GERMAN – ENGLISH
TECHNICAL AND ENGINEERING
DICTIONARY

D1727439

GERMAN – ENGLISH
TECHNICAL AND ENGINEERING
DICTIONARY

von

DR. LOUIS DE VRIES

vormals Professor an der Iowa State University

und

THEO M. HERRMANN

Nachdruck 1972
vollkommen überarbeitet und erheblich erweitert
1965

McGRAW-HILL BOOK COMPANY

NEW YORK LONDON SYDNEY TORONTO

OSCAR BRANDSTETTER VERLAG KG · WIESBADEN

Buch Nr. 0202

BROWN, BOVERI & CIE
Aktiengesellschaft
EA/EK
MANNHEIM

GERMAN – ENGLISH TECHNICAL AND ENGINEERING DICTIONARY

by

DR. LOUIS DE VRIES

formerly Professor, Iowa State University

and

THEO M. HERRMANN

Reprint 1972
completely revised and enlarged
1965

McGRAW-HILL BOOK COMPANY

NEW YORK LONDON SYDNEY TORONTO

OSCAR BRANDSTETTER VERLAG KG · WIESBADEN

"I shall not think my employment useless or ignoble if . . . my labors afford light to the repositories of science."

DR. SAMUEL JOHNSON

In diesem Wörterbuch werden, wie in allgemeinen Nachschlagwerken üblich, etwa bestehende Patente, Gebrauchsmuster oder Warenzeichen nicht erwähnt. Wenn ein solcher Hinweis fehlt, heißt das also nicht, daß eine Ware oder ein Warennamen frei ist.

In this dictionary as in general reference works existing patents, registered patents, trade marks etc. are not mentioned. If such a reference is absent, it does not mean that a commodity or tradename is "free".

German-English Technical and Engineering Dictionary, Second Edition
Copyright 1965 by the McGraw-Hill Publishing Company Limited, London.
All Rights Reserved. This book, or parts thereof, may not be reproduced in any form without permission of the publishers.
Library of Congress Catalog Card Number: 65-23218

ISBN 3 87097 042 1

Printed in the Federal Republic of Germany

Alleinauslieferung und Vertrieb für Deutschland Oscar Brandstetter Verlag KG, Wiesbaden
Exclusive rights of sale in Germany Oscar Brandstetter Verlag KG, Wiesbaden

16631

Gewidmet der Industrie,
die viele Anregungen zu dieser Ausgabe beisteuerte

Dedicated to Industry
which contributed so much in material and encouragement

VORWORT

Bereits fünf Jahre vor dem Erscheinen des ersten Bandes des *Technical and Engineering Dictionary* hatten die Vorbereitungen des Manuskriptes begonnen. Wenn ein allgemeines fremdsprachliches Wörterbuch immer wieder der Überarbeitung bedarf, weil jede Sprache lebt, überalterte Begriffe ausscheidet und neue schafft, so zwingt das ständige Anwachsen des technischen, naturwissenschaftlichen Stoffes in immer kürzer werdenden Zeiträumen zu einer Überarbeitung von Wörterbüchern, wie diesem *Technical and Engineering Dictionary*.

Um den aus dieser Erkenntnis resultierenden allseitigen Bedürfnissen zu entsprechen, wurde der deutsch-englische Band des *Technical and Engineering Dictionary* vollkommen überarbeitet, indem alte und inzwischen überholte Begriffe ausgesondert und das aus den Ergänzungsbänden hinzugefügt wurde, was inzwischen seine Gültigkeit bewiesen hat. Das Material hat eine lebendige Bereicherung durch Firmen der verschiedensten Industriezweige gefunden, die viele neue und neueste Begriffe aus ihrer Entwicklung beisteuerten. Diese Hilfe wird ebenso mit großer Dankbarkeit anerkannt, wie die unermüdliche und sachkundige Unterstützung, die die gesamte Arbeit durch die Tätigkeit des Mitautors erfuhr. Dank gebührt auch meiner Frau, die mit viel Fleiß und Umsicht dazu beigetragen hat, diese Aufgabe zu lösen.

Wohl wissend, daß trotz ernsthaftestem Bemühen der Autoren immer wieder Lücken geschlossen und Verbesserungen vorgenommen werden können, werden Anregungen jederzeit dankbar begrüßt.

Walldorf, August 1965

LOUIS DE VRIES

PREFACE

In 1950 the first volume of the *Technical and Engineering Dictionary* was published, although preparation of the manuscript started five years earlier.

Since that time tremendous advances have been made in science and technology. To meet the needs resulting from this ever-increasing development, the *German-English* volume has been completely revised, antiquated terms removed and the valid material of the supplement incorporated. In addition, the vocabulary has been considerably enhanced and brought up to date by the valuable and generous contributions from various branches of industry which supplied the newly-coined terminology from recent development and research.

This aid and support is very gratefully acknowledged, as are the untiring and competent support of the co-author and the work of Mrs. De Vries, who so meticulously prepared the manuscript for this comprehensive volume.

Since no work of this type is ever complete, the authors always welcome suggestions, corrections and contributions.

Walldorf, August 1965 Louis De Vries

MITARBEITER

Diese Aufgabe hätte nie ohne Hilfe und Mitarbeit der nachstehend aufgeführten Damen und Herren verwirklicht werden können, denen der Autor zu großem Dank verpflichtet ist.

H. B. Edwards, US Waterways Experimentation, Corps of Engineers, Vicksburg, Mississippi. Mr. Edwards gab die Anregung zu diesem Werk und überzeugte den Autor von seiner Notwendigkeit.

Die im folgenden aufgeführten Personen halfen mit ihren verschiedensten Beiträgen sehr und unterstützten die endgültige Fertigstellung bereitwilligst mit Rat und Anregung.

Carl V. Bertsche, Übersetzungsbüro für Recht und Wissenschaft
M. Y. Inomata, Berater der Japanischen Nationalen Eisenbahngesellschaft,
Lewis L. Sell, Autor von umfangreichen Stoffsammlungen in englischer, spanischer und portugiesischer Sprache
Max Wulfinghof · Edward Alt · Anton Fingerhuth · Franz Haid · Margot Hutt · O. M. Jörgensen · Gotthart Lenk · Fritz Niepert · Heinrich Pleines · Heinrich Resele · Lore Schlotz · Mr. Wattenberg · Karl-Heinz Winkelmann · A. M. Wittfoht · J. P. Wrede

COLLABORATORS

This task could not have been accomplished without the assistance and cooperation of men and women listed here to whom the author is deeply indebted.

H. B. Edwards, US Waterways Experimentation, Corps of Engineers, Vicksburg, Mississippi. Mr. Edwards originally recommended this work and persuaded the author to carry it out.

The following were most helpful with their valuable contributions, but above all because of their repeated words of encouragement and inspiration to carry on this work to its completion.

Carl V. Bertsche, Lawyers' and Merchants' Translation Bureau
M. Y. Inomata, Advisor, Japanese National Railways
Lewis L. Sell, the Author of internationally known dictionaries in English, French, Spanish and Portuguese
Max Wulfinghof · Edward Alt · Anton Fingerhuth · Franz Haid · Margot Hutt · O. M. Jörgensen · Gotthart Lenk · Fritz Niepert · Heinrich Pleines · Heinrich Resele · Lore Schlotz · Mr. Wattenberg · Karl-Heinz Winkelmann · A. M. Wittfoht · J. P. Wrede

A

a-Ader *f* tip wire, A-wire, T-wire

Aale *pl* thin wedges through wooden dowels

ab off, away ~ **Werk** exworks

Abakus *m* alignment, chart, nomogram

abalienieren to alienate

Abampere *n* abampere

abänderlich alterable, modifiable

abändern to alter, vary, change; (verbessern) improve; (teilweise) modify; (umarbeiten) revise, rectify, amend; (berichtigen) correct

Abänderung *f* alteration, modification, change, transformation, variation, revision, amendment, rectification

Abänderungs-antrag *m* amendment **-fähig** alterable, modifiable **-patent** *n* reissue patent

abarbeiten (ermüden) to overwork, work hard; (aus dem Groben) rough work, rough plane; (abnutzen) wear out, finish (a task)

Abarbeitungsnagel *m* finishing nail

a/b Arm minus-plus wiper, line wiper

Abart *f* variety, modification, variation, species, variant, degeneracy

abarten (entarten) to degenerate, (abweichen) deviate, vary

abatmen, abätmen to glow in a muffle, desiccate, anneal (superficially)

abätzen to remove with caustics, etch, corrode, cauterize

abbaken (Fahrwasser) to mark by stakes (or beacons), set buoys

Abbau *m* (Chem) disintegration, decomposition, separation, reduction; (Eiweiß) proteolysis; (Maschinen) dismounting, dismantling, disassembling; (Vernichtung) demolishing; (Abnutzung) attrition; (Gebäude) demolition; (Personal) staff reduction, dismissal, degradation ~ **mit Bergeversatz** mining with filling or stowing ~ **eines Flözes** working, cutting or winding of a seam or vein ~ **mit planmäßiger Geviertzimmerung** square sets ~ **in regelmäßigen Abständen** open stope with pillar ~ **unter Tage** underground winning or working **glockenartiger** ~ bell work **schachbrettförmiger** ~ square work ~ **der Stärke** peptonization

Abbaubetrieb *m* workings

abbauen (Grube) to work, exploit mine, quarry, demount, workout, exhaust; (Gebäude) take down, break up; (Maschine) take to pieces, demolish, disassemble, dismantle; (Chem) decompose, disintegrate, reduce, spilt up, analyze; (Ausgaben) retrench, cut; (Personal) cut down, dismiss, remove, discharge, lay off, reduce, weaken, faint **einen Firstenstoß** ~ to stope overhand **eine Grube** ~ to work a mine **eine Pumpe** ~ to remove a pump **stoßweise** ~ to stope out **einen Strossenstoß** ~ to stope underhand

Abbauen *n*, (Erschöpfung) ~ **eines Feldes** exhaustion of a mine

Abbaufeld *n* working field, mining region, panel, section

Abbaufirste *f*, **versatzlose** ~ open stope

Abbau-förderstrecke *f* winning headway **-fortschreitung** *f* advance on the face **-gerechtigkeit** *f* exploiting right (of a mine, land) **-hammer** *m* hulking hammer, coal picker, coal pick hammer, mechanical pick **-höhe** *f* lift **-meißel** *m* (rock) drill bit

abbäumen to take from the loom

Abbau-mittel *n* disintegrant **-ort** *m* stope, working place **-produkt** *f* derivative (product) **-punkt** m working face **-sohle** *f* level **-spitze** (Steinbrecher) demolishing point **-stelle** *f* winning face **-stempel** *m* cockersprag **-stoß** *m* face of workings, wall. forehead, adit end (min)

Abbau-strebe *f* longwall **-strecke** *f* board, chamber, stall, cross heading, opening **-streckenbänder** *pl* headway conveyors **-stufe** *f* stage of degradation **-system** *n* system of working (min) **-temperatur** *f* breaking-down or peptonization temperature **-verfahren** *n* mining or working method **-verhinderndes Mittel** antidisintegrant, stabilizer **-verlust** *m* waste in mining

abbauwürdig workable, exploitable, worth mining **-es Erz** pay or profitable ore **-es Erzvorkommen** workable ore field **-e Mächtigkeit** payable deposit **-e Schicht** productive bed **-e Steinkohlenlagerung** productive coal formation

Abbauzeit *f* tear-down time (work-factor)

abbefehlen to countermand

abbefördern to evacuate, transport

Abbeförderung *f* transportation, shipping

abbeizen to cauterize, pickle, scour, dip, remove the paint, lixiviate, macerate, remove with corrosives, taw **den Borax nach dem Löten** ~ to remove the borax by dilute sulfuric acid after soldering **mit Scheidewasser** ~ to remove with aqua fortis

Abbeizen *n* cauterization, pickling, dipping

Abbeiz-fluid *n* paint removing liquid, paint remover **-mittel** *n* pickling agent, corrosive, paint remover

abbersten to crack off, burst off, spring off

abberufen to call away, recall

abbestellen to countermand, cancel

Abbestellung *f* counterorder, cancellation

A-B-Betrieb *m* A-B method, normal junction working

Abbeugung *f* diffraction

abbewegen to move downward

Abbewegung *f* downward movement, lowering, out-movement

abbezahlen to pay off

Abbiegemaschine *f* bending machine

abbiegen to deflect, bend off or aside or downward, offset, curve, hook, snap or branch off, prevent, turn off (traffic) **etwas** ~ forestall, sidetrack

Abbiegestift *f* guide pin

Abbiegung *f* deflection, offset, bending, flexure, anticlinical flexure

Abbiegungswinkel *m* bending angle

Abbild *n* image, copy, likeness, conformal transformation, reflection **-barkeit zweier Flächen** possibility of mapping one surface into another (geom)
abbilden to copy, portray, depict, model, illustrate, image, picture, reproduce, emboss **sich ~** to be reflected or delineated
Abbilden *n* forming of an image (optics)
abbildend image-forming, reproductive, illustrative **-e Faktoren** image-forming factors **-e Ringelektrode** focusing ring **-es System** image-forming system (optics)
Abbildspule *f* image coil
Abbildung *f* picture, image, imagery, figure, projection, copy, representation, illustration, diagram, plate, cut, drawing, sketch, photograph, map **~ von Gebieten** mapping of regions **~ bei Brillengläsern** image formation **~ der projektiven Ebene auf sich** mapping of the projective plane into itself **~ durch parallele Normalen bzw. Tangentialebenen** mapping by means of parallel normals or tangent planes **~ des Torus auf sich** mapping of the torus into itself **~ durch Zentralperspektive** mapping by means of central perspective
Abbildung, geodätische ~ geodesic mapping; **geteilte ~** split focus (Walton method of scanning) **inhaltstreue ~** areapreserving mapping, true or accurate reproduction **komatische ~** comatic image **konforme ~** conformal mapping, conformable representation **längentreue ~** length-preserving mapping **nebenstehende ~** the near-by or accompanying illustration **punktförmige ~** point image **punktuelle ~** point focal vision or imagery **stetige bzw. topologische ~** continuous or topological mapping **latente ~** latent image formation **optische ~** optical mapping **streckentreue ~** projection without distortion of range
Abbildungs-eigenschaften *pl* characteristics of representation **-fehler** *m* defect of image (optics) aberration (optics) **-funktion** *f* function of representation **-gegenstand** *m* imaging object **-gesetz** *n* (von Abbe), (Abbe's) law of imagery **-gleichung** *f* imaging equation **-gruppe** *f* group of mappings **-gruppen** *f pl* groups of transformations **-güte** *f* difinition of image **-klassen** *f pl* classes of mappings **-magnet** *m* focusing magnet **-maßstab** *m* scale of reproduction, image or picture scale, scale of photograph, useful magnification (electron microscope) **-mittelpunkt** *m* center of image **-objektiv** *n* image forming objective **-optik** *f* imaging or focusing optics **-spule** *f* focusing coil **-system** *n* image-reproducing system **-tiefe** *f* depth of field **-tiefenskala** *f* (Tiefenschärfenskala) depth of field scale **-vermögen** *n* resolving power (optics) **-wärme** *f* heating
Abbimsen *n* buffing
abbimsen to abrade (rub) with pumice, pumice
Abbimser *m* stoner (tanning)
Abbinde-beschleuniger *m* accelerator, accelerating agent **-fähigkeit** *f* setting quality (cement) **-garn** *n* binding twine **-geschwindigkeit** *f* (Zement) rate of setting **-hammer** *m* little seam hammer
abbinden to unbind, tie (off), lash, set (concrete), harden, apply a tourniquet, loosen, bind, lace (cables), bond, block (chem.), seam, assemble, join (carp.), connect electrically to the metal structure of aircraft **die Kolumnenschnur ~** to untie the page cord (print.)
Abbinden *n* setting (of cement), untying, lossening, bonding
abbindend seeting **langsam -er Zement** slow-setting cement **rasch -er Zement** quick-setting cement
Abbinde-verhältnis *n* setting condition (cement) **-verlauf** *m* process of setting **-verspätendes Mittel** (Chemisches Produkt) retarder **-wärme** *f* (von Zement) heat of setting (of cement) **-zeit** *f* curing period, setting time
Abbindung *f* removal by ligature, setting
Abblase-druck *m* working pressure, blowing-off pressure, valving pressure, pressurized alarm (boilers) **-hahn** *m* blowoff valve **-leitung** *f* blowoff line, blowdown piping
abblasen to blast (castings), sandblast, blow or dust off, blow down, release gas, blow, (Farbton) turn pale (lose color), discharge a boiler or digester under pressure, valve gas **den Dampf ~** to blow off steam **mit Wasserdampf ~** to distill with steam
Abblasen *n* cleaning (iron)
Abblase-pistole *f* blow-gun, air pistol **-rohr** *n* escape pipe, exhaust pipe **-stutzen** *m* delivery pipe **-tank** *m* blow-down tank **-ventil** *n* blowoff or exhaust valve, bleeder valve **-ventilkammer** *f* exhaust-valve box **-vorrichtung** *f* blowoff device, blower
abblatten to remove the leaves, defoliate
Abblatten *n* defoliation, leaf pruning
Abblättern *n* spalling
abblättern to chip off, shell off, peel off, exfoliate, effloresce (paint films) flake (of a precipitate), spall (refractories), scale off (boiler scale)
abblättern, nicht ~ unstrippable, chip proof
Abblätterung *f* peeling off, scaling, lamination, exfoliation **~ der Schiene** exfoliation or scaling off of rail (metal)
abbleichen to bleach (fade)
Abblend-blech *n* dimming sheet **-einstellung** *f* dimming adjustment
abblenden to set the diaphragm, stop down (lens aperture), darken ship, dim, dip, or screen lights, mask off, occult, diaphragm, gate, blank, dowse (a beam), wipe, dissolve, fade, blackout **Scheinwerfer ~** to dim head lamps or searchlights
Abblend-faden *m* dimming filament **-fußschalter** *m* foot-operated dimming switch **-haube** *f* antiglare (dimming) cap **-kappe** *f* dim-out cap, head-light mask **-licht** *n* antidazzle light dim light **-schalter** *m* beam-deflector switch, dimming switch, anti dazzle switch **-umschalter** *m* antiglare switch
Abblendung *f* setting of diaphragm, dimming, stopping down (lens aperture), restricted lighting, screening (phot) **~ des Kristallbildes** stopping down of image of crystal
Abblendungsschalter *m* dimmer switch
Abblend-vorgang *m* dimming process (dimming action) **-vorrichtung** *f* anti-dazzle device, dimming device, screen, shade, dimmers (Auto)
abblicken to cease brightening, brighten, grow dull, tarnish (metal)

abblitzen to flash, misfire
abbluten to bleed (paper)
abbohren to bore, drill **die Stehbolzen ~** to bore out the stay bolts **ein Terrain ~** to explore the ground by bore holes
Abbohrer *m* long borer, long jumper (min)
Abbohrung *f* boring
abborken to strip bark from wood
Abborken *n* barking
abböschen to incline, slope, slant, give batter **steil ~** to slope steeply, cut steep down (building)
Abböschung *f* sloping
abbosseln to emboss
Abbrand *m* (Material) fire loss, waste; (Schmelzofen) melting loss; (Elektrode) burning off, consumption; (Chem) roasting, residue, scaling loss, furnace-loss, metal loss **effektiver ~** burn-up
Abbranddauer *f* burning length
Abbrandlänge, freie ~ uninterrupted feed-length
Abbrand-verlust *m* stand-by losses (of a power station) **-widerstand** *m* erosion resistor
abbrassen to brace full, fill the sails
abbrauchen to use up (wear out)
Abart *f* variety, variation, species
abarten to vary, degenerate
abbrechen (Haus) to demolish, dismantle, break up, pull or take down; (Vorgang) break off, cut, discontinue; (aufhören) cease, stop, break off **~** (an Menge) to reduce the quantity, truncate
abbrechendes Drehmoment break-away torque
Abbrecher *m* interrupter
Abbrechfehler *m* truncation error
Abbrechungssignal *n* breakdown signal
abbreiten, das Eisen ~ to stretch out or to beat out iron, flatten
abbremsen to brake, fishtail; race or run up (engine); suppress, decelerate, retard, slow down
Abbremsen *n* suppressing
Abbremser *m* suppressor
Abbrems-klotz *m* chockblock **-platz** *m* run-up area (of airport) **-vorrichtung** *f* arresting gear
Abbremsung *f* breaking, retarding, slowing down **-länge** *f* relaxation distance **-zeit** *f* relaxation time
Abbrenn-barkeit *f* combustibility **-bürste** *f* spark-contact brush or breaker, breaker point
abbrennen to burn off or down, deflagrate, cut (by oxyhydrogen), pickle, dip, calcine, spark (elec), miss fire **Messing ~** to pickle or dip brass **Stahl ~** to blaze off steel
Abbrenn-glocke *f* deflagrating jar **-kontaktstück** *n* spark-contact piece, sparker **-löffel** *m* deflagrating spoon **-schweißung** *f* fish welding, welding by sparks, flash butt welding **-schweißverfahren** *n* gas-welding method **-stumpfschweißung** *f* flash welding
Abbreviatur *f* abbreviation
Abbreviaturensatz *m* table of abbreviations
abbrevieren to abbreviate
abbringen to get off (weglenken), divert, deflect; (abraten), dissuade; remove, divert **ein gestrandetes Schiff ~** to float a stranded ship
Abbröckeln *n* crumbling
abbröckeln to peel off, scale, crumble (away), break off in bits, flake off.
Abbröckelung *f* crumbling **~ einer Böschung** slipping of a slope
Abbruch *m* (Beziehungen) breaking off, rupture, termination; (Schaden) damage, injury, wrecking, demolition, pulling down, fragment, discontinuance **~ der Küste** successful attack on the coast line **~ der Linie** dismantling of a line **~** tun, to injure, prejudice **~** reif, dilapidated
Abbruchs-arbeit *f* demolishing work **-kosten** *pl* dismantling charges **-regel** *f* stopping rule (reliability) **-ufer** *n* eroding (washing) bank **-unternehmen** *n* wrecking company **-wahrscheinlichkeit** *f* branching probability **-wert** *m* break-up value
abbrücken to break up, remove or dismantle a bridge
abbrühen to seethe, scald, boil out, parboil (cloth)
Abbrühen *n* boiling out
Abbrühkessel *m* scalding tub
abbrummen (slang), to make off speedily
abbuchen to write off
Abbuchen von Differenzen in Lagervorräten writing off stock differences
Abbuchung *f* depreciation (writing off)
Abbügeletikett *n* hot transfer
Abbürstemaschine *f* burring machine (for removing burrs, fluff, straws, etc)
abbürsten to brush off
Abcfolge *f* alphabetical order
Abcoulomb *n* abcoulomb
Abdach *n* lean-to (shed)
abdachen to slope away
abdachig sloping, slanting, inclined
Abdachung *f* (Gelände), slope, fall, escarpment (scarp), declivity (landscape), roofing, dip **~ eines Daches** declivity or slope of a roof **flache ~** glacis
Abdachungs-höhe *f* height of dip **-winkel** *m* angle of talus
Abdachverhältnis einer Böschung ratio of horizontal breadth to vertical height of a slope
abdämmen to dam, dam up **ein Flöz ~** to cut off a bed (geol)
Abdammtrupp *m* damming squad or detail
Abdämmung *f* insulation (acoustics), dam(ming), restraining, isolation, embankment, barrage
Abdampf *m* exhaust or waste steam, dry or dead steam, evaporating steam **-apparat** *m* evaporating apparatus **-becken** *n* evaporating basin **-düse** *f* steam exhaust nozzle
abdampfen to evaporate, damp, vaporize **~ lassen** to allow to evaporate, evaporate
Abdampfen *n* evaporation, volatilization, starting (a train)
abdämpfen to boil (down or out), evaporate, quench, scald, steam (down), volatilize, damp (charcoal); (Ton, Geräusche) attenuate, damp, deaden, soften, tone down; (Schwingungen) modulate vibraions
Abdämpfen *n* drying out, boiling out
Abdampf-energie *f* energy in the exhaust steam **-entöler** *m* exhaust-steam oil separator **-gefäß** *n* evaporating pan **-heizung** *f* waste-steam heating **-gehäuse** *n* exhaust chamber **-kessel** *m* evaporating boiler **-kolben** *m* evaporating flask **-kondenswasserabscheider** *m* exhaust-steam condensing-water separator **-krümmer** *m* elbow

of steam (exhaust system) **-leitungen** *f pl* exhaust pipe line **-ofen** *m* slip kiln

Abdampfpfanne *f* evaporating boiler or pan ~ **mit rotierenden Heizröhren in Käfigform** evaporating pan with rotating squirrel-cage heating pipes ~ **mit rotierender Heizspirale** evaporating pan with helical heating coil

Abdampf-rohr *n* exhaust, vent pipe **-rückstand** *m* solid residue from evaporation **-schale** *f* evaporating dish **-speicher** *m* exhaust steam accumulator **-stöpsel** *m* vent plug **-stutzen** *m* coupling pipe between turbine and condenser, exhaust-steam pipe **-trichter** *m* evaporating funnel **-triebtender** *m* exhaust-steam driven tender (for locomotives) **-turbine** *f* exhaust steam turbine

Abdampfung *f* evaporation, volatilization

Abdämpfung *f* damping, desiccation ~ **der Geräusche** reducing of noise(s)

Abdampfventil *n* waste valve, steam trap valve **-verwertung** *f* utilization of waste heat **-verwertungsanlage** *f* exhaust-steam utilizing plant **-vorrichtung** *f* evaporator **-vorwärmer** *m* exhaust-steam preheater

abdarren to dry, kiln-dry

Abdarr-horde *f* lower finishing hurdle **-temperatur** *f* final kilning temperature, finishing heat or temperature.

Abdeck-asphalt *m* masking asphalt **-aufzeichnung** *f* masking recording, matting **-band** *n* masking tape, cover band **-blech** *n* division plate, sheet cover, access plate, base plate, slideway guard, guardplate (dustplate) **-blende** *f* shutter, mask, shutter mask, diaphragm ring **-doppelzackenspur** *f* duplex variable-area track **-effekt** *m* sheltering effect **-einfachzackenspur** *f* unilateral variable-area track

abdecken (bedecken) to blind, cap, clead, conceal, cope, cover, plank, shield, mask; (freilegen) discover, remove, strip, uncover, unroof; (Linse) diaphragm; (Verpflichtungen) repay obligations; (Ätzen) provide a resist coat; (Haut) flay, skin; (abräumen) remove; (bedecken) cover; (Kredit) repay, pay back; (verdecken) mask, conceal, wash, uncover, cap, strip off or carry away (as roofs), eclipse, occult (lens), provide a resist coat (in metal etching) **mit Brettern** ~ to clead, plank **Fäden** ~ to strip fiber **ein Haus** ~ (das Dach abnehmen), to unroof a house

Abdecken mit Isolierstoff covering with insulating material

Abdecker *m* flayer, skinner

Abdeckerei *f* flaying house

Abdeck-flügel *m* masking or shutter blade, vane **-glas** *n* sight glass **-haube** *f* covering hood, cover **-hebel** *m* line feed lever **-jalousie** *f* (des Gebläses) louver (of a fan) **-klappe** *f* protective cover, dust cap, trap door (shutter), light flap (photo) **-lack** *m* masking lacquer **-leiste** *f* cover strip, capping, finishing strip. covering rail (border) **-masse** *f* means of protection **-papier** *n* paper cover, masking paper **-paste** *f* calking putty, masking paint **-plane** *f* tarpaulin

Abdeckplatte *f* cover plate, coping stone, floor plate, cover (manhole), lid (box), access plate (aviation), apron (rolling mill), masking plate ~ **für Wartungs- und Besichtigungsöffnung** access plate

Abdeckscheibe *f* spray or cover plate, shutter disk or stop disk with spiral slot, covering disc; (Lagerdichtung) washer; (Scheibenkupplung) end plate

Abdeck-schelle *f* covering clamp **-schild** *n* cover plate **-schirm** *m* vizor **-seite** *f* masked side (motion picture) **-stein** *m* capstone, coping **-streifen** *m* squeeze unit, barrier (motion picture) **-teil** *m* encasrment

Abdeckung *f* (Mauer) coping; (Planken) planking, capping, cover, guard, mask, stone paving, pitching, covering ~ **einer Drehscheibe** boarded floor of a turntable **Einfachzackenschrift mit** ~ unilateral variable-area track made with single-vane shutter ~ **der Zahnräder** protection of toothed wheels

Abdeckungsfrequenz *f* blanketing frequency

Abdeck-verfahren *n* shutter-mask method **-vorrichtung** *f* shutter control (as on carburetor), covering device

abdekantieren to decant, draw off

abdestillieren to distill off, distill, drive off, (Amalgam) retort

Abdichtbuchse *f* sealing bushing

abdichten (kalfatern) to calk; (Loch) plug up; (mit Kitt) lut, to seal, stuff, pack, waterproof, make tight **die Elektroden** ~ to pack the carbons of electrodes

Abdichten *n* sealing, jointing

abdichtende Naht sealing weld

Abdicht-filz *m* sealing felt **-klappe** *f* shutter **-masse** *f* sealing medium **-mittel** *n* sealing compound **-schale** *f* sealing dish **-scheibe** *f* joint washer **-stöpsel** *m* (für Kabelkanäle) duct plug

Abdichtung *f* calking (of a cask), luting; (Dichtfuge) joint, gasket, packing, sealing, waterproofing, rendering impervious; (Maschine) packing, tightness, jointing, hermetic plumbing ~ **gegen Ölaustritt** oil retention, sealing (packing) to prevent leakage of oil **metallische** ~ metal-to-metal joint

Abdichtungs-blech *n* tightening sheet, flushing plate **-graben** *m* cut-off trench **-gummierung** *f* rubber packing ring or gasket **-pappe** *f* tightening felt **-ring** *m* washer, sealing ring, expanding washer, gasket ring **-schleier** *m* grouted cut-off wall **-sporn** *m* (-mauer) cut-off wall **-teppich** *m* impervious blanket

abdocken to lay out (fabrics), unwind

Abdocker *m* layer-out (dyeing)

abdörren to dry (up), become parched, refine (met)

Abdörrofen *m* refining furnace

Abdraht *m* turnings

abdrängen to force away, shove away

Abdräng-kraft *f* drifting force **-ring** *m* fleeting ring

Abdrängung *f* deflection from course by wind, drift, leeway

Abdrängungs-berichtigung *f* drift correction **-messer** *m* drift indicator **-schreiber** *m* drift recorder (derivograph) **-winkel** *m* angle of drift

abdrechseln to remove in turning

Abdreh-apparat *m* truing device **-bank** *f* turner's lathe **-diamant** *m* diamond dresser (truing diamond) **-ebene** *f* truing plane

abdrehen (ab- aus-schalten) to shut off, switch off, turn off; (Kurs ändern) change the course, deviate; (Luftfahrt) go into a nose dive; (verdrehen) twist; (Gewinde) strip a thread; (Stirnflächen) face, face (lathe), remove by torsion, unscrew, desurface (products), twist off, dress

Abdrehen *n* turning off, truing, twisting off, turning (in lathe)

Abdreh-maschine *f* turning or finishing machine (lathe) **-rädchen** *n* pressing wheel **-richtung** *f* turn-off direction **-späne** *pl* turnings **-stahl** *m* turner's chisel, turning tool, lathe tool

Abdrehvorrichtung *f* wheel dresser **~ für den Kollektor** commutator turning device

Abdrehwerkzeug *n* dressing tool

Abdrift *f* drift (aviation, navy), leeway **-anzeiger** *m* drift indicator **-messer** *m* drift meter **-platz** *m* landing area, jump area for paratroops **-stab** *m* drift bar **-visier** *n* drift meter **-winkel** *m* drift angle

abdrosseln to stall or throttle (motor), throttle down, choke **vollständig ~** to choke out

Abdrosselung *f* throttling

Abdruck *m* mark, stamp, transfer (Buchdruck) copy, impression, imprint, print; (Gießtechnik) cast, mold, counterpart; (Phototechnik) print, photograph; (Nachdruck) reprint; (Korrekturabzug) proofsheet **~ durch Abwälzen** rolling print **~ auf Blättern** (Streifen), page (tape) printing **~ frischen Drucks auf der Gegenseite** set-off **~ im Fluge** flying print **~ einer Münze** ectype of a coin **~ mit der Schrift** print with the type **~ der Typen** reproduction of type faces **~ einer Versteinerung** fossil remains **unsauberer ~** smudgy impression

Abdruckbüchse *f* impression block

abdrucken to print, imprint, work off, impress, reproduce or copy (by printing or impression), stamp, set-off

abdrücken to impress, transfer; pull the trigger, fire; press (a button), release by pressure lever, or test; (abscheren) shear off, to drive out (by pressure), put on speed

Abdruckform *f* print

Abdrückkurve *f* back-off cam

Abdruckmethode *f* reproducing or imprinting method

Abdrück-mutter *f* draw-off nut **-scheibe** *f* forcing disc **-schraube** *f* lifting or puller screw, setscrew, key forcing screw, thrust screw, withdrawer screw

Abdruck-stempel *m* impression block **-träger** *m* print bearer **-verfahren** *n* impression method, method of copying, replica method **-versuch** *m* pressure testing

Abdrückvorrichtung *f* firing or release mechanism

Abdruschgewicht *n* thrashed weight

abdunkeln to deepen (print), darken, cut off or dim (light), occult, eclipse, obscure, blank or gate spots (television); (verdunkeln) black out, sadden

Abdunklungsmittel *n* darkening or saddening agent

abdunsten (abdünsten) to evaporate, vaporize

abduzieren to abduct

abdweilen to swab, dry with a mop

abebben to ebb (decline)

abebnen to level, decline, dwindle

abecken to chamfer

abeichen to calibrate, gauge, measure, adjust

abeisen to free from ice

Abelit *n* nitroglycerine

abelsche Gruppe commutative group

A-Belüftungsanlage *f* oxygen-pressure-regulation pipe

Abend-dämmerung *f* twilight after sunset, owl-light **-konzentration** *f* ionic concentration **-schicht** *f* night shift **-schule** *f* night school **-thermik** *f* terrestrial radiation, upwash due to heat rising in the evening **-weite** *f* western amplitude

aberkennen to annul, deprive, dispossess, revoke

Aberkennung *f* abjudication (of rights), dispossession, denial, deprivation, forfeiture, abrogation

Abernathyit *n* abernathyite

aberrant abnormal, exceptional

Aberration *f* aberration (phot) **~ außerhalb der Achse** extra-axial aberration **Kreis der geringsten ~** circle of least aberration **chromatische ~** chromatic aberration **sphärische ~** spherical aberration

Aberrationswinkel *m* angle of aberration

aberregen to de-energize, deactivate (elec.)

Aberregung *f* de-energization

Abessinierbrunnen *m* well with perforated pipe casing

abfachen to classify, partition, form compartments

abfackeln to burn off (oil), flare (of excess gas)

abfahrbares Farbwerk removable inking apparatus

abfahren to get under way, start; (Apparate) to remove

Abfahrt *f* start, take-off, departure, downhill run (skiing) **~ eines Wagens** start (starting) of a car

Abfahrts-gleis *n* departure track **-hafen** *m* port of departure **-ort** *m* point of departure **-signal** *n* ready-to-depart or clear signal (R. R.) **-zeit** *f* time of departure, starting, descent

Abfall *m* (Neigung, Schräge) slope, declination, decline, fall; (Spannung) drop in voltage; (Abfälle) waste, refuse, trash, rubbish, scrap, scraping, chippings, filings, shavings; (Erz) tailings; (Neigung) pitch, declivity, descent, fall, slope; (Abnahme) decrease, decrement, drop, deterioration; (Böschung) steep slope, descent, declivity, by-product (residue), discharge, roll-off (in frequency response), casse paper, lapse, disintegration, deads, drop, loss, droop, falling off (current) **ein Relais zum ~ bringen** to deenergize **steiler ~** steep fall, precipitation, precipice **vollständiger ~** decay

Abfall der Lumineszenz decay (of luminescence) **~ der Schallintensität** attenuation of sound **~ des Stromes** (Zeitkonstante) decay of current (time constant) **~ der Wärmewellenintensität erster Art** attenuation of first sound

Abfall-anlage *f* waste-utilization plant **-apparat** *m* apparatus for free fall **-asche** *f* riddlings **-aufbereitung** *f* waste recovery **-ausscheidung** *f* separation of waste **-ausstoßer** *m* scrapings ejector **-beize** *f* waste pickle liquor **-beseitigung**

f refuse disposal, fall-out disposal **-bunker** *m* (coking) breeze bunker

Abfälle *pl* scrap

Abfalleimer *m* waste bin

Abfalleisen *n* scrap iron, junk

abfallen to fall down; (Intensität) to attenuate, decay; (Relais) deenergize, relay, drop; (nachlassen) decrease, deteriorate; (ferner) fall off, decline, retract, slope (off), secede, relieve, release (drop), droop, loose (current), break; (absacken) sag; (d. Drehzahl d. Drehmoments) reduce, slow down; (schräg) slope off **steil ~** to precipitate **vollständig ~** to decay, drop down or off, release (a relay), slope down

Abfallen *n* fall, diminution, drop **~** (des Relais), release, releasing, restore

abfallend falling off, decaying; (Bilder) bled off; (geneigt) inclined

abfallend-er Absatz falling shoulder **-e Drehzahl** decreasing speed **-e oder geneigte Eiseneinlage** inclined reinforcement **-es Gelände** *n* sloping ground or terrain **-e Kurve** droop curve **langsam -es Relais** slow-to-release or slow-releasing relay **-es Ufer** *n* shelving shore

Abfallende *n* waste end

Abfall-energie *f* waste current or energy **-erzeugnis** *n* (meist nicht weiter verwertbares), waste product **-erzeugnis** *n* (weiter verwertbares), by-product, residuary product

Abfälleverwertung *f* waste utilization

Abfall-graben *m* tailrace **-grenze** *f* critical limit **-gummi** *m* waste rubber, scrap rubber **-gut** *n* waste washings **-haufen** *m* junk pile, scrap iron **-holz** *n* wood scraps or waste wood **-hülse** *f* sliding socket **-hütchen** *n* jetting cap

abfällig deciduous, disapproving

Abfall-kasten *m* waste bin, dust bin **-kohle** *f* waste coal **-koks** *m* stove coke, coke breeze **-lauge** *f* spent lye **-lutte** *f* overflow pipe

Abfall-marke *f* off-shade (dyeing)

Abfall-metall *n* scrap metal **-mauer** *f* downstream facing of weir or dam, forebay **-moment** *n* breakdown or stalling torque (polyphase motors), breakdown couple or point (sudden stoppage or stalling of polyphase motors), breakdown moment, torque **-prahm** *m* refuse lighter **-produkt** *n* waste product, by-product

Abfall-raum *m* waste chamber **-rinne** *f* refuse spout **-rohr** *n* discharge (drain) pipe, downspout, soil stack **-rutsche** *f* crop chute **-sammelanlage** *f* refuse-collecting plant **-säure** *f* residuary acid **-schneider** *m* scrap or waste cutter **-seife** *f* soap waste **-sortierer** *m* waste sorter **-stahl** *m* scrap steel

Abfallstoff *m* waste material or product, reclaimable waste **verwertbarer ~** by-product **radioaktiver ~** radioactive waste

Abfall-strom *m* waste current **-stück** *n* scantling, cutoff part **-vernichtungsanlage** *f* refuse- or sewage-disposal plant **-verwertung** *f* utilization of waste **-verwertungsanlage** *f* waste-utilizing plant **-verzögert** delayed-release **-verzögerung** *f* breaking delay, relay (electr), release lag (of relay) **-ware** *f* cullage

Abfall-wäscherei *f* waste washing **-wasser** *n* sewage **-wert** *m* drop-out (value), rate of decrease **-zeit** *f* drop-out time (relay)

Abfallzeit *f* decay time, decrease time, total hangover time, releasing time, time constant of fall **~ der Rückflanke** trailing edge rise time

Abfangbahn *f* part of trajectory with pull-out effect

abfangen to catch, capture; (abstützen) prop, support, brace, sustain; (Sturzflug) level off, flatten out, pull out (of a dive); (Stöße) absorb, cushion; (Kunden) entice away; (Flugzeug) intercept; (sammeln) collect, recover; (auffangen) intercept, screen off, brace, snatch from, level off (an aircraft) **Eisen ~** to tap the iron

Abfangen *n* pull-out, pulling up, flattening out (aviation), righting of aircraft, collecting, recovering (residues), catching (breaking), retaining, trapping; (Aushungern) *n* flare out; (Mauerwerk) *n* interception

abfangende Wirkung intercepting (catching) effect

Abfang-gabel *f* fork (rod elevator) **-graben** *m* intercepting ditch, catch-water ditch **-jäger** *m* interceptor **-kabel** *n* lift or flying wire **-kanal** *m* ring channel

Abfangkeil *m* casing slip **-heber** (Gestänge oder Rohrabfangkeilheber) slip elevator

Abfang-klappe *f* recovery flap **-radius** *m* pull-out radius **-seil** *n* check cable (aviat), safety stop cable **-strebe** *f* bracing strut, landing strut, wing support strut **-system** *n* intercepting system

Abfangung *f* underpinning

Abfang-ventil *n* interceptor valve **-verfahren** *n* construction using climbing rollers

Abfangvorrichtung *f* pull-out (device) **automatische ~** automatic pull-out, Plendell's adapter (on dive bombers)

Abfangwalze *f* climbing or front roller, roller bumper

Abfarad *n* abfarad

abfärben to lose color, stain, fade, discolor, decolor, bleed (of dyes), finish dying, rub-off, dye

Abfärben *n* bleeding (of dyes), rubbing off (of a coating)

abfasen to chamfer, slope, cant (timber), face, bevel

abfasern to ravel out, fray, fuzz; (Holz) lose fibers, unravel

abfassen (Brief) to intercept; (verfassen) compose, write; (aufsetzen) draft; (formulieren) word, formulate; (festhalten) arrest, catch, seize; (Bericht) compose, draw up, document, write, prepare, originate (a report); (abschrägen) chamfer, separate, bend, bevel or weld (metals), frame **neu ~** to reword

Abfassen *n* bending, beveling, catching

Abfassung *f* wording, formulation

Abfasung *f* (abfasen) beveling, chamfer

abfedern to equip with springs, absorb shocks, cushion (explosive), spring

Abfederung *f* padding, shock absorption, spring suspension (vehicle), springing, spring loading, springing (shock absorption by springs)

Abfederungs-kabel *n* shock-absorbing cable **-seil** *n* shock-absorber cord, elastic cord

abfegen to sweep (off)

abfeilen to file off or away, file down

Abfeilraspel *f* rasp (file)

abfertigen to dispatch, check (baggage), process

(for further disposition), expedite; (einen Anruf) to handle (a call)
Abfertiger *m* dispatcher
Abfertigung *f* dispatch **zollamtliche ~** customs entry, clearance
Abfertigungsgebäude *n* (Flugh) terminal building
Abfertigungs-schein *m* customs declaration **-stelle** *f* handling place, dispatch **-vorfeld** *n* service apron **-zeit** *f* handling time
abfetten to remove fat, degrease
abfeuern to discharge or fire (a gun)
Abfeuerung *f* firing
abfieren to pay out wire or rope from a reel **die Schoten ~** to case off sheets (naut)
abfilmen to film
abfiltern, abfiltrieren to filter, filter off, squeeze, strain off (by sieve, etc)
Abfiltrierung *f* filtration
abfinden to pay off **sich ~ mit** to reckon with, acquiesce in, reach an agreement with
Abfindung *f* reimbursement, indemnification, compensation (financial), settlement, lump sum settlement (insurance)
Abfindungs-geld *n* compensation, indemnity **-summe** *f* amount of compensation, indemnity, money paid in settlement (of claims, etc) **-vertrag** *m* agreement on compensation
abfinnen to scarf
abflachen to flatten, smooth (down), bevel, face, filter, shoal, broaden, make oblate, grade, chamfer, surface, truncate
Abflachen von Gewinden the truncating or flattening of threads
abflächen to attenuate, damp, face (in lathe)
Abflacher *m* voltage clipper (telegr)
Abflachschaltung *f* flattening arrangement (teleph)
Abflachstahl *m* side tool **linksseitiger ~** left-hand siding tool **rechtseitiger ~** right-hand siding tool
Abflachung *f* flattening, reduction, level of a crystal, bevel(ing), rounding off (a curve), leveling, smoothing, oblateness (at poles), truncation **~ der Spitzen** flattening of the peaks **~ einer Krümmung** easing of a bend **~ der Kugel** oblateness
Abflachungs-drossel *f* choke, retardation or attenuation coil, smoothing choke or coil **-kondensator** *m* smoothing or choke condenser
abflammen to singe **Leder ~** to tallow or grease leather over a charcoal fire
Abflammen *n* flamming
abflauen to abate fire, become weaker, lay, decrease (wind), sink, die down, lull
abfliegen to start, take off (airplane) **~ nach** to head for
abfließen to flow off or away, drain, stream, run, or leak off, flow out **~ lassen** to drain, drop (solution) by gravity
Abfließen durch natürliches Gefälle gravity feed **~ des Ladungsbildes** leakage (of the charge pattern)
abfließend defluent, decurrent **-es Wasser** tail water
Abfließspan *m* continuous chip
abfluchten to align, sight
Abfluchtung *f* alignment
Abflug *m* take-off, start, departure **~ mit Starthilfe** assisted take-off
Abflug-geschwindigkeit *f* take-off speed **-hafen** *m* airport of departure **-ort** *m* point of departure **-peilung** *f* back bearing, outbound bearing **-probe** *f* preflight check (rdo)
Abfluß *m* flow(ing)-off, discharge, runoff, drain, drainage, ebb, (opening) outlet, (outflowing) effluent, leak path (for grid current), demand flow, floor drain, outflow, sump **~ einer Talsperre** tail flow of a barrage (engin) **glatter ~** efflux, laminar flow in wake, smooth air-flow wake or wash **glatter ~ der Strömung** wash (aviation) **schießender ~** shooting flow **strömender ~** streaming flow
Abfluß-druck *m* flowing pressure **-gebiet** *n* catchment area or watershed **-geschwindigkeit** *f* velocity of waste flow, efflux, wake, slip stream, wash, or draining **-graben** *m* drainage ditch, gutter **-hahn** *m* discharge or drain cock or valve pet cock **-höhe** *f* discharge depth or head
Abfluß-kanal *m* drain ditch or channel, discharge culvert, drain passage **-kasten** *m* trap **-klappe** *f* drain plug **-kühler** *m* efflux condenser **-leckleitung** *f* drain **-leitung** *f* flow line or nipple, discharge pipe, drain **-loch** *n* drain hole, emptying hole
abflußlos without drainage **-es Gebiet** closed basin **-e Wanne** isolated basin
Abfluß-menge *f* river discharge **-mengenkurve** *f* discharge curve, hydrograph curve of discharges **-mengenverteilung** *f* division of the discharge **-nute** *f* flash groove **-öffnung** *f* discharge opening, outlet **-öffnungsgitter** *n* sink grid **-querschnitt** *m* cross section of stream discharge **-rinne** *f* drainage ditch, gutter, trough
Abflußrohr *n* outlet pipe or tube, waste (soil) pipe, discharge pipe, sewer, (drain) pipe, diverging cone **~ des verbrauchten Druckwassers** hydraulic waste pipe, hydraulic or low-pressure return pipe
Abfluß-rohrventil *n* overflow-pipe valve **-ventil** *n* discharge, delivery, escape, or drain valve **-vermögen** *n* reducing of the tidal capacity of an inlet **-wasser** *n* discharge water
Abfolge *f* origin (magmatic, sedimentary, or metamorphic processes)
abfordern to call to account (demand)
Abforderungsbrief *m* letter of recall
abformen to form, cast, mold (aviation)
Abfrage *f* interrogation **-amt** *n* answering board **-bake** *f* responder beacon **-apparat** *m* service instrument set, operator's telephone set, answering equipment, line-testing apparatus **-betrieb** *m* direct trunking
Abfrage-einrichtung *f* operator's telephone set **-empfänger** *m* responder (rdr) **-feld** *n* answering jackfield **-frequenz** *f* interrogation frequency (rdr) **-garnitur** *f* operator's set or telephone, speaking set **-gehäuse** *n* operator's telephone set **-impuls** *m* interrogation pulse **-kasten** *m* listening-in box **-klinke** *f* answering, home, or calling jack **-klinkenstreifen** *m* strip of answering or home jacks
abfragen to answer call at switchboard, inquire, interrogate, test the line (teleph), accept the call

Abfrage-platz *m* home position, answering (outgoing) position **-relais** *n* answering relay **-schalter** *m* listening or speaking key, answering switch **-schaltung** *f* answering circuit **-schnur** *f* answering wire or cord, switchboard wire **-sender** *m* interrogator (rdr) **-stecker** *m* answering plug **-stelle** *f* interrogator, inquiry station **-stellung** *f* switchboard position **-stromkreis** *m* operator's circuit **-system** *n* answering system

Abfragetaste *f* speaking key ~ (Amtsleitung, Meldeleitung) answering button (for trunk line)

Abfrageverschlüsselung *f* interrogation coding

Abfragung *f* questioning, interrogation, call (teleph), challenge (Rdr)

abfräsen to mill off, scalp

Abfräsmaschine *f* trimming machine

abfressen to corrode, eat away, consume, erode, remove by corrosive means

abfrieren to freeze off

abfrischen to renew, steep

Abfühleinrichtung *f* sensing unit

abfühlen to scan (with scanning disk), sense, examine by touch, select (sense)

Abfühler *m* card reader

Abfühl-hebel *m* contact lever **-klappe** *f* (Fernschreiber) retaining lid plate for perforated tapes **-nadel** *f* pecker, selecting needle, tape pin **-station** *f* reading station **-stift** *m* selector pin

Abfuhr *f* hauling away, removal, outlet **-anstalt** *f* sewage-removal plant

abführen to carry off or away, draw, lead, or take off, eliminate (heat), conduct, abstract, close quote marks (print)

Abführen des Hochwassers evacuation of flood-water spillways

Abfuhr-gebühr *f* carriage fee **-gelände** *n* disposal ground **-platte** *f* delivery sheet (of hopper) **-rollgang** *m* delivering live-roller table, runout with live rolls, delivery roller conveyor or gear **-stoff** *m* waste **Verarbeitung von Abfuhrstoffen** processing of waste materials **-system** *n* scavengering, cesspool system, refuse removal

Abführtisch *m* feed and delivery table (sugar mill)

Abführung *f* discharge, exhaust (steam, air, etc), evacuation, removal

Abführungskanal *m* outlet channel

Abfuhr-wagen *m* (Kehricht) waste-collecting cart **-walze** *f* delivery roller **-ziffer** *f* discharge coefficient

Abfüllanlage *f* racking or bottling plant (brewing)

Abfüllapparat *m* filling or racking apparatus, racker, decanting apparatus ~ **mit Gegendruck** back-pressure racking apparatus, counter-pressure racker

Abfüll-bock *m* racking bench or block, machine for drawing off **-bütte** *f* racking square **-darmschlauch** *m* racking gut (brewing) **-drücken** *n* filling pressure

abfüllen to empty, draw off, decant, fill up, rack **in Flaschen** ~ to bottle

Abfüllen *n* racking

Abfüller *m* siphon

Abfüll-hahn *m* filling tap **-keller** *m* filling or cleansing cellar **-maschine** *f* drawing-off or racking machine, filling machine **-raum** *m* filling or cleansing cellar

Abfüllschlauch *m* filling-up pipe, racking hose or pipe ~ **aus Darm** racking gut (brewing)

Abfüll-spund *m* drawing-off bung **-ständer** *m* racking bench or block **-station** *f* filling station **-stellen** *pl* filling points **-technik** *f* filling technique **-technische Erfordernisse** requirements of the filling technique

Abfüllung *f* filling, filling plant, decanting, tapping

Abfüll-ventil *n* (Lenkwaffe) oxygen replenisher valve (guided missile) **-vorrichtung** *f* racking apparatus, emptying contrivance **-wagen** *m* gasoline service truck

Abfunkeffekt *m* sparking (off) effect

abfüttern to feed, case, line

Abgabe *f* charge, fee, royalty, expense, tribute, rate, duty, tax, dues, sending, transmission (message), delivery, output, emission (of radiations, electrons, etc) **unter** ~ **von** by loss of, at the rate (fee) of ~ **der Steuersignale** provision of control signals

Abgabe-fähigkeit *f* ability to supply **-gerät** *n* output unit **-holz** *n* wood granted free of charge **-leistung** *f* operating speed

abgaben-frei free from duty **-pflichtig** liable to duty

Abgabe-rost *m* discharging tray **-spannung** *f* discharge voltage **-stelle** *f* supply station **-vorrichtung** *f* delivery (discharge) unit **-walze** *f* delivery roller

Abgang *m* riddlings, rejects, tailings, pairings, clippings waste, loss, escape, departure, feces, outflow, loss of energy

Abgangs-amt *n* departure station orginating office **-anstalt** *f* originating office or toll center **-bahnhof** *m* railway terminal **-bahnwinkel** *m* angle of departure (guided missile) **-dampf** *m* exhaust steam **-fehler** *m* jump (artil), vertical jump of a gun (ballistics), error in starting, error due to jump **-fehlerwinkel** *m* angle of jump (artil) **-geschwindigkeit** *f* velocity of departure **-gestänge** *n* distributing or rods pole **-gewichte** *pl* weights loaded **-kurs** *m* course at departure **-magnet** *m* starting magnet **-mikrophon** *n* sound-emission or impulse microphone **-platz** *m* outgoing or A position (teleph)

Abgangsplätze *m pl* A switchboard ~ **für Verkehr mit Wartezeit** (Regelfernplätze), point-to-point positions

Abgangs-richtung *f* line of departure (artil) **-rohr** *n* delivery tube, waste pipe **-vergütung** *f* withdrawal benefit (insurance) **-verkehr** *m* outgoing traffic **-winkel** *m* quadrant angle of departure or start **-zeit** *f* time of departure or dispatch

Abgas *n* exhaust gas or air, waste or flue gas **die Abgase entweichen** the burnt gases escape

Abgas-abführungsrohr *n* exhaust tail pipe **-abzug** *m* exhaust gas outlet **-ausgleichleitung** *f* exhaust balance line **-auslaß** *m* exhaust or waste gate **austrittsrohr** *n* waste gas escape tube **-beheizter Luftvorwärmer** exhaust-operated air preheater **-brüden** *n* gas or liquor emitted in discharging **-drosselklappe** *f* waste-gate throttle **-führung** *f* exhaust system **-gebläse** *n pl* exhaust gas-driven compressors

abgasgetriebener Turbokompressor exhaust turbosupercharger (aviation)

Abgas-ionisation *f* ionization by the exhaust gas **-kanal** *m* waste-gas flue or duct, exhaust flue **-kessel** *m* waste-heat boiler **-lader** *m* turbine-driven supercharger, exhaust supercharger **-leitschaufel** *f* exhaust stator plate **-leitung** *f* exhaust tail pipe, vent pipe **-prüfgerät** *n* exhaust-gas analyzer **-pyrometer** *m* exhaust-gas pyrometer

Abgas-regelklappe *f* control vent for exhaust gas, waste gate, flap on engine cowling **-reinigungsanlage** *f* waste-gas purifying plant **-rest** *m* residual exhaust gas **-rohr** *n* tail pipe **-rohrschlange** *f* exhaust gas cooling coil **-rückstoßer** *m* jet exhaust stack reactor **-sammelkanal** *m* waste-gas-collecting channel **-sammelleitung** *f* **-sammler** *m* exhaust manifold **-sammler** *m* exhaust collector **-schalldämpfer** *m* exhaust silencer **-speicherofen** *m* regenrative furnace, recuperator **-schornstein** *m* waste gas flue **-schubrohr** *n* ejector pipe

Abgas-strahlschub *m* exhaust-gas jet thrust **-strom** *m* exhaust blast **-stromimpuls** *m* exhaust blast momentum **-stutzen** *m* exhaust stack **-system** *n* exhaust system **-trockner** *m* waste flue-gas drier **-trübung** *f* exhaust dislocation, density of exhaust smoke **-turbine** *f* exhaust-gas or exhaust driven turbine

Abgasturbinen-gebläse *n* rotary-blower-type supercharger, turbo-supercharger **-schaufel** *f* exhaust gas turbine blade **-vorverdichter** *m* rotary induction system, exhaust-type supercharger

Abgas-turbolader *m* exhaust-driven supercharger, turbo-supercharger **-turbovorverdichter** *m* exhaust-type supercharger

Abgasung *f* discharge of exhaust gases

Abgas-ventil *n* blow-through valve **-verwertung** *f* waste-gas utilization **-verwertungsanlage** *f* waste- or flue-gas-utilizing plant **-vorverdichter** *m* turbo-compressor **-vorwärmer** *m* economizer (mach), reheater **-wärmeverwertung** *f* utilization of heat of exhaust gases

Abgautschapparat *m* coucher

abgautschen to couch

abgearbeitete Mutter finished nut

abgebaut worked out, exhausted

abgebeizt tanned

abgeben to give, give out; (Wärme) radiate, give off emit, generate, deliver, transfer, yield, lose, transmit (message) liberate, (Energie) release **Dampf.** ~ to generate or give off steam **den Strom** ~ to deliver current **Wärme** ~ to radiate heat

Abgeben *n* **der Abbindungswärme** dissipation of setting heat

abgeblaßt pallid, pale

abgebogen declinate, offset

abgebremst slowed-down

abgebrochen choppy (air wave)

abgebunden bound off, hard (cement)

abgedeckt boarded, covered, uncovered, untiled, boxed **-e Stelle** radio pocket or shadow, dead spot, concealed, burried

abgedichtet tightened, sealed, gasketad impermeable **mit Stampfmasse** ~ puddled with clay

abgedreht faced (on lathe), turned

abgedrosselt choked, throttled, derated (aviation)

abgeebnet leveled, declined, dwindled

abgefärbt decolored

abgefasert unraveled, having lost fibers or filaments

abgefast beveled, canted

abgefedert spring-mounted **-e starre Teile** rigid parts equipped with springs

abgeflacht flat(tened) **oben** ~ flat-topped **-er Bogen** depressed arch **-es Gewinde** truncated thread **an den Polen -e Kugel** oblate spheroid **-er Teil von Rundeisen** flat lug

abgefressen corroded

abgefüllt filled, packed, decanted

abgegangen dispatched signal (teleg), time of dispatch

abgegebene Leistung effective output (motors)

abgegerbt taken off by tanning

abgeglichen balanced, flush, equalized, aligned **-e Rahmenantenne** balanced loop (antenna)

abgegrenzt defined, definite **genau** ~ accurately defined, definite

abgegriffen worn, well-thumbed (book), tapped (wire)

abgehacktes Bild truncated picture

abgehärtet hardened

abgehen to depart, go off, pace, patrol, pass off, leave, start ~ **lassen** to forward, dispatch (goods) **reißend** ~ to take on rapidly (com)

abgehend outgoing (current) **-es Gespräch** outgoing call **-e Hitze** waste heat **-es Kabel** outlet cable **-e Leitung** outgoing line, outlet **-e Ortsverbindungsleitung** outgoing trunk **-e Plätze** A or outward board, outgoing positions, **-e Richtung** outgoing direction **-er Strom** outgoing current **-e Verbindung** outgoing trunk, outlet **-e Wirbelbahnen** trailing vortices (airfoil)

abgehoben lifted (off); contrasted; airborne

abgehört picked up, intercepted, monitored

abgejagt exhausted, overexerted, winded, worn-out

abgekantet chamfered, canted, beveled, subrounded **-er Balken** canted timber

abgekehrt (Richtung) looking away

abgeknickt (Röhre) bent (tube)

abgekocht boiled

abgekrackte Öle cracked oils

abgekratzter Kork scraped cork

abgekürzt abbreviated, shortened **-e Morsezahlen (-zeichen)** contracted Morse figures (signals) **-es Verfahren** abridged method

abgelagert seasoned (wood), deposited (geol), aged **-es, reifes Papier** seasoned paper

Abgelagerte *n* deposit

abgelassen tapped

abgelaufen run down (spring), expired (patent)

abgelegen remote (distant), matured

Abgelegenheit *f* isolation, remoteness

abgelegte Akten dead files

abgelehrt calibrated (gauge)

abgeleitet (Funktion) derived **-e Einheit** derived

unit **-e Funktion** derived function **-er Körper** derivate (chem)
Abgeleitete *n* derivative
abgelenkt deflected, cross cut, cut to size **nicht** (aus der Richtung) ~ undeflected
abgelesene Peilung observed bearing
abgelotet sounded
Abgeltung *f* settlement, compensation, compromise
abgemessen precise, dignified, stiff
abgeneigt unwilling, disinclined
abgenommen, von der Kontrolle ~ werden to pass inspection
abgenutzt worn-out, used up, worn down (said of sound head in tone recorder; (Bohrer usw) dull, blunt; (Isolierung) frayed **-e Schneide** blunt edge **-e Schrift** worn-out type
abgepaßtes Muster design with border **~ Warenstück** shaped article
abgeplattet oblate **~-rotationselliptisch** oblate spheroidal (Coordinates) **-er Kern** deformed nucleus **-es Rotationsellipsoid** oblate ellipsoid of revolution, flattened ellipsoid of rotation
abgepreßt squeezed
abgeprotzt unlimbered
abgepuffertes Luftpolster air buffer or cushion
abgepumpt pumped out
abgequetscht battered (type)
abgerahmt skimmed (off)
abgereichert-e Fraktion depleted fraction **-es Material** impoverished or depleted material
abgerissen torn, broken, abrupt, disjointed
abgerundet rounded off, fire-polished, dished **-e Kurbelwange** rounded cheek
abgerüstet laid up, disassembled
abgesackt sacculated, encysted
abgesaugt sucked or drawn off, evacuated
abgeschält peeled, stripped (off)
abgeschaltet disconnected, cut off **-e Regelung** *f* control loop which was opened
abgeschätzt rated, estimated, evaluated **~ auf** assessed at **-e Ankunftszeit** estimated time of arrival (aviation)
abgeschäumt skimmed
abgeschert stripped
abgeschieden separated **-er Stoff** precipitate
abgeschirmt screened, radio shielded, set tuned, adjusted **-es Einlaßventil** screened-air intake valve **-er Magnet** screened magneto **-e Niederführung** screened down-lead (radio) **-e Stelle** radio shadow or pocket, dead spot **-e Zündkerze** screened spark plug **-e Zündung** screened ignition
abgeschlackt slagged out
abgeschlagen fatigued
abgeschlämmt washed out
abgeschleuderte Lauge liquor discharge
abgeschlossen closed, terminated, sealed **in sich ~** self-contained **durch einen Widerstand ~** closed or terminated by a resistance **(ein) -es Ganzes** (a) self-contained unit **-er Innenraum** enclosed space **-e Sonde** shut-in or closed well **gegen Luft -es System** airtight system, dense air system
Abgeschlossenheit *f* seclusion
abgeschmirgelt rubbed or polished with emery
abgeschmolzen tipped off, sealed off (such as a fused shut electronic tube) **-e Röhre** sealed-off tube
abgeschnitten cut off **-er Anguß** scavenged sprue **-e Ecke** cut-off corner, truncated corner
abgeschnürt untied, tied off, enclosed (sea basin)
abgeschossene Hülsen empty cartridge cases
abgeschrägt beveled, skewed, chamfered, tapered, canted, sloped **(innen) -er Fangteil eines Hebers** (Fangklappe) bevelled clearing cam **-e Fuge** struck joint pointing, weathered pointing **-es Lineal** beveled rule, ruler, or straight edge **-er Pfosten** splayed jamb **-e Polränder** skewed pole tips **-es Schienenende** scarfed end of rail **-e Verbindung** splayed joint
abgeschreckt quenched **Stahl ~ und angelassen** steel quenched and drawn
abgeschrieben written off
abgeschwächt, nicht ~ unmitigated
abgeschweißtes Eisen refined wrought iron
abgesetzt reduced, recessed, discarded, discharged, thrown or written off, dismissed, deposed, deposited, detached, offset (aviation), set in type; (fortgenommen) removed **-er Beobachter** spotter (remote control) **-e Bohrung** stepped hole **-e Kernseife** settled or pitched curd soap **-e Schraube** necked-down bolt **scharf -e Stelle** sharp angle of steps or shoulders (mach) **-e Welle** shouldered rod
abgesichert (durch Sicherung) fused
abgesondert separated detached, discrete
abgespannt fatigued, relaxed, worn-out **-er Antennenmast** guyed antenna mast
Abgespanntheit *f* exhaustion
abgesperrt closed, no entry, no trespassing (on signs) **-er Dampf** cutoff steam
abgestanden stale
abgestellt parked
Abgestemme *n* (in den Firstenbauten), stull (min)
abgestimmt co-ordinated, adapted, tuned, in tune, syntonic **gleich ~** tuned alike **nicht ~** untuned, nonresonant, aperiodic, not in syntony or resonated **scharf ~** sharply tuned **unscharf ~** flatly tuned, broadly tuned **verschieden ~** differently tuned **auf Resonanz ~** tuned to resonance
abgestimmt-er Anodenkreis tuned anode circuit **-er Anruf** tuned ringing, harmonic ringing **-e Antenne** modulated antenna, periodic antenna **-er Dipol** tuned dipole or doublet **-e drahtlose Telegraphie** syntonized wireless telegraphy **-er Heizstrom** regulated filament current **-es Kabel** matched cable **-er Kreis** tuned circuit **-e Spule** loading coil **-er Summer** tuned buzzer **-er Verstärker** tuned amplifier
abgestochen tapped **-e Rohstahlmenge per Schmelze** tonnage of steel tapped per heat, steel poured
abgestoppt stopped
abgestorbenes Holz dead wood
abgestoßene Kante chamfered edge
abgestrahlt radiated
abgestrebt strut braced **-es Leitwerk** braced tail unit
abgestuft stepped, graded, graduated, shouldered off, scaled down, stepped down (of a pipe), staged **-e Bremswirkung** gradual breaking **-er Block** step block **nach oben -e Formation** stepped-up formation **nach unten -e Formation**

stepped-down formation **-er Widerstand** stepped resistance (elec)
abgestumpft dull(ed), truncated, blunted, dull, callous, blunt ended, with frustum **-er Kegel** truncated cone, frustrum of cone
abgetafelt delivered
abgetakelt unrigged
abgetastet sampled (TV), scanned, sensed **-es Gebiet** coverage
abgeteilt divided (up) **-er Raum** compartment
abgetötet killed, destroyed
abgetragen plotted (math), worn, threadbare, shabby
abgetrepptes Fundament footing
abgetrieben, durch den Strom (Schiff) ~ carried away by current or by tide (ship)
abgewandt turned off or away, averted **von der Luftschraube -e Seite des Motors** antipropeller end
abgewichene Bohrung deflected or deviated well
abgewickelt, unwound, wound off, rolled out **~ gezeichnet** represented as rolled out **-e Linie** evolute
abgewinkelt angular, warped **-e Form** angle-shaped form
abgewinnen to reclaim (land)
abgezapft tapped (off)
abgezogen retracted, withdrawn **-e Haut** (Fell, Leder) dressed skin
abgezweigt branched off
abgieren (Schiff) to sheer off or away
abgießen to pour, cast, found, teem (ingots), pour off, decant, spray from a plane **fallend ~** to top-pour **stehend ~** to pour on end **steigend ~** to bottom-pour **waagerecht ~** to pour horizontally
Abgießgerät *n* spray device
Abgießung *f* decantation
Abglanz *m* reflection **~ eines Öls** cast or bloom of an oil
abglänzen to oil, polish, finish
abglasen to glass or glaze
Abglasmaschine *f* glazing jack or machine
abglätten to smooth off, polish
Abgleich *m* adjustment, alignment; (Brücke) balance
Abgleich-bereich *m* balance range **-detektor** *m* null detector **-element** *n* ground equalizer conductor
abgleichen to equalize, balance, adjust, level, even, plane, square, equilibrate, lay flat, rectify (current), tune (synchronously), compensate, trim, align, calibrate **die Seiten ~** to align (type pages)
Abgleichen *n* balancing, alignment
Abgleicher *m* adjusting condenser, planisher, evener
Abgleich-fehler *m* unbalance, balance error, asymmetry **-filter** *n* ripple filter **-frequenz** *f* balancing frequeny, crossing-over frequency, tie-down point **-kasten** *m* vane alignment box **-kondensator** *m* padding or trimming capacitor, trimmer **-kurve** *f* equalization curve
Abgleich-länge *f* balance length **-latte** *f* (molding) strike **-mittel** *n* matching equipment (radar and elec) **-platte** *f* tuning spade, plate, or wand, corrector vane **-potentiometer** *n* adjusting or balancing potentiometer **-prüfer** *m* balancing tester
Abgleich-säge *f* smoothing saw **-schaltung für Verstärker** balancing two way repeaters **-signal** *n* compensating action **-spindel** *f* matching stub (radar and elec) **-spule** *f* alignment coil, cancellation coil (guided missiles) **-tisch** *m* trimming testboard
Abgleichung *f* alignment, padding, equalization, balance, balancing, leveling (removal of ground) **schlechte ~** unbalance, want of balance **~ der Frequenzempfindlichkeit** equalization, frequency response
Abgleich-verfahren *n* method of balancing, inductance variation, balance method **-vorrichtung** *f* balancing arrangement or circuit **-wicklung** *f* adjusting winding **-widerstand** *m* balancing or compensating resistance
abgleiten to sideslip (aviation), slide off, slip (off), creep
Abgleiten *n* sideslip (aviation)
Abgleit-fläche *f* surface of subsidence **-schiene** *f* bullet-deflector plate
Abgleitung *f* slippage, gliding (cryst), deformation, matching, plastic shear, yield criterion
abgliedern to disconnect, dismember
abglühen to anneal (metal), heat red hot, cool (off), cease glowing
Abgrabung *f* excavation
Abgrat-arbeit *f* trimming **-bank** *f* flash removing lathe **-einrichtung** *f* burring attachment, deburring attachment
abgraten to trim, burr
Abgrat-fräser *m* trimming cutter **-maschine** *f* scraping machine, trimming machine, flash trimmer **-matrize** *f* trimming die **-presse** *f* trimming machine, trimming press, burring press **-scheibe** *f* fettling wheel **-schere** *f* trimming shears **-schrott** *m* trimmings **-stempel** *m* trimmer punch
Abgratungspresse *f* burring machine
Abgrat-vorrichtung *f* deflasher **-werkzeug** *n* trimming tool
abgreifen to caliper, pick off, transcribe, take measurements, plot (with a compass), measure (a map offset), tune (radio), adjust, read (an instrument on a graph), tap (off) current, tap (a wire)
Abgreifen der Entfernung measuring map range with dividers or compass
Abgreifer *m* pickup, wiper, scanner, tapper
Abgreif-kippschaltung *f* reading flip-flop **-punkt** *m* tap, tapping point, balance point
abgrenzen to demarcate, divide by boundaries, separate (off), mark (off), delineate, circumscribe, bound, define or fix (limits), delimit, define
Abgrenzung *f* demarcation, definition, delimitation, partition
Abgriff *m* tap, tapping, calipering, pick-up (autom. contr) **-bügel** *m* compensating lever (radar)
Abgrund *m* abyss, precipice, fault
Abgrusung *f* crystalline decomposition
Abguß *m* casting, cast, founding, mold, paste, pouring off **mangelhaft ausgelaufener ~** short-run casting
Abgußgewicht eines Niederfrequenzinduktions-

ofens casting weight of a low-frequency induction furnace
Abgußschnauze *f* tap spout
abhaaren to unhair, scrape off hair
abhacken to chop or cut off, brush off (sugar)
Abhacken *n* cutting or brushing off
abhaken to unhook, check off (figures, numbers)
abhalten to hold off, restrain, check, prevent
abhämmern, grob ~ to hammer roughly, rough hammer
Abhandlung *f* article, treatise, discourse, paper, dissertation; transaction, proceedings
Abhang *m* slope, hillside, incline, escarpment
abhangen to trail (antenna)
abhängen to depend on, be dependent on, hang or lag behind, take off or down, overtake (an aircraft), unhook, hang up, disconnect, replace receiver, (slang) to put distance between **den Hörer ~** to remove the receiver **~ von** to derive from **voneinander ~** as a function of
abhängig dependent, sloping, inclined **linear ~** linearly dependent **~ sein von** to depend upon **voneinander ~** interdependent **-e Größe** *f* dependent variable **~ verzögerter Auslöser** inverse time-limit release **~ wirkend** acting independently, independent **-e Signale** interlock signals
Abhängige *f* dependent variable
Abhängigkeit *f* dependence, subjection, relationship, slope, disconnection **in ~ von** as a function of **gegenseitige ~** interdependence **lineare ~** linear dependence **einen Wert in ~ von einem anderen darstellen** to plot a value against another **~ von der Röhrenspannung** dependence on tube voltage **~ von der mittleren freien Weglänge** dependence on mean free path
Abhängigkeits-beziehung *f* functional relation **-faktor** *m* interaction factor **-zone** *f* domain of dependence
Abhängung *f* disconnection
abhärten to temper (steel), harden
abharzen, einen Baum ~ to remove resin from a tree.
Abhaspelmaschine *f* reeling machine
abhaspeln to reel off, wind off, unwind
Abhau, einen ~ machen to drive a gallery to the hade of a seam (min)
abhauen to cut off, knock off, leave the unit, dipple, work to the dip; (Bergbau) to cut down
Abhauen *n* pitting
abhäuten to skin, flay, excoriate, scum, free from scum (metel)
abhebbar removable
Abhebefallschirm *m* lift-off-type parachute
Abhebeformmaschine *f* flask-lift-type molding machine, draw machine (for patterns) **~ mit Abstreifkamm** flask-lift stripping machine **~ mit Druckluftpressung** flask-lift machine with air pressure or air squeezing **~ mit Handhebelpressung** flask-lifting machine with hand-lever pressure **~ mit Handstampfung** hand-ramming flask-lift machine **~ mit Wendeplatte** pattern-draw turn-over molding machine
Abhebe-kolben *m* draw piston **-kontakt** *m* take-off contact, time of take-off (elec) **-löffel** *m* cover remover, skimmer **-maß** *n* lifting gap
abheben (aufheben) to lift, raise, take or cut off, remove, uncover; (aufsteigen) pull up, become airborne, lift up; (Kontrast) contrast, set off; (abschlacken) dross; (abschäumen) skim off, draw off, relieve, retract, rise, to contrast **beim Start ~** to lift off (aviation) **vom Wasser ~** (Flugboot), to unstick (flying boat) **Geld ~** to draw money (from the bank) **den Hörer ~** to remove the receiver
Abheben *n* lifting, removal **~ des Hörers** removal of the receiver **selbsttätiges ~ des Werkzeuges beim Rückwärtsgange** automatic lifting of a tool on return stroke
Abheber *m* plow (to peel film from teeth)
abhebern to siphon off
Abhebe-säule *f* lifting rod **-signal** *n* take-off signal **-stange** *f* damper rod (piano) **-stift** *m* lifting pin or post, guide bolt or pin
Abhebe- und Durchzugformmaschine *f* flask-lift stripping-plate machine
Abhebe-vorrichtung *f* flask-lift mechanism, patterndraw mechanism, lifting device **-winkel** *m* relief angle **-zylinder** *m* draw cylinder, removable sheath, sliding sleeve
Abhebung *f* lifting, raising, draw, removal, withdrawal, retraction
abheften to detach from a holder or file, loosen, unhook, unbind, quilt (textiles)
abhelfen, einer Sache ~ to obviate, remedy **einem Übel(stande) ~** to redress a grievance
abhellen to clear, clarify
Abhieb *m* cut, hew (stone) **gänzlicher ~,** final felling
Abhilfe *f* relief, help, remedy, cure, redress, remedial action
Abhilfsmaßnahme *f* remedial measure
Abhitze *f* waste heat **-kanal** *m* waste-heat flue **-rückgewinnung** *f* waste-heat recovering **-verwertung** *f* waste-heat economy, flue-gas utilization, waste heat utilization **-verwertungsanlage** *f* waste heat recuperator
Abhitzkessel *m* waste-heat boiler, boiler that exploits energy contained in waste gases
Abhobelmaschine für Fässer cask cleaning-off or planing machine
abhobeln to plane, plane off **eine Weichenzunge ~** to plane a switch tongue (R.R.)
Abhobeln des Parketts (inlaid-) floor dressing
abholen to fetch, meet at station, collect
Abholung *f* hauling off, collection
Abholungspostamt *n* nondelivery post office
abholzen to deforest, cut down the trees
Abholzung *f* clearance
Abhör-apparat *m* listening gear, stethoscope, detector for use against submarines **-barkeit** *f* listening **-box** *f* monitoring box
abhorchen to overhear, learn by listening, listen to
Abhorchen von Flugzeugen acoustic fixing of aircraft, auditory locating, spotting, detecting or fixing aircraft position by ›sound-locater devices
Abhorch-gerät *n* monitor, check or pick-up microphonic device, stand-by circuit means **-stelle** *f* listening post or station **-trichter** *m* sound locater **-vorrichtung** *f* listening device, sound detector
Abhör-dienst *m* interception or tapping service **-empfänger** *m* monitor receiver
abhören to intercept (teleph.), tap a wire, listen

in (to), pick up, monitor **eine Telegraphenleitung ~** to tap a telegraph line **eine Unterhaltung ~** to intercept a conversation

Abhören *n* wire tapping, (program) monitoring (in broadcasting), eavesdropping **~ der Negative** direct sound reproduction from negatives **Maschine zum ~ von Tonfilmstreifen** machine for editing and rehearsing sound film.

Abhör-gefahr *f* danger of interception **-gerät** *n* sound locator or detector, radio locator (radar) **-kabine** (Radio) control cubicle **-kontrolle** *f* audio monitoring **-netz** *n* message-interception net **-station** *f* interception or listening station **-stelle** *f* listening post **-stromlauf** *m* listening or tapping circuit **-tätigkeit** *f* interception activity **-tisch** *m* sound-film-editing machine **-verfahren** *n* listening, tapping **-verstärker** *m* monitoring amplifier

Abhub *m* skimmings, draw

Abietinsäureäthylester *m* ethyl abietate

abirren to err, wander, deviate

Abirrung des Lichtes aberration of light

abisolieren to bare, skin, strip, tape, insulate

Abisolierer *m* wire skinner

Abisoliermaschine *f* stripper, wire shipping machine

abisolierter Draht *m* skinned wire

Abisolierung von Draht bare the wire (baring)

abjochen to unyoke

abkalken to remove lime

Abkalktisch *m* chalk bench

Abkant-arbeit *f* folding job **-bank** *f* folding press

abkanten to round off, chamfer, bevel, trim, level, take off edge, cant, fold, bend, subround, take off corners

Abkant-hobel *m* shooting plane, trimming tool **-klappe** *f* creasing support **-maschine** *f* folding or bending press **-presse** *f* power break, trimming press; (b. Blechen) folding press; (b. Profilen) bending press **-profil** *n* folded profile **-schiene** *f* creasing rule **-wälzfräser** *m* tooth chamfering hub **-winkel** *m* creasing angle

Abkantung mit innerem Falz edge turned over inside

abkappen to lop off (peaks or crests), clip, limit amplitude, cut off

Abkapper *m* amplitude or output limiter

Abkappschaltung *f* slicer

abkarren, die Erde ~ to wheel or to cart the ground

abkarten to prearrange, plan, plot

abkaufen to purchase

abkehlen to channel, groove

abkehren to dismiss, discharge, turn off, terminate an engagement, turn away or aside, divert, sweep or brush off **sich ~** to depart

Abkehrmaschine für Blattgold sweeping machine for gold leaf

Abkehrschein *m* license for a miner to quit

abketteln to hook up

abketten to unhook, unchain, hook up

abkimmen to chamfer the ends of the staves, form the chime (of a cask)

abkippen to tip, dump, pour, break away (aviation), dip-nose down (dive), pitch down

Abkippgeschwindigkeit *f* stalling speed (aviat)

Abkippmessung *f* stall test

abklappbar tilting, tiltable, hinged **~er Flügel** folding wing **~er Gehrungsanschlag** tilting miter-cutting guide

abklappen to swing or hinge down, out, or away, let down

Abklärapparat *m* decanter

abklären to clarify, decant, clear (up), filtrate

Abklärer *m* brightener (dyeing)

Abklär-flasche *f* decanting bottle **-topf** *m* decanting jar

Abklärung *f* clarification, decantation

Abklatsch *m* impression (print.), proof (cast)

abklatschen to stereotype, dab, reproduce, mark off, empty (chem.)

Abklatscher *m* dabber, proof printer, block-maker (print.)

Abklatschmaschine *f* dabbing machine

abkleiden to partition off, plaster

Abkleidung *f* insulation, lagging

abklemmen to disconnect from binding post, separate (by pressing), pinch off

Abkling-behälter *m* delay tank **-dauer** *f* dying-out time (sound)

abklingeln to ring off

abklingen to fade (out), decay, die down, away, or out

Abklingen *n* fading (of latent image) (phot.), dying out (sound), damping, decay, attenuation; **~ einer Schwingung** fading (radio)

abklingend evanescent **-e Kraft** damped sine vibration (asymptotic wave, vibration, oscillation)

Abklingkonstante *f* decay or damping constant

Abklingung des latenten Bildes latent image fading

Abklingzeit *f* fade-out, dying out, or decay time, time required for damping out of a vibration, cooling period, dead time **-konstante** *f* decay time

Abklopf-apparat *m* (molding) rapper **-bürste** *f* beating brush (print.)

abklopfen to scale off, chip off, descale, (molding) rap; (Kessel) descale, beat, knock off **das Hängende eines Flözes auf seine Festigkeit hin ~** to feel, sound the roof of a vein for its firmness (by knocking) (min.)

Abklopfer *m*, **Abklopfhammer** *m* scaling hammer or chipper

Abklopfvorrichtung *f* (molding) rapping device

abknebeln to unmesh

abkneifen to nip off, pinch off

Abkneifen von Gußtrichtern removing gates from castings

Abkneifer *m* cut-off

Abkneif-presse *f* gritting machine **-zange** *f* gate cutting pincers

abknicken to bend (tube) or deviate (a ray), snap or break off

abknipsen to pinch off

Abknöpfer *m* washer remover

abknüpfen to untie, take off, undo

abkochecht fast to boiling (as colors)

abkochen to boil, boil off, cook, degum **einen Sud stramm ~** to boil a strike of sugar

Abkoch-gerät *n* water-decoction apparatus **-mittel** *n* decocting medium

Abkochung *f* decoction

Abkochverlust *m* loss of weight in boiling off

Abkohlen *n* brushing, or breaking (min.), taking

Abkohler *m* coal remover
Abkohlung *f* partial decarburization on coal
abkommandieren to detach, detail
abkommandiert sein to be on detached duty **~ werden** to be detached
abkommen, vom Fahrweg ~ to drive off the road, deviate from course, lose the way
Abkommen *n* agreement, arrangement, deal, understanding, settlement, convention, contract, sight graticule or reticle (optics), point of aim, deviation **das ~ melden** to call the shot **ein ~ erfüllen** to implement an arrangement
Abkomm-fehler *m* coincidence error **-kamera** *f* aim checking camera
abkömmlich available
Abkömmling *m* derivative, descendant
Abkomponente *f* downward component
A/B-Kontaktbank *f* line bank (elec.)
abköpfen to top
abkoppeln to uncouple
Abkratzeisen *n* scraper
abkratzen to scrape off, (slang) die, scratch off
Abkratzen *n* scraping
Abkratzer *m* scraper of a conveyer, push plate
Abkreiden *n* (protective coatings) chalking, flaking
abkröpfen to offset (machine)
Abkröpfung *f* bending at angles
abkröseln to crumble
abkrücken to rake off
abkrümmen to bend off, fire, squeeze
abkrusten to scale (metal)
Abkühl-apparat *m* refrigerator
abkühlen to cool (off or down), chill, refrigerate, anneal **sich ~** to cool (down)
Abkühl-faß *n* annealing oven, cooling vat **-geschwindigkeit** *f* cooling speed (metallurgy) **-mittel** *n* cooling agent, cooling medium **-ofen** *m* annealing oven **-pause des Motors** cooling period of motor **-pumpe** *f* quench pump (for cooling pumping oil) (petroleum)
Abkühlung *f* cooling, cooling down, quenching, chilling, refrigeration, (occasionally) annealing, radiation (aviation) **beschleunigte ~** forced chill (foundry)
Abkühlungs-fläche *f* cooling surface, chilled margin **-geschwindigkeit** *f* rate of cooling **-kurve** *f* recalescence or cooling curve **-mittel** *n* refrigerant **-mittel** *n* coolant **-platz** *m* cooling down station **-prozeß** *m* cooling process **-spannung** *f* cooling strain **-verlust** *m* condensation losses **-zeit** *f* cooling period
Abkühl-verlust *m* loss from cooling **-vorrichtung** *f* cooling fixture **-zeit** *f* time taken for cooling off
Abkunft *f* agreement, breed, decent, race
abkuppelbare Trommel free drum
abkuppeln to throw out the clutch, disengage, disconnect, uncouple
Abkürzkreissägemaschine *f* cut-off circular saw
Abkürzsäge *f* crosscut saw **~ für Dauben** stave crosscut or shortening saw
abkürzen to abbreviate, abridge, shorten
Abkürzung *f* abbreviation, brevity, abridgment
Abkürzungs-symbole der Betriebsarten symbols denoting the type of service **-taste** *f* abbreviation key (typewriter) **-verfahren** *n* rapid (accelerated) method

ablackieren to remove varnish
Ablade-gebühr *f* landing charge **-hahn** *m* dump valve **-platz** *m* dump, dumping ground
abladen to discharge, unload, dump
Abladen *n* unloading, dumping
Ablader *m* unloader
Abladung *f* unloading, discharge
Abladungskosten *f pl* discharging expenses
Ablage *f* depot, repository, warehouse, storeroom, dump; delivery (print); file (of documents)
Ablage-anzeiger *m* deviation indicator **-fach** *n* card bin, pigeon hole **-instrument** *n* course deviation indicator **-magazin** *n* card receiver (punched cards) **-messung** *f* distance difference measurement (radar)
ablagern to deposit, store, age, season (wood), store in stock pile **~ lassen** to season, superseason **der Sand lagert sich ab** the sand is deposited
Ablagern des Holzes seasoning of timber
Ablagerost *m* depositing grid
Ablagerung *f* deposit, sediment, sedimentation, alluvium, alluviation, stratum, storage, aging, seasoning, depositing, precipitation, bed **-inselartige ~** island deposit
Ablagerungs-becken *n* settling chamber (pumps or dredgers) **-menge** *f* quantity of deposit **-zaun** *m* drift fence, snow fence
Ablage-schrank *m* filing cabinet **-stück** *n* file copy **-stapelmechanismus** *m* mechanisme for delivery pile
ablandig offshore **-er Wind** land wind
ablängen to saw square, crosscut, cut to length
Ablängsäge *f*, **rotierende ~** revolving crosscut saw
Abläng- und Zentriermaschine *f* cross-cut and centering machine
Ablass *m* drain, discharge, delivery, outlet, discount, allowance shunt **-düker** *m* regulating siphon (hydr.)
ablassen to drain, discharge, empty, tap, siphon or draw off; drive out, blow down; make an allowance; take off, deduct; deflate (tire), remove, dump; (senken) lower, **Roheisen ~** to run off iron
Ablassen *n* purging, bleeding
Ablass-farbe *f* temper color, oxidation tint **-grube** *f* sump or blowdown pit
Ablaß-hahn *m* delivery or discharge cock, blowoff or drawoff cock, drain cock, valve, or tap, stop and waste cock; (kleiner) pet cock
Ablaß-härtung *f* temper hardening **-kante** *f* trailing edge **-klappe** *f* blast gate **-kondensator** *m* dump condenser **-leitung** *f* main line current **-mittel** *n* tempering medium, drawing compound **-ofen** *m* tempering or drawing furnace **-öffnung** *f* outlet, discharge opening, cleanout **-öl** *n* tempering or drawing oil
Ablaß-pfropfen *m* drain plug **-rinne** *f* discharge spout **-rohr** *n* outlet tube, discharge pipe **-schlauch** *m* drain(age) hose **-schleuse** *f* sluiceway **-schraube** *f* drain plug, delivery screw **-schütz** *n* pond plug, scouring sluice, sluice board **-sprödigkeit** *f* temper brittleness
Ablaß-stopfen *m* drain or vent plug **-stufe** *f* tempering range **-stutzen** *m* pressure-tube joint

-**temperatur** *f* drawing temperature **-trichter** *m* emptying funnel **-ventil** *n* outlet or discharge valve, bleeder (drain valve), starting, safety, or blow-off valve **-vorrichtung** *f* discharging device **-wirkung** *f* drawing or tempering effect **-zapfen** *m* blowoff plug

ablasten to unload

Ablauf *m* outlet, drain, issue; (Arbeitsgang) work cycle, result, operating sequence; (Gewindebohrer) back taper; (Schneidwerkzeug) runoff of a cutting tool; (Flüssigkeiten) discharge, out flow; (Ablaß) discharge pipe, drain, outlet, waste pipe; (Ergebnis) issue, result, completion; (Frist) expiration, termination; (Elektronen) flight of electrons; (Gosse) gutter, sewer; (Verlauf) development, course, progress, flow, jet, tray downspout, outflow, expiration, lapse, start, launching rotation (of electrons), film feed (from magazine spool)

Ablauf *m* **dicker** ~ viscous molasses **eigentlicher** ~ actual movement of stern into the water (launching) **erster** ~ first run-off ~ **der Lieferzeit** expiration of delivery time ~ **des Wagenspiels** working play of the carriage **zeitlicher** ~ disappearance in (course of) time, time history

Ablaufanlage *f* humpyard (R.R.)

Ablaufapparat *m* launching cradle ~ **für Würze** *f* wort-drawing apparatus

Ablaufautomatic *f* automatic cycle control

Ablaufbahn *f* launching ways, runway **geradlinige** ~ launching slip having a constant (invariable) pitch or declivity (naval arch.)

Ablauf-berg *m* switching or double incline, hump **-blech** *n* discharge chute **-bogen** *m* runoff arc **-bohrung** *f* drain hole **-bremse** *f* retarder, slipper **-brett** *n* drain board **-deck** *n* flight deck

Ablaufen *n* running down, return(ing), expiration, taxiing (aviation) ~ **des Kabels** paying out of cable **schnelles** ~ **eines Uhrwerkes** bolting (watchworks)

ablaufen to flow or run off, expire, start, return (dial switch), drain, occur, wind, go on; (tropfen) to drip ~ **lassen** to release, let go, return (dial switch) **schnell** ~ to run off or down quickly, bolt (watchworks)

ablaufend, von selbst ~ self-sustaining **-e Polkante** trailing pole tip **-es Wasser** waste water, ebb tide

Ablauf-gerinne *n* discharge channel **-gerüst** *n* cradle, launching cradle

Ablauf-geschwindigkeit *f* run-off speed ~ (Stapellauf) launching speed

Ablauf-gewicht *n* launching weight **-glocke** *f* look box **-hahn** *m* drain cock (discharge cock) **-haspel** *f* supply drum, spool, bobbin, roll, uncoiler, pay-off reel

Ablauf-kamera *f* recording camera **-kammer** *f* outlet chamber **-kanal** *m* drain passage **-kasten** *m* uncoiling box, vacuum-pan-supply tank for runoff **-knagge** *f* slip dog **-kontrollprogramm** *n* path scheduling program **-krone** *f* swift **-kurve** *f* dropping flank (aviation) **-leitung** *f* waste or drain pipe **-linie** *f* drain line, starting line

Ablauf-öl *n* (Entparafinierung) foots oil (dewaxing) **-phase** *f* cycle of operation **-posten** *m* bridge-traffic control post (aviation) **-programm** *n* operating cycle **-punkt** *m* point of orientation, initial or starting point **-raum** *m* outlet chamber **-rinne** *f* runoff gutter, discharge channel, delivery chute **-rohr** *n* discharge pipe, outlet tube **-rohrbogen** *m* arch for drainage pipes **-rolle** *f* feed roller **-rollgang** *m* delivery roller conveyor **-rücken** *m* double incline or ridge

Ablaufschema *n* flow chart **-schlauch** *m* delivery hose **-schleuse** *f* tail lock (hydr.) **-schlitten** *m* (Lenkwaffe) launching cradle (guided missile) **-schurre** *f* discharge chute, runway **-seite** *f* trailing edge (aviat.)

Ablauf-stein *m* sink (stone) **-stift** *m* reversing pin **-strecke** *f* landing distance **-stutzen** *m* discharge pipe, drain, run-off socket **-termin** *m* expiration **-trennung** *f* classification of runnings **-trichter** *m* discharge funnel **-trommel** *f* pay-off spool

Ablauf-ventil *n* relief valve **-walze** *f* delivery roller **-wanne** *f* draining pan (oil pan) **-wasser** *n* effluent **-wasser der Diffusion** diffusion pulp water **-zahn** *m* back taper tooth

Ablaufzeit *f* return time (of a dial switch); ~ **des Nummernschalters** time of running down of the dial

Ablaufzeitpunkt *m* expiration

Ablauge *f* black, spent or waste liquor, washings

ablaugen to steep in lye, macerate, lixiviate

ablaugend saponifying

Ablaugmittel *n* saponifying medium

ablauschen to listen in, intercept, pickup (radio)

abläuten to ring off

abläutern to refine, purify, clarify, drain off, strain, filtrate, wash (ore)

Abläuterung *f* refining, purification, clarification, draining off, washing (ore)

Abläutezeichen *n* ring-off signal

abledern to wipe with chamois skin

Ablegeapparat *m* distributing apparatus (print.), plaiting machine ~ **für Lettern** distributing apparatus for types ~ **für Papierbogen** apparatus for laying-out sheets

Ablege-form *f* forme for distribution **-gefäß** *n* piling cistern **-karton** *m* file made of cardboard **-kasten** *m* delivery box, receiving box **-mappe** *f* file

Ablegen *n* depositing

ablegen to take off, let down, distribute (print.); (ausstoßen) to eject **einen Eid** ~ to take an oath **einen Satz** ~ to distribute a composition **falsch** ~ to file into wrong boxes or places **in Schwaden** ~ to lay in swaths (agr.)

Ableger *m* distributor (print.) **-antrieb** *m* distributor drive

Ablegerost *m* depositing grid, setting-down grid

Ableger-stange *f* distributing bar

Ablege-satz *m* dead matter **-schlitten** *m* distributor carriage **-span** *m* distribution rule **-tisch** *m* delivery board (table), stand, tray **-wagen** *m* distributing car **-walze** *f* delivery roller **-zahnstange** *f* toothed distributor bar

ablehnen to decline, reject, refuse, challenge, dismiss

Ablehnung *f* refusal, rejection

ablehren to gauge, true, dress, calibrate **eine Bohrung** ~ to caliper a hole against standard

ableimen to delaminate, unglue

Ableimen *n* deguming

ableitbar derivable

ableiten to lead off, turn aside; (Flüssigkeit) to drain off; (Flußstrom) divert; (Math.) differentiate; (Strom elektr.) lead away, leak off, shunt off; (Gedanken) divert, draw off, distract; (Ursprung) derive, deduce, trace; (folgern) conclude, deduce, derive, abstract; (Wärme) carry off (heat); (fehlleiten) distract, mislead; (ablenken) turn off, shunt off; (differenzieren) differentiate, pass off, conduct away, by-pass, dissipate or abduct (heat, etc.), shunt **den Strom in die Erde ~** to ground the current

Ableitblech *n* deflecting blade

Ableiter *m* arrester, charge eliminator, surge suppresser, conductor (elec.), differentiator, delivery gripper (print), lightning arrester **~ für Kondenswasser** trap

Ableiterstange *f* conductor bar

Ableit-kondensator *m* by-pass condenser or capacitor **-stange** *f* lightning conductor **-strom** *m* leakage current

Ableitung *f* (Elektr.) leakage, shunt conductance; (Math.) derivative, derivation; (Folgerung) deduction, inference; (Wärme) dissipation; (Schmierung) drain, determination, differential, coefficient, differentiation, quotient, leak, grounding, down-lead, lead-in (antenna), branch circuit, short circuit, issue (gas), withdrawal, offtake (tube), delivery pipe, diversion means (in apparatus), outlet, shunt, by-pass

Ableitung aus dem Energiesprungmodell derivation from energy gap model **~ durch den einlaufenden Flüssigkeitsstrahl** leakage through the incoming jet of liquid **~ einer Ladung** conductive discharge **~ je Längeneinheit** leakage per unit length **~ der Wärme** dissipation of the heat **~ großer Wassermengen** high discharge capacity (of a river) **Antenne mit ~** shunt-excited antenna **dritte ~ der Charakteristik** third differential of characteristic **mit ~ behaftet** leaky **dielektrische ~** dielectric leakance **mit erhöhter ~ belastet** leak-loaded **mit erhöhter ~ laden** to leak-load

Ableitungs-dämpfung *f* leakance loss **-draht** *m* shunt wire (elec.), connecting wire **-gesetz** *n* derivation law **-glied** *n* shunt element **-graben** *m* communication trench **-kanal** *m* draining channel, drain, ditch

Ableitungs-messer *m* leakage meter **-mittel** *n* derivative conductor **-öffnung** *f* deflecting louvers **-rohr** *n* outlet pipe, delivery pipe **-stollen** *m* diversion tunnel **-strom** *m* leak(age) or leakance current, stray current **-system für Regenwasser** drainage system for surface water **-widerstand** *m* leak(age) resistance, shunting resistor, bleeder resistor

Ableit-verlust *m* leak loss **-widerstand** *m* leakage resistance

Ablenk-apparatur *f* deflection apparatus **-astigmatismus** *m* deflection astigmatism **-barkeit** *f* deflectability, deviability **-blech** *n* baffle **-defokussierung** *f* deflection defocusing **-einheit** *f* deflector system **-elektrode** *f* deflecting electrode **-element** *n* deflecting member **-empfindlichkeit** *f* diffraction or deviation sensitivity, sensitivity of deflection (electronics)

ablenken to deflect, divert, avert, deviate, inflect, distract, diffract, turn or aside **den Lichtstrahl ~** to deflect, diffract (light ray) **die Magnetnadel ~** to deflect the magnetic needle **Schallwellen ~** to refract sound waves

ablenkend, nach rechts ~ dextrogyre **nach links ~** levogyre **-es Drehmoment** deflecting couple

Ablenker *m* baffle plate, deflector, diverter

Ablenk-fehler *m* deflection aberration, pattern distortion (CRT) **-fläche** *f* deflector, guide vane (jet) **-frequenz** *f* time-base frequency, sweep frequency **-führung** *f* switch (deflecting) side guard **-generator** *m* sweep generator (tv) **-gerät** *n* deflection apparatus, sweep unit, deflector means, time base, scan generator, diverter **-gitter** *n* baffle plate

Ablenk-induktivität *f* deflecting inductance **-joch** *n* deflection yoke **-kammer** *f* deflection chamber or space (in electron microscope) **-klappe** *f* (Flugzeug) deflector **-kreis** *m* sweep circuit **kreisvorspannung** *f* sweep circuit bias **-organ** *n* deflecting member

Ablenkplatte *f* deflecting, deflector or deflection plate (cathode-ray oscilloscope), deflection condenser, arc baffle, catcher, beam, baffle plate, splash plate **~ des Kühlers** radiator spreader **~ des Schmiersystems** splash plate

Ablenk-registrierung *f* deflection registering **-richtung** *f* deflecting direction **-rohr** *n* **-röhre** *f* deflecting tube (cathode-ray oscilloscope) **-rolle** *f* guide pulley, deflecting roller **-schaltung** *f* deflectional connection, deflectional system **-schuh** *m* deflecting piece

Ablenkspannung *f* deflecting voltage, sweep voltage **Symmetrierung der ~** balancing of the deflecting voltage

Ablenkspannungen, symmetrische ~ equal and opposite or symmetric sweep voltages or deflection potentials

Ablenk-spule *f* orbit shift coil, sweeping coil, deflecting or deflection coil **-stange** *f* deflecting bar (in transmission gear) **-strich** *m* deflection indicator (radar) **-strom** *m* deflecting current **-stück** *n* deflecting piece **-system** *n* deflecting or sweeping system

Ablenkung *f* turning off; (Magnetnadel) deviation, deflection; (Zerstreuung) distraction, diversion, inflection, diffraction (optics), aberration, side tracking, time base, branching off, bifurcation, derivation, bending, swing, sweep

Ablenkung *f* **des Lotes** deflection or deviation of the plumb line **~ nach links** backing, shifting counterclockwise, veer or deflection to the left **~ nach rechts** shifting clockwise, veer or deflection to the right **elektrische ~** electrostatic deflection **größte ~** amplitude of deflection **horizontale ~** horizontal or line scan, sweep or deflection

Ablenkungs-amplitude *f* amplitude of deflection **-änderung** *f* change of deviation **-anzeiger** *m* swinging base **-effekt** *m* deflecting effect **-elektrode** *f* deflecting electrode or plate **-empfindlichkeit** *f* deflection sensitivity (reciprocal of deflection factor) **-fehler** *m* zero error **-feld** *n* deflecting (electrostatic) field **-größe** *f* amount of deviation

Ablenkungs-keil *m* deflecting (deflection) wedge or prism, whipstock **-koeffizient** *f* deflection coefficient **-kondensator** *m* deflecting, deflector or deflection plate, deflection condenser **-kraft** *f* deflecting force **-linie** *f* deviation curve or line **-magnetfeld** *n* deflecting magnetic field **-messer** *m* deflectometer **-nachprüfung** *f* deviation check **-oszillator** *m* sweep oscillator **-platte** *f* deflecting plate **-prisma** *n* deviation prism

Ablenkungs-rolle *f* deviation roller **-spannung** *f* sweep voltage **-spule** *f* deflecting yoke, sweeping yoke or coil **-tafel** *f* deviation table **-vermögen** *n* rotatory power **-vervielfacher** *m* (optischer) optical) deflection multiplier **-wechsel** *m* vertical-deflection cycle, vertical or frame deflection, scan **-weite** *f* sweep amplitude **-wert** *m* amount of deviation, deviation figure **-widerstand** *m* resistance to turning **-winkel** *m* angle of deviation **-zahl** *f* coefficient of deviation or deflection

Ablenk-verstärker *m* time-base deflection amplifier (radar), deviation or sweep amplifier **-verzeichnung** *f* deflection distortion **-verzögerungsregler** *m* delaying sweep control **-vorrichtung** *f* deflection device **-werkzeuge** *pl* (Ausweichwerkzeuge) deflecting tools **-winkel** *m* angle of deflection, fleet angle

ablesbar legible, readable

Ablesbarkeit *f* reading indication ~ **des Instruments** instrument read-out

Ablese-einrichtung *f* reading apparatus, reading device **-fehler** *m* error in reading **-fenster** *n* reading window, screen **-fernrohr** *n* reading telescope **-genauigkeit** *f* accuracy of reading, reading presision **-gerät** *n* indicating instrument, indicator **-index** *m* reading index, pointer **-lupe** *f* reading magnifier, reading glass, magnifying glass **-marke** *f* pointer, reference point, index line or mark **-mikroskop** *n* reading microscope **-möglichkeit** *f* possibility or way of reading, legibility, readability

ablesen, eine Karte ~ to read (off or from) a map or chart **die Anzeige eines Meßgerätes** ~ to take a reading on an instrument **ein Meßgerät** ~ to read a value by an instrument **einen Winkel** ~ to read an angle

Ablesen *n* reading, observation, deduction **schnelles** ~ ready reading

Ableser *m* tape reader

Ablese-scheibe *f* (Peilen) dial of direction finder **-strich** *m* graduation mark, reading line **-trommel** *f* graduated or reading drum **-vorrichtung** *f* reading device **-zenithokular** *n* reading zenith eyepiece

Ablesung *f* reading, test or direct reading **eine** ~ **nehmen** to take a reading **fehlerhafte** ~ error reading **direkte** ~ direct transmission **unmittelbare** ~ direct reading ~ **in Skalenteilen** reading in scale division

Ablesungsfehler *m* error of reading

ableuchten to inspect, check with flashlight

Ableucht-halter *m* leak detector torch **-lampe** *f* inspection lamp, lamp for interior lighting **elektrische** ~ electric lamp for lighting off

Ablichtung *f* projection, photostatic copy, photostat

abliefern to deliver, supply

Ablieferung *f* delivery, supply

Ablieferungs-leitung *f* (Ausgangs-) delivery pipe **-walze** *f* delivery roller

abliegen to be spaced apart or away, differ from, set off

ablohen to bark

ablohnen to dismiss, pay off

ablöschen to quench (coke), water, slake (lime)

Ablöschen *n* quenching (coke), watering, slaking, frilling (of the emulsion, phot.)

Ablöschmittel *n* quenching agent, quenching medium

Ablöschung *f* extinguishing, quenching, extinction

Ablösearbeit *f* total internal work function

Ablösen *n* severing relief, redemption ~ **der Strömung** flow separation

ablösen to loosen, peel, strip (off), relieve (in service), separate, detach (aviation) **eine Schuld** ~ to discharge a debt **sich schichtweise** ~ to flake (aviation)

ablösend alternate (shift)

Ablöser *m* reliever

Ablösung *f* crack, parting; relief; dismissal for unfitness (aviation); cavitation (of propellers, pumps, etc.); separation of flow; eddy making (hydrodynamics); flow becoming nonlaminar, separation, burbling (aerodyn.), break-away, redemption, commutation ~ **von Elektronen** detachment of electrons ~ **der Wellenfronten** (bei Kugelwellentrichtern) launching the wave fronts

Ablösungs-arbeit *f* **-energie des Elektrons** total internal work function, excitation, or extraction energy **-fläche** *f* shake, joint (geol.) **-gebiet** *n* burbling region **-punkt** *m* separation point, transition point **-stelle** *f* point of shedding **-wert** *m* surrender value (comm.)

abloten to plumb, sound

Abloten *f* plumbing

ablöten to solder tightly, unsolder

Abluft *f* exhaust or exhaust air, used air, contaminated air, spent air

Abluftanlage *f* extraction system

Ablüfter *m* exhaust fan

Abluft-kammer *f* spent air chamber **-kanal** *m* air-outlet conduit **-leitung** *f* exhaust air duct **-lutte** *f* exhaust air duct or exit **-rohr** *n* exhaust air duct **-stutzen** *pl* ventilating outlets or stubs, ventilating exhausts **-ventilator** *m* exhaust fan

abmachen to arrange

Abmachung *f* agreement, contract, fixture, arrangement, convention, stipulation

abmagern to become emaciated, make lean

abmähen to crop

abmaischen to mash off

abmallen to mold

Abmangel *m* wantage

abmanteln to dismantle

Abmantelkopf *m* sheat stripping head

Abmantelung *f* dismantling

abmarken to demarcate

Abmarkung *f* demarcation

Abmaß *n* off size, of incorrect dimension, tolerance, allowance, deviation, variation (aviation), measurement, dimension ~ **der Nutbreite** keyway tolerance, variation of keyway width from standard (mech. engin.) **Plus- und Minus-** ~ tolerances, *i.e.*, plus and minus limits (mech. engin.) **oberes** ~ upper deviation (constr.), allowance above nominal size

unteres ~ lower deviation or variation **zulässiges ~** allowance
Abmaßgrenzen *pl* tolerance limits **~summierung** *f* accumulation of manufacturing tolerances, tolerance accumulation (avaition) **~zustand (oberer)** maximum material condition
abmatten to fatigue, tire
abmeißeln to chisel off
Abmeißeln *n* chipping
abmeßbar measurable
abmessen to measure (off or out), gauge **nach der Zeit ~** to time
Abmessen *n* metering
Abmeßpumpe *f* proportioning pump
Abmessung *f* dimension size, measuring, measurement, calibration **äußere ~** overall dimension **~ betreffend** dimensional **größte, gesamte ~** over-all dimension(s)
Abmessungs-bereich *m* range of gear sizes **-norm** *f* dimensional standard
abmildern soften (color, dyeing)
Abminderung *f* reduction
Abminderungsfaktor *m* (factor of) effiency, diminuation factor, reducing coefficient
abmontieren to dismount, dismantle, disassemble, remove (tires), strip
Abmontierung *f* dismantling
abmustern to lay or play off, evaluate; discharge (naut.), sample
Abnahme *f* (Entgegennahme) acceptance; (Verminderung) decrease, decline, diminution, decrement, reduction, degredation; (Schwundverlust) shrinkage, loss; (Geschwindigkeit) deceleration; (Entfernung) removal; (Übernahme) taking over; (Verschlechterung) decay, fall, drop, sale, lapse, draft, reduction of area, testing station **~ der Anlage** taking over the plant **~ der Helligkeit, Schärfe u.s.w., gegen den Rand des Bildes** decrease of brightness, sharp definition, etc., toward the margin of the picture **~ der Spannung** fall in tension (elec.) **bei ~ von** on purchasing **fortschreitende ~** progressive diminution
Abnahme-bedingung *f* acceptance specifications **-bereit** ready for delivery (acceptable) **-bericht** *m* acceptance report **-elektrode** *f* output or collector electrode **-folge** sequence of reductions **-flug** *m* acceptance fiying **-koeffizient** *m* coefficient of reduction **-kontrolle** *f* inspection control **-lauf** *m* acceptance run of engines, acceptance or specification test
Abnahmelehre *f* acceptance or inspection gauge **~ für Besteller** purchase inspection gauge, acceptance gauge
Abnahme-messung *f* acceptance or factory test **-möglichkeit** *f* acceptability **-reihe** *f* reduction schedule **-spule** *f* take-off spool **-stand für Lichtmaschinen** test stand for dynamos **-station** *f* receiving head end **-stelle** *f* delivery or receiving station, sound gate **-stempel** *m* inspector's acceptance stamp **-toleranz** *f* acceptance tolerance **-trommel** *f* delivery cylinder
Abnahme- und Bauaufsichtsingenieur *m* ground engineer
Abnahme-versuch *m* acceptance test **-verweigerung** *f* rejection **-vorrichtung** *f* take-away, hauloff **-zeugnis** *n* acceptance certificate **-zone** *f* delivery zone
Abnarbeisen *n* buffing slicker
abnarben to scrape, peel off
abnehmbar removable, detachable, demountable **-e Triebwerksverkleidung** detachable engine cowling **-es Verdeck** removable hood or top **-e Verkleidungsbleche** detachable panels
Abnehmbarkeit *f* detachability, removability, dismountability
abnehmen (entgegennehmen) to receive; (ablösen) detach; (abbauen) demount, dismount; (vermindern) decrease, lessen; (berauben) deprive; (ablehren) caliper; (kaufen) purchase; (Deckel usw.) remove; (prüfen) inspect; (Gewicht) lose weight; (Geschwindigkeit) slow down, decelerate; (Wasser) recede; (Strom) collect; (Qualität) deteriorate; (technische Erzeugnisse) accept, approve, test; (Spannung) drop in tension, take off, over, up, away, or on, remove, lower, decline, fall off, dwindle, unfix, wane, drop, reduce, tap, transfer (potential, etc.) **vom Boden ~** to take off **von Kontrolle ~** to pass inspection **eine Menge ~** to take off, take away **auf Null ~** to die away, decay, pick up
Abnehmen *n* unrigging, accepting, removing, decreasing **~ der Geschwindigkeit** deceleration, retardation **~ der Mischung** batching off
abnehmend decreasing **-e Bewegung** slackening motion **-e Changierung** decreasing stroke, traverse motion **-e Charakteristik** drooping characteristic **-er Querschnitt** taper (aviation) **Leitvorrichtung mit -em Querschnitt** contracting nozzle **-e Steigung** decreasing pitch
Abnehmer *m* customer, client, buyer, receiver, consumer, attendant, bankman, lender, collector brush of a dynamo
Abnehmer-arm *m* trolley pole or arm **-bürste** *f* collector brush
Abnehmerstange *f* trolley-pole or -arm contact rod **schwenkbare ~ mit zwei Abnehmerrollen** trolley overhead contact pivoted and with two wheels
Abnehmer-stelle *f* sound gate or pickup **-tausch** *m* exchange of customers
abneigen, sich ~ to turn away from, be disinclined
Abneigung *f* repugnance, declination, deviation
abnieten to unrivet, draw rivets
abnorm anomalous
abnormale Reflexionen sporadic reflections **-er Werkstoff** off gauge material
abnorme Verwerfung thrust fault (petroleum)
abnötigen to extort
abnutschen to filter by means of suction
Abnutschen *n* draining or filtering by means of a funnel
Abnutzbarkeit *f* wearing capacity, wearability, wearing quality or property, attrition quality
abnutzen to wear, wear out, off, or away, use up, deteriorate **sich ~** to wear out, fray **durch Reibung ~** to fret, gall
Abnutzung *f* (Abrieb) abrasion; (Zermürbung) attrition; (Abschreibung) depreciation, wear and tear, corrosion, pitting, erosion, scoring, scuff **~ durch Gebrauch** wear **~ der Lager** wear of the bearings **~ durch Reibung** fret, gall

(aviation) ~ **des Rohres** erosion of the bore
Abnutzungs-ausgleich *m* compensation for wear **-beständigkeit** *f* wearability, resistance to wear **-erscheinungen** *pl* phenomena of wear **-festigkeit** *f* resistance to wear and tear **-fläche** *f* utilization area **-geschwindigkeit** *f* speed of wear **-größe** *f* coefficient of wear **-maschine** *f* wear or abrasion testing machine
Abnutzungs-prüfdorn *m* wear-testing plug gauge **-prüfer** *m* wear-testing gauge **-prüfung** *f* wearing test **-satz** *m* yield or rate of depreciation **-spur** *f* trace of wear **-tiefe** *f* depth of wear **-widerstand** *m* resistance to wear or to abrasion
Aböl *n* waste oil
abölen to remove oil from
Abonnement *n* subscription
Abonnements-gebühr *f* subscription rate **-gespräch** *n* conversation by subscription
Abonnent *m* subscriber
abonnieren to subscribe
Abordnung *f* deputation, detachment, delegation
Abort *m* latrine, toilet **-anlage** *f* closet, water closet, lavatory **-grube** *f* cesspool **-kübel** *m* **für Bergwerke** privy tube for mines **-spülapparat** *m* flushing apparatus for toilet **-trichter** *m* closet hopper **-wagen** *m* toilet car
aboxydieren to oxidize off
Abpalen *n* picking, plucking
abpassen to measure, fit, adjust, cut to size, square, proportion **etwas** ~ to time a thing
Abperleffekt *m* water-repellent effect
Abpfählbuch *n* survey book (elec.)
abpfählen to peg or stake out
Abpfählen der Linie process of marking out a line by means of surveying rods
Abpflasterung *f* paving
Abpflöcken, eine Bahnlinie ~ to stake out a railway line
abplatten to flatten, oblate
Abplattung *f* flattening, collapsing (tires) ~ **(der Erde** *f*) ellipticity (of the earth)
Abplattungs-filter *n* flattening filter **-material** *n* flattening material **-theorie** *f* theory of ellipticity (Hertz) (phys. math.) **-zone** *f* flattening zone
abplatzen to peel or chip off, exfoliate, spall
abplatzsicher chip proof
abprägen to emboss
Abprall *m* resilience (aviation); rebound
abprallen to rebound, reflect, ricochet
Abprallen *n* rebounding, resiliency
Abpraller *m* ricochet, ricochet burst **-schießen** *n* ricochet fire **-wirkung** *f* ricochet effect
Abprallgeschwindigkeit *f* velocity of rebound or ricochet (ballistics)
Abprallung *f* rebound, resilience, reflection (optics)
Abprallungswinkel *m* angle of deflection
Abprall-weite *f* length of ricochet **-winkel** *m* angle of ricochet or rebound
Abpreß-brett *n* backing board
abpressen to press out, squeeze out or off **einen Buchrücken** ~ to back a book
Abpressung *f* hydraulic test
Abpreß-vorrichtung *f* pressure testing set **-walze** *f* presser
Abprodukt *n* waste product, by-product
Abprotzspritze *f* fire engine mounted on a truck
abpuffern to buffer (chem.)
abpumpen to pump out, pump down (vacuum system)
Abputz *m* plaster
abputzen to clean or dust (off), celanse, scour, howel (a cask) **einen Balken mit der Queraxt** ~ to dress a timber with the twibil **eine Mauer** ~ to plaster a wall
Abputzhammer *m* waller's hammer, walling hammer
Abquetscheffekt *m* squeezing effect
abquetschen to squeeze (out, off)
Abquetsch-fläche *f* flash edge or ridge, leak **-form** *f* flash mold **-fraktur** *f* fracture by crushing off **-kante** *f* shear edge **-nute** *f* flash groove **-rand** *m* flash ridge **-vorrichtung** *f* squeezing rollers **-walzen** *pl* squeeze rolls
abquicken to purify, separate (gold), refine (with mercury)
abrahmen to take out of a mounting frame, dismantle, skim (milk)
abrammen to ram, tamp
abrasieren to shave off
Abrasion *f* abrasion, erosion
Abrasions-ebene *f* level of abrasion **-fläche** *f* area of abrasion, plain of denudation
abraspeln to chip off, rasp
abraten to deprecate, dissuade
abrauchen to evaporate, fume off
abräuchern to fumigate (smoke)
abrauhen to chip, dress, trim roughly, fettle (castings)
Abraum *m* rubbish, rubble, waste, overburden, overlay shelf, barren rock, earth roof (geol.) **-absetzmaschine** *f* dump truck for transporting barren rock
Abräumarbeiten *pl* open cast mining, removal of barren rock
abraumen, abräumen to clear, remove
abräumen, eine Darre ~ to unload or discharge a kiln
Abräumen *n* stripping
Abräumer *m* floor clearer (of kiln)
Abraum-förderbrücke *f* conveying bridge for coal open working, overburden transporter bridge **-fördergeräte** *pl* over-burden removal equipment **-salz** *n* saline deposit **-sprengung** *f* stripping with explosives, blasting away of a shelf of rocks **-strossenband** *n* face conveyor **-schwenkbagger** *m* traversing and luffing excavator plant
Abräumung *f* emptying
abreagieren to bring a reaction to completion
Abreaktion *f* catharsis
abrechen to rake off
abrechnen to deduct, subtract, settle (account), make an accounting
Abrechner *m* money collector
Abrechnung *f* account, accounting, calculation, billing, clearing, balancing of account
Abrechnungs-nachweis *m* balance sheet, statement **-periode** *f* accounting period **-stelle** *f* clearing house **-unterlagen** *pl* accounting records
Abrecken *n* fulling
abregnen to spray gas from a plane
Abregung *f* deexcitation
Abregnungsmechanismus *m* deexcitation (me-

chanism)

abreiben to rub off, wear by rubbing, grind (colors), fray, abrade ~ **mit Bimsstein** to pounce ~ **mit Sandpapier** to sand-paper

Abreiben *n* abrasion

abreibend abrasive

Abreibe-prüfmaschine *f* abrasive-wear or abrasion tester **-vorrichtung für Malz** malt detrition apparatus

Abreibfestigkeit *f* resistance to abrasion

Abreibung *f* abrasion, attrition

Abreibungs-mittel *n* abrasive **-probe** *f* abrasion test

Abreibversuch *m* abrasion test

abreichern to deplete, strip

Abreicherung *f* depletion

Abreiß-arbeit *f* demolition work **-band** *n* breaking band **-block** *m* date block **-bogen** *m* interruption arc **-effekt** *m* discontinuity effect

abreißen to pull or take down, tear off or away, break down or away, rupture, extract (nails, spikes), separate; (Faden) to snap

Abreißen *n* change from laminar to turbulent flow (aerodyn.) ~ **der Funkverbindung** loss of radio contact ~ **des Lichtbogens** interruption, breaking of the arc ~ **der Saugsäule** breaking down of the suction column ~ **der Strömung** break away of flow ~ **der Strömung an rücklaufendem Blatt** retreating blade stall ~ **der Verbrennung** interrupted combustion

Abreißer *m* designer, rupturing device, tracing tool

Abreiß-feder *f* antagonistic, reaction, or retracting spring, rip cord or restoring spring **-funken** *m* contact-breaking spark, touch spark, spark jumping the gap **-funkenstrecke** *f* rotary spark gap, spark gap discharger **-gebiet** *n* area of separation, zone of burbling (aviation) **-grenze** *f* limit for disruption of flow **-hebel** *m* interrupter (motor), sparking tappet **-kante** *f* sharp edge **-klinke** *f* contact breaking catch **-knopf** *m* fuse-cord handle (hand grenade), rip-cord handle (parachute) **-kontakt** *m* arcing contact **-kupplung** *f* brake-away coupling **-leine** *f* rip cord **-magnetzünder** *m* make-and-break-type magneto

Abreißmechanismus, mechanischer ~ mechanical make and break

Abreiß-methode *f* adhesion method **-platte** *f* surface table or plate **-punkt** *m* stalling or burble point **-schlaufe** *f* firing cord loop **-schnur** *f* breaking cord or rip cord on parachute, fuse cord (hand grenade), lanyard **-span** *m* fragmental chip **-stecker** *m* magnetic plug **-steckergegenstück** *n* female part of magnetic plug

Abreißung *f* tearing off

Abreißungspunkt *m* burbling point, point of separation, discontinuity point (aerodyn.)

Abreiß-vorderschaft *f* automatic (push down) fore-end **-vorrichtung** *f* make-and-break mechanism, contact-breaking device **-walze** *f* web-breaking roller **-winkel** *m* stalling angle **-zünder** *m* friction igniter (pin of hand grenade), antagonistic ignition

Abreißzündmagnet *n* make-and-break magneto **Niederspannungsmagnet oder** ~ **mit Zündapparat** low-tension or make-and-break magneto with igniter

Abreißzündung *f* make-and-break ignition, touch-spark ignition, coil ignition

abreiten to ride along (the front), patrol on horseback

abresten to decant

Abrichtdiamant *f* truing diamond, diamond dresser

abrichten (anlernen) to train, drill; adjust, plane, straighten, fit (form), sharpen, trim, dress, true, surface; ~ (Schleifscheibe) to trim (grinding wheel) **Schleifsteine** ~ to trim up grindstones

Abrichter *m* dressing tool, wheel dresser, truing tool

Abricht-hammer *m* planing-hammer **-hobelmaschine** *f* planing machine, sizer **-leistung** *f* dressing capacity **-lineal** *n* straightedge **-maschine** *f* planing machine **-maschinenarbeiter** *m* rough planer **-platte** *f* surface plate **-schleifmaschine** *f* disk grinder **-vorrichtung** *f* truing attachment **-werkzeug** *n* dressing tool

Abrieb *m* wear, scour, abrasion, abrasive, breeze, fines, dust, slurry (coal) **mechanischer** ~ abrasion, attrition

abrieb-beständig wear-resistant **-prüfmaschine** *f* surface-endurance testing machine

abriebfest non-abrasive abrasion-proof **-es Buna** abrasion-proof buna rubber

Abriebfestigkeit *f* abrasive resistance, non-abrasive quality

abriegeln to cut off, block, bolt (breechblock); cordon off

Abriegelung *f* box barrage, cutting off, blocking

Abriegelungsfront *f* bolt position

abrieseln lassen to let trickle down

abrinden to decorticate, unbark, bark (off), excorticate

Abringeln *n* spontaneous breakage (of glass) in a horizontal fracture

Abriß *m* (Gebäude) pulling down, break down, demolition; (Skizze) sketch; (Entwurf) draft; (Übersicht) brief survey, outline; (Auszug) abstract, design, plan, synopsis, summary, scheme **elektromagnetischer** ~ break of magnetic flux

Abriß-punkt *m* bench mark (survey) **-selbstversteller** *m* automatic breaking timing device

abritzen to scratch off

Abritzstein *m* scratching stone

Abrohr *n* outlet or discharge pipe

Abroll-bewegung *f* rolling motion **-bock** *m* tipping bracket (R.R.) **-diagramm** *n* rolling test diagram

abrollen (wegrollen) roll away, roll off; (Photo) unwind, to unroll, uncoil, pay out, ride (on), roll on or off

Abrollen *n* peeling (of glazes), rolling motion

Abroller *m* transfer roller (feeder)

Abroll-haspel *f* uncoiler **-punkt** *m* (an d. Startbahn) turn-off point (on runway) **-spule** *f* revolving or rolling bobbin; (Laufspule) movable pirn **-stange** *f* roller bar

Abrollung *f* rolling action

Abroll-walze *f* pull-off roll **-welle** *f* unwinding shaft

abröschen to air (paper)

abrosten to rust off, corrode

abrösten to roast
Abröstung *f* (preliminary) roasting
abrücken to move off, depart, remove, clear, indent (a line), withdraw
Abrück-abschnitt *m* clearing section (elec.) **-relais** *n* relay of clearing section
Abruf *m* recall, call (comm.) order **auf ~** at or on call
Abrufauftrag *m* make and hold (paper mfg.)
abrufen to ring off, test the line, recall, repeat verbally, order
abrunden to round off or out, round, dress, true; (Zähne) **~** to chamfer **Ecken ~** to round off edges **eine Zahl ~** to express in round numbers or figures **nach unten oder oben ~** to eliminate odd numbers
Abrunden *n* finishing, rounding-off **~ von Gewinden** truncating or blunting of threads
Abrunder *m* wheel dresser
Abrund-fehler *m* error in rounding off **-fräser** *m* gear chamfering cutter **-maschine** *f* round corner cutter (print), rounding (off) machine **-stahl** *m* rounding tools **-wälzfräser** *m* tooth chamfering hob
Abrundung *f* rounding off or quarter circle, shoulder (or rounded part under bolthead), curvature, chamfer of tooth, radius of thread, fillet; (Walzkaliber) bellmouthing
Abrundungs-halbmesser *m* radius of curvature **-platte** *f* bull nosed tile **-radius** *m* radius of sphericity or curvature, contour radius **-vorschuß** *m* rounding advance (com.)
Abrundwerkzeug *n* rounding tools
abrußecht not crocking
abrußen to soot, crock (rub off).
abrüsten to dismantle, take apart, dismount, disassemble take down; disarm, demobilize
Abrüstung *f* demobilization, disarmament
Abrüst-wagen *m* breakdown truck **-zeit** *f* shutdown time (workfactor)
abrutschen to slide down, slip or glide (off), sideslip (aviation), stall **~ nach hinten, ~ über den Schwanz** to tail slide (aviation) **seitlich ~** to fall off, sideslip (of an airplane)
Abrutschen *n* sideslip, stall (aviation) **rückwärtiges ~** tail slide
Abrutsch-geschwindigkeit *f* velocity (rate) of side slipping **-instabilität** *f* spiral instability (aviation), yaw-roll instability **-winkel** *m* angle of sideslip
Absackanlage *f* sacking equipment
absacken to sag, sink (submarine), bog, drift, pitch down **mit der Flußströmung ~** to flow down a river with the tide
Absackschnecke *f* sack-filling screw
Absackung *f* sag, slump
Absack-vorrichtung *f* sacking mechanism, sack-filling device **-waage** *f* bagging scale
Absage *f* (eines Auftrages) cancellation (of an order)
absagen (Bestellung) to countermand (an order)
absägen to saw off **Holz quer ~** to cross-cut wood
absatteln to unsaddle, unseat, prop (building)
Absättigung *f* saturation, neutralization
Absättigungsprozeß *m* saturation process
Absatz *m* (Unterbrechung) intermission, pause, stop, interruption; (Verkauf) marketing, distribution, sale, disposal; (Abschnitt) break, section, period, paragraph; (Buch) paragraph; (Kesselstein) sediment; (Schuh) heel; (Stufe) stage; (Gestein) shelf, ledge; (Vertiefung) reduction, precipitate, setoff, onset, step, deposit, offset, recess, article, section, deposition, stair landing, outlet, tooth, wear and tear (film), shoulder, **~ finden** to be salable **einen ~ machen** to indent a line, start paragraph **mit einem ~ versehen** to reduce, recess, put on a heel **schlechten oder schwierigen ~ haben** to be of heavy or slow sale
Absatz-bassin *n* settling tank **-baustift** *m* heel nail, Larrabee pin **-becken** *n* settling basin **-bereich** *m* trading area **-bewegung** *f* disengagement, retreat **-bottich** *m* settling vat **-drehen** *n* shoulder turning **-drehwerkzeug** *n* roller box tool in turret **-drehvorrichtung** *f* roller box tool
Absätzen, in ~ alternately, intermittently
absatzfähig marketable, salable
Absatz-frontbeschneidemaschine *f* loose heel breasting machine **-gebiet** *n* supply area, outlet, market **-gefäß** *n* precipitation tank **-gestein** *n* sedimentary (stratified) rock
Absatz-kreis *m* area in which the product of a factory may be sold **-markt** *m* market, market outlet **-möglichkeit** *f* opening for the sale **-muffe** *f* reducing coupling box (eng.) **-säge** *f* tenon saw **-schwelle** *f* toothed or tripping bar **-steigerung** *f* sales promotion **-stift** *m* clout nail (boot) **-stockung** *f* standstill or stagnation in the market **-stück** *n* bushing **-tank** *m* settling tank **-teer** *m* by-product tar (coal tar) **-teich** *m* settling pond **-tendenz** *f* trend of sales **-weg** *m* traffic route, channel, outlet
absatzweise intermittent (motion pictures), by steps, by stages, at intervals, alternately, discontinuously, interrupted, gradually **~ bewegt** actuated or excited intermittently **~ Destillation** fractional distillation **~ Frieren** step freezing **~ Schweißung** intermittent welding, staggered weld **~ Summierung** intermitted, integration
Absatz-zeichen *n* break mark **-zylinder** *m* offset cylinder
absäuern to acidify, acidulate
Absäuerungsbad acidifying bath (acid bath)
absaufen (Motor) to flood (engine)
Absaug(e)-anlage *f* suction plant **-e-düse** *f* exhaust nozzle **-einrichtung** *f* suction device **-elektrode** *f* collector electrode
absaugen to suck off or out, exhaust (gas), draw or drain off, remove by suction, (treat with a) squeegee, syphon off
Absaugen *n* suction **~ der Grenzschicht** sucking away of boundary layer
Absauger *m* suction box, exhaust fan, exhauster or lifting jet, exhaust
Absaug-feld *n* positive field, suction field designed to draw away, drive or concentrate electrons **-flügel** *m* wing with boundary layer bleed **-flugzeug** *n* airplane with suction slot **-gebläse** *n* extractor fan, vacuum blower **-haube** *f* extractor cowl, suction hood **-kasten** *m* plenum chamber **-kolben** *m* suction or filter flask **-leitung** *f* drain or return pipe
Absaugemaschine zum Entnässen von Geweben aller Art hydrosuction machine for drying all

kinds of fabrics

Absaug(e)-pumpe *f* vacuum pump **-rohr** *n* suction tube **-sonde** *f* suction bell

Absaugung *f* exhaust, sucking off, removal by suction

Absaugungsanlage *f* exhaust installation or system, ventilation plant

Absaugvorrichtung *f* suction device (exhauster)

abschaben to scrape off, peel, grind off, abrade, skive, shave off

Abschaben *n* abrasion, scraping

Abschaber *m* scraper (of a conveyer), push plate

Abschabewerkzeug *n* scraping or scaling tool, scraper, skiver

Abschabsel *n* scrapings, shavings

Abschabspachtel *f* flexible knife

Abschabung *f* abrasion, abrasive

abschaffen to abolish, supersede, suppress, get rid of

Abschaffung *f* abolition, repeal, suppression

abschalen, Bruchsteine ~ to pare quarry stones

abschälen to pare, shell, flake off, peel, strip off, remove a layer **sich ~** to peel (aviation)

Abschäler *m* peeler

Abschaltabfall *m* (Lenkwaffe) thrust decrease at cutoff

abschaltbar disconnectible, severable, disengageable, optional (control)

Abschalt-batterie *f* cut out battery **-beiwert** *m* cut-off coefficient **-dauer** *f* cut-off period **-druck** *m* cut-off pressure

abschalten (Licht, Radio) to switch off, tune out; (Kontakt) break, disconnect, cut-off; (Maschine) turn off, put out of action, cut, disengage, stop, disconnect; (Getriebe) throw out of gear; (Kupplung) uncouple, declutch, disengage; (Wasser) shut off, arrest, detach, take off, cut out

Abschaltenergie *f* shut-down power

Abschalter *m* circuit breaker, switch, cut-out

Abschalt-funke *m* spark on breaking **-funkenstrecke** *f* earth arrester (electronics) **-funktion** *f* cut-off constant **-gerät** *n* disconnecting device **-geschwindigkeit** *f* cut-off speed **-größe** *f* cut-off constant **-hebel** *m* cut-off lever **-kennwert** *m* cut-off coefficient **-klappe** *f* cut-off valve **-klinke** *f* cut-off jack (teleph.) **-leistung** *f* rupturing, circuit opening or -breaking capacity, cut-off input

Abschaltrelais *n* cut-off relais, over-flux relay, disconnect relay **~ der Flip-Flop-Schaltung** disconnect relay of flip-flop circuit

Abschalt-sicherung *f* cut-out fuse **~** (einer Zelle) total operating time **-strom** *m* interrupting current **-stromstärke** *f* current on breaking **-stromstoß** *m* clearing pulse **-stufe** *f* cut-off stage **-taste** *f* disconnection key, cutout key **-temperatur** *f* cut-off temperature

Abschaltung *f* disconnection, arrest, switching off (elec.), all-busy circuit, uncoupling, disengagement **drahtlose ~** radio signal cut-off **automatische ~** forced release

Abschalt-ventil *n* by-pass valve **-verfahren** *n* shut-down procedure **-verstärker** *m* shut down amplifier **-vorspannung** *f* cut-off bias **-zeit** *f* clearance time, turn-off time, down time **-zelle** *f* spare cell

Abschälung *f* detaching (waterways)

abschärfen to chamfer, fair, scarf, slice

Abschärfmaschine *f* slicing machine **~ für Pappe** chamfering machine for pasteboard

abschattieren to shade off, adumbrate

Abschattierung *f* corner cutting (TV)

Abschattierungsstörsignal *n* spurious signal, shading signal (in iconoscope operation)

Abschattung *f* shading

Abschattungsverlust *m* shadow effect

abschätzen to value, estimate, tax, rate, appraise, evaluate, assess, appreciate, cast off (copy)

Abschätzung *f* estimation, evaluation, appreciation, assessment, computation, taxation

Abschaum *m* scum, dross, refuse

abschäumen to skim (off), scum, remove the dross, degrease, remove fat

Abschäum-hahn *m* surface blow-off cock **-löffel** *m* skimming ladle **-maschine** *f* skimming machine **-pfanne** *f* scumming or skimming pan

Abschäumung *f* skimming

Abschäumwanne *f* scumming or skimming pan

abscheidbar separable, precipitable

Abscheide-gefäß *n* separator **-kalorimeter** *m* separating calorimeter **-leistung** *f* dust extraction capacity

abscheiden to separate; (Metalle) refine; (Chem.) disengage, be precipitated; (Öl) separate; (aussondern) divide off, eliminate, extract, liberate; (ausseigern) segregate; (ausfällen) deposit, precipitate

Abscheideplatte *f* collecting plate

Abscheider *m* filter, settling chamber, stripper, trap (separating vessel), arrester, separator, skimmer, refiner, deflector (wave) trap; **~** (Öl) separator (oil)

Abscheidezone *f* separating zone

Abscheidung *f* separation, extraction, deposit, deposition, refining; liberation, dissociation precipitate, breakaway, discarding, scavenging, stripping

Abscheidungs-gefäß *n* sediment bowl **-geschwindigkeit** *f* rate of deposition **-mittel** *n* separating medium, precipitant **-produkt** *n* separation product **-stoff** *m* precipitate **-zentrum** *n* crystallisation center

Abscher-arbeit *f* shearing work **-block** *m* shearing block **-bolzen** *m* shearing pin or bolt

abscheren to shear off, shear, smash landing gear while landing, strip

Abscheren *n* shearing

Abscher-festigkeit *f* shearing strength, streamlined shearing **-glied** *n* shear member **-kupplung** *f* shear-pin clutch, safety coupling **-messer** *n* shearing blade **-querschnitt** *m* shearing cross section **-ring** *m* shearing collar **-span** *m* continuous chip **-stift** *m* shearing pin **-stiftsicherung** *f* safeguarding by shearing pin

Abscherung *f* shear, shearing **einschnittige ~** simple shearing **zweischnittige ~** double shearing

Abscherungs-beanspruchung *f* shearing strain **-festigkeit** *f* shearing strength **-riß** *m* shearing crack

Abscher-versuch *m* shearing test **-wert** *m* shear value **-wirkung** *f* shearing action or effect

Abscheu *m* aversion, abhorrence

abscheuern to scour, wear off, wear out, fray (cloth), chafe **sich ~** to fret

Abscheuern *n* abrasion (of insulation)
Abscheuerung *f* abrasion, scour
abschichten to separate into layers, stratify
abschicken to dispatch, send off
Abschiebehebel *m* shifting lever
abschieben to shove off, evacuate, deport
Abschieber *m* transfer (transferer), transfer conveyor
Abschiebevorrichtung für Walzwerke stripping device for rolling mills
Abschiebung *f* fault normal (petroleum), deportation
abschiefern to exfoliate, scale off
Abschieferung *f* exfoliation, scale
abschießbarer Getter flashing getter
abschießen to launch; flash (computer), fade (colors); shoot down, fire **~** (des Getters) to set off, cause vaporization (of a getter)
Abschirm-becher *m* shielding can **-becken** *n* screening can (elec.) **-bedingungen** *pl* requirements shielding **-blech** *n* screening plate (radar) **-büchse** *f* screening can **-deckel** *m* gate **-dublett** *n* screening doublet **-effekt Radius** cut-off distance
abschirmen to screen, block off, shield, preset, screen (out), blanket, adjust, set, tune (radio), guard
Abschirmen *n* screening **~ der Zündung** ignition screening
abschirmende Wirkung shielding effect
Abschirm-faktor *m* screening factor, shield factor **-gehäuse** *n* screening box (radar) **-fenster** *pl* shielded windows **-haube** *f* (radio) screen, screening or shielding box **-hülle** *f* screening cover **-hülse** *f* screening can **-kammer** shield chamber **-kappe** *f* cathode screen
Abschirm-koeffizient *m* absorption coefficient (screening function) **-konstante** *f* screening constant **-konus** *m* (der Bildröhre) conical magnetic shield **-korrektur** *f* screening correction **-mauer** *f* curtain wall **-rohr** *n* shield tube **-schlauch** *m* shielding tubing, shielding sleeve (electr.) **-spule** *f* field-neutralizing coil **-teile** *pl* radio interference screening parts **-topf** *m* screen can (radar)
Abschirmung *f* screening, shielding, screening box or shield, protection tuning, adjusting, setting (radio), clad, cladding, mask, protective screen **elektrische ~** electrical shielding **~ des Kernfeldes** atomic screening
Abschirmungs-faktor *m* shield factor **-kühlluft** *f* air cooling shield **-ringe** *pl* shield rings **-träger** *m* shield-base **-weise** *f* mode of suppression
Abschirm-wirkung *f* screening or guarding effect **-zahl** *f* screening number **-zement** *n* screening cement **-zylinder** *m* screen cylinder
abschirren to unharness
abschlacken to slag (off), tap slag, draw or skim off slag, rake out slag (or cinder), take off the slags, flush off.
Abschlack-öffnung *f* slag notch **-rinne** *f* slagging spout
Abschlackung *f* removal of slag, flush, runoff
Abschlag *m* discount, allowance, abatement, deduction, reduction **auf ~** on account
abschlagbarer Formkasten snap flask
Abschlag-drehzahl *f* backing-off speed **-einrichtung** *f* knocking-over device (weaving)
Abschlagemaschine *f* chopping machine (match mfg.)
abschlagen to knock or strike off, repulse, repel, reject; (eine Maschine) to take down, dismantle; (Matrize) to stereotype **Faden ~** to slough thread **Seil ~** to take off rope
Abschlagen und Aufwinden backing-off and winding-on
Abschlag(s)-exzenter *m* knocking-over cam (weaving) **-fortschaltkurve** *f* backing-off cam **-kamm** *m* knocking-over comb (weaving) **-kante einer Platte** knitting surface of a sinker **-kasten** *m* snap-flask (unit) **-lohn** *m* subsist **-rad** *n* cast-off burr (weaving) **-schiene** *f* knocking-over bar **-stellung** *f* cast-off position **-walze** *f* stripper roller **-zahlung** *f* part payment, payment on installment **-zeit** *f* backing-off time
Abschlamm *m* residue
Abschlämmapparat *m* blow-off valve
Abschlämmen *n* elutrition
abschlämmen to elutriate, wash (ore), purify
Abschlämmventil *n* blowoff (blowdown) valve
abschleifen to grind (down), mill, finish, polish, wear, tear down (old buildings), pumice; (Holz) to smooth, furbish; (abnutzen) abrade
Abschleifen *n* abrasion
abschleifend abrasive
Abschleifer *m* grinder
Abschleif-messer *n* grinding blade or knife **-versuch** *m* abrasion test
Abschlemmen *n* levigation
Abschlepp-band *n* car-towing steel band **-dienst** *m* recovery work, towing service
abschleppen to drag off, tow away
Abschleppen *n* towing (aviation)
Abschlepp-fahrzeug *n* wrecker salvage truck **-gerät** *n* towing equipment **-kraftwagen** *m* wrecking truck **-kran** *m* salvage crane, wrecking crane **-kommando** *n* towing detachment or detail, recovery party, wrecking section **-kupplung** *f* towing coupling, towing hook **-seil** *n* towing cable (rope) **-stange** *f* tow-rod **-wagen** *m* breakdown lorry, tow truck
Abschleudermaschine *f* hydroextractor
abschleudern to centrifuge, catapult (aviation), hydroextract (by centrifuge)
abschlichten, das Holz ~ to clean or finish off a planed surface of wood
Abschlichthammer *m* planishing hammer
abschließbare Tür lockable door
abschließen to close, lock, shut off, seal, stop, conclude, terminate, invest, surround, blank off (aviation) **dicht ~** to seal off **eine Anleihe ~** to negotiate a loan **die Bücher ~** to balance the books **eine Leitung durch ihren Wellenwiderstand ~** to terminate a line in its own impedance **einen Vertrag ~** to make an agreement or a contract
Abschließen *n* closing, barrage (of a river arm), raising
abschließend final
Abschließschraube *f* locking screw
Abschließung eines Meeresarms closing of an arm of the sea
Abschliff *m* wear, scour
Abschluß *m* (Gefäß) shutting off; (Beendigung) termination, conclusion; (Fertigmachen) com-

pletion; (Vertrag) contract; (Geschäft) transaction, deal; (Verkauf) sale, seal, joint, closure, conclusion, head, settlement, sealing (off), (fiscal) balance ~ **durch ein halbes Längs-(Quer-)glied** mid-series (mid-shunt) termination **gasdichter** ~ gastight seal **regelnder** ~ regulating barrage or dam **wasserdichter** ~ water seal

Abschluß-bericht *m* final report **-blech** *n* end cover or cap, protecting screen **-blende** *f* front diaphragm **-bogen des Flügels** curved wing tip (aviation) **-borte** *f* seaming lace **-damm** *m* retaining dike or level **-deckel** *m* cover plate, end plate **-dichtung** *f* seal, shut-off **-draht** *m* edge stiffening wire **-fehler** *m* closing error **-fenster eines Thermoelements** closing window of a thermocouple **-flansch** *m* end flange **-glas** *n* glass plug, end disk **-glashaube** *f* (bei Scheinwerfern) cover glass cowl

Abschluß-hahn *m* stopcock **-hülse** *f* terminal sleeve **-impedanz** *f* load impedance, terminal impedance **-kabel** *n* terminal cable **-kappe** *f* cap, cover strip, end cap, top cap, protecting cap **-kessel** *m* gyro compartment or case, enclosure **-kondensator** *m* terminating or block condenser **-kunstschaltung** *f* terminal network **-leiste** *f* trailing-edge strip

Abschlußmauer, gewölbte ~ semicircular head wall

Abschluß-meldung *f* final report **-membran** *m* sealing diaphragm **-muffe** *f* pothead (cable), cable head, cable-distribution plug, pothead jointing sleeve, terminal box **-mutter** *f* terminal (final) nut, cap nut or screw **-nadel** *f* needle (of a needle or tire valve) **-okklusion** *f* shutting off **-plättchen** *n* base cover **-platte** *f* stop plate **-prüfer** *m* auditor

Abschluß-rahmen *m* end frame **-rechnung** *f* final account or settlement **-ring** *m* end ring, shround ring of blades

Abschlußscheibe *f* shield, end plate, thrust (stop) washer ~ **aus Blauglas** (Kugelspiegelleuchte) light filter

Abschluß-schieber *m* stop or slide valve **-schild** *n* seal **-schirm** *m* end shield **-schraube** *f* plug **-schwelle** *f* guard wall **-stellung** *f* neutral position **-transformator** *m* **-übertrager** *m* terminal transformer **-wehr** *n* enclosing weir

Abschlußventil *n* cutoff or closing valve, paddle valve (hyd,) **automatisches** ~ automatic isolating valve

Abschluß-vorrichtung *f* closing device, closing-in arrangement, seal **-wand** *f* end plate **-werk** *n* gates for waterwork

Abschlußwiderstand *m* terminal resistance (electronics) ~ **einer Röhre** internal resistance of a tube, load resistance of a tube

Abschlußzapfen *m* delivery plug

abschmecken to judge by its flavor **mischen und** ~ to blend and flavor

abschmelzbar ablating

Abschmelz-brenner *m* falling-off or sealing off burner, tipping torch **-dauer** *f* fusing time **-draht** *m* safety fuse, cutout fuse, fuse or fusible wire

Abschmelzen *n* melting (away), smelting, fusing, flashing off, blowing ~ **einer Sicherung** blowing, fusing, or melting of a fuse

abschmelzen to melt (off), smelt, fuse (off), flash off, blow

abschmelzend ablating **-e Elektrode** *f* consumable electrode

Abschmelz-geschwindigkeit *f* burn-off rate **-schweißung** *f* flash or fusion welding, fluid welding **-schweißverfahren** *n* flash method of welding **-sicherung** *f* safety fuse, fuse, safety cutout, electrical fuse, fusible cutout **-stöpsel** *m* fusible plug **-streifen** *m* safety fuse, fuse strip **-strom** *m* fusing current **-stromstärke** *f* fusing current, blowing or striking point

Abschmelz-verfahren *n* flash-welding method, fusion welding **-zeit** *f* time of fusing

Abschmierblech *n* lubricating sheet

abschmieren to scrawl, scribble, to grease thoroughly, lubricate, set-off (slur)

Abschmieren *n* lubricating, greasing

Abschmierer *m* grease monkey

Abschmier-fett *n* lubricating grease **-gerät** *n* greasing set, lubricating equipment, lubricating set **-presse** *f* grease gun

abschmirgeln to grind or abrade with emery, polish, sandpaper **den Kollektor** ~ to sand or polish the commutator

Abschmutzbogen *m* set off sheet (print)

abschmutzen to set-off (print), soil, maculate, blot

Abschmutz-papier *n* blotting paper **-vorrichtung** *f* set-off device (print.)

abschnappen to snap off

Abschnapp-hebel *m* impulse starter lever **-kuppelung** *f* (beim Magnetzünder) impulse starter or coupling

Abschneide-apparat *m* cutting apparatus **-draht** *m* cutting wire **-frequenz** *f* cutoff frequency **-gefäß** *n* precipitation tank **-gesenk** *n* cutoff **-maschine** *f* cutting machine, cutter **-messer** *n* cutting blade, shearing blade

abschneiden to cut off, fare, come off (well), intercept, square off, remove (signal), set off (x-ray), shear off, separate (by cutting), clip, burn (cutting by oxyhydrogen) **die rohen Kanten** ~ to trim off the rough edges **eine Länge** ~ to intercept a length **den Weg** ~ to intercept **schräg** ~ to bevel ~ **mit** (bündig sein) to be flush with

Abschneiden *n* cutting off, amputation ~ **einer Krümmung** cutting out of a bend or curve ~ **von Silben und Worten** clipping, obliteration, or mutilation of speech

abschneidend mit, bündig ~ flush

Abschneide-radius *m* cut-off radius **-satz** *m* cut-off theorem **-schere** *f* shears **-schweifsäge** *f* cutting-off frame saw **-stahl** *m* cutting-off tool **-stempel** *m* cutting punch **-tisch** *m* cutting table **-wellenlänge** *f* cut-off wavelength **-winkel** *m* cutting angle

Abschneidung *f* interception

abschnellen (schnappen) to fly back, spring off

Abschnellfeder *f* starting spring

Abschnitt *m* (Geom.) segment; (Buch) section, paragraph, passage; (Teil) portion, part; (Abfall) clipping, waste, cuttings, cut, period, stage, sector, geologic shelf, interface, stretch, bay, reach, intercept **langer** ~ long length

Abschnitte, in ~ **zerlegen** to sectionize

Abschnitt(s)-baustab *m* sector construction

staff **-dämpfer** *m* span attenuator **-grenze** *f* sector boundary **-gestänge** *n* transposition pole (telegr.) **-karte** (perforiert) stub cart **-kontrolltafel** *f* sector control panel **-länge** *f* cutoff **-linie** *f* ornamental rule, cutting line (print.) **-punkt** *m* transposition point (teleph.) **-weise** *f* by sectors, in phase, in stages **-zeichen** *n* (Paragraph) section

abschnüren to mark or measure off with a cord, constrict, tie off, untie **das Holz ~** to line out stuff or timber

Abschnürung *f* chalking a line, marking off, cutting off

abschöpfen to skim off, crop, top, discard (the top of an ingot), ladle out, remove surface of molten metal

Abschöpf-löffel *m* cover remover, ladle (brewing) **-schere** *f* crop or cropping shears

abschotten to partition by means of bulkheads

Abschottung *f* compartmentalization (naut.)

abschrägen (abhalden) to slope, incline, bevel, chamfer, skew, scarf, level, taper, cant

Abschräg-hobel *n* shooting plane **-maschine** *f* bevelling machine

Abschrägung *f* bevel(ing), chamfer(ing), slope, facet **gemeißelte ~** chisel bevel

Abschrägungswinkel *m* scarfing angle (of wire ends)

Abschram *m* extremity (min.)

abschrämmen to cut, hew

abschrapen to scrape (plane) off

abschraubbar unscrewable, detachable **-er Augendeckel der Astro-Okulare** unscrewable eye cap for astronomical eyepieces

Abschraubblock *m* break-out block

abschrauben to unscrew, screw off, loosen (screw, nut) **eine Verbindung ~** to break a joint

Abschraubzange *f* break-out tongs

Abschreck-alterung *f* quench aging, hardening **-bad** *n* quenching bath **-behälter** *m* **-bottich** *m* quenching tank **-einrichtung** *f* quenching installation

abschrecken deter; quench (hot metal), chill, temper, harden metal (by sudden cooling) **das Roheisen ~** to chill iron

Abschrecken *n* quenching, chilling, tempering **~ in Blei** lead quenching or hardening **~ der Lötkolbenspitze** tip freezing (soldering defect) **~ in Luft** air tempering **~ in Wasser** water quenching or hardening

Abschreck-flüssigkeit *f* quenchant (aviation) **-form** *f* chilling form **-mittel** *n* quenching medium, compound, or solution, tempering medium or liquid **-plättchen** *n* iron chill **-probe** *f* spalling test **-punkt** *m* quenching point **-rost** *m* water screen **-spannung** *f* quenching stress **-tiefe** *f* depth of quenching or chilling

Abschreckung *f* quenching, chilling, hardening, temper, decalescence **stufenweises Härten mit unterbrochener ~** time quenching

Abschreck-vorgang *m* quenching process **-wirkung** *f* quenching or chilling effect

Abschreckzone, Neigung zur Bildung einer ~ chilling property

abschreiben to depreciate; duplicate, copy, write up **als Verlust ~** to write off as a loss

Abschreiben *n* writing up, copying

Abschreibung *f* copying, depreciation; amortization **~ und Verzinsung des Anlagekapitals** cost of interest and amortization of capital

abschreiten, eine Strecke ~ to pace a distance

Abschrift *f* copy **~ mit der Hand** handwritten or manuscript copy **beglaubigte ~** certified or legalized copy **gleichlautende ~** true copy **rechtsgültige ~** legalized copy

abschriftlich copied, in duplicate

Abschrot *m* cutter, bottom tool

abschroten to clip, chop off, crosscut, hew

Abschroten *n* fettling

Abschroter *m* anvil chisel

abschrubben to turn roughly, plane off

abschruppen to hew, rough-plane

Abschub *m* evacuation, deportation, transfer to the rear **-stelle** *f* evacuation center **-widerstand** *m* resistance

abschülpen to peel off (in patches), spall

abschuppen to scale or flake off

Abschürfung *f* scratch, abrasion

Abschuß *m* discharge or report of a gun, launch (of a rocket) **gleichzeitiger ~ mehrerer Bohrlöcher** battery of holes (blasting)

Abschuß-base *f* launching site **-bereich** *m* take-off region **-entfernung** *f* range to present position, present slant range **-höhe** altitude of target at firing point **-höhenwinkel** angular height of target when gun is fired

abschüssig steep, precipitous, sloping, abrupt, slanting **-e Bahnstrecke** downhill grade (R.R.) **-e Bahn** chute

Abschüssigkeit *f* declivity

Abschuß-kartenentfernung *f* horizontal range to target at firing point **-lafette** *f* laundier **-mannschaft** *f* launching team (g/m) **-ort** *m* launch site **-plattform** *f* launching platform **-punkt** *m* firing position **-rampe** *f* launching platform **-ring** *m* launch ring (g/m) **-rinne** *f* (Rakete) launching rail **-rohr** *n* projector **-seitenwinkel** *m* azimuth of target at firing point **-tisch** *m* launching table **-weite** *f* distance of departure **-winkel** *m* angle of departure

abschütteln to shake off or down

Abschützung *f* shielding, screening, regulation by valves

abschwächen to weaken, reduce, clear, soften, slacken, attenuate, diminish, mitigate, dilute (thin) **Farbe ~** lessen color

Abschwächer *m* reducer, reducing agent, brake, attenuator **selektiver ~** differential gain control, gain-sensitivity control **variabler ~** fader

Abschwächung *f* attenuation, reduction of intensity, weakening, fall, reduction (phot.), slackening, fatigue, decline in activity **~ des Seegangs** abatement of swell, expansion or reduction of waves

Abschwächungs-faktor *m* attenuation factor **-filter** *n* neutral density filter **-koeffizient** *m* attenuation coefficient or factor **-lösung** *f* reducer solution **-mittel** *n* diluent, thinner, reduction agent **-widerstand** *m* reducing resistance

abschwarten to square, edge (timber) decorticate

abschwefeln to desulfurize, free of sulfur (ores), calcine

Abschwefelung *f* desulfurization, calcination

abschweifen to deviate, digress, stray
Abschweifung *f* digression, excursion, straggling
abschweißen to cut by torch
Abschweißen *n* flame washing
Abschweißwärme *f* wash, cinder, or sweating heat
abschwelen to calcine, roast, carbonize under vacuum, distill under vacuum
abschwelken to wither (brewing)
abschwellen to shrink; (Geräusch) ebb away, decrease
Abschwellung *f* deswelling
abschwemmen to elutriate, rinse, wash (ore)
abschwenkbar releasable, movable, rocking
abschwenken to swing off (out) or sideways, branch off
abschwimmen to fade (print)
Abschwimmschicht *f* float fraction
abschwingen to centrifuge, hydroextract
abschwirren to centrifuge
abschwitzen to sweat off, depilate
Abschwörung *f* denial under oath, abjuration
Abschwung turning in flight operation, sharp bank
Abscisse *f* abscissa(e)
absedimentieren to sediment out
absehbar visible, conceivable, not too distant
absehen (von) to dispense with, disregard, let alone
Absehen *n* sight graticule
Absehlinie *f* collimation line
Abseide *f* flock silk
abseifen to soap
Abseifen der Schweißnähte air test with soap and water on welds
abseigern to liquate, separate by fusion, plumb, measure the perpendicular height
abseihen to filter off, strain, decant, draw, drain, percolate
Abseihhahn *m* cock with long pipe to strain off store casks
abseilen to rope down
Abseilschlinge *f* safety sling
abseits aside, apart **-liegend** remote
absenden to deliver, post, mail, send off, dispatch, forward
Absender *m* sender; dispatcher, consignor
Absendestelle *f* dispatching point, office or station of origin, sending point
Absendung *f* dispatch, shipment
absengen to singe (off), sear
absenkbar can be lowered
Absenkbarkeit *f* vertical adjustability
Absenkeinrichtung *f* raising and lowering mechanism
Absenken *n* lowering
absenken to sink, move down, lower, drop, settle, subside
Absenkformmaschine *f* drop-plate-type molding machine
Absenkung *f* settlement, subsidence, downthrow, drawdown ~ **des Grundwassers** *n* lowering of the water table ~ **in den Höhen** deaccentuation or attenuation of high frequencies, treble cut ~ **des Wasserspiegels** lowering of the level by the wind
Absenkungs-faktor *m* disadvantage factor (atom.) **-kurve** *f* curve of lowering of the groundwater level (by drainage wells, etc.)
Absenkvorrichtung *f* lowering mechanism or device
Absetzanlagen *pl* removing plants
absetzbar removable, marketable, taken on and off
Absetzbassin *n* settling tank **-becken** *n* subsiding, settling or receiving tank (sugar), settling chamber or room (crushing mill) **-behälter** *m* settling tank, thickener (flotation), settler, drainer, draining tank or chest **-bewegung** *f* withdrawal, disengagement **-bottich** *m* settling vat **-effekt** *m* precipitation effect
absetzen (verkaufen) to sell, dispose of; (Chem.) deposit, be precipitated, settle; (kontrastieren) set off (against), stand out (against); (unterbrechen) break off, discontinue, interrupt; (Maschinerie) turn a shoulder; (rechtwinklig ~) offset; (Angestellte) discharge, remove, dismiss; (Summe) deduct, deposit, precipitate, thicken, displace, set down (aviation), be grounded, lay off or plot (on a map or chart), shape course for, put down, **sich** ~ to increase distance between aircraft in flight, disengage, withdraw, deposit, settle ~ **lassen** to decant, settle ~ (im Wasser) to settle in water ~ (unter rechtem Winkel) to offset **das Muster** ~ to design (weaving) **ein Manuskript** ~ to set a copy
Absetzen *n* settling, sedimentation, deposition, thickening, removal, sale, disposal **durch** ~ **ausscheiden** to separate by sedimentation
Absetz-fläche *f* settling area **-gefäß** *n* settling tank, settler **-geräte** *pl* putting-down equipment **-geschwindigkeit** *f* settling speed **-kammer** *f* settling chamber (crushing mill) **-kasten** *m* settling tank **-maschine für den Abraumbetrieb** putting-down machine for transporting barren rock **-ort** *m* **-platz** *m* touch-down or deplaning point **-probe** *f* test for gas **-streifen** *m* belt (painting) **-tank** *m* settler, settling tank thickener **-teich** *m* settling pond
Absetzung *f* deposition, sedimentation, settling
Absetz-verhinderungsmittel *n* anti-settling agent **-vorrichtung** *f* release gear
absichern to fuse, protect by fuse
Absicherung *f* fuse protection, fusing
Absicht *f* intention, aim **eigene** ~ own plan
absichtlich purposely, deliberate
absickern to trickle down
absieben to screen (out), sieve, sift, riddle
Absieben *n*, **Absiebung** *f* screening, sieving, sifting, riddling
absieden to boil, extract by boiling
absinken to descend, sink, move down, bore, decline; ~ (Kurve) sag
Absinken *n* pass, subsidence ~ **der Spannung** dropping of the voltage
absinkende Gebiete sinking areas
absintern to leak, liquate
Absitzbehälter *m* settling tank, settler
absitzen to settle down, deposit, dismount ~ **lassen** to allow to settle, deposit or clarify
Absitz-behälter *m* precipitating tank **-grube** *f* sedimentation, clarification **-rohr** *n* deposition tube, settling cylinder **-verfahren** *n* gravity-settling process

absolut absolute, ultimate ~ **eichbares Meßgerät** absolute apparatus ~ **trocken** ovendry **-e Absorption** true absorption **-e Adresse** specific address **-er Alkohol** pure alcohol **-er Anstellwinkel** *m* absolute angle of attack (aviation) **-er Druck** absolute pressure (rolling), work of draft (pressure) **-e Einheit** absolute unit **-er Fahrtmesser** true air speedometer **-e Festigkeit** ultimate strength

absolut-e Feuchtigkeit absolute humidity **-e Fluggeschwindigkeit** air speed **-er Frequenzmesser** absolute-frequency meter **-es Gehör** *n* absolute pitch **-e Gipfelhöhe** absolute (theoretical) ceiling **-es Glied** absolute term **-er Heizeffekt** calorific value **-e Höhe** absolute altitude **-er Höhenmesser** terrain-clearance indicator, absolute altimeter

absolut-e Kraft absolute force **-es Kelvin-Elektrometer** attracted disk electrometer **-e Luftsättigung** absolute humidity **-es Maßsystem** absolute system or measurement (G.C.S. system, gram-centimeter-second system) **-e Temperatur** *f* degree Kelvin **-er Zahlenwert** nondimensional quantity

Absolut-berechnung *f* absolute terms **-blendung** *f* absolute dazzle **-geschwindigkeit** *f* absolute velocity ground speed (aviation) **-system** *n* absolute system (ballistics) **-tensor** *m* absolute tensor

Absolutwert *m* absolute value

Absolvent *m* graduate

absondern to separate, isolate, separate out, detach, segregate, eliminate, abstract, discriminate, secrete, dissociate

Absonderung *f* separation, isolation, segregation, jointing, extraction, elimination ~ **durch Kristallisation** segregation (in castings) **schiefrige** ~ slaty cleavage

Absonderungs-apparat *m* weather-forecasting equipment, meteorological apparatus **-fläche** *f* joint, breakage, fracture

Absorbens *n* absorbing substance

Absorber *m* absorber, absorbent

absorbier-bar absorbable **-barkeit** *f* absorbability, absorption (power), capacity

absorbieren to absorb ~ (an der Oberfläche), to occlude

absorbierend absorptive, absorbent **-er Abschwächer** absorptive attenuator **nicht -er Abschwächer** reactice attenuator **-er Körper** absorbing (medium) **-e Schicht** absorbing fluid or material

Absorptiometer *n* absorptiometer

absorptiometrische Methode absorption-measuring method

Absorption *f* absorption, absorption factor ~ (durch die Oberfläche) occlusion **dielektrische** ~ dielectric or electric absorption ~ **durch Defektelektronen** hole absorption ~ **durch Paarbildung** pair-production absorption ~ **ohne Spaltung** non fission absorption

Absorptionsanteil des Potentials absorption potential

Absorptions-analyse *f* analysis by absorption **-anlage** *f* absorption plant **-apparat** *m* absorbing apparatus, absorber **-element** *n* cartridge **-fähig** absorptive **-fähigkeit** absorptive power, power of absorption **-filter** *n* absorbing filter **-fläche** *f* capture area **-folie** catcher foil **-frequenzmesser** *m* absorption frequency

Absorptions-geschwindigkeit *f* speed of absorption **-grad** *m* coefficient of absorption, absorption rate **-isotherme** *f* absorption isotherm **-kante** *f* absorption discontinuity or limit

Absorptionskoeffizient *m* absorption coefficient, extinction coefficient **totaler linearer** ~ coefficient of linear absorption

Absorptions-kohle *f* activated charcoal or carbon **-kontinua** absorption spectra continuous **-kontinuum** *n* absorption band **-kraft** *f* absorptive power **-kreis** *m* absorbing or absorber circuit **-kristallspektrum** *n* crystal absorption spectrum **-kurve** *f* absorption curve **-küvette** *f* absorption cell

Absorptions-mittel *n* blocking medium, absorbing medium, absorbent, absorber **-modulation** *f* absorption modulation, Heising modulation **-öl** *n* absorbent oil

Absorptionsquerschnitt *m* effective area ~ **für Neutronen** neutron-absorption cross-section

Absorptions-regelung *f* absorption control **-rohr** *n* absorption column or tube **-röntgenspektren** *pl* absorption spectra of x-rays **-schwund** *m* fading by absorption **-spektroskopie** *f* absorption spectroscopy **-sprung** *m* absorption discontinuity **-streifen** *m* absorption bands or spectrum **-strom** *m* absorption current **-stromkreis** *m* absorbing circuit **-stufe** break through **-turm** *m* absorber or absorption tower

Absorptions-vermögen *n* absorption factor, absorption (absorptive) capacity, absorptive power **-vorlage** *f* absorption tube **-wellenmesser** *m* absorption wavemeter, grid-dip meter **-wert eines Glases** absorbing capacity of a lens

abspalten to split off, cleave, crack (oil), separate, break up, set free

Abspaltung *f* splitting off, cleavage, separation, cracking (oil)

Abspaltungsprodukt *n* separation product

abspanen to cut, chip, machine

Abspann *m* strain **-bügel** *m* anchoring bracket **-bund** *m* dead-end tie **-dachständer** *m* roof-end stand or post **-doppelstütze** *f* terminal double pin **-draht** *m* stay wire, guy wire, span wire, stretching wire, anchoring wire

abspannen to unbend, unhook, unload, unclamp; (Draht) terminate (a wire); (Strom) lower the pressure; (Technik) stay, brace, anchor; (abnehmen) unclamp, unhook, unhitch (animals), guy, strain back to, cut off, reduce, slacken, ease, relieve of tension or strain, relax, release **Dampf** ~ expand steam

Abspannen *n* staying

Abspanner *n* (step-down) transformer (elec.)

Abspann-gestänge *n* terminal pole **-hebel** *m* hammer release lever **-isolator** *m* (strain) insulator, terminal or shackle insulator **-isolatorstütze** *f* insulator pin **-kette** *f* guy **-klemme** *f* straining clamp, dead-end or anchor clamp **-konsole** *f* terminal bracket **-mast** *m* strutted, guyed, or stayed pole, dead-end tower, pylon (tower) **-material** *n* stays and guys **-mauerbügel** *m* span bracket

Abspann-öhre *f*, **-öse** *f* strain ear (elec. traction) **-pfahl** *m* span pole **-schiene** *f* straining tie **-seil** *n*

anchoring rope, guy or span rope or cable **-stange** *f* stay or terminal pole, strain pole or mast **-strecke** *f* span with anchoring or span pole (elec.) **-stütze** *f* terminal bracket (teleph.), terminal spindle

Abspann- und Verbindungsmaterial für Fahrleitungen material for termination and connection of trolley wires

Abspannung *f* anchoring, guy, removal, unloading, dead-ending, termination, span, staying, rigging (of radio masts, etc.); resonance (radio); binder, dead-end tie **~ der Leitungen** termination of wires on intermediate or terminal poles

Abspannungsgestänge *n* stay-poles terminal in telegraph poles

Abspannwerk *n* transformer station

Abspannzeit *f* unload time

Absperrarmatur *f* shut-off valve

absperrbar (which) can be closed **-er Leitungsstrang** pipe system with shutoff device

Absperr-bereich *m* antiresonance band **-damm** *m* dam **-drehschieber** *m* shut-off valve

absperren (isolieren) to isolate, confine; (Wasser, Gas) turn off, shut off; (abschließen) lock, close; (Dampf) shut off, cut off steam; (abdichten) seal (off), check, rail off, stop (engine), throttle down (gas), filter, suppress the echo, stop, stopper, cut out, cordon off

Absperren *n* closing or barrage (of a river arm)

Absperrer *m* suppressor

Absperr-flüssigkeit *f* confining or sealing liquid (as an oil, for use with water) **-gestell** *n* manhole or cable guard **-glied** *n* shut-off device, valve, sluice, electronic tube, cock, faucet, switch, cork, plug **-griff** *m* tap handle **-hahn** *m* (stop)-cock, shutoff nozzle, stopcock box, stop valve **-hülse** *f* throttle sleeve **-kegel** *m* valve cone **-klappe** *f* throttle valve **-klaue** *f* pawl **-kolben** *n* closing piston **-kreis** *m* antiresonant or antiecho circuit **-mittel** *n* scaler **-nadel** *f* closing needle **-nadelventil** *n* shutoff needle valve

Absperr- oder Regelorgan für eine Strömung valve

Absperr-organ *n* shutoff device, valve, sluice, electronic tube, cock, faucet, switch, stopper, cork, plug **-pflock** *m* shut-off plug **-schichtphotozelle** *f* rectifier photocell **-schieber** *m* (Tiefbohrg.) control gate, slide, gate, or sluice valve, wedge gate valve, gate-type shut-off valve, slide-valve damper, parallel-slide stop valve **-schlüssel** *m* **für Stoppventil** stop-valve key **-schraube** *f* stopper or plug screw **-signal** *n* block signal **-spindelverlängerung** *f* spindle extension **-sunk** *m* suction wave **-teil** *m* shutoff device, valve, sluice, electronic tube, cock, faucet, switch, stopper, cork, plug

Absperr- und Überlaufhahn *m* stop and waste cock

Absperrung *f* closing, cutoff

Absperr-ventil *n* stop, check, or shutoff valve, gate or cutout valve **-vorrichtung** *f* shutoff device, valve, sluice, electronic tube, cock, faucet, switch, stopper, cork, plug **-wirkung** *f* antiresonance device or apparatus

abspiegeln to mirror, reflect

Abspiel-dose *f* electric-phonograph sound box, pick-up **-einrichtung** *f* play-back unit

abspielen to play-back **sich ~** to take place, occur, be enacted **direktes ~** direct playback

Abspielen *n* reproduction

Abspiel-fehler *m* playback loss **-gerät** *n* reproducer **-geräusch** *n* needle scratch (phono) **-kopf** *m* play-back head **-nadel** *f* phonograph needle, stylus **-stärke** *f* play-back strength **-verlust** *m* tracing loss

abspitzen to dress

absplittern to splinter off, split off, spall

Absplittern *n* spalling (aviation)

Absplitterung *f* splintering, flaking, spallation

Absplitthebel *m* column splits

absprechen to pass judgment, deny, discuss

abspreizen to shore, strut, stay, support, prop

Abspreizung *f* stay

absprengen, mit Pulver ~ to blow off with gunpowder

Absprengschloß *n* press-off cam

Absprengung *f* separating control airplane from missile

absprenkeln to spray

absprießen to strut, brace (a frame)

Abspringen *n* bailing out (aviation) **~ des Blitzes** sideflashing of lightning **~ des Nietkopfes** bursting-off of the rivet head **~ des Tonschneiders** stylus jump

abspringen to fly off, crack off, peel off, pop off, rebound, bail out, abandon the airplane, jump off, snap off **mit dem Fallschirm ~** to bail out, descend by parachute

Abspring-ring *m* cracking-off ring **-zone** *f* (des Blitzes) rebounding zone

abspritzen to wash (off), spray off or over, cleanse, disgorge, spatter, wash with a spray

Abspritz-druck *m* ejecting pressure, spray pressure **-ring** *m* slinger ring (for propeller deicing fluid) **-rohr** *n* spurting (squirting) pipe **-vorrichtung** *f* spraying device

Absprühöl *n* chassis spraying oil

Absprung *m* jump-off, reflection (physics) **~ mit verzögerter Öffnung** delayed jump

abspulen to wind or reel off, uncoil

Abspulen *n* feeding film from magazine or feed spool, uncoiling

abspülen to wash (off), cleanse, rinse

Abspülen *n* rinsing **~ von Fasern** fiberising

Abspuler *m* reel handle

Abspüren *n* gas detection

abstammen to derive, descend, be derived

Abstand *m* (zeitlich) interval; (Spielraum) clearance; (Gewinde~) pitch; (Entfernung) distance; (Zwischenraum) space, range (rdr), difference, desisting, spacing, separation **in Abständen von . . . Kilometern** at . . . kilometer intervals **in (un)gleichen Abständen** (un)evenly spaced, equidistant **auf ~ gebracht** spaced out **in ~ halten** to separate, keep apart **~ nehmen von** to desist from

Abstand, geringer ~ proximity **gleicher ~** equidistance **hyperbolischer ~** hyperbolic distance **rechter** (verbesserter) **~** true distance **regelmäßiger ~** pitch (aviation) **mit vergrößertem ~ fahren** to proceed in open order

Abstand, ~ der Buhnen beträgt . . . Meter the groins (dikes) are . . . meters apart **~ nehmen von** to refrain or desist from **~ zwischen zwei Bändern** energy gap between two bands **~**

zwischen zwei Teilstrichen einer Strichplatte interval between two scale lines of a graticule **~ vom Pfeifpunkt** singing margin, margin of stability **~ der Leitungen vom Erdboden** clearance of pole lines **~ (je) zweier Schraubengänge** screw pitch **~ zwischen Radoberkante und Kotflügel** clearance (radially) between car wheel and guard **~ zwischen Wasser und Krone** freeboard **~ vom Rande** distance from the edge **~ zwischen Schweißnähten** pitch of weld

Abstand(s)-änderung *f* change in distance **-bedingung** *f* distance condition (phot.) **-begrenzung** *f* (Ladebegrenzung) clearance limitation **-buchse** *f* space bushing **-büchse** *f* spacer, spacer sleeve, distance piece **-fehler** *m* distance or depth error **-flansch** *m* filler piece (petroleum) **-fuß** *m* distance piece (foot)

Abstand(s)-geber *m* range transmission unit (rdr.) **-gleich** equidistant **-getreu** equidistant **-halter** *m* range spacer **-hülse** *f* spacer tube **-isolator** *m* distance piece, spacer, insulator **-keil** *m* spacing wedge **-kurzschluß** *m* short-line fault **-lehre** *f* feeler gauge, guard ring **-lehre für Elektroden** electrode gap gauge **-leiste** *f* spacing strip **-licht** *n* marker light

Abstand(s)-messer *m* distance, thickness or feeler gauge, position finder **-meßgerät** *n* distance measuring equipment **-messung** *f* range measurement **-niet** *m* separating rivet **-ring** *m* spacing sollar, ring, distance washer (ring), spacer, distance sleeve **-rohr** *n* distance piece, spacer sleeve, spreader tube **-rücklicht** *n* distance (convoy) light

Abstand(s)-säule *f* distance piece (radar) **-scheibe** *f* spacing washer, shim, space disk or plate **-schirm** range-height marker **-stange** *f* spacing bar **-steuerung** *f* distance control **-strebe** *f* drag strut

Abstandsstück *n* spacing piece, distance piece, spacer **~ zum Magnetrad** magneto-gear distance piece

Abstands-stütze *f* spreader **-tafel** *f* table of distances **-taste** *f* blank, spacing or spacer key **-unterscheidung** *f* range discrimination **-verhältnis** *n* distance ratio **-verringerung** *f* interval decrease **-zeichen** *n* space character, spacing signal **-zünder** *m* proximity fuse

abstanzen to punch off (cut off)

abstatten to render, convey, make

Abstaubband *n* dusting band

abstaubecht non-crocking (of colors)

abstauben to dust or clean (off), wipe free of dust, extract dust

Abstaub-maschine *f* bronzing machine **-pinsel** m dusting brush

Abstech-arbeiten *pl* parting-off operations **-bank** *f* cutting-off machine **-drehbank** *f* cropping bench, cutting-off lathe, trimming or slicing lathe **-eisen** *n* cutting tool

abstechen to draw-off, rack (liquid), run off (iron), part off, to cut off, tap (furnace), teem, trim (off), part **von etwas ~** to contrast

Abstechen *n* cutting off **~ von Flüssigkeiten in Gefäßen** dipping of liquids in vessels **~ der Schlacke** tapping slag

Abstecher *m* tapper (of metal), etcher, detour

Abstech-futter *n* stamping chuck **-kurve** *f* cutoff cam **-maschine** *f* cutting-off machine **-spieß** *m* tapping bar **-stahl** *m* cutting-off tool **-stahlhalter** *m* cutting(-off) tool post, cutting-off tool **-support** *m* cutoff (rest)

Abstechung *f* contrast

Abstech-vorgang *m* cutting of operations **-vorrichtung** *f* stop (or clutch) control **-werkzeug** *n* parting tool (aviation) **-wirkung** *f* tool parting

Absteck-arretierung für stufenweise Rampeneinstellung pin connection lock for stepwise setting

Absteckbolzen *m* connecting pin

abstecken to mark (off), lay or peg out, set or stake out, trace, make out **mit dem Fernrohr die Geraden ~** to range straight lines with a telescope **die Linie ~ oder ausplocken** to set out or peg out the line **ein Tau ~** to unlash or unbend a rope

Abstecken *n* setting out (surveying), plotting (a course) **~ eines Werkes** the layout of a work on the ground

Abstecker *m* aligner, plug (switch)

Absteck-fähnchen *n* surveyor's flag **-glied** *n* connecting link **-haken** *m* stake **-pfahl** *m* **-pflock** *m* iron pet, picket, stake, surveying rod **-stange** *f* stake, directing staff

Absteckung *f* (act of) tracing, marking, laying out, alignment

Abstehen *n* a cooling period (to permit glass to obtain a proper working temperature)

abstehen to slice (ingot), contrast with, be distant

abstehen lassen to let stand (cool), deadmelt, kill

abstehend distant, projecting, spreading **gleichweit ~** equidistant

Abstehenlassen *n* resting, deadmelting, killing

Absteif-balken *m* truss **-bohle** *f* poling plank, poling board

absteifen to stiffen, reinforce, support, strut, prop (mine), thicken, timber (a trench), shore, truss, stay, brace

Absteifung *f* shoring, shuttering, reinforcement, support, thickening, strut(ting) **~ eines Balkens** propping or staying of a beam **~ der Sprießung** strut

absteigen to dismount, descend

absteigend downhill, descending **-er Ast** descending branch of a trajectory **-e Differenz** backward difference **-er Zug** downtake flue

Abstellbahnhof *m* switching yard (R. R.)

abstellen to shut down or off, turn or take off, stop (engine), arrest (machinery), disconnect, switch off, detach, cut out of action, remove; park (a car); cut off (steam); throw off (roller), silence (audible signal)

Abstellen *n* stoppage

Absteller *m* dead bolt, automatic disconnecter or cut-off device (for soldering irons, etc.)

Abstell-fach *n* shelf **-feld** *n* dispersion (flying) field **-fläche** *f* stop surface **-gabel** *f* weft fork (textiles) **-gabelgitter** *n pl* weft-fork grates (textiles) **-gelände** *n* empty car yard **-geleise** *n* classification track (R. R.), siding **-gestänge** *n* stop motion rails **-gleis** *n* siding rail

Abstell-hahn *m* shuttoff cock or valve, regulating cock, stopcock **-hebel** *m* throw-off (regulating) lever, stopping lever **-kappe** *f* register **-kasten** *m*

stop-motion box **-klinke** *f* operating lever **-knopf** *m* stop or cancelling button **-kontakt** *m* stopping contact **-magnet** *m* cut-off magnet, stopping solenoid or magneto

Abstell-platz *m* parking place or area, dispersal area **-platte** *f* side rest **-raum** *m* store or lumber room **-relais** *n* stopping relay **-rost** *m* grid shelf **-schalter** *m* stop switch **-scheibe** *f* stop plate **-stange** *f* stopping rod **-stift** *m* operating pin **-system** *n* stopping mechanism

Abstellung *f* stopping, switching off (elec.), throw off **elektrische ~** shutting off of electric current **~ der Schiebemarken** disengagement of gauges

Abstell-ventil *n* stop valve **-verzögerungsrelais** *n* delay action stopping relay **-vorfeld** *n* parking apron **-vorrichtung** *f* stop(ping) device, locking device, closing apparatus, stop mechanism, release device (typewriter), **-zähler** *m* hank or meter indicator

abstemmen mit dem Meißel to chip out or off with the chisel

abstempeln to stamp

Abstempeln *n* stamping, marking

absterben to fade out, die down, wither

Absterbeordnung *f* life table

abstergieren to cleanse, treat with abstergents

Abstich *m* cutting-off separation, tapping, tap, runoff, contrast **alle . . . Stunden wird zum ~ geschritten** the pouring or casting takes place every . . . hours

Abstich-bühne *f* tapping platform **-generator** *m* wet-bottom producer (aviation) **-gewicht** *n* tap weight **-graben** *m* feeder, sow (foundry) **-grube** *f* sump, basin, pit (of hearth) **-herd** *m* pit (foundry) **-kanal** *m* runway, tap spout

Abstich-loch *n* taphole, metal notch **-öffnung** *f* taphole, tapping door, metal notch **-pfanne** *f* tap ladle **-rinne** *f* tap spout, runner gutter **-schlacke** *f* tapping slag, slag tapped out **-seite** *f* tapping side (cut-off-end) **-sohle** *f* pouring level **-spieß** *m* rake, tapping bar

Abstieg *m* drop, fall, descent, lowering, downward flight **-winkel** *m* angle of descent

Abstimm-änderung *f* tuning drift (due to temperature effects) **-anzeige** *f* tuning control, tuning crystal meter **-anzeiger** *m* tuning meter or indicator, visual tuning indicator, electric eye **-anzeigeröhre** *f* visual tuning, tuning indicator tube, electron-ray indicator tube, magic eye **-apparat** *m* tuner **-automatik** *f* automatic tuning means **-bereichüberstreichung** *f* scanning a tuning range **-einrichtung** *f* tuning device or means, tuning control, selector

abstimmbar tunable **-er Oszillator** variable-frequency oscillator **-er Steuersender** variable frequency oscillator

Abstimmbarkeit *f* gradation (photo), selectivity (radar)

Abstimm-bereich *m* tuning range **-blende** *f* synchronizing baffle **-druckknöpfe** *pl*, **(-drucktaster)** tuning pushbottons

abstimmen (Radio) to tune in; (aufeinander ~) harmonize, reconcile; (koordinieren) coordinate, bring into line; (zeitlich) time, synchronize, adjust; (Farben) shade off, come to an agreement, proportion, syntonize, tune, balance, counterbalance, vote, modulate **auf Resonanz ~** to resonate, tune to resonance **aufeinander ~** to tune one upon another

Abstimmen *n* tuning **unscharfes ~** flat tuning (teleph.)

Abstimmeter *n* tuning meter (radar)

Abstimm-fähigkeit *f* tuning property **-glimmröhre** *f* tuning-indicator glow tube, flashograph **-glühlampe** *f* glow lamp, dial light **-induktanz** *f* syntonizing, inductance **-kern** *m* tuning slug or core **-kette** *f* tuning arrangement comprising a plurality of oscillation circuits **-knopf** *m* tuning knob **-kolben** *m* plunger, piston

Abstimmkondensator *m* tuning condenser or capacitor **verlustarmer ~** low-loss tuning condenser

Abstimm-körper *m* slug tuner **-kreis** *m* tuned or tuning circuit, tank circuit **-kurve** *f* selectivity curve or characteristic, band-width curve **-melder** *m* tuning indicator **-meter** *n* tuning meter (radar) **-mittel** *n* tuning means **-pfeife** *f* matching stub **-platte** *f* tuning spade or plate, tuning wand

Abstimmschärfe *f* sharpness of tuning or of resonance, selectivity (degree of) **die ~ erhöhen** to improve the selectivity or precision of tuning

Abstimm-scheibe *f* tuning (synchronizing) plate **-skala** *f* tuning scale **-spruch** *m* tuning message **-spule** *f* tuner, tuning coil or inductance, syntonizing coil **-stichleitung** *f* stub tuner **-teil** *m* radio-frequency section of radar equipment **-ton** *m* note and wave of tuning

Abstimmung *f* adjustment, setting (of controller knobs), reconciliation, timing, coordination, paralysis circuit, tuning, modulation, syntonization, syntony, selection, accordance, formulation (of solvent or diluent mixtures), resonance **~ des Fernsehempfängers** tuning of the television receiver **~der Tonhöhe** sound tuning **~ von Tonhöhe und Welle** note and wave tuning **Vorhandensein der ~** syntony **~ durch veränderlichen Widerstand** resistance tuning, tuning by variable condenser **falsche ~** mistuning **feine ~** fine or sharp tuning **fühlbare ~** lazy tuning

Abstimmung, geheime ~ secret ballot **genaue ~** accurate tuning **stark gespreizte ~** flat tuning **grobe ~** rough or coarse tuning **induktive ~** permeability tuning **leise ~** silent tuning, quiet (automatic-valve-control) tuning **rohe ~** broad, coarse, or flat tuning **scharfe ~** sharp tuning, fine or precise tuning **schlechte ~** mistuning **ungenaue ~** off-resonance tuning **unscharfe ~** flat or imperfect tuning, broad tuning **selbsttätige ~** automatic tuning control

Abstimmungs-aggregat *n* tuning set or unit **-antenne** *f* balancing aerial **-anzeiger** *m* tuning indicator **-grad** *n* degree of tuning **-kreis** *m* balancing circuit **-kreuz** *n* tuning indicator (magic eye) **-stromkreis** *m* silent (quiet automatic-volume-control) tuning circuit

Abstimmvorrichtung *f* tuning apparatus **vielfache ~** multiple tuner **~ mit zwei Blindleitungen** double-stub tuner

Abstimm-versuch *m* synchronizing test, propellant mixing ratio test (missiles) **-zeiger** *m*

tuning indicator
abstirnen to face grind
abstocken granulate
abstoppen to stop the way (of a ship), time
Abstoppen von Zeitdauern stop-watch measurement of time intervals
abstöpseln to plug up or in
Abstoß *m* push-off
Abstoßen *n* knocking off
abstoßen to exclude, expel, eject, thrust, to knock or push off, repulse, sell (comm.), realize, shove off, cut by degrees, repel **sich gegenseitig ~** to repel mutually
abstoßend repulsory, repulsive, repelling
Abstoßen des Samenstengels cutting off the seed stalk
Abstoß-fett *n* table grease **-greifer** *m* frisket finger **-maschine** *f* grease jack
Abstoßung *f* pushing off, repulsion **gegenseitige ~** mutual repulsion
Abstoßungs-effekt *m* effect of repulsion **-kraft** *f* repulsive force or power, repulsion **-potential** *n* repulsion potential
abstrahieren to abstract
Abstrahl *m* reflected ray
Abstrahlbasis *f* sound base (tape rec.)
abstrahlen to blast, radiate, reflect
Abstrahler *m* radiator (alternating current, antenna)
Abstrahl-fläche *f* radiation or radiant surface (loud-speaker), reflecting surface or area **-richtung** *f* direction of beam (radar)
Abstrahlung *f* reflection, radiation
Abstrahlungs-erfassung *f* determination of radiation **-fläche** *f* radiating surface **-winkel** *m* angle of deflection or departure
Abstrahlwinkel *m* reflected ray angle
abstrakt abstract
Abstrakte *f* tracker, prolong (pipe organ)
Abstrebekraft *f* centrifugal force
abstreben to brace (aviation)
Abstrebung *f* buttress base; (Gebäude) raking shoring
Abstreich-apparat *m* scraper **-bürste** *f* brushing-off device **-daumen** *m* tripping or deflecting cam **-eisen** *n* scraper, skimmer (for removing slag from molten metal), sugar-mill scraper
abstreichen to scrape or strike off, strickle, skim (slag), scum, draw off, skin, lute, brush off; (auf Liste) cross off **die Walze ~** to scrape up the roll (print)
abstreichende Gase escaping gases
Abstreicher *m* scraper, skimmer, strike, wiper, rake, doctor (blade)
Abstreich-feder *f* sheet separator spring **-hacker** *m* oscillating evener **-holz** *n* straightedge **-latte** *f* (molding) strike, strickle **-lineal** *n* straightedge **-löffel** *m* skimmer, scummer **-maß** *n* strike measure **-messer** *n* scraping-off knife, scraper, doctor (mach), ductor (textiles) **-riemen** *m* strop **-teller** *m*, **-tisch** *m* disk feeder **-walze** *f* stripper roller
Abstreifanschlag um das Arbeitsstück vom Steigen mit dem Bohrer zu verhüten stripper stop (for a drill) preventing the piece from rising with the drill
Abstreifarm *m* wiper arm (of a switch)
abstreifbar strippable **-er Überzug** strip coating
Abstreifbohle *f* strike-off screed
abstreifen to strip or wipe (off), peel off, patrol, rub off
Abstreifen *n* stripping, peeling off
Abstreifer *m* skimmer, wiper, (ingot) stripper, cleaner, stripping fork **-form** *f* stripper plate mold **-platte** *f* stripper plate **-zange** *f* stripper or wiper tongs
Abstreif-formmaschine *f* stripping-plate molding machine, stripper **-kamm** *m* stripping plate **-kran** *m* stripping crane **-leiste** *f* stripping edge
Abstreifmeißel *m* guard, stripper guides **~ mit Federausgleichung** *f* guard balanced by a spring **~ mit Gewichtsausgleichung** *f* guard balanced by a counterweight
Abstreif-messer *n* rubber cleaner, feeding scoop, wiping knife, scraper, scraping knife, doctor blade (mach.) **-ölung** *f* wiper lubrication **-pinzetten** *pl* stripping tongs **-platte** *f* stripping plate **-rahmen** *m* stripping or stripper frame **-raum** *m* stripping room **-ring** *m* scraper ring **-teller** *m* rotating table with adjustable scraper **-tisch** *m* stripping table, **-vorrichtung** *f* pick-off **-walze** *f* doctor roll **-zange** *f* wire strippers
abstreuen to scatter, sprinkle
Abstrich *m* deduction, swab,scum, dross, skimming, litharge, down-stroke or trailing edge (of an impulse) **-blei** *n* lead skim **-lineal** *n* straightedge **-maß** *n* strike measure **-ofen** *m* drossing oven
Abstrom *m* wake, wash, slip stream, down-wash, downflow, down(ward) current (aerodyn), side stream
Abström-begrenzung *f* (GEM) restricted discharge **-druck** *m* flow-off (or exit) pressure
abströmen to flow away or off, pass off, escape, blow away (air or wind)
Abström-kante *f* trailing edge
Abströmung *f*, **freie ~** free discharge (GEM)
Abströmungswinkel *m* angle of down-wash
Abströmwinkel *m* exit angle (gas turbine)
abstrossen to work by graduation, cut by degrees
Abstufbarkeit *f* graduation
abstufen to grade, stage, step off, form steps, cut by degrees, graduate, shade (painting), vary
Abstufung *f* variation, progression, gradation, shade, degree, graduation or division into degrees **~der Helligkeitsunterschiede** gradation of tons **empfindungsgerechte ~** natural or subjective grading or spacing (in chromatic scale)
Abstufungs-methode *f* gradation method **-variation** *f* continuous variation **-ventil** *n* graduation valve
abstumpfen to deaden, dull, blunt, truncate (math.), neutralize, saturate (acids), correct
Abstumpfungs-fläche *f* truncating face (cryst.) **-kriterien** dulling characteristics **-wirkung** *f* dulling action
Absturz *m* fall, crash (aviation), drop, dive **zum ~ bringen** to bring down (aviation)
Absturzbauwerk *n* drop structure (hydr.)
abstürzen to dump, tumble down, crash (aviation)
Abstürzen *n* dumping **Höhenlinie, an der das ~ stattfindet** dumping level
Absturz-halde *f* dumping ground **-rinne** *f* chute **-schacht** *m* well, gully

Abstütz-basis *f* spring base **-block** *m* trestle support truss, buffer block **-bolzen** *m* stop bolt
abstützen to prop, strut, reinforce, brace, support, cut smaller, shorten; (Pfeiler) buttress
abstützende Teile staying members
Abstütz-gestänge *n* stay rods **-lager** *n* bracket, support, socket **-leiste** *f* impression support bar
Abstutzmaschine *f* shearing machine (textiles)
Abstützplatte *f* base plate
Abstützung *f* brace, support; (Gebäude) shoring ~ **der Druckstäbe** staying the compressional members
Abstützvorrichtung *f* support assembly
absuchen, das Gelände ~ to search the grounds
Absuchen *n* search, scan (radar), sweep, explore
Absuch-vorgang *m* hunting action **-wähler** *m* hunting selector
Absud *m* suds, decoction, extract
absüßen to sweeten, desugarize
Absüßer *m pl* sweet water
Absüß-kanal *m*. sweet-water channel **-kessel** *m* edulcorating-basin **-spindel** *f* sweet-water spindle **-pumpe** *f* sweet-water pump **-wasser** *n* sweet water
Abszisse *f* abscissa
Abszissen-achse *f* x-axis **-platte** *f* time-axis plate
abtafeln to plait down
Abtafel- oder Aufwickelvorrichtung *f* unwinding or unwrapping mechanism
Abtafelvorrichtung *f* cuttle motion
abtakeln to strip (a mast), dismantle
Abtast-band *n* scanning belt **-blende** scanning aperture or hole, scanning diaphragm **-blendung** *f* scanning **-bildzerleger** *m* flying spot scanner **-bündel** *n* scanning beam **-dose** *f* pickup unit, electric or pickup sound box **-einrichtung** *f* analyzer, scanning device at transmitting end, feeler device, sensing-device, pick-up
abtasten to make contact with, find, scan (TV), palpate, explore, move about, investigate by feel, hunt, sweep, pick up, probe, search, sense (comp.), read, convey, sample, caliper
Abtasten *n* scanning, exploring, analyzing, gauging; (Ton) tracking ~ **der Kippfunktion** scanning the sweep function (oscillography, electronics) **kreisförmiges** ~ circular scanning ~ **in entgegengesetzter Zeilenrichtung** oscillatory scanning
abtastender Lichtfleck scanning spot (television)
Abtaster *m* scanner, reader, spinner
Abtaster-ablenkgerät *n* scan generator unit **-kennlinie** *f* pick-up characteristic
abtastern to measure, caliper
Abtast-feld *n* scanning field, frame **-fläche** *f* scan area **-fleck** *m* scanning spot (radar, radio) **-frequenz** *f* scan frequency (= lines × frame frequency) **-gerät** *n* pickup (aviation) **-geschwindigkeit** *f* velocity of scanning, pickup velocity, pickup rate (phonograph) **-lichtstrahl** m scanning beam or scanning pencil of light **-linearität** *f* scanning linearity **-linie** *f* active line
Abtast-mikroskop *n* flying spot microscope, scanning microscope **-nadel** *f* phonograph needle **-öffnung** *f* aperture in scanning disk (television) **-optik** *f* scanning lens or optical system **-periode** *f* time base (radio) **-punkt** *m* scanning spot **-richtung** *f* direction of scanning **-röhre** (Fernsehen) camera tube (pick-up tube) **-scheibe** *f* scanning disk (television), exploring or spiral disk **-spalt** *m* scanning slot **-spalte** *f* sound-scanning slit **-stelle** *f* picture or film gate **-stift** m transmitting stylus **-strahl** *m* electron spot, beam or brush (iconoscope), scanning beam **-strahlstrom** *m* scanning beam current
Abtastung *f* scanning, exploring, exploration, sweeping out (of picture area); (Fernschreiber) sensing, exploring ~ **durch die Ablenkung des Bildes** scanning by deflection of the image ~ **nacheinanderfolgender Bildpunkte mit unsichtbaren ultraroten Strahlen** noctovisor scan (using infrared rays) ~ **mit gleichbleibender Geschwindigkeit** constant-speed scanning ~ **mit veränderlicher Geschwindigkeit** variable-speed scanning ~ **mit bewegter Rasterblende** scanning with a moving diaphragm **quadratische** ~ **nacheinanderfolgender Bildpunkte** square-law scanning **sprungweise** ~ **nacheinanderfolgender Bildpunkte** interlaced scanning **unmittelbar aufeinanderfolgende** ~ progressive, sequential, or straight scanning
Abtast-verstärker *m* preamplifier (reproducing amplifier) **-vorrichtung** *f* hunting device, scanner **-vorschub** *m* scanning traverse **-zeile** *f* scanning line or strip
Abtaueinrichtung *f* deicing or defrosting device for trolley wires
abtauen to defrost (refrigerators), thaw off
Abteil *n* division, compartment, leak in an electric current, separation, classify
abteilen to divide, classifff, departmentalize, separate **durch eine Wand** ~ to partition off
Abteilen *n* (in Fächer) compartition
Abteilung *f* department, section, series, compartment, division, unit, panel, heading, detachment, leakage (of current) ~ **eines Gestells** bay
Abteilungs-linie *f* dividing rule **-ventilator** *m* panel ventilating fan
Abteil-ventil *n* block valve **-vorrichtung** *f* separator
abtelegraphieren to transmit
Abteufarbeit *f* sinking work
abteufen to deepen, sink (a shaft), bore, surface (excavation) **den Schacht** ~ to sink the shaft
Abteufen *n* deepening, sinking (a shaft)
Abteuf-gerüst *n* sinking trestle **-kübel** *m* sinking bucket **-kabel** *n* shaft cable **-pumpe** *f* bore-hole pump
Abteufung *f* sinking (shaft)
abtippen to copy (by typing)
Abtitrierungspunkt *m* end point, completion of titration
abtönen to shade off, tint, tone down, soften, tune (teleg.)
Abtönen *n* shading (print)
Abtönfarbe *f* tinting color
Abtönung *f* gradation
Abtönungsfarbstoff *m* shading dyestuff
abtöten to extinguish, destroy, kill, mortify
Abtöten *n* extinction, destruction
Abtrag *m* deduction, cut (in earthwork), excavation, excavated material
abtragen to remove, carry (away), take down,

wreck, level, raze, plot or lay off, diminish in size; (Gebrauch), wear off, mark off

Abtragen *n* sputtering (of metals from filaments), erosion, using up of filaments, sloughing action ~ **eines Bauwerks** demolition of a building

Abtragevorrichtung *f* transferer

Abtraghöhe *f* height of dump, height of site

Abtragsböschung *f* slope of embankment

Abtragsmassen ermitteln to take out quantities (moving dirt or soil)

Abtragsvermögen *n* removing capacity

Abtragung *f* abrasion, denudation, erosion, ablation, disintegration, attrition, degradation, diminution in size, marking off, liquidation

Abtransport *m* evacuation, removal

Abtransporteur *m* discharge conveyor

abtransportieren to convey, ship, evacuate

Abtraufe der Dachrinne spout of a gutter, gargoyle

Abtraufen *f pl* eaves of a roof

Abtreibeapparat *m* still, decanter

Abtreibearbeit *f* (mit senkrechtem Anstecken der Pfähle), sinking by piling ~ **in losem Gebirge** piling through loose rock, sheeting pile

Abtreibe-herd *m* refining hearth **-kolonne** *f* exhausting column

abtreiben to force off, carry away, drive off, decant, expel (fumes), distill off, cupellate, separate, wash, scrub, clean up, sink by piling, drift, yaw **Gestein** ~ to take off the gangue **seewärts** ~ to fall to leeward

Abtreiben *n* drift

abtreibender Maschinenteil driver

Abtreibe-ofen *m* cupeling furnace, cupel furnace **-pfahl** *m* lath

Abtreiber *m* decanter, still

Abtreibesäule *f* column still

Abtreib-kapelle *f* refining cupel (metal) **-schmelze** *f* refining melt **-winkel** *m* angle of yaw (aviation)

abtrennbar (Formular) detachable (form)

abtrennen to cut off, dissociate, separate, sever

Abtrenner *m* separator

Abtrenn-relais *n* cutoff relay **-schalter** *m* splitting key

Abtrennung *f* separation, dissociation, cutoff, severance, division **vollkommene** ~ exhaustion

Abtrennungspunkt *m* cutoff point

abtreppen to cut steps **eine Mauer** ~ to wall in the form of stairs

Abtreppung *f* offset or step

abtreten to dismiss, cede, assign, convey, transfer ~ **lassen** to dismiss

Abtretender *m* assignor

Abtretung *f* assignment, assignation, cession

Abtretungs-erklärung *f* declaration of assignment **-urkunde** *f* deed of assignment or conveyance

Abtrieb *m* output, driven end of shaft, power take-off (mach.), downward pressure, drift, deviation, leeway, clear cutting (forest), secondary drive **Zuschlag für** ~ slack

Abtrieb(s)-anker *m* drogue, deviator, drag anchor **-flansch** *m* power take-off flange, tail flange, drive flange **-drehzahlregelung** *f* driving speed regulation **-geschwindigkeit** *f* speed of the driven side **-glied** *n* off-drive member **-hebel** *m* drift bar (aviation) **-kurbelarm** *m* output crank **-säule** *f* stripping section **-scheibe** *f* driven pulley **-schlag** *m* final stage (metal) **-seite** *f* power take-off side, output end (kinematics)

Abtrift *f* right of pasture, drift, leeway, deviation **-anzeiger** *m* drift indicator **-berichtigung** *f* drift correction **-geschwindigkeit** *f* lateral or drift velocity **-kompaß** *m* drift compass **-messer** *m* drift indicator or gauge drift meter **-ring** *m* azimuth ring, inner ring **-schreiber** *m* drift recorder (aviation) **-stab** *m* drift bar

Abtrift- und Übergrundgeschwindigkeitsmesser drift- and ground-speed indicator

Abtrift-visier *n* drift meter **-winkel** *m* drift angle (aviation)

abtripeln to rub with tripoli

abtrocknen to dry, wipe off

abtrommeln to uncoil

Abtropf-blech *n* drip pan **-brett** *n* dripping or dropping board **-brücke** *f* dripping rack

abtröpfeln to drip

abtropfen to trickle down, drip off, drain, drop off ~ **lassen** to allow to drain

Abtropfen (elektrostatisches) n de-tearing (electrostatic)

Abtropfer *m* drip-board

Abtropf-gefäß *n* colander **-gestell** *n* draining rack or stand **-kante** *f* drip(ing) edge **-kasten** *m* drain table, draining chest **-ring** *m* drip ring **-schale** *f* jar, drainer, drip pan, draining dish **-ständer** *m* draining stand **-tisch** *m* drain or drip table

abtrudeln (über den Schwanz), to go into a (tail) spin (aviation)

Abtrudeln *n* tail spin (aviation)

abtun to take off, abolish, dispose of, finish, kill ~ (von Schüssen), to fire

abtupfen to dab, wipe off

abtürmen to make off, leave

ab- und zunehmende Bewegung surging

A-B-Verkehr *m* trunk service

abvieren to square (lumber)

abvisieren to sight out, line out (surveying)

abwägen to weigh off, weigh, balance, take the level, judge **gegenseitig** ~ to balance up

Abwägeschaltung *f* comparator circuit organization

Abwalkmaschine *f* tire removing device

Abwälzbewegung *f* roll motion

abwalzen to compact with roller, roll down, ride on, roll, reduce (while rolling), mesh into

abwälzen to hob

Abwälz-federbock *m* slide shacklespring carrier **-fräsautomat** *m* automatic hobbing machine

Abwälzfräser *m* generating milling cutter hob cutter, hob, gear hobber, hob type milling cutter **-schärfmaschine** *f* hob sharpening machine **-schleifmaschine** *f* hob cutter grinder

Abwälzfräs-maschine *f* gear hobber, hob cutter, hobbing machine **-verfahren** *n* gear hobbing system, hob milling method

Abwälzhobeln *n* generating planing method **-hobelverfahren** *n* reciprocating-cutter generating methods **-lager** *n* sliding shackle bearing **-stößel** *m* tappet rod of eccentric-cam type

Abwälzung *f* development

Abwälzverfahren *n* hob method **nach dem** ~

herstellen to produce by self-generating method (milling machine)
Abwälz-versteller *m* hob-type advance mechanism
abwandelbar declinable, variable
abwandeln to decline, vary, alter, change, modify
Abwanderung *f* drift (radio) precession (in gyroscope) ~ **von Teilchen** depletion (of particles)
Abwandlung *f* modified arrangement, modification, variation
Abwärme *f* waste heat **-kessel** *m* exhaust-heat boiler **-kraftmaschine** *f* heating-power machine **-verlust** *m* waste-heat loss **-verwerter** *m* waste heat recuperator **-verwertung** *f* waste-heat utilization
abwarten to await, expect, anticipate, wait for
abwärts down, downward **-bewegen** to lower, move downward, descend **-bewegung** *f* descent, downward motion or movement, downstroke **-bö** *f* downward gust or air current **-gang** *m* fall (aviat.) downward stroke **-gebogen** (synklinal), synclinal **-gerichtet** in a downward position **-gehen** *n* fall **-gehende Destillation** distillation by descent **-gleiten** *n* diving, gliding (aviat.) **-hub** *m* return stroke, downward strike or stroke, dropping way (aviation) **-lüftung** *f* downward conveying
Abwärts-regulierung *f* step-down regulation **-schalten** to change to lower gear **-schweißen** *n* down-hand welding **-streichen** to travel or flow downward **-transformator** *m* step-down or reducing transformer **-transformieren** to step down (elec.), reduce **-transformierung** *f* step(ping) down **-wandler** *m* stepdown transformer
abwaschbar washable
Abwaschbecken *n* sink, wash basin
abwaschen to wash, wash off, cleanse, rinse
Abwaschen *n* ablution
Abwaschmittel *n* washing solution
Abwasser *n* waste water, sewage, backwater, overflow drain water **-aufbereitung** *f* waste water treatment (industrial) **-behandlung** *f* treatment of sewage effluents **-behandlungsanlage** *f* sewage-disposal plant **-beseitigung** *f* disposal of waste water **-chlorung** *f* chlorination of waste water **-kanal** *m* sewer **-kläranlage** *f* purification plant of waste water **-klärung** *f* waste-water clarification **-leitung** *f* sewer or overflow pipe
abwassern to take water off or on
abwässern to drain
Abwässern *n* drainage
Abwasser-reinigungsanlage *f* waste-water-purifying plant **-rücknahme** *f* reutilization of waste water
Abwässerung eines Simses weathering of a molding
Abwässerungsanlage *f* drainage system
Abwasser-verrieselung *f* irrigation of sewage **-verwertung** *f* salvage of sewage **-wesen** *n* sewerage, sewage disposal
abwechseln to alternate, interchange, vary, change
abwechselnd alternating, alternate, variable, reciprocating ~ **etwas tun** to alternate ~ **in entgegengesetzter Richtung arbeitend** push-pull
Abwechslung *f* variety, alternation, change, variation
abwecken to ring off
abwehen to clear up (meteor)
abwehren to ward off, protect, repulse
Abwehrmittel n prophylactic
abweichen (Magnet) to decline; (Optik) deflect; (Säge) cut untrue; (losweichen) soak, deviate (from the rates), depart differ, diverge, vary, deviate, incline **nach oben oder unten** ~ to vary (up or down)
abweichend anomalous, erratic, deviating, divergent, unlike, different, imperfect (paper mfg.) **-e Anfangsgeschwindigkeit** starting-velocity error **-es Bohren** sidetracking (petroleum) **-es Merkmal** difference
Abweichung *f* (Licht) aberration, deflection, declination (of light); (~ von der Regel) departure from, exception to the rule; (Unterschied) difference; (Maße) off-size; (Qualität) off grade; (zulässige ~) allowance, tolerance; (Optik) aberration, declination, deviation, variation, divergence, margin, discordancy, residual tolerance, softening-up process, fluctuation, derivation, offset, disparity, anomaly, swing, drift
Abweichung eines synchronen Apparates disturbance, perturbation ~ **von der Geraden** deviation from the straight line ~ **der Gewindesteigung vom Sollmass** difference of thread pitch from the real size ~ **des Kompasses** compass variation ~ **des Lichts** deflection of light ~ **vom Lot** out of plumb ~ **des Nullpunktes** zero error ~ **von der Regel** exception to the rule ~ **von der wahren Richtung** deviation from true bearing ~ **vom Sollwert** deviation from the desired value ~ **des Windes** deviation of wind
Abweichung, Größe der ~ amplitude of aberration **erlaubte oder gestattete** ~ tolerance (of deviation) **mittlere (quadratische, normale)** ~ average or mean deviation, standard deviation **seitliche sphärische** ~ tranverse spherical aberration **zulässige** ~ tolerance, allowance (teleph.)
Abweichungen, ~ **behandeln** to deal with discrepancies ~ **der Oberfläche von der Kugelgestalt** deviations of the surface from spherical shape
Abweichungs-anzeiger *m* deviation meter, deviation indicator or recorder **-faktor** *m* factor defining variation **-grad** *m* per cent drift **-größe** *f* deviation variable **-karte** *f* deviation card (aviation) **-korrektur** *f* achromatization (optics) **-messer** *m* driftmeter **-nadel** *f* dipping needle **-parallele** *f* parallel of departure (declination) **-rate** *f* lapse rate **-verhältnis** offset ratio
Abweichungswinkel *m* angle of deflection ~ **der Magnetnadel** magnetic azimuth
abweifen to reel off
Abweis(e)bleche *n pl* flashings
abweisen to repulse, attack, throw back, refuse, reject, repel ~ (eine Klage) to dismiss (a suit), nonsuit
abweisend repellent
Abweiser *m* fender, recoil guard, bumper, diverter, deflector bar, shoulder guard **hinterer** ~ rear bumper **vorderer** ~ front bumper
Abweis-messer *n* fleeting knife **-stein** *m* curbstone

Abweisung *f* rejection, rebuff, refusal ~ **des phasengleichen Signals** common-mode rejection, in-phase rejection
Abweisungsmaterial *n* anticipatory material or references, anticipations (in prior art)
abwelken to fade away, wither
Abwelkpresse *f* dewatering press
abwenden to divert, avert, turn off or away, avoid
abwerfbar droppable **-er Brennstoffbehälter** slip fuel tank (aviation) **-es Fahrgestell** droppable undercarriage (aviation) **-e Tür** push-out door
Abwerf-behälter *m* slip fuel tank (aviation) **-einrichtung** *f* arrangement to release switches
abwerfen to dump, yield, release, let go, to drop ~ **nach unten** to throw downwards
Abwerfen *n* breaking down (of rock), release (armature), runoff (slag)
Abwerf-klaue *f* claw for casting off **-leuchte** *f* flare **-ofen** *m* refining furnace **-pfanne** *f* refining pan, (tinning) list pot **-saum** *m* listmark **-system** *n* operator aid system **-vorrichtung** *f* discarding device
Abwerg *n* waste tow or oakum
Abwertung *f* devaluation, depreciation
abwesend absent, missing, away
Abwesender *m* absentee
Abwesenheit *f* absence
abwettern to blow away (weather), seal (a mine)
abwetzen to fray
Abwickelachse *f* feed spindle
abwickelbar developable **-e Fläche** developable surface
Abwickel-haspel *f* dispenser **-maschine** *f* untwisting machine
abwickeln to reel or wind off, unroll, unwind, uncoil, settle or handle (affais), perform, develop (cylinder), project into a plane, rectify (current), develop (photo.), wind up, wind off (a coil), rectify (math.), dispense; (haspeln) de-coil **ein Kabel** ~ to run out a cable, pay out (a cable)
Abwickelspule *f* feed reel (tape rec.), feed spool (film)
Abwickel- und Aufwickelhaspel *m* wind-off and wind-up reel
Abwickel-werk *n* unwinding mechanism **-vorrichtung** *f* winding-off motion
Abwicklung *f* winding off, settlement, liquidation, performance, settlement (of accounts), unwinding, development, handling, developed projection ~ **von Kurven** evolution (aviation) ~ (eines Körpers oder einer Fläche) development (geom.) ~ **des Randes** development of edge (cartography) ~ **der Rechnungen** payment of accounts ~ **eines Zylindermantels** development of a cylinder
Abwicklungs-bremse *f* feed-reel brake **-gruppe** *f* continuity suite **-halbmesser** *m* radius of development of spiral or spiral sinoid **-kurve** *f* involute (geom.) **-stelle** *f* demobilization office **-zeit** *f* handling time
Abwiegemaschine *f* weighing machine
abwiegen to weigh, dose
Abwind *m* descending air current, down current, downwash, sideslip (of an air screw) **-berichtigung** *f* downwash correction **-feld** *n* region of downward or descending currents **-gebiet** *n* downwind area **-verhältnis** *n* downwash and wake condition, slipstream characteristic (aviation) **-winkel** *m* downwash angle **-wirkung** *f* downwash effect
abwinden to wind off (up)
abwinkeln to distort, bend
abwischen to clean, wipe off, efface
abwittern to effloresce
Abwölbung *f* curvature
abwracken to dismantle, wreck, scrap, break up
Abwracken *n* wrecking, breaking up
Abwrack-metall *n* old metal (scrap) **-schiff** *n* scrapped or laid-up vessel
Abwrackung *f* dismantling, wrecking
Abwurf *m* launching, dropping (bombs), release **-abstand** *m* distance, between bombs in a stick **-band** *n* discharge belt **-behälter** *m* drop, slip, or (alternating current) belly tank, aerial delivery unit **-ende** *n* discharge end **-haube** *f* discharge spout **-gondel** *f* aerial-delivery container **-kontrolle** *f* dump check **-kurbel** *f* dump crank **-platz** *m* dropping range **-radiosonde** *f* dropsonde **-rampe** *f* sloping bench **-schaltkasten** *m* release switch box **-schurre** *f* discharge chute of an ore-handling bridge crane
Abwurf-stelle *f* dumping point, message-dropping ground, drop point **-tasche** *f* message bag (aviation) **-trommel** *f* discharger pulley **-versuch** *m* drop test **-wagen** *m* dump car, shuttle type discharger, tripper
abwürgen to stall an engine, pull (a bolt) apart by means of simultaneous shearing and tensile stresses
Abwürgeversuch *m* stripping test (of threads)
abzählbar countable, denumerable, enumerable (math.) ~ **unendlich-dimensional** enumerably infinite dimensional
Abzähleinrichtung *f* counting device
abzählen to count off
abzählende Geometrie enumerative geometry
Abzählwerk *n* counting device, counter
Abzapfbrunnen *m* bleeder well
Abzapfdampf *m* bled steam
abzapfen to tune (on or off) a radio, tap, draw off, bleed (a pipe)
Abzapfhahn *m* draw-off cock, drain valve
Abzapfungsverlust *m* tapping loss
abzäumen to unbridle
abzehren to consume, emaciate, corrode
Abzehrung *f* consumption, emaciation, corrosion
Abzeichen *n* insignia, markings (aviation), stamping, badge, mark, ensign
abzeichnen to copy, mark or chalk off
Abzieh-apparat *m* bottling or racking apparatus (brewing), proof press (print.) **-bad** (Entfärbungsbad) *n* stripping bath
abziehbar peelable, removable **-es Papier** transfer paper
Abzieh-bild *n* decalcomania picture, metachromotype, transfer picture **-bilderdruck** *m* transfer printing **-bildverfahren** *n* metachromotype process **-blase** *f* still, retort **-bogen** *m* proof-paper **-bürste** *f* beating or letter brush **-effekt** *m* stripping effect **-emulsionsschicht** *f* pellicle, stripping film
abziehen (entfernen) to draw off; (Reifen) remove; (vervielfältigen) mimeograph; (po-

lieren, schleifen) smooth, touch up; (Parkett) surface; (ableiten) drain; (abdrehen) true; (destillieren) destil, decant; (Rauch) escape, disperse; (Buchdruck) take a proof; (Math.) substract; (Messer) sharpen; (Wetzstein) whet; (Chem.) decant, elutriate, distill; (Gerben) pare, scrape; (Math.) substract, deduct; (Photo) print, rectify, strip, tap, copy, trim or true (a wheel), divert, skim, slag off, dress, dross, pass off (gas), detract, issue, leave, withdraw, stone (cutting edge)

abziehen, ~ (mit dem Ölstein) to sharpen, hone, whet, strop, stone **in Fahnen ~** to pull in slips, take a rough proof copy **einen Korrekturbogen ~** to pull a proof, work, strike, or take off a sheet **von der Kurbelwelle ~** to draw off, or remove from, the crankshaft **mit dem Lineal ~** to draw off (masonry) **einen Probedruck ~** to pull off a proof **unsauber ~** to smut, blot (print.) **nach unten ~** to draw away downwards

Abziehen *n* distillation, rectification, tapping, bottling, racking, slagging, drossing, stripping, issue, escape, deduction, substraction, honing, proofing (printing)

Abzieher *m* (am Schacht), banksman, racker (brewing), extractor

Abzieherin *f* bobbin doffer (textiles)

Abzieh-feder *f* pull-off spring **-feile** *f* smooth file **-formkasten** *m* snap flask **-futter** *n* pulling chuck **-gewinde** *n* detaching thread **-hülse** *f* withdrawal sleeve **-latte** *f* smoothing board **-maschine** *f* whetting machine **-messer** *n* back iron, cleaning knife, drawknife **-mittel** *n* rectifier, stripping agent

Abzieh-papier *n* proof paper, transfer-type (stripping) paper (photo) **-pflug** *m* draining plow **-platte** *f* drawing-off plate **-presse** *f* proof or galley press **-raum** *m* racking room (brewing)

Abzieh-schraube *f* puller screw **-stein** *m* whetstone, oilstone **-verfahren** *n* stripping process **-vorrichtung** *f* extractor, puller (aviation), withdrawer, detaching device; (für Schleifscheibe) wheel dresser or brace, truing device, dresser **-walze** *f* stripping roller **-werkzeug** *n* wheel dresser **-zange** *f* puller collet, extracting collet, pulling-off pliers **-zünder** *m* friction igniter

abzielen auf to tend

abzirkeln to compass, measure with compass

Abzug *m* (Auslaß) outlet, escape, drain, fume chamber, flue; (Chem.) hood; (Preis) deduction, pressproof; (Photo) print, copy, positive, reproduction; vent, drawing off, scum, dross, trigger, offtake, retreat, draft, contact, withdrawal **in ~ bringen** to deduct **~ von einem Negativ** copy, reproduction, photoprint **terminmäßiger ~** allotment

Abzüge *m pl* core ducts or ventilating channels (elec.), sharp slags **~ machen** to make prints, copy, multigraph

Abzug(s)-angel *f* trigger sear **-band** *n* transfer belt conveyor **-blei** *n* lead obtained from dross **-boden** *m* draw-off plate **-bogen** *m* firing spring (explosives) **-bügel** *m* trigger guard **-bühne** *f* landing stage, shaft landing, charging deck **-dampf** *m* exhaust steam **-draht** *m* shunt wire **-drehwerk** *n* can coiler **-dreieck** *n* lowering cam (switch cam) **-einrichtung** *f* (für Gase) ventilation **-fähig** deductable **-feder** *f* trigger spring

Abzugs-gabel *f* trigger-sear fork **-gas** *n* burnt gases, flue, exit, or waste gas, escaping or dead gas **-gewicht** *n* trigger pull **-graben** *m* drainage ditch, tailrace, catch pit **-griff** *m* lanyard handle **-grube** *f* sinkhole or trap **-hängebank** *f* delivery platform **-haspel** *f* decoiler **-haube** *f* hood **-hebel** *m* trigger arm, firing lever, cocking handle **-hechel** *f* coarse or roughing hackle

Abzugs-kabel *n* trigger or hauling-down cable **-kanal** *m* offtake, chimney flue, discharge pipe, culvert, sewer (main), sink, cesspool, escape channel **-kurve** *f* withdrawal cam **-leine** *f* firing line (explosives), lanyard **-loch** *n* weeper (bridge building) **-magnet** *m* trigger magnet **-öffnung** *f* outlet, discharge opening, vent **-papier** *n* dry-proofing paper **-papier** duplicating paper **-pulmaschine** *f* reeling frames and reels (unwinding)

Abzugs-rohr *n* **-röhre** *f* delivery or discharge pipe, offtake, drainpipe, vent stack (of arc lamp), waste pipe or tube, vent pipe, outlet **-rohrverschluß** *m* soil trap **-schacht** *m* draft flue **-schalter** *m* firing connector (explosives) **-schieber** *m* sluice valve **-schiene** *f* trigger bar **-schleuse** *f* sewer, sink, cloaca, cesspool **-schnur** *f* firing lanyard **-schrank** *m* hood **-sicherung** *f* safety catch

Abzugs-stange *f* sear, trigger arm **-stelle** *f* tapping point **-stift** *m* trigger pin **-stollen** *m* trigger sear, sear nose **-stück** *n* lanyard, firing-arm trigger piece **-tisch** *m* delivery table **-ventil** *n* outlet valve **-vorrichtung** *f* firing or trigger mechanism **-walze** *f* delivering bowl, take-up roller (knitting) **-welle** *f* drawoff roll, firing rod, trigger sleeve **-werke** *n pl* dross, scum works or plant

Abzweig *m* branch, leak, shunt, spur, tap, service line, feeder (power system) **-bund** *m* tapping or tap binding **-dose** *f* branch or connector box, junction box, conduit plate or box (lead-in wires), elector

Abzweige *f*, **halbschräge ~** Y-shaped branches **schräge ~** Y-shaped fittings

abzweigen to branch (off), shunt off, tee, tap **~** (von Strahlen), to split off or deviate (rays) **eine Anzapfung ~** to intercept water

Abzweig-flußmesser *m* shunt meter **-gestänge** *n* pole with cross arms **-getriebe** *n* auxiliary drive (jet) **-kabel** *n* stub or bifurcating cable, cable-joint box **-kasten** *m* cross-connection box, dividing or coupling box, junction manhole or box **-klemme** *f* branch terminal **klemmbrett** *n* cord terminal strip **-klinke** *f* branching jack **-kondensator** multiple-unit condenser

Abzweigleitung *f* branch circuit **kurze ~** spur line

Abzweig-muffe *f* parallel joint(ing) sleeve, dividing box, cable distributing plug, branch T (of a pipe) **-punkt** *m* distributing point, branching or branch-off point, tap **-reaktanzspulen** *f pl* feeder reactors **-rohr** *n* branch or saddle pipe **-schelle** *f* pipe saddle

Abzweig-spleißstelle *f* Y splice **-spule** *f* tapped or bridging coil, tapped inductance **-station** *f* junction station **-stelle** *f* switching point, branch, branch-off (R.R.) **-stollen** *m* branch gallery (min.) **-stromkreis** *m* derived circuit **-stück** *n* tee-branch **-stutzen** *m* branch piece, branch T **-technik** *f* tapping or splitting technique **-transformator** *m* tapped transformer

Abzweigübertrager, Vierer ~ *m* combining transformer

Abzweigung *f* branch, branching (off), branch pipe, arm shunt, tap, tapping, junction, bifurcation, derivation (elec.) branch line, radar branch, tie line, ramification, division (of a patent application) **~ einer Leitung** wire-netting tapping **~ von Leitungen** tappings

Abzweigungs-rohr *n* **-röhre** *f* branch (pipe-)line **-stelle** *f* branching-off point **-unterstation** *f* distributing or teeing-off substation **-verhältnis** *n* branching ratio **-widerstand** *m* shunt resistance

Abzweig-vorrichtung *f* branch block **-wicklung** *f* shunt coil **-widerstand** *m* leak resistance or leak coil, shunt resistance

abzwicken to pinch (a wire or hose), nip

Abzwirnen *n* (über den Kopf), upstroke twisting

Ac . . . for words beginning thus, see also Ak . . . and Az . . .

Acacin *n* gum arabic

Achat *m* agate **bunter ~** mochastone, dendritic agate **schwarzer ~** silicious schist

Achat-einsätze *m pl* agate (jewel) bearings, mountings, or settings **-fuß** *m* agate tip **-haltig** agatiferous **-glas** *n* alabaster-glass **-glattmaschine** *f* stone burnisher **-hütchen** *n* agate cup, jewel cup **-kugel** *f* agate ball **-mörser** *m* agate mortar **-schellack** *m* shellac substitute **-seidenpapier** *n* agate tissue paper

Achromasie *f* achromatism, achromatization, degree of achromatic correction

Achromat *m* achromat, achromatic objective (photo.)

achromatisch achromatic, colorless **-er Punkt** *m* white point

achromatisieren to achromatize

Achromatismus *m* achromatism

Achs-abstand *m* distance between axes or center, center distance, wheel or axle base **-abstrebung** *f* axle stay **-abtriebvorgelegewelle** *f* final drive shaft **-anschlag** *m* axle bumper

Achsantrieb (Traktoren) *m* differential (gear), axle drive **(s)-gehäuse** *n* final drive housing **(s)-ritzel** *n* axle drive pinion

Achs-band *n* axle clip **-bandhalter** *m* axle-clip holder **-belastung** *f* axle load or weight **-bolzen** *m* king pin, steering pivot pin **-brücke** *f* axle bracket **-büchse** *f* **(-buchse)** *f* axle-tree box steering swivel bush

Achsbüchsen-deckel *m* axle-box cover **-führung** *f* axle-box guide

Achs-bund *m* axle collar **-drehung** *f* rotation **-drehvorrichtung** *f* journal turning attachment **-druck** *m* axle load or pressure **-druckgesperre** *n* axle pressure locking gear

Achse *f* spindle, shaft(ing), axle (tree), arbor, axis, center, line, axial beam, trunnion, ordinate line (math.); (Unterdruckklappe) pivot pin **von ~ zu ~** center to center **per ~** by carriage, rail, car, truck **~ für periodische Blattverstellung** feathering axis **~ der Bildkammer** axis of camera **~** (ohne Drehmomentübertragung, im Gegensatz zur Welle) axle **mit einer Dynamowelle gekuppelten ~** axle coupled with dynamo shaft **~ mit Querkardanwellen** jointed cross shaft axle **~ der Rolle** bearing of roller **~ der Waage** center of oscillation pivot

Achse, außer ~ extraaxial, abaxial **bewegliche ~** radius axle, articulated axle, jointed axle, movable axle **die ~ entlasten** to take off weight from the axle **drehende ~** live axle, floating axle **dreiviertelfliegende ~** three-quarter-floating axle **durchgehende ~** passing axle, banjo-type axle **feststehende ~** solid or fixed axle, dead or stationary axle **fliegende ~** floating axle

Achse, gebrochene ~ divided axle **gekröpfte ~** cranked or dropped axle **gestürzte ~** cambered axle **geteilte ~** divided axle, split-type axle **gezogene ~** solid-drawn axle **große ~** major axis **halbfliegende ~** semifloating axle **halbfreitragende ~** semi-floating axle **kleine ~** minor axis **neutrale ~** *f* neutral fiber **parallaktische ~** equatorial or parallactic axis **vollfliegende ~** full-floating axle

Achsel *f* shoulder **-hoher Ausschluß** shoulder-high spaces (print) **-schrägung** *f* shoulder bevel **-zapfen** *m* shouldered tenon

Achsen *f pl* axes **sich schneidende ~** concurrent axes

Achsen-abschnitt *m* axis intercept, parameter, indices **-abstand** *m* distance between axes, center distance, axle or wheel base, center-to-center distance

Achsenabstech- und Zentrierbank *f* axle cutting-off and centering machine

Achsen-abzeiger *m* axis indicator **-ankerrelais** *n* axial-armature relay **-antrieb** *m* axle drive **-austrittspunkte** *m pl* points of emergence of the axes **-belastung** *f* load on axle **-bilder** *n pl* interference figures **-bock** *m* axle bracket **-bruch** *m* break in an axle

Achsende *n* axle end

Achsen-drehung *f* rotation of axes, circular motion **-durchstoßpunkt** *m* **mit der Platte** foot of the optical axis upon the plate, optical center of the plate **-ebene** *f* plane of (optical) axes **-ende** *n* axle-arm **-entfernt** abaxial, off axis **-entfernung** *f* center distance, wheel base **-federung** *f* axle springing **-gehäuse** *n* axle sleeve, axle box, or easing **-hals** *m* axle journal or neck, axle washer **-kappe** *f* axle cap **-kopf** *m* axle head, wheel seat

Achsenkreuz *n* (coordinate) system of axes, coordinate axes, system of coordinates, intersection of axes, normal class **senkrechtes ~** orthogonal axes

Achsen-lager *n* axle or journal bearing, bearing(s), trunnion bearing, axle box, shaft bearings **-lagerhals** *m* axle journal **-lagerung** *f* axial-armature **-längsdruck** *m* **-längsschub** *m* side thrust, axial thrust or pressure **-last** *f* axle load **-mächte** *f pl* axis powers **-moment** *n* axial momentum (of a couple) **-motor** *m* hub motor **-nagel** *m* axle or linch pin **-neigung** *f* inclination of axis **-rad** *n* axle wheel **-regler** *m* shaft governor **-reibung** *f* axle friction

Achsen-richtung *f* direction of the gyro axis, axial direction **-richtverfahren** *n* axle pointing system (missiles), crosshairs, crosslines **-rohr** *n* axial tube **-schalter** *m* axis switch, locking switch **-schenkel** *m* axle neck **-schiene** *f* horn plate **-schmiere** *f* axle grease **-schmieröl** *n* axle or journal box oil **-schnitt** *m* meridional section, axial section **-schnittpunkt** *m* shaft intersection **-sehprüfscheibe für astigmatische Augen** axis test disk for astigmatic eyes **-senkrechte** *f* vertical axis **-stand** *m* wheel base **-stift** *m* linch pin **-stütze** *f* axle support

achsensymmetrisch symmetrical about an axis, spherical **-er Strom** axis symmetrical flow

Achsen-system *n* **parallaktisches ~ mit Stundenkreis und Deklinationskreis** equatorial head with hour circle and declination circle **-träger** *m* axle bracket **-T-Stück** *n* axle tee (brake) **-triebmotor** *m* wheel motor **-vergrößerung** *f* longitudianl magnification **-verhältnis** *n* axial ratio **-verlängerung** *f* trailing shaft (ship) **-verschränkbarkeit** *f* radius of axle turn **-welle** *f* drive shaft **-winkel** *m* optic or axial angle **-zapfen** *m* axle neck or journal

Achs-feder *f* axle spring **-federung** *f* axle suspension **-ferne Strahlen** off-axis rays **-fett** *n* axle grease **-futter** *n* axletree bed (of wagon)

Achsgabel *f* horn plate **-backen** *f pl* guide plates **-steg** *m* pedestal tie bar or binder, horn-plate stay **-strebe** *f* axleguard strut

Achs-gehäuse *n* axle box, casing, axle sleeve or case **-generator für veränderliche Drehzahl** variable-speed axle-driven generator **-hals** *m* axle journal or neck, axle washer, axle journal steering knuckle **-halter** *m* axle guard or support **-höhe** *f* height of center

achsig axial

Achs-innenlagerstelle *f* inside journal **-kabel** *n* axle yoke **-kapsel** *f* hub cap **-kappenzähler** *m* axle cap recorder **-kegelrad** *n* bevel side gear **-kopf** *m* axle head or journal **-körper** body of the axle, axle beam **-kraft** *f* axial force

Achskröpfung *f* cambering of cranked axle **Innenkurbeln, die ~ erfordern** inside cranks that necessitate a cranked axle

Achslager *n* axle, journal, or shaft bearing **federndes ~** *n* elastic axle box

Achslager-ausschnitt *m* opening for axle-box guide (R.R.) **-buchse** *f* shaft bearing bush **-deckel** *m* wheel bearing cap

Achslagerführung *f* axle slide, journal-box guide **gerade ~** pedestal, horn-block pedestal (R.R.)

Achslager-gleitplatte *f* axle-box liner **-motor** *m* axle suspension motor **-schale** *f* axle-bearing step **-schraube** *f* adjusting screw (of axle box wedges) **-spindelbüchse** *f* wheel bearing spindle bushing

Achslagerstellkeil *m* axle-box adjusting wedge **-schraube** *f* adjusting screw of axle-box wedge

Achs-lagerung *f* axle mounting or bearing **-lagerunterkasten** *m* axle-box keep **-loch** *n* hole for axle, axle bore **-loses Fahrgestell** split undercarriage **-mitte des Bohrloches** center of borehole **-mitteldrehbank** *f* axle middle lathe **-mittelstück** *n* axle center piece

achsmittig symmetrical

Achs-montageständer *m* axle assembling stand **-motor** *m* direct-drive motor **-mutter** *f* collar or axle nut **-nagel** *m* forelock, linch or axle pin **-nahe Strahlen** par-axis rays **-parallel** concentric, axis parallel, paraxial **-pfanne** *f* axletree band **-recht** axial **-ring** *m* end or linch hoop, axle ring (wagon) **-rohr** *n* axle (housing) tube

Achs-satz *m* wheel and axle set **-satzschleifmaschine** *f* wheel and axle-set grinder **-scheibe** *f* axle flange (disk), axle plate **-schemel** *m* axletree bed bolster

Achsschenkel *m* axle journal or neck, steering knuckle, half of axle, swivel axle, journal-wheel or axle spindle, stub axle **-blech** *n* axletree clout, axle-tree wrapping-plate **-bolzen** *m* steering knuckle pin, king pin, axle spindle bolt **-bolzenbuchse** *f* king pin bushing **-bruch** *m* fracture of the steering knuckle **-drucklager** *n* axlespindle-bolt thrust bearing

Achsschenkel-lager *n* king pin bearing, steering knuckle bearing **-lagerbüchse** *f* spindlebolt-bearing box **-lenkung** *f* axle-pivot steering, steering-knuckle type of steering, Ackermann steering **-mutter** *f* spindle-bolt nut **-prägepoliermaschine** *f* machine for burnishing axle journals **-schruppdrehbank** *f* axle-roughing lathe **-träger** *m* axle-spindle-bolt assembly, steering head, steering knuckle carrier

Achs-schmierbüchse *f* axle grease-box **-schrägung** (Kupplung) straddling of axle (coupling) **-schwingschenkel** *m* wheel spindle **-sitz** *m* axle seat **-spiegeldrehbank** *f* lathe for facing axle ends **-spiel** *n* clearance (play) of the axle **-stabsignalrakete** *f* signal rocket with axial staff **-stand** *m* wheel base **-stoß** *m* axle-washer **-stummel** *m* axle journal, neck of axle, axle end **-stumpf** *m* stub shaft **-sturz** *m* axle camber or dip, pivot or kingpin inclination **-stutzen** *m* sleeve bearing **-stütze** *f* axle bracket, axle-tree stay

Achs-teilung *f* linear pitch **-trichter** *m* final drive housing, flared tube of axle **-untersetzung** *f* reduction of axle speed **-verkleidung** *f* axle streamlining **-verlagerung** *f* axle shift(ing) **-verlängerung** *f* axle extension **-versetzung** *f* axle misalignment **-verstrebung** *f* axle brace, stay rod

Achs-wechselvorrichtung *f* axle-changing device (R.R.) **-wechselwinden** *pl* axle changing winches **-welle** *f* shaft, axle driving shaft **-wellendichtung** *f* axle driving shaft gasket **-widerstand** *m* resistance of the axis **-winkel** *m* shaft angle (spiral bevel gear) **-winklig** axis arranged at an angle

Achs-zähleinrichtung *f pl* axle counter **-zapfen** *m* axle journal, axle-end pivot, kingpin (steering-knuckle pivot) **-zapfenlager** *n* knuckle support **-zapfensturz** *m* pivot or kingpin inclination **-zwinge** *f* axle coupling plate

Acht *f* attention, consideration, care, eight, buckled wheel; boycott **außer ~ lassen** to disregard, neglect

acht eight **~ in der Querlage** four-bank eight (aviation) **~ längs des Weges** eight along a road (aviation) **~ quer über den Weg** eight across a road (aviation) **~ um den Wendeturm** eight on pylon (aviation) **~ um zwei Wendetürme** eight around pylons (aviation)

Achteck *n* octagon **sich selbst ein- und umbeschriebenes ~** octagon inscribed into and circumscribed about itself

achteckig octagonal

Achtecksäule *f* octagon column

Achtel *n* eighth **-geviert** *n* hair space **-kohleneisen** *n* octoferric carbide **-kreis** *m* octant

achtelkreisförmige Komponenten octantal error components (direction finder)

achtelkreisige Peilfehler octagonal error (direction finding)

Achtel-meile (engl.) *f* furlong **-petit** *f* one point (print) **-schlag** *m* miter **-verfahren** *n* method by eighths **-winkellineal** *n* miter square

Achter *m* eight-wire core, quadruple twin, abaft, aft, figure eight **-aus** aft, abaft, astern **-bündel** *n* eight-wire core, quadruple twin **-deck** *n* quarterdeck, poop deck, aft(er) deck (small craft) **-deich** *m* back dike **-ebbe** *f* end of the ebb **-ebene** *f* plane view of antenna field pattern **-ende** *n* aft end **-figur** *f* figure of eight

Achter-holer *m* guy backstay **-kante** *f* trailing edge (aviation) **-kreis** *m* double- or superphantom circuit, double-phantom radar **-kreis** *m* phantom circuit (double) **-lastig** down by the stern **-laterne** *f* poop lantern **-leine** *f* stern line **-leitung** *f* ghost, double-phantom circuit, superphantom circuit

achterliche Kurslinie astern course, direct line away from transmitter

Achterliek *n* after leech rope

achtern aft, astern **nach ~** sternward

Achter-piek *f* afterpeak **-raum** *m* afterhold **-riemen** *m* stroke oar **-schale** *f* octet, ring of eight electrons **-schaltung** *f* quadruple twin circuit **-schiff** *n* stern, afterbody **-schraube** *f* octet ring **-spant** *n* after frame **-spule** *f* octagonal coil

Achtersteven *m* stern post **über den ~ auslaufen** to go out stern first

Achter-telegraphie *f* double phantom telegraphy **-untersetzer** *m* scale of eight circuit

achterverseilt quadruple pair

Achter-verseilung *f* eight fold twisting (cable) **-zählrohr** *n* scale of eight circuit

achtfach octuple, eightfold **-er Untersetzer** scale of eight

Achtfach-funkenzieher *m* eightfold spark drawer **-schreiber** *m* eight-point recorder **-telegraph** *m* octuplex telegraph **-pumpe** *f* octuple pump

Acht-flach *n* octahedron **-flächig** octahedral **-flächner** *m* octahedron **-ganggetriebe** *n* eight-speed transmission

Achtkant *m* octagon, octahedron **-eisen** *n* octagons, octagon stock

achtkantig octagonal

Achtkant-material *n* octagon stock or bars **-mutter** *f* octagonal nut **-schlitten** *m* octagon tool arm **-schlüssel** *m* octagonal spanner **-stab** *m* octagon bar **-stößel** *m* octagon ram

acht-läufig eight-barreled **-los** inattentive

Achtpolröhre *f* octode, eight-electrode type of tube or valve

Achtrollenmaschine *f* eight-reel press

achtsam attentive

Achtsamkeit *f* watchfulness, care

Achtschloßstrickmaschine *f* eight-lock knitting machine

achtseitig octahedral

Acht-spule *f* eight-film reel or spool **-stundentag** *m* eight-hour working day **-tageuhr** *f* eight-day clock

Achtung *f* attention, regard, respect, esteem, caution, danger, warning

Achtungs-signal *n* attention signal **-verletzung** *f* insubordination

achtwertig octavalent

Achtwinkelmaß *n* miter square

Achtzehnzylinder-Doppelsternmotor *m* two-row eighteen-cylinder radial engine **-W-Motor** *m* eighteen-cylinder inverted W-engine

Achtzylinder-motor *m* straight-eight engine **-reihenmotor** *m* eight-cylinder in-line engine **-sternmotor** *m* eight-cylinder radial engine

Acidalbumin *n* acid albumen

Acidimeter *n* acidity meter

Acker *m* field **-bau** *m* agriculture, farming, cultivation **-boden** *m* arable soil **-fräser** *m* tillage cutter **-furche** *f* furrow **-geräte** *n pl* farm implements **-land** *n* arable land or soil, farm land

ackern to plow, till

Acker-schleife *f* clod crusher **-schleppe** *f* sweeper, clod crusher **-schlepper** *m* tractor

Acker- und Federzahnegge spring and peg-tooth harrow

Acker-vorbau *m* catch crop **-wagen** *m* field cart, farm wagon **-walze** *f* field, land, or smooth roller, field cylinder roller

Acmegewinde *n* acme screw-thread

Acrylsäureester *m* acrylate

Actinidenreihe *f* actinide series

Adamellit *m* adamellite

Adamsit *n* adamsite

Adapterlagerdichtung *f* adapter bearing seal

adaptieren to adapt

adaptiert suitable

Adaptierung *f* adaptation

Adaptometer *n* adaptometer

Adaptor *m* phonographic pickup, adaptor

Adatom *n* adsorption atom

Adcock-Antenne *f* Adcock antenna

Adcock-Peiler *m*, *n* Adcock direction finder Adcock system **-Vierkursfunkfeuer** *n* Adcock radio range

Addend *m* addend

Addiereinrichtung *f* adder (info proc.)

addieren to add (up), sum (up)

addierend additive, cumulative **~ und subtrahierend** reversible **-er und subtrahierender Dekadenzähler** reversible decade counter

Addierer *m* adder

Addier-methode *f* method of continuous addition **-werk** *n* adder, adding device

Addition *f* addition

Additions-duplex *m* incremental duplex **-fehler** *m* mistake in adding **-gerät** *n* summation device **-konstante** *f* addition constant **-kontrollbuchsen** *pl* plus hubs **-kreis** *m* adder **-maschine** *f* adding machine **-prinzip** (Fernschreiber) aggregate motion principle **-produkt** *n* additive compound **-schaltung** *f* summer (comput.)

additiv additive, cumulative

additive Frequenzverschiebung incremental frequency shift **~ Multiplikation** multiplication by repeated additions

Additivität *f* additivity **~ der Drehwinkel**

additive property of plane rotations
Additiv-ausmagerung *f* additive depletion **-kreis** *m* adder, applique circuit
Additron *n* additron
Addukte *n* adduct
Ader *f* rod seam, vein; (Elektr.) core lead, conductor; leader, lode; core of a cable, wire, artery, flow (in marble); electric wire lead **a ~** tip wire, T wire **b ~** ring wire, B wire **c ~** private wire, C wire **~ zum Stöpselhals** ring wire, B wire **~ zum Stöpselkörper** sleeve or test wire, C wire, private wire **~ zur Stöpselspitze** tip wire, T wire **~ zum Stöpselhals** ring wire **an der Erde liegende ~** positive wire A **~ eines Kabels** lead of a cable **oberflächliche ~** superficial seam
Ader-bänder *pl* cable core tapes **-endhülse** *f* multicore cable end (elec.)
Aderholz *n*, **geadertes ~** veined wood
aderig streaky, veiny
Ader-kabel *n* cable core **-kreuzung** *f* crossing of wires
adern to vein, marble, streak
Adern ausprüfen to identify wires
Adern-bündel *n* group of conductors, strands of wire or rope, stranded wire, twisted wire **-kreuzungsverfahren für Kapazitätsausgleich** test-splicing method **-lage** *f* layer of cable conductors **-paar** *n* pair of cables **-paar** (zum Ausfüllen der Lücken der Kabelseele) worming pair **-zählfolge** *f* numbering of cable conductors (color scheme)
Ader-presse *f* tourniquet **-schnitt** *m* chordal or tangential cut or section **-stärke** *f* diameter of core
Aderung *f* marbling, mottling
Aderverseilmaschine *f* core laying-up machine
Adervierer *m* quad (elec.)
adhärieren to adhere
Adhäsion *f* adhesion, adherence
Adhäsions-fett adhesive grease **-grenze** *f* limit of adhesion **-kraft** *f* adhesive power or capacity, attacking force (origin of force) **-vermögen** *n* adhesiveness, adhesive power
adhäsiv adhesive
Adiabasiefaktor *m* adiabatic factor
Adiabate *f* adiabatic curve **-kalorimeter** *n* adiabatic calorimeter
Adiabaten-exponent *m* adiabatic exponent **-gleichung** *f* equation of adiabatic change of state, relation between pressure and density **-satz** *m* adiabatic theorem
adiabatisch adiabatic, isentropic **~ gehemmt** adiabatically arrested **-e Änderung** *f* adiabatic process of change (thermodyn.) **-e Bedingung** adiabatic conditions **-er Wirkungsgrad** adiabatic efficiency **-er Zustand der Luft** adiabatic lapse rate (meteor) **-e Zustandsänderung** adiabatic change of conditions
adiaphor adiaphorus
adiatherman heat-insulating
Adion *n* adion
adipidieren to grease
adjektive Farbstoffe adjective (indirect) dyestuffs
adjungiert adjoint (kernel) **-e Matrix** (math.) adjoint matrix
Adjunktion *f* adjunction
Adjustage *f* adjustment, straightening department, finishing shop **-maschine** *f* adjusting or adjustment machine
adjustieren to adjust, regulate, true; (Gewichte) gauge
Adjustierung *f* adjusting, adjustment-scale correction
adjustierbar adjustable
adjustieren to adjust, set
Adler *m* eagle **-stein** *m* eaglestone, fibrous red iron ore, kidney ore **-zange** *f* stonelifting tongs
administrativ administrative
Admiralitäts-metall *n* admiralty brass
Admission *f* admission
Admissions-druck *m* admission or inlet pressure **-kanal** *m* admission port **-linie** *f* admission line (exhaust) **-spannung** *f* admission tension or potential
Admittanz *f* admittance (radio)
adoptieren to adopt
Adrenalin *n* adrenalin
Adressant *m* sender, consignor, writer
Adressat *m* addressee
Adreßbuch *n* directory
Adresse *f* address, bucket **per ~** in care of **~ von ~** *f* indirect address (info proc.)
adressenfreier Befehl zero-address instruction
Adressen-leerstelle *f* address blank **-lesedraht** *m* address-read wire **-löser** *m* address decoder **-prüfung** *f* address search **-register** *n* B-register, B-line **-schaltkernsignal** *n* select switch-core output **-schreibdraht** *m* address-write wire **-speicherzellenzuordnung** *f* address cell pattern **-system** *n* selection system **-teil** *m* address part or code **-wahlschalter** *m* address selection switch **-wahlspur** *f* time-selection band **-zuweisung** *f* orienting (info proc.)
adressierbarer Speicher addressed memory
adressieren to address
Adressiermaschine *f* addressing machine
Adressierung *f* addressing, orienting (info proc.)
adrige Leitung *f* core cable
Adronolazetat *n* adronol acetate (cyclohexanol acetate)
Adsorbat *n* adsorbed substance
Adsorbens *n* adsorbent
Adsorber adsorbent
adsorbieren to adsorb
adsorbierte Schichten adsorbed layers **~ Substanz** *f* adsorbate
Adsorption *f* adsorption
Adsorptions-analyse *f* chromatographic analysis **-fähigkeit** *f* adsorbing capacity, adsorption property **-gesetz** *n* law of adsorption **-isotherme** *f* adsorption isotherm **-kohle** *f* activated charcoal **-schicht** *f* adsorption layer **-stoffe** *f* adsorption medium **-verdrängung** *f* adsorption displacement **-vermögen** *n* adsorbing power **-vorgänge** *pl* adsorption processes
Adstringenz *f* astringent affect
adstringierend astringent
Adurol *n* adurol (photographic developer)
Advektion *f* advection
Advektionsnebel *m* advection fog (meteor.)
adventiv adventive
Aelotropie *f* aelotropy

A-Entlüfter *m* oxygen vent valve
A-Entlüfterhauptventil *n* main oxygen valve
Aeration *f* aeration
aerob aerobic
Aerobe *f* aerobic cell
Aerodynamik *f* aerodynamics
aerodynamisch streamlined, aerodynamic **~ günstig** having a neat pure aerodynamic form **~ sauber** clean, properly streamlined **-er Ausgleich** aerodynamic balance **-e Eigenschaften** aerodynamic qualities **-e Feinheit** aerodynamic fineness **-er Gesamtwirkungsgrad** over-all aerodynamic efficiency **-e Linienführung** aerodynamic forms **-e Waage** windtunnel balance **-er Wirkungsgrad** aerodynamic efficiency
Aeroelastizität *f* aero-elasticity
Aerogel *n* aerogel
aerogen aerogenous
Aerogengas *n* aerogene gas
aerogeodätisches Gerät instrument for aerial survey
Aerographie *f* aerography
Aerokartograph *m* aerocartograph (machine plotting photogrammetric photograph)
Aerolimnologie *f* aerolimnology
Aerolith *m* aerolite
aerologisches Meßgerät instrument for aerological measuring
Aeromechanik *f* aeromechanics
Aerometeorograph *m* aerometeorograph
Aerometer *n* aerometer, hydrometer
Aeromobil *n* road-going airplane
Aeromühle *f* aeropulverizer
Aeronautik *f* aeronautics
Aerophon *n* aerophone
Aerophotogrammetrie *f* air photogrammetry, air phototopography
aerophotographisch aerophotographic
aerophysikalisches Meßverfahren method of aerophysical measurement
Aeroplan *m* airplane, aeroplane
Aerosiderit *m* aerosiderite
Aerosol *n* aerosol **-abscheidekammer** *f* aerosol separating chamber **-teilchen** *n* aerosol particle
Aerostat *n* aerostat
Aerostatik *f* aerostatics
aerostatisch aerostatic
Affen-sattel *m* (monkey saddle) hyperbolic paraboloid (geom.)
Affiche *f* poster, bill
Affichenpapier *n* posters, bill paper
affichieren to post bills, advertise
affin affinitive **-e Verzerrung** affine transformation **-er Zusammenhang** affine connection
Affinade *f* affinated or affination sugar
Affinations-ausbeute *f* affination output **-wert** *m* affining quality
affinierbar affinable
Affinierbarkeit *f* affinability
affinieren to affine, refine
Affiniermaische *f* raw-sugar mixer
Affinierung *f* refining, refinery
Affinität *f* affinity (chem.)
Affinitäts-achse *f* axis of affinity **-konstante** *f* affinity constant **-rest** *m* residual affinity
Affinoren *pl* affinors
affizieren to affect
afokales Vorsatzlinsensystem afocal ancillary lens system
A-förmiges Gestänge A-fixture
A-Formwinkel *m* negative dihedral angle
After *m* (Aufbereitung) tailings (min.) **-kegel** *m* conoid **-kiel** *m* falseheel, keel shoe **-kristall** *m* pseudomorph crystal **-kugel** *f* spheroid **-ramme** *f* pile block **-strom** *m* eddy, swell **-ventil** *n* automatic (check) valve
Agalit *n* agalite (fibrous magnesium silicate)
Agalmatolith *m* agalmatolite, figure stone
Agathendisäure *f* agathic acid
Agavenfaser *f* sisal-fiber
Agens *n* reagent, agent (chem.), medium
Agent *m* agent, salesman
Agentur *f* agency, representation
ageostrophisch geostrophic
Agglomerat *n* agglomerate, agglomerated cake, sintercake
Agglomeration *f* agglomeration
Agglomeratkuchen *m* agglomerated sinter cake
Agglomerieranlage *f* agglomerating plant
agglomerieren to agglomerate
Agglomerierverfahren *n* agglomerating process or method
Agglutination *f* agglutination
agglutinieren to agglutinate
Aggregat *n* aggregate; unit or set of machines, plant; multinominal, polynominal, average, installation; generating set; contraption **-beleuchtung** *f* set lighting **-betrieb** *m* plant operation **-gewicht** *n* weight of missile **-gleichung** *f* moment equation (missile)
Aggregation *f* aggregation
Aggregat-lagerwinkel *m* missile-angle **-motor** *m* motor of a unit **-schalter** *m* switch for generating set **-steuerung** *f* (missile) steering control
Aggregatzustand *m* physical condition, state of aggregation **fester ~** solid phase, solid state (physics) **flüssiger ~** liquid state **gasförmiger ~** gaseous state
Aggregatzustandsänderung *f* change of state of aggregate or of aggregation
Aggregierung *f* aggregation
aggressiv aggressive **-er Boden** aggressive soil **-e Gase** corrosive gases
Aggressivität *f* aggressiveness
Agio *n* prenium, agio
Ägirit *m* aegirine, aegirite
Agitations-flotator *m* agitation-type flotation machine **-maschine** *f* agitator **-zelle** *f* agitator box or cell
Agone *f* agonic curve or line
agonische Kurve agonic curve or line
Agraffe *f* brooch, clasp, stud (piano)
Agranulozytose *f* agranulocytosis
Agrometer *n* agrometer
AGW-Markierer *m* TGS-marker
Ahle *f* awl, broach, bodkin, reamer, prod
Ahming *f* draught mark(s)
ähnlich similar, resembling, analogous
Ähnlichkeit *f* similarity, similitude, likeness, resemblance
Ähnlichkeits-achsen von Kreisen und Kugeln axes of similitude of circles and spheres **-betrachtung** *f* dimensional analysis, consideration of

similitude **-geometrie** *f* geometry of (general) similarity **-gesetz** *n* law of similarity or similitude **-gesetze bei Modellversuchen über technische Feuerungen** law of similarity in model experiments on industrial firing **-mechanik** *f* mechanics of similitude **-prinzip** *n* dimensional analysis **-punkte** (*m pl*) **von Kreisen und Kugeln** points of similitude of circles and spheres **-regel** *f* similarity rule **-satz** *m* law of similarity, similarity theorem, final value theorem **-theorie** *f* similarity principle, similitude theory **-transformationen** *f pl* similarity transformations **-verhältnis** *n* ratio of similitude

Ahorn *n* maple **-holz** *n* maple wood **-säure** *f* aceric acid **-sirup** *m* maple sirup **-zucker** *m* maple sugar

Ähre *f* ear, spike, spicula

Ähren-heber *m* grain lifter **-köpfer** *m* header **-leser** *m* gleaner **-mähmaschine** *f* header **-mähvorrichtung für Binder** header attachment for binder (agr.) **-spindel** *f* ear spindle (grain)

Ahrentscher automatischer Bleistich Ahrent's siphon lead tap

Ährenwerk *n* herring-bone work

Aichmetall *n* Aich metal

Akajouholz *n* mahogany

Akanthus *m* acanthus

Akaroidharz *n* acaroid gum or resin, yellow grass-tree gum

Akazie *f* acacia

Akazien-gummi *m* gum arabic **-holz** *n* wood of acacia or locust **-öl** *n* acacia oil

akklimatisiert acclimatized

Akkometsammler *m* accomet accumulator (radio)

Akkomodations-apparat *m* accommodator **-breite** *f* amplitude of accommodation **-entspannung** *f* relaxing of adaptation **-fähigkeit** *f* power of accommodation **-kraft** *f* power of accommodation (optics) **-loses Auge** unaccommodated or fixed eye **-ruhe** *f* relaxed state of accommodation

akkommodieren to accommodate

Akkord *m* settlement, piece wages; contract, agreement accord (music) **im ~ arbeiten** to work by piece or by contract **in ~** by contract

Akkord-arbeit *f* piecework, contract or job work, task work **-berechnung** *f* rate fixing **-durchschnitt** *m* average incentive rate **-folge** *f* chord sequence

akkordieren to arrange, contract

Akkordion-balg *m* accordion bellows **-griff** *m* keyboard

Akkord-lohn *m* piecework rates, piece wage **-satz** *m* piece-per-hour rate **-schere** *f* production-wage discrepancy, rate cutting **-verdienst** *m* premium earnings **-wesen** *n* time study **-zeitregistrierapparat** *m* job-time recorder **-zettel** *m* job ticket **-zitter** *f* autoharp

akkreditieren to open a credit

Akkreditiv *n* letter of credit, credentials

Akku *m* (short for) accumulator, storage battery

akkumulative Meßmethode *f* cumulative method

Akkumulator *m* storage battery or cell, battery accumulator, secondary cell **~ bleiplatte** *f* accumulator lead plate **~ mit gelatiniertem Elektrolyt** unspillable accumulator **~ mit Säurefüllung** accumulator with liquid electrolyte **einen ~ laden** to charge an accumulator **kochender ~** agitated or gassing accumulator

Akkumulatorbatterie *f* storage battery

Akkumulatoren-antrieb *m* driving by accumulators **-batterie** *f* (battery of) storage battery, accumulator cells, accumulator battery **-element** *n* storage-battery cell **-fahrbetrieb** *m* storage-battery traction **-fahrzeug** *n* electrical vehicle **-ladeapparat** *m* accumulator charging apparatus **-platte** *f* storage-battery plate **-raum** *m* battery compartment (submarines) **-säure** *f* accumulator acid **-teile** *pl* accumulator parts

Akkumulator-gefäß *n* accumulator box or jar **-gestell** *n* battery rack **-gitterplatte** *f* accumulator grid plate **-glas** *n* glass accumulator box, accumulator jar **-kasten** *m* accumulator box or case **-klemme** *f* accumulator terminal **-lokomotive** *f* storage-battery locomotive **-platte** *f* (storage-battery) plate, grid **-raum** *m* battery compartment **-säure** *f* accumulator acid, storage-battery acid, electrolyte **-spannung** *f* storage-battery voltage or potential, cell voltage or potential **-zelle** *f* storage-battery cell **-zweifachzelle** *f* double accumulator cell

akkumulieren to accumulate

Akkumulierungs-effekt additivity effect, irradiation **-verfahren** *n* air-storing process

akkurat exact, punctual

Akkuraum battery compartment

aklinisch aclinic

Akonitin *n* aconitine

Akontozahlung *f* payment on account, installment

Akribometer *n* acribometer

Akridin-farbstoff *m* acridine color or dye **-säure** *f* acridic (acridinic) acid

Akrolein *n* acrolein

Akrylat *n* acrylate

Akryl-glas *n* acrylic glass **-harzkunststoffe** *m pl* acrylic plastics **-säure** *f* acrylic acid

Akte *f* document, record, paper file **zu den Akten** (*f pl*) to place on file

Aktenbündel *n* file

Aktendalarm *m* reel-end signal (film)

Akten-deckel *m* document cover, folder **-fach** *n* filing cabinet **-format** *n* foolscap-size **-klammer** *f* paper clip **-mappe** *f* briefcase, portfolio, satchel **-material** *n* official documents or their contents **-notiz** *f* memo **-schrank** *m* filing cabinet **-schwanz** *m* docket tab rider **-ständer** *m* filing cabinet

Akten-stoß *m* file, bundle, pile of documents **-stück** *n* document, act, deed, file **-tasche** *f* briefcase, portfolio **-umlaufaufzüge** *pl* file transporting elevators **-vermerk** *m* memorandum **-vernichter** *m* shredding machine (print) **-verzeichnis** *n* file index **-zeichen** *n* file number (of a patent), serial number or symbol, docket or reference number **-zeichnung** *f* drawing incorporated (in docket or case records)

Aktie *f* share **die Aktien stehen auf pari** shares are at par **~ mit Nennwert** par-value share **~ mit Stimmrecht** voting share

Aktienanteil *m*, **einen ~ übernehmen** to take over part of the stock

Aktien-bank *f* joint-stock bank **-besitzer** *m* stockholder **-einziehung** *f* redemption of shares **-gesellschaft** *f* joint-stock company, stock com-

pany, open corporation **-inhaber** *m* shareholder, stockholder **-kapital** *n* share or joint capital
Aktiniden *pl* actinide elements, actinides **-reihe** *f* actinide series
aktinisch actinic ~ **undurchlässig** adiactinic **-e (Licht)strahlen** actinic rays
Aktinität *f* actinity
Aktinium *n* actinium **-atom** *n* atom of actinium **-emanation** *f* actinon **-zerfallsreihe** *f* actinium series
Aktinogramm *n* actinogram **-graph** *m* actinograph **-uran** *n* actino uranium
Aktinolith *m* actinolite
Aktinometer *n* actinometer
Aktinon *n* actinon
Aktion *f* action, campaign
Aktionär *m* shareholder, stockholder
Aktions-bereich *m* radius of action, flying range (aviation), driving range, cruising radius, maximum range **-bereitschaft** *f* readiness for action **-freiheit** *f* freedom of action, freedom of maneuver **-komitee** *n* committee of action, acting committee **-radius** *m* radius of action, covered area (artil.), range of flying **-reichweite** *f* range of action (aviation) **-turbine** *f* action or impulse turbine **-verlauf** *m* course of action **-zentrum** (*n*) **der Atmosphäre** center of action of the atmosphere
aktiv active, regular, actinic (in radiation) **-e Masse** active material, active paste
Aktiva *n pl* assets
Aktivator *m* activator, sensitizer
Aktiven *pl* assets
aktivierbare Bestände inventory assets
aktivieren to activate; (kapitalisieren) to capitalize
Aktivieren (einer Kathode) activation (of a cathode)
aktivierendes Isotop *n* activating isotope
aktivierte Bleicherde activated clay or fuller's earth
Aktivierung *f* activation, capitalization, activity, firing ~ **durch Deuteronen** deuteron-induced activity ~ **des Überzuges** coating activation
Aktivierungs-analyse *f* activation analysis **-energie** *f* energy required to produce disintegration (combustion) of a molecule of an explosive, intensity of activation **-folie** *f* foil detector **-gleichung** *f* activation equation **-impuls** *m* indicator gate (rdr) **-mittel** *n* activator, activating agent **-querschnitt** *m* activation cross section
Aktivierungswärme *f*, **scheinbare** ~ **bei Zündung durch heiße Kugeln** apparent heat of ignition by hot pellets ~ **von Atom- und Radikalreaktionen** activation heat of atom and radical reactions
Aktivierungs-zahl *f* activation number
Aktivität *f* activity ~ **des Erdmagnetismus** terrestrial magnetic activity **optische** ~ cathode-ray tube **spezifische** ~ isotope specific activity
aktivitätsfrei-es Laboratorium cold laboratory **-er Raum** cold area
Aktivitäts-grenze *f* activity limit **-kontrolle** *f* monitoring
Aktivitätsverminderung *f* cooling ~ **der Spaltstoffe** fuel cooling
Aktivitätsverteilung *f* activity distribution
Aktivkohle *f* activated carbon **-filter** *n* activated charcoal filter
Aktiv-störung *f* radar jamming **-wert** *m* asset
Aktogramm *n* activity (curve) graph.
aktuell actual **-e Energie** *f* kinetic energy
Akumeter *n* acoumeter, acousimeter
A_1-Kurve *f* cumulative float curve
A_2-Kurve *f* cumulative sink curve
Akustik *f* acoustics ~ **eines Raumes** acoustic properties (of a room)
Akustikplatten *pl* acoustic boards
akustisch acoustic(al), aural, audible (signal) **-e Alarmvorrichtung** audible alarm **-e Ausgangskontrolle** output monitoring **-es Einbruchssignal** *n* acoustic intrusion detector **-e Empfindung** *f* acoustic perception **-e Erregung** acoustic excitation **-e Gegenwirkung** acoustic reactance **-e Größe** acoustical quantity or value **-er Speicher** *m* acoustic memory, sonic delay line
akustoelektrisch acoustoelectric **-es Verhältnis** (Sender, Mikrophon) acousto-electric index
akut acute
Akzelerator *m* accelerator
Akzelermeter *n* accelerometer (aviation), foot throttle
Akzept *n* acceptance, accepted bill, draft
akzeptieren to accept, honor
Akzeptor *m* acceptor (impurity)
Akzeptorenkonzentration *f* acceptor level
Akzeptor-niveau *n* acceptor level **-verunreinigung** *f* acceptor impurity
akzessorisch accessory **-er Parameter** *m* irreducible constant (of a differential equation)
akzentuieren to accentuate
Akzidenz-abteilung *f* jobbing department **-arbeit** *f* job work **-drucker** *m* job printer **-material** *n* jobbing fount **-schrift** *f* job types **-setzer** *m* jobbing compositor
Akzise *f* excise, internal revenue
Alabandin *m* alabandite
Alabaster *m* alabaster, compact gypsum **-beleuchtungsgegenstand** *m* alabaster lamp **-gips** *m* alabastrite
Alanine *n* alanine
Alarm *m* alarm, warning ~ **aus** all clear ~ **blasen** to sound the alarm **blinder** ~ false alarm
Alarm-abschalter *m* alarm (horn) stopping switch **-anlage** *f* alarm system or plant **-anzeige** *f* fault indication **-apparat** *m* alarm apparatus, alarm **-bereit** on the alert, ready for fault indication **-bereitschaft** *f* alarm readiness, alert, stand-by, preparation for action, test equipment **-bestimmungen** *f pl* alarm orders
Alarmeinrichtung mit Arbeitsstrom open-circuit alarm system ~ **mit Ruhestrom** closed-circuit alarm system
Alarm-ende *n* all-clear signal **-frist** *f* period of alarm (air defense) **-geber** *m* monitron **-generator** *m* alarm generator **-glocke** *f* alarm bell **-hebel** *m* communication cord (alarm in railroad cars)
alarmieren to alarm, summon
Alarmkontaktgabe *f* alarm contact making **-manometer** *n* pressure warning unit **-platz** *m* alarm assembly station, alarm station **-posten** *m* alarm sentry, air-raid warden **-prüfhahn** *m* alarm test cock
Alarmrelais *n* alarm relay, fault relay ~ **für „Hauptsperrkette gestört"** (MR) alarm relay

for "main lockout chain faulty" ~ **für ,,Markierer dauerbelegt"** alarm relay for "marker permanently engaged"

Alarm-ring *m* alarm ring, a circle with a radius of 100 kilometers with the defended objectives as its center **-sammelplatz** *m* alarm assembly post or station **-schalter** *m* alarm device **-schußgerät** *n* trip-wire alarm **-schwelle** *f* alarm threshold **-sicherung** *f* alarm fuse **-verriegelung** *f* alarm locking **-vorrichtung** *f* alarm device **-zeichen** *n* alarm signal

Alaskait *m* alaskaite

Alaun *n* alum **-artig** aluminous **-auflöser** *m* dissolver or dissolving chests **-brühe** *f* alum pickle, solution of alum and salt **-erde** (Tonerde) alumina, aluminium oxide **-gar** alum-tanned **-gips** *m* marble cement, artificial marble **-haltig** aluminous, aluminiferous **-sauer** aluminous **-schiefer** *m* alum slate, alum shale **-siederei** *f* alum works **-stein** *m* aluminous limestone, alunite, alum stone; (unechter) **-stein** ironstone concretion

Albedo *n* albedo (reflection factor of diffusely reflecting surfaces, esp. of a celestial object), a white structure, tissue, or material

Albertit *m* albertite

Albit *m* albite, pericline

Albitit *m* albitite

Albitzwilling *m* albite twinning

Albondur *n* a type of light-metal alloy with good elastic properties used as aircraft skin

Albuminat *n* albuminate

Albumin *n* albumen **-druck** *m* albumen printing

Albuminometer *n* albuminometer

Albuminpapier *n* albumenized paper **brillantes** ~ double albumenized paper (phot.)

Albumin-stoff *m* protein **-verfahren** *n* albumin process

Aldehyd *n* aldehyde

aldehydisch aldehydic

Aldol *n* aldol

Aldose *f* aldose

Aleurometer *n* aleurometer

Alexanderson Hochfrequenzmaschine Alexanderson alternator

Alexandrit *m* alexandrite

Alfalfa- und Grasdrillmaschine *f* alfalfa and grass drill

Alfalfazinken *m pl* alfalfa teeth

Alfapapier *n* esparto paper

Alfenid *n* alfenide

Alfol *n* aluminium foil

Algarobilla *n* algarovilla

Alge *f* alga

Algebra *f* algebra

algebraisch algebraic(al) **-e Flächen** algebraic surfaces **-e Funktion** algebraic function **-e Gleichung** algebraic equation

algebroide Funktionen algebroid functions

Alginat *n* alginate

Algolfarbstoff *m* algol color

Algorithmus *m* algorithm

Algraphie *f* algraphy

Alhidade *f* alidade, sight rule

Alhidaden-kreis *m* alidade circle **-libelle** *f* alidade bubble, telescope bubble **-transporteur** *m* alidade transporter

aliphatisch aliphatic

Alit *m* alite

Alitieren *n* aliting (a process of surface alloying iron with aluminum), aluminizing

alitieren to alite, aluminize, alitize

alitierter Stahl calorized or alited steel

Alizarin *n* alizarin **-farbe** *f* alizarin dye **-krapplack** *m* alizarine madder lake **-rot** alizarin red **-sulfosaures Natrium** alizarin sodium monosulfonate

alizyklisch alicyclic

Alkaleszenz *f* alkalinity, alkalescence

Alkali *n* alkali **-atom** *n* alkali atom **-beständig** alkaliproof **-beständigkeit** *f* resistance to alkali **-bildner** *m* alkaline **-bindemittel** *n* alkali binding agent **-blau** alkali blue **-echtheit** *f* fastness to alkali **-empfindlich** susceptible to alkali **-gehalt** *m* alkaline strength, alkalinity

Alkalihalogenid *n* alkali halide, synthetic optical crystal **-kontinua** *pl* continuous spectra of alkali halides **-kristall** *n* alkali-halide crystal **-schicht** *f* alkali-halide film

Alkali-kalkprovinzen *pl* calc-alkali provinces **-kontinua** *pl* alkali halides, continuous spectra **-kristalle** *pl* alkali halide crystals **-lauge** *f* lye, alkali solution **-löslich** alkali-soluble **-metall** *n* alkali metal

Alkalimetallgruppe *f* alkaline-metal or -earth group **Oxyde der** ~ oxides of the alkaline-earth group

Alkalimetallion *n* alkali-metal ion

Alkalimetallphotozelle *f* alkaline photocell

Alkalimetallproben, Vorbereitung von ~ preparation of alkali metal specimens

Alkalimeter *n* alkalimeter

alkalinisch alkaline

Alkalinität *f* alkalinity

Alkali-patrone *f* alkali cartridge **-photozelle** *f* alkaline photocell **-reife** *f* alkaline maturity, ripeness

alkalisch alkaline **-er Akkumulator** alkaline accumulator **-er Schlamm** lye sludge, alkaline mud

Alkali-schicht *f* alkali halide film

alkalisieren to alkalize

Alkalisierung *f* alkalinization

Alkalität *f* alkalinity

Alkalitäts-anzeiger *m* alkalinity tester **-rückgang** *m* retrogression of alkalinity

Alkali-zelle *f* alkali-metal photoemissive cell **-zellulose** *f* alkali cellulose **-zyanid** *n* alkali cyanide

Alkaloid *n* alkaloid

Alkamin *n* alkamine

Alkan *n* alkane

Alkannarot *n* anchusin

Alkladblech *n* alclad

Alkohol *m* alcohol **absoluter** ~ pure alcohol, anhydrous alcohol **einwertiger** ~ monohydric alcohol **fünfwertiger** ~ pentahydric alcohol **geschwefelter** ~ thio-alcohol

Alkoholat *n* alcoholate

Alkohol-auszug aus Pflanzen alcoholate of plants **-enthaltend** alcoholic **-ersatz** *m* adulterated alcohol **-frei** nonalcoholic **-gärung** *f* alcoholic fermentation **-gärungspilz** *m* alcoholic ferment **-gemisch** *n* alcohol-blended fuel **-haltig** alcoholic

Alkoholisierung *f* reduction into alcohol
alkoholisch alcoholic **-e Pikrinsäure** picral **-e Salpetersäure** nitol, (nitric acid), alcohol-nitric acid solution
Alkoholometer *n* alcoholometer
Alkohol-oxydation *f* alcohol oxidation **-sulfonat** *n* alcohol sulfonate **-treibstoff** *m* alcohol-blended fuel **-verdrängung** *f* alcoholization **-zusatz** *m* alcohol addition
Alkoven *m* alcove
Alkydal-öllack *m* alkydal oil varnish **-spritlack** *m* alkydal lacquer
Alkydharz *n* alkyd resin **-lack** *m* alkyd varnish, paint or enamel
Alkylhydroperoxyd *n* alkylhydroperoxide
alkylieren to introduce alkyl into
Alkylierung *f* alkylation
Alkylrest *m* alkyl
Allanit *m* allanite
Allantoin *n* allantoin
Alle *f* white or silver poplar
Allein-berechtigung *f* sole or exclusive right **-besitz** *m* exclusive property **-eigentümerschaft** *f* sole proprietorship **-fliegen** to fly solo
Alleinflug *m* solo flight
Allein-gerbstoff *m* self-tannin **-gerbung** *f* self-tannage **-handel** *m* monopoly **-hersteller** *m* sole manufacturer **-inhaber** *m* sole owner or holder **-stehend** detached, isolated **-verkauf** *m* exclusive sale **-vertreter** *m* monopolist, sole distributor, sole agent
allelomorpher Stoff allelomorph
allerletzt ultimate
allerhärtest very hardest (of all), most penetrating
Alleskleber *m* all-purpose adhesive
Alleszerkleinerer *m* universal chopper for fodder dehydrator
allfärbig panchromatic
Allgebrauchslampen *pl* multi-purpose lamps ~ **in Linienform** line shape general lighting lamps ~ **in Kerzenform** candle shape general lighting lamps ~ **in Röhrenform** tube shape general lighting lamps ~ **in Tropfenform** drop shape general lighting lamps
allgemein general, common, in general **-e Anlagen für die Behandlung** general treating units **-e Ansicht** general view **-e Geschäftsunkosten** overhead expenses **-e Gleichung der Meßbrücke** fundamental bridge equation ~ **gesprochen** generally speaking **-e Struktur** *f* gross structure (band spectrum) **-e Unkosten** *pl* overhead cost ~ **verbindlich** universally (generally) valid
allgemeingültig generally valid **-e Anordnungen** general orders
Allgemeingültigkeit *f* generality, general validity
Allgemeinheit *f* universality, generality **die ~ betreffend** generally
Allgemeinkosten *f pl* general expenditures or expenses, over-all expenses
Allgemeinveränderung *f* change of general conditions
Allglas-ausführung *f* all glass construction **-röhre** *f* all-glass tube or valve
Allianz *f* alliance
Alligator *m* alligator **-quetsche** *f* alligator or crocodile squeezer **-schere** *f* alligator or crocodile shears, lever shears **-zange** *f* alligator wrench
allitieren to coat with aluminium, aluminize
Allklauengetriebe *n* dog clutch constant mesh gearbox
All-Lagen Trägheitsplattform *f* all-altitude inertial platform
allmählich gradual(ly), progressive, slowly ~ **belasten** to subject to gradual application of load **-e Belastung** (Werkstoffprüfung), gradual application of stress **-e Kurve** easement **-e Richtungsänderung** gradual change of direction
Allnetzgerät *n* all-mains receiver
Allobar *m* allobar
allochromatisch allochromatic
allomorph allomorphic
Allonge *f* adapter, flyleaf, rider
Allophan *n* silicious aluminium
allotriomorph allotriomorphic, xenomorphic
allotrop allotropic
Allotropie *f* allotropy, allotropism
allotropisch allotropic
Allpaß *m* all-pass **-netzwerk** *n* all-pass or universal network
Allrad-antrieb *m* four-wheel or all-wheel drive **-lastkraftwagen** *m* all-wheel truck **-lenkung** *f* four-wheel steering
Allrichtungsschallquelle *f* simple sound source
allseitig universal, all-round ~ **bearbeitet** machined all over ~ **geschlossen** covered in all round
Allstrom *m* alternating current and direct current (A.C.–D.C. or a.c.–d.c.) **-betrieb** *m* operating alternating current or direct current **-empfänger** *m* all-mains or universal receiver **-gerät** *n* ac-dc-set **-motor** *m* universal motor, a.c. and d.c. motor **-netzteil** *n* alternating current-direct current power mains **-röhre** *f* alternating-current-direct-current (a.c.-d.c.) tube or valve
Allsynchrongetriebe *n* fully synchronized gear
alluvial alluvial
Alluvium *n* alluvion, alluvium
Allverbreitung *f* ubiquity
Allverstärker *m* universal amplifier
Allwellen-antenne *f* multiband antenna **-empfänger** *m* all-wave, multirange, or multiple-band receiver **-empfangsanlage** *f* all-wave receiving set **-pumpe** *f* fully synchronized gear **-rundempfangsantenne** *f* omnidirectional all-wave receiving antenna
Allwetter-aufbau (der Karosserie) *m* all-weather body **-straßen** *pl* all-weather roads **-einsatz** *m* all-weather operation
Allylaldehyd *n* allyl aldehyde
Allyl-alkohol *m* allylic alcohol **-bromid** *n* allyl bromide **-senföl** *n* allylisothiocyanate, artificial mustard oil **-sulfid** *n* allyl sulfide
Allzeichner *m* pantograph
Allzweck-bauart *f* all-purpose type **-diode** *f* general pupose diode **-maschine** *f* all-purpose machine **-meßbrücke** *f* universal bridge **-schrift** *f* all-purpose type (face) **-radar** *n* general purpose radar
Alm *n* aluminum
Almandin *m* almandine, almandite
Alni-magnet *m* alni-magnet **-magnetfluß** *m* alni

magnetic flux **-stahlmagnet** *m* alni steel magnet

Aloe-faser *f* aloe fiber **-holz** *n* aloe wood, calambac **-seil** *n* aloe rope

Aloxit *m* aloxite

Alpaka *n* alpaca (an alloy) **-besteck** *n* knife, fork, and spoon of alpaca metal **-weber** *m* alpaca weaver

Alpax *m* alpax

Alphabet *n* alphabet, code

Alpha-Beta Zählrohr *n* alpha-beta Geiger tube

alphabetische Reihenfolge alphabetic order

Alphabet-locher *m* alphabetical punch **-lochprüfer** *m* alphabetical verifier **-lochschriftübersetzer** *m* alphabetical interpreter **-mischeinrichtung** *f* alphabetical collating device **-perforiermaschine** *f* alphabet perforating machine **-schloß** *n* combination lock **-schreibende Tabelliermaschine** alphabetical accounting machine **-schreiblocher** *m* alphabetical printing punch **-schreibung** *f* alphabetic printing **-wiederholungslocher** *m* alphabetical duplicating punch

Alpha-emission *f* alpha change **-explosiondetektor** *m* alpha burst detector **-impulszähleinsatz** *m* alpha pulse counting insert **-naphthol** *n* alpha-naphthol **-naphthylamin** *n* alphanaphthylamine

alphanumerisch alphameric, alphanumeric(al) **-e Typenstangen** alphanumerical type bars

Alpha-spektrometer *n* alpha-ray spectrometer **-strahlen** *pl* alpha rays **-strahler** *m* alpha radiator, alpha emitter **-strahlspektrometer** *n* alpha-ray spectrometer **-strahlung** *f* alpha radiation

Alphateilchen *n* alpha particle **Beschießung mit ~** alpha bombardment **weitreichende ~** long-range alpha particle

Alphateilchen-einfang *m* alpha particle capture **-quelle** *f* alpha particle source

alphatopisch alphatopic

Alphatron *n* alphatron **-manometer** *n* alphatron gauge

Alpha-uran *n* alpha uranium **-zählrohr** *n* alpha counter tube

Alphazerfall *m* alpha decay or disintegration **~** (Behinderungsfaktor) alpha radioactivity hindrance (departure) factor

Alphazerfallsenergie *f* alpha disintegration energy

alsbald direct, immediate, at once

Alstonit *m* alstonite, bromlite

Alt *m* alto **tiefer ~** contralto

alt old, antique, old-fashioned, obsolete **-er Mann** old man, old excavation, old ground **-er Scheck** stale check

Altan *m* platform, balcony, flat, flat roof

Altar-geländer *n* altar rail **-nische** *f* apse, tribunal **-raum** *m* chancel

Alt-besitz *m* old holdings **-bücher** *n pl* old or secondhand books

Alteisen *n* scrap iron, junk **-händler** *m* junk dealer **-ofen** *m* fagoting furnace

Alter *n* age **von ungleichem ~** of different ages, unevenly aged

älter senior, older

altern to age, mature, (super)season, fatigue, tire, ageharden

Altern *n* aging, maturing, (super)seasoning, aging of brines or gels **zu starkes oder zu langes ~** (Werkstoff), overaging

Alternatia *n pl* alternatives

alternativ alternative

Alternator *m* alternator, alternating-current generator

alternieren to alternate

alternierend alternating, alternative, alternate **-e Bewegung** alternating motion **-e Entladung** alternating discharge

Altersbestimmung *f* determination of age, dating **~ von Gesteinen** geologic age determination **~ mit Hilfe von Isotopen** isotope dating

Alters-erhöhung *f* rating up in age **-gleichung** *f* age equation **-grenze** *f* age limit **-gruppe** *f* age group **-härtung** *f* age-hardening **-messung** *f* dating **-riß** *m* season crack **-sichtigkeit** *f* presbyopia

Altertumskunde *f* archeology

Alterung *f* aging, (super)seasoning **künstliche ~** aging operating, artificial aging **Selbst ~** aging at room temperature **~ verzögerndes Mittel** *n* anti-oxidant **~ eines Zählrohrs** hysteresis of a counter

Alterungs-beständigkeit *f* resistance to aging **-durchschlag** *m* aging puncture **-einfluß** *m* aging effect **-erscheinung** *f* aging effect **-freie Legierung** alloy that does not deteriorate with age **-grenze** *f* maximum brittleness, limit of brittleness **-härtung** *f* age-hardening **-kerbzähigkeit** *f* increase of impact strength by aging

Alterungs-probe *f* aging test **-riß** *m* season crack **-schutzmittel** *n* age resister, anti-oxidant (for rubber) **-sprödigkeit** *f* aging brittleness **-stabilisator** *m* anti-oxidant **-temperatur** *f* aging temperature of metals **-verfahren** *n* aging process

Alterungsversuch *m* aging test **Schnell ~** accelerated aging test

Alterungs-vorgang *m* aging process **-widerstand** *m* resistance to aging

Altgummi *n* used, scrap or waste rubber **-regenerieranlage** *f* rubber reclaiming plant

althergebracht customary, traditional, ancient

Altholz *n* old timber

Altimeter *n* height indicator, altimeter

Alt-material *n* junk, scrap, waste **-messing** *n* old or scrap brass **-metall** *m* scrap, secondary or old metal **-modisch** old-fashioned

Altocumulus *m* alto-cumulus (cloud)

Altöl *n* oil recovered from waste oils and fats (salvage products) **-aufbereitungsanlage** waste-oil regeneration plant

Altostratus *m* alto-stratus (cloud)

Altpapier *n* refuse, used or old waste paper **-reinigungsanlage** *f* waste-paper cleaning plant **-schneideanlage** *f* waste-paper cutting plant

Altrose *f* altrose

Altrot-grundierung *f* old red ground **-ölpräparation** *f* old red-oil preparation **-verfahren** *n* Turkey red dyeing

Alt-sand *m* old, used, or black sand **-stoffsammlung** *f* salvage of scrap materials, scrap drive **-wasser** *n* oxbow, dead channel, old river bed

Altwert *m* scrap value

Alu (= Aluminium) *n* aluminium

Alubandkappen *pl* aluminium foil strip

Aludel *m* aludel

Alukappen *pl* aluminium caps

Alulegierung *f* aluminum alloy
Alumetieren *n*, **Alumetierung** *f* aluminum plating
Aluminat *n* aluminate **-lauge** *f* aluminate liquor
Aluminazetat *n* aluminum acetate
aluminisieren to aluminize, coat with aluminum
Aluminium *n* aluminum **stearinsaures ~** aluminum stearate **~ aufspritzen und einbrennen** to aluminize **Aufspritzen von ~** aluminizing, spraying or coating with aluminum
Aluminium-ammonium *n* aluminium ammonium **-acetat** *n* aluminium acetate **-barren** *m* aluminium pig, ingot or bar **-bekleidung** *f* aluminium cover **-bindedraht** *m* aluminium binding wire **-bisulfit** *n* aluminium bisulfite **-blech** *n* aluminium sheet **-bor** *n* aluminium boride **-bronzeröhre** *f* aluminium bronze tube **-darstellung** *f* aluminium manufacture **-dichtung** *f* aluminium seal **-draht** *m* aluminium wire **-druck** *m* printing from aluminium plates **-einlage** *f* aluminium backing
Aluminiumeisen *n* ferroaluminium **-phosphat** *n* (wasserhaltiges) barrandite
Aluminium-erz *n* aluminium ore **-farbe** *f* aluminum paint **-fassung** *f* aluminum mounting **-feilspäne** *m pl* aluminum filings **-filtersatz** *m* aluminium absorption filter **-fluorwasserstoffsäure** *f* fluo-aluminic acid **-fluosilikat** *n* aluminum silicofluoride **-folie** *f* aluminium foil **-foliendruckfarbe** *f* aluminium foil printing ink **-folienkaschiermaschine** *f* aluminium laminating paper **-fritter** *m* aluminium coherer
Aluminium-gehalt *m* aluminium content **-gehäuse** *n* aluminium housing **-geschirr** *n* aluminum plate **-gewinnungseinrichtung** *f* equipment for producing aluminum **-gleichrichter** *m* aluminum rectifier **-granalien** *pl* aluminium shot **-grieß** *m* aluminum shot **-großgefäß** *n* large vessel of aluminum **-guß** *m* cast aluminum, aluminum casting **-haltig** containing aluminum, aluminiferous, aluminum-bearing **-hartlot** *n* aluminum solder **-hülse** *f* aluminium cartridge **-hütte** *f* aluminum works **-jodat** *n* aluminum iodate **-jodid** *n* aluminum iolide
Aluminium-kaliumsulfat *n* aluminum potassium sulfate **-knetlegierung** *f* malleable aluminum alloy **-kochgeschirr** *n* aluminum kitchen sets or kitchen utensils **-kokillenguß** *m* aluminum chill casting **-kolben** *m* aluminum piston **-kupferzinklegierung** *f* aluminum-copper-zinc alloy, aluminum brass **-kurbelgehäuse** *n* aluminum crankcase **-legierung** *f* aluminum alloy **-löten** *n* aluminum soldering **-messing** *n* aluminum brass **-motorenzylinder der Bauart Cross ohne Laufbüchse** Cross linerless aluminum cylinder
Aluminium-natriumchlorid *n* aluminium sodium chloride **-natriumsulfat** *n* aluminium sodium sulfate **-oxyd** *n* aluminium oxide, alumina **-oxydanteil des Katalysators** alumina portion of the catalyst **-oxydhydrat** *n* aluminum hydroxide, trihydrate, or hydrate **-pulver** *n* aluminum powder **-putzmittel** *n* aluminum polish **-rhodanid** *n* aluminum thiocyanate **-rohr** *n*, **-röhre** *f* aluminum tube or pipe **-sandguß** *m* aluminum sand casting **-schale** *f* aluminum tray **-schalenguß** *m* aluminum chill casting
Aluminiumschicht *f*, **mit einer aufgedampften ~ versehen** aluminized
Aluminium-schwimmer *m* aluminum float **-seil** *n* stranded aluminum wire **-silber** *n* aluminal silver, dyscrasite **-silikat** (mit natürlichem Kristallwassergehalt) hydrous alumina silicate **-stange** *f* aluminum rod **-staub** *m* aluminum dust **-thermische Schweißung** thermit welding dust **-thermische Schweißung** thermic welding **-töne** *m pl* aluminum reeds (accordion) **-überzug** *m* aluminum coat **-walzbarren** *m* aluminum-rolling ingot **-wicklung** *f* aluminium coil **-würfel** *m* aluminum cube **-zellengleichrichter** *m* aluminum-cell rectifier **-zement** *m* high-alumina cement
Aluminothermie *f* aluminothermy
aluminothermisch aluminothermic **-es Schweißverfahren** thermic (pressure) welding
Alundum *n* alundum **-ziegel** *m* alundum brick
Alunit *m* alunite
Alunogen *n* alunogen, native aluminum sulfate
Amalgam *n* amalgam, mercury alloy
Amalgamationsanlage *f* amalgamating plant
Amalgamator *m* amalgamator
Amalgam-ausbrenntopf *m* amalgam pot retort **-bad** *n* amalgamating (bath) solution **-fänger** *m* amalgam trap (stamp milling)
amalgamierbar amalgamable
amalgamieren to amalgamate
Amalgamier-herd *m* amalgamating table **-pfanne** *f* amalgamating pan **-tisch** *m* amalgamator
Amalgamierung *f* amalgamation
Amalgamierungsflüssigkeit *f* amalgamating liquid
Amalgam-presse *f* amalgam press **-silber** *n* native amalgam **-zusatz** *m* denuder
Amaranth (Ton) amaranth (shade)
Amaranthholz *n* mahogany
A-Mast *m* A pole (cross-braced)
Amateur (Funkamateur) *f* radio amateur (ham) **-lizenz** *f* amateur license **-photograph** *m* amateur photographer
Amatol *n* amatol
Amazonenstein *m* amazonite
ambipolar ambipolar **-e Diffusion** ambipolar diffusion
Amboß *m* anvil, primer anvil **~ der Zündglocke** detonator anvil
Amboß-bahn *f* anvil face **-einsatz** *m* anvil insertion piece, intermediate block **-förmiger Kumulo-nimbus** incus **-futter** *n* anvil bed, stock, or stand **-gesenk** *n* anvil tool, swage **-horn** *n* anvil horn or beak
Amboß-klotz *m* bedplate, base casting, anvil block **-kontakt** *n* anvil contact, buffer contact **-lager** *n* base casting, bedplate **-schraube** *f* threaded anvil **-stock** *m* anvil block **-stöckel** *n* anvil stake **-wolke** *f* anvil cloud
Ambra *f*, **graue ~** ambergris
Ambrafettsäure *f* ambreic acid
Ambroin *n* ambroin
ambulant ambulant
ambulatorisch ambulatory
Ambursensperre *f* Ambursen dam
Ambuskade *f* ambush
Ameise *f* ant
Ameisen-aldehyd *n* formaldehyde **-äther** *m* ethyl formate, formic ether **-geist** *m* formic spirit **-säure** *f* formic acid

ameisen-sau(e)r formate of **-es Ammon** ammonium formate **-es Äthyl** ethyl formate **-es Natron** sodium formate
Amelioration *f* amelioration
Amenium *n* a type of tertiary amine salts
Americium *n* americium
Amerikanisch-e Drahtlehre American wire gauge, Brown and Sharp wire gauge **-es Lindenholz** (Schwarz) basswood **-e Norm** U.S.standard **-es Ulmenholz** rock elm
Ametall *n* nonmetal
ametropfehlsichtig ametropic
Amiant *m* asbestos, mountain flax
Amid *n* amide **-gruppe** *f* amino group
amidieren to amidate
Amido-azobenzol *n* amidoazobenzene **-azotoluol** *n* amidoazotulene **-benzol** *n* aminobenzene **-charakter** *m* amidic character **-essigsäure** *f* aminoacetic acid **-kohlensäure** *f* carbamic acid, amidocarbonic acid **-phenol** *n* aminophenol **-säure** *f* amino acid **-schwefelsäure** *f* amidosulfuric acid (sulfamic acid) **-sulfosäure** *f* amidosulfuric acid, aminosulfonic acid
Amid-säure *f* amido acid, amic acid **-schnitzel** *n pl* amide chips (sugar mfg.) **-stickstoff** *m* amido nitrogen
Amin *n* amine
Aminoglutarsäure *f* glutamic acid, aminoglutaric acid
Aminographie *f* aminography
aminieren to aminate
Aminierung durch Aminolyse amination by ammonolysis
Amino-glutarsäure *f* glutamic acid, aminoglutaric acid **-gruppe** *f* amino group (amino acids) **-ketonisch** aminoketonic **-säure** *f* amino acid **-verbindung** amino compound
Aminsäure *f* amino acid, amic acid
Ammeter *n* ammeter
Ammon *m* ammonia, ammonium **überchlorsaures ~** ammonium perchlorate
Ammon-alaun *m* ammonia alum, aluminum ammonium sulfate **-chlorid** *n* ammonium chloride **-hydrosulfid** *n* ammonium hydrosulfide
Ammoniak *n* ammonia, ammonium hydroxyde **doppeltkohlensaures ~** ammonium or ammonia bicarbonate **essigsaures ~** ammonium or ammonia acetate **kohlensaures ~** ammonium or ammonia carbonate **milchsaures ~** ammonium or ammonia lactate **salzsaures ~** ammonium chloride **schwefelsaures ~** ammonium sulfate **überschwefelsaures ~** ammonium or ammonia persulfate **weinsteinsaures ~** ammonium or ammonia tartrate
Ammoniak-abscheidung *f* ammonia separation **-alaun** *m* ammonia alum, aluminum ammonium sulfate
ammoniakalisch ammoniacal
Ammoniak-anlage *f* ammonia works **-apparate** *pl* ammonia equipment **-ausbeute** *f* ammonia yield **-auslaßventil** *n* ammonia outlet valve **-betrieb** *m* ammonia works **-dissoziation** *f* ammonia dissociation **-flüssigkeit** *f* (Salmiakgeist) ammonia liquor **-gas** *n* ammonia (gas) **-gewinnung** *f* ammonia recovery **-haltig** ammoniacal **-kühlschlange** *f* ammonia refrigerating coil **-kupferchlorür** *n* ammoniacal cuprous chloride **-laugung** *f* ammonia leaching, gas-houseliquor leaching
Ammoniak-sauerstoffgemisch *n* ammonia-oxygen mixture **-sodaprozeß** *m* Solvay process (for the industrial preparation of soda) **-verdichter** *m* ammonia compressor **-wäsche** *f* ammonia scrubbing, ammonia washing process **-wascher** *m* ammonia (washer) scrubber
Ammoniakwasser *n* ammonia water, ammoniacal liquor **verdichtetes ~** concentrated ammonia water
Ammonium *n* ammonium **wolframsaures ~** ammonium tungstate
Ammonium-arseniat *n* ammonium arsenate **-chlorid** *n* ammonium chloride, sal ammoniac **-cobaltosulfat** *n* cobalt ammonium tuttonsalt **-formiat** *n* ammonium formate **-dihydrophosphat** *n* ammonium dihydrogen phosphate **-hydrosulfid** *n* sulfhydrate of ammonia **-hydroxyd** *n* ammonium hydroxide or hydrate **-imidosulfonat** *n* ammonium imidosulfonate **-pikrat** *n* ammonium picrate **-radikal** *n* radical of ammonium **-rhodanid** *n* ammonium sulfocyanate, ammonium thiocyanate
Ammonium-salpeter *m* ammonium nitrate **-sulfat** *n* ammonium sulfate **-sulfhydrat** *n* ammonium hydrosulfide **-sulfozyanid** *n* ammonium sulfocyanate, ammonium thiocyanate **-wolframat** *n* ammonium tungstate **-zinnchlorid** *n* pink salt
Ammon-kabonit *n* Ammon-Carbonite (trade name of an explosive)
Ammonolyse *f* ammonolysis
Ammon-pulver *n* ammonal **-salpeter** *n* ammonium nitrate explosive
A-Modulation *f* class A modulation
amorph amorphous **-er Kohlenstoff** amorphous carbon **-es Paraffin** amorphous wax **-e Unterlage** amorphous substratum
amorphisch amorphous
Amortisation *f* amortization, redemption
Amortisationsfund *m* sinking fund
amortisieren to amortize
Amortisierung *f* amortization
A-Motor *m*, **Motor in hängender V-Anordnung** inverted-V-type engine
Ampangabit *m* ampangabeite
Ampas *m* bagasse, trash
Ampelit *m* ampelite (a black coloring pigment)
Ampelodesma *n* Ampelodesma (an Italian herb used for cellulose)
Ampère *n* ampere, bolometer **-drähte** *m pl* ampere wires or conductors
Ampèremeter *n* ammeter, bolometer **-kasten** *m* ammeter box **-nebenwiderstand** *m* ammeter shunt **-umschalter** *m* ammeter selector switch
Ampèresche Schwimmerregel Ampère's rule
Ampère-stärke *f* amperage **-stunde** *f* ampere-hour **-stundenwirkungsgrad** *m* ampere-hour efficiency **-stundenzähler** *m* ampere-hour meter or quantity meter **-windung** *f* ampere turn **-windungszahl** *f* ampere turns, number of ampere turns **-windungsverstärkung** *f* ampere-turn gain **-zahl** *f* amperage, ampere-hour capacity
Amphibie *f* amphibian
Amphibienflugzeug *n* amphibian plane
amphibisch amphibious
Amphibium *n* amphibian (flying boat) **~ mit**

Schwimmern float-plane amphibian
Amphibium-flugboot *n* amphibian flying boat
Amphibol *m* amphibole
Amphibolit *n* amphibolite (hornblende schist)
Amphidromie *f* amphidromy **-punkt** *m* amphidromic point
Amphigenstoffe *pl* amphide bodies
amphoter amphoteric
amphoterisch amphoteric
Amphydromie *f* amphidromy **-punkt** *m* amphidromic point
Amplidyne *f* amplidyne
Amplidynmaschine *f* amplidyne generator **-system** *n* metadyne drive
Amplitude *f* amplitude, crest
Amplituden-abhängigkeit *f* amplitude dependence **-abnahme** *f* reduction in amplitude **-abschneider** *m* peak limiter, clipper, lopper **-abschwächung** *f* sideband attenuation **-änderung** *f* variation of amplitude **-anzeiger** *m* glow-tube amplitude, tuning or resistance indicator, flashograph **-aufschaukelung** *f* amplitude increase **-ausflug** *m* amplitude excursion **-aussteuerung** *f* amplitude range **-bedingung** (für die Eigenerregung) amplitude relationship **-begrenzer** *m* amplitude limiter or lopper, peak limiter, clipper or lopper, clipper circuit
Amplituden-diskriminator *m* kicksorter **-eichstufenwähler** *m* amplitude calibrator **-eichvorrichtung** *f* amplitude calibration unit **-entzerrung** *f* correction of amplitudes **-frequenzverzerrung** *f* amplitude-frequency distortion **-gang** *m* amplitude-frequency characteristic **-getreu** of equal amplitude, with amplitude fidelity **-glimmröhre** *f* glow-tube-amplitude, tuning or resonance indicator, flashograph
Amplituden-kurve *f* amplitude curve **-linearität** *f* linearity in amplitude **-modler** *m*, **-modlung** *f* amplitude modulator **-modulation** *f* A.M., amplitude modulation (radio) **-modulationsrauschpegel** *m* amplitude-modulation noise level
amplitudenmodulierter Sender amplitude-modulated transmitter
Amplituden-regelung *f* amplitude regulation, gain control **-schrift** *f* sound tracks (variable area) **-schwund** *m* amplitude fading **-selektion** *f* amplitude filter, amplitude separator or selector, amplitude-discrimination selector **-sieb** *n* amplitude separator, discriminator, filter, or selector
Amplitudenspitzen, Abschneiden der ~ clipping or lopping off of amplitude peaks or crests, by limiter means
Amplituden-spitzenwert *m* peak pulse amplitude **-treue** *f* amplitude response **-unterdrückungsgrad** *m* amplitude-suppression ratio
Amplitudenverhältnis *n* ratio of amplitudes, magnitude ratio **~ der stehenden Welle** standing wave ratio **~ der Zeichen zu den Luftstörungen** signal-to-static ratio
Amplituden-verstärkung *f* amplitude gain **-verzerrung** *f* amplitude nonlinear or wave-form distortion, fundamental component distortion
Amplitudenverzerrungscharakteristik *f* amplitude-distortion characteristic **-faktor** *m* amplitude-distortion factor
Amplituden-zu-Zeitumsetzung amplitude-to-time conversion
Ampulle *f* ampoule, ampulla
Ampullen-bedruckmaschine *f* ampoule printing machine **-halter** *m* ampoule holder **-öffner** *m* ampoule opener
Amt *n* office, station, telephone exchange, central office, bureau, board, administrative department or fuction, appointment, calling, density, authority **~ ohne Überweisungsverkehr** non-parent exchange **~ ohne Umrechner** trunk control center **~ mit künstlichen Verlängerungsleitungen** switching pad office **~ mit Verlängerungsleitungen** office with extension lines **das ~ anrufen** to ring the exchange **ein ~ in die Leitung eintreten lassen** to call in a repeater station **eigenes ~** home station **fernes ~** distant station **unüberwachtes ~** unattended office **von Amts wegen** as a matter of routine
amtlich official **~ anerkennen** to homologate **~ bestätigen** to approve **-e Anerkennung eines Rekordes** homologation of a record **-er Bescheid** patent-office action, decision, official notice or notification **-e Bestätigung** official confirmation **-e Zulassung** approval
Amts-anlage *f* internal plant **-anlassungsrelais** (Trennrelais) trunk link start relay (cut-off relay) **-anruf** *m* exchange call **-anrufrelais** *n* call accepting relay for incoming trunk calls **-anschließer** *m* adapter, telephone exchange, connecting device, post-office adapter for field telephone **-anschluß** *m* post-office exchange connection **-antritt** *m* entrance **-batterie** *f* exchange battery **-bezeichnung** *f* office code or prefix **-bezeichnungssystem** *n* office code system **-bezirk** *m* exchange area **-blatt** *n* official gazette or journal
Amts-dämpfung *f* loss within exchange, exchange loss **-einführung** *f* inauguration **-einheit** (*f*) **mit . . . Anschlüssen** unit of . . . lines **-einrichtung** *f* office equipment, exchange apparatus **-enthebung** *f* dismissal **-erde** *f* post-office earthing point **-freizeichen** *n* dialing tone **-führung** *f* administration **-Fünfzigergruppen-Wähler** *m* (AFGW) trunk-fifties-selector (TFS) **-gebäude** *n* office **-geheimnis** *n* official secret **-gespräch** *n* trunk call (P.A.B.X.) **-gewalt** *f* official power **-gruppenwähler** *m* (AGW) trunk-group selector (TGS)
Amts-kabel *n* office cable **-kennziffer** *f* trunk digit (P.A.B.X.) **-klinke** *f* exchange jack **-leitung** *f* (direct) exchange line, central-office trunk, individual line, junction from private-branch exchange to exchange, trunk, subscriber's line, post-office line **-markierer** *m* trunk marker **-mechaniker** *m* central-office maintenance man **-namen** *m pl* office code **-namenspeicher** *m* office-code register **-namenwähler** *m* code switch **-nebenstelle** *f* exchange extension set **-nummer** *f* exchange number
Amts-pflege *f* exchange maintenance work **-schalter** *m* exchange switch **-schlüssel** *m* office code **-seite** *f* (des Hauptverteilers), exchange side, vertical side (of main distributing frame) **-sprechberechtigte Nebenstelle** unrestricted extension, extension exchange facilities **-störungspersonal** *n* exchange-fault staff **-summerzeichen** *n* dialing tone **-taste** *f* office key **-tätigkeit** *f* office routine **-telegramm** *n* service message

Amts-übersichtsplan *m* communication chart **-verbindung** *f* exchange call **-verbindungsleitung** *f* interoffice trunk **-verdrahtung** *f* internal wiring **-verkabelung** *f* office wiring **-verlust** *m* loss of official position **-verwaltung** *f* administration **-wähler** *m* junction or office selector **-wähllampe** *f* digit-key strip transfer lamp **-wegen** (von) matter of routine (as a), official course (in) **-zeichen** *n* dial(ing) tone **-zeit** *f* tenure of office **-zusatz** *m* telephone-exchange attachment or auxiliary set for field telephone, apparatus connecting directly to switchboard

Amts-Zweihunderter-Gruppen-Wähler *m* (AZGW) trunk twohundreds-selector (TTS)

Amydalin *n* amydalin

Amyl *n* amyl **ameisensaures ~** amyl formiate

Amylalkohol *m* amyl alcohol

Amylen *n* amylene

Amyl-jodid *n* amyl iodide **-opektin** *n* amylopectin **-oxydhydrat** *n* amyl hydrate, amyl alcohol **-sulfhydrat** *n* amyl hydrosulfide **-zyclohexan** *n* amylcyclohexane

anabatisch anabatic

anachromatisch anachromatic

anaerob anaerobic

Anaerobe *f* anoxic cell

Anaglyphen-brillen *f pl* anaglyph viewers **-verfahren** *n* anaglyphic method

Analcim *n* analcite

anallaktischer Punkt anallactic point

analog analogous **-er Transistor** *m* analogous transmitter

Analogien für Strömungen analogier to mechanism of flow

Analogrechner *m* analog computer **-technik** *f* analogue technique

Analysator *m* analyzer **harmonischer ~** harmonic analyzer, periodometer (music)

Analysatornikol *n* analyzing Nicol

Analyse *f*, **Analysis** *f* analysis **~ und Körnung** analysis and grade **gärungsphysiologische ~** zymotechnical analysis **momentane ~** instantaneous sampling **~ des Tagesganges** analysis of the diurnal variation

Analysen-befund *m* result of analysis **-fehler** *m* analytical error **-fein** ready-ground for analysis **-feuchtigkeit** *f* total moisture contents of the sample **-probe** *f* analysis sample, analytical test **-rein** analytical-grade

Analysenwaage *f* analytical (chemical) balance **kurzarmige ~** short-beam analysis balance

analysierbar analyzable

analysieren to analyze

Analysierzähldruckgerät *n* analyzing counter with printed putput

Analytiker *m* analyst

analytisch analytic(al)

Anamorphogramm *n* mathematically transformed diagram

Anamorphose *f* anamorphosis

anamorphotisch-e Dehnung (1-fach) (2-fold) anamorphotic expansion **-es Vorsatzlinsensystem** *n* anamorphotic ancillary lens system

Anaphase *f* anaphase

Anaphorese *f* anaphoresis

anarbeiten to attach, join or work onto

anastatischer Druck anastatic printing

Anästhetikum *n* anaesthetic

Anastigmat *n* anastigmat

anastigmatisch anastigmatic **-e Einschlaglupe** anastigmatic folding magnifier

Anatas *m* anatase, octahedrite

anätzen to etch, corrode, cauterize superficially or slightly

Anätzen *n* etching **elektrolytisches ~** anodic etching

Anätzung *f* first etching

anbacken to cake upon, bake on, adhere, bake superficially, fix by firing

anbahnen to prepare the way for

Anbau *m* annex, addition to structure, attachment, cultivation **~ am Achsbund** shoulder of axle collar

Anbaublinkleuchte *f* attachable-tape blinker lamp

anbauen to grow, cultivate, attach, build on

Anbaufläche *f* acreage, area **bearbeitete ~** mounting pad **vorgezogene ~** raised pad

Anbauflansch *m* attaching pad, mounting flange

Anbaugerät *n* mounted implement **~ zum Schlepper** tractor attachment **~ für Raupenschlepper** attachment for crawler tractors

Anbau-gruppe *f* extension board **-kasten** *m* adjacent box **-konsole** *f* mounting pad **-mäher** *m* mounted mower, mower **-maß** *n* constructional dimension **-motore** *m pl* built-on motors **-mikroskop** *n* attachment microscope **-platte** *f* adjacent plate

Anbau-schiene *f* drawbar **-scheinwerfer** *m* attachable-type head lamp **-teile** *m pl* attaching parts **-versuch** *m* experiment in cultivation **-vorrichtung** *f* construction jig **-winker** *m* exterior model of direction finder

anberaumen to appoint, assign, fix **Termin zur Verhandlung einer Sache ~** to set or fix date for hearing a case

anbiegen to bend

anbieten to offer, proffer

Anbietwähler *m* trunk-offering selector

Anbinde-kreuz *n* toggle **-pfahl** *m* mooring pile

anbinden to tie to, lash

Anbinder (Kran) *m* slinger

Anbindezettel *m* tag

anblasen to blast, turn or put on the blast, blow in (in a blast furnace), blow against, wind on

Anblasen *n* (der Tanks eines U-Bootes), initial blowing of tanks of a submarine by compressed air after which turboblowers take over

Anblase-technik *f* blowing-in practice (blast furnace) **-winkel** *m* angle of attack

Anblas-geschwindigkeit *f* velocity in blower stream **-rand** *m* edge (leading or entering, aviation)

Anblasrichtung *f* direction of air flow **~ verschwindenden Auftriebs** direction of relative wind for zero lift

Anblaston *m* aelian tone

Anblaswinkel *m* air-flow angle

anblatten to halve, half-lap join

Anblattung *f* halved joint, halving, half-lap joint

anbläuen to (color) blue

Anblick *m* aspect

Anbohrapparat *m* boring rig, drilling device, drill rig

ambohren to drill, bore, scuttle, tap, start bore

Anbohrer *m* center bit or drill **~ von Versagern**

drilling out misfires (explosives)
Anbohr-hahn *m* boring cock **-maschine** *f* centering machine **-rohrschelle** *f* boring pipe box **-schieber** *m* boring valve
Anbohrung *f* center hole, boring
Anbohr-vorrichtung *f* pipe drilling appliance **-werkzeug** *n* boring tool
anbolzen to bolt
Anbrechbohrer *m* pitching-borer
anbrechen begin to break, discover, open, spoil
anbrennen (anzünden) to light, set fire to
Anbrenn-freudigkeit *f* readiness of combustion **-schweißung** *f* flash welding **-zeit** *f* flashing time, time of lighting up (foundry, street lights)
anbringen to mount, fit, attach (to), apply, make, place, fix
Anbringung *f* mounting, attachment, placing **~ eines Kopfes** heading **~ in einer bestimmten Lage** location, act of locating
Anbruch *m* open lode, opening (min.), beginning, commencement, opening, decay, first yield, incipient fracture (metal)
anbrühen to steep, infuse in hot water, scald
Andalusit *m* andalusite
Andauern einer Wirkung prolonged effect
andauernd permanent, continual
ander other, else, next, different **einer hinter dem anderen** tandem
anderen, zum ~ secondly
andererseits on the other side, on the other hand
ändern to correct, change, alter, rectify, amend **sich ~** to alter (oneself), vary, change **sich sprunghaft ~** to change suddenly **sich mit der ... Potenz ~** to vary at the ... power
anders otherwise, different
Andersonit *m* andersonite
Anderswertigkeit *f* being of different valence
anderthalb sesqui
Anderthalbdecker *m* sesquiplane
anderthalbfach one and a half times
Änderung *f* change, alteration, variation, deformation, amendment, correction, modification, transformation, reversal **prozentuale ~** percentage change **technische ~** engineering change **~ des Blatteinstellwinkels** change of blade pitch **~ des Drehvermögens** mutarotation **~ mit der Frequenz** variation with frequency **~ der Generatorspannung mit der Drehzahl** voltage variation with speed of a generator **~ einer Gesprächsanmeldung** change in instructions (in connection with a call)
Änderung der Stellgröße corrective action **~ der Verfahrensordnung** *f* modification of rules **~ vorbehalten** data subject to change without notice **~ der Wartezeit** modification of delay **~ des Wirkungsgrades eines elektroakustischen Apparates mit der Leistung** net loss variation with amplitude of an electroacoustic apparatus
Änderungen *f pl* changes **~ des magnetischen Erdfeldes** variations in the earth's magnetic field **~ des Kompasses** variations of compass diurnal
Änderungs-faktor *m* factor defining variation **-geschwindigkeit** *f* rate of acceleration or change of target speed, remaining velocity (ballistics), process reaction rate **-prüfung** *f* modification test **-tendenzfunktion** *f* function showing tendency to variation
Anderkonto *n* trust account
Andesit *n* andesite
andeuten to indicate
Andeutung *f* hint, indication
Andrang *m* rush
andrehen to turn on, start, tighten, screw on, crank, start an engine, switch on **~** (einen Ausbruch veranlassen) to kick off, start (an eruption)
Andrehen *n* joining a thread **~ der Ketten** chain twisting
Andreh-hülse *f* starting crank jaw **-klaue** *f* crank socket, starter clutch
Andrehkurbel *f* crank handle, starting crank **-griff** *m* starting handle, jaw or grip **-klaue** *f* starting-crank jaw, clutch for starting handle **-lagerstütze** *f* starting-crank bracket
Andreh-motor *m* starting motor **-ritzel** *n* turn pinion **-seite** *f* airscrew or propeller end **-vermögen** *n* maneuverability, ability to start (motor) **-vorrichtung** *f* starter, turning device **-welle** *f* starting crank shaft
Androgenesis *f* androgenesis
Androhung *f* warning, caution, notification (of a threatened action), threat **~ nachteiliger Folgen** threat of dire consequences
Andromedanebel *m* nebula of Andromeda (astron.)
Andruck *m* counter pressure, proof copy
Andrückbürste *f* pressing brush
andrücken to press on, force against, (slang) to power dive, put on speed
andrucken to proof
Andrück-etikett *n* self-adhesive label **-exzenter** *m* pressing excentric
Andruckfenster *n* pressure gate (film)
Andrück-hebel *m* pressing lever **-kippschalter** *m* momentary trigger switch **-kurve** *f* attach cam
Andruck-magnet *m* pressure solenoid (tape rec.) **-maschine** *f* proofing machine **-platte** *f* pressure plate **-presse** *f* proof press **-rolle** *f* back-up roller, pressure pulley, puck (tape rec.) **-schaltarm** *m* contact arm **-schiene** *f* (crossbar) connecting bar, pressure pad or guide **-vorrichtung** *f* auxiliary roller system **-walze** *f* feed roll **-zeit** *f* pressure applying period
Andrückwalze *f* auxiliary roller
aneignen, sich ~ to appropriate, adopt
aneinander-fügen to join together, frame **-geraten** to clash, come together **-gesprengte Prismen** broken contact (uncemented) prism (closely fitted together) **-grenzen** to join, be contiguous **-grenzend** adjacent, adjoining, superposed **-hängend** contiguous, sticking together **-kurbeln** (Spitzenstreifen) to sew together
Aneinander-lagerung *f* bond, joining **-prallen** *n* collision **-prallen** to collide **-reiben** *n* rubbing on each other, attrition **-reiten** to line up, to combine (Zahlen) **-rücken** *n* rapprochement **-stoßen** *n* continguity **-stoßen** to meet (by thrust or push)
anelastisch inelastic **-e Messungen** anelastic measurements
Anelastizität *f* anelasticity, inelasticity
Anelektrotonus *m* anelectrotonus

anellieren to anellate
Anemobiagraph *m* anemobiagraph
Anemograph *m*, **Windrad ~** fan-wheel anemograph, rotating wheel or wind vane, anemograph
Anemo-gramm *n* anemogram **-klinograph** *n* anemoclinograph **-messer** *n* anemometer, air meter, wind gauge **-skop** *n* anemoscope **-tachometer** *n* wind-velocity indicator
Anerbe *m* principal heir
Anerbieten *n* offer, tender
anerkannt accepted, standard, admitted, recognized, approved (listed) **-er Fachmann** accepted authority
anerkennen to acknowledge, recognize, appreciate, homologate a record, admit **amtlich ~** to homologate
Anerkennung *f* recognition, acknowledgment **~ eines Rekordes** acceptance of a record **amtliche ~ eines Rekordes** homologation of a record
Anerkennungs-gebühr *f* wayleave charges **-schreiben** *n* commendation, testimonial letter **-zahlung** *f* token payment
Aneroidbarometer *n* aneroid barometer, capsule aneroid **~ besonderer Art** statoscope (a very sensitive aneroid altimeter)
Aneroid-Luftdruckmesser aneroid berometer or altimeter **-manometer** *n* bellow gauge
anfachen to kindle, excite a wave, vibration, or oscillation
Anfach-gebläse *n* gas blower **-raum** *m* generator or working space (beam tube)
Anfachung *f* regenerative amplification, continuous excitation of waves (or point where oscillating begins), fanning, kindling, antidamping
Anfachungs-bedingung *f* oscillation condition, condition for self-oscillation **-mechanismus** *m* exciting mechanism (electronics) **-stadium** *n* initial state, non-fully development state
Anfachzeit *f* building-up period
Anfahr-beschleunigung *f* starting acceleration (of a locomotive) **-drehmoment** *n* starting torque
anfahren to bring up, drive up, move along, start, bring to speed, cut a lode, encounter, enter, start-up
Anfahr-gang *m* low gear **-hebel** *m* starting lever **-kosten** *f pl* cartage expenses **-kraft** *f* starting energy or force, tractive force **-luft** *f* starting air **-maß** *n* clearance **-methode** *f* start-up procedure **-moment** *n* starting moment **-schieber** *m* starting valve (slide valve) **-schwierigkeit** *f* launching difficulty (in rocketry) **-sohle** *f* entrance level **-stellung** *f* starting position **-strecke** *f* starting distance **-strom** *m* starting current **-stufe** *f* preliminary stage (in propulsion of rockets)
Anfahrt *f* descent (into a mine), drive, avenue **-rampe** *f* loading ramp of a ferry ship
Anfahr-ventil *n* starting valve **-vorgang** *m* combustion start, starting process or procedure **-vorrichtung** *f* starting device, starting gear (airplane) **-widerstand** *m* starting resistance **-wirbel** *m* starting or initial vortex **-zeit** *f* start-up time
Anfall *m* yield, impost, surprise attack, raid
anfallen to obtain, be obtained, produce, yield, result, accumulate, collect
anfällig allergic
Anfälligkeit *f* susceptibility (to disease)
anfalzen to rabbet
Anfang *m* start, beginning, commencement, origin, inception, outset **~ der äußeren Bogenfläche** spring (skewback) of extrados **~ der inneren Bogenfläche** spring (skewback) of intrados **am ~ stehend** initial **~ des Geigerbereichs** Geiger-müller threshold
anfangen to begin, start, commence **~ zu brennen** to catch fire
anfangend incipient
Anfänger *f* beginner, novice, learner **-ausbildung** *f* elementary flying training **-modell** *n* beginner's model **-segelflugzeug** *n* primary training glider
anfänglich initial **-e Rekombination** initial recombination **-e Schwierigkeiten** early difficulties **-es Seitenspiel** (Kolbenring) initial side clearance
Anfang(s)-adresse *f* initial address **-anschlagwert** *m* minimum resistance at starting position (variable resistor) **-auftriebsbeiwert** *m* initial lift coefficient or factor **-auslenkung** *f* initial displacement **-ausschlag** *m* initial amplitude **-bahn** *f* initial path **-beanspruchung** *f* initial strain **-bedingung** *f* initial condition **-belastung** *f* initial stress, initial load **-bohrer** *m* (Steinbrechen), hammer-shaped iron plug (quarrying), starting borer **-buchstabe** *m* initial letter, first letter
Anfang(s)-daten *pl* initial data **-drall** *m* initial twist **-drehzahl** *f* initial revolutions per minute **-drift** *f* initial drift (of photocell) **-druck** *m* kickoff pressure, initial pressure **-durchschlag** *m* initial breakdown **-eisen** *n* gathering iron **-empfindlichkeit** *f* start-of-scale sensitivity
Anfangsenergie *f* initial or starting energy **~ von Neutronen** initial energy of neutrons
Anfangs-ergebnis *n* first-runnings product **-erzeugnis** *n* first-runnings product **-fehler** *m* inherited error
Anfangsgeschwindigkeit *f* initial velocity (rocket) initial speed **~ eines Geschosses** muzzle velocity
Anfangs-gradient *m* initial gradient **-grund** *m* rudiment element **-intensität** *f* original intensity **-kapazität** *f* initial capacitance, minimum or zero capacity (radio) **-kolumne** *f* opening column **-konvergente** *f* convergently beginning series **-konzentration** *f* prefocusing **-kurs** *m* opening price or rate (exchange)
Anfangs-ladung *f* initial charge (blasting) **-lage** *f* initial position, starting point **-lagerspiel** *n* initial slackness **-längenkreis** *m* initial meridian **-leistung** *f* initial performance **-masse** *f* initial mass (of rocket) **-material** *n* raw material **-meridian** *n* zero meridian **öffnung** *f* full (maximum) aperture **-ordinate** *f* initial ordinate
Anfangsperiode des normalen Betriebes initial operation of the plan
Anfangs-permeabilität *f* initial permeability, permeability at low magnetizing forces **-potential** *n* starting potential **-punkt** *m* initial boiling point (petroleum), origin **-randsteller** *m* left-hand margin stop **-schenkel** *m* starting leg **-schlacke** *f* initial slag **-schub** *m* initial or starting thrust, lift-off thrust **-seite** *f* opening page **-siedepunkt** *m* initial boiling point **-span-**

nung *f* input voltage, initial (stress) voltage **-spektrum** *n* injected spectrum **-sperre** *f* incoming block (electr.) **-spiel** *n* initial slackness

Anfangs-stadium *n* initial stage **-standmelder** *m* starting condition (or position), gauge (missiles) **-stärke** *f* initial strength **-steigegeschwindigkeit** *f* initial climbing speed, rate of climb **-steigung** *f* initial pitch or slope **-stein** *m* second cheek stone **-stellung** *f* initial position **-störung** *f* initial disturbance **-strom** *m* initial current, starting, incipient, or original current **-stück** *n* initial part **-stufe** *f* initial step (radio) **-suszeptibilität** *f* initial susceptibility **-tagesförderung** *f* initial daily production **-verstärkung** *f* initial amplification **-verschiebung** *f* intiial displacement **-verschleiß** *m* initial wear **-volumen** *n* original volume

Anfangswert *m* initial condition, initial or early value ~ **der Flüchtigkeit auf der Verdampfungskurve eines Brennstoffes** front-end volatility of a fuel

Anfangswertaufgabe *f* initial value problem **-methode** *f* initial-value method

Anfangs-widerstand *m* initial resistance **-winkel** *m* angle of impulse **-zeichen** *n* start signal **-zeugnis** *n* first runnings product **-zustand** *m* initial state or condition

Anfärbbarkeit *f* dye affinity or absorption

anfärben to stain superficially, color

Anfärbevermögen *n* dye affinity or absorption

Anfärbung *f* first inking, dyeing

Anfasen *n* chamfering

anfassen to graps, touch, take hold of, pick up (arms), contact

anfechten to combat contest, assail, dispute **die Gültigkeit eines Patentes** ~ to challenge validity of a patent, argue nonvalidity

Anfechtungsprozeß *m* contested action

anfertigen to make, manufacture, prepare

Anfertigung *f* manufacture, making ~ **der Lageskizze** sketching

Anfettapparat *m* greasing apparatus

anfetten to lubricate, grease slightly

Anfeuchtapparat *m* moistener

anfeuchten to moisten, wet, dampen, sprinkle, temper (water content) ~ **in Sägespänen** to sawdust ~ **mit dem Schwamm** to sponge

Anfeuchter *m* damper, humectant

Anfeucht-feuerung *f* fulminate compound **-maschine** *f* dampers or damping rolls, spray damper, moistening machine

Anfeuchtung *f* pre-wetting

Anfeuchtwalze *f* damping roller

anfeuern to make a fire, set on fire

Anfeuerung *f* combustible composition

Anfeuerungssatz *m* tracer igniter, booster charge

anfilzen to harden

anfirnissen to (prime-)varnish

Anflächung *f* flat

Anflansch *m* (bei Geräten) flange type

anflanschen to flange, screw on

Anflanschsteuergerät *n* flange-mounted control valve

anflechten to join by twisting or plaiting

anflicken to patch on

anfliegen to fly on, effloresce, spring up spontaneously; fly toward, approach (aviation)

Anflug *m* approach; incrustation, coating, film, efflorescence, superficial layer (in sublimation), run, flight, sprinkling, touch

Anflug-ebene *f* approach or landing path **-fläche** *f* approach surface **-folge** *f* approach sequence

Anfluggrundlinie *f* flight base line, principal course of approach (extender) center line **beidrehen auf** ~ to turn to or steer for center of approach sector **-grundlinienbefeuerung** *f* base approach lighting

Anflug-kontrolle *f* approach control **-kontrollstelle** *f* approach control office **-leerlaufzustand** *m* approach idling conditions **-Leitfeuer** *pl* lead-in lights **-manöver** *n* approach procedure **-richtung** *f* direction of approach **-schneise** *f* approach sector or corridor **-sektor** *m* approach area **-weg** *m* approach path or way **-winkel** *m* approach angle **-winkelfeuer** *pl* angle-of-approach lights **-zeit** *f* duration of approach flight

Anfluß *m* onflow, alluvium, afflux, rise, swelling **-geschwindigkeit** *f* velocity of approach, afflux velocity (of fluids)

anfordern to demand, require, claim, requisition quisition

Anforderung *f* claim, demand, requirement, requisition **briefliche** ~ request

Anforderungen *f pl* specifications, requirements **den** ~ **entsprechen** to come within, or meet, the requirements **hohe** ~ exacting requirements ~ **stellen** to impose design objectives, set requirements on

Anforderungs-formular *n* request form **-nummer** *f* requisition (reference) number **-verflichtungen** *f pl* cash liabilities **-zeichen** *n* code number, order or requisition number or symbol

Anforderzeichen *n* requisition symbol

anformen to tip-stretch

Anfrage *f* inquiry, request **auf** ~ upon request

Anfrageapparat *m* listening-in equipment for inquiry purposes (teleph.)

anfragen to inquire, ask (for)

Anfraß *m* corrosion, pitting, staining, erosion

anfräsen to mill

anfressen to corrode, pit, stain, erode (cavitation), attack, eat away

Anfressung *f* erosion, corrosion, seizure **grübchenartige** ~ pitting **narbenartige** ~ honeycomb corrosion **örtliche** ~ pitting

Anfressungsbeständigkeit *f* resistance to corrosion or erosion

anfrischen to refresh, varnish, refine (metal)

anfügen to annex, attach, add, enclose

anfühlen to feel

Anfuhr *f* conveying, transporting

anführen to lead, lead on, cite, dupe, quote, mention

Anführer *m* (file) leader

Anfuhrgeld *n* cartage

Anführung *f* quotation, leadership, guidance

Anführungszeichen *n* quotation mark

anfüllen to charge, fill up, replete

Anfüllen der Pumpe priming of the pump

Anfüllung *f* filling, cramming, plenum

Anfüllventil *n* priming valve

anfunken to talk to by radiotelephone

Angabe *f* specification, estimate, information, report, instruction, indication, datum, statement, declaration, assertion, summary **beglaubigte ~** sworn or certified statement

Angaben *f pl* details, particulars, data, statements, allegations **bauliche ~** structural data **weitere ~** further particulars **~ beschaffen** to secure information **~ des Kunden** customer's specification

angängig approachable, possible, applicable, feasible

angearbeitetes Eisen scrap iron

angebaut annexed, built on to **-er Regler** attached governor

angeben to state, inform, report, instruct, declare, indicate, outline, point out, tell, allege, supply; (in großer Linie) outline

angeblich nominal, supposedly

Angeber *m* detector, indicator

angebohrter Radiusmittelpunkt *m* drill-marked center

Angebot *n* offer, supply, tender, proposal, bid or quotation (of price) **das billigste ~** the lowest bid **ein versiegeltes ~** a sealed offer or tender

angeboten innate

Angebots-aufforderung *f* bid invitation, invitation to tender for . . . (to request a tender for . . .) **-mappe** *f* information folder

angebracht timely, applicable, situated, suitable, in order **-e Steuerscheibe A** cam A mounted

angefacht induced

angefault rotten, rotting

angeflanscht flange connected or mounted **-er Antriebsmotor** *m* flanged motor **-es Gewinde** *n* flatted thread

angefordert called for

angefressen corroded, eroded, ulcerated

angefüllt replete

angegeben given, supplied

angeglichene Luftschraube nach der Schmierung wet balance of propeller after lubrication

angegossen cast integral, integrally cast, cast-on **-e Rippen** fins cast integral

angegriffen attacked

angehakt checked

angehen to approach, apply to, (Farbstoff) be absorbed

Angehen *n*, **selbstätiges ~** self-starting

angehend incipient, prospective, budding **-er Flugzeugführer** candidate pilot

Angehkurve der Lichtmaschine *f* starting curve of dynamo

angehören to belong or appertain to

Angehöriger *m* member, relative

Angeklagter *m* defendant, respondent

angekörnt punch-marked

angekreuzt checked

angekündigt announced **-er Verkaufspreis** posted selling price

Angel *f* pivot, axis, fishing rod or hook, hinge, tongue (of a file), tang (Tür-)**~**, hinge

angelagert associated **-e Elektronen** trapped electrons **-e Flüssigkeiten** associated liquids

angelassener Stahl annealed (drawn) steel

Angeld *n* first installment, deposit

Angeldraht *m* trip wire

angelegen important, of concern, interesting

Angelegenheit *f* matter, affair, subject, business, cause, case

angelegentlich earnest, urgent

angelehnt adjoining, in touch with, supported by, covered by, leaning (against), ajar (door) **-er Flügel** supported flank

Angeleisen *n* angle-iron

angelenkt (drehbar), pivoted, articulated, hinged **nachgiebig ~** flexibly jointed

angelernt semiskilled **-er Arbeiter** semiskilled worker or operator

Angel-nute *f* tang slot **-ring** *m* pin with eyebolt, pan, socket, sole **-spannung der Gattersägen** angle stress of frame on reciprocating saws

angelochter Lochstreifen (Fernschreib.) shapeless perforated tape

Angel-punkt *m* fulcrum, pivotal point **-schnurproblem** *n* fishline problem

Angelzapfen (*m*) **einer Türangel** pivot or axis of a hinge

angemachte Farben ready-made paints

angemachter Kalk slaked lime

angemeldet announced, applied for (patents), filed **-es Patent** patent pending **~ sein** to be on hand

angemessen conformable to, proportionate to, suitable, proper, apt, adequate, opposite to, appropriate, due, equal, expedient, just, fair, convenient, reasonable **~ sein** to suit

angemessene Sorgfalt reasonable diligence

angenähert approximate **-er Knotenpunkt** partial node **-er Meßbereich** approximate range of measurement **-e** (mittlere) **Nachbildung** compromise network

angenommen assuming, supposing, adopted; let (bei Formeln) **-er Anteil an der Durchgangsgebühr** hypothetical transit quota

angepaßt adapted **-er Abschlußwiderstand** nonreflecting termination, matched termination **-er Empfänger** matched receiver **-er Hohlleiter** matched waveguide **-e Leitung** matched (transmission) line **-e Richtleiter** matched crystal diodes (matched for uniformity) **-e T-Antenne** T-matched antenna **-es Verzweigungsglied** matched junction

Angerbung *f* superficial tanning, fermentation

angeregt excited, stimulated **-es Atom** *n* excited atom **-e Gruppe** *f* excitor (in dielectric breakdown) **-e Heliumzustände** *pl* excited helium states **-es Ion** excited ion **-es Molekül** activated molecule **-e Moleküle als Kettenträger** stimulated molecules as chain agents **-er Zustand** *m* excited state

angereichert enriched, doped **-e Frakrion** *f* enriched fraction **-er Reaktor** *m* enriched pile (reactor) **-es Uran** *n* enriched uranium **-e Zone** *f* seed area

angerostet slightly rusty

angerufene Leitung called line

angerufener Teilnehmer called (wanted, required) subscriber or party

angesaugte Luftmenge volume of air drawn in

angeschärft scarfed, thinned **Verbindung mit -en Enden** scarfed joint

angeschlossen connected, in circuit **-er Strom** bias of a circuit

angeschmiedete Wellenflansche forged on shaft collar

angeschnitten sein to be gated (die-casting)

angeschrägt beveled (points)
angeschraubt screwed on
angeschuhte Stange shoed or stub-reinforced pole
Angeschuldigter *m* accused defendant
angeschweißt welded
angeschwemmt alluvial **-er Boden** alluvium
angeschwollen bulged
angesetzt, rechtwinklig ~ an fixed at right angles to
angesichts owing to, in the face of
angespannt intense (Physik)
angespült alluvial
angestauchter Rand staved end
angestaut congested
angestellt employed
Angestellten-verband *m* employees' organization **-versicherung** *f* liability insurance for employees
Angestellter *m* employee
angestrebt aimed at **-e Keilbreite** desired wedge **-es Ziel** objective
angestrengter Betrieb des Motors high-duty running of an engine
angetan adapted, suitable
angetrieben driven **elektrisch ~** electrically operated **-e Pumpe** power pump **unmittelbar -er Lader** direct-driven blower
angewachsen adherent, attached
angewalzter Flansch *m* rolled-on flange
angewandt applied, practical **-e Methode der Wiederbewertung** method of reevaluation used **voll -es Ruder** *n* full rudder **-e Sätze** rates used
angewendet applied
angewiesen sein auf to be dependent on
angewöhnen to accustom, condition, adjust
Angewohnheit *f* mannerism, habit
angezapft tapped **-er Dampf** bled steam **-e Wicklung** tapped winding **in der Mitte -e Wicklung** center-tapped winding with midpoint tap **-er Widerstand** tapped resistance
angezeigt reported, indicated, advisable, announced **-e Fluggeschwindigkeit** indicated air speed **-e Leistung** indicated horse-power
angezogen dressed (with clothing), normally pulled up **mit den Fingern -e Schraubenmutter** finger-tight nut
angießen to pour or cast on, join by casting, color (by coat of clay)
Angießen *n* splashing, checking
angilben to develop a yellowish tinge
Angiocardiographie *f* angiocardiography
angleichen to assimilate, equate, correct, compensate, adapt
Angleicher *m* rectifier
Angleichfeder *f* adapter spring, assimilating spring
Angleichfrequenz *f* tuning knob
Angleichung *f* adjustment, adaptation, (approximate) matching (of brightness, color)
Angleich-ventil *n* adapting valve, assimilating valve **-vorrichtung** *f* adapting device **-weg** *m* compensating path, equalizing path, adapting travel
Anglesit *m* anglesite, lead vitriol, lead sulfate
angliedern to attach, incorporate, connect, annex, affiliate
Angliederung *f* coalition, union, affiliation, attachment
anglühen to heat, anneal
angreif-bar attackable, undermined **-barkeit** *f* chemical durability (of glass), attackability
angreifen (anfassen) to touch, handle; (Aufgabe) tackle, approach; (Werkstück) attack; (Kapital) draw on, dip into; (Chem.) corrode, attack; (unternehmen) set about, engage; (Last) apply, assault, affect, pit, catch, act upon **~** (Feile, Schneidwerkzeug) to bite **nicht ~** to behave inertly **~ der Kraft an einem Punkt** the force acts on a point
angreifend -es Ende eines Werkzeuges business end of a tool **-er Erddruck** *m* active earth pressure **-e Kraft** acting force
Angreifer *m* attacker, agressor
angrenzen to border on, join, butt against
angrenzend adjoining, adjacent, juxtaposed to, neighboring, contiguous, bordering on **-es Gebirge** adjoining soil or mountains (shaft sinking)
Angriff, chemischer ~ attack by chemical action, gas attack, corrosion
Angriffs-fähigkeit *f* susceptibility or capability to attack **-feld** *n* zone of attack **-fläche** *f* working surface **-form** *f* form of attack, attack formation **-freudig** aggressive
Angriffs-geschwindigkeit *f* rate (speed) of attack **-höhe** *f* working depth **-kraft** *f* momentum, aggressive or attacking power, striking potential **-linie** *f* (für eine Kraft) line of application
Angriffs-lustig aggressive **-mittel** *n pl* means of attack, corroding media or agents **-mittelpunkt** *m* center of attack or of pressure **-möglichkeit** *f* possibility of attack **-moment** *m* applied moment (mech. engin)
Angriffspunkt *m* point of application (of attack), place of application, applied moment, working point, point of engagement, attachment, action **~ der Kraft** point of or application of force or action, origin of force
Angriffsrichtung *f* direction of attack **~ des Luftschraubenschubes** thrust line
Angriffs-schenkel *m* actuating arm **-stelle** *f* point of attack, or of application, working face **-streifen** *m* sector of attack **-verfahren** *n* method of attack **-verlauf** *m* progress of attack **-versuch** *m* attempted attack **-winkel** *m* brake action **-zeit** *f* zero hour
Angst *f* anxiety, fear, anguish
Ångström Å angström Å
Ångströmeinheit *f* angstrom unit (A.U.)
Anguß *m* dead head, jet (plate), extension gate, pouring on, feedhead, lug, coupon (on castings), deadhead, boss, cleat **~ der gegossenen Typen** break of the types **~ entfernen** to degate
Anguß-abreißstift *m* sprue lock pin **-auswerferstift** *m* sprue lock pin **-buchse** *f* sprue bushing, feed bush, adapter **-buchsenhalter** *m* nozzle adapter **-kanal** *m* sprue runner **-kegel** *m* sprue slug, spur
angußlos without groove **-es Spritzen** direct injection molding
Angußstelle *f* gate mark
anhaben to wear (clothing) **einem etwas ~** to have a design upon somebody
anhaften to adhere, cling, stick to
Anhaften *n* adherence
anhaftend adherent, adhesive, inherent, be attached to

Anhaftung *f* adhesion, adherence
Anhaftungsfähigkeit *f* adhesion
anhaken to fasten with hooks, hook, hitch (couple), catch
Anhall *m* attack, transient
Anhallen *n* building up of acoustic energy
Anhalt *m* support, foothold, training publication, rough indication, guide; general principle for action or thought; pause, stoppage **~ gewinnen** to get a footing, gain a foundation or basis
anhaltbar can be stopped
anhalten to lock, adjust, set, stop, stay, brake, arrest, impede, dam, detain, hold, restrain, maintain stationary, fix, secure, continue, intercept, last, endure, persist
Anhalten *n* stoppage, stopping, arrest
anhaltend persistent, lasting, permanent, constant, continuous
Anhalte-punkt *m* fulcrum, stopping point or place **-potentialmethode** *f* stopping potential method **-verzögerung** *f* delayed stopping control
Anhaltevorrichtung *f* stopping device **~ eines Indikators** detent gear of an indicator
Anhaltspunkt *m* fitting point, guiding principle, indication, stopping, or essential point, fulcrum, clue, reference or datum point, guide, base, station, criterion, index **-punkte** *m pl* instructions (without force of orders)
Anhaltstift *m* stop pin (instruments)
Anhaltszahlen *pl* reference values
anhand (an Hand) with the aid of, by
Anhang *m* annex, addition, following, supplement, postscript, support, appendix, schedule
Anhänge-antenne *f* drag antenna **-gerät** *n* portable set, signal **-kalkulation** *f* tag-on calculation (permitted supplement to original price calculation) **-last** *f* trailer load
anhangen to adhere, hang on
anhängen to add, join, append, attach, adhere, annex, throw in, couple, connect, hang up or on, affix **sich ~** to cling, adhere, join, follow **den (Fern)hörer ~** to hang up the receiver, restore the circuit
Anhängen des Hörers hanging up the telephone **Vermessen durch ~** survey by controlled traverse
anhängend adherent, adhesive, cohesive
Anhängeplatte *f* movable plate (print)
Anhänger *m* trailer, follower, supporter, adherent, tag, partisan, bottom filler, hanger-on **~ für Kabeltransport** cable-reel trailer
Anhänger-achse *f* trailer axle **-beleuchtung** *f* trailer lights **-bremse** *f* trailer air brake **-bremsgestänge** *n* trailer brake linkage **-bremsventil** *n* trailer brake valve **-dreieckzeichen** *n* trailer triangle sign **-haken** *m* hitch hook **-kehrmaschine** *f* trailer sweeper **-kippvorrichtung** *f* trailer tipping device
Anhängerkupplung *f* rigid-type trailer coupling, trailer coupling, trailer hitch, tow coupling **~ drehbar** pivoted-type trailer coupling **~ gefedert** spring-type trailer coupling **~ schwenkbar** swinging-type trailer coupling **~ selbsttätig** automatic trailer coupling
Anhänger-kupplungskopf *m* tow coupling head **-leitung** *f* lead to the trailer **-lichtkupplung** *f* trailer-light coupling **-öse** *f* pintle hook **-schiene** *f* drawbar, tool bar, hitch rail **-schürfwagen** *pl* two-type scrapers
Anhänger-steckdose *f* trailer plug box or socket **-steuerventil** *n* trailer control or brake valve **-stütze** *f* hitch bracket **-vorrichtung** *f* trailer coupling **-zughaken** *m* two-hook for trailer
Anhänge-siegel *n* affixed seal **-straßenhobel** *m* two-type graders **-vorrichtung** *f* loading rack
Anhängewagen *m* trailer **~ mit Kippkasten** hopper trailer
Anhänge-zeichen *n* trailer sign or marker **-zettel** *m* tag
anhängig sein to be pending
Anhängsel *n* appendage, pendant
anharmonisch anharmonic **-e Terme** anharmonic terms or constants
Anharmonizität *f* anharmonicity **-konstanten** *pl* anharmonicity constants
anhaspen to hook, catch, fasten with iron bands
Anhaublech *n* (Mähmaschine) metal sweep (reaper)
Anhauen von Wetterbläsern cutting of blowers, feeders, or gas
anhäufen to pile or heap up, aggregate, accumulate, mass, condense **sich ~** to (ac)cumulate, condense
anhäufend (ac)cumulative
Anhäufung *f* accumulation, aggregation, agglomeration, agglomerate, massing, congestion, sinter cake, piling up, concentration, damming up, loading, storage, build up
Anhäufungs-zeichen *n* group busy signal **-zone** *f* zone of accumulation
Anhebeblock *m* jack, lifting pad
anheben to lift, hoist, prime, fetch, emphasize, accentuate, underscore (sounds or frequency bands)
Anhebe-stange *f* handling bar **-vorrichtung** *f* jack
Anhebezeit (Hubzeit) time of raise
Anhebung *f* emphasis, accentuation (elec.), lift, boost **~ der Bässe** bass lift **~ der hohen Frequenzen** high boost, high-frequency compensation **~ der Höhen** treble lift
Anhebungs-filter *n* emphasizer **-netzwerk** *n* accentuator
anheften to hook, fasten, attach
Anheftungslinie *f* line of junction
anheimfallen to subject to, revert to, become the property of
anheimstellen to leave to, give the choice of
anheizen to fire, heat up, start up or stoke up boilers, turn the heater on
Anheizen *n* heating up, preheating, initial heating (of a tube), kindling
Anheiz-periode *f* heating-up period **-ventilator** *m* starting fan **-wirkungsgrad** *m* heating-up efficiency **-zeit** *f* heating-up period, cathode-heating time, pre-heating time, time taken for heating up, warm-up time
anheuern to hire
anheulen to excite
Anhieb *m* first blow, cut, or felling
Anhöhe *f* rise, elevation, hill, slope
anholen to haul (tight), bring up
anholomen anholomonic
anhören to listen, tell by listening
Anhub *m* lift **-moment** *n* initial power **-stange des Ventils** valve push rod

Anhydrid *n* anhydride
anhydrisch anhydrous
Anhydrit *n* anhydrite, anhydrous gypsum
Anilin *n* aniline, aminobenzene, phenylamine, aniline oil **-chlorhydrat** *n* aniline hydrochloride
Anilin-druck *m* flexographic printing **-druckwerk** *n* aniline printing unit **-einbadschwarz** *n* one-dip aniline black **-farbe** *f*, **-farbstoff** *m* aniline dye **-formaldehyd** *n* aniline formaldehyde **-hydrochlorid** *n* aniline hydrochloride, aniline salt **-klotzschwarz** *n* slop-padded aniline black **-schwarzbeize** *f* aniline black mordant
Anilit *n* anilide
animalische Leimung animal gelatin, glue, sizing, tub sizing
Anion-Fehlstelle *f* anion vacancy
anionisch anionic
Anis *m* anise, aniseed **-aldehyd** *n* anisic aldehyde
Anisidin *n* anisidine
Anisol *n* anisole
anisomer anisomeric
Anisometropie (eine Ungleichheit der Fehlsichtigkeit beider Augen) anisotropia (defective sights are dissimilar in the two eyes)
anisotrop anisotropic, non-isotropic **-e Festkörper** anisotropic solids **-e Setzung** anisotropic consolidation **-e Verdichtung** anisotropic consolidation
Anisotropie *f* anisotropy **-koeffizient** *m* anisotropy coefficient **-kraft** *f* anisotropy energy **-wert** *m* anisotropy value
anisotropische Verzeichnung anisotropic distortion, shear distortion, distortion of orientation
Ankathete, die ~ zu the adjacent side to (in a right triangle)
Ankauf *m* buying or purchasing
Ankaufspreis *m* purchase or prime cost, cost price
ankeilen to fasten with a wedge
Anker *m* anchor(age), stay, guy, tie rod, keeper, tieplate rotor, escapement, grapnel, (dynamo) armature **~ eines Dauermagnetes** armature of a permenent magnet **~ mit Gegengewicht** gravity-controlled armature **~ mit Knäuelwicklung** wire-wound armature **~ mit Nuten** slot armature **~ eines Relais** armature or tongue of a relay **~ des Seiles** cable anchorage **~ mit Stabwicklung** bar-wound armature **~ mit Trommelwicklung** drum armature **~ mit kurzgeschlossener Wicklung** short-circuited or squirrel-cage rotor **feststehender** (umlaufender) **~** fixed (rotating) armature
Anker, den ~ fallen lassen to drop anchor **der ~ ist Kurz Stag** the the anchor is at short stay **den ~ lichten** to weigh anchor **die ~ seefest zurren** to secure anchors for sea **vor ~ liegen** to lie at anchor **zu ~ liegen** to ride at anchor **fester ~** fixed anchorage **mit zwei Ankern** *m pl* double-armature **unterständiger ~** overtype armature
Anker-achse *f* armature shaft (electr.) **-abfall** *m* detraction of armature **-anschlag** *m* armature stop screw **-antrieb** *m* armature drive **-anzug** *m* attraction of armature **-auslaufzeit** *f* time for armature to run out **-balken** *m* anchor stock **-bandage** *f* band of armature
ankerben to notch up
Anker-beting *f* mooring bitts **-bewegung** *f* armature travel **-bindedraht** *m* armature binding wire **-blech** *n* armature lamination, armature core disk **-block** *m* deadman (anchor block)
Anker-bohrung *f* armature bore or gap **-boje** *f* mooring buoy **-bolzen** *m* anchor(ing) bolt, lag screw; tie, long or holding-down bolt, tie or truss rod, truss bolt, stay, tie bar **-büchse** *f* armature spider **-bühne** *f* crooked wharf **-draht** *m* stay rope or wire, halyard **-einstellhebel** *m* armature bracket link **-eisen** *n* armature iron
Ankerflansch der Triebseite pinion-end core head **vorderer ~** armature-head flange
Anker-fallhebel *m* slipper handle **-feld** *n* armature field **-flott** *n* buoy (for seaplane) **-flunken** *m* anchor fluke **-formation** *f* anchoring formation **-fortsatz** *m* armature extension **-führungsbolzen** *m* armature guiding pin **-gang** *m* anchor escapement (clockwork) **-gegenwirkung** *f* armature reaction **-gerät** *n* mooring (material) **-geschirr** *n* anchor gear **-gesperre** *n* anchor escapement (clockwork) **-gleitlager** *n* armature plain bearing **-glied** *n* elementary coil of armature **-grund** *m* anchorage, berth (for ship) **-haken** *m* guy (wire) hook, stay or anchor hook **-halteschraube** *f* armature-holding screw **-hand** *f* flukes of an anchor **-hemmung** *f* anchor or lever escapement (clockwork) **-hub** *m* armature stroke, play of tongue **-isolation** *f* armature insulation
Ankerit *m* ankerite
Anker-kante *f* armature edge **-kausche** *f* guy or stay thimble **-keil** *m* armature key
Ankerkern *m* armature core **~ mit Ladewicklung** armature core with charging winding **~ mit Lichtwicklung** armature core with lighting winding **~ mit Zündwicklung** armature core with ignition winding
Anker-kette *f* bower anchor chain **-klemmen** *pl* armature end connections **-klotz** *m* fixed mooring, anchor, stay block **-klüse** *f* hawsepipe (naut.) **-körper** *m* rotor body, armature spider **-kraftfluß** *m* armature flux **-kraftlinie** *f* armature line of force **-kreuz** *n* anchor crown **-kurzschlußbremsung** *f* braking by short-circuiting armature **-lage** *f* site of an anchor light or buoy
Ankerlager für Wischermotor armature bearing for wiper motor
Anker-lagerblock *m* armature bearing bracket **-laschen** *f pl* anchoring clips **-laterne** *f* anchor light **-leiter** *m* armature conductor or wire **-licht** *n* anchor light **-lichtmaschine** *f* anchor capstan **-linie** *f* line of anchors **-luftspalt** *m* armature air gap **-mast** *m* mooring mast **-mastturm** *m* mooring tower **-material** *n* mooring gear **-mine** *f* anchored or moored mine
ankern to anchor
Ankern *n* mooring, anchoring (operation)
Ankernabe *f* armature spider, hub of armature
Ankernapparat *m* centering apparatus
Ankernebenschluß *m* armature shunt
ankernen to spot, center, punch, mark
Anker-nocken *f pl* lugs on bedplate (for fixing), foot or feet lugs **-nut** *f* armature slot **-nutenwellen** *f pl* (des Gleichstroms) slot ripple **-öse** *f* tie-down loop **-paket** *n* armature plates **-pfahl** *m* anchor pile or stake, stay block or rod,

anchoring picket, picker (electr.) **-peilung** *f* anchor bearing **-platte** *f* base shoe, foundation or plate washer, anchor or tie plate, backstay

Ankerplatten-auflagefläche *f* armature plate support **-einpaß** *m* armature plate spigot

Ankerplatz *m* anchorage **den ~ wechseln** to shift berth **nach dem ~ gehen** to stand toward the anchorage

Ankerpolschuh *m* armature pole shoe **-kante** *f* edge of the armature pole shoe

Ankerprüfgerät *n* armature tester, growler

Ankerprüfmaschine *f* anchor-testing machine **~ mit Laufgewichtswaage** anchor-testing machine with sliding-weight balance

Anker-raum *m* anchor compartment **-relais** *n* knife-edge relay **-ring** *m* mooring ring **-ritzel** *n* armature pinion **-rödel** *n* anchor-rack stick **-rohr** *n* axial conduit, stay tube **-rückdruckfeder** *f* armature return spring **-rückwirkung** *f* armature reaction

Ankerruhestellung *f* **Relais mit mittlerer neutraler ~** neutral relay, relay with differentially moving armature

Anker-rührer *m* horseshoe mixer, anchor agitator **-rute** *f* anchor shank **-säule** *f* buckstay **-schaft** *m* shank of anchor **-schäkel** *m* anchor shackle **-schraube** *f* armature, coach or lag screw, anchor bolt (screw), foundation or lewis bolt **-schuhkante** *f* edge of the armature shoe **-schutzpfahl** *m* stay guard **-schwerpunkt** *m* armature center of gravity **-segment** *n* armature segment **-seil** *n* guy, wire strand, stay (wire), mooring line **-seilrolle** *f* anchor-rope reel **-spannschraube** *f* stay tightener, swivel, slack puller **-spannung** *f* armature voltage **-spannungsverstellung** *f* variation of armature voltage

Anker-sperrhebel *m* armature locking lever **-spiel** *n* play of tongue, armature stroke **-spill** *n* windlass, capstan **-spillmotor** *m* anchor and capstan motor (submarines) **-spitze** *f* bill **-spule** *f* armature coil, element of a winding **-stab** *m* armature bar **-stange** *f* tie bar or rod **-steg** *m* armature bridge **-stegkette** *f* stud link chain **-stein** *m* mooring sinker, closer (brick) **-stelle** *f* **-stellung** *f* anchorage

Anker-stern *m* armature spider or cross **-stich** *m* anchor hitch **-streufluß** *m* armature-stray or -leakage flux **-streuung** *f* armature leakage **-strom** *m* armature current **-stütze** *f* guy attachment **-sucher** *m* grapnel **-tau** *n* anchor cable or line, mooring rope **-taumine** *f* moored mine **-trocknungsvorrichtung** *f* drying device for rotors

Anker-trommel *f* armature drum **-turm** *m* mooring tower **-uhr** *f* lever watch **-umformer** *m* rotary converter **-umlegefeder** *f* (Wecker) biasing spring (alarm clock) **-umlegung** *f* tripping (naut.) **-umschlag** *m* armature travel or excursion, transit of armature **-unruhe** *f* anchor escapement (clockwork) **-verteilerschutz** *m* armature diverter contactor **-vorsprünge** *m pl* armature projection (lug, shoulder) **-wache** *f* anchor watch **-wall** *m* anchor wall, tie wall

Anker-weg *m* armature travel **-welle** *f* armature (-shaft) spindle **-wickelmaschine** *f* armature winding machine **-wicklung** *f* armature (-winding) coil **-widerstand** *m* armature resistance **-winde** *f* capstan **-windung** *f* armature coil **-windungsschluß** *m* short circuit in armature coil **-zahn** *m* armature tooth **-zahnrad** *n* armature pinion (elec.) **-zweig** *m* path of armature winding

anketteln to stitch on

anketten to link, chain to, fasten with a chain

ankippen to tilt

ankitten to fasten with cement, cement or putty on

Anklage *f* indictment, charge, accusation, complaint

anklagen to accuse

Ankläger *m* accuser

Anklageschrift *f* statement of charges, complaint, bill of indictment

anklammern (an), to clamp (to), cleat (on), grapple (a submarine cable), cling tenaciously **sich ~** to cling

Anklammerungspunkt *m* holding-on point, strong point

Anklang *m* concord, accord, sympathy, tuned state **~ finden** to meet with approval, find acceptance, become popular

ankleben to glue on, paste on, adhere, stick, fasten with adhesive, cling

Ankleben *n* adherence, stick

anklebend agglutinative

ankleistern to paste on

anklemmen to press against

Anklemmrührer *m* portable mixer

anklingeln to ring up, call up, telephone

Anklingen *n* gradual rise or waxing, initial sounding, intonation

anklingendes Feld effective field (electron micros.)

Anklinggeschwindigkeit *f* speed of growth

Anklingzeit *f* starting or onset time (of a tone)

Anklopfmaschine *f* pounding-up machine

anknipsen to switch, turn on

anknöpfen to button

anknoten to knot

Anknoten der Ketten *f pl* chain twisting

Anknotenstelle *f* fastening place

anknüpfbar attachable **schnell -er Fallschirm** quick-connector-type parachute

anknüpfen, an etwas to tie to, start from, pursue (a discussion), carry further

Anknüpfung *f* fastening

Anknüpfungspunkt *m* starting point, point of contact.

ankochen to start boiling

ankohlen to char, carbonize (superficially, slightly, or partially)

Ankohlen *n* charring

ankommen to arrive

ankommend arriving, incoming (teleph.) **-es Gespräch** incoming call **-e Leitung** incoming (wire) line **-e Plätze** B or inward board **-er Strom** incoming current **-e Verbindungsleitung** incoming junction **-er Verkehr** incoming traffic (teleph.) **-e Welle** oncoming wave

anköpfen to head

Anköpfen *n* heading

Anköpfer *m* heading tool

Ankoppelkreis *m* coupling circuit (elec.)

ankoppeln to attach, couple

Ankoppelung *f* coupling (radio)

Ankörnbohrer *m* countersinking bit
ankörnen to center-punch, center, punch-mark, countersink
Ankörner *m* center punch
ankörnern to punch-mark
Ankörnmaschine *f* centering machine
Ankörnung *f* punch mark, center mark
ankrallen, sich ~ to cling to
ankrampen to cramp
Ankreis *m* encircle (math.)
ankreiseln to circle
ankreuzen to check (aviation)
anklümpeln to swage
ankündigen to announce, advise, proclaim, advertise, intimate
Ankündigung *f* announcement, notice, proclamation, prospectus, warning, bulletin ~ **des Dienstschlusses** notice of closing of service
Ankündigungs-kommando *n* preparatory command **-satz** *m* carrier sentence **-signal** *n* warning signal **-vorrichtung** *f* warning apparatus
Ankunft *f* arrival, advent ~ **und Abflug** arrival and departure
Ankunfts-anstalt *f* terminating office or toll center **-bahnsteig** *m* arrival platform **-blatt** *n* ticket for incoming call **-kurs** *m* course of arrival **-platz** *m* inward position (or B position), incoming position **-signal** *n* home signal **-verkehr** *m* incoming traffic **-zeit** *f* time of arrival **-zentrale** *f* terminating toll center (T.T.C.)
ankuppeln to couple, engage, connect, hitch or couple (to) ~ **an** couple up with
ankuppen to round-off end
Ankuppelung *f* coupling
Ankuppelungsgelenk *n* coupler knuckle
Ankuppmaschine *f* dressing machine
ankurbeln to start, crank
Anlage *f* (Bau) construction; (Einbau) installation; (Fabrik~) plant, works, establishment, installation; (Betriebs~) equipment, installation; (Maschinen~) plant, machinery; (Fähigkeiten) talent, ability, aptitude; (Kapital~) investment; (ferner:) mill, unit, enclosure, predisposition, rig, layout, apparatus, appliance, outfit, drawing, mechanism, sketch, foot (arch), emplacement, circuit, appendix, annex, supplement, aid, set
Anlage, ~ **eines Kanals** laying out a canal ~ **zum Mischen des Betons** concrete plant **bevorrechtigte** ~ privileged work (teleph.) **fliegende** ~ temporary plant, building (with equipment) structure **von außen unabhängige** ~ self-reliant plant **zeitweilige** ~ temporary plant
Anlage-abrechnung *f* plant and equipment accounting **-blatt** *n* supplementary page insert **-erstellung** *f* capital construction **-fläche** *f* contact surface **-gegenstände** *pl* assets of salvage value **-grenzen** *pl* plot limits **-heft** *n* appendix folio
Anlage-kante *f* lay edge, fitting edge, bearing surface, joined or matching surfaces **-kapital** *n* capital invested **-kosten** *f pl* first cost, purchasing cost, investment, establishment charge, cost of installation, construction, or maintenance
Anlagen *f pl* installations, system(s); (ornamental or pleasure) grounds facilities ~ **zum Fein-fraktionieren** rerunning stills (chem.) **komplette** ~ complete plants ~ **im Bau** works in progress
Anlagen-bildsteuerung *f* mimic diagram control **-planung** *f* system planning
Anlage-plan *m* lay-out plan **-risiko** *n* plant (investment) risks
anlagern to accumulate, store up, add on **sich** ~ to add to, deposit
Anlagerung *f* addition, juxtaposition, accumulation
Anlagerungs-erzeugnis *n* additive compound (chem.) **-koeffizient** *m* attachment coefficient **-reaktion** *f* addition reaction **-verbindung** *f* addition compound
Anlage-sand *m* facing sand **-teile** *pl* parts of the plant **-veränderungen** *pl* plant changes **-winkel** *m* angleplate (for setting up work) **-wirkungsgrad** *m* over-all or total efficiency
Anlande-brücke *f* landing stage **-vorrichtung** *f* works for berthing, wharf
Anlandung *f* blind landing (aviation), alluvial land ~ **an einem Ufer** accretion along a bank **unbedeichte** ~ unembanked alluvial land
anlangen to arrive
Anlaß *m* occasion, occurrence, starting, letting on, rise, cause, stimulus ~ **geben zu** to give rise to
Anlaß-ätzverfahren *n* method of determining content of austenite, ferrite, and carbide by acid etching in conjunction with color changes produced during tempering (metal.) **-automatik** *f* starting automatics **-beständigkeit** *f* retention of hardness **-dauer** *f* tempering time **-doppelmagnetschalter** *m* two-step magnetic-type starting switch **-drehmoment** *n* starting torque **-drehzahl** *f* starting speed **-druckknopf** *m* starter button, self-starting push button **-düse** *f* starting or inertia nozzle **-einspritzanlage** *f* starting or priming fuel injector **-einspritzleistungen** *f pl* primer tubing **-einspritzpumpe** *f* primer pump **-einspritzsystem** *n* doping system **-einspritzvorrichtung** *f* fuel-priming-system doper
anlassen to temper, draw (heat treatment of steel), gain (speed), anneal, start, put on, bring up steam, age-harden, reheat, crank, turn on ~ (Vergütung), to draw **den Motor** ~ to start or crank the engine **eine Pumpe** ~ to prime a pump
Anlassen *n* tempering, drawing (air cooling), annealing, toughening, starting, age-hardening ~ **in Blei** lead tempering ~ **des Motors** engine starting **schweres** ~ hard starting ~ **mit voller Spannung** across-the-line starting
Anlasser *m* starter (of a machine), starting level, automatic starter, starting magneto; (offen) open starter ~ **mit Drehzahlregelung** starter (for electric motors) with speed control ~ **mit Druckknopfbetätigung** push button operated starter ~ **eingekapselt** enclosed starter ~ **mit mechanischer Einrückung** starter with mechanical engagement ~ **mit ruckweiser Schaltung** starter with switching in jerks (electr.) ~ **mit Übersetzungsgetriebe** starter with reduction gearing
Anlasser-anker *m* starting motor armature **-betätigung** *f* starter operation **-druckknopf** *m* starter button **-hebel** *m* starter level **-kabel** *n*

starter cable **-kasten** *m* starter box **-klaue** *f* starter dog or jaw, driving dog **-klinke** *f* starter pawl **-kreis** *m* starting circuit

Anlasser-leitung *f* starter cable **-lichtmaschine** *f* combined lighting and starting dynamo **-prüfstand** *m* starter test bench **-prüfvorrichtung** *f* starter testing equipment **-ritzel** *n* starter gear or pinion

Anlasser-schalttafel *f* starter or starting panel **-stromkreis** *m* starting circuit **-welle** *f* starter shaft **-verkleidung** *f* starter housing or jacketing **-zahnkranz** *m* starter ring gear **-zahnrad** *n* starter gear

Anlaßfarbe *f* graining color, annealing or tempering color, oxidation ink **blaue ~** blued surface resulting from tempering

Anlaß-funkenlänge *f* length of starting spark **-fußschalter** *m* foot-operated starting switch **-gasleitungsrohr** *n* injection or priming pipe **-gefüge** *n* temper structure **-gemisch** *n* starting (induction) mixture **-gestänge** *n* starting gear

Anlaß-hahn *m* starting cock **-härte** *f* secondary hardness **-härtung** *f* artificial aging **-hebel** *m* starting lever **-hilfe** *f* starting assist or aid **-hilfsgerät** *n* auxiliary starting device **-hilfsvorrichtung** *f* starting device

Anlaß-kabel *n* starting cable or wire **-kante** *f* leading (entering) edge **-klaue** *f* starting dog **-knopf** *m* starter or starting button **-kondensator** *m* starting condenser (or capacitor) **-kontakt** *m* starter button **-kontaktstück** *n* starting brush

Anlaßkraftstoff *m* primer **~ einspritzen** to prime (motor)

Anlaßkraftstoff-einspritzvorrichtung *f* doper

Anlaß-kreis *m* starting circuit **-kurbel** *f* crank starter **-kurbelbolzen** *m* starting-crank jaw pin **-kurve** *f* annealing curve **-leitung** *f* starting circuit or pipe **-luftbehälter** *m* starting-air tank **-luftflasche** *f* startingair bottle **-luftkompressor** *m* starting-air compressor **-luftsteuerung** *f* distribution gear controlling the starting air **-magnet** *m* magneto booster, battery booster, start(ing) magneto **-magnetzünder** *m* booster magneto **-mittel** *n* tempering medium, priming agent **-moment** *n* starting torque **-motor** *m* starter motor **-nocken** *m* starting cam

Anlaß-ofen *m* tempering furnace **-patrone** *f* cartridge for cartridge starter **-pistole** *f* cartridge starter **-regler** *m* starter relay, solenoid switch **-relais** *n* start or starting relay **-ring am Schwungrad** starting-gear ring on flywheel **-ringleitung** *f* starter ring conduit **-ritzel** *n* starter pinion (jet) **-rohrleitung** *f* primer tubing **-rückschlagventil** *n* starter check valve

Anlaß-schalter *m* starting switch, starter **-schaltstange** *f* trigger **-schaltung** *f* starting wiring (diagram), starting-up connection (elec.) **-schlagweite (Zündapparat)** voltage at starting speed (magneto) **-spannung** *f* starting voltage **-spartransformator** *m* autotransformer starter **-sperrschutz** *m* starter safeguard relay **-sprödigkeit** *f* temper brittleness **-spule** *f* starting or booster coil

Anlaß-stellung *f* starting position **-stempel** *m* starting plunger **-steuerrelais** *n* starter control relay **-steuerung** *f* starting-air control, starter gear **-stift** *m* starting brush **-stoß** *m* starting impuls **-strecke, eines Pupinkabels** end section, first section **-strom** *m* electric torque, starting current **-stromkreis** *m* starting circuit **-stromstoß** *m* starting impulse **-stufe** *f* starter step, starting connection **-system** *n* starting system

Anlaß-temperatur *f* tempering heat or temperature, annealing or drawing temperature **-tor** *n* blast gate **-transformator** *m* autotransformer starter **-umschalter** *m* starting change-over switch

Anlaß- und Regelwalzen drum type starters and regulating starters

Anlassung *f* starting, start

Anlaßventil *n* starting-air valve, primer valve **-kegel** *m* cone of starting-air valve

Anlaß-versager *m* failure to start **-verzahnung** *f* starter gear **-vorgang** *m* tempering or starting operation **-vorrichtung** *f* starter, starting mechanism or equipment, device, gear or apparatus **-walzenschalter** *m* drum-type starting switch **-welle** *f* starter shaft **-wicklung** *f* starter winding **-widerstand** *m* starter or starting resistance, starting rheostat **-wirkung** *f* temper-effect

Anlaß-zahnkranz *m* starter gear ring **-zeit** *f* tempering period (metal.) **-zugschalter** *m* pull-type starting switch **-zündleistung** *f* starting ignition performance **-zündleitung** *f* starting ignition cable **-zündspule** *f* booster or starting-ignition coil **-zündung** *f* starting ignition

Anlauf *m* slope, incline, start (of run), starting, batter, rush, advance, take-off run, run (gunnery), take-off, visit (to a port), pick-up, acceleration **~ unter Vollast** starting with full load **in ~** in production **stoßfreier ~** starting without jolt or shock, smooth starting

Anlauf-belastung *f* starting load **-beständigkeit** *f* resistance to tarnish, tarnish-proofness, tarnish **-bewegung** *f* impulse motion **-bolzen** *m* counter bolt **-buchse** *f* butt collar, butting or rubbing bush **-charakteristik** *f* transfer characteristic **-daten** *pl* starting data, initiating data **-drehfeld** *n* starting rotating field **-drehmoment** *n* starting torque **-druck** *m* lifting pressure (valve of oil engine)

anlaufen (Metall) to tarnish, become coated or oxidized; (Maschinen) start up, start, run up, increase, touch or call at (port), accumulate, become dull or dim, buck against (a potential) **~ lassen** to set in motion **belastet ~** to start under load **unter (ohne) Last ~** to start under (without) load **die Gläser laufen an** the lenses are fogged or bedewed

Anlaufen *n* start(ing), frosting (of glass), tarnishing (of silver); (Farbe) blooming **~ von Metall** oxidation **~ der lackierten Gegenstände** bloom of varnished articles

anlaufend incident, incoming **-e Welle** indicent wave

Anlaufende einer Schiene facing end of a rail

anlaufendes Flugzeug approaching airplane

Anlauf-farbe *f* temper(ing) or annealing color, oxidation tint **-fläche** *f* butting face **-flansch** *m* check flange **-gebiet** *n* counter range **-gestell** *n* starting carriage or cradle (aviation) **-hafen** *m* port of call **-hebel** *m* starting lever **-kondensator** *m* starting condenser (or capacitor) **-kosten** *pl* initial costs **-kupplung** *f* starting clutch **-kurve** *f* advance cam **-länge** *f* terminal or first loading coil section, starting length **-leistung** *f* starting output or power **-nocken** *m* start cam

Anlauf-moment *n* starting torque or effect **-rad** *n* starting or landing wheel **-rampe** *f* starting ramp **-rechnung** *f* beginning or preliminary calculation **-reibung** *f* starting friction (metal.)

Anlaufring *m* butting or thrust ring, depth washer **~ aus Fiber für Zündverteiler** fiber disc for ignition distributor **~ (Ölrückförderring) für Zündverteiler** oil return ring for ignition distributor

Anlauf-schablone *f* lifting template **-scheibe** *f* butting ring, buffer disc, thrust washer, check or guard plate **-schritt** *m* start signal **-seite** *f* leading edge **-spannung** *f* starting voltage **-strecke** *f* starting or take-off run or distance

Anlaufstrom *m* residual current, initial-velocility current, starting current **-gebiet** *n* residual current state, range of the starting current, range or region of incipient current flow **-zustand** *m* residual current state

Anlauf-tisch *m* approach or entry table **-verhältnis** *n* starting condition or ratio **-vorgang des plastischen Fließens** incipient plastic flow **-vorgänge** *pl* transient problems **-vorrichtung** *f* starting arrangement (aviation) **-wert** *m* starting value, reaction value (aut. contr), reciprocal of process **-wickel** *m* starting winding **-widerstand** *m* starting resistance **-winkel** *m* angle of approach

Anlaufzeit *f* reaction time (aut. contr), response time, settling time, start-up time, machine inertia constant, period of starting engine, building-up time **kurze ~** short period of rise

Anlaufzustand *m* residual-current state

anläuten to ring or call up

Anlege-apparat *m* feeding apparatus, apparatus for laying on sheets **-brett** *n* feeding board **-brücke** *f* jetty **-dreieck** *n* course or scale triangle **-goniometer** *n* protractor, contract goniometer **-hafen** *m* port of call **-kassette** *f* clamp-on dark slide **-leiste** *f* registering straightedge **-marke** *f* lay gauge **-maschine** *f* spreading frame **-maßstab** *m* contact rule

anlegen to aim, invest, build, construct, dock, install, employ, establish, plot (a curve, data) **~ an** to join to **an die Leitung ~** to put (to), switch on (to), apply (to), join (to), throw (a line) onto, put ashore **Geld ~** to invest money **Lager ~** to lay out stores **ein Lineal ~** to set a ruler **eine Spannung ~** to apply a voltage, impress

Anlegen eines Bergarbeiters hiring, applying (a miner) **~ eines Flugplatzes** construction of an airdrome

Anlege-öl *n* oil base for varnish **-platte** *f* feed board **-platz** *m* berth (place for mooring) **-punkt** *m* orienting or reference point, aiming point

Anleger *m* layer-on, feeder (print.), (press) **-seitenteil** *n* side frame

Anlege-rahmen *m* registering frame, backing frame, go or not-go gauge **-schiene** *f* guide rail (print) **-seilöse** *f* mooring-rope eyelet **-steg** *m* head side (print.), side stick (print.) **-stelle** *f* berth, lay-by, pier, tie-up wharf **-thermometer** *n* contact thermometer **-tisch** *m* feed table or board, horse (print.) **-tischträger** *m* fixing plate **-vorrichtung** *f* feeding device **-wandler** *m* split-wire type transformer **-winkelmesser** *m* bevel protractor **-zange** *f* hook on meter

Anlegekarte *f* guiding or leading edge

anlehnen to lean against

Anlehre *f* (in-factory) training period

Anleihe *f* loan **-kapital** *n* loan capital

anleimen to glue on

Anleim-maschine *f* glueing machine **-vorrichtung** *f* glueing device

anleiten to guide, instruct, introduce

Anleitung *f* instruction, guide, guidance, key, regulation, conductance **schriftliche ~** written or printed guide, manual

Anlenkbolzen *m* articulated rod pin, knuckle, hinging bolt, link, or wrist pin, kingpin **~ für Nebenpleuel** articulated rod pin

anlenken to pivot, articulate, fulcrum, hinge **drehbar ~** to hinge

Anlenk-pleuel *n* articulated or link rod **-radius** *m* link radius

Anlenkungspunkt *f* pivotal point, fulcrum, hinge

Anlenkzapfen *m* pivot

anlernen to break in, instruct, train, drill

Anlernling *m* trainee, learner

Anlernzeit *f* training time

anleuchten to spot with beam of light, illuminate, pick up

anliefern to supply

Anlieferung *f* delivery, supply, consignment

Anlieferungszustand *m* state of material as supplied, condition of material at time of supply **im ~** as received

anliegen to lie against, fit **~ an** to abut, butt or rest against **dicht ~** to sit close

Anliegen *n* request, wish, application

anliegend adjacent, adjoining **-es Magnetfeld** applied magnetic field **-e Spannung** applied voltage

Anliegergrundstück *n* marginal property

Anliegestrich *m* thrust line, lubber line (compass)

anlötbar solderable

anlöten to solder, solder on

Anlötdraht *m* soldered-on lead

Anlötung *f* soldering

anlüften to lift up, (molding) to draw (the pattern) very slow at the start

anluven to bear up, beat to windward

Anmachebottich *m* mixing or preparing vat

anmachen to attach, prepare, mix, light, kindle **den Teig ~** to knead or make the dough

Anmachwasser *n* mixing water

Anmarschweg *m* approach, route of approach **An- und Abmarschweg** road approach

anmaßend pretentious

Anmaßzustand (unterer) minimum material condition

Anmelde-abteilung *f* record section **-anstalt** *f* originating exchange (teleph.) **-beamtin** *f* recording (table) operator **-gebühr** *f* registry fee **-leitung** *f* recording trunk

anmelden to announce, report, book **ein Gespräch ~** to place a toll call **ein Patent ~** to apply for a patent, apply for letters patent, file an application **sich ~** to report one's arrival, announce one's coming **Konkurs ~** to file petition in bankruptcy
Anmeldeplatz *m* registration office
Anmelder *m* applicant
Anmeldespitzenplatz *m* record-transfer position **Beamtin am ~** record-transfer operator
Anmelde-stelle *f* recording section **-taste** (für Amtsgespräch) button for pre-advising trunk calls **-tisch** *m* record table
Anmeldezeit *f* filing (booking) time, request time
Anmeldung *f* application (patents), booking, recording, filing **~ eines Fernsprechanschlusses** service application (teleph.) **~ von Reihengesprächen** sequence calling or calls **eine ~ zurückstellen** to hold a call **abgezweigte ~** divisional application
Anmeldungs-akten *m pl* file wrapper, application papers **-gegenstand** *m* object of invention
anmengen to mix, blend, temper
anmerken to mark, sign, designate, brand, stamp, note
Anmerkung *f* note, remark, comment, footnote, marginal note, annotation, memorandum
Anmerkungskreuz *n* dagger
Anmerkzeichen *n* reference mark (print)
anmessen to fit
anmontieren to mount, attach
anmoorig partly peat and partly mineral (soil)
anmustern, die Mannschaft ~ to enroll the crew
annageln to nail (to), spike
Annagung *f* pitting, corrosion
annähern, sich ~ to approach, draw near, approximate
annähernd approximate(ly), approaching, nearly
Annäherung *f* approximation, approach, exposure, situation of proximity **in erster ~** to a first approximation, first order treatment
Annäherungs-formel *f* approximation formula **-geschwindigkeit** *f* closure range, approximate velocity or speed **-grad** *m* degree of approach **-kurve** *f* approximate curve **-maßstab** *m* approximate scale **-richtung** *f* direction of approach **-schalter** *m* proximity switch
Annäherungs-verfahren *n* trial-and-error method, method of approximation **-verschluß** *m* approach locking device **-weg** *m* approach (road), line or route of approach **-weise** approximately **-wert** *m* approximate value, approximation **-winkel** *m* closure angle **-zünder** *m* proximity or influence fuse
Annahme *f* acceptance, receipt, collection, assumption, supposition, presumption, adoption, hypothesis, addition, admission **-amt** *n* accepting (collecting) office **-schalter** *m* counter **-stelle** *f* collecting, receiving, or recruiting office, acceptance center **-verweigerung** *f* refusal of acceptance **-wert** *m* assumed value **-zeit** *f* filing time, time handed in
Annalin (Weißerde) annaline (white clay)
annässen to wet, moisten, dampen
annehmbar acceptable, reasonable **-er Preis** reasonable or fair price
annehmen to accept, assume, collect, receive, suppose, adopt, presume **~** (Farbe) to take (ink)
Annehmlichkeit *f* comfort
anneigen to incline, converge
annektieren to annex
Annerodit *m* annerodite
annetzen to moisten, dampen (superficially)
Annetzer *m* mason's broom or brush
Annexion *f* annexation
annieten to rivet (on)
Anniet-lappen *m* rivet lap **-mutter** *f* rivet nut
Annihilationsgammaquant *m* annihilation gamma quantum
Annonce *f* advertisement
annoncieren to advertise
annullieren to cancel, annul, nullify
Annullierung *f* cancellation, nullification
anodal anodal
Anode *f* anode, positive electrode plate, collector (C.R.T.) **gekapselte ~** enclosed anode **geschwärzte ~** carbonized anode **luftdicht gekapselte ~** airtight anode **zweite ~** second anode, second accelerator, second gun **~ einer Elektronenröhre** plate, output electrode, wing **~ der Exitronröhre** exitation anode **~ einer Kathodenstrahlröhre** (TV) collector **innerer Leitwert einer ~** anode alternating-current conductance, reciprocal of internal resistance
Anoden-abfall *m* anode scrap **-absinkkurve** *f* anode or plate-current curve **-alarmrelais** *n* alarm relay for plate potential (teleph.) **-ansatzpunkt** *m* spot on anode (of an arc) **-anschluß** *m* anode lead **-aufhänger** *m* anode hanger **-aussortierung** *f* anode sorting
Anodenbasis-schaltung *f* grounded-anode circuit **-verstärker** cathode follower, grounded anode amplifier, cathode-coupled circuit
Anoden-batterie *f* high-voltage battery, battery supplying plate, anode or plate battery **-belastung** *f* anode loading, plate load **-besprechung** *f* plate or plate-circuit modulation **-blech** *n* anode plate or sheet metal **-blende** *f* anode diaphragm or partition **-bügel** *m* anode hanger or clamp
Anoden-dichte *f* anodic density **-dunkelraum** *m* anode dark space **-durchführung** *f* anode leading-in wire **-einheit** *f* anode insert **-fall** *m* anode drop or fall, potential fall **-flüssigkeit** *f* anolyte **-form** *f* anode mold **-fußkondensator** *m* plate bypass capacitor anode b.c.
Anoden-gitterkapazität *f* grid-plate capacitance, micromicrofarad of grid-plate capacitance **-gleichrichter** *m* anode or plate detector, plate-circuit or anode-bend detector **-gleichrichterspannung** plate direct current **-gleichrichtung** *f* anode or plate detection, anode or plate current rectification **-gleichspannung** *f* anode supply voltage, plate direct-current voltage or potential **-gleichstrom** *m* plate (anode) direct current, plate current, direct current
Anoden-hochfrequenzstrom *m* high-frequency anode current **-impedanz** *f* anode or plate load impedance **-innenleitwert** *m* anode AC conductance **-innenwiderstand** *m* anode AC resistance **-kappe** *f* anode side cap **-kennlinie** *f* anode bend
Anodenkreis *m* anode or plate circuit, anode-to-

filament or plate-to-filament circuit, discharge circuit **abgestimmter** ~ tuned anode or plate circuit **-abstimmung** *f* anode tuning **-spule** *f* plate coil

Anoden-kühlungsvermögen *n* anode cooling capacity **-laufzeitwinkel** *m* plate transition-time angle

Anodenleistung *f* plate circuit efficiency **zugeführte** ~ anode input power

Anoden-leitwert *m* plate conductance **-licht** *n* anodal light **-loch** *n* gun (in cathode-ray tube) **-lose Röhre** *f* plateless valve **-maschine** *f* anode generator **-mechanisch** electrolytic **-modulation** *f* plate modulation **-ohr** *n* anode lug

Anoden-rauschen *n* anode hum **-raum** *m* anode compartment **-reste** *m pl* anode remnants **-rückkopplung** *f* plate feedback coupling **-rückleitung** *f* plate return **-rückwirkung** *f* plate reaction, anode reactance, adjustable or variable condenser, anode or plate feedback **-ruheleistung** *f* plate input power **-ruhespannung** *f* no-signal anode plate-cathode voltage **-ruhestrom** *m* idle current at plate, feed current, zero signal direct anode current, anode rest current

Anoden-sammler *m* anode accumulator **-sättigung** *f* voltage saturation **-schale** *f* anode segment (of magnetron) **-schatten** *m* heel effect **-schlamm** *m* anode mud **-schutzgitter** *n* anode-screening grid, suppressor grid **-schutznetz** *n* anode-screening grid **-schutzwiderstand** *m* anode stopper **-schwanz** *m* anode bend (electr.) **-seite** *f* plate voltage

Anodenspannung *f* plate or anode voltage, plate or anode potential, plate volts, discharge voltage, high tension (HT), ultra voltage (C.R.T.) **kritische** ~ critical anode voltage

Anodenspannungs-apparat *m* high tension supply unit, plate voltage apparatus **-aussteuerung** *f* plate voltage excursion **-drossel** *f* smoothing choke **-kennlinie** *f* plate-voltage characteristic **-modulation** *f* choke or Heising modulation, constant-current modulation **-quelle** *f* positive supply, plate supply **-tastung** *f* high-tension keying, plate keying **-versorgung** *f* high-tension supply **-wicklung** *f* plate-voltage winding **-zuführung** *f* anode input lead

Anodenspeisung *f* anode or plate supply ~ (ohne Gleichspannung am Schwingkreis) parallel feed

Anoden-spitzenspannung *f* peak-anode-voltage radio **-spitzenstrom** *m* peak anode or plate current, peak forward anode-voltage **-spule** *f* plate coil **-stecker** *m* battery pricker **-strahlen** *pl* anode or canal rays, positive rays, corpuscular anode rays

Anodenstrom *m* space, plate or anode current, discharge current **-anodenspannungskennlinie** *f* plate-current-plate-voltage characteristic **-änderung** *f* plate-current variation **-aussteuerung** *f* plate-current excursion **-gitterspannungskennlinie** *f* grid-plate characteristic, plate-current-grid-voltage characteristic, grid-potential-anode-current characteristic **-gitterspannungskurve** *f* anode current grid voltage

Anodenstrom-kennlinie *f* plate characteristic **-kreis** *m* plate or anode circuit, plate filament circuit **-meßschalter** *m* plate-current measuring switch **-sparschaltung** *f* quiescent push-pull circuit **-stärke** *f* (spezifische ~) anodic density

Anoden-tastgerät *n* anode modulator (radar), anode switching device **-tastung** *f* anode modulation or keying, plate-voltage keying **-unruhe** *f* fluctuation of plate or anode feed current **-verbindungsstreifen** *m* anode strap **-verlustleistung** *f* plate dissipation, electric anode dissipation **-vorwiderstand** *m* anode-feed resistance **-wechselspannung** *f* plate alternating-current voltage or potential

Anodenwiderstand *m* anode or plate resistance (load) ~ **im Betriebszustand** dynamic plate resistance (radio)

Anoden-winkel *m* anode or target angle **-zündspannung** *f* anode breakdown voltage

anodisch anodic, anodal **-e Stromdichte** anode current density

Anodisierungsverfahren *n* anodising process

Anoin *n* anoin

anölen to (coat with) oil, grease, lubricate

Anolyt *m* anolyte

anomal anomalous, abnormal **-e Beugung** anomalous diffraction **-es magnetisches Moment** anomalous magnetic moment **-e Valenz** anomalous valence

Anomalie *f* anomaly

anomalistisch anomalistic

Anon *n* cyclohexanone

anoptisches System anoptic system

anordnen to arrange, group, design, set, adjust, dispose, order **übereinander** ~ to stack one above the other

Anordnung *f* order, instruction, arrangement, layout, settlement, direction, grouping, regulation, design, allocation, classification, system, disposal, installation, configuration, set-up disposition, adjustment or tuning of controller to process (automatic central) ~ (Seil) reaving of rope **kritische** ~ critical assembly ~ **der Ventile** valve location **klare** ~ neat grouping **Gerbersche** ~ Gerber design (a type of cantilever construction) **in hängender** ~ suspended **besondere Anordnungen** *f pl* special dispositions, administrative details

Anordnungs-axiome *n pl* axioms of order **-operator** *m* rearranging operator **-satz** *m* array theorem

anorganisch inorganic

anormal abnormal

Anorthit *m* anorthite, lime harmotome

Anpassung *f* integration

anpacken to tackle, hold **eine Aufgabe** ~ to tackle a problem

anpassen to proportion, adapt, fit, accommodate, match, adjust, acclimatize, blend, conform, correct, tune, suit **sich dem Gelände** ~ to adapt oneself to the ground

anpassende Oberfläche facing surface

Anpaß-form *f* forming die **-stichleitung** *f* matching stub

Anpaßstück *n* adaptor ~ (Leitung zur Phasenverschiebung) phasing section

Anpaßübertrager *m* (impedance) matching transformer

Anpassung *f* proportioning, adaptation, accommodation, matching, adjusting, fitting, tuning ~ **an den menschlichen Körper** body

conformity
Anpassungs-blende *f* matching plate, resonant diaphragm **-blindschwanz** *m* matching stub **-dämpfung** *f* matching or nonreflection attenuation **-fähig** flexible, adaptable
Anpassungsfähigkeit *f* accommodation power, versatility, adaptability, flexibility **~ im Betriebsverhalten** operational flexibility
Anpassungs-gerät *n* matching or adjusting unit (radar), adapter unit **-geschwindigkeit** *f* speed of accomodation **-kreis** *m* matching circuit **-schaltung** *f* accommodating connection **-stab** *m* shim rod **-stift** *m* matching pillar **-strom** *m* transient current **-stück** *n* matching bar (stub)
Anpassungs-teile *pl* instrument panel assembly **-transformator** *m* matching or impedance-matching transformer **-verhältnis** *n* matching condition **-vermögen** *n* adapting capacity
Anpaß-wischer *m* adapted wiper **-wischmotor** *m* adaptable-type wiper motor
anpeilen to bear, take a bearing
Anpeilen *n* radio direction finding, take bearings from or on (a radio station) **~ von Flugzeugen** aircraft interception
Anpeilung *f* bearing (aviation)
Anpfahl *m* spill, templet
anpfählen to fasten with pales or stakes
anpflöcken to pin (secure with split pins or bolts)
anpfropfen to assemble butt on butt
Anprall *m* impact, violent striking, shock
anprallen to impinge, strike **~ an** to strike against
anpreisen to praise recommend, mark goods with prices
Anpreß-balken *m* clamping bar (print) **-bund** *m* compressing collar **-deckel** *m* pressure cover **-druck** *m* surface or contact pressure, bearing presure
anpressen to press against
Anpreß-kraft *f* contact pressure **-platte** *f* driving plate, pressure plate **-stempel** *m* holder-on or stationary die, dolly **-teller** *m* pressure plate
Anpressung *f* tightening
Anpressungsdruck *m* contact or normal pressure
Anpreßvorrichtung *f* holding down attachment, pressure mechanism
Anprobe *f* fitting
anproben to try on, fit on
anprobieren to try or fit on
Anpumphebel *m* pump primer lever
anquicken to amalgamate
anraten to advocate, advise
anrauchen to (expose to) smoke
anräuchern to fumigate
Anräucherung *f* smoking, fumigation
anrauhen to abrade, roughen
Anraum *m* silver thaw, white frost, rime, glaze
anrechnen (Konto belasten) to charge to the account, pass to the debit
Anrechnung *f* charge, offset in **~ bringen** to charge, debit
Anrecht *n* right, claim, title
Anrede *f* address, speech
anreden to address
Anregekristalle *m pl* seed crystals, shock seed
anregen to stimulate, start up, propose, set going, prompt, suggest
Anregerrelais *n* exciting relay
Anregung *f* stimulation, encouragement, proposal, suggestion, inducement, excitation, impulse, stimulus, incitation, response, sounding
Anregungs-arbeit *f* excitation state (level) **-band** *n* excitation band **-bedingung** *f* excitation condition **-energie** *f* excitation or stimulation energy
Anregungs-faktor *m* excitation factor **-fehler** *m* excitation defect **-größe** *f* forward signal **-mittel** *n* stimulant
Anregungsspannung *f* excitation potential or voltage, preionization potential **~ der Eigenstrahlung** excitation voltage of characteristic radiation
Anregungs-stärke *f* work or strength function **-stoff** *m* stimulant, ferment **-stoß** *m* excitation collision or shock **-wahrscheinlichkeit** *f* excitation probability **-welle** *f* exciton
Anreibemaschine *f* roughening machine
anreiben to grind, rub on, press on (book cover), squeegee (phot.)
Anreiben *n* pasting
anreichern to enrich, concentrate, strengthen, grow rich (in) **sich ~** to accumulate, become richer in
Anreicherung *f* enrichment, concentration, sorting, grading
Anreicherungs-apparat *m* concentrator
Anreicherungsdüse *f* enrichment jet or nozzle **~ für Volleistung** power jet
Anreicherungs-faktor *m* enrichment or separation factor, concentration factor **-grad** *m* strength **-stellung des Gemischreglers für Nothöchstleistung** emergency position of automatic mixture control **-ventil** *n* enrichment valve
anreihen to arrange in, or attach to a series, align, string to, add to, sequence
anreißen to mark (out), scribe, trace, draw, plot, sketch, tear off, pluck (a string or chord)
Anreißen der Druckwalze ploughing-up of the roller
Anreißer *m* marker
Anreiß-gerät *n* tracer or marking device **-lehre** *f* marking or surface gauge **-nadel** *f* mark scraper, scriber, marking tool **-platte** *f* surface plate or table, marking plate **-schablone** *f* tracing, stencil, template or pattern **-teilmaschine** *f* graduating machine
Anreiß-spitze und Meßschnabel für Innenradius scribing point and fillet measuring jaw
Anreiß- und Prüfwerkzeuge marking and laying-out tools
Anreiß- und Richtwerkzeuge laying-out and marking tools
Anreiß-vorrichtung *f* jig, tracer device **-winkel** *m* square
anreizen to abet (law), incite, excite, energize
Anreiz-kontakt *m* dialing impulse (supervisory control) **-kreis** *m* control circuit, exciting circuit
Anreizung *f* abetment (law), incitement
anrichten to produce, cause, regulate, aim at, serve up (a meal), prepare, dress, mix, perform, sight, sight in, align, cause (damage)
Anrichter *m* assayer, dresser, converter, detector, oscillator

Anriß *m* flaw, crack, incipient (crack) flaw, cracking, break, surface crack **~ auf der Zugseite** starting crack on the side under tension **-sucher** *m* crack detector
anritzen to scratch
anrollen to taxi (aviation), roll along runway
Anroll-maschine *f* stitching machine **-vorrichtung** *f* stand for stitcher
anrosten to begin to rust, become fixed by rust, corrode
Anrostung *f* corrosion **~ des Rohres** rusting of the pipe
anrücken to march up, advance
Anrücksperre *f* approach locking
Anruf *m* signal call, challenge, telephone call **~ mit Gebühr** chargeable call **~ im Fernverkehr** toll or trunk call **~ mit Maschinenstrom** machine or power ringing **~ im Ortsverkehr** local call **~ im Vorortsverkehr** toll call to suburban area **den ~ wiederholen** to call again, recall **~ zwischen Teilnehmern einer Gesellschaftsleitung** reverting call
Anruf, abgestimmter ~ harmonic ringing **dringender ~** urgent or express call **hörbarer ~** audible signal **selbsttätiger ~** (ohne Rufschlüssel) keyless ringing, (mit Maschinenstrom) machine ringing **selektiver bzw. wahlweiser ~** selective ringing or calling **überzähliger ~** supernumerary call **vorberechtigter ~** priority call
Anruf-anreiz *m* calling condition **-antwort** *f* answer to telephone call **-anzeiger** *m* call indicator **-apparat** *m* call-signal apparatus **-aushilfe** *f* possibility of auxiliary operation **-beantworter** *m* telephone responder
Anrufbetrieb *m* straightforward trunking method, direct-trunking operation **~ auf Fernleitungen** trunk signaling working **~ auf Leitungen, die von einer Beamtin bedient werden** generator signaling working with individual line group
Anruf-einheit *f* subscriber's line or calling equipment (in an exchange) **-einrichtung für Übertragungen** calling device, silencer
anrufen to challenge, hail, call up, telephone **das Amt ~** to ring the exchange
Anrufen *n* ringing, calling
Anrufer *m* calling device **-magnet** *m* silencer magnet **-schränkchen** *n* silencer cabinet
Anruf-feststeller *m* (Teleph.) call detector, call identifier **-glühlampe** *f* calling lamp, line lamp **-induktor** *m* calling magneto **-klappe** *f* calling indicator, line drop, annunciator drop, switch-board drop annunciator (signal) **-klinke** *f* calling jack **-kontrollampe** *f* general call pilot lamp **-lampe** *f* calling lamp, line lamp, calling-in lamp **-lampenstreifen** *m* calling-lamp strip (teleph.) **-ordner** *m* call allotter **-organ** *n* subscriber's line or calling equipment (in an exchange)
Anrufrelais *n* ringing relay, line or call relay **~ für Kabelbetrieb** call relay for cable working
Anruf-schauzeichen *n* incoming-call signal light **-schrank** *m* calling concentrator (teleph.) **-signal** *n*calling or line signal **-sperre** *f* incoming-call blocking **-suchen** *n* finding action, finder switch
Anrufsucher *m* (line) finder, finder switch, call finder **~ mit Vorwähler** (ein ~ und ein Vorwähler), line finder with allotter switch **erster ~** subscriber's line finder, primary line switch
Anrufsuchergestell *n* finder rack
Anruftaste *f* starting key
Anruf-tisch *m* concentrating table (teleph.) **-verteiler** *m* call distributor, call receiving switch **-verteilungssystem** *n* call-distributing system (teleph.) **-wecker** *n* call bell **-welle** *f* calling wave **-wiederholung** *f* repeating of the calling lamp (teleph.)
Anrufzeichen *n* call signal, line signal, (drop) indicator **~ beim Vielfachschrank** home indicator
Anrufzeichenkästchen *n* indicator case (teleph.)
Anrufzusammenfassung *f* concentration of incoming calls (teleph.)
anrühren to stir, handle, mix, touch
Ansage *f* announcement, notification **-gerät** *n* answer-only machine
ansagen to announce
Ansager *m* announcer
ansammeln to accumulate, collect, gather, aggregate **sich ~** to collect, accumulate, build up
Ansammlung *f* accumulation, collection, aggregate, heat storage or retention (by adjacent masses), concentration (troops), aggregation
Ansammlungsapparat *m* condenser (elec.)
ansässig settled, domiciled, residing at
Ansatz *m* (s. ff. Zusammensetzungen oder Verbindungen); (Technik) attachment, connection, lug, shoulder, rim, rest, set off, arrangement; (Ansatzstück) extension, attachment, adjoint piece; (Stufe) shoulder, neck; (Mundstück) mouthpiece; (Geologie) deposit, sediment, crust; (Anlage) disposition; (Anlauf) start; (Verlängerungsstück) adjoint piece; (Voranschlag) appropriation; (Math.) statement, set up; (Schätzung) estimate, assessment; (Ansatzpunkt) starting point; (Chem.) formula, formulation, trial solution, preparation; (Kruste) deposit, crust, incrustation in boiler; (Formulierung) set-up, formulation (of equation), preparation (of emulsion)
Ansatz *m* ear, projection (anode), added piece, insertion, ingredient, mixture, scaffold (of a blast furnace), recess, expression, statement, charge, obstruction, prolongation, tail, run (in series of parallel experiments), side arm or appendage (of a bulb or tube), adapter (phot.), relation, loss, nipple, setting into action, evaluation, rate, price, quotation, wing, root, bulge, sortie, assumption, article, method, offset, onset **in ~ bringen** to reckon, take into account **~ einer Gleichung** laying down a formula or equation **zylindrischer ~** cylindrical projection
Ansatz-bad *n* initial bath **-behälter** *m* mixing vessel **-bildung** *f* cops building **-bottich** *m* preparing vessel
Ansätze *m pl* kidneys (of converters), accretions, scars (in furnace)
Ansatz-feile *f* flat file **-feld** *n* additional multiple (teleph.) **-fläche des Objektivgewindes** screw shoulder, screw collar or seat of objective amount **-flansch** *m* union flange **-flügel** *m* stub wing **-kamera** *f* attachable camera, camera

body **-kern** *m* starting nucleus **-konzentration** *f* initial concentration

Ansatz-lösung *f* starting solution **-platz** *m* extension multiple section (teleph.) **-punkt** *m* contact point (airplane landing, spot (of arc, on cathode), point of attachment or insertion, starting point **-ring** *m* check ring **-rohr** *n* attaching (connecting) tube, short pipe, nozzle, connecting or side tube **-säge** *f* tenon saw **-schleifen** *n* shouldered work grinding

Ansatzschrank *m* cable turning or dummy section (teleph.) **~ für ein Drittel des Vielfachfeldes** end section with one-third of the multiple

Ansatz-schraube *f* shoulder screw, setscrew **-spitze** *f* pointed spigot, cone end **-stück** *n* coupling or connecting piece, extension piece, adapter piece, socket, throat **-stutzen** *m* adapter piece **-tragflächen** *pl* stub wing **-tubus** *m* extension tube **-winkel** *m* agnle of incidence, clearance angle, rake of a tool

ansäuern to acidify, acidulate

Ansäuerung *f* acidification, acidifying

Ansauge-druck *m* intake pressure **-glocke** *f* suction bell **-hub** *m* suction stroke, charging period (gas engine) **-kanal** *m* suction duct **-leistung** *f* suction capacity **-luftleitung** *f* air suction line

ansaugen to suck in, draw in, draw off, absorb, inspire, aspirate **sich ~** to become attached by suction

Ansaugen *n* suction stroke, aspiration, sucking, adsorption, drawing in (air), intake (motors); (des Düsentriebwerks) ingestion (of jet engine)

Ansauger *m* breather

Ansauge-raum *m* suction-valve chamber **-rohr** *n* throttle **-schacht** *m* air-inlet duct **-takt** *m* intake or suction stroke **-ventil** *n* air-suction valve

Ansaug-filter *n* suction filter **-gerät** *n* aspirator **-geräuschdämpfer** *m* intake muffler **-gestänge** *n* suction rods, admission gear **-heber** *m* syphon **-hub** *m* intake or suction stroke **-hutze** *f* suction scoop **-kanal** *m* (Motorzylinder) induction or suction port **-krümmer** *m* intake elbow, air-intake horn

Ansaugleitung *f* intake pipe, suction line (pipe), induction manifold, intake duct **verzweigte ~** induction manifold

Ansaugluft *f* inflow, aspirated or intake air **-strömung** *f* indraft

Ansaugluftvorwärmer *m* carburetor-air heater **mit Auspuffgas arbeitender ~** air stove

Ansaug-menge *f* free air capacity **-öffnung** *f* intake, suction port **-periode** *f* suction stroke **-querschnitt** *m* intake cross-section, suction (cross) section **-raum der Dampfstrahlpumpe** steam cone of the injector

Ansaugrohr *n* inlet or intake manifold, induction or intake pipe, suction pipe, induction manifold **~ mit Verzweigungen** manifold **~ zur Ölpumpe** lubricating oil suction pipe

Ansaug-schacht *m* induction manifold **-schlot** *m* air chimney **-seite** *f* inlet or induction side (left side of engine) **-spannung** *f* inlet pressure **-spirale** *f* induction scroll **-stutzen** *m* intake stack **-system** *n* **des Motors unter Staudruck setzen** to ram an engine **-takt** *m* induction stroke

Ansaug- und Verdichtungshub umfassende Kurbelwellenumdrehung idle revolution

Ansaugung *f* suction adsorption

Ansaug-vakuum *n* aspiration vacuum **-ventil** *n* intake or inlet valve, suction or admission valve **-volumen** *n* inspired volume **-vorgang** *m* induction **-vorrichtung** *f* suction device

ansäuren to acidify, sour, acidulate

anschaffen to provide, purchase, procure, supply

Anschaffungs-kosten *f pl* prime cost, first cost **-preis** *m* purchase price

anschäften, ein Beil ~ to helve an ax

anschäkeln to shackle

Anschalte-klinke *f* service jack, operator's jack **-leitung** *f* transfer circuit

anschalten to connect, put through, switch on **mit Stöpseln ~** to plug up, wire up, tap (elec.) **sich ~** to tee in **an- und abschalten der Erde** to switch on and off the ground

Anschalterelais *n* connecting relay, switching relay **~ für Markierer** marker connecting relay **~ für Rufstrom und Hörzeichen** connecting relay for ringing current and tone signals

Anschalt-gerät für Morseleitungen switching device for connection with Morse lines, tapping device attachable set (elec.) **-leitung** *f* transfer circuit **-klinke** *f* operator's jack **-stöpsel** *m* operator's plug

Anschaltung *f* connection, connecting circuit

Anschaltvorrichtung *f* tapping or connecting device, control system

anschärfen to scarf, thin, neutralize, dull, deaden, sharpen

Anschärfmaschine *f* whetting or sharpening machine

anschaulich plain, distinct, clear **~ vorführen** to demonstrate

Anschauung *f* view, opinion

Anschauungsmittel *n* illustrative or demonstration material, visual-education material

Anschein *m* likelihood **den ~ haben** to seem

anscheren to warp (textiles)

anschichten to pile in layers, stratify

anschieben to push against, extend, lengthen

anschienen to splint

anschießen to crystallize, shoot, rush, test a gun, wound by shooting, start engine by compressed air

Anschießfaß *n* crystallizer

Anschirmkonstante *f* screening number

anschirren to harness

Anschlag *m* stroke (Anprall) impact; (Wecker) striking; (~ einer Taste) depression; (Plakat) poster, bill; (Bekanntmachung) notice, annoncement; (Technik) stop, detent; (Schätzung) estimate, valuation; (Berechnung) calculation; (in ~ bringen) take into account; (fester ~) positive stop; (~ b. Schreibmaschine) stroke; (Endanschlag) limit stop, back stop

Anschlag *m* fixing, blow, boss limitation or buffer (mech.) firing position, dog (mech.), base, head, catcher, jig, guide, stop gauge, stud, lug, fitting edge, matching or mating edge bearing, surface of shafting, deflection, plot, poster, present position, register, bulletin, ledge, head (underground work), attempted assassination, attempt to damage (a railroad), catch, latch ~ **und Hebel für die selbsttätige Auslösung des Rundtischselbstganges** rotary attachment feed-trip dog and lever ~ **des Klopfers** clicking ~ **für Leerlaufstellung** stop for idling position ~ **einer Taste** touch, depression of a key ~ **des Typenträgers** impact of the type bar ~ **für die selbsttätige Vorschubauslösung** automatic stop ~ **des Weckers** striking **in ~ bringen** to take into consideration **einstellbarer ~** adjustable stop **rückwärtiger ~** backstop **starker ~** hard stroke **ungefährer ~** approximate estimate **verschiebbarer ~** movable stop

Anschlag-bedienungsseite stop adjustment, operator's side **-bolzen** *m* stop pin, stock stop, trip dog **-buchse** *f* stop sleeve (bush) **-bund** *m* stop collar **-draht** *m* stop wire

Anschlagdrehen, mehrfaches ~ multiple tripping (to a line)

Anschläge *m pl* bearing surfaces of doors, windows, strokes ~ **zur Hubverstellung** stops for adjustment of stroke ~ **je Sekunde** number of strokes per second

Anschlageholz *n* mill clack

anschlagen s.a. Anschlag to strike, knock, beat against; (befestigen) fasten, fix, nail to; (Glocken) sound, ring; (Stunden) strike; (berechnen) calculate; (schätzen) estimate, value

anschlagen to butt, bounce, touch, depress, respond, blank (print), arrest (stop), rate, come to rest, estimate, click (ein Tau) make fast (a hauser to a bollard), post, loop by hand (textiles) ~ **gegen** to strike ~ (der Düsennadel) to bounce **die Lade ~** to beat the lathe **ein Schloß ~** to nail or fasten a lock (to a door) **eine Taste ~** to strike a key, tap ~ (Rotornabe an der Welle) to rock (rotor)

Anschlagen *n* (bill) posting

Anschläger *m* (bottom-)banksman, striker, cager, hanger-on, chainer **-signal** (Bergb.) onsetter signal

Anschlag-fäustel *n* breaking hammer **-fläche** *f* banking face jamb, stop face **-flansch** *m* limiting flange **-hebel** *m* trip lever, stop lever (print), suction cut-out lever (print) **-hocker** *m* abutment boss **-höhe** *f* breast height, elevation, height for firing

Anschlag-kamm *m* set-up comb **-kasten** *m* extension or detachable stock **-kette** *f* sling chain **-klötzchen** *n* stop blocks **-knagge** *f* slide dog **-kolben** *m* removable shoulder stock **-kraft** *f* impact force **-kreuz** *n* multiple stop device **-lamelle** *f* (clutch) stop disc **-leine** *f* lacing

Anschlagleiste *f* registering (holding) strap (bar or edge), registering or locating stop, rubbing face (jamb of recess), stern post **hölzerne ~** timber upright

Anschlag-liek *n* headrope (of sail) **-lineal** (beim Steigungsprüfer) backrest **-linie** *f* striking line (piano) **-loch** *n* stop hole **-magnet** *m* impact or percussion magnet **-maschine** *f* pin stenter **-mutter** *f* stop nut, impact nut

Anschlag-nase *f* stop dog, ejector nose **-nocken** *m* lug cam **-papier** *n* posters **-plättchen** *n* front guide plate **-platte** *f* impact or stop plate **-puffer** *m* bumper **-punkt** *m* impact or percussion point, landing **-raste** *f* quantity stop **-regler** *m* shut-off regulator **-regelung** *f* beat regulation **-regulierung** *f* (Tastenhebel) touch control

Anschlagring *m* stop ring for locking fulcrum (aviation), check ring, end collar ~ **mit Ausrückhebel** end collar for front guard with lever

Anschlagrolle *f* tappet roller **-säule** *f* advertising pillar (billboard)

Anschlagscheibe *f* bearing retainer ~ (Kompressor) guide washer ~ (Lockheedbremse) detent plate

Anschlagschiene *f* striker bar, adjoining, rigid, or stock rail **-schraube** *f* setscrew or stop screw ~ (für Mengenverstellhebel) stop screw for quantity-regulator handle (accelerator) **-sohle** *f* station in the shaft

Anschlag-sporn *m* screwed jack spur **-stange** *f* quantity stop rod, stop bar **-stärke** *f* force of blow (type-writer) **-stelle** *f* terminal (electr.), striking point **-stift** *m* stop or trip pin, positioning pin **-stück** *n* terminal (electr.), backstop, stop plate or piece, limiting stop **-tafel** *f* notice or bulletin board **-taste** *f* beat

Anschlagvorrichtung *f* arresting device ~ **für den Revolverschlitten** automatic stop device

Anschlag-winkel *m* front lay gauge, stop bracket, angle of elevation, back or try square, evaluation angle **-wirkung** *f* striking effect (typewriter) **-zapfen** *m* nipple **-zettel** *m* placard, broadside, poster **-zünder** *m* percussion fuse

anschlämmen to become muddy, deposit mud, suspend

anschleifen to grind, sharpen, grind partially

anschließbar suitable for connection

anschließen (anketten) to chain to; (Technik) connect, join (to), link up with; (Elektr.) connect, wire (to); (mit Stecker) plug in; (anfügen) add, join to, link up with, incorporate; (angrenzen) border on, be adjacent; (nachfolgen) follow, put through (to), wire (to), annex, attach, install, equip, enclose, close up, fasten on, fit **sich einer Ansicht ~** to agree with an opinion **eng ~** (Kleidung), to fit tightly (clothing) **sich ~** to join up with

anschließend subsequent

Anschließen und Abnehmen der Schläuche coupling and uncoupling hoses

Anschließer *m* adapter

Anschließ-feld *n* junction panel **-öl** *n* oil base for varnish

Anschliff *m* polished section, ground and polished surface (under microscopic examination), cut, polished specimen **-presse** *f* parallel mounter **-winkel** *m* grinding angle

anschlingen to sling

Anschlitzung *f* tongue-and-groove joint

Anschluß *m* (s. a. anschließen) connection; (Telef. Leitung) line, joint, contact, terminal, junction (with other troops), (wing-fuselage) union, crystallization, enclosure, annex, closed line of position, installation, fusion, recovery, support, gusset ~ **aufeinanderfolgender Aufnahmen** conjunction of successive photographs, photographic extension ~ **an das Fernsprechnetz** substation of telephone system ~ **des Flügels an den Rumpf** junction of the wing with the fuselage

Anschluß für einen Bildfolgeregler intervalometer connector receptable ~ **für Manometer-**

leitung connection for pressure gauge ~ **an das Netz** supply, wiring, communication ~ **und Stoßdeckung** connections and butt straps ~ **an 220 V** operates from 220 V **rückseitiger** ~ rear connection **vorderseitiger** ~ front connection

Anschlußapparat für Endoskopie electromedical apparatus for endoscopy

Anschluß-auge *n* connecting eye **-ausgleichsleitung** *f* balancing pipe connection **-bahn** *f* branch line, signal **-bahnhof** *m* junction (R.R.) **-bereich** *m* (multioffice) exchange area, local plant **-berufung** *f* cross appeal **-blatt** *n* contact or adjoining sheet **-blech** *n* joint plate, gusset **-bogen** *m* sweep **-bolzenschraube** *f* terminal screw **-büchse** *f* (connector) socket **-dichtung** *f* joint washer

Anschlußdose *f* connection box, connector receptacle, junction or plug box, wall socket **unverwechselbare** ~ noninterchangeable wall socket

Anschluß-dosenstöpsel *m* socket plug **-drähte** (bei Transistoren) pigtails **-druckluftbremse** *f* compressed air brake connection

Anschlüsse (zum Prüfen) circuit points

Anschluß-einheit *f* line unit or terminal (tel) **-ende der Schiene** junction rail end **-fahnen** *pl* connecting lugs **-feld** *n* junction panel **-fertig** ready for installation (print) **-flansch** *m* connection (mounting) flange, coupling flange

Anschluß-gehäuse *n* connecting or flange housing **-gebühr** (bei Gleisanlagen) siding charge **-geleise** *n* railway connection or siding, connecting track **-gerät** *n* connecting or connector set **-gewinde** *n* threaded connection **-gewinde für Röhren** screwed pipe connection **-gewindelehrzapfen** Not Go screw plug member **-großvorrichtung** *f* fitting jig or rig **-hahn** *m* connection cock

Anschluß-kabel *n* (connection) lead, by-pass or distributing cable, subscriber's cable **-kappe** *f* top-cap **-kasten** *m* service or junction box, terminal or connection box

Anschlußklemme *f* terminal, connector block connecting terminal, binding post ~ **für Hauptschalterbetätigung** terminals for operating the circuit breaker

Anschlußklemmen-brett *n* connecting or terminal block **-paar** *n* terminal pair **-leiste** *f* junction or terminal block

Anschluß-klinke *f* connection jack, (electr.) line or station-line jack **-kontakt** *m* connection contact **-kontakt an der Spitze des Glasballons** horns of a tube (techn. communications) **-kopf** *m* thermocouple joint, terminal head **-krümmer** *m* elbow connector

Anschluß-leiste *f* contact strip, connection block (elec.), terminal strip, terminal block (refrigerator) **-leistung** *f* connect load, subscriber's line **-leiter** *m* leads (terminals) **-leitung** *f* connection (pipe), connection (elec.), subscriber's line, branch line **-linie** *f* branch (feeder) line **-litze** *f* cord.

Anschluß-maße *pl* companion dimensions **-messung** *f* measuring by conjunction **-möglichkeit** *f* possibility to connect **-muffe** *f* junction box; (Tiefbohrg.) (top) collar **-mundstück** *n* connecting mouthpiece **-mutter** *f* union or connecting nut **-nippel** *m* connecting fitting **-nummer** *f* subscriber's number **verkettete Anschlußnummernverteilung** linked numbering system

Anschluß-öse *f* connecting ear, eyelet **-peitsche** *f* cable stub **-platte** connection board or plate **-pol** *m* terminal post **-prüfgerät** *n* test socket or connection **-punkt** *m* point of attachment, distribution point

Anschluß-relais *n* cut-through relay **-ring** *m* joining ring **-rohrleitung** *f* connecting pipe line **-rolle des Anschaltgerätes** condenser reel for switching device

Anschluß-säule *f* terminal post (brass) **-schelle** *f* clip (aviation) **-schema** *n* cable arrangement (photo) **-schiene** *f* connecting or terminal strip, connecting block or rail

Anschlußschnur *f* flexible lead or cord ~ **eines Meßgerätes** connection cable or cord, instrument cord

Anschlußschraube *f* terminal bolt, connecting or binding screw ~ **für Stromabnehmer** connecting screw for terminal

Anschluß-spant *n* connecting frame **-sperrung** *f* freeze out **-steckdose** *f* plug socket or receptacle, connection plug **-stecker** *m* wall plug, attaching plug **-steckkontakt** *m* plug socket or receptacle **-steg für Verdrahtung** supporting strip for connecting wires **-stelle** *f* connector plug, place of attachment **-streifen** *m* connection or terminal strip, foil tab

Anschlußstück *n* tube nozzle, hose nipple, nipple gooseneck, tuyere connection pipe, wing fillet, connecting piece, joint coupling, union ~ **für Ölrohr** oil pipe connector

Anschluß-stutzen *m* connection branch or piece, pipe connection, connecting socket, connecting adapter

Anschlußteil *m* matching part, terminal part, connecting part, connector ~ **der Garbe** margin of the sheaf of fire

Anschluß-stöpsel *m* **des Sprechzeuges** plug for operator's headset **-strecke** *f* feeder line **-teilnehmer** *m* subscriber with several lines **-trichter** *m* (Rendezvoustrichter) docking collar (spacecraft) **-tübbings** *pl* joining tubbing of mine shaft

Anschluß-vorrichtung *f* fitting jig or fixture **-vorrichtungen** *f pl* **der Schnur** cord terminal **-wert** *m* connected load or value **-zimmerung** *f* timbering joint **-zug** *m* flank platoon, corresponding train

anschmauchen to soot, smoke

anschmelzen to melt a fuse on, fuse, solder, join onto, begin to melt

Anschmelz-herd *m* smelting (melting) furnace **-maschine** *f* sealing machine **-rost** *m* melting rack (print)

anschmieden to forge together

anschmiegen to join closely, adapt **sich einer Geraden** ~ to conform to a straight line **sich** ~ to cling to (print)

Anschmiegung *f* osculation **enge** ~ intimate or snug adhesion, adherence, engagement or fit, close contact, hug

anschmieren to daub, grease

anschmoren to scorch

anschmutzen to stain (soil)

anschnallen to strap to **sich** ~ to strap oneself in

(aviation)

Anschnall-gurt *m* safety or seat belt **-riemen** *m* tying strap **-schnalle** *f* safety belt buckle **-sporn** *m* strapped jack spur **-vorrichtung** *f* safety belt assembly

Anschneide-linie *f* line of intersection **-ergebnis** *n* cross-bearing

anschneiden to cut, obtain a bearing on, chamfer (founding gate), raise (a question), begin, point, aim at, locate by intersections, make intersections, gate (die-casting) ~ (Auflage-fläche), to spot (a surface)

Anschneiden *n* cutting **Art des Anschneidens der Eingüsse** (Gießerei) gating (founding) ~ **von Stemmkanten** cutting the caulking edges, bevel cutting

Anschneide-senker *m* spot facing cutter **-theodolit** *m* transit theodolite **-verfahren** *n* sound and flash ranging

Anschnitt *m* gate (founding), gating, notch, jag, chamfer, bevel, channel, cross bearing, ingate, intersection ~ **einer Gewindeschneidbacke** throat on threading die **-gewindebohrer** chamfer, start, pointing (of a tap)

Anschnitt-länge *f* length of taper **-technik** *f* gating practice **-winkel** *m* lead angle

anschnüren to tie or lace on, fasten

Anschnürung *f* tying in (textiles)

anschoppen to form on infarct

Anschrägung *f* facet ~ (der Zähne bei Zahnkranz oder Zahnrad) chamfering angle (gear)

anschrauben to bolt to, screw on, fasten (screw)

Anschraub-fläche *f* screw-on surface **-flansch** *m* securing pad, threaded flange **-gewinde** *n* screw-on thread **-lappen** *m* screw-on lug **-leiste** *f* fastening rail **-loch** *n* threaded hole **-ring** *m* mounting ring (print), lens flange **-stück** *n* fixing piece

anschreiben to write down, to book

Anschrift *f* address

Anschriften-maschine *f* addressing machine **-maschinenschablone** *f* addressing-machine stencil **-übermittlung** *f* distribution list

Anschubvorrichtung *f* boosting device

anschuhen to shoe, lengthen

Anschulterung *f* shouldering

anschüren, das Feuer ~ to stir, stoke, or poke the fire

Anschuß *m* crystallization, sighting shot

anschütten to bank or fill up, heap up or pour out against, backfill

Anschüttung *f* embankment **kegelförmige** ~ fill, quarter cone filling

Anschütz-Punkter *m* yawing gauge designed by Anschütz a pendulum or gyropendulum recording gauge

anschwängern to saturate

Anschwänzkreuz *n* sprinkling pipe

anschwärzen to blacken, slander

anschweben to float in, swell, glide in

anschwefeln to sulfurize

anschweißen to weld on, weld to

Anschweiß-ende *n* iron stud, welding end **-stelle** *f* welding point

anschwellen to swell, increase, accumulate, bulge, rise, plumb

Anschwellen *n* bulge, hump ~ **des Stromes** rush of current

Anschwellprobe *f* bulging test

Anschwellung *f* swell, swelling, bulge

Anschwemmfilter *n* alluvial filter, matting filter

Anschwemmung *f* drift, deposit from water, alluvium, silting ~ **der Eiszeit** glacial drift

anschwimmen to swim or drift ashore

Anschwing-steilheit *f* oscillation build-up transconductance **-strom** *m* starting current, preoscillation current **-zeit** *f* build-up period

Anschwödebrei *m* strong liming paste

Anschwöden (mit Kalk und Arsenik) flooding

Ansegelungs-feuer *n* landing light **-marke** *f* landmark (navig.) **-tonne** *f* fairway buoy

Ansehen *n* view, aspect, appearance, authority, credit, reputation

ansehnlich handsome, considerable

anseilen to tie with or to a cable

ansenken to counterbore, spot face, countersink

Ansenken *n* spot facing

Ansenkung *f* countersinking

Ansetzblatt *n* plain edge (of a file), fly-leaf

ansetzen (anstücken) to add, piece on, (befestigen) fasten to, apply, put on; (bereiten) make, prepare; (Termin) appoint, fix, schedule (a date); (abschätzen) access, rate, value; (Preis) fix, quote; (Math., Gleichung) put up; (entwickeln) develop, produce; (versuchen) try; (Chem.) deposit; (anbauen) attach; (Rost) rust, to set up or on, mix, start, incrustate, launch, initiate, ram (a shell), crystallize, effloresçe, formulate, charge in a bill, strike (an arc) **Hebel** ~ **to** apply the lever **zur Landung** ~ to come in to land, set down (an airplane) **zu niedrig** ~ to underrate

Ansetzen *n* preparation (of a solution) ~ **des Satzes** mixing or preparing of composition (fireworks)

Ansetzereinrichtung *f* rammer

Ansetzstück *n* attached piece or part

Ansetzung *f* application, attachment

Ansicht *f* opinion, view, sight, elevation, judgment, clean proof (from machine), section ~ **im Aufriß** elevation ~ **im Grundriß** plan or top view ~ **im Seitenriß** side view or elevation

Ansicht *f* ~ **von einem Ende aus** end-on view ~ **in voller** (natürlicher) **Größe** full-size view ~ **im Schnitt** sectional view ~ **von oben** top-plan view ~ **von unten** inverted-plan view, worm's-eye view **die** ~ **vertreten** to predicate **zur** ~ **schicken** to send on approval **perspektivische** ~ perspective view **teilweise** ~ **in Schnittdarstellung, teilweise im Schnitt dargestellte** ~ part-sectional view **vergrößerte** ~ enlarged view

Ansichts-ebene *f* plane of projection

Ansichts-kopie *f* release print **-skizze** *f* panoramic sketch

ansiedeln to colonize, settle

ansieden to boil, start boiling

Ansiedescherben *m* scorifier, roasting or calcining test

Ansiedler *m* colonist, settler

Ansiedlung *f* settlement, colony

ansingen to excite (aviation)

Ansolvosäuren *f pl* complexes of organic acids with inorganic salts

anspannen to stretch, strain, hook, hitch (animals), tighten, bend, subject to current,

connect, turn on or tune in a radio
Anspannung *f* stretch, stress, strain, tension, exertion
anspielen auf to allude to, refer to, hint at
Anspielung *f* reference, allusion, hint
anspinnen to string up, begin to spin **einen Faden ~** to join a thread
Anspinner *m* piecer and doffer
Anspinnwalze *f* doffing (waste) roller
anspitzen to point, sharpen **~ im Gesenk** to swage, point
Anspitzer *m* (pencil) sharpener
Anspitzhammer *m* pointed hammer
Anspitzmaschine *f* pointing engine **~** (für Stangen) sharpening or swaging machine
Anspitzwalzwerk *n* **für Draht** rolling mill for sharpening wires
Anspitz-werk *n* (Kabel) pointing stand **-werkzeug** *n* pointing tool
anspleißen to joint, splice (cable)
Ansporn *m* incentive
anspornen to stimulate, spur, spur on, incite
Ansprache *f* address, speech, designation, inception or onset (radio)
Ansprech-bedingung *f* operate characteristic **-charakteristik** *f* response characteristic **-druck** *m* minimum pressure of response **-empfindlichkeit** *f* acoustic sensibility, sensitivity of response
ansprechen to adress, speak to, react, relay, operate (magnet), pull up, trip, cut out or trip (relay or release gear), blow, strike, melt (fuse), actuate (elec.), act (respond) **~ als** to address as, pronounce, call **~ auf** to respond to **~ in freier Luft** response in free space or air (of a microphone) **nur langsam ~** to be sluggish in response to **sofort ~** to give instant response **ein Relais ~ lassen** to operate a relay
Ansprechen *n* operation, blowing, fusing, melting, striking (fuse), actuating (elec.) **~** (eines Reglers) response (of a regulator) **~** (des Motors) **auf Verstellung der Drosselklappe** throttle response **lineares ~** linear response **sofortiges ~ des Motors auf Vollgasgeben** instant response of the engine to the throttle **zum ~ bringen** to cause to operate or respond (as a relay) **~ eines Relais** respond
ansprechend responsive to, operating, pleasant, attractive **schnell -es Relais** relay (quick operating) **langsam** (schnell) **~** slow (fast) operating **nur langsam ~ auf** sluggish in response to
Ansprech-funkfeuer responder beacon **-geschwindigkeit** *f* operating speed, speed of response, time of relay **-grenzen** *pl* differential gap, sensitivity limits **-kraft der Bremse** grip(ping) power of brake **-konstante** *f* sensitivity constant (microphone), microphone responsiveness
Ansprech-schwelle *f* control resolution **-stellung** *f* (Gerät) sensitive position (of motor or machine) **-strom** *m* operating current, actuating current **-stromstärke** *f* figure of merit (relay), striking point (fuse) **-stufe** *f* response stage **-vermögen** *n* susceptibility, ability to respond, operate, function (motor)
Ansprechverzögerung *f* **Relais mit ~** slow-operating relay
Ansprechwahrscheinlichkeit eines Zählrohres efficiency of countertube (likelihood to respond or register), response function
Ansprech-wert *m* response factor (aut. contr.), pick-up (value), threshold value **-zähler** *m* surge counter
Ansprechzeit *f* response time or lag, sensitive time, operating time, transit time (of armature)
ansprengen (Endmasse) to bring together (final mass of rocket at end of flight, aviation motors), wring
Anspreng-platte *pl* wring-on plates **-schicht** *f* wringing layer
Ansprengungsdistanz *f* wringing distance
Ansprengversuche *m pl* blast tests
anspringen to start, leap or jump at **in jeder Kurbelstellung ~** to start in any position of the crankshaft
Anspringen, leichtes ~ starting ability of an engine **schlechtes ~ des Motors** hard starting of the engine
Anspringwert *m* hop-on resistance
Anspruch *m* right, demand, require, claim (patent) title **in ~ nehmen** to lay claim to **~ haben auf** to be entitled to, deserve **~ geltend machen** to advance, prefer, raise (plead) a claim or point **in ~ nehmen** to avail, engage, claim, require, engross **nicht bestreitbarer ~** indisputable title
anspruchslos unassuming, unpretentious, simple, modest
anspruchsvoll pretentious, fastidious, exacting, hard to please
Anspülung *f* alluvium, washing (ashore)
anstacheln to stimulate (incite), instigate
anstählen to caseharden
Anstalt *f* office, station, institute, institution, establishment, works
anstandslos without hesitation or delay, ill-mannered, without inconvenience
Anstau *m* damming or piling up of water by any means, tidal effect, effect of rotation of the earth
anstauchen to upset, head, form heads (of screws, bolts), squeeze
Anstauchen *n* upsetting, driving, forming of collars (on wheel spokes) **~ eines Kopfes** heading
Anstauchung *f* upsetting (end of bar)
anstauen to dam up, flood **das Wasser ~** to pen, stem, dam up or retain the water
Anstauung *f* damming up, flooding, flooded area, stowing, retaining
anstechen to tap off (furnace), prime (pump), tie, fasten, hitch, pierce, open
Anstech-hahn *m* tap **-ventil** *n* priming valve
ansteckbar attachable, detachable, containable
Ansteck-blech *n* float plate **-dose** *f* socket, plug or wall socket
anstecken (ein Seil) to fix (a rope), tap, set fire to, infect, attach, fasten, hitch
ansteckend infectious, contagious, communicable
Ansteck-hahn *m* tap **-magazin** *n* detachable magazine **-pfahl** *m* board **-pfähle** *m pl* laths **-spund** *m* faucet plug
Ansteckung *f* infection, contagion
ansteckungshemmend anti-infectious

anstehen to outcrop, stand in line
anstehend cropping out **-er Talk** naturally occurring talc **-es Gestein** *n* solid rock, ore in sight, parent rock
ansteigen to rise, ascend, pass up, go up, advance
Ansteigen *n* rise, ascent **allgemeines ~** (des Luftdruckes) surge (of air pressure)
ansteigend ascending, sloping, rising, uphill **-e oder abfallende Flanke** (von Impulsen) leading or trailing edge (of impulses) **-es Förderband** inclined conveyor
Ansteigung *f* rise, ascension, elevated approach, ramp, grading
anstellbar adjustable
Anstellbarkeit *f* adjustability
Anstell-änderung *f* incidence variation, change in angle of incidence **-bottich** *m* gyle, starting tub or vessel
anstellen to appoint, start (an engine), employ, engage, pitch (brewing); turn on (radio)
Anstell-geber *m* pitch indicator **-geschwindigkeit** *f* screw-down speed
anstellig fit, practical, suitable
Anstell-leiter *f* fire-escape ládder **-mechanismus** *m* screw-down mechanism **-schraube** *f* **-spindel** *f* housing screw **-temperatur** *f* initial or starting temperature, pitching temperature
Anstellung *f* position, job, appointment, post, incidence, equipment, installation
Anstellungsschein *m* certificate for preferential employment of retired officers.
Anstellvorrichtung *f* adjusting equipment, housing screw; (Walzwerk) screwdown gear
Anstellwinkel *m* angle of incidence (aviation); (Tragfläche) angle of attack; chord incidence; angle of pitch; blade angle, setting angle **~ des Drehmeißels** clearance angle of turning steel **kritischer ~** critical angle of attack, stalling angle
Anstellwinkel-anzeiger *m* incidence indicator **-bereich** *m* incidence range **-schreiber** *m* angle-of-attack recorder
ansteuern to control, steer toward, head or make for, take bearings from, keep on course
Ansteuerungs-feuer *n* approach beacon **-funkfeuer** *n* localizer **-system** *n* selection system **-tonne** *f* route-marking buoy **-zeichen** *n* streamer **-zeit** *f* switching time
Anstich *m* bunghole, broaching (cask); (Walzwerk) first pass, starting material **-bohrloch** *n* stab hole **-hahn** *m* broaching tap
Anstieg *m* rise, climb, ascent, slope, rate of climb, gradient (math.) **~** (Gewinde) pitch (thread) **-beiwert** *m* climbing coefficient **-flanke** *f* wave front (surge front), ascending flank **-leitfähigkeit** *f* slope conductivity **-winkel** *m* angle of climb
Anstieg(s)zeit *f* rise time, transition time, building-up time **~ des äquivalenten Impulses** equivalent response pulse growth-time
anstiften to pin, peg
Anstifter *m* instigator
Anstiftung *f* instigation
anstimmen to tune in (elec.)
Anstoß *m* incentive, impulse, shock, jar, point of contact, starting point **~ geben** to offened **~ nehmen** to take exception to **bündiger ~** flush joint
Anstoßdruckschalter *m* flush-pressure switch
anstoßen to butt, to collide, strike (against), impinge, abut **einen Stromkreis ~** to impulse
Anstoßen *n* butting against, twisting (in felt-making) **~ der Schwingungen** release or starting of oscillations (increment of oscillation)
anstoßend adjoining, contiguous, impulsive
anstößig shocking, objectionable
Anstoß-impuls *m* trigger pulse **-marke** *f* side-mark (print) **-maschine** *f* planking machine, twister (in felt manufacture) **-pegel** *m* triggering level **-schalter** *m* push switch
anstrahlen to floodlight, irradiate
Anstrebekraft *f* centripetal force
anstreben to aim at, make efforts to
anstreichen to paint, coat, varnish, brush, tinge, seek firing support for weapon, mark
Anstreichen *n* stroking (a string), initial bowing (of a violin), s.a. Anstrich
Anstreicher *m* painter
Anstreich-gerät *n* spray diffuser for wall painting **-spritzpistole** *f* paint-spraying pistol
anstrengen to strain, exert **sich ~** to struggle, exert oneself
anstrengend taxing, exhausting
Anstrengung *f* exertion, strain, straining, stress, effort, endeavor, tension, labor
Anstrich *m* coat of paint, coloring, finish, covering, appearance, feel **einen ~ geben** to tinge **farbiger ~** protective coloration **feuersicherer ~** fire-resisting paint **deckender ~** covering coat **~ mit bituminösen Mastix** bitumastic coating
Anstrich-aufbau *m* coating paint system **-bindemittel** *n* binder used in the paint trade
Anstriche *pl* coating materials
Anstrichfarbe *f* paint, color, color of paint **magere ~** short-oil paint **halbfette ~** medium-oil paint **fette ~** long-oil paint
anstrichfertige Farbe (Lack) ready-mixed paint
Anstrich-masse *f* primer, coating (compound **-mittel** *pl* coating media **-stoff** *m* paint, varnish, lacquer, preservative
Anstrichverstellung *f* **von einem Punkt aus regelbare ~** contact controllable from one point
anströmen to blow or flow against
Anström-geschwindigkeit *f* velocity of flow from initial direction, velocity in blower stream (wind tunnels), flow or free-stream velocity, face velocity **-kante** *f* leading edge **-richtung** *f* (initial) direction of air flow, direction of relative wind, approach flow direction (turbines) **-seite** *f* leading edge
Anströmung *f* velocity head, oncoming flow, incident flow
Anströmungs-geschwindigkeit *f* afflux or approach velocity (electronics) **-richtung** *f* initial direction of flow
Anströmwinkel *m* angle of attack
anstückeln to piece together, patch
anstücken to joint, join, connect, piece
Anstückung *f* lengthening piece (carp.)
Ansturm *m* assault, rush
anstürmen to assault, attack, charge
anstürzen to come tumbling

anstutzen to curtail
ansuchen to request, apply
Ansuchen *n* **Ansuchung** *f* application, request
ansumpfen to inundate, swamp, become swampy
Ansumpfung *f* inundation, inundated area
antarktisch antarctic **-er zirkumpolarer Strom** antartic circumpolar current
antasten to touch (capital)
anteigen (Viskose), to premix (viscose), stir to a paste
Anteigmittel *n* pasting agent
Anteil *m* part, portion, share, component, quota, increment, constituent, interest, sympathy, stake **~ des Leistungsaufwandes für Kühlzwecke** (or Kühlung) fractional cooling-power loss
anteilig shared (electrons), component, pro rata, proportionate, in proportion
Anteil-nahme *f* interest **-schein** *m* certificate share
Anteilszahl *f* percentage
Anteilziffer *f* percentage share
Anteisosäuren *pl* anteisomeric acids
Antenne *f* antenna (US), aerial (Brit.) loop **~ mit Ableitung** shunt-excited antenna **~ mit gewelltem Hohlleiter** corrugated-surface antenna **der ~ zugeführte Leistung** antenna input **~ mit seitlichem Minimum** directive antenna **~ mit Mittelanschluß** antenna center-driven **~ mit Rundwirkung** omnidirectional antenna **nach zwei Seiten gerichtete ~** bidirectional antenna **~ mit stehenden Wellen** standing wave antenna, open antenna **~ auskurbeln** to lower the antenna, wind out the antenna **~ einziehen** to reel or haul in, wind in, retract antenna wire **abgeschirmte ~** shielded (down-lead) antenna, antistatic or screened antenna **abgestimmte ~** tuned antenna
Antenne, aperiodische ~ untuned or aperiodic antenna **ausgekurbelte ~** reeled out, lowered, or paid out antenna **dachförmige ~** roof-shaped antenna **eingebaute ~** built-in antenna **eingefahrene ~** retracted or drawn-in antenna **eingegrabene ~** buried antenna **vom Sender entkuppelte ~** balanced antenna **feine ~** fine-tuning antenna **freihängende ~** trailing wire antenna, trailing aerial
Antenne, geknickte ~ bent antenna **gerichtete ~** directive or directional antenna **geschlossene ~** closed antenna **gesonderte ~** tuned antenna **jeweilige ~** antenna of any desired length **künstliche ~** artifical or dummy antenna, mute or phantom aerial, tuning antenna **lineare ~** vertical-wire antenna **mehrdrähtige ~** multiple-wire antenna **mehrfach abgestimmte ~** multiple-tuned antenna
Antenne, offene ~ open antenna (radio); (stark) **richtfähige ~** (highly) directive antenna **schwundmindernde ~** fading-reducing antenna, antifading aerial **ungerichtete ~** nondirective, omnidirectional, equiradial or nondirectional antenna **verlängerte T-~** extended T-shaped antenna **verstimmte ~** mute, out of tune, or not functioning antenna **zweidrähtige ~** two-wire antenna
Antennen-abführung *f* antenna downlead **-abgleichmittel** *n* antenna syntonizing means **-ableitung** *f* antenna lead(-in), down-lead **-abnahme** *f* antenna lead-in (radio) **-abschwächer** *m* antenna attenuator **-abspannung** *f* **-abspannungskurve** *f* resonance curve
Antennenabstimm-häuschen *n* antenna tuning house, antenna house **-kondensator** *m* antenna tuning condenser or capacitor
Antennenabstimmspule *f* antenna tuning inductance, antenna tuning coil, antenna trailing inductance coil **Induktivität der ~** antenna inductivity
Antennen-abstimmung *f* antenna tuning **-abstimmungsgerät** *n* antenna tuning unit **-anfachung** *f* antenna excitation **-anführung** *f* antenna lead-in **-ankoppelung** *f* antenna coupling **-anlage** *f* antenna array (radar)
Antennenanordnung *f* curtain, end-on directional antenna **~ für Längsstrahlung** end-on directional (aerial) array (radio) **~ regelmäßiger Ausführung** array (normal aerial, not especially adapted for directional radio transmission) **~ für Querstrahlung** broadside array (broadside directional radio aerial) **~ mit hohem Richteffekt** superdirective array
Antennen-anpassung *f* antenna matching unit **-anpassungsgerät** *n* antenna-matching unit (radar) **-anschluß** *m* antenna connection **-anschlußbüchse** *f* antenna jack **-anzeigeskala** *f* antenna repeat dial **-aufhängung** *f* antenna suspension **-ausschaltgerät** *n* receiver-antenna switch **-bauvorschrift** *f* instruction for construction of antennas **-blindwiderstand** *m* antenna reactance **-buchse** *f* antenna socket **-büchse** *f* antenna jack **-bündelung** *f* directivity
Antennen-dämpfung *f* antenna decrement **-dipol** *m* dipole, doublet **-draht** *m* antenna wire **-drehzahl** *f* rotational speed of antenna **-drossel** *f* antenna chocke **-durchführung** *f* antenna duct or trunk **-durchhang** *m* antenna dip
Antennen-ei *n* antenna weight (radar) **-einführung** *f* antenna lead-in **-eingangswiderstand** *m* antenna feed impedance **-endgewicht** *n* fish (of trailing antenna) **-erder** *m* antenna ground plate **-energie** *f* antenna signal intensity **-ersatzstromkreis** *m* dummy, phantom, or mute antenna
Antennen-führungsrohr *n* guide tube for antenna **-gebilde** *n* antenna structure or network, antenna array or system **-gerät** *n* antenna outfit or equipment **-gerüst** *n* antenna support **-gruppe** *f* unit antenna array **-güte** *f* antenna field gain **-haftung** *f* **für Schäden** liability for damages caused by antennas **-haspel** *f* antenna winch or reel **-hebungsklinke** *f* antenna elevation pawl **-hochführung** *f* down-lead (of an antenna)
Antennen-induktivität *f* antenna inductance **-kapazität** *f* antenna capacitance **-kappe** *f* antenna base cover **-kennlinie** *f* antenna characteristics **-klemme** *f* antenna terminal **-kopplung** *f* antenna coupling, antenna-coupling control **-kreis** *m* antenna circuit
Antennenkreisleistung *f* peak power of transmitter **~ in unmoduliertem Zustand** unmodulated power of the transmitter
Antennenleistung *f* antenna power **zugeführte ~** antenna input
Antennen-leitung transmission line
Antennen-litze *f* antenna cording, or strand **-mast** *m* radio mast or tower, or antenna

mast **-nahfeld** *n* vicinity or short-range field of antenna

Antennennetz *n* **kontinuierliches lineares ~** continuous linear antenna array **~ mit Parasitärelementen** parasitic array **~ mit geringer räumlicher Trennung** close-spaced antenna array

Antennen-paar *n* pair of antennas twin antenna, dipole, doublet **-resonanzkurve** *f* antenna resonance curve **-richtdiagramm** *n* antenna directivity pattern **-ringleitung** *f* multiple-receiver connection to antenna **-rohr** *n* antenna tubing **-schacht** *m* aerial lead-in tube, antenna fair-lead or lead-in **-schalter mit Sicherung** antenna switch with fuse

Antennen-schluß *m* antenna connection **-schwingung** *f* vibration, swaying or swinging of antenna **-selbstinduktion** *f* antenna inductance **-spannung** *f* antenna voltage **-speiseleitung** *f* antenna feeder **-speisescheinwiderstand** *m* antenna feed-impedance

Antennenspeisung *f* excitation (electronics) **direkte ~** direct feed of the antenna

Antennen-spule *f* antenna coil or tuning **-stecker** *m* antenna spreader or plug **-stegleitung** *f* twin-lead transmission line **-stellung** *f* directional position of antenna

Antennenstrom *m* antenna current **-anzeiger** *m* antenna-current indicator, antenna ammeter

Antennenstufenschalter *m* antenna or aerial current loading switch

Antennen-system *n* directional antenna system **-tasche** *f* antenna housing (radio) **-trommel** *f* antenna winding drum or winch **-turm** *m* pylon **-übertrager** *m* antenna transformer **-umschalter** *m* antenna switch **-umschaltungsgerät** *n* identification-friend-or-foe receiver antenna switch **-verkleidung** *f* antenna fairing **-verkürzungskondensator** *m* (antenna) shortening or series condenser or capacitor

Antennen-verlängerungsspule *f* antenna loading coil, antenna-inductance coil **-verstärker** *m* antenna amplifier or booster **-verstärkung** *f* directive gain **-verteilung** *f* antenna distribution **-wahlschalter** *m* antenna selection switch **-winde** *f* antenna reel **-wirkungsgrad** *m* radiation efficiency **-zuleitung** *f* down-lead, lead-in wire, antenna-lead, feeder line, transmission line **-zündung** *f* brown type mine ignition, antenna firing (of mines)

anteponierend occurring prematurely

Anthrachinon *n* anthraquinone

Anthrakometer *n* anthracometer

Anthranilsäure *f* anthranilic acid

Anthrazen *n* anthracene **-öl** *n* anthracene oil

Anthrazit *m* anthracite **~** (im Gegensatz zur bituminösen Kohle) carbonite **~** (stengliger, mit Stangenkohle) columnar anthracite

Anthrazit-art *f* (kleine) barley coal, culm **-bildung** *f* anthracitization **-grus** *m* anthracite culm **-haltig** culmiferous

anthrazitisch anthracitic **-e Kohle** semianthracite, anthracitic coal

Anthrazit-kulm *m* anthracite culm **-schlamm** *m* **-schlammkohle** *f* anthracite silt or slush

Anthropometer *n* anthropometer

Anthygronflansche und Kabelstutzen anthygron flanges and cable sealing ends

Anthygronrohrdrähte *pl* anthygron armored wires and cables

Anti-automorphismus *m* anti-automorphism **-blendungsfarbe** *f* antiglare paint **-chlor** *n* antichlorine (sodium thiosulfate), sodium hyposulfite **-cordal** *n* anticordal, anti aluminium-magnesium-silicon alloy, **-crackmittel** *n* anti-cracking agent **-drönmasse** *f* antinoise compound, anti-hum noise **-effekt** *m* anti-effect **-fäulnisfarbe** *f* anti-fouling composition **-ferroelektrika** *f* antiferroelectrics

antiferroelektrisch antiferroelectric **-e Verschiebungen** antiferroelectric displacements

Antiflatterbock *m* antishimmy brace or shackle **-flimmervorrichtung** *f* antidazzle (dimmers) **-flußspatgitter** *n* antifluorite lattice

Antifriktions-lager *n* antifriction bearing **-metall** *n* nearing metal

Antikatalysator *m* anticatalyst

Antikathode *f* target, anticathode (of X-ray tube)

Antikathodenleuchten *n* anticathode luminescence

Antik-bronze *f* patina-covered bronze **-glas** *n* antique glass

antiklinal anticlinal

Antiklinale *f* anticline

Antiklinal-falte *f* anticlinal fold **-theorie** *f* anticlinal theory

Antiklinorium *n* anticlinorium

Antiklopf-brennstoff *m* antiknock fuel **-mittel** *n* antiknock (compound) **-zusatzmittel** *n* antiknock fuel dope

Anti-koagulationsmittel *n* anti-coagulant stabilizer **-kohärer** *m* anticoherer

Antikoinzidenz *f* anticoincidence **-anordnung** *f* anticoincidence arrangement or system **-messung** *f* anticoincidence measuring **-schaltung** *f* anticoincidence circuit, inhibiting gate **-verstärker** *m* anticoincidence amplifier

Antikompound-dynamo *f* differentially compounded dynamo **-wickelung** *f* differential compound winding

Anti-körper *m* antisubstance, antibody **-löcher** *pl* antiholes

anti-magnetisch antimagnetic, nonmagnetic

Anti-materie *f* antimatter

antimer antimer

Antimon *n* antimony **-abstich** *m* antimony skimmings **-arsen** *n* allemontite **-arsennickel** *n* niccolite **-artig** antimonial, antimonylike **-blei** *n* antimonial lead, lead antimony alloy **-blende** *f* kermesite **-blüte** *f* antimony bloom, valentinite **-chlorid** *n* antimony chloride, antimony pentachloride **-chlorür** *n* antimony chloride, antimony trichloride

Antimonerz *n* antimony ore **-verhüttung** *f* antimony metallurgy **-vorkommen** *n* antimony-ore deposit

Antimonid *n* antimonide

antimonige Säure antimonious acid

Antimon-fahlerz *n* tetrahedrite, antimonial gray copper **-glanz** *m* antimony glance, stibnite **-goldschwefel** (Lack) golden antimony sulfide **-haltig** antimonic, antimonious, antimonial

Antimonin (milchsaures Antimon) antimony lactate

antimonisch antimonial, antimonic, antimonious

Antimon-jodür *n* antimonious iodide **-kalium-oxalat** *n* antimony potassium oxalate **-kalium-tartrat** *n* antimony potassium tartrate **-kupfer-glanz** *m* antimonial copper glance **-nickelglanz** *m* ullmannite, nickel stibine **-oxychlorür** *n* antimony oxychloride **-oxyd** *n* antimony oxide, antimony trioxide

antimonsaures Natrium sodium antimoniate

Antimon-silber *n* antimonial silver, dyscrasite **-silberblende** *f* pyrargyrite **-stern** *m* antimony star **-sulfür** *n* antimonious sulfide, antimony trisulfide or pentasulfide **-trisulfid** *n* antimony trisulfide **-trisulfidsol** *n* gel or colloid of antimony trisulfide **-weiß** *n* antimony (white) trioxide **-zinnober** *m* kermes mineral, red antimony sulfide

Antineutrino *n* anti-neutrino (atom. phys.)

Antinode *f* anti-node

Anti-oxydantien *pl* antioxygenes **-oxydations-mittel** *n* oxidation inhibitor, antioxidant **-paralaxeneinrichtung** *f* antiparallax

antiparallel antiparallel

Antipassat *m* antitrades, countertrade

Antipode *m* optically opposite form

antipodisch antipodal

antippen to touch

Antiproten *n* negative proton, antiproton

Antiqua *f* roman type or character, brevier (print.)

Antiquariat *n* **Antiquariatsbuchhandlung** *f* second-hand bookshop

antiquarisch second-hand

Antiquaschrift *f* Roman type (face)

Antireflexbelege *pl* antireflex coatings

Antiresonanz *f* parallel resonance, antiresonance **-frequenz** *f* antiresonant frequency

Anti-rotation *f* reserve rotation, counterrotation **-schaummittel** *n* defoamer

antiseptisches Mittel antiseptic

antistatisches Tau antistatic (cartridge or wire trailing from airplane)

anti-Stokessche-Linien anti-Stokes lines

antisymmetrischer Tensor antisymmetric tensor

Antiteilchen *n* antiparticle

Antizentrum *n* anticenter

Antizyklon *m* anticyclone, area of high pressure, barometric maximum

antizyklonal anticyclonic(ally) **-stadium** *n* anticyclonic state

Antizyklotron *n* anticyclotron

antönen to tinge

Antrag *m* motion, complaint (law), proposal, proposition, suggestion, recommendation, request **~ aufnehmen** to secure a proposal **einen ~ stellen** to make an offer, put a motion

antragen to proffer

Antraglegierung *f* alloy available on request

Antragsformular *n* form of application, application blank

Antragsteller *m* applicant, petitioner

Antragsstellung *f* application

Antransport *m* transportation in motion toward

antreffen to encounter, meet

antreiben to propel, impel, prompt, push, urge, drive (on), start, operate, actuate, stimulate, hasten, rotate, run; (Motor) to activate, crank

antreibend impulsive **-e Kraft** exciting force **-es Maschinenteil** driver

Antreiber *m* pacemaker, impeller, driver, propeller (aviation)

Antreibesystem *n* sweating or slave-driving system

Antreibmaschine *f* **für Faßreifen** hoop-driving machine, trussing machine

antreten to take a position, take possession, set out (trip) **den Dienst ~** to enter service, report for work, assume duty **Beweis ~** to offer evidence

Anthranilsäure *f* anthranilic acid

Anthrazenöl *n* anthracene oil

Antrieb *m* drive (machine), start, impulse, impulsion, motive, motion, urge, motor, rotation, motive power, propulsion, impetus, gearing, momentum, control, fine tuning, actuator, operator (control valve), driving gear, input (kinematics) **~ durch Druckwasser** hydraulic-pressure drive **~ mit Fest- und Losscheibe** idler pulley **~ durch Reibräder** friction drive **~ mit Schaltkasten** press drive and main switch panel **~ durch Schwerkraft** gravity drive **~ durch Stufenscheibe** cone-pulley drive **~ mit Übersetzung ins Schnelle** speed-increaser drive **~ und Steuerungsmechanismus** gearing and controlling mechanism **~ des Zündverteilers** drive of the ignition distributor

Antrieb, mit ~ von oben top-driven **mit ~ von unten** underdriven **mit oberem** (unterem) **~** with driving gear above (below) **direkter ~** direct drive **doppelseitiger ~** bilateral drive **elastischer ~** nonrigid drive **federnder ~** spring drive **freischwingender ~** free-swinging drive

Antrieb, gemeinsamer ~ common drive **mechanischer ~** mechanical or machine drive **oberer ~** top drive **oberhalb gelagerter ~** overhead drive **rückwärtiger ~** rear drive **schlupffreier ~** nonslip, geared, or positive drive **unterer ~** bottom drive **zwangsläufiger ~** positive drive

Antriebsachse *f* propeller shaft, driving axle or shaft **direkte ~** live axle

Antriebs-aggregat *n* drive unit, moving part (of the plant), power package **-anker** *m* drag anchor **-anstieg** *m* power climb **-art** *f* driving system (method), kind of drive **-ausrüstung** *f* driving equipment **-block** *m* headstock **-bock** *m* gearing end frame; (für Pumpen) fulcrum for pumps **-bolzen** *m* driving pin **-element** *n* motor element (of loud-speaker) **-büchse** *f* driving bush

Antriebs-deckenvorgelege *n* overhead driving gear **-drehmoment** *n* driving torque **-drehzahl** *f* driving speed (r.p.m.) **-element** *n* driving mechanism or element **-energie** *f* motive energy **-flansch** *m* driving flange **-gabel** *f* driver **-gelenkwelle** *f* propeller shaft **-gestänge** *n* lever system **-gewicht** *n* driving weight **-gleichstrom-motor** *m* driving direct-current motor

Antrieb(s)-haspel *f* power take-up reel **-hebel** *m* operating lever, fine-tuning lever, driving or actuating lever **kasten** *m* gearbox **-kegelrad** *n* bevel pinion, bevel drive gear **-keilwelle** *f* multiple-splined driving shaft **-kette** *f* drive chain **-kettenrad** *n* drive or driving sprocket, driving chain wheel

Antriebs-klaue *f* clutch dog, claw coupling, driving jaw **-knopf** *m* driving knob **-kopf** *m*

drive coupling **-kraft** *f* driving force or power, motive power **-kurbel** *f* operating crank **-kupplung** *f* driving or starting clutch

Antriebs-lager *n* drive bearing **-leistung** *f* propulsive output, drive or generated power, efficiency (of pump) **-los** power off

Antriebsmaschine *f* driving engine, prime mover **halbstehende ~** semiportable engine

Antriebs-maschinerie *f* propelling machinery **-mechanismus** *m* motion (driving) mechanism **-mittel** *n* working fluid **-mittelpunkt** *m* center of thrust **-modell** *n* power- or motor-driven airplane model **-moment** *m* starting (driving) moment or torque

Antriebsmotor *m* mover, driving motor **-scheibe** *f* driving pulley **~ 2-fach kugelgelagert** motor with 2 ball bearings

Antriebs-mühle der Hilfsmotoren fan (of emergency motors, aviation) **-nocken** *m* driving cam **-organ** *n* driving mechanism, driving element **-platten der Schlagarme** picking plates of loom

Antriebsrad *n* drive (wheel) gear, pinion **federndes ~** spring drive **~ für Karren** bed drive gear **~ für Strudelrad** vee-belt drive agitator **~ zur Vertikaleinstellung** vertical driving-shaft gear

Antriebs-reibungskupplung *f* friction-starting clutch **-richtung** *f* direction of drive **-riemen** *m* driving belt **-riemenscheibe** *f* drive pulley **-ritzel** *n* driving pinion, pinion, starter **-rohrwelle** *f* tubular drive shaft **-rolle** *f* friction roller, driving pulley **-säule** *f* driving starting pillar

Antriebsscheibe *f* drive or driving pulley, main pulley, driving disc, driving wheel **~ für tote Spitzen** dead-center pulley **die ~ ausrücken** to throw driving pulley out of gear

Antriebsscheibenkonsole *f* drive-pulley support

Antriebs-schwenklager *n* swivel bearing of drive system **-schlüssel** *m* camera driving pin **-seil** *n* driving rope or string, pulley cord **-seite** *f* driving side, input end (kinematics) **-selbstversteller** *m* automatic regulator on drive, automatic timing device **-spindel** *f* driving spindle or shaft, operating screw

Antriebs-stahlhohlwelle hollow driving shaft **-stange** *f* feed rod, driving shaft or rod, actuating rod **-starter** *m* impulse starter **-station** *f* driving unit **-strahl** *m* propulsive jet **-stromkreis** *m* driving circuit **-stufenscheibe** *f* driving-cone pulley or step pulley **-stutzen** *m* drive bushing

Antriebs-teil *m* driving member, part of the drive **-trommel** *f* driving pulley, tin roller **-übersetzungsverhältnis** *n* transmission ratio of drive **-untersetzung** *f* speed (gear) reduction **-vorrichtung** *f* driving arrangement, operating (gear) machinery **-walze** *f* drive roller

Antriebswelle *f* driving or actuation shaft, clutch shaft, propeller or line shaft, main shaft **~ für den Rundtischvorschub** rotary-attachment feed rod **hohle ~** driving tube, fine-tuning shaft (radio)

Antriebswellen-büchse *f* driving-shaft bushing **-kuppelung** *f* driving-shaft coupling **-wellenstumpf** *m* gear box tunnel, transmission tunnel

Antriebs-werk *n* driving mechanism or gears **-wirkungsgrad** *m* propulsive efficiency **-zahnrad** *n* drive gear (transmission), pinion **-zapfen** *m* driver, drive journal **-zentrum** *n* center of thrust

Antritt *m* beginning, first step

Antrittsstufe *f* top-step landing

Antrocknen *n* surface drying (of lacquers)

Antwort *f* answer, reply, response **um ~ wird gebeten** a reply is requested **abschlägige ~** refusal, negative reply

Antwortbake *f* responder beacon, transponder

antworten to answer, reply, respond, plead **Teilnehmer antwortet nicht** there is no reply

Antwort-geber *m* revertive signal means, check-back or monitoring position indicator **-impulse** *pl* reply pulses **-klinke** *f* answering jack **-schein** *m* reply coupon **-schreiben** *n* (written) reply **-sender** *m* transponder, responder **-signal** *n* return light, answering signal **-stöpsel** *m* answering plug **-welle** *f* answering wave, assigned wave length **-zeichen** *n* answer signal

anvisieren to align sights on, take bearings on, sight, lay, take aim

Anvisieren *n* (eines Horizontalpunktes) sighting a point on the horizon (navig.)

Anvulkanisation *f* prevulcanization

anvulkanisieren to burn, prevulcanize, scorch

Anwachs *m* growth, increase, accretion

anwachsen to grow, increase, swell, rise

Anwachsen *n* rise, increase, swelling, growth **~ mit dem Quadrat von** increase in proportion with the square of **~ des Widerstands infolge von Fremdatomen** increment of resistivity due to impurities

Anwachs-kurve *f* growth curve **-zeit** growth time

anwählen to dial

Anwahlsteuerung *f* selective control

anwalken to plank

Anwallung *f* attack, fit, paroxysm

Anwalt *m* lawyer, attorney, counsel

Anwandlung *f* impulse, seizure, slight attack

Anwärmapparat *m* feed heater, preheater

Anwärme-brenner *m* preheating torch **-herd** *m* heating plate

anwärmen to warm up, heat (up), temper

Anwärmen, zum ~ des Motors erforderliche Zeit warming-up time of an engine

Anwärmer *m* heater

Anwärmeschuß *m* warming-up shot

Anwärmschlange *f* heating coil

Anwärmung *f* (pre)heating

Anwärmvorrichtung *f* (pre)heater

Anwärter *m* cadet, candidate, aspirant

Anwartschaft *f* reversion, candidacy, contingent revision

anwassern to alight on water, land, alight, descend on, or make contact with the water (airplane)

anwässern to moisten slightly, dampen

anwecken to ring (telephone), wake up

anweichen to soak, steep, soften

anweisen to instruct, advise, direct, order, appoint, point out, appropriate, transfer (money)

Anweisender *m* assignor

Anweisernetz *n* indicator net

Anweiseschein *m* assignment form

Anweisung *f* order, remittance, voucher, draft, instruction, direction, specification, allocation, assignation, allotment, charge **~ für einheit-**

liche Betriebsuntersuchungen instruction for uniform factory control **kurze** ~ folder **schriftliche** ~ order

anwendbar practical, usable, relevant, available, applicable ~ **sein** to apply

Anwendbarkeit *f* applicability, practicability **vielseitige** ~ maximum flexibility of usefulness

anwenden to use, employ, apply, utilize **sparsam** ~ to economize

Anwendung *f* use, application, practice, employment, administration, utilization, tuning in, exercise ~ **des Versuches** significance of test ~ **finden** to be used

Anwendungs-art *f* method of employment **-beispiel** *n* example of application **-bereich** *m* scope, range of application **-feld** *n* operational range **-form** *f* embodiment **-gebiet** *n* field of application, range of characteristics and uses (of practical application) **-grenzen** *pl* limits or range of applicability **-möglichkeit** *f* suitability, use, applicability **-vorschrift** *f* direction for use **-weise** *f* method of application **-zweck** *m* purpose

anwerben to recruit **sich** ~ **lassen** to enlist

anwerfen to crank (an engine), throw (an engine) into gear, start up, swing propeller, set in motion **Motor** ~ to start the engine

Anwerf-klaue *f* starter dog **-kurbel** *f* starting crank or handle **-motor** *m* starting motor

Anwerfvorrichtung, selbsttätige ~ automatic starting device

Anwesen *n* estate, premises

anwesend present

Anwesenden *m* or *f pl* die ~ those present

Anwesenheit *f* presence

Anwesenheits-karte *f* attendance card **-zeit** *f* attendance time

anwirken (Strumpf), to foot stockings

Anwitterung *f* incrustation, oxidation

Anwuchs *m* growth, increase, increment, accrescence, accretion

Anwurf *m* patch, rough cast, plaster(ing) **-kurbel** *f* starting switch, handle, or crank **-motor** *m* pony motor

anwürgen to grip, crimp, constrict, choke

Anzahl *f* number, quantity ~ **der Gänge auf den Zoll** threads (pipe) per inch ~ **von Teilen, die gleichzeitig bearbeitet werden** number of parts in a batch **geringe** ~ paucity **größere** ~ lot **zulässige** ~ allowance

anzahlen to pay on account, make a first installment

Anzahlung *f* part payment, first installment, down payment, deposit

Anzapf *m* tap(ping), leaker off, bleeder **-anpassung** *f* Delta-matching **-antenne, symmetrische** ~ Y antenna **-dampf** *m* bleeder steam, leakage or bleeder current **-dampfmaschine** *f* extracting or bleeder type steam engine

anzapfen to tap, tune in

Anzapfen *n* bleeding (steam)

Anzapf-leitung *f* power lead-in **-punkt** *m* pass-out point **-spule** *f* tapped coil

Anzapfstelle *f* tapping (point), tap **mittlere** ~ center tapping point

Anzapf-strom *m* leakage or bleeder current **-stufe** *f* tapping stage **-transformator** *m* split or tapped transformer **-turbine** *f* bleeder, extraction, pass-out, or by-pass turbine **-umschalter** *m* tap ,changer

Anzapfung *f* tap, taper, tapering, tapping (radio, radar), extraction, interstage leak-off

Anzapfungspunkt *m* tapping point

Anzapf-ventil *n* by-pass or bleeder valve **-widerstand** *m* tapped resistor

Anzeichen *n* indication, sign, symptom, warning, evidence **-gerät** *n* marking-off device

anzeichnen to mark, indicate, index, notice ~ **mit Reißnadel** to scribe

Anzeige *f* record, reading, notice, information, indication, advertisement, report, notification, warning, denunciation, signal, representation (electronics) **befristete** ~ notification within a given period **gedämpfte** ~ deadbeat, nonballistic or aperiodic reading **ungedämpfte** ~ ballistic reading or indication

Anzeige-bereich *m* indicating or instrument range **-dauer** *f* display time **-einschub** *m* plug-in indicator **-fehler** *m* indication error

Anzeigegerät *n* indicator, indicating instrument, indicator gauge ~ **der Wasserstandsfernmeldeanlage** remote-reading water-level indicator

Anzeige-geschwindigkeit *f* speed of indication **-gitter** *n* indicator grid **-instrument** *n* recording device, measuring unit, indicator **-lampe** *f* control or signal lamp, indicator lamp, pilot lamp **-lehre** *f* indicator gauge, main presentation unit **-leuchte** *f* signaling or indicating lamp

Anzeigemarke, schwarze ~ black dot pointer or mark (on dials) to read bearings

Anzeigemechanismus *m* registering (recording) mechanism

Anzeige-meßgerät *n* **-lehre** *f* indicator gauge **-vorrichtung mit Rückmeldeeinrichtung** (z.B. bei Einziehfahrwerk), telltale indicator

anzeigen (ankündigen) to annonce; (Meßinstrument) indicate, show; (Zeitung) advertise, publish, report, record, register, denounce, signal, detect **förmlich** ~ to notify

Anzeigen der Instrumente instrument reading

Anzeigenabzug *m* advertisement proof

anzeigend, fortlaufend ~ continuously indicating **-es Instrument** reading instrument **-er Meßapparat** indicating meter **-es Organ** index (meas-instr.)

Anzeigen-sammler *m* advertisement broker or canvasser **-setzer** *m* advertisement typesetter

Anzeigepflicht *f* obligation to report (a crime)

anzeigepflichtig notifiable

Anzeiger *m* indicator, informer, advertiser, exponent (math.), pointer, index, recorder, marker, detector, responder, dial ~ **für Landeklappenausschlag** flap-position indicator

Anzeiger-blatt *n* indicator dial **-boje** *f* marker buoy **-deckung** *f* signaling or marking disk **-feder** *f* indicator spring

Anzeigenröhre *f* tuning-indicator tube

Anzeigerschiene *f* indicator slide

Anzeige-skala *f* indicating scale **-skizze** *f* lay-out sketch **-spannung** *f* indication voltage, indicated voltage **-stange** *f* indicator bar **-tafel** *f* indicator board **-trägheit** *f* inertia of needle or pointer, indicator lag

Anzeige-verfahren *n* recording process **-verstärker** *m* directly indicating amplifier **-ver-**

zögerung *f* retarded indication

Anzeigevorrichtung *f* indicating (recording) device, indicator, landing-gear-position indicator, signaling or marking apparatus, visual reading instrument ~ **mit Rückmeldeeinrichtung für Betriebszustände** telltale (indicator)

Anzeige-widerstand *m* resistance indicator

Anzeigung *f* detection, indication **hörbare** (sichtbare) ~ audible (visual) detection

anzetteln to warp (textiles), to weave a plot

Anziehbolzen *m* clamping bolt

anziehen to pull, draw, screw up, tighten, set, start, attract, advance, go up, absorb, dress, screw down (nut), pull up (relay or armature) **fest** ~ to tighten

Anziehen *n* attraction, advancing (prices), tightening ~ (Mörtel) initial hardening ~ (Zement) setting ~ **der Rückkopplung** tightening feedback, making regenerative coupling closer

anziehend (at)tractive **-er Bereich** field of attraction

Anziehkraft *f* centripetal force, force of attraction

Anziehmaschinearbeitsreifen *m* truss hoop driving machine (brewing)

Anziehschrauben *f pl* turnbuckle or swivel screws, tightening screws

Anziehung *f* attraction, operation, working **Gegenstand der** ~ object of attraction

Anziehungs-effekt *m* effect of attraction **-gebiet** *n* sphere of attraction **-kraft** *f* attraction, force of attraction, attractive power or force, magnetism, adhesive force, gravitation **-punkt** *m* center of attraction or gravity **-zentrum** *n* center of attraction

anzielen (einen Gegenstand) to point, aim at, sight

Anzug *m* entrance, approach, draft, taper, suit, concave, quarter round, incline, tightening ~ **des Kalibers** taper of the pass **im** ~ **sein** to draw near, approach

Anzugsdorn zum Fräsdorn draw-in rod for arbor

Anzug(s)-drehmoment *n* starting torque, stall torque **-fläche** *f* magnetic surface **-gewinde** *n* thread for draw-in bolt **-gußmodell** *n* casting-model draft (power plant engin.) **-keil** *m* adjusting wedge, taper key **-kraft** *f* tractive effort at starting, initial power, starting torque **-kraftmesser** *m* torque meter

Anzugsmoment tightening torque, initial tension, initial moment of stress, starting torque

Anzugspol und Rückzugspol (Magnete) attracting pole and resetting pole

Anzugs-schraube *f* attachment screw (Mi) tripod screw (geo.) **-stellung** *f* attracted position (of a relay) **-strom** *m* starting current (of electr. motors) **-vermögen** *n* acceleration

anzugsverzögertes Relais time delay relay

Anzugsverzögerung *f* operate lag (of relay), delay in starting **Relais mit** ~ slow-operating relay

Anzugs-winkel *m* fleet angle **-zeit** *f* operating time

anzünden to ignite, kindle, light (up), start, strike (an arc)

Anzünden *n* lighting (of lights)

Anzünder *m* igniter, flame lighter

Anzündöffnung *f* lighting aperture

anzwecken to fasten with tacks

Anzwirnen *n* twisting in (textiles)

äolisch aeolian, wind-deposited **-es Geröll** aeolian rocks

Äols-glocke *f* aeolian bell **-harfe** *f* aeolian harp

Äolotropie *f* aeolotropy

Äolusball *m* aeolipile

Apatit *m* apatite

aperiod (Stromkreis) aperiodic (circuit)

aperiodisch aperiodic, dead-beat aperiodic ~ **ausschwingend** deadbeat (coming to a rest as the indicator of a highly damped galvanometer) ~ **gedämpftes Instrument** aperiodic instrument **-e Antenne** untuned antenna **-e Dämpfung** deadbeat (aviation) **-es Galvanometer** deadbeat glavanometer **-er Kompaß** aperiodic or deadbeat compass **-er Kreis** aperiodic circuit **-es Pendel** aperiodic pendulum **-e Sonde** untuned probe **-er Spannungsmesser** aperiodic voltmeter **-er Vorgang** *m* aperiodic phenomenon

Aperiodizität *f* aperiodicity

Apertometer *n* apertometer

Apertur *f* (focal) aperture, spot size ~ **des Brennpunkts** focal aperture

Apertur-ausbeute *f* aperture efficiency **-begrenzung** *f* aperture limitation **-blende** *f* aperture stop or diaphragm **-blendenkorrektur** *f* aperture corrector **-fläche** *f* aperture illumination **-meter** *n* apertometer **-verteilung** *f* aperture distribution

Apfel-äther *m* malic ether **-baumholz** *n* apple wood **-säure** *f* malic acid

Apfelsinenschalen Effekt, ~ **Erscheinung** orange-peel effect (of lacquers)

Aphongetriebe *n* synchromesh transmission, constant-mesh transmission

Aphrit *m* aphrite, slate spar, argentine

Aphrizit *m* aphrizite

Aphrodite code for a type of radar decoy

Aphrometer *n* aphrometer

Aplanasie *f* aplanatism

Aplanate *pl* aplanatic systems

aplanatisch aplanatic (optics) **-e Einschlaglupe** aplanatic folding magnifier **-e Lupe** (Leuchtlupe) aplanatic magnifier (illuminating magnifier) **-es Objektiv** aplanatic (rectilinear) lens or objective **-e asphärische Ophthalmoskoplinse** nonspherical aplanatic focusing lens

A-Platz *m* outgoing or A position

A-Platz mit Wählzusatz key pulsing A-position

A-Plätze *m pl* outgoing or A position

A-Platzschrank *m* A switchboard

Apochromat *m* apochromatic objective

apochromatisch apochromatic

Apogäum *m* apogee

Apogluzinsäure *f* apoglucic acid

apolar-e Flüssigkeit apolar liquid **-es Lösungsmittel** non-polar solvent

Apomekometer *n* apomecometer

Apostilb (German term corresponding to) lambert (illuminating engin. unit)

Apotheke *f* pharmacy, drugstore

Apotheker *m* pharmacist, druggist **-gewicht** *n* apothecaries' weight

Apparat *m* apparatus, equipment, instrument,

device, appliance, contrivance, accessory ~ **zum Anziehen von Drähten** apparatus for drawing wires ~ **zum elastischen Deformieren** apparatus for deforming elastically ~ **zum Messen der Hubkraft am Heck** stern-weighing device ~ **mit Ruhestellung** restore-to-normal switch ~ **ohne Ruhestellung** stay-put switch ~, **der Signale in Fächerform aussendet** fan marker ~ **zur Stromstoßunterdrückung** digit-absorbing selector **gegen falsche Bedienung gesicherter** ~ foolproof apparatus **schlagwettersicherer** ~ flameproof appliance ~ **mit Voreinstellung** preset apparatus

Apparat-aufbau *m* assemblage (of apparatus) **-aufsicht** *f* operator in charge **-beamter** *m* operator

Apparate-bau *m* manufacture of apparatus **-gamma** *n* apparatus gamma (electronics) **-gas** *n* generator gas **-schlüssel** *m* spanner **-teil** *m* accessory compartment **-zuleitung** *f* instrument or apparatus lead **-gehäuse** *n* housing or casing of the instrument, instrument case **-geräusch** *n* system noise (sound recorder)

apparativ belonging or pertaining to an apparatus

Apparat-karren *m* instrument cart **-klinke** *f* instrument jack **-körper** *m* body **-patent** *n* apparatus patent **-raum** *m* **-saal** *m* instrument (galley) room, switch room, auto room **-satz** *m* set, assembly **-teil** *m* item or part of apparatus

Apparattisch *m* instrument table **vierteiliger** ~ four-part operation table (teleph.)

Apparat-tornister *m* instrument case **-träger** *m* rear crankease section

Apparatur *f* equipment, mechanical outfit, apparatus, fittings, tackle (of any sort), instrumentality, device, mechanism, outfit, contrivance, appliance **-gamma** *n* apparatus gamma (electronics)

Apparatwecker *m* station ringer

Apparatzuleitungen *f pl* instrument leads

Appareils *m pl* lineman's climbers

Appell *m* roll call, assembly, inspection, muster, appeal ~ **abhalten** to call the roll

appellfähig proper, spick and span

Applanations-tonometer *n* applanation tonometer

Applikation *f* administration

applizieren to apply

apportieren to retrieve

Appret *n* finishing process, sizing material

Appretieren *n* dressing, finishing ~ **von Geweben** finishing of tissues **zweiseitiges** ~ **von Geweben** double sizing of fabrics

Appretierer *m* finisher

Apprettiermaschine *f* finish(ing) machine

Appretur *f* dressing or finish(ing), seasoning **-anstalt** *f* cloth-finishing establishment **-echt** fast to finishing or dressing **-fähigkeit** *f* capacity to take on finish **-körper** *m* loading agents on fillers (paper) **-leim** *m* dressing glue **-maschine** *f* finishing or dressing machine **-mittel** *n* finishing (sizing) preparation **-zusatzmittel** *n* chemical dressing agents

A-Produkt *n* half-finished steel product

Approximation im Mittel mean approximation

approximativ approximate

Apsiden *pl* apsides

Apsis *f* apsis

aptieren to adapt, convert (guns etc.)

Aquadag-belag *m* aquadag coating

Aquädukt *m* aqueduct, culvert

Aquarell-farbe *f* water color **-malerei** *f* water color painting

Äquator *m* equator **-bogen** *m* equatorial arc **-ebene** *f* earth's equator

äquatorial equatorial(ly) **-e Aufstellung** equatorial mounting **-e Gebiete** equatorial belt **-es Gradnetz** equatorial grid references system **-e (magnetische) Quantenzahl** total angular momentum quantum number

Äquatorial-reflektor *m* equatorial reflector **-refraktor** *m* equatorial refractor **-strom** *m* equatorial current

Äquator-minute *f* minute of the equator **-naht** *f* equatorial seam **-schnitt** *m* equatorial section

äquianharmonisch equianharmonic **-e Punkte** equianharmonic points

äquidistant equidistant **-e Abszissen** equally spaced points

äquilibrieren to equilibrate

äquimolekular equimolecular

äquinoktial equinoctial

Äquinoktial-punkt *m* equinoctial point **-sturm** *m* equinoctial gale or storm

Äquinoktium *n* equinox

Äquipartitionstheorem *n* equipartition theorem

Äquipotential-fläche *f* isopotential or equipotential surface or plane or contour **-kathode** *f* indirectly heated or equipotential cathode, unipotential **-linie** *f* equipotential line

äquipotentiell equipotential

Äquipräsenzprinzip *n* equipresence principle

Äquivalent *n* equivalent

äquivalent equivalent **-e Anstiegszeit** *f* equivalent build-up time **-e Breiten** equivalent widths **-e Erdoberfläche** equivalent earth plane **-e Menge** quantivalence **-e Punkte bei diskontinuierlichen Abbildungsgruppen** equivalent points with respect to discontinuous groups of mappings **-e Sinuswelle** equivalent sine wave **-er Störstrom** I-T product **-er Stromkreis** equivalent circuit

Äquivalent-gewicht *n* equivalent weight **-induktivität** *f* equivalent inductance **-kapazität** *f* equivalent capacity **-leitvermögen** *n* equivalent conductance **-volumen** *n* atomic volume **-widerstand** *m* equivalent weight (resistance)

Äquivalenz *f* equivalence **-betrag** *m* equivalent amout **-breite** *f* equivalent width **-punkt** *m* end point, point of equivalence **-schaltbild** *n* equivalent circuit **-verbot** *n* exclusion principle

Aquosystem *n* aquo system

Ar *n* are (metric unit)

Araben *n* araban

Arabingummi *n* gum arabic

Arabinose *f* arabinose

Arabinsäure *f* arabinic acid

Arabonsäure *f* arabonic acid

Arachid (Erdnußöl) *n* arachis oil, peanut oil

Aragonit *m* aragonite

Aragopunkt *m* Arago spot (aviation)

Araldit *n* araldite

Aräometer *n* areometer, densimeter, hydrometer, hydrostatic-level gauge

aräometrisch areometric, hydrometric
Aräopyknometer *n* areopycnometer
Arbeit *f* work, labor, job, task, operation, make, treatise, business, trouble, energy, investigation ~ (mit zwei Dritteln) double bank ~ (in der Grube) inside labor (min.) ~ **in Schichtlohn** *m* work by the day ~ **unter Tage** underground working **getriebene** ~ embossed work **physikalische** ~ energy **vorliegende** ~ the (subject) paper under discussion
arbeiten to operate, run, work, labor, function, act, perform, go **auf Menge** ~ to work for volume **sauber fertig** ~ to make a finishing cut **schwer** ~ to toil **unruhig** ~ to work unsteadily (engine)
Arbeiten *n* performance, functioning, operation, working, operating ~ **in beiden Richtungen** two-way working (duplex) ~ **in einer Richtung** (einseitiges ~) one-way working ~ **mit Verzögerung** delayed action ~ **ohne Verzögerung** quick action **-einseitiges** ~ **in Gegensprechschaltung** half-duplex working **einwandfreies** ~ efficiency **laufendes** ~ routine work **schlechtes** ~ (eines Gerätes) malfunctioning (of a device)
arbeitend operative **-e Maschinenteile** moving parts
Arbeiter *m* workman, laborer, hand, operator, helper, fitter **gelernter** ~ **des Maschinenbaues** machinist
Arbeit-geber *m* employer **-nehmer** *m* employee **-nehmererfindung** *f* employee invention
Arbeitsablauf *m* working methods or sequence, processing, procedure, cycle, course of manufacture, sequence of operations, run of working process **rationeller** ~ economical working methods
Arbeitsablauf-bildaufnahme *f* memo-motion study **-diagramm** *n* operational time sequence chart
Arbeits-abstand *m* working distance **-abteilung** *f* fatigue detail
arbeitsam industrious, diligent
Arbeits-anfall *m* work **-angebot** *n* supply of labor **-anschlag** *m* operating stop **-anweisungen** *pl* job instructions, operational layout or write-up **-anzug** *m* work clothing, fatigue uniform, overalls **-art** *f* occupation, kind of work **-aufnahme** *f* energy absorption **-auftrag** *m* work order **-auftragsnummer** *f* job number **-aufwand** *m* expenditure of energy, energy expended **-ausdruck** *m* expression representing the work **-bedarf** *m* energy or power requirement **-bedingung** *f* working condition
Arbeitsbedingungen, vorbildliche soziale ~ outstanding social working conditions
Arbeits-beginn *m* starting work **-belastung** *f* working load, live or rolling load **-bereich** *m* capacity, working scope, sphere of activity **-bereitschaft** *f* operational standard **-bewegung** *f* labor movement **-bestgestaltung** *f* methods engineering **-bestverfahren** *n* standard method **-bewerter** *m* job evaluator **-bewertung** *f* job evaluation or classification **-breite** *f* working width
Arbeitsbühne *f* working platform, scaffold, floor, derrick floor **in der Höhe verstellbare** ~ elevator
Arbeits-charakteristik *f* speed and torque characteristics (elec.)
Arbeitsdruck *m* working pressure (weight of blow), tool thrust, cutting pressure **mittlerer** ~ mean effective pressure **-anzeiger** *m* working-pressure gauge
Arbeits-ebene *f* working floor **-effekt** *m* power **-eichkreis** *m* working reference system, working standard **-einheit** *f* unit of work, unit of capacity **-einkommen** *n* earned income **-einsatz** *m* mobilization of labor, labor pool or supply **-einstellung** *f* strike **-elektromagnet** *m* working magnet
Arbeits-elemente *pl* operating features **-ende (eines Drehstahles)** nose (of a turner's chisel) **-eignung** *f* aptitude **-ersparnis** *f* labor saving **-fähig** able to work **-fähigkeit** *f* capacity for doing work, energy
Arbeits-feld *n* field or radius of action, endeavor **-festigkeit** *f* working strength, safe range of stress, fatigue limit, endurance limit of stress, fatigue strength **-fläche** *f* working or bearing surface, rubbing parts, working plane, wearing surface **-flugzeug** *n* airservice airplane **-flur** *m* working floor **-fluß** *m* flow of work **-flüssigkeit** *f* working fluid **-folge** *f* sequence (pass) of operation, cycle of work **-fuge** *f* expansion (construction) joint
Arbeitsgang *m* working operation, schedule, process or procedure, run, pass, or sequence of operation, working step or stage, course of manufacture **in einem** ~ in one operation **in einem** ~ **zueinander passend bearbeitet** machined together **in produktivem** ~ on stream
Arbeitgeberrecht an Arbeitsnehmer-Erfindung shop right
Arbeits-gebiet *n* field of activity, sphere of action **-gemeinschaft** *f* labor council, study group, pool of factories, cartel, working agreement **-gerade** *f* dynamic straight line, load line **-gerät** *n* implements, tools **-gerüst** *n* scaffold **-geschwindigkeit** *f* operating speed, rapidity of action, working speed, rate of production
Arbeits-gewinn *m* mechanical advantage **-gipfelhöhe** *f* peak performance altitude **-gleichung** *f* energy or power equation **-gliederung nach Eignungsstruktur** linking labor to suit structure **-grad** *m* efficiency of working **-grube** *f* inspection pit **-gruppe** *f* task group **-häufung** *f* (Stoßarbeit) peak load **-höhe** *f* peak performance, service altitude
Arbeitshub *m* power stroke, working or expansion stroke, fire stroke **die den** ~ **enthaltende Umdrehung des Motors** working revolution **-rad** *n* (Ölpumpe) operating cam (lubricator) **-scheibe** *f* (Schmierpumpe) delivery disc
Arbeits-hygiene *f* occupation hygiene **-inhalt** *m* energy storage, potential energy **-kammer** *f* working chamber **-kampf** *m* labor dispute **-kenngrößen** *f pl* performance characteristics **-kennlinie** *f* dynamic or performance characteristic, operating curve, working curve or characteristic **-kittel** *m*, **-kleidung** *f* work clothing, overalls **-kolben** *m* working or main piston, operating plunger (pump), main ram **-kolbendurchmesser** *m* operating piston diameter **-kolonne** *f* operating force **-kommando** *n* fatigue party
Arbeits-kontakt *m* operating point, operating or make contact **-kopie** *f* studio copy or print

kosten *pl* labor or operating cost, labor charges **-kraft** *f* worker, workman, hired help, manpower **-kräfte** *pl* labor **-kurbel** *f* switching handle **-kurve** *f* dynamic characteristic, working radius or courve, operating line

Arbeitslage *f* operative or operated position **~ auf der Röhrenkennlinie** working point of the valve characteristic

Arbeits-last *f* working load **-laufgang** *m* working aisle **-lehrdorn** *m* shop plug gauge **-lehre** *f* production gauge, working or shop gauge **-leisten** *pl* guide facings

Arbeits-leistung *f* working capacity, labor (work) or operation efficiency, output, power, achievement **~ beim Kartenziehen** card pulling volume

Arbeits-linie load line **-lohn** *m* earnings, wages, pay **-los** unemployed

Arbeits-magnet *n* clutch magnet **-mangel** *m* lack of work **-manometer** *n* working pressure gauge **-mann** *m* workman **-markt** *m* labor market **-maschine** *f* processing machine **-menge** *f* quantity of work **-methode** *f* method of working, operational method

Arbeits-milieu *n* work shift, work center, working environment **-ministerium** *n* ministry of labor **-mikroskop** *n* routine microscope **-modell** *n* working model **-muster** *n* sample of fabric **-nachweis** *m* labor exchange **-nocke** *f* working cam **-öffnung** *f* operating aperture, rabbling hole **-ordnung** *f* factory regulation

arbeitsparend labor saving

Arbeits-pause *f* rest period, mealtime **-pflicht** *f* liability to labor service **-phase** *f* duty factor **-plan** *m* production schedule or sheet, flow chart or sheet **-planung** *f* production planing

Arbeitsplatz *m* operator's position, operating position, job **~ mit n Leitungen** operator's position working *n* circuits **~ mit Rufanzeige** call-indicator position **-bewertung** job evaluation

Arbeits-prozentsatz *m* marking percentage **-prozeß** *m* method of operation, working process, procedure **-pumpe** *f* feed pump, operating pump

Arbeitspunkt *m* working point on characteristic curve (of valve) of tube, radar *q* point, quiescent point (of a valve) **Innenwiderstand im ~** ohms of internal resistance, ohmic internal resistance **statischer ~** quiescent point

Arbeits-quarzkeil *m* working wedge **-rad** *n* transmission or power gear

Arbeits-raum *m* generating space, working space **~ des Flammofens** body of a reverberatory furnace **beengter ~** cramped working space

Arbeits-reglermotor *m* operation governed motor **-reif** *m* retaining or truss hoop

Arbeitsreifenanziehmaschine *f* truss-hoop driving machine

Arbeits-rhythmus *m* operating rhythm **-rohr** *n* plunger barrel **-rückstand** *m* back log

Arbeits-Ruhe-Folge-Kontakt *m* make-before-break contact

Arbeits-schauuhr *f* kymograph **-scheinwerfer** *m* industrial spotlight, working floodlight **-schema** *n* schedule of operation **-schicht** *f* shift **-schieber** (Kompressor) working blade **-schiene** *f* power rail, marking stop (elec.) **-schlauch** *m* building bag

Arbeitsseite *f* output side

Arbeits-skala *f* working scale **-spannung** *f* working voltage operating current **-sparend** labor saving **-speicher** *m* working storage **-spiel** *n* cycle (operations), working cycle **-spindel** *f* main spindle **-spule** *f* operating coil **-station** *f* working station **-steilheit** *f* mutual conductance under dynamic conditions **-stelle** working place

Arbeitsstellung *f* operating or working position, operated or off-normal position **in der ~ befindlich** off normal

Arbeits-stoff *m* working medium **-streckung** *f* reduction of man-hours

Arbeitsstrom *m* working or watt current, operating or marking current, space current, cathode current **-auslöser** *m* tripping solenoid, overload release, overcurrent release **-betrieb** *m* open-circuit operation **-schaltung** *f* open-circuit connection **-system** *n* open-circuit system **-verfahren** *n* open-circuit signalling

Arbeits-stück *n* workpiece, job **-studie** *f* work analysis **-stufe** *f* stage of operation **-stunden** *pl* working hours, man hours **-stundenbericht** (Wochenzettel) *m* time sheet

Arbeits-tag *m* working day, workday **-tagung** *f* labor conference **-takt** *m* working or action cycle, working or power stroke, rhythm **-tasche** *f* docket **-techniker** *m* time and motion expert, time-study man **-teile** *m pl* working parts **-temperaturbereich** *m* operating range (cryst.) **-tempo** *n* steady pace, speed at which work is executed

Arbeits-tisch *m* worktable, workbench **-trübe** *f* undiluted heavy medium **-trupp** *m* work squad, fatigue party **-tüchtigkeit** *f* fitness for his work **-tür** *f* charging, working, or paddling door, rabbling hole **-unfähig** unfit for work **-uniform** *f* working uniform **-unterlage** *f* working material, document **-untersuchung** *f* process planning **-ventil** *n* working valve

Arbeitsverbrauch *m* expenditure of mechanical work **~ im Leergang** wasted energy (on no load)

Arbeits-vereinfachung *f* (Plan zur ~) work simplification program

Arbeits-verfahren *n* strain energy method, working method, working process (in engine), method of operation, technique, manufacturing process **-verhältnis** *n* agreement or contract for service **-verlust** *m* lost work **-vermögen** *n* working capacity, kinetic or potential energy, energy of deformation, capacity for performing work, energy, capacity for work, latent energy **-vertrag** *m* contract of employment **-verweigerung** *f* refusal to work, sit-down strike **-verwendungsfähig** fit for labor employment **-verzerrung** *f* operational distortion (telegr.)

Arbeits-vorbereiter *m* work planner, methods engineer **-vorbereitung** *f* production planing **-vorgang** *m* working cycle, operation **-walze** *f* live or work(ing) roll **-weg** *m* path of work, working traverse

Arbeits-weise *f* method of operation, procedure, practice **normale ~** standard practice

Arbeits-welle *f* signal marking or working wave, transmitting wave **-wert der Wärmeeinheit**

mechanical equivalent of heat **-wicklung** *f* power or output winding (of transducer) **-widerstand** *m* working resistance **-winkel** *m* operating angle

Arbeitszeit *f* working or operating time **-kontrollapparat** *m* time clock **-registrieruhr** *f* employee time recorder **-unterbrechung** *f* (coffee) break

Arbeits-zerlegung *f* element breakdown **-zettel** *m* time sheet **-zeug** *n* working clothes **-zylinder** *m* (testing machine) straining cylinder, working cylinder, jack (hydr.)

Arcatomschweißung *f* atomic hydrogen arc welding

Archaouloff Einrichtung Archaouloff system

Arche *f* soundboard

Archimedisches Axiom Archimedes' axiom

Archipel *m* archipelago

Architektur *f* architecture

Architrav *m* architrave

Archiv *n* archives, file **-exemplar** *n* file copy

Archivolte *f* archivolt

Archivstelle *f* record office

Arcus-funktion *f* inverse trigonometric function **-kosenkans** *m* inverse cosecant **-kotangens** *m* inverse cotangent **-sekans** *m* inverse secant

Ardometer *n* ardometer, radiation pyrometer

Areafunktion *f* area function

Areal *n* area **~ des Schraubenkreises** disk area of propeller

Arecolinbromid *n* arecoline bromide

Areometer *n* hydrometer, liquor gauge

Argentan *n* German silver **-schlaglot** *n* argentan solder

Argentindruck *m* bronze and silver printing

Argentometer *n* argentometer

Arginase *f* arginase

Argon *n* argon

Argonalgleichrichter *m* argonal rectifier

Argon-hochstrombogen *m* high-current argon arc **-schweißung** *f* argonic welding **-wolframbogenverfahren** *n* argon tungsten-arc process

argumentierbar arguable

Argus-pendel *n* argus contact lever **-rohr** *n* pulse motor

Arh (Arbeitsbühne) construction platform, scaffold

aride Schüttwannen rock debris in arid regions

Arithmetik *f* arithmetic

arithmetisch arithmetic(al) **~ geometrische Reihe** arithmetico-geometric mean series **-es Mittel** arithmetic mean **-er Mittelwert** *m* average value **-e Reihe** *f* arithmetic progression

Arithmometer *n* arithmometer

Arkanit *m* arcanite

Arkatomschweißen *n* atomic hydrogen welding

Arktik *m* smoke acid, for use in extremely cold weather

arktisch arctic **-e Kaltluft, -e Luft** arctic or polar air **-er Nebel** arctic smoke

Arkusfunktion *f* arcus function

Arl (Arbeitslehre) production gauge

Arldsche Kupferröhre copper jointing sleeve

Arm *m* arm, spoke (of wheel), channel, bracket, horn, web, limb **~ des Kreuzstückes** spider arm **~ zum Operieren** operating arm **~ einer Schrämmaschine** jib **~ einer Stimmgabel** prong of a tuning fork **blinder ~** false channel **langer ~ der Führung** (slang) fighter aircraft, bombers **langer ~ des Oberkommandos** (slang) bombers

arm poor, lean, low grade, coarse (ore), weak (said of mixtures) **~ an . . .** deficient in (poor in) **-es Gemisch** lean mixture

Armatur *f* armature, fitting, mounting, valve, steel reinforcement, armature controls (elec.), jacket for boiler, autoclaves

Armaturen für Luftdruckregulierung *f* airregulating accessories

Armaturenband *n* instrument panel

Armaturenbrett *n* instrument board or panel, dashboard **vom ~ aus regelbar** dash-controlled

Armaturenbrettleuchten *pl* instrument panel lighting fixtures

Armaturen-prüfbrett *n* instrument test board, reduction valve test panel **-stutzen** *m* adapter for fitting **-tafel** *f* control board, instrument panel

Arm-auflage *f* armrest, elbow rest **-ausladung** *f* overhang of arm

Armband *n* arm band, brassard **-kompaß** *m* wrist or bracelet compass **-uhr** *f* wrist watch

Arm-blei *n* refined lead **-bolzen** *m* running-up bolt

Armco Eisen *n* Armco or ingot iron

Arme *m pl* arms, brackets, horns

Armee *f* army **-ausrüstung** *f* army equipment

Ärmel *m* sleeve **-abzeichen** *n* sleeve patch **-aufschlag** *m* cuff **-kanal** *m* the English Channel **-patte** *f* cuff patch

Armfeile *f* arm file

Armführungs-prisma *n* **-wange** *f* arm ways (shop term)

Armgas *n* lean gas

Armgerüst *n* loop

Armhängelager *n* bracket drop hanger **~ mit Kugelbewegung und in der Höhe verstellbarer Lagerachse** adjustable ball-and-socket bracket drop hanger

armieren to equip, arm, reinforce (concrete), protect, sheath (cable)

armiert armor-plated, tipped, or shielded (as propeller tips), armored, sheathed, reinforced **-er Beton** reinforced concrete **-es Kabel** armored cable **-er Schlauch** armored hose

Armierung *f* armoring, reinforcement, sheath(ing), equipment, armament, armor for electrical cables **geschlossene ~** closed or locked armor **leichte ~** light armor **offene ~** open armor **schwere ~** heavy armor

Armierungs-kabel *n* armored cable **-scheibe** *f* armoring disc

Armkegelrad-Schutzdeckel *m* armmiter gear guard (radial drill)

Armklemm-hebel *m* arm-binder handle **-muttern** *f pl* arm-clamping nuts **-stück** *n* arm girdle

Armkran *m* hand crane

Armkreuz *n* set of arms, arm cross, spider (engin.) ring plate **-lager** *n* spider bearing **-ringe** *m pl* backing wires (paper)

Armkrispelholz (Pantoffelholz) arm graining board

Arm-lehne *f* armrest, elbow rail or cushion **-leuchter** *m* chandelier, bracket

Armoxyde *n pl* refining skimmings (low-grade

oxides)
Armprisonstift *m* arm dowel pin
Armreichschalter *m* mixture control
Arm-schiene *f* splint **-schneckenlager** *n* arm-worm box **-signal** *n* semaphore signal **-spiegel** *m* arm badge **-stern** *m* spider (of a wheel) **-stützen** *f pl* arm braces (harness) **-träger** *m* arm girdle
armtreiben to concentrate
Armut *f* poverty, want, tenor deficiency
Armutsgrenze *f* minimum standard of living
Arm-welle *f* arm shaft **-zahnstange** *f* arm rack **-zeichen** *n* arm and hand signal, arm signal
Arobe *f* stone or cembra pine
A Rohr *n* oxygen pipe (aviation)
Ärologie *f* aerology
Aroma *n* fragrance, flavor
Aromaten *pl* aromatics
aromatisch aromatic **-e Kohlenwasserstoffe** aromatic hydrocarbons **-e Reihe** aromatic series
aromatisieren to aromatize
Äronautik *f* aeronautics
äronautisch aeronautical
Aron-Gleichstromzähler *m* Aron meter (elec.)
Aronzähler *m* pendulum meter
ärophysikalisch aerophysical
arretierbarer Stoßriegel lockable joining member
Arretier-bolzen *m* locking bolt (torpedo), check bolt **-bügel** *m* stop lever
arretieren to lock, adjust, set, stop, brake, arrest, impede, dam, detain, hold back, restrain, maintain stationary, fix, secure
Arrettier-feder *f* check, control, detend or drawback spring **-greifer** *m* locking clan **-hebel** *m* adjusting (checking) lever, catch, stop(ing) or blocking lever **-kegel** *m* cone stop collar **-klinke** *f* safety catch **-knopf** *m* clamping or stop knob **-leiste** *f* detent rail, shift lock **-nase** *f* catch, retaining stud **-rad** *n* locking wheel **-riemen** *m* check strap (textiles) **-schraube** *f* stop screw or pin **-stange** *f* retaining pin, stop bar **-stift** *m* preventer, safety or retension pin, detent, blocking pin
Arretierung *f* arrest, adjustment, setting, stop(ping), detent, catch, stop
Arretierung(s)-hebel *m* blocking lever (general) **-klappe** *f* block flap **-kugel** *f* detent ball, lock ball **-lamelle** *f* terminal plate **-platte** *f* stop plate **-scheibe** *f* star wheel, locking disk **-stange** *f* stop bar
Arretiervorrichtung *f* device for stopping, locking, arresting, adjusting, or setting, controlling gear (of servomotor)
Arretierzahn *m* locking cog.
arrondieren to round off
Arrondierfräse *f* finishing-countersink
Arsen *n* arsenic **-abstrich** *m* arsenic skimmings
Arsenal *n* arsenal, naval dockyard
Arsen-blende *f* orpiment **-blüte** *f* arsenic bloom, arsenolite, pharmacolite, white arsenic **-eisen** *n* leucopyrite **-eisensinter** *m* pitticite **-erz** *n* arsenic ore **-fahlerz** *n* tennantite
arsen-frei arsenic-free **-führend** arseniferous **-haltig** arsenical, containing arsenic **-gitter** *n* arsenic lattice
arsenige Säure arsenious acid
arsenigsau(e)r arsenite of **-es Kupfer** copper arsenite **-es Natrium** sodium arsenite
Arsenik *n* arsenic **weißes ~** arsenic bloom, arsenolite
arsenikalisch arsenical, containing arsenic
Arsenik-antimon *n* allemontite **-äscher** *m* arsenic lime **-bleispat** *m* mimetite **-glas** *n* vitreous arsenic trioxide **-kalk** *m* arsenolite **-kobalt** *m* safflorite **-kupfer** *n* domeykite **-mangan** *n* kaneite **-nickel** *n* niccolite, arsenical or copper nickel **-säure** *f* arsenic acid
arseniksaures Salz arsenides
Arsenik-silber *n* arsenical silver **-silberblende** *f* proustite **-sinter** *m* scorodite **-spießglanz** *m* allemontite **-vitriol** *n* arsenic sulfate
Arsen-jodid *n* arsenic iodide **-kies** *m* arsenical (iron) pyrites, (prismatischer) arsenopyrite, mispickel **-kobalt** *m* **-kobaltkies** *m* skutterudite **-metall** *n* arsenic metal, (metallic) arsenide **mittel** *n* arsenical
Arsen-nickel *m* nickel arsenide, niccolite **-nickelglanz** *m* **-nickelkies** *m* gersdorffite **-ojodid** *n* arsenic triiodide **-oxyd** *n* arsenic oxide, arsenic trioxide **-pentasulfid** *n* arsenic pentasulfide **-säure** *f* arsenic acid
arsensau(e)r . . . arsenate of **-es Ammonium** ammonium arsenate **-es Blei** lead arsenate **-es Natrium** sodium chlorate **-es Natron** sodium arsenate
Arsen-spiegel *m* arsenic mirror
Arsensulfid *n* arsenic sulfide **gelbes ~** auripigment, arsenic trisulfide **rotes ~** realgar, arsenic bisulfide
Arsen-trijodid *n* arsenic triiodide **-trioxyd** *n* arsenic trioxide, arsenious acid **-trisulfid** *n* arsenious sulfide, orpiment, arsenic trisulfide **-wasserstoff** *m* arsenic hydride
Arsen-verbindung *f* arsenide
Arsin *n* arsine
Art *f* kind, species, manner, method, way, variety, sort, class, type, style, character, process, pattern, scheme, kindred **~ der Besselfunktion** kind of Bessel function **~ der** (induktiven) **Belastung** type of loading **~ der Funkstelle** class of station **~ oder Gütegrad einer Passung** grade of fit **~ und Weise** manner, way, method, fashion, mode, kind **die ~ des Grundes** nature of the bottom of sea **der üblichen ~** of customary type, custom-made **jeder ~** of every description **nach ~ des . . .** on the . . . plan, along the lines of . . .
arteigen characteristic, specific, true to type or race
Arterien-klemme *f* hemostatic forceps **-kompressorium** *n* tourniquet
Arteriographie *f* arteriography
artesisch-e Bedingung *f* artesian condition **-er Brunnen** artesian well **-er Druck** artesian pressure **-e Druckhöhe** artesian head
artfremd heterogeneous, unspecific, alien
Artgleichen *pl* (Komponenten in demselben Zustande) of the same type
artgemäß true to type, racially unobjectionable
Arthrographie *f* arthrography
Artikel *m* article, material, goods **gangbarer ~** goods of a ready sale, staple goods **-bestand** *m*

stock status **-karten** *pl* commodity cards
Artikulation *f* articulation
artikuliert articulate **-es Gelenk** universal joint
Artnummer *f* type or category number
artverwandt akin, kindred
Artwärme (spezifische Wärme) *f* specific heat, thermal capacity
Arznei *f* medicine, drug, medicament **-fertigware** *f* patent medicine **-kapsel** *f* medicinal or gelatin capsule **-kasten** *m* **-kiste** *f* medicine chest
arzneilich pharmaceutic, medicinal
Arzneimittel *n* medicine, remedy, medicament **-erzeugung** *f* production of pharmaceutical products **-industrie** *f* drug industry **-synthese** *f* drug synthesis (pharmaceutical)
Arzneipflanze *f* medicinal plant
Arzt *m* physician, medical officer **leitender ~** physician in charge of ward or of hospital
ärztlich medical **-e Behandlung** medical treatment or attendance **-e Untersuchung** medical or physical examination
Asbest *m* asbestos, earth flax, amianthus **-anzug** *m* asbestos suit **-artig** asbestoid **-aufschlemmung** *f* asbestos milk **-band** *n* asbestos ribbon **-dichtung** *f* asbestos washer, joint, packing, or gasket **-dichtungsmanschetten** *pl* asbestos gaskets
Asbestdrahtnetz *n* asbestos wire gauze **~ mit kugelförmiger Vertiefung** wire gauze with hemispherical asbestos center
Asbest-fasermehl *n* asbestos-fiber powder **-faserstoff** *m* asbestos fiber **-flocken** *f pl* asbestos wool **-füllung** *f* asbestos filling **-garn** *n* asbestos yarn **-geschützt** asbestos-protected **-gewebe** *n* asbestos cloth **-grube** *f* asbestos quarry **-handschuh** *m* asbestos glove **-holz** *n* asbestos lumber or wood **-leinwand** *f* asbestos canvas **-mehl** *n* powdered asbestos, asbestos flour
Asbestolith *n* short-fibered asbestos
Asbest-packung *f* asbestos packing **-pappe** *f* asbestos board **-platte** *f* asbestos pad or plate
Asbest-schicht *f* asbestos stratum **-schiefer** *m* asbestos slate **-schieferbrett** *n* asbestos-slate board, transom board, asbestos transom **-schirm** *m* asbestos screen **-schnur** *f* asbestos cord **-schürze** *f* asbestos apron **-schutzkleidung** *f* asbestos clothing **-tuch** *n* asbestos cloth **-umsponnen** asbestos covered **-vorgespinst** *n* asbestos slub **-wand** *f* transom boards **-wolle** *f* asbestos wool, cotton asbestos
Asbest-zement-dachplatten *pl* asbestos-cement roofing plates **-preßteile** *pl* pressed parts of asbestos cement **-wellplatten** *pl* corrugated sheets of asbestos cement
Asbest-zwischenstück *n* intermediate asbestos member
Asche *f* ash, slag, cinder, embers **~ ablöschen** to quench ashes
Asche-bestimmung *f* ash determination **-bildend** ash-forming **-bildner** *m* ash-constituent
aschefrei ash-free
Asche-gehalt *m* ash content
Aschen-abfuhr *f* removal of ashes or rubbish **-ablagerung** *f* slag deposit, deposition of ashes **-abzug** *m* cinder outlet **-arme Kohle** low-ash coal **-austragung** *f* removal of ashes, clinker or slag disposal **-ausziehöffnung** *f* opening (door) for withdrawing ashes **-bahn** *f* cinder track **-becher** *m* ash tray **-bestandteil** *n* ash content **-bestimmer** *m* ash apparatus **-entfernung** *f* removal of ashes
Aschen-fall *m* cinder fall, ashpit **-falle** *f* ash chute or pit **-fallklappe** *f* ash valve, ash damper, ash door, dumping grate **-fleckig** specked with sullage **-förderanlage** *f* ash conveyor, ash-handling plant **-frei** ash-free, ashless **-gehalt** *m* ash content or percentage **-gehaltsbestimmung** *f* ash determination **-grube** *f* ashpit, cinder pit **-koeffizient** *m* saline coefficient **-lauge** *f* lye from ashes **-ofen** *m* calcining furnace or oven **-raum** *m* ashpit **-stromregler** *m* ash fusing point
Aschen-salz *n* pearlash, potash **-schacht** *m* incinerator **-schicht** *f* ash-fraction **-schieber** *m* damper, check draft **-schmelzpunkt** *m* ash fusing point **-schmelzverhalten** *n* ash fusibility **-schnellbestimmer** *m* apparatus for rapid determination of ash **-schüssel** *f* ashpan **-sieder** *m* ashes boiler **-staub** *m* braze **-transportanlage** *f* ash-handling equipment **-verflüssigung** *f* clinkering, honey-combing **-wäsche** *f* ash washing
Äscher *m* slake-lime pit, tanner's pit **-brühe** *f* lime liquor
aschereich inferior (coal) **-e Kohle** *f* high-ash coal
Äscher-gang *m* set of lime pits **-grube** *f* lime pit
äschern to ash, reduce to ash, steep, (soak in) lime
Äscher-ofen *m* frit kiln **-trommel** *f* liming drum **-verfahren** *n* lime process **-werkstatt** *f* lime yard **-zange** *f* tanner's tong
Ascheziehen *n* ash removal
aschfahl ash-grey
Aschfall *m* ashpit **-klappe** *f* dumping grate
asch-farben ash shade **-grau** ash-gray **-haufen** *m* ash dump **-heißmaschine** *f* ash hoist **-prahm** *m* ash boat
A-Schrank *m* A-(switch)board
Aschschütte *f* ash shoot
Ascoloy *n* Ascoloy, American chrome steel
Ascorbinsäure *f* ascorbic acid
aseptisch aseptic
Askandruck *m* asphalt process
Äskulapstab *m* caduceus
Asordin *n* Asordin (chlorinated hydrocarbon)
Asparagin *n* asparagine **-säure** *f* aspartic acid
Aspe *f* aspen tree
Aspektverhältnis *n* aspect ration (aviation)
Asphalin *n* asphaline
Asphalt *m* asphalt, mineral pitch
Asphalt-anstrich *m* asphalt coating **-belag** *m* asphalt flooring or surfacing, black top paving **-benzollack** *m* asphalt varnish **-bewurf** *m* asphaltic plaster **-bildung** *f* inspissation **-dachfilz** *m* tarpaulin **-decke** *f* asphalt pavement, surfacing
Asphalten *n* asphaltene
Asphalt-estrich *m* asphalt floor **-farbe** *f* asphaltum paint, bituminous paint **-firnis** *m* black varnish **-filz** *m* asphalt-impregnated felt **-fußboden** *m* asphalt floor(ing) **-gestein** *n* crude asphalt **-guß** *m* asphaltic mastic
asphalthaltig containing asphalt, asphaltic, bituminiferous **-es Gestein** natural rock
asphaltieren to asphalt, coat with asphalt
asphaltisch asphaltic **-er Kohlenwasserstoff** as-

phaltic hydrocarbon

Asphalt-kitt *m* asphalt putty, asphalt cement **-klotz** *m* asphalt block **-kopierverfahren** *n* asphalt process (print) **-lack** *m* bituminous varnish, black japan **-mastik** mastic asphalt **-papier** *n* tar paper **-pappe** *f* asphalt board (tarroofing), roofing felt

Asphalt-pech *n* bituminous pitch **-pflaster** *n* asphalt paving or pavement **-platte** *f* asphalt block **-staubkorn** *n* asphalt grain **-stein** *m* asphalt, mineral pitch, crude asphalt **-straße** *f* asphalt(-paved) road **-tiefdruckfarbe** *f* asphalt intaglio printing ink **-überzug** *m* asphalt coat

asphärisch aspherical, nonspherical **~ gekreuzt** aspherical crossed

Aspinallhub *m* Aspinall stroke

Aspirations-reinigungsmaschine *f* receiving and milling machine, smutter **-psychrometer** *n* evaporation psychrometer, wet and dry bulb psychrometer

aspirieren to aspirate, draw (by suction)

Assekur-adeur *m* underwriter **-adeuranz** *f* assurance, insurance

Assekuranz *f* insurance

assekurieren to assure, insure

assimilierbar assimilable, capable of being assimilated

assimilieren to assimilate

Assistent *m* assistant

Assistenzarzt *m* intern, resident physician, assistant medical officer

assortieren to assort, sort

assouplieren to partially boil, render supple or pliable, half-boil (silk)

assoziieren to associate

Assurrelinie *f* combination rule (print)

Ast *m* branch (of a science), branch (limb of a tree), knot (in timber) **~ einer Kurve** leg of a curve **absteigender ~** descending branch (of a trajectory) **aufsteigender ~** ascending branch (of a trajectory)

astabil astable

Astasie *f* astatics, astatic condition

astasieren to astatize

Astasierung *f* astatizing, rendering astatic

Astatin *n* astatine

astatisch astatic **-e Belastung** astatic load **-es Nadelpaar** astatic pair or couple **-e Regelung** null off-set **-e Spulen** astatic coils **-es System** astatic system **-er Zustand** astaticism

Astatisierung *f* astatisation, astaticity

Astausflickautomat *m* automatic knot-hole pegging machine

Asterismus *m* asterism

Asteroid *m* asteroid

Ast-fänger *m* knot catcher **-frei** branchless, knotless **-gabel** *f* gun rest

Asthenosphäre *f* asthenosphere

Ästhesiometer *n* esthesiometer

Astholz *n* branch wood

ästig knotty, branchy

astigmatisch astigmatic **-er Bildfehler** astigmatic-image error or defect

Astigmatismus *m* astigmatism

Astknoten *m* branch knot

A-Stoff *m* oxygen (rockets) **-pumpe** *f* oxygen pump **-pumpenrad** *n* oxygen-pump propeller **-pumpenwelle** *f* oxygen-pump shaft **-tank** *m* oxygen tank

Astrachan, unechter ~ imitation astrakhan fur

astrachanisieren to curl

Astragal *n* fillet (beading, band, collar, molding)

Astralit *m* astralite

Astralon *n* astralon

astreich branchy

astrein branchless, without knots (lumber)

Astro abbreviation for astro or celestial navigator **-biologe** *m* astrobiologist **-dynamik** *f* astrodynamics

Astrograph *m* astrograph

Astroiden *n pl* astroids

astronomisch-e Navigation celestial navigation **-er Meßzug** astronomical-survey platoon

Astro-kamera *f* astro camera **-kompaß** *m* astrocompass

Astronaut *m* astronaut

Astro-navigation *f* astrogation **-peiler** *m* radiotelescope **-photographie** *f* astrophotography **-photometer** *n* astrometer

astrophysikalisch astrophysical

Astrophysiker *m* astrophysicist

Astuar *n* estuary

Astverhau *m* abatis

Asymeter *n* asymeter

Asymmetrie *f* asymmetry, dissymmetry **-fehler** *m* (optical) coma **-index** *m* asymmetry index **-potential** *n* asymmetry potential

asymmetrisch asymmetric(al) **-e Leitfähigkeit** asymmetrical, nonlinear, or unilateral conductance (of crystals)

asymmetrisch-heterostatische Schaltung asymmetrical heterostatic circuit

Asymptote *f* asymptote

Asymptoten-abbildung *f* asymptotic image **-brennweite** *f* asymptotic focal length **-linien** *f pl* asymptotic lines **-richtungen** *f pl* asymptotic directions **-wert** *m* asymptotic value

Asymptotik *f* asymptotic behavior

asymptotisch asymptote, asymptotic(al) **-e Spalterwartung** iterated fission expectation **-e Breite** asymptotic width **-e Darstellung** asymptotic representation **-e Gleichung** asymptotic expression **-e Spalterwartung** iterated fission probability **-es Verhalten** asymptotic behavior **-e Wasserstoffwellenfunktion** asymptotic hydrogen wave-function

asynchron asynchronous, nonsynchronous **-e Scheibenfunkenstrecke** asynchronous discharger

Asynchron-anwurfmotor *m* asynchronous starting motor **-betrieb** *m* variable cycle operation **-drehstromgenerator** *m* three-phase induction generator **-funkenstrecke** *f* nonsynchronous rotating spark gap **-generator** *m* asynchronous alternator **-kraftwerk** *n* fully automatic asynchronous power station

Asynchronmotor *m* asynchronous motor, indication motor **~ mit Käfigläufer** squirrel cage induction motor **~ mit Kurzschlußläufer** squirrel cage induction motor **~ mit Schleifringläufer** induction motor with wound rotor

Asynchron-multiplex *n* asynchronous multiplex **-rechner** *m* asynchronous computer **-schwingungsregler** *m* nonsynchronous pulsation-weld timer **-speicherwerk** *n* asynchronous remote-controlled power station

aszendenten Erzmineralien primary ore minerals
Atakamit *m* atacamite
Atabrin *n*, **Atebrin** *n* atabrine **-musonat** *n* atabrinmusonate
Ataxie *f* ataxia, irregularity
A_1 **Telegraphie, tonlos** A-1 on-off keying (CW)
A_2 **Telegraphie, tönend** A-2 tone keying (MCW)
A_3 **Telephonie** A-3 Telephony
Atelier *n* studio, stage, teletorium, telestudio **-direktor** *m* studio manager **-kamera** *f* studio camera **-schrift** *f* studio (transcription) film
Atem *m* breath, wind **-anlage** *f* oxygen equipment **-bar** respirable **-einsatz** *m* filter element in gas mask **-filter** *m* filter in gas mask **-gerät** *n* breathing apparatus, respirator (oxygen)
Atem-holen *n* respiration **-los** breathless **-luft** *f* ventilating air **-maske** *f* oxygen mask **-mundstück** *n* mouthpiece (mask) **-sack** *m* respirator bag, breathing bag **-schlauch** *m* breathing tube, hose on gas mask or other breathing apparatus
Atemschutz *m* **-apparat** *m* respirator **-gerät** *n* protective device exhaled air
Atemtätigkeit *f* breathing
Atemwiderstand *m* breathing resistance (gas mask) **-feldprüfer** *m* resistance gauge for filter drums (gas mask)
Ate-Nachfüllbehälter *m* breather reserve tank
Äthan *n* ethane **-disäure** *f* oxalic acid **-öl** *n* antifreeze (alcohol)
Äthanolaminseife *f* ethanolamine soap
Äthansäure *f* ethanoic acid
Äther *m* ether
ätherartig ethereal, etherous
ätherecht ether resistant
ätherifizieren to etherify, etherize
Ätherifizierung *f* etherification, etherization
ätherisch ethereal, ethereous, volatile **-es Öl** quickdrying or essential oil **-e Wellen** ether waves
ätherisieren to etherize
Ätherisierung *f* etherization
ätherlöslich ether soluble
atherman athermanous
athermisch athermal
Äther-mitbewegung *f* ether drift **-modell** *n* ether model **-relationen** *pl* ether relations **-sau** *f* (slang) radio operator **-säure** *f* ether acid **-verschiebung** *f* ether drift **-welle** *f* ether wave
Äthin *n* ethine, acetylene
Athodyd *n* athodyd, aerothermodynamic duct
Athodydenflug *m* ramjet flight
Äthrioskop *n* ethrioscope
Äthyl *n* ethyl **ameisensaures** ~ *n* ethyl formate
Äthyl-acetat *n* ethyl acetate, acetic ether, vinegar naphtha **-aldehyd** *n* ethylic or ethyl aldehyde **-alkohol** *m* ethyl or grain alcohol **-amin** *n* ethylamine **-arsindichlorid** *n* ethyldichlorarsine **-äther** ethyl ether, ether **-azetat** *n* ethyl acetate, acetic ether **-dichlorarsin** *n* ethyldichlorarsine
Äthylen *n* ethylene, olefiant gas **-bromid** *n* ethylene bromide, dibromethane **-chlorid** *n* ethyl chloride, ethylene chloride **-diamin** ethylene diamine **-diamintartrat** *n* ethylene diamine tartrate **-glykol** *n* ethylene glycol, Prestone **-höchstdruckkompressor** *m* ethylene maximum pressure compressor **-verbindung** *f* ethylene compound, olefiant gas
Äthyl-formiat *n* ethyl formate **-holz** *n* ethylated wood
Äthyl-i-butyrat *n* ethyl isobutyrate, isobutyric ether
Äthyliden *n* ethylidene **-chlorid** *n* ethylidene chloride
Äthyl-jodid *n* ethyl iodide, monoiodoethane **-sulfat** *n* ethyl sulfate **-weinsäure** *f* ethyl tartaric acid
Ätiologie *f* etiology
Atlant *m* atlas
atlantische Polarluftmasse polar Atlantic air mass
Atlantenformat *n* broad side or sheet
Atlantik-flug *m* Atlantic flight **-verkehr** *m* transatlantic traffic
Atlas *m* satin, atlas **-appretur** *f* satin finish **-erz** *n* malachite **-gips** *m* fibrous gypsum **-glanz** *m* satin luster **-holz** *n* satin wood **-papier** *n* glazed paper **-spat** *m* calcite, satin spar **-trikot** *m* diamond fabric **-vitriol** *n* zinc sulfate
atmen to breathe, respire, throb
Atmen *n* breathing ~ **des Films** in-and-out-of-focus effect ~ **des Kohlenmikrophons** breathing of microphone ~ **des Störgeräusches** fluctuations or waxing and waning of noise
atmend breathing **-e Membrane** flexible or non-reflecting diaphragm **-es Mikrophon** breathing microphone
Atmometer *n* atmometer, evaporimeter
Atmosphäre *f* atmosphere, atmospheric pressure, air
Atmosphären-druck *m* atmospheric pressure or tension **-dynamo** *n* atmospheric dynamo **-modell** *n* model of atmosphere **-schicht** *f* atmospheric layer **-überdruck** *m* (atü) atmospheric excess pressure
Atmosphärilien *f pl* atmospheric influences or agencies, weathering factors, intemperateness, elements
atmosphärisch atmospheric(al), aerial **-es Aufwallen** surge (meteor.) **-e Absorption** tropospheric absorption **-er Ansaugvorgang** atmopheric induction **-e Beständigkeit** air resistant **-es Pfeifen** whistling atmospherics **-e Risse** sun-cracks **-e Störungen** strays, X's, atmospherics, statics **-er Torpedo** compressed-air torpedo **-e Wärmedurchlässigkeit** atmospheric transmittance
Atmung *f* breathing, respiration ~ **des Kurbelgehäuses** breathing of crankcase
Atmungs-apparat *m* respirator, breathing apparatus, aerophore **-behälter für Tankgase** breathing ventilator or air valve of tank **-dach** *n* breather roof (of tank) **-gerät** *n* breathing apparatus, respirator, breathing appliance **-maske** *f* respirator **-messer** *m* spirometer **-öffnung** (Luftloch) ventilation hole **-raum** (Zündkerze) scavenging area **-schlauch** *m* breathing tube (oxygen apparatus) **-ventil** *n* vent valve, breather **-verschraubung** *f* breather
Atom *n* atom, corpuscle **-abstand** *m* interatomic distance **-antrieb** *m* nuclear propulsion
atomar atomic **-e Anordnung** atomic domain **-e Bindung** atomic bond **-es Bremsvermögen** atomic stopping power **-e Gewichtseinheit** a w u (atomic weight unit) **-e Maßeinheit** a m u (atomic mass unit) **-er Streufaktor** atomic scattering factor **-e Vorgänge** atomic processes

-e **Wasserstoffschweißung** (Wassergasschweißung) atomic-hydrogen arc welding
Atom *n*, **naktes ~** stripped atom
atomartig atomlike, atomic
Atom-auflöser *m* atom smasher **-batterie** *f* atomic battery **-bau** *m* atomic structure **-bezirk** *m* range of an atom **-bindende Kraft** atomic combining power, valence
Atombindungs-kraft *f* atomic valence **-vermögen** *n* atomic valence
atomdispers atomically dispersed
Atome, gleiche Schwingungen der ~ equal atomic vibrations **~ auf Zwischengitterplätzen** interstitial atoms
Atomeigenschaften *pl* atomic properties
Atomernergie (Kernenergie) *f* atomic energy (nuclear energy) **-gebiet** *n* field of atomic energy **-kraftwerk** *n* atomic power plant
Atom-explosion *f* atomic blast **-formfaktor** *m* atom form factor, atomic scattering or structure factor **-gewichteinheit** *f* atomic weight unit (a w u) **-gewichtstabelle** *f* table .of atomic weights **-geschoß** *n* atomic projectile **-gramm** *n* gram atom **~ haltig** atomic **-hülle** *f* atom shell **-hüllenniveau** *n* atomic level **-ionenanteil** *m* fraction of atomic ions **-ionenbildung** *f* production of atomic ions
atomisch, -er Ofen atomic, atomic furnace
Atomismus *m* atomism
Atomistik *f* atomistics
atomistisch atomic(al), corpuscular **-e Versetzung** atomic jump
Atomkern *m* atomic center, atomic core, atomic nucleus **ungerader ~** odd term of atom
Atomkerne aufbauen building up the nuclei of atoms
Atomkernspaltung *f* atom fission, splitting of atomic nucleus
Atomkraft-anlage *f* atomic power plant **-bändiger** *m* harnesser of atomic energy **-maschine** *f* atomic energy machine **-station** *f* atomic power station **-werk** *n* nuclear power plant
Atom-kugel *f* atomic sphere **-ladung** *f* atomic charge **-leitfähigkeit** *f* atomic conductance or conductivity
Atommasseneinheit *f* amu (atomic mass unit)
Atommeiler *m* nuclear pile or reactor, atomic pile **~ mit natürlichem Uran** natural uranium pile
Atom-modell *n* model for the atom **-nummer** *f* atomic number **-ordnung** *f* atomic arrangement **-ordnungszahl** *f* atomic number **-parameter** *pl* atomic parameters **-reaktor** *m* nuclear reactor **-rumpf** *m* atomic torso or hull **-sprengkopf** *m* atomic warhead **-schmelzwärme** *f* heat of fusion of atomic weight **-schwingung** *f* atomic vibration
Atomstrahl *m* atomic beam **-methode** *f* atomic beam method, molecular or atomicray method
Atom-streitmacht *f* atomic deterrent force **-technik** *f* atomic science, nucleonics
Atomterm mit geradzahligem Spin even term of atom
Atom-transmuttation *f* atomic transmutation **-treibstoff** *m* nuclear fuel
Atom-U-Boot nuclear submarine
Atom-umlagerung *f* discomposition, knocking-out effect **-umwandlung** *f* atom chipping or conversion **-verbindung** *f* atomic union **-verhältnis** atomic ratio **-verkettung** *f* atomic linkage **-verrückung** *f* (-verschiebung) atomic displacement **-verteilung** *f* atom distribution
Atom-wanderung *f* atomic migragtion **-wertigkeit** *f* atomicity, atomic valence
Atomzahl (ziffer) *f* atomic number **~ eines Moleküls** atomicity
Atom-zeitalter *n* atomic age **-zerfall** *m* disintegration of atom **-zerlegung** *f* nuclear fission, atom splitting
Atomzertrümmerung *f* atom splitting or smashing, nuclear transmutation
Atonalität *f* atonality
atramentieren (Phosphat) to protect a metal surface
attachiertes (eingefügtes) **Thermometer** attached thermometer to protect a metal surface
Attenuator *m* attenuator, fader
attenuieren to attenuate, dilute
Attest *n* testimonial, certificate
attestieren to testify, certify, attest
Attrappe *f* dummy (as parachute), mock-up
Attrappengewicht *n* drop keel
Attribut *n* symbol, attribute
Atropin *n* atropine
Atü (Atmosphärenüberdruck), atmospheric excess pressure, gauge pressure in atmospheres, usually in kg/cm^2
Ätz-alkalien *pl* caustic alkalies **-alkalisch** caustic alkaline **-ammoniak** *m* caustic ammonia **-anlage** *f* pickling plant **-artikel** *m* discharge style **-bad** *n* etching bath
ätzbar corrodible, corrosible
Ätzbarkeit *f* dischargeability
Ätz-baryt *n* barium hydroxide **-beizdruck** *m* discharge printing **-beize** *f* mordant, caustic, stain, discharge (in printing) **-beständig** discharge-resisting **-bild** *n* etch pattern **-blech** *n* etching sheet **-boden** *m* discharge ground
Ätz-dauer *f* time of etching **-druck** *m* discharge or style of printing, etching
Ätze *f* etch, etching, aqua fortis (art), etching solution
Ätzeinrichtung *f* etching equipment
ätzen to etch, corrode, macerate, cauterize, treat with mordants
Ätzen *n* etching, etching operation or treatment, corrosion **metallographisches ~ der Laufbüchse** etching of the barrel
ätzend corrosive, caustic **scharf ~** mordant (of dyes) **-er Kalk** quicklime, caustic lime
Ätzer *m* etcher
Ätz-erscheinung *f* phenomenon occurring in etching **-farbe** *f* etching ink **-figur** *f* etch pattern, etching figure (glass) **-flüssigkeit** *f* etching liquid or acid **-gas** *n* corrosive gas **-grübchen** *n* etching pit **-grund** *m* resist, protective coating (etching)
Ätz-kali *n* caustic potash or alkali, potassium hydroxide **-kalilauge** *f* caustic potash (lye) solution **-kalk** *m* caustic lime, quicklime **-kasten** *m* etching (box) trough **-kraft** *f* corrosive power, causticity **-lauge** *f* caustic (lye) solution **-leitverfahren** *n* etched wire technique **-lösung** *f* etching solution **-mittel** *n* etching (medium) reagent, corrosive substance, caustic **-muster** *n* discharge pattern **-natron** *n* sodium

hydroxide, caustic soda, lye

Ätz-paste *f* **für Glühlampen** etching paste for incandescent lamps **-probe** *f* etch test, etch (specimen), etching **-pulver** *n* caustic powder **-salz** *n* caustic salt **-schliff** *m* ground section prepared for etching of metals **-stift** *m* caustic or corrosive stick **-stoffe** *m pl* vesicants **-streifung** *f* etching bands **-sublimat** *n* mercuric chloride, corrosive sublimate **-tinte** *f* etching ink

Ätzung *f* etching, etching treatment or operation **~ mit Säure** acid etching **durch ~ mattiert** acid etched

Ätz-verfahren *n* etching method, etching **-versuch** *m* corrosion test **-vertiefung** *f* etching pit **vorrichtung** *f* etching device **-wasser** *n* etching solution (mordant) **-widerstand eines Metalles** corrosion resistance of a metal **-wirkung** *f* discharge effect, etching action

Aubo-fähre *f* (Außenbordmotorfähre), outboard motor ferry **-motor** *m* outboard motor

Audienz *f* hearing, reception

Audio-frequenz *f* audio frequency **-gramm** *n* audiogram **-meter** *n* audiometer

Audion *n* grid or grid-circuit detector, grid-leak and/or condenser detector, audion, detector tube, (thermionic) valve detector, detecting tube or valve, rectifier triode, second detector **rückgekoppeltes ~** regenerative grid-current detector, ultraudion **selbstschwingendes ~** autodyne

Audion-detektoren *m pl* detector tubes **-detektorröhre** *f* audion detector **-empfänger** *m* audion receiver **-gleichrichtung** *f* grid or grid-current detection, grid-leak, grid-condenser, or leaky-grid detection, grid or grid-circuit rectification, cumulative rectification **-kraft** *f* pentode, power-grid detector **-kreisabstimmung** *f* detector circuit tuning **-röhre** *f* detector tube **-schaltung** *f* audion circuit **-stufe** *f* audio-stage amplifier (elec. and radar)

Audionverstärker *m* amplifying detector **-röhre** *f* audion amplifier

Auditorium *n* audience

Auer-brenner *m* Welsbach burner **-licht** *n* Welsbach light **-strumpf** *m* Welsbach mantle **-verwerfungswinkel** *m* fault dip (geol)

Auf (on switches) "off", "open"

Auf-zu open-close, on-off

auf on, upon, in, toward, up, at, by **~ und nieder, ~ und ab** up and down **langsam ~** bend-up steadily

aufarbeiten to (re)work, recondition, recover, use up, finish, dress, work up (barograph), overhaul

Aufarbeiten *n* working up, using up

Aufarbeitung *f* reconditioning, electrolyte recovery

Aufarbeitungsverlust reprocessing loss

aufätzen to open with caustic, corrode (etch) upon

aufbänken to keep-up the fire, bank

Aufbanker *m* log roller

Aufbau *m* (Montage) assembly, erection, mounting; (Karosserie) body; (Chem.) synthesis; (Organisation) structure, system; (Anordnung) arrangement; (Gestaltung) design; (Bau) construction, installation, make-up, organization, topwork, layout, superstructure, composition, constitution, setup, reconstruction, rig, assemblage, building up; (Werkzeugmaschinen) set up

Aufbau *m*, **gedrungener ~** cramped construction **periodischer ~** (aus gleichen Gliedern bestehender) periodic (recurrent) structure **~ als geschlossene Einheit** unit construction **~ eines Magnetfeldes** experimental magnetic field **~ der Maschine** body design **~ des Rumpfes** structure of fuselage **~ der Selbsterregung** build-up of a selfexcited generator **~ aus mehreren Teilen** assemblage, assembly, building up **~ einer Verbindung** establishment of a connection

Aufbauarbeit *f* work of reconstruction and improvement

Aufbauart (der Antennen) mounting arrangement

aufbauchen to belly, swell, bulge out

Aufbauchung *f* bellying (fluffiness)

Aufbaudeck *n* spar deck, superstructure deck

Aufbaueinheiten für Werkzeugmaschinen standardized elements for unit-built machine tools

aufbauen to build up, construct, erect, compose, synthesize, install, design, assemble, mount, set up; (eine Anlage) **~** to rig up (construction work) **ein Magnetfeld ~** to set up or create a magnetic field **wieder ~** to rebuild

aufbauend constructive, structural, synthetic

Aufbau-gerät *n* instrument for surface mounting, built-on implement **-gußring** *m* adjusting tubing **-instrument** *n* salient instrument, surface type instrument **-komponente** *f* component of structure **-lehrgang** *m* training schedule or course **-lüfter** *m* ventilator of the superstructure **-maß** *n* setting dimension

aufbäumen to beam up, tilt up, buck (aviation)

Aufbäummaschine *f* winding-up machine

Aufbau-plan *m* schematic diagram (construction) **-rahmen** *m* body frame (construction) **-regler** *m* surface regulator

aufbauschen to puff up, exaggerate, inflate, swell, bulge

aufbauschend bulky

Aufbauschneide *f* (Drehstahl) pickup on the cutting edge, built-up edge

Aufbauschung *f* swelling, exaggeration

Aufbau-stahlhalter *m* duplex (double-deck) tool holder **-stand** *m* cabinet stand

Aufbauten *m pl* superstructure, (naval arch.) superstructural parts, set (film work)

Aufbau-werkzeug *n* double-deck tool **-zeit** building-up time, period of reconstruction

aufbereitbar washable (ores), suitable for reconditioning

Aufbereitbarkeit *f* washability (of ores)

aufbereiten to prepare, separate, refine, upgrade, wash or dress (ores), concentrate, work up

Aufbereiter *m* one who prepares, dresser

aufbereitet prepared **-es Erz** dressed ore **-es Kesselspeisewasser** treated boiler feed water **-es** (gut) **Lockergestein** graded (closely) soil

Aufbereitung *f* dressing, beneficiation, dressing floor, washing (ores), preparation, separation, treatment, sorting, grading, cleaning, purification **~ der Kohle** upgrading of coal

Aufbereitungs-anlage *f* separating plant, dressing, washing, or preparation plant **-herd** *m* concentration or dressing table **-konzentrat** *n* preparation concentrate **-kosten** *f pl* dressing expenses **-maschine** *f* preparatory-treatment-machine **-verfahren** *n* method of dressing or preparing **-walzwerk** *n* first crushing rollers, ore dressing mill
aufbessern to improve, strengthen
Aufbeton *m* concrete (slab) topping
aufbeulen to buckle
Aufbeulen des Randes ridging on the edges
Aufbeulung *f* indentation
aufbewahren to store, stock, keep, preserve, lodge
Aufbewahrung *f* storage, keeping, preservation **sichere** ~ safekeeping
Aufbewahrungs-behälter *m* storage vessel **-dauer** *f* duration of storage **-kasten** *m* storage case, cabinet **-kasten für Stöpsel** plug-protector pan **-temperatur** *f* storage temperature
aufbiegen to bend or turn up(ward)
aufbieten to mobilize, summon
Aufbildwerfer *m* epidiascope
aufbinden to untie, tie up (print)
aufblähen to blow, expand, swell up, bulge out, inflate, belly
Aufblähen *n* expansion, swelling
Aufblähung *f* inflation (aviation)
aufblasbares Boot inflatable boat or dinghy ~ **Gummischlauchboot** inflatable rubber dinghy
aufblasen to blow up, inflate, pump **mit Luft** ~ to inflate
Aufblasen *n* blowing (up), inflation
Aufblasevorrichtung *f* inflation device
aufblättern to exfoliate
aufbleien to lead fuel
aufblenden to dissolve or fade in (film projection)
Aufblick *m* fulguration, blick
aufblicken to brighten, look upward
aufblitzen to flash (up)
Aufblitzen *n* flash
Aufblühen *n* bloom
Aufblühung *f* efflorescence
Aufblockdiagramm *n* jacking diagram
aufbocken to jack up, prop up
aufbohren to drill out or up, (re)bore
Aufbohren *n* drilling, boring
aufbordeln to flange
Aufbohrspindel *f* bore grinding spindle
aufbrassen to square away
aufbrauchen to use up, consume, dissipate (energy), exhaust
aufbrausen to effervesce
Aufbrausen *n* effervescence
aufbrechen to strike camp, start, break or force open, break up, depart
Aufbrechen *n* breaking up, rise
Aufbrecher *m* breaker
Aufbreitmaschine *f* spreader (textiles)
aufbrennen to burn up
aufbringen to capture, apply (force), raise (up), afford, impress (signal), surface, coat, put on **eine Kraft** ~, **eine Last** ~ apply (a force), afford
Aufbringen *n* applying, application ~ **einer Belastung** application of a force ~ **eines harten Überzuges** hard surfacing
Aufbringung eines galvanischen Niederschlages als Korrosionsschutz fescolizing (aviation)
Aufbringungsumlage *f* contribution to be raised
aufbrisen to increase (of wind)
aufbrodeln to boil up (bubble up)
Aufbruch *m* departure, start, rise, uprising, awakening, consumption (depletion) **-proben, Untersuchung von** ~ investigation of samples of road carpets
Aufbruchs-ort *m* starting or departure point **-zeit** *f* departure time
aufbrücken to bridge
Aufbügelfilm *m* hot transfer film (print)
aufbügeln to iron
aufbumsen (slang) to collide, strike
aufbürsten to brush
Aufchromen *n* chromium plating for thickness
aufdämmen to bank (fire)
Aufdampfanlage *f* coating plant
aufdampfen to evaporate (vaporize), steam
aufdämpfen to deposit by evaporation, smoke or vaporize upon, evaporate on, to coat by vapor
Aufdämpfen *n* vaporizing operation, vaporization
Aufdampf-film *m* evaporated film **-kathoden** *pl* vaporizing or disintegrating cathodes (electronics), evaporation cathodes **-leiter** *m* evaporated line
Aufdämpfplatte *f* vaporizing plate
Aufdampf-schicht *f* evaporated film **-technik** *f* metalizing technic
Aufdämpfung *f* evaporation
aufdecken to discover, uncover, expose, detect, disclose
aufdirken to top up
aufdornen to punch **Löcher** ~ to enlarge holes with a drift
Aufdornen *n* expansion, extrusion
Aufdorngerät *n* flaring tool **-probe** *f* drifting test **-werkzeug** *n* reamer
Aufdornung *f* flare
Aufdornvorrichtung *f* expanding device ~ (Schärfmaschine) punching device
Aufdornwerkzeug *n* tube expander
aufdrallen to twist
aufdrängen to push on **sich** ~ to crowd, force, suggest oneself
aufdrehen to screw open, turn up or on edge, twist, step up ~ (ein Ende), to unlay (a rope), turn on (tap) **sich** ~ untwine, untwiste **Hahn** ~ to open the cock
Aufdrehen *n* fanning, shuffling (paper)
Aufdrehwinkel *m* angle of upturn
aufdringlich (Geruch) penetrant (odor)
Aufdruck *m* imprint
aufdrucken to print (on)
aufdrücken to impress, superimpose, impress (a potential upon), imprint, stamp upon **einem Stromkreis eine Spannung** ~ to impress a voltage upon a circuit
Aufdrücken *n* impression
Aufdrückvorrichtung *f* pressing (press-on) tool
aufdunsten to evaporate (vaporize), steam
Aufeinanderarbeiten *n* (Flächen) rubbing (surfaces)
aufeinander abgestimmt concerted ~ **arbeitende**

Teile striking parts
Aufeinanderfolge *f* succession, sequence, turn
aufeinanderfolgend consecutive, successive, sequential
aufeinander-liegende Flächen mating surfaces **-häufen** to heap (pile) up, stack (up) **-passen** to match, register (aviation)
Aufeinanderpassen *n*, **dichtes ~** snug fit
Aufeinander-schichten *n* superposition **-schichten** to pile up **-stapeln** to pile up (on each other) **-stoßen** to clash **-treffen** (Gegensätze) to slash
aufeisen to free from ice
Aufenthalt *m* stop, sojourn, whereabouts, halt, stay
Aufenthalts-dauer *f* hold-up time **-los** nonstop **-ort** *m* residence, domicile **-punkt** *m* place of residence or of temporary stop **-raum** *m* waiting room, rest room **-wahrscheinlichkeit** *f* (an der Oberfläche) surface probability
auferlegen to impose, inflict
auferlegte Arbeit task
Auferregung *f* build-up of a self-exited generator
Auferstehung *f* resurrection
auffächern to fan out, spread fanwise
Auffächern *n* fanning
auffädeln to thread string
auffahren to beat away the ground, drive a level (mining), come into action (artil.) **eine Strecke ~** to drive
Auffahrschiene *f* ramp
Auffahrt *f* ramp, platform, ascent **-blech** (Schlepper) sliding plate
auffallen to be conspicuous, fall on
auffallend striking, conspicuous, distinctive **-es Licht** incident light
auffällig conspicious, bold
Auffallwinkel *m* angle of incidence, glancing angle
Auffalzen *n* seaming-on
Auffang *m* trap **~ für die Ausscheidung** *f* knock-out box (petroleum)
Auffang-anode *f* collecting or gathering anode, target (in a multiplier), catcher (in beam tube) **-barke** *f* (Kristallisator) magma tank (crystallizer) **-behälter** *m* collecting vessel or tray, storage tank, drain pan **-blech** *n* drip pan **-draht** *m* receiving wire (antenna)
Auffangelektrode *f* electron collector, target electrode
Auffangelektrodenspannung *f* collecting potential, polarizing voltage
auffangen to collect, intercept, pick up (a signal), detect, absorb, catch or capture (electrons)
Auffänger *m* collector electrode, target (of cyclotron), catcher (in beam tube) **-dicke** *f* target thickness **-käfig** *m* collector electrode **-platte** *f* target or impactor plate, collector (electrode) **-plattenverlustleistung** *f* collector dissipation (of multiplier)
Auffang-gabel *f* (cylinder) catch **-gefäß** *n* collecting vessel, receiver **-gitter** *n* collector **-glas** *n* objective lens, glass container **-graben** *m* catch pit **-kasten** *m* trap box (print), receiving basket, container **-kolben** *m* receiving flask **-netz** *n* (catch) net
Auffang-öffnung *f* collecting mouth **-pfanne** *f* cutting tray **-querschnitt** *m* capture cross section **-rinne** *f* (Rundherd) gully (gutter), collecting launder **-schale** *f* collecting reservoir, drip pan **-schirm** *m* intercepting screen
Auffang-spule *f* search coil **-stab** *m* collecting staff (temporary) **-stange** *f* buffer bar, safety sear **-stift** *m* pilot pin **-trichter** *m* collecting cone (wind tunnel) **-trog** *m* catchall (tool machine) **-vorrichtung** *f* catching device, trap, buffer, absorbing device, (sheet) stopper (print), stacking tray
auffärben to lift (color)
Auffärbung *f* corrected white (paper)
auffasern to separate into fibers, unravel
Auffaßgerät *n* receiving (instrument) apparatus
auffassen to conceive, perceive, understand, pick up; defect (rdr); catch
Auffassung *f* conception, understanding, concept defection (rdr) **indeterministische ~** indeterministic conception or interpretation
Auffassungs-gabe *f* power of apprehension, perceptive faculty **-radar** *n* acquisition radar
Auffaßwinkel *m* angle for first indication (radar)
Auffederung *f* swelling, amount of swell
auffeuern to stroke up
Auffiederung *f* splitting of the radiation pattern into side-lobes
auffieren to check, ease away, freshen (a rope)
auffinden to discover, locate, find out
aufflackern to flare up, flash up
aufflammen to flare or flame up, deflagrate, blaze, flash
aufflechten to braid, twist, plait
auffordern to bid, urge, solicit
Aufforderung *f* invitation, request, demand, summons, instigation (law)
Aufforderungs-signal *n* dialling tone **-zeichen** *n* opening signal
Aufforsten von Ödland putting waste land into forest, reforestation
Aufforstung *f* afforestation
auffräsen to countersink
auffrischen to freshen up, revive (Batterie), regenerate, recuperate, brighten (color), re-tire, renew
Auffrischen *n* reprocessing, renewing, reviving, restoring, regeneration
Auffrischer *m* replenisher
Auffrischung *f* recuperation, renewal
Auffrischungsschulung refresher training
aufführen to itemize, list, enumerate, register, lead the web (paper mfg.), state, tabulate, summarize, build, erect **einzeln ~** to itemize
Aufführen *n* construction
Aufführung *f* performance, quotation, behavior, production (of a witness), broadcasting, receiving and transmitting
Aufführungsraum *m* large radio studio
Auffüllarmatur *m* filler-well adaptor assembly
auffüllen to fill (up), replenish, top up (elements), make up (with, to) **~ zur Marke** to make (fill) up to the mark
Auffüllen *n* filling, topping up; (b. Pumpen) prime **~ und Laden** topping-up (accumulator) **durch ~ zum Ansaugen vorbereiten** to prime (pump)
Auffüll-pumpe *f* refill pump **-trichter** *m* filling funnel
Auffüllung *f* filling, topping up, backfilling **durch Kippen gewonnene ~** tipped fill

Aufgabe *f* duty, task, mission, abandonment, problem, example (math.), theme, surrender, resignation, delivery

Aufgabe-band *n* belt feeder, feeding belt **-becherwerk** *n* charging or feeding elevator **-bunker** *m* feed hopper, receiving hopper **-gut** *n* feed, head, product treated

Aufgaben-bereich *n* duties, scope (of application) **-gebiet** *n* tactical employment, missions **-kreis** *m* duties (of a position) **-stellung** *f* problem, machining requirements, specifications, service requirements **-wert** *m* desired value (aut. contr.)

Aufgabe-öffner *m* loading opener **-platte** *f* feed plate **-plattenband** *n* apron feeder **-rost** *m* receiving tray **-rührwerk** *n* feeder with agitator **-rutsche** *f* delivery chute **-schaukelschieber** *m* shuttle injector **-schein** *m* receipt of delivery **-schieber** *m* delivery valve **-schlitten** *m* feeder skid **-schnecke** *f* feed screw

Aufgabe-seite *f* infeed side **-sollwert** *m* control point **-station** *f* loading station, take-up end **-stelle** *f* feed(ing) point **-stempel** *m* postmark **-tisch** *m* feeding disk **-trichter** *m* feed hopper, feeding funnel

Aufgabe-vorrichtung *f* feeding device, charging mechanism **-walze** *f* feeding roller **-wert** *m* desired value **-zeit** *f* code time, time of acceptance, time of origin **-zone** *f* feeding or intake station

Aufgang *m* ascension, upstroke (of piston), ascent, rise

aufgären to effervesce, ferment

aufgearbeitet clear, finished (task), worked up, treated (prepared) **-er Bestand** salvaged or second hand stock **-es Spaltmaterial** recycled fuel

aufgeben to charge, deliver, feed, give up, abandon, resign, surrender, relinquish, discontinue, mail, forfeit, renounce, waive, post (mail)

Aufgeber *m* charger, feeder, reacher (textiles), originator (signal)

Aufgebe-sohle *f* charging platform **-trichter** *m* feed hopper, distributor **-walze** *f* feed roll

aufgeblasen inflated, turgid, puffed up

Aufgeblasenheit *f* inflation, distention

aufgebläht bloated, vesicular

aufgebogen-er Stab bent up rod **-es Tragflächenende** washed-out wing tip

Aufgebot *n* conscription, calling out of troops, summons, public notice

Aufgebotsverfahren *n* public notice or notification

aufgedampft evaporated **-er Kohlewiderstand** vaporized carbon resistance, cracked-carbon resistance

aufgedrückt forced impressed; (Spannung) applied **-e Schwingungen** forced oscillations

aufgedunsen swollen, inflated, puffed up, swelled up

aufgeflanscht flange-mounted

aufgefärbtes Weiß neutralized, corrected white (paper)

aufgefordert solicited, challenged

aufgegossen (aufgießen), cast (on solid)

aufgehängt suspended ~ **an einem Faden** hung from a fibre

aufgehäuft piled up

aufgehen to go up, rise, swell, open, merge, evaporate, dissolve, germinate (seed), ferment, work ~ **in** to merge

Aufgehen des Kalkes ebullition of lime

aufgehende Zahl rational number or quantity

aufgeien to brail up, clew up

aufgejungferter Pfahl spliced pile

aufgekauft cornered (market speculation)

aufgekeilt keyed, secured by wedge

aufgeklärtes Tau coil

aufgeklebt bonded

aufgekohlt carbonised

aufgeladen charged **nicht** ~ no-pressure charged **-e Batterie** primed battery **mäßig -er Motor** medium supercharged motor **nicht -er Motor** unboosted engine

Aufgeld *n* premium, agio, discount

aufgelegt, ein Schiff ist ~ a barge (boat or vessel) is laid up (not working)

aufgelöst dissolved, disbanded, in open order **-e Fundamente** concrete foundation block sunk in drilled holes **-e Linienbilder** resolved line patterns **-e Staumauer** buttres dam **-er Stoff** solute **-er Zucker** melted sugar, dissolved sugar

aufgelötet (hart) brazed on, soldered on

aufgenommene Leistung energy input, input (of electric motors), power input

aufgeprägt-er Impuls superposed pulse **-e Spannung** *f* impressed voltage

aufgepreßte Briden turned or pressed flanges ~ **Narben** embossed grain

aufgerauht roughened **-er Stoff** sueded cloth

aufgerieben reamed (holes)

aufgerüstetes Gewicht all-up weight

aufgeschnitten cut open, split **-er Ring** split ring **-er Zylinder** slotted cylinder

aufgeschoben postponed

aufgeschraubt bolted, threaded (on) **warm** ~ **und geschrumpft** screwed and shrunk on **-e Messer** screwed blades

aufgeschrumpft *m* shrunk on, fitted by shrinking

aufgeschütteter Boden filled-in ground

aufgeschweißt welded (on)

aufgesetzt superimposed **-er Rammklotz** dolly **-er Schalter** surface mounted switch **-er Zahnkranz** forced-on gear ring, shrunk-on gear ring

aufgespalten extended (dislocation), cloven, split **-e Schreibweise** split notation

aufgespeichert latent

aufgespritzte Überzüge sprayed coatings of zinc, aluminium, lead

aufgespult spoded

aufgestapelt stacked

aufgestiftet pinned **-e Blechschablone** dowelled sheet templet

aufgetankt with full fuel tanks

aufgetautes Gebirge thawed soil

aufgeteilte Abbildung split focus (scanning method)

aufgetoppt topped

aufgetreten occurred **-e Unfälle** accidents that have occurred

aufgewalzte Rohre tubes expanded in

aufgewandte Sorgfalt accuracy

aufgeworfen elevated, thrown up

aufgewundener Exponentialtrichter twisted or

coiled exponential loud-speaker
aufgezeichnet indicated **-e Höhenleistung** indicated altitude **-e Pferdekraft** indicated horsepower
aufgezogen wound up (spring) **er Stein** worn-out die
aufgichten to charge (metal)
aufgießen to pour upon, sprinkle, infuse
Aufglasur *f* over-glaze
aufgleisen to rerail
Aufgleisung *f* rerailing
Aufgleiten *n* (warmer Luftmassen auf kalte) rise (of warm air masses over cooler ones)
Aufgleit-fläche *f* (Met.) surface of discontinuity **-front** *m* rising warm front **-wolke** ascending or rising cloud
aufgliedern to classify
Aufgliederung *f* breakdown
aufglühen to glow up (sun)
aufgraben, den Boden ~ to rake up the ground, dig up the earth
Aufgrabung *f* excavation
aufgreifen to adopt, pick up
Aufguß *m* cast-on mount (print) infussion (chem.) **-apparat** *m* sparger, sprinkling apparatus **-kopf** *m* dead head **-probe** *f* pouring test **-raum** *m* filling space **-verfahren** *n* infusion process
aufhaken to unhook, hook on, unclasp, unfasten, break open
Aufhaken *n* message pickup (aviation)
Aufhalte-kraft *f* power of resistance **-linie** *f* line of arrest, stop line
aufhalten to stop, detain, stem, check, arrest **sich ~** to dwell, reside, stay
Aufhalter *m* interruptor
aufhanfen (Isolatoren) to fix with hemp (insulators)
Aufhänge-achse *f* suspension pin **-band** *n* suspensory ligament **-boden** *m* drying place or room, hanging room **-brücke** *f* supporting bridge, upper support for frames **-bügel** *m* gimbals, trunnion arms of the compass, suspension stirrup or loop, loop hanger **-draht** *m* suspending or suspension wire **-eisen** *n* hanger rod, iron suspension tie, suspension iron **-faden** *m* suspension fiber **-gestänge** *n* suspension rods **-gestell** *n* suspensory mounting, suspension gear **-haken** *m* suspension or attachment hook
Aufhänge-haspel *f* piling-winch **-höhe** *f* height of suspension **-isolator** *m* suspension insulator (single hook) **-joch** *n* lifting sling or yolk **-ketten** *f pl* suspension chains **-lasche** *f* suspensing clip, suspension lug
aufhängen to suspend, hang up, hang **kardanisch ~** to suspend on gimbals, hang by gimbals **federnd ~** to spring, suspend on springs
Aufhänge-nasen *f pl* suspension lugs **-öse** *f* suspension eye or loop, lifting eye, lug **-pratzen am Kurbelgehäuse** bearer feet of crankcase **punkt** *m* point of suspension, fixed end (of cable), fulcrum of suspension
Aufhänger *m* hanger, rack, loftsman, drier, suspender (for aerial cables) **-blech** *n* hanger plate
Aufhängerahmen *m* mounting or suspension frame (radar)
Aufhänger-bolzenlager *n* locating bolt bearing **-haken** *m* hanger
Aufhänge-riemen *m* brace **-rolle** *f* suspension pulley
Aufhängerring *m* hanger
Aufhänge-saal *m* (paper) hanging room (print) **-schlaufe** *f* hoisting sling **-stange** *f* suspension link
Aufhängevorrichtung *f* hanging apparatus, mount, T bar, lifting or suspension gear
Aufhängezapfen *m* suspension pivot
Aufhängung *f* hanging, suspension, attachment, overhead suspension, mounting brackets **~ der Blöcke** block lifting **~ der Feder** suspension of the spring **gegenfädige ~** top-bottom suspension **~ für Generator** generator suspension **kardanische ~** compass gimbals, Cardanic suspension **~ für Motor** engine suspension **pendelnde ~** rocking suspension **starre ~** rigid suspension **stoßdämpfende ~ oder Lagerung** shock-absorbing mountings
Aufhängungs-draht *m* bearer or carrier wire **-ohr** *n* lug **-punkt** *m* point of suspension
Aufhärtbarkeit *f* potential hardness increase
Aufhärtung *f* hardening, hardness increment (weld)
aufhaspeln to reel (up or in), wind up, hoist, raise with a windlass
Aufhau *m* cutting upwards, up set
aufhauen to hit upward, (of files) cut, open, rise in the back (mining) **einen Abbau ~** to open a chamber **ein neues Feld ~** to cut new ground **~ von stumpfen Feilen** recutting of used files
Aufhauen *n* opening, rise, wall, sharpening anew
Aufhauer *m* cutting chisel
aufhäufen to heap (up), store, pile up, accumulate, bank, amass
Aufhäufung *f* accumulation, storing, packing or building up
Aufhaumaschine *f* nibbling or blanking machine
aufheben (aufbewahren) to keep, preserve; (lagern) store; (Versammlung) break up, dismiss; (Math.-Bruch) reduce; (Vertrag terminate; (Chem.) neutralize, cut off, withdraw a plug, counteract (neutralize), lift up, raise, outweigh, offset, abolish, kill, cancel, annul, invalidate, dissolve, nullify, compensate, discontinue, revoke, abate **eine Verbindung ~** to clear, suspend or take down a connection, release a call **eine Wirkung ~** to negative an effect, neutralize **einander ~** to cancel, annul each other **sich gegenseitig ~** mutually cancel (math., physics, electronics)
Aufheben *n* lifting **Motor zum ~** lifting motor
Aufhebung *f* clearing, neutralization, cancellation, abrogation, abolition, suspension
Aufhebezange *f* pickup tongs
aufheften to stitch or pin together
aufheißen to sway
Aufheiterung *f* clearing (met.)
aufheizen to heat up
Aufheiz-pastenkathode *f* self-heating oxide cathode **-wirkung** *f* reheat effect (jet)
Aufhelfung *f* lighter bar (paper)
aufhellen to clear up, clarify; make lighter, brighten (up), spotlight, eludicate; (der Eigenfarbe) decolorize **sich ~** to clear up (weather)

Aufheller *m* klieg light, brightener
Aufhellschirm *m* reflecting screen
Aufhellung *f* corrected white (paper), brightening **~ schwarzer Stellen** blooming, excessive brightness, loss of contrast (in picture)
Aufhellungs-dauer *f* illuminating time **-dicke** *f* clearing thickness **-lagen** *f pl* positions of maximum illumination **-organ** *n* intensity or brilliance modulation of control electrode
Aufhellvermögen *n* brightening power
Aufhieb *m* upset
aufhissen to hoist, pull or rise up
aufhocken to bunch up
aufhöhen, eine Mauer ~ to raise or run up a wall
aufholen to withdraw, fetch or pick up, gain on, trice
Aufholer *m* tripping line
aufholzen to mount (on wood)
aufhören to finish, discontinue, stop, end, cease
Aufhören *n* stopping, cessation
Aufkadung eines Deiches raising a dam
aufkämmen to cog, join by cogging
aufkanten to set on edge
aufkarden to burr (raise nap)
aufkarten to wind on cards
Aufkarter *m* cart winder (weaving)
aufkatten to cat (an anchor)
aufkaufen to corner, buy wholesale or on installment plan
Aufkäufer *m* buying speculator
aufkegeln (Kegelverfahren) to cone (coning)
aufkeilen to key on, wedge on, fit a key
Aufkeilung *f* keying
Aufkeilwinkel *m* angle of pitch (of an eccentric or cam)
aufkellen to wedge up
Aufkimmung *f* rise (naval arch.) **~ einer Bodenwrange** rising of a floor or of a floor timber (ship building) **~ einer Luft- oder Schiffsschraube** rise of a propeller
aufkippbar tiltable, tilting
aufkippen, vorn ~ to buck or tilt up in front (aviation)
aufkitten to cement on
Aufkittlinse *f* cementing lens, cemented bifocal
aufklaffen to (burst) open, rupture, split
aufklappbar hinged, capable of being swung open or raised (on hinges), turn-up, fold-out, swing-out **-er Ausleger** hinged apron **-er Kondensator** swing-out condenser **-es Lager** hinged-cap bearing (seat) **-e Stufe** fold-out tread (tip-up trad)
Aufklappdeckel *m* revolving cover
aufklappen to open up on hinges, lift up, drop (a leaf), to turn up, fold (swing) out, raise **das Verdeck ~** to put the hood up, raise the hood
aufklären to reconnoiter, scout, clarify, explain, clear up, observe, patrol, illuminate **sich ~** to clear, clear up, lighten
aufklärend informational
Aufklärung *f* clarification, enlightenment, clearing up, search
Aufklärungssatellit *m* reconnaissance satellite
aufklauen to join by a triangular notch, fix with a grapnel
aufklebbar adhesive
aufkleben to paste, paste up or on, gum (to) **Abzüge ~** to mount, paste upon copies
Aufkleber *m* labeller (label)
Aufklebe-karton *m* paste-on mount **-punktur** *f* needling (print) **-zettel** *m* sticker, label
aufkleistern to paste or glue on
aufklemmbar attachable
aufklingende Schwingungen oscillations increasing in amplitude
aufklinken to unlatch, unlock
aufklotzen to mount, block (print), pad
Aufklotzapparat *m* (block) mounting device
aufknacken to crack
aufknallen to bang open
aufknöpfen to unbutton, button on
aufknoten to untie
aufknüpfen to undo
aufkochen to boil up, boil, blow up
Aufkocher *m* blow-up tank, juice boiler, reboiler
Aufkochgefäß *n* boiling vessel
aufkohlen to recarburize, carburize, cement, cementite
Aufkohlung *f* recarburization, carburization, cementation
Aufkohlungs-mittel *n* (re)carburizing agent, (re)carburizer, cement **-periode** *f* carbon period
aufkommen to force ahead, pass **~ lassen** to fade in
Aufkomponente *f* upward component
aufköpfen to head
aufkratzen to scratch up, scratch, rake
aufkrempeln to roll up, turn up
aufkreuzen to beat to windward
aufkrücken (aufrühren) to stir up
Aufkugeln *n* press-finish
aufkündigen to give notice, recall
Aufkündigung *f* notice, warning, recall, revocation
aufkupfern to electroplate copper (print)
Aufkupferung *f* copper coating
Aufkupferungsanlage *f* copper depositing installation
aufkurbeln to wind up
Aufkurssignal *n* on-course signal (navig.)
aufladbares Element regenerable cell
Auflade-band *n* charging belt **-einrichtung** *f* supercharging equipment **-gebläse** *n* charging blower, booster, supercharger **-gerät** *n* charging set **-geschwindigkeit** *f* rate of charge (or discharge) **-kommando** *n* loading detail **-luftdruck** *m* charging pressure **-motor** *m* supercharged engine
aufladen to load, charge (elec.), recharge, burden, boost, supercharge; (Motore) to pressure-charge, turbo-charge
Aufladen *n* loading, charging, detonating charge, supercharge
Aufladeplatte *f* bolster plate
Auflader *m* loader
Auflade-strom *m* charging current **-verfahren** *n* charging process **-vorrichtung** *f* boost device
Aufladung *f* top charge (explosives), charge, detonating-charge boost **hoher Grad der ~** high degree of boost **mit und ohne ~** aspirated and pressure charged **Motor mit geringer ~** low-supercharged engine **Motor mit ~** supercharged engine **Motor ohne ~** uncharged engine
Aufladungsprozeß *m* charging process

Aufladewiderstand *m* charge resistance

Auflage *f* requirement, condition, obligation, run, circulation (print), overlay, support, rest, seat, edition, coating, tax **-bock** *m* horse (aviation) **-bogen** *m* arc of contact **-druck** *m* bearing or contact pressure, surface pressure, downward pressure (stylus in record player), tracking force (phono), needle force (phono) **-durchmesser** *m* supporting diameter **-filter** *n* filter medium, support

Auflagefläche *f* bearing area or table, bearing or contact surface, seat, attaching pad, bedding **~ rings um ein Loch mit Senker glatt und eben fräsen** to spotface **eine ~ anschneiden** to spot a surface

Auflage-flansch *m* supporting flange **-höhe** *f* edition (print) **-knagge** *f* (Windmühle) bearer (windmill), supporting bracket **-kraft** *f* reaction force, bearing load **-länge** *f* length of surface support, take-off runway

Auflageleiste *f* seating or registering shoulder (ledge, rim) **zugeschärfte ~** bevelled lath

Auflagemetall *n* cladding material

Auflagendruck *m* running off single editions (print.)

Auflage-platte *f* supporting plate **-punkt** *m* center of tire impact, point of support **-rand** *m* supporting edge

Auflager *n* pedestal, support, abutment, bearing, hanger bar, saddle, truck, seat, stop, trunnion, track, bearing surface **am ~ verstärken** to reinforce at the bearing **festes ~** (Schiene) fixed rail

Auflager-bedingung *f* condition of support, cantilever or bearing condition(s) (arch., statics) **-blech** *n* face plate **-bolzen** *m* supporting bolt **-druck** *m* thrust, bearing pressure or reaction, pressure on the support **-entfernung** *f* distance between supports

Auflagerfläche *f* seating, bearing area, area of rest, supporting area **kugelig gebildete ~** spherical seating

Auflager-gegendruck *m* counter-boost pressure **-gelenk** *n* bearing hinge **-halten** *n* storing, storage **-konsole** *f* bearing bracket **-kraft** *f* reaction of or on support **-leiste** *f* bearing strip

auflagern to bed, support, store, superpose

Auflager-platte *f* wall plate, bed plate **-punkt** *m* bearing point **-reaktion** *f* reaction of or bearing pressure on supports, reaction at the abutment, supporting reaction **-stein** *m* foundation or base stone **-verschiebung** *f* displacement of the support

Auflagerung *f* foundation, support, bearing, storage, superposition

Auflage-sattel *m* rear tip frame support (guided missile) **-scheibe** *f* spacer, washer **-schiene** *f* locating fence **-schuh** *m* supporting shoe **-stelle** *f* point of support **-strang** *m* paper web (machine) **-tisch** *m* table, supporting table **-winkel** *m* supporting angle, mounting bracket

Auflandung *f* aggradation

Auflanger *m* futtock

Aufläppen *n* lapping

auflassen to abandon a mine, allow to ascend (of balloons)

auflässig abandoned

Auflast surcharge or applied load on the surface (ports)

Auflauf *m* forward end (paper mfg.), rising scaffold bridge **~** (einer Stromschiene) leoding ramp **-bremse** *f* overrunning brake **-bremskopf** *m* override brake head **-druck** *m* (Anhänger) running-up pressure (trailer)

auflaufen to increase, run up, germinate (seed)

Auflaufen *n* (des Rades) mounting (of wheel) **~ des Films** take-up (by spool) of film strip **~ der Gleichlauffehler** compounding or integration of differences of synchronism

auflaufende Polkante *f* leading pole tip or horn

Aufläufer *m* feeder or sow (foundry), wrap (single filaments) **-gehäuse** *n* incline housing

Auflauf-fläche *f* abutting surface **-haspel** *f* winding, gathering or collecting drum, windlass, capstan, reel, spool, sheave, bobbin, cop, roll **-hebel** *m* roller lever **-kontakt** *m* limit switch **-kurve** *f* (Nocken) lifting flank, incline **-nase** *f* run-off piece **-nocken** *m* stop cam, arresting or stopping cam **-punkt** *m* first point of contact

Auflauf-rahmen *m* deckle frame **-rolle** *f* take-up reel **-rollgang** *m* approach roller conveyor, live-roller feed bed **-schiene** *f* conductor-rail ramp **-stück** *n* knuckle lug on guncarriage frame **-walze** *f* receiving roller **-zunge** *f* ramp for climbing

Auflege-apparat *m* feeder **-block** *m* V-block **-fläche** *f* bearing surface **-gewicht** *n* flat weight **-kasten** *m* rest block **-maschine** *f* spreading machine

auflegen to lay on or up, apply, place on, deposit, start construction **den Hörer ~** to replace the receiver, hang up **ein Buch neu ~** to reprint or republish a book

Auflegen *n* replacement, restoring

Aufleger *m* card feeder (text), lifter, layer, semitrailer

Auflege-rahmen *m* stiffening frame **-schuß** *m* mud capping **-tisch** *m* feed-table

auflehnen to revolt, mutiny

Auflehnung *f* resistance, revolt, mutiny

aufleimen to glue on

Aufleiter *m* guide

auflesen to pick up, gather

Aufleuchtdauer *f* illuminated or light period

aufleuchten to light (up), flash (up), emit flashes, shine, glow

Aufleuchten *n* lighting, flashing, illumination, gun flash, flaring **zum ~ bringen** to flash up

Aufleuchtlampen *f pl* indicator lamps

Auflicht *n* aximuthal or top illumination, light from vertical sources, vertical illumination, incident light **-beleuchtung** *f* direct illumination, epi-illumination **-elektronenmikroskop** *n* direct light electron microscope

auflichten to clear

Auflicht-kondensator *m* incident light condenser **-mikroskop** *n* incidental light microscope **-wechselkondensator** *m* incident-light changeover condensor

Auflieferung *f* delivery

Aufliegeachse (Tankwagen) supporting axle

aufliegen to rest on, be supported

auflockern to break up, loosen up, vent, disintegrate, relax, aerate, open up, slacken,

separate, aerate (the mixture) **das Gefüge ~** to loosen up the structure
Auflockerung *f* loosening, aeration, disintegration
Auflockerungs-apparat *m* aerator, aerating apparatus **-maschine** *f* ploughing machine **-sprengung** *f* breaking-in shot
auflodern to flash or emit flashes
auflösbar soluble, resolvable **-er Abstand** *m* resolving distance
Auflösbarkeit *f* solubility
Auflösbarkeitsgrenze *f* solubility limit, disappearing point
Auflöse-behälter *m* dissolver, dissolving chest **-knopf** *m* release knob
auflösen (öffnen) loosen, untie; (entwirren) disentangle; (verflüssigen) dissolve, melt; (zerlegen) disintegrate, break up, resolve; (zersetzen) decompose; (Aufgabe) solve; (Chem.) analyse; (Math.-Bruch) reduce; (Beziehungen) break up; (Vertrag) annul, cancel; (Geschäft) liquidate, solve, dissipate, dissociate, disband, liquefy, release, open (connections), atomize **~ eine Gleichung nach** *n* to solve an equation with respect to *n* **~ in seine Bestandteile** to disintegrate **eine Verbindung ~** to clear out, release
Auflösen *n* solution, solving, dissolving, release
auflösend, sich ~ dissolving, dissipating
auflösende Kraft resolving power (optics)
Auflösepfanne *f* melting pan, melter
Auflöser *m* resolver, solvent
Auflöserrelais *n* clear-out relay
auflöslich soluble
Auflöslichkeit *f* solubility
Auflösung *f* (Lösung) solution; (Zerlegung) decomposition, disintegration; (Chem.) analysis; (Vertrag) cancellation, disbanding, scattering, dissolution, loosening, solubility, undoing, dissociation, re-solution, analyzation, release, clear(ing) out, expansion (math.), friability, mellowness, liquidation, disappearance; (Fernsehen) definition, resolution (of the field emission); (einer Aufnahme) resolution (of a micrograph)
Auflösung, gute ~ full resolution (TV) **hohe ~** high resolution **in ~ begriffen sein** to be in the process of dissolution **rückwärtige ~** back release **vorzeitige ~** premature release **Aufnahmen mit großer ~** photographs faithful to minute details **~ in die Bestandteile** disintegration **~ von Gleichungen** reduction **~ einer Gleichung nach** *n* solution of an equation for *n* **~ des Lichtes** decomposition of light **~ einer Versetzung** break-away of dislocation
auflösungsbegrenzender Faktor limiting resolution factor
Auflösungs-beiwert *m* dissociation coefficient **-grad** *m* degree of disintegration **-grenze** *f* limit of resolution, revolving limit **-mittel** *n* solvent **-pfanne** *f* clarifier **-stab** *m* demobilization staff
Auflösungs-vermögen *n* dissolving, solvent or resolving power (of telescopes, photographic, and shortwave telescope), re-solution, resolving property, capacity of solution or dissolution, persistence of the spot (cathode-ray oscillograph), fineness of grain in film, acuity of image of camera, resolving power, power of analysis, possible definition
Auflösungs-wärme *f* heat of solution **-zeichen** *n* a natural (music) **-zeit** *f* resolving or resolution time **-zustand** *m* state of decomposition
auflöten to solder on, unsolder, braze
Auflötflansche *m* soldered or brazed flange
aufmachen to open up, undo, turn on, raise (steam)
Aufmachen eines Schachtes clearing out of a shaft
Aufmachung *f* scenery (film), settings, composition, layout, make-up, design
Aufmachungs-einheit *f* package **-kosten** *f pl* cost for making up (textiles)
aufmagnetisieren to magnetize
Aufmagnetisierung *f* magnetization (mechanical)
aufmaischen to mix
Aufmaischen *n* second mashing
aufmalen to paint
Aufmasse *f* offsets
aufmauern to brick up
aufmeißeln to open with a chisel
aufmerksam attentive, alert, absorbing
Aufmerksamkeit *f* attention, watchfulness, attentiveness, alertness, vigilance **erhöhte ~** increased vigilance or alertness
Aufmerksamkeits-lampe *f* chargeable time signal or lamp **-wanderung** *f* wandering of attention **-umfang** *m* span of attention
Aufmessung *f* measurement
aufmischen to mix up
aufmodulieren to modulate upon
aufmontieren to assemble, erect, fit, set up
aufnadeln to needle
aufnageln to nail on
aufnähen to sew on
Aufnahme *f* (Einbau) incorporation, mounting, installation; (Aufsaugung) absorption; (Einverleibung) assimilation; (Einleitung) starting, initiation; (Eingliederung) integration, incorporation; (Einbeziehung) inclusion; (Zulassung) admission; (Einschreibung) registration, enrollment; (Inventar) inventory; (Ton) recording; (Topographie) survey, plotting; (Werkstück) holding fixture; (Werkzeug) tool carrier, input (elec.), recording (elec.), uptake or detection, delaying position, receiver, photograph, reception, taking or exposure (photographs), shot (motion picture), insertion, photographic or phonographic shooting or taking (of pictures), taking up, plotting (curves), covering, target, reserve, withdrawal, establishment of contact; **~** (der Fertigung) starting of (or taking up) the production **~** (Sitz von Werkzeugen) receptacle **~** (des Tatbestands) fact-finding
Aufnahme, ~ direkt vom Empfänger off-the-air recording **~ einer Fernsehsendung** telerecording **~ nach dem Gehör** reception by sounder or buzzer **~ des Geländes** survey, mapping, aerial photograph **~ einer Kurve** (durch ein Instrument) plotting of a curve **~ nach Lage und Höhe** survey(ing) for position and elevation **~ für Stecker** receptacle
Aufnahme, freundliche ~ welcome, warm reception **kinematographische ~** moving picture **luftphotogrammetrische ~** aerophotogramme-

tric survey **magnetische ~** magnetic susceptibility **photogrammetrische ~** photogrammetric survey **photographische ~** photograph, photographic image **photographische ~** (Vorgang) impression of a photograph, exposure **stereophotogrammetrische ~** stereophotogrammetric survey **tachymetrische ~** tacheometric survey **technische ~** technical survey, engineering survey **terrestrische ~** terrestrial survey, ground photograph **topographische ~** topographic survey **verschwenkte ~** tilted photograph

Aufnahme-abstand *m* base **-anordnung** *f* arrangement of the survey **-apparat** *m* recording instrument, camera **-beamter** *m* checker **-bedingungen** *f pl* stipulations for acceptance of a manuscript or merchandise **-behälter** *m* receiving drum or buoy **bildweite** *f* principal distance of the photograph **-boden** *m* drawoff pan **-breite** *f* width of strip photographed **-brennweite** *f* focal length of the photograph **-brücke** *f* recording bridge

Aufnahmecharakteristik, spektrale ~ pick-up spectral characteristic

Aufnahme-dorn *m* receiving lug, arbor **-entzerrer** *m* pre-record tape equalizer

aufnahmefähig susceptible, absorbable, absorptive

Aufnahmefähigkeit *f* absorption power, consuming power, capacity, receptivity, efficiency, pickup performance (of antenna) **~ der Linie** maximum capacity of the line

Aufnahme-faktor *m* pickup factor **-filter** *f* taking filter **-format** *n* size of photograph **-galvanometer** (Lichthahn) recording galvanometer (sound film) **-gelände** *n* location (film)

Aufnahmegerät *n* surveying apparatus, camera, input or recording unit **~ für Verstellinie** pick-up device for adjusting line

Aufnahme-geschwindigkeit *f* speed of exposure **-haken** *m* pickup hook **-höhe** *f* flying height **-intervall** *n* time interval between successive photographs

Aufnahme-kamera *f* pickup camera, surveying-camera unit **-kasten** *m* receiver **-kolben** *m* absorption flask **-kontrolle** *f* recording monitoring **-kopf** *m* recording head (tape recorder) **-kreis** *m* pick-up circuit **-lampen** *f* studio lights **-leistung** *f* performance of the survey, radiographic output **-leiter** *m* chief cameraman **-leuchten** *pl* lighting fixtures for studio lighting

Aufnahme-lichtfilter *n* photographic lightfilter **-listen** *pl* stocktaking sheets **-loch** *n* receiving hole, location hole **-magnet** *m* recording or pickup magnet **-maßstab** *m* scale of the survey **-mikrophon** *n* pickup transmitter

Aufnahmen *f pl* photographs **~ machen** to take photographs **gleichmäßig geneigte ~** symmetrically tilted photographs **linksverschwenkte ~** leftaverted photographs **rechtsverschwenkte ~** rightaverted photographs **ungleichmäßig geneigte ~** asymmetrically tilted photographs **vertikalkonvergente ~** oblique-convergent photographs

Aufnahme-objekt *n* object to be photographed **-objektiv** *n* picture-taking lens, photographic field lens

Aufnahmeort *m* pick-up point (TV), camera station **~ in der Luft** air position or station

Aufnahme-platte *f* platter (16-inch electric transcription record) **-prüfung** *f* entrance examination **-punkt** *m* reference point (survey) **-raum** *m* recording room, studio (of broadcast transmitter), teletorium, telestudio **-relais** *n* receiving relay **-richtung** *f* direction of object to be photographed **-ring** *m* receiving ring

Aufnahmeröhre *f* camera tube, pick-up tube, supporting tube of concentric cable **~ ohne Speicherung** non-storage camera tube

Aufnahmesegment *n* receiving segment

Aufnahmespitze *f* absorption point **umlaufende ~** live center

Aufnahme-spule *f* take-up spool **-standpunkt** *m* camera station **-station** *f* take-up, receiving, or head end **-stelle** *f* location (film shooting), receiving or translating place (telegraphy), recruiting center **-stellung** *f* delaying, rallying, or covering position **-streifen** *m* teleprinter, signal tape (telegr.) **-strom** *m* radiographic current **-stromkreis** *m* input circuit **-tasche** *f* storage bin **-technik** *f* technical proceeding of the survey **-techniker** *m* camera technician **-teil** *m* input unit

Aufnahmetopf für Scheinwerfereinsatz headlamp unit

Aufnahme-traverse *f* axle supports **-tubus** *m* direction cone

Aufnahme- und Wiedergabegerät *n* record/playback unit

Aufnahmeverfahren *n* pick-up method

Aufnahmevermögen *n* absorption capacity, receptivity, susceptibility **von hohem** (geringem) **~** high (low) capacity

Aufnahme-verstärker *m* recording amplifier **-vorrichtung** *f* speech recorder, pick-up attachment, supporting device **-vorsatz** *m* taking attachment **-wagen** *m* television or electron camera truck, video bus, televising car **-walze** *f* pick-up roll **-winkel** *m* shooting angle, pick-up angle **-zähler** *m* exposure counter **-zählwerk** *n* serial counter assembly **-zapfen** *m* tang, square **-zeit** *f* time of exposure

aufnehmen (aufsaugen) to absorb; (enthalten) hold, carry, contain; (eingliedern) include, integrate, incorporate; (eintragen) enter (inventory) take stock; (beginnen) start, take up; (wieder ~) resume, trap, record (sound), take or shoot (pictures), copy (messages), accommodate, draw, survey, receive, photograph, detect, intercept (radio), raise, borrow, sketch, pick-up, lift, challenge, record, establish, lodge, matriculate, trace, plot (graphs), remove, take (current) **~** (in Bearbeitungsvorrichtung) to allocate **eine Grube ~** to survey a mine **mit dem Kompaß ~** to dial **begierig ~** to swallow **Fahrt ~** to gain speed **Verbindung ~** to make contact, establish communication

Aufnehmen *n* reception, tracing, plotting, removal, picking up, recording

aufnehmend absorbing, receiving **-er Teil** female piece **-er oder führender Teil** target **Wärme ~** endothermic

Aufnehmer *m* receiver, absorber, container, scoop

aufnieten to rivet on, unrivet

auf- oder abfahren to move in either direction

Aufpaarung *f* disjunction
aufpassen to mind, pay attention, watch, be on the alert, fit, register (print)
aufpausen to copy (print)
aufpflanzen to mount, erect, set up
aufpfropfen to graft, splice
Aufpfropfung *f* pruning, grafting
aufpinseln to apply by brush
aufplatzen to burst open, blow up, break open
Aufplatzungsprobe *f* burst test
aufpolieren to refinish
aufprägen (Spannung) to impress(on), to superpose a voltage
Aufprägung *f* embossing, imprint
Aufprall *m* bound, impact, bombardment, impingement, striking (of electrons), rebound, knock-on
aufprallen to strike the ground, strike, hit, bounce, impinge
aufprallend falling
Aufprallfläche *f* target (for electrons)
Aufpreis *m* extra price (added to base price), surcharge
aufpressen to force on, press on, imprint
Aufprojektion *f* front projection
aufprotzen to limber, couple
Aufpudern *n* dusting
aufpumpen to inflate, blow up
Aufpumpen *n* pumping ~ **der Reifen** inflation of tires
Aufpunkt *m* plotted point, space point, field point; (Navigation) receiving point (direction findings)
Aufputzen *n* cleaning, dressing up
Aufputz-montage *f* surface mounting **-steckdose** *f* surface socket **-kombination** *f* combination for surface mounting
aufquellen to swell up, swell, well up
Aufquellen *n* bubbling up, creep, swelling ~ **des Liegenden** (Bg) creep
aufraffen to recover
aufrahmen to tenter
Aufrahmen *n* tentering (cloth fabrication)
Aufrahmungsmittel *n* creaming agent, emulsifier
Aufrahmzeit *f* duration of the stability of a disperse system (such as an aerosol or hydrosol)
aufrakeln to scrape (on)
Aufrauhbürste *f* rotary sweeper (used in road construction)
aufrauhen to nap, roughen, get rough, granulate, grind superficially, knurl, rag, sand-paper (print), teasel
Aufrauhen *n* roughening, buffing ~ **des Brennfleckes** *n* crater formation
Aufrauhmaschine *f* buffing machine
Aufrauhung *f* roughening, wrinkling; (Säge) rough cutting edge ~ **des Brennflecks** crater formation (abrasion)
Aufrauhverfahren *n* roughening process
Aufräumarbeit *f* clearing, reaming
aufräumen to mop up, clear, carry off, remove, clean, ream **das taube Gestein** ~ to clear the debris or rock **einen Stollen** ~ to clear an adit
Aufräumen *n* salvaging
Aufräumer *m* sweeper, stocker, reamer
Aufräumung *f* mopping up, clearing up
Aufräumungsarbeiten *f pl* salvage work
Aufräumzeit *f* clean-up time (workfactor)
aufrechnen to reckon up, charge (to an account), integrate
Aufrechnung *f* balance, bill, settlement, addition
aufrecht straight, upright, honest, vertical, erect, endwise **-e Falte** symmetrical fold ~ **gießen** to cast upright
aufrechterhalten to maintain, keep alive (an application or patent), uphold
Aufrechterhalten *n* maintenance
Aufrechterhaltung *f* maintenance, support, upkeep ~ **der öffentlichen Ordnung** maintenance of law and order
aufrechtstehend arranged upright, upright **-e Säule** upright **-er Trommelmischer** end-over-end type drum mixer
aufregen to excite, enrage, arouse
aufregend exciting
Aufregung *f* excitement
Aufreibedurchmesser *m* reaming diameter
aufreiben to rub open, grind, destroy, annihilate, ream (out), broach, drift, open out
Aufreiben *n* reaming
Aufreiber *m* reamer
Aufreibe- und Ausreibemaschine *f* reaming and scraping machine
Aufreibevorrichtung *f* reaming attachment
Aufreibung des Wasserspiegels raising of the level (by the wind)
aufreihen to thread (on), arrange, line up, sequence
Aufreiher *m* sequencer
außreißen to pull apart, tear up, crack, chap, split, plot, sketch, lay out, draw out, line, break part way, tear open, rip, take up, trace, open
Aufreißen *n*, **kurzzeitiges** ~ **der Drosselklappe** snatch operation of the throttle
Aufreißer *m* scarifier
Aufreißhammer *m* ripping hammer (pneumatic) jackhammer for wrecking, pavement breaker
Aufreiß-stahl *m* scarifier
Aufreißungsvorrichtung *f* release gear
Aufreißwand *f* ripping panel
Aufreutern von Rübenblättern frame stacking of beet tops
Aufrichtemoment *m* metacenter
aufrichten to right, erect, set up, raise, straighten out, level, right the path of flight, point **die Klappe** ~ to restore the shutter
Aufrichten *n* raising
aufrichtendes Moment righting or restoring moment
Aufrichteprisma *m* image-rotation correcting prism, erecting prism
aufrichtig sincere, honest, frank, candid
Aufrichtmotor *m* precession motor, autopilot
Aufrichtübersprechen *n* erection cross-talk
Aufrichtung *f* erection, raising ~ **der Schichten** uplift of strata
Aufrichtungs-blende *f* erector stop **-prisma** *n* erecting prism **-vermögen** *n* static stability
Aufrichtvermögen *n* righting capacity (of a ship)
aufriegeln to unbolt
Aufriß *m* design, sketch, draft, elevation, vertical projection, section, or plan, front-elevation drawing, elevation of a building, layout

-zeichenvorrichtung *f* device for the drawing of plans of elevation **Ansicht in ~ und Schnitt** sectional elevation or view
Aufrißebene *f* vertical projection plane
aufritzen to tear up, scratch
aufrollen to clear, roll up, push back, roll back, coil, unroll, coil up, reel in, wire, wind up
Aufroller *m* stitcher stand, fleece roller, roller (winder)
Aufroll-maschine *f* coiling machine, reeling machine **-spule** *f* winding-on bobbin **-stuhl** *m* beaming machine
Aufrollung *f* rolling up
Aufrollungswalze *f* delivery reel
Aufrollwalze *f* batch(ing) roller, (beaming roller)
aufrücken to close up, advance, move up **~ lassen** to promote
Aufruf *m* proclamation, call, summons, subpoene
aufrufen to call up
Aufruf-leitung *f* read address line **-zahl** *f* call number
aufruhend supported
Aufruhr *m* revolt, mutiny, riot, insurrection
aufrührbar stirrable, agitable
aufrühren to stir (up), agitate, disturb (sediment)
Aufrührer *m* stirrer, agitator
aufrunden to even, round off, bring to the nearest round figure, approximate (math.) **eine Dezimale ~** to approximate a decimal
aufrüsten to arm, rearm, assemble, equip, rig
Aufrüsten *n* rigging
Aufrüstung *f* rearmament, plank scaffolding on a pontoon, armament
Aufrüstungsposition *f* rigging position
Aufrüstzeit *f* make-ready time (workfactor)
aufrütteln to rouse, shake up
aufsagen to give warning
aufsägen to saw
aufsammeln to pick-up, collect
Aufsattel *m* turntable (semi-trailer truck) **-druck** *m* king-pin load, fifth-wheel load **-vorrichtung** *f* fifth-wheel device; (Sattelschlepper) pivot coupling gear
Aufsattlungspunkt *m* (Sattelschlepper) pivot point
Aufsatz *m* fixture, attachment, headpiece, riser, top, cap, treatise, offtake, article, cowl, mounting, essay, ornament, gun sight, mount, optical or tangent sight, telescope mount, composition, any part put or set on, neck, dome **~ der Stange** finial, headpiece **~ stellen** to set the sight **~ für Aufsatzkopf** cylinder head box
Aufsatzamboß zum Biegen von Werkstücken creasing stake
Aufsatz-backe *f* face, jaw **-brett** *n* keyboard (print), cap **-band** *n* pin hinge **-büchse** *f* sight socket **-einsteller** *m* sight setter **-einteilung** *f* elevation graduations **-entfernung** *f* corrected range **-erhöhung** *f* corrected elevation **-fehler** *m* error in range **-fernrohr** *n* telescopic sight **-form** *f* forming die, rearing form, setting up or raising apparatus
Aufsatz-gehäuse *n* sight case, sight-mount housing, elevation-scale drum on dial sight **-hammer** *m* snap head die, cup-shaped die **-herd** *m* set-up range **-höhe** *f* elevation **-hülse** *f* backsight socket **-kasten** *m* mountable case **-klappe** *f* extension flap **-klaue** *f* top jaw **-knaggen** *pl* catches
Aufsatzkopiereinheit, schwenkbar detachable swiveling copying unit
Aufsatz-kränze *m pl* tubing rings **-libelle** *f* striding level **-ring** *m* adapter ring **-rohr** *n* upper portion of casing of drainage well, lengthening pipe
Aufsatz-schieber *m* sight (deflection) leaf, (rear sight) slide **-schlüssel** *m* socket wrench **-stab** *m* sight bar, tangent sight **-stange** *f* sight adjustment, sightbar, tangent sight **-stativ** *n* stockhead **-stück für Ankerachse** attachable piece for armature shaft **-stützen** *pl* catches, supports **-teilung** *f* range scale **-träger** *m* sight bracket or supports **-trieb** *m* elevation mechanism or handwheel on dial sight **-trommel** *f* angle-of-elevation dial, elevating drum **-verbesserung** *f* spotting correction (range)
Aufsatzwinkel *m* angle of elevation, tangent of elevation, superelevation under firing-table conditions **-trieb** *m* angle-of-elevation mechanism or gear
Aufsatzzeiger *m* sight indicator, telescope mount, reference pointer
aufsäubern to clean up
Aufsaugemasse *f* absorption mass
aufsaugen to absorb, suck up, soak, aspirate
aufsaugend absorbent **-es Mittel** absorbent
Aufsaugevermögen *n* absorption capacity, absorption power
Aufsaugung *f* absorption, suction, occlusion, imbibition
Aufsaugungsfähigkeit *f* absorptive capacity
aufschablonieren to stencil on
aufschalten to superimpose (a voltage) modulate, mix signals (guided missiles), control (automatic pilot)
Aufschalten (Teleph.) switching-in, listening-in
Aufschalterrelais *n* cutting-in relay (for preference service) **~ für Hausmarkierer** cut-in relay for local marker
Aufschaltezeichen *n* offering signal
Aufschaltgröße *f* signal mixing ration, magnitude of the command given (missiles) **-motor** *m* signal mixing motor (missiles)
Aufschaltung *f* intrusion, superimposition, modulation, signal mixing (ratio) (missiles), addition or imposition of a signal **~ der Steuermaschine** mixing ratio in the guide beam
Aufschaltwert *m* modulating coefficient, modulation factor
aufschärfen to prime
Aufschärfung *f* sharpening anew
aufschaukeln to amplify (waves)
Aufschaukeln *n* resonant rise, build up or increase of amplification (of oscillations, in proper phase) **~ der Schwingung** self-reinforcing or amplitude increase of a vibration **~ der Schwingungsanschläge** accumulation of amplitudes
Aufschaukelung des Signals resonant rise of a signal, step-up ratio of the signal
Aufschaukel-vorgang *m* building-up process **-zeit** *f* building-up time, time constant of resonant amplification
aufschäumen to foam up, froth, effervesce

Aufschäumen *n* excessive boiling, violent bubbling, effervescence, raise, foaming, frothing
aufscheren to warp
aufschichten to pile up, stack, staple, stratify, layer
Aufschichtung *f* stratification
aufschieben to delay, postpone, push open, defer **Förderwagen ~** to add tubs, insert tubs
Aufschieben *n* loading
Aufschieber *m* hanger-on
Aufschiebeschlaufe *f* slide, runner
Aufschiebung *f* postponement, adjournment, suspension, arrest (of judgment)
aufschiefern, sich (Holz) **~** to split up in shivers
aufschießen to coil or range (cable), rope, flemish down
Aufschießen *n* coiling
aufschirren to harness
aufschlacken to be reduced to dross
Aufschlag *m* mark-up, surcharge, impact, rebound, extra charge of fee, overcharge, facing, advance, rise, increase, excise, percussion, hit, cuff
Aufschlaganzeiger *m* indicator of impact
aufschlagen to impact, break open, open, increase, advence, strike (projectile), impinge, erect, hit, pitch, poach, brush out (paper) **ein Zelt ~** to pitch a tent; (ein Ende) **~** to unlay (rope)
Aufschlag-farbe *f* (Hängefarbe) suspender **-fläche** *f* impact surface **-gewinn** *m* loading profit
Aufschlagpunkt *m* point of impact, objective point **~ verlegen** to shift point of impact
Aufschlag-schutz *m* fire-prevention mechanism for crashes (aviation) **-tellerhorn** *n* stricking disc-type horn **-ventil** *n* kickoff valve **-wasser** *n* moving water **-weite** *f* horizontal distance from point of burst to point of impact, burst interval **-winkel** *m* angle of impact
Aufschlagzünder *m* percussion fuse, impact detonator **~ mit Verzögerung** delay fuse **~ ohne Verzögerung** nondelay fuse
Aufschlagzündung *f* ignition due to impact, ground burst, percussion ignition
aufschlämmen to suspend, reduce to slime, make into a paste
Aufschlämmung (von Ton) clay sludge
Aufschlämmungen *f pl* suspensions (colloid (chem.)
aufschleifen to match (electric current) **ein Stück ~** to grind on a piece
Aufschlemmung *f* solution, suspension
Aufschlemmverfahren *n* flotation method
Aufschleppe *f* slipway
aufschleppen to draw, haul up
Aufschlepphelling *f* hauling-up slip, slipway, slip for small craft, patent slip
aufschlicken to silt up
Aufschlickung *f* silting up
aufschließbar capable of being opened, unlockable, exploitable, decomposable
aufschließen to decompose, digest, open, unlock, tap, develop (mine), disintegrate, hydrolyze (starch), crush (cool), explain, disclose, render soluble, explore, dissolve, break (up or down), close ranks
Aufschließung *f* decomposition, digestion, opening
aufschlitzen to rip (open), slit
Aufschluß *m* treatment, digestion, decomposition, explanation, information, indication, exposure, outcrop, check (information), disclosure, discovery, criterion, data **~ des Rohberylls** dressing of the raw beryl
Aufschluß-bohrung *f* wildcat well, trial boring **~ einer Tiefbohranlage** deep-well drilling plant
Aufschlüsse *m pl* indications (oil)
aufschlüsseln to decode, classify **~ nach** to break down by
Aufschlüsselung *f* breakdown
Aufschluß-mittel *n* means of attack (chem.), hydrolizing agent (for sizes) **-raum** *m* part of prospected volume subject to current or displacement lines **-reich** very informative
Aufschlußverfahren *n* fusion process, hydrolizing process
aufschmelzen to melt on, sinter, fuse
Aufschmelzen *n* melting on, sintering, fusing
aufschneiden to cut or rip open
aufschnellen to jerk up, rebound
aufschnüren to trace in full size
aufschöpfen to scoop or dip up
aufschottern to gravel, coat or cover with small brocken stone
Aufschotterung *f* graveling, coating with broken rock
aufschraubbar capable of being screwed on
aufschrauben to thread on, screw on, unscrew **eine Mutter ~** to do up a nut
Aufschraubring *m* attachment ring
aufschreiben to write down, record
Aufschreiber *m* recorder
Aufschreibung *f* recording
Aufschrift *f* inscription, legend, address, label **mit einer ~ versehen** to address, label
aufschroten to mount by parbuckle, parbuckle
aufschrumpfen to shrink on, press on (barrel)
Aufschrumpfen *n* heat shrinking, shrink fitting
Aufschrumpfmethode *f* shrink-fitting method
Aufschrumpfung *f* shrunk fit
aufschrunden to cause to chap or crack
Aufschub *m* postponement, delay, suspense, adjournment, time extension, stay, prolongation, deferment, respite, suspension, moratorium **-vorrichtung, mechanische** automatic onsetting machine
aufschüren to stir up, poke, stoke
aufschütteln to shake up
aufschütten to pile, charge, coal, fill, deposit, feed (furnace) **Erde ~** to deposit the earth **trocken ~** to heap in a dry state **lose ~** to bulk
Aufschütten des Steinschlags coating with broken stones
Aufschütt-platte *f* fire plate **-rumpf** *m* feed hopper **-trichter** *m* (feeding) hopper
Aufschüttung *f* barrier, fill
Aufschüttungskegel *m* cone of debris
aufschwämmen to deposit (silt)
aufschwefeln to treat with sulfur, sulfurate
Aufschweißbiegeversuch *m* bending tests on built-up welded joints
aufschweißen to weld on, build up (by welding), solder, deposit, fuse, shut up **elektrisches ~** electrowelding

Aufschweißen *n* welding
Aufschweißlegierung *f* hard-facing alloy **-presse** *f* welding press
aufschwellen to swell up
aufschwemmen to deposit, float, wash
Aufschwemmung *f* deposit
Aufschwimmen *n* pivoting point in launching
Aufschwung *m* improvement, recovery, expansion **geschäftlicher ~** boom
Aufseher *m* supervisor, inspector, checker, keeper, warden, foreman, deputy
Aufsetzband *n* loop and hook, hinge with hook
aufsetzbar-er Kreuztisch attachable mechanical stage **-er Rundtisch** detachable circular table **-er Schablonenhalter** copy strip holder
Aufsetzbogenanleger *m* low pile feeder
aufsetzen to cover-print, pile, put on (paper), readjust (tape rec.), erect, superimpose, set up, word, draw up, put on, occur, touch down **gleich ~** phase, bring into phase; (ein Rohr) ~ to add (pipe)
Aufsetzen *n* cowling, keep, touching ground, lowering **~ der Stühle auf Querschwellen** fastening the chairs to the ties
Aufsetzkamera *f* camera attachment **~ mit Belichtungsmeßeinrichtung** camera attachment with exposure meter equipment
Aufsetz-kasten *m* jigger (dyeing), superimposed box **-licht** *n* contact or set-down light **-probe** *f* gas mask drill **-punkt** *m* landing point, touchdown point **-rahmen** *m* filling frame **-vorrichtung** *f* cage seat, holding apparatus, setting-up device **-zone** *f* touchdown zone
Aufsicht *f* supervision, control, inspection, top view, plan, plain view, care **-führender** *m* supervisor
Aufsichts-abteilung *f* supervisor's section **-beamter** *m*, **-beamtin** *f* supervisor, chief operator
Aufsichtsbehörde *f* supervising authority, supervision
Aufsichts-betrachtung *f* direct or frontal viewing (television) **-dienst** *m* supervisory work **-farbe** *f* reflected color **-platz** *m* chief operator's desk
Aufsichtsrat *m* board of directors **-mitglied** *n* director of the board **-vorsitzender** *m* chairman (of board of directors)
Aufsichts-sucher *m* view finder **-tisch** *m* chief operator's desk, monitoring desk **-turm** *m* control tower
aufsieden to boil up
Aufsilizieren *n* siliconizing
aufsitzen to mount, sit, seat **einen Bolzen ~ lassen** to jump a pin **das Ziel ~ lassen** to hold below the target in aiming, put the target
Aufsitzen des Ventils valve seating
aufsitzend, gut -es Ventil well-seated valve
Aufsitzfläche *f* valve seat **~ eines Klappventils** valve seat of a flap valve **~ eines Kugelventils** valva seat of a ball valve
aufspachteln to float
Aufspalt *m* catalysis
aufspalten to split up **in kleinste Teilchen ~** to atomize
Aufspalten *n* splitting up, slotting, cracking **~ von Eiweißsubstanzen** deproteinization
Aufspaltöl *n* cracked oil
Aufspaltung *f* splitting, splitting up, spalling, cleavage, exhaustion (potential energy), separation, division, dissociation **~ der Rotationsbänder** splitting of rotational lines
Aufspaltungs-bilder *n pl* splitting patterns (optics) **-erscheinung** *f* splitting phenomenon **-faktor** *m* splitting factor
Aufspann-block *m* vise, clamping plate or support **-bolzen** *m* work arbor
Aufspanndorn *m* mandrel, work holding arbor **verstellbarer ~** expanding mandrel
aufspannen to set, fix, clamp, stretch, spread out, unfold, mount (reel), tenter
Aufspanner *m* step-up transformer (elec.)
Aufspann-fläche *f* mounting table **-frosch** *m* clamp **-flansch** *m* fixing flange, clamping plate **-futter** *n* chuck (machine)
Aufspann-kasten *m* table of box type, slotted (for a drill) **-klaue** *f* clamp **-kopf** *m* work head **-maschine** *f* expanding machine **-platte** *f* adapter or clamping plate, fixing plate, bolster plate, die carrier plate **-schlitz** *m* fixing or T- slot, bolt slot **-schlitze oder -nuten** *pl* clamping grooves or slots **-spindel** *f* work holding spindle **-spindelstock** *m* work head **-tisch** *m* fixture, work table
Aufspannung *f* setting
Aufspannvorrichtung *f* clamping device, jig **elektromagnetische ~** magnetic chuck
Aufspann-werkzeug *n* clamping tool **-winkel** *m* angle plates, clamping angle **-zeit** *f* setting-up time
aufspeichern to store (up), warehouse, accumulate, stock, register, impound
Aufspeicherung *f* accumulation, storage, storing **~ des Wassers** impounding of water
aufsperren to spread apart, open wide, unlock
aufspießen, einen Stecknadelkopf ~ to string a pin
Aufspindelmaschine (zum Aufpressen) forcing machine (for printing rollers)
aufspleißen to fan out (a cable)
Aufpleißung *f* fanning out
aufsplittern to splinter, subdivide
Aufsprech-entzerrer *m* recording equalizer (tape rec.) **-kopf** *m* recording head
aufspreizbar capable of expanding
aufspringen to crack, split, rebound, burst open
aufspritzen to spray on, spray
Aufspritzen *n* (Metall) metallization **~ von Aluminium** aluminizing **~ flüssigen Metalles auf eine Oberfläche mittels Preßluft** metallization
aufsprudeln to bubble-up
Aufsprudeln *n* effervescence
aufspulen to spool, coil, wind (up, onto)
Aufspulen *n* coiling, winding
Aufspuler *m* reel
Aufspülung *f* hydraulic fill
Aufspulung, schnelle ~ fast forward
aufspunden to unbung
Aufstampfboden *m* bottom, turnover or joint board
aufstampfen to stamp on, tamp down, bank up, ram, ram up **eine Gußform ~** to ram up a mold
aufstapeln to pile up, stack, heap up, store up
Aufstapler *m* piler, stower
Aufstaplung *f* accumulation, storing, stack
Aufstau eines Flusses banking-up of a river

Aufstauelevator *m* piling or stowing elevator
Aufstäubebürste *f* dusting brush
aufstäuben (einen Überzug) to spray, dust, or atomize (a coat or film), powder
aufstauchen to upset, shorten, weld short and thick, dam up
aufstauen to retain, impound
aufstechen to pierce, perforate, puncture, fix (print)
Aufstechnadel *f* fixing needle
aufsteckbar attachable **-e Kappe** slip-on cap
Aufsteck-achse *f* extension shaft **-antenne** *f* plug-in antenna **-backe** *f* detachable cheek pad **-dorn** *m* arbor
Aufsteckdorne für Fräser arbors for shell end mills
aufstecken to slip on, hoist, put up, give in or up, insert, mount
Aufstecken *n* overplugging
Aufstecker *m* plug-in connection (elect.), stud inserter
Aufsteckfräser *m* shell end mill, arbor **~ mit Spiralzähnen** spiral-cut shell end mill
Aufsteck-fuß (Scheinwerfer) mounting socket **-gatter** *n* (bei der Spinnmaschine) creel (of a spinning frame, textiles), vertical creel **-glas** *n* slip-on lens segment **-griff** *m* insertion handle **-hals** *m* mounting neck
Aufsteckhalter *m* arbor (mounting), holder **~ für Reibahlen und Senker** arbors for shell reamers, countersinks and counterbores
Aufsteck-hebel *m* slip-on lever **-hülse** *f* extension tube **-kabelschuh** *m* slip-on cable socket **-kappe** *f* slip-on cap **-kurbel** *f* cranked handle **-nabensenker** *m* spot facers **-öse** *f* plug eye **-rahmen** *m* creel frame
Aufsteckreibahle *f* shell reamer **~ mit nachstellbaren Messern** adjustable-blade shell reamer
Aufsteckrohr *n* extension tube or rod **-schablone** *f* prong templet **-schlüssel** *m* socket wrench, box key **-senker** *m* shell drill, spot facer **-spindel** *f* skewer **-spule** *f* plug-in coil **-system** *n* spindle system **-wechselrad** *n* loose change gear **-werkzeug** *n* shell tool **-zubehör** *n* attachable accessories
aufstehen to rise, get up, stand up
aufsteigen to rise, ascend, go up, move up, pass up, travel up, bubble up, climb (aviat.), take to the air
Aufsteigen *n* elevation, ascension, rise
aufsteigend mounting, rising, ascending **-er Ast** ascending branch of trajectory **-e Differenz** forward difference **-e Komponente** upward component **-er Luftstrom** *m* up current **-e Strömung** upward current of air, upwind, upcurrent of air
Aufsteig-leiter *f* boarding ladder **-rohr** *n* rising pipe **-schacht** *m* climbing or gun shaft **-stelle** *f* base of ascent **-tritt** (Tankwagen) step bracket
Aufstellbahnhof *m* switching yard, make-up railroad yard
aufstellen (Bauten) erect; (Maschinen) assemble, set up, instal (specify) itemize; (Problem) state; (System) establish; (Tabelle) compile, mount, arrange, fit up, put up, draw up, make up, allocate, post, emplace, park, distribute, constitute
Aufsteller *m* erector
Aufstell-gleis *n* passing or switch siding (R.R.), make-up track **-plakat** *n* showcard **-platte** *f* base plate, adjustment plate **-punkt** *m* location
Aufstellung (Anordnung) arrangement; (Liste) schedule, list, statement; (Tabelle) tabulation, tabel; (Übersicht) survey; (Montage) assembly; (Maschine) erection, setting up; (Anlage) installation, specification, fitting (up), allocation, exposure, formation, distribution, disposition, establishment, graph, plan, formula, mounting position, record (accounts), compilation
Aufstellung am Betriebsort erection in the field **~ im Freien** outdoor location **Gleitbahn für ~** stop groove **~ im Innenraum** indoor location **~ der Inventarlisten** preparation of inventories **~ der Rechnungen** establishment or opening up of accounts
Aufstellung, flügelweise ~ units on line **gegliederte ~** successive order **jährliche statistische ~** annual returns **kordonartige ~** line of posts **schachbrettförmige ~** echelon formation **treppenweise ~** disposition in depth **zahlenmäßige ~** tabulation
Aufstellungs-befehl *m* initial organization order **-kosten** *f pl* cost of erection or installation **-ort** *m* site, location **-plan** *m* foundation or installation plan **-platz** *m* place of installation
aufstemmen tp pry open, open with chisel
aufstempeln to stamp on
Aufstieg *m* ascent (balloon), step, footstep (aviation), upstroke (of piston) **kapillarer ~** capillary rise **kurzer ~** pull-up (aviation)
Aufstieg(s)-bahn *f* climbing path (of rockets) **-bühne** *f* access platform **-flug** *m* ascent, climb (aviation) **-geschwindigkeit** *f* rate of climb **-kanal** *m* cable shaft or chute **-leiter** *m* climbing or mounting ladder
Aufstieg(s)-ort *m* place or point of departure **-platz** *m* ascension place, take-off field **-schacht** *m* climbing shaft **-spielraum** *m* margin of lift **-theorie** *f* theory of lift
Aufstieg- und Sinkgeschwindigkeit *f* speed of ascent and descent
Aufstieg-vorrichtung *f* high-lift devices **-winkel** *m* climbing angle **-zeit** *f* time of rise or ascent (of bubbles) (colloid chem.)
aufstiften to pin (to)
aufstöbern to ferret out
aufstocken to raise, ad a story
Aufstockregler *m* stack controller
aufstollen to stake
Aufstoßeinrichtung *f* transferring device
aufstoßen to push up, push open, transfer
Aufstoßvorrichtung *f* decking plant
aufstrahlen to shine
Aufstrahlstoff *m* fluorescent substance
aufstreben to have a tendency to rise
aufstrecken to hoist (put up), stretch a line or wire
aufstreichen to give off the dash signal, spread on, brush on, stain (paper)
Aufstreichmaschine *f* spreading machine
aufstreifen to slip on, thread on (to)
aufstreuen to spread over, sprinkle, strew
Aufstreupulver *n* sprinkling powder
Aufstrich *m* smear, leading edge or upstroke (of an impulse); (Lack) staining

Aufstrom *m* upcurrent
Aufströmung *f* upwash (meteor.)
Aufstromvergaser *m* updraft carburetor
aufstuhlen, die Schwellen einschneiden und ~ to adz and to fix the chairs on the ties
aufstülpen to turn up (the brim)
Aufstürzung *f* spoil bank, side piling (R.R.)
aufstützen to shore up, support
aufsuchen to search, locate, see, find, explore
Aufsuchen *n* discovery, search, finding
Aufsuchung *f* prospecting, exploration, scouting
Aufsummen *n* porpoise (aviation)
auftafeln to plait down
auftakeln to rig
Auftakt *m* initial phase
auftaljen to bouse
auftanken to refuel
Auftankvorrichtung *f* refueling device
Auftastgenerator *m* gate generator
Auftastimpuls *m* gating pulse **-auslösediode** *f* gate trigger diode **-kreis** *m* double limiter, gate of entry, window (radar)
auftauchen to (rise to the) surface, emerge, appear, arise (question) **das U-Boot taucht auf** the submarine surfaces
Auftauchen *n* surfacing of a submarine **zum ~ bereitmachen** to rig for surface
auftauen to melt, thaw
Auftauen, ~ der Bohrlöcher thawing boreholes **~ tiefgekühlter Lebensmittel** food defrosting
Auftaugerät *n* thawing device
Auftauung *f* thawing
Aufteileinrichtung *f* equalizing device
aufteilen to distribute, split up **prozentuales ~** percentual break down
Aufteilmuffe *f* cable distributing sleeve
Aufteilung *f* break-down, division, sectioning, distribution
Aufteilungs-filter *n* crossover network (sound production) **-kabel** *n* distributing cable **-verhältnis** *n* potentiometer ratio
auftiefen to emboss
Auftiefmeißel *m* drift
Auftourenkommen des Motors picking up of motor
Auftrag *m* (Beauftragung) commission, charge; (Bestellung) order; (Bau) contract; (Weisung) direction, instruction; (Farbe) application, laying on, embankment, fill(ing) (in earthwork), contract, coat (of paint), mission, task **~ erledigt** mission accomplished **Lichtbild ~** photographic mission **im ~** by order of (above a signature on a document), in charge **einen ~ erteilen** to issue an order **erster ~ von Lack** bottom coat
Aufträge-bestand *m* orders on hand **-geschwindigkeit** *f* rate of deposition
Auftragemaschine *f*, **Zement-~** cement laying-on machine
auftragen, Auftrag (Farben) to coat, lay on, apply; (Straßenbau) fill, embank, plot or trace (curves), cover, face, illustrate graphically, add, charge, put on, charge (a furnace), protract (geom.) **eine Aufmessung ~** to protract a survey **die Farbe auf die Form ~** to roll the form, take ink **Kurvenwerte ~** to plot against **Schweißraupe ~** to build up a bead
Auftragen *n* application (color) **~ von Hartmetall** hard facing
Auftrageröllchen *n* ink roller, ink wheel
Auftrag-geber *m* employer, one who has work done by contract, customer, client, principal, mandator, orderer, contractor **-maschine** *f* coating machine **-nehmer** *m* contractor **-rollen** *f pl* application rollers, inking rollers **-schweißen** to fill up irregularities
Auftrags-abteilung *f* order department **-dienst** *m* service interception, absentee service **-erteilung** *f* distribution of orders, assignment of a mission, placing an order **-karte** *f* flight diagram **-lenkung** *f* allocation of business and government order according to a general plan **-lenkungsbüro** *n* office for the distribution of orders **-nummer** *f* order number **-rückstand** *m* accumulation of unfilled orders **-schüssel** *f* dip tank **-schicht** *f* coating thickness **-schweißen** *n* building-up welding, electro-slag welding, hardfacing, resurfacing **-umfang** *m* size of order **-weise** *f* in accordance with instructions **-zettel** *m* order slip or sheet
Auftragung *f* plotting (of a map), inking (color)
Auftragwalze *f* application roll, casting roll, inking roller or cylinder, printing roller, inker
Auftragwalzen-lager *n* journal box **-rolle** *f* runner for inking rollers **-schloß** *n* journal box
aufträufeln to trickle down drop by drop
Auftreffelektrode *f* target electrode
auftreffen to strike, impinge (upon), abut (against), encounter **~ von Zahn auf Zahn** butting of teeth
Auftreffen *n* impingement, impact **~ der Elektronen** electron bombardment
auftreffend incident (optics)
Auftreffenergie *f* striking energy
Auftrefffläche *f*, **flüssige ~** liquid target
Auftreff-gelände *n* area of impact **-geschwindigkeit** *f* striking, impact, or final velocity **-platte** *f* target **-punkt** *m* point of impact
Auftreffwinkel *m* angle of impact or incidence **schräger ~** oblique incidence angle
Auftreffwucht *f* force of impact
auftreibbar expanding
Auftreibeisen *n* blowpipe
auftreiben to force on or up, drive on, ascend, travel up, blow up, buoy up
Auftreiben *n* expanding **~ eines Loches** opening out a hole
Auftreiber *m* reamer
Auftreibung des Bodens sinking of the subsoil
auftrennen to sever, rip up or open **eine Leitung ~** to interrupt a line (elec.)
Auftrenn-technik *f* sectional toll switching (aut. telephony) **-zeit** *f* splitting time
auftreten to occur, appear, crop up, accrue, be apparent, be liberated
Auftreten *n* occurence, appearance, bearing, demeanor **~ einer saugheberartigen Wirkung** siphoning **zufälliges ~** (einer Erscheinung) occurrence
Auftrieb *m* uplift, buoyancy, flow, lift (aviation), upward (hydraulic) pressure on foundations, draft (of chimney), force, upthrust, aerodynamic lift, ascendency **statischer ~** buoyant lift, buoyancy **dynamischer ~** positive buoyancy or

lift
auftrieberzeugende Strebe *f* lift strut
Auftrieb(s)-achse *f* lift axis, **-änderung** *f* lift change or variation **-beiwert** *m* lift or buoyancy coeffiient **-bestimmung** *f* lift indication **-beizahl** *f* lift factor
auftriebserhöhend lift-increasing, lift-boosting, liftaugmenting **-e Einrichtung** lift-increasing device
Auftrieb(s)-erhöhung *f* increase of lift **-erzeugung** *f* coefficient of lift **-formel** *f* equation of lift, lift formula **-koeffizient** *m* lift coefficient **-komponente** *f* coefficient of lift (aviation) **-korrektur** *f* correction of buoyancy **-kraft** *f* buoyant force, upward or lifting force **-kurve** *f* curve of buoyancy
Auftrieb(s)-methode *f* float or buoyant-force method (hydrometer) **-mine** *f* buoyant moored mine **-mittel** *n* buoying agent, lifting medium **-mittelpunkt** *m* center of buoyancy, center of displacement, center of lift **-nullpunkt** *m* zero angle of lift **-ofen** *m* glory hole, an auxiliary furnace for finishing glassware **-parabel** *f* lift parabola **-resultierende** *f* resultant of lift **-richtung** *f* direction of lift **-schwankung** *f* fluctuation of lift, lift change or variation **-schwerpunkt** *m* center of buoyancy
Auftrieb(s)-spindellager *n* elevating screw bearing **-tank** *m* buoyancy tank **-theorie** *f* theory of lift **-veränderlich** variable lift **-vermehrung** *f* increase of lift **-verminderung** *f* decrease of lift **-verteilung** *f* lift distribution **-vorrichtung** *f* high-lift devices
Auftriebs-waage *f* lift balance **-wasser** *n* upwelling **-wirbel** *m* lift vortex **-zahl** *f* lift coefficient (aviation) **-zentrum** *n* center of buoyancy or lift
Auftritt *m* tread, tread width (of stairs), banquette (fort.), fire step (trench), berm, step, platform, foothold **-stufe** *f* banquette **-stütze** *f* step bracket
auftrocknen to dry, dry up
auftropfen to apply by dropping
Auftropflegierung *f* metalizing alloy
auftuchen to furl
auftürmen, sich ~ to tower, pile up, accumulate
auf- und abbauen, sich ~ to pile-off and pile-on
Auf- und Abbewegung *f* up-and-down movement, heaving motion
Auf- und Abspanner *m* (regulating) transformer (elec.)
Auf- und Abwärtsbewegung *f* moving up and down up-and-down motion
Auf- und Abwindhaspel *f* wheeled cable drum carriage
Auf- und Abziehen *n* mounting and dismantling
Auf- und Abziehpressen mounting and demounting presses
auf- und niedergehende Sonde hunting probe
Auf- und Zuklappen *n* opening and closing
aufvulkanisieren to vulcanize on
aufwachen to awake, wake up
aufwalken to wet back
aufwallen to bubble, effervesce, boil up
Aufwallen *n* raise, violent agitation, wildness, bubbling up, boiling, gassing **atmosphärisches ~** surge
Aufwallung *f* wildness, bubbling, ebullition, effervescence
aufwältigen to clear, clear up a mine
Aufwältigung *f* clearing out
aufwalzen to roll on, ink up (form) **ein Kesselrohr ~** to expand a boiler tube
Aufwalz-flansch *m* expanded flange **-maschine** *f* expanding machine **-vorrichtung** *f* roll coater
Aufwand *m* expenditure, expenses, consumption, display, input, effort **~ an Arbeit** wasting of time **technischer ~** technical resources
Aufwandsentschädigung *f* compensation for expenses, allowance
aufwärmen to warm up, heat slightly
Aufwärmen *n* warm up
Aufwärmer *m* reboiler
aufwarten to serve, wait upon
Aufwärter *m* attendant, steward **-in** *f* stewardess
aufwärtige Wendung über dem Landungspunkt overhead approach
aufwärts up, upward **-biegen** to turn up **-bewegen** to raise upward, move up **-bewegung** *f* upward motion, ascent, upward movement or tendency, upstroke **-flug** *m* climbing flight **-gang** *m* (Kolben) upward stroke **-gehen** *n* up-stroke **-gerichteter (Luft-)Strom** ascending current **-hub** *m* upward stroke, upstroke, ascent **-lüftung** *f* upcast ventilation
aufwärts-schalten to change to higher gear **-schweißen** to weld up-hand **-seilung** *f* inclined upward **-strebend** buoyant **-strömen** to flow upward **-strömung** *f* upward flow **-transformator** *m* step-up transformer **-transformieren** to step up **-transformierung** *f* step up **-trudeln** *n* upward spin **-wandler** *m* step-up transformer (radio)
aufwaschen to wash up
Aufwaschmaschine *f* washing-up machine
aufwecken to wake up, rouse
aufweichen to soften, soak, moisten
aufweichend emollient, softening
aufweisen to show, exhibit, have, experience
Aufweitedorn *m* flaring expander
aufweiten to expand, bulge, ream up, enlarge, open put
Aufweite-presse *f* reaming press **-probe** *f* drift test, bulging test
aufweitern to expand **ein Rohr ~** to open out a pipe (mouth)
Aufweite- und Bördelmaschine *f* socketting and flanging machine
Aufweite-walzwerk *n* becking mill, expanding mill **-werkzeug** *n* flaring tool
Aufweitung *f* recess, expansion, bulge out
Aufweitversuch *m* bulging test; (Rohre) drift test
aufwenden to spend, expend, employ
Aufwendung *f* expenditure
Aufwendungen *pl* oberheads
Aufwendungsposten *pl* expense items
aufwerfen to throw up, charge, pile up **sich ~** to warp, presume
Aufwerfhammer *m* helve hammer, lift hammer, tilt hammer, trip hammer, fly hammer, forge hammer
aufwerten to revalorize, reassess
Aufwertung *f* reevaluation, reassessment, stabilization (currency)
Aufwickel-apparat *m* take-up roller **-friktion** *f*

reeling friction **-hülse** *f* winding sleeve **-länge** *f* coiling length (of drum) **-maschine** *f* reeling machine

aufwickeln to spool, coil, wind (up, onto), wrap up or upon, take up (film), unwind, unwrap

Aufwickel-punkt *m* winding point **-rolle** *f* batching roller **-spule** *f* take-up reel (motion pictures), winding spool or bobbin **-trommel** *f* aerial drum **-vorrichtung** *f* winding-on device (motion) **-walze** *f* re-winding roller **-werk** *n* rewinding devise

Aufwicklung *f* rolling-up arrangement

aufwiegen to outweigh, counterbalance, compensate for (make up for)

Aufwind *m* ascending air current, anabatic wind, upcurrent, upwash, upwind, upslope wind, updraft **-bö** *f* bump

Aufwinde-draht *m* faller-wire **-drehzahl** *f* winding-on speed **-fortschaltkurve** *f* winding-on cam **-haspel** *f* winding winch

aufwinden to lift (up), jack up, wind up or onto, hoist, reel

Aufwinderbewegung *f* faller motion

Aufwinde-röhre *f* bobbin, cop, prim **-trommel** *f* winch **-vorrichtung** *f* jacking equipment **-welle** *f* faller shaft

Aufwind-feld *n* region of upward or ascending currents **-gebiet** *n* region of upward ascending currents

Aufwindgeschwindigkeit *f* (lineare Zunahme des Aufwindes) linear increase of velocity of ascending or upward currents

Aufwindungsverhältnis *n* winding condition

Aufwind-wert *m* amount of ascending or upward current **-zone** *f* upwind region

aufwirbeln to whirl up, raise (dust etc.)

aufwischen to mop

Aufwischlappen *m* swab

aufwölben to bulge

Aufwölbung *f* anticlinal bulges, arching (geol.)

Aufwolfung *f* upwarping (of strata)

Aufwurf *m* parapet, mound **-hammer** *m pl* **mit Gummipuffer** rubber-cushion helve hammers

aufzählen to enumerate, list, itemize

Aufzählung *f* enumeration, summarization, addition, summation, total, specification

aufzehren to absorb, consume, dissipate

Aufzehrgrad *m* degree of consumption or absorption

Aufzehrung *f* absorption, consumption, dissipation

Aufzeichenvorrichtung *f* recording apparatus

aufzeichnen to plot, draw, outline, record (instruments), register, sketch, note, indicate, trace **eine Schaulinie ~** to establish a curve **Stromlinien ~** to map or plot tubes or lines of force

Aufzeichnen *n* plotting

aufzeichnendes Thermometer recording thermometer

Aufzeichnung *f* outline, drawing, notation, record, sketch, memorandum, notification, recordings or minutes of proceedings, plot (sketch), recording (of observations) **unmittelbare ~** direct recording **~ des Belegungszählers** call-count record **~ der Gesprächsanmeldungen** booking, recording of calls **~ des Verkehrsmeßgerätes** traffic record, call-count record

Aufzeichnungs-dauer *f* duration of recording **-dichte** *f* recording density **-kammer** *f* recording chamber (in electron microscope) **-konstante** *f* recording constant **-kontrolle** *f* monitoring (of sound recording or sound tracks) **-kopf** *m* recording head **-kopfpolspalt** *m* recording head pol gap

Aufzeichnungslampe, Aeo ~ alkaline-earth-oxide lamp or light

Aufzeichnungs-objektiv *n* recording objective **-röhre** *f* recording tube **-schlitz oder -spalt** *m* recording slit or aperture

Aufzeichnungsträger *m* record or track support (sound on film, disk) **~ in der Bildtelegraphie** record means (tape), recording medium, in facsimile-record member (drum)

Aufzeichnungsumfang *m* recording range

Aufzeichnungs- und Wiedergabe-Bandgeschwindigkeitsabweichungsmeeser *m* tape fluttermeter

Aufzeichnungsverfahren *n* recording principle

Aufzieh-achse *f* winding stem **-apparat für Hefe** yeast-raising apparatus

aufziehbar retractable **-es Fahrgestell** retractable landing gear

Aufzieheisen *n* tire lever

aufziehen to draw up, pull up; (hochziehen) lift, hoist; (öffnen) open, draw open; (Reifen) fit on; (Unternehmen) arrange, organize; (Wählscheibe) pull round (the dial), wind up, screw up, stall, force on, shrink on, draw near, form, mount or paste (pictures), reeve (a wire line), pull round (dial), approach (said of bad weather), attach, stretch (sheet) **schnell ~** to rush on

Aufziehen *n* winding up; (eines Farbstoffes) absorption

Aufzieh-fenster *n* sash window, cased sash, slide window **-geschwindigkeit** *f* speed of absorption **-hammer** *m* chasing hammer **-hebel** *m* lever ratchet **-karton** *m* mounting board **-leine** *f* release cord, static line (parachute)

Aufzieh-ring *m* pull ring **-schnüre** *pl* simple cords **-stange** *f* drawing rod **-stift** tightening toggle, draw pin **-vermögen** *n* affinity **-vorrichtung** *f* hoisting apparatus, tension device (for rubber motor) **-werk** *n* winding-up mechanism

Aufzipfelung *f* lobing (of antenna pattern), side lobes

Aufzischen *n* fizzing

aufzischen to fizz

Auf-Zu open-close, on-off

Aufzug *m* (Fahrstuhl) elevator, lift, hoist, packing (cylinder), slope of parapet, elevation, second coat (on wall), crane, cage, parade **~ mit seitlichem Verschluß** side-door elevator **schräger ~** inclined elevator

Aufzug(s)-bewegung *f* winding cycle **-bogen** *m* packing sheet **-brücke** *f* drawbridge **-bühne** *f* elevator platform **-gerüst** *n* elevator frame, hoist structure **-haken** *m* hoisting hook **-hebel** *m* tilting lever

Aufzug(s)-kabine *f* lift car, elevator cage **-kasten** *m* hoisting bucket **-klappe** *f* tympan clamp, cylinder dressing clamp **-kloben** *m* hoisting block **-knopf** *m* winding knob **-kombination** *f* cylinder packing **-lehre** *f* cylinder packing gauge **-leine** *f* rip cord, release cord (parachute) **-motor** *m* hoisting motor **-maschine**

f hoisting engine, winchoperating engine **-mechanismus** *m* winding mechanism

Aufzug(s)-öse hoisting device **-papier** *n* mounting paper tympan **-schacht** *m* elevator shaft **-schiene** *f* packing clamp **-seil** *n* hoisting rope, lift or elevator hoisting rope or cable **-spannvorrichtung** *f* stretching device **-sperre** *f* stop work **-stärke** *f* packing thickness **-stellung** *f* point in the winding cycle **-steuerleitung** *f* lift control cable **-steuerung** *f* elevator-control gear **-tür** *f* lift door **-wagen** *m* hoist carriage **-winde** *f* hoisting winch

Aufzweigung *f* branching

aufzwingen to force upon

Aug (Ausnietgroßvorrichtung) riveting jig or rig

Augapfel *m* eyeball, bulbus (electronics)

Augbändsel *m* seizing throat

Augbolzen *m* eyebolt

Auge *n* eye, eyelet, lug, boss ~ **der Führung** (slang) reconnaissance aircraft ~ **des Sturms** eye of the storm (meteor.) **akkomodationsloses** ~ unaccommodated or fixed eye **alterssichtiges** ~ presbyopic eye **berichtigtes** ~ corrected eye **bewaffnetes** ~ aided eye **aus dem** ~ **verlieren** to lose sight of **mit bloßen** ~ with the naked eye **dunkel adaptiertes** ~ dark-adapted eye **elektrisches** ~ photoelectric eye

Auge, entspanntes ~ relaxed eye **fehlsichtiges** ~ defectively sighted eye, ametropic eye **fernakkomodiertes** ~ relaxed eye **fernsichtiges** ~ farsighted eye, hyperopic eye **kurzsichtiges** ~ shortsighted eye, myopic eye **magisches** ~ magic eye, visual tuning indicator **mittleres normales** ~ average eye (standard eye for photometry) **nahsichtiges** ~ nearsighted eye, myopic eye **rechtsichtiges** ~ normal-sighted eye, emmetropic eye **unbewaffnetes** ~ unaided eye, naked eye **weitsichtiges** ~ farsighted eye, hyperopic eye

Augen *n pl* eyes **in die** ~ **fallend** conspicuous **in die** ~ **springend** salient

Augen-abstand *m* interocular distance, interpupillary distance **-achat** *m* cats eye, eyestone **-achse** *f* optic axis **-abstandsmesser** *m* interpupillary distance gauge **-anpassung** *f* eye adaption (to wave length of light), eye accomodation (to changes of distance) **-anstrengung** *f* eyestrain **-ärztliches Besteck** ophthalmic diagnostic set **-aufklärung** *f* visual reconnaissance **-beobachtung** *f* visual observation **-bestrahlungsgerät** *n* eye-radiation apparatus **-blick** *m* instant, moment

augenblicklich instantly, at present, instantaneous, momentary **-e Rotationsachse** axis of instantaneous rotation

Augenblicks-aufnahme *f* instantaneous photograph, snapshot **-belastung** *f* momentary or instantaneous load **-bild** *n* snapshot **-leistung** *f* instantaneous power **-pegel** *m* actual level **-schalter** *m* quick-break switch **-spannung** *f* instantaneous voltage

Augenblicks-stereoaufnahme *f* instantaneous stereo photograph **-strom** *m* instantaneous current **-verschluß** *m* instantaneous shutter (of a camera) **-wert** *m* instantaneous value, momentary value **-wirkung** *f* instantaneous action or effect **-ziel** *n* fleeting target or objective, momentary or transient target **-zünder** *m* instantaneous (high-sensitive) fuse

Augen-bolzen *m* eyebolt, screw ring **-bolzenmuffe** *f* eyebolt sleeve **-brechungsmesser** *m* skiascope, retinoscope **-diagnostiker** *m* ophthalmic (eye) diagnostician **-drehpunkt** *m* center of rotation of the eye **-eigenlicht** *n* self-light, intrinsic light of eye or retina, eye's own light **-empfindlichkeit** *f* intensity discrimination, contrast sensitivity **-erkundung** *f* visual reconnaissance **-fällig** evident **-farbenempfindlichkeit** *f* color or spectral sensitivity of eye, spectral response of eye **-fenster** *n* eyepiece (gas mask) **-glas** *n* sight glass

Augen-hintergrund *m* fundus of the eye **-höhe** *f* eye level, range of vision of officer on bridge or from conning tower **-höhle** *f* socket of eye, orbit, orbital cavity **-hügel** *m pl* palpebral lobes of the eyes **-kreis** *m* exit pupil **-korrektionsfehler** *m* color-correction filter **-lager** *n* solid journal bearing **-lehre** *f* ophthalmology **-lichtempfindlichkeit** *f* luminosity response of eye **-lid** *n* eyelid **-linse** *f* eye lens **-linsenfaserung** *f* fibrillation of lens

Augenmaß *n* measuring by sight, measure taken by the eye **nach dem** ~ **zeichnen** to draw by sight **nach** ~ **gerade** straight to the eye

Augenmaßaufnahme *f* free sketch

Augen-medien *pl* ocular media **-merk** *n* point of view, aim, attention **-messer** *m* ophthalmometer, optometer **-muschel** *f* cup of the eyepiece, eyecup, eye guard, eyeshield **-optik** *f* ophthalmic articles **-pulver** *n* very small print **-punkt** *m* station point, point of sight, eyepoint, exit pupil, eyepit **-reizstoff** *m* lachrymator, tear gas **-ring** *m* eyepiece frame (gas mask) **-schärfe** *f* visual acuity (TV)

Augenschein *m* appearance, evidence, sense of sight **in** ~ **nehmen** to inspect, look at closely

augenscheinlich obvious, apparent, seeming, visible, probable, self-evident, ocular

Augen-schirm *m* (reader's) shade **-schlitz** *m* viewing slit **-schraube** *f* eyebolt **-schützer** *pl* goggles **-spiegel** *m* ophthalmoscope, skiascope **-stäbchen** *n pl* cones (of nerve endings) **-stern** *m* pupil **-täuschung** *f* optical illusion **-textur** *f* orbicular structure **-trägheit** *f* persistence of vision (TV) **-verbindung** *f* visual communication **-zäpfchen** *pl* rods (of nerve endings) **-zerstreuungsbilder** *n pl* blur circles of eye **-zeuge** *m* eyewitness **-zittern** *n* nystagmus

Auger-Ausbeute *f* Auger yield **-Effekt** *m* Auger effect **-Koeffizient** *m* Auger coefficient **-Übergang** *m* Auger transition

Augit *m* augite **körniger** ~ coccolite

augitartig augitic

Augpunkt *m* south pole

Augspleiß *m*, **Augspleißung** *f* eye splice

Augustinprozeß *m* Augustin (brine-leaching) process

auktionieren to auction

A- und B-Betrieb im Fernverkehr no-delay working, A-board toll traffic

A- und B-Leitungsdraht line wire

Auralnull *f* aural null

Auramin *n* auramine

Aureole *f* show, glory, aureole, corona, firedamp cap

Aureomyzin *n* aureomycin

Aurichlorwasserstoffsäure *f* chloroauric acid

Auripigment *n* orpiment, yellow arsenic sulfide
Auriverbindung *f* auric compound
Auro-chlorid *n* aurous chloride **-kaliumzyanid** *n* potassium aurocyanide
aus off (on a switchboard)
ausaalen to flush out (drains)
ausarbeiten to work out, prepare, elaborate, make up, draft, carve, make perfect
Ausarbeiten des Vorprojektes preliminary engineering for the project
Ausarbeitung *f* elaboration, preparation, finish and finishing of machine parts
ausarten to degenerate
ausästen to trim (trees), to prune (electr. lines)
Ausästen *n* pruning
Ausästwerkzeug *n* tree trimmer
Ausatemventil *n* exhaling valve, flutter valve (gas mask)
ausäthern to shake out with ether
ausatmen to expire
ausätzen to cauterize, destroy by caustic
Ausbacken *n* baking (of insulating coils)
ausbaggern to dredge, excavate, dig out, mark with buoys
Ausbaggern *f* **eines Kanals** dredging a canal
ausbalancieren to balance out, counterbalance, balance, compensate
ausbalancierter Anker balanced armature
Ausbalancierung *f* balancing, compensation (electr.)
Ausbau *m* (Fertigstellung) completion; (Vergrößerung) extension, enlargement; (Entwicklung) development, improvement; (Abbau) removal, dismounting, consolidation, construction, establishment, disassembly, dismantling, logging, timbering, walling, removing **~ mittels Holzpfeilern** pigsty timbering **~ rechteckiger, mit behauenen Balken** chock, square timber **~ wasserdichter** crib tubbing **beim ~ der Bank** when removing shelf, ground **erster ~** first section to be constructed **im ersten ~** on first establishment
Ausbauarbeiten *pl* bit charging
ausbaubar extensible, detachable **-er Steuerknüppel** control stick **-er Steuerungsknüppel** control column
Ausbaubelastung (Straßen) desgin loading (roads)
ausbauchen to bulge, bulge out, belly out camber **sich ~** to widen, bulge, swell, hollow out
Ausbauchung *f* bulging out, bulging, batter, bulge, oil can (aviation), swell, hollow, groove, bellying, widening, expansion **~ eines Ganges** widening of a lode
Ausbauchungsfaktor *m* fullness factor, curve factor
ausbauen (fertigstellen) to complete; (vergrößern) extend, enlarge; (entwickeln) improve, develop; (festigen) consolidate; (abbauen) remove, dismount, disassemble, to dismantle, equip, snub (pressure), demount
ausbaufähig, ~ für 25 Teilnehmer (Telef.) extensible to 25 lines **nicht ~** not extensible **-e Doppelsteuerung** detachable dual controls
Ausbau-großvorrichtung *f* large construction fixture jig or rig **-höhe** *f* overhead space
Ausbauleistung *f* ultimate capacity **~ eines Kraftwerkes** capacity of a power station when completed
Ausbaumaterial eines Schachtes shaft-lining material
Ausbau-möglichkeit *f* accommodation for an ultimate growth **-plan** *m* development study **-stufe** *f* serial-model modification **-wassermenge** *f* design flow (hydraulic power st.) **-werkstoff** *m* lining material
ausbedingen to stipulate
ausbeißen to crop out (oil)
ausbeizen to stain, cauterize
ausbessern to repair, amend, recondition, reline, patch, redress, improve, rectify, fettle
Ausbesserung *f* repair, relining, patching, remarking **einstweilige ~** temporary repair
Ausbesserungen mit federförmigen Rand "feather-edge" patches
Ausbesserungs-abteilung *f* repair gang **-arbeit** *f* repair work **-bedürftig** in need of repair **-fähig** reparable **-grube** *f* inspection pit **-kraftfahrzeug** *n* repair car **-zeit** *f* system improvement time **-zeitfaktor** *m* per cent time out
ausbeulen to flatten, planish, buckle, plane, buckle out, bulge, straighten, beat out, shallow, round out, take out dents (in a metal part)
Ausbeulen *n* buckling
Ausbeulung *f* buckling (of plates), dent
Ausbeute *f* yield, output, gain, profit, recovery, efficiency **~ liefern** to produce output **photoelektrische ~** photoelectric emissivity or yield **~ pro Stufe** fractional yield
Ausbeute-erhöhung *f* increased output or yield **-formel** *f* formula for calculation of yield **-gleichung** *f* gain equation **-grad** *m* yield
ausbeuteln to sift
Ausbeute-matrix *f* efficiency matrix **-mengen** *pl* yields **-messungen** *pl* yield measurements
ausbeuten to work, exploit, deplete
Ausbeuter *m* exploiter
Ausbeute-tabelle *f* yield table **-tensor** *m* efficiency tensor
Ausbeuteverteilung *f*, **spektrale lichtelektrische ~** color sensitivity or response, spectrophotoelectrical sensitivity
Ausbeutezeche *f* dividend mine, productive mine
Ausbeutung *f* exploitation, working
Ausbeutungsplätze *m pl*, **ergiebige ~** payable places
ausbezahlen to pay in full
ausbiegen to bend out, deflect, turn out
Ausbiegestelle *f* splitting-up line, turnout (R.R.)
Ausbiegung *f* deflection
ausbieten to offer for sale
ausbilden to form, improve, perfect, train, develop, drill, instruct, educate
Ausbilder *m* instructor
Ausbildung *f* formation, development, perfection, construction, manufacture, training, education, drill **~ und Anordnung eines verzweigten Rohrleitungssystems** manifolding of pipe-line system **~ am Doppelsteuer** dual instruction **aerodynamisch günstige ~** cleanness (aerodyn.)
Ausbildungs-abteilung *f* division for training **-anweisung** *f* training order **-einrichtung** *f* training apparatus or facility **-gerät** *n* training

equipment or instrument **-handbuch** *n* training manual **-kursus** *m* course of instruction

Ausbildungs-plan *m* training schedule **-richtlinie** *f* training outline or regulations **-schiff** *n* training ship **-stab** *m* training staff **-stand** *m* state of training **-stelle** *f* training center **-stufe** *f* training phase **-vorschrift** *f* training manual, drill regulations

ausbinden to loosen, untie, assemble, frame (in building)

Ausbindeschnur *f* page cord (print)

Ausbiß *m* basset, escarpment, ourtcrop ~ **eines Kohlenflößes** outcrop coal

Ausblähung *f* efflorescence

Ausblase-apparat *m* dust extractor, bellows (print) **-bohrung** *f* exhaust bore **-butte** *f* blow pit, tank, vat **-dampf** *m* exhaust steam **-düse** *f* blast jet (nozzle) **-hahn** *m* blowoff cock **-leitung** *f* blowoff pipe **-luft** *f* exhaust air **-mundstück** *n* exhaust nipple

Ausblasen *n* blowing out

ausblasen to blow (out), blow down, exhaust, deflate, dust off, clean off, discharge a boiler or digester under pressure

Ausbläser *m* blown-out shot, weak charge

Ausblase-stutzen *m* outlet connecting piece **-ventil** *n* blowout valve, outlet or sluice valve **-verteiler** *m* blow-out or blowing-down distributor (submarine)

Ausblas-fläche *f* escape surface **-öffnung** *f* blow-out port (rocket), blow-off outlet **-pistole** *f* blowout gun **-rohr** *n* blast pipe **-stutzen** *m* extractor socket

ausblatten to jak, calk

ausbleiben to stay away, fail to come **die Zündungen bleiben aus** the ignition fails

Ausbleiben *n* absence

ausbleichen to bleach out

Ausbleichen *n* bleaching

Ausbleichverfahren *n* bleaching-out process

ausbleien to lead (joints) line with lead, shield (in radiography), provide with a lead coating

ausblenden to mask with apertured diaphragm or stop, limit the field, diaphragm out, cut down aperture of a stop, iris out, circle out, cut out (tape rec.), fade-out (film)

Ausblenden *n* fade out (elec.), fade down (elec.)

Ausblend-mittel *n* limiting aperture, screening, masking or stopping means **-steuerung** *f* obturator or cutoff modulation **-stufe** *f* double limiter gate (radar), gate

Ausblendung *f* scattering (of rays)

Ausblick *m* objective lens, outlook, view, prospect **freier** ~ unobstructed view

Ausblick-kopf *m* (eines Sehrohrs) reflector head **-öffnung** *f* base reflector window **-prismengehäuse** *n* objective-prism housing **-rohr** *n* objective-lens tube or adapter **-stutzen** *m* objective-lens socket

ausblühen to come up to the grass, be in efflorescence, bloom

Ausbluten *n* (Farbe) bleeding

ausbluten (Lack) to bleed

Ausblühen *n* blooming, bleed

Ausblühung *f* effiorescence, blistering (in welding)

ausböden, ein Faß ~ to head a cask

Ausbogemaschine *f* scalloping or festoon frame

ausbogen to (cut a) channel

Ausbohr-arbeit *f* boring (operation) **-drehbank** *f* boring lathe

ausbohren to bore (out), drill out

Ausbohr-maschine *f* boring machine **-spindel** *f* boring or cutting bar **-stahl** *m* (inside) boring tool

Ausbohrung *f* bore

Ausbohrvorrichtung *f* reboring equipment

ausbojen to buoy (a channel)

ausbooten to disembark

Ausbootung *f* debarkation

Ausbrand *m* (Kondensator) combustion, final combustion, cleared short circuit (capacitor) **-stelle** *f* (Kondensator) cleared spot (capacitor) **-versuch** *m* scaling test

ausbrechen to break out or off, rake out, quarry (out), clear (furnace), veer off the course, begin, break away

Ausbrechen *n* swerve (in taking off)

ausbreiten to hammer, flatten, plate out, spread out, permeate, spread over, expand, extend, spread (of pressure), unfold, diffuse, propagate (waves), scatter **offen** ~ to display **sich** ~ to expand **sich ausbreitende Welle** traveling wave

Ausbreite-probe *f* hammering test, flow test, plating-out or flattening test

Ausbreiter *m* opening rail

Ausbreit-maschine *f* spreader (expander) **-maßprüfung** *f* slump test (cement)

Ausbreitung *f* spread, spreading, expansion, diffusion, propagation, extension, enlargement, radiation, fanning out ~ **drahtloser Wellen längs der Erdoberfläche** wave propagation along the earth's surface

Ausbreitungs-bedingungen *pl* propagation conditions **-bezirk** *m* area of spreading or diffusion **-erscheinung** *f* propagation characteristic **-faktor** *m* propagation factor **-form** *f* mode of propagation **-formel** *f* radio-transmission formula **-geschwindigkeit** *f* velocity of propagation (of waves), propagation velocity **-konstante** *f* propagation constant or coefficient

Ausbreitungs-methode *f* propagation method **-richtung** *f* direction of propagation **-strom** *m* dispersion current **-verhältnisse** *n* propagation conditions **-vorgang** *m* propagation phenomenon or action **-weg** *m* path of propagation **-widerstand** *m* diffusion resistance, resistance of earth plate

Ausbreit-versuch *m* spreading test **-walze** *f* expansion roller

ausbrennen to burn out, cut out (by autogenous method), blow out (mining), weld, score, eliminate (by burning)

Ausbrennen *n* burnout (elec.), erosion (of a gun barrel)

Ausbrennernergie *f* burning-out energy

Ausbrenner *m* flash combustion unit

Ausbrenn-grad *m* combustion degree or efficiency **-schacht** *m* combustible pit **-topf** *m* pot retort

Ausbrennung *f* barrel erosion or enlargement, bore, erosion

Ausbrennvorgang *m* burning-out process

ausbringen to yield, produce, bring out, take away, drive out (print)

Ausbringen *n* yield, output, production, produce, recovery, capacity

Ausbringung *f* output, capacity, finish, recovery, production **~ pro Stunde** gears per hour
ausbröckeln to crack (steel)
Ausbröckelung *f* crumbling
ausbröseln to chisel off
Ausbruch *m* break, outbreak, eruption, flow, gusher, blowout, inrush, excavation
Ausbruchs-drosselhahn *m* flow nipple or bean **-kopf** *m* flow head **-produktion** *f* flush production **-ventil** *n* blow-out preventer or valve **-versuch** *m* sally, sortie
ausbrühen to scald
Ausbrütapparat *m* incubator
ausbuchen to get off the books
ausbüchsen, ausbuchsen to bush (bearing), box, place in a box **ein Rad ~** to box a wheel
ausbuchten to warp, bulge **sich ~** to form bays
Ausbuchtung *f* throat depth, salient, convexity, bulge **~ der Mündung oder Lippe** droop of muzzle of gun **~** (am Metall), bulging (of metal), oil can (aviation)
ausbuckeln to emboss
ausbuddeln to dig up
ausbürsten to brush thoroughly
ausdämpfen to steam, evaporate, smoke out, cease steaming, steam out
Ausdampfung *f* evaporation
Ausdämpfwasser *n* steaming-out liquor
ausdarren to kiln
Ausdauer *f* endurance, steadiness, stamina, tenacity
ausdauern to endure, last
ausdauernd assiduous
ausdehnbar dilatable, expansive, expansible, extensible, ductile
Ausdehnbarkeit *f* expansibility, dilatability, extensibility
ausdehnen to expand, stretch, extend, elongate, enlarge, dilate
Ausdehner *m* expanser
Ausdehnschleife *f* compensating loop or bend (steam pipes)
Ausdehnung *f* (Erweiterung) extension, expansion, spread; (Umfang, Bereich) extent, range; (Dehnung) elongation, stretching; (Math.) dimension, increase in volume; (Verformung) deformation; (Gase) expansion; (feste Körper) dilation, expansion; (Raum) contents, latitude, scope, distention, frontage, attenuation **~ eines Hafens** extent of a port (port area) **~ der Turbulenzelemente** scale of turbulence (wind tunnels) **seitliche ~** lateral deformation
Ausdehnungs-arbeit *f* work performed during expansion **-behälter** *m* surge tank **-beiwert** *m* coefficient of expansion **-dichtung** *f* expansion joint **-drang** *m* tendency to expand **-fuge** *f* expansion joint **-gefäß** *n* expansion tank **-hub** *m* expansion or power stroke **-koeffizient** *m* coefficient of expansion or dilation **-kraft** *f* expansive force **-kupplung** *f* expansion coupling, cutoff coupling, expansion clutch
Ausdehnungs-lager *n* expansion bearing **-messer** *m* extensometer, dilatometer **-raum** *m* expansion chamber **-riemenscheibe** *f* expanding pulley **-ring** *m* expander **-ringstück** *n* expansion ring **-rohrbogen** *m* expansion loop **-rohrverbindung** *f* expansion pipe joint **-scharnier** *n* hinge bellows unit **-schwingungsart** *f* extentional mode of vibration **-spiel** *n* clearence, play
Ausdehnungs-stoß *m*, **-stück** *n*, **-verbindung** *f* expansion joint **-verflüssiger** *m* expansion liquefier **-verhältnis** *n* ratio of expansion **-vermögen** *m* ability to expand or extend **-zahl** *f* coefficient of expansion **-ziffer** *f* coefficient of thermal expansion
ausdenken to conceive
ausdeuten to interpret, explain, decipher
Ausdeutung *f* interpretation, evaluation, explanation
ausdocken to undock
ausdornen to drift (a hole)
ausdörren to scorch
ausdrechseln to turn out
Ausdreh-apparat *m* boring machine
ausdrehen to turn off, turn out, (turn) hollow, bore
Ausdrehstahl *m* boring tool
Ausdrehung *f* recess, bore, groove
Ausdrehvorrichtung *f* inside turning equipment
Ausdruck *m* expression, term (of an equation), denonation (of a factor) **aus zwei Gliedern bestehender ~** binomial (math.)
ausdrucken to finish printing, complete printing
ausdrücken to press out, force out, squeeze out, push out, express **zahlenmäßig ~** to evaluate
Ausdrucksform *f* extracting mandrel
Ausdruckleitung *f* discharge pressure line (submarine)
ausdrücklich expressly, explicit
ausdruckslose Färbung *f* undefinable shade
Ausdrück-maschine *f* charging or pushing machine, coke pusher, mechanical pusher **-rahmen** *m* knock-out frame **-stange** *f* pushing ram or arm
ausdrucksvoll expressive **-e Färbung** *f* striking shade
Ausdrucksweise *f* expression
Ausdrückverteiler *m* high-pressure air-line blowing system
ausdünnen to thin out
ausdünsten to evaporate, exhale
Ausdünstung *f* evaporation, exhalation, perspiration
Ausdünstungsmesser *m* evaporimeter
ausebnen to level out
ausecken to chamfer, bevel
aus-ein off-on
Auseinander-bau *m* dismantling **-bersten** *n* distruption **-brechen** to breakdown **-drängen** to disrupt **-fahren** to break up, separate, diverge **-fallen** to fall to pieces, disintegrate, spread **-falten** to unfold **-gehen** to diverge, separate, fall apart, break up
Auseinandergehen *n* divergence
auseinandergehend divergent **-e Werte** divergent or discrepant values
auseinandergezeichnete Teile (Zeichnung) exploded view (diagram)
auseinandergezogen drawn or pulled apart **Darstellung in -er Anordnung** exploded view
auseinanderhalten to keep separate or apart
Auseinanderklaffen des Schweißspaltes spreading of weld seams during welding
auseinander-klappen to unfold, spread **-laufen** to diverge
Auseinanderlaufen *n* divergence **~ eines Buckels**

spread of hump

auseinander-legen to space apart **-nehmbar** capable of being taken apart, collapsible **-nehmen** to diassemble, dismantle strip, undo, take to pieces, take apart, take down, dismember, dismount **-reißen** to tear down or apart, disrupt, break up **-rollmaschine** *f* uncoiler, unwinder **-schichten** *n* stripping **-setzen** to explain

Auseinander-setzung *f* explanation, analysis, discussion, argument **-spreizen** to spread (expand) **-sprengen** to dynamite, blast (asunder) **-stellung der Bestandteile** disintegration **-strebend** divergent **-treiben** to disperse, widen **-weichen** to deviate, diverge, separate **-weichen** *n* divergence, deviation, separation **-wickeln** to disentangle **-ziehen** to deploy, pull apart, extend, spread (tactically), spread apart **-zupfen** to pull asunder

Ausentwicklung *f* full development

auserkoren chosen, elected

auserlesen choise, exquisite, celected

auserwählt select

ausexponiert fully exposed

ausfahrbar horizontally drawing out, withdrawable **-er Auslegetisch** retractable delivery board **-er Mast** dismountable mast

Ausfahrbewegung *f* (Waggonkipper) removal of empty cars

ausfahren to ride, climb up, extend, drop, put out (to sea), drive out, lower (flaps or the undercarriage) **das Fahrwerk ~** to extend the undercarriage

Ausfahren *n* driving, move out, swing out **~ des Auslegers** letting out the jib **~** (der Bergleute) ascent **~ durch Eigengewicht** extension under own weight **automatisches ~** automatic extension **~ des Glühgutes** removal of the annealed material **zum ~ auf volle Höhe** (Lichtmast) for fully extended position of the floodlight mast

Ausfahr-gleis *n* departure track **-katze** *f*, **-schiene** *f* extension crane

Ausfahrt *f* departure **-geschwindigkeit** *f* speed of the out-going carriage **-peilung** *f* outbound bearing

Ausfahrungsrohr *n* outlet or exhaust pipe

Ausfahrweg *m* track or road through portal of mine

Ausfahrzylinder *m* extension cylinder

Ausfall *m* sortie, sally, to be out of action, deficit, attrition, cutting out of the circuit, deficiency, result, precipitation, precipitate, loss, long lunge or thrust, casualty, fall-out, loss in men and material, breakdown, drop (in current), stoppage (factory), shortage, failure, gun out of battery **~ eines oder mehrerer Triebwerke beim mehrmotorigen Flugzeug** partial failure of one or several motors of a multimotored airplane **elektrischer ~** electric shock (electronics)

Ausfäll-apparat *m* precipitator, precipitron (electronic) **-bar** precipitate

Ausfall-bogen *m* clean machine proof **-bündelzeiger** *m* back pointer **-bürgschaft** *f* letter of indemnity, collateral security **-eisen** *n* offgrade iron

Ausfälle (mikrotome) skips

ausfallen to make a sortie, drop out, be a casualty, fall out, turn out, get out of commission (motor), precipitate, deposit; (einer Färbung) to turn out **gänzlich ~** to fail altogether

Ausfallen *n* flare of ship's ribs, frames, stem, and stern posts **~ eines Motors** engine failure

Ausfällen *n* precipitation, deposit, precipitate

ausfallender Lichtstrahl emergent light ray

Ausfall(s)-erscheinung *f* abrogation **-erwartung** *f* expected failure time **-hafen** *m* naval base **-muster** *n* type sample **-öffnung** *f* discharge opening **-richtung** *f* direction of reflection **-rutsche** *f* billet chute off heat **-schütze** *f* discharge sluice **-straße** *f* arterial road **-tor** *n* starting point of attack **-winkel** *m* angle of reflection **-zeit** *f* down-time, outage time

Ausfällung *f* precipitation

Ausfallwinkel *m* angle of reflection or emergence

Ausfalzung *f* fluting mortise

ausfärben to give the last dye

Ausfaserapparat *m* clearing attachment

ausfasern to feaze **nicht ~** non-fraying

Ausfaulbehälter *m* putrefaction container

ausfaulen to digest

ausfechten to fight to a decision

ausfegen to sweep or clean out, scavenge (gases)

ausfeilen to file out, indent

ausfertigen to make out (report), copy, draw up, issue

Ausfertigung *f* copy, drawing up a report, official copy **in dreifacher ~** in triplicate **in zweifacher ~** in duplicate **siebenfache ~** septuplicate

ausfetten to extract or grease, scour, deoil

Ausfeuern *n* (beim Schleifen ohne Vorschub auslaufen lassen bis Funken verschwinden), sparking out

ausfiltern to filter out, exclude

ausfindigmachen to discover, find out, trace, ascertain, to locate

ausfindig zu machen suchen to seek

ausflaggen to full-dress ship

ausflecken to retouch (print)

ausflicken to patch, reline, repair

Ausflicken *n* relining, (re)patching, repair

ausfließen to flow out, discharge, issue, emanate **aus kleinen Öffnungen ~** to bleed

ausfließend outflowing, effluent

Ausflockbarkeit der Farbstoffe capacity of dyestuffs to flocculate out, work performed by dyes during flocculation

ausflocken to (de)flocculate, separate in flakes, separate at the flocculent state, separate as a flocculent, precipitate

Ausflocken *n* flocculation

Ausflockung *f* (de)flocculation, coagulation

Ausflockungsgeschwindigkeit *f* flaking or flocking speed

Ausflucht *f* evasion, excuse, subterfuge

ausfluchten to align, jut out, line out

Ausfluchtung *f* alignment

Ausflugschneise *f* departure corridor

Ausfluß *m* flow, outflow, efflux, effluent, discharge (of water), outlet, emanation, mouth, drain **~ unter Wasser** submerged discharge

Ausfluß-druck *m* open pressure **-einschnitt** *m* contraction coefficient **-filter** *n* outlet filter **-geschwindigkeit** *f* rate of flow, discharge velocity **-hahn** *m* bibcock, discharge cock **-kanal** *m* channel, outlet, passage **-koeffizient** *m* coefficient of discharge **-kopf** *m* flow head **-loch** *n* outlet, discharge opening, orifice **-menge** *f* quantity discharged **-methode** *f* efflux **-monitor** *m* effluent monitor **-mündung** *f* lip of a casting ladle

Ausfluß-öffnung *f* discharge gate, outlet, orifice, teeming nozzle **-rinne** *f* discharging spout or chute **-rohr** *n* gutter, outflow tube, discharge or waste pipe **-schnauze** *f* outlet nozzle, lip **-strahl** *m* discharge jet **-ton** *m* jet tone, slit tone **-ventil** *n* discharge valve **-zahl** *f* discharge coefficient **-zeit** *f* discharge time

Ausflutung *f* channel

ausfördern to extract

ausformen to lace out, form out (a cable)

Ausformen *n* lacing out, forming out, blocking

ausforschen to cross-question, sound out, investigate

ausfragen to question, interrogate

ausfransen to fray

Ausfräsen (von Löchern) sinking

ausfräsen to mill out or ream, notch or recess (in milling machine)

Ausfräskopf *m* routing head

ausfressen to erode

Ausfressung *f* scouring, erosion, pitting

ausfrieren to freeze out (in liquid-air trap)

Ausfrier-falle *f* refrigerated (mercury vapor) trap **-gefäß** *n* freezing container

ausfugen to point up brickwork, cement

Ausfuhr *f* export(ation), export trade

Ausführband *n* delivery tape

ausführbar exportable, feasible, practicable

Ausführbarkeit *f* practicability, feasability

Ausfuhrbewilligung *f* permit or license to export

ausführen to execute, construct, effect, carry out (tests), perform, accomplish, export, pattern, manufacture **Arbeiten ungeschickt und ohne Sachkenntnis ~** to fumble

Ausführender einer Analyse analyst

ausführender Ingenieur project engineer

Ausführer *m* contractor

Ausfuhrgeschäft *n* export trade or business

Ausfuhr-handel *m* export trade **-land** *n* export country

ausführlich detailed, circumstantial, explicit

Ausfuhrprämie *f* bounty on exportation

Ausführrolle *f* delivery (tension) roller (print)

Ausfuhrschein *m* export permit or certificate

Ausführsignal *n* signal to go ahead or carry on

Ausfuhrtätigkeit *f* export activity

Ausführung *f* carrying out; (Plan, Auftrag) execution; (Vertrag) performance; (Bau) construction; (Bauart) make, finish, style, model; (Fertigstellung) completion; (Konstruktion) design; (Qualität) workmanship; (Maschinen) type, construction, type, installation, comment, outfit, version, specification, solving of a mathematical problem, erection (of buildings), perpetration, disposition, arrangement, exportation, exercise, version, discourse, explanation, detailed statement, pattern, delivery guide, leading out, production, argument, idea, fabrication, leadin

Ausführung (einer Reparatur) execution (of a repair) **äußerliche ~** finish **die ~ des Werkes ist unterbrochen** the work is interrupted or temporarily stopped **in zweifacher ~** in duplicate **zur ~ bringen** to put into effect, put into execution

Ausführungen *f pl* details, types **~ in Meehanite** engineering grades of Meehanite

Ausführungs-art *f* embodiment, method, version **-arten** *f pl* finishes (mahogany, chromium, rough, smooth), types (of wheels, ships, etc.) **-beispiel** *n* application, example of operation, exemplified embodiment, form of construction (cited by way of example in patent specifications) **-datum** *n* date of reduction to practice, date of execution or fabrication **-form** *f* formula, style, type model, specific embodiment **-fuge** *f* construction joint

Ausführungs-kabel *n* leading-out cable (elec.) **-kennzeichen** *n* design characteristic **-kommando** *n* command of execution **-maß** *n* dimension of the design **-material** *n* material for construction **-methode** *f* executive method

Ausführungsraum *m*, **großer ~** large studio

Ausführung-verfahren *n* technique **-walzen** *f pl* pinch rolls **-zeichnung** *f* constructional or working drawing **-zeit einer Verbindung** connection time, time of setting up a call **-zwang** *m* compulsory working (of a patent) **-zylinder** *m* delivery cylinder

Ausfuhr-verbot *n* embargo **-vergütung** *f* tax rebate on export

Ausführzylinder *m* delivery cylinder (print.)

Ausfüllblock *m* spacer

ausfüllen to fill (in), fill up, provide, furnish **mit Abraum ~** rocking the well

Ausfüll-masse *f* filling, stuffing **-öffnung** *f* outlet

Ausfüllung *f* filling out, filling (for wood surfaces), content, lining **~ des Gewölbzwickels** span drill

Ausfüllungsgrad *m* (der Luftschraubenkreisfläche durch die massiven Schraubenblätter) solidity

ausfurchen to nick out

ausfüttern to line, fettle, case, bush, pad, upholster **~ mit** to bush with

Ausfütterung *f* lining, fettling **~ mit Röhren** casing (tubing) **versteifende ~** backing

Ausgabe *f* expense, expenditure, outlay, input, edition, issue, issuance, distribution, delivery, output **-beleg** *m* issue voucher **-frist** *f* period of issue **-gerät** *n* output equipment **-geschwindigkeit** *f* readout rate **-magazin** *n* distributing warehouse **-maschine** *f* output equipment

Ausgaben *f pl* charges or costs **laufende ~** running costs **unvorhergesehene ~** contingencies

Ausgaben-buch *n* cashbook **-kontrolle** *f* expenditure control

Ausgabe-programm *n* output routine (info proc.) **-speicher** *m* output block, external memory **-stelle** *f* distributing point **-tisch** *m* cupboard **-zeit** *f* time of issuance, time of release **-werk** *n* output unit (comp.)

Ausgang *m* departure, outlet, egress, end, exit, outcome, result, output, termination, outflow, issue, delivery section, forerunner **Schalter mit fünf Ausgängen** five-point switch

Ausgangs- initial, starting, raw casting, unmachined

Ausgangsadmittanz *f* output admittance **wirk-**

same ~ effective output admittance

Ausgangs-amplitude *f* output amplitude **-analyse** *f* initial analysis **-atom** *n* parent atom **-bandleitung** *f* delivery tape guide (print) **-basis** *f* starting point **-baumuster** *n* prototype **-befehl** *m* exit instruction **-begriff** *m* original term **-bildwähler** *m* master switching unit **-blech** *n* exhaust pipe **-buchse** *f* exit hub, outlet, output socket

Ausgangs-elektrode *f* output electrode **-element** *n* parent element **-energie** *f* output power **-energieregelung** *f* regulation of output **-erzeugnis** *n* initial product **-filter** *n* output filter **-flughafen** *m* airport of departure **-form** *f* fundamental or basic shape of form **-front** *f* initial position (attack) **-funktion** *f* trial function

Ausgangs-gestein *n* parent rock **-gleichungen** *f pl* starting or initial equations **-graben** *m* jump-off trench **-größe** *f* output quantity, output variable **-größen** *pl* input data **-hafen** *m* port of departure **-härte** *f* initial hardness **-herd** *m* beginning, origin, source **-impedanz** *f* output impedance, sending-end impedance **-impuls** *m* output pulse

Ausgangs-kapazität *f* output capacitance **-kegel** *m* (Düse) exit cone **-klemme** *f* output terminal noise, backfire, output **-kolumne** *f* short page **-kontrollgerät** *n* output monitor **-kraftstoff** *m* basic gasoline **-kreis** *m* output circuit **-kreisimpedanz** *f* output impedance **-lage** *f* assult position, starting or original position

Ausgangsleistung *f* (maximum undistorted) power output, output power ~ **des Bildgleichrichters** video output ~ **für Dauerbetrieb** continuous output

Ausgangs-leitung *f* outgoing circuit **-leitwert** *m* output admittance or conductance **-linie** *f* line of departure, jump-off line, datum line **-lösung** *f* starting solution **-maß** *n* initial dimension **-material** *n* raw material, original or primitive material, base material, starting material, feed stock **-monitor** *m* actual monitor **-nuklid** *n* parent nuclide

Ausgangs-öffnung *f* exit port **-ort** *m* point of departure **-pegel** *m* recording level **-platz** *m* outgoing position **-plätze** *m pl* A or outward board **-präparat** *n* basic preparation used as a starting point (chem.) **-produkt** *n* raw product, original constituent initial material

Ausgangs-punkt *m* starting point, origin, source, common point ~ **des Zielstrahls** emergent ray point

Ausgangs-pupille *f* exit pupil (phys.) **-rauschleistung** noise output power **-resonator** *m* output resonator **-richtung** *f* zero line, initial direction **-rohr** *n* outlet pipe, discharge pipe **-ronde** *f* initial blank **-scheinwiderstand** *m* output impedance (radio) **-schlitz** *m* exit slit (spectrograph)

Ausgangsschmierstoff *m*, **ungemischter** ~ base oil

Ausgangs-signal *n* output signal **-signalwandler** *m* monitoring element **-spalt** *m* exit slit, output aperture

Ausgangsspannung *f* output voltage ~ **des Aufzeichnungskopfes** recording head output voltage

Ausgangs-spannungsmesser *m* visual indicator, output voltage meter, output-balance meter **-speicher** *m* buffer storage **-sperrimpuls** *m* modulator blocking pulse (radar) **-stellung** *f* starting position, home position (of a wiper), normal position, initial or jumping-off position, line of departure (in attack) **-stoff** *m* initial substance, raw material **-störspannung** *f* output noise voltage

Ausgangs-strom *m* output current **-stromkreis** *m* output circuit, plate-filament circuit **-stromsprung** *m* snap action **-stufe** *f* output stage **-tastimpuls** *m* modulator output pulse (radar) **-teil** *m* (starting) output part **-transformator** *m* output transformer, outlet transformer **-trommel** *f* plotting drum (of flak computer), outgoing data, drum of Malsi, converter, plotting drum of antiaircraft computer **-übertrager** *m* output transformer, outlet transformer

Ausgangs- und Eingangsspannung *f* output and input voltage

Ausgangs-verbindung *f* outgoing call **-verstärker** *m* output amplifier **-wähler** *m* outgoing selector **-walze** *f* delivery roll **-wechselstrom** *m* output alternating current **-welle** *f* output shaft **-werkstoff** *m* raw material, original (base) metal, basic materials **-wert** *m* original datum **-wicklung** *f* starting winding or coil, first winding or coil, secondary winding or coil, output winding

Ausgangs-widerstand *m* output impedance, output resistor **-zeile** *f* last line (print.) **-zellulose** *f* original cellulose, basic cellulose (colloid chem.) (pulp mfg.) **-zoll** *m* export duty **-zustand** *m* initial state

ausgaren to refine, extract (gaseous or liquid)

ausgären to ferment well, cease fermenting

Ausgarzeit *f* killing period, quiescent period (steel melting)

ausgearbeitet, sorgfältig ~ elaborate

ausgebaut completed (as applied to construction or design) **voll** ~ fully equipped

ausgeben to spend, issue, distribute

Ausgeben von Fahrkarten sale of (transportation) tickets

ausgebildet trained, constructed, designed

ausgeblendeter, sehr fein ~ **Elektronenstrahl** narrowly defined electron beam

ausgebohrt drilled **voll** ~ fully bored

ausgebreitet splayed (a pipe mouth), extended

ausgebuchtete Rohre bulbous pipes or tubes

ausgebundener (Stehsatz) tied-up

ausgedehnt extensive, large, wide, vast, comprehensive

ausgedruckt, gerade ~ just come off the press

ausgedrückt expressed **anders** ~ stated another way

ausgefahren extended (said of the undercarriage) **-es Fahrgestell** extended undercarriage **-e Meterzahl** payed-out or reeled-out yardage **-e Straße** road broken up by traffic, road in bad repair

ausgefallen eccentric, unusual, odd **-e Größen** odd sizes **-er Motor** dead engine

ausgeflocktes Sol flocculated sol

ausgefluchtete Linie ranged line

ausgeformtes Kabel cable fan or form

ausgefräst milled out or reamed

ausgefressene Kontakte pitted contacts, worn contacts

ausgeführte Verbindung effective call
ausgefüttert lined
ausgegeben patent and printed copies issued
ausgeglichen regulated, equalized, compensated, balanced, even **nicht ~** unbalanced **~ werden durch . . .** to be counter-balanced by . . . **~ durch Gegengewicht** neutralized by a counterweight **-e Belastung** *f* balanced load (of a triphase system) **-e Bewegung** averaged motion, smoothed motion **-e Bewegung und Störbewegung** mean and eddy motion **-e Konstante** adjusted constant **-e und Störbewegung** mean and eddy motion **-er Verstärker** *m* balanced amplifier **-e Wasserstände** water pressures balanced
Ausgeglichenheit *f* good balance (uniformity)
ausgeglüht annealed **~ werden** to be made red-hot **-er Sand** dry sand (foundry)
ausgegossen compound-filled (electr.) **-e Lagerschale** bush with cast-in liner
ausgehalst outward-flanged **-er Kesselboden** boiler with bottom end flanged outward
ausgeheizt baked out
ausgehen to originate, emanate, disappear, pinch out, end, make even, run short, go out, become extinguished, start, issue from **mit der Seite ~ lassen** to make up the page (print.) **zu Tage ~** to crop out (geol.) **~ von . . .** to originate at . . .
Ausgehen *n* (von einem Punkte), departure
ausgehend endling, waning **-er Verkehr** originating traffic
Ausgehende *n* basset, outcropping
ausgehoben drafted
ausgehöhlt hollow(ed), cupped, cored
ausgekehlt fluted, chamfered
ausgekippt discharged
ausgekleidet lined
ausgeklinkt disengaged
ausgeklügelt engineered, managed, elaborate, skilfully arranged
ausgekreuzt cross-braced
ausgekuppelt out of mesh, disengaged
ausgelaufen worn hollow, worn-out; (Lager) burnt out (bearing) **-es Gleitlager** worn-out bearing **-es Kugellager** ball bearing worn or run out **-e Säure** spilled electrolyte
ausgelaugt lixiviated **-e Gerberlohe** lixiviated tan **-e Lohe** spent tan-bark **-es Schnitzel** beet pulp
ausgelegt laid open to public inspection (patents), covered **-e Leistung** maximum continuous rating
ausgeleiertes Gewinde nut with slipped thread
ausgelernt haben to have served one's apprenticeship
ausgelesene Dublette matched doublets
ausgelichteter Raum clearance
ausgelöst liberated **~ durch Störungen** shock-exited
ausgemergelt exhaust, worm, decrepit
ausgemustert discharged (soldier), rejected as unfit
ausgenommen except(ing) **~ von** exept from
ausgepeilte Richtung bearing (geog.)
ausgeprägt characteristic, distinct, defined, marked, decided, distinguished, peculiar, singular, particular, significant, excellent, salient (poles) **-er Pol** salient pole
ausgepumpt evacuated, pumped out
ausgeräumte Ofensohle cleaned-up bottom
ausgerben to tan
Ausgerbung *f* final tanning
ausgereift developed **-e Konstruktion** matured construction (design)
ausgerichtet aligned **schlecht ~** improperly trued, out of alignment
ausgerissenes Gewinde stripped thread
ausgerolltes Furnierholz unrolled veneers
ausgerückt out of gear, disengaged
ausgerüstet mit equipped, fitted, or provided with **~ mit Gitternetz** latticed
ausgesaugt (mixture) drawn off
ausgeschaltet switched off or out, out of gear, out of action **~ sein** to be out, out of action, not operating, disconnected
ausgeschieden werden to exude
ausgeschlagen deflected **mit Blech -e Kiste** tin-lined case **~ mit Blei** lead-lined **-es Lager** worn bearing
ausgeschleuderter Materialblock hydro-extracted block
ausgeschliffen ground out
ausgeschlitzt slotted or hollowed out
ausgeschlossen impossible, out of the question **-e Werte** rejected values, rejected data
ausgeschrägt splayed
ausgeschruppt rough hewn, roughed out, roughly made in general
ausgeschwärmt extended
ausgeschweift sinuated **-er Balken** routed beam **-es Profil** routed section
ausgeschwenkt swivelled
ausgesetzt liable, subject to **~ sein** to be exposed, undergo **-e Summe** allowance
Ausgesetztsein *n* weather exposure, liability
Ausgesiebtes *n* screenings
ausgespannte Saite stretched or tensioned cord or string
ausgespart hollow **-es Bett** gap bed **-es Kurbelblatt** crank disk provided with an opening
ausgesperrt locked out
ausgespiegelte Wasserstände water pressures balanced
ausgesprochen decided, outspoken
ausgestalten to develop or shape
Ausgestaltung *f* development, shaping perfection, refinement
ausgestanzt, rund ~ punched-out round
ausgestattet mit provided with
ausgestellt on exhibition, issued (passes, permits) **-er Gegenstand** exhibit
ausgesteuert, schwach -er Tonstreifen low-modulation sound track **~ werden** (Gitter) to be swung
ausgestrahlt radiated
ausgestrichen expunged
ausgesucht picked, select
ausgesüßtes Benzin sweetened gasoline
ausgetastet limited (TV) **-es Bildsignal** video signal with blanking **-es Videosignal** blanked picture signal
ausgetauschte Wärmemenge quantity of heat exchanged
ausgetuchtes Loch bushed hole
ausgeübt practiced, exercised
ausgewachsen grown out

ausgewählt select **-er Zeitwert** select time (work-factor)
ausgewalzt cogged (of an ingot)
ausgewogen ballasted up, weighed off, trimmed (in stability) (aviation)
ausgeworfene Teile scrapped parts
ausgewuchtet balanced **-er Motor** balanced motor **-e Schleudermassen** balanced centrifugal weights, balanced centrifugal masses
ausgezackt toothed, indented, jagged, dented **-e** (ausgezahnte) **Linie** jagged, serrated, notched, dented, or dentated line
ausgezeichnet excellent, distinguished, distinct, market, singular, significant, particular **-er Punkt** excellent or singular point **-e Punkte** cardinal points (opt.)
ausgezogen solid (not dotted line), shown in full, racked **-e Glasröhre** capillary tube **-e Kurve** solid curve **-e Linie** solid or full line, unbroken line (in graphs, drawings)
ausgiebig abundant
Ausgiebigkeit *f* spreading rate, viscosity (of gels, starch), yield value (of paints), spreading or covering power (for paints), productiveness, fertility, abundance, yield ~ (Deckkraft von Farbe und Lack) spreading power, covering power
ausgießen to pour out, run out, teem, line; (Beton) to grout; (isolieren) to fill up **mit Blei** ~ to lead **Lager** ~ to line bearings **ein Lager neu** ~ to remetal a bearing **mit Weißmetall** ~ to reline, remetal
Ausgießen des Kabels sealing end of cable ~ **der Lager** remetalling bearings
Ausgießungsofen *m* effusion, oven
ausgipsen to cover with plaster
ausglätten to smooth, flatten (graphs)
Ausgleich *m* rectification, compensation, balancing, adjustment, phasing, equalization, balance, settlement (of accounts), equilibrium, compromise, self-regulation ~ **in der Belastung der einzelnen Plätze** balancing of operators' loads ~ **der Ladungen** equalization of charges **aerodynamischer** ~ aerodynamic balance **energiewirtschaftlicher** ~ economical equalization of energy **zum** ~ **bringen** to balance **Dauer des Ausgleiches bei Stromschließung** transient period (elec.)
ausgleichbar adjustable
ausgleichen to balance, settle, equalize, compensate (for), adjust, level, outweigh, balance out, take up wear, assimilate, counterbalance, compromise, align, bias out (by counterforce), space evently, even out ~ **durch eine Gegenkraft** to bias out, counterbalance **neu** ~ to rebalance
Ausgleichen *n* balancing, compensation, equalization, radar equilibrator, equilibration ~ **einer Leitung** balancing of a circuit ~ **von Schallwellen** neutralization of sound waves **neues** ~ rebalancing, rebalance
ausgleichend equilibrant **-er Erdschluß** ground counterpoise (radio) **-er Strom** equalizing or rectifying current
Ausgleicher *m* equalizer, compensator, ratchet-stop control **-arm** *m* equilibrator arm or anchor **-lager** *n* equilibrator seat
Ausgleich(s)-achse *f* differential pinion shaft **-aggregat** *n* compensation set **-anzeiger** *m* balance indicator **-apparat** *m* equalizer **-auge** *n* equalizing port **-becken** *n* equalizing basin (pondage) **-behälter** *m* expansion tank, fluid reservoir, header tank, compensating or equalizing tank, gasometer **-bewegung** *f* compensating movement **-bogen** *m* compensating layer **-bohrung** *f* balance hole **-bunker** *m* catch bin
Ausgleich(s)-draht *m* equalizing or adjustment wire **-druck** *m* potential difference, equalizing pressure **-düse** *f* nozzle, compensating jet (carburetor) **-effekt** *m* transient phenomenon **-entzerrung** *f* complementary recording **-farbe** *f* complementary color **-feder** *f* equalizer spring, centering spring **-fehler** *m* correction error **-filter** *n* compensating filter, balanced filter **-fläche** *f* balancing surface (aviation), balance tab, trim tab, isostatic surface **-flosse** *f* compensating surface
Ausgleich(s)-gefäß *n* expansion tank **-gehänge** *n* compensating suspension gear **-gehäuse** *n* differential housing **-geschwindigkeit** *f* balancing speed, compensating speed
Ausgleichsgetriebe *n* differential gear(ing) **selbstsperrendes** ~ differential gear with self-locking device
Ausgleichsgetriebe-gehäuse *n* differential cage **-rad** *n* differential gear **-sperre** *f* differential lock, differential locking assembly **-sperrhebel** *m* differential lock lever
Ausgleich(s)-gewicht *n* counterbalance or damper weight, counter-weight, compensating weight **-grad** *m* gain factor (aut. contr.) **-grube** *f* soaking pit **-hebel** *m* equalizer, compensating beam or lever **-impuls** *m* equalizing pulse
Ausgleich(s)-kammer *f* equalizing or compensating chamber **-kapazität** *f* balancing capacity **-kegelrad** *n* differential bevel gear, differential pinion **-kolben** *m* compensating piston **-kondensator** *m* balancing capacity, smoothing condenser **-körper** *m* compensating body **-kreis** *m* balancing circuit, corrector circuit **-kurve** *f* fitting curve (math.), compensating curve
Ausgleichs-ladung *f* equalizing charge **-leitung** *f* balancing pipe, compensating pipe **-linie** *f* trend line **-loch** *n* balance hole **-luftdraht** *m* balancing aerial
Ausgleich(s)-magnetometer *n* null astatic magnetometer **-maschine** *f* direct-current balancer **-messung** *f* compensation measurement **-möglichkeit** *f* compensating device **-netzwerk** *n* equalization network, correcting network **-optik** *f* compensating optics **-pleuel** *n* connecting-rod system with corrected dead-center angles
Ausgleich(s)-rad *n* adjuster wheel, compensating gear **-rechnung** *f* balancing calculation **-rennen** *n* handicap race **-ring** *f* shim, spacing washer, equalizing ring **-rohr** *n* balance pipe, equalizing tube or pipe **-rohr** *n* (hydraulischer Druck) stand-pipe, expansion pipe **-rolle** *f* compensating roller **-ruder** *n* balanced control surface
Ausgleich(s)-schaltung *f* quiescent push-pull switch, compensating circuit ~ **ohne Gleichstromkomponente** quiescent push pull
Ausgleich(s)-schaufel *f* diffuser vane, straightening vane **-scheibe** *f* shim, compensating

disc or washer, equalizer disc **-schicht** *f* equalizing layer, filler course **-schleife** *f* expansion loop (steam pipes) **-schwungscheibe** *f* rotary stabilizer (motion-picture projector), impedance wheel **-spannung** *f* transient voltage **-sperre** *f* differential gear-setting mechanism, differential lock **-spirale** *f* expansion coil **-spule** *f* equalizing or rectifying coil

Ausgleich(s)-stab *m* shim rod **-stange** *f* adjusting rod, equalizer beam **-stern** *m* differential spider **-stopfbüchse** *f* expansion, stuffing box

Ausgleich(s)strom *m* transient current, compensating or equalizing current **-anzeiger** *m* balance indicator, three-wire system **-kreis** *m* compensating circuit **-stoß** *m* equalizing current impact or surge

Ausgleich(s)-stück *n* levelling piece **-tiefe** *f* compensation depth **-topf** *m* balance tank **-transformator,** (-übertrager) *m* hybrid transformer or coil, balanced or differential transformer **-umformer** *m* balancing transformer

Ausgleichung *f* balance, balancing, equilibration, graduation (math.), compensation, equalization, adjustment, adjusting (method of least squares) **~ des toten Ganges** *m* taking up the backlash (of threads) **schlechte ~** want of balance, unbalance

Ausgleichungs-fehler *m* balance error, unbalance **-längsmagnet** *m* compensating fore-aft magnet **-lehrsatz** *m* compensation theorem **-magnet** *m* compensating magnet **-quermagnet** *m* compensating thwartship or transverse magnet **-schaltung** *f* equalizing network **-stand** *m* (propeller) balancing machine **-strom** *m* transient (electr.) **-strömung** *f* compensatory current

Ausgleich(s)-ventil *n* balancing or equalizing valve **-verbindung** *f* equipotential connection **-verdampfer** *m* equalizing evaporator **-verfahren** *n* compensation method **-vermögen** *n* self-regulation (autom. contr.)

Ausgleichsvorgang *m* transient effect or phenomenon or recovery, transient (radio), recovery curve **~ bei Stromschließung** (Stromunterbrechung) make (break) transient

Ausgleich(s)-vorrichtung *f* compensator **-waage** *f* adjusting scales **-wagen** *m* balance car; (Kran) compensating truck **-wattmeter** *n* composite-coil wattmeter **-welle** *f* differential shaft **-werk** *n* base-load station **-wert** *m* adjusted value, steady-state gain (aut. contr.)

Ausgleichswerte der kleinsten Quadrate adjusted values of least-squares

Ausgleich(s)-wichte (Trennwichte HP) effective separating density **-widerstand** *m* compensating, balancing, ballasting, phase or balance resistance, compensating resistor **-windung** *f* pigtail (aviation) **-zahl** *f* compensating factor **-zahnrad** *n* idler sprocket **-zeit** *f* equalizing, compensating or balancing time, soaking time, recovery time (autom. contr.) **-zellen** *f pl* accumulator end or balancing cells **-zoll** *m* countervailing duty **-zusatzmaschine** *f* balancing booster **-zustand** *m* equilibrium state **-zylinder** *m* counterbalance cylinder

ausgleiten to slip, skid

Ausgleiten *n* slipping, skidding **seitliches ~** sideslip (of an airplane)

Ausgleitzeiger *m* sideslip indicator (aviation), equalizer

ausgliedern to disincorporate, segregate

Ausgliederung *f* segregation (administrative) separation

Ausgliederungskosten *pl* items of expenditure and revenue

ausglühen to anneal, normalize, burn out, calcine, temper, roast, soften (steel), heat red-hot

Ausglühen *n* (full) annealing, process annealing, normalizing **durch ~ spannungsfrei machen** to stress anneal

Ausglüher *m* annealer, blancher

Ausglüh-flammofen *m*, **-ofen** *m* annealing furnace **-verfahren** *n* annealing method or process

ausgraben to excavate, dig (out)

Ausgrabung *f* excavation

ausgreifend extensive **weit ~** far-reaching

Ausguck *m* lookout, periscope **-plattform** *f* observation platform **-posten** *m* lookout post, observation post, lookout station (on ship)

Ausgucksmann *m* lookout

Ausguß *m* outlet, drain, spout, discharge, pouring out, delivery, effusion, lip, nozzle, sink, discharge connection, beak **-höhe** *f* height of delivery **-kasten** *m* drain box, spout, discharge **-kopf** *m* pipe (hydraulic-)casing-head **-lage** *f* turned-down position **-lippe** *f* pouring or teeming spout (of a crucible)

Ausgußmasse *f* box or filling compound **~ für Kabel** cable compound

Ausguß-öffnung (einer Gießpfanne) *f* lip of a casting ladle **-pfanne** *f* casting or pouring ladle, ingot mold **-raum des Kondensators** hot well **-rinne** *f* pouring spout **-röhre** *n* pouring spout, shoe, waste or overflow pipe, delivery pipe **-schale** *f* spout, sink, basin **-scheibe** *f* cast-lens blank **-schnauze** *f* outlet nozzle, drawn-out lip, pouring nozzle, lip, or mouth **-stutzen** *m* discharge connection **-tülle** *f* spout **-ventil** *n* delivery, discharge or escape valve

aushacken to hew out

Aushacker *m* comb (textiles)

aushaken to uncouple, unhook, unhitch

aushalsen to neck out, open

Aushalsen *n* necking (mechn.)

Aushalsestahl *m* necking tool

Aushalsungsarbeit *f* necking operation

aushalten to endure, bear, stand, pick out, sort, last, hold out, withstand **den Druck ~** to take the thrust, hold it

Aushalten *n* (der Berge in der Grube) separation, extent (geol.), endurance

aushämmern to batter, hammer even or flat

aushandeln to bargain

aushändigen to hand over, turn over, pass over

Aushändigung *f* handing in or filing (of a message), handing over, delivery

Aushang *m* placard, poster

Aushänge-bogen *m* specimen sheet (print), clean sheet (print.) **-exemplar** *n* copy given to the author **-tafel** *f* display board

aushängen to lift (the telephone), remove (aus den Angeln) unhinge

Aushängeschild *n* sign, signboard, signpost

aushärtbar age-hardening

aushärten to cure, age (metal), harden, set
Aushärten *n* artificial aging
Aushärtung *f* recrystallization hardening (in case of aluminium alloys), age-hardening, solidification
Aushärtungsgrenze *f* limit of age-hardening or aging
aushauchen to exhale
Aushaueisen *n* drift
aushauen to carve, rough out, sculpture
Aushauer *m* hewing chisel, cutter, punch
Aushau-maschine *f* nibbing or blanking machine **-schere** *f* stamping press, nibbling machine
ausheben to draw out, lift out or off, remove, withdraw, draw, dig (trench), excavate under water, lift clear of (pawl), enroll, conscript, draft, mop up, reduce a fraction to lowest terms, unhinge (a door)
Ausheben *n* lifting, raising, withdrawal
Aushebe-platte *f* lifting plate, rapping plate **-kette** *f* lifting chain
Ausheber *m* lifter, knock-out (metal), (Preß- und Stanztechn.) ejector, knock-out **-rahmen** *m pl* nipper frames (textiles)
Aushebe-span *m* composing rule, setting rule **-schaufel** *f* pick-up shovel **-stift** *m* ejector pin **-verfahren** *n* hand-lifting process **-vorrichtung** *f* lifting device or contrivance, roller
Aushebung *f* conscription, draft, enrollment
ausheilen to cure completely, heal up
ausheizen to bake out, heat, anneal
Ausheiztemperatur *f* baking-out temperature
Aushelf spare, auxiliary
Aushilfe *f* makeshift, improvisation, teamwork, expedient, substitute, auxiliary, temporary assistance
Aushilfs-adern *pl* auxiliary lines (electr.) **-anlasser** *m* emergency starter **-arbeit** *f* odd jobs, temporary work **-klinke** *f* auxiliary or ancillary jack **-kraftwerk** *n* emergency power station **-stelle** *f* relief or emergency station **-weise** temporarily
aushobeln to plane
aushöhlen to hollow (out), burrow, excavate, groove, hole, channel, cave
Aushöhlung *f* groove
ausholen ro swing, make a wide envelopment, haul out, lunge
Ausholen des Bohrgeräts pulling tools
Ausholer *m* halyard, outhaul, questioner
Ausholring *m* traveler (mech.)
Aushornmesser *n* horning knife
Aushub *m* lift, draw, withdrawal, removal, excavated material, excavation ~ **eines Kanals** excavating a canal **-material** *n* borrow material
aushülsen to shell, hull
aushungern to flare out (aviat.)
ausixen to double V-groove (welding)
auskämmen to comb out, mop up
auskarren to wheel out, discharge with a wheelbarrow
auskaufen to buy up
auskehlen to chamfer, flute, channel, groove
Auskehlfräser *m* grooving cutter (tongue-and-groove woodwork)
Auskehlung *f* channel, chamfer, groove, flute, niche, fillet ~ **zwischen Flügel und Rumpf** fillet between wing and fuselage
auskehren to clean out
auskeilen to wedge out, thin out, pinch out **sich** ~ to dwindle, wedge out
Auskeilen *n* balk
Auskeilung *f* dwindling away, wedging away
auskeimen to germinate, cease germinating
auskellen to ladle (out)
auskellern to clear cellar
auskerben to scallop (textiles)
auskernen to stone (fruit)
Auskernmaschine *f* stoning machine (fruit pip or stone extractor)
auskippen to dump out, pour out
Auskippstellung *f* inverted position, tipped or tilting position, pouring position
auskitten to fill (with cement), cement, putty
ausklammern to factor out (math.)
ausklappbar swinging out, capable of being swung out or dropped (on hinges) **-er Halter** swing-out holder
ausklappen to turn (swing) out, fold out (down, up) unfold, spread
Ausklappen *n* swinging out
Ausklarieren *n* clearance (ship)
Ausklarierung *f* clearance outward
ausklauben to pick out, sort out, select
auskleiden to cover, line, pave, coat, equip, plate, case, line up, brasque, clothe
Auskleidung *f* lagging, coating, lining, fillet (war) **feuerfeste** ~ fireproof casing (of a blast furnace)
Ausklingeln der Adern circuit identification
ausklinkbar disengageable
ausklinken to release, throw out, disengage, unlatch, cope, trip, trigger, throw out (of gear)
Ausklink-hebel *m* stripper lever **-maschine** *f* coping machine, notching machine **-mechanismus** *m* trip gear **-nocken** *n* tripping or deflecting cam **-relais** *n* tripping relay **-steuerung** *f* trip gear (steam distribution)
Ausklinkung *f* coping or blocking (of steel beams), release
Ausklinkung *pl* block-outs
Ausklinkvorrichtung *f* mechanism for releasing tow cable from sailplane, release system or gear, coping attachment
ausklopfen to beat or knock out, scale off **den Kessel** ~ to scale the boiler
ausklügeln to plot, engineer
ausknicken to buckle, bend sharp, bend
Ausknicken aus Trägerebene buckling out of the plane of the girder
Ausknickung *f* transverse failure, buckling, bending (at a sharp angle)
auskochen to blow out (mining), decoct, extract, boil, boil out or off
Auskocher *m* boiler, extractor
Auskohlung *f* total decarburization
auskolken to undermine, erode, wash away
Auskolkung *f* depression washed out of river bed by current, erosion, scour, hole, pool (in a river), cratering, loading
Auskommen *n* living, subsistence, sufficiency, livelihood
auskömmlich ample
auskopieren to copy, print (photo)
Auskopierpapier *n* printing(-out) paper

Auskoppelfeld *n* output field, absorbing or uncoupling field, delivery field

auskoppeln to tune out, balance out, neutralize, decouple (to suppress or lessen feedback)

Auskoppel-raum *m* catcher space, output gap **-spalt** *m* output gap

Auskoppelung *f* tuning out, balancing out, neutralization

Auskopplungsraum *m* catcher space

auskragen to corbel, jut out, cantilever

auskragende Spundwand cantilever sheet piles

Auskragung *f* bracket, projection, cantilever, corbelling

auskratzen to scrape out, scratch out, rake out, rabble out

Auskratzer für Rillenschienen scrapers for ground rails

auskreuzen to V-groove, weld, chase, (Adernpaare) to test splice, cross-joint, vee out.

Auskreuzen *n* test splicing (method), cross-jointing

Auskreuzlötstelle *f* test splice

Auskreuzung *f* bracing (aviation), cross-bracing, transposition

auskriechen to creep out

auskristallisieren to crystallize (out), sugar

Auskristallisieren *n* crystallizing, sugaring

auskrücken to rake out

Auskultation *f*, **Auskultieren** *n* auscultation

auskunden to survey (a line)

auskundschaften to explore, spy, scout

Auskundschaftung *f* reconnaissance, reconnoitering

Auskundung *f* surveying

Auskunft *f* information, intelligence

Auskunftei *f* information bureau

Auskunfts-beamter *m* inquiry clerk, information operator **-blatt** *n* inquiry docket **-stelle** *f* information bureau or desk

auskuppelbar capable of being thrown out of gear, disconnectable, disengaging **-e Doppelsteuerung** disconnectable dual control

auskuppeln to disengage (a clutch), release, uncouple, disconnect

Auskupp(e)lung *f* disconnection, disengagement, uncoupling

Auskupplungsvorrichtung *f* disengaging gear

auskurbeln to reel out, lower, pay out (the aerial)

Ausladebahnhof *m* railhead, detraining station, freight yards **~ für den Nachschub** railhead for supplies, supply-unloading depot

Auslade-bericht *m* cargo outtake certificate **-brücke** *f* handling or loading platform **-einheit** *f* unloading unit **-gebiet** *n* unloading or detrucking area **-gebläse** *n* air-compressor booster **-kommando** *n* unloading detail

ausladen to discharge, unload, project, detrain, deliver at the surface, detruck

ausladend projecting, outrigging

Ausladeplatz *m* unloading or detrucking point

Auslader *m* conducting arc, stevedore

Auslade-rampe *f* unloading platform **-spitze** *f* railhead, truck head **-station** *f* railhead **-stelle** *f* unloading or detrucking point **-übersicht** *f* detraining or unloading table

Ausladung *f* (einer Bohrmaschine) working range, working zone, drilling area; (radial) radius; (Auskragung) projection; (Wagen) unloading; (Drehkran) working angle, radial range, radius, length of action, detraining, outer (or cantilever) arm of the titan (crane), length of overhang, sweep, overhang (aviation), discharging, reach, radius of travel or jib, length of jib, maximum distance spindle to table, spindle center to column face, swing, working radius, gap, throat; (Brücke) cantilever **~ einer Radialbohrmaschine** sweep (mech.)

Ausladungs-gebühr *f* wharfage **-platz** *m* wharf

Auslage *f* expense, outlay, disbursement, display

Auslageplan *m* layout plan

auslagern to adsorb (at points of attachment)

Auslagerung *f* precipitation, removing of stocks from vulnerable places

Ausland *n* foreign country **im ~** abroad

Ausländer *m* foreigner, alien

ausländisch alien, foreign

Auslands-dienst *m* foreign service **-geschäft** *n* foreign business **-gespräch** *n* international call **-leitung** *f* international line or circuit **-lieferung** *f* foreign delivery, delivery to foreign markets **-nachricht** *f* information received from abroad, foreign news **-presse** *f* foreign press **-schrifttum** *n* foreign literature **-telegramm** *n* foreign message **-versand** *m* foreign shipping **-vertreter** *m* foreign agent

auslängen to push on the works

Auslängen *n* tendency of profiled metal pile to deform, twist, or otherwise lose original shape, pile driving

Auslaß *m* outlet, discharge, delivery, exhaust, exit, exhaust valve

auslaßbar extensible (said of landing gear)

Auslaß-deckung *f* exhaust lap, inside lap **-drossel** *f* blast gate **-druckwelle** *f* exhaust pressure wave **-ellbogen** *m* discharge knee

auslassen to omit, release, leave out, skip, blow off (steam), expand, let out, discharge, exhaust **sich ~** to expatiate, expand, make extended remarks, dilate, extenuate **mehr Tau ~** to slaken (rope)

Auslaß-energie *f* total exhaust energy **-exzenter** *m* exhaust eccenter, eduction or exhaust eccentric **-gehäuse** *n* delivery valve chamber **-gestänge** *n* exhaust rods or gear **-geschwindigkeit** *f* release velocity **-führungen** *f pl* delivery guides **-hahn** *m* discharge **-hub** *m* exhaust stroke **-kanal** *m* outlet or exhaust passage **-klappe** *f* outlet, discharge, or exhaust flap **-krümmer** *m* exhaust manifold

Auslaß-nocken *m* exhaust cam, outlet cam **-nockenwelle** *f* exhaust camshaft **-öffnung** *f* outlet orifice **-rohr** *n* delivery pipe **-röhre** *f* vent **-schieber** *m* outlet slide **-schleuse** *f* outlet **-schlitz** *m* (Kühlluft) exit slot **-seite** *f* exhaust or outlet valve **-seitige Zündkerze** exhaust plug **-steuerung** *f* exhaust-gear mechanism, exhaust valve **-stutzen** *m* exhaust stack, outlet connection or branch **-tor** *n* blast gate

Auslassung *f* omission

Auslassungszeichen *n* apostrophe (print)

Auslaßventil *n* escape valve, delivery valve, exhaust or outlet valve, discharge **~ für Luft** air vent

Auslaßventilkammer *f* exhaust port

auslasten to center, balance, equalize loads
Auslastung *f* burden, charge, load
Auslastungsgrad *m* rate of utilization
Auslauf *m* (Wasser) out flow, discharge; (Auslaß) outlet, drain, gate, deceleration, standoff, continuation, projection, mouth (of a river), landing run (aviation), taxiing, free floating of a ship as it leaves the launching slip (more precisely, from the start of free floating up to complete stoppage of the vessel, run-down (TV) delivery side ~ **von der Rolle** point where film strip leaves drum ~ **mit Schauglas** bull's-eye discharge, light feed ~ **der Waschtrommel** eyes of the drums (paper) **in** ~ production discontinued
Auslauf-bahn *f* expansion orbit **-bauwerk** *n* outlet structure **-becher** *m* (Farbe) outflow cup
auslaufen (ausrinnen) to run out, flow out; (Gefäß) leak out; (Flugzeug) taxi; (Farbe) run, blur; (allmählich ~) slow down; (Kabel) end; (Lager) wear out; (spitz ~) taper off, discharge, issue, bleed, die out, trickle, complete a run after landing, put to sea; (Motor) ~ to run down, stop gradually **Produktion ~ lassen** to taper off production
Auslaufen *n* coasting ~ **des Motors** motoring ~ **des Lagers** running-out (or burning-out) of the bearing ~ **des Schiffes** *n* slowing down of a ship
auslaufend outgoing, outward bound, ending **in eine Düse** ~ ending in a nozzle **nicht** ~ non-bleeding **-e Welle** propagating wave
Auslaufende *n* delivery or discharge end
Ausläufer *m* branch, dropper, tongue, spur, tail, extension, streamer, offshoot
Auslauf-fläche *f* drainage area **-flasche** *f* overflow flask **-gelände** *n* run-out (area) **-geschwindigkeit** *f* speed of landing run **-gestell** *n* **für Flaschen** bottle draining truck **-gleichung** *f* equation for slowing down **-hahn** *m* drain cock **-kanal** *m* discharge culvert **-kurve** *f* coasting curve, deceleration curve **-länge** *f* length of end section, length of landing run **-licht** *n* run-out light
Auslauf-manöver *n* escape maneuver **-öffnung** *f* outlet opening **-pipette** *f* calibrated delivery pipette **-probe** *f* pouring test **-raum** *m* delivery space, volute chamber **-rille** *f* run-out groove (phono), concentric groove (phono) **-rohr** *n* outlet pipe, discharge pipe **-rutsche** *f* discharge chute
Auslauf-scheibe *f* free-run test inertia disk **-schurre** *f* discharge chute **-seite** *f* delivery side, delivery end **-spitze** *f* discharge tip **-steuerdaumen** *m* slowing-down control cam
Auslaufstrecke *f* landing run, landing distance ~ **mit Bremsen** landing run with brakes ~ **mit Landeklappen** landing run with flaps
Auslaufstutzen *m* outlet connection ~ **mit Schauglas** sight discharge
Auslauf-tisch *m* delivery table **-trichter** *m* outlet funnel, discharge funnel **-ventil** *n* tap **-verfahren** *n* retardation method, inertia method **-versuch** *m* running-out test, deceleration test (balloons)
Auslaufzeit (Motor) *f* slowing time ~ (Viskositätmessung) efflux time
Auslaugbarkeit *f* solubility (of glass)
Auslaugeapparat *m* extraction apparatus
auslaugen to leach (out), extract, wash out, steam, fuse, construe
Auslaugen *n* leaching
Auslaugerei *f* leaching plant, washer plant
Auslaugerückstand leached pulps
Auslaugung *f* leaching, (wet) extraction, elution
Auslaugungstest *m* (Gummi, bei Schläuchen) (gum) leaching test
ausleeren to empty, evacuate, drain
Ausleer-halle *f* knock-out shop **-rüttler** *m* emptying jigger **-stelle** *f* discharge point, dump
Ausleerung *f* emptying
Auslegeapparat *m* delivery apparatus
Auslegearm *m* jib ~ **des Antriebslagers** projecting arm of the driving and bearing
Auslegemaschine *f* paying-out (reel) machine
auslegen to pay out, construe, interpret, publish, lay (cables), explain, expose, extend, lay out money, lay open (a patent), design, plan **mit Holzwolle** ~ to palletize
Auslegen *n* dismantling (a gun), interpretation, explanation ~ **der Leitung** paying out the line
Auslegepappe *f* dressing board
Ausleger *m* arm, overhang beam (of a rotating crane) boom, derrick, outrigger, jig loom, bracket, transom, hanger (on mast), mine chute, crosspiece, crossbar, crossbeam, spar, transverse, joist transverse, (sheet) delivery; (Brücke) cantilever; (Kran) boom, jib
Ausleger, aufklappbarer ~ hinged apron extension **drehbarer** ~ swing boom, revolving jib **einziehbarer** ~ level luffing jib **freitragender** ~ cantilever **gitterförmiger** ~ lattice-type crane arm **starrer** ~ fixed jib **umsteuerbarer** ~ reversible delivery (print.) **verstellbarer** ~ luffing jib
Ausleger-antrieb *m* jib derricking **-arm** *m* jib trolley capacity, arm of a machine tool **-balken** *m* pin-jointed or cantilever beam **-baum** *m* boom **-bock** *m* A-frame **-bockkran** *m* cantilever crane **-bohrmaschine** *f* radial boring machine **-brücke** *f* cantilever bridge **-dach** *n* cantilever roof **-drehscheibenkran** *m* derrick-type crane, moving vertically and revolving **-drehwand** *f* delivery support bracket
Auslegerechenwelle *f* delivery shaft
Ausleger-fahrgestell *n* outboard part of landing gear **-feder** *f* cantilever spring, outrigger spring **-fuß** *m* foot of jib **-gegengewicht** *n* counterweight of a crane or derrick **-gerüst** *n* flying scaffold **-getriebe** *n* outrigger gear or drive **-hebewerk** *n* boom elevator
Ausleger-kopf *m* jib head (of a crane) **-kran** *m* jib crane, derrick-type revolving crane, cantilever **-laufkatze** *f* derrick or crane traveling on rails **-leiter** *f* ladder monted on derrick **-mast** *m* bracket pole, pole with bracket **-nietmaschine** *f* beam-type riveting machine **-rolle** *f* jib sheave, jibhead sheave (crane)
Ausleger-seitenteil *m* delivery side frame **-stanzmaschine** *f* beam-type automatic punching machine **-stativ** *n* boom stand **-strebe** *f* overhang strut **-wagen** *m* delivery carriage **-werkzeug** *n* horn die **-wippkran** *m* derrick
Auslege-tisch *m* delivery table **-trommel** *f* payingout drum **-zeichen** *n* ground panel
Auslegung *f* laying, publication, interpretation, explanation, comment, construction (of an

act) **falsche** ~ misinterpretation, erroneous interpretation or construction ~ **der Anlage oder Konstruktion** plant layout or design ~ **der Nut** the lining of the slot

Auslegungspunkt *m* point of interpretation, design (starting) point

ausleiern to wear out

ausleihen to lend

auslenken to defect, bank, incline, travel out, compensate (guided missiles)

Auslenkhärte *f* deflection hardness

Auslenkkraft (Schreiber) rebalancing force **seitliche** ~ side thrust (acoust.)

Auslenkung *f* deflection or deflecting from true path, deviation, lateral deflection **seitliche** ~ (d. Grammophonnadel) lateral excursion

Auslese *f* selection, sorting, prime **-fähigkeit** *f* selectivity **-knopf** *m* selector, switch

Auslesen *n* signal reading

auslesen to pick out, select, sort, read through, separate, classify, grade, read out

Ausleser *m* separator, sifter

Auslese- und Sortiermaschine *f* selecting and sifting machinery

Ausleuchtapparat für Fässer cask-illuminating apparatus

ausleuchten project (screen) **ein Faß** ~ to illuminate a cask

Ausleuchten *n* optical stimulation

Ausleuchtlampe *f*, **elektrische** ~ electric lamp for lighting

Ausleuchtung *f* illumination, stimulation ~ **und Tilgung** extinction or quenching (of fluorescence), evanescence **gleichmäßige** ~ even illumination

auslichten to thin out

ausliefern to deliver up, relinquish, give, give off, impart, surrender, extradite, supply

Auslieferung *f* surrender, extradition, delivery, exposure, distribution

Auslieferungsvertrag *m* extradition treaty

Auslieger *m* coast-guard vessel

Ausliterung *f* measuring content in liters

auslochen to mortise

auslöffeln to scoop out, remove with a spoon

auslohnen to pay off

auslösbar removable, soluble

auslöschen to darken, extinguish, quench, blow out, delete, erase, blot, obliterate, cancel, put out

Auslöschmagnet *n* obliteration magnet, obliterating pole piece

Auslöschung *f* (X ray) interference, darkening, extinction, null point, quenching ~ **der Bahndrehimpulse** quenching of the orbital moments

Auslöschungs-lage *f* extinction position **-schiefe** *f* extinction angle **-satz** *m* extinction theorem **-schräge** *f* extinction angle

Auslöschzone *f* dead spot, region of silence

Auslöse-ader *f* release wire **-anschlag** *m* trip dog **-arbeit** *f* total internal work function **-batterie** *f* tripping battery **-charakteristik** *f* characteristic of circuit control (elec.) **-daumen** *m* resetting cam, releasing cam **-einrichtung** *f* release gear or mechanism **-elektrode** *f* release (emitting) electrode **-elektron** *n* triggering electron **-feder** *f* release or tripping spring **-fehler** *m* failure to release **-funke** *m* trip spark

Auslöse-gestänge *n* release rod **-grenzstrom** *m* minimum tripping current **-griff** *m* release handle **-haken** *m* detaching hook, clips for monkey (trip gear), drop action of pile driver **-hebel** *m* release lever, trip lever, detent lever **-impuls** *m* trigger pulse (electron.) **-kennlinie** *f* tripping characteristic **-klinke** *f* trip-releasing catch (setting off the trigger) **-knagge** *f* coupling tappet **-knaggen** *m* trip dog **-knopf** *m* release button **-kontakt** *m* release contact **-kreis** *m* transfer circuit

Auslösemagnet *m* release magnet, trigger magnet, trip magnet ~ **und Fortschub** release and spacing magnet

Auslösemagnetdruck *m* printing trip magnet

Auslöse-mechanismus *m* trip mechanism **-moment** *m* instant of exposure or shutter release **-muffe** *f* release sleeve

auslosen to raffle, draw by lots

auslösen to loosen, release; (auskuppeln) disengage, throw out of gear; (Elektr.) break the circuit, render operative, trip, ungear, dissolve out, relieve, trigger, disconnect, release (shutter), reset, emit, give off (electrons); (ausrücken) ~ to release; (einrücken) ~ to trip, start; (eine Wirkung) ~ to produce an effect **langsam auslösend** slow to release **plötzlich** ~ to trip

Auslösen (einer Ltg.) *n* to trip, release, interrupt (a line)

Auslöse-nase *f* cam for cut-out, releasing lug (lobe) **-nocken** *m* releasing cam

Auslöse- oder Steuerstange *f* trip rod

Auslöse-propeller *m* rotary distributor (multiple-spark photography) **-punkt** *m* bomb-release point, release point

Auslöser *m* release knob, lever, trigger, tripping device; (Fernschreiber) carriage return lock bar

Auslöserelais *n* tripping relay, clearout relay, releasing relay

Auslöser-fläche *f* liberating area **-knopf** *m* jack or escapement button, set-off button (piano) **-spule** *f* trip coil

Auslöse-schalter *m* trip switch **-schaltkasten** *m* release switchbox **-scheibe** *f* release disk **-schere der Kunstramme** drop action of pile driver **-spindel** *f* trip spindle **-spule** *f* trip coil **-stab** *m* trigger bar (print) **-stange** *f* release bar, trip bar **-stift** *m* rod (loose hand rod for tripping or moving a gear)

Auslösestrom *m* releasing current **-stoß** *m* starting impulse **-kreis** *m* trip circuit

Auslösesynchronimpuls *m* tripping pulse (radar)

Auslösetaste *f* release key ~ **für Magnettasten** release button for magnetic buttons

Auslöse-überwachung *f* release guard **-verzögerung** *f* release retardation **-vorrichtung** *f* releasing or tripping device, tumbler, unlocking mechanism, release (trigger) mechanism, bomb release control

Auslöse-welle *f* releasing axle, tripping bar ~ **von Auslösewippe gesteuert** trip spindle controlled by release catch

Auslöse-zeit *f* delay-time action, time lag (total period of), lag of release **-zeitpunkt** *m* bomb-release moment

Auslosung *f* allotment

Auslösung *f* trip(ping), starting, release, releasing, resetting, stop, launching, uncoupling, hole, depression, detaching, redemption, detent, escapement (watch), opening, trip (elec.), cutout, drawing, clearing, automatic circuit control mechanism **~ der Energie** release of energy **~** (Ausrückung) **der Kupplung** release of the coupling

Auslösung, abhängig verzögerte ~ inverse time element **mit (un)abhängig verzögerter ~** (definite) inverse time-limit relay or release

Auslösungs-anschlag *m* trip dog **-feder** *f* escapement spring, release or trip spring **-haken** *m* nipper of a pile driver **-knopf** *m* jack, escapement or set-off button or knob **-punkt** *m* trip point **-zeichen** *n* release guard signal **-zeit** *f* time or period of throw-out (switch)

ausloten to plumb, sound

Ausloten einer Wand battering of a wall

auslüften to air, renew the air, ventilate

Auslug *m* lookout

ausmachen to put out, arrange, discover, constitute, determine, total, make

Ausmachen *n* perception of a light (maritime signals)

ausmahlen to grind, mill

Ausmahlprodukt *n* attrition product

Ausmahlung *f* comminution, grinding

ausmalen to paint, imagine

Ausmaß *n* extent, dimension, size, measurement, over-all length, amount, amplitude

Ausmaße *pl* overall dimensions

ausmauern to wall up, brick up, line with brick

Ausmauerung *f* brick lining, brickwork, masonry, stone cradling **wasserdichte ~ eines Schachtes** coffering

ausmeißeln to sculpture, chase, chisel

ausmerzen to eliminate, eradicate, remove

ausmessen to measure, gauge, survey, span.

Ausmeß-gerät *n* admeasuring or measuring apparatus, measuring machine **-platte** *f* gauge plate

Ausmessung *f* admeasurement, measurement **~ der Position** plotting of position

Ausmeßverfahren *n* method of admeasurement or measurement

ausmitteln to form the average, identify, determine

ausmittig eccentric, off-center **-e Druckbelastung** asymmetrical compressive stress

Ausmultiplizieren der Klammer multiplying out the expression or quantity in brackets

ausmünden to discharge, lead into, open, empty, end

Ausmündung *f* orifice, outlet, exit, discharging hole, mouth (print), nozzle **~ eines Kanals** the outlet of a canal (into a river)

ausmünzen to coin, mint

ausmustern to discharge, reject

Ausmusterung *f* sampling

Ausmusterungsschein *m* certificate of rejection

ausnagen to gnaw, nibble, eat into, corrode

Ausnagung *f* gnawing from inside out, corrosion

Ausnahme *f* exception **mit ~ von** except(ing) **ohne ~** invariably

Ausnahme-fall *m* exceptional case, exception **-gespräch** *n* urgent call **-hauptanschluß** *m* main plugout connection (signal) **-querverbindung** *f* cross plug-out connection (signal) **-querverbindungen** *f pl* special cross connections **-zustand** *m* state of emergency

ausnahmslos invariable

ausnahmsweise by way of exception, for once

ausnehmen to exempt, take out, select, except

Ausnehmung *f* clearance, recess

Ausniet-großvorrichtung *f* riveting jig or rig **-vorrichtung** *f* riveting fixture

ausnuten to groove

ausnutzbare Ladefähigkeit disposable load

ausnutzen to exploit, take advantage of, utilize, exhaust, turn to profit, make the most of **bis zur Grenze der Leistungsfähigkeit ~** to strain to the utmost limit of the capacity

Ausnutzung *f* exploitation, utilization, efficiency, efficient utilization, workload **~ günstiger Gelegenheiten** utilization of opportunities

Ausnutzungs-faktor *m* unit capacity factor, over-all or commercial officiency, utilization or exploitation factor **-grad** *m* utilization factor, coefficient of utilization **-koeffizient** *m* utilization coefficient **-zahl** *f* unit-capacity factor

ausörtern to take the squaring

ausösen to bail out (water)

auspacken to unpack

Auspackrost *m* emptying grid

auspeilen to examine or sound (the ground), test by sound (ranging equipment)

auspellen to husk

auspendeln to oscillate

Auspendeln *n* swing **~ des Motors** final oscillating, stopping oscillation of motor

auspfählen to pile

auspfänden to distrain

auspfeifen to blow out (mining)

auspflastern to pave (out)

auspichen to pitch, tar

auspinseln to paint, swab, blot out

ausplatten to flatten out, plate out

Ausplatten *n* plating out, flattening

Ausplatzungen *pl* spalling (enamel)

ausplentern to prick out (forest)

auspolstern to upholster, pad, quilt

Auspolsterung *f* lagging, lining

ausprägen to coin, mint

Ausprägungskategorien *pl* categories of definition

auspressen to squeeze out, press out, force out, crush

Auspressen *n* extrusion

Auspreß-maschine *f* squeezer **-sonde** *f* outlet well, ejection well **-walzen** *pl* washing or pulping rolls (first process)

ausproben to test, sample, try out

ausprobieren to test out, try out, try, experiment

Ausprobieren *n* testing, trying, cut-and-try method

Ausprobiermethode *f* cut and try method

ausprüfen to debug **Adern ~** to identify wires

Auspuff *m* outlet, exhaust, exit, escape, outflow **~ mit Abgasschubausnutzung** ejector exhaust **mit ~ arbeiten** to work with open exhaust **freier ~** open exhaust **rauchfreier ~** clean exhaust

Auspuff-blitze *pl* exhaust ports **-dampf** *m* escape

steam **-dampfmaschine** *f* noncondensing steam engine **-dampfturbine** *f* steam turbine (exhaust type) **-dichtung** *f* silencer, muffler **-drehschieber** *m* rotary exhaust valve **-druck** *m* terminal pressure

auspuffen to exhaust, escape, discharge

Auspuffen *n* exhaust stroke **freies ~** exhausting to atmosphere

Auspuff-flammendämpfer *m* exhaust-flame damper **-filter** *n* exhaust strainer **-flansch** *m* exhaust flange **-freihebel** *m* cutout lever **-führung** *f* piping of the exhaust gases **-funkenkorb** *m* exhaust spark catcher **-flammendämpfer** *m* exhaust-flame damper **-führung** *f* piping of the exhaust gases **-gas** *n* exhaust gas **-gaszerleger** *m* exhaust-gas analyzer **-gegendruck** *m* exhaust back pressure **-geräusch** *n* exhaust noise **-geschwindigkeit** *f* exhaust-gas velocity **-gestänge** *n* exhaust rods or gear **-hub** *m* exhaust stroke

Auspuff-kammer *f* exhaust chamber **-kanal** *m* exhaucht port or duct **Auspuff-kessel** *m* exhaust chamber **-klappe** *f* cutout (exhaust), exhaust valve **-knallen** *n* backfire, exhaust detonation **-kondensation** *f* condensation of the exhaust gases **-kopf** *m* exhaust head **-krümmer** *m* exhaust pipe or stack, exhaust manifold **-kühlung** *f* cooling of the exhaust gases

Auspuff-leitung *f* exhaust pipe, line, manifold or duct **-maschine** *f* non-condensing engine **-öffnung** *f* exhaust opening **-periode** period of exhaust, exhaust stroke **-pfeife** *f* exhaust alarm **-ring** *m* exhaust collector ring **-rohr** *n* exhaust pipe, exhaust manifold

Auspuffröhre *f* exhaust stack **~ zum Auspufftopf** manifold

Auspuffrohrschelle *f* exhaust-manifold clamp

Auspuffsammler *m* exhaust manifold, receiver, exhaust collector **ringförmiger ~** exhaust ring **-rohr** *n* exhaust manifold, outlet manifold

Auspuff-sammelring *m* (Sternmotor) exhaust collector ring **-schalldämpfer** *m* exhaust silencer or muffler **-schelle** *f* exhaust manifold clamp **-schlitz** *m* exhaust port **-schweif** *m* vapor trail (engines) **-seite** *f* port side **-steuerachse** *f* exhaust-cam axle **-steuerwelle** *f* exhaust camshaft **-stutzen** *m* exhaust manifold or stack, short stack, stub exhaust pipe, exhaust port or connection **-system** *n* exhaust system or arrangement **-takt** *m* exhaust stroke, exhaust cycle, last explosion in the engine **-topf** *m* exhaust muffler, chamber, head, or silencer

Auspuffventil *n* exhaust valve **-bolzen** *m* exhaust-valve pin **-drücker** *m* exhaust-valve lift **-feder** *f* exhaust-valve spring **-führung** *f* exhaust-valve guide **-kanone** *f* exhaust valve, sleeve **-mitnehmer** *m* exhaust-valve lifter **-spindel** *f*, **-stange** *f* exhaust valve stem

Auspuff-widerstand *m* exhaust resistance, back pressure (of exhaust) **-wolke** *f* exhaust smoke **-wulst** *m* exhaust-valve chamber or chest (internal-combustion engines)

auspumpen to pump out, evacuate, exhaust, run down

Auspumpen *n* unwatering, running down, exhaustion, evacuation

Auspumpung *f* exhaustion, rarefaction, pumping (out)

Auspumpzeit *f* pump-down time

auspunktieren to run out (with leaders)

Ausputz *m* card waste

ausputzen to clean (out), trim, polish, snag

Ausputz-kratze *f* cleaning brush **-loch** *n* slush hole **-walze** *f* stripping roller

ausquadrieren to square out

ausquetschen to flow out laterally, squeeze out, ring out, squeegee

Ausquetschwalze *f* squeezing roller

ausradieren to erase, scrape out, obliterate

Ausradiervorrichtung *f* sound eraser

ausrändeln to pink

ausrangieren to sort out, discard, shunt out

ausräuchern to smoke out, fumigate

Ausräumbohrer *m* square tap reamer

ausräumen to broach, draw out, rake out, clinker, ream, clear out (stoppage), remove, mop up, discharge (the centrifugal)

Ausräumen *n* discharging

Ausräumer *m* fluke **~ für Bohrlöcher** drag

Ausräum-maschine *f* cleanser **-schnecke** *f* drag twist

ausrasten release (tape rec.)

ausrauschen lassen to let go

ausrechenbar calculable

ausrechnen to calculate, compute, run out

Ausrechnung *f* computation, calculation

ausrecken to stretch, extend, lengthen, rack **das Tuch ~** to smooth the cloth

Ausrecken (*n*) **des Drahtes** rectification of wire

ausreffen to shake out a reef, unreeve

ausregeln to level, control, stabilize

Ausregelung der Abweichung deviation control

Ausregelzeit *f* decline period of control potential, transient load response

Ausregulator *m* throttle-valve

ausreiben to ream, erase, rub out **Fässer ~** to rub the pitch out of the screw bung

Ausreiber *m* reamer, contersink

ausreichend sufficient, adequate, decent **-e Güte** acceptable quality level **nicht ~** scanty, insufficient

ausreifen to flute, channel, rifle

Ausreifung *f* maturation, maturing

ausreißen to pluck (out), desert, spread (a sail), tear out

Ausreißer *m* plucker (one who plucks out), wild or stray shot, outliers (quality control)

Ausreißer *pl* outliers (quality control)

ausrenken to sprain, dislocate

Ausrichtbeil *n* cone block

Ausrichtemarke *f* guide mark

ausrichten to discover, explore (min.), level, dress, align, straighten, adjust, true up, perform, coordinate, indoctrinate, orient **~** (fluchten), to straighten out, place in position **~ in Linie** to align, level, line up **ein Lager ~** to true a bearing **sich ~** to align **sich nach links oder rechts ~** to dress left or right

Ausrichten *n* alignment, straightening, adjustment, focusing, dressing, leveling, fitting, truing up **~ der Federn eines Relais** aligning of springs of a relay **Stativ zum ~ von zylindrischen Körpern auf der Werkzeugmaschine** stand for checking cylindrical pieces on the machine tool

Ausricht-keile *m pl* wedge strips, fitting wedge pieces **Ausricht-lochung** *f* register punching **-schablone** *f* aligning jig **-strecke** *f* advance heading (min.)

Ausrichtung *f* alignment, orientation, straightening, focusing (print), exploring (min.) **die ~ prüfen** to check alignment **falsche ~** misalignment (of image or track) **genaue ~** accurate alignment **schlechte ~** misalignment **~ der Kernmomente** orientation of nuclear moments

Ausrichtungsarbeit *f* exploration work, prospecting work

Ausrichtwalzen *f pl* straightening rolls

ausringen to wring

Ausringen des Seidengarns silk wringing

ausrinnen to run or leak out

ausrippen to strip, unrib

Ausrisse *m pl* tears or partings of material in fatigue

ausroden to root out, clear (a forest)

ausrollen to roll, unroll, stop rolling, roll to a stop **ein Kabel ~** to run out a cable

Ausrollen *n* landing run (aviation)

Ausroll-geschwindigkeit *f* speed of the landing run, landing speed **-grenze** *f* plastic limit **-strecke** *f* (beim Landen), length of landing run of aircraft **-winkel** *m* landing angle **-zeit** *f* stick time (aviation)

ausrosten to clinker, remove slag

ausrotten to exterminate, purge, root out, wipe out, crush, annihilate

Ausrotter *m pl* grubbers and weeders (agr.)

Ausrottung *f* extinction

ausrückbar disconnectable **-e Kupplung** coupling capable of being disengaged, disconnectable coupling

Ausrück-bolzen *m* release pin **-büchse** *f* throwout sleeve (of gear clutch) **-bügel** *m* disengaging strap

ausrücken to throw out, declutch, disengage, shift, release, trip, evacuate, run away, throw out of gear, stop, disconnect, move up, unmesh, march out, depart **~** (Getriebe) to throw out **den Riemen ~** to throw off the belt

Ausrücken *n* release, launching, uncoupling, disengaging (Zahnräder) **~** demeshing gears **augenblickliches Einrücken und ~** instantaneous engaging and release

Ausrücker *m* (belt) shifter, disengaging gear, stopper, releasing lever **-bügel** *m* shifter yoke **-gabel** *f* shifter fork or finger, disengaging or disconnecting fork **-welle** *f* shipper shaft, belt shifter bar

Ausrück-feder *f* release spring **-gabel** *f* disengaging fork **-gang** *m* stopping (print) **-glied** *n* stop link **-hebel** *m* disengaging lever, lifter, clutch lever, belt shifter **-hebewelle** *f* disengagement lever spindle **-klaue** *f* clutch coupling box **-klinke** *f* release trigger **-kloben** *m* table feed trip block **-kupplung** *f* disconnecting clutch

Ausrück-lager *n* release bearing **-muffe** *f* throwout bearing or sliding sleeve, release bearing for clutch **-schiene** *f* disengaging bar **-spindel** *f* stop spindle **-stange** *f* disengaging rod **-stärke** *f* initial strength **-stellung** *f* disengaged position

Ausrückung *f* throwing out of gear, disconnection, disengagement

Ausrück-vorrichtung *f* disengaging device, disengaging or tripping gear, (belt) shifter, shifting device **-welle** *f* disengaging shaft

ausrufen lassen to page (some out)

Ausrufungszeichen *n* exclamation point

Ausrundbohrer *m* auger

ausrunden to round

Ausrundung *f* rounding off, fillet, smoothing out

Ausrupferin *f* plucking woman (textiles)

ausrüsten to equip, remove scaffolding or forms, fit out, supply, furnish

Ausrüster *m* finisher

Ausrüstung *f* equipment, outfit, apparatus, fitting, armature, rig, finishing (paper), appliance, device, mechanism, furniture, material **~ für Fußantrieb** foot-power attachment **~ von Gestängen** arming of poles **~ für erste Hilfe** first-aid outfit **elektrische ~ mit Kontrollern** electric control gear **feine ~** (Kessel) fittings **grobe ~** (Kessel) fixtures **serienmäßig eingebaute ~** regular equipment

Ausrüstungs-gegenstand *m* article of equipment, distributing asset **-gerät** *n* accessory equipment **-hafen** *m* fitting-out wharf **-nachweis** *m* equipment status report **-platz** *m* supply base **-stück** *n* accessory piece of equipment **-verfahren** *n* finishing process **-verzeichnis** *n* equipment inventory **-vorschrift** *f* installation or equipment specification

ausrutschen to slip, glide

Ausrutschen *n* sideslipping

Aussaat *f* sowing

aussäbeln to hock (bar)

aussacken to empty a bag (sack)

aussäen to sow, drill, disseminate

Aussage *f* statement, deposition, testimony, declaration, affidavit, affirmation, evidence

aussagen to testify, declare, assert, state, give evidence

aussägen to saw out

Aussagender *m* declarant, deponent, witness

aussaigern to segregate, liquate, sweat out (tin)

Aussaigerung *f* sweating

aussalzen to salt out (Seife) **~** grain (out)

Aussalzstärke salting strength

Aussalzungskoeffizient *m* salting-out coefficient

aussäuern to deacidulate

aussaugen to exhaust, drain out, suck out **~** (eine Flotte) to remove by suction

Aussaugpumpe *f* vacuum pump

ausschaben, (den Kessel) **~** to clean or scrape (a boiler)

Ausschaber *m* scraper

ausschachten to excavate, tunnel

Ausschachtung *f* excavation

ausschäkeln to unshackle

ausschalen to remove forms (from concrete), dismantle

Ausschalen *n* stripping the forms

ausschaltbar disengegeable, disconnectible

Ausschaltbewegung auslösen to trip out (aviation)

Ausschalthebel *m* throw-out lever

ausschalten (Sache, Angelegenheit) to dispose of; (korrigieren) correct, compensate for; (Licht) switch off, turn out; (Strom) cut out; (Kupplung) throw out, disengage, break, eliminate, correct, cut off, disconnect, avoid, put out, take off, release, throw out, turn off, exclude, trip (the current), separate, open the circuit, break contact, switch out of circuit **sich ~** to trip out (aviation) **einen Gang ~** to throw out of gear **durch Übergehen einer Be-**

grenzung ~ to override (aviation) **die Zündung** ~ to disconnect the ignition

Ausschalten *n* disconnection, opening of a circuit, switching off (out), disconnecting ~ **der Grundstufe** calibration correction, correction for velocity error ~ **des Schallverzuges** acoustic correction ~ **der Temperatureinflüsse** elasticity correction on gun ~ **des Windes** wind correction ~ **der besonderen und Witterungseinflüsse** rectification of error of the moment, correction for interior and exterior ballistic factors **ruckweises** ~ cutting out or disconnection by reversing, jerking stop

Ausschalter *m* circuit breaker, cutout, switch, disconnecting switch ~ **eingestellt für ... Sekunden Auslösezeit** time lag set for ... seconds

Ausschalte-sicherung *f* disconnecting switch fuse **-stab** *m* shut-off rod **-vorrichtung** *f* stopping device

Ausschalt-feder *f* cut-off spring **-hebel** *m* release lever **-leistung** *f* breaking capacity **-rille** *f* throw-out groove (phono) **-signalstift** *m* shut-off indicating pin **-spule** *f* trip coil **-stellung** *f* switch-off position **-strecke** *f* length of break

Ausschaltstrom *m* breaking current **zulässiger** ~ circuit-breaker capacity

Ausschalt-tafel *f* switch panel **-taste** *f* circuit-breaking key **-vermögen** *n* breaking capacity **-verzögerung** *f* disconnection delay

Ausschaltung *f* elimination, exclusion, circuit break, switching off, disconnection, excavation, framework cutout ~ **wertloser Erzeugnisse** elimination of valueless products, disposal of waste products ~ **der Schnittbildversetzung** halving adjustment on range finder

Ausschaltvorrichtung bei Übergeschwindigkeit overspeed governor

Ausschalung *f* sheeting, boarding, encasing, lathing, lining

ausscharen to ramify

ausschärfen to bevel, deaden, dull, scarf (edges), sharpen ~ (abstumpfen) to neutralize

Ausschärf-fräsmaschine *f* scarf-milling machine **-hobelmaschine** *f* scarf-planing machine **-maschine** *f* scarfing machine

ausscharten to notch

ausschaufeln to shovel out

ausscheiden to eliminate, separate; (ausschließen) remove, exclude; (Math.) eliminate; (ausziehen) extract; (fällen) settle out, precipitate; (ausseigern) segregate; (absetzen) settle, deposit, discard, sort out, liberate, secrete, retire, reserve, detail, put out of action, detach, drop out, condense ~ (Teile einer Anmeldung), to divide an application for letters patent **als Ausschuß** ~ to scrap, reject **sich** ~ to precipate, settle down or out

Ausscheiden *n* setting out ~ **des Salzes** separation of the salt

Ausscheidetafel *f* decrement table

Ausscheide- und Ladeverluste *pl* pumping losses

Ausscheidewahrscheinlichkeit *f* rate of withdrawal

Ausscheidung *f* exudation, separation, elimination, segregation, generation, removal, precipitation, dissociation, precipitate, deposit, efflorescence

Ausscheidungs-effekt *m* filtering, separating, or excluding action or effect **-härtung** *f* age-hardening, precipitation hardening, dispersion hardening **-mittel** *n* separating agent, precipitant **-produkt** *n* by-product **-prüfung** *f* eliminating test **-punkt** *m* point of separating out **-rennen** *n* elimination run

ausschenken to retail, dispense, put on draught

ausscheren to leave a formation, fall out, run off, leave station in a formation

ausscheuern to scour, scrub, wear out by friction

ausschicken to send out, dispatch, detail, detach

ausschiebbar telescopic

ausschieben to exhaust

Ausschießbrett *n* imposing board (print)

ausschießen to impose (print.), puff (said of the wind), interleave (print)

Ausschießen *n* puffing out ~ **der Diffuseure** discharging ~ **des Stevens** rake ~ **des Windes** veering

Ausschießplatte *f* imposing surface

ausschiffen to debark, disembark

Ausschiffung *f* debarkation

ausschirren to unharness

ausschlachten to scrap, salvage **die Form** ~ to pull the form to pieces (print.)

ausschlacken to slag, tap slag, draw off, remove or skim off slag, rake out slag or cinder, clinker (clean out)

Ausschlag *m* (Zeiger) deflection, deviation; (Pendel) swing; (Schwingungsweite) amplitude; (~ der Waage) turn of the scale; (~ einer Schwingung) amplitude, efflorescence, turn, movement, result, thrust, removal, scum, lining, exudation, eruption, throw, reading, displacement of phase, decisive factor, angular displacement, stop, beat, rash result, excursion, kick, travel (of a coil diaphragm, instrument needle, or beam), decision, level, magnitude ~ (Ausblühen) efflorescence exudation **den** ~ **geben** to decide ~ **eines Anzeigegerätes** deflection of an indicator ~ **des Geigers** deflection of the pointer ~ **der Räder** steering lock ~ **nach beiden Seiten** deflection in both directions ~ **der Schwingung** amplitude of a vibration ~ **des Ventils** valve opening ~ **eines Zeigers** beat **einseitiger** ~ scale with zero at end, deflection in one direction **gleichmäßiger** ~ steady deflection

Ausschlag-begrenzung *f* limit of deflection (wheels) **-bereich** *m* range of deflection of control surface **-bildung** *f* spotting out **-bogen** *m* arc of rotation, arc of amplitude of the oscillation of a pendulum **-bottich** *m* hop back, underback **-eisen** *n* punch

ausschlägeln, einen Edelstein ~ to hollow a precious stone

ausschlagen to knock out; (Mine) crush and sift; (ablehnen) refuse, pass up; (Zeiger) deflect; (Waage) turn; (Pendel) swing; (ablaufen) result in, turn out throw (out), flatten, cover, take out a clearing cistern, line (a box with zinc), exude, extend (flaps), effloresce, open out, descend (scales) **nach rückwärts** ~ to deflect backward **zu weit** ~ to overthrow

Ausschlagen *n* deflection, swinging, throwing, lining **zu weites** ~ overthrowing

Ausschläger *m* finisher scutcher

Ausschlagfaktor *m* deflection factor

ausschlaggebend determinative, decisive, telling, crucial **-er Faktor** *m* determining factor

Ausschlag-kompensator *m* deflection potentiometer **-kraft** *f* deflecting force **-laternen** *pl* side and buffer lanterns **-maschine** *f* reading and stamping machine **-methode** *f* deflection method **-verhütung** *f* antiscum **-weg** *m* angle range **-weite** *f* amplitude

Ausschlagwinkel *m* angle of deflection ~ **des Schiffes** angle of deviation of a ship

Ausschlagwinkelbereich *m* range of angular deflection (of control surface)

ausschlämmen, Teiche ~ to clear pools from mud

Ausschlämmen *n* elutriation

ausschleifen to whet, grind (out), wear out, rebore **kugelförmig** ~ to grind out into a spherical curvature

Ausschleifung *f* pitching

Ausschleudermaschine *f* centrifuge, draining machine

ausschleudern to centrifuge, drain, spin out, hydroextract

ausschleusen to remove

Ausschleusen *n* discharging

Ausschleusungsvorrichtung *f* (Förderanl.) delivery device

ausschlichten to plane, dress, ground (with the moon-knife)

Ausschließapparat *m* justification device (print)

ausschließen to disqualify, exclude, preclude. justify (print.), interdict, bar

ausschließend prohibitive

ausschließlich with exception of, exclusive, excluding

Ausschließlichkeit *f* uniqueness

Ausschließlichkeitsrechte *pl* exclusivity rights

Ausschließquerstück *n* quad (print)

Ausschließung *f* exclusion, exemption, disqualification

Ausschließungs-gründe *m pl* reasons for exclusion **-prinzip** *n* exclusion or equivalence principle **-regel** *f* exclusion rule **-schein** *m* certificate of exclusion from military service for those not worthy

Ausschliff (bei Bifokalgläser) portion which is cut out to produce segment

Ausschlinger Versuch free rolling test (for ships)

Ausschlitz *m* outlet

ausschlitzen, im offenen Schacht ~ to construct in open cutting

Ausschluß *m* disconnection, exclusion, spaces (print.), determination, switch off **-brille** (für ein Auge) "barlight" spectacles **-dose** *f* switch box

ausschlüsseln to decode

Ausschluß-feder *f* disconnecting spring **-gebiet** *n* exclave **-kasten** *m* space (quad) case **-keil** *m* justification wedge **-kontakt** *m* locking contact **-material** *n* spacing material

Ausschlußrelais mit gegenseitigem Ausschluß relay with alternating reciprocal action

Ausschluß-sphäre *f* sphere of exclusion **-zeiger** *m* justifying (scale) pointer

ausschmelzen to melt out, melt, fuse off, render

Ausschmelzen *n* (Fett) dry rendering

ausschmieden to forge, forge out, hammer, draw out, extend, beat out

ausschmiegen to chamfer, splay

ausschmieren to grease, lubricate, smear

Ausschmückung *f* decoration

ausschnappen to snap out, release

ausschneiden to cut out

Ausschneiden mit Führungsgerät für das Schneidewerkzeug routing for cutting tool

Ausschnitt *m* cutout, notch, hole, opening, cutaway portion, louver, aperture, recording window, sector, segment, hollow slot; newspaper clipping **-handel** *m* retail trade **-skizze** *f* detail sketch

Ausschnürer *m* one who unties, tier up (textiles)

ausschöpfen to ladle out, empty, teem

Ausschöpfen *n* scooping ~ **einer Baugrube** drainage of an excavation. draining a spring

Ausschöpfung *f* drainage, burnout

ausschrägen to splay, slant, bevel

Ausschram *m* carving

ausschrämen to hole, carve

ausschrapen to scrape out

ausschrauben to screw off, screw out, unscrew

Ausschraubwerkzeug für Spundringe bush wrench

ausschreiben to announce, work out

Ausschreiben der Anfragen und Bestellungen making out of inquiries and orders

Ausschreibung *f* advertising (for bids). submission request for proposal, proposal request

Ausschreibungsverfahren *n*, **öffentliches** ~ competitive procurement procedure

ausschreiten to pace, step out

ausschroten to husk

ausschrumpfen to outshrink

Ausschruppen *n* roughing out

Ausschub *m* exhaust, oscillation **-druck** *m* squeezing-out pressure **-hub** *m* **-periode** *f* exhaust stroke **-stern** *m* discharge star **-winkel** *m* angle of oscillation

ausschüren, das Feuer ~ to clean (the fires)

Ausschuß *m* commission, board, committee, low-quality goods, casse paper, spoilage, offcuts, waste, scrap, refuse, rejects, discard, rejected material, rejection, spoiled casting, point where bullet leaves the body, broke, brokes, broken (paper mfg.) ~ **für Einheiten und Formeln** committee on units and formulas, standards or standardization committee ~ **durch Nacharbeit gebrauchsfähig machen** to salvage **als** ~ **ausscheiden** to reject, scrap

Ausschuß-bogen *m* spoil sheet **-kurve** *f* percentage table of rejects **-lehre** *f* not-go gauge **-liste** *f* scrap list **-papier** *n* mackled sheets, waste paper **-rate** *f* part rejects rate **-stück** *n* waster (metal) reject, scrap **-ware** *f* damaged goods **-wolle** *f* flock, bad wool

Ausschußziffer im Verhältnis zum Ausbringen scrap-to-finish product ratio

Ausschüttanlage *f* supply mechanism ~ **für Säcke** sack-shaking plant

ausschütteln to shake out

ausschütten to dump out, pour out, empty, tip, diffuse, spill (acid)

Ausschütt-höhe *f* dumping height **-rinne** *f* delivery chute

Ausschütt- und Absackwaage dumping and sacking scale

Ausschüttung *f* payment (of dividends), dumping

Ausschüttweite *f* dumping radius
Ausschwebelänge *f* length of leveling off
ausschweben to flatten out (aviation) **~ lassen** to flatten out, hold off
Ausschwebestrecke *f* length of leveling off
ausschwefeln to impregnate with sulfur, fumigate with sulfur
ausschweifen to splay out, beat out, scallop
Ausschweißen *n* rendering
Ausschweißung *f* weld deposit
Ausschwellprobe *f* bulging or expanding test (tubes)
ausschwemmen to flush out (drains)
Ausschwemmen *n* flushing
Ausschwemmungsboden *m* eluvial soil
ausschwenkbar can be swung out **-er Einlagedorn** swing-out mandrel
ausschwenken to swing over, swing out (away), shake, traverse, rinse (whirl)
Ausschwenkmaschine *f* centrifuge, hydroextractor
Ausschwenkung aus der Mittellage rotational deviation
Ausschwingdauer *f* dying-out or decay time
ausschwingen to die out, die away, die down, decay, fade out
Ausschwingen *n* decay, dying out, free vibrations
Ausschwing-grad *m* rate of decay **-konstante** *f* dying-out constant (transient) **-kurve** *f* deflection curve **-maschine** *f* centrifuge **-platte** *f* swing-out plate **-strom** *m* decay current, decaying current (of transients) **-versuch** *m* test by free oscillation
Ausschwingungs-kurve *f* curve of extinction of rolling **-versuch** *m* free-vibration test, free-oscillation test **-verzerrung** *f* decay nonlinear distortion, facsimile transient distortion **-verzug** *m* hang-over (electronics), tailing, excessive prolongation of decay of wave tail **-zeit** *f* time of decay (radar)
Ausschwing-verfahren extinction of oscillation procedure **-vorgang** *m* dying-out process, decay process, dying-out transient **-zeit** *f* dying-down time, time of decay (of an oscillation)
ausschwirren to whiz out, centrifuge
Ausschwitzen *n* sweating (of lacquers), seep; (von Farbe) floating; (Leim) glue penetration
Ausschwitzung *f* exudation, oozing out
Ausschwungvorgang *m* dying-out process decay process
aussedimentieren to sediment out
aussehen to appear, look (out) **gut ~** to be neat in appearance
Aussehen *n* appearance, look, make-up, finish **~ des Gebirges unter den Anschwemmungen** subdrift contour **~ des Gefüges** structural features **gutes ~** good finish
ausseigern to segregate, liquate, sweat out (tin), lignate
Ausseigerung *f* segregation, liquation
außen outward
Außenabmessung *f* external-dimension measurement
Außenabtrieb *m* power take-off, transfer case
Außen-anlage *f* external plant, outdoor equipment **-ansicht** *f* outside view **-anstrich** *m* outside coating **-antenne** *f* exterior antenna, outdoor or outside or open antenna **-antriebsgehäuse** *n* power take-off case **-armierung** *f* external frame **-aufhängung** *f* external stowage or surpension **-aufnahme** *f* outdoor or exterior picture or shot, outdoor scene, screen pattern photographed with outside camera
Außen-backenbremse *f* external shoe brake, external contraction or contracting brake **-bahn** *f* outer orbit **-ballistik** *f* exterior ballistics **-bandbremse** *f* external contracting (band)-brake, outer band brake **-befestigung** *f* outworks **-bekleidung** *f* outer lining **-belag** *m* outer coating, outer cover(ing), outer layer **-belüftung** (Motor) fan-cooled **-besatzbeutel** *m* external tamping bag **-beschaffenheit** *f* finish appearance **-bezirk** *m* outskirts **-boden** *m* outer shell (missiles) **-bohrrohr** *n* outer barrel **-bohrung** *f* outpost well
außenbord external (battery), outboard **~ stabilisierender Schwimmer** outboard stabilizing float
Außenbord-lager *n* outboard bearing **-motor** *m* outboard motor **-scharnier** *n* outboard hinge fitting
Außen-böschung *f* counterscarp **-bremse** *f* outer brake
aussenden to emit, send out, radiate, transmit, dispatch, give off, issue, disseminate (of standard frequencies), emerge
aussendend emissive
Außendienst, Störungssucher im ~ external faultsman
Außendruckkörper *m pl* bulges
Aussendung *f* transmission (radio), act of dispatching, emission (of a sound)
Außen-durchmesser *m* external or outside diameter **-einpaß** *m* outside register **-endlager** *n* outboard thrust bearing
Außenfläche *f* outer surface, facing of pitching, pitched face **~ eines Körpers** periphery
Außen-flügel *m* outboard wing, outer main plane **-fort** *n* outer fortification **-fräser** *f* hollow mill
aussengen to singe
Außengewässer *pl* exterritorial waters
Außengewinde *n* outside screw thread, male screw thread, external thread **-durchmesser** *m* major diameter **-schneidemaschine** *f* screw cutting machine, external thread cutting machine
Außengewinde- und Profilschleifmaschine *f* external thread and form grinding machine
Außen-gitter *n* outward or exterior grid **-glied** *n* outside link **-glocke** *f* outer globe, outer bell jar **-grenzlehre** *f* snap gauge **-hafen** *m* outer harbor **-handel** *m* exports
Außenhaut *f* covering or skin (aviation), outer covering, wing fabric (aviation), outer skin, hull plating (navig.); shell, ship's skin, outer or lower gates **tragende ~** with stressed skin
Außenhaut-boden *m* external bilge skin (of a ship) **-dichtung** *f* membrane waterproofing **-leitkante** *f* leading edge skin
Außen-hülle *f* outer cover **-isolator** *m* outdoor or overhand insulator **-kabel** *n* outside or external cable **-kaliber** *n* outside caliper **-kante** *f* top edge **-kegel** *m* outer cone; (Keillochbohrer) outside taper (cotter hole drill)
aussenken to countersink
Außen-kette *f* (der Anflugfeuerung) wing bar

(of approach lighting) **-kerbe** *f* external notch, notched edge (of plates) **-klüver** *m* flying jib, outer jib **-kontaktsockel** *m* side-contact base, external contact base **-kopieren** *n* external copying

Aussenkung *f*, **kegelige ~** countersink hole **kreisförmige ~** circular countersinking

Außen-kurbel *f* crank lever, outside crank **-lack** *m* varnish for outdoor use **-lamelle** *f* driven disc; (Kupplung) external disc **-lager** *n* outside box, external or outer bearing **-landung** *f* off-field landing (aviation), landing outside an airfield **-längskopieren** *n* external copying **-laufbahn** *f* outer race (way) **-läufer** *m* outside rotor **-läufermotor** *m* motor of the externalrotor type **-laufring** *m* outer race **-leiter** *m* outer main, outer (conductor or wire) **-leiterspannung** *f* voltage on outside lines of three-wire system **-leitung** *f* external leads

Außenleuchten *f pl* exterior illumination, outdoor lights fixture **~ mit Emaillereflektoren** outdoor luminaries with vitreous enamel reflectors **~ mit Glasglocken** outdoor luminaries with protecting glass

außenliegend external

Außenlinie *f* contour, outline

Außenluft *f* outer or outside air **-temperatur** *f* outside-air temperature **-thermometer** *n* outside-airtemperature gauge

Außenluftdruck *n* barometric pressure **-thermometer** *n* free-air thermometer

Außen-lunker *m* surface defect, surface blowhole **-manometer** *n* sight gauge **-mantel** *m* outer jacket, outer liner **-maß** *n* over-all dimension, outside measurement, external measurement **-mauer** *f* outside wall **-mauerwerk** *n* external brickwork **-messung** *f* external (outside) measurement, outside (external) gauging **-meßvorrichtung** *f* outdoor metering device **-mittig** eccentric, off-center **-muffe** *f* fullhole, tool joint **-nebenstelle** *f* off-premises extension station, external extension

Außenpol-dynamo *n* end or external pole dynamo **-generator** *m* external pole generator

Außen-posten *m* advance post **-quellenbestrahlung** *f* external radiation **-rad** *n* outside wheel

Außenradius *m* tip radius, maximum radius **~ der Hülle** outer radius of shell

Außen-rahmen *m* external loop **-rand** *m* outer border **-räummaschine** *f* surface broaching machine **-räumung** *f* (Bearbeitungsverfahren) surface broaching **-reede** *f* open roadstead (offering little shelter) **-ring** *m* retaining ring, outer race, outer ring **-rolle** *f* outside roll **-rumpf** *m* outer hull **-rundmessung** *f* measuring of outside circumference **-rundschleifmaschine** *f* plain grinding machine **-rüttler** *m* outside vibrator

Außen-sammler *m* outer duct, external exhaust collector, ring (jet) **-schenkel** *m* outer leg or limb **-schicht** *f* outer layer **-schieber** *m* outer slide, outer sleeve (on engine) **-schleifmaschine** *f* external grinding machine **-schleifenflug** *m* outside loop **-seegerring** *m* outer seal ring

Außenseite *f* outside, surface, periphery **an der ~ befindlich** peripheral

Außenseiter *m* independent, outsider, layman

außenseitig external, outdoor

Außen-sicherungsring external safety ring **-spannturm** *m* king post, wing or outer pylon **-spant** *n* frame of the outer hull of a submarine **-speicher** *m* external memory (print), external (secondary) storage **-stände** *pl* outstanding debts or liabilities

Außenstehender *m* outsider

Außen-stelle *f* outpost, field office, outlying station or post **-steuerröhre** *f* external control tube **-steuerung** *f* external controls **-stiel** *m* outer post **-strähler** *m* inside and outside chaser **-strebe** *f* outer strut **-strom** *m* foreign current, parasitic current **-taster** *m* outside calipers, firm-joint calipers

Außenteiler *m* divider **verlängerter ~** supplemental divider

Außen-tor *n* flood-tide gate **-träger** *m* outside girder **-trommel** *f* warping end of winch **-überfang** *m* exterior flash **-überschlag** *m* outside roll **-übertragung** *f* outdoor pickup, field broadcasting **-überzug** (abnehmbar) outer cover (removable)

Außen- und Seitenbordmotoren outboard and sideboard motors

Außen-verspannung *f* exterior bracing **-verstrebung** *f* external bracing or strutting **-verzahntes Zahnrad** external gear **-verzahnung** *f* external toothing of gears **-vorschubeinrichtung** *f* outside feeding attachment **-wache** *f* exterior guard **-wand** *f* outer wall, outside wall, surface **-wandungen** *pl* (Kompressor) walls of interior cooling

Außen-wange *f* (Treppe) outer string **-wärme** *f* outer or outside temperature **-wäsche** *f* pressure wash **-wecker** *m* extension bell **-welt** *f* external world, ambient **-werke** *n pl* outer works **-widerstand** *m* load resistance

Außenwinkel eines Dreiecks exterior angle of a triangle

Außen-winkelprofil *n* chine strip **-wirkung** *f* external effect **-zahnkranz** *m* outside gear ring **-zentriersitz** *m* outside register **-zone** *f* external zone **-zugabe** *f* oversize **-zwickel** *m* outer cable filler **-zylinder** *m* outside cylinder (locomotive)

außer unless, besides, except, outer, outward, external **~ Achse** extra-axial, abaxial **~ Aktion setzen** to cut out of action **~ Arbeit setzen** to lay off **~ Betrieb** not in use, out of order **~ Dienst** retirement **~ Eingriff bringen** to disengage, throw out of gear **~ Strom setzen** to put out of circuit, cut out, deenergize **~ Wettbewerb** out of the running

äußer-e Ausbuchtung *f* fillet (outside) **-er Block** outer bracket **-e Eigenform** true external form **-e Form** outside appearance **-e Haspelstütze** outside reel support **-es Produkt** cross product (vector) **-e Schicht** top layer **-e Weite** outer diameter **-er Widerstand** external field influence **-er Wirkungsgrad** *m* external or ballistic efficiency

außerachsig eccentric

außerachtlassen to disregard, neglect, leave out of consideration

außeraxial extra-axial **-er Spiegelabschnitt** extra-axial mirror zone **-e Strahlen** extra-axial rays

außerballistisch pertaining to exterior ballistics

Außerbetriebsetzung *f* placing out of operation, laying off of works for repairs or other purposes, complete breakdown (mach.), switching off

Außerbetriebszeit *f* standby unattended time, down time

Außerdienststellung *f* putting out of commission, laying off of work, retirement

Außereingriffkommen *n* (von Zahnrädern), demeshing

Äußeres outward appearance (exterior)

Außer-fokusbild *n* out-of-focus picture **-gerichtlich** extrajudicial, out of court **-gewöhnlich** unusual, unconventional

außerhalb outside; beyond **~ der Antiklinie gelegener Schacht** offset well **außen oder ~ befindlich** outside **~ des Bereichs** out of range **~ des Bereichs des Kerns befindlich** extranuclear

außerirdische Störungen extraterrestrial- or interstellar-space noise or disturbances

Außer-kraftsetzung *f* abrogation, rescession **-kurssetzung** *f* withdrawal from circulation

äußerlich external, exterior, outward, outboard

außermittig eccentric, eccentrical(ly), off-center **-e Lage** eccentricity

Außermittigkeit *f* eccentricity

äußern to express

außerordentlich extraordinary, extreme, exceptional, outstanding **-e Aufwendungen** extraneous items **-e Komponente** extraordinary component (of rays)

außerplanmäßig exceeding authorized basic allowance or strength, not in accordance with plans, extraordinary, itinerant, unscheduled (comput.)

außerstande unable **~ sein** to be unable

äußerst utmost **-es Ende** extremity **-e Kraft** maximum power **-e Kraft laufen** to run full speed ahead **bis auf das -e Maß ausnutzen** to wear down to the utmost **-er Preis** the lowest price **-e Schicht** boundary film

Außertrittfallen *n* out of parallel, taking out, falling out-of-step, breaking step **~ der Teilraster beim Zeilensprungverfahren** pairing off (of fractional scan) in interlaced scanning method

Außertrittfallmoment *m* pull-out torque (electr. mach.)

aussetzen to put out, set out; (unterbrechen) intermit, interrupt, break up; (Tätigkeit) discontinue, stop; (aufschieben) defer, postpone; (verschieben) put off; (vertagen) postpone; (versagen) fail, expose, get out, criticize, object to, suspend, lower (boats), post (an outpost detachment), quit, miss, give out, offer a prize, hoist out, hold in abeyance, soak **der Luft ~** to expose to the air

Aussetzen *n* exposure, failure, cessation, posting, time off **~ des Druckes** failure of pressure **~ der Schwingungen** failure of oscillation **~ der Zündkerze** misfiring

aussetzend discontinuous, intermittent **zeitweilig ~** intermittent **-e Belastung** intermittent load **-er Betrieb mit gleichbleibender Belastung** intermittent service

Aussetzer *m* skip, misfire, miss, failure, idle stroke, slips (ignition) **-betrieb** *m* intermitted service **-regelung** *f* hit-and-miss governing **-ring** *f* shifting-ring

Aussetzleistung *f* interrupted capacity

Aussetzung *f* exposure, adjournment, discontinuance, deferment, stay (of proceedings), arrest (of judgment) **~ des Verfahrens** suspension of the proceedings

aussetzungsfreie Überschläge (Zündung) regular sparking (ignition)

Aussicht *f* chance, perspective, prospect, outlook, view **in ~ stehend** in expectation of, prospective

Aussichts-dichte *f* reflection or specular density **-fernrohr** *n* observation telescope **-los** hopeless **-punkt** *m* vantage point

aussichtsreich promising, prospective **-e Stelle** progressive position

Aussichtsturm *m* observation tower

aussickern to trickle out, percolate, sinter, ooze out

Aussickerung *f* exosmosis

aussieben to screen out, screen, sieve (out), sift (out), filter (out), select, boil thoroughly, boil out

aussinnen to devise, think out, think up

aussintern to sinter

aussoggen to precipitate in crystals

aussöhnen to reconcile

Aussöhnung *f* conciliation

aussondern to separate (out), eliminate, sort

Aussonderung *f* separation, elimination

Aussonderungs-befehl *m* reject instruction **-fach** *n* reject pocket **-nachweisung** *f* disposal certificate **-reif** fit for elimination

aussortieren to sort out, sort, pick out, single out

Aussortierung *f* sorting

Assoziations-festigkeit *f* firmness of association **-flüssigkeit** *f* associated liquids **-forschung** *f* study of association **-halbleiter** *m* reserve semiconductor **-system** *n* system of associative fibers

ausspachteln to trowel off

ausspähen to scout, reconnoiter, spy, pry

Ausspähung *f* espionage, reconnaissance, spying

ausspannen to extend, stretch, spread, slacken, string (wires), release

Ausspannen *n* papering-out

aussparen to recess, spare, hollow out, leave untouched, bypass, remove material from, set aside (marginal portions for sound track on film), clear out (blacks)

Aussparung *f* recess, notch, fillet, relief, hollow, cutout, section (aviation), opening, safety limits (to prevent important buildings, installations or troops from being fired upon), groove, channel, lockout, clearance, cutting away, enlarging, raking out, void **~ für die Zündkerze** passage for the plug **halfkugelförmige ~ im Kolbenboden** hemispherical depression in the piston crown

Aussparungs-faktor *m* void coefficient **-öffnung** *f* cupel

aussperren to lock out, space (print)

Aussperrkondensator *m* blocking condenser

Aussperrung *f* lockout, exclusion **~ der Arbeiter durch den Unternehmer** lockout of workers by the employer

Aussprache *f* pronunciation, enunciation, dis-

cussion, debate, exchange of views **undeutliche ~** inarticulateness
ausspitzen to cut, pick out
aussprechen to pronounce, express, declare **deutlich ~** to pronounce, articulate
ausspreizen to splay
ausspringen to spring out, spring off, fly off, crack, jump out
ausspringend salient, protruding, projecting, jutting **-er Pol** *m* salient pole **-er Winkel** *m* salient (angle)
ausspritzen to flush out (drains), squirt (out), wash by squirting, inject
Ausspritzöffnung *f* nozzle (jet)
Ausspritzung *f* washing or cleansing by syringing, ejaculation
Ausspruch *m* verdict
Aussprung *m* stepped edges **-winkel** *m* angle of reflection
Ausspüldüse. schwenkbare (Entaschung) oscillating sluicing nozzle
ausspülen to rinse out, wash out, flush out
Ausspülen *n* flushing
Ausspüler *m* flushing-out apparatus
Ausspülhub *n* scavenging stroke **-schleusen** *pl* flushing and scouring sluices
Ausspülung *f* flushing out, corrosion **~ des Arbeitszylinders** scavenging of the working cylinder
(aus)spünden to groove for tongue-and-groove joint, plug a hole
ausspuren to disengage
Ausstäbung *f* cabling
ausstaffieren to provide, garnish, trim
ausstampfen to stamp, ram up, ram, line up, line
Ausstampfung *f* ramming, stamping, lining (up)
Ausstand *m* strike, outstanding debt, liability
ausständig sein (Arbeiter) to be out on strike
Ausstanzeisen *n* punch
ausstanzen to blank (out), punch out
Ausstanzen *n* punching out
Ausstanz-maschine *f* punching machine **-presse** *f* stamping-out press **-stück** *n* punching forme
ausstatten to equip, provide with, substitute, furnish (supply) (mit etwas) **~** endow
Ausstattung *f* equipment, outfit, layout, kit, issue, settings, set, composition
Ausstattungs-band *n* decorative ribbon **-papier** *n* fancy paper **-stück** *n* fitment
ausstäuben to dust or extract dust
Ausstechbremse *f* paying-out brake
ausstechen to pay out cable, slaken (a chain), cut away
Ausstechmeißel *m* plugging chisel
ausstecken to stake out, to pay out (cable)
ausstehen to stand, endure; (Forderungen) stand out, be outstanding (claims)
ausstehende Gelder outstanding debts
aussteifen to stiffen, strengthen, reinforce, strut, brace
Aussteifung *f* reinforcing, stiffening, stiffener, framework, routing (of beams), web, strengthening
Aussteifungs-ring *m* circular or ring-shaped stiffener, annular stiffener **-winkel** *m* stiffener
Aussteifungsstrebe zur Aufnahme der Kräfte der Blattebene stiff drag brace
Aussteigeluke *f* roof trap door
aussteigen to disembark, alight, get off, abandon the plane; (aus dem Flugzeug) **~** to disembark, bail out (aus dem Führersitz) **~** to dismount
Aussteigeklappe *f* exit door
ausstellen to exhibit **~ einer Urkunde** to execute a document
„Aus"-Stellung (des Schalters) open position (of the switch) off-position (of relay)
Ausstellung *f* drawing up, exhibition, show, fair, display **Flugzeug ~** aircraft exhibition **Luftfahrt ~** aeronautical exhibition
Ausstellungs-halle *f* exhibition hall **-modell** *n* exhibition model **-stand** *m* display booth
ausstemmen to mortise
Ausstemmung *f* chiseling out
Aussteuer-bereich *m* range of modulation **-fähigkeit** *f* modulability **-instrument** *n* (Mischpult) volume indicator (mixer console)
aussteuern to modulate, control, balance out **~** (im Kartenmischer) to match
Aussteuerung *f* modulation, control, tone control, level control **prozentuale ~** percentage modulation **vollständige ~** complete modulation **~ in einer Koordinate** single coordinate control **bei voller ~ des Verstärkers** with the amplifier driven to full output
Aussteuerungs-abhängigkeit *f* amplitude-response (testing of carbon granule transmitter) **-anzeige** *f* recording level meter, volume indicator (tape rec.) **-anzeiger** volume indicator, level meter (sound recording), recording level indicator (tape rec.) **-bereich** *m* drive range, grid swing, grid base, grid space (el. tube), range below point where overload begins **-grad** *m* percentage, degree of or depth of modulation factor, carrier amplitude (in telemetric or teletransmission work) **-grenze** *f* overload point
Aussteuerungs-intervall *n* control range, drive range **-kennlinie** *f* drive characteristic (el. tube) **-koeffizient** *m* percentage, degree of or depth of modulation
Aussteuerungskontrolle *f* recording level indication (tape rec.) **~ mit Neonröhre** neon-tube volume indicator
Aussteuerungs-kontrollgerät *n* modulation meter, load indicator **-messer** *m* volume indicator
ausstemmen to chisel out
Ausstieg *m* exit
ausstimmen to tune out
ausstollen to stake
ausstopfen to stuff, pad
ausstöpselbarer Rheostat plug-in rheostat
ausstöpseln to unplug, unstop
Ausstoß *m* (Produktion) expulsion, discharge, output **-beiwert** *m* exit shock coefficient **-büchse** *f* smoke canister ejected from projectile on burst **-dorn** *m* ejection mandrel, plunger **-düse** *f* discharge or ejector nozzle, reaction or jet nozzle **-einrichtung** *f* discharge fittings (torpedo)
ausstoßen to eject, expel, emit, push out, throw out, extrude, discharge, work out, eliminate
Ausstoßen *n* scavenging (gases), expelling, exhaust stroke, expulsion
Ausstoßer *m* rejector, rejector circuit, ejector
Ausstoß-formmaschine *f* core machine **-hahn** *m* discharge valve, purge or surge cock **-hobel** *m*

grooving plane **-hub** *m* exhaust stroke **-kamm** *m* stripping comb **-kolben** *m* ejecting piston **-kreis** *m* rejector circuit **-ladung** *f* bursting or explosion, charge **-leistung** *f* high production rate **-maschine** *f* setting-out machine, ejecting machine, coke pusher

Ausstoß-öffnung *f* discharge orifice **-platte** *f* pusher (ejector) blade **-produkt** *n* waste product **-rohr** *n* discharge pipe, ejector tube

Ausstoß-seite *f* discharge side, discharge end **~ des Verdichters** (Kühlschrank) exhaust side of compressor (refrigerator)

Ausstoß-schlitten *m* ejector (pushing) slide **-stange** *f* pusher (ejector) bar **-stempel** *m* pushing ram, discharging stamp

Ausstoßung *f* rejection, expulsion, cashiering, extrusion

Ausstoß-ventilator *m* delivery fan **-vorrichtung** *f* discharge apparatus (torpedo), ejector **-werkzeug** *n* drift

Ausstrahl *m* emission

ausstrahlen to radiate, emit

ausstrahlend emissive **-e Hitze** radiant heat

Ausstrahl-spitze *f* terminal point

Ausstrahlung *f* radiation, emanation, emission of rays, oscillations, vibrations, and waves **~ der Oszillatorschwingungen** radiation of the oscillations generated in the oscillator **~ in den Raum** radiation into space

Ausstrahlungs-bedingung *f* radiation condition **-fläche** *f* radiating surface **-kurve** emission characteristic **-richtung** *f* direction of light, radiation **-verluste** *m pl* radiation losses **-vermögen** *n* radiating power (or capacity), emissive power **-winkel** *m* angle of emission

ausstreben to strut, brace

ausstrecken to stretch, extend, elongate

Ausstreicheisen *n* straightening rod

ausstreichen to strike out, smooth, smooth out, spread out, level, erase, slur (founding), paint, obliterate, cancel, distribute (color), crop out (geol.)

Ausstreichen *n* outcrop, brushing

Ausstreich-feile *f* equalling file **-messer** *n* smoothing or leveling blade, scraper **-rad** *n* stroke wheel **-walzen** *f pl* scrimp rollers

ausstreuen to scatter, disseminate, spread

Ausstreuung *f* diffuser, diffusion, dissemination

Ausstrich *m* stream-tin (metal), outcrop

Ausströmdüse *f* discharge nozzle **~** (Astron.) efflux nozzle, exhaust nozzle (rocket)

Ausströmelektrode *f* exit electrode

ausströmen to flow out, pass out, go out, pour, issue, escape, discharge, emanate, run out (leak) **~ lassen** to emit, discharge, pour **zischend ~** to chug

Ausströmen *n* emanation, flowing out

ausströmend effluent **-es Mittel** effluent

Ausström-erscheinungen *f pl* effusion phenomena **-gas** *n* exhaust (of rocket) **-geschwindigkeit** *f* discharge velocity **-hub** *m* exhaust (scavening) stroke **-laterne** *f* outflow port lantern **-öffnung** *f* outlet or discharge opening **-raum** *m* delivery space, volute, chamber, diffuser **-regler** *m* throttle-valve **-trichter** *m* discharge funnel

Ausströmung *f* outflow, issue, escape, discharge, flow, emanation, exhaust (steam), emission **~ unter Druck** discharge

Ausströmungs-dampf *m* exhaust steam **-geschwindigkeit** *f* extruding speed, discharge velocity **-hub** *m* exhaust stroke **-messer** *n* effusiometer **öffnung** *f* outlet or discharge opening **-regulator** *m* throttle valve **-rohr** *n* exhaust pipe, delivery pipe, outlet tube

Ausström-ventil *n* outlet valve **-verfahren** *n* outflow method **-verlust** *m* discharge loss

ausstufen to cut into steps

Ausstülpung *f* offshoot, evagination, protuberance

ausstürzen to dump, empty, discharge, rush out

ausstützen to prop, stay

aussuchen to select, choose, sort, pick out

aussüßen to edulcorate, leach, wash

austäfeln to panel, wainscot

Austäfelungsarbeit *f* inlaying

austarieren to tare

Austarieren *n* calibrate, tare

austasten to block blank, cut off or gate (pencil or beam on flyback), blackout (by blanking signal), key off (a carrier)

Austasten *n* black-out (TV) **~ von Impulsen** gating of pulses

Austast-gemisch *n* black-out pulse **-gerät** *n* blanking device **-impuls** (Wegtastimpuls) blanking pulse, masking pulse **-intervall** *n* blanking interval **-lücke** *f* blanking interval **-pegel** *m* blanking level, black-out level **-signal** *n* blanking pulse or signal, black-out signal (TV) **-spannung** *f* black-out voltage

Austastung *f* blanking (TV), keying out

Austast-wert *m* blanking level **-zeichen** *n* blanking signal (impulse) **-zeit** *f* suppression period

Austauchung *f* emersion, out of water

austauen to thaw out

Austausch *m* substitute, exchange (as of ions), interchange, relief **~ des Brennstoffes** fuel unit changes **~ freier Leistung** free-energy change

Austausch-anlage *f* conversion plant **-bar** interchangeable, exchangeable **-barkeit** *f* interchangeability **-beschränkung** *f* exchange narrowing **-dienst** *m* exchange service

austauschen to exchange, interchange

Austauschenergie *f* exchange energy

Austauscher *m* exchanger, interchanger **-wertetabellen** *pl* exchanger rating sheets **-wirkungsgrad** *m* interchanger efficiency

austausch-fähig exchangeable (positive ions)

Austausch-faktor *m* fraction exchange **-geschwindigkeit** *f* rate of exchange **-halbwertzeit** half-time of exchange **-integral** *n* exchange integral **-kräfte** *f pl* exchange forces or energies **-ladung** *f* exchange charge **-lecksuchröhre** *f* spare leak detector tube **-lot** *n* substitute solder

Austausch-objektiv *n* interchangeable lens **-operator** *m* charge-exchange operator **-reaktion** *f* substitute reaction, exchange reaction **-relation** *f* commutation rule (magnetism) **-reparatur** *f* standard repair **-scheinwerfer** *m* interchange head lamp

Austausch-stahl *m* substitute steel **-stoff** *m* substitute material, ersatz **-stück** *n* duplicate or spare part **-term** exchange term **-triebwerk** *n* interchangeable power unit **-ware** *f* substitute, ersatz **-wechselwirkung** *f* exchange interaction **-werkstoff** *m* replacement materials

austeilen to distribute, dispense, allot, deal

Austeiler *m* distributor
Austempering *m* austempering, gaining of an austenitic structure
Austenit *n* austenite, gamma iron, various forms of steel, cementite, pearlite, mixed crystals **-stahl** *m* austenitic steel
austenitisch austenitic **-e rostfreie Stähle** austenite antirust steels, austenitic stainless steels
Austenitumwandlung *f* conversion of austenite (metal.)
austiefen to hollow out or cup
austilgen to efface
Austin-Cohensche Formel *f* Austin-Cohen transmission formula
austoben to crease, raving
austönen to shade
austordieren to destroy the torsion (of a fiber)
Austrag *m* throughput **~ aus dem Pochtrog** discharge from stamping trough
austragen to carry out, deliver, distribute, report, decide, discharge, fight a battle to a decision
Austrag(s)-eingang *m* influx of orders **-ende** *n* discharge end, delivery end **-höhe** *f* height of discharge **öffnung** discharge opening, nozzle or outlet
Austragsrad mit Siebschaufeln wheel with perforated flights
Austrag(s)-rinne *f* discharge trough **-rohr** *n* discharge pipe **-schieber** *m* refuse gate **-schurre** *f* discharge chute **-sieb** *n* discharge screen **-vorrichtung** *f* discharger
Austragung *f* discharge
Australisches Eisenholz Australian ironwood
Austrebermaschine *f* spent-grains remover
austrebern to remove the spent grains
austreiben to drive out or off, oust, expel, eject, clean up
Austreiber *m* center key, drill drift, expeller
Austreibkeil *m* drift key
Austreibung *f* expulsion, eviction
austreten to step out, issue, go out, leave, emerge, overflow, retire, withdraw; (Öl) to leak out (oil)
austretende Kante eines Propellerflügels trailing edge of a propeller blade
austretende Lichtbüschel emerging light beam
austretendes Licht emergent light
Austrieb *m* (molding), flash, excess rubber
Austriebsrille *f* (molding) flash, groove, escape groove
austrimmen to trim
Austritt *m* exit, outlet, egress, escape, issue, vent, discharge, exhaust, withdrawal, retirement, efflux **freier ~** straight-through outlet
Austritts-arbeit *f* work function (electronics), electron affinity **-blende** *f* exit slit **-(dampf)-spannung** *f* back pressure (of exhaust) **-dicke** *f* delivery thickness **-dosis** *f* exit dose **-durchmesser** *m* effective diameter
Austrittsdüse *f* outlet nozzle **~ des Schaumgemisches** emulsion outlet
Austritt(s)-energie *f* total exhaust energy **-feld** *n* exit portal **-fenster** *n* tube window, exit window **-gefälle** *n* exit gradient **-geschwindigkeit** *f* exhaust velocity of turbines (gas), exit velocity or speed, muzzle velocity (of guns), exhaust speed, delivery speed **-kanal** *m* exhaust or evacuation port **-kante** *f* trailing edge, inlet or outlet edge **-kegel** *m* exhaust cone (jet) **-klappe der Kühldurchlüftung** gill exit
Austritt(s)-leitapparat *m* exhaust conducting device (jet), exhaust diffuser **-leitkranz** *m* exhaust nozzle ring **-öffnung** *f* exhaust port, orifice, discharge point, outlet from discharge culverts, light (entry) passage, open end **-potential** *n* exit potential **-querschnitt** *m* exhaust aperture **-schaufel** *f* exhaust stator, blade (gas turbine) **-schlitze** *pl* discharge vents or ports **-seite** *f* outlet or delivery end or side, catcher's side (met.)
austrittseitiger Federungskörper metal bellows on delivery side
Austritt(s)-spirale *f* spiral volute **-strahl** *m* emergent ray **-stufe** *f* landing step (of stairs) **-stutzen** *m* outlet pipe connection, water outlet (to water pump), outlet flange **-temperatur** *f* outlet temperature, exhaust temperature (power plant) **-ventil** *n* outlet valve **-verlust** *m* discharge or exit loss **-verschiebung** *f* exit displacement **-wärmegrad** *m* outlet temperature **-winkel** *m* angle of emergence
austrocknen to dry (up), dry out, desiccate, drain, exsiccate **Holz ~ lassen** to season wood
Austrocknen *n* drying (up or out), seasoning, desiccating
austrocknendes Mittel desiccant
Austrockner *m* drier, desiccator
Austrocknung *f* drying, draining, desiccation, drainage, exsiccation
auströpfeln to drip out, trickle out
Austuchung *f* bushing
austüfteln to think up, scheme
austupfen to remove by sponging or mopping
austuschen to ink (in)
ausüben to exert, exercise, practice, carry out, execute **ein Verfahren ~** (benutzen) (Patent) to perform a system
Ausübung *f* maintenance of service (nontechnical), practice, exercise, execution **~** (eines Gedankens) carrying into practice or effect, execute (an idea) **~ fällig** (Patent) working due **in ~ des Dienstes** in line of duty
Aus- und Abgießgerät *n* liquid- and gas-spraying apparatus on a plane
aus- und einbauen to remove and remount
Aus- und Einlaßventil *n* exhaust and air-intake valve
Aus- und Einschwenken *n* swinging out and in
Aus- und Vorrichtungsarbeiten *f pl* opening and forewinning
aus- und wieder einrücken to start and stop
ausvauen to V-groove (welding)
Ausverkauf *m* clearance sale, selling off
ausvieren to square out
Auswaage *f* (weighed) analytical product
auswachsen to germinate, sprout, reach full growth, heal up, grow crooked
auswägen to weigh out, tare, counterbalance, calibrate
Auswahl *f* selection, choice, variety, collection **mit ~ und Unterscheidung verfahrend oder erfolgend** selective
auswählen to choose, select, elect
Auswahleinheit (im Kartenmischer) feed control unit
Auswahl-passung *f* selective assembly **-prinzip** *n*

-regel *f* selection principle, selection rule (in electron transition) **-reihe** *f* selected combinations **-tabellen** *pl* summary tables **-verhältnis** *n* selection ratio **-verstärker** *m* push-pull amplifier **-vorrichtung** *f* selecting device

auswälzbar rollable

auswalzen to roll out, roll down, rough down, cog, sheet out, bloom; (Blech oder Band auf geringere Dicke) ~ to roll down (tin plate) **die Luppen** ~ to bloom, to rough down the blooms

Auswalzen *n* rolling, flaring or bellmouth (petroleum)

auswandern to get out of range (rdr.)

Auswandern *n* shift of beam or beacon course

Auswanderung *f* migration

Auswanderungs-messer *m* range corrector, lead computer **-strecke** *f* component of target travel during time of flight of projectile, receding leg of target course, target course or leg between present and future positions, linear travel of target **-zeit** *f* angular or lead rate or time

auswärmen to heat, anneal

Auswärmofen *m* annealing furnace

auswärtig foreign **-e Angelegenheiten** foreign affairs

auswärts out of town, outward **-drehen** to turn outwards, supinate

Auswärts-kehrung *f* eversion **-transformator** *m* step-up transformer

auswaschbar washable, removable by washing

auswaschen to clean, wash out, wash, scrub (out), rinse, erode, leach

Auswaschen *n* panning out, washing

Auswasch-flasche *f* wash bottle **-relief** *n* washed-out relief (the coating that remains after hardening and development by light) (phot.) **-tisch** *m* washing (table) bench

Auswaschung *f* elutriation, erosion

auswässern to soak, steep, macerate

Auswässerung *f* emersion

auswattieren to pad

auswechselbar interchangeable, replaceable, renewable, exchangeable, removable **-er Behälter** change-can (tank) **-es Futterrohr** loose liner, removable liner **-es Seelenrohr** removable liner **-er Spulensatz** interchangeable coil set **-e Werkzeuge** change parts **-e Zylinderbüchse** removable liner

Auswechselbarkeit *f* interchangeability, exchangeability

auswechseln to replace, interchange, (ex)change, doff, substitute **beliebig** ~ change at random

Auswechseln *n* replacing, replacement ~ (von Hölzern), relieving timbers ~ (der Zimmerung) retimbering

Auswechs(e)lung *f* replacement, exchange, renewal, change, interchange

Auswechslungsfähigkeit *f* replaceability, facility of replacement

Ausweg *m* alternative, expedient, way out, vent **das Wasser sucht sich einen** ~ the water seeks an outlet

Ausweichbewegung *f* tactical movement to avoid contact, evading movement, withdrawing movement to new position, move of deflection or declination

Ausweiche *f* turnout, shunt

ausweichen to turn aside, evade, avoid, elude, withdraw, fall back, give way, shunt onto a siding

Ausweichen *n* cleavage (of rock upon blasting), shifting **seitliches** ~ lateral yielding

ausweichende Antwort evasive reply

Ausweich-flugplatz *m* alternate aerodrome **-frequenz** *f* alternative frequency **-geschwindigkeit** *f* velocity of deflection, speed of declination **-gleis** *n* shunting line, siding, turnout track, by-pass tracks **-kanal** *m* alternative channel **-kraftstoff** *m* alternate or substitute fuel **-leitung** *f* by-pass line **-leitweg** *m* alternate routing **-lösung** *f* substitute

Ausweich-platz (Verladegleis) passing place, siding **-probleme** *n pl* problems of digression **-punkt** *m* yield point **-regeln** *f pl* airtraffic regulations **-richtung** *f* direction of deflextion or declination **-stelle** *f* shunting, by-pass, lay by, passing place, tie-up basin, siding, turnout **-stellung** *f* alternate position **-welle** *f* alternative wave **-ziel** *n* alternate or secondary target

Ausweichung *f* offset, passing place **plastische** ~ plastic flow **seitliche** ~ lateral flow, lateral deformation

Ausweich-vermittlung *f* emergency exchange, alternate routing, auxiliary telephone line, signal **-welle** *f* secondary frequency, alternative frequency or wave (radar)

Ausweis *m* certificate, proof of identity, identification, papers, pass, permit, return

ausweisen to expel, make it evident **sich** ~ to identify oneself

Ausweis-halter *m* license folder **-karte** *f* pass, permit, identification card **-papier** *n* affidavit, document, identification papers

Ausweisung *f* expulsion

ausweitbar extensible (as in the case of an accordionlike crystal lattice), expanding

ausweiten to widen, expand, extend, dilate, enlarge, bulge, stretch

Ausweiterungswinkel *m* taper (the angle at which some types of rocket nozzles open out from the throat)

Ausweitung *f* enlargement (of a vent or orifice)

auswendig outside ~ **angebracht** mounted externally ~ **lernen** to commit to memory

auswerfen to throw out, eject, scrap, reject, shoot, discharge material, splutter

Auswerfen *n* spewing

Auswerfer *m* ejector, throw out, extractor, knock-out **-bolzen** *m* retaining or knock-out pin **-lager** *n* ejector seat **-muffe** *f* ejector sleeve **-stange** *f* knock-out bar **-stift** *m* ejector **-vorrichtung** *f* ejector mechanism **-vorstecker** *m* ejector securing bolt

Auswerfgreifer *m* delivery gripper

Auswerfung *f* rejection

auswertbar plottable

Auswerte-bereitschaft *f* operational readiness of plotters **-brennweite** *f* focal length of plotting lens **-gerät** *n* protractor, reduction instrument, plotting apparatus, production analyzer, evaluation equipment **-geschwindigkeit** *f* speed of plotting maps **-impuls** *m* gating or strobing pulse **-impulsgenerator** *m* gating pulse generator **-leistung** *f* output of plotting maps **-lineal** *n* computing slide rule for transfer of sound- and

flashranging data to control chart **-maßstab** *m* plotting scale
auswerten (Angaben, Resultate) to evaluate, analyze; (schätzen) estimate; (ausnützen) utilize; (Patente) exploit, compile results, plot, interpret, draw a map, discuss **~** (Meßergebnisse) to analyze (measurement results)
Auswerten von Luftbildern interpretation of aerial photographs, plotting
Auswerteobjektiv *n* plotting lens
Auswerter *m* plotter
Auswerte-objektiv *n* plotting lens **-station** *f* time-ranging station **-stelle** *f* computing station (sound and flash ranging) or plotting station, exploitation section **-tisch** *m* plotting table **-verfahren** *n* plotting or evaluation method **-vordruck** *m* evaluation form, recording blank **-zug** *m* plotting section
Auswertung *f* evaluation, plotting of curves, plotting (of photogrammetric data), interpratation, analysis, computation, collation, solution, valuation, assay, appraisal **~ der Lage** estimate of the situation **~ der erhaltenen Versuchsergebnisse** analysis of the records obtained **punktweise ~** point-by-point evaluation **zeichnerische Lösung oder ~** graphical solution
Auswertungs-instrument *n* protractor, reduction instrument **-stufe** *f* evaluation stage
auswichten to center, balance
Auswichten *n* centering, balance
Auswicken *n* picking, burring
auswiegen to weigh out, tare, balance out, counterbalance, balance the airplane in construction
Auswiegen *n* aerodynamic balance
auswinden to wrench out, unscrew, wring out (press out)
Auswinde-maschine *f* drying rolls or press **-vorrichtung** *f* wringer
auswinkeln to take the squaring
auswintern to weather, season
auswirken to become perceptible or effective, assume significance **sich ~** to take effect, work out
Auswirkung *f* reflection, result, effect, consequence
auswischen to wipe off, obliterate, sponge out
auswittern to weather, season (wood)
Auswittern *n* (von Salzen) efflorescence
Auswitterung *f* weathering, seasoning, efflorescence
auswringen to wring, squeeze
Auswuchs *m* outgrowth, protuberance; (unregelmäßiger) **~** excrescence
Auswüchse bilden to fan out (storage-cell plates)
Auswuchtdorn *m* balancing mandrel
auswuchten to balance out, counterbalance, compensate, equilibrate
Auswuchten *n* balancing **~ der Luftschraube** balancing of the propeller
Auswucht-großvorrichtung *f* power-balancing jig or rig **-maschine** *f* balancing machine **-stand** *m* balancing stand **-stück** *n* balance piece or material
Auswuchtung *f* balancing, balance **~ der Oberwalze** dynamic balancing of the upper roll **dynamische ~** running balance **statische ~** gravity balance
Auswuchtungsverhältnis *n* mechanical balance
Auswuchtvorrichtung *f* balancing fixture
Auswurf *m* discharge, throwing out, ejection, delivery point of a conveyer, ejecta **-bogen** *m* cancel **-gestein** *n* eruptive rock **-haken** *m* cramp iron **-haube** *f* delivery hood **-kamin** (Konverter) spark escape **-rohr** *n* discharge pipe
Auswürfling *f* ejected block, ejectum
Auswurföffnung *f* ejector or ejection opening
Auswurf- und Aufblasversuch *m* ejection and inflation test
Auszackeisen *n* pinking iron
auszacken to indent, notch, tooth, scallop, jag, serrate, dentate
Auszackmaschine *f* scalloping or festoon frame
Auszackung *f* notching, denticulation, indenting
auszählen to count **statistisch ~** to sort
Auszahlung *f* payment
Auszählung *f* counting out
Auszahlungsnachweis *m* disbursement return
Auszählvorrichtung *f* counter, meter
Auszahnung am Typenhebel slit of the type bar
auszehren to consume, impoverish, exhaust
auszeichnen to mark out, distinguish, accentuate (display) **sich ~** to distinguish oneself, be remarkable
Auszeichnen, scharfes ~ einer Fläche durch Objektiv sharp focusing by lens of image in angle of field
Auszeichnung *f* distinction, decoration, medal, display setting (type), citation
Auszeichnungsschrift *f* capital letters, display type
auszentrifugen to centrifuge
Ausziehschalter *m* draw-out-type circuit breaker
ausziehbar telescopic, removable, extensible **-e Antriebswelle** telescopic feed shaft **-e Gelenkwelle** telescopic shaft **-es Kernrohr** removable core bit **-er Meißel** collapsible bit
Ausziehbarkeit *f* ductility
ausziehen to draw out, pull, stretch, extract, abstract, rake out, remove, move, eliminate, ink (drawings) **mit Tusche ~** to trace with India ink
Ausziehen *n* drawing, withdrawal, removal, extraction, macerating, maceration **~! Laufen! Los!** Pull! Run! Release! (command in sailplant) **~ eines Pfahles** pile extraction drawing **~ einer Spundbohle** extracting a sheet pile
ausziehender Schacht upcast ventilating shaft
Auszieher *m* extractor
Auszieh-fallschirm *m* auxiliary parachute **-flügel** *m* telescopic or variable span wing **-geleise** *n*, **-gleis** *n* lead track (R.R.) **-hebel** *m* withdrawing lever **-kralle** *f* extractor barb or hook **-leiter** *f* extension ladder **-öffnung** *f* withdrawing or raking-out opening or door **-rohr** *n* telescopic tube **-schacht** *m* return shaft
Auszieh-schnecke *f* drawing-out worm **-schraube** withdrawing screw **-sicherung** *f* pull-out or push-in fuse (elec.) **-strom** *m* upcast ventilation, return **-tubus** *m* drawtube (of microscope) **-tür** *f* withdrawal door **-tusche** *f* drawing ink (Indian ink) **-type** *f* pull-out and push-in type (switch) **-zahn** *m* extractor hook or tooth
Ausziehung *f* extraction, extension
Auszieh-verfahren *n* exhaust process, extractor,

puller **-vorrichtung** *f* drawing device **-werkzeug** *n* extracting tool

Auszimmerung *f* timbering of galleries

Auszug *m* extract, summary, abstract (of an article), separation (color phot.), departure, extension, extraction, compendium, abridgment, draw tube, excerpt, stretch **gekürzter ~** abridgment **einen ~ machen** (verringern) to abridge

Auszugsmittel *n* contrivance for extraction

auszugsweise in extracts, in part, partially, in selection **~ wiedergeben** to abridge

auszupfen to pick, cull, bur

auszwängen to force out

auszusetzen, ohne ~ without interrupting

autark self-sufficient

Autarkie *f* autarchy

authentisch authentic

authentisieren to authenticate

Autismus *m* autism, autistic, thinking

Auto-abbruch *m* demolition of cars **-alarmgerät** *n* automatic alarm receiver **-anhänger** *m* trailer **-aufbaukran** *m* motor-car crane **-bagger** *m* truck excavators **-bahn** *f* (main) automobile highway, express highway, arterial or cross-country highway

autobarotrop autobarotropic

Autobarotropie *f* autobarotropy

Auto-batterie *f* automobile battery **-beschlag** *m* automobile fitting **-bus** *m* motorbus

Autochrom *n* autochrome **-platte** *f* autochrome plate

autochthon autochthonous, in situ

Autoclav *n* digester

autodidaktisch self-taught

Autodyn *n* endodyne **-empfang** *m* autodyne reception **-empfänger** *m* autodyne oscillator or receiver, car radio, receiver

autoelektrische Entladung field emission

Autoelektronenemission *f* autoelectronic emission, field or cold emission of electrons

Auto-empfänger *m* car radio receiver **-entstörkondensator** *m* vehicular radio interference (noise) suppression capacitor **-fette** *pl* motor greases **-flugzeug** *n* air car, road-going aircraft **-frettage** *n* cold-drawing, autofrettage **-frettiert** cold-worked, self-hooped (gun barrel)

Autogal A an aluminum alloy

Autogas *n* acetylene a name for waste gas from coal hydrogenation

autogen autogenous, oxyacetylene **~ geschweißt** autogenously welded **-e Oberflächenhärtung** flame hardening (by oxyacetylene flame) (met.) **-es Schneiden** autogenous cutting **-er Schweißapparat** oxyacetylene cutter **-e Schweißung** autogenous welding, gas welding, oxyacetylene welding, lead burning

Autogene *f* fusion

Autogen-gas *n* dissolved acetylene **-gerät** *n* gas-welding apparatus **-gasflasche** *f* acetylene gastank **-schläuche** *pl* hoses for autogenous welding **-schneidbrenner** *m* autogenous cutting torch, gas cutting machine **-schnitt** *m* gas cutting

Autogen-schweißbrenner *m* gas welder, oxyacetylene torch or welding set **-schweißen** *n* oxyacetylene or autogenous welding **-schweißplatte** *f* autogenous welding plate **-schweißung** *f* autogenous welding **-technik** *f* autogenous-welding technique

Autogiro *n* autogiro, gyroplane **~ mit Direktsteuerung** direct-control autogiro **~ für Senkrechtaufstieg und Landung** direct take-off and landing autogiro

Autographie *f* autography, autographical printing **-farbe** *f* autographic color **-papier** *n* autographic printing paper

autographiert autographic, autographical

Autographiertinte *f* autographic ink

Autoheterodyn *n* autoheterodyne

autoinduktiv autoinductive

Auto-instandsetzungskran *m* motor-car repair crane **-ionisation** *f* autoionization **-jigger** *m* autojigger (electr.)

Autokartograph *m* stereoscopic plotting machine

Autokatalyse *f* autocatalysis

Autoklav *m* autoclave, digester

Autoklaven-presse *f* autoclave press, vulcanizing press **-spaltung** splitting up (fats) in the autoclave **-verfahren** *n* autoclave method, method used to determine alkali in glass manufacturing

Autoklemmlampe *f* auto clamping lamp

Autokollimation *f* autocollimation

Autokollimations-fernrohr *n* autocollimator, autocollimating telescope **-kamera** *f* autocollimation camera

Autokollimator *m* autocollimator

Autokolonne *f* motor-vehicle column, motor-march column

Autokorrelations-funktion *f* auto-correlation function

Autokorrelogramm *n* auto-correlogram

Autokrane *pl* mobile cranes

Autolampe *f* headlight

Autolyse *f* autolysis

Automalith *m* automalite

Automat *m* automatic machine, automaton, automatic screw machine, automatic circuit breaker, automatic cut-out

Automaten-amt *n* automatic exchange **-dreherei** *f* automatic lathes **-fernrohr** *n* automatic telescope **-legierung** *f* machining alloy stock **-leitung** *f* coin-box circuit **-messing** *n* machining brass

Automaten-nebenamt *n* automatic branch exchange **-rollenkarton** *m* reeled card for automatic machines **-schalterregelung** *f* contactor control **-stahl** *m* (mit kurzbrechendem Span) free-cutting steel, automatic steel **-teile** *pl* repetition work **-weichstahl** *m* milked steel for automatic lathes, free cutting steel **-zähler** *m* prepayment meter

Automatik *f* automatic (sharp) tuning means **~ mit Anlaßventil** automatics with starter valve **~ mit Auffüllventil** automatics with charging valve

Automatik-ausschalter *m* automatics cut-out switch **-betrieb** *m* automatic operation **-betrieb für Aggregat** automatic operation for (gen.) set **-umschalter** *m* automatics changeover switch

Automation *f* automation

automatisch automatic, self-acting **~ wirkend** automatically acting **~ einstellbarer Fangteil** automatic tuck bar **-e Abschaltung** *f* auto-stop **-es Abstimmgerät** servocoupler (antenna) **-es**

Amt mit Durchgangsverkehr auto-switching center

automatisch-er Azimutanzeiger *m* omnibearing indicator (navig.) **-er Befehlsgeber** automatic indicator **-er Bleistich** siphon lead tap **-e Farbtonregelung** ACC (automatic chrominance control) **-er Fallschirm** automatically opening parachute **-e Fehlerkorrektur** automatic error correction

automatisch-e Gittervorspannung automatic or self-biasing of grid **-er Kinoschrank** automatic motion-picture projector **-er Kursanzeiger** offset-course computer **-e Kurssteuerung** automatic or mechanical pilot

automatisch-e Nullstellung clearing device **-er Ölumlauf** automatic oil-pressure lubrication **-e Phasenregelung** (APC) automatic phase control (TV) **-e Profildrehbank** automatic jig lathe

automatisch-es Regelsystem automatic control system **-er Regler** automatic controller **-er Ruf** keyless ringing **-e Rundnahtschweißmaschine** *f* automatic circular seam welding machine **-e Schaltung** automatic gear change **-e Schaltkupplung** automatically operated coupling **-er Schutzdeckel** forced action guard lid **-e Steuerung** automatic pilot **-es System** dial system

automatisch-er Treffanzeiger automatic spotter, auto-spotter **-er Verschluß** automatic shutter **-e Vielstahlfertigdrehbank** automatic multiple cutter finishing lathe **-er Vorschub** automatic feed **-e Vorschubeinrichtung** automatic carriage **-e Winde** *f* automatic cathead **-er Zeitstempel** time check

automatisieren to automate

automatisiert automated

Automatisierung *f* automatic control, automation, automatic working

Automobil *n* passenger car, automobile **-anruf** *m* taxicab call **-bau** *m* automotive industry **-blech** *n* automobile-body sheet steel **-brücke** *f* rear axle differential casing **-fabrik** *f* motor-car factory **-teil** *m* automobile part

Automolit *m* zinc spinel, gahnite, automolite

automorph automorphic

Automorphismus einer Konfiguration automorphism of a configuration

Auto-Münzfernsprecher *m* drive-in coin telephone

autonom autonomous **-e Einheit** self-contained unit **-er Übertrag** self-instructed carry

Autooxydation *f* self-oxidation

Autopoliermittel *n* motorcar polish

Autopolimerisation *f* self-polymerization

Autoradiogramm *n* auto-radiograph

Autoradiographie *f* autoradiography

Autoradiozerhacker *m* car radio vibrator transformer

autorisieren to authorize

Autor *m* author

Autorenrecht *n* copyright

Autorität *f* authority, credit

Autorotation *f* autorotation

Autoruf *m* taxicab call, special telephone system for hailing taxis

Auto-schalter *m* drive-in counter (of bank) **-schlepp** *m* wrecking car, wrecker, automatic towing apparatus, towing by automobile, method of catapulting gliders by motorcar and cable **-schleppen** *n* catapulting of gliders by motor and cable **-schleppstart** *m* auto-towed start or take-off **-schmieröl** *n* motor lubricant **-schmierstoffe** *pl* motor oils and greases **-schütter** *m* tipper **-start** *m* launch by automobile tow **-transformator** *m* autotransformer

Autostereogramm *n* autostereogram

Auto-störsuchgerät *n* automobile fault-finder **-transduktor** *m* auto-transductor

Autotypie *f* half-tone etching, autotypy **-andruckpresse** *f* block proofing press **-ätzfarbe** *f* process engraving ink **-druck** *m* printing of half-tone etchings or engravings **-farbe** *f* autotype printing ink **-platte** *f* autotype plate **-raster** *m* halftone screen

Auto-verkehr *m* motor traffic **-winde** *f* motorcar jack **-windenstart** *m* launch by automobile winch

Autoxydation *f* autoxidation

Autoxydator *m* autoxidator

Autunit *m* uranite, autunite

Auxanometer *n* auxanometer

Auxiliarmaschine *f* auxiliary engine

Auxochrom *n* auxoxhrome

auxochrome Gruppe (Chem.) auxochromous group

Auxometer *n* auxiometer

avalieren to stand security, guarantee

avancieren to be promoted

Aventurinfeldspat *m* sunstone, adventurine feldspar

Aventurisieren *n* punctiform flashing

A Verstärker *m* A battery, filament battery, class A amplifier

Aviatik *f* aviation

Avidität *f* avidity

Avionallegierungen *f pl* aluminum-copper-magnesium alloys for aircraft construction, light metals

Avis *m* information, advice

avisieren to advise, notify, inform

Aviso *m* dispatch boat, fleet, station tender

Aviage *f* finishing, preparation, coating (e. g. on tire cord)

avivierecht (Seide) fast to scrooping (brightening)

avivieren to finish

Aviviermittel *n* scrooping agent

A1-Wert *m* inductance rating (in henrys per 1,000 turns)

A W Zahl (Amperewindungszahl) number of ampere turns

axial axial **-e Fokussierung** axial focussing **-er Tensor** axial tensor

Axial-beanspruchung *f* axial stress or load **-belastung** *f* axial load, thrust load

Axialdruck *m* axial or thrust load, end thrust, axial pressure **unausgeglichener ~** unbalanced end thrust

Axialdrucklager *n* thrust bearing

axial durchströmt axial-flow

axialelastischer Schneckenförderer axially-flexible screw conveyor

Axial-feder *f* axial spring **-gebläse** *n* axial-flow fan, axial blower, axial compressor **-gegendruckturbine** *f* axial back-pressure turbine **-geschwindigkeit** *f* axial velocity
Axialität *f* alignment
Axial-kompressor *m* axial-flow compressor (jet), gas turbine **-kraft** *f* axial force, longitudinal force, normal force **-kugellager** *n* axial ball bearing **-kühler** *m* axial flow radiator **-lader** *m* axial supercharger (aviation) **-lager** *n* thrust bearing **-luft** *f* axial-clearance tolerance **-pumpe** *f* axial-flow pump
Axial-rad *n* axial rotor **-radialverdichter** *m* mixed flow compressor **-rillenkugellager** axial grooved ball bearing **-schub** *m* side thrust, axial thrust or pressure, end thrust **-seil** *n* axial wire or cable **-spiel** *n* end clearance, end float, axial or end play **-steigung** *f* axial pitch **-stromturbine** *f* axial-flow turbine **-stufe** *f* axial stage
axialsymmetrisch axial(ly) symmetric **-e Strömung** axial flow
Axial-turbine *f* axial-flow-type turbine (jet), gasturbine **-ventilator** *m* axial-flow fan **-verdichter** *m* axial (flow) compressor **-verfahren** *n* axial feed method **-verschiebung** *f* axial movement, lateral thrust (of turbines)
axial versetzen to displace in axial direction
Axial-verspannung *f* axial bracing or wiring **-vorstufe** *f* axial inducer stage **-zug** *m* axial tension **-zylindermotor** *m* barrel-type motor, axial-cylinder engine
Axinit *m* axinite
Axiomatik *f* axiomatics, axiomatic theory
axiomatischer Begriff axiomatic concept
Axiome, ebene ~ axioms of plane geometry **räumliche ~** axioms of solid geometry
Axiometer *n* axiometer, telltale gauge
Axonometrie *f* axonometry
axonometrisch axonometric
Axt *f* adz, ax, hatchet
Ayrtonscher Nebenschluß *m* Ayrton shunt, universal shunt box, compensating resistance
Azelainsäure *f* azelaic acid
Azenaphthen *n* acenaphthene
Azenium *n* a triaryl azine compound
azentrisch acentric
azeotropisch azeotropic
Azeotroppunkt *m* point of inflection
A Zerstäuber *m* oxygen fuel sprayer
Azetaldehyd *n* acetic aldehyde
Azetamid *n* acetamide
Azetanilid *n* acetanilide
Azetat *n* acetate **-faser** *f* a type of artificial wool manufactured from beech **-kunstseide** *f* acetate rayon **-lack** *m* acetate dope **-zellwolle** *f* acetate spun rayon **-zellulosefilm** *m* cellulose acetate film
azeteliertes Lignin acetylized lignin
Azetessigäther *m* acetonacetic ester
Azetil-film *m* acetate film stock **-zellulose** *f* cellulose acetate
Azetimeter *n* acetimeter
Azet-itril *n* acetonitrile
Azeton *n* acetone
Azetosyringon *n* acetovanillone
Azetyl *n* acetyl **-chlorid** *n* acetyl chloride
Azetylen *n* acetylene **-anlasser** *m* acetylene starter **-befeuerung** *f* acetylene lighting **-beleuchtung** *f* acetylene lighting system **-dichlorid** *n* ethylene dichloride, dichlorethylene **-druckminderer** *m* acetylene regulator **-entwickler** *m* acetylene generator **-erzeugungsapparat** acetylene generator **-flasche** *f* acethylene cylinder
Azetylen-gas *n* acetylene gas **-geruch** *m* odor of acetylene **-glühlicht** *n* incandescent acetylene lighting **-glühlichtbrenner** *m* incandescent acetylene burner **-hartlötausrüstung** *f* acetylene brazing output **-leuchtfeuer** *n* acetylene flare light **-preßgaserzeuger** *m* acetylene pressure generator **-reinigungsmasse** *f* acetylene purifying agent
Azetylensauerstoff-brenner *m* oxyacetylene blowpipe or torch **-gas** *n* oxyacetylene **-schneidbrenner** oxyacetylene cutting torch **-schweißung** *f* oxyacetylene welding
Azetylen-schneideanlage *f* acetylene cutting plant **-scheinwerfer** *m* acetylene headlight **-schweißbrenner** *m* oxyacetylene welding torch **-schweißung** *f* acetylene welding **-sicherheitsvorlage** *f* water-seal weld
azetylierbar acetylable
azetylieren to acetylate
Azetylierung *f* acetylation
Azetyl-saccharose *f* sucrose octa-acetate **-säure** *f* acetic acid **-zellulose** *f* acetyl cellulose
Azid *n* trinitride, azide, hydrazoate
azidifizieren to acidify, sour
Azidität *f* acidity
azidolytischer Abbau acidolytic degradation, hydrolyric degradation by means of acids
Azidul *n* hyperoxygenated salt
Azimut *m* azimuth, bearing **~ der Aufnahmerichtung** azimuth of the plate perpendicular **~, bezogen auf die Hauptvertikalebene der Aufnahme** ground plumb bearing (geod.)
azimutabhängig azimuthal
azimutal azimuthal **-e Quantenzahl** orbital or second quantum number
Azimutal-projektion *f* azimuthal projection **-schwingung** *f* azimuthal mode
Azimut-bogen *m* arc of azimuth **-diagramm** *n* azimuth diagram **-entfernungsmesser** *m* depression range or position finder **-kreisel** *m* azimuth gyro **-peilvorrichtung** *f* azimuth indicating goniometer **-streuung** *f* azimut spread **-wert** *m* azimuth value (radar) **-winkel** *m* azimuth angle **-zeiger** *m* azimuth finder
Azingruppe *f* azine group
Azobenzol *n* azobenzol, azobenzene
Azofarbstoff *m* azo dyestuff
Azokörper *m* azo compound, azo derivative
Azot *n* nitrogen
Azo-verbindung *f* azo compound **-zyklisch** azocyclic
Azoxygruppe *f* azoxy group
azur (blau) sky blue
Azurstein *m* lapis lazuli
azyklisch acyclic

B

BA (Betriebsamt *n*) operations office

Babbeln *n* babble (teleph.)

Babbittmetall *n* bearing or white metal, Babbitt or Britannia metal

B-Abfragebetrieb *m* ring-down junction

Bach *m* stream, brook, rivulet

Bachdurchlaß *m* culvert

Back *m* vat (dyeing)

Back *f* forecastle, locker, partition, berth

Backbord *n* port, larboard, port side **~ achteraus** port aft **~ voraus** on the port bow

Backbord-dalbe *f* port dolphin or pale **-halsen** *f pl* tack, starboard, port **-korrektor** *m* port corrector **-kurve** *f* port (left-hand) curve **-licht** *n* port light **-maschine** *f* port engine

Backbordmotor *m* port engine **der innere ~** port inner engine

Backbord-seite *f* portside **-seitenlicht** *n* port light **-zeichen** *n* port signal

backbrassen to heave to, brace back

Backe *f*, **Backen** *m* wedge grip, wedge, jaw (holding fixture), die, bit, check, flange, joint, endpiece **mit ~ belegt** put on beacons **~ an Drahtstiftmaschinen** jaw for wire rail machine **einteilige ~** solid die **verschiebbare ~** sliding jaw

backen to bake, cake, bind, cement, roast, burn (coke)

Backen *n* clinkering, coking, caking (coal or sugar) **-abstand** *m* jaw distance **-bohrer** *m* pipe stock tap, master tap **-brecher** *m* jawbreaker, jaw crusher **-bremse** *f* shoe brake, stem for casing dogs, block brake, friction brake

backend baking, caking, binding, cementing **-e Kohle** caking coal, bituminous coal

Backenfänger *m* casing spear

Backenfutter *n* jaw chuck **auswechselbares ~** jaw liner

Backen-gewindebohrer *m* die hob for cutting open dies **-kupplung** *f* jaw clutch **-lager** *n* collet **-meißel** *m* bit, wing bit **-paar** *n* set of dies, set of jaws **-quetsche** *f* jaw crusher **-schiene** *f* stock rail **-schleifvorrichtung** *f* grinding attachment (for threading dies) **-setzstock** *m* jaw type steady, friction pads **-schraube** *f* wedge bolt **-stück** *n* check strap

back-fähig capable of baking (or caking) **-fähigkeit** *f* coking capacity, caking property or quality, binding or cementing property, coking index, coking property or quality **-haube** *f* baking hood **-kohle** *f* bituminous-coal, caking coal, fat coal **-maschine** *f* baking machine **-mulde** *f* kneading trough **-ofen** *m* baking oven, oven **-pulver** *n* baking powder **-spiere** *f* boom, defense boom, boat boom, swinging boom **-stag** *m* backstay

Backstein *m* burnt brick **-mauer** *f* (fire)brick wall **-mauerwerk** *n* brickwork **-ofen** *m* brick kiln **-raster** *m* brick screen **-schicht** *f* course of bricks

Back-torf *m* turf cake **-trog** *m* baking trough, kneading trough **-vermögen** *n* coking quality

Bad *n* bath, cell, tank **ein ~ ansetzen** to prepare a bath **~ zum Beizen** pickling bath **~ beschicken** to charge a bath **galvanisches ~** electroplating bath, galvanic vat **das ~ ist zu metallarm** the bath has become impoverished **~ bei steter (unveränderlicher) Temperatur** constant-temperature bath

Badbewegung *f* agitation of bath, swirling of metal, stirring effect (in induction furnace), circulation of electrolyte

Bade-einrichtung *f* bathroom installation **-kaue** *f* pit bath, washhouse **-leitung** *f* pipe line to baths and showers

Badeofenbleche und -bänder sheets and strip for Geysers

b-Ader *f* (Teleph.) ring wire, R wire

Bäder-anordnung *f* cell-group arrangement (electrolysis) **-dampfer** *m* high-speed coasting vessel

Bad-flüssigkeit *f* bath solution **-kasten** *m* (electrolysis) cell **-nebel** *m* bath vapor

Badnitrieren *n* salt bath nitriding

Bad-probe *f* bath sample **-reaktion** *f* bath reaction **-spannung** *f* (electrolysis) bath potential, bath voltage, cell potential or voltage, tank potential or voltage **-spiegel** *m* bath level or surface **-strecke** *f* (des Fadens) bath travel (of thread)

Badstrom *m* bath current **-regler für Elektrolyse** regulators for electrolysis circuits

Baduhr *f* electroplasting clock

Bad- und Klosettpumpen *f pl* sanitary pumps

Bad-widerstand *m* tank resistance **-zementieren** *n* liquid carburizing (met.)

Bagasse *f* crushed sugar cane, residue or waste bagasse, residue after the sap has been pressed from sugar cane **-lignin** *n* bagasse lignin **-zellstoff** *m* bagasse cellulose

Bagatelle *f* bagatelle, trifle, small claim

Bagger *m* dredge, excavating machine, steam shovel, excavator, dredger, shovel, drag **-achse** *f* center line (c/l) of excavator **-betrieb** *m* dredging service **-bohrer** *m* dredging bit **-bohrung** *f* drilling by dredging

Baggerbolzen *m* dredger joint pin **-ring** *m* ring for dredging bolt

Bagger-boot *n* dredger **-eimer** *m* bucket **-grube** *f* pulp silo **-gut** *n* dredged material, the spoil **-kasten** *m* dredger bucket **-kette** *f* dredging chain **-kopf** *m* suction head **-maschine** *f* dredge

baggern to dig, excavate, dredge, dray

Bagger-schaufel *f* dredger bucket **-prahm** *m* ballast dredger, mud lighter **-schute** *f* barge **-stich** *m* paddock **-teile** *m pl* dredgingmachine parts

Baggerung *f* dredging

Baguios baguios

Bahamaholz *n* Brazil wood

bähen to foment, sweat

Bahn *f* (Physik) path, orbit (celestial body or satellite), trajectory, way, course, ray, race track (nucl.), track, railroad, run, groove (of a hammer), face, gore, channel, sheet; (Papier) web, tape; (Dachpappe) course (of roofing felt)

Bahn, antriebsfreie ~ free-flight trajectory, portion of the trajectory of rockets after combustion cutoff **die ~ berechnen** to calculate the trajectory **sich ~ brechen** to push one's way through **direkte ~** direct ray **die ~ einhalten** to maintain the trajectory **gedeckte ~** shooting gallery **in geschlossener ~** over a closed circuit **neutrale ~** nonpermanent runway

Bahn eines Elektrons electron (ion) trajectory **~ der Flüssigkeitsteilchen** stream line **~ eines Ions** ion trajectory **~ des Lichtzentrums** photocentric orbit

Bahn-abzweigung *f* branching **-achse** *f* axis parallel to the path, flight axis **-analyse** *f* analysis of path **-anlagen** *f pl* railroad buildings, properties or installations **-anschluß** *m* rail connection **-ausrüstungsteile** *m pl* railway equipment **-bau** *m* railway construction **-berührende** *f* tangent of motion **-beschleunigung** *f* acceration along the path **-betriebswerkstatt** *f* railway repairshop **-bewegung** *f* orbital motion (of a planet)

bahnbrechend pioneering, radically new

Bahn-brecher *m* pioneer **-dickenregelung** *f* web thickness control **-damm** *m* railroad embankment

Bahndrehimpuls *m* orbital angular momentum **-quadrat** *n* square of the orbital angular momentum **-quantenzahl** *f* orbital quantum number

Bahn-druck *m* pressure perpendicular to the road exerted by a vehicle **-durchlauf** *m* sheet passage **-durchmesser** *m* diameter of orbit **-ebene** *f* trajectory plane **-eigentum** *n* railway property **-einlenkung** *f* approach to standard path of beam-guided missiles with damped oscillating trajectory **-elektronen** *n pl* orbital electrons

bahnen to prepare or pave the way, beat, smooth, clear (a way or path)

Bahnen-streckenmaschine *f* belt stretching machine **-trockner** *m* web drier (sheeting drier)

bahnfeste Achse air axis (aerodyn.)

Bahn-frachten *f pl* rates of freight **-frachtsätze** *m pl* railway rates **-frachttarif** *m* railway tariff **-frei** free on rail, free on board **-gebiet** *n* railroad right of way **-gelände** *n* right-of-way of railroad **-geschwindigkeit** *f* velocity in trajectory, velocity of flight **-gleis** *n* line of rails **-graben** *m* side ditch **-größen** *f pl* ballistic variables **-hammer** *m* face hammer

Bahnhof *m* (railroad) station

Bahnhofs-leistung *f* station capacity **-vorstand** *m* stationmaster

Bahnhöhe *f* orbiting altitude (g/m), height of the strip

Bahnhöhen-neigung *f* orbit inclination (g/m) **-stabilisierung** *f* orbital stabilization (g/m)

bahnig flat, even

Bahn-impuls *m* orbital moment **-kette** *f* spiked chain **-knoten** *m* railroad junction **-körper** *m* roadbed (R.R.) **-kreuzung** *f* traverse **-krone** *f* crown of roadbed (R.R.) **-krümmung** *f* route or track curvature **-kurve** *f* track curve, path line

bahnlagernd deposited at railway station

Bahn-länge *f* length path, pitch (bombing practice) **-moment** *m* orbital moment **-motoren** *m pl* railway motors **-neigung** *f* inclination of flight path, inclination of trajectory, path angle, tilt (g/m) **-neigungswinkel** *m* inclination angle of the flight path

Bahn-netz *n* railroad net or system **-normale** *f* perpendicular to the trajectory plane **-oberbau** *m* superstructure (R.R.) **-parallel** parallel to or along the path **-planum** *n* roadbed foundation (R.R.) **-punkte** *pl* line points **-räumer** *m* rail guard **-richtung** *f* direction of track, trajectory path track, direction of motion or flight, flight path

Bahn-schaltanlage *f* railway (electrical) switchgear **-schlägel** *m* face hammer **-schlinge** *f* orbital loop **-schranke** *f* crossing gate **-schutz** *n* railroad police force composed of railroad employees (Germany) **-schwelle** *f* sleeper **-schwingung** *f* trajectory oscillation **-senkrecht** path normal, at right angle to flight path

Bahn-spannungsregelung *f* control of web tension **-spur** *f* track formation, trace of trajectory **-spurkleckse** *pl* track blobs **-stabilisierung** *f* orbital stabilization **-stabilität** *f* orbital stability

Bahnsteig *m* railroad platform **-rufanlage** *f* railway call system **-unterführung** *f* platform underpass

Bahn-stetigkeit *f* stability of trajectory **-strecke** *f* railway line, division **-stromversorgung** *f* traction power supply **-tangente** *f* tangent to course (of a ship) **-tangentenneigungswinkel** *m* path angle **-teil** *m* cell size **-transport** *m* railroad transportation **-überführung** *f* undergrade arch crossing **-übergang** *m* grade crossing, level crossing **-umkehrprinzip** *n* path-reversal principle **-unterführung** *f* underpass, traffic tunnel

Bahn-valenz *f* orbital valence **-verbindung** *f* train connection, railroad line, railroad communication **-verbreiterung** *f* flareout **-verfolgung** *f* space tracking (of rocket) **-verfolgungsstation** *f* space tracking station **-verkehr** *m* rail(road) traffic **-verladen** loaded on railcar **-verlauf** *m* form of trajectory behavior of ballistic variables, ray path, ray tracing, trajectory **-vermessung** *f* survey of the trajectory, trajectory or path computation **-verpackt** packed for transport by rail **-versand** *m* shipping by rail

Bahn-werte *pl* ballistic values **-widerstand** *m* series resistance of bulk of semiconductor, bulk resistance **-winkel** *m* angle of position **-winkeländerung** *f* variation in path angle **-wurzel** *f* root of the path **-zustand** *m* orbital state

Bahre *f* stretcher

Bähung *f* fomentation, sweating

Bai *f* bay (small gulf)

Bailey-Ofen *m* Bailey (resistance) furnace

Bajonett *n* bayonet **-anschluß** *m* bayonet-type fitting **-auspuffrohrsystem** *n* bayonet stacks **-fassung** *f* swan socket, bayonet socket, **-griff** *m* bayonet grip **-korn** *n* locking ring pin **-kupplung** *f* bayonet catch or clutch **-rahmen** *m* bayonet frame **-rohr** *n* closed tube

Bajonettscheibe *f* bayonet plate **-scheibenbefestigung** *f* bayonet mounting, bayonet plate fixing **-sockel** *m* bayonet base **-stoß** *m* bayonet thrust

-verbindung *f* bayonet joint **-verschluß** *m* slide lock, slide catch, bayonet catch, joint, or lock, bayonet union (as used in bayonet-type lamp holders), bayonett unit (lamps), slide-type spring lock

Bake *f* (radio) beacon, navigational aid, landmark, signal light ~ **für Kursanzeige** course-indicating beacon

bakelisierter Faserstoff phenol fiber

Bakelit-federhalter *m* bakelite fountain pen **-formstück** *n* bakelite molding

bakelitgebundene Schleifscheibe bakelite-bonded grinding

Bakelitklötzchen *n* small bakelite block

Bakelitmodelle mit Aluminiumbewehrung armored bakelite models

Bakelit-rändelschraube rilled bakelite screw **-scheibe** *f* (Lichtscheibe) plastic lens

Baken-antenne *f* beam antenna, beacon antenna, radio-range antenna **-boje** *f* beacon buoy **-empfang** *m* radio-beacon reception **-empfänger** *m* radio-beacon receiver **-kurs** *m* beacon course **-leitstrahl** *m* radio range leg **-licht** *n* signal light **-stab** *m* antenna component **-system für Blindlandung** blind approach beacon system (BABS) **-tonne** *f* beacon buoy

Bakterien *n pl* bacteria **-filternutschen** *f pl* bacteria suction filters **-krieg** *m* bacterial warfare

Bakteriologe *m* bacteriologist

bakteriologisch bacteriological

Bakteriose *f* gummy disease

bakterizid bactericidal **-e Wirkung** bactericide effect

Balance *f* balance, equipoise **-gewicht** *n* counter weight **-rad** *n* balance wheel **-ruder** *n* balanced rudder

Balanzier *m* beam, balancing lever, walking beam **-block** *m* trestle-balance standard **-bock** *m* a type of stand for balancing propellers **-bügel** *m* gimbal frame **-dampfmaschine** *f* beam engine **-draht** *m* balancing wire (elec.)

balanzieren to balance

Balanzier-feder *f* balance spring **-kolben** *m* balancing piston of turbine **-latte** *f* balance rod **-maschine** *f* beam engine **-mutter** *f* balance weight, balance nut **-ring** *m* gimbal frame **-rohr** *n* **und Verlängerungsrohr eines Fernrohres** balancing and extension tube of a telescope **-säge** *f* radius crosscut saw machine **-trog** *m* balance trough, tank

Balata *f* balata **-riemen** *m* balata belt **-riemenleder** *n* balata belting

Balbachprozeß *m* Balbach (electrolytic refining) process

Baldachin *m* canopy, cabane, center section (of wing); (Teil der Lampe) fixture flange **-holm** *m*, **-strebe** *f* center-section strut, cabane strut

Balg *m* bellows (photo.) **-auszug** *m* bellow extension of camera **-dichtung** *f* bellows joint (sealing)

Balgen *m* bellows (camera) **-auszug** *m* bellows extension **-kammer** *f* camera adapter **-stütze** *f* bellows support

Balg-falten *pl* bellows folds **-kamera** *f* extensible camera, bellows camera **-linse** *f* bellows ring (packings) **-membran** *f* bellows

Balken *m* log, beam, balk, girder, joist, dash, spar; (TV) spike, bar ~ **zum Festspannen** clamping girder ~ **bündig überschneiden** to scarf timbers **abgekanteter** ~ cant timber **ausgefalzter** ~ grooved beam **einfacher** ~ simple beam **eingespannter** ~ fixed beam **verdübelter** ~ joggled-built beam **verschränkter** ~ scarfed-built beam **verzahnter** ~ indented-built beam **zusammengesetzter** ~ built-up beam

Balken-bahn *f* timber roadway **-belag** *m* planking **-belastung** *f* beam loading **-biegepresse** *f* beam-bending press **-biegung** *f* bending of beams, deflection of a beam **-bremse** *f* wheel brakes with shoes **-brücke** *f* girder bridge **-decke** *f* span ceiling, ceiling of timbers **-fach** *n* tail bay **-falz** *m* channel for beams **-floß** *n* log raft

Balken-generator *m* bar generator **-gerüst** *n* scaffolding of girders **-gleisbremse** *f* beam-type retarder **-herd** *m* beam hearth **-holm** *m* straight spar **-krümmung** *f* curvature of beams **-lage** *f* framing of joists **-mitte** *f* middle of the beam **-muster** *n* bar pattern **-nadel** *f* (hydro-electric works) needle beam **-probe** *f* beam test **-pumpe** *f* beam pump **-rost** *m* grating of timbers **-rührer** *m* straight arm paddle agitator **-schalung** *f* girder casing

Balkensperre *f* timber road block, nuts and booms (navy) **schwimmende** ~ floating boom

Balken-stapel *m* log crib, timber crib **-stütze** *f* prop **-testbild** *n* bar test pattern **-theorie** *f* theory of beams **-träger** *m* straight girder or beam **-unterkante** *f* lower edge of beam **-verhau** *n* timber obstacle **-verhauträger** *m* straight girder or beam **-waage** *f* steelyard, beam balance **-werk** *n* rafters, beams **-zeiger** *m* beam-shaped pointer **-zug** *m* tie beam

Balkon *m* balcony, gun turret on aircraft

Balkweger *m* clamp, shelf

Ball *m* ball, globe

Ballast *m* ballast **fliegender** ~ shifting ballast

Ballast-betrieb *m* ballasting (pumps for adjusting ballast) **-gewinnung** *f* water recovery **-klötze** *m pl* ballast weights (secured to the keel of a submarine) **-reich** high in inerts **-röhre** *f* absorber tube or valve, ballast tube **-schaufel** *f* charging scoop **-tank** *m* ballast tank **-tankauslaßventil** *n* ballast-tank vent valve **-tankflutventil** *n* ballast-tank flood valve **-widerstand** *m* ballast resistance, loading resistance, ballast resistor

Ballaufnahme *f* bulb exposure **-auslöser** *m* ball release

Bälle *m pl* balls, clay ballots (ceramics)

Balleisen *n* ball pane iron **gekröpftes** ~ offset bent chisel

Ballempfang *m* ball reception (elec.), relay reception, relay television

Ballempfänger *m* retransmission receiver **-sender** *m* radio relay station

ballen to form balls, conglomerate, bale, package, cake, pack together

Ballen *m* bale, hoof ball, bit bar, saddle bar, pack, body, bundle (batch)

Ballen *n* baling

Ballen-band *n* baling band **-bindeapparat** *m* bale tie maker **-brecher** *m* bale breaker **-brett** *n* baling board **-eisen** *n* dressing chisel **-griff** *m* ball grip, machine handle **-lage** *f* palm rest

-länge *f* surface length of roll
Ballen-messer *m* body gauge **-messer** *n* bale knife **-mühle** *f* ball crusher (ball mill) **-oberfläche** *f* working surface **-öffner** *m* bale opener **-packmaschine** *f* baling-machine **-packpresse** *f* baling press **-presse** *f* baling press **-reifen** *m* baling hoop
Ballgesenk *n* bottom fuller
Ballhammer *m* ball hammer, top fuller **-unterteil** *n* bottom fuller
ballig crowned, spherical, lumpy, cambered roll **~ drehen** to crown **~ gedreht** (Riemenscheibe) bulged, convexly turned (strap wheel)
Ballig-drehen *n* spherical turning **-drehvorrichtung** *f* convex turning attachment
Balligkeit *f* amount of crown, bulging, crowning **~ der Walzen** camber of rolls
Ballig-schleifeinrichtung *f* cambering attachment **-verzahnung** *f* cutting crowned teeth, crowned tooth bevel gears, crowned gear
Ballingspindel *n* balling spindle
Ballistik *f* ballistics
ballistisch ballistic **-er Flug** ballistic flight **-es Luftgewicht** ballistic air density **-e Rakete** ballistic missile (IBCM) **-e Tageseinflüsse** ballistic density and wind factors
Ballistit *f* ballistite
Ballon *m* carboy, balloon (flask), bulb, demijohn **einen ~ mit frischem Gas füllen** gassing a balloon
Ballon-abfüller *m* pump-equipped balloon flask **-abstieg** *m* balloon descent **-abweiser** *m* antiballoon device **-ader** *f* balloon conductor **-amme** *f* reserve or supply balloon **-aufnahme** *f* balloon survey **-aufstieg** *m* balloon ascent **-aufstiegplatz** *m* balloon take-off site
Ballon-bahn *f* panal, fabric gore **-entleerungsapparat** *m* carboy-emptying apparatus
Ballonett *n* ballonet **unpralles ~** flabby ballonet
Ballon-flasche *f* carboy **-führer** *m* balloon pilot **-gurt** *m* balloon cable, rigging band on captive balloon **-halle** *f* hangar, shed **-hülle** *f* envelope gas bag, balloon envelope **-kipper** *m* carboy tilter **-korb** *m* balloon basket, nacelle **-mannschaft** *f* balloon crew **-netz** *n* balloon net **-registriertheodolit** *m* pilot balloon theodolite **-reifen** *m* balloon tire **-schirm** *m* ballute (of space craft) **-schirmreißleine** *f* ballute pack rip cord
Ballon-seide *f* balloon silk **-sender** *m* balloon-borne transmitter **-sonde** *f* sounding or registering balloon, balloon sonde, radio sonde (meteor.), rabal **-sondierung** *f* sounding the atmosphere with balloons to determine wind direction, barometric pressure, and other data (meteor.) **-sperre** *f* balloon barrage **-station** *f* captive-balloon station **-stoff** *m* balloon fabric **-theodolit** *m* balloon theodolite **-variometer** *m* balloon statoscope **-ventil** *n* main gas valve (balloon) **-winde** *f* balloon winch
Ballsenden *n* reradiation, rebroadcasting, radio repeating
Ballsender *m*, **Ballsendestation** *f* relay or relaying station, rebroadcast transmitter or station, station belonging to a network
Ballsendestelle *f*, **Ballstation** *f* radio-repeating station
Ball-sendung *f* relay broadcast **-toppzeichen** *n* spherical top mark
Ballung *f* agglomeration, sinter cake, bunching, packing **~ im Bremsfeld** reflex bunching
Ballungs-fähigkeit *f* coalescing or spheroidizing property (cryst.), balling or caking property **-maß** *n* bunching parameter
Ball-verschluß *m* pneumatic shutter (camera) **-werk** *n* skull cracker
Balme *f* rock niche or shelter, re-entrant
Balsa *n* balsa wood **-flugmodell** *n* all-balsa model **-holz** *n* balsa wood
Balsam *m* balsam
Balsam-harz *n* gum rosin **-papel** *f* balsam poplar, tacamahac **-tanne** *f* balsam fir, Norway spruce, spruce
Baltasekunden *f pl* ballistic density and wind factors in time-of-flight seconds, meteor seconds, meteor correction per second of flight (artil.) **-verfahren** *n* procedure in correcting for ballistic density and wind
Balustrade *f* balustrade
Bamagschachtverfahren *n* Bamag-shaft process, Bamag method
Bambus *m*, **-holz** bamboo **-rohr** *n* malacca cane
Bananen-baum *m* banana tree **-stecker** *m* banana plug, split (banana-shaped) plug, banana pin, spring-contact plug **-steckerverbindung** *f* banana plug connection
Band *m* volume, binding
Band *n* ribbon, tape; (Bindfaden) string, cord; (Befestigung) tie, bond; (Binde) bandage; (Magnetophon) recording tape; (Faß) hoop; (Förderband) conveyer, strap, strip, band (ring), grip (suspender for loading torpedoes), (conveyer) belt, molding (inside flask jacket), recording, isopleth, graph, web (of cloth), driving band, binder, brace
Band *n*, **mit ~ bewickeln** to tape (together) **~ ohne Ende** endless belt **besetztes ~** full band **elastisches ~** elastic web **gefülltes ~** filled band **harmonisches ~** harmonic or overtone band (optics) **am laufenden ~** serially, by the belt conveyor system, mass production, on the assembly line **laufendes ~** endless belt system, continuous production, belt-type ticket carrier **verbotenes ~** forbidden band, energy gap **das ~ wandert** the strip creeps
Band-abhebevorrichtung tape lifting device **-ablage** *f* tape delivery, coiling
Bandabschattierung *f* degradation of bands **nach rot oder violett ~** degradation of bands to red or violet
Band-absperre *f* band-eliminator filter **-abstand** *m* energy gap (semiconductors) **-absteller** *m* stop motion **-abstreifer** *m* belt scraper **-abzugswalze** *f* delivery roller **-achat** *m* ribbon agate
Bandage *f* bandage, dressing, binding, band; (Reifen) tire, rim (wheels)
Bandagen-draht *m* tie-wire **-drehbank** *f* tire turning mill **-eisen** *n* tire steel or iron **-glühofen** *m* tire heating furnace **-halter** *m* binding wire clip **-schweißung** *f* building up of wheel tires **-walzerei** *f* tire-rolling practice **-walzwerk** *n* tire-rolling mill
bandagieren to fit with tires, bandage, wrap or tie with ribbon or tape
Bandagierung *f* retaining ring, shroud ring
Band-anfang *m* front end of assembly line

-anlage *f* belt conveyor system **-antenne** *f* tape antenna, band or ribbon antenna **-antrieb** *m* tape drive **-antriebsachse** *f* driving spindle (tape rec.), driving shaft (tape rec.) **-arbeit** *f* moving-belt production **-aufgabe** *f* apron feeder, belt feeder **-aufhängung** *f* strip suspension **-aufnahme** *f* tape recording

Bandbenutzung *f*, **gemeinschaftliche ~** band-sharing

band-bewehrt band armored **-bewicklung** *f* winding with cotton rope **-blitz** *m* ribbon lightning

Bandbreite *f* band width, frequency range (radio); (bei Walzen) rolling width

Bandbreite(n)-einstellung *f* frequency-range control, band-width adjuster **-regler** *m* band-width control **-regelung** *f* band spread or adjustment **-schalter** *m* band-selector switch (electronics) **-verfahren** *n* band-width method

Bandbremse *f* band brake, strap brake, frequency control

Bandbremskuppelung *f* frequency-control coupling

Bändchen-galvanometer *n* twisted strip or band galvanometer **-mikrophon** *n* velocity microphone, ribbon or tape microphone (tape rec.)

Band-chronograph *m* graphic recorder **-dehnung** *f* band spreading (radio) **-dickenmessung** *f* measurement of strip thickness **-durchlaßbereich** *m* band pass

Banddurchzieh-glühen *n* continuous-strip annealing **-ofen** *m* continuous-strip furnace

Bande *f* cushion

Band-einengung *f* squeezing or compression of band **-einlage** *f* belt ply **-einlegeschlitz** *m* drop-in tape loading slot **-einrichter** *m* ribbon loom gaiter **-einrichtung** *f* belt conveyor capacity

Bandeisen *n* hoop iron, strip, band, or strap iron, steel flat (strip of small rectangular section) **-bewehrung** *f* hoop-iron sheathing, tape armoring **-haspel** *f* hoop-iron reel **-reif** *m* band iron hoop **-schleudervorrichtung** *f* tumbling device for hoop iron **-schrappvorrichtung** *f* roughing device for hoop iron **-spannapparat** steel strapping stretcher with sealer **-straße** *f* flat iron train **-verschnürgerät** *n* strapping tool

Bandempfang *m* reception by tape

Banden-ausfilterung *f* band elimination **-besetzungsgrad** *m* degree of filling of bands

Bandende *n* rear end of assembly line

Banden-dicke *f* finished strip thickness **-durchlässigkeit** *f* band pass **-kante** *f* band edge **-kopf** *m* band head, band edge (spectral analysis) **-spektrum** *n* band spectrum **-träger** *m* chain agents **-zug** *m* band progression **-zweig** *m* branch, part of series of lines forming a band

bänderarmer Falzapparat folder with few tapes

Bänder-bremsschirm *m* ribbon brake parachute **-führung** *f* tape guides (print) **-kitt** *m* tape cement **-modell** *n* collective electron, treatment band theory, band model

Banderole *f* revenue stamp

Bänderton *m* varved clay

Bänderung *f* banded structure, stratification

Band-fabrikation *f* production-line fabrication or manufacture **-feder** *f* coil spring, tripping spring **-fehlstelle** *f* bad spot (tape rec.)

Bandfilter *n* wave-form selector, band (pass) filter, wave-band filter, acceptor circuit (electronics), band selector (circuit), preselector **~ von großer Lochbreite** broad band filter **zweikreisiger ~** intermediate-frequency transformer

bandfilter-gekoppelt band-pass coupled **-kreise** *m pl* band-filter circuits **-spule** *f* band-pass filter coil

Band-folie *f* strip, foil **-fördereinrichtung** *f* belt conveyor

Bandförderer *m* band conveyer, belt carrier or conveyer **ortsfester ~** stationary belt conveyer **schrägliegender ~** inclined belt conveyer

bandförmig band-shaped **-e Materialien** strip materials

Band-führung *f* guiding of the sliver **-führungsplatte** *f* feed plate **-gerät** *n* tape recorder **-geschwindigkeit** *f* tape speed **-geschwindigkeitsumschalter** *m* speed selector (tape rec.) **-gestell** (Förderanlage) belt frame **-gewicht** *f* sliver weight **-haken** bridle wire, tie hook **-heftmaschine** *f* strip stitcher

Bandhub *m* ribbon control mechanism **-ausschalthebel** (Fernschreiber) ribbon lockout bar

Band-jaspis *m* striped jasper **-kabel** *n* ribbon (-shaped) cable, flat cable, switchboard cable **-kante** *f* band edge, band head **-kette** *f* belt coupling, band chain, rim clutch, band expansion clutch **-klebevorrichtung** *f* tape splicing equipment **-kontrolle** *f* (Mischpult) input monitoring (mixer console) **-körnung** *f* grain of grinding band **-kupplung** *f* belt coupling, rim clutch, band expansion clutch **-kurve** *f* trajectory

Bandlauf *m* tape run (tape rec.) **-leitkontrolle** *f* belt trailing idler **-leitung** *f* strip line, micro-strip-line **-leitungsmaschine** *f* lapping engine (textiles) **-leserichtung** *f* tape travel **-maß** *n* tape, tape measure, measuring tape **-material** *n* coiled stock, sheet material **-meißel** *m* forked chisel **-messer(spalt)maschine** *f* belt knife (splitting) machine **-mikrophon** *n* electromagnetic transmitter, ribbon or band microphone **-mitte** *f* middle of band **-montage** *f* belt assembly, line assembly

Bandolier *n* bandoleer

Bandöse *f* bridge guide

Bandpanzerleitung *f* band armored cable, BX cable

Bandpaß *m*, **-filter** *m* band pass, band-pass filter

Band-post *f* band conveyer or carrier, belt-type ticket carrier **-rauschen** *n* tape background noise **-rauschzahl** *f* average noise factor **-reif** *m* hoop **-rolle** *f* belt idler, conveyor drum, tape pulley **-ringscheider** *m* belt ring separator **-rücksetzen** backspace (tape rec.) **-rückspulen** *n* rewind **-rückzug** *m* tape backspacing **-rührer** *m* spiral agitator

Band-säge *f* belt saw, band iron **-sägeblatt** *n* endless saw blade, band saw balde **-schaltung** *f* ribbon reverse mechanism **-scharnier** *n* strap hinge **-scheibe** *f* band wheel **-scheibennabe** *f* belt pulley **-scheider** *m* belt separator **-schelle** *f* clip **-schläger** *m* presser (book binding) **-schleifer** *m* belt sander

Bandschleifmaschine *f* belt grinder; (Sandpapier f-Holzverarbeitung) belt sander

Band-schlupfkontrollgerät *n* belt slip control unit

-(schnecken)mischer ribbon mixer **-schnitt** *m* editing of the tape **-schraube** *f* helix of tape-wire **-schrumpfung** *f* shortening of ligament **-schutzschiene** *f* protective edge rail **-seil** *n* flat rope, flat cable, band rope **-seiltrommel** *f* bobbin, drum, flat-cable drum

Bändsel *n* lashing, seizing **-leine** *f* seizing line

Band-separator *m* belt separator **-sieb** *n* traveling screen **-span** *m* ribbon chip **-spannung** *f* tape tension, brake-band voltage stress **-speicher** *m* tape store (info proc.) **-sperre** *f* band-rejection filter, band-elimination filter, band stop (radio) **-sperrfilter** *n* band stop filter, filter for band elimination **-spieler** *m* tape recording player, rerecorder, band of rerecorders **-sprecher** *m* ribbon loudspeaker **-spreizung** *f* band spread (radio) **-sprosse** *f* frame (tape rec.)

Bandspule *f* ribbon coil, tape spool, reel (tape rec.), spool (tape rec.) **hochkant-** (flach) **gewickelte ~** edgewise (flatwise) wound ribbon coil

Bandstahl *m* strip steel, band steel, strips, bands, hoop steel **-glühen im offenen Bund** open coil annealing **-schnitte** *m pl* punching tools of steel strip **-straße bzw. -walzwerk** *n* strip mill, hoop mill

Band-stärke *f* gauge **-straße** *f* belt conveyor flight **-streifig** streaked, banded **-strömung** *f* band voltage, laminar flow, depth (layer) of volume flow **-stuhl** *m* ribbon loom (textiles) **-teller** *m* reel **-theorie** *f* band theory **-träger** *m* belt beam **-traggerüst** *n* bed frame **-transporteur** *m* belt conveyer **-trockner** *m* conveyer drying machine, belt-type dehydrator, roll or belt dryer, belt-conveyor dryer **-tunnelgefrierapparat** *m* belt type freezing tunnel

Band-übertrager *m* ribbon feeder **-umführungsriemen** *m* belt wrapper **-umkehrachse** *f* ribbon reverse shaft **-umkehrung** *f* speech band inversion (secret telephony)

Bandumschaltung, automatische ~ automatic ribbon reverse **handbetätigte ~** hand controlled ribbon reverse

Band-umsetzer *m* frequency changer **-umsetzung** *f* frequency frogging **-umwicklung** *f* tape shrouding, taping **-veredelungsanlage** *f* strip-finishing and surface treatment plant **-verschluß** *m* strip locking **-verständlichkeit** *f* band articulation **-verstärker** *m* band amplifier **-verzögerung** *f* tape delay **-vorschub** *m* tape feed (comput)

Band-waage *f* conveyor type weigher **-walze** *f* tape roller, strip mill roller **-walzerei** *f* hoop milling, strip milling **-weite** *f* band width (radio) **-wendel** *f* strip helix **-wendelkabel** *n* tape helix coaxial cable **-wickel** *m* reel **-wickelmaschine** *f* strip winding machine **-wickler** *f* taping machine, strip winder, ribbon folder **-widerstand** *m* adhesive-tape resistor **-wischhebel** *m* band wiper arm **-wulst** *f* strip bulging

Band-zählwerk *n* position indicator (tape rec.), tape counter **-zug** *m* tape tension, tension of magnetic tape **-zugumschaltung** *f* tape tension adjustment **-zünder** *m* tape fuse

Banjerdeck *n* lower deck

Banjoachse *f* banjo axle

Bank *f* bank, layer, stratum, bench, parapet, shoal, measure (min.), bed, stand **liegendste ~** bottom measure (min.) **optische ~** optical bench

Bankazinn *n* Bance tin

Bankeisen *n* cramp iron for wood

Bankett *n* side slope, footings (especially under a wall), shoulder, earthwork, terrace **inneres ~** berm

Bank-formerei *f* bench molding work **-geschäft** *n* bank, bank business **-hammer** *m* bench hammer **-horn** *n* beak iron, two-beaked anvil

bankig bedded

Bank-kloben *m* table hand vise **-knecht** *m* support stock or vise **-maschine** *f* bench machine **-meißel** *m* cold shisel **-recht** perpendicular to stratification **-säge** *f* bench saw **-schraube** *f* bench (srew) vise **-schraubstock** *m* bench vise **-spitzenapparat** *m* bench centering device **-zwinge** *f* bench vise

Bankung *f* banking, bedlike jointing (geol.)

B-Anlasser *m* Bosch pinion shift starter, Rushmore type starter

Bann *m* spell, ban **-gut** *n* contraband **-ware** *f* contraband cargo

Bar *n* (atmosphärische Einheit) bar (Physics) a unit of pressure equal to 1.000.000 dynes per square centimeter

bar cash **gegen ~ verkaufte Ware** goods sold for cash **-es Geld** cash money

Bär *m* rammer, light pile driver, hammer of a pile driver, tup, skull, ram (of a press) **~** (Diesel) bulldozer (Diesel)

Baracke *f* hut, barrack

Baracken-bau *m* barrack construction **-lager** *n* barrack camp or encampment **-unterkunft** *f* hutted encampment

Baratt *m* barter

Baratte *f* drum, baratte (sulfiding)

Bäraufhaltevorrichtung *f* hammer-head stop

Barbermeldung *f* meteorological telegram

Barbestand *m* cash in hand

Barbitursäure *f* barbituric acid

Barege (Art Gaze) barege

Bareis *n* smooth ice (not snow-covered)

Baretter *m* voltage regulator, resistor, barretter

Barettfeile *f* cant file, small pointed file

Barfrost *m* blackfrost

Bärführung *f* hammer tup guide

Bärgewicht *n* driving weight of a pile driver, ram weight

Barium *n* barium

Barium-hydrat *n*, **-hydroxyd** *n* barium hydroxide **-hyperoxyd** *n* barium peroxide, barium dioxide **-oxyd** *n* barium oxide, baryta **-oxydhydrat** *n* barium hydroxide **-peroxyd** *n* barium peroxide **-platinzyanür** *n* barium platinocyanide **-rhodanid** *n* barium thiocyanate

Barium-sulfat *n* barium sulfate, blanc fixe, permanent white, barite, sulfate of barium **-sulfid** *n* barium sulfide **-sulfit** *n* barium sulfite **-sulfozyanid** *n* barium sulfocyanate **-superoxyd** *n* barium peroxide, barium dioxide **-thiosulfat** *n* barium thiosulfate, barium hydrosulfite **-wolframat** *n* barium tungstate

Barkasse *f* motor launch (navig.)

Barkaution *f* cash deposit

Barke *f* tank, tub, vat, bark, boat

Barkhausen-Kurz-Schaltung *f* Barkhausen-Kurz

circuit
Barkhausen-Kurz-Schwingungen *f pl* Barkhausen-Kurz oscillations
Barkhausen-Kurzwellen *f pl* microwaves, microrays, quasioptical waves
Barkhausen-Phon Barkhausen-phon (a sound-level unit, acoustics)
Barkhausen-Sprung *m* Barkhausen effect or jump
Bärkolben *m* hammer piston
Barkometer *n m* barkometer
Bärlappsamen *m* lycopodium spores
Bärme *f* barm, yeast
Barn *n* barn (physics)
Barnstein *m* brick
Barogramm *n* barogram
Barograph *m* barograph
Barographenblatt *n* barographic chart
baroklin baroclinic
Baroklinievektor *m* baroclinicity vector
Barometer *n* barometer **luftleeres ~** aneroid **registrierendes ~** barograph
Barometer-dose *f* bellows **-druck** *m* barometer pressure **-höhe** *f* barometric height **-korrektur** *f* barometric check (direction finder) **-relais** *n* barometric switch (radar) **-röhre** *f* barometer tube **-säule** *f* barometric column **-skale** *f* barometer scale **-stand** *m* barometric pressure, barometer reading
barometrisch barometric **-er Druckregler** *m* barometric pressure control **-es Gefälle** pressure gradient **-er Höhenmesser** *m* pressure altimeter **-e Höhenmessung** leveling by means barometer **-er Luftdruckanstieg** barometric pressure gradient **-e Navigation** *f* pressure-pattern navigation **-e Reglerdose** *f* control aneroid
Baromorphose *f* morphological changes due to effects of gravitation
Baroskop *n* baroscope, open end barometer
Barotaxis *f* locomotor behavior due to varying pressure
barotrop barotropic
Barotropie *f* barotropy
Barozyklonometer *n* barocyclonometer
Barre *f* bar (high sea bed parallel with the shore), sand bar, harbor bar shoal, billet
Barrel *n* barrel **-meile** *f* (Maßeinheit) barrel mile
Barren *m* bar, ingot, billet **-silber** *n* bar silver **-zink** *n* bar zinc
Barretter *m* ballast resistor, barretter
Barriere *f* barrier, extensive natural obstacle
Barrikade *f* barricade
Bart, *m* bur, bit, beard, fin, fash, seam **-bildung** *f* (Magnetpulver) formation of whisker- or beardlike clusters of filings or Magnaflux powders; (Maschinenwesen) formation of burrs **-kühler** *m* barb- or beard-type radiator
Baryt *m* heavy spar, native sulfate of barium, baryta, barite, barium oxide **unreiner ~** cawk **zyansaures ~** barium cyanate
baryt-artig barytic **-erde** *f* baryta, barium oxide
Barytflußspat *n* barytic fluor spar **-papier und -karton** baryta paper and board **-weiß** *n* enamel white **-zinkweiß** *n* lithopone
Baryt-gelb *n* barium yellow **-hydrat** *n* barium hydroxide **-kreuzstein** *m* harmotome **-lauge** *f* barium hydroxide solution **-weiß** *n* blanc fixe, permanent white, barium sulfate
Baryum *n* barium **-azid** *n* barium azide **-nitrat** *n* barium nitrate **-superoxyd** *n* barium peroxide
baryzentrisch barycentric
Baryzentrum *n* center of gravity
Barzahlung *f* payment in cash
Bärzylinder *m* hammer or tup cylinder
Basalborste *f* basal bristle
Basalt *m* basalt, toadstone, whinstone
Basalt-felsen *m* basaltic rock **-mehl** *n* ground basalt **-tuff** *m* trap tuff, whin **-verwerfung** *f* basalt wall
Base *f* base (chem.)
Basenaustausch *m* exchange of bases (chem.)
basen-bildend basifying, base-forming **-bildner** *m* base former, basifier **-druck** *m* base printing **-überschuß** *m* excess base
Basicität *f* basicity
basieren to base, be based
BA-Signal *n* blanked television signal (BA-signal)
Basilika *f* basilica (arch.)
Basis *f* base, base line, basis, bottom, radix (math.)
basisch basic **~zugestellt** basic lined **-es Bleikarbonat** white lead **~ chromsaures Salz** subchromate **~ essigsaures Salz** subacetate **~ essigschwefelsaure Tonerde** basic aluminium acetatesulfate **~ salpetersaures Salz** subnitrate **~ schwefelsaure Tonerde** basic aliminium sulfate **~ -es Gestein** basic rocks **-e Last** basic load **~ -er Stahl** basic steel
Basis-einstellung *f* setting of the base, base adjustment **-elektrode** *f* base electrode **-entfernungsmesser** *m* base range finder **-fläche** *f* basal plane (cryst.) **-flächenzentriert** end centered **-frequenzbereich** *m* baseband **-grundschaltung** *f* grounded base connection, common base connection **-innenwiderstand** *m* internal base resistance
Basis-klemme *f* base lead **-kreis** *m* time-base circuit **-komma** *n* radix point **-kontakt** *m* base terminal **-kristall** *m* parent crystal **-länge** *f* base length (of the mount of a photogrammetric or surveying camera) **-latte** *f* stadia rod **-lineal** *n* base ruler, base-line arm **-line** *f* base line (rdr) **-meßapparat** *m* base-measuring apparatus **-meßlatte** *f* base-measuring subtense bar, stadia **-messung** *f* base measuring
Basis-platte *f* stadia rod subtense staff **-projektion** *f* base projection **-raster** *m* basic grid **-schreibweise** *f* radix notation **-station** *f* standard port **-vektor** *m* unit-cell vector **-verhältnis** *n* base ratio (aviation) **-wagen** *m* transversal, base carriage
Basiswinkel im gleichschenkligen Dreieck base angles in an isosceles triangle
Basis-wolke *f* base surge **-zelle** *f* unit cell **-zentriert** base centered **-zweig** *m* base branch **-zone** *f* base (semiconductors), base region
Basität *f*, **Basizität** *f* basicity
Basizitätstheorie *f* theory of valences
Basküle *f* break-down frame, swivel **-kloben** *m* staple **-verschluß** *m* breakdown or lifter action
basophiles Körnchen basophil granule
Baßanhebung *f* bass boosting, bass compensation, tone-control means to accentuate,

emphasis on bass tones **automatische ~** automatic bass compensation (a.b.c.)
Baß-balken *m* bass bar (string instrument) **-entzerrer** *m* bass compensator
BAS-Signal *n* (TV) composite signal
Bassorin *n* (chem.) bassorin
Bassin *n* tank, basin, reservoir, bowl, chamber, cistern **-versuch** *m* model basin test **-wagen** *m* tank car
Baß-kasten *m* bass box (musical instruments) **-pfeife** *f* bassoon **-reflektierend** bass-reflex **-wiedergabe** *f* bass response
Bast *m* basswood, bast
Bastard-feile *f* bastard file **-schloß** *n* backspring lock **-treibstoff** *m* hybrid propellant
Bast-band *n* bast packaging tape (bast band) **-bindegewebe** *n* bast parenchyma
Bastelbegabung *f* talent for technical hobbies, mechanical skill in puttering
Bastelbuch *n* an amateur and experimenter's radio technician's handbook
basteln to gadget (do it yourself)
Basteln *n* craftwork
Bastfaser *f* bast fiber **-arten** *f pl* types of bast fibers
Bastit *m* bastite, schiller spar
Bastler *m* radio technician and repairman (a term that came in with radio, corresponds to American designation for amateurs "ham"), amateur, fan, home mechanic, amateur craftsman, hobbyist
Bast-matte *f* mat (rush or cane) **-papier** *n* manila paper **-seide** *f* silk in the gum **-seife** *f* degumming soap **-seil** *n* bass (or esparto) rope **-tau** *n* coir rope **-zellulose** *f* cutocellulose
Batist *m* cambric
Batschöl *n* batch (batching) oil
Batterie *f* battery, pile, (coke-furnace) block, set **A ~** filament battery, heater battery **B ~** B battery, high-voltage battery **~ in Dauerladeschaltung** floating battery, continuously connected battery connected to a discharge circuit
Batterie, eine ~ anlegen to apply a battery **aus einer ~ betreiben** to run from a battery **die ~ laden** (aufladen) to charge a battery **geerdete ~** earthed or grounded battery **gemeinsame ~** common, central, or universal battery **geteilte ~** split battery **-abdeckung** *f* battery cover **-abschalter** *m* battery cut-out switch
Batterieanschluß-klemme *f* battery connecting terminal **-klemmenbrett** *n* terminal board for battery connections **-platte** *f* battery plate terminal
Batterieanruf *m* battery ringing **Fernsprecher mit ~** battery-ringing telephone
Batterie-deckel *m* battery container cover **-draht** *m* battery wire **-elektrode** *f* battery electrode **-element** *n* battery cell **-empfänger** *m* battery receiver, battery-operated receiver slider coil **-entladung** *f* battery discharge **-entlüftungsventil** *n* battery vent valve
Batterie-galvanometer *n* battery gauge **-gespeist** (Funkempfänger) battery operated **-gestell** *n* battery stand, rack, or frame **-glas** *n* battery jar **-größe** *f* capacity (size) of battery **-hauptschalter** battery main switch **-heber** *m* battery syringe **-heizung** *f* battery heating **-kasten** *m* battery box, battery container **-kennlinie** *f* characteristic curve of battery **-klemme** *f* battery terminal connection (clip) **-klinke** *f* battery or power jack **-kohle** *f* battery carbon **-kran** *m* loading crane **-kurzschluß** *m* battery short (circuit)
Batterielade-anlage *f* battery charging equipment **-gerät** *n* battery booster, battery charger **-gleichrichter** *m* battery-charger rectifier **-raum** *m* battery charging shop **-satz** *m* battery charger, battery charging set **-station** *f* battery charging station **-tafel** *f* battery charging board **-tisch** *m* battery charging bench **-wicklung** *f* winding for battery charging
Batterie-ladung *f* battery charge **-lampe** *f* battery lamp, flashlight **-leitung** *f* battery lead **-mitte** *f* battery mid-point, center of the gun's zero point **-nullpunkt** *m* battery's zero point **-ofen** *m* (coking) bank furnace **-pfanne** *f* battery pan (sugar concentrating) **-pol** *m* battery pole or terminals **-prüfer** *m* battery tester or gauge, accumulator tester (instrument) **-raum** *m* battery room **-regulierschalter** *m* accumulator switch
Batterie-schaber *m* battery knife **-schalter** *m* accumulator switch, battery switch **-schlosser** *m* battery artificer, gunsmith **-schnelladegerät** *n* battery fast charger **-schrank** *m* battery box or case **-sicherung** *f* battery fuse **-spannung** *f* battery voltage **-stand** *m*, **stellung** *f* battery position **-strom** *m* battery current, plate current **-tafel** *f* battery manning table **-Tonbandgerät** *n* self-powered recorder **-träger** *m* battery carrier
Batterie-umschalter *m* battery change-over switch **-unterbrecher** battery contact breaker **-unterlage** *f* battery pad **-unterteil** *m* battery container, bottom part **-wärter** *m* battery attendant **-wechsel** *m* battery commutator **-widerstand** *m* battery resistance **-zähler** *m* battery indicator **-zelle** *f* battery cell **-zuführung** *f*, **-zuleitung** *f* battery lead **-zündanlage** *f* battery ignition equipment **-zündung** *f* battery ignition, coil-ignition system **-zündverteilerkopf** *m* distributor head **-zusatzmaschine** *f* battery booster
Batteurknopf *m* beater button
Bau *m* structure, construction, building, manfacture, making **im ~** under erection, under construction **gedrungener ~** compactness **geschlossener ~** close-order construction
Bau-abschnitt *m* stage (of construction) **-abteilung** *f* entrenching detachment, construction detachment, boundary, panel **-akkord** *m* building contract **-akustik** *f* architectural acoustics **-amt** *n* construction office **-anschlag** *m* building costs or estimate **-anweisung** *f* installation construction **-arbeit** *f* construction work **-arbeiter** *m* wireman, construction worker
Bauart *f* construction, design, structure, formula **gedrängte ~** compact construction or design **herkömmliche ~** orthodox design **liegende ~** horizontal type **stehende ~** vertical type **übliche ~** orthodox design
Bau-aufseher *m* inspector **-aufsicht** *f* construction supervision, aeronautical inspection, directorate **-aufwand** *m* capital investment, cost of

construction **-aufzug** *m* building elevator **-ausführung** *f* construction of a work **-bagger** *m* excavator **-behörde** *f* (public) building authorities **-beschreibung** *f* specification

Baubetrieb überwachen to supervise construction in process

Bau-blei *n* builder's lead **-breite** *f* overall (construction) width

Bauch *m* antinode, loop, belly, abdomen, retort bulb **~ einer Schwingung** bulge, loop, antinode of a vibration, internode of an oscillation

Bauch-behälter *m* (Flugzeug) ventral tank **-freiheit** *f* bulk clearance, ground clearance (vehicle)

bauchen to swell out, make bulge

Bauchgurt *m* belly band (of safety belt)

bauchig bellied, bulgy

Bauch-kühler *m* underslung or belly radiator **-landung** *f* wheels-up landing, belly landing (aviation) **-prozeß** *m* (alkali) kier boiling process **-säge** *f* felling saw **-schwingung** *f* antinode (loop) **-seite** *f* belly

Bauchung *f* swelling, convexity, bilge

Bauchzange *f* crucible tongs

Baud *n* baud (mod.)

Bau-direktor *m* building superintendent **-dock** *n* shipbuilding dock

Baudotgeber *m* baudot keyboard **-system** *n* Baudot system **-telegraph** *m* Baudot telegraph

Bau-drehkran *m* rotating crane **-ebene** *f* plane of site **-einheiten** *pl* individual parts of the apparatus **-eisen** *n* structural iron **-elemente** *pl* constructional units, structural elements

bauen to build, construct, cultivate, erect, design, work **gleich ~** to construct on similar lines

Bauen *n* construction

Bauentwurf *m* construction plan, project

Bauer *m* farmer, constructor

Bauern-ofen *m* single block furnace (met.) **-regel** *f* weather maxim **-säge** *f* crosscut saw (with two handles) **-schlepper** *m* farm tractor

Bau-erz *n* silver ore, native ore **-fach** *n* building trade **-fähig** workable, exploitable **-fällig** dilapidated, decaying **-fehler** *m* imperfection, fault of or in construction **-feld** *n* working **-festigkeit** *f* structural strength **-flucht** *f* alignment of buildings **-fluchtlinie** *f* line of direction, straight length, straight line, range, row, flush, flushing

Bauform *f* type of construction **mehrholmige ~** multispar construction **technisch gut durchdachte ~** sound engineering structure

Bau-formel *f* design formula **-fortschritte** *pl* construction progress **-fotos** *pl* construction photographs **-fuge** *f* construction joint **-führer** *m* construction superintendent, foreman **-genehmigungsbehörden** *f pl* authorities empowered to grant permission to construct **-gerätezug** *m* construction equipment platoon **-gerüst** *n* structural frame, scaffold(ing) **-geschichte** *f* case history

Bau-gewerbe *n* building trade **-gewerklich** architectural **-gewicht** *n* structural weight **-gips** *m* builder's gypsum **-glas** *n* building glass **-glaser** *m* constructional glazier **-glied** *n* structural unit, section of structure **-größe** *f* model

Baugrube *f* excavation (for structure), back filling, refilling, trench, basin (structural) **abgesteifte ~** timbered trench **Trockenlegung in offener ~** drainage in the open

Baugruben-aufzug *m* elevator for foundation pit **-verkleidung** *f* foundation trench sheeting

Baugrund *m* foundation soil, building ground or site **-forschung** *f* investigation of foundation **-pressung** *f* pressure on foundation soil **-untersuchung** *f* investigation of foundation soil

Bau-gruppe *f* assembly, subassembly, structural components **-guß** *m* structural casting **-hafen** *m* shipbuilding port **-hammer** *m* construction (builder's) hammer **-handwerk** *n* building trade **-herr** *m* employer, owner (of building under construction) **-hof** *m* building yard, equipment pool, plant depot, contractor's yard

Bauhöhe *f* over-all or total height, headroom; (gesenkt) overall height (lowered); (Laufkrane usw.) headroom **die ~ vergrößerndes Zwischenstück** riser

Bau-holz *n* (structural) lumber building lumber, timber **-horizont** *m* building line, index for building and contracting **-ingenieur** *m* civil engineer, resident engineer **-jahr** *n* year of manufacture, year of construction **-kabel** *n* interruption cable **-kasteneinheit** *f* assembly of unit parts **-kastenprinzip** *n* mechanical assembly technique (MAT) **-kastensystem** *n* assembly of prefabricated machine parts **-klammer** *f* dog **-klotz** *m* building block **-kolonne** *f* construction unit or gang **-kompanie** *f* construction or entrenching company **-konstruktion** *f* construction

Bau-kontrolle *f* job control, inspection **-kosten** *pl* costs of construction, production costs **-kran** *m* building crane, construction-site crane **-kunst** *f* art of construction, architecture **-kurs** *m* direction in building, course in construction **-lager** *n* storage or store for building materials **-länge** *f* over-all or total length, face to face (petroleum) **-leistungen** *pl* building work **-leiter** *m* superintendent of construction **-leiter** *f* extension ladder **-leitung** *f* supervision of construction

baulich constructional, structural **-e Anordnung** *f* structural arrangement **-e Kennzeichen** design features

Baulichkeiten *pl* buildings, structures, edifices

Bau-linie *f* building line **-lizenz** *f* construction license **-los** *n* allotment

Baum *m* tree, beam **Bäume ausästen** to trim trees

baumähnlich treelike, arborescent, dendriform

Baumannsche Schwefelprobe Baumann sulfur print

Baum-antenne *f* fishbone antenna **-arbeit** *f* beam work **-arm** *m* (Hebebaum) beam arm

Bau-maß *n* installation measurement, structural dimensions **-mast** *m* derrick pole **-material** *n* building material

Baum-beobachtung *f* observation from a tree **-beobachtungsstand** *m* observation post in a tree **-bewachsung** *f* foliage

Baumégrad *m* degree Baumé

Baumeister *m* builder, building contractor, architect

baumeln to dangle, swing trail

bäumen to wind up on a beam **die Kette ~** to beam the warp

Bau-merkmale *pl* design or constructional features

Baumé-skala *f* Baumé scale **-spindel** *f* Baumé spindle **-standard** *m* American standard scale for density

baum-förmig dendritic, tree-like **-gerade** straight as a rail or tree **-grenze** *f* timber line **-gruppe** *f* group or clump of trees, copse **-harz** *n* resinous exudate on outside of trees, wood resin **-krone** *f* treetop **-lagerung** *f* (Hebebaum) beam bearing support

Bäum-maschine *f* beaming machine

Baum-messer *m* dendrometer

Baum-mitnehmer *m* beam chuck

Baum-öl *n* linseed oil

Bau-mörtel *m* common mortar

Baum-rinde *f* bark, rind **-säge** *f* wood, rippling or pit saw **-schälmesser** *n* trunk stripping knives **-schere** *f* tree pruner **-schraube** *f* tree screw **-seide** *f* mercerized cotton

Baumsetzmaschine *f* Baum jig

Baumsperre *f* dead abatis, tree entanglement **leichte ~** light dead abatis

Baum-stamm *m* trunk (of a tree) **-stammkufe** *f* log runner **-stein** *m* dendrite **-stuhl** *m* beaming frame or machine **-stumpf** *m* tree stump **-trägerisolator** *m* suspended insulator **-trommel** *f* pressure drum **-trumm** *n* log

Baumuster *n* prototype, building specimen, (aircraft) type of construction **~ für bestimmten Verwendungszweck** specific type of construction

Baumuster-bezeichnung *f* model designation or number **-prüfung** *f* type test **-zulassung** *f* type approval

Baum-verankerung *f* tree anchorage **-verhau** *m* abatis, line abatis **-wachs** *n* grafting wax **-welle** *f* winch

Baumwollabfall *m* cotton waste, cotton linters **-reißerei** *f* cotton-hard-waste breaking **-sortierer** *m* cotton-waste hand

Baumwoll-abgang *m* cotton waste **-aufbereitungsanlage** *f* cotton-dressing installation **-ausbreiter** *m* cotton-lap-machine minder, cotton lapper **-öffner** *m* cotton-bale picker, cotton-bale breaker

Baumwollband *n*, **ungeglättetes ~** uncalendered cotton tape

Baumwoll-bremsband *n* cotton brake lining **-dämpfer** *m* cotton steamer **-dichtung** *f* cotton packing **-draht** *m* cotton-covered wire **-drell** *m* **-drillich** *m* cotton drill

Baumwolldrillmaschine *f* cotton planter **~ mit Sitz** riding cotton planter

Baumwolle *f* cotton **die ~ entkörnen** to gin cotton **mit ~ umsponnen** cotton-covered **doppelt umsponnen mit ~** double-cotton-covered **einfach umsponnen mit ~** single-cotton-covered **gezupfte ~** picked cotton **isoliert mit ~** cotton-covered **kurzstapelige ~** short-staple cotton

baumwollen cotton

Baumwoll-entkörnungsmaschine *f* cotton gin **-faden** *m* cotton thread **-fallschirm** *m* cotton parachut **-faser** *f* cotton fiber **-feinstrecker** *m* cotton speeder tenter **-filtertuch** *n* cotton filter cloth **-garn** *n* cotton twine, cotton yarn **-gaze** *f* tarlatan **-gewebe** *n* cotton duck, canvas, cotton fabric or texture

Baumwoll-gurt *m* brake band of cotton strap **-hartgewebe** *f* cotton fiber (pressed plastic, used for fabrication of gears) **-haspelei** *f* cotton winding **-holz** *n* cottonwood **-kabel** *n* cotton-covered cable **-karden** *n* cotton-carding process **-kratze** *f* cotton card or gin **-leine** *f* cotton cord of line **-maschine** *f* cotton machine

Baumwollpflanzer *m* cotton planter **~ mit Führersitz** riding cotton planter

Baumwoll-putzwolle *f* cotton waste **-reißer** *m* cotton hard-waste-breaker tenter **-riemen** *m* cotton belt(ing), canvas belt **-rupfer** *m* cotton-picker tenter **-saatöl** *n* cottonseed oil, cotton oil **-samenöl** *n* cottonseed oil **-schlagmaschinearbeiter** *m* cotton shaker **-schnitzel** *pl* chopped cotton cloth **-schnur** *f* cotton twine or yarn

Baumwoll-seidenkabel *n* silk and cotton-covered cable **-seil** *n* cotton rope **-stramin** *m* canvas **-strecker** *m* cotton-drawing frame tenter **-strickerei** *f* cotton hosiery **-tau** *n*, **-trosse** *f* cotton rope **-tuchriemen** *m* cotton belt **-überspinner** *m* cotton threader **-umklöppelung** *f* cotton-braided covering, braiding of cotton **-umspinnung** *f* cotton covering

Baumwoll- und Maisanhäufler *m* cotton and corn lister

Baumwoll- und Maisdrillmaschine *f* cotton and corn drill

Baumwoll-vollender *m* cotton-finisher minder **-vorgarnspinner** *m* cotton-roving frame tenter **-wolfer** *m* cotton willower or deviler **-zellstoff** *m* cotton linters pulp **-zwirner** *m* cotton twister

Baumwurzel *f* tree root

Bau-nivellier *n* builders level **-nummer** *f* work's number **-ordnungswesen** *n* road-construction program **-pappe** *f* building paper or boards **-plan** *m* blueprint, construction plan **-platz** *m* building or construction site, building yard **-polizei** *f* (public) building authorities

baupolizeiliche Vorschrift building code (by law)

Bau-praxis *f* construction engineering **-programm** *n* building program, construction schedule, production program **-rahmen** *m* fuse and test panel **-rechte** *pl* constructional rights **-reihe** *f* model, range, class or series (of fabricated products) **-riß** *m* (building) plan, blueprint **-rolle** *f* gin' block **-sachverständiger** *m* building expert **-sand** *m* building sand, mortar sand

Bausch *m* wadding, plug, antinode **in ~ und Bogen** wholesale

Bau-schaltbild *n* wiring layout

Bausch-elastizität *f* resistance to creasing, wrinkle-proofness, undulation recovery

Bau-schema *n* connection diagram

bauschen, sich ~ to swell, bag, bulge, puff up, refine (tin)

bauschig bulky (flossy)

Bauschinger Effekt *m* prestressing

Bauschinger Rollenapparat *m* Bauschinger multiplying lever extensometer

Bau-schraube *f* square-cap screw **-schreinerei** *f* joinery for buildings

Bauscht *m* post (a pile of sheets of wet pulp) (paper mfg.), a size of paper

Bauschung *f* swelling, protuberance
Bau-schutt *m* rubble, rubbish **-schutzbereich** *m* building restrictions zone around airports
bauseits on the part of the builder
Bau-sicherheit *f* factor of safety **-sohle** *f* level (min.) **-spitze** *f* forward end of a telephone line under construction (signal) **-stab** *m* construction staff
Baustahl *m* structural steel **legierte Baustähle** structural alloy steels
Bau-stahlgewebe *n* reinforcement wire mesh **-stange** *f* line pole, lance pole **-stärke** *f* structural strength **-statik** *f* theory of structure
Baustein *m* brick, building stone or block
Baustelle *f* building site or yard, construction site, building, project
Baustoff *m* material for construction, engineering material, building or structural **-abnahme bei der Lieferung** acceptance of material **-prüfmaschine** *f* building material testing machine
Bau-strecke *f* building section **-stufe** *f* construction stage **-tagebuch** *n* logbook **-technik** *f* structural engineering **-techniker** *m* builder
Bauteil *m*, *n* member (aviation), part, construction unit, structural member or part, prefabricated piece **Flugmodell ~** model-airplane components **tragendes oder Kräfte aufnehmendes ~** structural member
Bauteile *pl* component parts **gedrückte ~** compression members **~ aus Rohren** tubular structural members
Bauteil-gruppe *f* subassembly or unit of structural parts **-terrain** *n* building-site topography
Bauten *m pl* structures **-schutzmittel** *n* building preservative
Bau-terrain *n* building site **-tiefe** *f* width (or sections) (depth) **-tischler** *m* building joiner **-tischlerei** *f* house carpentry, joinery for buildings **-trupp** *m* construction squad, gang, or unit, repair gang **-truppwagen** *m* tool car **-überwachung** *f* construction supervision **-unternehmer** *m* (general) building contractor **-unternehmung** *f* contracting firm **-urkunde** *f* certificate of construction
Bau-verfahren *n* brick building method, construction method **-vertrag** *m* building (project) contract **-vorhaben** *n* building project **-vorrichtung** *f* assembly jig, jig **-vorschrift** *f* building regulations, construction requirements or specification **-weise** *f* method of construction, type of construction
Bauwerk *n* building, structure, edifice, construction, design **-sohle** *f* base of structure, foundation level or footing
Bauwerks-fuge *f* structural joint **-teil** *n* structural part or member
Bau-wesen *n* construction engineering, building construction or industry **-wettbewerb** *m* (Modelle) constructional competition (models) **-winde** *f* socket jack, builder's hoist
bauwürdig payable, workable **-es Vorkommen** workable deposits
Bauwürdigkeit *f* worthiness of being worked (min.)
Bauxit *m* bauxite **-ofen** *m* bauxite kiln
Bau-zahl *f* design factor, product of power loading and root of wing loading **-zaun** *m* billboard **-zeichnung** *f* construction drawing, buildung plan
Bauzeug *n* construction material, line material **eisernes ~** ironwork
Bau-ziegel *m* (building) brick **-zimmerer** *m* house carpenter **-zug** *m* construction unit **-zweck** *m* construction purpose, building purpose
Bayleyit *m* bayleyite
beabsichtigen to intend, plan, contemplate
Beagid *n* an inflammable product composed of carbide and other substances, used in acetylene lamps
Beamter *m* civil servant, (public) official civil-service employee, operator, executive, clerk **leitender ~** officer in charge **technischer ~** engineering officer
Beanspruchbarkeit *f* capacity to withstand stresses or take loads
beanspruchen to claim, demand; (Gebrauch machen) make use of; (Technik) stress, strain, load, apply stresses, require, pretend
beanspruchend requiring, claiming **viel Platz ~** cumbersome
beansprucht, auf Scherung ~ loaded in shear **hoch ~** high-duty; (Maschinenteile) heavily stressed
Beanspruchung *f* claim, pretention; (Anstrengung) strain; (Spannung) stress, strain, load; (Verschleiß) wear and tear, demand (upon), press, service, shear, stressing, loading, duty, external force, application, straining, force, rating, load, **~ auf Abscherung** shearing strain **~ auf Biegung durch den Winddruck** bending stress by wind pressure **~ (einer Mauer)** forces acting on a wall **auf gleichmäßige ~ hin konstruiert** designed for stress uniformity **stoßweise ~** pulsating or intermittent stress **übermäßige ~** overstress, overstrain **unangemessene ~** undue strain **zulässige ~** safe working stress, permissible load
Beanspruchungs-art *f* kind of stressing **-grenze** *f* limit of stress, limiting range of stress
beanstanden to object to, protest against, challenge, exclude, reject, decline, refuse acceptance
Beanstandung *f* rejection, objection, complaint, refusal, accusation
Beanstandungen *f pl* **geltend machen** to bring complaints to notice
beantragen to demand, apply for, move, propose, petition, make a motion
beantworten to answer (a call)
bearbeitbar machinable, workable, treatable **gut ~** readily workable **-er weicher Werkstoff** soft machinable material
Bearbeitbarkeit *f* machinability, machining quality, machining property, tooling quality, workability, manageability **spananhebende ~** free-cutting machinability
bearbeiten to work, treat, finish, process, machine, dress, tool **allseitig ~** to machine all over **kalt ~** to cold-work **leicht zu ~** easily machined **spanabhebend ~** to machine **warm ~** to hot-work **zusammen ~** to machine together
Bearbeiten *n* machining, dressing
Bearbeiter *m* reviewer, reviser, researcher
bearbeitet worked, tooled, machined **teilweise ~**

partly machined **-es Bauholz** lumber **-er Bolzen** bright (machined) bolt, finished bolt **-e Mutter** machined nut, finished nut

Bearbeitung *f* working, (mechanical) treatment, processing, machining, dressing, tooling, finish, make, preparation, finishing, handling, shifting, editing, workmanship, manufacture, converting (print), conditioning **chemische ~** chemical processing **durch maschinelle ~ herstellen** to fabricate **spanabhebende ~** steel cutting, metal cutting

Bearbeitungs-betrieb *m* processing shop **-fähigkeit** *f* machinability, workability **-fehler** *m* faulty machining **-fläche** *f* working surface **-gang** *m* phase of operation **-grad** *f* workability **-güte** *f* finish, workmanship, machining quality **-kosten** *pl* machining costs **-maschine** *f* processing machine **-maß** *n* finished dimension

Bearbeitungs-narben *pl* processing scars **-plan** *m* (Fertigung) operation sheet **-rauhigkeit** *f* processing roughness **-spuren** *pl* finish (processing) traces **-straße** *f* processing line **-verfahren** *n* tooling methods, manufacturing operation **-vorgang** *m* machining operation

Bearbeitungsvorrichtung *f* fixture **zusätzliche ~** attachment

Bearbeitungs-zeichen machining symbols **-werkstatt** *f* machine shop

Bearbeitungszeit *f* processing period **~ verringern** to cut operating time

Bearbeitungs-zugabe *f*, **-zuschlag** *m* machining allowance (for extra thickness), bonus (for employee) **-zweige** *f pl* branches of machining practice

Beaufort Skala *f* Beaufort scale

Beaufort Wetterskala Beaufort notation

Beaufort Windstärkeskala Beaufort scale of wind force

Beaufortsche Windskala Beaufort scale of wind intensities

beaufschlagen to act upon, admit; (belasten in der Elektrotechnik) to load

beaufschlagt, vom Fahrtwind ~ facing forward **-e Gleichdruckturbine** partial admission impulse turbine

Beaufschlagung *f* electric stress (placed on an insulator link or unit), admission (as of turbines), acoustic action or sound pressure (brought on microphone), attack of fluid about an airfoil, admission of fluid to turbine blades, impingement, impacting (by electrons)

beaufsichtigen to supervise, control, inspect

Beaufsichtigung *f* supervision, inspection, control

beauftragen to order, commission, charge, direct, entrust with, give or assign a task

Beauftragter *m* mandatary, representative, deputy, attorney, agent, delegate, commissioner

Bebakung *f* beaconing, setting or planting of beacons

Bebänderung *f* tape lapping

bebauen to cultivate

bebaute Felder cultivated fields **~ Fläche** built-up or tilled ground area **-es Gelände** built-up area

Bebauungs-grenze *f* (Bg) line of demarcation **-plan** *m* plan for housebuilding, master-plan

beben to quiver, vibrate

Beben *n* vibration, tremor, quivering, earthquake **-messer** *m*, **-zeiger** *m* seismograph, seismometer

bebildern to illustrate

bebohlen to plank over, cover with boards

Bebohlung *f* furnishing with boards

beborten to trim

Bebung *f* vibration

Becher *m* beaker, bucket, goblet, cup, bowl **-ausschnitt** *m* shaped-out portion, cup notch, a Pelton turbine bucket **-befestigung** *f* bucket attachment **-block** *m* encased fixed tubular paper or mica-wound or -wrapped condenser **-förmig** cup-shaped **-glas** *n* beaker

Becher-glaskolben *m* beaker flask, Erlenmeyer flask **-kette** *f* conveyor chain **-kolben** *m* Erlenmeyer flask **-kondensator** *m* metal-cased capacitor, paper condenser **-lampe** *f* cup-shaped bulb **-maschine** *f* cup-making machine **-rad** *n* bucket wheel (actual bucket or dredger form) **-radflügel** *m* hydrometric gauge with cup-type water wheel **-scheibe** *f* cup wheel **-transporteur** *m* bucket conveyer

Becherwerk *n* bucket conveyer or elevator **~ für senkrechte Förderung** vertical bucket elevator **~ mit Kettenführung** chain-type bucket elevator or conveyer **~ mit Rückführung** bucket elevator or conveyer with return run, continuous bucket elevator

Becherwerkaufgabevorrichtung *f* charging device for elevators

Becherwerke *n pl* bucket-type machines, excavators, dredges, ditchers, ore and cargo chain-bucket conveyers

Becherwerkgrube *f* elevator pit

Becherwerkskopf *m* bucket-elevator boot

Beckbetrieb *m* high intensity carbon service

Becken *n* basin, reservoir, tank, trough, sump, pan, pool, pond, wave, launching basin, vessel, coal field, pelvis, cymbal **~ für ein Pumpspeicherwerk** basin for a pump storage station

Becken-griff *m* sunken door handle **-messer** *m* pelvimeter **-neigungsmesser** cliseometer **-urinal** *n* pedestal urinal

Becquereleffekt *m* photovoltaic effect, Becquerel effect

Becquerelit *m* becquerelite

bedachen to roof

bedacht deliberate, considerate, intent on

Bedachung *f* roofing

Bedachungs-bleche *pl* roofing sheets **-material** *n* roofing material

bedämpfen to dampen, load

Bedampfen *n* vapor-deposition

Bedämpfung *f* resistance, damping, attenuation **~ des Gitterkreises** damping, grid circuit is damped down

Bedampfungsanlage *f* vaporization plant

Bedarf *m* (large) requirement, need, want, demand, consumption, exigency **~ decken** to satisfy the demand **nach ~** as occasion demands

Bedarfs-anforderung *f* purchase request, requisition **-artikel** *m* commodity **-deckung** *f* satisfaction of needs or wants (e.g., of a consumer of electricity

Bedarfsfall *m* case of need, emergency

Bedarfs-gegenstand *m* requirement, necessary

article or object **-nachweis** *m* purchase permit **-sammelrelais** *n* demand totalizing relay **-schein** *m* certificate of need, in lieu of priority for certain household goods **-spitzen** *pl* peak requirements

bedecken to blanket, cover **sich ~** to cover

bedeckt overcast, cloudy, covered, overgrown **~ mit Cäsium** cesiated **fast ~** broken (sky) **~ sein** (vom Wasser im Bad) to be immersed **-e Flügelspitze** tipped propeller **-er Güterwagen** boxcar **-er Himmel** overcast sky

Bedeckung *f* cover convoy, escort, guard, covering, capping, coverage (rdr.) **~ des Netzes** coverage factor

Bedeckungs-grad *m* degree of coverage **-theorie** *f* film theory (of passivation of metals) **-veränderliche** *f* eclipsing binary

bedenken to take into consideration

Bedenken *n* consideration, hesitation, objection

bedenklich doubtful, critical, hazardous, risky, serious, grave, delicate, precarious, ticklish

Bedenklichkeit *f* hesitation

Bedenkzeit *f* respite, time for reflection

bedeuten to mean, signify, denote, imply

bedeutend considerable, important, significant

Bedeutung *f* meaning, significance (of test), importance, consideration **von ~ sein** to matter, be of importance **~ beimessen** to attache significance

Bedeutungs-feld *n* semantic range **-los** insignificant, inconsiderable

bedielen to plank, cover with boards, boards up, floor

Bedielung *f* deck or flooring of a bridge

bedienbar manipulable, operable

Bedienbarkeit *f* manipulability, maneuverability, operation

bedienen to attend (to), work, operate, manipulate, handle, service, serve, make use (of), employ **~ eine Leitung, einen Schrank** to be assigned to a circuit or position

Bediener *m* controller, operator

Bedien-gerät *n* control unit **-gestänge** *n* control-lever system **-gestängehebel** *m* control lever (jet) **-hebel** *m* control lever **-pult** *n* control desk **-schraube** *f* set screw **-teil** *m* control desk **-tisch** *m* control board

Bedienung *f* attendance (to), operation, manipulation, control, handling, service, gun crew, servicing **Zentrale für die ~ der Maschinen** machine-controlling cabin or -control room

Bedienungs-anleitung *f* working (operation) instructions **-anweisungen** *pl* operational instructions **-apparatur** *f* operation apparatus **-armatur** *f* control **-ausgang** *m* service gangway or walk

Bedienungsbrücke, obere ~ overhead bridge, upper bridge

Bedienungs-bühne *f* service platform, platform for the operator **-einrichtung** *f* controls control device, operating device **-element** *n* operating element **-entlastung** *f* relief of strain (on pilot or operator) **-erleichterung** *f* easy observation **-fehler** *m* operating field, (pilot's) error **-feld** *n* control panel **-gang** *m* service passage **-gerät** *n* modulation unit, tuning or control unit (radio), operating unit, main control panel of radar or radio equipment **-gestänge** *n* control linkage **-gestänge** *n* (des Motors) controls (of motor)

Bedienungs-griffe *pl* controls, pedals and levers **-hahn** *m* working valve **-haken** *m* cant hook

Bedienungshandgriff *m*, **(-handlung)** *f* control move (manipulation) **~(-teil)** control (element), control handle, lever

Bedienungs-hebel control lever, hand lever, operating handle or lever **-kette** *f* maneuvering chain **-knopf** *m* control knob, operating knob **-kosten** *f pl* cost of attendance or of operation, working coasts **-mann** *m* attendant, operator **-mannschaft** *f* operating crew, squad, gun-crew personnel

Bedienungs-organ *n* control **-person** *f* operator, attendant **-personal** *n* operating personnel **-platte** *f* operating or control panel **-platz** *m* operating position **-podest** *m* service platform **-pult** *n* control desk (transm.), control panel **-rad** *n* operating handwheel **-rampe** *f* catwalk **-raum** *m* observation stand, work or control room

Bedienungs-säule *f* floor stands **-schalter** *m* control or operating switch (electr.) **-schema** *n* general layout of models **-schlüssel** *m* wrench **-seite** *f* service side, operator's stand **-stand** *m* operating station, platform **-stange** *f* controls (of the engine) **-station** *f* attendant's set (P.A.B.X.)

Bedienungs-steg *m* (service) walkway, service bridge **-tafel** *f* service board, switchboard **-tisch** *m* operating desk **-treppe** *f* servicing ladder **-vorgang** *m* operating process **-vorrichtung** *f* operation details, maneuvering apparatus **-vorschrift** *f* working instructions, directions for use **-wagen** *m* traveling crane **-weg** *m* servicing step **-winde** *f* maneuvering winch **-zeit** *f* handling time

bedingen to condition, stipulate, agree upon, contract for, imply

bedingt conditional, subject to, metastable, limited, required **-es Gegensprechen** semi-duplex operation **-es Haltesignal** *n* permissive or slow-down signal **-e Raumfolge** permissive block **-er Sprung** conditional jump **-er Sprungbefehl** conditional jump order **-e Verschlußeinrichtung** conditional interlock

Bedingung *f* condition, stipulation, limitation, restriction, postulate, requirement, term **besondere ~** clause

Bedingungen *pl* (Zahlungs-, Lieferungs) terms **~ aufstellen** to make terms or conditions **unbillige ~** unreasonable terms **unter den folgenden ~** subject to the following qualifications **die im Werk erforderlichen ~** "on site" requirements

Bedingungs-gleichung *f* equation of condition **-los** unconditional

bedrahten to wire (up)

Bedrahtungsplan *m* wiring diagram

bedrängen to oppress, harass, distress

bedrohen to threaten

bedrohlich threatening

Bedrohung *f* threat

Bedrucken *n* printing

bedrucken to print over or on

bedruckt printed on

bedrückt oppressed, depressed

Bedrückung *f* oppression
Bedson Drahtstraße *f* Bedson (continuous) rod mill ~ **Straße** *f* Bedson (continuous) mill train
bedürfen to need, require
Bedürfnis *n* need, want, requirement, lack, use
beeidigen to swear to, confirm by oath
Beeidigung *f* confirmation by oath
beeilen, sich ~ to hurry, speed up, hasten
Beeinflußbarkeit *f* suggestibility
beeinflussen to influence, control, affect, induce
Beeinflussung *f* influencing, modulation, control, affection, coordination (power and telephone line), influence, interference ~ **durch die Sprache** voice control ~ (Induktion) **durch Telegraphie** crossfire, induction influence by means of telegraphy **elektromagnetische** ~ (Induktion) electromagnetic induction **elektrostatische** ~ electric influence, static induction **fortgesetzte** ~ continued interaction **gegenseitige** ~ interaction (between), mutual action **gegenseitige** ~ **von Starkstromleitungen und Schwachstromleitungen** inductive effects between high-voltage and low-voltage lines **induktorische** ~ inductive interference, inductive trouble **störende** ~ interference
Beeinflussung-faktor *m* percentage, degree of, or depth of modulation **-röhre** *f* modulator valve or tube, modulation tube
beeinträchtigen to impair, injure, prejudice, encroach upon, infringe, detract from, affect, compromise (e.g. the quality), deteriorate, jeopardise
beeinträchtigt impaired, hindered, handicapped
Beeinträchtigung *f* infringement, injury, impairment, prejudice, influence
beeisen to cover ice, cover or sheathe with iron
beendigen to finish, end
Beendigungszeichen *n* sign-off signal
beengen to narrow, cramp, straiten, oppress
befähigen to qualify, enable
befähigt capable of, qualified
Befähigung *f* qualification, capability **die** ~ **einbüßen** to lose qualification, be disqualified
Befähigungszeugnis *n* certificate of competency
befahrbar passable
Befahrbarkeit *f* accessibility
befahren to travel, run over **eine Grube** ~ inspect (the workings of) a mine **einen Schacht** ~ to descend into a shaft
Befall *m*, **schädlicher** ~ contamination (atom. phys.)
befallen to affect, fall upon, overtake ~ **werden von** to come down with
befassen, sich ~ **mit** to attend to, have dealings with, occupy or concern onself with
Befehl *m* order, command, instruction, (operational) control signal, command signal **adressenfreier** ~ zero-address instruction ~ **in Dienstsachen** official order **einen** ~ **überschreiten** to exced one's orders **schnelle und eindeutige Übermitt(e)lung von Befehlen** speedy and distinct transmission of instructions
befehligen to command, be in command of
Befehls-adresse *f* instruction address, location order (info proc.) **-bibliothek** *f* program routine library **-code** *f* instruction code
Befehlsfolge *f* coding, control or instruction sequence **relative** ~ relative coding **-register** *n* sequence control register (info proc.)
Befehlsfunkgerät *n* command set
Befehlsgeräte (Druckknopftaster, Schwenktaster) control stations (momentary-contact pushbuttons and twist keys)
Befehls-liste *f* order code **-netz** *n* command or control net **-nummer** *f* operation number **-raum** *m* control room **-register** *n* control or order register **-rohr** *n* pilot or master thyratron, the tube through which orders are transmitted from bridge to engine room (on a ship) **-schalter** *m* master switch, electrically controlled **-scheibe** *f* master cam disc **-schema** *n* flow chart
Befehls-sprache *f* terminology of orders **-stand** *m* command post **-stelle** *f* command post, any agency vested with government authority, **-stellwerk** *n* station block (R. R.) **-technik** *f* technique of orders **-turm** *m* control tower
Befehls-übermittler *m* runner **-übermittlung** *f* transmission of orders, inter-communication **-übermittlungsapparat** *m* signal distributor **-übertragung zwischen Flugzeugen** interaircraft voice or command communication **-übertragungsanlage** *f* firing-control-station transmitter **-verhältnisse** *n pl* chain of command **-verzug** *m* dead time (gun)
Befehls-weg *m* chain of command, command channel **-wort** *n* instruction word (com.) **-zähler** *m* order counter, program counter, sequence control register (info proc.) **-zeile** *f* coding line
befeilen to touch up
befelgen, ein Rad ~ to rim a wheel
befestigen to fasten (to), fix, clamp, secure, tighten, strengthen, fortify, mount ~ **mit Klammern** to cleat
befestigt fast, fortified, attached to, fastened, held, solid (with) **-e Piste** paved runway
Befestigung *f* anchorage, attachment, protection, reinforcement, revetment, fortification, fastening, fixing, cleating, tightening, consolidation, clamping **zur** ~ **dienendes Bauteil** retainer **gelenkige** ~ flexible fixing or fastening ~ **des Kanalbettes** lining of the bed (of the bottom) ~ **der Laschen an den Schienenenden** fastening fishplates to the ends of the rail ~ **im Mauerwerk** sealing in **permanente** ~ permanent fortification
Befestigungs-anschluß mounting attachment **-arm** *m* bracket, mounting arm **-art** *f* type of mounting (fixing method) **-band** *n* fixing tape **-bock** *m* clamping stand **-bolzen** *m* clamping bolt, mounting stud **-bügel** *m* fixing bracket or bridle, bow (of a sinker), fixing strap **-fläche** *f* clamping face **-flansch** *m* mounting or attachment flange
Befestigungs-eisen *n* fixing strap (lug) **-glied** *n* attachment link or member, coupling link or member **-kette am Nadelkopf** small chain for hanging curtain from head of needles **-klemme** *f* screw terminal **-knagge** *f* fixing ot attaching lug, holding lug **-lappen** *m* fastening or fixing lug
Befestigungs-lasche *f* fitting plate, attachment collar, mounting strap **-leine** *f* lashing, securing cord **-leiste** *f* attachment rail **-loch** *n* mounting hole, fixing or fastening hole **-material** small

iron wave, mounting material **-mittel** *n* fastener, fastenings **-möglichkeit** *f* fastening possibility **-mutter** *f* retaining, clamping or lock nut **-nadel** *f* fastening pin **-öse** *f* eyelet attachment

Befestigungs-pflaster *n* patch **-platte** *f* bracket or fastening plate **-pratze** *f* fixing clamp **-punkt** *m* fastening point **-riegel** *m* fixing catch **-ring** *m* ring fastener, securing ring **-schelle** *f* mounting bracket, fixing clip or strap **-schiene** *f* attachment or mounting rail **-schnur** *f* fastening cord

Befestigungsschraube *f* clamping bolt, assembly screw, fixing bolt, setscrew, tightening, fastening, or fixing screw ~ **für Zylinder** cylinder holding down bolt

Befestigungs-streifen *m* fastening or fixing strip **-teil** *m* fixing or fastening part (fitting) **-vorrichtung** *f* fastening means (fastenings) **-wand** *f* mounting wall **-wandstärke** mounting wall thickness

Befestigungs-werk *n* fortification **-winkel** *m* fastening angle, connection angle, support bracket **-zone** *f* fortified zone

befetten to lubricate, grease

befeuchten to wet, moisten, damp, water

Befeuchtung *f* humidification, (humidifying)

Befeuchtungs-anlage *f* moistening plant **-kammer** *f* (Luft) air-moistening chamber **-kasten** *m* moistening chamber **-maschine für Garne** wetting machine for yarns **-mittel** *n* (zum Konditionieren) conditioning agent **-spule** *f* conditioning bobbin (textiles)

befeuern to mark light with lights, to light

Befeuerung *f* heating, firing, lighting, navigation lights

Befeuerungshilfe *f* lighting aid

befiedert feathered

befinden to find, deem adjudge

befingern to touch, handle, palpate

befirsten to ridge a roof, lay a ridge

beflechten to plait or braid around **mit Stroh** ~ to straw

Beflechtung *f* braid

beflecken to stain, spot, blur

befliegen (eine Strecke) to fly

beflissen anxious, eager, zealous, studious, intent

Beflockung (elektrostatische) covering with fibers (electrostatic)

Beflockungsgerät *n* flocking apparatus

befohlener Übertrag separately instructed carry

Befolgung *f* following, carrying out **peinlich genaue** ~ **einer Vorschrift** rigid adherence to an instruction or a prescription

befördern to convey, transfer, transport, haul, ship, deliver, forward, transmit, advance, promote **im Rang** ~ to promote

Befördern von Fernsprüchen und Funksprüchen transmission of telephone and radio messages

Beförderung *f* conveyance, transport, forwarding, dispatch, delivery, transformer, promotion, transmission, transportation ~ **der Blöcke** transport of blocks ~ **dem Dienstalter nach** promotion by seniority ~ **auf Grund der Auswahl** promotion by selction ~ **von Personen** passenger service

Beförderungs-anlage *f* conveyor plant, equipment for transportation **-frist** *f* time of delivery, delivery date **-liste** *f* promotion list **-mittel** *n* means of transportation, vehicle, material-handling equipment, conveying machinery **-tuch** *n* traveling apron **-vermerk** *m* routing instructions **-weite** *f* mileage

Beforstung *f* afforestation

befrachten to ship by freight

Befrachter *m* charterer

Befrachtungskontrakt *m* **für eine lange Dauer** time charter

Befrachtungsvertrag *m* freight contract

befragen to consult

Befragung *f* consultation, questioning

befreien to set free, liberate, free, relieve, rid ~ **von der Umhüllung** to strip, unwrap **von Gerüchen** ~ to deodorize

befreit freed, liberated

Befreiung *f* liberation, exemption, release, act of freeing

befrieden to fence in

befriedigen to satisfy, appease, gratify

befriedigend satisfactory

Befriedigung *f* satisfaction

befrieren to cover with ice

befristet delayed, without time limit

Befristung *f* time limit

befruchten to make worthwhile contributions, further

Befruchtung *f* fertilization

Befugnis *f* authority, power, privilege

Befugnisse *pl*, **übertragene** ~ powers vested

befugt authorized, competent, entitled ~ **sein** to be competent to do

Befühlungskräfte *pl* tactile force

Befund *m* finding(s), result, outcome, state, verification

Befundaufnahme *f* analysis test ~ **eines zerlegten Motors** teardown inspection, analysis test

Befundbogen *m* auditing or inspection sheet, check sheet

Befunde *m pl* findings, data

Befund-prüfung *f* inspection **-schein** *m* certificate of examination

befürchten to fear, suspect

befürworten to recommend, advocate, stand for

begabt gifted, talented

Begabung *f* talent

begasen to attack with gas

Begasung *f* laying of gas obstacle

Begebenheit *f* event, occurrence

begegnen to meet, encounter

Begegnung *f* meeting

Begegnungs-periode *f* relative period **-vorgang** *m* approach

begehbar passable, negotiable, walkable

Begehbarkeit der Meßstrecke patrolling of the measuring distance

begehen to commit (an act), inspect, patrol (lines on foot)

Begehen *n* patrolling

begehren to wish, desire, want

Begehung *f* perpetration, commission (crime), pacing off, patrolling ~ **des Geländes** reconnaissance

begeistern to enthuse, inspire

begichten to burden, charge

Begichtung *f* top charging, charging operation, filling, burdening ~ **mit zwei Aufzügen** double-skip charging ~ **von Hand** barrow charging

Begichtungsanlage *f* charging unit, charging gear or installation ~ **mit Kippgefäß** skip-charging gear ~ **mit Kübel** bucket-charging gear

Begichtungs-bühne *f* charging floor **-einrichtung** *f* charging device or arrangement **-wagen** *m* charging car **-zone** (Kupolofen) charging zone

begierig eager, greedy ~ **aufnehmen** to swallow

begießen to wet, moisten, water, irrigate, coat (film)

Beginn *m* beginning, start, origin, source, initiation ~ **des Abbindens** initial set ~ **des Eisgangs** debacle ~ **des Siedens** *n* initial boiling point

beginnen to start, begin, originate, initiate, commence

beginnend incipient **eben** ~ incipient **-e Glut** first visible red, black red

Beginnzeichen *n* answer signal

begipsen to plaster

beglasen to glaze

Beglasung *f* glazing (putting in windowpanes), varnish, icing, enamel, glass, silicate mixture, frosting

beglaubigen to certify, verify, confirm, attest, testify

beglaubigte Abschrift certified, legalized, authentic, or attested copy **beglaubigt, korrekt und wohlbegründet, Bezahlung nicht erhalten** certified correct and just, payment not received

Beglaubigung *f* authentication, certification, confirmation, verification

Beglaubigungsschreiben *n* credentials, letter of credit

begleichen to settle, square, balance

Begleichung *f* settlement ~ **der Rechnungen** settlement of accounts

Begleit-brief *m* covering letter **-element** *n* metalloid

begleiten to accompany, escort, convoy

Begleiten zum Fernsehbild *n* sound or audio action accompanying television

begleitend accompanying **-es Dreikant einer Raumkurve** moving trihedral of a curve in space

Begleiter *m* companion, indicator, escort, assistant driver, associate, satellite

Begleit-erscheinung *f* attendant, accompanying, or secondary phenomenon or action, satellite effect, symptom **-feuer** *n* accompanying fire

Begleitflöz *n* accompanying bed **kleines** ~ rider

Begleit-heft *n* logbook (in mass-per-unit-time contexts) **-heizung** *f* steam trace **-körper** *m* accompanying substance or body, impurity, foreign substance or admixture **-linien** *f pl* satellite lines

Begleit-metall *n* accompanying metal, foreign metal, metal impurity **-mineral** *n* accompanying mineral **-papier** *n* bill of lading **-saiten** *f pl* accompaniment strings **-schein** *m* packing list, waybill, docket **-schiff** *n* auxiliary vessel, escort vessel **-schreiben** *n* covering letter **-schutz** *m* escort, fighter excort **-sitz** *m* auxiliary seat (next to driver) **-stoff** *m* accompanying body or substance, impurity, foreign substance

Begleit-strecke *f* counterhead; subsidiary gallery **-symptom** *m* concomitant symptom **-umstand** *m* attendant circumstance

Begleitung *f* escort, convoy

Begleit-welle *f* associated wave **-wort** *n* explanatory remark **-zettel** *m* emergency medical tag **-zug** *m* convoy

begradigen to level, shorten the front line, retreat

begreifen to understand, conceive, grasp

begrenzen to limit, terminate, bound, define, circumscribe

begrenzend limiting, terminal

Begrenzer *m* (signal) limiter, limiting device, delimiter (info proc.) ~ **der Sprachwellen-amplitude** speech clipper

Begrenzer-diode *f* limiter diode **-kennlinie** *f* limiter characteristic **-kreis** *m* clipper, clipping circuit **-röhre** *f* clipper tube, limiter valve **-schaltung** *f* clamping circuit **-stufe** *f* limiting stage

begrenzt limited, (de)finite, local, concentrated ~ **beständige Phase** metastable phase **-te Verstärkung** finite gain

Begrenzung *f* limitation, localization, boundary, limit, termination, definition ~ **der Fahrzeuge** material gauge ~ **der Ladung** loading gauge ~ **der Last** load limit ~ **der Normalbreite** limitation of the normal width ~ **der Stromschiene** third-rail gauge ~ **des Tiefganges** limitation of the draft

Begrenzungsanschlag *m* (back)stop, limiting means **verstellbarer** ~ stop dog

Begrenzungs-bake *f* boundary beacon, boundary-marker beacon **-drossel** *f* (current-)limiting coil

Begrenzungsfläche *f* area of contact **untere** ~ bottom surface

Begrenzungs-gerät *n* boundary marker, marker beacon, signal limiter **-hebel** *m* traversing clamp, stop lever **-kante** *f* boundary edge **-kugel** *f* gauge knob **-lampe** *f* position light, gauge or limit lamp, width-indicating lamp **-leuchten** *f* gauge lamp, obstacle light, marking lamp, limiting lamp **-leuchten** *n* boundary illumination searchlight, illumination of sector boundaries **-licht** *n* boundary light **-linie** *f* boundary line

Begrenzungs-oberfläche *f* boundary surface **-reiter** *m* boundary marking **-ring** *m* (Haspel) balloon catch (reel), set collar, outer ring **schalter** *m* limit switch **-schiene** *f* limiting bar **-schraube** *f* limit screw **-seil** *n* check cable

Begrenzungs-stab *m* limit bar, clearance indicator rod **-symbol** *n* delimiter, (info proc.) **-widerstand** *m* limiting resistance **-zeit** containment time

Begriff *m* idea, concept(ion), term, motion, precept, catchword (by-word) **ist zu einem** ~ **geworden** is now accepted as a standard, is a by-word ~ (der Serienresonanz) concept (of series resonance)

begriffen, im Bau ~ in construction, in the process of being constructed **auf der Rückreise** ~ homeward bound

begrifflich conceptually, theoretically, conceivably

Begriffs-bestimmung *f* definition **-fach** *n* category **-festlegung** *f*, **-festsetzung** *f* definition **-klasse** *f* category **-teller** (Eisenbahnsignale) aspect control relays **-vermögen** *n* intelligence **-verwechslung** *f* confusion of ideas **-verwirrung** *f*

confusion of ideas **-zeichen** *n* sign symbol
begründen to establish, found, constitute, substantiate, create, (Ausführung) prove, give reasons for
begründet (wohlbegründet) well founded (in fact and law)
Begründung *f* validity, reason, motivation, foundation, (Ausführungen) argument proof **~ eines Einspruches** argumentation (in support of an opposition)
Begründungsfrist *f* period for giving grounds (law)
begünstigen to favor
Begünstigter beneficiary
Begünstigung *f* privileges
Begußmasse *f* slip, engobe (ceramics)
begutachten to give an expert opinion **~ lassen** to submit to an expert
Begutachter *m* expert
Begutachtung *f* appraisal (judgment)
behaart hairy, hirsute
Behaglichkeits-wert *m* comfort factor
behalten to keep, retain
Behalten *n* retention
Behälter *m* receptacle, container, vessel, trough, tank, reservoir, hopper, bin, bunker, pocket, basin, store, well **~ für Brennstoff** fuel tank **~ zum Speisen der Brunnen** feeder reservoir for wells **geschützter ~** self-sealing tank **selbstabdichtender, beschußsicherer ~** bullet-proof self-sealing tank **trichterförmiger ~** hopper **~ für Wascheinrichtung** sludge basin
Behälter-ausgang *m* container outlet **-bau** *m* container making **-behäutung** *f* tank skin **-blech** *n* tank plate **-böden** *m pl* tank heads or ends, boiler heads **-deckel** *m* container cover **-druck** *m* tank pressure **-entlüftung** *f* tank ventilation **-haube** *f* (Metallhaube) domed (bell) cover **-haut** *f*, **-hautblech** *n* tank skin **-inhalt** *m* tank capacity **-innenseite** *f* half-shell interior
Behälter-lager *n*, **-park** *m* tank farm **-schuß** *m* cylindrical part of prollant tanks guided missiles **-schutz** *m* protection of fuel deposits **-spitze** *f* front section of rocket containing instrument and pressure-tank compartments **-standanzeiger** *m* tank gauge **-standsonde** *f* oxygen-indicator gauge **-wagen** *m* tank car **-wanderung** *f* wall of a container
Behältnis *n* container, case, box, bin, store, magazine, cage
behandelbar manipulable, treatable, tractable, workable, processable
behandeln to treat, manipulate, handle, work **mit Verstand ~** to manipulate **einen Werkstoff ~** to process a material **schwer zu ~** intractable, unwieldy
Behandlung *f* handling, treatment, processing, manipulation **~ mit Lauge** alkali treatment **~ mit Säure** acid treatment **~ mit Schwefelsäure** sulfuric acid treating **ambulante ~** ambulatory treatment **herabwürdigende ~** degrading treatment **bei richtiger ~** given reasonable care **vorschriftswidrige ~** treatment contrary to regulations, abuse
Behandlungs-mittel *n* agent, reagent **-schäden** *pl* process defects **-station** *f* cleaning station **-vorschrift** *f* instruction **-weise** *f* manner of treatment, procedure **-werk** *n* treating plant
Behang *m* decoration, hangings, drapings, trimming
behängen to hang on, attach, decorate, drape, trim
beharren to continue, persist, persevere, be stable
beharrlich constant, insistent, pertinacious, stubborn
Beharrlichkeit *f* persistence, perseverence, steadiness
Beharrlichkeitsgrenze *f* (Klimaanlage) comfort zone
Beharrung *f* perseverance, persistence, stability
Beharrungs-drehzahl *f* settled speed **-kennwerte** *pl* steady-state characteristics **-kraft** *f* inertia **-moment** *m* moment of inertia, rotational inertia **-punkt** *m* center of inertia, center of mass, centroid **-temperatur** *f* inertia temperature, permanent temperature **-verhalten** *n* steady-state behaviour (aut. contr.)
Beharrungsvermögen *n* inertia, moment (of inertia), vis inertiae **~ der Masse** mass inertia
Beharrungs-wirkung *f* inertia effect **-zustand** *m* permanence, state of inertia or of rest, regimen, ready state, state of equilibrium, state of resistance, resistance (of a machine), persistence, freedom from transients, steady-state condition, equilibrium condition; (Turbinenregler) settled speed
behauen to trim, dress, chip, cultivate, square, adze **-er Bruchstein** ashlar **-es Geröllmauerwerk** squared flint work
behaupten to maintain, assert, allege, state, aver, declare, vindicate, predicate, affirm, assent
Behauptung *f* claim
Behausung *f* dwelling lace, lodging
Behäutung *f* covering skin
beheben to put an end to, eliminate, remove, correct (jam or stoppage); (Fehler) to clear, rectify faults or trouble
Behebung *f* (des Fehlers) elimination of defect **~ der Panne** servicing
beheizen to heat **zu stark ~** to overheat
beheizt fired, heated **schwach ~** dull **stark ~** bright
Beheizung *f* firing, heating
Beheizungsfrage *f* heating problem
Behelf *m* expedient, makeshift, subterfuge, emergency
behelfend, behelfs- auxiliary, improvised
Behelfs-antenne *f* auxiliary antenna, makeshift, temporary, or emergency antenna or aerial **-bauten** *pl* temporary structures **-befestigung** *f* temporary or emergency fortification **-brücke** *f* emergency bridge **-brückenbau** *m* emergency-bridge construction **-fähre** *f* makeshift or emergency ferry **-floßsack** *m* pneumatic assault boat **-flugplatz** *m* auxiliary landing site **-gasschütz** *n* emergency gas protection
Behelfs-konstruktion *f* makeshift construction, emergency construction **-landebrücke** *f* makeshift landing stage **-lösung** *f* expedient **-mäßig** makeshift, temporary, in the nature of an expedient, provisional **-material** *n* emergency construction material **-mittel** *n* expedient **-schlitten** *m* improvised sledge **-schwimmwerk für Landflugzeuge** flotation gear **-werkzeug** *n* makeshift tools

beherbergen to harbor, lodge, quarter, shelter
beherrschen to cope with (e.g. a complex problem), control
beherrschend commanding, dominating
Beherrschung *f* rule, sway, domination, control, supremacy
Beherrschungszeit *f* containment time
behindern to obstruct, hinder, restrain, detain (Bewegung) interfire with
behindert heavy-handed **-e Rotation** hindered or inhibited rotation (of molecules)
Behinderung *f* hindrance, hindering, inhibition, restraint, impediment, obstacle **räumliche ~** steric hindrance
Behm Lot *n* sound-ranging altimeter (aviation), depth indicator, fathometer, depth sounder (sonic), echo depth sounder, sonic altimeter **~ Lotpatrone** *f* Behm detonating cartridge **~ Ohrlot** *n* Behm echo-sounding machine, Behm ear lead **~ Zeitmesser** *m* microchronometer, Behm period meter
behobeln to plane, chip
beholmen, die Pfähle ~ to cap the piles
beholzen to plant trees
behorchen to listen to or in, overhear
Behörde *f* authority, government(al) agency
behördlich zugelassen authorized, officially sanctioned **-e Vorschriften** public regulations
behüten to guard
behutsam cautious, careful
bei in the case of, at, near, with, by **~ weitem** by far
beibehalten to retain, maintain, keep
Beibehaltung *f* retention
Beiblatt *n* supplement (to a journal)
Beiboot *n* dinghy
beibringen to inflict (losses, etc.) **etwas ~** to impart (knowledge)
Beibringung *f* production, adduction
Beibringungsmittel *n* vehicle for drugs
beidäugig binocular
beiderseitig on both sides; (gemeinsam) mutual, common; (gegenseitig) reciprocal; (Vertrag) bilateral **-e Auslösung** joint party control **-er Druck** duplex printing
beiderseits on both sides of, mutual(ly) **~ verwendbarer Stoff** reversible cloth
beidhändig ambidextrous
Beidraht *m* supplementary earth wire
beidrecht reversible (two-sided)
beidrehen to heave to (navig.)
beidseitig on both sides, bilateral(ly) **~ offener Zylinder** double-ended cylinder
beidwegs reversible
Beiende *n* front warp
Beifahrer *m* rear rider, sidecar rider, assistant driver, pillion rider, auxiliary rider, co-driver
beifolgend enclosed, attached, accompanying, annexed
beifügen to include, add to, supplement
Beifügung *f* addition, notation
Beigabe *f* adjusting strip
beigeben to attach to, allot to, acquiesce
beigedreht hove to, brought to **-es Schiff** ship brought or hove to
beigefügt additional
beigeklappt folded
beigeordnet coordinated **-er Flugzeugführer** copilot
beihalten to retain
Beiheft *n* supplement
Beihilfe *f* subsidy, grant
Beikasten *m* attachment case
Beiklang *m* consonance
beiklappbar folding **-e Flügel** folding wings
beiklappen to fold
Beikreis *m* epicycle
Beil *n* hatchet, ax, adz
Beiladung *f* igniter, igniting charge, priming charge
Beilage *f* annex, enclosure, appendix, supplement, spacer, schedule; (Zwischenstück) shim **dünne ~** shim (plate)
Beilage-blech *n* shim, shim plate **-bündel** *n* shim **-folie** *f* shim (plate) **-keil** *m* gib **-platte** *f* shim (plate) **-ring** *m* shim ring **-scheibe** *f* shim, washer
Beiläuferexzenter *m* auxiliary cam
Beilauffaden *m* intermediate layer, (Kabel) tracer
Beilaufzwickel *m* center cable filler
Beilegefolie *f*, **geschichtete ~** laminated shim
beilegen to attribute **einen Wert ~** to assign a value (to)
Beilegering *f* spacer, collar (print)
Beilegescheibe *f* ring-type shim (washer), shim (plate) **geschichtete ~ aus dünnen Folien** peeling shim
Beilegplatte shim plate
beiliegend enclosed
Beilpicke *f* pickax
Beilstein *m* jade, nephrite
Beiluft *f* secondary air
beimengen to admix, add
Beimengung *f* mixture, pyritous impurity, addition, impurity, atmospheric pollution (meteor.)
beimessen to attach, attribute, impute
beimischen to admix, intermix, intermingle, add.
Beimischer *m* feeding shoe, adder (TV)
Beimischung *f* admixture, addition
beimischungs-frei free from contamination or impurities **-stoff** *m* addition agent
Bein *n* leg, bone, rib, spur, leg
beinahe almost, well-nigh, nearly
Beinährstoff *m* accessory food stuff, vitamine
Bein-feile *f* scalping iron **-gurtschlaufe** *f* leg strap (on parachute) **-leder** *n* leather puttee **-säge** *f* bone saw **-schwarz** *n* animal or bone charcoal, bone black
Beinstandausgleich *m* cross-leveling of the piece
Beintaste *f* bone key
beiordnen to coordinate, arrange, assign, relegate
Beiprodukt *n* by-product
Beirat *m* advisory body, committee
Beiregelplatte *f* corrector vane
Beisatz *m* admixture, addition
Beischiff *n* depot ship
beischließen to enclose, contribute (funds)
Beischluß *m* enclosure
beiseitelegen to junk
Beisitzer *m* aid, assessor
Beispiel *n* example, instance, illustration **-los** unprecedented, unexampled, unparalleled
beispielsweise by way of example, for instance, exemplifield
Beißbacken *pl* (Prüfmaschine) serrated wedges

beißen to bite **sich ~** (Farben) to clash
beißend pungent, acrid, caustic, mordant (dyes)
Beißer *m* biter, quarreler, man-eater
Beiß-keil *m* wedge grip with serrated grooves **-zange** *f* pincers, pliers, tongs, clippers, cutting pliers, electrician's side-cutter pliers, pair of pincers
Beistand *m* assistance, help, aid, stand-by
beistehen to help, assist, aid
Beistellmöglichkeit *f* tool adjustment
Beistellung *f* in-feed, feed adjustment
Beisteuer *f* subsidy, grant
beistimmen to accede, assent or agree to, acquiesce in
Beitau *n* spring line (navy)
Beitel *m* (chipping) chisel **-hefte** *pl* chisel handles
Beiton *m* second (in accoustics)
Beitrag *m* subscription, share, part
beitragen to aid, help, contribute, add to, cooperate
beitragend conducive
Beitrags-deckungsverfahren *n* method of providing cover by contributions **-fläche** *f* contributing (drainage) area
beitreiben to recover, collect, exact, requisition, commandeer
Beitreibung *f* requisition, requisitioning, recovery, collection
Beitreibungsschein *m* requisition receipt
beitreten to join
Beitritt *m* accedence, concurrence, enrollment **~ zum Abonnement** service application **~ zum Verfahren** intervention
Beiwacht *f* bivouac
Beiwagen *m* sidecar, trailer coach **-krad** *n*, **-maschine** *f* sidecar motorcycle
Beiweg *m* by-pass
Beiwert *m* coefficient, factor, mathematical constant, index, parameter, coordinate **~** (Peilung) correction value (to compensate bearing errors) **~ der Schwellung** coefficient of swelling **~ der Ungleichmäßigkeit** coefficient of irregularity
beiwohnen to attend
Beizabwasser *n* waste pickling water
Beizahl *f* (numerical) coefficient, factor
Beiz-anlage *f* pickling plant **-artikel** *m* mordant style **-bad** *n* pickling bath **-behälter** *m* pickling vat **-behandlung** *f* pickling **-blase** *f* pickling blister **-brüchigkeit** *f* acid brittleness **-brühe** *f* oozing, ooze, tan pickle **-bütte** *f* drench pit
Beize *f* corrosive, pickle, caustic, mordant (chem.), bate, stain, etching acid or solution
beizeiten on time, early
beizen to stain, tan, corrode, scour, pickle, disinfect, dress, etch, stain (glass with a metal), mordant, cauterize
Beizen *n* corrosion, pickling, staining, etching, fix, pickle
beizend corroding, corrosive, caustic, pickling, mordant (of dyes)
Beizen-dampffarbe *f* mordant steam color **-druck** *m* mordant printing **-druckartikel** *m* mordant printed style **-farbstoff** *m* mordant dyestuff **-klotzartikel** *m* mordant-padded style
Beizerei *f* pickling house or department
Beiz-flotte *f* mordanting bath or liquor **-flüssigkeit** *f* pickling fluid **-grund** *m* mordanted bottom **-korb** *m* pickling basket **-kraft** *f* corrosive power, caustic power, mordant action **-lösung** *f* pickling solution **-mittel** *n* disinfectant, speed dressing, mordant, corrosive, caustic **-sprödigkeit** *f* acid brittleness **-tönung** *f* mordant toning
Beizung *f* disinfection, seed dressing
Beiz-vergoldung *f* pigment gilding **-zusatz** *m* pickling compound, inhibitor
bekalken to lime, cement
bekalmt becalmed
bekämpfen to combat, fight
Bekämpfung von Lärm noise abatement
bekannt known **~ wegen** noted for **allgemein ~** notorious **-es Gebiet** proven territory
Bekanntgabe *f* publicity, announcement **~ von Mitteilungen** to disseminate information
bekanntgeben to announce, make, public, report
Bekanntgeben *n* announcement, admission, acknowledgment
bekanntmachen to publish, make known, advertise, announce
Bekanntmachung *f* notification, publication, notice, proclamation
Bekanntmachungsgebühr *f* lay-out fee, announcement fee
bekanten to chamfer
bekennen to confess, admit
bekiesen, das Pflaster ~ to gravel the pavement
Beklagter *m* accused, defendant, respondent
bekleben to paste on, label, placard
Beklebe-papier *n* liming (cover) paper (print) **-zettel** *m* label
beklecksen to soil, blur, blot, stain, daub
bekleiden to cover (with paint, insulation), coat, line, face, box, sheathe, clothe, revet
Bekleidung *f* casing, lining, jacketing, covering (wings), sheathing, revetment, clothing, uniform
Bekleidungs-blech *n* cover or coating or lining sheat, (Hochhaus) curtain wall sheet **-entgiftung** *f* clothing decontamination **-erde** *f* top soil, surface soil **-sack** *m* duffel bag **-stück** *n* article of clothing
Bekleidungs-vorschrift *f* dress regulations **-wirtschaft** *f* clothing industry
Beklemmung *f* anguish, anxiety
beklopfen to test by knocking, percuss
bekneifen to jam
bekohlen, ein Schiff ~ to coal a ship
Bekohlungs-anlage *f* firing machine, coaling plant or installation **-hafen** *m* coal bunkering port or wharf **-station** *f* coaling station
bekommen to get, receive
Beköstigung *f* board, food, mess
Beköstigungs-geld *n* garrison ration **-mittel** *n* ration supply, subsistence supply
bekräftigen to aggravate, confirm, emphasize, strengthen, corroborate
Bekräftigung *f* corroboration, substantiation, aggravation
bekratzen to scratch, scrape
Bekrönung *f* crown of the arch, crown
Bekrönungsdreieck *n* triangular section added to top of triangular dam to provide a horizontal crest
bekrusten to (in)crust
bekunden to show, give evidence
Bel *n* bel

Beladebühne *f* loading platform
beladen to load, load up, charge, fill, activate, sensitize (a surface), loaded
Beladen *n* loading (operation)
Belade-plan *m* loading diagram, loading table, stowage chart for vehicles **-rampe** *f* loading bay **-schurren** *f pl* loading chutes of an ore-handling bridge crane **-station** *f* loading station, take-up end, head end, receiving end **-stelle** *f* loading and unloading wharf **-zeit** *f* loading time
Beladung der Schiffe loading of ships
Beladungsbeschränkungen *pl* load limits
Belag *m* coat, cover, covering, plating, lining, overlay (harness), planking, (bridge) plank, incrustation, paving, coating, surfacing, surface (road), pavement, layer (film); (Fußboden) flooring **ohne** ~ without surfacing
Belag-bogen *m* covering sheet **-brettchen** *n* wood lagging
Belag-fläche *f* coating surface **-frei** free from coating **-korrosion** *f* deposit attack **-pfanne** *f* coating pan **-platte** *f* coverning plate **-ring** *m* facing, lining **-verlust** *m* surface leakage loss (dielectric)
Belang *m* importance **von** ~ of importance **nicht von** ~ of no importance, insignificant
belangen, gerichtlich ~ to bring legal action against
belanglos irrelevant, inconsiderable, unimportant, dummy (info proc.) **-e Fehler** irregularities
belassen to leave (as it was), put up with
Belastbarkeit *f* capacitance, loading or carrying capacity, load
belasten to load, weight, burden, charge, debit, strain, encumber **mit Ableitung** ~ to leak load **mit Querspulen** ~ to lump load **gleichförmig** ~ to load continuously **induktiv** ~ to load inductively **punktförmig** ~ to lump load
Belasten *n* loading
belastet loaded **für Hochfrequenz** ~ loaded for carrier **leicht** ~ lightly loaded **mittelstark** ~ medium heavily loaded **stark** ~ heavily loaded **stetig** ~ continuously loaded **von unten** ~ load acting at the bottom **auf Druck -er Stab** bar or rod loaded for pressure column
belästigen to molest, annoy, bother
Belästigung *f* annoyance, molestation, nuisance, bother, trouble
Belastung *f* stress, strain, load, loading, charge, burden(ing), dead load, current density, unit stress, application of load, bearing pressure, level of drive (cryst.) ~ **mit Ableitung** leak load(ing) ~ **durch Eigengewicht** dead load ~ **der Flächeneinheit** unit stress ~ **eines Grundstückes** encumbrance ~ **pro Pferdestärke** power loading (aeronautics) ~ **je Quadratmeter** loading per square meter ~ **mit Querspulen** lumped leak load(ing) ~ **der Wähler** selector carrying capacity
Belastung, allmähliche ~ (Werkstoffprüfung) gradual application of stress **ausgeglichene** ~ balanced load **aussetzende** ~ intermittent load **bewegliche** ~ live load **bleibende** ~ basic load **drehsymmetrische** ~ axially symmetrical load **elastische** ~ elastic strain **gleichförmige** ~ continuously or evenly distributed load **induktive** ~ inductive or inductance load **kapazitive** ~ condenser load **punktförmige** ~ lumped (series) load **ruhende** ~ dead load
Belastung, spezifische ~ unit stress **spezifische ruhende** ~ dead load **spezifische zulässige** ~ safe load **statische** ~ static load, dead load **stoßweise** ~ intermittent shock load, pulsating load, vibratory shock load **wechselnde** ~ live load **zulässige** ~ safe load **zunehmende** ~ increasing load
belastungsabhängig dependent on load
Belastungs-abschnitt *m* loading section **-annahme** *f* assumed load **-anzeiger** *m* load indicator, drillometer (petroleum) **-art** *f* type of stress, strain, or load **-ausgleich** *m* load compensation or equalization **-bereich** *m* range of stress, load range
Belastungscharakteristik für reine Blindlast zero power-factor characteristic
Belastungs-dauer load duration, duration of load application **-diagramm** *n* load diagram **-dreieck** *n* load triangle **-einrichtung** tensioning device **-erhöhung** *f* increase in load **-fähigkeit** *f* load capacity **-faktor** (des Kraftwerks) *m* coefficient of utilization or load factor
Belastungsfall *m* type of stress (aviation), type of loading, loading case
Belastungs-fläche *f* load area **-folgen** *pl* load spectra, loading sequence **-gänge** *m pl* load changes, repetitions or cycles **-gebirge** *n* seasonal load curve, annual load curve (elec.) **-geschwindigkeit** *f* rate of load application **-gewicht** *n* balance weight, counterweight, loading weight, dead weight, aerial weight of trailing antenna
Belastungsglieder *n pl* load coefficient, identical with the cross-line distances, load terms (of an equation)
Belastungs-grad *m* load factor **-grenze** *f* maximum load, load limit, load capacity; (Elektronenröhre) dissipation limit **-koeffizient** *m* load factor
Belastungskreisausbeute *f* load-circuit efficiency
Belastungs-kurve *f* load diagram, load(ing) curve or line **-linie** *f* load axis, load curve or line **-mechanik** *f* load system **-metamorphose** *f* regional metamorphism **-möglichkeit** *f* load capacity
Belastungs- oder Antriebsmaschine *f* regulating machine (Scherbius set)
Belastungsprobe *f* load test, static test ~ **bis zum Bruch** *m* load test up to breaking, breaking load test
Belastungs-prüfung *f* loading or static test **-rahmen** *m* loading frame **-rekord** *m* load record **-richtung** *f* loading direction **-rolle** *f* loading or weighted tension roller **-scheibchen** *n* loading disc **-scheide** *f* reversing point of shear action **-schemata** *pl* loading diagrams **-schwankung** *f* load variation, surging (elec.), load fluctuation
Belastungs-spannung *f* working tension, effective pull, load tension or voltage **-spitze** *f* load peak, maximum load **-spule** *f* loading coil, loading endurance **-stoß** *m* considerable load variation, load surge **-strom** *m* load current **-stufe** load grade
Belastungstabelle *f* stress table (wires) ~ **für isolierte Leitungen** permissible current-carrying capacities of insulated conductors

Belastungs-tal *n* off-peak **-teller** *m* cover plate **-ventil** *n* loaded valve **-verhältnis** *n* ratio of load

Belastungsverhältnisse des Netzes load conditions of network

Belastungs-vermögen *n* loading capacity **-versuch** *m* static test, slow test **-verteilung** *f* load distribution **-wahlschalter** load selector switch **-wechsel** *m* load change, reversal of stress **-wert** *m* load value

Belastungs-widerstand *m* load(ing) resistor, load(ing) resistance **-wiederholung** *f* cycle of stress **-zahl oder -ziffer** *f* load factor or rating **-zeitverhältnis** *n* duty factor **-zunahme** *f* load increase **-zustand** *m* load condition

Belastvorrichtung *f* loading device, loading frame (photoelasticity)

belatten to lath

belaubt leafy, covered with leaves (tree)

belaufen, sich ~ auf to amount to

beleben to enliven, brighten (freshen up) **die Gärung ~** to animate the fermentation

belebter Schlamm activated sludge

Belebtschlammprozeß *m* activated-sludge process

Belebung *f* improvement

Belebungsmittel *n* restorative

beledert leather-covered

Beleg *m* proof, voucher, record, document

Belegaufstellung *f* supporting schedule

belegen to occupy, cover, coat, line, belay, incrust, employ workmen in a mine, shell, silver (a mirror) **mit Gebühren ~** to charge **unnütz ~** to tie up **Zeitdauer ~** to hold (communication)

Belegen *n* busying, seizure, marking engaged

Beleg-exemplar *n* voucher copy **-klampe** *f* belaying cleat **-kontierung** *f* voucher accounting **-nadel** *f* belaying pin, cleat **-nagel** *m* belaying pin (naut.)

Belegschaft *f* employees, workers, crew, personnel

Belegschaftshöchstgrenze *f* manpower ceiling

Beleg-signal *n* seizing signal **-stelle** *f* authoritative quotation

belegt busy, engaged **~ halten** to hold

Belegtisch *m* silvering table (glass mfg.)

Belegt-lampe *f* busy lamp (trunk or service line) **-zeichen** *n* busy-signal (teleph.)

Belegung *f* (Platz) reservation; (Telef.) seizing; (Beweis) verification; (Beispiel) illustration, plate, coatings, seizure, billeting, busying, coverage, holding, shelling, coat (of condenser), plating, deposit, film, covering, density (of electrons in beam), occupancy **~ eines Kondensators** plate or vane of a condenser **~ des Fernschranks** engagement of the trunk switchboard **~ des Fleckes** impingement on the spot (cathode) **~ der Teilnehmerleitung durch die Fernbeamtin** holding a subscriber line by toll operator **magnetische ~** magnetic induction, charge, or field, seat of magnetic flux

Belegungen *f pl* condenser plates (elec.)

Belegungsdauer *f* holding time **~ in vom Hundert** circuit usage

Belegungs-fähigkeit *f* billeting capacity **-funktion** *f* surface-distribution function **-hilfsrelais bei Gebührenerfassung** auxiliary busying relay for automatic message accounting **-minute** *f* message minute **-plan** *m* allocation scheme

Belegungsrelais *n* busying relay

Belegungs-sperrelais *n* guard relay against intrusion of other calls **-stärke** *f* density of gas obstacle **-stunde** *f* telephone traffic unit or call (other than Bell)

Belegungszähler *m* call-count meter, overflow meter **~ für Leitungen des Regelwegs** late-choice call meter

Belegungszeit *f* occupation time

belehren to teach

Belehrung *f* instruction

Belehrungstafel *f* instruction plate

Beleimapparat *m* gluing apparatus

beleimen to glue

Belemnit *m* belemnite, thunderstone

belesen to burl, pick, cull

beleuchten to illuminate, light, floodlight

Beleuchten *n* lighting

Beleuchter *m* pathfinder, light electrician, scaffold or top-light controller, lighting operator (in theatre)

Beleuchtung *f* illumination, lighting, glow, lighting system, irradiance (in lux or candle-meter units) **eingeschränkte ~** partial blackout **gerade ~** direct illumination **senkrechte ~** scaffold lighting, overhead lighting **spaltfreie ~** apertureless illumination

Beleuchtungs-anhänger *m* searchlight trailer **-anlage** *m* searchlight trailer, lighting equipment or system **-apparat** *m* lighting fixture, aerophore **-armaturen** *f pl* lighting fittings **-aufsatz** *m* lamp attachment **-ausrüstung** *f* illuminating outfit

Beleuchtungs-balken *m* (Scheinwerfer) light beam, light trough **-brücke** *f* travelling light crane, gantries (film) **-büschel** *n* illuminating pencil of rays

Beleuchtungseinrichtung illuminating equipment or plant

Beleuchtungs-fenster *n* lighting aperture **-gerät** *n* lighting or illumination instrument **-grad** *m* degree of illumination **-grenze** *f* boundary or limit of illumination **-intensität** intensity of illumination **-kegel** *m* cone of light

Beleuchtungskörper *m* lighting fixture or unit, lamp, illuminator **~ für Leuchtstoffröhre** fluorescent fitting

Beleuchtungs-kuppel *f* glass globe **-lampe** *f* illuminating lamp **-linse** *f* condensing or illuminating lens, bull's eye lens **-messer** *m* lux meter, illumination meter **-messung** *f* measurement of illumination, photometric measurement **-mittel** *n* means of illumination, illuminant

Beleuchtungs-prisma *n* illuminating prism **-schalter** *m* lighting switch **-schalttafel** *f* lighting panel **-schirm** *m* (lighting) reflector **-schwerpunkt** *m* luminous center of gravity **-spiegel** *m* illuminating mirror

Beleuchtungsstärke *f* illumination, intensity of illumination, brightness, illumination at a point on a surface, ratio of luminous flux to area of element of surface in lux units, illumination level, screen brightness (CRT) **Kurve gleicher ~** isophot curve **-messer** *m*, **photometer** *n* illumination photometer, illuminometer, lux meter

Beleuchtungs-tafel *f* lighting panel **-technik** *f* lighting engineering **-transformator** *m* lighting transformer **-trommel** *f* exposure drum, recording drum **-trupp** *m* searchlight squad or section **-untersatz** *m* illuminating base, substage lamp unit **-verhältnis** *n* lighting conditions **-wagen** *m* searchlight wagon **-zweck** *m* illuminating or lighting purpose

belgische Drahtstraße Belgian rod mill, looping mill

belgischer Ofen Belgian furnace

belichten to expose to light, irradiate

belichtet illuminated, exposed (phot.)

Belichtung *f* illumination, exposure (phot.), exposure to light

Belichtungs-dauer *f* duration or time of exposure **-differenz** difference in lighting, exposure difference (photo) **-fenster** *n* aperture (in a plate), photocell window **-geschwindigkeit** *f* printing speed **-kanal** *m* film track, film channel (camera) **-karte** *f* exposure chart **-kasten** *m* exposure box **-klappe** *f* exposure shutter **-lampe** *f* exciter lamp **-maß** *n* exposure level **-meßeinrichtung** *f* exposure meter equipment

Belichtungs-messer *m* illumination meter, amplifier exposure meter **-messer** *m* cinophot, brightness or turbidity meter **-probe** *f* exposure test (light test) **-quelle** *f* light source **-reihenschieber** *m* series exposure slide, exposure recording slide **-riß** *m* sun cracking (of rubber) **-rolle** *f* printing drum, sound-recording drum, scanning point, translation point (in sound-film reproduction)

Belichtungs-schaltuhr *f* exposure clock **-schieber** *m* exposure lid or shutter **-spielraum** *m* latitude or range of exposure **-stärke** *f* intensity or strength of lighting **-stelle** *f* sound gate **-stufe** *f* stage of exposure (photo) **-tabelle** *f* exposure chart, exposure-time table **-technik** *f* lighting engineering **-trommel** *f* exposure drum, recording drum (sound film)

Belichtungs-uhr *f* exposure timer **-zahntrommel** *f* printing sprocket, main sprocket **-zeit** *f* exposure time **-zeitenring** *m* shutter speed setting ring **-zylinder** *m* printing cylinder

Belieben *n* discretion, selection **nach ~** at will, at random **nach ~ einschaltbarer Lader** engageable at-will blower

beliebig arbitrary, any, anybody, haphazard, (at) random, any . . . at all, any . . . whatever, optional, discretionary, at liberty **~ auswechseln** change at random **~ lange** indefinitely long **~ senkrecht belastet** loaded with any type vertical loading or load coefficient **~ senkrecht von unten** (von oben) **belastet** loaded with any type vertical loading acting at the bottom (at the top) of the member (sometimes loading coefficient) **~** (waagrecht) **aber gleich belastet** loaded with any (horizontal) loading, both members carrying the same load (or load coefficient) **~** (waagrecht, senkrecht) **aber symmetrisch zur Rahmenmitte belastet** loaded with any type (horizontal, vertical) loading, acting symmetrically about the center line of the frame (also load coefficient) **~ waagrecht belastet** loaded with any type horizontal loading (or load coefficient)

beliebig-e Zahl random number **-er Zugriff** random access (comput.)

beliebt liked, popular, favored

Beliebtheit *f* popularity, vogue

beliefern to supply (a customer), deliver, feed

Belieferung der Teilnehmer mit Fernsprechbüchern telephone-directory distribution

Belit *m* belite

Beller *m* barker

Bellini-Tosi System *n* Bellini-Tosi system

Bells Roheisenentphospherungsverfahren *n* Bell's pigwashing or dephosphorizing process

Belohnung *f* reward, commendation, recompense

Belonit *m* acicular bismuth, needle ore

belüften to pressurize the oxygen tank of rockets, ventilate **~** (Druckanzug, Astron.) to aerate

belüftet, -er Beton air entrained concrete **mit -em Gehäuse** double-casing (machine) **mit -em Rippengehäuse** ventilated ribbed surface (machine)

Belüftung *f* ventilation, vent, aeration **regelbare ~** controllable ventilation

Belüftungs-anlage *f* ventilating system **-element** *n* aeration cell **-haube** *f* air scoop **-kappe** *f* air-vent protector, air cap **-klappen** *f pl* cowling flaps **-leitung** *f* pressure-regulator pipe **-mittel** *n* air entraining agent **-rohr** *n* air line or tube **-schraube** *f* air inlet valve (of carburetor) **-spalt** *m* ventilating slot

bemalen to paint, color, besmear

bemängeln to find fault with

bemannen to man

bemannte Station attented or manned station

Bemannung *f* crew, manning, complement

bemänteln to disguise, smooth over

bemerken to state, note, mention, notice, perceive, observe, remark **nicht ~** to overlook

bemerkenswert remarkable, noticeable, noteworthy, notable, marked

Bemerkung *f* remark, note, notation, comment, observation

bemessen to subject to measurement, measure, ascertain, adjust by measuring, apportion, rate, proportion, to regulate, seize, dimension **neu ~** to redimension **zeitlich ~** to time

bemessen determined, measured, adjusted, rated for or at **-e Feder** dimensioned top spring

Bemessung *f* determination of size, dimensioning, rating, proportioning, choosing, dimension, size, proportions **reichliche ~ von Konstruktionsteilen** conservative design

Bemessungs-fluggeschwindigkeit *f* design airspeed **-regel** *f* rule for proportioning **-tafel** *f* design table

bemörteln to plaster

bemühen, sich ~ to endeavor

bemustern to sample

Bemusterung *f* sampling, inspection

Bemusterungsmethode *f* method of sample taking

benachbart neighboring, adjacent, adjoining, contiguous **-e Windungen** neighboring turns

Benachbarte *f* (Reihe), adjacent row in any array

benachrichtigen to inform

Benachrichtigung *f* advice, notice, information, message, transmission of information

Benachrichtigungsgebühr *f* report charge

Benachteiligter *m* aggrieved party

Benachteiligung *f* detriment, injury, impairing **~ der hohen Frequenzen** deaccentuation, de-

emphasizing, slighting or partial suppression of high frequencies ~ **der hohen Töne** high note attenuation
Benadelung *f* pinning
benannt defined (math.) **-e Größe** *f* dimensional variable
benarbt scarred, cicatricial
benässen to wet
Bendix Getriebe *n* Bendix gear
benebeln to cover with fog, screen
benehmen, sich ~ to behave
Benehmen *n* behavior, demeanor
benennen, genau ~ to specify
Benennung *f* nomenclature, (Terminologie) term, naming, denomination, designation (of instruments)
benetzbar wettable, capable of being wetted or moistened
Benetzbarkeit *f* wettability
benetzen to wet, moisten, sprinkle
benetzende Flüssigkeit wetting liquid
Benetzer *m* surface-active agent
benetzt wetted **-e Fläche** wetted area **-e Oberfläche** wetted surface
Benetzung *f* wetting
Benetzungs-fähigkeit *f* moistening power **-wärme** *f* heat of wetting
bengalische Beleuchtung Bengal lights
Bengel *m* bar (print)
Benommenheit *f* numbness, stupor
benötigen to need, demand, require **keine Wartung** ~ demanding no maintenance
benötigt required **-es Vorvakuum** required forepressure
Bensäure *f* benic acid, behenic acid
Bentonit *n* bentonite
benummern to number
Benummerung *f* numbering
benutzen to use, take advantage of, utilize, employ, avail, profit
Benutzer *m pl* (telephone) users, public, subscribers
Benutzung *f* assignment of an international circuit, use, employment, utilization, improvement, advantage ~ **eines Patentes** working or reduction to practice of a patent ~ **von Umwegen** indirect routing by path **vor (nach)** ~ before (after) use
Benutzungs-absicht *f* utilization intention (trade mark) **-anweisung** *f* instruction **-gebühr** *f* royalty, technical know-how fees
Benzalchlorid *n* benzal chloride
Benzaldehyd *n* benzaldehyde
Benzamid *n* benzamide
Benzanilid *n* benzanilide
Benzanthren *n* benzanthrene
Benzene (Steinkohlenbenzol), benzol (from hard-coal distillation)
Benzidin *n* benzidine, para-diamino-diphenyl
Benzil *n* benzil **-säure** *f* benzilic acid
Benzin *m* fuel, gasoline, benzine ~ **für die Luftfahrt** aviation gasoline ~ **mit hoher Oktanzahl** high-octane gasoline
Benzin-abscheider *m* fuel or benzine separator **-aggregat** *n* gasoline electric generator or power unit **-behälter** *m* gasoline tank **-betrieb** *m* gasoline propulsion for engines **-druckmesser** *m* fuel gauge, gasoline-pressure gauge **-einführungsnadel** *f* fuel-inlet-valve needle **-einspritzverfahren** *n* gasoline-injection system
benzinelektrisch -e Aggregate electric generator sets **-er Stromerzeuger** petrol (or gasoline) engine driven generator
Benzin-filter *m* gasoline filter **-förderung** *f* fuel supply petrol feed **-gießer** *m* gasoline tank hose **-hahn** *m* fuel cock **-hydrieranlage** *f* gasoline hydro-treater **-injektor** *m* fuel injector **-kanne** *f* gasoline can **-kanister** *m* gasoline container, drum or jerry can **-kohlenwasserstoff** *m* petroleum hydrocarbon
Benzin-leck *n* fuel leak **-leitung** *f* fuel pipe line **-lösung** *f* naphtha solution **-manometer** *n* gasolinepressure gauge (aviation) **-messer** *m* fuel gauge **-motor** *m* gasoline motor, gasoline engine
Benzinpumpe *f* fuel pump, priming pump, gasoline pump ~ **mit sichtbarem Meßglas** gasoline pump with liquid level controller
Benzin-raffinieranlage *f* **(-Raffinerie)** gasoline refining plant **-reiniger** *m* fuel filter, gasoline separator **-rohr** *n* fuel pipe **-sack** *m* gasoline chamber **-schlepper** *m* gasoline tractor **-seife** *f* dry cleaning soap **-standanzeiger** *m* gasoline gauge **-standmesser** *m* fuel gauge, gasoline gauge **-störung** *f* fuel trouble **-strömungsmesser** *m* gasoline flowmeter
Benzintank *m* fuel tank, gasoline tank **fahrbarer** ~ gasoline wheel tank
Benzin-tankaufbau *m* petrol tank body **-tankstelle** *f* gasoline station **-uhr** *f* gasoline-tank meter, fuel gauge **-verbrauch** *m* gasoline consumption **-vernebler** *m* helical distributor, fuel pulverizing scroll **-vorrat** *m* gasoline supply **-waage** *f* gasoline balance or scale **-zapfsäule** *f* roadside gasoline pump **-zufuhr** *f* gasoline feed
Benzochinon *n* benzoquinone
Benzoe *n* benzoin (gum) **-äther** *m* ethyl benzoate, benzoic ether **-äthylester** *n* ethyl benzoate **-säure** *f* benzoic acid
benzoesaures benzoate ~ **Ammonium** ammonium benzoate ~ **Natrium** sodium benzoate
Benzoin *n* benzoin
benzoiniert benzoinated, benzoated
Benzol *n* benzene, phenyl hydride, benzol coal naphtha ~ **abtreiben** to debenzolize
Benzol-abtreiber *m* benzol still **-gemisch** *n* benzol mixture **-gewinnung** *f* benzol recovery, **-gewinnungsanlage** *f* benzol-recuperation plant **-kern** *m* benzene nucleus **-kohlenwasserstoff** *m* benzene hydrocarbon **-maschine** *f* engine operating on benzene
Benzol-reihe *f* benzene series **-sulfochlorid** *n* benzene sulfonylchloride **-sulfonsäure** *f* phenylsulfonic acid, benzene sulfonic acid **-vorerzeugnis** *n* crude benzene **-wäsche** *f* benzene recovery plant, debenzolation **-wäscher** *m* benzene scrubber or washer **-waschöl** *n* wash oil
Benzo-naphtha *n f* betanaphthol benzoate **-nitril** *n* phenyl (iso)cyanide, benzonitrile
Benzopersäure *f* benzoper acid
Benzo-phenol *n* carbolic acid (phenol) **-phenon** *n* benzophenone, diphenyl ketone
Benzoyl-bromid *n* benzoyl bromide **-chlorid** *n* benzoyl chloride
bezoylieren to benzoylate

Benzoylwasserstoff *m* benzoyl hydride, benzaldehyde, almond oil
Benzyl *m* benzyl **-amin** *n* benzylamine
Benzylidenchlorid *n* benzyl chloride
Benzyl-zellulose *f* benzyl cellulose (lacquer base developed in Germany consisting of treating cellulose by etherification with benzyl alcohol) **-zyanid** *n* benzyl cyanide
beobachten to observe, watch, detect
Beobachter *m* spotter, lookout, observer, radar operator **abgesetzter ~** spotter, remote control
Beobachter-fernrohr *n* spotting scope on height finder **-raum** *m* observer's cockpit **-sitz** *m* observer's seat or cockpit **-stand** *m* observer's cockpit
Beobachtung *f* observation, detecting, study, examination **~ von seitlicher Beobachtungsstelle** flank spotting **~ der Längenabweichung** horizontal spotting **seitliche ~** lateral observation **subjektive ~** visual observation **vorbedingte ~** conditional observation
Beobachtungs-blatt *n* circuit-usage record **-bogen** *m* observation sheet **-einrichtung** *f* visual control facility **-fehler** *m* error in or of observation, personal error **-feld** *n* observation panel (aviation) **-fenster** *n* bezel, observation window, peephole, **-fernrohr** *n* observation telescope **-fläche** scanned area
Beobachtungs-gabe *f* power of observation **-gerät** *n* observation instrument, scanning unit **-gleichung** observation equation **-haube** *f* observation panel **-kammer** *f* observation chamber **-korb** *m* observation basket (balloon) **-kuppel** *f* cupola (used for observation)
Beobachtungs-loch scanning hole **-mittel** *n* tool for observation **-objektiv** viewing lens or objective **-ort** *m* station (photogrammetry, trig.) **-platz** *m* service observing desk **-punkt** *m* point of observation
Beobachtungs-raum *m* searching sector, observation area **-reihe** *f* series of observations **-rohr** *n* trench periscope, spotting telescope, observation tube (in electron microscope) **-scharte** *f* embrasure, loophole **-schirm** *m* plan display (rdr.) **-spiegel** *m* periscope **-stand** *m* observation post **-stelle** *f* observation point **-streifen** *m* zone of observation **-system** *n* visual system
Beobachtungs-teil *m* main, fine-range, or split presentation unit of radar equipment **-turm** *m* cupola (used for observation)
beölen to oil
beordern to order, command
bepacken to load, burden
Bepackung *f* load, outfit, kit
bepflanztes Feld cultivated field
bepflastern to plaster
bepichen to pitch
beplanken to cover with metal or wood (aviation)
Beplankung *f* planking, covering, sheeting (as with plywood), wing skin, covering with metal or wood **mittragende ~** stressed skin
Beplankungsgroßvorrichtung *f* covering machine, planking fixture
Beplattung *f* plating, sheathing, skin (of a ship)
bepneut inflated, air-filled
bepudern to dust, apply powder to
bepunkten to stipple
bequarzt quartz treated
bequem comfortable, easy, convenient
Bequemlichkeit *f* convenience, comfort
berändeln to edge
Berandung *f* boundary, bounds
Berandungslinie einer Kurvenschar envelope of a family of curves
Berandungsschärfe *f* edge sharpness
Berapp *m* coarse or rough plaster, roughcast
berappen to roughcast
berasen to fire at, pepper
beratend advisory, consulting **-er Ingenieur** consulting engineer
Beratung *f* recommendation, advisory deliberation, advice, consultation, counsel
Beratungs-dienst *m* consulting service, **-gegenstand** *m* agendum, item of business **-stelle** *f* advisory board, consulting office **-wetterwarte** *f* advisory meteorological observatory
beräuchern to fumigate, disinfect
berauhen to roughen
Berauhwehrung *f* facing with fascines
berechenbar calculable, computable, appraisable
berechnen to calculate, compute, figure out, charge, quote, estimate, design, reckon **einfach (doppelt, dreifach) ~** to charge one, two, three fees **genau ~** to cut fine
Berechner *m* calculator, estimator
berechnet intended, computed, charged, designed **-e Geschwindigkeit** designed speed **nicht -es Gespräch** free call
Berechnung *f* cost study, estimate, calculation, computation, charge, rate, account, design, reckoning, proportioning **~ des Eintretens** computing inception **~ der Schaltung** design of the circuit **~ der Talsperren** design of dams **ohne ~** freee of charge **zahlenmäßige ~** numerical calculation (math.)
berechnungsfähig susceptible to design
Berechnungs-formel *f* equation **-grundlage** *f* computation base **-hochwasser** *n* computed high water **-weise** *f* method of calculation
berechtigen to entitle, authorize, justify
berechtigt authorized, qualified, entitled **-er Anlaß** valid cause (legal proceedings) **-er Teilnehmer** (Teilnehmerschaltung) priority line circuit
Berechtigung *f* authorization, justification, right
Berechtigungsrelais *n* admission relay, discriminating relay **~ für gerufenen Tln (B)** discriminating relay for called party
Berechtigungsschein *m* priority
Beregner *m* sprinkler
Beregnung *f* overhead irrigation, sprinkling, rain, exposure test
Beregnungs-anlage *f* sprinkling system **probe** *f* rain-exposure-test specimen **-verfahren** *n* sprinkler method, spraying method **-versuch** *m* rain test, wet test (of insulator)
Bereich *m* zone, area, scope, limit, sphere, range, band, branch (of manufacture), reach (of a beam, gun, girder), extent, frequency, sweep **außer ~** out of one's sphere, out of reach, beyond range **im ~ von** within the limits or range of **mittlerer ~** midrange
Bereich, ~ der Drehzahlverstellung speed changer range **~ der Durchlässigkeit** range of

transmittancy ~ **mittlerer Feldstärke** medium signal area ~ **einer Kurve** portion of a curve

Bereich(s)-band *n* band-range radio **-blende** *f* range, final range value **-fernamt** (Telef.) sectional center (SC) **-kontrolle** *f* area control (in aviation) **-schalter** *m* band switch **-umfang** *m* range span **-umschalter** *m* range selector **-temperaturwert** *m* span temperature coefficient

bereifen to rime, cover with hoar frost, hoop (cask), cover with rime, put on a tire

Bereifung *f* tires, set of tires, tire setting

Bereifungsart *f* kind of tire

bereift rimy (meteor.)

Bereinigung *f* clean-up ~ **des Minimums** zero clearing (direction finder)

bereisen to travel to, visit, inspect

bereißen to rip

bereit ready, prepared, stand-by

bereiten to prepare, make ready, make, break (a horse)

bereit-gestellt made ready **-machen** to make ready, prepare

bereithalten to keep ready, provide for

Bereitschaft *f* readiniss, preparedness, lowest alert condition in batteries, stand-by (switch) **in** ~ in readiness, in support, at stand-by **ständige** ~ utility operating method

Bereitschafts-anlage *f* stand-by plant **-dienst** *m* stand-by service

Bereitschaftsstellung *f* initial setting **in** ~ **bringen** to return to the working position

Bereitschaftstasche *f* carrying case

bereitstehen to stand by, be available

bereitstellen to put in readiness, make available, prepare

Bereitstellung *f* disposition of troops, preparation, putting in readiness ~ **eines Gesprächs** maturation of a call ~ **der Kräfte** combat preparation of forces

Bereitstellungen, gesetzliche ~ legal provisions ~ **und Eventualverpflichtungen** provisions and accruals

Bereitstellungs-befehl *m* assembly order **-platz** *m* assembly position, assembly point **-raum** *m* assembly area

Bereitung *f* preparation, manufacture

Bereitungsweise *f* method of preparation

bereitwillig willing, ready

Bereitwilligkeit *f* willingness, readiness

Berg *m* mountain, hill, mount, gobbing, tailings, mine filling ~ (einer Kurve) peak, crest ~ **eines Papierholländers** breasting backfall

berg-ab downhill **-abhang** *m* mountain declivity **-ader** *f* vein, lode **-akademie** *f* school of mines **-alaun** *m* rock alum **-amt** *n* mine office **-an** uphill

Berg-arbeit *f* mining **-arbeiter** *m* miner **-arbeitersiedlung** *f* mining camp **-art** *f* gang, gangue, vein stuff, matrix **-assessor** *m* junior mining inspector **-auf** uphill **-ausrüstung** *f* mining equipment

Bergbau *m* mining, working of mines **-freiheit** *f* permission to mine **-gesellschaft** *f* mining company

bergbauliches Vorkommen mineralogical occurence

Bergbau-sachverständiger *m* mining expert **-tagesanlage** *f* aboveground (mine) **-verwaltung** *f* mines department **-werkzeugstahl** *m* tool steel for the mining industry

Berg-blau *n* azurite, copper carbonate **-braun** *n* umber **-büro** *n* mine office **-butter** *f* mountain or rock butter, halotrichite, impure iron alum, iron or zinc sulfate **-eisen** *n* picker, wedge

Berge *m pl* refuse, mine waste, deads, muck, mullock **-dienst** *m* recovery service, salvage-collecting service **-eigentümer** *m* owner of mines **-geld** *n* salvage money or charges **-gerinne** *n* tailings launder **-inspektor** *m* mine viewer **-kipper** *m* tipper **-klein** *n* deads **-kolonne** *f* recovery or salvage column **-mauer** *f* dry walling, pack wall **-mittel** *n* band, stone band **-mühle** *f* subterranean quarry

bergen to save, rescue

Bergen *n* recovery, salvage

Bergenge *n* defile

Berge-pächter *m* lessee **-pachtzins** *m* rent of a mine **-pfeiler** *m* pillar

Bergermischung *f* Berger-type smoke agent mixture composed of two parts of zinc dust to three parts of hexachlorethane

Berges-Trieb *m* Berges drive

Berge-tasche *f* waste pocket **-unternehmer** *m* adventurer, lessee **-verleihung** *f* grant of the minerals **-vergasung** *f* refuse gasification **-versatz** *m* tailings for mine filling, (mine) filling, gobbing, debris, pack stowing **-versatzmaschinen** *pl* stowing machines **-versatzpfeiler** *m* cog

Bergfall *m* landslide

Bergfahrt *f* hill climb, ascent, on gradients (referring to performance of wireless telegraph)

Berg-fäustel *n* ragging hammer **-fett** *n* mountain tallow, ozocerite **-feuchtigkeit** *f* quarry water **-fleisch** *n* mountain flesh (asbestos) **-fluß** *m* colored quartz **-föhn** *m* foehn **-führerabzeichen** *n* mountain-guide badge **-gang** *m* vein, lode **-gelb** *n* ocher, iron ocher, red ocher **-gerät** *n* recovery equipment, salvage-collecting equipment

Berggerechtsame *f* right or privilege to mine **zusammengelegte** ~ amalgamated claims

Berg-gericht *n* barmote **-gesetz** *n* mining law **-gipfel** *m* mountaintop, mountain summit or peak **-glimmer** *m* margarite **-glas** *n* rock crystal **-gold** *n* free gold **-grat** *m* ridge, crest **-grün** *n* mineral green, green verditer **-gruppe** *f* protected category

Berg-haar *n* fibrous asbestos **-halde** *f* spoil bank, slags dump, waste heap or dump **-hammer** *m* mattock **-hang** *m* hillside, mountain slope **-hauptmann** *m* chief inspector of mines **-holz** *n* timber, fender, wale (of a ship) **-ingenieur** *m* mining engineer

bergig hilly, mountainous

berginisieren (von Bergius) to hydrogenate

Berg-inspektor *m* superintendent **-joch** *n* saddle **-kalk** *m* mountain-limestone **-kamm** *m* crest **-kegel** *m* conical (mountain) peak **-kessel** *m* mountain hollow **-ketten** *pl* mountain chains **-kiefer** *m* mountain pine **-kiesel** *m* rock flint **-kluft** *f* gorge, ravine **-knappschaft** *f* body of miners **-kohle** *f* lignite, brown coal **-kork** *m* a type of asbestos

Berg-kommando *n* collecting unit, salvage party, recovery party **-kompanie** *f* tunneling company, mining company **-kristall** *m* rock crystal, quartz **-kupfer** *n* native copper **-kuppe** *f* dome-shaped top or summit of a mountain **-lazur** *f* azurite **-leder** *n* a type of asbestos **-lehne** *f* mountain side **-letten** *m pl* clay **-leute** *pl* miners, mining engineers

Berg-mann *m* miner, collier, digger, pitman, mineworker **-mehl** *n* infusorial earth, diatomaceous earth, kieselguhr, fossil meal **-milch** *f* rock milk, agaric mineral, earthy calcium carbonate

Bergnebel *m* mist **dicker ~ mit Nieselregen** Scotch mist

Berg-naphtha *n* crude oil, petroleum **-nase** *f* mountain spur **-öl** *n* petroleum **-papier** *n* a type of asbestos **-pech** *n* bitumen, mineral pitch, asphalt **-rat** *m* board of mining company, senior inspector **-recht** *n* mining law

bergrechtliche Pachtverträge mining leases

Berg-revierbeamter *m* mining inspector **-rot** *n* realgar, Indian red **-rücken** *m* ridge **-rutsch** *m* landslide **-salz** *n* rock salt **-schaden** *m* damage due to mining operations, surface damage **-schlucht** *f* ravine **-schwaden** *m* firedamp

Bergseite *f* upstream (of dam) **abgetreppte ~ des Wehrkörpers** upstream stepped face (of dam)

Berg-striche *m pl* hachures **-strichelung** *f* hatching, hachure **-strom** *m* mountain stream, torrent **-sturz** *m* landslide, mountain creep **-stütze** *f* backstay, skid, sprag (automobiles) **-talg** *m* hatchettine, mineral tallow or wax, ozocerite paraffin **-teer** *m* mineral tar, pissasphalt, maltha, asphalt, bitumen **-trog** *m* miner's trough

Berg- und Talbahn *f* cable car, funicular

Berg- und Talwind *m* mountain and valley breezes

Bergung *f* salvage

Bergungen *f pl* salvage operations on disabled ships (naut.)

Bergungs-anlage *f* salvage plant **-arbeiten** *f pl* salvage work (navy), rescue operation **-dienst** *m* recovery service **-fähig** recoverable (aviat.) **-gerät** *n* recovery device, crash equipment **-kolonne** *f* salvage or recovery column **-schiff** *n* rescue or salvage vessel **-versuch** *m* attempted salvage

Berg-waage *f* clinometer, batter level **-wachs** *n* mineral wax, ozocerite **-wand** *f* precipice, mountain side

Bergwerk *n* mine, pit **ein ~ bauhaft halten** to keep a mine in repair **ein ~ fündig machen** to discover a mine

Bergwerks-abgaben *f pl* contributions by mines, mines' taxes **-aktien** *f pl* mining shares, mining stocks **-anlage** *f* mining installation **-anspruch** *m* claim **-arbeiter** *m* miner **-direktor** *m* mine-owner's agent **-eingang** *m* adit **-gesellschaft** *f* mining company **-ingenieur** *m* mining engineer

Berg-wind *m* mountain breeze **-wirtschaft** *f* mining activity **-wolle** *f* mountain wool, a type of asbestos **-zinn** *n* vein tin, mined tin, cassiterite **-zinnober** *m* native cinnabar **-zug** *m* mountain range **-zunder** *m* a type of asbestos

Bericht *m* report, information, news, advice, account, paper, print, review, communiqué **~ über die Bewegung der höheren Winde** winds-aloft reports **~ erstatten** to make a report, report **zusammenfassender ~** survey report, review, summarizing article

Berichte über die Wetterlage weather condition reports

berichten to report, inform, relate

Berichter *m* correspondent, reporter

Berichterstatter *m* reporter

Berichterstattung *f* reporting, report

berichtigen to set right, correct, rectify, adjust, amend, redress

berichtigend corrective **-es Glas** correcting lens

berichtigt corrected **-es Auge** corrected eye **durch Streupunkte gelegte, -e Kurve** a faired curve

Berichtigung *f* correction, rectification, adjustment, amendment **~ der Verzerrung** correction of distortion

Berichtigungs-beiwert *m* corrective factor **-faktor** *m* correction factor **-gerät** *n* adjustment gear for range finder, compensation means (cam, etc., in direction finding) **-latte** *f* adjusting lath or bar for range finder **-linse** *f* collimator **-marke** *f* correction mark **-meßreihe** *f* adjusting reading on range finder **-regler** *m* regulator between angular height of control point and angular height of target

Berichtigungs-schraube *f* adjusting screw **-taste** *f* reset key **-verfahren** *n* correction methods, theory of approximations **-walze** *f* correction wedge or adjustment drum (range finder) **-wert** *m* correction value, correction factor **-winkel** *m* angle of correction **-zeichen** *n* correcting signal

Berichts-instruktion *f* training regulations for reports **-jahr** *n* fiscal year

beriechen to sniff at, scent

berieseln to spray, wash, scrub, water, irrigate, sprinkle, cause to flow or trickle over, douche

Berieselung *f* spraying, watering, scrubbing, trickling, irrigation; (Kühlturm) sprinkling system

Berieselungs-anlage *f* sprinkling system for fire fighting, irrigation works **-apparat** *m* sprinkler **-brause** *f* sprinkler (drencher) **-bütte** *f* wash box **-graben** *m* watering ditch **-kondensator** atmospheric condenser, surface spray cooler

Berieselungskühler *m* **mit Rundrohrflächen** round-type drip cooler

Berieselungs-luftkühler *m* spray type air cooler **-methode** *f* flooding method **-rohr** *n* perforated pipe **-verdampfer** *m* spray type cooler **-turm** *m* wash tower, scrubbing tower, scrubber, washer, spray tower, wash cloumn

Berieselungsverflüssiger *m* humidifier for ventilator or air conditioner **~ mit liegenden Rohren** spray condenser with horizontal pipes **~ mit stehenden Rohren** spray condenser with vertical tubes

Berieselungsvorrichtung *f* spraying device

beringen to ring **einen Pfahl ~** to hoop a pile

Berkelium *n* berkelium

Berlinerblau *n* Prussian blue, Berlin blue

Berme *f* berm, bench, terrace **bepflanzte ~** berm planted with reeds

Bernotar bernotar, a polarizing filter

Bernoulli's Lehrsatz Bernoulli's theorem

Bernstein *m* amber (yellow) **-alaun** *m* aluminous amber

bernsteinartig amberlike

Bernstein-lack *m* amber varnish **-öl** *n* amber oil **-säure** *f* succinic acid

Berstdruck *m* bursting strength (of paper, etc.), breaking limit, bursting limit, explosion or cracking limit **-prüfung** *f* bursting strain or strength

bersten to burst, explode, detonate, crack

Bersten *n* bursting, disruption

Berst-festigkeit *f* bursting strength **-scheibe** *f* rupture or safety disk **-zahl** *f* burst factor

Bertolin code for hydrazine hydrate (a rocket propellant)

Bertrand-Thiel-Verfahren *n* Bertrand-Thiel process

berücksichtigen to consider, take into account, take care of, allow for

Berücksichtigung *f* consideration, regard, allowance, significance ~ **der Ströme** regard to currents ~ **der Tageseinflüsse** allowance for the error of the day **unter ~ ausreichender Sicherheit** conservative

Beruf *m* vocation, occupation, profession, trade, department ~ **ausüben** to practice one's profession, profess **bürgerlicher** ~ civilian occupation

berufen zu entitled to

Berufener *m* authorized person

beruflich professional

berufsmäßig professional

Berufsausbildung *f* vocational training

berufsbedingte Bestrahlung occupational exposure

Berufs-beratung *f* vocational guidance **-bild** *n* professional specifications and qualifications **-bildung** *f* vocational training or education **-eignungsprüfung** *f* vocational or aptitude test **-ekzem** *n* occupational eczema **-fahrer** *m* professional driver **-geheimnis** *n* professional discretion **-genossenschaft** *f* employers' liability insurenace, trade union

Berufs-krankheit *f* occupational disease **-mäßig** professional **-noxe** *f* occupational disease or hazard (such as chemicals or noxious gases) **-pflicht** *f* duty **-pilot** *m* professional or commercial pilot **-tätig** practicing **-unfähigkeit** *f* professional inability **-zeichner** *m* professional draftsman

Berufung *f* call, vocation, appeal (law), brief for appeal; (auf einen Posten) appointment ~ **einlegen** (gegen) to appeal, take or lodge an appeal (from)

Berufungs-abteilung *f* appeal division or department **-begründung** *f* arguments and grounds for appeal, confirmation of appeal **-beklagter** *m* defendant in appeals court, respondent in an appealed cause **-gericht** *n* jury of appeal **-grund** *m* ground of appeal

Berufungsinstanz *f*, **zuständig sein als** ~ to have appellate jurisdiction

Berufungs-klage *f* appeal **-kläger** *m* appellant, appellor, appealer **-recht** *n* right of appeal **-schrift** *f* petition on appeal

beruhen auf to be based on, due or owing to, derived from, conditioned by, predicated upon, to rest on

beruhigen to kill (melt), quiet, steady, stabilize, smooth, calm **sich** ~ to abate (chem.), become calm **sich ~ lassen** to make bull (foundry)

beruhigt quiet, dead **-er Stahl** killed steel **-er Vergütungsautomatenstahl** killed or deoxidized temperhardening automatic screw machine

Beruhigung *f* quieting, killing, destruction (of kinetic energy), stabilizing (weight)

Beruhigungs-becken *n* wave trap **-behälter** *m* surge tank

Beruhigungsdrossel *f* antihunt transformer ~ **für die Druckmesser** pressure gauge throttle

Beruhigungs-einrichtung *f* steadying device **-element** *n* damping element **-flügel** *m* intermediate blade, antiflicker blade **-frequenz** *f* fusion frequency, critical no-flicker frequency (motion pictures) **-glied** *n* steadying circuit, smoothing network **-kammer** *f* stilling basin, water cushion

Beruhigungs-kapazität *f* smoothing capacitance **-kondensator** *m* smoothing capacitor **-kreis** *m* smoothing circuit or network, steadying circuit, antihunting circuit **-mittel** *n* sedative agent **-rohr** *n* smoothing pipe **-rolle** *f* damping pulley **-raum** *m* plenum chamber

Beruhigungs-strecke *f* calm region, region of steady flow **-substanz** *f* deoxidizer **-vorrichtung** steadying device, arc silencer **-widerstand** *m* steadying or smoothing resistance **-zeit** *f* stabilization period **-zuschlag** *m* deoxidizing additive

berührbar touchable

berühren to touch, refer to briefly, strike, be in contact **sich** ~ to meet

berührend tangent

Berührende *f* tangent

Berührlinie *f* line of contact

Berührung *f* touch(ing), contact, contiguity, cross ~ **längs einer Linie** line contact ~ **zwischen Stöpselspitz und Berührungsschaft** tip-and-sleeve contact **gegen** (zufällige) ~ **geschützt** semienclosed

Berührungs-belastung *f* contact load **-bogen** *m* tangent or contact arc **-dauer** *f* time of contact **-dichtungen** *f pl* sealed contact joints **-ebene** *f* tangential plane **-elektrizität** *f* contact electricity **-fläche** *f* contact (sur)face, area of contact, contact plane, line of contact interface **-gefahr** *f* risk or hazard of (electric) shock

Berührungs-beheizung *f* contact heating (heated clothing or pads) **-kapillarradikale** *n pl* meniscular formations **-korrosion** *f* contact corrosion **-linie** *f* spiral line, line of contact, tangent compass, tangent galvanometer

berührungsloses Messen non-contact gauging

Berührungs-normale *f* normal to point of contact **-punkt** *m* point of contact, touching point, point of tangency or osculation

Berührungsschutz *m* contact safety device, protection against electric-shock hazard **mit** ~ screen-protected (machine) ~ **bei Motoren** protection against accidental contact

Berührungsschutz-kapazität *f* capacitance for shock protection **-kappe** insulating (protection) cap **-kondensator** *m* capacitor for shock protection, contact safety condenser **-schalter** *m* protective switchgear against contact voltage

berührungssicherer Stecker shockproof plug

Berührungs-spannung *f* contact potential **-spannungsschutz** *m* protection against electric-shock hazard **-stelle** *f* place of contact, osculation point (between two curves), point of contact **-stellen** *pl* (Fingerabdruck) finger marks **-systementwickler** *m* contact generator **-transformation** *f* contact transformation, tangential transformation **-warngerät** *n* high-voltage warning device **-widerstand** *m* resistance of contact, compensating or steadying resistance **-zeichen** *n pl* touch signals **-zündung** *f* contact fire

berunzeln to wrinkle, corrugate

berußen to smoke, soot

berüsten to scaffold, stage

Beryll *m* beryl **blättriger ~** disthene, cyanite

Beryll-erde *f* beryllia, glucina, beryllium oxide **-hydrat** *n* beryllium hydroxide

Beryllium *n* beryllium, glucinum

Berylliumoxyd *n* beryllia

Bes (Beschneideschablone) trim or cutting pattern template

besagen to indicate, say, attest

besämen to seed

Besan *m* spanker, driver **-baum** *m* spanker boom **-bramstenge** *f* mizzentopgallant mast

besanden to sand

Besandung *f*, **Prüfung durch ~** sand test

Besan-mars *m* mizzentop **-mast** *m* mizzenmast

Besatz *m* stemming, tamping, relining (of furnace), braid, trimming, packing about an explosive charge **-streifen** *m* cap band, stripe

Besatzung *f* garrison, crew, complement, personnel **fliegende ~** flight crew

besäumen to edge, square, shear, hem, border, trim, square (sheets)

Besäum-maschine *f* trimming cutter **-säge** *f* trimming saw **-schere** *f* trimming shears

beschädigen to damage, impair, injure, mutilate, gall

beschädigt damaged

Beschädigung *f* damage, injury, mutilation

Beschädigungszeit *f* damage time

beschaffen to supply, procure, provide, get

Beschaffenheit *f* state, condition, nature, quality, character, composition **nach der ~** qualitative

beschaffenheitsmäßig qualitatively

Beschaffung *f* supply, providing, remittance, procurement **~ von Ausrüstungsmaterial** procurement of equipment **~ Versand und Prüfung** procurement, expediting and inspection

Beschaffungsamt *n* procurement office

beschäftigen to employ, occupy, concern **sich ~** to be busy or occupied, busy oneself

beschäftigt employed

Beschäftigung *f* occupation, business

Beschäftigungs-grad *m* activity **-losigkeit** *f* inactivity

beschalen to board

beschälen to peel

Beschallung *f* acoustic irradiation, radiate or cause sound or ultra-sound waves to act or impinge upon

Beschallungsgerät *n* sound or sonic appliance

beschalten to wire (up or for)

Beschaltung *f* wiring **vorder- (rück)seitige ~** surface (panel) wiring (of a switchboard)

Beschaltungsplan *m* wiring scheme or plan

beschatten to shadow, shade

Beschauer *m* observer

beschaufeln to manage with blade

beschaufeltes Rad bladed wheel (turbine)

Beschaufelung *f* blading, buckets or blades of a turbine

Bescheid *m* answer, reply, information, action (law) **abschlägiger ~** adverse action or decision, refusal, disallowing action (patent)

Bescheiddienst *m* changed number interception

bescheiden modest, humble

Bescheidenheit *f* modesty

Bescheid-gebühr *f* report charge **-leitung** *f* information trunk, intercepting trunk

bescheinen to shine upon, illuminate

bescheinigen to attest, certify

bescheren to shear, give

beschichten to emulsify, treat, coat (a film with emulsion), form a layer or a film, apply emulsion

Beschichtung *f* coating

Beschichtungs-kalander *m* coating calender **-loch** *n* drop-out (tape rec.) **-stoffe** *m pl* (emulsion) coating materials (photo.)

Beschicken *n*, **durch ~** by inserting

beschicken to load, charge, feed, fill, exhibit, expose

beschickte Leitung current-carrying line

Beschickung *f* loading, infeed, charging, burdening, charge, melting stock, burden, feed, quadrantal error, correction or compensation (in direction-finding work), radio compass calibration **~ die das Metall nicht zu strengflüssig macht** charge making the metal bath not too tough **~ auf gleiche Temperatur** reduction to equal temperature

Beschickungs-anlage *f* mechanical charger, charging equipment, feeding installation **-boden** *m* mixing shed (met.) **-bühne** *f* charging or loading platform **-gut** *n* melting stock, charge, burden **-kran** *m* charging crane **-material** *n* melting stock, charge, burden

Beschickungs-mulde *f* charging box **-oberfläche** *f* charging surface, stock line **-öffnung** *f* charging door or opening **-raum** *m* charging room **-rinne** *f* charging chute **-seite** *f* charging end **-trichter** *m* (Kohle) feed hopper **-vorrichtung** *f* charging device or appliance, feed unit **-wagen** *m* loading car

Beschienung *f* band equipment, rail, splints

beschießen to shell, bombard, fire on, bombard (with electrons, etc.) **der Länge nach ~** to enfilade, rake with fire

Beschießung *f* bombardment **~ mit Neutronen** neutron bombardment

Beschießungsschaden *m* bombardment damage

beschiffbar navigable

Beschilderung *f* marking, labeling

beschirmen to shield or cover

Beschirmung *f* protection

Beschirrung *f* harness

Beschlag *m* (Beschläge) metal fitings, hard ware; (Kisten) bond; (Rückstand) deposit; (auf Metall) tarnish; (Chem.) efflorescence; (Schimmel) mold, armature, horseshoeing, bloom, tarnish on glass, coating; (Zellenbau) metal fastening, mount(ing), garniture; (Außen-) layer; (Innen-) lining **mit ~ belegen** to seize, attach, arrest **in ~** under arrest **in ~ nehmen** to occupy, seize (by legal process), take over

Beschläge *m pl* sublimates, encrustations, metal fittings, hardware, fixtures

beschlagen to fit, cover, become coated, tarnish, film, oxidize, effloresce, give an incrustation, sheathe, mist, well up on, well-read, conversant with, fouling (photo) **mit Feuchtigkeit ~** to become covered with moisture **die Ware beschlägt** the goods sweat

Beschlagen *n* fog formation (on window) **~ der Lampenbirnen** age coating of lamp bulbs

Beschlagenheit *f* experience, alertness

Beschlag-klotz *m* packing block **-legung** *f* seizure, attachment **-nahme** *f* seizure, confiscation, expropriation, foreclosure, embargo, attachment **-nahmerecht** *n* right of attachment **-nehmen** to seize, confiscate **-schmied** *m* blacksmith **-teile** *n pl* fittings **-zeising** *f* gasket

Beschlagung *f* hooping

beschleichen to sneak up to, creep upon, stalk

beschleunigen to accelerate, hasten, speed up, rush, expedite, force

Beschleuniger *m* accelerator, catalyzer, catalyst, activator **chemischer ~** catalyst, catalyzer

Beschleuniger-pumpe *f* accelerating pump **-pumpenkolben** *m* mass-discharge piston **-regler** *m* acceleration regulator **-röhre** *f* accelerating tube **-wirkung** *f* accelerator activity

beschleunigt accelerated, speedy **-er Alterungsversuch** accelerated aging test **-er Ermüdungsversuch** *m* accellerated fatigue test **-er Fernverkehr** *m* combined-line and -recording service **-e Leistungsabnahme** emergency trip **-er Motor** *m* hooped-up engine **-es Teilchen** accelerated particle **-e Verbrennung** *f* accelerated combustion **-e Zuführung** high-speed feed

Beschleunigung *f* acceleration, speeding up **negative ~** deceleration, retardation

Beschleunigungsanlage accelerator **~ für hohe Energien** high-energy (particle) accelerator

Beschleunigungs-anode *f* second anode, second accelerator, second gun, gun anode **-aufnehmer** *m* acceleration pickup **-aufschaltung** *f* mixing ratio for angular acceleration signal in steering control of guided missiles **-einrichtung** *f* high-potential transformer and vacuum tube **-elektrode** *f* accelerator electrode **-erträglichkeit** *f* acceleration endurance

Beschleunigungs-feder *f* accelerator spring **-feld** *n* accelerating field **-formel** *f* acceleration formula **-fühler** *m* acceleration gauge **-fußhebel** *m* accelerator pedal **-geber** *m* (NF-Beschleunigungsgeber) L.F. acceleration pickup **-gitter** *n* accelerating grid, accelerator grid (cathode-ray tube), screen grid (of tetrode) **-gleichung** *f* equation of motion **-hebel** *m* accelerator pedal, linkage lever **-identitäten** *pl* acceleration identities **-integrationsgerät** *n* accelerometer

Beschleunigungs-kammer *f* accelerating chamber **-kennlinie** *f* acceleration characteristics (kinematics) **-kraft** *f* accelerative force **-kurve** *f* acceleration curve **-linse** *f* **aus zwei Lochelektroden** double-aperture accelerator lens **-los** accelerationless

Beschleunigungs-maschine *f* accelerator **-maße** *n pl* measures of acceleration **-messer** *m* accelerometer **-meßgerät** *n* accelerometer **-meßkopf** *m* electromagnetic accelerometer **-meßtisch** *m* acceleration-measuring table **-mittel** *n* accelerator **-möglichkeit** *f* pickup (of production) **-moment** *n* accelerating moment

Beschleunigungs-pedal *n* accelerator, foot feed **-pendel** *n* acceleration pickup pendulum **-phase** *f* acceleration period **-pumpe** *f* acceleration pump **-raum** *m* acceleration space **-rohr** *n* accelerating tube

Beschleunigungs-schreiber *m* recording accelerometer **-spannung** *f* accelerating voltage, gun potential, accelerator potential, beam voltage **-stange** *f* hurryup stick **-strecke** *f* distance of acceleration **-untersuchung** *f* acceleration or high speed test (on pilots) **-ventil** *n* acceleration control valve

Beschleunigungsverhalten des Motors throttle response of motor

Beschleunigungs-vermögen *n* maneuverability **-verträglichkeit** *f* adaptability to acceleration

Beschleunigungswicklung des Gulstadrelais acceleratiol coil of the Gulstad relay

Beschleunigungs-widerstand *m* forcing resistance **-wirkung** *f* acceleration effect **-zeiger** *m pl* acceleration instruments (aviation) **-zeit** *f* period of acceleration **-zentrum** *n* center of acceleration

beschließen to resolve, decide, decree, conclude, determine, vote

Beschluß *m* decision, decree, resolution, conclusion, close, action (of patent office), order (of a court of law) **~ fassen** ro decree **~ mit einfacher Mehrheit** resolution with bare majority

beschlußfähig forming a quorum

Beschlußfassung *f* (-nahme) coming to a decision

beschmieren (mit Fett) to grease, lubricate, oil, smear, daub

beschmutzen to soil, dirty

beschmutzt (verschmutzt) fouled

Beschmutzung *f* fouling

Beschneide-bank *f* dressing bench **-brett** *n* reglet **-glas** *n* trimming glass, print trimmer **-hobel** *m* plow knife, plow **-hobel** *m* edging planer, edger, trimming knife **-klotz** *m* trimming block or die **-maschine** *f* (automatic) cutter **-messer** *n* trimming knife, edging tool

beschneiden to cut, trim, clip, cut off, curtail, square, shear, cut smaller, shorten, fettle, prune (electr. lines)

Beschneiden eines Blechstapels *m* stack cutting

Beschneideschablone *f* trim or cutting pattern, template

Beschneidung *f* clipping (loss of initial or final speech sounds)

Beschnitt *m* trimming (trim)

beschnitten cut, trimmed **zu stark ~** bled (a pamphlet cut down too much) **-es Format** trimmed size **-e Platte** *f* plate cut to size

Beschnittsteg *m* side stick (print.)

beschnüren to tie (up), fasten with cords

beschottern, eine Straße ~ to gravel a street, ballast or turnpike a road

Beschotterung *f* metal, graveling, ballasting

beschränken to confine, restrict (to), reduce, limit, contract (shorten), hem in

beschränkt limited, bounded, restricted, confined **-e Sicht** low visibility

Beschränktheit *f* limitation

Beschränkung *f* restriction, restraint, limitation, confinement, reduction

beschreiben to describe

beschreibend descriptive

Beschreibung *f* description, portrayal, characterization, specification (of a patent), outline, sketch ~ **von Bildern auf Schirm** picture tracing, re-creation or delineation on screen **ausführliche** ~ detailed description **eingehende** ~ specification **weitgehende** ~ broad or detailed specification ~ **des Gegenstandes** (in Budgetlisten) description of asset

Beschreibungseinleitung *f* (Pat.) introduction to the specification

beschreiten to walk on, take a course

beschriften to label, designate, write on (something) **eine Zeichnung** ~ to letter a drawing

Beschriften *n* making a record or sound track upon, impressing a film or blank with acoustic actions ~ **im Elektrosignierverfahren** marking by the electro-marking method

Beschriftung *f* designation, label, lettering, inscription (legend) ~ **einer Zeichnung** legend, inscription, recording (on film)

Beschriftungsformel *f* formula of designation (or inscription)

beschroten to edge, trim (met.)

beschuhen, einen Pfahl ~ to shoe a pile

beschuldigen to charge (law), accuse

Beschuldigter *m* (the) accused

Beschuldigung *f* accusation

Beschuß-teilchen *n* bombarding particles

beschütten to pour on, cover with

beschützen to protect

Beschützung *f* protection

Beschwerde *f* complaint, difficulty, hardship, grievance, appeal, trouble, ailment ~ **einleiten** to complain, accuse ~ **erheben** to lodge a complaint

Beschwerde-abteilung *f* appeals department, Board of Appeal **-buch** *n* register of complaints **-einrede** *f* rejoinder (in an appeal) **-fähig** appellant **-gegner** *m* respondent **-gericht** *n* court of appeals

Beschwerde-ordnung *f* complaint (appeal) regulations **-schrift** *f* appellatory plaint, appeal papers **-stelle** *f* complaint section, complaint desk **-verfahren** *n* injunction method (patent), appeal action or procedure

beschweren to weight, load, burden; complain, **sich** ~ to complain

beschwerlich difficult, cumbersome, troublesome, complicated, intricate

Beschwerlichkeit *f* difficulty

beschwertes Papier charged paper

Beschwerung *f* weighting (of silk), loading, burdening, disturbance, annoyance, encumbrance, impedance

Beschwerungs-appretur *f* (-masse) weighting size **-mittel** *n* weighting or filling agent, loading material, filler **-rohr** *n*, **-stück** *n* counterpoise, counterweight

Beschwerwalze *f* tension roller

beschwingen to stimulate

beschwören to take an oath, sign an affidavit, declare under oath

beseelen to animate, enliven

besehen (Ware) to examine **sich** ~ to look at

beseitigen to eliminate, remove, obviate, neutralize (artil.), clear (faults) **eine Störung** ~ to clear a fault

Beseitigen *n* ~ **eines Wracks** raising or removal of a wreck ~ **von Eigenspannungen** (durch Erwärmen), strain relief ~ **von Hemmungen** immediate action (ordnance term)

Beseitigung *f* elimination, removal, settlement (of quarrels), clearing ~ **radioaktiver Abfälle** waste disposal (atom) ~ **störender Schirmaufladungen** elimination of disturbing screen charges ~ **von Sperren** clearing of obstacles

Beselersteg *m* trestle footbridge

Besen *m* broom, besom

Besen-borste *f* broom bristle **-stiel** *m* broom handle

besengen to burn slightly, singe

besetzen to occupy, garrison, man, ram, tamp, populate, to needle (with spikes) **ein Bohrloch** ~ to tamp a hole

besetzt attended, staffed, busy (teleph.), engaged, occupied, invaded ~ **halten** to hold or guard (a circuit) ~ **sein, durch eigenen Anruf** to be caller, line is busy by one's own call **als** ~ **kennzeichnen** to busy, mark engaged **eine Leitung** (oder eine Teilnehmerleitung) ~ **halten** to hold a circuit or a subscriber's line **-es Band** full band **-e Leitung** busy line **-er Platz** occupied position, staffed position **-e Schale** completed shell **-e Verbindungsleitung** busy trunk

Besetzt-anzeige *f* (optische) visual busy signal **-einrichtung** *f* make-busy arrangement **-erde** *f* busy earth **-fall** *m* engagement (teleph.) **-flackerzeichen** *n* engaged signal

besetzthalten einer Leitung to hold a circuit, holding a line

Besetzthaltung *f* holding a subscriber line (by toll operator) **selbsttätige** ~ automatic holding device

Besetzt-klinke *f* busy back jack, jack for busy tone **-lampe** *f* engaged lamp, busy lamp, visual busy lamp **-leistung** *f* blocked traffic **-machen** to hold or guard (a circuit), busy **-meldung** *f* busy signal or response **-prüfen** *n* (durch Berühren der Leitungsklinke mit der Stöpselspitze), busy test

Besetztprüfung *f* busy test, engaged test, checking ~ **mit Flackerzeichen** flashing signal ~ **mit Summerton** busy test with tone signal **akustische** ~ audible test **Knackgeräusch bei der** ~ engaged click **optische** ~ visual busy signal **optische** ~ **mit Druckknopf** visual engaged test with key control

Besetzt-relais *n* busy(-test) relay **-schauzeichen** *n* busy-signal light

Besetztsein *n* engagement, engaged (condition) **auf** ~ **prüfen** to verify a busy report

Besetztsignal *n* engaged signal

Besetztspannung *f* engaged battery, busying potential ~ **anlegen** to establish the busy condition, apply busying potential

Besetzt-stellung *f* busy condition **-ton** *m* busy (back) tone

Besetztzeichen *n* busy signal, busy-back signal (teleph.) ~ **belegen** to mark engaged, busy, seize **optisches** ~ visual engaged signal

Besetztzustand *m* busy (engaged) position, busy condition

Besetzung *f* staff, personnel, occupation, hard facing, cast (moving picture)
Besetzungsgrad der Banden degree of filling of bands
Besetzungsverbot der vollbesetzten Quantenzustände exclusion principle of occupied electron states
Besetzungs-verhältnisse *n pl* size of audience (in a playhouse) **-vorschrift** *f* occupation rule **-wahrscheinlichkeit** *f* occupancy probability
Besetzungszahl *f* occupation (phonon) number ~ **der Elektronen in einem Niveau** extent to which level is populated by electrons
besichtigen to inspect, view, survey, examine
Besichtigung *f* inspection, examination, surveying, review
Besichtigungs-fenster *n*, **-loch** *n* sighthole (furnaces, etc.) **-panel** *n* inspection panel
besiedeln to colonize, settler
Besiedlung *f* colonization, settlement
besiegeln to (affix a) seal, make final, consummate
Besitz *m* possession, ownership ~ **ergreifen** to take possession, seize, appropriate
Besitzeinweisung *f* assignment of ownership, transfer of possession
besitzen to own, possess
besitzend concentric
Besitz-entziehung *f* dispossession, expropriation
Besitzer *m* owner, possessor, holder
Besitz-ergreifung *f* occupancy, seizure **-nahme** *f* taking possession **-stand** *m* ownership **-steuer** *f* property tax **-urkunde** *f* title deed
Besitztum *n* property, possessions
Besohlanstalt *f* sole-repairing factory
besohlen to sole
Besohlung *f* (vulkanisieren) topcap
Besoldung *f* payment, pay, wages
Besoldungs-dienstalter *n* seniority for computation of pay **-einbehaltung** *f* detention of pay **-einbuße** *f* loss of pay **-gesetz** *n* pay law **-vorschrift** *f* pay regulation **-wesen** *n* pay and allowance administration
besonder particular, special **-e Anordnung** administrative details in combat orders **-e Dienstzweige** special services **-e Einflüsse** interior ballistic factors **bei -em Einsatz** on active duty during special commitment **-es Leitungsbündel** individual trunk group **-e und Witterungseinflüsse** exterior and interior ballistics
besondern, im ~ especially
Besonderheit *f* peculiarity, particularity, property, speciality, specialty, characteristic, feature
Besonderheiten der Konstruktion special design features
besonders particular, peculiar, special, in particular ~ **starke Linie** enhanced line
Besonnenheit *f* sobriety
Besonnung *f* insolation
besorgen to procure, get, take care of, provide
Besorgnis *f* alarm
Besorgung *f* procurement
bespannen to cover (as a wing with fabric), (mit Saiten) string
Bespannerei *f* covering or fabric shop
Bespann-fahrzeug *n* trailer **-stoff** *m* fabric
bespannt horse-drawn, covered
Bespannung *f* fabric, covering (aviation), draft horses, wing covering, baffle cloth, packing (print.) ~ **einer Batterie** battery horses ~ **der Filtertrommel** filter drum cover **verstellbare** ~ **eines Führersitzes** covering for cockpit
Bespannungs-lack *m* airplane dope **-stoff** *m* (airplane) fabric, covering material
bespicken to stud
Bespiegelung *f* reflection
bespinnen to cover wire (with cotton, etc.)
bespitzen, einen Stein ~ to hew an ashlar with the pickhammer
besponnen covered (wire), braided **-er Draht** spun over wire **-es Kabel** *n* wrapped cable
besprechen to discuss, talk over, arrange, control; (Sender) to voice-modulate
Besprechung *f* discussion, talk, conversation, conference, critique, voice control ~ **mit Eisendrossel** modulation by voice action with magnetic modulator ~ **einer Röhre** voice control
Besprechungs-anlage *f* sound pickup outfit **-bericht** *m* conference report **-exemplar** *n* review copy **-mikrophon** *n* ordinary microphone, sound pickup microphone, sound collector **-niederschrift** *f* minutes **-punkt** *m* point where sound action is impressed **-raum** *m* sound studio (radio), conference room
besprengen to sprinkle, spray, water
Besprengen *n* sprinkling
bespritzen to sprinkle, spatter
besprochen speech-modulated, voice-actuated **-er Modulator** voice-impressed or voice-actuated modulator
besprühen to spray
Besprühmittel *n* spraying medium
bespulen to branch off, coil-load, pupinize, provide with winding, load a cable
bespult -e Leitung loaded transmission line **-er Widerstand** cryotron
bespülen, mit Öl ~ to supply with oil
Bespulung *f* coil loading, pupinization, provision for winding coil or loading means ~ **eines Relais** relay windings **leichte** ~ extra light loading **mittlere** ~ medium-weight loading **sehr leichte** ~ **für Musikübertragung** program circuit loading ~ **eines Relais** relay windings
bespült wetted, watered
Bespulungsplan *m* loading scheme
Bespurungsmaschine *f* tracking apparatus
Bessel-Funktion erster Art Bessel function of the first kind
Besselsche Funktion Bessel's function
Bessemer-anlage *f* Bessemer plant, Bessemer installation or mill **-betrieb** *m* Bessemer work or operation plant
Bessemerbirne *f* Bessemer converter **-stahl** *m* Bessemer converter steel, Bessemer steel **-verfahren** *n* Bessemer converter process
Bessemerei *f* Bessemer foundry, Bessemer plant
Bessemer-eisen *n* Bessemer iron or steel **-flußeisen** *n* Bessemer ingot iron, Bessemer low-carbon steel
bessemern to Bessemerize
Bessemern *n* Bessemerizing
Bessemer-roheisen *n* Bessemer pig iron **-schmelze** *f* Bessemer blow, Bessemer heat
Bessemerstahl *m*, **saurer** ~ acid Bessemer steel

Bessemerverfahren *n* Bessemer (converting) process, air-refining process, pneumatic process

bessere Sorte superior grade

bessern to mend, improve **sich ~** to improve

Besserung *f* improvement, betterment, recovery, correction (law)

best- most effective

bestallen to install, invest (with)

Bestand *m* stock, amount, durability, stability, inventory, existence, duration, supply, strength (of a unit), continuance, consistency, balance, cash in hand, stand (forest), value, reserve, holding **stofflicher ~** material constituents

Bestände *pl* material stocks **~ an Verpackungen** packing stocks **~ an verpackten Waren** packed stocks **~ an unverpackten Waren** bulk stocks

beständig fast (colors), steady, constant, stable, resistant, durable, permanent, continuous, invariable, steadfast, lasting, settled, proof **~ gegen physikalische Einflüsse** exposure-proof material **kälte ~** antifreezing **rost ~** stainless **-e Phase** stable phase

Beständiger *m* stabilizer

Beständigkeit *f* constancy, invariability, continuity, permanence, stability, steadiness, durability, persistence, constancy, perseverance, resistance **chemische ~** chemical resistance; (mechanische) **~** (mechanical) properties **~ der Frequenz** frequency stability **~ verleihendes Mittel** stabilizer

Beständigmachen *n* stabilization

Bestandsaufnahme *f* inventory, stocktaking **physische oder effektive ~** physical verification or stocktaking **~ durch Zählung** physical verification

Bestands-aufstellungen *pl* stock records **-bewegung nach Sorten** stock movements by grades **-buch** *n* inventory, stock or store book **-karte** *f* balance card, map of stock (forest) **-konten** *pl* stock accounts **-liste** *f* inventory of supplies, equipment, property book **-meldung** *f* stock statement **-nachweisung** *f* stock inventory, stock report

Bestandteil *m* constituent, ingredient, component part, substance, mater **brennbarer ~** combustible or inflammable constituent **fremder ~** foreign matter or substance **unverbrennlicher ~** incombustible constituent **wesentlicher ~** element

Bestandteile *m pl*, **in seine ~ auflösen** to disintegrate **mineralische ~** mineral matter

Bestandteillisten *pl* parts lists

Bestandsüberprüfungen und Bestätigung stock checking and certification

Bestandsübersicht *f*, **monatliche ~** monthly stock summary

Bestands-unterlagen *pl* stock records **-verminderung** *f* stock decrease

bestätigen to confirm

bestätigte Bestellung official confirmatory order

Bestätigung *f* confirmation, statement, acknowledgment **betriebliche ~** routine acknowledgment

Bestätigungsurteil *f* confirmatory decision

bestäuben to dust, powder; (m. Flüssigkeit) spray

Bestäubungs-apparat *m* dusting apparatus **-gerät** *n* powder outfit **-vorrichtung** *f* dust kit

Bestauslese *f* selection (of the fittest)

Bestechung *f* bribe, bribery, graft (slang)

Besteck *n* instruments (med.), cutlery, instrument case, position, sight (astron.), dead reckoning, ship's position, set of instruments or utensils fix (navig.) **-berechnung** *f* dead reckoning **-breite** *f* latitude of fix, reckoned latitude

bestecken to stick on

Besteck-fehler *m* error in fix or reckoning **-führung** *f* dead reckoning **-länge** *f* longitude of fix, reckoned longitude **-ort** *m* position of fix or reckoning, point of reckoning **-rechnung** *f* fixing a position, reckoning (ship's position by dead reckoning), dead reckoning **-stanzen** *f pl* blanking dies

Besteckungskosten *f* trimming expense

Besteckversetzung *f* difference between dead and observed reckoning

bestehen to exist, be composed of, endure, stand, pass an examination **~ auf** to insist on **~ in** to consist in

Bestehen *n* existence, validity

bestehend consisting (of) **aus Eisen ~** iron **aus zwei Metallen ~** bimetallic **aus einem Stück ~** (mit etwas), integral

bestehende (geführte, laufende) **Konten** current accounts in operation

besteigen to climb, board, go on board, mount, emplane **ein Flugzeug ~** to emplane

besteinen to stone (pavement)

Bestell-angaben *pl* details for ordering **-bar** deliverable (as mail) **-buch** *n* order book

bestellen to order, (telegrams) deliver (up), assign (a representative), cultivate (a field)

Besteller *m* customer, purchaser, messenger, calling subscriber (teleph.)

Bestell-formular *n* order form **-gebühr** *f* charge fee, postage, delivery expense **-liste** *f* code number, catalogue number, purchase order number **-maß** *n* specified dimension **-nummer** *f* requisition number **-schein** *m* order sheet or form, requisition

Bestellung *f* order, delivery, assignment, cultivation, requisition, indent **auf ~ gemacht** custom-made **auf ~ machen** to custom-make

Bestellungsabteilung *f* procurement department, purchasing department **-urkunde** *f* certificate of appointment

Bestell-vordruck *m* order form, order sheet **-wesen** *n* ordering **-wort** *n* code word **-zeichen** *n* ordering reference **-zeit** *f* delivery period, time of ordering, sowing time **-zettel** *m* order form

bestenfalls at best

bestens in the best way, very much

besteuern to tax

Besteuerung *f* taxation

Bestform-Glas *n* bestform lens

bestielen to helve, equip with a handle

Bestiften *n* studding

bestiftet studded **-e Schlagwelle** *f* picking shaft

bestimmbar predictable, estimable, definable, subject to influence **nicht im voraus ~** unpredictable

bestimmen to determine, state, analyze, decide, stipulate, fix, define, specify, plot (curve)

bestimmt fixed, definite, certain, precise, specific,

determined, decided ~ **für** meant to, intended for, destined for ~ **sein für** adapted **-er Zeitpunkt** specified date, predetermined moment
Bestimmtheit *f* precision, definiteness, certainty, reasonable assumption
Bestimmung *f* (Verfügung) disposition; (Ermittlung) determination; (Chem.) definition; (zahlenmäßige ~) evaluation; (Vorschrift) regulation, direction; (Vertrag) term, stipulation; (Beruf) vocation, analysis, specification, finding, designation, destination, purpose, indication, clause, provision ~ **des Flammpunktes** flash test ~ **der Gesprächsdauer** timing of calls (teleph.) ~ **der Leistung auf Grund des Ladedruckes** manifold density method ~ **des Stockpunktes** pour test ~ **des Trübpunktes und des Erstarrungspunktes** cloud and pour test ~ **des Wirkungsgrades** measurement of efficiency
Bestimmungen *f pl* specifications, code, ordinance, conditions, terms **amtliche ~ für die Zivilluftfahrt** civil air regulations
Bestimmungs-anstalt *f* terminating office **-apparat** *m* apparatus meter
Bestimmungs-dreieck *n*, **schlankes ~** slender definition triangle
Bestimmungs-flugplatz *m* airport of destination **-funkstelle** radiostation of destination **-gemäß** as authorized according **-gleichung** *f* defining equation, equation of condition, qualifying or definitive equation **-größe** *f* defining quantity, determinant, value to be determined
Bestimmungs-hafen *m* port of destination **-kontrolle** *f* measurement control **-land** *n* country of destination **-methode** *f* method of determination, method of analysis **-ort** *m* (point of) destination, destination station **-stelle** *f* station of destination **-stück** *n* characteristic, factor, parameter, operating datum, determinant **-verfahren** *n* determination procedure
Bestlast *f* economical rating or load
Bestleistung *f* record, best performance **eine ~ aufstellen** to set a record
Bestmelierte *f* (Kohlensorte) best quality coal
bestmelierte Eßkohle a short-flaming semibituminous coal of selected sizes
bestoßen to slot, trim, shave (print.)
Bestoßen der Schnitzelmesser sloting of the knives
Bestoß-feile *f* planing file **-hobel** *m* trimming plane
Bestoßmaschine *f* wood trimmer ~ **für Schnitzelmesser** slotting machine for paring knives or choppers
bestrafen to punish
Bestrafung *f* punishment
bestrahlen to irradiate, illuminate, light, expose
Bestrahlung *f* insolation, exposure to (solar) radiation, irradiation, process of irradiation, illumination, radiation ~ **fester Körper** irradiation of solids
Bestrahlungs-anlage (sand) blasting equipment **-biologie** radiobiology **-dosis** *f* exposure to radiation **-erholung** *f* radiation annealing **-feld** *n* radiation field **-intensität** *f* radiation intensity **-kanal** *m* beam hole
Bestrahlungs-lampen *pl* irradiation lamps **-nachweis** *m* detection of beta radiation **-schäden in Festkörpern** radiation damage in solids **-system** *n* irradiation system **-tubus** *m* localizer, treatment cone, X-ray therapy applicator **-zweck** *m* purpose of irradiation, of illumination, or of exposure to rays **-zeit** *f* time of exposure
Bestrebung *f* effort, endeavor ~ **fördern** to sponsor
bestreichbar variable, capable of spreading, brushing, or greasing **-er Wellenbereich** variable wave length **kontinuierlich -er Wellenbereich** continuously variable wave length
bestreichen to coat, smear, paint, spread, stroke (magnet), sweep over, brush (in chilling), reek, sweep (fire), rake (fire), enfilade, graze, cover, wipe (over), sweep out, scan, explore (the picture area or screen with beam, pencil, or spot), cover (a range), contact; (Luft) to sweep (air) ~ **mit** to smear, spread, grease, brush, paint
Bestreichungs-bogen *m* arc of fire or of training **-winkel** *m* angle of traverse
bestreikt strikebound
bestreitbar disputable, contestable
bestreiten to contest ~ (Kosten) to defray
bestreuen to strew, sprinkle, powder, spread over
bestrichen passed **-er Raum** danger zone, beaten zone **-er Raum der Kerngabe** effective beaten zone, 85 per cent of total zone
bestroppen to strop
Bestrüppung *f* bush (in sheave of bar)
Bestückung *f* armament, guns, ordnance ~ (eines Gerätes mit Röhren oder Transistoren) complement, line-up
Bestürzung *f* alarm, consternation, dismay, perplexity, stupefaction, confusion, abashment **in ~ versetzen** to startle
Best-verfahren *f* method of achieving the optimum of production **-wert** *m* optimum, most favorable, best, optimum value **-wirkungsgrad** *m* optimum efficiency
Bestzeit-programm *n* optimally coded program (info proc.) **-programmierung** *f* minimum-access programming
Besucher *m* visitor **-terrasse** *f* public gallery
Besuchskarte *f* business (calling) card
besudeln to dirty, sully, defile, deface, contaminate (soil)
Beta-aktivitäten *f pl* beta radiation (sources) **-abschreckung** *f* beta quench **-dickenmesser** *m* beta-absorption gauge **-eisen** *n* beta iron
Betäfelung mit Platten dressing with slabs
Betafit *m* blomstrandite, betafite
Betain *n* betaine
betakeln to rig
Betakelung *f* rigging (of ship or airplane)
Betanaphtol-eisfarben *pl* beta-naphthol-ice colors **-natron** *n* sodium salt of beta-naphthol **-präparation** *f* beta-naphthol preparation
Betanaphtylamin betanaphthylamine
betanken to fill up
Betankung *f* refuelling
Betankungs-flugzeug *n* (aviat.) tanker transport **-kuppelung** *f* filler neck coupling rockets **-leitung** *f* filling hose **-öffnung** *f* fuel inlet **-schlauch** *m* filler hose **-stutzen** *m* filler neck, shaped filler pipe for fuel **-ventil** *n* oxygen filler

valve
Beta-schirm *m* beta screen **-spektrum** *n* beta-ray spectrum
betasten to touch, feel, handle, palpate
Betastrahlen *m pl* beta rays **-schutzscheibe** *f* beta-ray protection screen **-schutztischaufsatz** *m* beta-ray protectiontable top
Beta-strahler *m* beta emitter, beta radiation **-strahlspektrometer** *m* beta-ray spectrometer **-strahlung** *f* beta-ray emission **-teilchen** *n* beta particle
Betastung *f* sense of touch, palpation
betätigen to manipulate, operate, actuate, prove, manifest, energize, start, control, set free, release trigger
Betätigerkolben *m* control piston
betätigt actuated, operated, manipulated **durch Gestänge ~** operated by means of tie rods **durch Kabel ~** operated by cables **zwangsläufig ~** positively actuated
Betätigung *f* manipulation, operation, actuation, control, activity **~ nur wenn Maschine frei** operate only when engine in clear **doppelte ~** (Lockheed) duo-service
Betätigungs-flügel *m* tail of the wicket (weirs) **-glieder** (elastische **~**) resilient interponent members **-hebel** *m* actuating lever, linkage lever, control lever **-impuls** *m* activating impulse
Betätigungs-knopf *m* motion (manipulating), head, button, knob, control head; (für Schalter zum Ziehen) operating knob (for pulltype switch) **-kraft** *f* operating force, control force **-nocken** *m* trip stop **-organ** *n* actuator, actuating appliance
Betätigungs-schalter *m* actuation switch, trip switch, mechanically operated switch **-spule** *f* working, tripping or differential coil **-stange** *f* operating bar, operating rod, actuating strut **-übertragungsfunktion** *f* actuating transfer function **-vorrichtung** *f* control mechanism **-winkel** *m* buffer **-zylinder** *m* operating cylinder
betatopisch betatopic
Betatron *n* betatron **-elektronenschleuder** *f* doughnut tube **-kern** *m* betatron core **-magnet** *n* betatron magnet **-schwingungen** *pl* betatron-oscillations **-strahlung** *f* betatron radiation
betäuben to anesthetize, stun, deafen
Betäubung *f* black-out effect
Betäubungsmittel *n* anesthetic, narcotic
betauen to bedew, dew
Beta-umwandlung *f* beta transformation, beta process
Beta-Uran *n* beta-uranium
Beta-Uranophan *n* beta-uranophane, beta-uranotile
Betazerfall *m* beta decay, beta disintegration
Betazerfalls-elektron *n* beta-decay electron **-energie** *f* beta-disintegration energy
beteeren to tar
beteiligen, sich ~ to participate, take part, partake
beteiligt concerned, intersted
Beteiligter *m* accessory, legal partner, party concerned, interested, or involved
Beteiligung *f* participation, share
Beteiligungen *pl* investments
Beteiligungszahl *f* quota
beteuern to assert, protest
Beteuerung *f* assertion, assurance
Bethe-Effekt *m* Lamb shift
Bethel-Kreosot-Imprägnierverfahren *n* Bethel process of creosote impregnation
Bethe-Weizäcker oder Kohlenstoffzyklus carbon-cycle, carbon nitrogene cycle
Beting *f* bitt, carrick bitt **einen Törn um die ~ nehmen** to bitt
betitelt titled, entitled, headed
Beton *m* concrete **aus ~ bestehend** concrete **den ~ verkleiden** to coat the concrete **armierter, bewehrter ~** reinforced concrete **gestampfter ~** rammed concrete **vorgespannter ~** pre-stressed concrete
Beton-abschirmung concrete shield **-armierdraht** *m* concrete reinforcing wire **-bahn** *f* concrete strip **-balken** *m* concrete slab, beam, or girder **-bau** *m* concrete construction or building **-bauten** *m pl* concrete structures **-bauwerk** *n* concrete structure **-bedeckung** *f* concrete cover **-beschuß** *m* probe proof of concrete **-bettung** *f* concrete base, foundation, or bed **-block** *m* concrete block **-Bogenstaumauer** *f* concrete arch dam **-bombe** *f* concrete bomb **-bordstein** *m* concrete kerb
Beton-bruch *m* concrete fracture, concrete break **-brücke** *f* concrete bridge **-bunker** *m* concrete bunker or pillbox **-decke** *f* concrete floor, (runway) concrete apron **-deckplatte** *f* concrete cover **-deckung** *f* concrete covering or shelter **-deformationsgeber** *m* concrete deformation pick-up **-eisen** *m* reinforcing iron (for concrete) **-eisenschere** *f* shearing machine for cutting reinforcement of concrete **-fertigpfahl** *m* precast-concrete pile **-fuge** *f* (concrete) joint **-gosse** *f* concrete channel
betonen to emphasize, accentuate, lay stress on
Beton-fläche *f* concrete area **-fundament** *n* concrete bed or foundation **-fußboden** *m* concrete floor **-gestell** *n* concrete support **-gewölbe** *n* concrete arch
betonieren to (reinforce with) concrete
Betonieren *n* concreting, concretion
betoniert built of concrete, reinforced with concrete
Beton-kasten *m* concrete box **-kipper** *m* concrete buggy **-kübel** *m* skip with or for concrete **-maschine** *f* concrete mixer
Betonmasse *f* concrete mass **erdfeuchte ~** damp concrete mass
Beton-mast *m* concrete pole **-mischer** *m* **-mischmaschine** *f*, **-mischwerk** *n* concrete mixer
betonnen to buoy
Betonnung *f* setting or planting of beacons
Beton-panzer *m* concrete shield **-pfahl** *m* concrete pile **-pfeiler** *m* concrete column **-pfeilerstaumauer** concrete buttress dam **-pflaster** *n* concrete paving **-platte** *f* concrete slab **-plattenbelag** *m* concrete slab paving **-presse** *f* concrete press **-prüfmaschine** *f* concrete testing machine **-pumpe** *f* concrete pump
Beton-rammpfahl *m* concrete pile **-rohr** *n* concrete pipe **-rostplatte** *f* concrete grillage **-säule** *f* concrete pillar or support **-schicht** *f* layer of concrete **-schirm** concrete shield **-schotter** *m* gravel for concrete mixing **-schwergeschwichtsmauer** *f* concrete gravity dam **-seilspule** *f* cast-in-concrete current-limiting reactor **-sockel** *m*

concrete foundation
Betonsohle *f* concrete floor **Verzahnung der ~** key (river weirs)
Beton-sperre *f* concrete obstacle **-spule** *f* concrete reactor **-stärke** *f* thickness of concrete **-stampfer** *m* concrete ram **-stein** *m* concrete block, artificial stone **-stirnplatten** *f pl* concrete plates **-straße** *f* concrete road
Betonstraßendecke *f*, **gedichtete ~** concrete road surface padded down **profilgerechte ~** concrete road surface true to profile **wellenfreie ~** concrete road surface without undulations
Beton-turm *m* concrete turret **-ummantelung** *f* concrete jacket
Betonung *f* emphasis, accentuation, action or stimulus (brought upon)
Betonungs-anzeiger *m* stress lamp (acoust.) **-zeichen** *n* stress mark
Beton-unterstand *m* concrete dugout, concrete shelter **-verarbeitung** *f* concrete working, concrete treatment **-wehr** *n* concrete weir **-werk** *n* concrete work, concrete fortification **-werkstein** *m* concrete ashlar **-zuschlag** *m* concrete aggregate **-zuschlagstoff** *m* balast
Betracht *m* consideration, respect **in ~ ziehen** to take into consideration, allow for
betrachten to contemplate, regard, consider, view, examine
beträchtlich considerable, important
Betrachtung *f* visual observation, observation, viewing, consideration, reflection, view, analysis **unmittelbare ~** direct viewing
Betrachtungs-abstand *m* viewing distance **-apparat** *m* viewing apparatus, kinetoscope **-basis** *f* observation base **-einrichtung** *f* viewing box **-lupe** *f* observation magnifier **-mikroskop für Negative** negative viewing microscope **-parallaxe** *f* observation parallax
Betrachtungs-richtung *f* sight line, line or direction of regard **-schirm** *m* Röntgen screen (X ray) **-stellung** *f* observing position of a photograph (positive position) **-system** *n* visual system **-tisch** *m* film-viewing machine **-verhältnis** *n* aspect ratio **-winkel** *m* viewing angle **-zeichen** *n* reference letter, reference numeral, symbol
Betrag *m* amount, sum, total, value, magnitude, modulus **~** (Mass), rate or percentage **~ der Doppelbrechung** birefringence **~ und Phase** magnitude and phase **der fällige ~** amount due
betragen to amount to **sich ~** to behave
Betragen *n* behavior, demeanor, conduct
Beträger *m* transformer
Betrag(s)-abgleich *m* quantity balance **-feld** *n* amount field
betrauen to entrust with
beträufeln to besprinkle
betraut entrusted
Betrauung *f* charge trust
Betreff *m* reference, regard, concern, re (on documents and letters)
betreffen to pertain to, strike, attack
betreffend concerning, with reference to, respective, regarding, in re
betreiben to run, work, conduct, operate, energize, exploit **mit Arbeitsstrom ~** to work or operate on open circuit **aus einer Batterie ~** to run by or form a battery **mit Ruhestrom ~** to operate on closed circuit **nach einem selbsttätigen System ~** to operate on an automatic system
betreten to tread or enter upon, step on
Betretung *f* entrance, entry
betreuen to take care of, attend, look after
Betreuung *f* maintenance, attendance
Betreuungsabteilung *f* welfare unit, morale unit
Betrieb *m* (Leitung) management, running, operation; (Unternehmen) business, enterprise, firm, concern; (Fabrik) factory, manufacturing plant; (Werkstatt) workshop; (Herstellungsgang) manufacture; (Arbeitsweise) operation, working; (Betriebsamkeit) activity, performance, exploitation, traffic, practice, plant, mill, shop, trade, establishment, service, duty (of a machine)
Betrieb, A-B- ~ A-board toll operation **A- und B- ~, im Fernverkehr** *m* A-board toll traffic **~ über A- und B-Plätze** A-board toll operation **~ mit erzwungener Erregung** constrained current operation **~ mit natürlicher Erregung** free current operation **außer ~ befindliche Leitung** dead line
Betrieb, ~ über Ortsverbindungsleitungen local interoffice trunking **~ auf den Privatleitungen** private-wire service **durch Störung außer ~ gesetzt** disturbed **~ mit selbsttätiger hörbarer Zeichengebung für die Beamtin des Ankunftsplatzes** straight-forward operation
Betrieb, den ~ aufnehmen to make the morning circuit test **außer ~ setzen** to put out of gear, out of action, service, operation **gemischter ~** mixed system **im ~** in gear, in service, on, working, in action **in ~ sein** to run, work, be in operation
Betrieb, in ~ setzen to set to work, put into service, start, exploit **wieder in ~ setzen** to reopen **intermittierender ~** discontinuous running **aus dem ~ ziehen** to withdraw from service
betrieben driven **~ aus** run from **~ mit Motor** power-driven
betrieblich operational, operative, functional, working, concerning actual use in service **-er Mangel** *m* operational snag **-e Mitbestimmung** joint consultation of management and labor force
Betriebs- industrial **-abrechnung** *f* cost accounting **-abteilung** *f* operations section, management, service section, production department **-abwicklung** *f* handling (operating methods) **-amt** *n* operations office **-angaben** *f pl* shop data **-anlage** *f* plant, machinery, equipment, installation **-anleitung** *f* operating instructions
Betriebs-annehmlichkeiten *f pl* smooth operation **-anstalten** (beim Zoll) bonded plants **-anweisung** *f* maintenance instructions, directions, instructions to operator **-apparat** *m* working set, working instrument **-appell** *m* collection in plant **-art** *f* service, drive, method of operation, duty (of a machine) **-artenschalter** *m* operating switch, function selector switch, performance switch **-arzt** *m* factory or plant physician
Betriebs-ausdruck *m* technical or shop term **-ausgaben** *f pl* operating expenses **-ausrüstung** *f* installation accessories, shop or running equipment **-auswerter** *m* traffic analyst **-bean-**

spruchung *f* service conditions, shop condition or requirement, service stress, operating load **-beanspruchungslisten** *pl* rating sheets

Betriebsbedingungen *f pl* operating, working or service condition(s), plant condition

Betriebs-begehung *f* inspection tour **-behälter** *m* service tank, feed tank **-belastung** *f* working load, live load **-bereich von Motoren** working range of motors **-bereit** ready for work **-bereitschaft** *f* readiness for use, proper functioning, operating condition

Betriebs-bericht *m* operating statement **-besichtigung** *f* visit to the works **-bestellschein** *m* factory order blank **-bestimmungen** *f. pl* regulations for plant operation **-blatt** *n* service bulletin, instructions **-blind** having a onetrack mind **-bremse** *f* service brake **-brüche** *m pl* service fractures **-brücke** *f* service bridge **-buch** *n* station logbook, station log register **-budget** *n* operating budget

Betriebs-chemiker *m* industrial chemist, works chemist **-dampf** *m* process steam **-dämpfung** *f* operative attenuation, effective attenuation, line losses, loss factor **-daten** *pl* operating conditions, working data **-datenschieber** *m* computer for flight data **-datentafel** *f* data card **-dauer** *f* time of operation, lenght of operation, working time **-dienst** *m* traffic department (teleph. or teleg.)

Betriebs-dienstleistung *f* load (of men or machinery) **-direktion** *f* works management **-direktor** *m* works superintendent, managing director, production manager **-drehzahl** *f* normal speed **-druck** *m* operating or working pressure or tension

betriebseigene Programmierung open shop ~ **Prüfungen** internal audits ~ **Untersuchungsmethoden** company methods

Betriebs-eigengewicht *n* service deadweight **-eigenschaften** *pl* operating characteristics, working qualities **-einheit** *f* operations unit **-einnahmen** *pl* operating income, gross receipts **-einrichtung** *f* operating installation, operating device or facilities, plant **-empfänger** *m* auxiliary wireless-telegraph receiver, commercial receiver **-erfahrung** *f* practical experience, operating experience

Betriebs-erfordernis *n* service requirement **-ergebnis** *n* operating result **-erweiterung** *f* extension of works **-factor** *m* traffic factor **-fähig** clear, perfect, in (good) working order, operative, in running order, operable, workable

Betriebsfähigkeit *f* working order, clearness **Prüfung auf** ~ clear test

Betriebsfaktor (effektiver) operating ratio

Betriebsfälle *m pl* industrial instances **Leistung in allen vorkommenden Betriebsfällen** all-around performance

Betriebs-feld *n* field of operation, compartment of a set in a guided missile **-fehler** operational error

Betriebsfernsprech-anlage *f* service telephone plant **-leitung** *f* service telephone line

betriebsfertig ready for use, for service, for operation, for the road ~ **machen** to tune up (engine) **-e Magnetfeldröhre** packaged magnetron **-es Programm** running program

Betriebsfestigkeitsversuch *m* serviceability test

-forschung *f* production research **-fortsetzungsmöglichkeit** *f* fall-back possibility

betriebsfremde Programmierung closed shop ~ **Prüfer** external auditors ~ **Revisionen** external audits

Betriebsfrequenz *f* normal frequency, operating frequency (electronics)

betriebsführend managing **-e Anstalt** controlling office **-e Beamtin** controlling operator **-e Zentrale** controlling office

Betriebs-führer *m* (general) manager, acting manager **-führung** *f* (plant) management **-funkenlänge** *f* length of operation spark **-funkspruch** *m* ordinary radio message (no priority) **-gas** *n* fuel gas **-gegendruck** *m* working back pressure **-geheimnis** *n* trade secret, shop secret **-geschwindigkeit** *f* (commercial) working speed, operating speed

Betriebs-gespräch *n* speech channel **-gewicht** *n* service weight, weight loaded, weight in running order **-gipfelhöhe** *f* service ceiling (aviat.) **-güte** *f* grade or quality of service **-hebel** *m* operating lever **-hindernd** acting impedimentally upon operation

Betriebshöhe *f* operational altitude **der ~ entsprechender Unterdruck** altitude depression

Betriebs-ingenieur *m* manufacturing engineer, works engineer, plant engineer **-inspektion** *f* motor-transport inspection **-instandhaltung** plant maintenance

Betriebskapazität *f* mutual capacity, wire-to-wire capacity ~ **einer Doppel- oder Viererleitung** mutual capacitance or capacity of a pair of a phantom ~ **der Viererkreise** pair-to-pair capacity

Betriebs-kapital *n* working capital **-kennzahlen** *pl* operating figures or characteristics **-kennzeichen** *n* operating signal **-klar** in order, ready for operation **-klima** *n* shop morale **-kompanie** *f* operating company, airfield ground staff, ground crew **-kondensator** *m* motor operating capacitor, running capacitor **-konto** (Ertragsrechnung) trading account **-kontrolle** *f* control of operation **-kontrollfraktometer** process vapor fractometer

Betriebs-korrosionsversuch *m* service corrosion test **-kosten** *pl* working costs, factory and manufacturing costs, running charge, operating costs **-kraft** *f* utilities, motive power **-kraftabteilung** *f* utilities department **-labor** *n* refinery laboratory **-last** *f* consumable load **-laufzeit** *f* delay or over-all transmission time, time of propagation **-lautsprecheranlage** *f* works or plant public-address system

Betriebs-lebensdauer *f* operational life **-leistung** *f* service performance, production, output, operating or manufacturing efficiency **-leiter** *m* master mechanic, superintendent, manager, technical director **-leitung** *f* plant or shop management **-luft** *f* air draught **-magnet** *n* running magneto **-mann** *m* operating man **-mannschaft** *f* operating crew

betriebsmäßig workable, commercial **-e Verwendung** operative use

Betriebsmeister *m* chief operator, foreman **technischer** ~ engineering superintendent

Betriebs-merkmale *n pl* operating characteristics **-meßgerät** *n* industrial measuring instrument

Betriebsmittel *n pl* rolling stock, machinery materials **-charakteristika** *pl* utility characteristics **-rohrleitungen** *pl* utility piping **-vorbereitung** *f* preparation of production facilities **-zeit** *f* available machine time, available process time

Betriebs-oberingenieur *m* superintendent, senior engineer **-ölfüllung** *f* quantity of oil in engine necessary for operation **-ordnung** *f* operating regulations **-pause** *f* interval, stoppage, shutdown **-periode** *f* period of service **-personal** *n* operating force or staff

Betriebs-plan *m* plan of operations (management), sketch **-praxis** *f* shop or manufacturing practice, operating practice **-prüfung** *f* works test **-punkt** *m* operating level, operating point, heading; (Bg) getting face **-qualität** *f* transmission rating **-radiographie** *f* industrial radiography **-rat** *m* workers' council

Betriebs-raum *m* operating room, manual switchroom **-raumbedarf** *m* floor space **-rechnungen** *pl* operating calculations **-refraktometer** *n* industrial refractometer **-regeln** *f pl* operating rules or practices, standards of operation **-regelung** *f* management or arrangement of a workshop **-reife** *f* service or practical stage (fully developed)

Betriebs-saal *m* room of operations **-schalter** *m* operating switch **-schaubild** *n* graphic panel, process diagram **-schlosserei** *f* mechanical service shop **-schluß** *m* shutting down **-schwierigkeit** *f* operating difficulty **-schwingversuch** *m* fatigue test under actual service conditions **-sender** *m* commercial transmitting station

betriebssicher reliable (in operation), safe to operate

Betriebs-sicherheit *f* operating reliability (safety), constancy of performance **-sollstrom** *m* rated current

Betriebsspannung *f* operating voltage, operating pressure **mechanische ~** operating strain

Betriebs-spesen *pl* operating costs **-spiel** *n* (Maschinenteile) working clearance **-spule** *f* operating coil **-spulewicklung** *f* operating coil winding **-spruch** *m* procedure message **-stärke** *f* operating field strength **-steilheit** *f* (einer Verstärkerröhre), mutual conductance or slope (of the characteristic curve of a valve) **-stelle** *f* operating site, servicing station **-stillegung** *f* shutdown **-stillstand** *m* operating stoppage **-stockungen** *pl* **ausschalten** to eliminate disturbances in the smooth working of a plant

Betriebsstoff *m* fuel, working material, power fuel, fuel and oil **-ausgabestelle** *f* distribution point, gasoline and lubricants **-ergänzung** *f* refueling **-kesselkraftwagen** *m* gasoline tank truck **-kolonne** *f* gasoline and lubricants supply column **-lager** *n* gasoline and lubricant bulk-storage plant **-messer** *m* fuel gauge

Betriebsstoff-verbrauch *m* fuel consumption **-verbrauchssatz** *m* rate of fuel consumption **-versorgung** *f* fuel supply **-vorratsmesser** *m* fuel-level gauge **-wagen** *m* tank truck **-zusatzmittel** *n* dope for aviation gasoline, additive (fuel)

Betriebs-störung *f* operating trouble, breakdown, shutdown, stoppage, disturbance, fault, interference, jamming **-strom** *m* working current **-stunde** *f* working hour; (Motor) running hour **-stundenzähler** *m* service hour meter, hour counter, running-time meter, elapsed-time meter

Betriebs-tag *m* operating day **-tank** *m* service tank **-techniker** *m* operator **-temperatur** *f* operating temperature, cool running of an engine **-tisch** *m* working table

Betriebs-überschüsse *m pl* net receipts, surplus **-überwachung** *f* production supervision, plant supervision, repair service, service control **-überwachungsgerät** *n* shop control instrument **-umstellung** *f* work stoppage, rearranging machinery in a plant

Betriebs- und Geschäftsausstattung operating facilities and office equipment **~ und Solldrücke und -temperaturen** operating and design pressures and temperatures

Betriebs-unfall *m* accident, shop or mill accident **-unklar** unserviceable **-unterbrechung** *f* interruption of operation, shutdown **-unterlage** *f* telephone service plan containing network diagram, directory of personnel, codes and code names, a duty roster **-unterlagen** *f pl* working records **-unternehmen** *n* enterprise **-ventilspiel** *n* actual operating valve clearance

Betriebs-vereinbarung *f* shop agreement **-verfassungsgesetz** *n* works countil law **-verhalten** *n* behaviour (of a gear), action **-verhältnisse** *n pl* service, shop, or plant conditions, rating of an apparatus or a machine **-verluste** *m pl* working losses **-vermögen** *n* net assets **-verstärkung** *f* overall gain **-versuch** *m* field test **-verzerrung** *f* service distortion **-vorschrift** *f* service instruction, operating code, regulations **-vorschriften** *f pl* specifications, prescriptions, or rules to be observed in operating (ship, plane, plant, etc.)

betriebswarm, bei -em Motor under hot running conditions

Betriebs-wärmegrad *m* working or running temperature **-wasser** *n* water for industrial use **-wasserstand** *m* operating (water) level **-weise** *f* method of operation, practice, mode of operation **-welle** *f* signal wave **-wellenlängen** *f pl* operating wave lengths (of a radio direction finder) **-werkstatt** *f* workshop **-werte** *m pl* operating data

betriebswirtschaftliche Kennzahlen financial index (numbers)

Betriebs-wirtschaftler *m* manufacturing engineer **-wirtschaftlichkeit** *f* economy of work's operation **-wirtschaftsstelle** *f* production control office **-wissenschaft** *f* industrial engineering **-wissenschaftlich** technically trained, pertaining to industrial engineering, efficient

Betriebs-zeit *f* working hours, working time, business hours **-zeitfaktor** *m* unit operating factor **-zentrale** *f* central radio office, central traffic, operating exchange **-zugehörigkeit** service with the company

betriebszulässig-e Temperatur safe operating temperature

Betriebs-zusammenfassung *f* concentrated operation **-zustand** *m* working order, operating or working condition **-zuverlässigkeit** *f* reliability in service **-zweig** *m* branch of manufacture

betroffen aggrieved, concerned **nicht ~** unaffected

Betrug *m* fraud, defraudation, deceit, swindle
Betrüger *m* swindler, impostor, cheat
Betrügerei *f* trickery, fraud
betrügerisch fraudulent
Bett *n* layer, bed, base, berth, lathe bed; (gekröpftes) gap bed
Bett-bahn *f* bed ways **-balken** *m* track **-bildend** bed forming (discharge), (soil mechanics) **-breite** (Drehbank) width of bed
betten to embed, bed, seat
Bett-fräsemaschine *f* bedplate miller **-führungen** *f pl* guideways on the bed; (Drehbank) ways (of the bed), guideways, outside ways **-führungsbahnen** *f pl* bed guideways, slideways, bedways **-koks** *m* bed coke **-konsol** *n* bed bracket **-kröpfung** *f* bed gap **-oberkante** *f* top edge of guide ways (mech.) **-schicht** *f* lower side of the lode
Bettschlitten *m* turning carriage, carriage, saddle **Leisten zum Festhalten von einem ~ auf der Flachführung** gibs
Bettschlitten-flügel *m* wing of saddle **-führung** *f* carriage guide **-weg** *m* saddle traverse
Bettsetzen *n* (Aufbereitung) ragging
Bettung *f* outrigger base, roadbed, bedplate, foundation, bedding, bed, platform (gun), setting, support **auf elastisch nachgiebiger ~** reposing on an elastic half plane
Bettungs-koffer *m* coffer, coffering, boxing **-loch** *n* gun-platform excavation **-ring** *m* race (of gun) **-staffel** *f* platform detail **-tiefe** *f* depth of trench **-ziffer** *f* ratio of soil pressure to settlement, coefficient of subgrade reaction, soil coefficient, ground constant, bedding value
betünchen to whitewash
betupfen to dab, dip, tip, spot, stipple, touch
Betupfen der Zündhölzchen dipping the matches into the inflammable compound
Beuche *f* buck, lye
beuchen to buck, soak, scour
Beuch-faß *n* bucking tub **-lauge** *f* bucking lye
beugbar flexible
Beugemittel *n* coercive measure, measure to bring to terms
beugen to bend, deflect, diffract, (acust., light, radio) inflect
Beugen *n*, **Beugung** *f* bending, diffraction, inflection, flexure, refraction
beugsam flexible, pliant, diffracting
Beugung *f* diffraction **~ des Lichts** diffraction of light **~ des Schalls** diffraction of sound
Beugungsapparatur *f* inflection apparatus
Beugungsbild *n* diffraction pattern, picture or image **~ aufnehmen** to record a diffraction pattern
Beugungsbündel *n* diffraction beam **-diagramm** *n* diffraction pattern **-erscheinung** *f* phenomenon of diffraction (phys.), diffraction pattern **-farben** *f pl* prismatic colors **-figur** *f* diffraction pattern **-fransen** *f pl* diffraction fringes **-geometrie** *f* diffraction geometry **-gitter** *n* ultrasonic crossgrating (acoust.), diffraction screen **-ring** *m* diffraction ring
Beugungs-saum *m* diffraction fringe **-scheibchen** *n* diffraction disk **-spektrum** *n* diffraction spectrum **-streifen** *m* diffraction fringes or lines (optics) **-streuung** shadow scattering **-stripping** *n* diffraction stripping **-tensor** *m* deflection tensor **-winkel** *m* diffraction angle
Beulbeiwert *m* buckling coefficient
Beule *f* indentation, bump, bulge, dint, swelling, bruise **eine ~ machen** to turn outside the wake
Beulen *n* local buckling
beulensteif buckling resistant
Beulen-klopfer *m* hammer for removing bumps **-messung** *f* buckling or distortion test
Beul-festigkeit *f* buckling strength or resistance **-grenze** *f* buckling or wrinkling limit
beulig full of bumps, covered with boils
Beul-spannung *f* denting stress, local buckling stress **-steifigkeit** *f* blister resistance
Beulung *f* bulging
Be- und Entlüftungsanlage *f* airing plant
Be- und Entlüftungsventil *n* pressure and vacuum relief valve
beunruhigen to disturb, harass, cause uneasiness, alarm
beunruhigend disquieting, harassing, alarming
beunruhigter Stahl wild steel
Beunruhigung *f* harassment, uneasiness, disturbance, alarm
beurkunden to verify, authenticate, legalize, record
Beurkundung *f* recording, registration, documentary verification
beurlauben to grant leave of absence
beurlaubt on leave
beurteilen to judge, estimate, value, criticize, gauge, rate
beurteilt nach judged by, judging from
Beurteilung *f* judgment, valuation, estimation, classification **~ der Lage** estimate of the situation
Beurteilungs-größen *pl* appraisal rating **-maßstab** *m* criterion for judgment, scale for evaluation **-merkmal** *n* criterion **-notiz** *f* summary of character assessment
Beute *f* booty, loot, large trough, beehive
Beutel *m* bag, pouch, sack **-elektrode** *f* bag electrode **-element** *n* sack cell **-filter** *f* bag filter **-futter** *n* bag lining **-gaze** *f* bolting silk (silk gauze) **-kartusche** *f* bag ammunition **-maschine** *f* bolting mill, sifting machine
beuteln to bolt, sift
Beutel-papier *n* bag paper **-schweißen** *n* bag sealing **-sieb** *n* bolting sieve, bolter **-verschließmaschiene** *f* bag sealing machine
Bevatron *n* bevatron
bevölkern to populate, people
Bevölkerung *f* population, populace
Bevölkerungsdichte *f* density of population
bevollmächtigen to assign, authorize, empower
bevollmächtigt authorized **nicht ~** noncommissioned **-er Gesandter** minister (diplomatic)
Bevollmächtigter *m* authorized agent, plenipotentiary, assignee, trustee, attorney, power holder, proxy, mandatory proxy
Bevollmächtigung *f* assignment, assignation, authorization
Bevorratung *f* stockage, supply
bevorrechtigte Anlage privileged work
bevorstehen to lie ahecd
bevorstehend imminent
bevorworten to preface
bevorzugen to prefer, favor
bevorzugt preferred **-e Kristallachsenrichtung**

preferred crystallographic axis orientation **-e Orientierung** nonrandom orientation, privileged orientation **nicht -e Orientierung** randomly oriented, random orientation

Bevorzugung *f* preference, accentuation, emphasizing **energetische ~** energy preference

bewachen to keep watch, watch, guard

Bewacher *m* custodian, guard; convoying vessel, patrol boat

bewachsen overgrown, covered with foliage

Bewachung *f* watch, supervision, guard, custody

Bewachungsfahrzeug *n* convoying or patrolling vessel

bewaffnen to arm

bewaffnet armed **-es Auge** aided eye

Bewaffnung *f* arms, arming, armament, gun power

bewahren to conserve, preserve, keep, save

bewähren to function, prove good or useful, stand the test, give satisfactory results, prove (itself) **sich vielfach ~** to prove itself time and again

bewährt approved, successful, reliable, time-tried

Bewahrung *f* conservation, protection

Bewährung *f* proving of fitness, competence, durability, verification, trial, performance test

bewalden to afforest, overgrow with wood

bewaldet wooded

Bewallung *f* embakment

bewältigen to overcome, master, handle, cover

Bewältigung *f* coverage

bewandert skilled, versed in, proficient, knowledged

bewässern to irrigate, water, moisten

Bewässerung *f* watering, irrigation

Bewässerungs-graben *m* irrigation channel or ditch **-schaufeln** *f pl* irrigating shovels **-schleuse** *f* irrigation lock

bewegbar movable, mobile

bewegen to move, stir, agitate, travel **frei ~** flutter freely (tape rec.) **zu weit ~** to overshoot, overthrow **im Kreise ~** to gyrate

bewegend moving, motive

Beweggrund *m* motive

beweglich movable, mobile, portable **-e Anlagen** travelling plants **-e Anlagewerte** *pl* movables **-es Auflager** (Schiene) movable rail, expansion bearing **-e Belastung** *f* live load **-e Bodenfunkstelle** *f* mobile surface (radio) station **-e Deichselvorrichtung** pivot-tongue attachment

beweglich-e Flugfunkstelle *f* aeronautical mobile station **-e Flußsohle** shifting river bed **-e Formrahmen** floating chase **-e Funkstelle** *f* mobile radio station **-e Güter** movables **-e Hebelvorrichtung** *f* pivot lever attachment **-es Hindernis** portable obstacle **-es einschaliges Hyperboloid** collapsible hyperboloid of one sheet

beweglich-es Komma *n* floating point (info proc.) **-er Kontakt** movable contact **-e Kontaktbrücke** *f* moving contact bridge **-e Kontaktfeder** moving contact spring **-es Kreisschnittmodell, des dreiachsigen Ellipsoids** collapsible model of a general ellipsoid consisting of circular sections **-e Kupplung** *f* flexible coupling **-e Ladung** moving charge **-e Last** moving load, live load

beweglich-e Massen rotating and reciprocating parts **-es Meßgerät** portable metering unit **-es entfesseltes Mikrophon** portable or following microphone **-es Organ** moving element, moving-coil galvanometer **-es hyperbolisches Paraboloid** collapsible hyperbolic paraboloid **-er Poller** movable bollard

beweglich-e Rolle *f* loose or flying pulley **-er Rost** revolving grate **-e Spule** *f* moving coil **-es System** moving system **-er Teil** moving part or section, rotating and reciprocating part **-es Ziel** moving target

Beweglichkeit *f* mobility, flexibility, fluidity (being the reciprocal of dynamic viscosity); (von freien Trägern) mobility (of liberated carriers)

beweglichkeitsgeregelt mobility-controlled

Beweglichkeits-gleichung *f* mobility equation **-koeffizient** *m* mobility coefficient **-tensor** *m* mobility tensor

bewegt moving

Bewegtsehen *n* seeing objects at rest as moving

Bewegung *f* movement, agitation, activity, motion, traveling, migration, motion, stir, travel, action (in film projection) **~ der Ebene in sich** motion of the plane into itself **~ im Kreise** gyration **~ des Liegenden** (Bg) creep **~ in nur einer Richtung** unidirectional motion

Bewegung, ebene ~ plane motion **in ~ setzen** to put into motion, actuate **eine ~ ausführen** to execute a maneuver or movement **fortschreitende ~** progression, translation, progressive motion **gleichförmig beschleunigte ~** uniformly accelerated motion **hin- und hergehende ~** reciprocating motion (movement), to-and-fro, rocking, or oscillating movement, shuttling motion

Bewegung, hüpfende ~ skipping motion **krummlinige ~** movement in a curved line **periodische ~** periodical motion **ruckartige ~** jerk **rückläufige ~** retrogression **schnelle unregelmäßige ~** flutter(ing) **sinusförmige ~** harmonic, plain harmonic, or sine movement **rein sinusförmige ~** simple harmonic motion

Bewegung *f*, **thermische ~** thermal agitation **wirbelfreie ~** potential motion, streamline motion **zu- und abnehmende ~** surge **zu weite ~** (des Zeigers usw.) overthrow(ing), overshoot(ing) (of the indicator or pointer) **zwangsläufige ~** positive movement

Bewegungs-achse *f* axis of rotation **-amplitude** *f* velocity amplitude **-antrieb** *m* motive power, motion drive **-apparat** *m* motor apparatus **-ataxie** *f* motor ataxia **-bahn** *f* track of travel, path of motion **-bestrahlung** moving beam radiation **-bild** *n* pattern of motion **-buch** *n* record of transactions

Bewegungs-ebene *f* plane of motion **-eindruck** *m* sensation or illusion of motion **-elektrizitätslehre** *f* electrokinetics **-element** *n* moving part, controls **-empfindung** *f* sensation of movement kinesthesis **-empfänger** *m* velocity microphone, pickup or detector of motion **-energie** *f* kinetic or motional energy **-erscheinung** *f* motion phenomenon, stirring effect

bewegungs-fähig capable of movement, locomotive **-feld** motional field **-fläche** *f* movement area (airport) **-freiheit** *f* freedom of maneuver, of movement, or of action, room to move

-fuge *f* expansion joint **-geschwindigkeit** *f* velocity of motion, traverse speed **-gesetze** *pl* laws of motion **-gleichung** *f* equation of motion, dynamical equation, law of motion, ponderomotive law **-größe** *f* momentum (mass × velocity), impulse, amount of motion, kinetic or motional quantity or magnitude

Bewegungsgruppen *f pl* groups of motions, translation groups **diskontinuierliche und kristallographische ~** discontinuous and crystallographic groups

Bewegungs-halluzination kinesthetic hallucination **-hemmung** *f* impediment to movement, inhibition **-impedanz** *f* motional impedance **-klasse** *f* motion classe **-knopf** *m* motion head or knob **-knoten** *pl* nodes of vibration **-kontrolle** *f* flight control **-kraft** *f* motive power or force **-lehre** *f* kinematics, dynamics, mechanics, kinetics **-linie** *f* curve of flight path **-los** dead in the water, motionless **-losigkeit** *f* inaction

Bewegungs-maschine *f* prime mover **-mechanismus** *m* working gear, operating machinery **-mikrophon** *n* velocity microphone, pressure-gradient microphone **-moment** *n* momentum of a body **-nachahmung** *f* echokinesis **-organ** *n* motion element, mechanism or means

Bewegungsrichtung *f* guide motion **Wähler mit einer ~** single-motion selector

Bewegungs-rohr *n* mobility tube **-schaufeln** *f pl* impeller blades of a turbine **-schema** *n* motion pattern **-schraube** *f* lead screw, motion screw **-sitz** *m* clearance fit, loose fit **-sperre** *f* travel stop **-spiel** *n* clearance of motion **-spindel** *f* screw drive **-staat** *m* state of flux **-studie** *f* motion study **-stufe** *f* stage of motion, phase progress

Bewegungs-type *f* motion type **-übergang** *m* motional transient **-übersicht** *f* movement plan or timetable **-übertragung** *f* transmission of motion **-umkehr** *f* reversal, change of movement **-unfähig** incapable of moving, immobilized, stuck, stalled **-unschärfe** *f* movement blur **-vorgang** *f* motional or cinematographic action, phenomenon of motion or movement

Bewegungsvorrichtung *f* working gear or operating mechanism **hydraulische ~** hydraulic operation

Bewegungs-zähigkeit *f* kinematic viscosity **-zeit** *f* moving time (work-factor) **-zeittabelle** *f* moving-time table **-zustand** *m* state of motion

bewehren to reinforce, strengthen, arm, armor, sheath

bewehrt armed, armored, sheathed **-er Beton** reinforced concrete **-es Kabel** armored cable

Bewehrung *f* (steel) reinforcement (in concrete), shielding of cables with wire mesh, armature, (of a cable) sheath(ing), wrapping, reinforcing, fittings (hardware, of an insulator) (metal) armoring **~ in Bandform** tape armoring **~ von Drahtgeflecht** reinforcing of wire netting **geschlossene ~** closed or locked armor, lapped armoring **leichte ~** light armor **offene ~** open armor **schwere ~** heavy armor

Bewehrungs-draht *m* armoring or sheathing wire, **-eisen** *n* reinforcing bar(s) (reinforced-concrete construction) **-maschine** *f* armoring machine **-netz** (im Voraus hergestelltes) fabric reinforcement, steel fabric

Beweis *m* proof, evidence, exhibit (law), argument **~ der Abbruch tut** impeaching evidence, prejudicial to validity **~ erbringen** to produce evidence **~ führen** to demonstrate, prove **als ~ vorlegen** to tender in evidence **strenger ~** rigorous proof

Beweisbeschluß *m* direction or order for evidence

beweisen to prove, demonstrate, verify

Beweis-fehler *m* error of demonstration **-führung** *f* demonstration, argumentation, method of proof **-grund** *m* argument **-kraft** *f* conclusiveness, evidential value, conclusive force **-kräftig** conclusive, convincing **-last** *f* burden of proof **-material** *n* written evidence, (documentary) evidence, evidential material, testimony, or proof

Beweis-recht *n* law of evidence **-mittel** *n* proof, evidence (of proof) **-satz** *m* theorem **-stelle** *f* authority (valid) reference **-stück** *n* exhibit, document, proof **-wert** *m* evidential value

bewerben, sich ~ um to apply for

Bewerber *m* applicant, candidate, competitor

Bewerbung *f* application (for a position)

Bewerbungsschreiben *n* letter of application

bewerfen to plaster

bewerkstelligen to effect, perform, accomplish, get done, do, make

bewerkstelligt accomplished, done

bewerten to assign a value to, weight, estimate (value)

bewertet-er Eigenverbrauch valued own consumption **-e Gegenstände** (Posten) value items

Bewertung *f* valuation, value, qualification, evaluation, rating **numerische ~** numerical rating **positive ~** merit rating **~ der Endbestände** valuation of closing stocks

Bewertungs-ausgleich *m* valuation adjustment **-bericht** *m* valuation report **-faktor** *m* valuation factor **-filter** *n* weighting network **-gesetz** *n* valuation law **-grundlage** *f* basis of valuation **-klasse** *f* degree of priority or value as applied to objects to be defended **-kurve** *f* evaluation curve **-merkmal** *n* job factor

Bewertungs- oder Berichtigungsreserven valuation or qualifying reserves

Bewertungs-prüfung *f* judgment test, random sampling **-stichtag** *m* date of valuation

Bewertungszahl *f* figure of merit, valuation figure **~ für die Bestandteile einer noch ungebleiten Kraftstoffmischung** clear blending value

bewettern to weather a storm, ventilate, expose to weather

Bewetterung *f* ventilation (in mine), air conditioning, exposing to weather, forced ventilation, reserve power **~ von Grubenbauten** ventilation of mines

Bewetterungs-anlage *f* air conditioning plant **-probe** *f*, **-prüfung** *f* weather-exposure test, weathering test

bewickeln to wind, wrap round, envelop, wrap (up), whip, cover wire (with cotton), tape **mit Band ~** to tape

Bewickeln *n* winding

Bewicklung *f* wrapping, winding (coils), relay windings, wrapping (up), whipping, taping

Bewicklungstau *n* winding rope

bewilligen to allow, grant, permit, allot

bewilligt-e Erzeugung allowable production **-es**

registriertes Aktienkapital authorized share capital **-e** (zugewiesene) **Dividende** appropriated dividend
Bewilligung *f* consent, allowance, approval, license, concession, permission, grant
bewirken to effect, cause, bring about, secure, lead to, give rise to
bewirtschaften to manage, superintend, till (land), cultivate (soil)
Bewirtschafter *m* operator, manager
Bewirtschaftung *f* control, rationing, regulation of scarce supplies, control and rationing
Bewirtung *f* entertainment
Bewitterung *f* weathering
Bewitterungs-fähigkeit *f* weatherability **-leitung** airing tube **-probe** *f* weather-exposure test **-verhalten** *n* weather resistance **-versuch** *m* weathering test
bewohnbar inhabitable
bewohnen to occupy, inhabit
bewölken to cloud, darken
bewölkt overcast, cloudy
Bewölkung *f* cloudiness
Bewölkungs-grad *m*, **-größe** *f* degree of cloudiness, magnitude or extent of cloudiness **-höhe** *f* ceiling **-karte** *f* cloud map
Bewurf *m* coarse plaster, rough plaster, rough cast
bewußt conscious **-los** unconscious **-losigkeit** *f* unconsciousness, insensibility
Bewußtsein *n* consciousness **~ verlieren** to lose consciousness, faint
bezackt jagged, indented
bezahlbar payable
bezahlen to pay; (Kosten) defray
bezahlt, sich ~ machen to pay (off) **-e Antwort** prepaid reply
Bezahlung *f* settlement, payment **~ nach dem Gewicht** payment by weight or on tonnage basis **~ nach dem Zuckergehalt** payment on sugar-content basis
Bezahlungsdatum *n* date of payment
Bezahnung *f* teething, toothing, teeth
bezeichnen to mark, designate, signify, indicate, denote, note, term, label, name
bezeichnend significant, indicative, characteristic
Bezeichnung *f* mark, brand, designation, name, marking, term, indication, expression, nomenclature, label, notation, symbol, relation(ship), connection, denotation, sign, labeling (for identification), color coding (of conductors), notation (math.), specifications **genaue ~** specification, rating (e.g. voltage rating) **~ der Arbeit** job title (classification) **~ der Funkwellen** designation of radio-electric waves
Bezeichnungs-erklärung legend (on map) **-nagel** *m* (Leitung), distinguishing mark, numbering nail, letter nail (electric line or lead) **-schild** *n* designation card, label, name-plate **-streifen** *m* designation or marking strip **-system** *n* notation **-weise** *f* manner or method of notation
bezeigen to show, express, manifest
bezetteln to label, put stickers
bezeugen to certify, witness
bezichtigen to accuse of, charge with
beziehen to take possession of, draw (rations), cover (with), order, buy, relate, refer, purchase, mount guard, occupy a position, collect pay, subscribe to (magazine) **sich ~ auf** to refer to **sich beziehend auf** relative to
Bezieherabteilung *f* subscription department
Beziehung *f* reference, regard, respect, relation, connection, relationship, interrelationship, correlation, equation **in dieser ~** in this respect or regard **in ~ setzen** to relate to **in ~ stehen** to be in relation with **in** (wechselseitige) **~ setzen** to correlate **gespannte ~** strained relations
Beziehungs-assoziation association by relation **-wahn** *m* delusions of reference or interpretation
beziehungsweise respectively, relatively, or, or else, as the case may be, and/or, . . . or . . . or both, and, or rather
beziffern to number, mark with ciphers
Bezifferung *f* numbering, numeration, calculation, indexing, figures, lettering **dekadische ~** decimal numbering
bezinnen to castellate
Bezirk *m* district, precinct, confines, zone, area **~ der gebührenfreien Telegrammzustellung** free delivery zone for telegrams
Bezirks-amt *n* main district exchange **-kabel** *n* exchange or trunk cable **-kontrollzentrale** *f* (Flugsicherung) area control centre (ACC) **-leiter** *m* regional manager **-netz** *n* tandem area **-steuerstelle** *f* area control point **-verkehr** *m* junction or toll traffic **-wähler** *m* code selector
bezogen drawn, ordered, referred to, (furnitures) upholstered **~ auf** relative to, related to **-e Farben** related colors **-e Geschwindigkeit** relative velocity **-es Gewicht** (Wichte) specific gravity **-e Größe** *f* relative value, non-dimensional value or variable
Bezug *m* reference, relation, hood (maritime), covering, cover, datum, respect, acquisition of rationed goods, washer; (Erwerb) purchase **~ für Otterschwanzstück** attachments to tailpiece of otter (nav.) **~ für Schneideapparat** attachments to cutter **~ haben auf** to relate to, bear **~ habend** relevant **in ~ auf** with reference to, referring to **mit ~ auf** relating to, with reference to
bezüglich relative, with reference (to), as to, relative to, concerning, about **auf einen Winkel ~** angular
Bezugnahme *f* reference (to)
Bezugs-achse *f* axis of reference, reference axis **-anweisung** *f* order form or blank **-artikulationsäquivalent** *n* articulation reference equivalent
Bezugsatmosphäre *f* **fundamentale ~** basic reference atmosphere
Bezugs-ausbeute *f* reference performance **-bedingungen** *f pl* terms or conditions of delivery, trade terms **-berechtigung** *f* entitlement, priority
Bezugsdämpfung *f* transmission or volume equivalent, volume loss, reference equivalent **~ je Längeneinheit** volume loss per unit length **~ eines Übertragungssystems** reference equivalent, volume equivalent
Bezugs-daten *pl* reference record **-dipol** *n* reference dipole **-drehzahl** *f* theoretical rate of revolution **-düse** *f* **für Eichzwecke** reference jet **-ebene** *f* datum level, plane of reference, datum plane, reference level, fiducial level **-elektrode**

f reference electrode, comparison electrode
Bezugs-feuchtigkeit *f* reference humidity **-fläche** *f* datum level or plane **-flügelfläche** *f* (aerodyn.) design wing area
Bezugsgenerator *m* **quarzgesteuerter ~** quartz-reference oscillator
Bezugs-größe *f* reference magnitude, reference quantity **-haken** *m* reference hook (in drawing) **-höhe** *f* reference altitude, datum altitude **-horizont** *m* datum line, horizon, datum level (soil mech.) **-kern** reference core **-konfiguration** *f* reference configuration **-koordinate** *f* reference coordinate **-kraftstoff** *m* reference fuel
Bezugskreis *m* reference circuit
Bezugs-lautstärke *f* reference telephonic power (RTP) **-linie** *f* reference axis or line; (Zeichnung) datum line **-maß** *n* datum dimension, reference dimension **-netz** *n* grid of reference **-norm** *f* reference standard **-normale** *f* reference standard
Bezugs-pegel *m* relative level **-preis** *m* cost, cost price **-profil** *n* basic profile **-punkt** *m* reference or datum point, bench, landmark, station, fiducial point **-quelle** *f* reference source, source of supply **-recht** *n* claim, right, option, subscription right
Bezugsrichtung einer Antenne zero line
Bezugs-schwingung *f* reference signal **-spannung** (Bezugspotential) reference voltage level **-staudruck** *m* standard dynamic pressure referred to initial velocity to equal 100 meter-seconds and air density on ground **-steigung** *f* (eines Propellers) standard pitch **-strahlungskeule** *f* reference lobe (ant.) **-strom-kreis** *m* reference circuit **-system** *n* frame of reference, reference system, standard or norm (used for comparison), reference source
Bezugs-temperatur *f* reference temperature, initial temperature, normal temperature **-ton** *m* reference tone **-verzerrungsmesser** *m* start-stop distortion meter **-wert** *m* relative value, reference value **-zahlen** (in Zeichnungen) reference numerals, keying references **-zeichen** *n* (bei Formelgrößen), reference character or designation, reference symbol (numeral or letter)
bezweifeln to doubt, call in question
bezwingen to reduce, overcome
bibasisch (zweibasisch) bibasic
Biberschwanz *m* plain tail **-bündel** *n* beaver-tail beam **-säge** *f* whipsaw
Biberwehr *n* beaver dam
Bibliothek *f* library
Bibliotheksprogramm *n* library subroutine (info proc.)
Bibliothekar *m* librarian
Bicarbonathärte *f* bicarbonate hardness
Bicharakteristik *f* bi-characteristic
Bichlorid *n* bichloride
Bichromat-gefäß *n* bichromate cell **-kolloid-kopierprozeß** *n* bichromate-emulsion reproduction process **-titration** *f* bichromate titration
bichromsaures Kali(um) potassium bichromate
Bickel *m* pickax
Bidipentode *f* duodiode tetrode with suppressor grid, duodiode pentode
Biditriode *f* duodiode triode, double diode triode
biegbar pliable, flexible **-e Schnur** flexible cord
Biegbarkeit *f* pliability, flexibility
Biege-apparat *m* bender, bending apparatus **-automat** *m* automatic bending machine **-backe** *f* bending jaw **-balken** *m* transverse beam, cradle **-beanspruchung** *f* bending strain or stress, bending, flexure, bending load **-belastung** *f* bending strain (load), transverse loading **-block** *m* bending block
Biegebruchfestigkeit *f* bending strength **~ im Schwellbereich** fatigue strength under repeated (fluctuating) bending stresses
Biegedauerfestigkeit im Schwellbereich fatigue strength under pulsating bending stresses
Biege-dauerhaltbarkeit *f* endurance of rigidity **-dorn** *m* bending mandrel **-druck** *m* bending pressure, bending strain **-ebene** *f* plane of flexure **-eigenschaften** *pl* flexural properties **-eigenschwingung** *f* natural frequency in bending **-ermüdungsversuch** *m* transverse-fatigue test
Biege-fähigkeit *f* bending property **-feder** *f* spiral spring **-fest** stiffened against bending **-festigkeit** *f* bending or fatigue strength, transverse strength, flexure, stiffness, rigidity, bending property, resistance to bending strain **-fließgrenze** *f* flexure yield point **-form** *f* bending or flexing die **-formung** *f* bending (flexure) strain
Biege-gehänge *n* bending cradle **-gesenk** *n* snaker **-gesenke** *n pl* forming dies **-gleitung** *f* flexural gliding **-grenze** *f* (beim Biegeversuch) bending limit **-halbmesser** *m* bending radius **-kraft** *f* bending force **-kristall** *n* bender crystal
biege-kritische Drehzahl *f* critical bending speed
Biege-länge *f* length subjected to bending **-last** *f* bending load **-linie** *f* deflection curve bending line **-maschine** *f* (iron) bending machine, bulldozer, transverse testing machine, doubling machine **-modell** *n* bending block (or die)
Biegemoment *n* bending couple, moment of flexure, bending moment, flexural torque **~ um Achse x-x** bending moment referred to axis x-x
biegen to bend, deflect, inflect, curve, camber, diffract, refract, flex, warp
Biegen *n* bending, inflecting
Biege-pfeil *m* ratio of deflection to width between supports **-pfeilmesser** *m* deflectometer, flexure level gauge **-plan** (Statik) deflection diagram **-platte** *f* diaphragm
Biegepresse *f* bending press **horizontale ~** bulldozer
Biege-probe *f* bending or bend test **-probekörper** *m* bending-test specimen **-prüfung** *f* bending test **-prüfungsmaschine** *f* transverse-bending-test machine
Bieger *m* bender, crow
Biege-rißbildung *f* flex cracking (rubber) **-rohr** *n* torsion tube **-schlagversuch** *m* bending-impact test **-schwellfestigkeit** *f* pulsating fatigue strength under bending stresses **-schwingung** *f* flexural wave, flexural vibration bending oscillation **-schwingungsfestigkeit** *f* repeated-bending-stress strength, bending-fatigue range **-schwingungsmaschine** *f* bending vibration or repeated-bending-stress testing machine **-span-**

nung *f* bending stress or strain, bending resilience, transverse strain or stress, transverse-bending resilience, modulus of rupture **-spannungsgröße** *f* intensity of bending stress **-stanze** *f* power brake **-steif** resistant to bending

Biege-steifigkeit *f* bending resistance, flexural stiffness **-stelle** *f* bending point **-stempel** *m* bending ram or die **-tisch** *m* bending table **-versuch** *m* transverse-bending test, cross-breaking test, transverse test, deflection test **-vorrichtung** *f* bending device, bending fixture, bending-test shackle **-walze** *f* bending roll, bending machine **-walzmaschine** *f* bending roll

Biege-wange *f* bending beam **-wechselbeanspruchung** *f* alternating bending load **-wechselfestigkeit** *f* fatigue strength under repeated (reversed) bending stresses, reversed or alternating bending strength **-wechselspannung** *f* alternating bending stress **-wellen** *pl* flexural waves **-wellenvorsatz** *m* flexible shaft attachment

Biege-werkzeug *n* bending tool **-winkel** *m* bending angle, cold bend expressed in degrees of a circle (fatigue-testing unit) **-wulst** *m* fold (bending crease) **-zahl** *f* bending value **-zange** *f* bending pliers or tongs **-zugfestigkeit** *f* (Rohr) bending strength **-zugspannung** *f* flexural tensile stress **-zylinder** *m* bending cylinder

Bieg-festigkeit *f* buckling strength, bending strength, rigidity **-linie** *f* elastic curve

biegsam flexible, pliant, pliable, bendable, ductile, supple **-e Leitung** flexible tubing **-es Rohr** flexible hose **-es Sprachrohr** gosport, flexible speaking tube (aviation) **-es Stahldrahtseil** flexible steel wire rope **-e Strebe** flexible stay bolt **-e Verbindung** flexible joint, slip joint **-e Welle** flexible shaft(ing) **-e Zapfenegge** peg-tooth harrow

Biegsamkeit *f* flexibility, ductility, pliability

biegsam machen to ductilize (as a tungsten wire)

Biegung *f* bend, bending, flexure, deflection (spring), curve, curvature, flection, (point of) inflection, bend (break possible), sag, set **~ machen** to turn off (course)

Biegungs-art *f* bending mode **-ausschlag** *m* deflection **-beanspruchung** *f* bending or flexural stress **-belastung** *f* bending stress **-dauerschwingfestigkeit** *f* flexural fatigue strength **-ebene** *f* plane of flexure **-einräumung** *f* bend allowance **-empfindlich** pliable **-fähig** flexible, pliable, ductile

Biegungsfedern *pl* **gewundene ~** spiral springs, helical torsion springs

biegungs-fest moment-resisting **-festigkeit** *f* resisting moment, bending strength, transverse strength, resistance to bending, tensile strength **-halbmesser** *m* bending radius, radius of curvature **-kraft** *f* bending stress **-messer** *m* deflectometer, deflection indicator

Biegungs-moment *n* bending moment **-linie** *f* bending line, curve of deflection **-pfeil** *m* maximum deflection, amount or direction of deflection, deflection of a girder **-polygon** *n* polygon of flexure **-radius** *m* bending radius **-riß** *m* bending crack **-schwingung** *f* bending or flexural vibration, flexure mode **-schwingungsart** *f* flexural mode of vibration **-schwingungsfestigkeit** *f* bending-fatigue strength **-schraubenfeder** *f* helical torsion spring

Biegungs-spannung *f* operating voltage, bending stress or strain, bending resilience, transverse stress or strain, transverse-bending resilience **-steif** resistant to bending **-steifigkeit** *f* bending resistance or stiffness **-vermögen** *n* pliability, flexibility **-versuch** *m* flexing test **-wechsel** *m* repeated flexing

Biegungswelle *f* flexural wave **~ längs eines Stabes** flexural wave along a rod

Biegungs-widerstand *m* resistance to bending **-zuschuß** *m* bend allowance

Bieg-walze *f* bending press or rolls (bending plates for shipbuilding) **-walzwerk** *n* bending machine **-wechselfestigkeit** *f* bending-change strength, bending-strength under alternating loading **-welle** *f* flexible shaft

Bienenharz *m* bee glue, propolis

bienenkorbartiges Gitter honeycomb grid

Bienenkorb-koksofen *m* beehive coke oven **-kühler** *m* honeycomb radiator **-lampe** *f* beehive neon lamp **-ofen** *m* beehive furnace, beehive (coke) oven

Bienen-wabe *f* honeycomb **-wachs** *n* beeswax **-zucker** *m* sugar for feeding bees

Bier-brauen *n* brewing **-pech** *n* brewers' pitch **-spiegel** *m* beer level **-trebermelasse** *f* brewers' grain molasses **-würze** *f* beer wort **-würzekühler** *m* beer-wort cooler

Biete (press) *f* cage

bieten to offer, proffer, bid, show

Bietungsgarantie *f* tender guarantee

Bif (Biegeform) bending or flexing die

Bifeder *f* bimetal spring (bi-spring)

bifilar double wound, bifilar, noninductively wound **-e Wicklung** double winding, bifilar winding, two-wire winding, noninductive winding, dual-strand winding

Bifilar-antenne *f* two-wire antenna **-aufhängung** *f* bifilar or double suspension **-brücke** *f* bifilar bridge

Bifilardraht *m* bifilar wire, twisted pair **-wicklung** *f* bifilar winding

Bifilar-elektrometer *n* Wulf electrometer **-gewickelt** double wound, wound in duplicate **-wicklung** *f* bifilar winding **-widerstand** *m* non-inductive resistance, bifilar resistor, double-wound resistor

bifokal bifocal **-e Brillengläser** bifocal lenses

Bigramm *n* two-digit group (comp.)

Bikalziumsilikat *n* dicalcium silicate

Bikarbonat *n* bicarbonate

bikonkave Linse double concave lens, concavo-concave lens

bikonvexes Profil biconvex airfoil section

Bikonvexlinse *f* biconvex lens (optics)

Bilanz *f* balance sheet **~ ziehen** to strike a balance

Bilanz-analyse *f* analytical study of a balance sheet **-gesetze** *pl* balance laws **-gleichung** *f* balance equation **-kurs** *m* rate of exchange **-status** *m* statement of resources and liabilities **-stichtag** *m* balance sheet date

Bild *n* image, figure, picture, idea, diagram, design (pattern), display (e.g. on C.R.O.); (auf Filmstreifen) frame, video **~ von natürlicher Größe** image of natural size **~ auf Reiter** image on saddle stand **~ im Ton** vision on sound **abgeleitetes ~, zum Unterschied vom Urbild** (Kontaktkopien) derived image in contradistinction to original image

Bild, aufgerichtetes, aufrechtes ~ erect(ed) image, rectified image **bewegtes ~** moving picture (radio) **detailreiches ~** contrasty picture (rich in details and contrasts) **flaches ~** very soft picture, flat picture **flaues ~** non-contrasty picture or image **gerastetes ~** halftone

Bild, hartes ~ contrasty, crisp or harsh picture or image, hard image, high contrast image (TV) **hochzeiliges ~** high-definition image or picture (television) **lichtschwaches ~** low-luminosity picture **reelles, umgekehrtes ~** real reversed image **ruhendes ~** still, still picture, unanimated picture, ordinary photograph **scharf eingestelltes ~** sharp picture, sharply focused image

Bild, scharfes ~ sharply defined image, distinct image **sprechendes ~** talking-motion picture **auf dem Kopf stehendes ~** inverted image **tönungsreiches ~** picture with proper shading values and contrast **umgekehrtes ~** reversed or inverted image **unbewegtes ~** still picture, unanimated picture **unscharfes ~** not sharply defined image, indistinct image

Bild, unverzeichnetes, unverzerrtes ~ orthoscopic image, undistorted picture **verbranntes ~** overexposed print **vergrößertes ~** enlarged image **verkleinertes ~** reduced image **verschwommenes ~** blurred image **vollständiges ~** frame **weiches ~** weak or soft picture, uncontrasty picture

Bild-ablenkgerät *n* deflection apparatus, unit **-ablenkjoch** *n* image-deflection yoke **-ablenkstufe** *f* scanning stage **-ablenkung** *f* frame or picture scan **-abstand** *m* distance of the object photo) **-abszisse** *f* abscissa of an image point **-abtaster** *m* televisor, television scanning device **-abtastrohr** *n* image pick-up tube, inconoscope

Bildabtasterröhre *f* image pick-up tube **~ mit mechanischer Blende** Farnsworth dissector of electron camera, magnetic scanner **doppelseitige ~** two-sided mosaic pick-up tube

Bild-abtaststelle *f* picture or film gate (motion pictures) **-abtastung** *f* scanning, exploring, analyzing (of the picture), frame or picture scan **-abtastung** *f* picture-gate **-abtastvorrichtung** *f* analyzer, scanning device at the transmitter end **-abteilung** *f* serial photo-section **-abzug** *m* print **-achsen** *f pl* plate axes, axes of the image **-anlage** *f* facsimile apparatus or installation (radio) **-anode** *f* barrier grid mosaic

Bild-anschluß *m* photographic extension **-aufbau** *m* picture synthesis, build-up of picture (line by line) **-auffänger** *m* scanning device **-aufklärung** *f* photographic reconnaissance **-auflösung** *f* picture definition, scan, picture resolution

Bildaufnahme, Kofferapparat für ~ box equipment, trunk unit for shooting pictures

Bildaufnahmeröhre *f* camera tube, image orthicon **~ mit einer zusammenhängenden Photokathode** dissector tube

Bildaufnahmevorbereitung *f* lining up for shooting pictures

bildaufrichtend image erecting **-es Hornhautmikroskop** image-erecting corneal microscope **-es Mikroskop** image-erecting microscope

Bild-aufrichtung *f* image erection, rectification, or inversion **-aufzeichnung** *f* picture re-creation, tracing, or delineation **-aufzeichnungsanlage** *f* picture recording equipement **-aufzeichnungsverstärker** *m* picture amplifier cubicle **-ausleuchtung** *f* flashing of image **-ausschnitt** *m* scrap, frame (of camera), image area (on scanning disk), picture detail **-austastsynchronsignal** *n* (TV) composite signal **-austastung** *f* frame suppression **-austastzeichen** *n* vertical blanking impulse

Bild-auswerter *m* photo interpreter **-auswertung** *f* interpretation of or plotting from aerial photographs **-band** *n* image band **-bandbreite** *f* vision bandwidth **-bearbeitungsgerät** *n* photographic processing apparatus **-bericht** *m* pictorial (report) feature **-berichter** *m* photographic reporter, war photographer **-berichterstatter** press photographer **-beschreibung** *f* picture tracing, re-creation or delineation **-betragungsgerät** *n* facsimile equipment **-breiteregelung** *f* width control

Bildbrennpunkt *m* **bildseitiger oder hinterer ~** rear focus

Bild-bühne *f* aperture, film trap **-bühneneinstellung** *f* framing, racking (by framing device) **-charakter** *m* pictorial character, key of a picture or image **-dauer** *f* image duration, picture period **-detail** *n* image detail **-diapositiv** *n* diapositive **-dienst** *m* pictorial or photographic service **-drehung** *f* image rotation **-druckpresse** *f* press for illustration printing **-ebene** *f* plane of the paper or of the projection, image plane **-ebnung** *f* flattening of the image field **-eindruck** *m* presentation (Tv) **-einstelllampe** *f* framing lamp

Bild-einstellschaltung *f* framer **-einstellung** *f* centering, height or horizontal control, framing (TV), focusing **-einstellungsspule** *f* frame coil **-element** *n* picture element, image element, scanning element, mesh (of screen), scanning spot **-empfang** *m* **mit Braunscher Röhre** image reception with Braun's cathode-ray tube **-empfänger** *m* picture receiver or reconstructor, television receiver, picture-viewing tube **-empfangsstelle** *f* picture or facsimile (telegraphic) receiving station or office, recording point

bilden to form, shape, build up, work, make, construct, constitute, fashion **sich ~** to be formed, be set up **Kurve ~** to plot a curve

bildende Künste creative arts

Bild-endröhre *f* video tube **-endstufe** *f* image power amplifier stage (TV)

Bild-entwerfung *f* formation of an image, imagery, imaging **-erkundung** *f* photographic reconnaissance, photographic survey

Bilder-beilage *f* picture supplement **-bogen** *m* picture sheet **-dienst** *m* newsphoto service **-druck** *m* printing of illustrative matter **-form** *f* halftone form **-leisten** *pl* picture molding **-öse** *f* picture eye

Bilder-rahmen *m* frame **-rahmenbruch** *m* picture-frame-type fracture, fracture of black-heart malleable iron **-reich** well illustrated **-residuum** *n* residual image **-werk** *n* illustrated volume **-tafel** *f* picture panel **-schrift** *f* hieroglyphics

(print)

Bild-erzeugung *f* reproduction of the image, reconstruction of the image, scanning, exploring, scansion, formation of an image, imagery, picture (re-)creation, picture tracing **-fähig** plastic

Bildfang *m* **vertikaler ~** vertical hold

Bild-fänger *m* cinematograph, camera for taking pictures, surveying apparatus, image receiver or collector, collector (radio) video pick-up camera, television camera **-fängerröhre** *f* camera tube (pick-up tube) **-fangrohr** *n* image-receiver tube

Bildfehler *m* picture distortion, image defects **astigmatischer ~** astigmatic image error

Bildfeinheit *f* detail (degree of) definition of picture

Bildfeld *n* image field, frame, scanning field, screen, radar, angle of view, picture area **-ausleuchtung** *f* picture field illumination **-ebnung** *f* (anastigmatic) plane imagery, flattening of the image field, elimination of curvature (optics) **-größe** *f* width-of-field **-krümmung** *f* curvature of image field **-marke** *f* measuring mark, collimating point **-rahmen** *m* image frame **-wölbung** (TV) image field curvature **-zerleger** *m* picture scanner, picture dissector, picture-exploring means (television) **-zerlegung** *f* image-field dissection, scanning (radio and television, signal engineering), image (field) definition

Bildfenster *n* picture gate, aperture (motion pictures), image aperture, picture screen, film gate, trap **~ mit zwei Ausschnitten** film gate with two frames

Bildfenster-ausschnitt *m* aperture mask opening **-linsen** *pl* picture gate lenses

Bild-fernschreiber *m* panoramic teletype, range display writer (electronics) **-fernübertragung** *f* picture transmission **-fläche** *f* image plane, image area, picture field (TV), entire faceplate area **-flachheit** *f* **-flauheit** *f* flat, soft or non-contrasty quality of a picture, limy condition, fuzziness

Bild-flieger *m* aerial photographer **-flug** *m* photographic flight **-folge** *f* (Zeitfolge aufeinanderfolgender Aufnahmen) time interval between successive photographs, sequence or series of optic or pictorial actions (motion pictures) **-folgefrequenz** *f* picture frequency, frame frequency **-folgeregler** *m* picture-interval regulator

Bildformat *n* size of image or picture, size of print (photo.), picture ratio, aspect ratio, picture shape or format, frame size or format **~** (Abmessungen des Emulsionsträgers—Platte, Film) size of image (dimensions of carrier of sensitive layer—plate, film) (photogrammetry)

Bildfrequenz *f* video frequency, vision or frame frequency, picture frequency, repetition rate (television) visual frequency

Bildfrequenz-störung *f* image interference **-verstärker** *m* amplifier for frame saw-tooth time base

Bildfunk *m* radio transmission of pictures, television, radiophotograph, image or photoradio transmission, wired picture, facsimile transmission **-anlage** *f* facsimile apparatus, radio-picture transmitter **-einstellvorrichtung** *f* video framer **-gerät** *n* phototelegraphic apparatus

Bild-funktion *f* laplace transform of function **-geber** *m* pick-up camera, picture source **-geräte** *pl* picture units, picture sets (monitors) **-geräusch** *n* frame noise (motion pictures) **-geschwindigkeit** *f* image speed **-gießerei** *f* bronze-statue foundry **-gleichlaufzeichen** *n* vertical synchronizing impulse **-gleichrichter** *m* video detector **-gleichrichtung** *f* video detection **-greifer** *m* in-and-out claw (of threading mechanism)

Bildgröße *f* size of image or picture, format of picture **nutzbare ~** usable size of the photograph **Linse für veränderliche ~ und Brennweite** zooming lens for variable magnification and variable focus

Bild-güte *f* picture quality (figure of) merit or quality of picture **-halt** *m* picture lock **-halter** *m* (für Fotos usw.) picture holder **-hauerbeitel** *m* carving tools **-hauptpunkt** *m* principal point on image **-hauptsenkrechte** *f* **-hauptvertikale** *f* principal line **-hauptwaagerechte** *f* axis of tilt

Bildhelligkeit *f* brightness or distinctness of image, illumination or brilliance of picture **mittlere ~** average picture level (APL) (TV)

Bild-helligkeitsregler *m* brightness knob **-helligkeitssignale** *n pl* video signals, shading-value signals (television) **-hintergrund** *m* picture background **-hintergrundmarke** *f* background collimating point

Bildhöhe und Zeilenlänge *f* aspect ratio, height of image and line length

Bild-horizont *m* horizon trace **-impuls** *m* picture synchronizing signal or impulse, frame impulse, frame synchronizing pulse **-impulslampe** *f* frame-impulse lamp **-ingenieur** *m* video engineer **-inhalt** *m* picture content or subject matter, picture information **-kammer** *f* camera, aerocamera, aerial camera **-kanal** *m* picture or vision channel

Bildkante *f* **verwischte ~** trailing edge (TV)

Bild-kantenschärfe *f* resolution on border **-kantenverhältnis** *n* aspect ratio

Bildkarte *f* photographic map

Bildkartiergeräte *n pl* plotting apparatus **~ für Bildpaare** plotting apparatus for pairs of photographs **~ für Einzelbilder** single-photograph plotting apparatus

Bild-kartierung *f* plotting of plans or maps from photographs, mapping from photographs **-kippeinsatz** *m* incipient frame flyback or beam return (television) **-kipper** *m* frame time base

Bildkipp-frequenz *f* image (frame) sweep frequency **-generator** *m* framing oscillator **-gerät** *n* frame-sweep apparatus **-schwingung** *f* frame or picture time-base oscillation or impulse **-spannung** *f* frame sweep voltage **-punkt** *m* image sweep point, point or moment of image change

Bild-knotenpunkt *m* rear nodal point **-konservierung** *f* (Fehler) image retention (TV) **-kontrolle am Geber** image control at the transmitter **-kontrollempfänger** *m* monitor **-kontrollgerät** *n* picture and waveform monitor **-koordinate** *f* plate, image or picture coordinate **-koordinatensystem** *n* collimating axes, plate coordinate system

Bild-kraft *f* image force or potential **-kraftberechnung** *f* image-force calculation **-kreis** *m* view (photo), image circle, representative circle **-kreismittelpunkt** *m* center of image **-kristallgleichrichter** *m* crystal video rectifier **-künstler** *m* photographer **-lagekarte** *f* map composed of aerial photographs **-ladung** *f* picture charge

bildlich graphic, graphical, figurative, diagrammatic **~ darstellen** to depict **-e Darstellung** *f* pictorial representation

Bild-linie *f* focal line, image line **-los** amorphous, noncrystalline **-lotpunkt** *m* plate plumb point, nadir or the image, point of image perpendicular **-lupe** *f* picture viewer

Bildmarke *f* collimating point, trade sign

Bildmarken am Ophthalmometer mires

Bildmarken-anordnung *f* arrangement of collimation points **-verbindungsgeraden** *f pl* lines connecting collimation points **-viereck** *n* quadrangle formed by collimation points

Bild-maske *f* framing mask **-mäßig** pictorial (phot.), (made) in accordance with illustration **-maßstab** *m* scale of image, picture, or photograph **-material** *n* photogenic subject (matter) **-meister** *m* director of photography, picture chief or director **-meldung** *f* photographic report **-messer** *m* view meter (phot.) **-meßgeräte** *n pl* image-, picture-, or plate-measuring apparatus, photogrammetric apparatus **-meßtheodolit** *n* photogoniometer **-meßverfahren** *n* photographic recorder system

Bildmessung *f* image, picture, or plate measuring, photogrammetry **~ nach Porro** Porro's photogoniometric method

Bild-meßwesen *n* photogrammetry **-mischer** *m* video mixer **-mischpult** *n* video consolette or video mixer

Bildmittelpunkt *m* center of image, picture, or plate **optischer ~** center of optical image, picture, or plate

Bild-mitteneinstellung *f* vertical centering control **-modelung** *f* picture modulation **-modulation** *f* image or pattern modulation, picture signal modulation **-modulationsfrequenz** *f* video, image or picture frequency **-monitor** *m* picture monitor (TV)

Bildmuster (zum Prüfen der Bildgüte) test pattern **-generator** *m* test pattern generator (TV) pattern-signal generator

Bildnachleuchten *n* afterglow, phosphorescence of picture

Bildnachstellung *f* framing, phasing, racking (motion pictures, television), centering control (television) **falsche ~** misframing, out-of-frame condition

Bild-nadir *m* plate plumb point, nadir of the image, point of image perpendicular **-neigung** *f* tilt of the vertical photograph

Bildnis *n* portrait, picture, photograph

Bild-nummer *f* number of the picture or photograph, number of illustration **-ordinate** *f* ordinate of the image

Bildpaar *n* **stereoskopisches ~** pair of stereoscopic pictures

Bild-parallele *f* photo-parallel **-plan** *m* picture or photographic plan, controlled mosaic **-planskizze** *f* partially controlled (sketched) mosaic (aviation) **-plastik** *f* plastic, relief, or stereoscopic effect, distortion of television image in form of multiple contours of diminishing intensity, ghost picture **-prägung** *f* picture embossing

Bildpunkt *m* picture or scanning element, mesh (of screen), image (spot) element, image point, point image, video frequency, picture-unit or elementary area, picture level or point or dot, scanning point **hellster ~** high light, bright light **dunkelster ~** shadow **nachleuchtender ~** phosphorescent picture point

Bildpunkt-abtaster *m* analyzer, scanning device at the transmitting end, scanning key or switch, video switch **-dauer** *f* persistence or duration of image spot **-frequenz** *f* image or picture frequency, video frequency (TV) **-größe** *f* image-spot size **-kraft** *f* image force **-signal** *n* video signal, electrical impulse resulting from elementary area

Bildpunkt-verlagerung *f* spot shift (causing plastic effect, television), diffusion of the point image **-verteiler** *m* video distributor, picture scanner (at receiving end) **-verteilung** *f* reproduction or reconstruction of image, scanning, exploring, scansion, scanning device at the receiving end **-verzerrung** *f* aperture distortion **-zahl** *f* number of image or picture elements

Bild-qualität *f* definition (film) **-quelle** *f* image source, virtual source **-rand** *m* margin of image **-raster** *m* grating, scanning, scanning field, picture raster (television), (halftone) screen **-raum** *m* image space **-reaktor** image reactor **-reihe** *f* strip mosaic, sequence of pictorial actions, frames or pictures (moving pictures)

Bildröhre *f* kinescope, kine (TV), picture tube (TV), recording tube monitor **~ mit Konusteil aus Metall** metal cone kinescope

Bild-rücklauf *m* image or frame flyback **-rundfunkempfänger** *m* wireless picture telegraph

bildsam plastic, ductile, moldable **in der Wärme ~** thermoplastic

Bildsamkeit *f* plasticity, capability of being kneaded, fashioned, formed or molded (by pressure and/or heat application), formability, moldability, fictility

Bild-satz *m* progressive set of photographs **-säule** *f* statue **-schale** *f* image shell **-schallplatte** *f* sound and picture on disk **-schaltung** *f* feed or movement of frame (motion pictures), frame ratcheting, frame time base (television) **-schärfe** *f* image or picture definition, focus, contrast, quality of the image **-schaukeln** *n* image-drift **-scherung** *f* shearing of an image

Bildschirm *m* projection screen, picture screen picture area, fluorescent screen, tube screen, plan-position indicator; (Radar) scope **~ mit aufgedampfter Aluminiumhaut** aluminized screen

Bildschirm-maßstab *m* display scale (Rdr) **-träger** *m* display console (Rdr)

Bildschlitzausrüstung zur mechanischen Radialtriangulation equipment for the slotted-templet method

Bild-schreiber *m* recorder **-schreibrohr** *n* image-producing tube **-schreibröhre** *f* televisor tube, viewing tube, picture-reproducing tube **-schritt** *m* frame gauge **-schwingungen** *f pl* picture or video impulses or signals **-seitenverhältnis** *n* picture-aspect ratio

bildseitig-er Brennpunkt focus on the image side **-e Grundfläche** upper end of lens cone **-er (hinterer) Hauptpunkt** (Projektionszentrum) internal perspective center **-er Knotenpunkt** rear nodal point **-es Stutzenende** upper end of lens cone

Bild-sendeempfangsanlage *f* facsimile transceiver set, radio-picture set **-sendegeräte** *pl* picture transmitters **-sendeleistung** *f* visual-transmitter power **-senden** to transmit picture **-sender** *m* image or video or facsimile transmitter, picture transmitter, TV-transmitter **-senkrechte** *f* parallel to the principal line

Bildsignal *n* video or vision or picture signal **~ (BA)-Wähler** video signal patching panel **~ mit Abtastung** blanked picture (video) signal

Bildsignaleingang *m* picture-signal input

Bildskizze *f* photographic sketch, uncontrolled mosaic

Bildspannung *f* image or picture voltage **Untergehen der ~** swamping of video or picture signal

Bildspeicherröhre *f* image-storing tube, charge or signal storage tube, normal iconoscope, graphecon

Bildsperre *f* picture trap (TV)

Bildsprung *m* picture-repetition frequency, picture cycle, break or shift of vision **Unmerklichkeit des Bildsprunges bei einer Zweistärkenbrille** absence of any break of vision in a bifocal glass

Bild-spurzeit *f* development factor **-stecher** *m* engraver **-stein** *m* agalmatolite, figure stone **-stelle** *f* photographic station, picture scanner telephoto station (facsimile) **-steuerung** *f* picture control (TV) **-stock** *m* cliché, cut, bracket, stereotype, block (printing office) **-stöße** *m pl* frame impulses **-strahl** *m* image ray, ray through a point image

Bildstreifen aufeinanderfolgender Aufnahmen strip of successive photographs

Bildstricheinstellung *f* phasing or framing of picture **fehlerhafte oder falsche ~** misframing, out-of-frame condition

Bildstrich-geräusch *n* frame-line noise **-lage** *f* position of the picture frame bars **-verstellung** *f* adjustment framing, picture phaseing

Bildstrom *m* reactive current, video or picture current **-frequenzen** *f pl* frequencies of image current **-stärke** *f* intensity of image current **-stürzung** *f* toppled condition of pictures

Bild-sturz *m* **-stürzen** *n* somersaulting or tumbling of the images **-sucher** *m* finder frame, view finder (phot.) **-synchron** picture synchronized

Bildsynchronisier-impuls *m* picture-synchronizing signal or impulse, frame-synchronizing impulse or pulse, low-synchronizing impulse **-lücke** *f* synchronizing band, or gap, blank bar (between successive frames)

Bildsynchronisierung *f* picture synchronization

Bildsynchronisierungsimpulsverstärker *m* frame-synchronizing-impulse or -pulse amplifier

Bild-synthese *f* reproduction or reconstruction of image, scanning, exploring, scansion **-tafel** *f* plane of projection **-tanzen** *n* unsteadiness or jumping of picture **-teile** *m pl* **verschiedener Gliederung** picture portions of dissimilar nature, classification, composition, or make-up

Bild-telegramm *n* phototelegram, facsimile telegram **-telegraph** *m* picture telegraph

Bildtelegraphenanlage *f* **Einrichtung einer ~** receiver station for a picture telegraph installation

Bild-telegraphengerät *n* photoelectric apparatus, picture telegraph apparatus **-telegraphie** *f* image or picture telegraphy, wired or radio phototelegraphy, radio or wire transmission of pictures, facsimile, wirephoto, telephotography

Bild-theodolit *m* photogoniometer **-tiefe** *f* pictorial depth **-tonabstand** *m* lead-lag relation between picture and sound **-töne** *pl* tonal values (shades)

Bildträger *m* image-film or image-carrier sound film, plate or film carrier (TV) **-frequenz** *f* picture carrier frequency **-scheibe** *f* disk shaped photo-carrier

Bild-transportrolle *f* picture feed roller **-triangulation** *f* triangulation from photographs **-überblendungvorrichtung** *f* picture-changeover **-überträger** *m* television apparatus, picture transmitter

Bildübertragung *f* picture or image transmission, facsimile or telephoto transmission **elektromechanische und elektrochemische ~** picture, photographic or facsimile transmission by electromechanical or electrochemical means

Bildübertragungsgerät *n* picture telegraph apparatus, phototelegraphy, facsimile equipment or set

bildumkehrendes Linsensystem, verstellbares ~ variable-image inverting system of lenses

Bildumkehrung *f* image reversion, image inversion, solarization

Bild- und Zeilenoszillogramm *n* frame and line oscillogram

Bildung *f* structure, shape, formation, development, organization, rimming action **~ von Kristallisationskernen** nucleation

Bildungs-dauer *f* formative time **-element** *n* formative element **-energie** *f* energy of formation or of generation, binding or bond energy **-fähig** capable of development **-gang** *m* course of instruction **-gesetz** *n* principles **-gleichung** *f* equation of formation, structural equation **-grad** *m* degree of formation **-kraft** *f* plastic force **-stufe** *f* educational age, stage of development **-vorgang** *m* process of formation

Bildungswärme *f* heat of formation, enthalpy **~ von Fehlordnungen** heat of formation of defects

Bildungsweise *f* manner or mode of formation

Bild-unschärfe *f* lack of picture definition **-unterschrift** *f* caption **-verbreiterung** *f* image spread **-verfahrensmesser** *m* photogrammetry **-verdopplung** *f* split image **-verdrehung** *f* image rotation

Bildverschiebung *f* slow drift or hunting of image **seitliche ~** lateral shift of image

Bildverstärker *m* video (-frequency) amplifier, image or picture amplifier, head amplifier, image intensifier, image-intensifying screen

Bild-verstärkung *f* image picture amplification or intensification **-verstärkungsregelung** *f* contrast control **-verstellung** *f* framing of image (motion pictures), framing adjustment **-verstellungsknopf** *m* image-framing knob **-verstellungswelle** *f* image-framing shaft **-verwackelung** *f* image-frame unsteadiness **-verzerrung** *f* image or picture distortion, field distortion, jiggers (in facsimile) **-vordergrundmarke** *f* foreground collimating point **-vorschubbewegung** *f* frame-sweep scansion

Bild-waagerechte *f* parallel to the axis of tilt **-wähler** *m* image selector, display selector **-walze** *f* picture cylinder **-wand** *m* projection or moving-picture screen

Bildwandler *m* supericonoscope (image tube), picture-forming tube on infrared spotter, image changer or converter (television), electronic lens, optical lens converter, infrared viewer, metascope **-röhre** *f* image-viewing tube, image-converter tube iconoscope (telev.)

Bildwandleuchtdichte *f* brightness or luminous density of screen

Bildwechsel *n* repetition of pictures, image changes (frame change), picture cycle **stetiger ~** continuous, steady, or nonintermittent feed or motion of film

Bildwechsel-frequenz *f* frame or frame-repetition frequency, image or picture frequency, number of frames per second **-frequenzregelung** *f* field frequency control **-impuls** *m* frame or image impulse **-zahl** *f* image or frame frequency, scanning rate, number of successive images (television) **-zeit** *f* image period or time, feeding time, picture cycle, moving period (moving pictures)

Bildweichheit *f* bloom (TV)

bildweise Filmschaltung intermittent film feed, discontinuous film movement

Bildweite *f* principal distance, perspective, image distance, distance between screen and lens, image intercept, width of (illustration) picture

Bildweitensteuerung *f* (Entzerrungsgerät) control of principal distance (rectifier)

Bildwellenspannung *f* video-signal wave potential

Bildwerfer *m* projector (phot.), cinematograph picture projector **-lampe** *m* projection lamp

Bild-wiederaufbau *m* reconstruction (of a facsimile picture) **-wiedergabe** *f* reproduction or reconstruction of image, scanning, exploring, scansion

Bildwinkel *m* angle of image or of view **~ des Objektivs** angular field of the lens **nutzbarer ~** effective angular field of image

Bildwirkung *f*, **plastische ~** illusion of depth (of picture), stereoscopic effect

Bild-wölbung *f* aberration of form (phot.), curvature of field or of image **-wurfelektrode** *f* target electrode **-wurfkammer** *f* camera of projection **-zahl** *f* frame or frame-repetition frequency, image or picture frequency **-zähler** *m* frame counter or indicator

Bild-zeichen *n* design mark **-zeile** *f* line (in scanning with cathode-ray tube in television), line (radio), wire line, picture line, picture strip (television), scanning line **-zeilendurchlauf** *m* line transversal **-zeilenfrequenzverstärker** *m* vision IF amplifier **-zeitbasis** *f* picture output **-zerdrehung** *f* rotational, tangential, or orientational distortion, twist of image **-zerleger** *m* picture analyzer, scanner, or explorer, scanning device at the transmitting end, dissector (of Farnsworth) **-zerlegerröhre** *f* image dissector

Bildzerlegung *f* scanning, scansion, exploring, or analyzing of picture **mechanisch-optische ~** mechanical-optical image scanning (dissection)

Bildzerlegungsvorrichtung *f* analyzer, scanning device at the transmitting end

Bild-ziehen *n* photographic travel ghost **-zittern** *n* unsteadiness or jumping of picture **-zurichteverfahren** process for dressing pictures

Bildzusammensetzung *f* reproduction or reconstruction of image, scanning, exploring, scansion **mechanisch-optische ~** mechanical-optical composition of the image

Bildzusammensetzvorrichtung *f* scanning device at the receiving end, picture-reproduction means, picture recreator or delineator, picture scanner

Bild-zusammenstellung *f* picture synthesis **-zwischenfrequenz** *f* image intermediate frequency **-zylinder** *m* engraving cylinder

Bilge *f* floorheads, bilge **-brunnen** *m* bilge well **-wasserhilfspumpe** *f* emergency bilge pump **-wasserpumpe** *f* bilge pump

Bilinearform *f* bilinear form **bilinearskalar** bilinear scalar

Billard-kreide *f* billiard-cue chalk **-kugel** *f* billiard ball

Billietit *m* billietite

Billet *n* ticket

billig cheap, inexpensive

billigen to approve, sanction

Billigkeitsverfahren *n* equity suit

Billigung *f* approval, approbation, consent, acquiescence, assent

Bilux-Lampe *f* two-filament bulb (Bilux)

Bimester bimensal or bimonthly period

Bimetall *n* bimetal, bimetallism **-aktinometer** *m* bimetal actinometer **-bügel** *m* bimetal strip **-draht** *m* bimetallic wire, copper-clad steel wire **-feder** *f* bimetal spring **-instrument** bimetallic instrument

bimetallisch bimetallic

Bimetall-relais *n* bimetal relay **-streifen** *m* bimetallic strip, trip, or tripping gear **-thermograph** *m* bimetallic thermograph

bimorph bimorph

Bims-beton *m* pumice concrete **-dieler** *pl* pumice slabs

bimsen to polish with pumice

Bims-maschine *f* buffing wheel, grinding machine **-sand** *m* pumice sand **-staub** *m* pumice powder

Bimsstein *m* pumice **-artig, -ähnlich** pumiceous **-ersatz** *m* pumice substitute **-mehl** *n* pumice powder **-papier** *n* pumice paper **-seife** *f* pumice (stone) soap

Binantenschachtel *f* box with a two-segment electrometer system

binär binary **-e Darstellungsweise** binary notation **~ gelochte Karte** binary punched card **-e Legierung** binary alloy **-es System** binary system, two-component system **-er Untersetzer** scale of two circuits **-e Verbindung** *f* binary compound **-er Zähler** binary scaler **-e Zählstufe** flip-flop circuit

Binär-code binary code **-dezimalkonvertierung** *f* binary-to-decimal conversion **-darstellung** *f* binary notation **-element** *n* binary cell

binärgesetzte Dezimalschreibweise *f* binary code decimal notation

Binär-komma *n* binary point **-schreibweise** *f* binary notation **-setzung** *f* binary notation **-speicherelement** *n* two-state-device **-stellendichte** *f* bit density **-stellenzahl** *f* binary digits **-zahl** *f* binary number **-zähler** *m* scale-of-two counter, binary counter **-ziffer** *f* binary digit **-zifferndichte** bit density

binaural binaural **-e Ortung** binaural location

Binaural-prinzip *n* binaural principle (in sound locating) **-verfahren** *n* binaural method in sound locating

Binde *f* bandage, binding, band, sash **-apparat** *m* binding attachment **-band** *n* binding tape **-blech** *n* brace plate **-bücher** *pl* cording quires **-draht** *m* binding wire, binder, tie, lashing, or baling wire **-faden** *m* connecting thread **-fähigkeit** *f* binding property or quality, bonding power, bonding-capacity property, strength, or quality **-festigkeit** *f* adhesion

Binde-garn *n* (binder) twine **-gewebe** *n* connective tissue **-glied** *n* (connecting) link, connecting part or member **-holz** *n* lacing **-kette** *f* connecting chain, stitching warp **-kraft** *f* cohesion, binding power, setting strength **-leine** *f* binding cord **-mäher** *m* grain binder, harvester and binding machine **-maschine** *f* binder (agr.) **-material** *n* binder

Bindemittel *n* binding means or agent, binding material, cement, agglutinate, binder, bond, bonding agent, cementing agent or material, vehicle (alum), material cement, insulating material **~ nach Abbinden** matrix **-emulsion** *f* emulsion binder **-gehalt** *m* cementing agent **-suspension** *f* binder suspension

binden to bind, cement, bond, tie, tie up, combine, unite, absorb, lace, engage, set, harden, consolidate, store up, retain, contain, compact

bindend binding, obligatory; bonding, adhesive

Bindepunkt *m* binding point (interlacing point)

Binder *m* frame, bent, truss, header (brick), girder, binding stone, bond, necktie **-balken** *m* principal or main beam or girder, binding joist, main truss, poop, or couple **-betätigungsmagnet** *m* solenoid **-decke** *f* binder cover

Binderbügel *m* heel strap

Bindereifen *m* wheel rim

Binderfarbe *f* rubproof paint, emulsion paint

Binderiemen *m* thong, strap, leather belt

Binder-obergurt *m* top flange of truss **-querträger** *m* transverse girder **-schicht** *f* course of headers, heading course **-sparren** *m* principal rafter **-stein** *m* header

Binde-satz *m* (Ankündigungssatz) carrier sentence **-stab** *m* bonding tie **-steiger** *m pl* shrink bobs, bind risers **-strang** *m* trace, tug **-strich** *m* hyphen **-ton** *m* bonding or plastic clay, clay bond, ball clay **-tuch** (Riemen) *n* cotton duck, canvas

Binde-vermögen *n* binding power property, or quality, bonding capacity **-vorrichtung** *f* binding attachment **-zeit** *f* time required for concrete to set, time of set, setting time **-zwirn** *m* tying thread, unbleached hemp cord, twine, pack cord

Bindfaden *m* string, packthread, twine, cord, binding thread **-knäuel** *n* ball of twine **-korb** *m* twine holder or basket **-rolle** *f* roll of twine

bindig cohesive **nicht ~** (kohäsionslos) cohesionless (materials), non-cohesive **Steine mit -em Boden** stone with binding materials

Bindsel *n* lashing seizing

Bindung *f* absorption, binding, union, penetration weld, association, affinity (Biol.) (Verkettung, Reihe) linkage; (chemische) combination, compound, chemical bond (von Gasen) mixing; (Handelswesen) tying up, inactivation; (keramische) vitrified bond, bond(ing); (Struktur, Gefüge, Aufbau) texture; (techn.) fusion; (Verpflichtungen) engagement, obligation, commitment; (Weberei) cross-weaving

Bindung (des Luftkabels am Tragseil) marline tie, (von Gasen) absorption

Bindung, ~ (bei Elektronen) covalent bonding **kovalente ~** covalent bond **~ im oberen** (seitlichen) **Drahtlager** top(side) binding **~ bei Schleifscheiben** bonding with grinding wheels **~ des atmosphärischen Stickstoffes** nitrogen fixation **~** (Tuch) construction (fabric)

Bindungs-art *f* bond type **-bahn** *f* bond orbital **-effekt** *m* interlacing effect **-eigenschaft** *f* bond property

Bindungsenergie *f* bond energy, binding energy, combination energy, bond strength, cohesive energy, separation energy, ionization potential **~ pro Teilchen** packing fraction

Bindungs-kraft *f* linkage force **-lehre** *f* theory of interlacing **-mittel** *n* binding means or agent, binding material, cement, agglutinate, binder, bond, bonding agent **-moment** *n* bond moment **-polarisierbarkeit** *f* bond polarizability **-refraktion** *f* bond refraction **-stärke** *f* bonding strength **-verfahren** *n* binding process **-wärme** *f* heat of absorption, heat of combination **-wechsel** *m* change of weave **-zustand** *m* state of binding

Bineutron *n* bineutron

Binge *f* kettle-shaped deepening, funnel-shaped pit

binnen within **-bords** inboard **-deich** *m* inner dam **-dock** *n* inner dock **-druck** *m* presure within or between **-eis** *n* continental icecap **-gang** *m* inside stroke **-gewässer** *n* interior or inland water(s) **-grenze** *f* regional frontier **-hafen** *m* inner harbor, estuary or river port, dock, locked basin **-handel** *m* home or domestic trade **-haupt** *n* inner (or upper) gates **-klima** *n* continental climate **-klüver** *m* inner jib

Binnen-land *n* inland, interior **-ländisch** situated inland, in the interior, continental **-pfähle** *m pl* filling timbers **-schiffahrt** *f* inland shipping or navigation **-see** *m* inland sea, lake **-spant** *m* rider plate **-tief** *n* drain or small canal in a town **-tiefland** *n* inland lowlands **-tor** *n* ebbtide gates **-verkehr** *m* home or inland traffic **-volk** *n* inland population **-währung** *f* inland currency (not for international trade) **-wasserstraße** *f* inland waterway **-wirtschaft** *f* home or internal economy

Binode *f* binode, diode triode **-röhre** *f* diode triode

binokular binocular **-er Schrägtubus** inclined binocular tube

Binokularspule *f* binocular coil

Binom *n* binomial

Binominal-antennennetz *n* binominal antenna array **-reihe** *f* binomial series **-torder** *m* binominal twist **-verteilung** binominal distribution **-winkelsystem** binomial corner

binomischer (Lehr)satz, binomial theorem

binormal binormal

Binse *f* rattan, rush

Binsen-korb *m* rush basket, hamper **-matte** *f* mat of rush

Biochemie *f* biochemistry

biochemisch biochemical

bioklimatische Bedeutung bioclimatic significance

biologisch-e Erneuerung turnover **-e Halbwertzeit** biological half life **-er Konzentrationsfaktor** biological concentration factor **-er Strahlungseffekt** biological effects of radiation

Biolumineszenz *f* bioluminescence

Biophysik *f* biophysics

Biose *f* disaccharid

Biot-Savart'sches Gesetz Biot-Savart law

Bipartitionswinkel *m* bepartition angle

Bipolarität *f* bipolarity

Bipolarkoordinate *f* bipolar coordinate

Bipotentialgleichung *f* bipotential equation

Biprisma *n* biprism **-versuch** *m* biprism method

Biquadrat *n* fourth power

Biquarz *m* biquartz

biquinäre Schreibweise biquinary notation

Biquinär-code *m* biquinary code **-setzung** *f* biquinary notation

Birke *f* birch

birken, aus Birke(nholz) of birch

Birkengang Ofen Birkengang furnace

Birkenholz *n* birch wood

Birkenholzteerseife *f* birch tar soap

Birken-maser *f* curled birchwood **-sperrholz** *n* birch plywood **-teeröl** *n* birch-tar oil

Birmingham Normallehre für Bleche und Bandeisen Birmingham sheet- and hoop-iron standard gauge

Birnbaumholz *n* pearwood

Birne *f* pear, vessel, electric bulb, converter ~ (Tiefbohren), casing-spud straightener; (Seil) rope socket

Birnen-ausschalter *m* pear switch **-fassung** *f* bulb socket **-förmig** pear- or converter-shaped **-lampe** *f* pear-shaped lamp (bulb) **-prozeß** *m* Bessemer or air-refining process, acid and basic hearth-converting process **-ring** *m* trunnion ring **-schalter** *m* pear switch **-schiene** *f* pear-head rail

Birner *m* swadge

Birntaster *m* pear-key

bis up to, to, till, until, as far as

Biscuitpackpapier *n* biscuit caps

Bisektrix *f* bisector

bisher hitherto, to the present, so far, previous, former

bisherig hitherto existing

Bisilikat *n* bisilicate

Bissen *m* bite

Bist *m* (Biegestanze) power brake

bistabil bistable **-es Bauelement** two-state device **-e Kippschaltung** *f* two-condition trigger circuit **-er Oszillator** flip-flop oscillator

Bisterbraun *n* bister

bisterfarbiger Ton bister shade

Bistouri *m* bistoury

Bisulfit-lauge *f* bisulfite waste liquor **-zinkstaubküpe** *f* bisulfite-zinc vat

Bit *n* bit (comput.), binary digit (gen.)

Bitte *f* petition, request, prayer

bitten to ask, ask for, request **dringend ~** to entreat, solicit

bitter bitter, acrimonious

Bitter-erde *f* magnesia, magnesium oxide **-fenchelöl** *n* common fennel oil **-holz** *n* quassia, bitterwood **-kalk** *m* **-kalkspat** *m* dolomite, muricalcite, magnesium limestone

Bitterkeit *f* bitterness

Bitter-mandelöl *n* oil of bitter almonds, benzaldehyde **-salz** *n* Epsom salt, magnesium sulfate **-säure** *f* picric acid, trinitrophenol, trinitrophenic acid

Bitter'sche Streifen Bitter (powder) patterns, Bitter bands

Bitterspat *m* magnesium carbonate, rhomb spar, magnesite, dolomite

Bittschrift *f* petition

Bittsteller *m* petitioner

Bitumastic-anstrich *m* paint made of bituminous mastic **-belag** *m* layer of bitumastic (pitch mastic)

Bitumen *n* bituminous earth, bitumen **-anstrich** *m* bitumen or bituminous coat, asphalt coating

bitumenartige Isolation bituminous insulation

Bitumen-beton *m* bituminous concrete **-bewurf** *m* asphaltic plaster **-dichtung** *f* bituminous seal **-erhitzer** *m* bitumen heater **-farbe** *f* bituminous paint

bitumen-gebundener Straßenunterbau bitumen-bound road bases **-haltig** bituminiferous, rich in bitumen **-pappe** *f* bituminous felt

bitumig bituminous

bituminierte Wellpappe type of bituminized corrugated pulpboard

Bituminierung *f* bituminization

bituminös bituminous **-er Lack** bituminous coating composition **-er Mastix** bitumastic **-er Stoff** bituminous material

bivalenter Code two-condition cable code

Bivektor *m* bivector

Bivektorenraum *m* bivector space

bizarres Echo spill-over echo

bizyklisch bicyclic

B-K-Schwingungen *f pl* Barkhausen-Kurz oscillations

Blach-feld *n* tableland, plateau **-mahl** *n* iron dross, slag **-stab** *m* bare wire electrode

Blackband *m* blackband, blackband ironstone

Blahe *f* sackcloth, canvas

blähen to inflate, swell, expand

Blähen *n* (Ton) bloating

Bläh-index *m* swelling index **-mittel** *n* inflating agent or medium, blowing agent **-neigung** *f* swelling (foundry) **-pore** *f* bubble-hole **-probe** *f* swelling test **-ton** *m* expanded clay, bloating clay **-zahl** *f* swelling index

Blähungsgrad *m* expanding or swelling property,

degree of inflation or imbibition

blaken to smolder, smoke

blanc fixe blanc fixe, permanent white, pearl white, barite

blanchieren to blanch, whiten, bleach

Blanchierstahl *m* whitening blade or steel

Blanchimeter blanchimeter

Blank *n* blank, spacing signal

blank clean, smooth, polished, clear, naked, exposed, bare (wire); (Metall) bright, untarnished ~ **machen** (Draht) to scrape and clean brightly, scour (a wire) ~ **gezogenes Material** bright-drawn material **-er Draht** bare, bright, or naked wire **-es Kabel** bare cable **-er Leiter** bare conductor or wire **-e Profile** bright drawn sections **-e und gedrehte Schrauben** bright and turned bolts and screws **-es Seil** bare cable

Blank-ätzen *n* electrolytic polishing **-beizen** *n* pickling **-brennen** to bright-burn **-draht** *m* raw wire **-elektrode** *f* bare electrode, uncoated electrode

blänken to polish (clean), make shiny

Blankett *n* blank (form)

Blankfilm *m* film base **gelatinebeschichteter** ~ gelatin-coated film base **unbeschichteter** ~ plain, uncoated film base

Blankfiltration *f* bright filtrate

blank-geglüht bright-annealed **-gewalzt** bright (cold-)rolled **-gezogen** bright-drawn, cold-drawn **-glühen** *n* bright annealing

Blankglühofen *m* bright annealing furnace

Blankhärte- und Glühofen *m* nonoxydizing annealing and hardening furnace

blank kochen to boil blank

Blanklack *m* clear varnish

blank machen to glaze, polish

blanko uncovered, blank **-formular** *n* blank form **-geschäft** *n* short sale, sale in blank **-vollmacht** *f* unlimited power of attorney, blank letter of attorney

Blank-präge *f* blanking die or cutter **-putzen** to polish **-scheibe** *f* clear glass screen **-scheit** *n* busk, miter sill of a canal lock **-schlagen** to blank **-schleifen** *n* smooth grinding **-seite** *f* blank page, blank or unused side (paper), cellulose face or side (of film)

Blank-stahl *m* bright steel **-stoßzylinder** *m* glazing cylinder **-strahlen** *n* grit blasting **-taste** *f* blank key **-tran** *m* pure cod oil **-verdrahtung** *f* strapping, piano wiring **-wischen** to wipe (clean)

Blas-apparat *m* blast apparatus **-arbeit** *f* blasting operation **-balg** *m* bellows

Bläschen *n* (small) bubble, vesicle

Blas-düse *f* blast nozzle, blast gun, sandblast nozzle, discharge nozzle **-düsenkopf** *m* blast-nozzle tip **-düsenöffnung** *f* blast-nozzle orifice

Blase *f* bubble, blowhole, blister, flaw, honeycomb, bag, bell, still, seed, gaseous inclusion (in glass), bladder ~ **der Libelle** bubble of level ~ **in Metall** blasthole

Blaseapparat *m* blower, blast apparatus

Blasebalg *m* bellows ~ **mit Tretvorrichtung** foot blower

Blasebalg-kamera *f* bellows-body camera **-schwengel** *m* breakstaff or rocker of a smith's bellows

Blase-dauer *f* time of blowing **-einrichtung** *f* blower **-form** *f* tuyère arch **-formung** *f* blistering **-geräusch** *n* roaring noise caused by blast (during boil) **-hals** *m* (eines Ventilators), chimney **-lampe** *f* blast lamp **-loch** *n* tuyère hole, blasthole **-meister** *m* blower (Bessemer), foreman in charge of blower

blasen to blow, blast, sound, smelt (blast furnace), inject (steam) **mit Heißwind** ~ to blow with hot air, blow hot **mit Kaltwind** ~ to blow with cold air, blow cold

Blasen *n* (Gaseinschlüsse) blisters

Blase(n)-abschneider *m* bubble separator **-ähnlich** vesicular, ampullaceous **-anzeiger** *m* bubble indicator **-bewegung** *f* movement of the bubble

Blasenbildung *f* formation of blowholes, blister or bubble formation, blistering (paint, metal, photography), cavitation, occlusion of gases ~ **an Ionen** bubble nucleation by ions

blasende Kerze *f* blowing plug

blasen-frei nonporous, dense, bubble-free **-gerät** *n* bladder diaphragm **-hohlraum** *m* blowhole **kammer** *f* bubble chamber **-kette** *f* chain of bubbles (filtration) **-kupfer** *m* blister copper **-loser Stahl** nonblistered steel

Blasen-radius *m* bubble radius **-raum** *m* blowhole **-sextant** *m* bubble sextant **-stahl** *m* blister(ed), cement or converted steel **-wachstum** *n* bubble growth **-weg** *m* bubble movement **-ziehend** blistering, vesicant **-zieher** *m* vesicant **-zusammensturz** *m* bubble collapse (cavitation)

Blase-ofen *m* blow furnace **-probe** *f* bubble test

Bläser *m* ventilator, blower, fan, feeder of gas, exhaust fan **rotierender** ~ rotary blower

Bläserführung *f* guide for blower bar

Blase-rohr *n* blowpipe, blast pipe, tuyère **-stellung** *f* blowing position **-verfahren** *n* blowing process **-vorgang** *m* blow **-zeit** *f* time of blast, time of blowing

Blas-flasche *f* gas cylinder **-form** *f* blow mold **-formen** *n* blow molding **-formmaschine** *f* blow molding machine **-formverfahren** *n* blow molding **-geschwindigkeit** *f* rate of blowing **-gut** *n* material to be blasted

Blashaus *n* blast room, sandblast cabinet ~ **mit Drehboden** turntable cabinet for sandblast ~ **mit Drehtisch** rotary-table blast cabinet

blasig bubbly, honeycombed, spongy, blowy, blown, porous, blistery, mushy, blistered, vesicular ~ **werden** to get blisters **-er Guß** blistered casting, casting with blowholes

Blas-instrument *n* wind instrument **-kopf** *m* blow(ing) head **-lampe** *f* blast lamp **-loch** *n* blow-hole **-luft** *f* air blast (relative) wind **-magnet** *n* blowing magnet, flame-control magnet **-maschine** *f* blower (spreader) **-mundstück** *n* blast nozzle **-ofen** *m* blast, blowing, wind, or single-piece furnace **-öffnung** *f* blast opening, tuyère opening or hole

Blas-pistole *f* air gun, compressed-air cleaner **-probe** *f* blow test, bubble test **-prüfstand** *m* test stand with air flow to stimulate flight, blower test plant **-querschnitt** *m* total blast-nozzle area, total tuyère area **-raum** *m* blast chamber, blast cabinet **-rohr** *n* blast, blow, or discharging pipe, tuyère iron, air blast tube

blaß pale, dim

Blas-sand *m* blasting sand, abrasive **-schlitz** *m* air jet
Blässe *f* paleness
blaßgedruckte Stelle imperfect ink coverage (print)
Blas-spule *f* blow-out coil **-strom** *m* air stream
Blas- und Saugluftregulierung *f* blast air and vacuum adjustment knobs
Blasung *f* arc quenching
Blas-ventilator *m* blowing fan **-verfahren** *n* method of gas attack **-versatz** *m* pneumatic stowing or packing
Blas-versatzrohre *pl* pneumatic stowing pipes
Blas-wirkung *f* arc blow, action of blast, blowing effect **-zylinder** *m* dust bellows
Blatt *n* (Papier) sheet; (Seite) page; (technisch) plate, lamina; (Metall) foil, leaf, blade (oar), breast strap (harness), lamella, shoulder, foil, folio, blade (of knife switch), lamination (of a magnetic core); (Papier) sheet, page; (Messer) blade **~ Papier** slip **leeres ~** (paper) blank **welkes ~** withered or falling leaf, stunt flying
Blatt-aluminium *n* aluminium foil **-anschluß** *m* rotor blade retention **-adapter** *m* adapter, blade grip **-anstellwinkel** *m* blade pitch
Blattaufhängungssystem *n*, **gelenkiges ~** articulated system
Blattbenetzung *f* liquid propeller anti-icing
Blattbiegung senkrecht zur Drehebene beamwise bending
Blatt-binden *n* reed binding **-breite** *f* width of propeller blade **-breitenverhältnis** *n* blade-width ratio of propeller
Blättchen *n* thin layer, scale, lamina, lamella, foil, slip, small leaf, flake **-artig** lamellar, laminated, laminiform, lamelliform **-bildung** *f* scaling (paint)
Blättchenform, in ~ in the form of flakes or leaves
blättchen-förmig flake-shaped **-gefüge** *n* laminated structure **-pulver** *n* flake powder (with little smoke) (explosives), flaked gunpowder, flake or leaf powder **-verschluß** *m* slotted or lamellar shutter
Blatt-dichte *f* solidity of blades **-druck** *m* page printing **-drucker** *m* page printer, page printing apparatus **-drucktelegraph** *m* page-printing telegraph **-einrichter** *m* harness fixer **-einsetzen** *n* reed mounting **-einstellung** *f* pitch of blades
Blatteinstellwinkel *m*, **kleiner ~** low pitch
Blatt-einteilung *f* index **-eisen** *n* sheet iron
Blattel *f* disk of pig iron
Blatt-elektrometer *m* leaf electrometer or electroscope **-element** *n* blade element **-enden** *n pl* blade tips of propeller **-erde** *f* leaf mold
Blätter *n pl* bars, fly bars, roll bars (paper), blades (knife) **~ mit hoher Massenträgheit** high inertia blades
Blätter-bruch *m* cleavage, cleaving **-bürste** *f* foil brush, laminated brush **-erz** *n* foliated tellurium, nagyagite **-förmig** in thin sheets, leaf-shaped (laminated)
blätt(e)rig laminated, lamellar, foliated, flaky
Blätter-karde *f* sheet card (textiles) **-kern** *m* laminated core **-kernspule** *f* laminated iron-core coil **-kies** *m* lamellar pyrites, marcasite **-kohle** *f* slate coal, foliated coal, paper coal **-kupplung** *f* lamellar coupling
blättern to laminate, flake, scale, peel
Blätter-schwamm *m* agaric, mushroom **-tellur** *m* foliated tellurium, nagyagite
Blättervisier *n* sight leaf
Blätterung *f* lamination
Blätterzeolith *m* foliated zeolite, heulandite
Blätterzerreißmaschine *f*, **Rüben ~** turnip-tops-plucking machine
Blattfaser *f* leaf fiber
Blattfeder *f* flat spring, leaf (type) spring, plate spring, laminated spring, reed, blade, spring clip, flat air valve spring (print) **-biegemaschine** *f* laminated-spring bending machine **-bündel** *n* stack of plate springs
Blattfedern mit progressiver Charakteristik leaf springs with progressive spring characteristic **einlagige ~** single leaf springs
Blattfedernprüfmaschine *f* laminated spring testing machine
Blattfeder-scheibe *f* flat spring washer **-sporn** *m* leaf-spring tail skid **-summer** *m* electromagnetic oscillator **-werk** *n* laminated plated spring
Blatt-fernschreiber *m* page teleprinter **-fläche** *f* blade area (of propeller) **-flächenbelastung** *f* load per unit area of (propeller) blade surface **-form** *f* blade form **-fuge** *f* scarf joint **-führung** *f* guide for band saw **-fußmanschette** *f* (Luftschraube) blade-shank cuff **-geschwindigkeit** *f* speed of blade, propeller speed
Blattgold *n* leaf gold, gold leaf or foil **-abkehrmaschine** *f* sweeping machine for gold leaf **-anreibemaschine** *f* grinding machine for gold leaf **-druck** *m* gold leaf printing **-grundöl** *n* oil base for varnish on which to apply gold leaf **-schlägerei** *f* gold beating
Blatt-grün *n* chlorophyll **-gummi** *m* sheet rubber **-haller** *m* Blatthaller speaker (radio) **-hinterkante** *f* trailing edge of airfoil **-kantenbeschlag** *m* blade edge tipping or sheathing **-kiel** *m* flat cotter **-kohle** *f* slate coal, foliated or paper coal **-kupfer** *n* sheet copper, copper foil **-kurve** *f* folium **-lack** *m* shellac **-laufeinstellung** *f* tracking operations
Blatt-meißel *m* (Bohrer) drag bit **-metall** *n* foil or sheet metal **-nabeneinheit** *f* blade-hub unit **-neigung** *f* propeller-blade rake
Blattnasen-ausgleichshorn *n* leading edge control horn
Blattnerphon *n* blattnerphone
Blatt-ordner *m* file (print) **-querschnitt** *m* blade section or profile
blättrig laminated, lamellar, foliated
Blatt-rübentrockner *m* desiccation of untopped beets **-rührer** *m* flat blade paddle agitator **-säge** *f* pad saw **-schellack** *m* flake shellac **-schichtung** *f* stratification **-schreiber** *m* page printer (teletype) **-silber** *n* silver leaf, beaten silver
Blatt-spitze *f* blade tip **~ der Luftschraube** propeller tip
Blattspitzen-beschlag blade tip metal sheathing, blade tipping **-querschnitt** *m* tip cross section **-umfangsgeschwindigkeit** *f* blade peripheral velocity **-wirbel** *m* blade-tip vortex or eddy
Blatt-stärke *f* blade thickness **-stechen** *n* passing threads into combs **-stecher** *n* reed hook (textiles) **-steigung** *f* pitch (propeller) **-stellung** *f* blade position

Blatt-steuerungshebel *m* pitch control lever **-steuerungshorn** *n* pitch horn **-stoß** *m* scarfed joint **-stück** *n* capping plate, coping piece or plate **-tiefe** *f* blade chord

Blattung *f* scarf(ing)

Blattverbiegung in Drehebene chordwise bending

Blatt-verbindung *f* scarf joint **-verdrehung** *f* blade twist **-vergoldung** *f* gold blocking, gilding with gold leaf **-verstärkungsplatte** *f* butt plate

Blattverstell-lager *n* pitch change bearing **-einrichtung** (Blattsteuerung) pitch change control **-horn** *n* blade pitch horn **-trommel** pitch change drum

Blatt-verstellung *f* pitch change (control) **-verwindung** *f* blade twist **-völligkeit** *f* solidity ratio **-vorderkante** *f* blade leading edge **-vorschub** *m* page feed, paging up **-widerstandsstrebe** *f* blade drag brace

Blattwinkel *m* blade angle ~ **periodisch verstellen** to feather

Blattwinkelverstellung *f* pitch control **periodische** ~ cyclic pitch **Lager für periodische** ~ feathering bearings

Blatt-winkelverstellvorrichtung *f* pitch-control mechanism **-wirbel** *m* blade vortex or eddy

Blattwurzel *f* thickened portion of a propeller blade where it enters the hub, blade root **-lager** *n* blade root bearings **-verkleidung** *f* blade shank cuff

Blatt-zahl *f* number of blades **-zapfen** *m* slipper block or shoe **-zeichen** *n* bookmark **-zinn** *n* tin foil

blau blue **-er Himmel** blue sky **-es Himmelslicht** blue of the sky **-er Ton** blue clay **-er Ziegel** blue brick

Blau-anlaufen *n* blueing **-auszug** *m* blue record **-bad** *n* blueing bath **-beimischer** *m* blue adder (TV) **-blankes Blech** polished blue sheet **-blindheit** *f* blue-blindness **-brenner** *m* Bunsen burner **-bruch** *m* blue shortness, blue brittleness **-brüchig** blue short, blue brittle **-brüchigkeit** *f* blue shortness, blue brittleness **-bruchversuch** *m* blue fracture test

Blau-druck *m* indigo print, blueprint drawing **-druckplatte** *f* blue (plate) printer

Bläue *f* blue (color), blueness, blueing

blauempfindlich blue-sensitive

bläuen to blue, tint

Blauempfindlichkeit *f* sensivity to blue

Bläuen *n* bluish tinge, blueing

Blau-entladung *f* blue discharge **-eisenerde** *f* **-eisenerz** *n* **-eisenspat** *m* blue iron earth, vivianite, ferric phosphate **-erz** *n* vivianite, brown ore **-farbenglas** *n* ultramine, smalt, potash-cobalt glass **-fäule** *f* blue rot **-filter** *n* blue filter, viewing filter (photo.) **-gas** *n* blue or oil gas

Blau-, Gelb, Rotglaskalotte blue, yellow, red glass hood (calotte) screen

blau-glas *n* blue glass **-glühend** blue-hot **-glut** *f* white glow **-grau** livid

Blauholz *n* logwood **-extrakt** (gereinigt) hematine **-schwarz** *n* log wood black **-späne** *pl* logwood ships

Blau-kugel *f* bluestone **-küpe** *f* indigo vat **-lack** (Kopie) *f* cold top **-lias** *n* blue lias

bläulich bluish

Bläumaschine zum Anlassen von Eisenteilen blueing machine for tempering iron pieces

Blau-negativpapier *n* blueprint paper **-ofen** *m* shaft furnace, blast furnace, flowing furnace **-öl** *n* blue oil **-papier** *n* blueprint paper

Blaupause *f* blueprint **eine** ~ **herstellen** to blueprint

Blaupausenpapier *n* printing or copying papers (blue or white prints)

Blau-salz *n* potassium ferrocyanide **-säure** *f* hydrocyanic or prussic acid, ferrocyanide **-saures Kali** *n* potassium ferrocyanide **-saures Salz** (Cyanid) cyanide (prussiate) **-scheibe** *f* blue filter **-schreiber** *m* dark-trace CRo **-schrift-oszillograph** *m* blue-writing oscillograph **-schriftröhre** *f* dark-trace tube sciatron

Blau-spat *m* vivianite **-spiegel** *m* blue light mirror **-sprödigkeit** *f* blue brittleness **-stein** *m* blue vitriol, lapis lazuli, vivianite **-stich** *m* blue tint **-stichig** with bluish haze or tint **-stift** *m* blue pencil

Blaustrahlsystem *n* (Elektronenstrahlsystem für blau leuchtende Teile des Bildschirms) blue electron gun (TV)

Blau-vitriol *n* sulfate of copper **-warm** blue heat **-wärme** *f* blue or temper heat of iron **-wassergas** *n* Blau water gas, Blaugas

Blech *n* plate, sheet, sheet metal or iron, foil, tin sheeting, lamella, lamination of metal ~ **bis 5 mm** sheet ~ **über 5 mm** plate ~ **1. Güte** primes ~ **2. Güte** menders, seconds **aus** ~ **gestanzt** blanked out from sheet metal **doppelseitig plattiertes** ~ sandwiched metal **dickes** ~ plate **dünnes** ~ thin sheet, light-gauge sheet, sheet

Blech, einmal dekapiertes ~ single-pickled sheet ~ **erster Wahl** prime sheet ~ **zweiter Wahl** mender **gelochtes** ~ perforated sheet **gekantetes** ~ bent plate, folded sheet **geriffeltes** ~ riffled sheet iron **gewehrschußsicheres** ~ bulletproof plating **hochglanzpoliertes** ~ planished sheet, bright-finished sheet **kastengeglühtes** ~ box-annealed sheet, close-annealed sheet **schwarzes** ~ black-iron plate, (ordinary) black sheet steel **verzinktes** ~ galvanized sheet metal **weißes** ~ tin plate

Blech-abfälle *m pl* clippings **-abstand** *m* gap between sheets **-anker** *m* gusset stays of boiler **-arbeit** *f* platework **-ausführung** *f* sheet metal manufacture **-aushauer** *m* sheet metal punch **-ausleger** *m* box-section-type jib **-ausschnitt** *m* **-ausstoß** *m* blank (metall.) **-balken** *m* plate girder

Blech-bearbeitungsanlage *f* sheet-metal-working plant **-bearbeitungsmaschine** *f* plate-working machine **-behälter** *m* sheet-metal tank, metal container **-bekleidung** *f* plating **-belag** *m* plate covering **-beplankung** *f* metal skin **-besäummaschine** *f* plate-edge planing machine **-besäumung** *f* plate edge planing **-beschlag** *m* **zur Drahtbefestigung** wiring plate (aviation) **-beschlagen** covered or plated with metal

Blech-biegemaschine *f* plate-bending machine, plate-bending rolls, brake, sheet doubler, sheet folder **-blasinstrument** *n* brass wind instrument **-bördelmaschine** *f* plate-flanging machine, sheet-bordering machine **-büchse** *f* tin box, tin can **-büchsenmacher** *m* tin-box maker **-bürstmaschine** *f* plate brushing machine **-dach** *n* sheet metal roof **-deckel** *m* sheet-metal cover **-dicke** *f* gauge or thickness of a sheet or plate

Blech-doppler *m* sheet-doubling machine, sheet doubler **-dose** *f* tin can, tin box **-dosenlack** *m* lacquer for tin cans **-duo** *n* two-high plate mill **-eisen** *n* sheet iron

Blechdruck *m* tin or sheet-metal printing **-farbe** *f* tin-plate ink **-firnis** *m* tin printing varnish **-maschine** *f* tin printing machine **-rotationsmaschine** rotary tin printing press

Bleche *pl* plates and sheets ~ **in Stanz- und Tiefziehgüte** plates in stamping or deep-drawing quality

Blecheinsatz *m*, **mit** ~ tin lined

Blechemballage *f* sheet metal container, tin box, canister

blechen, blechern to tin-plate

blechern tinny (sound)

Blecherzeugnisse *n pl* metal-plate products

Blech-etikett *n* metal tag **-faltemaschine** *f* tin-making machine, tin-plate folder **-festhaltung** *f* holding-down clamp for plates **-flasche** *f* oil can, tin vessel or container with a narrow neck **-folie** *f* tinfoil **-gefäß** *n* tin or tin-plated container, can **-gehäuse** *n* sheet-metal case or housing **-gerüst** *n* plate- or sheet-mill stand **-geschirr** *n* hollow ware, tin vessels and plates **-glühofen** *n* furnace for heating plates **-gurtförderer** *m* steel belt-apron conveyer

Blech-hafen *m* tin can **-halter** *m* blank holder **-haut** *f* plating **-hülle** *f* sheet-metal casing **-hülse** *f* sheet metal sleeve **-instrument** *n* brass (instrument) **-kamin** *m* steel chimney **-kanister** *m* metal container **-kanne** *f* tin can, canister

Blech-kantenhobelmaschine *f* plate-edge planing machine, plate planers **-kapsel** *f* sheet metal cap **-kassette** *f* sheet-metal plateholder **-kasten** *m* sheet-metal box, tin box **-kern** *m* laminated core **-klemme** *f* sheet metal clip **-konstruktion** *f* sheet-metal structure **-körper** *m* shell

Blech-lack *m* tin plate enamel or laquer, varnish for sheet-metal tin plate **-lackiermaschine** *f* sheet-metal varnishing machine **-lager** *n* sheet metal store **-lehre** *f* metal gauge, plate gauge, feeler gauge **-lochmaschine** *f* plate-punching machine **-lochsieb** *m* perforated plate sieve, metal screen

Blech-mantel *m* sheet-iron lining or cover, sheet-metal shell or cylinder, steel jacket **-marke** *f* tin control plate **-material** *n* sheet metal **-messing** *f* sheet brass **-mulde** *f* sheet-metal trough

Blechner *m* tinsmith

Blech-niet *m* brazier-type rivet **-ofen** *m* sheet furnace **-packen** *m* sheet pack **-packung** *f* tin (metal) container **-paket** *n* bundle of laminations, stack of sheets **-panzer** *m* sheet-metal or steel casing (furnace) **-plakat** *n* metal sheet poster **-platte** *f* tin plate **-pratze** *f* plate clamp **-prüfapparat** *m* sheet-metal-testing apparatus, ductility-testing-machine, cupping machine

Blech-rand *m* metal rim edge **-reversierduo** *n* two-high reversing plate mill **-richtmaschine** *f* plate-straightening machine, sheet leveler, plate-straightening roll **-rinne** *f* plate-metal chute, drain-pipe **-rohr** *n*, **-röhre** *f* sheet-metal tube, sheet-iron pipe

Blechrundmaschine *f* **Dreiwalzen** ~ three-roller plate-bending machine

Blech-schablone *f* pass template **-schachtel** *f* can **-schaufel** *f* sheet metal blade

Blechschere *f* plate-cutting or plate-shearing machine or attachment, sheet-iron shears, tinner's snips ~ **mit geschlossenem Gestell** gate or guillotine shears

Blechschleif- und -poliermaschine plate grinding and polishing machine

Blech-scherenmesser *n* shear blade **-schlußring** *f* plate closer or holder, plate closing die **-schmied** *m* tinner, tinsmith **-schneidemaschine** sheet metal cutter **-schnitt** *m* electrical sheet-steel lamination **-schnitzel** *n* shred of plate

Blech-schornstein *m* steel chimney **-schraube** *f* self-tapping screw **-schrott** *m* sheet metal scrap **-schuh** (Eisen) sheet-iron shoe **-schutz** *m* apron (automobile) **-schutzgehäuse** *n* sheet steel enclosure **-schweißung** *f* plate welding

Blech-sicherung *f* lead-strip fuse **-sieb** *n* metal screen **-spannen** *n* sheet or plate straightening **-spannmaschine** *f* sheet-straightening machine **-stab** *m* sheet bar **-stahl** *m* sheet steel

Blech-stanzen *f pl* sheet trimmings **-stanzwerkzeug** *n* blanking tool **-stapel** *m* **beschneiden** stack cutting **-stärke** *f* gauge or thickness of a sheet or plate **-stoß** *m* butt (joint) **-straße** *f* sheet-rolling train, plate-mill train **-strecke** *f* sheet- or plate-mill train **-streicher** *m* plate painter **-streifen** *m* sheet-metal strip, sheet or skelp, strip stock

Blech-sturz *m* sheet pack **-sturzwärmofen** *m* sheet-pack heating furnace **-tafel** *f* sheet or sheet-metal plate or iron, sheet panel, panel stock, plate panel of metal or aluminium alloys **-träger** *m* plate girder, plate gland **-trichter** *m* tin funnel **-trio** *n* three-high plate mill **-trommel** *f* sheet-metal drum

blechumhüllt sheathed

Blech- und Drahtindustrie *f* sheet-and-wire industry

Blechverkleidung *f* sheeting

Blechverrohrung *f*, **genietete** ~ riveted tube

Blech-verschalung *f* sheet metal covering **-verkleidung** *f* sheet metal cover **-verschluß** *m* locking sheet-iron disk **-verzinnungsofen** *m* plate-tinning furnace **-walze** *f* plate roll **Blechwalz- und Richtmaschine** *f* sheetmetal straightening and rolling machine

Blechwalzwerk *n* plate-rolling mill, sheet-rolling mill; (fein) *n* sheet mill; (grob) *n* plate mill

Blech-wand *f* sheet metal plate **-ware** *f* tinware **-warenerzeugnisse** *pl* sheet products **-wärmer** *m* sheet heater **-wärmofen** *m* sheet furnace **-wender** *m* manipulator for turning sheets **-zwischenlage** *f* shim

Blei *n* lead **mit** ~ **ausgeschlagen** lead-lined **fein verteiltes** ~ lead in continuous phase **gediegenes** ~ native lead **schwefelsaures** ~ sulfate of lead **unterschwefligsaures** ~ lead hyposulfite **wolframsaures** ~ lead tungstate

Blei-abfall *m* scrap lead **-abgang** *m* lead dross, lead scoria **-abguß** *m* lead cast **-abschirmung** *f* lead shielding, collimating shield (collimator) **-abschlußmuffe** *f* leaden end box of cable **-ader** *f* lead vein **-akkumulator** *m* lead storage battery, storage cell, lead accumulator **-aktiviert** lead activated **-amalgam** *n* lead amalgam

Blei-anode *f* lead anode **-ansatz** *m* lead crust **-antimonerz** *n* zinkenite **-antimonlegierung** *f* lead-antimony alloy **-äquivalent** *n* lead equivalent, protective value **-arbeit** *f* lead smelting, plumbing **-arsenglanz** *m* sartorite **-arsenik** *m* leard arsenate, lead arsenide **-arsenit** *n* lead arsenite **-art** *f* kind or variety of lead

bleiartig leadlike, leady, plumbeous

Blei-asbest *m* lead asbestos **-asche** *f* lead dross, ashes or suboxide, litharge **-aufteilungsmuffe** *f* leaden dividing box of cable, indoor lead distribution sleeve **-ausbringen** *n* lead yield **-ausgekleidet** lead-lined or covered

Blei-auskleidung *f*, **-ausschlag** *m* lead lining (accumulators) **-azetat** *n* lead acetate **-azid** *n* lead azide **-backe** *f* lead jaw socket, leaden jaw, lead clamp **-badeofen** *m* lead-bath furnace **-ballast** *n* lead weight **-barren** *m* pig of lead, lead pig **-batterie** *f* lead battery

bleiben to stay, remain **im Freien ~** to be left in the open air **an der Leitung ~** to hold the line (teleph.)

bleibend lasting, permanent, constant, consistent **verformt ~** permanently deformed **-e Belastung** basic load **-e Dehnung, -e Durchbiegung** permanent set **-e Formänderung** permanent set or distortion **-e Regelabweichung** permanent offset, sustained deviation

Blei-benzin *n* (lead) doped gasoline, tetraethyl lead fuel **-bergwerk** *n* lead mine **-blech** *n* lead sheet **-blende** *f* tube diaphragm

Bleiblock *m* lead bricks, Trauzl block (explosives), lead pig **-ausbauchung** *f* Trauzl block expansion (explosives), buckling or bulging of lead blocks used for testing explosives

Blei-blüte *f* mimetite **-boden** *m* lead weight in the bottom of the compass bowl **boratglas** *n* lead borate glass **-brocken** *m pl* lump of lead **-bronze** *f* lead bronze **-bronzelager** *n* lead bronze bearing **-büchse** *f* lead box or case **-bügel** *m* lead spring

bleich pale

Bleich-anlage *f* bleaching plant **-anstalt** *f* bleachery **-apparat** *m* color-removal or bleaching apparatus **-artikel** *m* bleach style **-beize** *f* bleachings mordant **-bottich** *m* bleaching chest

Bleiche *f* bleaching, bleach

bleich-echt fast to bleaching, unbleachable **-echtheit** *f* ability of a fabric to resist or withstand bleaching **-effekt** *m* bleach effect

bleichen to bleach, whiten, lose color, fade

Bleichen *n* decolorizing, deblooming, discharge **~ der Papiermasse** potching **~ des Zellstoffes** bleaching of cellulose (rayon)

Bleicherde *f* fuller's earth, clay, bleaching earth(s) **aktive ~** active bleaching earth **mit ~ behandeltes Öl** contacted oil

Bleicherdebehandlung *f* clay treatment

Bleicherei *f* bleaching

Bleichergehilfe *m* bleacher's helper, drainerman

Bleich-fleck *m* bleaching stain or spot **-flotte** *f* bleaching liquor **-flüssigkeit** *f* bleaching liquor, bleach **-gold** *n* pale gold **-holländer** *m* poaching or bleaching engine **-kalk** *m* chloride of lime, bleaching powder, calcium hypochlorite

Bleichlorid *n* lead chloride

Bleich-mittel *n* bleaching agent, bleach, chloride of lime **-pulver** *n* bleaching powder, chloride of lime, calcium hypochlorite

Bleichromat *n* lead chromate

Bleich-säure *f* chlorine, chloric acid **-soda** *f* bleaching soda, sodium hypochlorite

Bleichung *f* bleaching

Bleichverfahren *n* bleaching process

Blei-dampf *m* lead vapor or fume **-datierungsmethode** *f* lead dating method **-dichtung** *f* lead packing **-dicke** *f* surrounding lead shielding **-dioxyd** *n* lead dioxide, lead peroxide **-draht** *m* lead wire **-einlage** *f* inside lead lining **-eisenstein** *m* iron-lead matte **-elektrolyse** *f* electrolytic refining of lead

Bleiempfindlichkeit eines Kraftstoffes lead response of a fuel

bleien to lead, plumb

Bleierde *f* earthy cerussite

bleiern leaden, lead, leady

Bleierz *n* lead ore **-funken** *m pl* small pieces of lead ore **-gedinge** *n* bing tale, tale **-röstung** *f* lead-ore roasting **-stück** *n* lead pea

Blei-essig *m* basic (solution of) lead acetate, lead subacetate **-essigklärung** *f* wet-lead clarification **-fahlerz** *n* bournonite **-farbe** *f* lead paint **-farben, -farbig** lead-colored **-feder** *f* lead pencil **-feile** *f* shave hook, lead file **-ferrit** *n* lead ferrite

Blei-folie *f* lead foil **-form** *f* lead mold **-frei** free from lead **-fuge** *f* leaded joint (calked) **-führend** plumbiferous, lead-bearing **-füllung** *f* lead charge **-fuß** *m* metal mount, lead base

Blei-gang *m* lead vein **-gans** *f* pig lead **-gefüttert** lead-lined **-gehalt** *m* lead content or percentage **-gelb** *n* massicot, lead chromate, yellow lead **-gesenk** *n* lead die **-gewicht** *n* lead weight **-gewinnung** *f* lead extraction **-gießer** *m* plumber **-gießerarbeit** *f* plumbing (with lead) **-gitter** *n* lead grid

Bleiglanz *m* galena, lead sulfide **-detektor** *m* galena or lead sulfide detector **-kristall** *m* galena crystal

Blei-glas *n* lead glass, lead silicate, anglesite **-glasur** *f* lead glaze **-glaszähler** *m* lead glass counter

Bleiglätte *f* lead monoxide, litharge **gelbe ~** litharge, lead monoxide **rote ~** massicot

Blei-glimmer *m* micaceous form of cerussite **-grau** lead-gray **-grieß** *m* lead gravel **-grube** *f* lead mine

Bleigummi *n* lead rubber, plumbo resinite, lead-pencil eraser, opaque rubber **-schürze** *f* lead-rubber apron, protective apron

blei-haltig plumbic, plumbiferous **-handkreisel** *m* spinning top **-halogenide** *pl* lead halides **-härtung** *f* lead hardening

Bleihorn-erz *n* **-spat** *m* phosgenite

Bleihütte *f* lead-refining plant, lead smeltery

bleiisch leady, leadlike **-es Bodenzink** leady spelter

Blei-jodat *n* lead iodate **-kabel** *n* lead(-covered) cable **-kabellöter** *m* lead-cable jointer **-kalk** *m* lead calx, lead oxide **-kammerkrystalle** *n pl* lead-chamber crystals **-kammerschlamm** *m* sludge in the lead chamber of photoelectric cells **-kappe** *f* lead cap

Bleikarbonat *n* lead carbonate, cerussite **basisches ~** white lead

Blei-kathode *f* lead cathode **-kern** *m* lead core **-kolik** *f* lead colic **-kondensatorenmuffen** *pl*

lead condenser sleeves **-könig** *m* lead regulus **-kraftstoff** *m* tetraethyl lead fuel **-krankheit** *f* lead poisoning **-krätze** *f* lead dross **-kugel** *f* lead ball, lead bullet

Blei-lasur *f* linarite **-leder** *n* silver with a high lead content **-legierung** *f* lead alloy **-leiste** *f* connecting or terminal bar **-linie** *f* (Spektrum) lead line (spectrum) **-lot** *n* lead solder, soft solder, plumb line **-löter** *m* lead burner, plumber **-löterei** *f* **-lötung** *f* lead soldering **-lötgerät** *n* lead soldering apparatus **-lötverfahren** *n* lead-soldering process

Bleimantel *m* lead sheath(ing) or covering, lead jacket **mit einem ~ umpreßt** lead-sheathed **mit einem neuen ~ versehen** to (re)lead

Bleimantel-abstreifmaschine *f* lead sheath stripping machine **-verbinder** *m* bonding ribbon (copper) (teleph.), bonding strip

Blei-matrize *f* lead-molding matrix **-mehl** *n* lead meal or dust **-mennige** *f* red lead, minium **-mennigegrundierung** *f* red lead coating

Bleimine *f* lead mine **unergiebige ~** poor or nonproductive lead mine

Bleimolybdat *n* lead molybdate

Bleimuffe *f* lead sleeve **Lötwulst der ~** plumber's wiped joint

Blei-mulde *f* lead pig **-niederschlag** *m* precipitated lead, lead precipitate **-niere** *f* bindheimite **-ofen** *m* lead-smelting furnace **-oleat** *n* lead oleate

Bleioxyd *n* lead oxide, litharge, massicot, lead monoxide, red lead **kohlensaures ~** carbonate of lead **rotes ~** minium, red lead oxide **titansaures ~** lead titanate

Blei-oxydhydrat *n* lead hydroxide **-oxydsalz** *n* lead salt **-oxydul** *n* lead suboxide **-oxyduloxyd** *n* minium **-palmitat** *n* lead palmitate **-papier** *n* lead paper **-peroxyd** *n* lead peroxide or dioxide

Blei-pflaster *n* lead plaster **-phosphit** *n* lead phosphite **-platte** *f* lead plate **-plattenprobe** *f* lead-plate test (explosives) **-plombe** *f* lead seal (for a meter, etc.) **-plumbat** *n* red lead oxide, minium **-prägung** *f* molding-in lead **-presse** *f* lead press

Blei-produktion *f* lead production or output **-prozeß** *m* lead-chamber process **-quader** *m* lead blocks **-raffination** *f* lead refinery or refining plant **-raffinerie** *f* lead refinery or refining plant **-raspel** *f* lead or coarse rasp **-rauch** *m* lead fume or smoke **-reich** leady, rich in lead **-rhodanid** *n* lead sulfocyanate **-rohr** *n* lead pipe or tube **-rohrausbohrer** *m* inside lead tube scrapers

Bleirohrkabel *n* lead-covered cable **~ zwischen Überführungskasten und Freileitung** pothead tail, tail end **zweiadriges** (vieradriges) **~** lead-covered twin- (four-) wire cable, two- (four-) wire lead cable

Blei-rohrpresse *f* lead-pipe press **-röstprozeß** *m* lead-roasting process **-rot** *n* red lead, minium **-sack** *m* lightened silver dross **-safran** *m* orange lead **-salizylat** *n* lead salicylate **-salpeter** *m* lead nitrate

Blei-salz *n* lead salt **-sammler** *m* (lead) storage cell or battery, lead sulfuric acid cell, lead accumulator **-säure** *f* plumbic acid **-schachtofen** *m* lead blast furnace **-schale** *f* lead dish or basin **-schaum** *m* lead dross or ashes **-scheibe** *f* lead packing ring **-scheren** *pl* plumbers' lead cutters

Bleischirm *m* lead screen **für Strahlung undurchlässiger ~** lead screen opaque to radiations

Blei-schlacke *f* lead slag **-schlamm** (-schlick) *m* lead deposit, lead sludge, slime or mud **-schlange** *f* lead coil **-schmelzherd** *m* lead-smelting hearth **-schnitt** *m* lead engraving **-schrot** *n* lead shot **-schutz** *m* lead protection **-schwamm** *m* spongy or sponge lead, lead sponge, mossy lead

Blei-schwärze *f* black spar **-schweif** *m* slickensides, compact galena **-seele** *f* lead lining, lead tube drawn through iron pipe as liner for hot sea-water lines of large diameter **-selenid** *n* selenium lead **-sicherung** *f* lead (safety) fuse, fusible plug **-silikatglas** *n* lead silicate glass **-späne** *pl* abraded lead particles

Bleispat *m* lead spar, cerussite **roter ~** crocoite

Blei-speise *f* lead speiss **-spiegel** *m* specular galena, slickensides **-spritzer** *m* lead or bullet spatter **-staub** *m* lead dust **-staubmühlen** *pl* lead-powder mills **-staubsammler** *m* lead-dust storage cell **-stearat** *n* lead stearate **-stein** *m* leady matte **-stemmer** *pl* lead caulking chisels

Bleistift *m* lead pencil **-einsatz** *m* pencil point, pencil bow **-fräser** *m* lead-pencil sharpener **-gummi** *m* pencil eraser **-kreuze** *n pl* penciled crosses **-lack** *m* pencil lacquer **-mine** *f* pencil lead **-röhre** *f* pencil tube **-skizze** *f* pencil sketch or drawing **-spitzer** *m* pencil sharpener or pointer **-zeichnung** *f* pencil drawing

Blei-strangpresse *f* lead extursion press **-streifen** *m* strip of lead **-styphnat** *n* trinitroresorcinate of lead **-sulfat** *n* lead sulfate, anglesite- **-sulfid** *n* lead sulfide **-sulfidtyphalbleiter** *m* lead sulfide type semiconductor **-superoxyd** *n* lead peroxide **-tetraäthyl** *n* lead tetraethyl **-tetraazetat** *n* lead tetraacetate **-tetroxyd** *n* red lead oxide, minium **-trinitroresorzinat** *n* trinitroresorcinate of lead **-überzug** *m* lead coating

bleiumhülltes Kabel lead-sheathed cable

bleiummanteltes Kabel lead-insulated cable

Blei-verbindung *f* lead compound **-vergiftung** *f* lead poisoning **-verhüttung** *f* lead smelting **-verkleidung** *f* lead lining **-verschluß** *m* leading **-verstemmung** *f* lead caulking **-verteilungsmuffen** *pl* lead distribution sleeves **-vitriol** *n* lead vitriol, lead-sulfate, anglesite **-vitriolspat** *m* anglesite

Blei-wasser *n* lead water, Goulard water **-weiß** *n* white lead **-weißfarbe** *f* white lead paint **-weißstein** *m* cerussite **-wolle** *f* lead wool **-wismut** *n* lead bismuth **-wolframat** *n* lead tungstate

bleizinnlegiertes Weißblech terne plate

Blei-zinnlot *n* lead-tin solder **-zinnober** *m* red lead, minium **-zucker** *m* acetate of lead

Blend-abdeckung *f* shutter cover **-blech** *n* flame damper, deflector plate

Blendanstrich *m* camouflage, dazzle paint **-beleuchtungsfarbe** *f* anti-dazzling light intensity **-boden** *m* dead floor **-bogen** *m* shallow arch **-deckel** *m* blank cover

Blende *f* light stop, diaphragm, aperture (stop), slit, shield, shutter, glance, orifice (in nozzles, screen), eyecatcher, hood, lens aperture, screening, orifice plate, restrictor **Lage der ~** mounting of the screen

Blende-konzentrat *n* blende concentrate **-messer** *m* diameter of the baffle

blenden to blind, screen, dazzle, glare, dim

Blenden *pl* inserts (Geiger)

Blenden-abstand *m* disk spacing **-ausschnitt** *m* aperture, slit **-bild** *n* image of stop

blendend dazzling, glaring **-er Glanz** (Blendung) glare **-er Lichtstrahl** light beam of intensive, intrinsic brilliancy

Blenden-durchmesser *m* diameter of diaphragm (optics) **-ebene** *f* diaphragm plane **-einrichtung** *f* diaphragm **-einsatz** *m* diaphragm holder **-einstellring** *m* diaphragm adjusting ring **-einstellung** *f* (action of) setting of diaphragm, stop down (aperture of lens); (Auslösehebel) trigger **-flügel** *m* shutter blade **-gehäuse** *n* shutter housing, baffle chamber

Blenden-hebel *m* shutter lever **-korn** *n* hooded front sight **-kupplung** *f* aperture coupling **-lamelle** *f* diaphragm leaf **-loch** *n* anode aperture (cathode-ray tube) **-nachstellung** *f* phasing of shutter **-nippel** *m* domed cover glass **-öffnung** *f* aperture (of diaphragm or stop), insert hole **-paar** *n* pair of diaphragms **-rohr** *n* screening tube

Blendenscheibe *f* blade (disk) of the diaphragm, horizontal edge (film recording), auxiliary rotary shutter disk with spiral slot (for quadruple scanning) **kreisförmige ~ in Rohrleitungen** *f* orifice plate in pipe lines (automobile)

Blenden-schirm *m* gobo (acoust.), motion pictures) **-träger** *m* diaphragm support **-trommel** *f* scanning drum

Blenden-revolver *m* diaphragm turret **-satz** *m* diaphragm set **-skala** *f* diaphragm scale **-vorwahl** *f* pre-selection of aperture **-vorwahleinrichtung** *f* pre-selector for single lens **-wert** *m* diaphragm interval

Blender *m* dazzler

Blenderöstofen *m* blende-roasting furnace

Blenderrahmen *m* shutter frame

Blendescheibe *f* antiglare shield or pane

Blend-farbstoffe *pl* colors for sighting purposes **-fassade** *f* blind wall, dead face **-fenster** *n* blind window **-feuer** *n* flare **-frei** glare-free

Blend-glas *n* moderating glass, dimmer (optics) **-gläser** *n pl* anti-glare glasses **-glaskappe** *f* moderating glass revolver

Blend-holz *n* facing board (carp.) **-kappe** *f* headlight shield **-körper** *m* frangible-glass smoke grenade **-laterne** *f* dark (of a lantern), dark lantern **-leder** *pl* blinkers **-leistung** *f* dimming effect **-licht** *n* headlight

Blendling *m* mixture

Blend-löffel *m* antidazzling cap, headlight shield **-photometer** *m* diaphragm photometer **-rahmen** *m* blinker, blind frame **-ring** *m* dimming ring **-scheibe** *f* disk diaphragm, stop

Blendschieber *m* sliding diaphragm **mikrometrisch verstellbarer ~** micrometrically movable slide

Blendschirm *m* gobo (for sound absorption, motion pictures) **~ für Positionslicht** light screen or shade for side light

Blendschutz *m* protection from glare, antidazzle device **-brille** *f* antidazzle goggles or glasses, antiglare goggles

Blendschützer *m* antiglare shield or screen

Blendschutz-gläser *pl* antiglare glass **-kappe** *f* anti-dazzle louver (louvre) or cap **-raster** *m* anti-glare screen **-scheibe** *f* antidazzling or antiglare screen, antidazzle glass

Blendschutzvorrichtung bei Scheinwerfern headlight dimmer

Blendung *f* dazzle source, glare, blinding, dazzle (of eye) **akustische ~** aural dazzling **~ ausschalten** to eliminate glare

Blendungs-faktor *m* dazzle factor **-frei** nondazzling, nonglare **-schießen** *n* smoke-screening fire **-schirm** *m* antidazzle or antiglare screen **-schutz** *m* antidazzle devises, glare prevention

Blend-verfahren *n* diaphragm method (for pencil modulation) **-wand** *f* facing **-werk** *n* camouflage **-wirkung** *f* glaring light of arc **-ziegel** *m* facing brick

Blick *m* look, glance, view **-bewegung** *f* visual movement **-ebene** *f* plane of vision

blicken to brighten, blick, look, view, glance

Blickfang *m* something to catch the eye (*e.g.*, a pretty girl smilingly displaying wares in advertising), eye-catcher **-blech** *n* shinning sheet

Blickfeld *n* field of view (optics), range of vision **~ des Oszillogrammes** field of view of oscillogram **beidäugiges ~** binocular field of view

Blick-feldblende *f* field stop **-gold** *n* refined gold containing silver **-linie** *f* line of vision or of sight **-punkt** *m* point of view **-richtung** *f* line of vision, direction of view or sight, direction of regard, sight line

Blickschulung *f* eye training

Blickschulungssignal *n* beacon light

Blick-silber *n* refined pure silver **-weite** *f* sight distance **-winkel** *m* angle of view

blind blind, blank, feigned, wattless, dummy **~ flanschen** to blind flange, blank flange **-er Alarm** false alarm **-er Bogen** blank sheet **-e (trockene) Bohrung** dry hole **-es Ende** *f* dead end **-er Flansch** blank flange **-es Kaliber** inoperative pass (in rolling) **-es Loch** dead hole

blind -e Mauer blind wall **-e Mutung** demand for concession without previous discovery **-er Schlag** ineffective blow **-es Stanzen** touch typewriting **-e Stelle** *f* **im Funkempfang** blind spot **-er Versuch** blank test **-er Widerstand** reactance resistance, capacity resistance

Blind-achse *f* loose axle, countershaft axle **-anteil** *m* reactive component **-band** *m* dummy (of a Book) **-baum** *m* blind beam **-bedienung** *f* touch operation **-belastung** *f* reactive load, dummy load **-belegung** *f* dummy connection **-boden** *m* dead or counter floor **-bohrung** *f* blind hole **-buchse** *f* dummy socket or jack

Blinddeckel *m* blank cover

Blind-diode *f* capacitive diode **-druck** *m* relief printing (embossing) **-einstellung** *f* setting on blind flying

Blindendruck *m* embossed printing for blind

Blindenschrift *f* Braille

Blind-feuer *n* blank fire **-flansch** *m* blank or blind flange **-fliegen** *n* **flug** *m* instrument or blind flying

Blindflug-gerät *n*, **-gerätausrüstung** *f* blind-flying equipment **-haube** *f* blind-flying hood **-instrumente** *n pl* blind-flying instruments **-kurve** *f* blind-flying bank or curve, blind turn **-landung** *f* instrument landing **-lehrgerät** *n* training equipment for instrument flying **-plan** *m* instrument-flight plan **-schule** *f* instrument flight school

Blind-folge *f* succession of flashes, frequency of flashes **-funk** *m* broadcast method (wireless telegraph) **-funkverkehr** *m* blind wireless traffic **-geladen** loaded with inert filling **-geschwindigkeit** *f* blind speed (rdr) **-gußzeile** *f* blank slug **-härteprüfung** *f* blank hardness test **-holz** *n* veneer **-kassette** *f* blind holder

Blindkerze *f* dummy plug **~ für Versand** shipping plug

Blind-kilovoltampere *n* kilovoltampere reactive **-kilowatt** *n* kilovar (kvar), reactive kilovoltampere **-klemme** *f* unused terminal

Blindkolben der Ölschmierpumpe dummy plunger of lubricating pump

Blind-komponente *f* reactive, wattless, idle, or quadrature component **-kreis** *m* reactance circle **-kurbeln** *n* blindfold operation of crank wheels

Blindlande-anlage *f* instrument landing system (ILS) **-gerät** *n* instrument landing equipment **-system** *n* instrument landing system

Blindlandung *f* blind landing

Blindlandungs-einrichtung *f* blind-landing system **-gerät** *n* blind-landing device

Blindlast *f* reactive load **-einsteller** *m* reactive load adjuster **-transduktor** *m* transductor reactor **-widerstand** *m* reactive load resistance

Blindleistung *f* apparent power, reactive wattless or idle power

Blindleistungs-bedarf *m* kilovar requirements **-maschine** *f* compensator, synchronous or asynchronous condenser, rotary phase converter, phase converter, phase changer **-messer** *m* varmeter

Blindleistungsregelung, selbsttätige ~ kilovar control, automatic

Blindleistungs-relais *n* relay responsive to kilovars **-zähler** *m* var-hour meter, reactive energy meter

Blindleitung *f* dummy line **~ zur Anpassung** non-dissipative stub

Blindleitwert *m* susceptance

blindlings at random

Blindloch *n* dummy hole (tape rec.)

blind machen, das Glas ~ ~ to blunt glass

Blind-material *n* spacing material (print) **-modulator** *m* reactance modelator **-muster** *n* dummy

Blind-ort *n* dummy drift, gateway **-ortversatz** *m* dummy packing, strip-and-blind-stall or strip-and-dummy-stall packing (stowage) **-platte** *f* blind printing plate **-präge** *f* blank swage **-prägung** *f* blind (blocking) embossing **-probe** *f* blank determination, blank test sample

Blind-rahmen *m* window frame **-röhre** *f* reactance valve **-rohrmodulator** *m* reactance tube modulator **-schacht** *m* blind shaft, drop staple, winze, pit head **-schaltbild** *n* mimic (connection) diagram **-scharfgestänge** *n* fuse-arming gear **-scheibe** *f* blank flange

blind-schlagen to leave blank **-schlagen** *n* racing of the propeller **-schloß** *n* mortic lock (doors) **-schwanz** *m* reactance, arrangement to make resistance alternately zero and infinite, (in dipole feeder operation) stub **-sicherung** *f* dummy fuse **-spannung** *f* reactive or reactance voltage

Blindspannungskomponente *f* reactive, wattless, idle, or quadrature component of voltage, wattless component of electromotive force

Blind-spitze *f* dummy warhead **-stecker** *m* **-stich** *m* dummy pass (rolling mill) **-stopfen** *m* **-stöpsel** *m* dummy or blind plug **-strecke** *f* dummy road **-strom** *m* reactive, idle, wattless, or reactance current **-stromaufnahme** *f* drawing or taking of wattless, idle, or reactive current **-stromkompensation** *f* compensation of reactive current, power-factor improvement

Blindstromkomponente *f* reactive, wattless, idle, or quadrature component of the current

Blind-strommesser *m* wattless current meter **-stück** (Pumpe) *n* dummy piece **-titration** *f* blank titration **-übermittlung** *f* blind transmission **-verankerung** *f* blind anchorage **-verbrauchsschwerpunkt** *m* point of concentration of the inductive load **-verbrauchszähler** *m* reactive energy meter, var-hour meter, sine or wattless component meter **-verkehr** *m* blind traffic

Blind-versuch *m* blank test or determination **-voltampere** reactive volt-ampere **-walze** *f* idle roll **-welle** *f* loose axle or shaft, countershaft axle **-wellenschieber** *m* idle-phase shifter

Blindwert *m* numerical result of blank test, blank (value) **~ elektrischer Größen** wattless or imaginary component of electric values

Blindwiderstand *m* resistance, reactance (elec.) **mit ~ behafteter Stromkreis** reactive circuit **akustischer ~** acoustic reactance **induktiver ~** inductive, inductance, or positive reactance, inductance **kapazitiver ~** capacity, capacitive, or condensive reactance, capacitance, negative reactance, condensance

Blindwiderstands-isolator *m* capacitance bushing **-kennlinie** *f* reactance characteristic **-verhältnis** *n* Q factor, quality factor

Blindzettel *m* dummy ticket (for statistical purposes)

Blink-anlage *f* blinker system **-apparat** *m* lamp-signal apparatus **-aufsteller** *m* demonstration stand for blinkers **-bake** *f* flash beacon **-batterie** *f* blinker-signal battery **-betrieb** *m* signaling service **-bremsleuchte** *f* combined blinker and stop lamp **-einrichtung** *f* blinking or flickering device

blinken to signal (with lamps), blink, flash, flicker **~ über eine Zwischenstelle** to relay blinker signaling

Blinken *n* flash(ing), signal-lamp transmission, blinking **durch ~ das Amt zum Eintreten veranlassen** to flash in the exchange

Blinker *m* blinker-signal operator, signal lamp, flashing light (indicator), signal flasher

Blinkerei *f* blinker signaling

Blinker-relais *n* flasher relay **-schalter** *m* blinker switch **-stand** *m* blinker-signaling post (coast defense) **-verbindung** *f* blinker-signal communication

Blinkfernrohr *n* signaling telescope

Blinkfeuer *n* revolving light or beacon, intermittent or flashing light (duration of light shorter than duration of obscurity), blinker light, flashing beacon, series of flashes lasting more than two seconds **-bake** *f* revolving beacon

Blink-folge *f* flash period **-frequenz** *f* blinker frequency **-garbe** *f* flash **-geber** *m* blinker unit **-gerät** *n* blinker-signal equipment, blinker apparatus or beacon, lamp-signaling apparatus **-kennung** *f* light or lamp signal **-lampe** *f* flash or blinker lamp, flasher **-leuchte** *f* blink lamp, blinker jump, flashing light, flash lamp

Blink-licht *n* blinker light, flashing light **-lichtapparat** *n* occulter **-linie** *f* signaling line **-meldung** *f* blinker message **-mikroskop** *n* blink or flicker microscope

Blinkrelais *n* flasher relay **-schlußleuchte** *f* combined flash and tail lamp **-signal** *n* flash signal **-stadtleuchte** *f* combined blinker and parking lamp **-tasten** *n* tapping out on signaling lamp **-verkehr** *m* signal traffic **-vermittlung** *f* retransmitting station

Blink-schaltung *f* blinking arrangement, ratchet circuit scheme **-signal** *n* flashing-light signal **-spruch** *m* blinker-signal message **-station** *f* **-stelle** *f* blinker-signal station **-taster** *m* key for signaling lamp **-verbindung** *f* signal-lamp communication **-verfahren** *n* system of blinker signaling, blinking method

Blinkzeichen *n* (lamp) flashing, flash or flickering signal, blinker signal ~ **geben** to flash

Blip *m* **in der zweiten Abtastung erscheinender** ~ second time round blip ~, **kurzer Impuls** pip

Blitz *m* lightning, flash, statics (film) **der** ~ **schlägt ein** the lightning strikes **rücklaufender** ~ return lightning stroke

Blitzableiter *m* lightning conductor, arrester, or rod, voltage-discharge gap, spark-gap discharger ~ **mit Sicherung** lightning fuses and protector blocks,

Blitzableiter-draht *m* lightning conductor wire **-kabel** *n* lightning conductor **-schelle** *f* lightning-arrester collar **-seil** *n* lightning-conductor cable **-streifen** *m* protector strip

Blitz-anfälligkeit *f* lightning expectancy **-anflugleuchten** *pl* flashing approach lights **-artig** lightninglike **-aufnahme** *f* flash radiography

Blitzbahn *f* track or path of lightning **verschlungene** ~ tortuous path of lightning flash

Blitz-beleuchtung *f* flash illumination **-bündel** *n* lightning-flash cluster

blitzen to flash or emit flashes ~ **und donnern** fulminate

blitzend glary

Blitz-entladung *f* lightning discharge **-feuer** *n* flashing light, long flashes **-flugzeug** *n* flash-services plane **-folge** *f* rate of flash **-funk** *m* (urgent) radiogram **-gefahr** *f* danger of lightning **-gespräch** *n* lightning call **-kessel** *m* flash boiler **-lampe** *f* flashlight, flash bulb, magnesium light

Blitzlicht *n* flashlight (phot.), flash bulb, magnesium light **-anschluß** *m* flash contact **-ausrüstung** *f* flash equipment ("strobe" connection) **-geräte** *pl* flashlight equipment **-lampe** *f* flash bulb, magnesium powder burner, flashlight lamp (bulb) **-luftbild** *n* aerial flashlight photograph **-zeichen** *n* flashing of flashlight signal

Blitz-nest *n* the region in which lightning strikes with high frequency **-röhre** *f* flash tube **-pfeil** *m* danger arrow **-rohrzange** *f* electrician's pliers, slip-joint pliers **-photographie** *f* photography of lightning **-schlag** *m* lightning stroke, flash, or discharge, lightning bolt **-schnell** quick as lightning

Blitzschutz *m* protection against lightning, lightning arrester or protector **-draht** *m* ground wire **-kabel** *ü* (lightning) protective cable **-seil** *n* (ground) wire **-sicherungen** *f pl* lightning-arrester equipment **-spirale** *f* inductance spiral **-stange** *f* lightning rod **-vorrichtung** *f* lightning protector or arrester

Blitzsicherung *f* (lightning) arrester

Blitzstörung, einpolige ~ unidirectional lightning disturbance

Blitz-strahl *m* lightning flash, thunderbolt **-zange** *f* gripping pliers, locking pliers, rapid action pliers, self-gripping general purpose pliers **-zug** *m* (special) express (train)

Blizzard *m* blizzard

Blocher *m* electric floor polisher

Block *m* (Holz) log; (Fels) block, boulder; (Kühler) (pulley) block; (Metall) ingot, pig; (Linotype/Typograph) slug; (Papier) pad; (Hebewerkzeug) pulley, hoist, block, block (of purchase), tree trunk (railway track, pulley) **einscheibiger** ~ single pully block **fester** ~ fixed block **gehefteter** ~ stitched pack **gewalzter** ~ bloom **unruhig vergossener** ~ rimmed steel ingot **vorgewalzter** ~ bloom, cagged ingot **zweischeibiger** ~ double pully block

Block-abschnitt *m* block section (R. R.) **-abstand** *m* distance between two block stations, block gap **-abständer** *m* train staff instrument **-abstreifer** *m* ingot stripper **-abstreifkran** *m* stripper crane, ingot-stripping crane

Blockade *f* blockade, turned letter (print)

Block-anlage *f* block-system plant **-armatur** *f* block armature **-auflegevorrichtung** *f* putting on device for ingots **-ausdrücker** *m* ingot pusher **-auszieher** *m* ingot-drawing-out or -withdrawing device **-ausziehkatze** *f* ingot withdrawing machine **-ausziehkran** *m* ingot withdrawer **-bandsäger** *m* muley sawer **-basisgrundschaltung** *f* (Transistoren) groundet base arrangement

Block-batterie *f* block battery **-bauweise** *f* unit construction **-betrieb** *m* block operations **-blei** *n* pig lead **-brecher** *m* breaker block **-brechpresse** *f* ingot-breaker press, breaking-down mill press **-bruchbau** *m* block caving **-buchstabe** *m* block letter **-chargierkran** *m* billet charging crane, ingot charger

Blöckchen *n* ingot, pig (iron)

Block-drahtheftmaschine *f* block wire-stitching machine **-dreherei** *f* ingot turning **-druck** *m* block printing or print **-drücker** *m* ingot pusher **-duo** *n* two-high blooming mill

Blöcke *m pl* sheave blocks

Block-einrichtung *f* block apparatus **-einsetzkran** *m* ingot-charging crane **-einsetzmaschine** *f* ingot charger **-einsetzwagen** *m* ingot-charging car **-einziehwerk** *n* (Kran) luffing gear block **-eis** *n* block ice **-eisen** *n* ingot iron, ingot steel, pig, pig iron **-empfang** *m* party reception, block reception, communal reception

blocken to block, cog

Blocken *n* blocking

Block-ende *n* bloom end, bloom crop end **-erzeugung** *f* ingot production

Blockfeld *n* block system **-freileitungsdraht** *m* block system overhead wires

Block-fernsprecher *m* block telephone **-form** *f* ingot mold, cast-iron mold **-fundamente** *n* monolithic foundations **-fuß** *m* bottom of an ingot, large end of an ingot **-gatter** *n* sawmill with one saw

Block-gefüge *n* macrostructure of an ingot **-gerüst** *n* blooming-mill stand, roughing stand, cogging stand, bloomer **-greifer** *m* ingot gripper **-gußstück** *n* monoblock casting **-hahn** *m* stopcock **-halde** *f* coating of blocks **-haken** *m* tackle hook **-hebetisch** *m* ingot tilter **-herzstück** *n* solid crossing (R. R.) **-holz** *m* logwood **-hütte** *f* block signal box (R. R.) **-hydraulik** *f* hydraulic lift unit

Blockierdraht *m* inhibit wire

blockieren to block (up), stopper, jam (radio), bar, deny, to take or put out of service, to turn letters (print)

blockierend blocking

Blockier-grenze *f* blocking limit **-schalter** *m* blocking switch **-schaltung** *f* clamping circuit, paralysis circuit

blockiert tied up, locked, disabled **-e Steuerung** locked controls

Blockiersystem *n* transfer blocking (in power-line protection)

Blockierung *f* blocking, locking

Blockierungs-effekt *m* blocking effect **-grad** *m* blocking ratio **-potential** *n* stopping potential **stromkreis** *m* blocking-current circuit

Blockierzeit *f* paralysis time

Block-kaliber *n* blooming pass, cogging pass **-kasten** *m* multiple container **-kastenbatterie** *f* block-type battery **-kern** *m* central portion, ingot core **-kette** *f* block chain **-kettenrad** *n* block-chain sprocket **-kettenradwälzfräser** *m* block-chain-sprocket hob **-kipper** *m* ingot-tipping device, ingot tilter **-klemme** *f* terminal block **-kondensator** *m* block(ing) or stopping condenser, fixed or variable capacitor, fixed condenser, blocking, stopping, or insulating capacitor

Blockkopf *m* top end of an ingot, ingot crop end **-beheizung** *f* ingot-head heating device

Block-kraftwerk *n* unit (system) power station **-kran** *m* ingot crane, block transport crane **-kruste** *f* ingot skin **-kühler** *m* core radiator **-lagen** *f pl* courses of blocks, blockwork **-lager** *n* bloom and slab yard, thrust block, pad thrust bearing **-lagersitz** *m* thrust block seating **-leitung** *f* line wire

Block-meißel *m* hardy, anvil cutter, blacksmith's chisel **-mitte** *f* center portion of ingot **-motor** *m* engine with one-piece cylinder **-mühle** *f* grinding mill **-nagel** *m* axle of pulley, block pin **-nickel** *m* pig nickel, nickel ingots

Block- oder Schollenlava *f* block lava

Block-presse *f* billet press **-preßverfahren** *n* fluid-compression process **-rand** *m* edge or exterior part of an ingot **-reifen** *m* block tire **-reihe** *f* tier, row or course of blocks **-relais** *n* track relay **-relaxation** *f* block relaxation **-reversierduo** *n* two-high reversing blooming mill **-rolle** *f* pulley

Blockrüsterei *f* **pneumatische ~** pneumatic ingot-dressing shop

Block-säge *f* logsaw, pitsaw **-satz** *m* grouped style **-säulenbauweise** *f* unit-column design **-schaltbild** *n* block (wiring) diagram, block schematic **-schaltplan** *m* diagram of connections for railroad stations **-scheibe** *f* pulley, sheave, wheel **-schere** *f* bloom shears, ingot shears **-schichten** *f pl* pier of blocks **-schiene** *f* filled-section rail **-schloß** *n* block lock (signal gear) **-schneidemaschine** *f* block slicing machine **-schnitt** *m* die **-schrank** *m* block instrument case

Block-schrift *f* block signals, block type or letters, Egyptian type **-schruppbank** *f* ingot-roughing lathe **-seigerung** *f* segregation in an ingot, ingotism **-sicherung** *f* safety block provisions **-signal** *n* signal indicating position of points, block signal **-speiseleitung** *f* signal-feeder line **-sperrholz** *n* reinforced plywood, a special plywood **-sprache** *f* assembly language **-stab** *m* train staff **-stahlhalter** *m* toolpost **-stanze** *f* block stamp (for cutting out lids etc)

Block-station *f* signal box, blocking-signal station **-stelle** (Eisenbahn) block station, track sectioning cabin **-stichel** *m* box tool **-stichelhaus** *n* box for tool block, block tool box **-straße** *f* cogging- or blooming-mill train **-strecke** *f* cogging-mill train, blooming-mill train, section block and blocking (traction) **-stripper** *m* ingot stripper **-strom** *m* blocking current

Block-stufe *f* solid tread **-system** *n* block system (R. R.) **-taste** *f* knob, button **-teilmaschine** *f* ingot-slicing machine **-trio** *n* three-high blooming mill or bloomer **-übertragung** *f* block access **-umspanner** *m* unit-connected transformer (in unit power station)

Blockung *f* lock-and-block system

Blockverlegung *f* **vor Kopf** setting in advance (as the work advances operating from the part already built)

Block-verschluß *m* breechblock mechanism **-verwerfung** *f* block faulting **-vorrollvorrichtung** *f* ingot-conveying device **-wagen** *m pl* bloom buggies **-wall** *m* block barrier or wall **-walze** *f* ingot-rolling mill, bloomer, blooming or cogging roll **-walzenständer** *m* blooming-mill housing **-walzgerüst** *n* blooming-mill stand

Block-walzkaliber *n* blooming pass, cogging pass **-walzstraße** *f* blooming or cogging-roll train **-walzwerk** *n* cogging mill, blooming mill **-wand** *f* log wall **-wandverschiebung** *f* domain-wall switching **-wärmeofen** *m* bloom or ingot reheating furnace **-wender** *m* manipulator, ingot tilter **-werk** *n* block on a railroad track **-wurf** *m* riprap

Block-zange *f* ingot stirrup, ingot tongs **-zeichnung** *f* schematic or diagrammatic illustration, block diagram **-zeit** *f* block to block time **-zinn** *n* block tin

Blomstrandit *m* blomstrandite

bloß mere, exposed, bare, naked **-legen** to (lay) bare, expose, clear, visualize (test) **-stellen** to compromise (code, etc.), expose

Blubbern (Funktechnik) motor-boating

Blühen *n* blooming

Blumendraht *m* florists' wire

Blut *n* blood **-armut** *f* anemia

Blutdruckmesser *m*, **elektronischer ~** blood

pressure follower
Blutdruckwechsel *m* changing blood pressure
Bluten *n* bleeding, extraction
Blütengold *n* gold leaf or foil
Blut-erguß *m* hemorrhage **-farbemesser** *m* plethysmograph (monitors color changes), electroarteriograph **-farbstoff** *m* blood pigment, hemoglobin **flüssigkeit** *f* blood fluid, plasma, or serum **-gefäß** *n* blood vessel **-gefäßklemme** *f* hemostatic forceps **-gerinnung** *f* blood coagulation **-gerinsel** *n* blood clot **-getränkt** blood-soaked **-glanz** *m* blood seasoning **-gruppe** *f* blood group or type **-holz** *n* logwood **-kohle** *f* blood charcoal
Blutkörperchen *n* blood corpuscle **rotes ~** erythrocyte **weißes ~** leucocyte
Blutkörperchen-zähler *m* hemocytometer, blood counter **-zählkammer** *f* hemocytometer, blood-counter chamber **-zählung** *f* blood count
Blutlaugensalz *n* potassium ferrocyanide, prussiate **rotes ~** potassium ferricyanide
Blutmelasse *f* blood molasses
Blutplättchen *n* thrombocyte, platelet **-zählung** platelet count
Blut-regen *m* blood rain, red rain **-spender** *m* blood donor **-stein** *m* hematite, bloodstone, red iron ore, red mine stone, red slag ironstone
blutstillend styptic **-es Mittel** styptic
Blutsturz *m* hemorrhage
Bluttransfusion *f* blood transfusion
Blutung *f* bleeding, hemorrhage
Bluntersuchung auf Radioaktivität blood-counts
Blut-vergiftung *f* blood poisoning **-verwertungsanlage** *f* blood processing plant **-wolle** *f* skin, pelt, fellmongered, or plucked wool
B-Modulation *f* class B modulation
B-Modulator *m* class B modulator
Bö *f* squall, gust, bump **~ mit breiter Front** line squall **schwere ~** violent gust, heavy squall
Bobine *f* bobbin, reel, winding drum (pit haulage)
Bobinen-papier *n* coils (paper) **-spulmaschine** *f* winding machine for bobbins
Bock *m* (Technik) jack, stand, trestle, support frame, horse; (Regal, Gestell) rack, stool, lug, gin pole, frame, chock, shear legs, pedestal, bent, box of a vehicle, pile (bridge), crutch mounting (engine) **-bein** *n* trestle leg, standard footing **-brücke** *f* trestle bridge
Böckchen *n* small support or base, guide block, clutch
Bockdalben *m* buck dowel, kingpin
bocken to buck, sulk, pitch (naut.)
Bocken *n* **bei niedriger Drehzahl** low-speed buck
Bock-fräse *f* horizontal machine **-fräsmaschine** *f* single-spindle upright shaper **-gerät** *n* trestle gear **-gestänge** *n* pole strutted in pyramidal form **-holm** *m* transom
bockig (Wetter) bumpy
Bockigkeit *f* bumpiness, turbulence
Bockkonstruktion *f* trestle
Bockkran *m* gantry crane, gantry, transfer gantry **feststehender ~** stationary transfer gantry
Bock-lager *n* pedestal bearing **-leiter** *f* double ladder **-schere** *f* bench shears **-schnellsteg** *m* trestle footbridge **-schnürbund** *m* square lashing **-setzen** *n* setting of piles **-sprengwerk** *n* simple improvised truss (building), lock-spar support **-strecke** *f* trestle bay **-stütze** *f* trestle bearer, lean-to trussed strut **-verstellung** *f* scaffolding trestle **-wagen** *m* box cart **-winde** *f* hoisting crab, winch
Boden *m* (Erde) ground, soil, earth; (Gefäß) bottom; (Zimmer) floor; (Dach) attic, garret, loft; base, plate (distilling column), plug, bottom board or plate, head, tray, invert land, boiler head, bulkhead, underlay (print) blotch design, prints
Boden, ~ und Daubenfügemaschine head-and-stave jointing machine **~ des Gehäuses** bottom of casing or housing **~ zur Luftpumpe** back end cover for air pump **~ des Rumpfes** floor of fuselage
Boden, am ~ on or near the ground, in the attic **angeschwemmter ~** alluvial deposits **bewachsener, schmutziger ~** foul bottom **~, beweglicher ~** shifting soil **bindiger ~** cohesive soil **doppelter ~** false bottom **ebener ~** level floor **den ~ entrümpeln** to clear the attic **eingehalster ~** boiler end flanged inward **fester steiniger ~** hard stony ground **gebördelter ~** flanged end
Boden, gewachsener ~ natural, overgrown, or undisturbed soil, bush, vegetable mold, natural ground level **gewölbter ~** arched back (music) **~ gewinnen** to gain ground, make headway **oberer ~** tank top of a type of guided missile **rutschender ~** slipping earthwork **sich setzender ~** compressible soil **tiefgewölbter ~** deep-dished boiler head **~ tränken** to grout the floor **unterer ~** tank bottom of a type of guided missile **weggespülter ~** eroded soil **vom ~ reflektierte Wellen** ground reflecter waves
Boden-abfragestelle *f* (Radar) ground interrogator **-ablagerung** *f* stock pile, deposit ground or tip
Bodenablaß *m* bottom cleanout **-flansch** *f* **und Stopfen** cleanout flange and plug
Bodenabrichtmaschine *f* head-straightening machine
Bodenabricht- und Fügemaschine *f* head-straightening and jointing machine
Boden-absorption *f* ground absorption **-abstand** *m* ground clearance (of propeller) **-analyse** *f* soil analysis
Bodenanlage *f* ground installation
Boden-anlasser *m* ground starter **-anstrich** *m* floor painting, antifouling composition **-antenne** *f* ground or earth antenna, underground or buried antenna **-art** *f* type of soil **-aushub** *m* spoil **-auszug** *m* lens extension
Boden-beanspruchung *f* ground pressure, soil requirement **-bearbeitung** *f* cultivation
Bodenbearbeitungszuggerät *n* draught machines for soil tilling
Boden-bedienung *f* ground crew **-beheizt** bottom heated **-beheizung** *f* bottom heating **-beize** *f* floor stain **-belag** *m* boarding, bottom or floor covering, matting; (Gummi) rubber flooring **-belastungswerte** *m pl* (genaue) soil bearing values (proper) **-beleuchtung** *f* ground illumination
Bodenbenderit *m* bodenbenderite
Boden-beobachtungsmeldung *f* surface-obser-

vation report **-beschaffenheit** *f* nature or composition of the soil or ground, structure of the surface **-bestellung** *f* cultivation **-betrieb** *m* ground handling (aviation) **-beutel** *m* flat-bottom bag

Boden-bewachsung *f* vegetation **-bewachsungswasser** *n* vegetation moisture, water of vegetation **-bewegung** *f* earthwork, soil creep, ground movement

bodenbildender Vorgang soil-forming process

Boden-bildung *f* formation of the soil **-blech** *n* bottom plate, base-tray **-bö** *f* ground gust **-bohrwerk** *n* floor-type boring machine

Boden/Bord ground-to-air ~ **Verkehr** ground-to-air communication

Boden-brennofen *m* bottom-drying kiln, bottom-heating furnace **-brett** *n* baseboard, floorboard

Bodenbretterabrichthobel- und Fügemaschine *f* head-straightening and -jointing machine

Bodenbretterfügemaschine *f* head-jointing machine

Boden-deckplatte *f* bottom cover **-dichte** *f* density of soil **-dienst** *m* ground radio service **-drähte** *m pl* backing, backing wires

Bodendruck *m* ground pressure, (active) earth pressure, load on soil **spezifischer** ~ specific ground pressure, ground pressure per unit area

Bodendruck-geber *m* ground pressure pick up **-pressung** *f* compression of ground or soil

Boden-dunst *m* ground mist or haze **-ebner** *m pl* levelers **-echo** *n* ground return **-effektfahrzeug** *n* (BEF) ground effect machine (GEM) **-einfluß** *m* ground effect **-einsatzwagen** *m* **für Konverter** truck for converters, bottom jackcar **-einsenkung** *f* subsidence, surface fall **-einsetzmaschine** *f* bottom-charging machine **-elektrode** *f* bottom electrode, hearth electrode, **empfänger** *m* airborne receiver

Bodenentlader *m*, **Standbahn mit** ~ rail with bottom-discharge tubs

Boden-entleerer *m* bottom-discharge car or wagon **-entleererlastwagen** *m* bottom dump truck **-entleerung** *f* bottom discharge **-entwässerungsanlage** *f* soil-draining plant **-erhebung** *f* upheaval, soil elevation, rise **-erschöpfung** *f* soil exhaustion **-falte** *f* furrow, gully

Boden-falz *m* bottom fold **-feuchte** *f* moisture of soil **-feuchtigkeit** *f* ground humidity **-fläche** *f* ground surface, floor space, bottom surface **-flansch** *f* bottom flange **-fluß** *m* soil movement **-fräse** *f* ground mill, motor cultivator with rotary knives, rotary hoe, tiller, soil pulverizer

Bodenfreiheit *f* ground clearance (of tank) terrain clearance ~ **der Luftschraube** propeller clearance

Boden-frost *m* ground frost, hoarfrost **-fügemaschine** *f* head-jointing machine **-funkdienst** *m* ground radio service **-funker** *m* ground radio operator **-funkfeuer** *n* ground radio beacon **-funkgerät** *n* ground radio equipment

Bodenfunkstelle *f* aeronautical station, air-ground communication station **feste** ~ FAX (aeronautical fixed station)

Bodenfunkstellen-Rufzeichen *n* ground-station call sign or signal

Boden-gare *f* mellowness of the soil **-gekriech** *n* soil movement or creep **-gerät** *n* instrument on the ground **-geschoß** *n* garret story **-geschwindigkeit** *f* ground speed (of an airplane), speed at ground level

Boden-gestaltung *f* configuration or formation of ground, terrain, features **-gestell** *n* floor or low stand **-gesteuert** surface-to-air guided **-gewicht** *n* weight stand **-haftung** *f* road traction, ground adhesion (hang-on) **-hals** *m* any sort of outlet branch at or near bottom of layout **-heftung** *f* bottom stitching **-heizung** *f* heating from bottom **-hilfen** *pl* ground aids **-hobelmaschine** *f* head-planing machine

Bodenhöhe *f* ground level, floor level **unter** ~ **liegendes Erdgeschoß** basement

Boden-holz *n* heading **-isolation** ground insulation

Bodenkammer *f* base of shell **-ladung** *f* base charge **-schrapnell** *n* base spray

Boden-kanzel *f* ball turret, belly or ventral turret **-kappe** *f* tray cap **-kennziffern** *f pl* soil constants, soil coefficients, soil modulus **-kippe** *f* place of discharge, tip, spoil bank, stock pile **-kippen** *n* tipping, dumping, or discharging excavated material **-klappe** *f* ash door, hinged-bottom door, drop bottom, bottom gate, cover slide, breech door (torpedo) **-klappenträger** *m* drop-door girder **-kolloid** *n* soil colloid **-kolonne** *f* plate column

Boden-kontakt *m* hearth contact, bottom contact **-körper** *m* solid phase **-korrosion** *f* soil corrosion **-kräfte** (Boden- oder Wasserkräfte) ground reactions **-kunde** *f* soil science **-kurs** *m* track **-lack** *m* floor varnish **-lader** *m* supercharger with low-blower ratio blower, low-level blower **-lademotor** *m* ground supercharged engine **-lafette** *f* gunner's or belly blister, ventral gun mount, floor gun mounting, bulge to house gunner's partition

Bodenleerlaufzustand *m* (eines Flugzeugmotors) ground idling conditions

Bodenlehre *f* soil science

Bodenleistung *f* ground-level power **ideale** ~ sea-level equivalent of power

Boden-leitblech *n* paper guide **-leitung** *f* floor leads **-leitwertmeßgerät** *n* soil conductivity meter **-leitzunge** *f* cardboard slide **-leuchten** *n* ground illumination **-luftdichte** *f* ground-air density **-luftdruck** *m* air pressure at ground level **-lüftungsgerät** *n* soil-ventilating device **-luke** *f* mudhole (boilers) **-markierung** *f* ground marking, the practice of dropping flares from plane preliminary to operations **-mechanik** *f* soil mechanics **-motor** *m* low supercharged engine, sea-level-rated engine **-musterapparat** *m* bottom-hole-sample packer

bodennah near the ground **-er Kanal** ground-based duct, surface duct

Bodennähe *f* ground level **in** ~ near the ground

Bodennähendruck *m* power at the ground

Boden-nährstoff *m* soil nutrient **-navigation** *f* pilotage **-nebel** *m* ground fog, mist **-neigung** *f* gradient **-oberfläche** *f* surface **-öl** *n* floor oil **-organisation** *f* air-corps ground organization

Boden-ovalschneidemaschine *f* head ovaling machine **-pappe** *f* mulch paper **-peilapparat** *m* ground-station direction finder **-peiler** *m* ground direction finder **-peilstelle** *f* ground radio bearing station, direction-finder wireless station, ground direction-finder station **-personal** *n* ground personnel, ground crew or staff **-physik** *f* soil physics

Boden-platte *f* base or bottom plate, tuyère plate, drop bottom, bedplate; (Bagger) tread, mats **-pressung** *f* pressure on soil, consolidation of the subsoil (by weight) **-profil** *n* relief surface, profile of surface **-probe** *f* soil sample **-produkt** *n* (Destilliersäule) bottoms **-punkt** *m* pegging, survey, or reference point, bench mark **-querschnitt** *m* chine (seaplane)

Bodenrad *n*, **großes** ~ center or minute wheel (watch-making)

Bodenrahmen *m* longitudinal sill

Boden-rand *m* rim or flange of cartridge case **-reaktion** *f* soil reaction **-reflexion** *f* ground reflection **-reflexionsfaktor** *m* ground reflection factor **-reibung** *f* bottom friction, road-surface friction **-reibungszahl** *f* **-reibungsziffer** *f* coefficient of ground friction **-reißer** *m* bottom tearer (said of a cartridge or shell case cracked during firing) **-resonanz** *f* ground resonance **-ring** *f* tray ring

Boden-rohre *n pl* floor tubes **-rollen** *pl* ground rolls **-rollräder** *pl* handling wheels **-rost** *m* floor grating, bottom grid (refrigerator) **-rückstreuung** *f* ground back scatter **-rundschneidemaschine** *f* head-rounding machine **-rundnaht** (Kessel) end seam

Bodensatz *m* bottom settlings or sediments, ground deposit ~ **nach der Destillation von Rohöl** crude bottom ~ **und Wasser** bottoms sediments and water

Boden-sau *f* salamander, furnace sow, bear, horse **-saugvermögen** *n* soil suction **-schale** *f* pan, tray **-schall** *m* sound transmitted by solid bodies, solid-borne sound **-scharre** *f* bent shovel **-schätze** *m pl* wealth under ground, mineral resources or wealth, earth's natural recources **-schaufel** *f* bent shovel **-scheinwerfer** *m* ground projector

Bodenschicht *f* lowest stratum, filtering material **die zu prüfende** ~ the soil under test

Boden-schraube *f* bottom bolt or screw **-schwanz** *m* tail (bomb) **-schwelle** *f* ground beam or timber, tie **-segment** *n* soil segment **-seitig** near or on the ground **-sender** *m* ground-station transmitter

Bodensenkung *f* ground subsidence or submergence, sagging, low spot or depression, mining subsidence, creep, ground giving way, depression of ground

Bodensicht *f* ground visibility **auf** ~ in sight of the ground (aviat.)

Boden-speisung *f* ground power supply to guided missile **-spieker** *m* brad, slender nail **-stampfmaschine** *f* plug-ramming machine **-stand** *m* belly-gun position **-ständig** native, stable, permanent, static, stationary **-stärke** *f* thickness at bottom **-stärkenmessung** *f* measuring of base

Boden-start *m* rise off ground **-steckdose** *f* floor outlet **-stein** *m* hearth bottom, bedstone **-stelle** *f* ground station **-stoß** *m* ground impact or thrust **-strahl** *m* surface, direct, or ground ray **-strahlung** *f* ground radiation **-strom** *m* bottom current (oceanog.) **-struktur** *f* soil texture

Bodenstück *n* breech plate, base plate **-sperre** *f* base-plate latch

Boden-technologie *f* soil technology **-teig** *m* bottom paste, underdough **-teilchen** *n pl* soil particles **-temperatur** *f* soil or ground temperature **-thermik** *f* thermic upwash near ground **-tisch** *m* hopper apron **-tragfähigkeit** *f* soil bearing **-transport** *m* transportation of excavated material **-treffbild** *n* covered-area diagram, dispersion pattern, horizontal shot, group, 100 per cent diagram, probability diagram

Boden-treffer *m* base-impact hit **-treppe** *f* garret staircase **-trichter** *m* hopper bottom **-trockengewicht** *n* dry weight of soil **-tür** *f* loft or garret door **-übergang** *m* section between base and side wall on shell or cartridge cases **-unterstützung** *f* tray support **-untersuchung** *f* soil research, investigation of soil

Bodenventil *n* bottom blow valve, foot valve, bottom valve, dump valve, Kingston valve, sea cock **-kegel** *m* bottom-valve poppet

Boden-verdichter *m* road grader and tamper **-verdrängung** *f* displacement of soil **-verfestigung** *f* soil stabilization or consolidation **-verhältnisse** *n pl* soil conditions **-vermörtelung** *f* soil-cement stabilization **-verschluß** *m* breech door, rear door **-versenkt** underground **-verstärkung** *f* underground pole reinforcement **-versorgungsaggregat** *n* ground power unit (aviat.) **-versuch** *m* experimental test of rockets on ground **-walze** (Druck) blotch roller **-wanne** *f* bathtub gunner's pit, base or floor pan

Boden-wärme *f* ground temperature **-welle** *f* ground or surface wave, direct wave (that hugs earth's curvature), undulation of ground, fundamental wave **-wellenempfangszone** *f* ground-wave reception zone **-wellenpeiler** *m* ground-wave direction finder **-wetterkarte** *f* ground weather map or chart **-wind** *m* ground or surface wind

Boden-wirkungsgrad *m* plate efficiency **-wölbplatten** *pl* bottom dishes **-wrange** *f* floor, transom, floorplate (of a ship) **-wrangenplatten** *f pl* floorplate transoms **-ziegel** *m* paving tile **-ziel** *n* ground objective, ground target **-zünder** *m* base percussion fuse, base detonator, base fuse of a shell (artil.)

Bodmerei *f* bottomry

Böen-band *n* squall belt, zone of wind gusts **-front** *f* secondary squall front **-gefühl** *n* bumpiness **-kopf** *m* squall head **-linie** *f* squall line, isobar **-messer** *m* gust meter **-schleppe** *f* vapor trail (engines) **-schreiber** *m* gust recorder **-windkanal** *m* gust tunnel **-wolke** *f* squall cloud

Bogen *m* arc (math.), arch, elbow, bend, curvature, rounding, bow, curve, sheet (of paper) limb, clip **abgeflachter** ~ depressed arch **ausgeschrägter** ~ splayed arch **langer** ~ long elbow **umspannter** ~ arc of contact

Bogen-ableger *m* layboy (print.) **-ableiter** *m* arc arrester **-abnehmer** *m* taker-off (print.) **-abstand** *m* pitch or distance along an arc **-abstreifer** *m* sheet remover **-abzug** *m* steady-brace **-anfang** *m* front edge of sheet **-anlegeapparat** *m* sheet feeding apparatus **-anleger** *m* sheet feeding apparatus **-anlegerschläuche** *pl* feeder hoses

Bogen-anschlag *m* poster advertising **-ausleger** *m* flyer sheet deliverer **-auswerfer** *m* sheet fly

-bahn *f* trajectory **-baustein** *m* arch brick **-bildend** arcing (metal) **-bildung** *f* arcing, formation of arcs **-blitzableiter** *m* arc arrester **-bremse** *f* sheet slow-down **-brücke** *f* arched bridge

Bogen-diagramm *n* arc plot **-einheit** *f* radian **-element** *n* element of arc **-ende** *n* rear end of the sheet **-endsignal** *n* end of page signal **-entladung** *f* arc discharge **-entladungskontinuum** *n* arc discharge continuum **-fachwerk** *n* arch truss **-fänger** *m* taker-in (print), taker-off flyers **-federventilkapsel** *f* bowspring valve cup

Bogenfläche *f* face of an arch **äußere ~** extrados **innere ~** intrados

Bogen-flamme *f* arc flame **-förmig** curved, arched **-frosch** *m* bow frog (string instrument)

Bogenführung *f* side guide bearing **pneumatische ~** pneumatic feeding arrangement (print.)

Bogen-führungsfeder *f* sheet guide spring **-fußpunkt** *m* arc root **-gang** *m* arcade **-geradeleger** *m* jogger (print.) **-geradestreifer** *m* sheet smoother **-gerüst** *n* soffit scaffolding

Bogen-halter *m* drop fingers, paper holder **-hebel** *m* bent crank **-höhe** (Geom.) *f* height of arc, rise **-kalander** *m* sheet calender **-kämpfer** *m* archer, impost or springer of an arch **-kathode** *f* arc cathode **-korrektur** *f* proofed sheets

Bogenlampe *f* arc lamp, acetylene **~ mit breitwinklig gestellten Kohlen** scissors-type arc lamp

Bogenlampen-abzugsrohr *n* vent stack of arc lamp **-drosselspule** *f* impedance (choking) coil **-kohle** *f* carbon (electric arc light) **-sender** *m* arc **-spiegel** *m* arc-lamp mirror **-zubehör** *n* arc-lamp accessories

Bogen-länge *f* arc length (of an oscillation arch) **-lehre** *f* center, bow member (building) **-leibung** *f* intrados or soffit of an arch **-licht** *n* arc light (elec.) **-lineal** *n* bow, French curve **-linie** *f* arcuate, arc, or curved line **-maschine** *f* sheet fed press **-maß** *n* circular measure, arc measure, measurement (of an angle) in radius **-minute** *f* angle minute

Bogen-offsetmaschine *f* sheet-fed offset press **-pfeiler** *m* flying buttress **-reihenstaumauer** *f* multiple arch dam **-rippe** *f* groined arch **-rohr** *n* angle pipe, curved pipe, bent pipe, elbow (pipe) **-rotationsmaschine** *f* sheet-fed rotary machine **-rückschlag** *m* arc back

Bogensäge *f* bow saw; (Holzsäge) coping saw; (Metallsäge) hacksaw **mechanische ~** power hacksaw

Bogensatz *m* quires **drahtgehefteter ~** wire-stitched quires **fadengehefteter ~** sewed quires

Bogen-säule *f* arc column **-schalung** *f* arch centering **-scheide** *f* arc sheath **-scheitel** *m* crown, top, key or apex of arch **-schiebeapparat** *m* sheet pusher **-schieberblech** *n* jogger plate

Bogen-schluß *m* keystone, heading stone **-schneider** *m* sheet cutter **-schneidmaschine** *f* sheet cutter **-schnur** *f* bow string **-schub** *m* horizontal or tangential thrust or stress **-schuß** *m* high-angle shot or fire, indirect fire

Bogen-schweißung *f* arc welding, metal arc welding **-sehne** *f* chord of an arc **-sehnenträger** *m* polygonal bow-string girder **-sekunde** *f* second of arc **-skala** *f* curved scale **-spannweite** *f* arch span **-spannung** *f* arc voltage **-spektrum** *n* arc spectrum **-spitze** *f* ogive, point of projectile ogive **-staumauer** *f* arch dam

Bogen-stich *m* height of an arch **-streicher** *m* sheet steadier **-strom** *m* arc (lamp) current **-träger** *m* arched girder **-übergabe** *f* sheet transfer **-übergang** *m* sheet passage **-verankerung** *f* grappling of arch **-verband** *m* arch bond **-verluste** *pl* arc-drop loss

Bogen-verzahnung *f* curved teeth, spiral-toothed bevel gears **-viertel** *n* quadrant of a circular arch **-weite** *f* span, width (arch) **-widerlager** *n* arch abutment **-zähler** *m* sheet counter **-zeichen** *n* sheet signature **-zirkel** *m* wing callipers **-zuleitungsbänder** *pl* feeding tapes (print.) **-zündung** *f* arc ignition

Bohle *f* (thick) plank, board, batten, deal

Bohlen-bahn *f* pile road **-belag** *m* bordage, plank flooring, floor, planking, sheathing, deck(ing) **-fußboden** *m* plank floor **-weg** *m* plank road

Bohl-wand *f* wall of planks or timbers, bulkhead, timbered wall **-werk** *n* piling, bulkhead

Bohnenpflanzmaschine *f* bean planter

Bohnen- und Erbsendreschvorrichtung *f* bean-and-pea threshing

Bohner-maschine *f* floor polisher **-masse** *f* floor-polishing paste, polish for floors **-wachs** *n* floor wax **-wachszerstäuber** *m* wax sprayer and atomizer

Bohnerz *n* (oolithisches Eisenerz) pea, bog, bean ore, oölitic ore

Bohr zum Schmieren der Achsen tube or device for lubricating axles

Bohr-anlage *f* **-apparat** *m* boring plant, drilling boring apparatus, drilling rig **-arbeit** *f* drilling work or operation, drilling **-arm** *m* spud **-aufseher** *m* tool pusher **-ausrüstung** *f* boring rig, drill kit **-bank** *f* boring frame, wrench board, drill press **-bericht** *m* boring journal, log **-birne** *f* casing-spud straightener, swage **-bock** *m* boring saddle **-bogen** *m* drill bow **-brücke** *f* drilling bridge **-brunnen** *m* bored well, artesian well **-brunnenpumpe** *f* artesian pump

Bohrbüchse *f* drill-jig bush, bushing, drill socket **~ für Bohrvorrichtung** drill-jig bush

Bohr-bühne *f* derrick platform **-bündel** *n* boring clamp **-deckel** *m* casing cap **-dock** *n* walking-beam post **-dreher** *m* breast drill

Bohrdruck *m* drill thrust or pressure **-kontrolle** *f* drilling control **-messer** *m* drillometer

Bohr-egge *f* drill **-einsatz** *m* bit **-eisen** *n* auger bit, iron drill

bohren to bore, drill, pierce, punch (holes) **mit Fräser ~** to mill

Bohren *n* boring, drill(ing) (a new hole) with twist drill, boring (cored holes)

Bohrer *m* borer, drill, auger, drill bit, boring mill, gimlet, bit drill, tap **~ für Bohrkurbel** bits for handbrace **~ mit Einsätzen** insert bit **~ für hartes Gestein** hard-formation cutting head **~ mit Konusschaft** taper-shank drills **~ mit zylindrischem Schaft** straight-shank drill **~ mit drei Schneiden** three-lipped drill **~ für Strebenschrauben und Stutzen** auger **~ für Streckenbetrieb** tunnel drill

Bohrer, flacher ~ bull bit **halbrunder ~** half-round reamer bit **sich selbsttätig verschiebender ~** self-feeding rock drill **zweimännischer ~** double-handed borer

Bohrer-angel *f* tang (of a drill) **-einsteckende** *n*

chisel shank **-führungsstücke** *n pl* auger stem guides **-halter** *m* steel retainer **-hülse** *f* drill sleeve **-lehre** *f* wire or drill gauge plate **-nute** *f* flute of drill **-satz** *m* drill sets **-schneide** *f* boring bit **-spitze** *f* drill point, drill bit **-stauchmaschine** *f* drill upsetting machine **-type** *f* auger type **-zapfen** *m* drill tang, shank of bit

Bohr-fänger *m* fishing grab **-fäustel** *n* miner's hammer **-fett** *n* cutting oil **-fräser** *m* countersink **-führer** *m* driller **-futter** *m* boring socket, drill chuck, tap holder, (boring) jig **-futterkegel** *m* drill socket **-garnitur** *f* drilling outfit **-gebläse** *n* drill(ing) blower **-gerät** *n* drill rigs **-gerätefuß** *m* boring-tool support **-gerätekupplung** *f* drilling-tool joint **-gerüst** *n* breastplate, bore frame, boring trestle, derrick

Bohrgestänge *n* bore rods, drill poles, drill pipe, boring tools **-gewinde** *n* drill pipe threads

Bohr-gestell *n* bore frame, drilling rig **-gezähe** *n* drilling tools or implements **-grat** *m* burr **-guß** *m* low-grade malleable iron of easily drillable character **-gut** *n* drill chips

Bohr-haken *m* tool hook; (Tiefbohrg.) casing hook **-halter** *m* drill socket **-hammer** *m* hammer drill **-haspel** *m* draw spool, windlass for drilling **-hauer** *m* driller, helper **-hebel** *m* bore lever, spring pole **-hülse** *f* taper sleeve **-käfer** *m* wood-boring beetle

Bohrkern *m* boring kernel, drill core, boring sample **-hülle** *f* core shell **-zieher** *m* core extractor

Bohr-kette *f* **mit Wirbel** drill chain and swivel **-keule** *f* drill club **-klein** *n* borings, drillings **-knarre** *f* rack brace, rock drill, ratchet drill **-kolben** *m* boring rod, cutter block **-kolonne** *f* oil-well casing, string of casing, water string **-kopf** *m* casing head, bearings (of a drilling engine), boring head, cutter head, drill head, drill chuck **-kopfschaft** *m* boring head shank **-kran** *m* drilling rig **krangerüst** *n* drilling-rig frame

Bohr-kranteile *n pl* rig irons **-krone** *f* core bit, drill, cutter head, annular bit **-kronengewindenippel** *m* threaded drill-bit nipple **-krücke** *f* boring brace **-krückel** *m* brace head **-kurbel** *f* crank of main shaft, hand brace **-ladung** *f* blasting charge **-lehre** *f* drilled jig, boring template **-leier** *f* brace **-leistung** *f* drilling capacity **leistungsversuch** *m* hardness testing of material under drill

Bohrloch *n* boring, borehole, auger hole, shot hole, well, drill hole **aus dem ~ herauskommen** to come out of a well **ein ~ schaukeln** to rock a well **Anstich ~ Entspannungs-~** stab hole **Grenz-~, Nachbar-~** offsetting well **wildes ~** wild well

Bohrloch-abmessungen *pl* well dimensions **-achse** *f* center of bore **-ausräumer** *m* reamer **-distanz** *f* bore-hole spacing

Bohrlöcher absenken (tiefboren) to sink wells

Bohrloch-futterrohr *n* well casing **-glätter** *m* instrument for straightening a bore **-kopf** *m* outlet of well **-kristall** *n* well crystal **-neigungsmesser** *m* (Tiefbohranl.) hole deviation measuring device **-mund** *m* mouth of a bore **-öffnung** *f* collar, heel of a well

Bohrloch-pfeife *f* blown-out hole **-pumpe** *f* borehole pump **-querschnitt** *m* (nutzbarer), available width of a bore **-schießen** *n* borehole shooting, well-shooting **-schutzrohr** *n* conductor **-tiefe** *f* depth of borehole **-untersuchung** *f* borehole logging **-untersuchungsmethode** *f* bore hole logging method **-wand** *f* walls of borehole

Bohr-löffel *m* drilling spoon, bailer, shell, sludger **-mannschaft** *f* drilling crew

Bohrmaschine *f* drilling or boring machine, drill, driller, rock drill, drill press, perforating machine, trepan, boring mill, borer **~ zur Prüfung der Bearbeitungsfähigkeit von Guß** drill-hardness-testing machine **rotierende ~ mit Diamanten gespitzt** rotary drill rig with diamond-crowned points **mehrspindlige ~** multiple-drill press

Bohr-maschinenfutter *n* chuck **-mast** *m* derrick **-mehl** *n* borings, cuttings, drillings, boring dust **-milch** *f* drill milk

Bohrmeißel *m* bore or drill bit **~ mit zentraler Wasserspülung** trepan with central water clearing **flacher ~** flat bit **gerader ~** straight bit **schiefer ~** one-sided bit

Bohrmeißel-haken *m* fishing hook for bits **-kanal** *m* hole of a hollow bit

Bohr-meister *m* driller, foreman driller **-mine** *f* driller mine **-nadel** *f* picker, gad (tool, textiles) **-öl** *n* soluble oil **-ort** *n* bottom of borehole **-patrone** *f* blasting or explosive cartridge **-pfahl** *m* bored pile **-pflug** *m* seed-drill plough **-pinole** *f* boring quill **-prisma** *n* V block

Bohr-probe *f* drill test **-probenbüchse** *f* tube sample boring **-profil** *n* log **-protokoll** *n* boring log **-pumpe** *f* deep pump **-punkt** *m* (Tiefbohrg.) drilling site **-punktbestimmung** *f* locating a bore **-rapport** *m* boring journal, log **-ratsche** *f* ratchet brace, ratchet drill **-rechen** *m* boring rake **-reitstock** *m* boring head, drilling tailstock

Bohrrohr *n* casing, casing pipe, borehole tube or lining **-abfangkeil** *m* drill-pipe slips **-benzin** *n* casing-head gasoline **-druck** *m* casing pressure

Bohrröhre *f* boring tube **~ mit stark gewölbten Muffen** casing with bulging collars **~ mit tonnenförmigen Muffen** casing with bell-mouthed collars **patentgeschweißte, verschraubte ~** patent-welded casing

Bohr-röhrenkolonne *f* **-röhrenzug** *m* string of casing **-rohrkopf** *m* driving cap **-rohrstopfbüchse** *f* stuffing box for casing **-rolle** *f* crown pulley or sheave **-schablone** *f* drilling jib, drill template **-schacht** *m* shaft put down by boring **-schappe** *f* auger, auger bit **-schaufel** *f* spud **-schaufelschuh** *m* spudding shoe **-scheibe** *f* boring block **-schere** *f* jars

Bohrsches Atommodell *n* Bohr atom, Bohr model

Bohrsches Magneton *n* electronic Bohr magneton

Bohrschlamm *m* drilling mud, sludge cutting **schieferhaltiger ~** shale mud

Bohr-schlauch *m* boring hose **-schlitten** *m* sliding drill head or arm, carriage of a boring machine, boring slide **-schmant** *m* boring silt, slime, sludge, drilling mud, cuttings of a boring **-schneide** *f* bit, cutter of the borer **-schuh** *m* drive shoe **-schuß** *m* shot (blasting) **-schwengel** *m* walking beam

Bohr-seil *n* drilling line, drilling rope **-seiltrommel** *f* **-seilwinde** *f* bull wheel **-sohle** *f* bottom of borehole **-späne** *m pl* borings, drillings, chips **-spaten** *m* spud

Bohrspindel *f* box, cutter bar of a boring machine or spindle; (kugelgelagert) drilling spindle runs in ball bearings **-ausladung** *f* distance from center of drill spindle to column **-führung** *f* drill-spindle guide **-hub** *m* travel of drill spindle **-rad** *n* drilling spindle gear wheel

Bohr-spitze *f* auger bit **-stahl** *m* boring tool, drill steel **-stahlhalter** *m* boring-tool holder **-stampfer** *m* stemmer **-ständer** *m* drill stand, upright

Bohrstange *f* drilling pipe, boring bar, drill rod, pole ~ **mit aufgeschweißtem Förderwedel** drill rod with welded-on delivery worm

Bohrstangen-aufnahme *f* boring bar receptacle **-führung** *f* pilot bush for boring bar **-halter** *m* boring-tool holder or snout **-obersupport** *m* boring bar top slide **-stahl** *m* sucker-rod steel **-verbindung** *f* sucker-rod joint

Bohr-stelle *f* drilling site **-stichel** *m* boring cutter or blade, cutter blades **-stock** *m* boring rod **-strang** *m* drilling shaft or string **-stütze** *f* drilling support **-tafel** *f* boring platform **-tagesbericht** *m* log, boring journal **-taucher** *m* conductor **-technik** *f* drilling engineering **-tiefe** *f* depth of boring or bore **-tisch** *m* drilling bench **-transportwagen** *m* truck for conveyance of drilling tools **-trübe** *f* boring mud or sludge

Bohrturm *m* derrick (drilling), frame of boring rig, boring tower ~ **für Erdölbohrung** oil-well derrick **einen** ~ **walzen** to skid the derrick

Bohrturmgebälk *n* lumber for derrick

Bohr- und Drehwerk *n* boring and turning mill

Bohr- und Fräswerke *pl* combined boring and milling machines

Bohr- und Schießarbeit *f* blasting, shooting

Bohr- und Schießzeug *n* blasting tools

Bohr- und Senkvorrichtung *f* drilling and counterboring fixture

Bohrung *f* bore, borehole, diameter of bore, boring, drill, well, bore (cylinder), making a boring, drilling, caliber, shaft, drill hole ~ **mit Kernbüchsen** tube sample boring ~ **eines Lagers** diamter of a bearing **die** ~ **schlichten** to finish the hole **abgesetzte** ~ stepped hole **flache** ~ shallow boring **radiale** ~ radial bore **schräge** ~ slope boring **verrohrte** ~ cased-in bore

Bohrungs-lehre *f* plug gauge, internal cylindrical gauge, internal caliper gauge **-mischöse** *f* straight-bore mixing nozzle **-mittenabstand** *m* drilling center **-orthotest** *m* orthotest bore gauge

Bohr-unternehmer *m* contractor of wells, boring or drilling contractor **-versuch** *m* boring or drill test, experimental or test boring **-vorrichtung** *f* drilling or boring jig, drilling device, tapping attachment **-wagen** *m* drill cradle **-wasser** *n* diluted soluble oil **-weg** *m* travel of drill spindle **-welle** *f* cutter bar, drilling shaft **-werk** *n* boring mill; (Tiefbohranl.) drilling output, drilling aggregate **-werkzeug** *n* boring tool

Bohr-widder *m* (hydraulischer), hydraulic ram **-winde** *f* draw works, bit brace, ratchet brace **-winder** *m* hand or boring brace, breast drill **-wirbel** *m* swivel, swivel head **-wurm** *m* woodworm **-zwinge** *f* drilling ferrule

böig bumpy, gusty, squally **-e Luft** bumpy air

Böigkeit *f* bumpiness, turbulence

Boje *f* buoy **an der** ~ **festmachen** to secure to a buoy **an die** ~ **gehen** to pick up a buoy **von einer** ~ **loswerfen** to cast off from a buoy

Bojen-laterne *f* buoy lantern **-tau** *n* buoy rope

Boleine *f* bowline

Bölinie *f* squall line

Böller *m* bollard

Bollwerk *n* quay, wharf, camp sheathing bulwark

Bolometer *n* bolometer, barretter **-abschluß** *m* bolometer mount **-diagramm** *n* bolograph **-strahlungsmessung** *f* bolometer detection

bolometrisch bolometric(al) **-e Korrektur** bolometric correction

Boltzmannsche Gleichung *f* Boltzmann equation

Bolusmaterial *n* Bolus material

Bolzen *m* pin, bolt, billet, screw, plug gauge, gudgeon, striker, firing pin, pole pin (wagon), post, prop, stay, pivot stud, threaded shouldered pin

Bolzen, ~ **zum Abzugstück** trigger pin ~ **mit rechtwinklig eingebogenem (Anker) Ende** lug bolt ~ **mit gespaltenem** (Anker) **Ende und Keil** fox bolt ~ **mit flachem Kopf** flat-headed bolt ~ **mit versenktem Kopf** countersunk bolt ~ **mit Kopf und Splintloch** pin with head and hole for split pin, cotter pin ~ **zur Luftabstellung** suction control spindle ~ **zur Pumpe** pump crank pin ~ **zum Spannstück** cocking lever pin

Bolzen, ~ **mit Splint** pin with cotter, cotter bolt ~ **mit Vorlegescheibe und Mutter** bolt **durchgehender** ~ through bolt **einsteckbarer** ~ loose or stop pin **geschlitzter** ~ slotted bolt **glatter, nicht abgesetzter** ~ plain bolt ~ **mit flachem Verlängerungsstück** bat bolt **versplinteter** ~ cottered pin ~ **im Winkelhebel** pin in bellcrank

Bolzen-abschneider *m* bolt clipper **-durchmesser** *m* bolt diameter **-ende** *n* point of bolt **-federscheibe** *f* firing-pin spring washer **-gelenk** *n* pin joint

Bolzengewinde *n* male thread; (auf Drehbänken) external thread, screw thread **-schneidemaschine** *f* bolt thread cutting machine

Bolzen-kette *f* riveted drive chain, bolt chain **-kronenschläger** *m* bolt-crown-beater

Bolzenkupplung *f* bolt clutch, pin coupling **elastische** ~ flexible pin coupling

Bolzen-lager *n* hinged support, trunnion bearing **-länge** *f* length under head **-loch** *n* pin hole **-material** *n* bolt and nut articles **-meßgerät** *n* measuring instrument for cylindrical work **-mutter** *f* bolt or stud nut **-riegel** *m* cylindrical padlock

Bolzen-schaftfräsemaschine *f* bolt-milling machine **-scheibe** *f* bolt washer **-schießapparat** *m* bolt setting guns **-schießgerät** *n* cartridge-powered tool, bolt driving gun **-schläger** *m* bolt beater **-schlüssel** *m* (bolt) spanner, wrench **-schneider** *m* bolt clipper

Bolzenschraube *f* expansion bolt ~ **zum Montieren** assembling bolt

Bolzen-schrotzimmerung *f* shaft timbering **-schwächung** *f* bolt deduction **-schweißer** *m* stud welder **-schweißpatronen** *pl* stud welding cartridges **-schweißpistole** stud welding gun

-schweißverfahren *n* stud welding process **-setzer** *m* stud driver, setter **-ventil** *n* bolt valve **-verbindung** *f* bolted union **-verriegelung** *f* pin-type locking system **-verschraubung** *f* bolt screwing, bolting **-zahnkranz** *m* pin wheel, crown wheel, lantern gear

Bolzer *m* etching needle

Bombage *f* lapping (wrapping), knob (on rolls, etc.) **mit Bombagen überzogen** knobbed (as a roll on a textile-finishing machine), bulging of food tins

bombagieren to wrap with cloth

Bombardement *n* bombardment

bombardieren to bombard

Bombardierung *f* bombing, bombardment

Bombaxwolle *f* kapok

Bomben-kalorimeter *n* bomb-type calorimeter **-rohre** *n pl* carius tubes **-sauerstoff** *m* tank oxygen

Bombier-maschine *f* dishing machine **-presse** *f* end closing press

Bondermaschine *f* bonderizing machine

bondern bonderize

Bondern *n* bonderizing

Bondur *n* aluminum-copper-magnesium alloy

Boosterspannung *f* boost voltage

Boot *n* boat, body or hull (aviation), working barge **ein ~ anrufen** to hail a boat **ein ~ aussetzen** to lower a boat **ein ~ einsetzen** to hoist a boat

Bootheißvorrichtung *f* gear for launching small boats (booms, derricks, or davits)

Boot-nagel *m* boat spike **-rumpf** *m* hull **-stufe** *f* hull step

Boots-anker *m* grapnel **-bauer** *m* boatbuilder **-besatzung** *f* boat's crew **-breite** *f* beam **-breitenbelastung** *f* beam loading **-bug** *m* bow of the boat **-davit** *m* davit **-deck** *n* boat deck **-gräting** *f* boat's grating

Boots-haken *m* boat hook **-heißmaschine** *f* boat hoist **-hißstropp** *m* boat slings **-kadett** *m* midshipman of boat **-klampen** *f pl* gripes (naut.) **-körper** *m* hull **-krabben** *f pl* gripes (naut.) **-lack** *m* spar varnish **-mann** *m* boatswain, seaman

Bootsmanns-hellegatt *n* boatswain's store **-maat** *m* (der Wache), boatswain's mate (quartermaster of the watch)

Boots-posten *m* boat watch (sentry) **-ring** *m* mooring ring **-sonnensegel** *n* boat's awning **-steurer** *m* coxswain **-stropp** *m* boat slings **-takel** *n* boat's tackle **-weise** boat by boat **-werft** *f* shipyard, boat-building workings **-winde** *f* ship's winch **-zubehörteile** *pl* marine supplies

Bor *n* boron, borine

Boral *n* boral **-schirm** *m* boral shield

Borat *n* borate

Boräthan *n* boroethane

Borax *m* borax, borate of soda **-kalk** *m* calcium borate **-säure** *f* boric acid **-spat** *m* boracite **-weinstein** *m* boryl potassium tartrate

Borazit *m* boracite

Bor-benzoesäure *f* borobenzoic acid **-bromid** *n* borobromide **-butan** *n* borobutane

Bord *m* board (ship, plane, etc.), border, edge, rim; (Kesselboden) contact surface; (in Zusammensetzungen) airborne **an ~** aboard **~ an ~** alongside **~ zu ~** interaircraft **~ zu ~ Kennung** aircraft-to-aircraft identification **~ zu Boden** air to ground **an ~ gehen** to embark **über ~ fallen** to fall overboard **über ~ werfen** to jettison, throw overboard **loser ~** loose flange **umgezogener ~** flange

Bord-ablenkung *f* distortion of bearing on site, aircraft error **-abtastgerät** *n* airborne scanner (rdr)

Bordanlage *f* aircraft radio set (rdr)

Bord-anlasser *m* cockpit starter **-anschluß** *m* intake connection (oil, etc.) **-antenne** *f* ships antenna **-besatzung** *f* air crew

Bord-betrieb *m* marine service **-brett** *n* wind board **-buch** *n* logbook (navig. and aviation)

Bord/Boden air-to-ground, air-to-ground communication **-sprechverkehr** *m* air-to-ground radio telephony, communication with aircraft

Borde *f* molding

Bordeaux-Farbton *m* claret shade

Bordeffekt *m* board effect, ship field error (in direction-finding work), quadrantal error (due to structural parts, metal)

Bördel *n* flange **-arbeit** *f* flanged sheetwork

Bördelblech *n* flanged sheet **~ aus Flußeisen** flanged mild-steel plate

Bördel-breite *f* heigh of the border **-einrichtung** *f* flanging attachment **-eisen** *n* bordering tool **-flanschrohr** *n* flanged pipe with loose back flange **-gerät für Rohrenden** pipe-end opener, pipe-flanging tool **-kräfte** *pl* flanging forces **-loch** *n* round-edged hole **-maschine** *f* bordering or flanging or beading machine **-matrize** *f* beading die

bördeln to flange, border, bead, edge, rim

Bördel-naht *f* double flanged seam **-nahtschweißung** *f* flange-joint welding **-niete** *f* joggled rivet **-nietung** *f* flange riveting **-probe** *f* flanging test **-rand** *m* bead, flanged or beaded edge **-schweißnaht** *f* flange butt-welding joint **-schweißung** *f* double-flanged butt weld or square-edge joint **-stoß** *m* double-flanged butt joint

Bördel- und Flanschpresse *f* flanging press

Bördel-verbindung *f* jointed-flange connection **-versuch** *m* bead test **-walze** *f* flanging roll

Bord-empfänger *m* airborne receiver **-empfangsgerät** *n* airplane receiving set **-fernsprechanlage** *f* intercommunication plane installation **-feuerlöscher** *m* board fire extinguisher

Bordfunk-anlage *f* ship or aircraft radio installation or equipment **-einrichtung** *f* radio equipment of plane or vessel

Bordfunker *m* flight radio operator, wireless officer of aircraft

Bordfunk-gerät *n* airborne radio **-peiler** *m* airborne radio direction-finder, ship's radio range finder **-stelle** *f* airborne radio direction-finder, station on board, airplane radio station

Bordgebühr *n* ship or aircraft charges

Bordgerät *n* flight instrument or equipment **~ zur Flugüberwachung** flying instrument

Bord-gespräch *n* aircraft intercommunication **-hilfsaggregat** *n* marine auxiliary set **-höhe** *f* freeboard (ship) **-höhenanzeiger** *m* terrain clearance indicator **-instrument** *n* aircraft-type instrument **-kanone** *f* aircraft cannon **-kompaß** *m* ship's compass

Bord-mannschaft *f* air crew **-mechaniker** *m* flight

engineer or mechanic **-navigator** *m* flight navigator

Bordnetz *n* power supply for plane communication apparatus, mains power supply, aircraft electric wiring system other than radio **-ausfall** *m* failure in aircraft wiring (elec.)

Bord-notaggregat *n* marine emergency set **-peilanlage** *f* ship or aircraft direction-finder gear **-peiler** *m* ship direction-finding station, ship's radio direction finder, radio compass **-peilgerät** *n* aircraft or airborne direction-finder **-peilstelle** *f* ship direction-finding station, ship's radio direction finder **-peilung** *f* heading marker or indicator **-pfahl** *m* gauged pile of a cofferdam, standard pile **-prüfgerät** *n* in-flight check-out unit (aviat.) **-pumpen** *f pl* ship's pumps **-radar** *n* airborne radar **-rakete** *f* airborne rocket **-rand** *m* flange, rim **-registrierung** *f* missile-mounted recording instrument **-reif** improvement of a device to a degree where its use on shipboard is justified

Bord-sammelschiene *f* missile-mounted terminal board **-scheibe** *f* flanged-coupling pulley **-schwelle** *f* curb, curbstone, sole bar **-seitig** missile-mounted on board **-sender** *m* airborne transmitter **-spiegel** *m* rear-view mirror (aviation)

Bord-sprechanlage *f* aircraft intercommunication system, radio interphone system **-sprechgerät** *n* intercommunication telephone, interphone **-spruch** *m* ship-to-ship or plane-to-plane communication **-stromsammler** *m* aircraft battery (elec.) **-stein** *m* curb, curbstone **-störsender** *m* airborne communication jammer **-suchgerät** *n* air-borne search apparatus (radar) **-tagesbericht** *m* logbook **-techniker** *m* flight mechanic engineer **-telephon** *n* interphone, intercommunication telephone **-uhr** *f* dashboard clock (aviation)

Bordüre *f* border (edging)

Bordürenband *n* trimming ribbon

Bord-verständigung *f* aircraft intercommunication (radio), interphone communication **-verständigungsanlage** *f* intercommunication system **-voll** *m* bankfull (soil mech.)

Bord-wand *f* side of ship **-wände** *pl* side and tail boards **-wart** *m* flight engineer **-werkzeugtasche** *f* service tool kit, flight kit **-winkel** *m* safety toe angle **-wippkran** *m* level luffing deck crane

Borfluorwasserstoffsäure *f* hydrofluoboric acid

borflußsauer fluoboric

Borflußsäure *f* fluoboric acid

Borgbrasse *f* preventer brace

borgen to borrow

Borger *m* borrower, lender

Borium *n* boron **-fluorid** *n* boron fluorid, fluoroborate **-zählrohr** *n* boron counter tube

Borkarbid *n* boron carbide

Borke *f* bark, bark wood

borken to decorticate

Bork(en)holz *n* bark, bark wood

Bornit *m* bornite

Borokalzit *n* borocalcite

Boronatrokalzit *m* ulexite

Borsalbe *f* boric acid ointment

Borsäure *f* boric acid **-anhydrid** *n* boric anhydride **-getränkt** soaked in boric acid **-lösung** *f* boric acid solution

borsaures borate ~ **Ammonium** ammonium borate ~ **Kalium** potassium borate ~ **Kupfer** copper borate

Borschirm *m* boron shield or target

Börse *f* stock exchange

Börsenamt *n* commercial or stock-exchange switch-board or office

Börsen-bericht *m* stock exchange report **-drucker** *m* stock ticker **-geschäft** *n* exchanging of money **-gespräch** *n* stock-exchange call **-sprechstelle** *f* stock-exchange telephone station

Borstahl *m* boron steel

Borste *f* bristle

Borsten-scheibe *f* buffing brush **-zurichterei** *f* bristle-finishing works

Bor-stickstoff *m* boron nitride **-sulfid** *n* boron sulfide

Bort *m* bort

Borte *f* galloon, trimming, ribbon ~ **von Blech** sheet iron (edging)

Bortelantrieb *m* bead drive, rim drive

börteln to bend the edges of a sheet, flange (on larger objects), border, bead

Börtelpresse *f* trimming press, flanging or crimping press

Borten-wirker *m* galloon or lacemaker, trimming or loop maker **-wirkerei** *f* lace working or workshop

Bortrimethyl-Zähler *m* boron-tri-methyl counter

Bortrioxyd *n* boric oxide

Borverbindung *f* boron compound

Borwasserumschlag *m* dressing or application of aqueous solution of boric acid

Borwolframsäure *f* borotungstic acid

bösartig malicious, wicked, malignant

Bosch Einspritzdüse Bosch injection nozzle

böschen to slope, batter out, batter, chamfer

Bosch-Kontroller *m* Bosch sight controller

Bosch Öler *m* Bosch lubricator-oiler ~ **Schütz** *n* heavy-duty relay made by Bosch

Böschung *f* slope, incline, embankment, talus, batter, scarp, bevel, chamfering, bank, ramp, escarpment, elevation, glacis ~ **im Abtrag** negative slope ~ **im Auftrag** positive slope ~ **aus Feinsand** fine sand slope **flache** ~ gentle slope **gebrochene** ~ broken slope **gepflasterte** ~ pitched or paved slope **gewölbte** ~ convex slope **natürliche** ~ natural slope

Böschungs-anlage *f* batter **-befestigung** *f* slope stabilization **-fläche** *f* surface of constant slope **-fuß** *m* base or foot of slope **-kante** *f* military crest, sloping or coved edges **-krone** *f* topographical crest **-linie** *f* slope line **-mauer** *f* toe wall

Böschungsneigung *f* batter or facing of weir or dam **mittlere** ~ mean inclination or slope of bank

Böschungs-pflaster *n* paving of a bank **-rutschung** *f* slope failure **-system** *n* bank slope system **-verkleidung** *f* revetment **-waage** *f* clinometer

Böschungswinkel *m* angle of repose of (the natural) slope, angle of slope, gradient **natürlicher** ~ angle of repose

Bosch-Zosch-Zündmagnet *m* Bosch-Zosch magneto

böse bad, evil, wicked, malicious, angry, harmful, cross, displeased **-s Wetter** bad weather, afterdamp, chokedamp

Boson *n* boson
bosseln to patch up, mold, emboss
Bosshammer *m* large, bush, or boss hammer, sledge hammer
Bossier-durchschlag *m* embossing punch (metal) **-eisen** *n* embossing iron, gouge
bossieren to bulge, emboss **einen Bruchstein ~** to ax or dress a quarrystone
Bossierhammer *m* stonemason's hammer
bossiert hammer dressed
Bossierwachs *n* molding wax
Bostwickgitter *n* sliding latticework or grid, sliding door
Bote *m* messenger
Boten-gang *m* messenger trip **-lohn** *m* porterage **-rufanlage** *f* messenger call installation
Böttcher *m* cooper
Bottich *m* tank, vat, tub, vessel, keeve, tun
Bottichgärung *f* tun fermentation **offene ~** fermentation in open tubs
Bottich-geläger *n* tun sediment (brewing) **-mantel** *m* tun casing or jacket **-schwimmer** *m* attemperator **-seiher** *m* tun drainer
boucherisieren to boucherize
Boucherisierung *f* boucherization
Bourdon Röhre *f* Bourdon tube **~ Druckmesser** *m* **~ Manometer** *n* Bourdon pressure gauge or manometer
Bourdonsche Röhrenfeder Bourdon tube
Bournonit *m* bournonite
Bourrettegarn *n* bourrette yarn
Bovenstumpen *m* boven body
Bowden, ~ Kabel *n* **~ Steuerzug** *m* Bowden (cable)
Bowdenzug *m* Bowden control cable in flexible steel conduit, Bowden wire **-schalter** *m* cable and conduit operated switch
Boxeranordnung *f* **4-Zylinder** four-cylinder opposed arrangement
Boxerbauart, Motor der ~ opposed cylinder-type engine
Boxermotor *m* double-piston engine, flat twin engine, opposed cylinder-type engine
Boxpalette *f* box pallet
Boylesches Gesetz Boyle's law
B-Platz *m* inward position, B position, B switchboard
B-Platzschrank *m* incoming or B position
brach idle
Brachystochrone *f* brachistochrone
Brackwasser *n* brackish water
Bradfield Isolator *m* Bradfield insulator
Bragg-Grayscher Hohlraum Bragg-Gray cavity
Braggsche Streuung Bragg scattering, ordered scattering
Braggscher Winkel glancing angle
Bragit *m* bragite
Brahne, Brahme *f* plumb bob
braken to break the flax
Brakenstange *f* brake shaft
brakisch brackish
Bram *m* topgallant
Bramah Schloß *n* Bramah lock
Bramme *f* iron slab, slab or flat bloom, slab ingot, cast or plate slab
Brammen *n* slabbing **-auflegevorrichtung** *f* putting on device for slabs **-form** *f* ingot slab mold **-schere** *f* slab shears **-straße** *f* slabbing-mill train **-tiefofen** *m* slab-heating furnace **-walze** *f* slabbing roll, blooming mill **-walzwerk** *n* slabbing mill
Bramraa *f* topgallant yard
Branche *f* branch, division of a field (such as amateur photography)
Branchenverzeichnis *n* classified telephone directory
Brand *m* fire, burning, combustion, calcination, burnt out, charge, batch **in ~ setzen, in ~ stecken** to set afire
Brand-bekämpfung *f* fire fighting **-binde** *f* absorbent gauze treated with bismuth for burns **-damm** *m* fire dam **-eisen** *n* burnt iron, branding iron
branden to break (of sea)
Brandenburger *m* (slang), hot bearing
Brander *m* fuse (elec.), fuse (for detonating charge)
Brand-fackel *f* incendiary torch **-fälle** *m pl* fires **-feld** *n* fire zone **-fest** fireproof **-flasche** *f* frangible grenade, incendiary bottle, Molotov cocktail **-fleck** *m* scald **-flecken** *m* roughened surface (on glass) **-gefahr** *f* danger of fire **-gefährdete Zone** *f* designated fire zone **-geschoß** *n* incendiary bullet or projectile, incendiary shell or missile
Brand-gold *n* refined gold **-hahn** *m* safety (pet)-cock (in gasoline engine), fire cock **-herd** *m* furnace **-kruste** *f* scale **-lackiert** burnt-in lacquered **-loch** *n* vent hole (of blasting cap), fire plate **-lunte** *f* slow match
Brand-masse *f* incendiary composition **-mauer** *f* fireproof wall **-meister** *m* fire marshal **-messer** *m* pyrometer **-mittel** *n* incendiary agent **-öl** *n* oil obtained by destructive distillation **-pappe** *f* pressing board **-probe** *f* fire test, fire assay **-rißbildung** *f* heat or fire cracking
Brand-satz *m* powder train **-schaden** *m* fire damage **-schäden** *m pl* incendiary damage **-schiefer** *m* bituminous shale, bass **-schott** *n* fireproof bulkhead, fire wall **-schottstecker** *m* fire-wall bulkhead plug **-schutz** *m* fire protection **-silber** *n* refined silver **-sohle** *f* inner sole, insole **-spant** *m* fireproof bulkhead **-stein** *m* brick **-stellen** *pl* burnt spots **-stifter** *m* incendiary **-stifterisch** incendiary **-stiftung** *f* arson **-stoff** *m* incendiary agent **-träge** flash resistant **-tür** *f* fire door
Brandt'sche Weiche *f* Brandt's separating filter
Brandung *f* surf, surge, breakers
Brandungs-gürtel *m* bar (roller of breaking waves) **-kehle** *f* channel formed by breakers
Brandungsreiter *m* **Wirkung des Flugbootkiels als ~** keel of flying boat causing surfboard effect
Brandungsschwebung *f* surf beat
Brand-vorrat *m* water stored for fire fighting **-wirkung** *f* incendiary effect **-wunde** *f* burn, scald
Brandzeichen *n* brand, mark made with a hot iron **mit einem ~ versehen** to brand
Brandziegel *m* firebrick
Bränke *f* yeast tub
Brannerit *m* brannerite
Brannthefe *f* spent yeast
Braschen *f pl* ashing, slag, cinders, scoria (metal.), dross (iron)
Brasmoskop *n* brasmoscope

Brassbaum *m* outrigger (for direction finder)
Brasse *f* brace
Brassinsäure *f* brassic acid
Bratgerät *n* baking appliance
Brat-ofenwärmeisolation *f* oven-heat insulation **-pfanne** *f* frying or roasting pan **-pfannengeräusch** *n* frying noise **-rohr** *n* roasting oven **-rost** *m* grill
Bratspieß *m* spit **-drehvorrichtung** *f* winding turnspit
Bratspill *n* windlass
Bratzen *m* bracket
Braubottich *m* brewing cup or tun, mash tun
Brauch *m* habit, custom, practice, usage **-bar** useful, of use, fit, suitable, serviceable, usable, passable, adaptable
Brauchbarkeit *f* fitness, usefulness, utility, practicability, usability, serviceability, adaptability **in der ~ beeinträchtigen** to vitiate
Brauchbarkeitsprüfung der Vakuumröhren tube testing
brauchen to need, want, use, require
Brauen *n* brewing
Brauerei *f* brewery **-rührwerk** *n* brewery stirring device
Brauerpech *n* brewer's pitch
Brau-kessel *m* brew kettle **-krücke** *f* hand rake
braun brown **-er Rauch** *m* brown smoke
Braunbleierz *n* pyromorphite
Brauneisen *n* brown ore **-erz** *n* brown iron ore, brown hematite, brown ore, ochery brown iron ore **-mulm** *m* limonite, earthy brown hematite **-stein** *m* brown iron ore, brown hematite, brown ore
bräunen to burnish **sich ~** to darken, turn dark
Braun-erz *n* brown iron ore, brown hematite, limonite **-holzpapier** *n* brazilwood paper, browns, nature brown **-holzstoff** *m* brown mechanical pulp
Braunit *m* braunite
Braunkalk *m* brown spar, pearl spar
Braunkohle *f* brown coal, lignite, ligneous or soft coal **erdige ~** earthy brown coal **gemeine ~** common brown coal **mulmige ~** pulverulent or earthy brown coal **ölreiche ~** bituminous lignite
Braunkohlen-aufbereitungsanlage *f* lignite dressing plant **-brikett** *n* brown-coal briquette, lignite briquette **-bruchschlitzmaschine** *f* machine for mining lignite **-feuerung** *f* brown-coal or lignite firing **-gas** *n* brown-coal gas **-grubenmaschine** *f* lignite-mining machine **-halbkoks** *m* partially carbonized lignite, semicoke from brown coal
Braunkohlen-klein *n* lignite breeze **-koks** *m* carbonized lignite **-kraftwerk** *n* lignite power plant **-lager** *n* lignite field **-pech** *n* lignite pitch **-sandstein** *m* brown-coal grit **-schiefer** *m* schistous lignite **-schwelkraftwerk** *n* lignite low-temperature carbonization power station **-schwelerei** *f* lignite-carbonization plant
Braunkohlen-schwelung *f* carbonization of lignite, lignite coking **-staub** *m* powdered brown coal or lignite **-teer** *m* lignite tar **-teeröl** *n* lignite-tar oil **-tiefbau** *m* lignite mining **-vergasung** *f* coking or distilling of lignite, peats, etc. **-vorkommen** *n* lignite beds
Braunkräusen *f pl* fuzzy heads
bräunlich brownish
Braun-macher *m* browner **-pause** *f* Vandyke print **-stichig** brownish **-tran** *m* thick cod oil
Braunsche Röhre Braun tube, cathode-ray tube (C.R.T.)
Braunschliff *m* brown mechanical pulp
Braunschweiger Grün Brunswick green
Braunspat *m* dolomite, ankerite, brown spar
Braunstein *m* pyrolusite, natural manganese dioxide, manganese(-ore), manganite, pebble manganese **künstlicher ~** manganese peroxide, artifical manganese dioxide **roter ~** rhodochrosite **schwarzer ~** hausmannite
Braunstein-beutel *m* manganese dioxide sack (in mask) **-kies** *m* alabandite **-zylinder** *m* manganese dioxide cylinder
Braupfanne *f* brewing pan
Brause *f* sprinkler, rose, douche, sprinkling can, spray, shower head; (mehrfädige Düse) multiple nozzle **-bad** *n* shower bath
brausen to roar, buzz, froth, boom, effervesce (chem.)
Brausen *n* roaring
Brause-pulver *n* effervescent powder (Seydlitz powder) **-salz** *n* effervescent salt **-sieb** *n* rinsing screen **-trübe** *f* rinsing medium **-vorrichtung** *f* spraying device **-wasser** *n* soda water
Brau-welt *f* brewing industry **-zucker** *m* brewer's sugar
brav brave, honest, well-behaved, fresh, strong
Breccie *f* breccia
Brecciengefüge *n* breccia structure
Brech-achse *f* breaking shaft **-anlage** *f* breaking or crushing plant (Erzaufbereitung)
Brechbacke *f* breaker or crusher jaw **geriffelte ~** checkered jaw
brech-bar breakable, frangible, fragile, brittle **-barkeit** *f* fragility, frangibility **-block** *m* (des Walzwerks) breaking piece **-bolzen** *m* shearing pin
Breche *f* brake
Brecheisen *n* crowbar, wrecking bar, pinch bar, jimmy, ripping chisel **~ mit Kuhfuß** crowbar with split end
brechen (reißen) to rupture; (zertrümmern) smash to pieces; (mahlen) crush; (Papier) fold, crease; (Steine) break, quarry; (Lichtstrahl) refract; (Vertrag) break, violate; (Widerstand) crush, break the back of **~** (Wort) to divide **~** diffract, fracture, fail, buck, vomit, burst, fractionize, split (rays)
Brechen *n* breakage, fracture, splitting, crushing, milling
brechend refracting **-e Brennfläche** diacaustic **-es Medium** refractive medium
Brecher *m* breaker, crushing machine, crusher **~ für Pilé** Pilé sugar crusher **unruhige See mit kurzen Brechern** choppy sea
Brecher-anlage *f* crushing plant **-mantel** *m* crusher housing **-typ** *m* breaker type
Brech-gut *n* material for jaw or disk crushing **-hammer** *m* pick or stone hammer, pick mattock **-haus** *n* breaker or crushing plant **-kegel** *m* crushing head, breaking cone **-kies** *m* crushed gravel **-klaue** *f* crowbar **-kohle** *f* broken or crushed coal **-koks** *m* egg coke, crushed or screened oven coke **-körper** *m* brake body
Brechkraft *f* power of refraction **-einheit** *f* diopter (optics) **-lose Wirkung** zero power

Brech-mantel *m* shell of the breaker **-maschine** *f* breaker, disintegrator, crushing machine **-maul** *n* crushing mouth **-messer** *m* crushing gauge, breakers **-mittel** *n* emetic **-nuß** *f* nux vomica

Brech- oder Rodepflug *m* breaker plow

Brechplatte *f* jaw plate **umlaufende ~** travelling breaker plate

Brech-punkt *m* breaker point (elec.), breaking point (chem.), point of charge, crank point **-ring** *m* breaking or crushing ring **-scherbolzen** *m* notched bolt **-schnecke** *f* grinding or crusher worm **-spaltweite** *f* discharge setting **-spindel** *f* (des Walzwerks) breaking shaft **-stange** *f* pinch bar, crowbar, pincher, ringer, wrecking bar **-topf** (Walzwerk) breaker

Brechung *f* fracture, breaking, diffraction, refraction (optics) **~ der Gasströmung** interruption of the gas flow **~ von Röntgenstrahlen** refraction of X-rays **~ an Tröpfchen** refraction by droplets **~ von Ultraschallwellen** refraction of ultrasound waves **~ einer Welle** refraction of a traveling wave

Brechungs-achse *f* axis of refraction

Brechungsanteil des Potentials refractive potential

Brechungs-brennfläche *f* diacaustic **-ebene** *f* plane of refraction **-einheit** *f* diopter, dioptry **-erscheinung** *f* refraction **-exponent** *m* index of refraction, refractivity **-geschwindigkeit** *f* setting performance **-gesetz** *n* law of refraction **-glied** *n* fraction term **-index** *m* index of refraction, refractive index **-indexbestimmung** *f* refractometry **-indexrealteil** *n* real part of the refractive index

Brechungs-koeffizient *m* index of refraction **-konstante** *f* ultra-sonic grating constant (acoust.), refraction constant **-messer** *m* refraction meter, refractometer **-modul** *m* refractive modulus **-quotient** *m* index of refraction **-strahl** *m* refracted ray **-streuung** *f* diffraction scattering, shadow scattering **-system** *n* refracting system **-verhältnis** *n* **-verhältniszahl** *f* index of refraction **-vermögen** *n* index of refraction, refractive power, refractivity **-welle** *f* refracted wave

Brechungswinkel *m* angle of refraction **~ bei Polygonzugmessung** polygonal angle

Brechungszahl *f* refractive index

Brech-walze *f* roller crusher **-walzwerk** *n* crushing mill or plant **-weinstein** *m* antimony potassium tartrate **-werk** *n* crusher **-wurz** *f* ipecac **-zahlmesser** *m* refractometer

Brei *m* pulp, paste, mash **zu ~ zerquetschen** to mash

Breiapparat *m* pulper or masher (sugar working)

breiartig, breiig pulpy, pappy, pasty

Breikutsche *f* massecuite wagon

Breimühle *f* beating engine (pulps, etc.)

breit wide, in width, broad, lengthened **-e Seite** broad dimension **-es Mattblech** *n* longterne plate

Breit-abquetschvorrichtung *f* squeezing roller for open width squeezing **-auffahren** *n* widening out (min.)

Breitband *n* wide strip, broadband, wideband

Breitbandachse *f* wide-band axis **~ von Orange nach Zyan** orange-cyan-wideband (O.C.W.)

Breitband-antenne *f* broad- or wideband antenna (radio) **-dipol** *m* wideband dipole **-eigenschaft** *f* wide-band property **-empfänger** *m* broad- or wideband receiver **-empfängersperrröhre** *f* bandpass cell **-film** *m* large screen picture **-filter** *n* wide bandpass filter **-geräusch** *n* broad-band noise

breitbandiger Chrominanz-Primärreiz fine chrominance bandwidth

Breitband-kabel *n* high frequency carrier cable, wide-band cable **-Koaxialübertrager** *m* wide band coaxial transformer **-kreis** *m* broad-band circuit **-oszillograph** *m* wide-band oscillograph **-tannenbaumantenne** *f* wide-band curtain array **-übertragung** *f* broad-band conveyor **-walzwerk** *n* wide strip mill, broad strip mill

Breit-beil *n* adz, broad ax **-beinig** straddle-legged **-bettfelge** *f* wide base rim

Breite *f* latitude, width, gauge, breadth, beam of a vessel **~ in der Ekliptik** latitude in ecliptic **~ der Flagge** hoist of flag **~ eines Gestirnes** angle of declination of a star **~ über Spant** molded breadth (maritime signals) **~ der Stäbe** width of members **~ über Stützen** width over bearers

Breite, der ~ nach broadwise **geographische ~** latitude **gesamte ~** over-all span, distance from tip to tip of an airfoil **mittragende ~** effective width of reinforcement **nördliche ~** northern latitude **nutzbare ~** working width

Breiteisen *n* universal mill plate, cross chisel, (sheet) bar, semifinished flat; broad tool

breiten to flatten, widen, extend, spread

Breiten *n* broadening, flattening, spreading

Breiten-änderung *f* change of latitude; variation in spread **-ausdehnung** *f* divergence of lines of latitude, extension of width **-berichtigung** *f* correction of latitude (navig.) **-effekt** *m* latitude effect (cosmic rays) **-eingang** *m* **der Zeuge** shrinking or contraction of cloth in width

Breiten-flug *m* latitude flying **-gliederung** *f* distribution, formation, or organization in width

Breitengrad *m* parallel or degree of latitude **nördlicher** (südlicher) **~** latitude . . . degree, north (south)

Breitengrade *pl* degrees or parallels of latitude **Die südlichen vierziger ~ der stürmischen Westwinde** the roaring forties

Breiten-gradunterschied *m* difference in latitude **-höhe** *f* meridian altitude **-kreis** *m* parallel of latitude **-kreisfaser** *f* horizontal fiber, fiber of latitudes on the surface of a shell (sphere cylinder hemisphere, dished boiler, tank head, etc.) **-maß** *n* horizontal dimension, width (breadth) gauge or gauging instrument **-metazentrum** *n* transverse metacenter **-minute** *f* minute of latitude **-parallel** *n* parallel of latitude **-richtung** *f* lateral sense **-schwankung** *f* latitude variation **-skala** *f* scale of latitude **-streuung** *f* lateral dispersion, spread, area of lateral dispersion

Breiten-unterschied *m* difference in latitude **-wert** *m* azimuth value (of vision) **-wirkung** *f* spreading effect, effect of side spray (artil.)

breitestes Maximum maximum response

Breit-falter *m* cuttler **-flanschig** wide-flanged

-flanschträger *m* wide- or broad-flanged beam **-fußschiene** *f* wide-bottom flange rail **-hacke** *f* mattock **-hammer** *m* set or sledge hammer **-haue** *f* mattock **-karbonisiermaschine** *f* open width carbonizing machine **-keil** *m* broad wedge formation **-kopfstifte** *pl* nails with large head **-laufen** to run in full width **-meißel** *m* large bit

Breitsaatsämaschine *f* broadcast seeder

Breitsaatsä- und Hackmaschine *f* hoe broadcast seeder

Breitsämaschine *f* seed drill, scattering (agr.), broadcast seeder

Breitsä- und Hackmaschine *f* hoe broadcast seeder

Breitsattel *m* swaging die

Breit-säureanlage *f* full width acidulating device **-säureeinrichtung** *f* machine for full-width acid impregnation

Breit-schläger *m* flattener **-schleuder** *f* full width hydroextractor **-schlitzdüse** *f* fishtail die

Breitschneidestahl *m* **zum Vorstechen** broad-nose or stocking tool

Breitseite *f* breadth, broadside **-stapel** *m* broad-side slip

Breitseit-pforte *f* broadside port **-rohr** *n* beam tube (torpedo)

breitseits broadside on

Breitspur *f* wide gauge

breitspuriges Fahrgestell wide-track under-carriage

Breit-stellspindel *f* width adjusting spindle **-strahler** *m* fog lamp, broad or wide beam headlight, widerange speaker **-strecken** to tighten in the width **-streckegalisiermaschine** *f* broad-drawing equalizing machine

Breitung *f* spread, broadening

Breitungs-arbeit *f* spreading work **-wirkung** *f* spreading effect or action

Breit-walzgerüst *n* spreader stand **-waschmaschine** *f* **mit Dreiwalzensystem** washing machine in full width with three rollers or with triple rolling system **-wimpel** *m* commodore's broad pennant **-ziehpressen** *pl* double-crank drawing presses

Brekzie *f* agglomerate, breccia

Brems-abdeckblech *n* drum plate **-achse** *f* braking axle **-anordnung** *f* retarding circuit **-anschlußdose** *f* socket for brake circuit **-antrieb** *m* brake control **-äquivalenz** *f* equivalent stopping power **-arbeit** *f* work of braking, braking energy or effect **-arm** *m* brake arm **-audion** *n* brake-field oscillator

Brems-ausgleich *m* brake equalization **-ausgleicher** *m* brake equalizer **-ausgleichhebel** *m* brake-compensating lever **-ausgleichwelle** *f* brake-compensating shaft **-ausrüstung** *f* brake equipment **-backe** *f* brake shoe, brakehead, brake cheek, brake clutch

Bremsbacken-belag *m* brake-shoe lining **-halter** *m* brake-shoe holder **-klötze** *m* chocks **-lagerbolzen** *m pl* brake-shoe mounting bolts **-licht** *f* brake-shoe stoplight **-pedal** *n* brake pedal **-probe** *f* brake test **-rad** *n* braked wheel **-rückholfeder** *f* brake-shoe return spring **-rückzugfeder** *f* brake-shoe check spring **-spiel** *n* brake shoe clearance **-träger** *m* brake shoe carrier **-vorrichtung** *f* braking device

Bremsbahn *f* brake distance

Bremsband *n* brake band or strap, friction band, brake(-band) lining, brake collar, sheet smoother **~ aus Baumwollgurten** brake band of cotton straps

Bremsbandbelag *m* brake-band lining

bremsbar capable of being braked **-e Räder** wheels with brakes

Brems-bedienung *f* brake operation **-befestigungsflansch** *m* flange for fastening the brake drum **-befestigungsring** *f* brake fastening flange **-belag** *m* brake liner or lining **-belastung** *f* brake load **-bereich** *m* range of brake **-bereitschaft** *f* braking **-berg** *m* inclined plane, braking incline, slope (min.) **-betätigung** *f* brake control or operation **-betätigungshebel** *m* brake-operating lever **-blinkschlußleuchte** *f* combined stop, tail and blinker lamp **-block** *m* brakehead, brake shoe

Brems-bock *m* brake anchor plate, brake box **-bolzen** *m* brake screw **-brutto** *n* gross weight to be braked **-büchse** *f* brake socket, brake bushing **-bügel** *m* brake arm, brake lever **-dauer** *f* braking period **-daumen** *m* brake cam **-deckplatte** *f* brake backing plate, brake cover plate **-dichte** *f* slowing-down density **-dorn** *m* trail spade

Brems-draht *m* brake cable (such as is stretched across flight deck of aircraft carriers) **-drehmoment** *m* braking torque **-dreieck** *n* brake triangle, brake truss bar or beam **-druck** *m* brake pressure **-druckregler** *m* **einer Fördermaschine** self-adjusting brake gear of a winding machine **-dynamo** *n* dynamometric dynamo **-dynamometer** *n* absorption or brake dynamometer

Bremse *f* brake, buffer, drag wheel, arresting gear, suppressor, control **~** (Auflaufbremse) running-up brake **~** (Öldruck) hydraulic brake **~ für ein Flugzeug** parking brake for an airplane **die ~ rutscht** the brake slips **~ anziehen** to brake **~ lösen** to release the brake **~ lüften** to bleed the brakes (car), apply the brakes (RR)

Brems-einstellung *f* brake adjustment, brake regulation **-elektrode** *f* reflecting or retarding-field electrode (in positive-grid tube) (TV)

bremsen (Bremse anziehen) to brake, set the brakes, apply the brakes; (abbremsen) brake the speed, apply brake, lock, adjust, stop, arrest, impede, dam, detain, hold back, restrain, maintain stationary, fix, secure, check (the motion), suppress, control, decelerate **mit voller Kraft ~** to jam brakes **~ durch Gegenstrom** plugging

Bremsenberechnung *f* calculation of brakes

Bremsenergie *f* work or energy of braking

Bremsentlüftung *f* breeding of the brake

Bremser *m* brakeman

Brems-fallschirm *m* A-type of parachute, braking or drag parachute **-feder** *f* brake (release) spring **-federzangen** *pl* brake spring pliers

Bremsfeld *n* reflecting field (vacuum-tube, engin.), retarding field (in electron-oscillation tube) **-audion** *n* positive-grid detector, electron-oscillation detector or rectifier **-elektrode** *f* retarding-field or reflecting electrode **-generator** *m* negative transconductance generator or oscillator, positive-grid or retarding-field oscillator **-oszillator** *m* positive-grid oscillator, retarding-field oscillator **-röhre** *f* brake-field tube, retarding field tube **-schaltung** *f* retarding-field or positive-grid circuit scheme, oscillating-electron or electron-oscillation scheme with reflecting electrode, suppressor, control, circuit in which magnetization does not proceed at uniform rate **-schwingung** *f* retarding field oscillation

Brems-filz *m* tow brush **-fläche** *f* braking area, brake drum surface, slowing-down area **-flächeneinheit** *f* brake surface unit **-flöße** *m pl* braking kites (used by the Germans in launching the Scharnhorst) **-flüssigkeit** *f* recoil liquid, brake fluid (hydraulic), buffer fluid **-förderer** *m* retarding conveyor

Brems-führung *f* brake guide **-fußhebel** *m* brake pedal **-fußpumpe** *f* brake foot pump **-fußhebelübersetzung** *f* brake pedal gear **-fußhebelwelle** *f* brake pedal shaft

Brems-futter *n* brake lining **-gabel** *f* slotted jaw for brakes **-gehänge** *n* brake hanger **-gehäuse** *n* brake housing **-gelenkstück** *n* brake-articulation piece **-gesenk** *n* braking decline **-gestänge** *n* brake-rod linkage or system **-gestell** *n* carriage **-gewicht** *n* counterpoise, counterbalance

Bremsgitter *n* suppressor, cathode, or earthed grid, retarding or grounded grid **-modulation** *f* suppressor grid modulation **-regelröhre** *f* exponential pentode **-röhre** *f* pentode **-tastung** *f* suppressor-grid keying

Brems-glieder *pl* brake shoes **-griff** *m* brake-applying handle **-handhebel** *m* brake hand lever **-hang** *m* braking incline

Bremshebel *m* stop or brake lever, torque arm, hand brake; (Fernschreiber) dashpot lever **-arm** *m* brake lever arm **-führung** *f* brake lever guide **-wange** *f* brake lever side plate

Brems-holz *n* wooden brake shoe **-kabel** *n* brake cable **-kammer** *f* stilling basin **-keil** *m* chock, scotch **-kennzeichenleuchte** *f* combined stop and number plate lamp **-kern** *m* slowing-down kernel **-kessel** *m* air receiver **-kette** *f* brake chain

Brems-klappe *f* air brake, air deflector **-klappenapparatur** *f* brake flap device on guided missiles **-klatsche** *f* brake for airplane engine **-klaue** *f* brake-shoe holder **-klotz** *m* brake shoe, brake block, chock block (aviation), skid board, wheel chock, chocks **-klotzhalter** *m* shoe holder of brake **-knebel** *m* braking bar **-knüppel** *m* braking club **-kolben** *m* brake piston **-konus** *m* inverted brake cone **-kopf** *m* braking head

Bremskraft *f* brake pressure, brake horsepower, braking force **-begrenzer** *m* braking power limiting device **-minderer** *m* brake reducing valve (reducer) **-übertragung** *f* braking power transmission

Brems-kreis *m* negative-anode or negative-plate circuit **-kratzbänder** *pl* retarding scraper conveyor **-kuppelung** *f* brake coupling **-kurbel** *f* brake crank **-länge** *f* slowing-down length **-längenmesser** *m* brake meter **-lasche** *f* brake pull rod **-laterne** *f* stop lamp **-leder** *n* brake leather **-leerweg** *m* free pedal travel

Brems-leiste *f* tension bar, tension rod, brake rod **-leistung** *f* brake horsepower, brake power **-leitung** *f* brake line, brake-pressure lead **-leuchte** *f* stop light **-licht** *n* stop light **-lichtschalter** *m* stop light switch **-lösevorrichtung** *f* brake release device **-lösezylinder** *m* brake release cylinder

Bremsluft-behälter *m* compressed-air brake cylinder **-bohrungen** *pl* air bleeders (motor)

Bremslüfteinrichtung brake lifting set

Bremslufteintritt *m* balance air entry (motor)

Bremslüfter *m* brake solenoid, brake magnets (elec.)

Bremsluftkanal *m* air blend hole (motor)

Bremslüftmagnet *m* brake-lifting magnet

Bremsluftschraube *f* brake propeller (aviation), dummy airscrew, fan brake, static airscrew **geeichte ~** calibrated fan brake **vierflügelige ~** four-bladed fan brake

Bremsluft-steuerkolben *m* bleeder air-control piston **-system** *n* compressed-air system

Brems-magnet *m* brake magnet **-moment** *n* braking couple (of a continuously rotating instrument), brake or retarding torque (of a meter) **-nachstellschraube** *f* brake adjusting screw **-nachstellung** *f* brake adjustment, brake wear adjuster **-nachstellvorrichtung** *f* brake adjuster **-nocke** *f* brake cam **-nockenwelle** *f* brake camshaft **-ölbehälter** *m* buffer oil chamber **-pedal** *n* brake pedal **-pedaldruck** *m* brake pedal pressure **-pedaleinsteller** *m* brake pedal adjuster

Bremspferdekraft *f* **-stärke** *f* brake horsepower

Brems-potential *n* retarding or stopping potential **-propeller** *m* reversible pitch propeller **-prozeß** *m* slowing down process **-quelle** *f* brake cross shaft **-querschnitt** *m* stopping cross section **-rakete** *f* retro-rocket (of spacecraft) **-rad** *n* brake wheel **-regulierlager** *n* brake-adjusting bearing **-riegel** *m* brake bar **-ring** *f* brake ring or band

Brems-röhre *f* brake-field valve or tube, Barkhausen-Kurz valve, retarding-field tube, retarded-field triode, plate characteristic **-rohrwelle** *f* brake tube **-rollenhebel** *m* braking roller lever **-schalter** *m* control switch **-schaltung** *f* control connection, switch connection, brake gear **-scheibe** *f* brake pressure plate, friction disk, brake pulley **-schilde** *n pl* brake masks **-schirm** *m* drag parachute **-schlauch** *m* hose for hydraulic brake, brake hose **-schlußlaterne** *f* **-schlußleuchte** *f* stop and tail lamp

Brems-schlußnummernlaterne *f* combined stop, tail and number plate lamp **-schub** *m* reverse thrust **-schuh** *m* brake shoe, brakehead **-schuhprinzip** *n* brake-shoe principle **-schütz** *m* (zur Gangschaltung) brake contactor (for speed selection) **-seil** *n* brake wire or cable **-spannung** *f* brake tension, negative-anode potential (in electron-oscillation tube) **-sperre** *f* brake ratchet **-spinne** *f* brake spider **-spur** *f* skid mark (road), braking trace **-stellung** *f* brake (braking) position

Bremsstand *m* brake-testing stand, dynamometer test stand **~ mit elektrischer Leistungsaufnahme** electric dynamometer

Brems-stange *f* tension bar or rod, brake rod **-stapel** *m* brake clevice **-steuerung** *f* brake control **-stoff** *m* moderator (material added to adjust speed of the neutrons causing fission) **-stoffgitter** *n* moderator lattice **-stoß** *m* brake knock **-strahlen** *m pl* radiative stopping, rays caused by particle retardation **-strahlung** *f* continuous radiation, radiation in a continuous spectrum, white, heterochromatic, or deceleration radiation, radiative stopping

Brems-strecke *f* stopping distance, arresting gear **-strom** *m* damped current **-stützlager** *n* brake-support bearing **-substanz** *f* moderator material **-system** *n* braking system **-träger** *m* brake anchor pin, brake bracket **-tritt** *m* brake pedal **-trommel** *f* brake drum

Brems- und Bremsluftmagnete *pl* brake and brake-lifting magnets

Brems- und Rückfahr-Lichtschalter *m* stop and reversing light switch

Brems- und Schlußleuchter *pl* stop and tail lights

Bremsung *f* braking (action), retardation, deceleration ~ **der Elektronen** reflection, deflection (in magnetron), deceleration or retardation of electrons ~ **von Neutronen** moderation of neutrons **elektrische** ~ electric braking, apparatus that absorbs electric energy

Brems-ventil *n* brake valve **-verfahren** *pl* braking methods (elec.) **-verhältnis** *n* moderating ratio **-verlustzeit** *f* brake lag

Brems-vermögen *n* stopping power (of photographic emulsion), braking or retarding power

brems-verstärkend self-energizing braking **-verstärker** *m* brake energizer **-verschluß** *m* brake lock **-verzögerung** *f* braking retardation **-vorrichtung** *f* brake, recoil buffer (of gun) **-wagen** *m* guard's van **-walze** *f* braking roller **-wasser** *n* water used in brake **-weg** *m* stopping distance, length of brake path ~ (Weg der Bremshebel) idle path

Brems-welle *f* brake shaft **-werk** *n* braking gear **-widerstand** *m* damping resistance (elec.), braking resistance of friction **-winkel** *m* brake angle, bell-crank handle

Bremswirkung *f* braking action, retardation, deceleration, braking or brake effect, friction action ~ **der negativen Raumladung** repelling action of electron charge, negative space charge

Brems-zahl *f* stopping number **-zaum** *m* Prony brake **-zeug** *n* rail brake **-zug** *m* back tension, back pull **-zugschere** *f* brake rod **-zugstange** *f* brake-lever connecting rod, brake bar **-zwischenhebel** *m* pivot lever for rear brake **-zwischenwelle** *f* intermediate brake shaft

Bremszylinder *m* recoil brake cylinder (artil.), dashpot, cataract cylinder; (Fernschreiber) friction cylinder ~ **mit Ölfüllung** oil dashpot **Relais mit** ~ dashpot relay

Brenkas *n* East India tin

Brenn-abstandspunkt *m* focal distance **-achse** *f* focal axis

brennbar combustible, inflammable, burnable **-er Bestandteil** combustible or inflammable constituent

Brennbares *n* combustibles

Brennbarkeit *f* combustibility

Brenn-bereich *m* operating range (as of a glow tube) **-blase** *f* alembic (still) **-bock** *m* boiling and crabbing machine **-dauer** *f* duration of burning, burning period (of an incandescent lamp), hours of lighting, powered phase (of rocket)

Brennebene *f* focal plane **hintere** ~ back focal plane **vordere** ~ front focal plane

Brenneisen *n* branding iron

brennen (Kalk) to burn, calcine; (Porzellan) burn, bake, fire roast, sinter, clinker, char, smart **dicht** ~ to vitrify (ceramics) **den Faden** ~ to singe or gas the thread

Brennen *n* burning, calcining, calcination, roasting, sintering, charring, distillation, illumination (lamps)

brennend burning, alight, glary, on fire ~ **abstürzen** to go down in flames (aviat.)

Brenner *m* burner, torch, blowpipe, heated filament; (Uranbrenner) pile **-anlage** *f* burner unit, burner system **-anordnung** *f* burner arrangement **-austrittsöffnung** *f* burner orifice **-düse** *f* burner nozzle, burner mouth, jet, flame-cutting nozzle, weld

Brennerei *f* distillery **-kühler** *m* distillery attemperator **-trebermelasse** *f* distiller's grain molasses

Brenner-griff *m* torch handle **-härtungsverfahren** *n* local hardening **-kenngröße** *f* burner characteristic, fuel-air ratio **-kopf** *m* burner tip, torch head **-leistung** *f* burner capacity or efficiency **-motor** *m* combustion engine **-mund** *m* **-mundstück** *n* burner tip or nozzle **-rohr** *n* burner tube or pipe **-spitze** *f* burner tip **-zange** *f* burner pliers

brennfähig combustible

Brennfläche *f* focal surface, caustic surface (optics) ~ **einer Fläche** *f* focal surface of a surface **brechende** ~ caustic surface (optics) **reflektierende, rückstrahlende** ~ catacaustic surface

Brennfleck *m* focus (of X rays), focal spot, spot (beam pencil), area of impact of the anticathode, (focused) spot **-ausdehnung** *f* dish of confusion (radius) **-charakteristik** *f* focal spot characteristic

Brenn-gase *n pl* fuel gases, combustible gases **-gemisch** *n* induction mixture **-geschwindigkeit** *f* velocity of flame propagation, rate of combustion, burning rate (rocket) **-glas** *n* burning glass, convex lens **-härten** *n* Double-Duro hardening (motors) **-höhe** *f* height of flame **-holz** *n* firewood

Brenn-kalender *m* table of lighting-up times (aviation) **-kammer** *f* combustion chamber, firebox, carbonizing chamber, thrust chamber **-kammereinsatz** *m* combustion-chamber liner (jet) **-kapsel** *f* (Keramik) saggar **-kegel** *m* flame cone (of a Bunsen burner), Seger cone, fusion cone, pyrometric cone **-kolonnen** *f pl* ethyl alcohol stills **-kopf** *m* (Rakete) head element (of a rocket combustion unit)

Brennkraft *f* intensity of combustion **-maschine** *f* internal-combustion or gasoline engine, fuel-burning engine or machine **-turbine** *f* combustion turbine

Brenn-kugel *f* spherical line of combustion when burning a mixture of combustible gases **-länge** *f* time of burning, fuse setting **-längenscheibe** *f* fuse indicator **-längenschieber** *m* time-train indicator (fuse), corrector **-linie** *f* focal or image line **-luftventilator** *m* combustion air fan **-material** *n* fuel **-ofen** *m* furnace, calcining kiln or furnace, roasting furnace, (baking) oven, burning oven or kiln

Brennöl *n* fuel oil, burning oil, lamp oil **-behälter** *m* oil service tank **-filter** *n* fuel oil filter **-vorwärmer** *m* fuel oil preheater

Brenn-periode *f* combustion period **-probe** *f* burning quality or test **prozeß** *m* roasting, calcining, or baking process, sintering or combustive process

Brennpunkt *m* focus, focusing or focal point, burning or fire point, aerodynamic center, point of burst, cathode or electron beam **auf den ~ einstellen** to focus **im ~ vereinigen** to focus **vorderer ~** first focal point

Brennpunktabstand *m* focal distance

Brennpunkte *pl* foci **~ einer Flächennormalen** foci of a surface normal **~ eines Kegelschnittes** foci of a conic **mit zwei Brennpunkten** bifocal

Brennpunktebene *f* focal plane

Brenn-rahmen *m* testing screen **-raum** *m* combustion chamber **-rohr** *n* combustion cowl (jet) **-schacht** *m* combustion chamber

Brennschluß *m* propellant cutoff (in guided missiles), burnout, flameout **Flug nach ~** coasting flight

Brennschluß-anlage *f* combustion cutoff system in guided missiles **-empfänger** *m* cutoff-evaluation receiver (guided missiles) **-empfängerwagen** *m* cutoff-evaluation truck (guided missiles) **-frequenz** *f* combustion cutoff frequency **-gabe** *f* cutoff-signal transmission (guided missiles) **-geschwindigkeit** *f* cutoff velocity (g/m), burnout speed **-gewicht** *n* weight of the guided missile at combustion cutoff termination **-integral** *n* combustion-cutoff integral **-kommando** *n* cutoff signal (g/m) **-kontakt** *m* cutoff contact **-punkt** *m* combustion-cutoff point

Brennschluß-signal *n* combustion-cutoff signal **-stellung** *f* combustion-cutoff signal site (guided missiles) **-streuung** *f* variation in combustion-cutoff point (guided missiles) **-vermessung** *f* cutoff control **-weite** *f* abscissa of point of cutoff **-winkel** *m* cutoff angle

Brenn-schneiden *n* gas or flame cutting **-schneider** *m* (oxy-) acetylene cutter **-schnittspalt** *m* kerf **-schweißen** *n* flash welding **-schwindung** *f* shrinkage in firing (ceramics) **-spannung** *f* constant-glow or normal-running (glow-tube) potential, operating voltage, working, maintaining or burning voltage, arc-drop (voltage) **-spiegel** *m* reflector sheet **-spiritus** *m* fuel alcohol **-stahl** *m* blister steel **-stand** *m* combustion test stand, static test stand (rockets)

Brennstaub *m* pulverized or powdered fuel, fuel dust **-anlage** *f* fuel-pulverizing mill, pulverized-coal plant **-befeuert** dust-fuel-fired **-feuerung** *f* coal-dust firing, powdered-coal firing

Brenn-stempel *m* marking or branding iron, burning brand **-stift** *m* cautery

Brennstoff *m* fuel **~ einnehmen** to fuel (ship) **jüngerer ~** fuel of recent geological formation **verkohlter ~** carbonized fuel **~ für einen Forschungsreaktor** fuel for a research reactor

Brennstoff-absperrhahn *m* fuel stop cock **-aufbereitung** *f* preparation of fuel **-aufnahme** *f* refueling **-aufwand** *m* fuel consumption **-ausnutzung** *f* utilization of fuel **-band** *n* fuel tape

Brennstoffbehälter *m* fuel reservoir, tank, or bin **abwerfbarer ~** slip fuel tank

Brennstoff-behälterauslaßröhre *f* fuel-tank vent **-beschickung** *f* fuel charging **-charge** *f* fuel charge **-chemie** *f* fuel or petroleum chemistry **-dampfgemisch** *n* mixture of fuel vapor **-drucksystem** *n* fuel-pressure system **-einblasung** *f* fuel injection **-einspritzdüse** *f* fuel nozzle **-einspritzer** *m* fuel injector **-einspritzpumpe** *f* fuel-injection pump **-einspritzung** *f* injection of fuel **-einspritzvorrichtung** *f* fuel injector **-element** *n* fuel cell (spacecraft) **-ersparnis** *f* fuel saving

Brennstoff-filter *n* fuel filter, fuel strainer **-förderpumpe** fuel oil transfer pump, fuel feed pump **-füllstutzen** *m* fuel filler cap **-gestell** *n* fuel rack **-gemisch** *n* fuel mixture **-gewicht** *n* weight of fuel or oil, fuel load **-kanal** fuel channel **-lager** *n* gasoline or fuel dump **-lagerung** *f* fuel storage **-leitung** *f* fuel system, fuel-supply line **-leitungsschema** *n* fuel-system diagram **-luftgemisch** *n* fuel mixed with air

Brennstoff-mangel *m* fuel shortage **-messer** *m* fuel gauge **-nebel** *n* combustion mist **-nebenwegregler** *m* fuel by-pass regulator **-nocken** *m* fuel cam **-öl** *n* fuel oil **-platte** *f* fuel plate **-pumpe** *f* gasoline or fuel pump **-pumpenlaufbüchse** *f* fuel-pump liner **-pumpenstößel** *m* fuel-pump tappet **-quelle** *f* fuel source

Brennstoff-reiniger *m* fuel filter **-reserve** *f* fuel reserve **-schicht** *f* fuel bed **-schlauch** *m* fuel hose **-schleier** *m* fuel spray entering cylinder of Diesel engine **-schnellentleerung** *f* fuel jettisoning **-schüttung** *f* charging of fuel **-schwelung** *f* carbonization of solid fuels

Brennstoff-sparer *m* fuel economizer **-speisevorrichtung** *f* fuel-feeding apparatus or feeder **-spiegel** *m* fuel level **-strahl** *m* fuel jet **-tagesbehälter** *m* daily supply tank for fuel oil, primary fuel tank

Brennstofftank *m* fuel tank **-schott** *m* fuel-tank baffle **-wagen** *m* gasoline-tank truck

Brennstoff-technik *f* fuel engineering **-uhr** *f* fuel-level gauge **-umwandlungsverfahren** *n* process of fuel conversion

Brennstoff und Luftmischungzerleger *m* fuel-air-mixture analyzer

Brennstoffventil *n* fuel-oil valve

Brennstoffverbrauch *m* fuel consumption **-messer** *m* fuel-consumption gauge, fuel-flow meter **-sprobe** *f* fuel-consumption test, fuel burnt per kilo of water evaporated

Brennstoff-verschwendung *f* waste of fuel **-voreilung** *f* fuel lead **-vorrat** *m* fuel supply **-vorratsbehälter** *m* fuel-oil supply tank **-vorratsmesser** *m* fuel-level gauge **-vorrichtung** *f* fuel system **-vorwärmer** *m* fuel hot spot **-wärme** *f* heat generated by fuel **-wiederaufbereitung** fuel reprocessing **-wirtschaft** *f* fuel economy **-zahl** *f* ratio of propellant weight to net weight of rocket

Brennstoffzuführung *f* fuel feed **~ durch Gefälle** fuel feed by gravity

Brenn-strahl *m* focal radius (ellipse) **-strahlhärtung** *f* flame hardening **-strahlung** *f* heterochromatic radiation (white) **-stunde** *f* burning or lighting hour, lighting-up time **-temperatur** *f* baking or burning temperature **-verlauf** *m* combustion process **-verlust** *m* ignition loss **-versuch** *m* burning test

Brennweite *f* focal length, focal distance, con-

vergence distance **Linse für veränderliche ~ und Bildgröße** zooming lens for variable focus and variable magnification, zoom lens **hintere ~** back focal length **konstante ~** fixed or infinity focus
Brennweiten-einstellung *f* setting of the focal length **-korrektion für Ultrarot** infrared focus calibration **-messer** *m* focometer
Brenn-wert *m* fuel value, calorific value **-widerstand** *m* combustion drag
Brennzeit *f* combustion period **~ des Zünders** fuse length
Brennzone *f* combustion zone
Brennzünder *m* fuse, fuse train, time fuse **-schuß** *m* time fire
Brenz-essigäther *m* acetone **-gallussäure** *f* pyrogallic acid **-katechin** *n* pyrocatechin, pyrocatechol **-katechingerbstoff** *m* catechol tannin **-öl** *n* crude pyrocatechol 111
brenzlich(er Geruch) empyreumatic (smell)
Brenz-säure *f* pyro acid, pyro-gallol **-terebinsäure** *f* pyroterebic acid
Bresche *f* breccia, breach, opening wedge **eine ~ legen, schießen** to breach **in die ~ springen** to mount the breach
Brett *n* board, panel, shelf, deal, plank **~ gehobelt** planed board **~ rauh** rough board
Brettchen skeleton board
Bretter-bahn *f* boardwalk, plank walk **-bekleidung** *f* plank revetment **-bock** *m* plank trestle **-dach** *n* board roof **-fußboden** *m* boarded floor(ing) **-hobelmaschine** *f* thicknessing machine for planks **-lager** *n* timber store
Bretterschalung eines Daches boarding of a roof
Bretter-schuppen *m* wooden shed **-stapel** *m* plank crib **-tafel** *f* plank floor **-teppich** *m* plank flooring **-tür** *f* wood-board flap **-verkleidung** *f* boarding **-verschlag** *m* partition of boards **-zaun** *m* boarding fence, billboard
Brettfallhammer *m* board drop hammer
Brettsäge *f*, **verjüngte ~** straight pit saw
Brett-schaltung *f* breadboard or experimental setup **-stückmine** *f* duckboard mine, pressure-board mine **-verkleidung** *f* sheating
Brewsters Brewster (units used to express value of the photoelastic coefficient C determined by Felon)
Brief *m* letter **-ablegekasten** *m* desk tray **-aufstellmaschine** *f* letter facing machine **-beschwerer** *m* letter weight **-beutel** *m* mailbag **-bogen** *m* sheet of stationary **-einwurf** *m* slot of mailbox, mail slot **-fach** *n* post-office box **-kasten** *m* letter box, mailbox **-karte** *f* letter card **-kopf** *m* letter head **-kurs** *m* selling rate
brieflich by letter, in writing
Brief-mappe *f* portfolio, writing case **-marke** *f* (postage) stamp
Briefmarken-druck *m* postage stamp printing **-leiterplatte** *f* postage stamp board **-walze** *f* postage-stamp guards
Brief-ordner *m* letter-file **-papier** *n* note paper, stationary **-post** *f* mail **-sortieranlage** *f* letter sorter **-tasche** *f* wallet **-telegramm** *n* night telegraph letter **-träger** *m* postman **-verschluß** *m* flap **-waage** *f* letter scale or balance **-wahl** *f* ballot-by-mail
Briefwechsel *m* correspondence
Brigade *f* brigade
Brightstock *m* bright stock (oil)
Brikett *n* briquette, pressed coal **-element** *n* agglomerate cell **-fabrik** *f* briquetting plant **-herstellung** *f* briquette manufacture
Brikettier-anlage *f* **-anstalt** *f* briquette or briquetting plant
brikettieren to briquette
Brikettier-fähigkeit *f* briquetting property **-presse** *f* briquetting press
Brikettierung *f* briquetting
Brikettierungsanlage *f* briquetting plant
Brikettierverfahren *n* briquetting process
Brikettpresse *f* briquette or briquetting press
Brillant-grün *n* brilliant green **-lack** *m* high-gloss varnish **-weiß** *n* brilliant white (a variety of calcium sulfate)
Brillanz *f* bounce (in sound reproduction), brilliancy
Brille *f* spectacles, glasses, goggles **~** (oder Lünette), center rest (engin.) **~ der Stopfbüchse** gland of stuffing box (aviation) **feststehende ~** steady rest **mitlaufende ~** follower (aviation)
Brillen-gestell *n* spectacle frame **-glas** *n* spectacle lens
Brillengläser *pl* **durchbogene ~** meniscus spectacle glasses **punktuell abbildende ~** point-focal glasses
Brillen-glaskondensor *m* spectacle condenser **-glassalbe** *f* antidim compound **-lupe** *f* spectacle magnifier **-ofen** *m* spectacle furnace, furnace with two pits **-träger** *m* wearer of glasses
Brinell Einheit *f* Brinell unit (metal.) **~ Härte** *f* Brinell hardness (hardness test for metals) **~ Härteprobe** *f* Brinell hardness test
brinellieren to brinell
Brinell Kugeldruckprobe *f* Brinell ball-hardness test **~ Meßverfahren** *n* Brinell hardness test **~ Presse** *f* **mit Hebelwaage** dead-weight Brinell machine, lever-type Brinell machine **~ Probe** *f* Brinell test
Brinellsche Härtezahl *f* **Brinell Zahl** *f* Brinell hardness number or coefficient of hardness
bringen to bring
brisant high explosive **-e Sprengstoffe** brisant explosives
Brisanz *f* high explosive, shattering power, damage to gun barrels by too powerful explosives **-wirkung** *f* explosive effect
Brise *f* breeze **leichte ~** gentle breeze
Bristol Karton *m* **~ Papier** *n* Bristol board
Britisch-e Normallehre British Standard Gauge (B.S.G.) **-e Wärmeeinheit** British Thermal Unit (B.T.U.)
Brixgrad *m* degree Brix
Briz *m* loess
Brockantit *m* brochantite
bröck(e)lig crumbly, brittle, friable, fragile
bröckeln to crumble
Brocken *m* chippings, cobble, lump, fragment, piece, (slang) large ship or heavy projectile **-fänger** *m* calyx **-gespenst** *n* Brocken specter, glory **-gestein** *n* breccia **-span** *m* segmental chip **-torf** *m* lump peat
Brodel *m* vapor, steam, bubbling
brodeln to bubble, boil
Brodeln *n* boiling (noise), alternating-current hum

Brodelstörung *f* alternating-current hum, level characteristic
Brodem *m* steam, fumes, vapor, exhalation
Bröggerit *m* bröggerite
Brom *n* bromine **-acetylbromid** *n* bromoacetyl bromide **-ammonium** *n* ammonium bromide
Bromat *n* bromate
Brom-äther *m* **-äthyl** *n* ethyl bromide **-äthylen** *n* ethylene bromide **-benzoesäure** *f* bromobenzoic acid **-benzol** *n* bromobenzene **-benzylzyanid** *n* brombenzyl cyanide **-eisen** *n* iron bromide **-fluor** *n* bromine fluoride **-hydrat** *n* hydrobromide, bromine hydrate
Bromid *n* bromide **-papier** *n* bromide paper
Bromierung *f* bromination
Brom-kalium *n* potassium bromide **-kresolpurpur** *m* bromcresol purple **-naphthalin** *n* bromonaphthalene **-natrium** *n* sodium bromide **-öldruckpapier** *m* bromoil printing paper
Bromozyanidprozeß *m* bromocyanide process
Brom-phenolblau *n* bromine-phenol blue (chem.) **-phosphor** *m* phosphorus bromide
bromsaures bromate **~ Kali** potassium bromate **~ Natron** *n* sodium bromate
Bromsilber-druck *m* silver bromide printing **-emulsion** *f* silver bromide emulsion **-papier** *n* **-gelatinepapier** *n* bromide paper (phot.) **-positiv** *m* silver bromide positive
Brom-silizium *n* silicon bromide **-spat** *m* bromyrite **-verbindung** *f* bromide **-wasserstoff** *m* hydrogen bromide, hydrobromic acid **-wasserstoffsäure** *f* hydrobromic acid **-wismut** *m* bismuth bromide **-zyan** *n* cyanogen bromide, bromocyanogen
Brons Motor *m* Brons engine
Bronze *f* bronze, gun or bell metal **selbstschmierende ~** oilite
Bronze-arbeit *f* bronzework, metalwork **-bezug** *m* bronze sleeve, bronze plating or coating
Bronzebüchsen *f pl* bronze bushed bearings **mit ~ versehen** to bush with steel casting bronze
Bronzedraht *m* bronze wire
Bronzedruck *m* metallic printing **-farbe** *f* metallic ink **-firnis** *m* bronze printing varnish
Bronze-farbe *f* bronze pigment **-gehäuse** *n* bronze-casing **-gelenk** *n* bronze hinge or joint **-gießerei** *f* brass or bronze foundry **-glanz** *m* bronze lustre **-klötze** *pl* bronze blocks **-lack** *m* lacquer for bronze, bronze-pigmented or bronzing lacquer **-lager** *n* bronze bearing **-lagerschale** *f* bronze bearing bush
bronzener Schimmer bronzy sheen
Bronze-pulver *n* bronze powder **-schraubendraht** *m* bronze screw wire **-schrift** *f* bronze type **-tinktur** *f* bronzing varnish **-unterdruckfarbe** *f* bronzing medium **-ziseleur** *m* bronze chaser
bronzieren to bronze
Bronzieren *n* blooming (defect in maroons), painting with bronze **bronzierend** bronzy
Bronzierungserscheinung *f* bronzy appearance
Bronzitfels *m* bronzite
broschieren to stitch, sew (binding)
Broschieren *n* brocading
broschiert stitched, paper-bound
Broschierwebstuhl *m* swivel loom
Broschur *f* stitching
Broschüre *f* leaflet, pamphlet, booklet, de luxe edition, prospectus, catalogue **seitlich geheftete ~** booklet stitched sideways
Brot *n* loaf (of bread, sugar) **-form** *f* loaf mold **-röster** (elektrischer) *m* electric toaster **-säge** *f* saw for loaf sugar **-schleuder** *f* loaf-sugar centrifugal **-zucker** *m* loaf sugar
Brotmesser *n* bread knife
Brownmillerit-Zement *m* Brownmillerite cement
Brownsche Bewegung Brownian motion, Brownian movement, random walk
Bruce-Antenne *f* Bruce or Grecian type antenna
Bruch *m* (Brechen) break, breaking; (Stahl) failure, break; (Gefüge) structure; (Riß) crack, crevice, fissure; (Maschine) failure, break down; (Flugzeug) smash up, crack up; (zerbrochenes) breakage; (Math.) fraction (Knochen) fracture, rupture, quarry, breach, crash, (slang) trash, damaged plane, cleft, scrap, fragment, breakdown, crease, crimp, waste **beginnender ~** incipient failure **echter ~** proper fraction (math.) **fortschreitender ~** progressive failure **gemeiner ~** vulgar or common fraction **gemischter ~** mixed number **ein ~ des Abkommens** a breach of the agreement **~ am Fuße einer Rutschung** base failure **muscheliger ~ des Porzellans** conchoidal fracture of porcelain **speckiger ~** lardaceous fracture **unechter ~** improper fraction **zu Bruche bauen** to bring down the roof (min.) **zu Bruche gehen** to break down, fall in (min.)
Bruch-arbeit *f* energy of fracture **-ablenkung** *f* fractured deflection
Brucharten *pl* **des Stahles** brittle, tough, and hybrid fractures of steel
Bruch-aussehen *n* appearance of fracture **-band** *n* truss **-bau** *m* caving system **-beanspruchung** *f* breaking stress **-bedingung** *f* failure condition **-belastung** *f* breaking load, maximum load, ultimate stress **-belastungsprobe** stress-to-rupture **-bildung** *f* fracture **-dehnung** *f* elongation on or at break or fracture, failure load, elongation, breaking elongation, total extension, breaking tension, stretch (paper)
Bruch-dicke *f* throat (welding) **-ebene** *f* plane of fracture **-eisen** *n* iron scrap, scrap iron **-element** *n* crushable leg **-entstehung** *f* fracture origin **-faktor** *m* breaking factor, initial striking energy to fracture, single-blow impact value **-faltengebirge** *n* mountains formed of disrupted folds **-feld** *n* cavities
bruchfest resistant to fracture or rupture, tenacious, resisting breaking
Bruchfestigkeit *f* resistance to rupture, strength, breaking strength or load or stress, tensile strength, ultimate strength
Bruchfläche *f* fracture (pig iron), fractured surface or plane, surface or area of fracture, plane of failure **faserige ~** fibrous fracture **feinkörnige ~** fine-grained, smooth, or even fracture **grobkörnige ~** coarse-grained, granular-crystalline, or bright-crystalline fracture **irreguläre ~** irregular or uneven fracture **muschelige ~** conchoidal fracture **splitterige ~** splintery fracture, barked or fibrous fracture
Bruch-flächenaussehen *n* appearance of fracture **-fuge** *f* joint of rupture **-gefahr** *f* risk of breakage, danger of breaking **-gefüge** *n* structural fracture **-gestein** *n* quarry rocks **-gewicht** *n*

fractional weight **-gramm** *n* fraction of a gram **-grenze** *f* point of maximum load, ultimate stress limit, breaking limit or strain, rupture limit, strength

brüchig brittle, short, fragile, friable, flawed, unsound, hot, cracky

Brüchigkeit *f* shortness, brittleness, fragility, friability

Brüchigkeitsgebiet *n* range of brittleness

Brüchigwerden *n* embrittlement

Bruch-kupfer *n* copper scrap **-landeeignung** *f* crash ability **-landung** *f* crash-landing

Bruchlast *f* breaking load or strain, breaking weight, mean tensile strain, maximum load, total load at fracture, breakage load, ultimate load (aircraft), ultimate strength **-spielzahl** *f* number of cycles to failure, life to fracture **-wechselzahlen** *f pl* number of load cycles at which fracture occurs

Bruch-linie *f* fault line, rupture line **-lochwicklung** *f* fractional-slot winding **-los** without shearing **-metall** *n* scrap metal **-modul** *n* modulus of rupture

Bruch-neigung *f* tendency to fracture **-platten** *f pl* bursting disks **-probe** *f* breaking or breakdown test, specimen for strength test **-punkt** *m* breaking or yield point, brittle point (of glass) **-querschnitt** *m* weld size **-rechnung** *f* calculation involving fractions **-riß** *m* (failure) crack **-schlitzmaschine** *f* mining machine that cuts and breaks coal in low-level lignite mines **-schrottofen** *m* breakdown furnace

bruchsicher resistant to fracture or rupture **-er Behälter** crashproof tank

Bruch-sicherheit *f* safety against fracture **-sicherung** *f* safeguarding or security against breakage **-silber** *n* scrap silver

Bruchspannung *f* ultimate stress or strength, breaking stress or strain **wahre** ~ true ultimate stress, true stress of fracture

Bruchstein *m* quarry or rubble stone, stones, ashlar or dressed stone, broken stone **-bettung** *f* rock filling

Bruchsteine *m pl* stone(s) **geschüttete** ~ rock filling **vorspringende** ~ projecting stones **trocken verlegte** ~ (dry) stone

Bruchsteinfüllung *f* rock filling, rubble bed

Bruchsteinmauerwerk *n* ashlar masonry, rubble masonry **rohes** (felsenartiges) ~ rock-faced rubble **(unregelmäßiges)** ~ **mit Steinlagen** level bedded rubble, random rubble in course ~ **mit dünnen Steinlagen** flat bedded rubble

Bruchstein-schüttung *f* dry-stone reventment, riprap, rubble **-unterlage** *f* rubble bed

Bruchstelle *f* site of break(ing), of fracture, or of rupture, diaclase, breaking, crack, seam, fissure ~ **im Deich** breach in a dike or embankment

Bruch-strich *m* bar of fraction, crossline, fraction stroke **-stück** *n* fragment **-stücke** *n* fission products, fragments, fracture or ruptre pieces

Bruchteil *m* fragment, fraction, section, fractional or aliquot part ~ **der Zeit** fraction of time

Bruch-versuch *m* fracture test **-widerstand** *m* breaking strain or strength, tensile strength, ultimate strength **-zeichen** *n* fraction mark **-ziffern** *pl* fractions

Brucit *m* brucite

Brücke *f* bridge, arch, platform, runner, runner gate, viaduct, crossbar, rider (piano) ~ **des Stöpsels** contact plate ~ **mit festen Stützen** fixed bridge ~ **mit schwimmenden Stützen** floating bridge ~ **des Tors** top deck of the caisson **in** ~ **liegen** to be in bridge (teleph.) **in** ~ **geschaltet** in leak, teed or bridged across **in** ~ **schalten** to bridge, tee (across) (teleph.)

Brücke, bewegliche ~ opening or movable bridge **einfache** ~ single bridge **fahrbare** ~ traveling bridge **fliegende** ~ swing or flying bridge **magnetische** ~ permeability bridge **Wheatstonesche** ~ Wheatstone bridge

Brücken-abgleich *m* balanced bridge **-achse** *f* bridge center line **-anordnung** *f* bridge circuit (arrangement) **-anschaltehilfsrelais** (BR_1) auxiliary holding bar switching relay **-anschalterelais** (BR) *n* holding bar switching relay **-antrieb** *m* bridge drive

Brückenarm *m* bridge arm, duplex or bridge coils **feste Brückenarme** ratio arms

Brücken-ausgang *m* bridge exit **-ausgleich** *m* bridge balance **-ausgleichstrom** *m* bridge-balancing current **-bahn** *f* bridge causeway **-bau** *m* bridge construction, building, or design **-bauanstalten** *f pl* bridgebuilders (office or establishment) **-bauer** *m* bridge designer, bridgebuilder

Brücken-baugerät *n* bridgebuilding equipment **-baum** *m* sleeper **-belag** *m* bridge planks **-besatzung** *f* watch on a bridge **-bildung** *f* arching, bridge formation, gap bridging **-bock** *m* trestle of a bridge **-boden** *m* platform, platform flooring **-bogen** *m* arch, gullet, or bay of a bridge **-boot** *n* pontoon **-damm** *m* approach embankment **-detector** chain-gated analyser

Brückendraht *m* bridge wire ~ **mit Gleitkontakt** (differential) slide wire

Brücken-drehkran *m* rotary bridge crane **-endwiderlager** *n* abutment **-fahrbahn** *f* bridge roadway **-fahrwerk** *n* transporter travel gear **-fahrzeug** *n* bay section **-feld** *n* bay of bridge **-fertigung** *f* platform production **-floß** *n* bridge raft, floating support **-frontschott** *n* forward or weather bridge bulkhead **-fuß** *m* leg of the crane

Brücken-gegensprechschaltung *f* bridge duplex connection **-gegensprechsystem** *n* bridge duplex system **-geländer** *n* bridge railing **-gerät** *n* bridging equipment **-gewölbe** *n* bridge arch, bridge vault **-gleichgewicht** *n* bridge balance, duplex balance **-gleichrichter** *m* bridge rectifier **-glühzünder** *m* bridge-wire cap (explosives) **-hammer** *m* two-standard hammer **-hilfsrelais** *n* assistant holding bar relay

Brücken-H-Schaltung *f* **Entzerrungskette mit** ~ H-type attenuator network (balanced)

Brücken-isolationsmesser *m* bridge megger **-kabelkran** *m* cableway bridge crane **-kasten** *m* post-office box of Wheatstone bridge **-kolonne** *f* bridge train **-kommandant** *m* bridge commander (engin.) **-kompression** *f* compression of vapor by its own pressure **-kopf** *m* bridgehead **-kopflinie** *f* bridgehead line **-kopfstellung** *f* bridgehead position **-körper** *m* bridge wall

Brücken-kran *m* traveling crane, bridge crane

-kreis *m* bridge circuit **-last** *f* bridge load **-leitung** *f* laddered circuit **-linie** *f* bridge line (engin.) **-magnet** *m* holding bar magnet, bridge magnet **-mauerrohre** *n pl* bridge-wall tubes **-megger** *m* bridge megger **-messung** *f* bridge test, bridge measurement **-nock** *n* wing of bridge **-oberbau** *m* superstructure of bridge

Brücken-pfeiler *m* bridge pile, pier **-regler** *m* potentiometer controller **-relais** *n* bridge relay **-rückkopplung** *f* bridge feedback **-schaltung** *f* bridge circuit or connection, bridge structure or arrangement **-scheitel** *m* bridge apex **-schiene** *f* U rail **-schiff** *n* pontoon **-schlag** *m* bridge-building, bridging **-schlüssel** *m* bridge key (elec.) **-schwelle** *f* curb beam **-skizze** *f* bridge diagram

Brücken-spannung *f* bridge span **-speisung** *f* feeding by bridges (teleph.) **-spitze** *f* open ends of bridge **-steg** *m* footbridge **-stein** *m* float (in a glass tank) **-stelle** *f* bridge site **-stoß** *m* bridge joint (rails) **-strecke** *f* bay **-stützweite** *f* span of bridge **-system** *n* a system of range finding for antiaircraft batteries based on a Wheatstone bridge **-teil** *n* bridge member or part **-träger** *m* bridge boom, bridge girder

Brücken-T-Schaltung *f* **Entzerrungskette mit ~** T-type attenuation network (unbalanced)

Brücken-schiene *f* bridge rail **-troß** *m* bridge train **-trupp** *m* bridge-construction party **-überbau** *m* bridge superstructure or substructure **-überführung** *f* bridge crossing **-überträger** *m* differential transformer **-unterbau** *m* foundation substructure of bridge **-verfahren** *n* bridge method **-verhältnisarme** *m pl* ratio arms of bridge **-verstärker** *m* bridge amplifier **-verzweigung** *f* hybrid T

Brücken-waage *f* platform balance, scale beam, weighbridge **-wache** *f* watch on the bridge, lookout on the bridge **-wagen** *m* bridge truck **-walzen** *f pl* rollers for a bridge **-weite** *f* span **-widerlager** *n* abutment **-widerstand** *m* bridge resistance **-zweig** *m* bridge branch, arm of the bridge (elec. engin.)

Brüden *f* vapors **-dampf** *m* vapor **-gebläse** *n* vapor fan **-kompression** *f* vapor compression **-kondensator** *m* vapor condenser **-pumpe** *f* vapor-pump evaporators, distilling unit, vapor concentrate pump **-raum** *m* vapor chamber **-rohr** *n* vapor pipe, exit pipe **-schieber** *m* vapor slide valve **-wasser** *n* condenser water

Brühe *f* liquor

brühen to scald

Brühenmesser *m* barkometer

Brüh-fabrik *f* factory with scalding process **-raum** *m* scalding chamber **-saft** *m* scalding juice **-schnitzel** *m* Steffen sugar pulp

brüllen to roar, shout, bellow

Brumm (Welligkeit) *m* ripple **-balken** *m* hum bar **-effekt** *m* hum effect

brummen to hum

Brummen *n* alternating-current hum, hum(ming) buzzing noise

Brumm-filter *n* ripple filter **-frequenz** *f* hum frequency **-kasten** *m* bass keys **-kompensationsspule** hum bucking coil (elec.)

Brummschleife *f*, **galvanische ~** conductive ripple pickup

Brumm-spannung *f* hum voltage (elec.), hum potential, ripple potential, ripple voltage **-spannungsverhältnis** *n* ripple ratio, percent ripple voltage **-spur** *f* **-streifen** *m* buzz track, hum (broad bands on screen of cathode-ray tube) **-tastenfeder** *f* spring for bass keys (accordion) **-ton** *m* alternating-current hum, hum **-welligkeit** *f* hum ripple **-zeichen** *n* buzzer signal

Brünierbeize *f* bronzing pickle

brünieren to brown, bronze, burnish, black finishing

Brünieren *n* gun-barrel oxydizing

Brünierung *f* browning antirust treatment or coating on rifle- or gun-barrel burnishing; (von Holz) *f* burnettising (of timber)

Brunnen *m* well, spring, well point (soil mech.), shaft, fountain **-abdeckung** *f* roof of manhole **-abschluß** *m* well curbing **-absenkung** *f* drilling of a borehole or well, driving a well point **-auslauf** *m* well outlet **-ausschachter** *m* well sinker **-baukommando** *n* well-sinking and construction detachment

Brunnen-bohranlage *f* well-boring plant **-bohrer** *m* well-boring drill **-brüstung** *f* **-einfassung** *f* curb or lining of a well **-feld** *n* well pit **-gräting** *f* screw well's grating **-gründung** *f* foundation on wells, sunk by loading (monolith foundation) **-kranz** *m* cutting edge at bottom of well casing, head around a well

Brunnen-macher *m* well sinker **-mantel** *m* lining of a well **-schacht** *m* well shaft **-schalung** *f* well lining (casing) **-schwengel** *m* draw beam of a well, pump handle **-stube** *f* well chamber **-sumpf** *m* discharging trough, discharging basin **-trommel** *f* barrel of well winch **-wasser** *n* well water

Brust *f* breast, front, gain, front or facade (wall), hearth opening (blast furnace) **geschlossene ~** closed front, closed fore part **offene ~** open front, open fore part

Brust-baum *m* breastbeam (naut.), breast roll (textiles) **-beutel** *m* money bag **-blatt** *n* breastplate (harness) **-bohrer** *m* breast drill, brace, hand brace **-fallschirm** *m* chest-pack parachute **-fernsprecher** *m* head and chest set, chest-type telephone signal

Brustfläche einer spiralverzahnten Führungsreibahle lips of a pilot type spiral fluted reamer

Brust-hammer *m* belly helve **-holz** *n* neck yoke, poling board **-klappe** *f* trace toggle (harness) **-kühler** *m* nose or bow radiator

Brust-lehne *f* balustrade **-leier** *f* hand or boring brace, breast drill, carpenter's brace, brace, crank brace **-mauer** *m* parapet **-mikrophon** *n* breastplate transmitter, breastplate microphone **-panzer** *m* breastplate **-platte** *f* breastplate (for drilling) **-riegel** *m* straining beam **-scheibe** *f* silhouette target (head and shoulder) **-schild** *m* breastplate **-stütze** *f* breast support

Brüstung *f* railing, handrail, guardrail, parapet, window railing

Brust-walze *f* breast roll **-wehr** *f* parapet, breastwork, parapet wall **-wehrkrone** *f* fire crest **-werk** *n* parapet, breastwork **-winkel** *m* front or top rake **-zacken** *m* fore plate

brütbar fertile

Brüten *n* fertilization

Brut-gewinn *m* breeding gain **-mantel** breeder blanket **-material** breeder material **-ofen** *m* incubator

Brutreaktor *m* breeding reactor, breeder reactor (produces more fuel than it burns) **langsamer ~** thermal breeder **schneller ~** fast breeder

Brutstoffe *pl* fertile materials (Isotopes transmuted into nuclear fuel by bombarding with neutrons)

brutto gross (weight) **-absackwaage** *f* sack gross weigher **-belastung** *f* gross load **-betrag** *m* gross amount **-erlös** *m* gross proceds **-ertrag** *m* gross receipts, earnings, or profit **-formel** *f* gross or over-all formula **-gewicht** *n* gross weight **-gewinn** *m* gross profit **-prämie** *f* office premium **-reaktionen** *f pl* gross reactions **-registertonnen** *f pl* gross registered tons **-tonnengehalt** *m* gross tonnage **-verdienst** *m* gross earnings **-zugänge** *pl* gross additions

Brut-verhältnis *n* breeding ratio **-zyklus** *m* breeding cycle

B-Schirm *m* range bearing display

B-Schrank *m* B (switch) board

B-stoff *m* code for hydrazine hydrate, a rocket propellant, also symbol for bromaceton, a type of rocket fuel, alcohol **-behälter** *m* fuel tank **-betankungsschlauch** *m* fuel filler hose **-druckleitung** *f* fuel feed line **-düse** *f* fuel-spray-nozzle multiple in some rockets **-einlaufsicke** *f* fuel-intake fold, fuel-distributing ring **-einlaufstutzen** *m* fuel-intake connection **-empfangswagen** *m* alcohol transloading vehicle

B-stoff-entleerungsventil *n* fuel drain valve **-enttanken** *n* fuel draining **-enttankungsventil** *n* alcohol release valve **-hauptventil** *n* main fuel valve **-kesselkraftwagen** *m* fuel tank truck **-leckleitung** *f* fuel leak line **-pumpe** *f* fuel pump **-pumpenmaschinensatz** *m* fuel-pump assembly **-rohr** *n* alcohol pipe

B-stoff-saugstutzen *m* fuel-intake port **-steigeleitung** *f* fuel ascending line **-tank** *m* fuel tank **-tanken** *n* fuel filling **-tankwagen** *m* fuel tank truck **-umwälzleitung** *f* fuel return or fuel bypass line **-vorventil** *n* preliminary fuel valve, pressure-operated alcohol valve **-zerstäubersystem** *n* fuel-atomizer system

Buch *n* book, volume, journal, log **-ausstattung** *f* make-up of a book **-beschlag** *m* metal work (corners) **-beschneidemaschine** *f* book trimming machine **-besprechung** *f* book review **-binde** *f* jacket **-binden** *n* bookbinding **-binderei** *f* bookbinding

Buchbinder-kattun *m* calico **-leinen** *n* book cloth **-pappe** *f* bender's board, bookbinding board **-schriften** *pl* bookbinder's type **-werkzeuge** *pl* bookbinder's tools

Buch-decke (Buchdeckel) book cover **-druck** *m* printing, typography **-druckätzung** *f* halftone engraving **-drucker** *m* printer **-druckerahlen** *pl* printer's broaches **-druckerei** *f* printing office, typography **-druckereieinrichtung** *f* printing equipment **-druckerkunst** *f* printing craft **-druckerwappen** *n* printer's emblem **-druckrollenrotation** *f* web-fed rotary letter press **-druckschnellpressen** *pl* letterpress high-speed printing machines **-druckwalzenmasse** *f* printing roller composition

Buche *f* beech

Bucheckernöl *n* beech (nut) oil

Bucheinbände *pl* book covers

buchen to book, record, count up, enter, register

Buchen-holz *n* beechwood **-holzzellstoffabrik** *f* factory that manufactures artificial wool from beech pulp, a cellulose product **-kohle** *f* beech charcoal **-pech** *n* beech-tar pitch

Bücherbrett *n* bookshelf

Bücherei *f* library

Bücher-gestell *n* bookcase, bookshelf **-revision** *f* audit **-schrank** *m* bookcase **-schutzdecke** *f* book corner

Buch-führer *m* **-halter** *m* bookkeeper **-führung** *f* accounting (book-keeping) **-gold** *n* leaf gold **-haltung** *f* accounting department

Buchhaltungsabteilung *f*, **Leiter der ~** comptroller

Buch-haltungsmaschine *f* accounting machine **-haltungsunterlagen** *pl* accounting records **-handel** *m* bookselling, bookseller's trade, retail book trade **-händler** *m* retail bookseller **-handlung** *f* book store, bookseller's shop, bookshop **-heften** *n* book stitching **-heftmaschine** *f* book sewing machine

Buchholzrelais *n* Buchholz protective relay, gaspressure relay

Büchi Aufladung *f* Büchi supercharging

Buchrücken *m* back of a book

Buchsbaum *m* box (shrub or tree) **-holz** *n* boxwood

Büchsbohren *n* bailer boring

Buchse *f* (Technik) bush(ing); (Muffe) sleeve; (Zylinder) liner; (Fett) cup; (Elektr.) socket

Buchse *f* hub, jack, mechanical sleeve, worm drive, shaft insert, bush (for flywheel), bearing **~ für Bananenstecker** pin jack **~ zum Walzenstuhl** bush for roller carriage

Büchse *f* box, case, container; (Blech) tin (box), can, canister; (Salben) pot jar; (Milit.) rifle, carbine; (Verpack.) tin, pot, can

Büchse *f* sleeve, barrel, bush, bushing, gas-mask carrier, filter canister, socket **~ für Fettschmierung** cup for grease lubrication, grease cup **selbsttätig schmierende ~** self-oiling bushing

Büchsen-fanghaken *m* bailer fishing hook **-filter** *m* canister filter **-gruppe** *f* socket strip (elec.) **-kamera** *f* box camera **-kette** *f* steel-bushed roller chain

Buchsenleitung *f* sleeve conductor, socket or jack line

Büchsen-macher *m* armorer, warrant ordnance officer, gunsmith **-metall** *n* Babbit or white metal **-öffner** *m* can opener, (slang) hawker hurricane

Buchsen-platte *f* socket panel **-ventil** *n* sleeve socket

Buchsring *m* axle ring, packing ring, bushing

Buchstabe *m* letter **fetter ~** bold face type **großer ~** capital (letter)

Buchstaben *pl* characters, printing type, letters, capitals, lower case characters **-abstand** *m* letter space, letter blank **-ausstoßer** *m* typepusher **-auswechselung** *f* interchangeability of types **-bezeichnung** *f* lettering, notation (math. formula) **-blank** *n* letter blank or space **-blanktaste** *f* letter-blank key **-fehler** *m* typographical error **-gruppe** *f* code group, word **-holer** *m* type-carrier **-inversion** *f* letters shift **-leerschrift** *f* letter space or blank

Buchstaben-rechnung *f* algebra **-schreibempfang**

m teleprinter or visual reception **-stempel** *m* lettering punch **-tafel** *f* phonetic alphabet **-trommel** *f* letter drum **-umschaltung** *f* letter shift (signal), unshift **-vorschub** *m* letter feed **-wechsel** *m* letter shift (signal), unshift **-weiß** *n* letter blank or space **-zählvorrichtung** *f* letter-counting device

buchstabieren to spell, speak phonetically

Buchstabier-tafel *f* phonetic alphabet **-verfahren** *n* spelling system

Bucht *f* line of repeater bays, bay, inlet, bight, creek, cove, gulf, thwartship convex arch of deck, bilge, round

Buchtspleiß *m* cut splice

Buchung *f* accounting, posting

Buchungs-angaben *pl* data **-beleg** *m* voucher **-formular** *n* accounting form **-maschinen** *pl* accounting machines **-methode** (Verbuchungsmethode) booking method **-papier** *n* ledger paper **-papier und -karton** paper and card-board for bookkeeping purposes **-pult** *n* desk set, remote interrogation set **-verfahren** *n* booking procedure

Buch-verleger *m* publisher **-wert** *m* book value

Buckel *m* hump, humpback, back, bulge, knuckle (min.) **~ einer Kurve** hump or bulge of a curve

Buckel-maß (Bricketpresse) taper **-platte** *f* buckle plate **-schweißmaschine** *f* projection welder

Bude *f* shed

budgetierte Kosten revenue expenditure

Büffelleder *n* buffalo skin

Buffer *m* pad, buffer, cushion, dashpot **-feder** *f* buffer spring **-kontakt** *m* buffer contact **-tank** *m* surge tank

Bug *m* bow (navy), prow, stem, nose (aviation), bows (seaplane), bend **über den andern ~** on the opposite tack **vor dem ~** on the bow

Bug-anker bow anchor **-auftriebtank** *m* bow buoyancy tank **-bewaffnung** *f* front armament

Bügel *m* (Kleider) hanger; (Band) strap; (Handgriff) handle; (Klammer) clamp, bracket; (Schloß) shakle; (Stromabnehmer) collector; (Säge) frame; (Nietmaschine) yoke, bale; bow, bail, yoke, stirrup, saddle bracket (microscope), staple, clip, clevis, blink, tie, ring, hoop, trigger guard, transverse, crossbeam, crosstie, rod, bar, loop, triangular or pear-shaped lifting eye, curved piece of metal, bout (string instrument), handle of a pail or bucket, holder, bend, hand bracket, stay bar, harness (of headphones), loop (of magnetron)

Bügel einer Brille temple **~ mit Einlage** *f* temples with wire core **~ auf Exzenterkörper** straps on eccentrics **~ für Seitenschutz** side guard rail **~** (Stromabnehmer), bow (current collector) **durch einen ~ verbunden** clamped or strapped (together) **eiserner ~** metal straps

Bügel-blech *n* trim tab **-bolzen** *m* U bolt **-druckapparat** *m* transfer printing apparatus **-druckmaschine** *f* selvedge printing machine **-echtheit** *f* fastness to hot pressing **-eisen** *n* flatiron **-elektrode** *f* bow-type electrode **-feder für Scheinwerfer** fastening spring for head lamp

Bügel-gatter *n* bow-saw frame **-gleitbacke** *f* horn block, pedestal **-haken** *m* shackle hook **-hakenauge** *n* shackle hook or eye **-holz** *m* wooden-block (for polishing glassware) **kaltschere** *f* strap cold shears **-kontakt** *m* bow contact (elec.) **-maschine** *f* ironer, ironing machine **-meßschraube** *f* (Mikrometer) external micrometer

bügeln to iron, smooth

Bügel-papier *n* transfer paper **-regeltransformatoren** stage lighting regulating **-säge** *f* hack saw, bow saw, framed crosscut saw **-sägemaschinen** *pl* power hacksaws **-schleifkontakt** *m* sliding bow (elec.) **-schraube** *f* stirrup bolt, U bolt, stable bolt, strap bolt, sling bolt **-stangen** *f pl* holding-down bars **-teilung** *f* stirrup spacing **-versuch** *m* yoke test **-weite** *f* hasp width

Bug-fenster *n* nose window **-flagge** *f* jack **-gebläse** *n* (Flugzeug) nose fan **-geschütz** *n* bow or front gun **-kanzel** *f* bow cockpit (aviation)

Bug-kappe *f* bow cap **-kühler** *m* nose radiator **-landung** *f* bowlanding **-lastig** bow- or nose-heavy, trim by the bow **-lastigkeit** *f* bow heaviness (aviation) **-licht** *n* headlight, front light **-panzer** *m* bow armor

Bugrad *n* front wheel, nose wheel **-fahrwerk** *n* tricycle undercarriage, nose wheel landing gear

Bug-radargerät *n* nose radar **-röhre** *f* bow torpedo tube **-ruder** *n* active rudder **-schwer** bow-heavy **-seitenleine** *f* yaw line

bugsieren, ein Fahrzeug ~ to tow a vessel

Bugsiertau *n* towrope

Bug-spriet *n* bowsprit **-stand** *m* chin turret forwardgunner station, nose-gun station

Bugwelle eines Geschosses nose wave of a projectile

Bug-wellenproblem *n* prow problem **-wulst** *f* bulbous bow

Buhne *f* groin, spurdike, diversion dam, dike

Bühne *f* stage, arena, platform, trestle, gallery, sollar stopping place, scaffolding **fliegende ~** flying cradle, flying sollar **obere ~** upper platform **untere ~** lower platform

Bühnen-arbeiter *m* scene shifter **-aufsteller** *m* set dresser **-belag** *m* platform flooring **-beleuchtung** *f* stage lighting, footlights (theater) **-einbauten** *m pl* groin structures

Buhnen-feld *n* area between two groins or dikes **-kopf** *m* head of a groin, dike

Bühnenlautsprecher *m* projection-screen loudspeaker

Bühnenlicht-effekte *m pl* stage-lighting effects **-regulator** *m* dimmer or multicontact dimmer (theater), dimmer switch **-stellwerk** *n* dimmer board **-wechselstromsteller** *m* Bordoni regulating transformer

Bühnenmikrophon *n* stage microphone

Buhnenpfähle *m pl* stakes, pickets

Bühnenstellwerk *n* dimmer control

Buhnenwurzel *f* root of a groin, dike

Bühnloch *n* hitch, holing

Bulin *f* bowline

Bull-auge *n* porthole, deadeye, scuttle **-dog** tractor (Bulldog) **-dozer** *m* (Planierraupe) bulldozer

Bu-Kamm (Fernschreiber) function lever-letters (Ltrs)

Bummerangverfahren *n* oboe system

Bummelzug *m* slow train

Bumslandung *f* rough landing, heavy landing
Buna (Handelsbezeichnung) synthetic rubber, butadiene natrium **-reifen** *m* buna tire
Bund *m* (Band) band, tie; (einer Welle) collar; (Anschlag) rod-stop; (Flansch) flange, shoulder, shackle, bunch, binding, swelling, federation, lashing (rope), coil, shelf
Bund-abbau *m* coil build-down **-aufbau** *m* coil build-up **-bolzen** *m* collar stud, flange bolt, ball bearing stud, shouldered bolt, journal bolt **-buchse** *f* flange bushing
Bunddurchmesserausgleich *m* (bei abnehmendem Bund) compensation for coil build-down ~ (bei zunehmendem Bund) compensation for coil build-up
Bunde und Knoten knots and ties
Bündel *n* bundle, bunch; (längliches) sheaf; (Strahlen) beam; (Ionen) stream; (Noten) parcel, package; bale, group, crossbar, file (paper), pack, pencil, cone (of rays), wave packets ~ **abschneiden** to flush **vom ~ gelenktes Projektil** beam rider ~ **von Kanälen** group of channels
Bündel-achse *f* beam axis **-apparat** *m* bunching attachment **-breite** *f* apex angle **-durchschnitt** *m* aperture of the beam **-einschnürung** *f* intersection (in the beam) **-endröhre** *f* beam-power valve or tube
Bündeler *m* buncher
Bündel-erzeugungssysteme *pl* beam producing systems **-feuer** *n* leading light (single) **-holz** *n* bundled wood **-knoten** *m* cross-over **-leistung** *f* beam power **-leiter** *m* bundle conductor (of powerline) **-maschine** *f* buncher
bündeln to bundle, bunch (together), focus, concentrate, cluster (of rocket)
Bündel-potential *n* electron-stream potential **-presse** *f* baling press **-querschnitt** *n* aperture of the beam **-schraube** *f* clamp screw, screw for wooden casing clamp **-staffelung** *f* group grading
Bündelung *f* beaming, concentrating, bundling, focusing, directivity (electronics), bunching (of electrons in Klystron), concentration, ensuring beam or directive-antenna effect, grouping ~ **des Lichts** concentration of the light rays **scharfe** ~ great directivity
Bündelungs-anlage *f* beaming device **-anode** *f* focusing anode **-elektrode** focusing electrode **-faktor** *m* directivity factor (of antenna) **-gewinn** *m* directive gain **-grad** *m* sound power concentration (acoust) **-index** directivity index **-spule** *f* focusing coil **-trichter** *m* directing horn
Bündel-verbreiterung durch Eigenladung space charge beam spreading **-zentrierung** *f* camera alignment
Bundes-bahn *f* Federal railway
Bund-flansch *m* union, coupling flange **-gatter** *n* multiple-blade frame saw **-gewicht** *n* coil weight **-haken** *m* swelling guard
bündig succinct, brief, concise, summarized, valid, flush, snug, compact ~ **abschneidend** flush ~ **machen** to make flush with **-e (Tür) Stufe** reveal step
Bündigkeit *f* compactness
Bund-lager *n* collar end bearing **-los** flangeless **-mutter** *f* collar nut, flange nut, lock nut
Bündnis *n* alliance
Bundpfahl *m* **mit Nuten** rabbeted corner pile
Bund-ring *m* end ring or collar **-rolle** *f* flanged roller **-schraube** *f* collar screw **-schwelle** *f* ground plate or sill of a framework
Bündsel *n* seizing
Bundstahl *m* fagot steel, fagot of steel bars
Bunker *m* bin, bunker, silo, small fortification ~ **für Verstärker** bay or rack of amplifiers ~ **für Zuschläge** flux bin
Bunker-anlage *f* group of bunkers **-bänder** *pl* bunker belts **-entlüftung** *f* bunker ventilation **-kohle** *f* steam coal, bunker coal **-linie** *f* line of pillboxes, line of concrete dugouts **-lüftung** *f* bunker ventilation
bunkern to bunker
Bunker-räumwagen *m* bin emptying truck **-stand** *m* concrete emplacement **-stellung** *f* bunker position **-verschluß** *m* bunker gate
Bunsen Brenner *m* Bunsen burner ~ **Element** *n* Bunsen cell ~ **Flamme** *f* Bunsen flame ~ **Photometer** *m* Bunsen or grease-spot photometer
bunt varicolored, motley ~ **bemalt** dazzle-painted **-e Farben** hue or chromatic colors **-er Lappen** colored-cloth garnish, garland **-er Rand** (Farbsaum) color fringe (TV)
Bunt-ätzdruck *m* colored discharge print **-ätze** *pl* color(ed) discharge **-ätzeffekt** *m* color discharge effect **-ätzfarbe** *f* color discharge paste **-bild** *n* color picture (TV) **-bleiche** *f* branning **-druck** *m* color or decorative printing, colored impression, chromotypography **-farbenanstrich** *m* protective coloration (camouflage) **-feuer** *n* poison gases that attack respiratory organs **-glaspapier** *n* diaphanic paper **-glasrohpapier** *n* diaphanic base paper
Buntheit *f* chrominance (TV)
Bunt-hilfsträger *m* chrominance subcarrier (TV) **-information** *f* chrominance information (TV) **-kreuze** *n pl* colored crosses used to identify gas shells **-metall** *n* nonferrous metal **-munition** *f* colored-cross gas shells **-papiermaschine** *f* coating machine for stained paper **-pappe** *f* colored board **-regler** *m* color control (TV) **-reserve** *f* colored resist **-sandstein** *m* new red sandstone, variegated or mottled sandstone
buntscheckig motley **-schillernd** shatoyant
Buntschießen *n* simultaneous or alternate shelling with high-explosive and chemical shells
Buntsignal *n* chrominance signal (TV) **kombiniertes** ~ combined chrominance signal (TV)
Bunt-signalsperre *f* chrominance signal elimination (TV) **-signalumsetzer** *m* chromacoder **-spannungsregler** *m* color control (TV) **-stift** *m* colored pencil
Bunzen *m* eye (of type) **-arbeit** *f* chased work **-auslegekarton** *m* felt board for printing shops **-tiefe** *f* depth of set
Bürde *f* burden, load, apparant ohmic resistance (elec.)
Bürette *f* burette, buret
Büretten-ausflußspitze *f* burette tip **-gestell** *n* burette stand **-hahn** *m* burette valve **-klemme** *f* burette clamp **-schwimmer** *m* burette float
Bürge *m* guarantor
Burg *f* castle **-artig** castlelike, towering
bürgen to guarantee

Bürger *m* citizen
bürgerlich civil, civic **-e Dämmerung** *f* civil twilight **-es Recht** Civil law
Bürgersteig *m* sidewalk, footway
Bürgschaft *f* bail, security, guarantee, pledge **~ gewähren** to grant security
Bürgschaftsleistung *f* suretyship
Bürgschafts- und Haftungsverhältnisse contigent liabilities
Burgunderpech *n* white resin
Burnett-Verfahren *n* method of wood preservation using zinc chloride
Büro *n* office, bureau, place of business **-arbeit** *f* clerical work **-bedarf** *m* office requisites **-einrichtung** *f* office furniture **-klammer** *f* paper clip or fastener, office clip **-material** *n* stationery and office supplies
Bürste *f* brush, wiper **Kohlen-~** brush (carbon) **dauernd aufliegende ~** brush in permanent contact **untere ~** reading brush **die Bürsten verstellen** to shift the brushes **a/b Bürsten** line wipers **versetzte ~** staggered brush
bürsten to brush, sweep
Bürsten *n* brushing **-abhebevorrichtung** *f* brush-raising gear, brush-lifting device **-abzug** *m* copyproof, brushproof (galley proof) **-arm** *m* brush or brush gear, trailer, brush rocker (straight arm), brush or selector rod, brush shaft **-armspindel** *f* brush or wiper shaft **-auflagedruck** *m* brush contact pressure **-brücke** *f* rocker for brushes (radial type) **-brückenträger** *m* support for electrical brush holder ring
Bürsten-deckel *m* clamping plate **-detacheur** *m* brush detacher **-detektor** *m* cat-whisker detector **-draht** *m* brush wire **-druck** *m* brush printing **-einzieher** *m* brush fitter **-entladung** *f* brush form of discharge, brush discharge (between glow discharge and sparking)
Bürstenfeder für Kohlebürste compressing spring for carbon brush
Bürsten-fenster *n* brush opening **-feuchter** *m* brush damper **-feuer** *n* sparking of brushes **-halter** *m* brush holder (elec.) **-halterring** *m* brush-holder ring **-halslöffelbohrer** *m* brace spoon bits for brush blocks
Bürsten-holzbohrer *m* brushwood borer **-joch** *n* brush yoke (elec.) **-kontakt** *m* brush form of contact **-kontrolle** *f* brush compare check **-paar** *n* coupled brushes, pair of brushes **-rahmen** *m* brush carriage **-reibungsverlust** *m* brush friction loss (elec.) **-sammelring** *m* collector ring **-scheibe** *f* circular brush, wheel brush
Bürsten-schlüssel *m* brush-holder key **-schnecke** *f* brushing worm **-spitze** *f* tip of brush **-stellhebel** *m* lever for adjusting brushes **-stellung** *f* brush position **-stift** *m* brush-holder rod **-streichmaschine** *f* brush spreader **-strich** *m* brush coat **-träger** *m* brush (gear), brush carriage, brush ring or collar, wiper shaft, brush or selector rod, line brush or wiper, brush spring or support **-trägergestell** *n* brush rack
Bürsten-verschiebung *f* brush shift, lead of brushes, adjustment of position of brushes **-verschiebungswinkel** *m* brush displacement **-verstellung** *f* brush shifting, lead of brushes **-vorschub** *m* forward lead of brushes **-vorrichtung** *f* brush contrivance **-wähler** *m* brush selector, trip rod or spindle **-walze** *f* brush roller (pulp and paper) **-welle** *f* wiper shaft, brush rod **-winkel** *m* angle of brushes or of brush load (with commutator)
Bürstvorrichtung *f* brushing device
Busche *f* hoop
Buschegge *f* bush or wood harrow
Büschel *m* cluster (of crystals), pencil of rays, tuft, sheaf, bunch, beam (light), mop **sich in Büscheln entladen** to brush
Büschel-entladung *f* brush discharge **-funken** *m* brush spark **-kohle** *f* foliated or slaty coal **-licht** *n* brush light **-querschnitt** *m* beam cross section
Busch-hopsen *n* hedgehop **-hopserflugzeug** *n* hedgehopper airplane **-packung** *f* fascines **-rodepflug** *m* brush-breaker plow **-wehr** *n* brush weir **-würste** *f pl* bundles of fascines
Büse *f* lance
Bussole *f* magnetic or box compass, compass, dial **Kreis ~** circular compass **Röhren ~** trough compass
Bussolen-gehäuse *n* compass case, compass housing **-instrument** *n* theodolite with compass **-kreis** *m* compass circle, compass card **-richtkreis** *m* aiming circle **-ring** *m* compass ring **-zug** *m* compass traverse
Butadien *n* butadiene **-kautschuk** *m* butadiene rubber
Butan *n* butane
Butanol *n* butanol **-azetonvergärung** *f* butanol-acetone ferment
Butan-oxydation *f* butane oxidation **-wiedergewinnung** *f* butane recovery
Bütte *f* tub, bucket, scuttle, vat, tank, chest
Bütten-brett *n* plank **-karton** *m* handmade board **-leimung** *f* pulp sizing **-ofen** *m* pot furnace (for melting glass) **-papier** *n* handmade paper, mold-made paper **-presse** *f* pulp press (for paper) **-rand** *m* deckle edge **-randpapier** *n* Dutch paper, deckle-edged paper **-randkreismesser** *n* circular deckle edge knife **-stuhl** *m* couch-stool
Butter-äther *m* ethyl butyrate **-echt** grease proof **-faß** *n* churn, tub of butter **-gangkupplungsschale** *f* clutching disk of churning speed **-hahn** *m* butter valve **-milch** *f* buttermilk **-sauer** butyrate of . . .
Butter-säure *f* butyric acid **-säureäther** *m* ethyl butyrate **-säureäthylester** *n* butyric acid
buttersaures butyrate **~ Ammonium** *n* ammonium butyrate **~ Äthyl** *n* ethyl butyrate
Butterverpackungspapier *n* wax- or greaseproof paper
Bütt-geselle *m* dipper, vatman **-krück** *m* paddle(s), stick
Büttner *m* cooper
Butyl-aldehyd *n* butylaldehyde **-cyclohexan** *n* butylcyclohexane **-stearat** *n* butyl stearate
Butylen *n* butylene (gas)
Butylverbindungen *f* butyl compounds
Butyraldehyd *n* butyraldehyde **-peroxyd** *n* butyraldehyde peroxide
Butyrat *n* butyrate
Butyrometer *n* butyrometer
Butz *m*, **Butze** *f*, **Butzen** *m* bunch, patch, pocket of ore

Butzen-scheibe *f* bull's-eye glass **-scheibenlinse** *f* bull's-eye lens
B-Verstärker *m* class B amplifier, quiescent push-pull
Bypass-kondensator *m* by-pass capacitor **-ventil** by-pass valve
Byssolith *n* asbestos

C

c-Ader *f* C wire, sleeve or test wire, private wire
Cadmieren *n* cadmium plating
Cadmium *n* cadmium **-band** *n* cadmium strip **-grenze** *f* cadmium cut-off **-kontinua** *pl* cadmium spectra, continuous
Cadreantenne *f* frame or loop antenna
Calan *m* (Isolierstoff) calan
Calandria Kochapparat *m* calandria pan
Calcium Silizium *n* dope (calcium silicate) (foundry)
Calcul *n* calculation
Calit *m* calite
Callier Faktor *m* Callier factor (of print contrast)
Callow Sieb *n* Callow (traveling belt) screen
Calomel *n* calomel, mercurous chloride
calorimetrisch calorimetric
Calorisation *f* calorizing (calorized steel)
Calorstat *m* thermostat
Camera (*f*) **clara** camera lucida
Camlockbefestigung *f* camlock mounting
Campane *f* bell jar
Candela *f* (Lichtstärkeeinheit) candela (cd)
Candeler *m* candle
Cannelkohle *f* cannel coal
capillaraktiv surface-active
Capronsäure *f* caproic acid
Caprylsäure *f* caprylic acid
Carbaminsäure *f* carbamic acid
Carbanilsäure *f* carbanilic acid
Carbenium *m* a type of triphenylmethyl salts
Carbid *n* carbide
Carbol-kalk *m* carbolated lime **-säure** *f* carbolic acid
Carbonathärte (Wasser) hardness due to carbonates, temperary hardness
Carbonisieranlage *f* carbonizing plant
Carbonspat *m* spathic carbonate
Carburationsapparat *m* (Vergaser) carburetter
carburieren to carburet
Carcel-brenner *m* carcel burner **-lampe** *f* carcel lamp or burner
c-Arm *m* private wiper
Carnauba-säure *f* carnaubic acid **-wachs** *n* carnauba wax
Carneol *m* carnelian
Carnotit *n* carnotite
Carotin *n* carotene
Carnot Prozeß *m* Carnot cycle
Carnotscher Kreisprozeß *m* Carnot cycle
Caron Verfahren *n* Caron process
Carreau *n* square check
cartesische Fläche Cartesian surface
Cäsium *n* cesium **-alaun** *m* cesium alum **-bedeckt** cesiated
Cäsiumchlorid *n*, **flächenzentriertes ~** face centered cesium chloride
Cäsium-chloridgitter *n* cesium-chloride-structure **-lichtbogen** *m* cesium arc **-schichten auf Wolfram** cesium films on tungsten (properties) **-silber-kathode** *f* cesium oxide-on-silver **-zelle** *f* cesium cell
Cassegrain Spiegelteleskop *n* Cassegrain reflector
Cassiopeium *n* lutetium
Catechu *n* cashew
Categorien (*f pl*) **der Bruchsteine** classes or categories of rock filling
Catkin-röhre *f* catkin valve
Cauer-Filter *n* cauer filter
C-Ausbringen *n* carbon-yield
Cazo-Prozeß *m* Cazo process (hot-pan amalgamation)
C-Barren *m* foundry ingot
C-Berge *pl* carbon refuse
C-Bürste *f* private wiper
CCIR-Norm *f* CCIR standard
CCM combined crypto machine
Cearawachs *n* Carnauba wax
Ceder *f* cedar
Celit *m* celite
Cellit *n* secondary cellulose acetate
Cellon *n* type of coating for the skin, fabric dope, artificial material similar to cellophane **-lack** *m* cellulose acetate lacquer or dope **-lampe** *f* prismatic light
Celluloid-überzug *m* celluloid-coating
Cellulose *f* wood fiber **reine ~** chemical cotton
Cellulose-azetatseide cellulose acetate rayon **-folie** *f* cellophane **-lack** *m* cellulose lacquer **-nitratseide** *f* cellulose nitrate rayon **-zahl** *f* cellulose number
Celsius centigrade **-grad** *m* degree centigrade **-skala** *f* centigrade (scale)
Centradian *n* centraradian (one-hundredth radian)
Centralrakel *n* front doctor
Cer *m* cerium **-erde** *f* cerium earth **-erz** *n* cerium ore, cerite
Ceraunograph *m* ceraunograph
Ceresin *n* ceresin, earth wax
Cer-Gehalt *m* cerium content **-Isotop** *n* cerium isotope
Cerichlorid *n* ceric chloride
Cerinstein *m* cerite
Cerioxyd *n* ceric oxide
Ceritverbindung *f* ceric compound
Cermetall *n* cerium
Cermischmetall *n* misch metal
cernieren to besiege
Cerosalz *n* cerous salt
Cerotinsäure *f* cerotic acid
Ceroverbindung *f* cerous compound
Cer-oxyd *n* cerium oxide **-oxydul** *n* cerium protoxide
Cerussit *m* cerussite, lead carbonate
Ce-stoff *m* cyanogen bromide
Cetan-wert *m* cetane number **-zahl** *f* cetane number or rating

Cetanzahlbestimmung (*f*) **im laufenden Motor** (Zündverzugsverfahren) running cetane rating **~ beim Start aus dem kalten Zustand** (Anlaßverfahren) cold cetane rating
Cetyl *n* cetyl
Cetylen *n* cetene
Cetyl-essigsäure *f* stearic acid **-säure** *f* cetylic acid, palmitic acid
Ceylongraphit *m* Ceylon (graphite) plumbago
C-förmige Schraubzwinge C clamp
C-Gestell *n* testing apparatus for all radio antennas
C-Glied *n* C network
cgs-System *n* cgs-system
Chabotte *f* anvil bed, base casting, bedplate **~ eines Dampfhammers** anvil of a steam hammer
Chagrin *n* pebble **(-leder)** *n* shagreen
chagrinieren to grain
Chagrinierrolle *f* pebbling roller
Chalcedon *m* chalcedony
Chalcopyrit *m* chalcopyrite, copper pyrites
Chalkolith *m* chalcolite
Chalkosin *m* chalcocite
Chalkotrichit *m* capillary red oxide of copper, chalcotrichite, plush copper
Chamäleon *n* chameleon mineral, potassium permanganate **-lösung** *f* potassium permanganate solution
Chamoiston *m* buff shade
Chamosit *m* chamoisite ore
Chamottestein *m* firebrick
Chancel *f* degree of fineness of sulfur on the Chancel sulfurimeter
Chandelle *f* chandelle, zoom
changierend chatoyant
Changierung *f* travers motion, iridizing
Chapelet-Ofen *m* Chapelet furnace
Charakter *m* character, peculiarity, qualification, honorary rank carrying specific seniority but not the pay **-eigenschaft** *f* characteristics
Charakterisierung *f* characterization, conferment of honorary rank carrying specific seniority but not the pay, brevet
Charakteristik *f* characteristic property, characteristic curve **~ der Röhre** grid-plate or plate-current, grid-voltage characteristic, grid-potential anode-current characteristic, transfer, mutual, or anode characteristic **~ Wellenwiderstand** characteristic impedance, surge impedance, characteristic resistance **~ der spektralen Empfindlichkeit** current-wavelength characteristic (of a photocell), color-sensitivity curve, color-response curve **fallende ~** dropping characteristic, falling characteristic **quadratische ~** square-law characteristic
charakteristisch characteristic **-e Größe der Röhre** parameter of a thermionic valve, vacuum-tube constant
Charge *f* charge, heat, batch (viscose); (Seide) *f* weighting
Chargen-betrieb *m* batch process **-dauer** *f* duration of heat **-fertigung** *f* batch production **-gang** *m* heat, heat run, smelting process **-größe** *f* batch sizes **-mischer** *m* batch mixer **-probe** *f* sample of molten metal
Chargierbühne *f* charging platform or floor
chargieren to charge, load, feed; (Seide) weight (the silk)
Chargierer *m* charging-machine operator
Chargier-kran *m* charging crane **-maschine** *f* charging machine **-mulde** *f* charging box **-schwengel** *m* balanced peel, charging peel **-vorrichtung** *f* charging appliance, tipping cradle **-zeit** *f* stand-by time (with furnace)
Charpy Rundkerbe Charpy notch
Charpyscher Pendelhammer Charpy impact-testing machine
Charpy-Schlagversuch *m* Izod-test
chartern ohne Besatzung to demise
Charterflug *m* charter flight
Chassis *n* chassis; (Foulard) color box (trough) **ausschwenkbares ~** swing-out chassis **-anschluß** *m* chassis connection **-antenne** *f* undercar antenna **-rahmen** *m* color box frame **-rolle** *f* furnisher
Chatterton-Masse *f* Chatterton's compound
Chaussee *f* causeway, highway, main road **-meile** *f* mile, as a measure (equal to 7,4 kilometers) **-walze** *f* road roller
chaussieren to macadamize
Chaussierung *f* macadam, macadamization
Chef *m* chief, principal, commander **-konstrukteur** *m* chief designer **-mathematiker** *m* chief actuary **-pilot** *m* chief pilot
Chemie *f* chemistry **-fasern** *pl* man-made fibers **-ingenieurwesen** chemical engineering
Chemigraph *m* process engraver
Chemigraphie *f* process engraving
chemigraphisch photomechanical
Chemikalien *n pl* chemicals **-fabrik** *f* chemical plant
chemikalisch chemical(ly)
Chemiker *m* chemist
Chemilumineszenz *f* chemiluminescence
chemisch chemical **~ gebunden** chemically vombined or fixed **-e Anlage** chemical plant **-er Aufbau** chemical construction **-e Bindung** chemical bond **-es Fräsen** chemical milling **-e** (Isotopen-)**Trennung** chemical separation (of isotopes) **-er Kraftstoffmotor** chemical-fuel motor, rocket motor **-es Potential** (Elektronen) chemical potential **-e Rückwandlung** chemical retransformation
chemisch rein chemically pure or clean
Chemismus *m* chemism, chemical process
Chemolumineszenz-Kontinuum *n* chemoluminescence continuum
Chemotechnik *f* chemical engineering
chemotechnisch chemotechnical
Cheralit *m* cheralite
Chiastolith *m* chiastolite
Chicle *n* chicle
Chiffonieren *n* crushing
Chiffrat *n* ciphered message
Chiffre *f* cipher, cipher code **-adresse** *f* box number **-schlüssel** *m* cipher(ing) code **-schrift** *f* cipher **-telegramm** *n* ciphered message
chiffrieren to cipher, code, encipher
Chiffrier-maschine *f* ciphering machine **-schlüssel** *m* code key **-schrift** *f* cipher writing
chiffrierte Anzeige *f* box number advertisement
Chiffriertext *m* ciphering message
Chiffrierung *f* encipherment, coding
chilenische Mühle Chilean mill
Chilesalpeter *m* Chile saltpeter, sodium nitrate, Chile niter

Chimäre *f* chimera, quest, phantom
China-rinde *f* cinchona bark, Peruvian bark **-säure** *f* quinic acid **-ton** *m* China clay, kaolin
chinesischer Gebläseofen Chinese blast furnace
Chinhydron *n* quinhydrone **-elektrode** *f* quinhydrone electrode
Chinin *n* quinine
Chinkolobwit *m* chinkolobwite
Chinolin *n* quinoline **-säure** *f* quinolinic acid
Chinon *n* quinone
Chinookwind *m* chinook
Chinopyridin *n* quinopyridine
Chinoxalin *n* quinoxaline
Chiralität *f* chirality
Chireix-gardine *f* Chireix antenna **-modulation** *f* outphasing modulation
Chirurg *m* surgeon
Chloanthit *m* chloanthite
Chlor *n* chlorine (gas) **-allyl** *n* allyl chloride **-amin** *n* chloramine **-ammonium** *n* ammonium chloride, sal ammoniac **-amyl** *n* chloroamyl, amyl chloride **-arsenik** *n* chloride of arsenic
Chlorat *n* chlorate **-ätze** *f* chlorate discharge
Chlor-äthyl *n* chloroethane, ethyl chloride **-äthyliden** *n* ethylidene chloride
Chloration *f* chlorination
Chlorationstrommel *f* chlorination barrel
Chloratsprengmittel *n* chlorate explosive
Chlorazetol *n* acetone chloride
Chlorazetophenon *n* chloracetophenone **-chlorpikrinlösung** *f* chloracetophenone solution
Chlor-benzoesäure *f* chlorobenzoic acid **-benzol** *n* chlorobenzene **-benzyl** *n* benzyl chloride **-bleichlauge** *f* sodium hypochlorite (liquor) **-bleispat** *m* phosgenite **-bromsilber** *n* silver chlorobromide, embolite **-calcium** *n* calcium chloride **-chrom** *n* chromium chloride, chromic chloride **-chrombeize** *f* chloride of chrome mordant **-chromsäure** *f* chlorochromic acid **-cyan** *n* cyanogen chloride **-echt** fast to chlorine **-eisen** *n* iron or ferric chloride **-eisenoxyd** *n* ferric chloride **-eisenoxydul** *n* ferrous chloride
chloren to chlorinate
Chlor-entwickler *m* chlorine generator **-entwicklung** *f* generation or formation of chlorine **-essigsäure** *f* chloracetic acid **-gas** *n* chlorine (gas) **-gehalt** *n* chlorinity **-hydrat** *n* chlorhydrate, hydrochloride
Chlorid *n* chloride **-lauge** *f* chloride solution **-sammler** *m* chloride storage cell **-schlacke** *f* chloride cake **-verdampfungsprozeß** *m* chloride volatilizing process
chlorieren to chlorinate
Chlorierung *f* chlorination, chloridization
chlorierungs-fähig chloridizable **-mittel** *n* chlorinating agent
chlorig chlorous **-säure** *f* chlorous acid
Chlorin *n* chlorine (gas)
Chlorit *m* chlorite, ripidolite
chloritisch chloritic
Chlorit-schiefer *m* chlorite slate **-spat** *m* spathic chlorite
Chlor-jod *m* iodine chloride, iodine monochloride **-kali** *n* potassium chloride, potassium hypochlorite **-kalium** *n* potassium chloride **-kalk** *m* chloride of lime, bleaching powder, calcium chloride, calcium hypochlorite **-kalkbleiche** *f* bleaching with calcium hypochlorite **-kalklösung** *f* bleach, bleaching liquid **-kalzium** *n* calcium chloride **-kautschuk** *m* chlorinated rubber
Chlor-knallgasexplosion *f* chlorine-oxygen-hydrogen explosion **-kobalt** *m* cobalt chloride **-kohlenoxyd** *n* phosgene (gas), carbonyl chloride **-kohlensäure** *f* chlorocarbonic acid **-kohlensäureamid** *n* carbamyl chloride **-kohlenstoff** *m* carbon chloride, carbon tetrachloride **-lauge** *f* chloride of lime, bleach **-magnesium** *n* magnesium chloride
Chlor-messer *m* chlorometer **-monoxyd** *n* chlorine monoxide **-natrium** *n* sodium chloride **-natron** *n* chloride of soda, sodium hypochlorite
Chloro-Dihydrophenarsazin *n* chloro-dihydrophenarsazine
Chlor-pikrin *n* chloropicrin **-platinsäure** *f* chloroplatinic acid **-sauerstoffbleiche** *f* chlorine-peroxide bleach **-säure** *f* chloric acid **-säureanhydrid** *n* chloric anhydride
chlorsaur-es Ammonium ammonium chlorate **-es Kali** potassium chlorate **-e Tonerde** aluminium chloride
Chlor-schwefel *m* sulfur monochloride, sulfur chloride **-silber** *n* silver chloride **-silizium** *n* silicon tetrachloride **-stickstoff** *m* nitrogen chloride **-strontium** *n* strontium chloride, muriate **-sulfonsäure** *f* chlorosulfonic acid **-trifluorid** *n* chlorine trifluoride
Chlorung von Wasser chlorination of water
Chlorür *n* protochloride, chloride **-säure** *f* chlorous acid
Chlorvinyldichlorarsin *n* lewisite
Chlor-verflüssigungsanlage *f* chlorine liquefying plant **-wasserstoff** *m* hydrochloric acid, hydrogen chloride **-wasserstoffäther** *m* ethyl chloride **-wasserstoffsäure** *f* hydrochloric acid **-wismut** *n* bismuth chloride, bismuth trichloride **-zinn** *m* stannic chloride
Cholestanol *n* cholestanol
Cholesterin *n* cholesterin
Cholin *n* choline
chopperstabilisiert chopper-stabilized
Chor *m* choir, assembly of strings (music)
Christbaum *m* Christmas tree **-beleuchtung** *f* Christmas-tree illumination
Christensen-Wähler *m* Christensen selector
Chrom *n* chromium, chrome
Chromalaun *n* chrome alum, chromium potassium sulfate **eingebettetes** ~ diluted chromium alum
Chromat *n* chromate
Chromatid *n* chromatid
Chromatidenteilung *f* chromatid break
Chromatin *n* chromatin
chromatisch chromatic **-e Abweichung, -er Fehler** chromatic aberration **-e Aberration** chromatic aberration **-e Farbabweichung** chromatic aberration **-er Schaum** chromatic soft focus or bleeding ~ **korrigiert** chromatically corrected, nonchromatic, achromatic
Chromatographie- oder Elektrophorese-Papierstreifen *m* chromatographic or electrophoresic paper strips
Chrom-azetat *n* chromium acetate **-chlorür** *n* chromous chloride **-chromat** *n* chromium chromate, chromic chromate **-eisen** *n* chromic

iron, ferrochromium, chromite **-eisenstein** *m* chrome iron ore, chromite **-eiweißkopierlösung** *f* chrome-alumen solution **-empfindlichkeit** *f* sensibility to chrome **-erz** *n* chrome ore, chromite

Chrom-fluorid *n* chromium fluoride, chromic fluoride **-fluorür** *n* chromous fluoride **-gallerte** *f* chrome gelatin **-gelatine** *f* bichromated gelatine **-gelb** *n* chrome yellow, lead chromate **-grün** *n* chrome green, chromium oxide **-haltig** chromic, chromiferous **-hydroxyd** *n* chromium hydroxide, chromic hydroxide **-hydroxydul** *n* chromus hydroxide

chromieren to sensitize chrome

Chromierungsbrühe *f* chrome tan liquor

Chromi-kaliumsulfat *n* chromic potassium sulfate **-salz** *n* chromic salt

Chromit *m* chrome iron ore, chromite

Chromi-verbindung *f* chromic compound **-zyankalium** *n* chromic potassium cyanide

Chromjodid *n* chromic iodide

Chrom-kali *n* chromate of potassium, potassium dichromate **gelbes ~** potassium chromate **rotes ~** potassium dichromate

Chrom-kalium *n* chromium-potassium **-karbid** *n* chromium carbide, chromic carbide **-leder** *n* chrome leather **-molybdänstahl** *m* chrome molybdenum steel **-molybdat** *n* chromium molybdate, chromic molybdate

Chromnickel *n* chrome nickel, Nichrome **-draht** *m* nichrome wire **-rohr** *n* nichrome tube **-stahl** *m* chrome-nickel steel

Chromo-chlorid *n* chromous chloride **-ersatzkarton** *m* chrome imitation board **-karton** *m* chromoboard **-löschkarton** *m* chromo blotting board **-oxalat** *n* chromium oxalate, chromic oxalate **-oxydchlorid** *n* chromium oxychloride, chromyl chloride **-oxyd** *n* chromium oxide, chromic oxide **-oxydhydrat** *n* chromium hydroxide, chromic hydroxide **-oxydnatron** *n* sodium chromite **-papier** *n* chromo paper **-phorelektronen** *pl* chromophoric electrons

Chromoskop *n* chromoscope, color kinescope, color (picture) tube

Chromosom *n* chromosome

Chromosomen-aberration *f* chromosome aberration **-ausfall** *m* chromosome delection **-austausch** *m* chromosome exchange **-bruch** *m* chromosome break **-teilung** *f* chromosome break

Chromosphäre *f* chromosphere

Chrom-oxydsalz *n* chromic salt **-oxydul** *n* chromous oxide **-oxydulverbindung** *f* chromous compound **-oxyfluorid** *n* chromium oxyfluoride **-ring** *m* chrome plated piston ring **-rot** *n* chrome red, red lead chromate (a dye) **-salpetersäure** *f* chromonitric acid **-salz** *n* chromium salt, chromate

Chromsäure *f* chromic acid **-anhydrid** *n* chromic anhydride **-element** *n* chromic acid cell, bichromate cell

chromsaures Ammon ammonium chromate

chromsaures Bleioxyd *n* lead chromate

Chrom-schwarz *n* chrome black **-schwefelsäure** *f* chromosulfuric acid **-siliziumstahl** *m* chromiumsilicon steel **-stahl** *m* chrome steel, chromium steel **-wolframstahl** *m* chrome-tungsten steel

Chromylchlorid *n* chromyl chloride, chromium oxychloride

Chromzyanid *n* chromium cyanide, chromic cyanide

Chronaximeter *n* chronaximeter

Chronik *f* chronicle

Chronocylograph *m* chronocylograph

chronoelektrische Registrierung chronoelectrical recording

Chronogramm *n* chronogram

Chronograph *m* chronograph

Chronoisotherme *f* chronoisotherm

Chronometer *m* chronometer, stop watch

Chronoskop *n* chronoscope

Chronotron *n* chronotron

Chrysoberyll *m* chrysoberyl

Chrysoidin *n* chrysoidine

Chrysokollerz *n* chrysocolla ore

Cicero *f* pica (print.)

Cina (abbr.) standard air as defined by Commission Internationale de Navigation Aérienne **-Atmosphärenhöhe** *f* density altitude

Cinchoninhydrochlorid *n* cinchonine hydrochloride

Cinnamylsäure *f* cinnamylic acid, cinnamic acid

Citeia (abbr.) Comité International Technique d'Experts Juridiques Aériens

Citomat *n* code for an automatic frequency-selector device

Citronensäure *f* citric acid

Clamping-Schaltung *f* clamp

Clapot *n* rope washer

Clarkeit *m* clarkeite

Clark-Element *n* (Latimer) Clark cell

c-Leitung *f* third conductor, C wire, private wire

Clerget-Divisor *m* Clerget divisor **~ Verfahren** *n* Clerget method

Cletrac-Lenkgetriebe *n* Cletrac steering mechanism

Cleveit *m* cleveite

Cliché *n* (printing) block

Clinton-Erz *n* Clinton ore, flaxseed ore

Clipper *m* clipper **~ mit Ansprechschwelle** amplitude gate

Clogston-Kabel *m* Clogston cable

Clophenkondensator *m* clophene capacitor

Cluster Integral *n* cluster integral **-Zählung** *f* cluster counting

Cm symbol of coefficient used in determining the pressure in sections

Code *m* code **~ für beschränkte Zugänglichkeit** barred code

Code-bake *f* code beacon **-markierung** *f* label coding **-name** *m* code sign **-prüfung** *f* code check

Coder *m* coder

Codewandler *m* code converter

codieren to code, (info proc.)

Codierer *m* coder

Codier-maschine *f* inscriber **-schaltung** *f* matrix encoder

codiert-e Befehlsfolge coding **-e Befehlsreihe** coding **-e Befehlszeile** coding line **-es Dezimal** coded decimal **-e Dezimalziffer** (*n*) coded decimal digit

Codierung *f* coding

Codress *n* (Spruchform) codress

Coffinit *m* coffinite

Coke *m* coke

Colby-Ofen *m* Colby furnace
Cölestinblau *n* sky blue
Collabrieren *n* collapse
collidieren to collide, foul
Collinscher Hilfspunkt auxiliary point, survey
Collodium-deckfarben *pl* nitrocellulose finishes **-papier** *n* collodium paper
Colloidale Öle *n pl* colloidal lubricants
Colloresin *n* methyl cellulose
Colloxylin *n* collodion
Colophonium *n* colophony
Colpitts-Schaltung *f* Colpitts oscillator circuit
Columbit *m* columbite
Compiler *m* compiler **~ erzeugendes Programm** compiling routine
Compobüchse *f* compo-type bush
Compound-dynamomaschine *f* compound-wound generator **-erregung** *f* compound excitation **-motor** *m* compound-wound motor **-panzerplatte** *f* compound armor plate **-stahl** *m* hardened steel **-verschluß** *m* compound shutter **-wicklung** *f* compound winding
Compton-effekt *m* Compton effect **-ionisationskammer** *f* Compton meter **-streuung** *f* Compton scattering **-verschiebung** *f* Compton shift
Compurverschluß *m* compur shutter
Conchieren *n* a tumbling treatment (in a conche) (especially in chocolate manufacture)
Condensa *f* condensa
conditionieren to condition
Conehülse *f* cone core
Conform *f* conformal survey
conglobieren to heap up, conglomerate
conphas inphase (condition), inphase coincidence
Contact-ruß *m* a contact black
Continu-breitwaschmaschine *f* continuous open width washer **-dämpfer** *m* continuous steamer
Contraplex-Mühle *f* contraplex mill (disintegrator)
Contrerakel *n* lint doctor
Conveyor *m* conveyor **-anlage** *f* conveyor machinery
conzentrisch concentric
Coolbaugh-Prozeß Coolbaugh (sulfate-roasting) process
Corazit *m* coracite
Cord-bindung *f* corduroy weave **-gewebe** *n* breaker cord strip, cord fabric **-reifen** *m* cord tire **-samt** *m* corduroy
Corioliskraft *f* coriolis force
Corona-Entladung *f* coronal discharge
Coronium-Linie *f* coronium line
Cosausdruck *m* cosine term
cosec^2-Antenne cosecant-squared antenna
Cosekans *m*, **Cosekante** *f* cosecant
Cosinus *m* cosine **-entzerrer** *m* aperture corrector **-reihe** *f* cosine series
Cosmotron *n* cosmotron
Cosynsscher Kreuztisch *m* Cosyns stage
Cotangens *m* cotangent
Cotangente *f* cotangent
Cotg cotangent α
cottonisieren to cotonize
Cottonstrumpfware full-fashioned hosiery
Cottrell-Verfahren *n* Cottrell (electrical precipitation) process
Coulomb *n* coulomb **-abstoßung** *f* coulombian repulsion **-kraft** *f* Coulomb energy **-messer** *m* coulomb meter **-meter** *m* voltameter
Coulomb-sches Gesetz Coulomb's law **-scher Potentialwall** *m* Coulomb barrier **-sche Streuung** *f* Rutherford scattering, Coulomb scattering **-sche Waage** *f* Coulomb's balance
Coulombzähler *m* coulomb meter
Coulometer *n* coulometer
Coupé *n* compartment
coupieren to weaken the coloring power
Coupüre *f* reduced print
Covellit *m* covellite
Cowper *m* Cowper stove, hot-air stove **-Coles-Methode** *f* Cowper-Coles (cold-galvanizing) method **-esse** *f* Cowper-stove chimney
„C"-Prozeß *m* C process (process for extracting toluene from coal gas)
crabbecht fast to crabbing
crabben to crab
Crackingprozeß *m* cracking process
Cresylsäure *f* cresylic acid
Cristobalitgitter *n* cristobalite lattice
Cr-Ni-Mo-Stahl *m* chrome nickel molybdenum steel
Crocus Martis *n* Crocus Martis, colcothar, red iron oxide
Crokustuch *n* crocus cloth
Crookessche Röhre *f* Crookes tube
cross-country Walzwerk cross-country rolling mill (continuous-type mill with stands arranged in two or more separate lines)
Crossing-over *m* crossing over
Croton-chloralhydrat *n* croton chloralhydrate, butyl chloralhydrate **-säure** *f* crotonic acid
C-Schirm *m* C display
C-Stoff *m* code for hydrazin hydrate and alcohol, code for a type of rocket fuel
Cumalinsäure *f* cumalic acid
Cumarinsäure *f* cumarinic acid
Cuminsäure *f* cuminic acid, cumic acid
Cumol *n* cumene, cumol
Cumulus *m* cumulus **-bildung** *f* cumulus formation
Cuno-Filter *n* Auto-Klean-Filter
Cuno-Ölfilter (*m*) **ohne Querschnittsverringerung** fullflow Cuno oil filter
Cuno-Spaltfilter *m* Cuno oil filter
Cupramafaser *f* a type of artificial wool manufactured from beech
Cupri-chlorid *n* cupric chloride **-oxyd** *n* cupric oxide
Cuprit *m* cuprite
Cupriverbindung *f* cupric compound
Cupro-chlorid *n* cuprous chloride **-jodid** *n* cuprous iodide
Cupronelement *n* copper oxide cell (elec.)
Cuprooxyd *n* cuprous oxide
Cuproxam *n* cuprammonium
Cuproxtrockengleichrichter *m* copper oxide rectifier, cuprous oxide rectifier
Curbsenden *n* curbed signaling, curbing
Curcuma *f* curcuma
Curiescher Punkt Curie point
Curit *n* curite
Curium *n* curium **-isotop** *n* curium isotope
Cuvelage *f* tubbing **gußeiserne ~** cast-iron tubbing **gußstählerne ~** cast-steel tubbing **schwimmende ~** submerged tubbing **Setzen der ~** setting of the tubbing

Cuvelage-deckel *m* cover of shaft tubbing **-zimmerung** *f* crib tubbing
Cuvette *f* trough, bulb, narrow test flume
C-Verstärker *m* class C amplifier radio
Cyan *n* cyanogen **-chlorarsin** *n* diphenylcyanarsine
Cyanamid *n* cyanamide **-natrium** *n* sodium cyanamide
Cyan-bad *n* cyanide bath **-diskrepanz** *f* cyanogen discrepancy **-eisenkalium** *n* potassium ferrocyanide **-gas** *n* cyanogen **-härtung** *f* cyaniding, cyanide hardening **-kupfer** *n* cyanide of copper
Cyanit *m* cyanite, disthene
Cyankali(um) *n* cyanide of potash
Cyanogen *n* cyanogen, cyanogen gas
cyansauer cyanate
Cyan-Sauerstoff-(Stickstoff-) **Gemische** cyanogen-oxygen(-nitrogen) mixtures
Cyan-säure *f* cyanic acid **-wasserstoffsäure** *f* hydrocyanic acid, prussic acid
Cyclohexadien *n* cyclohexadiene
Cyclohexan *n* cyclohexane
Cyclohexen *n* cyclohexene
Cycloidhöhe *f* cycloidal height
Cyclopentadien *n* cyclopentadiene
Cyclopentan *n* cyclopentane
Cyclopentano-Perhydro-Phenatren *n* cyclo-pentane-perhydro-phenathrene
Cyclopenten *n* cyclopentene
Cyclopropan *n* cyclopropane
Cyclotron *n* cyclotron (magnetic resonance accelerator using two D's and a spiral beam)
Cylpeps *n pl* short cylindrical shapes for use in ball mills
Cymol *n* cymol (methyl-1-propylbenzol)
Cypernholz *n* rosewood
Cypervitriol *m* old name for copper sulfate
Cyrtolith *m* cyrtolite
Cyrtometer *n* cyrtometer

D

Daak *m* fog
daaken to come over foggy
Dach *n* roof, dome, ceiling (aviation), shed, back, top, canopy, head, bell **gebrochenes ~** curb roof **tonnenförmiges ~** arched roof, barrel roof **zweihängiges ~** ridged roof
Dach-abfallrohr *n* downspout **-abspanngestänge** *n* roof standard, house pole **-amboß** *m* slater's anvil **-antenne** *f* roof antenna, roof-type aerial radio **-artig** rooflike, roof-shaped **-aufbau** *m* monitor part of roof **-aufsatz** *m* skylight turret **-aufsetzer** *m* skylight turret, **-aussteigluke** *f* trap door on roof **-bau** *m* roofing
Dachbedeckung-Impregniermittel *n* roof saturant
Dach-bedeckungsmaterial *n* roofing material **-begriff** *m* general concept or designation **-belag** *m* roofing **-binder** *m* roof truss or bent **-binderauflager** *n* roof truss bearing **-binderbalken** *m* tie or chief beam **-bock** *m* truss of roofing **-boden** *m* loft **-bretter** *n pl* roof boarding **-bunker** *m* overhead bunkers (single bunker near roof)
Dachdecker *m* roofer **-arbeit** *f* roofing **-ausrüstung** *f* slater's tools **-hammer** *m* slater's hammer
Dach-druck *m* top pressure (min.) **-eindeckung** *f* roofing **-falzziegel** *m* grooved roof tile **-fenster** *n* dormer window **-first** *m* ridge **-fläche** *f* superface (geol.)
dachförmig roof-shaped **-e Transportkette** roof-top or bevel-top transfer chain **-er Verbrennungsraum** penthouse combustion chamber
Dach-füße *m pl* eaves of a roof **-gaube** *f* roof cowl **-gebälk** *n* roof timber, roof beams **-gebinde** *n* roof truss **-gebirge** *n* roof, roof rock **-gehölz** *n* roof timbers **-gerüst** *n* frame of a roof **-geschoß** *n* garret story, attic **-gesimsstütze** *f* special roof bracket for subscriber's circuits, roof standard
Dach-gestänge *n* house pole, roof standard, overhouse structure **-gestein** *n* overlying rock **-haut** *f* roofing, roof sheating, roof membrane **-kantprisma** *n* pentaprism
Dachkapazität *f* top (loading) capacity **Antenne mit ~** top-loaded antenna
Dach-kehle *f* (roof) valley **-klappe** *f* folding dormer window **-kohle** *f* upper coal
Dach-latte *f* roof batten, square lath **-lattung** *f* slating, roof laths **-luke** *f* eyelet, eyelet hole, lower or dormer window, luthern, turret hatch, opening in the roof **-lukenglimmer** *m* skylight mica **-pappe** *f* tar paper or board, roofing pasteboard or felt, roll roofing **-pfanne** *f* roofing or pan tile **-pfette** *f* purlin, templet **-platte** *f* purlin **-polsterung** *f* roof pads **-prismenführung** *f* inverted guideways
Dach-rahmen *m* roof principal, purlin **-reiter** *m* ridge turret, louver turret **-rinne** *f* gutter, eaves **-rippenmesser** *n* rib-roof or ridge knife **-rippenschnitzel** *n* ridge slices **-rohre** *n pl* roof tubes **-röhre** *f* gutter, rain, or waste pipe
Dachs-bau *m* badger hole, dugout **-beil** *n* adz
Dach-schalung *f* roof boarding **-schaube** *f* straw sheaf, bundle of reed or wisp of straw for thatching, tippet **-schiefer** *m* roofing slate **-schindel** *f* shingle, clapboard, weatherboard
Dachschräge *f* tilt; (von Impuls) pulse tilt
Dach-schuh *m* roof protecting shoe **-schwelle** *f* pole plate
Dachs-haarpinsel *m* badger-hair pencil or brush
Dach-silo *m* roofed bin **-sparren** *m* rafter, spar **-spitze** *f* ridge of a roof **-sprosse** (*f*) **für Glasdächer** trellis for glass roofs
Dach-ständer *m* roof pole, roof standard **-stein** *m* roofing tile **-stube** *f* attic chamber **-stuhl** *m* roof truss or framing **-stütze** *f* roof bracket (elec.) **-stützpunkt** *m* roof support (elec.) **-träger** *m* short tubular pole affixed to walls for carrying wires on façades **-traufe** *f* eaves
Dach- und Mauerständer *m* rigid support
Dachung *f* roofing
Dach-unterzug *m* roof joists or sill **-ventilator** *m* roof ventilator **-verkleidung** *f* top timbering (min.) **-verschalung** *f* ashlaring **-verzimmerung** *f* top timbering (min.) **-vorsprung** *m* eave **-wehr** *f* bear-trap dam **-winkel** *m* maximum elevation, roof angle **-wippe** *f* porter bar **-wute** *f* side curve of roof **-ziegel** *m* (roofing) tile, shingle **-zinne** *f*

ridge piece of a house
Dackel *m* bloom, loop, lump, ingot
dadurch inasmuch, that way, in that way, thereby, by way of, by that means, through
dahingleiten to glide
dahin-rasen to rush **-schwinden** to fade
Dahmenit *n* dahmenit (explosive)
Dakeit *m* schroeckingerite
Dakryozystographie *f* dacryocystograph
daktyloskopieren to fingerprint
Dalben *f pl*, **Dallen** *m* dolphins, mooring posts, bollards
Daltonsches Gesetz Dalton's theory
Damaszenerstahl *m* damask or Damascus steel
damaszieren to damask, damascene
Damaszierung *f* damascening
Damast *m* damask, damascening **-gaze** *f* gauze with damask figures **-stahl** *m* damask, or Damascus, steel
damit so that, that, therewith, with it, with this
Damm *m* dike, dam, weir, bank, sea wall, fill, bulkhead, level, margin or narrow strip (phonograph disks), barrier; (Eisenbahn) embankment ~ **der Straße** roadway
Dammarharz *n* Dammar resin or gum
Dammarharz *n* Dammar resin, gum
Dammbalken *m* bulkhead, stop log **-verschluß** *m* dam-beam seal **-wehr** *f* stop-log dam
Damm-bruch *m* bursting of a dike **-elektrode** *f* perineal electrode
dämmen to dam, dam up, stop up, build a dam, curb, insulate
Dämmerlicht *n* dim light; dusk, twilight
Dämmerung *f* twilight, dawn, dusk
Dämmerungs-bogen *m* twilight arch **-effekt** *m* twilight effect (radio), night effect polarization error **-erscheinung** *f* night effect on direction finder **-farben** *f pl* sunrise and sunset colors **-schalter** *m* twilight switch **-schein** *m* twilight glow **-strahlen** *m pl* crepuscular rays **-zone** *f* twilight zone
Damm-falze *m pl* stop-log grooves or recesses, vertical beams of cofferdam **-fuß** *m* toe of the dam **-glätter** *m* ridge buster **-grube** *f* foundry pit **-kern** *m* core **-körper** *m* dam embankment
Dammkulturhackmaschine *f* lister cultivator ~ **mit Rädern** wheeled lister cultivator **-Schlitten** sled lister cultivator
Dammkulturpflug *m* lister plow ~ **für losen Boden** loose-ground lister plow ~ **mit Baumwoll und Maisdrill** cotton and corn lister ~ **und Maisdrill** corn lister **kombinierter** ~ **und Maisdrill** combined lister
Dämm-masse (Tamper) *f* tamper (reflector), reflector (tamper) **-platte** *f* insulating slab
Damm-riff *m* barrier reef **-rohr** *n* discharge pipe
Dämmschicht *f* insulating course, layer
Damm-schüttung *f* embankment **-schüttungsarbeiten** *pl* construction of slopes **-schutz** *m* bank defenses, protecting walls, defenses **-setzer** *m* paver, pavior
Dämmstoff *m* insulating material
Dämmstoffe *pl* aggregates
Dammstraße *f* highroad, causeway
Dämmung *f* insulation, impermeabilization, damming, diking, isolation
Dämm-wandplatte *f* insulating wall board **-wirkung** *f* insulating effect **-zahl** *f* sound insulation factor (acoust.)
Dampf *m* steam, vapor, fume, smoke, exhalation, attenuation ~ **ablassen** to let the steam off or out ~ **aufhaben** to have steam up ~ **aufmachen** to raise steam **direkter** ~ live steam ~ **einspritzen** to steam **gedrosselter** ~ throttled steam
Dampf, gesättigter ~ saturated steam **indirekter** ~ latent steam **nasser** ~ wet steam **trockener** ~ dry steam **überhitzter** ~ superheated steam, dry steam **ungesättigter** ~ surcharged steam, overheated steam
Dampf-abblaserohr *n* steam-escape pipe **-abblaseventil** *n* blow-through valve **-ablaßschlauch** *m* condensing tube **-ableitungsrohr** *n* waste-steam pipe, steam eduction pipe **-absaugung** *f* steam exhaust **-abscheider** *m* steam separator **-abschluß** *m* steam veil sealing **-absperrschieber** *m* gate-type steam-shutoff valve, parallel-slide steam stop valve, steam-slide stop valve, steam gate valve **-absperrung** *f* cutting off the steam **-absperrventil** *n* steam stop valve **-abzugsrohr** *n* steam-outlet pipe **-anlage** *f* steam installation, steam-generating plant
Dämpfanlage *f* steaming plant
Dampf-anschluß *m* steam connection **-antrieb** *m* steam drive **-armatur** *f* steam fitting **-ausgleich** *m* steam balance hole **-auspuff** *m* steam exhaust **-aussprühstation** *f* steam spraying station **-ausströmungskanal** *m* steam-exhaust port **-austritt** *m* steam vent, vapor outlet **-austrittsdruck** *m* exhaust pressure **-austrittsstutzen** *m* steam exhaust pipe **-betrieb** *m* steam power **-bildung** *f* steam generation **-blase** *f* steam or vapor bubble, steam-heated still, steam void
Dampfblasenbildung *f* formation of steam, bubbles; (in der Kraftstoffleitung) fuel vapor lock **Unterbrechung des Flüssigkeitsstromes durch** ~ vapor lock
Dampf-boden *m* jacketed bottom **-boot** *n* steamboat **-bremsventil** *n* steam-brake valve **-büchse** *f* steam chest **-chloren** *n* steam chemicking **-decke** *f* steam washing **-dicht** steam-tight or -proof, vaportight or -proof **-dichtemesser** *m* dasymeter **-dichtung** *f* steam packing **-dom** *m* steam dome, expansion tank, accumulator
Dampfdruck *m* vapor pressure or tension, steam pressure or compression **-bild** *n* steam diagram **-gleichgewicht** *n* vapor pressure equilibrium **-messer** *m* steam gauge, monometer, tensimeter **-minderventil** *n* steam-pressure reducing valve **-reduzieranlage** *f* steam-pressure reducing set
Dampfdruckregelventil *n* steam pressure reducing valve ~ **mit Ölsteuerung** oil-relay steam pressure reducing valve
Dampfdruck-regler *m* steam pressure governor **-turbine** *f* steam turbine (impulse type) **-übersetzer** *m* steam-pressure intensifier **-verminderer** *m* steam reducer **-zünder** *m* vapor-pressure igniter
Dampf-durchgangshahn *m* straightway steam cock **-düse** *f* steam nozzle
Dämpfe *m pl* vapors, steam, fumes
dampf-echt fast to steaming **-einblasedüse** *f* steam injector **-eingangskanal** *m* steam-admitting pipe
Dampfeinlaß *m* admission port, steam port or

inlet **-rohr** *n* steam-admitting pipe **-ventil** *n* steam-admission valve

Dampf-einströmungskanal *m* steam-inlet port **-eintritt** *m* steam admission or inlet **-eintrittsspannung** *f* admission pressure of steam **-elektrisiermaschine** *f* hydroelectric machine **-emulgierungszahl** *f* steam-emulsion number

dämpfen (mit Dampf behandeln) to steam; (abschwächen) damp; (Ton) deaden, muffle, subdue; (Physik) alternate; (Licht, Farbe) subdue, soften; (Flugwesen) stabilize; (Schwingungen) absorb; (löschen) quench, put out; (unterdrücken) subpress; (polstern) absorb, smother, extinguish, stew, bank (a blast furnace or ship), attenuate, evapurate, fume, smoke, dampen (silence), silence, die away, decay, mute (musical instrument) **vollständig ~** to damp out **gedämpft werden** to attenuate

Dämpfen *n* damping down, banking (a blast furnace) **~ unter Druck** pressure steaming

Dampf-entnahme *f* drawing off of steam **-entöler** *m* oil separator for steam **-entpichmaschine** *f* steam pitching device **-entwässerer** *m* steam desiccator or drier **-entwicklung** *f* steam generation **-entwicklungsverfahren** *n* steam developing process

Dampfer *m* steamship, steamer

Dämpfer *m* (Lautsprecher) baffle; (Schall) silencer, muffler; (Stoß) shock-absorber; (Flugwesen) stabilizer; (Atomphysik) moderator; (Kocher) pressure (steam) cooker, autoclave, attenuator, bumper, deafener, antihum, sourdine, damper, dashpot, steamer (steaming), mute (musical instrument) **~ für die Rollbewegung** antiroll device **dynamischer ~** dynamic torsional balancer **rotierender ~** rotary stabilizer (film feed)

Dämpfer-drähte *m pl* armor rods **-fahne** *f* damping vane **-feder** *f* damping spring **-kammer** *f* damping chamber **-wicklung** *f* amortisseur winding, damping winding

Dampf-erzeuger *m* steam generator **-erzeugung** *f* steam rasing, steam generation; (Kessel) evaporating capacity **-esel** *m* steam floor clearer **-esse** *f* chimney stalk or shaft **-expansionszerstäuber** *m* steam atomizing oil burner **-feuchtigkeit** *f* quality of vapor **-feuchtkasten** *m* steam damping box **-feuerspritze** *f* steam fire engine **-fördermaschine** *f* hauling steam engine **-form** *f* vapor phase

dampfförmig vaporous **-es Kältemittel** *n* vaporized refrigerant

dampf-frei free of vapor **-gebläse** *n* steam blast, steam blower or blowing engine **-gekühlt** steam-cooled **-geschwindigkeit** *f* steam velocity **-getriebene Hebewerke** steam driven hoist **-getrocknet** steam-dried **-glocke** *f* steam dome (hood) **-göpel** *m* steam winder **-hahn** *m* steam cock **-haltig** containing steam, humid, moist

Dampf-hammer *m* steam hammer **-hammerschmiede** *f* large-steam-forgings manufacture **-haube** *f* steaming cone or dome **-heizung** *f* steam heating **-hemd** *n* cylinder jacket, steam case **-hülle** *f* gas envelope, steam jacket, vaporous envelope or sheath, vapor shroud **-injektor** *m* steam injector **-kabel** *n* steam rig **-kanal** *m* passage for steam, steam port **-kasten** *m* steaming chamber (steam ager)

Dampfkessel *m* boiler, steam or generator boiler **-anlage** *f* boiler plant **-armaturen** *f pl* steam-boiler fittings **-bekleidung** *f* boiler casing **-blech** *n* boiler plate **-feuerung** *f* boiler firing **-füße** *m pl* boiler holder **-kohle** *f* steam coal **-siederohr** *n* boiler tube **-speisepumpe** *f* boiler feed pump

Dämpfkissen *n* driving cushion

Dampf-klappe *f* steam trap **-klärpfanne** (*f*) **mit fester Heizspirale** steam clarifier with fixed heating coil **-kochanlage** *f* steam-cooking installation **-kochkessel** *m* autoclave **-kochtopf** *m* steam digester **-kohle** *f* steam coal **-koks** *m* steam coke

Dampfkolben *m* steam piston **-liderung** *f* steam-piston packing **-packung** *f* leather gasket **-gebläse** *n* steam blowing engine

Dampfkompressions-kältemaschinen *pl* compressed vapor refrigerators **-system** *n* compressed vapor system

Dampfkraft *m* steam power **-anlage** *f* steam power plant **-werk** *n* steam power station **-zentrale** *f* central or main steam power plant

Dampf-kran *m* steam crane **-kranlöffelbagger** *m* steam-crane navvy, steam shovel **-kühlung** *f* steam-cooling system, vapor cooling **-leistung** *f* steaming capacity **-leitung** *f* steam piping, steam conduit, steam line **-luftejektor** *m* steam-jet air pump

Dampfmantel *m* annular boiler, steam jacket **mit ~ versehen** steam jacketed

Dampfmaschine *f* steam engine **~ mit rohrförmiger Kolbenstange** trunk engine **einzylindrige ~** single-cylinder steam engine

Dämpfmaschine *f* steaming machine

Dampfmaschinen-antrieb *m* steam-engine drive **-kessel** *m* steam boiler **-öl** *n* steam-engine oil

Dampf-mengenmessung *f* steam metering **-messer** *m* steam or pressure gauge, manometer, tensimeter

Dämpfmittel *n* attenuator

Dampf-motor *m* steam engine **-motormodell** *n* steam-motor model **-muldentrockner** *m* steam trough drier **-pfeife** *f* whistle (steam) **-pfeifenventil** *n* steam-whistle valve **-phase** *f* vapor phase **-pinasse** (*f*) **vom Dienst** duty steamboat **-pufferregelventil** *n* dash relief valve **-pumpe** *f* steam pump

Dampf- (oder Druckluft-)Rammbär mit einzelner Wirkung single-acting steam (or compressed air) hammer

Dampf-ramme *f* steam ram, steam pile driver **-rammwinde** *f* steam-pile-driving hoist **-raum** *m* steam space **-regulator** *m* steam governor **-reibung** *f* steam friction **-reiniger** *m* steam purifier, steam clarifier **-reinigungssieb** *m* steam strainer **-rohr** *n* steam pipe, steam tube, steam throttle **-röhrentrockner** *m* steam tube dryer **-röste** (Flachs) steam retting **-rotte** (*f*) **des Flachses** warm-water retting of flax **-rübenheber** *m* steam-driven beet lifter **-rückschlagventil** *n* steam check valve

Dampf-sack *m* vapor lock **-säge** *f* steam-powered sawmill **-sammler** *m* steam collector, steam chamber or accumulator **-sandstrahlgebläse** *n* steam-jet sandblast **-sättiger** *m* steam saturator **-schale** *f* evaporating dish or basin **-schaufel** *f* steam shovel **-schieber** *m* (steam) slide valve, steam sluice valve **-schiff** *n* steamship, steamer, steamboat **-schlange** *f* steam coil **-schmier-apparat** *m* steam lubrication apparatus, duplex **-schwarz** *n* steam black **-schwelung** *f* destructive distillation with steam **-schwitze** *f* steam sweating

Dampfspannung *f* steam or vapor tension (pressure)

Dampfspannungs-messer *m* vaporimeter **-thermometer** *n* vapor pressure thermometer

Dampf-speicher *m* steam accumulator **-speisepumpe** *f* steam injector, donkey pump **-sperre** *f* steam or vapor lock **-spirale** *f* steam coil **-spritze** *f* steam fire engine **-sprudler** *m* steam douche **-sprühe** *f*, **-sprühregen** *m* cascade **-spule** *f* steam coil **-sterilisator** *m* steam sterilizer **-stoß** *m* steam jet

Dampfstrahl *m* vapor beam, steam jet **-apparat** *m* steam injector

Dampfstrahler *m* steam ejector, steam jet

Dampfstrahl-gebläse *n* steam-jet blower, injector **-luftpumpe** *f* steam air ejector, steam-jet air pump **-luftsauger** *m* steam operated air ejector **-probe** *f* steam jet test **-pumpe** *f* steam ejector, ejector booster pump, ejector diffusion pump (mercury) **-rauchrohrreiniger** *m* steam-jet flue-cleaning apparatus **-rührgebläse** *n* steam-mixing jet

Dampfstrahlsauger und barometrische Kondensatoren vacuum jets and barometrics

Dampfstrahl-ventil *n* steam jet valve **-verdichter** *m* ejector condenser **-zerstäubung** *f* steam atomization

Dampf-straßenwalze *f* steam roller **-straßenzugmaschine** *f* street steam tractor **-strecke** *f* radius of action of steam **-strommethode** *f* streaming-vapor method **-stutzen** *m* steam dome **-sudwerk** *n* steam brewing plant **-tandemwalze** *f* tandem steam road roller

Dampftemperatur *f* steam temperature **-messer** *m* steam temperature indicator **-regelventil** *n* desuperheat control valve

Dampf-topf *m* digester, steam apparatus **-traktor** *m* steam tractor, traction engine **-trebertrocken-apparat** *m* steam draff-drying apparatus **-trecker** *m* steam tractor **-treibapparat** *m* steam intensifier **-trichter** *m* steam funnel **-triebwerk** *n* steam power plant **-trockenmaschine** *f* cylinder drying machine **-trockner** *m* steam drying apparatus **-trommel** *f* drying cylinder (steam cylinder) **-turbine** *f* steam turbine

Dampfturbinen-anlauf *m* turbine run-up **-antrieb** *m* steam turbine drive **-öl** *n* steam-turbine oil **gebläse** *n* steam turboblower **-läufer** *m* steam-turbine rotor **-prüfstand** *m* steam-turbine test bed

Dampf-überdruck *m* steam pressure above atmospheric, effective pressure as shown by the manometer **-überhitzer** *m* steam superheater **-überhitzung** *f* superheating of the steam **-umformer** *m* desuperheater **-umformventil** *n* steam converting valve **-umsteuerung** *f* steam reversing gear

Dämpfung *f* (Energie) loss; (Kernphysik) attenuation; (Schwingungskreis) damping; (Flugwesen) stabilization; (Nachlassen) slowing down, absorption, transmission loss or equivalent, cushioning, damping decrement, vibratin damping properties, leak (electronics), loss (of energy), dissipation, drop, impedance, decrement, steam processing, cushioning, internal friction, damping capacity, stray field (radio), leakage (radio), muting, muffling (acoust) **~ der Echoströme** active return loss **~ je Längeneinheit** attenuation constant, attenuation per unit length

Dämpfung, aperiodische ~ deadbeat **geometrische ~** geometrical attenuation **kilometrische ~** attenuation per kilometer of line **mechanische ~** mechanical resistance or impedance **räumliche ~** attenuation, weakening **relative ~** relative equivalent, relative efficiency **sekundäre ~** current supply loss **spezifische ~** attenuation constant **zeitliche ~** damping **zulässige ~ der Teilnehmerleitung auf der Empfangs-**(Sende-)**seite** local line receiving (sending) allowance

Dämpfung durch Abgase flame attenuation **~ der Echoströme** active return loss, echo attenuation **~ eines Schwingungskreises** flattening **gute ~ eines Spiegelgalvanometers** a well stabilized mirror galvanometer

Dämpfungsänderung mit der übertragenen Leistung net loss variation with amplitude

Dämpfungs-anzeiger(messer) *m* transmission measuring set **-arm** low-loss **-armut** *f* low losses

Dämpfungs-aufteilung zwischen 2 Teilnehmern loss allocation

Dämpfungs-ausgleich *m* attenuation equalization **-ausgleicher** *m* attenuation equalizer, equalizing network, compensating network **-behälter** *m* damping cup **-bereich** *n* attenuating band, region

Dämpfungsdekrement *n* decrement of damping, or of attenuation **scheinbares logarithmisches ~** equivalent logarithmic decrement

Dämpfungs-diode *f* (TV) damping diode **-einrichtung** *f* attenuation device **-entzerrer** *m* (line) attenuation equalizer, equalizing network, compensating network **-entzerrung** *f* attenuation equalization or correction **-exponent** *n* attenuation or damping constant **-fähigkeit** *f* damping, property, or capacity, damping power, property, or capacity **-fahne** *f* damping lug **-faktor** *m* damping coefficient or constant, decay coefficient, damping or attenuation factor **-feder** *f* equalizing spring (damping spring)

Dämpfungs-fläche *f* stabilizing surface, tail-plane stabilizer, damping surface (aviation) **-flosse** *f* tailplane stabilizer **-flügel** *m* damping vane **-frequenzkurve** *f* attenuation-frequency curve **-gang** *m* frequency response or characteristic of attenuation

Dämpfungsglied *n* attenuator, damping element, attenuator pad (elec.)

Dämpfungs-glimmer *m* anti-vibration mica, damping mica **-grad** *m* degree of damping, damping factor, damping ratio, attenuation ratio **-kennlinie** *f* characteristic curve of attenuation, damping curve (elec.)

Dämpfungs-klotz *m* damping plate **-konstante** *f* attenuation constant, attenuation per unit length, damping factor or coefficient **-kraft** *f* damping force **-kreisel** *m* damping gyro **-kurve** *f* attenuation curve

Dämpfungsleiter in Abzweigschaltung *f* ladder

attenuation

Dämpfungs-maß *n* attenuation equivalent or constant, total transmission equivalent, total attenuation, unit of attenuation (in decibels or nepers), attenuation standard **-manometer** *n* membrane gauge, surface gauge **-material** *n* attenuator

Dämpfungsmeßeinrichtung oder Dämpfungsmesser transmission measuring set

Dämpfungs-messer *m* transmission-efficiency-measuring set, attenuation-measuring device, decremeter, damping meter, over-all (toll-circuit) transmission test **-messung** *f* attenuation measurement, transmission test **-mittel** *n* sound damper **-moment** *n* damping torque, damping couple (of a deflecting instrument) **-netzwerk** *n* attenuator (network) attenuation (network)

Dämpfungs-parameter *n* damping parameter **-periode** *f* quench period **-plättchen** *n* resistance vane **-pol** *m* damping pole, attenuation peak, point of attenuation

Dämpfungs-reduktion *f* regenerative amplification, damping reduction, regeneration, gain, deattenuation **-regler** *m* damping gyro regulator, autopilot, high frequenzy attenuator, attenuation control (by hand), attenuation regulator (automatic)

Dämpfungsröhre *f* damping diode; (im Zeilenablenkkreis) damping tube

Dämpfungs-schalter *m* attenuation switch (elec.) (in autom. Abstimmsystem) muting switch **-schaltkennzeichen** *n* pad control signal **-schaltung** *f* anti-sidentone circuit **-spule** *f* damping or amortisseur coil **-streifen** *m* damping strip **-trommel** *f* drag-cup

Dämpfungs-ventil *n* damping valve **-verhältnis** *n* subsidence ratio, decrement, ratio of attenuation **-verlauf** *m* attenuation curve or characteristics, dependency of attenuation on frequency

Dämpfungsverminderung *f* regeneration, gain, improvement, regenerative amplification, damping reduction, deattenuation **erhöhte oder übertriebene ~** superregeneration

Dämpfungsvermögen *n* damping power or property

Dämpfungsverzerrung *f* distortion of amplitude, frequency, or tone **~ einer Leitung** *f* amplitude resistance

Dämpfungs-vorrichtung *f* damping device, damper, dashpot **-wahl** *f* manual control for damping signal **-wert** *m* decrement, value of damping or of attenuation **-wicklung** *f* damping or amortisseur winding **-widerstand** *m* loss resistance, damping resistance; nonreactive, effective, dissipative, or ohmic resistance, attenuator

Dämpfungs-winkel *m* phase-angle difference, loss angle **-wirkung** *f* quench action **-zahl** *f* attenuation factor, damping factor **-zeiger** *m* transmission measuring set **-zeitkonstante** *f* damping time constant **-ziffer** *f* damping constant or factor, damping or decay coefficient, attenuation coefficient **-zylinder** *m* damping cylinder

Dampf-ventil *n* vapor nozzle **-ventil** *n* steam valve **-verbrauch** *m* steam consumption **-verbrauchversuch** *m* water-rate test (turbine) **-verfahren** *n* steaming process **-verteiler** *m* steam distributor **-verteilung** *f* distribution of steam **-vulkanisation** *f* steam cure

Dampf-wagen *m* steam truck **-wäscherei** *f* steam laundry **-wassertopf** *m* steam trap

Dämpfwiderstand *m* damping resistance

Dampf-winde *f* steam winch **-wolke** *f* vapor cloud **-zähler** *m* steam meter or counter, recording manometer **-zeiger** *m* steam gauge

Dämpfzeit *f* steaming period

Dampf-zentrale *f* steam or thermal station **-zersetzung** *f* decomposition of steam **-zerstäuber** *f* steam atomizer **-zerstäubung** *f* steam atomizing **-zerstäubungsbrenner** *m* steam-atomizer burner **-ziegelei** *f* brick steam works

Dampf-zuführung *f* steam supply, steam conductor or lead-to pipe **-zulaßventil** *n* steam regulator or throttle **-zuleitungsrohr** *n* steam-supply line **-zuwagen** *m* steam tractor **-zutritt** *m* access of steam **-zylinder** *m* steam cylinder **-zylinderöl** *n* steam-cylinder oil

daneben beside, near (it); next to (it)

Danek-Beutelfilter *n* danek (bag filter)

Daniell-Element *n* Daniell's cell

Danly-Bremse *f* Danly brake **-Kupplung** *f* Danly clutch

daraufhinarbeiten to work away at it

darbieten to offer, tender, entertain (radio)

Darbietung *f* entertainment (radio, acoustic or visual), program (material), performance

Darbysche Kohlung *f* Darby's recarburization

darlegen to point out, unfold

Darlegung *f* statement, demonstration

Darmsaite *f* gut string

Darr-anlage *f* kiln plant **-bühne** *f* drying kiln

Darre *f* liquation hearth, kiln, drying room or kiln **~ mit einer Horde** one-floored kiln **mit getrennten Horden kombinierte ~** kiln combined with separated hurdles

Darre-abräumer *m* kiln-floor clearer **-gewicht** *n* kiln-dry or oven-dry weight

darren to liquate (copper), dry, kiln-dry

Darr-esel *m* mechanical floor clearer **-haus** *n* drying chamber or place **-holz** *n* kiln-dried wood **-kammer** *f* drying room **-kupfer** *n* liquated copper **-ofen** *m* kiln, drying oven, liquation hearth **-ordnung** *f* kiln regulation **-probe** *f* kiln-drying test **-sau** *f* kiln warming tub, kiln sow

D'Arsonval Galvanometer *n* moving-coil or magnet galvanometer, D'Arsonval galvanometer

darstellbar respresentable, which can be prepared

darstellen to produce, manufacture, construct, represent, decribe, prepare, display **~ (als Kurve)** to plot (a curve), graph, depict **graphisch ~** to represent graphically **schematisch ~** to skeletonize **mit starken** (schwachen) **Linien ~** to show heavy (light) **einen Wert in Abhängigkeit von einem andern ~** to plot a value against another **vektoriell ~** to represent vectorially

darstellend representing, representative **-e Beobachtung** representative observation **-e Geometrie** descriptive geometry **-er Maßstab** representative scale

Darstellung *f* manufacture, production, construction, representation, graph, description, preparation, plotting (a curve), exhibition, display (math.) **~ in auseinandergezogener Anordnung** exploded view **graphische ~** graphical representation **konkrete** ~ hardware representation (info proc.) ~ **des Raumes** realization of space **vektorielle** ~ vector representation

Darstellungs-linien *f pl* projectors **-raum** *m* space of representation **-theorie** *f* representation theory **-verfahren** *n* method of obtaining **-weise** *f* method of preparation, manner of representation, style

dartun to show

darübergelagert overlying

darunterliegend subjacent, underlying

Dasein *n* being, existence

Daten *n pl* data, facts, dates, characteristics **äußere** ~ outer orientation **innere** ~ inner orientation (camera)

Daten-bericht *m* data report **-blatt** *n* specification sheet **-erfassung** *f* data acquisition **-fluß** *m* data flow **-listen** *pl* data sheets **-sammlung** *f* data collection **-schild** *n* rating plate (on machines)

Daten-speicher *m* data logger **-steuerung** *f* programming, numerical control **-übermittlungs-Direktschaltung** *f* data collection transfer hookup **-verarbeiter** *m* data processor

Datenverarbeitung *f* data processing **mit laufender** ~ on-line data reduction **elektronische** ~ electronic data processing

Datenverarbeitungsanlage *f* sequential computer

Datenverarbeitungssystem *n* data handling system **geschlossenes** ~ integrated data processing system

Datenverschmelzung *f* file consolidation **-verteilung** *f* data distribution

datieren to date

Datierung mit Hilfe von Isotopen isotopic dating

Datum *n* date **-anzeigeruhr** *f* date-indicating watch **-grenze** *f* date line, limiting date line, date-limit line **-stempel** *m* date stamp

Datumwechsel *m*, **Linie des Datumwechsels** international date line

Daube *f* hoop, stave

Dauben-abkürzsäge *f* stave crosscut saw, stave-shortening saw **-abrichtmaschine** *f* stave-dressing machine **-auskleidung** *f* stave lining **-fügen** to joint staves

Daubenfüge-, Nut- und Federmaschine *f* stave, grooving, and tonguing machine

Daubenreflektor *m* barrel-stave reflector

Dauben- und Bodenfügemaschine *f* stave- and head-jointing machine

Dauben-zurichtmaschine *f* staving machine (for casks and barrels)

Dauer *f* duration, endurance, continuance, permanence, period ~ **des Anwachsens** time of growth ~ **des natürlichen Ausflusses** flowing life **auf die** ~ for a long time, in the long run **für die** ~ **dieses Abkommens** during the term of this agreement

Dauer-abblendung *f* continuous dimming **-abbremsung** *f* endurance or continuous test **-abfallbeseitigung** *f* permanent disposal **-abstand** *m* distance of flying on a beam **-abzug** *m* trigger for full-automatic fire **-anmeldung** *f* call booked by prearrangement **-anriß** *m* fatigue crack **-anschlag** *m* repeat typing **-anschlagssperre** *f* non-repeat action (office machines) **-anschlagssperrkreis** *m* antirepeat circuit

Dauerbeanspruchung *f* repetition of stress, fatigue loading, continuous load or stress **pulsierende** ~ repetition of dynamic stress **ruhende** ~ static loading stress

Dauer-befehl *m* standing order **-belegung** *f* permanent call **-belastbarkeit** *f* continuous loadability

Dauerbelastung *f* continuous load or charge, permanent load; (elektrische) fatigue loading; (Kessel) continuous rating

Dauer-benutzung *f* continuous service **-beschuß** *m* permanent bombardement

Dauer-betrieb *m* commercial continuous service (C.C.S.), full load, continuous operation or service, continuity of operation, continuous working, rating, or load ~ **mit gleichbleibender Belastung** continuous service, continuous duty ~ **mit periodisch veränderlicher Belastung** periodic service

Dauerbetriebs-beanspruchung *f* permanent operating pressure **-bereitschaft** *f* ready for operation

Dauerbiege-beanspruchung *f* repetition of bending stress **-festigkeit** *f* bending-stress durability, flexural fatigue strength **-maschine** *f* fatigue bending machine **-probe** *f* fatigue bending-test specimen **-prüfmaschine** *f* flexibility tester

Dauerbiege-versuch *m* fatigue bending test, repeated bending-stress test, endurance bend(ing) test, endurance transverse-stress test ~ **mit Stabumdrehung** rotating-bar fatigue test

Dauerbiegung *f* fatigue bending

Dauerbrand *m* continuous combustion **-bogenlampe** *f* long-burning arc lamp, enclosed arc lamp **-fackel** *f* long-burning torch **-herd** *m* slow-combustion cooker **-lichtbogenlampe** *f* enclosed arc lamp **-ofen** *m* slow-combustion stove

Dauerbrenner *m* permenent call, false or permenent signal, slow burning stove

Dauerbruch *m* fatigue fracture, breakdown, eleastic breakdown, endurance failure, fatigue crack or failure, repeated stress failure **-beginn** *m* begin of fatigue failure

Dauerbruchgefahr *f*, **Bereich der** ~ range of damage

Dauer-bruchgrenze *f* endurance limits **-(dreh)-moment** *n* continuous torque **-druckleistung** *f* average capacity (printing) **-echo** *n* permanent or fixed echo **-einstellung** *f* permanent set-up **-elektrode** *f* continuous electrode **-element** *n* inert cell **-entladung** *f* permanent discharge (elec), steady discharge **-entlüftung** *f* continuous air venting **-erdschluß** *m* sustained earth fault **-erwärmung** *f* continuous-duty temperature rise

Dauerexperiment *n*, **langes** ~ long-term run

Dauer-fährbetrieb *m* permanent ferrying operations **-fahrt** *f* long-distance cruise or trial, endurance trial

Dauerfestigkeit *f* fatigue limit, creep strength, limiting range of stress, fatigue strength or life, endurance limit (of stress), endure strength ~ **im Druck-schwellbereich** fatigue strength under pulsating (oscillating, fluctuating) compressive stress ~ **im Zugwechselbereich** fatigue strength of alternating tensils stresses

Dauerfestigkeits-grenze *f* endurance or fatigue limit, fatigue strength **-prüfmaschine** *f* endurence-testing machine

Dauerfestigkeits-schaubild *n* fatigue strength-diagram, diagram for effect of range of stress on fatigue strength **~ nach Gerber** Gerber's diagram (parabola) **~ nach Goodman** Goodman's diagram (for effect of range of stress)

Dauerfestigkeits-verhältnis *n* fatigue ratio

Dauer-feuer *n* continuous or sustained fire, fixed light (lighthouse), permanent light **-fluß** *m* permanent flux (telegr.)

Dauer-form *f* permanent mold, long-life mold **-formguß** *m* permanent mold casting **-formgußteil** *n* gravity casting **-formmaschine** *f* permanent molding machine **-frost** *m* permafrost **-genauigkeit** *f* sustained accuracy **-geräusch** *n* continuous noise **-geschwindigkeit** *f* maintainable speed **-gestänge** *n* permanent telephone-pole line signal **-gleichgewicht** *n* radioactive or secular equilibrium **-gleichstrom** *m* permanent direct current **-glühen** to soak **-guß** *m* gravity die casting, permanent casting

dauerhaft durable, lasting, strong, permanent, enduring, stable, fast

Dauerhaftigkeit *f* permanence, lasting quality, durability, stability, endurance **~ der Regulierung** permanence of regulation

Dauerhaltbarkeit *f* fatigue limit or strength, endurance strength, serviceability, service life, fatigue strength of large structure, fatigue durability

Dauer-implantation *f* permanent implant **-kalender** *m* perpetual calendar **Dauerkerbschlagversuch** *m* notched-bar impact-endurance test

Dauerkontakt-geber *m* permanent contactor **-schalter** *m* maintained contact push button **-schaltgerät** *n* salvo-release equipment

Dauerkoronadurchbruch *m* steady corona **Einsetzen des ~** onset of steady corona

Dauerkurzschlußstrom *m* sustained short-circuit current

Dauer-ladung *f* continuous charging (loading), trickle charge (elec.) **-last** *f* permanent load, dead load

Dauerlauf *m* continuous running, endurance test **~** (von unbestimmter Dauer) **bis zur Zerstörung eines wichtigen Motorteils** destruction test (mach.)

Dauerlauf-kondensator *m* continuous running condenser (or capacitor) **-prüfbank für Lichtmaschinen** continuous run test stand for dynamos **-wickel** *m* continuous running winding

Dauerleistung *f* endurance, lasting power, continuous output or power, normal rating, feat of endurance, cruising power; (elektr.) continuous rating **erhöhte ~** emergency cruising output (higher cruising power than normal) **erhöhte ~ für Notfälle** continued emergency power **höchste ~** maximum continuous power **höchstzulässige ~** maximum cruising power **verfügbare ~** power available for continuous cruising

Dauerleistungsgleichdruckhöhe *f* critical cruising altitude

Dauer-licht *n* steady light, light is steady-on, continuous beam of light **-linien** *f pl* permanent telephone lines **-magnet** *m* permanent magnet **-magnetisierung** *f* permanent magnetization **-magnetmaschine** *f* permanent-magnet machine **-magnetstahl** *m* permanent-magnet steel **-minus** *n* steady negative polarity (telegr.)

dauern to last, continue, endure, keep, take **länger ~ als** outlast, outlive

dauernd permanent, lasting, constant, continuous **~ einstellbar** continuously adjustable **~ gekuppelt** fixedly (permanently) connected **~ zunehmen** ever increasing (e. g. for power) **-e Formänderung oder Deformation** permanent deformation **-e Ungleichförmigkeit** droop or permanently drooping voltage characteristic (governor) **-e Ungleichförmigkeit des Reglers** governor droop characteristics **-e Verformung** *f* permanent set

Dauernennleistung *f*, **höchste ~** maximum continuous rating

Dauer-papier *n* ready sensitized paper (phot.) **-parker** *m* day parker **-plakat** *n* standard poster **-präparat** *n* permanent slide culture **-probe** *f* long-distance trial, endurance test **-prozeß** *m* duration process (in phosphorescence decay) **-prüfmaschine** *f* fatigue-testing machine

Dauer-prüfung *f* endurance, continuous, or fatigue test **-rauchpeilboje** *f* navigational smoke buoy **-registrierung** *f* long-period recording **-rekord** *m* time or endurance record, duration record **-riß** *m* fatigue crack(ing) **-schalung** *f* re-usable shuttering

Dauerschaltung *f*, **Batterie in ~** floating battery

Dauerschirmung *f*, **Lager mit ~** life-time grease lubricated bearing

Dauer-schlag *m* continuous stroke **-schlagarbeit** *f* repeated impact energy

Dauerschlagbiegefestigkeit *f* repeated-impact bending strength, repeated-transverse-stress strength

Dauerschlagbiegeversuch *m* repeated-impact bending test, fatigue bend test, repeated-transverse-stress test, flexural-impact fatigue test **~ mit Stabumdrehung** rotating-bar-impact fatigue test

Dauerschlag-festigkeit *f* fatigue impact strength, repeated-impact strength, impact-endurance test **-haltbarkeit** *f* impact-fatigue endurance **-probe** *f* continuous, fatigue-shock, or impact test **-versuch** *m* repeated-impact test, fatigue impact test **-werk** *n* repeated transverse stress, repeated-impact testing machine, continuous or fatigue-impact-test machine **-zugversuch** *m* repeated-impact tension test

Dauer-schmierlager *n* continuous lubrication bearing **-schmierung** *f* permanent lubrication **-schweißbetrieb** *m* continuous welding

Dauerschwing-beanspruchung *f* fatigue loading, alternating (cyclic) stress **-bruch** *m* fatigue (vibration), failure (fracture) **-festigkeit** *f* fatigue strength, fatigue (endurance) limit of stress

Dauerschwingung *f* continuous oscillation, phugoid motion, hunting (in airship)

Dauerschwingungs-beanspruchung *f* repetition of dynamic stress

Dauerschwingversuch *m* fatigue test

Dauer-spannung *f* continuous voltage, non-intermittent voltage **-speicher** *m* permanent storage, non-volatile storage, permanent memory **-stahlmagnet** *m* permanent steel magnet **-standbruchbelastung** *f* permanent breaking load

Dauerstandfestigkeit *f* creep (resistance) limit, limiting creep stress, (long-time) creep strenght, endurance strength, stress, or limit, fatigue strength, rigidity, resistance to creep, fatigue stress **Prüfung der ~** long-time creep test

Dauer-standversuch *m* creep or fatigue test **-stellung** *f* permanent position **-störung** *f* continuous interference, continuous disturbance

Dauerstrich *m* continuous-dash or continuous-wave signal, equisignal zone, long dash, permanent note **-sender** *m* continuous-signal transmitter (a radar jammer) **-störsender** *m* continuous-wave jammer

Dauerstrom *m* permanent current, continuous flow, persistent current **-verfahren** *n* tone-idle system **-wahl** *f* continuous tone signaling

Dauer-taste *f* all blank repeat key **-tauchversuch** *m* continuous immersion test

Dauerton *m* continuous or permanent note, tone, sound or signal, sine wave tone

Dauer-überwachung *f* permanent supervision **-verbindung** *f* night-service connection (as applied to P.B.X.'s) **-verbraucher** *m* permanent consumer

Dauerverdrehungs-probe *f* endurance-torsion-test specimen **-versuch** *m* repeated-torsion test, torsion-endurance test

Dauerversuch *m* endurance or fatigue test, vibratory or repetitive-stress test, static, dynamic, or long-duration test **~ mit pulsierender Beanspruchung** dynamic-endurance test, repeated-stress test **~ mit ruhender Beanspruchung** static-load fatigue or endurance test **~ mit wechselnder Beanspruchung** alternating-repeated-stress test

Dauerversuchsbiegeprobe *f* endurance-bending-test specimen

Dauerversuchsmaschine *f* endurance- or fatigue-testing machine, repeated-stress testing machine **~ für Drehschwingungsbeanspruchung** testing machine for repetition of torsional stress **~ für pulsierende Beanspruchung** repeated-dynamic-stress testing machine **~ für ruhende Beanspruchung** machine for static-endurance tests **~ für wechselnde Beanspruchung** endurance- or fatigue-testing machine for alternating stresses **~ für wechselnde Schlagbeanspruchung** fatigue-testing machine for alternating-impact stresses **~ für Zugbeanspruchung** repeated direct-stress or repeated-tension testing machine

Dauerversuchszugprobe *f* static-tensile-test specimen

Dauer-vorschub *m* permanent feed **-vorschuß** *m* money advances **-waren** *f pl* preserves **-wärmfestigkeit** *f* thermal endurance properties

Dauerwechsel-beanspruchung *f* prolonged alternating loading, alternating repetition of stress, cyclic fatigue loading **-festigkeit** *f* prolonged-alternating-stess strength, long-time alternating-strength stress **-schlagversuch** *m* alternating-impact test **-schlagwerk** *n* alternating-impact machine

Dauer-weltrekord *m* world's endurance record **-wert** *m* steady (state) value **-windeprobe** *f* endurance-torsion-test specimen **-wirkung** *f* lasting or permanent effect **-zugfestigkeit** *f* endurance tensile strength (of overhead lines) **-zugversuch** *m* repeated-tension test, endurance-tension test, repeated-direct-stress test **-zustand** *m* steady state, permanent state

Daumen *m* wiper shaft, thumb, cam, tappet, dog (aeronautics), cog **axial wirkender ~** face cam **versetzte ~** staggered cams

Daumen-antrieb *m* cam gear **-breite** *f* thumb's width (range estimation) **-drücker** *m* frame handle **-falle** *f* thumb latch **-form** *f* shape of cam **-hebel** *m* joystick **-kasten** *n* cam box **-mutter** *f* thumb nut **-nocke** *f* cam **-platte** *f* thumb plate

Daumen-rad *n* thumb wheel, cogwheel, sprocket (wheel) **-regel** *f* thumb rule **-scheibe** *f* cam (wheel), disk with lobes **-schraube** *f* thumb-screw, wing screw **-sprung** *f* thumb jump, thumb's width method of range determination **-steuerung** *f* cam gear **-welle** *f* camshaft, tumbler shaft, thumb shaft

Däumling *m* cam, knob, little thumb

Davit *m* davit **-backstag** *n* davit guy

Davidit *m* davidite

Davyn *m* nephelite, eleolite

Davysche Lampe safety lamp

dazugehörige Maschinenanlage *f* component machinery

dazwischengelegt interposed

Dazwischen-kunft *f* intervention **-liegend** intermediary, intervening **-schalten** to interpose (interpolate) **-sprechen** *n* interruption of speech, break-in procedure **-treten** to interfere, intercede, intervene **-tretend** intervening, mesne

D-behälter *m* pressure-tank nitrogen contained in and used on certain types of guided missiles

DBGM = **Deutsches Bundes-Gebrauchs-Muster** *f* Federal German Registered Design

DBP = **Deutsches Bundes-Patent** *f* Federal German Patent

DBPa = **Deutsches Bundes-Patent angemeldet** Federal German Patent pending

Deblockierung *f* unblocking

debouchieren to debouch

Debye-Scherrer-Ring *m* Debye-Scherrer ring or circle (powder pattern), Hull ring

Decahydronaphthalin *n* decahydronaphthalene

Decan *n* decane

Decapieren *n* pickling

dechiffrieren to decipher, decode

Dechsel *m* adz

Decibel *n* decibel (db, dB)

Deck *n* bridge (of a ship), half deck (literally projecting), floor, deck(ing) **begehbares ~** walkable deck

Deck-ablauf *m* wash or purging sirup **-abstand** *m* distance between wings (aviation) **-anruf** *m* code call **-anstrich** *m* finishing or top coat **-apparat** *m* claying apparatus **-appretur** *f* top finish **-asphaltschicht** *f* asphalt surfacing **-aufbau** *m* superstructure (navy) **-aufstrichmittel** *n* top-coating material **-ausrüstung** *f* deck equipment or gear

Deck-bad *n* covering bath **-balken** *m* deck-beam **-band** *n* (Turbine) shroud band **-bandrolle** *f* cover belt holding roller **-bewegung** *f* covering motion

Deckblatt *n* supplementary cover or base sheet, wrapper (cigar), veneer **durchsichtiges ~** transparent cover sheet (radio)

Deckblech *n* cover sheet

Decke *f* (Oberfläche) surface; (Zimmer ~) ceiling; (Hülle) envelope; (Überzug) lining, cover, hood, blanket, tarpaulin, roof (gallery, dugout), tire show, tire cover, coat, skull, covering, integument, mat, slab, nappe, rug, cleansing (sugar), washing, belly (string instrument) ~ **der Arbeitskammer** ceiling of caisson working chamber **an der ~ montiert** motor mounted overhead **blinde ~** inserted ceiling **gerippte ~** groined or ribbed ceiling

Deckel *m* filler cap (press), roof (furnace), cover, lid, bonnet, cap, shutter, top, apron (artil.) ~ **mit Gewinde** threaded cap ~ **mit Scharnieren** hinged cover **abnehmbarer ~** removable cover

Deckel-anschlag *m* cover buffer **-antrieb** *m* flat drive **-aufleger** *m* lid layer **-auflegevorrichtung** arrangement for delivering the lids (to the churns) **-ausrüstung** *f* cover equipment **-elektrode** *f* (metallic) counter electrode (at the rectifying junction) **flug** *m* top fly

Deckel-gewicht *n* tympan weight **-gleitfläche** *f* flat **-halter** (Federträger) cap holder (spring holder) **-hebel** *m* top lever **-hut** *m* top disc **-knauf** *m* lid knob **-lager** *n* pedestal bearing

deckeln to provide with lid or cover

Deckel-öler *m* lid oil cup **-platte** *f* cover plate **-presse** *f* arming press **-rahmen** *m* frame for manhole cover, cap frame **-rand** *m* cover edge **-raste** *f* lid arrester (tape rec.) **-riegel** *m* cover-plate catch **-riemen** *m* cover strap **-ring** (Scheibenfassung) lens socket (rim) **-satinage** *f* board glazed or glazing (paper mfg.)

Deckel-schieber *m* cover valve **-schleifvorrichtung** *f* flat grinding arrangement **-schmiergefäß** *n* lubricator for top head **-schraube** *f* cover bolt or screw cap screw **-sperre** *f* cover-plate lock **-stiftschraube** *f* cover stud **-stuhl** *m* gallows (print.) **-teller** *m* top disc

Deckelverriegelung *f* lid catch ~ **der Schleuder** cover lock of the centrifuge

Deckel-verschluß *m* lid-locking device **-verschraubung** *f* head bolting, cover joint **-wulst** *m* cover beading **-zapfen** *m* cover pivot

decken cover, protect **sich ~ mit** to cover oneself with, coincide with (geom.) **sich nicht ~** to differ, diverge **sich teilweise ~** to overlap

Decken *n* claying, bottoming, washing, covering, purging (sugar) **-balken** *m* overhead beam **-behandlung** *f* treatment of ceilings **-bürste** *f* ceiling brush

deckend opaque (color) **-e Farbe** mass color **-es Pigment** hiding pigment

Decken-druckmaschine *f* blanket printing machine **-durchführung** *f* ceiling duct **-einbaumaterial** *n* (Straße) surfacing material **-fächer** *m* ceiling fan **-fassung** *f* ceiling-lamp holder **-fertiger** *m* road finisher, finishing machine **-fühler** *m* radiation detector

Decken-gewölbe *n* roof arch, arched roof **-gurt** *m* surcingle (harness) **-heizung** *f* radiant heating, panel heating, ceiling panel heating **-hohlraum** *m* ceiling void **-hohlstein** *m* hollow filler tile

Decken-kühlsystem *n* ceiling type coil **-lampe** *f* interior light, roof-light, dome light **-laufkatze** *f* overhead trolley **-laufkran** *m* ceiling crab **-leiste** *f* covering strip **-leuchte** *f* ceiling light or lamp, roof light

Decken-licht *n* skylight, dome light, tonneau light **-lichtspiegler** *m* ceiling reflector **-mietapparat** *m* crown-plate riveting apparatus **-oberlicht** *n* skylight **-projektor** *m* ceiling projector (to determine cloud height) **-putz** *m* ceiling plaster(ing) **-schaden** *m* (Straße) pavement distress **-schalung** *f* floor slab form **-schicht** *f* upper layer **-schiene** *f* monorail **-sinkkasten** *m* ceiling sink water trap

Decken-stärke *f* thickness of roof, strength of roof **-strahlungsheizung** *f* overhead radiation heating system **-strich** (beim Lederlackieren) daub **-stück** *n* top sill of frame **-träger** *m* top fixing bracket, roof beam, girder, I beam **-transmission** *f* overhead transmission or shafting **-transport** *m* overhead transportation **-ventilator** *m* ceiling ventilator **-verteiler** *m* ceiling spreader **-vorgelege** *n* overhead transmission gear, countershaft for ceiling suspension **-zeug** *n* shaggy coverlet, rough covering

Decker *m* tickler (textiles) **-druck** *m* blotch print

deckfähig (Lack) of good covering power

Deck-fähigkeit *f* opaqueness (color), hiding or covering power (distinction not always precise), coverage, covering capacity **-fähigkeitsmesser** *m* cryptometer **-faltengebirge** *n* mountains formed of overthrust or recumbent folds **-farbe** *f* body color, opaque pigment, opaque ink (color) **-farbenzurichtung** *f* dressing with pigment finishes

Deck-fenster *n* skylight **-firnis** *m* protecting varnish **-fläche** *f* top surface or area, lap or cover of slide valve **-flüssigkeit** *f* wash liquor **-gebirge** *n* overburden (min.), roof rock, overlying rocks **-geschütz** *n* deck gun

Deckglas *n* glass slip, cover glass, lamp cap, glass cover, skylight ~ **einer Linse** anterior surface of a lens

Deckgläschen *n* cover glass (of microscope)

Deckglasdicke *f* coverslip thickness

Deckglastaster *m* cover-glass gauge

Deck-grün *n* Paris green **-haus** *n* deckhouse **-hilfsmaschinen** *pl* deck auxiliaries **-hütchen** *n* capsule (explosives) **-kalk** *m* burnt gypsum

Deck-karte *f* multiple deck card **-kette** *f* covering warp, narrowing chain **-kläre** *f*, **-klärsel** *n* wash liquor, covering liquor **-kraft** *n* hiding, concealing, or covering power (of paints), coverage, density (phot.), opacity, coating properties **-kraftmesser** *m* cryptometer **-lack** *m* coating laquer (for outside painting) **-ladung** *f* deck cargo **-landeflugzeug** *n* deck-landing plane (navy), carrier-borne aircraft

Deck-leiste *f* cornice mold, cover bar, rib flange, rod or triangle covering a joint **-licht** *n* skylight **-linse** *f* lamp cap, jewel **-lochkarte** *f* deck card **-lohe** *f* heading **-maschine** *f* tickler machine (textiles) **-matte** *f* mattress pegged to the ground **-mittel** *n* covering material, resist, protective coat, ground

Deck-name *m* trade, code, or cover name, pseudonym, code word **-namenverzeichnis** *n* list of code names **-operation** *f* symmetry operations (of the lattice), covering operation (X-ray practice)

Deckpapp *m* resist paste, reserve

Deckpappe *f*, **geölte ~** oiled board

Deck-pappdruck *m* resist printing **-peilung** *f* leading line, transit or alignment bearing **-plättchen** *n* cover slides **-platte** *f* cover (plate), top plate, coping, adjustment plate **-plattenbelag** *m* paving **-quader** *n* coping, ashlar (dressed), stone coping **-rahmen** *m* manhole frame **-raupe** *f* top layer of a weld **-rechen** *m* sheet smoother **-riegel** *m* cover-plate latch **-ring** *m* hub ring (rotor), bottom ring

Decksaufklärer *m* sweeper

Deckschaufel *f* folding tool

Deckscheibe *f* (Kompr.) blade end, blade tips, plate, cover plate, cover washer

Deckschicht *f* surface film, overburden (U.S.), top coating (lacquer), surface layer, top stratum, topsoil, protective layer, surface formation **Stärke der ~** thickness of overburden (min.)

Deck-schiene *f* cover-rail **-schleuder** *m* centrifuge for washing sugar **-schwelle** *f* cap, capping, capping piece, head beam **-sirup** *m* wash sirup, wash, covering sirup **-span** *m* veneer **-stein** *m* coping

Deckung *f* cover, corering, shelter, protection, guard (fencing), mask, concealment, coincidence, registry, congruence (geom.), intensity or coverage (optics), stereoscopic contact (in range finder), registration (TV), opaqueness (color) **~ der beiden Leuchtfelder** coincidence of the two fields of illumination **zur ~ bringen** to bring coincidence

Deckungs-aviso *n* reimbursement advice **-fehler** *m* compensation error **-kapital** *n* policy reserve, cover(age) **-material** *n* roofing material **-rückstellungssoll** *n* reserve for cover (place to reserve) **-spiegel** *m* trench periscope **-stärke** *f* thickness or strenght of cover

Deckungszusage, vorläufige ~ interim cover note

Deckungs-winkel *m* minimum elevation, angle of minimum elevation or of clearance **-winkelmesser** *m* minimum-range clinometer, site-to-mask clinometer, angle-of-sight instrument

Deck-vermögen effective coverage, hiding power, covering ability **-vorrichtung** *f* device for narrowing (textiles), washing device (sugar) **-walze** *f* surface roller (hydr.), standing wave, inking roller **-weiß** *n* zinc white, white lead **-weißfarben** *f pl* (Lack) oil paints produced with the assistance of white pigments **-werk** *n* blinds (fort.), mattress pegged to the ground **-winkel** *m* splice angle **-ziegel** *m* capping brick, gutter tile

decodieren to decode

Decodierschaltung *f* decoding circuit, function circuit

Decodierung *f* code translation

Deemphase *f* de-emphasis

Defekation *f* clarifying, clearing

defekt defective

Defekt *m* breakdown failure, imperfection **-bogen** *m* faulty sheet

Defektelektron *n* electron vacancy, hole (in electron valence band), (positive) hole

Defektelektronen *n pl* (Löcher) positive holes, deficit electrons **-leitung** *f* hold conduction (trans.)

Defektenkasten *m* font-case

Defekt-(halb)leiter *m* (Mangelleiter) deficit conductor, defect conductor, p-type conductor **-halbleitung** *f* defect conduction, conduction by holes, p-type conduction **-leiter** *m* p-type semiconductor **-leitung** *f* (Transistoren) conductivity by holes

Defensive *f* defensive

definierter (Kristall-)Gitterreflex *m* selected (crystal) lattice reflex

Definition *f* definition

Definitions-bereich *m* domain of definition **-gemäß** by definition **-gleichung** *f* defining or definition equation

deflagrieren to deflagrate

Deflektor *m* deflector

defokussierende Phaseneffekte defocussing phase effect

Defokussierung *f* defocussing **~ infolge Ablenkung** deflection defocussing **~ durch Raumladung** space-charge debunching

Defokusstrich-Verfahren *n* defocus-dash mode

Deformation *f* strain composition, distortion, deformation, strain, stress, change of form **ebene ~** plane strain **~ einer Fläche in sich** deformation of a surface into itself

Deformations-bänder *pl* deformation bands **energie** *f* strain energy **-geschwindigkeit** *f* rate of strain **-geschwindigkeitstensor** *m* rate-of-deformation tensor **-maß** *n* measure of deformation **-mechanismus** *m* mechanism of deformation **-messer** *m* extensometer **-messung** *f* strain measurement

Deformations-tensor *m* deformation or strain tensor **-theorie** *f* strain theory **-verteilung** *f* strain-distribution **-widerstand** *m* resistance to deformation

Deformierbarkeit *f* deformability (of nuclei)

deformieren to deform, distort, strain, lose shape

deformiert-e Fläche deformed surface, figured surface **-es Okular** eyepiece with aspherica surface

Deformierung *f* deformation, strain

Deformierungsenergie bei Spaltung deformation energy of fission

degagieren to relieve

degaussieren to degauss

Degenerierung *f* degeneration

Degenrohr *n* telescopic pipe

Degorgieranlage *f* disgorging plant

Degradation *f* degradation, demotion

degradieren to break, reduce in rank

degraissieren to degrease

Degras *n* degras, stuff

degressive Abschreibung (im Sinne von Wertminderung) diminishing value

degummierecht fast to boiling off

degummieren (Seide) to degum

dehnbar ductile, elastic, extensible, flexible, expansible, dilatable, malleable, tensible **~ machen** to ductilize (wire) **-e Böden** dilative (dilatable) soil

Dehnbarkeit *f* ductility, elasticity, extensibility, flexibility, expansibility, dilatability, malleability

Dehnbarkeitsmesser *m* ductilimeter, dilatometer, extensometer

Dehnbereich *m* elongation portion

dehnen to extend, elongate, stretch, stress, rack,

expand, strain **sich ~** to expand
Dehner *m* expander
Dehn-festigkeit *f* tensile strength **-fuge** *f* expansion joint **-geschwindigkeit** *f* creep rate **-grenze** *f* (bei hochfesten Stählen) yield strength **-kraft** *f* power of expansion **-maß** *n* strain magnitude, modulus of elasticity **-schaftsdurchmesser** *m* minimum body diameter **-schraube** *f* necked-down bolt **-steife** *f* modulus or coefficient of elasticity **-streifenbrücke** *f* strain gauge bridge
Dehnung *f* elongation, extension, expansion, dilation, tension, stretch(ing), stress, elasticity, strain(ing), plastic flow **bleibende ~** permanent extension or set **elastische ~** elastic elongation, stretch **~ von Drähten** elongation of wires
Dehnungs-ausgleicher *m* bellows **-fähigkeit** *f* elasticity, extensibility, flexibility, expansibility, dilatability **-faktor** *m* stretch factor, factor of expansion **-fuge** *f* expansion joint **-geschwindigkeit** *f* strain rate, strain velocity, elongation speed **-grenze** *f* ultimate strength, elastic limit
Dehnungs-koeffizient *m* modulus of extension **-körper** *m* expansion joint **-kraft** *f* force of expansion **-kurve** *f* strain curve
Dehnungs-länge *f* linear extension **-linie** *f* stress-strain curve, strain curve **-meßbrücke** *f* strain bridge
Dehnungsmesser *m* extension indicator, tensiometer, extensometer, strain-measuring instrument, strain gauge, dilatometer, expansion or elongation meter, ductilimeter **~ mit schwingenden Saiten** vibrating string extensometers
Dehnungsmeßlineal *n* elongation ruler
Dehnungsmeßstreifen *m* resistive wire strain, wire strain gauge
Dehnungsmeßstreifen-beschleunigungsmesser *m* strain gauge accelerometer (gyro) **-rosette** *f* strain gauge rosette
Dehnungs-meßtechnik *f* strain measurement technics **-meßuhr** *f* elongation dial indicator **-messung** *f* strain control
Dehnungsmessungen bei Flüssiggastankwagen tests of the liquid gas vehicle
Dehnungs-modul(us) *m* modulus of extension or of elasticity
Dehnungs- oder Dilatationsfuge *f* expansion joint
Dehnungs-prüfung *f* elongation test **-ring** *m* expansion seat ring **-riß** *m* expansion crack **-schiene** *f* expansion strip **-schlitz** *m* slip joint **-schwingung** *f* longitudinal or extensional vibration **-spannung** *f* tensile stress or strain
Dehnung-Spannung-Verhältnis *n* stress-strain ratio
Dehnungsstück *n* expansion piece
Dehnungs-verlauf *m* progress of elongation **-vermögen** *n* ductility **-wärme** *f* heat of elastic extension **-welle** *f* dilational wave, extensional wave **-wert** *m* elongation value **-zahl** *f* strain coefficient (reciprocal of modulus of elasticity), coefficient of elongation **-zeigerapparat** *m* elongation indicator
Dehydratisierung *f* dehydration
Dehydrenium-Farbstoffe *m pl* a class of xanthenium or pyrenium dyes (carbenium salts) made by dehydrogenation
dehydrieren to dehydrate, dehydrogenize
Dehydrierung *f* dehydrogenation, dehydration **~ von Kohlenwasserstoffen durch H- und D-Atome** dehydration of hydrocarbons by H and D atoms
Dehydrocholesterin *n* dehydro cholesterol
Dehydrogenisierungskatalyse *f* dehydrogenizing catalysis
Deich *m* bank, dike, levee, embankment, dam **~ oder Dammböschung** slope of an embankment or dike
Deich-bruch *m* breach of a dike, failing or breaking of a dike or embankment **-fuß** *m* toe of a dike or slope, riverside toe of a dike **-kappe** *f* summit or top of a dike **-krone** *f* top of a dike or slope, crest
Deichsel *f* center pole (wagon), wagon shaft, pole **~ für Anhänger** twobar **kombinierte Ein- und Zweispännerdeichsel** combination thill and pole (wagon)
Deichsel-ausgleichvorrichtung *f* adjustable pole support **-bolzen** *m* pole pin (wagon) **-einrichtungen** *f pl* tongue attachment (wagon) **-kette** *f* pole chain (wagon) **-kopf** *m* pole end (wagon) **-rolle** *f* castor wheel (wagon) **-schlepp** *m* pole tow (wagon) **-stumpf** *m* stub pole (wagon) **-stütze** *f* pole prop (wagon), two bar support **-träger** *m* castor wheel (wagon)
Deichsiel *n* overflow of dike
D-Einfluß (Vorhalt) derivative action, rate action (in controller) **~ Koeffizient** *m* derivative action coefficient
Deisterherd *m* Deister table
dejustiert out of adjustment
Dejustierung *f* disadjustment **~ gegenüber der optischen, mechanischen oder magnetischen Achse** loss of boresight
Dekade *f* decade, level
Dekaden-relais *n* group relay **-rheostat** *m* decimal rheostat **-stufe** *f* decade stage **-teiler** *m* decade divider **-untersetzer** *m* scale of ten circuit **-vielfach** *n* level multiple **-widerstand** *m* decade resistance box, decimal resistance **-zähleinrichtung** *f* decade scaler
Dekadenzähler *m* decade counter **addierender und subtrahierender ~** reversible decade counter
Dekaden-zählröhre *f* decade counter tube **-zuschlag** *m* add carry (for decade counting)
dekadisch, ~ einstellbarer Steuervorsatz crystal-governed drive unit **-e Darstellungsweise** decimal notation **-e Logarithmen** common logarithms **-er Untersetzer** decade scaler
Dekagramm *n* decagram
Dekaleszenz *f* decalescence
Dekameter *m n* decameter, dielectrometer **-wellen** *pl* decametric waves
Dekantierapparat *m* decantation apparatus
dekantieren to decant, levigate
Dekantieren *n* decantation, levigation
Dekantier-gefäß *n* decanter **-glas** *n* decanting glass **-topf** *m* decanting jar **-zylinder** *m* decanting cylinder **-zentrifuge** *f* decanting centrifuge **-zylinder** *m* decanting cylinder
dekapieren to pickle
dekapierte Bleche pickled sheets
dekarbonisieren to decarbonize, decarburize
Dekare *f* decare
Dekatier-anstalt *f* sponging establishment **-apparat** *m* steaming apparatus
dekatieren to hot-press (cloth), steam, sponge,

shrink, decatize

Dekatier-falte *f* decatizing mark **-kalander** *m* steaming calender

Dekatiermaschine *f* shrinking machine

Dekatierwickelmaschine (*f*) **zum Aufwickeln der Stoffe mit Zwischenläufertuch** batching machine for the decatizer for batching of goods with wrapper

Dekatron *n* decatron

dekaturecht fast to decatizing

Deklination *f* declination (of the compass), magnetic variation

Deklinations-getriebe *n* declination gear **-kreis** *m* declination circle **-linie** *f* line of dip **-messer** *m* declinometer **-nadel** *f* declinometer **-parallelen** *f pl* parallels of declination **-tiden** *pl* declination tides **-winkel** *m* angle of declination

Deklinatorium *n* declination compass

Dekoder *m* decoder

Dekohärer *m* tapper, decoherer

Dekoktionsverfahren *n* decoction method

Dekompressions-hebel *m* decompressor **-einrichtung** *f* half-compression device **-nocken** *m* half-compression or decompression cam

dekonzentriert defocused, dispersed, out of focus, debunched

Dekopiersäge *f* jig saw

Dekor *n* still, design; scenery (studio)

Dekorations-platte *f* spandrel **-schild** *n* trim **-stoffe** *pl* furnishing fabrics

Dekors *pl* properties

Dekrement *n* damping decrement, decrement **scheinbares logarithmisches ~** equivalent logarithmic decrement

Dekrementmesser *m*, **Dekremeter** *n* decremeter, attenuation-measuring device

Dekupier-maschine *f* nibbling machine **-säge** *f* nibbling saw, scroll saw

Delco-Zündung *f* Delco ignition system

Delfter Porzellan *n* delftware

Delle *f* dent depression, dip in a curve

Delorenzit *m* delorenzite

Delta-anpassung *f* Delta-matching **-Antenne** Delta-matched impedance antenna, Y-antenna **-flügel** *m* delta wing

deltaförmig delta shaped

Deltafunktion *f* delta function **Ableitung der ~** delta function derivative

Delta-metall *n* delta metal (a brass alloy) **-papier** *n* gelatin chloride paper **-rauschen** *n* delta noise **-schaltung** *f* delta connection, mesh connection **-symbol** *n* delta **-verfahren** *n* toe negative method (phot.)

Deltoid *n* deltoid (math.)

Demagnetisierungs-faktor *m* demagnetizing factor

Dematerialisation *f* dematerialization

Demodulation *f* detection, rectification, demodulation

Demodulationseinrichtung *f* decoding cabinet

Demodulator *m* demodulator, translating circuit **gleichlaufender ~** synchronous detector (TV)

demodulieren to rectify, demodulate

Demolierung *f* demolition

Demonstration *f* demonstration, feint, show **-okular** *n* tutor eyepiece

demonstrieren to demonstrate

Demontage *f* dismantling, disassembly, demounting

demontieren to dismount, dismantle, disassemble, take apart, strip, undo, break up or down, knock down

demontiert knocked down

denaturieren to denature, denaturize

denaturierter Alkohol methylated spirit

Denaturierung *f* denaturation

Denaturierungsmittel *n* denaturant, denaturizing agent

Dendrit *m* dendrite, dendritic or fir crystal, crystallite, arborescent, treelike, or fern-leaf crystal

Dendritenverästelung *f* branching dendrites

dendritisch dendritic, arborescent

Dengel-amboß *m* scythe anvil **-bahn** *f* beat of a scythe **-gerät** *n* scythe-sharpening appliance **-hammer** *m* scythe hammer

dengeln, die Sense ~ to sharpen a scythe by hammering

Denier *n* count (silk and art silk)

Denitrieranlage *f* denitrating plant

Denitrierung *f* denitration

Denkmal *n* monument, bench mark

Densimeter *n* densimeter

densimetrische Methode densimetric method

Densität *f* density

Densitometer *n* density meter, densitometer

Deoxidation *f* deoxidation

Deperdussin Steuerung dep control (deperdussin) (wheel control, aviation)

Depesche *f* telegram, dispatch

Depeschen-flugzeug *n* dispatch carrier (airplane) **-schlüssel** *m* telegraphic ciphers, code

depeschieren to telegraph, cable, wire

Dephlegmator *m* dephlegmator, water separator, fractionating column

Deplacement *n* displacement (navy) **-schwerpunkt** *m* center of buoyancy

Deplattung *f* fuse cap

Depolarisation *f* depolarization

Depolarisationsgrad *m* degree of depolarization, depolarization factor

Depolarisator *m* depolarizer

depolarisieren to depolarize

Depositen-kasse *f* deposit department, trust money **-konto** *n* deposit account **-schein** *m* deposit receipt, bill of deposit

Depositum *n* deposit

Depot *n* deposit, depot, dump, warehouse, storehouse **-schiff** *n* storeship, harbor ship **-schiffsverband** *m* train (navy)

Depression *f* depression

Depressions-bahn *f* path or track of the depression **-entfernungsmesser** *m* depression telemeter **-gewölk** *n* depression clouds **-kern** *n* core of depression **-winkel** *m* dip (horizon) **-zentrum** *n* center of the low or depression **-zone** *f* suction zone, zone of negative pressure

Deputat-holz *n* wood granted free of charge **-kohle** *f* supply of coal free to miners

derb massive, rough, solid, compact, dense, strong, firm, sturdy **-gehalt** *m* actual volume

Derbheit *f* ruggedness, robustness, solidity, strength

Derb-holz *n* close-grained wood **-stückig** lumpy, large-sized

Derivat *n* derivative

Derivation *f* drift (artil.)
derivieren to derive
Derivograph *m* drift recorder, recording driftmeter
Derrick-abspannung *f* derrick rigging **-kran mit Ankerseilen** derrick supported by guys
Desaggregation *f* disintegration
Desakkomodation *f*, **zeitliche ~** magnetic aging
Desaktivierung *f* deactivation
desarsenizieren to remove arsenic
desaxierte Kurbelwelle offset crankshaft
desensibilisieren to make insensitive
desensibilisierende Farbe desensitizing dye
Designation *f* designation, assignment to a post
Desinfektion *f* disinfection
Desinfektions-kammer *f* disinfecting chamber **-mittel** *n* deodorant, disinfectant
desinfizieren to disinfect
desinfizierend deodorant
Desintegrator *m* disintegrator, cage mill
desinteressieren, sich ~ to stand aloof
Desodorieranlagen *f pl* deodorizers
desodorisieren to deodorize
Desorption *f* desorption
Desoxydation *f* deoxidation
Desoxydations-mittel *n* deoxidant, deoxidizer, deoxidizing agent **-schlacke** *f* deoxidizing slag, deoxidizing flux **-wirkung** *f* deoxidizing action
desoxydieren to deoxidize
Dessin *n* design, pattern
Dessinateur *m* designer
Dessindruck *m* pattern printing
Dessiniermaschine *f* punching machine
dessiniertes Gewebe fancy cloth
Dessinierwalzwerk *n* Dessinier rolling mill
Dessin-maschine *f* figuring machine **-walze** *f* engraving roller
Destillat *n* distillate **~ für Maschinenreinigung** engine distillate
Destillat-eis *n* crystal(line) ice
Destillateur *m* distiller
Destillatgewinnung *f* recovery of distillate
Destillation *f* distillation, carbonization (by-products preparation) **~ mit Wasserdampf** steam distillation **stetige ~** continuous distillation
Destillations-anlage *f* distilling plant **-benzin** *n* straight-run gasoline **-bereich** *m* distillation range **-gas** *n* by-product or coke-oven gas **-gefäß** *n* distilling vessel **-kokerei** *f* by-product coke-oven plant or practice, by-product coking **-kolben** *m* distilling flask **-ofen** *m* distilling furnace, by-product coke oven **-probe** *f* distillation test **-produkt** overhead product **-rohr** *n* distillation or distilling tube **-rückstand** *m* distillation residue, bottom settlings or sediment, tailings
Destillat-sammelgefäß *n* run-down drum or tank **-überlappung** *f* distillation overlap
Destillier-apparat *m* distilling apparatus, still, distiller, distilling plant **-aufsatz** *m* fractionating column, ball-top attachment **-bar** distillable **-batterien** *pl* distilling batteries **-betrieb** *m* refinery **-blase** *f* distilling vessel, retort, still
destillieren to distill
Destillier-filter *m* distilling filter **-gefäß** *n* distilling vessel **-kessel** *m* still **-kolben** *m* alembic, distilling retort **-ofen** *m* distilling furnace **-säule** *f* column still, distillation column
destilliert distilled
Destillierung *f* distillation
destruktiv-er Betrieb destructive mode **-es Lesen** destructive reading or readout
Detacheur *m* stain remover
detachieren to detach
Detachiermittel *n* spot removing agent
Detachur *f* spotting
Detailkonstrukteur *m* draftsman
Detailkontrast-verringerung *f* reduced detail contrast
Detaillieren *n* detail drawing
detailreiches Bild picture rich in detail and contrasts
Detail-skizze *f* part drawing **-wiedergabe** *f* detail rendition (TV) **-zeichenpapier** *n* tracing paper, transparent drawing paper **-zeichnung** *f* part or detail drawing
Detektion *f* detection
Detektor *m* detector, demodulator, responder **elektrolytischer ~** electrolytic detector or responder **erster ~** first detector, heterodyne, conversion, or radio-frequency detector **linearer ~** linear detector or rectifier, straight-line detector **quadratischer ~** square-law detector or rectifier **quantitativ arbeitender ~** integrating detector **zweiter ~** second or audio detector
Detektor-apparat *m* detector receiver **-arbeitsspannung** *f* detector operating current **-blende** *f* detector aperture
Detektorenempfänger *m* detector or crystal receiver (radio), thermionic valve, galena (etc.) receiver
Detektor-fernhörerkreis *m* detector-phone circuit **-gerät** *n* detector receiving set **-gesetz** *n* detector law **-gitter** *n* detecting grating **-kreis** *m* detector circuit **-röhre** *f* detector valve or tube, rectifying tube, valve, or audion **-schaltung** *f* detector circuit **-wirkung** *f* detector or detecting action
Determinante *f* determinant (math.)
Determinantensatz *m* determinant theorem
determinierende Gleichung indicial equation
Detonation *f* detonation, explosion **~ unter Einschluß** enclosed detonation (grenades or underwater explosions)
Detonations-aufnahmen *f pl* detonation photographs **-drucke** *m pl* detonation pressures, blast pressure **-geschwindigkeit** *f* detonation velocity **-grenzen** *f pl* detonation limits **-kapsel** *f* detonating tube or fuse **-leuchter** *m* luminous phenomenon or light produced during detonation **-welle** *f* detonation wave
detonieren to detonate, explode
detonierend detonating **-e Strecke** detonating column **-er Verstärker** heterodyne amplifier **-e Zündschnur** cordeau (detonating fuse)
Deul *m* billet, lump, bloom, ball, loop, ingot
deuten to interpret, explain, indicate
deuterierte Emulsion deuterium loaded emulsion
Deuterium *n* deuterium **-atom** *n* deuterium atom
Deuteron *n* deuteron
Deuteronen-beschuß *m* deuteron bombardment **-bildung** *f* deuteron formation
Deuteron-photoeffekt *m* deuteron photodisintegration (at high energies)
Deuteroprisma *n* prism of the second order
deutlich distinct, intelligible, clear, plain, arti-

culate, unmistakable ~ **bezeichnend** prominently marked ~ **sichtbar** conspicuous **-e Aussprache** clear pronunciation, good articulation
Deutlichkeit *f* clearness, definition, articulation
Deuton *n* deuteron
Deutpatrone *f* indicator cartridge
Deutrid *m* deuteride
deutsch German **-es Bundespatent** (D.R.P.) (German Patent) **-es Gebrauchsmuster** German utility model **-e Industrienorm** (DIN) German industrial standard **-e gesetzliche Zeit** German standard time
Deutsche Normal-Profile NP-sections
Deutscher Verdingungsausschuß German Contract Committee
Deutschießung *f* marking fire
Deutung *f* interpretation, explanation, evaluation
Deviation *f* deviation, deflection ~ **bestimmen** to swing for deviation
Deviations-änderung *f* change of deviation **-kontrolle** *f* deviation check **-lehre** *f* theory of compass deviation **-linie** *f* deviation curve or line **-moment** *n* product of inertia
Deviations-nachprüfung *f* deviation check **-pfahl** *m* deviation mark, pole, or post **-tabelle** *f* table of deviation **-tafel** *f* deviation clock **-wert** *m* amount of deviation, deviation figure **-winkel** *m* angle of deviation
Devise *f* foreign bill, bill or money of exchange, trademark
Devisen-ausländer *m* persons considered foreigners under the German foreign exchange regulations **-bescheinigung** *f* exchange voucher, foreign exchange certificate **-betriebsfonds** *pl* foreign exchange operations fund **-eingang** *m* receipts of foreign exchange **-export** *m* export of foreign exchange **-händler** *m* foreign-exchange broker **-rechtlich** under foreign currency regulations **-stelle** *f* foreign exchange office **-terminkauf** *m* forward currency purchase **-zentrale** *f* office of currency control
Dewar Gefäß *n* Dewar vessel or flask
Dewindit *m* dewindite
Dexel *m* adz
Dextran *n* dextran
Dextrin *n* dextrin, artificial gum
dezentralisieren to decentralize
dezentrierte Speisung offset feed
Dezentrierung *f* decentration, decentering, eccentricity
Dezibel *n* decibel (db. dB) **-meter** *n* decibelmeter, volume indicator **-skala** *f* decibel scale
Dezi-bereich *m* ultra-high frequency **-gramm** *n* decigram **-kreis** *m* decimeter circle or circuit **-liter** *n* deciliter
Dezilog *m* decilog
Dezimal-bezeichnung *f* decimal notation **-bruch** *m* decimal fraction
Dezimale aufrunden to approximate a decimal **auf die erste** ~ to a first order
dezimal decimal **-e Ordnung** decade **-e Schreibweise** decimal notation **-er Untersetzer** decade scaler **-es Zahlensystem** decimal number system
Dezimal-binärkonvertierung *f* decimal-to-binary conversion **-kerze** *f* standard candle **-klassifikation** *f* decimal index system or classification **-komma** *n* decimal point **-lehre** *f* decimal gauge **-logarithmus** *m* common logarithm **-maß** *n* metric measure, decimal measure **-rechnung** *f* metric calculation
Dezimal-setzung *f* decimal notation **-schreibweise** *f* decimal notation **-stelle** *f* decimal place, decimal **-system** *n* decimal system or base **-titer** *n* decimal count **-waage** *f* decimal scales
Dezimalzahl, dual dargestellte ~ binary ordered decimal number
Dezimal-zählror *n* decade counter tube **-ziffer** *f* decimal digit
Dezimeter *n* decimeter **-gebiet** *n* decimeter range **-gerät** *n* decimeter apparatus **-welle** *f* ultra high frequency (UHF)
Dezimeterwellen *pl* microwaves (for waves below twenty centimeters), microrays, quasi-optical waves, decimeter wave lengths (radar) **-frequenz** *f* ultra high frequency
Dezi-neper *n* decineper **-strecken** *pl* UHF links **-wellen** *f* microwaves, microrays, quasioptical waves (electromagnetic waves between one meter and ten centimeters)
Dextrinbinder *m* cereal binder
Dhau *f* dhow
Dia *n* slide (photo), photographic transparency **-abtastgerät** *n* slide scanner **-anbaugerät** *n* attachment slidelantern **-anlage** *f* slide changing (scanning) equipment
Diabas *m* diabase, greenstone **-schiefer** *m* green slate
Diabetometer *n* diabetometer
Diacetyl *n* diacetyl **-dioxim** *n* diacetyl (dioxime), glyoxime
Diadochit *m* diadochite
Dia-Einrichtung *f* still-view projection attachment
Diagenese *f* diagenesis, induration
Diagnose-möglichkeit *f* possibility (use) to diagnose **-programm** *n* diagnostic routine (info proc.)
Diagnostikröhre *f* diagnostic tube
Diagometer *n* diagometer
diagonal diagonal ~ **stehende Lochung** perforation placed in diagonals
Diagonal-ausschluß *m* angular spaces and quads **-bewehrung** *f* diagonal reinforcement **-beziehungen** *f pl* diagonal relationships (in periodic system) **-bindung** *f* diagonal weave
Diagonale *f* diagonal
Diagonalschnittpunkt *m* point of intersection of diagonals
Diagonal-gruppierung *f* wiring in diagonal pairs
Diagonalisieren *n* diagonalization
Diagonal-kupplung *f* diagonal bogie coupling **-papiere** *n pl* angle-cut papers **-schichtung** *f* current or false bedding **-schlag** *m* diagonal layer (arrangement of the double fabric used in gas bags, dirigibles, (etc.) **-schneidemaschine** *f* bias cutting hole, bias or angle cutter, diagonal cutting machine **-stab** *m* diagonal member
Diagonal-stoff *m* biased or diagonal fabric **-strebe** *f* diagonal strut or member, diagonal brace, strut **-streifen** *pl* cross stripes **-verband** *m* framework, diagonal bracing **-verdichter** *m* mixed-flow compressor **-verspannung** *f* wire cross bracing **-versteifung** *f* braced-beam con-

struction, equipped with diagonal web members **-verwerfung** *f* diagonal fault **-verziehung** *f* twisting

Diagramm *n* curve, chart of a recording instrument, diagram, graph **völliges ~** fat diagram

Diagramm-apparat *m* diagram recorder, autographic recording apparatus **-ausfüllung** *f* gapfiller **-blatt** *n* card **-fläche** *f* area of diagram (engine indicator) **-papier für Indikator** indicator card **-rollen und -scheiben** reels and discs for recording instruments **-schreiber** *m* diagram recorder; (streifen) (recorder) chart, strip chart **-trommel** *f* chart bearing drum

Diakaustik *f* diacaustic (curve or surface)

Diakyl-monohydroxyperoxyd *n* dialkylmonohydroxyperoxide **-peroxyd** *n* dialkylperoxide

Dialogit *m* dialogite, rhodochrosite

Dialysator *m* dialyzer

Dialyse *f* dialysis

Dialysierapparat *m* dialyser

dialysieren to dialyze

dialysisch dialytic

Diamagazin *n* slide magazine

diamagnetisch diamagnetic **-er Körper** diadiamagnetic body **-er Stoff** diamagnetic substance

Diamagnetismus *m* diamagnetism

Diamant *m* diamond, moat, glass cutter **-artige Verbindung** adamantine compound **-bohrer** *m* diamond drill **-bohrkrone** *f* diamond annular bit, diamond rockdrill crown **-bort** *m* diamond bort

Diamant-drehstrahl *m* diamond turning tool **-erweiterungsbohrer** *m* diamond reamer **-fangkrone** *f* diamond fishing crown **-feinstbohrwerke** *pl* diamond fine-boring, machines **-gerüst** *n* atomic structure of diamond **-gitter** *n* diamond-structure, diamond lattice (structure) **-glanz** *m* adamantine luster **-grau** *n* zinc gray **-halter zum Abdrehen der Schleifscheibe** diamond toolholder

Diamantine aus Glas diamond dust

Diamant-kegel *m* diamond cone **-kernbohrer** *m* diamond-core boring bit **-kollbohrer** *m* solid diamond bit **-krone** *f* diamond bit **-mörser** *m* diamond mortar **-prüfspitze** *f* (hardness tester), diamond sphero-conical penetrator **-pyramidenhärte** *f* diamond pyramid hardness

Diamant-säge *f* diamond saw **-schleifer** *m* diamond cutter **-schleifscheibe** *f* diamond grinding wheel **-spat** *m* common corundum, adamantine spar **-spitzstahl** *m* diamond-point tool **-splitter** *pl* diamond chips **-struktur** *f* diamond structure **-ziehsteine** *pl* diamond drawing dies **-zug von Drähten** diamond wire drawing

Diamaterial *n* slides

diametral diametral **~ entgegengesetzt, gegenüber-**(liegend) diametrically opposite, diametrical

Diametralpitchgewinde *n* diametral pitch threads

Diamido-benzol *n* diaminobenzene **-toluol** *n* diaminotoluene

Diamin *m* diamine

Dianisidin *n* dianisidine

Diaphanie *f* diaphane, transparent picture

Diaphanometer *n* diaphanometer

Diaphanoskop *n* diaphanoscope.

Diaphon *n* diaphone

Diaphonie *f* cross talk, babble

Diaphragm *n* diaphragm, electrolytic diaphragm, baffle, mask, membrane, shutter **-anode** *f* apertured anode or stop **-saugpumpe** *f* diaphragm suction pump

Diapositiv *n* lantern-slide, diapositive, diapositive, transparent positive **-einrichtung** *f* diapositive attachment **-halter** *m* lantern slide holder **-projektion** *f* lantern-slide projection **-werbung** *f* lantern slide advertising

Diapyr *n* diaper

Diarähmchen *pl* slides

Diaskleral-kegel *m* cone with bent point **-leuchte** *f* diascleral lamp

Diaskop *n* diascope

Diaspor *m* diaspore

Diastafor *n* diastafor

Diastase *f* diastase

diastasereich buoyant

diastatisch diastatic

Diastimeter *n* diastimeter

Diastrophismus *m* diastrophism

Diathermansie *f* diathermancy

Diathermie *f* diathermy

Diäthyl-amin *n* diethylamine **-anilin** *n* diethylaniline, dimethylamidobenzol **-äther** *m* diethylether **-cyclohexan** *n* diethylcyclohexane **-hexan** *n* diethylhexane

diäthylmalonsaures Äthyl diethylmalonic ester

Diatomeen-erde *f*, **-pelit** *m* diatomaceous or infusorial earth **-steine** *pl* kieselguhr bricks

Diatomitschicht *f* chemical filter layer (diatomite), diatomite layer

Diatomschlamm *m* diatom ooze

Dia-übertragungsanlagen *pl* slide scanning equipment **-wechsel** *m* slide changing **-wechseleinrichtung** *f* slide (changer) changing arrangement

Diazetonalkohol *m* diacetone alcohol

Diazobenzol *n* diazobenzene

Diazobelag *m* diazo coating

Diazoniumverbindung *f* diazonium compound

diazotierbar diazotizable

Diazotierung *f* diazotizing, diazotization

Dibbelmaschine *f* dibbling machine, spacing drill, seed drill, scatterer (agr.)

dibbeln to dibble

Dibenzyl *n* dibenzyl

Dibrom-äthan *n* dibromethane, ethylene bromide **-benzol** *n* dibromobenzene

Dibutyläther *n* dibutylether

Dichlor-äthylen *n* dichlorethylene, ethylene dichloride **-äthylsulfid** *n* dichloroethyl sulfide, mustard gas **-benzol** *n* dichlorobenzene **-methan** *n* dichloromethane, methylene chloride

dichotomisch dichotomic

Dichroismus *m* dichroism

Dichroit *m* iolite, dichroite, cordierite

dichroitisch dichroic **-er Schleier** dichroic or dichromatic fog, silver or red fog

Dichromat *n* bichromate

dicht dense, tight, compact, close, firm, massive, leakproof, consistent, sealed, hermetic; (wasser- oder gas ~) impervious **~ über den Boden fliegen** to hedgehop **~ bei** close, close by **~ bevölkerte Gebiete** densely populated areas **~ brennen** to vitrify (ceramics) **~ gestellte Kette** closely set warp **~ machen** to tighten, calk, make impermeable ~ (bei Metallguß) sound (metal) ~ (Papier) close-texture, thick, or heavy paper **vollständig** ~ hermetic(al) **zu** ~ overdense **-e Ware** close goods (textiles)

Dicht in situ density in situ

Dicht-brücke *f* sealing yoke **-druck** *m* leakage pressure

Dichte *f* packing density (comp.), density, compactness, closeness, firmness, tightness, thickness, solidity **feine** ~ fine-grained density ~ **der angeregten Atome** (eines Gases) excited-atom density (of a gas) ~ **einer Kreislagerung** density of a packing of circles **absolute** ~ specific gravity referred to water at 4 degrees centigrade **elektrische** ~ electric density **mittlere** ~ average density **orthobare** ~ critical density

Dichte-abfall *m* decrease or slope of the density **-änderungen** *pl* density fluctuations **-anisotropie** *f* density anisotropy **-bestimmung** *f* density or gravity determination

Dichte-effekt *m* density effect **-feld** *n* density distribution or field **-formel** *f* density formula **-fühler** density detector gauge **-funktion** *f* density function **-gitter** *n* density grid, density control or regulating grid **-grad** *m* degree of density

Dichteisen *n* calking iron, tight-making iron

Dichte-matrix density matrix **-meßanlage** measurement of density **-messer** *m* densimeter, hydrometer, aerometer, viscometer

Dichtemessung *f*, **photographische** ~ densitometry, photodensitometry, photographic density measurement

Dichtemodulation *f* density modulation, charge-density modulation

dichten to tighten, lute, pack, seal, compact, condense, calk, fit tightly, densify, contrive, devise

Dichten *n* sealing, jointing ~ **einer Quelle** plugging up or sealing a spring

Dichte-operator *m* density operator **-reguliergitter** *n* density grid, density-regulator or control grid **-schrift** *f* variable-density sound track, variable-density recording **-schwankung** *f* density fluctuation **-skala** *f* density scale

dichteste Kugelpackung close-packed structure

Dichte-übergangskurve density transition curve **-unterschied** *m* density variation **-verhältnis** *n* relative density **-verteilung** *f* distribution or variation of density **-zahl** *f* specific gravity

Dicht-flansch *m* gasket **-fläche** *f* sealing surface **-gepackt** close-packed **-gewebt** tightly woven **-gummi** *m* (für elekt. Kabel) rubber grommet, sealing strip **-halten** *n* valve gas tightness **-hammer** *m* calking mallet

Dichtheit *f*, **Dichtigkeit** *f* soundness, sealing, density, firmness, closeness, compactness, tightness, solidity, watertightness ~ **der Maße** mass density **auf** ~ **prüfen** to test for leaks

Dichtheitsprüfung *f* leakage test

Dichtigkeits-messer *m* densimeter, hydrometer, aerometer, viscometer **-verlust** *m* loss due to leakage, diminution of density

Dichtkegel *m* grummet, sealing ferrule, stuffing cone ~ **aus Gummi** valve pad

Dicht-leiste *f* packing strip **-linie** *f* sealing band **-lippe** *f* packing washer **-manschette** *f* sealing sleeve, sleeve (motor) **-maschine** *f* roller expander **-masse** *f* jointing compound, sealing material **-meißel** *m* calking chisel **-mittel** *n* jointing solution

Dicht-naht *f* tight weld **-nippel** *n* sealing nipple **-packung** *f* packing **-platte** *f* sealing plate (gasket) **-pulververpackung** *f* sealing-powder packing **-rahmen** *m* sealing frame **-ränder** *pl* sealing rims

Dichtring *m* seal, sealing, sealing washer, sealing ring, gasket ~ **für Öl** (kolbenringähnlich), piston-ring-type oil seal

Dicht-scheibe *f* sealing disc, packing washer **-schließend** tight **-schnur** *f* gasket cord **-stoffe** *pl* jointing materials

dichtstehend closely spaced

Dicht- und Festnaht *f* composite weld

Dichtung *f* bond, sealing, waterproofing, compacting, rendering impervious, packing, stuffing, jointing, luting, joint, consolidation, gasket-sealing washer, proofing (material), seal, cementing ~ **für Gehäusehälfte** (Kupplungsseite) gasket for housing half-member (clutch side) ~ **für Gehäusehälfte** (Magnetseite) gasket for housing halfmember (timing side) ~ **eines Kolbens** leathering or packing of a piston

Dichtungs-abschluß *m* (spring-water) seal **-abschlußkappe** *f* dust cap **-bahn** *f* building paper **-band** *n* jointing ring **-blatt** *n* impermeabilizing sheet **-blech** *n* skin plate **-buchse** *f* packing sleeve **-bund** *m* socket **-deckel** *m* sealing cover

Dichtungs-einsatzspitze *f* labyrinth gland point **-element** *n* gasket element, sealing element **-fadenandrückmaschine** *f* packing-ring press **-fett** *n* joint grease **-fläche** *f* joint face, sealing surface, faying surface **-flansch** *m* sealing flange

Dichtungsgruppe *f* gasket group **-halter** *m* seal retainer, journal gasket retainer **-haut** *f* damp-proof membrane **-jalousie** *f* stanching blind, watertight curtain **-kappe** *f* sealing cap **-kegel** *m* sealing ferrule, packing cone

Dichtungs-läppchen (*n*) **für Spunde** linen cap or patch for screw bungs **-leder** *n* washer leather

Dichtungs-leiste *f* sealing ledge, face of joint **hölzerne** ~ timber stanching frame, water seal, or stop, wooden waterproofing

Dichtungs-manschette *f* control device, gasket **-masse** *f* sealing compound

Dichtungs-material *n* seal, packing material, cementing material, luting material, clay filling, sealing material; (nachgiebig) resilient gasket material

Dichtungsmittel *n* packing, jointing, proofing, lute, cementing agent or medium, method for impermeabilizing ~ **gegen Flüssigkeitsdurchtritt** antileak cement

Dichtungs-pappe *f* gasket board **-platte** *f* packing sheet

Dichtungsring *m* gasket ring, sealing ring washer, packing, joint, or stanching ring, watertight ring or seal, oil seal, journal bearing seal ~ **aus Aluminium** aluminium seal

Dichtungs-scheibe *f* washer, packing ring, gasket **-schicht** *f* tightening or proofing layer (gas, water) **-schirm** *m* curtains (watertight) **-schloß** *n* piston-ring lock **-schnur** *f* sealing strip, packing cord **-schraube** *f* sealing screw

Dichtungs-schutzkappe *f* gasket or dust cap **-schweißung** *f* calk weld **-schwierigkeit** *f* difficulty with washers **-spalte** *f* sealing gap **-spundwand** *f* sheet pile screen **-stab** *m* impermeabilizing bar **-stange** *f* rod for sealing **-stelle** *f* sealing point **-stoff** *m* packing or cementing material, luting material, calking, plumbing material (vacuum work) **-streifen** *m* sealing tape **-strick** *m* sealing rope (cord) **-tiefe** *f* depth of packing

dick thick, stout, corpulent, heavy **-er Dipol** fat dipole **-e Schicht** (Röntgenspektrum) thick target **-e Stelle** *f* high spot

dickdrähtig of heavy-gauge wire, thick-ply, thick-stranded

Dickdruckpapiere *n pl* bulk paper

Dicke *f* thickness, consistency, volume, gauge, density **~ der adsorbierten Schicht** adsorption space **~ des Eises** thickness of ice **~ der Platte** thickness of (crystal) flake (geol.) **~ der Schicht** thickness of layer **~ der Schweißnaht** throat or thickness of welded seam

Dicken-abnahme *f* reduction (in thickness) **-belegung** *f* profile coordinates measured from mean line **-lehre** *f* thickness gauge **-empfindlichkeit** *f* flaw sensitivity **-gradient** *m* thickness gradient **-meßanlage** *f* gauge for measurement of thickness

Dickenmesser *m* micrometer, pachymeter, thickness or amplifying gauge, calipers **~ mit Durchstrahlung** transmission gauge

Dicken-messung *f* microlimit control, thickness gauge **-schwingungen** *f* transverse vibrations, thickness vibrations (cryst.) **-stufe** *f* thickness gradient **-vergleichsmessung** *f* comparative measuring of thickness **-verhältnis** *n* (Profil) thickness-chord ratio **-verteilung** *f* thickness distribution

dick-flüssig semifluid, viscous, viscid **-flüssigkeit** *f* consistency, viscousness, viscidity **-griffiges Papier** bulky paper **-mantelelektrode** *f* heavily coated electrode

Dickicht *n* thicket

Dick-maische *f* thick mash **-mittel** *n* covering material **-öl** *n* bodied oil, stand oil **-quetsche** *f* first mold of vellum

Dicksaft *m* thick juice, sirup **-aufkocher** *m* thick-juice blowup **-decke** *f* thick-juice washing **-einziehkasten** m vacuum-pan supply tank for thick juice **-saturation** *f* thick-juice carbonation **-sud** *m* strike of thick juice

dick-schalig husky, thick-skinned **-schlamm** *m* thick mud **-spülung** *f* fluid mud

Dickte *f* layer or lamina of wood, thickness

Dickteer *m* heavy tar

Dickten-hobel *m* panel planing machine **-hobelmaschine** *f* thicknessing machine for planks, lamina-planing or -thicknessing machine **-lehre** *f* thickness gauge

Dick-trübe *f* regenerated dense medium **-wandig** heavy- or thick-walled

Diderichit *m* diderichite

Didotpunktmaß *n* Didot point system

Didym *n* didymium

Diebel *m* dowel, pin, peg, dowel pin, key

Diebstahl *m* theft, larceny **-sicherung** *f* burgler alarm

Dieder . . . dihedron . . . **-klassen** *pl* dihedral classes

diedrischer Winkel dihedral angle

Diele *f* flooring board, deal, plank, deal board

Dielektrikum *n* dielectric **festes ~** solid dielectric **künstliches ~** artificial dielectric **schlechtes ~** poor dielectric

dielektrisch dielectric(al) **-e Festigkeit** disruprive, electric, or dielectric strength, dielectric rigidity **-e Hysterese** dielectric hysteresis **-e Konstante** permittivity, specific inductive capacity

dielektrisch-e Leitung dielectric path **-e Nachwirkung** dielectric viscosity **-er Stabstrahler** dielectric rod-radiator **-er Verlustwinkel** phase-angle difference (of a condenser) **-e Widerstandsfähigkeit** elastance

Dielektrizitäts-konstante *f* specific inductive capacity, dielectric constant or coefficient, permittivity, inductive capacity, inductivity, negative charge **relative ~** specific inductive capacity

dielen, den Fußboden ~ to board the floor

Dielen *n* boarding **-balken** *m* joist, boarding joist **-bandsäge** (*f*) **mit schnellgreifendem Sattelgetriebe** log saw with quick-grip feed saddle gear (band saw) **-(fuß)boden** *m*, **gefugter ~** plain jointed floor **-lager** *n* boarding or bridging joist

Dielkometrie *f* coined word for measurements of dielectric properties

Dielung *f* boarding, boarded floor **verkeilte ~** wedged floor

dienen als to serve, as or for

dienlich serviceable, fit, useful, conducive

Dienst *m* duty, service **-abfrageklinke** *f* service answering jack **-abzeichen** *n* service badge, chevron **-alter** *n* seniority **-altersgrenze** *f* age limit **-ältester** *m* senior officer **-anruf** *m* official or service call **-anruflampe** *f* order wire lamp **-anrufschalter** *m* service-call key **-anschluß** *m* official or service telephone **-anweisung** *f* service regulation or instruction, instructions for working or practices **-ausrüstung** *f* service equipment **-beobachtungsergebnisse** service observing summary

dienst-bereit ready for service **-bescheinigung** *f* certificate of service

Dienst-farbe *f* service color **-fähig** serviceable **-gespräch** *n* service call, official message **-gruppe** *f* operator's team **-gewalt** *f* authority **-gewicht** *n* gross or loaded weight, weight in working order **-gipfelhöhe** *f* service ceiling (aviation)

Dienstgruppe *f* group assigned to duty, operators' tour or shift

Diensthandlung *f* act performed in line of duty **zur Vornahme** (oder Unterlassung) **einer ~ nötigen** to urge or compel execution (or omission) of act in line of duty

Dienst-herr *m* employer, master **-klinken** *f pl* service jacks **-last** *f* service load

Dienst-kanal *m* order channel **-leistung** *f* performance, efficiency in service, duty

Dienstleitung *f* order wire circuit, interposition trunk, order wire, speaker wire, call wire, service circuit **~** (Verbindungsleitung), order-wire junction **~** (zwischen zwei Plätzen eines Amtes) transfer circuit **~** (Sammeldienst) split order wire **unmittelbare ~** straight order wire

Dienstleitungs-betrieb *m* order-wire operation, trunking, or system, call-circuit method **-feld** *n*

order-wire panel **-taste** *f* order-wire or assignment key, call-circuit key

Dienstleitung zwischen Fernämtern service circuit between trunk exchange

Dienstleitungsverteiler *m*, **selbsttätiger ~** automatic order-wire distributor

Dienstleistungswähler *m* order-wire distributor

dienstlich official, authorized **~ weggesandt werden** to be sent away on duty **-e Aufzeichnungen** statement of calls handled at a position **-er Vorfall** service irregularity

Dienst-lohn *m* wages **-notiz** *f* service advice

Dienst-personal *n* personnel, staff **-plan** *m* service or daily training schedule (navy), assignment of hours, duty roster, timetable **-prämie** *f* service bonus **-raum** *m* service room **-sache** *f* official business, pertaining to the service **-schicht** *f* period or shift of duty or business hours, operators' tour or shift

Dienst-schreiben *n* official correspondence **-siegel** *n* official seal **-signal** *n* transfer signal **-stelle** *f* office, civil service assignment **-stellung** *f* appointment **-stempel** *m* official stamp

Dienststunden *f* business hours **~ einer Fernsprechanstalt** hours of service of a central telephone office

Dienst-tafel *f* duty roster **-taste** *f* order-wire button

Diensttasten-leitungen *f pl* service key(ing) circuit **-streifen** *m* order-wire button strip

Dienst-telegramm *n* service message **-titel** *m* official title **-überwachung** *f* service observation **-überwachungsplatz** *m* observation desk

Dienst-verkehr *m* official traffic, service-control channel **-vermerke** *m pl* statement of calls handled at a position, service indications **-verrichtung** *f* maintenance of service (nontechnical) **-vertrag** *m* contract for service, contract between employer and employee **-vorkommnis** *n* service irregularity or error **-vorschrift** *f* service rules, instructions, regulations, service manual, official working rule or regulation

Dienst-wähler *m* special code selector, service connector or switch **-weg** *m* official channels **-zeichengeber** *m* autocontrol (teleph.) **-zeit** *f* duty hours **-zeugnis** *n* service certificate, reference

Dienstzweig *m* branch of service, department **besonderer ~** special service

diesbezüglich referring or relating (thereto), corresponding

Diesel-aggregat *n* Diesel-generating set **-brennstoff** *m* Diesel fuel **-drehkran** *m* Diesel rail crane **-elektrischer Antrieb** *m* Diesel electirc drive **-fahrzeug** *n* automotive Diesel vehicle **-flugmotor** *m* Diesel aero engine

Diesel-gleichstromaggregat *n* Diesel D.C. generating set **-horst-Martin-Kabel** *n* multiple-twin cable **-horst-Martin-Verfeilung** *f* multiple-twin formation **-indizes** *m pl* Diesel indices **-kraftstoffe** *m pl* Diesel fuels **-kran** *m* Diesel crane **-kühllastwagen** *m* Diesel reefer **-lastwagen** *m* Diesel engine truck **-luftverdichter** *m* Diesel air compressor

Dieselmotor *m* Diesel engine **-dreiradwalze** *f* three-wheel Diesel motor roller **kompressorloser ortsfester ~** airlines-injection stationary Diesel engine **umsteuerbarer ~** reversible Diesel engine

Dieselmotoren-betrieb *m* Diesel-engine practice **-brennstoff** *m* Diesel-engine oil **-schmieröl** *n* Diesel lubricating oil

Diesel-motorkran *m* Diesel-engine crane **-öl** *n* Diesel oil **-prozeß** *m* Diesel or constant-pressure cycle **-schlepper** *m* Diesel tractor **-treibstoff** *m* Diesel (engine) fuel **-triebwagen** *m* Diesel rail coach **-umstellzünder** *m* Diesel convertible ignition unit **-verbrennung** *f* Diesel combustion **-verfahren** *n* Diesel principle **-zahl** *f* Diesel index number

diesig misty **-es Wetter** haze

Diessigsäure *f* diacetic acid

Dietrich *m* picklock, skeleton or false key

Differdingerträger *m* wide-flanged steel I beam

Differential *n* differential, increment, differential or infinitesimal quantity **~ zur Aufnahme des Erdtastendrucks** differential relay for accepting and evaluating ground button pulse

Differential-achse *f* live axle **-antrieb** *m* differential drive **-antriebskegelrad** *m* (großes) differential-axle-drive bevel gear **-betätigung** *f* differential operation **-bewegung** *f* differential action **-blutbild** *n* differential white count **-blutkörperchenzähler** *m* blood cell differential counter **-bremse** *f* differential brake **-brücke** *f* differential bridge **-differenzengleichung** *f* differential-difference equation

Differential-drossel *f* differential reactor **-drosselung** *f* differential reactance **-druck** *m* differential pressure **-druck-Durchflußmengenmesser** *m* variable-head flowmeter **-druckmesser** *m* differential manometer

Differential-einfluß *m* derivative action **-empfänger** *m* differential receiver **-flaschenzug** *m* differential pulleys, differential chain block **-fleier** *m* differential fly frame **-galvanomesser** *m* differential galvanometer **-gegensprechsystem** *n* differential duplex system **-gehäuse** *n* differential casing or housing **-getriebe** *n* differential gear(ing)

differential gewickelt differentially wound

Differential-gleichung *f* differential equation **-gleichungslöser** *m* differential analyzer **-glied** *n* hybrid set, differential element **-hebel** *m* compound lever **-ionisationskammer** *f* differential ionization chamber **-kalorimeter** *n* differential calorimeter **-kondensator** *m* differential capacitor, differential (twin) condenser **-kreuz** *n* differential spider

Differential-lagerkasten *m* differential carrier **-laufwindbewegung** *f* **an einer Spinnmaschine** differential winding motion (tectiles) **-manometer** *n* differential manometer or gauge **-melder** *m* differential alarm **-nachlaßvorrichtung** *f* differential feed controlling device **-pumpe** *f* multistage or multicellular pump **-pupilloskop** *n* differential pupilloscope **-querruder** *n* differential aileron **Querrudersteuerung** differential-aileron control

Differentialquotient *m* derivative, differential coefficient or quotient **~ *n*ter Ordnung** differential coefficient of the *n*th order **zeitlicher ~** derivative with respect to time

Differential-quotientengeber *m* differential-quotient transmitter

Differential-rad *n* differential wheel, planetary gear **-rechnung** *f* differential calculus **-reduktion** *f* differential reduction **-regelfaktor** derivative control factor **-regelung** derivative control **-regelwerk** *n* differential regulator **-relais** *n* differential relay **-ritzel** *m* differential pinion **-rolle** *f* differential pulley or sheave **-schaltung** *f* differential arrangement or connection **-schrumpfung** *f* differential contraction **-seitenwelle** *f* axle shaft

Differential-sender *m* differential transmitter **-sperre** *f* differential lock **-stirnrad** *n* ring gear **-synchroempfänger** *m* synchro differential receiver **-transformator** *m* differential transformer or repeating coil **-übertrager** *m* (dreispuliger) hybrid coil, differential transformer **-verdünnungswärme** *f* differential heat of dilution **-verfahren** *n* differential method

Differentialvorschub *m* differential feed ~ **des Morselochers** differential (tape) feed of Wheatstone perforator

Differential-vortrieb *m* differential feed **-welle** *f* differential shaft **-wicklung** *f* differential winding **-wirkung** *f* differential action **-zähltafel** *f* differential counting chart **-zeuge** *n pl* **mit gradliniger Zahnung** chain blocks spur-geared **-zugmesser** *m* differential draft gauge

Differentiation *f* differentiation

Differentiator *m* differentiator

differentiell, -e Erholungsrate differential recovery rate **-er Ionisationskoeffizient** specific ionization coefficient **-e Suszeptibilität und Permeabilität** differential susceptibility and permeability

Differenz *f* difference, balance **halbe** ~ semidifference **-druck** *m* pressure differential ~ **der Modulationstiefe** difference in depth of modulation

Differenzabweichungsanzeiger *m* differential deviation indicator

Differenzdruck *m* differential pressure

Differenzen-gleichung *f* difference equation **-rechnung** *f* method of differences, differential calculus, step-by-step calculation **-verfahren** difference equations

Differenz-faktor *m* hybrid balance **-frequenz** *f* beat frequency, difference or differential frequency

Differenziation *f* differentiation

differenzierbar differentiable

differenzieren to differentiate (with respect to) **nach . . . differenzieren** to differentiate with respect to

differenzierender Einfluß derivative action, rate action

Differenzier-gerät *n* differentiator **-kreis** *m* peaking network **-schaltung** *f* differentiating circuit **-spule** *f* peaker strip

Differenzierung *f* differentiation

Differenz-meßanlage *f* differential gauge, differential gauge equipment **-mutter** *f* differential nut **-rechnung** *f* calculus of differences **-schaltung** differential connection **-schemaverfahren** *n* difference scheme method **-spannung** *f*, **-strom** *m* bias of a circuit

Differenzton *m* intermodulation frequency, difference or differential tone **Erzeugung von einem** ~ intermodulation (radio)

Differenz-tonfaktor *m* coefficient of differential tones **-trägerverfahren** *n* intercarrier system **-verstärker** *m* sum-and-difference amplifier **-waage** *f* differential balance **-zugmesser** *m* differential draught gauge

Diffraktion *f* diffraction **-gitter** *n* diffraction grating

diffundieren to diffuse

diffundiert legiert (Transistor) post diffusion alloyed

diffus scattered, diffused **-e Lichtreflexion** diffused reflection of light **-e Schallreflexion** diffused reflection of sound

Diffusat *n* diffusate

Diffusereinsatz *m* diffuser neckpiece

Diffuseur *m* diffuser, diffusion cell, blow pit, tank, vat

Diffusion *f* diffusion, interfusion, interpenetration (soldering)

Diffusionsapparat *m*, ~ **mit unterer Entleerung** diffusion apparatus with bottom discharge ~ **mit unterem hydraulischem Mannlochverschluß** diffusion apparatus with hydraulic device for closing bottom manholes

Diffusionsbatterie *f*, **verkürzte** ~ shortened diffusion battery

Diffusions-dauer *f* time of diffusion **-effekt** *m* diffusion phenomenon **-fähig** diffusible **-fläche** *f* diffusion area **-flächentransistor** *m* grown-diffused transistor

Diffusions-gefäß *n* diffusion cell **-gerät** *n* apparatus for measuring permeability, diffusion apparatus, permeameter **-geschwindigkeit** *f* rate or speed of diffusion **-gleichgewicht** *n* equilibrium of diffusion **-gleichung** *f* diffusion equation

Diffusions-integralkern *m* diffusion kernel **-kammer** *f* spray chamber **-kapazität** *f* diffusion capacitance

Diffusions-länge *f* diffusion length **-lichthof** *m* diffusion halo (halation) **-nebelkammer** *f* diffusion cloud chamber **-pumpe** *f* (oil) diffusion pump **-querschnitt** *m* diffusion cross section **-reflektor** *m* diffuser types of shade (phys.) **-saftvorwärmer** *m* diffusion-juice preheater **-schicht** *f* diffused junction

Diffusionsschnitzel, ausgelaugte ~ pulp **unausgelaugte** ~ cossettes

Diffusions-spannung *f* diffusion voltage, height of the potential barrier **-sprung** *m* diffusional jog **-strom** *m* current due to the concentration gradient **-stromdichte** *f* diffusion current density

Diffusionstensor im Geschwindigkeitsraum diffusion in velocity tensor

Diffusions-transistor *m* diffusion layer transistor **-vektor** *m* diffusion vector **-verfahren** *n* osmosis **-verlust** *m* loss through or due to diffusion **-vermögen** *n* diffusivity, diffusibility **-wand** *f* diffusion barrier **-wärme** *f* diffusion heat (gas) **-wasser** *n* diffusion waste water **-weg** *m* diffusion path

Diffusität *f* diffusity

Diffusor *m* diffuser, diffusion, diffusibility, delivery space, volute chamber ~ (Lader) vaned diffuser plate

Diffusor-boden *m* diffuser bottom **-düse** *f* divergent nozzle **-haube** *f* diffuser top **-leitschaufel** *f*

diffuser deflection vane **-schaufel** *f* diffuser or diffusion vane (jet) **-thermometer** *n* diffuser thermometer
Digallussäure *f* gallotannic acid
digerieren to digest
Digerierflasche *f* digestion bottle
Digerierung *f* digestion
Digestionskolben *m* digesting flask
Digestor *m* digester
Digestorium *n* chimney
digital darstellen to digitize **-e Rechenanlage** calculator (info proc.)
Digital-anzeige *f* digital display **-ohmmeter** *n* digital ohmmeter **-rechenmaschine** *f* digital computer **-rechner** *m* digital computer
digitieren to digitize (comput)
Digitonin *n* digitonine
Diglykol-nitratblättchenpulver *n* diglycolnitrate flake powder **-röhrenpulver** *n* diglycol tubular powder (a propelling charge)
digonal twofold
DI-Gruppe *f* DI-pole array (signal)
Dihedralwinkel *m* dihedral angle
dihedrisch dihedral
dihydratisch dihydric
Dihydro-agnosterinazetat *n* dihydro agnosterol acetate **-derivat** *n* dihydro derivate
Dijod-anilin *n* aniline diiodide **-methan** *n* methylene iodide
Diktaphonplatte *f* transcription record
diktieren to dictate
Diktier-gerät *n* dictating machine **-maschine** *f* dictograph
Dilatanz *f* dilatancy
Dilatation *f* dilatation, elongation, expansion
Dilatationsvorrichtung *f* expansion point
dilatierend, nicht -es Gußeisen nongrowth cast iron
Dilatometer *n* dilatometer
diluvial, diluvisch diluvial
Dimension *f* dimension, size
dimensional dimensional
dimensionieren to dimension
dimensioniert dimensioned, of ample size
Dimensionierung *f* dimensioning, sizing, design, power ranges
Dimensions-betrachtung *f* method of dimension similitude consideration **-gleichung** *f* dimensional equation **-konstante** *f* dimension constant
dimensionslos dimensionless, non-dimensionalized **-e Größe** nondimensional quantity **-e Veränderliche** dimensionless variable
Dimeren (chem.) *n* dimerics, dimers
Dimethyl-amidoazobenzol *n* dimethylaminoazobenzene **-aminchlorhydrat** *n* **-aminhydrochlorid** *n* dimethylamine hydrochloride **-anilin** *n* dimethylaniline **-benzol** *n* dimethylbenzene **-glyoxim** *n* dimethyl glyoxime, diacetyldioxime
dimethyliert dimethylated
Dimethylsulfat *n* dimethyl sulfate
dimetrisch dimetric
dimorph dimorphous
Dimorphie *f* dimorphism
DIN (Deutsche Industrie-Norm) German Industrial Standards
DIN-Format *n* standard paper-size
Dinaphthyl *n* dinaphthyl
Dinaphthylin *n* dinaphthyline
Dinas-stein *m* Dinas brick **-ton** *m* Dinas clay
Ding *n* thing, matter; object (opt.)
Dingbrennpunkt *m*, **dingseitiger oder vorderer ~** front focus
Ding-ebene *f* object plane **-glas** *n* objective (lens)
Dingi *n* dinghy, skiff
dingliche Sicherheit material security
Ding-punkt *m* object point, point object **-raum** *m* object space
dingseitig on the object side (opt.) **-er Brennpunkt** focus on the object side **-er** (vorderer) **Hauptpunkt** (Aero.) external perspective center **-er Knotenpunkt** front nodal point
Dingweite *f* object distance
Dinitroglyzerinsprengstoff *m* dinitroglycerin explosive
Dinitrotoluol *n* dinitrotoluol **-base** *f* explosives with toluol bases
DIN-Passung *f* German Industrial Standard fitting
Dinylin *n* dehydrodinaphthylenediamine
Diode *f* diode, two-electrode tube, Fleming valve **~ mit flachen parallelen Elektroden** planar diode **äquivalente ~** equivalent diode of a triode **gesättigte ~** saturated diode
Diode-Heptode *f* diode heptode
Diode-Pentode *f* diode pentode
Dioden-außenwiderstand *m* diode load resistance **-gleichrichter** *m* diode detector **-gleichrichtung** *f* diode detection or rectification **-gleichstrom** *m* noise current **-schaltung** *f* diode circuit (elec.)
Diodenspannung *f*, **äquivalente ~** equivalent diode voltage
Dioden-strecke *f* diode path **-typ** *m* diode type
Diopter *n* diopter, sight, sight vane, alidade, orthoptic **-faden** *m* diopter thread or hair **-kimme** *f* back sight **-kompaß** *m* miner's dial **-korn** *n* front (fore) sight **-lineal** *n* alidade (ruler), index **-schlitz** *m* diopter slit
Dioptometer *n* dioptometer
Dioptrie *f* sight, sight vane, diopter, orthoptic, alidade
Dioptrien- einstellung *f* diopter focusing mount **-ring** *m* knurled head with diopters **-teilung** *f* diopter scale
Dioptrik *f* dioptrics (refraction branch of optics)
dioptrisch dioptric
Diorit *m* greenstone, diorite
Diotron *n* diotron
Dioxanzusatz *m* dioxane addition
Dioxychinolin *n* dihydroxyquinone
Dioxyd *n* dioxide
Dioxylbenzol *n* dihydroxybenzene
Dioxy-naphthalin *n* dihydroxynaphthalene **-tuluol** *n* dihydroxytoluene
Dipenten *n* dipentene
Diphensäure *f* diphenic acid
Diphenyl-amin *n* diphenylamine **-aminchlorarsin** *n*, **-chlorarsin** *n* adamiste, diphenylchloroarsine
Diplex-betrieb *m* diplex operation **-funkübertragung** *f* diplex radio transmission **-system** *n* diplex system **-telegraph** *m* diplex telegraph **-verkehr** *m* diplex transmission
diploide Zelle diploid cell
Diplom *n* diploma, certificate **-ingenieur** *m* graduated engineer **-papier** *n* a type of paper

(substitute for rice paper)

Dipol *m* dipole, doublet **Hertzscher ~** Hertzian doublet **~ mit Schlitz-Speisung** slot-fed dipole

Dipol-anordnung *f* dipole array (antenna) **-anschlußklemme** *f* dipole connector **-antenne** *f* dipole antenna

Dipole, in einer Linie angeordnete ~ collinear antenna

Dipol-ebene *f* broadside array **-ebenenanordnung** *f* curtain array **-einstellung** *f* dipole adjustment **-flächendichte** *f* dipole surface density **-gruppe** *f* dipole array

Dipol-näherung *f* dipole approximation **-quellenbelegung** *f* dipole source covering **-rahmen** *m* loop **-reihe** *f* linear array **-schicht** *f* electric double or dipole layer **-schleifenpaar** *n* dipole pair

Dipol-singularität *f* dipole singularity **-strömung** *f* dipole current flow **-wand** *f* curtain array (antenna) **-welle** *f* dipole wave **-zeile** *f* line array **-zone** *f* electric double or dipole layer, dipole zone

Dipper *m* tickler, flusher **-relais** *n* dipper relay

Dirac-Funktion *f* Dirac's function

direkt direct, conductive, primary; (Licht) incident (light) **~ umsteuerbarer Dieselmotor** directly reversible Diesel engine **~ -geheizte Gleichrichterröhre** filamentary rectifying tube **~ angetriebene Luftschraube** direct-driven propeller **~-einstellbarer Wähler** *m* directly controlled selector switch

direkt-er Durchsatz once-through operation **-e Kuppelung** direct coupling (by resistance) **-es Licht** direct lateral light **-e Lichtbogenerhitzung** direct arc heating **-er Motor** ungeared motor **-er Regler** self-acting controller **-e Selbsterregung** *f* auto-self-excitation **-e Wirkung** direct acting **-e Zwischenhebelverbindung** positive sub-lever connection

Direkt-ablesung *f* direct reading **-antrieb** *m* (Tex.) surface drive (of the package itself)

direktanzeigender Peiler direct-reading direction-finder

Direkt-druck *m* direct printing **-einspritzung** *f* direct fuel injection **-farben** *pl* flushed colors

Direktion *f* management

Direktions-betrieb *m* main office **-kraft** *f* directing, directive, or versorial force **-schaufeln** *f pl* guide vanes (turbine)

Direktive *f* directive, mission-type combat order, dipole antenna

Direkt-lautsprecher *m* direct loudspeaker **-messung** *f* direct measurement

Direktor *m* director, (ant., ant. tel.) **technischer ~** engineering manager **~ mit Tragrohr** director with tubular support

Direktor-amt *n* director exchange **-gradient** *m* director gradient **-system** *n* director, controller, or translator system

Direktrix *f* directrix

Direkt-röhre *f* direct view tube **-schaltung** *f* direct control **-schreiber** *m* cable code direct printer **-schreibung** *f* direct recording **-sichtbildröhre** *f* kinescope **-sichtempfänger** *m* direct-vision receiver

Direkt-sprechen *n* direct communication **-steuerung** *f* direct control **-teilverfahren** *n* direct indexing **-verbindung** *f* (Funk) point-to-point communication **-verkehr** *m* (Fernschreiber) point-to-point service **-verstärker** *m* straight-ahead amplifier **-wirkende Pumpe** direct-acting pump

dirigieren to conduct, manage

dirigiertes Bohren directional drilling

Dirk *f* topping lift

Disacharat *n* disaccharate

Disacharid *n* disaccharid

Disagio *n* discount

Diskant *m* descant, treble

Diskon-Antenne *f* discone antenna

diskontinuierlich discontinuous, intermittent **-e Anlage** batch process, batch operation **-e Bewegungsgruppen** discontinuous groups of motions

Diskontinuität *f* discontinuity

Diskontinuitätsfläche *f* surface of discontinuity

diskordant unconformable, dissonant

Diskordanz *f* unconformity, dissonance

Diskrasit *m* dyscrasite

Diskrepanz *f* discrepancy

diskret discreet, distinct **-e Elektronen** mono-energetic electrons

Diskriminante *f* discriminant **~ einer Algebra** discriminant of an algebra

Diskrimination *f* discrimination

Diskriminator *m* discriminator (rdo.)

Diskriminator-ausgang *m* discriminator output **-impuls** *m* discriminator pulse **-röhre** *f* discriminator

diskriminieren to discriminate

Diskusegge *f* disc harrow

Diskussion *f* discussion, controversy

diskutieren to discuss, argue

Dislokation *f* stationing of troops (peacetime), dislocation

dispergieren to disperse

Dispergier-fähigkeit *f* dispersing effect **-stoff** *m* dispersing agent

Dispergierungsmittel *n* deflocculation agent

dispergiert dispersed

dispers dispersive, dispersed, disperse

Dispersion *f* dispersion

Dispersions-grad *m* dispersion rate **-kraft** *f* dispersion force **-messung** *f* dispersion measurement **-mittel** *n* deflocculation agent, dispersion medium **-prisma** *n* dispersion prism **-terme** *pl* dispersion terms **-vermögen** *n* dispersive power

Dispersität *f* dispersion

Dispersoid *n* disperse system **-analyse** *f* dispersoid analysis

Disponent *m* dispatcher (operations department)

disponieren to manage

disponierte Bestände stocks earmarked for sale

Disposition *f* arrangement, disposal, management

Disproportionierung *f* rearrangement, disproportionation

disruptiv disruptive

Dissertation *f* thesis

Dissipationsfunktion *f* dissipation function

dissipativ linear dissipative linear

Dissipativität *f* dissipativity

Dissousgas *n* dissolved acetylene cylinder gas

Dissoziation *f* dissociation **elektrolytische ~** electrolytic or ionic dissociation

Dissoziations-feldeffekt *m* dissociation field

effect **-gleichgewicht** *n* dissociation equilibrium **-grad** *m* coefficient or degree of dissociation **-isotherme** *f* dissociation isotherm **-halbleiter** *m* exhaustion semiconductor **-vermögen** *n* dissociation power **-vorgang** *m* dissociation process **-wärme** *f* heat of dissociation
dissoziativ dissociative
dissoziierbar separable, dissociable
dissoziieren to dissociate
Dissoziierung *f* dissociation
Dissymmetrie *f* dissymmetry
Distanz *f* distance, pitch (distance or degree) **-block** *m* spacer block **-bolzen** *m* distance pin, journal shaft **-büchse** *f* distance washer, spacer sleeve, bearing spacer **-einstellungsapparat** *m* distance gear (torpedo) **-faden** *m* stadia line **-füllgerät** *n* remote control filling equipment **-halter** *m* spacer, separator, spacing means **-isolator** *m* spacing or standoff insulator **-latte** *f* distance staff, surveyor's rod, stadia **-messer** *m* range finder, telemeter, diastimeter
Distanz-relais *n* distance relay **-ring** *m* distance piece, spacer, spacer ring, distance washer **-rohr** *n* distance collar, spacer (tube) **-scheibe** *f* distance washer, spacer **-schraube** *f* distance bolt **-strich** *m* stadia line, subtense line **-stück** *n* distance or separator piece, spacer **-vorrichtung** *f* countermechanism **-zeiger** *m* distance indicator
Disthen *m* disthene, cyanite
Distributeurmaschine *f* dispenser unit
Distributivgesetz *n* distributive law
Distrikt *m* district, region, zone
Disulfaminsäure *f* disulfamic acid
Disulfosäure *f* disulfonic acid
Disziplin *f* discipline
Dithionsäure *f* dithionic acid
ditschen to ditch (aviation)
Dityndallismus *m* diffraction polarization
divariant bivariant, divariant
divergent diverging, divergent
Divergenz *f* divergence **-fall** *m* case of divergence **-formal** *f* expansion formula
divergenzfrei solenoidal **-es Feld** solenoidal field
Divergenz-koeffizient *m* divergence coefficient **-winkel** *m* angle of divergence
divergieren to diverge (from)
divergierend diverging, divergent
Diversion *f* diversion
Diversityempfang *m* diversity reception
Diviationsmomente *pl* products of inertia
dividieren to divide
Division *f* division (math.)
Divisor *m* divisor
Diwolframsäure *f* ditungstic acid
Djalmait *m* djalmaite
DKT (Dikaliumtartrat) dipotassium tartrate
D-Legierung *f* pressure die-cast alloy
D.M.-Vierer *m* multiple twin quad
Döbel *n* dowel, dowel pin, plug, peg
Docht *m* wick **-baumwolle** *f* **-garn** *n* wick yarn **-kohle** *f* cored carbon **-kohlestoff** *m* arc lamp carbon **-lehre** *f* wick-trimming gauge **-öler** *m* wick oiler, wick lubricator, siphon lubricator
Docht-schere *f* curved scissors (for wick trimming) **-schmierapparat** *m* wick lubricator **-schmierung** *f* wick lubricator or feed system **-spieß** *m* wick wire, dipping rod **-träger** *m* wick holder **-verdampfer** *m* wick carburetor
Dock *n* dock, dockyard, pier, landing stage **-anlage** *f* dock installation
Döckchen *n* stud
Docke *f* bundle (skeins), mandrel
docken to wind, dock, bind
Docken-feder *f* poppet spring **-knüpferin** *f* hank knotter **-maschine** *f* braiding or plaiting machine **-stock** *f* fixed mandrel **-wagen** *m* feeder frame (for logs)
Dockerin *f* hank winder
Dock-gebühren *f pl* dockage, dock dues **-hafen** *m* dock harbor **-haupt** *n* entrance gate (of dry dock) **-kammer** *f* interior of dry dock **-kran** *m* dock crane **-problem** *n* dock problem **-pumpe** *f* dock pump **-schiff** *n* floating dock **-schleuse** *f* single entrance, single gate (ebbtide gates) dry-dock and locks
Dock-sohle *f* floor of dry dock **-tor** *n* caisson (navy) **-verlängerung** *f* extension of dry dock **-verschluß** *m* sluice of the dock **-verschluß-ponton** *n* caisson **-vorhafen** *m* basin into which the dry dock opens **-wand** *f* side wall
Dodekaeder *n* dodecahedron **-gleitung** *f* dodecahedral slip
dodekaedrisch dodecahedral
Doggerstahl *m* dogger steel (inferior steel, retaining magnetism)
Doghouse *n* doghouse (charging bay of a glass tank)
Döglingstran *m* bottlenose whale blubber, arctic sperm oil
dokimastisch docimastic
Doktrin *f* doctrine
Dokumentarfilm *m* documentary reel
Dokumentationsgeräte *pl* document recorders
dokumentenecht (Kugelschreiber) document proof
Dokumententinte *f* redord ink
Dolch *m* dagger, poniard, dirk
Doldrums *n* doldrums, calm belt
Dolerit *n* dolerite
Dolier-eisen *n* buffing slicker **-walze** *f* buffing cylinder
Doline *f* sink hole
Dollbord *m* gunwale
Dolle *f* thole, tholepin, crutch, rowlock, nick **-bord** *m* gunwale
Dolly, **~ vorfahren** dolly in **~ zurückfahren** dolly out
Dolmetscher *m* interpreter
Dolomit *m* dolomite, magnesian limestone **gebrannter ~** calcined dolomitic **totgebrannter ~** deadburned dolomite
Dolomit-anlage *f* dolomite plant **-brennofen** *m* dolomite-calcining kiln, dolomite kiln or cupola furnace **-haltig** dolomitic **-herd** *m* dolomite bottom **-kalk** *m* magnesian limestone, dolomitic lime **-mehl** *n* dolomite powder **-spat** *m* dolomite **-stein** *m* dolomite brick **-zustellung** *f* dolomite lining
Dom *m* dome, steam dome
Domänen-grenzflächen *pl* domain boundaries **-größe** *f* domain size
Dom-boden *m* dome bottom **-druck** *m* dome pressure **-gas** *n* dome gas
dominierende Wellenlänge (Farbe) dominant wavelength

Domizilprinzip *n* rule of domicile
Dommantel *m*, **geschweißter ~** welded dome body
Dom-pfaffenorgel *f* bird organ **-sitz** *m* dome seating **-stutzen** *m* socket on dome **-winkelring** *m* dome-base angle ring
Donator (Elektronen-Donator) donator, donor
Donatoren-konzentration *f* doping level (semiconductors) **-niveau** *n* donor level **-wanderung** *f* donor migration
Donatorverunreinigung *f* donor impurity
Donner *m* thunder, thunderclap **-bö** *f* black squall **-effekt** *m* thunder effect (photographic distortion in variable-area recording) **-keil** *m* thunderbolt
donnern to thunder
Donner-schlag *m* thunder, thunderclap **-stein** *m* ceraunia, thunderstone
Dop *m* dab
Dopen *n* doping
Doppel *n* duplicate
doppel- double, twin, duplicate
Döppel *m* punch
Doppel-ableger *m* double distributor **-abtrift** *f* double drift
doppelachsiges Fahrgestell split-axle-type landing gear
Doppelader *f* twin wire or leader, two-wire core **gekreuzte ~** crossed or transposed pair (teleph.) **verdrallte ~** twisted pair or loop (teleph.)
Doppeladerleitungsabschnitt *m* carrier line section
doppeladrig two-wire, pair (of), twin, bifilar **-es Kabel** twin or bifilar cable
Doppel-anker *m* V or double stay, H-section armature **-ankerrelais** *n* double-armature relay **-anruf** *m* call switched by an A to a B operator to whom the subscriber passes his request **-anschalteklinke** *f* operator's jack **-anschnitt** *m* two-station pilot-balloon spotting **-antimonfluorid** *n* double antimony fluoride **-antrieb** *m* double drive, double reduction final drive **-arbeit** *f* duplication of effort **-arbeitskontakt** *m* double-make contact
doppelarmig two-armed, double-armed **-er Hebel** two-armed lever
Doppel-armkneter *m* double arm kneader **-atomig** biatomic **-auflauf** *m* dual take-up **-auflauftrommel** *f* two-spool take-up
Doppel-aufnahme *f* duplex shot **-ausleger** *m* double bracket **-ausschalter** *m* double cutout **-außenräummaschine** *f* dual-ram vertical surface, broaching machine
Doppel-backenbremse *f* double shoe, double-jawed, or cheek brake **-bahn** *f* double-track or two-way railway line **-bandgelenk** *n* double link **-basisdiode** *f* double-base diode **-batterie** *f* double battery (two batteries operating as a tactical unit) **-begrenzer** *m* double limiter **-belegung** *f* double seizure (tel.) **-belichtung** *f* double exposure
Doppel-beobachtungsfernrohr *n* binocular observation telescope **-bereifung** *f* double or dual tires **-beschichteter Film** double-coated film stock, sandwich film **-besteuerung** *f* double taxation **-besteuerungsabkommen** *n* double taxation agreement **-bestimmung** *f* repeat determination **-betrieb** *m* duplex operation, duplex system **-betriebsschaltung** *f* composite connection **-beugung** *f* diffraction polarization **-biegung** *f* bending in two directions **-bifilargravimeter** *m* double-bifilar gravimeter
Doppelbild *n* echo images **-einrichtung** *f* double-image device **-entfernungsmesser** *m* double-image range finder **-mikrometer** double-image micrometer **-theodolit** *m* photogoniometer for pairs of photographs **-vorsatz** *m* front attachment prism **-werfer** *m* double projector, camera plastica **-wurf** *m* double projection
Doppel-bindung *f* double bond **-bindungsregel** *f* double-bond rule **-blatt** *n* four-page folder **-blendenmethode** *f* double-slit method **-blickzielfernrohr** *n* double direct-sighting telescope **-blinkleuchte** *f* twin blinker **-blockkondensatoren** *pl* double-block condensers (ocean cable) **-boden** *m* double bottom **-bodenzelle** *f* double-bottom compartment
Doppel-bogen *m* double bend, double elbow (pipe) **-bogenfalzmaschine** *f* two-sheet folder **-bogenkalander** *m* twin calender for glazing paper sheets **-bogenlampe** *f* double carbon-arc lamp **-bohrsystem** *n* dual drilling system **-bördelflanschrohr** *n* double bordered flange pipe
doppel-brechend doubly refracting **-brechung** *f* double refraction birefringence **-brücke** *f* double bridge (Kelvin) **-brückenverstärker** *m* double-bridge two-way repeater **-bügel** *m* brace **-bügelaufhängung** *f* suspension in double bows **-bürstensatz** *m* double set of brushes
Doppel-chlorid *n* dichloride, double chloride **-chlorzinn** *n* stannic chloride, (tetrachloride of tin) **-cylinderheuauflader** *m* double-cylinder hay loader **-dach** *n* false roof work **-darre** *f* tow-floored kiln
Doppeldaumen *m* shuttle cam **~ für Hin- und Rückgang** shuttle cam for reciprocating motion
Doppeldecke *f* false ceiling
Doppeldecker *m* biplane **~ mit gleichgroßen Flächen** equal-span biplane
Doppeldecker-bauart *f* biplane formula or construction **-flugmodell** *n* biplane model
Doppeldeckflachpalette *f* double decked flat pallet
Doppeldiagonalwalzenstuhl *m* double-diagonal roller mill
Doppeldiode *f* double diode, duodiode **-pentode** *f* double diode pentode **-triode** *f* double diode triode
doppeldrähtig double-wire, two-wire **-e Leitung** metallic circuit
Doppeldrahtzwirnmaschine double-twisting machine
Doppel-drehkondensator *m* double-gauged variable capacitor or condenser **-drehteil** *m* compound swivel base **-drillingspreßpumpe** *f* double three-throw pressure pump **-drossel** *f* double reactor, double choke
Doppeldruck *m* slur (music), mackle **-kaltpresse** *f* double-blow cold up-setting machine **-lager** *m* double thrust bearing **-luftmesser** *m* dual airpressure gauge **-maschine** *f* duplex printing machine **-messer** *m* two-scale pressure gauge **-minderventil** *n* two-stage reducing valve **-reduzierventil** *n* double stage (regulator)

reducing valve

Doppeldublettantenne *f* double-doublet antenna

Doppelduo *n* Dowlais mill ~ **mit Vorgerüst** *n* double two-housing mill with roughing train

Doppelduo-straße *f* continuous rolling train, two-high mill **-walzwerke** *pl* double two-high mill, dowlas mill

Doppel-Duro-Härtung *f* Double-Duro-hardening

Doppel-düsenvergaser *m* double-jet carburetor **-eindeutig** one-to-one-sequential **-echopanorama** *n* double echo display **-einschlag** *m* splice **-einschlaglupe** *f* double folding magnifier **-eisen für Fügblöcke** double iron for cooper's plane **-empfang** *m* dual or double reception **-endbolzen** *m* double-end bolt **-ender** *m* double-ended boiler

Doppelerdschluß *m* ground leakage on two phases (elec.) **-erfassung beim widerstandsabhängigen Zeitstaffelschutz** controlling double ground conditions in time-graded, distance-dependent protective systems

Doppel-erregerwicklung *f* double-type excitating winding **-fach** *n* double shed **-fadenaufhängung** *f* bifilar suspension **-fadenglühlampe** *f* double-contact bulb **-fädig** bifilar **-fähre** *f* doubly supported raft **-fahrleitung** *f* twin contact wire **-faltversuch** *m* double bend test **-falzapparat** *m* double folder **-falznummer** *f* double fold number **-falzzahl** *f* double folds (for films, etc.) **-farbig** dichromatic (dichroic) **-farbigkeit** *f* dichroism

Doppel-feder für Drehgestelle elliptical bogie spring for rotating platforms (locomotive) **-fenster** *n* storm sash **-fernglas** *n* field glass, binocular **-fernrohr** *n* double or binocular telescope, battery commander's telescope, field glass **-fernrohrlupe** *f* binocular telescopic magnifiers **-feuergaserzeuger** *m* double fire gas producer **-feuergenerator** *m* double-zone producer **-filter** *n* two-stage filter **-flächige Waren** double-sided goods **-flansch** *m* companion flange **-flanschig** double-flanged **-florig** double pile

Doppel-flügel *m* double section wing (aviation) **-flügeltür** *f* double sliding door **-flugkettenformation** *f* two-flight squadron formation **-flugzeug** *n* composite aircraft **-fluß** *m* double flow **-flutig** double-suction **-fokusröhre** *f* double-focus tube **-frequenzmesser** *m* double frequency meter **-führungskette** *f* double slide crank chain **-funke** *m* duplex sparking

Doppel-gabelhebel *m* double-yoke lever **-gänger-aufnahme** *f* dual-role work

doppelgängig bifilar, bifurcate, forked, branching **-e Gewinde** double thread **-e Schnecke** double lead screw

Doppel-gärverfahren *n* double fermentation process **-gas** *n* combination of water gas and distillation gas **-gatter** *n* frame saw with two blades **-geber** *m* **mit elektrischer Geberkuppelung** synchronizer for two guns with electrical coupling **-gefüge** *n* duplex structure **-gegenschreiben** *n* quadruplex telegraphy **-gegensprechbetrieb** *m* quadruplex working (teleph.)

Doppelgegensprechen *n* quadruplex system ~ **für Gabelverkehr** split quadruplex ~ **für Staffelverkehr** extended quadruplex

Doppel-gegensprechsatz quadruplex system **-gegensprechsystem** *n* quadruplex system **-geleise** *n* double track **-gelenk** *n* double joint, universal joint **-gesenkhammer** *m* double drop hammer

Doppel-gestaltung *f* dimorphism **-gestänge** *n* H pole, coupled poles, double pole **-gesteuerte Heptode** dual control heptode **-gewebe** *n* reversible cloth **-gewindeschraube** *f* double-threaded screw

Doppelgitterröhre *f* four-electrode or screen-grid vacuum tube, double-grid valve or tube, tetrode, spacecharge tetrode, twin-grid tube, bigrid valve ~ (in Schutznetzschaltung) pliodynatron

Doppel-gitterverfahren *n* double grating method **-glas** *n* binocular **-glasspiegel** *m* double-glass mirror **-gleichrichter** *m* full-wave rectifier **-gleisig** with double tracks **-gleitung** *f* duplex slip

Doppel-glocke *f* double shed or petticoat insulator (single or double petticoat) **-glockenanlage** *f* double bell jar plant **-glockenisolator** *m* double-shed or petticoat insulator **-hahn** *m* two-way cock **-haken** *m* sheet hook double **-härtung** *f* double hardening

Doppel-haue *f* double, forked, or tow-pronged hoes **-hebel** *m* driving crank, double lever, twin pedal **-hebelschalter** *m* double-lever switch **-hebelübersetzung** *f* double lever transmission **-herzstück** *n* diamond crossing, double frog

Doppel-hobeleisen *n* thin straight double plane cutter **-holländer** *m* duplex beating engine **-hordig** two-floored **-hörig** binaural **-hub** *m* up-and-down stroke **-hubzeit** *f* double stroke time **-hülle** *f* double hull **-impulsgeber** *m* twin-synchronizing pulse generator **-impulsverfahren** *n* double-impulse method **-integral** *n* double integral **-ionisationskammer** *f* double ionisation chamber **-isolator** *m* transposition insulator **-jigger** *m* double jig

Doppelkäfig-läufer *m* double cage rotor **-motor** *m* double cage motor engine **-wicklung** *f* double squirrel-cage winding

Doppel-kalander *m* tandem calender **-kamera** *f* double camera, stereoscopic (stereo) camera **-kammer** *f* two-lens camera, double chamber **-kammerofen** *m* double-chamber-type tunnel kiln **-kamm-Magnetron** *n* interdigital magnetron **-kaspelmikrophon** *n* double-button transmitter

Doppel-karnieseisen *n* reed plane iron with square and cove **-kassette** *f* two-plate holder **-kantig** double edged **-kapazität** *f* dual capacitance **-kapselmikrophon** *n* double-button carbon microphone **-kastenspeiser** *m* double hopper feeder

Doppelkegel *m* double cone **-antenne** *f* double-cone or cage antenna **-kolbenventil** *n* double-cone piston (or plunger) valve **-kreiselmischer** *m* double-cone impeller mixer **-kreiselrührer** *m* double-cone impeller **-kupplung** *f* double-tapered muff coupling **-ring** *m* double bevel ring **-trommelmischer** *m* double-cone mixer

Doppelkeil *m* folding wedge, gib an cotter **-haue** *f* double-pointed pick, mandrel, universal pick **-polarisationsapparat** *m* double-wedge saccharimeter **-riemen** *m* twin V-belt **-spanten** *n* hardchine hull

Doppelkern-bohrer *m* double-core barrel drill

-bohrgarnitur *f* double core drilling equipment **-dünnfilmspeicher** *m* bicore thin-film memory, double core thin-film memory **-rohr** *n* double-core barrel

Doppel-kessel *m* jacketted vessel **-kettenstichnähmaschine** *f* double chain-stitch sewing machine **-kiellinie** *f* double column (navy), ships in double column **-klammer** *f* bus-bar clamp **-klang** *m* echoed sound, hearing sound twice **-klauenwinde** *f* jack with two hooks

Doppel-klemme *f* double terminal **-klinke** *f* double or operator's jack **-knie** *n* staple knee **-kniestück** *n* return bend (pipe) **-knippmaschine** *f* double-acting cutting machine **-knoten** *m* double-loop knot, binode **-kohlemikrophon** *n* push-pull carbon microphone or transmitter

doppelkohlensaure(s) bicarbonate of

Doppelkolben *m* twin piston **-Dieselmotor** *m* double-piston or opposed-piston Diesel engine **-maschine** *f* opposed-piston engine **-motor** *m* double-piston or twin-piston engine

Doppel-kollektormotor *m* double-commutator motor **-komplettgießmaschine** *f* automatic double-casting machine **-kondensator** *m* twin condenser **-kontakt** *m* double or collateral contact **-kontrasteinlauftechnik** *f* double-contrast enema technique

Doppel-kontrolle *f* dual control **-konusantenne** *f* biconical antenna, double-cone or cage antenna **-kopf(fern)hörer** *m* headphones **-kopfschiene** *f* bullhead or bulbhead rail **-kraftmessung** *f* double measurement of charge

Doppel-krampe *f* double link **-kreischarakteristik** *f* figure-of-eight polar diagram (direction finder) **-kreisdiagramm** *n* figure-of-eight diagram, tangent-circle pattern **-krempelführer** *m* double card tenter (textiles) **-kreuzgelenk** *n* universal joint **-kreuzrahmenantenne** *f* double-cross coil antenna **-kreuzsupport** double-compound slide rest **-kristall** *n* twin crystal

Doppel-kugellager *n* double-row ball bearing **-kugelrückschlagventil** *n* double-ball non-return (or check) valve **-kühlfalle** *f* tow-stage cold trap **-kurbel** *f* two-throw crankshaft **-kurbelrechen** *m* double propelling rake **-kurbelumschalter** *m* double-lever switch

Doppel-lafette *f* double mounting (of gun) **-läufig** double-barreled **-laut** *m* diphthong **-läuter** *m* Bright's bells, two sounders **-läutewerk** *n* double-stroke bell **-leerstelle** *f* double void **-leiter** *m* twin conductor

Doppelleitung *f* double or twin conductor, double lead, duplex conductor wire, twin or loop(ed) circuit, two-wire metallic circuit **Widerstand je Meile ~** resistance per loop mile

Doppelleitungs-betrieb *m* two-wire operation **-linie** *f* two-wire route **-widerstand** *m* loop resistance

Doppellenker-kran *m* double guide crane **-wippdrehkran** *m* double-link level luffing crane

Doppel-leuchte *f* twin optical apparatus (maritime signals) **-linie** *f* double line or rule, doublet (optics) **-linse** *f* double lens, doublet **-lochung** *f* double punch **-lötungen** *f pl* double seals **-luftschraube** *f* tandem-design propeller **-lupe** *f* double magnifier

Doppel-magazinsetzmaschine *f* two-magazine composing machine **-magnetschalter** *m* two-step magnetic switch **-mantel** *m* double casing or jacket **-markierung** *f* double mark **-masche** *f* double stitch **-maßstab** *m* two-scale rule **-mast** *m* double pole

Doppelmattglas *n*, **blaues ~** double ground blue glass

doppel-mäuliger Schraubenschlüssel double-head wrench **-messer** *n* double knife **-messerschalter** *m* double-throw knife switch **-metalldraht** *m* bimetallic wire **-mikrophon** *n* double-button transmitter, push-pull transmitter **-mikroskop** *n* double microscope, stereo-microscope **-modulation** *f* double or dual modulation **-Morse-Sicherheitsschaltung** *f* broken circuit working **-muldenkneter** *m* divided trough kneader

doppeln to double, duplicate, copy, sheathe (ships, etc.)

Doppeln *n* doubling

Doppel-nadelabstrecken *pl* intersecting gill boxes **-nadeltelegraph** *m* double-needle telegraph **-nietung** *f* double-riveting **-nippel mit Sechskant** hexagonal nipple **-nutmotor** *m* double squirrel cage motor **-objektiv** *n* double lens **-ofen** *m* pair furnace **-parry** *m* double closure, double-bell-and-hopper arrangement **-pedalharfe** *f* double-action harp **-peilung** *f* twin bearings (radio), bearing channel (radio)

Doppel-pendel *n* double governor or pendulum **-pentagonprisma** *n* double penta prism **-pentodenendröhre** *f* double output pentode **-pfahl** *m* double wringing post **-picke** *f* double pick **-planrätter** *m* double sieve, duplex shaking table **-platten** *f pl* twin plates or crystals, composite crystal, biquartz **-plattenkristall** *m* bimorph crystal, divided plate crystal, biquartz **-pneu** *m* twin or double pneumatic tires **-pol** *m* dipole (radio)

doppelpolig bipolar, double-pole, double-polar **-e Umschaltung** double commutation

Doppel-polwechsler *m* double-pole alternator (radio) **-polzündung** *f* double-pole ignition

Doppelpotentiometer *n* dual potentiometer **~ mit konzentrischen Achsen** dual potentiometer with concentric control spindles

Doppel-presse *f* double press **-prisma** *n* double prism **-projektion** *f* double projection **-projektor** *m* double projector, camera plastica **-propeller** *m pl* coaxial contrarotating propellers **-puddelofen** *m* double or double-puddle furnace **-pumpe** *f* twin pumps

Doppel-punkt *m* colon (punct.) **-punkteinschaltung im Raum** double-point interpolation in space **-quarzkeil** *m* double quartz wedge

Doppel-rad *n* double driving gear, twin wheel **-radfahrgestell** *n* double or dual wheel undercarriage **-rahmenpeiler** *m* double frame direction finder **-raffinierstahl** *m* double-refined steel **-raspel** *f* two-winged rasp

Doppel-rechenbewegung *f* mangle rack motion **-reflektorflutlicht** *n* twin floodlight **-regal** *n* double rack **-regler** *m* double-type regulator, duplex governor **-reifen** *m* dual tire

Doppelreihe *f* double series (math.), double file

Doppel-reihenbefeuerung *f* double row lighting **-reihenmaschine** *f* twin-cylinder or double-tandem engine (four cylinders altogether) **-richtröhre** *f* duodiode **-richtungshörer** *m* twin sound locator **-riemen** *m* double-layer or two-ply belt **-riemenscheibe** *f* twin belt pulley

Doppelring-lehre für Grenzmessung der Dicke limit gauges for outside maximum and minimum **-oberflächenspannungsmesser** *m* twin-ring-type surface tensiometer **-schlüssel** *m* double head box wrench **-trensengebiß** *n* double-ring snaffle bit **-visier** *n* double-ring sight

Doppelröhre *f* double casing, twin tube

Doppelröhrenschaltung *f* tandem-tube (push-pull) circuit organization

Doppelrohr-mühle *f* combination mill **-rahmen** *m* (motorcycle) duplex frame **-verflüssiger** *m* double-pipe condenser **-verstärker** *m* two-valve repeater **-zwischenverstärker** *m* two-valve two-wire repeater (teleph.)

Doppelrolle *f*, **schnelle ~** double snap roll (aviation)

Doppel-rollenkupplung *f* double roller clutch **-röntgenblitzröhre** *f* double X-ray flash tube **-rost** *m* double grate **-röstung** *f* double roasting, double sintering **-rücklaufrad** *n* cluster gear **-ruder** *n* twin rudder **-ruderig** double-banking **-rührer** *m* double-motion agitator **-rundbohrer** *m* double reamer, double round bit

doppelsägeförmige Spannung double-sawtooth potential

Doppel-salz *n* double salt **-sammelschienen** *pl* double bus bars **-saugrohr** *n* double or double-throat Venturi tube **-schachtanlage** *f* double-pit plant **-schalter** *m* duplex switch **-schaufel** *f* double bucket (turbine) **-schaufelpflug** *m* double-shovel plow **-schauflig** double-blade **-scheren** *pl* double-cutting shears **-scheibenegge** *f* tandem-disk harrow

Doppel-scheibenfräser *m* interlocking side milling cutter, straddle cutter **-schicht** *f* double layer, double striation **-schichtfilm** *m* sandwich or double-coated film **-schichtlinse** *f* double-layer lens **-schichtmodell** *n* two layer model **-schichtschirm** *m* double-layer screen

Doppel-schieber *m* double slide **-schiebermotor** *m* double-sleeve valve engine **-schirm** *m* cascade-type screen **-schirting** *m* cretonne **-schlagwecker** *m* double-stroke bell **-schleife** *f* double loop **-schleifenwicklung mit Parallelverbindungen** double-loop winding with parallel connections (elec.) **-schleifständer** *m* double wheel grinder

doppelschlicht superfine

Doppel-schlichtfeile *f* dead-smooth file **-schließkontakt** *m* double-make contact **-relais** *n* double-make relays **-schlittenkassette** *f* double dark slide **-schloßventil** *n* lockout valve

Doppelschluß-dynamomaschine *f* compound-wound generator **-erregung** *f* compound excitation **-generator** *m* double-wound generator **-maschine** *f* compound dynamo **-motor** *m* compound-wound motor **-verhalten** *n* compound characteristic **-wicklung** *f* compound winding

Doppel-schmiege *f* combination bevel **-schmierölfilter** *n* reversible double lube oil filter **-schnecke** *f* twin-screw conveyer **-schneckenextruder** *m* twin-screw extruder **-schneckenförmig** double-helical **-schneckenmischer** *m* double screw mixer

Doppelschneidewiegemesser *n* two-bladed mincing knife

doppelschichtig with double cross section (as a U stirrup)

Doppelschnur *f* double flexible (elec.), twin flex, two-wire conductor

Doppel-schrägkugellager *n* double bevel ball bearing

Doppelschrauben *pl* twin screw **-richtmaschine** *f* twin-screw elevating mechanism **-schiff** *n* twin-screw ship **-schlüssel** *m* double-head wrench

Doppel-schreiben *n* diplex telegraphy **-schritt** *m* stride **-schußgeber** *m* synchronizer for two guns **-schütz** *n* double gate or sluice **-schützenwehr** *n* double-sluice weir **-schwächungswiderstand** *m* double gain controller **-schwefeleisen** *n* iron pyrites **-schwefelzinn** *n* stannic bisulfide

doppelschwefelsauer bisulfite of

Doppel-schwengel *m* double tree **-schwimmer** *m* twin float **-schwinge** *f* double compensating lever **-schwingenbrecher** *m* double-swing jaw crusher

Doppelsechs, Schlaefische ~ Schlaefi's double six

Doppel-seilförderung *f* main-and-tail-rope haulage **-seitensteuer** *n* twin rudders

doppelseitig bilateral, to both sides, double-faced, double-sided; (Stoff) reversible **-e Bildabtaströhre** two-sided mosaic pickup tube **-es Gestell** double-sided rack **-e Kopierdrehmaschine** double-ended copying lathe **-e Mosaikröhre** image-multiplier iconoscope **-er Zeigerausschlag** deflection in either direction

Doppel-senden *n* double transmission **-sichtigkeit** *f* diplopia **-signalzone** *f* bisignal zone **-sinnig** ambiguous, equivocal, uncertain, double meaning **-sitz** *m* double seat, tandem seat **-sitzer** *m* two-seater (aviation)

doppel-sitzig double-seated **-sitzventil** *n* double-seat valve, hollow-disk reversing valve **-skala** *f* double scale (instruments) **-spaltferritkern** *m* double gap ferrite core

Doppel-spat *m* Iceland spar **-spatenmeißel** *m* double-star bit **-speiche** *f* double spoke **-sperrklinke** *f* double dog, (in a Strowger selector) pair of pawls, double pawls, double detent **-spiegel** *m* double aerial array **-spindel** *f* double spindle **-spiralbohrer** *m* double-cutting or double-spiral bit (two spiral grooves) **-spitzhacke** *f* double pick **-sprechbetrieb** *m* phantom telephone operation

Doppel-sprechen *n* two-way telephone conversation, phantom telephony, phantoming **-sprechringübertrager** *m* phantom repeating coil **-sprechschaltung** *f* phantom or duplex telephone connection, phantom circuit **-sprengkabel** *n* duplex blasting ignition cable, twin detonating wires (blasting), two-conductor firing wire **-spulenkette** *f* double high-pass filter **-spulspinnmaschine** *f* nonidle spinning machine **-spülsteine** *pl* double sinks **-spur** *f* half track (tape rec.), twin track **-spuriger Tonstreifen** double-edged variable-width sound track or record

Doppelständer *m* broad pendant **-exzenterpresse** *f* double-sided eccentric press **-schleifmaschine** *f* planer type grinding machine **-kurbelpresse** *f* straight-sided crank press

Doppelstangenlinie *f* H-pole or H-fixture line

Doppel-S-Taster *m* double-Scal(l)ipers, double S compass
Doppel-stativ *n* double stand **-stecker** *m* multipoint plug, biplug, double, two-pin, or two-way plug **-steppstich** *m* double lock stitch
Doppelstern *m* binaries, double star **-kabel** *n* spiral-eight cable, quad pair cable, star quad cable **-vierer** *m* quad (star)
Doppelsternmotor *m* double-row radial engine, double-bank radial engine, two-row radial engine ~ **mit gegeneinander versetzten Zylindersternen** staggered radial engine
Doppelstern-schaltung *f* duplex star connection **-vierer** *m* pairs cabled in quad-pair formation (teleph.)
Doppelsteuer *n* dual control **-flugzeug** *n* duo-control airplane **-röhre** *f* double control tube, power pentode (cathode grid connected with control grid rather than with cathode)
Doppelsteuerung *f* dual control (aviation) **ausbaubare** ~ removable dual control **auskuppelbare** ~ disconnectable dual control
Doppel-steuervorrichtung *f* dual control **-stiftstecker** *m* two-pin plug **-stopfhacke** *f* double pick **-stöpsel** *m* double plug, two-way plug **-stoßschwingsieb** *n* double shaking screen **-strahlröhre** *f* split-beam cathode ray-tube, double shaking screen, double-beam (cathode-ray) tube **-streuversuch** *m* double-scattering experiment **-strickmaschine** *f* knitting machine with double mechanism
Doppelstrom *m* double current **-betrieb** *m* transmission by double current, double-current operation **-gegensprechen auf Doppelleitungen** metallic polar duplex **-gegensprechsystem** *n* polar duplex system **-gegensprechübertragung** *f* duplex repeater **-taste** *f* double current key **-telegraphierzeichen** *n* double-current telegraph signal **-übertragung** *f* double-current translation
Doppelstütze *f* double (pin) pole **U-, J-, S-förmige** ~ double U, J, or S insulator spindle
Doppel-stutzen *m* double connecting piece, double union
Doppel-suchfernrohr *n* sighting or exploring binoculars, double-finder telescope **-sudwerk** *n* double brewing plant
Doppelsuper-effekt *m* double-super effect **-empfang** *m* double super-heterodyne reception
Doppelsupport *m* two compound rests ~ **mit getrennten Unterschiebern** connected rests on separate slides
Doppel-synchronumrichter *m* twin synchronizing commutator **-tandemsatz** *m* dual-tandem design
Doppeltantimonfluorid *n* bifluoride of antimony
doppelt double, duplex, twin, dual, two-ply, twofold, twice, double duplicate ~ **ausführen** to duplicate ~ **begossener Film** double-emulsion film ~ **breit** double-wide ~ **gekröpft** double throw ~ **sublimiert** resublimed ~ **wirkend** double acting
doppelt-e Belichtung double exposure **-er Betazerfall** double-beta disintegration or decay **-e (oder mehrfache) Drehung** crosses inserted in twist system **-e Genauigkeit** *f* double precision **-es Gewinde** double thread **-e Gewindesteigung** *f* double screw thread **-e Haltbarkeit** *f* double life **-es Krümmer-T-Stück** sweep T
doppelt-e Lauffläche double tread **-er Lochbandvorschub** dual feed tape carriage **-es oder zweifaches Mahlen** double grinding **-e Pumpe** duplex pump **-e Schaltkreise** duplicate circuitry **-es Seitenleitwerk** dual fins and rudders
doppelt-er Viertelwellenübertrager double quarter-wave transformer **-e Vorsteckeinrichtung** double front feed **-er Wandknoten** *m* double shroud knot **-e Zahnzange** double rack
Doppel-T-Anker *m* H armature, shuttle armature (magneto)
Doppeltarif *m* double tariff **-zähler** *m* two-rate meter, double-tariff meter
doppeltberührend bitangent
doppeltbrechend birefringent, birefractive **-er Kristall** double-refracting crystal
doppeltchromsaures Kali bichromate of potash
Doppel-T-Eisen *n* H-section iron, I beam, double-T iron, T iron
Doppel-T-Eisenträger *m* double-T gland
Doppeltensor *m* double tensor
doppeltgelagert with a double bearing
doppeltgerichtet bothway, two-way **-e Verbindungsleitung** bothway junction, two-way trunk circuit
doppelt-geschweißtes Eisen double-refined iron **-gespinst** *n* double rove **-haken** *m* (Kran) ramshorn hook **-hochrund** convexo-convex **-hohl** concavo-concave
doppelt-kieselsaurer Kalk dicalcium silicate
doppeltkohlensaures Natron sodium bicarbonate
doppeltkonisch biconical **-e Muffe mit Einschnitten** coupling with recessed ends
doppeltlogarithmische Koordinaten log-log coordinates
Doppeltmahlen *n* double grinding
Doppel-T-Netzwerk *n* parallel-T network, twin-T-network
Doppelton-detektor *m* two-tone detector **-druck** *m* double-tone printing **-druckfarbe** *f* double-tone printing ink **-effekt** *m* (Lack) double-tone effect **-farbe** *f* (Lack) double-tone color **-horn** *n* bitone horn **-WT** (Wechselstromtelegraphie) two-tone voice-frequency telegraphy
Doppeltopfmanschette *f* double cup-shaped gasket
Doppel-T-Profil *n* channel section
Doppel-T-Querschnitt *m* I section
Doppel-transporteur *m* station pointer **-treibstoff** *m* bi-propellant (rocket) **-trennkontakt** *m* double-break contact
Doppeltrichter-apparat *m* cup and cone charger (blast furnace) **-förmiges Rohr** converging and diverging nozzle
Doppeltriode *f* duo-triode
Doppeltriowalzwerk *n* three-high rolling mill
doppeltrümmig-e Förderung double track conveying **-er Schrägaufzug** double-track skip hoist, double-track hoist bridge
Doppel-T-Schiene *f* double-T rail, T rail
Doppel-T-Stück *n* crossover T
Doppel-T-Träger *m* I beam, I girder, double-T girder
Doppel-tubus *m* binocular tube **-tunnel** *m* twin tunnel **-tür** *f* twin door, double or two-wing door **-turm** *m* twin turret (navy), two-gun turret
Doppel-T-Verteilungsstück *f* four-way T

doppeltweinsaures Kali potassium bitartrate, cream of tartar
doppeltwirkend double-acting **-e Maschine** double-acting engine **-e Pumpe** double-acting pump **-er Zylinder** double-acting cylinder
Doppelüberlagerungseffekt *m* double super effect
Doppelüberschlagen, schnelles ~ double snap roll
Doppel-übersetzung *f* two-speed gear **-übersetzungsgetriebe** *n* double-gear train, double-reduction gear **-U-Eisenrahmen** *m* two-channel type frame **-umfassung** *f* double envelopment **-umkehrprisma** *n* inversion prism (reverses in both axes of image) **-umschalter** *m* double commutator, double switch
Doppel- und Fehllochaussuchvorrichtung *f* double punch and blank column detection
Doppelung *f* lamination
Doppelunterbrecher *m* double-lever contact breaker
Doppelunterbrechungs-klinke *f* double-break jack **-relais** *n* double-break relay **-verbindung** *f* double connection **-wandig** double- or hollow-walled
Doppel-U-Stoß *m* double-U butt joint
Doppel-V-Antenne *f* double-V antenna, doublet
Doppel-ventil *n* two-way valve **-venturirohr** *n* double or double-throat Venturi tube **-verflüssiger** *m* double condenser **-vergaser** *m* duplex carburetor **-verhältnis** *n* cross ratio, anharmonic ratio **-verkehr** *m* duplex or two-way communication **-verkehrszusatz** *m* transmitting and receiving attachment (radio) **-verschluß** *m* double closure, double bell-and-hopper arrangement
Doppel-visierfernrohr *n* binocular gun sight **-vokal** *m* diphthong **-voltmeter** double voltmeter
Doppelvorwahl *f*, **gemischte** ~ partly double preselection
Doppel-wägung *f* double weighing **-währung** *f* bimetallism **-walzenkanal** *m* double cylinder channel **-walzenmühle** *f* double-roll crusher **-walzenscheider** double roller separator **-walzentrockner** *m* twin-drum drier **-wand** *f* jacket, double wall **-wandig** double-walled **-wandiger Kessel** *m* steam-jacketed pan **-wandung** *f* jacketed wall
Doppelweg-gleichrichter *m* (der Wellen), full-wave rectifier **-gleichrichterröhre** *f* full-wave rectifying valve **-gleichrichtung** *f* full-wave rectification **-schaltung** *f* double or full-wave rectifier circuit organization
Doppel-weiche *f* dual directing means (for routing purposes), double switch **-wendel** *n* wound coil **-wendelglühdraht** *m* coiled-coil filament **-wendelsystem** *n* biplane filament system **-werkbank** *f* double bench **-wicklung** *f* shunt or compound winding **-wicklungsspule** *f* double-winding reactor **-winde** *f* double acting hoist, double winch
Doppel-windelprisma *n* line ranger **-windkanal** *m* double wind channel or tunnel **-winkellasche** *f* double-angle fishplate **-winkelmesser** *m* double protractor or goniometer **-wirkender Motor** double-acting engine
Doppel-zackenschrift mit Abdeckung duplex variable-area track, bilateral track recording with double-vane shutter, double-edged variable width track **-zahnrad** *n* double gear wheel **-zahnradpumpe** *f* double gear pump **-zahnstange** *f* impression operating rack **-zahnstangenbewegung** *f* double-rack motion **-zeichen** *n* double or echo signals, split response, double blip on radar **-zeichenkontrolle** *f* double-mark check **-zeile** *f* double line
Doppel-zellenschalter *m* two-point end cell or emergency cell switch, double regulating switch, double battery or cell switch **-zentner** *m* two hundredweight, 100 kilograms **-ziehfeder** *f* double-line ruling pen **-zug** *m* two-step drawing **-zugriff** *m* dual access **-zuleitungskabel** *n* twin feeder cable
Doppelzünder *m* combination fuse, double or dual ignition, time or percussion fuse ~ **S/60** clockwork time percussion fuse ~ **und Zeitzünder** combination fuse
Doppel-zündmagnet *m* dual (ignition) magneto **-zündung** *f* dual ignition **-zündungssystem** *n* dual-ignition system **-zungenpfeife** *f* double-tongued flute
Doppelzweckantenne *f* diplexer ~ **in Brückenschaltung** bridge diplexer
Doppel-zweckgeschütz *n* dual-purpose gun **-zweipoldreipolröhre** *f* duodiode-triode tube
Doppel-zweipolröhre *f* two-electrode tube, duodiode **-zweipolvierpolröhre** *f* duodiode-tetrode tube **-zweiwalzenstraße** *f* continuous rolling train **-zwilling** *m* two-pair core **-zwirner** *m* doubler and twister **-zylinder** *m* twin cylinder **-zylinderwalze** *f* **mit zwei Hauptwalzenpaaren** double fulling machine with two main pairs of rollers
Döpper *m* riveting set or snap, anvil
Doppler *m* reproducer **-breite** *f* Doppler broadening **-effekt** *m* Doppler effect, Doppler shift
Doppler-frequenz *f* Doppler frequency **-Radar mit ungedämpften Wellen** continuous-wave (C.W.), Doppler radar **-Verbreiterung** Doppler broadening
Dopplung *f* double precision
Dorn *m* taper plug, spindle, thorn, spine, triblet, pin, punch, spike, drift, bolt, tongue, mandrel, tap cinder, puddling slag (of copper), slag, cotter, peg, core bar, spur, shaft, wrench ~ **zum Ausdornen** punch for expanding ~ **mit federnder Mitnehmerscheibe** spring-tensioned driving plate ~ **eines Scharnierbandes** bolt of a hinge **flacher** ~ flat triblet **fliegender** ~ floating mandrel
dornartig spiked
Dorn-aufbereitung *f* mandrel dressing **-ausziehvorrichtung** *f* mandrel stripper **-durchmesser** *m* mandrel diameter **-elektrode** *f* contact bar
dornen to expand by mandrel, indent, open out (a hole)
Dornen *n* drifting (punching or spreading) **-krone** *f* crown of thorns (appearance of certain type of pulse jamming on radar sets)
Dörnerschlacke *f* tap cinder, puddling slag, (metal) bulldog
Dorn-fänger *m* fishing-tool socket, socket with valve **-hammer** *m* punch or drift hammer, drift punch
dornig thorny

Dorn-leitungsschuhe *pl* prod-type terminals **-niet** *m* pop rivet **-presse** *f* mandrel or arbor press **-ringe** *m pl* ring gauges **-sammelrost** *m* broach collecting grid **-schloß** *n* pin lock (doors) **-stab** *m* mandrel bar **-stange** *f* mandrel rod **-stauchpresse** *f* mandrel upsetting press **-umwickelprobe** *f* mandrel coiling test **-verriegelung** *f* hold-up attachment (lock)

Dörr-anstalt für Obst fruit-drying plant **-apparat** *m* desiccating device

dörren to desiccate, dry, scorch, kiln-dry **Holz ~** to dry wood (in a stove), stove wood, season wood artificially

Dörr-ofen *m* drying oven **-schrank** *m* (elektrischer) dehydrator

Dorsalkapsel *f* dorsal cup

Dose *f* plug socket, socket, holder, box, can, cell, container, capsule, diaphragm

Dosenabschneide- und Bördelmaschine *f* tin-cutting and -edging machine

Dosen-aneroid *n* aneroid, barometer, capsule aneroid **-barometer** *n* aneroid barometer **-einheit** *f* resistance unit **-endverschluß** *m* boxhead **-entwicklung** *f* (daylight) tank development (phot.) **-fernhörer** *m* watch or box receiver, watchcase telephone **-fertigungsmaschine** *f* machine for making tin boxes **-gesteuert** capsule-controlled (aviation)

Dosen-höhenmesser *m* aneroid altimeter **-horizont** *m* enclosed or box horizon **-kammer** *f* diaphragm chamber (motor) **-libelle** *f* leveling indicator, circular spirit level, leveler, spherical or box level, spirit-level clinometer, box or circular bubble **-membran** *f* capsule, capsular element **-membranzugmesser** *m* capsule diaphragm draught gauge **-relais** *n* box relay **-schließer** *m* hermetical fitter **-senker** *m* recess cutter **-telephon** *n* watch receiver **-wecker** *m* circular bell

Dosieranlage *f* dosing or proportioning plant

dosieren to dose

Dosier-gefäß *n* apportioning vessel **-leistung** *f* dose rate, dosage rate **-maschine** *f* powder-weighing or dosing machine **-meßgerät** *n* dose meter **-pumpe** *f* dosing pump, metering pump **-schnecke** *f* proportioning screw **-tank** *m* metering tank

dosiert in measured quantities, quantitatively regulated, dosed

Dosierventil *f* dosaging valve

Dosierung *f* dosage, dosage rate

Dosierungsgitter *n* dosage grid

Dosimeter *n* dosimeter (roentgen dose)

Dosis *f* dose **gesamte absorbierte ~** integral absorbed dose

Dosis-einheit *f* unit of dosage **-fraktionierung** *f* dose fractionation **-gleichung** *f* equation of dose **-konstante der Gammastrahlung** specific gamma-ray emission **-leistung** *f* dose rate

Dosis-leistungskammer *f* dose value chamber **-leistungsanzeige** *f* dose value indication **-leistungsmeßgerät** *n* dose value measurement **-messer** *m* quantimeter, dosimeter **-protrahierung** *f* dose protraction **-wirkungskurve** *f* dose-effect curve

Dostenöl *n* origanum oil

dotiert doped

Dotierung *f* doping (of semiconductors)

Dotierungsausgleich *m* doping compensation

Doublé *n* rolled gold

Doubeln *n* duplicating

doublieren to double

Doublierstange *f* doubling rod

Dowmetall *n* Dowmetal

Dowsongas *n* Dowson gas, semiwater or power gas

Drache *m* dragon, kite

Drachen *m* kite **-antenne** *f* kite antenna (radio) **-aufstieg** *m* kite ascent **-ballon** *m* sausage or kite balloon **-fesselballon** *m* captive kite balloon **-flugzeug** *n* fixed-wing aircraft **-leine** *f* kite sweep **-schnur** *f* kite string **-spann** *m* kite span **-start** *m* kite start (of airplane models) **-stropp** *m* kite strop **-theorie** *f* dynamic-lift or kite theory **-warte** *f* sounding-balloon station (meteor.)

Dragganker *m*, **Dragge** *f* grapnel

Draht *m* wire, leader, conductor, filament, thread, (slang) cash **abisdierter ~** skinned wire **~ abwickeln** to pay out wire **~ legen** to wire (elec.) **a-(b) ~** a (b) wire, a (b) limb or leg **ausgeglühter ~** annealed wire **bewehrter ~** sheathed wire **blanker ~** bare wire, bare conductor

Draht, den ~ umklöppeln to cover wire with braid **den ~ umspinnen** to cover wire **dünner ~** fine wire, small-gauge wire **durchgehender ~** through wire **einen ~ führen, verlegen** to run a wire **einen ~ ziehen** to string a wire **einfach (doppelt, dreifach) umsponnener ~** single-(double-, triple-)covered wire **feuersicherer ~** flameproof or fireproof wire

Draht, gelitzter ~ stranded wire **gewobener ~** woven wire **gezogener ~** drawn wire **hartgezogener ~** hard-drawn wire **von innen längsrissiger ~** cuppy wire **isolierter ~** insulated or covered wire **mit Gummi isolierter ~** rubber-covered wire **mit Seide isolierter ~** silk-covered wire **nackter ~** bare wire

Draht, papierisolierter ~ paper-insulated wire **schwingender ~** filament swing (magnetron) **spannungsführender ~** live, charged, or hot wire **starker ~** heavy-gauge wire **stromführender ~** current-carrying or live wire **umklöppelter ~** braided wire **umsponnener ~** covered wire **mit Baumwolle umsponnener ~** cotton-covered wire

Draht, unter elektrischer Spannung stehender ~ live wire **unterteilter ~** composite or stranded wire **verdrillter ~** twisted or snaked wire **verkupferter ~** copper-clad or coppered wire **verseilter ~** twisted wire **verzinkter ~** galvanized or zinc-coated wire **verzinnter ~** tinned wire **zweimal gezogener ~** two-draft wire

Draht-abfall *m* scrap wire **-abschneider** *m* wire cutter, nippers **-anker** *m* guy wire, stay, stranded-wire stay **-anschrift** *f* telegraphic or cable address **-anspitzmaschine** *f* wire-sharpening machine **-antenne** *f* wire aerial **-arbeit** *f* filigree **-aufhängung** *f* wire suspension **-auslösehebel** *m* wire-release lever **-auslöser** *m* cable-release **-auslösung** *f* (Verschluß) Bowden-wire shutter) release, wire release **-band** *n* wire tape **-barren** *m* wire bar, wire ingot **-berührung** *f* contact with wire

Drahtbetriebe *pl*, **Zwei ~** two-wire operation

Draht-bewehrung *f* wire armoring or sheathing

-biegegerät *n* wire-bending apparatus **-biegemaschine** *f* wire bending machine **-bindezange** *f* wire-binding pliers **-bogen** *m* wire spring **-bruch** *m* open, break (teleph. line) **-bruchrelais** *n* wire or line-break relay **-bügel** *m* wire strap (wire bow) **-bund** *m* wire or cable lashing **-bündeltransportkran** *m* wire-coil handling crane **-bürste** *f* wire brush

Draht-dicke *f* **(-durchmesser** *m***)** gauge or diameter of wire **-drehwiderstand** *m* wire-wound variable resistor **-einlage** *f* wire core or reinforcement, wire inlet or insertion **-einlauf** *m* wire feed **-einlegemaschine** *f* wiring machine **-einlegen** *n* wiring **-einzäunung** *f* wire fence or enclosure **-eisen** *n* wire rod, iron for wire **-emailiermaschine** *f* wire enameling machine

Draht-erzeugnis *n* wire product **-feder** *f* wire spring **-federstab** (Drehstabfeder) torsion rod (spring), torsion bar spring **-fernsprechen** *n* wire telephony **-fertigstraße** *f* wire rod finishing mill **-festwiderstand** *m* fixed wire resistance **-filter** *n* wire filter

Draht-flechtmaschine *f* wire-braiding or wire-netting machine **-form** *f* laid mold **-förmig** filamentary **-führerrahmen** *m* wire guide frame **-führung** *f* wire-rod guide **-führungsfeder** *f* feeding spring **-führungsschloß** *n* wire guiding lock

Drahtfunk *m* carrier transmission, wired wireless, wired or line radio, wire program distribution, radio diffusion (wire broadcast), wire broadcasting, broadcast or radio relay, rediffusion **-endschaltung** *f* carrier terminal circuit **-leitung** *f* carrier line or circuit **-netz** *n* distribution network **-system** *n* wire carrier system **-technik** *f* wire carrier art

Draht-fußmatte *f* wire foot mat or scraper **-gabel** *f* crook stick (for laying or hoisting wires) **-gabeln** (Vier)-**Einheitsgabeln** four-wire fork, unit forks, hybrid coils **-gaze** *f* wire gauze or mesh, wire cloth **-gebunden** wire-connected **-gebung** *f* twisting **-geflecht** *n* metal-protecting cage, wire netting or cloth, gauze wire **-geflechtzaun** *m* wire fencing **-gehefteter Bogensatz** wire-stitched quires **-gelenkt** wire guided **-gestell** *n* wire frame

Drahtgewebe *f* wire gauze, meshing, netting, or cloth ~ **mit eingepreßter Asbestschicht in der Mitte** wire gauze with flat asbestos center

Draht-gewebeeinlage *f* wire netting insertion **-gitter** *n* wire grating or grid, screen, wiring mat, lattice, metal gauze, wire grating **-gitterflechter** *m* wire lattice maker **-glas** *n* wire glass, wire-reinforced glass **-glühen** *n* wire annealing **-gurtband** *n* wire tissue belt **-haft** *m* (wire) hook **-halter** *m* terminal (elec.), binding post **-handbürste** *f* wire hand brush **-handtäckse** *pl* wire hand tacks **-härtemesser** *m* wire penetrometer **-härterei** *f* wire-hardening plant

Drahthaspel *f* wire reel or rod, reel, rod reel, pay-out reel ~ **mit Drehung des Drahtringes im Aufnahmekorb** pouring rod reel ~ **mit rotierendem Führungsrohr** pipe reel

Drahthebel *m* wire arm (wiper) ~ **mit Wischgummi** wire arm with wiping rubber

Draht-heftapparat *m* wire-stitching apparatus **-heftklammer** *f* binder, wire staple **-heftung** *f* wire-stitching

Drahthindernis *n* wire entanglement, protective wire **durchlaufendes** ~ continuous wire entanglement

Draht-horde *f* wire kiln floor, wire hurdle **-hose** *f* tree-guard **-igel** *m* gooseberry (type of obstacle) **-kabel** *n* wire rope **-kaliber** *n* wire-rod pass, wire gauge or size **-kanal** *m* wire channel **-kern** *m* wire core **-kernspule** *f* (iron) wire-core coil **-kissen** *n* wire cushion

Draht-klammer *f* wire staple, wire cramp or clamp **-klampe** *f* staple **-klemme** *f* terminal, binding post, eccentric clamp, wire connector **-klemmhebel** *m* wire clamp lever **-kluppe** *f* pliers, pointing clamp **-knüppel** *m* wire rod **-kopf** *m* wire-head **-kopfgehäuse** *n* wire-head casing **-korb** *m* wire basket **-kreuzung** *f* cross (ing), wire crossing, transposition of (line) wires, crossover **-lackiermaschine** *f* wire lacquering machine **-lage** *f* lay of wire

Drahtlager *n* neck groove ~ **des Isolators** insulator groove ~ **der Doppelglocke** insulator groove **oberes** (seitliches) ~ top (neck) groove

Draht-lampe *f* drawn filament lamp **-lehre** *f* wire gauge **-leier** *f* drawing frame (for wire) **-leitung** *f* wiring, conducting wire, wire line

Draht-litze *f* wire strand, stranded wire **-litzenmaschine** *f* wire-stranding machine **-litzenseele** *f* wire strand core

drahtlos wireless, radio ~ **gesteuert** radio-controlled **-es Fernsehen** television **-e Nachricht** wireless message **-e Ortsbestimmung** radio direction finding **-e Peilung** radio bearing **-e Steuerung** radio control **-e Telefonie** radio telephony **-e Telegraphie** wireless telegraphy **-e Übertragung der Bildströme** wireless transmission of image currents

Draht-löter *m* wire brazer **-luftschild** *n* name plate on plaited wirework **-magnetophon** *n* magnetic wire recorder **-maschengitter** *n* wire netting **-maß** *n* gauge or thickness of wire **-matte** *f* wiremesh mat **-meßbrücke** *f* slide-wire bridge (elec.) **-messer** *m* wire gauge **-meßvorrichtung** *f* wire-gauging device **-mitnehmer** *m* wire transport

Drahtnachricht *f* telegram

Drahtnachrichten-mittel *n* means of wire communication **-netz** *n* wire net or system **-verbindung** *f* telephone communication

Drahtnägel *n pl* wire nails

Drahtnetz *n* network system of wires, wire net ~ **zum Tarnen** camouflage wire netting

Drahtnetz-elektrode *f* wire gauze, electrode **-hülse** *f* guard of wire netting or gauze (for gauge glass) **-kappe** *f* gauze top **-reflektor** *m* grating reflector

Draht-nummer *f* gauge or thickness of wire **-öse** *f* staple, wire eyelet **-ösenlitze** *f* mail heald (textiles) **-querschnitt** *m* cross section **-reiterklemme** *f* staple pliers **-reuse** *f* wire bow net **-richtapparat** *m* wire straightener **-ring** *m* ring or coil of wire

Draht-rohr *n* wire-wrapped gun, wire-wound barrel **-rolle** *f* wire roll (entanglement), concertina, coil of wire **-rundfunk** *m* wire broadcasting, broadcast or radio relay, rediffusion, line radio **-rundspruch** *m* program transmission over wires **-rundspruchanlage** *f* electrophone or transmission system **-saite** *f* music wire, wire string

Drahtschale *f* wire gauze ~ **mit eingepreßter Asbestschicht** wire gauze with hemispherical asbestos center

Draht-schälmaschine *f* wire-peeling machine **-schenkel** *m* couple wire **-schere** *f* wire shears or cutter, nippers **-scheurer** *m* furbisher **-schirm** *m* wire screen

Drahtschleife *f* wire loop, wire winding or turn ~ **für verkorkte Flaschen** wire noose for corked bottles

Draht-schlinge *f* wire sling, trip wire (entanglement), wire loop or snare **-schloß** *n* clip, cable, wire **-schluß** *m* wiring plate, lock wire **-schneider** *m* knife, wire cutter **-schneidezange** *f* nippers **-schotter** *m* crushed rock wrapped in wire mesh (for river-control work) **-schraube** *f* helix of thin wire

Drahtschutz *m* wire shield **-kappe** *f* wire cage **-korb** *m* wire guard

Draht-seele *f* wire center or core **-segel** *pl* roll vanes

Drahtseil *n* wire rope or line, stranded wire, wire or suspension cable, cable ~ **zur Aufhängung der Rollenbahn** suspension cable of roller train ~ **mit Hanfseele** wire rope with hemp center or hemp core **dreilitziges** ~ three-strand wire rope **geflochtenes** ~ stranded wire rope

Drahtseilanker *m* wire-rope or stranded-wire stay, guy

Drahtseilbahn *f* aerial or wire ropeway, (wire) cable railway ~ **für Materialien** supply cableway **elektrische** ~ telpher line

Drahtseil-block *m* wire-rope pulley **-fett** *n* wire-rope compound (grease) **-flaschenzug** *m* cable hoist, wire-rope block **-hindernis** *n* cable block, wire-cable obstacle **-kausche** *f* rope eye **-klammer** *f* wire-line clamp **-klemme** *f* cable clamp, wire-rope clamp **-kloben** *m* steel-wire block, cable block

Drahtseil-kopf *m* type wire rope holder **-kübel** *m* cable or swing bucket **-rolle** *f*, **-scheibe** *f* wire-rope sheave **-schlaufe** *f* wire rope sling **-schloß** *n* cable joint, clip, clamp **-trieb** *m* wire-rope or cable drive **-umlenkrolle** *f* deflection sheave **-zug** *m* wire pull

Draht-sicherung *f* wire fuse, snaked wire **-sieb** *n* wire strainer or screen, wire or wire-netting sieve **-siebkorb** *m* wire screen basket **-sonde zur Flammentemperaturmessung** wire probe for measuring flame temperature **-spankiste** (Drahtbundkiste) wirebound box **-spanner** *m* wire stretcher, wire grip **-spannschloß** *n* wire tightener **-speiche** *f* spoke (of wire wheel) **-speichenrad** *n* wire or wire-spoke wheel **-spirale** *f* wire spiral or helix, wire coil, spiral or helical wire **-spule** *f* wire coil or spool, solenoid **-spulenfeder** *f* bobbin spring **-spulenhalter** *m* bobbin holder

Draht-stab *m* wire rod **-stange** *f* wire rod **-stärke** *f* wire gauge, diameter or thickness of wire **-stärkentabelle** *f* wire-gauge table, wire gauge **-stellwiderstände** *m pl* regulating wire resistances **-stift** *m* wire nail or pin **-strang** *n* strand (of cable or rope) **-straße** *f* rod mill, rod-mill or wire-rod rolling train, wire rolling mill, wire or metal mesh road **-strecke** *f* wire-rod-mill train, looping-mill train **-stück** *n* filament

Draht-tabelle *f* wire-gauge table, wire gauge **-telegraphie** *f* wire telegraphy **-telephonie** *f* wire telephony **-thermoelement** *n* wire thermocouple **-torsionsgerät** *n* wire-twisting apparatus **-trage** *f* drum barrow **-träger** *m* wire or cable supports **-trimmer** *m* wire-wound trimmer **-trosse** *f* wire rope or hawser **-tuch** *n* wire netting or network **-uhrkupplung** *f* twist wheel clutsch **-umflechtung** *f* wire braiding **-umklöppelung** *f* braided metal covering **-umspinner** *m* fancy threader **-umspulgerät** *n* wire-coating or wire-winding apparatus **-umwicklung** *f* wire framing

draht- und drahtloser Verkehr wirebound and wireless operation

Drahtung *f* telegram, radiogram

Draht-verbindung *f* (direct) wire communication, wire connection, wiring, joint or wire binding, armoring **-verbindungshülse** *f* jointing sleeve

Draht-verhau *m* barbed-wire barrier or entanglement **-verlegung** *f* wire winding

Drahtverschluß *m* wiring clip **-kabel** *n* locked-wire rope

Draht-verschnürer *m* cork wirer **-verseiler** *m* cable-machine driver **-verseilmaschine** *f* wire stranding machine **-verspannt** wire-braced **-verspannung** *f* wire bracing **-verwicklung** *f* wire wire entanglement, cross (teleph.) **-verwindungsgerät** *n* wire-twisting apparatus **-verzinkung** *f* wire zincification or galvanization

Draht-verzinnerei *f* wire-tinning plant **-vorschubhebel** *m* wire feed lever **-walze** *f* reinforced concertina roll, wire roll **-walzen** *n* wire-rod milling, rod or wire milling **-walzenhindernis** *n* concertina roll **-walzer** *m* wire roller **-walzerei** *f* rodmilling plant **-walzung** *f* rod milling

Drahtwalzwerk *n* (wire-)rod mill, wire mill ~ **mit mechanischen Ein- und Ausführungen** guide mill

Draht-waren *pl* wire ware, articles, or goods **-wellentelegraphie** *f* wired radio, wired wave telegraphy **-wickel** *m* wire strand **-wicklung** *f* wire coiling, turn of wire **-widerstand** *m* wire-wound resistance (elec.) **-windung** *f* winding of wire **-wischhebel** *m* wire wiper arm **-wort** *n* cable address

Drahtzange *f* flat wire pincers, pliers, nippers, wire cutters ~ **mit flachem Maul** flat-nosed pliers

Draht-zaun *m* double-apron entanglement or fence, wire fence **-ziehbank** *f* wire-drawing bench **-zieheisen** *n* wire drawing die **-ziehen** *n* wire drawing **-zieher** *m* wire drawer **-zieherei** *f* wire mill, wire-drawing plant, wire-rod rolling mill **-ziehmaschine** *f* wire drawing machine **-ziehstrumpf** *m* wire grip **-ziehwerk** *n* drawing mill (for wires)

Draht-zuführung *f* wire feeding **-zuführungsautomat** *m* automatic wire feed **-zuführungswalze** *f* wire feeding roller

Drahtzug *m* pull of wire, drawing wire, draw bench for wire drawing, wire line; (Kühlerabdeckung) radiator blind **-kraft** *f* pull of wire **-seil** *n* wire haulage rope **-tabelle** *f* wire-stress table

Draht-zurichter *m* wire dresser **-zwecken** *pl* small wire tacks **-zwinge** *f* wire ferrule **-zylinder** *m* **einer Sicherheitslampe** wire gauze of a safety lamp

Drainage *f* draining, drainage ~ **mittels Preßluftinjektion** drainage by compressed air, repressuring
Drainage-löcher in Mauern weep holes **-röhren** drainpipes
Draingraben *m* drainage ditch
drainieren to drain (off)
Drainieren *n* draining, drainage
Drainierspalten *m* drain spade
Drainröhre *f* drainpipe
Draisine *f* railway trolley
drakonitisch draconitic
Drall *m* rifling (gun), pitch, twist, lay, untwist, angular momentum, spin, twist(ed) spin (of (electrons), couple, torque, spiral thread, torsional force, moment of momentum (phys.) **einfacher** ~ twisting (continuous twisting) **gleichbleibender** ~ uniform rifling **zunehmender** ~ increasing twist (rifling)
Drall-abweichung *f* drift due to rotation of projectile **-achse** *f* gyro vector axis **-änderung** *f* rate change of couple **-apparat** *m* twist counter
drallarm with a low number of twists, nonrotating **-es Stahlseil** steel rope with moderate twist
Drall-ausgleicher *m* twist compensator **-bereich** *m* range of lays **-blech** *n* swirl vane (jet) **-büchse** *f* twisting guide **-düse** *f* swirl nozzle (rocket), turbulence nozzle (jet) **-einsatz** *m* swirl vanes or baffles (jet)
drallfrei nonkinking, nontwisting, unrifled **-es Seil** *n* non rotating or non-spinning rope **-e Strömung** *f* irrational flow
Drall-freiheit *f* absence of twist **-führung** *f* twisting guide **-lage** *f* length of lay or twist **-länge** *f* length of rifling **-loses Kabel** nonspinning wire rope, (longlay) wire rope **-luftruder** *n* drift controls **-nut** *f* helical groove **-prüfung** *f* torque test **-regelung** *f* vane control (in fan) **-schlag** *m* rotary blow
Drall-spindel *f* twist spindle **-stabilisierung** *f* spin stabilization **-steigungswinkel** *m* angle of twist **-verbesserung** *f* drift correction **-winkel** *m* angle of rifling or of twist **-wirkung** *f* twist effect of slipstream **-zug** *m* groove
Drän *m* drainage tube, drain
Dränage *f* stone drain, draining, drainage
dränen to drain, irrigate
Drang *m* urge, impulse
Drängelampe im Fernverkehr group busy signal or lamp
Drängelsignal *n* signal to speed up the operation
drängen to urge, crowd
dränieren to drain
Drän-leitung *f* drain pipe **-netz** *n* drain net **-röhre** *f* drain, drainpipe
Dränung *f* drainage
drapieren to drape
Draufsicht *f* plan view, topview
draußen abroad, outside, in the offing
Drechselbank *f* lathe (wood-working)
drechseln to turn
Drechsler *m* turner (wood-working) **-beitel** *m* turning chisel
Drechslerei *f* turnery (wood-working)
Dreck *m* dirt, filth, dung, (slang) fog, muggy weather, or thick cloud **-eisen** *n* pig iron **-schleudern** *pl* mudslinging
D-Regelung *f* derivative control
Dregganker *m* drag, grapnel, creeper
dreggen to grapple, drag (for)
Dreggen *n* grappling
Dregg-haken *m* creeper, grapnel **-tau** *n* grapnel rope (of boat)
Dreh . . . rotary, rotatory, revolving, torsional, turning
Drehachse *f* axis or center of rotation, oscillation, torsion, joint or swivel pin, pivot, revolution axis, fulcrum, hinge **krystallographische** ~ axis of rotation, in crystallography
Dreh-achsmitte des Teilkopfes swivel axis of index head **-anker** *m* pivoted armature (loudspeaker) **-ankerrelais** *n* rotating armature relay **-ankersystem** *n* pivoted armature system **-anodenröhre** *f* rotating anode tube **-anodenröntgenröhre** *f* rotating anode X-ray tube **-anschluß** *m* swing joint
Dreh-antenne *f* rotary antenna **-antriebsaufnahme** *f* rotating input (kinematics) **-apparat** *m* rotary rig **-arbeit** *f* lathe work **-arm** *m* moving or rotating arm, torque arm, jib arm of a crane **-ausgleich** *m* torque compensation **-ausleger** *m* swiwelling-jib, swiwelling boom
Dreh-bake *f* rotating beacon **-balken** *m* pivoting arm
Drehbank *f* turning or turner's lathe **kleine** ~ bench lathe **auf der** ~ **bearbeiten** to lathe ~ **mit Drehscheibe** turntable lathe ~ **für Futterarbeit** chuck lathe ~ **mit Kröpfung** engine gap lathe ~ **für Metallbearbeitung** metalworking lathe ~ **von 25 cm Spitzenhöhe** a 25 centimeter lathe ~ ~ **für Stangenarbeit** bar stock lathe
Drehbank-bau *m* copying lathe design **-bett** *n* lathe bed **-bettverlängerung** *f* lathe bed extension **-fuß** *m* bed-box or box-type leg **-futter** *n* lathe chuck, chuck **-herz** *n* lathe dog **-kopf** *m* lathe headstock **-körner** *m* lathe center
Drehbank-mikroskop *n* optical thread tool gauge **-rauter** *m* shaving machine **-spannfutter** *n* geared scroll lathe chucks **-spindel** *f* lathe spindle, mandrel **-spindelstock** *m* lathe headstock **-spitze** *f* lathe center **-support** *m* lathe carriage **-zubehör** *n* lathe accessories
drehbar rotating, rotary, revolving, reversible, swiveling ~ **angelenkt** pivoted ~ **angeordnet** pivotally attached ~ **eingesetzt,** ~ **gelagert** pivoted ~ **verbunden** pivoted (spinned)
drehbar, ~ **gelagerte Achswelle** rotatable axle shaft **-er Ausleger** swing boom ~ **gelagerter Hebel** pivoted lever, fulcrumed lever **-e Rahmenantenne** rotating loop antenna **-e Stütze** pivoted leg **-er Verstärker** rotating amplifier **-e Walzen** revolving rolls
drehbar lagern to pivot (in, on)
Dreh-beanspruchung *f* torsional stress or strain, torsion **-bereich** *m* turning capacity **-beschleunigung** *f* spin **-bestreben** *n* tendency to rotate, turning tendency **-bewegung** *f* rotary motion, rotation, revolution **-bild** *n* turning finish **-bläser** *m* revolving blower **-blende** *f* rotary shield
Dreh-blinkfeuer *n* flashing light **-boden** *m* turntable **-bodensand-Strahlapparat** *m* turntable sandblast cabinet **-bohrer** *m* rotary drill, rotary drilling bit, Archimedean drill **-bohrmaschine** *f* spiral drilling machine

Dreh-, Bohr- und Abstechbank *f* turning, boring, and cutting-off machine or bench

Dreh-bolzen *m* fulcrum pin, pivot pin or bolt **-bottich** *m* rotating tub **-brett** *n* templet, pattern **-brücke** *f* swing bridge, turn bridge **-buch** *n* scenario, shooting script, screen play **-bügelaufhängung** *f* revolving-shackle suspension **-bündel** *n* rotary boring clamp **-bürste** *f* rotary cleaning brush **-diagramm** *n* rotation diagram (radio) **-dose** *f* crank box **-drähte** *pl* warping wires (aerodyn.) **-drossel** *f* variometer

Drehdorn *m* lathe mandrel ~ (einfach) plain solid mandrel ~ (spreizbar) expanding mandrel ~ **mit Konusscheibe** cone mandrel

Drehdurchführung *f* rotary transmission

Drehdurchmesser *m* turning diameter ~ **ü. d. Bett** *m* swing over bed ~ (üb. Bettschlitten) swing over saddle ~ **von Drehbank** swing turning diameter ~ **für Futterarbeit** diameter of chuck work ~ **i. d. Kröpfung** swing over gap ~ (über Quersupportschlitten) swing over cross slide rest

Drehdurchmesserbereich *m* maximum turning diameter

Dreheisen-einheitsmeßwerk *n* moving-iron type of voltmeter or ammeter **-instrument** *n* moving-iron instrument **-oszillograph** *m* soft-iron oscillograph **-spannungsanzeiger** *m* moving-iron voltmeter

Dreh-elektromagnet *m* rotary (electro)magnet **-ellipsoid** *n* ellipsoid, oblate and oblong

drehen to revolve, rotate, turn, twist, roll, turn on edge, tack (naut.), to swing, shift; (formdrehen) to form; (plandrehen) to face **sich** ~ to swing round

drehen, ~ der Platinenexcenter rotating jack cam ~ **um X Grad** swivel through x degrees **auf Maß** ~ turn to template **rechts** ~ to veer (of wind) **zu kurz** ~ to turn inside the wake **sich** ~ to turn, revolve, rotate, gyrate, whirl **sich in Angeln** ~ to swing **sich auf einem Zapfen** ~ to turn upon a pivot

Drehen *n* turning, torsion, revolving, rotating, twisting, turning on edge, spin ~ (Formdrehen) *n* forming ~ (Plandrehen) facing

drehend rotating, turning, rotary **-e Achse** driving or live axle **-e Funkenstrecke** rotary spark gap **-er Unterschneider** wall scraper

Dreher *m* turner, lathe hand or operator; (Läufer) *m* traveler

Dreherei *f* turning section

Drehergebnis *n* rotary result

Dreherwirkung *f* leno effect

Dreh-faß *n* tumbler (drum) **-feder** *f* torsion spring **-federwaage** *f* torsion balance **-fehler** *m* (Magnet-Kompaß) turning error

Drehfeld *n* rotating or rotary field **-ablenkung** *f* rotating-field deflection **-admittanz** *f* cyclic admittance **-antrieb** *m* rotating field motor **-erzeugung** *f* rotary-field generation **-geber** *m* rotating field instrument

Drehfeld-impedanz *f* cyclic impedance **-instrument** *n* rotating-field instrument **-richtungsanzeiger** *m* three-phase sequence indicator **-schwingung** *f* rotating-field oscillation **-spule** *f* chocke **-transformator** *m* rotating field transformer **-umformer** *m* rotary field converter

Dreh-festigkeit *f* torsional strength, twisting strength **-festigkeitsmaschine** *f* torsion-testing machine **-feuer** *n* revolving light, rotating beacon **-filter** *n* rotary filter **-fläche** *f* surface of revolution **-flammofen** *m* revolving reverberatory furnace **-flansch** *m* rotary flange **-flügel** *m* rotating airfoil or wing, rotor, turning sash, window valve

Dreh-flügelflugzeug *n* rotating wing aircraft, helicopter, gyroplane ~ **mit beim Fluge frei umlaufenden Drehflügeln** rotaplane

Dreh-flügelpropeller *m*, **-flügelschraube** *f* reversible propeller **-flügelpumpe** *f* vane-type pump **-führung** *f* twisting guide **-funkfeuer** *n* rotating radio beacon or radio range, omnidirectional radio range **-futter** *n* lathe chuck **-gasgriff** *m* twist grip throttle control

Dreh-gelenk *n* swivel (joint), swiveling piece or link, hinge joint **-geschützt** curve-compensated (electronics) **-geschwindigkeit** *f* rotative or turning speed, rate of revolution, speed of rotation **-geschwindigkeitstensor** *m* spin tensor **-gestänge** *n* drill poles

Drehgestell *n* pivot mounting, truck, turn-over manipulator, bogie (R.R.); (Lauf ~) trailing bogie; (Maschinen ~) power bogie; (Trieb ~) traction bogie, driving bogie **-achsenstand** *m* bogie wheelbase **-bremse** *f* bogie brake **-zapfenlager** *n* center plate

Dreh-getriebe *n* turning gear **-gleichstromumformer** *m* motor converter **-gleitwiderstand** *m* variable resistor **-grenze** *f* yield point of torsional shear **-griff** *m* control grip **-halbautomat** *m* semi-automatic lathe **-halle** *f* revolving-type hangar **-herd** *m* revolving table, rotating buddle **-herdofen** *m* rotary furnace **-herz** *n* lathe dog **-hülse** *f* turn sleeve

Drehimpuls *m* angular momentum, moment of momentum **-bilanz** *f* balance of moment of momentum **-matrizelemente** *pl* angular momentum matrix elements **-quantenzahl** *f* rotational quantum number

Dreh-invarianz *f* rotational invariance **-inversionsachse** *f* rotary inversion axis **-kabel** *n pl* warping wires (aviation) **-kante** *f* edge about which rotation takes place **-keil** *m* rotating wedge (optics) **-keilkupplung** *f* rolling-key clutch, pin clutch

Dreh-kessel *m* rotary-type boiler **-kette** *f* crossing warp **-klappe** *f* swivel damper, hinged valve **-klappenabdeckung** *f*, **-klappenjalousie** *f* flap or vantype shutter **-klemme** *f* turning clip **-klinke** *f* turning pawl **-knicken** *n* torsional buckling **-knopf** *m* milled head, control button, rotary knob, rotary button (tape rec.)

Drehko *m* variable condenser, rotating-plate condenser

Drehkocher *m* rotary boiler

Drehkolben *m* rotary piston **-antriebsmotor** *m* rotary-piston driven motor **-gebläse** *n* rotary compressor **-lader** *m* displacement supercharger **-motor** *m* (Wankelmotor) internal combustion engine with revolving piston **-verdichter** *m* rotating piston compressor **-pumpe** *f* rotary pump

Dreh-kompensator *m* rotary compensator **-komponente** *f* rotating component

Drehkondensator *m* adjustable disc condenser,

variable capacitor, variable or turning condenser, rotating-plate condenser **frequenzgleicher** ~ straight-line frequency condenser

Dreh-konus *m* turning taper **-kopf** *m* turret (head), capstan of lathe, rotary head **-kopplung** *f* rotating joint

Drehkörper *m* body of revolution, rotor ~ **mit ringförmigem Querschnitt** torus

Dreh-kraft *f* torque, torsional force, rotary or turning force **-kraftlinie** *f* diagram of crank effort

Drehkran *m* swing or rotary crane, revolving or all-round crane ~ **mit festem Ausleger** slewing crane with fixed jib ~ **in Säulenbauart** column-guided slewing crane

Drehkranz *m* rotating track, turntable, ring mount; (bei Sattelschlepper) fifth wheel (semitrailer); (Kran) slewing track ring

Drehkreis *m* radius of turn, turning circle **-fläche** *f* disk area (of propeller)

Drehkreuz *n* capstan handle, turnstile, continuous twist (electronics), spider ~ **zum schnellen Einstellen der Bohrspindel** spindle quick-motion turnstile ~ **für den Revolverschlitten** turnstile

Dreh-kreuzachse *f* center of a telegraph system **-kristall** *m* rotating, oscillating, or revolving crystal **-kristallmethode** *f* rotating crystal method **-kübel** *m* revolving bucket **-kugellager** *n* swiveling ball bearings **-kugeltype** *f* shot drill **-kuppel** *f* revolving turret

Dreh-kupplung *f* revolving turret **-lade** *f* lathe **-ladewebstuhl** *m* circular box-type loom **-lager** *n* pivot bearing **-länge** *f* length to be turned **-längenbereich** *m* maximum turning length

Dreh-laufkatze *f* underhung revolving jib, swinging crane, traveling on overhead rails **-laufkran** *m* propelled swinging crane **-leistung** *f* torque **-leiter** *m* (Motor) motor antenna ladder or extension ladder **-leiter** *f* turntable firemen's ladder

Dreh-lichtschalter *m* lever lighting-switch **-lichtscheinwerfer** *m* revolving searchlight or beacon light **-lichtsignal** *n* revolving beacon

Drehling *m* lathe tool, lantern, pinion, crank

Drehmagnet *m* step-by-step magnet, rotary magnet **-instrument** *n* moving-needle galvanometer, moving-magnet instrument **-maschine** *f* turning machine **-matrixelement** *n* angular-momentum matrix element

Drehmeißel *m* turning tool ~ **mit Hartmetallschneiden** carbide-tipped turning tool

Drehmelder *m* function generator, synchro **-motor** *m* dualsyn (gyro)

Dreh-messer *n* lathe tool, knife tool, cutting tool, turning tool **-modul** *m* modulus of torsional shear **-mitte** *f* turning center

Drehmoment *n* torque, torsional or twisting moment, starting or propeller torque (aviation), moment of rotation, angular or rolling momentum ~ **des Motors** engine torque **ablenkendes** ~ deflecting couple **bezogenes** ~ torque-weight ratio

Drehmomentaufnehmer *m* torque pickup **-ausgleich** *m* torque compensation **-begrenzungskupplung** *f* overload clutch **-bemessung** *f* torque rating **-dose** *f* torque gauge

Drehmoment-erzeuger *m* torque motor, torquer **-geber** *m* torque pickup **-kasten** *m* torque box **-kolben** *m* torque piston **-kompensator** *m* torque-balance system **-meßgerät** *n* torque indicator **-messer** *m* torquemeter

Drehmoment-meßnabe *f* torque metering hub, torque indicator **-meßschlüssel** *m* torque-metering, spanner torque wrench **-schlüssel** *m* torque wrench **-schraubenschlüssel** *m* tension wrench **-überlastkupplung** *f* torque overload release clutch

Drehmoment-übertragungszylinder *m* torque cylinder **-verlauf** *m* flow of the torque **-verstärker** *m* torque amplifier **-waage** *f* torque dynamometer **-wandler** *m* torque converter

Dreh-mühle *f* gyratory crusher **-nockenschalter** *m* rotary snap switch **-ofen** *m* rotary or revolving furnace, rotary calciner or kiln **-pendelbewegung** *f* rotary pendulum movement **-pendeltachometer** *n* rotary pendulum tachometer or speedometer

Dreh-pfahl *m* laying pole (ropemaker's) **-pfanne** *f* bearing socket (railway turntables), center pin socket **-pflug** *m* rotary tiller **-phasenschieber** *m* rotary phase shifter

Drehplatte *f* flat plate, turntable, lathe faceplate, propeller torque ~ **für die selbsttätige Auslösung des Tischvorschubes** feed-trip plate

Drehplattenkondensator *m* rotating-plate condenser

Dreh-pol *m* center of rotation, rotating field pole **-polarisation** *f* rotatory polarization, optical rotation **-prisma** *n* rotating prism **-puddelofen** *m* rotary or revolving puddling furnace

Drehpunkt *m* center or point of rotation or of revolution, fulcrum (point), center of gyration or of motion, pivot **fester** ~ fixed fulcrum **krystallographischer** ~ center of rotation, in crystallography

Dreh-punktabstand *m* distance between the centers of rotation **-radius** *m* (Bagger) rotating deck radius

Drehrahmen *m* rotatable coil, moving or rotating frame **-antenne** *f* rotating loop antenna (radio) **-peiler** *m* rotating-loop direction-finding antenna **-peilfunksender** *m* rotating radio or loop beacon **-peilverfahren** *n* rotating-frame direction-finding principle

Dreh-raster *m* circular screen **-reep** *n* tye **-regler** *m* selsyn-type regulator (self-synchronous), induction impedance, induction regulator **-resonanz** *f* torsional oscillation resonance **-richtantenne mit kleinem Elementenabstand** close-spaced rotary beam antenna

Dreh-richter *m* threephase inverter **-richtung** *f* sense or direction of rotation **-richtstrahler** *m* rotary beam (antenna) **-richtungsumkehr** *f* reversal of rotation, leadscrew reversal **-riefe** *f* turning groove **-riegel** *m* hasp (French window)

Dreh-ring *m* turntable racer, turntable ring or scarf mount, circular rack **-ring** (Drehhaken) swivel **-ringwippe** *f* rocking turntable **-röhre** *f* turning gouge **-rohrofen** *m* (cylindrical) rotary kiln, rotating cylindrical kiln, revolving cylindrical furnace, rotary drier, revolving tubular furnace

Drehrollendruck *m* slewing wheel pressure

Drehrost *m* revolving grate **-gaserzeuger** *m* rotary-grid or -grate generator, revolving-rate gas producer **-generator** *m* revolving-grate producer

Dreh-sandstein *m* buffing wheel **-schalter** *m* rotary or revolving switch, selector or spindle switch **-schaltung** *f* rotary switch **-scharnier** *n* swivel hinge **-schaufel** *f* turbine vane or bucket

Drehscheibe *f* turntable, rotary table, gate end plate, dial ~ **mit Querbewegung** cross sliding turntable

Drehscheiben-Fluglehrapparat *m* Link trainer **-grube** *f* pit of turntable

Drehscheibenkarde *f* revolving flat card (textiles) **selbstreinigende** ~ self-stripping revolving flat card

Drehscheiben-kran *m* self-propelling swinging crane **-lafette** *f* turntable gun carriage

Drehscheibenverschluß *m* rotating-disk shutter ~ **mit Umkehrscheiben** reversing-disk shutter

Dreh-scheinwerfer *m* rotating beacon light **-schemel** *m* swiveling bolster, (pivoted) bogie **-schemellenkung** *f* pivoted bogie steering, fifth-wheel steering

Drehschieber *m* swivel damper, rotary slide valve **flacher** ~ rotary disk valve **zylindrischer** ~ distributing valve ~ **zum Steuergerät** rotary spool for control valve

Drehschieber-pumpe *f* rotary sliding vane type compressor, rotary vane pump **-steuerung** *f* rotary slide-valve steering **-vakuumpumpe** *f* rotary slide valve vacuum pump **-ventil** *n* rotary-spool valve **-weiche** (Rohrpost) rotary slide valve switch

Drehschlag-bewegung *f* rotary blow motion **-rollenkupplung** *f* rotary blow roller coupling

Dreh-schlitten *m* swivel(ing) or pivoted carriage (of a machine tool) **-schlüssel** *m* turn handle **-schlüsselkranz** *m* wrench circle **-schnitt** *m* turning cut **-schranke** *f* swing gate **-schritt** *m* rotary step

Dreh-schurre *f* revolving chute **-schütz** *m* butterfly valve **-schützklappe** *f* flap or pivot-leaf gate **-schwingabtrieb** *m* oscillating output (kinematics) **-schwingkreisel** *m* twist gyro **-schwingung** *f* rotary oscillation, torsional vibration, oscillation about a center **-schwingung der Welle** torsional vibration of shaft

Drehschwingungs-beanspruchung *f* repetition of torsional stress **-dämpfer** *m* torsional-vibration balancer **-dämpfergewicht** *n* torsional-vibration damping weight **-festigkeit** *f* torsional-fatigue or torsional-endurance limit **-maschine** *f* endurance-testing machine for repeated torsion **-probe** *f* repeated-torsional-test specimen **-prüfmaschine** *f* torsional-vibration testing machine **-rahmen** *m* tilting stage **-schreiber** *m* recording torsion meter **-versuch** *m* repeated-torsion test

Dreh-schwingversuch *m* oscillation or alternating-torsion test **-sieb** *n* rotary screen (sieve), rolling screen (flour milling), revolving screen (min.)

Drehsinn *m* sense or direction of rotation; (umkehrbarer) reversible rotation; (nicht umkehrbarer) irreversible rotation **-schwellenkurve** rotational threshold curve

Dreh-sitz *m* running fit **-sitzspiel** *n* running clearance **-späne** *pl* drillings, borings, turnings **-spannung** *f* (intensity of) torsional stress, strain, or resilience, twisting strain

Dreh-sockel *m* swivel base **-spannungsgleicher** *m* variable condenser **-spannungsteiler** *m* variable potentiometer **-spektrogramm** *n* rotation spectrograph **-spiegel** *m* revolving mirror **-spiegelachsen** *f pl* rotary alternating axis **-spiegelinstrument** *n* rotating mirror instrument **-spiegelung** *f* combined rotation and reflection (crysr.), rotary reflection **-spindle** *f* rotating spindle, adjustment shaft **-spitze** *f* turning center **-spulanzeigeinstrument** *n* moving-coil indicating instrument

Drehspule *f* moving, rotating, or rotor coil, suspended rotating coil (elec.), deflecting magnet **mit einem Lager versehene** ~ unipivotal moving coil

Drehspulenstrommesser *m* moving-coil ammeter

Drehspul-galvanometer *n* moving-coil galvanometer, D'Arsonval or magnet galvanometer **-instrument** *n* moving-coil instrument (elec.) **-meßinstrument** *n* moving-coil meter **-meßwerk** *n* moving coil measuring system **-motor** *m* triphase motor **-relais** *n* **-schütz** *m* moving-coil relay (electronics) **-schnellschrieber** *m* moving-coil telewriter **-schreiber** *m* moving coil recorder **-strommesser** *m* moving-coil ammeter **-tonabnehmer** *m* moving-coil pick-up **-variometer** *n* rotating-coil variometer **-zeigergalvanometer** *n* moving-coil pointer galvanometer

Drehstab-abfederung *f* torsion bar suspension **-dauerfestigkeitsprüfmaschine** *f* rotating-beam testing machine **-feder** *f* torsion rod (spring), torsion-bar spring

Drehstahl *m* turning, cutting, or lathe tool, turning knife, tool bit **eckiggeschliffener** ~ diamond-pointed cutting tool **rundgeschliffener** ~ round-nosed cutting tool

Dreh-stahlhalter *m* lathe toolholder **-stahlspindel** *f* cutter spindle **-stand** *m* rotating cabin

drehsteif stiff against torsion **-e Flügelnase** leading edge stiff against torsion

Dreh-stern *m* star-type reel-stand **-stichel** *m* graver, turning graver

Drehstift *m* rotary pin, tommy bar, mandrel, arbor ~ (Rundtisch v. Werkzeugmaschine) rotary table

Dreh-stock *m* winch, lever **-stoß** *m* rotary impulse

Drehstrahl (gekröpfter) off-set tool; (gerader) ~ straight tool ~ *m* (linker) left hand turning tool ~ (rechter) right hand turning tool

Drehstreifenabschwächer *m* rotary attenuator

Drehstrom *m* three-phase or rotary current, polyphase alternating current **-anlasser** *m* three-phase-starter **-dreileiterzähler** *m* three-phase three-wire meter **-dynamo** *n* three-phase generator **-erregermaschine** *f* three-phase A. C. exciter **-flanschmotor** *m* flange-mounted three-phase motor **-generator** *m* three-phase-current generator, a. c. alternator **-gleichstromeinankerumformer** *m* rotary-current continuous-current converter **-gleichstromumformer** *m* rotary-current continuous-current dynamotor, motor converter

Drehstrom-kollektormotor *m* three-phase commutator motor **-kurzschlußmotor** *m* three-phase squirrel cage motor **-leistungsmesser** *m* three-phase-current output meter **-motor** *m* polyphase induction motor, alternative motor, three-phase motor **-netz** *n* three-phase mains **-niederspannungsanlage** *f* three-phase low-voltage plant **-ofen** *m* three-phase furnace current **-ölumformer** *m* three-phase-current oil transformer

Drehstrom-reihenschlußkurzschlußmotor *m* three-phase series-wound short-circuit motor **-reihenschlußmotor** *m* three-phase series commutator motor

Drehstrom-repulsionsmotor *m* three-phase repulsion motor **-reversieranlasser** *m* three-phase reversing starter **-schalter** *m* three-phase switch **-schwungradgenerator** *m* three-phase-current flywheel generator **-spannungsquelle** *f* three-phase voltage source **-system** *n* three-phase or three-wire system **-transformator** *m* three-phase transformer **-vierleitersystem** *n* three-phase four-wire system

Drehstrom-vierleiterzähler *m* three-phase four-wire meter **-wattmeter bei ungleichbelasteten Stromkreisen** three-phase wattmeter on unbalanced circuit **-zähler** *m* three-phase electricity meter

Dreh-stuhl *m* swivel or revolving chair **-sturm** *m* revolving storm, twister **-support** *m* swivel head, holder, slide rest, turned piece **-symmetrie** *f* rotational symmetry **-symmetrisch** axially symmetric **-tastenschalter** *m* rotary pushbutton switch

Drehteil *n* turned piece, turned part, swivel **~ des Werkzeughalters** swivel of toolholder **geformter ~** profile turned piece

Drehteiluntersatz *m* swivel base

Drehteller *m* coiler plate **~ einer Zuteilvorrichtung** rotary mixing table, turntable (radiogram)

Drehtide *f* rotatory or amphidromic tide

Drehtisch *m* rotary, rotary or turning table, swivel carriage, revolving platform, rotating stage, rotator (optics) **-anlage** *f* rotary-table mill **-fräsmaschine** rotary milling machine

Drehtisch-gebläse *n* rotary-table sandblast machine **-presse** *f* rotating-table press **-sandstrahlapparat** *m* rotary-table sandblast machine **-sandstrahlgebläsehaus** *n* turntable sandblast chamber **-wirbelstrahler** *m* rotary table sandblaster **-zuckerpresse** *f* sugar press with rotary table

Drehtopf *m* revolving can **-ständer** *m* coiler stand

Drehtor *n* sluice door, turning lock door **-schleuse** *f* sluice or lock with turning doors

Drehtransformator *m* adjustable transformer, converter, induction regulator

Drehtrichter *m* reciprocating trumpet

Drehtrommel *f* rotary or rotating drum, rotary kiln, revolving breech, rotating barrel **-röstofen** *m* rotary calcining kiln **-sandstrahlgebläse** *n* revolving-barrel sandblast machine, sandblast barrel mill

Dreh-tür *f* hinged or turning door **-turm** *m* revolving turret **-umformer** *m* rotary converter **-umschalter** *m* turning change-over switch

Dreh- und Hobelstahlschleifmaschine *f* lathe and planer tool grinder

Dreh- und Schiebedrossel *f* variometer

dreh- und zentrierbarer Kreuztisch revolving and centering mechanical (compound) stage

Drehung *f* revolution, rotation, turn, turning, angular motion, torsion, twist(ing), pivoting, torque, gyration, barreling (in power-line transposing) **~ des Achsenkreuzes** rotation of axes **~ der Ebene** plane rotation **~ des Geschosses** rotation of projectile **~ im Uhrzeigersinn** clockwise rotation **einfache ~** twisting (continuous twisting) **magneto-optische ~** magneto-optical or magnetic rotation, Faraday effect **optische ~** optical rotation, rotatory polarization

Drehungs-achse *f* axis of revolution or of rotation, turning axis **-änderung** *f* change in rotation **-beanspruchung** *f* torsional stress **-bereich** *m* twist range **-dispersion** *f* rotatory dispersion **-feder** *f* torsion spring **-festigkeit** *f* torsional strength **-frei** steady, nonvortical, irrotational, rotation-free

Drehungs-grad *m* degree of turn **-instabilität** *f* torsional instability **-kasten** *m* torque box **-koma** *n* rotation coma **-kraft** *f* torque, torsional force **-kreis** *m* circle **-kristall** *m* twister crystal **-messer** *m* radius, turning gyrometer **-moment** *n* torsional or twisting moment, starting torque, moment of rotation **-richtung** *f* twist direction **-schwingung** *f* torsional vibation

Drehungssinn, positiver ~ positive rotation

Drehungsvermögen *n* rotary power **Umkehrung oder Wechsel des Drehungsvermögens** mutarotation

Drehungs-versuch *m* twisting or torsion test **-verzeichnung** *f* rotational distortion **-wähler** *m* rotary switch **-widerstand** *m* torsional or twisting resistance **-windmesser** *m* rotating anemometer **-winkel** *m* angle of twist or of torque, torsion or turning angle, angle or stage of rotation **-zähler** *m* twist counter **-zeiger** *m* turn indicator

Dreh-unterteil *m* swivel(ing) base **-variometer** *n* rotating-coil variometer, contact rectifier, crystal detector **-verschluß** *m* turn button, turning lock **-versuch** *m* turning test **-verteiler** *m* rotary scanning and switch unit (radar) **-verwerfung** *f* fault due to torsion **-vorrichtung** *f* swivel head, barring gear, lathe fixture, turning mechanism (device) **-vorschub** *m* rotary feed **-vorwähler** *m* rotary (pre)selector or line switch **-waage** *f* torsion balance

Drehwähler *m* vertical and rotary selector or switch, spindle switch **~ (mit einer Einstellrichtung)** uniselector **~ als Vorwähler** preselecting rotary line switch

Drehwähler-system *n* rotary system **-verteiler** *m* uniselector distribution frame **-zahlengeber** *m* sender with rotary switch

Dreh-wandler *m* induction-voltage regulator **-wanne** *f* revolving pot (for glass-blowing machines) **-webstuhl** *m* box loom (textiles) **-weiche** *f* turning points, sector turntable **-welle** *f* rotary selector

Drehwerk *n* slewing gear, rotation gear, rotating mechanism (lens clock), turning machine **-kritzel** *n* pinion of slewing gear

Dreh-werkzeuge *pl* lathe tools **-wert** *m* **-wertigkeit** *f* number of turns **-widerstand** *m* rheostat, variable resistor **-widerstandsröhre** *f* torque tube **-winkel** *m* angle of rotation **-wirbel** *m* swivel, twister **-wuchs** *m* **-wüchsigkeit** *f* twisted growth, spiral grain **-wucht** *f* rotational inertia

Drehzahl *f* number or rate of revolutions, speed, rotational speed, speed of rotations **~ per Minute** revolutions per minute (Motor) **~ im Leerlauf am Boden** ground speed **Luftschraube gleichbleibender ~** constant-speed airscrew **die ~ des Motors auf 1,000 Umdrehungen per Minute einregeln** to give the engine 1,000 revolutions per minute **Motor mit konstanter ~** *m* constant-speed engine **auf ~ kommen** to run up to speed **mit zu hoher ~** overrevving, overspeed **mit zu niedriger ~** underrevving, underspeed **hohe ~** high number of revolutions **synchrone ~** synchronous revolutions per minute **~ vor dem Umschalten einregulieren** to set speed before changing over

Drehzahl-abfall (-anstieg) *m* speed drop (rise) **-änderung** *f* speed variation **-anzeige** *f* revolutions-per-minute reading **-ausgleich** *m* speed compensator **-begrenzung** *f* limitation on speed **-bereich** *n* speed range of engine **-dynamo** *m* speed dynamo

Drehzahlen der Schruppreihe roughing speed

Drehzahlen-bereich *m* number of feed rates, speed range, spindle speed range **-schaubilder** *pl* spindle speed tables **-schreiber** *m* recording tachometer

Drehzahlen und Vorschübe in beliebiger Zuordnung speeds and feed rates for independent selection

Drehzähler *m* tachometer, revolution counter

Drehzahl-erhöhung *f* increasing speed **-geber** *m* tachometer, impulse transmitter for revolution indicator **-mangel** *m* speed deficiency **-messer** *m* tachometer, speedometer, revolution indicator, speed counter, tachoscope **-messung** *f* measuring of revolutions **-regelnde Antriebskraft** speed-controlling driving power

Drehzahlregler *m* speed governor, speed-regulating device **~ mit Drehzahlverstellvorrichtung** speed regulator with speed adjusting device **~ mit Sicherung gegen Überdrehzahl** overspeed safety governor **~ für Verstellschraube gleichbleibender Drehzahl** constant-speed governor

Drehzahlreg(e)lung *f* speed control, speed regulation **Motor mit ~** variable-speed motor

Drehzahl-reihen *pl* speed ranges **-relais** *n* speed relay **-schalter** *m* speed switch **-schild** *n* speed indicator **-schreiber** *m* tachograph **-schütz** *m* speed contactor **-schwankung** *f* speed variation **-steuerrelais** *n* speed control relay **-verhalten** *n* speed characteristics **-verminderung** *f* speed reduction

Drehzahlverstell-einrichtung *f* control unit for varying speed **-hebel** *m* speed-control lever **-motor** *m* speed adjusting motor

Drehzahl-verstellung *f* speed changer **-verstellvorrichtung** *f* speed adjusting device **-vorschubwähler** *m* speed and feed selector **-wächter** *m* speed controller or guard **-wächter** *m* overspeed monitor **-wahlhebel** *m* speed-selector lever **-wählskala** *f* speed selection dial **-warngerät** *n* overspeed indicator

Dreh-zahn *m* tool bit **-zapfen** *m* pivot, trunnion, gudgeon, bearing, journal (of an axle), turning pin **-zapfenabstand** *m* kingpin center, truck center (R. R.) **-zapfenlager** *n* center plate or bearing for bogie pin **-zeug** *n* turning tools **-zündbrücke** *f* spark gap (rotary)

Dreiachsen-steuerung *f* three-dimensional or three-plane autopilot **-trimmschalter** *m* three-way trim switch (elec.)

Dreiachser *m* six-wheel vehicle

dreiachsig triaxial, with three axis **-es Ellipsoid** general ellipsoid

Dreiadressenbefehl *m* three-address instruction

dreiadrig triple core, triplet, three-wire **-es Kabel** three-conductor (lead) cable, three-wire conductor **-e Schnur** three-wire or triple-core cord **-e Verbindungsleitung** three-wire trunk

Drei-amperemeterverfahren *n* three-ammeter method **-armklemme** *f* three-legged tongs **-atomig** triatomic **-backen, -bohrfutter** *n* three-jaw drill chucks

Dreibackenfutter *n* scroll or three-jaw chuck **~** (m. Handspannung) three-jaw hand operated chuck **~** (zentr. spannend) self-centering three-jaw chuck

dreibasisch tribasic

Dreibein *n* trihedral, shear legs, tripod, boring tripod **~ begleitendes** moving trihedral

Dreibein-anlasser *m* tripod starter **-fahrwerk** *n* tricycle landing gear

dreibeiniger Bock tripod support

Dreibein-lafette *f* tripod mount **-mast** *m* tripod mast **-stativ** *n* tripod

Dreiblattverstellschraube *f* three-bladd controllable propeller

Drei-bock *m* tripod cable support **-brenner** *m* triple burner **-bürstenmaschine** *f* third brush dynamo **-decker** *m* triplane **-dekadenstufenwiderstand** *m* three-decade resistance

dreidimensional tridimensional **-es Fernsehen** stereoscopic television **-e Krümmung** compound curvature (or curve) **-e Strömung** three-dimensional flow

Dreidimensionalität *f* tridimensionality (stereoscopic property, optics)

drei-drähtig threefold, of three threads **-drahtsystem** *n* three-wire system **-düsenzerstäuber** *m* three-nozzle atomizer

Dreieck *n* triangle **~ in der elliptischen Ebene** triangle in elliptic plane **Außenwinkel von einem ~** exterior angle of triangle **Winkelsumme in einem ~** sum of angles of triangle **fehlerzeigendes ~** triangle of error **gleichseitiges ~** equilateral triangle **kongruentes ~** congruent triangle **rechtwinkliges ~** right-angled triangle **sphärisches ~** spherical triangle **ungleichseitiges ~** scalenous triangle

Dreieck(s)-antenne *f* multiwire-triatic antenna, triangle antenna **-aufhängung** *f* three-point suspension **-aufnahme** *f* triangulation **-balkensperre** *f* triangular timber obstacle **-berechnung** *f* trigonometry **-bügel** *m* triangular frame or stirrup

Dreieck(s)-feder *f* triangular spring **-flügel** *m* triangular or delta wing, tapered wing **-geschäft** *n* triangular barter (requiring no foreign exchange) **-gitter** *n* triangular lattice **-glied** *n* delta circuit, mesh **-impuls** *m* triangular pulse

dreieckig triangular, three-cornered **-er Ring** D ring

Dreieck(s)-keil *m* triangular wedge **-kerben** *pl* triangular notches **-kette** *f* chain of triangulation **-koordinat** *m* trilinear coordinate **-kurve** *f* triangle curve

Dreieck(s)-lehre *f* trigonometry **-marke** *f* triangular mark **-membrane** *f* delta-diaphragm **-messung** *f* triangulation, trigonometry **-netz** *n* net or triangulation **-punkt** *m* triangulation point, trigonometrically fixed point, triple point, triangulation station **-punktkreis** *m* Colpitts oscillator

Dreieck-querlenker *m* triangular transversal swinging arm **-rahmen** *m* triangular frame **-rechner** *m* course and speed calculator, triangulator (for trigonometric calculations) **-reflektorantenne** *f* trigonal reflector antenna

Dreieckschaltung *f* triangle connection, delta or mesh connection, delta circuit **in ~** mesh-connected, delta-connected

Dreieck-schütze triangular sluice **-spannung** *f* delta voltage **-spitze** *f* triangular point **-spule** *f* triangular coil **-sternschalter** *m* delta-star switch **-sternverbindung** *f* star-delta connection **-symmetrie** *f* triangle symmetry

Dreieck-wicklung haben to be delta wound **-zeichen** *n* triangular sign (signal) **-zeichenleuchte** *f* triangular sign indicator lamp **-zielen** *n* triangulation (aiming exercise), sighting triangle

Dreielektroden-glimmrelais *n* glow-triode relay **-rohr** *n* **-röhre** *f* triode, triple-electrode tube (radio), audion

Dreielement-Einkontakt-Knickregler *m* three-element one-contact voltage and current regulator **-regler** *m* three-element regulator

Dreier *m* (drei Punkte oder Tüpfel verschiedener Leuchtstoffe) triad **-alphabet** *n* three-unit or ternary code **-fächer** *n* spread salvo of threes (torpedo) **-gemisch** *n* triple fuel mixture (50 per cent gasoline, 40 per cent benzol, 10 per cent alcohol) **-impuls** *m* three-momentum **-stöße** *m* triple collisions, threefold collisions **-stoßpartner** *m* partner in a triple collision

Dreietagenofen *m* three-storied furnace

dreifach (f. Instrumente) 3-point, threefold, triple, treble **~ orthogonale Flächensysteme** triply orthogonal systems of surfaces **-e Ausfertigung** triplicate **-e Kohlensäuresaturation** triple carbonation **-e Leuchte** triform optical apparatus **-e Oberharmonische** triple-harmonic **-er Okularrevolver** *m* triple eyepiece revolver **-er Streifenfilter** *m* tricolor banded filter **-e Stufenscheibe** *f* three step cone pully **-e Vorsteckeinrichtung** triple front feed

Dreifach-aufspaltung *f* triple split **-bindung** *f* triple bond(ing) **-diode-Triode** *f* triple diode triode **-dipol** *m* tridipole antenna **-drehkondensator** *m* three-gang condenser

Dreifach-drossel *f* triple reactor, triple choke **-druckknopf** *m* triple push button **-düse** *f* triple nozzle **-frei** trivariant **-garn** *n* three-threaded yarn **-kran** *m* triple crane **-rechtwinklig** trirectangular

Dreifach-röhre *f* three-unit or three-purpose tube **-schnur** *f* triple flexible (elec.) **-stecker** *m* three-pin plug, triplug **-übersetzungsnabe** *f* hub with three-speed gear

Dreifachungsfrequenztransformator *m* frequency trebler

Dreifach-verbindung *f* ternary compound **-verstärker** *m* three-stage amplifier **-vorgelege** *n* three-speed backgears **-wurzel** *f* triple root **-zünder** *m* combination fuse superquick delay and time

Drei-fadenmethode *f* three-wire-method **-fadenlampe** *f* three-filament lamp **-farbband** *n* three-colored ribbon

Dreifarben-aufnahmekamera *f* three-color camera **-druck** *m* three-color printing **-druckfarbe** *f* three-color printing ink **-leuchtdichte** *f* tricolor reflection-density value **-raster** *m* three-color screen **-röhre** *f* tricolor cinescope, tricolor tube **-tiefdruck** *m* three-color photogravure **-trennung** *f* three-color separation **-verfahren** *n* three-color process

Drei-fingerregel *f* three-finger rule, right-hand or thumb rule, Fleming's rule **-flächig** three-faced, tetrahedral **-flammig** three-flame, three-flamed **-flammrohrkessel** *m* three-flame-tube kettle **-flügelige Luftschraube** three-bladed propeller

Dreiflügel-meißel *m* three wing bit **-schraube** *f* three-bladed propeller

Dreifuß *m* shear legs **~** (Stativ) tripod, spider stand **~** (Zwischenstück zwischen Stativ und Theodolit), tribrach, three-screw base

Dreifuß-anlasser *m* tripod starter **-aufsatzstück** *n* tripod extension piece **-bohrer** *m* tripod drill **-lafette** *f* tripod mount **-lupe** *f* tripod magnifier **-ring** *m* tripod ring

Dreiganggetriebe *n* three-speed transmission

dreigängiges Gewinde *n* triple thread

Drei-gelenkbogen *m* three-hinged arch **-gitterröhre** *f* three-grid tube

dreiglied(e)rig three-membered, trinominal **-e Division** triangular division **-e Farbgleichung** three-color or three-stimulus equation

Drei-halskolben *m* three-necked flask **-holmig** with three spars **-hordendarre** *f* three-floored kiln **-kammersystem** *n* three-chamber system

Dreikanal-Koinzidenz-Antikoinzidenz-Verstärker treble-channel coincidense-anticoincidence amplifier **-verfahren** *n* three-channel method

Dreikant trihedral **begleitendes ~** moving trihedral

Dreikant-beschlag *m* triangular cornerpiece **-feile** *f* triangular file **-haltespeer** *m* triangular shaft

dreikantig three-cornered, triangular, three-square

Dreikant-mundstück *n* triangular opening **-riemen** *m* V-belt **-schaber** *m* triangular scraper **-schiene** *f* triangular bar **-schnitzel** *pl* triangular slices **-speer** *m* triangular spindle **-spitze** *f* three-square tip **-winkel** *m* trihedral angle

Drei-klangsignal *n* three-tone signal **-klinkenschloß** *n* three-point lock **-knopfschalter** *m* three-button switch (elec.) **-kolbenpumpe** *f* triple-plunger or three-piston pump **-komponentenwaage** *f* three-component balance **-körperverdampfapparat** *m* triple-effect evaporator

Dreikreisel-anordnung *f* three-gyro system, triple-gyro arrangement **-kompaß** *m* triple gyrocompass **-mutterkompaß** *m* triple gyro master compass

Drei-kreisempfänger *m* **-kreiser** *m* three-circuit

receiver or set **-kurbelige Welle** *f* three-throw crank-shaft **-kurvenschreiber** *m* three-point curve-drawing recorder **-ladungsträgermodell** *n* three-carrier model **-lagerzwillingsmaschine** *f* twin-cylinder engine with triple bearing **-lamellig** three-bar

Dreileiter *m* triple or three-wire lead **-drehstrom** *m* three-wire three-phase a-c **-dynamo** *f* three-wire generator **-kabel** *n* triple-core cable **-netz** *n* three-wire supply system **-system** *n* three-wire system with direct or alternating current

Dreimaischverfahren *n* three-mash process

Drei-mantelkabel *n* SL cable (three-conductor cable with three lead sheaths, one per conductor) **-maschinensatz** *m* three-engine set **-messerautomat** *m* automatic three-knife trimmer **-messerschnellschneider** *m* high-speed triple-blade trimmer

Drei-motorenlaufkran *m* three-motored or three-engined traveling crane **-motorig** trimotor, three-engined **-nadelstuhl** *m* three-needle frame (textiles) **-nahtmeßmethode** *f* three wire method **-nockenschraube** *f* trilobe screw **-nutig** three-groove **-nutkurzschlußanker** *m* three-ring short-circuit armature

dreiparametrige Wellenfunktionen three-parameter wave function

Dreiphasen-dynamo *f* three-phase generator **-gleichgewicht** *n* three-phase equilibrium **-gleichrichter** *m* three-phase rectifier **-kontaktzone** three-phase confluent zone **-motor** *m* three-phase motor **-netz** *n* three-phase network **-ofen** *m* three-phase furnace

Dreiphasen-schaltung *f* three-phase connection (elec.) **-schweißbetrieb** *m* three-phase welding service **-strom** *m* three-phase current, triphase current **-system** *n* three-phase system **-vierleiternetz** *n* three-phase network with four wires **-(wechsel)strom** *m* three-phase (alternating) current **-wechselstrommotor** *m* three-phase alternating motor **-zuführung** *f* three-phase supply

dreiphasig three-phase, triphase **-er Stoßkurzschlußstrom** *m* (einphasiger) maximum asymmetric three-phase short-circuit current (single-phase) **-er Wechseltrom** three-phase alternating current

Dreiphononen-prozeß *m* three-phonon process **-wechselwirkung** *f* effect of three-phonon interaction

dreipolig three-polar, three-pole **-er Normstecker** *m* three-pin plug

Dreipolröhre *f* triode, three-electrode tube

Dreipunkt-aufhängung *f* three-point suspension **-auflage** *f* three-point contact on the ground **-kreis** *m* **-kreisschwingungserzeuger** *m* Hartley or Colpitts oscillator **-lagerung** *f* three-point bearing **-landung** *f* three-point landing (aviation) **-regler** *m* three-term controller **-schaltung** *f* three-point (connection) Hartley or Colpitts circuit, Hartley oscillator **-spatium** *n* three-point space

Dreiquantenvernichtung *f* three-photon annihilation

Drei-rad *n* tricycle **-räderpumpe** *f* three-gear pump **-radfahrgestell** *n* three-wheeled undercarriage

dreirädrig tricycle **-es Fahrgestell** tricycle landing gear **-er Transportwagen** three-wheel load-carrying truck

Drei-reihenstandmotor *m* arrow engine, three-bank upright engine **-riemenscheibenantrieb** *m* triple-pulley drive **-rillendrehstern** *m* three reel stand **-röhrenempfänger** *m* three-valve receiver **-rollenmaschine** *f* three-reel machine **-schäftiges Kabel** three-strand cable

Dreischar-pflug *m* three-furrow plow **-vorrichtung** *f* third plow attachment

Drei-schenkeldrossel *f* three-legged reactor or choke coil **-schenkelig** three-legged **-schicht** three-ply **-schichteneinsatz** *m* three-layer filter (gas mask) **-schichtig** (Sperrholz) three-ply **-schienengeleise** *n* three-rail track, triple-rail line **-schiffig** three-bayed **-schlauchbrenner** *m* double-oxygen hose-cutting torch **-schneidenbohrer** *m* three-lip drill **-schneider** *m* three-knife trimmer **-schneidiger Schaber** three-square scraper **-seemeilenzone** *f* three-mile limit

dreiseitig three-sided, trilateral, triangular **-er Winkel** trihedral angle

Dreiselbstanschlußsystem three-wire automatic telephone system

dreisilbig trisyllabic

Drei-sitzer *m* three-seater airplane **-sitzig** three-seat, three-seated, having three places **-spitzzirkel** *m* three-leg compasses **-spule** *f* triple coil

dreispaltig three-column

Dreispindel-Reihenbohrmaschine *f* three-way series drilling machine

Dreispitzenfunkenzieher *m* three-point spark drawer, three-point test gap

Dreistab-kopplung *f* tri-rod coupler **-stachel** *m* fork (agr.) **-stellig** three-figure, to three decimal places **-steuerflugzeug** *n* three-control airplane **-stieler** *m* three-bay, three-strutter, three-bay biplane (aviation)

Dreistift-sicherheitssteckvorrichtungen *f pl* three-pin safety sockets and plugs **-sockel** *m* three-pin base

dreistöckig three-storied

Dreistoff-legierung *f* ternary alloy, three-component alloy **-system** *n* ternary or three-component system

Drei-strahlproblem *n* three-beam problem **-strahler** *m* three-beam headlight **-strom** *m* three-phase current

Dreistufen-heizung *f* three-stage heating device **-lesesignalverstärker** *m* three-stage sense amplifier **-scheibenantrieb** three-step pulley drive

dreistufig with three steps, three-stage

dreiteilig tripartite, in three parts or sections **-es Objektiv** three-lens objective, three-lens combination, three-component lens **-er Stecker** three-point plug, three-way plug

Dreiteilung *f* trisection, tri-equipartition

Drei-trägerbauart *f* three-girder design **-überschußcode** *m* excess-three code

dreiviertel elliptische Federn three-quarter elliptic springs **-fliegende Achse** three-quarter floating axle **-rückansicht** *f* three-quarter rear view

Dreivoltmeterverfahren *n* three-voltmeter method

Dreiwalzen-blechbiegemaschine *f* three-roller plate-bending machine **-kompensator** *m* three-roller compensating device **-maschine** *f* triple-roller machine **-mühle** *f* **für Zuckerrohr** three-roller cane mill **-quetschsystem** *n* squeeze unit of three rollers each **-reibemaschine** *f* three-roller grinding mill **-stuhl** *m* three-roll mill **-zuckermühle** *f* three-roll sugar mill

Dreiwalzwerkfarbenreibmaschine *f* three-roller refiner for colors

Dreiweg(e) three-way

Dreiwege-bohrwerk *n* three-way boring mill **-bohr- und Plandrehwerk** *n* three-way boring and facing mill **-flanschenhahn** *m* three-way flange cock **-hahn** *m* selector valve, three-way (stop)cock or tap **-hahnküken** *n* plug of three-way cock **-schalter** *m* three-way switch **-stück** *n* three-way pipe

Dreiweg-ventil *n* three-way valve **-verbindung** *f* three-way connection **-weiche** *f* three-way aerial frog

dreiwertig trivalent **-es Element** trivalent element, triad

Dreiwicklungstransformator *m* hybrid transformer

dreiwinklig triangular

Dreizack *m* three-prong

dreizählig ternary, trigonal (cryst.), threefold, triple **-e Harmonische** triple harmonic

dreizähnige Pinzette forceps with three teeth

Dreizylinder *m* three-cylinder **-motor** *m* three-cylinder engine **-preßluftmotor** *m* three-cylinder compressed-air motor **-sternmotor** *m* three-cylinder inverted engine

Drell *m* cotton drill **-bogen** *m* drill bow

Drellennaht *f* projection weld

Drempel *m* sill for sealing base of gates, miter sill, miter sill's foundation **-quader** *n* quoins of pointing or miter sill **-schleuse** *f* lock with cheek gates **-vorsprung** *m* rise of pointing or miter sill

Drescher *m* pulp machinery for paper

Dresch-maschine *f* thresher **-tenne** *f* threshing floor **-trommel** *f* thrashing drum

dressieren to finish, planish, dress, train (animals)

Dressier-gerüst *n* skin-pass stand **-stich** *m* skin-pass **-walzwerk** *n* temper pass mill

Drift-energie *f* drift energy **-frei** drift-free **-geschwindigkeit** *f* drift velocity **-kraft** *f* drifting force **-transistor** *m* drift transistor **-strömung** *f* drift, drift current

Drillich *m* drill (cloth), ticking, canvas, denim **-anzug** *m* fatigue or work uniform, denims

Drill-achse *f* rotator (quantum theory) **-anzug** *m* fatigue suit

Drillbohrer *m* drill, crankshaft **-einsatz** *m* drill bit

Drillbohr-fänger *m* drill-bit grab **-speer** *m* twist-drill spear

drillen to drill, turn, twist **-egge** *f* drill harrow

Drill-eisen *n* twisted bars **-gerät** *n* twisting apparatus (textiles)

drillierter Federdraht three-strand plated wire (armament)

Drilling *m* triplet, sporting gun with three barrels

Drillings-behälter *m* triple barrel tank **-fenster** *n* triple lancet window **-festigkeit** *f* twisting strength **-maschine** *f* three-cylinder engine, expansion machine

Drillingspreßpumpe *f* **doppelte ~** double three-throw, three-piston, or three-plunger pressure pump

Drillingsstecker *m* three-pin plug, plug with three current consumption places

Drillings-turm *m* three-gun turret, triple turret **-walzwerk** *n* trio rollers, trio mill

Drillmaschine *f* drill machine, drill **~ mit Hackschare** hoe drill **~ mit Schuh** shoe drill

Drill-maschinenvorrichtung *f* drill jig **-moment** *n* twisting moment

Drillometer *m* drilling weight indicator

Drill-sämaschine *f* drill plow **-säge** *f* hack saw **-schar** *f* seed drill **-schreiber** *m* torsion meter **-stab** *m* torsion bar or rod (vehicle) **-steifigkeit** *f* torsional stiffness or rigidity

Drillung *f* torsion, twist, torsion or twisting couple

Drillungs-kristall *m* twister crystal **-modulus** *m* torsion or shear modulus, rigidity modulus **-schwingungen** *pl* torsional vibrations

Drill-verformung *f* torsional deformation **-weite** *f* drill spacing **-wulststahl** *m* twisted concrete cross section steel

dringen to urge

dringend urgent, pressing, express **~ bitten** to appeal **-es Gespräch** express call **-es Notsignal** SOS **-es Staatsgespräch** government priority call **-es Telegramm** urgent message

dringlich urgent pressing

Dringlichkeit *f* priority, urgency

Dringlichkeits-grad *m* (degree of) priority **-liste** *f* priority schedule or list **-meldung** *f* urgent message **-stufe** *f* degree of necessity or importance, a measure the extent to which protection is necessary for an objective **-stufe** *f* precedence, priority number or rating **-zeichen** *n* urgency signal

dritte Saturation third carbonation

Drittel *n* gang, third **-bogen** *m* third of a sheet (print.) **-führer** *m* deputy of sinkers **-punkte** *pl* third points **-spatium** *n* third space

dritteltägig diurnal, three times daily **-e Welle** eight-hourly wave

Drittelverfahren *n* method by thirds

Drittelwicklung *f* tertiary winding

dritter Ausschnitt *m* third ply

Drittwicklung *f* tertiary winding (of a transformer)

Drogerie *f* pharmacy

dröhnen to boom, utter low dull sound, drone

dromochronische Kurve time-distance curve or graph

Drop *m* lozenge

Droschke *f* taxicab

Drossel *f* choke, reactive, impedance, or retardation coil, reactor, throttle, damper, pressure-regulating valve, inductor, tickler coil (regeneration) **~ für Dreileitermaschinen** equalizing coil **~ mit Luftkern** air-core inductor **~ mit veränderlicher Induktivität** swinging choke **~ öffnen** to open, open up an engine **~ ganz öffnen** to shove the throttle full open **~ schließen** (drosseln) to throttle back **eisenfreie ~** air-core coil or choke **teilweise geöffnete ~** part-open throttle **voll geöffnete ~** full-open throttle

Drossel-absperrklappe *f* throttle-clack valve **-achse** *f* throttle shaft **-anschlag** *m* throttle stop **-bar** throttleable **-bohrung** *f* choke bore **-büchse** *f* throttle bush **-düse** *f* throttle nozzle **-einlaß** *m* throttle opening

Drosseleinstellung, unveränderte ~ fixed throttle

Drossel-gerät *n* head meter **-griff** *m* throttle handle or grip **-hebel** *m* throttle lever **-kalorimeter** *m* throttling calorimeter **-kette** *f* low-pass filter **-klappe** *f* throttle valve or flap, butterfly valve (gate), damper, accelerator

Drosselklappen-achse *f* throttle-valve spindle **-heber** *m* throttle lever **-ventil** *n* butterfly valve **-welle** *f* throttle shaft

Drossel-kompaß *m* flux-gate compass **-kondensator** *m* combined choke and condenser suppressor **-kreis** *m* multiple, branched, or parallel resonant circuit, rejector or stopper circuit **-modulation** *f* modulation due to iron saturation

drosseln to throttle, baffle, choke, iron out **~** (Schub) to shut off (thrust)

Drosselöffnung, mit verminderter ~ partially throttled

Drossel-organ (Kühlmaschine) refrigerant-metering device, throttling member **-regulierung** *f* throttle governing **-relais** *n* high-impedance relay **-röhre** *f* choking tube **-satz** *m* rejector circuit, noise killer **-schalter** *m* tone-reducer switch **-scheibe** *f* orifice plate **-spindel** *f* throttle spindle or shaft **-spinner** *m* throttle frame tenter **-stoß** *m* impedance bond

Drosselspule *f* impedance coil, inductance (coil), reactive or reaction coil, retard(ation) coil, reactor, inductor, choke, impedance **veränderliche ~** reactance regulator

Drossel-spulenverstärker *m* choke-coupled or impedance-coupled amplifier **-stelle** *f* restrictor **-steuerung** *f* throttle control **-stoß** *m* inductive rail connection **-stuhl** *m* throttle frame **-tür** *f* wicket or gauge door **-überdeckung** *f* throttle cover

Drosselung *f* throttling, curb **~ im Auslaß** wire drawing in exhaust **~ im Einlaß** wire drawing in intake **~ des Kühlluftstromes** choking effect on the flow

Drosselungsarbeit *f* work of throttling

Drossel-ventil *n* throttle, choker or butterfly valve, power control **-verbindung** *f* choke joint **-verstärker** *m* choke-coupled or impedance-coupled amplifier **-welle** *f* throttle shaft **-wirkung** *f* attenuation (filter, etc.), choking or throttle effect (on), damping action

Druck *m* printing, presswork, pressure, thrust, print, compression, head, draft, load, tension, impression **~** (axial) *m* journal load, thrust **~ auf Gummi** offset printing **~ in mm Quecksilbersäule** pressure in terms of millimeters of mercury **~ abfangen** *n* inching (slow action) **einen ~ abziehen** to pull off, take a proof **auf ~ beansprucht** in compression **sich im ~ befinden** to be in press

Druck, einfacher ~ simple stress **indirekter ~** side pressure **hydrostatischer ~** hydrostatic pressure **mittlerer indizierter und effektiver ~** medium indicated and medium effective pressure **~ konstant halten** to maintain equal pressure **unter ~ setzen** to pressurize **statischer ~** static pressure **stichähnlicher ~** engravinglike print **weicher ~** soft impression (print.) **(Mehrfarben-~)** color print **(Tief-~)** *m* rotary photogravure

Druckabfall *m* drop in pressure **~ am Zylinder** air-pressure drop across the cylinder

druck-abfallverhinderter Einbau antiflash baffling **-abhängig** pressure-responsive, pressure-dependent, being a function of pressure **-abhängigkeit** *f* pressure dependence **-ablassen** *n* breathing (releasing pressure in crankcase) **-absperrventil** *n* discharge stop valve **-absteller** *m* throw-off, cylinder trip (print.) **-abstellung** *f* stopping of machine

Druck-abteufung *f* pneumatic shaft sinking **-abwicklung** *f* printing progress **-achse** *f* printing shaft **-achsensperre** *f* printing clutch throw-out lever **-akkumulator** *m* pressure accumulator **-alarm** *m* pressure alarm **-alarmeinrichtung** *f* pressure-warning unit **-amplitude** *f* compressive amplitude, pressure, compression **-analyse** *f* stress analysis **-analytiker** *m* stress analyst **-änderung** *f* change of pressure

Druck-anfang *m* start of pressure **-anlage** *f* feed gauge **-ansammlung** *f* stress concentration **-ansatz** *m* print(ing) color or paste **-anstieg** *m* pressure rise **-anstiegsgeschwindigkeit** *f* rate of pressure rise **-anzeige** *f* pressure reading, pressure indication **-anzeiger** *m* **-anzeigerohr** *n* pressure gauge or tube **-apparat** *m* printing apparatus, pressure or tank apparatus **anzug** *m* (Höhenflug) pressure suit **-arbeit** *f* presswork

Druck-arm *m* printing bail arm **-artikel** *m* print style **-auflage** *f* edition **-aufnahmeröhrchen** *n* pressure probe (in article on tilted weir plates)

Druckausbreitung *f* propagation of pressure (wave), pressure spread **geradlinige ~** rectilinear pressure spread

Druckausfall *m* finished product (print.)

Druckausgleich *m* equalization of pressure, pressure balance, allowance for elevation (oil engines, etc.) **Kolben mit ~** balanced piston

Druckausgleich-behälter *m* pressure-equalizing reservoir **-einrichtung** *f* compensating device for pressure, pressure-balancing device **-kolben** *m* dummy piston **-flasche** *f* levelling bottle **-öffnung** *f* breather, vent **-verfahren** *n* (Indikatoreichung) balanced-pressure method

Druck-auslösemagnet *m* printing trip magnet **-auslösung** *f* pressure release

Druck-automat *m* automatic press **-balken** *m* clamping bar **-band** *n* printing tape

Drückbank *f* spinning lathe

Druck-baum *m* forcing lever **-beanspruchung** *f* compressive-load application, compression or crushing stress, pressure load **-becken** *n* diffused-air tank **-begrenzungsventil** *n* relief-valve jet **-behälter** *m* pressure tank, monte-jus, suction and forcing apparatus, acid egg **-belastung** *f* compressive load, compressive-load application, compression stress

Druckbelüftungs-blech *n* pressure-type baffle or deflector **-kühlung** *f* **-kühlverfahren** *n* pressure cooling **-system** *m* pressurization system

Druck-benzinuhr *f* air-pressure or hydrostatic gauge **-beständigkeit** *f* bursting pressure

Druckbestäuber *m* print sprayers **-spritzmittel** *n* contents for pressure sprayers

Druck-bestimmung *f* impression setting **-betan-**

kung *f* (Astron.) pressure fuelling (spacecraft) **-beton** *m* compressed concrete

Druckbild *n* printing style **~ des Dampfes** steam diagram

Druck-birne *f* monte-jus, acid egg **-blatt** *n* separate leaflet **-bogen** *m* printed sheet **-bohlenmine** *f* pressure-plank mine **-bolzen** *m* wearing button, plunger, clamping or thrust bolt **-bohrung** *f* pressure hole **-breite** *f* printing width

Druck-brett *n* (Handdruck) printing board **-brettmine** *f* pressure-board mine **-buchstaben** *pl* printed characters **-bügel** *m* (Fernschreiber) printing bail, pressure stirrup **-bügelregler** *m* pressure-bar controller

Druck-daumen *m* printing cam **-dauer** *f* pressure period **-decke** *f* printer's blanket **-deformation** *f* inflation deflection **-dehnung** *f* flexural strength **-dicht** tight, pressurized **-dichtebeziehung** *f* pressure density relation **-differenzgeber** *m* pressure-difference transducer

Druckdose *f* hydraulic intensifier, capsule, siphon, pressure element or box, bellows **barometrische ~** barometric bellows

Druckdosen *pl* crushers, crusher gauges (hollow cylinders, used to measure remote effects of underwater explosions) **-messung** *f* measurement (of pressures in underwater explosions) with crusher gauges **-steuerung** *f* capsule control

Druckdrehfilter *n* rotary pressure filter

Druck-düse *f* discharge (pressure) nozzle, combining or mixing nozzle (injectors) **-ebene** *f* thrust plane

Druck-eichung *f* pressure calibration **-eigenspannung** *f* residual compressive stress **-einfluß** *m* pressure effect **-einheit** *f* printing unit **-einrichtung** *f* printing arrangement **-einspritzung** *f* solid injection

Druck-einstellhebel *m* impression control lever **-einstellschraube** *f* pressure adjusting screw **-einstellung** *f* pressure adjustment **-elastizität** *f* elasticity of compression **-elektrisch** piezoelectric **-elektrizität** *f* piezoelectricity **-empfang** *m* printing or typescript reception **-empfänger** *m* pressure(-responsive) microphone, printing-receiving apparatus

Druckempfindlichkeit *f* pressure sensitivity, pressure response

drucken to print

drücken to press, squeeze, wring, push, put the nose down (aviation), compress, spin, thrust, bear, depress (a key) **schwer ~** to weigh heavily (e.g. on the cost price) **sich ~** (slang) to malinger, shirk one's duty **auf Maß ~** press to gauge

Drücken *n* pressing, thrusting, bearing, depression **~ der Diffusionsbatterie** pressure in the battery **~ auf der Drehbank** to spin

drückend heavy, sultry, oppressive **-es Gebirge** sticky formation **-er Handlocher** printing perforator **-er Schiefer** heaving shale

Druckende (print) *n* deadline

Druckentgaser *m* pressure de-aerator

druckentlastet balanced

Druckentlastung *f* release of pressure, pressure relief

Druckentlastungsventil pressure relief valve

Druckentspannung *f* pressure drop, pressure release

Drucker *m* printer, printing apparatus

Drücker *m* trigger, latch, pusher, thumb nut (sight leaf)

Druckerballen *m* leather ball

Druckerei *f* printing office or factory **-artikel** *m* print style **-bedarf** *m* printer's supply **-betrieb** *m* printing plant **-erhöhungspumpe** *f* booster pump **-fachgeschäft** *n* printer's supply house **-faktor** *m* overseer (print,) **-hilfsprodukt** *n* printing auxiliary **-setzmaschine** *f* composing machine for printing offices

Drucker-empfanglocher *m* printing reperforator **-falle** *f* printer latch (telegr.)

Druck-erhitzung *f* heating under pressure **-erhöher** *m* intensifier, pressure step-up means **-erhöhung** *f* increase of pressure

Druckermarke *f* printer's mark

Druckermüdungsversuch *m* compression-fatigue or compression-endurance test

Druckerpresse *f* printing or letter press

Drückerschalter mit Feststellvorrichtung trigger switch with lock

Druckerschwärze *f* printing ink, carbon black **-öl** *n* printing-ink oil

Druck-erzeuger *m* thrust generator **-erzeugung** *f* pressurizing **-erzeugungsanlage** *f* pressure unit

druck-fähig printable **-fähigkeit** *f* printing property **-falle(nschiene)** (Fernschreiber) printing bail (track). print releasing bar **-farbe** *f* mimeograph ink, printing ink

Druck-faß *n* blow case **-feder** *f* pressure or compression spring **-federn** *n* spring action **-fehler** *m* erratum, error, misprint **-feld** *n* printing area **-fenster** *m* pressure plate or gate (motion pictures) **-fertig** ready for printing

druckfest resistant to compression **~ gekapselt** air-tight (machine)

druckfest-er Behälter *m* pressure resistant container **-er Motor** flameproof motor **-es Schutzrohr** well (e.g. of thermometer) **-e Sonderausführung** pressure-resistant type **-e Umhüllung** pressurized casing

Druck-festigkeit *f* compressive, compression or crushing strength, resistance to compression, to crushing, or to pressure **-fettpresse** *f* grease gun **-feuerbeständigkeit** *f* refractoriness under load

Druck-figur *f* pressure diagram **-filter** *m* pressure filter **-filz** *m* blanket (print.), printing felt **-fläche** *f* printing surface, area of pressure, bearing-surface area **-flansch** *m* pressure flange **-flügel** *m* pressure vane **-flüssigkeit** *f* pressure fluid, hydraulic fluid

Druck-folge *f* printing sequence **-förderung** *f* pressure feed **-formenschneider** *m* block cutter **-fortpflanzungsgesetz** *n* law of the transmissibility of pressure **-freistrahlgebläse** *n* pressure-type hose sandblast tank machine **-fundament** *n* type bed

Druckgas *n* pressure gas (such as nitrogen used to force the propellants of the liquid-fuel rocket into the blast chamber during firing) **-anlage** *f* pressure-gas plant **-anschluß** *m* pressure gas connection **-armatur** *f* pressure gas fitting **-düse** *f* compressed gas nozzle (rocket) **-einsatzverfahren** *n* gas casehardening process **-generator** *m* pressure gas producer, gas generator with suction and with pressure **-schalter** *m* gas-blast or air-blast switch, autopneumatic circuit breaker **-tank** *m* gas pressure tank

Druck-geber *m* pressure pick-off **-gebiet** *n* pressure area, compressed region **-gebung** *f* roller pressure

Druckgefälle *n* pressure gradient or drop, pressure or differential head, isobaric slope **dynamisches ~** dynamic head **statisches ~** static head

Druck-gefäß *n* pressure box, pressure vessel **-genehmigung** *f* permission to print **-geschwindigkeit** *f* printing speed **-gewerbe** *n* printing (trade) craft **-gießen** *n* die casting

Druckgleichgewicht, osmotisches ~ osmotic equilibrium

Druck-glied *n* compression member **-gradienten-mikrophon** *m* pressure-gradient or velocity microphone **-grenze** *f* pressure limit **-gurt** *m* upper chord, compression member or chord **-guß** *m* die cast metal **-gußforschung** *f* die-casting research

Druck-hahn *m* compression cock, pressure tap **-hälfte** *f* pressure half coupling **-halterung** *f* pressure mounting (cryst.) **-haltung** *f* pressure resistance **-hammer** *m* printing hammer **-härte** *f* indentation hardness **-haut** *f* pressure film

Druck-hebel *m* printing lever, pressure lever **-hebelböckchen** *n* operating lever fulcrum **-heber** *m* siphon for aerated water **-heft** *n* brochure, pamphlet, booklet **-hilfsmittel** *n* printing medium

Druckhöhe *f* pressure head (of water), discharge head height of water, pressure altitude **statische ~** static head

Druckhöhen-gefälle *n* hydraulic gradient, pressure height gradient, pressure altitude gradient **-messer** *m* pressure altimeter **-verlust** *m* loss of head

Druck-hub *m* discharge or compression stroke **-hülse** *f* pressure sleeve **-indikator** *m* pressure indicator **-kabine** *f* pressurized cabin

Druckkammer *m* pressure chamber **-lautsprecher** *m* pressure-chamber or pneumatic loudspeaker **-prüfungsmethode** *f* pressure-chamber conditioning

Druck-kasten *m* pneumatic caisson **-kegel** *m* pressure cone **-kern** *m* pressure core **-kessel** *m* air-pressure tank, header **-klemme** *f* press clamp (elec.)

Druckknopf *m* patent fastener, control knob, press fastener, push (key), push or press button, pressure head **~ zur Hupe** horn (operator) button

Druckknopf-abstimmung push-button tuning **-betätigung** *f* push button control **-empfänger** *m* push-button or press-button receiver set, receiver with automatic tuning means **-gesteuert** push button-operated **-gesteuerter Regelmotor** push-button-controlled variable-speed motor **-melder** *m* manual alarm box

Druckknopf-schalter *m* push-button (type) switch **-schalter einpolig** push button single circuit **-schaltung** *f* push-button control **-sperre** *f* plunger lock **-starter** *m* push-button starter **-steuerung** *f* push-button control **-tafel** *f* push-button switch-board **-ventil** *n* button-type blowcock **-verschluß** *m* snap-button fastener

Druckkocher *m* pressure digester

Druckkoeffizient *m* pressure coefficient **~ der Kompressibilität** dependence on pressure of compressibility

Druck-kolben *m* pressure arm, piston digestion flask, piston, ram, plunger **-komponente** *f* component of compressive force **-kontrolle** *f* pressure control **-kontrolluhr** *f* pressure gauge **-konvektion** *f* forced convection **-kopf** *m* numbering box **-körper** *m* pressure hull, indentor (rubber) **-kosten** *f pl* printing costs

Druckkraft *f* compressive force or stress, crushing stress, pressure, thrust **-festigkeit** *f* compression force or strength **-geber** *m* load cell **-meßdose** *f* load cell **-messer** *m* thrust-measuring apparatus, pressure or thrust gauge **-messung** *f* measurement of thrust or of compression **-prüfer** *m* compression-stress tester

Druck-krümmer *m* pressure elbow **-kufe** *f* pressure pad (motion pictures) **-kugel** *f* ball thrust **-kugellager** *n* ball race (thrust), thrust ball bearing **-kühlung** *f* compression refrigeration **-kurbellager** *n* pressure crank-end bearing **-kurve** *f* pressure curve, printing and function cam

Drucklager *n* abutment, spigot, thrust bearing or block, thrust race **~ zur Aufnahme des Luftschraubenschubes** propeller-thrust bearing

Druck-lagerbügel *m* thrust shoe **-lagerkamm** *m* thrust collar **-last** *f* working load **-legung** *f* impression, going to press **-lehre** *f* pressure gauge

Druckleistung *f* printing capacity; (Kompr.) delivery output

Druckleistungsprobe *f* sample print

Druck-lehre *f* pressure gauge **-leitbleche** *pl* pressure or intercylinder baffles **-leitung** *f* compressed-air line or pipe, delivery pipe, pressure line **-letter** *f* type **-linie** *f* hydraulic gradient, potential line, pressure curve, axis of pressure, line of impression

drucklos pressureless

Druckluft *f* compressed air, pressure air **durch ~ betätigt** pneumatic

Druckluft-akkumulator *m* compressed-air accumulator **-anhängerbremsenschluß** *m* compressed air trailer brake coupling **-anlage** *f* compressed-air plant, desiccator **-anlasser** *m* compressed-air starter **-anlaßgefäß** *n* compressed-air receiver for starting **-anlaßvorrichtung** *f* compressed air starting device

Druckluft-anschluß *m* compressed air connection **-anschlußventil** *n* compressed air pipe-connection valve, pressure-control valve **-antrieb** *m* pneumatic drive **-behälter** *m* compressed-air container **-betätigtes Spannfutter** pneumatic chuck **-betrieb** *m* compressed-air service **-bläser** *m* compressed-air blower **-bohrer** *m* pneumatic drill

Druckluft-bremsausrüstung *f* air-brake assembly **-bremsbehälter** *m* compressed-air tank for brake **-bremse** *f* compressed-air brake **-bremskreis** *m* pneumatic braking circuit **-bremsschläuche** *pl* compressed-air brake hoses **-bügelbetätigung für Stromabnehmer** hoop actuated by compressed air for overhead contact **-einkammerbremsverstärker** *m* pneumatic single-chamber brake energizer **-einspritzung** *f* air injection **-empfänger** (Rohrpost) pressure receiving valve **-enteiser** *m* pneumatic deicer **-erzeuger** *m* air compressor **-fangvorrichtung** *f* pneumatic catch **-flasche** *f* gas cylinder, compressed-air bottle **-förderer** *m* compressed-air conveyer

Druckluft-förderverfahren *n* (für Hebung von Flüssigkeiten), airlift **-futter** *n* air-operated chuck **-gerät** *n* compressed air installation **-gesteinstaubförderanlage** *f* pneumatic conveying plant for stone powder **-gesteuert** pneumatically controlled **-gründung** *f* foundation work under compressed air **-hammer** *m* pneumatic or compressed-air hammer **-haspel** *m* pneumatic winch **-hebelschalter** *m* pneumatic lever switch **-heber** *m* air lift **-heberpumpe** *f* compressed-air lift pump **-hebezeug** *n* air hoist

Druckluft-horn *n* pneumatic horn **-kanal** *m* forced draught duct **-kasten** *m* caissan **-kessel** *m* pressure tank (of a sandblast-tank machine), blast-pressure tank **-klopfapparat** *m* pneumatic rapper **-kolben** *m* air operated piston

Druckluft-kondensator *m* compressed-air condenser **-kontrollrelais** *n* compressed air control relay **-kühlung** *f* forced-draft cooling **-leitung** *f* compressed-air line or pipe **-mangel** *m* lack of compressed air **-meißel** *m* pneumatic chipping hammer **-motor** *m* compressed-air or pneumatic motor **-niethammer** *m* pneumatic riveter **-nietung** *f* pneumatic riveting **-öldruckbremse** *f* air-hydraulic brake **-preßformmaschine** *f* air squeezer **-preßvorrichtung** *f* air jar squeezer **-prüfung** *f* air-pressure test

Druckluft-ramme *f* pneumatic pile driver **-raum** *m* compressed-air chamber **-rüttler** *m* air-jarring machine **-schalter** *m* (cross) air-blast switch, autopneumatic circuit breaker **-scheibenwischer** *m* pneumatic windshield wiper **-schlagwerkzeug** *n* percussion pneumatic tool **-schlauch** *m* compressed-air tube or hose **-schraube** *f* pusher airscrew **-servobremsanlage** *f* pneumatic servo-brake system

Druckluft-spannfutter *n* pneumatic chuck **-spritzapparat** *m* aerograph **-strahlgerät** *n* compressed-air jet or spray apparatus **-steuerkolben** *m* compressed air control piston **-strom** *m* compressed-air stream, forced draft

Druckluft-stutzen *m* compressed-air valve **-übernahme** *f* compressed-air cock **-ventilator** *m* blower **-ventilklappe** (Rohrpost) air-pressure valve flap **-versatz** *m* pneumatic stowage **-versatzmaschine** *f* pneumatic stower **-verteilerstutzen** *m* compressed-air distributor **-vibrator** *m* compressed-air vibrator **-vorratsbehälter** *m* air receiver **-vorschubeinrichtung** *f* pneumatic feed mechanism

Druckluft-warngerät *n* pneumatic warning unit **-wasserkessel** *m* presser (water) tank **-werkzeug** *n* pneumatic or compressed-air tool **-wischer** *m* pneumatic window wiper **-zahnradmotoren** *m pl* gear-wheel air turbines **-zerstäuber** *m* compressed-air atomizer **-zuführung** *f* compressed-air supply **-zuleitung** *f* compressed-air line **-zylinder** *m* compressed-air cylinder, air cylinder

Druck-magnet *m* striker magnet, printing magnet **-manometer** *m* pressure manometer or gauge

Druckmaschine *f* printing press **zweiseitige ~** duplex or two-face printing machine

Druckmeßdose *f* pressure cell, compression standardizing box, piezoelectric gauge, pressure pickup

Druckmesser *m* liquid or fluid manometer, pressure gauge or meter, piezometer **~ und Gefrierpunktmesser** manocryometer **osmotischer ~** osmometer

Druckmesser-anschluß *m* pressure-gauge connection **-rohr** *n* manometer, pressure tube **-ventil** *n* pressure-gauge valve

Druck-meßfeder *f* compression-measuring spring **-meßgerät** *n* piezometer (for water pressure), pressure meter **-messing** *n* pressed brass **-meßsonde** *f* pressure-sampling device **-messung** *f* measurement of pressure **-meßzelle** *f* pressure element **-mikrophon** *n* pressure microphone

Druck-minderanlage *f* pressure reducing set **-minderer** *m* pressure-reducing valve, pressure reducer **-minderung** *f* pressure decrease or drop, pressure loss **-minderungsventil** *n* reducing valve **-minderventil** *n* pressure-relief valve, pressure-reducing-valve regulator

Druck-minimum *n* minimum pressure **-mitte** *f* pressure center **-mittel** *n* pressure medium **-mittelpunkt** *m* center of pressure **-model** (Handdruck) printing block **-muster** *n* printing design, printing specimen **-muttern** *pl* thrust nuts

Druck-nachlaß *m* pressure drop **-nase** *f* trigger cam **-nippel** *m* pressing nipple **-nippelrändel** *n* pressure nipple knurl **-öffnung** *f* pressure orifice or head

Drucköl *n* pressure oil **Rohr für ~** pipe for oil under pressure

Drucköl-abfluß *m* oil-pressure discharge **-anlage** *f* telemotor **-behälter** *m* hydraulic oil reservoir **-bremse** *f* hydraulic brake

Drucköler *m* force feed oiler

Drucköl-flasche *f* air-loaded accumulator **-gesteuert** hydrocontrolled, hydrocontrollable **-gesteuerte Verstelluftschraube** hydrocontrollable propeller **-lager** *n* forced-lubrication bearing **-pumpe** *f* pressure oil (telemotor) **-schmierung** *f* pressure lubrication

Druckölung *f* forced- or pressure-feed lubrication

Drucköl-ventil *n* oil-pressure valve **-winde** *f* oil-pressure winch **-zufluß** *m* oil-pressure supply **-zuleitung** *f* oil-pressure lead

Druck-organ (Fernschreiber) printing device, type bar **-oxydation** *f* oxidation under high pressure **-pegelmesser** *m* volume unit meter **-pfahl** *m* pressure, bearing, or strut pile **-plättchen** *n* stellite **-platte** *f* pressure plate, printing or engraving plate, fastening plate **-platte** *f* spacer **-polieren** *n* pressure polishing

Druck-porenzifferdiagramm *n* pressure-void ratio curve **-probe** *f* compression or crushing-test specimen, compression or crushing test **-probekörper** *m* compression-test specimen

Druckpropellerflugzeug *n* pusher aeroplane

Druck-prüfer für Luftreifen tire gauge **-prüfgerät** *n* pressure gauge **-prüfung** *f* pressure test **-prüfungsmaschine** *f* compression-testing machine **-pumpe** *f* forcing, pressure, or condensing pump

Druckpunkt *m* pressure point or center, aerodynamic center (aviation) center of pressure ~ **nehmen** (slang) to shirk one's duty
Druckpunkt-abstand *m* ratio of distance of pressure center from mouth of venturi to caliber **-lage** *f* center of pressure **-verlegung** *f* center-of-pressure movement **-wanderung** *f* shift of aerodynamic center (aviation)
Druck-rad mit offener Mitte open-center press wheel **-räder** *n pl* wheel weights **-rahmen** *m* film trap (projection work), clamping frame **-rand** *m* pressure rim **-raster** *m* printer's screen **-raum** *m* surge chamber **-räume** *pl* pressure space **-reduktionsapparat** *m* pressure reducer **-regelung** *f* pressure control **-registrierung** *f* pressure recording
Druck-regler *m* pressure-regulating valve, pressure regulator or reducer, (tire) gauges **-reglung** *f* **-regulierung** *f* regulation of pressure **-regulierapparat** *m* pressure regulator **-regulierung** *f* pressure control **-regulierventil** *n* pressure-regulating valve **-reguliervorrichtung** *f* pressure regulating device **-reif** ready for press **-relais** *n* printing relay **-relaxation** *f* pressure relaxation **-ring** *m* thrust collar, thrust ring
Druckrohr *n* pressure pipe or tube, penstock, discharge or delivery pipe **-anschluß** *m* inlet union, delivery pipe connection **-bahn** *f* pressure-pipe line **-leitung** *f* discharge pipe
Druckrohr-stutzen *m* inlet union, pressure pipe connection or socket **-temperatur** *f* discharge temperature **-winkelanschluß** *m* pressure pipe elbow
Druckrolle *f* platen, impression roller, gang press wheel (agr.), presser or pad roll (film feed) ~ **mit offener Mitte** open-center press wheel **massive** ~ solid press wheel
Druckrollen für Geleiserückmaschinen pressure rolls for rail-straightening machines
Druckrollenvorrichtung *f* press-wheel attachment
Druck-rückgang *m* depression **-rückgewinn** *m* pressure recovery **-sache** *f* printed matter **-sammler** *m* pressure accumulator **-sandstrahlgebläse** *n* pressure-type sandblast machine **-säule** pressure column or head, holding-down beam, delivery head **-schalter** *m* pressure switch, push button **-schaltung** *f* automatic feed (of machine tool) **-schaltungsmagnet** *m* printing circuit magnet **-schank** *m* siphon for carbonated water
Druck-scheibe *f* thrust washer **-schieber** *m* pressure valve **-schiene** *f* pressure shoe (film projection), sliding rail **-schlauch** *m* delivery hose, pressure hose or tubing **-schmierapparat** *m* lubricator **-schmierbüchse** *f* compression grease gun **-schmierkopf** *m* pressure lubricator, pressure grease fitting **-schmierpresse** *f* grease gun **-schmierung** *f* forced(-feed) lubrication, shot-lubrication system
Druckschnecke *f* pressure worm
Druckschraube *f* thumbscrew, pressing screw, thrust bolt, attachment screw, pusher-type propeller, set-screw, airscrew ~ **mit am Ende angedrehtem Druckzapfen** dog-point (set) screw ~ **mit Kegelzapfen** hanger-point setscrew ~ **mit Kugelkuppe** ball-point setscrew ~ **mit Linsenkuppe** round-point setscrew ~ **mit Spitze** cone-point setscrew ~ **mit Zapfen** pivot-point setscrew
Druckschrauber *m* pusher airplane
Druckschreiber *m* manograph ~ **von geringer Trägheit der beweglichen Teile** low-inertia manograph
Druckschrift *f* printed characters, print, printed work **amtliche Druckschriftenvertriebsstelle des Englischen Schatzamtes** H. M. Stationery Office
Druck-schulter *f* pressure shoulder **-schutzspirale** *f* compressive protection spiral **-schwankung** *f* fluctuation of pressure **-schwellbereich** *m* range for pulsating (fluctuating) compressive stresses **-schwimmer** *m* pressure float **-schwingungen** *f pl* compressional vibrations **-seidenpapier** *n* tissue-paper
Druckseite *f* printed page, bottom camber (of wing), pressure side or surface, delivery side ~ **beim Kolben** thrust side (piston) ~ **des Luftschraubenflügels** propeller-blade face, propeller thrust or driving face ~ **der Pumpe** delivery side of a pump ~ **des Schraubenflügels** propeller-blade face
Druck-sonde *f* static tube, pressure head **-sondung** *f* sounding **-spaltung** *f* compressive cleaving **-spannung** *f* push collet chocking, compressive or crushing stress, or compressive resilience strain, crushing strain **-spannungsgröße** *f* intensity of compressive stress
Druck-speicher *m* pressure reservoir **-speisung** *f* pressure feed **-spindel** *f* housing screw or pin **-sprung** *m* pressure drop or jump **-stab** *m* stay crutch, spur (of a pole), compression member, strut **-stange** *f* plunger, pressing rod, spindle, connecting rod **-stapler** *m* pile delivery **-stärkeregulierung** *f* impressional force regulation **-starrluftschiff** *n* pressure rigid airship
druckstauende Wirkung (Druckstauwirkung) **der Einströmleitung** booster action of intake manifold
Druckstauung *f* sound pressure increase
Druck-steg *m* pressure or harmonic bar (piano) **-steigerer** (Zündkerzenprüfgerät) compression booster **-steigerung** *f* increase of pressure **-steigung** *f* pressure gradient **-steigerungspumpe** *f* booster pump **-stellbolzen** *m* pressure-regulating bolt **-stellbügel** *m* pressure adjusting handle **-stelle** *f* pressure mark, compression mark, pressure point
Druck-stellvorrichtung *f* pressure adjusting device **-stellwelle** *f* eccentric shaft for impression **-stelze** *f* press rod **-stempel** *m* pressure stamp, piston ram, (testing machine) pressure foot **-steuerung** *f* pressure control **-steuerventil** *n* pressure-control valve **-stift** *m* pressure pin
Druckstock *m* printing block, cliché, stereotype ~ **für Strichätzung** line block
Druckstock-prüfapparat *m* plate testing device
Druck-stöpsel *m* plunger, key **-störung** *f* pressure perturbation
Druckstoß *m* shock pressure, pressure surge, water hammer ~ **des Bogens** thrust or pressure of arch
Druck-stößel *m* push rod, tappet **-strahl** *m* jet of water **-strahlpumpe** *f* injector **-strebe** *f* prop, diagonal strut
Druckstreckgrenze *f* compressive yield strength

Druckstück *n* thrust piece, printed matter, sear-release lever, contact piece or trigger, internal vane (rocket), pressure plate **-halterung** *f* jet-vane support

Druckstufe *f* draft or pressure stage **hohe ~** (Lader) high-level blower, high pressure stage

Druck-stutzen *m* pressure connection, pressure-inlet nipple **-system** *n* pressure system **-tank** *m* pressure tank **-taste** *f* key, push-button **-tastenabstimmung** push-button tuning **-tastenaggregat** *n* press button plug (tape rec.) **-taster** *m* sending key **-telegraph** *m* printing telegraph, type printer, teleprinter

Druck-tiegel *m* platen **-tinktur** *f* ink reducer **-tinte** *f* printing ink **-tisch** *m* printing table **-träger** *m* printing carrier **-trajektorie** *f* compression trajectory **-tuch** *n* blanket (print.)

Druck-überschreitung *f* exceeding of pressure **-überschuß** *m* blow off pressure **-übersetzungsverhältnis** *n* pressure-transmittance ratio **-übertragungsfaktor** pressure response

Druck-umlauf *m* force circulation **-umlaufschmierung** *f* pressure lubrication, forced-feed lubrication, circulating forced lubrication

Druck- und Gefrierpunktsmesser *m* manocryometer

Druck- und Saugleitung *f* pressure and suction system

Druck- und Setzmaschine *f* printer and typesetter

Druck- und Stanzautomaten *m pl* automatic printing and punching machines

Drückung der Gewindekernausrundung compression of the root

Druck-unterschied *m* pressure gradient, differential pressure **-unterschiedsmesser** *m* pressure-difference gauge

Druckventil *n* pressure, discharge, delivery, outlet, or exhaust valve **fahrendes ~** traveling valve **rückläufiges ~** return-pressure valve

Druckventil-einsatz *m* (motor) cage of delivery valve **-feder** *f* pressure-valve or delivery-valve spring **-federraum** *m* spring chamber of delivery valve **-kegel** *m* cone of delivery valve

Druck-veränderung *f* change in pressure **-verbreiterung** *f* pressure broadening (gas spectrum) **-verfahren** *n* printing process **-verformung** *f* compression strain **-vergaser** *m* pressure-type carburetor **-vergleich** *m* dublication check (comput.) **-verhältnis** *n* compression ratio, pressure ratio **-verkokung** *f* coking under pressure

Druck-verlauf *m* pressure or stress distribution **-verlust** *m* pressure loss or drop **-vermehrung** *f* **für die Luftstromgeschwindigkeit** ramming **-verminderung** *f* pressure drop or loss, decrease of pressure, depression, flash **-verminderungsventil** *n* pressure-reducing or pressure-release valve, pressure regulator **-verschiebung** *f* pressure shift (spectral lines)

Druckverschiebungs-Phasendifferenz *f* pressure-displacement phase shift

Druckverschraubung *f* pressure screw joint

Druckversuch *m* compression and tension test, pressure test, crushing test **~ mit behinderter Seitenausdehnung** consolidation test, confined-compression test **~ mit unbehinderter Seitenausdehnung** unconfined-compression test

Druck-verteilung *f* pressure or stress distribution **-verteilungsmesser** *m* pressure-distribution meter **-verteilungsvermögen** *n* stress dispersion capacity **-viskosität** *f* pressure viscosity

Druck-vorgang *m* act or process of printing **-vorlage** *f* manuscript **-vorrichtung** *f* compression arrangement or apparatus, printing device, bulging device **-waage** *f* piston manometer **-walke** *f* crank fulling mill **-walze** *f* pressure roller, dandy roll (paper) printing roller or cylinder **-wäsche** *f* pressure wash

Druck-walze (Fernschreiber) platen **-walzengraveur** *m* roll-engraver **-ware** *f* printed styles

Druckwasser *n* pressure or power water, hydraulic supply, high-pressure pipes **mit ~ spülen** (einspritzen), to jet

Druckwasser-akkumulator *m* hydraulic accumulator **-behälter** *m* compressed-water reservoir

Druckwasserantrieb *m* hydraulic pressure **Torbewegung mit ~** hydraulic operation of gates

Druckwasser-betrieb *m* hydraulic-flask-lifting molding machine **-entaschung** wet-type clinker remover **-hahn** *m* compression-gauge cock **-hebezeug** *m* hydraulic hoist **-kessel** *m* pressure-water tank **-kolben** *m* hydraulic piston **-kran** *m* hydraulic crane **-leitung** *f* hydraulic main or pipes

Druckwasser-nietung *f* hydraulic riveting **-pumpe** *f* hydraulic pump **-reaktor** *m* pressurized water reactor (PWR) (atom. phys.) **-schutz** *m* water-tight protection **-sparventil** *n* economical-pressure-water valve **-speicher** *m* hydraulic accumulator **-winde** *f* hydraulic jack **-zylinder** *m* hydraulic-gate jack

Druck-wechsel *m* change in pressure (+ to —) **-welle** *f* pressure wave, compressional wave **-wellenkopf** *m* cusp of pressure wave

Druckwerk *n* printing mechanism, pressure engine or pump, coining press, mint **-anordnung** *f* arrangement of printing units **-einkapselung** *f* enclosed printing unit **-schild** *n* press frame

Druck-widerstand *m* pressure drag, compressive strength **-windkessel** *m* blast-pressure tank **-wirkung** *f* pressure effect

Drückzange *f* forming pliers

Druck-zapfen *m* thrust journal **-zeile** *f* line of print **-zeit** *f* impression time (print) **-zentrum** *n* center of thrust **-zerstäuber** *m* mechanical atomizer burner, pressure spray gun **-zone** *f* zone of pressure

Druckzug-mikrophon *n* double-button transmitter, push-pull transmitter **-ventilation** *f* forced ventilation **-verstärker** *m* push-pull amplifier

Druck-zünder *m* pressure firing device, pressure or push igniter **-zuschaltung** *f* push-pull circuit (elec.) **-zwiebel** *f* pressure bulb **-zwillingsbildung** *f* compressive twin formation

Druckzylinder pressure cylinder, master cylinder (brake), hydraulic cylinder **-bearbeitung** *f* machining of printing rolls **-bekleidung** *f* impression cylinder dressing **-bezug** *m* impression cylinder covering **-gehäuse** *n* pressure cylinder casing **-greifer** *m* impression cylinder gripper **-köpfe** *pl* pressure cylinder heads

Drumme *f* wooden culvert

drunter und drüber topsy-turvy, upside-down

Druschgewicht *n* thrashed weight
Druse *f* drusy cavity, vug, nodule, druse **große** ~ vug **linsenförmige** ~ lenticular vug
Drusen enthaltend vuggy
Drusenraum *m* cavity, drusy cavity
drusig drusy
Dschungel *m* jungle
Dschunke *f* junk
D-Spannung *f* D voltage
dual, -es Netzwerk reciprocal network **-er Tensor** dual of a tensor
Dual-gitter *n* dual lattice **-glied** *n* structurally dual network
dualinvariante Konfiguration dually invariant configuration
Dualität *f* duality
Dualitätsprinzip *n* (ebenes) duality principle (in the plane) ~ (räumliches) duality principle (in space)
Dual-komponente *f* dual component **-untersetzer** *m* flip-flop circuit **-voruntersetzer** *m* dual prereducer **-zahl** *f* binary number **-zerfall** *m* multiple decay
Duanten *pl* duants (cyclotron), dees **-elektrometer** duant electrometer
dubbeln, dubben to duplicate
Dübel *m* peg, (wall) plug, treenail, socket, dowel, dowel pin, tap bolt, stud, tenon
dübeln to dowel
Dübelschweißung *f* slot welding
Dublett-abstand *m* doublet spacing, doublet difference **-aufspaltung** *f* doublet splitting
Dublette *f* doublet
Dublettenaufspaltung *f* doublet separation (spectrum)
dublieren to double, line
Dublieren *n* mackling (print.), double impression
dublierend walzen to roll double
Dublierer *m* doubler (textiles)
Dubliermaschine *f* doubling machine (frame)
Dubliermeß- und Wickelmaschine *f* rigging, measuring, and rolling machine
Dublierverfahren *n* doubling process
Ducht *f* crossbeam, thwart, strand (of cable) **-rohr** *n* winch tube for anchor rope
Duckdalben *f pl* dolphins, mooring posts, bollards
ducken, sich ~ to duck
Dücker *m* sluice pipe (road), inverted siphon, culvert siphon
Duckstein *m* trass
duff dead, dull
Duffmaschine *f* continuous finishing machine
Dufrenit *m* green iron ore, dufrenite
Duft *m* scent, fragrance, odor **-anhang** *m* silver thaw, white frost, rime **-auszug** *m* scent extract
duften to be vaporous or misty
Düker *m* siphon
duktil ductile
Duktilität *f* ductility (test)
Duktilometer *n* ductilimeter
Duktor *m* ductor roller **-handrad** *n* hand-wheel **-lineal** *n* duct blade **-schaltung** *f* duct switch **-walze** *f* fountain roller complete
Düllbeitel *m* socket chisel
Dülle *f* socket
Dulling *n* dulling (suppression of audio frequency by dubbing or scoring, motion pictures)
Düll-lochbeitel *m* mortise chisel with socket **-stechbeitel** *m* firmer chisel with socket
Dulzin *n* dulcin
Dumontit *m* dumontite
dumpf (speech) drummy, heavy, dull ~ **klingen** to sound heavy (drummy), booming
Dumpfheit *f* heaviness, drumminess, dullness
dumpfig musty
Düne *f* (sand) dune, sand hill
Dünen-aufforstung *f* protection of dunes by tree planting **-bau** *m* dune protection **-bepflanzung** *f* protection of dunes by planting **-böschung** *f* slope of the dune **-kamm** *m* crest of the dune **-schutzwerk** *n* fortification or defense of dunes **-steilküste** *f* steep coast covered with dunes
Dung *m* manure, dung
Düngekalk *m* lime powder, manuring lime
Düngemittel *n* manure, fertilizer **-fertigungsanlage** *f* fertilizer-producing plant, manure-manufacturing plant
düngen to manure, fertilize, dress
Dünger *m* fertilizer, manure **-bedürfnis** *n* manurial requirement **-mischmühle** *f* fertilizer mixer
Düngerstreu-apparat *m* **-einrichtung** *f* fertilizer-dispersing attachment or device
Düngerstreuer *m* fertilizer sower or spreader, manure spreader ~ **und Getreidedrillmaschine** fertilizer-dispersing and grain drill machine
Düngerstreumaschine *f* manure distributor or drill
Düngerzufuhrapparat *m* **automatischer** ~ apron of fertilizer spreader
Düngpulver *n* sewage powder, poudrette
Dunkel *n* darkness, gloom, dusk **Modulierung auf** ~ modulation to dark condition
dunkel dark, obscure **-adaptation** *f* **-anpassung** *f* dark adaptation, scotopia **-entladung** *f* dark discharge **-farbig** dark-colored
Dunkelfeld *n* dark ground or field **-abbildung** *f* dark-field illumination **-bänder** *pl* dark band zone **-beleuchtung** *f* dark-field illumination **-beleuchtungseinrichtung** *f* dark-ground illumination attachment **-beobachtung** *f* dark-field observation **-birne** *f* concentrated-filament (lamp) bulb **-blende** *f* dark-ground stop **-einrichtung** *f* dark-field equipment **-verfahren** *n* dark contrast method
dunkelgetönte Farbe shade
Dunkelheit *f* darkness, obscurity
Dunkel-kammer *f* darkroom, camera obscura **-methode** *f* observation in darkness
dunkeln to darken, get dark
Dunkel-öl *n* black oil **-pause** *f* dark period, cutoff or obscuring period (motion pictures) **-pegel** *m* black level
Dunkelpunkt *m* center of target pip, dark spot, blackout marker (radar) **-stufe** *f* dimming switch, dimmer
Dunkelraum *m* dark space **Crookesscher** ~ Crookes space
dunkelrot dull or dim red, dark red (hot metal) **-glühend** dull red hot **-glut** *f* dim or dull red heat
Dunkelschalter *m* dimmer switch, dimmer

Dunkelschrift-röhre *f* dark trace tube (skiatron) **-röhrenbild** *n* skiatron display **-schirm** *m* dark-trace screen

Dunkel-stellungen *pl* dark positions (geol.) **-strahlung** *f* obscure radiation, heat radiation, invisible (actinic) radiation beyond the violet **-strom** *m* dark current (photoelectric cell) **-stromsignal** *n* dark-spot signal **-stufe** *f* (Farbe) depth of shade **-suche** *f* dark search of searchlights

Dunkel-suchgerät *n* night binoculars, dark searching instrument **-suchmann** *m* dark searcher **-tran** *m* dark brown cod oil

Dunkelungsbad *n* saddening liquor

Dunkel-wasserzeichen *n* intaglio **-wertsteuerung** *f* adjustment to value of darkness **-widerstand** *m* dark resistance **-zeit** *f* dark interval or period **-zelle** *f* dark cell

dunkle Entladung silent discharge

dünn thin, dilute, slender, fine, rare (air), tenuous, feeble **~ getauchte Elektrode** washed electrode **-es Blech** light-gauge sheet, thin sheet **-er Draht** cylindrical wire **-er Flügel** thin section wing **-e Folien** thin films **-er Mörtel** grout, slurry **-es Profil** thin profile **-er werden** (allmählich) to taper away

Dünn-blechschweißung *f* light-gauge sheet-steel welding **-brett** *n* half plank, half-inch plank, shelf **-drähtig** small-gauge wire, fine-stranded **-druckpapier** *n* thin printing paper

Dünnfilm-dickenmessung *f* thin film thickness measurement **-matrix** *f* film arrays **-speicher** *m* thin-film memory **-stapelschichtspeicher** *m* stacked-planes thin-film memory **-transistor** *m* thin-film transistor **-vorschrift** *f* thin-film specification

dünnflüssig watery, dilute, highly fluid, thin **-es Öl** light or lightweight oil **-e Schlacke** fluid or thin slag, honeycomb or flue-sheet clinker

Dünn-flüssigkeit *f* fluidity, low viscosity

dünn-geschichteter Ton varved clay **-getaucht** washed **-hobeln** to lessen by planing

Dunnit *n* explosive D

Dünnpergamin *n* glassine

Dünnquetsche *f* second mold of vellum

Dünnsaft *m* thin or clarified juice **-aufkocher** *m* thin juice blow-up tank **-endschwefelung** *f* **-schlußschwefelung** *f* final sulfitation of thin juice

dünn-schalig thin-skinned **-schliff** *m* microsection, thin section (of rock or metal for microscopic examination), transparent cut **-schnitt** *m* veneer, thin-section **-schuppig** in thin scales

dünnste Kugellagerung most rarefied packing of spheres

Dünnteer *m* fluid tar

Dünntrübe *f* dilute medium

Dünntuchband *n* gauze ribbon

Dünnung *f* throat (carp.)

dünnwandig thin-walled **-er Guß** thin-section or thin-walled castings

Dünnwandigkeit *f* thinness of walls

Dunst *m* vapor, steam, fume, damp, mist, haze **-absauganlage** *f* vapor-exhaust system **-abzug** *m* vapor escape, hood (for fumes) **-abzugsrohr** *m* vent pipe **-bildung** *f* haze formation (explosives), vapor formation, mist

dunsten to evaporate, steam

Dunst-grenze *f* limit of mist or haze **-haube** *f* vaporhood **-hülle** *f* vaporous envelope, atmosphere

dunstig hazy, misty

Dunst-kamin *m* ventilating chimney **-kreis** *m* atmosphere **-loch** *n* air hole or vent **-los** fumeless **Dunst-messer** *m* atmidometer, evaporimeter, atmometer **-mittel** (Lederindustrie) mulling agent **-nebel** *m* mist due to water vapor, fog or vapor mist

Dunstrohr *n* ventilating pipe **~ der Scheidepfanne** stack of the carbonator

Dunst-schlot *m* ventilator tube or chimney **-schwitze** *f* steam sweat (steaming) **-streuung** *f* haze scattering **-teilchen** *n* moisture particle **-trommel** *f* smoke drum **-wirkung** *f* mulling effect **-wolke** *f* cloud of haze, vapor mist

Dünung *f* ground swell, surf

Duo *n* two-high rolling mill **-anordnung** *f* two-high mill arrangement **-blechstraße** *f* two-high plate- (or sheet-)rolling train **-blechwalzwerk** *n* two-high plate mill **-blockstraße** *f* two-high blooming-mill train, two-high cogging-mill train **-blockwalzwerk** *n* two-high blooming mill, two-high coogging mill

duodezimale Schreibweise duodecimal notation

Duodiode *f* duo-diode, double diode **~ mit gemeinsamer Kathode** twin diode

Duo-feinblechstraße *f* two-high sheet-mill train **-feinblechwalzwerk** *n* two-high sheet-rolling mill **-fertiggerüst** *n* two-high finishing stand **-fertigstraße** *f* two-high finishing-mill train **-fertigstrecke** *f* two-high finishing stands in train **-filter** (Zweifach-Kraftstoff-Filter) duo filter (series connect twin-type fuel filter) **-gerüst** *n* two-high stand (metal.) **-kontrolle** *f* twin check **-maßwalzwerk** *n* two-high sizing mill **-mittelstraße** *f* two-high intermediate roll train

Duoreversier-blechstraße *f* two-high recersing plate-rolling train **-blechwalzwerk** *n* two-high reversing plate mill **-blockstraße** *f* two-high reversing blooming train **-blockwalzwerk** *n* two-high reversing blooming mill **-gerüst** *n* two-high reversing stand **-straße** *f* two-high reversing-mill train **-streckgerüst** *n* two-high reversing stand of rolls for roughing **-walzwerk** *n* two-high reversing mill

Duo-schaltung *f* two-lamp circuit, lead-lag circuit, duo circuit **-stopfenwalzwerk** *n* two-high piercing mill **-straße** *f* two-high rolling-mill train **-streckwalze** *f* two high rougher

duotrizinäre Schreibweise duotricenary notation

Duo-universalstraße *f* two-high universal mill train **-universalwalzwerk** *n* two-high universal mill **-vorstrecke** *f* two-high roughing stands in trains **-walzgerüst** *n* two-high rolling-mill stand **-walzstraße** *f* two-high rolling train **-walzstrecke** *f* two-high mill train

Duowalzwerk *n* two-high rolling mill, two-high mill **~ mit Anordnung zum Überheben des Walzgutes** pull-over mill **~ mit gleichbleibender Drehrichtung der Walzen** two-high nonreversing mill

Dupemulsion *f* duplicating emulsion

Dupinsche Zykliden Dupin's cyclids
Dupinscher Satz über dreifach orthogonale Flächensysteme Dupin's theorem on triply orthogonal systems of surfaces
Dupkontrolle *f* twin-check (comp.)
Duplex-abgleich *m* **-abgleichung** *f* duplex balance **-autotypie** *f* duplex halftone
duplex betreiben to duplex
Duplexbetrieb *m* duplex operation or working **einseitiger ~** half-duplex operation
Duplex-dampfpumpe *f* duplex steam-force pump **-entstäubungseinrichtung** *f* duplex dusting equipment **-karton und -pappe** duplex board **-kolbenringe** *pl* duplex piston rings **-leitung** *f* duplex circuit **-nachbildung** *f* duplex artifical circuit **-papier** *n* duplex paper
Duplex-pumpe *f* duplex pump **-rasteraufnahme** *f* duplex halftone photography **-rechenwerk** duplex register **-schneidkuppe** *f* double pipe stock **-verbindung** *f* duplex (communication) **-verfahren** *n* duplex process, combined Bessemer and Martin processes, duplex system
Duplexverkehr *m* duplex operation or working **drahtloser ~** radio duplex service **Leitung für ~** duplex circuit
duplieren to double, mackle (print.)
Duplierwickelmaschine *f* double winder (textiles)
Duplikat *n* duplicate **-kontrolle** *f* duplication check **-negativ** *n* picture dupe negative **-prüfung** *f* twin check **-vergleich** *m* duplication check
duplizieren to duplicate, duplex
Duplizierung *f* duplication
Dupnegativ *n* duplicating negative
Düppel *n* (U. S.) chaff sticks (Engl.) tinsel, window (metallic strips used to interfere with radar) **-straße** *f* window cloud, chaff cloud
Düppelung *f* chaff dropping
Duppositivfilm *m* duplicating positive stock, master positive
Dur *n* (Tonart) major (musical pitch or mode)
Dural *n* duralumin **-beplankung** *f* duralumin covering
Duralblech *n* sheet duralumin **plattiertes ~** alclad
Dural-holm *m* duralumin spar **-niete** *f* duarlumin rivet **-rohr** *n* duralumin tube
Duralumin *n* duralumin **~ mit Außenschicht aus Reinaluminium** alclad
Duraluminium *n* duralumin
Duralumin-profil *n* duralumin section **-rippe** *f* duralumin rib **-rumpf** *m* duralumin fuselage
Duralwellblech *n* corrugated sheet duralumin
durch through, by, across, during, owing to, by means of **~ und ~** thoroughly
durcharbeiten to complete, work through **sich ~** to force one's way through
durchaus quite, thoroughly, absolutely, at all **~ zuverlässig** thoroughly reliable
Durch-balken *m* winter (print.) **-belichten** to fully expose or irradiate **-biegen** to bend, deflect, sag
Durchbiegen *n* deflection **vorheriges ~ einer Feder** predeflecting of a spring **~ der Tragfedern** bending of the bearing springs
Durchbiege-versuch *m* deflection test **-platte** *f* sagging plate
Durchbiegung *f* bowing under load, sag, bending, deflection, flexure, thorough bend, break, coflexure, dip (of line wire) **bleibende ~** permanent set **elastische ~** transverse elasticity **~ einer Linse** bending, depth of curvature, coflexure
Durchbiegungs-diagramm *n* load-deflection diagram **-fähig** deflectable, flexible **-festigkeit** *f* cross-breaking or transverse-bending strength **-geschwindigkeit** *f* rate of deflection **-grad** *m* degree of bending **-linie** *f* line of deflection **-messer** *m* deflection indicator, deflectometer **-spannung** *f* transverse stress, strain, or resilience **-widerstand** *m* resistance to bending **-winkel** *m* angle of bending (of test piece)
durchbilden to design, develop, improve
Durchbildung *f* arrangement, designing **konstruktive ~** design
Durchblasdüse *f* blower nozzle
Durch-blasehahn *m* purging cock **-blasen** to blow through, blow by (said of piston rings)
Durchblasen *n* sparging, blow by **~ des Kolbens** gas blow, piston blow, piston-ring blow by
Durchblick-öffnung *f* observation (inspection) aperture, sighting aperture **-vorrichtung** *f* dioptric device
durch-bohren to perforate, bore, pierce, drill, punch, penetrate **-bohrt** perforated, punctured, punched, bored **-bohrung** *f* perforation **-brechen** to break (through), pierce **-brechmeißel** *m* plugging chisel
Durchbrechung *f* perforation, open work
Durchbrennen *n* fusing, blowing, melting, striking, burning out or through
durchbrennen (Sicherung) to fuse, blow, melt, strike, (Spulen) burn out or through
durchbrochen punctured, pierced, perforated, open-worked, broken, interrupted **~ gearbeitet** through carved (textiles) **-es Gewebe** openwork fabric **-e Kettenware** lace warp fabric (textiles) **-er Pumpenkolben** hollow piston **-er Riester** slot mold attachment **-es Wehr** carved weir
Durchbruch *m* rupture (of insulation), breakdown, break off, puncture, break-through, opening, crevasse, eruption, escape, penetration, any change for the better, disruptive discharge (electr.) **~** (bei Geiger-Müller-Zähler) discharge
Durchbruch(s)-entladung *f* disruptive discharge, spark discharge **-erfolg** *m* tactical success of break-through **-feldstärke** *f* dielectric strength **-spannung** *f* breakdown voltage **-stelle** *f* point of break-through **-stoß** *m* burst pulse (radar) **-verhalten** *n* breakdown (transistor)
durchdacht planned
durchdiffundiert diffused
Durchdrehanlasser *m* cranking starter
Durchdrehen der Räder wheel spin
durchdrehen to hunt over a complete level, overflow, swing the propeller, make a complete or full revolution **~** (Luftschraube), to pull through (propeller) **den Motor ~** to turn over or crank an engine
Durchdrehen *n* full rotation (of a selector) **Motor durch ~ losbrechen** to free an engine
Durchdrehlauf *m* (Fremdantrieb), belting-in run
Durchdrehung eines Wählers full rotation of a selector
Durchdrehungsvorrichtung *f* hand starter, turning gear **~ für eingelagerte Motoren** turning-over device for stored engines **von Hand be-**

tätigte ~ hand-turning or manually operated gear

durch-dringbar permeable, penetrable **-dringbarkeit** *f* permeability, porosity **-dringen** to penetrate, permeate, force one's way through, pierce, pervade **-dringen** *n* penetration, safe delivery (of a message)

durch-dringend perspicacious, sharp, penetrant, penetrating **-er Schauer** penetrating shower

Durch-dringfähigkeit *f* penetrability **-dringlich** permeable, pervious **-dringlichkeit** *f* permeability **-dringung** *f* osmosis, diffusion, penetration, permeation

Durchdringungs-frequenz *f* penetration or critical frequency **-linien** *f pl* lines of self-intersection **-potential** *n* penetration potential **-vermögen** *n* penetrability, penetrative ability, permeability

Durchdringungszwillinge *m pl* penetrating twins

Durchdringwahrscheinlichkeit *f* penetration probability, transmission coefficient

Durch-druck *m* penetration of prints **-drungen** traversed (by light) **-drücken** to push, press or force through

Durcheinander *n* confusion, mixup, bedlam **-fallen** to tumble (over) **-fliegen** to move about (at will) **-wirbeln des Wassers** churning of water (as by a baffled pump)

durcheilen to pass through or over

durchfahren to traverse, pass or run through

Durchfahrt *f* thoroughfare, passage, diffusion **-breite unter einer Brücke** width of navigable passage under a bridge, horizontal clearance **-höhe** *f* vertical clearance

Durch-fall *m* portion passing through screen, screenings, siftings **-fallasche** *f* riddlings **-fallen** to fall or pass through, clear, be transmitted (current), pancake (aviation) **-fallendes Licht** permeating or transmitted light **-fallkohle** *f* riddlings **-federn** to spring, act as a spring **-federung** *f* resilience, elasticity, deflection, sagging

Durch-färbevermögen *n* property of dying through **-faulen** to putrefy (rot through) **-feuchten** to soak, wet, moisten thoroughly **-feuchtung** *f* amount of water held in rock **-filtern** to filtrate, filter **-flechten** to interlace, interweave **-fliegen** to traverse **-fließen** to flow through, pass, traverse (by flowing) **-fließung** *f* diffusion **-flochten** interwoven

Durchfluß *m* flowing through, passage **bettbildender ~** bed-forming discharge **den ~ bis zum Tropfen reduzieren** to reduce the flow to a trickle

Durchfluß-anzeiger *m* sight discharge indicator, flow indicator **-betrieb** *m* flow-through principle **-bolzen** *m* hollow bolt **-elektrode** *f* flow-type electrode

Durchflüsse *m pl* discharges **Frequenz der ~** discharge frequency **Linie der registrierten ~** rating curve of discharges

Durchfluß-erhitzer *m* flow heater **-filtration** *f* continuous filtration **-freier Querschnitt** unrestricted passage area (aviation)

Durchflußgeschwindigkeit *f* **mittlere ~** mean velocity of flow, rate of flow or of circulation

Durchfluß-kante *f* edge (trailing or rear edge) **-koeffizient** *m* discharge coefficient **-kolorimeter** *m* flow colorimeter **-kühlung** *f* flow cooling **-küvette** *f* flow cell **-leistung** *f* rate of flow

Durchflußmenge *f* rate or quantity of flow

Durchflußmengen-meßblende *f* static plate **-meßgerät** *n* flowmeter *n* **-messer** *m* volumeter **-messung** *f* flow measurement **-regler** *m* flow-volume regulator

Durchfluß-messer *m* flowmeter, inferential meter **-mischer** *m* pipeline mixer, flowmixer **-öffnung** *f* flow passage, sluiceway (opening), discharge opening **-probenwechsler** *m* automatic sample ohanger **-profil** *n* water way (bridge) **-Pyrheliometer** water-flow pyrheliometer

Durchflußquerschnitt *m* cross section of passage **freier ~** unrestricted passage area, free opening

Durchfluß-regler *m* flow controller **-regulierung** *f* flow regulation **-richtungsanzeiger** *m* sight flow or flow-direction indicator **-rohr** *n* discharge duct, jet **-strom** *m* current (flow) **-wascher** *m* bubbling washer (gas bubbles through from below) **-wege** flow paths **-zähler** flow meter **-zählrohr** *n* flow counter **-zeit** *f* time of flow **-zentrifuge** *f* flow-through centrifuge

Durch-flutung *f* circulation (magnetic potential), flow (of radio frequency) **-flutungsgesetz** *n* Laplace's law, Biot-Savart's law **-forsten** to thin (a forest) **-fracht** *f* through loading **-fressen** to erode, cut or eat through, corrode **-fressen** *n* erosion, corrosion **-fuhr** *f* transit **-führbar** practicable, feasible **-führbarkeit** *f* practicability

durchführen to carry through, perform, pass through (wire), lead or convey through, execute, accomplish, conduct **Vermessungen ~** to conduct surveys

Durch-führkessel *m* second-washpot compartment (metal) **-fuhrkosten** *pl* transit expenses **-führung** *f* performance, execution, accomplishment, leading, (bushing) insulator, wall entrance, bushing, duct (elec.), lead-in wire

Durchführungs-bolzen *m* duct bolt (elec.) **-filter** *n* lead-through filter **-gummi** *n* lead-in transition rubber **-hülse** *f* grommet **-isolator** *m* wall entrance insulator, bushing insulator, wall-tube insulator, leading-in insulator (antenna) **-kabel** *n* leading-out cable (elec.) **-kondensator** *m* feed-through capacitor, screen mounting condenser

durchfurchen to furrow plow

Durchführungs-loch *n* lead-in hole **-rohr** *n* wall tube (elec.) **-schraube** *f* transition screw (bolt screw) **-stift** *m* leading-in pin **-stromwandler** *m* bushing-type current transformer **-verordnung** *f* implementing ordinance

Durchfuhrzoll *m* transit duty

Durchgabe *f* transmission

Durchgang *m* passage, gangway, aisle, transit (rolling), pass, travel, thoroughfare **~** (Bearbeitung), travel **~ des Kolbens** piston passage

durchgängig generally, usually, on the average **~ gebraucht** used throughout

Durchgangsamt *n* switching point, tandem, central office, transit office **zwischenstaatliches ~** international transit exchange

Durchgangs-anstalt *f* through-switching exchange **-anteil** transit quota **-bahnhof** *m* through station (R. R.) **-blatt** *n* transit ticket (teleph.)

-bohrung *f* through-hole (bolt hole) **-blockwerk** *n* section block **-buch** *n* transit book (teleph.) **-dichtung** *f* grommet (grummet) **-draht** *m* through-wire **-fernamt** *n* zone center (teleph.) **-fernleitung** *f* through toll line, through circuit **-fernschrank** *m* through switchboard **-fernspruch** *m* through telephone call, long-distance direct-wire telephone call **-frequenz** *f* penetration frequency

Durchgangsgebühr *f* transit charge **angenommene ~** hypothetical transit charge

Durchgangs-geschwindigkeit *f* rate of travel **-gespräch** *n* through-call **-gewindebohrer** *m* through hole typ **-gut** *n* transit goods **-hahn** *m* straight-way or two-way cock **-küken** *n* plug of two-way cock **-handel** *m* transit trade

Durchgangs-leitung *f* through or transit circuit through line **-loch** *n* through bore **-lochzapfen** *m* throughhole pilot guide **-luftfilter** *m* straight-through air filter **-ofen** *m* through-type oven **-öffnung** *f* opening of passage, width of passage, port, slot **-platz** *m* tandem or through position **-profil** *n* clearance diagram, clearing gauge, passage section

Durchgangs-prüfung *f* continuity check **-querschnitt** *m* cross-sectional area of passage; (Klimaanlage) free area **-richtung** *f* forward or low-resistance direction (rectifier) **-schein** *m* pass, permit (for transit)

Durchgangsschieber *m* gate or straight-way valve **~ mit Bügel** clamp gate valve

Durchgangs-schrank *m* through switchboard **-sieb** *m* limiting screen **-stelle** *f* passing place **-stellung** *f* (eines Verbindungsschalters) through position **-transformer** *m* by-pass transformer **-ventil** *n* straightway or globe valve, through-way or two-way valve

Durchgangsverbindung *f* built-up connection (in international service, one using more than one international circuit) **~ über drei zwischenstaatliche Leitungen** three-switch connection

Durchgangsverbindungs-Schnurpaar through-position cord pair

Durchgangs-verkehr *m* through or transit traffic, transit (trade) **-versuch** *m* transmission experiment **-vermittlung** *f* long-distance telephone exchange **-verwaltung** *f* long-distance telephone administration **-wahl** *f* tandem dialling, tandem selection **-wähler** *m* tandem selector **-weg** *m* transit route

Durchgangs-weite *f* passage width **-wellenmesser** transmission frequency meter **-widerstand** *m* conductance (of valve), current-flow resistance, resistance opposition to electric flow, insulation resistance, volume resistance (exclusive of surface resistance) **-zentrale** *f* transit exchange **-zoll** *m* transit duty **-zug** *m* through or nonstop train

durchgearbeitet worked **stark -er Werkstoff** heavily worked material

durch-geben to transmit (message), filter, strain **-gebogene Gläser** bent lenses **-gebrannt** burnt out or blown (fuse), fused (coil) **-gedreht** rotated **-gefärbt** colored throughout **-gehdrehzahl** *f* runaway speed **-gehen** to run away, bolt, stampede, pass or go through, race (motor)

Durchgehen *n* (Bohrgerät), dropping (punch) **~ einer Maschine** overspeeding or racing of a machine

durchgehend continuous, permanent, piercing, passing through, transmitted (light) **-er Dienst** twenty-four-hour service **-er Draht** through wire **-es Feuerrohr** internal flue **-e Leitung** through or transit line **-es Licht** transmitted light **-e Schweißung** continuous weld **-er Träger** center T cross brace **-er Unterschieber** extended cross slide **-es Verdeck** full-length top **-e Welle** continuous or traversing shaft **-er Zug** nonstop or through train

durch-gelassenes Licht transmitted light **-gelassene Welle** transmitted wave (acoust.)

durchgelocht-er Lochstreifen through perforated tape **-er Streifen** fully perforated tape

durch-geschaltet (cut) through (teleph.) **-gescheuerte Stelle** bare spot **-geschlagen** burnt-out, punctured (elec.) **-geschmiedet** forged through, finished wrought **-gesetzt** interspersed, gained ground **-gespült** flushed **-getreten** (Hebel ganz **~**) pedal fully depressed **-gießen** to pour through, filter, strain

durchglühen to soak, heat red-hot

durchgreifend radical, intensive, thorough, penetrative

Durchgriff *m* inverse amplification factor (radio), reciprocal of amplification factor, penetration (magnification) coefficient, shielding factor, passage grid controllance, grid penetration factor, grid transparency, transgrid action **~ des Schirmgitters** "throughgrip", reciprocal of screen grid amplification factor

Durchgrifflinse *f* aperture lens

Durchgriffsfaktor *m* amplification factor (through grip)

Durchgriffskapazität *f* through-capacitance

Durch-guß *m* filter, strainer, filtration, gutter **-halten** to maintain course and speed, weather (a storm) **-haltevermögen** *n* stamina **-hang** *m* sag, slack **-hängen** to sag, dip, droop **-hängen** *n* sagging **-hängenetz** *n* entire pipe system

Durchhangsregelung *f* adjustment of tension in wires

Durchhang-tabelle *f* table of sags **-verfahren** *n* toe method of recording (underexposure of film)

Durch-härten *n* (Farbe) hard drying **-härtung** *f* through, depth, or penetration hardening **-hau** *m* lane or path cut through a forest **-heftung** *f* stabbing **-hieb** *m* improvement cutting passage **-kneten** to pug, knead thoroughly, squeeze

durch-kochen to boil briskly or thoroughly **-kohlung** *f* carbonization **-konstruieren** (neu) to re-design **-konstruierte Maschine** well-constructed machine **-kopieren** to copy or print through **-krählen** to rabble

durchkreuzen to cross, traverse, intersect **Pläne ~** to frustrate (plans)

Durchkreuzungszwillinge *pl* cruciform twins (cryst.)

durch-kriechen to creep (through) **-krümmen** to press the trigger, squeeze **-laden** to load, charge (magazines) **-laschen** to lash

Durchlaß *m* filter, sieve, passage, discharge opening, outlet, transmission, culvert, port, sluice pipe (road), opening section (swing bridge) **-band** *n* pass band **-bereich** (bei Richtleiter) forward region **-bereich** *n* band width, transmission range, band-pass width of a filter (radio) **-breite** *f* width of band pass

durchlassen to filter, let through, pass, transmit, strain

durchlassend (Licht) previous to light

Durchlaß-frequenz *f* pass wave **-gebiet** *n* transmission band **(Rein-) -grad** *m* transmittance

durchlässig permeable, pervious, penetrable, leaky (insulator) (Licht ~) translucent (Luft ~) (Wasser ~) porous **-er Baugrund** *m* pervious subsoil **-er Kreis** acceptor circuit

Durchlässigkeit *f* perviousness (sand), permeability, penetrability, venting quality or property, porosity, transparency, transmission factor, transmitting power or property; (d. Atmosphäre) transmissivity (of the atmosphere) **~ für ultrarote Strahlen** diathermancy **elektrische ~** dielectric constant **magnetische ~** permeability, magnetic inductivity

Durchlässigkeits-apparat *m* permeameter **-beiwert** *m* coefficient of permeability

Durchlässigkeitsbereich *m* range of free transmission, transmission range **~ eines Filters** pass band or range, free-transmission range, filter range, transmission band

Durchlässigkeits-faktor *m* transmission coefficient **-gebiet** (Licht) transmission range **-grad** *f* efficiency of transmission (of a shutter) degree of permeability **-grade** grades of porosity, filtering grades **-koeffizient** *m* coefficient of permeability **-kurve** *f* transmission curve **-messer** *m* permeameter **-modell** *n* permeability model **-nummer** filtering number **-versuch** *m* permeability test

Durchlaß-kennlinie *f* transmission characteristics **-kurve** *f* response curve, selectivity curve (of a direction-finding receiver) **-öffnung** *f* porthole, leak hole, hatch, manhole, lead aperture **-periode** *f* gating period **-posten** *m* examining post

Durchlaß-richtung *f* forward direction, low-resistance direction (of a rectifier), conducting direction, pass direction, direction of transmission **-schaltung** *f* gate or gating circuit **-schein** *m* pass, permit **-spannung** *f* forward voltage **-strom** *m* forward current **-treffplatte** *f* transmission target

Durchlassung, gestreute ~ diffusion by transmission

Durchlassungsgradmesser *m* diaphanometer

Durchlaß-ventil *n* gate valve **-wehr** *n* sluice weir **-weite** *f* transmission range **-widerstand** *m* forward resistance (dry rectifier), transmitting resistance

Durchlauf *m* complete sweep (mine sweeping), passage or running through (of a film), sweep (a line) **-balken** *m* continuous beam **-beizanlage** *f* continuous pickling plant

durchlaufen to filter, run through, pass (through), pay off (tape rec.)

Durchlaufen *n* traversing **~ der Wassermenge** water passage

durchlaufend flowing, continuous **~ numerieren** to number continuously **-er Balken** *m* continuous beam, girder **-er Betrieb** continuously running operation **-er Flügel** continuous wing **-e Naht** continuous weld **-e Platte** *f* continuous slab

durchlaufend-er Posten (Buchhaltung) transit entry **-e Schweißnaht** straight line of weld **-e Strecke** distance sailed or covered **-er Träger** continuous beam **-e Warenbestände** stocks of goods in transit **-e Wassermenge** quantity of circulating water

Durchläufer *m* fatigue tested (fatigued) specimen without rupture

Durchlauferhitzer *m* continuous flow heater, multi-point gas water heater

Durchlauf-fertigung *f* line-production system **-filter** *n* gravity filter, through-run filter **-gefäß** *n* flow chamber **-geschwindigkeit** *f* running speed, (speed of passage) **-gleis** *n* through-track **-kopieren** *n* continuous copying

Durchlauf-kopiermaschine *f* continuous film printer **-kühlung** *f* non-circulating water cooling **-magazinvorräte** *m pl* materials in transit **-messer** *m* delivery meter **-ofen** *m* continuous-heating furnace, pusher-type furnace **-öl** *n* flux oil **-wechselventil** *n* automatic short-circuit valve

Durchlaufzeit *f* transit time **-röhren** *pl* velocity-modulation tubes

durchlecken to leak through

durchleiten to conduct, send through, pass through

durch-lesen to read through, go over, peruse **-leuchtend** transparent, diaphanous

Durchleuchtung *f* fluoroscopy, any penetration by rays, radioscopy, transillumination **~ mit Roentgenstrahlen** (diagnostic) radioscopy

Durchleuchtungs-abtastung *f* scanning by illumination **-apparat** *m* radioscope, fluoroscope **-bild** *n* X-ray photograph **-einrichtung** *f* illuminated pannel **-entnahme** *f* fluoroscopic picture **-gerät** fluoroscope, diaphanoscope, roentgenoscope **-kasten** *m* radioscope box, film viewer (phot.) **-kopie** *f* transparent copy **-lampe** *f* transillumination lamp **-tisch** *m* radioscope table

Durchlicht *n* transillumination, transmitted light **-kugeltisch** transillumination ball stage

durch-lochen to perforate, punch (holes) **-löchern** to perforate, pierce, punch (holes)

durchlöchert punctured, perforated, pierced, apertured, having holes or pits **-er Bügel** beehive shelf (gas drying) **-er Hilfsflügel** perforated wing flap **Casing mit -em Rohr** perforated pipe casing, perforator

Durch-löcherung *f* **-lochung** *f* perforation **-ladeeinrichtung** *f* cocking apparatus **-lüften** to ventilate, vent, air, aerate **-lüftungskammer** *f* aerating compartment **-mengen** to intermix, blend

durchmessen to measure throughout, traverse; (einen Motor) **leistungsmäßig ~** to calibrate (a motor)

Durchmesser *m* diameter **innerer ~** caliper **lichter ~** inside diameter **nutzbarer ~** effective diameter

Durchmesser-abnahme *f* draft (wire drawing) **-abweichung** *f* variations in diameter **-bereich** *m* diameter **-genauigkeit** *f* accuracy of the work diameter **-spannung** *f* diametral voltage **-teilung** *f* modulus with gears, diametral pitch **-verminderung** *f* draft (wire drawing) **-verteilung** *f* size distribution **-wicklung** *f* drum winding with diametral pitch, full-pitch winding

durch-mischen to mix thoroughly, intermix, blend **-mischung** *f* intermixture, intimate mixture **-modulierung des Senders** operating transmitter at high modulation percentage **-mustern** to survey, review, catalogue, count **-musterung des Spektrums** passing the spectrum in review **-nässen** to soak, wet, moisten thoroughly, saturate **-näßt** soaked **-nässung** *f* soaking, saturation

durchörtern, das Gebirge ~ to cut across or intersect the ground, drive a heating through the ground

Durch-örterung *f* intersection, cutting across **-pausen** to trace, make a carbon copy **-pauspapier** *n* tracing paper **-perlungselektrode** *f* bubbling-type electrode **-pressen** to press, force, or squeeze through, strain **-projektion** *f* back projection, diaprojection, rear projection **-projektionswand** *f* translucent screen **-prüfen** to examine, test, overhaul **-prüfen der Linie** examination of the line (on completion of construction) (teleph.) **-prüfung** *f* leapfrog test (computer)

Durch-punkt *m* point of intersection of plane of target and plane of sighting, point at which trajectory intersects plane of aerial target perpendicular to line of sighting **-queren** to cross, traverse **-querung** *f* crossing **-rechnen** to calculate (again) **-rechnung** *f* full solution, detailed calculation **-reißen** to tear asunder, break, jerk the trigger (mil.) **-rosten** to rust (through) **-rufen** to ring through, pass the word

Durchrufen *n* through ringing **~ in Schleifenschaltung** loop ringing **~ in Simultanschaltung** composite (through) ringing **~ in Simultanschaltung mit Erdrückleitung** differential earth ringing

Durchrufrelais *n* (through-)ringing relay, signaling relay **Rufen mit ~** relayed ringing

Durchrufschaltung *f* ringing-through scheme

durchrühren to stir thoroughly, mix, agitate

Durchrutschweg (Eisenbahn) overrun length, braking distance, incoming route ahead of starting signal

durchsacken to stall, pancake (aviation)

Durchsack-geschwindigkeit *f* critical or stalling speed **-landung** *f* pancake landing **-warngerät** *n* stall or warning device

durchsagen to pass the word

Durchsatz *m* throughput of a unit, weight rate of flow (elec.), charge (furnace), drive throughput of a machine or unit **~ eines strömenden Mittels** weight rate of flow

Durchsatz-geschwindigkeit *f* rate of travel or of driving, traveling speed **-leistung** *f* throughput capacity **-quote** *f* throughput quota **-verhältnis** *n* by-pass ratio (rocket) **-zeit** *f* time per charge, rate of charging

durchsaugen to suck through

Durchsäuerung *f* acidulating

durchschalten to cut through, put or connect through, extend to **eine Teilnehmerleitung zum ersten Gruppenwähler ~** to extend a subscriber's circuit to the first group selector

Durchschalterelais *n* cut-through or connecting-through relay

Durch-schaltung *f* cutting-through or connecting-through extension **-schaltversuch** *m* test run (guided missiles) **-schalt(e)zeichen** *n* ringing tone **-scheinen** to shine through **-scheinend** translucent, transparent, diaphanous **-scheren** to reeve **-scheuern** to chafe (through)

durchschießen to interleave (print.)

Durchschlag *m* arc through, overshoot, nail set, punch (drift), filter, strainer, carbon copy, puncture, breakdown (elec.), breakoff, intersection, disruptive discharge, cutting across (petroleum) **~ einmaliger** burst pulse **~ durch Erhitzung** heat breakdown **gußeiserner ~** cast-iron strainer **~ amorpher Substanzen** breakdown in amorphous media

durchschlagbar penetrable, reversible **-es Fernrohr** (Theodolit) transit telescope (theodolite)

durchschlagen to come through, sink, break, punch, perforate, penetrate, disrupt, break down, puncture

Durchschlagen *n* puncturing, breaking-down, break-down, disruption, penetration **~** (Farbe) grinding through **~ der Brenngase** penetration of fuel gases **~ des Fernrohres** transitting of the telescope **~ der Gleichstromkomponente** direct-current component reaches screen by way of synchronizing pulses **~ vom Nachbarsender** interference by neighboring station in volume, neighboring station's break-through or swamp signals

durch-schlagend telling, marked, decisive **-schläger** *m* punch drift

Durchschlag(s)-bedingung *f* breakdown condition **-feldstärke** *f* dielectric strength, breakdown field-strength

Durchschlagsfestigkeit *f* electrical-insulation value, disruptive, electric, or dielectric strength or rigidity, rupturing strength, breakdown (resistance) potential or voltage **~ von Transformatorenölen** dielectric strength of transformer oils

Durchschlag(s)-geschwindigkeit *f* propagation speed, rate of insulation breakdown **-hammer** *m* punch or drift hammer **-kanal** *m* breakdown filament **-kraft** *f* piercing effect (explosives), puncture resistance (papier), breakdown (elec.), penetrating power, dielectric strength (der Stimme) permeating efficiency of the voice **-leistung** *f* penetration (of a projectile) **-meßtisch** *m* breakdown bench **-papier** *n* carbon paper, copy paper **-probe** *f* breakdown or piercing test (insulation)

Durchschlag(s)-punkt *m* point of penetration or intersection **-sicher** leakage-proof (secure against puncture) **-spannung** *f* disruptive voltage, breakdown, rupturing, or puncture voltage, flashover potential **~ einer Relaisröhre** trigger breakdown voltage

Durchschlags-stelle *f* point of puncture, pinhole (elec.) **-strom** *m* spark current **-versuch** *m* breaking-down test **-wirkung** *f* punching effect

Durch-schleifen *n* looping-in, abrasion **-schleifungskondensator** *m* pass through capacitor

durchschleusen to pass through **ein Schiff ~** to pass a vessel through a lock

Durch-schleusung *f* taking (a boat) through a lock **-schlupf** *m* narrow passage, (secret) escape **-schlüpfen** to creep or slip through, escape **-schmelzen** to fuse, blow, melt **-schmelzen** *n*

fusing, blowing, melting **-schmelzschweißen** *n* melt-through welding **-schmelzspule** *f* blowout coil **-schmelzung** *f* burnout, blow, blowout, fusion, melting **-schneiden** to cut through or across, cut up, intersect, transverse **-schneidungssprung** *m* intersection jog (cryst.)

Durchschnitt *m* average, diameter, cross section, section, mean, intersection, profile **annähernder ~** rough average **den ~ bilden** (or nehmen), to average **über dem ~** above the average **~ zweier Mengen** section of two sets

durchschnitten intersected, broken

durchschnittlich average, mean, on an average **~ betragend** averaging **-er Werktagsverkehr** traffic per average business day

Durchschnitts-alter *n* average age **-ausbringung** *f* average output **-belastung** *f* average load **-bestimmung** *f* average analysis or determination, averaging **-betrieb** *m* (Mittelbetrieb) average shop **-brett** *n* half plank, half-inch plank or shelf **-dichte** *f* sectional density (rocket weight versus air resistance) **-einkommen** *n* average earnings **-ertrag** *m* mean yield

Durchschnitts-frequenz *f* mean frequency **-geschwindigkeit** *f* average speed, mean velocity **-kosten** *pl* average cost **-kraft** *f* average force **-krümmung** *f* mean camber **-leistung** *f* average capacity or output, average performance **-linie** *f* line of intersection

Durchschnittsmaß *n* average measure **auf ein ~ bringen** to equate

Durchschnitt(s)-molekulargewicht *n* average molecular weight **-muster** *n* average or all-level sample **-neigung** *f* ordinary gradient **-panzerstärke** *f* average thickness of armor **-polymerisationsgrad** *m* average degree of polymerization **-probe** *f* average sample **-qualität** *f* average quality **-sätze** (von Kosten) short cuts **-system** *n* score-cut principle, system of or using averages **-titer** *m* average number **-verbrauch** *m* average consumption **-verminderung** *f* reduction of area (electronics) **-wert** *m* average or mean value, equated value

Durchschnittszahl *f* average number, mean (number) **eine echte ~** a true average figure

Durchschnitts-zeichnung *f* cross-section drawing **-zeit** *f* average time

durchschossen leaded (print.)

Durchschreibe-block *m* carbon-copy block, duplicate pad **-buch** *n* transfer copying book, duplicating book **-feder** *f* manifold pen **-papier** *n* carbon paper **-stift** *m* pencil for making carbon copies **-verfahren** *n* carbon duplicate system

durchschreiten to traverse, walk or pass through

Durchschrift *f* duplicate copy, carbon copy

Durchschuß *m* space, white line, blank, margin, leads, slugs (print.) **-apparat** *m* inlaying apparatus (textiles) **-blatt** *n* interleave **-bogen** *m* interleaving sheet **-linie** *f* space line

durch-schütteln to shake thoroughly, agitate, vibrate thoroughly, toss **-schweißen** to weld through **-schwingen** to swing through **-schwitzen** to ooze through (sweat through)

durchsehen to peruse, examine, look over, go over, review, revise **flüchtig ~** to examine (papers) superficially or carelessly

durch-seihen to strain, filter, percolate **-seihen** *n* colation, colature

Durchsenkung *f* sag, slack

durchsetzen to permeate, infiltrate, intermingle, sieve, sift, carry through, penetrate, intersperse, mix, cross, jig, pervade, travel or streak through

durchsetzt penetrated **~ mit** dispersed by **der Fluß durchsetzt die Windungen** the flux threads with the turns

Durchsicht *f* inspection, revision, perusal, check up, review; (optische) *f* optical visibility

durchsichtig translucent, transparent, clear, manifest, lucid, limpid **-es Filtrat** clear filtrate **-e Tragflächen** transparent wings **-er Werkstoff** transparent plastic material

Durchsichtigkeit *f* transparency, clearness, translucency

Durchsichts-betrachtung *f* rear viewing (of pictures) **-bild** *n* diapositive, lantern slide, glass transparency (picture thrown from rear on frosted-glass pane), translucent picture **-dichte** *f* transparent density (motion pictures) **-farbe** *f* transmitted color **-kathode** *f* transparent photocathode **-schirm** *m* transparent screen (television) **-sucher** *m* direct-view or eye-level finder

durchsickern to seep or trickle through, leak out, percolate, ooze **nach unten ~** to work down (liquids)

Durch-sickern *n* infiltration, percolation, seepage **-sickerung** *f* leak(age), percolation **-sieben** to screen, sieve out, sift, riddle **-sieben** *n* sieving, sifting **-siebt** riddled like a sieve **-sinken** to pass through **-sintern** to trickle through, percolate

durch-sommern to season in summer (tile) **-spießungsfalte** *f* diaper (special folding produced by an intruding plastic core piercing the sediments with a punch, petroleum) **-sprechen** to telephone **-sprechstellung** *f* through position (teleph.) **-spülen** to scavenge, rinse (flush) **-start** *m* balked landing, pull up

durchstarten (Flugzg.) to go around again

Durchstarten *n* scrambled or hurried take-off, wave-off, overshoot

durch-stechen to pierce, stab, cut through **-stechen** *n* pricking out (of a nipple) **-steckstift** *m* through-pin

Durchsteck-wanddurchführung *f* wall bushing insert **-wandler** *m* bushing transformer

durchsteuern, stark ~ to drive hard (transister)

Durchstich *m* cutoff, intercepting cut, excavation, cutting, tunnel (R. R.), cut **-böschung** *f* face of a slope (railway cutting)

Durchstoß *m* intersection, penetration by assault **-stoßen** to pierce, push through, penetrate, fly through (a cloud bank)

Durchstoß-landung *f* landing through clouds **-maschine** *f* punching machine **-ofen** *m* gravity-discharge furnace **-punkt** *m* point of intersection (of a line with a plane), (X-ray) perforation or piercing point **-verfahren** *n* cloud breaking procedure

Durchschreibpapier *n* carbon paper

durchschreiten to traverse, walk or pass through

Durchstrahlungs-beugung *f* transmission diffraction **-methode** *f* irradiation method **-spektrograph** *m* transmission spectrograph **-über-**

mikroskop *n* transmission-type electron or ultramicroscope **-verfahren** *n* transmission method (using tin foil) (ultramicroscopy)

durch-streichen to cross out, cancel, pass, travel, or flow through, pass in and out, circulate through **-streichende Linie** trajectory **-strom** *m* multiphase current **-strömen** to stream or flow through, pass or seep through **-strömgefäß** *n* flow assembly **-strömquerschnitt** *m* valve opening area **-strömung** *f* seepage, flow

Durchströmungs-geschwindigkeit *f* rate of flow **-kanal** *m* port (mach.) **-kalorimeter** *n* continuous flow calorimeter **-linie** *f* topmost flow line, line of seepage, phreatic line **-system** *n* flow system

Durchstromzentrifuge *f* concurrent centrifuge

durch-suchen to search **-teufen** to penetrate (in depth) **-teufen einer Schicht** shaft sinking through a stratum or layer **-tränken** to saturate, impregnate, soak, bond **-tränken mit Wasser** water logging **-tränken** *n* proofing **-tränkt** impregnated **-treiben** to drive or force through, drift

Durchtreiber *m* punch, backing-out or drift punch **runder ~** round-eye punch

durchtreten to pass through

Durchtrittsöffnung *f* opening, cutaway for ejected cartridge cases

Durchtrittsquerschnitt *m* cross-sectional area of nozzle aperture or orifice **freier ~ zwischen Druckleitblechen und Zylindern** leakage area between cylinder walls and baffles **Filter ohne Verminderung des Durchtrittsquerschnittes** full-flow filter

durch-trocknen to complete drying (of a lacquer), dry thoroughly **-tunneln** to tunnel **-verbinden** to cut or connect through, put or extend through (a call) **-verbindung** *f* through connection **-verbindungsstecker** interconnecting plug **-verbindungsstreifen** *m* connecting strip **-vulkanisation** *f* through vulcanization **-wachsen** to interpenetrate, intermingle, grow through **-wachsungszwillinge** *pl* penetration twins (geol.) **-wählen** to dial through **-wählen** *n* through-dialing **-wandern** to diffuse

Durchwahl zur Nebenstelle (direct) inward dialling

Durchwahl in abgehender Richtung outward dialling

Durch-wärmdauer *f* soaking time **-wärmung** *f* soaking, heating **-waschen** to wash thoroughly **-wässern** to soak **-waten** to ford, wade through **-weichung** *f* soaking **-weichungsgrube** *f* soaking pit **-werfen** to bolt or sift, traject **-wintern** to season in winter (tile)

Durchwirbelung *f* swirling motion, turbulence **~ der Luft** turbulence or turbulent motion of the air

durch-wirkt embroidered **-wurf** *m* screen, sieve **-zeichnen** to trace, calk, draw through transparent paper **-zeichenpapier** *n* tracing paper **-zeichnung** *f* deep dimension picture, tracing **-ziehen** to trace, strip, drag or pass through, pull out of a drive **-ziehband** *n* fishing wire **-zieherwicklung** *f* pull-through winding

Durchzieh-formmaschine *f* stripping-plate machine **-glas** *n* slide **-platte** *f* stripping plate **-verfahren** *n* stripping process **-vermögen** *n* stamina **-vorrichtung** *f* drawing device

Durchzug *m* traction power, draft, pulling or drawing through, passage, circulation; girder, support, drawing frames (textiles) **-formmaschine** *f* stripping-plate machine **-matrize** *f* wire-drawing die

Durchzug(s)-dauer *f* duration of passage **-kraft** *f* pulling power, tractive force or power **-moment** *n* lugging capacity of a engine **-platte** *f* stripping plate **-schaltung** *f* system of progressive gear **-vermögen** *n* hard pulling

Durchzündung *f* arc-through

dürftig poor (of gases, vacuum, etc.), scanty

Dürftigkeit *f* need, insufficiency, poverty

Durokavimeter *n* durometer

Duroplast *n* thermosetting plastics

dürr dry, dead, barren, lean, arid, torrid

Dürre *f* drought, aridity, dryness

Duschbad *n* shower bath

Düse *f* blast pipe, jet, nozzle bell pipe, tuyere, spray, nozzle, orifice, carburetor, nose pipe, ejector, nipple, tip, vent, spray, Venturi tube **~** (aus welcher der Strahl austritt) jet **~ des Blasebalges** tuyère **~ der Drosselplatten-bauart** small jet of the plate type **~ des Schmiedefeuers** tuyère **~ des Windkanals** throat of the tunnel **nach außen erweiterte ~** flared nozzle **schwenkbare ~** swivelling nozzle

Düsen-abdeckung *f* nozzle flap **-absperrschieber** *m* tuyère gate **-anordnung** *f* tuyère arrangement **-ansatz** *m* nozzle adapter **-antrieb** *m* jet propulsion, propulsion (aviation) **-ausflußleistung des Vergasers** carburetor metering **-auspufftopf** *m* nozzle exhaust box or muffler

Düsenaustritt *m* tuyère outlet, nozzle arrangement

Düsenaustritts-fläche *f* jet orifice **-kante** *f* edge of the nozzle exit **-öffnung** *f* jet orifice

Düsen-auswerfer *m* nozzle ejector **-ausziehvorrichtung** *f* implements for dismantling a nozzle **-beiwert** *m* nozzle coefficient **-belüftung** *f* nozzle type stenter **-bericht** *m* jet report (sheet) **-boden** *m* tuyère bottom, plate or plug **-bohrung** *f* nozzle hole, base of nozzle, jet **-buchse** *f* nozzle **-druck** *m* nozzle pressure (jet pressure) **-einsatz** *m* nib **-einspritzdruck** *m* injection pressure **-einstellung** *f* jet setting

Düsen-eintritt *m* nozzle inlet **-ende** *f* backing out, exit section **-endfläche** *f* mouth of Venturi tube **-fächer** *m* ducted fan **-feder** *f* injector spring, nozzle spring **-fixierung** *f* nozzle fixing **-flügel** *m* slotted wing, auxiliary airfoil stabilizer **-flugzeug** *n* jet(-propelled) aircraft **-größe** *f* tipsize **-gruppe** *f* nozzle group **-gruppensteuerung** *f* governing by opening series of nozzles in rotation **-hals** *m* throat (rocket)

Düsenhalter *m* nozzle holder **-flansch** *m* injector yoke **-flanschprofil** *n* nozzle holder flange profile **-körper** *m* nozzle holder body

Düsen-höhe *f* tuyère level **-hütchen** *n* jet cap, emulsion tube (in carburetor) **-jäger** *m* jet-(propelled) fighter aircraft **-kaliber** *n* jet size **-kammer** *f* nozzle chamber, box, humidifier (washer)

Düsen-kanal *m* nozzle duct, die approach (channel) **-kasten** *m* nozzle casing or box **-kegel** *m* cone, swirl plug (jet) **-klappe** *f* nozzle flap **-kopf** *m* nozzle tip **-körper** *m* die base (body), nozzle head or body **-korrektor** *m* fuel-jet adjuster (aviation), mixture-control-device **-kranz** *m* nozzle scroll

Düsenkühler *m* nozzle, jet, tunnel-type or ducted radiator **Kühlung durch ~** duct cooling **Lufteintritt in einem ~** induction of duct

Düsen-kühlung *f* ducted cooling system **-lehre** *f* nozzle gauge **-leuchtlupe** *f* nozzle magnifying torch **-libelle** *f* box bubble, circular bubble **-luftstrommesser** *m* Pitot-Venturi air-speed indicator **-mantel** *m* combustion cowl, injector bushing **-maschine** *f* jet aircraft **-messer** *m* nozzle meter **-mischertyp** *m* orifice type blender **-mündung** *f* end of nozzle **-mündungsfläche** *f* nozzle outlet area **-mutter** *f* nut

Düsen-nacharbeitsgerät *n* nozzle-reconditioning equipment **-nadel** *f* jet or nozzle needle, conical member of discharge, jet needle valve, nozzle bullet, nozzle pin **-nadelsitz** *m* nozzle needle seat **-nadelverstellwelle** *f* nozzle-control-shaft jet **-öffnung** *f* jet orifice **-öffnungsdruck** *m* nozzle opening pressure

Düsen-paßstück *n* nozzle adapter **-pilz** *m* nozzle pintle **-plättchen** *n* nozzle **-platte** diaphragm, nozzle plate or ring, atomizer plate **-prüfstand** *m* nozzle test(ing) stand **-prüfvorrichtung** *f* nozzle tester **-pumpe** *f* jet pump

Düsen putzen to poke tuyères

Düsen-querschnitt *m* tuyère area **-regler** *m* nozzle regulator **-reihe** *f* row of tires or of nozzles, tuyères **-reiniger** *m* cleaning tool for the nozzle **-reinigungswerkzeug** *n* nozzle cleaning outfit **-ring** *m* nozzle ring (turbines) **-rohr** *n* jet tube, tuyère pipe, nozzle holder

Düsen-scheibe *f* nozzle plate **-schlitz** *m* nozzle slot **-schraube** *f* nozzle screw **-steuerkolben** *m* jet-operated pistion

Düsen-spaltverstellung *f* adjustment of the extrusion orifice **-spitze** *f* nozzle tip **-spritzkopf** *m* spray nozzle head, jet spraying head **-stock** *m* burner nozzle assembly, tuyère connection or stock, nozzle or blast connection **-stockklappe** *f* tuyère cap or latch **-stockregler** *m* tuyère controller

Düsen-strahl *m* nozzle jet **-strahler** *m* nozzle, spout (antenna) **-strahltriebwerk** *n* (ram) jet engine **-strömung** *f* nozzle flow **-system** *n* tuyère system **-töne** *pl* jet tones

Düsen-träger *m* jet or nozzle carrier **-treibstoffe** *m pl* jet fuels **-ventil** *n* nozzle valve, governor valve **-vergaser** *m* spray or jet carburetor **-verschmutzung** *f* clogging, fouling of nozzle

Düsen-wand *f* (die) hole wall, ram jet wall **-winkel** *m* exit cone angle **-wirkungsgrad** *m* nozzle efficiency **-zapfen** *m* nozzle pin **-zerstäuber** *m* jet dispersor **-zunge** *f* nozzle flap **-zwischenboden** *m* nozzle diaphragm

düster obscure, dull, overcast

Dute, Düte *f* assay crucible, glass cylinder, paper bag

Duzdraht *m* Bowden wire

Duzgestänge flexible control cables

Duzzing *n* flexible control

dwars athwart, across, abeam of **-balken** *m* crossbeam **-feste** *f* breastrope

Dwarslinie *f* loxodromic spiral, rhumb line, in line, abreast **~ bilden** to form line abreast

Dwars-naht *f* butt joint **-saling** *f* cross tree **-schiffs** athwartship **-see** *f* athwart or broadside sea, beam sea **-wind** *m* cross wind

Dweil *n* mop

dweilen to swab, dry with a mop

D-Wert *m* quadrantal error (aviation)

D-Wirkung zweiter Ableitung second derivative action

dyadisch dual

Dyn *n* dyne

Dynameter *n* dynameter

Dynamik *f* dynamic range, dynamic volume range, dynamics, contrast or sound-volume ratio between lowest and highest intensities of notes or passages **~ fester Körper** geodynamics **~ flüssiger Körper** hydrodynamics **~ luftförmiger Körper** aerodynamics

Dynamikbegrenzer *m* volume-range limiter; (bei Verstärkeranlage) intensity-range limiter

Dynamikdehner *m* automatic volume-expander

Dynamik-einebnung *f* dynamic compression **-einregelung** *f* adjustment of contrast **-entzerrer** *m* dynamic expander **-entzerrung** *f* gamma correction **-linie** *f* volume-range or contrast characteristic **-presser** *m* compressor (in volume-range control) **-pressung** *f* volume range compression **-regelung** *f* control of volume range

Dynamik-regler *m* compandor, volume- or dynamic-range control means, contrast regulator **-steigerung** *f* volume or contrast expansion, dynamic-range expansion **-verengung** *f* compression, stricture, constriction of volume **-verringerung** *f* volume contraction **-verzerrer** *m* dynamic compressor

dynamisch dynamic(al) **~ ausgewuchtet** dynamically balanced **-e Abkühlung** dynamic cooling **-er Antrieb** (Stoß) dynamic thrust **-er Arbeitspunkt** working point **-er Auftrieb** dynamic lift, buoyancy **-e Austrittsfläche** *f* jet orifice **-e Beanspruchung** repeated or dynamic stresses **-e Belastung** dynamic load **-e Festigkeit** dynamic strength **-es Gleichgewicht** stability, dynamical equilibrium

dynamisch-er Grenzstrom limiting dynamic current **-e Kenngröße** dynamic characteristics **-e Koerzitivkraft** dynamic coercive force **-e Kühlung und Erwärmung** dynamic cooling and heating **-e Lichtempfindlichkeit** *f* dynamic luminous sensitivity **-e Luftkräfte** *pl* aerodynamic forces **-es Mikrophon** *n* moving coil microphone, dynamic microphone **-e Öffnung** *f* jet orifice

dynamisch-e Regelung *f* kinetic-control system **-e Reibung** dynamical friction **-er Segelflug** dynamic soaring (glider flight) **-er Speicher** dynamic storage **-e Stabilität** *f* transient or dynamic stability **-es Teilprogramm** dynamic subroutine (comput.)

Dynamit *n* dynamite, giant powder

Dynamo *m* generator, dynamo **~** (elektrischer Motor) electric motor **~ mit gemischter Wicklung** compound dynamo **(halb)gekapselter ~** (semi-)enclosed dynamo

Dynamo-anker *m* dynamo armature **-antrieb** *m* dynamo drive **-blech** *n* dynamo sheer iron, laminations

dynamoelektrisch dynamoelectric **-er Verstärker** dynamo-electric amplifier

Dynamo-karren *m* supply cart **-meterleistungsmesser** *m* dynamometer-wattmeter

Dynamomaschine *f* generator, dynamo **direkt gekuppelte ~** direct-driven dynamo **fremderregte ~** separately excited dynamo

Dynamometer *n* dynamometer

dynamometrisch dynamometric **-er Motorzähler** Thomson meter

Dynamo-monteur *m* dynamo fitter **-öl** *n* dynamo oil **-rad** *n* dynamo gear **-riemen** *m* dynamo strap **-riemenverschluß** *m* dynamo-strap-end clip **-ritzelwelle** *f* dynamo pinion shaft **-scheibe** *f* dynamo pulley **-schleiffeder** *f* dynamo collector brush

Dynamotor *m* dynamotor

Dynatron-oszillator *m* dynatron oscillator **-schwingung** *f* dynatron oscillation **-struktur** *f* dynode structure **-wirkung** *f* dynatron effect, dynatron characteristic

Dynastarter *m* starter generator

Dynatron *n* dynatron **-art** *f* dynatron mode **-generator** *m* **-summer** *m* dynatron oscillator **-verfahren** *n* dynatron method

Dyne *f* dyne

Dyotron *n* dyotron

Dysprosium *n* dysprosium

D-Zug *m* express train

E

Ebbe *f* ebb or low tide **~ und Flut** ebb and flow **letzte ~** end of the ebb **~ und Flutgebiet** *n* tidal territory

Ebbeflut Korrosionsversuch tidal corrosion test **~ Prüfstand** tidal test stand

Ebbe-rinne *f* ebb or ebb-tide channel **-seite** *f* ebb side of a dam **-strom** *m* ebb-tide current, ebb **-tor** *n* ebb-tide gates

Ebbe- und Flutmaschine *f* tidal-power installation

Ebbe- und Flutmesser *m* tide gauge

Ebbe- und Fluttor *n* ebb-and-flow gate

Ebbewassermenge *f* volume of water discharging on ebb tide, volume of ebb

Ebbstrom *m* outgoing or ebb stream

eben plane, flat, level, even, two-dimensional **~ senkrecht** flat vertical **-e Anordnung** plane arrangement **-e Fläche** plane surface, plane **-e Glasscheibe** plane lens **-e Grundplatte** level base plate **-e Konfigurationen** plane configurations **-e Kurven** plane curves **-es Netz eines Polyeders** plane net of a polyhedron **-es Netzwerk** planar network **-es Punktgitter** plane point lattice **-e Straße** (gerade Strecke) level tangent railrod **-e Strömung** two-dimensional or plane flow **-e Welle** plane wave

Eben-bild *n* image, likeness, similarity **-bürtig** equally efficient, of equal quantity

ebendrehen to smooth (plane)

Ebene *f* optical flat, plane, plane surface, plain, flat country, water table, tier, range (electr.) **in einer ~ mit** flush with, coplanar **elliptische ~** elliptic plane **euklidische ~** Euclidean plane **hyperbolische ~** hyperbolic plane **in gleicher ~ liegend** flush, coplanar **optische ~** optical plane or flat **projektive ~** projective plane **schiefe ~** inclined plane **unendlich ferne ~** plane at infinity **Geometrie der ~** plane geometry, planimetry

Ebenen-büschel *n* cluster of plane surfaces **-paar** *n* pair of planes **-schar** *f* family of plane surfaces

ebenerdig flush with the ground

Ebeneverspannung *f* plane bracing

ebenflächig having a plane surface

Ebenflügler *m* planiwing (missile)

Ebenführung *f* linkage for tracing a plane

Ebenheit *f* planeness, flatness, smoothness, evenness

Ebenholz *n* ebony

Ebenmaß *n* symmetry, proportion **-fläche** *f* plane of symmetry

ebenmäßig even, equal, symmetrical, proportionate

ebenpolarisiert plane-polarized

Ebenströmung *f* plane flow, two-dimensional flow

ebnen to level, flatten, smooth, plane, even

Ebnen *n* fileting

Ebnung des Bodens leveling or removal of ground

Ebonit *n* ebonite **-gehäuse** *n* ebonite case **-kaspel** *f* ebonite box or case **-schutzglocke** *f* ebonite guard insulator

ebullieren to boil up, break out

Ebullio-meter *n* ebulliometer **-skop** *n* ebullioscope

Eccles-Jordan-Schalter *m* Eccles-Jordan trigger

Echelettegitter *n* echelette (phys.)

Echo *n* (telephonic) echo, reverberation, multipath effect, fold-over multipath effect, multiple image, double image, ghost (TV) **künstliches ~** plume, feather **stufenförmiges ~** echelon formation of multiple echoes **Form des Echos** presentation (rdr)

Echo-absperrer *m* echo suppressor **-effekt** *m* doubling effect, echo effect **-empfänger** *m* echo receiver **-falle** *f* power equalizer **-fläche** *f* radar cross-section **-hohlraumresonator** *m* echo box **-intensität** *f* intensity of echo **-kompensation** *f* echo cancellation **-kontrolle** *f* echo checking **-laufzeit** *f* echo transmission time

Echolot *n* sonic altimeter, sonic depth finder, fathometer **~** (mit Ultraschall) supersonic echo sounding

Echolotung *f* echo or reflection sounding, radar or radio locator, sonar work (predicated upon echo principle) **~ der Ionosphäre** sounding the ionosphere

Echo-messer *m* echo-attenuation measuring set **-messung** *f* (TV) reflection measurement **-mikrophon** *n* echo microphone **-paar** *n* paired echo **-probe** *f* echo checking **-rückkunft** *f* return echo

Echosperre *f* echo suppressor **stetig arbeitende ~** valve-type (or metal-rectifier-type) echo suppressor ~ **löschen** to turn off or switch-out the echo suppressor ~ **zünden** to turn on or switch-in the echo suppressor

Echo-sperrer *m* echo suppressor, echo killer **-störung** *f* echo trouble, disturbance due to echo **-strom** *m* echo current **-stromdämpfung** *f* echo (current) attenuation, active return loss of echo **-teilung** *f* echo splitting **-unterdrücker** *m* echo suppressor **-unterdrückung** *f* echo suppression, echo killing, damping of reverberations **verlust** *m* reflection loss **-weg** *m* echo path **-weite** *f* echo area, effective scattering cross section of radar target **-welle** *f* echo or reflected wave, sky wave **-werk** *m* swell organ **-wirkung** *f* echo effect

echt genuine, real, effective, true, pure, fast (colors), ingrained, proof **-er Bruch** simple or common fraction, proper fraction **-er Gang** *m* fissure vein **-e Längenmessung** direct measurement of length **-er Spaltengang** true fissure vein

Echt-base *f* fast color base **-beizenfarbstoff** *m* fast mordant dyestuff **-färben** to dye fast **-druckfarbe** *f* fast printing color

Echtheit *f* fastness (dye), genuineness, authenticity

Echtheits-anspruch *m* fastness demand(ed) or required **-grad** *m* fastness grade

Echt-zeit *f* real time **-zeitmesser** *m* real time computer (astronout.)

Eck *n*, **über** ~ across, crosswise, diagonal **vollständiges räumliches n-~** complete n-gon in space

Eck-anker *m* corner brace **-anschluß** *m* corner (angle) connection **-aussteifung** *f* (Kastenträger) corner truss **-balken** *m* corner post **-band** *n* angle iron, corner plate **-blech** *n* gusset or corner plate, knee bracket **-bohle** *f* taper sheet pile **-brett** *n* corner shelf

Ecke *f* angle, corner, summit (of a crystal), quoin ~ **der Schleuseneinfahrt** rounded corner **ausspringende** ~ external angle, arris, corner **verbrochene** ~ blunt angle, obtuse corner

Eckeisen *n* angle iron

ecken to tilt, turn slightly on edge, angle off, corner on, get out of line or alignment, jamb; (eines Randes) to jam

Ecken *pl* corners, angles **umgeschlagene** ~ dogeared

Ecken der Welle canting of the shaft ~ **beim Fahren** canting while moving

Ecken-abrundmaschine *f* round cornering machine **-abstand** *m* distance between corners **-ausstanzmaschine** *f* corner punching machine **-ausstoßmaschine** *f* corner cutting machine **-bearbeitungsmaschine** *f* corner-working machine (print.) **-biegemaschine** *f* angle-forming machine **-brenner** *m* tangential corner burner, canting burner **-einziehmaschine** *f* cornering machine **-feuerung** *f* corner firing

Ecken-haftklammern *pl* corner staples **-heftung** *f* corner stitching **-markierung** *f* corner mark(s) **maß** *n* with across corners **-radius** *m* radius of curvature of a corner

Ecken-rundstanzmaschine *f* round corner punching machine **-rundstoßmaschine** *f* cornering machine, round-corner-beveling machine (print) **-schärfe** *f* corner detail, definition of or at the edges **-schliff** *m* corner cut **-schließpapier** *n* corner sealing paper **-stanzmaschine** *f* corner punching machine **-verbindemaschine** *f* corner mounting machine **-verzierung** *f* corner ornament

Eckerdoppe *f* valonia

Eck-feile *f* triangular file **-first** *m* hip, corner ridge (of building) **-flügel** *m* raised wing (of building) **-frequenz** *f* pulsation, angular velocity or frequency, sharp cutoff **-hahn** *m* angle cock **-holz** *n* squared timber

eckig angular, cornered **-e Klammer** square bracket, square parenthesis

Eckigkeit *f* angularity, clumsiness

Eck-kappe *f* covering strip **-klammer** *f* corner or border clamp

Eckleiste *f* corner fillet ~ **für Decken** cove

Eck-mast *m* angle post **-moment** *n* moment at the joint **-naht** *f* corner joint (weld) **-pfeiler** *m* newel corner pillar, jambstone, stone stud, butt pier **-pforte** *f* angle or indented port **-platte am Rahmen** gusset plate **-platz** *m* corner seat **-punkt** *m* joint **-quadrat** *n* mitted quad

Eck-radius *m* flanging radius **-rahmen** *m* side frame **-ring aus Gußstahl** cast-steel stiffening ring **-rohrzange** *f* elbow (tube) pliers **-rückschlagventil** *n* angular non-return valve **-runge** *f* end stanchion **-säule** *f* corner pillar, corner angular column **-schiene** *f* angle bar, iron corner cramp **-schweißung** *f* corner joint welding **sitzplatte** *f* gusset

Eckstein *m* quoin, cornerstone ~ **mit Hohlkehle** hollow quoin

Eck-stahl *m* corner tool (angular tool) **-stichbalken** *m* tie beam

Eckstück *n* corner bracket, elbow piece **kleines** ~ scantling

Eck-ventil *n* angle valve **-verband** *m* edge joint, edge bond, connection of corners **-verstärkung** *f* fillet **-verstrebung** *f* gusset stay **-verzapfung** *f* edge joint **-wasserzeichen** *n* corner mark **-ziegel** *m* quoin brick

edel noble (metals), rare or inert (gases), rich (mine), precious (gems or stones), electropositive, vital **-erde** *f* rare earth **-erz** *n* rich ore

Edelgas *n* rare or inert gas, noble gas **-blitzableiter** *m* vacuum lightning protector **-bogen** *m pl* arcs in rare gases **-füllung** *f* rare-gas filling **-gefüllt** inert gas filled **-gleichrichter** *m* rare-gas rectifier **-glühkathodengleichrichter** *m* rare-gas or tungar rectifier

Edelgas-kontinua *f* continuous rare gas spectra **-kristalle** *n pl* rare gas crystals **-photozelle** *f* rare-gas photoelectric cell **-röhre** *f* rare-gas tube **-sicherung** *f* rare-gas lightning arrester, surge arrestor (rare gas)

Edel-gleitsitz *m* medium force fit **-guß** *m* fine casting **-holz** *n* ornamental wood, fine wood **-kontakte** *pl* precious metal contacts **-korund** *n* electro-corundum

Edelkunstharz *n* synthetic resin, cast resin

Edelmetall *n* noble or precious metal **-gehalt pro Tonne** output of pure noble metal per ton of ore **-probe** *f* precious-metal assaying **-sammler** *m* precious-metal collector **-scheider** *m* precious-metal refiner **-schrott** *m* pure scrap

Edel-opal *m* precious or noble opal **-passung** *f* close or force fit **-putz** *m* facing plastering, plaster for facing **-rost** *m* patina **-schiebesitz** *m* heavy force fit **-schrott** *m* pure scrap **-splitt** *m* double-broken chippings

Edelstahl *m* fine steel, high-grade or high-quality steel, refined or superior alloy steel **unlegierter ~** plain superrefined steel

Edelstahl-ausführung *f* stainless steel model **-blech** *n* superrefined steel plate **-blöcke** *pl* refined steel ingots **-guß** *m* highgrade cast steel **-halbzeug** *n* semiproduct of supperrefined steel

Edelstein *m* jewel, gem **-kunde** *f* gemmology **-lager** *n* (Meßgerät) jewel bearing

Edison-batterie *f* Edison storage battery **-effekt** *m* Edison effect **-fassung mit Aufhängehaken** Edison lamp holder with suspension hook **-sammler** *m* Edison storage cell or battery, iron-nickel accumulator

E-Ebene *f* guide-beam plane

E-Ebenen-Linse *f* E-plane lens

Effekt *m* effect, power **~ der Hyperfeinstruktur** effect of hyperfine structure **~ einer langen Leitung** long-line effect, frequency hysteresis **~ der hinteren Schwarzschulter,Schwarztreppe** back-porch effect **~ der schnellen Spaltung** (Vervielfachung) fast fission effect (fast multiplication effect)

Effekt-anlage *f* sound effect system **-beleuchtung** *f* effect lighting, spot or fancy lighting **-bogenlampe** *f* flame lamp, arc lamp with carbon electrodes

Effekten *pl* (Bank) securities, stocks **-börse** *f* stock exchange

Effektenergien asymmetrischer Kreiselmoleküle effect energies of the gyrating asymetric molecules

Effekten-handel *m* exchange of, or dealing in, stocks **-makler** *m* stockbroker

Effektfaden *m* effect threads (rayon, etc., with special dyeing propertics)

effektiv effective **-e Atomladung** effective atomic charge **-e Ausgangsadmittanz** effective output admittance **-er Betriebsfaktor** operation ratio **-e Eingangsimpedanz** effective input impedance **-er Energiegewinn** net energy gain **-e Entionisationszeit** effective deionization time

effektiv, -e Höhe (einer Antenne) effective height (of an antenna), radiation height **-e Höhe** (der ionisierten Schicht) virtual height (of ionized layer), effective height **-er Kolbendruck** effective pressure of piston **-e Ladung** effective charge **-er Laufwinkel** effective bunching **-e Leistung** effective capacity, actual power

effektiv -e Pferdestärke actual metric horsepower, brake horsepower **-e Propellerleistung** thrust horsepower **-e Radiumquantität** *f* effective radium content **-er Raumwinkel** effective solid angle **-er Spaltleitwert** effective gap capacitance **-er Trennfaktor einer Stufe** effective simple process factor **-e Weglänge** effective rotation **-e Wellenlänge** effective wavelength

Effektiv-höhe *f* (einer Antenne) effective height (of an antenna), radiation height **-leistung** *f* brake horsepower **-potential** *f* effective potential **-spannung** *f* effective or root-mean-square voltage **-stärke** *f* effective strenght, effectives **-strom** *m* effective or root-mean-square current **-voltmesser** *m* true r.m.s. voltmeter

Effektivwert *m* effective or root-mean-square value, virtual value **~ einer periodischen Größe** effective value of a periodic quantity

Effektkanal nicht durchlaufend beschriftet FX channel is not continuously modulated

Effekt-kohle *f* flame carbon **-lampe** *f* studio light (ordinary table lamp, motion pictures) **-lichtbogenlampe** *f* arc with colored effect **-spur** *f* buzz track (film) **-szenen** *pl* scenic or light effects

efferveszieren to effervesce

Effloreszenz *f* efflorescence

effloreszieren to effloresce

Effluvien *n pl* electric wind

Effusion *f* effusion, escape

Effusivgestein *n* volcanic rock

egalisieren to equalize, level, flatten

Egalisiergerüst *n* (Kaltwalzen) skin-pass stand; (Warmwalzen) skin-pass edging stand

egalisieren to shake out (straighten)

Egalisierer *m* levelling agent

Egalisier-farbstoff *m* levelling dyestuff **-kluppen** *pl* equalizing screw stocks **-lack** *m* topcoat for leather (a lacquer) **-maschine** *f* conditioning machine, levelling machine **-schwierigkeiten** *pl* difficulties levelling

Egalisierung *f* equalization

Egalisierwalzmaschine *f* equalizing rolling mill

Egalität *f* equality, sameness, uniformity, evenness

Egge *f* harrow, plank with projecting nails (used as obstacle)

eggen to harrow

Eggen *n* harrowing

Egrainieren *n* ginning

egrenieren, die Baumwolle ~ to clean or gin the cotton

Egrenier-kreissäge *f* gin saw for cotton cleaning **-maschine** *f* gin, cotton gin

Eguttör *m* dropper, dropping tube

Ehren-erklärung *f* apology **-mitglied** *n* honorary member **-preis** *m* prize cup **-rat** *m* honorary council(lor), court of honor

Ei *n* egg **-ablage** *f* egg laying or deposit

Eibenholz *n* yew

Eich-absorptionskurve *f* calibration absorption curve **-abwanderung** *f* calibration variations **-amt** *n* gauging or calibration office, bureau of standards

Eichapparate für Thermometer apparatus for calibrating thermometers

Eich-bedingung *f* gauge condition **-deckel** *m* equivalent standard sample **-daten** *pl* calibration **-düse** *f* reference jet

Eiche *f* oak

eichel-förmig gestalteter Teil acorn-shaped part, gland **-mutter** *f* nut **-röhre** *f* acorn tube

eichen to gauge, calibrate, standardize, adjust, measure, test, stamp, log

Eichen *n* calibration **~ eines Instrumentes** calibrating an instrument

Eichen-faßholz *n* oak wood for cask-making **-galle** *f* gall nut **-gerbsäure** *f* quercitannic acid

Eichenholz *n* oak wood **-extrakt** *m* oak extract **-schalttafel** *f* switchboard in oak

Eichen-kontrolle *f* calibration check (electronics) **-krummholz** *n* compass oak timber **-langholz** *n*

straight oak timber **-laubkranz** *m* wreath of oak leaves, oak-leaf cluster **-lohgrubengerbung** *f* oak tanning

Eicher *m* assessor, calibrator, gauge

eichfähig gauged **-e Wiegevorrichtung** weighing device working to fire tolerances

Eich-faktor *m* gauge factor **-fehler** *m* trouble in calibration, calibration error **-folie** *f* calibrated foil **-frequenz** *f* calibration frequency, standard frequency **-geber** *m* standard signal generator (missilies) **-gebühr** *f* gauger's fee **-genauigkeit** *f* calibration accuracy **-impulsgenerator** *m* generator for calibrating **-instrument** *n* calibration instrument, calibrating apparatus, test gauge **-invarianz** *f* gauge invariance

Eich-kabel *n* calibration cable **-kondensator** *m* standard or calibration condenser, calibration capacitor **-kontrolle** *f* calibration check **-kreis** *m* calibration circuit **-kreismikrophon** *n* standard-circuit transmitter **-kreistelephon** *n* standard-circuit receiver **-kurve** *f* calibration curve

Eich-lampe *f* standard lamp (for tests) **-lauf** *m* calibration test **-leitungsprüfer** *m* tester for calibration circuit **-lösungen** *f pl* calibration solutions **-maß** *n* standard (measure), gauge **-meister** *m* gauger, adjuster **-mikrophon** *n* standard microphone or transmitter **-nebenschluß** *m* calibration shunt **-normal** *n* standard **-ordnung** *f* regulations for gauging weights and measure

Eich-pfahl *m* calibration post, maximum permissible elevation of reservoir water surface **-pfropfen** *m* gauging plug **-phasenschieber** *m* zero setting, phase shifter **-probe** *f* calibration sample **-pumpe** *f* master test pump **-reizkurven** *pl* visibility curves (electronics)

Eich-schraube *f* gauge propeller **-signal** *n* test signal **-spannung** *f* calibration voltage **-spannungsregler** *m* calibration-voltage regulator **-stelle** *f* gauge shop **-strich** *m* measuring line, gradation **-stromregler** *m* calibration-current regulator **-substanz** *f* gauge substance **-tabelle** *f* table or certificate of correction, calibration table **-tafel** *f* calibration chart (radar) **-transformation** *f* gauge transformation

Eichung *f* calibration, gauging, standardization, verification, standard **~ der Kontrollstäbe** control rod calibration **~ eines Meßgeräts** calibration of testing instrument

Eichungs-kondensator *m* calibration condenser **-kovarianz** *f* gauge covariance

Eich-unterlage *f* calibration curves (radar) **-verfahren** *n* method of calibration **-versuch** *m* calibration test **-vorrichtung** *f* calibrating equipment, checking arrangement **-widerstand** *m* calibrating resistance **-zahl** *f* galvanometer constant **-zähler** *m* calibration meters **-zirkel** *m* calibration circle

eidliche Versicherung affidavit, sworn statement, testimony, declaration

Eidesleistung *f* attestation

eidesstattliche Erklärung *f* affirmation (affidavit) in lieu of oath

Eier-antenne *f* weighted or trailing antenna **-briketts** *pl* oval briquettes **-isolator** *m* egg insulator **-kette** *f* chain of egg insulators **-kohle** *f* egg coal **-schalenglanz** *m* egg-shell luster or polish **-schalenmattierung** *f* eggshell finish

eiförmig egg-shaped, oval, elliptical **-er Körper** ovoid

Eiformlampe *f* oval lamp or bulb

eigen proper, one's own, individual, special, peculiar, characteristic, specific **-er Antrieb** self-contained drive **-es Feld** self-consistent field **-e Lager** own depots **-e Nockenwelle** built-in camshaft

Eigen-abstoßung der Elektronenwolke repelling action of electron charge, negative space charge **-amt** *n* home exchange **-antrieb** *m* self-contained drive, self-propulsion **-arbeit** *f* no-load capacity **-art** *f* originality, individuality, peculiarity, characteristic **-artig** peculiar, specific, unique, characteristic, remarkable **-bedarf** *m* internal consumption **-bedarfssatz** *m* station service unit **-bedarfsversorgung** (v. Kraftwerk) station service system, auxiliary service supply

Eigen-befugnis (im Budget) routine expenditure **-belastung** *f* dead-load **-belüftet** self-cooled, self ventilated **-belüftung** *f* self-ventilation **-bewegung** *f* proper motion, characteristic motion, mode of oscillation **-charakteristik** *f* inherent characteristic **-dämpfung** *f* self-damping, inherent damping

Eigen-drehbewegung *f* self-motivated spin **-drehgeschwindigkeit** *f* speed of autorotation **-drehimpuls** *m* (Phys.) self-motivated spin, characteristic angular momentum **-drehmoment** *n* intrinsic angular momentum **-drehung** *f* autorotation

Eigen-energie *f* characteristic or proper energy, self-energy, intrinsic energy **-entstörung** *f* short-distance radio shielding, close-range radio shielding **-erregermaschine** *f* self exciter **-erregung** *f* individual exitation, pilot-exciter exitation, self-exitation

eigenerregter Schwingkreis free-running oscillator **~ Sender** self-excited sender

Eigen-erwärmung *f* self-heating **-fahrwerk** *n* self-propelled travelling gear **-farbe** *f* inherent (natural) color **-feld** *n* self-consistent field **-filterung** *f* inherent filtration **-fortbewegung** *f* self-propelling

Eigenfrequenz *f* eigenfrequency, proper frequency, fundamental (natural) frequency, inherent or characteristic frequency **~ des Sperrkreises** antiresonance frequency

Eigen-funktion *f* eigenfunction, characteristic function, proper function **-ganggeschwindigkeit** *f* proper rate **-(gegen)kopplung** *f* natural negative feedback

Eigengeräusch *n* set noise, inherent film noise, intrinsic noise **~ einer Entladungsröhre** tube noise

Eigengeschwindigkeit *f* (initial) velocity (phys.), airspeed (aviation) **wahre ~** true airspeed

Eigengeschwindigkeits-geber *m* automatic airspeed control **-ausgleich** *m* own-speed compensation

Eigengesetzlichkeit *f* any tendency to follow a fundamental law unaffected by external variables

eigen-gesteuert inherent control **-gewicht** *n* own weight, true specific weight, net or dead weight, specific gravity, tare, dead load **größe** *f* characteristic variable, proper variable **-halb-**

leiter *m* intrinsic semi-conductor

eigenhändig personally, single-handed

Eigenheit *f* peculiarity, property, singularity

Eigen-impedanz *f* self-impedance **-induktion** *f* self-induction **-induktivität** *f* internal inductance, natural inductance **-instabilität** *f* inherent instability

Eigenkapazität *f* natural capacitance, self-capacity, self-capacitance (distributed capacity) ~ **der Spule** coil capacity, self-capacity of a coil

Eigen-kapazitätseffekt *m* proximity effect **-kapital** *n* own capital (private) net worth **-klirrfaktor** *m* inherent distortion factor **-klirrdämpfung** *f* residual distortion **-kontrolle** inherent control **-kreiselwirkung** *f* self-gyro-interaction **-kühlung** *f* (d. Trafos) natural cooling **-ladung** *f* space charge, self charge **-last** *f* individual or dead weight **-leitend** intrinsic (trans.) **-leitung** *f* intrinsic conduction **-leitungstemperaturgebiet** *n* intrinsic temperature range

Eigenlicht des Auges eye's own light, self-light or intrinsic light of retina

Eigenlüftung *f* self-ventilation

eigenmächtig unauthorized, arbitrary, on one's own authority ~ **handeln** to act on one's own authority, act without authority

eigenmagnetisch self-magnetic

Eigenpeilen auf Funkfeuer to home on a beacon, come in on the beam

Eigenpeilgerät *n* radio compass

Eigenpeilung *f* bearings determined from the airplane (aviation), self-bearing, direction finding by taking bearings from an aircraft on two or more direction finders, bearings taken by airplane on two or more known radio stations to determine position ~ (auf Funkfeuer), homing (on a beacon)

Eigen-peilverfahren *n* bearings taken aboard an airplane **-periode** *f* natural period (of oscillation), characteristic period **-pfiffe** *pl* self whistles **-potential** *n* self-potential **-rauschen** *n* background noise, basic noise, self-noise, (in electron tubes and resistors) granular noise; (von Elektronenröhren oder Widerständen) granular noise (electronics) **-reibung** *f* internal friction **-richtung** *f* direction or heading relative to the air

Eigenschaft *f* quality, attribute, peculiarity, chemical or physical property, feature, characteristic, character, condition ~ **des offenen Kraftflusses** open-flux structure

Eigenschaften, störungsunempfindliche physikalische ~ perturbation insensitive physical properties

Eigenschatten *m* cast on an object, an object's own shadow

Eigenschwingung *f* natural motion, vibration, or oscillation, natural period or (oscillation) frequency, vibrational mode **Pendel ohne** ~ recording pendulum without natural frequency

Eigenschwingungen des Materialfeldes proper states of the field of matter

Eigenschwingungs-form *f* individual or natural shape of vibration **-frei** aperiodic, deadbeat (phys.) **-periode** *f* natural period of oscillation **-zahl** *f* natural frequency or period

eigensicher intrinsically safe **-e Stromkreise** intrinsically safe circuits

Eigen-spannung *f* residual stress, inherent or internal tension or strain, induced voltage, body stress **-stabil** inherently stable **-stabilität** *f* inherent stability, natural (dynamic) stability **-stabilisierung** *f* self stabilization **-ständig** independent **-steif** inherently rigid **-steuerung** *f* automatic control **-stoff** basic substance, base material

Eigen-störstellenleitung *f* electronic conduction caused by intrinsic impurities **-störung** *f* internal trouble **-strahlung** *f* fluorescent or characteristic radiation **-streuung** *f* natural divergence, self-scattering **-symmetrie** *f* specific symmetry, characteristic or proper symmetry **-temperatur** *f* eigen-temperature **-theorie** *f* intrinsic theory

eigentlich intrinsic, specific, proper, properly speaking, actually

Eigenträgheit *f* intertia

Eigentum *n* property, belongings

Eigentumsvorbehalt *m* lien

Eigentümer *m* proprietor, owner

eigentümlich peculiar, inherent, characteristic, specific

Eigentümlichkeit *f* strangeness, peculiarity, characteristic, inherent feature, property

Eigentumsrecht *n* ownership, proprietary or property right, proprietorship

Eigen-vektor *m* characteristic vector, proper vector **-ventiliert** self-cooled **-veränderung** *f* individual change **-verbrauch** *m* internal or power consumption, tare, own use, consumption **-verbrauchsablesung** *f* tare reading **-verbrauchsbestimmung** *f* tare reading **-vergrößerung** *f* actual magnification or enlargement

Eigenverlust *m* internal loss, natural leak ~ **des Kondensators** inherent (or natural) loss of condenser (or capacitor)

Eigenversorgung *f* self-sufficiency, station service (power station)

Eigenverständigung *f* intercommunication (intercom)

Eigen-verzerrung *f* distortion proper to **-verzögerung** *f* inherent or natural lag **-viskosität** *f* specific viscosity, intrinsic viscosity **-volumen** *n* original, specific or natural volume

Eigenwärme *f* sensible or specific heat, body or animal heat ~ **eines Körpers** total heat of a body

Eigenwelle *f*, **Eigenwellenlänge** *f* natural wavelength, electron resonant wave length ~ **eines Luftleiters** (ohne zusätzliche Schaltmittel) unloaded wave length of an aerial

Eigenwellenlänge *f* natural wave length

Eigenwert *m* eigen value (molecular phys., magnetism), characteristic number or value, representative, typical, or inherent value **-aufgabe** *f* characteristic value problem, eigenvalue problem **-problem** *n* eigenvalue problem, proper value problem

Eigen-widerstand *m* (internal) resistance **-willig** arbitrary **-zeit** *f* proper time, time element (of autom. circuit breaker) **-zeitkonstante** *f* residual time constant **-zündung** *f* compression ignition (engine) **-zündungsmotor** *m* compression-ignition motor **-zustand** *m* eigen state, proper state, mode

eignen to suit, be suitable, be qualified, be adapted **sich ~ für** to be suitable for

Eignung *f* suitability, applicability, usability, fitness, aptitude, acceptability

Eignungs-prüfung *f* ability or psychological test, consistency check, qualification test **-untersuchung** *f* psychological examination

Ei-Isolator *m* (Antenne) egg insulator

Eikonal *n* two-point characteristic function **-funktion** *f* eikonal function

Eikonogen *n* eikonogen

Eiland *n* island, isle

Eil-beförderung *f* express delivery **-bewegung** *f* rapid power or quick-return traverse, rapid-return motion **-bote** *m* express (messenger) **-brief** *m* special-delivery letter **-fracht** *f* express goods or freight

Eilgang *m* rapid power or quick-return traverse, rapid-return motion **~ in allen Bewegungsrichtungen** rapid power traverse in all directions of movement

Eilgang-geschwindigkeit *f* rapid traverse rate **-getriebe** *n* step-up gear **-hebel** *m* high-speed lever **-kupplung** *f* quick motion coupling **-motor** *m* quick traverse motor **-pumpe** *f* rapid traverse pump **-sicherheitsschaltung** *f* quick-motion safety trip **-stellung** *f* quick-motion position **-ventil** *n* rapid traverse valve **-welle** *f* rapid power traverse shaft

Eilgut *n* express goods **-beförderung** *f* parcels porterage

Eilgüter-boot *n* express cargo boat **-zug** *m* express freight train

Eilgut-gebührensatz *m* express-freight tariff **-verkehr** *m* express-freight traffic

Eil-regler *m* quick-acting regulator **-rückgang** *m* rapid power or quick-return traverse, rapid-return motion **-rücklauf** *m* rapid-return motion **-rücklaufschieber** *m* rapid return valve **-tarifsatz** *m* express rate **-zug** *m* fast or express train

Eimer *m* pail, bucket **-bagger** *m* bucket or ladder dredge **-kette** *f* bucket chain **-kettenbagger** *m* bucket-conveyer excavator or dredge **-kettenförderer** *m* bucket chain conveyor **-kettenleiter** *f* bucket tender **-kunst** *f* bucket elevator or lift **-leiterbagger** *m* bucket (conveyor) dredge **-rad** *n* blade or bucket wheel (turbine) **-rinne** *f* bucket gutter or channel **-trockenbagger** *m* bucket-land dredge **-trommel** *f* dredging tumbler **-weise** by the bucket **-werk** *n* bucket elevator, noria

ein a, an, single, one, (Schaltstellung) on **~ für allemal** once and for all

Einachs-anhänger *m* two-wheel trailer **-fahrzeug** *n* single-axle vehicle

einachsig uniaxial **-e Straße** single-line mill train

Einachsigkeit *f* uniaxiality

Einachs-lagerung *f* suspension with one degree of freedom **-schlepper** *m* single-axle tractor, uniaxial-wheel tractor

Ein-Adreß one-address, single-address **-befehl** *m* one or single-address instruction **-system** *n* single-address system

einadrig single-core, single-wire **-es Kabel** single-core(d) cable

Einankersystem *n* single armature system

Einankerumformer *m* rotary or synchronous converter, dynamotor **~** (Drehstrom-Gleichstrom), motor-converter dynamotor

Einanoden-stromrichtergefäß *n* single-anode rectifier vessel **-ventil** *n* single-anode rectifier

einarbeiten to work in(to), break in, force in, thrust in, train, get familiar with

Einarbeiten, gegenseitiges ~ coordination of new methods

Einarbeitungszeit *f* on-the-job training period

einarmig one-armed **-e Ausstanzmaschine** *f* one-armed (open-front) punching press **-er Hebel** *m* one-arm lever, simple bed lowering lever **-er Kneter** single arm kneader **-e Spindelpresse mit Reibungsantrieb** overhanging screw press with friction drive

einäschern to calcine, cremate, incinerate

Einäscherungsofen *m* incinerator, crematory

Einatmenventil *n* inhaling valve (gas mask)

einatomar, einatomig monoatomic

einätzen to engrave, etch

einäugig monocular **-es Sehen** monocular or nonstereoscopie vision

ein–aus on–off

Einaus-schalter *m* off-on switch **-schaltung** on off type of servo **-tastung** *f* on-off keying

Einbad-anilinschwarz *n* one-dip aniline black **-chromierfarbstoff** *m* single-bath chrome dyestuff **-färbeverfahren** *n* one-bath dyeing process **-gerbung** *f* single-bath tanning

einbahnige Maschine single-line machine

Einbahn-katze *f* (Winde) monorail motor hoist (crab) **-straße** *f* one-way street **-verkehr** *m* one-way traffic

Einband *m* binding, cover **-decke** *f* cover (binding) **-leinen** *n* binding cloth **-projektor** *m* single-film projector **-rücken** *m* book backing **-übertragung** *f* single-side-band transmission

einbasisch monobasic **-e Säure** monobasic acid

Einbau *m* mounting, assembly, insertion, installation, inclusion, fitting, inner player (piano) **~ von Reaktanzspulen** installation of reactors **beweglicher ~** movable mounting **elastischer ~ mittels Gummipuffer** rubber-buffer mounting **fester ~** fixed mounting

Einbau-aggregat *n* built-in unit **-anleitung** *f* fitting instruction **-anordnung** *f* installation **-antenne** *f* built-in antenna **-art** *f* type of installation **-bedingungen** *pl* conditions for mounting (or installation) **-bereich** *m* installation zone **-blinkleuchte** *f* built-in blinker light **-bremslaterne** *f* built-in stop lamp **-schema** *n* installation diagram

einbauen to build in, fit in, install, mount, set, insert, dig in **in etwas ~** incorporate

Einbau-fähre *f* construction float **-gerät** *n* flush mounting instrument **-großvorrichtung** *f* installation jig or rig **-hülse** *f* mounting sleeve **-kippschalter** *m* toggle-type switch **-koeffizient** *m* distribution coefficient **-lage** *f* position of device, fitting position **-länge** *f* laid length **-maße** *pl* installation dimensions **-mappe** *f* installation folder **-meßkopf** *m* built-in gauge head

einbäumig single-beam

Einbau-mikroskop für Werkzeugmaschinen machine tool microscope **-motor** *m* motor for independent electric drive, conversion engine, built-in motor **-plan** *m* installation drawing

Einbauplatte *f* adapter plate, ~ **für Sternmotoren** mounting plate or flange
Einbau-rahmen *m* mounting frame **-ring** *f* flush ring **-rückfahrleuchte** *f* built-in rear light or reversing light **-schalter** *m* built-in coverless switch **-scheinwerfer** *m* flush-fitting headlamp, built-in head lamp **-schlußlaterne** *f* built-in tail lamp **-spiel** *n* assembly clearance **-stelle** *f* point of insertion **-stellung des Motors** installation position of motor **-stück** *n* piece of installation, part of construction or structure, chock **-stutzen** *m* coupling flange, nipple (aviat.) **-teil** *m* detachable accessory
Einbauten *pl* components, installations, armor **Heckzelle ohne** ~ tail hull guided missiles
Einbau-verhältnis *n* conditions of installation or of fitting **-vorrichtung** *f* mount, mounting fixture **-vorschlag** *m* fitting proposal or suggestion **-vorschrift** *f* directions for installing **-wassergehalt** *m* placement, moisture (water content) **-werke** *pl* built-in movements **-zeichnung** *f* installation drawing or diagram, assembly drawing **-zustand** *m* assembled condition
einbegreifen to include, imply **mit** ~ to implicate
einbegriffen implied, including
einbehalten to withhold
Einbehaltung *f* detention
Einbein-fahrgestell *n* cantilever landing gear (aviation), landing gear or wheels with independent legs, single-strut landing gear **-fahrwerk** *n* single-strut landing gear
Einbereich *n* single span
Einbereichsuper *m* superheterodyne receiver superhet
einberufen to convene
einbeschrieben inscribed **-e Kreislinie** inscribed circumference **-es Vieleck** inscribed polyhedron **-er Winkel** *m* included angle
einbetonieren to embed in concrete, concrete
einbetonierter Mast mast or pole set in concrete
einbetten to embed, insert, place in matrix
Einbetten *n* embedding, potting
Einbett-harz *n* embedding resin **-mittel** *n* embedding medium **-probe** *f* packing test **-schaltelemente** *pl* potted circuit elements **-schaltung** *f* potted circuit board
Einbettung *f* bedding, potting; (Polster) embedding
Einbettungs-material *n* matrix or embedding material **-medium** *n* mounting (embedding) **-theorie** *f* imbedding theory **-tiefe** *f* depth of embedding, covering of bars
Einbeulapparat *m* bulge-testing apparatus
einbeulen to bulge, dent
Einbeulung *f* blister dent, indentation
Einbeulungsprüfung *f*, **Einbeulversuch** *m* bulging test
einbezogen integrated, included
einbiegen to bend in, turn down, deflect, sag
Einbiegung *f* curvature, inflection, sagging, deflection, flexure
Einbildmessung *f* single-photograph measuring
Einbindelinie *f* tie line
einbinden to bind, melt, tie in
Einbinde-stelle *f* splice point **-stoff** *m* binding material **-tiefe** *f* anchoring depth
Einbindungsgrad *m* fusion rate, rate of retension
Einblasdruckregler *m* air-injection pressure-control valve
Einblase-düse *f* injection nozzle, injector **-gefäß** *n* injection-air receiver **-leitung** *f* air injection, injection conduit
Einblaseluft *f* injection air **-behälter** *m* injection-air reservoir **-kompressor** *m* **-pumpe** *f* injection-air compressor
Einblase-maschine *f* (Diesel) engine for air injection of fuel **-mühle** *f* direct-feeding mill
einblasen to blast in, blow in (into), inject, throw into, bubble through, insufflate
Einblasen *n* blowing in, injection
Einblaser *m* insufflator
Einblasevorrichtung *f* blowing device (for charging shaft furnaces)
einblatten, die Schwellen ~ to adze the ties
Einblattluftschraube *f* single-blade (airscrew) propeller
einblenden to gate (electronics), fade-in
Einblenden der Mikrophone fade-in and mixing of microphones
Einblendung *f* concentration (of rays), adjustment, focusing
Einblick *m* insight, eyepiece (optics), dial sight **-kopf** (des Sehrohrs) eyepiece end **-linse** *f* eyepiece lens **-prisma** *n* deflection prism **-richtung** *f* direction of inspection **-rohr** *n* eyepiece tube, viewing tube **-stutzen** *m* eyepiece socket or mount **-tubus für Sucher** viewing visar for finder
Einblitzfeuer *n* single-flash beacon
einbördeln to roll in (flange)
Einbördeln *n* sintering
Einbrand *m* penetration by burning, penetration (in welding) **-kerbe** *f* penetration notch, undercut **-tiefe** *f* (depth of) penetration of burning or fusion
einbrechen to break in or. open, give way, fall in or down
Einbrecherglocke *f* burglar alarm
einbrennbare Abziehbilder kiln-proof decalcomanias
Einbrennemaille *f* stoving enamel
einbrennen to burn in, cauterize, brand, pass through the muffle, penetrate, weld, anneal; (Fett) to stuff hot; (keramische Farben und Emaillen) to stove (ceramic colors and enamel)
Einbrennen *n* burning, poisoning **durch** ~ **beschädigen** to darken by burning
Einbrenn-farbe *f* annealing color, baking finish **-firnis** *m* stove varnish **-lack** *m* annealing lacquer, baking enamel, stoving enamel **-lackierung** *f* stove-enamelling **-lampe** *f* blast lamp **-maschine** *f* crabbing machine **-muffel** *f* decorating lehr
Einbrenn-ofen *m* burning-in oven, glory hole (glass mfg.), an auxiliary furnace for finishing glassware **-rückstand** *m* stoving residue **-stelle** *f* burned-in spot **-temperatur** (Lacke) stoving temperature **-verfahren** *n* stoving process, hot stuffing process **-zange** *f* tongs for burning-in **-zeit** *f* heating period (electronics), time to warm up
einbriefen, die Stecknadeln ~ to paper the pins
eindringbar (wiederbringbar) recoverable
Einbringemanöver *n* berthing maneuver (of airship)

einbringen to bring in or home, capture, seize, yield, place, gain, take in (a line) **eine Brücke ~** to raise the trusses of a bridge **den Kolben ~** to put in the piston **in Schichten ~** to place in layers

Einbringen *n* inserting **~ des Betons mittels Rutschen** pouring concrete by chute **~ des Betons von einer Laufbühne** pouring concrete from walkway

einbringend productive

Einbringverfahren *n* application methods

Einbruch *m* break, breaking in, burglary, inroad, penetration, raid, in-rush (of water) **-alarm** *m* burglar alarm **-melder** *m* burglar alarm **-periode** *f* surge period **-schuß** *m* breaking-in shot

einbruchsicher safe against pilferage **-es Fenster** burglarproof window

Einbruch-stelle *f* point of penetration **-wecker** *m* burglar-alarm bell

Einbuchtung *f* niche, bay, salient, recess, bight, indentation

einbühnen to notch

Einbuße *f* loss, damage

einbüßen to lose, forfeit

eindämmen to confine by dikes, dam in or up, embank

Eindämmen einer Quelle damming off a spring

Eindämmung *f* embankment, check, restriction

Eindampfapparat *m* evaporating apparatus

eindampfen to evaporate, concentrate (by evaporation), boil down, steam, vaporize

Eindampfen *n* evaporation, vaporization

Eindampf-gerät *n* evaporator, drying apparatus with evaporation **-rückstand** *m* total solids (refinery) **-schale** *f* evaporator, drier, drying cup with evaporation

Eindämpfung *f* steaming, evaporation, inherent damping

eindecken to roof, cover up **sich ~** to provide oneself with, lay in (provisions)

Eindeck-flachpalette *f* single decked flat pallet **-rahmen** *m* covering frame

Eindeckung *f* roofing, (overhead) cover, recess

eindeutig plain, well-defined, unambiguous, indisputable, specific, unmistakable, unique (math.), clear, one-valued, unequivocal **-e Peilseite** absolute direction (sounding) **-e Richtungsanzeige** unidirectional direction finding

Eindeutigkeit *f* uniqueness, unambiguity **umkehrbare ~** one-to-one correspondence

Eindeutigkeits-prinzip *n* exclusion or equivalence principle **-satz** *m* uniqueness theorem **-theorie** *f* uniqueness theory

Eindicke *f* inspissation

eindicken to thicken, concentrate, liver (paints), body (drying oils), inspissate, boil down, condense, reduce by boiling

Eindicken *n* thickening

Eindicker *m* thickener, concentrator **-überlauf** *m* thickener overflow

Eindick-filter *n* thickening filter **-trommel für Zellulose** thickening drum for wood pulp

Eindickung *f* thickening, livering (paints), bodying (oils)

Eindickungsmittel *n* thickening substance

Eindick-zyklon *m* cyclone thickener **-zylinder** *m* concentrator

eindimensional unidimensional, one-dimensional **-e Bewegung** lineal motion **-er Fall** in the one dimensional case **-e Fehlordnung** *f* one-dimensional disorder

Eindraht-antenne *f* single wire antenna **-aufhängung** *f* unifilar or simple suspension

eindrähtig unifilar, single wired **-e Leitung** ground return circuit, single wire (line)

Eindraht-fernsteuerung *f* single-pilot remote control **-lampe** *f* single filament lamp, one-filament bulb **-leitung** *f* single wire circuit, longitudial circuit **-speiseleitung** *f* single-wire feeder **-wellenleiter** *m* guide wire

eindrehen to indent, recess, tap (a screw thread), strain, cut-in (in two-motion selector)

Eindreher *m* inserter (tool)

Eindrehschnecke *f* feed screw

Eindrehung *f* recess, tapping, indent, extractor groove in a cartridge case

eindrillen to drill

Eindringbleibende *f* depth of impression (on hardness testing)

eindringen to break into, penetrate, enter, pierce, infiltrate, ingress, soak or leak (in, into) **mit Gewalt ~** to intrude

Eindringen *n* intrusion, ingress, leakage, penetration (in, into) **durch Feuer gebildetes ~** igneous intrusion (petroleum) **gewaltsames ~** forced entry **~ der Sonde** progress in penetration

Eindring-gesetz *n* penetration law **-körper** *m* the ball or pointed body to be forced into the material being tested

eindringlich impressive, forcible, penetrating

Eindringtiefe *f* depth of penetration or of impression, radius of action, range **~ der primären Absorption** range of primary absorption **~ von der mittleren freien Weglänge** penetration depth on mean free path

Eindringung *f* penetration

Eindringungs-bereich *m* zone of penetration **-fähigkeit** *f* penetrativeness **-protokoll** penetration record **-tiefe** *f* depth of penetration or of impression, radius of action of bombers **-verfahren** *n* indentation process or test **-versuch** *m* (cone) penetration test **-widerstand** *m* resistance to sinking

Eindruck *m* impression, mark, stamp, imprint, indent, insert; (Markierung) impression, mark, stamp; (Stoß) *m* dent **~ (durch Schlag oder Stoß erzeugt)** dent

Eindrückdorn *m* (pressing-in) mandrel

Eindruckdurchmesser *m* diameter of impression

eindrucken to ground in, reenter (cloth print.), impress (imprint) insert

eindrücken to impress, crush, force into, compress, press, flatten, stamp

Eindruck(s)-empfänglichkeit *f* impressibility **-farbe** *f* color to fit in **-fläche** *f* area of impression, area of indentation **-form** *f* skeleton form **-gleichheit** *f* equality of sensation or inpression **-härte** *f* indentation hardness

Eindruck-kalotte *f* indentation cup, ball impression, mark or print of test ball **-kaltpresse** *f* single-blow cold upsetting machine **-messer** *m* penetrometer **-mitte** *f* center of indentation

Eindrück-pfaffe (Pfaffe, Kunststoffe) hob, mas-

ter hob (plastics) **-ring** *m* inserted ring
eindrucks-fähig impressionable
Eindruck-schmierung *f* shot-lubrication system **-stempel** *m* indenting tool **-tiefe** *f* indentation depth **-tiefenmesser** *m* indentation-depth gauge, imprint-depth indicator, penetrometer **-tiefenmeßuhr** *f* indentation-depth dial indicator, indentation-depth dial gauge
Eindrückung *f* collapsing
Eindruckverfahren *n* indentation test, ball test, Brinell hardness-test method
Eindruckwerk, dreiwalziges ~ printing unit of three rollers
einebnen to level, flatten, plane, lay flat, even, smooth, spread and level
Einebnen *n* surfacing, leveling
Einebnung *f* leveling, equalization, smoothing
eineindeutige Zuordnung one-to-one correlation or correspondence
Einelektronenzustand *m* one-electron state
einendig single-ended
einengen to concentrate, compress, narrow down, hem in, boil down
Einengung *f* limitation, narrowing, shrinking **~ durch Gefrieren** concentration by freezing
Einengungsverhältnis *n* concentration ratio
Einer *m* unit (math.), units' digit **-ausgabe** *f* one output **-dekade** *f* units stage
Einergang-Kurbel und -welle *f* single-picture crank and shaft (motion pictures)
Einer-stelle *f* unit place **-stufe** *f* units' digit **-wahl** *f* dialing of units **-wählen** to dial units' digit **-wellen** *f* ultra-short waves **-zelt** *n* lean-to tent, one-man shelter tent **-ziffer** *f* digit in the units place
Einetagen-ofen *m* one-story furnace **-presse** *f* single daylight press
einfach simple, single, single-ply, elementary, plain, easy, ordinary, straightforward **~ brechend** single refracting (opt.) **~ entstört** with single interference suppression **~ gestaltet** plain (shaped or formed) **~ kugelig** single ball **~ primitiv** primitive (cell) **~ verboten** first forbidden **~ verzweigt** single-branched **~ zusammenhängend** simply connected
einfach abgeschlossene Schalen single closed shells (nuclei) **~ destilliertes** (nicht gekracktes) **Benzin** straight-run fuel **~ offene Steuerung** open-loop control **~ wirkender Arbeitskolben** single-acting lift piston **~ wirkender Motor** single-acting engine
einfach-e Abschrägung single bevel **-er Drall** continuous twisting **-e Einschlaglupe** single-folding magnifier **-e Flügelklappe** plain flap **-e Marke** (Farbstoff) single strength brand **-er Prozeß** simple process
einfach-e Schiebung simple movement **-e Schraube** single-threaded screw **-er Schraubenschlüssel** single-ended spanner **-er Schraubstock** plain vise **-e Stangenlinie** single-pole line **-er Stoff** plain cloth or plain fabric **-e Strömung** laminar flow **-es Ziel** simple target **-e Zugspannung** simple tension
Einfach-anschnitt *m* single-station pilot-balloon spotting **-antenne** *f* plain antenna **-band** *n* single-meche **-bereifung** *f* single rear wheels **-betrieb** *m* simplex operation or working **-brücke** *f* simple bridge (teleph.) **-chlorzinn** *n* tin protochloride or crystals **-chlorjod** *n* iodine monochloride **-chlorschwefel** *m* monochloride (protochloride) of sulfur
Einfach-diode *f* single diode **-dipol** *n* simple dipole **-drossel** *f* single reactor, single choke **-druckmesser** *m* single-type pressure gauge (manometer) **-einzelkassette** *f* single plateholder **-filter** *n* one-layer filter **-form** *f* single cavity mold
einfachfrei univariant, monovariant, having one degree of freedom **-es Gleichgewicht** monovariant or univariant equilibrium
Einfach-gleitung *f* simple glide **-glockenisolator** *m* single-cup insulator
Einfach-hindernisleuchte *f* single obstruction light **-hobeleisen** *n* uncut straight plane cutter **-kabel** *n* single cable **-kamera** *f* single-lens camera, single chamber **-kammer** *f* camera for single photographs **-kupplung** *f* single roller clutch **-leitung** *f* single-wire circuit, simplex circuit, single-core circuit, earth-return circuit **-meßkammer** *f* photogrammetric camera for single photographs **-nadelzeiger** *m* simplex needle indicator **-nietung** *f* single riveting **-nocken** *m* single lobe cam
Einfach-punktschreiber *m* single dotted line recorder **-reihenmeßkammer** *f* single-lens (aerial) survey camera **-riemen** *m* single-ply belt **-ringschlüssel** *m* single head box wrench **-rollenketter** *m* simplex roller chain **-saugrohr** *n* single-throat Venturi tube **-schaltung** *f* simplex circuit or system **-schicht** *f* monolayer, monomolecular layer, unilayer **-schneide** *f* single cutting edge **-schraubenschlüssel** *m* single-head wrench, single-ended spanner **-schreiber** *m* single-record instrument
Einfach-schwefeleisen *n* protosulfide of iron, ferrous sulfide **-signal** *n* singel-component signal **-streuung** *f* single scattering **-strom** *m* neutral current, single current **-strombetrieb** *m* transmission by simplex current **-stromsignalisierung** *f* single-current signalling **-tarif** *m* flat rate (tariff) **-telegraph** *m* single-channel or simplex-operated telegraph **-telegraphie** *f* simplex telegraphy **-umsponnen** single-covered **-unterbrecher** *m* single-lever contact breaker
Einfach-verbindung *f* simplex communication **-verkehr** *m* simplex operation or working **-waagerechtfräsmaschine** *f* plain horizontal milling machine **-walzenmühle** *f* single-roll crusher **-wechselventil** *n* spring-loaded shuttle valve
einfachwirkend single-acting **-e Maschine** single-acting engine **-e Pumpe** single-acting pump **-er Zylinder** single-acting cylinder
Einfachzacken-schrift mit Abdeckung unilateral variable-area track with single-vane shutter **-spur** *f* unilateral variable-area track
Einfach-zeilensprung *m* interlaced scanning, single interlacing **-zellenschalter** *m* one-point end-cell or emergency-cell switch **-zündung** *f* normal-type ignition
Einfachzweckeinfachbereichinstrument *n* single-range meter
einfädeln to mount **sich ~** to thread a needle, join or get into line, thread (up) film
Einfädelschlitz *m* cog (tape rec.), ridge (tape rec.)

Einfaden-aufhängung *f* unifilar suspension **-glühlampe** *f* one-filament bulb
einfädig unifilar **-e Aufhängung** unifilar suspension
einfahren to descend (into a mine), go underground, tune up (a motor), float prepared bridge sections into place, road test (car) **den Brand ~** to put or set bricks in the kiln
Einfahren des Turbogeneratorläufers bringing in the rotor of the turbogenerator
Einfahrer *m* subinspector (min.), road test driver
Einfahr-fahrzeug *n* road test vehicle **-geleise** incoming track **-signal** *n* home signal **-straße** *f* test road
Einfahrt *f* entrance (vehicle), inlet, mouth (waterway), descent (into a mine), retraction (of landing gear, etc.), driveway, in-movement **-geleise** *n* incoming or arrival track **-peilung** *f* inbound bearing **-schleuse** *f* entrance lock **-signal** *n* home or station signal **-zeichen** *n* green traffic light, right-of-way signal
Einfahr-vorschrift *f* run-in instruction **-zeit des Motors** running-in period of engine
Einfall *m* falling in, fall, idea, notion, inroad, incidence (phys.), pitch, invasion **schiefer oder streifender ~** grazing, oblique, or glancing incidence **senkrechter ~** vertical incidence
einfallen to fall in, into, or upon, interrupt, occur, flow down, dip (min.), drop, raid, invade, join, snap (in, into) (bolt), to incide (phys.), come in (waves)
Einfallen *n* snapping in, incidence, inclination, underlie, dip, pitch, collapse, implosion **~ eines Ganges** hade of fault **~ der Schichten** inclination of strata, dip **gegen die Senkrechte ~** hade **gegen die Waagerechte ~** dip
einfallend incoming, oncoming, incident **-es Licht** incident light **-e Ortsstrecke** (Bg) brow **-er Strahl** impinging beam **-e Strecke** (Bg) down-inclined gate **-es Teilchen** colliding, bombarding or incident particle **-e Welle** incident wave
Einfall(s)-dosis *f* incoming dose **-ebene** *f* plane of incidence **-feld** *n* gate of entry, entry portal **-geschwindigkeit** *f* bombardment velocity **-höhe** *f* height of incidence (optics) **-lot** *n* axis of incidence, perpendicular, normal (line)
Einfallsrichtung *f* direction of incidence **schwankende ~** wandering direction of arrival
Einfall(s)-schacht *m* drop shaft **-strahl** *m* incident beam **-vorrichtung** *f* engaging clutch
Einfallswinkel *m* angle of incidence, rigger's angle **den ~ ändern** to feather **den ~ verändern** (gegen den Luftstrom) to unfeather **den ~ vergrößern** to increase the angle of incidence
einfaltige Gruppe one-dimensional group
einfalzen to fold in
Einfang *m* capture **dielektronischer ~** dielectronic capture **~ eines Hüllenelektrons** orbital electron capture **~ zur Spaltung** capture-to-fission
Einfangausbeute *f* capture efficiency
Einfangbereich *m* lock-in range (rdo.)
einfangen to capture, captivate, trap (electrons)
Einfang-faktor *m* capture coefficient **-gammaquant** *n* capture gamma radiation **-gammastrahlung** capture gamma radiation
Einfangquerschnitt *f* capture cross section **~ für Neutronen** neutron-capture cross-section
Einfangzentrum *n* trap
einfärben to ink, ink up
Einfärben *n* inking
Einfarben-bogenoffset *m* single color sheet-fed offset press **-druck** *m* single-color printing, monochrome printing **-punktschreiber** *m* single-color dotted-line recorder **-übertragung** *f* monochromatic transmission
Einfärbevermögen (Druckfärbevermögen) *n* penetrating properties
einfarbig monochromatic **-es Licht** monochrome, monochromatic light
Einfärbung *f* inking, steeping in dye, dyeing, staining, imbition
einfassen to border, edge, frame, hem, trim, enclose, bind, trap
Einfaß-maschine *f* bordering machine **-leisten** *f pl* binding strips **-schaufel** *f* shovel for barreling
Einfaß- und Fälzelpapier *n* trimming and folding paper
Einfassung *f* enclosure, curb, wall, border, jamb, window sill, skirting
Einfassungs-borte *f* binding border **-mauer** *f* enclosing wall **-stück** *n* repetition border
Einfederung *f* stroke (e.g., of a telescopic shock absorber)
Einfeiler *m* groover
Einfeilung *f* notch
Einfeinerung *f* elimination of finishing process
Einfeldeinkontakt-regler *m* single-field single-contact regulator **~ mit Neigkennlinie** single-field single-contact regulator with drooping characteristic curve
Einfeld-regler *m* single-field regulator **-Zweielement-Zweikontaktregler** single-field-two-element tow-contact regulator **-Zweikontaktregler** *m* two-contact single field regulator
einfetten to lubricate, grease, oil
Einfettung *f* greasing, lubrication, oiling
Einfiltrierung *f* infiltration
Einflammenrohrkessel *m* cornish boiler
einflammig single-flame
Einflammrohrkessel *m* one-flue boiler
Einflankenwerkzeug *n* one-sided cutter
Einflanschstück *n* flanged spigot
einflechten to interweave
Einfliegen *n* trial flight
Einflieger *m* test pilot
Einfließgeschwindigkeit *f* rate of inflow
einflößen to administer
einfluchten to align, arrange **einen Stab ~** to range in a pole
Einfluchten *n* marking out
Einflüchter *m* alignment tool
Einfluchtung *f* alignment, line-up
Einflug *m* entry by air
einflügelig single-blade **-es Fenster** single-sashed window **-e Luftschraube** single-blade (airscrew) propeller
Einflug-erlaubnis *f* permit for entry by air **-genehmigung** *f* entry clearance (aviation) **-richtung** *f* direction of approach (in airplane landing) **-schneise** *f* approach track or path

-sektor *m* approach sector **-sender** *m* marker beacon (aviation) **-zeichen** *n* marker **Haupt~** (HEZ) middle marker (MM) **Vor~** (VEZ) outer marker (OM) **Platz~** (PEZ) inner marker (IM)

Einfluß *m* influence, influx, inflow, action, bearing, effect **~ der Temperatur** temperature effect **~ auf den Wechselstromwiderstand** effect on alternating-current resistance **gesetzwidriger ~** illegal influence **ungünstiger ~** penalty

Einfluß-bereich *m* influential reach or sphere, radius of action **-bilanz** *f* importance function

Einflüsse *pl* effects, attack **besondere ~** special factors

Einfluß-fläche *f* actuator disk **-funktion** *f* correlation function, importance function **-größe** *f* limiting quantity **-höhe** *f* range of influence **-linie** *f* influence line **-reich** influential **-rinne** *f* loading trough, gutter, trench **-rohr** *n* inlet pipe or tube **-schleuse** *f* inlet sluice **-zahl** *f* weighting factor (ballistics) **-zone** *f* radius of influence

einfordern to call in, demand

einformen to mold

einförmig uniform, monotonous

Einformung *f* forming in

Einfräsung *f* milled slot or recess

Einfrequenz-fernwahl *f* alternating-current dialing **-signal** *n* simple signal **-system** *n* single-frequency operation

einfressen to corrode, erode, pit

Einfressung *f* corrosion, erosion, pitting

einfriedigen to fence in, enclose, corral

Einfriedigung *f* fence, enclosure, corral

einfrieren to freeze (in or up), congeal, be frozen in (a vessel)

Einfrieren *n* freezing **~ des Spannungszustandes** stress freezing

einfritten to frit

Einfügedämpfung *f* insertion attenuation

einfügen to insert, secure, interpose, fit in, rabbet, intercalculate

Einfügen *n*, **Einfügung** *f* insertion, interposition **~ eines Getriebes** fitting in

Einfügung *f* adjustment

Einfügungs-gewinn *m* insertion gain **-verlust** *m* insertion loss

Einfuhr *f* import(ation)

Einführbänder *n pl* guiding tapes

einführen to lead in, import, introduce, insert, direct upon, feed into, initiate, thread (up) film **den Stöpsel in eine Klinke ~** to plug in

Einführen *n* insertion, inlet, lead-in, entrance, introduction

Einfuhr-hafen *m* port of entry **-handel** *m* import trade **-quoten** *pl* import quotas **-schein** *m* bill of entry

Einführtisch *m* feed board

Einführung *f* entering, entering guide, import, insertion, inlet, introduction, injection, lead-in adoption **~ von Stoffen** ingestion **~ des Wahlbetriebes** introduction of automatic working

Einführungsbacke *f* entry guide jaw **-brunnen** *m* leading-in manhole **-doppelstütze** *f* leading-in double bracket (elec.) **-draht** *m* lead-in wire, drop wire, lead-in **-druck** *m* air-injection pressure **-gestänge** *n* lead-in pole (elec.)

Einführungsisolator *m* lead-in insulator, feedthrough insulator, bushing **~ mit Vergußkammer** pothead insulator

Einführungs-kabel *n* (Spulenkasten) stub cable; (Luftleitungen) terminal cable, lead-in cable **-kanal** *m* **für Hauseinführungen** conduit for lead-in cables (teleph.) **-kasten für Leitungen** entrance box for lines **-kondensator** *m* feedthrough capacitor **-leitung** *f* telephone drop, leading cable **-nadel** *f* needle of gasoline inlet valve **-öffnung** *f* inlet

Einführungspfeife *f* inlet funnel **~ aus Porzellan** porcelain tube (teleph.)

Einführungs-preis *m* introductory price **-presse** *f* entry guide press **-rinne** *f* feed or entring channel or trough **-rohr** *n* intake, inlet tube **-schreiben** *n* introduction **-stangen** *pl* terminal poles **-stelle** *f* point of introduction, entrance **-stützen** *m* lead-in tube **-verlust** *m* insertion loss **-walzen** *pl* feed rollers or feeders (textiles)

Einfuhr-verbot *n* prohibition of importation **-waren** *pl* imports **-zoll** *m* entrance, import, or customs duty

Einfüllarmaturen *pl* battery-filling accessories

einfüllen to fill in or up, pour in, charge, feed, put in

Einfüller *m* loader

Einfüll-hahn *m* feed cock **-kasten** *m* fill box **-loch** *n* filling hole **-meßgefäß** *n* measure **-öffnung** *f* filling hole, feed opening **-pipette** *f* filling pipette **-rumpf** *m* hopper **-schraube** *f* filler plug, filler screw **-stoff** *m* packing **-stutzen** *m* filler socket, filler connection, filling vent or tube, filler neck, inlet, (tank) filler cap **-topf** *m* replenishing cup **-trichter** *m* funnel tube

Einfüllung *f* filler vent

Einfüllverschluß *m* filler cap **-kraftstoffsieb** *n* filler cap filter **-oberteil** *m* filler cap top part

Einfüll-verschraubung *f* screwed filler cap **-vorrichtung** *f* feeding (filling) device

Einfunkenzündung *f* single-spark ignition

Eingabe *f* amendment, application or petition (patents), input (in computer) **-gerät** *n* input equipment

eingabeln to bracket

Eingabelung *f* bracket, bracketing

Eingabe-speicher *m* input (storage), input block **-speicherung** *f* input voltage **-werk** *n* input unit (comp.)

Eingang *m* entrance, receipt, inlet, input **~ eines Anrufes** receipt of a telephone call **~ (Gewebe)** shrinkage (fabric) **verbotener ~** no admittance

eingängig single, single-thread (mech) **-e Ankerwicklung** singly reentrant armature winding **-es Gewinde** single thread **-e Parallelwicklung** simple parallel winding (simplex lap)

Eingangs-abschwächer *m* input attenuator **-admittanz** *f* input admittance **-amplitude** *f* input amplitude **-Ausgangs-Intervall** *n* transducer pulse delay **-bedämpfung** *f* input resistance or damping **-beleuchtung** *f* illumination of the entrance **-buchse** *f* entry hub **-daten für Ausgleichsrechnung** input data for least squares adjustment **-differenzverstärker** *m* difference amplifier **-druck** *m* in-feed pressure

Eingangs-einschub *m* plug-in input **-elektrode** *f* input elektrode **-empfindlichkeit** *f* input sensitivity **-feld** *n* entrance field **-geschwindigkeit** *n* input rate **-gitterkapazität** input grid capacity **-größe** *f* input variable, input quantity **-hohl-**

raum *m* input bunker **-impedanz** input impedance, insertion loss

Eingangs-kanal für Dampf steam-admitting pipe **-kanalspin** *m* entrance channel spin **-kapazität** *f* input capacitance (of an electronic valve or tube) **-kegel** *m* entrance cone **-klemme** *f* input terminal **-kreis** *m* input circuit, grid-(to-) filament circuit **-kreisimpedanz** *f* input impedance **-leistung** *f* input (gen.) **-leitung** *f* incoming circuit **-leitwert** *m* input conductivity **-lichter** *pl* contact lights

Eingangs-manifest *n* bill of entry **-öffnung** *f* entrance **-pegel** *m* input level **-plätze** *pl* incoming positions, B or inward board, B switchboard **-pupille** *f* entrance pupill **-rauschen** *n* noise input **-rauschtemperatur** *f* effective input noise **-resonator** *m* buncher, input resonator

Eingangs-schaltung *f* input circuit **-scheinleitwert** *m* input admittance **-scheinwiderstand** *m* input impedance (radio) **-scheinwiderstandsklemmen** *pl* input-impedance terminals (radio) **-schlitz** *m* entrance slit

eingangsseitige Verschiebung input displacement (kinematics)

Eingangssignal *n* input signal **Größe des ~** input rate (inertial navig.)

Eingangssignal-anschluß *m* input connector **-bereich** *n* input range **-wandler** *m* input computer

Eingangs-spalt *m* input gap **-spannung** *f* input voltage, reception range **-speicher** *m* buffer storage, input block **-stollen** *m* entrance gallery or tunnel (min.) **-strom** *m* input current **-stromkreis** *m* input circuit **-tisch** *m* lattice feed **-transformator** *m* input transformer **-und-Ausgangszeichen** *n* entrance-exit sign **-umschalter** *m* input selector **-verbindung** *f* incoming call **-verstärker** *m* input amplifier **-vorverstärker** *m* input preamplifier

Eingangs-wähler *m* incoming selector **-walze** *f* feed roller **-wechselspannung** *f* input alternating-current voltage, A.C input voltage **-wechselstrom** *m* input alternating current **-welle** *f* primary shaft **-werte** *pl* initial data **-wicklungen** *pl* signal windings **-widerstand** *m* input resistance or impedance, antenna impedance, insertion loss **-wirkleitwert** *m* input conductance, input active admittance

Eingangs-zeit *f* (bei der Durchgangsanstalt) filling time **-zeitkonstante** *f* input time constant **-zentrum für Defektelektronen** hole trap **-zündung** *f* detonator charge, booster or priming charge **-zylinder** *m* delivery roll

eingeätzt engraved **-e Linien** etched lines

eingebaut installed, arranged, mounted, fitted, incorporated **~ in einem Apparat** mounted, fitted, or incorporated on, to, or in an apparatus **~** (Maschinenbau) flush mounting **-er elektrischer Anlasser** integral electric starter **-e Antenne** built-in antenna **-er Antrieb** built-in drive **fest -e Kanone** fixed cannon **-er Schalter** *m* inset mounted switch **-er Speicher** internal storage **-es** (elektrisches) **Thermometer** internal detector of temperature

eingeben to administer, prompt

eingebettet imbedded **-er Dübel** bed plug dowel **-e Kristalle** diluted crystals **-e gedruckte Schaltung** sealed circuit

eingebeult dented

eingebleiter Bolzen leaded-in bolt

eingeborener Kautschuk native rubber

eingebrannter Sand burnt sand **~ Fleck, Fläche verringerter Leuchthelligkeit** (auf dem Schirm der Bildröhre) ion spot

eingebunden bound

eingedickte Trübe regenerated dense medium

eingedrückt crushed, bulged in **-es Rohr** bulged tube (boilers)

eingedrungenes Gestein intrusive rock

eingeeist ice-bound

eingeengt local, confined, compressed, cramped **-er Kanal** *m* throttled passage

eingefahren-e Antenne retracted, drawn-in, or reeled in antenna **-es Fahrwerk** retracted landing gear

eingefangen trapped

eingefedert closed (as a compensator jack), compressed (said of shock absorber)

eingefressene Isolation burnt insulation

eingefroren latent, dormant

eingefügt inserted

eingeführte Kohle imported coal

eingegangen incurred, agreed, arrived, entered, decayed, perished

eingegossen cast integral, fused

eingehalster Boden boiler end flanged inward

eingehängter Heizkörper floating calandria

eingehen to shrink, come to hand, come in, cease, enter (obligations), agree, contract, perish **auf etwas näher ~** to consider something more in detail **in eine Formel ~** to enter into a formula **in eine Gleichung ~** to enter into, occur, or appear in an equation **in ganze Zahlen ~** to yield integers

Eingehen *n* shrinkage **~ der Niete bei Abkühlung** contraction of cooling rivet

eingehend incoming, detailed, full, through, exhaustive **~ behandeln** (in einem Aufsatz) to deal descriptively with **~ prüfen** to scrutinize

eingehülltes Plutonium covered plutonium foil

eingehülster Detektor covered foil detector

eingekapselt encased, encapsulated

eingekerbt incised, notched, nicked

eingekittete Linse cemented lens

eingeklemmt fastened, clamped, pinched **-er Quarz** clamped crystal

eingeklinkt engaged, latched

(ein)geknickt cracked

eingekoppelt coupled in

eingekuppelt in mesh (engaged)

eingelagert embedded

eingelassen inserted, embedded, inset; (in die Wand) flush mounted **-es Querruder** ailerons inset from wing tips **-er Schalter** flush-type switch **-e Schraube** countersunk screw **-er Zapfen** gudgeon

eingelaufen (Motor) broken in

eingeleitete Energie energy input

eingelötet soldered, solder-mounted (crystal)

Eingemeindung *f* annexation

eingemietete Schnitzel siloed pulp

eingenommener Raum space occupied

eingepaßt fitted **eng ~** fit snugly **-e Schraube** fitted or reamed bolt **-er Teil** *m* component part

eingepflastertes Geleise track set in paving

eingeprägt-er Gleichstrom load-independent d-c,

impressed d-c **-er Stoß** applied shock
eingerastet notched-in, tuned in (specially)
eingeräumt conceded
eingereicht handed in, presented, filed (patent)
eingerichtet installed, fitted, laid (artil.), unidirectional
eingeritzte Marke scribed line or mark, scratch-mark
eingerückt introduced (into), inserted (advertisement), locked (mach.), inducted (mil.), in gear, engaged
eingerüstiges Walzwerk single-stand mill
eingerüttelt vibrated
eingesackt sacked
eingesägt serrated
eingesandet embedded (mooring sinker)
eingesäuertes Schnitzel siloed pulp
eingeschabt, aufeinander ~ scraped to fit each other
eingeschaltet closed, in action, in operation (elec.) **~ sein** to be in or connected (elec.) **~ werden** to come into circuit **ein Meßgerät ~ lassen** to leave an instrument on **-e Regelung** connected control **-er Verstärker** through-line repeater (permantly connected in circuit)
eingeschlagen (von aufeinander arbeitenden Teilen) pounded; (Maschinennummer) stamped
eingeschliffen ground **-e Hohlkehle** hollow-ground edge
eingeschlossen enclosed, housed **~** (Flüssigkeiten, Luftblasen) trapped (liquids, air bubbles) **-es Gas** occluded gas **-e Produktion** closed-in production **-er Wasserstoff** occluded hydrogen
eingeschnitten serrated
eingeschnürt necked-down **-e Gassäule** pinched gas **-er Teil** necked-down portion
eingeschurrt enclosed in chute
eingeschüttet thrown into **~ angeschweißtes Material** weld metal
eingeschoben interposed
eingeschraubt screwed in
eingeschrieben registered, inscribed **-er Brief** registered letter **-er Brief mit Rückschein** registered letter with advice of delivery
eingeschrumpft, warm ~ pressed and shrunk (into) (aviation)
eingeschwenkt swung up **im -em Zustand** in swung-in position
eingeschwungener Strom steady-state current **~ Zustand** steady state (of current, oscillation, etc.)
eingesetzt inserted **-er Kurbelzapfen** inserted crankpin **-es Messer** inserted blade **-es Paßstück** *n* inserted adapter **-er Zahn beim Rad** cog **-er Zapfen** gudgeon pin **-e Zylinderlaufbüchse** *f* cylinder liner
eingespannt with fixed ends, held, cantilever (airplane construction), fully restrained, fixed **-er Balken** pinended or fixed beam, beam restrained at one end **-er Freiträger** clamped cantilever
eingesprengt interspersed (by sprinkling), disseminated
eingestehen to confess, admit
eingestellt fixed, cropped up, turned up, appeared, adjusted, stopped **nicht mehr richtig ~** out of adjustment **zeitweilig ~** temporarily suspended **-er Schwimmer** adjustable float
eingestrahltes Licht incident or exciting light
eingestreut thrown in
eingestrichene Oktave one-stroked octave
eingetaucht immerged **-er Körper** immersed or submerged body or object
eingeteilt classified, classed, subdivided, divided
eingetragen registered, licensed, certified
eingewalzt expanded into
eingewanderte Schicht *f* diffused layer (trans.)
eingewaschener Boden hydraulic fill
eingewurzelt rooted, inveterate
eingezahltes Kapital paid-in or paid-up capital
eingezogen retracted, drawn in **-es Fahrgestell** retracted undercarriage **-e Marginalien** cut-in marginal zones **-e Röhre** casing with inserted joints
eingießen to cast integral, pour in
Eingießer *m* ladle pourer
Eingießung *f* pouring in, infusion, transfusion
Eingitterröhre *f* single-grid tube or valve, triode, three-electrode tube
Eingeleisebahn *f* single-track railroad
eingleisig monorail, single-track
eingliederige Zahlengröße monomial
eingliedern to assign, incorporate, make a part of, classify
Eingliederung *f* assignment, incorporation, organic arrangement, classification
eingraben to inter, hide, burrow, sink, entrench **sich ~** to dig in
Eingrabetiefe *f* burying depth
eingravieren to engrave
eingreifen (Anker) to catch; (Technik) engage; (Getriebe) gear into, mesh, mate; (vermittelnd) intervene; (störend) interfere; force, interlock, act, take a hand in, come to the aid of **in ein Gespräch ~** to enter, interfere in, or interrupt a conversation
Eingreifen *n* gearing, mating, intervention, interference **~ der Greifer** in-and-out movement or engagement of claws **~ von Zahnrädern** gearing in or enlargement
eingreifend in gear, engaged (mach.)
eingrenzen to locate, localize
Eingrenzen *n*, **Eingrenzung** *f* localization, location **~ von Fehlern** tracking down seat or source of interference or trouble, localization of trouble
Eingrenzung *f* (von Fehlern) sectionalization
Eingrenzungs-messung *f* localization test **-verfahren** *n* location method
Eingriff *m* gearing, mesh, (Zahnrad) engagement, catch, contact, meshing, (chemical) action **~ (unbefugter) bei Maschinen** tampering of unauthorized persons **außer ~** clear (teleph.) **in ~ bleiben** to remain in gear **außer ~ bringen** to throw out of gear **in ~ bringen** to throw into gear **außer ~ kommen** to disengage (motor) **in ~ bringen** to force into engagement **zum ~ kommen** to bind (motor) **in ~ stehen** to gear, mesh, be in gear, engage, mate
Eingriff-abstimmung *f* one-knob tuning **-bedienung der drei Abstimmkreise** three-tuning-bands reception
Eingriffe des Sees marine encroachment
Eingriffs-bereich *n* zone of contact **-bogen** *m* arc of contact **-dauer** *f* period of contact or of

engagement
Eingriffsfläche *f* zone of contact ~ **eines Zahnradzahnes** working face of the tooth of a gear
Eingriffs-funktion *f* influencing function **-länge** *f* angle of action of gear **-linie** *f* (Zahnrad) line of action, line or path of contact, pressure line
Eingriffs-signal *n* instruction signal **-spulenwechsel** *m* one-knob-coil adjustment or tuning **-strecke** *f* working depth **-tiefe** *f* depth of engagement of gear
Eingriffswinkel *m* angle of action, angle of mesh, pressure angle (metal.) ~ **der Zahnflanke** pressure, obliquity, or generating angle of gear-tooth profile
Eingriffs-wirkung *f* engaging (gear) action **-zahn** *m* entering gear tooth **-zirkel** *m* depthing tool
Eingruppenmodell *n* one-group model
Einguck *m* inspection hole
Einguß *m* mold, ingot, infusion, pouring in, gate (hopper), pour (in founding), (pouring) gate, runner, running, sprue, feeder, basin **-abschneider** *m* git or sprue cutter **-kanal** *m* downgate, ingress or inlet gate, runner, runner gate, sprue **-kappe** *f* filler cap **-lauf** *m* downgate, ingress or inlet gate, ingate, runner, runner gate, sprue **-loch** *n* sprue hole or opening **-mündung** *f* pouring or sprue-opening gate
Einguß-öffnung *f* pouring-in hole **-rohr** *n* central gate **-schnauze** *f* charging spout **-sieb** *n* inlet strainer **-stelle** *f* gate **-stock** *m* gate or runner stick **-stutzen** *m* inlet connecting branch or tube, filler tube **-sumpf** *m* runner or pouring basin **-trichter** *m* gate, pouring or ingress gate, funnel, sprue opening, downgate, runner, sprue, git, ingate, runner gate or trumpet **-tümpel** *m* pouring or flood basin **-verschlußbolzen** *m* sprue lock pin
einhacken to cut up or in, chop up, roughen
einhägen to fence in, enclose, suspend
einhaken to hook (to), hitch, clasp, clench, engage
Einhalsung *f* inward flange
Einhalt *m* stop, arrest ~ **tun** to stop, check, suppress, restrain, arrest
Einhaltbefehl *m* injunction, interdict
Einhalteaugenblick *m* moment of stop
einhalten to adhere to (directions), preserve, check, restrain, stop, stick, keep (promise), match, meet, follow (course)
einhämmern to draw in by hammering
Einhand-bedienung *f* one-hand operation **-brenner** *m* one-hand burner
Einhänge-befestigung *f* suspension fastening **-blende** *f* inset diaphragm **-bügel** *m* clevis hook **-deckelring** (Breitstrahler) suspended cover ring (broad beam lamp) **-gewicht** *n* set-up weight **-maschine** *f* wrapping machine, casing-in machine
einhängen to replace, restore (the receiver), clear, hang, send, case in; (Telef.) clear the line; (in eine Lösung) to suspend
Einhängen *n* replacement, restoring, clearing ~ **des Hörers** hanging up or replacing telephone receiver
Einhänger *m* riser pipe (in drainage well), back joiner (bookbinding)
Einhängestück *n* swivel
Einhärtbarkeit *f* potential hardness increase
Einhärtetiefe *f* hardening depth
einhauen, ein Loch in Stein ~ to sink a hole in stone
Einhauen *n* ragging (roll surface)
Einhebel-schaltung für Tischvorschübe directional single-lever control of table feed **-schlitzsteuerung** *f* single lever slot control **-schnellschalteinrichtung** *f* single-lever quick-action control **-steuerung** *f* single-lever control
einheben, die Form ~ to lay on form (print.) to put the form (in the press)
einheften to stitch in, file
Einheftkante des Blattes binding edge of the sheet
einhegen to fence
einheimisch domestic, native, homemade, interior ~ **machen** to acclimatize **-es Erz** native ore
Einheimischer *m* native
Einheit *f* unit, unity, standard, integral part **abgeleitete** ~ derived unit **elektromagnetische** ~ electromagnetic unit **elektrostatische** ~ electrostatic unit ~ **für sich** self-contained subunit **zu einer geschlossenen** ~ **machen** to incorporate ~ **des Atomgewichts** atomic weight unit ~ **der Lichtintensität** unit light intensity **eine** ~ **der Masse** *f* slug
Einheit-bedienungsgerät *n* operation unit, supply and auxiliary circuit **-betriebsstoffverbrauch** *m* fuel consumption per unit horsepower-hour
Einheiten-einsatz *m* unit rack stop bar **-fläche** *f* unit area
Einheitenform *f* multi-cavity die (die-casting) ~ **mit mehreren Formhohlräumen** nest die (die-casting)
Einheiten-länge *f* unit lenght **-rand** *m* unit border **skala** *f* unit indicator **-system** *n* system of units **-widerstand** *m* unit rack stop
einheitlich uniform, homogeneous **-e Beschleunigung** uniform acceleration **-er Datenträger** common information carrier **eine -ere Streuung der Ergebnisse** a better standard deviation
Einheitlichkeit *f* uniformity, homogeneity
Einheits-bauart *f* standard type (construction) **-bedienungsgerät** *n* supply and auxiliary circuit panel (radio) **-belastung** *f* basic load **-betriebstoffverbrauch** *m* fuel consumption per unit horsepower-hour, specific fuel consumption **-bohrung** *f* basic hole, standard bore, unit-bore system **-code** *m* equal length multi-unit code (tra.) **-diagramm** *n* unit diagram **-drehbank** *f* standard lathe **-element** *n* unit element **-empfindlichkeit** *f* unit sensitivity **-erzeugung** *f* standardized production
Einheits-fläche *f* unit form **-flächenwinkel** *m* steradian **-flanschverbindung** *f* unit flange connection **-flugmotor** *m* general-purpose aero engine **-form** *f* unit form **-frequenz** *f* standard frequency **-funktion** *f* unit function **-gestänge** *n* combination rods **-gestell** *n* unit rack **-gewicht** *n* weight (of engine per horsepower), specific gravity **-gewinde** *n* standard thread
Einheits-gitter *n* unit lattice **-grund** *m* single undercoater **-induktivität** *f* unit inductance **-kanister** *m* standard gasoline container, unit container **-klassifikation** *f* unified system of filing **-klemme** *f* universal rail anchor **-koeffizient der Tidehöhe eines Hafens** semirange of

the tide at a port, on a day of mean equinoctial springs **-kondensator** *m* standard condenser (or capacitor) **-kostenvergleich** *m* unit cost comparison

Einheits-kraftverbrauch *m* specific fuel consumption **-kreis** *m* circle of unit radius **-kugel** *f* unit sphere **-kupplung** *f* standard coupling, standard clutch **-ladung** *f* unit charge **-luftdichte** *f* standard density of air **-maß** *n* unit of measurement **-öle** *pl* standardized oil types **-pol** *m* (magnetischer) unit (magnetic) pole **-preis** *m* unit or standard price **-prinzip** *n* unit principle **-prozess** *m* unit process **-punkt** *m* unit or principal point

Einheits-querschnitt *m* unit section or area of section **-rahmen für die Gurtfüllmaschine** frame for belt-loading machine **-relais** *n* universal relay **-scheibe** *f* standard target **-schlüssel** *m* special wrench **-schnurpaar** *n* universal cord pair **-schrank** *m* unit cubicle **-sieb** *n* standard sieve **-spin** *m* unit spin **-sprung** *m* unit step **-stoß** *m* constant impact **-tensor** *m* unit (or identify) tensor **-transformation** *f* unit transformation **-typ** *m* standard type

Einheits-vektor der Polarisation polarization unit vector **-verstärker** *m* standard or basic repeater unit **-volumen** *n* unit volume **-welle** *f* basic shaft, unit shaft system **-wert** *m* unit value **-wurzeln** *pl* cubic roots **-zeit** *f* legal or uniform time, standard time **-zeitzone** *f* standard-time zone **-zelle** *f* unit or elementary cell, unit crystal, lattice unit **-zone** *f* standard-time zone **-zünder** *m* combination or standard fuse

einheizen to heat (fire)

einhellig unanimous

einherdiger Ofen single-hearth furnace

Einhiebverfahren *n* impact-hardness or dynamic-hardness test

einhieven to heave (short), heave in cable

einhobeln to cut the nick

einhöckrig one-lobed

einholen to haul in or down, overtake, catch up with, collect, bring in

Einholen des Luftschiffes towing or recovery of the airship

Einholmbauart *f* single-spar type

einholmig monospar

Einhordendarre *f* one-floored kiln

ein-hordig one-floored **-hörig** monaural **-hüftig** with one post

Einhüllbedingung *f* condition of envelopping

einhüllen to encase, envelop, coat, enwrap, cover, shroud, sheathe

Einhüllende *f* envelope, contour, outline

Einhülsen *n* canning

einige several, few, some

einigen to unite, agree, come to terms

einigermaßen to or in some degree

Einigung *f* agreement, settlement, understanding

einimpfen to inoculate, vaccinate

Einjustierung *f* system line-ups

einkalken to treat in lime, soak in lime water

Einkammer-apparat *m* single chamber machine **-bremse** *f* one-chamber brake **-bremsverstärker** *m* single-chamber brake energizer **-druckluftbremsventil** *n* single-chamber pneumatic brake valve **-sandstrahlapparat** *m* single-compartment sandblast-tank machine **-trockner** *m* single chamber drying apparatus **-vakuumfüller** *m* single chamber vacuum filler

Einkanal *m* single channel (teleph.) **-analysator** *m* single-channel analyser **-diskriminatoreinschub** *m* plug-in single-channel discriminator **-einseitenbandgerät** *n* single-channel single-side-band equipment **-spectrometer** *m* single-channel spectrometer **-tastung** *f* single-channel pulsing (television) **-übertragung** *f* single-channel transmission **-verfahren** *n* single-channel method

Einkapselmikrophon *n* single-button carbon microphone

einkapseln to encase, enclose, cover

Einkapselung *f* casing

einkarren to cart

einkassieren to collect money

einkaufen to buy, purchase

Einkäufer *m* purchasing executive, buyer

Einkaufs-abteilung *f* purchasing department **-büro** *n* procurement service agency **-direktor** *m* purchasing manager **-preis** *m* purchase price

einkehlen to groove, provide with a gutter, channel, chamfer, flute

einkeilen to (in)dent, nick, groove, notch, wedge, quoin

einkellern to lay in

Einkerbbiegeversuch *m* notched-bar bending test

einkerben to notch, indent, nick, jog, roughen; (Walzen) to score, pit

Einkerben *n* notch(ing), indent(ing), nicking, ragging, roughening, indentation, groove

Einkerbung *f* indent, gagger, notching, nick, indentation, denting

Einkerbungswerkzeug *n* indenting tool

einkernig mononuclear, single-cored

Einkessel single-enclosure (multipolar switch) **-schalter** *m* single **-tank** *m* switch or circuit breaker

einkippen to level, put, pour, dump in

Einkipptrieb *m* elevating mechanism (trench mortar), leveling mechanism

einkitten to putty, to cement

einklagbar actionable

einklammern to include in parentheses

Einklang *m* harmony, syntony, agreement, unison, lead, consonance, concord, accord **in ~ bringen** to reconcile **in ~ sein** to agree

einklappbar swinging, folding, hinged

einklappen to turn (swing) in, retract, index (into position)

einklarieren to clear in

Einklarierung *f* clearance inward, entry, bill of entry

einkleben to glue in

einkleiden to coat (chem.)

einklemmen, sich ~ to get, pinch, squeeze, clamp

Einklemmen *n* fastening

einklinken to throw in, fall in, fall into a notch, latch, clench, catch, lock, engage (in a catch)

Einklink-feder *f* click spring **-haken** *m* notch hook

Einknallverfahren *n* sound-ranging method of fixing position of microphones (radio)

einknicken to fold, bend in

Einknopf-abstimmung *f*, **-bedienung** *f* single-dial, single-control, or single-span tuning, single-

knob controlling **-kontrolle** *f* uniselector, unicontrol **-steuerung** *f* single push-button control
einknotig single-noded
einknüpfen to knot (tie)
einkochen to boil down, evaporate, concentrate
Einkolben-handschmierpumpe *f* single-piston hand-operated oil pump **-pumpe** *f* single plunger pump **-schmierpumpe** *f* single-plunger lubricating pump **-verteilerpumpe** *f* single-plunger districutor pump
Einkommen *n* income **-steuer** *f* income tax
einkomponenter Schreiber yawing gauge of gyropendulum type
Einkontakt *m* single-contact **-einfeldregler** *m* single-contact onefield regulator **-zweifeldregler** *m* single-contact twofield regulator
einkopieren to overprint, double print
Einkoppel-sonde *f* exciting probe (meas.) **-strecke** *f* buncher space
Einkorbbetrieb *m* singe cage operation
Einkreisel-anordnung *f* single-gyro system **-kompaß** *m* monogyrocompass, single gyrocompass
Einkreis-empfang *m* single-circuit or primary reception **-empfänger** *m* single-circuit or primary receiver, one-circuit set, ultraaudion
einkreisen to envelop, surround, encircle, invest
Einkreiser *m* single-circuit receiver, one-circuit set
einkreisiges Kristallgoniometer crystal goniometer with one circle
Ein- oder Zweikreisgoniometer *n* one- or two-circle goniometer
Einkreistriftröhre *f* single-circuit drift tube
Einkreisung *f* encirclement
Einkristall *m* single crystal, monocrystal **-faden** *m* single-crystal or monocrystal filament **-oberflächen** *pl* single crystal surfaces **-proben** *f pl* single crystal specimens **-züchtung** *f* single-crystal growth
Einkünfte *pl* revenue
einkuppeln to entrain, throw in gear, clutch, couple
Einkurbel-dampfmaschine *f* single-crank steam engine **-verbunddampfmaschine** *f* single-crank compound steam engine
Einkurven-regler *m* single-point recording controller **-schreiber** *m* single-point curve-drawing recorder
einladen to invite, load, entrain, entruck
Einladen *n* loading
Einladeübersicht *f* entraining or entrucking table or survey
Einlage *f* enclosure, charge, filler, deposit, liner, lining, inlay, center, insertion, insert, printing frame (photo.), dark slide for camera insertion
Einlagen (aus gesintertem Hartmetall) inserts (from cemented carbide)
Einlagenschalter *m* limit switch
Einlageripper *m* filler stripper (tobacco)
einlagern to encase, embed, store up, incorporate
Einlagerohr *n* liner (in gun barrel)
Einlagerung *f* embedment, cushioning, occlusion, inclusion, storage, warehousing, incorporation, quartering (mil.) **kurzzeitige ~** short-time storage
Einlagerungs-fremdatom *n* interstitial impurity (atom) **-rate** *f* rate of incorporation (cryst.) **-verbindung** *f* intercalation compound
einlagige Spule single-layer coil
Einlaß *m* entrance, inlet, admission **-bauwerk** *n* intake (structure) **-bohrung** *f* intake well **-drallkanal** *m* helical inlet port **-druck** *m* admission or intake pressure
einlassen to admit, let in, lower, mortise, sink or trim in, embed **sich ~** (in) to engage (in), enter (into a discussion), be connected (with)
Einlassen *n* running, running in (tools, casing), admission (to), engagement (in)
Einlaß-ende *n* feeding end **-farbe** (Antikleder) graining color **-feld** *n* inlet limit **-fläche** inlet face **-führung** *f* receiving guide **-führungskanal** *m* intake header **-galgen** *m* cross-bar **-gestänge** *n* admission gear, suction rods **-hebel** *m* inlet-cam roller lever **-hub** *m* induction stroke **-kanal** *m* intake tube, inlet port **-kante** *f* admission edge (slide valves), inlet edge
Einlaß-karte *f* ticket **-kegel** *m* admission-valve cone **-kette** *f* lowering chain **-kopf** *m* multiple inlet head **-lagernde** *n* bushed inlet end **-leitschaufel** *f* air-intake guide vane (jet) **-leitung** *f* inlet piping, manifold (inlet), induction system **-nocken** *m* inlet or admission cam
Einlaßöffnung *f* admission port, inlet port or opening, intake, inlet **~ für Öl** oil inlet
Einlaß-organe inlet valves **-periode** *f* period of admission
Einlaßrohr *n* admission, inlet, or supply pipe **-leitung** *f* suction piping
Einlaß-scheibe *f* admission cam (gas and oil engines) **-schieber** *m* inlet sliding plug **-schlitz** *m* scavenging or inlet port, admission aperture or port (engines) **-seite** *f* inlet or induction side, left side of engine **-seitige Zündkerze** inlet plug **-sonde** *f* input well **-steuerung** *f* admission gear, inlet governor **-steuerwelle** *f* inlet camshaft **-stück** *n* insert
Einlaßstutzen *m*, **~ des Kühlers** air-intake casing (jet), water inlet of radiator
Einlaßtuch *n* feeding cloth
Einlaß- und Auslaßtemperatur *f* inlet and outlet temperatures
Einlaßventil *n* inlet or intake valve, supply valve **~ für Luft** air-intake valve
Einlaßventil-kammer *f* intake-valve chamber **-keil** *m* inlet-valve cotter **-rolle** *f* admission-valve roller **-spindel** *m* inlet-valve stem **-stange** *f* admission-valve rod **-verbindungshebel** *m* inlet-cam roller lever **-verschraubung** *f* inlet-valve cap **-winkel** *m* angle of admission or inlet of the steam (turbines)
Einlaßwalze *f* feeding roller
Einlauf inlet, influx, intake (for steam, water), culvert, convergence, entrance, running in, green run, feed side; (v. Motoren) inlet, intake, run-in **~ einer Schleuderpumpe** eye or inlet (of a centrifuge or compressor)
Einlauf-armatur *f* inflow fittings **-bauwerk** *n* intake structure **-bohrung** *f* intake **-büchse** *f* inlet box **-düse** *f* eye or inlet (of a centrifuge, compressor, etc.)
einlaufen to shrink, contract, enter, arrive, run in, flow in **~ lassen** to let run in, run in **den Motor ~ lassen** to let the motor run itself in
Einlaufen *n* (Verschleiß) settling down **durch ~ entstandene Oberflächenbeschaffenheit** running-

in surface finish
einlaufend running in, incoming **-e Felder** incoming fields **-e Kugelwelle** incoming spherical wave
Einlaufgitter *n* trash rack
einläufig single-barreled, unicursal, single-tracked, single-channeled
Einlauf-kanal *m* culvert **-leitkranz** *m* air intake casing (rocket) **-leitschaufel** *f* intake stator (jet) **-protokoll** *n* running-in test log sheet **-punkt auf die Rolle** point where film is fed onto drum **-rille** *f* starting groove (phono.), lead-in spiral (phono.), lead-in groove (record disc) **-rinne** *f* gate or gullet (for pouring metal) **-rohr** *n* inlet or supply pipe
Einlauf-schacht *m* sump **-schlacke** *f* melt-down slag **-schnecke** *f* feed worm **-seiher** *m* inlet strainer **-seite** *f* feed or threading end (motion pictures), entry side, entry end **-steckseiher** *m* inlet strainer for insertion
Einlaufstelle *f*, **engste ~** throat (of container or pipe)
Einlauf-stutzen *m* intake, intake branch **-trichter** *m* feed or mill hopper, intake, inflow funnel **-trompete** *f* (Schalltrichter) bellmouth **-vorgang** *m* bedding-in process, running in **-widerstand** *m* intake drag (aerodyn.) **-zeit** *f* running-in time
Einlege-arbeit *f* inlaid work **-block** *m* snatch block **-kamm** *m* threading comb **-kassette** *f* slide-in plateholder
Einlege-keil *m* inserting quoin, laid-in key, round-ended taper-sunk key **~ mit runden Enden** round-ended sunk key
einlegen to insert, put in, embed, secure, fit, enchase, load **Berufung ~** to lodge or take an appeal **Film ~** to thread up the film **Platten in Kassetten ~** to charge the magazine (phot.), load the dark slides
Einlegen des Bandes tape loading **~ des Films** threading of the film
Einleger *m* inserter, layer-on, feeder (print.) **regulärer ~** plain feed table
Einlege-rähmchen *n* small insertion frame **-rahmen** *m* plate carrier **-rohr** *n* subcaliber barrel, liner (artil.) **-scheibe** *f* washer **-schlauch** *m* laid-in float **-schranke** *f* rod barrier **-sohle** *f* insole **-stücke** *pl* adjusting strips or wedges **-tisch** *m* feed board **-vorbau** *m* the charging bay of a glass tank
einlegiert alloyed
Einlegung *f* insertion
einleimen to glue in
einleiten to pass or lead in, feed into, conduct in, start, open, commence, induce, initiate, introduce
einleitend incipient **-er Schritt** initiative
Einleiter-antenne *f* single-wire antenna **-faltdipol** *m* simple folded dipole **-kabel** *n* single or simple cable (one conductor only)
Einleitung *f* initiation, originating, incipient (explosives), prelude, introduction
Einleitung(s)formel zur Beschreibung preamble of specification
Einleitungs-rippe *f* end or root rib **-spant** *n* end bulkhead
einlenken to guide into path or into line of sight
Einlenk-kondensator *m* inflector **-programm** *n* formula for guidance into line of sight, guided missiles **-rechengerät** *n* vectoring computer **-rechner** *m* computer for guidance into line of sight
Einlesen *n* reading-in
einliefern to deliver
Einlinien-Schaltbild *n* one-line diagram
Einlinsen-dach *n* single-blister roof **-objektiv** *n* single-lens objective
Einloch-befestigung *f* one-hole or single hole mounting **-düse** *f* single-hole nozzle, one-hole nozzle (single jet injection)
einlochen, einen Zapfen ~ to mortise a tenon
einlösbar negotiable
einlösen to redeem **einen Wechsel ~** to honor a draft
einloten to plumb-line, try with the plummet, plumb
einlöten to solder (in) **in eine Ausdrehung ~** to solder into a turned groove
Einlötstück *n* soldered member
einlullen to drop (of wind)
einmachen to knead (dough), preserve (fruit)
Einmachtechnik *f* canning technology
einmaischen to mash, mix, dough in
einmal once, at one time, at one pass **auf ~** suddenly, all at once
Einmaleinskörper *m* multiplier
einmalig single, solitary, unique, happening but once, non-recurrent, non-repetitive **-e Abfindung** lump-sum payment **-er Vorgang** non-recurrent, unique, or singular action or phenomenon, single event
Einmalschmelzerei *f* refinery
Einmann-lochwerk *n* single-operator punching machine **-telegraph** *m* single-operator telegraph (instrument)
einmaschieren to march in, enter
Einmastantenne *f* single-tower antenna
einmauern to brick (up), embed, wall up or in
Einmauerung *f* immuration, embedding
einmengen to intermix, intermingle, interfere (with)
einmessen to locate (a point) by surveying
Einmesser-schnelldreischneider *m* rapid three-side trimmer with one knife only
einmieten to clamp, silo
einmischen to mix, intermix, blend **sich ~** to interfere, meddle with
Einmischung *f* interference, intervention
einmitten to center, adjust (lens)
Einmitten *n* centering
einmontiert, fertig ~ ready fitted
Einmotoren *pl* built-in motors
einmotorig single-engined
einmünden to flow, empty, or discharge (into)
Einmündung *f* side-road crossing, mouth of river, estuary, lake basin
Einnadel-telegraph *m* single-needle telegraph **-rose** *f* single-needle compass rose or card
Einnahme *f* receipt, reception, acceptance, capture, occupation, seizure **-schein** *m* receipt
Einnahmen aus Beteiligungen proceeds from investments
einnebeln to surround with or lay a smoke screen, blanket **sich ~** to put up a smoke screen
einnehmen to receive, take in, occupy, conquer, capture **für sich ~** to capivate

einnehmend, die Mitte ~ median
Einnietdruckknöpfe *pl* press buttons
einnieten to rivet
einnisten, sich ~ to settle into place, nest
Einniveauformel *f* single level formula
Einnivellieren von Punkten taking the levels of points
ein- oder ausatmen to inspire, expire, breathe
ein- oder zweireihig in one or two rows
einölen to oil
einordnen to classify, file, arrange in columns
Einordnungsstellung *f* position of grating resulting in a one-order spectrum
einpacken to pack, pack up, wrap up
Einpackstelle *f* packing point
einparametrische Familienscharen one-parameter family of curves
Einpaß *m* adapting (fitting)
einpassen to adjust, set, fit, adapt, trim in, true
Einpassen *n* truing **~ am Bildkartiergerät** machine setting of photographs
Einpaß-größen *pl* fits, tolerances (geom.) **-rohr** *n* register tube **-stelle** *f* fitting-in place **-verfahren** *n* method of adjustment, setting (on points of control) **-zugabe** *f* margin of manufacture
Einpegelung *f* leveling, level adjustment
einpeilen to take a radio bearing, locate (by direction finder) **~ Funksender mit Richtempfänger** to take bearings from, or tune in, a radio transmitter with directional receiver
Einpendeln *n* hunting
einpfählen to fence or hedge with pales or stakes, palisade
Einpfeifen *n* beat-frequency oscillation
einpfeifen to whistle-in intermediate frequency, backtune (radio)
Einphasen-anlasser *m* single-phase starter **-bahn** *f* single-phase electric railway **-bahnspeiseleitung** *f* single-phase electric-railway power circuit **-bahnstrom** *m* single-phase current for railroad supply **-generator** *m* single-phase generator **-gleichrichter** *m* single-phase rectifier **-induktionsmotor** *m* single-phase induction motor **-lauf** *m* single phasing **-motor** *m* single-phase motor
Einphasen-strom *m* monophase or single-phase current **-stromkleintransformator** *m* small single-phase-current transformer **-stromzähler** *m* single-phase meter **-system** *n* single-phase system (soil mech.) **-transformator** *m* single-phase transformer **-vollwegschaltung** *f* single-phase full-wave connection (elec.) **-wechselstrom** *m* single-phase alternating current **-wechselstrommotor** *m* single-phase alternating-current motor, monophase alternomotor **-zähler** *m* single-phase meter **-zuführung** *f* single phase supply
einphasig single-phase, monophase, one-phase
Einplattentrockenkupplung *f* single-plate dry clutch
einpolig single-pole, unipolar (apparatus) **-e Blitzstörung** unidirectional lightning disturbance **-er Fernhörer** single-pole receiver **-er Schalter (unter Verputz)** one-pole switch **-e Umschaltung** single commutation
Einpolluftleiter *m* Marconi antenna, quarter-wave vertical antenna
einprägen to impress, imprint, emboss (sound track on film)
einpressen to force in, press, compress
Einpressung *f* indentation
Einpreßvorgang *m* pressing operation
Einprismaspektrograph *m* single-prism spectrograph
einpudern to dust, powder
Einpulsverfahren *n* single-pulse or monopulse method (electronics)
einpumpen to pump in, inject
Einpunkt-schreiber *m* single-point recorder **-spatium** *n* one-point space
Einquellempfänger *m* solodyne receiver
einquellen to steep, soak (brewing)
Einradfahrgestell *n* single-wheel undercarriage (sailplane)
einrahmen to border
einrammen to sink by driving, drive in (piles)
Einrammglocke *f* driving socket
einrasten to engage, lock, ram home, snap, shut, catch, register
Einrast-knopf *m* lock knob **-taste** *f* lock-down button
einräumen to furnish, yield, allow, stow away
Einräumung *f* storage, concession, allowance
einrechnen to reckon, include in or take into account, consider
einreffen to reef (a sail), take in a reef
einregeln to regulate, adjust, to time
Einregelschalter *m* single-throw switch (elec.)
Einregelung der Dynamik adjustment of volume range or contrast
Einregelungszeit *f* building up or waxing period (control potential)
einregulieren to adjust, regulate
Einregulieren eines Motors tuning of an engine
Einregulierungsspannung *f* adjusting voltage
Einregulierung *f* adjustment
einreiben to rub in, smear
einreichen to file, hand in, present, petition, apply for
Einreichung *f* submission
einreihen to enroll, align, range, classify
einreihig in one row, single row **-e Nietung** single-row riveting **-es Querlager** (Kugellager) single-row rigidball journal bearing **-es Spannhülsenlager** (Kugellager) single-row rigid-ball journal bearing with taper clamping sleeve **-er Sternmotor** single-row radial engine
Einreihung *f* enrollment, alignment
einreißen to tear, rend, demolish, spread, scratsch (with scriber)
Einreißen *n* tearing
Einreiß-festigkeit *f* tearing strength or resistance **-platte** *f* bursting plate (in intercart hydraulic system, safety device for excessive pressure)
Einrichte-arbeit *f* setting, setup **-kosten** *pl* setting cost
einrichten (Haus) to fit up, fix up, decorate, furnish; (Geschäft) establish, set up, found; (technisch) install, equip; (justieren) adjust; (Maschine) set, to organize, arrange, prepare, set (a broken limb), tool, fit, attach
Einrichten *n* setting up **~ einer Karte** orientation of a map **~ einer Stellung** preparation or improvement of a position **~ einer Werkzeugmaschine** tooling

Einrichter *m* toolsetter, setter, installer, wireman
Einrichterei *f* setting-up department
Einrichtezeit *f* tool-setting or setting-up time
Einrichtung *f* arrangement, organization, set up; (Bauart) design; (Gründung) establishment, setting-up; (technisch) equipment, facilities; (Einstellung) setting; (Anlage) plant, installation; (Vorrichtung) apparatus, appliance, mechanism; furnishing, outfit, facility, appliance, instrument, installation, institution, system, **~ für das Balligverfahren** crowning attachment **~ für Bandvereinigung** sliver doubling attachment **~ für selbsttätige Beschleunigung** automatic speed control **~ zum Eggen** harrow equipment **~ für Höhenatmung** breathing apparatus for stratosphere flying **~ für regelmäßige Prüfungen** automatic routine test equipment **~ eines Teilnehmeranschlusses** installation of a subscriber's telephone **~ für Tonfrequenzfernwahl** voice-frequency selective signaling system **~ für Unterlagerungstelegraphie** composite set **~ für halbindustrielle Versuche** pilot plant **zusätzliche ~** auxiliary attachment **~ zur Störbefreiung** (teleph.) anti-paresitic device
Einrichtungen *pl* facilities
Einrichtungs-gebühr *f* installation charge **-gegenstand** *m* equipment object **-kosten** *pl* establishment charges, equipment costs **-leiter** *m* isolator **-wandler** *m* unidirectional transducer
Einriegelschloß *m* dead lock
Einrinnenofen *m* single-ring-type furnace
Einriemchenhochverzugsstreckwerk *n* single apron high draft system
Einrillentieflochbohrer *m* single lipped rifle deep hole drill
Einriß *m* fissure, flaw (defect), tear
einritzen to scratch, engrave
Einröhren-empfänger *m* single-valve receiver **-gerät** *n* one valve receiving set **-kessel** *m* mono-tube boiler **-kippanordnung** *f* single-tube (deflecting-arrangement) sweep circuit **-verstärker** *m* single-valve (intermediate) repeater, single-relay (intermediate) repeater, single-valve amplifier, one-valve (two-way) repeater
Einrohr-kanal *m* single duct conduit
einrollen to roll
Einrollen *n* curling (of or in paper), rolling up **~ der Leisten** rolling of the selvedges
Einrollen-antrieb *m* single-drum drive **-drahtführer** *m* single-roller wire guide
Einroll-gewebe *f* intermediate **-maschine** *f* loose coiler
einrosten to rust (in)
einrücken to throw in, engage, shift, trip, start, insert, couple, mesh, interlock **einen Gang ~** to put in a gear **~** (der Pumpe) to put in gear
Einrücken *n* starting up, indentation; (einer Kuppelung) engaging, coupling
Einrücker *m* shifter
Einrückgestänge *n* starting gear
Einrückhebel *m* trip(ping) lever, engaging or starting lever **~ zur Reibungskuppelung für das Vorgelege** friction-clutch hand lever **vorgelegter ~** back gear lever
Einrück-klaue *f* engaging claw **-kolben** *m* engaging piston (jet) **-kupplung** *f* engaging clutch **-magnet** *n* start, trip or trigger magnet **-magnetschalter** *m* starting magnetic switch
Einrückung *f* engagement, shifting, insertion, connection, starting, setting in operation
Einrück-vorrichtung *f* coupling or engaging gear, starter device **-welle** *f* starting shaft
einruderig single-banking
einrühren to stir in or up
Einrumpfflugzeug *n* single-fuselage plane
Einrüstung *f* arrangement, fittings
Einsackelevator *m* sacking elevator
einsacken to bag
Einsacken *n* bagging
Einsacker *m* bagger
Einsack-plattform *f* bagging platform **-trichter** *m* bagging hopper
Einsackung *f* slump
Einsalzen der Felle salting the hides
Einsattlung *f* crevasse or dip (of a resonance or other curve), peak-to-valley ratio (TV)
Einsatz *m* (Gefäß) insert; (Metall) charge; (Anteil) share; (Verwendung) application, use; (Auftrag) mission; (Anstrengung) effort, intonation (acoustics), onset, incipiency, insertion, inset, initiation, bushing (retainer), assembly (mech.), take-off, stake, charge (of a furnace); cemented zone, extension (pair of compasses), inventory, participation; (Dichtungslabyrinth) shoe; (Kessel) element; (Ofen) charge; (Tiefbohranlage) bushing; (Zylinder) liner
Einsatz, auswechselbarer ~ replaceable inset **bei besonderem ~** on active duty, during special commitment **fester ~** cold charge **~ fliegen** to fly a sortie **~ für getrennt aufgestellte Leuchten** mirror device **im ~ härten** to case-harden **harter ~ der Schwingungen** hard start of oscillations **heißer ~** hot metal **im ~** in action **kalter ~** cold metal, cold iron **~ pro Partie** charge per batch **warmer ~** hot metal **weicher ~ der Schwingungen** gentle or smooth start of oscillations
Einsatz-aggregat *n* operative missile **-anode** *f* insertible anode **-backen** *f pl* false jaws **-bereich** *m* range of application **-besprechung** *f* orders conference, briefing **-blende** *f* interchangeable diaphragm (optics) **-bohrer** *m* drill, bit **-brücke** *f* gap bridge, bridge piece; (Drehkran) gap piece filler block **-brückenbohrvorrichtung** *f* gap piece drilling fixture **-büchse** *f* reducer, taper sleeve **-dauer** *f* charging time **-deckel** *m* inserted cover **-dichte** *f* number of stations satisfactorily operable inside a given wave band
Einsatz-dichtung *f* gasket **-drehstrahl** *m* (f. Stahlhalter) tool holder bit **-effekt** *m* thresold effect (of electr. valves) **-fähig** available for assignment, commitment or employment **-fähigkeit** *f* casehardenability, adaptability **-futter** *n* reduction cone **-gewichte** *pl* set of weights (one fitting inside the other) **-glühofen** *m* case-hardening furnace **-glühung** *f* case annealing **-gut** *n* charging material **-härtbarkeit** *f* carburizing property, case-hardenability, case-hardening property
einsatzhärten to caseharden
Einsatz-härten *n* casehardening, carburizing, cementation, cyaniding **-härter** *m* casehardener
Einsatz-härtung *f* casehardening, surface, partial, or superficial cementation, armorizing **~ durch Aufkohlung** carburization

Einsatz-höhe *f* pile height **-hülse** *f* taper sleeve **-kapsel** *f* transmitter inset or button **-kasten** *m* casehardening box **-klemmen** *pl* joint and junction terminals **-kontrolle** *f* continuity control **-kopf** *m* (bei Ultrathermostat) insert vessel **-körper** *m* brake body **-material** *n* casehardening material

Einsatzmesser *m* Venturi meter ~ (ungeschliffen f. Stahlhalter) blank cutter bit ~ (zum Einsetzen in Stahlhalter) tool holder bit

Einsatz-mittel *n* casehardening compound, cementing medium cement, carburizer **-möglichkeit** *f* operational possibility **-ofen** *m* casehardening or cementation furnace **-öffnung** *f* feeding gate or mouth of a furnace **-plättchen** *n* right raising cam **-platte** *f* intermediary plate **-produkt** *m* charging stock **-pulver** *n* casehardening compound or powder **-pumpe** *f* encasement pump **-punkt** *m* zero of operating range

Einsatz-ring *m* insert ring **-rohr** *n* liner pipe **-röhre** *f* insert tube **-schale** *f* insertion step **-schalter** *m* insert switch **-schicht** *f* hardening layer (metal.) **-schuh** *m* fuse holder (elec.) **-sicherung** *f* pull-out or push-in fuse (elec.) **-spannung** *f* spark or flashover potential, breakdown or starting potential, cutoff voltage, operating voltage **-spulenrahmen** *m* insert coil form **-stahl** carburizing or casehardening steel; (geschl. f. Stahlhalter) cutter bit ground to form **-stangen** *pl* shifting rods **-stück** *n* insert, distance piece

Einsatz-stutzen *m* connecting branch **-tiefe** *f* depth of case **-topf** *m* casehardening, cementing, carburizing, annealing, or packing pot, filter-element container **-tür** *f* charging door **-türschwelle** *f* charging-door sill

Einsatz- und Erweiterungsmöglichkeiten extendible applications

Einsatz- und Vergütungsstähle case hardening and heat treatable steels

Einsatz-verfahren *n* pack-hardening process **-verhältnisse** *n pl* make-up of charge, components of charge **-werkstoff** *m* charge (metal) **-werkzeug** *n* insertable tool **-zirkel** *m* compass with detachable legs **-zylinder** *m* cylinder liner

einsäuern to ensilage

Einsaugdüse *f* suction nozzle

Einsaugemittel *m* absorbent, adsorbent

einsaugen to suck in or up, soak up, draw in, absorb, swallow, imbibe

einsaugend absorbent

Einsaugtakt *m* induction or intake stroke (gas)

Einsaugung *f* aspiration (sucking-in)

Einsaugungsfärbung *f* absorption coloring

Einsäulentrenner *m* single-pillar isolator

Einsäurebottich *m* acid vat

einsäurig monoacid

einschaben to bed (surfaces or brasses) **das Lager ~** to scrape the bearing

einschachteln to put in a box (box)

einschalen to encase

Einschaler *m* form setter

einschalig of one sheet (geom.), univalve **-es Hyperboloid** hyperboloid of one sheet **-er Wecker** single-dome bell

einschaltbar can be introduced

Einschalt-brett *n* starting panel **-blatt** *n* insertion leaf **-dauer** *f* duration of connection (operation), duration of voltage application, duty cycle **-drehzahl** *f* cutting-in speed **-druck** *m* cutting-in pressure **-dynamometer** *n* transmission dynamometer

Einschalteklinke für Abfrageapparate operator's jack (teleph.)

einschalten to connect (in), switch on or in, cut in, insert, plug in, join up, engage, throw on, turn on, interline, interpolate, put into gear, come, cut, put into circuit **nach dem Start ~** switch on after starting **mit Stöpseln ~** to plug in **~ einen Winkel** to subtend an angle **durch Ziehen von Stöpseln ~** to unplug

Einschalten *n* throwing in, engaging, clutching

Einschalter *m* (closing) switch, circuit closer, contactor

Einschalt-hebel *m* starting lever **-knopf** *m* closing push-button **-kreis** *m* closing circuit **-rastung** *f* cut-in notch **-relais** *n* tripping relay, cut-in relay **-relaisstellung** *f* on position **-röhre** *f* contact tube

Einschalt-spannung *f* cut-in tension, cutting-in voltage **-spitze** *f* surge, transient peak **-spitzenstrom** *m* starting current peak **-stellung** *f* on position, closed position **-stoß** *m* cut-in current rush **-strom** *m* inrush current, starting current **-stromstärke** *f* current intensity at make **-stromspitze** *f* switch-on peak **-überströme** *pl* current surge

Einschaltung *f* switching in, interpolation, current rise, word or phrase in parenthesis, introduction, switching-on, insertion ~ (im Text) paraphrase **~ der Spule** re-engagement of the winding unit **~ von Verstärkern bei den Durchgangsfernämtern mit Wahlbetrieb** repeater insertion on automatic long-distance tandem exchanges **selbsttätige ~ von Verstärkern durch Fernwahl der Beamtin** automatic insertion of repeaters with operator dialing

Einschaltungs-dynamometer *m* transmission dynamometer **-zeichen** *n* insertion mark

Einschalt-verzögerungsrelais *n* connection time lag relay **-vorgang** *m* transient, insertion process **-weg** *m* switching travel

einschanzen to dig in, entrench

einschärfen to impress upon

einschätzen to assess (tax), estimate, rate, value

Einschätzung *f* rating, assessment, appreciation **~ basiert auf Instrumenterfahrung** instrument rating **~ gemäß der Pferdekraft** horsepower rating

einschaufeln to shovel into, fill in

Einschauloch *n* inspection hole (aviation)

Einscheibe *f* constant-speed or single pulley

Einscheiben-antrieb *m* single-pulley drive **-drucklager** *m* single-disk thrust bearing **-kupplung** *f* plate clutch, single-disc clutch **-riemenantrieb** *m* single pulley belt drive **-trockenkupplung** *f* single-plate dry clutch

einscheibiger Block single block

einschenkelig with one thigh or arm, single-bar, single-leg

einscheren to mortise, edge into line, reeve

einschichten to embed, arrange in layers, stratify, interleave

Einschicht-film *m* single-layer film **-isolierhülle** *f* one-layer insulating cover **-wicklung** *f* one-layer coiling, single coiling (winding)

einschiebbar (Stativ) extensible, movable **-e Bodentreppe** *f* folding ladder staircase
Einschiebegestänge *n* sweep's rods
einschieben to push in (insert)
Einschieber-motor *m* single-sleeve valve engine **-steuerung** *f* poppet valve
Einschiebstütze *f* transposition bracket
Einschiebschablone *f* dovetail templet
Einschienen-bahn *f* monorailway **-förderbahn** *f* monorail conveyer **-greiferkatze auf Hochbahn** monorail bucket crab running on an overhead track **-hängekatze** *f* monorail traveling crab **-hochbahn** *f* overhead single-rail track **-kran** *m* monorail hoist **-laufbahn** *f* monorail track **-laufkatze** *f* monorail crab
einschienig single-rail **-e Kreuzkopfführung** single-slide bar guides **-e Schwebebahn** monorail track or railway
einschießen to try out, range (of a gun), deposit, to lift a form into the press, pick (shoot in)
Einschießen *n* imposing, interleaving
Einschießvorrichtung *f* interleaving device
einschiffen to embark (passengers)
Einschiffgerät *n* single-ship sweep
einschiffig (building) with one aisle
Einschiffung *f* embarkation
Einschiffungsgebühr *f* loading tax
Einschlag *m* driving in (of a nail), woof (textiles), intermixture, turning circle **-begrenzung** *f* turning limit stop
einschlagen drive in or beat in (nail), wrap (package), begin or work a mine, stave in, (Blitz) to strike (lightning)
Einschlagen *n* pounding (of valve seats), penetration **~ der Ventilsitze** (durch das Hämmern des Ventils) pocketing of valve seats
Einschlag-faden *m* weft **-fassung** *f* folding mount **-gabel** *f* weft fork **-garnspulen** *n* weft winding **-glocke** *f* single-stroke bell
einschlägig respective, appropriate
Einschlag-lupe *f* folding magnifying glass **-maschine** *f* wrapping machinery **-multivibrator** *m* single-shot multivibrator **-papier** *n* packing or wrapping paper **-seide** *f* tram, weft silk **-stelle** *f* striking point, point of burst **-vorrichtung** *f* stamping device **-wecker** *m* single-stroke bell **-winkel der Lenkung** angle of lock
einschlaufen to loop in
einschleichender Reiz *m* accumulating stimulus
Einschleifdorn *m* grinding mandrel
einschleifen to grind, cut, or lap in (valve), loop in (an office), true **~** (in ein Gehäuse) to enclose, incase **~** (Verbindung) to loop (into the connection)
Einschleifen *n* edging and glazing (fitting), grinding, reseating, truing **~ einer Leitung** connecting a line into a telephone circuit **~** (Ventilsitz) lapping-in
einschleifig single-loop (servo)
Einschleif-masse *f* grinding paste **-öl** *n* running-in oil **-paste** *f* grinding compound
Einschleusen *n* charging
Einschleusung *f* damming up, unconditional transfer
Einschleusvorrichtung für Platten air-lock device for plates (electron micros.)
einschließen to enclose, include, surround, embed, occlude, lock or seal in, incorporate, confine (in a borehole), form (an angle), entrap, weld, matrix, to insert in brackets, put-in parentheses
Einschließ-kamm *m* web holder (textiles) **-kehle der Platine** sinker throat
einschließlich including, inclusive of
Einschließ-platine *f* holding down sinker **-stellung** *f* latch clearing position
Einschließung *f* enclosure, housing, occlusion
Einschließungssatz *m* inclusion theorem
Einschliff *m* countersink
Einschluß *m* incorporation, inclusion, occlusion, enclosure, ingredient **-medium** *n* inclusion agent **-röhre** *f* sealed tube
einschmalzen to lubricate with grease
Einschmelzdraht *m* fused-in wire, sealed-in wire
einschmelzen to smelt, melt, seal (glass), seal in (a wire or lead in a tube)
Einschmelzen *n* smelting, melting
Einschmelz-maschine *f* sealing-in machine **-pfanne** *f* melting pan, melter **-probe** *f* melt-down test, first or preliminary test, furnace-control test **-schlacke** *f* first or oxidizing slag, white slag **-sirup** *m* remelt sirup or liquor
Einschmelzstelle *f* seal **~ des Glühfadens** filament seal
Einschmelztiefe *f* depth of fusion
Einschmelzung *f* sealing (elec.)
einschmieren to lubricate, grease, oil, smear **den Motor ~** to slush an engine
einschnappen to snap (in, into), catch, fall in, click
Einschnappfeder *f* catch spring
Einschnecken-plastifikator *m* single-screw plasticizer **-spritzgießmaschine** *f* single screw injection molding machine
Einschneide-apparat *m* cutting apparatus **-fräser** *m* single-lip cutter
einschneiden (einkerben) to notch; (auszacken) indent, diminish, splice in, score, scratch, carve, cut up or in, tap, intersect, take cross bearings, engrave **rückwärts ~** to resect **vorwärts ~** to intersect
Einschneiden *n* intersecting, resecting **~ nach drei Punkten** three-point resection **~ auf Richtungslinie** point determination along an orienting line
Einschneidephotogrammetrie *f* photographic intersection, photogrammetry by intersection
einschneien to snow in or under
Einschnitt *m* cut, notch, groove, kerf, slot, indentation, excavation, incision, recess, mortise, embrasure, porthole, cutoff (spectrum) **~ in der Resonanzkurve eines Quarzes** crevasse in the resonance curve of a quartz **offener ~** open cut **mit Einschnitten versehen** to notch, groove, slot, gash
Einschnittarbeit *f* cutting, cut work
einschnittig (bolt or rivet) in single shear, with single cross section, single lip **-e Abscherung** simple shear **-e Nietung** single-shear riveting
Einschnitts-böschung *f* face of a slope (railway cutting) **-stollen beim Tunnelbau** advance heading (tunneling) **-tiefe** *f* depth of cut
einschnittig single-cut
Einschnurbetrieb *m* single-cord operation (teleph.)

Einschnüreffekt *m* pinch effect
einschnüren to contract in area, narrow down, swage, lace **sich ~** (Zugversuch) to bottle (tensile test)
Einschnürrolle *f* (Förderband) snub pulley
Einschnur-schaltung *f* single cord **-system** *n* single cord (system)
Einschnürung *f* reduction or contraction of area, shrinkage, recess, constriction, nick, chocking, necking, wire-drawing effect, bind-up, waist **~** (Filmeinschnürung) squeezing or compression of film **~ eines Rohres** throat of a pipe **~** (eines Ventilschaftes) necked-down portion of a pipe **mit einer ~ versehen** necked-down portion **~ in eine aufgespaltene Versetzung** constriction of an extended dislocation
Einschnürungs-blende *f* crossover aperture **-effekt** *m* pinch effect (elec.) **-energie** *f* constriction energy **-modell** *n* constriction model **-punkt** *m* crossover (in electron optics) **-querschnitt** *m* cross-sectional area of contraction
einschränken to restrict (to), modify, reduce, prorate
Einschränkung *f* limitation, modification, restraint, restriction, reduction, reservation
Einschränkungsmaßnahme *f* austerity
Einschraubautomat *m* screw-in type circuit breaker
einschrauben to screw in place, screw into, down, or on, thread into
Einschraubende der Stiftschraube threaded end of the stud
Einschraubenklemme *f* single-screw clamp or chuck
Einschraub-gewinde *n* (screw-in) thread **-länge** *f* length of engagement, reach of screw **-maschine** *f* screw driver **-stück** *n* external screw part, adaptor; (Zylinderkopf) pressure relief plug **-stutzen** *m* threaded bushing, threaded socket, screw union **-verschraubung** *f* pipe union **-winkelstutzen** *m* threaded angle connection piece (or socket) **-zapfen** *m* screwed male
einschreiben to register, shrink, inscribe, write (in)
Einschreiben *n* registration, entry
einschrumpfen to shrink, contract, shrivel
Einschrumpfung *f* shrinkage
Einschub *m* sound floor, false ceiling, cabinet rack, slide-in unit **-bauweise** *f* plug-in design **-brett** sound boarding
Einschübe mit Steckverbindung plug-in chassis
Einschub-einheit *f* slide-in or plug-in unit or module or tray **-rückseite** *f* rear of the plug-in units **-steckeinheiten** *pl* plug-in units **-stern** *m* feed star **-system** *n* slide-in tray system
einschüren to compress
Einschuß *m* weft, woof
Einschüsse *pl* (Gas) impurities; (Gestein) inclusions; (kalte) cold shuts
Einschußspule *f* cop (textiles)
einschütten to feed, charge, pour in
Einschütt-kasten *m* feeding box or hopper, feeder pot **-öffnung** *f* charging opening, feeding hole
Einschüttung *f* feeding, charging
einschützig one shuttle
Einschwalben *n* dovetailing
einschwärzen to ink up
Einschwebetrichter *m* lead-in funnel (aviation)
Einschweifung des Sägezahnes gullet of a saw tooth
einschweißen to weld
Einschweißstutzen *m* weld-in flange
einschwenkbar retractable
einschwenken to swing on, pivot **seitlich ~** to pivot sideways, fan out
Einschwimmerflugzeug *n* single-float plane
Einschwingdauer *f* building-up time
einschwingen to build up, turn in (a boat) **~ auf** to resonate to (a wavelength)
Einschwingen *n* building-up (process), reentry oscillation **~ des Schreibimpulses** write transient
Einschwingenbrecher *m* single-toggle jaw crusher
Einschwing-periode *f* transient period **-strom** *m* building-up or transient current
Einschwingung *f* initial transient, natural oscillation, transient oscillation
Einschwing-verhalten *n* transient behaviour, transient response (servo) **-vorgang** *m* building-up transient oscillation or process, transient phenomenon, onset or initiation of impulse, enabling transient **-zeit** *f* building-up time, transient time or period, rise time, time constant of rise **-zustand** *m* transient state
Einschwung *m* undershoot **-vorgang** *m* building-up process
einsehen to look into, inspect, peruse, understand, see
Einseitenband *n* single-side-band (s.s.b., SSB) **-betrieb** *m* single-side-band operation (teleph.) **-empfänger** *m* single-side-band receiver **-gerät** *n* single-side-band unit **-kurzwellensender** *m* SSB short-wave transmitter **-modulation** *f* single-side-band modulation **-senden** *n* single-side-band transmission **-sender** *m* single-side-band transmitter **-system** *n* single-band system **-übertragung** *f* single-side-band transmission **-verzerrung** *f* single side band distortion **-weiterverkehrs-Empfangsanlage** *f* single-side-band longdistance receiving equipment
einseitig one-sided, unilateral, subjective, unidirectional, to one side **~ gerichtete Antenne** unidirectional antenna **~ gerichteter Impuls** unidirectional pulse **~ unendlich ausgedehnter Körper** semi-infinite solid **~ oder in einer Richtung betriebene Leitung** one-way circuit **~ unendliche Spule** semiinfinite coil **~ geschlossener Zylinder** closedend cylinder **~ einstellen** to bias **~ gerichtet** unidirectional **~ glatt** machine-glazed **~ offen** unilaterally open **~ unendlich** semi-infinite **~ vorgespannt** unilaterally biased (of grid, magnet) **~ wirkend** unilateral, unidirectional, bias
einseitig-er Anpressungsdruck single sided (or unilateral) pressure application **-e Appretur** *f* one-side finish **-es Arbeiten** operation to one side **-er Druck** directional pressure **-e Flächen** one-sided surfaces **-e Flottenzirkulation** one-way circulation **-es Gegensprechen** half duplex operation **-e Kehlnahtschweißung** *f* single-fillet weld **-er Kompressor** single-entry compressor
einseitig-er Multivibrator one-shot multivibrator, single-shot multivibrator **-er Rahmen** single-sided rack **-e Ruhelage** side stability **-er**

Scheibenfräser half-side mill -e **Traverse** side arm -er **Umschlag** pressing, thick, tough or tinted cover -er **V-Stoß** single level of butt joint -e **Wirkung** bias

einsenden to remit, submit, forward

einsenken to immerse, plunge, dip (into), sink, countersink

Einsenken *n* (Gesenkfertigung) cold hobbing

Einsenkpressen *n* hot dimpling

Einsenkung *f* depression, crevasse, dip, sinking, fall of a ship's deck ~ **der Scheitellinie** saddle (low part of anticline)

Einsetzband *n* lapp, butt (hinge)

einsetzbare Schneidezunge adjustable cutter

einsetzen (einfügen) to insert; (stiften) institute; (Geld) stake; (in ein Amt) install, appoint; (anwenden) use, employ, apply; (Arbeitskräfte) assign; (Leben) risk, stake; (sich ~) stand up for; (Schmelzgut) charge; (Aufkohlung) carbonize, cement, case-harden, set or put in, include, plane, secure, fix, place in position, carburize, substitute or introduce (a value), start, use **sich für etwas** ~ sponsor **einen Stecker** ~ to insert a plug

Einsetzen *n* charging, setting in, inception, (of metals) casehardening, entering of flood, insertion, substitution, start, onset, carburizing inset (super-fluidity) ~ **von Glas(scheiben)** glazing ~ **der Ionisierung** onset of ionization ~ **und Verkeilen der Glasringe** focusing of prismatic elements of an optic ~ **der Zündung** initiation or incipience of striking or firing **wiederholtes** ~ iteration

Einsetz-kran *m* charging crane **-maschine** *f* charging machine **-mulde** *f* charging bucket **-ring** *m* insert ring **-seite** *f* charging side **-tür** *f* charging door **-wagen** *m* (Konverter) jack car

Einsetzung *f* substitution

Einsetz-vorrichtung *f* charging device (rolling mill) **-zähne** *pl* set teeth

Einsicht *f* insight, perusal, inspection, understanding

einsickern to infiltrate, soak or ooze in

Einsickern *n* filtering, infiltration

Einsickerung *f* infiltration

Einsickerungszeit *f* soaking-in period

einsinken to sink in

Einsinkpunkt *m* sinking point

Einsitz *m* single-seated

Einsitzer *m* single-seater

einsitzig single-seating

Einsitz-regelventil *n* single-set regulating valve **-ventil** *n* single-seat valve

einspaltig single-column

Einspannbacken *pl* chuck or contact jaws

einspannen to chuck, fix, clamp, insert, stretch (in a frame)

Einspannen *n* gripping, chucking, holding, clamping, stretching ~ **der Rundplatten** lock-up the round plates

Einspänner-waage *f* singletree **-wagen** *m* one-horse wagon

Einspann-gehäuse *n* clamping housing **-hacke** *f* chuck jaw, wedge grip **-halter** *m* clamping holder

einspänniger Transportwagen one-horse (hauling) wagon

Einspann-klaue *f* wedge grip, clamping chuck **-klemme** *f* grip, jaw (testing machine) **-konus** *m* clamp cone

Einspannkopf *m* clamp, shackle, gripping or clamping head or chuck, specimen holder, grip ~ **für Biegeversuche** bending-test shackle, gripping device for bending tests, transverse-bending-test shackle ~ **für Gewindeköpfe** specimen holder for screwed test pieces ~ **für Ketten** pulling head for chains ~ **für Stabköpfe** specimen holder for headed test pieces ~ **mit kugelförmigem Widerlager** spherically seated grip holder ~ **für Zugversuche** tension shackle

Einspann-länge *f* length of shank chucked, distance between clamps, span **-moment** *m* fixed-end moment **-querschnitt** *m* fixation-clamping section

Einspannrand, gewellter ~ corrugated suspension means (of loud-speaker cone)

Einspann-schweißvorrichtung *f* clamp welding machine **-stelle** *f* point of support, clamping place, fixing point

Einspannung *f* gripping, clamping, setting, fixing, insertion, restraint (at ends) ~ **der Probe** specimen holder, gripping (clamping) head

Einspannungs-moment *m* (fixed) end moment, moment on the support or on the pin joint **-weise** *f* method of gripping

Einspannvorrichtung *f* jig, gripping or clamping device, shackle, chuck, chucking device ~ **für Druckfedern** gripping device for compression springs ~ **für Handlister** one-horse attachment for walking lister ~ **für Kettenzugversuche** gripping device for testing chains in tension ~ **für Zugfedern** pulling hook for tension springs

Einspann-werkzeug *n* clamping tool **-wirkung** *f* effect of end restraint (e.g., where piling is driven into soil)

einsparen to reduce cost, economize

Einsparung *f* cost reduction, economy, saving

einspeisen (Spannung) to inject ~ **in** to feed into, apply to

Einspeisestelle *f* junction point

Einspeisung *f* feed

einsperren to shut in, imprison, impound

Einspiegeln von . . . imaging of

einspielen to balance, break in, bring to the center, center of its run **sich** ~ to balance out

Einspielen der Libelle leveling, cross-leveling ~ (lassen) **der Libellenblase** centering of the bubble of water level

Einspielfehler *m* centering error

Einspindel-automat *m* single-spindle automatic **-wagenheber** *m* jack screw

Einspitzenlagerung *f* unipivot bearing

einspleißen to splice

Einsprache *f* protest, intercession

einsprengen to sprinkle, intersperse, interstratify, disseminate, burst open

Einsprenger *m* sprinkler

Einsprengling *m* phenocryst.

Einsprengmaschine *f* sprinkling engine

einsprenkeln to intersperse, disseminate

Einspringbereich *m* lock in range

einspringen to jump in, intervene, shrink (of fibers), contract, spring in, reenter (of an angle)

einspringend-e Ecke re-entrant angle **-er Winkel** reentrant

Einspritz *m* jet **-anlasser** *m* engine primer **-ausrüstung** *f* injection equipment **-beginnverstellung** *f* injection timing gear **-dauer** *f* duration of injection **-druck** *m* injection pressure

Einspritzdüse *f* injection nozzle or valve, discharge or fuel-injection nozzle, burner, injector, spray (jet) **elektromagnetisch gesteuerte ~** electromagnetic spray valve

einspritzen to inject, grout

Einspritzen *n*, **Loch zum ~** drill hole for grouting **~ von Anlaßkraftstoff in den Motor** engine priming

Einspritzer *m* injector

Einspritz-folge *f* injection order **-geschwindigkeit** *f* rate of injection, rate of die casting **-hahn** *m* injection cock **-handverstellhebel** *m* injection control hand lever **-kondensator** *m* injection or jet condenser **-kühlung** *f* injection cooling **-loch** *n* grouting hole **-motor** *m* fuel-injection engine **-moment** *m* injection timing **-öffnung** *f* inlet or injection port (for propellants into rocket motor) **-pumpe** *f* injection or priming pump, injector **-pumpenantrieb** *m* injection pump drive **-pumpenantriebswelle** *f* injection pump drive shaft **-pumpenrad** *n* injector-pump wheel

Einspritzpunkt *m* site of injection **Vorrichtung zur Regelung des Einspritzpunktes** injection timing gear (motor, engine)

Einspritz-rohr *n* grouting tube, injection pipe **-röhre** *f* injector pipe **-strahl** *m* injection jet (injection spray) **-system** *n* propellant injector (rocket)

Einspritzung *f* injection, syringing

Einspritz-ventil *n* grouting, atomizer, injection or sprayer valve **-verfahren** *n* combustion method, combustion principle, combustion system **-vergaser** *m* spray or atomizing carburetor **-verzug** *m* injection lag **-vorgang** *m* injection process

Einspritzvorrichtung *f* primer **~ für Öl** oil-injection device

Einspritz-wasser *n* spray water **-wasserzufuhr** *f* water injection **-zeitversteller** *m* injection timing control **-zeitverstellhebel** *m* injection advance lever timing control

Einspruch *m* objection, protest, plea, demurrer; (Widerspruch) plea (jur.), opposition (patent) **~ erheben** to raise an opposition **~ unterstützen** to argue in support of an opposition

Einspruchs-frist *f* opposition period **-material** *n* alleged anticipating matter (patent law) **-verfahren** *n* opposition proceedings

Einsprung *m* (Gewebe) contraction, shrinkage (of fabric)

einspülen (bei Rammen) to jet

Einspulen-transformator *m* autotransformer **-trommel** *f* one-knob coil changing **-wecker** *m* single-coil ringer

einspulig single-coil

einspunden to bung

Einspunkt *m* cross-over point

Einspurbewegung *f* meshing movement

einspuren to mesh (engage) **einen Mast ~** to step a mast

Einspurhebel *m* meshing lever

einspurig single-track (R.R.) **-er Tonstreifen** single-edged variable-width sound track or record

Einspur-magnetschalter *m* meshing magnetic switch **-richtung** *f* meshing direction **-trieb** *m* meshing drive

einstampfen to tamp, ram, stamp down, rod, repulp (paper)

Einstampfen *n* ramming, stamping, reduction (paper)

Einstandentfernungsmesser *m* single-station rangefinder

Einständer-dampfhammer *m* single-frame steam hammer **-exzenterpresse** *f* open-front eccentric press **-hammer** *m* single-frame hammer **-hobelmaschine** *f* open-side planer **-presse** *f* single column press **-schleifmaschine** *f* open-side grinding machine

Einstandspreis *m* cost price

einstäuben to dust, powder

Einstäuben *n* dusting, powdering

Einstaub-kasten *m* dusting box **-mittel** *n* (in molding) parting medium

Einstauchungstiefe *f* depth of penetration

Einstech-bogen *m* tympan sheet (print.) **-arbeiten** *pl* plunge-cutting operations, recessing-off operations

einstechen to groove, puncture, punch, cut in, dig, recess

Einstechen *n* recessing, plunge-cutting

Einstech-innenschleifmaschine *f* plunge-cut internal grinder **-schleifen** *n* plunge-cut grinding **-stahl** *m* nicking, cutting-off, or recessing tool **-tiefe** *f* depth of in-feed **-tiefenskala** *f* depth feed scale **-verfahren** *n* gashing method **-vorrichtung** *f* recessing tool **-vorschub** *m* recessing feed **-vorschubregelung** *f* depth feed control

einsteckbar insertable **-er Bolzen** loose or stop pin

Einsteck-blende *f* slip-in diaphragm **-block** *m* plug-in unit **-bogen** *m* insert sheet

einstecken to insert, slip in, bend or clinch cables; (in e. Gehäuse) to case

Einstecken *n* plugging in, inserting

Einsteck-ende *n* (Bohrer) shank **-fassung** *f* slip-on mount **-griff** *m* removable handle **-hals** *m* inserting neck **-kastenschloß** *n* rim knob lock **-klappe** *f* flap (inserting) **-klebeverbindung** *f* shrunk-on pipe joint **-kupplungsteil** *m* male coupling **-kurbel** *f* inserting crank **-lauf** *m* liner **-loch** *n* flap-slot

Einsteck-maske *f* diaphragm **-pflanzmaschine** *f* runner planter **-reifenluftpumpe** *f* tire inflator assembly **-riegel** *m* mortise knob latch **-riegelschloß** *n* mortise belt **-schaltkarte** *f* plug-in circuit card **-schlitz** *m* slot (inserting) **-schloß** *n* mortise dead lock or bolt **-schlüssel** *m* socket wrench; (doppelseitig) double end socket wrench

Einsteck-seiher *m* plug-in inlet strainer **-seite** *f* roller's side **-sicherung** *f* pull-out or push-in fuse **-sockel** *m* socket (candlestick type) **-spule** *f* plug-in coil **-werke** *pl* built-in movements **-werkzeug** *n* inserting tool **-werkzeuge für Innennuten** recessing tools for internal slots

Einsteigeisen *n* (für Kabelschachte) manhole steps

einsteigen to get in(to), enter, embark, break into (a house)

Einsteigerelais *n* trunk entering relay

Einsteig-leiter *f* entrance ladder **-loch** *n* manhole

-luke *f* entrance or access hatch **-öffnung** *f* manhole culvert or opening, cleaning door **-schacht** *m* inspection shaft, manhole **-tür** *f* entrance door

Einsteinium-Isotopen einsteinium isotopes

Einstellanschlag *m* quantity stop

einstellbar adjustable **-er Anschlag** adjustable stop **-er Haspelzug** *m* adjustable reel tension **-e Holzschraube** wooden adjustable-pitch propeller **-es Komma** *n* adjustable point (info proc.) **-e Luftschraube** variable-pitch propeller **-e Schraube** (am Boden) adjustable-pitch (airscrew) propeller **-e Sonde** tuning probe

Einstell-barkeit *f* adjustability **-bereich** *n* range of adjustment or of setting **-bohrung** *f* adjusting hole **-bolzen** *m* adjustment bolt **-buchse** *f* adjusting (control) bush **-bügel** *m* (Fernschreiber) adjusting loop **-dauer** *f* response time **-deckel** *m* adjustment cover **-dorn** *m* adjusting mandrel **-drehung** *f* setting, adjusting, rotation **-ebene** *f* focusing plane, plane of reference

Einstellehre *f* adjusting or setting gauge **schraubzwingenähnliche ~** adjusting gauge of a screw-clamp shape

einstellen (Arbeitskräfte) to hire, employ; (Mechanik) position, adjust; (Radio) tune in; (Chem.) standardize; (Zeit) time; (Betrieb) put into service; (aufgeben) give up, stop, discontinue, leave off; (Zahlung) suspend, stop; (Arbeit) strike, walk out; (Betrieb) suspend work, shut down; (sich ~ auf) adjust; (vorbereiten) prepare for; (~ auf) to bring up to, to set, regulate, locate, adapt, fix, align, postpone, defer, lay up, put up, put in, cease, engage, aim, point (optics), position, dial or set up a number, focus **auf eine Ansprechstromstärke von** *n* **MA ~** to margin or pull up an *n* milliampere **die Arbeit ~** to strike, stop work **den Betrieb ~** to suspend work, stop the work **in den Brennpunkt ~** to focus (lamps) **Feuer ~** to cease fire

einstellen, auf Null ~ to set to zero **ein Relais weniger empfindlich ~** to decrease the sensitivity of a relay **die Schützen ~** to stop the flood gates **auf einen Unterschied ~** to margin **Wagen ~** to put in a garage **die Zahlungen ~** to suspend payment

einstellen, fein ~ to point precisely **grob ~** to point roughly **mittig ~** to center **neu ~** to readjust **neutral ~** to set neutral, adjust neutrally **normal ~** to set at normal **scharf ~** to focus

Einstellen *n* alignment, setting up, adjustment, engagement, focusing **~ von Hand** manual control **~ der Libelle** centering of the bubble level **~ der Ventile** timing of the valves **~ der Werkzeuge** tool adjustment **selbsttätiges ~** self-alignment

Einstell-entfernung *f* distance (focusing)

Einsteller *m* setter (tools), positioning device, adjuster

Einstellerei *f* setting-up department

Einstell-fassung *f* focusing mount (of lens) **-feder** *f* equalizer spring **-fehler** *m* error in focusing, faulty focusing or spot control, decrease of spot with intensity increase, large diffuse speck on screen in gasfocused picture-reproducing tube, adjustment aberration **-fernrohr** *n* focusing telescope

einstellfeste Gläser lens corrected for image shell error

Einstellfenster *n* inspection window

Einstellfinger zum Ausrichten der Schneidbrust cutter lip aligning gauge

Einstell-fuß *m* adjusting foot **-genauigkeit** *f* precision of adjustment **-geschwindigkeit** *f* setting speed **-gewindelehren** *pl* thread setting gauges **-glied** *n* setting member **-griff** *m* adjusting lever **-hebel** *m* adjusting lever, Hughes' unison lever, zero-adjusting lever **-hülse** *f* adjustable holder, focusing sleeve **-indexplatte** *f* adjustment index plate

Einstell-knaggen zum Tischvorschub fixed-table feed trips **-knopf** *m* thumb wheel, preset knob, focusing knob (of camera), setting knob or head, pinion **-kosten** *pl* setting cost (tools) **-kreis** *m* adjustment circle **-kreuz** *n* adjusting cross **-kurve** *f* sensing cam **-lehre** *f* feeder gauge, setting gauge, master gauge **-lehrring** *m* ring gauge, template **-leiste** *f* adjusting gib

Einstell-lupe *f* focusing magnifier, adjustable magnifier **-magnet** *m* setting magnet **-marke** *f* focusing, sighting, or adjustment mark, index, adjustable marker, timing, reference, or measuring mark, gauge mark, index dot (on dial), wander mark (of telescope), setting mark; (b. Kompaß) lubber line **-markierung** *f* adjusting mark **-maß** *n* standard (for setting), reference gauge **-mattscheibe** *f* ground-glass focusing screen **-mikroskop** *n* focusing microscope **-möglichkeit** *f* range of adjustment **-mutter** *f* adjustment or regulating nut (screw), set nut

Einstell-nadel *f* adjustment needle **-okular** *n* focusing eyepiece, spotting ocular **-plan** *m* tooling diagram, tool layout **-platte** *f* adjusting plate **-potentiometer** *m* setting or adjusting (potentiometer) control **-propeller** *m* adjustable-pitch propeller **-rad** *n* preset disk **-rasten** *pl* quantity stops **-raum** *m* garage **-ring** *m* adjusting ring, setting collar **-rohr** *n* sliding tube **-scheibe** *f* dial, timing disk (aviation) **-schieber** *m* adjusting slide, adjusting pilot valve; (Rauchgase) regulating damper **-schiene** (Kreuzschinenschalter) selecting bar (crossbar switch) **-schlüssel** *m* adjusting wrench **-schnecke** *f* roller setting worm, positioning screw

Einstell-schraube *f* setscrew, adjusting or leveling screw, adjustable or multiposition propeller **-schraubensperrmutter** adjusting screw lock nut **-sektor** *m* timing or regulating sector **-skala** *f* control dial, focusing scale, tuning scale **-sperrstift** *m* adjustment lockings pin **-spindel** *f* setting spindle, adjusting screw **-stange** *f* adjusting rod (aviation) **-steuerungen** *pl* setting controls **-stift** *m* adjusting pin **-tafel** *f* focusing board, test chart **-teilung für Senkrechtschwenklager** vertical swivel mount setting scale **-tiefe** *f* (für Stangen) depth of pole hole **-tubus** *m* micrometer adjustment (electron microscope), adjusting tube

Einstellung *f* (Arbeiter) engagement; (Mechanik) adjustment, setting, control, calibration; (Chem.) standardization; (Beendigung) cessation, discontinuance; (Betrieb) stoppage; (Zahlungen) suspension; (Ansicht) view, approach, regulation, focusing, correction, timing, tool layout, tooling diagram **„Ein"-Stellung** (des Schalters) closed position (of switch)

Einstellung des Betriebes einer Grube suspension or stoppage of mine work **~ für die Gegenlagerständer auf dem Bett** adjustment for back rest on bed **~ des Höhenmessers** altimeter setting **~ der Mischung** formulating the mixing **~ einer Nummer** dialing **~ des Platinenexzenters** jack cam adjustment **~ der Querverreibung am Zylinderfarbwerk** adjustment of vibration motion at rotary unit **~ der Senker** setting for the stitch cam **~ der Steuerung** timing adjustment **~** (Steuerzeiten) timing (valve timing) **~** (auf unendlich) infinity focus **kritische ~** critical or delicate adjustment, setting, or focusing

Einstellungs-bestreben *n* tendency to set itself **-differenz** *f* difference in focal adjustment (optics) **-ebene** *f* focusing plane **-fläche** *f* surface of reference **-geschwindigkeit** *f* time constant **-merkmal** *n* adjustment feature **-plan** *m* tooling diagram **-widerstand** *m* variable resistance

Einstell-vorrichtung *f* setting device, focusing mechanism, adjustment **-walze** *f* adjusting roller **-weg** *m* selecting path, (common) dialing trunk, impulse circuit **-weite** *f* range of setting, focal range **-werk** *n* setting register **-wert** *m* control value, cutoff coefficient **-wicklung** *f* set winding **-widerstand** *m* setting resistor, adjustable resistor (converter)

Einstellwinkel *m* angle of incidence (U.S.), adjustable rake (angle), rigging angle of incidence, indicated angle **~ des Werkstückträgers beim Spiralschleifen** work ficture setting angles for spiral grinding work

Einstell-zapfen *m* adjusting pivot **-zeichnung** *f* tooling diagram, tool layout **-zeit** *f* time constant, time travel (recorder), adjustment time, relaxation time; (eines Galvanometers) damping time

Einstellzeiger *m* adjustment or timing needle **~** (zur Einstellung der Steuerzeiten) timing pointer (valve timing)

Einstellzeit *f* time of operation

einstemmen to mortise, caulk

einstempeln to stamp in

Einstempelplattformhebebühne *f* single-jack platform elevator

einstemplig single-head

einsteppen to stitch

Einsternmotor *m* single-row radial engine

einsteuern to proceed at blank speed, steer into (harbor, etc.)

Einsteuerung *f* picking up target (aviation)

Einstich *m* pass (in rolling), puncture, perforation, recess **-farbe** *f* effect color **-seite** *f* entering side (in rolling), roller's side **-stahl** *m* parting tool

Einstieg *m* entry **~ und Ausstieg** entry and exit

Einstieg-klappe *f* hatch cover **-luke** *f* entrance hatch

Einstieler *m* single-bay machine (aviation)

einstielig single-bay **-er gestaffelter Doppeldecker** single-bay staggered biplane

einstimmig unanimous, monophonic, one-voiced

Einstimmungsrad *n* tone wheel

Einstockantenne *f* single type antenna

einstöckig one-story (building)

einstöpseln to plug in

einstößelbarer Tastenlocher plug-in keyboard perforator

einstoßen to push in, ram in, slot

Einstoß-schlitten *m* decking carriage, onsetting carriage **-vorrichtung** *f* pusher (in rolling), knocking-in device, lehr stacker (glass)

Einstrahl-funkstelle *f* beam station **-rohr** *n* single-beam tube (radar) **-sender** *m* beam transmitter, unidirectional transmitter **-system** *n* beam system

Einstrahlung *f* insolation, solarization, irridiation

Einstrahlungsverlust *m* loss by absorption of radiant heat

Einstreich-feile *f* slitting or feather-edged file **-mittel für Formen** coating agent for molds **-säge** *f* slitting saw

einstreuen to strew, sprinkle, interperse; (Material) feed (into the bowl)

Einstreumaterial *n* dusting material

Einstreuung *f* stray effect **~ von Störungen durch fremde Stromquellen** (Funktechnik) pickup from external electrical sources (radio)

Einstrich *m* divider, partition timber

Einström-druck *m* flow-in pressure **-düse** *f* inlet nozzle

einströmen to flow in, stream in, pass into

einströmender Dampf flowing-in vapor

Einström-hub *m* intake stroke **-kasten** *m* inlet chamber **-leitung** *f* induction system, intake manifold **-öffnung** *f* inlet port **-schlitz** *m* inlet port **-system** *n* induction system

Einstromtriebwerk *n* pure jet

Einströmung *f* induction, inflow, suction, indraft

Einströmungs-druck *m* inlet pressure **-öffnung** *f* inlet, intake **-querschnitt** *m* cross-sectional area of inlet **-rohr** *n* inlet pipe, intake

Einströmventil *n* inlet or intake valve

einstückig in one piece

einstufen to grade (by quality), classify

Einstufen-gebläse *n* one-stage blower **-dauerschwingversuch** *m* fatigue test in one load stage (step) **-lader** *m* single-stage blower **-mahlung** *f* single-passage grinding **-mahlwerk** *n* single-stage grinding mill **-zerkleinerer** *m* single-passage crusher

einstufig single-stage, single-step **-er Kompressor** single-stage compressor or supercharger **-er Verstärker** one-stage amplifier

Einstufung *f* classification

Einsturz *m* collapse, cave-in **-beben** *n* subsidence earthquake **-trichter** *m* sink hole

einstürzen to throw in, fall in, collapse, cave in

Einsturzgeschwindigkeit *f* reentry velocity

einstweilige Verfügung temporary, provisional, or interim injunction, provisional decree

einsumpfen to wet, soak, digest with water

eintasten to key on or in, imprint

eintauchen to immerse, dip, soak, sink in, steep, plunge, submerge, pitch (of ships), telescope (a coil)

Eintauchen *n* plunging, submerging, immersion, dipping **~ mit schwingendem Mastkran** setting by pontoon or floating sheers

Eintauchende *n* fire or dipping end
Eintaucher *m* dipper, vatman
Eintauch-fläche *f* immersed part of a filter surface **-gitter** *n* wet lattice **-kolorimeter** *m* dipping colorimeter **-marke** *f* immersion mark **-plattierung** *f* dipor immersion plating (galvan.) **-pyrometer** *n* dipping pyrometer
Eintauchrefraktometer *m* dipping or immersion refractometer **~ mit Durchflußküvette** immersion refractometer with flow-cell attachment
Eintauch-rohr *n* immersion pipe **-schmierung** *f* flood lubrication **-sonar** *n* dunking sonar **-thermometer** *n* total-immersion thermometer
Eintauchtiefe *f* depth of immersion, submergence **~ des Thermometers** depth of immersion of the thermometer
Eintauchtrommel *f* dipping drum
Eintauchung *f* submergence, immersion
Eintauch-verfahren *n* immersion method **-walze** *f* (Druck) dip roller (immersion roller) **-zähler** *m* immersion counter **-zeit** *f* immersion time
einteeren to tar
einteigen to dough in, mash in
Einteigen *n* doughing in, mashing in
einteilbar divisible
Einteilchen-dichte *f* singlet density **-modell** *n* single-particle model, model of nucleus **-niveau** *n* single particle level **-schalenmodell** *n* single-particle shell model **-übergang** *m* single particle transition **-verteilungsfunktion** *f* singlet distribution function **-wellenfunktion** *f* single particle wave function
einteilen to divide, subdivide, graduate, index, grade, classify, time, space, distribute, separate
einteilig one-part, single, in one piece, integral **-es** (ungeteiltes) **Hauptpleuel** solid master connecting rod **-es Lager** solid bearing
Einteilung *f* division, subdivision, graduation, indexing, classification, grading
Einteilungsplan *m* grading chart
Eintiefung *f* erosion
Ein-ton *m* single tone
eintönen to tint
eintönig monotone
Einton-ruf *m* single-tone ringing **-verfahren** *n* single-tone keying
Eintouren-maschine *f* single-revolution machine **-presse** *f* single-revolution press
Eintrag *m* charge, feed, entry, furnish (paper mfg.), weft, input
Eintragebuch *n* register, logbook (power station)
eintragen to enter, record, register, feed, post, carry in **~** (in einen Plan) to enter into, mark on, plot on (a plan)
Eintragende *n* feed or charge end
Einträgerlaufkran *m* single-beam traveling crane
Eintrag-faden *m* shoot, thread of the weft **-garn** *n* filling (in fabric)
einträglich remunerative, commercial (of efficiencies)
Eintrags-ende *n* feed end **-öffnung** *f* feed entrance, aperture, feeding **-schnecke** *f* feed screw or worm **-spule** *f* cop (textiles)
Eintragung *f* registration, record, entry, notation
Eintragungs-bescheinigung *f* certificate of registry **-gebühr** *f* registry fee **-schein** *m* registration certificate **-urkunde** *f* certificate of registration **-zwang** *m* compulsory registration
einträcken to imbibe, dip, soak, impregnate
Eintreibdorn *m* expander, (driving-in) mandrel
eintreibbar recoverable
eintreiben to drive (in), run into
eintreten to enter, set in, commence, occur, enlist **~ für . . .** advocate **in eine Leitung ~** to come in on a circuit, ingress
eintretend entering **in den Zylinder -es Gemisch** ingoing charge
Eintritt *m* admission, ingress, entry, entrance, inlet, intake **~ verboten** keep out, no admittance **störungsfreier ~** unobstructed entry **stoßfreier ~** shock-free entry **~ verbotenes Gebiet** exclusion area
Eintritts-blatt *n* entry vane **-blende** *f* input diaphragm or capacity disk (klystron) **-dicke** *f* intering thickness **-druck** *m* admission pressure **-feld** *n* area of applicator at skin surface **-flughafen** *m* airport of entry **-geschwindigkeit** *f* speed of entering, approach or inlet velocity **-kanal** *m* admission channel, inlet port **-kante** *f* leading or entering edge of wing (aviation), inlet edge of blade **-kreisschlitz** *m* annular opening
Eintrittsöffnung *f* intake port, throat **~ des Laders** eye of the supercharger
Eintritts-phase *f* entrance phase **-potential** *n* input potential **-preis** *m* entrance fee, price of admission **-pupille** *f* entrance pupil **-querschnitt** *m* inlet cross section **-reflektor** *m* (Autokartograph) ingress reflector **-rohr** *n* admission pipe **-schaufel** *f* entry fan **-schleuse** *f* air lock **-seite** *f* entering side (in rolling), pressure side of a valve
Eintritts-spalt *m* incident ray, entrance slit **-spannung** *f* admission potential **-stelle** *f* inlet spot (place) **-stutzen** *m* inlet-pipe connection, filler neck, inlet, intake flange **-temperatur** *f* inlet temperature
Eintritts-ventil *n* induction or inlet valve **-verlust** *m* entrance loss **-wärmegrad** *m* inlet temperature **-winkel** *m* entering angle, angle of contact
eintrocknen to dry (up)
eintröpfeln to drop in
eintrümmig single-track, single-strand **-er Schacht** single shaft **-er Schrägaufzug** single-track hoist bridge, single-skip hoist **-es Seil** one-sided rope
ein- und ausfahren advance and retract (boom)
Ein- und Ausführwalzen *pl* feeding and delivery rollers
Ein- und Ausgang *m* feed and delivery sides
ein- und ausklappbar swing-out, swinging, folding
Ein- und Auslaß *m* input or output
Ein- und Auslaßventil *n* poppet valves
Ein- und Auslaufwinkel *m* approach and run-off angle
Ein- und Auslegen *n* (der Walzen) placing and removing (of the rollers)
ein- und ausrücken to start and stop, connect and disconnect, engage and disengage
Ein- und Ausrückhebel *m* starting and stopping lever
Ein- und Ausrückkuppelung *f* clutch (coupling)
ein- und ausschaltbar engaging and disengaging
Ein- und Ausschalten *n* starting and stopping **schnelles ~** quick action and release

Ein- und Ausschalthebel *m* start and stop control lever
Ein- und Ausschalterknopf *m* start-stop button
Ein- und Ausschaltung starting and stopping
Ein- und Ausschwenken *n* moving in and out
Ein- und Ausschwingen *n* transient phenomenon, equilibrating process, make-and-break transients **Verzerrung durch ~** transient distortion (nonlinear), build-up and decay (in alternating current, fascimile, etc., associated with hangover, tailing, underthrow, and overthrow)
Ein- und Ausspannen der Tuche papering-in and papering-out the cloth
ein- und doppelseitig single- and double-ended
ein-und-einachsig orthorhombic (cryst.)
Ein- und Mehrschneidenfräser *m* single-lip and multiplefluted cutters
Ein- und Mehrspindelbohrmaschinen *pl* one and multi spindle machines
ein- und zweiatomig mono- and diatomic
Einvergütung *f* tempering
Einvernehmen *n* agreement, understanding
einverstanden sein to agree to, acquiesce
Einverständnis *n* agreement, conformity, accordance
Einwaage *f* weighed sample or object, weight of sample or object
einwachsen to wax
einwägen to weigh in
Einwägung *f* amount weighed out, leveling
einwalken to plank
Einwalken *n* shrinkage
einwalzen to roll in, expand in
Einwalzen *n* rolling
Einwalzen-brecher *m* single-roll crusher **-trockner** *m* drum drier (single drum drier), drier with single roller
Einwalzstempel *m* rolling die
Einwalzung *f* (Blockfehler) scrab mark
Einwand *f* objection, demurrer
einwandern to diffuse, immigrate
Einwanderung *f* diffusion
einwandfrei unobjectionable, irreproachable, satisfactory, acceptable, tolerable, efficient, troubleproof, without distortion (TV), distortionless **~ arbeiten** to work correctly **technisch ~** consistent with sound engineering **-e Abfüllung** proper filling **-e Erdung** *f* faultness grounding (elec.) **-e Lagerung** accurate mounting **-e Leitung** circuit in good order
einwechseln to exchange, change, give in exchange
einwecken to preserve
Einwegeverstärker *m* one-way or simplex repeater
Einweggebinde *n* lost container
Einweggleichrichter *m* half-wave rectifier **~ der Wellen** full-wave rectifier
Einweg-gleichrichterröhre *f* half-wave rectifying valve **-gleichrichterschaltung** *f* half-wave rectifier circuit **-gleichrichtung** *f* half-wave, single-wave, or one-way rectification **-gleichschalter** *m* half-wave rectifier **-hahn** *m* stopcock
einwegig one-way, simplex, single-channel **-er Telegraph** single-channel telegraph
Einweg-leiter *m* unilines **-leitung** *f* unidirectional circuit, one-way circuit **-schalter** *m* discriminating, seeking, or selecting switch **-umschalter** *m* single-way switch **-vielspindel-Bohrmaschine** *f* single-way multi-spindle drilling machine **-wähler** *m* rotary switch, uniselector
Einweich-apparat für Flaschen bottle-soaking apparatus **-bottich** *m* (Säure) acid-steeping bowl **-bütte** *f* macerator
einweichen to soak, digest, steep, macerate
Einweich-grube *f* retting pit **-trommel** *f* cone breaker
Einweichung *f* maceration
einweisen to train, (Flugzeug mit Radar) to vector
Einweiser *m* guide
Einweisung *f* instruction, regulation, induction, assignment, direction, familiarization
einweißen to powder with magnesia
Einwellen-betrieb *m* single-wave operation **-blockkraftwerk** *n* single-shaft unit system power station
einwellig sinusoidal, simple-harmonic, single-phase, reliable, constant, unchanged
Einwelligkeit *f* single-cycle state (or condition)
Einwendung *f* plea, defense, objection, demurrer
einwertig monovalent, univalent, single-valued **-er Alkohol** monohydric or monovalent alcohol **-es Radikal** univalent radical **-e Salze** one-to-one salts
einwickeln to wrap up or in, enclose, muffle
Einwickelpapier *n* wrapping paper
Einwicklung *f* wrapping, packing
einwiegen to weigh in, level **die Werksteine ~** to set the quarrystones horizontal
einwilligen to consent, agree or accede to, comply with
Einwilligung *f* compliance, approval, consent, permission
einwinden to weigh (anchor) **das Ankertau ~** to heave the cable
Einwinker *m* (Flughafen) marshaler
einwirken to act, react (on), interfere (with), affect **~ auf** to bear upon **aufeinander ~** to interact **auf jemanden ungünstig ~** to impress somebody unfavorably, penalize **~ lassen** to allow to react (chem.), be exposed to
Einwirkung *f* action, reaction, interference (with), influence, effect **gegenseitige ~** mutual influence, interaction
Einwirkungszeit *f* (Versuche) induction period (experimenting with engines)
Einwohnerschaft *f* population, inhabitants
einwölben to vault, (over)arch
Einwölbung *f* down warping (of strata)
Einwurf *m* slit, slot, hopper **-apparat** *m*, **-entwickler** *m* carbide-to-water generator **-grube** *f* receiving pit **-klappe** *f* charging opening **-öffnung** *f* charging opening **-rost** *m* dumping grid **-trichter** *m* feed or track hopper, bin **-zucker** *m* remelt sugar
Einwurzeln *n* taking root
Einzackenschrift *f* single-edged variable-width sound track or record
einzahlen to pay in
Einzählerhebelkontrollkasse *f* simple-lever cash register
Einzahlung *f* payment, installment
einzahnen to indent
einzahniger Gewindestahl single-point threading tool

Einzahn-scheibe *f* drive wheel (motion pictures) **-stift** *m* striking roller (motion pictures)
einzapfen to mortise
einzäunen to enclose, fence in, rail off
Einzäunung *f* enclosure, stockade, compound
Einzeichen *n* single-signal
einzeichnen to plot, draw in, mark, enter into
Einzel-abfederung *f* independent suspension (aviation) **-abnahme** *f* reduction per pass **-abschnittfilter** *m* single-section filter **-abstimmstichleitung** *f* single-stub tuner **-abwurf** *m* individual or single release **-akkord** *m* individual piece work **-alarmlampe** *f* (EA) unit fuse alarm lamp **-anfertigung** *f* single piece production **-anführung** *f*, **-angabe** *f* specification **-anlage** *f* unit plant, separate plant
Einzelanruf mit bestimmten Frequenzen harmonic selective ringing **~ bei Gemeinschaftsleitungen** selective ringing **~ mit verabredeten Zeichen** semiselective ringing
Einzel-anrufer *m* selector (calling apparatus) telegraph selector **-anschlußteilnehmer** *m* individualline subscriber, single line subscriber
Einzelantrieb *m* single drive, separate drive, individual control, singly operated drive, direct motor drive **~** (Werkzeugmaschine) self-contained drive (tool machine) **riemenloser ~** direct self-contained drive
Einzel-arbeit *f* output per unit **-aufhängung** *f* single, independent or individual suspension **-aufnahme** *f* single photograph or view **-ausbildung** *f* individual training **-ausgang** *m* single (separate) delivery **-batterie** *f* single or component battery **-befehl** *m* fragmentary or extract order **-beratung** *f* individual information **-bereichmeßgerät** *n* single range instrument **-bestimmung** *f* separate operation (chem.) **-bezirk** *m* single region **-bild** *n* **einer Bildreihe** individual picture or unit frame in a series or sequence **-bildgerät** *n* single-photograph plotting apparatus
Einzel-blitzfeuer *n* light with flashes at regular intervals **-brenner** *m* burner with nonvariable head, nonvariable head torch **-chassis** *n* individual chassis, unit chassis **-darstellung** *f* single representation, separate treatise, monograph **-deviation** *f* single component of deviation, individual deviation or deflection **-diffusionsstufe** *f* single diffusion stage **-drehstahl** *m* single cutting tool **-druckgang** *m* individual operation **-elektron** *n* unpaired electron **-elektronensystem** *n* lone electron system **-entstörung** *f* (single screening) single radio shielding **-exemplar** *n* single copy
Einzel-faden *m* single filament **-fahrer** *m* single or independently routed ship **-feld** *n* **mit Meßinstrumenten** instrument panel (elec.) **-fertigschneider** *m* single finishing cutter **-fertigung** *f* single-part production **-feuer** *n* independent firing, single fire, single-shot or semiautomatic fire **-filmelement** *n* single film element **-flug** *m* solo flight
Einzelfundament *n* footing **flaches ~** shallow footing
Einzel-fundation *f* spot footing **-funkenstrecke** *f* single spark gap **-gang** *m* list speed **-gänger** *m* outsider (one who is by himself, apart from others, linguistically or otherwise) **-ganggeschwindigkeit** *f* list speed **-gebläse** *n* individual blower or supercharger **-gebühr** *f* message rate, measured rate **-gebührenanschluß** *m* message-rate subscription **-geleise** *n* single track **-gesprächgebühr** *f* message rate **-glocke** *f* single shed insulator **-gußverfahren** *n* separate casting method **-handel** *m* retail business
Einzelheit *f* individual item, detail, particular, singleness, minutiae
Einzelheiten-Kontrastverhältnis *n* detail constrast ratio
Einzel-hülle *f* single hull **-impulszählung** *f* counting individual pulses **-kabel** *n* single conductor or cable **-kammer** *f* camera for single photographs **-kartenprüfung** *f* single card checking **-kassette** *f* single-plate dark slide **-klang** *m* (sounding of an) individual note
Einzelkompensation *f* individual-capacitor method; (von Motoren) individual-motor power-factor improvement
Einzel-kontrast *m* detail contrast **-kostenaufstellung** *f* schedule of individual costs **-kraft** *f* concentrated force or load, point force **-kreis** *m* single circuit **-kristall** *m* single or unit crystal **-lader** *m* single-loader, single-shot weapon **-last** *f* concentrated load (on beam), single or point load **-leiter** *m* single conductor **-leitung** *f* ground-return circuit, grounded line, single circuit, single (wire) line **-leitungslinie** *f* single-wire route
Einzellenfernseher *m* single-cell television apparatus
einzellig monocellular, unicellular
Einzel-linse *f* unipotential lens (electron microscope), unit lens (of focusing field) **-lohnkosten** *pl* productive labor cost, direct labor cost **-lupe** *f* single magnifier, magnifier unit **-magazin** *n* single container **-maschine** *f* single unit **-matrix** *f* idempotent or unit matrix, idempotent, primitive idempotent **-mittel** *n* individual means
einzeln particular, individual, single, separate, detached, isolated, odd **~ angeben** to specify **~ aufführen** to itemize **~ in Ansatz bringen** to cost individually **~ stehend, Motor mit ~ stehenden Zylindern** motor with separate cylinders **-e Stücke** odd parts
Einzel-nummer *f* single copy **-objektiv** *n* single lens (objective) **-peilung** *f* taking bearings from one object **-postenvorschub** *m* single item ejection **-preis** *m* price of a single copy **-preßling** *m* single pressing **-probe** *f* individual sample, increment, check by back substitution **-prospekte** *pl* detailed descriptive material or literature **-prüfung** *f* routine test **-pumpenelement** *n* pump unit **-punktschweißung** *f* individual spot welding
Einzel-radbelastung *f* single-wheel load (SIWL) **-radlast** *f* single isolated wheel load **-rauhigkeiten** *pl* single roughness **-regler** *m* channel control **-riemchenflorteilchen** *n* individual tape divider **-riemen** *m* single belt **-saturation** *f* batch carbonation **-schallquelle** *f* single-sound source **-scheibenantrieb** *m* single-pulley drive **-schlag** *m* single blow **-schlagstärke** *f* single stroke force
Einzel-schnitt *m* single or individual cut **-schnittverfahren** *n* single-intersection method **-schnur** *f* single cord, monocord **-schraube** *f* adjusting

screw **-schritt** *m* individual stage **-schrittsteuerung** *f* individual step control **-schuß** *m* single shot or round **-schutz** *m* individual protection **-schweißbrenner** *m* non variable head welding torch **-schweißumformer** *m* single-operator welding machine

Einzel-schwimmer *m* single float **-schwingung** *f* individual oscillation **-sparren** *m* single spar **-sprung** *m* single leap or jump, bound **-spule** *f* coil (of a distributed winding) **-ständer** *m* single frame **-steigungsfehler** *m* individual pitch error **-steuerung** *f* individual steering or flying control **-störung** *f* isolated or single disturbance **-stöße** *pl* single collisions **-strahler** *m* individual radiator **-streuung** *f* single scattering (of electrons) **-strom** *m* single current **-stütze** *f* single pole or support **-tarifzählung** *f* single-fee metering

Einzelteil *n* piece part, component or spare part, member ~ **von Paaren** an odd piece of pairs

Einzelteilbenennung *f* nomenclature

Einzelteilchen *n* odd particle

Einzelteilverfahren *n* single-dividing method, single-indexing process

Einzel-tier *m* filament, denier **-transport** *m* individual transport **-treibstoff** *m* mono-propellant (rocket) **-triebeinstellung der Okulare eines Feldstechers** separate focusing to the eyepieces of a field glass **-übergangstransistor** *m* unijunction transistor

Einzel- und Zwillungsbehälter *pl* single and twin barrel tanks

Einzel-vergrößerung *f* component magnification **-verlegung** *f* (Leitung) single wiring **-verlustverfahren** *n* loss-summation method

Einzelversetzung in einem unendlich ausgedehnten Kristall single dislocation of an infinite crystal

Einzel-verstellung *f* separate adjustment, individual traverse, individual or independent adjustment **-versuch** *m* single test **-verzahnung** *f* single gearing **-vorgang** *m* single or separate process, action, event, or reaction **-welle** *f* solitary wave **-wickel** *m* single winding **-wirkungsgrad** *m* efficiency per unit **-wurf** *m* individual or single release (bombing) **-zähler** *m*, **-zählwerk** *n* discharge register **-zeichendrucker** *m* single action printer **-zeichnung** *f* detail drawing **-ziel** *n* point target

einzementieren to cement, cause to float in cement

einziehbar retractable, retractile **-er Antennenmast** retractable antenna mast **-es Fahrgestell** retractable undercarriage **nicht -es Fahrwerk** fixed undercarriage **-er Kühler** draw-out or retractable radiator **-es Fahrwerk** retractable landing gear

Einzieh-dose *f* drawing-in box **-draht** *m* draw wire **-drehmoment** *n* draw-in torque

einziehen to draw in; (Mechanik) retract; (einbauen) insert; (Erkundigung) inquire, gather information; (Flüssigkeit) soak in, be absorbed; (Geld) collect, haul, pull in, wind or reel in (antenna), carry (threads), withdraw, conscript, confiscate, cash, contract, arrest, suppress, turn down, decrease, call in, swage, reduce (diameter), indent, introduce ~ **eines Bandes** piecing of the sliver ~ **lassen** to allow to soak

Einziehen *n* indentation, pulling in, drawing in ~ **des Fahrwerkes** retraction of landing gear

einziehender Schacht (Bg) downcast shaft

Einzieh-fahrgestell *n* retractable undercarriage **-fahrwerk** *m* retractable landing gear **-falte** *f* drawing tear (metal.) **-geschwindigkeit** *f* web-feeding speed **-getriebe** *n* (Kran) luffing gear, derricking gear **-haken** *m* heddle or drawing hook **-haspel** *f* feeding-in winch **-kasten** *m* vaccum-pan supply tank **-kran** *m* luffing crane, level luffing crane **-matrizen für Patronenhülsen** drawing dies for cartidge shells **-messer** *n* reed hook (textiles)

Einzieh-schacht *m* downcast shaft **-schraube** *f* screw point (of a bit) **-stellung** *f* retracted position **-strebe** *f* retracting strut, radius rod **-streben** *n* retracting link **-strecke** *f* intake **-strom** *m* downcast, intake air **-strumpf** *m* cable grip **-trommel** *f* luffing drum

Einziehung *f* infiltration, absorption, abolition, collection (mony), conscription, broad channel, flat flute or hollow, quirk or recess head

Einziehungsmittel *n* absorbent

Einzieh-vorrichtung *f* retracting mechanism **-walzen** *pl* feed rollers, feeders **-werk** *n* luffing gear **-werkzeug** *n* drawing die **-winde des Schleppschaufelbaggers** winch of the dragline for pulling in the ropes

einzig alone, only, sole, single **-artig** unique

Einzigkeitstheorem *n* uniqueness

Einzug *m* drawing up, taking in, entry, indentation, feeding apparatus

einzügig single-duct (cable), single way **-es Formstück** single tile, single-duct concrete block **-er Kanal** single-way duct

Einzugs-gebiet *n* catchment (drainage) area, watershed, cross-sectional area of undistorted portion of field (direction-finding frame) **-magnetschalter** *m* draw-in type magnetic switch **-richtmaschine** *f* feeder leveller **-ventil** *n* charging valve **-wicklung** *f* draw-in coil **-zylinder** *m* feed roller

einzwängen to wedge or force in

einzwingen to force in

Einzweck-gerät *n* single purpose unit **-maschine** *f* single-purpose machine **-rechner** *m* single purpose computer **-sendermaschine** *f* special single-purpose machine

Einzylinder-auspuffdampfmaschine *f* single-cylinder-exhaust steam engine **-dampfmaschine** *f* single-cylinder steam engine **-Dieselmotor** *m* single-cylinder Diesel engine **-gebläse** *n* single-cylinder blower **-magnetzünder** *m* single-cylinder magneto **-motor** *m* single-cylinder test unit or motor **-prüfstand** *m* single-cylinder test bed or test bench **-tauchkolbenverdichter** *m* single-cylinder plunger-type compressor **-trockner** *m* single-cylinder drier (yankee drier) **-verdichter** *m* single-cylinder type compressor **-verteilerpumpe** *f* single-plunger distributor-type pump **-zweitaktmotor** *m* single-cylinder two-cycle engine

Eiquerschnitt *m* egg-shaped section

Eirich-Gegenstrom-Schnellmischer *m* rotary pan mixer, Lancaster (Plow tube) counter current pan mixer

Eirich-Mischer (Mischkneter) *m* muller mixer

eirund oval, egg-shaped

Eis *n* ice **-abgang** *m* clearing of ice **-anker** *m* ice anchor **-ansatz** *m* ice accretion **-artig** icy, glacial **-bahn** *f* skating rink, track on the ice **-balken** *m* fender beam **-bank** *f* pack ice **-barre** *f* ice barrage, ice dam, ice jam

Eis-baum *m* floating ice boom or barricade **-belag** *m* ice coating **-belastung** *f* ice load (elec.) **-beobachtungsstation** *f* ice- or iceberg-observation station **-berg** *m* iceberg, block of ice **-bildung** *f* ice formation **-bildungswarnapparat** *m* ice-warning indicator **-blau** glacier blue **-blink** *m* iceblink

Eisblumen-glas *n* fristed glass **-lack** *m* frosted finish **-lackierung** *f* crackle finish

Eis-brechen *n* ice breaking **-brecher** *m* icebreaker (vessel), ice-breaking structure to protect bridges, ice apron **-brechpflug** *m* ice-breaking ram **-decke** *f* ice sheet or coating **-dienst** *m* iceberg patrol

Eisen *n* iron, steel, iron instrument **~ abfangen** to tap iron (foundry) **geschmiedetes ~, getriebenes ~** wrought iron **halbiertes ~** mottled iron **hartgeschlagenes ~** cold- or cool-hammered iron, hammer-hardened iron

Eisen, kadmiertes ~ cadmiated iron **schmiedbares ~** wrought or malleable iron, forging steel, wrought steel **technisches ~** commercial iron **teigiges ~** pasty iron **weiches ~** soft or magnetic iron

Eisen-abbrand *m* iron waste **-abfall** *m* scrap iron, iron scrap **-abscheider** *m* ore extractor, tramp iron separator **-abscheidung** *f* iron separation **-ähnlich** ironlike, ferruginous, chalybeate **-algen** *pl* iron algae **-amiant** *m* fibrous silica, asbestos **-ammonalaun** *m* ammonium ferric alum

Eisen-antimon *n* ferruginous antimony **-antimonerz** *n*, **-antimonglanz** *m* berthierite **-apatit** *n* triplite **-armierung** *f* iron reinforcement (structural) **-artig** ironlike, ferruginous, chalybeate **-asbest** *m* fibrous silica **-atom** *n* iron atom **-aufnahme** *f* absorption of iron

Eisenausbau *m*, **hufeisenförmiger ~** steel arches, horseshoe girders

Eisenbahn *f* railroad, railway **ein- (zwei-)gleisige ~** single- (double-)track railroad **elektrisierte ~** electrified railway

Eisenbahn-anlage *f* railroad installation (buildings and property) **-anschluß** *m* railroad junction, siding, or connection **-bau** *m* railroad construction **-bautechnik** *f* permanent way construction (RR) **-beförderung** *f* railroad transportation **-betrieb** *m* railroad service, traffic, or operation

Eisenbahn-damm *m* railroad embankment **-einschnitt** *m* railway cutting **-endpunkt** *m* railroad terminal, railhead **-fähre** *f* railroad ferry **-funkdienst** *m* railroad radio service **-gelände** *n* railroad right of way **-geleise** *n* railroad track **-gesellschaft** *f* railroad company

Eisenbahn-hof *m* railroad yard or station **-kesselwagen** *m* tank car **-klaue** *f* spur track **-knotenpunkt** *m* railroad junction **-küchenwagen** *m* kitchen car **-kuppelung** *f* railroad coupling **-kuppelungsspindelgewinde** *n* coupling spindle thread for railroad work

Eisenbahn-linie *f* railroad, railway line or track **-nachschublinie** *f* railroad supply line **-oberbaumaschine** *f* machinery for constructing a permanent way for railroad **-radreifen** *m* railway tire **-schiene** *f* rail (R.R.) **-schienenwalzwerk** *n* rail rolling mill

Eisenbahn-schotter *m* railroad ballast **-schutz** *m* semimilitary corps for railroad protection **-schwelle** *f* tie (R.R.), sleeper (R.R.) **-sicherungsanlage** *f* railroad safeguarding plant, installation of railroad safety appliances **-sicherungswesen** *n* railway safety installations **-signalanlagen** *pl* railway signalling system **-stellwerk** *n* railroad signal tower, switch-control room **-strecke** *f* railroad, railway line or track **-tankstelle** *f* railroad tank station, gasoline and lubricant railhead, bulk reduction point **-tankwagen** *m* tank car **-tarif** *m* railroad-rate schedule **-tragfeder** *f* bearing spring for railroad carriages

Eisenbahn-transportfolge *f* rail-road-transport timetable **-überführung** *f* railroad overbridge **-übergang** *m* crossing over the railroad **-unterbau** *m* railroad earthworks, substructure for railroads **-verbindung** *f* connecting railroad, railroad connection **-verkehr** *m* railroad traffic **-verwaltung** *f* railroad management

Eisenbahnwagen *m* railroad car **~ mit seitlicher Entladung** side-dump car **geschlossener ~** boxcar

Eisenbahnwagenarmatur *f* fittings for railroad cars

Eisenbahn-wegschranke *f* barrier or gate of railroad **-werkstätte** *f*, **-werke** *pl* railroad material works or shops **-zentrale** *f* traction (tramway) or railroad central station **-zubringerlinie** *f* auxiliary field railroad

Eisenband *n* iron hoop, ferrule **-umspinnung** *f* iron taping, iron-tape winding

Eisenbakterien *pl* thread bacteria, iron bacteria (geol.)

Eisenbau *m* iron or steel construction **-unternehmer** *m* structural-ironwork contractor **-zeug für Telefonleitungen** iron material for telephone lines

Eisenbearbeitungsmaschine für Kraftbetrieb power-driven machine for constructional engineering

Eisen-bedarf *m* iron requirement **-begleiter** *m* material or elements accompanying iron, iron companions or associates **-beize** *f* iron mordant or liquor **-beschlag** *m* ironwork, iron mounting, lifting lug, ferrule, framework **-beschwerung** *f* weighting with iron **-bestimmung** *f* determination of iron

Eisenbeton *m* reinforced concrete **-bau** *m* reinforced-concrete construction **-brücke** *f* reinforced-concrete bridge **-konstruktion** *f* reinforced concrete construction **-kuppel** *f* reinforced-concrete turret **-mast** *m* reinforced-concrete pole **-pfahl** *m* reinforced concrete pile **-spundwand** *f* sheet piling of reinforced concrete **-stange** *f* reinforced-concrete pole

eisen-bewehrt ironclad, iron-sheathed **-bitterkalk** *m* ferruginous dolomite, ferromagnesium, limestone **-blatt** *n* iron lamina(tion)

Eisenblätterkern *m* laminated-iron core **-spule** *f* laminated-iron-core coil

Eisenblau *n* vivianite, phosphate of iron, blue

iron earth **-erde** *f* earthy vivianite, blue iron earth **-holzschwarz** *n* iron-logwood black **-negativpapier** *n* ferro prussiate negative paper **-papier** *n* blueprint paper **-säure** *f* ferrocyanic acid **-saures Kali** potassium ferrocyanide **-spat** *m* vivianite, blue iron earth

Eisenblech *n* sheet iron, iron plate, iron lamina **ausgeglühtes ~** annealed sheet iron **getriebenes ~** embossed or dished iron plate **verzinktes ~** zincked sheet iron **verzinntes ~, weißes ~** tin plate

Eisenblech-bramme *f* slab **-kern** *m* laminated-iron core **-mantel** *m* iron shell **-membran** *f* ferrotype diaphragm, sheet-iron diaphragm **-muffe** *f* ironplate box **-säule** *f* magnetic laminated shunt **-schalung** *f* sheet-iron mold **-ummantelung** *f* sheet-iron jacketing

Eisen-blende *f* pitchblende **-block** *m* (iron) block, bloom, ingot **-blumen** *pl* iron flowers, ferric chloride **-blüte** *f* flos ferri **-bor** *n* iron boride **-bromürbromid** *n* ferrosoferric bromide **-bronze** *f* iron bronze **-brühe** *f* iron mordant or liquor **-bügel** *m* iron staple or yoke

Eisen-carbonat *n* ferrous or iron carbonate **-chlorid** *n* iron perchloride, ferric chloride **-chlorürchlorid** *n* ferrosoferric chloride **-chlorwasserstoff** *m* ferrichloric acid **-chrom** *n* ferrochromium, chromite **-chromschwarz** *n* iron-chrome black **-chrysolith** *m* hyalosiderite, fayalite **-dibromid** *n* ferrous bromide, ferrobromide **-dichlorid** *n* ferrous or iron chloride **-dijodid** *n* ferrous or iron iodide **-disulfid** *n* iron disulfide, iron pyrite **-dorn** *m* iron mandrel

Eisendraht *m* iron or steel wire **galvanisierter oder verzinkter ~** galvanized-iron wire

Eisendraht-beflechtung *f* whipping (cable) **-geflecht** *n* iron-wire mesh **-gewebe** *n* wire netting or network **-kernspule** *f* iron wire core coil **-netz** *n* iron gauze **-seil** *n* iron cable **-umspinnung** *f* iron-wire winding, iron whipping **-widerstand** *m* iron wire resistance

Eisendrehspäne *pl* iron turnings or chips

Eisendrossel *f* iron-cored choke coil or inductance **Besprechung mit ~** modulation by voice action with magnetic modulator

Eisen-einlage *f* steel or iron reinforcement, steel insert, armoring **-element** *n* iron cell **-empfindlichkeit** *f* susceptibility to iron **-epidot** *m* epidote **-erde** *f* iron mold

Eisenerz *n* iron ore **-ablagerung** *f* iron-ore deposit **-lehm** *m* clay band (clay ironstone) **-vorkommen** *n* iron ore deposit

Eisen-fachwerk *n* iron framework **-fällung** *f* iron precipitation **-fänger** *m* grappling hook, grip for tools **-farbe** *f* iron color **-farbig** iron-colored **-faß** *n* steel barrel **-fassung** *f* iron mounting or lining

Eisenfeder *f*, **mit** (eingesetzter) **~** iron tongued

Eisen-feilicht *n* iron filing **-feilspäne** *pl* iron filings **-feinschlacke** *f* iron-refinery slag **-firnis** *m* (Lack) varnish for iron goods **-flasche** *f* iron flask or cylinder **-fleck** *m* iron spot or stain **-fleckig** iron-stained, iron-spotted **-flüssigkeit** *f* iron liquid

eisenfrei iron-free, ironless **-e Drossel** air-core coil **-er Kupferdraht** non-ferrous copper wire **-er Magnet** air-care magnet **-e Spulen** ironfree coils, air-cored (choke) coils

Eisen-frischerei *f* iron refimery, iron refining or puddling **-frischflammofen** *m* puddling furnace **-frischschlacke** *f* refinery cinders **-führend** ferriferous, iron-bearing **-galluspapier** *n* black line paper **-gang** *m* iron vein or lode **-gans** *f* iron pig **-garn** *n* iron wire **-gaze** *f* iron gauze **-gefäß** *n* iron tank or tray **-gehalt** *m* iron content, steel area (in reinforced-concrete section) **-gehäuse** *n* iron case

eisengekapselt ironclad, iron-encased or -shielded **-e Schaltanlage** enclosed switchgear

Eisen-gelb *n* iron yellow **-gerippe** *n* iron frame

eisengeschlossen iron-cored, ferric, closed core **-er Apparat** ferrodynamic instrument **-es Dynamometer** ferrodynamic instrument

Eisen-gerbung *f* iron tannage **-gewebe** *n* iron reinforcement (structural) **-gießer** *m* foundry man **-gießerei** *f* iron foundry **-gilbe** *f* yellow ocher **-gittermast** *m* steel-lattice mast **-glanz** *m* specular iron ore, oligiste iron ore, hematite **-glanzerz** *n* yellow ocher **-glas** *n* mica, fayalite **-glasur** *f* iron glaze or varnish **-glimmer** *m* iron mica, micaceous iron ore, hematite, göthite

Eisen-glimmerschiefer *m* itabirite **-goniometer** *m* iron-cored goniometer **-granat** *m* almandite, iron garnet **-grau** iron-gray **-graupen** *pl* granular bog-iron ore **-grube** *f* iron(-ore) mine **-grund** *m* iron liquor **-gummi** *m* iron rubber **-guß** *m* iron castings, cast iron **-gymnit** *m* deweylite

eisen-haltig containing iron, ferruginous, ferric, ferriferous, ferrous **-hammerschlag** *m* iron scale **-hardt** *m*, **-hart** *m* ferriferous gold sand **-hart** hard as iron **-härtemittel** *n* iron-tempering material **-haube** *f* iron cap **-hochbau** *m* (iron-) steel-skeleton construction, steel-frame superstructure **-holz** *n* iron bark **-hut** *m* gossan, monkshood, aconite **-hütte** *f* ironworks **-hüttenwesen** *n* metallurgy of iron

Eisen-hutwurzel *f* aconite root **-hydroxyd** *n* iron hydroxide **-hymnit** *m* deweylite **-induktion** *f* induction in iron **-joch** *n* iron yoke **-jodat** *n* ferric or iron iodate **-jodürjodid** *n* ferrosoferric iodide **-kalium** *n* potassium ferrate **-kalk** *m* calcined iron, hydrated iron peroxide **-kamin** *m* steel stack **-karbid** *n* cementite

Eisenkern *m* iron core or mass **geblätterter ~** laminated iron core **geschlossener ~** closed iron core **unterteilter ~** divided iron-core

Eisenkern-abstimmung *f* slug tuning **-induktivität** *f* iron-core inductance **-spule** *f* iron-core(d) coil, iron dust cored coil

Eisen-kies *m* iron disulfide, iron pyrites **-kiesel** *m* ferruginous quartz **-kitt** *m* iron cement; (Rostkitt) iron rust cement **-klumpen** *m* iron block, sow or pig (metal.) **-kobaltkies** *m* **-kobalterz** *n* spathiopyrites, safflorite

Eisenkohlenoxyd *n* iron carboxide

Eisenkohlenstoff-bestimmungsapparat *m* apparatus for the determination of carbon in iron **-legierungen** *pl* iron-carbon alloys

Eisen-konsole *f* iron bracket **-konstruktion** *f* steel construction **-konstruktionswerkstätte** *f* structural-steel works **-körper** *m* steel hull **-kraftfluß** *m* (magnetic) flux in iron

Eisenkreis *m* ferric magnetic circuit, iron circuit **geschlossener** (offener) **~** closed (open)

magnetic or iron circuit

Eisen-kupferkies *m* chalcopyrite **-lack** *m* iron varnish **-lebererz** *n* hepatic iron ore **-legierung** *f* iron composition, ferroalloy **-lichtfunken** *m* iron-arc spark **-liste** *f* steel list, bar list (schedule)

eisenlos ironless, coreless, air core **-e Endstufen** transformerless output stages

Eisen-luppe *f* iron loop or bloom **-magnetisch** ferromagnetic

Eisenmangan *n* ferromanganese **wolframsaures ~** ferromanganese tungstate

Eisen-mangel *m* lack of iron, deficiency in iron **-mann** *m* scaly red hematite

Eisenmantel *m* iron jacket **mit einem ~ versehen** iron-jacketed

Eisen-massekern *m* iron powder core (teleph.)

Eisen-massel *f* iron pig **-mast** *m* iron pole **-menge** *f* amount of iron **-mennige** *f* red ocher, iron ochre, red lead **-meißel** *m* cold chisel **-meßgerät** *n* permeameter **-metall** *n* ferrous metal **-metallurgie** *f* siderurgy **-mohr** *m* black iron oxide, martite **-monoxyd** *n* protoxide of iron **-muffe** *f* iron box

Eisen-nickelakkumulator *m* iron-nickel storage battery, Edison accumulator **-nickelkies** *m* pentlandite **-nickelsammler** *m* iron-nickel accumulator **-niederschlag** *m* precipitate of iron, iron deposit **-ocker** *m* iron ocher

Eisen- oder Stahleinlage *f* reinforcement or reinforcing steel

Eisen-oolith *m* oölitic ironstone **-oxalat** *n* ferric oxalate **-oxyd** *n* iron or ferric oxide **-oxydkitt** *m* rust cement **-oxydreich** rich in iron oxide **-oxydschichten** *pl* iron oxide layers

Eisenoxydul *n* ferrous oxide **-oxyd** *n* magnetic iron oxide **-verbindung** *f* ferrous compound

Eisen-paket *n* core **-panzer** *m* cemented armor, iron shield or screen **-panzerung** *f* iron shield **-pecherz** *n* pitticite **-pentacarbonyl** *n* ferropentacarbonyl **-peridot** *n* fayalite **-phosphor** *n* iron phosphide **-Portlandzement** *n* siderurgical cement, iron Portland cement **-pulver** *n* iron dust

Eisenpulverkern *m* iron-powder core, compressed-iron-dust core **gepreßter ~** compressed-iron-powder core

Eisen-pulverkernspule *f* iron-powder coil, iron-dust coil **-pulververfahren** *n* magnaflux inspection method **-quarz** *m* ferriferous quartz **-querschnitt** *m* iron cross section **-quetscher** *m* iron flattener **-rahm** *m* limonite **-rahmen** *m* iron frame, iron-cored frame (direction finder) **-reich** rich in iron **-reihe** *f* iron series, iron group

Eisen-resin *n*, **resinit** *m* humboldtine **-reste** *pl* skulls **-rhodonit** *m* rhodonite **-ring** *m* iron ring, iron torus, ferrule **-rinne** *f* iron troughing **-röhre** *f*, **-rohr** *n* iron tube, pipe, or tubing **-rohrstrang** *m* iron-pipe conduit **-rost** *m* iron rust **-rostfarbe** *f* iron oxide paint **-rostwasser** *n* iron liquor **-rot** *n* colcothar **-salz** *n* iron salt

Eisen-sand *m* ferruginous sand **-sau** *f* iron sow or bear (metal.), iron pig **-säule** *f* iron standard or column **-schale** *f* (mit Stiel) iron dish, ladel, or cup (with handle) **-schaum** *m* scaly red iron ore **-schiene** *f* rail **-schlacke** *f* iron slag, refinery cinders **-schluß** *m* path closed, or passing, through iron, magnetic shunt **-schmelze** *f* iron smelting, smeltery, or founding

Eisen-schmelzhütte *f* iron foundry **-schörl** *m* bog-iron ore **-schrott** *m* scrap iron **-schüssig** ferruginous, ferriferous **-schutzfarbe** *f* paint for protecting iron **-schutzmittel** *n* antirusting agent **-schwarz** *n* iron black, lampblack, graphite **-schwärze** *f* graphite, black-lead powder, earthy magnetite **-sinter** *m* pitticite

Eisensorte *f* grade of iron or steel **schmiedbare ~** forging-grade steel

Eisen-späne *pl* iron borings, turnings, filings, or chips **-spinell** *n* spinel of iron **-spule** *f* iron-cored coil **-spundwände** *pl* steel-sheet piling **-ständer** *m* iron standard or column

Eisenstaub *m* iron dust **-kern** *m* compressed-iron-powder core, iron-dust core **-kernspule** *f* iron-dust-core coil

Eisenstein *m* iron ore, ironstone **spatiger ~** spathic iron ore, siderite

Eisenstein-feld *n* allotment for iron ore **-mark** *n* lithomarge containing iron **-röster** *m* iron-ore calciner

Eisen-strom *m* stream of metal **-sublimat** *n* iron sublimate, ferric chloride **-sulfat** *n* green vitriol, iron or ferrous sulfate, hydrous ferrous sulfate **-sulfid** *n* iron or ferric sulfide **-sulfozyanid** *n* ferric sulfocyanate, ferric thiocyanate **-sulfür** *n* ferrous sulfide **-sumpferz** *n* bog-iron ore **-täfelung** *f* iron roofing and siding **-teil** *m* iron part

eisentfernender Gummimechanismus overshoes (aviation), ice-removing rubber device

Eisen-tiegel *m* iron crucible **-tinte** *f* iron ink **-titan** *n* ferrotitanium, ilmenite **-ton** *m* iron clay, clay ironstone **-tongranat** *m* almandite **-träger** *m* iron girder **-transformer** *m* iron-core transformer **-umgeben** ironclad **-umspinnung** *f* iron whipping, winding, taping, or wrapping **-umsponnen** iron-whipped

Eisen- und Gittermaster *pl* iron and lattice masts

Eisen-unterlagesteg *m* iron furniture **-untersuchung** *f* examination of iron, iron analysis **-urdoxwiderstand** *m* uranium dioxide resistance, iron-hydrogen resistance **-valerianat** *n* iron valerate, ferric valerate **-vanadin** *n* ferrovanadium **-verarbeitende Industrie** industry using iron or steel **-verbindung** *f* iron compound **-verhüttung** *f* iron smelting **-verluste** *pl* iron or core losses **-verlustmessung** *f* iron loss measurement

eisenverstärkter Beton reinforced concrete

Eisenvitriol *n* green vitriol, hydrous ferrous sulfate **natürliches ~** melanterite

Eisenvitriol-kalkkupe *f* ferrous sulfate-lime vat **-zinnsalzkupe** *f* ferrous sulfate-tin crystals vat

Eisen-vollsetze *f* iron driver, iron set hammer **-vorbereitung** *f* pre-processing of steel material **-walze** *f* iron roller **-walzwerk** *n* iron-rolling mill **-waren** *pl* hardware **-wasserbau** *m* hydraulic ironwork

Eisenwasserstoff-stromregulatorröhre *f* iron-filament ballast lamp, iron ballast tube **-widerstand** *m* iron-hydrogen resistence **-widerstandslampe** *f* iron-filament ballast lamp **-widerstandsröhre** *f* iron-hydrogen resistance lamp

Eisen-weg *m* ferromagnetic circuit, iron circuit or path **-werk** *n* ironworks, metalwork **-wick-**

lung *f* iron winding or whipping

Eisenwiderstand *m* resistance of iron **Lampe beruhend auf** ~ iron-filament ballast lamp **magnetischer** ~ magnetic reluctance or resistance of iron

Eisen-wolfram *n* ferrotungsten **-wolframat** *n* iron tungstate **-zement** *m* ferroconcrete, rust cement **-zinkblende** *f* marmatite **-zinkspat** *m* ferruginous calamine **-zinnerz** *n* ferriferous cassiterite

Eisen-zwinge *f* clamping ring **-zyanfarbe** *f* iron-cyanogen pigment **-zyankalium** *n* potassium ferrocyanide **-zyanür** *n* ferrous cyanide **-zyanürzinkoxyd** *n* zinc ferrocyanide **-zyanverbindung** *f* iron-cyanogen compound, ferrocyanogen or ferricyanogen compound

eisern (of) iron, ferrous **-es Bauzeug** iron work **-e Scheuerleiste** fender iron

Eis-erzeuger *m* ice freezing tank **-erzeugungsmaschine** *f* ice machine **-essig** *m* glacial acetic acid **-fänger** *m* ice trap **-feld** *n* ice field, ice pack **-frei** free from ice **-fühlergerät** *n*, **-fühlgerät** *n* ice detector **-gang** *m* drift(ing) ice **-glas** *n* frosted glass **-hülle** *f* coat of ice

eisig icy, glacial

Eis-kalorimeter *m* ice calorimeter **-kalt** ice-cold **-keim** *m* sublimation center (in ice formation) **-keller** *m* ice cellar, icehouse **-kerne** *pl* ice nuclei **-klappe** *f* ice valve, flap or skimmer on a gate of a movable dam, ice gate **-kluft** *f* frost shake or cleft in wood **-klüftig** pertaining to ice, frost cleft **-klumpen** *m* lump of ice **-kristall** *m* ice crystal **-last** *f* ice load **-leistung** *f* icemaking capacity, ice production **-maschine** *f* ice machine, freezer

Eis-maschinenanlage *f* ice-machine manufacturing plant **-maschinenöl** *n* ice-machine oil **-mühle** *f* ice crusher **-nachrichtendienst** *m* ice-information service, iceberg service **-nadeln** *pl* ice needles **-nebel** *n* ice fog **-pfanne mit Stopfenausguß** teeming ladle **-pickel** *m* ice adz or ax **-punkt** *m* freezing point **-pyrheliometer** *n* ice-pyrheliometer **-reflexion am Horizont** iceblink **-regen** *m* ice rain **-rutsche** *f* ice chute **-schild** *n* ice sheet

Eis-schmelze *f* ice-break **-scholle** *f* block of ice, ice floe, floating ice **-schrank** *m* icebox **-schublade** *f* ice cube tray **-schutz** *m* protector or protection against ice, deicer **-schwimmer** *m* ice float, bucket attemperator **-spat** *m* rhyacolite **-sporn** *m* ice spade (trail spade) **-sprengen** *n* breaking up of ice by explosives **-stein** *m* cryolite **-stopfung** *f* packing or stoppage of ice **-stoß** *m* ice jam or impact **-trieb** *m* ice flow **-überzug** *m* ice coating

Eis- und Kühlanlage *f* ice and cooling installation

Eis- und Kühlmaschinen *pl* refrigerating machinery

Eis-warngerät *n* ice-warning unit or device **-warnungsapparat** *m* ice-warning indicator **-warte** *f* ice-observation post **-wasserkasten** *m* ice-water tank **-zapfen** *m* icicle **-zeit** *f* ice age **-zelle** *f* ice can, ice mold **-zerkleinerungsmaschine** *f* ice-crushing machine

Eiweiß *n* albumen, albumin **-abbau** *m* proteolysis **-abbauprodukt** *n* albumen decomposition product **-artig** albuminous **-fänger** *m* albumin filter **-körper** *m* protein material **-kunststoffe** *pl* protein plastics **-leim** *m* albumen glue **-stoffwechsel** *m* protein metabolism

Ejektor *m* ejector

Ekato-Korbkreiselmischer *m* cyclone impeller mixer **-Rührer** *m* portable propeller mixer **-Trommelkreiselrührer** *m* rotor cage impeller

E-Kern *m* three-limb core, E-core

Eklimeter *n* eclimeter

Eklipse-bauart *f* eclipse system **-ringe** *pl* eclipse rings

Ekliptik (Sonnenbahn) *f* ecliptic **-koordinaten** *pl* ecliptical coordinates **-kugel** *f* equator-ecliptic (ball) body

Ekrasit *n* ecrasite

Ekrüseide *f* crude silk

Elaidinsäure *f* elaidic acid

Elainsäure *f* oleic acid

Eläolith *m* nepheline, eleolite

Eläometer *n* eleometer

Elastik-bereifung *f* cushion-tire equipment **-kopf** *m* elastic head **-muffe** *f* flexible coupling

elastisch elastic, springy, flexible, resilient ~ **aufgehängter Motor** flexibly mounted engine ~ **gestreut** elastically scattered ~ **verschraubt** screwed with spring action

elastisch-e Aufhängung *f* elastic suspension system, flexible suspension **-er Belastungsversuch** elastic test **-e Dehnung** elastic elongation **-e Formänderung** elastic deformation or strain **-es Gewebe** (gummilos) elastic non-rubber fabrics **-e Grenze** *f* elastic limit **-e Linie** elastic curve (mech.) **-e Nachwirkung** elastic afterworking or aftereffect, afterflow, refreshment, recovery, plastic-flow persistence **-es Rohr** flexible pipe

elastisch-e Scheibenkupplung flexible disk coupling **-er Schmirgelkörper** *m* elastic abrasive head **-e Spannung** *f* elastic stress **-er Spannungszustand** elastic stress **-er Stoß** elastic collision **-e Streuung** (Wirkungsquerschnitt) elastic scattering (cross section) **-er Strom** *m* elastic flow **-es Vorgelege** elastic driving gear **-e Wellen** elastic or stress waves **-er Widerstand** *m* elastic resistance

Elastizität *f* elasticity, flexibility, resilience; (des Motors) flexibility **unvollkommene** ~ imperfect elasticity **vollkommene** ~ perfect elasticity

Elastizitäts-beiwert *m* coefficient of elasticity **-gebiet** *n* elastic range **-gesetz** *n* elasticity-law, Hooke's law **-gleichung** *f* slope deflection equation **-grad** *m* degree of elasticity, elastic ratio **-grenze** *f* elastic limit, limit of (linear) elasticity, yield strength **-koeffizient** *m* modulus of elasticity, coefficient of elasticity **-maß** *n* modulus or valve of elasticity **-messer** *m* elastometer, torsometer

Elastizitätsmodul *m* modulus of elasticity, coefficient of elasticity, Young's modulus, modulus of rigidity or of stiffness, spring constant ~ **für Druck** modulus of compression, bulk modulus, volumetric modulus of elasticity ~ **für Schub** modulus of elasticity for (or in) shear, modulus of shear, shearing modulus of elasticity ~ **für Zug** modulus of elasticity for (or in) tension, modulus of direct elasticity

Elastizitäts-müdigkeit *f* elastic fatigue **-theorie** *f* theory of elasticity **-verstärker** *m* elasticator **-zahl** *f*, **-ziffer** *f* modulus or coefficient of

elasticity, Young's modulus
Elastkuppelung *f* flexible coupling
Elasto-dynamik *n* dynamic elasticity **-gramm** *n* diffraction diagram
Elatationswirkungs-querschnitt *m* elatation cross section
Eldro-gerät *n* electro-hydraulic brake lifter, Eldro unit **-lüfter** *m* (AEG) eldro thruster
E-Latte *f* aiming stake or post
Elefantenrüsselrutsche *f* elephant-trunk chute
elegant attractive, smooth (styling)
Elektret *n* electret
elektrifizieren to electrify
Elektrifizierung *f* electrification
Elektriker *m* electrician **-trupp** *m* electrician squad
elektrisch electric(al), electrified **~ beheizter Enteiser** electrical heating deicer system **~ einziehbares Fahrgestell** electrically operated retractable undercarriage **~ leitfähige Gummischläuche** *pl* electrically bonded rubber hoses **~ betätigte Klappen** electrically operated flaps **~ verstellbare Schraube** electrically controlled variable-pitch airscrew **~ heizbares Staurohr** electrically heated Pitot tube
elektrisch angetrieben electrically driven **~ betätigt** electrically operated or actuated **~ betrieben** electrically operated **~ gekuppelt** electrically connected **~ geschweißt** electrically welded **~ symmetrisch** homopolar **gleichnamig ~** similary electrified or charged **~ leitend** electrically conductive; (Reifen) static discharge (of tires) **negativ ~** electronegative **positiv ~** electropositive **ungleichnamig ~** oppositely electrified or charged **~ werden** to acquire static electricity
elektrisch-e Abfühlung electrical sensing **-e Ablenkung** electric deflection **-e Abschaltung** radio-signal cutoff (guided missiles) **-e Analogie** electrical analogy **-er Anlasser** *m* starting magneto, booster **-e Anpassung** *f* electrical matching **-er Antrieb** electric-motor-operated or -driven **-e Arbeit** (Joule, Wattstunde) electrical energy **-e Ausrüstung** *f* electrical equipment
elektrisch-e Beleuchtung electric lighting **-er Blattantrieb** electric chart drive **-er Bohrer** electromechanical brush **-er Dipol** electric dipole **-e Einstellung** electric focusing **-es Elementarquantum** electronic charge, elementary charge **-e Energie** potential energy **-e Entladung** electric discharge **-es Entladungsgefäß** electronic discharge vessel
elektrisch-es Feld electric field, field of force **-e Feldstärke** electric field strength, electric force **-er freistrahlender Körper** electric radiator **-er Hammer** interrupter **-e Kurzzeitmeßgeräte** electric microtime measuring devices **-e Metallbogenschweißung** metallic arc welding **-e Normaluhr** electric master clock **-er Salzgehaltmesser** electrical salinometer **-e Verzögerungsleitung** electric delay line
elektrisierbar electrifiable
elektrisieren to electrify
Elektrisieren durch Influenz electrostatic induction
elektrisiert electrified
Elektrisierung *f* electrification
Elektrizität *f* electricity **gebundene ~** dissimulated or bound electricity **gleichnamige ~** electricity of same sign **ungleichnamige ~** electricity of opposite sign
Elektrizitäts-ableitungsvorrichtung *f* electrical discharger gear **-erzeugung** *f* generation of electricity **-gesellschaft** electric power company **-ladung** *f* charge of electricity **-leiter** *m* conductor **-leitung** *f* electrical conduction
Elektrizitätsmenge *f* quantity of electricity **Einheit der ~** unit quantity of electricity
Elektrizitäts-messer *m* electrometer **-selbstverkäufer** *m* prepayment or coin-in-the-slot electric meter **-träger** *m* charged particle **-versorgung** *f* electric supply **-versorgungsunternehmen** power company, electricity-supply company **-waage** *f* electrometer **-werk** *n* electric-power company or station, electric central station **-zähler** *m* electric meter, electricity-supply meter **-zeiger** *m* electroscope
Elektro-abscheider *n* electrical dust collector, electric precipitator **-aggregate** *pl* electric generator sets **-akustik** *f* electroacoustics **-Analogon** *n* electro-analogue **-analyse** *f* electroanalysis **-analytisch** electroanalytical **-antrieb** *m* electric propulsion or power **-aufzug** *m* electric hoist **-beleuchtungsglas** *n* glass for electric lighting purposes **-bleche** *pl* sheets for electrical industry **-bus** *m* electric bus **-chemie** *f* electrochemistry **-chemiker** *m* electrochemist
elektrochemisch electrochemical **-es Potential** Fermi level (in semi-conductors) **-e Spannungsreihe** electrochemical series
Elektrode *f* electrode (of a storage battery) plate, applicator **~ mit flachem Ende** (Zündkerze) flat-topped electrode (spark plug) **~ mit Gashäutchen** gas electrode **~ mit gasumhülltem Lichtbogen** shielded arc electrode **blanke ~** bare electrode **-blechumhüllte ~** sheathed electrode **getauchte ~** coated electrode **nackte ~** plain rod **negative ~** negative electrode, cathode **positive ~** positive electrode, anode **ummantelte ~, umwickelte ~** covered, coated, or sheathed electrode **verstellbare ~** sliding electrode
Elektroden-abbrand *m* consumption of electrodes **-abdichtung** *f* electrode economizer, electrode gland **-abstand** *m* electrode gap, spark gap, electrode spacing; (Funkenstrecke) gap separation, auxiliary gap **-abstandslehre** *f* (Zündkerze) electrode gap gauge **-admittanz** *f* electrode admittance **-anordnung** *f* electrode arrangement **-anschluß** *m* horns of a tube or valve, electrode contact or connection
Elektrodenanschlußstück *n* electrode clamp, electrode terminal **wassergekühltes ~** electrode economizer, water-cooled electrode collar
Elektroden-arm *m* electrode arm, horn (welding) **-ausleger** *m* electrode arm **-biegevorrichtung** *f* electrode bending device **-blindleitwert** *m* electrode susceptance **-blindwiderstand** *m* electrode reactance **-druck** *m* electrode force, net electrode pressure, tip pressure **-durchführung** *f* electrode collar (metal.) **-ende** *n* electrode end, terminal (of an arc) **-fahrsäule** *f* electrode support or mast (electric furnaces) **-fassung** *f* electrode holder, clamp, or collar **-fläche** *f* electrode surface, electrode area **-form**

f shape of electrodes **-führung** *f* electrode control **-gleichspannung** *f* supply voltage

Elektroden-halter *m* electrode holder or support **-herdofen** *m* electrode hearth furnace **-kapazität** *f* interelectrode capacity **-kitt** *m* electrode or electrode compound **-kopf** *m* electrode head, upper end of electrode **-korrosion** *f* corrosion of electrodes

elektrodenlos electrodeless, devoid of, or without, electrodes **-e Röhre** nullode

Elektroden-mantel *m* electrode shell **-masse** *f* compounds for electrodes **-mehl** *n* crushed electrodes **-metall** *n* filler metal **-regeler** *m* electrode regulator, electrode control device **-regelung** *f* regulation of electrodes **-regelvorrichtung** *f* electrode control device **-regulierung** *f* electrode regulation or control **-reste** *pl* short electrode ends, electrode waste **-röhre** *f* electrode tube

Elektroden-schaltung *f* electrode connection **-scheinleitwert** *m* electrode admittance **-scheinwiderstand** *m* electrode impedance **-schluß** *m* electrode short circuit **-schweißung** *f* electrowelding **-spanner** *m* electrode (wrench) **-spannung** *f* electrode potential **-spitze** *f* electrode tips (spot welder)

Elektroden-ständer *m* electrode mast or support **-stellungsregelung** *f* electrode control **-stellungsregler** *m* electrode adjusting gear **-stift** *m* electrode rod **-stützenstrahlung** *f* stem radiation **-träger** *m* electrode support **-tragkonstruktion** *f* electrode support **-tragvorrichtung** *f* electrode-carrying superstructure **-verlustleistung** *f* electrode dissipation **-verschleiß** electrode wear **-verstellung** *f* electrode regulation **-vorspannung** *f* electrode bias **-wasserkühlmantel** *m* water-circulation jacket surrounding the electrodes **-wirkleitwert** *m* electrode conductance **-zange** *f* electrode holder

Elektrodialyse *f* electrodialysis

elektrodisch electrodic

Elektro-drehbohrmaschine *f* rotary electric drill **-dynamik** *f* electrodynamics

elektrodynamisch electrodynamic **-er Fernhörer** moving conductor receiver **-er Lautsprecher** moving coil loudspeaker **-er Motorzähler** Thomson-meter

Elektro-eisen *n* electric steel **-enzephalogramm** *n* E. E. G. electroencephalogram **-erosivbearbeitung** *f* spark machining

elektroerosives Bohren spark drilling

Elektro-fahrwerk *n* electric traversing gear **-filter** *n* electrical or electrostatic precipitator (for gas cleaning), electrostatic filter **-flaschenzug** *m* electric hoist or pulley **-flußstahl** *m* electric steel **-gebläse** *n* electrically driven blower

Elektro-handbohrmaschine *f* portable electric drill **-hängebahn** *f* motor-driven overhead trolley conveyer, electric trolley system **-hartguß** *m* electrochilling (met.) **-hartgußgießerei** *f* electro chilled-iron foundry **-herdofen** *m* electric-hearth furnace **-hochofen** *m* electric shaft furnace, electric smelting furnace **-hub** *m* power lift **-hubwagen** *m* electric elevating-platform truck, power-lift truck **-hubwerk** *n* electric hoisting gear **-induktiv** electroinductive **-ingenieur** *m* electrical engineer **-installateur** *m* electrician fitter

elektrokalorisch thermo-electric(al), electrocaloric

elektrokapillar electrocapillary

Elektro-kapillarität *f* electrocapillarity **-kardiogramm** (EKG) *n* electrocardiogram

Elektrokarren *m* electrical industrial or general-utility truck, electric freight truck, electric trolley ~ **mit Kippmulde** electric dump truck

Elektro-karrenanhänger *m* electric-truck trailer **-krankarren** *m* electric-crane truck, mobile crane **-kinetik** *f* electrokinetic **-korund** *m* fusel alumina, aluminous abrasive **-kraftstoffventil** *n* solenoid fuel valve **-kultur** *f* electroculture **-kymograph** *m* electrokymograph **-lackpappe** *f* varnished paper board **-lamellenkupplungsprüfstand** *m* electro-magnetic multidisc test rig **-lot** *n* electrical depth sounder **-lötkolben** *m* soldering iron **-lumineszenz** *f* electroluminesccence

Elektrolyse *f* electrolysis **schmelzflüssige** ~ smelting-flux electrolysis

Elektrolysen-bad *n* electrolytic bath or cell **-behälter** *m* electrolysis tank **-betrieb** *m* electrolytic refining practice **-endlauge** *f* spent electrolyte **-schlamm** *m* electrolytic slime **-zelle** *f* reduction pot, electrolytic cell

Elektrolyseprozeß *m* electrolytic refining process

Elektrolyser *m* **Elektrolyseur** *m* electrolyzer, electrolyzer's outfit

elektrolysieren to electrolyze

Elektrolysiergefäß *n* electrolytic vessel

Elektrolysierung *f* electrolyzation

Electrolysiszelle *f* electrolytic cell, reduction pot

Elektrolyt *m* electrolyte **kieselflußsaurer** ~ fluosilicate electrolyte

Elektrolyt-detektor *m* electrolytic detector **-eisen** *n* electrolytic iron **-gleichrichter** *m* electrolytic rectifier

elektrolytisch electrolytic(al) ~ **aufgebracht** electrolytically deposited (films) ~ **aufgebracht gedruckte Schaltung** plated circuit

elektrolytisch-es Anätzen anodic etching **-es Bad** galvanic bath **-e Bleiraffination** electrolytic lead refining **-es Dekapieren** electrochemical pickling **-e Fällung** precipitation by electrolysis, electrodeposition **-er Lösungsdruck** electrolytic solution pressure **-e** (Metall-) **Raffination** electrolytic refining **-er Niederschlag** electrolytic deposit

elektrolytisch-e Raffination electrolytic refining or parting **-es Reinigen** electrochemical pickling **-e Überspannung** electrolytic excess voltage **-es Ventil** electrolytic rectifier or valve **-er Wellenanzeiger** electrolytic detector **-e Zelle** *f* electrolytic detector **-e Zersetzung** electrolytic or ionic dissociation **-e Zerstörung** electrolytic corrosion

Elektrolyt-kondensator *m* electrolytic capacitor **-kupfer** *n* electrolytic copper **-profilkupferrohre** *pl* sectional electrolytic copper tubes **-unterbrecher** *m* electrolytic interrupter **-zähler** *m* electrolytic meter **-zelle** *f* photoelectrolytic cell, electrolytic photocell, photolytic, photovoltaic, Becquerel, or liquid cell **-zinn** *n* electrolytic tin

Elektromagnet *m* solenoid, electromagnet **Maschine mit** ~ dynamo-electric machine

Elektromagnetanker *m* electromagnet armature

elektromagnetisch electromagnetic **-er Abriß** break of magnetic separation (of isotopes) **-e Aufspannvorrichtung** electromagnetic holding device **-e Backenbremse** solenoid block brake **-e Einheit** electromagnetic unit **-er Schaltschütz** electromagnetic contactor, solenoid contactor **-e Schienenbremse** electromagnetic slipper brake

Elektromagnetismus *m* electromagnetism

Elektromagnet-kern *m* electromagnet core **-kupplung** *f* electromagnetic clutch **-spule** *f* electromagnet coil **-ventil** *n* solenoid valve **-wicklung** *f* electromagnet winding

Elektro-mechanik *f* electromechanics **-mechaniker** *m* electrician

elektromechanisch electromechanic(al) **-er Umwandlungsfaktor** electromechanical force factor **-er Wandler** electromechanical transducer

Elektro-metall *n* electron (a metal) **-metallurge** *m* electrometallurgist **-medizin** *f* medical electronics **-meterröhre** *f* electrometer valve **-monteur** *m* electrician

Elektromotor *m* electromotor, electric motor **eingekapselter ~** iron-clad electric motor

Elektromotorantrieb *m* electric-motor drive

Elektromotorenöl *n* electric-motor oil

elektromotorisch electromotive **-e Gegenkraft** counterelectromotive force **-e Rückkoppelung mit Hilfsfrequenz** superregenerative reception **-e Kraft** electromotive force **-e von rechteckiger Kurvenform** square-topped electromotive force **-e Schwebung mit besonderem Überlagerer** separate heterodyne reception **-e der Selbstinduktion** electromotive force of self-induction **periodische -e Kraft** periodic electromotive force **rein sinusförmige -e Kraft** pure sine electromotive force **zusammengesetzte -e Kraft** composite electromotive force

Elektron *n* electron **Bahn eines ~** electron trajectory **~ mit Eigendrehimpuls** spinning electron

Elektron-ätzplatte *f* electron etching plate **-autotypie** *f* electron halftone

Elektronegativität *f* electronegativy

Elektron-Elektron-Zusammenstöße effektiver Wirkungsquerschnitt effective cross-section for electron electron collisions

Elektronen *pl* electrons **angelagerte ~** trapped electrons **angestoßene ~** knock-on electrons **auslösende ~** triggering electrons **diskrete ~** mono-energetic electrons **kernferne ~** outer (level) electrons, conduction, valence, peripheral, orbital, or planetary electrons **kernnahe ~** inner or fixed electrons **klebende ~** captured electrons, electrons sticking to electronegative gases or surfaces **kreisende ~** orbital electrons **positive ~** positrons, positive electrons **rückwärts gesteuerte ~** back-scattered electrons **schwere ~** heavy electrons, barytrons, dynatrons, mesotrons, penetrons, X particles

Elektronen, Stöße zwischen ~ electron collisions **Streuung von ~** scattering of electrons

Elektronenabbildung *f* electron image

Elektronenabgabe, glühelektrische ~ thermionic emission

Elektronen-abgabefläche *f* electron-emission or -emitting area **-absaugung** *f* electron collection **-abtaststrahl** *m* electron scanning spot or brush, electron pencil or beam **-affinitätsspektren** *pl* electron affinity spectra **-anlagerung** *f* electron attachment

Elektronenanordnung *f*, **Wechselwirkung zwischen ~** configuration interaction (electronics)

Elektronen-anregung *f* electronic excitation **-auffang** *m* electron capture **-aufprall** *m* cathodic bombardment **-ausbeute** *f* (-auslösung *f*) electron emission or efficiency **-außendend** electron emitting **-austrittsarbeit** *f* work function of electrons

Elektronen-bahn *f* electron path, orbit, or trajectory, flight of electrons **-bandenspektren** *pl* electronic band spectra **-belastung** *f* electron loading **-belegung** *f* density of electrons (in beam) **-beraubtes Atom** stripped atom **-beschießung** *f* electron bombardment **-beugung** *f* electron diffraction **-beugungsaufnahme** *f* exposure of electron diffraction **-beugungsdiagramm** *n* electronic-diffraction diagram **-beugungsgitter** *n* electron diffraction lattice **-beugungskammer** *f* electron-diffraction camera

Elektronen-beute *f* electron efficiency **-bild 0** electron-current image, cathode-ray tube display **-bildfang** *m* electron image pickup **-bildröhre** *f* electron-image tube **-bildzerleger** *m* electron-image dissector **-blech** *n* sheet electrons **-blitz** *m* electron burst, electronic flash

Elektronen-bohrmaschine electron drill **-bohrverfahren** *n* electron drilling process **-bremsung** *f* reflection, deflection (in magnetron), retardation or deceleration of electrons **-bündel** *n* electron beam, cathode ray or beam **-dichte** *f* electron density **-drall** *m* electron spin **-durchlässig** electron-transmitting (permeable) **-einfang** *m* electron capture or trapping, electron attachment

Elektronenemission *f* electron emission **glühelektrische ~** thermionic emission, temperature emission of electrons, electron evaporation **lichtelektrische ~** photoelectric emission, photoemissive or external photoelectric effect, Hallwachs effect

elektronenemittierendes Metall metallic electron emitter

Elektronenenergie *f* electron energy, electron affinity

Elektronenentladung *f* electron discharge **~** (Glühentladung), thermionic discharge **monoenergetische ~** monoenergetic electron discharge

Elektronen-fänger *m* (impurity) acceptor **-fleck** *m* electron or scanning spot **-fluß** *m* flow of electrons **-flußdiskontinuität** *f* electronic shot effect **-gas** *n* electron gas **-geschwindigkeit** *f* velocity of electrons **-gitterstrom** *m* grid current **-gruppierung** *f* phase focusing (in beam tubes)

Elektronen-haftstellen *pl* electron traps **-hülle** *f* gyration, outer electrons, electron shell or cloud **-hüllenradius** (mittlerer) *m* gyration radius **-intensität** *f* electron beam intensity **-interferometrie** *f* interferometry of electrons **-kartenabbildung** *f* auto radar plot **-kontinuum** *n* free-bond transition spectrum **-konzentration** *f* electron density or focusing **-kreis** *m* orbit or shell of electrons **-kupplung** *f* electron coupling

Elektronen-ladung *f* electronic charge **-laufzeit** *f* transition time, electron transit time, orbit time of electron **-lawine** *f* avalanche of electrons **-lehre** *f* electronics **-linearbeschleuniger** *m* linear electron accelerator **-linse** *f* electronic lens (electromagnetic or electrostatic) **-mangelleitung** *f* hold conduction (trans.) **-masse** *f* mass of the electrons

elektronenmikroskopische Aufnahme *f* electron micrograph

Elektronen-mikroskopselbstleuchtverfahren *n* self-luminous or self-emission electron microscope **-niederschlag** *m* electrode-position **-niveau** *n* electron level **-optik** *f* electron optics

elektronenoptisch electron-optical **~ korrigiert** electron-optically corrected

Elektronen-ort *m* electron position or locus **-pendelschwingungen** *pl* pendulum motions of electrons **-pendelung** *f* pendulum motion of electrons, oscillating of electrons **-physik** *f* electronics **-plasma** *n* residual electrons, electron plasma **-quelle** *f* electron (emission) source, electron emitter **-rastermikroskop** *n* raster microscope, electron-scan microscope **-rechenanlage** *f* electronic computers **-rechner mit steuerbarer Rechenfolge** selective sequence electronic calculator **-relais** *n* electron relay, valve relay, thermionic or discharge relay **-rohr** *n* electron gun

Elektronenröhre *f* thermionic valve, tube or vacuum tube, electronic or ionic valve, electron tube, audion **~ die gleichzeitig als Mischröhre und als Überlagerungsoszillator arbeitet** converter tube

Elektronenröhren-gerät *n* thermionic apparatus **-gleichrichter** *m* electron tube rectifier **-klemme** *f* electron tube terminal

Elektronen-rumpf *m* core, kernel, stable electron group **-schalen** *pl* electron shells **-schalter** *m* electron switch (radio) **-schicht** *f* electron sheath **-schleuder** *f* electron gun, betatron, electron accelerator **-schwarm** *m* cloud of electrons **-schweißnaht** *f* arc-welded joint **-schwingungen** *pl* electron oscillations **-sicherung** *f* fusetron **-sonde** *f* electron probe

Elektronen-spender *m* electron donor (of impurities) **-spinresonanz** *f* electron spin resonance **-spritze** *f* electron gun **-sprungspektrum** *n* electron transition (or jump) spectrum **-stauung** *f* electron cloud or accumulation **-steuerung** *f* electronic control, thymotrol panel **-stoß** *m* electron impact **-stoßspektrum** *n* electron impact spectrum

Elektronenstrahl *m* electron beam or ray, cathode ray or beam, electron stream **abtastender ~** scanning electron beam **~ teilende Elektrode** splitting electrode

Elektronenstrahl-abtaster *m* iconoscope, electron-scanning pencil, beam, spot, brush, or lever **-bündel** *n* electron beam

Elektronenstrahlengang *m* electron-ray path

Elektronenstrahl-erzeuger *m* electron gun **-krümmungsspule** *f* bending coil **-oszillograph** *m* cathode-ray oscillograph **-peiler** *m* cathode-ray direction finder **-röhre** beam deflection tube cathode-ray tube, electron-beam tube, Braun tube, thermionic tube, cathode-ray tuning-indicator tube **-schweißen** *n* electron beam welding **-system** *n* system of beam, electron gub system

Elektronen-straße *f* arc core **-strecke** *f* electron path **-strom** *m* ionic current, stream of electrons, electronic or space current **-stromdichte** *f* density of electron current **-strommodulation** *f* electron quantity modulation **-strömung** *f* electron stream

Elektronentanz *m* pendulum motion or oscillatory movements of electrons **elektrischer ~** Barkhausen-Kurz oscillations

Elektronentanzschwingungen *pl* pendulum motion of electrons

Elektronen-technik *f* electronics **-term** *m* electron term **-trägheit** *f* electron inertia **-turbine** *f* cyclotron and inverted forms thereof **-übergang** *m* electron promotion **-übergangswahrscheinlichkeit** *f* electron transition probability **-überholungsgebiet** *n* electron catch-up or over-take region **-überkreuzungsstelle** *f* crossover of electrons **-übermikroskop** *n* electronic supermicroscope, electronic ultramicroscope

Elektronen- und Gitterkomponente electronic and lattice components

Elektronen- und Gitterwellen, Wechselwirkung zwischen ~ interaction between electrons

Elektronen-unterhülle *f* subshell (of electrons) **-ventil** *n* electronic or ionic valve **-verdampfung** *f* thermionic emission, temperature emission of electrons, electron evaporation **-vervielfacher** *m* (Photozelle) electron-multiplier tube (photocell), photomultiplier **-vervielfachung** *f* electron amplification **-vervielfachungsröhre** *f* electron multiplier tube

Elektronenwechselwirkung *f*, **kurzreichweitige ~** electron interaction short range

Elektronen-welle *f* electron or phase wave **-wellenröhre** electron wave tube **-wirkungsgrad** *m* emission efficiency

Elektronenwolke *f* cloud of electrons **Eigenabstoßung der ~** repelling action of electron charge, negative space charge

Elektronen-wucht *f* collision or bombardment force of electrons **-zeugungsgitter** *n* electronic diffraction grating **-zertrümmerung** electrodisintegration **-zufuhr** *f* electron input **-zustand** *m* electron(ic) state **-zustandssumme** *f* electronic partition function

Elektrongußstück *n* electron casting

Elektronik *f* electronics

Elektroniker *m* electronics engineer

Elektronik-geräteschacht *m* (Astron.) electrical bay **-teil** *n* electronic package

Elektron-Ion-Rekombination *f* electron-ion recombination

Elektron-Ion-Wandrekombination *f* electron-ion wall recombination

elektronisch electronic

Elektron-klischee *n* electron (block) plate **-kurbelgehäuse** *n* electron crankcase

Elektronogen *n* electronogen

Elektronographie *f* electronography

Elektronoskopie *f* electron spectroscopy

Elektron-Phonon-Wechselwirkungsenergie *f* electron-phonon interaction energy

Elektron-Phonon-Wechselwirkungsparameter *n* electron-phonon interaction parameter

Elektron-richtstrahler *m* beam or cathode-ray tube **-röhren** *pl* electron tubes **-strichätzung** *f* electron line-plate **-warmpreßteile** *m pl* electron warm-pressed parts

Elektro-ofen *m* electric furnace **-ofenspannung** *f* electric-furnace voltage **-optik** *f* electrooptics **-optischer Verschluß** electrooptic shutter **-osmose** *f* electroosmosis **-pendelzentrifuge** *f* electrically driven pendulum hydroextractor

Elektropher *m* electrophorus

Elektro-phononwechselwirkungsenergie *f* electro-phonon interaction energy **-phorese** *f* electrophoresis **-phoresezelle** *f* electrophoresis cell **-physik** *f* electrophysics **-physikalisch** electrophysical **-plattieren** to electroplate **-plattierung** *f* electroplating **-plattierverfahren** *n* electroplating process

elektropneumatisch electropneumatic **-er Fahrschalter** electro-pneumatic controller **-er Regler** pneumatic controller with an electrical measuring element

Elektro-porzellan *n* electrotechnical porcelain **-raffination** *f* electrorefining **-reduktionsofen** *m* electric (ore) reduction furnace **-remissionsphotometer** *n* photoelectric reflection photometer **-roheisen** *n* electric pig **-schachtofen** *m* electric shaft furnace **-schaltbild** *n* wiring diagram **-schlackeschweißen** *n* electro-slag welding **-schmelzanlage** *f* electric smelting plant **-schmelzofen** *m* electric melting or smelting furnace **-schmelzschweißung** *f* electric-arc welding **-schweißen** *n* electric welding **-schweißer** *m* arc welder **-speicher** *m* electricity container, battery box

Elektroskop *n* electroscope

Elektrostahl *m* electric-furnace steel, electric steel **-anlage** *f* electric steel plant **-halbzeug** *n* semiproduct of electric steel **-ofen** *m* electric melting furnace **-schmelzen** *n* electric-furnace melting, manufacture of electric steel **-verfahren** *n* electric steelmaking process, electrometallurgy of iron and steel **-werk** *n* electric steel plant

Elektrostatik *f* electrostatics

elektrostatisch electrostatic(al) ~ **geschirmt** electrostatically shielded or screened **-es C.G.S.-System** electrostatic centimeter-gram-second system **-es Arbeitsverfahren** *n* electrostatic precipitation **-e Eichung** electrostatic calibration **-e Einheit** electrostatic unit **-er Kreisel** *m* electrically suspended gyro **-e Ladungen entfernen** to destaticize **-er Lautsprecher** electrostatic loudspeaker, condenser loudspeaker, capacitor loud-speaker **-es Meßsystem** electrostatic system of measurement **-es Spiegelbild** electrical image of a conductor as to earth

Elektro-stauchmaschine *f* electric upsetting machine **-striktion** *f* electrostriction **-tauchkolbenverdichter** *m* reciprocating motor compressor **-tauchpumpe** *f* electric immersion pump **-technik** *f* electrical engineering **-techniker** *m* electrical engineer, electrician **-technisch** electrotechnical

elektrotensometrische Waage electrical strain-gauge scale

elektro-thermisch electrothermal **-tonus** *n* electrotonus **-werte** *pl* shares of electrical concerns **-winde** *f* electric hoist **-wirtschaft** *f* public electricity supply **-zug** *m* electric hoist **-zugkarren** *m* tractor

Element *n* element, principle, battery, cell (elec.), thermocouple ~ **mit einer Flüssigkeit** single fluid cell ~ **mit Luft als Depolarisator** cell with air depolarizer **ein** ~ **ansetzen** to set up a cell **galvanisches** ~ primary or galvanic cell **geschlossenes** ~ closed-circuit cell **linienreiches** ~ (Spektroskopie), element with large number of spectrum lines **nasses** ~ wet cell, hydroelectric cell **thermoelektrisches** ~ thermocouple **umkehrbares** ~ reversible cell **zweiwertiges** ~ dyad

elementar elementary, elemental

Elementar-analyse *f* ultimate analysis **-bereich** *m* (Zelle) unit cell **-kondensator** *m* elementary condenser **-ladung** *f* elemental charge, electronic charge **-magnet** *m* molecular magnet **-quantum** *n* atomic charge

Elementarteilchen mit positiver oder negativer Ladung meson

Elementar-teilertheorie *f* theory of elementary divisor **-welle** *f* elementary wavelet, Huygens' wavelets **-zelle** *f* unit cell, elementary cell, lattice unit

Elementbecher *m* battery box, cell container

Elemente, ganzzahlige ~ elements integral

Elementen-bündelverflüssiger *m* countercurrent condenser of the multipass type **-messung** *f* stoichiometry **-kühler** *m* sectionalized or cellulartype radiator **-verflüssiger** *m* multishell condenser

Element-glas *n* battery or element jar, element glass **-kohle** *f* battery carbon **-prüfer** *m* battery tester, battery voltmeter **-schlamm** *m* battery mud

Element- und Verbindungshalbleiter *m* element and compound-semiconductor

Elemiharz *n* elemi (gum)

Elevationswinkel *m* angle of elevation or of tangent

Elevator *m* elevator ~ **für Schubbinder,** ~ **für Stoßbinder** elevator for push binder

Elevator-becher *m* elevator bucket or scoop **-behälter** *m* elevator boot

Elevatorenkette *f* elevator chain

Elevator-gehäuse *n* elevator casing **-gurt** *m* elevator belt **-schlotte** *f* elevator trunking **-tuch** *n* elevator canvas

Elfenbein *n* ivory

Eliasit *m* eliasite

Elimination *f* elimination

eliminieren to eliminate, avoid

Elit *n* Elit

Ellbogen *m* elbow

Elle *f* ell, yard

Ellipse *f* ellipse

Ellipsen-abschnitt *m* segment of an ellipse **-bahn** *f* elliptical orbit **-förmig** ellipse-shaped **-querschnitt** *f* elliptical cross section

Ellipsenzirkel *m* trammel ~ **mit Gleitführung** egg calipers with slider

Ellipsoid *n* ellipsoid, spheroid **dreiachsiges** ~ general ellipsoid **Rotations** ~ ellipsoid of revolution

Elliptikfeder *f* elliptic spring

elliptisch elliptic(al), ellipsoidal **-e Ebene** elliptic plane **-e Flügel** elliptical wings **-e Gewölbe**

three-centered (elliptic) arch **-e Integrale** elliptic integrals **-e Krümmung** elliptic curvature **-es Paraboloid** elliptic paraboloid **-er Raum** elliptic space **-er Rumpf** elliptical fuselage

Elliptizität *f* ellipticity

Ellira-schweißung *f* Unionmelt welding method (automatic) **-verfahren** *n* Unionmelt process

Ellsworthit *m* ellsworthite

Elmsfeuer *n* St. Elmo's fire

Eloxal-verfahren *n* electrolytic surface oxidation of metals in an oxalic or sulfuric acid bath, eloxation

Eloxalschicht *f* eloxation layer anodized oxyde layer **-überzug** *m* eloxal coating, anodic or oxide coating

eloxieren to eloxadize, treat by eloxal process

Eloxieren *n* anodic treatment

eloxiert anodised

Elsenholz *n* alder wood

Eluierung *f* elutriation

Elutionsverfahren *n* elution process

elutrieren to elutriate, wash

Eluvialboden *m* residual soil

Email *n* **Emaille** *f* enamel (vitreous or organic) **mit ~ überziehen** to enamel

Email-blech *n* enameled sheet **-draht** *m* enamel-covered wire, enamel-insulated wire, enameled wire **-farbe** *f* enamel (color) paint **-glas** *n* enamel glass, fusible glass **-lack** *m* enamel varnish

Emaille-lackierung *f* japanning **-leuchtofen** *m* enamelled electric fire **-skala** *f* enamel gauge

emaillieren to enamel

Emaillierofen *m* enameling oven

emailliert enameled, enamel-coated

Emaillier-überzug *m* enamel coat **-verfahren** *m* enameling process **-werk** *n* metal enameling manufacture

Email-litze *f* enameled strand **-schild** *n* enameled plate

Emanation *f* emanation (chem.) **abgeklungene ~** emanation with diminished or decaying radioactivity

Emanations-koeffizient emanating power **-messer** *m* emanometer

emanieren to emanate

E-Maschine *f* electric motor

E-Maschinenraum *m* electric-motor room

Emballage *f* packing, package **-papier** *n* wrapping paper

emballieren to box, case, pack for shipment, bale

Emballiermaschine *f* baling machine

Embargo *n* embargo

Embolit *m* embolite

Embryonalkammer *f* initial shell

E-messer *m* range-finder operator, height-finder sergeant

E-meßgerät *n* range finder, altimeter, height finder

Emi-ausschleifer antenna-tuning unit

Emilit *n* emilite

Emission *f* emission, issue **glühelektrische ~** thermionic emission **~ von Neutronen** emission of neutrons

Emissionsbande, kurzwelliger Ausläufer emission band, high energy tail

Emissions-fähigkeit *f* emission capability **-fläche** *f* emitting area or surface, radiating surface (of a cooler) **-geschwindigkeit** *f* velocity of emission **-gesetz** *n* three-halves power law, $^3/_2$ law, emission law **-kennlinie** *f* emission characteristic, emission curve **-koeffizient** *m* emission coefficient **-kontinuum** *n* continuous emission spectrum **-kristallspektren** *pl* emission spectra of crystals

Emissions-mechanismus *m* emissive mechanism **-meßgerät** *n* emission measuring device **-messung** *f* measurement of emission **-rauschstrom** *m* total emission noise **-rückgang** *m* deterioration of emission **-schicht** *f* emitting layer **-stärke** *f* emissivity **-steuerung** *f* emission control **-strom** *m* space current, cathode current, total emission current, electronic current **-vermögen** *n* emissive power, emissivity, radiating capacity

Emitter *m* emitter **~ von verzögerten Neutronen** delayed neutron emitter

Emitter-basisschaltung (Transistoren) grounded emitter arrangement **-grundschaltung** common emitter circuit **-klemme** *f* emitter lead **-schicht** *f* emitter junction **-übergang** *m* emitter junction **-wirkungsgrad** *m* emitter efficiency **-zone** *f* emitter region **-zweig** *m* emitter branch

emittierende Elektrode emitting electrode **~ Oberfläche** *f* emitting surface **~ Thoriumschicht auf Wolfram** thoriated tungsten emitter

emittiert emitted

E-modul *n* modulus of elasticity

E.M.K. (elektromotorische Kraft) E.M.F. (electromotive force)

EMK des Luftspaltfeldes Potier's electromotive force

Emmensit *n* emmensite

Emn-Typ *m* Emn mode

Emotivität *f* temper

Empfang *m* reception, receipt **auf ~ bleiben** to stand by **~ mit schwingendem Audion im Schwebungsnull** homodyne or zero-beat reception **drahtloser ~** wireless or radio reception **gerichteter ~** directional or directive reception **~ mit Kardioidantenne** cardioid reception **~ durch wilde Kopplung** stray pick up **Stellung auf ~** stand-by position

empfangen to receive, listen, to pick up

empfangender Tank receiving vessel

Empfänger *m* receiver, radio or wireless receiver, receiving set or system, addressee, consignee, collector, pickup (microphone) **~** (Adressat), adressee, recipient, recorder, detector; (b. Meßinstrument) indicator **~ für Allstrombetrieb** all-mains receiver **~ für Gleichstrom, ~ für Gleichstrom-Netzanschluß** direct-current-operated or mains receiver, direct-current receiver **~ mit thermischem Hörer** thermal telephone receiver **~ mit Rückkopplung** receiver with feed back **~ für Schallplattenwiedergabe** radio gramophone, radiogram

Empfänger, ~ für Wechselstrom, ~ für Wechselstrombetrieb alternating-current-operated or mains receiver, alternating-current receiver **~ für Wechselstrom-Netzanschluß** alternating-current-operated or mains receiver, alternating-current receiver **~ für gedämpfte** (ungedämpfte) **Wellen** spark (continuous-wave) receiver **ausbalancierter ~** balanced receiver **photographischer ~** photographical recorder **verdrahteter ~** fully wired receiver set **Pumpen des**

Empfängers motorboating

Empfänger-abstimmung *f* receiver tuning **-achse** *f* receiving shaft; (Fernschr.) main shaft **-antenne** *f* receiver antenna **-blechgestell** *n* metal chassis **-dekrement** *n* receiver decrement **-dipol** *n* identification-friend-or-foe receiver dipole **-Eigenstrahlung** *f* receiver radiation **-fernhörer** *m* telephone receiver for wireless **-fläche** *f* radiation-sensitive surface, record sheet **-gehäuse** *n* receiver cabinet **-kreis** *m* receiver circuit **-rahmen** *m* receiver mounting frame, loop antenna

Empfänger-magnet *m* receiving magnet **-meßsender** *m* R. F. service oscillator **-motor** *m* receiver motor **-pegel** *m* reception level **-rauschen** *n* receiver noise **-reichweite** *f* range of receiver, distance-getting ability of radio set **-röhre** *f* radiotelegraphic valve, receiving valve

Empfänger-schaltung *f* receiver circuit, receiver connections **-selektivität** selectivity of receivers **-senderkombination** *f* microtelephone, transceiver radio set **-sockel** (Fernschreib.) typing unit base **-sperröhre** *f* transmit receive switch **-sperrzelle** *f* T-R cell **-station** *f* receiver station **-tafel** *f* receiving board (screen) **-umformer** *m* receiver converter **-verdrosselung** *f* receiver choke radio **-verstärker** *m* receiving or reception amplifier **-vorröhre** *f* input value for receiver **-wagen** *m* cutoff evaluation truck (guided missiles) **-wellenerreger** *m* receiver vibrator unit **-zusatzgeräte** *pl* receiver accessories

Empfangfeldstärke *f* incoming-signal level

empfänglich appreciative, grateful, receptive, responsive, susceptible, sensitive

Empfänglichkeit *f* susceptibility, receptivity, responsiveness

Empfangs-abteilung *f* radio-receiver detail **-anlage** *f* receiving system or set, installation radio

Empfangsantenne *f* receiving antenna, wave collector **vom Sender entkoppelte ~** balanced-receiver antenna (uncoupled from transmitter)

Empfangs-anzeige *f* acknowledgment of receipt **-apparat** *m* receiver **-apparatur** *f* receiver chassis, receiving equipment **-bandbreite** *f* band pass **-bandfilter** *n* receiving band filter pass **-behälter** *m* receiver **-berechtigter** *m* beneficiary **-bereich** *m* range or zone of reception **-bereitschaft** *f* listening watch **-bescheinigung** *f* receipt, receipt voucher **-bestätigung** *f* acknowledgment **-bild** *n* recorded copy (in facsimile) **-bürsten** *pl* receiving brushes

Empfangseinrichtung *f* receiving device **~ einer Bildtelegraphenanlage** receiver station for a picture-telegraph installation

Empfangs-ende *n* receiving end (of a line) **-energie** *f* receiving energy **-erde** *f* receiving ground **-feldstärke** *f* received field strength **-fernhörer** *m* wireless-telephone receiver **-frequenz** *f* receiving frequency **-gebäude** *n* tackle block **-gebiet** *n* service area (in broadcasting) **-gerät** *n* receiver, radio or wireless receiver, receiving set **-gleichrichter** *m* receiver rectifier (radio) **-gleichrichterröhre** *f* audion

Empfangs-höchststärke *f* maximum reception **-horn** *n* feedhorn **-kasten** *m* receptacle (electricity) **-kurve** *f* arrival curve **-lage** *f* signal area **-lautstärke** *f* volume of reception **-leistung** *f* received or incoming power **-loch** *n* blind spot, radio shadow or pocket **-locher** *m* receiving perforator, reperforator, reperforating attachment **-lochstreifen** *m* perforated receive tape **-luftdraht** *m* receiving aerial **-luftleiter** *m* receiving antenna or wire **-magnet mit Teilkreis** receiver magnet with graduated scale, teleprinter **-messung** *f* receiving or reception measurement **-minimum** *n* minimum reception

Empfangs-platte *f* withdrawal plate **-pegel** *m* receiving level **-rahmen** *m* receiving loop **-relais** *n* receiving relay **-ring** *m* receiving ring **-röhre** *f* receiving valve or tube **-satz** *m* receiving set **-schaltung** *f* receiving circuit **-scheibe** *f* receiving disk **-schein** *m* receipt **-schienensatz** (Fernschreiber) set of assembly of code bars **-segment** *n* receiving segment **-seite** *f* receiving end **-silo** *n* receiving silo

Empfangsspannung *f* receiving voltage **gerichtete ~** directional, incoming, or signal potential

Empfangs-spiegel *m* receiving reflector **-station** *f* receiving station **-stelle** *f* receiving station (electronic current) **-steller** *m* receiver-adjustment device **-stellung** *f* receiving condition, stand-by position **-störung** *f* reception interference, jamming **-störungen** *pl* **durch atmosphärische Entladung** statics **-streifen** *m* receiving tape **-stromkreis** *m* input circuit **-system** *n* receiving system **-teil** *m* receiver aerial **-teiler** *m* receiving distributor **-teilwagen** *m* transloading vehicle **-trichter** *m* hopper (receiver funnel or trough)

Empfangs- und Verstärkerröhren *pl* tubes for receivers and amplifiers

Empfangs-verhältnisse *pl* receiving conditions **-vermittler** *m* detector **-verstärker** *m* receiver-amplifier radio **-verstärkung** *f* receiving or reception amplification **-versuch** *m* reception test **-verteiler** *m* receiving selector or distributor **-vorrichtung** *f* receiver arrangement **-wahlschalter** *m* reception-selection switch, receiving selector **-welle** *f* received wave, receiving frequency **-zentrale** *f* receiving station **-zone** *f* reception zone

empfehlen to recommend, commend

empfehlenswert recommendable, suitable

Empfehlung *f* recommendation

empfinden to sense, perceive, feel, apprehend, experience, have consciousness

Empfinden, allgemeines ~ consensus, sensitiveness at all points

empfindlich (Organ) sensible, susceptible, (Bauart) delicate, (Instrumente) sensitive, responsive, reactive, be a function of, be dependent on **~ für** (ansprechend auf) responsive to **~ gegen** critical to **~ machen** to sensitize **-er Aufschlagzünder** superquick impact fuse **-er Kopfzünder** all-ways fuse **-er Zünder** superquick, graze, or sensitive fuse

Empfindlichkeit *f* sensitiveness, sensitivity, sensibility, delicacy, responsiveness, efficiency, yield, output, susceptibility **~ einer Echosperre** sensitivity of an echo-suppressor **~ gegen Kaltverformung** cold sensitivity **~ beim relativen Pegel Null** zero-level sensitivity **~ der Photozelle** sensitivity of the photoelectric cell **~ pro mm** openness of scale **~ der Regulierung** delicacy of regulatory device **~ im diffusen**

Schallfeld random-incidence response ~ **gegen Schlag** sensitiveness to impact **monochromatische** ~ monochromatic sensitivity **spektrale** ~ color sensitivity or response, spectrophotoelectric sensitivity

Empfindlichkeits-achse *f* sensitive axis (of a gyro) **-bereich** *m* range of sensitiveness **-faktor** *m* multiplying power **-grad** *m* sensitiveness, degree of sensitivity **-grenze** *f* limit of sensitivity **-kehrwert** *m* sensibility reciprocal value **-kurve** *f* response characteristic or curve **-maß** *n* noise factor, sensitive measure **-messer** *m* sensitometer **-messung** *f* sensitometric measurement **-mischer** *m* low-noise mixer

Empfindlichkeits-probe *f* sensivity test **-profil** *n* sensitivity profile **-prüfer** *m* testing device for receiver sensitivity **-prüfung** *f* sensitivity test **-regler** *m* sensitivity regulator **-regelung** *f* sensitivity control **-schwankung** *f* fluctuation of sensitivity (radar) **-schwelle** *f* threshold sensitivity **-übertragungsfaktor** *m* sensitivity response **-veränderung** *f* sensitivity drift

Empfindlichkeitsverteilung, spektrale ~ color sensitivity or response, spectrophotoelectric sensitivity, sensitivity distribution, spectral response (of eye)

Empfindlichkeits-zahl *f* light value (photo), sensitivity ratio **-ziffer** *f* sensitivity factor

Empfindlich-machen *n* sensitizing **-machung** *f* sensitization, activation, sensibilization

Empfindung *f* perception, feeling, sensation **-erde** *f* receiver ground (connection)

Empfindungsdauer *f* propensity **-fähig** sensitive **-gemäße Farbstufe -gerechte Abstufung** subjective or natural grading or spacing (chromatic scale) **-gerechte Farbstufe** subjective chromatic scale value **-grenze des Ohres** loudness contour of ear, auditory-sensation area **-lautstärke** *f* response of ear to signal strength, sensible loudness of sound **-vermögen** *n* maximum input voltage, sensitivity **-zunahme** *f* sensation increment

Emphase *f* emphasis

empirisch empiric(al) ~ **bestimmt** empirically determined (work function) **-es Ermittlungsverfahren** cut and try method **-e Formel** composition formula, empirical formula **-e Lösung** by trial and error **-e Massenformel** empirical mass formula

Emplektit *m* emplectite

empor up, upward, aloft

emporragen to tower

Empore *f* choir loft, gallery

Empor-heben *n* elevation **-kommen** to rise, emerge, mount, ascend **-richten** to raise up **-schnellen** *n* upward flick **-schrauben** to spiral up **-steigen** to rise up, travel upward, pass up, ascend **-steigen** *n* rise, climb, emersion

Emscherbrunnen *m* Imhoff tank

emsig busy, active, industrious, assiduous

Emulgator *m* emulsifier

Emulgierbarkeit *f* emulsibility

emulgieren to emulsify

Emulgieren *n* emulsifying

Emulgier-fähigkeit *f* emulsifying capacity **-maschine** *f* emulsifier **-mittel** *n* emulsifier

Emulgierung *f* emulsification

Emulgierungs-körper *m* emulsifying agent **-öl** *n* emulsifying oil

Emulsierbarkeit *f* emulsifiability

Emulsion *f* emulsion **-aufstreicher** *m* emulsion coater

emulsionieren to emulsify

Emulsionierung *f* emulsification

Emulsions-bildner *m* emulsifier, emulsifying agent **-bildung** *f* emulsification **-brechen** *n* demulsifying **-paket** *n* emulsion stack **-reinigung** *f* background eradication **-schicht** *f* emulsion layer **-seite** *f* face (of film) bearing emulsion, sensitized face (photo.) **-steilheit** *f* steepness of gradation **-tiefdruck** *m* emulsion intaglio printing **-verfahren** *n* emulsion process **-versuch** *m* emulsion test

enantiomorph enantiomorphic, enantiomorphous

enantiotrop enantiotropic

Enceinte *f* enceinte

Encym-entschlichtung *f* encym desizing **-präparat** *n* encym preparation

Enalith *m* enalite

enantiomorph enantiomorphic

End-abnahme *f* final test **-abstellschalter** *m* limit stop switch **-abstellvorrichtung** *f* limit stop mechanism or device **-abweichung** *f* steady-state deviation **-alkalität** *f* end or residual alkalinity **-amplitude** *f* end or terminal amplitude, output, final **-amt** *n* terminal office or station, central exchange **-anflug** *m* final approach **-anlage** *f* terminal equipment **-anode** *f* final anode

End-anschlag *m* limit stop, end stop, travel stop **-anschlagswert** *m* minimum resistance at starting position **-ansicht** *f* end view **-anstalt** *f* terminal exchange, central exchange (teleph) **-antrieb** *m* final drive **-apparat** *m* end or terminal apparatus **-arbeitsgang** *m* final operation

End-aufbau *m* final assembly **-auflager** *n* end supports, shore piling, abutment **-ausbau** *m* (equipped to) ultimate capacity **-ausklinkung** *f* final safety trip **-auslauf** *m* exit or delivery end **-ausschalter** *m* limit switch **-ausschlag** *m* full deflection or excursion, limiting deflection **-auswerter** *m* intelligence collator **-auswertung** *f* final analysis or sifting of intelligence

End-bahnhof *m* terminal (station) railhead **-ballistik** *f* terminal ballistics **-band** *n* identification trailer (film) **-bar** terminable **-bearbeiten** to finish, complete **-bearbeitung** *f* finishing process **-begrenzungsschalter** *m* limit switch **-bestand** *m* closing stock **-bohrer** *m* finishing or long jumper **-bild** *n* final picture (end image) **-bildleuchtschirm** *m* final image luminescent screen **-bund** *m* dead-end binding (elec.)

Enddichtung, feste ~ upset end joint

Enddrall *m* terminal twist **-winkel** *m* angle of twist at end of path

Enddrehzahl *f* final number of revolutions **-bereich** *m* maximum speed range **-feder** *f* maximum speed spring **-regler** *m* maximum speed governor

Enddruck *m* end thrust, final pressure; (Luftkompressor) *m* delivery pressure **-kugellager** *n* ball thrust bearing

Ende *n* end, finish, conclusion, wing, flank, extremity, terminal, termination, limit ~ **des Blasens** wind off **mit dem** ~ **nach vorn** endwise

äußerstes ~ extremity **glattes** ~ (eines Muffenrohres), spigot **hinteres** ~ further end **offenes** ~ **des Kolbens** skirt end of a piston **unteres** ~ bottom, butt (end) **verjüngtes** ~ tapered end **zubereitetes** ~ treated butt

End-eck *n* summit, terminal angle **-einrichtung** *f* terminal (of carrier system) **-element** *n* terminating element

endenschleifen to face (mech.)

End-erfolg *m* net result **-ergebnis** *n* final result **-erzeugnis** *n* finish, final or finished product **-feinheit** *f* final size desired **-feld** *n* end span **-fernamt** *n* toll center (TO) **-festigkeit** *f* ultimate strength **-fläche** *f* end face **-flanke** *f* trailing wave front **-flansch** *m* terminal flange **-flügel** *m* flange, outer wing **-flughafen** *m* **-flugplatz** *m* air terminal **-fräsmaschine** *f* rotary planer, end milling machine

End-gebühr *f* terminal charge **-gerüst** *n* finishing stand **-geschwindigkeit** *f* final velocity, striking velocity **-gespräch** *n* in-call terminal call **-gestänge** *n* end pole, stayed terminal pole **-gestell** *n* off-end stand output cabinet **-gewicht** *n* fish of a trailing antenna **-gleichgewicht** *n* final balance **-glied** *n* terminal member **-größe** *f* output quantity

endgültig ultimate, final **in die -e Lage** in final position

End-hafen *m* terminal port **-haken** *m* rubber (fixing) hook **-hülle** *f* grummet

endigen to end, terminate, finish, cease **an Klinken** ~ to be terminated on jacks

End-impedanz *f* terminal, end or load impedance **-isolator** *m* lead-in insulator **-kabel** *n* terminal cable **-kaliber** *n* last pass, finishing pass **-kapazität** *f* top capacity, terminating or end capacity **-kappe** *f* end cap, end plate **-kondensator** *m* terminating condenser or capacitor **-kontrolle** *f* final inspection **-kontrollpunkt** *m* final control desk **-kopf** (bei E-Messern) end head **-koppelschleife** *f* segment-fed loop **-krater** *m* end crater **-kühler** *m* aftercooler **-kunstschaltung** *f* terminal circuit network

End-lackierung *f* final camouflage paint **-lage** *f* final position, extreme or end position, full throttle **-lagenschalter** *m* limit switch, safety switch **-lager** *n* end bearing **-lagerbüchse** *f* flywheel box **-last** *f* applied at end of load **-lauge** *f* final liquor, discard solution, foul electrolyte **-leiste** *f* trailing edge of a wing (aviation) **-leistendruckmaschine** *f* piece-end printing machine

endlich final, ultimate, limited, finite

endlichdimensional finite dimensional

endliche Sperrschicht limited reverse impedance

Endlichkeit *f* finiteness

endlos unending, endless, infinite **-e Feinbewegung** continuous slow motion (optics) **-er Filmstreifen** endless film strip **-es Kabel** bull rope **-e Kette** chain belt **-es Papier** reel paper **-es Schleifband** (Metall) endless abrasive belt **-es Seil** endless rope or cable, dead line **-es Sieb** drainage sieve **-e Transportkette** (automatischer Düngerzufuhrapparat) apron (farm mach.)

Endlosformulare *pl* continuous forms, endless office forms

End-marke *f* gauge point **-maß** *n* end measure, end-measuring rod, precision-gauge block, end block, slip gauge **-masse** *f* final mass of rocket at end of flight

Endmaßeinsatz *m* end-measuring rod **sphärischer** ~ end-measuring rod with spherical end

Endmaß-halter *m* end measuring block **-käfig** *m* gauge block cage **-komparator** *m* gauge block interferometer **-messung** *f* (Inko) contact correction error **-lehre** *f* end-measure gauge **-satz** *m* set of gauge blocks **-stufen** *pl* gauge intervals

End-mast *m* terminal tower, terminal or end pole **-melasse** *f* blackstrap molasses **-monitor** *m* master monitor **-montage** *f* final assembly **-moräne** *f* terminal moraine **-nische** *f* end recess **-nuance** *f* final shade **-öffnung** *f* end span **-ordinate** *f* final ordinate

endogen endogenous

Endolymphe *f* endolymph, fluid of the semicircular canal

Endomorphismus *m* endomorphism

Endosität *f* endosity

Endosmose *f* endosmosis

endosmotisch endosmosic

endotherm endothermic, endoergic

End-penthode *f* output pentode **-platte** *f* (Schiff) end strake **-polklemme** *f* end terminal **-prisma** *n* base prism **-produkt** *n* finished or final product **-punkt** *m* end point, extremity, terminal, terminus; (einer Kurve) final point **-querschnitt** *m* cross section of mouth of nozzle **-querschwelle** *f* nose sill

End-randsteller *m* (Schlußrandsteller) margin stop right **-regelfeder** *f* spring for maximum speed governing **-regelung** *f* maximum-speed governing **-regelungsgerät** *n* final control element **-regler** *m* constant speed governor **-reinigung** *f* final cleaning **-resultat** *n* net result **-rille** *f* (Phono.) concentric groove **-ring** *f* ferrule, end inhibitor

Endröhre *f* final stage valve, output valve or tube, power tube, loud-speaker tube, terminal valve ~ **mit Elektronenbündelung** beam-power valve

End-satz *m* terminal repeater, final set, terminal unit or equipment **-schäkel** *m* end shackle **-schalter** *m* limit switch **-schaltsatz** *m* terminal repeater **-schaltung** *f* terminal circuit **-scheibe** *f* end plate, vertical fin; (am Leitwerk) outboard fin **-schirm** *m* final screen **-schlacke** *f* final slag **-schwefelung** *f* final desulfurization **-schwelle** *f* end sill **-siedepunkt** *m* end point (distillation), final boiling point **-spannung** *f* final voltage, output voltage **-spektrum** *n* emergent spectrum **-spiel** *n* axial play, end play, backlash, final (sports), and clearance **-springwert** *m* minimum resistance at end position

End-stabilität *f* ultimate strength **-station** *f* terminus, railhead, end station, terminal **-stauchung** *f* ultimate crushing stress **-stein** *m* finishing die

Endstelle *f* terminal, terminal station ~ **einer Simultanleitung** composite set

End-stellung *f* final position, extreme or end position (aviation) **-stich** *m* final pass, finishing or edging pass **-stiel** *m* outboard strut **-stöpsel** *m* end cap **-streifen** *m* trailer (of a film) **-strom** *m* output current **-strosse** *f* end bench

Endstück *n* tail (Pol einer Leitung) adjusting nut ~ **einer Mole** terminal or end section

End-stufe *f* output stage, end stage, top stage (of rocket) **-stufenmodulation** *f* high-level or high-power modulation **-taster** *m* limit switch **-tetrode** *f* (Elektronenbündelung) beam power tetrode **-tiefe** *f* tip chord **-totaldruck** *m* total ultimate vacuum **-träger** *m* end truss **-trieb** *m* final drive **-satz** *m* final drive **-welle** *f* final drive shaft **-triode** *f* output triode **-tülle** *f* terminal bushing, ferrule **-übertrag** *m* carry-over **-umschalter** *m* limit switch

Endung *f* termination, ending

End-urteil *n* final judgment **-verbindung** *f* butt joint **-verbraucher** *m* ultimate user **-vergrößerung** *f* final magnification **-verlust** *m* end or terminal loss **-verschluß** *m* (box) terminal, cable head or socket, sealing end, termination of a cable, cable box, end arrangement

End-verschraubung *f* thread(ed) cap ~ **für die Dornanzugstange** spindle drawbar cap

Endverstärker *m* terminal or station amplifier, terminal repeater, power or output amplifier **-schaltung** *f* terminal-repeater circuit **-stufe** *f* final amplifier stage, power-amplifier stage

End-versteifung *f* end rib (aviation) **-verzweiger** *m* terminal block, distribution terminal **-wähler** *m* (EW) terminal selector (TeS) **-wert** *m* final value, performance, resultant or ultimate value, output value, equilibrium value **-wicklung** *f* end winding, end turns (elec.) **-widerlager** *n* abutment, side wall **-widerstand** *m* terminal resistance **-wucht** *f* remaining energy

End-zapfen *m* end journal **-zelle** *f* terminal cell **-ziel** *n* final objective **-zusammenschweißvorrichtung** *f* final-welding jig **-zustand** *m* terminal state, final condition or state **-zweck** *m* final purpose

energetische Bevorzugung energy preference (radio)

Energie *f* energy, force, power ~ **der Bewegung** kinetic energy ~ **der Lage** potential energy **zurückgewonnene** ~ regenerated or restored energy

Energieabgabe *f* energy release ~ **je Längeneinheit** linear energy transfer

Energie-abnahme *f* decrease in energy **-änderung** *f* current or power fluctation **-aufnahme** *f* energy absorption, energy input or consumption **-aufspeicherung** *f* accumulation of energy storage **-aufwand** *m* expenditure of energy **-ausstrahlung** *f* radiation of energy **-austausch** *m* energy exchange, exchange of power

Energie-band *n* energy range or band **band-verbreiterung** *f* energy band broadening **-bedarf** *m* power requirements, loading **-berg** *m* energy hill or barrier **-betrag** *m* amount of energy **-betriebe** *pl* utilities **-dichte** *f* density of energy **-eigendichte** *f* proper energy density **-erhaltung** *f* energy conservation or preservation

Energie-fluß *m* energy flow **-form** *f* form of energy **-freigabe** *f* energy release **-frequenzbeziehung** *f* energy relation **-gewinn** *m* energy gain **-gewinnungseinrichtung** *f* power-harnessing equipment **-gleichrichtung** *f* energy equation **-haltig** energy-containing

Energie-impulssätze *pl* energy momentum theorems **-impulstensor** *m* energy momentum tensor **-inhalt** *m* energy content, stored-up energie **-leistung** *f* energy output, (energy) feeder lead, feeder down-lead, transmission line **-leitung** *f* transmission line, feeder cable or line, aerial feeder **-leitungskosten** *f pl* cost of transmission of energy **-lieferung** *f* liberation of atomic energy **-linie** *f* energy gradient **-los** nondissipative, wattless **-lückenmodell** *n* energy-gap model

Energie-massenbeziehung *f* relationship between energy and mass **-messer** *m* wattmeter, ergometer **-messungen** *f pl* energy measurements **-nachfuhr** *f* additional supply of power **-netz** *n* national grid **-niveau** *n* energy level, quantum state **-quantum** *n* energy quantum **-quelle** *f* source of energy **-reich** full of energy, energy-rich, energetic, energy-bearing **-rückgewinnung durch Bremsen** energy recuperation by (regenerative) braking **-satz** *m* law of conservation of energy **-schaltung** *f* oscillatory circuit **-schema** *n* energy-level diagram **-schwelle** *f* threshold of energy, energy barrier

Energie-spannungskomplex *m* energy-stress complex **-spektrum der Spaltneutronen** fission spectrum **-sprung** *f* energy gap **-strom** *m* energy flow, equalizing current **-stromdichte** *f* energy flux density **-strömung** *f* equalizing current **-stufe** *f* energy level or term, quantum state, state of energy **-stufendiagramm** *n* centroid diagram **-summenspektrum** *n* co-cumulative energy spectrum

Energie-termverschiebung *f* energy shift **-überfluß** *m* reusable waste heat or energy **-übertragung** *f* transfer of energy **-umfang** *f* mutation of energy **-umsatz** *m* transformation of energy **-umsetzung** *f* conversion of energy **-umwandler** *m* transducer **-umwandlung** *f* transformation of energy

Energieverbrauch *m* (Elektrizität) electric demand, demand for electrical energy

Energieverbrauch *m* energy or power consumption, dissipation, loss of energy **ohne** ~ nondissipative wattless

Energie-verlust *m* loss of energy or of power **-vernichter** *m* energy dissipator **-vernichtung** *f* dissipation of energy **-vernichtungseinrichtung** *f* baffle piers, energy-dissipating device **-verschwendung** *f* wasting of energy **-versorgungseinrichtung** *f* energy supply equipment **-verteilung** *f* energy distribution **-verteilungskurve** *f* curve of spectrum **-wall** *m* energy wall, potential barrier

Energie-verzehrung *f* dissipation of energy **-vorrat** *m* power supply **-wirtschaft** *f* power economy **-wirtschaftlicher Ausgleich** equalization of energy **-zähler** *m* energy meter **-zentrale** *f* power station **-zerstreuung** *f* dissipation of energy **-zufuhr** *f* supply of energy or of power

enfilieren to enfilade

Enfilierung *f* raking, enfilading

eng narrow, close, tight, intimate, confined

engbenachbarte Frequenz closely-spaced frequency

Enge *f* narrows, straits, defile, narrowness, closeness, tightness ~ **steile Spirale** tight spiral

enger machen to tighten

Enghalsflasche *f* narrow-necked or narrow-mouthed bottle

enghalsig narrow-mouthed or -necked
engjähriges Holz close-grain wood
Engjustierung *f* adjustment
Englage *f* limiting position
Engländer *m* monkey wrench, universal screw wrench, spanner (for nut)
Englergrad *m* (EG) degree "Engler"
englisch English, British **-es Rot** crocus (polishing powder) **-es Salz** Epsom salt **-er Schraubenschlüssel** universal, combination, or spanner wrench **-e Wärmeeinheit** British thermal unit
Englischrot *n* crocus, rouge (polishing powder)
englochig fine-meshed
englumig with a narrow internal diameter
engmaschig narrow-meshed, close-meshed, fine-meshed, fine **-es Festpunktnetz** *n* close-mesh control network **durch einen -en Filter gedrückt** close-filtered **-es Sieb** fine-mesh screen
Engobe (Keramik) *f* engobe
Engobiermaschinen *pl* engobing machines
Engpaß *m* narrow pass, defile (on maps), wire-drawing effect ~ (z. B. der Erzeugung) bottleneck
Engpaßgerät *n* equipment in short supply
Engramm *n* engram, trace
engröhriger Kessel small-tube boiler
engros wholesale **-preis** *m* wholesale price
Engschrift *f* condensed type
engsitziger Aufbau close-coupled body
engspaltig narrow-spaced
engster Querschnitt *m* bottleneck
Engstspalt *m* minimum gap
Enigma *n* (cipher machine) equipment in signal corps
Enklave *f* enclave
Enneode *f* enneode
Enometrie *f* volumetric determination of unsaturation
ensilieren to ensile
entaktivieren (Radium), to deactivate
Entaktivierung *f* deactivation
entalkoholisieren to extract alcohol, dealcoholize
entarretieren to unlock
entarsenizieren to remove arsenic
entarten to degenerate, decay, deteriorate
entartet degenerate, abnormal, debased **-es Elektronengas** degenerate electron gas **-er Elektronenzustand** degenerate electron state **-e Terme** degenerate levels
Entartung *f* degeneration, decay, abnormality, degeneracy
Entartungs-kriterium *n* criterion of degeneracy **-temperatur** *f* degeneracy temperature
Entaschung *f* ash removal
Entaschungsanlage *f* ash handling plant
Entasphaltierung *f* deasphaltizing
entästen to free from branches
entäußern to discard, part with
Entbasten der Stengel decortication, green and chemical cleansing of stems (stalks)
entbehren to lack, dispense with **entbehrlich** dispensable, needless
entbinden to release, liberate, set free, expel, give birth
Entbindung *f* release, liberation
Entbindungs-flasche *f* generating flask **-rohr** *n* delivery tube
entbittern to eliminate bitter substances or principles
entbleien to remove lead (metal.)
entbleite Lösung deleaded solution
entblocken to clear, free the line, line free
Entblockierung *f* receiver gating (rdr.)
entblockt clear (R. R.)
Entblockung *f* clearing a section (of track)
entblößen to expose, denude, bare, strip
entblößt bare, naked, exposed
entbromen to debrominate
Entbrummer *m* antihum device, hum eliminator, hum balancing potentiometer
Entbrumm-kondensator *m* anti-hum capacitor **-potentiometer** *n* hum balancing potentiometer
Entbündeln *n* debunching (in klystron), unbunching, defocusing
Entbutanisierungsapparat *m* debutanizer
entchloren to dechlorinate
Entchromungsbad *n* dechroming bath
entcoden to decode
entdämpfen to reduce the damping, improve
Entdämpfung *f* correction, amplification, repeater or transmission gain, improvement, damping reduction, deattenuation, regenerative amplification, regeneration, reversal of damping
Entdämpfungs-frequenzkurve *f* gain-frequency curve **-messer** *m* gain-measuring device
entdecken to detect, discover, find
Entdecker *m* discoverer, explorer
Entdeckung *f* detection, discovery
Entdoublierungsvorrichtung *f* undoubling angle
Entdüppelung *f* elimination of jamming effects (radar)
Ente *f* duck; canard, false report
enteignen to expropriate, dispossess
Enteignung *f* expropriation
enteisen to deice
enteisenen to eliminate iron from
Enteisenung *f* removal of iron
Enteiser *m* deicer, ice guard ~ **in der Flügelnase** ice guard on the leading edge (aviat.)
Enteiserpumpe *f* deicing pump
enteisnen to remove iron
Enteisungs-anlage de-icing equipment de-icer system **-flüssigkeit** *f* deicing fluid **-gerät** *n* deicer **-mittel** *n* anti-icer solution **-vorrichtung** *f* deicer
Entelektrikator *m* antistatic device
entemulgieren to demulsify
Entemulgierversuch *m* demulsibility test
Enten-flugzeug *n* tail-first airplane, canard (airplane) **-fußelektrode** *f* duck foot electrode **-modell** *n* canard-type aircraft **-muschel** *f* barnacle
Enterhaken *m* boarding grapnel
entern to board
entfachen to ignite, kindle, blow into flame
Entfall *m* discard, waste, scrap, yield
entfallen to become scrap, be wasted, lose (a chance), drop out, fall
entfalten to unfold, display, evolve, develop, deploy
Entfaltung *f* development
Entfaltungs-geschwindigkeit *f* (Fallschirm) opening speed (parachute) **-punkt** *m* point of development or of deployment; (Fallschirm)

point of opening, point of deployment (parachute) **-stoß** *m* (Fallschirm) opening shock (parachute) **-stoßschreiber** *m* opening-shock indicator (parachute), parachute-testing device **-zeit** *f* opening time (parachute)
Entfaltvorrichtung *f* spreading device
Entfärbelösung *f* de-inking solution
entfärben to decolorize, bleach
Entfärbung *f* decolorization, bleaching
entfärbungsfreies Glas stabilized glass
Entfärbungs-kohle *f* decolorizing carbon **-mittel** *n* decolorizing or bleaching agent, decolorant **-vermögen** *n* decolorizing power **-zahl** *f* discoloration factor (of oil)
entfasern to remove fibers
entfernbar detachable
entfernen to remove, take off or away **von seinem Platz ~** to dislodge
Entferner *m* eliminator
Entfernung *f* removal, distance, range (rdr.) **~ zwischen den Anlaufrädern** tread (R. R.) **~ in geschlossener Bahn** distance over a closed circuit **~ messende Fäden** (Tachymeter) stadia lines **die ~ abgreifen** (Karte) to measure distance with compasses, stake off the distance **~ in gerader Linie** distance in straight line **~ in gebrochener Linie** distance in broken line **~ in der Luftlinie** air-line distance
Entfernung, auf große ~ at long range **auf richtige ~ einstellen** to focus **in unendlicher ~ liegend** situated at an infinite distance **eigenmächtige ~** absent without leave **mittlere ~** medium range (up to 800 meters) **nächste ~** close range (up to 100 meters) **nahe ~** close range (up to 400 meters) **tatsächliche ~** true distance **unerlaubte ~** absence without leave **weite ~** long range (over 800 meters) **zurückgelegte ~** distance run
Entfernungen (Abstände) **im großen Zirkel** great-circle distance
Entfernungs-ablage *f* range reading **-änderung** *f* range correction **-angabe** *f* range reading **-anzeigegerät** *n* range-indicator unit, fine-ranging unit **-anzeiger** *m* range clock **-auflösungsvermögen** *n* range resolution **-berechner** *m* range computer **-brücke** *f* distance piece (phot.) **-differenz** *f* (slant) range difference **-einstellung** *f* distance focusing device, range setting **-ermittlung** *f* range determination **-fehler** *m* distance error, error in depth, range error **-feinmeßröhre** *f* fine-range oscilloscope, cathode-ray tube
Entfernungs-gerät *n* range finder **-geschwindigkeit** *f* rate of change of range **-gesetz** *n* law of radiation (electronics), telemetric law, law of the index of remoteness, law governing fragmentation radius in bombing **-kraft** *f* centrifugal force **-kreise** (geodätische) distance-circles (geodesic) **-lineal** *n* (Vermessung) stadiometric straightedge, range ruler (war) **-marke** *f* range indicator **-maßstab** *m* telemetric scale **-meßausbildung** *f* range-taking instruction **-messen** *n* telemetry
Entfernungsmesser *m* range finder, range-finding apparatus, telemeter **~ mit senkrechter Basis** depression telemeter **einstationärer ~** single-station range finder **stereoskopischer ~** stereoscopic range finder
Entfernungs-meßfaden *m* (Vermessung), stadia line **-meßgerät** *n* range finder, altimeter, distance measuring equipment **-meßkontrollanlage** *f* range finder, corrector and adjuster
Entfernungs-messung *f* distance measurement, range finding, range determination **-mittler** *m* range averager **-nachlauf** *m* automatic distance control (radar) **-quadratgesetz** *n* inverse square law **-rekord** *m* (Segelflug) distance record, long-distance record **-schätzen** *n* range estimation **-schätzer** *m* range taker **-schätzgerät** *n* range-estimating instrument
Entfernungs-schleier *m* distance fog **-skala** *f* range scale distance scale **-spinne** *f* range estimator, range spider **-streuung** *f* long-distance scattering **-tabelle** *f* distance chart **-teilung** *f* range scale **-trommel** *f* range drum, range knob **-übersichtsgerät** *n* ranging unit **-uhr** *f* range clock **-unterschied** *m* range difference, rate **-vorgang** *m* removal **-vorhalt** *m* range lead, slant, range difference or correction
entfesseltes bewegliches Mikrophon following microphone
Entfestigung *f* softening
entfetten to degrease, scour (wool)
Entfetten *n* degreasing, scouring
Entfettung *f* degreasing, removal of fat **~ im Stück** piece scouring (textiles)
Entfettungs-anlage *f* degreasing unit **-apparat** *m* fat extraction apparatus **-maschine** *f* steeping machine (textiles) **-masse** *f* degreasing composition **-mittel** *n* degreasing agent
entfeuchten to demist, dehumidize, extract moisture
entfeuchtete Luft dehydrated air
Entfeuchtung *f* dehydration (squeezing effect)
Entfieberung *f* defervescence
entflammbar inflammable **schwer ~** flame-resistant
Entflammbarkeit *f* inflammability
Entflammbarkeitsprüfung *f* ignition test
entflammen to set alight, fire up
Entflammen *n* ignition
Entflammung *f* inflammation, ignition **zur ~ bringen** to ignite
Entflammungs-probe *f* flash test **-punkt** *m* flash point **-temperatur** *f* flash point
Entflechtung *f* disentanglement, decentralization
Entfleischzylinder *m* fleshing cylinder
entfliegen to fly away
entfließen to emanate, flow from
entflocken to deflocculate
entformen to open the mold
Entformungsmittel *n* mold release medium
entfremden to alienate **~ von . . .** to wean away from
entfritten to decohere
Entfritter *m* decoherer, tapper, scrambler, signal (teleph.)
Entfrittung *f* decoherence
Entfroster *m* defroster **-düse** *f* defroster nozzle **-gebläse** *n* defroster blower **-schlauch** defroster hose
entfuseln, den Branntwein ~ to free spirits from amylic alcohol
entgasen to degas, decontaminate, extract gas, distill, clean up, remove gases
Entgaser *m* fume extractor, exhaust, gas expeller; (Speisewasser) deaerator

entgast, -e Lösung degassed solution **-er Stahl** dead steel, killed steel

Entgasung *f* degasification, volatilization, dry or destructive distillation, carbonization, coking, deaeration, degassing, outgassing (of el. tubes)

Entgasungs-anlage *f* degasifying plant, degasser, (bei Speisewasseraufbereitung) de-aerating plant **-erzeugnis** *n* distillation **-gas** *n* coke-oven gas **-mittel** *n* degasing agent **-rohr** *n* extension for vent **-speicher** *m* deaerator **-stutzen** *m* vent outlet **-wärme** *f* heat of degasification

entgegenarbeiten to counteract, buck, work against

entgegendrehen, dem Wind ~ to head into the wind

entgegengesetzt opposite, inverse, contrary, opposed, contrasted **~ induziert** inversely induced **~ wirkend** antagonistic **dem Uhrzeiger ~** counterclockwise **-er Kurs über Grund** reciprocal track **-e Pole** opposite or unlike poles **-er Schlittengang** *m* return stroke **in -em Sinne** on the other hand, in contrary direction **-e Steuerung** opposite control **-e Ströme** opposed currents **-e Vorzeichen** *pl* opposite signs, reversed signs **-er Winkel** *m* vertical angle

entgegengesetzt gerichtet opposed, in opposition, in opposite direction

entgegenhalten to oppose, (Patent) cite

Entgegenhaltung *f* prior art (reference), checking against prior art, anticipation, anticipatory disclosure, (Patent) citation

entgegenhandeln to counter

entgegenkommen to meet

entgegen sehen to expect, look forward to

entgegensetzen to oppose, contrast **Widerstand ~** to put up opposition

Entgegensetzung *f* opposition

entgegenstellen to oppose, contrast

entgegentreten to face, stand up to

entgegenwirken to oppose, counteract, inhibit, act or work against **der Resonanz ~** to be antiresonant

entgegenwirkend opposed, opposing

entgehen to escape, elude, evade

entgeisten to dealcoholize

Entgeistung *f* stripping of alcohol

Entgelt *n* remuneration

entgelten to pay for, recompense, get even with

entgerben to free from tannic acid

entgiften to disinfect, decontaminate, degas

Entgiftung *f* decontamination, degassing detoxication

Entgiftungs-dienst *m* decontamination or degassing service **-gerät** *n* decontamination or degassing apparatus **-mittel** *n* decontaminating or degassing agent **-stoff** *m* decontamination agent

Entgiftungstrommel *f* decontamination sprinkling drum

Entgitterung *f* removel of fences

entglasen to devitrify

Entglasung *f* devitrification

entgleisen to be derailed, jump tracks

Entgleisung *f* derailment

entgolden to extract gold

entgraten to remove burrs, ridges, or fins, trim

Entgraten *n* deburring

Entgrater *m* burr removing device

Entgrat-fräser *m* burring reamer **-maschine** *f* trimming machine

Enthaar- und Glattmaschine *f* picking or plucking machine (hair and hides)

Enthaarung *f* depilation

Enthalpie *f* enthalpy **von der gleichen ~** isenthalpic

enthalten to contain, yield, comprise **sich ~** to refrain

enthärten to soften, anneal

Enthärtung *n* softening

Enthärtungsanlage *f* water softener

entharzen to extract resin

Entharzung *f* extraction of resin

enthaupten to behead

Enthauptung *f* decapitation, beheading

entheben to relieve, replace, dismiss

enthüllen to disclose

enthülsen to husk, shell

Enthülser *m* sheller

Enthülsungsmaschine *f* stripping machine, hulling mill

enthydrieren to dehydrate

entionisieren to deionize, scavenge

Entionisierung *f* deionization, scavenging

Entionisierungs-feld clearing field **-geschwindigkeit** *f* de-ionization rate **-gitter** *n* de-ionization grid **-potential** *n* de-ionization potential **-zeit** *f* de-ionization time, clearing time

entisolieren to bare

Entisolierer *m* wire skinner, insulation stripping tool

entkalken to decalcify, delime

Entkalkungsmittel *n* deliming agent

Entkarbonisierungsanlage *f* decarbonization plant

entkeiltes Rad slipped wheel

entkeimen to destroy or remove bacteria, disinfect **~** (dauerhaft machen), to sterilize

entkeimend sterilising

Entkeimung *f* disinfection, sterilization

Entkeimungs-apparat *m* degerminator **-filter** *n* sterilising filter **-schichten** *f* sterilising filter sheet

Entkernmaschine *f* stoning machine

Entketten *f* picking, burring

entklammern to unlock

Entkletten der Wolle wool picking

Entklettung *f* burring action

Entknurrungswiderstand *m* antigrowl resistance, resistor designed to suppress growling noise due to radio frequency

entkohlen to decarburize, decarbonize

Entkohlung *f* decarburization, decarbonization **~ aufhalten** to arrest carbon drop

entkommen to escape, flee, get away

Entkommen *n* escape

Entkompressionshebel *m* decompression lever

entkonservieren deprocessing

Entkoppeler *m* decoupling network

entkoppeln to tune out, neutralize, balance out, uncouple, decouple

entkoppelte Antenne balanced antenna

Entkoppelung *f* tuning out, neutralization, balancing out, decoupling, uncoupling, disconnection **~ von Störern** balancing-out of jamming

Entkopplungs-glied *n* declutching member **-kondensator** *m* decoupling condenser **-kreis** *m* anti-resonant circuit **-schaltung** *f* decoupling network **-widerstand** *m* decoupling resistance

entkörnen to gin, thresh

entkräften to debilitate, enervate, enfeeble, exhaust, invalidate

entkräftigen to exhaust, debilitate, weaken, vitiate, invalidate

Entkräftung *f* inanition (caused by hunger), enfeeblement, debility, exhaustion

entkrusten to descale

entkupfern to extract copper, remove copper by drossing

entkuppeln to uncouple, disengage, disconnect, declutch

Entkupplung *f* uncoupling, declutching, disengagement, release, throwing out of gear, neutralization, disconnection, disengaging clutch

Entkupplungs-hebel *m* declutching lever **-kurve** *f* throw-out cam

Entlade-anlage *f* unloading machinery **-brücke** *f* unloading bridge, handling bridge **-dauer** *f* time of discharge **-einrichtung** *f* eliminator of static electricity **-fähigkeit** *f* discharge rate or capacity **-feld** *n* explosive field (elec.) **-geschwindigkeit** *f* rate of charge or discharge **-grenzspannung** *f* discharge limit **-hafen** *m* delivery port **-hebel** *m* discharge lever **-hub** *m* exhaust stroke **-kennlinie** *f* discharge characteristic (line or curve) **-kosten** *f pl* discharging expenses **-kurve** *f* current-voltage characteristic (of the two-electrode valve), discharge curve **-methode** *f* method of discharging **-leistung** *f* unloading rate

entladen to unload (a gun or camera), discharge (electric battery), empty (a shell), dump **sich** ~ to discharge, (in Büscheln) brush

Entladen *n* discharging, discharge

Entlader *m* discharger, dumpcart, extractor, destaticizer

Entlade-schaltung *f* circuit means causing fast rise of saw-tooth potential **-spannung** *f* discharge voltage or potential **-spannungswandler** *m* discharge potential transformer **-stab** *m* unloading staff **-stange** *f* clearing rod (firearms) **-stärke** *f* rate of discharge **-station** *f* discharging station **-stelle** *f* unloading and loading wharf, unloading point

Entlade-stock *m* cartridge extractor, unloading rod **-stoßschweißung** *f* electrostatic percussion welding **-strom** *m* discharge current **-stromstärke** *f* discharge rate of current **-verzug** *m* time lag **-vorgang** *m* discharge process or procedure **-vorrichtung** *f* discharge device, discharger **-widerstand** *m* discharge resistor (bleeder resistor with condensors) **-zeit** *f* time for emptying

Entladung *f* unloading, discharge **aperiodische** ~ aperiodic, dead-beat, impulsive, nonoscillatory, or unidirectional discharge **autoelektrische** ~ field emission **kathodische** ~ cathodic discharge **kontrahierte** ~ contracted discharge **oszillatorische** ~ **oszillierende** ~ oscillating or oscillatory discharge **selbständige** ~ self-sustained, spontaneous, or unassisted discharge **stille** ~ corona, silent discharge **strahlartige** ~ needle-point, corona, or streamer discharge, leader-stroke discharge **überspannte** ~ overvolted discharge **unselbständige** ~ assisted or non-self-sustained discharge **Zündbedingung für** ~ threshold relation for streamer discharge

Entladungscharakteristik *f* discharge characteristic ~ **einer Diode** current-voltage characteristic (of the two-electrode valve)

Entladungs-dauer *f* discharge time **-erscheinung** *f* phenomenon of discharge **-frequenz** *f* discharge frequency **-funke(n)** *m* disruption spark **-gebilde** *n* discharge (figure)

Entladungsgefäß *n* (electron-)discharge tube, discharge vessel, gas tube, gas-discharge tube **elektrisches** ~ electronic-discharge vessel ~ **mit flüssiger Kathode** pool-rectifier

entladungsgeheizte Kathode ionic-heated cathode

Entladungs-gesetz *n* three-halves-power law, $^3/_2$ law, emission law **-kreis** *m* discharge circuit **-kurve** *f* curve of discharge **-lampe** *f* discharge lamp **-leuchtstreifen** *m* luminous streamers **-methode** *f* loss of charge method **-nachglimmen** *n* discharge afterglow **-potential** *n* discharge potential **-raum** *m* discharge space **-relais** *n* (gas-)discharge relay **-rohr** *n* **-röhre** *f* discharge tube

Entladungs-schalter *m* discharge key **-spannung** *f* discharge potential **-seil** *n* suspending wire **-steilheit** *f* discharge slope **-stoß** *m* discharge surge, burst, pulse, corona **-strecke** *f* discharge gap or space **-strom** *m* space, cathode, total-emission, or discharge current **-stromkreis** *m* discharging circuit **-verbindung** *f* discharge connection **-verzug** *m* discharge delay **-weg** *m* discharge path, rectifier **-widerstand** *m* discharge resistance or resistor **-zeit** *f* time of discharge

entlang along **-gleiten** to ride **-streichen** (of gases) to flow or pass along **-streifen** to brush, wipe (over), skirt, graze

entlassen to dismiss, discharge, set free, release, relieve, disband, demobilize

Entlassung *f* dismissal, discharge, release

Entlassungsgesuch *n* resignation ~ **einreichen** to resign

entlasten to release, relieve, remove (a load), unload, ease, discharge **eine Leitung** ~ to relieve a circuit of some of its traffic

entlastet balanced (as ailerons) **-er Kolbenschieber** balanced piston valve **-er magnetischer Lautsprecher** balanced-armature magnetic loud-speaker **-es Ruder** balanced surface (aviation) **-er Schieber** balanced valve

Entlastung *f* release, relief, removal of the load, unloading, unburdening ~ **der Druckleitung** discharging of the delivery pipe ~ **vom Seitenschub** balancing for the thrust

Entlastungs-art *f* method of relieving the pressure **-bogen** *m* relieving arch **-einrichtung** *f* pressure-relieving device **-feder** *f* discharging spring, relief spring **-fläche** *f* balancing surface **-getriebe** *n* release gear **-gewicht** *n* discharge weight **-kanal** *m* by-wash, by pass **-kerbe** *f* relief notch **-klappe** *f* overflow valve **-kolben** *m* relieving piston **-kraft** *f* relieving force **-kurve** *f* rebound curve

Entlastungs-leitung *f* discharge line **-loch** *n* discharge hole, relief port **-platte** *f* balance plate, reliefing plate **-ruder** *n* balancing tab **-scheibe** (Pumpe) *f* balancing disc **-schiebegewicht** *n* sliding counterpoise **-seil** catenary suspension, support strand, additional steel suspension **-straße** *f* by-pass (road) **-ventil** *n* relief wave, release or by-pass valve (Hochofen) bleeder valve **-verdrehung** *f* relieve distortion **-vorrichtung** *f* relieving or blocking gear, counterbalance **-wehr** *m* spillway weir **-werk** *n* evacuation of floodwater, spillways

entledigen to discharge, get rid of

entleeren to empty, discharge, dump, exhaust, deflate, drain, unload (Gase) evacuate

Entleeren *n* emptying

Entleerpumpe *f* draining pump

entleerte Glühbirne exhausted lamp bulb

Entleerung *f* discharge, emptying, exhaustion; (mech.) discharge, drain; (Greifer) dumping **~ einer Baggerschute** pumping the material from a barge **untere ~** bottom discharge

Entleerungs-effekt *m* dispersal effect **-gerät** *n* draining device **-hahn** *m* drain cock **-klappe** *f* discharge door **-leitung** *f* delivery pipe, drain duct **-loch** *n* deflation sleeve **-öffnung** *f* discharge gate or outlet **-schlauch** *m* deflating sleeve **-schraube mit Überdruckventil** blow-off valve (drain plug) **-ventil** *n* drain valve

Entleerungsvorrichtung *f* drain device **~ für Gefälle** gravity emptying device

Entleerungszeit *f* deflation time, time required for emptying

entlehnen to borrow

Entleiher *m* borrower

entleimen to delaminate, degum (desize)

entleuchten to make nonluminous, shine, radiate

entlohnen to pay off

entlüften to remove air, ventilate, vent, evacuate, air (batteries)

Entlüfter *m* exhauster, exhaust fan, ventilator, safety valve, vent valve, breather, de-aerator **~ mit Handbetrieb** hand ventilator **~ mit Motorantrieb** motor ventilator

Entlüfter-klappe *f* breather, ventilator, air louver **-leitung** *f* vent line **-rohr** *n* breather pipe **-schraube** *f* vent screw **-stutzen** *m* vent plug

Entlüftung *f* ventilation, vent(ing), pressure release

Entlüftungs-anlage *f* air conditioning plant, ventilating system **-behälter** *m* deaerator tank **-dom** *m* discharge dome for vents **-drossel** *f* bleeder throttle **-druck** *m* venting pressure **-einrichtung** *f* ventilation system **-einsatz** *m* air escape cage **-filter** *n* vent filter **-hahn** *m* (air) relief cock, relief valve, air release and drain cock **-hutze** *f* gas-shaft or exhaust-gas hood, ventilation cap, suction hood **-kanal** *m* air duct **-klappe** *f* vent valve, air evacuation valve, breather

Entlüftungs-laufrad *n* ventilator impeller **-leitung** *f* air vent pipe, breather pipe or line, vent line, air pipe **-loch** *n* vent hole **-öffnung** *f* vent, breather **-pumpe** *f* air pump (laboratory) **-rohr** *n* air-vent pipe, ventilating duct, blowpipe, pressure relief pipe, air discharge pipe **-schieber** *m* slide valve for the air **-schlauch** *m* relief hose, bleeder or breather tube

Entlüftungs-schlitz *m* ventilator **-schornstein** *m* ventilating shaft **-schraube** *f* venting screw, release screw, vent plug, vent branch **-stutzen** *m* air vent, breather, vent branch **-verschluß** (Batterie) gas relief stopper (battery) **-ventil** *n* (air-)vent valve, relief or air-vent cock, air-escape, air-relief, or air-exhaust valve **-vorrichtung** *f* breather **-zweck** *m* venting purpose

entmagnetisieren to demagnetize, degauss, de-energize

entmagnetisierter Probekörper demagnetized sample

Entmagnetisieren *n* demagnetization

Entmagnetisierer *m* demagnetizer

Entmagnetisierung *f* demagnetization

Entmagnetisierungsfaktor *m* demagnetizing factor

entmastet dismasted

Entmetallisierungsbad *n* liberator or depositing-out tank

Entmineralisierung *f* demineralization

entmischen to separate into parts, dissociate, disintegrate, decompose, liquate, core

Entmischer *m* (Fernschreiber) decoder

entmischt immiscible

Entmischung *f* separation, dissociation, disintegration, decomposition, liquation, coring, precipitation, segregation (of aggregate or sand from cement) **~ des Möllers** separation of constituents

Entmischungsvorgang *m* separation process

Entmodeler *m* demodulator

entmodeln to demodulate (radio)

Entmodelung *f* **Entmodulierung** *f* demodulation, detection, rectification

Entnahme *f* extraction (draining) removal **-dampf** *m* bled steam **-elektrode** *f* output electrode, catcher (in beam tube) **-gerät** *n* **für Bodenproben** soil sampler, sampling tool **-häufigkeit** (Proben) *f* frequency of sampling **-klemmen** *pl* output terminals **-kondensatorturbine** *f* pass-out condensing turbine **-kreis** *m* output circuit, load circuit **-pipette** *f* sampling pipe **-punkt** *m* output terminals, tapping point

Entnahme-rohr *n* pressure probe, sampling tube **-röhrchen** *n* pressure probe in tilted weir-plate article **-scheibe** *f* bunker gate **-schein** *m* requisition form, withdrawal form **-seite** *f* receiver end

Entnahmesonde *f*, **geteilte aufklappbare ~** split spoon

Entnahme-stelle *f* borrow pit or borrow area, place where samples are taken, place where pressures are taken, tapping point, extraction place **-störung** *f* sampling disturbance **-stromkreis** *m* receiver circuit **-stutzen** *m* drain spout **-stufe** *f* tapping stage **-sunk** *m* drawdown wave **-turbine** *f* bleeder turbine, pass-out turbine **-turm** *m* outlet tower **-ventil** *n* extraction (bleeder) valve, tapping-point valve **-verschluß** *m* offtake gate

Entnässen von Geweben drying fabrics

entnebeln to take moisture out of gases, disperse fumes, clear of fog or mist

Entnebelung *f* fume removal

Entnebelungsanlage *f* fume dispersion equipment

entnehmbar removable **höchste längere Zeit -e Leistung** maximum except take-off power

entnehmen to remove, take from, bleed, tap (as air from a compressor) extract, absorb, pick up, catch or abstract (energy from an electron beam), derive or infer from ~ **mit Pipette** to pipette out
Entnehmen *n* bleeding
entnerven to enervate, unnerve, weaken
entnieten to remove rivets, unrivet
entnommene Leistung output
Entnullen *n* zero suppression
entölen to remove the oil, de-oil
Entöler *m* oil separator
entölt free of oil
Entorientierung *f* disorientation
Entparaffinierung *f* dew point, de-waxing, waxing
entphosphor(e)n to dephosphorize
Entphosphorung *f* dephosphorization, phosphorus drop
entpichen to unpitch
entplomben to unseal
Entpolymerisation *f* depolymerization
Entpropanisierung *f* depropanizer
entpülpen to depulp
Entquellen *n* shrinkage
Entrahmungsmaschine *f* cream separator
Entrastung *f* disengaging, lowering
entraten to dessuade
entrechten to deprive of rights
entreffen to inflate (a parachute), unreef
entregen to de-energize
Entregerwiderstand *m* de-energizing resistor
entreißen to snatch, tear away
entriegeln to unlock, unlatch, release the catch, trigger, release, trip
Entriegelung *f* unlocking device, release
Entriegelungs-magnet *m* unlocking magnet **-stange** *f* release rod
entrieseln to trickle away
entrinden to bark, decorticate
entrinnen to escape
entrollen to unfurl, uncase
Entropie *f* entropy **von gleicher** ~ isentropic **unveränderliche** ~ constant entropy
Entropie-analogon *n* entropy analog **-änderung** *f* entropy variation **-dichte** *f* entropy density **-druck** *m* disorder pressure **-stromdichte** *f* entropy flow
entrosten to remove rust
Entrostungs-mittel *n* rust remover **-werkzeug** *n* scaling tool
entrümpeln to clear of rubbish and easily ignited loose material **den Boden** ~ to clear the attic
Entrümpelung *f* clearing of inflammable material
entrunzeln to unwrinkle
entsanden to desand
Entsandung *f* desilting, removal of sand
Entsalzungs-anlage *f* sludge-fittings **-wasser** *n* sludge
Entsatz *m* relief, relieving force **-versuch** *m* attempt to relieve
entsäuern to deacidify, neutralize, edulcorate
entsäuerter Raffinationsabfall disacidified or deacidized tar
Entsäuerung *f* deacidizing
Entsäuerungstrog *m* deacidizing vessel
entschädigen to indemnify, remunerate, make amends
Entschädigung *f* indemnity, compensation, damages, reimbursement, allowance, consideration ~ **festsetzen** to assess or fix damage (indemnity) ~ **zuerkennen** to award damages
entschädigungspflichtig sein to be liable to indemnity
entschalen (Seide) to boil off (degum)
entschälen, die Seite ~ to scour the silk
Entschäler *m* sheller
entschälte Seide scoured silk
entschärfen to render safe, unprime, disarm, defuse, deactivate
entschäumen to skim
Entschäumungsschleuder *f* centrifugal oil foam remover, deaerator
Entscheid *m* decision
entscheiden to decide
Entscheidung *f* decision, crisis, sentence, verdict, judgment **eine** ~ **bei höherer Instanz** decision in a higher court
Entscheidungs-element *n* decision element (comput.) **-gehalt** *n* decision content (Comput.) **-gerät** *n* decision element **-kern** *m* crux of a decision **-los** indecisive
Entscheinen *n* deblooming
Entscheinungsfarbe *f* deblooming color
entschichten to remove coating
entschieden decided, determined
Entschiedenheit *f* decisiveness
entschlacken to free from dross or slag, remove or rake out slag, draw off slag or clinker, deslag
Entschlacker *m* slag-removing plant
Entschlackung *f* removal of slag or of cinder
entschlammen to free from mud, remove the sludge
Entschlämmungssieb *n* de-sliming screen
entschlaufen to unloop
entschleiern to unveil, reveal
entschleimen to deslime, remove slime
Entschleimung *n* desliming, removal of slime or coagulated material
entschlichten to desize (fabrics)
Entschlichtungsbad *n* desizing bath
entschlickern to dross
entschließen, sich ~ to decide, resolve, determine
Entschließung *f* resolution
entschlossen resolute, determined, firm, decided
Entschlossenheit *f* determination, resoluteness
Entschluß *m* decision, resolution **strategischer** ~ strategic decision
entschlüsseln to decode, decipher, decrypt
Entschlüsselung *f* decoding, ungarbling, deciphering, breaking a (secret) code
Entschlußfassung *f* decision, formulation of decision
Entschlußkraft *f* power of decision
Entschlüßler *m* decoder
entschöpfen to draw, derive, obtain
entschuldigen to excuse **sich** ~ to apologize
Entschuldigung *f* apology, excuse
Entschuppen *n* flocculation, deflocculation
entschwärzen to clean (wash) the form
entschwefeln to desulfurize
Entschwefelung *f* desulfurization, desulfurizing, sulfur removal, sweetening, doctored solution,

sulfur drop
Entschwefelungsmittel *n* desulfurizer, desulfurizing agent
Entschweißung der Wolle wool scouring
entschwelen to distil
entsenden to dispatch, hurl, let fly, send off
entsetzen to relieve, displace
Entsetzung *f* dismissal, relief
entseuchen to disinfect, sterilize
Entseuchen *n*, **Entseuchung** *f* disinfection, decontamination, sterilization
Entseuchungs-filter *n* decontamination filter **-gerät** *n* disinfector **-mittel** *n* disinfecting agent **-schrank** *m* disinfecting chamber
entsichern to release safety catch, disengage or release the safety arm or activate, cock, prepare for firing
Entsicherungsflügel *m* arming vane
entsiegeln to unseal
entsilbern to desilver, desilverize
Entsilberung *f* desilverization, desilvering
Entsilberungs-anlage *f* desilverization plant **-arbeit** *f* desilvering operation
entsilizieren to desiliconize
Entsilizierung *f* desiliconization
entsockelt with socket (base) removed
Entspanneinrichtung *f* tension removing device
entspannen (die Federspannung) to release the tension, uncock, relax, anneal, slacken, relieve a spring, remove stress, temper, (geschweißte Bauteile) stress-relieve
Entspannen einer Feder relaxing, relieving, or untensioning of a spring
entspannt slack
Entspannung *f* slackening, relaxing (of springs), relaxation, expansion (of steam), annealing, removal of stress, seasoning (a gauge block), pressure release or drop, tension release
Entspannungs-abkühlung *f* cooling due to expansion **-bohrlöcher** *pl* stab holes **-gefäß** *n* blow-off tank, let-down vessel **-glühen** *n* stress-relieving anneal(ing) **-kammer** *f* flash drum, flash chamber **-kühler** *m* expansion cooler **-raum** *m* expansion chamber
Entspannungs-topf *m* flash trap **-trocknen** *n* flash drying **-trommel** *f* flash drum **-turm** *m* flash tower **-ventil** *n* relief valve, expansion valve **-verdampfer** *m* flashing chamber **-verhältnis** *n* expansion ratio **-verhieb** *m* stress-relieving lift
Entspiegelung *f* dereflection
entsperren to unlatch, open, unseal, unlock, break
entsprechen to correspond, meet, come up (to), conform to, match, mate, comply with, agree, satisfy (math.) **der Belastung ~** to be in conformity with the load **einer Gleichung ~** to fit an equation
Entsprechen *n* depicting
entsprechend corresponding (to), adequate, according to, analogous (math.), in conformity with, suitable **dem Wunsch des Kunden ~** to customer's requirements
Entsprechung *f* equivalent, denotation, analogy
entspringen to spring, rise, issue
entsprühen to spit forth
entspulen to deload
entspunden to extract bungs
entstammen to stem from, be derived from, descend from, originate
entstanden aus . . . arising out of **durch sich selbst ~** autogenous
entstänkern to deodorize
Entstänkerung *f* deodorizing, deodorization
Entstänkerungspatrone *f* deodorizing cartridge
entstauben to remove dust, dust off
Entstauber *m* cleaner for machinery, compressed-air apparatus
Entstaubung *f* dust exhaust, dust collection, dust separation, removal, or arrest
Entstaubungsanlage *f* dust-arrester installation, dust arrester, dust-collecting equipment **~ mit Staubfilter aus Stoff** cloth-screen dust arrester
Entstaubungs-kammer *f* dust-collecting chamber de-dusting screen **-vorrichtung** *f* dust-separating or dust-collecting appliance
entstehen to arise, originate, begin, form, result
Entstehen *n*, **im ~ begriffen** nascent **~ von Beanspruchungen** setting up of stresses
entstehend resulting, growing, in process of formation
Entstehung *f* formation, origin, development, genesis **~ von Rissen** development of cracks
Entstehungs-bedingung *f* formation condition, mode of origin **-geschichte** *f* genesis **-ort** *m* origin, source, or seat of generation or production **-potential** *n* appearance potential, ionization potential **-ursache** *f* original cause **-vorgang** *m* process of formation **-zentrum** *n* center of origin **-zustand** *m* nascent state
Entsteiner *m* eliminator and stoner
entstellen to mutilate, alter, distort, deform
Entstellung *f* mutilation, alteration, deformation
Entstör-anlage *f* interference protection **-art** *f* mode of suppression **-barkeit** *f* interference suppressibility **-diode** *f* interference inverter (TV) **-drossel** *f* suppressor choke
entstören to screen (radio), eliminate (defects or stoppages), clear interference, suppress, shield, antijam
Entstörer *m* interference eliminator or suppressor, filter, shield
Entstör-geflecht *n* screening metal braid **-gerät** *n* anti-interference device **-geschirr** *n* shielding harness, radio shielding device **-grad** *m* degree of radio noise suppression **-kappe** *f* ignition shield, screening cap **-kondensator** *m* anti-interference condenser **-mittel** *n* (wireless) interference suppressor **-muffe** *f* screening sleeve
Entstör-netzwerk *n* noise killer **-platte** *f* interference suppressor plate **-röhre** *f* rectifier tube **-schlauch** *m* shielding tube **-stecker** *m* suppressor plug **-stutzen** *m* interference suppression socket
entstört, voll ~ all interference eliminated
Entstörung *f* noise suppression, interference elimination, shielding
Entstörungs-drossel *f* radio interference suppression reactor (choke) **-gerät** *n* interference suppressor **-kondensator** *m* anti-interference condenser, radio interference, (noise) suppression capacitor **-messung** *f* interference elimination measuring **-mittel** *n* radio interference equipment suppression **-trupp** *m* line

crew **-verfahren** *n* antijamming technique **-vorschaltgerät** *n* radio interference (noise) suppressor

Entstör-widerstand *m* resistor suppressor **-wirkung** *f* screening effect

entströmen to flow, stream, escape or issue from **~ lassen** (Gas) to release gas

Entstümmelungstafel *f* permutation table

entsumpfen to drain swamps

Enttankeinrichtung *f* defuelling facility

enttanken to defuel

Enttankungsventil *n* fuel-release valve

entteeren to detar, separate tar

Entteerung *f* detarring, tar separation

Enttrübung *f* sharpening of minimum, deblurring, fast time control (rdr)

Enttrübungsrahmen *m* frame designed to make zero or minimum point sharp, zero cleaning or sharpening frame **-sieb** *n* drainage screen

Endverkehr *m* terminal traffic

Entvulkanisation *f* devulcanization, devulcanizing

Entvulkanisationskessel *m* digester

entwaffnen to disarm

entwalden to deforst

Entwarnung *f* all-clear signal

Entwässerer *m* water separator, drainage appliance

entwässern to drain, dewater, dehydrate, concentrate, tap

entwässert drained, dehydrated, anhydrous, concentrated **der Boden wird allmählich ~** the ground dries out gradually **-er Beton** vacuum concrete

Entwässerung *f* drainage, dewatering, dehydration, concentration, draining (off) **Graben ~** drainage by ditches or gutters

Entwässerungs-anlage *f* canalization, drainage system, sump hole, spillway **-apparat** *m* drying, dehydrating, or desiccating apparatus **-auspuff** *m* drain for engine exhaust box **-becherwerk** *n* drainage elevator **-brunnen** *m* drainage wells **-filz** *m* draining felt **-graben** *m* drainage ditch **-hahn** *m* drain cock **-kanal** *m* by-wash by-pass **-kolonnen** *pl* dehydrating columns

Entwässerungs-leitung *f* drain pipe line **-maschine** *f* wet machine, pulp machine **-mühle** *f* noria **-presse** *f* squeezing roller **-pumpe** *f* drainage pump **-rohr** *n* drainpipe, pipe drain, weep hole **-schleuder** de-watering centrifuge **-schleuse** *f* drainage valve

Entwässerungs-sieb *n* de-watering screen, drainage band or screen **-stollen** *m* culvert, drainage gallery, drainage tunnel **-teppich** *m* drainage blanket **-turm** *m* dewatering tower **-vorrichtung** *f* drainage appliance, water separator **-walze** *f* dandy roll **-zylinder** *m* concentrator

Entweder-oder-satz *m* alternative

entweichen to pass off, escape, disappear

Entweichen *n* escape (of a gas), evasion **~ des Dampfes** puff of steam

Entweichung *f* escape, eduction, leak

Entweichungsventil *n* escape, drain, or outlet valve, vent valve

entwenden to steal

entwerfen (konstruktiv) to design, construct, plan, project, devise, draw up, draft, trace (out), sketch, map, (zeichnerisch) outline, contrive, lay out, focus, form (an image) **eine Anlage ~** to design an installation **in großen Zügen ~** to outline

Entwerfen *n* designation, planning, selection, plotting

Entwerfer *m* designer

entwerten to depreciate, cancel, (durch Stempel) to deface

Entwertung *f* depreciation

Entwertungssatz *m* rate of depreciation

entwesen to disinfect, sterilize

Entwesen *n* disinfecting, sterilizing

Entwesung *f* delousing **~ von Ungeziefer** disinfection

entwickelbar developable

entwickeln to liberate, evolve, generate, develop, expand, gather (speed), disengage

entwickelte Funktion explicit function

Entwickler *m* generator, developer (phot.) **-behälter** *m* generator **-bottich** *n* developing tank **-gefäß** *n* area of development **-lösung** *f* developing solution (photo) **-schale** *f* developing tray

Entwicklung *f* deployment, development, evolution, formation, expansion, generation (of gases) **~ des Flugwesens** development of aviation **~ eines Zyklons** (Wirbelsturmes) cyclogenesis **zeitliche ~** time element in the development of

Entwicklungs-abteilung *f* research division, department of development, design department **-arbeit** *f* development(al) work **-bad** *n* developing bath **-bereich** *m* development area, possibility of development **-faktor** *m* development factor, time of appearance **-foulard** *n* developing padding machine **-flüssigkeit** *f* developing agent, developer, developing liquid **-gang** *m* course of development **-kassette** *f* developing tank or vessel **-linie** *f* line of development **-parameter** *n* expansion parameter **-periode** *f* period of evolution **-programm** *n* development program

Entwicklungs-rahmen *m* developing rack **-richtung** *f* trend **-satz** *m* expansion theorem **-schale** *f* developing tray, developing dish or pan **-stadium** *n* stage of (progress) development **-steilheit** *f* slope (of a Hurter and Driffield curve) **-stillstand** *m* arrest in development **-tempo** *n* acceleration of development **-träge** slow to develop **-trog** *m* developing tank or pan **-werk** *n* development laboratory

entwischen to get away, escape

entwirren to disentangle, scutch, unravel

Entwurf *m* draft, design, project, proposition, plan, layout, sketch, outline, drawing model, type, pattern, scheme

Entwurf(s)-bestandteile *pl* design elements **-frage** *f* design problem (engin.) **-ingenieur** *m* project (design) engineer **-minimumgewicht** *n* minimum design weight **-parameter** design parameter **-schub** *m* rated thrust (g/m) **-teil** *m* projected area **-werkstätte** *f* drafting office **-zeichnung** *f* draft, sketch

entwurzeln to uproot

entzerren to correct (a distortion) or eliminate distortion, rectify, regenerate, equalize, compensate; **~** (Luftbildaufnahmen), reestablish

entzerrend-e Übertragung regenerative repeater

-er Verstärker compensating, correcting, equalizing repeater
Entzerrer *m* regenerative repeater (teleg.) correcting device, antidistortion device, equalizer, rectifier, corrective network, attenuator (sound recording and reproduction), attenuation compensator ~ **zum Anheben und Senken** compensator to accentuate and deaccentuate frequencies or bands
Entzerrer-anordnung *f* **-einrichtung** *f* distortion-correcting device, antidistortion device **-drossel** *f* (TV) peaking coil **-kette** *f* correcting or corrective network **-kurve** *f* attenuation characteristic of equalization **-schaltung** *f* compensating or correcting circuit
Entzerrspule *f* peaking coil (TV)
Entzerrung *f* rectifying, rectification, regeneration (radio), equalization, correcting of distortion, correction (of aerial photographs), transforming (phot.), suppression (of interference) ~ (Dynamik) expansion (by an expander) ~ **von Geometriefehlern** (TV) correction of geometrical distortions
Entzerrungs-anordnung *f* distortion-corrector device or compensator, antidistortion device **-bereich** *m* frequency range of equalization **-drossel** *f* antiresonant coil **-einrichtung** *f* distortion-correcting device **-filter** *n* filter-type equalizer, equalizing net-work, four-terminal-type equalizer
Entzerrungsgerät *n* rectifier, rectifying apparatus, rectifying camera (aerial phot.) **halbautomatisches** ~ semiautomatic rectifier **teilautomatisches** ~ partly automatic rectifier
Entzerrungs-grenze *f* frequency limit of equalization **-grundlage** *f* basis for rectification **-kammer** *f* rectifying camera
Entzerrungskette *f* filter-type equalizer ~ **mit Brücken-H-Schaltung** H-type network attenuator (balanced) ~ **mit Brücken-T-Schaltung** T-type network attenuator (unbalanced)
Entzerrungs-kreis *m* (zum Hervorheben einiger Frequenzbereiche) balancing network (to accentuate or underscore certain bands) **-optik** *f* anamorphic optics **-photogrammetrie** *f* rectifying photogrammetry **-schalter** *m* antidistortion switch **-unterlage** *f* basis for rectification **-verstärker** *m* regenerative repeater
entziehen to withdraw, deprive of, extract, remove, abstract, rid **sich** ~ to elude, avoid, evade, disengage
Entzieher *m* entrainer
Entziehung *f* abstraction, extraction, withdrawal
entziffern to decipher, decode
Entzifferung *f* decoding, deciphering
Entzifferungsdienst *m* decoding service
entzinken to dezinc
Entzinkung *f* dezincking
entzinnen to detin
Entzinnung *f* detinning
Entzuckerung *f* extraction of sugar, desugarizing, desaccharification
entzündbar combustible, inflammable
Entzündbarkeit *f* inflammability
entzünden to kindle, ignite, (Holz) inflame, light, set fire to
entzundern to scour, pickle, descale
Entzunderung *f* scaling off, descaling
Entzunderungswärme *f* wash heat, cinder heat, sweating heat
entzündlich inflammable
Entzündlichkeit *f* ignitability, inflammability, pyrophoric property
Entzündung *f* ignition, kindling, inflammation
Entzündungs-funke *m* ignition spark **-gefahr** *f* ignition hazard **-gemisch** *n* explosive mixture **-probe** *f* ignition test **-punkt** *m* kindling or burning point, flare or flash point (of oil) **-stelle** *f* ignition point **-temperatur** *f* ignition temperature, kindling temperature
entzurren to unlock, unclamp
entzwei-brechen to break across **-gehen** to break **-schlagen** to break into pieces, break in two **-schneiden** to cut in two
Enzym *n* enzyme **rohrzuckerspaltendes** ~ sucrose-splitting enzyme
enzymatisch enzymatic **-e Spaltung** enzymatic splitting
Eosin *n* eosine
eosinophil eosinophil
Eozän *n* eocene
Ephantinit *m* ephantinite
Ephemeriden *pl* ephemerides
Epidemie *f* epidemic
Epidiaskop *n* epidiascope
Epikadmium *n* epicadmium
Episkop *n* reflecting projector, episcope
Epitasimeter *n* epitasimeter
Epitaxialtransistor *m* epitaxial transistor
Epitrochoide *f* epitrochoid
Epizentrum *n* epicenter
Epizogenik *n* epizogenics
epizyklisch epicyclic
Epizykloid *f* epicycloid
Epsom Salz Epsom salt, magnesium sulfate
equipotentiale Oberflächen equipotential surfaces
Erachten *n* judgment, opinion **meines Erachtens** in my opinion or judgment
erbauen to erect, design, build, construct
Erbauer *m* designer, constructor, builder, founder
Erbauung *f* construction
erbeuten to capture
Erbinerde *f* erbium oxide
erbitten to ask for, request
Erbium *n* erbium
erblasen to blast, blow
erblassen to fade, pale, die out, expire
Erblindung *f* loss of sight
erbohren to find by boring
Erbpacht *f* long lease, hereditary tenure, copyhold
erbreiten to broaden
erbringen to produce, adduce
Erbsen-größe *f* pea size **-kohle** *f* pea coal **-säeapparat** *m* pea attachment **-stein** *m* pisolite
Erbskohle *f* pea coal
Erb-stollen *m* main adit for draining a mine **-teufe** *f* depth to the adit for draining a mine **-zins** *m* hereditary rent **-zinsvertrag** *m* ground rent, leasehold
erschweren to aggravate
Erd-ableiter *m* earth arrester **-abplattung** *f* earth's oblateness **-abplattungsnäherung** *f* earth flattening approximation **-absorption** *f*

ground absorption **-achse** *f* earth's axis
erdacht thought of
Erdader *f* ground wire
Erdalkali *n* alkaline earth **-kontinua** *pl* continuous alkaline earth spectra **-metall** *n* alkaline-earth metal **-oxyd** *n* alkaline earth oxide **-salz** *n* alkaline salt
alkalisch alkaline-earth
Erd-anker *m* ground anchor (aviation) **-anschluß** *m* ground, ground connection, earth connection **-anschlußkasten** *m* feeder plug box on the ground **-antenne** *f* ground or underground or buried antenna **-anziehung** *f* gravitation **-anziehungskraft** *f* gravitational force
Erd-äquator *m* terrestrial or earth's equator **-arbeit** *f* digging, earthworks, excavation work **-artig** earthy, earthlike **-asphalt** *m* earthy asphalt **-asymmetrisch** unbalanced to ground **-atmosphäre** *f* atmosphere of the earth, terrestrial atmosphere **-aufklärung** *f* ground reconnaissance **-auflager** *n* end supports, shore piling **-aufschüttung** *f* earth fill
Erdaufwurf *m* heap of earth, mound, parapet, berm, embankment **durchlaufender ~** continuous parapet
Erd-bagger *m* dredger for clearing dry earth **-bahn** *f* earth's orbit, terrestrial orbit **-ball** *m* earth **-band** *n* telluric band **-bau** *m* earthwork, earth construction, earthwork engineering
Erdbeben *n* earthquake **-anzeiger** *m* seismograph **-kunde** *f* seismology **-messer** *m* seismometer, seismograph **-strahlen** *pl* seismic rays **-warte** *f* seismological observatory
Erd-beobachtung *f* ground observation **-beschleunigung** *f* acceleration due to gravity **-bewegungen** *pl* ground leveling, dirtmoving (US) earthmoving, soil shifting operations
Erdbild-aufnahme *f* terrestrial survey, ground photograph **-aufnahmegerät** *n* field apparatus for ground photogrammetry **-messung** *f* ground or terrestrial photogrammetry, phototopography
Erdboden *m* ground, soil, earth's surface **-absorption** *f* ground absorption **-erschütterung** *f* ground unrest, ground resistance **-widerstand** *m* ground-resistance unrest
Erdbogen *m* inverted arch
Erdbohrer *m* earth auger, earth borer, auger, pipe pusher, churn, drill, auger bit **~ mit Stoßbewegung** thrust borer
Erdbohrung *f* trial boring
Erdböschung *f*, **natürliche ~** natural slope of the earth or soil
Erd-buchse *f* grounding sleeve **-damm** *m* embankment, earth bank or dam
Erddraht *m* earth or ground wire **mit einem ~ versehen** to ground-wire
Erddraht-netz *n* ground network, ground mat **-schleifenmessung** *f* loop test
Erd-drehung *f* rotation of the earth, earth rate **-druck** *m* earth or soil pressure, active earth pressure, thrust **-koeffizient** *m* coefficient of earth
Erde *f* ground, earth, soil **an ~ liegende Ader** positive wire **an ~ legen** to (put to) earth, ground **an ~ liegend** grounded, earthed **die ~ umkreisen** to orbit **um die ~ kreisendes Echo** round-the-world echo **in die ~ verlegen** to bury **mit ~ verbinden** to connect to earth or ground **seltene ~** rare earth
Erd-einschiebziel *n* ground-registration target **-einstellung** *f* setting (radar) **-elastizität** *f* earth elasticity **-elektrode** *f* earth or ground plate
erden to ground, earth, put to earth **die Leitung ~** (an Erde legen) to ground the line
Erden *n* earthing, grounding **-schluß** *m* ground connection
erden-fern remote from the ground or the earth's surface **-nah** near the ground or the earth's surface
Erder *m* ground (elec.), earth plate, ground plate or wire **-platte** *f* ground rod, pipe or plate, earth plate **-widerstand** *m* ground resistance
Erd-fall *m* depression **-farbe** *f* earthy or mineral color
Erdfehler *m* earth fault **-schleife** *f* earth loop (teleph.)
Erdfehlerschleifenmessung *f* loop test **~ nach Varley** Varley loop test
Erd-feld der Schwerkraft earth's gravitational field **-ferne** *f* distance from the earth **-fernrohr** *n* terrestrial telescope **-fernsprechverbindung** *f* ground-return telephone circuit **-feste Achse** earth axis (aerodyn.) **-feuchte** (Betonmasse) of low water content (concrete), damp **-fließen** *n* soilfluction (slow creeping of wet soil)
erdfrei ungrounded **-e Spannung** floating voltage
Erdfunken *n* earth telegraphy (using the ground as a conductor) **-stecke** *f* earth terminal arrester
Erdfunkerdienst *m* ground wireless service
Erdfunkerei *f* earth wireless telegraphy
Erdfunkstelle *f* ground signal station
Erdgas *n* natural gasoline, natural gas, casing-head gas, marsh gas **-beförderung** *f* natural gas transmission **-benzin** *n* natural or casing-head gasoline **-energie** *f* natural gas energy **-feld** *n* gas field **-förderung** *f* natural gas extraction **-leitungen** *pl* natural gas pipe lines **-quelle** *f* natural-gas well or source **-schürfrechte** *pl* natural gas rights
erd-gebunden restricted to the ground, grounded, earth-minded **-geräusch** *n* earth noise **-geschoß** *n* ground floor, basement **-geschoßstrom** *m* fault current, current to earth **-gezeiten** *pl* earth bodily tides **-glas** *n* selenite **-glasur** *f* earth glaze **-gleiche** *f* ground level **-gleicher** *m* terrestrial or earth's equator **-grube** *f* burrow, pit **-gürtel** *m* zone
Erd-halbkugel *f* hemisphere **-halbmesser** *m* equatorial semidiameter **-harz** *n* bitumen, resinous earth, asphalt **-harzig** asphaltic, bituminous **-haue** *f* mattock, pickax **-hebenmesser** *m* seismometer, seismograph **-höhle** *f* (underground) cave **-hörer** *m* geophone
erdig earthy **-e Braunkohle** earthy brown coal, easily slacking lignite coal
Erd-induktion *f* earth induction **-induktionskompaß** *m* earth-inductor compass, flux-gate compass, gyrosyne compass **-induktor** *m* induction compass, earth inductor **-innere** *n* interior of the earth
Erdkabel *n* buried cable, ground cable, underground cable, earthing cable, leader cable **-leitung** *f* underground line

Erd-kalk *m* limestone **-kampfflugzeug** strike aircraft **-kapazität** *f* earth capacity, wire-to-earth capacity **-karte** *f* geographical map **-keil** *m* soil wedge **-kern** *m* earth's cone **-klemme** *f* ground or earth(y) terminal, ground clamp **-kobalt** *m* earthy co l alt, asbolite **-kohle** *f* earthy coal, lignitic earth **-kontakt** *m* grounding contact **-körper** *m* terrestrial body **-kraft** *f* gravity **-kreis** *m* (earth's) sphere, globe, (civilized) world **-kreislinie** *f* horizon **-krumme** *f* topsoil **-krümmung** *f* curvature or bulge of the earth **-krümmungslineal** *n* depression-position finder, altitude-correction ruler **-kruste** *f* earth's crust **-kugel** *f* globe

Erdkunde *f* geography **mathematische ~** geodesy, geophysics, mathematical geography

Erd-landebremse *f* ground brake **-längenkreis** *m* meridian of longitude, meridian **-leiter** *m* ground wire

Erdleitung *f* ground or earth wire, ground lead, earth or ground connection, earth circuit

Erdleitungs-draht *m* ground wire, antijamming **-klemme** *f* earthing terminal **-prüfer** *m* earth tester **-rohr** *n* ground pipe (radio) underground pipe **-stromkreis** *m* grounding circuit **-unterbrecher** *m* ground arrester

Erdlot *n* bearing perpendicular to the earth (aerial phot.)

Erdmagnetfeld *n* terrestrial magnetic field, geomagnetic field

erdmagnetisch earth-magnetic, terrestrial-magnetic, geomagnetic **-es Feld** terrestrial magnetic field, geomagnetic field

Erd-magnetismus *m* terrestrial magnetism **-masse** *f* earth mass **-meridian** *n* meridian of the earth **-messer** *m* geodesist, surveyor **-messung** *f* geodesy, surveying

Erdmeß-instrument *n* instrument of geodesy **-kunst** *f* geodesy

Erd-metall *n* earth metal **-mine** *f* ground mine, land mine **-mineral** *n* earthy mineral **-mittagskreis** *m* meridian of longitude **-mittelpunkt** *m* center of the earth **-nähe** *f* perigee **-netz** ground network, ground mat

Erdnuß-dreschvorrichtung *f* **-säapparat** *m* peanutsowing attachment **-schalenmelasse** *f* peanut-shell molasses

Erdoberfläche *f* surface of the earth, ground plane

Erdoberflächenlehre *f* geomorphomology

Erdöl *n* petroleum (mineral oil), naphtha, crude oil, crude petroleum **-benzin** *n* benzine **-bohrung** *f* oil well **-destillat** *n* distillation product of petroleum **-raffinerieanlagen** *pl* petroleum refinery plants

Erdorganisation *f* ground organization

Erdortung *f* pilotage

Erdpech *n* mineral pitch, bitumen, (natural) asphalt **-artig** bituminous **-haltig** containing asphalt, asphaltic

Erd-peilgerät *n* earth direction finder **-pfahl** *m* ground peg or stake **-pflock** *m* ground peg or stake **-platte** *f* earth plate **-plattenstrom** *m* ground current **-pol** *m* earth pole **-potential** *n* earth potential, ground potential **-punkt** *m* point of the earth **-raupe** *f* earthworm, surface grub, cutworm

Erdreich *n* ground **goldführendes ~** pay dirt

Erd-rinde *f* earth's crust **-rohr** *n* soil pipe, underground pipe **-rohrleitung** *f* underground piping

erdrosseln to throttle, strangle

erdrücken to stifle, repress, smother, overwhelm

Erdrückleitung *f*, **Stromkreis mit ~** earth-return or grounded circuit

Erdrutsch *m* slide, sliding, landslide

Erdsappe *f* sap (min.) **flüchtige ~** hasty sap

Erd-satellit *m* earth satellite **-schaber** *m* bent shovel **-schalter** *m* grounding switch **-schatten** *m* earth's shadow **-schelle** *f* earth clip, ground clamp **-schiene** *f* ground bar **-schleife** *f* earth circuit, ground circuit

Erdschluß *m* ground leak or accidental ground, ground(ing), earth(ing), short circuit to ground, ground connection, ground binding post, fault indicator **ausgleichender ~** ground counterpoise **satter ~** dead ground **mittels ~ telegrafieren** to telegraph by line grounding **vollständiger ~** dead grounding **zeitweiser ~** intermittent or interrupted earth circuit

Erdschluß-anzeiger *m* earth-leakage indicator, indicator for earthen electric contact **-bestimmung** *f* ground location **-fehler** *m* ground fault **-löschspule** *f* Petersen coil **-löschvorrichtung** *f* ground-fault neutralizer **-messer** *m* earth-leakage meter **-prüfer** *m* leakage indicator or tester, ground detector **-stange** *f* ground rod **-strom** *m* short circuit to ground, loss current to earth **-wischer** *m* transient earth fault

Erdschollenquetsche *f* clod crusher

Erd-schraube *f* earth screw **-schuß** *m* active earth pressure, earth movement, ground shot **-schwere** *f* gravity (force of) **-seil** *n* earth wire, overhead earthing conductor **-seilklemme** *f* earth wire connector **-senkung** *f* subsidence of the earth **-sicht** *f* visual reference to the ground (terrain) **-sporn** *m* trail spade **-sprechgerät** *n* hand-generator-powered field telephone **-spieß** *m* ground spike **-spulen** *pl* short circuit to earth chokes and coils

Erd-stampfe *f* earth rammer, beetle (instrument) **-stampfer** *m* paving tamp, earth rammer **-station** *f* ground station **-stecker** *m* ground(ing) rod (elec.) **-stein** *m* eaglestone **-stelle** *f* ground station **-stoffe** *m pl* earth materials, soils **-störung** *f* earth disturbance **-stoß** *m* (earth) tremor or seism **-streckenmessung** *f* measurement of distance at earth's surface, ground distance measurement **-strich** *m* zone, region

Erdstrom *m* earth or stray current **-ausgleicher** *m* earth-current equalizer **-schleife** *f* metallic circuit against earth current **-schürfung** *f* earth-current prospecting

Erd-stufe *f* terrace **-sturz** *m* landslide **-sucher** *m* earth leakage detector

erdsymmetrisch balanced to ground **-e Leitung** balanced line

Erd-system *n* ground-return or composite signaling system, earth-return automatic system **-talg** *m* mineral tallow **-taste** *f* grounding key **-teer** *m* mineral tar, maltha **-teil** *m* continent **-telegraphie** *f* earth telegraphy (using the ground as a conductor) **-telegraphieverbindung** *f* ground-return telegraph circuit **-transport** *m* transportation of excavated material **-truppen** *f pl* ground forces **-überwachungseinrichtung** *f* ground-fault super-

vising equipment
Erdumdrehung *f* rotation of the earth (upon its axis)
Erdumlauf-bahn *f* earth orbit **-signal** *n* **-zeichen** *n* round-the-world signal
Erdung *f* ground (elec.), grounding (aviation), earth(ing), grounding device **~ von Betriebsbatterien** grounding of working batteries **einwandfreie ~** unexceptionable earthing (elec.)
Erdungs-ader *f* ground conductor **-anker** *m* grounding anchor antenna **-anschluß** *m* static bonding connection **-buchse** *f* ground bushing **-bügel** *m* cradle guard **-drossel** *f* drainage coil **-funkenstrecke für Hochspannungsleitungen** spark gap to earth in connection with high-tension wires **-grad** *m* earthing percentage **-kabel** *n* grounding cable **-klemme** *f* grounding terminal **-kohle** *f* earthing brush
Erdungs-leitung *f* ground wire or grounding circuit **-litze** *f* grounding strand **-messer** *m* earth tester **-schalter** *m* ground switch, earthing switch, arcing-ground suppressor **-schelle** *f* grounding clamp **-schiene** *f* earth bar **-schleife** *f* multiple earthing point **-schraube** *f* earthing screw, ground terminal
Erdungs-spule *f* arc suppression coil **-stift** *m* earthing pin **-streifen** *m* earth strip **-strom** *m* grounding current **-taste** *f* earthing key **-trenner** *m* earthing insulator **-vorrichtungen** *pl* earthing devices **-widerstand** *m* earthing or ground resistance **-zeichen** *n* symbol for earth
Erd-verbindung *f* ground or earth connection **-verbindungskurzschließer** *m* earth arrester **-vergleichsziel** *n* auxiliary ground target, ground-registration target **-verkehrsnetz** *n* global communication network **-verlegt** underground **-verlegung** *f* underground laying **-vermessung** *f* topographic survey **-vorlage** *f* earth parapet (in front of concrete wall) **-wachs** *n* ozocerite, native paraffin **-wall** *m* embankment, earth wall
Erdwärme-messer *m* geothermometer **-tiefenstufe** *f* geothermal gradient
Erd-welle *f* ground wave **-werk** *n* earthwork **-widerstand** *m* (passive) earth pressure, resistance offered by earth to being displaced **-widerstandsmesser** *m* earth resistance meter **-winde** *f* winch, capstan
Erd-zone *f* ground-line section **-zuleitung** *f* ground lead (elec.) **-zunge** *f* neck of land
ereignen, sich ~ to happen, occur, come to pass
Ereignis *n* event, occurrence, action, phenomenon **einmaliges ~** nonrecurrent, unique, or singular event or action
ereignis-los uneventful **-reich** eventful
ereilen to overtake, catch up with
ererben to inherit
erfahren experienced, seasoned, skilled, expert
Erfahrenheit *f* skill, experience
Erfahrung *f* experience, knowledge, practice, skill, observation **aus der ~ folgernd** a posteriori
Erfahrungs-austausch *m* exchange of experience **-bericht** *m* test report **-daten** *pl* empirical data
Erfahrungs-ergebnis *n* empirical result **-gemäß, -mäßig** empirical, known from experience **-sache** *f* matter of experience, matter of practice **-satz** *m* experimental theorem **-tatsache** *f* matter of experience, empirical, experimental, or practical facts or data **-wahrscheinlichkeit** *f* empirical propability **-wert** *m* empirical value **-winkel** *m* angle of reception **-zahl** *f* coefficient (from experiment or experience)
erfaßbar controllable, determinable **zahlenmäßig ~** numerically evaluable
erfassen to comprehend, grip, bite, grasp, seize, detect, pick up, engage, determine, entangle
Erfassungs-bereich *m* coverage (radar) **-winkel** *m* angle of reception **-wesen** *n* recruiting service
erfinden to invent, contrive, devise
Erfinder *m* inventor, discoverer **-eigenschaft** *f* inventorship **-geist** *m* inventive genius, creative conception **-gemeinschaft** *f* joint inventors
erfinderisch inventive, ingenious
Erfinder-patent *n* patent **-schutz** *m* patent **-zuwendung** *f* award to the inventor
Erfindung *f* invention, contrivance, device
Erfindungs-beschreibung *f* description, inventor's consent form **-gedanke** *m* basic or underlying idea of an invention **-gegenstand** *m* object of invention, disclosure **-geltungsbereich** *m* scope of invention or patent **-höhe** *f* level of invention **-kraft** *f* inventive faculty, ingenuity **-patent** *n* patent for invention, letters patent **-reich** prolific **-schritt** *m* progress in an invention
erflogen reached by flying **-e Meßwerte** data obtained during flight
Erfolg *m* success, result, achievement **~ haben** to succed (in a venture) **taktischer ~** tactical success, tactical result
erfolgen to succeed, result (from), take place
erfolglos unsuccessful, fruitless
Erfolglosigkeit *f* failure
erfolgreich successful
Erfolgs-faktor *m* achievement factor **-haftung** *f* responsibility for consequences **-kontrolle** *f* follow-up study **-prinzip** *n* trial and error principle **-sicher** sure-fire **-rechnung** *f* trading account
erfolgversprechend promising
erforderlich requisite, necessary, required **fester als ~** overstrength **-e Pistenlänge** *f* actual length of runway **-e Startlaufstrecke** *f* (eines Flugzeuges) take-off run required
Erforderliche, das für die Durchführung ~ wherewithal
erforderlichenfalls in case of need, if necessary
erfordern to demand, require, call for, render necessary, necessitate
Erfordernis *n* requirement, exigency, requisite, condition, demand
erforschen to investigate, examine, explore, research **bis ins einzelne ~** to scrutinize
Erforscher *m* investigator, explorer
Erforschung *f* exploration, investigation, research
Erforschungswindung *f* search coil
erfreulich enjoyable, gratifying
erfrieren to freeze, freeze to death
erfrischen to freshen (up), cool, refresh
Erfrischung *f* refreshment
erfüllen to fill (up), fulfill, satisfy (math.), impregnate, perform, comply (with), measure up to **eine Beziehung ~** to satisfy or fit a relation
Erfüllung *f* fulfillment, execution (action)
Erg *n* (cgs-Einheit der Arbeit) erg

ergänzen to replenish, complete, supplement, add to, restore, integrate

ergänzend complementary, supplementary

ergänzt completed

Ergänzung *f* completion, (zu 180°) supplement, (zu 90°) complement, (Comput.) replenishment, reserves, integration, addendum, annex

Ergänzungs-band *m* supplementary volume **-batterie** *f* holding battery, buffer or auxiliary battery **-bedarf** *m* supplementary supplies, deficiency shortage, replacement, requirements **-farbe** *f* complementary color **-geräte** *pl* accessories **-impedanz** *f* supplementary impedance **-kegel des Kegelrades** back cone of bevel gear **-kondensator** building-out capacitor

Ergänzungs-maßnahme *f* compensating measure **-planquadrat** *n* auxiliary map grids **-reihe** *f* complemental series **-schnitt** *m* supplementary fount **-speicher** *m* backing storage **-stelle** *f* replacement center **-stirnrad** *n* complementary spur gear **-stoff** *m* vitamin **-teil** *m* spare part, supplement, amendment **-trichter** *m* supplemental hopper **-winkel** *m* complementary angle, complement, supplement

ergeben to yield, show, accrue, ensure, offer, result, arise, give **sich ~** to surrender, capitulate, result, arise **sich ~ aus** to result from

ergeben loyal, devoted, humble

Ergebnis *n* result, consequence, product, outcome, amount, yield **ein ~ liefern** to yield (or produce) a result

Ergebnis-kraft *f* resultant (phys.) **-los** without result, fruitless

Ergebnisse *pl*, **gemeinsam erzielte ~** joint results **~ von Untersuchungsarbeiten** findings of studies

ergiebig productive, profitable, plentiful, fertile, abundant

Ergiebigkeit *f* yieldingness, productiveness, fertility **~** (eines Farbstoffs) tinctorial power **~** (einer Schallquelle) strength of a sound source

ergießen to pour metal **sich in etwas ~** to discharge into

Ergmesser *m* ergmeter

Ergodenproblem *n* ergodic problem

Ergodensatz *m* ergodic hypothesis

Ergometer *n* ergometer

ergreifen to seize, apprehend, affect

ergründen to find out, investigate, research, fathom

Erguß *m* overflow, discharge, effusion **-gesteine** *pl* extrusive (effusive) rocks

erhaben raised, elevated; (berühmt) eminent, illustrious; (großartig) grand, magnificent; (**~** über) superior to relief, convex, projecting, embossed, plastic, exalted, outstanding **~ herausarbeiten** to emboss **-e Arbeit** embossed work **-es Muster** raised design **-e Schrift** raised characters **-e Walzenmarke** *f* high spot

Erhabenheit *f* elevation, relief; eminence, grandeur

Erhalt *m* receipt (aviation)

erhalten to receive, obtain, maintain, preserve, keep (up) **~ bleiben** to be retained (of a quality)

erhaltend preserving

erhältlich available, procurable **im Handel ~** commercially available

Erhaltung *f* maintenance, preservation, conservation **~ der Masse** conservation of the mass **~ der Tiefen** maintenance of the depth

Erhaltungs-gesetz *n* law of conservation **-kosten** *pl* maintenance charge **-ladung** *f* compensating (trickle) charge **-satz** *m* conservation theorem **-zustand** *m* maintenance standard

erhärten to harden, verify, confirm, state, set, aver

Erhärten *n* setting

Erhärtung *f* hardening, declaration

Erhärtungs-probe *f* hardening test (or sample) **-verlauf** *m* process of setting

erheben to raise (math.), lift, charge, levy, exalt, make a claim, bring or file a suit or an action **sich in die Luft ~** to soar **in die** *n***te Potenz ~** to raise to the *n*th power

erheblich considerable, remarkable, important, especial

Erhebung *f* (Boden) elevation, rising ground; (Beförderung) elevation, promotion; (Ermittlung) investigation, inquiry, rebellion, official survey, raising (a question), canvassing, projection, rise, peak, point **~ einer Schallquelle** elevation of a source of sound

Erhebungen *pl* statistics, data

Erhebungswinkel *m* angle of gradient, of slope, or of elevation, quadrant angle **~** (des landenden Flugzeugs) angle of gradient

erhellen to illuminate, light up, brighten, clear up

erhitzen to heat, grow hot, ignite, anneal **sich ~** to get hot, heat (up)

Erhitzen *n* heating

Erhitzer *m* heater, still

erhitzt heated, hot, preheated

Erhitzung *f* heating (up), warming

Erhitzungs-geschwindigkeit *f* rate of heating **-gleichung** *f* heating equation **-kammer** *f* heating chamber, hearth, laboratory **-versuch mit Schwefelsäure** (sulfuric) acid heat test **-widerstand** *m* heat resistance

erhobene oder vertiefte Radien concave or convex radii

erhöhen to increase, advance, (Wert, Ton) raise, intensify, extend (credit), elevate, step up

erhöht elevated, increased

Erhöhung *f* increase, advance, boost, intensification, bulge (in curve), (quadrant) elevation, commading ground, prominence, lobe (as of a cam) **~ des Wassers** raising of the water level **schußtafelmäßige ~** firing-table elevation

Erhöhungs-fehler *m* elevation error **-skala** *f* elevation scale **-winkel** *m* quadrant elevation, angle of elevation **-zeichen** *n* sharp (music)

erholen, sich ~ (Batterie) to recover, recuperate

Erholung *f* recovery, recuperation **~ des Akku** recharge of battery

Erholungs-fähigkeit *f* recuperative capacity **-geschwindigkeit** *f* recovery rate **-glühen** *n* recovery annealing **-pause** *f* relief period **-platz** *m* recreation ground **-raum** *m* (der Beamtinnen), (operators') recreation room **-temperatur** *f* recovery temperature **-zeit** *f* time of recovery or of recuperation, settling time

Erholzuschlag *m* fatigue allowance

Ericsson-blechprüfapparat *m* Ericsson sheet-metal-testing apparatus, Ericsson cupping or ductility machine **-prüfer** *m* Ericsson cupping machine **-prüfung** *f* Ericsson cupping test **-tiefung** *f* Ericsson cupping **-tiefziehprobe** *f* Ericsson cupping or ductility test **-versuch** *m* Ericsson test **-wähler** *m* Ericsson selector

Ericsson-Zentral-Batterie-System *n* bridged-impedance common-battery system

erinnern to remind, draw attention to **sich ~** to remember, recollect, recall

Erinnerung *f* remembrance, recollection, reminiscence **die ~ betreffend** reminiscent

Eriometer *n* eriometer (optics)

erkalten to cool (down), chill, grow cold, solidify

erkälten to cool, chill **sich ~** to catch cold

Erkaltungsmethode *f* method of cooling

erkämpfen to gain by force

erkennbar distinguishable, marked **-er Grund** obvious reason

Erkennbarkeit *f* recognition

erkennen to recognize, know, detect, distinguish, acknowledge, realize, find (law)

Erkennen *n* perception

Erkenntnis *f* knowledge, (re)cognition, realization, finding or sentence (law), insight

Erkennung *f* recognition, make, trade name

Erkennungs-licht *n* recognition light **-marke** *f* identification tag **-signal** *n* identification or recognition signal **-tuch** *n* identification panel, ground panel

Erkennungszeichen *n* airplane marking, identification mark, challenge (mil.) **~** (z. B. für aufgetretene Störung) sign, indication (engine trouble)

Erker *m* bay window, jutty, bay-window-type gun mount in front right sponson **-brüstung** *f* railing of balustrade

erklärbar explicable

erklären to explain, clear (up), account for, declare, define

erklärlich explainable

Erklärung *f* statement, explanation, comment, interpretation, elucidation, deposition, definition **eidesstattliche ~** affidavit of execution, affirmation in lieu of oath

erklimmen to reach (by climbing)

erkoppelte Fahrt speed by dead reckoning

erkranken to become sick

erkunden to reconnoiter, explore, scout, gain information

Erkunder *m* scout, reconnaissance airplane

erkundigen, sich ~ to inquire

Erkundigung *f* inquiry, search

Erkundung *f* reconnaissance

Erkundungs-ergebnis *n* reconnaissance report **-flug** *m* reconnaissance flight

Erkundungs-organ *n* reconnaissance element **-prisma** *n* reconnoitering prism

Erlähmung *f* fatigue (of metals)

erlängen (von Strecken), to drive galleries (min.)

Erlaß *m* order, decree, warrant, remission, allowance, discount, pardon

erlassen to issue orders, remit, absolve (from debts, etc.)

erlauben to allow, permit, let, authorize

Erlaubnis *f* allowance, license, permit, permission **-inhaber** *m* licensee

Erlaubnisschein *m* permit, leave, pass **~ für den Transportflugzeugführer** transport-pilot rating

erlaubt permitted **-es Energieniveau** permitted level, permitted quantum state or energy zone **-e Maßabweichung** tolerance **-er Übergang** permitted transition

erläutert illustrated

Erläuterung *f* explanation, elucidation, legend

erledigen to settle, handle, finish, take care of, execute **Arbeiten schnell ~** to dispatch

erledigend settling, accomplishing **zu -e Punkte** agenda

Erledigung *f* handling, settling

Erledigungsschein *m* receipt, release

erleichtern to lighten, relieve, alleviate, ease, facilitate

Erleichterung *f* relief, help, alleviation, facility, lightening of an airplane due to using up fuel

Erleichterungs-bohrung *f* drilling for lightness **-loch** *n* lightening hole (metal. constr.) **-steg** *m* lightened web

erleiden to suffer **Schaden ~** to suffer damage

Erlen-holz *n* alder wood **-schichtholz** *n* alder plywood

Erlenmeyer-Kolben *m* Erlenmeyer flask

erlesen to select

erleuchten to illuminate

Erleuchtung *f* light, illumination

Erlös *m* proceeds realized by a sale **-minderung** *f* reduction in proceeds **-rechnung** *f* profitability statement **-zahl** *f* proceeds figure

erloschen dull, dead, expired (patents), extinct

erlöschen to be extinguished, cease to exist, die, expire (patents), grow dull, slake (lime), darken, blow out

Erlöschen *n* darkening, extinguishing, expiration, extinction **~ der Besetzlampen** extinguishing of the engaged lamps **~ eines Patentes** expiry, expiration, or annulment of a patent **zum ~ bringen** to darken, extinguish **plötzliches ~ der Zündflamme** (eines Düsenmotors) flame-out

Erlöschung *f* extinction, null point

erlösen to deliver, rescue, redeem

ermächtigen to empower, authorize

Ermächtigung *f* authorization, warrant, authority

ermangeln to lack, be deficient in

Ermangelung *f* **in ~ von** in default of, in the absence of, failing

ermäßigen to reduce, lower (speed)

ermäßigte Gebühr reduced rate

Ermäßigung *f* reduction, discount, rebate, allowance, decrease

ermatten to tire, wear down

Ermessen *n* judgment, discretion **nach freiem ~** arbitrary

ermitteln to find out, determine, ascertain

Ermittelung *f* inquiry, investigation, determination, discovery **~ des Drehpunktes** determination of the center of rotation

Ermittlungen *f pl* findings

Ermittlungsverfahren *n*, **empirisches ~** cut-and-try method, trial-and-error method

ermöglichen to render possible

ermüden to fatigue, exhaust, tire

ermüdend tiring, tedious

Ermüdung *f* fatigue (as of metals), sluggishness, inertia, tiredness

Ermüdungs-anzeichen *n* sign of fatigue **-ausgleichszuschlag** *m* compensating relaxation allowance **-beständig** antifatigue **-bruch** *m* fatigue failure, fatigue break-down, repeated-stress failure **-erscheinung** *f* (bei dem Photoeffekt) photoelectric fatigue **-festigkeit** *f* fatigue strength, endurance limit **-frei** fatigue-proof **-grenze** *f* endurance limit, fatigue limit or range, safe range of stress **-kurzversuch** *m* accelerated fatigue test

Ermüdungs-prüfung *f* fatigue test **-riß** *m* endurance crack, fatigue crack **-schutzmittel** *n* fatigue inhibitor **-spur** *f* stress trace **-stärke** *f* fatigue strength **-striemen** *pl* fatigue striations **-verhältnis** *n* endurance ratio **-verlauf** *m* progress of fatigue **-versuch** *m* endurance test, fatigue test **-widerstand** *m* fatigue resistance

ernähren to feed, nourish

Ernährung *f* nutrition

Ernährungs-stoff *m* nutritive (alimentary) substance

ernannt appointed (to brevet rank)

ernennen to assign, name, appoint

Ernennung *f* assignation, appointment to brevet rank

Erneuerer *m* renewer

erneuern to restore, renew, regenerate, prolong

Erneuerung *f* renewal, revamping, renovation **~ der Lauffläche** retreading

Erneuerungs-gebühr *f* renewal fee **-geschwindigkeit** *f* turnover rate **-kosten** *pl* renewal cost **-prozeß** *m* birth-and-death process **-schein** *m* certificate renewal **-zeit** *f* turnover time

erneut renewed

erniedrigen to lower, to reduce (as temperature), decrease

Erniedrigung *f* lowering, humiliation, depression (chem.)

Erniedrigungszeichen *n* flat (music)

ernst serious, grave

Ernst *m* graveness, seriousness, earnestness **-haft** earnest, serious, grave **-haftigkeit** *f* earnestness, seriousness **-lich** seriously

Ernte *f* crop, harvest **-einschränkung** *f* crop restriction **-maschine** *f* harvester

ernten to harvest, reap

Ernte-schätzung *f* crop estimate **-zeit** *f* harvest time

erodieren to erode

eröffnen to open **den Betrieb einer Grube ~** to open a mine **ein Werk ~** to start a work

Eröffnung von Sprechbeziehungen opening of telephone service

Eröffnungs-funke *m* opening (initial) spark **-weite** *f* opening or width of port opened

erörterbar discussable, arguable, disputable

erörtern to discuss, debate, argue **für und wider ~** to argue

Erörterung *f* discussion, debate

Erosion *f* erosion

erpressen to extort, press out of, extract

Erpressung *f* extortion, blackmail

erproben to test, try (out), prove (ordnance)

Erprobung *f* test(ing), trying, trying out (in connection with ordnance material), proving (of armor plate ballistically tested), attacking, trial, experiment **in der ~** undergoing tests

Erprobungs-ausschuß *m* trials committee **-flug** *m* test flight **-frequenz** *f* test-missile frequency **-gerät** *n* test missile **-kommando** *n* experimental unit or detachment (mil.) **-läufe** *pl* test runs **-pilot** *m* test pilot **-stelle** *f* experimental or test station, testing department or laboratory

erratisch erratic

Erratum *n* misprint

errechnen to calculate, compute, figure (out)

errechnete Analyse calculated analysis

Errechnung *f* calculation, computation

erregbar sensitive, excitable

Erregbarkeit *f* excitability, sensitiveness, activity of crystals (electronics)

erregen to excite, stimulate, agitate, stir up, energize, provoke, actuate **-de Kraft** exciting force

Erreger *m* exciter, excitant **-anode** *f* ignition anode, exciting anode **-bürste** *f* exciter brush **-dipol** *m* energized dipole **-feld** *n* exciter panel or field **-fluß** *m* exciting flux **-flussigkeit** *f* exciting fluid **-funkenstrecke** *f* exciting spark gap **-frequenz** *f* frequency of excitation **-gruppe** *f* exciter set

Erreger-kreis *m* exciting or energizing circuit **-kreistastung** *f* control of excitation **-lampe** *f* exciter or exciting lamp (motion pictures) **-leistung** *f* excitation output **-maschine** *f* exciter **-(maschinen)satz** *m* excitation set **-maschinensteckdose** *f* exciter socket

Erreger-masse *f* excitant **-netz** *n* field circuit **-paste** *f* white or exciting paste **-relais** exciter relay **-röhre** *f* exciter tube **-satz** *m* excitation set **-schwingungen** *pl* exciting oscillations **-spannung** *f* exciting or energizing voltage **-spule** *f* operating winding **-strom** *m* induction current, exciting current, field or energizing current **-stromkreis** *m* exciter circuit **-teil** *m* field spider with pole ring (electr.) **-verlust** *m* exciter loss **-wicklung** *f* field coil or winding, exciting winding, magnetizing or magnet coil, induction or excitation winding, exciter coil **-wirkung** *f* excitation

erregt werden to pull up, energize

Erregung *f* excitation, stimulation, agitation, commotion, energization **~ eines Relais** energizing of a relay

Erregungs-diagramm *n* relay-working diagram **-energie** *f* excitation energy' **-geschwindigkeit** *f* voltage response of an exciter **-kreis** *m* energizing circuit **-lampe** *f* exciter or exciting lamp **-leistung** *f* energizing power **-linie** *f* line of induction **-ursache** *f* excitation **-zahl** *f* coefficient of induction

erreichbar attainable, obtainable

Erreichbarkeit *f* availability (tel.)

erreichen to attain, obtain, reach (high speeds, pressures)

errichten to erect, construct, build up, mount, install **ein Lot, eine Senkrechte ~** to erect a perpendicular

Errichtung *f* assembly, erection, mounting, construction, installment, installation **~ eines Gerüstes** scaffolding

Errichtungsprotokoll *n* minutes of proceedings

errufen to call, gain the attention

Ersatz *m* substitute, spare, supplement, reserve,

replacement, compensation, renewal, draft (of mil. reserves) **-abschlußeinheit** spare termination set **-ader** *f* spare conductor (cable) **-anker** *m* spare armature **-anlage** *f* emergency set, spare set **-anspruch** *m* indemnity claim **-antenne** *f* artificial or dummy antenna, mute, phantom, or reserve aerial **-apparat** *m* spare instrument **-ausrüstung** *f* spare equipment

Ersatz-batterie *f* spare battery **-bequemlichkeit** *f* facility of replacement **-bereifung** *f* spare-tire equipment **-beschaffung** *f* replacement supply **-bestandteil** *m* spare part **-bestückung** *f* spare part replacement **-bild** *n* equivalent-circuit diagram **-brennweite** *f* (Entzerrungsgerät), amended focal length (rectifier)

Ersatz-dämpfung *f* equivalent articulation loss **-elektron** *n* equivalent or replacing electron **-fähigkeit** *f* capability or susceptibility of being replaced, equivalency **-fahrer** *m* substitute driver **-flügeltiefe** *f* mean aerodynamic chord **-funkstelle** *f* secondary radio station

Ersatzgerät *n* (battery) eliminators **~ für Anodenbatterie** B-battery eliminator, B eliminator **~ für Batterie** battery eliminator

Ersatz-glas *n* duplicate lens **-gleichrichter** *m* substitutional rectifier **-glühkörper** *m* spare glower **-größe** *f* controlled variable **-handlung** *f* substitute action **-hebel** *m* spare bar **-hilfsanlage** *f* emergency set, equipment, or plant **-kapazität** *f* equivalent capacity **-karte** *f* provisional or substitute map **-kettengarn** *n* spare warp thread **-kreis** *m* equivalent circuit

Ersatz-leder *n* imitation leather **-leistung** *f* reparation **-leitung** *f* defect conduction **-lieferschein** *m* substitute form **-lieferung** *f* replacement, substitute **-magazin** *n* reserve depot **-mann** *m* substitute, deputy **-messer** *n* spare knife

Ersatz-mine *f* (Füllbleistift) spare lead **-mittel** *n* substitute, surrogate **-motor** *m* replacement engine **-pflicht** *f* liability **-pflichtig** liable **-platte** *f* spare plate **-rad** *n* spare wheel or tire **-reifen** *m* spare tire **-reifensicherung** *f* spare wheel lock **-röhre** *f* replacement tube

Ersatz-schaltbild *n* equivalent-circuit diagram **-schaltschema** *n* equivalent circuit or system **-schaltung** *f* equivalent circuit or network **-schema** *n* equivalent-circuit scheme **-seelenrohr** *n* spare tube (artil.), spare liner (aviation) **-spannung** *f* total electromotive force **-stab** *m* spare member **-sternschaltung** *f* star connection equivalent **-stoff** *m* substitute **-stromkreis** *m* equivalent circuit **-stück** *n* spare part

Ersatzteil *m* spare part, substitute, replacement, repair, or reserve part, fittings **-bedarf** *m* need for replacements **-fertigung** *f* spare parts manufacture **-lager** *n* spare-parts depot **-liste** *f* list of spare parts, spare-parts catalogue

Ersatz-verbindlichkeit für Bruch obligation to make good any loss by breakage **-wasser** *n* make-up water (feed or accumulators) **-weg** *m* alternate route **-widerstand** *m* equivalent resistance or resistor

erschaffen to create, produce

erschallen to resound, echo

erscheinen to appear

Erscheinung *f* appearance, phenomenon, action, event, manifestation **äußere ~** feature, aspect, outward appearance **in ~ treten** to appear

Erscheinungs-bild *n* hypothetical postulate **-datum** *n* publication date **-form** *f* manifestation, phase, state, physical appearance **-land** *n* country of publication **-ort** *m* place of publication **-potential** appearance potential **-spannung** *f* appearance-potential

Erschießen *n* **~ der Entfernung** ranging fire

erschlaffen to relax, weaken, slaken

erschließen to disclose, open, discover

Erschließung mit Säure (von Ölgruben) acidizing of wells

Erschließungsstollen *m* exploratory drift

erschmelzen to smelt, melt

Erschmelzung *f* smelting, melting **~ im Lichtbogen** electric arc melting

erschmolzen molten

erschöpfen to exhaust, run down, wear out, use up **sich ~** to exhaust oneself, disappear, pinch out

erschöpfend exhaustive, depleting

erschöpft depleted, spent **-e Batterie** run-down battery

Erschöpfung *f* exhaustion, running down, depletion **~ der Batterie** battery discharge, running down of a battery

Erschöpfungsrandschicht *f* depletion layer, exhaustion layer

erschroten to discover

erschürfen to discover

erschüttern to shake, chatter, vibrate, jar, unnerve, shock

Erschütterung *f* vibration, shock, percussion, jarring, chatter, tremor, concussion, shake, shaking **~ des Bodens** subsoiling (agric.), vibration of soil

Erschütterungs-beständigkeit *f* impact and vibration resistance **-dämpfung** *f* shock absorption **-fest** vibration-proof, shockproof

erschütterungsfrei free from vibration, shockless, resilient, shock-absorbent, non-vibratile **-e Unterlage** *f* resilient support

Erschütterungs-halbmesser *m* radius of shock **-kontakt** *m* percussion contact, vibration contact **-ladung** *f* cracking charge **-messer** *m* vibration meter **-schutz** *m* protection against vibration **-sicher** shakeproof, shock-proof, vibration-proof **-zeiger** *m* seismograph **-zünder** *m* vibration fuse

erschweren to render difficult, aggravate, complicate, make heavy, impede, load (weight)

Erschwernis *f* aggravating condition

erschwerter Beton loaded concrete

Erschwerung *f* aggravation, penalty, impediment

Erschwerungsmittel *n* weighting agent

erschwingen to afford, manage

ersehen (aus) to note (from)

ersetzbar renewable, replaceable

ersetzen to replace, substitute (math.), supersede, refund, make good, compensate, renew, supplant **eine fehlerhafte Leitung ~** to make good a faulty circuit **~ durch** to supersede by

Ersetzung *f* renewal, replacement

ersoffen (Schacht) drowned, submerged (pit or mine)

ersparen to save, economize

Ersparnis *f* saving, economy

erstarken to strengthen
erstarren (Metall) to solidify, freeze (liquids), congeal (fat), harden, set (cement), coagulate
Erstarren *n*, **gerichtetes ~** normal freezing
erstarrt solid(ified)
Erstarrung *f* freezing, solidification, congealing, hardening, setting
Erstarrungs-bereich *m* solidification range **-gestein** *n* igneous rock **-intervall** *n* solidification period, interruption of cooling **-kammer** *f* hardening room **-kurve** *f* freezing-point curve, solidification curve **-linie** *f* line of solidification **-probe** *f* setting test (cement)
Erstarrungs-punkt *m* solidification or solidifying point, set point, freezing, congealing, or coagulation point **-raum** *m* hardening room **-schwindung** *f* solidification shrinkage **-temperatur** *f* solidification or congealing temperature **-verfahren** *n* freezing method **-wärme** *f* heat of fusion or solidification **-zone** *f* solidification range
erstatten to restore, return **einen Bericht ~** to report **eine Gebühr ~** to rebate a charge
Erstattungspflicht *f* liability to make restitution
Erstausführung *f* prototype, original type
Erstausrüstung *f* first equipment
Erst-ausscheidungen *pl* first minerals to separate out, earliest separation products **-ausstattung** *f* initial issue **-belastung** *f* initial load **-bestückung** *f* first equipment
erstehen to purchase (by bidding), arise, originate
ersteigen to climb, mount, ascend
erstellen to plot a curve
erster, ~ Gang starting gear **~ Zug** (beim Kaltziehen) ripping, rumpling
Ersterzeugnis *n* first product
Erstflug *m* maiden flight
ersticken to choke, asphyxiate, smother, decay, stifle, suffocate **im Keime ~** to nip in the bud
erstickend asphyxiating
Erstickung *f* asphyxiation, suffocation
erstklassig first-class, first-rate, high-grade, prime **-e Referenzen** highest or best references
Erstkreis *m* primary circuit
Erst-luftzufuhr *f* primary air supply **-montage** *f* green assembly **-planung** *f* initial program
Erstprodukt-füllmasse *f* first fill mass, high-grade massecuite **-maische** *f* first-product crystallizer **-vakuum** *n* first-product vacuum pan
Erstprüfung *f* virgin test
erstrangig of first importance
erstreben to strive (for), aspire (to)
erstrecken to extend, stretch **sich ~** to range, bear, stretch, extend, reach
Erstreckung *f* extension, extent, reach
Erst-strom *m* transmitter current, primary current **-stufentriebsatz** *m* first-stage power plant
Erst-wicklung *f* primary (coil) winding **-zucker** *m* first-product sugar
Erstzusammenbau *m* new assembly (of an engine) **~ eines Motors** new assembly of an engine
Ersuchen *n* request, demand **~ um Auskunft** information call **~ um Gehör** file application or petition to be heard
Ersuchung *f* research, request
ertasten to find or detect by feel or touch, palpate
erteilen to give, furnish, bestow, grant, impart, (eine Freigabe) issue (aviat.)
erteilt granted (patents)
Erteilung eines Patentes grant or allowance of letters patent
Erteilungs-akten *f* documentary record (of patents), file wrapper **-bericht** *m* notice of allowance
ertönen to sound, resound (acoust)
Ertrag *m* yield, profit, proceeds, revenue
ertragen to stand, bear, endure, suffer
Ertragen *n* bearing
erträglich tolerable
Erträglichkeit *f* toleration
Erträglichkeitsgrenze *f* limit of tolerance
Ertrags-ausfall *m* loss of yield **-fähig** productive **-fähigkeit** *f* productive capacity **-feststellung** *f* determination of yield **-lage** *f* productivity situation (economic situation) **-rechnung** *f* profitability statement **-reich** profitable **-saldo** *m* balance of profit
Ertragswert *m* capitalized value of property **voraussichtlicher ~** expectation value
ertränken to drown
ertrinken to drown
eruieren to ascertain, find out
Eruption *f* eruption **freie ~** open flow
Eruptiv-gänge *pl* igneous dikes or veins **-gestein** *n* eruptive, volcanic, or igneous rock
erwägen to consider, weigh
Erwägung *f* consideration, contemplation **in ~ ziehen** to contemplate
erwähnen to mention
Erwähnung *f* mention
erwärmen to heat, warm, warm up
Erwärmen *n* heating **~ und Abschrecken** solution heat-treatment
Erwärmer *m* heater
erwärmte Verbindungsstelle thermo-junction
Erwärmung *f* heating, warming, temperature rise (heating) **~ des Gebläsewindes** preheating of the blast (smelting)
Erwärmungs-dauer *f* time of heating **-kraft** *f* heating power, calorific power **-lauf** *m* heat run **-umlauf** *m* joulean effect, thermal or heat loss **-verlust** *m* joulean effect, thermal or heat loss
erwarten to expect, await, anticipate
Erwartung *f* expectation, anticipation
Erwartungswert *m* expected or anticipated value
erweichen to soften, fuse, sinter, plasticize
Erweichung *f* softening, fusing, sintering
Erweichungs-mittel *n* emolient, softener **-punkt** *m* fusion point, softening or sintering point, deformation point **-temperatur** *f* fusing temperature, upsetting temperature
Erweis *m* proof, demonstration **-bar** provable
erweitern to widen, extend, enlarge, expand, ream, broaden, complete, underream, multiply through, dilate, spread **nach außen ~** to open out, flare
erweitert expanded **-e Pupille** dilated pupil **-e Selbsthilfe** supplemented, large-scale, localized, or community passive air defense
Erweiterung *f* widening, expansion, extension, enlargement, completion, elaboration, flaring **~ bestehender Betriebe** enlarging old shops

Erweiterungs-bau *m* addition **-ausbau** *m* plant extension **-bohrer** *m* broaching or eccentric bit, reamer, post-hole auger **-büchse** *f* enlarging bailer **-faktor** *m* multiplying power (of a galvanometer shunt) **-instrument** *n* reaming instrument **-keilhaue** *f* pick **-programm** *n* expansion program **-schacht** *m* enlarging shaft **-verhältnis** *n* ration of expansion (in a nozzle) **-winkel** *m* angle of delation, angle of divergency or expansion

Erwerb *m* acquisition, earning, industry, occupation, profit, returns, wages

erwerben to earn, obtain, acquire

Erwerber *m* purchaser, transferee

Erwerbs-fähigkeit *f* ability to earn a living **-losenunterstützung** *f* unemployment allowance, dole **-loser** *m* unemployed **-losigkeit** *f* unemployment **-mittel** *pl* subsistence, resources **-tätig** gainfully employed, industrious **-tätigkeit** *f* trade, industry **-zweig** *m* branch of trade or industry

Erwerbung *f* acquisition

Erwerbungskosten *pl* acquisition cost, purchase cost or price

erwidern to reply, retaliate, answer, reciprocate

Erwiderung *f* reply, retaliation, answer, rejoinder, replication (of plaintiff to defendant's answer)

erwirken to effect, achieve

Erythemdosis *f* erythema dose

Erythrosin *n* erythrosin

Erz *n* ore **~ pochen** to crush ore **~ zugeben** to ore down **abbauwürdiges ~** pay ore **anstehendes ~** ore in sight **hochhaltiges ~** high-grade ore **minderhaltiges ~** low-grade ore **reichhaltiges ~** high-grade ore **selbstgehendes ~** self-fluxing ore **strengflüssiges ~** refractory ore **sulfidisches ~** sulfide ore

Erz-abfälle *pl* tailings **-ader** *f* ore vein, ore lode, lode seam **-arbeit** *f* tin-concentrate smelting **-aufbereitung** *f* cleansing, preparation, or dressing of ores **-aufbereitungsanlage** *f* ore-dressing plant **-ausfuhr** *f* ore export

Erzausscheidung, gangartige ~ vein **lagenartige ~** flatwork

Erz-behälter *m* ore bin, ore bunker, ore-storage pocket **-bergbau** *m* ore mining **-bergwerk** *n* ore mine **-bewertung** *f* ore valuation, determination of the character of ore **-bezeichnung** *f* classification of ore **-bohrmaschine** *f* ore-boring machine

Erz-brecher *m* ore crusher, ore breaker **-brikettierung** *f* ore briquetting **-brikettpresse** *f* ore-briquetting press **-brocken** *m* lump of ore **-bruch** *m* ore mine **-bunker** *m* ore bunker, ore bin **-butze** *f* chamber of ore **-charge** *f* ore charge **-enthaltend** ore-bearing

Erz-eindicker *m* ore thickener

erzen brazen; (Erz zusetzen) to ore

erzeugen to produce, make, induce, generate (gases), raise (steam), create, set up, breed, cause, result in

erzeugend producing, generating, generant **Wärme ~** exothermic **-e Funktion** generating function **-e Linie** generatrix (math.) **-es Programm** compiling routine, generating routine (info proc.)

Erzeugende *f* generatrix **~ des Ergänzungskegels** generating line of the back cone

Erzeuger *m* (Hersteller) manufacturer, producer (generator) **-anlage** *f* generating unit **-seite** *f* generator end **-werk** *n* manufacturing plant

Erzeugnis *n* product, produce, make, manufacture, fabric, article; (Monopol) *n* proprietary article **deutsches ~** of German make, German factory product **flaches ~** flat stock **minderwertiges ~** of inferior make

Erzeugung *f* production, manufacture, fabrication, generation, activation **~ von Differenztönen** intermodulation **~ von Luftleere** evacuation **~ von Neutronen** activation by neutrons **abnehmende ~** falling-off production

Erzeugungs-apparat *m* generator **-art** *f* method of production **-bereich** *n* program **-druck** *m* dynamic pressure **-kosten** *f pl* production costs **-leistung** *f* output capacity **-linie** *f* generatrix

Erzeugungs-menge *f* output **-operator** *m* creation operator **-satz** *m* rate of production **-steigerung** *f* growth in production **-vorhaben** *n* production plan **-wirkungsgrad** *m* generating efficiency

Erz-fall *m* ore shoot **-farbe** *f* bronze color **-feld** *n* allotment of ore, ore deposit **-formation** *f* ore formation **-frischreaktion** *f* ore boil **-füllrumpf** *m* ore bin **-gang** *m* lead, lode reef, ore vein, lodestone, or lode **-gattung** *f* class of ore **-geben** *n* ore yielding

Erz-gedingehauer *m* tributer **-gemisch** *n* ore mixture **-gicht** *f* ore charge **-gießerei** *f* brass foundry **-greifer** *m* ore grab **-greifermesser** *n* dredge-bucket teeth, ore grab **-grube** *f* mine **-haltig** ore-bearing **-handel** *m* ore traffic **-haufen** *m* ore pile or heap

erziehen to educate, rear, train

erzieherisch educational, pedagogical

Erziehungsbeihilfe *f* education allowance

erzielen to gain, attain, obtain, achieve, procure, yield

Erzielung *f* attainment, realization, extraction

erzittern to vibrate

Erz-kai *m* ore-shipping quay **-karre** *f* ore barrow **-kauf** *m* ticketing, ore purchase **-kern** *m* lumps or knots (in calcined ore) **-klauber** *m* ore picker **-klein** *m* broken ore, ore fines **-klumpen** *pl* bunches **-korn** *m* grain of ore

Erzkörper *m* ore body **reicher ~** bonanza ore body

Erz-kübel *m* ore bucket **-kübelkran** *m* ore-bucket-handling crane **-ladung** *f* ore load, ore cargo

Erzlager *m* ore deposit, ore bed **-platz** *m* ore yard **-stätte** *f* ore deposit, ore bed

Erz-laugerei *f* ore-leaching plant, ore-leaching practice **-laugung** *f* ore leaching **-leer** barren **-leseband** *n* ore-picking belt **-maß** *n* basket, bucket **-möller** *m* ore burden **-möllerung** *f* ore burdening **-mühle** *f* ore pulverizer **-mutter** *f* ore matrix **-nest** *n* ore pocket **-nieren** *pl* ore nodules

Erz- oder Ölader *f* stringer

Erz-pfeiler *m* pillar of ore **-platten** *pl* cakes of ore **-platz** *m* ore-dumping yard, ore yard **-pocheisen** *n* bucking iron **-pochen** *n* ore crushing **-pocher** *m* ore crusher or stamper, stampman, bucker, spaller **-probe** *f* specimen of ore, ore assaying **-puddeln** *n* ore puddling **-quetsch-**

maschine *f* crusher -**reduktion** *f* reduction of ore -**röstofen** *m* ore-drying kiln

Erz-röstung *f* ore roasting -**rutsche** *f* ore chute -**säule** *f* ore column -**schaufel** *f* ore shovel -**scheider** *m* ore separator -**scheidung** *f* sorting of ores -**schlacke** *f* ore slag -**schlamm** *m* ore sludge, ore slurry, ore wash, ore slime -**schlämmen** *n* washing of ores -**schlämmer** *m* ore washer

Erz-schlauch *m* ore pipe, ore chimney -**schlich** *m* concentrates of ore -**schmelzen** *n* ore smelting, pig-and-ore process -**schmelzofen** *m* ore-smelting furnace -**schnur** *f* string of ore -**seife** *f* placer deposit, placer bed -**sieb** *n* ore separator -**sonderung** *f* ore refining -**sortierung** *f* ore sorting, ore separation -**stahlverfahren** *n* pig-and-ore process -**stock** *m* ore deposit -**stück** *n* ore lump

Erzstücke *pl* (lose, an der Oberfläche) float ore **~ die sich auf dem Siebboden abgesetzt haben** raggings

Erz-stufe *f* specimen -**tagebau** *m* open-pit ore mining -**tasche** *f* ore-storage picket or bunker -**taschenverschluß** *m* ore-bin gate, ore-pocket gate -**trübe** *f* ore pulp, overflow of ore, waste ore

Erztrumm *m* branch or course of ore **derbes ~** ore sheet **flaches ~** bed of ore, floor

Erz-trümmer *pl* stringer leads -**verarbeitung** *f* ore smelting or working -**verfahren** *n* ore process -**verhüttung** *f* ore treatment -**verladeanlage** *f* ore-handling equipment or machinery -**verladebrücke** *f* ore-loading bridge -**verladung** *f* ore loading -**vorkommen** *n* ore deposit -**wäsche** *f* ore-washing room -**waschen** *n* ore washing -**wäscherei** *f* ore-washing plant -**waschmaschine** *f* ore-washing machine

erzwingen to force, gain by force

erzwungen forced **-e Schwingungen** forced or constrained vibrations, forced oscillations **-er Übergang** forced or nonspontaneous transition **Amplitude der -en Schwingungen** amplitude of nonharmonic or forced vibrations

Erz-zerkleinerungsanlage *f* ore-breaking plant, ore-crusher plant -**zerlegung** *f* ore extraction

Esche *f* ash tree

Eschenholz *n* ash (wood)

E-Schirm *m* E scope

Eschweger Seife *f* a mixture of neat nigre obtained by adding electrolyte to a soap nigre and cooling

Eschynit *m* eschynite

e.s.E. (elektrostatische Einheit) electrostatic unit (esu)

Esel *m* wooden strut or stay, drainage horn; donkey

Eselshaupt *n* masthead cap

Eselsohr *n* dog's-ear, crease

Eselsohrumkehrstück *n* mule-type header

Eskalade *f* scaling of fortification

Eskaladiergerüst *n* scaling equipment

Eskarpe *f* forward slope of trench

Eskarpenkaponniere *f* caponier

Esortin code for nitrogen tetraoxide

Espenholzschliff *m* asp wood pulp

Esse *f* stack, chimney, smokestack

Esseisen *n* tuyère

essen to eat

Essen-gas *n* flue gas, stack gas -**kehrer** *m* chimney sweeper -**klappe** *f* stack damper -**kohle** *f* forge coal

Essensback *f* mess table

Essen-schaft *m* chimney stack -**schieber** *m* (stack) damper -**temperatur** *f* stack temperature -**ventil** *n* chimney valve

Essenz *f* essence

Essenzug *m* stack draft, chimney draft

Esserkuppelung *f* type of coupling for airplane towing

Essig *m* vinegar -**äther** *m* acetic ether, ethyl acetate -**geist** *m* acetone -**prüfer** *m* acetimeter, vinegar tester

essig-sauer, -saur acetate of **-es Ammon** ammonium acetate **-es Bleioxyd** lead acetate **-es Kali** potassium acetate **-er Kalk** calcium acetate **-es Kupferoxyd** copper acetate **-es Manganoxydul** manganese acetate **-es Natron** sodium acetate **-e Tonerde** aluminum acetate **-es Uranoxyd** uranium acetate

Essigsäure *f* acetic acid -**amid** *n* acetamide -**amylester** *n* amyl acetate -**anhydrid** *n* acetic anhydride -**äthylester** *n* ethyl acetate -**chlorid** *n* acetyl chloride

Essigtropfenprobe *f* vinegar-spot test

Eßkohle *f* forge coal, semibituminous coal of medium rank (semifat, short-flaming, smokeless)

Eßkohlenschlamm *m* steam coal slurry

Ester *m* ester -**gummi** *n* ester gum -**lack** *m* ester varnish

E-Stoff *m* surrogate

Estrich *m* (floor) fiinish -**gips** *m* Keene's cement, flooring plaster

Etage *f* level sole; (Förderkorb) *f* deck

Etagen-abzweigkasten *m* junction box arranged in tiers -**gasheber** *m* stage lift -**gestell** *n* tier stand or frame -**höhe** *f* daylight -**kessel** *m* battery boiler, multiple-stage boiler -**maschine** *f* deck machine -**ofen** *m* kiln with overlying beds, story furnace -**presse** *f* multilayer (hydraulic) press, cage oil press, box or plate press -**räder** *pl* staggered gear rims -**rost** *m* step grate -**spannrahmen** *m* horizontal hot-air tentering machine

Etagen- und Firstenbruchbau (vereinigter) combined shrinkage-and-caving method

Etagenventil *n* multiseated valve

Etagere *f* rack, stand, shelf, support

Etalonapparat *m* reference or standard instrument, reference standard, calibrated instrument

etappenweise by stages

Etat *m* budget **monatlicher ~** monthly allowance

etatmäßig provided by the budget

Etatposten *m* budget item

Etats-festsetzung *f* determination of the yield -**stärke** *f* required strength

Ethylenkohlenwasserstoff *m* ethylenic hydrocarbon

Etikett *n* label, tag

Etikettendraht *m* tag wire

etikettieren to label

Etikettiermaschine *f* labeling machine

Etmal *n* day's run

Etui *n* case, box -**beschläge** *m pl* case fittings

Eudiometer *n* eudiometer, absorption tube

Eugenglanz *m* polybasite

Eukalyptusöl *n* eucalyptus oil
euklidisch Euclidean **~-geometrisch** euclidean geometric **-es Bezugssystem** Euclidean frame **-e Ebene** Euclidean plane **-es Raum-Zeit-Kontinuum** Euclidean space-time
Eulerscher Polyedersatz Euler's theorem on polyhedra
Eulytin *m* eulytite, bismuth silicate
Eurekasystem *n* eureka
Euritporphyr *m* feldspar, quartz porphyry
Europasockel *m* European base
Europium *n* europium
europiumaktiviert europium activated
eustatisch eustatic
Eutektikum *n* eutectic, eutectic mixture
eutektisch eutectic **-es Gemisch** eutectic mixture
Eutektoid *n* eutectoid
eutektoidisch eutectoid
Eutropie *f* eutropy (cryst.)
Euxenit *m* euxenite, polycrase
Evakuieranlage *f* evacuating system
evakuieren to evacuate
evakuiert evacuated **-es Gehäuse** evacuated vessel or housing **-e Lampe** exhausted lamp bulb
Evakuierung *f* evacuation
Evektion *f* evection
Evektionstiden *pl* evectional tides
eventuell possible, eventual(ly), optional(ly), contingent(ly), if desired or necessary, ultimate(ly)
E-Verdichter *m* electric compressor
Evolute *f* evolute (math.)
Evolvente *f* evolvent, involute
Evolventenfläche *f* **schraubenförmige ~** involute helicoid surface
Evolventen-profil *n* involute profile **-prüfgerät** *n* gear involute **-rad** *n* involute gear **-schnecke** *f* involute worm **-schrägzahnrad** *n* involute helical gear **-schraube** *f* involute screw **-verzahnung** *f* involute-tooth system or gear **-zahn** *m* involute tooth **-zahnkegelrad** *n* bevel gear with involute-tooth spiral
evolventisch involute
evolvieren to evolve
EV (Empfangsverstärker) receiving amplifier
EW (Einweg-Gleichrichtung) half-wave rectification
Ewartskette *f* Ewart chain
ewiger Schnee perpetual snow
E-Winkel *m* E corner
Examen *n*, **ein ~ machen** (ablegen) to take an examination
Exaktguß *m* precision castings
Exaktheit *f* exactitude
Exanthem *n* exanthema
Exemplar *n* specimen, sample, pattern, copy
exerzieren to drill, march
Exerzier-form *f* drill formation **-geschoß** *n* dummy projectile **-halle** *f* drill hall **-haus** *n* armory **-kopfzünder** *m* practice nose fuse, delay-action fuse **-ladung** *f* practice charge **-marsch** *m* practice march, goose step **-munition** *f* drill ammunition, dummy or blank ammunition **-ordnung** *f* drill formation, drill regulation **-patrone** *f* dummy cartridge, blank, drill
Exerzierplatz *m* drill ground, parade ground
Exerzier-vorschrift *f* drill regulations **-zündspitze** *f* arrow point, arrow head, exercise nose
Exhaustor *m* exhauster, exhaust fan
Exhaust-rohr *n* exhaust pipe **-ventilator** *m* suction ventilating fan
Existenz *f* existence, position, post
Exciton *n* exciton
Excitron *n* excitron
Existenz-beweis *m* existence proof **-satz** *m* existence theorem
Exkavator *m* excavator, chain dredger, bucket conveyer, grab or grab bucket, scoop shovel, navvy
exklusives Oder or else circuit (comput.)
Exkretion *f* excretion
Exolierung *f* anodic treatment, anodizing
Exosmose *f* exosmosis
exospor exosporal
exotherm, exothermisch exothermic
Expander *m*, **-verstärker** *m* expander
expandieren to expand
Expandierprobe *f* bulging or expanding test (tubes)
Expansion *f* expansion
Expansions-bandbremse *f* expanding-band brake **-büchse** *f* tube ferrule (for condensers) **-dampfmaschine** *f* steam engine working expansively **-dorn** *m* expansion mandrel, expanding chuck **-düse** *f* expanding nozzle **-enddruck** *m* final expansion pressure **-endspannung** *f* expansion end tension **-gasturbine** *f* explosion gas turbine **-gleitbacke** *f* expansion sliding block
Expansions-hebel *m* detent lever **-hub** *m* expansion stroke, power stroke **-kämme** *pl* expanding combs **-kammer** *f* expansion chamber **-keilriemenscheibe** *f* expansion V-belt pulley **-kulisse** *f* expansion link **-kuppelung** *f* expansion joint **-rohr** *n* expansion pipe **-röhrengreifer** *m* expanding-type tubing packer
Expansions-schalter *m* air-blast circuit breaker, expansion circuit breaker or switch **-schieber** *m* expansion slide valve **-schlag** *m* expansion stroke **-schnecke** *f* worm wheel of expansion **-schraubenbohrer** *m* expansion tap **-stange** *f* detent lever **-steuerung** *f* expansion gear **-stufe** *f* expansion stage **-ventil** *n* cutoff valve (with expansion) **-verbindung** *f* expansion joint **-verhältnis** *n* ratio of expansion **-vorrichtung** *f* expansion gear **-welle** *f* expansive wave
expansiv expansive **-kraft** *f* expansive force
Expedient *m* clerk, dispatcher
expedieren to dispatch
Expeditions-beamter *m* shipping clerk
Experiment *n* experiment
experimentell experimental
Experimentieranlage *f* test rig
experimentieren to experiment, try, test
Experimentier-lizenz *f* experimenter's license **-tisch** *m* testing table
Experimentierung *f* experimentation
Expertise *f* examination by experts
explizit explicit, direct
explodierbar explosive, explodable
explodieren to explode, detonate

Explorationsbohrloch *n* exploratory borehole
explosibel explodable, capable of explosion
Explosion *f* explosion, shot, detonation
explosions-artig explosive **-druck** *m* blast pressure, explosion pressure in engines **-druckwelle** *f* blast **-fähigkeit** *f* explosiveness **-gefahr** *f* explosion hazard
explosionsgefährlicher Betriebsraum confined space liable to contain explosive mixtures
Explosions-gemisch *n* explosive mixture **-geschützt** explosion-proof (apparatus), fireproof, flame-proof **-grenzen** *pl* explosion limits **-kalorimeter** *n* bomb calorimeter, combustion bomb **-kammer** *f* explosion chamber **-kappe** *f* explosion relief valve **-klappe** *f* bleeder valve explosion door **-motor** *m* internal-combustion engine **-periode** *f* explosion stroke **-ramme** *f* pile driver earth tamper **-raum** *m* explosion chamber **-schutz** *m* flame trape
explosionssicher explosion-proof **-e Anlage** explosion-proof plant **-es Gefäß** explosion-proof vessel or tank, nonexploding reservoir **-er Heizkörper** explosion-proof heating member
Explosions-sicherheit *f* safety against explosion accidents **-takt** *m* work stroke, explosion stroke **-tür** *f* explosion door **-verbinden** explosive bonding **-verhütung** *f* explosion prevention **-zentren** *pl* detonation inducers **-zünder** *m* detonating primer, mine exploder
explosiv explosive **-er Laut** explosive sound
Explosiv-formgebung *f* explosive forming **-konsonant** *m* explosive sound **-verbrennung** *f* combustion by explosion
Exponent *m* power, exponent, index, exponent of power ~ **der Polytrope** polytropic exponent
exponential exponential **-ausdruck** *m* exponential expression
Exponentialgesetz *n* exponential law **nach einem** ~ exponentially
Exponential-hexode *f* variable-mu hexode **-hochfrequenzpenthode** *f* variable-mu high-frequency pentode **-kasten** *m* exponential well **-kurve** *f* exponential curve **-linie** *f* exponential curve **-penthode** *f* variable-mu high-frequency pentode **-röhre** *f* variable-mu valve or tube, exponential, supercontrol, or multi-mu tube, variable mutual-conductance valve, valve with variable slope, remote-cutoff tube **-schirmgitterröhre** *f* **-tetrode** *f* variable-mu tetrode, variable-mu screen-grid tube
Exponential-trichter *m* exponential horn, logarithmic horn **aufgewundener** ~ twisted, coiled, or curled exponential horn **gefalteter** ~ folded exponential horn
exponentiell exponential **-er Flankenabfall** exponential tail
exponieren to expose
Export *m* export trade **-artikel** *m pl* exports, articles of export **-ausführung** *f* export version
Exporteur *m* exporter
Export-geschäft *n* export trade **-vergütung** *f* bounty
Exposition *f* exposure
Expositions-uhr *f* exposure meter **-zeit** *f* time or duration of exposure, exposure scale
Expreßgut *n* goods shipped by express
Exsiccator *m* desiccator, exsiccator **-einsatz** *m* desiccator plate
exstirpieren to exstirpate
Exsudat *n* exudate, exudation
extemporieren to extemporize, improvise
Extensometer *m* extensometer, strainmeter
externe Posten *pl* extraneous items
Extinktion *f* absorbance
Extinktions-gleichung *f* extinction equation **-koeffizient** *m* total-reflection coefficient, extinction coefficient **-modul** *n* absorbance index length of absorbing path **-schreiber** extinction market
extra special, extra, additional ~ **matt** rough matt
Extrabenzin *m* supergasoline
extrahierbar extractible
extrahieren to eliminate, extract, lixiviate
Extrahochspannung *f* extra-high tension
Extrakosten *pl* additional cost, extra cost
Extrakt *m* extract, abstract, excerpt **-ausbeute** *f* extract yield **-bemesser** *m* extract-measuring instrument
Extraktgehalt *m* extract contents, gravity **scheinbarer** ~ apparent extract or gravity
Extraktions-anlage *f* extraction or extracting plant, extractor equipment **-apparat** *m* extractor **-hülse** *f* extraction cartridge or shell, extraction thimble **-kolben** *m* extraction flask **-mittel** *n* extraction solvent **-probe** *f* extraction test **-schicht** *f* extract layer **-weise** *f* extraction method
Extraktivstoff *m* extractive matter
Extra-lösung *f* extra solution **-polation** *f* extrapolation
Extrapolations-abstand *m* augmentation distance **-formal** *f* extrapolation formula **-kammer** extrapolation chamber
extrapolieren to exterpolate
extrapoliert-e Reaktorbegrenzung extrapolated boundary **-e Reichweite** extrapolated range
extrastarkes Doppelrohr double-extra-strong pipe
extraterrestrisch extraterrestrial
extraweicher Stahl dead-soft steel
Extrazeit *f* overtime
Extremale *f* extremal
Extremal-eigenschaft *f* extremal property **-normale** *f* transversal **-problem** *n* extremum problem
Extreme *pl* extremes
Extremierung *f* finding extreme values
extremkurze Wellen ultrashort waves
Extremwert *m* extreme value
extrospektiv behavioristic
Extruderschnecke *f* extrusion screw
Extremal-eigenschaft *f* extremal property **-nor-**
Extrudieren *n* extrusion (plastics)
Exzenter *m* eccentric, cam, disk with lobes ~ **zur Arretur** internal cam operating propeller motion ~ **für Druckzylinder** eccentric collar ~ **für Rundwirkmaschinen** eccentric of shearing machine, eccentrics ~ **für Saugerschwingung** cam for sucker bar swing ~ **für Vorgreiferbewegung** opening cam for swinging grippers
Exzenter-abgratpresse *f* eccentric trimming press **-abkneifpresse** *f* eccentric gitting press **-antrieb** *m* eccentric drive **-bolzen** *m* eccentric

pin or stud **-buchse** *f* eccentric bushing **-büchse** *f* eccentric box or case **-bügel** *m* eccentric collar strap **-dipol** *m* off-center dipole **-druck** *m* eccentric pressure **-einlage** *f*, **-futter** *n* liner of eccentric strap

Exzenter-hebel *m* eccentric lever **-hülse** *f* eccentric housing, eccentric sleeve **-lager** *m* eccentric bearing **-lagerauge** *n* eccentric strap **-meißel** *m* eccentric bit, one-sided bit **-mittellage** *f* middle position of eccentric

Exzenter-paar *n* pair of cam **-presse** *f* eccentric press **-pumpe** *f* eccentric pump **-rad** *n* cam gear **-ring** *m* eccentric hoop **-rolle** *f* cam follower, follower of eccentric disk **-scheibe** *f* eccentric sheave or disk **-skaleneinstellung** *f* scaled cam setting motion **-stein** (Gasmaschine) *m* eccentric guide block **-stiftschraube** *f* eccentric stud **-welle** *f* eccentric shaft **-zahnrad** *n* eccentric gear wheel **-ziehpreßmaschine** *f* toggle drawing press

Exzentrik-rad *n* eccentric wheel **-regulator** *m* eccentric governor

exzentrisch eccentric, nonconcentric **-e Belastung** eccentric load

Exzentrizität *f* eccentricity

Exzentrizitäts-fehler *m* eccentricity error **-winkel** *m* angle of eccentricity

Exzitron (Gasröhre) excitron

F

Fabrik *f* factory, manufacturing plant, mill, plant, works **-anlage** *f* manufacturing plant

Fabrikant *m* manufacturer, mill owner

Fabrikarbeiter *m* factory hand

Fabrikat *n* make, manufacture, product, article

Fabrikation *f* manufacture, fabrication, making, production, run **glatte ~,** straightforward working **laufende ~,** course of manufacture

Fabrikations-abfälle *pl* broke, broken, brokes, waste (paper mfg.) **-abteilung** *f* manufacturing department **-anforderung** *f* fabrication requirements **-anlage** *f* production equipment **-aufstellung** *f* manufacturing arrangement **-bauten** *pl* production units, process plants **-echtheit** *f* fastness to processing **-freigabe** *f* admission of manufacturing **-gießerei** *f* tonnage foundry

Fabrikations-länge *f* manufacturing length, drum length (of a cable) **-leiter** *m* superintendent **-nummer** *f* stock number, serial number **-programm** *n* manufacturing schedule **-vorgang** *m* fabricating operation, manufacturing operation **-werkzeug** *n* tool of fabrication

Fabrik-betrieb *m* industrial plant **-direktor** *m* superintendent **-gebäude** *n* factory building **-hof** *m* factory yard **-kondensat** *n* processing steam condensate **-kosten** *m pl* factory costs **-lager** *n* factory stores **-leiter** *m* superintendent, factory manager

Fabrik-marke *f* trade-mark **-mäßig herstellen** to manufacture (as in a factory) **-messung** *f* factory test, production test **-normen** *f pl* works standards **-preis** *m* factory price **-prüfstand** *m* chassis dynamometer **-schild** *n* maker's name plate

Fabriksdirektor *m* superintendent, factory manager

Fabrikwaren *f pl* manufactured goods

Fabrikzeichen *n* manufacturer's mark, trademark **~ anmelden** to register a trade-mark

fabrizieren to make, manufacture, produce, fabricate **am laufenden Band ~** to manufacture on a conveyer belt, produce on a large scale

Facette *f* bevel

Facetten-fräser *m* bevelling machine **-halter** *m* flange **-hobel** *m* bevelling machine

facettieren to bevel

facettiert-es Glas cut glass **-e Linse** bevel-edged lens

Fach *n* (Abteil) compartment, partition, division; (Deckenfeld) coffer, department, branch; (Geschäft) trade, business; (Unterricht) subject; (beruflich) profession, field (of study), shelf, occupation, shelving, bay, panel (of art), art, filing cabinet, lock box (post office), drawer, pigeonhole, receptacle, specialty, line, field of competency, branch of knowledge

-fach -fold **40fache Verstärkung** 40-fold amplification

Fach-abteilung *f* professional service unit **-arbeit** *f* skilled or specialized work **-arbeiter** *m* technical worker, skilled worker or laborer, specialist, technician **-aufsatz** *m* scientific article or paper **-ausbildung** *f* technical education, schooling, or training **-ausdruck** *m* technical term or expression **-ausdrücke** *pl* terminology

Fach-baum *m* sill or crest of the weir **-bearbeiter** *m* technician specialist, staff officer or official in charge of some technical branch or administrative department **-berater** *m* technical adviser **-bildung** *f* technical or professional education **-blatt** *n* technical paper or publication **-buch** *n* handbook, text book **-bücherei** *f* special library

fachen, Garn ~ to ply yarn

Fächer *m* ventilator, fan, blower **elektrischer ~** motor fan, electric fan

Fächer-antenne *f* fan or curtain antenna, fan(-shaped) or harp antenna **-aufblendung** *f* fan fade-in **-blende** *f* fan-fading shutter **-brenner** *m* fantail burner, batswing burner **-brücke** *f* radiating bridge **-falte** *f* fan-shaped fold **-flügel** *m* leaf of fan-shaped gate **-förmig auseinanderziehen** to spread out on a line of bearing **-funkfeuer** *n* fan marker beacon **-gestell** *n* rack shelving

fächerig cellular, locular

Fächer-kammer *f* fan-type combustion chamber **-leuchte** *f* divergent beam light **-luftleiter** *m* fan-shaped aerial **-markierungsbake** *f* fan marker **-motor** *m* fan engine, W-type engine, double-V engine

fächerndes, stark ~ Prisma highly dispersive prism

Fächer-platte *f* gusset plate (ship) **-scheibe** *f* washer (fan-disk)

Fächerung *f* chromatic dispersion

Fächer-tor *n* fan-shaped gate or sector gate **-turn** *m* fan turn (turning the aircraft suddenly in the plane of its wings after loss in altitude in perpendicular climb to go into a nose dive) **-zurichter** *m* fan fitter

fach-gemäß workmanlike **-größe** *f* celebrity **-händler** *m* stockist **-ingenieur** *m* expert or special engineer **-kenntnis** *f* professional knowledge **-kraft** *f* expert, specialist, trained man, skilled labor

Fachkreisen, in ~ among experts

fach-kundig expert, competent **-lehrer** *m* technical instructor **-leute** *pl* trained workers, experts, specialists

fachlich professional, technical

Fach-literatur *f* technical literature or press **-mann** *m* specialist, expert, professional man **-männisch** expert, competent **-maschine** *f* multiple spooling machine **-norm** *f* technical standard **-normenausschuß** *m* engineering standards committee **-ordnung** *f* classification **-photograph** *m* professional photographer **-presse** *f* technical press or literature

Fach-schrifttum n technical literature **-schule** *f* service school, trade school, technical school **-simpeln** to talk shop **-sparte** *f* professional speciality **-sprache** *f* technical terminology or language, professional terminology **-technisch** professional engineering **-trupp** *m* technical troop, engineer platoon, specialist squad (repair, dynamite, etc.) **-verständiger** *m* specialist, expert **-wählertastatur** *f* classification keyboard **-wand** *f* bay work, lath-and -plaster wall **-welt** f technical world

Fachwerk *n* trussing, framing, truss, framework, structure, skeleton, paneling, latticework, checkerwork **rohrgeflochtenes ~** framework of tubes

Fachwerk-ausleger *m* lattice jib **-balken** *m* truss girder **-bauart** *f* method of allotting woods to a number of periods **-bogen** *m* trussed arch **-brücke** *f* truss bridge, latticed-girder bridge **-feld** *n* bay, panel **-gestell** *n* lattice frame (machines) **-glied** *n* truss rods (under trussed beam) **-holm** *m* truss spar girder, spar trussed beam **-kanal** *m* checker passage **-körper** *m* checkerwork

Fachwerk(s)-mauerung *f* checkering **-rippe** *f* channel rib **-rost** *m* checkerwork grillage **-rumpf** *m* framework body or fuselage **-schacht** *m* checker passage, checker-work stack **-stab** *m* frame member **-stein** *m* checker-brick **-strebe** *f* lattice tie, diagonal member **-träger** *m* lattice girder, frame girder, bridge superstructure, truss, structural built-up beam

Fach-wissenschaft *f* branch of science **-wort** *n* technical term

Fachzeitschrift *f* technical journal or paper, trade journal

Fackel *f* torch flare **-entladung** *f* torch form of discharge **-erscheinung** *f* flicker effect (of a cathode) **-feuer** *n* blue light **-kohle** *f* cannel coal

fackeln to flicker, flare, be fickle, hesitate

Fackelventil n escape valve

fade stale, insipid

Faden *m* thread fiber, filament, fathom, yarn, wire, hairline, string cord, grain **~ im Okular** thread hair, wire, web of a graticule **thorhaltiger** (thorierter) **~** thoriated filament

Faden-anleger *m* piecer (textiles) **-anreicher** *m* reacher (textiles) **-aufhängung** *f* fiber suspension **-beleuchtung** *f* illumination of fiducial lines, filar illumination **-bremse** *f* yarn brake, thread brake **-dicketaster** *m* calipers with jaws to measure thread gauge capacitively **-diopter** *n* cross-wire sight, cross-hair diopter **-distanz** *f* thread interval, interval between graticule wires **-distanzmesser** *m* thread interval meter **-einleger** *m* thread feeder **-einschußzusatz** thread interlacing attachment **-einziehen** *n* drawing-in (textiles) **-einzug** *m* draft, pass **-elektrometer** *n* thread or filament electrometer **-endenabstand** end-to-end distance

Faden-fangvorrichtung *f* catch-thread device (automatic stop for broken thread) (textiles) **-festigkeitsprüfer** *m* thread-strength tester (textiles)

fadenförmig vee-shaped, filamentary, fibrous, thread-shaped **-e Entladung** linear pinch discharge

Faden-führer *m* thread guide, guide **-führung** *f* thread guidance **-führungsnut** *f* yarn-guiding groove **-galvanometer** *n* thread galvanometer, string galvanometer **-gehefteter Bogensatz** served quires **-gerade** (as) straight as a die **-glas** *n* reticulated glass, spun glass, filigree glass **-gras** *n* esparto (the fiber) **-hänger** *m* thread carrier, bobbin, spindle **-heftmaschine** *f* thread-stitching machine (print), thread-swing machine **-helligkeit** *f* brightness of the crosslines (optics)

Faden-kabel *n* coaxial or concentric cable with silk-thread-supported central conductor **-kandis** *m* thread candy **-kathode** *f* filamentary cathode **-klauber** *m* thread picker **-kochen** n boiling to string proof

Fadenkonstruktion *f* tracing by means of a string **~ der Ellipse** tracing of an ellipse **~ des Ellipsoids** tracing of the ellipsoid **~ der Evolventen** tracing of the involutes **~ des Kreises** tracing of the circle **~ der Krümmungslinien auf dem Ellipsoid** tracing of the lines of curvature on an ellipsoid

Faden-korrektion *f* stem or column correction **-korrosion** *f* filiform corrosion

Fadenkreuz *n* crossweb, cross wire, crosslines, graticule, cross hairs, reticule, cross spider, crossed threads, spider lines, hairlines, reticle **beleuchtetes ~** illuminated cross wires, graticule

Fadenkreuz-einlesemaschine *f* leasing machine **-lupe** *f* reticle magnifier, reticle glass, reticle lens **-messer** *m* cross-wire meter **-mikrometer** *n* cross-wire micrometer **-platte** *f* graticule

Faden-länge *f* length of filament **-leiter** *m* thread take-up lever, thread guide **-loser Kandis** candy sugar grown without threads **-maß** *n* measurement in fathoms or dimensions **-messer** *n* twine knife (sewing machine) **-meter** *n* fathometer **-mikrometer** *m* filar micrometer **-molekül** *m* filamentary molecule

Faden-papier *n* cloth-centered paper **-platte** *f* grid, graticule **-probe** *f* string-proof test **-problem** *n* string problem **-prüfer** *m* checker, yarn counter **-pulver** *n* nodular powder **-recht** straight **-rolle** *f* tape bar **-schatteninstrument** *n* string-shadow instrument **-scheinig** sleazy, threadbare **-schneider** *m* carpet knife **-schwimmuhr** *f* float fuel gauge **-spanner** *m* thread-tension device **-spannung** *f* filament voltage **-spannvorrichtung** *f* filament tension or stretching device

Faden-stärke *f* tensile strength **-strahl** *m* thread beam (fuzzy hoelike pencil of nonuniform cross section in gas-focused cathode-ray tube) **-strahlen** *pl* pencil rays (electrons) **-strahlentladung** *f* thread-ray discharge **-strich** *m* spider line **-strom** *m* filament current, heating current, heat current, cathode current **-strömung** *f* laminar flow **-stück** *n* reticule support (optics), front-sight piece **-teilstangen** *pl* shed rods (of a loom, textiles) **-transistor** *m* filamentary transistor **-umschnürung** *f* serving of thread **-wächter** *m* knock-off action **-wächterbügel** *m* tension spring arrestor **-widerstand** *m* filament resistance of a tube filament (radio frequency) **-zähler** *m* linen tester, thread counter **-zeiger** *m* hair pointer

fadenziehend ropy **-es Fett** fiber grease **-es Staufferfett** fiber grease

Fading *n* fading **-ausgleich** *m* automatic volume control (AVC) **-automatik** *f* automatic-volume-control means **-effekt** *m* fading effect **-hexode** *f* fading hexode **-mischhexode** *f* automatic-volume-control mixer hexode **-regelung** *f* automatic volume control

Fadon *n* fathom

Fagott *n* bassoon **-wasserabguß** *m* bassoon siphon

Fähigkeit *f* capability, ability, quality, capacity **~ des Festhaltens** tenacity **~ stereoskopisch zu sehen** stereoscopic sense, aptitude for stereoscopic vision

Fähigkeitsnachweis *m* qualifying reference

fahl fallow, fawn, ashy, earth-colored, faded

Fahl-band *n* Fahlband **-erz** *n* gray copper ore, tetrahedrite

Fähnchenwattmeter *n* vane wattmeter

Fahne *f* flag, colors, standard, lug, vane, ensign (flag), flag guidon, soldering lug, lug of a battery plate (einer Feder) web (of a feather) (Druckerei) galley proof **stromführende ~** current-carrying lug **in Fahnen abziehen** to take a rough proof, copy in slips, pull in slips

Fahnen-abschwächer *m* vane attenuator **-abzieher** *m* proof puller (print) **-band** *n* pennant, battle honors **-bildung** *f* signal inertia drag **-abzug** *m* galley proof **-durchmesser** (Kollektor) diameter of lug (commutator) **-korrektur** *f* proof **-magnetron** *n* vane magnetron **-stellung** *f* (des Propellers) feathered pitch

Fahr-abteilung *f* transport section **-arm** *m* hinged tracing lever (of planimeter) **-aufnahme** *f* running, follow, or traveling shot **-auftrag** *m* drive mission, driving order **-ausbildung** *f* driving drill **-ausweis** travel order or permit

Fahrbahn *f* track, runway, overhead runway, beam track, travel beam, roadway, lane, roadway over a bridge, trackway, way of a railway **-träger** *m* roadway beam, crane balks, overhead carrier rail, floorbeam, roadway girder

fahrbar passable, navigable, transportable, portable, movable, mobile, traveling as a conveyer, practicable **-e Anlage** portable plant **-e Benzinpumpe** portable pump **-e Einrichtung** movable installation **-es Gießrohr** movable sprayer, movable rose **-es Mischpult** dolly or car-type mixer, tea-wagon console mixer **-er Montagebock** *m* dolly **-er Motor** portable engine **-er Pflug** wheeled plow

Fahr-barkeit *f* portability, movability **-befähigungsnachweis** *m* driver qualification record **-befehl** *m* travel order, transportation order **-benzin** *n* standard gasoline (for cars) **-bequemlichkeit** *f* riding comfort, driving convenience **-bereich** *n* cruising radius, radius of action, range of action, operating range, traveling distance **-bereit** ready to move **-bereitschaft** *f* transport pool, readiness for moving off alert, driving order **-bereitung** *f* portable position **-bericht** *m* traffic report

Fahrbetrieb, elektrischer ~ electric traction

Fährbetrieb *m* ferrying operation(s)

Fahr-bewegung *f* travelling motion **-bühne** *f* traversing platform, elevator car **-bremse** *f* brake, wheel brake **-brücke** *f* rising scaffold bridge

Fährbrücke *f* ferry bridge

Fahrdamm *m* roadway, highway

Fahrdraht *m* trolley wire, contact wire (aerial) **-aufhängung** *f* trolley-wire suspension, trolley span wire **-isolator** *m* trolley- or contact-wire insulator **-klemme** *f* ear (a metal fitting) **-lokomotive** *f* trolley locomotive **-oberleitung** *f* aerial contact line **-spannung** *f* contact-line voltage **-weiche** *f* trolley frog

Fähre *f* ferry, ferryboat traject

Fahr-eigenschaft *f* driving quality **-einrichtung** *f* traversing mechanism

fahren to ride, navigate, steer, run, move, travel

Fahren *n* (des Bergmanns) climbing, riding

fahrendes Ziel moving target

Fahrenheitskala *f* Fahrenheit scale

Fahrer *m* chauffeur, driver **-haus** *n* driver's compartment, cab

Fahrerin *f* woman driver

Fahrer-optik *f* driver's periscope **-sehklappe** *f* driver's visor (on tanks)

fahr-fertig ready for driving **-fläche** *f* tread (of wheels, rails, etc.) **-fußhebel** *m* foot pedal

Fahrgast *m* passenger **-hafen** *m* passenger berth

Fahrgastraum *m* **aufgeladener ~** pressurized cabin

Fahr-gelegenheit *f* conveyance (riding, driving) **-gerät** *n* propelling equipment **-geschwindigkeit** *f* traveling speed, speed of a boat or barge, permissible speed

Fahrgestell *n* undercarriage, chassis, underframe, carriage for removal, wheel frame, truck **~ mit durchgehender Achse** cross-axle undercarriage **~ mit Hosen** trousered undercarriage **~ mit Schneekufen** ski undercarriage **~ einziehen** to upgear, to retract the undercarriage **abwerfbares ~** detachable undercarriage

Fahrgestell, achsloses ~ tripod undercarriage **einziehbares ~** retractable undercarriage **einziehbares ~, in die Motorgondeln** undercarriage retracting into the engine nacelles **einziehbares ~, in die Rumpfseiten** undercarriage retracting into the sides of the fuselage **einziehbares ~, seitwärts in die Tragflächen** undercarriage retracting sideways into the wings **einziehbares rückziehbares ~** retractable or retractile undercarriage **festes ~** fixed undercarriage

Fahrgestell-abfederung *f* springing of the undercarriage **-achse** *f* undercarriage axle **-anzeiger** *m* undercarriage position indicator **-auskreuzung** *f* undercarriage bracing **-beine** *pl* undercarriage leg **-bügel** *m* undercarriage stirrup **-einstellung** *f* undercarriage adjustment **-einziehhebel** *m* undercarriage release and stowage lever, retractable-undercarriage lever **-einziehschacht** *m* hole for the retractable undercarriage **-einziehung** *f* retraction of undercarriage

Fahrgestell-federung *f* undercarriage springing **-flügel** *m* streamlined undercarriage axle **-hälfte** *f* undercarriage half **-hinterstrebe** *f* rear undercarriage strut or leg **-maße** *f* chassis earth (ground) **-rahmen** *m* chassis frame

Fahrgestell-schenkel *m* undercarriage strut **-schuh** *m* undercarriage socket **-spur** *f* track of the undercarriage **-stellung** *f* positioning of undercarriage

Fahrgestellstrebe *f* undercarriage strut **hintere ~** rear undercarriage strut

Fahrgestell-strebenschuh *m* strut socket **-tragfähigkeit** *f* chassis carrying capacity **-verkleidung** *f* undercarriage fairing, undercarriage fairing **-verspannung** *f* undercarriage bracing **-vorderstrebe** *f* front undercarriage strut **-winde** *f* undercarriage winch

fahrgliederweiser Ausbau disassembly into individual ferries

Fahr-halle *f* traveling or service shed **-hauer** *m* deputy **-höhe** *f* cruising altitude **-kante, der Schiene** running edge or inner edge of rail **-karte** *f* ticket, transportation ticket

Fahrkartenschalter *m* ticket window

Fahr-kolonne *f* supply train **-korb** *m* cage (pits, mines) **-kostenentschädigung** *f* travel allowance **-kran** *m* traveling crane **-küche** *f* rolling kitchen **-kurve** *f* track curve **-lässig** negligent

Fahr-lässigkeit *f* negligence, carelessness **-leder** *n* leather apron **-lehrer** *m* driving instructor **-leitung** *f* trolley wire (elec.), catenary, contact line **-leitungsisolatoren** *pl* overhead-line insulators **-linienmeßgerät** *n* speed-time measuring device **-loch** *n* manhole (of an engine) **-motor** *m* traction motor, portable motor **-motorenlüftersatz** *m* traction-motor blower set **-motorentrennschütze** *m* traction-motor isolating contactors **-ordnung** *f* traffic regulation **-personal** *n* flying or flight or airship personnel

Fahrplan *m* timetable, schedule (train) **-mäßiger Zug** scheduled train

Fahr-preisanzeiger *m* taximeter **-prüfung** *f* driving test

Fahrrad *n* bicycle **-antrieb** *m* cycle-driving gear **-bestandteile** *pl* parts or supplies for bicycles, cycle fittings **-gestell** *n* bicycle frame **-lenkstange** *f* cycle handle bar **-röhre** *f* bicycle tubing **-schlüssel** *m* adjustable pocket spanner **-tretkurbel** *f* cycle tread crank

Fahr-richtung *f* travel direction **-rinne** *f* channel passage (between the banks), rut **-rohr** (Rohrpost) *n* pneumatic tube **-säule** *f* job crane (for electrodes) **-schacht** *m* circulation shaft, ladder shaft, ladderway **-schalter** *m* controller **-schalterkontakt** *m* controller contact **-schalterwiderstand** *m* controller resistance **-schalthebel** *m* switch lever **-schaltung** *f* circuit diagram for travel

Fahr-schautafel *f* illuminated track diagram **-schemel** *m* equalising truck **-schiene** *f* rail, track **-schienenisolator** *m* third rail insulator **-seil** *n* ferry cable, ferry rope, trail **-seilgerät** *n* ferry cable gear **-sicherheit** *f* driving safety **-sperre** *f* automatic stop device **-stativ** *n* movable tripod

Fährstelle *f* ferry site, embarkation point

Fahr-stellung *f* traveling position **-stift** *m* tracing or tracking point (of planimeter) **-strahl** *m* radius vector, guide beam **-straße** *f* track, road, highway, roadway, horse road **-straßensignalschalter** *m* itinerary lever **-straßensteller** m route setting relay **-strecke** *f* range of action, entry, steaming radius **-strom** *m* traction current **-stufen** *pl* working points **-stuhl** *m* elevator (cabin), lift, hoist **-stuhlbrücke** *f* lift bridge **-stuhllandung** *f* descent by stages, rocking-chair landing **-stutzen** *m* raised manhole (engine) **-stützpunkt** *m* (airship) base

Fahrt *f* trip, drive, journey, route, headway, course or way (of a ship), ladder (way in mine), speed **~ über den Achtersteven haben** to have sternway **~ über Grund** ground speed, relative airspeed **~ achteraus haben** to have sternway **~ aufnehmen** to gather speed **~ voraus halten** to keep headway **~ vermindern** to slacken speed **freie ~** free pass **freie ~ geben** to clear the line **ökonomische ~** cruising speed **in ~** underway (aviat.)

Fahrtafel *f* table of railway movements and marches

Fahrt-antrieb *m* travel drive **-ballast** *m* ballast for cruising **-befehl** *m* signal from air-speed pickup (auto pilot) **-bereich** *m* (flying) range, radius of operation **-bestimmung** *f* finding or determination of course **-dauer** *f* duration of flight **-dreieck** *n* course or speed triangle, wind triangle **-eigenschaften** *pl* conditions under way

Fährte *f* track, trail, trace

Fahrtenbuch *n* log book

Fahrt-erschütterung *f* driving shocks or vibration **-fehler** *m* course error **-geber** *m* air-speed indicator, alleron pickup, autopilot **-geschwindigkeit** *f* speed (of travel), flight speed **-haken** *m* ladder hook **-halten** to maintain speed **-haspe** *f* ladder hasp

Fahrtiefe, nutzbare ~ depth of the navigable channel

Fahrt-liste *f* travel order, entraining table **-licht** n driving light **-meßanlage** *f* airspeed indicating system **-messer** *m* (mit Staurohr) pilot static airspeed indicator **-messeranzeige** *f* airspeed indicator reading **-nachweis** *m* trip ticket or certificate **-nummer** *f* consignment or flight number **-regler** *m* speed governor for cars **-richtung** *f* direction of journey

Fahrtrichtungs-änderung *f* change of the driving direction **-anlaßschalter** *m* direction and starting switch **-anzeigeleuchte** *f* direction indicator switch (traffic or control switch) **-anzeiger** *m* direction indicator (signal) **-haltung** *f* ability to hold a course **-schalter** *m* commutator switch, reversing switch

Fahrtrichtungswechsel *m* **stoßfreier ~** smooth change of direction without shocks

Fahrt-schreiber *m* tachograph, recording air-speed indicator, tachometer course recorder **-stellung** *f* running position **-stufe** *f* rate (e. g., revolutions per minute of engine) **-tafel** *f* speed table **-widerstand** *m* rolling resistance, tractive resistance

Fahrtwind *m* air-stream, air flow, relative wind, slip stream **Kühler ganz im freien ~** fully exposed radiator **Widerstand der Luftschraube eines ausgefallenen Motors, die vom ~ angetrieben wird,** windmilling drag

Fahrtwindgenerator *m* wind-driven generator

Fahr-übung *f* cruising practice, cruising maneuver, driving drill, driving lesson **-unterweisung** *f* driving instruction **-versuch** *m* drive test, transportation test **-vorrichtung** *f* moving gear **-vorschrift** *f* traffic regulation **-wegsuche** *f* routing

Fahrwasser *n* (navigation) channel, fairway channel **das ~ räumen** to sweep a channel

Fahrwasserbezeichnung *f* waterway marking

Fahrweg *m* roadway, dirt road

Fahrwerk *n* landing gear, (aviation) chassis, alighting gear **das ~ ausfahren** to extend or lower the landing gear

Fahrwerk(s)-achse *f* landing-gear axle **-anzeiger** *m* landing-gear-position indicator **-bock** *m* landing-gear truss **-bremse** *f* landing-gear brake **-brücke** *f* landing gear yoke **-federbein** *n* landing-gear strut, shock-absorber strut

Fahrwerk(s)-gerät *n* understructure (aviation) **-kettentrieb** *m* chain-drive propelling mechanism **-klappe** *f* landing-gear door, landing-gear well flap **-rahmen** *m* chassis frame **-strebe** *f* landing-gear strut **-teil** *m* landing-gear part **-tor** *n* landing-gear door **-träger** *m* bogie girder

Fahrwiderstand *m* road resistance, resistance to rolling, resistance to motion, resistance to the rolling of a car, drag when taxiing, resistance to taxiing, tractional resistance

Fahrzeit *f* driving time, running schedule (Rohrpost) carrier running time **-übersicht** *f* timetable

Fahrzeug *n* power-propelled vehicle, vessel (navy), car, (power) craft (marine, land, or air) **-batterie** *f* traction battery **-dampfmaschine** *f* automobile steam engine **-funk** (Autobahnfunk) *m* moving-vehicle communication **-kolonne** *f* column of vehicles, train of vehicles **-leitungen** *pl* wires for vehicles **-motor** *m* automotive engine **-überhang** *m* overhang angle of approach **-wanne** *f* tank hull

Fakokitt *m* a type of cement for plexiplass

Faksimile *n* facsimile (FAX) **-telegraphie** *f* phototelegraphy, picture telegraphy

faksimilieren to imitate flawlessly

Fakten *pl* facts

Faktis *m* **brauner ~** black substitute

Faktor *m* factor, multiplier, agent, coefficient, foreman, submultiple (of a number) **~ der gerichteten Reflexion** regular reflection factor **~ einer Zahl** submultiple **ausschlaggebender ~** decisive factor **gemeinsamer ~** common factor

Faktorei *f* trading company, colonial plant or agency

Faktorenzerlegung *f* factorisation

Faktorielle *f* factorial

Faktorisierungsmethode *m* factorization method

Faktotum *n* handy man

Faktum *n* fact

Faktura *f* invoice

fakturieren to invoice

Fakturieren *n* invoicing

Fakturist *m* invoice clerk

Fakultät *f* factorial function, faculty (university)

fakultativ optional, nonobligatory, noncompulsory, permissive **-klausel** *f* optional clause **-schalter** *m* option switch

falb pale yellow, cream (colored), fallow

Fall *m* fall, case, event, decline, drop, dive, inclination, fall or head of water or weir **~ im beengten Raume** hindered falling **zu ~ bringen** to tumble

Fall-anlasser *m* drop starter **-apparat** *m* slipping apparatus

Fällbad *n* setting bath, coagulating bath

Fallbahn *f* trajectory

Fallbär *m* falling tup, tup, ram, rammer, drop-hammer ram, monkey

fällbar precipitable

Fällbarkeit *f* precipitability

Fall-behälter *m* gravity tank, header tank **-benzin** *n* emergency fuel **-benzinförderung** *f* gravity gas-feed **-benzintank** *m* gravity tank **-beschleunigung** *f* gravitational constant, acceleration due to gravity **-blattuhr** *f* read-out clock **-block** *m* breechblock **-blockverschluß** *m* drop-block breech mechanism, vertical sliding breechblock **-bö** *f* air pocket (descending gust), down gust, downdraft **-bremsbar** fall breaking **-bremse** *f* lift brake **-brücke** *f* drawbridge, snare, trap

Fallbügel *m* chopper type monitoring (automatic control) **-abtastung** *f* chopper type monitoring **-instrument** *n* instrument with locking device **-regler** *m* hoop drop relay (elektr. Meßgeräte) chopper bar controller **-relais** *n* hoop-drop relay **-schreiber** *m* gravity-type scribe, chopper-bar recorder, pen recorder

Fall-büchse *f* valve socket **-bühne** *f* drop (stage) **-dauer** *f* time of fall **-drähte** *m pl* drop wires (textiles) **-druck** *m* gravity

Falle *f* trap, snare, pitfall, latch, catch, sluice gate, leaf, bolt, valve **im ~** in case of **~ mit niedrigem Widerstand** low-resistance trap

Fälle *pl* cases, falls

Fall-eisen *n* latch **-leitung** *f* gravity-feed pipe

fallen to fall, sink, go down, decrease, decline, drop, descend **~ lassen** to abandon (a patent, an application), drop (procedure), dump

Fallen *n* underlie, dip **~ des Wassers** fall of the water, ebb

fällen to fell, cut down, precipitate, drop, pass (judgment), pass **ein Lot ~** to drop a perpendicular **ein Urteil ~** to render a judgment, decision, sentence, verdict, or award, issue a decree

Fallenachse *f* latch shaft, catch, pivot

fallend falling **~ (ab)gießen** to top-pour, top-cast, cast from the top **~ gegossen** top-poured **-es Blatt** falling leaf (a flying maneuver) **-e Charakteristik** drooping characteristic, falling characteristic **-er Guß** top pouring, top casting **-e Tendenz** downward tendency **-es Wasser** ebb tide

Fallende *n* descending gallery

Fallen-hammer *m* stop block **-scheibe** *f* stop disc **-zug** *m* sluice gate

Fall-fangschere *f* fishing jars **-fenster** *n* sash

window **-folge** *f* order of drop **-förderanlage** *f* gravity feed system (aviat.) **-geschwindigkeit** *f* falling speed, speed of fall **-gesetz** *n* law of falling bodies **-gewicht** *n* falling weight, balance weight, floating weight (Hammer) tup weight **-gewichtsversuch** *m* falling weight test **-gleiter** *m* parachute brake **-grube** *f* obstacle trench **-haken** *m* tumbling hook **-hakenkupplung** *f* catch-hook coupling

Fallhammer *m* falling weight (explosives), drop hammer, indenting hammer, hammer drop **mit dem ~ geformt** drop-forged

Fall-hammer-gesenk *n* drop-forging **-probe** *f* falling-weight test (explosives) **-schmieden** *pl* drop forging **-versuch** *m* drop test, drop-hammer test

Fallhärte *f* impact-ball hardness **-prüfer** *m* ball tester, hardness-drop tester

Fallhaspel *f* collapsible reel **-hebel** *m* clasp handle

Fallhöhe *f* height of fall, height of drop, drop height, fall or weight (of water) head **~** (Absatzgefäße) sedimentation depth

fallieren to become bankrupt or insolvent, fail

fällig due, payable **~ werden** to fall due

Fälligkeit *f* settling velocity (falling velocity), expiration on maturity (of notes)

Fälligkeits-datum *n* due date, date of maturity **-termin** *m* date of maturity

Falliment (Fallissement) *n* bankruptcy, failure

Fallinie der Lagerstätte direction of full dip of the mineral deposit

Fallinien *pl* lines of steepest gradient, lines of dip

Fallinstrument *n* slipping instrument

Fäll-kasten *m* precipitation box, zinc box **-kessel** *m* precipitating vessel, hydrolyzer

Fallklappe *f* (drop) shutter, drop indicator, trap board **~ mit elektrischer** (mechanischer) **Rückstellung** electrical (mechanical) replacement drop indicator

Fall-klappenauslöser *m* fire-shutter control **-klappenrelais** *n* drop indicator relay **-klotz** *m* monkey (of a pile driver) **-koks** *m* coke recovered **-kolben** *m* dropping piston **-kraftstoffanlage** *f* gravity (feed) fuel, system **-kraftstofftank** *m* gravity-type fuel tank **-kugel** *f* drop weight, load to be dropped by the magnet

Fallkurve *f* trajectory **Wurfbahn der ~** flight path of the bomb, trajectory of the bomb

Fallmasche *f* ladder

Fällmittel *n* precipitant, precipitating agent

Fall-moment *n* gravitational momentum **-öl** *n* oil feed by gravity **-pendel** *n* friction pendulum (explosives) **-probe** *f* falling-weight test, drop test, drop-weight test, dynamic test

Fällprodukt *n* precipitate

Fall-punkt *m* point of fall, level point (ballistics) **-raum** *m* cathode drop or fall space **-rinne** *f* chute

Fallreep *n* gangway (ladder) **das ~ hinaufgehen** to ascend the gangway **achtere** (vordere) **~** after (forward) gangway

Fallrichtung *f* down dip **der ~ entgegen** up dip

Fall-riegel *m* falling latch **-rohr** *n* gravity tube, down pipe, outlet pipe, barometric tube **-röhren** *f pl* fall tubes, drop casing

Fallscheibe *f* falling disk, drop shutter, annunciator disk **Wecker mit ~** indicator bell

Fallscheiben-apparat *m* annunciator board **-kasten** *m* indicator board **-tafel** *f* annunciator board (drop indicator)

Fallschieber *m* sliding damper **-verschluß** *m* drop shutter

Fallschirm *m* parachute **~ mit Handauslösung** *f* manually operated parachute **einen ~ abrutschen lassen** sideslipping a parachute **mit dem ~ abspringen** to parachute, bail out **der ~ geht auf** the parachute opens **den ~ öffnen** to release (open) the parachute **der ~ öffnet sich** the parachute opens **sich mit dem ~ retten** to save oneself by parachute

Fallschirm-abspringer *m* parachute jumper, parachutist **-absprung** *m* parachute jump or descent **-absprungturm** *m* controlled parachute tower **-anzug** *m* parachute parasuit **-auslösung** *f* parachute release **-ausstoß** *m* release of parachute **-behälter** *m* chute boot of a sounding rocket **-dach** *n* parachute canopy

Fallschirm-kappe *f* parachute canopy **-last** *f* delivery unit **-leinen** *f pl* parachute cords, rigging lines **-leuchte** *f* parachute flare **-leuchtpatrone** *f* parachute-flare cartridge **-luftloch** *n* parachute vent **-pack** *m* parachute pack

Fallschirmpatrone *f* parachute cartridge **~ für Windmessung** parachute cartridge for measuring wind velocity

Fallschirm-puppengerät *n* parachute test stand for use with dummies **-rakete** *f* parachute flare or rocket signal **-reißleine** *f* parachute rip cord **-schule** *f* parachute (training) school, school of parachutists **-sitz** *m* parachute seat **-springen** *n* parachute jumping

Fall-schloß *n* trunk lock, lock with falling latch, spring lock (doors) **-schmieden** *n* drop forging **-schnecke** *f* drop or trip worm **-schutzvorrichtung** *f* safety apparatus for cages **-speisung** *f* gravity feed **-stange** *f* catch rod **-stifterdungsschalter** *m* drop-pin earthing-switch **-stift-schalter** *m* drop-pin switch **-streifen** *pl* fall-streaks, streamer (cloud) **-strick** *m* snare, noose, gin **-stromvergaser** *m* inverted-type carburetor, downdraft carburetor **-stück** *n* dropping piece **-stütze** *f* sprag, drop type of sprag, drop-gate sluice **-systemplattenwechsel** *m* drop system of record changing

Fall-tafel *f* bomb-trajectory table **-tank** *m* header tank, gravity tank **-tropfenanzeiger** *m* falling drop indicator **-tür** *f* trap door, parachute opening (in floor of aircraft), escape hatch

Fällung *f* precipitation, precipitating, dropping **elektrolytische ~** precipitation by electrolysis, electrodeposition

Fällungs-mittel *n* precipitant, precipitating agent **-reagenz** *f* precipitating reagent

Fall-verschluß *m* drop shutter **-versuch** *m* impact test **-vorrichtung** *f* drop unit (a booster rocket jettisonable after exhaustion of propellant)

Fallwasser *n* falling water, hot-well water, tail-tank water **-kasten** *m* hot well, seal tank **-rohr** *n* barometric tube, barometric leg pipe, barometric tail pipe

Fallweg *m* trail of fall (of a bomb)

Fallwerk *n* pile driver, blow-impact machine, drop-testing machine, vertical-drop machine, tumbler gear, stamp, drop work, pig breaker, power hammers, impact-testing apparatus, monkey (of a pile driver)

Fallwerkskran *m* ram crane
Fall-wind *m* katabatic wind, down gust of wind **-winkel** *m* hade of the fault, angle of pitch, fall, or inclination **-winkelmesser** *m* clinometer **-wucht** *f* force of the fall, impact **-zeit** *f* falling time **-zerreißversuch** *m* tensile-impact test **-zuleitung** *f* gravity feed **-zünder** *m* percussion fuze
falsch wrong, false, incorrect, deceitful, dead (of materials, points), dummy, imitation **~ berechnen** to miscalculate **-e Anschnitte** careless cutting of gates **-e Ausrichtung** misalignment (of image or track) **-e Flügelrippe** former (a shaping strip of a plane) **-er Holm** false spar **-er Lautlosigkeitskegel** false cone of silence **-es Licht** light fog, leakage light, stray light (in film printing) **-e Linie** *f* ghost (optics)
falsch-er ~ Meltau false mildew, downy mildew **-e Naht** mock-seam **-er Nebel** mock fog **-e Rippe** false rib, stiffening rib, rib stiffening **-e Strahlung** stray radiation, stray rays **-es Teil** false mold **~ Verbindung** wrong connection **-e Zählimpulse** spurious counts **-er Zirrus** false cirrus
Falsch-abstimmung *f* mistuning, off-resonance condition **-anpassung des Widerstandes** mismatching of impedance, mismatched impedance **-anpassungsfaktor** *m* mismatching factor, reflection factor, transition factor **-anruf** *m* wrong number call **-echos** *pl* indirect echoes **-einstellung** *f* maladjustment
fälschen to falsify, adulterate, forge, counterfeit
Fälscher *m* forger
falsch-lastig incorrectly trimmed **-lochungen** *pl* errors in card punching **-luft** *f* infiltrated air, by-padded air
falschphasig misphased, dephased, out of phase **-e Elektronen** electrons of unfavorable phase
Falsch-sehen *n* visual hallucination **-stöpseln** to insert plug in wrong jack
Fälschung *f* distortion, vitiation, falsification, adulteration, fraud, forgery, counterfeiting
Fälschungsmittel *n* adulterant
Falsch-wahl *f* faulty selection **-weisung** *f* error in indication
Falsifikat *n* falsificate
faltbar foldable, collapsible
Faltbarkeit *f* foldability
Falt-beanspruchung *f* folding stress **-blatt** *n* leaflet folder
Faltboot *n* collapsible (rubber) boat, folding boat, collapsible dinghy, faltboat **-brücke** *f* bridge of collapsible boats
Falt-dichtring *m* (für Kerzen) folded packing
Falt-broschüre *f* folder leaflet **-dichtring** *m* (für Kerzen) folded packing ring (for spark plugs) **-dipol** (Radio) folded dipole
Falte *f* fold, flexure, curvature, hinge, joint, crease, wrinkle, lap, hollow, slip, (absichtlich gelegte) pleat, ply (fold, coat, thickness) **überkippte ~** inverted fold, reversed fold
fälteln to pleat, cockle, crinkle, pucker
Faltemaschine *f* frilling machine, folding machine
falten to fold, pleat, double, bend over, crease (zusammen **~**) double
Falten *n* beaming (textiles) **-achse** *f* anticlinal line or axis **-balg** *m* bellows, siphon
Faltenbalgabdichtung, Stopfbüchse mit ~ siphon gland
Falten-beutel *m* gusset bag **-bildung** *f* folding, pleating, wrinkling **-bogen** *m* creased bend **-brennkammer** *f* clawbaffle combustion chamber **-bündel** *n* anticlinorium **-filter** *n* folded filter, prefolded filter, pleated filter, fluted filter **-frei** smooth, free from creases
Falten-gebirge *n* mountains formed of folds, fold mountains **-halter** *m* annular holder **-hohlraum** *m* folded cavity **-horn** *n* folded, coiled, curled or twisted horn (of a loudspeaker) **-kamm** *m* comb for beaming (textiles) **-körper** *m* sheet baffle **-krause** *f* frill **-krümmer** *m* creased bend **-lautsprecher** *m* folded-horn loudspeaker **-legemaschine** *f* pleating machine
falten-reich folded, creased, wrinkled **-rohr** *n* flexible pipe **-rohrbogen** *m* creased bend **-schenkel** *m* flank of a fold (in geology) **-schlagen** *n* creasing **-schlauch** *m* pleated or corrugated hose or tube, accordion tube **-verteilungswalze** *f* cylinder with pleat distributing device **-werfen** *n* puckering, shrivelling, creasing
Falter *m* folder, creaser
Falt-garage *f* collapsible garage **-hobel** *m* grooving plane
faltig wrinkled, puckered, having folds, pleats, or creases
Falt-karton *m* cardboard for folding boxes **-leiste** *f* folding strip **-prospekt** *m* folder, leaflet **-punkt** *m* plait point **-schachtel** *f* folding box **-schaufel** *f* folded or bent blade, sheetformed blade **-schichten** folding sheets **-stanzmaterial** *n* punching material for folding boxes **-tür** (Garage) overhead door
Faltung *f* folding, doubling, wrinkling, pleating, fold, bending **~ von Funktionen** folding (convolution) of functions **~ einer Lagerstätte** plication **~ der Schichten** fold (of strata)
Faltungs-integral *n* convolution integral **-satz für Transformationen** *m* convolution theorem for transforms **-summe** *f* convolution sum (math.) **-überschiebung** *f* overthrust of folds
Faltversuch *m* folding test, doubling test, bend-over test **-werk** *n* folded plate structure, prismatic structure
Falz *m* rabbet, groove, notch, recess, channel, fold, edge hammered down, folding border, flute **-anlage** *f* folding lay
Falzapparat, bänderarmer ~ folder with few tapes
Falz-beständigkeit *f* folding endurance (of film) **-blech** *n* metal sheet with good bend properties **-bock** *m* shaving beam **-bruch** *m* fold (break) **-deckel** *m* grooved cover **-einbrennmaschine** *f* folding machine **-eisen** *n* curriers' knife
Fälzel *n* slip-fold
Fälzen *n* bar folding
falzen to groove, notch, rabbet, bead, fold, joggle
Falz-fähigkeit *f* foldableness **-festigkeit** *f* folding endurance or strength **-fräser** *m* notching cutter, rebating cutter (woodwork) **-fuge** *f* rebated joint (half lap) **-gesenk** *n* seaming die **-hobel** *m* fillister (plane) rabbet plane **-klappe** *f* folding blade
Falz-linie *f* folding direction **-maschine** *f* beading press, tin-box jointing machine (clasp joint) **-membran** *f* nonrigid noncircular cone (with curved radiating surface) **-naht** *f* folded seam **-pfahl** *m* sheet piles and piling **-rahmen** *m*

grooved chase **-rohr** *n* (B. X.) cable tube, rabbet pipe, slip joint tubing **-rolle** *f* flanging roller

Falz-schiene *f* tram rail, tramroad **-trichter** *m* former **-verbindung** *f* scarf joint **-verschlußmaschine** *f* tin-box jointing machine (clasp joint) **-widerstand** *m* folding resistance **-zange** *f* pliers, folding tongs **-ziegel** *m* interlocking (roofing) tile, ridge, hollow, or gutter tile

Familienscharen, einparametrische ~ one-parameter family of curves

Fanal *n* light signal, beacon

Fanfarenanlage *f* fanfare set

Fang *m* intake **-anode** *f* collecting or gathering anode **-apparat** *m* fishing apparatus **-arbeit** *f* fishing, fishing job **-band** *n* catch band, strap (for steering lock) **-bereich** *m* pull-in range **-birne** *f* mandrel socket **-blech** *n* baffle sheet (in a magnetron) **-büchse** *f* fishing-valve socket **-bügel** *m* check or stop (for arresting tool or spring), fishing stirrup **-buhne** *f* weir, dike, dam, breakwater

Fangdamm *m* cofferdam **oberer ~** upstream cofferdam **unterer ~** downstream cofferdam

Fang-diffusore *f* intake diffusory **-diode** *f* suppression diode **-dorn** *m* fishing tap, tap catcher **-draht** *m* guard wire **-düse** *f* mixing nozzle (steam jet), combining nozzle, female nozzle, mixing cone (injector) **-einrichtung** *f* number checking arrangement, interception equipment (tel.), cardigan arrangement **-elektrode** *f* target

fangen to catch, seize, capture, interept mischievous calls, entrap (water, oil, etc.), receive, take, captivate, collect, trap, secure

Fänger *m* catcher, worm screw, grab, dish **-glocke** *f* valve guard **-teller** *m* catcher plate

Fang-feder *f* spring catcher, cushioning spring **-frosch** *m* catching piece **-gabel** *f* catch wrench **-gabelförderstuhl** *f* trap-fork elevator **-garn** *n* hand net **-gerät** *n* fishing tool, worm screw **-gestänge** *n* fishing rods **-gitter** *n* suppressor grid, cathode grid, grounded or earthed grid, interceptor grid **-gleis** *n* safety siding, trap spur **-glocke** *f* die coupling, bell screw, bellmouthed fishing socket **-graben** *m* side ditch **-gurt** *m* suspension belt

Fang-haken *m* fishing hook, wall hook, grapnel, grip or gripping device, jaw, indicator clip, catch hook (Bohrgerät) extractor, grapple **-hebel** *m* cardigan cam lever **-hund** *m* jar latch **-hülse** *f* fishing socket **-instrument** *n* gripping instrument

Fang-kabel *n* drag wire (aviation) **-keil** *m* stem for casing dogs, cotter **-kette** *f* safety chain **-kettenware** *f* double-rib warp goods **-klappe** *f* mousetrap **-klotz** *m* grip block

Fang-kluppe *f* die coupling, clamp **-korb** *m* protecting screen, coupling cage **-kraft** *f* brake power **-krone** *f* fishing socket

Fang-leine *f* grappling rope, parachute cords, rigging lines, shroud line (parachute), suspension line, painter **-mittel** *n* getter(ing substance) bait **-netz** *n* harbor net, antisubmarine net **-netz** *n* aircraft arrester net **-nippel** *m* die nipple **-pflanze** *f* catch crop **-platte** *f* target or impactor plate, latch plate (textiles) **-pol** *m* acceptor pole **-presse** *f* anchor press

Fang-rachen *m* alligator grab **-rahmen** *m* fender **-raum** *m* pocket, collecting pocket **-rechen** *m* grate **-rille** *f* catching groove **-ring** *m* fishing ring **-rohr** *n* dip pipe (pickup or scoop) **-rost** *m* recovery grate, slag screen **-rutschschere** *f* fishing jars

Fang-schale *f* collecting pan **-schere** *f* grip or gripping device, jaw, fishing jars for ropes **-schirm** *m* collecting diaphragm **-schlaufe** *f* check cable, safety stop cable **-schnur** *f* aiguillette, fourragère **-schraube** *f* locking screw (on gear) **-schwerstange** *f* sinker bar **-spiegel** *m* collecting mirror **-stange des Blitzableiters** lightning rod **-stelle** *f* trap (trans.) tuck position, trapping spot (trans.) **-stiel** *m* combined flying and landing strut **-stoff** *m* getter **-stoß** *m* parry **-strebe** *f* combined flying and landing strut **-stuhl** *m* double-rib frame

Fang-teil eines Hebers separate clearing cam **-trichter** (Entaschg.) housing over point of discharge from hopper to sluiceway, collecting funnel **-vorrichtung** *f* arrangement for the interception of mischievous calls, grip or gripping device, jaw, safety apparatus of cages, safety catches **-werkzeug** *n* fishing tool **-zange** *f* pickup grab, fishing tongs **-zapfen** *m* male fishing trip **-zaun** *m* protective hedge or fence **-zeug** *n* safety clutch or brake of lift **-zylinder** *m* enshrouding cylinder

Fantasie-einfassung *f* fancy frame **-wirker** *m* fancy or coat stitcher

Fantol *m* code for furforyl alcohol

Farad *n* farad

Faraday-scher Dunkelraum Faraday dark space **-sches Gefäß** Faraday ice pail, Faraday cylinder **-sche Gesetze** Faraday's laws of electrolysis **-scher Käfig** Faraday ice pail, Faraday screen, shield, or collector

Faradisation *f* faradization

faradisch faradic **-er Strom** faradic current

Farb-abbrennmundstück *n* paint burning tip **-absatz** *m* dyeing difference **-abstellung** *f* ink supply shut-off **-abstimmung** *f* gradation of color shades **-abstreichrakel** *f* color doctor **-abweichung** *f* chromatic aberration (TV)

Farb-angleichung *f* color matching, color comparison **-anpassung** *f* color match **-anstrich** *m* coat of color or paint, painting **-an- und abstellung** *f* ink supply cut-out and reset **-arm** having few colors, gray **-atlas** *m* color scale, color chart **-ätzer** *m* color process etcher

Farb-aufnahme *f* colored image **-aufnahmevermögen** *n* absorptive power for dyestuffs **-auftragung** *f* inking **-ausgleich** *m* color balancing (of color film) **-auszug** *m* color separation

Farbauszug *m* color record, chromatic selection **negativer ~** separation negative

Farbauszüge *pl* color component (images), partial color (images)

Farbbad *n* dyebath, dyeliquor

Farbbalken-generator *m* (Meßgerät) color bar generator **-muster** (auf dem Bildschirm für Meßzwecke) color bar pattern (TV) **-signal** *n* color bar signal (TV)

Farbband *n* typewriter ribbon, ink ribbon **abgelaufenes ~** unwound ribbon

Farbband-führung *f* ribbon guide **-hub** *m* ribbon lift mechanism **-hubhebel** *m* ribbon oscillator lever **-spule** *f* ribbon spool **-transport** *m* ribbon feed **-umschaltung** *f* color ribbon reverse **-vor-**

schub *m* ink-ribbon feed **-wechsel** *m* ink-ribbon change or reversal

färbbar colorable

Farb-behälter *m* ink reservoir **-beständigkeit** *f* fastness of color **-bestimmung** *f* color determination **-beutel** *m* fluorescein bag **-bild** *n* color picture (TV) **-coder** *m* color coder

Farb-deckfähigkeit *f* concealing, covering, or hiding power (of paint), opacity **-deckschicht** *f* color coat **-decoder** *m* color decoder **-demodulator** *m* color demodulator (TV) **-diaabtaster** *m* color slide camera **-differenzsignal** *n* color-difference signal **-drilling (aus** verschiedenen Leuchtstoffstreifen) **color triple (TV) -drucken** to color print **-druckstock** *m* color block

Farbe *f* color, paint, pigment, stain, hue, tint, refining skimmings (in lead refining), ink, dye, shade (dark), tone **anstrichfertige** ~ ready mixed paint ~ **auftragen** to apply color, ink **bezogene** ~ related color **bunte** ~ hue color, chromatic color **hervorstechende** ~ sharp color **spritlösliche** ~ alcohol-soluble color(ing) **unauslöschbare** ~ indelible ink **unbezogene** ~ unrelated color **unbunte** ~ hueless color, achromatic color, color devoid of hue **unechte** ~ fugitive or not fast color **unzerstörbare** ~ indelible ink ~ **für Rotationsdruck** rotary machine ink

Färbeband *n* dye band

farbecht fast-dyed, of fast color

Färbefoulard *n* dyeing pad

farbehaltend keeping color

Färbe-haspel *f* dyeing paddle **-hülse** *f* dye tube

Farbeisen *n* slice (print)

Färbe-kessel *m* dyeing vat **-kraft** *f* tinting strength, dyeing power, tinctorial **-mittel** *n* dye(stuff), coloring agent

Farb-empfänger *m* color receiver (TV) **-empfindlichkeit** *f* color sensitivity **-empfindung** *f* color sensation or perception **-fadenversuch** *m* dye experiment

färben to paint, color, stain, dye

Farben-abbeizmittel *n* paint remover **-abstreichmesser** *n* (color) doctor **-abstufung** *f* gradation of colors **-abtötung** *f* color tinting (color shading) **-abweichung** *f* chromatic aberration **-änderung** *f* change of color **-anzeiger** *m* color indicator **-aufnahme** *f* color picure **-auftrag** *m* laying on of colors **-ausgleich** *m* (zur Erzeugung von Grauwerten) color balance **-auszugfilter** *m* selective filter, selective screen

Farben-band *n* spectrum **-bild** *n* (color(ed) image, spectrum **-bindemittel** *n* color agglutinant **-blind** color-blind **-blindheitsprüfung** color perception test **-bogen** *m* iris **-brechung** *f* color refraction **-chemie** *f* color chemistry **-chemiker** paint chemist **-code** *f* color code

färbend dyeing, coloring

Farben-dreieck *n* color triangle **-druck** *m* lithochromy, color printing, impression of colors

farbenempfindlich color-sensitive, orthochromatic **-es Zäpfchen** color-distinguishing cone (of eye)

Farbenempfindlichkeit *f* chromatic sensitivity ~ **des Auges** color sensitivity or spectral response of the eye

Farben-empfindlichkeitsverteilung *f* color sensitivity or spectral response of the eye **-empfindung** *f* color sensation, chromatic sensation **-erzeugend** color producing, chromogenic **-fabrik** *f* color manufactory, manufacture of inks **-fächer** *m* spectrum **-fehler** *m* chromatic defect, color defect, chromatic aberration **-fehlsichtigkeit** *f* color-vision deficiency **-filmaufnahme** *f* color photograph **-flimmern** *n* color flicker **-folge** *f* color scheme **-froh** colorful, delighting in color **-fülle** *f* abundance of color

Farben-gebung *f* coloration **-gefühl** *n* color sense **-glas** *n* colored glass **-gleichheit** *f* chromatic identity **-gleichung** *f* color equation **-grad** *m* chroma **-hören** *n* colored hearing **-karte** *f* color chart **-korrektion** *f* achromatization **-kreisel** *m* color wheel or top, color mixer (optics) **-kunstdruck** *m* colored plate

Farben-lage *f* laying on of colors **-lehre** *f* science of color, chromatics **-leiter** *f* color scale **-libelle** *f* color level (TV) **-lichtdruck** *m* heliographic printing, collotype **-lichtechtheitsprüfer** *m* fadeometer **-lichtprüfung** *f* color perception test **-lithographie** *f* color lithography **-lösung** *f* color, staining solution

Farben-mannigfaltigkeit *f* multiplicity of color **-maß** *n* colorimeter **-meßapparat** *m* colorimeter, color measurer **-messer** *m* chromatometer, colorimeter, tintometer **-messung** *f* colorimetry, chromatometry, chromatometrics **-mischmaschine** *f* dye-stuff mixing machine **-mühle** *f* paint grinder (machine) **-muster** *n* color specimen

Farben-oktaeder *m* color pyramid **-ordnung** *f* color sequence **-platte** *f* color plate **-problem** *n* color problem **-rad** *n* rainbow wheel **-reiber** *m* grinder for paint, color grinder **-reibmaschine** *f* paint grinder, ink- or color-grinding machine **-reinheit** *f* chromatic purity **-reste** *pl* residual chromatic aberration, uncorrected color **-richtig** orthochromatic (phot.)

Farben-sättigung *f* chroma-saturation **-saum** *m* color fringe **-schalten** *n* color switching **-schattierung** *f* gradation of shade **-scheibe** *f* color disk **-schichtfilm** *m* dye-coated film **-schiller** *m* (-schillern *n*) iridescence **-schmelzofen** *m* color enameling furnace

Farben-sehen *n* color perception, color vision **-siebmaschine** *f* color straining machine **-sinn** *m* color sense **-skala** *f* chromaticity scale, color scale, color chart **-spektrum** *n* color spectrum, chromatic spectrum **-sperre** *f* color killer **-spiel** *n* iridescence, opalescence **-spritzapparat** *m* spray-painting apparatus, cementing apparatus

Farben-steindruck *m* chromolithography (print.) **-stellung** *f* composition of colors **-stufe** *f* color gradation, shade, tint **-stufenmesser** *m* tintometer **-tafel** *f* color chart **-tiefdruck** *m* photogravure color printing **-treue** *f* color fidelity (TV) **-tüchtigkeit** *f* true color perception, color vision **-überzug** *m* coat (of paint) **-umschlag** *m* color change

Farben- und Lackindustrie *f* paint and lacquer industries

Farben-unterscheidung *f* color discrimination **-untüchtigkeit** *f* color blindness **-veränderung** *f* change of color, discoloration **-verdünner** *m* thinner **-vergleich** *m* color matching, color comparing **-verreibmaschine** *f* ink mill **-ver-**

reibung *f* distribution of ink **-viereck** *n* color square

Farben-wahrnehmung *f* color vision, color perception **-walze** *f* ink roller, inker (textiles) **-wechsel** *m* change of color **-wiedergabe** *f* color reproduction **-wirkung** *f* color effect **-zerlegung** *f* color-break-up (TV) **-zerstreuung** *f* chromatism, color dispersion, chromatic aberration (optics) **-zinkoxyd** *n* leader zinc oxyde **-zusatz** *m* ink compound (reducer)

Färbe-pinsel *m* paint brush

Färber *m* dyer

Farberde *f* colored clay, coloring earth **-gewinnung** *f* mineral-pigment quarry

Färberei *f* dyeing, dye works

Färberröte *f* madder

Färbe-sieb *n* color strainer **-tabletten** *pl* Varitone tablets **-vermögen** *n* coloring power (coloring strength) **-zylinder** *m* doctor (scraper for starch, etc., on textiles)

Farb-fehler *m* chromatic aberration **-fehlerfrei** achromatic **-fernseh-bildröhre** *f* chromoscope, color picture tube, color kinescope **-fernsehen** *n* color television **-film** *m* technicolor movie, dye film **-film-betrachtungsgerät** *n* color transparency viewer **-filter** *m* color filter, colored filter **-flotte** *f* dye liquor **-folie** *f* color foil

Farb-gebung *f* ductor movement, inking (print) **-gefäß** *n* inkwell **-gitter** *n* color grating, color grid **-glas** *m* colored glass, stained glass, colored filter **-glasrevolver** *m* colored glass revolver **-gleichlauf** *m* color synchronism (TV)

Farbgleichung, dreigliederige ~ three-color equation

Farb-holz *n* dyewood **-hören** *n* colored hearing

farbig colored **-e Ziele** colored objects

Farb-index *m* color index **-information** (Helligkeit, Buntheit) color information (TV), (luminance, chrominance)

Farbkasten *m* inkwell **-seitenteil** *m* end plate for ink duct **-walze** *f* duct roller

Farb-kelle *f* ink slice **-kennzeichnung** *f* color coding **-kissen** *n* ink(ing) pad **-klotz** *m* ductor key **-komponente** *f* color or image component **-koordinatentransformation** *f* color-co-ordinate transformation **-kopie** *f* color print **-körper** *m* color solids, body of a paint, pigment **-korrigiert** color-corrected achromatized

Färbkraft *f* coloring power

Farb-kreide *f* colored crayon **-kreis** *m* color spectrum

Färbküpen *pl* dyeing and color vats

Farb-lampe *f* safe light **-läufer** *m* brayer, ink block, stage **-leiter** *f* color scale

Farblicht-orgel *f* device for projecting colored ornaments **-signale** *pl* (Eisenb.) colorlight signal

farblos colorless, achromatic, hueless **-es Paraffinöl** white oil

Farb-löser *m* ink medium **-losigkeit** *f* absence of color achromatism **-lösung** *f* staining solution (micros.) **-maschine** *f* padding machine **-maserung** *f* color graining **-maßsystem** *n* chromaticity scale system, color chart, CIE (Commission Internationale d'Eclairage) diagram **-matrix** *f* color matrix (TV)

Farb-menge *f* quantity of (ink) color **-meßapparat** *m* colorimeter, color-measuring apparatus **-messend** colorimetric **-messer** *m* colorimeter **-messerschraube** *f* ductor-knife screw **-messerstellschraube** *f* ink regulating screw **-messung** *f* colorimetry, color measurement **-mischer** *m* color wheel or top, color mixer (optics) **-mischmaschine** *f* color-mixing machine, paint mixer **-mischskala** *f* scale for ink mixing **-mischwerte** *pl* color mixture data

Farb-mittel *n* coloring matter **-modulator** *m* color modulator (TV) **-mühle** *f* grinder for paint **-muster** *n* color sample **-nebel** *m* paint mist **-nebelhaltig** containing paint mist **-norm** *f* color standard

Farb-paste *f* paste paint **-photographie** *f* chromophotograph **-photometrie** *f* color photometry **-präparat** *n* color material **-rad** *n*, **-rädchen** *n* ink(ing) wheel, ink disk, inking roller **-rakel** *n* color doctor **-randeffekt** *m* color fringing (TV)

Farbraster *m* color embossing **-aufnahme** *f* colorscreen photography **-platte** *f* colorscreen plate

Farb-raum *m* color space **-regulierung** *f* ink feed roller adjustment **-reibemaschien** *f* color-grinding mill, paint roller mill **-reinheitsspule** *f* color purity coil (TV) **-retusche** *f* color retouching **-richtig** orthochromatic, isochromatic **-ringsystem** *n* color cycle system **-rolle** *f*, **-röllchen** *n* ink(ing) roller, inker, inking wheel **-rührwerk** *n* ink agitator

Farb-satz *m* set of color plates **-saum** *m* color fringe **-säure** *f* color acid **-schaltfolge** *f* color sampling sequence (TV) **-schaltfrequenz** *f* color sampling (rate) frequency (TV) **-schattierung** *f* color shade **-scheibe** *f* color screen **-schirm** *m* color picture screen **-schleier** *m* chemical fog **-schlierenverfahren** *n* color schlieren method

Farbschreiber *m* Morse receiver, inker, inkwriter, writer, printer **~ mit vorgeschaltetem Relais** local inker **unmittelbar in die Leitung geschalteter ~** direct inker

Farb-schriftröhre *f* dark trace tube **-schutzüberzug** *m* coats of paint **-schwellenwert** *m* liminal value or threshold of intensity of a color **-sehprüfung** *f* chromatopsia test **-skala** *f* color chart **-spachtel** *m* palette knife, spatula **-sperre** *f* color killer (TV) **-spritzanlage** *f* spray-painting unit

Farbspritzkabine *f* paint spraying booth **~ mit Trockenabscheidung** spray booth (dry type)

Farbspritzpistole *f* paint spray gun **nebelfreie ~** smoke preventing spraying gun

Farb-stärke *f* chroma **-stichig** stained **-stift** *m* colored pencil **-stiftminen** *pl* colored pencil leads

Farbstoff *m* coloring matter or substance, dye, pigment, color, dyestuff, stain **-zusatzgefäß** *n* container (provided) for adding dye-stuffe **-zusatztrichter** *m* funnel for adding dyestuff

Farbstreifen *m* color band **-regulierung** *f* ink feed regulation

Farbstufe *f* color gradation, tint, shade **empfindungsgemäße ~** subjective chromaticity scale value

Farb-synchronisierschaltung *f* color synchronizer **-synchronsignalbasis** color burst pedestal

Farb-tafel *f* pattern-sheet **-tarnung** *f* color camouflage **-teller** *m* ink disc **-temperatur** *f* color temperature **-tisch** *m* color making table, ink slab **-toleranz** *f* color tolerance

Farbton *m* chroma (TV), color, hue, tint, shade (Farbwert und Sättigungsgrad) chromaticity (hue and saturation), (TV) **-diagramm** (aller möglichen Farbtöne) chromaticity diagram (TV) **-empfindlichkeit des Auges** chromaticity acuity (TV) **-gleiches reines Gelb** psychologically unique yellow **-karten** *pl* shade cards **-regler** *m* chroma control (TV) **-regelung** *f* color phase control **-richtig** orthochromatic

Farb-tönung *f* degree of coloring, shade, hue **-träger** *m* chrominance-carrier **-trägerunterdrücker** color killer **-treue** *f* color fidelity (of color film) **-übergang** *m* color transition (TV) **-übersättigung** *f* color overload (TV) **-überzug** *m* paint coat **-umschlag** *m* color change, color reversion, change of color, discoloration

Färbung *f* coloration, coloring, staining, dyeing, color, dye, hue **~ des Schalles** timbre, tone or sound color, quality **dunkelgetönte ~** shade

Färbungs-mittel *n* coloring agent **-schaltverfahren** color-switching procedure

Farb-unruhe *f* uneven dyeing **-unterschied** *m* color difference, color intensity (in heat-treating), dyeing difference **-unterscheidungsvermögen** *n* color-discrimination faculty **-valenz** *f* color stimulus specification **-vergleicher** *m* color comparator **-verreibtisch** *m* ink grinding table **-verreibungsversorgungsanlage** *f* ink supply **-verschmelzung** *f* color contamination

Farbwalze *f* ink roller, inker (teleg.), inking roller (print.), ink drum **-wechsel** *m* change of color iridescence, opalescence **-werk** *n* inking device **-werkschiene mit Blasrohr** *f* roller track with blowtube

Farbwert *m* chromaticity value, color value (gleichbedeutend mit dominant wavelength) hue (TV) **-regler** *m* hue control (TV) **-verschiebung** *f* color contamination (TV)

Farb-wiedergabe *f* color rendition (TV), color reproduction **-wiedergabetreue** *f* color fidelity (TV) **-zahl** *f* dye number **-zentren** *pl* Farnsworth centers **-zerstäuber** *m* aerograph, atomizer **-zufuhr** *f* ink feed **-zylinder** *m* inking cylinder

Farewell Sand *m* Farewell sand or rock, lowest rock holding oil

Farin *n* brown sugar

Farinatom *n* grain tester, section cutter for grain examination

Farnboro-Indikator *m* Farnboro indicator

Farnsworth-sche Bildfangröhre Farnsworth image dissector tube **-scher Vervielfacher** Farnsworth multiplier tube

Faschine *f* fascine, fagot, mattress (for foundations)

Faschinen-ausfüllung *f* fascine filling, fagot fitting **-bahn** *f* fascine footpath, fascine road **-bekleidung** *f* fascine revetment **-bock** *m* fascine trestle **-damm** *m* fascine dam, raised fascine road (war) **-lage** *f* fascine work **-messer** *n* brush hook, hedging bill **-packung** *f* fascines **-packwerk** *n* fascine work **-verblendung** *f* fascine revetment **-werk** *n* fascine work (hydr.)

Fase *f* chamfer, bevel

fasen to chamfer

Faser *f* streak, seam, thread, fiber, filament, grain, strand, hard vein **neutrale ~** (Festigkeitslehre) neutral axis **quer zur ~** across the grain

Faser-absaugung *f* removal of fibers by suction **-ähnlich** fiberlike, fibroid **-aragonit** *m* flos ferri **-artig** fibrous **-asbest** *m* fibrous asbestos **-bandwinkel** *m* lap, ribbon lap (first stage of drawing and combing, textiles) **-braunkohle** *f* fibrous lignite **-brei** *m* fiber slurry **-brücke** *f* filament **-büschel** *m* fiber tuft

Fäserchen *n* fibrilla

Faserdämmstoffe *pl* fibrous insulating materials

Faserfänger *m* pulp catcher **-fritte** *f* fritted glass plate provided for catching fibers **-kapsel** *f* fiber-catching capsule

Faser-festigkeit *f* strength of fiber **-flug** *m* blowing off fuzz **-förmig** fibrous, filiform **-frei** non-fibrous **-gehalt** *m* fiber yield **-gewinnung** *f* production of fibers

faserig fibrous, grained, fuzzy, fuzziness, fibery, funicular **-es Gefüge** texture, fibrous structure **-e Struktur** fibrous structure, fibriform structure, capillary structure, bacillary structure

Faserigkeit *f* fuzzy, fuzziness

Faser-kalk *m* agalite, fibrous limestone, satin spar **-kiesel** *m* fibrolite **-kohle** *f* fibrous coal (soft, humified, bituminous coal), mineral charcoal **-kreuzung** *f* decussation **-kunde** *f* technology of fibers

fasern to tease, separate thread, revel out

Faser-papier *n* mottled paper **-platte** *f* fiberboard **-prüfung** *f* fiber test **-pulver** *n* powdered fiber **-reifen** *m* fiber ring **-richtung** *f* direction of grain **-sättigung** *f* fiber saturation **-schicht** *f* surface **-seele** *f* fiber (core) **-stärke** *f* fiber strenght **-staub** *m* fiber dust **-steinkohle** *f* fibrous coal, fusain **-stoff** *m* fibrous material (chem.)

Faserstoff-beflechtung *f* fiber braid, fiber, fibrine **-gewerbe** *n* textile industry **-industrie** *f* textile industry **-kabel** *n* fibercovered cable **-technik** *f* technology of textiles **-veredlungsindustrie** *f* industry of finishing textile fibers

Faser-streifen *m* ghost line, ghost **-struktur** *f* fibering, fibrous structure, fiber structure, bacillary structure **-tonerde** *f* aluminium oxide **-torf** *m* surface peat, fibrous peat

Faserung *f* texture, fibering, fibrillation, grain

Faser-verfestigung *f* fiber hardening **-verlauf** *m* grain flow, flow lines, run of the fiber or grain **-vlies** *n* non-woven fabric **-wickel** *n* fiber lap **-zahldiagramm** *n* cumulative frequency curve

Faß *n* cask, drum, barrel, tub, vat, keg, brewer's vat, (slang) a large or capital ship **ein ~ ausreiben** to rub the pitch out of a cask **vom ~** on draught

Faßabfüllapparat *m* cask-decanting or -emptying apparatus

Fassade *f* front or façade wall

Fassaden-beleuchtung *f* flood lighting **-farben** *pl* plaster paints, stucco paints **-klinker** *m* facing clinker (brick) **-verkleidung** *f* facing

Faß-äscher *m* drum lime **-aufsatzform** *f* cask setting up or raising apparatus **-aufschlagfender** *m* barrel fender **-band** *n* cask hoop **-binden** *n* hooping **-binder** *m* cooper **-bleche** *pl* barrel sheets **-boden** *m* (cask)-head **-boje** *f* barrel buoy

Fäßchen *n* drum, small cask

Faß-daube *f* stave (barrel) **-daubenfügemaschine** *f* stave-jointing machine **-elevator** *m* barrel elevator

fassen to seize, grasp, take; (fangen) catch, apprehend, seize; (geistig) understand, grasp; (aufnehmen) hold, accommodate; (enthalten) contain; (in sich ~) include, comprise; (Werkzeug) bite, grasp, grip, catch, mount, comprehend, draw, identify, frame, get hold, embrace, set (inserted parts or precious stones)

Fassen *n* seizure, grip

Faßentleerungsvorrichtung *f* barrel drainer **tragbare ~** portable barrel drainer

Faß-färbung *f* drum dyeing **-füllstelle** *f* barreling station **-gar** drumtanned **-geläger** *n* bottoms, cask deposit or sediment **-haken** *pl* cooper's hooks **-krippe** *f* barrel cradle **-krösemaschine** *f* cask-croze or cask-groove cutting machine, cask-crozing or cask-grooving machine **-kühler** *m* drum or barrel radiator **-lager** *n* roller race **-loch** *n* bunghole

Fasson *f* form, shape, design, contour, section, cut, style, shaped **-arbeit** *f* form work **-draht** *m* special, figured, profiled, or section wire, sectional, shaped, or fashioned wire **-drehbank** *f* forming lathe, profiling lathe, screw machine **-drehen** to profile **-eisen** *n* rolled-steel member, profile iron, fashioned or figured bar iron, section(al) iron, section steel, structural steel, structural shape section **-enddruck** *m* forming end-pressure **-fräser** *m* form cutter, profile cutter **-hobelmesser** *m* beader knife or bit (plane)

Fassonier-arbeit *f* shaping, forming profiling or forming operation **-einrichtung** *f* forming or profiling attachment

fassonieren to form, shape, profile

Fassonieren *n* forming

Fassonniermaschine *f* copying machine (woodwork)

Fassonpressen *n* stamping, forming

Fassonrohr *n* adapting piece, make-up piece **vierfaches ~** four-way conduit (elec.)

Fasson-schiene *f* form plate **-schlüssel** *m* special spanner **-schmieden** *n* swage work **-schnitt** *m* forming cut **-stahl** *m* forming tool, shaping tool **-stein** *m* shape **-stifte** *pl* special nails **-stück** *n* sample, special piece **-support** *m* forming rest **-teil** *m* sectional part

Faß-schmiere *f* drum stuffing **-schraube** *f* grip screw **-picher** *m* dauber

Faßreifen *m* cask hoop, barrel hoop **-auftreibmaschine** *f* hoop-driving machine, trussing machine **-bandstahl** *m* supporting hoop for barrels

Faß-riegel *m* crossbeam of a cask **-schienen** *f pl* barrel track **-schienenklotz** *m* barrel stop **-schlupfen** to wash casks **-schwanken** to clean(se) or rinse casks **-spange** *f* cask clasp **-spangenhalter** *m* cask clasp holder **-spannkette** *f* chain to prevent expansion of store casks **-spund** *m* barrel bung, faucet **-stab** *m* cask stave **-tonne** *f* barrel buoy **-trichter** *m* barrel dash

Fassung *f* (Technik) frame, mounting, support (Wortlaut) wording, formulation, version, composure (Zeichnung) *f* chase, holder, socket, fitting, capacity, attachment, self-control, setting (jewel), lampholder, lamp socket, style, curb (general, mechanical), valve holder **~ für Kristalle** crystal (oscillator or resonator) mount or holder **~ eines Objektives** lens mounting, mount, barrel of lens or objective **~ mit Schalter** key socket **aus der ~ bringen** to upset

Fassungs-adern *pl* lamp cords **-kraft** *f* power of comprehension, capacity **-los** disconcerted, confused

Fassungs-raum *m* contents, capacity, seating capacity **-ring** *m* (Kugellager) holding ring for ball bearing **-rohr** *n* well tube **-teller** *m* bulb socket **-tragarm** *m* conennction to the lampholders **-träger** (Lampenfassung) lamp-socket holder

Fassungsvermögen *n* (carrying) capacity, equipped capacity, capacity (of a tank), tankage capacity, holding capacity, volumetric capacity **~ der Kassette** loading capacity of the magazine **gesamtes ~** total holding capacity

Faß-zwickel *m* try cock, bundle of files or of papers

fast almost, nearly **~ bedeckt** broken (meteor) **~ schlichte Abbildung** almost "schlicht" mapping (math.), conformal mapping

Fastebene *f* peneplain (geol.)

Fata Morgana *f* mirage, looming

Fatamorganabild *n* mirage

fauchen to spit and mew (like a cat), hiss (like a steam engine), make a noise like a projectile, chug

faul rotten, bad, decaying, brittle, lazy, indolent, foul (of pipes, ships) **-äscher** *m* rotten lime **-behälter** *m* septic tank **-brand** *m* smut **-bruch** *m* shortness, brittleness (met) **-brüchig** rotten, short-brittle, burnt (of a metal) **-brüchigkeit** *f* rottenness, shortness, brittleness **-flecke** *pl* stains caused by putrefaction **-gas** *n* sewage gas **-grube** *f* fermenting pit

Fäule *f* rottenness, rot, rotten hole

faulen to digest with water, rot, decay, putrefy, decompose, get rotten

Faulen *n* rotting

Faulgas *n* marsh or sewer gas, methane

Faulheit *f* idleness

Fäulnis *f* decay, putrefaction, rot, rotting, rottenness, putrefaction **-bekämpfend** antiseptic **-erreger** *m* agent of putrefaction **-hemmend** antiseptic **-hindernd** antiseptic **-sichere Farbe** *f* anti-fouling paint **-verhütend** anti-fouling preservative **-widrig** antirot, rot-preventing, antiseptic **-wirkend** putrefactive

Faulraum für Schlamm sludge-digestion tank

Faulschlamm *m* sapropel (putrid mud), sediment containing decaying organisms, sludge, debris

faulsichere Farbe *f* antifouling paint

Faust *f* fist **-achse** *f* Mercedes type of front axle, solid end axle, reversed Elliot-type axle

Fäustel *n* double-face hammer, hand hammer, mallet, hammer sledge

Faust-formel *f* rough calculation, formula for a rough approximation, rule of thumb **-hammer** *m* small hand hammer **-handschuh** *m* mitten **-hobel** *m* plane (hand or machine planes) **-leier** *f* brace, hand brace, breast borer, crank brace **-leierbohrer** *m* bitstock drill, breast drill **-regel** *f* rule of thumb, rough rule, rough-and-ready rule **-regelmethode** *f* rule-of-thumb method **-riemen** *m* bayonet knot, sword knot **-schußwaffe** *f* hand firearm **-skizze** *f* rough sketch

FAZ (Fernrufzeichen) trunk calling signal

Fazettenglas *n* beveled glass

fazettieren to bevel-edge, facet

Fazit *n* sum, result

fechten to fence, fight

Feder *f* spring, pen, feather, capacitance (elec.)

spline, key, tenon, torque, rib ~ (Bolzen) *f* spring peg ~ **für Keilnut** spring, feather, spline ~ **und Nut** tongue and groove ~ **in Nut mit planen Enden** plain feather ~ **in Nut mit runden Enden** round-ended feather **A** ~ a spring, short spring (of the jack) **B** ~ b spring (long spring)

Feder, an einer ~ angebracht spring-supported **eine ~ anspannen** to bend, tighten or tension a spring **durch eine ~ festgehalten** spring-clamped **eine ~ entspannen** to relax a spring, relieve or untension **feine ~** hairspring **gespannte ~** spring in tension **mit einem Gewicht versehene ~** weighted spring **schwache ~** spring of low rate **(eine) ~ spannen** to extend a spring

Feder-abstreifer *m* spring-mounted scraper **-achse** *f* quill gear **-achsantrieb** *m* quill-gear drive (locom.) **-angel** *f* spring hinge **-anlasser** *m* spring-type starter **-anschlag** *m* spring stop **-anschlagpuffer** *m* buffer **-anschlußklemme** *f* spring terminal plug **-antrieb** *m* spring action or activation

Feder-apparat *m* spring holder attachment **-arm** *m* dump iron **-artig** springlike, bouncing **-aufhängung** *f* spring suspension (of cars, various) **-auflage** *f* spring pad **-auge** *n* spring eye **-ausgleich** *m* balance by spring compensation **-ausgleicher** *m* spring equilibratior

Feder-balg *m* spring bellows **-balgdichtung** *f* syphon bellows **-balkenmantel** *m* spring-pole jacket **-ball** *m* shuttlecock

Federband *n* flat keep spring **-kupplung** *f* spider coupling, coil clutch, spring friction clutch **-stahl** *m* spring-steel cross bands

Feder-barometer *n* aneroid barometer **-befestigung** *f* spring connection **-befestigungsstift** *m* spring center bolt

Federbein *n* shock-absorbing strut (aviation), compression leg, spring leg, shock-absorber leg, shock or compression strut, oleo strut, parts of undercarriage enclosing springs and oil-pressure pipe **-belastet** spring-loaded **-berechnung** *f* computation of spring **-füllventil** *n* oleo strut filling valve **-stütze** *f* resilient leg support

federbelastet spring-loaded

Federblatt *n* spring leaf, leaf of a spring, spring plate **-rippe** *f* rib or spring plate **-spreizer** *m* spring leaf opener, spring separator **-werkzeug** *n* spring separator tool

Federblech *n* spring plate

Federbock *m* spring bracket (vehicle), bracket or spring carrier, spring hanger, spring clamp ~ **für Stromabnehmer** trolley base

Feder-bohrer *m* spring bit **-bolzen** *m* spring shackle bolt, hinge pin, pin bolt, spring bolt **-bremse** *f* spring brake **-bride** *f* spring stirrup, bridle or buckle, spring U clamp **-bruchsicherung** *f* prevention against spring fracure **-buchse** *f* spring bush, spring eye bushing **-büchse** *f* spring seat or clamp, spring bailer, spring bar box, eye of laminated springs **-bügel** *m* spring U bolts, spring saddle, spring clip

Federbund *m* spring shackle, spring clip **-abziehhammer** *m* spring-band dismantling or dismounting hammer **-abziehpresse** *f* press for dismounting bands from laminated springs **-aufziehpresse** *f* spring-band mounting press **-stütze** *f* spring hanger **-zapfen** *m* bearing or nipple of spring buckle

Feder-büschel *m* plume **-dämpfer** *m* concussion spring **-deckel** *m* spring cap **-deckelöler** *m* spring-lid oil cup **-deckelschmiernippel** *m* spring cap oiler **-dehnung** *f* spring extension **-dichtung** *f* spring washer **-dorn** *m* expanding mandrel **-draht** *m* spring wire **-draht-bügel** *m* spring wire bow or stirrup **-draht-relais** *n* wire spring relay

Federdruck *m* spring pressure **-hülse** *f* spring sleeve (cylinder) **-messer** *m* spring manometer **-schmierbüchse** *f* spring-compression grease cup **-sonde** *f* spring-pressure sounding apparatus

Feder-durchbiegung *f* spring deflection **-eigenschaft** *f* spring or elastic quality **-einlagen** *pl* inner springs **-einrichtung** *f* spring mechanism **-einstellung** *f* spring setting **-elastizität** *f* springiness

Federende *n* end of the spring **gerolltes ~** spring with rolled end **gestauchtes ~** spring with upset end

Feder-erz *n* feather ore, heteromorphite **-fahne** *f* feather beard **-falle** *f* spring trap **-fesselung** *f* elastic suspension **-fesselungskraft** *f* elastic or spring restraining force **-formmaschine** *f* spring bending machine **-freilauf** *m* spring free wheeling **-führend** in charge

Feder-gabel *f* spring fork **-gamasche** *f* (Federschutz) spring cover, spring gaiter **-gedämpft** spring cushioned **-gehänge** *n* spring suspension **-gehäuse** *n* spring housing **-gips** *m* fibrous gypsum **-haken** *m* spring catch or hook **-halter** *m* penholder, spring retainer **-hammer** *m* spring or dead-stroke hammer **-hängebolzen** *m* adjusting spring link or hanger **-heber** *m* spring lever or lifter

Federhand *f* spring seat, spring carrier arm (open and closed types), carrier arm of leaf spring, spring bracket ~ (vorne und hinten) dumb iron (front and back)

Federhänger *m* spring shackle

federhart springy, elastic, cold-hammered, spring hard ~ **werden** to become spring hard **-e Eigenschaft** resiliency, quality of a hard spring

Feder-härte *f* spring or elastic temper **-haus** *n* spring drum, spring barrel, spring box **-hobel** *f* dovetail plane (for grooves) **-hülse** *f* spring cage **-innentaster** *pl* inside spring calipers **-kaliber** *n* toolmaker's calipers **-kammer** *f* pocket for a valve stem or for a spring **-kappe** *f* spring cover **-kapsel** *f* spring seat or clamp **-kapselmaschine** *f* spring capping machine **-kasten** *m* spring band, buckle, shackle; pencil box **-kissen** *n* spring cushion

Feder-klammer *f* spring leaf retainer, spring clip, clamping spring **-klappe** *f* spring flap **-klappenventil** *n* spring flapper valve **-klemme** *f* (spring) clip **-klinke** *f* spring catch **-kolben** *m* firing pin, spring plunger, breechblock, end piece, spring block **-konstante** *f* force constant, elasticity constant, spring rate, spring stiffness

Feder-kontakt *m* switch jack, spring contact **-kopf** *m* magazine spring-base stud (pistol), spring stud, follower-spring stud **-korn** *n* folding-spring front sight **-kraft** *f* spring tension, elasticity, elastic force, resilience of a spring, tension, springiness **-kraftantrieb** *m* clockwork train, spring motor, clockwork (motor) drive **-kräftig** elastic **-kraftregler** *m* spring governor **-kreuz** *n* star tensioner **-krümmer** *m* spring-supported bend, camber of spring **-kufe** *f* spring skid **-kupplung** *f* spring clutch, resilient coupling **-lade** *f* flier lathe **-lager** *n* spring bearing

Federlänge *f* spring length **ungespannte ~** unloaded spring length

Feder-lasche *f* spring shackle, shackle **-laschenbolzen** *m* shackle pin **-laschentragbock** *m* spring shackle bracket **-lehre** *f* pressure gauge **-leicht** featherweight **-leiste** *f* spring contact strip (elec.) **-lot** *n* tension-spring **-luftdruckmesser** *m* aneroid barometer **-manometer** *n* spring manometer, spring-pressure gauge **-messer** *n* penknife **-messing** *n* spring brass **-motor** *m* spring-(wound) motor **-muffe** *f* spring shock absorber **-muffengehäuse** *n* spring cup

federn to be elastic, spring, feather (oars, paddles, fan blades)

Federn *n* (den Einfallswinkel ändern), feather (to change the angle of incidence)

Federnabe *f* flexible hub

Federnbündel *n* set of springs

federnd springy, elastic(al), flexible, resilient, yielding, cushioned, supple **~ eingespannt** spring-clamped **~ montiert** shock-mounted **-e Aufhängung** spring suspension **-e Fassung** *f* (v. Röhren) cushioned socket **-er Fadenführer** spring thread guide **-e Formänderung** elastic deformation **-er Futterring** spring collet **-er Greifer** spring gripper

federnd-e Haltevorrichtung spring bar **-er Kontakt** flexible contact, spring contact, contact spring **-es Lager** spring bearing **-e Leitrolle** spring-loaded idler **-e Nase** elastic shoulder (lug) **-e Platte** diaphragm

federnd-e Röhrenfassung cushioned tube holder or socket **-er Röhrenhalter** cushioned tube holder or socket, antimicrophonic valve holder **-e Spannpatrone** spring collet **-er Tisch** springy stage **-e Unterlagscheibe** spring washer **-er Zahn** ratchet spring **-e Zahnscheibe** toothed spring disk

Federn-paket *n* spring pile, bank, set of springs **-paketkupplung** *f* laminated-spring coupling **-satz** *m* spring assembly, spring bank

Feder-nute *f* spline, groove **-öler** *m* spring lubricator **-platte** *f* spring plate, membrane **-plattengehäuse** *n* diaphragm case **-plattenventil** *n* leaf valve (referring to the leaf) **-pose** *f* quill **-prüfapparat** *m* spring-testing apparatus **-prüfmaschine** *f* spring-testing machine **-pufferhalter** *m* socket plate for rubber pad

Feder-rad *n* spring pulley **-raster** *m* spring catch, spring detent **-regler** *m* spring-loaded governor **-regulator** *m* spring governor **-riegel** *m* jack latch **-ring** *m* spring washer, lock washer, spring ring, grower, split lock washer **-rohr** *n* expansion pipe, bourdon tube **-rohrbogen** *m* expansion U bend (steam pipes) **-rollenlager** *n* spring roller bearing **-rost** *m* spring catch **-sattel** *m* spring-pivot seat **-satz** *m* spring assembly, spring bank **-säulensatz** *m* spring guide

Feder-schalter *m* clip-spring switch, snap switch, spring-controlled switch, switch with spring contacts **-scharnier** *n* spring hinge **-scheibe** *f* spring plate, lock washer (spring washer) **-schelle** *f* spring fastener **-schiene** *f* needle-spring slide **-schlagstuhl** *m* spring pick loom

Feder-schloß *n* spring lock (doors), latch lock **-schmierapparat** *m* spring lubricator **-schmierbüchse** *f* spring-compression grease cup, spring lubricator **-schmierkeil** *m* spring lubrication key **-schneide** *f* spring cutters **-schnepper** *m* spring trigger **-schraube** *f* spring bolt **-schraubvisier** *n* adjustable spring rear sight **-schuh** *m* spring extremity shoe or piece **-schutz** *m* spring gaiter **-schutzgamasche** *f* spring protecting sleeve **-schutzhülle** *f* spring gaiter

Feder-seite *f* spring end (side) **-sitz** *m* spring perch, spring seat **-sitzscheibe** *f* spring-seating washer **-skizze** *f* pen-and-ink sketch

Federspann-griff *m* spring-stretching handle **motor** *m* clockwork (motor) **-platte** *f* spring clamp plate **-schraube** *f* tension screw, spring tensioning screw **-werk** *n* spring resetting gear

Federspannung *f* tension of spring, spring tension **unter ~ stehend** spring-loaded

Federspeicher-bremse *f* (automatic safety brake, spring-loaded brake **-bremszylinder** *m* spring-loaded brake cylinder, automatic safety brake cylinder

Feder-spiel *n* range or play of spring **-spitze** *f* nib point **-spitzzirkel** *m* spring dividers **-splint** *m* spring cotter pin **-sporn** *m* folding-tail spade, sprung tail skid **-stabstahl** *m* spring steel bar

Federstahl *m* spring steel, turner's spring tool **-band** *n* spring steel band or strip **-draht** *m* spring wire **-drahtgewebe** *f* spring-steel wire gauze

Feder-stange *f* spring rod (bolt), guide rod, spring pole **-steife** *f* spring rate **-steifigkeit** *f* rigidity of the spring **-stift** *m* spring pin, spring eye bolt **-stoßdämpfer** *m* shock absorber (spring type) **-stoßfänger** *m* spring shock absorber

Feder-strebe *f* flexible spar, telescopic leg (aviation), shock-absorber leg, compression strut **-strich** *m* stroke of the pen **-stuhl** *m* carrier arm of leaf spring, spring hanger **-stütze** *f* thrust pin **-stützenführung** *f* spring hanger guide

Feder-taster *m* spring calipers **-teilzirkel** *m* spring dividers **-teller** *m* spring washer, spring rest, spring guide, helical spring plate, spring cap or collar, valve spring retainer **-topfantrieb** *m* quill-gear drive **-träger** *m* spring support **-tragzapfen** *m* spring bracket **-trommel** *f* spring drum, spring barrel **-tülle** *f* spring sleeve **-uhrwerk** *n* spring-driven clock-work

Federung *f* springiness, springing, spring, elasticity (of flexure), deflection property, spring action, (spring) suspension, compliance, mechanical capacitance **~ mit Quer- und Längsfedern** three point spring suspension, platform spring

Federungs-arbeit *f* work of elastic strain cushioning action **-art** *f* spring suspension **-blech** *n* bellows **-block** *m* bellows, elastic diaphragm (jet) **-charakteristik** *f* spring characteristic **-grenze** *f* yield point (according to application) **-körper** *m* metal bellows **-kraft** *f* force of spring, elasticity **-vermögen** *n* springiness, resilience **-weg** *m* travel stroke **-widerstand** *m* compliance, mechanical capacitance **-zustand** *m* state of suspension

Feder-unterbrecher *m* spring operated breaker

-**unterlegscheibe** *f* spring washer -**verkleidung** *f* spring cover -**verschlußbolzen** *m* spring couple pin, spring dynamometer -**verstellmotor** *m* spring adjusting motor -**visier** *n* spring leaf sight -**vorholer** *m* spring counterrecoil mechanism, spring recuperator -**waage** *f* spring balance, balance spring, spring dynamometer, spring scale -**walzenmühle** *f* spring roller mill

Federweg *m* pitch of spring, travel stroke, telescopic shock course (said of springs), spring deflection, spring excursion or elongation **großer** ~ long course

Feder-weiche *f* switch with spring tongs -**weiß** *n* French chalk, soap stone -**welle** *f* flexible spindle -**werk** *n* spring mechanism -**wickelmaschine** *f* coiling machine -**wickelvorrichtung** *f* spring winding device -**widerlager** *n* bearing bracket for spring bar -**wiege** *f* spring hanger or cradle -**windung** *f* coil or turn of the spring -**wirbel** *n* spring swivel -**wirkung** *f* spring action or reaction, springiness -**wolke** *f* cirrus cloud, mare's-tail -**wulst** *f* ridged or raised end

Federzahn-egge *f* spring-tooth harrow -**kultivator** *m* spring-tooth cultivator -**sätze** *pl* spring-tooth gangs

Feder-zange *f* pincers, tweezers, small nippers (jeweler's), spring pliers -**zeichnung** *f* pen and ink drawing -**zirkel** *m* spring compasses, spring divider -**zug** *m* stroke, flourish (of pen) -**zwischenlage** *f* intermediate spring leaf

Federzylinder *m* spring housing (gun)

fedrig elastic, flexible

Fedrigkeit *f* elasticity, flexibility

Feeder *m* feeder, delivery mechanism (on a glass furnace), transmission line

Fegesand *m* scouring sand

Fegsel *n* sweppings

Fehl-abgleichung *f* faulty alignment, misalignment -**anflug** *m* missed approach -**anpassung** *f* mismatching, defective focus -**anpassungsfaktor** *m* mismatching factor, reflection factor, transition factor -**anpassungszeiger** *m* reflectometer -**anruf** *m* false-start call, permanent signal, lost call -**anweisung** *f* incorrect indication or reading, misreading -**anzeige** *f* negative report, mistaken indication blank, nil return, indication error (rdr)

Fehl-arbeit *f* wrong work -**art** *f* type of fault (radar) -**ausrichtung** *f* misalignment -**band** *n* imperfect tape -**bar** fallible -**bauerscheinung** *f* mosaic structure (of metal crystals) -**bedarf** *m* deficiency -**bedienungsrelais** *n* wrong connection indicating relay -**belegung** *f* false seizure (tel.) -**bestand** *m* shortage discrepancy -**betrag** *m* deficiency, deficit, shortage, loss

Fehl-boden *m* sound floor, false ceiling or floor -**bogen** *m* imperfect sheet -**bohrung** *f* failure to drill oil -**druck** *m* misprint, error -**drucken** to misprint -**einsatz** *m* abortive sortie -**einstellung** *f* misadjustment, wrong setting -**eintragung** *f* erroneous entry

fehlen to fail, miss, be absent, err, lack

Fehlen *n* failure, defect, shutting down, stoppage

Fehlentfernung *f* miss distance

Fehler *m* (Mangel) shortcoming, defect; (Makel) blemish, flaw; (Technik) defect, fault, flaw, miss; (Versehen) mistake; (Irrtum) error, blunder; (Mangel) deficiency, shortcoming, defect, imperfection; (Nachteil) drawback, disadvantage; (Ungenauigkeit) incorrectness, inaccuracy, failure, (in wood) balk, distortion, aberration (in lenses), trouble (in circuits) ~ **in einem Amt** exchange troubles ~ **in der Gebührenberechnung** mistake in charging ~ **auf einer Leitung** fault on a line

Fehler, ~ **beheben** rectify trouble, clear faults ~ **beseitigen** to remove faults ~ **eingrenzen** to locate faults ~ **suchen** to trace faults **chromatischer** ~ chromatic aberration **mittlerer** ~ mean error, mean value (cost) **stroboskopischer** ~ stroboscopic aberration **wahrscheinlicher** ~ probable error **zulässiger** ~ allowable error

Fehler-abgleichsmethode *f* consumation of error -**abschätzung** *f* estimation of errors -**ader** *f* faulty wire -**anzeigefeld** *n* leakage-indicator panel -**anzeigelampe** *f* error-indicator light -**ausgleichsrechnung** *f* computation of an adjustment -**ausgleichung** *f* adjustment of observations, compensation of errors -**beseitigung** *f* removal of faults, curing or elimination of errors or of defects -**anzeige** *f* (selbsttätige) automatic error detection -**ausgleichung** *f* adjustment of errors -**begrenzung** *f* limit of error -**berichtigung** *f* correction of error -**bestimmung** *f* error determination

Fehler-dämpfung *f* return loss, balance attenuation -**dreieck** *n* triangle of error -**einfluß** *m* effect of errors -**einflußzahl** *f* weight of an error (math.) -**eingrenzung** *f* fault location, fault localization, tracking down seat or source of interference or trouble, localizing trouble, fault sectionalizing -**ellipsoid** *n* ellipsoid of error -**errechnung** *f* error-finding calculation -**fortpflanzung** *f* error propagation

fehlerfrei faultless, sound, perfect, unflawed, accurate, correct, free from flaws, faults, or defects, unmarred, aplanatic (free from spherical aberration), aberrationless (of a lens) **fast** ~ without appreciable error

Fehler-freiheit *f* accuracy -**funktion** *f* error function, error equation -**gesetz** *n* normal law of errors -**gewicht** *n* weight of an error (math.) -**gleichung** *f* observational equation, working equation, error equation -**glocke** *f* automatic trouble signal -**grenze** *f* limit of error, permissible variation -**größe** *f* magnitude of error

fehlerhaft defective, faulty, unsound, incorrect, erroneous, imperfect, flawed, vicious, impaired, having flaws -**e Ablesung** (eines Meßgerätes), error reading

Fehler-integral *n* error function, error integral -**lampe** *f* trouble localizer light -**linie** *f* curve of error -**los** perfect, flawless -**losigkeit** *f* soundness, exactitude -**matrix** *f* error matrix -**methode** *f* trial and and error method

Fehlerort, ~ **an unterirdischen Kabeln** cable fault or puncture -**bestimmung** *f* localization of a fault -**meßbrücke** *f* fault-localizing bridge -**messung** *f* fault-location test, localization test

Fehler-orthogonalität *f* orthogonality of error -**ortung** *f* fault locating -**ortungsgerät** *n* line fault locator -**probe** *f* blot test -**prüfgerät** *n* defects detecting device -**quadratmethode** *f* least squares method -**quelle** *f* source of error -**scheibchen** *n* circle of confusion, apertural effect

Fehlerscheinung *f* defect (phenomenon)
Fehlerschutz *m* leakage protection **-einrichtung** *f* fault-clearing device
Fehlerstelle *f* place of error **mit ~ behaftet** unsound
Fehler (Störungs)quelle *f* source of error (disturbance)
Fehler-strecke *f* faulty section **-strom** *m* fault current **-stromschutzschalter** *m* earth-leakage circuit breaker **-suche** *f* error detection **-suchen** *n* error detection, faulting **-sucher** *m* aniseikon, electronic crack detector, electromagnetic flaw detector, magnaflux inspection means **-suchgerät** *n* trouble shooter **-suchprogramm** *n* diagnostic routine **-suchtabelle** *f* adjustment instructions
Fehlertafel *f* error chart, table of errors **graphische ~** graph of errors, diagram of errors
Fehler-tiefenbestimmung *f* depth determination of flaws, stereoscopic radiography for locating defects **-toleranz** *f* tolerance (of error) **-verteilungskurve** *f* error-distribution curve **-widerstand** *m* fault resistance **-winkel** *m* angle of deviation **-zettel** *m* (minor) repair slip
Fehl-farbe *f* off color **-feuerung** *f* misfire **-fuß** *m* throwout, reject **-gänger** *m* miss **-gehen** to miss one's way, err, fail **-geleiteter Spruch** misrouted message
fehlgeordnet disordered (crystal) **ideal ~** ideally imperfect (crystal)
Fehl-gewicht *n* shortweight **-griff** *m* blunder, mistake, error of judgment, wrong manipulation **-guß** *m* spoiled casting **-gußstück** *n* waster casting, waste casting, misrun casting, faulty casting
Fehl-handlung *f* blunder, wrong action, mistake **-investitionen** *pl* misapplied or misdirected investments **-klassieren** to mis-classify **-lage** *f* angular deviation **-leistung** *f* malfunction **-leiten** to misroute **-leitung** *f* misrouting **-messung** *f* incorrect (erroneous) measurement
Fehlordung *f* (lattice) disorder **~ durch Fremdatome** substitutional disorder
Fehlordnungerscheinung, thermische ~ formation of holes (cryst)
Fehlordnungs-korrelationen *pl* disorder correlations **-stelle** *f* lattice defect or imperfection, irregularity, distortion atom **-streuung** *f* disorder scattering
Fehl-ort *m* location of a fault (radar) **-prägung** *f* faulty stamping **-reaktion** *f* wrong reaction **-rechnung** *f* miscalculation **-schaltung** *f* wrong connection, faulty control **-schlagen** to fail, prove a failure, miscarry **-schnitt** *m* faulty cut **-schritt** *m* misstep, faux pas, trespass, transgression **-schuß** *m* misfire, miss, misconclusion, wrong inference **-schweißung** *f* defective or unsound weld
fehlsichtig ametropic, defectively sighted **-es Auge** defectively sighted eye, ametropic eye
Fehl-sichtigkeit *f* defect or deficiency of sight **-startentriegelung** *f* false start release **-startrelais** *f* false start relay **-stelle** *f* gap, flow, location of error or defect (in casting), defect, fault, crack, blowhole, deficiency, imperfection **-stellen** *n* failure **-stellenbehandlung** *f* defect treatment **-stellenerzeugung** *f* defect generation **Fehl-stoß** *m* spurious pulse **-strom** (Relais) non-operate current **-strom** *m* minimum operating current, failing current **-teil** *m* missing or deficient part **-treffer** *m* near miss **-treten** to trip, stumble, slip **-tritt** *m* misstep, stumble, slip
Fehl-überdeckung *f* (der Farben auf dem Bildschirm) misregistration (TV) **-verbindung** *f* defective joint **-weisung** *f* direction-finding error, errors in taking bearings **-winkel** *m* phase-displacement angle, shift angle **-wurf** *m* miss (cast) **-zerspringer** *m* weak burst **-zünden** to misfire
Fehlzündung *f* backfire, misfire (ignition), misfiring, backlash, failure to fire or ignite (rectifier, ignitron) **Motor mit Fehlzündungen** balky engine
Fehn *n* peat locality, peat deposit
Feilbank *f* bench (mach.) **-bar** machinable **-block** *m* filing block **-bürste** *f* wire brush
Feile *f* file, ratchet **eine ~ aufhauen** to recut a file **eine ~ verschmieren** to choke teeth of a file **dickflache ~** cotter or pillar file **einhiebige ~** single-cut file
feilen to file
Feilen *n* shaping **-angel** *f* file tang **-aufhauen** *n* file cutting anew **-bürste** *f* file cleaner, file brush, file card **-hart** file-hard
Feilen-härte *f* file hardness **-haue** *f* file-cutting tool **-hauer** *m* file cutter
Feilen-hauermeißel *m* file-cutting chisel **-haumaschine** *f* file cutting machine **-heft** *n* file handle **-hieb** *m* cut of file **-karde** *f*, **-kratzbürste** *f* file cleaners **-probe** *f* file test **-prüfmaschine** *f* file-testing machine **-stahl** *m* file steel **-strich** *m* touch
Feil-futter *n* filling block or board **-halten** *n* delivery on sale (of goods), exposing or exhibiting for sale **-hieb** *m* notch **-holz** *n* filling block or board
Feilicht *n* filings, filing dust
Feil-kloben *m* hand vise, pin vise, filing vise **-kluppe** *f* sloping clamp **-maschine** *f* shaper **-maschinenfeile** *f* file for filing machines **-scheibe** *f* circular file
Feilsel *n* filings, filing dust
Feil-späne *pl* filings **-staub** *m* file dust, filings **-strich** *m*, **-stück** *n* file stroke
fein delicate, fine, refined **~ regelbar** accurately controllable **~ verteilt** highly dispersed, finely distributed **-er Regen** drizzle **-er Sand** close sand
Fein-abgleich *m* vernier tuning, precision adjustment **-ablauf** *m* high green sirup **-abstimmung** *f* fine tuning, sharp tuning, vernier control **-abtastung** *f* close scanning **-antrieb** *m* vernier drive **-anzeige** *f* microindication **-arbeit** *f* fine work, (re)fining **-ätzung** *f* fine etching **-ausrüstung** *f* (Kessel) fittings **-bereichsbeugung** *f* selected area diffraction, fine range diffraction
Feinbewegung *f* slow motion, fine motion **endlose ~** continuous screw feature
Feinbewegungsschraube *f* slow-motion screw
Feinblech *n* thin (under 4.5 mm.) metal plate, thin-gauge plate, sheet, thin plate or sheet **-anlage** *f* sheet mill **-gerüst** *n* sheet-mill stand **-straße** *f* sheet-rolling train or mill **-walze** *f* sheet roll **-walzerei** *f* sheet rolling **-walzwerke** *n pl* (thin-)sheet-rolling mill, sheet mills
Fein-bohrblock *m* fine boring block, precision boring machine **-bohren** *n* precision drilling

Feinbohr-maschine *f* precision drill **-messer** *n* fineboring tool **-stahl** *m* precision cutter **-werk** *n* fineboring machine

Fein-brecher *m* fine crusher **-brennen** *n* refining (met) **-bruch** *m* fine granulation **-bürsten** *pl* fine brushes **-dessiniert(e) (Oberfläche)** finely figured (surface) **-dispers** finely dispersed

Feindraht *m* fine wire, small-gauge wire **-führer** *m* fine wire guide **-wickelmaschine** *f* fine wire coil winding machine

Fein-drehbank *f* precision turning lathe **-drehen** *n* precision turning

Feindruck-manometer *n* micromanometer **-messer** *m* differential manometer, multiplying manometer, micromanometer

Feine *n* fineness ~ *pl* fines

fein-einstellen to adjust carefully **-einstellen** *n* finest adjustment **-einsteller** *m* vernier

Feineinstell-kondensator *m* vernier control condenser, vernier tuning condenser **-schraube** *f* fine-adjusting screw **-skala** *f* micrometer scale

Feineinstellung *f* microadjustment device, fine tuning or setting, precision adjustment, fine control or adjustment, vernier (dial) adjustment or tuning

Feineisen *n* refined iron, light-section steel **-straße** *f* rolling train for light sections, small-section mill train **-walzwerk** *n* mill for rolling light sections

feinen to refine, purify, fine

Feinen *n* refining

Feinentzerrer *m* twist equalizer

Feinern *n* refining (of steel)

Feinerz *n* fine ore **-ofen** *m* fine-ore furnace

Fein-faserig fine-fibrous, fine-fibered, fine-grained **-feile** *f* fine file **-feuer** *n* finery fire, finery hearth, knobbling fire, refinery **-filter** *n* fine-mesh filter **-filterschichten** *pl* fine filter sheets **-filtrierender Anteil** fine-filtering component **-fleier** *m* finishing fly frame **-fluten** fine adjustment for flooding (submarines)

Feinfokus *m* fractional focus **-durchleuchtungsgeräte** *pl* fine focus diaphanoscopes

Fein-förderkohle *f* fine small coal **-fühlig** delicately sensitive **-fühligkeit** *f* sensitiveness **-fühligkeit der Bremse** sensitivity (responsiveness or smoothness) of the brake **-gang** (Elektrozug) *m* creeping speed, inching speed **-gefüge** *f* fine structure, microstructure **-gehalt** *m* standard, fineness **-gehaltstempel** *m* hallmark **-gemahlen** powdered

Feingemisch *n* lean mixture **stärkstes** ~ (von Brennstoff und Luft) lean best power mixture

fein-geriffelt finely fluted **-gesiebt** fine-screened **-gestuft** fine progression **-gepulvert** finely powdered, pulverized, comminuted, or atomized **-gesiebt** fine screened **-gewebe** *n* tissue **-gewinde** *n* fine thread, small work **-gewindeschraube** *f* finely threaded screw **-gewindespindel** *f* fine pitch screw **-gezähnte Säge** fine-toothed saw

Fein-gießtechnik *f* investment casting **-gips** *m* finely-ground gypsum, land plaster **-gleitung** *f* microslip **-gliedrig** of short pitch (said of tracks) **-gold** *n* refined or pure gold **-goldgewicht** *n* gold carat

fein-grob Höhenmesser sensitive-coarse altimeter

Fein-guß *m* high quality castings **-gut** *n* refined or good material

Feinheit *f* refinement (as ingenious detail); (des Bildes) detail or (degree of) definition of picture or image ~ (des Kornes) fineness, grist, size

Feinheiten *pl* fine details

Feinheits-bezeichnung des Streichwollgarns sizing of the carded yarn **-grad** *m* degree of fineness **-koeffizient** *m* fineness coefficient **-messer** *m* granulometer **-probe** *f* fineness test **-stufe** *f* fineness grade **-nummer** *f* count or number (of yarn)

Fein-herd *m* refining hearth **-hieb** *m* finishing cut **-höhenmeßeinrichtung** *f* precision heightmeasuring device **-höhenmesser** *m* statoscope, sensitive or precision altimeter, (aneroid) barometer measuring atmospheric pressure at airdrome not reduced to sea level **-horizontierung** *f* accurate levelling **-hubsteuerung** *f* precision hoist **-hubwerk** *n* precision hoisting gear **-intervall** *n* smallest interval **-justieren** to adjust finely **-kennung** *f* fine beam (in radio-controlled navigation)

Feinkartonage *f* fine cardboard box

Feinkohle *f* fine coal, small coal, coal slack, slack, coal dust, fines, screenings, silt, duff, fine smudge **gewaschene** ~ fine small duff **ungewaschene** ~ unwashed slack

Fein-kohlensumpf *m* fine-coal sump **-koks** *m* rubbly culm coke **-kontakt** *m* precision contact

Fein-korn *n* fine grain, fine sight **-eisen** *n* fine-grained iron, close-grained iron **-entwickler** *m* fine-grain developer **-film** *m* fine-grain film **-grenzen-Wanderung** *f* subgrain growth **-guß** *m* close-grained cast iron **-puddeln** *n* puddling of fine-grained iron **-setzmaschine** *f* fine-grain washing machine

feinkörnig fine-granular, close-grained, fine-grained, compact-grained **-er Sandstein** grit-stone

Fein-körnigkeit *f* fine-grain quality **-kornmaschine** *f* fine coal jig **-krempel** *m* finishing carder (textiles) **-kristallin(isch)** finely crystalline, compact-grained

Fein-kupfer *n* refined copper **-lagerung** *f* very small bearing, instrument bearing **-leinen** *n* fine linen **-leinwandweber** *m* lawn or cambric weaver **-lunker** *m* pinhole **-lunkerung** *f* porosity **-machen** *n* refining **-mahlanlage** *f* grinding plant

feinmahlen to pulverize, powder, grind fine, triturate

Fein-mahlen *n* fine grinding, pulverizing, powdering, fine crushing, brushing, brushout **-mahlgut** *n* material to be pulverized **-mahlung** *f* fine grinding **-maschig** fine-meshed **-mechanik** *f* precision or fine mechanics

Feinmechaniker-bohrmaschine *f* mechanic's drilling machine **-drehbank** *f* precision lathe **-tischdrehbank** *f* mechanic's bench lathe **-werkzeuge** *pl* mechanic's tools

feinmechanisch precision **-e Arbeit** precise mechanical work

Feinmeßdiagramm *n* stress-strain diagram

feinmessen to measure accurately

Feinmesser *m* micrometer

Feinmeß-geräte *pl* precision measuring instruments **-lehre** *f* micrometer caliper or gauge **-manometer** *n* sensitive pressure gauge **-raum** *m* view room **-schieber** *m* micrometer slide

-schraube *f* micrometer-gauge screw **-schraublehre** *f* micrometer calipers, micrometer caliper gauge **-tiefenlehre** *f* micrometer depth gauge

Fein-messung *f* precision measurement, micrometric measurement **-metall** *n* refined metal **-mühle** *f* pulveriser **-nivellierlatte** *f* high-precision leveling staff **-ofen** *m* finery hearth, refining furnace **-ortung** *f* accurate scanning

Fein-papier *n* bond paper **-papiermaschine** *f* highgrade paper machine **-passung** *f* free fit **-porig** fine-pored, finely porous, fine-grained **-profilierung** *f* fine section **-prozeß** *m* refining process **-puddeln** *n* refining puddling **-pulverig** pulverulent

Fein-raspel *f* fine rasp, grater file **-rasterung** *f* high-definition scan (of picture) **-rastig** with fine screen **-regelstab** *m* fine-regulating rod **-regelung** *f* fine regulation, vernier control **-regelungsorgan** *n* micromanipulator **-regler** *m* precision regulator **-regulierung** *f* sharp tuning (of radio), precision adjustment **-richtung** *f* fine adjustment

Fein-säge *f* sash saw **-scheren** to shear fine **-schlacke** *f* refinery slag **-schlag** *m* fines **-schleifen** *n* precision grinding, fine polishing **-schlichten** *n* fine finishing **-schlichtfeile** *f* superfine or dead-smooth file **-schliff** *m* finishing **-schnittkreissägemaschine** *f* circular saw for thin boards

Fein-schraube *f* fine adjustment screw **-schraublehre** *f* micrometer screw gauge **-schrot** *n* fine grist **-schuppige magnetische Struktur** fine-scaled magnetic structure **-sehrohr** *n* microscope **-sicherung** *f* heat coil, microfuse, glow-tube type, etc., of lighting arrestor, fine-wire fuse

Feinsicherungs-einsatz *m*, **-patrone** *f* heat coil (fuse)

Fein-sieb *n* fine or finishing screen **-silber** *n* refined or pure silver **-sinn** *m* tact, delicacy **-skala** *f* precision scale **-spaltmaschine** *f* fine splitting machine **-spannungsschutz** *m* low-current protector (teleg.) **-spindelbank** *f* finishing flier frame (textiles) **-spinnmaschine** *f* finishing machine, spinning frame **-spinnverzug** *m* spinning draft **-spitzen** to (point) sharpen **-splitt** *m* stone chippings **-sprit** *m* rectified alcohol

Feinstahl *m* double-refined steel **-walzwerk** *n* small section rolling mill

Feinstbearbeitung *f* microfinish

Feinst-bearbeitungsmaschine *f* superfinishing machine **-bohrwerke** *pl* super-finish boring mills **-dispers** most finely dispersed **-dreharbeiten** *f* precision turning (tools) **-drehbänke** *pl* super-finishing lathes **-drehen** *n* superfinish turning

Feinstein *m* refined garnierite for gaining copper

Feinsteinstellung *f* micrometer setting or adjustment

Feinsteinzeug *n* fine stoneware

feinstellen to adjust

Fein-stellen *n* fine adjustment (of a tool or cutter) **-steller** *m* vernier (arrangement)

Feinstell-schraube *f* micrometer screw (gauge), finely adjusting screw, vernier **-skala** *f* slow-motion dial, vernier dial **-spindel** *f* fine adjustment screw **-trieb** *m* precision-adjustment drive

Feinstellung *f* fine adjustment (of a tool or cutter)

Feinstellvorrichtung *f* vernier (arrangement), fine adjustment device

Feinsteuer-druckhalter *m* precision load regulator **-ventil** *f* precision control valve

Feinst-filter *n* superfine (very fine) filter **-fräsmaschine** *f* precision milling machine **-mahlung** *f* pulverization **-mahlvorrichtung** *f* micronizer

Feinstrahl-anordnung *f* (Elektronen) high resolution camera **-kondensor** *m* precision ray condenser **-methode** *f* microbial technique

Fein-straßen *pl* small section mills **-strecker** *m* fine drawer **-streifig** laminated

Feinstruktur *f* microstructure, fine structure **-aufspaltung** *f* fine stucture splitting **-dublett** *n* fine structure doublet **-quantenzahl** *f* fine quantum number **-untersuchung** *f* microscopy

feinst-schleifen to microfinish, superfinish **-schleifen** *n* super-finish grinding

Feinstufenregelung *f* sensitive control

feinstufig delicately stepped, sensitive **-e Ausführung** delicately stepped type **-e Regulierung** sensitive control

Feinstziehschleifen *n* superfinish(ing)

Feintaster *m* sensitive tracer **-gehäuse** *n* tracer housing **-weg** *m* tracer travel

Fein-teilkreis *m* fine graduated circle **-teilung** *f* micrometer scale **-treiben** *n* refining **-trieb** *m* fine motion **-trennung** *f* sensitivity of selection (in tuning)

Fein- und Mittelblechbearbeitung *f* thin and medium sheet metal working

Feinung *f* refining

Feinungs-periode *f* refining period, deoxidation period **-schlacke** *f* final slag

Fein-vakuum *n* medium-high vacuum range **-verschiebung** *f* fine displacement **-verstellbarer Schlitten** micrometer adjustment slide

Feinverstellung, Klemmung der ~ clamp for fine adjustment **~** (der Schrauben) *f* micrometer adjustment

fein-verteilt finely divided, in continuous phase (aviation) **-verteilung des Eisens** fine division **-vorschub** *m* fine feed **-werktechnik** *f* precision engineering **-walze** *f* finishing rolling mills **-walzen** *n* fine crushing **-walzwerk** *n* finishing rolls **-wanderung** *f* metal migration **-zellig** fine-celled **-zerkleinern** *n* fine grinding or crushing, comminution, finely dividing **-zerkleinerung** *f* fine grinding, fine crushing, regrinding, grinding **-zerkleinerungsmühle** *f* grinding mill **-zerreibemaschine** *f* **für Farben und Lacke** machine for rasping colors, paints, and varnishes to perfect fineness **-zerteilt** finely divided

Feinzeug *n* stuff **-holländer** *m* beating engine, beater, finisher (paper mfg.)

Fein-ziehschleifen *n* superfinishing precision honing **-ziehschleifmaschine** *f* superhoning machine **-zink** *m* high-grade zinc **-zinn** *n* fine or ringing or sonorous tin **-zug** *m* finishing pass (drawing), finishing block, finishing die **-zustellung** *f* screw-type spindle depth stop

Feld *n* array (info proc.), field; (Grund) ground, soil; (Füllung) panel, compartment; (Gebiet) domain, field, department, zone, section, battlefield, bay, panel, span, country, scope, sphere, land (of rifling), division, partition, pane, frame (film pictures); **~** (Fläche) **der Flossen** fin area (aviation) **~ eines Fachwerk-**

trägers panel of a trussed beam **das ~ behaupten** to control the field

Feld, äußeres ~ extraneous field **bewegliches ~** moving field **elektrostatisches ~** electrostatic field, static field **erdmagnetisches ~** terrestrial magnetic field, earth's magnetic field, geomagnetic field **feststehendes ~** fixed field **freies ~** unproclaimed ground (min.) **das lange ~ des Rohrs** chase of the gun barrel **offenes ~** uncovered part of a slab or tile **quellenfreies ~** solenoidal field **ruhendes ~** fixed field, static field **schwingendes ~** oscillating field, oscillatory field

Feld, totes ~ dead zone (of ribbon microphone) plane of ribbon **überlagertes ~** super(im)-posed field **umlaufendes ~** rotating field, rotary field **unausgerichtetes ~** reserves, unworked country (min.) **veränderliches ~** variable field **wanderndes ~** moving field, traveling field **wanderndes ~, aus zwei senkrechten Komponenten** quadrature field **wirbelfreies ~** irrotational field **wölbungsfreies ~** flattened field **zusammengesetztes ~** composite field **~** (eines Linienfeldes) **in Felder unterteilen** to panel

Feld-abhängigkeit *f* field dependence **-amperemeter** *n* field ammeter **-anlasser** *m* field starter **-arbeit** *f* field work, groundwork **-arbeiter** *m* farm laborer **-ausgleichwicklung** *f* field compensating winding **-berechnung** *f* computation of field **-bereinigung** *f* land amalgamation **-besteck** *n* field (instrument) case **-bild** *n* field map (physics) field pattern **-bild der Materie** field aspect of matter **-bogen** *m* high-field-emission arc

Feld-desorption *f* field desorption **-ecken** *pl* corners of the field **-durchgriff** *m* action of field through aperture lens (optics) **-ebenungslinse** *f* field flattener (optics) **-einsatz** *m* field work **-eisenbahn** *f* field railroad, narrow-gauge railroad

Feldelektronen *pl* field electrons **-emission** *f* autoelectronic, cold, or field emission

Feld-element *n* field cell, cell for field telegraph **-entwässerung** *f* marsh drying **-entregungsschalter** *m* field de-excitation switch

Felder *pl* lands, fields **~ und Züge** flats and grooves in rifling of barrel, lands and grooves

Feld-bau *m* paneling **-decke** *f* ceiling with bays, coffered ceiling **-einschnitt** *m* marking **-einteilung** *f* division in squares **-feile** *f* file for removing burred edges of rifling

Felder-latte *f* checkerboard staff **-quetschung** *f* burred edges of barrel rifling

Felderregerspule *f* field (exciting) coil

Felderregung *f* field excitation

Felderscheibe *f* target divided into squares

Feldes-breite *f* breast, breast side of work **-länge** *f* length, run

Feld-exponent *m* field index **-fahrzeug** *n* field vehicle

Feldfernkabel *n* two-strand field cable, field trunk cable or wire **-kraftwagen** *m* field-trunk-cable-truck **-trupp** *m* wire-laying detail for placing two-strand field cable, wire-laying team

Feldfern-schreiber *m* portable teletype **-sprecher** *m* field telephone

Feld-flasche *f* canteen **-flußkabel** *n* field subfluvial cable **-folgesystem** *n* field sequential system **-frei** field-free **-funkentelegraphie** *f* military (service) radio telegraphy, noncivilian wireless **-funksprecher** *m* field radio telephone, portable radio, walkie-talkie, field radio set **-funksprechgerät** *n* field radio set

Feld-gerät *n* field implements, field equipment **-gleichungen** *f pl* Maxwell's equations, equations of field **-handapparat** *m* field handset, war telephone handset

Feld-induktionsspule *f* flip coil **-instandsetzung** *f* line maintenance **-intensität** *f* field intensity, intensity of fild, field strength, strenght of field **-ionenemission** *f* field ion emission **-ionenmassenspektroskopie** *f* field ion mass spectroscopy **-justiervorrichtung** *f* field adjusting device (phot.)

Feldkabel *n* field cable **-ader** *f* field-wire strand **-bau** *m* laying of field cables, field-wire laying **-leitung** *f* field-cable line, field-wire line

Feld-kappen *f pl* retaining rings **-kessel** *m* camp kettle **-klappenschrank** *m* field-telephone exchange, portable switchboard **-klemme** *f* field terminal **-kochherd** *m* field range **-komponente** *f* component field

Feld-krümmungskorrektur *f* field flattening **-krümmungsverzerrung** *f* distortion due to curvature or lack of flatness, curvilinear distortion **-kultivator** *m* field cultivator **-laboratorium** *n* field laboratory **-lager** *n* military camp, bivouac **-länge** *f* lenth of section, span length **-leitungsbau** *m* field-line construction **-linie** *f* line of flux, line of force (elec.)

Feldlinien-dichte *f* magnetic flux **-röhre** *f* tube of flux

Feldlinienvektor *m* line of flux

Feldlinse *f* field lens, condensing lens

feldlose Emission zero field emission

Feld-magnet *m* field magnet (elec.), alternator or dynamo magnet **-messen** *n* surveying

Feld-messer *n* land surveyor, surveyor, geometry **-messerkette** *f* surveyor's chain **-meßinstrumente** *n pl* surveying instruments **-meßkästchen** *n* field testing set **-messung** *f* plotting field map or configuration of electrostatic field, land surveying or measurement **-mitte** *f* center of span

Feldort *m* end of a level **-strecke** *f* level drift

Feld-periskop *n* field periscope **-photogrammeter** *m* field photogrammeter **-phototheodolit** *m* field phototheodolite

Feld-profil *n* field pattern **-prüfschrank** *m* field testing set, field test panel **-punkt** *m* field stop **-quant** *n* field quantum **-quantisierung** *f* field quantization

Feld-rain *m* fence row, uncultivated strip at edge of field **-regler** *m* field rheostat, field regulator **-regelung** *f* field variation **-regulator** *m* field regulator **-regulierschalter** *m* field regulating switch **-regulierung** *f* field regulation **-regulierwiderstand** *m* field regulator

Feld-richtung *f* field direction **-ringübertrager** *m* field repeating coil (elec.), field toroidal repeater coil **-röhre** *f* tube of flux **-schritt** *m* field pitch (elec.) **-schütz** *m* field relay **-schutzwiderstand** *m* field protection resistor **-schwächung** *f* weakening of the field **-sicherung** *f* field fuse **-sicherungskästchen** *n* field fuse box

Feldspat *m* feldspar **dichter ~** felsite **glasiger ~**

glassy feldspar **Abart des Feldspates** moonstone
feldspat-artig feldspathic **-gestein** *n* feldspathic rock **-haltig** feldspathic
Feldspeicher *m* field depot **-prüfungsanweisung** *f* testing instruction for field storage
Feldsprünge *pl* field changes
Feldspule *f* field coil, field winding, exciting winding, magnetizing coil, magnet coil **~ eines elektrodynamischen Lautsprechers** field coil of a moving-coil speaker
Feldstärke *f* field intensity, intensity of field, field strength, strength of field, field density, intensity of magnetic field, magnetizing force, flux density **~ des Fernsehsenders** field intensity of the television transmitter **~ des aufzunehmenden Senders** field strength of the incoming signal (at the receiving site) **elektrische ~** intensity of electric field, strength of electric field, electric-field strength, electric force
Feldstärke-änderung *f* variation of field intensity **-messer** *m* field intensity meter **-meßgerät** *n* field-intensity meter, field-strength measuring set **-messung** *f* field-intensity measurement, field strength measurement
Feldstärken-diagramm *n* radiation characteristic, radiation pattern, field pattern **-mühle** *f* electrostatic induction voltmeter **-profil** *n* field pattern
Feldstärkeschwankungen *f pl* variation of field intensity
Feldstativ *n* field tripod **~ mit verstellbaren Spreizen** field tripod with adjustable stays
Feld-stecher *m* field glass, binocular (glasses), fieldglass magnifier **-stechlupe** *f* field glass magnifier **-stein** *m* great rubble stone, cobblestone
Feldstrom *m* field emission, field current (emission of electrons due to an electric field) **-kreis** *m* field current **-verstärkung** *f* field amplification
Feld-system *n* field system **-teilchen** *n* fundamental field particle **-trichtertheorie** *f* field funnel theory
Feld- und Raumladeverhältnis *n* field and space charge ratio (teleph.)
Feld-unterbrechungsschalter mit Dämpfungswiderstand field break switch with damping rheostat **-unvollkommenheit** *f* field imperfection **-verfahren** *n* legal procedure in the field, summary court procedure **-verlauf** *m* field-strength distribution, field shape, feld map, field pattern, field configuration **-vermessung** *f* survey of field
Feld-verspannung *f* secondary diagonal wiring (airship) **-verstärker** *m* fieldistor **-verstärkung** *f* field amplification **-verteilung** *f* field (strength) distribution **-verzerrung** *f* field distortion, field deformation
Feld-weg *m* dirt road, cross-country field path **-weite** *f* span (dimension) **-welle** *f* field wave **-wellenwiderstand** characteristic wave impedance **-werk** *n* fieldwork **-werkstatt** *f* field workshop **-werkstätte** *f* field repair shop **-werkstattzug** *m* field workshop platoon
Feld-wert *m* field value **-wetterstation** *f* **-wetterstelle** *f*, **-wetterwarte** *f* field meteorological station, field weather station **-wicklung** *f* field coil, field winding, exciting winding, magnetizing coil, magnet coil, compound winding **widerstand** *m* field rheostat, field regulator **-zerfall** *m* field decay

Felge *f* felly, rim (of tire or wheel), rim of wheel generally **abnehmbare ~** detachable or demountable rim **die ~ aufziehen** to fit the rim on
felgen to fit (a wheel) with fellies
Felgen-abziehhebel *m* rim tool **-artig** rim type **-band** *n* tire flap, rim tape **-boden** *m* base of rim **-bolzen** *m* rim bolt **-größe** *f* rim size **-hauer** *m* wheelwright **-horn** *n* wheel flange
Felgen-kante *f* bull-wheel flanges **-keil** *m* rim wedge **-kranz** *m* rim (of wheel) **-läufer** *m* circumferential runner **-montiereisen** *n* rim tool **-ohr** *n* flange (fixed) clinch
Felgen-rand *m* rim edge **-richtamboß** *m* rim truing anvil **-ring** *m* rim ring **-rundstauchmaschine** *f* rim sizing machine **-scheibe** *f* disk rim or circumference **-schulter** *f* shoulder of rim **-stoß** *m* wheel-rim joint, felloe joint **-walze** *f* tire roll
Felit *m* felite
Fell *n* hide, skin
Fels *m* rock, stone, reef **-artig** rocklike **-block** *m* boulder, rock **-boden** *m* rock soil, bedrock, rocky ground **-bruch** *m* quarry
Felsen *m* rock, stone, reef, cliff **-ader** *f* rock seam or vein **-bein** *n* petrous portion of temporal bone **-fest** unshakable, firm as a rock **-klippe** *f* bluff **-kluft** *f* chasm **-meer** *n* bedrock-fragments and rocks **-nest** *n* rockbound hamlet or position **-riff** *n* reef **-wand** *f* precipice, crag
Fels-geröll *n* boulders, rock debris, detritus **-gestein** *n* rock material **-glimmer** *m* mica **-grund** *m* rocky bottom
felsig clifted, clifty, rocky
Fels-küste *f* cliff **-öl** *n* petroleum **-rutsch** *m* rock slide **-trümmer** *f* rock waist **-untergrund** *m* bedrock
Feluke *f* felucca
femisch femic
Fenchelöl *n* fennel oil
Fender *m* fender (of boat) **-eisen** *n* fender iron **-tau** *n* swifter (of boat), rope fender
Fenster *n* window, sight peep, lighting aperture, gate (motion picture), projection aperture (film projector), window (in envelope of a cell, iconoscope, etc.), bezel (in casing or panel or radio apparatus) **~ mit drei Doppellichtern** three twin window **~ einer Photozelle** window of a photocell **in der Höhe verschiebbares ~** sash window **nach außen aufschlagendes ~** window opening to the outside **blindes ~** dead, blank, or mock window **einflügeliges ~** single-sashed window **schräges ~** skylight, skylight window
Fenster-anschlag *m* window rabbet **-bank** *f* window seat, sill, or bench **-bilder** *pl* window transparencies **-blende** *f* blind for a window, apertural stop, diaphragm **-bogen** *m* arch **-brett** *n* sill **-briefumschlag** *m* window or transparent envelope **-brüstung** *f* window ledge or sill, elbow rest, breast height, parapet, breastwork **-dichter** *m* weather stripping, draft preventer **-druck** *m* gate pressure, gate friction **-durchlässigkeit** *f* passage (of betarays)
Fenster-einfassung *f* window case, sash frame **-eisen** *n* iron window bar **-enteiser** *m* window deicer **-fach** *n* window-pane, window square, sash square **-fassung** *f* (Scheinwerfer) lens rim **-fläche** *f* window surface (area) **-flügel** *m* wing, valve, or casement of a window **-flügelrahmen**

m valve or sash wing, wing frame **-führung** *f* aperture guide **-füllung** *f* window sash **-futter** *n* case of a window **-gerähme** *n* framework or complete framing of a window **-gesims** *n* molding at the head or foot of a window, window sill **-gestell** *n* window case, sash frame **-gewände** *f* jamb stone **-glas** *n* plate glass, window glass **-glimmer** *m* muscovite

Fenster-heber *m* window lifter **-jalousie** *f* Venetian blind **-kitt** *m* glazier's putty **-klappen** *pl* window louvres **-konsole** *f* corbel under a window jamb **-kopiermaschine** *f* step printer, intermittent printer **-krampe** *f* casement staple **-kreuz** *n* window frame **-kurbel** *f* window crank

Fenster-laden *m* window shutter **-lauf** *m* window frame **-leder** *n* chamois leather **-lenkzielschiff** *n* wireless-controlled target ship **-linse** *f* aperture lens **-los** windowless

Fenster-nische *f* bay of a window **-pfosten** *m* window post, wooden window jamb **-platte** *f* aperture plate **-rahmen** *m* window frame, sash **-reiter** *m* window rider, transparent index label **-riegel** *m* window catch **-riemen** *m* sash strap, window strap (R.R.) **-ring** *m* eyepiece gasket (mask), window ring **-rolladen** *m* rolling window blind or window curtain **-rolle** *f* antirattle roller (for window)

Fenster-scheibe *f* windowpane **-schieber** *m* sliding sash of a sash window **-schluß** *m* head of a window, window head **-schmiege** *f* embrasure of a window **-schwelle** *f* window sill, bench, or ledge **-skala** *f* window dial **-sohle** *f* window still, window ledge

Fenster-sprosse *f*, **-stange** *f* window bar **-steller** *m* windscreen adjustor **-stock** *m* jamb, window case, sash frame **-stollen** *m* lateral tunnel used to permit access to, or driving of, main tunnel from intermediate points **-sturz** *m*, **-träger** *m*, **-überlage** *f* lintel (beam over window), window head **-umschlag** *m* window envelope **-verstärker** *m* window amplifier **-vorhang** *m* curtain **-wirbel** *m* turnbuckle or turn button of a window, sash bolt **-zarge** *f* window case, sash frame

Ferberit *m* ferberite

Ferch *m* chokedamp

Ferghanit *m* ferghanite

Fergusonit *m* fergusonite

Ferment *n* ferment

fermentieren to ferment

Fermentwirkung *f* fermentation, ferment action

Fermi *n* fermi **-kante** *f* Fermi level **-oberfläche** *f* Fermi surface **-potential** *n* (in Metallen) top of fermi distribution

Fermische Verteilung Fermi distribution

Fermium *n* fermium

fern far, distant, remote

Fernabfrageklinke *f* trunk or toll answering jack

Fernablesung *f* remote reading **Meßgerät mit ~ bzw. Fernanzeige** remote indicating instrument

Fernabstellrelais *n* remote stopping relay

Fernamt *n* trunk exchange, toll exchange, line positions, long-distance switchboard, toll central office, toll office, local and long-distance telephone **~ mit Anrufsuchern** trunk exchange with automatic call distribution **äußerstes ~ in einer Verbindung** toll center at origin or terminal

Fernamts-anschluß *m* trunk telephone station **-aufsicht** *f* trunk supervision **-auskunft(stelle)** *f* trunk inquiry, toll information desk, trunk-directory inquiry **-beamtin** *f* trunk operator, long-distance operator **-einrichtung** *f* toll-office equipment **-meldeleitung** *f* trunk record circuit **-meldestelle** *f* trunk record section **-schaltung** *f* trunk or long-distance circuit **-trennung** *f* breaking of local calls for toll calls through clearing

Fern-anemometer *m* remote-control anemometer **-anlage** *f* telephone plant **-anlasser** *m* remote-control starter **-anlaßrelais** *n* remote starting relay

Fernanruf *m* trunk call, trunk signaling, local or long-distance call **-zeichen** *n* trunk or long-distance call signal

Fern-anschluß *m* trunk connection **-antrieb** *m* remote control, remote drive **-antriebsteuerung** *f* remote control or activation **-anzeige** *f* distant transmission, tele-indicating

Fernanzeigegerät *n* apparatus for distant transmission **schreibendes ~** telewriter **Geber eines Fernanzeigegerätes** remote-control head

fern-anzeigen to transmit to a distance **-anzeiger** *n* telemeter **-aufnahme** *f* distance shot, telephoto(graph) **-ausbreitung** *f* long-distance propagation of radio wave **-auslöser** *m* distance release **-ausschaltung** *f* remote action release

Fern-beamtin *f* toll operator, long-distance operator **-beben** *n* distant earthquake **-bedienbar** suitable for remote control **-bedieneinsatz** *m* remote control panel **-bediengerät** *n* remote-control apparatus **-bedienpult** *n* remote-control desk **-bedient** remote-controlled **-bedienung** *f* remote control, distant control **-bedienungstafel** *f* remote control panel

fernbesetzt toll busy, engaged on trunk call, busy on toll connection **-lampe** *f* group busy lamp **-sein** *n* toll-busy condition **-zeichen** *n* signal for busy trunk lines

Fern-besprechgerät *n* remote-control unit **-besprechung** *f* remote-control operation, long distance conversation **-betätigt** remotely controlled, distance-controlled **-betrieb** *m* action at a distance, distance traffic **-betriebsüberwachung** *f* toll-service supervision

Fernbild *n* telephoto, television picture, televised picture **-großaufnahme** *f* projection video picture (of large size) **-schrift** *f* phototelegraphy, picture telegraphy, facsimile **-sendung** *f* teleiconography **-übertragung** *f* television

Fern-blick *m* farsightedness **-blitzanzeiger** *m* keraunophone **-brecher** *m* telebreaking

Ferndienst-klinke *f* trunk order-wire jack **-lampe** *f* order-wire lamp **-leitung** *f* interposition trunk at toll board

Fern-drehzahlmesser *m* distant-reading tachometer, distance revolution counter, dashboard tachometer teletachometer **-drehzahlverstellvorrichtung** *f* remote speed regulator **-drucker** *m* printing telegraph, longdistance type printer, teleprinter, teletype apparatus, stock ticker, teletyper, Siemens printer

Ferndurchgangs-platz *m* through switching position **-schrank** *m* through switching board

Ferne *f* (Windform) tuyère

Fern-eichung *f* remote calibration control **-einstellung** *f* remote control, long-range focus

-empfang *m* distant reception, long-distance reception, distant-station reception **-empfangszone** *f* reception zone beyond the skip distance
Fernen-boden *m* (in a converter) tuyère plug **-dunst** *m* distant fog
Fernentstörung *f* distant radio shielding
ferner moreover, furthermore
Fern-fahrer *m* long distance driver **-fahrtanzeiger** *m* distant-reading-speed indicator (aviation) **-fahrtmesser** *m* telespeedometer, teleairspeed indicator **-feld** *n* remote radiation field **-feuchtigkeitsmesser** *m* telepsychrometer
Fernflug *m* long-distance flight **-sicherung** *f* long-distance air traffic control
Fern-fokuskathode *f* tele-focus cathode **-funk** *m* transoceanic or long-distance broadcast **-funkfeuerstelle** *f* long-range radio beacon station
Ferngang *m* overdrive **-getriebe** *n* overdrive gear
Ferngas *n* grid gas, long-distance gas **-versorgungsanlage** *f* long-distance gas-supply plant **-wirtschaft** *f* grid gas supply
Ferngeber für Druckdifferenzmesser teletransmitter for differential pressure meters
Fern-gebührentafel *f* toll-rate table or chart **-gegenstand** *m* distant object **-gehilfin** *f* trunk operator, toll operator **-gelenkt** remote-controlled
Ferngespräch *n* telephone call, long-distance telephone call, toll message, toll-line conversation, telephone conversation **~ zu bestimmter Zeit** fixed-time call **dringendes ~** urgent telephone call **gewöhnliches ~** routine call
ferngesteuert remotely controlled, pilot-operated (regulating valve) **-es Flugzeug** teleguided aircraft **-e Rakete** remote-guided rocket **-es Segelflugmodell** radio-controlled glider model **-es Unterwerk** tele-controlled substation
ferngetastet remote-controlled or transmitted
Ferngewitter *n* distant thunderstorm
Fern-glas *n* field glass, spy glass, telescope, binoculars **-gläser** *pl* binoculars **-glaslibelle** *f* surveyor's level, leveling instrument **-greifer** *m* remote handling tongs master slave manipulator **-gruppenumschalter** *m* remote group switch
Fern-heizungsanlage *f* long-distance heating system **-heizwerk** *n* central heating station **-höranschluß** *m* headphone connector
Fernhörer *m* telephone receiver, telephone, hand receiver **doppelpoliger ~** double-pole or bipolar receiver **einpoliger ~** single-pole receiver **elektrodynamischer ~** moving-conductor receiver **elektromagnetischer ~ mit Eisenanker** moving-iron receiver **verzerrungsfreier ~** pantelephone
Fernhörer-kapsel *f* receiver case **-kissen** *n* telephone cushion **-normal** *n* receiver standard **-schnur** *f* telephone cord
Fernhydraulik *f* hydraulic remote control
Fernkabel *n* trunk cable, long-distance cable, toll cable, trunk telephone cable, long-distance telephone cable, trunk wire **-leitung** *f* (mit Sprechstromverstärkern) (repeatered) toll-cable circuit **-linie** *f* toll-cable circuit **-löter** *m* trunk-cable jointer **-netz** *n* toll-cable system, long-distance cable system
Fern-kamera *f* tele-camera **-kinematographie** *f* film television, telecinematography
Fernkino *n* film television, telecinematography, telecast, intermediate-film system (television) **-sender** *m* film transmitter, long-distance or remote television
Fernklappe *f* trunk or long-distance drop
Fernklinken-feld *n* trunk-jack panel **-lampe** *f* trunk or long-distance jack lamp **-leitungen** *pl* long-distance jack lines
Fern-kompaß *m* telecompass, remote compass **-kraftwerk** *n* long-distance supply work
Fernkurs *m* correspondence course **-kreisel** *m* gyrocompass
Fernleitboot *n* wireless-controlled target tender
fernleiten to transmit to a distance
Fernleitung *f* trunk line, long-distance line, toll line, long-distance circuit, toll circuit, telephone trunk line, station-to-station telephone line (Germany), intercity telephone line (Germany **~ ohne Verstärker** nonrepeatered toll circuit **durchgehende ~** direct international circuit
Fernleitungs-bezirkskabel *n* trunk-zone cable **-endkabel** *n* toll-entrance or terminal cable **-endverstärker** *m* terminal repeater **-gesellschaft** *f* long-lines company **-kabel** *n* exchange cable, cable toll **-klinke** *f* toll-line jack **-linie** *f* toll line, trunk route **-netz** *n* toll plant, trunk system, toll network, station-to-station telephone-line net (Germany), telephone system or network
Fernleitungs-rohre *pl* long-distance mains **-schaltplan** *m* toll switching plan **-schnur** *f* trunk cord **-schrank** *m*, **-tafel** *f* telephone-trunk-line board **-verstärker** *pl* trunk line repeaters **-wähler** *m* toll connector, longdistance connector **-welle** *f* remote-control shaft or beam **-zwischenkabel** *n* toll intermediate cable
Fernlenk-flugzeug *n* remote-control plane, telecontrolled aircraft **-kommandoempfänger** *m* remote-control receiver **-pult** *n* control desk, radio-control desk for guided missiles
Fern-lenkung *f* remote control, radio control **-lenkwaffe** *f* guided missile **-lesen** *n* reading(s) at a distance
Fernlicht *n* bright light, head light, high beam, upper beam, long distance headlight **-anzeigelampe** *f* main (or country) beam indicator light **-anzeigerleuchte** *f* control lamp for high beam, head light control lamp **-bündel** *n* main (or country) light beam **-einstellung** *f* main (or country) beam adjustment **-faden** *m* main (or country) beam filament
Fern-linie *f* trunk line, long-distance line, toll-line amplitude-modulation power detection **-linse** *f* telephoto lens
Fernmelde-anlage *f* remote signaling plant, installation signaling plant, communication facility **-aufzeichnung** *f* telecommunication log **-betriebszentrale** *f* communication center **-dienst** *m* telecommunication service **-einrichtung** *f* communication facility **-freileitung** *f* overhead communication line **-funker** *m* signaler **-kabel** *n* cable for weak currents **-leitung** *f* communication circuit or line, signal circuit or line **-luftkabel** *n* aerial telecommunication cables **-nebenstelle** *f* tributary station **-netz** *n* radio network, telecommunication network or system
Fernmelder *m* communicator (elektr.) **~ für den**

Flüssigkeitsstand remote level indicator
Fernmelde-satellit *m* communications satellite **-schaltplatte** *f* communications switch-ing panel **-technik** *f* (tele-) communication (elec.) **-wesen** *n* telecommunication
Fern-meldung *f* remote signaling **-messer** *m* range finder, range-finder operator, telemeter
Fern-meßeinrichtung *f* telemetering equipment
Fernmeßgerät *n* range finder, telemeter ~ **mit Fernablesung** telegauge, telemeter, remote-indicating instrument
Fernmeßinstrument *n* transmitting-type gauge ~ **mit elektrischer Übertragung** electric-type telegauge
Fernmeßsummengeber *m* telemetric integrator **-meßtechnik** *f* telemetry **-messung** *f* remote measurement, telemetering
fernmündlich by telephone **-e Mitteilung** telephone message forwarded by subscriber for delivery to nonsubscriber from telephone exchange, by messenger
Fern-nachwähler *m* long-distance switch **-nebensprechen** *n* far-end crosstalk **-objekt** *n* distant object **-objektiv** *n* telephoto lens **-ordnung** *f* long range order
Fernordnungs-grad *m* long-range degree **-erscheinung** *f* order-disorder phenomenon
Fern-photographie *f* phototelegraphy, picture telegraphy, fascimile, telephotography **-photographisch** telephotographical
Fernplatz *m* toll position, trunk position **-rufleitung** *f* switching trunk
Fern-programm *n* radiodistribution **-punkt** *m* (Stereoaufnahmen) distant point, far point (optics) **-prüfschrank** *m* trunk or toll test board **-psychrometer** *n* telepsychrometer **-räumgerät** *n* remote-controlled sweeping device **-regelung** *f* remote-control gear **-regulierung** *f* remote regulation **-richtungsanlage** *f* directional radio unit, direction-finder equipment
Fernrohr *n* telescope ~ **mit Entfernung messenden Fäden** telescope with stadia lines **durchschlagbares** ~ transit telescope **kurzbrennweitiges** ~ telescope of short focal length **parallaktisches** ~ equatorial telescope
Fernrohr-arme *pl* tubes of battery commander's telescope, telescope tubes **-aufnahme** *f* telephoto **-aufsatz** *m* telescopic sight **-besetzt** equipped with telescopic sight **-brille** *f* telescopic spectacles **-brillenprobsystem** *n* telescopic spectacle-trial combination **-büchse** *f* rifle with telescopic sight, telescope tube or barrel **-hals** *m* neck of telescope, telescope center section **-hülse** *f* telescope tube, telescope housing
Fernrohr-kopf *m* telescope head **-körper** *m* body of telescope, telescope tube, body of binoculars **-lager** *n* telescope seat **-leistung** *f* (Bildkartiergeräte) optical performance, telescopic performance (phot.) **-linse** *f* telescopic magnifier **-objektiv** *n* telescope lens **-post** *f* pneumatic dispatch **-schlüssel** *m* telescope adjustment screw **-steg** *m* telescope support **-träger** *m* telescope support, telescope stand or carrier **-visier** *m* telescopic sights **-wiege** *f* telescope cradle
Fern-punkt *m* far point of the eye **-ruf** *m* long-distance call
Fernschalt-apparat *m* remote switch **-gerät** *n* subscriber box **-(zusatz)gerät** *n* dial unit, additional box for local perforating
Fern-schalter *m* remote-control switch, remotely controlled switch, teleswitch, contactor **-schaltung** *f* distant or remote control
Fernschrank *m* long-distance or trunk (telephone) switchboard, toll switchboard, trunk exchange switchboard **-beamtin** *f* long-distance operator
Fern-schreibapparat *m* teletypewriter **-schreibemeßgerät** *n* telewriter **-schreiben** *n* transmission of readings, teleprint, telex
Fern-schreiber *m* telegraph, teletype, teletypewriter, telegraph printer, telegraph operator **-Tastgerät** *n* teletype keying unit
Fernschreib-funker *m* teleprinter operator **-gerät** *n* teletype writer apparatus or equipment **-kraftwagen** *m* teleprint truck or lorry **-leitung** *f* teletype writer circuit
Fernschreib-maschine *f* teletype writer, teleprinter **-mechaniker** *m* teleprinter mechanic **-meßgestell** *n* teletype control panel **-netz** *n* teletype network **-speichervermittlung** *f* teleprinter tape switching center **-vermittlung** *f* teleprinter switching center, teleprinter exchange or connection **-vermittlungsanlagen** *pl* telex (teleprint) exchange systems **-wagen** *m* teleprint truck or lorry, teletype truck **-werk** *n* **eines Meßgerätes** remote-recording system
fernschriftlich by teleprint
Fernschweißsteuerung *f* remote welding control
Fernseh-abtaster *m* televisor, scanner (at sending end) **-abtastung** *f* telecine scan of film
Fernsehaufnahme *f* television pickup **-raum** *m* televisionstudio **-röhre** *f* iconoscope, camera tube **-wagen** *m* television reporting van, television or electron (pickup) camera truck, video bus, televising car
Fernsehbild *n* television image **plastisches** ~ stereoscopic or three-dimensional video picture
Fernseh-bildraster *m* television frame **-einrichtung** *f* television system **-empfang** *m* television reception **-empfänger** *m* television receiver, picture-reproducing device, teleview apparatus
fernsehen to televise, teleview, watch television
Fernsehen *n* television ~ **im Dunkeln** noctovision ~ **geringer Güte** low-definition television ~ **hoher Güte** high-definition television **direktes** ~ direct pickup and viewing **drahtloses** ~ radiovision **farbiges** ~ color television **mechanisches** ~ television by mechanical methods **plastisches** ~ stereoscopic television
Fernseher *m* television apparatus, television transmitter, video or television camera, televisor
Fernseh-frequenz *f* video frequency **-funk** *m* telecast television
Fernsehgeber mit elektrischer Abtastung television transmitter with electric scanning
Fernseh-gerät *n* television set **-gittergeber** *m* cross-bar generator
Fernsehkabel *n* television cable **-übertragung** *f* television-cable transmission
Fernseh-kanal *m* television channel **-kolben** *m* television tubes **-kompaß** *m* telecompaß **-norm** *f* television standard **-raster** *m* television grating, scanning surface, unmodulated screen pattern **-reichweite** *f* television range **-relaiskette** *f* television relay link **-relaisstrecke** television station

link **-röhre** *f* television tube **-röhrenprüfer** *m* monoscope, monotron, phasmajector **-rundfunk** *m* televsion broadcasting, viscual broadcasting

Fernseh-sender *m* television transmitter (comprises strictly both video and aural signal transmitters) **-senderöhre** *f* television-transmission pickup tube **-sendung** *f* television broadcast, telecast, television transmission **-signal** *n* video signal, picture signal, television signal

Fernseh-spiel *n* telecast, TV-show **-sprechen** *n* television speech, television combined with telephone service **-sprecher** *m* television telephone, video telephone **-sprechnetz** *n* system for television speech, television combined with telephone service **-strecke** *f* television stretch, TV-link **-sucherröhre** *f* viewfinder **-synchronisierung** *f* television synchronization

Fernseh-telephon *n* television telephone, video telephone **-turm** *m* TV tower **-übertragung** *f* television transmission

Fernseh- und Bildübertragung *f* transmission of pictures and images

Fernseh-verbindung *f* television connection **-vermittlung** *f* community television **-verkehrslenkung** *f* television monitoring **-wandlerorgane** *pl* photocells and light relays **-zerlegerröhre** *f* television dissector tube **-zwischenfilmsender** *m* intermediate-film transmitter

Fernsender *m* remote transmitter ~ (beim Messen und Regeln) transmitter

Fernsicht *f* visual range, distant or perspective view or visibility **beschränkte** ~ limited view

Fernsignal *n* distance signal

fernsprech- telephonic **-abschlußkabel** *n* telephone end cable **-abteilung** *f* telephone detail

Fernsprechamt *n* local telephone exchange, exchange, (telephone) central office ~ **privat mit mehreren Vermittlungsstellen** multioffice exchange **fliegendes** ~ temporary exchange **halbautomatisches oder halbselbsttätiges** ~ semiautomatic exchange **öffentliches** ~ public exchange **unbedientes** ~ unattended exchange

Fernsprechamt-anschluß *m* telephone station **-apparat** *m* telephone instrument or outfit **-automat** *m* coin-collector telephone station, pay station **-betrieb** *m* telephone service **-buch** *n* telephone directory **-dienst** *m* telephone service **-doppelleitung** *f* metallic telephone circuit, two-wire telephone circuit, telephone loop

Fernsprechanlage *f* telephone installation, telephone plant or equipment, exchange

Fernsprechanschluß *m* subscription or contract, telephone connection (war) **vorübergender** ~ temporary service contract

Fernsprechanschluß-kabel *n* subscriber's cable **-trupp** *m* communication-construction squad, telephone-installation unit

Fernsprechanstalt *f* telephone office

Fernsprechapparat *m* telephone set (or telephone) ~ **mit Batterieanruf** (Ortsbatterie) local battery telephone set with battery ringing ~ **für Handbetrieb** manual telephone set ~ **mit Induktoranruf** magnetotelephone set ~ **mit Induktor- und Sommeranruf** (Ortsbatterie) local battery telephone set (magneto and buzzer calling) ~ **mit festem Mikrophon** desk stand or wall telephone set ~ **mit Ortsbatterie** localbattery telephone set ~ **ohne Rückhördämpfung** (ohne Geräuschdämpfung) side-tone telephone set ~ **mit Summeranruf** (Ortsbatterie) local battery telephone set (buzzer calling) ~ **für Wahlbetrieb** dial telephone set ~ **mit Zentralbatterie** common battery telephone set

Fernsprech-bautrupp *m* telephone-construction crew **-bauwagen** *m* telephone-construction truck

Fernsprechbetrieb *m* telephone operation ~ **mit Durchgangsvermittlung** tandem operation ~ **mit selbsttätiger Durchgangsvermittlung** *f* dial-system tandem operation

Fernsprechbetriebs-funker *m* radiotelephony operator **-kraftwagen** *m* telephone-operations truck, mobile telephone exchange **-trupp** *m* telephone-operations squad (team) **-wagen** *m* telephone-operations truck **-zug** *m* telephone-operating platoon

Fernsprech-bezugsleistung *f* reference telephonic power **-boje** *f* telephone buoy **-buch** *n* telephone directory **-bündel** *n* telephone channel group **-doppelleitung** *f* metallic telephone circuit **-eichkreis** *m* telephone (transmission) reference system, telephone reference system

Fernsprecheinrichtung, gesamte ~ inside plant

Fernsprechempfangsgerät *n* telephone receiver

fernsprechen to telephone

Fernsprechen *n* telephony **drahtloses** ~ wireless or radiotelephony

Fernsprechendverstärker *m* telephone terminal repeater

Fernsprecher *m* telephone, telephone station ~ **für Batterie- (Induktor-) Anruf** battery-ringing (magneto-) telephone station ~ **für zehn Linien** ten-way telephone station ~ **mit Schutzschaltung gegen Mikrophongeräusch** anti-side-tone telephone set

Fernsprecherschlüssel *m* telephone code

Fernsprechformfaktor *m* telephone-voltage form factor (of an electric line), telephone-influence factor ~ **der Spannung** voltage telephone-influence factor ~ **des Stromes** current telephone-influence factor

Fernsprech-frequenz *f* telephone frequency **-gerät** *n* telephone equipment **-hauptanschluß** *m* main set, (subscriber's) main station **-kabel** *n* telephone cable **-kanal** *m* telephone channel **-klappenschrank** *m* telephone switchboard

Fernsprech-kabel für Orts- und Fernverkehr subscriber and trunk cables **-klappen-schrank** *m* telephone switchboard **-kleinlampen** *pl* lamps for telephone switchborards **-kundendienst** (-auftragsdienst) absent subscriber service

Fernsprechleitung *f* telephone circuit, telephone line, telephone wire ~ **für den inneren Verkehr** domestic telephone circuit **(un)gekreuzte** ~ (non)transposed telephone line **hochspannungsgeschützte** ~ telephone line with protection against high tension **verdrallte** ~ twisted telephone circuit **zwischenstaatliche** ~ international telephone circuit

Fernsprech-meßtechnik *f* telephonometry **-mikrophon** *n* telephone transmitter **-nebenstelle** *f* telephone extension set **-nebenstellenanlage** *f* private branch exchange

Fernsprechnetz *n* telephone network, (outside) telephone plant, telephone system, wire net (war) ~ **mit Handbetrieb** manual-telephone system ~ **mit mehreren Vermittlungsämtern** multioffice exchange ~ **mit Wahlbetrieb** dial-telephone system

Fernsprech-normalsystem *n* reference telephone system **-reihenanlage** *f* intercommunication or housetelephone plant **-relais** *n* telephone relay, telephonic relay **-ringübertrager** *m* toriodal repeating coil **-rohrdrähte** *pl* telephone conduit wires **-seekabel** *n* submarine telephone cable

Fernsprech-schlüssel *m* telephone code **-schnellverkehr** *m* express (no-delay) telephone service **-schrank** *m* telephone switchboard **-sperre** *f* withdrawal of telephone service, disconnection **-stelle** *f* telephone station **-störfaktor** *m* telephone-interference factor **-störung** *f* telephone breakdown **-system** *n* telephone system

Fernsprech-tafel *f* telephone board **-tarif** *m* telephone tariff **-teilnehmerverzeichnis** *n* telephone directory **-telegrammaufnahme** *f* phonogram section **-tornister** *m* pack telephone, portable telephone **-trupp** *m* telephone-operations squad, telephone section

Fernsprech-übertrager *m* telephone transformer, repeating coil

Fernsprech-übertragungsmaßregeln *f* transmission layout **-übertragungstechnik** *f* telephone-transmission technique **-unteramt** *n* subexchange **-verbindung** *f* telephone communication(s) **-vergleichsstromkreis** *m* standard reference telephone circuit **-verkehr** *m* telephone traffic **-verkehrsschreiber** *m* telephone-traffic recorder **-vermittlung** *f* telephone exchange, telephone connection, telephone or switching central **-vermittlungsamt mit Zentralbatteriebetrieb** common-battery central office **-vermittlungsstelle** *f* telephone exchange, central office (U.S.A.), telephone central office

Fernsprechverstärker *m* telephone repeater **-amt** *n* telephone-repeater station **-betrieb** *m* telephonerepeater operation **-röhre** *f* telephone amplifying valve, telephone-repeater tube

Fernsprech-verzeichnis *n* telephone directory **-wagen** *m* telephone wagon or truck **-weg** *m* telephone channel **-weitverkehr** *m* long-distance telephone service **-wesen** *n* telephony

Fernsprechzelle *f* telephone cabin(et), telephone booth **öffentliche** ~ public telephone station **schalldichte** ~ soundproof cabinet

Fernsprech-zentrale *f* telephone exchange **-zone** *f* telephone zone **-zonenhauptpunkt** *m* telephone-zone center **-zwischenverstärker** *m* telephone intermediate repeater

Fern-spruch *m* telephone call, telephone message, telephone transcription **-startanschluß** *m* remote starting connection **-stelle** *f* trunk exchange

Fernsteuer-anlage *f* remote-control plant **-einrichtung** *f* remote-control device **-gerät** *n* remote controller

Fernsteuerung *f* supervisory control, remote control, distant control, remote-control-gear, distance, telemetric, or remotecontrol action (by selsyn-type motor) **von Zwischenämtern** ~ tandem toll-circuit dialing

Fernsteuerungs-kabel *n* keying cable **-leitung** *f* keying line **-möglichkeit** *f* remote control **-ventil** *n* remote-control valve

Fernsteuervorrichtung mit Rückmeldung telerepeating device

Fernstoß *m* distant collision

Fernstsuchanlage *f* ultra-long-range search radar

Fern-suchgerät *n* early-warning radar set **-synchronisierung** *f* step-by-step synchronizing **-tachometer** *n* tachometer **-taster** *m* remote control **-tastgerät** *n* remote-control-key radio **-tastkabel** *n* keying cable **-tastung** *f* remote control, remote keying **-teil** *m* distanc portion **-telephonie** *f* toll telephony

Fernthermometer *n* instrument-board thermometer, distance thermometer, telethermometer, distant-reading pyrometer, water-temperature gauge **-anschluß** *m* remote-reading thermometer connection

Fern-tisch *m* trunk or long-distance table **-transport** *m* long-distance haulage work **-trennschalter** *m* remote-controlled master switch **-trieb** *m* remote control **-tross** *m* third-echelon supply train

Fernübertragung *f* (elektrische) remote control, long-range transmission **Wettermeßinstrument mit funkentelegraphischer** ~ radiotelemeteorographic or telemetric instrument, radiosonde

Fernübertragungsgerät *n* apparatus for long-range transmission

Fern-überwachung *f* remote supervision **-überwachungslampe** *f* toll call pilot lamp

Fern- und Ortsamt, vereinigtes ~ combined trunk and local exchanges

Fernunterricht *m* instruction by correspondence

Fernv (Fernverkehr) toll or long-distance traffic, long-distance communication and travel

Fern-verbindung *f* long-distance conversation, toll call, trunk communication, trunk line **-verkehr** *m* toll or long-distance traffic, long-distance communication and traval

Fernverkehrsbereich *m* telephone trunk zone

Fernverkehrstraße *f* trunkline road, trunk road

Fernverkehrszone *f* telephone trunk zone

Fernvermittlungs-leitung *f* toll-switching trunk, trunk-junction circuit **-platz** *m* toll-switching position

Fern-versorgung *f* long-distance supply **-vorbereitet** prepared for long-distance call **-vorbereitungsschaltung** *f* toll preparing connection (circuit)

Fernwahl *f* long-distance selection, toll switching, toll-line dialing ~ **über ein Durchgangsamt** through-dialing over trunk or toll circuits ~ **mit vier Frequenzen** four-frequency dialing or key sending ~ **mit Nummernscheibe oder Tastensatz** dialing or key pulsing

Fernwahlleitung *f* dial toll circuit

Fern-welle *f* extension shaft **-widerstand** *m* line resistance **-windmeßanlage** *f* remote-control anemometer **-wirkeinrichtung** *f* remote action equipment **-wirk-Impuls** *m* telecontrol pulse **-wirktechnik** *f* telemetry and remote control **-wirkzone** *f* remote effective zone **-wirkung** *f* distant or remote effect, radiation effect, action at a distance, telemetric action **-wirkungstheorie** *f* action at a distance

Fern-zähler *m* remote recorder **-zählwerk für Wassermesser** telecounter for water meters **-zeichnung** *f* perspective drawing **-zeiger** *m* long-distance indicator **-zünder** *m* fuse for distance **-zündgerät** *n* remote-firing device, device for long-range initiation of detonation

Ferranti-Ofen *m* Ferranti furnace
Ferri-bromid *n* ferric bromide **-chlorwasserstoffsäure** *f* ferrichloric acid **-ferrooxyd** *n* ferrosoferric oxide **-ferrozyanid** *n* ferric ferrocyanide, Prussian blue **-kaliumferrozyanid** *n* ferric potassium ferrocyanide **-rhodanid** *n* ferric thiocyanate, ferric sulfocyanate
Ferrit *n* ferrite **-antenne** *f* ferrite antenna **-bügel** *m* ferrite core (erase head)
ferritisch ferritic
Ferri-zyan *n* ferric cyanogen **-zyankalium** *n*
Ferritstreifen *pl* lines of ferrite, bands of ferrite potassium ferricyanide **-zyannatrium** *n* sodium ferricyanide **-zyansilber** *n* silver ferricyanide **-zyanverbindung** *f* ferricyanide, ferricyanic compound **-zyanwasserstoffsäure** *f* ferricyanic acid
Ferro-aluminium *n* ferroaluminum **-bromid** *n* ferrous bromide **-chrom** *n* ferrochrome, chromic iron, chromit, ferrochromium **-columbium** *n* ferrocolumbium **-elektriken** *pl* (hysteresis) ferroelectrics **-ferrioxyd** *n* ferrosoferric oxide **-fluxgerät** *n* ferro-flux tester **-magnetica** (Neutronenbewegung) ferromagnetics (neutron diffraction) **-kaliumsulfat** *n* ferrous potassium sulfate **-kohlentitan** *n* ferro-carbon-titanium **-legierung** *f* ferroalloy
ferro-magnetisch ferromagnetic **-magnetismus** *m* ferromagnetism **-molybdän** *n* ferromolybdenum **-oxyd** *n* ferrous oxide, magnetic iron ore, protoxide of iron **-silizium** *n* ferrosilicon, high-silicon softener, softener, silvery pig iron **-wolfram** *n* ferrotungsten **-zirkon** *n* ferrozirconium **-zyan** *n* ferrocyanogen
Ferro-zyanbarium *n* barium ferrocyanide **-zyanid** *n* ferrocyanide, sulfocyanide, ferrous cyanide **-zyankalzium** *n* calcium ferrocyanide **-zyankupfer** *n* cupric ferrocyanide **-zyannatrium** *n* sodium ferrocyanide **-zyanverbindung** *f* ferrocyanide **-zyanwasserstoffsäure** *f* ferrocyanic acid **-zyanzink** *n* zinc ferrocyanide
Ferse *f* heel
fertig finished, ready, perfect, proficient **~ gemacht** finished **~ gegossen** precast (pile)
Fertiganstrich *m* finish coat
Fertigaufschlagzünder *m* fixed percussion fuse
Fertig-bauhalle *f* assembly shop or room **-bauweise** *f* precast construction **-bearbeiten** to finish **-bearbeitung** *f* final machining **-betonplatte** *f* precast slab **-bohren** to finish bore **-bolzen** *m* safety pin **-decke** *f* precast floor **-drehbank** *f* finishing lathe **-drehen** *n* finish turning **-drehstahl** *m* turner's finishing tools
fertigen to finish, make, do, process, manufacture, prepare, dispatch
Fertiger *m* finisher, maker
Fertig-erzeugnis *n* finished article, finished product, manufactured goods **-fabrikat** *n* finished product **-facettiert** bevel-edged **-form** *f* finishing mold (glassbottle making) **-fräsen** *n* finish milling or cutting **-fräser** *m* finishing cutter, finish-milling or cutting **-frischen** *n* final purification **-frischofen** *m* finishing furnace **-gemacht** prepared **-gerüst** *n* finishing stand of rolls **-gesenk** *n* finisher (die) **-gestellt** finished **-gewalzt** finished rolled **-gruppe** *f* sub-assembly
Fertig-hobeln *n* finish planing **-kaliber** *n* finishing pass
Fertigkeit *f* dexterity, fluency, skill
fertig-kochen to boil off (sugar, silk, etc.) **-konzentrat** *n* finished concentrate **-machen** to finish, dress, finish type
Fertigmachmaschine *f* finishing machine
Fertigmaß *n* finished size **auf ~ bearbeiten** to finish to size
Fertig-material *n* finished product **-montage** *f* final assembly **-polieren** *n* polishing, planishing, final finishing, finishing to size **-polierkaliber** *n* last (planishing) pass, final-polish pass **-probe** *f* final test (smelting) **-produkt** *n* finished product **profil** *n* finished section **-reibahle** *f* finishing reamer **-reiben** to finish-ream **-schlacke** *f* white slag (electrometal)
Fertig-schleifen *n* finish grinding **-schlichten** to planish, finish, finish to size **-schlichten** *n* polishing, planishing, final finishing, finishing to size **-schlichtkaliber** *n* last planishing pass, last pass, final polish pass **-schlichtschnitt** *m* finishing cut **-schlichtstich** *m* last finishing pass, final polishing pass **-schneideisen** *n* bottoming die **-schneiden** *n* finishing (of threads) **-schneider** *m* bottoming tap **-schnitt** *m* finishing cut **-schweißen** *n* final welding
Fertig-signal *n* (Bergb.) all-clear signal, OK-signal (U.S.) **-sinterung** *f* final sintering operation **-staucher** *m* finishing edger **-stauchstempel** *n* header **-stellen** to finish, complete **-stellung** *f* finish, completion
Fertigstellungs-berichte *pl* completion reports **-daten** *pl* completion dates **-meldungen** *pl* completion reports
Fertig-stich *m* finishing pass, shaping pass **-stoffauslauf** *m* completed material discharge **-strang** *m* finishing-roll line **-straße** *f* finishing-mill train, finishing train **-strecke** *f* finishing rolls or train, finishing stands in train, finishing-mill train **-teil** *m* finished part **-teillager** *n* finished stores
Fertigung *f* fabrication, production, yield, output, finish, manufacture **zerspannende ~** cutting (steel) **fließende ~** progressive assembly **wirtschaftliche ~** economical manufacture
Fertigungs-ablaufdiagramm *n* flow chart, flow diagram **-ablaufstudie** *f* chronological study **-anlaufszeit** *f* lead time **-auftrag** *m* production order **-aufwand** *m* production requirement or cost **-betrieb** *m* industry **-engpaß** *m* production bottleneck **-fachmann** *m* production engineer
Fertigungs-fehler *m* manufacturing defect **-folge** *f* manufacturing program **-halle** *f* factory, workshop, finishing shop **-jahr** *n* year of manufacture **-kapazität** *f* production capacity **-kosten** *pl* production costs **-menge** *f* unit of production **-nummer** *f* serial number
Fertigungsplanung *f* production engineering **Abteilung für ~** production engineering department
Fertigungs-programm *n* production program **-prüfer** *m* works inspector **-reife** *f* production stage or testing **-solleistung** *f* scheduled production rate **-steuerung** *f* process control **-straße** *f* production line, conveyer system **-technik** *f* finishing technique
fertigungstechnische Gründe functional efficiency
Fertigungs-teil *m* finished or production part **-toleranz** *f* manufacturing tolerance **-verlage-**

rung *f* dispersal of manufacturing facilities **-vorbereitung** *f* manufacturing preparation **-zeit** *f* production time

Fertig-verarbeitung *f* finishing system (unit) **-walken** to plank up **-walze** *f* finishing roll **-walzen** to finish, roll to final gauge, finish-rolling **-wälzfräser** *m* finishing hob **-walzstraße** *f* finishing roll (or mill) train **-ware** *f* finished product **-warenbestand** *m* finished stock **-zug** *m* finishing pass (drawing) **-zugstempel** *m* finish draw punch **-zünder** *m* fixed fuse, ready-fixed fuse

Ferulasäure *f* ferulic acid

Fescolisieren *n* fescolizing

Fessel *f* caging (gyro), pastern, handcuffs, condenser (elec.) **-ballon** *m* captive balloon, kite balloon, observation balloon **-drachen** *m* captive kite **-flugzeug** *n* captive plane **-gelenk** *n* fetlock joint

Fesseligkeit *f* structural strength

Fessel-kabel *n* main hauling line, morring line **-kegel** *m* mooring cone **-kraftanzeiger** *m* mooring-cable strain indicator, mooring-force indicator

fesseln to fetter, captivate, chain, contain, fix, pin down, tie up

Fesseln *pl* fetters, shackles, irons

Fessel-punkt *m* mooring or anchoring point **-seil** *n* main hauling line **-start** *m* anchored start **-tau** *n* ground or mooring cable

Fesselung *f* pinning down, containing, restraint (gyro), slaving (gyro), cager (guided missiles)

Fesselungs-hebel *m* cager weight (guided missiles) **-kontakt** *m* gyro contact for restoring **-leine** *f* picketing-line attachments (aviation) **-spule** *f* caging coil

Fesselung *f* capacity

fest firm, solid; (hart) compact, hard; (widerstandsfähig) strong, sturdy; (starr) fixed, rigid; (Technik) stationary; (straff) tight; (dauernd) permanent; (unerschütterlich) firm, steady, unshakable; (dauerhaft) stable, durable; (Gehalt) fixed, fast, secure, established, locked, unvarying, proof ~ **abgestimmt** having fixed frequency, fixed-tuned ~ **an** integral with ~ **anziehen** (Schraube) to tighten (a screw) ~ **eingebaut** fixed ~ **werden** to set, become solidified **das Lager brennt** ~ the bearing seizes

fest-e Anlagen stationary plants **-er Brennstoff** solid fuel **-e Frequenz** fixed frequency (radar) **-er Index** fixed index **-e** (verklebte) **Kolbenringe** dead rings **-e Kopplung** *f* close coupling, strong coupling

fest-e Linie im Raum stabilized line **-e Luftschraube** fixed-pitch propeller **-e Steigung** fixed pitch **-e und bewegliche Anlagen** fixed assets and movables **-e Verlegung** stationary installation **-e Zeileneinstellung** fixed-line posting

fest-abstand *m* fixed distance **-abstandsfeuer** *pl* fixed distance lights **-amorph** solid-amorphous (state) **-antenne** *f* fixed antenna **-antennenlehre** *f* stress analysis

festbacken to cake together (by heat or pressure), bake together, frit together, clinker

Festbacken *n* caking, baking, fritting (together)

fest-binden to seize, tie up, fasten **-bleiben** to hold **-bett** *n* packet bed **-bettadsorber** *m* fixed bed adsorption unit **-block** *m* stationary block **-brennen** to burn to (ashes, death), sinter, seize (bearing) **-detektor** *m* contact or crystal detector **-drehmoment** *n* tightening torque

Feste *f* density, dimness, solidity

fest-eingebauter Ballast *m* fixed ballast **-eingebautes Lager** *n* staked bearings **-einstellung** *f* fixed setting

festfahren, sich ~ to deadlock

Festfahrwerk *n* fixed landing gear

Festfeuer *n* fixed light ~ **mit Blitzen** fixed and flashing light

festformatiger Falzapparat stationary folder

Festfrequenzen *pl* spot frequencies

festfressen to seize, jam, freeze **sich** ~ to seize (engine)

Fest-fressen *n* seizing, jamming **-frieren** to freeze fast **-gebremst** securely braked **-gefressen** seized up (engine)

festgehalten locked **-e Lage** constant missile angle **-es Ruder** fixed controls

fest-gekeilt wedged **-geklemmt** clamped **-gekoppelt** tightly coupled **-gelagert** firmly consolidated, compact, dead, fixed **-gelegt** definite, fixed, preset **-geschlagen** tight-spun (said of ropes) **-geschraubt** bolted, screwed

festgesetzt preset, settled, fixed (radar) **-es Gewicht** fixed weight **-e Temperatur** declared temperature **-e Zeit zum Entladen eines Schiffes** lay day

fest-gestellt fixed **-geworden** congealed **-gezogen** tightened **-haften** to adhere, stick to **-haftend** very adhesive **-haken** to hook in, bite, catch, hold **-haltefeder** *f* stop spring **-haltehebel** *m* stop lever

festhalten to lock, adjust, set, stop, brake, arrest, impede, dam, detain, hold back, restrain, maintain stationary, fix, secure, retain, hold **photographisch** ~ to record photographically (on record sheet)

Festhalte-platte *f* clevis plate **-stift** *m* detent pin **-stromkreis** *m* maintenance circuit **-vorrichtung** *f* locking device **zahn** *m* locking cog

Festhaltungsvermögen *n* retentivity (of adsorbents)

Festherd *m* stationary furnace bottom

festigen to consolidate, make fast or firm, fix establish, confirm

Festigkeit *f* ruggedness, strength, (tensile) solidity, stability, density, persistency, resistance (mech.), rigidity, firmness, tightness, tenacity, stiffness, sturdiness, compactness, consistency ~ **für 0,2% bleibende Dehnung** 0.2 strength ~ **des Holzes** strength of wood ~ **der Stoffe** strength of materials ~ **des Werkstoffes** resistance of the material **dielektrische** ~ dielectric strength, elastance **dynamische** ~ dynamic strength **elektrische** ~ electrical strength **mit hoher** ~ high-grade **höhere** ~ higher tensile values **die** ~ **reicht aus** the strength guarantees a safe working

Festigkeits-berechnung *f* stability computation (analysis), stress calculation **-eigenschaften** *pl* physical properties **-grad** *m* degree of firmness **-grenze** *f* limit of stability or density, breaking point, limit of resistance **-guß** *m* high-strength cast iron **-hypothese** *f* strength hypothesis **-koeffizient** *n* coefficient or modulus of resistance **-kurve** *f* stress curve, strength characteristic

-lehre *f* theoretical mechanics, (science of the) strength of materials, stress analysis **-modulus** *m* strength modulus **-nachweis** *m* stress analysis

Festigkeits-probe *f* testing of hardness **-prüfer** *m* strength tester **-prüfmaschine** *f* strength-testing machine **-prüfung** *f* strength test **-rechnung** *f* stress analysis **-schweißung** *f* strength weld **-skala** *f* strength scale **-steigerung des Werkstoffes durch Vorbeanspruchung** prestressing **-untersuchung** *f* stress analysis, strength test, tenacity test **-werte** *m pl* ultimate stress values, strength factors **-zahl** *f* stability ratio, consistency factor, strength coefficient, ultimate stress, coefficient or modulus of resistance **-ziffer** *f* coefficient or modulus of resistance

Festigung *f* strain hardening (forging)

festkeilen to wedge, wedge up, key (mach.) fasten by wedges, jam **auf der Welle ~** to key to the shaft

fest-klammern to clamp, grip in **-klampen** to cleat, screw fasten **-kleben** to stick fast **-kleben der Kolbenringe** ring sticking

festklemmen to clamp, tie up, jam **sich ~** to wedge, jam (tightly)

Fest-klemmen *n* jamming, wedging, blocking **-klemmvorrichtung** *f* clamping mechanism, traversing lock **-knebeln** to toggle

Festkomma *n* fixed point (data processing) **-darstellung** fixed-point representation **-rechnung** *f* fixed-point computation (comp.)

fest-kommen to run aground **-kondensator** *m* fixed or nonvariable condenser or capacitor

Festkörper *m* solid-state body **-begrenzung** *f* solid boundary **-modell** *n* models of solid **-oberfläche** *f* solid surface **-physik** *f* solid-state physics **-problem** *n* problem of solid bodies

festkrampen to cleat

Fest-kuppelung *f* tight coupling **-land** *n* mainland, continent

festlaufen, sich ~ to get stuck, bog down, stall, jam tight, seize, grip (of bearings)

Festläufer (Walzwerk) *m* cobbles; (Gießen) sticker

Festlegemittel *n* device for stopping, locking, arresting, adjusting, or setting

festlegen (bestimmen) to determine, fix, establish; (Termin) schedule; (Vertrag) stipulate; (Regel) lay down, define, fasten, clamp, secure in position, lock, anchor, formulate, arrest, stop, plot, locate, adjust, set **durch Linien ~** to delineate

Festlege-punkt *m* reference point, basic laying point **-spiegel** *m* sighting mirror **-zahl** *f* deflection reading, new reading in adjusting the piece

Fest-legung *f* localization, fixing, determination, making fast, agreement, accord, laying down (rules), immobilization **-liegend** fixed (stationary) **-lohn** *m* fixed wages

Fest-los-scheibe *f* fast and loose pulley

Festmache-boje *f* mooring buoy **-bügel** *m* mooring ring

festmachen to bed (mach.), belay, berth, consolidate, solidify, make concrete or firm, fasten, secure, attach, fix, lash, make fast, moor

Festmachen *n* solidification, tying

Fest-machepfahl *m* mooring pile, structure for mooring pier **-platz** *m* berth (place for moorings)

Festmacher *m* mooring line **-boje** *f* mooring buoy

Festmache-ring *m* mooring ring **-tau** *n* cable, hawser **-tonne** *f* mooring buoy **-vorrichtungen** *pl* mooring gear or equipment

Fest-marke *f* permanent echo **-maß** *n* solid measure **-meter** *m* solid or cubic meter **-nageln** to nail

Festnaht *f* strength weld

Fest- oder Vollscheibe *f* fast pulley

Festonwolke *f* festoon cloud

Fest-preis *m* fixed price **-pressen** to squeeze, press home **-propeller** *m* fixed pitch propeller

Festpunkt *m* fixed point, ground point of control, anchorage, reference, fixed datum or bench mark, elevation (above a certain point, surveying, etc.), fixed target, datum, section point

Fest-(Fix-)punkt *m* reference point **~ für Leitungskreuzungen** for line crossings **~ für Spulenabstände** for loading coil spacing

Festpunkt-bestimmung *f* triangulation, levelling **-netz** *n* framework of fixed points, control-point net

Fest-rahmenantenne *f* fixed loop antenna **-rammen** to tamp **-reibung** *f* solid friction **-reyon** *n* high strength rayon **-rolle** *f* fixed pulley **-rosten** to rust into **-rostgaserzeuger** *m* fixed (or stationary) grate-type gas producer, dry bottom gas producer

Fest-schablonen *pl* single-purpose templets **-scheibe** *f* tight pulley, fixed or fast pulley **-scheibenantrieb** *m* tight-pulley drive **-schießen** to seat the base plate by firing **-schlagen** to fasten with blows, drive home **-schnallen** to buckle on, strap **-schnallvorrichtung** *f* safety-belt assembly, parachute harness **-schnüren** to lace up **-schrauben** to fasten with screws, screw on (up or tightly), bolt, secure by bolts, tighten

festsetzen to fix (reinforcement), stipulate, determine, define, clog, seize, gain a foothold, assess (charges), settle, establish **sich ~** to settle **vorher ~** pre-establish

Festsetzung *f* timing of calls, determination, stipulation, definition, clogging, fixing, appointment, terms

Festsetzvorrichtung *f* locking gear

Festsitz *m* medium-force fit, interference fit, tight fit, close fit, driving fit (petroleum), snug fit

festsitzen to be jammed tight, be stuck

Festsitzen des Sicherheitsventils auf dem Sitz sticking of the safety valve to its seat

festspannen to clamp or stretch tightly

Festspannen *n* gripping, chucking, holding, clamping, stretching

Festspann-mutter *f* draw-in nut (clamping nut) **-schraube** *f* draw-in spindle

Festspannung *f* fixed voltage

Festspannvorrichtung *f* clamping device

festspiekern to nail

feststampfen to tamp firm, ram, pun, beat down, stamp

Fest-stampfen *n* tamping, punning, packing, ramming up, tamping down, stamping down **-stauen** *n* scaffold, scaffolding, obstruction in blast furnace

fest-stecken to stitch **-stehen** to be certain, stand fast, be settled, stand still

feststehend stationary, fixed, stable, established, firm, fast **-e Achse** solid, fixed, dead, or stationary axle **-er Anker mit Wicklung** stationary armature with winding **-er Anschlag für die Auslösung der selbsttätigen Vertikalbewegung** vertical feed-trip blocks **-e Brille oder Lünette** steady rest **-er Fadenführer** stationary thread guide **-es Handrad** rising wheel (valve) **-e Kraft** fixed force **-er Magnet** stationary magnet **-e Maschine** stationary engine **-es Messer** dead knife **-e Pumpe** fixed pump **-e Spitze** dead center **-e Teile** *m pl* fixed parts **-er Zeiger** marking pointer

feststellbar determinable, ascertainable, lockable (in position), fixable, securable **-er Lagerverschleiß** perceptible bearing wear

Feststell-bock *m* locking bracket **-bolzen** *m* locking pin, locking bolt **-bremse** *f* manually operated brake, locking bracke, parking brake **-buchse** *f* locking socket

feststellen establish, state; (erklären) declare; (ermitteln) find out, detect; (bestimmen) determine; (Lage) locate; (spannen) clamp, lock; (beobachten) notice, observe, confirm, fix, settle, discover, determine, log a station, ascertain, localize (a fault), adjust, set, brake, arrest, impede, dam, detain, hold back, restrain, maintain stationary, to stop, secure (in position), to verify, to identify **Fehler ~** to state, locate (faults) **die (Uhr)zeit ~** to determine the time

Feststeller *m* shift lock, end stop

Feststell-hebel *m* binder **-kegel** *m* cone stop collar **-klammer** *f* fixing clip **-klinke** *f* locking pawl **-knagge** *f* stop **-knopf** *m* lock knob **-mutter** *f* lock nut **-pinzette** *f* fixation forceps **-platte** *f* fixing plate

Feststell-riegel *m* fixing bolt **-schieber** *m* blocking slide **-schraube** *f* setscrew, lock bolt, locking screw, anchoring screw **-segment** *n* notched locking quadrant **-stift** *n* index, locking pin **-stöpsel** *m* locking pin **-taste** *f* shift lock key

Feststellung *f* establishment, findings; (Festklemmung) clamping, locking in position, securing; (Vorrichtung) detent, locking device, statement, location, stopping, verification, timing, identification, determination, confirmation, stopwork (watch), establishment, stop, stoppage, arresting, lock **~ der Giftgase** detection of poison gases **~ der Lichtstärke** candle-power test **~ des stationären Schubs** static-thrust test **~ vom Sender durch Peilungen** logging a station by means of direction finder

Feststellungs-klage *f* declaratory action **-urteil** *n* declaratory judgment

Feststellvorrichtung *f* blocking gear, locking gear or device, relieving gear, control clamping device

Feststoff-abscheidung *f* removal of solids **-anteile** *pl* solid matter content

Feststoffe hard substances, solid matter **~ körnige** granular solids

Feststoff-förderleistung *f* solids pipeline **-gewinnung** *f* reclaiming of solid matter **-marschantrieb** *m* soild propellant system (of spacecraft) **-partikel** *n* particulate solid **-rakete** *f* (Astron.) solid fuel rocket, solid-propellant booster rocket **-raketenmotor** *m* solid rocket motor

Fest-substanz *f* solid phase, solids **-tag** *m* holiday

Festtreibstoff *m* (Astron.) solid propellant **-zündraketensatz** *m* solid propellant rocket boosters

festtreten to tamp

Fest- und Leerlaufscheibe *f* fast and loose pulley **und Losriemenscheibe** *f* fast and loose pulley **und Losscheibe** *f* fast and loose pulley

Festungs-reihe *f* chain of fortifications **-verband** *m* diagonal bond (masonry)

Fest-verhältnis *n* locked ratio **-verlegt** metal-braided and connected (of cable) **-verspannt** fixed **-weich** semisolid **-welle** *f* fixed wave **-werden** *n* freezing solid in boring, sticking, thickening, solidification, coagulation

Festwert *m* constant (math.), coefficient **unveränderlicher ~** constant (of meter or instrument)

Festwertregelung *f* continuous value control, fixed point control (aut. contr), regulation with fixed set point, set-value control

Festwiderstand *m* (Gegenstand) fixed resistor; (Eigenschaft) fixed resistance

Fest-zacke *f* permanent echo (radar) **-zahl** *f* constant

Festzeichen *n* permanent echo (radar) **-befreiung** *f* fixed-echo elimination **-löscher** *m* (rdr.) moving target indicator (MTI) **-unterdrückung** *f* permanent echo cancellation (rdr.)

Festzeitgespräch *n* appointment message

fest-ziehen to tighten (a screw, bolt), secure, screw down (a nut), fasten, draw fast **-ziehmoment** *n* tightening torque **-zündung** *f* fixed ignition **-zurren** to lash, clamp securely

Fetch *f* fetch, extent of the open sea

Fett *n* grease, lubricant, fat (of clay), glut **~ für Ausschalter** switch grease **~ für Heißwalzen** hot-roll neck grease **~ für Kaltwalzen** cold-roll neck grease **~ für Kugellager** ball-bearing grease **~ zur Schmierung des Achsenlagers** axle-box grease, railroad journal grease **~ einspritzen** to grease, lubricate **konsistentes ~** consistent lubricant **säurefreies ~** noncorrosive grease **tierisches ~** animal grease

fett greasy, oily, fat, fatty, rich, fertile, aliphatic, profitable, obese, bituminous **~ gedruckt** in bold-face type **-es Gemisch** rich mixture **-er Lack** oily lacquer

Fett-abscheider *m* grease extractor or separator **-anstrich** *m* grease film **-artig** fatty, greasy (lipoid) **-avivage** *f* brightening with fat **-basis** *f* fatty basis **-bestandteil** *m* fatty substance **-büchse** *f* grease cup, lubricator **-buchse** *f* lubricator

fettdicht greaseproof, fat-tight **-es Papier** butter paper, greaseproof paper

Fett-druck *m* bold-face type **-dunst** *m* greasy mist **-echt** grease-proof

fetten to grease, oil, lubricate, stuff

Fett-fang *m* grease trap, grease separator **-fänger** *m* grease filter (for greasy water) **-feine Linie** shaded rule **-fleckphotometer** *n* Bunsen or grease-spot photometer **-förderkohle** *f* fat semibituminous run-of-mine coal **-frei** grease-free **-gar** oil-tanned **-gas** *n* oil gas **-gedruckt** printed in bold **-gehalt** *m* fat content **-gemisch** *n* mixtures of fats **-glanz** *m* fatty aspect, greasy luster

fett-haltig fatty **-härtung** *f* fat hardening **-harzreserve** *f* fat resin resist

Fett-hüllen *pl* greaseproof bags **-hülse** *f* grease wrapper

fettig greasy, oily, fatty, unctuous, adipose ~ **anfühlen** to feel greasy

Fettigkeit *f* fattiness, lubricity, oiliness, unctuousness (plastic, soapy)

Fett-kalk *m* fat, burnt, or white lime **-kammer** *f* grease chamber, grease pocket **-kasten** *m* grease box **-kessel** *m* fat boiler, tinman's pot **-kohle** *f* fat coal, caking coal, coking coal, bituminous coal **-kohlenwasserstoff** *m* aliphatic hydrocarbon **-körper** *m* aliphathic compound **-licker** *m* fat-liquor **-loch** *n* natural oil seepage **-löser** *m* (Phräparat) fat solvent **-löslich** soluble in fat **-lösungsmittel** *n* grease solvent

Fett-menge *f* quantity of fat **-nippel** *n* grease gun **-öl** *n* fatty oil

Fetton *m* fuller's earth, diatomaceous earth

Fett-papier *n* greaseproof paper **-presse** *f* grease gun **-preßnippel** *n* alemite fitting **-pumpe** *f* grease gun **-puddeln** *n* (of iron) pig boiling, wet puddling **-quarz** *m* resinous quartz **-reihe** *f* aliphatic series **-rückförderring** *m* grease return ring **-sauer** sebacic, sebate of

Fettsäure *f* fatty acid, sebacic acid **-destillieranlage** *f* fatty-acid still

Fett-schliff *n* greased (ground-in) joint **-schmelzer** *m* grease boiler **-schmiere** *f* fat liquor **-schmierer** *m* greaser **-schmierpresse** *f* grease gun **-schmierpumpe** *f* grease pump **-schmierung** *f* grease lubrication, greasing **-spaltend** fat cleaving, lipolytic **-spaltung** *f* cleavage of fat, lipolysis **-spritze** *f* grease gun **-schwarz** *m* fat soluble black

Fett-seife *f* fat dissolving soap **-stein** *m* eleolite, nephelite, nepheline **-stecher** *m* fat knife **-stift** *m* colored wax pencil **-stoff** *m* fatty matter **-tasche** *f* grease pocket **-ton** *m* fuller's earth **-überzug** *m* grease coating

Fett- und Ölbeständigkeit *f* grease resistance

Fettung *f* greasing, lubrication, oiling

Fett-verbindung *f* aliphatic compound **-wachs** *n* adipocere **-walke** *f* kicking process **-zumeßventil** *n* grease-proportioning valve **-zusatz bei der Saturation** addition of oil in saturation

Fetzen *m* rag, shred

feucht wet, damp, moist, humid **-e Appretur** damp finish **-es Kugelthermometer** wet-bulb thermometer **-e Luft** humid or moist air, damp air **-e adiabatische Maßveränderung** wet adiabatic lapse rate **-e Oberfläche** wetted surface **-er Ölsumpf** wet sump **-er Raum** damp room **-er adiabatischer Zustand der Luft** wet adiabatic lapse rate

feucht dämpfen to steam in moist steam

feuchtadiabatisch moistadiabatic (lapse)

Feucht-apparat *m* wetting machine **-brett** *n* wetting board **-druck** *m* humidity content

Feuchte *f* moistness, moisture, dampness **-gewicht** *n* drained weight **-graderhöhung** *f* humidification **-messer** *m* humidity meter, hygrometer, psychrometer

feuchten to moisten, dampen, wet, damp, mollify

Feuchte-regelung *f* moisture control **-schreiber** *m* humidity recorder

Feucht-filz *m* moleskin **-glätte** *f* dampers, damping rolls, nip rolls, water finish, smoothing rolls (paper) **-glättwerk** *n* breaker stack (paper mfg.) **-haltung** *f* (Beton) moist curing (concrete)

Feuchtheit *f* dampness, moisture, humidity

Feuchtigkeit *f* dampness, humidity, moisture, moistness, wetness ~ **austreiben** to expel humidity

Feuchtigkeits-abdichtung *f* vapor barrier **-anzeiger** *m* hygroscope **-aufnahme** *f* moisture pick-up, absorption of moisture soakage (as of a hull) **-ausgleich** *m* humidity compensation **-beständig** dampproof **-bestimmung** *f* moisture determination

feuchtigkeits-dicht dampproof **-einflüsse** *pl* humidity effects **-empfindlich** mosture sensitive **-entzug** *m* dehumidifaction **-fest** moisture-resistant or -resisting **-geber** *m* humidity cell **-gehalt** *m* moisture content or percentage, humidity content **-grad** *m* moisture content **-gradmesser** *m* moisture meter **-korrosion** *f* aqueous corrosion

Feuchtigkeitsmesser *m* hygrometer, hygroscope, psychrometer, wet- and dry-bulb thermometer **registrierender** ~ hygrograph

Feuchtigkeits-meßgerät *n* moisture measuring device **-nebenschluß** *m* humidity derivation **-regelung** *f* air-conditioning **-rest** *m* residue of moisture **-schreiber** *m* hygrograph **-schutz** *m* humidity protection **-sicher** dampproof, moistureproof, nonhygroscopic **-temperatur** *f* wet and dry bulb temperature **-wasser** *n* moisture **-zeiger** *m* hygroscope **-zustand** *m* state of humidity

feuchtigkeitvertreibend acting as a hygrofuge

feucht-kalt clammy **-kammer** *f* wetting room **-labilität** *f* conditional instabilit, hygroscopic instability **-lagerversuch** *m* damp storage tests, high fumidity and condensation test **-maschine** *f* wetting machine **-presse** *f* dampers, damping rolls **-proben** *pl* moisture tests **-raumleitung** *f* conductor for moist places, dampproof installation cable **-raumprüfung** *f* humid room test **-raum- und Mantelleitungen** *pl* dampproof and non-metallic sheathed wires **-schalter** *m* tropical or feet switch

Feucht-schutzisolation *f* moisture-proof insulation **-stein** *m* press (print.) **-temperatur** (Klimaanlage) *f* wet bulb temperature **-thermometer** *n* wet bulb thermometer **-tisch** *m* wetting table

Feuchtung *f* wetting, moistening

Feucht-walzenschlauch *m* cylinder moistening hose **-walzenstoff** *m* moleskin **-warm** muggy (met.), with warm moist temperature **-wasser** *n* damping solution **-wasserfarbe** *f* water color **-werk** *n* damping device

Feuer *n* fire, conflagration; light, signal light, luminous signal, beacon, (radio) beam, station, radio range ~ (als Seezeichen), light (of lighthouse), light (a navigation light) ~ **anmachen** to set, light, or kindle a fire ~ **anschüren** to poke the fire

Feuer, bengalisches ~ false flames ~ **fangen** to catch or take fire **durch** ~ **gebildet** igneous ~ **kreuzen** to cross-fire **unter** ~ **nehmen** to fire upon, open fire on, shell-strafe ~ **schüren** to stir, stoke, or tease the fire ~ **verteilen** to distribute fire **das ~ vorverlegen** to lengthen range, lift fire, advance fire ~ **zusammenfassen** to concentrate fire

Feuer-abriegelung *f* box barrage **-anzeiger** *m* fire detector **-anzünder** *m* lighter **-art** *f* method of fire **-arten** *pl* classification of fire **-bake** *f* light beacon

Feuer-begriffe *pl* fire classification **-beheizt** fuel-fired **-bekämpfung** *f* fire fighting **-beobachtung** *f* observation of fire **-bereich** *n* field of fire, fire zone

feuerberührt (surface) exposed to the fire **-e Heizfläche** convection heat surface

Feuerbeschränkung *f* firing limitation

feuerbeständig refractory, fire-resisting, fire-proof, heat-resistant, fixed **-er Guß** heatproof cast iron **-er Ziegel** firebrick

Feuer-beständigkeit *f* refractoriness, heat resistance, refractory property, refractory quality, power of resisting heat, fireproofness **-bestattungsanstalt** *f* crematorium

Feuerblech *n* furnace plates ~ **aus Flußeisen** mild steel plate flanged for fireboxes

Feuer-blende *f* fireblende, pyrostilpnite **-bock** *m* fire bridge **-brücke** *f* bridge of boiler furnace, fire bridge, (front) bridge wall, flame bridge **-brückenkühlrohre** firebridge water boxes **-brunst** *f* great fire

Feuerbuchs-bodenring *m* firebox bottom flange **-bohrmaschine** *f* firebox drilling machine **-decke** *f* firebox crown

Feuerbüchse *f* combustion chamber, firebox (of boiler), locomotive furnace, furnace **-strebe** *f* firebox stay

Feuerbuchs-kessel *m* internal-flue boiler **-mantel** *m* firebox shell **-rohrwand** *f* front wall of firebox **-rückwand** *f* back plate of a firebox

Feuer-dämpfer *m* flash hider **-einheit** *f* fire unit **-einstellung** *f* cessation of fire **-emaillierung** *f* vitreous-enamelling **-empfindlich** sensitive to fire or heat **-erlaubnis** *n* permission to fire **-eröffnung** *f* opening or commencement of fire **-farben** fiery red

feuerfest incombustible, refractory, fireproof, heatproof **-er Anstrich** fireproof coating or dope **-er Anzug** fireproof clothing or suit **-er Baustoff** refractory or fireproof building material **-es Futter** refractory lining **-er Kitt** fireproof cement

feuerfest-e Materialien refractory products **-er Mörtel** refractory mortar **-er Stein** firebrick, refractory stone **-er Ton** fire clay, firebrick **-e Wand** firebrick wall **-er Zement** refractory cement **-er Ziegel** firebrick

Feuerfestigkeit *f* refractoriness

Feuerfläche (Heizfläche) heating surface

feuerflüssig liquid to melting temperature, liquid at high temperature, molten, fused **-e Elektrolyse** electrolytic furnace operation

Feuer-fühler *m* fire detector **-gase** *pl* fire gases, furnace gases, burnt gases, flame gases, waste gases, products of combustion, flue gases, combustion gases **-gasrest** *m* residual combustion gas **-gefahr** *f* fire hazard, fire risk **-gefährlich** hazardous, inflammable, combustible **-gefährlichkeit** *f* (in)flammability, liability, fire hazard **-geschränk** *n* furnace front

feuergetrocknet fire-dried, fire-fried **-e Schnitzel** fire-fried beet pulp

Feuer-gewicht *n* density of fire **-grube** *f* ash hole or pit **-hahn** *m* fireplug, fire hydrant, fire cock **-haken** *m* fire rake, poker, stoker's poker bar **-harke** *f* fire rake **-haut** *f* lining (especially in rocket-combustion chambers)

feuerhemmend fire-resistive **-e Farbe** fire-retardant paint

Feuer-kammer *f* firebox of boiler **-kampf** *m* fire fight, duel, or duel weapons **-kanal** *m* flue **-kasten** *m* combustion chamber **-kette** *f* skirmish line, line of skirmishers **-kiste** *f* furnace, firebox **-kitt** *m* clay or fireproof mortar (for setting firebricks)

Feuer-kraft *f* fire power **-krücke** *f* furnace rake, rabble, fire rake **-kugel** *f* meteor **-lärm** *m* fire alarm **-leitanlage** *f* fire control system **-leiter** *m* fire escape

Feuerlösch-anlage *f* fire-extinguishing equipment, fire extinguisher **-apparat** *m* fire extinguisher **-boot** *n* fire-float (boat), fire-float pump **-brause** *f* sprinkler **-decke** *f* fire-extinguishing cover

Feuerlöscher *m* fire extinguisher

Feuerlösch-flüssigkeit *f* fire-extinguishing fluid **-gerät** *n* fire-extinguishing appliances **-hauptleitung** *f* fire main **-hydrant** fire hydrant **-mittel** *n* fire-extinguishing medium **-ordnung** *f* fire-prevention plan **-pumpe** *f* fire-extinguishing pump **-schaum** *m* Foamite (fire-extinguishing foam) **-sprengapparat** *m* automatic sprinkler **-steigerohr** *n* rising main **-stutzen** *m* rising-main hose connection **-system** *n* sprinkler system **-wasser** *n* fire water

Feuer-löten *n* muffle brazing **-lötung** *f* sweating **-meldeapparat** *m* fire alarm (instrument)

Feuermelder *m* fire detector, fire alarm (signal box) **-leitung** *f* fire-alarm circuit

Feuermeldestelle *f* fire station

feuern to fire, heat, burn, spark, flash

Feuern *n* flashing, sparking, arcing

Feuer-ordnung *f* method of fire **-patsche** *f* fire swatter used in fire fighting **-pause** *f* firing pause, interval in firing, cease firing **-pausenwert** *m* stand-by datum

Feuer-pfosten *m* fireplug, fire hydrant **-plan** *m* firing chart, coordinated fire plan

Feuer-politur *f* fire-polish (of glassware) **-probe** *f* fire test **-punkt** *m* fire point (aviation), focus (optics), hearth (min.) **-quelle** *f* source of fire

Feuerraum *m* combustion chamber, fireplace, firebox, furnace, hearth **-belastung** *f* furnace-heat capacity, heat release per unit grate area **-decke** *f* furnace roof **-kühlsystem** *n* furnace water walls

Feuer-regelung *f* regulation of fire **-reihe** *f* (d. Befeuerung) row of lights (of lighting system) **-richtung** *f* direction of fire **-riegel** *m* box barrage **-ring** *m* fire ring **-risiko** *n* fire risk

Feuerrohr *n* flue (metal tube in boiler), fire tube **-bürste** *f* flue or tube brush **-kessel** *m* fire-tube boiler

Feuer-rost *m* grate, fire grate **-rüpel** *m* chimney sweeper **-säule** *f* column of flames **-schaufel** *f* fire shovel **-schein** *m* gun flash, glare of fire **-schiff** *n* floating light, lightship (mar.) **-schlag** *m* burst of fire, rafale, sudden concentration **-schlauch** *m* fire hose **-schott** *m* firewall

Feuerschutz-kanal *m* fire-protection flue **-polizei**

f fire-protection police **-trommel** *f* safety magazine (of film projector)

Feuer-schwaden *m* firedamp **-schwamm** *m* tinder **-schweißung** *f* forge welding **-schwindung** *f* fire shrinkage **-setzen** *n* fire setting

Feuersgefahr *f* fire risk, fire hazard

feuersicher flameproof, fire-resisting, fireproof, fire-resistant, incombustible, refractory (to fire) **-machen** to flameproof

Feuer-signal *n* fire-alarm signal, fire call **-sirene** *f* fire alarm siren **-sperre** *f* barrage, protective barrage, final protective fire **-spritze** *f* fire-engine, fire hose, fire extinguisher **-spritzen-schlauch** *m* fire hose **-steg** *m* (Kolben) (piston) top land **-steigerung** *f* increased rate or intensification of fire **-stein** *m* flint, silex, firestone, firebrick **-steinpulver** *n* powdered flint **-stelle** *f* firebox

Feuer-trockner *m* apparatus for direct drying by means of furnace gases **-trocknung** *f* direct drying **-trotz** *m* fireproof (in compound words) **-tür** *f* fire door, stoking door, coaling door, furnace door **-turm** *m* lighthouse **-überlegenheit** *f* fire superiority

Feuerung *f* heating, firing, fireplace, firebox, fire, furnace, hearth; (Gas- und Ölfeuerung) *f* firing equipment **~ mit Druckluft** forced-draft furnace **~ für die Toppingsanlage, für die Krackanlage** topping, cracking furnace **~ der Zirkulationsanlage für dunkles Öl** black-oil circulation furnace

Feuerungen *pl* combustion accessories

Feuerungs-anlage *f* fire equipment, furnace, hearth, fireplace **-bau** *m* heating-plant construction **-kunde** *f* fuel engineering **-material** *n* fuel **-mörtel** *m* firclay mortar **-raum** *m* boileroom **-rost** *m* fire grate, furnace grate **-rückstände** *pl* furnace residue **-technik** *f* firing practice, fuel engineering **-technisch** pyrotechnic(al) **-tür** *f* fire door, stoking door, coaling door **-unterstützung** *f* supporting fire **-verfahren** *n* method of heating firing or stoking **-zug** *m* heating flue

feuer-vergoldet fire-gilt **-verkadmen** to hot cadmium-plate **-verlötet** sweated together **-versicherung** *f* fire insurance **-versilberung** *f* silver coating, hot-dip silver-plating

feuer-verzinken to (hot) galvanize, pot galvanize **-verzinken** *n* pot galvanizing, hot galvanizing **-verzinkung** *f* hot galvanizing, pot galvanizing, hot galvanization, pot galvanization **-verzinnen** *n* hot tinning, tin coating **-verzinnt** fire-tinned **-verzinnung** *f* hot tin plating, hot-dip tinning **-wache** *f* fire station, fire guard **-wand** *f* (combustion) chamber wall

Feuerwehr *f* fire bridgade, fire department **-anschluß** *m* fire hydrant **-posten** *m* fire station **-telegraph** *m* fire-alarm telegraph

Feuer-weiß *n* surface foam (on glassware) **-werk** *n* fireworks **-werker** *m* ordnance sergeant, artificer, member of a bomb-disposal squad, demolitions expert **-werkhellegat** *n* gunners' store **-werkskörper** *m* pyrotechnic composition **-wirkung** *f* fire effect

Feuer-zange *f* fire tongs **-zarge** *f* box of fire door **-zement** *m* refractory mortar **-zersplitterung** *f* dissipation of fire

Feuerzeug *n* tinderbox, cigar or pocket lighter, cigarette lighter **-lunte** *f* match cord

Feuer-ziegel *m* fire bricks **-zug** *m* heating flue, flue, draft chimney

feurig fiery

F-Farbzentrum *n* F-center

F-Haube *f* cowling

Fiatofen *m*, **Fiat** *m* (direct-arc nonconducting hearth-type) furnace

Fiber *f* fiber **-bolzen** *m* fiber pin **-dichtung** *f* fiber washer **-hülse** *f* fiber sleeve **-keil** *m* fiber wedge **-klötzchen** *n* fiber button **-leinenscheibe** *f* fibrous linen disc **-packung** *f* fiber packing **-rad** *n* fiber pinion

Fiberring *m* fiber ring **Mutter mit Sicherung durch elastische Verformung eines Fiberringes** elastic stop nut

Fiber-ritzel *n* fiber pinion **-rohr** tubes made of fiber **-rohrstrang** *m* fiber duct, fiber conduit **-scheibe** *f* fiber plate, disk **-zahnrad** *n* fiber pinion

Fibrille *f* fibrel

Fibroin *n* fibroin

fibrös fibrous

Fibrox *n* Fibrox (a fibrous oxycarbide of silicon)

Fichte *f* pine, spruce

Fichtenharz *n* pine resin, spruce resin **trockenes ~** white resin

Fichten-holz *n* pinewood, balsam (fir), deal or plank **-nadel** *f* pine needle

Ficierungspaar *n* standard couple (spectrum analysis)

Fid *m* or *f* splicing fid

Fieberbaum(-holz) *m* gumwood

Fieber-messer *m*, **-thermometer** *n* clinical thermometer

Fiedelbogen *m* fiddle bow, fiddle drill, drill bow

Fiederstreifung *f* orientation of striae

Fiederungsstrich *m* tail stroke

fieren to lower, veer off, slacken, ease away, pay out (a cable) **die Stenge ~** to strike the topmast **zu Wasser ~** to lower (boat)

Figur *f* shape, figure, diagram **stehende ~** stationary pattern or figure

Figuren-druck *m* figure printing **-verzeichnis** *n* index of figures **-wechsel** *m* shift (signal), inversion

Figurscheibe *f* silhouette target **-schuß** *m* figuring weft

fiktiv fictive, imaginary, fictitious **-es Vermittlungsamt** hypothetical central office

Filet *n* network, netting, doffer **-trommel** *f* doffer (textiles)

Filiale *f* subsidiary, branch establishment

Filigran *n* filigree

Film *m* film **doppelbeschichteter ~** sandwich film, double-coated film **gegossener ~** coated film **glasklarer ~** pellucid film stock **mehrfachbeschichteter ~** double-coated film, sandwich film **plastischer ~** stereoscopic film, plastic film **unverbrennbarer ~** slow-burning film, safety film **verregneter ~** rainy film

Film-abheber *m* plow (to peel film from teeth) **-absatz** *m* packing, wear and tear **-abtaster** *m* film scanner, telecine equipment **-abtastung** *f* telecine transmission, film scanning **-abwickler** *m* magazine drum, feeding reel **-architektur** *f* setting and composition **-atmen** *n* in-and-out-of-focus effects **-auflaufspule** *f* film-take-up spool or reel **-aufnahmekammer** *f* cinematograph, moving- or motion-picture camera **-aufwickelspule** *f* film-take-up spool or reel **-aufwickelvorrichtung** *f* film-winding mechanism **-bahn** *f* film track, film channel

Film-band *n* film tape, film band, film strip **-bandführung** *f* aperture guide **-baukunst** *f* setting and composition **-belichtungsstelle** *f* film gate **-bewegung** *f* intermittent film feed or movement **-bildner** *m* (Farbe) film-former **-bildschicht** *f* film emulsion, film coat **-bildweise** *f* intermittent film feed or movement **-blitz** *m* statics (motion-picture film) **-doppeln** *n* film duplicating **-druck** *m* screen printing, film printing

Film-ebene *f* plane of the film **-einfädelung** *f* **-einführung** *f* threading of film **-einschnürung** *f* squeezing or compression of film **-einzelmessung** *f* single measurements on film **-entwickelungsvorrichtung** *f* film-processing equipment **-fenster** *n* film gate, film trap **-fernsehabtastung** *f* telecine scan **-fernsehsystem** *n* intermediate film television system **-fläche** *f* surface of film **-format** *n* film size **-fortschaltung** *f* film feed, film motion, film travel **-führung** *f* film feed, film guiding, film gate **-führungsrolle** *f* film take-up spool

Film-geber *m* film transmitter, film pickup, film scanner, telecinematographic device **-gießlösung** *f* film casting solution **-justierung** *f* registration of film **-kameralaufwerk** *n* camera-film-feed mechanism **-kammer** *f* film camera, roll-film camera **-kanal** *m* film track, film channel **-kassette** *f* film magazine (roll film) **-kern** *m* reel, spool **-kittlehre** *f* film-splicing gauge **-klebemittel** *n* film adhesive **-kufen** *pl* film slide

Film-lauf *m* film run, film track, film travel, film path **-laufkontrolle** *f* film-run control **-laufwerk** *n* film drive, film-fed mechanism **-magazin** *n* film magazine **-masken** *pl* masking frames **-merkscheibe** *f* film indicator **-messer** *m*, **-meterzähler** *m* footage counter

Film-packkassette *f* film-pack magazine **-projektionsfenster** *n* aperture, gate **-rahmen** *m* focal film register **-rand** *m* film edge **-registerhaltigkeit** *f* registration or stability of film **-regler** *m* film-traction regulator (stabilizer) **-reihenbildkammer** *f*, **-reihenkammer** *f* serial-film camera **-rolle** *f* film take-up spool or reel **-rollenschneidmaschine** *f* film-roll cutting machine **-schablone** *f* film screen **-schale** *f* film cup

Film-schaltung *f* film feed or movement **bildweise ~** intermittent film motion, discontinouus film feed

Film-schichtseite *f* emulsion side of film **-schleife** *f* film loop **-schneiden** *n* film editing **-schwanz** *m* trailer runout (piece of blank film at end) **-schwärzung** *f* film density **-sensitometer** *m* sensitometer, timer **-spannung** *f* film tension, film traction **-speicher** *m* film memory **-spule** *f* film spool **-spulenhalter** *m* film-roll holder **-steilheit** *f* contrast of film **-stelle** *f* film station **-streifen** *m* film strip **-träger** *m* film carrier, film base, film support

Filmtransport *m* film feed, forward movement of the film **-anlage** *f* film-drive spocket **-mechanismus** *m* film-movement mechanism **-rolle** *f* film (-feed) sprocket, film drive sprocket

Film-trommel *f* film drum (phot.) **-tür** *f* film gate **übertragung** *f* telecine transmission, film scanning **-übertragungsanlage** *f* flying spot film scanners **-uhr** *f* footage counter

Film- und Freilichtaufnahmen *pl* film and outdoor direct pickups

Film- und Tonbandschnitt *m* film and sound cutting

Film-verarbeitung *f* film processing **-verblitzung** *f* dendriform exposure of film **-verleih** *m* film lending (institute) **-vertrieb** *m* release of film, distribution of film **-vorführapparat** *m* motion-picture projector **-vorführung** *f* film demonstration, film projection, film exposure (in gate) **-vorlauf** *m* lead or precession of sound recording **-vorratsspule** *f* film-magazine roll, magazine **-vorschub** *m* film feed **-wirkung** *f* merit or quality of picture **-wölbung** *f* film buckling **-zähler** *m* footage counter **-zug** *m* film pull

Filter *m* electric-wave filter, filter, sifter, strainer **akustischer ~** acoustic filter **aschenfreier ~** ashless filter **rotarmer ~** red-abstracting filter **tonrichtiger ~** true-color filter, pure-color filter, orthochromatic filter **~ mit induktivem Eingang** choke-input filter **~ mit kapazitivem Eingang** capacitor-input filter

Filter-abgriff *m* filter arrangement **-ablaß** *m* filter drawoff

Filterabschluß *m* filter termination **~ durch ein halbes Längsglied** mid-series filter termination **~ durch ein halbes Querglied** mid-shunt filter termination

Filter-abschnitt *m* filter section **-belag** *m* filter floor or plate **-blatt** *n* filter paper **-brandhahn** *m* filter-safety-cock fitting (armature) **-becken** *n* filtering basin **-betätigung** *f* filter handle **-bett** *n* filter bed

Filterbeutel *m* filter bag **ein Satz ~** set of filter bags

Filter-bewegung *f* seepage flow **-brücke** *f* filter bracket

Filterbrunnen *m* spring well, well point **-aggregat** *n* battery of filter wells, well points **-rohr** *n* artesian casing

Filter-büchse *f* canister (mask), gas-mask canister **-deckel** *m* filter cup, filter cover **-drossel** *f* filter choke **-durchlaßbereich** *m* filter pass band **-effekt** *m* filtering effect **-eingang** *m* input filter **-einheit** *f* filter unit **-einlage** *f* filter cone **-einsatz** *m* strainer, filter element or unit, container, filtering apparatus **-element** *n* filter element

filter-fähiger Werkstoff permeable material **-faktor** *m* filter factor, screen factor **-federungswiderstand** *m* compliance (of mechanical filter) **-feinheit** *f* grade of filtration **-fläche** *f* filter area **-folie** *f* filter foil **-gehäuse** *n* filter housing, filter case, arrester case, filter container; (Kraftheber) oil-filter bowl (hydraulic lift unit) **-gehäusedeckel** *m* cleaner cap **-geschwindigkeit** *f* filtration velocity **-gesetz** *n* filter law (Darcy's law) **-gewebe** *n* filter gauze, filter mesh, filtering tissue **-glied** *n* filter section, filter mesh, filter unit **-glocke** *f* filter hood **-gur** *f* diatomaceous **~ gut** *n* filtrate

Filter-halter *m* filter bracket, filter holder **-häutchen** *n* filtering pellicle **-hilfsmittel** *n* filtering aids **-kammer** *f* filter chamber **-kasten** *m* filter box **-kegel** *m* filter cone **-kerze** *f* filter cartridge **-kessel** *m* filtering tank **-kies** *m* filter gravel

-kohle *f* filter(ing) charcoal **-kolonne** *f* water-purification column **-korb** *m* filtering basket, filter strainer **-körper** *m* filter pad **-kreis** *m* filter(ing) circuit **-kreuzschiene** *f* filter crossbar

Filterkuchen *m* filter cake, press cake, slack wax, crude scale wax **-abnahmevorrichtung** *f* filter-press cake-removing device

Filter-lage *f* filter layer **-leistung** *f* filtering efficiency, filter output, filter performance **-lochlage** *f* position of transmission range **-masse** *f* filter block **-massenwiderstand** *m* inertness (of mechanical filter) **-medien** *pl* filter media **-mittel** *n* filter aid

filtern to filter

Filtern *n* straining

filternde Näherungen filtering approximations

Filterpapier *n* filter paper **-einsatz** *m* paper element

Filter-patrone *f* filter end can, cleaner element, filter element, filter cartridge **-platte** *f* filter plate **-plattenpaket** *n* filter plates **-posten** *m* (CFP) control filter post (CFP)

Filterpresse *f* filter press **~ überziehen** to dress the filter press **~ mit seitlichem Schlammkanal** filter press with side-feed channel **~ mit zentraler Schlammzuführung** filter press with central feed **~ mit hydraulischem Verschluß** filter press with hydraulic closing device

Filterpressen-anordnung in parallel as in filter presses **-papier** *n* paper for filter presses

Filter-quarz *m* filter crystal **-rahmen** *m* filter frame **-rammspitze** *f* filtering driving shoe **-reinigung** *f* filtering system **-reinigungsflüssigkeit** *f* filter cleaning liquid **-rohr** *n* lower, perforated portion of casing of drainage well (sometimes slotted instead of perforated), screen pipe, filter pipe, filtering tube **-rohrbrunnen** *m* filtering fountain **-röhre** *f* filter tube **-sack** *m* cock bagging, filter bag **-satz** *m* filter element

Filter-ring *m* filter holder ring **-rückstand** *m* filtration residue **-sack** *m* filtering bag **-schacht** *m* filter cavity **-schale** *f* filter plate with raised edges **-scheibe** *f* filter plate **-schicht** *f* filter bed, filtering layer **-schichtensorten** types of filter sheets **-schieber** *m* filter insert **-schlamm** *m* filter mud **-schlauch** *m* cock bagging, filter hose, filter spout **-schleim** *m* filter pulp **-schmieröl** *n* filter lubricating oil **-schoner** *m* filter cone

Filter-sicherung *f* filter safety device **-sieb** *n* filter screen, gauze filter **-kette** *f* band-pass filter, wave-band filter **-sperrbereich** *m* filter attenuation band **-spirale** *f* filter spiral **-stab** *m* filter tube **-stativ** *n* filter stand **-steilheit** *f* sharpness (of cutoff) of selecting network, slope **-stein** *m* filtering stone, dripstone **-stoff** *m* filtering medium, filter cloth **-stütze** *f* filter support **-tasche** *f* filter pocket or cell, filter pouch

filtertechnisches Laboratorium technical filter laboratory

Filter-topf *m* filtering jug **-träger** *m* filter bracket **-trägerplatte** *f* filter carrier plate **-tragring** *m* filter jumper ring **-trichter** *m* filter funnel, filtering funnel **-trog** *m* filter trough **-trommel** *f* filter drum

Filtertuch *n* filter cloth, filtering cloth, cloth filter

Filtertücher *pl* filter cloth(s) **Auswechseln der ~** changing of filter cloth **Hartwerden der ~** hardening of filter cloth

Filtertuch-unterlage *f* filter cloth support **-verbrauch** *m* filter cloth consumption

Filterung *f* filtering

Filter-verrohrung *f* perforated casing **-versuch** *m* seepage test **-vorsatz** *m* filter, air filter in gas masks **-wasser** *n* filtrate **-wechsel** *m* filter replacement **-weiche** *f* notch diplexer **-widerstand** *m* filter resistance **-wirkung** *f* filtering action **-zelle** *f* filter element **-ziermutter** *f* filter acorn **-zusatz** *m* filter aid **-zylinder** *m* filter cylinder

Filtrat *n* filtrate **-abführrohr** *n* pipe for filtrate outflow

Filtration *f* filtration

Filtrations-aufgabe *f* filtering operation, filtration task **-druck** *m* filtering pressure **-erleichterung** *f* facilitating filtration **-geschwindigkeit** *f* rate of filtration **-schicht** *f* filter bed or layer **-unterbrechung** breaks in filtration **-verlauf** *m* filtration

Filtrat-kreiselpumpe *f* filtrate centrifugal pump **-leistung** *f* filtrate output **-menge** *f* filtrate quantity **-saugleitung** *f* filtrate suction pipe

Filtricht *n* filtrate

Filtrier-apparat *m* percolator, filtering apparatus **-bar** filterable **-barkeit** *f* filtering property, filtrability **-beutel** *m* percolator, filtering bag

filtrieren to filter, strain

Filtrierer *m* filterer

Filtrier-gestell *n* filter stand **-konus** *m* filtering cone, filter cone **-leinen** *n* filtering cloth **-schale** *f* filtering dish **-scheibe** *f* filtering disc **-sieb** *n* perforated filter plate, filtering sieve **-stativ** *n* filter stand **-trichter** *m* filter funnel, filtering funnel, percolator **-tuch** *n* filtering cloth

Filtrierung *f* filtration, filtering, straining, percolation

Filz *m* felt **mit ~ ausgelegt oder unterlegt** felted

Filz-ärmel *m* felt sleeve **-aufzug** *m* felt dressing **-barkeit** *f* felting property **-dichtung** *f* felt pad **-dichtungsring** *m* felt seal retainer **-einsatz** *m* felt element

Filzen *n* felting

Filz-kufe *f* felt pad **-leitwalze** *f* felt guide roll or roller **-mantel** *m* felt jacket **-maschine** *f* jig (textiles) **-mühle** *f* fulling mills **-pappe** *f* felt board **-pfropfen** *m* wad **-platte** *f* felt washer, felt pad or plate **-platteneinsatz** *m* felt pad or felt plate insert **-plattenfilter** *m* felt plate filter **-polierscheibe** *f* felt polishing wheel, buffing wheel **-polster** *n* felt cushion **-ring** *m* felt seal, felt ring, felt washer

Filzrohr-einsatz *m* felt-tube insert **-filter** *n* felt-tube filter **-sackfilter** *n* combined felttube and cloth-sack filter **-sternfilter** *m* combined felt-tube and radial-type filter **-zellenfilter** *n* combined felt-tube and cell filter

Filz-röllchen *n* felt pad (tape rec.) **-sauger** *m* felt suction (paper mach.) **-schaber** *m* guard board **-scheibe** *f* felt washer or disk **-schleifteller** *m* felt grinding disk **-schuh** *m*, **-stiefel** *m* felt boot **-stock** *m* polishing tool, burnisher **-stopfen** *m* felt spigot **-streifen** *m* felt strip

Filz-teller *m* felt disc **-umkleidung** *f* felt covering (boilers, cables, and pipes) **-unterlage** *f* felt (under)layer, felt pad **-unterlegscheibe** *f* felt washer or disk **-walker** *m* felt fuller **-walze** *f*

dabber

Fimmel *m* gad, wedge of iron, miner's wedge

Finalstock *m* tailpiece

finanziell financial

Finder *m* finder **-recht** *n* right of the discoverer or finder **-teilkreis** *m* finder circle

Findigkeit *f* ingenuity

Findling *m* erratic block, perched blocks

Findlingsquarzit *m* boulders of quartzite

Finesse *f* finesse, cunning

Finger *m pl* grappling irons, fingers **-abdruck** *m* fingerprint **-anschlag** *m* finger stop (of dial switch) **-balken** *m* cutter bar (mower) **-bildner** *m* digitorium (for piano practicing) **-fertig** deterous

fingerförmig finger-shaped **-es Befestigungspflaster** finger patch

Finger-fräseinrichtung *f* end-milling attachment **-fräser** *m* milling cutter (end-on type of rod form, for holes and slots), end mill, end-milling cutter **-futter** *n* finger stall **-griff** *m* finger grip **-haken** *m* tappet hock **-hebelwelle** *f* steering-knuckle shaft

Fingerhut *m* thimble, finger pad **-ionisierungskammer** *f* thimble ionizing chamber **-zerstäuber** *m* thimble-type diffuser

Finger-kammer *f* finger-type (combustion) chamber **-kontakt** *m* finger contact (controller's) **-krone** *f* finger bit

Fingerling *m* finger stall, finger cot, pintle (of rudder)

Finger-nagellimbus *m* border of the fingernail **-öffnung** *f* finger hole **-probe** *f* touch, rule of thumb **-ring** *m* baffle ring, finger ring **-rührer** *m* finger paddle agitator **-satz** *m* fingering **-scheibe** *f* dial (teleph.), pencil wheel, finger disk or wheel, dial switch **-schutzvorrichtung** *f* finger protector for feeders (print.) **-spitzengefühl** *n* instinct, intuition, tactile sensitiveness, discretion **-stein** *m* belemnite, fingerstone **-strickmaschine** *f* glove-finger knitting machine **-trichter** *m* finger-shaped gate (in casting) **-zeig** *m* hint, indication, cue, pointer

fingieren to feign, simulate, invent

fingiert dummy, feigned

Finknetzkasten *m* hammock netting

Finlekstal (Swedish), fineness number

Finne *f* fin, flash (of a hammer) pane, peen, pane (of a hammer) ~ **des Hammers** hammer peen **mit der** ~ **hämmern** to peen

Finnenzelt *n* plywood shelter for winter operations

Finnfischtran *m* finback whale oil

finster dark, obscure, dim

Finsternis *f* eclipse, darkness, obscurity, dimness

Finte *f* false attack, trick, ruse

Firma *f* firm, company

Firmen-schild *n* maker's name plate, commercial sign **-zeichen** *n* trade mark **-zeitschrift** *f* house magazin

Firn *m* glacier snowfield **-eis** *n* glacier ice **-feld** *n* snowfield

Firnis *m* varnish (woodworking), primer, dope ~ **kochen** to boil (linseed oil) upon litharge

Firnis-anlage *f* varnish-making plant **-bindemittel** *n* oil-varnish vehicle **-farbe** *f* varnish paint **-gehalt** *m* varnish content **-hülse** *f* varnish or doped envelope **-papier** *n* oiled paper, wallpaper

firnissen to varnish, lacquer

First *m* roof of gallery (min.), ridge, coping **-abdeckung** *f* ridged coping **-balken** *m*, **-baum** *m* ridge beam (buildings or cars) **-blech** *n* ridging plate **-brause** *f* (open) sprinkler **-brett** *n* top sheet, tympan (print.)

Firste *f* roof (min.) head, ascending step, back, top ~ **eines Stollens** back or roof of a gallery (min.) **die** ~ **nachreißen** to stow away the roof (min.)

First-eindeckung *f* ridging **-eisen** *n* cap plate

Firstenbau *m* overhand stoping, overhead stoping ~ (vereinigter) **und Etagenbruchbau** combined shrinkage and caving method ~ **mit geneigter Firste** rill stoping ~ **mit Versatz** cut-and-fill stoping ~ **mit waagrechter Firste** flat back stoping **einen** ~ **abbauen** to stope overhand

Firsten-bohrloch *n* back borehole **-druck** *m* super incumbent pressure of the ground **-erz** *n* roof ore **-stempel** *m* stay for timbering of the roof, propshore **-stirn** *f* face of the ascending step **-stoß** *m* ascending step, overhand stope **-strecke** *f* brattice way **-weise** upward

firstförmige Abdeckung ridged coping

First-haube *f* coping or ridge of a roof **-kamm** *m* crest **-leitung** *f* ridge circuit **-linie** *f* coping or ridge of a roof **-lot** *n* overhead plumb **-pfahl** *m* top plank **-pfette** *f* ridge purlin or lead **-punkt** *m* apex, roof point **-stange** *f* ridge rod or beam **-träger** *m* top center-line girder **-ziegel** *m* ridge tile

Fischaugenstein *m* apophyllite

Fischband *n* fish joint (mech) **-säge** *f* pin hinge saw

Fischbauch-antenne *f* fish-belly antenna **-klappe** *f* fishbelly flap **-mast** *m* double-tapered tower, cantilever tower **-profil** *n* fish-bellied **-träger** *m* fish-bellied girder **-trägerbrücke** *f* fish-bellied girder bridge

Fischdampfer *m* trawler

Fischerei *f* fishing, fishery **-becken** *n* fish dock **-erzeugnis** *n* fishing product **-gerät** *n* fishing tackle **-hafen** *m* fishing (or fishery) harbor **-schutzboot** *n* fishery patrol boat

Fischerverfahren *n* Fischer blind-landing method

Fisch-fang *m* fishing, catch **-geräte** *f* fishbone **-grätenantenne** *f* fistibone antenna **-grätenhindernis** *n* fishbone obstacle pattern **-gratverband** *m* herring-bone bond **-haken** *m* barbed hook, fishhook **-halle** *f* fish market **-konservenfabrik** *f* fish curing house **-leim** *m* isinglass, fish glue **-leiter** *f* fish ladder

fischmaulförmig fish-mouth shaped **-e Spleißung** fish-mouth splice

Fisch-öl *n* train oil, fish oil **-paß** *m* fish ladder, grating (for fish, or in a well) **-platte** *f* fishplate

Fischschwanz-bohrer *m* fishtail bit **-brenner** *m* fishtail burner (gas), bat's-wing burner **-flugmanöver** *n* fishtailing **-kneter** *m* fishtail type kneader **-meißel** *m* fishtail bit

Fisch-tran *m* fish oil, train oil **-weg** *m* grating (for fish, or in a well)

Fisettholz *n* young fustic, fustet, zantewood

Fisklappe *f* F-sharp key

Fiskus *m* fisc, exchequer, treasury

Fissium *n* fissium

Fitschenband (Fenster) butt hinge

Fittichziegel *m* pantile
Fittings *pl* fittings
Fitzband *n* tie band
Fitze *f* groove (including grooving, fluting, or channeling generally)
fitzen to lace **-arbeiterin** *f* skein examiner **-stock** *m* lease bar or rod, lease pins
Fitz-feile *f* needle file **-garn** *n* lacing yarn
fix fixed, firm, fast (made permanent, not to be removed) **-es Salz** fixed salt
Fixativ *n* fixative
Fix-bleiche *f* hypochlorite of lime bleach **-echo** *n* permanent echo **-färberei** *f* fast dyeing **-geschäft** *n* transaction on account (exchange)
Fixier-bad *n* fixing bath, fixer **-bügel** *f* holding strap
fixieren to fix, lock in position, fix
Fixier-flüssigkeit *f* fixing liquid, fixing liquor **-leuchte** *f* fixation lamp **-loch** *n* fixed or locating hole **-lösung** *f* fixing solution **-mittel** *n* fixing agent, fixative, fixer **-natron** *n* hypo, sodium hyposulfite, sodium thiosulfate **-salz** *n* fixing salt **-schraube** *f* wedge bolt, fixing screw **-stift** *m* guide pin, dowel pin
fixiert fixed, settled, established **-er Kathodenfleck des Quecksilberlichtbogens** anchored spot of mercury arc
Fixierton *m* fixing clay
Fixierung *f* fixing, fixation
Fixierungs-paar *n* standard couple (spectral analysis) **-schloß** *n* lock
Fixpunkt *m* (hydraulic engineering) anchor (of penstocks), fixed point, ground point of control, fixed end (of a cable), set point, bench mark **~ einer Abbildung** fixed point of a mapping
Fixpunkt-bogenlampe *f* focusing arc lamp **-differentialbogenlampe** *f* self-focusing differential arc lamp **-nebenschlußbogenlampe** *f* self-focusing shunt arc lamp **-satz** *m* fixed point theorem
Fix-scheibe *f* fast pulley **-sternkugel** *f* fixed-star body, fixed-star ball **-sternhimmel** *m* the fixed stars or heavenly bodies, starry heaven **-wert** *m* fixed value
Fjord *m* fiord
Fizeausches Rad chopper disk
flach shallow, flat, level, plain, plane, squat, even, without contrast, with low gamma (picture), flattopped (curve) **~ auffallend** incident at small angle, oblique **~ auffallender Strahl** ray incident at small or oblique angle, oblique ray **~ auftreffend** incident at small angle, oblique **~ werden** to level off, flatten out, slope, become less steep, be smoothed **zu ~** too low a gamma **-er Boden** flat top **-er Bogen** platband arch, flat arch **-e Böschung** gentle slope **mit der -en Hand leicht schlagen** to dab **-e Krümmung** slow sweep **-e Kurve** flat turn **-er Motor** flat-type engine **-e Mulde** *f* shallow depression **-er Rundkopf** thin brazier rivet **-e Vorlage** flat copy **-e Sporen** flat lugs
Flach-amboß *m* flat anvil **-anker** *m* flat armature **-anlasser** *m* face place starter **-antenne** *f* flat-top antenna, plane antenna
flacharbeitende Hackmaschine surface cultivator
flach-auffallend incident at small angle **-aufnahme** *f* photograph with approximately horizontal axis, high oblique photograph **-auftreffend** incident at small angle, oblique **-bagger** *m* surface digging machine
Flachbahn *f* flat bedway, flat trajectory **-anlasser** *m* face plate starter **-kaliber** *n* bull-head pass **-regler** *m* (Mischpult) waferswitch, sliding controls (mixer console)
Flachband *n* (conveyor) flat belt **-teilspulen** *f pl* ribbon flat coils **-windungen** *pl* flat-strip windings
Flach-bau *m* flat planting **-becken** *n* basin **-bettfelge** *f* flat-base rim **-beutel** *m* plane bolter **-biegeprobe** *f* flat-bending test **-biegetorsionsmaschine** *f* flat bending torsion testing machine **-block** *m* flat-shaped ingot, crosscut ingot
Flachboden *m* flattop (piston) **-kolben** *m* flat-topped piston **-selbstentlader** *m* track wheel flat dump car
flach-bodig flat-floored, flat-top **-bogen** *m* segmental arch **-bohrer** *m* flat drill **-bundmutter** *f* flat collar nut **-brenner** *m* fishtail burner (gas), flat or wing burner **-brunnen** *m* surface well
Flach-dexel *pl* carpenters'adzes **-dichtung** *f* flat gasket ring
Flachdibbel-apparat *m* flat-drop attachment **-maisdrill** *m* flat-drop corn planter
Flachdraht *m* flat wire **-bewehrung** *f* flat-wire sheathing **-kabel** *n* flat wire rope **-seil** *n* flat wire rope
flachdrehen to surface (mech.), face (in lathe)
Flachdruck *m* surface printing (as distinguished from relief and intaglio printing), flattening pressure, lithoprinting
flachdrücken to flatten
Flachdrücken *n* shallow forming
Flachdruck-maschine *f* platen machine **-presse** *f* flat-bed press **-rotationsmaschine** *f* flat-bed web machine, flat-bed rotary machine **-verfahren** *n* planographic process
Fläche *f* area, surface, plane, face, facet, zone, plain, level, sheet, flatness **~ der Fuge** face of joint **~ gleichen Potentials** equipotential surface **~ konstanten Potentials** equipotential surface, isopotential surface **abwickelbare ~** surface, developable **bearbeitete ~** machined or tooled surface **bebaute ~** effective floor space **cartesische ~** Cartesian surface **deformierte ~** deformed or figured surface
Fläche, ebene ~ plane surface, dead level, level surface **gekielte ~** V-bottom surface **geneigte ~** gradient, inclined plane, unlevel surface **regelmäßige ~** regular geometrical outline **stereoskopisch gedeckte ~** stereoscopically covered surface **tragende ~** supporting surface, lifting surface, land area of bearing **untere ~** sole **windschiefe ~** skew surface
Flacheisen *n* flat iron, flat steel, flat bar, rectangular or square (steel) bars, iron, flat bars, flats **-halter** *m* flat iron holder **-profil** *n* flat-iron section **-schere** *f* flat-iron shearing machine **-verankerung** *f* retaining plate **-walze** *f* plate-mill roll **-walzen** *n* plate rolling
flachen to flatten, level
Flachen *n* damping, attenuation
Flächen *pl* surfaces **~ konstanter Breite** surfaces of constant width **~ konstanter Gaussscher Krümmung** surfaces of constant Gaussian curvature **~ konstanter Helligkeit** surfaces of sonstant brightness **~ konstanter mittlerer**

Krümmung surfaces of constant mean curvature ~ **dritter Ordnung** surfaces of the third order ~ **höherer als dritter Ordnung** surfaces of order higher than the third

Flächen, ~ **vierter Ordnung** surfaces of fourth order ~ **zweiter Ordnung** (konfokale) surfaces of second order (confocal) ~ **im projektiven Raum** surfaces in the projective space **abwickelbare** ~ developable surfaces **algebraische** ~ algebraic surfaces **aufeinander arbeitende** ~ mating surfaces, rubbing surfaces **berandete** ~ surfaces with a boundary

Flächen-aberration *f* zonal aberration (optics) **-abstand** *m* wing gap **-abweichung** *f* zonal aberration (optics) **-analyse** *f* area analysis

Flächenantenne flattop antenna, plane antenna, sheet antenna **horizontale** ~ horizontal plane antenna

Flächen-anordnung *f* broadside array **-anziehung** *f* surface attraction, adhesion, adsorption **-artige Strombahn** current sheet, laminar or areal path of current **-aufnahmen** *pl* areal surveys, leveling operation **-ausdehnung** *f* square dimensions **-ausgleich** *m* aerodynamic balance **-ausmessung** *f* planimetering **-bearbeitung** *f* finish of surface in plastics **-bedarf** *m* floor space required **-belastung** *f* wing loading, load in pounds per square foot of wing area, lift per unit area, load per unit surface, wing load, surface loading **-berechnung** *f* plane and elevational measurements **-berieselung** *f* surface cooling **-berieselungsapparat** *m* surface cooler

Flächen-berührung *f* surface contact **-bestimmung** *f* plane and elevational measurements **-blitz** *m* sheet lightning **-brand** *m* area conflagration **-bürste** *f* surface brush

Flächen-dichte *f* density by surface (elec.) **-dilatation** *f* deformation of areas **-drahthindernis** *n* multiple-belt (concertina) entanglement **-druck** *m* pressure per unit area, surface pressure, surface friction

Flächeneinheit *f* unit area, unit of area, unit of surface **Reaktanz pro** ~ unit-area reactance

Flächeneinheitsbelastung *f* loading per unit area, unit load **-druck** *m* specific pressure on ground **-last** *f* loading per unit area, unit load (aviat.)

Flächen-elemente *pl* surface elements, elementary areas, unit areas **-erhaltung** *f* conservation of areas (in kinematics) **-erhaltungsgesetz** *n* principle of conservation of area **-fliegen** *n* plane flying **-förmig** areal, laminar, of sheetlike nature or form **-fräsen** *n* surface milling **-fräser** *m* face-milling cutter, surface cutter

Flächen-gebilde *n* a flat shaped article (a sheet or web of paper) **-getreu** of equal area (of a map or chart) **-gewicht** *n* weight per unit area

Flächengewichts-meßanlage *f* weight per unit area gauge **-schwankungen** *pl* variations in weight per unit area

Flächengitter *n* two-lattice (cryst.), layer lattice **-wirkung** *f* plane effect (cryst.)

Flächen-glätte *f* surface smoothness **-gleichrichter** *m* surface-contact rectifier, junktion diode **-glimmlampe** *f* surface glow lamp, flat-plate glow lamp, glow lamp or neon lamp with plate-shaped cathode, plate neon light

flächenhaft areal, laminar **-e Berührung** surface or areal contact **-e Rauhigkeiten** distributed roughness **-e Spule** laminar or striplike coil, nonfilamentary coil

Flächen-helle *f* brightness, brilliance, luminous brightness of a surface, intrinsic brilliance **-helligkeit** *f* surface brightness, luminous brightness of a surface, intrinsic brilliance **-inhalt** *m* (wing) area, surface area **-inhaltmesser** *m* planimeter **-inhaltseinheit** *f* unit of area **-integral** *n* area integral **-karte** *f* plane chart **-kathode** *f* plate-shaped cathode, large-surface cathode **-klasse** *f* class of surfaces

Flächenkontakt *m* junction **-photozelle** *f* junction photocell

Flächen-kraft *f* surface force **-krümmung** *f* curvature of a surface, co-flexure bending **-kühlung** *f* cooling by outspread surface

Flächenkurve *f* surface curve or curvature **Tiefe der** ~ camber

Flächen-lampe *f* pillar of lamps or luminous sources **-last** *f* area load **-lautsprecher** *m* surface loudspeaker, cabinet speaker **-leistung** *f* power-area ratio, wing power, horsepower per square foot of wing area, power per unit surface **-leuchte** *f* pillar of lamps or luminous sources **-maschine** *f* fixed wing aircraft

Flächen-maß *n* superficial measure, square measure, surface measure(ment) **-maßstab** *m* surface scale **-messer** *m* planimeter, integraph (for curves) **-meßplan** *m* plotting board (flash ranging) **-messung** *f* planimetry, measurement of areas **-metrik** *f* surface metric **-mittelpunkt** *m* center of area, centroid **-motor** *m* fan engine **-muster** *n* background pattern

Flächen-navigation *f* long range navigation (radar) **-navigationsgerät** *n* surface-navigation apparatus **-nebel** *m* area smoke screen **-normale** *f* surface normal **-pilot** *m* fixed-wing pilot **-pol** *m* pole of the face **-polarisation** *f* plane polarization

Flächen-porosität *f* effective pore area **-pressung** *f* pressure per unit of area, face pressure, surface pressure, contact pressure **-projektion** *f* developed surface **-quotient** *m* area quotient

Flächenraum *m* area, surface ~ **in Morgen** acreage

Flächen-reduktion *f* reduction of area **-reich** polyhedral, with many faces or sides **-satz** *m* theorem of conservation of areas **-schaber** *m* planer **-schleifen** *n* surface grinding **-schleifmaschine** *f* surface grinder, grinders or sharpeners and rectifiers (emery or grit, for tools, etc.) **-schliff** *m* surface grinding

Flächenschwerpunkt *m* center of gravity of a surface, centroid ~ **eines Querschnittes** centroid

Flächen-sehne *f* chord of a plane (aviation) **-skala** *f* scale of surfaces or of quantities **-spachtel** (Lack) surface filler **-spiere** *f* member or crosspiece (aviation) **-strahler** *m* (BEF) plenum chamber (GEM) **-strom** *m* surface current

Flächenstück *n* surface element, unit area, elementary area **orientiertes** ~ oriented surface

Flächen-symmetrie *f* plane symmetry **-system** *n* system of surface

Flächen-teilchen *n* surface element **-teilung** *f* plain division, division of area **-trägheitsmoment** *n* angular impulse, polar moment of inertia (acoust) **-tragwerk** *n* plane (load)-bearing structure, load-bearing slab **-transistor** *m* junction transistor

flächentreu of equal area (map or chart) **-es Abbildungsnetz** equal area map (math) **-e Projektion** equal-area projection (in mapping)

Flächen-treue *f* identity (map), equiareal, area-preserving, equivalent **-veränderlich** of variable area **-verhältnis** *n* aspect ratio **-verwindung** *f* wing warping **-vibration** *f* surface noise **-wagen** *m* wing truck **-wert** *m* surface value (of pulp or cellulose) **-widerstand** *m* surface resistance **-winde** *pl* surface winds **-winkel** *m* interfacial angle, plane angle, dihedral **-wirkungsgrad** *m* efficiency of illumination, aperture efficiency (antenna) **-wölbung** *f* wing camber or curvature

flächenzentriert face-centered (cryst) **-es Raumgitter** face-centered lattice space

Flächen-zentrierung *f* centered face **-zentrum** *m* center of area **-ziel** *n* extensive target, area farget

flach-erhaben bas-relief **-facette** *f* flat bevel **-fallendes Land** lode of medium dip (geol.)

Flach-feder *f* flat spring, leaf or grasshopper spring **-federspirale** *f* flat spiral spring **-feile** *f* flat file **-film** *m* plain film, nonplastic film, nonstereoscopic film **-finnhammer** *m* peen hammer

Flachflansch *m* plain coupling or connector

Flach-flanschverbindung *f* butt joint, plain connector **-formmaschine** *f* flat-bed machine **-fräser** *m* flat router **-fundation** (Gründung) mat foundation, shallow foundation, spread foundation **-fuß** *m* flat foot **-gang** *m* flat threaded screw

flachgängig square-threaded **-es Gewinde** square thread

flachgeneigte Steinverkleidung stone paving of gentle slope

flachgeschweißt lap-welded

flachgewalzte Erzeugnisse flat rolled products

flachgewickelt flatvise wound (electr) **-er Typ** flat-grid type

Flachgewinde *n* square (screw) thread, flat thread (mach.)

flachgewunden planispiral

Flach-glas *n* plate glass **-glaserzeugung** *f* plate glass production **-gießinstrument** *n* flat plate caster **-greifer** *m* surface digger, flat lugs **-gründung** *f* flat or slab foundation **-gummidichtring** *m* flat rubber gasket ring

Flach-halbrundstahl *m* half-oval steel **-hacke** *f* flat mattock **-hämmern** to peen **-haue** *f* pick, mattock, broad pick **-heftung** *f* flat stitching

Flachheit *f* flat or noncontrasty quality or condition (phot.), flatness

Flachherdmischer *m* flat-furnace mixer flat-hearth type mixer

flächig areal, laminar **-er Winkel** plane angle **-es Werkstück** flat part

Flach-kabel *n* ribbon(-shaped) cable, flat cable, flat (switchboard) cable **-kabelstecker** *m* flat cable plug **-kaliber** *n* flat groove, box pass **-kamera** *f* flat camera

Flachkeil *m* parallel key, flat key (shaft), flat plain key **-riemen** *m* flat V-belt **-verschluß** *m* square drop-block breech mechanism, sliding square-wedge breechlock

Flachkern *m* flat core **-kipper** *m* flat tilter **-klemme** *f* flat terminal (elec.) **-knüppel** *m* sheet bar, slab billet

Flach-kolben *m* flat-topped piston **-zweitakter** *m* two-cycle engine with flat-type crown pistons

Flachkopf *m* flat head

flachköpfig-er Bolzen flat-headed bolt **-es Niet** flat (or pan) headed rivet **-e Schraube** flat headed screw

Flachkopfniet *m* flat-head rivet

Flachkopf-nietung *f* pan riveting **-schiene** *f* flat-headed rail **-schraube** *f* low-head screw, pan head (cheese head) screw

Flach-kupfer *n* flat copper bar or strip **-kuppel** *f* low dome **-kurve** *f* flat turn **-küste** *f* low-lying coast **-land** *n* flat country, flats, plain **-landung** *f* two-point landing **-lasche** *f* (flat) butt strap, flat joint, flush joint **-laschendeckel** *m* flat joint cover **-lautsprecher** *m* flat or pan-cake or wafer loudspeaker **-lehrdorn** *m* flat-type plug gauge **-liegende Paketierung** flat box pile **-litzenseil** *n* flat strand rope

Flach-material *n* flat stock or material **-meißel** *m* chipping chisel, flat chisel, fitter's ordinary flat cold chisel **-moor** *n* low-lying bog **-muschelig** flatly conchoidal **-mutter** *f* plain nut **-naht** *f* flush weld

flachnebeneinander on the flat

Flächner *m* polyhedron

Flach-nutfräsen *n* slab milling **-offsetpresse** *f* flat bed offset machine **-passung** *f* flat fit **-pfanne** *f* grooved or gutter tile **-pinsel** *m* flat brush **-profilinstrument** *n* flat-section instrument (elec.), flat edgewise pattern meter **-querschnitt** *m* flat cross section **-reflektorantenne** *f* plane reflector antenna

Flach-regler *m* drum governor **-relais** *n* flat-type relay **-relief** *n* bas-relief **-riemen** *m* flat belt **-riemenantrieb** *m* flat belt drive **-ringanker** *m* disk armature **-ringschieber** *m* flat-ring side valve

Flach-röhre *f* flat TV tube **-rohrkühler** *m* flat-tube radiator **-rohrpostanlagen** *pl* pneumatic tube systems (PTS) with flat carriers **-rolle** *f* flat idler **-rund** with flat bottom **-rundkopf** *m* cup head, oval or mushroom head

Flachrundschraube *f* carriage bolt, truss head screw **~ mit Vierkant** carriage bolt with square neck

Flachs *m* flax, jute, yarn **mit Tannin getränkter ~** tanned jute

Flachs-aufleger *m* flax spreader **-bindeeinrichtung** *f* flax buncher **-breche** *f* flax brake

Flach-schaber *m* flat scraper **-schalttafel** *f* flat switchboard **-scheibe** *f* flat-face pulley

Flachschieber *m* flat slide valve, gate-type slide valve **-steuerung** *f* slide-valve gear

Flach-schiene *f* plate rail, strap rail, flat rail **-schlagen** to flatten (by impact)

flach-schleifen to surfacegrind **-schleifmaschine** *f* surface grinding machine **-schlichtfeile** *f* flat smooth file

flachschmieden, das Eisen ~ to beat out iron

Flach-schneidehackmesser *m* duckfoot **-schnitt** *m* horizontal section

Flachsschwadenablage *f* flax-swathing attachment

Flach-schweißen *n* lap welding **-schweißung** *f* lap-welding

Flachsee *f* shallow sea **-kabel** *n* intermediate-type submarine cable

Flachseil *n* flat rope or cable **-trommel** *f* bobbin, drum, flat-rope drum, flat-winding drum or coil

Flachseiten *pl* plane surfaces (tools)

Flachsgarn *n* jute yarn **-gewebe** *n* linen goods **-häufler** *m* (Flachsbindeeinrichtung), flax buncher **-hechelmaschine** *f* intersecting gills, circular gills, smoothing gills (textiles), lockering rollers **-hechler** *m* combs or combers for flax

Flach-sieb *n* horizontal screen **-siebeputzmaschine** *f* purifier with automatic brush clearing of the bolt sheet (flour milling) **-sitzdüse** *f* flat seat nozzle **-sockelbauart** *f* flat-base-type instrument (elec.) **-spanfräsen** *n* shallow slab-milling cut **-spirale** *f* flat spiral

Flachspitze *f* pick or pickax (one end flat-edged) **~ einer Feder** oval point (spring)

Flachspitzfeile *f* flat file

Flachspule *f* flat coil, disk coil, pancake coil **quadratische ~** flat-square coil, square place coil, pancake coil

Flachspülklosett *n* water closet with flat wash down

Flachsriffeln *n* flax rippling **-röste** *f* retting pit (ropemaking) **-strecker** *m* flax drawer

Flachstab *m* flat bar, plain bar **-probe** *f* plate specimen **-streichblech** *n* (durchbrochener Riester) flatmold attachment

Flach-stahl *m* flat-bar steel **-stahlhalter** *m* flat blade holder **-stange** *f* bar of flat section **-stanze** *f* shallow punch press **-stecker** *m* plug **-steg** *m* flat bridge **-stein** *m* amianthus

Flach-stereotypieapparat *m* flatplate stereotyping apparatus **-steuerung** *f* slide-valve gear **-stich** *m* flat pass, slab pass **-stichel** *m* flat scorper **-stiftstecker** *m* flat pin

Flachstrahl-brenner *m* flat-section jet burner **-verteiler** *m* air cap for fan spray (print)

Flach-strebe *f* flat strut **-streicher** *m* flat squeegee, strickler **-strickmaschinen** *pl* straight and circular knitters **-stromvergaser** *m* transverse draft carburetor **-strömung** *f* turbulent flow **-stumpffeile** *f* taper square file

Flachs-vorhechler *m* flax rougher **-werg** *n* cleaning waste

Flach-teilspulen *pl* flat coils **-träger** *m* flat support

Flachtorf *m* bottom peat

Flachtropfpflanzmaschine *f* flat-drop corn planter

Flachtrudeln *n* flat spin (aviation)

Flach- und Bandseil *n* band rope

Flachung *f* flatness

Flach-verbunderregung *f* level-compound excitation **-wagen** *m* gondola car **-wähler** *m* panel selector **-walze** *f* slabbing-mill roll **-walzen** *n* roughing flat, slabbing **-walzen** to roll flat, rough-flat, slab **-wandig** (Kokillen) plane sided **-wassertonne** *f* flat-bottom buoy **-wellige Lagerung** undulating seams **-winkel** *pl* solid steel squares

Flachwulst-eisen *pl* flat bulbs **-profil** *n* bulb section **-stahl** *m* bulb plate

Flachzange *f* tweezers, flatnose pliers, flat-jawed pliers **~ mit langer Maul- und Nadelspitze** chain-nose pliers **~ mit Seitenschneider** side-cutting pliers

Flach-zeiger *m* flat pointer **-zerreißstab** *m* flat tensile test bar **-ziegel** *m* flat, plain, or roofing tile **-zylinderschraube** *f* panhead screw

Flacker-, Aufschalte- und Irrungstaste (FL) flashing, cut-in and error button

Flacker-effekt *m* flicker effect **-feuer** *n* flare **-fotometer** *n* flicker photometer **-frequenz** *f* flicker frequency **-lampe** *f* flickering lamp **-licht** *n* flashing light **-lichtanlage** *f* flashing light system

flackern to flash, flicker (teleg.), flare, to scatter

Flackern *n* flickering, flash(ing) **~ oder Zucken der Flamme** flickering of the flame **~ des Lichtes** flashing (flickering) of light

Flacker-photometer *n* flicker photometer **-probe** *f* (Glühbirnen) spot test **-relais** *n* flashing relay **-schwund** *m* flicker fading (rdo) **-signal** *n* flickering (flashing) signal **-taste** *f* flicker-signal calling

Flackerzeichen *n* flickering or flashing signal **~ geben** to recall or flash operator **durch ~ zum Eintreten veranlassen** to flash in(to circuit)

Flackmaschine *f* beater (weaving)

Fladen- oder Stricklava *f* ropy lava

Flader *m* raised grain or vein, irregular vein, flat grain

fladerig mottled (cast iron, etc.)

Fladerschnitt *m* chordal or tangential cut or section

Flagge *f* hook (spinning defect)

Flagge *f* flag, standard **die ~ dippen** to dip (a flag) **die ~ halbstocks setzen** to half-mast the colors **die ~ hissen** to hoist the colors **die ~ niederholen** to lower the colors

Flaggen-signal *n* code signal, flag signal **-spind** *m* flag locker **-stange** *f* **-stock** *m* flagstaff, flagpole **-winker** *m* semaphore

Flaggleine *f* halyard

flambieren to singe

Flamm-abriß *m* burn out, flame out **-blaser** *m* blasting or blowing magnet **-bogen** *m* flaming arc

Flamme *f* flame, blaze **aufleuchtende ~** luminous flame **brausende ~** roaring flame **flackernde ~** flickering flame **nichtleuchtende ~** roaring flame **oxydierende ~** oxidizing flame **reduzierende ~** carbonizing flame, reducing flame

Flammen, in ~ aflame **in ~ aufgehen** to burst into flame

flammen to flame, burn, glow **-abdeckung** *f* fireproofing flame dampener **-aufnahmen** *pl* flame pictures **-ausbreitung** *f* flame propagation **-beständig** flameproof, flame-resistant **-bewegungen** *pl* flame movements

Flammenbogen *m* arc, flaming arc, flame arc, electric arc **-erdschluß** *m* arcing ground **-kohlenstift** *m* flaming carbon

flammen-dämpfend flame baffling **-dämpfer** *m* flame damper, flame baffle **-durchschlag** *m* flashback **-effekt** *m* (Zebra) flame effect (dyeing) **-emissionskontinuum** *n* flame emission continuum **-einstellung** *f* flame baffling, flame adjustment **-entwicklung** *f* flame formation **-farbig** flamelike, flame-colored **-färbung** *f* flame coloration **-form** *f* flame height **-fortpflanzung** *f* flame propagation **-front** *f* flame front **-führung** *f* flame baffling, direction of flame path, method of travel of the flames, heat regulation, regulation of flames

Flammen-glühen *n* (Härterei) flame softening

-härten *n* flame hardening **-härtmaschine** *f* flame hardening machine **-härtung** *f* flame hardening **-hindernis** *n* flame obstacle

Flammen-ionisationsdetektor *m* flame ionization detector **-kollektor** *m* flame collector **-los** flameless **-mikrophon** *n* flame microphone, flame transmitter **-mittel** *n* incendiary agent **-ofen** *m* reverberatory (puddling) furnace, air furnace **-öl** *n* flame-thrower fuel **-photometer** *n* flame photometer **-photometrischer Zusatz** flame photometry attachment

Flammen-richtung *f* direction of flames **-ring** *m* flame vortex **-rohr** *n* flame tube (g/m) **-rohrkessel** *m* internal firebox boiler, flue boiler **-rückschlag** *m* flashback, flareback, backfiring

Flammenrückschlagsicherung *f* (in der Ladeleitung), flame trap **gitterförmige ~** backfire grid

Flammen-rückschlagsieb *n* backfire grid **-saum** *m* feather of a flame **-schutz** *m* flame trap **-spaltrohr** *n* flame-splitting tube **-spektrum** *n* flame-emission spectrum **-strahl** *m* flame jet, jet of liquid fire **-strahlbohrer** *m* plasma-jet boring **-temperatur** *f* flame temperature **-vernichter** *m* flame baffle **-verzehr** *m* flame baffle **-weg** *m* path of the flames **-wirbel** *m* flame vortex

Flammen-zone *f* zone of flame **-zug** *m* flame flue **-zündung** *f* flame ignition

Flammenzusatzgerät zum Spektralphotometer flame attachment for spectrophotometer

Flammenzwirn *m* flake twist with long or short slubs

Flammhärten *n* flam hardening

flammicht watered (of fabrics), veined or grained (of wood)

flammig flamelike, flaming

Flamm-kammer *f* firebox **-kohle** *f* long, luminousflaming semibituminous coal of high rank, steam coal, flaming coal **-maschine** *f* singeing machine **-nußkohle** *f* long- and luminous-flaming semibituminous nut coal of high rank

Flammofen *m* reverberatory (puddling) furnace, air furnace **-arbeit** *f* reverberatory smelting **-betrieb** *m* reverberatory-furnace practice **-herd** *m* reverberatory hearth **-schlacke** *f* air-furnace slag **-schmelzen** *n* reverberatory smelting

Flammplattierverfahren *n* flame plating process

Flammpunkt *m* flash point, fire point, flashing point, kindling temperature, point of ignition, kindling point **~ im offenen Tiegel** open-cup flash point

Flammpunkt-apparat *m* flash-point apparatus **-bestimmung** *f* flash test **-prüfer** *m* flash-point tester

Flammrohr *n* fire tube, flue (of boiler, metal tube in boiler), flame tube **-futter** *n* fire-tube lining **-kessel** *m* fire-tube boiler, tubular boiler, internal furnace boiler, flue boiler

Flammrohrsiederohrkessel *m*, **ausziehbarer ~** multitubular boiler with removable firebox and smoke tubes

Flamm-rückschlagsicherung *f* flame trap **-schutzmittel** *n* fireproofing agent **-sicher** (Schlagwettersicher) noninflammable, fire proof, flame proof **-sperre** *f* flame arrester

Flamm-spritzgerät *n* flame spraying equipment **-spritzverzinkung** *f* metal sprayed zinc coating **-strahlen** *n* (metal) scarfing

Flandernzaun *m* double-apron fence or entanglement

Flanell *m* flannel **-polierscheibe** *f* flannel polishing wheel

Flangenanschluß *m* flanged union

Flanke *f* flank, side **die ~ aufdecken** to expose the flank **hohle ~** concave flank **offene ~** open flank

Flanken-ausbauchung *f* main breadth (ship) **-bewegung** *f* flanking movement **-deckung** *f* flank protection

Flankendurchmesser *m* (Gewinde) thread-pitch diameter **~ des Muttergewindes** effective diameter of female thread, pitch diameter of tapped hole

Flanken-eintrittspiel *n* edge-contact at beginning of mesh **-höhe** *f* step width **-kehlnaht** *f* fillet in parallel shear **-marsch** *m* flanking march **-maß** *n* effective or pitch diameter **-naht** *f* side seam, side weld **-richtungsfehler** *m* directional error of the tooth flank

Flanken-schutz *m* flank protection **-spiel** *n* flank clearance, backlash (of screw thread) **-stauung** *f* side leakage **-steilheit** *f* width of transition interval, steepness of sides or slopes of a curve **-stellung** *f* flanking position **-streuung** *f* side leakage, side stray, end stray

Flankenwinkel *m* included angle of thread **~ des Schraubengewindes** angle of screw thread

flankieren to flank, outflank

Flansch *m* flange, socket, vane **~ für Einlaßöffnung** inlet flange **~ für Entlüftungsleitung** vent flange **~ für Sammelschienen** bus-bar clamp **aufgelöteter ~** brazed-on flange **fester ~** fixed flange **gewölbter ~** radiused flange

Flansch-absperrschieber *m* flange gate valve **-anlasser** *m* flanged starter **-auflagefläche** *f* flange surface **-befestigung** *f* flanged coupling, fixing by flange **-bolzen** *m* flange bolt, spigot for gear **-buchse** *f* flanged bush

Flansch-dichtung *f* gasket, flange packing, joint washer, flange packing, joint packing, gasket **-dose** *f* connector receptacle (flush mounting), (flanged) connector **-drehbank** *f* flange-planing and -trimming machine **-drehsuport** *m* flange-turning jig **-druckrohr** *n* flanged pressure pipe **-einpaß** *m* flange spigot

Flanschen siehe Flansch

flanschen to flange, flange the edge over

Flanschett *n* flanged coupling

Flansch-fläche *f* flange facing **-gummireifen** *m* rubber coupling member

Flanschhahn *n* flange-type cock **~ mit gebogenem Auslauf** flange-type cock with bent outlet **~ mit Überwurfmutter** flange-type cock with cap screw

Flansch-kappe *f* flange box **-kopplung** *f* flanged connector, flange coupling **-krümmer** *m* flanged bends **-kupplung** *f* flange coupling, disk or plate coupling **-lager** *n* side-bracket bearing, flanged bearing, position of flange **-länge** *f* length of flange **-lappen** *m* flange lug **-los** flangeless

Flansch-maschine *f* flanging machine **-mitnehmer** *m* flange dog, flange yoke **-muffe** *f* flange socket **-nabe** *f* flanged hub **-packung** *f* joint packing (for pipes) **-partie** *f* web flange **-pumpe** *f* flanged-on pump

Flansch-reifen *m* tire of a coupling **-ring** *m* shrouding ring **-rohr** *n* flanged tube or tubing

-röhre *f* flanged pipe, welded or cast on **-rohrleitung** *f* flanged pipeline

Flansch-scheibe *f* flange pulley **-schraube** *f* flange bolt, bolt of flange **-schraubenschlüssel** *m* flange wrench **-stärke** *f* thickness of flange **-stoßscheibe** *f* flange axle collar **-stück** *n* muff **-stutzen** *m* flange tube or connection **-symmetrielinie** *f* symmetrical line of flange

Flansch-T-Stücke *n pl* flanged T's

Flansch-verbindung *f* flanged joint or coupling, flanged coupling joint **-verschraubung** *f* bolted flanges, flange joint **-walzmaschine** *f* flange rolling machine **-werkzeug** *n* flange tool **-welle** *f* flanged shaft **-zwischenlage** *f* waveguide shim

Fläschchen *n* small bottle, flask, phial, vial

Flasche *f* bottle, flask, jar, cylinder (for gas), casting box (in founding), flask, block (mech.), tackle, faucet, canteen, sharpening tool; (Hebezug) *f* pulley block **~ des Flaschenzuges** block **feste ~** crown block **auf Flaschen füllen** to bottle **~ mit großer Öffnung** wide necked bottle

Flaschen-abfüllraum *m* bottling room **-abtropfgestell** *n* bottle-draining truck **-ausgießer** *m* bottle emptier **-auslaufgestell** *n* bottle-draining truck **-azetylen** *n* cylinder gas **-batterie** *f* battery of bottle cells **-bodenformer** *m* bottle-bottom molder **-bruch** *m* breakage (bottles) **-bügel** *m* bail of patent stopper

Flaschen-einweichapparat *m* bottle-soaking apparatus **-form** *f* molds in bottlemaking **-führungskurve** *f* bottle guiding curve **-füllmaschine** *f* bottle-filling machine (for mineral water) **-gas** *n* cylinder gas **-gasabfüllung** *f* cylinder gas bottling **-gestell** *n* racks for tools, bottles, etc. **-gießmaschine** *f* bottle-casting machine **-größe** *f* bottle size **-gruppe** *f* cylinder bank

Flaschenhals-durchmesser *m* bottleneck diameter **-kokille** *f* bottleneck ingot mold

Flaschenhalter *m* flask holder **-gurt** *m* bottleneck hand strap **-strange** *f* flask-holder axle

Flaschen-hebelverschluß *m* bottle stopper with lever **-hülse** *f* bottle wrapper **-hub** *m* bottle lift **-inhalt** *m* capacity of bottle, bottle contents **-kapsel** *f* bottle cupsule **-kasten** *m* block-and tackle box **-korkmaschine** *f* bottle-corking machine **-kürbis** *m* bottle gourd

Flaschen-material *n* type of bottle **-mundstückformer** *m* bottle-ring maker **-mündung** *f* bottle mouth **-preßmaschine** *f* bottle-molding press **-reif** fit for bottling **-reinigungsmaschine** *f* bottle-cleaning machine **-rost** *m* battery of cylinders or bottles

Flaschen-sauerstoff *m* oxygen in cylinders **-scherben** broken glass **-schlußventil** *n* cylinder valve, cylinder-pressure regulator **-schwefler** *m* bottle sulfuriser **-stern** *m* bottle star **-teller** *m* bottle plate **-transporteinrichtung** *f* jar conveyor

Flaschen-ventil *n* valve of cylinder or bottle **-verschluß** *m* bottle shutter or stopper, closing device for bottles, cork **-winde** *f* bottle jack (lifting), locomotive jackscrew

Flaschenzug *m* single, double, or treble block, hoist, block and tackle, tackle, block, pulley, winding tackle, tackle block, set of pulleys **~ mit elektrischem Antrieb** electric chain hoist **~ mit verlängerter Antriebswelle** extension handwheel block **~ zum Aufheben** lifting tackle **~ mit eingebauter Laufkatze** trolley block **~ mit Stirnradplanetengetriebe** spurgeared chain block with planetary-gear system

Flaschenzug-bügelhaken *m* block shackle **-kette** *f* hoist chain, pulley chain **-kloben** *m* hoisting tackle **-leine** *f* block and tackle **-radverschluß** *m* catch for pulley block **-seil** *n* hoisting cable, hoist rope **-transporteur** *m* bottle conveyor **-trommel** *f* calf wheel

Flaser *f* flaser, streak

Flatter *m* directional oscillation flutter **-bock** *m* vibration clamp **-effekt** *m* flutter effect, undulation effect

Flatterer *m* flapping object

flatterhaft inconstant

flatterig wobbling, fluttering

Flatterjalousie *f* automatic ventilating louvre

flattern (Welle) to whirl, to flutter, flicker (of light), wave **~** (Räder) to wobble (wheels)

Flattern *n* pulsation, shimmying, whirling **~ der Kolbenringe** piston-ring flutter **~ der Räder** shimmy **~ von Schwenkrollen** shimmy **~ der Tragflügel** wing flutter

Flatter-ruß *m* lampblack **-schwingung** *f* buffeting flutter **-widerhall** *m* multiple reflection, flutter echo **-wirkung** *f* flutter(ing) effect

flau flat, without contrast, limy or blooming condition, fuzzy (of picture), poor (of gases, vacuum, etc.) **~ werden** to lull, flatten out **-es Bild** weak image

Flaum *m* fuzz **-feder** *f* downy feather or plume **-fett** *n* neutral lard (chem.) **-flocke** *f* fluff

Flausch *m* pad

Flaute *f* calm, lull, dead calm

Flechströmung *f* turbulent flow

Flechte *f* plait (cords, jute), lichen

flechten to twist, braid, strand, plait, interweave

Flecht-maschine *f* braiding machine **-stoff** *m* plaiting material

Flechtung *f* pleat, pleating or plaiting machine

Flechtungszahl *f* number of strands

Flecht-waren *pl* wicker goods **-weide** *f* water willow **-werk** *n*, **zaun** *m* wattlework

Fleck *m* spot, stain, patch, flaw, defect, speck **-analyse** *f* spot analysis **-belegung** *f* impingement on the (cathode) spot **-durchmesser** *m* spot diameter **-effekt** *m* patch effect

flecken to stain, spot, speckle, mottle, patch

Flecken *m* stain, blemish, blot, flaw, spot, defect

flecken-empfindlich susceptible to staining or spotting **-los** stainless, unblemished

Flecken-entfernungsmittel *n* stain remover

flecken-frei spotless, stainless **-gebiet** *n* patch area **-losigkeit** *f* stainlessness **-probe** *f* spot test **-theorie** *f* patch theory (of metals)

Fleck-fieber *n* spotted fever, typhus **-gerät** *n* spotting device, spotter **-helligkeit** *f* brightness of spot

fleckig spotted, stained, speckled, mottled **~ machen** to spot **fleckiges Bild** spottiness

Fleck-schärfe *f* (sharpness of) spot focus **-schiefer** *m* fleckschiefer (slate with minute spots), patched slate **-schuß** *m* point blank (shot) **-unschärfe bei Ablenkung** deflection defocusing **-verformung** *f* spot distortion **-verzerrung** *f* deflection aberration, spot distortion **-wasser** *n* scouring water

Fledermausbrenner *m* batswing burner

Fleet *n* watercourse, canal

Fleier *m* fly-frame tenter **-antriebsrädchen** *n* driving wheel for fliers **-gehilfe** *m* fly-frame helper **-spindel** *f* spindle for fly frames
Fleierei *f* reving processes
Fleisch-hackmaschine *f* meat grinder or chopper **-hackmesser** *n* meat-chopper knife **-kammer** *f* larder **-kohle** *f* flesh or meat charcoal **-konserven** *f pl* canned meat **-kühlanlage** *f* preservation of meat by cold storage **-pökler** *m* meat salter **-seite des Riemens** rough or flesh side of the belt **-wunde** *f* flesh wound
fleißig hard-working, industrious, diligent, assiduous
Flettner-hilfsruder *n* Flettner balance, servotab (naut.) **-ruder** *n* servorudder (control surface) (naut.) **-seitenruder** *n* servorudder (naut.)
flexibel flexible
Flexibelbogen *m* flexible bend
flexible Bolzenkupplung flexible pin coupling
flexible Decke (Flughafen) flexible pavement
Flexur *f* anticlinal flexure
Flick-arbeit *f* repair or patching work, patchwork **-daube** *f* bent stave for repairs
flicken to repair, patch, reline, mend
Flicken *n* repairing, patch(ing), relining
Flickerei *f* patching
Flicker-peilung *f* flicker direction-finding method **-photometer** *m* flicker photometer
Flick-kasten *m* sewing kit, repair, outfit **-masse** *f* patching material, ganister **-schaufel** *f* spoon with bowl (for relining furnace) **-standlinie** *f* patch-line base (photo.) **-stelle** *f* (Straße) patch **-stube** *f* repair shop, tailor shop **-zeug** *n* sewing kit, repair outfit
Fliege *f* fly, traveler, runner (textiles) **-draht** *m* flying wire
fliegen to fly, pilot **dicht über den Boden ~** to hedgehop **Einsatz ~** to fly a sortie **gegen den Wind ~** to fly upwind **mit dem Wind ~** to fly with tail wind **über das Ziel ~** to overshoot (flying) **blind ~** to fly blind
Fliegen im Verband formation flying
fliegend flying **~ angeordnet** in overhung position, overhung **~ gelagert** taper bore mounted, overhung **-e Anlage** temporary plant **-e Anordnung** overhung arrangement **-er Dorn** flying pin **-er Flügel** flying wing **-e Kathode** floating cathode **-er Kreisel** (Kompressor) overhung impeller **-es maßstäbliches Modell** flying scale model **-es Personal** flying personnel **-e Schere** flying shears
Fliegen-kopf *m* turned character (print.) **-leim** *m* flypaper adhesive **-papier** *n* flypaper **-pilz** *m* **-schwamm** *m* fly agaric or amanita **-stein** *m* white arsenic, flaky or native arsenic
Flieger *m* flier, aviator, flying machine
Flieger-aufnahme *f* aerial picture or photograph **-ausdrücke** *m pl* aeronautical terms (including slang) **-ausrüstung** *f* aviator outfit **-bekleidung** *f* aviator's uniform or clothing **-benzin** *n* aviation fuel **-beobachtung** *f* aircraft spotting
Flieger-bild *n* aerial photograph **-brille** *f* flying goggles **-drehstütze** *f* swivel extension for antiaircraft machine gun **-dreibein** *n* tripod mounting for antiaircraft machine gun
Fliegerei *f* aviation, flying
Fliegerfilm *m* aerofilm (phot.)
Flieger-film *m* aerofilm (phot.)
Flieger-handkamera *f* aerial portable camera **-handschuhe** *m* flying gloves **-haube** *f* flying helmet **-horizont** *m* artificial horizon, horizontal flight indicator
Fliegerhorst *m* air base, airfield, airport, service aerodrome
Fliegerin *f* woman pilot, aviatrix
fliegerisch pertaining to flying or aviation **-e Fähigkeit** flying capacity or ability
Flieger-karte *f* aeronautical chart **-krankheit** *f* airsickness
Flieger-notsignal *n* airplane distress signal **-personal** *n* air-force personnel **-schule** *f* flying school **-schutz** *m* antiaircraft defense **-schutzanzug** *m* flying suit or kit **-sichtstreifen** *m* ground panel (aviation) **-stiefel** *pl* flying boots
Flieger-störer *m*, **-störstelle** *f* airplane-jamming station **-tauglichkeit** *f* fitness for flying **-technisches Personal** air technicians **-untersuchungsstelle** *f* medical authority determining fitness for flying
Flieger-wache *f* air guard, aircraft observation
Flieg-lack *m* airplane dope **-werkstoff** *m* aircraft material
Flieh-backe *f* centrifugal arming device (fuse) **-backenfeder** *f* interrupter spring (fuse) **-beschleunigung** *f* centrifugal acceleration **-bolzen** *m* interrupter pin (fuse)
fliehen to flee, escape
Flieh-geschwindigkeit *f* escape velocity (the velocity at which an object would escape the gravitational attraction of a given astronomical body) **-gewicht** *n* flyball, centrifugal weight or force, fly weight
Fliehgewichts-antrieb *m* centrifugal-weight-drive type of fuse mechanism **-ausschlag** *m* centrifugal weight deflection (or deviation) **-bolzen** *m* flyweight trunnion **-kupplung** *f* centrifugal clutch **-regler** *m* centrifugal governor **-träger** *m* centrifugal weight carrier
Fliehkraft *f* centrifugal force, flywheel force **-anlasser** *m* inertia starter **-backe** *f* centrifugal wedge block **-beschleunigung** *f* radial or centrifugal acceleration **-erreger** *m* out-of-balance exciter **-feinregler** *m* precision-type centrifugal governor
Fliehkraft-gebläse *n* centrifugal type supercharger **-geschwindigkeitsmesser** *m* centrifugal-type speedometer **-kupplung** *f* centrifugal clutch **-pendel** *n* dynamic counterweight, governor centrifugal pendulum **-regler** *m* centrifugal governor or flyball **-schalter** *m* centrifugal contactor, centrifugal switch **-tachometer** *n* centrifugal-force tachometer **-versteller** *m* centrifugal timer or governor **-verstellung** centrifugal (automatic) timing control **-zünder** *m* centrifugal fuse
Fliehpendel *n* fly weight (jet) **-drehzahlmesser** *m* inertia revolution counter, speed counter, centrifugal-pendulum-type tachometer **-tachometer** *n* mechanical centrifugal tachometer
Fliesboden *m* flagged floor, flagging
Fliese *f* flag, tile, flagstone
Fliesen-abdeckung *f* tile creasing **-fußboden** *m* tile floor(ing) **-legerarbeiten** *pl* tile layers' work **-pflaster** *n* flagged floor, flagging **-waren** *pl* tiled articles

Fließ-arbeit *f* continuous production, assembly-line work, continuous operation, progressive manufacture or assembly **-arbeitseinrichtung** *f* progressive assembly-conveyer machinery
Fließband *n* progressive assembly line **-anlage** *f* belt carrier system **-fertigung** *f* conveyer-line production **-montage** *f* progressive assembly
Fließ-band für Zusammenbau assembly line **-bedingung** *f* yield condition **-behinderung** *f* inhibition of plastic deformation **-belastung** *f* yield load **-bereich** *m* plastic range **-betrieb** *m* continuous operation **-bett** *n* mill race, fluidized bed **-bettrockner** *m* fluidized bed drier
Fließ-bild *n* flow diagramm **-blatt** *n* blotter **-dehnung** *f* yield strain **-diagramm** *n* flow diagram **-drehen** *n* shear spinning, flow turning **-druck** *m* hydraulic pressure, pressure of fluidity **-eigenschaften** *pl* rheological properties
fließen to flow, circulate, run, pass (in, to, into)
Fließen *n* flowing, flow with velocity less than the critical value, flow, circulation **~ der Drucke** bleeding of the prints **Wissenschaft der Verformung unter ~** rheology **plastisches ~** viscous, streamline, laminar, or steady flow
fließend flowing, yielding, fluid, liquid **-e Fertigung** progressive assembly **-er Zusammenbau** *m* progressive assembly
Fließ-erscheinung *f* phenomenon of flow **-fähigkeit** *f* flowability, fusibility, ability or tendency to flow **-feder** *f* fountain pen
Fließfertigung *f* line-production system, assembly- or conveyer-line production **~ von Kleinmotoren** assembly-line production of small motors
Fließ-figuren *pl* flow or stretcher lines, lines of stress surface bands, strain figures **-funktion** *f* yield function **-gelenk** *n* yield hinge **-gerecht** fluidlike **-grenze** *f* stretching-strain limit, yield point or value, liquid or flow limit **-grenzenversuche** *pl* liquid-flow-limit tests **-gußformverfahren** flow molding
Fließindex (-zahl) *f* liquidity index **-koeffizient** *m* coefficient of discharge **-kohle** *f* colloidal fuel, colloidal coal **-körper** *m* fluid or liquid body or substance **-kraft** *f* yield force **-kunde** *f* rheology
Fließ-linien *pl* flow lines **-markierung** *f* flow mark **-mischer** *m* continuous mixer (continuous kneader mixer) **-moment** *n* yield bending moment **-ofen** *m* pyrites kiln
Fließpapier *n* blotting paper **-unterlage** *f* layer of gray paper
Fließ-pressen *n* extrusion molding **-probe** *f* flow or pouring test, flow sample **-punkt** *m* melting point, flow point, yield point or value **-rechteck** *n* yield rectangle **-richtung** *f* direction of flow
Fließ-sand *m* quicksand, drifting sand **-scheide** *f* no-slip point **-schema** *n* flow diagram **-schwimmsand** *m* quicksand **-span** *m* continuous chip **-spannung** *f* yield stress
Fließspannungs-ort *m* yield locus **-sprung** *m* change in flow stress **-verhältnis** *n* flow stress ratio
Fließ-strömung *f* quiet flow **-ton** *m* quick clay **-vermögen in der Kälte** cold flow **-verzug** *m* yield or flow distortion or deformation **-vorgang** *m* flow process **-widerstand** *m* resistance to flow, flow stress yield resistance **-zahl** *f* flow number
flimmerfrei flickerless **-e Verschlußblende** non-flicker shutter **-e Wiedergabe** flicker-free reproduction
Flimmer-freiheit *f* freeness from flicker **-frequenz** *f* fusion, no-flicker, or critical-flicker frequency **-messer** *m* scintillometer
flimmern to flicker, shine, glimmer, twinkle, scintillate
Flimmern *n* shimmer, scintillation, flicker, twinkling **Beseitigung des Flimmerns** elimination of flicker
Flimmer-peilung *f* loop-reversing or switch method, flicker direction-finding method **-phänomen** *n* flicker-phenomenon **-photometer** *n* flicker photometer **-schalter** *m* flicker-switch
flink speedy, smart **-sicherung** *f* quick-action fuse
Flinse *f* flaw
Flint *n* flint
Flinte *f* rifle, musket
Flinten-lauf *m* gun barrel **-schloß** *n* gunlock **-schrot** *n* small or quail shot, gunshot **-schuß** *m* gunshot
Flintglas *n* flint glass **-prisma** *n* flint-glass prism
Flint-mühle *f* flint tube mill **-sand** *m* flint sand **-stein** *m* flint, boulder flint **-steinmühle** *f* plebble-mill
Flip-Flopgenerator *m* monostable multivibrator
Flip-Floprelais *n* flip-flop-relay
Flip-Flopschaltung *f* flip-flop circuit, staticisor
Flirr *n* spathic iron ore
Flitter *m* spangle, tinsel, finery
flittern to glisten, glitter, sparkle, scintillate
Flittersand *m* micaceous sand
Flitzwagen *m* fast vehicle, jeep
Flocke *f* flock, flake, floccule
flocken to flake, form flakes or flocks, flocculate
Flocken *pl* flakes (fisheyes), clot **-abscheider** *m* flake discharger **-artig** flocculent, flaky **-asbest** *m* flaked asbestos **-bildung** *f* flocculation, coagulation **-eiserzeuger** *m* flake-ice maker **-empfindlichkeit** *f* susceptibility to flakes **-graphit** *m* flaky graphite **-riß** *m* flake **-rissig** flaky, flakily **-struktur** *f* flocculent structure **-versuch** *m* flock test **-verteilung** *f* flocculent structure **-walze** *f* corn and grain milling, flaking mill
Flockfangnadel *f* roll-picker needle
flockig flacky, flocky, flocculent **~ machen** to flocculate **-e Schicht** fluff
Flockigkeit *f* flocculence
Flockung *f* flocculation, deflocculation
Flödel *n* purfling (violin)
Flor *m* nap (textiles), gauze, tiffany, crepe
Florett *n* floret, foil **-seide** *f* raw unwound silk, floss
Floriannetz *n* Florian net, direct, direct lines to aircraft-reporting central station
Flor-papier *n* tissue paper **-post** *f* onion skin **-postpapier** *n* airmail paper, onion skin **-quetsche** *f* web squeezing machine **-schlauch** *m* pile tube **-schuß** *m* weft pile **-stoff** *m* crape, gauze, tiffany
Flor- und Durchschlagpost onion skin and copy paper
Floß *n* pig (metal.), raft, float
flößbar navigable for rafts, floatable
Floßbaumholz *n* balsa wood
Floß-boot *n* air raft, lifesaving raft **-brücke** *f*

floating bridge

Flosse *f* fin, blade; float, pig (metal.); fixed or stabilizing surface **~ kreuzförmig** (Rakete) cruciform fin

Floßeisen *n* white pig iron

flößen to float, infuse, refine (metal)

Flossen-antenne *f* skid-fin antenna (of aircraft) **-bett** *n* pig mold **-druckpunkt** *m* center of pressure of fixed tail surface **-ende** *n* tail plane tip, stabilizer tip **-endkappe** *f* cover-strip of tailplane tip **-gedämpfte Rakete** fin-stabilized rocket nonrotating in flight **-geschoß** *n* fin-stabilized missile

Flossen-kiel *m* fin keel **-kühler** *m* side radiator **-stummel** *m* wing-float stump, hydrostabilizer (aviation) **-träger** *m* fin carrier **-verstellgerät** *n* fin-adjusting instrument **-verstellung** *f* adjustment or trimming of the fixed-tail surfaces

Flößer *m* raftsman

Floß-feder *f* timber float, fin **-gasse** *f* raft channel or pass

Flößholz *n* float wood, raft wood, driftwood

Floß-loch *n* mouth of a furnace **-nagel** *m* rafter or tenpenny nail **-ofen** *m* blast furnace **-rechen** *m* grating for floating wood **-sack** *m* pneumatic assault boat

Flotation *f* flotation, floating

Flotations-anlage *f* flotation plant **-blende** *f* flotation blende **-fähig** floatable **-konzentrat** *n* flotation concentrate **-maschine** *f* flotation machine **-öl** *n* flotation oil **-verfahren** *n* flotation or washing process

Flotator *m* flotation machine

Flöte *f* flute, flageolet **~ mit Stimmzug** flute with tuning slide

flotierbar floatable

flotieren to float

Flotierungsmittel *n* flotation agent

Flotte *f* scouring solution; fleet, navy; mixture (of liquids)

Flotten-abflußventil *n* discharge flap **-abkommen** *n* naval agreement **-abteilung** *f* naval detachment **-behälter** *m* tank **-beschränkungsvertrag** *m* naval limitation treaty, agreement on naval-armament limitation **-bewegung** *f* circulation of dye liquor

Flotten-richtung *f* direction of flow **-station** *f* naval home base **-strom** *m* flow **-stützpunkt** *m* naval base or district **-umwälzung** *f* bath circulation **-verhältnis** *n* bath ratio, consistency (of pulp) (textiles)

Flottille *f* flotilla

Flott-stahl *m* ingot steel **-wassertiefe** *f* vertical distance between ship bottom and channel bed

Flöz *n* rock bed, layer, seam, stratum, deposit **das ~ streicht zu Tage aus** the vein crops **ein ~ erschürfen** to uncover a layer **ein ~ lösen** to drain a seam or bed **flach einfallendes ~** gently dipping seam **rechtes ~** edge seam (geol.) **schwebendes ~** dilated seam **stehendes ~** edge seam (geol.) **steiles ~** steep dipping seam

Flöz-abbau *m* work(ing) of a vein (min.) **-arm** poor in seams **-bau** *m* working of a bed **-flügel** *m* wing of working **-führendes Steinkohlengebirge** hardcoal-bearing strata **-gebirge** *n* secondary rock **-mächtigkeit** *f* thickness of deposit **-reichtum** *m* abundance of seams **-sattel** *m* saddle (geol.)

Fluatlösung *f* a waterproofing solution

Flucht *f* alignment, flight, escape, row, line **die ~ ergreifen** to flee **in die ~ schlagen** to put to flight

flucht-artig flightlike, hasty **-ebene** *f* vanishing plane

fluchten to align, be in alignment

Fluchten *n*, **zum ~ bringen** to align, fay, line up

Fluchtentafel *f* straight-line or self-computing chart

Flucht-fernrohr *n* straight line setting telescope **-gerade** *f* vanishing line **-gerecht** truly aligned, flush (with) **-geschwindigkeitsgrenze** *f* escape speed **-holz** *n* aligning board, (sprit) level, rule

flüchtig volatile, transient; fugitive; fleeting, cursory; superficial, hasty **~ entwerfen** to sketch, make a rough outline **nicht ~** fixed, nonvolatile **-er Anteil einer Mischung** volatile spirit, volatile ingredient(s) of a mixture **-er Bestandteil** volatile constituent **-er Blick** glance **-es Naphtha** solvent naphtha **-es Öl** essential oil **-e Spaltprodukte** volatile fission **-e Spannung** transient voltage **-er Stromstoß** transient impulse **-e Vermessung** rough survey (geol.) **-er Vorgang** transient phenomenon, equilibrating process

Flüchtigkeit *f* volatility, nonpersistence, transiency, fugacity, evanescence, carelessness

Flüchtigkeits-fehler *m* inadvertant mistake **-zahl** *f* volatility number

Fluchtlinie *f* vanishing line, straight or building line

Fluchtlinien-diagramm *n* alignment diagram **-nomogramm** *n* alignment nomogram **-plan** *m* frontage alignment **-tafel** *f* nomograph, nomographic diagram, alignment chart, alignment table

fluchtlos bauen to build slovenly

Fluchtort *m* adit window (min.)

Fluchtpunkt *m* vanishing point **-steuerung** *f* (Entzerrungsgerät) vanishing-point control (rectifier)

flucht-recht correctly or truly aligned, flush **-schleuse** *f* outlet sluice **-stab** *m* ranging rod, surveyor's or field rod

Fluchtungsfehler *m* misalignment

Fluder *m* waste weir, millrace, power canal

Flug *m* flight or flying (aviation) **~ im Bogen des größten Kreises** Great Circle flying **~ am Doppelsteuer** dual-control flying **~ ohne Halt** nonstop flight **~ in ruhiger Luft** flying in still air **~ in gerader Richtung** Great Circle or straight-line flying **~ mit Vollgas** flight with wide-open throttle **~ über der Wetterzone** overweather flight **überzogener ~** stall (aviation) **vorgerückter überzogener ~** advanced stall **vor dem ~** pre-flight

Flug-abschnitt *m* stage of flight **-anmeldung** *f* flight notification **-anzeiger** *m* flight indicator **-apparat** *m* flying machine **-asche** *f* flue dust, fly or quick ash (sugar refining) **-aschefänger** *m* flue-dust catcher **-aschenabscheider** *m* flue dust separator **-aschenabzug** *m* quick-ash outlet **-aufgabe** *f* flight mission **-ausbildung** *f* flight training

Flugaufnahmen *pl*, **Entzerrung von ~** restitution of aerial photographs

Flugaussage *f* ground to air radio telephone

Flugbahn *f* path of a projectile, trajectory, flight path **absteigender Ast der ~** descendent branch of trajectory **gestreckte, rasante ~** flat trajectory **mittlere ~** mean trajectory **Scheitel der ~** trajectory zenith

Flugbahn-anzeiger *m* track guide **-bild** *n* trajectory diagram **-ebene** *f* trajectory plane **-geschwindigkeit** *f* flight-path speed **-korrektur** *f* flight path correction **-neigungswinkel** *m* inclination angle of flight path **-projektion** *f* projection of flight path **-richtung** *f* direction of flight or flight path **-tangente** *f* tangent of flight path **-winkel** *m* flight-path angle

Flug-ballast *m* shifting ballast **-bedingungen** *pl* flying conditions **-begeistert** air-minded **-belastungen** *f pl* flight loads **-benzin** *n* aviation gasoline **-beratung** *f* briefing (on flight) **-beratungsdienst** *m* aeronautical information service (AJS)

Flugbereich *n* flying or cruising range, range or radius of action or of flight

Flugbereichlicht *n* flying range light, light covering the radius of operation

flugbereit ready to take off, ready for flying

Flug-besatzung *f* flight crew **-beschränkungsgebiet** *n* restricted area **-besprechung** *f* briefing of flight crews **-besprechungsraum** *m* briefing room **-betrieb** *m* flight operations, air traffic or activity **-betriebshandbuch** *n* flight operations manual **-(bewegungs)kontrolle** *f* air traffic control

Flugboot *n* seaplane, flying boat **-körper** *m*, **-rumpf** *m* hull of seaplane or flying boat

Flug-buch *n* logbook **-dach** *n* lean-to roof **-dauer** *f* duration of flight

Flugdeck *n* landing deck, flight deck **-kreuzer** *m* cruiser with flight deck

Flug-dienst *m* flying service or duty **-dienstberater** *m* dispatcher **-dienstausrüstung** *f* airfield service equipment **-disziplin** *f* flight discipline **-dynamik** *f* flight dynamics **-ebene** *f* plane of flight, slant plane through guns to path of target **-eigenschaften** *pl* flying qualities, flight characteristics or properties

Flügel *m* wing, lobe, vane, leaf, impeller, blade, airfoil, (aerodyn.) flank, flap, fluke (of an anchor), grand piano **~ des Patentlogs** rotator (ship's log) **~** (fest oder beweglich) **eines Quadrantenelektrometers** vanes (fixed or moving) of a quadrant electrometer **~ eines Rührwerkes** beater **~ mit Verjüngung** tapered wing **~ einer Zentrifugalsichtmaschine** beater of a centrifugal machine **~ Zerfaserer** blade shredder **Überschlag über den ~** wing over **auf den ~ stellen** to go into a steep bank

Flügel, abnehmbarer ~ detachable wing **durchgehender ~** one-piece wing **einholmiger ~** single-sparred wing **freitragender ~** cantilever wing **gehobener ~ einer Verwerfung** uplift (aviation) **gesunkener ~ einer Verwerfung** downthrow (aviation) **gewölbter ~** cambered wing (airplane), curved sail (windmill) **glatter ~** smooth sail

Flügel, halbfreitragender ~ semicantilever wing (aviation) **hohler ~ mit Preßfinger** hollow flier with spring finger **mehrholmiger ~** multispar wing (aviation) **~ negativer Pfeilform** swept-forward wing **offener ~** exposed flank or wing **verstrebter ~** strutted or braced wing **verwindbarer ~** warping or winding wing **voller ~** solid flier (textiles) **zusammenlegbarer ~** folding wing **zweiholmiger ~** two-spar wing

Flügel-abstand *m* wing gap (aviation) **-abstrom** *m* downwash **-anker** *m* vane armature **-ankerrelais** *n* vane-armature relay **-anlenkung** *f* wing pivot **-anordnung** *f* wing arrangement **-ansatz** *m* wing stub or root **-anschluß** *m* wing root, junction, or attachment

Flügel-anstellung *f* wing incidence or altitude **-aufbau** *m* wing structure **-ausschnitt** *m* sectional cutouf of wing **-balken** *m* vane beam **-bauart** *f* wing design **-befestigung** *f* support or fixing **-behälter** *m* wing gasoline tank **-behäutung** *f* wing skin or covering **-benzin** *n* gasoline carried in the wing **-beplankung** *f* wing covering or planking **-beschläge** *pl* wing fittings **-bespannung** *f* wing planking or covering, skin of fabric

Flügel-biegung *f* wing row **-blech** *n* stabilizing fin **-blende** *f* cutting blade (film) **-bohrer** *m* collapsible or enlarging bit **-breite** *f* span (of airplane) **-bremse** *f* fan brake **-bruch** *m* propeller rupture, wing failure **-dicke** *f* wing thickness **-duralumingerüst** *n* duralumin framework of a wing

Flügel-einsatz *m* dirt cage (centrifuge) **-einstellwinkel** *m* angle of wing setting **-einteilung** *f* wing sections **-eintrittskante** *f* leading or entering edge (aviation)

Flügelende *n* wing tip **-sackflug** *m* tip stall

Flügelend-fackel *f* wing-tip flare **-querruder** *n* wing-tip aileron **-scheibe** *f* end or wing-tip plate

Flügel-enteisung *f* deicing of aircraft wings **-fachwerk** *n* wing truss **-feld** *n* wing panel **-fenster** *n* casement window, French casement

Flügelfläche *f* wing surface or area, lifting surface **abgewickelte ~** developed blade area of propeller

Flügel-flächeninhalt *m* wing area **-flächenkühler** *m* wing radiator **-flattern** *n* wing flutter **-form** *f* wing shape or profile **-gebläse** *n* fan, ventilator, fan blower; (Flugzeug) wing fan **-gerippe** *n* wing skeleton **-gesteuert** wing-controlled **-gondel** *f* wing nacelle **-grundriß** *m* wing plan, form or contour **-hahn** *m* butterfly cock, winged tap

Flügelhalter, dreiarmiger ~ für Luftschiffpropeller support for a three-bladed air screw

Flügel-handgriff *m* wing-tip hand grip or handle **-häufler** *m* wing hillers (agr. mach.) **-haut** *f* wing fabric **-hinterkante** *f* trailing edge of wing **-holm** *m* wing spar or beam **-horn** *n* bugle, vocal horn

flügelig winged, bladed

Flügel-kanal *m* wing duct **-keil** *m* winged wedge **-kielflosse** *f* skid fin **-klappe** *f* wing flap **-klemme** *f* round-nosed clamps

Flügelknetmaschine *f* kneading and mixing machine **~ mit Wipptrog** combination kneader and mixer with tilting-type trough body

Flügel-kolben *m* piston (oil-driven vane piston), fly piston **-kolonne** *f* flank or wing column **-kompaß** *m* wing compass **-kopf** *m* winged head **-körper** *m* airfoil **-kreuz** *n* winged cross **-kufe** *f* wing skid, wing-tip ground support **-kühler** *m* wing or surface radiator

flügel-lastig wing-heavy **-leuchtpatrone** *f* wing-tip flare **-mauer** *f* wing walls **-messer** *m* vane-type fluid meter **-messung** *f* current-meter measurement (hydr.) **-metallgerüst** *n* metal framework of a wing **-mischmaschine** *f* paddle-blade-type mixing machine

Flügelmittelstück *n* wing center section **~ fest am Rumpf** wing center section built integral with the fuselage

Flügel-mittelteil *m* center plane section of wing **-moment** *m* wing momentum

Flügelmutter *f* winged or butterfly nut, wing or fly nut, thumb nut **~ mit Stoßarmen** fan with four whiskers, screw fan

flügeln to wing

Flügel-nase *f* nose of wing, leading wing edge **-nute** *f* wing slot **-oberseite** *f* upper (side) surface of wing **-ort** *m* side gallery, auxiliary drain, side drift **-profil** *n* airfoil or wing profile **-profildicke** *f* wing-profile thickness **-pumpe** *f* oscillating pump, rotary or semirotary pump, fly pump **-querschnitt** *m* wing section or profile, airfoil section

Flügelrad *n* impeller or runner, fan or worm wheel, screw wheel or propeller **-anemometer** *n* anemometer of windmill type, fan-wheel anemometer **-antrieb** *m* impeller drive **-flugzeug** *n* paddle-wheel airplane **-ölpumpe** *f* vane-type scavenge oil pump **-pumpe** *f* vane-type pump **-wassermesser** *m* vane water meter **-windmesser** *m* anemometer of windmill type

Flügel-rahmen *m* sash (window sash) **-rippe** *f* wing rib **-rippenkappe** *f* cap strip **-schaft** *m* fin or shaft (mortar shell) **-schalttafel** *f* bracket-type board (hinged panels) **-schiene** *f* guardrail **-schlitz** *m* wing slot

Flügelschnitt *m* airfoil section, wing section or profile **bikonvexer ~** biconvex airfoil profile

Flügelschnittwinkel *m* angle between zero-chord and zero-lift incidence

Flügelschränkung *f* decalage **negative ~** washin **positive ~** washout

Flügel-schraube *f* wing bolt or nut, winged screw, butterfly or wing-headed bolt, thumb or butterfly screw **-schraubenmutter** *f* butterfly nut **-schwimmer** *m* wing-tip float **-schwingung** *f* wing flutter **-sehne** *f* wing chord, chord line **-signal** *n* semaphore signal **-sonde** *f* (-messer) vane apparatus

Flügelspalt *m* wing slot **-spannweite** *f* wing span **-spant** *m* wing rib **-sparren** *m* wing spar **-spill** *n* vane spindle (windmill) **-spindel** *m* flyer spindle **-spinner** *m* fly-frame spinner **-spitze** *f* wing tip

Flügelspitzen-auftriebsverlust *m* wing-tip loss (uplift of airplane) **-umriß** *m* wing-tip rake **-verwindung nach oben** washin **-verwindung nach unten** washout **-wirbel** *m* wing-tip vortex

Flügel-stachel *m* sting (aviation) **-stange** *f* winged pole **-stellung** *f* vane setting **-steuerung** *f* wing or interplane control **-stiel** *m* wing or interplane strut **-strebe** *f* wing strut

Flügelstreckung *f* span-chord or aspect ratio **unendliche ~** infinite span (aerodyn.)

Flügel-stuhl *m* vane spindle **-stummel** *m* wing stub **-stützschwimmer** *m* wing-tip float **-tank** *m* wing tank

Flügeltiefe *f* wing chord **mittlere ~** mean wing chord

Flügel-träger *m* hinged back-plate **-trommel** *f* vane drum **-tülle** *f* wing socket **-tür** *f* folding door, door with two leaves **-übergang** *m* wing fillet **-überhang** *m* wing overhang **-umriß** *m* rake of wing tip, wing plan or contour **-unterseite** *f* under (side) surface of wing

Flügel-ventil *n* butterfly valve **-verbindungsdraht** *m* interaileron wire **-verdrehung** *f* wing twisting or distortion **-verjüngung** *f* wing taper **-verspannung** *f*, **-verstrebung** *f* wing bracing

Flügelverwindung *f* wing twist **~ nach oben** washin **~ nach unten** washout

Flügel-vorderkante *f* leading edge of wing **-weite** *f* top rail of valve (window) **-welle** *f* axletree, wind shaft, vane spindle **-widerstand** *m* wing drag **-wölbung** *f* camber **-wurzel** *f* wing root **-zelle** *f* cell, cellule **-zug** *m* flank platoon **-zuspitzung** *f* wing taper

Flug-erfahrung *f* flying experience **-erprobung** *f* flight testing **-fähig** able or capable to fly, airworthy **-feld** *n* airfield **-feldtankwagen** *m* aircraft refueller **-fernmeldedienst** *m* aeronautical telecommunication service **-fernmeldewesen** *n* aeronautical telecommunications

flugfertig ab Herstellerwerk f.a.f. fly-away-factory

Flug-figuren *pl* acrobatic figures (aviation), maneuver flying pattern **-fläche** *f* flight level **-form** *f*, **-formation** *f* flying formation

Flugfunk *m* aircraft or aeronautical radio **-dienst** *m* aircraft or aeronautical radio service **-forschungsanstalt** *f* aircraft radio research institute

Flugfunkstelle *f*, **bewegliche ~** aeronautical mobile station

Flugfunk-verbindung *f* air-ground communication **-verkehr** *m* air-ground communication, air-ground traffic **-wart** *m* aeronautical radio maintenance mechanic

Fluggast *m* airplane passenger **-kabine** *f*, **-raum** *m* passenger cabin (aviation) **-raumlüftung** *f* ventilation of passenger cabin

Flug-gelände *n* field for glider training, flying terrain **-geschwader** *n* squadron

Fluggeschwindigkeit *f* air speed, (rate of) flying speed, traveling velocity (electrons, etc.) **~ gegenüber dem Erdboden** ground speed **~ über Grund** ground speed, absolute speed **~ auf Grund der Staudruckmesseranzeige** indicated air speed **~ gegenüber der umgebenden Luft** air speed with reference to surrounding air **veranschlagte ~** construction speed **wirkliche ~** true air speed

Fluggewicht *n* gross loading, loaded weight, gross weight, weight in flying order

Flughafen *m* airport **-oberflächenradar** *n* taxiradar

Flug-halle *f* hangar **-haltung** *f* flying position **-handbuch** *n* flight manual **-hefe** *f* light yeast

Flughöhe *f* cruising altitude, ceiling, flight or plane altitude or height, ordinate of trajectory (ballistics), maximum ceiling **~ über Grund** flying height above ground, relative flying height **~ entsprechend der Luftdichte** airplane altitude relative to atmospheric density **absolute ~** absolute flying altitude, flying altitude above mean sea level **höchste ~** absolute ceiling **niedrige ~** low ceiling **relative ~** flying height aboveground, relative flying height

Flughöhen-anzeiger *m* ceiling height indicator **-ballon** *m* ceiling balloon **-strahl** *m* ceiling light

Flug-hydraulik *f* aero-hydraulics **-information** *f* flight information **-instrumente** *pl* flight instruments **-kapitän** *m* aircraft captain **-karte** *f* aeronautical map or chart **-kilometer** *pl* (Statistik) kilometers flown **-klar** ready to fly

Flugklarheit, Prüfung auf ~ preflight check

Flug-kleidung *f* flying clothing **-kleie** *f* beeswing bran **-klimatologie** *f* aeronautical climatology **-klimatologisch** aeronautical climatological **-kolbenmaschine** *f* free-piston engine **-kolbenmotor** *m* (Freikolben) free-piston-type engine **-kosten** *pl* air passage

Flug-kraftstoff *m* aviation or aircraft fuel **-kunststück** *n* flying stunt **-kursbuch** *n* air guide

Flug-lage *f* flight attitude, attitude of flight **-lagenanzeiger** *m* turn-and-bank indicator

Fluglandung, überzogene ~ stall landing

Fluglast-fälle *pl* flight load(ing) conditions **-vielfaches** *n* manoeuvring load factor

Flug-lehre *f* aerodynamics, aeronautics, theory of flight **-lehrer** *m* flight instructor **-leistungsschreiber** *m* flight recorder **-leiter** *m* air traffic controller or control officer **-leistungen** *pl* aeroplane performances **-leistungsmesser** *m* flying performance testing apparatus **-leitung** *f* flight operations office

Flug-linie *f* airline, line of flight **-liniendienst** *m* airline service **-liniennetz** *n* air-line system

Flug-maschine *f* aircraft, flying machine **-mechanik** *f* mechanics of flight **-mechanische Zeiteinheit** unit of aerodynamic time (aerodyn)

Flugmelde-dienst *m* aircraft warning service **-netz** *n* aircraft control and warning network, air-raid warning net **-posten** *m* aircraft observation guard **-stelle** *f* flight-reporting station **-zentrale** *f* aircraft reporting center

Flugmeldung *f* air report

Flugmodell *n* plane model, flying model, model plane **~ mit einziehbarem Fahrgestell** flying model with retractable undercarriage

Flugmodell-bau *m* airplane-model construction **-sport** *m* model-airplane flying **-wettbewerb** *m* model-aircraft competition

Flugmotor *m* aeroplane engine or motor **~ für niedrige Nennhöhe** sea-level rated engine

Flugmutterschiff *n* aircraft depot ship

Flugnavigations-einrichtung *f* air navigation facility **-funkdienst** *m* aeronautical radio navigation service

Flug-navigator *m* flight navigator **-neigungswinkel** *m* angle of dive **-nummer** *f* (Kennummer) flight identification

Flugordnung *f* flying regulations **gelöste ~** route formation

Flugort *m* (flying) position (of an aircraft) **-pionier** *m* aviation pioneer

Flugplan *m* flight plan

flugplanmäßig scheduled (flight) **-e Geschwindigkeit** scheduled speed of aircraft **-er Luftverkehr** scheduled air service

Flugplanvordruck *m* flight plan form

Flugplatz *m* aerodrome, airdrome **auf dem ~ rollen** to taxi **~ mit Verkehrskontrolle** controlled aerodrome

Flugplatz-ausrüstung *f* aerodrome equipment **-befeuerungsanlage** *f* aerodrome lighting system **-bezugspunkt** *m* aerodrome reference point (ARP) **-bezugstemperatur** *f* aerodrome reference temperature **-drehfunkfeuer** *n* terminal VOR (TVOR) **-entwurf** *m* aerodrome design **-erkennungszeichen** *n* aerodrome identification sign

Flugplatz-gebühren *pl* aerodrome tariffs **-gebäude** *n* terminal building **-höhe** *f* aerodrome elevation **-lage** *f* aerodrome site **-leuchtfeuer** *n* aerodrome beacon **-licht** *n* aerodrome floodlight **-verkehr** *m* aerodrome traffic **-wettermindestbedingungen** *pl* aerodrome meteorological minima

Flug-post *f* air mail **-postpapier** *n* airmail paper **-problem** *n* navigational or aeronautical or flying problem **-radius** *m* flying range, range of action **-regeln** *pl* flight rules **-regler** *m* autopilot **-reichweite** *f* flying range **-reisebuch** *n* flight log book **-rekord** *m* aviation record

Flugrichtung *f* course of flight, direction of flight **~ über Grund** direction of flight over ground, track made good

Flug-risiko *n* flying risk **-rost** *m* very thick film of rust **-route** *f* air route **-routennetz** *n* network of air routes **-rundsendedienst** *m* aeronautical broadcasting service **-sand** *m* quicksand, shifting sand, drift or blown sand **-scheibe** *f* flying target **-schein** *m* air-travel ticket **-scheinheft** *n* bulk travel voucher **-schiff** *n* flying boat or ship, air liner **-schlepp** *n* airplane towing

Flug-schneise *f* (flight) corridor **-schnelligkeit** *f* flying speed **-schrauber** *m* gyrodyne **-schreiber** *m* flight recorder **-schrift** *f* pamphlet **-schule** *f* flying school **-schüler** *m* flying student or cadet, student flier **-schulung** *f* flight instruction

Flug-sicherheit *f* flight safety **-sicherheitsdienst** *m* aircraft safety service **-sicherheitsmeldung** *f* flight safety message

Flugsicherung *f* air traffic control (ATC)

Flugsicherungs-anlage *f* installation for air traffic control **-dienst** *m* air traffic control service **-kontrollbezirk** *m* control area (CTA) **-kontrolldienst** *m* air traffic control service **-kontrollzentrale** *f* air traffic control center (ACC) **-kontrollzone** *f* control zone (CTR) **-verkehrsdienste** *pl* air traffic services

Flug-sicht *f* flight visibility **-sinne** *pl* flying senses or instinct **-sport** *m* sport(ing) flying **-sportlicher Wettbewerb** sporting-flying competition **-stabil** stable in flight **-stau** *m* ram pressure due to flight, dynamic pressure **-staudruck** *m* aerodynamic or ramming pressure

Flugstaub *m* smoke or flue dust, flying or fine dust **-kammer** *f* dust chamber, smoke chamber **-kondensation** *f* flue-dust condensation

Flug-staudruck *m* aerodynamic pressure **-steig** *m* ramp

Flug-stellung *f* flying position, flight attitude **-störung** *f* flight interruption or disturbance **-strecke** *f* air route, route of light

Flugstrecken-befeuerung *f* airway or route lighting **-feuer** *n* **-leuchtturm** *m* airway or route beacon **-netz** *n* network of air routes

Flugstunde *f* flying hour, flying time

Flugstützpunkt *m* air base, catapult ship for postal aircraft **schwimmender ~** refueling and catapult-launching ship, floating air base, depot ship

Flug-tag *m* air day, flying day, air display **-technik** *f* aeronautics, aeronautical or flying technique **-überwachung** *f* flight supervision **-überwachungsgerät** *n*, **-überwachungsinstrument** *n* flight instrument **-unfall** *m* flying accident **-unterricht** *m* flight training, flying instruction **-veranstaltung** *f* aviation meeting, air display **-verhalten** *n* flying characteristics **-verkehr** *m* air traffic

Flugverkehrs-freigabe *f* air traffic control clearance **-kontrolle** *f* air traffic control **-lotse** *m* air traffic controller

Flug-verlaufkurve *f* time fuel graph **-versuchsstation** *f* airplane-testing station **-vorbereitung** *f* preflight action, preparation for flight **-vorführung** *f* air exhibition or display **-wache** *f* air guard, air observation, visual observation section **-weg** *m* path or course of flight, track, airway, air route, advisory route

Flugweg-daten *f* flight path data **-rechengerät** *n* flight-path computer **-schreiber** *m* flight-log

Flug-weite *f* flying range, linear height of burst, range (of projectile or airplane)

Flugwendung mit Hilfe der Instrumente instrument turn

Flugwerk *n* air frame (air-plane without engines) **~ und Leitwerk eines Flugbootes** aerostructure of a flying boat

Flug-wesen *n* aviation, aeronautics, aerial navigation **-wettbewerb** *m* flying competition

Flugwetter *n* flying weather **-beratung** *f*, **-dienst** *m* aeronautical or meteorological weather service **-kunde** *f* aeronautical meteorology **-warte** *f* aviation weather station, meteorological station

Flugwind *m* relative wind for flying

Flugwindrichtung verschwindenden Auftriebes direction of relative wind for zero lift

Flug-winkel *m* angle of flight

Flugzeit *f* time of flight, flying time, flight time of a projectile

Flugzeitkurve *f* time-of-flight curve

Flugzeug *n* airplane, aeroplane **~ zu ~** air-air signal **~ mit zwei Bootskörpern** twin-hulled flying boat **~ mit Druckschraube** pusher-type airplane **~ mit veränderlicher Flügelfläche** airplane with variable lifting surface **~ mit verstellbaren Flügeln** variable-wing airplane **~ eines Flugzeugträgers** ship-borne airplane, carrier plane

Flugzeug, ~ mit zusätzlichen Kraftstoffbehältern airplane with auxiliary fuel tanks **~ in Pfeilform** airplane with sweepback **~ mit gestorbenem Propeller landen** dead-stick landing **~ mit Schneekufen** airplane on skis **~ im Schwebeflug** hovering airplane **mit dem ~ einen Sprung machen** (hochziehen) to zoom **~ mit nicht abnehmbaren Tragflächen** fixedwing airplane

Flugzeug, das ~ abfangen to level off **das ~ hebt ab** the airplane takes off **das ~ herum schwingen** to swing the airplane **das ~ sinkt** the airplane loses flying speed **das ~ steigt** the airplane climbs **das ~ steil hochreißen** to zoom **das ~ übersteuern** to overcontrol **das ~ überziehen** to stall the airplane **das ~ zerschmeißen** (slang) to crash an airplane **das ~ zerstören** to destroy an airplane **das ~ ziehen** to pull out

Flugzeug, anlaufendes ~ approaching airplane **führerloses ~** remote-control airplane **mehrmotoriges ~** multi engined airplane **mehrsitziges ~** multiseater **nicht genehmigtes ~** uncertified airplane **schwanzgesteuertes ~** tail-steering airplane **schwanzloses ~** tailless airplane **staubstreuendes ~** duster airplane (for insecticide dispersion) **trudelsicheres ~** nonspinning airplane **verspannungsloses ~** braceless airplane **zweimotoriges ~** twin-engined airplane **zweisitziges ~** two-seater

Flugzeug-abhörapparat *m* airplane sound locator or detector **-achse** *f* axis of aircraft **-antenne** *f* airplane antenna **-aufbauteile** *m pl* **mit dem Auge abmessen** sighting out of wind, aligning structures by eye **-aufhalter** *m* airplane arrester

Flugzeug-aufnahme *f* aerial view, aerial or airplane photograph **-aufsetzpunkt** *m* ground-contact point, touchdown point **-ausstellung** *f* aircraft exhibition **-bau** *m* aircraft construction, aviation industry **-baubedarf** *m* materials for construction of airplanes **-befehlsübertragung** *f* interaircraft voice or command communication **-beheizung** *f* airplane heating **-bein** *n* undercarriage strut, landing-gear strut

Flugzeug-beobachter *m* observer navigator **-bergetrupp** *m* airplane-salvage unit **-besatzung** *f* airplane crew **-bespannstoff** *m* airplane fabric **-bestückung** *f* airplane armament **-bewegung** *f* motion of airplane **-bildpersonal** *n* aerial photographers

Flugzeugbombe *f*, **höchst wirksame ~** most effective aerial bomb

Flugzeug-bordstation *f* airplane wireless set **-eigengeschwindigkeit** *f* true air speed of airplane, own speed **-empfänger** *m* aircraft receiver or receiving set **-erfassung** *f* airplane recognition **-erkennungsdienst** *m* aircraft-recognition service **-fabrik** *f* airplane factory **-fahrgestell** *n* carriage for aircraft **-feinmechaniker** *m* aircraft-instrument mechanic

flugzeugfest fixed in aircraft or body **-e Achse** body axis

Flugzeugflattern *n* airplane flutter

Flugzeugführer *m* airplane pilot or navigator **der zweite ~** copilot

Flugzeugführer-prüfung *f* pilot's license test **-schein** *m* pilot's license or certificate **-schule** *f* pilot's school

Flugzeug-führung *f* piloting of an airplane **-funkgerät** *n* airplane-radio equipment or apparatus **-funkpersonal** *n* aircraft-radio-servicing personnel **-funkstelle** *f* aircraft radio station **-funkwart** *m* aircraft radio-mechanic ground staff **-gerät** *n* aerial-gas-pressure sprinkler **-geschwindigkeitslineal** *n* airplane-velocity slide rule

Flugzeug-gewicht in Abwind download (aviation) **-gleichgewicht** *n* balance or trim of an airplane **-halle** *f* hangar **-höhe** *f* height of airplane **-holm** *m* airplane spar **-industrie** *f* aviation industry **-instrumente** *n pl* airplane or aircraft instruments **-kette** *f* flight of planes, flight of three planes **-klempner** *m* aircraft tinsmith or sheet-metal worker

Flugzeug-kommandant *m* commander of aircraft **-länge** *f* length of airplane **-laufradkeil** *m* airplane chock **-leinen** *n* airplane linen **-leistung** *f* airplane performance

Flugzeug-masse *f* mass of the aircraft **-mechaniker** *m* flight mechanic **-modell** *n* model airplane

Flugzeugmutterschiff *n* aircraft carrier, seaplane tender **~ für Wasserflugzeuge** seaplane parent ship

Flugzeug-reparatur *f* aircraft repair **-reserve** *f* airplane reserves **-rumpf** *m* fuselage, frame of airplane **-rüstpersonal** *n* aircraft armorer artificers or armament crew **-sattler** *m* aircraft leatherworker **-schieben** *n* crabbing of an airplane **-schiff** *n* aircraft carrier **-schlepp** *m* towing by aircraft **-schleppstart** *m* aerotow

Flugzeug-schleuder *f* airplane catapult or catapulting cradle **-schleuderschiff** *n* seaplane tender with catapult facilities **-schleuse** *f* aircraft routing center **-schuppen** *m* hangar **-schwerölmotor** *m* Diesel-type aircraft engine **-schwerpunkt** *m* center of gravity of airplane **-selbststeuergerät** (automatic pilot), gyroscope **-sender** *m* aircraft radio transmitter

Flugzeug-station *f* aircraft station **-steuerung** *f* airplane or flight control **-stirn** *f* nose of airplane **-stützpunkt** *m* airplane base, base airport **-tender** *m* seaplane tender, aircraft tender **-tischler** *m* aircraft carpenter **-träger** *m* aircraft carrier **-trägerschiff** *n* aircraft carrier **-traverse** *f* airplane cross-spar

Flugzeug-verband *m* airplane formation **-wart** *m* aircraft mechanic **-wartung** *f* airplane maintenance **-werk** *n* aircraft works or plant **-zelle** *f* aircraft frame **-zellengerüst** *n* airplane structure **-zerstäubungsgerät** *n* aerial gaspressure sprinkler **-zubehör** *n* aircraft accessories or parts

Flugziel *n* air or flying target or objective **-verfolgung** *f* (mit Suchradar) search-radar tracking

Flugzustand *m* flight position, flying condition

Fluh *f* mass of rock, precipice, stratum, concrete

fluhen to concrete, cement

fluid fluid

Fluidal-struktur *f* fluidal structure **-textur** *f* flow structure

Fluidkompaß *m* fluid or liquid compass, immersed compass

Fluidum *n* fluid

Flukkan *n* gouge (min.), water seepage into underground workings

Fluktuation *f* fluctuation

fluktuieren to fluctuate

Fluktuieren *n* fluctuation

Fluor *m* fluorine **-aluminium** *n* aluminium fluoride **-chrom** *n* chromium fluoride

Fluoreszein *n* fluorescein, diresorcinolphthalein

Fluoreszenz *f* fluorescence **-ausbeute** *f* fluorescence yield, fluorescence **-auslöschung** *f* fluorescence quenching or extinction, evanescence **-bildhelligkeit** *f* fluorescence brightness **-erregender Stoff** fluorogen **-erzeugend** fluorogenic **-farbe** *f* luminous paint

Fluoreszenz-leuchte *f* microscope fluorescence lamp **-leuchten** *n* fluorescent glow **-messer** *m* fluorometer, phosphoroscope **-schirm** *m* fluorescent or phosphorescent screen **-strich** *m* fluorescent screen tracing or line **-strom** *m* fluorescence yield **-unterdrückung** *f* quenching or killing of fluorescence

fluoreszieren to fluoresce, scintillate (when excited by α rays), luminesce

fluoreszierender Stoff fluorescent substance

Fluorid *n* fluoride

Fluorimetrie *f* fluorimetry

Fluorit *m* fluorspar

Fluoritlinsensystem *n* semiapochromatic-lens system

Fluor-kalium *n* potassium fluoride **-kalzium** *n* calcium fluoride, fluorite **-messer** *m* fluorimeter **-salz** *n* fluoride **-schwefel** *m* sulfur fluoride **-silikat** *n* fluosilicate **-wasserstoff** *m*, **-wasserstoffsäure** *f* hydrofluoric acid

fluotieren to form fluosilicate

Flur *m* meadow, territory; hall, vestibule, floor tile, floor, roller path (milling) **-balken** *m* roller path (milling) **-bedienungsstand** *m* floor control panel **-ebene** *f* floor level or line, ground level **-fördermittel** *n* handcart, wheelbarrow, cart **-karte** *f* field map **-namen** *pl* names of parcels (of land) **-platte** *f* floor plate **-schaden** *m* damage to cultivated fields **-steuerstand** *m* **der Presse** press control panel **-vermessung** *f* field measurung, surveying

Fuse *f* slub

Fluß *m* river, stream, flow, flux, fusion, canal, circulation, current, drift (of electrons) **~ in mehrfach verbundenen Körpern** flow in multiply bodies **~ eines Vektors** flux of a vector **magnetischer ~** magnetic flux **wirksamer ~** net flux

Fluß-abschnitt *m* reach of the river **-abwärts** downstream **-anzapfung** *f* river capture **-arm** *m* branch or arm of a river **-aufwärts** upstream **-ausbauchung** *f* river widening **-bett** *n* river bed, natural bed, channel (of fairway) **-breite** *f* river width **-breitenmesser** *m* river-width measuring instrument **-damm** *m* mole, wharf, dam, dike, bank, pier, jetty **-diagramm** *n* flow chart (info proc.) **-dichte** *f* flux density

Flußeisen *n* ingot steel or iron, converter iron, very low-carbon steel, soft or mild steel, structural iron **unberuhigtes ~** rimming steel

Flußeisen-blech *n* steel plate, mild-steel sheet **-gußwaren** *pl* cast-steel parts **-rohr** *n* mild-steel pipe **-schrott** *m* soft-steel scrap

Fluß-elastizität *f* fugitive elasticity **-erde** *f* earthy fluor, fluor earth **-erkundung** *f* river reconnaissance **-faktor** *m* advantage factor **-gabelung** *f* fork of a river **-gebiet** *n* drainage area **-hafen** *m* estuary, river port **-haltung** *f* reach of river

flüssig fluid, liquid, molten **~ machen, ~ werden** to liquefy, melt **nicht ~** fixed (chem.)

flüssig-er Ablauf (Filter) liquid filtrate **-er Brei** slurry **-er Brennstoff** liquid fuel **-er Brennstoffmesser** liquidometer **-er Einsatz** fluid-metal charge **-er Erdkern** liquid core **-e Kathode** pool cathode **-es Kühlmittel** liquid coolant

flüssig-e Mittel disposable fund (ready money) **-er Mörtel** grout **-es Pech** liquid asphalt **-e Phase** liquid zone **-e Raffinade** liquid sugar **-e Schlacke** fluid clinker **-e Schwindung** liquid shrinkage

Flüssiggas *n* liquid bottled motor fuel (such as propane, butane), liquid petroleum gas

Flüssigkeit *f* fluid, liquid, liquor, fluidity **eine ~ durchschütteln** to churn **die ~ verdrängen** to displace the liquid **milchige ~** emulsion **reibungsfreie ~** inviscid fluid **zerstäubte ~** degree of fluidity, viscosity

Flüssigkeits-abscheider *m* trap (petroleum), siphon **-absperrventil** *n* liquid shut-off valve or stop valve **-anlasser** *m* liquid starter **-anlaßwiderstand** *m* liquid-starting resistance **-antrieb** *m* fluid drive **-anzeiger** *m* gauge equipment **-ausgleicher** *m* fluid-type equilibrator (artil.), fluid equalizer **-bad** *n* liquid or fluid bath **-bahn** *f* path of liquid **-barometer** *n* liquid barometer

Flüssigkeitsbehälter *m* container for liquids **obenliegender ~** header

flüssigkeitsberührte Teile parts on contact with liquid

Flüssigkeits-bewegung im Inneren internal fluid motion **-brechung** *f* liquid reflection **-bremse** *f* hydraulic brake **-dämpfer** *m* viscous damper **-dämpfung** *f* liquid damping, fluid damping or dashpot action **-dichtemesser** *m* hydrometer, liquid density meter, areometer **-drehmomentwandler** *m* fluid torque converter **-druck** *m* hydrostatic pressure or head, fluid or hydraulic pressure **-druckgeber** *m* liquid-pressure pick-up

Flüssigkeits-druckmesser *m* piezometer, liquid manometer, liquid-pressure gauge **-durchflußzählrohr** *n* liquid-flow counter **-durchsatz** *m* rate of flow **-entlastung** liquid pressure relief **-fänger** *m* (für Gasbrunnen) flowhead **-feuerlöscher** *m* liquid extinguisher **-gekühlt** liquid-cooled **-gesteuert** hydraulically controlled **-getriebe** *n* hydraulic transmission or drive, fluid flywheel or drive **-grad** *m* (degree of) fluidity, viscosity **-gradmesser** viscosimeter

Flüssigkeits-heber *m* liquid siphon **-höhe** *f* liquid head **interferometer** *n* interferometer for liquids **-keilwirkung** *f* surfboard effect **-kompaß** *m* fluid, floating, or immersed compass, liquid-type compass, spirit compass **-kraftspeicher** *m* liquid accumulator **-kreislauf** *m* liquid cycle **-kühler** *m* liquid radiator or cooler, fluid or liquid cooling **-kühlung** *f* liquid cooling **-kuppelung** *f* fluid flywheel, fluid coupling, hydraulic clutch

Flüssigkeits-leitung *f* fluid pipe **-linse** *f* (oil or water) immersion objective **-maß** *n* liquid measure **-masse** *f* bulk liquid **-messer** *m* liquid meter, flowmeter **-mischer** *m* flow mixer (pipeline mixer) **-motor** *m* hydraulic motor

Flüssigkeits-pegelmanometer *n* liquid level manometer **pfeife** *f* liquid whistle **-phase** *f* liquid phase **-pressung** *f* fluid or hydraulic pressure **-prisma** *n* liquid prism **-probeentnehmer** *m* formation tester **-rakete** *f* liquid propelled rocket **-raum** *m* liquid space **-regelgetriebe** *n* hydraulic variable speed transmission

Flüssigkeits-reibung *f* liquid or fluid friction **-rektifizierheizer** *m* rectifying wash heater (for a rum still) **-rest** *m* liquid remnant **-säule** *f* head of liquid **-schicht** *f* liquid layer **-schieber** *m* liquid slide valve **-spiegel** *m* liquid level or surface; (Reflexion) liquid mirror reflection

Flüssigkeitsstand *m* level of liquid **-anzeiger** *m* liquid-level indicator **-glas** *n* liquid level gauge glass **-messer** *m* liquid level gauge **-regler** *m* liquid-level controller or regulator **-schreiber** *m* liquid level recorder

Flüssigkeitsstatoskop *n* aneroid-liquid statoscope

Flüssigkeitsstrahl *m* liquid jet **-mikrophon** *n* liquid-jet transmitter or microphone **-relais** *n* jet relay (for submarine cables)

Flüssigkeitsstrom *m* stream of liquid **der ~ reißt ab** the stream of liquid is interrupted

Flüssigkeits-stromumlenkung *f* flow direction change **-strömung** *f* fluid flow **-zintillatorzähler** *m* liquid scintillation counter **-thermometer** *n* spirit thermometer **-übertragung** *f* hydraulic transmission **-umkehranlaßwiderstand** *m* liquid-reversing and -starting resistance

Flüssigkeits-verlauf *m* flow of liquid **-verschleppung** *f* carrying liquid over **-vorlage** *f* sealing liquid **-wärme** *f* latent heat of liquid **-welle** *f* fluid wave **-widerstand** *m* flow resistance, internal-head loss, liquid or water resistance **-zähler** *m* liquid counter **-zählrohre** *pl* fluid counters

Flüssigkeitszerstäuber *m* atomizer (sprayer), spray tank, liquid-fuel nozzle **~ für Entgiftung** portable spray decontamination tank

Flüssigkeits-zuführung supply of liquid **-zünder** *m* liquid fuse

Flüssig-kühlung *f* liquid cooling **-machen** to fluidify **-machung** *f* liquefaction, melting **-maß** *n*, **-messer** *m* liquid measure **-metalldampf** *m* liquid metal vapor **-raketenmotor** *m* liquid rocket motor **-spaltstoffreaktor** *m* fluidized reactor **-werden** *n* fusion, fusing, dissolution (liquefaction) **-werdend** liquescent

Fluß-kabel *n* (sub)marine cable, (under)river cable, subfluvial cable **-kalkstein** *m* flux stone **-kies** *m* gravel, coarse or fine sea gravel or sand **-korrektion** *f* improvement of river channels **-kraftwerk** *n* river-run power plant **-kreuzung** *f* river crossing, traverse **-kreuzungsmast** *m* river crossing tower **-lauf** *m* river course **-leitwert** *m* forward conductance **-linie** *f* river line

Fluß-messer *m* flux or magnetic flux meter **-metall** *n* fluid metal **-mittel** *n* flux, fluxing agent or material, welding flux **-mündung** *f* mouth of river **-netz** *n* network of streams and torrents **-niederung** *f* river flats, river valley **-ofen** *m* smelting furnace

Flußplan *m* (Ablaufplan) flow chart (comp.) **-pulver** *n* flux powder **-quelle** *f* origin or head of a river **-regelung** *f* improvement of rivers and modification of the bed **-regulierung** *f* improvement of a river channel **-richtung** *f* direction of river flux, low-resistance or forward direction (of a dry or oxide rectifier) **-röhre** *f* tube of flow, stream tube

Fluß-sand *m* river sand, gravel **-säure** *f* hydrofluoric acid **-sau(e)rer Kalk** calcium fluoride **-schleife** *f* river meander **-schmiedeeisen** *n* malleable ingot iron **-schotter** *m* gravel, coarse or fine sea gravel or sand **-schweißen** *n* quasi-arc process (welding) **-sohle** *f* bed of river **-spaltung** *f* branching of a river

Flußspat *m* fluorite, limestone flux, calcium fluoride **-gitter** *n* fluorite lattice **-grube** *f* fluor spar quarry **-imprägnierungsmasse** *f* silico-

varnish **-leuchtstoffe** *pl* fluorite phosphors **-linse** *f* fluorite lens **-mehl** *n* finely ground fluorite **-mühle** *f* mill for fluorite **-platte** *f* fluorite plate

Flußsperre *f* river block (obstacle)

Flußstahl *m* mild steel, ingot steel or iron, very low-carbon or soft steel ~ **mit hohem Kohlenstoffinhalt** high-carbon steel, ingot steel **warmverformter** ~ wrought steel

Flußstahl-arten *f pl* types or grades of ingot steel **-blech** *n* soft-steel sheet **-erzeugung** *f* manufacture of soft or mild steel **-sorten** *f* low-carbon-steel grade **-erzeugung** *f* **auf offenem Herd** production of ingot steel in an open hearth **-rohr** *n* steel pipe **-scheibe** *f* soft-steel disk **-schlauch** *m* soft-steel flexible tube

Flußstrecke *f* straight reach of river **gekrümmte** ~ sinuous (winding) section of river

Fluß-strom *m* forward current **-system** *n* network of streams and torrents **-trübe** *f* turbid river water, river material **-überführung** *f* river crossing of cables **-übergang** *m* river crossing, ford, place where the current passes from one bank to the other

Flußufer *n* river bank **Wind gegen** ~ wind toward the bank

Fluß-vektor *m* flow vector **-ventil** *n* foot valve **-verbindung** *f* flux turn, linkage, turn flux **-verkettung** *f* flux linkage **-verteilung** *f* neutron flux distribution **-verunreinigung** *f* river pollution **-wasser** *n* river water, fresh water **-wasserbau** *m* fluviatic hydraulics **-wasserstoffsäure** *f* hydrofluoric acid **-wechseldichte** *f* density of flux changes (tape rec.) **-wehr** *n* river weir **-widerstand** *m* forward resistance

Flußwölbung *f*, **geometrische** ~ buckling (geometric)

Flußzeit *f* "on" period (el-tube)

flüstern to whisper

Flüsterpumpe *f* whispering pump

Flut *f* flood, deluge, high tide, tidal flow, flood tide **wilde** ~ waste water **das Einsetzen der** ~ entering of flood

Flut-auslaß *m* flank or saddle escape (hydr.) **-bassin** *n* tidal basin **-becken** *n* wet dock, closed basin, tidal basin **-brecher** *m* groin, breakwater **-brücke** *f* flood arch **-dock** *n* tidal basin or dock

fluten to flood tanks (of submarine)

Fluter *n* kennel

Flut-gang *m* channel, mill trough, millrace **-gerinne** *n* flume, gutter **-gold** *n* float gold **-grenze** *f* tidehead, upstream limit of tidewater, high-water mark **-größe** *f* range of tide **-hafen** *m* tidal harbor **-hahn** *m* flood cock, flooding valve **-höhe** *f* height of the tide **-höhenlinie** *f* lines of simultaneous high tides

Flut-intervall *n* range of tide **-kammer** *f* up-river sluice chamber of a lock **-klappe** *f* flooding flap **-kurve** *f* (örtliche) local tidal diagram **-licht** *n* floodlight **-lichtanlage** *f* floodlighting installation **-messer** *m* tide gauge **-öffnung** *f* flood span, high-water arch

Flutometer *n* floodometer, draught gauge

Flut-raum einer Brücke waterway of a bridge **-recht** flush **-rinne** *f* flood-tide or flood channel **-schleuse** *f* tide lock **-schütze** *m* stop plank **-strom** *m* flood-tide current, flood **-stundenlinie** *f* line of simultaneous high tide

Fluttereffekt *m* flutter effect

Flut-tor *n* flood gate, water gate (of a mill or pond) **-uhr** *f* tide gauge **-ventil** *n* flooding valve **-wassermarke** *f* high-water mark **-wassermenge** *f* volume of water entering on the flood tide, volume of the flood **-welle** *f* tide wave or advancing front of the incoming tide **-werk** *n* wash ore **-zeiger** *m* marigraph

Flux *m* flux

fluxen to flux

Fluxmeter *n* fluxmeter

F_1 Morse-Telegrafie durch Frequenzumtastung F-1 Frequency shift telegraphy (Morse)

FM-Sender frequency-modulated transmitter

FM-Sendermonitor *m* frequency modulator

Fochermotor *m* V-type engine

Fock *f* foresail, foremast **-braß** *f* forebrace **-bukgording** *f* fore buntline **-buktalje** *f* fore bunt whip **-bulin** *f* fore bowline **-geitau** *n* fore clew garnet **-hals** *m* foretack **-laterne** *f* masthead lantern or light

Fockleesegel *n* fore or lower studding sail **-fall** *m* fore-studding-sail halyard

Fock-mars *m* foretop **-mast** *m* foremast **-rüst** *f* fore channels **-schot** *f* foresail sheet **-stag** *n* forestay

Foettinger Getriebe, Foettinger transformator

Föhn *m* foehn, chinook, hot-air blower **-gerät** *n* antiaircraft-rocket projector **-luft** *f* foehn air

Föhre *f* fir, red fir, Scotch pine

Föhrenholz *n* (wood of) pitch pine, fir, or deal

Fokal-distanz *f* focal distance **-ebene** *f* focal plane **-fläche** *f* focal surface **-kurven einer Fläche zweiter Ordnung** focal curves of a surface of second order **-punkt** *m* focal point, isocenter, metapole (phot.)

Fokalpunktstriangulation *f* triangulation from equal-angle points (radial triangulation)

Fokalschlitzverschluß *m* focal-plane shutter

Fokometer *n* focometer, focimeter

Fokus *m* focal spot, anode or cathode spot, focus **-Defokus-Verfahren** *n* focus-defocus mode **-differenz** *f* difference of focus **-ebene** *f* focus plane **-einstellungsfeld** *n* focussing field **-lampe** *f* focusing lamp **-nahe Seite** focus end

Fokusmesser *m* focimeter, focometer **-weite** *f* focal length

Fokusplattenabstand target-plate distance

Fokussier-anode *f* focus anode (TV) **-bedingung** *f* focussing condition

fokussieren to focus

Fokussier-fehler *m* focussing defect **-hülse** *f* focussing ring **-knopf** *m* focussing control, focussing head or knob **-linse** *f* focussing lens **-spule** *f* focusing coil

Fokussierung eines Elektronenstrahles focusing or concentration of electron beam

Fokussierungs-einrichtung *f* concentrating cup **-einstellung** *f* focusing adjustment **-feld** *n* focusing field **-linse** *f* focusing lens

Fokustiefe *f* depth of focus or of field

Folge *f* sequence, succession, series, sequel, order, continuity, result, future, conclusion ~ **leisten** to comply with **zur** ~ **haben** to entail

folgeabhängig sequentiel

Folge-abtastung *f* sequential scanning (TV) **-Arbeits-Ruhekontakt** *m* make-before-break contact **-aufnahme** *f* travel shot **-automatik** *f*

automatic controls, consecutive connection
Folge-bedingung *f* consequential condition (math.) **-bild** *n* successive picture **-bildanschluß** *m* conjunction of successive photographs, photographic extension **-gesetz** *n* alternation law **-karte** *f* trailer card **-kern** *m* product nucleus **-kolben** *m* (Regeltechnik) follow-up piston **-kopieren** *n* follow-on copying, multistage copying **-kopierverfahren** *n* multistage method
Folgekontakt *m* make-before-break contact, sequence or continuity-preserving contact, trailing contact
Folgekontakte (Öffnen vor Schließen) break-before-make contact
Folgekontakte (Schließen vor Öffnen) make-before-break contact
Folge-ladung *f* explosive charge set off by detonation of another charge, induced-detonation charge **-leistung** *f* complicance, obedience
folgen to succeed, follow, obey, result **eine Kurve ~** to conform to a curve (of railway track)
Folgen *n* tracking (radar)
Folge-nummern *pl* consecutive or collective number **-ordnung** *f* progression **-pol** *m* consequent pole **-produkt** *n* metabolon **-prüfprogramm** *n* sequence-checking routine **-punkt** *m* consequent point or pole
Folger *m* leaper, loper, successor
Folge-reaktion *f* consecutive (consequent) reaction, secondary reaction **-recht** logical, consequent, consistant **-regelung** *f* program control, follower control, servomechanism, servo follower **-richtig** logical, sound **-richtigkeit** *f* logic, consistency **-rohr** *n* piloted thyratron
folgern to infer, conclude, deduce,
Folgerung *f* deduction, inference, conclusion, induction, corollary
Folgesatz *m* corollary (math.)
Folgeschalter *m* sequence switch **~ und Relaissatz für Leitungswähler** final sequence switch and relay set
Folge-schalterkamm *m* sequence-switch cam **-schaltung** *f* sequence control or operation **-schnitt** *m* jig saw, multiple press tools, follow dies **-steuerung** *f* follow-up control, remote control **-stufe** *f* subsequent stage **-versuch** *m* sequential test **-weg** *m* contact follow **-werkzeug** *n* follow-on tool
Folgezeiger *m* pointer, direction indicator, follow-the-pointer mechanism in data, transmission system **-antrieb** *m* continuous-pointing traversing wheel, follow-the-pointer drive **-einrichtung** *f* pointing mechanism, follow-the-pointer mechanism **-empfänger** *m* receiver, fuse, indicator, follow-the-pointer-type fuse setter **-system** *n* follow-up system
Foliant *m* folio volume
Folie *f* supporting film, foil, sheet of plotting drum
Folien *pl* (plastics) sheeting, windows **aus dünnen ~ bestehend** laminated
Folien-aktivierung *f* foil activation **-band** *n* foil strip **-bürsten** *pl* brushes (elec.) **-dicke** *f* thickness of film **-durchmesser** *m* record (disk) diameter
Folien-geräusch *n* window noise (electronics) **-kalander** *m* film or foil calender **-kondensator** *m* foil condenser or capacitor **-papier** *n* foil paper **-papierkondensator** *m* foil-paper capacitor **-prägemaschine** *f* foil-embossing machine
Folien-rollenkaschiermaschine *f* foil-laminating machine **-stärke** *f* foil thickness, film gauge **-störung** *f* window jamming **-walzwerk** *n* foil mills **-warmprägepresse** hot foil stamping press
foliieren to page (a book), silver (a mirror)
Folio *n* page, film, foil **-element** *n* film element **-format** *n* in folio, folio size **-schiff** *n* folio galley
Fonciermaschine *f* grounding or paper-staining machine
Fond *n* fund(s), capital
Fond *m* background **-farben** *pl* ground colors or shades **-muster** *n* ground design
Fontaktoskop *n* fontactoscope
Fontäne *f* fountain, column of water and spray **-effekt** *m* fountain-effect
forcieren to force, overtax, overload
Forcier-krankheit *f* strain disease (metals) **-maschine** *f* spinning machine
forciert severe, forced **-er Betrieb** forced work
Förderabgabe *f* duty, lot
Förderanlage *f* load-carrying equipment, transportation or haulage equipment, conveying machinery, conveying plant, conveyer system **ortsfeste ~** fixed conveying plant
Förder-apparat *m* conveyer **-arbeit** *f* hoisting work **-aufseher** *m* tram clearer **-ausfall** *m* loss in output **-bahn** *f* narrow-gauge field railroad, conveyer belt or track, roadway, wagon-way, miners' tram
Förderband *n* conveyer belt, belt or band conveyer, belt-type ticket carrier, picking belt (conveyers and crushers), production line **-ausleger** *m* extended derrick-type belt conveyer **-stapler** *m* belt conveyer
förderbar transportable, portable
Förder-beginn *m* begin of delivery **-behälter** *m* suction chamber (of carburetor) **-betrieb** *m* hauling practice **-büchse** *f* pneumatic traveler, conveying capsule
Förder-druck *m* discharge or lifting pressure (pumps), discharge head, feed pressure **-druckveränderung** *f* variation of the feed pressure **-düse** *f* (Erdöl) flow nipple **-einrichtung** *f* ticket-distributing system, transporter, winding gear, hauling (conveying) installation **-ende** *n* end of delivery or feeding
Förderer *m* conveyer, transporter, promoter, accelerator
Förder-gefäß *n* skip, conveyer bucket or vessel, charging carriage **-gerät** *n* conveyer **-gerippe** *n* drawing frame, cage (min.) **-gerüst** *n* headframe (min.), hoist structure **-geschwindigkeit** *f* winding or conveying speed (min.) **-gestell** *n* cage, drawing frame **-grus** *m* rough smalls **-gruskohle** *f* mine slack **-gut** *n* material delivered, output (min.), goods to be transported
Förder-haken *m* crane hook, bank hook, hoisting hook, hoisting block **-haspel** *m* pit-head winch, elevator gear, hauling windlass, winding engine **-höhe** *f* total or delivery head, lift, vertical projection of conveyer length, hoisting depth, pressure head **-hub** *m* turn **-hund** *m* tub, miner's truck **-karren** *m* trolley
Förder-kabel *n* hauling rope or cable **-kasten** *m* cage (of a goods lift), dray **-kette** *f* transfer

chain, conveying (machinery) chain **-klinke** *f* transport pawl **-kolben** *m* plunger **-kohle** *f* rough coal, run-of-mine coal, through-and-through coal **-kohlensieb** *n* raw coal screen **-kontrolle** *f* feed(ing) check

Förderkorb *m* drawing or mine cage, cage (pits, mines), dumping cage **-aufsetzstößel** *m* decking ram **-aufsetzvorrichtung** *f* holding apparatus for elevator cages **-fangvorrichtung** *f* catch device for elevator cages **-kran** *m* hoist **-kranwinde** *f* windlass **-kreis** *m* feed cycle **-kübel** *m* conveyer or elevator bucket, bucket, skip

Förderleute *pl* (Bg.) trammers

Förderleistung *f* conveying or elevating capacity, hauling output, feed performance **~ des Gebläses** delivery efficiency of blower **~ einer Pumpe** delivery of a pump

Förderleistungs-charakteristik *f* displacement characteristic **-kennlinie** *f* speed-delivery characteristic (pump)

Förderleitung *f* conveyer (pipe) line, conveying main, transport line, feed pipe

förderlich conducive

Förder-luft *f* delivery air **-mann** *m* buggyman, barrowman, filler, putter, hewing putter, roller, trammer (min) **-marken** *pl* tockens

Fördermaschine *f* winding engine, hoist, carrier **~ bedienen** to work a hoist

Fördermaschinen-gebäude *n* enginehouse **-sicherheitsapparat** *m* safety apparatus for winding engines

Fördermedium *n* flow medium

Fördermenge *f* discharge, delivery, quantity being transported, capacity **sekundliche ~ oder Durchflußmenge** weight velocity of flow, quantity delivered per second

Förder-mengenverlauf *m* speed-delivery characteristics **-mittel** *n* means of transportation, transportation or conveying device **-motor** *m* winding motor

fordern to ask, demand, request

fördern to convey, haul, transport, mine, promote, favor, draw, hoist, raise, advance, require, further, help, hasten

Fördernis *f* help, furtherance

Förder-organ *n* conveying agent **-öse** *f* hoisting loop **-pumpe** *f* feed or booster pump, fuel pump **-quantum** *n* output **-rechen** *m* rake conveyer **-riemen** *m* conveyer belt **-rinne** *f* conveyer chute or trough **-rinnenschubstange** *f* connecting rod for conveying troughs **-rohr** *n*, **-röhre** *f* screw, spirel, or helical elevator, conveying tube or tubing, tube conveyer **-rolle** *f* conveyor roller **-rutsche** *f* conveyer chute

Förder-schacht *m* hoisting or hauling shaft, pit gear, head framework, cage guide, hoisting gear, trolley **-schale** *f* cage (pits, mines), drawing frame **-schnecke** *f* screw or worm conveyer, feeding screw, revolving worm, conveyer screw or worm, spiral conveyer **-schwinge** *f* reciprocating plate feeder **-seil** *n* hoisting rope, hoisting cable **-seilscheibe** *f* head-gear pulley **-seite** *f* pressure side of a valve, delivery side of a pump **-sohle** *f* (Bergwerk) winding level

Förder-spiel *n* cycle of wind **-spitze** *f* temporary overload **-stand** *m* conveyer **-stollen** *pl* mine adits, galleries **-strang** *m* barrow tram

Förderstrecke *f* barrow-way, haulage-way, tram road, conveying track **~ mit maschineller Förderung** engine road **flach einfallende ~** inclined mother gate or gallery

Förder-stuhl *m* catching-rod elevator, rod swivel **-system** *n* conveying system **-technik** *f* mechanical conveying and handling **-teufe** *f* depth (of a pit) **-tisch** *m* assembly line **-trommel** *f* calf wheel, hoisting drum, drum, spool, winding drum of barrel **-turm** *m* winding tower, hoist or lift frame

Förder- und Hubgerät conveyer and lifting machine

Forderung *f* claim, requirement, demand, request, outstanding debt **eine ~ stellen** to postulate **der ~ entsprechen** to meet the demand

Förderung *f* advancement, promotion, conveyance, haulage, transfer, output, yield, delivery, transport, feed, supply, raising, drawing of minerals, furthering **~ im Abbauen** haulage in exhaustions (min.) **~ durch Schwere** gravity feed **~ unter Tage, unterirdische ~** underground conveyance or hauling **zweitrümmige ~** double hoisting

Förderungs-anlage *f* conveyor or feed system **-bestreben** *n* promotive effort or endeavor **-gas** *n* delivery gas **-leistungskurve** displacement curve **-system** *n* conveying system

Förder-ventil *n* discharge valve (under pressure) **-vorgang** *m* feed or delivery process **-vorrichtung** *f* conveying machinery

Förderwagen *m* truck, cart, barrow, car, tram, tub, wagon, transport or transfer car, delivery wagon or car, hopper-type truck **-beschlagteil** *m* fitting of delivery wagon **-zähleinrichtung** *f* counting apparatus for miner's trucks

Förder-walze *f* conveyor roller **-weg** *m* conveying route, engine plane **-welle** *f* main shaft **-werk** *n* elevator, screw jack, gin, lever, hoist, winch, lifting arrangement, lift **-widerstand** *m* supply resistance **-winde** *f* hoisting jack, hauling winch **-zeit** *f* hoisting time **-zug** *m* lift, wind

Forelleneisen *n* mottled pig iron

Forke *f* fork, crutcher (met.)

Forkel *f* furca

Form *f* form, figure, mold, shape, matrix, chill, contour, outline, tuyère, die, type **~ ganz im Boden** bedded-in mold **~ für Laufflächenerneuerung von Reifen** retreading mold **~ aus grünem Sand** greensand mold **~ der Verkabelung** cable form **eine ~ ablegen** to distribute the letters of a form **die ~ auflösen** to untie the form **die ~ ausheben** to lift out the form

Form, aerodynamisch günstige ~ pure aerodynamic form **äußere ~** fashion **eiserne ~** chill form **gebrannte ~** dry-sand mold **gerüttelte ~** jar-rammed or jarred mold **geschlossene ~** complete form, closed tuyère **geschweifte ~** curved form **günstige ~** optimum form **mangelhaft ausgelaufene ~** misrun **offene ~** open sand mold **verlorene ~** (of molding) sand mold **eine ~ pressen** to die cast

formal formal, classical (educ.), theoretical (tech. lit.)

Formaldehyd *n* formaldehyde

Formänderung *f* deformation, change of shape, strain, distortion, warp **bleibende ~** permanent set or distortion, overstrain, plastic strain **federnde ~** elastic deformation **gesamte ~** range of deformation **homogene ~** homogeneous strain

Formänderungs-arbeit *f* deformation energy, work of deformation, strain **-bereich** *m* region of deformation or of change of form **-fähig** capable of changing form, plastic **-fähigkeit** *f* ductility, deformability, rheologic or flow property **-festigkeit** *f* mean tensile strength **-vermögen** *n* capacity for deformation, deformability, plasticity **-widerstand** *m* deformation resistance **-wirkungsgrad** *m* forming efficiency **-zahl** *f* Poisson's number

Formanit *m* formanite

Formanlage *f* molding equipment

Formant *m* harmonic determining timbre or tone color, formant

Formanteil des Gesamtwiderstandes form pressure drag

Formanten *pl* formers, formants **~ eines Klanges** characteristic frequencies of a sound

Formarbeit *f* molding operation, molding, molding job or process

Format *n* format, form, shape, size **das ~ abschlagen** to take off the furniture (print.) **~ machen** to make up the margin, gauge a form

Format-ausrichtung *f* imposition (graph.) **-bildung** imposition (print.) **-blatt** *n* template (print.) **-buch** *n* dummy (print.) **-ecke** *f* corner of the negative **-einrichtung** *f* imposition (print.)

Formation *f* formation, age (geol.), system **bodenständige ~** fixed unit

Formationen *pl* units

Formationsfliegen *n* formation flying

Formations-flug *m* formation flight **-lampe** *f* formation lights or flying lamps **-segelflug** *m* soaring flight in formation

Format-machen *n* imposition (print.) **-platte** *f* imposing surface **-quadrate** *pl* gutter sticks (print.) **-schneider** *m* guillotine cutting machine **-steuerung** *f* format control **-veränderung** *f* change of measure **-zeiger** *m* measure indicator **-zylinder** *m* size cylinder

Form-auge *n* eye of the tuyère, tuyère hole **-back** *n* mold cistern (sugar mfg) **-bank** *f* molding bench **-bar** plastic, moldable, fictile

Formbarkeit *f* plasticity, (de)formability, workability, malleability, ductility

Form-belag *m* cover (paper mfg.) **-beständig** of stable, constant, or permanent shape **-beständigkeit** *f* stability of shape, nondeformability **-bildung** *f* shaping **-blatt** *n* prescribed form

Form-blech *n* shaped plate, baffle deflector **-blende** *f* special diaphragm **-block** *m* presser board, ramming block **-boden** *m* false bottom, odd side **-bohrer** *m* form drilling and boring tool **-brett** *n* molding board **-buchse** *f* mold (briquette press)

Form-deckel *m* deckle (strap or wire) **-draht** *m* shaped wire, section or sectional wire **-drehen** *n* forming **-drehsupport** *m* forming rest **-drehteil** *m* profile-turned piece **-ebene** *f* tuyère level or region **-einpaßvorrichtung** *f* form positioning device **-einrichtung** *f* molding equipment or appliance, imposition (print.)

Formeisen *n* section iron or steel, structural steel, structural shape, profile iron, rolled sections **-kalibrierung** *f* design of grooves for sectional iron **-profil** *n* structural-steel shape, section of shaped steel **-schere** *f* section-iron shears or cutter **-träger** *m* joist **-walzwerk** *n* section rolling mill

Formel *f* formula **-ausdrücke** *pl* formulas, terms, expressions **-bild** *n* structural formula **-gewicht** *n* formula weight

formell formal

Formelwertung *f* reduction by formula

Formelzeichen *n* symbol **~ mit Strichindex** primed symbol

formen to shape, form, mold

Formen *n* shaping, forming, molding **~ halb im Boden** bedding-in molding **~ nach Modell** plate or pattern molding

Formen-ausschießer *m* form setter (print.) **-eingießer** *m* pourer (foundry) **-gießer** *m* mold maker **-gleich** conformal **-guß** *m* mold castings **-halter** *m* mold catch **-regal** *n* form rack

Formen-schließen *n* locking of the form **-schluß** *m* mold clamping **-schlüssel** *m* quoin key **-schwindmaß** *n* molding (mold) shrinkage **-trockenofen** *m* mold-drying oven **-zonenring** *m* tuyère belt

Former *m* dipper, vatman, molder

Formerei *f* molding shop, molding operation or practice, pattern molding **-technik** *f* molding art

Former-messer *n* molder's punch **-nagel** *m* sand pin (aviation) **-pech** *n* molder's pitch **-pinsel** *m* molder's brush **-schaufel** *f* square foundry shovel **-sieb** *n* molder's sieve or riddle **-stift** *m* sand pin, molding pin, stake, nail, or sprig **-stoff** *m* molding or plastic material **-werkzeug** *n* former's or molder's tools

Form-erz *n* rich silver ore **-faktor** *m* form factor (of a symmetrical alternating quantity), multiplicity or stress-concentration factor, aspect ratio (picture) **-faktormeßgerät** *n* form factor meter **-feder** *f* spring **-fehler** *m* formal defect, informality **-festigkeit** *f* stability of shape, nondeformability **-fläche** *f* mold face **-flasche** *f* molding box, foundry or molding flask **-fräser** *m* form or profile cutter **-füllungsvermögen** *n* mold-filling capacity **-gebewerkzeug** *n* blanking tool

Formgebung *f* profiling, designing of section, fashioning, molding **aerodynamisch günstige ~** pure aerodynamic form **spanabhebende ~** shaping or fashioning by machining with removal of material by cutting tools

Form-gemäuer *n* tuyère arch **-genauigkeit** *f* accuracy of shape **-genauigkeitstoleranz** *f* accuracy tolerance **-gerecht, -getreu** true to shape or form, undistorted, having fidelity, faithful (in amplitude or phase of signals) **-gesenk** *n* former **-gestaltung** *f* design **-gewölbe** *n* tuyère wall **-gips** *m* pottery plaster

Formguß *m* shaped castings, dead mold casting **-erzeugnisse aus Rotguß** sandcastings in gunmetal **-kolbenring** *m* form-cast piston ring

Form-hälfte *f* mold part **-halle** *f* molding hall **-haltend** rigid **-halter** *m* form lock **-haltungsdraht** *m* fairing wire **-hammer** *m* blackjack (a type of hammer used in forming sheet metal to a die) **-heizung** *f* mold cure **-herstellung** *f*

preparation of molds (founding)
Formiat *n* formate
formieren to form
Formieren *n* formation
Formier-rahmen *m* forming rack **-spannung** *f* forming voltage, forming potential
formierte Platte formed plate
Formierung *f* forming (of a valve or cell), formation, activation, sensitization
Formierungsstrom *m* baking current (mercury rectifier practice)
förmig of the shape or type of
Form-kaliber *n* shaping pass, section or sectional groove **-kappe** *f*, **-kapsel** *f* shell of a mold
Formkasten *m* molding or casting box, foundry or molding flask, tuyère block, box or flask for casting, check ~ **mit Sandrippe** flask with sand rib or with flange ~ **mit Stiftenführung** flask with pinhold **aufklappbarer** ~ snap flask
Formkasten-ausleerer *m* mold box dumper **-band** *n* flask band, inside flask jacket **-boden** *m* flask-bottom board or plate **-brett** *n* flask or mold board **-festhalter** *m* flask clamp **-füllsand** *m* body or backing sand **-gehäuse** *n* tuyère arc cooler **-hälfte** *f* half-part molding box, flask section, box part
Formkasten-lappen *m* flask lug, lug of a molding box **-presse** *f* clamp, molding box **-schore** *f* flask bar **-stift** *m* molding-box or flask pin **-teil** *n* molding-box part **-traverse** *f* flask bar **-wagen** *m* runout table
Form-kern *m* molded core **-korrektor** *m* shape correction **-kurve** *f* forming cam **-lehm** *m* casting loam **-lehre** *f* profile gauge **-leiste** *f* molding
förmlich formal
Förmlichkeit *f* formality
Formlineal *n* template
Formling *m* briquette, casting, molded article or blank
Form-linie *f* joint (foundry) **-lippe** *f* tuyère, tuyère lip (met.)
formlos informal, shapeless, formless, amorphous
Formmantel *m* mantel, coat (foundry)
Formmaschine *f* molding machine ~ **mit Druckluftpressung** air-operated squeezing machine, air squeezer ~ **mit Druckluftrüttler** air-jarring molding machine ~ **mit Formkastenwagen** molding machine with runout table ~ **für kastenlosen Guß** molding machine for use with snap flasks ~ **mit Handpressung** hand-power squeezing molding machine, handsqueezing machine ~ **mit selbsttätiger Modellaushebung** molding machine with power lift ~ **mit ausschwingbarem Preßhaupt** molding machine with swing-out-type squeezing head ~ **mit Stiftenabhebung** flask-lift machine ~ **mit Wendeplatte** turnover molding machine ~ **für Zucker** sugar-molding machine
Form-maschinenanlage *f* molding machinery **-maschinenbetrieb** *m* molding-machine practice or work **-masse** *f* molding batch, dry sand **-modellrad** *m* pattern gear or wheel **-nagel** *m* foundry nail **-naht** *f* mold mark (on glassware) **-nase** *f* slag nose, slag tube **-nischenkasten** *m* tuyère-cooler housing
Form-öffnungshub *n* mold opening **-parameter** shape factor **-platte** *f* match plate, pattern plate **-plattenhalter** *m* former plate holder **-platz** *m* molding floor (founding) **-pressen** *n* compression molding **-preßholz** *n* molded plywood **-preßstoffe** *pl* compression molded plastics **-preßstück** *n* molded part
Formprofil *n* shaped section, sectional form **-eisen** *n* sectional steel, structural shapes **-walzwerk** *n* section mill
Form-puder *n* molding powder **-rahmen** *m* case, box (foundry) **-raum** *m* molding floor **-reihe** *f* row of tuyères **-rippe** *f* leading-edge strip, cap strip, wing-rib former **-rollengegenhalter** (b. Drehen m. Formstahl) roller shaving holder **-rüssel** *m* nose or furnace end of tuyère
Formsand *m* molding sand **ausgeglühter** ~ dry sand **feingesiebter** ~ facing sand **fetter** ~ dry or loamy sand **magerer** ~, **nasser** ~ green sand **trockener** ~ parting sand
Formsand-aufbereitung *f* preparation of molding sand **-kern** *m* molding-sand core **-lager** *n* molding-sand pit or quarry **-schüttelsiebmaschine** *f* reciprocating molding-sand riddle
Form-schablone *f* mold **-scheibe** *f* grinding wheel, cam disk **-scheibenstahl** *m* circular disc tool **-scheidung** *f* parting of a mold, joint line of a mold **-schleifscheibe** *f* shaped grinding wheel **-schlichte** *f* mold-finishing smoke black **-schließkraft** *f* locking pressure **-schluß** *m* closing shape (met.) **-schlüssig** form-closed or form-locking
formschlüssige Sicherung der Schraube positive locking of bolt
Form-schmieden *n* precision forging **-schneider** *m* form or print cutter **-schön** attractive **-schwindung** *f* shrinkage **-schwingungen** *pl* contour vibrations **-schwerpunkt** *m* center of buoyancy (aviation) **-spindel** *f* mold spindle **-spulenwicklung** *f* performed winding **-stabil** inherently stable
Form-stabilität *f* inherent or natural stability **-stahl** *m* forming or shaping tool, profile tool steel, structural or section steel **-stahlwalzwerk** *n* structural mill **-stampfmaschine** *f* stamping, tamping, or packing machine (to tamp molds, etc.) **-stanze** *f* forming die **-stecher** *m* clearing iron **-stein** *m* brick arch, shaped brick, profilated brick **-stich** *m* shaping pass **-stift** *m* medium-sized square nail **-stirnsenker** *m* formed countersink
Formstück *n* molded body, cast, sample, specimen, fitting, adapting piece, shaped part, template ~ (Isolierform) molded insulation ~ (Tonform) tile, clay conduit, earthenware block ~ (Zementform) concrete block
Formstückkanal *m* block conduit **irdener** ~ earthenware-block conduit
Form-technik *f* molding technique, mechanics of mold making, patternmaking practice **-teil** *m* shape or part of a mold **-teile** *pl* shaped parts **-tisch** *m* mold table, box table **-träger** *m* joist **-trockenofen** *m* mold-drying oven
Formtrog *m* mold cistern
Formular *n* questionnaire, form, blank form **-führungseinrichtungen** *pl* form feeding devices **-rolle** *f* (paper) web
formulieren to draw up (a letter)
Formulierung *f* formulation

Form- und Ablagebeleuchtung *f* lighting for form and delivery

Form- und Kernsand für Gußzwecke sand for casting purposes

Formung *f* forming, formation, shaping

Formunterteil *m* bottom box (drag)

Form-veränderung *f* form change, deformation, evolution in tactics **Grundsatz der geringsten ~** principle of least work

Form-veränderungsvermögen *n* formability, plastic workability, deformability **-veränderungswiderstand** *m* resistance to deformation **-verfahren** *n* molding process **-verzerrung** *f* harmonic distortion

Form-walze *f* grooved roll **-walzwerk** *n* girder and section mill **-wand** *f* mold face **-wechsel** *m* change of form **-weise** *f* molding method, method of molding without flasks **-wert** *m* coefficient of form ballistics **-widerstand** *m* body resistance, streamline resistance of a ship, drag form (aerodyn.)

Formylsäure *f* formic acid

Form-zacken *m* tuyère plate **-zahl** *f* form factor, stress concentration factor, form quotient **-ziegel** *m* profilated brick, molded brick **-ziffer** *f* shape factor, theoretical stress-concentration factor **-zone** *f* tuyère zone **-zustand** *m* physical condition **-zylinder** *m* stereo cylinder

forschen to study, conduct research, investigate, explore, search

Forscher *m* explorer, investigator, scientific researcher, experimenter

Forschung *f* investigation, research, study

Forschungs-abteilung *f* research department **-amt** *n* research directorate or bureau **-anstalt** *f* research institute, laboratory **-arbeit** *f* research work **-aufgabe** *f* research work **-bericht** *m* research paper or report **-ergebnis** *n* result of research **-flughafen** *m* research airport **-führung** *f* research control

Forschungs-gebiet *n* research field or domain **-geist** *m* inquisitiveness, inquiring or searching spirit **-ingenieur** *m* research engineer **-institut** *n* research institute **-reaktor** *m* research reactor **-spule** *f* search coil **-stollen** *m* exploratory drift (gallery) **-untersuchung** *f* reconnaissance survey

Forst *m* forest **den ~ unterstellen** to manage through forest officers **staatlicher ~** state forest

Forstaufseher *m* forest ranger

Förster *m* forester, forest ranger

Försterei *f* forester's house (located within forest), forester's district

Forst-haus *n* forest-ranger's house, name of a type of radar search equipment **-überwachungsflugzeug** *n* forest-patrol plane **-vermessung** *f* forest surveying

Forstgabelmaße *pl* log rules

Fort-bestand *m* continuance, continuous existence **-bestehen** to continue, live on, endure

fortbewegen to move **sich durch Schwerkraft ~** to gravitate, ride

Fortbewegung *f* propulsion, movement

Fortbewegungsgeschwindigkeit *f* rate of travel

Fortbildung *f* advanced or vocational training **~ der Lehrlinge** additional education given to apprentices

Fortbildungs-leiter *m* vocational-school superintendent **-schule** *f* trade or vocational school

Fort-dauer *f* continuity, permanence **-dauernd** continuous, permanent **-diffundierung** *f* diffusing away **-druck** *m* separate print

Forter-Ventil *n* Forter (reversing) valve, mushroom-type valve

Fortfall, in ~ kommen to fall off or away, cease, be abolished

fort-führen to carry away, convey, continue, prosecute

Fortführungstuch ohne Ende endless blanket

fort-geschritten advanced **-glimmen** (to continue) to smolder

fortheben to remove, lift **sich ~** to cancel out or eliminate (a factor)

fortkochen to boil off (chem.)

fortlaufend continuous, current, successive, constant, nonintermittent **~ numeriert** numbered consecutively **-er Polygonzug** gapless traverser chain **-e Rechnung** continuing computation **-e Reihe** unbrocken, uninterrupted, or continuous sequence or series

fort-leiten to conduct, convey, carry off **-leitung** *f* conduction, transfer, conveyance **-luft** *f* exhaust air **-oxydieren** to oxidize off **-pflanzen** to propagate, transmit

fortpflanzend, sich von selbst ~ self-propagating

Fortpflanzung *f* propagation, communication, convection, transmission **~ der Bewegung** communication of motion **~ der Flutwelle** translation of tidal wave **~ je Längeneinheit** propagation constant per unit length (teleph.) **~** (Verbreitung) **elektrischer Wellen** propagation of waves (elec.) **auf ~ beruhend** convective

Fortpflanzungsgeschwindigkeit *f* speed of propagation **~ des Schalles** velocity of propagation of sound **~ einer periodischen Welle** velocity of a periodic wave **~ der Wellen** velocity of wave propagation

Fortpflanzungs-gesetz *n* propagation law **-größe** *f* propagation constant, (hyperbolical) line angle, complex attenuation constant **-konstante** *f* propagation constant (per unit length), coefficient of transfer constant **-maß** *n* (hyperbolical) line angle **-richtung** *f* direction of propagation

fort-räumen to remove, clear away **-rücken** to shift, move away, move forward

Fortrückexzenter *m* feed eccentric (textiles)

Fortrückung *f* shifting, advance, feed, removal

Fortsatz *m* extension prolongation

fortschaffen to transport, pass off or away

Fortschaffung *f* removal, dismissal, transportation

Fortschalt-achse *f* ratched shaft **-einrichtung** *f* continuous-switching or -shifting device **-impulse** *pl* stepping pulses **-kupplung** *f* clutch **-kurve** *f* cop building cam disc **-scheibe** *f* cam disc

fortschalten to step on or up

Fortschalten des Films forward movement of the film

Fortschalt-magnet *m* feeding or stepping magnet **-relais** *n* accelerating relay, stepping or impulsing switch or relay

Fortschaltung *f* continuous-switching operation, cop building motion **~ des Filmes** film pull-down

Fortschaltungsmechanik *f* trip-free mechanism
Fortschalt-vorrichtung *f*, **-werk** *n* stepping device
Fortschauflungsofen *m* (ore roasting) reverberatory calciner or roaster (a rocking self-dumping type of grate furnace)
Fortschell-klingel *f* constantly active bell **-wecker** *m* continuously ringing alarm
Fort-schlagen *n* removal (of clinker) **-schleichen** to sneak away **-schreiten** to progress, advance, proceed
Fortschreitend *n* progression, advance, proceeding **~ bei gewöhnlicher Flamme** progress with ordinary flame (min.)
fortschreitend progressive, advancing, gradual, lineal **-e Abnahme** progressive diminution **-e Bewegung** translatory motion **-e Reihe** progression (math.) **-er Verhieb** heading advances **-e Welle** traveling, advancing, or progressive wave, transconductance
Fortschreitungs-bewegung *f* translational or propagational movement, stepping **-geschwindigkeit** *f* speed of progression or of travel **-richtung** *f* direction of propagation (waves, etc.)
Fortschritt *m* progress, improvement, advance, effective pitch progress
fortschrittlich progressive, liberal **-e Konstruktionseinzelheiten** (AV) design advances
Fortschritts-berichte *pl* progress reports **-geschwindigkeit einer Welle** velocity of translation of a wave or undulation **-grad der Luftschraube** propeller modulus, ratio of forward peripheral speed of propeller **-steigung** *f* effective pitch of a propeller **-winkel** *m* angle of advance **-zeitverfahren** *n* cumulative timing
Fort-schubmagnet *m* spacing magnet **-schwemmen** to wash away
fortsetzen to continue, carry on **das Arbeitsverhältnis ~** to continue service or work relations
Fortsetzung *f* continuation, prosecution, pursuit
Fortsetzungsprinzip *n* continuation principle
fort-spülen to wash away **-stellhebel** *m* indexing lever **-streben** to advance, try to get away
fortstrebend, vom Mittelpunkt ~ centrifugal
Fort-tragen *n* **(-waschen** *n***)** ablation **-treiben** to drive on, propel, expel
fortwährend continuous, perpetual, constant **-e Schwingung** buffeting
fortwälzen to roll
Fossil *n* fossil
fossil petrified **-es Wasser** connate water
fossil-führende Gesteine fossiliferous rocks **-inhalt** *m* fossil content
Föttinger-getriebe *n* Foettinger fluid torque converter
Foucaultströme *pl* eddy currents, Foucault currents
Fourdriniertrockner *m* Fourdriner drier
Fourieranalyse *f* Fourier's analysis
Fourier-sche Reihe Fourier's series **-scher Satz** Fournier's theorem **-sche Zerlegung** Fourier's analysis
Fourmarierit *m* fourmarierite
Fournier *n* veneer
fournieren to veneer
Fournier-holz *n* plywood, veneer **-klebrolle** *f* gummed veneer tape **-platte** *f* veneer
Fowlerklappe *f* Fowler flap
Fracht *f* cargo, freight, rate of freight, shipment, load(ing) **-abfertigung** *f* freight handling **-abteil** *n* freight or mail compartment **-beförderung** *f* freight transport **-beförderungsbehälter** *m* (Hubschrauber) cargo carrier **-brief** *m* consignment note, bill of lading, waybill **-dampfer** *m* cargo steamer, freighter
frachten to freight, ship, load, consign
Frachtenbeförderung *f* transportation of freight
Frachter *m* freighter
Fracht-fahrt *f* freight or transport flight **-flug** *m* cargo flight **-flugboot** *n* cargo flying boat **-flugzeug** *n* freight-carrying aircraft, cargo-transport airplane, flying boxcar **-frei** carriage paid, free of delivery charge **-geld** *n* freightage, cartage, transport charges
Frachtgut *n* ordinary freight **-verkehr** *m* freight traffic
Fracht-kosten *pl* freight rates or charges **-lagerung** *f* freight or cargo storage **-raum** *m* cargo compartment, freight capacity **-satz** freight rate or tariff **-schiff** *n* freighter **-verteilung** *f* cargo distribution
Frachtwagen *m* gondola **offener ~** gondola
Fracht-zettel *m* bill of lading **-zuschlag** *m* additional or extra freight
Frage *f* question, query, problem **in ~ kommend** eligible
Frage/Antwort-Gerät *n* interrogator-responder (Rdr)
Frage-bogen *m* questionnaire, list of queries **-recht** *n* right to cross-examine **-stellung** *f* questioning, interrogatory **-zeichen** *n* question mark
fragil fragile, easily broken, delicate
fraglich doubtful, questionable, out of line (gun.)
Fragment *n* chip, fragment
fragmentarisch fragmentary
Fraktion *f* fraction
Fraktionier-bodenglocke *f* bubble cap **-destillation** *f* fractional distillation
fraktionieren to fractionate
Fraktionieren *n* fractional distillation
Fraktionier-kolonne *f* fractionating column **-kondensation** *f* fractional condensation **-säule** *f* fractionating column **-turm** *m* bubble tower
fraktioniert fractional
Fraktionierung *f* fractionating, fractionation
Fraktionskolben *m* fractional-distillation flask
Frakto-numbus *m* scud **-stratus** *m* fractostratus
Fraktur *f* Gothic letter, German text, fracture **-schrift** *f* Gothic or German type or writing, Gothic character
Frame *n* frame (torpedo)
Francisturbine *f* Francis turbine
Frankesche Maschine Franke machine
frankieren to frank, pay for, prepay
Frankiermaschine *f* franking machine
Frankipfahl *m* Franki pile
Franklinisation *f* Franklinization (elec.)
Franklinit *m* franklinite
franko (frei) franco (free), prepaid
Franse *f* fringe, fuzz
Franz *m* (slang) flier, aviator, observer, navigator **-band** *m* calf binding **-branntwein** *m* French brandy, cognac

franzen to fix a position, find one's position, take bearings, navigate, wander off course (aviation)

Franzose *m* (Werkzeug) monkey wrench

Fräsarbeit *f* milling work ~ **mit Führung des Werkstückes von Hand** routing

Fräs-arten *pl* milling methods **-automat** *m* automatic milling machine **-bank** *f* milling machine **-bild** *n* milled surface **-blech** *n* trick plate **-dorn** *m* mandrel for shaping machine, cutter arbor **-dornringe** *pl* spacing collars for cutter arbors

Fräse *f* metal-cutting machine, milling cutter, milling tool

fräsen to mill (glass, metal), to cut (in circles), face, shape, gall ~ **von Stirnflächen** to spot face

Fräsen *n* mill(ing), cutting, facing ~ **nach Abwälzverfahren** hobbing ~ **eingängig** single start cutter ~ **im Gegenlauf** push-cut milling ~ **von Keilnuten** keyway-milling ~ **von Keilnuten mit ziehendem Schnitt** key-seating ~ **paralleler Stirnflächen** end milling

Fräser *m* milling cutter or tool, cutter, metal-cutting-machine operator, miller ~ **für halbkreisförmige Profile** concave or convex cutter ~ **mit hinterdrehten Schneidezähnen** form cutter, backed-off cutter ~ **für Wechselverzahnung** alternate-tooth cutter ~ **mit gefrästen Zähnen** profile cutter ~ **für Zahnräder** gear cutter

Fräser, einfacher ~ plain milling cutter **hinterdrehter** ~ backed-off or formed cutter **hinterschliffener** ~ eccentric relief cutter **linksschneidender** ~ left-hand cutter **zusammengesetzter** ~ gang or ganged cutters

Fräser-antriebsrad *n* milling-cutter driving gear **-auslauf** *m* runout of cutter **-drehzahl** *f* cutter velocity **-durchmesser** *m* cutter diameter

Fräserei *f* milling shop, milling work

Fräser-hinterschleifeinrichtung *f* milling-cutter relief-grinding attachment **-kette** *f* chain cutter (endless band of cutting teeth) **-messer** *n* cutter blade **-satz** *m* gang cutters **-schärfautomat** *m* automatic grinder for cutter **-schleiflehre** *f* cutter-clearance gauge **-schlitten** *m* milling carriage **-stärke** *f* width of milling cutter **-vorrichtung** *f* milling jig **-zahn** *m* tooth of milling cutter **-zapfen** *m* milling arbor or head

Fräs-gang *m* milling operation **-kopf** *m* cutter block, cutterhead, milling head **-krone** *f* milling crown **-kühlmittel** *n* coolant for milling

Fräsmaschine *f* milling or shaping machine, miller, shaper ~ **mit ausfahrbaren Ständern** milling machine with adjustable housings

Fräs-messer *n* cutter **-nute** *f* milled groove **-scheibe** *f* disk or wheel type of milling cutter **-schuh** *m* milling shoe **-schlitten** *m* milling carriage or support **-späne** *pl* millings

Frässpindel *f* cutter or milling spindle **schwenkbare** ~ swiveling milling spindle

Frässpindel-getriebe *n* milling spindle gearing **-hülse** *f* cutter spindle sleeve **-kopf** *m* milling spindle head **-lagerung** *f* milling spindle mounting **-nase** *f* milling-spindle end **-schaltung** *f* control of milling spindle **-schlitten** *m* milling spindle slide **-ständer** *m* milling spindle column **-stock** *m* milling spindle head **-wendegetriebe** *n* milling spindle reversing machanism

Fräs-stahlspindel *f* cutter steel spindle **-stichelschleifvorrichtung** *f* single lip cutter grinding attachment ~**- und Sägeketten** *pl* mortising and saw chains **-vorgang** *m* milling operation **-vorrichtung** *f* milling fixture **-weg** *m* milling path, milling travel **-werkstatt** *f* pattern or modeling shop **-werkzeug** *n* milling tool, milling cutter

Frauenglas *n* mica

Fraunhoferlinien *pl* Fraunhofer (absorption) lines

Fregatte *f* frigate

frei free, at liberty, at large, vacant, exempt, open, outspoken, uncontrolled, independent, uncombined, liberal, clear ~ **mit dem Auge** with the baked eye ~ **Ausladungsplatz,** ~ **auf dem Kai** free alongside ship ~**, franko Bord** free on board ~ **machen** to free, to frank (telegrams) ~ **suchen** to hunt, find ~ **wählen** to hunt, find ~ **werden** to become free or liberated

frei-er Hafen outer harbor **-e Luft** open air **-er Platz** hole (nuclear theory) **-er Raum** free space, clearance **-e Schwingung** free oscillation **-e Unterkunft** quarters in kind **-e Verbesserung** arbitrary correction **-e Wahl** hunting (operation) **mittlere -e Weglänge** mean free (length of) path

Frei-antenne *f* exterior or outdoor antenna **-arche** *f* paddle hole, clough arch, waste gate, flank or saddle escape (hydr.) **-auslösung** *f* trip-free release (elec.) **-auspuffhebel** *m* cutout lever

Freiballon *m* free balloon **-führer** *m* free balloon pilot

freibauen to cover its costs

freibeweglich floating **-e Aufhängung** flexible suspension (of trolley wire)

freibleibend subject to being sold, without engagement, not binding, not taken

Freibohrer *m* reamer

Freibord *n* freeboard **mit großem** ~ high out of water

Frei-brauen *n* privilege formerly granted to brew beer **-brief** *m* charter, permit license, patent **-dampf** *m* live steam **-drehen** to face (in lathe) **-drehung** *f* recess

Frei-erklärung *f* freeing (from legal charges or arrest) **-exemplar** *n* free copy **-fahrend** external (radiators) **-fahrt** *f* free trip, free flight (of propellers) **-fahrtturbine** *f* free turbine

Freifall *m* free fall **-apparat** *m* free-fall apparatus **-bewegung** *f* vertical motion **-bogenlampe** *f* gravity-feed arc lamp **-bohrer** *m* free-falling cutter **-bohrer** (selbsttätiger) automatic free-fall bit **-geschwindigkeit** *f* terminal velocity **-höhe** *f* height of free fall **-mischer** *m* hopper or barrel mixer with staggered baffles **-steuerung** *f* dropvalve gear

Frei-feld *n* uncovered part of a slab or tile **-fläche** *f* open space; (Flugplatz) clearway

freifliegen to float freely **-es Anlasserritzel** overhung starter pinion

Freiflug *m* free flight **-gewicht** *n* free flight weight **-kolbenmaschine** *f* air-cushioned free-piston-type engine **-kolbenverdichter** *m* free-piston engine compressor

Frei-flußventil *n* full-bore valve **-formschmieden** *n* hammer forging, hand forging

Frei-frei-Absorptionsübergänge free-free electron transition **-frei-Elektronenübergänge** free-free electron transition **-frei-Strahlung** *f* free-free-radiation

Freigabe *f* liberation, release, unblocking, disengagement, opening, clearance (aviat.) **-block** *m* clearing block **-schutzschalter** *m* interlock switch **-signal** *n* clear signal **-system** *n* transfer tripping (powerline protection) **-taste** *f* releasing key

Freigang des Kolbens floating of piston, free flow

Freigangstellung *f* floating position, free-flow position

frei-geben to release, disconnect, liberate, free, clear the line **-gebig** generous, liberal **-gebigkeit** *f* generosity, liberality **-gebinde** *n* common truss **-gegeben** released by censor **-gelände** *n* (Messe) open-air ground, open-air exhibition space **-gepäck** *n* free baggage **-gerinne** *n* gate of mill dam **-gewachsener Kristall** free crystal **-gold** *n* free or native gold

Frei-hafen *m* free port **-halter** *m* fender **-handel** *m* free trade **-handelszone** *f* customs-free trade zone

freihändig with the arm(s) free, offhand, hands off **~ fliegen** to fly with hands off, fly without use of controls **~ verkauft** sold privately

Freihand-nivellierinstrument *n* hand level **-schmiedestück** *n* hand forging **-walzen** *n* rolling by hand **-winkelmesser** *m* angle of sight instrument **-zeichnung** *f* freehand drawing

freihängend suspended in air, trailing

Freiheit *f* liberty, freedom, tactical mobility **operative ~** operational freedom of maneuver, operational mobility

Freiheitsgrad *m* degree of freedom, axis of freedom (of gyro) **~ des freien Elektrons** electronic mode **innerer ~** internal degree of freedom

Freiheitsgradzahl *f* variance (of a system)

Frei-hub *m* dead movement (motion) **-kolbenmanometer** *n* free piston gauge **-kolbenmotor** *m* free-piston engine

freikommen, vom Flugzeug ~ to get free of the aircraft

Frei-kux *m* free share, preference share **-lager** *n* bonded warehouse **-lagerung** *f* outside storage **-lampe** *f* idle indicating signal **-länge** *f* unsupported length or span, overhang **-laß** *m* release gear **-lassen** to release, leave blank **-laßventil** *n* no-load valve

Freilauf *m* a stable or free-running switching operation termed relaxation oscillation, free-wheeling, coasting, by-pass opening **Luftschraube mit ~** freewheeling propeller

Freilauf-achse *f* free-wheeling axle **-bremse** *f* freewheeling brake, coaster brake **-buchse** *f* clutch housing **-einrichtung** *f* (Walzwerk) idle running device, idle running gear

freilaufen to run light or without fuel

freilaufend freewheeling

Freilauf-getriebe *n* free running drive **-kuppelung** *f* overruning, freewheel, or roller clutch, slip coupling **-kurbel** *f* freewheel crank **-muffe** *f* free-wheeling sleeve **-rad** *n* freewheel bicycle **-scheibe** *f* free wheel disc **-system** *n* free-running **-trockner** *pl* free-run driers **-überholkupplung** *f* freewheel overrunning clutch **-zahnrad** *n* free-wheeling gear

freilegen to expose

Freilegen der Geleise lifting the track

Freileitung *f* open-air piping, open-air transmission line, overhead or open line

Freileitungs-abzweigklemmen *pl* overhead line connectors **-anlage** *f* aerial network **-armaturen** *pl* overhead-line fittings **-bau** *m* open-line construction **-einführung** *f* aerial leading **-höchstspannungsisolatoren** *pl* overhead line insulators for maximum voltage **-isolator** *m* outdoor or overhead insulator **-kabel** *n* overhead cable

Freileitungs-linie *f* openwire line or circuit, overhead line **-nachbildung** *f* open-line balancing network **-sicherung** *f* aerial cutout **-trennschalter** *m* overhead line isolator **-verteilungspunkt** *m* overhead distribution point

Freilicht-aufnahme *f* outdoor or exterior shooting or shot **-bühne** *f* open-air theater

freiliegen to be exposed, be unencumbered

freiliegend overhung

Freiluft-anlage *f* outdoor substation **-bewitterung** *f* open-air weathering test **-durchführung** *f* open-air wall duct, leadin outdoor bushing (insulator) **-kessel** *m* outdoor boiler **-isolator** *m* outdoor insulator

Freiluft-lagerung *f* outdoor exposure **-leitung** *f* overhead line **-schaltanlagen für Hochspannung** outdoor substations for high-tension **-transformatorenanlage** *f* open-air transformer plant **-umspannwerk** *n* outdoor transformer station **-unterwerk** *n* out-door sub-station **-windkanal** *m* open-air wind tunnel

freimachen to clear (the way), free, liberate, exempt, set free, extricate, rid

Freimeldelampe *f* visual busy-lamp

Frei-nabe *f* freewheel hub

Freiraum-ausbreitungsdiagramm *n* free space pattern **-feldstärke** *f* free space field intensity

Frei-sachen *pl* unrestricted or unclassified documents **-schneidebohrer** *m* free-cutting bit, reamer **-schnitt** *m* shears **-schürfen** *n* free prospecting **-schürfgebiet** *n* free-prospecting territory **-schütze** *f* gate of a mill dam **-schweben** to be suspended **-schwingender Antrieb** free-swinging drive

Freischwinger *m*, **~ Lautsprecher** *m* free-swinging loud-speaker

Freisignal *n* clear signal, line clear

Freispiegelstollen *m* nonpressure tunnel

freisprechen to acquit

Freisprechung *f* card of freedom (after serving apprenticeship)

freistehen to stand off, be exposed, be isolated or detached, be free

fteistehend exposed, detached, independent, free-standing, self-supporting **-er ventilierter Kamin** self-supporting ventilated stack **-e Linse** (nicht verkittet) uncemented lens **-er Säulendrehkran** isolated pillar crane **-er Schornstein** self-supporting chimney

Freistelle für Studium scholarship

Freistellungsbescheid *m* self-imposed assessment (tax term)

Freistrahl *m* free jet **-druckgasschalter** *m* free-jet air blast breaker **-gebläse** *n* hose sandblast, hose-type-sandblast tank machine **-gelüfteter Überfall** free (aerated) jet **-kanal** *m* free-jet tunnel **-rohr** *n* hose-type sandblast gun **-tunnel** *m* open-jet wind channel **-turbine** *f* impulse turbine, Pelton wheel, free-jet turbine, free-deviation-action turbine **-windkanal** *m* open-jet wind tunnel, open wind tunnel

Freistrich *m* relief groove

freitragend cantilever (construction type), self-supporting **-er Eindecker** cantilever monoplane **-es Fahrgestell** cantilever undercarriage **-er Flügel** cantilever wing, continuous wing **-er Rahmen** *m* cantilever frame **-er Tiefdecker** low-wing cantilever monoplane **-e Welle** cantilever shaft

Frei-träger *m* overhanging or cantilever beam, cantilever, simple beam **-treppe** *f* flier, perron **-übungen** *f pl* calisthenics, setting-up exercises **-wache** *f* dogwatch **-wahl** *f* (Teleph.) hunting operation **-wählen** to hunt over a bank **-wahlzeit** *f* selector hunting time **-wasser** *n* clear water (civil eng.) **-werden** *n* vacancy (liberation of smoke, etc.) **-werdend** nascent

Freiwerden von Energie energy release

freiwerdende Elektronen released electrons

freiwillig voluntary, volunteer-controlled, spontaneous **-es Trudeln** controlled spin

Freiwinkel *m* setting angle; (Drehstahl) front clearance angle; (d. Nebenschneide) side clearance angle; (b. Räumnadel) backoff angle, rake angle (Schneidestahl) clearance angle ~ **der Hauptschneide** front clearance angle ~ **der Nebenschneide** (Drehstahl) side clearance angle

Freizeichen *n* ringing tone, audible ringing signal, dial hum ~ (rückwärtiges Zeichen für den abgehenden Ruf), audible ringing signal

Freizeit *f* free time, recreation, recess

Freizügigkeit *f* freedom to move from place to place

fremd strange, alien, foreign ~ **gesteuert** separately excited **-e Felder** external fields

Fremd-antrieb *m* separate drive **-atom** *n* foreign atom, impurity atom **-atomzusatz** *m* addition of impurity **-belüftung** *f* independant air cooling **-bestandteil** *m* foreign matter or substance, extraneous or external matter **-bezug** *m* **von Strom** purchase of current **-elektron** *n* stray electron

Fremderregermaschine *f* separate excitor

fremderregt separately excited **-e Dynamomaschine** separately excited generator **-er Magnet** electromagnet, nonpermanent magnet **-e Schwingröhre, -er Sender** master-excited oscillator or transmitter

Fremd-erregung *f* independent excitation, foreign or separate excitation **-fabrikat** *n* outside make **-fehler** *m* error from external sources

Fremdfelder, magnetische ~ foreign magnetic fields

Fremd-fertigung *f* foreign manufacture **-führung** *f* separate commutation

Fremdgas *n* foreign gas (not domestic) **-zusatz** *m* foreign-gas additions

fremdgelüftet artificially or externally ventilated

Fremd-geräusche *pl* extraneous noises

fremdgesteuert separately controlled or excited **-e unselbständige Kippmethode** distant-operated non-self-running time-base method **-er Multivibrator** synchronized multivibrator **-e Steuerstufe** crystal-stabilized master stage

Fremd-induktion *f* external induction **-ion** *n* impurity ion **-kapital** *n* borrowed or outside capital **-keim** *m* foreign nuclei **-kerzen** *pl* outside made spark plugs

Fremdkörper *m* foreign body **-sonde** *f* bullet probe (med.)

Fremd-kühlung *f* separately cooled **-ladung** *f* independent or separate charging **-ländisch** of foreign manufacture **-licht** *n* outside light, light relay, Kerr cell **-modulation** *f* separate modulation **-peilung** *f* ground direction finding **-peilverfahren** *n* radio bearing from ground station **-rost** *m* extraneous rust

Fremdschicht *f* film of foreign material **-verfahren** *n* self-luminous or self-emissive method (using electrons)

Fremd-spannung *f* external voltage, hum and noise **-spannungsabstand** *m* noise level **-spannungsmesser** *m* sound level meter **-speicherung** *f* secondary storage **-sprache** *f* foreign language

Fremdsprachensatz und -druck *m* foreign language type-setting and printing

Fremd-spülung *f* separate scavenging **-steuerung** *f* separate excitation **-stoff** *m* foreign body or matter, foreign substance **-stoffig** heterogeneous **-stoffigkeit** *f* heterogeneity **-stoffkonzentration** *f* impurity concentration

Fremd-störstelle *f* impurity, impurity center or level **-störung** *f* (Radio) garble **-strom** *m* foreign (stray) current, sneak current **-substanz** *f* impurity **-synchronisierung** *f* remote-synchronization **-töne** *pl* alien frequencies or tones **-überlagerer** *m* separate heterodyne (local oscillator) **-zündung** *f* external auto-ignition, applied ignition

Frenkelfehlordnung *f* Frenkel disorder, Frenkel defect, Schottky defect

Freon *n* freon **-prüflampe** *f* halide torch

frequentieren to frequent

Frequenz *f* cycle, frequency (radio), periodicity ~ **der Ablenkspannungen** frequency of deflecting voltages **durch Absorption begrenzte** ~ absorption limiting frequency **eine** ~ **nach einer anderen einstellen** to adjust one frequency to another, synchronize **die** ~ **prüfen** to check the frequency **in der** ~ **übereinstimmen** to be of the same frequency ~ **null** zero frequency

Frequenz, gerastete ~ spot frequency **von gleicher** ~ equifrequent **hohe** ~ high frequency, radio frequency **mittlere** ~ medium frequency, mid-frequency **technische** ~ commercial or industrial frequency **ultrahohe -en** ultra-high frequencies

Frequenz-abbau *m* frequency division or submultiplication **-abgrenzung** *f* frequency dependence **-abhängig** variable with frequency, dependent on frequency, resonant **-abhängigkeit** *f* variability with frequency, dependency on frequency, having a frequency effect **-absenkung** *f* frequency decrease **-abstand** *m* distance between frequencies, frequency spacing, band width, interference-guard band, tolerance frequency **-abstimmung** *f* frequency tuning **-abweichung** *f* deviation, drift, swing, tilt of frequency **-abweichungsschwelle** *f* deviation sensitivity **-amplitude** *f* amplitude proportional to frequency

Frequenzanalyse *f* frequency analysis ~ **einer Wellenform** wave-shape analysis

Frequenz-änderung *f* frequency change **-angabe** *f* frequency designation **-angaben** *pl* frequency data **-angleich** *m* frequency control (radar), vernier tuning **-angleicher** *m* tuning knob, frequency rectifier **-anzeiger** *m* frequency indicator **-ausgleich** *m* frequency adjustment **-band** *n* frequency band **-bandausbeute** wide-band ratio **-bandbegrenzung** *f* frequency distortion noise impairment **-bandbreite** *f* frequency band width **-begrenzung** *f* limitation of frequency band

Frequenzbereich *m* frequency range ~ (Nachbildungsbereich), frequency range of simulation ~ (Sprechbereich) speech frequency range **durchgelassener** ~ transmitted band of frequencies

Frequenzbereich-anzeiger *m* frequency-range indicator **-filter** *n* band-pass filter **-überstreichung durch Kondensator** frequency range or band swept, scanned, or covered by a condenser or capacitor **-umschalter** *m* frequency-range switch

frequenz-benachbart having adjacent frequency **-brücke** *f* frequency bridge **-charakteristik** frequency response

Frequenz-demodulator *m* frequency demodulator **-detektor** *m* discriminator **-drehzahlmesser** *m* frequency-revolution speed counter, tachometer **-durchlässigkeit** *f* band width (of a filter), transmission range, frequency-passing range or characteristic **-durchlaßkurve** *f* transient response curve

Frequenz-eichung *f* frequency calibration **-einheit** *f* unit of frequency **-einstellung** *f* frequency setting or control, tuning control, frequency adjustment **-einteiler** *m* frequency divider **-empfindlichkeit** *f* frequency sensitivity **-empfindlichkeitskennlinie** *f* frequency-response characteristic **-entdämpfungskurve** *f* frequency-gain curve **-entzerrung** *f* response equalization **-erhöhung** *f* frequency rise **-erniedrung** *f* frequency division

Frequenz-feineinstellung *f* tuning control **-filter** *n* band-pass filter

Frequenzgang *m* frequency(-response) curve or characteristic, amplitude characteristic, frequency effect **starker ~ der Amplitude** marked dependence of amplitude upon frequency **~ der Höhen** high-end response, treble response **~ des Regelkreises** total open-loop frequency response **~ der Regelung** closed-loop frequency response

Frequenzgang-normung *f* standardization of frequency-response curve **-untersuchung** *f* frequency response investigation (aut. contr.)

Frequenz-gemisch *n* frequency spectrum **-genauigkeit** *f* precision or stability, frequency stability **-generator** *m* (high-)frequency generator **-gerader Kondensator** straight-line frequency condenser **-gesteuerte Senderöhre** frequency-stabilized transmitter tube **-gewobbelt** frequency swept **-gleichung** *f* frequency equation **-gleiten** *n* frequency change

Frequenz-hub *m* frequency fluctuation or deviation, swing, or variation **-inkonstanz** *f* frequency sliding mode shift **-intervall** *n* frequency range

Frequenz-kanal *m* frequency channel, frequency band **-kennlinie** *f* frequency response curve or characteristic, amplitude characteristic **-komponente** *f* component frequency **-konstanthaltung** *f* frequency stabilization **-konstanz** *f* constancy or stability of frequency **-kontrolle** *f* frequency control or check **-kontrollgerät** *n* wavemeter **-korrektur** *f* calibration adjustment

Frequenzkurve *f* frequency-response curve or characteristic, amplitude characteristic ~ (Dämpfungskurve) attenuation-frequency curve

Frequenzkurven-schreiber *m* sweep frequency oscillograph **-trimmung** *f* tight alignment

Frequenz-meßbrücke *f* frequency-measuring bridge **-messer** *m* frequency meter, wavemeter, ondometer **-messerumschalter** *m* frequency-meter change-over switch **-meßwandler** *m* frequency transfer units **-modelung** *f* frequency modulation **-modler** *m* frequency modulator **-modulation** *f* frequency modulation **-modulierte Steuerstufe** (eines Senders) frequency modulated exiter **-multiplexsystem** *n* frequency-division multiplex **-multiplikation** *f* frequency multiplication

Frequenz-nachlauf *m* automatic frequency control (AFC) **-normal** *n* frequency standard **-pendelung** *f* frequency alteration **-prüfer** *m* frequency tester, wave meter **-prüfgerät** *n* frequency tester, wavemeter **-prüfung** *f* frequency calibration **-raster** *m* frequency allocation scheme **-regler** *m* frequency regulator **-reihe** *f* series of frequencies

Frequenz-schema *n* frequency-average plan **-schnitt** *m* crossover of frequencies (sound film) **-schreiber** *m* frequency recorder **-schwankung** *f* variation of frequency, lilt or drift of frequency, frequency flutter or departure, swinging (momentary variation of received frequency) **-schwingungssteuerung** *f* beat-frequency oscillator **-selektion** *f* frequency selection **-sieb** *n* electric-wave filter, frequency sifter **-sieblochbreite** *f* transmitted band, filter band width, spacing between cutoff points **-skala** *f* frequency spectrum or scale

Frequenz-speicher *m* frequency memory **-spektrograph** *m* panoramic monitor **-spektrum** *n* frequency spectrum **-sprung** *m* sudden change of frequency **-stabilisierung** *f* frequency control **-stabilität** *f* frequency stability **-steigerung** *f* frequency multiplication **-steuerung** *f* frequency stabilization **-störung** *f* outside interference (wireless telegraph)

Frequenz-tafel *f* frequency record **-teiler** *m* frequency divider or submultiplier, tone divider **-teilerschaltung** *f* step divider circuit **-teilerstufe** *f* frequency-divider stage **-teilung** *f* frequency division **-toleranz** *f* frequency tolerance **-transformator** *m* frequency changer or converter (static) frequency transformer **-transformierung** *f* **-transponierung** *f* frequency translation

Frequenz-überhöhung *f* excess frequency rise **-übersetzer** *m* frequency charger **-übersetzung** *f* frequency transformation **-umfang** *m* frequency coverage **-umformer** *m* frequency changer or converter, (static) frequency transformer **-umformung** *f* frequency transformation **-umkehrung** *f* frequency inversion **-umschaltrelais** *n* frequency change-over relay **-umsetzer** *m* frequency transducer **-umtastung** *f* frequency shift keying

frequenz-unabhängig independent of frequency, free from frequency effect **-unabhängigkeit** *f* independence of frequency, invariability with frequency **-unsicherheit** *f* frequency error **-unterscheidung** *f* frequency discrimination

Frequenz-verdoppeler *m* frequency doubler **-verdoppelung** *f* doubling of frequency **-verdreifacher** *m* frequency tripler **-verdreifachung** *f* frequency triplication **-verhältnis** *n* frequency-response ratio **-verlauf** *m* slow frequency drift

Frequenz-verschiebung *f* frequency distortion, tone distortion **-verschränkung** *f* frequency interlacing (TV) **-vervielfacher** *m* frequency multiplier **-vervielfachung** *f* frequency multiplication **-vervielfachungsklystron** *n* frequency-multiplier klystron **-verwerfung** *f* slow frequency drift **-verzerrung** *f* frequency distortion, non-uniform frequency response, attenuation distortion **-vielfach** *n* frequency division multiplex

Frequenzwandler *m* frequency changer or converter, frequency transformer or multiplier **ruhender ~** static frequency changer

Frequenz-wandlung *f* frequency transformation or change, heterodyne or superheterodyne action, **-weiche** *f* separating or dividing filter or network separator (synchronizing and video signals in television), comprising limiter tube and network **-wende** *f* frequency inverter **-wiedergabe** *f* frequency-response characteristic **-zeiger** *m* frequency meter **-zuteilung** *f* frequency assignment

Fresko *n* fresco

Fresneleinheit *f* fresnel

fressen to corrode, scour, wear, erode, cut (slag or cinders), bind (machines), seize **das Lager ~** to seize the bearing

Fressen (Lager) *n* scuffing, seizing; (Riefenbildung) scoring **~ der Oberfläche** (durch Druck) galling

Freß-erscheinung *f* galling **-neigung** *f* scuffing tendency (metal.) **-schaden** *m* corrosion **-spuren** *pl* seizing marks

Frett *n* gimlet

Frettage *f* hooping, shrinkage

Frettbohrer *m* gimlet of auger type

Frette *f* ferrule, hoop or ring of a gun

fretten to ferrule

Frettsäge *f* curvilinear or fret saw

Frickofen *m* Frick (induction) furnace

Freund-Feind-Kennung *f* identification, friend or foe (IFF)

Friedens-gebrauch *m* peacetime use **-mäßig** as in peacetime **-richter** *m* justice of the peace

Friemel-kanter *m* friemel tilter **-maschine** *f* reeling machine

friemeln (Stangen) to straighten, reel

Frieranlage *f* refrigerator

frieren to freeze, be cold

Frieren *n* freeze, freezing

Frierpunkt *m* freezing point (of the thermometer)

Fries *m* frieze, molding **-fußboden** *m* cased, framed, or clamped floor **-glieder** *pl* border of a door panel **-leiste** *f* molding

Frigen *m* freon (elect.) **-beständiger Lackdraht** freon-proof varnished wire **-betrieb** *m* freon operation or service **-füllung** *f* freon filling

Friktion *f* friction; (trocken) solid friction

Friktions-antrieb *m* friction drive **-aufwickelapparat** *m* frictional winding-on machine **-aufzug** *m* friction hoist **-automatik** *f* permanently adjusted brake **-eindrückhebel** *m* friction-clutch lever **-einrückmutter** *f* feed friction nut **-förderung** *f* friction wheel **-getriebe** *n* friction gearing **-hülse** *f* friction socket

Friktions-kegel *m* friction clutch **-kupplung** *f* friction coupling **-pulver** *n* fulminating powder **-rad** *n* friction wheel or pulley **-räder** *n pl* friction gearing **-regler** *m* **-regulator** *m* friction governor **-rolle** *f* friction pulley or wheel

Friktions-säulenpresse *f* friction pillar (screw) press **-scheibe** *f* friction disk, friction plate **-scheibengetriebe** *n* friction gearing **-schiene** *f* friction track **-schlagrohr** *n* friction tube **-schmiedehammer** *m* friction forging hammer **-spindelpresse** *f* friction screw press

Friktions-vorgelege *n* friction countershaft **-vorschub** *m* friction feed action **-wendegetriebe** *n* friction reversing gear **-wendekuppelung** *f* friction reversing gear **-winde** *f* friction winch or windlass, friction-geared winch **-zünder** *m* friction igniter, priming tube **-zündschraube** *f* friction primer **-zündung** *f* friction priming

Frimmeln (ein Polierverfahren) buffing

frisch fresh, new, vigorous, cool, recent **-e Beschickung** fresh feed (petroleum) **-er Farbton** lively shade **-e Schnitzel** cossettes

Frisch-arbeit *f* finding process, fining, refining, purifying, fining process (metal.) **-aufnahme** *f* new recording, re-recording or new pickup of film **-balge** *f* steeping tub **-birne** *f* converter, converting vessel **-blei** *n* refined, soft, or merchant lead

Frischdampf *m* live steam **-druck** *m* initial steam pressure **-düse** *f* live-steam nozzle **-einlaß** *m* live-steam inlet **-gehäuse** *n* live steam cylinder **-leitung** *f* live-steam line, live-steam piping **-ringrohr** *n* annular live-steam main **-ventil** *n* live-steam valve

Frische *f* freshness, recentness, vigor

Frischeisen *n* refined iron

frischen to fine, refine, purify, decarburize, oxidize, anneal, reduce

Frischen *n* fining, refining, purification, decarburization, oxidation, blowing, converting, annealing, reduction, puddling (in ironworks) **~ des Eisens** refining the steel

Frischer *m* finer, refiner, converter

Frischereiroheisen *n* forge pig iron, pig iron for refining

Frisch-erz *n* raw ore **-esse** *f* finery fire

Frischfeuer *n* refining or running-out fire, refinery, refining hearth, charcoal furnace or hearth **-eisen** *n* fined or refined iron, charcoal iron, charcoal-hearth iron

Frischgas *n* carburated fuel

Frischherd *m* refining or running-out fire, refinery, refining hearth, charcoal furnace or hearth **-verfahren** *n* refinery or purification process

Frischhütte *f* smelting finery, refinery

Frischluft *f* intake air, fresh air (petroleum) **-eintritt** *m* fresh-air entrance **-eintrittrohr** *n* fresh-air intake tube **-fänger** *m* air scoop **-kanal** *m* fresh air duct

Frisch-metall *n* refined or virgin metal **-ofen** *m* refining or purifying furnace **-öl** *n* clean or fresh oil **-ölsaugleitung** *f* fresh-oil suction pipe **-periode** *f* oxidizing or oxidation period **-prozeß** *m* finery process **-sand** *m* newly mixed sand, new sand

Frischschlacke *f* oxidizing slag, refinery cinder **gare ~** rich slag **rohe ~** poor slag

Frisch-stahl *m* purified steal **-trübe** *f* make-up medium

Frischung *f* refining, refinement, purification, blowing, oxidation

Frischungs-ofen *m* refining furnace **-prozeß** *m* **-verfahren** *n* refining or fining process, purifying method, oxidizing or converting process

Frischwasser *n* fresh water, raw water **-kasten** *m* fresh-water storage tank **-kühlung** *f* fresh-water cooling

Frischwerk *n* refinery

Frischwirkung *f* oxidizing or purifying reaction

Frisehilfsflügel *m* frise aileron

frisiert specially tuned-up electronics

Frist *f* term, delay, respite, dead line, period of time, grace, limitation, moratorium **innerhalb der ~** within the time **eine ~ setzen** to set a certain time

Fristen-heft *n* maintenance logbook **-stelle** *f* term station **-weise** at stated intervals **-wesen** *n* establishing deadlines

frist-gemäß within specified time **-gerecht** in time, within time limit **-gesuch** *n* dilatory plea **-gewährung** *f* prolongation, extension of time, grant of respite **-kalender** *m* calender of dates due **-los** without time-limit or notice

Fristung *f* respite, delay, prolongation (min.)

Fristverlängerung *f* respite, grace, time extension

Frittbohrer *m* gimlet

Fritte *f* frit, batch

fritten to frit, sinter, cohere, concrete

Fritten *n* fritting, sintering

Fritter *m* **-empfänger** *m* coherer **-form** *f* type of coherer **-klemme** *f* coherer terminal **-schutz** *m* lightning arrester **-sicherung** *f* coherer-type acoustic shock reducer, coherer protector

Fritterung *f* coherence

Fritterwiderstand *m* coherer resistance

Fritt-ofen *m* fire or calcar arch **-porzellan** *n* soft or frit porcelain **-röhre** *f* coherer

Frittung *f* fritting, sintering, coherence, decoherence

Fritzscheit *m* fritzscheite

Front *f* front, face, fore part **breite ~** wide front

frontale Halbkugellinse hemispheric front lens (electronics)

Frontalzyklon *m* frontal cyclone

Front-antrieb *m* front-wheel drive **-aufwind** *m* upwash **-ausdehnung** *f* extent of front **-ausgangstellung** *f* line of departure **-bildung** *f* frontal formation **-blasen** to sound the alert or the attention **-böe** *f* line squall, cold-front squall **-bogen** *m* front arc, curved front line **-bogenausleger** *m* front delivery (print.)

Fronten-flug *m* **-segeln** *n* frontal soaring

Front-fensterzählrohr end-window counter **-lader** *m* front loader **-linsenmeniskus** *f* front meniscus **-platte** (TV) faceplate, front panel **-verkleidung** *f* front panel

Frontogenese *f* frontogenesis

Frontolysis *f* frontolysis

Front-vorsprung *m* salient **-welle** *f* impact wave, bow wave

Frosch *m* frog (of violin bow), cam, dog, (adjustable) stop (in machines), ladder peg, catch, pan (print.), nut, pin, arm, tappet, sliding bar **-beinwicklung** *f* frog-leg winding

Fröschel *n* ladder peg or wedge

Frosch-klappe *f* special flap valve **-klemme** *f* Dutch tongs, eccentric grip, grip gear of lift, wedge, toggle action or eccentric hand vice, wire strecher **-lauchpilz** *m* frog spawn, Leuconostoc **-perspektive** *f* worm's-eye view **-platte** *f* bolster (plate)

Frost *m* frost, chill, cold, freezing **-beständigkeit** *f* resistance to frost, freezeproofness **-dunst** *m* frost smoke

frösteln to shiver, feel chilly

frost-frei frost-proof **-gefahr** *f* danger of frost heave or action **-graupeln** *n* anti-icer **-hebung** *f* frost heave **-mischung** *f* freezing mixture **-muster** (b. Blech) even-spangled **-nebel** *m* frost smoke **-punkt** *m* freeze or freezing point **-riß** *m* frost shake or cleft in wood **-rissig** frost-cracked **-salbe** *f* chilblain ointment **-schnitt** *m* frozen section

Frostschutz-fett *n* nonfreezing or antifreezing lubricant **-lösung** *f* antifreeze compound **-mischung** *f* antifreeze solution or mixture **-mittel** *n* antifreezing solution or agent, nonfreezing or antifreeze mixture **-pumpe** *f* defrosting pump **-salbe** *f* antifrostbite ointment **-scheibe** *f* antifrost screen, frost shield, defrosting shields **-vorbereitung** *f* antifreezing preparation

frost-sicher nonfreezable, frost-resistant **-spalte** *f* fissure caused by frost **-sprengung** *f* burst due to frost **-versuch** *m* freezing test **-wetter** *n* frosty weather **-wirkung** *f* effect or action of frost **-zeit** *f* frost period

Frotté *m* sponge cloth

Frottierartikel *m* rubbing or massaging implement

frottieren to rub, chafe, or gall (wires, ropes, etc.)

Frottierhandtuch *n* rough towel

Froude-scher Satz Froude principle of wind-tunnel tests **-sche Zahl** similarity equation for dimensioning airplane models

Frucht *f* fruit **eingemachte ~** preserved fruit **einheimische ~** indigenous fruit **gedörrte ~** dried fruit **harte ~** hard grain **verzuckerte ~** fruit preserved in sugar

Frucht-äther *m* fruit ether **-bar** fertile, fruitful, prolific, rich (land) **-eiserzeuger** *m* icer, sherbet machine **-folge** *f* crop rotation **-gehänge** *n* festoon of fruit **-haus** *n* **-kammer** *f* corn magazine, granary **-kelterer** *m* fruit presser

Frucht-konservenfabrikant *m* manufacturer of

fruit preserves **-los** fruitless, barren, useless, unavailing **-schiefer** *m* fruchtschiefer (in which the spots resemble ears of corn) (geol.) **-spindel** *f* rachis **-versteinerung** *f* carpolite **-wechsel** *m* crop rotation **-zucker** *m* levulose

früh early, speedy

Früh-einspritzung *f* advanced injection **-einstellung** *f* advanced ignition

Frühlings-äquinoktium *n* vernal equinox **-holz** *n* spring wood or timber **-nachtgleiche** *f* vernal equinox

Früh-messung *f* (regelmäßige) morning (routine) test **-schicht** *f* morning shift **-schosser** *m* early bolter **-sprenger** *m* premature burst **-stück** *n* breakfast **-warnung** *f* (Rdr) distant early warning (DEW)

frühzeitig early (of motions or time), premature **-e Abnutzung** premature wear

Frühzünder *m* premature (torpedo)

Frühzündung *f* premature shot or ignition, preignition, advanced or early ignition, spark advance, backfire **äußerste ~** fully advanced ignition **~ geht nach hinten los** to backfire

Frühzündungs-anlage *f* position of advanced ignition **-druck** *m* preignition, advance ignition **-hebel** *m* sparking-advance lever

F-schicht *f* F layer of the ionosphere

F-Schirm *m* F scope

FS-Tonsender *m* television-sound transmitter

F_1-Tonlose Telegraphie *f* F_1-Telegraphy without modulation

Fuchs *m* flue, air duct, chimney intake at base, trestle, jack, unmeltable piece of iron, uptake (of boilers), fox, freshman, fluke, bay horse, belly, linnet hole **-ambra** *m* black amber

Fuchsanschluß-krümmer *m* smoke nozzle elbow, smoke hood elbow **-stutzen** *m* smoke hood

Fuchs-brücke *f* flue bridge, back bridge wall **-ende** *n* flue end **-gas** *n* flue gas

Fuchsin *n* fuchsin

Fuchsje *f* Spanish fox (naut.)

Fuchs-kanal *m* boiler flue, uptake **-loch** *n* fox-hole, niche **-öffnung** *f* flue opening, floss hole, draft hole **-schwanz** *m* pruning saw, hand saw, crosscut saw, hacksaw **-schwanzsäge** *f* handsaw pad or fox saw, whipsaw, crosscut saw **-verluste** *pl* flue losses (brick flue)

Fuder *n* cartload

Fugasse *f* fougasse

Fügbalken *m* main hood beam (windmill)

Fügblock *m* cooper's plane **-doppeleisen** *n* double iron for cooper's plane

Fuge *f* joint, seam, fugue, rabbet, gap, junction, interstice, groove, slit **~ der Verkleidung** joint of facing **abgefaßte ~** chamfered joint **bündige ~** flush joint **übereinandergelegte ~** capped joint **überfalzte ~** rebated or foliated joint

Füge-bank *f* copper's plane, whisk, jointer **-hobel** *m* long plane

Fugeisen *n* jointer

Fügemaschine *f* jointing machine

fugen to joint, rabbet

Fugen *n* jointing, slips **~ im Bohlenbelag** spacings in open deckings

fügen to join **ein Brett ~** to shoot or smooth the edge of a board

Fugen-abstand *m* joint spacing **-ausstreicher** *m* mortar worker **-dicht** tightly-joined, flush(ed) **-dichtung** *f* impermeabilizing of joints (highway construction) **-einschnitt** *m* rebated joint (half lap) **-falz** *m* edge hammered down, folding border

Fugen-gelenk *n* articulation joint **-heizung** *f* (Klebstoff) joint heating **-keil** *m* key of joint **-kelle** *f* small jointing or joint trowel **-kitt** *m* gap filling adhesive **-leiste** *f* rod or tringle covering a joint

fugenlos jointless **-e Ausmauerung** seamless lining

Fugen-schneidgerät *n* carborundum saw **-schraube** *f* assembling bolt **-schwelle** *f* joint tie **-sicher** tightly joined **-verstreichen** *n* pointing up the joints **-weite** *f* interstitial distance

Fügesäge *f* jointing saw

Füghobel *m* long plane

Fugkelle *f* jointer, trowel

fügsam flexible

Fügung *f* joining, joint, articulation, combination

Fühlanordnung *f* sensing device (servo)

fühlbar sensible, tangible, perceptible **-e Abstimmung** tuning condenser sensibly detained or braked **-e Marke** tangible mark, prick mark **-e Wärme** sensible heat

Fühlblech *n* thickness feeler, feeler gauge

fühlen to feel

Fühler *m* test point, tracer, transmitter, sensing or detecting element, feelers (fitter's gauge strips), finger gauges (for thickness) **~ einer Fühlersteuerung** *m* explorator, form tracer **~** (beim Meßgerät) sensitive element

fühler-gesteuert tracer-controlled **-kondensator** *m* scanning or pickup condenser **-kopf** *m* (Fühlersteuerung) tracer head **-lehre** *f* thickness gauge, slip gauge **-schneide** *f* stylus tip **-spindel** *f* tracer spindle **-steuerung** *f* tracer control

Fühlfinger *m* (profile) tracer **~ einer Fühlersteuerung** *m* explorator, form tracer

Fühl-fläche *f* feel or probe surface **-gerät** *n* detector **-glied** *n* sensitive element, the member sensing the condition to be controlled (e.g., the bulb of a thermometer) **-hebel** *m* (test) indicator, dial gauge, tactile, feeler, contactor, or probing lever, scanner, pickup means, indicator of micrometric caliper **-index** (Schaltschutz) feeling index **-kopf** *m* tracer head **-körper** *m* feeling body

Fühl-lehre *f* thickness gauge, feeler, feeler gauge **-nadel** *f* selecting needle or pin **-ort** *m* sensing point **-ratsche** *f* micrometer friction thimble **-raum** *m* space within reach **-rohr** *n* feeling tube **-schiene** *f* detector bar (railway signaling) **-schraube** *f* friction thimble **-stab** *m* stick gauge **-stift** *m* (profile) tracer, tracer stylus

Fühlung *f* contact, touch, feel **~ aufnehmen** to make contact **~ halten** to keep in touch, to maintain contact

Fühlung-halter *m* connecting file, contact plane, aircraft maintaining contact with enemy, shadower **-nahme** *f* establishment of contact, liaison

Fuhramt *n* transport office

Fuhre *f* load, transport, vehicle, wagon, cart

führen to lead, convey, steer, drive, run (wires), command, track a target, channel, support, hold (command); (Richtung) direct; (geleiten) conduct, guide; (steuern) guide, pilot; (verwalten) manage, control; (Bücher) keep books; (Geschäft) manage, carry on; (Ware auf Lager) carry in stock; (elektr. Strom) carry, conduct; (Aufsicht) superintend

führend leading, containing **-e Nullen** *f pl* leading zero (info proc.)

Führer *m* commander, leader, guide, driver, starter, pilot, chauffeur, engine driver, conductor

Führer-besprechung *f* conference, executive meeting **-bremsventil** *n* driver's brake valve **-gondel** *f* control car or gondola

Führer-haus *n* driver's cab **-kabine** *f* pilot's cabin or compartment **-kanzel** *f* pilot's cockpit, control cabin **-kompaß** *m* pilot's compass **-los** pilotless **-losigkeit** *f* absence or lack of leadership **-maschine** *f* commutating machine

Führerraum *m* pilot's cockpit or compartment, control cabin **-beheizung** *f* cockpit heating **-überdachung** *f* cockpit roof

Führer-schaft *f* leadership, group of leaders **-schein** *m* pilot's or driver's license, operator's permit **-scheintasche** *f* pass holder (for driver's license)

Führersitz *m* (pilot's) cockpit, driver's or pilot's seat **geschlossener ~** cabin **verstellbarer ~** adjustable pilot's or driver's seat

Führersitz-haube *f* cockpit cowling **-katze** *f* crane operator's cabin (suspended and traveling on rail) **-verkleidung** *f* hood, canopy, or enclosure of cockpit

Führerstand *m* pilot's or driver's compartment, operator's platform, control cabin, cab, pilot's cockpit, tank commander's position **-laufkatze** *f* telpher or crab fitted with driver's stand

Führertochterkompaß *m* pilot's repeater compass

Führerzügel *m* lead rein

Fuhr-faß *n* carriage cask **-gelegenheit** *f* chance conveyance **-lohn** *m* freight, cartage, carriage **-mann** *m* driver of an electric tram or locomobile **-park** *m* wagon park

Führstange *f* guide pole of a pack animal

Führung *f* slaving (gyro) guide, guideways, slideways; (Leitung) direction; (Unternehmen) control; (Lenken) driving, steering leadership, guidance, command, conduct, navigation, piloting, bars, slide, lead(ing), conduction, pin guide, pinholder, management, conduit, command post, headquarters, rotating band of projectiles **~ des Flugzeuges** air-plane piloting **die ~ übernehmen** to take the lead (sport)

Führung, feinfühlige ~ sensitive operation **hintere ~** rear guide **mittlere ~** medium-sized force **obere ~** higher command (forces from division upward) **persönliche ~** personal record **seitliche ~** lateral guidance (of airplane) **untere ~** lower command **zwangsläufige ~** restricted guidance

Führungen an Werkzeugmaschinen ways (tool machines or machine tools)

Führungs-arm (Fräsmaschine) *m* guide lug **-armklemmschraube** *f* arm-clamp screw **-backe** *f* guide jaw or rod, die guide, guard fence **-bahn** *f* guideway, way, track **-bahnen-Schleifmaschine** *f* slideway grinding machine, latherbed ways grinder **-band** *n* driving band, rotating band (of projectile), control strip (of a printer) **-bänder** *pl* leading-through tape (paper mfg) **-bandschutz** *m* rope grommet **-beschlag** *m* guiding stud (guided missiles)

Führungs-blech *n* guide plate **-bock** *m* guide casing (guided missiles) **-bogen** *m* **des Steuerungshebels** guide of reversing lever (locomotive) **-bolzen** *m* guide bolt **-bolzenbuchse** *f* guide pin bushing **-brille** *f* back rest **-buch** *n* guidebook, service and personal record **-buchse** *f* guide box, bushing guide, guide sleeve or bush **-bügel** *m* guide fork **-dorn** *m* pilot bar **-düse** *f* pilot jet **-einrichtung** *f* locating arrangement **-eisen** *n* iron guide **-fase** (b. Räumnadel) straight land

Führungsfelder *f* slide (guide) spring **~ einer Schiebetür** tongue of a sliding door

Führungs-feld *n* guide field **-finger** *m* guide finger

Führungsfläche *f* guide surface, surface of lands **seitliche ~** lateral bearing surface

Führungs-flansch *m* guide flange **-gabel** *f* guide fork **-gerüst** *n* template **-größe** *f* command variable, reference input **-grundsatz** *m* principle of leadership **-hals** *m* guiding shoulder **-hebel** *m* control lever **-hülse** *f* guide bearing, bush, or iron, traversing slide **-kabel** *f* guide rope **-kamm der Zugstäbe** pull bar guide **-kanal** *m* film track or channel

Führungskante *f* guiding edge, edge of lands (in gun barrel) **~ der Felder in der Geschützseele** driving edge of the lands in bore of gun

Führungs-kapsel *f* command capsule **-kasten** *m* guide cage **-keil** *m* guide piece **-klaue** *f* guide claw, assembly guide claw **-klötzchen** *n* guide block **-knaggen** *m* guiding projection **-körper** *m* guide, sleeve **-kranz** *m* guide ring **-krümmung** *f* beam-guided curvature **-krummzapfen** *m* radius bar **-kunst** *f* art of leadership or of command **-kurve** *f* guide curve

Führungs-lager *n* guide bearing **-leiste** *f* cam groove or ribbed guide in breechblock **-lineal** *n* guide arm, guiding rule gib **-litze** *f* guide rope

Führungsloch *n* feed hole, pilot hole, guide hole, guide perforation (for engagement of sprocket) **~ in der Mitte des Stanzstreifens** central feed hole of the perforated tape

Führungsloch-abstand *m* feed-hole space (teleph.) **-reihe** *f* row of feed holes

Führungs-mannschaft *f* crew **-marke** *f* guide mark **-meißel** *m* pilot bit **-mittel** *n* means or organ of leadership **-muffe** *f* stabilizer, guide sleeve **-nase** *f* locating nose (aviation) **-netz** *n* command telephone, net communication between high echelons **-nocken** *m* guide cam

Führungsnute *f* guide groove **T-förmige ~** T guide channel

Führungs-öse *f* guide eye **-pfahl** *m* guide pile, king pile **-pilz** *m* guide cone **-platte der Raupe** guide plate of caterpillar track **-prismen** *pl* vees, V-ways **-punkte** *pl* leaders

Führungs-querhaupt *n* traversee guide, guide traverse **-rad** *n* guide wheel **-rahmen** *m* guide frame, shift rail frame **-regler** *m* master controller **-rille** *f* track or groove (of phonograph record) **-ring** *m* rotating band, guide ring,

driving band (on ammunition or gun)
Führungsrinne *f* trough-line guide ~ **der Schütze** stop grooves for sluice
Führungsrohr *n* conductor, guide tube, tubular guide, stern tube (for diving rod) ~ **und Schutzschild** guiding shield
Führungs-röhre *f* liner **-röhrenzug** *m* string of conductors
Führungsrolle *f* guiding pulley, guide or contact roller, fair-lead, guide pulley, snatch-post pulley, friction roll or pulley (for friction hammer), sprocket wheel (of film feed) ~ (zum Regeln des Drahtdurchhanges) snatch block ~ (Förderanlage) *f* idler
Führungs-rollenlager *n* roller bearing **-säule** *f* column sleeve **-schablone einer Kopiereinrichtung** master cam **-schaft** *m* guide shaft (aviation) **-schale** *f* guide basin **-schaltung** *f* (LKW-Getriebe) gate **-schaufel** *f* guide blade, spoon (torpedo) **-schaufelring** *m* turbine ring (of guide blade) **-scheibe** *f* disk of turbine guide blades, guide washer **-schiene** *f* guide rail, guide bar, conductor, track **-schlitten** *m* guide block, slide (carriage)
Führungs-schlitz *m* selector shaft guide **-schloßteil** *n* filling-in cam **-schnitte für die Schloßindustrie** jigs or templates in lockmaking **-schraube** *f* lead screw **-schuh** *m* guide socket (box) **-schuhe** launshing lugs **-schwänze** *pl* dovetail guides
Führungs-seil *n* guide rope **-spindel** *f* leading spindle **-stab** *m* operations staff **-staffel** *f* leading or command echelon **-stange** *f* steering (guide) rod, strain rod, guide bar (round or square), sliding bar **-steine** *f* guide pieces **-stift** *m* rewind shaft (photo), guide steam or pin, flask pin, foundry pin **-stopfen** *m* guide pin
Führungs-stück *n* guide piece, traversing arc, feed guide (of gun), (T guide) **-stützen** *f pl* guide braces **-system** *n* guidance **-teil** *n* adapter **-traverse** *f* traverse guide, guide traverse **-vermittlung** *f* command telephone central **-vorrichtung** *f* guiding device **-walze** *f* guide roll or roller **-warze** *f* guide lug **-winkel** *m* guide piece **-winkeleisen** *n* guide angle iron **-wulst** *f* bourrelet, rear bourrelet
Führungszapfen *m* pilot, guide pilot ~ **mit Gewindeansatz** screwed spigot
Führungs-zeichen *n* driving signal (mil.) **-zeugnis** *n* service record, certificate of conduct **-zunge** *f* guiding tongue (on a frog) **-zylinder** *m* guide cylinder
Fuhrwerk *n* (horse-drawn) vehicle, wagon, cart, carriage **-träger** *m* cellular girder **-waage** *f* weighing machine for cars
Fuhrwesen *n* transport service
Fulchronograph *m* fulchronograph
Füllanlage *f* filling plant
Füllansatz *m* appendix, inlet fitting, filling sleeve, inflation nipple or manifold (balloon), inflation sleeve, neck **-leine** *f* filling-sleeve cord or line **-ring** *m* filling-sleeve circle or ring **-schere** *f* valve arms (scissors), spring of sleeve valve **-ventil** *n* balloon tail valve, filling-sleeve valve
Füll-anschluß *m* filling connection (filler) coupling **-anzeige** *f* stop-gap advertisement **-anzeiger** *m* (Tankw.) tank full indicator **-artikel** *m* filler
Füll-batterie *f* inert battery **-baum** *m* first frame of a mine shaft **-becken** *n* receiver, skipping teache (sugar mfg.) **-behälter** *m* hopper, filling bowl **-beton** *m* lean concrete used because of weight or to fill space **-bleistift** *m* patent lead pencil, filling pencil **-brett** *n* panel board **-deckel** *m* filler cap **-diagramm** *n* charging diagram **-drehzahl** *f* speed of rotation while filling the centrifugal (sugar mfg.) **-druck** *m* inflation pressure **-effekt** *m* filling effect
Fülle *f* plenty, abundance, filling
Füll-einlage *f* filler **-einlaß** *m* fill hole **-eisen** *n* calking chisel (for use on metal edges proper)
Fülleitung *f* filling pipe
Füllelement *n* dry cell, desiccated or add-water cell (elec.)
füllen to fill, stuff, load, gas (a balloon); (Kühlmaschine) ~ to charge refrigeration unit
Füllen *n* priming, charging
füllendes Mittel filler
Füller *m* filler (in smoothing surfaces for paint), charger
Füllerde *f* filling earth
Fuller-erde *f* fuller's earth
Füllerfuß *m* filler base
Fuller-mühle *f* fuller (ring roller) mill
Füller-oberteil *n* filler top **-teil** *m* filling unit
Füllextrakt *m* filling extract
Füll-faktor *m* space factor, activity, coefficient **-fassung** *f* mounting cell (optics)
Füllfeder *f* fountain pen **-halter** *m* fountain pen **-halterklappe** *f* cap of fountain pen
Füll-flasche *f* filling cylinder **-flüssigkeit** *f* immersion liquid (microscope) **-funkspruch** *m* dummy beacon radio message, dummy wireless-telegraph message "spoof" **-gas** *n* lifting or buoyant gas (balloon), supporting gas (mil.) **-gasgewicht** *n* weight of lifting or inflation gas **-gewicht** *n* filling weight **-gefäß** *n* hopper, charging bucket **-grad** *m* degree of admission **-grenze** *f* filling limit **-grube** *f* side cutting **-gut** *n* liquid filled
Füllhahn *m* feed cock **-steuerung** *f* filling valve control
Füll-halterdosimeter *n* pen-shaped dosimeter **-händel** *m* nozzle of charging pipe **-hebelanschlag** *m* dial indicator stop **-höhe** *f* filling height **-höhengenauigkeit** *f* filling level accuracy **-holz** *n* white (print.)
Füll-kanal *m* filling, chute **-kasten** *m* hopper **-kastenverfahren** *n* filling-chest process (R.R.) **-keil** *m* (fitter) wedge **-klappe** *f* charging door or flap, fill cap **-klotz** *m* filler (aviation) **-kohle** *f* cobble coal, lump coal **-koks** *m* bed coke **-konstante** *f* bulk factor **-kopf** *m* charging head **-korb** *m* coal basket, measure, or skip (min.)
Füllkörper *m* filling or packing material, filling body **-kolonne** *f* packed column **-säule** *f* packed tower
Füll-kraft *f* thickness, filling properties **-kugel** *f* shrapnel ball **-kurve** *f* single-loop oscillogram **-leistung** *f* filling efficiency **-leitung** *f* filling pipe line
Fülloch *n* fill hole **-abdeckung** *f* fill-hole cover **-schraube** *f* screw cap for filling hole, filling-hole screw or plug
Füll-löffel *m* foundry or casting ladle **-maschine**

f filling or charging machine

Füllmasse *f* massecuite, fillmass, filling compound, filler (sugar mfg.), filling or filling-in paste, putty (for castings), sealing composition (for joint boxes) **-kasten** *m* massecuite tank **-knoten** *m* sweets, balls of massecuite **-kutsche** *f* massecuite wagon **-schieber** *m* massecuite-emptying gate **-schieberventil** *n* massecuite slide discharge valve **-schnecke** *f* massecuite screw conveyer **-schurre** *f* massecuite chute

Füll-material *n* fill, filler, filling material **-mauer** *f* rubble walling, coffer, baked wall **-menge** *f* filling capacity **-mittel** *n* filling agent, filler, filling, stuffing, or loading material **-netz** *n* inflation net **-niet** *n* dummy rivet **-ofen** *m* slow-combustion stove, charging stove **-öffnung** *f* charging port or hole, trunnel head, fill hole, pour-in hole, filling-hole, mouth of furnace **-ort** *m* ingate plot, heapstead, landing, assembling point, pit bottom

Füll-perspektive *f* plenary perspective **-pfahl eines Fangdammes** filling pile of a cofferdam **-pfanne** *f* fill pan **-platte** *f* filler plate, loading shoe **-platz** *m* inflation station, air pump **-pulver** *n* powder charge, explosive powder, TNT

Füll-rahmen *m* sand frame (in core making) **-raum** *m* space for plugging cable termination, sheeting or sheathing, loading chamber, transfer chamber **-rohr** *n* fill or feed pipe (in charging converters), overhead chute **-rumpf** *m* hopper, charging, loading, or feed hopper, loading bin, hopper tank **-sand** *m* body, backing, or packing sand **-säure** *f* accumulator acid

Füllschacht *m* hopper, charging hopper **-feuerung** *f* self-feeding furnace

Füll-schlauch *m* inflation tube **-schraube** *f* filler (screw) plug, filler cap, priming plug **-schriftplatte** *f* variable micro-groove record **-schuß** *m* wadding pick **-schwall** *m* water bore **-spant** *n* filling timber or frame **-sparren** *m* chief or binding rafter **-stab** *m* web member (of truss) **-station** *f* **-stelle** *f* filling station **-stoff** *m* filler gas-shell filler, ingredient

Füllsel *n* filling

Füll-stellung *f* filling position **-stoff** *m* loading material, filler **-stopfen** *m* fill plug **-strich** *m* filling mark, gauge mark or line **-stube** *f* filling room **-stück** *n* spool piece, fairing, filler **-stutzen** *m* gas-cylinder manifold, filler cap **-stutzflaschenventil** *n* bottle valve **-ton** *m* filler clay **-trichter** *m* hopper, bin, feeder or charging hopper, filling funnel **-tulle** *f* funnel, spout **-tüte** *f* nursing tube

Füll- und Peilverschlüsse *pl* fill and dip caps

Füllung *f* fuel injection (Diesel engine), loading, bottling operation, charge, filling, inflation, capacity, getter, cutoff, stuffing, panel, packing **Frischluft ~** freshair charge **~ des Senkkastens** filling a caisson (concrete) **~** (Speisung) batch, charge **~** (einer Täfelung) panel **blinde ~** false panel **bündige ~** flush panel **eingestemmte ~** cased panel **veränderliche ~** variable admission

Füllungs-abschluß *m* cutoff (steam) **-anzeiger** *m* fluid level gauge **-begrenzer** *m* warning gauge **-bremse** *f* air vent **-dauer** *f* duration of filling **-druck** *m* filling or inflation pressure **-eisen** *n* fuller (naut.) **-führung** *f* injection control

Füllungs-gewicht *n* weight of balloon gas, inflation weight **-glieder** *pl* border of a door panel **-grad** *m* volumetric efficiency, degree of admission **-hebel** *m* floating lever (in Diesel) **-höhe** *f* depth of charge **-lattentuch** *n* creeper or filling lattice (tex.) **-leiste** *f* molding (wood) **-leitung** *f* filling pipe (petroleum)

Füllungs-material *n* clay filling **-menge** *f* quantity of filling **-mittel** *n* precipitating agent **-pedal** *n* accelerator pedal **-regelung** *f* feed or filling regulation **-regulierhebel** *m* idling stop lever **-regulierung** *f* fuel inlet control, injection control **-rohr** *n* filling tube

Füllungs-schlauch *m* inflation sleeve **-schluß** *m* cutoff point (steam) **-stab** *m* web member (of truss) **-strecke** *f* admission (part of the) stroke **-tür** *f* panel door **-verhältnis** *n* filling ratio **-wärme** *f* temperature of inflation gas

Füllventil *n* fill-up valve **-sitz** *m* muzzle of charging valve

Füll-verschraubung *f* filling screw, filler cap **-vorgang** *m* filling process **-vorrichtung** *f* filling device, feeder, charging hopper **-waage** *f* inflation balance or scale, automatic lift indicator **-wagen** *m* charging or hopper truck, hopper car, wagon tippler **-wand** *f* panel **-wanne** *f* fill pan **-wirkung** *f* feeding action (filling effect) **-zapfen** *m* filling plug

fulminant fulminating, threatening

fulminieren to fulminate

Fummeln *n* fumble

Fund *m* find, invention, discovery

Fundament *n* fundament, foundation, bed, seat, base, bottom plate, basis, bedplate **~ des Strebepfeilers** footing of buttress

Fundamentabsatz *m* base of foundation

fundamental fundamental, basic **-abstand** *m* fundamental interval **-bereich einer diskontinuierlichen Abbildungsgruppe** fundamental domain of a discontinuous group of transformations **-gesetz** *n* law (phys.) **-größe** fundamental entity **-gruppe einer Fläche** fundamental group of a surface **-schwingung** *f* first or fundamental wave of harmonic, sinusoidal wave

Fundament-anker *m* anchor bolt, foundation bolt **-aushub** *m* excavation (of foundation) **-belastungsschema** *n* foundation loading diagram **-block** *m* foundation (or toe) block or course **-bolzen** *m* lag screws, holding-down or foundation bolt **-graben** *m* footing trench, foundation ditch **-größe** *f* bed size

fundamentieren to lay the foundation

Fundamentierung *f* foundation

Fundament-klotz *m* foundation cap or block **-lehre** *f* template for laying down a bedplate **-mauer** *f* foundation wall **-platte** *f* foundation or base plate, slab foundation **-rahmen** *m* bedplate, raft, frame **-ring** *m* base ring

Fundament-schablone *f* template for laying down a bedplate **-schiene** *f* foundation slide rail **-schraube** *f* foundation or anchor bolt, lag screw **-sockel** *m* foundation base or stone **-sohle** *f* foundation base or slab, main foundation **-stein** *m* foundation stone **-zeichnung** *f* foundation sketch or plan

Fund-bericht *m* post-mortem report **-grube** *f* load work, founder shaft, discovery shaft

fundieren to found, endow, consolidate

Fundierung *f* foundation

fündig yielding, rich
Fündigkeit *f* discovery of a mineral (min.)
Fundort *m* source or plate of discovery
Fundpunkt *m* point of discovery **~ weggeschwemmter Erze** fret
Fundus *m* base, ground
fünf-atomig pentatomic **~ zum Quadrat** five square
Fünfeck *n* pentagon **räumliches vollständiges ~** pentagon, complete in space
Fünfecke, wechselseitig umschriebene pentagons, mutually circumscribed one about the other
fünfeckig pentagonal
Fünfelektrodenröhre *f* pentode
Fünfer-alphabet *n* five-unit code or alphabet **-schwarmwinkel** *m* wedge formation of five airplanes **-teiler** *m* division of five
Fünffach-kupplung *f* quintuple coupling **-punkt** *m* quintuple point **-zug-Anzeiger** *m* five-point draft gauge
fünffältig fivefold
Fünfflächer *m* pentahedron
fünfgliedriger Mischer five-channel mixer
fünfkantig pentagonal
Fünfkant-reibahle *f* hexagon and pentagon broaches **-revolverkopf** *m* pentagon turret
Fünfkörperverdampfapparat *m* quintuple-effect evaporator
Fünfleiter-netz *n* five-wire network **-system** *n* five-wire system with direct current
Fünflinsenobjektiv five-lens objective, five-lens combination
fünfmal gelagerte Kurbelwelle five-bearing crankshaft
fünfmotorig five-engined
Fünfpol-endröhre *f* output pendtode
fünfpolig (bei Steckkontakt) five-pole, five-way
Fünfpol-regelröhre *f* variable-mu-high-frequency pentode **-röhre** *f* pentode, five-electrode tube, pentode valve or tube **-schirmregelröhre** *f* variable-mu-high-frequency pentode **-schirmröhre** *f* high-frequency pentode
fünfseitig pentahedral
Fünfzehnnutanker *m* fifteen-slot armature
Fünfziger-Gruppen-Wähler *m* fifties-selector (FGS)
Fünfsekundenruf *m* machine ringing
Fünfsteckersockel *m* five-pin or five-prong base
Fünfströmealphabet *n* five-unit code or alphabet
Fünfstufenschwächer *m* five-step weakener (phot.)
Fünftastengeber *m* five-key transmitter
fünfteilig five-point, having five parts
Fünfwalzenmühle *f* five-roller sugar-cane mill
Fünfwalzwerk *n* five-roller mill
fünfwertig pentavalent
Fünfzylindersternmotor *m* five-cylinder radial engine
fungieren to behave
Funikularbereich *m* funicular region
Funk *m* radio
Funkabkürzung *f* radio abbreviation, procedure sign, code group
Funkabschirmung *f* spark-plug shield **~ der Zündeinrichtung** ignition screening
Funk-anlage *f* radio or wireless facility, wireless or radio station **-amateur** *m* "ham" **-apparat** *m* wireless apparatus or set **-aufklärung** *f* radio intelligence or interception **-ausrüstung** *f* radio or wireless equipment **-ausstellung** *f* radio show, wireless exhibition **-auswertestelle** *f* signal intelligence station
Funkbake *f* radio beacon, marker beacon **~ zur Kennzeichnung und Eingrenzung** marker beacon **umlaufende ~** revolving radio beacon
Funk-bastler *m* radio amateur **-befehl** *m* radio command or order **-beobachtung** *f* radio observation **-beobachtungsgerät** *n* radar search receiver, radio **-bereitschaft** *f* radio alert
Funkbeschickung *f* radio-beam deviation (at point of impact on plane), direction-finder deviation, quadrantal error, correction for deviation of direction-finder bearing, calibration
Funkbeschickungs-aufnahme *f* calibration of direction finder **-drahtschleife** *f* quadrantal-error compensating or clearing loop **-kurvenscheibe** *f* compensator cam, zero-clearing cam
Funk-beschränkung *f* limited radio silence, limitation of radio traffic **-besteck** *n* radio fix **-betrieb** *m* radio service, radio traffic or operation, radio
Funkbetriebs-flug *m* radio-testing flight **-kraftwagen** *m* mobile radio-operations unit or truck, wireless maintenance truck **-stelle** *f* radio-operations station **-unterlage** *f* signal-operation instruction **-zeichen** *n* prosign
Funk-bild *n* radio picture, wired photograph, radio-photogram **-bildgerät** *n* wireless picture telegraph **-boje** *f* radio buoy **-brief** *m* radio letter-telegram **-brücke** *f* radio link or relay **-buch** *n* radio log **-büschel** *n* wireless beam
Funk-dämpfung *f* spark damping **-dauerbereitschaft** *f* continuous radio alert **-dienstgeräte** *pl* radio-communication sets
Funkdienst *m* radio service **fester ~** radio service between permanent stations
Funk-doppelverkehr *m* simultaneous two-way radio communication or traffic **-drosselspule** *f* air-gap reactance coil
Funke(n) *m* spark **tönender ~** musical spark **überspringender ~** jump spark
Funk-echolot *n* ground-clearance indicator
funkeigener Pilot system pilot tone
Funk-eigensteuerung *f* radio autocontrol, loop navigation, (radio)direction-finding **-einrichtungen** *pl* radio or wireless apparatus or equipment, radio facilities **-einsatz** *m* employment of radio
Funkel-effekt *m* flicker effect, Schottky effect, sparkling, scintillation, glitter, low-frequency effect of local emission density (of electrons) **-feuer** *n* quick-flashing light
funkeln to sparkle, glitter, scintillate, twinkle
Funkeln *n* scintillation, twinkling
Funkelrauschen *n* flicker effect
Funkempfang *m* radio or wireless reception
Funkempfänger *m* radio or wireless receiver, receiving set, radio station
funken to radio, telegraph, spark, fire (artil.), (slang) flash
Funken *n* sparking, wireless transmission, spark, flash
Funken *pl*, **gesteuerte ~** timed sparks **~ sprühen** to sparkle
Funken-abstand *m* spark gap (magneto) **-an-**

zeiger *m* resonator **-ausbläser** *m* spark blowout **-auswurf** *m* emission of sparks, sparks emitted **-bahn** *f* path of spark **-bake** *f* radio beam **-bild** *n* appearance of sparks **-bildende Stelle** spark generating spot **-bildung** *f* formation or production of sparks, sparking **-bläser** *m* spark guard **-brücke** *f* spark gap

Funken-dämpfung *f* spark damping **-dauer** *f* time (duration) of the spark **-entladung** *f* disruptive discharge, spark discharge **-entladungsaufbauzeit** *f* formation time of spark discharge

Funken-entstörer *m* suppressor screen, shield, static, eliminator, wireless-telegraphy screening **-entstörung** *f* screening **-entzieher** *m* arcing contact **-erzeuger** *m* spark generator **-fänger** *m* spark arrester or catcher (on a locomotive), spark-condensing chamber **-felge** *f* succession of sparks

funkenfrei nonarcing (metals), sparkless, nonsparking **-e Unterbrechung** clean break

Funken-garbe *f* shower of sparks **-geber** *m* spark coil or transmitter, Ruhmkorff coil

Funkeninduktor *m* spark or induction coil, Ruhmkorff coil **~ mit Hammerunterbrecher** hammerbreak spark coil

Funken-kammer *m* spark arrester **-kanal** *m* spark track **-kinematograph** *m* flash motion picture **-kompaß** *m* radio compass **-kontinuum** *n* spark discharge continuum **-lage** *f* spark position **-länge** *f* spark length, sparking distance **-leiter** *m* spark conductor **-linie** *f* spark line **-los** sparkless (elec.)

Funkenlöscher *m* spark extinguisher, spark blowout or quench, arcing contact, spark killer or arrester **-kasten** *m* spark suppressor **-kondensator** *m* spark-quenching condenser **-kreiswerte** *pl* spark-quench circuit values **-magnet** *m* spark-extinguisher magnet **-spule** *f* spark-suppressor coil, magnetic blowout coil

Funkenlöschkreis *m* sparkquench circuit

Funkenlöschung *f* spark extinguishing

Funkenlöschwiderstandswert *m* quenched-spark resistance value

Funken-losigkeit *f* nonsparking (elec.) **-mikrometer** *n* micrometric spark discharger, spark micrometer, micrometric spark gap

Funken- oder Licht- und Bogenentladung *f* spark or arc discharge

Funken-potential *n* spark potential **-probe** *f* spark test **-puster** *m* (slang) radio operator **-rauschen** *n* flicker effect, background noise of radio **-rechen** *m* frame for arcing plates **-regen** *m* shower of sparks **-rost** *m* cinder frame, spark collector **-sammler** *m* spark condenser **-schirm** *m* jump-spark system **-schlagweite** *f* equivalent spark, sparking distance **-schutz** *m* spark killer **-schwächer** *m* spark reducer **-schwanzbildung** *f* spark-tail formation

Funkensender *m* (wireless) spark transmitter **tönender ~** musical spark transmitter

Funken-sieb *n* cinder frame, spark collector or catcher **-skala** *f* scale of sparks **-spannung** *f* spark potential **-spektrallinie** *f* spark radiation due to multiple ionization of the emitting atom **-spektrum** *n* spark spectrum **-sprühen** *n* scintillation, sparking

Funkenstation *f*, **schwere ~** high-power radio station

Funkenstöpsel *m* sparking plug

Funkenstrecke *f* spark gap (length), discharger sparking distance **feste ~** plain spark discharger **feststehende ~** static or stationary spark gap **rotierende ~** rotary spark gap **rotierende ~ für die Erzeugung ungedämpfter Wellen** timed spark discharger **rotierende oder umlaufende ~** disk discharger, rotary spark gap **tönende ~** resonance spark gap **umlaufende ~** rotary spark gap **unterteilte ~** multiple spark gap **~ im Nebenschluß** parallel spark gap **~ in Reihe** series spark gap

Funkenstrecken-blitzableiter *m* spark-gap type of arrester **-elektrode** *f* spark-gap face, spark knob, spark-gap terminal

Funkenstrecker *m* spark-gap disk, spark spacer

Funkentelegraphie *f* wireless (telegraphy), radio (telegraphy) **Versagen der ~** breakdown of wireless communication

Funkentelegraphie-Anlage *f* wireless installation **-Ausrüstung** *f* wireless equipment

funkentelegrafische Bordanlage airplane radio set

Funkentelephonie *f* radiotelephony

Funkentladung *f* spark discharge

Funken-ton *m* spark note **-trübung** code for antijamming devices

Funk-entstörer *m* suppressor screen, (shield) static eliminator **-entstörmittel** *n* radio interference control equipment **-entstört** radio-screened, shielded for radio interference **-entstörung** *f* elimination of radio interference, radio interference suppression

Funken-überschlag *m* spark-gap breakdown, flashover, sparkover **-übergang** *m* sparking **-verhindernd** spark suppressing **-versetzung** *f* angular offset of sparks **-verzögerung** *f* spark lag **-werfer** *n* scintillation **-widerstand** *m* spark resistance **-wurf** *m* throwing out of sparks

Funken-zahl *f* spark rate or frequency **-zähler** *m* spark counter **-zeitlupe** *f* high-speed spark camera **-zeitlupenaufnahme** *f* high-speed spark photograph **-ziehen** *n* spark drawing **-zieher** *m* discharger, spark drawer **-zieherscheibe** *f* disc of the rotary spark gap **-zünder** *m* jump-spark cap (high-tension cap) (explosives), spark igniter

Funkenzündung *f* spark ignition **Motor mit ~** electric-ignition engine

Funker *m* radio or wireless operator, signaler **-kabine** *f* radio operator's office, radio cabin

Funkerkennungsgerät *n* (IFF) identification friend or foe

Funker-raum *m* radio operator's compartment, radio cabin **-stand** *m* wireless station **-tisch** *m* radio operator's table

Funkfahrzeug *n* radio wagon

Funk-fehlweisung *f* radio-wave deviation, radio-direction-finder error, directional or quadrantal error, compass deviation, distortion of bearing **-fernführung** *f* wireless remote control **-fernschreiben** *n* radio telegraphy **-fernschreiber** *m* radio teletype (RATT) **-fernsprechanlage** *f* radio-telephone set or installation **-fernsprechen** *n* radiotelephone, wireless telephony **-fernsprechtrieb** *m* radiotelephone technique **-fernsprechverbindung** *f* radiotelephone circuit

-fernsteuerung *f* radio-telecontrol
Funkfeststation *f* non-mobile radio station
Funkfeuer *n* radio beacon, radio-beacon station, radio marker beacon, radio range **-empfänger** *m* radio-beacon receiver **-kennung** *f* radio beacon identification **-meßanlage** *f* UHF telemetry chain **-sender** *m* radio-beacon transmitter
Funkfliegen *n* radio flying
Funkfrequenz *f* radio frequency
Funkfrequenz-bereich *m* radio-frequency range **-kanal** *n* radio channel
Funk-freund *m* radio or wireless amateur, "ham" operator **-gabelverkehr** *m* radio communication by bifurcation **-geber** *m* radio transmitter **-geheimnis** *n* radio secrecy or secret
Funkgerät *n* radio outfit or set, wireless set or apparatus, radio equipment, transmitter and receiver, communication apparatus, radio station, radar set, radio altimeter **~ auf einen Sender einstellen** to tune in
Funk-gerätemechaniker *m* radio repairman **-gerätespulen** *pl* radio-receiver coils **-gespräch** *n* radio conversation **-gesteuert** radio-controlled **-haus** *n* broadcasting station **-hilfe** *f* radio aid **-höhenmesser** *m* radio altimeter
Funk-horchdienst *m* radio-listening or radio-intercept service **-horchempfänger** *m* radio-listening receiver **-horchkraftwagen** *m* radio-intercept(ion) truck **-horchstelle** *f* radio- intercept station **-induktor** *m* spark coil
Funk-kabine *f* radio compartment **-kanal** *m* radio channel, characteristic frequency band **-kennungsgerät** *n* identification friend or foe **-kerze** *f* spark plug, igniter plug (jet) **-kiste** *f* radio chest or case
Funk-kommando *n* radio command **-kommandoführung** *f* radio guidance (g/m) **-kommandosender** *m* (Astron.) command link transmitter **-kompaß** *m* automatic direction finder (ADF) radio or wireless compass, radiogoniometer **-kraftfahrzeug** *n* radio-communication motor vehicle **-kraftwagen** *m* radio (commando) truck or car
Funk-lade *f* radio index **-landeanlage** *f* instrument landing system **-leitung** *f* wireless-telegraph control **-lenkung** *f* radio guidance **-liebhaber** *m* radio or wireless amateur, radio enthusiast **-linie** *f* radio circuit or link, radio line, two-station net **-lösung** *f* blow out **-lot** *n* sonic altimeter
Funkmast *m* radio mast or tower, antenna mast, mast-type antenna **freitragender ~** self-supporting radio tower
Funkmastkraftwagen *m* (mobile) radio-antenna truck or unit
Funk-mechaniker *m* radio technician **-meldung** *f* wireless telegram, radio message
Funkmeß-koppelraum *m* radar information center **-landeanlage** *f* precision approach radar **-täuschungsgerät** *n* camouflage radar used in jamming **-technik** *f* radar (radio detecting and ranging)
Funkmessung *f* radio location
Funkmeß-verfahren *n* radio range-finding **-ziel** *n* radar target
Funk-mutung *f* radio prospecting, radio metal locating **-nachricht** *f* radio message or communication **-navigation** *f* radio navigation **-navigationseinrichtungen** *pl* radio navigation aids **-navigationshilfe** *f* radio navigational aid
Funknetz *n* radio system or network **~ für den Verkehr Bodenbord** air-ground net
Funknot-boje *f* jettisonable emergency, radio buoy **-signal** *n* radio distress signal
Funk-offizier *m* radio or wireless officier **-ortungsdienst** *m* radio location service **-ortungsstelle** *f* radio location station
Funkpeil-anlage *f* radio direction finding station **-anzeigegerät** *n* radio-direction-finder indicator **-dienst** *m* radio-direction-finding service **-einrichtung** *f* radio direction finder
Funkpeilen *n* radio direction-finding
Funkpeiler *m* (radio) direction finder, radio compass, radiogoniometer, directional radio transmitter
Funkpeil-reichweite *f* directional-radio range **-scheibe** *f* bearing-plate of radio direction finder **-schwund** *m* radio fade-out or fading
Funkpeil-skala *f* scale for direction-finding instrument **-stelle** *f* radio-direction-finding station or post **-tochterkompaß** *m* direction-finder repeater compass
Funkpeilung *f* radio bearing, radar bearing **korrigierte ~** corrected radio bearing
Funkpeilungskarte *f* radio-direction-finding chart
Funkpeilwesen *n* radio direction-finding
Funk-platte *f* radio or direction-finder log, spark plate (condenser of automobile radio) **-prüfer** *m* radio-testing set, radio tester **-pult** *n* radio-control desk **-querverbindung** *f* intercommunication channel **-raum** *m* radio room, wireless-telegraph office **-recht** *n* laws and regulations relating to radiotelegraphy **-richtweisung** *f* radio alignment
Funk-ruf *m* radio call **-rufzeichen** *n* radio call, sign **-schatten** *m* dead spot, radio shadow or pocket **-schutzummantelung** *f* anti-interference shrouding **-schwingungszahl** *f* radio frequency **-schwund** *m* fading, fade-out (of radio signals)
Funksehgerät *n* UHF sight unit
Funkseitenpeilung *f* directional radio bearing **beschickte oder verbesserte ~** true or corrected radio bearing **unverbesserte oder abgelesene ~** uncorrected or charted radio bearing
Funk-selbststeuerung *f* radio-autocontrol **-sendemonitor** *m* radio monitor
Funksenden *n* radio transmission
Funksender *m* radio or wireless transmitter, sender, broadcasting station **Einpeilen eines Richtempfängers auf einen ~** tuning in a transmitter station with directional receiver, to take bearings
Funksenderempfänger *m* wireless transmitter-receiver (in radar)
Funk-sendezentrale *f* radio-transmitting center **-sendung** *f* radio transmission **-signal** *n* radio (electric) signal
Funk-skizze *f* radio-net diagram, radio-communication diagram **-sonderkommando** special radio detachment
Funksonde *f* radiometeorograph, radio sonde (meteor.)
Funksprache *f* radiotelephony
Funksprech-anlage *f* radiotelephone system

-boot *n* radiotelegraph guard

funksprechen to radiotelephone

Funksprechen *n* radiotelephony, voice transmission by radio, radiotelephone communication

Funksprech-gerät *n* handie-talkie, radio telephone, radiotelephony set **-stromkreis** *m* radiotelephone circuit **-übermittlung** *f* voice-radio communication **-verbindung** *f* radiotelephone circuit, radio link **-weg** *m* radio link

Funkspruch *m* wireless or radio message, radiogram, radiotelephone message, radio signal **~ mit verschlüsselter Anschrift** codress message **geschlüsselter ~** radio-code message **offener ~** radio message in clear

Funkspruch-kopf *m* heading or preamble on radio message or signal **-übersicht** *f* radio-signal unit journal or number sheet **-vermittlung** *f* radio-message relay (station), radio-message transmission

Funkspruchweg *m* radio channel **auf dem ~** by or via radio

Funk-staffel *f* echelon of radio units, radio detachment **-standlinie** *f* radio reference line

Funkstation *f* radio or wireless station **fahrbare ~** cart-type radio station

Funkstelle *f* radio or wireless station **bewegliche ~** mobile radio station **feste ~** fixed radio station **ortsfeste ~** fixed station

Funk-steuerung *f* radiocontrol **-stille** *f* radio or wireless silence

Funkstör-dienst *m* radar-jamming service **-leitkompanie** *f* radio-jamming control company **-meßgerät** *n* interference measuring apparatus **-sender** *m* jammer radar

Funkstör- und Abwehrdienst *m* radio-countermeasures service

Funkstörung *f* radio interference or jamming

Funk-strahl *m* radio beam **-strecke** *f* spark gap **-streifenwagen** *m* radio patrol car **-streuung** *f* abnormal radiation **-tafel** *f* radio-code table **-tagebuch** *n* logbook, radio log **-tasten** *n* radiotelegraphy, keying **-täuschung** *f* deliberate transmission of false radio messages, radio deception **-täuschungsgerät** *n* radio decoy set, radar **-technik** *f* radio art, radio engineering, radio technics **-techniker** *m* radio engineer or technician

funktechnisch radio **-e Spulen** radio coils

Funk-telegramm *n* radio(tele)gram **-telegraph** *m* wireless telegraph **-telegraphenanlage** *f* radiotelegraph plant **-telegraphenbetrieb** *m* radiotelegraphy

Funktelegraphie *f* radiotelegraphy, wireless or continuous-wave telegraphy **~ mit gedämpften Wellen** spark telegraphy **abgestimmte ~** syntonic wireless telegraphy **gerichtete ~** directional wireless telegraphy

Funktelegraphie-gast *m* wireless operator (lowest rank in signals branch) **-sender** *m* radiotelegraphic transmitter

Funktelegraphie- und -telephoniegerät *n* wireless-telegraphy and radiotelephony apparatus

funktelegraphisch radiotelegraphic **-e Verbindung** radiotelegraphic connection, radio-signal communication (channel)

Funktelephon *m* radiotelephone, wireless telephone

Funktelephonie *f* radiotelephony, wireless telephony **-sender** *m* radiotelephonic transmitter

funktelephonisch radio(tele)phonic

Funktion *f* action, function, operation, service, office **eine ~ übernehmen** to take charge of a function **abgeleitete ~** derived function **einwertige ~** single-valued function **gerade ~** even function **hyperbolische ~** hyperbolic function **reziproke ~** inverse function **unentwickelte ~** implicit function **ungerade ~** odd function **universelle ~** universal function **zugeordnete ~** associated function

Funktional-ableitung *f* functional derivative **-determinante** *f* functional determinant **-differentialgleichung** *f* functional-differential equation

Funktionell *n* operation

funktionell functional **-e Ziffer** function digits

Funktionentheorie *f* theory of functions

funktionieren to function, work, operate, run, act

Funktionierung *f* functioning

Funktions-bedingung *f* operating condition **-bereit** ready for use **-erprobung** *f* operational test **-fähig** operable **-gabel** *f* function lever **-geber** *m* function generator **-mäßig** functionally **-multiplizierer** *m* function multipier

Funktions-prüfung *f* operational test **-schalter** *m* function switch **-schaltung** *f* control action **-störung** *f* malfunction (info proc.) **-tafel** *f* function table (info proc.) **-taste** *f* operating key (tape rec.) **-tisch** *m* plotting board **-trieb** *m* input table

Funk-trägerfrequenz *f* radio-carrier frequency **-trübung** *f* uncleared zero, blurring or lack of precision **-trupp** *m* radio detachment or section **-turm** *m* radio mast or tower **-übertragung** *f* radio relay **-überwachung** *f* radio monitoring, wireless-telegraphy security **-übung** *f* radio-communication exercise

Funk-urheberrecht *n* copyright in broadcasting **-verbot** *n* radio silence **-verfahren** *n* radio procedure

Funkverkehr *m* radio or wireless communication, radio traffic **einseitiger ~** one-way radio communication

Funkverkehrs-abkürzung *f* radio brevity **-art** *f* type of radio-network traffic **-buch** *n* radio log **-formen** *f pl* types or methods of radio communication **-karte** *f* radio-network chart **-linie** *f* radio circuit or link **-verbindung** *f* radio communication

Funk-verkehrzeichen *n pl* operating signals **-vermessung** *f* electrical trajectory tracing **-verordnung** *f* decree of protection of wireless service **-verschleierung** *f* radio coding **-wachboot** *n* wireless-telegraph guard boat **-wagen** *m* radio wagon, car, or truck **-warnung** *f* radio detection **-wart** *m* radio mechanic or technician

Funkwechsel-sprechen *n* simplex (voice communication) **-verkehr** *m* simplex operation

Funkweg *m* radio channel **auf dem ~** by or via radio

Funkwelle *f* radio wave

Funkwellen-ausbreitung *f* radiowave propagation **-bezeichnung** *f* designation of radio waves

-spektrum *n* radio spectrum

Funk-werbung *f* radio advertising **-werkstatt** *f* radio-maintenance shop or workshop **-wesen** *n* radio or wireless communication, radio engineering, radio technology **-wetterdienst** *m* radio or wireless meteorological service **-wetterwarte** *f* weather station, radio weather-broadcasting station **-wiederholer** *m* wireless-telegraphy link

Funk-zeit *f* photometer **-zeitzeichen** *n* radio time signal **-zelle** *f* radio compartment **-zentrale** *f* central radio station **-zielgerät** *n* radio-aiming device radio **-zucht** *f* radio (communication) discipline **-zug** *m* mobile wireless-telegraph unit **-zusatzgerät** *n* auxiliary radio apparatus, radio and radar accessory set or accessories

Furage *f* forage

furagieren to forage

Furagierleine *f* picket line

Furan *n* furan

Furche *f* furrow, drill, channel, groove, pass, radius, interstice, rill, rut, scour, wrinkle, ruling or line (of diffraction grating)

furchen to nick out, plow

Furchen-egge *f* drill harrow **-pflug** *m* ride plow **-rain** *m* ridge between furrows **-zieher** *m* ridge plow

furchig furrowed, grooved

Furchung *f* furrowing, grooving, segmentation, cleavage

Furier *m* quartermaster sergeant

Furnier *n* **-blatt** *n* veneer, plywood **-bockschlüssel** *m* glue clamp wrenches **-bockspindeln** *pl* glue clamp spindles **-dicke** *f* thickness of veneer, ply

furnieren to veneer, inlay

Furnierholz *n* veneer (wood), plywood sheet **ausgerolltes ~** unrolled veneers

Furnier-kreissäge *f* veneering circular saw **-messer** *n* veneer knife (plane) **-platten** *pl* veneer sheets **-presse** *f* veneer press **-presser** *m* veneer clamper **-rahmensäge** *f* veneer frame saw **-säge** *f* veneering or web saw, frame saw, veneer saw

Furnier-schabhobel *pl* veneer spoke shaves **-schälmaschine** *f* wood-peeling machine (rotary planer for peeling off veneer sheets) **-schneidemaschine** *f* veneer-saw frame, veneer-cutting machine **-schreiner** *m* veneerer **-sitz** *m* plated seat **-stärke** *f* thickness of veneer **-verschalung** *f* veneer shell, laminated covering **-zulagen** *pl* veneering sheets **-zusammensetzmaschine** *f* veneer assembling machine

Fürsorge *f* care, (public) welfare

Furt *f* ford, crossing, point of shallow depth between reversed curves in river course

fuselhaltig containing fusel (oil)

Fuselöl *n* fusel oil

Fusion *f* fusion

fusionieren to merge (comput.)

Fusionierung *f* merger

Fusionspunkt *m* fusion point

Fuß *m* foot, footing, base, pedestal, root, bottom, support, heel (of mast), pinch, press, squash, stem or foot (of a lamp, tube, or valve) **~ einer Böschung** horizontal measure of a slope **~ des Bügels für Befestigung in Mauerwerk** expansion anchor **~ des Kühlers** radiator bracket **~ der Schiene** lower flange, patten or foot of rail, base **~ des Supports** foot of the rest **Stelle, an der man ~ fassen kann** foothold **umgestülpter ~** re-entrant squash or press

Fußablend-schalter *m* foot-operated dimming switch **-umschalter** *m* foot-operated antidazzle switch

Fuß-abrundung *f* root radius (of gear) tooth fillet **-abstreifer** *m* shoe scraper **-anker** *m* stay fixed to pole at ground level **-anlasser** *m* foot starter **-anlaßschalter** *m* foot-operated starting switch **-antrieb** *m* foot power attachment, foot drive **-auflage** *f* pedal

Fuß-ball *m* football **-bank** *f* footstool, footstep **-bedient** pedal-operated **-bedienung** *f* foot operation **-bedienungsbügel** *m* pedal **-bedienungshebel** *m* foot operation lever **-bekleidung** *f* footwear

Fuß-betätigung *f* foot operation **-betätigungshebel** *m* pedal **-betrieb** *m* treadle operation or drive **-blatt** *n* sole of foot **-blech** *n* floor plate, foot plate **-block** *m* snatch block

Fußboden *m* floor, ground, flooring, floor board **den ~ aufreißen** to remove the flooring **stumpfgefügter ~** straight-joint floor

Fußboden-balken *m* floor beam **-belag** *m* floor covering, flooring, paving, pavement **-blech** *n* flooring, floor plate **-brett** *n* flooring plank, floor boards **-decklack** *m* floor varnish **-kitt** *m* wooden flooring putty **-kontakt** *m* floor contact **-kontrollgerät** *n* floor monitor

Fußboden-lager *n* floor beam or sill **-leiste** *f* floor strop, skirting board **-nagel** *m* brad **-öl** *n* floor saturant **-parkettschleifpapier** *n* parquetry abrasive paper **-platte** *f* floor plate, flooring slab or tile, flagstone **-pressen** *pl* flooring clamps **-schleifmaschine** *f* floor grinding machine **-schwelle** *f* floor beam **-unterlagspappe** *f* underlay feltboard

Fuß-breite der Schiene width of base of rail **-bremse** *f* foot brake **-bremshebel** *m* brake pedal **-brett** *n* footrest, footboard, bottom board

Füßchen *pl* feet of a plate **-füllung** *f* bulb filling

Fuß-decke *f* front of the foot **-drehbank** *f* foot lathe **-druckknopftaste** *f* pedal pressure switch **-durchmesser** *m* root diameter (of gear) **-einrückung** *f* pedal engagement **-einspannung** *f* fixed support

fußen to base

Fußflantsche *m* bottom flange, flange with feet

Fußgänger *m* pedestrian **-brücke** *f* footbridge **-unterführung** *f* pedestrian subway

Fuß-gashebel *m* foot throttle **-gelenk** *n* ankle joint, hinged support **-geschaltet** foot-operated

Fußgestell *n* socle, pedestal **~ einer Säule** pedestal base of a column

Fußhebel *m* foot pedal, foot lever, pedal treadle **~ für Rückwärtsfahrt** reserve pedal **nachstellbarer ~** adjustable pedal

Fußhebel-lagerblock *m* pedal bracket **-lagerung** *f* foot controls **-presse** *f* treadle press **-welle** *f* pedal shaft **-werk** *n* foot controls

Fuß-höhe (Zahnrad) *f* dedendum of a tooth **-kappe** *f* foot capping **-kegelwinkel** *m* dedendum angle **-kerze** *f* foot-candle **-kraft** *f* foot pressure **-kratzeisen** *n* door scraper **-kreis** *m* root line, dedendum line or circle **-kreisdurch-**

messer *m* diameter of root circle **-krümmer** *m* foot bend

Fuß-ladeumschalter *m* foot operated starting switch **-lager** *n* (foot)step bearing, vertical bearing, step, pivot bearing **-lasche** *f* bedplate, foot fishplate **-laschenverbindung** *f* bedplate-type joint, foot-fishing joint **-latte** *f* ledger (trestle), stretcher footboard (in boat), sill **-leiste** *f* skirting, footrest **-libelle** *f* foot bubble **-lichter** *pl* foot lights (border lights) **-linie** *f* foot rule, dedendum line **-lose Röhre** loktal tube

Fuß-maß *n* measurement in feet, foot measure or measurement **-matte** *f* door mat **-mauer** *f* foot wall (of embankment) **-motor** *m* foot-mounted (standard) motor **-note** *f* footnote **-öse** *f* foot eye, base lug

Fuß-pedal *n* foot pedal **-pendelpresse** *f* foot-lever press **-pfad** *m* attendant path (R.R.) **-pfahl** *m* templet **-pfund** *n* foot-pound **-platte** *f* base plate (camera), shoe, sole plate or underplate of an oil press, footplate float

Fußpunkt *m* foot, nadir, base **Fußpunkte auf gleicher Höhe** supports at the same elevation **mit verschieden hohen Fußpunkten** with supports at different elevations ~ **des Lotes** foot of a perpendicular

Fußpunkt-isolator *m* base insulator **-konstruktion der Kegelschnitte** tracing of conics by means of pedal points **-kurve** *f* pedal locus, pedal (or podal) locus curve **-linie** *f* podal line **-widerstand** *m* center-base impedance, terminal impedance or base loading (of antenna)

Fuß-rahmen *m* pole plate **-raste** *f* foot-rest **-regelschalter** *m* pedal control circuit **-ring** *m* base ring **-rippe** *f* web, web plate

Fußrolle *f* tail pulley ~ **eines Stativs** foot caster of a stand

Fuß-rücken *m* dorsal surface of the foot **-rückschlagventil** *n* foot valve **-sack** *m* foot muff **-schalter** *m* foot(-operated) switch, foot starter (elec.) **-schaltleiste** *f* footbar **-schaltung** *f* pedal switch, foot shifter **-scheibe** *f* footplate, pedal disk **-schemel** *m* footstool, stool **-schicht** *f* eaves or barge course, heads (roof) **-schiene** *f* footrail **-schlingenmine** *f* foot snare mine

Fußschraube *f* binding bolt ~ **eines Stativs** foot screw of a stand

Fuß-schutz *m* protection of the stock (elec.) **-setzlinie** *f* foot white (print.) **-sicher** sure-footed **-sockel** *m* wainscoted socle **-spiel** *n* bottom clearance **-spindelpresse** *f* foot press

Fuß-steg *m* step (aluminium mfg.) **-steig** *m* apron (aviation), footpath, sidewalk **-steuer** *n* foot-control **-stück** *n* socle, base, pedestal **-stütze** *f* footrest **-taste** *f* foot switch **-tau** *n* stay tackle **-teller** *m* float, plate, jack float

Fußtritt *m* foot pedal, foot lever, footstep, foot treadle, kick **-betätigung** *f* treadle operation **-bremse** *f* foot-operated brake **-schalter** *m* treadle switch

Fuß-umschalter *m* floor contact, foot-operated switch **-unterbrecher** *m* foot interrupter **-unterlage** *f* pedestal, base

Fußventil *n* foot valve (of air pump, feed pump), retaining valve **Sieb am** ~ foot-valve screen

Fuß-verdrehung *f* spraining of the foot **-wärmer** *m* foot warmer **-weg** *m* service walk-way, footpath **-winde** *f* hand jack

Fußwinkel *m* base ring ~ **des Kegelrades** dedendum angle of bevel gear ~ **eines Stativs** tread of a tripod

Fuß-zeichen *n* index **-zeiger** *m* subscript

Fustage *f* barrels, casks, containers, empties

Futter *n* lining, chuck or collet (mach.), case, coating, covering, forage, food, feed, mounting, fodder, bushing (metalwork), packing, filling piece, liner, fixture, jig

Futteral *n* case, box, cover, sheath, scabbard

Futter-aufspannung *f* chucking **-automat** *n* automatic chuck lathe **-backe** *f* chuck jaw **-blech** *n* fill plate **-gehäuse** *n* collet (mach.) **-haltbarkeit** *f* life of lining **-holz** *n* wood packing (filling) piece, blocking piece, furring, shim, puncheon, timber sheating or fenders, frame shim **-hölzer** *pl* timber fillets **-kissen** *n* driving cushion **-klinge** *f* chopper, chopping blade, chopping or straw knife

Futter-lade *f* chaff cutter **-lauf** *m* liner **-leinen** *n* linen lining **-masse** *f* lining material **-mauer** *f* retaining or protecting wall, brickwork lining

füttern to line, bush, feed, wedge, underlay

Füttern eines Bohrloches lining a bore hole

Futter-platten *f pl* chuck plates, vise jaws, clamping chuck (for bench lathes) **-rahmen** *m* casement, sash frame **-ring** *m* collet, or small chuck **-rohr** *n* liner (artil.), guide brush, inner tube (of a gun), casing, protective tube, casing pipe, barrel liner, inner barrel, removable liner

Futterröhren-strang *m* string of casing tubes **-zug** *m* string of casing

Futterrohr-flantsche *f* casing flange **-haken** *m* casing hook **-heber** *m* casing jack **-preßkopf** *m* pressing head of casing **-rammhaupt** *n* driving head of casing **-spalter** *m* casing knife **-rohrstück** *n* casing string

Futter-rübe *f* fooder beet, mangold **-scheibe** *f* adapter, backplate **-schneider** *m* ensilage cutter **-seidenpapier** *n* lining tissues **-sperrverbindung** *f* casing joint **-spalt** *m* lining split **-stein** *m* lining brick

Futterstoff *m* lining (clothing) **glänzender** ~ sateen

Futter-stück *n* line plate, liner, packing, bushing **-stücke** *n pl* make-up pieces **-stufe** *f* riser (of a staircase) **-turm** *m* tower silo

Fütterung *f* wedge, key, lining (print.)

Fütterungsstoff *m* lining material

Futterwagen *m* forage wagon

G

Gabe *f* dose

Gabbro *m* diallage rock, gabbro **-chaussierung** *f* macadam road

Gabe *f* dose

Gabel *f* (Telef.) cradle; (Deichsel) shaft, fork (rod elevator), prong, bracket (artil.), bifurcation (foundry ladle), shank, slit, slotted jaw, two- or four-wire connection, branch connection **~ eines Spinnrades** heck of a spinning wheel **~ des Tischfernsprechers** cradle (teleph.) **~ zur Zugstange** connecting fork **doppelseitige ~** double-end shank (ladle) **zweizinkige ~** double-pronged fork

Gabel-achse *f* forked axle **-amt** *n* bifurcation station **-anker** *m* forked tie **-antrieb** *m* (Seilbahn) rope fork drive **-arm** *m* fork arm **-artig** forked, furcated, bifurcate **-aufhängung in Gabelaufhängung gelagertes Fernrohr** telescope mounted on trunnions in fork bearing **-aufnahme** *f* forked bed **-auge** *n* eye of an eyebolt, eye of the fork (cycles) **-ausführung** *f* V-shape **-balken** *m* (Dampfmaschine) bedplate with crosshead guides **-baum** *m* shaft of a forked thill

Gabelspannung *f*, **dreifache ~** treble draft

Gabel-bieger *m* shaft bender **-bilden** *n* **-bildung** *f* bracketing method of adjustment of fire, bracketing **-blitz** *m* forked lightning **-bock** *m* forked stand, bracket for bell crank **-bolzen** *m* shackle bolt, clevis pin, fork pin **-deichsel** *f* pair of shafts, thill **-diopter** *m* forked peep sight **-drahtführer** *m* fork wire guide **-fahrt** *f* splitting or straddling of points **-falle** *f* fork member **-feile** *f* tongue file **-förmig** forked **-führung** *f* fork guide

Gabelgelenk *n* fork joining, link joint **-bolzen** *m* pin of forked (knuckle) joint **-stück** *n* forked link

Gabel-halter für Scheinwerfer forked headlight bracket **-haken** *m* claw hook **-haue** *f* double, forked or two-pronged hoe **-hebel** *m* forked lever, cut-out (slotted) lever **-hebelwelle** *f* forked steering-arm shaft **-heft** *n* double-pronged tiller **-heuwender** *m* fork-type tedder **-holz** *n* futtock crotch **-hubkarren** *m* fork-lift truck **-klammer** *f* forked clamp

Gabelkopf *m* forkhead (of connecting rod), yoke, clevis; (Verbindungsstück) yoke end (joint) **-bolzen** *m* clevis pin

Gabel-kreuz *n* pall **-lafette** *f* gun carriage with shafts **-lager** *n*, **-lagerung** *f* trunnion bearing, fork bearing **-lehre** *f* external caliper gauge **-leine** *f* branching line **-maße** *pl* log calipers **-mehl** *n* superfine flour **-montierung** *f* fork (type) mounting **-motor** *m* V-type engine

gabeln to bifurcate, fork, bracket (artil.) **sich ~** to intersect, fork, bifurcate

Gabel-niete *f* bifurcated rivet **-öse** *f* eye of connecting rod **-pfanne** *f* shank ladle, foundry or casting ladle (large) **-pleuel** *n*, **-pleuelstange** *f* forked connecting rod **-rahmen** *m* forked bed **-rechen** *m* rake

Gabelriegel einer Gabeldeichsel shaft bar of a forked thill

Gabelriegelband *n* strap of the limber tail

Gabelrohr *n* (flanged) Y piece, forked or bifurcated pipe, tube **-schaft** *m* shaft of a forked thill **-niete** *f* bifurcated tubular rivet

Gabel-rollendrahtführer *f* triple wire guide **-rührer** *m* fork-shaped agitator **-schalter** *m* telephone switch hook

Gabelschaltung *f* four-wire terminating set, matched transformers, matching repeating coils **~** (Gegensprechgabel) split (duplex) connection **Mehrfachtelegraph in ~** forked multiplex telegraph

Gabel-schaufel *f* fork shovel **-scheide** *f* fork girder or blade **-schlüssel** *m* fork wrench or spanner, structural wrench, fork spanner, open-end wrench, engineers wrench (spanner) **-schraubenschlüssel** *m* open end wrench **-schuh** *m* forked fitting, jaw fitting, clevis **-schwanz** *m* twin tail **-spannschloß** *n* forked or clevis endturnbuckle **-stahl** *m* fork steel **-stange** *f* fork rod, forked connecting rod **-stapler** *m* fork-lift, fork truck, high-lift fork stacking truck, fork lift truck type conveyancer **-stiel** *m* Y-strut, forked strut **-stiftschlüssel** *m* straddle wrench

Gabelstück *n* end piece fork (for spring), two-way breeches piece **~ der Pleuelstange** crosstail butt, strap, or stud

Gabelstütze *f* bipod, forked prop, cradle rest (teleph.) **~ für Laufbretter** fork for running boards

Gabel-symmetrie *f* hybrid balance **-teilung** *f* furcation, bifurcation **-träger** *m* cradle carrier, fork support **-tragriemen** *m* backband **-transportmechanismus** *m* system of forks **-übertrager** *m* hybrid transformer **-übertragung** *f* forked repeater **-umschalter** *m* cradle switch, hook switch

Gabel- und Endschaltungen *pl* hybrid and terminating networks

Gabelung *f* bracket (artil.), forking, bifurcation

Gabel-verbindung *f* slit and tongue, two-way communication **-verbindungsstange** *f* fork connecting rod **-verkehr** *m* two-way (radio) communication **-verstärker** *m* hybrid repeater **-visier** *n* forked sight **-wagen** *m* wagon with shafts, thill wagon, fork truck **-welle** *f* forked (steering-arm) shaft **-werk** *n* fork mechanism **-zapfen** *m* crosshead pin **-zinken** *pl* fork tines, tuning-fork prong or tine

Gadolinerde *f* gadolinite, gadolinium oxide

Gadoliniumnitrat *n* gadolinium nitrate

Gaffel *f* gaff, dog hook **-fall** *n* peak or throat halyard **-klaue** *f* gaff jaw **-liek** *n* gaff-head rope **-nock** *f* gaff end or peak **-rack** *n* gaff-jaw rope

Gagat *m* jet (mineral)

galaktisch galactic **-e Helligkeit** Galaxy brightness

Galaktometer *n* lactoscope, lactodensimeter, lactometer

Galakturonsäure *f* galacturonic acid

Galalith *n* galalith

Galanteriewaren *pl* fancy goods

Galeerenofen zur Läuterung des Schwefels furnace for the distillation of sulfur

galenisches Präparat galenical preparation

Galenit *n* galena

Galerie *f* gallery, step, drift

Galgen *m* gallows, bracket, girder; (Tiefbohrer) gin-pole **-amboß** *m* beakiron, anvil with one arm

Galipot *n* galipot, white resin

Gallapfel *m* gallnut **-aufguß** *m* infusion of gall-(nuts) **-auszug** *m* gall extract **-gerbsäure** *f* gallotannic acid **-säure** *f* gallic acid

Galle *f* gall, bitterness, salt water, undissolved sulfates in glass

Gallen-gerbstoff *m* gall tannin **-seife** *f* gall soap

Gallerieanordnung *f* gallery ports

gallern to refine metal

Gallert *n* gel, gelatine, jelly **-ähnlich** jelly-like,

gelatinous **-artig** gelatinous, colloidal
gallertig slimy
gallert-artig gelatinous, jellylike **-masse** *f* jelly-like substance **-säure** *f* pectic acid **-substanz** *f* colloid
Gallesche Kette roller chain
Gallion *n* cutwater, beakhead, nose of a ship, figurehead
Gallions-leiste *f* headrail (ships) **-stütze** *f* head timbers
Galliot *f* lugger
Gallitzenstein *m* goslarite
Gallium *n* gallium **-chlorid** *n* gallium chloride
Gallkette *f* stud chain
Gallone *f* gallon 4,54 l
Gallsche Gelenkkette Gall steel bushed chain, Gall-chain-link belting
Gallsche Kette Gall chain, band or roller chain
Gallus-gerbsäure *f* gallotannic acid **-säure** *f* gallic acid **-tinte** *f* gallic acid iron ink
Galmei *m* calamine, cadmia, zinc spar, smithsonite **-grau** *n* zinc gray
Galoppieren *n* galloping, pitching motion
Galtonpfeife *f* Galton pipe
Galvanisation *f* galvanization
galvanisch galvanic(al), conductive ~ **gefällt** electrodeposited ~ **getrennt** physically separated ~ **hergestellt** electroplated ~ **niedergeschlagen** to electrodeposit ~ **verbunden** conductively connected ~ **verzinnen** to tin-plate
galvanisch-e Anlage galvanic plant **-es Bad** electroplating bath **-es Element** galvanic cell or battery, voltaic cell or couple **-e Kette** voltaic cell or couple **-e Kuppelung** galvanic coupling, resistance coupling **-e Metallisierung** galvanic metallization **-e Metallüberziehung** electroplating **-er Niederschlag** electrodeposit **-e Plattierung** electroplating **-e Säule** pile **-er Überzug** electrodeposit **-e Verbindung** physical connection **-er Zinküberzug** zinc electrodeposited
Galvaniseur *m* galvanizer
Galvanisier-anlage *f*, **-anstalt** *f* galvanizing or electroplating plant
galvanisieren to electroplate, galvanize
Galvanisieren *n* electroplating, galvanizing, galvanoplastics
Galvanisierprozeß *m* plating or galvanizing process
galvanisiert galvanized **-es Eisen** galvanized iron **-es Rohr** galvanized pipe
Galvanisierung *f* galvanization, electrodeposition, electroplating
Galvanisierwerkstatt *f* electroplating shop
Galvanismus *m* galvanism, current electricity
Galvanispannung *f* Galvani potential, contact potential
Galvano *n* electrotype, electroplate **-biegeapparat** *m* apparatus for bending electrotypes **-chromie** *f* galvanic coloring **-graphische Abbildung** electrotype **-kaustik** *f* galvanic etching **-kohle** *f* coppered carbon **-magnetisch** galvanomagnetic
Galvanomesser mit unmittelbarer Ablesung direct-reading galvanometer
Galvanometer *m* galvanometer **kompensierter** ~ rheograph in which inertia and damping are compensated
Galvanometer-ablesegerät *n* galvanometer indicator **-konstante** *f* galvanometer constant **-kreis** *m* galvanometer circuit **-nebenschluß** *m* galvanometer shunt **-spiegel** *m* galvanometer mirror **-spule** *f* galvanometer coil
Galvano-metrie *f* galvanometry **-metrisch** galvanomagnetic **-plastik** *f* galvanoplastic (art), electroplating **-plastiker** *m* electrotyper
galvanoplastisch electroplating, galvanoplastic **-es Bad** electroplating bath
Galvanoplattierung *f* electroplating
Galvanoskop *n* galvanoscope, current detector
Galvanopyrometer *n* magnetic pyrometer
Galvanostegie *f* galvanoplastics, electroplating, electrodeposition
Galvano-technik *f* electroplating, galvanoplastics **-typie** *f* electro-typing
Gamaschen *pl* leggings, gaiters, puttees
Gamma gamma **-eisen** *n* gamma iron **-funktion** *f* gamma function **-korrektur** *f* gamma correction **-regelung** *f* gamma correction **-spektroskopie** *f* gamma spectroscopy **-strahlen** *pl* gamma rays **-wert** *m* gamma value, interval factor **-zählrohr** *n* gamma counter
gammeln to loiter, loaf
Gang *m* (Bewegung) motion; (Maschine) movement, running, operation, action; (Haus corridor, hall; (Röhre) duct; (Gewinde) worm, thread; (Motorgeschwindigkeit) speed, gear; (Bergbau) tunnel, gallery; (Bahn) course, walk, gait, passage, gangway, procedure, pitch (of thread), variation (of a curve), dike, working (of a machine), way, process, play, trend, drift, heat run, heat (of a melt), run (of a furnace), pass (in rolling), seam (min.), lode, spire (of a screw), function, response (characteristic) ~ **auf** ~ interval between one thread (of screw) and the next or between two coils of a spring ~ **mit hochwertigen Erzen** live hole ~ **eines Gewindes** pitch or thread of a screw ~ **einer geräuschlosen Kette** motion of a silent chain ~ **eines Ofens** working of a furnace ~ **zum Operieren der Tore** walkway for operating bridges ~ **eines Schmelzofens** run of a smelter (blast) furnace **toter** ~ **einer Schraube** backlash or lost motion of a screw **der** ~ **ändert das Streichen** the lode changes its course **nach der Tiefe sich auskeilender** ~ gash vein
Gänge auf einen Zoll threads per inch
Gang, in ~ **bringen** to actuate, start **einen** ~ **einrücken** to put into a gear **auf leichten** ~ **prüfen** to check for freedom **außer** ~ **sein** to be out of gear, idle **außer** ~ **setzen** to put out of operation or service, stop the engine **in** ~ **setzen** to start, throw in gear, put into action, engage **im** ~ **sein** to be working, work, be in operation **plötzlich in** ~ **setzen** to trip **plötzlich außer** ~ **setzen** to trip out **vom ersten auf den zweiten** ~ **übergehen** to change over from first to second speed **den** ~ **verlangsamen** to slow down the engine **ein** ~ **verwirft einen anderen** one lode is faulted by the other **der** ~ **wird mächtiger** the lode grows
Gang, abgebauter ~ exhausted vein **dritter** ~ third speed **durchsetzender** ~ cross course **echter** ~ fissure vein **erster** ~ starting gear **flacher** ~ flats (geol.) **flachfallender** ~ lode of medium dip **frei von totem** ~ free from end play, no backlash **garer** ~ good working
Gang, geheimer ~ private corridor **gelöster** ~

levelfree vein **geräuschloser ~** noiseless running (engine) **geräuschvoller ~** noisy running (engine) **heißer ~** hot working **kalter ~** cold working **leerer ~** backlash **leichter ~** soft or smooth running **offener ~** cavernous lode **rauher ~ des Motors** rough engine operation **gleich schneller ~** isochronism **ruhiger ~** silent, quiet, or noiseless running **seigerer ~** almost vertical lode **spielfreier ~** movement free from play **tauber ~** dead or poor lode **tonnlägiger ~** lode of steep dip

Gang, toter ~ backlash, lost motion, steering play, dead path (thermometer), dead running, dead run, dead travel **übersetzender oder anscharender ~** counterlode **unmittelbarer ~** direct drive **unregelmäßiger, unterbrochener ~** irregular lode, flying reef **unruhiger ~** noisy running **unterer ~** low gear **in vollem ~** at full speed **zügiger ~** intimate or positive threading of gear

Gang-änderung *f* change in speed **-anordnung** *f* gear-change diagram **-art** *f* gangue, dross or earthy dilution of ore, gait, matrix **-anzeigeleuchte** *f* speed indicator light

gangbar commercial, current, marketable, passable, salable, practicable **-e Ware** goods of a ready sale

gangbarste Sorten leading species

Gang-begrenzung *f* side wall of a vein **-bergbau** *m* working of lodes **-breite der Schraube** width of the thread **-einstellung** *f* running fit (aviation) **-erz** *n* vein ore, loadstone **-führungsplatte** *f* gate selector **-füllung** *f* vein infilling **-gefolgschaft** *f* vein accompaniments **-genauigkeit** *f* accuracy (said of clocks) **-geschwindigkeit** *f* rate **-gestein** *n* gangue, vein stuff, dross or earthy dilution of ore **-gesteine** *pl* dike rocks **-hauer** *m* lode miner **-hebel** *m* shift lever, speed lever

Ganghöhe *f* axial spacing of turns (pitch), pitch (of a winding, screw, thread, or spiral), amplitude **~ der Schraube, ~ des Schraubengewindes** pitch of the screw thread **~ des Spins bei Detonationen** pitch of spin in detonations **~ der Windungen** pitch of turns

gängig marketable, salable, current, threaded, pitched **~ machen** to play in, work in **-er Typ** current types

Gängigkeit *f* number of starts

Gang-kondensator *m* gang condenser **-konstanz** *f* constant speed (drive) **-kontrolle** *f* working control (watch) **-körper** *m* lode matter **-lette** *f* gouge **-linie** *f* progress line **-masse** *f* gangue rock or material **-mittel** *n* shoot (min.) **-netz** *n* network of veins

Gang-pflug ohne Sitz walking plow **-pfosten** *m* baluster **-reserve** *f* running reserve **-richtung** *f* thread direction **-rolle** *f* pivoted dial on a speedometer **-schaltanlage** *f* speed selection system **-schalten** *n* speed changing **-schaltgetriebe** *n* gear switch mechanism **-schaltsteueranlage** *f* speed selection control system **-schaltung** *f* gear shift **-setzen** *n* escapement setting **-spalte** *f* vein fissure, abra

Gangspill *n* capstan **-kopf** *m* sapstan drumhead

Gang-stein *m* gangue **-teilchen** *n* gangue particle **-trumm** *n* secondary lode, branch of a vein **-umkehrprinzip** *n* path reversed principle **-unterschied** *m* phase or path difference, relative retardation

Gang-verschiebung *f* phase displacement **-verzögerung** *f* cycle delay **-verzweigung** *f* network of lodes **-wählhebel** *m* gear-control hand lever **-wähler** *m* gear selector, speed selector (preselector) **-wand** *f* lode wall **-wechsel** *m* changewheel gear (speed), change of speed, gear shift **-wechselgetriebe** *n* speed-change gear, gear shift **-werk** *n* machine driving gear

Gangzahl *f* threads per unit, number of gears **~ des Gewindeteiles eines Gewindebohrers** threaded portion of a tap **~ eines Wälzfräsers oder einer Schnecke** number of starts of a hob or a worm

Gangzug *m* range of veins

Ganister *m* ganister, dinas

Gans *f* a pig or crude lump of different metals

Gänsefuß *m* patch (for cordage of airship), crow'sfoot (aviation), rigging patch, spider patch **-schar** *f* duckfoot (agric. mach.)

Gänsehals (Federstahl) goose-neck tool (springtool)

ganz all, whole, wholly, complete, entire, total, integral **~ bedeckt** totally overcast **~ groß** very big or important **nicht ~** fractional **~ rechts** extreme clockwise (position of knob) **-e Höhe** over-all height **-e Ladung** full cargo **-es Vielfaches** integral multiple **-e Zahl** whole number, integer, integral number

ganzautomatisch fully automatic

Ganzes *n* total, totality, whole, entirety

Ganz-fabrikat *n* finished article **-feld** *n* total field **-geviertstück** *n* emquad **-glasspritzen** *pl* all-glass syringes

Ganzheit *f* totality, whole, aggregation

Ganzholz *n* round or unhewn timber **-bauweise** *f* all-wood construction **-flugzeug** *n* airplane of allwood construction

Ganz-kasten *m* stuff chest **-lederband** *m* calf binding, calf-bound volume

gänzlich entire, thorough, whole, total

Ganzlochwicklung *f* integer-slot winding

ganzmattierte Lampe all-frosted lamp

Ganzmetall *n* all metal, duralumin **-bauart** *f* **-bauweise** *f* all-metal construction **-flugzeug** *n* all-metal airplane **-wand** *f* all-metal (projection) screen

Ganz-montage *f* complete assembly **-polkegel** *m* body cone, conical dipole **-rational** rational integral **-seitig** full-page

ganzselbsttätige Maschine fully automatic machine

Ganzstahl *m* all-steel **-bau** *m* all-steel body **-bauweise** *f* all-steel construction **-gehäuse** *n* all-steel casing **-karosserie** *f* all-steel body

ganztägig diurnal

Ganzton *m* whole tone

ganzzahlig integral **-e Ladung** integral spin, charge **-e vielfache Resonanz** submultiple resonance

Ganzzahligkeit *f* integralness, property of being an integer

Ganzzeug *n* whole stuff, pulp, paper pulp, finished product **-holländer** *m* beating engine, beater, finisher **-kasten** *m* stuff chest

gar refined, carbonized, coked, done, quite, very **~ aufbrechen** to break up the lump (metal.) **Stahl ~ machen** to refine steel **vollständig ~** burned off

Garage *f* garage
Gäranlage *f* fermenting plant
Garantie *f* guarantee, security, warrant **-leistung** *f* suretyship
garantieren to guarantee, warrant
garantierter Brennstoffverbrauch guaranteed full load fuel consumption
Garantie-schein *m* certificate of warranty, letter of indemnity, bond **-spiegel** *m* guaranteed mirror **-wert** *m* guaranteed value **-zink** *n* a commercial brand of zinc
Garanzin *n* garancine
gärbar fermentable
Garbe *f* pile, fagot, cone or sheaf of fire, sheaf, ray, cone of dispersion
Gärbecken *n* receptable for beer working out of the bunghole
gärben to refine
Garben-auflader *m* bundle loader **-band** *n* wisp of straw for tying sheaves **-binder** *m* grain binder, reaper, binder **-hocker** *m* grain shocker **-schiefer** *m* garbenschiefer (a spotted rock in which the spots resemble caraway seeds) **-selbstbinder** *m* sheaf-binding engine **-träger** *m* conveyer bundle carrier, grain lifter, elevator
Gärbottich *m* fermentation vat
Gar-brand *m* finishing burn (ceramics) **-brenne** *f* fired to maturity (ceramics) **-brennen** *n* hardening on
Gärbstahl *m* wrought or sheer steel, refined steel
Gär-bütte *f* fermenter, fermenting round **-dauer** *f* time of fermentation
Garderobe *f* wardrobe, vestiary **-webstuhl** *m* curtain-lace machine **-zugvorrichtung** *f* curtain-drawing device
Gardine *f* curtain
Gare *f* refined or finished state, temper (of metal)
Gareisen *n* trial rod
garen to refine, coke
gären to ferment, froth, effervesce
Garen der Metalle refining metals
Garerz *n* roasted ore
Gär-erzeugnis *n* fermentation product **-fähig** fermentable, fermentative **-faulverfahren** *n* fermentation-putrefaction process **-futterbehälter** *m* fermenting container for food
Gargang *m* refining process **~ des Hochofens** steady working of the blast furnace
Gargel *f* chime, croze (the groove itself) **-kamm** *m* grooving comb, notcher or crozer (cooper's)
gargeln, ein Faß ~ to notch or to groove a cask, to make the chimes of a cask
Gargelsäge *f* grooving saw
Garherd *m* refining hearth
Gärkeller *m* fermentation cellar, fermenting room
Gärkraft *f* fermentative energy or power **-bestimmung** *f* fermentative test
Gär-küfe *f* grape trough (press) **-kupfer** *n* refined copper, rosette copper
Gär-messer *m* zymometer **-mittel** *n* ferment
Garn *n* yarn, twine, thread, net **geschleiftes ~** double mule twist **gezwirntes ~** doubled yarn **meliertes ~** melange yarn
Garn-anfeuchtmaschine *f* conditioning machine **-anknüpferin** *f* yarn mender **-appretur** *f* yarn finishing **-aufhänger** *m* yarn taker-off **-aufkarter** *m* card winder **-aufwindemaschine** *f* drawing-in frame **-ausgeber** *m* yarn carrier
Garn-baum *m* warp or yarn beam **-bürstmaschine** *f* yarn-brushing machine **-dichtung** *f* yarn packing **-eisen** *n* refined iron **elastizitätsmesser** *m* apparatus for testing elasticity of yarn **-festigkeitsprüfer** *m* yarn-strength tester **-glätter** *m* hank polisher
Garnhaspel *f* reeling frames and reels (unwinding), yarn reel **-maschine** *f* yarn-winding machine
garnieren to trim
Garnierit *m* garnierite
Garnierung *f* bushing, lining
Garnison *f* garrison
Garnitur *f* fittings, mountings, furniture set, garniture, suit, set, trimmings **~ der Trommel** cylinder clothing
Garniturteile *pl* fittings
Garn-kiste *f* case of yarn **-knötchen** *n* little knot in silk yarn **-kötzer** *m* cop **-merzerisiermaschine** *f* hank mercerizing machine **-rolle** *f* spool of thread yarn, reel, core, reel of cotton **-rollenkern** *m* yarnreel core **-rollenröhre** *f* cotton-reel valve **-schlichtung** *f* yarn sizing **-streckmaschine** *f* yarn-tentering machine
Garn-trense *f* yarn worming **-verdämpfer** *m* yarn steamer **-wechseleinrichtung** *f* yarn-changing attachment **-weife** *f* reel **-winde** *f* reel **-windemaschine für die Textilindustrie** winding machine for textile industry **-zwirner** *m* twister
Garprobe *f* refining assay
Garretstraße *f* Garret (looping-rod) mill
Gar-rösten *n* finishing roasting **-schaum** *m* kish **-scheibe** *f* plate of refined copper, rose copper disk **-schlacke** *f* refining slag **-schlackenboden** *m* refining-slag bed
Gär-stoff *m* ferment **-tank** *m* fermenting tank **-tätigkeit** *f* fermentative activity **-teich** *m* fermentation pond
Gartenbau *m* gardening, horticulture **-betrieb** *m* market gardening
Garten-fräse *f* rotary tiller for gardens **-geräte** *pl* gardening tools **-kunst** *f* horticulture **-messer** *n* pruning knife
Gärtner *m* gardener
Gärtnerei *f* gardening nursery
Gärtnerschere *f* pruner, pruning tool
Garung *f* coking
Gärung *f* fermentation **in ~ übergehen** to enter into fermentation
Garungsdauer *f* coking time
Gärungs-alkohol *m* ethyl alcohol **-chemie** *f* fermentation chemistry **-erregend** zymogenic **-erreger** *m* ferment **-erscheinung** *f* anomaly during the fermentation **-fähigkeit** *f* fermentability **-hemmend** antizymotic, fermentation-inhibiting **-lehre** *f* zymology **-messer** *m* zymometer **-physiologie** *f* zymotechnology **-pilz** *m* ferment **-stoff** *m* zyme, ferment **-technik** *f* zymotechnology
Gärwärme *f* heat of fermentation
Gas *n* gas **~ absaugen** to draw off gas **~ entwickeln** to evolve gas **~ ganz wegnehmen** to close the throttle **~ geben** to open (out the) throttle, open up the engine **~ zurücknehmen** to throttle back, throttle down the engine
Gas, absorbiertes ~ absorbed gas **armes ~, ge-**

ringwertiges ~ poor or lean gas **heizkräftiges** ~ gas of high calorific value **hochwertiges** ~ rich gas **inertes** ~ rare gas **künstliches** ~ artificial or manufactured gas **okkludiertes** ~ occluded gas **verdünntes** ~ rarefied gas **zerknallbares** ~ explosive gas

Gas-abblaseverfahren *n* gas-release method **abdichtung** *f* gas check **-abführung** *f* gas outlet or exhaust, gas escape **-abflußrohr** *n* bleeder pipe to let off gas **-abfuhr** *f* venting **-abgabe** *f* emission of gas **-abgang** *m* gas issue, withdrawal or offtake, gas delivery **-ableitung** *f* gas take-off (in pipe), downcomer (of blast furnace) **-absaugungsanlage** *f* gas-suction plant **-abscheider** *m* gas separator, gas trap, vapor eliminator **-abteil** *n* gas compartment

Gasabzug *m* gas outlet or drain **-öffnung** *f* gas-draining vent

gasähnlich gaseous

Gas-analyse *f* gas analysis **-anfall** *m* gas yield **-anker** *m* gas anchor **-anlasser** *m* gas starter **-ansammlung** *f* accumulation of gas **-anstalt** *f* gas plant, retort-coke plant, retort-coke plant, gas-making plant

Gasanstalts-koks *m* gashouse coke **-retorte** *f* gashouse retort

Gas-antrieb *m* water-gas drive **-anwärmegehäuse** *n* gas-heating jacket **-anwärmer** *m* heating jacket **-anzeiger** *m* gas-detector kit or set **-anzug** *m* gas-protection suit **-anzünder** *m* gas lighter or igniter **-arm** *m* gas bracket

gasarm deficient in gas **-es Gemisch** weak gas mixture **-e Kohle** nongasceous coal

Gasarmatur *f* gas fitting

gasartig gaseous, gasiform **-er Brennstoff** gaseous fuel

Gas-atmosphäre *f* gaseous atmosphere **-aufnahme** *f* occlusion or absorption of gas

Gasaufzehrung *f* getter(ing), absorption of gases **plötzliche** ~ cleanup, sudden gas absorption

Gas-ausbeute *f* gas output or yield **-ausbruch** *m* gas outburst or eruption, (violent) liberation or escape of gas **ausgang** *m* gas outlet **-ausströmung** *f* efflux of gas **-austauch** *m* exchange or escape of gas **-ausgang** *m* gas outlet **-auscleanup** or expulsion, outgasing, degasing, gettering **-austritt** *m* gas leakage **-austrittsöffnung** *f* gas outlet **-automat** *m* slot or automatic gas apparatus, mechanical gas seller

Gas-badeofen *m* gas stove for baths, gas geyser

Gasballast-pumpe *f* gas ballest pump **-einrichtung** *f* gas ballast device **-steuerung** *f* gas ballast regulator **-ventil** *n* gas ballast valve

Gas-ballung *f* gas concentration **-bedarf** *m* natural gas requirements **-befeuerung** *f* gas lighting **-beförderung** *f* natural gas transportation **-behaftete Oberfläche** *f* gas-contaminated surface, surface with adsorbed gas **-behälter** *m* gasometer, gasholder, gas tank **-beheizt** gas-fired **-bekleidung** *f* protective clothing **-beleuchtung** *f* gas lighting **-bereitschaft** *f* gas alert, precaution against gas

Gas-beschädigter *m* gas casualty **-beschaffenheit** *f* gas quality **-betätigung** *f* gas throttle **-betonstein** *m* aerated cement block **-bildung** *f* gasification **-bindung** *f* getter(ing) **-bläschen** *pl* gas bubbles **-blase** *f* gas bubble, blowhole (in casting), gas cavity, gas hole or pocket

Gasblasen-bildung *f* cavitation, occlusion of gases **-seigerung** *f* spot segregation, blowhole segregate **-schwingung** *f* oscillation of gas globe **-strömungsmesser** *m* bubble gauge

Gas-bohrung *f* gas well **-bombe** *f* gas cylinder, gas bomb, chemical bomb **-bohrturm** *m* gas drilling derrick **-brand** *m* gas gangrene **-brenner** *m* gas burner **-brennerzange** *f* burner pliers **-brennschnitt** *m* gas cut

Gas-brille *f* gas goggles **-bügeleisen** *n* gas flatiron **-bürette** *f* gas burette **-dicht** gastight, impermeable to air, evaporation-proof

Gasdichte *f* density of a gas **-messer** *m* gas-density meter or gauge, dasymeter

Gas-dichtigkeit *f* impermeability to gas **-diffusion** *f* gaseous diffusion **-diffusionsverfahren** *n* gaseous diffusion method **-drehgriff** *m* (Motorrad) twist grip throttle control **-drosselgestänge** *n* gas-throttle controls **-drosselklappe** *f* gas-throttle valve **-drosselung** *f* gas throttling

Gasdruck *m* gas pressure, blowback **-fernzünder** *m* gas-pressure igniter at distance **-minderer** *m* gas-pressure reducing valve **-lader** *m* gas-operated gun, blowback-operated weapon **-messer** *m* gas-pressure meter **-meßgerät** *n* gas-pressure gauge **-prüfung** *f* gas-pressure test **-regler** *m* gas-pressure regulator

Gas-durchflußionisationskammer *f* gas flow ionization chamber **-durchflußzählrohr** *n* gas-flow counter **-durchgang** *m* gas passage **-durchlässig** permeable to gas **-durchlässigkeit** *f* permeability to gas **-durchlauferhitzer** *m* multi-point gas water heater **-düse** *f* nozzle, gas jet, gas-cylinder nozzle **-dynamik** *f* dynamics of gases **-dynamo** *m* gas engine generator **-einlaß** *m* suction nozzle or head (gas intake) **-einpreßbohrung** *f* inlet well **-einrichtung** *f* gas fitting

Gas-einsatz *m* employment of gas, chemical warfare **-einsatzhärtung** *f* gas casehardening process **-einsatzofen** *m* gas-fired heat treating furnace **-einschluß** *m* occlusion of gas, blowhole (metal.) **-einsteller** *m* gas regulator

gasen to gas, evolve gas

Gasen *n* steaming (in water-gas process), steaming period ~ (im Ruhezustand) gassing

gasend gassing

Gas-entartung *f* gas degeneracy **-entbindungsflasche** *f* gas bottle **-entladung** *f* gas discharge

Gasentladungs-gefäß *n* gas tube, gas-discharge tube, thyratron **-lampe** *f* glow lamp, glow-discharge tube or lamp, luminous-discharge lamp **-plasma** *n* gas discharge plasma **-relais** *n* gasfilled relay, gas-discharge relay **-rohr** *n* gas-discharge tube or valve **-röhre** *f* (für Lichtblitze) flash tube **-röhre** *f* gas-filled valve **-strecke** *f* gas-discharge path **-ventil** *n* (Ionenventil) gas-filled rectifier

Gas-entlastung *f* gas pressure relief **-entlüftungsschacht** *m* exhaust-gas trunk (airship) **-entnahmestutzen** *m* gas-intake pipe **-entschwefler** *m* gas desulfurisation plant **-entwickler** *m* gas producer or generator **-entwicklung** *f* formation or generation of gas, gassing, giving off of gas **-entwicklungsapparat** *m* gas generator **-entziehungsvorrichtung** *f* apparatus for taking off gases **-ergiebigkeit** *f* gas yield **-erkennungsdienst** *m* gas-detecting service **-erkennungs-**

mittel *n* gas detector

Gaserzeuger *m* gas producer or generator ~ **mit drehbarem Rost** rotary-grate-type gas producer ~ **mit festem Rost** dry-bottom or fixed-grate-type gas producer, simple stationary gas producer ~ **ohne Rost** wet-bottom gas producer ~ **mit drehbarem Schacht** rotary-body-type gas producer ~ **mit Schrägrost** inclined-grate-type gas producer **geblasener** ~ pressure gas producer **gezogener** ~ suction gas producer **rostloser** ~ wet-bottom gas producer

Gaserzeuger-anlage *f* gas-producer unit or plant **-gas** *n* producer gas **-grube** *f* gas-producer pit **-mantel** *m* gas-producer shell **-wirkungsgrad** *m* gas-producer efficiency

Gas-erzeugung *f* gas generation or production, gasification **-erzeugungsanlage** *f* gas plant, gas-producing plant **-fabrik** *f* gasworks **-fach** *n* gas engineering **-fachmann** *m* gas engineer **-faktor** *m* gassing factor **-fang** *m* gas collector, gas take **-feld** *n* gas field

Gasfernversorgungs-anlage *f*, **-netz** *n* gas plant for long-distance supply

gas-feuern to gas fire **-feuerung** *f* gas furnace, gas firing **-filter** *m* gas filter **-flammenprobe** *f* gas-flash test **-flammförderkohle** *f* long-flaming run-of-the-mine gas coal **-flammkohle** *f* long-flame gas coal, open-burning coal **-flammofen** *m* gas-fired air furnace, gas-fired reverberatory furnace **-flammofenfrischen** *n* gas puddling **-flasche** *f* gas cylinder or bottle

Gasflaschen-behälter *m* gas-flask container **-glocke** *f* gas bell **-mantel** *m* cylinder envelope, weld **-pore** *f* cylinder pocket, blowhole **-schweißverfahren** *n* cylinder welding **-überschuß** *m* excess of gas **-ventil** *n* valve of gas container **-verbrauch** *m* gas consumption

Gas-fokussierung *f* gas focusing **-fördergebläse** *n* gas feed blower **-förderkohle** *f* run-of-the-mine gas coal, gas coal

gasförmig gaseous **-es Öl** (Öl in der Gasphase) oil in the form of a vapor **-es Wasser** water in gaseous state

gas-frei free of gases **-freiheit** *f* absence of gases **-frischen** *n* gas puddling **-führend** gassy, gas containing **-führung** *f* gas distribution, direction of gas flow, gas-heating operation or regulation **-führungssystem** *n* gas-inlet system **-füllung** *f* gas filling, gas content **-füllzählrohr** *n* gas filling counter tube **-funde** *pl* gas discoveries

Gasfußhebel *m* accelerator pedal **-feder** *f* accelerator-control rod **-welle** *f* accelerator-pedal shaft

Gas-fußtritt *m* accelerator pedal **-fußwelle** *f* accelerator shaft **-gebläse** *n* gas-driven engine blower, gas blower, high-pressure exhauster **-gebläselampe** *f* gas-blast burner **-gebläsemaschine** *f* gas engine driven blower **-gebührenerheber** *m* gas-rate collector **-gefahr** *f* danger of gas **-gefeuert** gas-fired

gasgefüllt gas-filled (of a lamp bulb) **-e Birne** gas-filled bulb **-e Lampe** gas-filled lamp **-e Röhre** gascontent tube, gas-filled tube, gaseous tube

Gas-gehalt *m* gas content, gas factor, gas-oil ratio **-gehäuse** *n* gas-filled housing **-geheizter Muffelofen** gas-fired muffle furnace **-gelagerter Kreisel** *m* gas bearing gyro **-gemisch** *n* gas mixture or compound, gaseous mixture, fuel mixed with air **-generator** *m* gas producer or generator **-geruch** *m* smell of gas **-geschützt** gas-proofed **-gestänge** *n* throttle control rod

Gasgewinde *n* gas-pipe thread **-bohrer** *m* **-schneidebohrer** *m* gas-pipe tap **-schneidekluppe** *f* gas-thread pipe stock **-schneidemaschine** *f* diestock for gas pipes

Gas-gewinnung *f* gas generation or production **-glocke** *f* gasholder, gas bell (small holder)

Gasglühlicht *n* incandescent gas light **-beleuchtung** *f* incandescent gas lighting **-brenner** *m* incandescent gas burner

Gas-grus *m* **-gruskohle** *f* gas slack **-hahn** *m* gas tap, gas cock **-haltig** gaseous **-hammer** *m* gas hammer **-handschuh** *m* gas-protection glove **-härteofen** *m* gas-fired furnace for hardening **-hauptleitungen** *pl* gas mains **-haus** *n* gas-filled housing **-haushalt** *m* gas content

Gashebel *m* accelerator, (gas) throttle, throttle lever ~ **am Führersitz** (Flugzeug) pilot's throttle lever

Gashebelbock *m* throttle quadrant or box

Gas-heberanlage *f* gas lift **-heizofen** *m* gas stove **-heizung** *f* gas heating **-heizwert** *m* heating value of gas **-heizwertzahl** *f* calorific value of gas, heating value per unit weight of gas **-hub** *m* gas lift **-hülle** *f* gas bag (ballonn), gaseous envelope

gasig gaseous

Gas-inhalt *m* gas content or capacity, gas-oil ratio **-installationswerk** *n* gas-fitting work **-installatör** *m* gas fitter **-kalorimeter** *m* gas calorimeter **-kältemaschine** *f* gas refrigerating machine **-kammer** *f* gas chamber, gas-checker chamber, gas-regenerating chamber **-kammerofen** *m* gas-chamber kiln

Gas-kanal *m* gas conduit, duct, or flue **-kessel** *m* gas boiler **-kissen** *n* gas cushion **-kluppe** *f* gas-pipe stock **-kocher** *m* (slang) engine **-koeffizient** *m* gassing factor **-kohle** *f* gas coal (high-grade bituminous coal) **-koks** *m* gas coke, retort-oven coke, retort coke **-konstante** *f* gas constant

Gas-konzentration *f*, **-konzentrierung** *f* gas focusing or concentration, ionic focusing **-kraftmaschine** *f* gas engine **-krank** gas-poisoned, gassed **-kranz** *m* gas ring (heater) **-ladepumpe** *f* gas-compression pump **-leitung** *f* gas main, line, or pipe, gas conduit or flue, gas-flue leading

Gasleitungs-armatur *f* gas-main fitting **-rohr** *n* gas main, gas pipe

Gas-lenkwand *f* baffle **-lötkolben** *m* gas soldering copper **-luftfahrzeug** *n* aerostat, lighter-than-air craft **-machen** *n* manufacture of gas **-mantel** *m* gas envelope **-maschine** *f* gas engine **-maschinengebläse** *n* gas-blowing engine **-maske** *f* gas mask, breather

Gas-meßapparat *m*, **-messer** *m* gas meter, gasometer **-messerschieber** *m* gasmeter slide valves **-meßrohr** *n* gas-measuring tube **-mischung** *f* gas mixture **-motor** *m* gas engine or machine **-nachfüllen** *n* topping up, refilling **-nebel** *m* gas spray **-niederdruckspeicherung** *f* low-pressure gas storage **-ofen** *m* gas furnace (coke oven) **-ofenbau** *m* gas-oven construction

Gasogen *n* producer-gas fuel (produced from wood charcoal or coal in the vehicle)

Gasöl *n* oil fuel, gas oil, Diesel fuel

Gasolin *n* gasoline, petroleum ether

Gasölverhältnis *n* gas-oil ratio

Gasometer *m* gasometer, gasholder, gas receiver

Gas-pedal *n* accelerator pedal **-pendelleitung** *f* compensation pipe **-periode** *f* steaming, steaming period **-permeabilität** *f* permeability to gas **-phase** *f* gas phase **-pipette** *f* gas-sampling tube, gas pipette **-polarisation** *f* gas polarization **-pore** *f* blowhole, pocket, pinhole, pipe **-probenahmegerät** *n* scanning gear **-prüfer** *m* eudiometer **-pumpe** *f* gas pump **-pyrometer** *m* gas pyrometer **-quelle** *f* gas source, (natural-)gas well

Gasraum *m* vapor space, gas-testing compartment, gas chamber **-probe** *f*, **-prüfung** *f* gas-chamber test

Gas-regler *m*, **-regulator** *m* gas regulator or governor, throttle **-regulierungsfußhebel** *m* accelerator control pedal

gasreich rich in gas **-e Kohle** gas coal

Gas-reinheit *f* purity of the gas **-reiniger** *m* gas cleaner, washer, or purifier, scrubber, disintegrator **-reinigung** *f* gas cleaning, conditioning, or separation **-reinigungsanlage** *f* gas-cleaning plant or installation **-reinigungswasser** *n* gas liquor **-reste** *pl* gas residue **-retorte** *f* gas retort **-retortenbetrieb** *m* gas-retort operation or practice **-richtung** *f* gas flow **-ring** *m* (Kolben) pressure (piston) ring **-rohr** *n* **-röhre** *f* gas pipe or tube

Gasrohr-leitung *f* gas piping **-schneidekluppe** *f* diestock **-schraubstock** *m* gas-tube or -pipe vice **-stiel** *m* gas-pipe handle **-zange** *f* gas pliers, plumber's pliers, gas fitters

Gas-röstofen *m* gas-fired calcining kiln **-rückstand** *m* residual gas

Gasruß *m* carbon (gas) black **aktiver ~** impingement black

Gas-sack *m* gasbag **-sammelleitung** *f* gas collecting main **-sammelrohr** *n* gas-collecting tube, gas-sample collector **-sammler** *m* gasholder, gasometer **-sauger** *m* gas exhauster

Gasschalter *m* gas-blast switch **-löschrohr** *n* extinguishing tube for gas-blast switch

Gas-schieber *m* gas sluice or slide valve, gate-type gas-regulating valve **-schlauch** *m* gas tube **-schleuse** *f* air lock, gas trap

Gasschmelzschweißung *f* autogenous welding, gas-torch welding, gas welding, oxyacetylene welding

Gasschürfrecht *m* gas leases

Gasschutz *m* (anti)gas protection, chemical defense **-mittel** *n* material for protection against gas

Gas-schwaden *pl* gas fumes **-schweißer** *m* gas welder **-schweißung** *f*, **-schweißverfahren** *n* gas welding, torch or autogenous welding **-schwingungen** *pl* gas vibrations

Gasse *f* alley, street

Gas-selbstanzünder *m* automatic gas lighter **-senge** (Gassengmaschine) gas singeing machine

gas-sicher gasproof **-sicherheitsapparat** *m* gas-safety device **-sieb** *n* gas filter

Gas-spannung *f* gas tension or pressure **-spannungsmesser** *m* crusher gauge **-sperre** *f* gas barrier, vapor lock, contaminated area **-spindel des Gashebels** throttle hand-lever tube **-spüren** *n* gas detection by smelling **-spürer** *m* gas sentry, gas-detector apparatus

Gasspür-mittel *n* gas-detection compound **-trupp** *m* gas-detection squad

Gas-steuerantrieb *m* gas control **-stiefel** *pl* gas-protection boots **-strecke** *f* gaseous path or gap (in a tube) **-strom** *m* flow of gas, gas current or stream **-stromstärke** *f* amount of flow **-strömung** *f* gas current or flow **-strömungsregelung** *f* gas-flow control **-strumpf** *m* gas mantle **-sumpf** *m* gas pocket

Gas-technik *f* gas engineering **-techniker** *m* gas engineer **-teer** *m* coal(-gas) tar, producer-gas tar **-teilungsröhre** *f* gas distributor, gas-distributing pipe

Gasthermometer *n* gas thermometer

Gas-tonne *f* gas buoy **-triode** *f* gas relay **-tritt** *m* accelerator pedal **-trockenofen** *m* gas fired drying furnace (or oven) **-trockner** *m* gas-drying apparatus

Gastropodenschale *f* gastropod shell

Gastsitz *m* passenger seat

Gastunit *m* gastunite

Gasturbine *f* gas turbine

Gas-überdruck *m* positive gas pressure **-überschuß** *m* excess of gas **-uhr** *f* gas meter **-umhang** *m* gas-protection cloak

Gas- und Massendrehkraft *f* torque due to gas and inertia forces, aerodynamic and inertia forces in turns

gasundurchlässig impermeable to gas, gastight **-e Gummischicht** gas-retaining rubber film

Gas-untersuchung *f* gas analysis **-ventil** *n* gas valve **-verbundnetz** *n* interlinked (interconnected) gas grid system **-verdichter** *m* gas compressor **-verflüssigungsanlage** *f* gas-liquefying plant **-vergiftet** poisoned by gas, gassed **-vergiftung** *f* gas poisoning or contamination

Gas-verschluß *m* gas seal, bell and hopper, cup-and-cone arrangement (furnace) **-verschlußschraube** *f* gland screw **-versorgung** *f* delivery (supply) of gas **-versorgungssystem** *n* gas grid system **-verstärkung** *f* gas magnification, gas amplification **-verteilungskanal** *m* gas-distributing channel **-volum(en)** *n* gas volume **-volumeter** *n* gas volumeter **-volumetrisch** gasometric **-vorhang** *m* gas curtain **-vorlage** *f* gas-offtake main **-vulkanisation** *f* gas cure

Gas-waage *f* gas balance or scale **-walzenzugmaschine** *f* gas-rolling-mill engine **-wärmespeicher** *m* gas regenerator **-warner** *m* gas-warning sentry **-warnung** *f* gas warning **-waschapparat** *m*, **-wäscher** *m* gas washer, scrubber or purifier, disintegrator, gaspurifying apparatus **-waschflasche** *f* gas-washing bottle **-waschvorrichtung** *f* gas scrubber

Gaswasser *n* weak ammonia water or liquor **verdünntes ~** diluted ammoniacal water

Gaswechsel-arbeit *f* gas-changing process **-eigenschaften** *f pl* **des Motors** breathing characteristics of a motor **-klappe** *f* gas-reversing valve, reversing gas valve

Gas-werk *n* gasworks, gashouse, gas plant **-wirbelbewegung** *f* vortex motion or turbulent movement of gas **-wolke** *f* cloud of gas **-zähler** *m* gas meter **-zange** *f* gas pliers or tongs **-zelle** *f* gas-filled photocell, gas phototube, gasbag, ballonet, cell, cellule, gas-filled photoemission cell **-zellenalarm** *m* pressure alarm **-zucht** *f* gas discipline **-zufuhr** *f* gas supply

Gaszuführung, zwangsläufige ~ forced induction

Gaszuführungs-rohr *n* gas-supply pipe, gas intake

-zug *m* gas flue, gas up-and-down-take flue
Gas-zünder *m* gas igniter **-zusammensetzung** *f* composition of gas **-zusatzmaschine** *f* gas booster **-zutritt** *m* gas supply
Gat(t) *n*, **Gatjen** *n* eyelet, hole
Gatsch *m* slack wax (of crude scale), crude paraffin
Gatter *n* crossbars, grating, grillage, lattice, frame, trellis, hatch, gate (el.) **-balken** *m* railway gate
gattern, das Zinn ~ to refine tin
Gatter-quersäge *f* crosscut frame saw **-rahmen** *m* saw frame **-säge** *f* gang saw, frame or reciprocating saw, log frame saw **-sägeblätter** *pl* mill saw blades **-säule** *f* saw guides **-tisch** *m* creel plate **-tor** *n* gate (general terms) barrier or spar gate
gattieren to mix, sort, classify, calculate or make up a charge
Gattierung *f* mixture, charge, mix, mixing, sorting, burden
Gattierungs-berechnung *f* calculation of mixture **-laufgewichtswaage** *f* scale transfer car for weighing up charges **-waage** *f* charging scales, burden balance **-wagen** *m* charging car
Gattung *f* species, genus, class, sort, kind, rubric, arm of the service, gender, breed
Gattungsname *m* class name, generic name
Gaufre *m* pebble (rayon mfg.)
Gaufrieranstalt *f* goffering, cloth-printing or -embossing plant
Gaufrieren *n* goffering, embossing
Gaufrier-gravierung *f* die engraving **-kalander** *m* embossing calender **-maschine** *f* embossing machine **-presse** *f* embossing press (metal) **-walze** *f* engraved brass cylinder
Gauß *n* gauss
Gaußmeter *n* Gauß'meter
Gaußokular *n* Gauß'ocular
Gaußsche Näherung *f* Gaussian approximation
Gaußsches Verteilungsnetz *n* nomogram, nomograph, graph of aritmetrical probabilities
Gaußsche Zahlenebene *f* complex-number plane, G-plane
Gaußverteilung *f* Gaussian-distribution
Gautiergitter *n* Gautier grid
Gautschbrett *n* plank
gautschen, Papier ~ to couch paper sheets
Gautscher *m* coucher
Gayerde *f* native saltpeter, saltpeter sweepings
Gaylüssit *m* gaylussite
Gaysalpeter *m* native or swept saltpeter, saltpeter sweepings
Gaze *f* gauze **baumwollene ~** cotton gauze **broschierte ~** figured gauze
Gaze-aufspannvorrichtung *f* gauze stretching device **-band** *n* gauze ribbon **-binde** *f* gauze bandage **-boden** *m* gauze bottom **-bürste** *f* gauze brush **-geschirr** *m* gauze loom **-gewebe** *n* gauze **-papier** *n* tissue paper **-schaft** *m* leaf of the gauze loom **-sieb** *n* gauze sieve **-verband** *m* gauze dressing or bandage
Geäder *n* veined structure, marbling, grain, network
geädert, streaky, veined, mottled (cast iron)
gealtert aged
Gebälk *n* frame(work), beams, joists
geballt concentrated -e Ladung demolition charge of T.N.T., pole charge
gebankt bedded
Gebäude *n* structure, building, **-gruppe** *f* group or block of houses **-trockner** *m* salamander
gebauter Balken oder Träger built-up girder
gebaute und halbgebaute Kurbelwelle built-up and semibuilt crankshaft
Gebeeinrichtung *f* transmitter apparatus
gebeizt (Holz) stained; (Metall) pickled
geben to transmit, send, give (off or up), impart, signal, put on **sich ~** to cede, give way **Gas ~** to give gas, open the throttle **Vollgas ~** to open the throttle wide
Geber *m* (Morse-key) sender or transmitter, selsyn, azimuth and elevation indicator (radar), any kind of originator of signals, reproducer (acoust.) **~ eines Fernanzeigegerätes** remote-control head **~** (eines Meßgerätes) transmitting-type device, transmitter, pickup **~ für Wasserstandsfernmelder** transmitter for water-level teleindicators
Geber-amt *n* transmitting station **-anlage** *f* selsyn **-anlagehöhe** *f* elevation selsyn **-element** *n* transducer **-ende** *n* sending end **-gerät zur Messung von Schwingungsbeanspruchungen** vibration strain pickup **-schalter für Leuchtweiteregler** cutout switch for lightrange regulator **-seite** *f* (einer Meßeinrichtung) transmitting end **-station** *f* transmitting station **-stecker** *m* transmitter plug **-strom** *m* signal current **-welle** *f* transmitting wave (radio) **-wicklung** *f* pick-up winding
Gebetempo *n* rate of sending
gebeugtes Licht diffracted light
Gebevorrichtung *f* transmitter arrangement
Gebiet *n* district, field, territory, region, province area, zone **~ der mittleren Energie** intermediate energy region **~ des reinen Gefühles** range of pure sensation **komplexes ~** complex domain (math.) **reelles ~** real domain (math.) **~ der Vergütung** range of heat treatment
Gebiets-feld *n* square mining claim, extended concession **-kollokation** *f* domain collocation **-teil** *m* area, district, region, zone
Gebilde *n* figure, image, formation, structure, system, organization, form
gebildet learned, educated, cultured
gebilligt approved, accepted
Gebinde *n* bundle, truss, hoop (cask), barrel **-sparren** *m* tie beam
Gebirge *n* country, measures, mountains, mountain range **festes ~** solid rock, bedrock **mildes ~** soft rock **nachfälliges ~** caving rock **quellendes ~** heaving rock **schwimmendes ~** running rock
gebirgig mountainous
Gebirgs-bahn *f* alpine or mountain railway **-bewegungen** *pl* roof movements, moving ground **-bildend** mountain-building **-druck** *m* roof pressure, pressure of sail, rock pressure **-druckkontrolle** *f* roof control **-falte** *f* fold **-fluß** *m* mountain stream or torrent **-formation** *f* system of beds
Gebirgs-gelände *n* mountain terrain, hilly or mountainous ground **-hang** *m* mountain-side **-höhe** *f* height of mountains **-joch** *n* mountain pass **-kamm** *m* ridge, mountain crest **-lagerung** *f* rock arrangement **-kunde** *f* orography

Gebirgs-masse *f* massif **-paß** *m* col, mountain pass **-rücken** *m* mountain ridge **-sattel** *m* anticline, upbending fold, anticlinal ridge **-schläge** *pl* rock bursts **-schicht** *f* strata **-schichtung** *f* rock stratification **-schlag** *m* fall of country, rock burst **-spalten** *pl* (kleine), pin cracks **-sperre** *f* (geological) formation shutoff **-störung** *f* orogenic disturbance **-zug** *m* mountain chain

Gebiß *n* denture, set of teeth, bit (harness) **-feder** *f* denture spring

Gebläse *n* blower, ventilator, fan, blast (machine), wind stacker, blast lamp, jet, supercharger, compressor, air blast (gun) **das ~ abstellen** to stop the blast **das ~ anlassen** to set the blast to work **das ~ arbeitet** the blast is on **durch ~ gekühlter Motor** blower-cooled engine **mehrstufiges ~** multistage blower **Pumpen eines Gebläses** surging

Gebläse-anlage *f* blowing plant **-bediener** *m* blower-regulating man **-brenner** *m* blowpipe **-drosselschieber** *m* blower-throttle slide valve **-druck** *m* blast pressure **-druckstutzen** *m* blower-pressure pipe, butt-pressure inlet **-eintritt** *m* compressor inlet **-enddruck** *m* compressor discharge pressure **-flamme** *f* blow torch **-flügel** *m* blower vane, fan blade **-förderhöhe** *f* adiabatic compressor head

Gebläse-gehäuse *n* blower casing **-gitter** *n* compressor stator or diffuser **-haus** *n* blower house **-kammer** *f* blower chamber **-kapsel** *f* (Entfroster) blower casing **-kasten** *m* blast cabinet **-kies** *m* gravel for blast engines, blasting grit **-kühlung** *f* forced-air cooling **-kupolofen** *m* blast cupola

Gebläse-lampe *f* blow-pipe, blast lamp **-läufer** *m* compressor impeller **-leitung** *f* blast-pipe leading **-lötlampe** *f* soldering lamp **-luft** *f* air blast, blast air **-maschine** *f* blowing or blast engine, blower (engine) **-maschinenhaus** *n* blowing-engine or blower-engine house **-maschinenwärter** *m* blower engineer **-messer** *m* blast or draft meter **-motor** *m* forced-induction engine, supercharged engine, blower motor

geblasen blown **-er Generator** pressure-gas producer **-es Glas** blown glass

Gebläse-ofen *m* blast furnace **-öffnung** *f* fan outlet **-prüfstand** *m* compressor test stand **-rad** *n* impeller, fanwheel blower **-ringfläche** *f* annular flow-area **-rohr** *n* blower pipe **-röhre** *f* blast pipe **-sand** *m* sandblasting sand, blasting or blast sand, abrasive **-sandsichter** *m* abrasive separator **-schachtofen** *m* blast furnace

Gebläse-separator *m* blower or ventilator separator (grain) **-strahl** *m* fan air **-stufe** *f* compressor stage **-stutzen** *m* nozzle blower **-ventil** *n* blowing valve **-vorverdichter** *m* blower-type supercharger **-welle** *f* blower shaft **-werk** *n* blower fan, blast apparatus **-wind** *m* air blast, fan blast, air flow **-wirkungsgrad** *m* compressor efficiency **-zunge** *f* air delector **-zylinder** *m* blowing cylinder, blast cylinder

geblättert laminated, foliated **-es Eisen** laminated iron

geblauter Zucker blued sugar

gebleichtes Öl bleached oil

gebleit leaded (said of fuel and metal)

geblockt blocked

gebogen (biegen) curved, bent, buckled, cranked, hooked **-e Bohrung** curved well **-er Flansch** *m* saddle flange **-es Rohr** curved or bent pipe **-e Schere** curved scissors **-er Träger** *m* bow girder **-er Zentrierstahl** spotting tool **-e Zuschnitte** *pl* curved shapes

gebondert bonderized **-er Stahl** bonderized steel

gebördelter Boden flanged end

geböschte Mauer sloping wall

gebrannt (brennen) burnt, calcined **-er Borax** calcined borax **-er Kalk** burnt or calcined lime, quicklime **-e Magnesia** calcined magnesia, magnesium oxide

Gebräu *n* brew, brewing, quantity brewed, draught

Gebrauch *m* usage, custom, practice, way, application, employment, utilization **außer ~ gekommen** obsolete **außer ~ setzen** to discard **gewerblicher ~** industrial utilization

gebrauchen to use, apply, employ, utilize, handle

gebräuchlich usual, customary **-e praktische Einheiten** usual practical units **-es Geräuschmaß** noise unit

Gebräuchlichkeit *f* currency, (common) use, vogue

Gebrauchsanweisung *f* printed instructions, directions for use, operating instructions

Gebrauchsbeanspruchung *f* actual service conditions

gebrauchsfähig usable, ready for use, operative **~ machen** to render fit

gebrauchsfertig ready-made, prepared, ready for use, readied **-e Ablieferung** turn-key job

Gebrauchs-gegenstand *m* commodity **-geschirr** *n* utility dishes **-gipfelhöhe** *f* practical or service ceiling **-graphik** *f* advertising art **-güter** *pl* staple products, commodities **-höhe** *f* operational height **-hoher Ständer** *m* frame of convenient working height **-kopie** *f* usable or working copy **-ladung** *f* normal charge **-last** *f* working load, service load **-mikroskop** *n* general-purpose microscope

Gebrauchsmuster *n* design patent, working model, registered design or pattern, utility-model patent **eingetragenes ~** patented provisionally (trade-mark or model filed)

Gebrauchs-musterschutz *m* legal protection of registered designs, patent of utilization **-prüfung** *f* service test **-spannung** *f* working stress **-tüchtigkeit** *f* durability in wear, wearibility

gebrauchsunfähig not fit for use

Gebrauchs-vorschrift *f* directions for use **-wagen** *m* utility car **-wasser** *n* water for general use, service water **-wert** *m* serviceability, function value

gebraucht used, secondhand **-es Öl** used oil

Gebrause *n* roaring, rushing

Gebrechen *n* defect, infirmity **Vorschützung von ~** malingering, simulation

gebrechlich invalid, frail, delicate

gebremst-er Auslauf *m* braked run (aviation) **-e Pferdestärke** brake horsepower

gebrochen (brechen) crushed, fractional, divided **-e Farbe** broken shade **-e Form** broken mold **-es Härten** interrupted hardening or quenching (met.) **-e Kanten** chamfered edges **-er Kern** broken core **-e Linienzüge** polygonal lines **-er Strahl** refracted ray **-e Verrohrung** parted casing **-e Wolle** transmitted wave, refracted wave

Gebrumme *n* hum (of alternators)
gebuchtet wavy
Gebühr *f* fee, rate, tariff, duty, tax, dues **mit einer ~ belegen** to charge **eine ~ erheben** to levy a charge **ermäßigte ~** deferred rate **~ erstatten** to refund a charge **die ~ festsetzen** to determine the rate **eine ~ festsetzen** to assess a charge **volle ~** full rate **Telegramm zu ermäßigter ~** deferred telegram
Gebühren *pl* advisory fees **-ansage** *f* rate notification **-anzeiger** *m* (call) rate indicator
Gebührenbemessung *f* determination of charges **~ nach der Dauer** charging by time **~ nach der Entfernung** charging by distance
Gebühren-betrag *m* amount of charge **-einheit** *f* tariff unit **-erfassung** *f* rate registration, call metering **-ermäßigung** *f* allowance, remission of fees or rates, reduction in charges **-ermittlung** *f* assessing or computing of charges
gebührenfrei tax-free **-er Anruf** free call
Gebühren-freiheit *f* exemption from charge or fee **-minuten** *f* charged minutes, (perfect) paid time
Gebührennachlaß *m* discount, allowance **einen ~ gewähren** to make an allowance on a charge
gebührenpflichtig chargeable **-er Anruf** paid call, call liable to a charge **-e Gesprächsdauer** chargeable time
Gebührensatz *m* rate of charges
Gebührenschuldner *m* defaulting (telephone) subscriber **~** (Teilnehmer mit der Gebührenzahlung im Rückstand) subscriber in arrears (of payment)
Gebühren-tabelle *f* scale of rates **-tarif** *m* tariff **-zähler** *m* rate meter **-zeit** *f* perfect paid time **-zone** *f* exchange area
Gebührnisse *pl* allowances, rates
Gebund *n* hank, skein
gebündelt clustered **-e Ausstrahlung** (elektr.) beamed transmission **-er und gerichteter Strahl** focused beam
gebunden (binden) bound, fixed, latent, attached to, combined with **-e Energie** latent energie **-er Kohlenstoff** combined carbon **-e Ladung** bound charge **-er Rang** tied rank **-e Wärme** latent heat **-es Wasser** combined water **-er Wirbel** bound vortex
gebunkert bunkered
gebürstet wire-brush-finished **-es Papier** brush enamel
Geburts-jahrgang *m* age class **-ort** *m* birthplace **-tag** *m* birthday **-urkunde** *f* birth certificate
Gebüsch *n* underbrush, bushes, coppice, shrubbery
gebüschig bushy
gedacht (denken) imaginary, fictitious, conceived, assumed
Gedächtnis *n* memory (comput)
gedämpft damped, attenuated, vaporized, deadbeat (elec.), aperiodic **~ werden** to attenuate, be damped, die down **schwach ~** slightly or weakly damped **stark ~** strongly or highly damped **-e Anzeige** deadbeat, aperiodic, or nonballistic reading **-er Kompaß** aperiodic compass **-er Raum** moderately live room **-e Schwingungen** damped oscillations **-er Sender** spark transmitter **-e Wellen** damped waves, discontinuous waves, type-B waves
Gedanke *m* idea, thought **einen Gedanken fassen** to conceive an idea
Gedanken-austausch *m* exchange of ideas **-einheit** *f* order or logic of thought **-folge** *f* train of thought **-kreis** *m* intellectual horizon, range of thought or ideas **-strich** *m* dash (in a sentence), break, mark of suspension
gedeckt concealed, covered, decked, defiladed, masked, sheltered **-e Bahn** shooting gallery, alley for rifle practice **-e Batterie** masked battery **-er Garbton** covered shade **-e Lichter** covered lights **-e Pfeife** stopped pipe **-e Stellung** cover position **-er Raum** dead space, safety zone
Gedeihen *n* prosperity, success, thriving, growth **~ des Kalkes** increasing or swelling of lime
gedenken to remember, bear in mind
gediegen pure, native, (ores, metals), true, genuine, solid, curious **-es Gold** pure gold, native gold **-es Kupfer** native copper
Gedinge *n* piecework **-abnahme** *f* measuring day **-arbeit** *f* contract work, piecework **-lohn** *m* piecework wage, payment by job **-nehmer** *m* bargain master, taker **-stufe** *f* job mark **-zeichen** *n* draft mark
gedrängt compact (of machines, grain), close (together), compendious, of restricted dimensions **~ aufgebaut, ~ gebaut** small in bulk **-e Übersicht** summary
Gedrängtheit *f* closeness, compactness, a certain stretch or distance, spacing
gedrechselt turned
gedreht twisted **-er Bolzen** turned bolt **-er Eisenstab** twisted bar **-e Kette** twist-link chain
gedrillte Schnur lacing cord or twine
Gedrit *m* gedrite
gedrosselt partially throttled **-er Dampf** throttled steam
gedrückt crushed, depressed; (Fluglage) nose-down **-e Fläche** contact area, projected area in contact with rolls **-es Gewinde** pressed (sheet-metal) thread **-e Länge** contact length **-e Kurve** driving turn
gedruckte Daten printed data **~ Schaltung** printed circuit
gedrungen (dringen) sturdy, compact, close (together)
gedübelt doweled
geebnet flattened **-es Bildfeld** flattened image field
geeckt angled, cornered, angular
geeicht standard, gauged, calibrated **-er Detektor** scaled detector **-e Lampe** stamped lamp **-e Strichmarken** *pl* gauging lines
geeignet adapted, suitable, fit, proper, convenient
Geeignetheit *f* suitability, fitness
Gee-H-Verfahren *n* Gee-H-system
geerdet earthed, grounded, earth-connected **a-Zweig ~** A leg earthed **-er Kreis** ground circuit **-er Mittelleiter** grounded neutral **-er Nullpunkt** grounded neutral point **-es Schutznetz** earthed cradling
Gefach *n* drawer, partition, shelving
gefachtes Garn plied yarn
Gefahr *f* danger, risk, peril, hazard, menace

gefährden to endanger, imperil, risk, compromise
gefährdende Lichtquellen dangerous light (aviat)
Gefährdung *f* endangering, danger
Gefahren-feuer *n* hazard beacon **-gebiet** *n* danger area or zone **-klasse** *f* dangerous-materials class (*e.g.*, that comprising inflammable liquids) **-meldung** *f* warning of danger, danger report **-raum** *m* danger area **-winkel** *m* critical or danger angle **-zeichen** *n* danger signal **-zeit** *f* time of congestion (tel.) **-zone** *f* zone of danger
Gefahrknopf *m* emergency stop button
gefährlich risky, dangerous **-er Hügel, -e Steigung** dangerous hill
Gefährlichkeit *f* danger
gefahr-los safe (from) **-losigkeit** *f* absence of danger **-meldeanlage** *f* danger-alarm system **-meldung** *f* danger signal **-moment** *m* critical speed, burble point **-punkt** *m* critical or danger point **-quelle** *f* source of danger **-signal** *n* danger signal
Gefährt *n* vehicle, carriage, track (min.)
Gefäll-beton *m* levelling concrete, filling concrete **-bruch** *m* change of gradient
Gefälle *n* fall, head, drop, incline, slope, gradient, pitch, depression, descent, inclination **durch ~** by gravity **geodätisches ~** geodetic head **verfügbares ~** available head **verlorenes ~** lost head
Gefälle-änderung *f* slope change **-anzeiger** *m* flow indicator **-bahn** *f* inclined plane **-druck** *m* hydrostatic pressure or head **-messer** *m* gradient recorder, gradometer, clinometer
gefallen fallen, dead, killed
Gefälle-speicher *m* variable-pressure **-tank** *m* gravity tank **-verlust** *m* head loss, loss of fall (of water) **-wechsel** *m* point where declivity changes
Gefällhöhe *f* hydraulic height or head (of water)
Gefälligkeits-akzept *n*, **-wechsel** *m* accommodation bill
Gefällinie *f* line of inclination, hydraulic axis
Gefälls-gang *m* gradient variation **-kurve** *f* gradient curve **-messer** *m* clinometer
Gefällstrecke *f* incline or drop of runway
gefällt, frisch ~ freshly precipitated **-er Stamm** log
gefaltet-er Dipol folded dipole antenna **-er Exponentialtrichter** folded exponential horn (of loud-speaker)
gefalzt joined, folded, notched
gefärbt colored, dyed, pigmented **-es Glas** stained glass
gefasert grained **längs ~** straight-grained **-es Rohr** raveled cane
Gefäß *n* container, jar, pot, vessel, tank, skip, receptacle **~ mit Bodenentleerer** bottom-dumping skip **~ mit Dampfmantel** steam-jacketed kettle **~ mit Kopfkippung** overturning skip **hölzernes ~** kit **kugelförmiges ~** bulb **poröses ~** porous pot **Faraday'sches ~** Faraday ice pail or cylinder
Gefäß-barometer *n* bulb or cistern barometer **-diffusion** *f* jar diffusion **-förderung** *f* skip winding **-förderung** *f* (Schacht) shaft bucket conveyance **-halter** *m* vessel holder **-heberbarometer** *n* combination cistern and siphon barometer **-luftdruckmesser** *m* cistern barometer **-ofen** *m* closed, hearth, or retort furnace, pot, crucible, or converting furnace, receptacle furnace **-reflex** *m* vasomotor reflex
gefaßt composed, restrained, held, comprehended, grasped **-e Linse** mounted lens
Gefäßversuch *m* pot experiment
Gefäßwirkungsgrad *m* bulb efficiency (rectifier)
gefedert flexible, elastic, shock-mounted, spring-suspended, sprung
gefertigt, aus einem einzigen Stück ~ made of a single piece
gefettetes Öl compound oil
gefiedert (Kondensator) feathered
gefirnißtes Packpapier varnished packing paper
geflammt watered, waved
geflanscht flanged
Geflecht *n* plait (cords, jute), mesh, network, reticulation **feines** (**grobes**) **~** fine (coarse) mesh
Geflechtdraht *m* netting wire
gefleckt stained, spotty, spotted, marbled
geflickt patched
Geflimmer *n* flickering, sparkling
geflochten (flechten) interwoven, plaited, braided **-e Seidenschnur** braided silk cord **-er Riemen** twist belt
Gefluder *n* channel, launder, water kennel, flume
Gefolgschaft *f* retinue, staff, crew, workers of a factory
Gefolgschaftsmitglieder *pl* employees
gefordert required
geformt premolded, profiled
gefräßig greedy, voracious
Gefräßigkeit *f* greediness, voracity
gefräst milled **-es Gewinde** milled thread **-er Zahn** cut tooth
Gefrier-anlage *f* freezing or refrigerating plant **-apparat** *m* freezing apparatus, freezer
gefrierbar congealable, coagulable, freezable
gefrieren to freeze, congeal, refrigerate, frost
Gefrieren *n* freezing, congelation **zum ~ bringen** to refrigerate **~ bei tiefer Temperatur** sharp freezing
gefrierender Nebeldunst freezing mist
Gefrierer für Eisbecher freezer for ice goblets
Gefrierfach *n* freezer compartment **-verdampfer** *m* full width freezer evaporator with compartment
Gefrier-grenze *f* freezing level **-kerne** *pl* freezing nuclei **-maschine** *f* refrigerator, freezing apparatus **-mikrotom** *n* quickfreezing microtome **-mischung** *f* freezing mixture
Gefrierpunkt *m* freezing point, congealing point, ice point **-erniedrigung** *f* freezing point depression **-lehre** *f* cryoscopics
Gefrierpunktmesser *m* cryometer **~ und Druckmesser** manocryometer
Gefrier-rohr *n*, **-röhre** *f* freezing pipe **-schacht** *m* frozen or freezing shaft **-schnitt** *m* frozen section **-schrank** *m* refrigerator, icebox **-schutz** *m* protection from freezing, antifreeze **-schützer** *m* anti-icer **-schutzlösung** *f* antifreezing solution **-schutzmittel** *m* antifreeze agent or solution **-temperatur** *f* freezing point **-trockner** *m* vacuum freeze drier **-trocknung** *f* freeze-drying
Gefrierung *f* refrigeration

Gefrierverfahren *n* freezing process
Gefrisch *n* regenerate material (rubber, oil, etc.)
gefrittet fused
Gefüge *n* structure, texture, grain, bed, stratum, matrix **dichtes ~** close-grained structure **gleichmäßig dichtes ~** close texture uniform throughout **das grobe ~ betreffend** macroscopic **grobes ~** coarse- or open-grain structure **strahliges ~** radiating structure
Gefüge-abbildung *f* photograph of structural defects **-änderung** *f* structural change **-anormalität** *f* structural abnormality **-anordnung** *f* structural arrangement **-art** *f* type of structure **-aufbau** *m* structural composition or constitution **-aufnahme** *f* metallograph **-ausbildung** *f* arrangement of structure **-beständigkeit** *f* structural stability **-bestandteil** *m* structural constituent **-bild** *n* metallograph, micrograph
Gefüge-fehler *m* structural defect **-lehre** *f* metallography **-mikrobild** *n* photomicrograph **-los** structureless **-neubildung** *f*, **-umwandlung** *f* structural transformation, phase change **-umwandlungsgeschwindigkeit** *f* speed of structural change **-untersuchungen** *pl* structure examinations **-veränderung** *f* structural change **-verfeinerung** *f* refinement of structur
gefügig tame, tractable, adaptable, pliant
gefügt, sorgfältig ~ carefully jointed
Gefühl *n* feeling, sensation, touch **-los** unfeeling, hard, apathetic
Gefühls-hebel *m* feed-bar lever **-ratsche** *f* ratchet stop **-schraube** *f* thumb screw **-wellen** *pl* guided waves
geführt guided
gefüllt filled **mit Luft ~** air-filled **-er Latex** compounded latex (loaded latex) **-e Mischung** loaded stock or mixing **-e Säule** packed column
gefurcht grooved **-er Zylinder** scored cylinder
gefüttert lined
gegabelt forked, branched, bifurcated, siamesed **-e Laderohre** siamesed induction pipes
gegeben given **-e Größe** datum
Gegebenheit *f* structural conditions, reality fact, data, situation
gegen against, to, toward, opposed to, compared with, counter **~ chemischen Angriff widerstandsfähiges Glas** chemically resistant glass **~ den Wind** into (up) the wind
Gegenabdruck *m* counterproof or impression (print.) **einen ~ machen oder herstellen** to counterdraw (print.)
Gegen-abzug *m* counter-proof **-amperewindungen** *pl* back or counter ampere turns **-amt** *n* distant office or other office in the circuit (teleph.) **-angebot** *n* counteroffer **-antrag** *m* counterproposal **-antwort** *f* rejoinder, reply **-arbeit** *f* negative work due to back pressure **-arbeiten** to buck, oppose, counteract, work in opposition **-auftrag** *m* counterorder **-ausgleich** *m* counterbalance **-ausleger** *m* opposite-end derrick **-auslese** *f* adverse selection **-balancier** *m* bridle rod
Gegenbefehl *m* counterorder **einen ~ geben** to countermand
Gegen-beleuchtung *f* back(ground) illumination **-bewegung** *f* countermotion, countermovement
Gegenbeweis, direkter ~ rebutting testimony or evidence
Gegen-bezug *m* correlation **-bild** *n* counterpart, antitype, replica **-bildentfernungsmesser** *m* rangefinder with split or devided image **-bildlich** antitypical **-block** *m* counterblock or support **-böschung** *f* counterslope, counterscarp **-bremse** *f* back brake, counterbrake
Gegend *f* region, area, zone, section, district, vicinity **~ der Windstillen** intertropical front
Gegendämmerung *f* antitwilight, countertwilight
Gegendampf *m* back steam **~ geben** to cushion with steam
Gegendampfbremse *f* countersteam brake
Gegen-detektor *m* double detector **-diagonale** *f* counterbrace, diagonal **-dichtung** *f* lock washer **-dienst** *m* service rendered in return **-draht** *m* landing wire **-drall** *m* back twist **-drehung** *f* counterrotation
Gegendruck *m* back pressure, counterpressure, reaction **~ bei Ölbohrungen** choke (oil drilling)
Gegendruck-abfüllapparat *m* counterpressure racker **-betrieb** *m* noncondensing operation **-dampfturbine** *f* back pressure turbine **-entnahmeturbine** *f* backpressure pass-off turbine **-faßfüllapparat** *m* counterpressure racking apparatus **-feder** *f* back pressure spring, counter spring **-flaschenfüllapparat** *m* back-pressure bottle filler **-füllapparat** *m* counterpressure filling apparatus **-hebel** *m* counterlever **-kammer** *f* counterpressure chamber **-kolben** *m* dummy or balancing piston (steam turbines)
Gegendruck-maschine *f* back-pressure engine **-regelventil** *n* back-pressure regulating valve **-schmieden** *n* forging against back pressure **-spreize** *f* counterbrace **-turbine** *f* impulse turbine, steam turbine (back-pressure type) **-unterlagsscheiben** *pl* thrust washers **-ventil** *n* counterpressure valve **-walze** *f* back pressure roller **-zylinder** *m* inking or impression roll (print.)
gegeneinander head-on **~ geschaltet** opposing, connected differentially, connected in opposition **~ gestellt** confronted (with), compared **~ in Reihe** series-opposed **~ arbeitendes Rührwerk** stirring blades working in opposite direction, counteracting stirring mechanism **~ schalten** connect in opposition, connect differentially **~ stauchen** to force together under pressure **~ stellen** to toe in **~ versetzte Zahnreihen** rows of teeth displaced relatively to each other **~ versetzte Zahnscheiben** staggered driving pinions
Gegen-einschnitt *m* resection (survey) **-elektrode** *f* counterelectrode, signal plate or metallic screen (forming foundation of mosaic in television tube)
gegenelektromotorische Kraft back- or counter-electromotive force
Gegen-email *n* enamel laid on the back of a plate **-emission** *f* back emission **-farbe** *f* contrast of colors, complementary color **-färbung** *f* contrast coloring **-feder** *f* opposing or reacting spring, counterspring, return spring, control spring **-federhaus** *n* spring cover or housing **-feld** *n* opposing field (longitudinal field, elec.) **-feldmethode** *f* retarding potential method **-fernsehen** *n* two-way television **-flanke des Zahnes** mating tooth profil **-flansch** *m* counterflange, companion flange

Gegen-flußsystem *n* return-flow system **-fluß-turbine** *f* contraflow turbine (jet) **-forderung** *f* counterclaim, offset, setoff, cross demand **-form** *f* key form **-fritter** *m* anti-coherer **-führung** *f* back rest for swing tool, countersupport, counterstay; (Revolver) back rest for turret **-führungsfläche** *f* mating surface **-führungsrolle** *f* back guide roller

Gegen-funk *m* antispark disc, pare-flash **-funkstelle** *f* called or answering station, opposite number, repeating station **-furnieren** to veneer on both sides, to counterveneer **-fußpunkt** *m* antipode **-gabe** *f* antidote

gegengekuppelter Verstärker feed-back amplifier

gegengeschaltet counterconnected, duplex-connected **-e Sammlerzelle** countercell

Gegengetriebe *n* differential gear

Gegengewicht *n* counterpoise, earth screen, counterweight, balancing capacity, counterbalance, balance weight **~ von Beton** concrete counterweight **~ im Bremsberg** back balance, gravity plane **~ aus Stahl mit Bleizusatzgewicht** lead-loaded steel balance weight **das ~ halten** to counterbalance **festes ~** rigidly mounted counterweight **pendelndes ~** balance-weight vibration absorber, dynamic counterweight **ungeerdetes ~** earth screen

Gegengewichte der Kurbelwelle balance weights of the crankshaft **~ des Nadelventils** balance weights of needle valve

Gegengewichts-antenne *f* screened antenna **-anschluß** *m* counterpoise connector **-ausleger** *m* counterweight boom **-balancier** *m* counterbalance **-bolzen** *m* counterweight bolt **-kette** *f* counterweight chain **-nase** *f* counterweight carrier catch **-rad** *n* counterwheel **-schleife** *f* counterweight or counterpoise loop **-versuchsapparat** *m* dead-weight tester **-wagen** *m* balance car, dummy

Gegen-gift *n* antibody, antidote **-hall** *m* resonance, echo **-halt** *m* support, prop, backing

gegenhalten to hold up (for riveting), counterhold

Gegenhalter *m* arm brackets (arbor supports), dolly (for riveting), head cup, holding-up hammer; (Normalzubehör) overarm (standard equipment) **-führungsarm** *m* (Fräsemaschine) overarm **-stützen** *pl* arm braces (harness)

Gegen-hang *m* counterslope **-hebedraht** *m* antilift wire (aviation) **-impedanz** *f* negative-sequence field impedance **-induktion** *f* mutual induction, back induction **-induktivität** *f* mutual induction, impedance **-induktivitätskoeffizient** *m* coefficient of mutual inductance **-ionen** *pl* opposed ions **-kabel** *n* landing wire, antilift wire, counterwire (aviation) **-kammer** *f* opposite camera of station **-kapazität** *f* mutual capacitance or capacity

Gegen-keil *m* fox wedge, gib, folding wedge, tightening key, counterwedge **-kettenrad** *n* counterchain wheel **-klage** *f* countercharge or suit, cross claim **-klaue** *f* mating clutch **-klinke** *f* rachet pawl **-kolben** *m* opposed piston **-klopfmittel** *n* antiknock constituent, antidetonant, antidetonation compound **-kolbenmotor** *m* double-piston engine, opposed-piston engine **-kompoundierung** *f* differential excitation **-kontakt** *m* cooperating contact or terminal, opposite contact, fixed contact

Gegenkopplung *f* degenerative feedback, inverse feedback, negative feedback

Gegenkopplungs-faktor *m* coefficient of negative feedback **-schaltung** *f* inverse (negative) feedback circuit **-widerstand** *m* feedback resistance

Gegenkörner *m* tail piece

Gegenkraft *f* counteracting force, reacting force, opposing force, bias **durch eine ~ ausgleichen** to bias out

Gegen-krümmung *f* reverse curve **-kufe** *f* counterpad **-kuppelung** *f* restoring mechanism or action, reverse or negative feedback, degeneration **-kupplungshälfte** *f* counter-coupling half, counter-clutch half **-kurbel** *f* return crank **-kurbellager** *n* bearing of the countercrank **-kurs** *m* opposite course (aviat.) **-kurvenbahn** *f* counter-curving rail **-lage** *f* stiffening piece (teleph.)

Gegenlager *n* outer support, abutment, any relatively immovable point or surface sustaining pressure **~ für Schlagbolzen** striker spring stop

Gegenlager-büchse *f* opposed bearing bush **-leistenschraube** *f* back-rest gib screw

Gegenlagerständer *m* end support **-Feststellschraube** *f* back-rest clamp bolt

Gegenlauf *m* reverse motiven, countercurrent, counterrotation **-fräsen** *n* conventional milling, up-milling process **-graben** *m* counter-approach (trench)

gegenläufig countercurrent, oppositely directed or oriented, of contrary sense, contrarotating

gegenläufigdrehende Propeller *pl* (nicht koaxial) handed propellers

gegenläufig-e Bewegung double motion **-er Doppelrührer** *m* double-motion agitator **-e Kolben** opposite pistons **-er Kolben** piston working in opposite direction **-e Luftschraube** contrarotating propeller **Motor mit -en Kolben** opposed-pistontype engine **-e** (Gegenkolben-) **Maschine** opposed-piston engine

Gegenläufigkeit *f* opposition, opposition of phases

Gegenlauf-motor *m* differential or birotary turbine **-pressen** *n* reverse extruding (cold forming) **-schraube** *f* contrarotating propeller **-turbine** *f* birotary turbine, differential turbine

Gegen-laut *m* echo **-lehrdorn** *m* mating plug gauge **-lehre** *f* master gauge **-leistung** *f* equivalence, service in return **-lenker** *m* radius rod **-lenkerschaft** *m* way shaft

Gegenlicht *n* counterlight, sunlight against the attacker, defender or observer **-aufnahme** *f* exposure against the sun (photo) **-blende** *f* weather shade; (Film) gobo (acoust).

Gegen-lösung *f* countersign **-luftwirbel** *m* anticyclone **-magnetisierende Windungen** demagnetising turns **-magnetisierung** *f* back magnetization **-maßnahme** *f* countermeasure **-mauer** *f* counterwall, countermure

Gegen-messer *m* counterknife **-mine** *f* countermine **-mischbar** consolute **-mitsprechen** *n* side-to-phantom far-end cross talk (teleph.) **-mittel** *n* prophylactic antidote **-modulation** *f* push-pull modulation, modulation in opposition **-mutter** *f* check nut, lock nut or washer, binding nut, jam nut, clamping screw **-nebengespräch** *n* cross talk **-nebensprechdämpfung** *f* far-end cross-talk attenuation

Gegen-nebensprechen *n* far-end cross talk (teleph.) **-neigung** *f* reverse gradient **-ort** *n* counterexcavation, countergangway **-partei** *f* opponent, antagonist, opposite party, adversary **-passatwind** *m* antitrades, countertrade **-pfeiler** *m* buttress, corner arch, counterfort (hydraul) **-phase** *f* opposition, phase opposition **-phasigkeit** *f* phase opposition

gegenphasisch inphase-opposed, 180 degrees out of phase **-e Bereiche** antiphase domains

Gegen-platte *f* counter punch **-pol** *m* antipole, reciprocal pole **-polung** *f* opposition of polarity, opposite or reverse polarity **-posten** *m* setoff, offset, cross entry **-probe** *f* check determination or test, revision of test, contrasting sample **-profil** *n* male screed, screed whose edge protrudes in the shape of a male templet, counterprofile, mating profile **-puffer** *m* stopblock **-punze** *f*, **-punzen** *m* counterpunch

Gegen-qualitäten *pl* corresponding grades **-rakel einer Walzendruckmaschine** lint doctor **-rad** *n* mating gear or wheel **-rechnung** *f* blancing of accounts, setoff, counterclaim or reckoning **-rimesse** *f* counter- or return remittance **-richtung** *f* opposite direction **-ring** *f* counterring

Gegensatz *m* contrast, opposition, contradistinction, return, antithesis **im ~ zu** contrary to, in contrast with **einen ~ bilden** to contrast

gegensätzlich antithetic

Gegen-schaber *m* hut doctor (textiles) **-schalten** to cross-connect **-schaltmaschine** *f* booster to reduce volts **-schaltung** *f* differential circuit, differential or duplex connection, counterconnection **-schaltungsmethode** *f* opposition method **-scheibe** *f* driven pulley, washer **-schein** *m* antizodiacal light, reflection, reverberation **-scheinleitwert** *m* transadmittance **-schiene** *f* check rail **-schlag** *m* backlash or backpressure (apart from play) **-schläger** *m* counterfaller (textiles) **-schleuse** *f* countersluice **-schlüssel** *m* locking key **-schraffieren** to cross hatch

Gegen-schräge *f* counterbrace, diagonal **-schraube** *f* counter-rotation propeller, counter screw **-schreibbetrieb** *m* duplex working (telegraphy) **-schreiben** *n* duplex system of writing, full-duplex operation **-schrift** *f* written reply, rejoinder **-schriftanzeige** *f* back-to-back pip matching (radar) **-schuld** *f* reciprocal or mutual debt, counterclaim **-schütze** *m* wicket, tail gate **-schwelle** *f* stilling weir or sill **-see** *f* head sea **-sehen** *n* twoway television **-seil** *n* stagger wire, landing wire

gegenseitig reciprocal, mutual, opposite, two-way **~ ausschließen** mutually exclusive **~ sich hebende Farben** complementary shades **-e Abhängigkeit** *f* interdependence **-e Beeinflussung** mutual interference **-e Beeinflussung von Tragflügel und Rumpf** body-wing interference **-e Ersetzung** reciprocal replacement **-er Flächeneinfluß** biplane effect **-er Hinweis** cross reference **-e Induktion** mutual induction (between circuits) **-e Lizenzerteilung** cross licensing **-e Peilung** reciprocal bearing **-e Sprechverbindung** two-way telephone circuit **-e Überlagerung** self-shadowing **-e Wechselwirkung** *f* mutual interaction

Gegenseitigkeit *f* reciprocity

Gegenseitigkeitsgeschäft *n* barter (in foreign trade) requiring no foreign exchange

Gegensignal *n* answering signal, reply

Gegensinn, im ~ zum Uhrzeiger counterclockwise

Gegensinngetriebe *n* counterrotating drive

gegensinnig opposing, irrational, devoid of sense, nonsensical, illogical **~ in Reihe geschaltet** opposing in series **-e Parallelschaltung** back-to-back connection

Gegen-sonne *f* anthelion, cast, parhelion **-spannung** *f* inverse- or reverse-grid or backlash potential or voltage (radio) **-spannungsdraht** *m* countervoltage conductor **-spant** *n* reversed frame **-spitze** *f* tail center

Gegensprechanlage *f* two-way intercom (system)

Gegensprechbetrieb *m* (full) duplex operation **einseitiger ~** half duplex operation

Gegensprecheinrichtung *f* duplex installation (teleph.)

gegensprechen to duplex (teleph.)

Gegensprechen *n* two-way telephone conversation, duplex process, duplex telegraphy, duplex(ing), two-way working; (Rundfunkstudio) talk-back **~ in Staffelschaltung** echelon duplex

Gegensprechenübertragung *f* duplex repeater

Gegensprecher *m* two-way telephone

Gegensprech-leitung *f* duplex circuit **-satz** *m* duplex set, terminal duplex repeater set **-schaltsatz** *m* duplex set

Gegensprechschaltung *f* duplex connection or circuit **einseitiger Betrieb in ~** half-duplex operation

Gegensprech-system *n* duplex system **-taste** *f* reversing key **-taster** *m* duplex key **-telegraphie** *f* duplex telegraphy **-verkehr** *m* duplex or two way communication

Gegen-spulung *f* reverse circulation **-spur** *f* (Straße) opposing lane

Gegenstand *m* subject (matter), object, item, substance, article **geheimer ~** classified military item, secret item **körperlicher ~** solid or three-dimensional object **Stellung von Gegenständen zueinander** configuration

Gegen-ständer *m* countersupport **-ständige Augenlage** aligned lugs **-ständlich** perceptual, clear, objective **-standpunkt** *m* (einer stereophotogrammetrischen Aufnahme) opposite station (photogrammetry)

Gegenstands-breite *f* width of object **-glas** *n* object glass **-los** annulled, canceled, baseless, groundless, unfounded **-punkt** *m* object point, point object (phot.) **-weite** *f* object distance, distance from electron source (aperture or crossover) to lens

Gegen-stanze *f* counterpunch, grooving or creasing block, swage block **-station** *f* counterstation **-stecker** *m* matching plug **-stelle** *f* called station (radio) **-stempel** *m* counterpunch **-steuern** to adjust the rudder in failure of an engine **-steuern** *n* trimming with one or more engines inoperative **-steuerung** *f* push-pull modulation **-stoff** *m* antisubstance, antibody, antidote **-stollen** *m* countermine **-stößel** *m* plunger

Gegen-strahl *m* reflected ray, reflection **-strebe** *f*

compression member or strut, counterbrace

Gegenstrahlung *f* atmospheric radiation

Gegenstrom *m* counterflow, countercurrent, reverse(d) current **-austauscher** *m* counter-current interchanger **-bremsung** *f* countertorque control **-einspritzung** *f* counterflowing injection **-fluß** *m* countercurrent flow **-kessel** *f* countercurrent boiler

Gegenstromkondensator *m* reflux-type condenser **~ mit Wasserfänger** countercurrent condenser with water basin or catcher

Gegenstromluft- und Gasvorwärmer *m* recuperator

Gegenstrom-mischer *m* ribbon blender **-prinzip** *m* counterflow, countercurrent, or counterstream principle **-regenkondensator** *m* countercurrent rain-type condenser **-relais** *n* reverse-current relay **-röhrenkühlgerät** *n* countercurrent pipe cooler **-rolle** *f* electromagnetic shunt **-tellermischer** *m* countercurrent pan mixer

Gegenströmung *f* counterflow, countercurrent, eddy

Gegenstromverfahren *n* countercurrent process **Kondensator nach dem ~** condenser of reflux type

Gegenstromvorwärmer *m* countercurrent heater

Gegenstromwärmeaustauscher *m* counter-flow heat exchanger

Gegenstück *n* counterpart, match **-hälfte** *f* male or female half

Gegen-stufenscheibe *f* countershaft pulley **-stütze** *f* buttress, counterstay

Gegentakt *m* push-pull **-anordnung** *f* push-pull arrangement **-arbeiten** *n* push-pull operation, work in phase opposition **-audion** *n* push-pull grid, detector **-aufzeichnung** *f* (pull-down) claw, push-pull recording (motion pictures) **-ausgang** *m* push-pull output **-B-Modulation** *f* class B modulation **-bremsfeldaudion** *n* electron-oscillation detector or rectifier

Gegentakt-detektionsschaltung *f* push-pull detection circuit **-detektor** *m* push-pull detector **-eingangskreis** *m* push-pull input circuit **-endpentode** *f* push-pull pentode **-endröhre** *f* push-pull output control **-endstufe** *f* push-pull power stage **-erregung** *f* push-pull energization

Gegentakt-generator *m* push-pull oscillator **-gleichrichter** *m* push-pull detector **-kippgerät** *n* push-pull time base **-mikrophon** *n* push-pull microphone **-mischstufe** *f* push-pull mixing stage **-modulator** *m* push-pull modulator **-neutralisation** *f* cross-neutralization **-noiseless** *n* split-wave noiseless recording **-oszillator** *m* push-pull oscillator **-rohr** *n* push-pull valve

Gegentakt-schalter *m* push-pull breaker **-schaltung** *f* push-pull arrangement, connection, or circuit, push-pull switch **-schrift** *f* push-pull tract **-stufe** *f* push-pull stage **-transformator** *m* push-pull transformer **-übertrager** *m* push-pull transformer **-verkehr** *m* push-pull communication **-verstärker** *m* push-pull amplifier **-verstärkerschaltung** *f* push-pull amplifier circuit

Gegenteil *n* contrary, opposite, reverse, antithesis, converse **ins ~ verkehren** to negate an effect

Gegentor *n* gate strut, bracket

Gegen-träger *m* opposed contact holder **-trichter** *m* countersocket

gegenüber opposite, compared with **-gestellt** compared **-liegen** (Seite und Winkel) subtend **-liegend** opposed, opposite **-sprechen** *n* side-to-side far-end cross talk **-stehen** to stand opposite or opposed, contrast, be compared with **-stehend** opposite, abeam **-stellen** to oppose, compare, contrast, confront **-stellung** *f* confrontation, comparison

Gegenuhrzeigersinn, im ~ counterclockwise

Gegen-umdruck *m* reversed reprint **-vakuum** *n* anti-vacuum

Gegenverbund-dynamo *m* differential compound-(wound) dynamo **-erregung** *f* differential excitation **-motor** *m* differential compound-wound motor **-wicklung** *f* differential compound winding

Gegenverkehr *m* duplex operation or working, traffic from the opposite direction (mil.) **~ auf gleicher Frequenz** duplex operation on a single frequency

Gegen-verkehrssystem *n* intercommunication system **-verpflichtung** *f* counterobligation **-versuch** *m* control experiment, constrasting or check test **-vorschlag** *m* counteroffer **-vorstecker** *m* counterbolt **-vorstellung** *f* counterproposal **-wall** *m* counterscarp **-walze der Gaufriermaschine** paper cylinder of an embossing or a goffering machine **-wart** *f* presence, present time **-wartswert** *m* presentday value

Gegen-wechsel *m* cross- or counterbill, counterdraft **-wehr** *f* resistance **-welle** *f* countershaft, second-motion shaft **-wellengetriebe** *n* countershaft gear **-wert** *m* equivalent, countervalue **-wicht** *n* ground screen **-wickelung** *f* opposing winding **-wind** *m* head wind **-winderbewegung** *f* counter faller motion **-winderwelle** *f* counter faller shaft **-windung** *f* opposing winding, bucking coil

Gegen-winkel *m* opposite angle **-wirken** to counteract, react **-wirkend** reactive, antagonistic, reciprocating **-wirkleitwert** *m* intrinsic transconductance (trans.) **-wirkung** *f* reaction, reactance, counteraction, countereffect, recoil, kick **-zapfen** *m* anvil, fixed end **-zeichnen** to countersign **-zeichnung** *f* (Unterschrift) countersignature **-zeiger** *m* pointer indicator **-zeigersinn** *m* counterclockwise direction **-zelle** *f* counter electromotive force, (battery) cell

Gegenzug *m* countermove, back-pull (wire mfre)

Gegenzugdraht *m* antidrag wire (aviation)

Gegenzwilling *m* opposed horizontally, engines working on the same crankshaft

gegerbt tanned

gegißt calculated, estimated **-es Besteck** (position by) dead reckoning **-e Besteckrechnung** dead reckoning **-er Standort** estimated portion or position

geglättet smoothed

gegliedert organized, arranged in order, distributed, articulated, elbowed **tief ~** distributed in depth, disposed in depth **verschieden -e Bildteile** picture portions of different nature, composition, or organization

geglüht annealed, at high temperature **~ mit**

nachfolgender Abkühlung an der Luft normalizing (siderurgy)

Gegner-pfeil *m* path-of-flight pointer **-punkt** *m* present position, anticipated position of target at moment of burst (antiaircraft artil.)

gegossen (gießen) cast **aus Gips ~** molded from gypsum (of ornamental or fancy work, cornices) **in einem Stück ~** cast integral **fallend ~** top-poured **stehend ~** vertically cast **-er Film** coated film **-e Raffinade** cast raffinade **-er Zahn** cast tooth

gegründet auf based upon, predicated on, resulting from, conditioned by

gegürtet belted

Gehalt *n* (Inhalt) contents; (Chem.) concentration; (Bestandteile) content, proportion; (Münze) standard, strength, percentage, capacity, ingredients, tenure, yield **~** *n* pay, wages, allowance, salary **~ beziehen** to earn a salary **auf ~ Anspruch haben** to be entitled to salary **~ an Wasser und Absatz** (contents or percentage of) water and sediment

gehalten obliged, reserved, confined

gehalt-los superficial, valueless, worthless **-reich** solid, valuable

Gehalts-abzug *m* deduction from salary **-aufbesserung** *f* raise in salary **-wert** *m* quality factor **-zulage** *f* increase of salary, bonus

gehaltvoll rich, substantial, valuable

Gehänge *n* pendant, bail, hangers, suspension, attachment, hanger attachment, precipice, traverse, lifter, slope, declivity, festoon, suspension gear, hinge plate, suspension runner **-lehm** *m* residual clay **-schutt** *m* rock debris (from landslide) **-ton** *m* residual clay **-welle** *f* hangershaft

gehärtet hardened, casehardened, tempered, quenched **im Einsatz ~** casehardened **-es Eisen** chilled iron **-es Öl** hydrogenated oil **-er Pflugkörper** chilled bottom **-er Stahl** hardened or heat-treated steel

geharzt resin-coated (as nails) **-e Pappe** molding blank

gehauen-e Backen serrated jaws **-e Verzahnung** chiselled toothing

gehäufte Leistung heaped capacity

Gehäuse *n* case, housing, chamber, cabinet, (outer) casing, crankcase, jacket, cage, rotation box; (Zündkerzen) shell **~ mit Büchsen** body with bushes **~ mit Deckel** gear case with cover **~ für Kabelendstück** cable terminator, cable-end bell **~ eines elektrischen Motors** casing (electric motor) **rundes ~** shell **mit einem ~ versehen** to encase

Gehäuse-abstand *m* clearance between outer race and ball bearing **-anlaßwiderstand** *m* primary starter **-auge** *n* casing lug **-auslöser** *m* body shutter release (photo.) **-block** *m* cylinder block, housing **-boden** *m* bottom of shell **-bohrung** *f* stator bore **-bügel** *m* bow or ring of case **-deckel** *m* casing cover; (Kupplungsseite) housing cover (timing side) **-feder** *f* case spring (watch) **-fuß** *m* stand support, housing base

Gehäuse-hälfte *f* half of casing, housing half-member (clutch side) **-hals** *m* housing collar **-kappe** *f* spring cap **-kopf** *m* pendant **-Luftfilter** *m* cylinder-cased air filter **-masse** *f* (Lichtmaschine) yoke frame, yoke earth (dynamo) **-mittelteil** *m* middle part of casing **-nase** *f* front cover **-nenndurchmesser** *m* nominal diameter of case **-oberteil** *n* crankcase upper half, liner **-schaufel** *f* casing vane **-scheitel** *m* housing crest **-schilder** *pl* end caps

Gehäuse-spindel *f* boxed spindle **-teil zur Befestigung des Flugmotors am Traggerüst** mounting section of airplane engine **-unterteil** *n* crankcase lower half **-wand** *f* housing wall **-wandung** *f* casing shell

Gehbahn *f* sidewalk, footpath

gehbar practicable, passable

geheftet sewed, stitched, in paper cover (binding) **-er Block** stitched pack

Gehege *n* fence, enclosure

geheim secret, clandestine, confidential, classified

Geheim-analytik *f* cryptanalysis **-fernschreiber** *m* secret teleprinter or teletyper **-haltung** *f* secrecy, privacy **-haltungspflicht** *f* obligation of secrecy **-haltungssystem** *n* privacy system **-haltungsvorschrift** *f* instruction relative secrecy **-kamera** *f* concealed camera

Geheimnis *n* secret, mystery **~** (Nachrichtengeheimnis) secrecy (press news)

Geheim-prüfzähler *m* secret controlling counter **-schaltungsrelais** *n* secrecy relay **-schloß** *n* trick, puzzle, or combination lock (doors) **-schreiben** *n* crytograph **-schreibmaschine** *f* cipher-code typewriter

Geheimschrift *f* secret writing, code, cipher writing, cryptography **-analyse** *f*, **-entzifferung** *f* cryptanalysis

Geheim-sender *m* clandestine radio transmitter **-sprache** *f* code language **-sprecheinrichtung** *f* installation for secret conversations **-stelle** *f* wireless-telegraph secret listening post **-telephonie** *f* garbled, scrambled, or secret telephony **-text** *m* cipher text **-verfügung** *f* secret order **-wort** *n* cipher key **-zeichen** *n* secret symbol, code **-zusatz** *m* secret attachment for teleprinters

geheizt heated **indirekt -e Röhre** heater-type or indirectly heated tube

gehemmt held back (*e.g.*, a trigger)

gehen go, move, walk, pass, run, work **leer ~** to run idle **nicht weit genug ~** to undershoot (navy) **ins Ziel ~** to come, aim

Gehilfe *m* assistant, helper, attendant, aide-de-camp, officer serving with the staff of a specific commander **technischer ~** technical or engineering assistant

Gehirn *n* brain **-erschütterung** *f* concussion of the brain **-spannung** *f* brain voltage

gehobelte Bohle (Planke) dressed plank (board)

gehoben (heben) heaved, lifted, upset, raised **-er Beamter** senior official

Gehöft *n* farm

Gehölz *n* woods, copse

gehont honed

Gehör *n* hearing, auditory, acoustic, audio, aural **um ~ ersuchen** to file application or petition to be heard, petition for an audience **absolutes, echtes ~** genuine absolute pitch **nach dem ~** by ear

Gehöranzeige *f* audio signal

gehorchen to mind, obey, be responsive

Gehörempfindungsskala *f* auditory or aural sensation scale

gehören to belong (to)
Gehörgangfernhörer *m* telephone olive for insertion into ear
gehörig proper, appropriate, fit, due, duly, pertinent **zur Erde ~** terrestrial **zur Luft ~** aerial **zur See ~** maritime
Gehör-lehre *f* acoustics **-maskierung** *f* auditory masking, clouding **-messer** *m* audiometer **-peilung** *f* acoustic direction finding, bearing taken by ear, aural bearing
gehorsam obedient, submissive
Gehör-schädigung *f* hearing impairment **-schärfe** *f* acuity of hearing **-schärfemessung** *f* audiometry **-schützer** *m* ear plug **-signal** *n* audible or sound signal **-telegraphie** *f* acoustic telegraphy **-zielflug** *m* aural homing (aviat.)
Gehrdreieck *n*, **festes ~** miter square
Gehre *f* miter, bevel
gehren to miter
Gehren *m* bevel, gore, gusset, miter
Gehr-fuge *f* miter joint **-lade** *f* miter box **-maß** *n* miter rule, bevel, protractor **-stoß** *m* miter joint
Gehrung *f* miter(ing), bevel
Gehrungsanschlag *m* miter-cutting guide **abklappbarer ~** tilting miter-cutting guide
Gehrungs-fuge *f* miter joint **-hobel** *m* miter plane **-linien** *pl* mitred rules **-maß** *n* bevel rule **-quadrat** *n* mitred quad **-säge** *f* miter-box saw
Gehrungs-schere *f* miter-cutting shears **-schneider** *m* mitring cutter **-schnitt** *m* miter cut **-schweißung** *f* miter weld **-stanzmaschine** *f* miter-cutting machine **-stichel** *m* miter knife, plane **-stoßlade** *f* mitering machine **-winkel** *m* miter square **-zinke** *f* miter-dovetail **-zwingen** *pl* miter clamps
Geh-Steh-Apparat *m* start-stop apparatus, start-stop type of telegraph printer **-Prinzip** *n* start-stop system **-telegraph** *m* start-stop telegraph **-verteiler** *m* start-stop distributor **-welle** *f* start-stop spindle
Gehweg *m* sidewalk, path
Gei *f* guy wire **-baum** *m* derrick guy
Geigen-harz *n* rosin, colophony **-lack** *m* violin varnish
Geiger-Müller-Zähler *m* Geiger-Müller-counter
Geigerscher Spitzenzähler *m* Geiger counter with end window
Geiser *m* geyser
Geißelfuß *m* catch
Geißfuß *m* crooked pincher, crowbar, spike drawer **gebogener ~** bent parting tool **gerader ~** straight parting tool
Geißkopf *m* head
Geißlerröhre *f* Geißler tube
Geist *m* mind, morale, spirit, ghost, extract (substance or liquid)
geistige, ~ Gärung vinous fermentation **~ Tauglichkeit** mental fitness
geistreich ingenious
gekalkter Saft limed juice
gekämmte Rolle grooved roller
gekantet-es Blech bent plate, folded sheet **-e Eisenkonstruktion** structure bent from steel section
gekappte Schwelle lopped tie
gekapselt enclosed, encased **luftdicht ~** airtight, explosionproof **-e Filmführung** cased-in film guide **-e Schaltanlage** cellular switchboard
gekästeltes Papier squared paper
gekehltes Rohr grooved pipe
gekeilt wedged (joint)
gekennzeichnet (durch) characterized (by)
gekerbt toothed, indented **-er Quadrant** notched quadrant **-er Probestab** notched test specimen **-e Rolle** *f* grooved pulley
gekielte Fläche V-bottom surface
gekippt tilted, inclined
Geklapper *n* rattle
geklappt (in Lagen) lapped **-er Querschnitt** collapsed ribbon-shaped cross section
geklärte Lösung defecated (sugar mfg.)
geklebt glued, pasted **-er Karton** cardboard **-es Papier** sized paper
geklinkert clinker-built
geklöppelt braided
geknäuelt agglomerate, convoluted, coiled
geknetetes Aluminium wrought aluminum
geknickt bent down, buckled, collapsed, folded, subdued **-er Radiokurs** bent course (radio)
Geknister *n* crackling, rustling, crunching
geknöpftes Messer probe-ended knife
gekocht scoured, boiled
gekohltes Eisen carburized iron
geköpert twilled
gekoppelt coupled, connected **durch gemeinsame Kapazität ~** autocapacity-coupled **autoinduktiv ~** autoinductively coupled **kapazitiv ~** capacitycoupled **rück ~** back-coupled **widerstands ~** resistance-coupled **-e Kreise** coupled circuits **Gebilde aus -en Kreisen** coupled-circuit chain **-er Standort** position according to dead reckoning
gekordelt milled
gekörnt granulated, granular
gekracktes Benzin cracked gasoline
Gekrätz *n* waste, refuse, discard, dross, slag **-aschen** *pl* drosses
gekräuselt choppy, rippled
gekreuzt crossed **a-gekreuzt und b-Zweig gekreuzt** a and b legs crossed **-e Doppelader** crossed or transposed pair **Linie mit -en Leitungen** transposition line **-er Riemen** crossed belt
Gekriech *n* creep, creep wash
gekritzte Geschiebe striated rock pavements
gekröpft offset, cranked, crumped, edged, underslung, bent, cropped **vierfach ~** four-throw **zweifach ~** two-throw crank **-es Bett** (Drehbank) gap bed **-er Durchschlag** cranked punch **-es Flacheisen** cranked flat iron **-er Gewindebohrerhalter** knee tap holder **einfach -e Kurbelwelle** single-throw crankshaft **-es Rohr** S bend **-er Schruppstahl** cranked roughing tool **-e Unterwelle** gap undershaft **-e Welle** *f* crankshaft
Gekrösestein *m* tripestone
gekrümmt curved, curviliear, buckled, warped, tortuous **-e Oberfläche** curved surface **-es Rohr** curved or bent pipe, (pipe) bend
gekühlt refrigerated **-er Windtunnel** refrigerated wind tunnel
gekümpelt-e Böden dished ends **-es Stück** beaten or shaped piece
gekupfert coppered **-e Stahlbleche** coppered steel plates
gekuppelt coupled, connected **~ durch Räder-**

getriebe geared together

Gel *n* gel

geladen charged, live, loaded, armed, activated **-er Draht** live wire **-er Zustand** charged condition (of storage cells)

Geläger *n* cask deposit, sediment **-filterpresse** *f* sediment filter press

gelagert supported, stored, seasoned **drehbar ~** fulcrumed (at), pivoted (on)

Gelände *n* country(side), region, topography, terrain, ground, landscape, land **abfallendes ~** falling slope **aufsteigendes ~** rising slope **bedecktes ~** defiladed slope, covered terrain **bestrichenes ~** beaten zone **deckungsloses ~** open ground, open terrain **durchschnittenes ~** dissected country

Gelände, ebenes ~ flat ground **flachwelliges ~** open undulating ground **freies ~** open country **gitterloses ~** barrier without railings **hügeliges ~** undulating ground **schwieriges ~** difficult terrain **unebenes ~** broken ground **welliges ~** hilly country

Gelände-abschnitt *m* area, sector, terrain, compartment **-anpassung** *f* adaptation to terrain, blending with the ground **-arbeit** *f* field work, field operations **-aufnahme** *f* ground survey or photograph, terrestrial photography **-ausnutzung** *f* utilization of terrain **-ausschnitt** *m* ground zone or sector, coverage **-auswertung** *f* terrain appreciation

Gelände-beschaffenheit *f* nature of the terrain **-bö** *f* ground gust **-darstellung** *f* map representation, topographical or terrain representation **-durchschnitt** *m* profile

Geländeebbe *f* ground squall

Gelände-ebene *f* ground plane **-einrichtungen** *pl* field works **-erkundung** *f* ground or terrain reconnaissance **-fähig** adapted for cross-country driving **-fahren** *n* cross-country driving **-fahrzeug** *n* cross-country vehicle **-falte** *f* fold (topog.) **-formen** *f pl* terrain features

Gelände-gang *m* traction gear, underdrive, auxiliary gear **-gängig** capable of cross-country travel, having cross-country mobility, suitable for cross-country work or driving **-gängigkeit** *f* cross country operation **-gegenstand** *m* terrain feature, landmark **-gestalt** *f* configuration of ground, ground shape **-gestaltung** *f* configuration of terrain, terrain features **-hindernis** *n* natural obstacle, terrain obstacle **-inspektoren** *pl* area superintendants **-kammer** *f* field camera, terrestrial photographic camera

Gelände-kette *f* track put on rear wheels of track-wheel vehicles, traction band **-kraftfahrzeug** *n* cross-country car **-kunde** *f* topography **-nachbildung** *f* simulation of terrain **-nadir** *m* ground plumb point **-neigung** *f* slope, gradient **-oberfläche** *f* ground level **-orientierung** *f* orientation of terrain, orientation by map **-photogrammetrie** *f* ground or terrestrial photogrammetry **-punkt** *m* reference point, terrain point, ground feature, landmark **-punkthöhe** *f* height of feature

Geländer *n* rail, railing, handrail, trellis, guardrail, balustrade

Geländeraum *m* terrain area

Geländerdocke *f* rail post

Gelände-reifen *m* ground-grip tire

Geländer-holz *n* railing **-leine** *f* rail rope, guard rope **-pfosten** *m* baluster, rail post **-säule** *f* banister **-schiene** *f* guard rails **-stange** *f* railing, handrail **-stütze** *f* railing post, standard, handrail post

Gelände-scheibe *f* landscape target **-schutz** *m* defilade, natural protection **-skizze** *f* ground sketch, military sketch **-spiegel** *m* periscope **-streifen** *m* stretch of country, strip of ground, terrain sector **-teil** *m* area, sector **-verhältnisse** *pl* ground or terrain conditions **-vermessung** *f* terrain survey **-wagen** *m* jeep, cross-country truck **-welle** *f* rideau

Geländewinkel *m* angle of site or slope **negativer ~** angle of depression, negative angle of site

Geländewinkel-libelle *f* angle-of-site level **-messer** *m* angle-of-site instrument, clinometer **-meßvorrichtung** *f* angle-of-site mechanism

gelangen, dahin ~ to arrive at a destination **zu etwas ~** to arrive at an object or decision

gelappter Querschnitt lobed cross section

gelartig gel-like, gelatinous, colloidal, slimy

Gelaß *n* room, space, accommodation

gelassen tranquil

Gelatine *f* gelatin **-artig** gelatinous **-flitter** *m* gelatin spangle **-folie** *f* sheet gelatin **-herstellungsanlage** *f* gelatin-producing plant **-paushaut** *f* gelatine film for tracing **-pauspapier** *n* gelatin tracing paper **-plattenkühlapparat** *m* congealing apparatus for gelatin plates **-scheibe** *f* color screen **-schichtgerbung** *f* gelatine hardening **-überzug** *m* gelatin coating **-walze** *f* composition roller

gelatinieren to gelatinize

Gelatinier(ungs)mittel *n* gelatinizer

gelatinös gelatinous

Gelatit *n* a type of rock-blasting explosive

geläutertes Roheisen refined pig iron

Gelb *n*, **englisches ~** yellow oxychloride of lead

gelb yellow **-e Arsenblende** orpiment, auripigment **-es Arsensulfid** yellow arsenic sulfide, auripigment, orpiment **-es Bleioxyd** litharge, yellow lead oxide **-es Blutlaugensalz** potassium ferrocyanide **-es Präzipitat** yellow precipitate, yellow mercuric oxide

Gelb-blättrigkeit *f* yellow solution **-bleierz** *n* yellow lead ore, wulfenite **-brennanlage** *f* brass-dipping plant **-brennsäure** *f* aqua fortis **-eisenstein** *m* xanthosiderite **-erde** *f* yellow earth **-filter** *m* yellow screen or filter **-fleckenkrankheit** *f* yellow-spot disease **-gießer** *m* brassfounder **-gießerei** *f* brass foundry **-glut** *f* yellow heat, bright orange **-guß** *m* (yellow) brass **-holz** *n* fustic (wood)

Gelbildung *f* gel formation

Gel-Bildungstemperatur *f* gelling point

gelblich yellowish **-grau** drab

Gelb-kali *n* potassium ferrocyanide **-kupfer** *n* yellow brass, brass **-kupfererz** *n* chalcopyrite **-rot** amber (reddish yellow) **-scheibe** *f* yellow screen **-streifenkrankheit** *f* mosaic disease **-stich** *m* yellowisch tinge **-stichig** yellowish **-tannenholz** *n* yellow pine

Geld *n* money, coin, cash **-abfindung** *f* money allowance, reimbursement, cash settlement **-angelegenheit** *f* money matter **-anlage** *f* investment of capital **-anweisung** *f* money order **-ausgabe** *f* disbursement, expense, expenditure

Geldautomateneinrichtung des Fernrohres slot-paying mechanism of telescope

Geld-bestände *pl* cash in hand **-einwurf** *m* coin slot **-entschädigung** *f* reimbursement **-forderung** *f* money due **-handel** *m* exchange, banking **-kurs** *m* money rate, rate of exchange, bid price, banker's buying rate **-mittel** *n pl* means, resources **-not** *f* tightness or want of money **-posten** *m* sum of money **-preis** *m* cash prize

Geldschrank *m* (fireproof) safe **-beschläge** *pl* fittings for safes **-blech** *n* plate for safes **-platten** *f pl* safe plates **-sicherung** *f* safety contact for safe

Geld-sendung *f* remittance **-strafe** *f* fine (by law) **-stück** *n* coin **-umlauf** *m* circulation of money **-umsatz** *m* money turnover, returns **-verlegenheit** *f* pecuniary difficulties, financial embarrassment **-wert** *m* monetary worth, assets **-wesen** *n* financial business **-wirtschaft** *f* trade on a monetary basis **-zuwendungen** *pl* gratuities

Gelee *n* jelly

gelegen (liegen) situated **daran ~ sein** to matter

Gelegenheit *f* opportunity

Gelegenheitskauf *m* bargain

gelegentlich occasional

gelehrt learned, scholarly

Gelehrter *m* scientist, scholar

geleimtes Papier sized paper

Geleine *n* shroud lines (parachute), rigging (balloon)

Geleise *n* rail, track, permanent way, bed (R.R.) **-anlage** *f* railroad layout or yard **-anschluß** *m* railroad-line junction **-breite** *f* track width, gauge **-relais** *n* track relay **-stromkreis** *m* track circuit (elec.) **-tafel** *f* track diagram **-winkel** *m* track angle

geleistete Arbeitsstunden houres worked

Geleit *n* escort, convoy, safeguard **-boot** *n* chaser convoying boat (navy)

geleiten to convoy, escort, conduct

geleitete Schwingungsart *f* trapped mode

Geleitwort *n* preface, introduction

Gelenk *n* joint, link, hinge, knuckle, toggle, articulation, hinged bearing, flexible coupling **festes ~** hinged support

Gelenk-anschluß *m* hinge fitting **-arm** *m* hinged or slewing bracket (gas, electric) **-auge** *n* shackle toggle joint **-ausleger** *m* articulated or hinged arm **-band** *n* link **-becher** *m* hinged bucket **-binde** *f* joint bandage **-binden** *pl* ankle-wrap puttes

Gelenk-bogenbrücke *f* hinged-arch bridge **-bolzen** *m* joint bolt or pin, flexible stay bolt **-egge** *f* articulated harrow **-flansch** *m* joint flange **-förmig** joint shaped **-gabel** *f* fork-type joint **-gehäuse** *n* universal-joint housing **-glückshaken** *m* link hook **-hebel** *m* toggle joint

gelenkig flexible, pliable, jointed, articulated, supple, linked **~ am Flugzeuggerippe lagern** to mount flexibly onto fuselage **~ gelagert** pin-jointed (statics), with hinged supports **-er Stoßriegel** hinged joining member **-e Welle** *f* universal-joint shaft

Gelenk-kette *f* bank chain, link chain, sprocket chain, flat-link articulated chain **-klemme** *f* socketed grip or terminal (movable in socket) **-kondensator** *m* swingout condenser **-krümmer** *m* joint bend **-kugel** *f* spherical part (of universal joint) **-kupplung** *f* hinge coupling or articulated joint coupling, Hooke's joint, universal joint **-lager** *n* ball-and-socket joint **-lasche** *f* joint plate **-leuchte** *f* machine lamp **-maßstab** *m* folding ruler

Gelenk-mechanismen *pl* linkages **-muffe** *f* link box **-öse** *f* swivel eye or ring **-pfosten** *m* loose-jointed post **-platte** *f* wrist plate **-punkt** *m* joint, fulcrum, hinge **-puppe** *f* swivel doll **-quarz** *m* itacolumite, flexible sandstone

Gelenk-riemen *m* wrist strap **-rohr** *n* articulated pipe Cardan tube, drive, shaft, housing **-rohre** *pl* grasshopper or swing joints **-rotorsystem** *n* articulated rotor system **-säge** *f* hinge saw **-schaftbolzen** *m* link-rod pin **-scheibe** *f* shaft plate **-schiebersteuerung** *f* noneccentric valve gear **-schlauch** *m* flexible steam pipe (articulated) **-schraube** *f* swing bolt, hinged bolt, shackle bolt (swiveling) **-schraubstock** *m* hinged vice

Gelenk-schwingensteuerung *f* articulated link gearing (valve-gear drive) **-seilscheibe** *f* joint pulley **-spindel** *f* articulated spindle **-spindelbohrkopf** *m* articulated drilling head **-spindelbohrmaschine** *f* multiple-drill press **-spreizringkupplung** *f* articulated-jaw friction clutch **-stange** *f* hinge rod, link rod, handle bar, hinged tie bar **-stangenführung** *f* guide links **-stelle** *f* moving joint **-strebe** *f* hinged frame (with knuckle joint) **-stück** *n* toggle lever, joint, articulation piece, connecting piece **-stutzpappe** *f* shank board

gelenkt guided, controlled

Gelenk-teil *m* coupling crosshead pin (in Diesel) pivoting part **-träger** *m* support for joint **-trägerbrücke** *f* hinged girder bridge **-verbinder** *m* knuckle joint **-verbindung** *f* hinge connection, swivel connection or union, moving or swing joint **-wand** *f* link baffle **-viereck** *n* link quadrilateral bellcrank throttle control **-welle** *f* drive shaft, Cardan wave, universal-joint shaft **-wellenrohr** *n* drive-shaft housing **-wellenverbindung** *f* binding by means of cardan (shafts) **-zahnstange** *f* jointed rack **-zapfen** *m* link or hinge pin **-zug** *m* articulated train

gelernt skilled

Geleucht *n* armature, fitting

Gelferz *n* copper pyrites

Gelfkupfer *m* copper pyrites, chalcopyrite

geliefert, im Kasten ~ furnished mounted in a cabinet

gelitzt stranded

gellend shrill, yelling, tingling

gelocht perforated, holed **-es Blech** perforated plate or sheet

gelockerte Stelle (Gefüge) discontinuity

gelöscht extinguished, erased (magn. tape) **-er Funken** quenched spark **-er Kalk** slaked lime, slack lime **-er Zement** hydrated cement

gelöst dissolved, disengaged (machin) **-e Ordnung** a type of extended order in flight formation

gelötet soldered **-es Rohr** soldered or brazed pipe

Gel-Sol-Transformation solation

gelten to be valid, be current, hold, apply to, remain true **es ~** are valid, be alive, be in force **~ lassen** to assume

geltend-e Abmachungen valid, applicable, accepted, arrangements in force **-e Definition** accepted definition **-e Zahl oder Ziffer** significant digit (comp.)

Geltendmachen *n* (Anspruch) assertion, advance or make a claim

Geltung *f* validity **in ~ sein** to prevail **~ verschaffen** to enforce

Geltungsbereich *m* validity; (Norm) scope **~ einer Erfindung** scope or command of an invention

Geltungsgebiet *n* jurisdictional area

gelüftet ventilated

gemahlen ground, milled

Gemarkung *f* boundary, landmark

gemasert mottled (cast iron), speckled, streaked, veined, grained **-es Papier** grained paper

gemäß according to

Gemäßheit, in ~ in accordance

gemäßigt temperate, mild, moderate

Gemäuer *n* brickwork, masonry

gemauert built with brick **-er Kanal** brick channel **-er Stein** hand-laid rock in courses

gemein common, low, vulgar **-e Braunkohle** dense lignite, low-rank subbituminous coal **-er Bruch** simple fraction

Gemeinde *f* municipality, township, community, congregation, parish

Gemein-kosten *pl* overhead cost **-lade** *f* half-plank, half-inch plank, shelf **-nutz** *m* common weal or interest

gemeinnützig of public utility, beneficial to all, co-operative, non-profit (making) organization

gemeinsam common, joint, in common, cooperative, shared **-es Ausmaß** *n* joint measurement **-es Gebläse** central blower or supercharger **-er Nenner** common denominator **-e Regelung** unit control **-e Verbindung** common connection **-e Wege, zur Übermittlung der Zeichen** common signaling paths **-er Widerstand** joint resistance **-er Zweig** common branch (electr)

Gemeinschaft *f* community, partnership, cooperation

gemeinschaftlich common, mutual, collective, joint **~ und einzeln** jointly and severally **~ betrieben** geared and locked together, ganged **-e Erfinder** joint inventors **-er Teiler** common divisor

Gemeinschafts-anschluß *m* party line, connection **-anschlußleitung für Landteilnehmer** rural party line **-antenne** *f* party antenna, block antenna **-antennenanlage** *f* master antenna system **-arbeit** *f* cooperation, joint work, cooperative effort **-aufgabe** *f* common task **-empfänger** *m* political receiver (teleph.) **-gründung** *f* cooperative (enterprise) **-leistung** *f* collective performance **-leitung** *f* party line (tel) **-sender** *m* chain broadcast station **-übertragung** *f* panel of relay sets **-verkehr** *m* series-type supervisory system **-werbung** *f* collective advertising

gemeinverständlich popularly

Gemeinwesen *n* community, common wealth

Gemenge *n* mixture, rich mixture, batch (glass) **-anteil** *m* ingredient of a mixture **-haus** *n* (Glasindustrie) glass batch house

Gemengsel *n* medley, hodge-podge, confusion

Gemeng-stoff *m* ingredient **-teil** *m* constituent **-teilchen** *pl* mixed particles

gemessen measured **von A aus ~** measured from A **-e Dehnungen** determined stresses **-e Pferdestärke** indicated horsepower

Gemeßröhre *f* detector, mixer

Gemisch *n* composition, compound, mixture **-anreicherungsgrad** *m* mixture strength **-ausgleichvorrichtung** *f* strangler (of carburetor) **-beheizer** *m* mixture hot spot **-bildner** *m* mixture-generating apparatus, emulsifier

Gemischbildung *f* mixture formation; (äußere ~) carburetion; (innere ~) fuel injection

Gemisch-eintrittsöffnung im Zylinder intake port **-einstellung** *f* mixture setting **-grenze für Eintreten von Explosion** mixture limit for the appearance of explosion

Gemisch-komponenten *pl* spectral components **-regelung** *f* quantitative governing mixture control **-regler** *m* mixture corrector, mixture controls **-regulierung** *f* mixture control **-schmierung** *f* (Oberschmierung) petrol lubrication **-stärkemeßgerät** *n* aero-mixture indicator **-steuerung** *f* mixture control

gemischt mixed, combined **~ schalten** to connect in multiple arc **-er Betrieb** mixed service **-e Doppelvorwahl** preselection (partly double) **-e Gesamtheit** mixed ensemble **-er Halbleiter** mixed semi-conductor **-e Ladung** mixed cargo **-e Schaltung** series-multiple or multiple-arc connection, parallel-series connection

gemischt-er Schmelzfluß mixed melt **-e Stimme** multation stops (organ) **-e Verbrennung** mixed combustion, mixed cycle **-er Verkehr** mixed service **-e Verstellung** *f* mixed semiautomatic advance **-e Wicklung** *f* shunt or compound winding

Gemischt-basisschreibweise *f* mixed-base notation **-bau** *m* stick and wire construction (aviation), composite construction **-bauweise** *f* method of mixed construction (*i.e.*, wood and metal) **-beaufschlagte Turbine** mixed-pressure turbine **-falzung** *f* miscellaneous folding **-körnig** of various grain sizes **-paariges Kabel** combined or composite cable **-regler** *m* mixture control

gemischverdichtende Maschine gas engine, explosion engine

Gemischtverhältnis, theoretisches ~ mixture ratio for complete combustion

Gemisch-verteiler *m* direct-driven blower, paddle fan **-verteilung** *f* distribution **-vorwärmeinrichtung** *f* hot-spotting arrangement **-vorwärmer** *m* hot spot **-vorwärmer** *m* pre-heater of mixture **-vorwärmung** *f* preheating of gas mixture **-wert** *m* mixture strength **-zuführung** *f* mixture admission or supply **-zusammensetzung** *f* mixture strength **-zutritt** *m* mixture admission or inlet

gemittelt average **-e Operationszeit** average calculating operation **-e Zentralfelder** mean central fields

gemittet centered

gemodelt modulated **-er Strom** modulated current **-e ungedämpfte Welle** modulated continuous wave

Gemsleder *n* shammy, chamois leather, wash leather

gemustert fancy, figured, diapered, flowered **-er Deckbogen** pattern sheet

gen (gegen) toward

Gen *n* gene (biology)
genagelt pinned
genarbt grained
genau exact, particular, strict, precise, true, close (imitation), faithful (reproduction) **auf mm ~** to the nearest mm **~ auf zwei Dezimalstellen** correct to two decimal places **~ genommen** strictly speaking **~ wie oben** the same as (the value, formulas) above **-e Bezeichnung** (Pflichtenblatt) rating (*e.g.*, voltage rating of condenser), specification **-es Maß** true size, accurate dimension **-e Mitte** dead center
Genaudrahtzieherei *f* precision-wire-drawing works
Genauigkeit *f* exactitude, precision, closeness, faithfulness, accuracy **~** (Treue der Wiedergabe) fidelity **mit ~** accurately **erreichte ~** attained accuracy **fünfstellige ~** five-figure accuracy **verlangte ~** required or requisitioned accuracy **Bereich größter ~** (Meßtechn.) effective range
Genauigkeits-arbeit *f* precision work **-drehbank** *f* super-finishing lathe **-feile** *f* adjusting file **-grad** *m* degree of accuracy **-grenze** *f* precision limit **-grenzen** *pl* limits of accuracy **-guß** *m* precision castings **-höhenmesser** *m* precision altimeter **-landung** *f* accuracy landing, spot landing **-maß** *n* degree of error **-messer** *m* performance meter **-meßwerkzeug** *n* accurate-measuring instrument
Genauigkeits-ordnung *f* order of accuracy **-polieren** *n* fine polishing **-schnelldrehbank** *f* high-speed precision lathe **-schnitt** *m* precision cut **-stufen** *pl* grades of accuracy **-untersuchung** *f* investigation of the accuracy **-verlust** *m* loss of accuracy (info proc.) **-verzahnung** *f* precision gear **-werkzeug** *n* precision tool
Genauschmieden *n* precision forgings
genehmigen to approve, accept, sanction, allow, authorize, accede, permit
genehmigt approved **nicht ~** disapproved, uncertified **-er Flugplan** approved flight plan
Genehmigung *f* approval, permission, agreement, authorization, consent, allowance, sanction **amtliche ~** license **dienstliche ~** official authorization or approval
Genehmigungs-druck (Kessel) *m* maximum working pressure **-verfahren** *n* authorisation procedure
geneigt inclined, sloping, tilted, slanting, sloped **~ um** set at an angle **-er Boden** sloping bottom **-er Flansch** sloping flange **-e Luftbilder mit Nadirdistanz bis** obliques with nadir distances to **-er Pfahl** battered pile **-e Retorte** inclined retort **-e Sohle** inclined apron **-es U-Rohr** inclined U tube **-e Wellenstirn** tilted wave front
Geneigtaufnahme *f* oblique exposure
General-abfrage *f* general interrogation **-bevollmächtigter** *m* commissioner, general chargé d'affaires **-direktor** *m* general manager, president **-durchschaltung** *f* final test **-gedinge** *n* bargain by the job or lump
General-karte *f* general map **-kommissar** *m* commissioner-general **-konsul** *n* consul general
Generalstabskarte *f* generalstaff map (scale 1:100,000), ordnance or strategic map
General-umschalter *m* universal switch (elec.) **-unkosten** *pl* general expenses, overhead expenses **-versammlung** *f* general meeting **-vollmacht** *f* full power of attorney
Generator *m* producer, dynamo; (Gleichstrom) generator; (Wechselstrom) alternator **~ mit Fremderregung** separately excited alternator **~ für die Gittervorspannung** bias generator **~ mit gleichförmigem Luftspalt** nonsalient pole generator **~ mit an den Polkanten erweitertem Luftspalt** salient-pole generator **~ mit drehbarem Rost** rotary-grate-type producer **~ mit fixem Rost** fixed-grate-type producer, dry-bottom gas producer, simple stationary gas producer
Generator, ~ mit drehbarem Schacht rotary-body-type producer **~ mit Scheibenanker** disk-type alternator **~ mit Schrägrost** inclined-grate-type producer **~ für zwei Spannungen** double-voltage generator **~ durch Windschraube angetrieben** windmill-driven generator **geblasener ~** pressure-gas producer **gezogener ~** suction-gas producer
Generator-aggregat *n* gas generator **-anhänger** *m* generator trailer **-anlage** *f* generator plant or unit **-armatur** *f* generator fittings **-diagramm** *n* load impedance diagram **-gas** *n* producer or generator gas, suction gas **-gasanlage** *f* producer-gas plant **-gasbetrieb** *m* producer-gas operation **-gaserzeuger** *m* gas producer **-gasflamme** *f* producer-gas flame **-gruppe** *f* generating set
Generator-kreis *m* undamped circuit **-läufer** *m* generator rotor **-mantel** *m* producer shell **-röhre** *f* oscillator valve or tube, oscillating or generating valve, oscillation valve **-satz** *m* generating set, or electric generator **-schacht** *m* producer shaft or body **-schütz überlastet** generator contactor overloaded **-(schütz)-schalter** *m* generator switch **-sicherung** *f* generator fuse **-sockel** *m* producer base **-steckdose** *f* generator socket **-stückkohle** *f* screened producer coal **-überwachung** *f* generator control **-unterteil** *n* bottom section of a gas producer
genesen to recover, convalesce
Genesung *f* convalescence, recovery
Genetik *f* genetics
genetisch genetic
Genfer Abkommen *n* Geneva convention
Genfer Rotes Kreuz Geneva Red Cross
Genferkreuz *n* Geneva cross
Gengas *n* producer gas
Genick *n* nack, nape
genießbar edible, palatable
genießen to enjoy, eat
genietet riveted
Genmutation *f* gene mutation
genormt standardized
Genosse *m* associate, companion, comrade, chum
Genossenschaft *f* association, companionship, cooperative, company
genug enough, sufficient
genügen to suffice, come up (to), conform to, meet, be enough, satisfy, meet demands
gemügend enough, satisfactory, sufficient, ample
Genugtuung *f* satisfaction, atonement
Genuß *m* enjoyment, gratification **-mittel** *n pl* (wie Tabak) semi-luxuries (like tabacco)
genutet slotted, grooved, fluted **-e Welle** shaft with keyway, slot, or groove
Genveränderung *f* gene change mutation

geoantiklinal geoanticline
Geochemie *f* geochemistry
geochemisch geochemical **-e Basis** geochemical basis
Geochronologie *f* geochronology
Geodäsie *f* geodesy
Geodät *m* land surveyor
geodätisch geodetical ~ **parallel** geodesic parallel **-e Abbildung** geodesic mapping **-e Bauweise** geodetic construction **-e Krümmung** geodesic curvature **-e Linien** geodesic lines, geodesics
geöffnet open, open-circuited, standing on open circuit, at full interval, extended
geognostische Wissenschaften geognosy
Geographie *f* geography
geographisch geographical ~ **Nord** geographic or true north **-e Breite** latitude **geographische Höhe** *f* elevation **-e Länge** longitude **-er Norden** geographical north **-e Örter** geographic position
Geoid-bestimmung *f* geoid determination **-undulation** *f* geoid warping
Geolog(e) *m* geologist
Geologie *f* geology
geologisch geological **-e Beschaffenheit** structure **-es Profil** geological section
Geometer *m* geometrician, surveyor
Geometrie *f* geometry **-brumm** *m* geometry hum **-fehler** *m* geometric distortion
geometrisch geometric(al) ~ **iteriert** geometrical iterated **-e Bewegungslehre** graphic kinematics **-e Fernrohrlichtstärke** geometrical luminosity relative brightness **-e Grundform** geometrical fundamental **-es Mittel** geometric mean **-er Mittelpunkt** geometric center **mittlerer -er Abstand** mean geometric distance **-e Reihe** geometrical progression **-e Steigung** geometric pitch
Geometrisierung der Wellenmechanik geometric derivation of wave equation
Geomorphologie *f* topographical features
Geophon *n* geophone
Geophotogrammetrie *f* ground or terrestrial photogrammetry
Geophysik *f* geophysics
geophysikalisch geophysical **-e Forschung** geophysical method of prospecting
geophysische Untersuchung geophysical exploration
Geopolitik *f* geopolitics
geopotentieller Normfuß standard geopotential foot
geordnet orderly, systematic **regellos** ~ with random orientation **-e Mischphase** nonstochiometric compound **-er Zustand** orderly state or arrangement, perfect configuration
geortetes Ziel plot
geostrophisch geostrophic
Geosynklinal *n* geosyncline
geothermisch geothermic **-e Tiefenstufe** thermal gradient, temperature gradient
Geothermometer *n* geothermometer
geozentrisch geocentric
gepaart paired
Gepäck *n* pack, kit, baggage, luggage, impedimenta **-abfertigung** *f* dispatching of luggage **-abteil** *n* baggage compartment **-annahme** *f* acceptance of baggage **-aufgabe** *f* checking of baggage **-brett** *n*, **-galerie** *f*, **-halter** *m* baggage rack **-brücke** (Auto) luggage rack **-koffer** *m* (baggage) trunk **-netz** *n* parcel rack **-raum** *m* baggage compartment, hold
gepackt, dicht ~ close-packed
Gepäck-transportband *n* baggage conveyer belt **-troß** *m* baggage train, baggage transport, baggage convoy **-wagen** *m* baggage car, van (truck)
gepanzert shielded, armored, metal- or armor-clad, armor-plated **-e wenig streuende Spule** iron-core deflecting yoke
gepeiltes Besteck position by bearing
gepeilter Sender turned-in beacon or transmitter
gepfeilter Flügel swept-back wing
gepflastert paved **-er Deich** stone dike
gepfuscht bungled
geplante Leistung design power
geplatzter Reifen burst or punctured tire
gepökelt salted, pickled, or preserved (goods)
gepolstert padded
gepolt poled, polar, polarized **-es Relais** polarized relay
Gepräge *n* stamping, marking, impression, distinction, coinage, character
geprägt coined, stamped, pressed to shape, shaped **-e Folie** embossed foil
gepreßt pressed, stamped (metal), punched **grob** ~ coarse, coarsely powdered, slightly crushed
geprüft tested, examined
gepuffert (werden) (to be) floated **-e Batterie** buffer battery **-e Lösung** buffered solution
gepulvert powdered
gepumpter Beton pumped concrete
gequantelt quantized
gequirlter Satz broken matter
Geradbiegen *n* straightening, straight bending
Gerade *f* (straight) line, equation in straight form, even integer **in einer Geraden** in alignment (with) **unendlich ferne** ~ straight line at infinity
gerade straight, even (number), just, direct, erect, flush ~ **machen** to dress, straighten ~ **richten** to straighten ~ **Aufsteigung** (des Gestirns) right ascension ~ **Beleuchtung** direct illumination ~ **senkrechte Bohrung** straight well **-r und ebener Flug** straight and level flight ~ **auf den Strand laufen** to beach (a ship), run end on to shore ~ **einfallendes Licht** straight light, perpendicularly incident light **eine** ~ **Linie bilden** to make or draw a straight line **in eine** ~ **Linie bringen** to align with ~ **Muffe mit zweifach konischem Gewinde** coupling with plain ends ~ **Muffe mit Rechts- und Linksgewinde** coupling right and left
gerader-gerader Kern even-even nucleus
gerade-s Prisma right prism **-r Riegel** straight pole brace ~ **Strecke** tangent section (R.R.) ~ **Stütze** insulator pin **-s Verhältnis** direct ratio **-s Vielfaches** even multiple ~ **Zahl** even number **-r Zylinder** right cylinder
gerade ausrichten to level
geradeaus straight on, straight ahead, straight out, rectilinear
Geradeaus-anflug *m* straight-in approach **-empfänger** *m* straight receiver (radar), tuned radio-frequency receiver, simple detector-type receiver, straight-circuit receiver **-entfernung** *f* slant distance **-fliegen** to fly straight **-flug** *m* straight

flight **-frequenz** *f* tuned radio frequency **-spritzkopf** *m* straight head

Gerade-biegen *n* straightening **-facettehobel** *m* bevel planer **-flußsystem** *n* straight-flow system (gas turbines) **-führung** *f* alignment **-führungshebel** *m* levelling lever

Geradeisen *n* drawing or planishing knife

gerade-klopfen to knock straight **-kochen** (Borsten) *n* straight boiling **-laufen** to tighten up

Gerade-legen der Drähte straightening of the wire **-messer** *n* drawknife, plane

Geraden, windschiefe ~ skew lines

Geradenbüschel *m* (one-parameter) family of lines

gerade-richten to straighten **-richten** *n* straightening **-schneiden** to trim **-schnitt** *m* straight cut **-steller** *m* recalling fork **-stoßer** *m* jogger **-strekken** *n* straight, stretching, straightening **-ungerade-Kern** even-odd nucleus **-ungeradekontrolle** *f* odd-even check **-verzahntes Kegelrad** straight bevel gear **-verzahnung** *f* spur tooth **-ziehen** *n* straightening

Geradführung *f* (crosshead) guide, sliding bar, linkage for tracing a straight line **~** (Kreuzkopf) slide bar, (crosshead) guides

Geradführungsbacke *f* guide blocks

Geradhängevorrichtung *f* pitching tool

geradkörnig straight grained

Geradlauf-apparat *m* gyroscope (Obry's gear) **-versager** *m* gyroscope failure

geradleiten to rectify

geradlinig rectilinear, straight-lined, linear, in direct proportion **-e Beziehung** straight-line relationship **-er Gleichrichter** straight-line detector

Geradlinigkeit *f* linearity, straightness

Geradschliff *m* (Sägezähne) straight cut (saw teeth) **-maschine** *f* (Säge) straight-edge tooth-sharpening machine

Geradseit-felge *f* straight-side rim **-reifen** *m* straight-side tire

geradsichtiges Prisma direct-vision prism

Geradsichtspektroskop *n* direct-vision spectroscope

Geradstoßhobel *m* planer

geradverzahnt straight-fluted (plain teeth) **-es Kegelrad** straight bevel gear

Geradverzahnung *f* straight-tooth bevels

geradwertig of even valence **-e Gruppen** even-valent groups

geradzahlig even-numbered **-er Zeilensprung** evenline interlace

gerammt rammed (in) **die Spundbohlen sind dicht ~** the sheet piling is driven with plain joints

gerändelt, gerändert edged, milled, knurled

Gerassel *n* clatter

gerastert-es Bild half tone process image **-e Schicht, -er Schirm** mosaic screen (TV), photo-sensitized mosaic

gerastet rested, spot-set (frequency) **-e Frequenz** spot frequency

Gerät *n* (Werkzeug) tolls, utensils; (Ausrüstung) out fit; (Meßgerät) instrument; (Vorrichtung) fixture, device, appliance; (Schaltgerät) switch gear, apparatus, implement, equipment, gear, armature, (farming) implements, (fishing) tackle, box bill, dolly (min.), aggregate (*e.g.*, a guided missile, supersonic glider, rocket, etc.) **~ G** code for a type of guided missile

Gerät, ~ zum Aufzeichnen von Gesprächen telephone-voice recorder **~ zur Aufzeichnung der Oberflächenbeschaffenheit** contourograph **~ zur Bestimmung des Brechpunktes** device to determinate the breaking point **~ klar zum Einnehmen** prepared to bring in or to sweep **~ zur Feststellung von Rissen in metallischen Werkstoffen** flaw detector **~ mit Induktionsheizung** induction-heating apparatus

Gerät, ~ mit Lichtbogenheizung arc-heating apparatus **~ zum Stopfen des Geleises** tamping bar **~ mit Widerstandsheizung** resistance-heating apparatus **~ bis Wirbelschäkel ausbringen** to get out sweep as far as swivel shackle **~ anfordern** to request equipment **sprachbetätigtes ~** voice-operated device

Gerät-art *f* type of equipment **-ausstattung** *f* allotment of equipment

Geräte *pl* (allgemeine Ausrüstung) general apparatus and equipment **~ einregeln** to time instruments **mechanisch arbeitende ~** mechanically operating instruments **~ für Gewindelehren- und Koordinatenmessungen** instruments for measuring threads, gauges and coordinates **~ für Oberflächenprüfungen** instruments for surface testing

Geräte-anordnung *f* layout of equipment **-anschlußkabel** *n* instrument connection cable **-anschlußschnur** *f* flexible cable **-antriebgehäuse** *n* accessories-drive housing **-antriebritzel** *n* auxiliary-drive gear **-ausgabestelle** *f* equipment issuing point **-bau** *m* apparatus construction **-brett** *n* instrument board or panel **-brettbeleuchtung** *f* instrument panel illumination **-dose** *f* plug box **-durchsicht** *f* inspection of equipment or ordnance

Geräteeinheit *f* unit assemblage **(her)ausziehbare ~** draw-out type of equipment

Geräte-einzelstecker *m* single-plug apparatus (elec.) **-entgiftung** *f* decontamination of equipment **-glas** *n* glass suitable for laboratory ware, apparatus glass (stock) **-gruppe** *f* type of equipment **-heberanlage** *f* hydraulic lift **-kapsel** *f* instrument caspule (of spacecraft) **-kasten** *m* toolbox **-kennwerte** *pl* instrument parameters **-korb** *m* instrument basket or cage **-licht** *n* instrument light

geraten to get into **in einen Hinterhalt ~** to be ambushed **in Produktion ~** to start combustion **in eine petroleumhaltige Schicht ~** (to) drill in

Geräte-nachweis *m* equipment schedule **-platte** *f* instrument panel **-programm** *n* instrument program

Geräteraum *m* tool-storage room, central compartment (rocket) **hinterer ~** (zwischen Brandschott und Motor) engine rear compartment

Geräteraumgerippe *n* central-compartment shell (rocket)

Geräte-relais *n* integrator relay **-rückseite** *f* rear panel of the apparatus **-schalter** *m* plug switch, appliance switch **-schild** *m* instrument name plate **-schrank** *m* tool locker, apparatus compartment locker **-steckdose** *f* utensil socket **-stecker** *m* coupler plug, apparatus plug, utensil plug **-steckeranschluß** *m* instrument plug connections **-steckvorrichtung** *f* coupler plug and socket connection, coupler

Gerätetasche *f*, **vollständige ~ für Löter** splicer's tool bag **vollständige ~ für Störungssucher** lineman's or mechanic's tool bag

Geräte-teil *m* accessory **-tisch** *m* instrument table **-träger** *m* auxiliary gearbox, accessory section or rack **-transportwagen** *m* cart for tools **-überwachungsbuch** *n* equipment-control log, equipment checking book **-verdrahtung** *f* equipment wiring **-wagen** *m* equipment wagon or truck **-wirbel** *m* tool swivel

Gerät-inspizient *m* equipment inspector **-klasse** *f* class of equipment **-koffer** *m* toolbox

Gerätkraftwagen *m* equipment truck

Gerät-lehre *f* tool gauge **-nullpunkt** *m* zero-point director **-nummer** *f* serial number **-sammelstelle** *f* equipment-collecting point, ordnance-collecting point **-satz** *m* unit of equipment

Gerätsblock *m* plugging or blocking unit, Bucker unit

Gerät-schaft *f* apparatus, implements, tools, utensils, appliance **-schlüssel** *m* tool wrench **-stück** *n* piece or item of equipment

gerättert separated, sifted (min.)

Gerätverwalter *m* storekeeper

gerauht napped (fabrics)

geraum ample, considerable

geräumig large, roomy, spacious **-er Rumpf** roomy fuselage

Geräusch *n* noise, sound, sonic impulses **~ durch Einschwingvorgänge** noise due to transients **~ durch Mithören** noise caused by listening in **vom ~ abgeschlossen** soundproof **kratzendes ~** scratchy noise (phono)

Geräusch-abstand *m* signal-to-noise ratio **-analysator** *m* noise analyzer

geräuscharm of low noise, noiseless, silent, silenced **-e Übertragung** low-noise transmission

Geräusch-artung *f* noise camouflage, any noise-producing means intended to deceive enemy as to position of guns, advance of tanks, etc. **-bekämpfung** *f* noise abatement, suppression, or attenuation

Geräuschbeseitigung *f* blooping elimination **automatische ~** silent tuning, noise suppression, noise gate

geräuschbewertet measured with psophometric filter

Geräuschboje *f* hydrophone buoy

geräuschdämpfend antinoise, silencing **-es Material** soundproofing material

Geräuschdämpfer *m* muffler (noise damper)

Geräuschdämpfung *f* soundproofing, silencing **Verfahren zur ~** soundproofing method

Geräuschdämpfungsverfahren *n* quieting method

Geräusche durch Einschwingvorgänge transient noises

geräuschelektromotorische Kraft psophometric electromotive force

Geräusch-empfänger *m* (navy) hydrophone, underwater receiver **-film** *m* effect film **-filter** *n* noise suppressor; (Krachfilter *n*) scratch filter (phono)

geräuschfrei-e Abstimmung interstation noise suppression **-e Leitung** quiet circuit **-kasten** *m* equivalent acoustics

geräuschlos quiet, silent, noiseless **-er Gang** noiseless running **-er dritter Gang** silent third speed

Geräuschlosigkeit *f* silence, noiselessness, quietness, calm(ness)

Geräusch-menge *f* noise intensity **-messer** *m* noise meter, noise-measuring set, sound-level meter, acoustimeter **-minderer** *m* noise reducer **-muster** *n* noise pattern **-normal** *n* noise standard **-ortung** *f* hydrophone contact **-pegel** *m* noise level **-quelle** *f* source of noise or of sonic vibrations **-schluckend** sound-proofed **-sicher** soundproof **-spannung** *f* psophometric potential difference, psophometric voltage, noise voltage

Geräusch-spannungsmesser *m*, **-spannungszeiger** *m* noise meter, applause meter (radio broadcasting) **-spiegel** *m* noise suppressor or level **-spur** *f* buzz track (film) **-stärke** *f* noise intensity **-störung** *f* noise jamming **-tarnung** *f* noise camouflage **-tastung** *f* key clicks **-unsymmetriemesser** *m* disturbing-unbalance-measuring set **-unterdrückungsstromkreis** *m* silencing, noise reduction, or suppression circuit **-verdeckung** *f* overriding of noise **-vernichter** *m* noise killer

geräuschvoll noisy **-e Leitung** noisy circuit

gerautetes Glas lozenged glass

Gerb-anlage *f* tanning plant **-eisen** *n* wrought iron, burnisher, shaving knife

gerben to refine (metals), fine, tan (leather), curry, dress (hides) **den Stahl ~** to pile and weld the steel

Gerber *m* tanner

Gerberei *f* tannery, tanning

Gerber-gelenkholm *m* Gerber hinge, pinpointed spar **-gelenkträger** *m* girder with Gerber joints, Gerber beam

Gerbersche Anordnung Gerber design (a type of cantilever construction)

Gerberträger *m* cantilever structure, pin-jointed or cantilever beam, cantilever spar

Gerb-holzraspelmaschine *f* wood chopper **-leim** *m* tannic acid glue **-säure** *f* tannic acid, tannin **-säuremesser** *m* tannometer

gerbsaures Ammonium ammonium tannate

Gerb-stahl *m* shear steel, refined iron, wrought steel **-stoff** *m* tanning substance, tannin

Gerbung *f* (re)fining (met), tanning

gerecht just, righteous, lawful **~ werden** to satisfy, give consideration to **der Aufgabe ~ werden** to be equal to the task

gerechtfertigen to justify

Gerechtigkeit *f* justice, equity, equitableness

Gerechtsame *f* privilege, right, title

gereckt-er Einfaden spun filament **-e Probe** *f* stretched specimen

geregelt regulated, adjusted **-e Größe** controlled variable **-e Kreuzung** signalized intersection **-er Verkehr** smooth traffic

gereifelt serrated, grooved, milled, knurled, fluted

gereinigt refined, purified **-er Branntwein** rectified alcohol

gergeln, ein Faß ~ to notch or groove a cask, make the chimbs of a cask

gerichtet directive, directed, directional, poled, trued, adjusted, corrected **~ sein** to be directed or pointing (at), tend **einseitig ~** unidirectional

gerichtet-e Ausstrahlung (elektr.) beamed transmission **-e Empfangsspannung** directional signal or incoming potential **-er Kathodenstrahl** focused cathode ray **-e Kupplungsspule** directional coupler **-er Lautsprecher** directional loudspeaker **-e Leistung** (bei Antennen) power radiated in main direction **-es Licht** parallel light (rays) **-er Luftstrahl** directionally controlled high-velocity air jet **-es Mikrophon** directional microphone **-e Reflexion** regular refelction **-er Sender** directional transmitter **-er Verkehr** use of two groups of lines on the same route **-er Widerstand** reactive resistance

gerichtlich judicial, judiciary ~ **belangen** to bring legal or judiciary action ~ **verfolgen** to sue

gerichtliches Verfahren einleiten to institute (legal)proceedings against

Gerichtsbarkeit erster Instanz original jurisdiction

Gerichts-akten *pl* (legal) records **-befehl** *m* writ, warrant **-beisitzer** *m* assessor, associate judge **-beschluß** *m* decision, sentence, or decree of the court **-bezirk** *m* court circuit or district **-chemie** *f* forensic chemistry

Gerichtshof *m* court of justice **zuständiger ~** court of competent jurisdiction

Gerichts-kosten *pl* legal expenses **-stand** *m* competency of a court, jurisdiction **-verfahren** *n* legal proceedings **-verhandlung** *f* hearing, trial

gerieft serrated, corrugated, knurled, fluted, milled, grooved

Geriesel *n* trickling, drizzling, murmur (of water)

geriffelt grooved, milled, serrated, corrugated, fluted, ribbed (pavement), knurled **-e Walzen** chilled rolls

gerillt profiled, grooved, fluted **-e Antriebsscheibe** tug rim **-e Mutter** knurled nut

gering small, slight, unimportant, trifling, minute, low, slow (of speed) ~ **beanspruchte Teile** light-duty parts **-er Aufschlag** slight extra cost **-es Gewicht** lightness **-e Landegeschwindigkeit** slow landing speed **-e Sinkgeschwindigkeit** slow sinking speed **-e Spanabnahme** shallow cut **-er Verbrauch** low consumption

geringelt curled

geringfügig trifling, small, unimportant, insignificant **-e Schwankungen auffangen** to adjust minor fluctuations

Gering-fügigkeit *f* littleness **-haltig** low-grade, of low standard, worthless, of low content **-mächtig** thin (seams) **-schätzen** to disregard **-schätzung** *f* scorn, contempt, disdain

geringst minimum, lowest **-geschwindigkeit** *f* minimum speed

Geringstmaß *n* minimum measure

Geringstwert *m* minimum value

geringwertig low-grade, inferior, imperfect, poor (of gases, vacuum) **-es Gas** poor or lean gas

gerinnbares Eiweiß coagulable albumin

Gerinne *n* gutter, channel, sluice, ditch, flume, trough, drain, conduit, launder (mining conduit) **gekrümmtes ~** circular channel **gerades ~** straight channel **kreisförmiges ~** circular channel

gerinnen to coagulate, curdle, thicken, grow viscid

Gerinnen *n* coagulation, cutting (of oils, sugars)

Gerinnhaue *f* pickax

Gerinnsel *n* coagulum, curds

Gerinn-stoff *m* coagulant, coagulator **-stücke** *pl* drain metal

Gerinnung *f* coagulation

Gerippe *n* framework, skeleton, outline **-abteil** *m* bay **-bau** *m* skeleton, structure **-punkt** *m* structural pivot or joint **-unterteilung** *f* subdivision of framework or hull structure

gerippt gilled, ribbed, flanged, serrated, grooved, corrugated, finned **-e Form** laid mold **-e Papiere** laid papers **außen -es Rohr** externally ribbed or finned pipe

Gerippunkt *m* structural pivot or joint

gerissen (reißen) chapped, flawed, sprung, cleft (wall), cracked (metal or glass), chinked (wood) **-e Kurve** dotted-line curve, broken-line curve or graph **-e Rolle** sudden or abrupt roll in the direction of flight **-e Verrohrung** parted casing

geritztes Fadenkreuz graticule

Germanatleuchtstoffe germanate phosphors

Germanium *n* germanium **-chlorür** *m* germanous chloride **-oxydul** *m* germanous oxide **-sperrschichten** germanium blocking layers **-sulfür** *m* germanous sulfide

Germverfahren *n* germ process (petroleum)

Geröll *n* rubble stone, pebble, boulder, alluvial **aus ~ bestehend** detrital **äolisches ~** aeolian rocks **goldhaltiges ~** auriferous, alluvial

Geröll-bohrer *m* ram's-horn **-mauerwerk** *n* flint work **-sand** *m* detrital sand **-schicht** *f* layer of rubble

gerollt lifted (lacquer) **-es Federauge** curled over or rolled spring eye **-es Gewinde** rolled thread

geronnen (gerinnen) curdled, clotted, coagulated

geröstet roasted, calcined

Gersdorffit *m* gersdorffite

Gerstenputz- und Sortiermaschine *f* barley cleaner and separator

Geruch *m* scent, smell, odor **-bekämpfungsstoff** *m* deodorant **-belästigung** *f* odorous annoyance **-dicht** smell-tight, smell-proof

Gerüche *m pl* scents, odors **von Gerüchen befreien** to deodorize

geruchfrei machen to deodorize

geruchlos odorless, inodorous **-machen** *n* deodorization

Geruch-messer *m* olfactometer **-stoff** *m* smelling substance **-verschluß** *m* odor seal, interceptor of odors, drain trap, stench trap

gerundet rounded **-e Kanten** round edges

Gerüst *n* (Bau) scaffolding, trestle; (Arbeitsbühne) stage, platform; (Eisenbau) steel frame, steel structure, (supporting) framework or structure, housing, staging, stand, rack, skeleton ~ **des Luftschiffes** framework of an airship **schwimmendes ~** floating (temporary) staging ~ **mit Rohrstützen** structure with pipe supports

Gerüst-anordnung *f* frame or framework arrangement, arrangement of rolling stands **-bau** *m* skeleton structure **-block** *m* trestle **-brücke** *f* trestle-work bridge, construction trestle **-eiweiß** *n* scleroprotein **-gabel** *f* pole fingers **-halter** *m* lashing, device for carrying centering **-konstruktion** *f* scaffolding **-kran** *m* gantry crane **-pfosten** *m* frame post **-ring** *m* thrust ring structure **-rippe** *f* rib of a semicircle (centering) **-säule** *f* supporting column **-ständer** *m* frame stand, roll-stand housing, housing bearer **-stange** *f* putlog, scaffolding pole, imp, stilt **-zurrung** *f* scaffold lashing

gesalzen salted or preserved (goods)

gesamt entire, total, general, complete, gross, altogether, aggregate **-e Spannweite** overall spread or span

Gesamt-ablenkung *f* total or resultant deviation **-absatz** *m* total sale **-abweichung** *f* total departure or declination **-anlage** *f* general view **-anlagekosten** *f pl* capital cost or first cost of installation **-anlageplan** *m* general plan **-anordnung** *f* complete arrangement **-anschluß** *m* total connections

Gesamt-ansicht *f* general view, total view, assembly view **-arbeitszeit** *f* floor-to-floor time **-asche** *f* total ash **-aufschaltung** *f* resultant steering signal **-auftrieb** *m* gross lift, total lift **-aufwand** *m* total expense **-aufwind** *m* total upcurrent **-ausfall** *m* total losses **-ausgabe** *f* complete works, total expenditure **-ausschaltung** *f* inclusive correction, resultant steering signal

Gesamtauswanderungs-strecke *f* distance from reference point to future position, distance target travels during time of flight of the projectile plus dead time or distance from present to future position **-zeit** *f* time of flight from reference point to future position, time necessary for plane to fly from present to future position

Gesamt-bedarf *m* total consumption **-befehl** *m* complete field order **-behandlungszeit** *f* overall treatment time **-belastung** *f* total load **-belegschaft** *f* total of employees **-belegungszähler** *m* all-trunks-busy register **-berge** *pl* total refuse **-bereich der Meßuhrablesung** *f* total indicator reading **-berichtigung** *f* total correction **-betrag** *m* sum total **-bewölkung** *f* total cloudiness **-brechung** *f* total refraction **-breite** *f* over-all width **-bruchlast** *f* total load at fracture

Gesamtdämpfung *f* total loss, attenuation length, transmission efficiency, total transmission equivalent, total cable equivalent **zulässige ~** total permissible transmission equivalent

Gesamt-dämpfungswiderstand *m* total damping resistance **-darstellung** *f* general review **-dauer** *f* total duration **-dehnung** *f* total extension or expansion **-deviation** *f* total or resultant deviation **-dissoziationsgrad** *m* total degree of dissociation **-dosis** *f* cumulative dose **-drehimpulsquantenzahl** *f* total angular momentum quantum number **-druck** *m* total pressure **-durchflußmenge** *f* total oil flow **-durchflutung** *f* ampere-conductors **-durchsatz** *m* total amount of flow

Gesamte *n* the whole, total, resultant

Gesamt-echtheitseigenschaften *pl* all-round fastness properties **-eigenschaften** *pl* all-round properties **-einnahme** *f* total receipts **-einströmquerschnitt** *m* cross-section of total inflow **-empfindlichkeit** *f* overall or total sensitivity **-entropie** *f* total entropy **-erhöhung** *f* quadrant elevation, quadrant angle of elevation **-ertrag** *m* entire proceeds **-fading** *n* total fading **-fahrwiderstand** *m* total resisting effort **-fahrzeit** *f* total travel time **-fehler** *m* total error **-felddosis** *f* total field dose **-feuchtigkeit** *f* total moisture **-fläche** *f* total area **-flankenspiel** *n* overall backlash

Gesamt-flügelfläche *f* total wing area **-flügeltiefe** *f* chord of combination of wings **-fluggewicht** *n* all-up weight **-flugstrecke** *f* maximum range (of aircraft) **-flugzeit** *f* total flying time **-fluß** *m* total flux **-gebühr** *f* through rate **-gerät** *n* total instrument apparatus, assembled missile **-gesellschaft** *f* (Dachgesellschaft) holding company **-gewicht** *n* gross vehicle weight (GVW) total weight, gross weight (aviat) **-härte** *f* total hardness

Gesamtheit *f* totality, all, the whole, entirety, generality, assembly **~ der abgehenden Verbindungsleitungen** trunk group fully available to outward positions **~ der Einrichtungen** total facilities **~ der Leitungselektronen** assembly of conduction electrons

Gesamt-helligkeit *f* total intensity **-höhe** *f* overall height **-hub** *m* total lift or travel of crane hook **-hubraum** *m* (Motor) total piston displacement **-impuls** *m* total impulse **-integral** *n* total integral **-kilometerzähler** *m* total mileage odometer **-kohlenstoffgehalt** *m* total carbon content **-kraft** *f* resultant or total force **-krümmung** *f* total curvature **-ladungszahl** *f* total charge **-lage** *f* total or over all situation **-länge** *f* total or over all length

Gesamt-last *f* total load, useful load **-lastschalter** *m* total load switch **-leistung** *f* over-all efficiency, whole effect, total or combined output **-leitwerktiefe** *f* total chord of tail unit **-leuchtkraft** *f* overall-luminosity **-lichtstrom** *m* total light flux **-lösliche** *n* total soluble matter **-mächtigkeit** *f* over-all thickness **-maschinenleistung** *f* total power output of the engines **-maß** *n* overall dimension **-meßfehler** *m* total gauging error, error of measurement **-nebensprechkopplung** *f* interaction crosstalk coupling

Gesamt-oberfläche *f* total area **-objektiv** *n* combined lens **-plan** *m* master plan **-polare** *f* gross polar **-produktion** *f* ultimate production **-produktionswert** *m* total production figures **-querschnitt von Kernprozessen** total cross section of nuclear reactions **-querschnittfläche** *f* total sectional or cross-section area **-reflexion** *f* integral reflection **-rohrerhöhung** *f* quadrant elevation, total elevation **-rumpffläche** *f* total area of fuselage bottom

Gesamt-satz *m* over-all rate **-saugwirkung** *f* total suction action (of a chimney or stack), total heat **-schaltbild** *n* full connections **-schrittverfahren** *n* total step method **-schußweite** *f* maximum range **-schwebungsfrequenz** *f* beat-frequency component **-seilkraft** *f* total cable force **-seitenrichtung** *f* total traverse or deflection **-skala** *f* total range **-spannquerschnitt** *m* total cutting capacity **-spannung** *f* over-all voltage, total strain (tension) **-spannweite** *f* span of a wing unit **-spin** *m* total spin **-stärke** *f* total strength **-stoß** *m* total impact, complete splice at one section

Gesamt-strafe *f* total sentence (law) **-strahlung** *f* total radiation **-strahlungspyrometer** *n* ardometer, (total-)radiation pyrometer **-streckweite** *f* maximum range of draft **-strom** *m* total current **-stromschalter** *m* total current switch **-summe** *f* (grand) total **-tragkraft** *f* gross buoyancy **-trockensubstanz** *f* total solids **-übersetzung** *f* entire reduction ratio **-übertragungsmaß** *n* transmission efficiency

Gesamtübertragungswinkel *m* entire transmission angle **abtriebseitig wirksamer ~** final output transmission angle

Gesamt-unkosten *pl* total expense, total cost **-untersetzung** *f* total reduction **-unternehmer** *n* general contractor **-ventilöffnungszeit** *f* total valve-lift period **-verbesserung** *f* total correction **-verhalten** *n* general behavior **-verlust** *m* total loss **-verlustverfahren** *n* determination of efficiency by total losses **-versicherungswert** *m* total amount of insurance **-verstärkung** *f* over-all amplification or gain **-verzerrung** *f* total distortion **-vielfachfeld** *n* complete multiple **-vorhaltwinkel** *m* total angle of lead, principal lateral-deflection angle

Gesamt-wärme *f* total heat **-wassergehalt** *m* total moisture contents **-weg** *m* total travel **-weglänge** *f* integrated range **-weite** *f* over-all width **-wertung** *f* total value **-widerstand** *m* total drag or resistance, reactance **-widerstandsmoment** *n* total moment of resistance **-winkel** *m* total angle

Gesamt-wirkung *f* total effect **-wirkungsgrad** *m* total or over-all efficiency, commercial efficiency **-wirkungsquerschnittsmessung** *f* total cross section measurement **-wirtschaftlichkeit** *f* total economy **-zahl** *f* total number **-zylinderhubraum** *m* total cylinder displacement **-zylinderinhalt** *m* total cylinder capacity

gesättigt saturated **-er Dampf** saturated steam **-e Kohlenwasserstoffe** saturated hydrocarbons **-er adiabatischer Zustand der Luft** saturated adiabatic lapse rate

Geschabsel *n* scrapings, shavings

geschachtelt stacked

Geschädigter *m* aggrieved or injured party

Geschäft *n* business, transaction, firm, trade, commerce

geschäftig busy, active, industrious

Geschäftigkeit *f* activity

geschäftlich relating to business, commercial

Geschäfts-abschluß *m* conclusion of business **-angelegenheit** *f* business matter **-anschluß** *m* business telephone (subscriber's telephone on business premises) **-anteil** *m* share in a business **-anweisung** *f* (für die Bahnbevollmächtigten), regulations (for railway-traffic officers) **-aufschwung** *m* business upswing **-beginn** *m* opening of business **-belebung** *f* revival in business **-bericht** *m* annual report

Geschäfts-drang *m* pressure of business **-führende Verwaltung** managing administration **-führer** *m* managing director **-führung** *f* management (board) **-gang** *m* working, course of business, routine **-gebäude** *f* office building **-jahr** *n* financial year, fiscal year **-karte** *f* business card **-kundig** experienced, able, smart

Geschäfts-lage *f* market, business, trade, commercial status **-leiter** *m* business manager **-leitung** *f* company management **-linie** *f* commercial (air) line **-los** lifeless, stagnant, inactive (exchange) **-papier** *n* commercial paper or document **-reisender** *m* traveling salesman **-stelle** *f* office **-straße** *f* business street or thorough-fare **-stille** *f* dullness or stagnation of business **-stunden** *pl* office hours

Geschäfts-träger chargé d'affaires, (business) representative or agent **-viertel** *n* business district **-vorgang** *m* business transaction **-wagen** *m* commercial car, delivery truck **-wert** *m* goodwill **-zeichen** *n* reference mark (on documents) **-zimmer** *n* office

geschälter Stabstahl bright turned bars, peeled bars

geschaltet inserted, interpolated, connected **~ sein auf** to be connected to **über einen Widerstand ~** connected across a resistance

geschätzt-e Abweichung estimated error **-es Kabel** composite cable **-e Lebensdauer** (eines Gegenstands) estimated life **-e Werte** estimated values

gescheckt piebald, mixed, mingled, cross-hatched

geschehen to happen, occur

Geschehnis *n* action, event, happening, occurrence, phenomenon

gescheitert wrecked

Geschenk *n* gift, present, donation

Geschichte *f* story, history **Faden einer ~ oder Rede** clue

geschichtet stratified, laminated, flaky, stacked, coated, sandwiched (of plates) **-es Dielektrikum** *n* solid and air dielectric **-e Haufenwolke** strato-cumulus cloud **-es** (blätteriges) **Holz** laminated wood **-e Kathode** coated cathode **-e Lagerstätte** stratified deposit

Geschick *n* fate, destiny, aptitude, skill

Geschicklichkeit *f* cleverness, dexterity, adroitness, skill, expertness

Geschicklichkeits-flug *m* aptitude flight **-leistung** *f* skilled performance or production **-prüfung** *f* aptitude test

geschickt skillful, clever, able, adept, subtle

Geschiebe *n* sedimentary material transported along stream bed by flowing water, bed load, gravel and small boulders, detritus **Zunahme der ~** access of bed load

Geschiebe-ablagerung *f* solid deposit **-blöcke** *pl* erratic blocks, boulders **-fracht** *f* bed-load transport (solids discharge) **-führung** *f* bed-load transport, solid content, movement of boulders **-lehm** *m* boulder clay, glacial loam **-mergel** *m* glacial marl, boulder clay **-wall** *m* boulder wall

geschiedener Saft defecated juice

geschiefert foliated

geschirmt screened, shielded **-es Gitter** screened grid

Geschirr *n* harness, gear, utensils, crockery, vessel, apparatus, equipment **-einzug** *m* draft, pass **-macher** *m* harness maker **-spülmaschine** *f* dish washing machine **-tau** *n* trace, tug **-trockner** *m* dish dryer

geschlagen driven, struck **-es Blech** hammered plate **-er Niet** driven rivet **noch nicht -er Niet** unclinched rivet **-e Saite** percussed string or chord

geschlämmte Kreide whitewash

Geschlecht *n* gender, genus

geschleift werden, vom Fallschirm ~ to be dragged by the parachute

geschleppt towed **ein Schiff wird ~** a vessel is towed **-e Zielscheibe** drogue (aviat)

geschliffen (schleifen) ground, cut, finished flat (plate) **-er Diamant** cut diamond **-es Glas** cut glass **-es Holz** mechanical wood pulp **-e Kernseife** settled- or pitched-curd soap **-er Rüben-**

brei pulp finely divided by means of a rasp

geschlitzt slotted, split **-e Fangbüchse** cherry picker **-er Kern** split core **-es Rohr** slotted pipe **-er Stöpsel** split plug **-e Unterlagscheibe** split washer **-er Zylinderkopf** slotted cheese head (cylinder)

geschlossen (schließen) closed, enclosed, complete, locked, concentrated, compact, combined, in cipher (navy) ~ **fahren** to sail in close order ~ **kreisend** moving in a closed cycle ~ **werden** to close **in sich** ~ closed upon itself, self-contained ~ **mit äußerer Eigenbelüftung** (Eigenventilation) ventilated frame machine **-es Aggregat** complete unit **-er Aufbau** self-contained construction **-er Bau** close-order construction **-e Bauform** compact design or construction **-er Behälter** closed or box container **-e Bewehrung** closed armoring **-er Bügel** link

geschlossen-e Dampfschlange closed coil **-es Datenverarbeitungssystem** integrated data processing system **-er Dynamo** totally enclosed dynamo **-e Düse** closed nozzle **-er Eisenweg** closed core **-es Exerzieren** close-order drill **-es Flugzeug** enclosed-cabin airplane **-e Form** closed mold **-er Führersitz** enclosed pilot's cockpit **-es Gärgefäß** closed fermenter **-es Gefäß** (für die Bestimmung des Flammpunktes) closed tester (flash point) **-e Kabine** enclosed cabin **-es Kaliber** box pass, closed pass **-er Kreislauf** closed loop

geschlossen-es Laufrad closed impeller **-e Maische** closed crystallizer **-er Motor** enclosed-type motor **-e Ordnung** close-order type of flight formation **-es Polygon** closed circuits **-er Raum** enclosure **-er Regelkreis** closed loop **-e Schleife** closed loop **-es Seil** endless rope or cable **-er Strahl** solid jet **-er Stromkreis** closed circuit **-er Tiegel** closed cup **-es Trefferbild** consistent pattern (of hits) **-e Vollwandkonstruktion** full-web plate construction **-e Zapfendüse** (Einspritzdüse) needle-valve spray nozzle with pilot pin **-er Zylinder** blind-end cylinder

Geschlossenheit des Aufbaus compactness (of construction)

geschlungen (schlingen) sinuous

geschlüsselt encoded, secret **-er Funkspruch** radio code message

Geschmack *m* taste, flavor, savor, relish

geschmacklos tasteless, insipid, flavorless

Geschmacksmuster *n* design patent

Geschmeide *n* trinkets, jewelry

geschmeidig ductile, soft, flexible, supple, unctuous, malleable

Geschmeidigkeit *f* flexibility, pliability, ductility, malleability, plasticity, smoothness

Geschmeidigkeitseigenschaft *f* plastic quality

geschmiedet forged **-es Eisen** wrought iron **-e Flansche** forged-steel flanges **-e Metallschraube** forged-metal propeller **-er Nagel** wrought nail, spike **-er Stahlblock** body of hammered steel

geschmiert lubricated, greased **-es Kegelventil** lubricated plug valve **-e Platte** Faure plate (pasted plate)

geschmolzen (schmelzen) molten, fused, smelted **-es Aluminiumoxyd** fused alumina

geschnitten (schneiden) cut **-es Gewinde** cut thread **-e Kante** sheared edge, cut edge **-e Länge** cut length **-e Zähne** cut gear **-e Unterlagscheibe** cut washer

geschnitztes Holz carved wood

Geschoß *n* projectile, bullet, shell, missile, round (of ammunition), floor or story, shell ~ **mit abschraubbarem Boden** shell with detachable base ~ **mit abschraubbarem Kopf** shell with detachable head **zu kurz gehendes** ~ short (artil.)

Geschoß-abweichung *f* absolute deviation **-anfangsgeschwindigkeit** muzzle velocity **-anlage** *f* stock groove, clearance space **-art** *f* type of projectile **-aufschlag** *m* impact of projectile, point of impact **-bahn** *f* trajectory (of projectile), course, ballistic curve

Geschoß-drehbank *f* projectile lathe **-drehung** *f* spin of projectile **-durchmesser** *m* diameter of projectile

Geschoß-einschlag *m* impact of projectile, point of impact **-fang** *m* backstop (target) **-feldereinschnitt** *m* marking **-form** *f* shape of projectile **-führung** *f* forcing or seating of projectile **-führungsband** *n* rotating band (ammunition, gun barrel) **-füllung** *f* projectile charge

Geschoß-geschwindigkeit *f* ballistic velocity **-gewicht** *n* weight of projectile **-heber** *m* shell hook, handle for removing shells, clip, gun hoist, grab **-höhlung** *f* shell cavity **-hülle** *f* body of shell or projectile, cartridge **-hülse** *f* cartridge case

Geschoß-kammer *f* shell chamber **-kern** *m* core of projectile **-kopf** *m* head of projectile **-körper** *m* body of shell **-kran** *m* gun hoist

Geschoß-mantel *m* projectile or shell jacket **-ring** *m* rotating band **-spitze** *f* point or nose of projectile, ogive of shell **-teilchen** bombarding particle

Geschränk *n* half front, crossed piece

geschränkt crossed, dihedral **-er Hohlleiter** twist **-e Röllchen** angle-axis rollers **-er Sägezahn** sawtooth with side set

geschraubt screwed, threaded (rods and sockets) **-e Verbindung** (Stahlbau) bolted joint, bolted connection

geschroppt, geschruppt coarsely cut out

geschult skilled, trained

geschuppt ragged

Geschür *n* dross, residuum

Geschütte *n* mixed gangues

geschüttelter Beton vibrated concrete

Geschütz *n* gun, cannon **-bronze** *f*, **-bronzeguß** *m* gun metal **-gießerei** *f* gun foundry

geschützt protected, armored, bulletproof, metal-clad ~ (gesetzlich geschützter Name) registered (name) **-er Kraftstoffbehälter** self-sealing fuel tank **-er Behälter** self-sealing tank **-er Hafen** sheltered harbor **-es Kugellager** shielded ball bearing

Geschwader *n* wing (aviation) **-flug** *f* formation flying

geschwefelt-e Schnitzel sulfured cossettes **-es Öl** sulfonated oil

geschweift cranked, curved **-es T-Stück** (flanged) short-sweep twin elbow, (flanged) double-sweep T.

geschweißt fused, welded, brazed **-er Benzintank** welded gasoline tank **-e Flansche** welded neck flange **-e Rahmenkonstruktion** *f* welded framing **-es Rohr** butt-welded pipe **-e Rohrkonstruktion** *f* welded tubular structure **-er Stahl** corrugated steel **-es Stahlrohr** welded steel tubing

geschwelkt air-dried, withered

geschwind quick, rapid, swift, fast

Geschwindigkeit *f* velocity, speed **gleiche ~** isochronism **~ halten** to keep headway **kritische ~** critical speed (V_1) **an ~ übertreffen** to outspeed **dem gewollten Wert entsprechende ~** on speed

Geschwindigkeit, ~ in Bodennähe ground speed **~ über Grund** ground speed, absolute speed **~ über Grundstrecke** speed over a straight-line course **~ gegenüber umgebender Luft** air speed **~ zur Luft** indicated air speed **~ der Schallwelle** sound wave **~ bei Schlüpfung Null** pitch speed of a propeller **relative ~ bezogen auf ungestörte Strömung** relative velocity based on smooth flow **~ der seismischen Wellen** velocity of seismic waves **~ der Wellenfront** (Wellenstirn), velocity of propagation of wave front **~ der Zufallsauswanderung** random drift rate (gyro)

Geschwindigkeit, bezogene ~ relative velocity **durchschnittliche ~** mean or average speed **gleichförmige ~** constant or uniform speed **mit hoher ~** at high speed **kennzeichnende ~** characteristic velocity of flow **kritische ~** stalling speed **mittlere ~** average velocity, drift speed **relative ~** ground speed (aviation) **ungeordnete ~** velocity of agitation **wirkliche ~** actual velocity **zulässige ~** speed limit (allowed)

Geschwindigkeits-abfall *m* loss of speed **-abhängigkeit** *f* velocity dependence **-abnahme** *f* decrease of velocity **-abstufung** *f* velocity staging **-abtastung** *f* variable-speed scan **-amplitude** *f* colume current **-analyse** *f* velocity analysis

Geschwindigkeitsänderung *f* gear changing, variation of the speed **~ infolge von Versetzung** velocity change caused by dislocation

Geschwindigkeits-anzeiger *m* speed indicator, speedometer **-auflösung** *f* velocity resolution **-aufschaltung** *f* mixing ratio for angular velocity signal (missiles) **-aufteilung** *f* velocity ratio **-ausgleich** *m* velocity diffusion or equalization **-ausdehnung** *f* extension in velocity **-aussteuerung** *f* depth of velocity modulation **-begrenzer** *m* speed-limiting device **-bereich** *m* speed range **-bremse** *f* centrifugal brake **-dreieck** *n* velocity vector diagram, triangle of velocities

Geschwindigkeits-ebene *f* velocity plane **-einflußfunktion** *f* velocity correlation function **-einheit** *f* unit of speed **-einstellung** *f* speed regulator **-empfindlich** velocity sensitive **-erhöhung** *f* increase in speed **-feld** *n* velocity field **flug** *m* speed flight **-fokussierend** velocity focussing

Geschwindigkeits-gesetz *n* velocity law **-gesteuerter Elektronenstrahl** velocity-modulated electron beam or pencil (klystron) **-gesteuerter Servomotor** rate-type servomotor **-getriebe** *n* speed gear **-gewinn** *m* increase in speed **-gitter** *n* accelerator grid **-gleichhaltungsvorrichtung** *f* speed matching gear **-gradient** *m* velocity gradient **-grenze** *n* speed limit **-hebel** *m* speed lever **-höhe** *f* velocity head **-kurve** *f* speed graph, rate curve

Geschwindigkeitsleistungsdiagramm für Hubschrauber helicopter speed power polar

Geschwindigkeitsmesser *m* speed indicator, tachometer, speedometer, kymograph, measurement of current velocity, tachygraph **relativer ~** ground-speed meter

Geschwindigkeits-messerantrieb *m* speedometer assembly **-messung** *f* speed measurement **-meßwinkel** *m* angle of reference for integration of acceleration **-mikrophon** *n* pressure-gradient microphone, velocity microphone **-minderapparat** *m* speed reducer **-modulation** *f* velocity modulation **-potential** *n* velocity potential **-profil** *n* velocity distribution in a duct, velocity profile development **-prüfung** *f* eliminating test **-quadrat** *n* squared speed

Geschwindigkeits-rad *n* double-row velocity wheel **-raum** *m* momentum space, velocity space **-regelnde Wirkung** speed-regulating action **-regelung** *f* speed control **-regler** *m* (speed) governor or regulator, runaway governor **-regulator** *m* speed governor **-regulierung** *f* speed regulation **-rekord** *m* speed record **-reziproke** *f* inverse speed-rate curve **-schreiber** *m* tachograph

Geschwindigkeits-schwankungen *pl* speed fluctuations or variations, wows (electronics), flutter, gargle, whiskers **-schaubild** *n* speed diagram **-schild** *m* speed plate **-selektor** *m* velocity selector **-servosteuerung** *f* servo speed control **-sicherheitsausschalter** *m* overspeed governor **-sinn** *m* speed sense **-sortierung** *f* velocity sorting **-spanne** *f* speed range between high speed and landing speed **-spektrograph** *n* velocity spectrograph or analyzer **-sprung** *m* velocity jump

Geschwindigkeits-steigerung *f* acceleration, speed increase **-steuerung** *f* velocity modulation **-stufe** *f* velocity (stage) step **-sucher** *m* speed finder **-tonabnehmer** *m* velocity pick-up **-umstellungsvorrichtung** *m* change-speed gear **-vektor** *m* velocity vector **-verhältnis** *n* speed ratio **-verlauf** *m* speed variation

Geschwindigkeits-verlust *m* pancaking (in landing), stalling (in flight), loss of velocity **-verminderung** *f* velocity reduction **-versteller** *m* speed regulator **-versuchsflugzeug** *n* high-speed research plane **-verteilung** *f* velocity distribution, distribution of energy

Geschwindigkeitswechsel *m* change of speed **Hebel für den ~** speed-change lever

Geschwindigkeitswechsel-gehäuse *n* speed-box case **-getriebe** *n* change-speed gear **-wechselrad** *n* speed change gear

Geschwindigkeits-weglänge *f* velocity range curve **-weltrekord** *m* world's speed record **-wettbewerb** *m* speed competition **-zunahme** *f* velocity increase **-zuwachs** *m* velocity increase

Geschwindschritt *m* double-time (step)

Geschworener *m* juryman

Geschwulst *f* swelling, tumor

geschwungen (schwingen) swung

Geschwür *n* ulcer, abscess, boil, infection

gesegelter Kompaßkurs compass course made good

gesehnte Wickelung short-pitched winding, chord winding

Gesell(e) *m* journeyman
Gesellschaft *f* association, company, corporation, society, union, undertaking (especially public utility) ~ **mit beschränkter Haftung** limited-liability company, incorporated concern, corporation ~ **für Triebwagen-Ingenieure** Society of Automotive Engineers
Gesellschafter, stiller ~ sleeping partner
Gesellschafts-anschluß *m* party line **-anzug** *n* formal dress, dress uniform
Gesellschaftsleitung *f* (multi-)party line ~ **für 4 Anschlüsse** four-party line **Rückruf auf die** ~ reverting call
Gesenk *n* die, forging die, die-block swage, seat stone, swage, sump, pit, drain pit ~ (Bg.) upcast, downcast **im** ~ **schmieden** to drop-forge, swage **zweiteiliges** ~ open die
Gesenk-amboß *m* grooved anvil **-arbeit** *f* die work, swaging **-bau** *m* manufacture of dies **-block** *m* drop-forging block **-drücken** *n* swaging
Gesenke *n* mold, punch, boss, die, depression (of floor or ground)
Gesenk-einsatz *m* mold insert **-form** *f* die **-fräser** *m* die-sinking cutter **-fräserei** *f* die milling, die sinking **-fräsmaschine** *f* die-sinker **-fuge** *f* flash **-geschmiedet** drop-forged **-gußstück** *n* die-casting
Gesenk-hammer *m* swaging hammer, drop hammer **-hoblerei** *f* die shaping **-kopiermaschine** *f* die-sinking machine **-kopierfräsautomat** *m* automatic die sinking machine **-macher** *m* die maker **-macherei** *f* die tracing and finishing shop
Gesenkmacherschraubstock *m* moldmaker's vice
Gesenk-oberteil *m* upper die **-platte** *f* swage block **-presse** *f* forging press **-preßteil** *m* swage-pressed or die-pressed part **-schlosserei** *f* die tooling shop
Gesenk-schmiede *f* drop forge **-schmiedearbeit** *f* swaging, die-work **-schmieden** to drop-forge **-schmieden** *n* drop-forging **-schmiederei** *f* die forging, drop forging **-schmiederohling** *m* rough drop forging **-schmiedestück** *n* drop forging, swaged forging
Gesenk-stahlblock *m* die-block **-stähle** *pl* die steels **-tiefe** *f* depth of recess **-unterteil** *n* lower die **-verschluß** *m* wear on swage **-vertiefung** *f* die cavity
Gesetz *n* law, rule, principle, statute ~ **von Biot und Savarat** Biot and Savarat law ~ **von der Erhaltung der Energie** law of conservation of energy ~ **von der Erhaltung der Masse** law of conservation of matter ~ **der Erstbelastung** virgin curve ~ **vom abnehmenden Ertragszuwachs** law of diminishing returns **(einem)** ~ **folgen** to obey a law **erstes** ~ **der Anziehungskraft** first law of magnetism $^{3}/_{2}$ ~ $^{3}/_{2}$ power law **Lambert'sches** ~ emission law, Lambert's law ~ **der Nichtüberkreuzung** non-crossing rule **Ohmsches** ~ Ohm's law
Gesetz-blatt (staatlich) *n* gazette **-buch** *n* code, statute book **-entwurf** *m* bill, legislative proposal
Gesetzes-auslegung *f* law interpretation **-begründung** *f* official explanation of the law **-lücke** *f* legal loophole
gesetz-gebende Behörde legislative authority or body **-gebungsbefugnis** *f* legislative powers
gesetzlich lawful, legal, statutory ~ **geschützt** warranted, patented ~ **geschützter Name** copyrighted or registered name ~ **geschütztes Verfahren** patented procedure ~ **vorgeschrieben** statutory
gesetzlich-e Bestimmung legal requirement **-es Hindernis** statutory bar **-e englische Meile** statute mile **-e Regelungen** regulations having the force of law **-e Reserven** statutory reserve **-e Uhrzeit** standard time, legal time **-es Zahlungsmittel** legal tender
gesetzmäßig legal, according to law, lawful, on a definite plan in accordance with theoretical principles
Gesetzmäßigkeit *f* mathematical interrelationship, lawfulness, legality, legitimacy, procedure, according to statutes
gesetzt settled, composed, set in type
Gesetz-übertretung *f* violation **-vorschrift** *f* decree, rule, regulation **-widrig** unlawful, illegal
gesichert safe, secured ~ **sein** to hold security **-e Mutter** locked nut, jam nut
Gesicht *n* face, sight
Gesichts-achse *f* axis of vision, optic or visual axis **-ausdruck** *m* facial expression **-bildung** *f* physiognomy **-eindruck** *m* visual impression **-farbe** *f* color, complexion
Gesichtsfeld *n* field of view or vision, visibility **objektives** ~ objective field of view, objective angular field **subjektives** ~ subjective field of view, subjective angular field
Gesichtsfeld-beleuchtungseinrichtung *f* illumination attachment to field of view **-beschränkung** *f* field of view limitation **-blende** *f* field stop **-linie eines Fernrohres** visual line of a telescope **-messer** *m* goniometer **-winkel** *m* visual field angle
Gesichts-kreis *m* field of view, circle of the horizon **-linie** *f* collimation **-maske** *f* protective mask, face shield **-naht** *f* facial suture **-punkt** *m* point of view, principle, feature, aspect **-schärfe** *f* visual acuity **-schutz** *m* face shield **-sinn** *m* sight, vision **-strahl** *m* visual ray **-täuschung** *f* optical illusion **-vordrucke zum Projektionsperimeter** charts for the projection perimeter **-wert** *m* face value, facial brightness **-winkel** *m* angle of field of vision, angle of view or of sight, optic angle
gesiebt filtered, screened, sieved, sifted, separated **-e Kohle** screened coal
Gesims *n* cornice, molding **ansteigendes** ~ raking molding
Gesinter *n* agglomerated cake, sinter cake, agglomeration
gesintert-es Hartmetall cemented carbide product **-e Hartmetallsorte** hard-cemented-carbide grade **-es Metallkarbid** sintered (cemented) metal carbide
gesondert isolated
gespalten clifted, clifty, split **-er Bronzering mit Zeiger** split brass ring and pointers **das -e S** split S **-er Stahlkeil** split steel key
Gespann *n* stool (of an ingot mold), bottom plate, team (animals), fagot (for smelting), bundle of iron bars, truss, fellow or companion (print.) **-gießen** *n* group or bottom casting **-guß** *m* bottom pouring of multiple molds

-hacke *f* horse hoe **-platte** *f* casting plate **-rodepflug** *m* horse-drawn lifting plow **-schaft** *f* co-operating unit, work association

gespannt tense, cocked (firearms), tight, taut, stretched **-er Grundwasserspiegel** *m* perched water table

Gespanntheit *f* tension

Gespannungsmesser *m* crusher gauge

gespeicherte Information record (comput)

gespeist fed **mit Gleichstrom ~** supplied by continuous current

Gespensterstrom *m* ghost current

Gesperr *n* excapement, catch, ratchet, clickwork **~ mit fester und loser Klinke** fast and loose escapement

Gesperre *n* locking mechanism or gear, ratchet gear, safety catch

gesperrt blocked, barred, checked, closed, suppressed **-e Verzahnung** locked teeth

gespiegelte Welle reflected wave

Gespinst *n* spinning package, web, fabric, spun yarn or fabric, thread, yarn goods **-hülle** *f* spun casting **-umflechtung** *f* braiding with spun yarn

gesponnen (spinnen) spun (yarn) **-es Glas** fiber glass

Gespräch *n* conversation, call, connection, message, discussion **~ mit Gebührenansage** call with request for charges **~ mit Herbeiruf** messenger call **~ zwischen zwei Sprechstellen** station-to-station call **~ mit Voranmeldung** prearranged call (with operator) **~ über . . .** through connection via . . . **zu dem ein ~ an der Reihe ist** turn of call

Gespräch, ein ~ anmelden to book, file, place a toll call **~ beenden** terminate a call **ein ~ einleiten** to originate or initiate a call **ein ~ über drei Minuten verlängern** to extend a call beyond three minutes **ein ~ zählen** to record a call on the meter, meter a call **abgehendes ~** outgoing call **ankommendes ~** incoming call **dringendes ~** express call, urgent call **gebührenpflichtiges ~** chargeable call **zwischenstaatliches ~** international message

Gesprächs-abwickelung *f* handling of traffic or of calls **-anmelden** *n* toll recording, booking of a call

Gesprächsanmeldung *f* registration of a call **eine ~ weitermelden oder weitergeben** to pass a call again **gestrichene ~** canceled call

Gesprächs-art *f* type of call **-aufforderung** *f* notification of personal call

Gesprächsaufnahmeeinrichtung *f* telephone voice recorder

Gesprächsbeginn *m* **Zeit des ~** starting time of a conversation

Gesprächs-blatt *f* ticket, toll ticket, call-order ticket **-buch** *n* incoming register

Gesprächsdauer *f* duration of a call length of conversation **die ~ vereinbaren oder vergleichen** to agree on the chargeable duration of a call or the total daily chargeable minutes

Gesprächs-dichte *f* frequency of conversations **-einheit** *f* conversation or traffic unit, initial period **-frequenz** *f* frequency of conversations **-gebühr** *f* message rate or fee **-gebührentarif** *m* measured-rate tariff **-gebührenteilnehmer** *m* measured-rate subscriber **-minuten** *pl* duration of message in minuttes, ticket time **-pausen** *pl* intervals of no speech **-speicherung** *f* call accumulation **-schluß** *m* completion of call

Gesprächsuhr *f* timing device (teleph.) **~ mit Lampensignal** time-check lamp

Gesprächsverbindung *f* telephone communication or connection **eine ~ herstellen** to complete a call

Gesprächszähler *m* (conversation) meter, service meter, message register

Gesprächszählung *f* (call) metering **~ durch Zuschalten einer Zählspannung** booster-battery metering

Gesprächszeit *f* ticket time **durchschnittliche ~** average ticket time

Gesprächszeit-messer *m* timing register **-uhr** *f* chargeable time clock

Gesprächszettel *m* (toll) ticket **~ einordnen** to step in tickets

gespreizt spread, stilted, affected

gesprengt burst, cambered, semi-elliptical **-es Rad** split wheel **-er Ring** split ring

gesprenkelt speckled, spotted, stained, sprinkled, mottled, freckled

gespritzt squirted, extruded, sprayed, atomized **-er Glühfaden** squirted filament **-es Metall** die-cast metal

gesprungen (springen), cracked, split **-er Isolator** cracked insulator

gespult wound on spools or bobbins

gespült washed, hydraulic (fill dam)

gespundet bunged, stoppered, grooved (for slides)

Gest *f* yeast, barm

Gestade *n* coast, shore, beach

gestaffelt staggered, graded in echelon formation **nach der Tiefe ~** distributed in depth **-e Koppelleitung** echelon strapping **-e Kreise** staggered circuits **-er Mehrfachtelegraph** series or echelon multiplex telegraph **-e Sitze** staggered seats **-e Walzstraße** staggered rolling train

gestakt, ein Schiff wird ~ a barge is poled along (by a barge pole)

Gestalt *f* design, construction, shape, form, contour, stature **~ der Flugbahn** curve of the trajectory

gestalten to form, shape, mold, arrange, design, construct

Gestalter *m* draftsman, designer, constructor

gestaltet formed, shaped **aerodynamisch günstig ~** clean

Gestaltfestigkeit *f* design strength, form stability

gestaltlos amorphous, formless, shapeless, noncrystalline

Gestalts-unterschiede *pl* **der Ladung** shape variations of the (explosive) charge and projectile **-veränderung** *f* structural change, change of form or of shape, deformation

Gestaltung *f* (Formgebung) shaping; (Entwurf) design; (Bau) construction, structure, formation, shape, condition, appearance, figure, fashioning, organization **~ der Küste** indentation of the coast line (turning, break in the coast line)

Gestaltungs-merkmale *pl* design features **-vermögen** *n* variability

gestampft (Boden), tamped (soil) **-er Beton** rammed concrete **-er Lehmboden** baked dirt

Gestänge *n* (Maschine) linkage; (Technik) rods, bars structure, antlers, stakes, (main) spears, poll, push rod, support, lever system, gear ~ **mit Blattschloßverbindung** miser rods ~ **mit glatten Verbindungen** flush-joint drill pipe **massives** ~ solid rods **volles** ~ solid rods

Gestänge-abfangkeil *m* drill pipe slips **-antrieb** *m* lever system **-aufzug** *m* rod elevator **-ausreißer** *m* twist-off, break of the shaft in the interior of the boring (petroleum) **-ausrüstung** *f* pole fittings **-befestigung** *f* rod couplings **-belastung** *f* strain of pole, prop, stay, support **bohren** *n* rod boring **-bruch** *m* twist-off, break in the piping, breaking of the drill stem **-bühne** *f* safety board, floor, or platform (oil drilling) **-bündel** *n* pole clamp

Gestänge-drehkopf *m* pole swivel **-drucker** *m* pipe pusher **-elevator** *m* drill pipe elevator **-fahrstuhl** *m* drill pipe elevator **-falldorn** *m* rod tap **-fänger** *m* pole socket **-fanggerät** *n* catching-rod elevator **-fanggerätsförderstuhl** *m* fishing hook for poles **-fangkrone** *f* fishing socket for poles **-führung** *f* rod guide **-gabel** *f* catch wrench for poles **-gegengewicht** *n* counterweight for rods

Gestänge-hänger *m* beam hanger **-höhe** *f* line of rods **-keilfänger** *m* overshot **-kreuz** *n* triangle, cross lever **-leger** *m* rodman **-leitung** *f* pole line **-loch** *n* linkage hole **-nachstellvorrichtung** *f* slack adjuster **-rechen** *m* pole fingers, finger board

Gestängerohr *n* hollow rods **-drehbank** *f* lathe for hollow rods **-drehschlüssel** *m* knock wrench **-fangkrone** *f* fishing socket for hollow rods **-führung** *f* guide for hollow rods **-gewinde** *n* drill pipe thread, tool joints **-klammer** *f* hollow-rod clamp **-schneidezeug** *n* hollow-rod cutter **-spülkopf** *m* flushing head for hollow rods

Gestängerohr- und Muffengang *m* hollow-rod-collar thread

Gestänge-schläge *pl* knocking in the piping **-schloß** *n* joint of rods **-schlüssel** *m* rod wrench **-schneidezeug** *n* rod cutter **-schoner** *m* protector **-schutzaufziehvorrichtung** *f* expander for drill pipe protector **-schützer** *m* drill pipe protector **-schwinge** *f* swing

Gestängesteuerung *f* rod guide **auslösende** ~ slipper-out guide

Gestänge-stopbüchse *f* stuffing box for hollow rods **-stoß** *m* rod joint **-stück** *n* section of pole **-übertragung** *f* transmission by rods **-verbinder** *m* tool joint **-verbindung** *f* tool joint, tie rod **-wagen** *m* rod cart **-wirbel** *m* rod swivel **-zangen** *pl* tongs for drill pipe **-ziehen** *n* raising of rods **-zug** *m* string of drill pipes

Gestank *m* stench

gestanzt punched, blanked out from **-e Bleche** stamped plate, punched laminations **-er Stahl** stamped steel

gestapelt piled (up)

gestatten to allow, grant, let, permit

gestaucht jolted, tied (in bundles)

gestaut damned up (waters), stowed away **in den Bunkern** ~ trimmed (in bunkers)

Gestehungs-kosten *pl* manufacturing expenses, cost of production, factory cost **-preis** *m* production costs, cost price

gesteigert increased **-e Durchlässigkeit** enhanced permeability

Gestein *n* ground, rock, stone **das** ~ **setzt ab** the gangue changes ~ **abtreiben** to take off the gangue **anstehendes** ~ cropping, outcrop (in geology) **erzführendes** ~ stoping ground, ore-bearing rock **festes** ~ stonehead, bedrock **festes** ~ **unter alluvialer Ablagerung** main bottom **festes** ~ **unter dem Abraumgebirge** fast stonehead, bedrock **taubes** ~ deads, rubbish, stuff, trade, barren ground

Gesteins-bearbeitungsmaschine *f* stone-working machine **-beschreibung** *f* petrography **-bildung** *f* rock formation **-bohranlage** *f* rock-drilling plant **-bohren** *n* rock drilling

Gesteinsbohrer *m* rock drill, rock borer ~ **für hartes Gestein** granite drill ~ **für mildes Gestein** miner's drill

Gesteinsbohrer-schärfmaschine *f* rock-drill sharpening machine **-stauchmaschine** *f* rock-drill upsetting machine

Gesteins-bohrhammer *m* rock (or quarry) drilling hammer **-bohrmaschine** *f* rock perforator **-bohrtechnik** *f* rock drilling **-bohrung** *f* rock drilling **-dünnschliff** *m* thin-ground stone plate **-einheit** *f* lithologic unit **-gang** *m* vein of rock, dike **-hauer** *m* stone or hard-ground miner, stoneman **-kunde** *f* petrography, mineralogy, lithology, geognosy **-lehre** *f* mineralogy **-linien** *pl* minerals lines **-masse** *f* rock **-mühle** *f* subterranean quarry, rock-crushing mill

Gesteins-proben *pl* samples of the aggregate **-sprengmittel** *n* rock-blasting explosive **-schicht** *f* layer of rock, girdle, stratum **-schlacke** *f* scoria **-schutt** *m* detritus

Gestein(s)staub *m* stone dust, mineral dust **-förderanlage** *f* conveying plant for stone powder **-mahlanlage** *f* stone-powder pulverizing plant

Gesteins-stäubung *f* stone dusting **-verwitterung** *f* rock weathering or decay **-wand** *f* stone wall

Gestell *n* (Regal) stand, shelf, rack; (Bock) trestle, horse; (Technik) support; (Gerippe) frame; (Metallurgie) hearth, rig, crucible, well, bed, scaffold, understructure, stillage, chassis, tripod, stage, column, mount, panels, jack ~ **für selbsttätige Fernsprechzentralen** rack for automatic telephone exchanges ~ (Verstärkergestell) (repeater . . .) bay **einseitiges** ~ single-sided rack **freitragendes** ~ self-supporting rack **randloses** ~ rimless holder (glasses)

Gestell-bein *n* leg of a tripod **-belastung** *f* berth load **-boden** *m* (blast-furnace) hearth bottom **-einheit** *f* rack section **-federung** *f* springing of undercarriage **-förderanlage** *f* cage winding plant **-förderung** *f* frame winding **-fuß** *m* base of frame **-hobel** *m* (eiserner) iron-frame plane **-konstruktion** *f* rack construction **-kopf** *m* stand head **-mantel** (Hochofen) hearth jacket **-melden** to report faulty (teleph.) **-panzer** *m* (blast-furnace) hearth casting, hearth jacket

Gestell-rahmen *m* rack panel **-reihe** *f* (Verstärker) line of repeater bays **-säge** *f* wood or frame saw **-schrank** *m* relay-rack cabinet

Gestellung *f* appearance, presentation

Gestell-verdrahtung *f* rack wiring **-wand** *f* supporting frame **-weite** *f* width of framing

gestepptes Bremsband stitched brake lining

gesternt starred
gesteuert controlled, guided, steered, synchronized **-es Einlaßventil** mechanically operated admission valve **-e Funken** timed sparks **-e Impulseingänge** controlled zone entry hubs **-e Klappe** controlled valve **-e Rakete** controlled rocket **-er Übertrag** separately instructed carry **-es Ventil** positively controlled valve **-e Zündung** timed ignition
gestielt helved, stalked, pedunculated
Gestirn-halbmesser *m* radius of star **-höhe** *f* star's altitude **-peilung** *f* bearing by stars
gestochen (stechen) pricked, stung **-e Schärfe** microscopic sharpness (phot.)
gestorben (sterben) dead, deceased **-er Motor** dead engine **mit -em Propeller landen** to make a deadstick landing
gestört faulty, out of order, disturbed, perturbed **-es Einersignal** disturbed-one output **-es Nullsignal** disturbed-zero output
Gestörtsummerzeichen *n* out-of-order tone
gestoßen pounded
gestrandet stranded, aground
Gesträuch *n* underbrush, shrubbery
gestreckt elongated, stretched, flat ~ **gewalzt** stretch-rolled **-e Flugbahn** flat trajectory **-e Ladung** elongated charge **-e Länge** total length, stretched length **-es Rotationsellipsoid** prolate ellipsoid **-er Winkel** straight angle, 180-degree angle
gestreift striped, striated, streaked, banded
gestreut, elastisch und unelastisch ~ elastically and inelastically scattered **-e Durchlassung** diffusion by transmission **-e Reflexion** diffusion by reflection, diffuse-reflection factor **-er Strahl** scattered beam **-e Welle** scattered wave
gestrichelt dotted (e.g. line on graph) **-e Kurve** dashed curve **-e Linie** broken, dotted line **-e Schaulinie** dash-line curve
gestrichen (streichen) rubbed or touched lightly along the surface **frisch** ~ wet paint **-es Korn** medium or pointed gun sight **-es Papier** enamel paper, coated paper
gestrickte Mineralformen skeletal mineral forms
Gestübbe *n* coal dust breeze (met)
Gestrüpp *n* underbrush, brush
gestundete Prämie outstanding premium
gestürzt transposed (math.), tumbled, overthrown **-e Achse** *f* cambered axle **-e Ladung** *f* bulk cargo
gestützt supported, propped up **beiderseitig -es Schwungrad** flywheel between two bearings
Gesuch *n* request, petition, application **-steller** *m* applicant, petitioner
gesucht wanted, in demand **-er Wert** unknown value
Gesumme *n* hum
gesund healthy, sound, well, hale **-es Gewebe** living tissue **-er Guß** sound casting **-er Organismus** living organism **-e Strömung** unseparated flow
Gesundheit *f* health
gesundheitlich hygienic, sanitary
Gesundheits-amt *n* board of health **-buch** *n* individual-medical-record book **-dienst** *m* medical service, sanitary corps, public health service **-fürsorge** *f* sanitary precaution **-gefährdung** *f* health hazards **-ingenieur** *m* sanitary engineer **-pflege** *f* hygiene **-schädlich** injurious to health **-technik** *f* sanitary engineering **-wesen** *n* sanitation **-zustand** *m* physical condition
gesunken (sinken) lowered, thrown (down)
Getäfel *n* wainscot, wainscoting, paneling, inlaying
getäfelt paneled **-e Decke** paneled or boarded ceiling
getarnt camouflaged
getastet keyed (telegr.)
getaucht immersed, coated (said of electrode)
geteert tarred **-er Hanf** tarred hemp **-e Straße** tarred road
geteilt divided, separated, split **-e Achse** split axle **-e Batterie** split battery **-e Fahrgestellachse** split landing-gear axle **-es Rad** built-up wheel **-e Riemenscheibe** split pulley **-er Ring** split ring, segmented **-er Tubusauszug** graduated drawtube
getöntes Papier tinted paper
getränkt impregnated, soaked, saturated
Getreide *n* grain, corn **extra Tank für** ~ (Ergänzungstrichter) supplemental hopper
Getreidedrillmaschine *f* grain drill ~ **mit Düngerstreuvorrichtung** fertilizer drill **einfache** ~ plain grain drill
Getreide-elevator *m* grain elevator **-feld** *n* grain field **-grube** *f* silo **-heber** *m* grain elevator **-kasten** *m* **mit Registrierungsapparat** grain box with register
getreidelt, ein Schiff wird ~ a barge is horse-drawn
Getreide-mäher *m* reaper for wheat **-mahlen** *n* corn-and-grain milling **-maschinen** *pl* harvesters and reapers **-mischvorrichtung** *f* grain mixer **-mühle** *f* flour mill **-netzapparat** *m* wheat moistener **-reinigungsmaschine** *f* grain-cleaning machine
Getreide-saugaufzug *m* pneumatic (suction) elevator **-schälmaschine** *f* wheat scourer **-speicher** *m* grain elevator **-spitzmaschine** *f* corn-milling machine **-trocknerbrennkammer** *f* grain drier firebox shell **-umschlaganlage** *f* corn-transshipping plant **-waage** *f* grain scales
getrennt divided, separate(d), disconnected, cut off **-er Bau** extended-order construction
Getrenntlageverfahren *n* segregated-band system
getreu loyal, true, faithful **-e Wiedergabe** *f* faithful reproduction, fidelity in reproduction, good definition of image (television)
Getriebe *n* gearing, gear unit; (Räder) gears; (Kraftübertragung) power (gear) transmission; (Antriebsrad) pinion; (Antriebsorgan) drive unit; (Vorschub ~) feedbox, gear (meshing), machine(ry), harness (textiles), control, gear train ~ **mit ständigem Eingriff** constant-mesh gear ~ **mit Klauenschaltung** gearing with jaw-type clutch ~ **mit Pfeilverzahnung** herringbone gearing ~ **mit Schrägverzahnung** helical gearing ~ **mit Übersetzung ins Langsame** speed-reducer drive ~ **zur Verstellung des Reitstockes auf dem Bett** tailstock pinion ~ **mit Winkelverzahnung** double helical gearing
Getriebe, konisches ~ bevel gear **mit** ~ **versehen** to gear **ein** ~ **schalten** to shift a gear **leicht zu schaltendes** ~ easily shifted gear **selbstsperrendes** ~ self-locking gear **stufenloses** ~ variable-ratio gear **stufenlos regelbares** ~

continuously variable drive **zwangsläufiges und stufenlos regelbares ~** positive infinitely variable gear

Getriebe-ableger *m* reaping attachment **-aggregat** *n* gearing unit **-anordnung** *f* gearing arrangement **-antriebswelle** *f* main shaft, transmission shaft **-arbeit in losem Gebirge** piling through quicksand **-arm** *m* gear lever **-armkugel** *f* change-speed-lever ball **-aufhängung** *f* transmission or gear-set case suspension **-ausrücken** *n* release drive or gear

Getriebe-bremse *f* flywheel brake, transmission brake **-bremstrommel** *f* transmission brake drum **-deckel** *m* gear cover **-fett** *n* transmission lubricant, pinion grease **-flansch** *m* transmission case or gear box flange **-flüssigkeit** *f* gear fluid (automatic transmission fluid) **-gang** *m* stage, speed

Getriebegehäuse *n* gear cover, case, or housing, transmission housing, gearbox **Vorderteil des Getriebegehäuses** nose of the gear case

Getriebe-gestell *n* gear frame **-hauptwelle** *f* transmission main shaft

Getriebekasten *m* gearbox, gear case **~ mit Fußschaltung** foot-change gearbox

Getriebe-kastenunterlage *f* gear seat (car frame) **-kette** *f* drive chain **-kippvorrichtung** *f* gear-tipping appliance, gear-tilting device **-kräfte** *pl* gearing loads **-lader** *m* gear-driven or engine-driven supercharger, gear-drive supercharger **-läufer** *m* change gear **-leerlauf** *m* gear idling **-lehre** *f* kinetics, kinematics

getriebelos gearless, ungeared **-er Heuauflader** gearless hay loader **-er Motor** ungeared engine **-er Sternmotor** ungeared radial engine

Getriebemotor *m* geared engine

getrieben (treiben) driven **-e Arbeit** raised work (in relief) **-es Kegelrad** bevel gear **-e Scheibe** follower wheel or pulley **-e Welle** driven shaft

Getriebe-nebenwelle *f* lay-shaft **-öl** *n* transmission lubricant **-pfahl** *m* shore **-plan** *m* layout gearing work diagram **-pumpe** *f* gear pump **-querhaupt** *n* revolving frame **-räder** *n pl* gears, gear wheels **-regelvorrichtung** *f* regulation device of the hydraulic gears

Getriebe-schalthebel *m* gear shift lever **-schaltschütz** *m* propulsion-unit contractor (guided missiles) **-schaltung** *f* gear shifting **-schloß** *n* transmission lock, change-speed gear lock **-schnecke** *f* worm gear **-schonend** gear-preserving **-schubweg** *m* pinion travel **-sperre** *f* gear lock **-spindel** *f* driving spindle

Getriebestern, dreiarmiger ~ three-way-type spider

Getriebe-stufenscheibe *f* transmission step pulley **-teil des Motors** nose section of a motor **-turbine** *f* geared turbine, prime movers **-übersetzung** *f* multiplication **-übersetzungsverhältnis** *n* gear ratio **-umschaltung** *f* gearshift **-vorlegewelle** *f* countershaft

Getriebewelle *f* gear shaft, transmission shaft **dritte ~** third-motion shaft

Getriebezahnrad *n* gear wheel **Vorrichtung zum selbsttätigen Ein- und Ausrücken von einem ~** automatic meshing and demeshing device

Getriebezimmerung *f* framework inside a pit or well

Getriebsgehäuse *n* gearbox **-bremse** *f* Cardan shaft brake

getrocknet dried, seasoned, baked **-e vollwertige Zuckerrübenschnitzel** dried sugar-beet cossettes

getroffenes Teilchen bombarded particle

getrübt opal (glass)

Getter *n* getter, lamp filling **~ abschießen** to set off or cause vaporization of getter

Getter-metallspiegel *m* film of getter metal **-metallverdampfer** *m* getter metal vaporizer **-pille** *f* getter tab, patch, or pill **-spiegel** *m* getter patch or film

getüpfelt speckled

getupft (Oberfläche) of swirl finish

geübt practiced, dexterous, skilled **~ im Verkauf** trained in selling

geviert square, quaternary, quarter-sawn

Geviert *n* frame, set of timbers, square, em quadrat (print.) **-meter** *m* square meter **-punkt** *m* leaders

Gewächs *n* growth, plant

gewachsen (applied to soil) undisturbed **~ sein** to be a match for, be able to cope with **-er Balken** built-up girder or beam **-er Boden** natural, overgrown soil, solid ground **-er Fels** solid rock **-e Schicht** grown junction

Gewächshaus *n* greenhouse

gewachst waxed

gewaffelt wafered

gewagt risky, daring

gewählt selected

Gewähr *f* guarantee, surety, warranty, bail **ohne ~** unwarranted, without assuming any obligations

gewährbar allowable, grantable

gewähren to grant, give, allow, afford, furnish, guarantee, be surety for, warrant, grant a patent

gewährleisten to guarantee, warrant, assure, vouchsafe

Gewährleistung *f* warranty

Gewährleistungsanspruch *m* guarantee claim

Gewahrsam *n* custody, prison, surety, safety, proviso

Gewährsmann *m* guarantor, bailor, informant, bailsman

Gewährung *f* grant(ing)

gewalkt planked

Gewalt *f* force, power, might **~ haben über** to control **höhere ~** act of God

Gewaltbruch *m* forced rupture

gewaltig powerful, mighty, potent, strong

Gewaltprobe *f* violent proof

gewaltsam by force, forceful **etwas ~ tun** to use force or violence **-e Erkundung** reconnaissance in force

Gewalt-tat *f* outrage, violence, brutality **-tätigkeit** *f* violence **-versuch** *m* forced proof

gewalzt milled, rolled (on) **-er Erddamm** earth-fill dam **-es Gewinde** rolled thread **-es Glas** rolled glass **-e Graupappe** friction board **-er Gummi** milled rubber **-e Profile** rolled shapes **-er Träger** (aus Stahl) rolled steel joist

Gewand *n* garment, vestment, garb

Gewändanker *m* cramp iron for fastening the jamb-stones on the wall

Gewände *n* jamb

gewandt nimble, adroit, skilled

Gewandtheit *f* cleverness, dexterity, agility
Gewässer *n* waters, watercourse, stream, flood **-beschreibung** *f* hydrolysis **-kunde** *f* hydrology
Gewebe *m* tissue, texture, textile fabric, cloth, gauze, web, netting **loses** ~ open weaving
Gewebe-äquivalent *n* tissue equivalent **-dosis** *f* tissue dose **-einführapparat** *m* entering arrangement for fabric **-einlage** *f* plies of fabric
Gewebegebilde *n* **winzige** ~ ultramicrons (of eye tissue)
Gewebe-haftung *f* adhesive properties **-kunstleder** *n* artificial leather cloth **-lage** (bei Reifen) ply **-legemaschine** *f* cloth-folding machine
gewebelose Isolierschläuche insulating tubings without fabrics
Gewebe-papier *n* cloth-centered paper **-pisang** *m* manila hemp **-pressen** *n* cloth pressing **-prüfmaschine** *f* tissue-testing machine **-prüfung** *f* fabric examination
Gewebe-reifen *m* fabric ring **-riemen** *m* tissue belt **-schirm** *m* solid-type fabric parachute **-schlauch** *m* braided hose **-schnitzel** *pl* macerated fabric **-vorrollapparat** *m* let-off stripper
Gewehr *n* rifle **-abzug** *m* trigger release **-auflage** *f* parapet, fire crest
Gewehr-kolben *m* butt of rifle **-kuppelungstück** *n* bayonet coupling, barrel-locking stud **-lauf** *m* gun barrel, rifle barrel **-laufbohrer** *m* gunbarrel drill **-mieke** *f* **-mücke** *f* arms rack
Gewehr-putzstock *m* rifle cleaner **-pyramide** *f* pile of arms **-riemen** *m* rifle sling **-schaft** *m* gunstock **-schloß** *n* lock (of rifle), bolt
Gewehrschuß *m* rifleshot **-sicheres Blech** bulletproof plating
Gewehrverschluß *m* breechblock ~ **mit Schließmechanismus** breech of rifle with closing mechanism **-schraube** *f* breechblock screw
Gewehrversuch *m* rifle test
gewellt wavy, corrugated, undulated; (b. Teilkammer) sinuous **-e Barometerdose** corrugated pressure capsule or box, corrugated barometric cell **-er Einspannrand** corrugated suspension means (of cone) **-e Konusspitze** apex step
Gewerbe *n* trade, profession, occupation, branch, department or line (of business) **-art** *f* trade, handicraft **-ausstellung** *f* industrial exhibition **-hygienische Anlage** industrial hygienic plant **-ingenieur** *m* industrial engineer **-ordnung** *f* industrial legislation **-schule** *f* technical school or college **-treibender** *m* tradesman, craftsman **-unfallversicherungsschein** *m* employer's liability policy **-verein** *m* tradesmen's union **-zweig** *m* trade, handicraft
gewerblich industrial, concerning trade or profession **-e Meßgeräte** *pl* industrial measuring instruments
gewerbsmäßig professional
Gewerkschaft *f* (trade) union **-vertrag** *m* cartel contract
Gewicht *n* weight, stress, weighting, specific density ~ **der Luft** air weight ~ **des Pendels** bob ~ **je Pferdestärke** weight per horsepower **absolutes spezifisches** ~ absolute specific gravity **äußerstes** ~ limit load **geeichtes** ~ stamped or standard weight **scheinbares spezifisches** ~ apparent specific gravity **übliches** ~ standard weight **verschiebbares** ~ sliding weight
gewichtlicher Ausgleich static balance
Gewichtsabgang *m* short weight
gewichtsabhängige Friktion weight-loaded friction
Gewichts-abnahme *f* decrease in weight **-analyse** *f* gravimetric analysis **-analytisch** gravimetric **-angabe** *f* weight indication
Gewichtsantrieb, Uhrwerk mit ~ weight-driven clock
Gewichts-aräometer *m* hydrometer **-ausbringen** *n* yield by weight **-ausgleich** *m* balance of weight, mass balance **-ausgleicher** *m* weight equalizer **-ausgleichsgläser** *pl* weight compensating lenses **-ausgleichung** *f* balance of weight **-belastet** gravity type, weighted **-belastung** *f* dead load, dead weight (safety valves and presses) **-beschleunigung** *f* acceleration due to gravity or weight **-bremse** *f* weight brake
Gewichts-dichte *f* specific weight **-dosierung** *f* weight batching **-einheit** *f* unit of weight **-einsparung** *f* saving of weight **-erhöhung** *f* weight increase **-ersparnis** *f* saving in weight **-feile** *f* rough file **-gefühl** *n* sense of weight **-hebel** *m* weight lever **-hebeleinrichtung** *f* weight-lever system **-kasten** *m* weight box **-konstanz** *f* constant weight
Gewichts-last *f* dead weight **-losigkeit** *f* weightlessness **-manko** *n* short weight, underweight **-mittel** *n* weight average **-noten** *pl* weight notice **-prozent** *n* percentage by weight **-prozentskala** *f* weight-percentage scale **-regler** *m* weight governor
Gewichts-sammler *m* weight accumulator **-satz** *m* set of weights **-schale** *f* seat for loose poises **-scheibe** *f* wheel weight **-spannungsmesser** *m* gravity ammeter voltmeter **-staumauer** *f* gravity dam **-strommesser** *m* gravity ammeter, voltmeter **-stück** *n* weight piece (individual) weight **-teil** *n* part by weight **-tonne** *f* weight ton **-träger** *m* weight holder **-trägerhaken** *m* weight stand hook **-trimmen** *n* trimming by weights **-umrechnung** *f* conversion of weight
Gewichts-verhältnis *n* quantivalent ratio, proportion by weight, weight ratio **-verlust** *m* loss in weight **-vermehrung** *f* increase in weight **-verminderung** *f* reduction in weight **-verschiebung** *f* sliding weight **-verteilung** *f* weight-distribution balance **-voltameter** *n* weight voltameter **-vorschub** *m* weight-operated feed, weight feed **-zahl** *f* weight factor **-zunahme** *f* gain or increase in weight **-zusammensetzung** *f* composition by weight
gewickelt wound **lagenweise** ~ layer-wound **auf ein Ohm** ~ wound to a resistance of an ohm **in Serie** ~ series-wound **-es Rohr** rolled laminated tube, wrapped tube **-er Hochdruckbehälter** strip-wound high-pressure vessel
Gewinde *n* winding, coil, skein, thread (screw), spire, worm (gear) ~ **bohren** to tap (screw a hole) ~ **fräsen** to mill threads ~ **schneiden** to tap, thread, cut screws ~ **spritzen** to die-cast threads **mit** ~ **versehen** screwed, threaded
Gewinde, doppelgängiges ~ double thread **eingängiges** ~ single thread **flaches** ~ square thread **flachgängiges** ~ square thread **grobgängiges** ~ coarse pitch thread, coarse thread

konisches ~ tapered thread **mehrfaches** ~ multiplex thread **mehrgängiges** ~ multiple thread **scharfgängiges** ~ fine thread, sharp-V thread, angular or triangular thread **steilgängiges** ~ coarse thread **trapezförmiges** ~ tetragonal thread **versehen mit** ~ threaded **zylindrisches** ~ straight (joint)

Gewinde mittels Fräser thread milling ~ **mittels Schneideisen** thread cutting ~ **mittels Strehler** thread chasing ~ **nach dem Wälzverfahren** thread hobbing

Gewinde-abgleichkern *m* thread-balancing or -adjusting core **-abwälzfräser** *m* thread hob, threading hob, thread milling hob **-ansatz** *m* thread lug **-anschluß** *m* threaded pipe connection **-art** *f* type of thread **-auge** *n* threaded eye **-auslauf** *m* runout of thread, thread chamfer **-auslaufwinkel** *m* chamfer angle of the thread **-außendurchmesser** *m* major thread diameter **-außentaster** *m* outside-thread calipers

Gewinde-backen *m* threading die, (screw) die **-bereich** *m* screw, cutting range **-anschnitt** *m* chamfer (of a tap), pointing (of a tap) **-bohrautomat** *m* automatic tapping machine **-bohren** *n* tapping

Gewindebohrer *m* tap, screw tap, tap drill ~ **für Grundlöcher oder Sacklöcher** bottoming tap

Gewindebohrerbruch *m* tap breakage

Gewindebohrerhalter *m* tap holder **gekröpfter** ~ knee tap holder

Gewinde-bohrerlehre *f* tap gauge **-bohrmaschine** *f* tapping machine **-bohrung** *f* taphole, tapped hole **-bohrvorrichtung** *f* tapping attachment, tapping fixture

Gewindebolzen *m* plug bolt, thread bolt ~ **U-förmig gebogen** U-bolt

Gewindebolzen-kerndurchmesser *m* minor thread diameter **-verschluß** *m* coupling pin with nut lock

Gewinde-buchse *f* threaded or screwed bush or bushing, screw socket **-deckel** *m* cover nut **-drehbank** *f* thread-cutting lathe **-drehmaschine** *f* pipe-threading machine **-drehstahl** *m* thread tool **-drückmaschine** *f* thread-bulging machine

Gewinde-drücke-, Sicken- und Beschneidemaschine *f* threading, beading, and trimming machine

Gewinde-durchmesser *m* thread diameter **-einschraubsitz** *m* threaded seat **-eisen** *n* screw die, diestock, screw plate, die plate **-fänger** *m* die nipple **-fassung für Zündkerzen** plug adapter **flanke** *f* side or flank of thread **-flankendurchmesser** *m* root thread diameter, effective thread diameter **-flansch** *m* threaded or screwed flange

Gewinde-formfräser *m* single form cutter **-fortsatz** *m* threaded extension **-fräsen** *n* thread milling **-fräsmaschine** *f* thread-milling machine **-fräsvorrichtung** *f* thread milling attachment **-fuß** *m* thread bottom or base, root of thread **-futter** *n* threaded female chuck

Gewinde-gabelstahl *m* double-point threading chaser **-gang** *m* course of thread, thread, pitch of screw thread **-ganganzeiger** *m* thread-cutting indicator **-gelenk** *n* threaded knuckle **-glas** *n* tube with screw cap **-grenzmaß** *n* thread limit **-größe** *f* (in mm) thread diameter (in millimeters) **-herstellungsmaschine** *f* thread-cutting machine **-hinterstechen** *n* grooving at a back of thread **-höhe** *f* screw pitch **-hülse** *f* threaded sleeve

Gewinde-innentaster *m* inside-thread calipers **-kaliber** *n* thread gauge, screw-pitch gauge **-kanal** *m* thread groove **-kasten** *m* screw-cutting gearbox **-kerndurchmesser** *m* thread-core diameter **-kluppe** *f* screwstock **-kontrollapparat** *m* screw-thread comparator **-kopf** (b. Prüfmaschine) *m* clamping head for accommodating heads with threads **-kopfprobe** *f* threaded test piece **-kupplung** *f* screw joint

Gewinde-länge *f* length of thread **-lappmaschine** *f* thread lapping machine **-lehrdorn** *m* thread plug gauge **-lehre** *f* thread gauge, screw-thread gauge (fingers) **-lehrmutter** *f* template gauge **-lehrring** *m* ring thread gauge **-leitbacke** *f* follower **-leitpatrone** *f* leader **-loch** *n* tapped or threaded hole **-meßkomparator** *m* optical-screw-thread-measuring machine **-messung** *f* screw-thread measuring

Gewindemuffe *f* threaded sleeve, screwed socket or sleeve, collar with thread, coupling for tube conduit **gespaltene** ~ split collar

Gewinde-nachbohrer *m* plug tap (for screwing) **-nachschneider** *m* tap bottoming **-nachschnitt** *m* chasing of screw thread, tap bottoming **-nenndurchmesser** *m* full thread **-nippel** *n* thread nipple **-normblatt** *n* thread standards, specifications for standard threads **-normen** *pl* screw-thread standards **-nute** *f* flute **-nutenfräser** *m* flute cutter **-öse** *f* screw ring, eyebolt

Gewindepassung *f* (fein) close fit of thread ~ (mittel) free fit ~ (mittel bis fein) medium fit

Gewinde-patrone *f* mandrel **-profil** *n* (screw-) thread profile **-profilmikroskop** *n* thread contour microscope **-projektionsapparat** *m* thread profile projector **-rille** *f* thread groove **-rillenfräser** *m* thread-milling cutter, multiple form cutter **-ring** *m* threaded ring, nut, tap (for screw or bolt) **-rohr** *n* screwed or threaded, tube **-rohreinführung** *f* threaded conduit hub **-rohrleitung** *f* screwed pipeline **-rollbacke** *f* flat die for thread rolling **-rollmaschine** *f* thread rolling machine **-rollwerkzeug** *n* threading die tapper

Gewinde-schablone *f* screw-pitch gauge **-schleifautomat** *m* automatic thread grinding machine **-schleifmaschine** *f* thread-grinding machine **-schleifen** *n* thread-grinding

Gewindeschneid(e)-arbeit *f* threading (operation), tapping (operation) **-anzeiger** thread cutting indicator

Gewindeschneideapparat, außen threading operation ~ **innen** tapping operation

Gewindeschneid(e)-backe *f* **oder -backen** *m* threading die, screw plate, screw-cutting die **-backenschleifvorrichtung** *f* grinding attachment for threading dies **-bohrer** *m* tap (screw or screwing tap) **-drehbank** *f* screw-cutting lathe

Gewindeschneideeinrichtung *f* screw-cutting attachment ~ **für Linksgewinde** left-hand threading attachment

Gewindeschneid(e)-eisen *n* die plate, threading die, screw die, screw plate **-gang** *m* threading operation **-garnitur** *f* screw plate set

Gewindeschneidekopf *m* threading die head ~

(selbstauslösender für Außengewinde) self opening die head ~ **für Außengewinde** die head chaser ~ **für Innengewinde** collapsible tap

Gewindeschneid(e)-kopfbacken *m* die head chaser **-kluppe** *f* (screwing) diestock, screw plate, holder for (screwing) dies **-kuppe** *f* die stock **-maschine** *f* thread-cutting, tapping or threading machine, reamer, bolt (pipe) screwing machine

Gewindeschneiden *n* tapping, thread cutting, threading, reaming, metal cutting ~ (mit dem Schneideeisen) screwing ~ **mit Fräser** thread milling

Gewindeschneid(e)-öl *n* screw-cutting oil **-platte** *f* screw(ing) plate

Gewindeschneider *m* tap thread, screw plate

Gewindeschneidestahl *m* threading tool, screw-cutting tool **einseitiger** ~ single-point threading tool

Gewindeschneid(e)-werkzeug *n* threading tool, screw plate **-zahn** *m* thread chaser, tool chaser **-zeug** *n* (Kluppe mit Schneidebacken) stocks and dies **-zug** *m* stock and dies

Gewindeschraublehre *f* screw-thread micrometer calipers ~ **mit Fühlhebel** indicating screw-thread calipers

Gewinde-schulterstahl *m* shouldered thread chaser **-schutzkappe** *f* thread-cutting protective cap

Gewindeschutzmuffe, äußere ~ protecting box **innere** ~ protective cap (for thread cutting)

Gewindespindel *f* threaded or screwed spindle, worm-gear spindle ~ **für Vertikalverstellung** elevating screw

Gewinde-spitze *f* crest **-spitzstahl** *m* single-point threading tool, threading tool chaser **-stab** *m* threaded rod or pin

Gewindestahl *m* thread or threading tool, thread cutter, chaser (for screw threads) **gekröpfter** ~ bent threading tool

Gewindestahl als Spitzstahl single-point threading tool ~ **als Schulterstahl** shouldered thread chaser ~ **für Innengewinde** inside threading tool

Gewinde-stange *f* threaded pin or rod **-stärke** *f* size or diameter of thread

Gewindesteigung *f* pitch (of a screw), thread pitch, lead **große** ~ steep thread pitch

Gewinde-steigungslehre *f* screw-pitch gauge **-stern** *m* chasing star

Gewindestift *m* headless screw, grub screw, stud bolt (fixed), screwed pin, threaded rod or pin ~ **mit Innensechskant** Allen set screw ~ **mit Kegelkuppe** slotted cup point set screw ~ **mit Kugelansatz** grub screw with spherical end ~ **mit Spitze** threaded pin with tapering end ~ **mit Zapfen** slotted dog point set screw

Gewinde-stopfen *m* screw cap **-stöpsel** *m* screw or screwed plug **-strähler** *m* **strehler** *m* chasing tool, thread chaser **-stück** *n* threaded coupling **-stutzen** *m* threaded pipe, adapter nipple **-system** *n* thread system **-taster** *m* thread calipers **-teilung** *f* pitch of thread **-tiefe** *f* depth of thread **-toleranz** *f* thread tolerance **-übergangstaille** *f* rounded circumferential groove **-uhr** *f* chasing dial

Gewinde-verbindung *f* screw-coupling **-walzbacke** *f* thread-rolling die **-walze** *f* rolling thread cutter **-wälzfräser** *m* thread hob **-walzmaschine** *f* thread-rolling machine **-walzrolle** *f* cylindrical die for thread rolling **-werkzeug** *n* threading tool **-wirbelkopf** *m* thread cut whirling toolholder **-zahnhalter** *m* threaded-tool holder **-zapfen** *m* pin with tread, threaded journal, spigot

gewinkeltes Verbindungsstück elbow connection

Gewinn *m* profit, gain, advantage, benefit **am** ~ **beteiligt sein** to share in profits **veranschlagter** ~ estimated profits

Gewinn-abfuhr *f* surrender of profits **-anteil** *m* divided bonus, share of the profits

gewinnbares Kohlenvorkommen coal deposits that can be extracted

Gewinn-beteiligung *f* profit sharing **-bringend** profitable, advantageous

gewinnen to win, gain, earn, acquire, produce, extract, exploit, attain **Erze** ~ to raise or extract ore

Gewinner *m* (Wettbewerb) winner

Gewinn-faktor *m* gain factor **-marge** *f* margin of profit **-saldo** *m* balance of profit **-spanne** *f* margin of profit

Gewinn- und Verlustrechnung *f* profit and loss statement

Gewinnung *f* extraction, winning, recovery, production, reclamation, breaking, yield, output, exploitation ~ **im Tagebau** open-cut mining ~ **im Tiefbau** under-ground mining

Gewinnungsanlage *f* recovery or byproduct plant

gewinnungsberechtigt sein to be entitled to win

Gewinnungs-kosten *pl* winning expenses **-methode** *f* mining working **-verfahren** *n* extraction process, method of mining or of manufacture

Gewinn-verteilung *f* disposal of profits **-zerlegung** *f* analysis of profit

Gewirk *n* texture, weaf, weft

gewirkter Stoff knitted fabric

gewischte Zeichnung dabbed drawing

gewissenhafte Übersetzung faithful translation

Gewitter *n* thunderstorm, electrical storm **-bildung** *f* formation of a thunderstorm **-bö** *f* black squall, thundersquall **-drohend** ugly or threatening (sky) **-flug** *m* frontal soaring **-front** *f* front of thunderstorms **-frontenflug** *m* flight in front of a thunderstorm **-herd** *m* center of the thunderstorm

Gewitter-kragen *m* vault of cloud, arched squall **-neigung** *f* tendency to thunderstorm **-regen** *m* thundershower **-sack** *m* thunderstorm sack, heart of the thunderstorm **-störung** *f* atmospherics, static **-stufe** *f* stage of thunderstorm **-sturm** *m* thunderstorm **-wirbel** *m* thunderstorm whirl or vortex

Gewitterwolken *pl* cumulo-nimbus clouds, thunderclouds

gewobbelt swept (referring, e.g., to the frequency sweep in identification friend or foe), wobbulated (radar)

gewogen (wiegen) weighed

gewöhnen to accustom, break in, acclimatize

Gewohnheit *f* habit, custom, usage, common practice

Gewohnheitsrecht *n* common law

gewöhnlich normal, general, standard, common **für** ~ normally **-er Drahtbund** tie (teleph.) **-e**

Drehzahl rated revolutions **-es Eisen** ordinary iron **-es Ferngespräch** routine call **-er Gebrauch** usual standard **-e Havarie** general or average damage **-er Kohlenstoffstahl** straight carbon steel **-e Permeabilität** normal permeability

gewohnt (gewöhnen) accustomed

Gewöhnung *f* acclimatization

Gewölbe *n* arch, arched roof or crown, roof arch, vault, vaulted ceiling, roof ring **-anker** *m* tie anchor **-backstein** *m* brick arch **-bildung** *f* arching **-bogen** *m* span, archwork, arch of a vault **-bogenröhre** *f* roof-tubes **-dach** *n* dome-shaped roof, arched roof **-druck** *m* arch pressure **-fach** *n* vaulted cell **-kern** *m* arch core

Gewölbe-pfeiler *m* flying buttress **-reihensperre** *f* multiple-arch dam **-rippe** *f* nerve or rib of a vault **-schenkel** *m* arch limb **-spannung** *f* roof strengthening **-spannweite** *f* width of the vault **-stein** *m* roof brick, arch brick **-träger** *m* vault support **-wirkung** *f* arch action, arching **-zwikkel** *m* spandrel

gewölbt arched, convex, domed, dome-shaped, vaulted, arcuate **-er Boden** curved, rounded, or dished head **-e Böschung** convex slope **-e Decke** turtleback **-es Ende** (Rohr) dished end **-es Fach** arched shed **-er Flansch** heads with threads **kugelförmig -e Lamellen** dished laminae **-es Mauerwerk** vaulting **-er Rücken** rounded back

gewollt wanted, intended **nicht -e Aussendung** unwanted emission

gewonnen (gewinnen) obtained, excavated **-es Schleudergut** solid material obtained **~** (z.B. Schub) delivered (thrust)

geworfen (werfen) warped (wood), thrown

gewuchtete rotierende Körper dynamically balanced rotating masses

gewunden (winden) tortuous, twisted, coiled, wound **-e Biegungsfedern** spiral springs, helical-torsion springs

gewürfelt checkered (various patterns)

Geyserit *m* siliceous sinter of the geyser

gezackt ragged (in outline), serrate, forked (lightning) **-e Linie** jagged line, serrated or notched line, dentated or dented line

Gezäh(e) *n* tools, implements, rakes, instruments

Gezähne *n* gear, tools **-kasten** *m* toolbox, tool chest **-kiste** *f* miner's box

gezahnt toothed, cogged, serrated, indented, denticulate **-e Pinzette** forceps with teeth **-er Querschnitt** serrated cross section **-e Schiene** toothed rail **-e Stange** toothed rack, ratch

gezapftes Holz tongued wood

gezeichnet signed, drawn

Gezeiten *pl* tides **die ~ betreffend** tidal

Gezeiten-bewegung *f* tidal impulse **-beschleunigung** *f* tidal component **-erscheinungen** *pl* tidal phenomena **-erzeugende Kraft** tide producing force **-feuer** *n* tide or tidal light **-fluß** *m* tidal river **-gravimeter** *n* tidal gravimeter **-konstante** *f* tide constant **-kraftwerk** *n* tidal power plant **-messer** *m* thalassometer, tide-gauge

Gezeiten-rechenmaschine *f* tide-calculating machine **-reibung** *f* tidal friction **-signal** *n* tide signal **-strom** *m* tidal current **-strömung** *f* ebb and flow of tide, tidal currents **-tafel** *f* tide table **-vermessung** *f* tide measurement **-wechsel** *m* turning of the tides **-welle** *f* tidal wave

Gezeug *n* utensils, tools, implements **-strecke** *f* level gangway, main gangway, gallery (of a mine)

Gezimmer *n* timberwork, framework

gezinkt pronged

gezogen (ziehen) pulled, sucked, attracted, drawn (out), rifled, twisted, drawn cold; (Fluglage) nose-up **~ auf** drawn on **hart ~** hard-drawn **-e Achse** solid-drawn axle **-e Dose** drawn container **-er Draht** drawn wire **dreimal -er Draht** three-draft wire **-er Flußeisendraht** drawn iron wire **-er Generator** suction gas producer

gezogen-e Hülsen seamless sockets **-er Hohlkörper** hollow-drawn article **-er Holm** extruded spar **-e Kurve** climbing turn **-er Lauf** rifled barrel **-es Licht** dipped candle, dip **-e Röhre** drawn tube **-er Stahl** drawn steel **-e Transistoren** grown junction transistors **-es Ziel** towed target

gezündet ionized

gezupfte Saite plucked string or chord

gezwirnt twined

gezwungen (zwingen) (en)forced **zur Landung ~** forced to land

G-Faktor *m* G factor or value, interval rule

g-g-Kerne even-even nuclei

Gicht *f* throat (of furnace), top, mouth, charge, burden **-anzeiger** *m* indicator on the top of a blast furnace, stock line gauge **-aufzug** *m* furnace hoist, furnace-charging gear **-aufzugwinde** *f* furnace-hoisting machine **-boden** *f* **-brücke** *f* charging platform (of blast furnace) **-bühne** *f* charging platform (of blast furnace), charging floor **-bühnenkran** *m* furnace charging crane **-ebene** *f* charging platform (of blast furnace) **-einwurfsöffnung** *f* charging door (of blast furnace)

gichten to charge the furnace

Gichtenzähler *m* furnace-filling counter **registrierender ~** recording furnace-filling counter

Gicht-fahrzeug *n* furnace-charging carriage **-flamme** *f* (furnace-)top flame

Gichtgas *n* top gas, stack gas, outlet gas, blast-furnace gas, waste gas (from blast furnace), throat gas **-abzugsrohr** *n* gas offtake, uptake, or downtake, downcomer tube, downcomer **-gebläse** *n* gas-engine blower, gas-driven blowing engine **-entziehung** *f* taking off the gases of blast furnaces **-fang** *m* gas take of blast furnace **-leitung** *f* blast-furnace gas main, crude-gas main

Gichtgas-maschine *f* blast-furnace-gas engine, crude-gas machine **-reiniger** *m* blast-furnace-gas cleaner **-reinigung** *f* cleaning of blast-furnace gas, crude-gas cleaning **-reinigungsanlage** *f* crude-gas-cleaning plant **-rohrventil** *n* bleeder valve **-staub** *m* flue dust

Gicht-glocke *f* furnace-top bell, bell-type distributing gear **-glockenwinde** *f* bell-operating gear, throat-stopper winch **-kübel** *m* charging, hoisting, or distributor bucket **-mann** *m* charger, charging man, dumper (blast furnace) **-mantel** *m* mouth screen, wind wall on the mouth of a blast furnace **-maß** *n* charging gauge

Gicht-mauer *f* wind wall on the mouth of a blast furnace **-messer** *m* measuring rod for the descent of the charges **-öffnung** *f* furnace throat or top, top opening, charging hole, charging door **-pfropfen** *m* furnace-throat stopper **-rauch** *m* top smoke **-schirm** *m* wind screen of a blast furnace **-schwamm** *m* solid incrustation near top of furnace, furnace cadmia or calamine

Gichtstaub *m* (blast-furnace) flue dust **-abscheidung** *f* flue-dust separation **-brikettierungsanlage** *f* flue-dust briquetting plant

Gicht-temperatur *f* throat or top temperature **-treppe** *f* top stairs of a blast furnace **-trichter** *m* furnace-top hopper **-turm** *m* charging tower

Gichtung *f* charging

Gichtverschluß *m* furnace-top distributor or distributing gear, bell-and-hopper arrangement, cup-and-cone arrangement **doppelter ~** double-bell-hopper arrangement, cover and bells (of blast furnace)

Gicht-wagen *m* furnace-charging or hoist carriage, skip, furnace carriage **-weite** *f* diameter of furnace throat **-winde** *f* bell-operating gear, bell hoist

Gickel *m* axis of a hinge, pivot

Giebel *m* gable **-dach** *n* gable roof **-fenster** *n* gabled or dormer window **-mauer** *f* gable wall **-rolle** *f* sheave pulley **-wand** *f* gable wall

Giekbaum *m* main boom

gieken to jib, shift

Gien *n* deck tackle, purchases **-block** *m* winding-tackle block

giepen to gibe

Gier-achse *f* axis of yaw **-bewegung** *f* yawing motion in yaw **-brücke** *f* flying or swing bridge, trail flying bridge

gieren to yaw (naut, aviat)

Gieren *n* yawing, trail ferrying

Gierfähre *f* flying ferry, trail ferry

gierig greedy

Gier-mast *m* horse (hydr.) **-moment** *m* yawing moment **-schlag** *m* yawing **-schlagmesser** *n* yawmeter **-schwingung** *f* yawing, oscillatory yaw **-tau** *n* towing cable

Gierung *f* miter, mitered joint, yaw, lurch

Gierungs-messer *m* yawmeter **-winkel** *m* angle of yaw

Gierwinkel *m* yawing angle

Gieß-anlage *f* casting implements **-apparat** *m* congealing apparatus **-arbeit** *f* casting operation **-arm** *m* casting arm **-ausrüstung** *f* pouring outfit **-bach** *m* torrent **-band** *n* casting strand, pouring conveyer **-bar** capable of being poured or cast, fit for founding or casting **-barkeit** *f* capacity for being poured, castability **-becken** *n* sink

Gießbett *n* casting or pouring bed, pig bed **-aufbereitungsmaschine** *f* pig-bed dressing machine **-kran** *m* (overhead) crane for pig bed

Gieß-blech *n* casting tool **-bühne** *f* pouring or teeming platform **-dauer** *f* duration of pouring **-einrichtung** *f* casting equipment, pouring outfit

gießen to cast, pour (out), found, mold, spill, teem, coat (a film) **im Herd ~** to cast in open sand **in Kokillen ~** to chill **mit dem Steigrohr ~** to cast from the bottom **fallend ~** to top-pour, top-cast, pour from the top **massiv ~** to cast solid **nach oben ~** to cast up **stehend ~** to pour or cast on end **steigend ~** to bottom-pour, bottom-cast **waagerecht ~** to pour or cast horizontally

Gießen *n* casting, teeming, pouring, leaking **~** (Auslaufen von Flüssigkeiten) leaking **~ der Blöcke** teeming **~ im Gespann** group casting, bottom casting **~ mittels Gießlöffel** hand ladling **~ mittels Gießwagen** car casting **~ an der Trennlinie** gating at the joint

Gießer *m* caster, pourer, founder, melter

Gießerei *f* foundry, foundry work, casting **-anlage** *f* foundry plant **-bedarf** *m* foundry material **-bedarfsartikel** *m* foundry requisite **-betrieb** *m* foundry practice **-drehkran** *m* foundry jib crane **-einrichtung** *f* foundry device or equipment **-eisen** *n* foundry iron, foundry pig **-flammofen** *m* foundry furnace **-form** *f* mold (foundry)

Gießerei-formmaschine *f* foundry molding machine **-formmasse** *f* molding sand for iron **-holzkohlenroheisen** *n* foundry charcoal pig **-ingenieur** *m* foundry engineer, foundryman **-inspektor** *m* foundry supervisor **-karren** *m* foundry cart or barrow **-koks** *m* foundry coke **-kran** *m* casting crane (foundry) **-kupolofen** *m* foundry cupola **-kursus** *m* foundry course **-laufkran** *m* foundry traveling crane **-leiter** *m* foundry superintendent **-löffel** *m* ladle (metallurgy)

Gießerei-mann *m* foundryman, iron founder **-maschine** *f* foundry machine **-modelltischler** *m* foundry patternmaker **-ofen** *m* foundry furnace, iron-melting furnace **-roheisen** *n* foundry or casting pig iron **-sand** *m* foundry sand, molding sand **-schachtofen** *m* foundry cupola **-sohle** *f* foundry floor, foundry-floor level **-technik** *f* foundry practice **-wesen** *n* founding, foundry matters, foundry practice or work, foundry field

Gießerschwärze *f* black(en)ing, black wash, founder's black, facing

gieß-fähig capable of being cast **-fähigkeit** *f* capacity for being poured or cast, casting properties **-fertig** ready for pouring **-fläche** *f* casting area

Gießform *f* mold or form for block-making, ingot mold, casting mold **-achse** *f* mold shaft **-einsatzstück** *n* insert piece for casting mold **-nute** *f* casting mold groove **-seitenteile** *pl* mold side pieces **-wischer** *m* mold wiper

Gieß-gabel *f* crucible shank **-gerät** *n* stereo caster **-geschwindigkeit** *f* rate of pouring **-gespann** *n* stool (foundry) **-graben** *m* pit (foundry work) **-grube** *f* casting or foundry pit, teeming box **-grubenkran** *m* casting-pit crane, center casting crane

Gieß-halle *f* casting house, pig-casting yard **-hals** *m* pot throat **-harz** *n* casting resin **-harzwandler** *m* molded resin transformer **-hülse** *f* mold for composition inking rollers **-hütte** *f* foundry, casting house **-kanne** *f* watering can **-karren** *m* filler on wheels **-kasten** *m* casting mold, box or frame of a mold **-katze** ladle crab

-**kelle** *f* casting ladle -**kern** *m* casting (mold) core

Gieß-koks *m* foundry coke -**kolonne** *f* pouring gang or crew -**kokilleneinsatz** *m* casting chill insertion -**kopf** *m* jet, runner, deadhead -**kran** *m* foundry crane -**kunst** *f* founder's art, founding -**lade** *f* casting mold -**ling** *m* powder casting -**lingkopf** *m* gates and risers -**loch** *n* sprue or runner opening, teeming nozzle -**lochstein** *m* sleeve brick, fire-clay nozzle, firebrick sleeve, teeming nozzle -**löffel** *m* (casting) ladle, pouring cup -**maschine** *f* (pig) casting machine

Gießmetall *n* casting metal **von ~ umschlossener Kern** housing core

Gieß-modell *n* mold (foundry) -**mundlöcher** *pl* casting holes -**mundwischer** *m* pot mouth wiper -**muschel** *f* casting nozzle -**mutter** *f* mold, (casting) matrix -**ofen** *m* founding furnace -**periode** *f* casting time

Gießpfanne *f* casting or pouring ladle, foundry or teeming ladle, ladle **~ mit Ausgußschnauze** lip-pour or top-pour ladle **~ mit Gehänge und Wagen** cranetruck ladle **~ mit Getriebekippvorrichtung** geared ladle, ladle with tipping-gear appliance **~ mit Handkippvorrichtung** shank ladle, hand-tipping-type ladle **~ mit Krangehänge** crane ladle **~ mit Schnauzenausguß** lip-pour or top-pour ladle **~ mit Stopfenausguß** bottom-pour ladle, teeming ladle, stopper ladle **~ mit Wagen** truck or buggy ladle

Gießpfannen-ausguß *m* ladle lip, nozzle of a ladle -**auskleidung** *f* ladle lining -**behälter** *m* ladle bowl -**bügel** *m* ladle bail

Gießpfannengabel *f* ladle shank **doppelseitige ~** double-end ladle shank

Gießpfannengehänge *n* ladle bail

Gießpfanneninhalt *m* ladle capacity **~ nach der Ausschmierung** ladle capacity inside of lining

Gießpfannen-kran *m* ladle crane -**schnauze** *f* ladle lip or nozzle -**tiegel** *m* ladle bowl -**tragschere** *f* ladle shank -**wagen** *m* ladle truck or barrow

Gieß-pfropfen *m* ladle plug -**platz** *m* casting pit, foundry pit, teeming box -**probe** *f* pour(ing) test -**punkt** *m* pour point -**rad** *n* mold disc -**radachse** *f* mold disc axis -**rahmen** *m* casting frame -**rinne** *f* pouring spout -**sand** *m* molding sand

Gieß-schale *f* mold shell -**schnauze** *f* pouring lip or nozzle -**schweißung** *f* cast weld -**setzmaschine** *f* composition caster -**stelle** *f* point of pouring, casting pit -**stellung** *f* pouring position -**stern** *m* star wheel

Gieß-stift *m* securing pin -**stöpsel** *m* core print (foundry), plug -**strecke** *f* casting line -**tafel** *f* casting plate -**technik** *f* pouring technique or practice -**temperatur** *f* casting or pouring temperature -**topf** *m* pouring pot or jar -**trichter** *m* pouring gate, gate, ingress gate, downgate, sprue, runner, sprue opening, conical feeder, gate connecting rod or driving rod -**topfrollenhebel** *m* melting pot lever -**trommel** *f* casting drum

Gießstümpel *m* pouring or runner basin **~ mit Schaumfang** skimming basin

Gieß-verfahren *n* casting process or procedure -**vorrichtung** *f* casting equipment -**wagen** *m* casting buggy, hot-metal-ladle truck -**winkel** *m* casting square -**zange** *f* crucible tongs -**zapfen** *m* runner stick (met.) -**zeit** *f* pouring time

Gift *n* poison, venom -**äscher** *m* arsenic lime -**fang** *m* poison tower -**gas** *n* poison gas, lethal or asphyxiating gas

giftig poisonous, venomous, toxic

Giftigkeit *f* toxicity

Gift-kies *m* arsenopyrite -**mehl** *n* white arsenic powder, arsenious anhydride -**nebel** *m* toxic smoke -**nebelwolke** *f* gas cloud -**rauch** *m* irritant smoke -**rauchkerze** *f* toxic-smoke candle, gas candle

Gift-stein *m* arsenical cadmia, white arsenic -**stoff** *m* toxic agent -**turm** *m* poison tower -**wirkung** *f* toxic effect

Giga-Elektronenvolt *n* billion electron volts

Gigantolith *m* gigantolite

Gilbe *f* yellow ocher

gilben, das Pergament ~ to dye parchment yellow

Gilbert *n* gilbert (unit of magnetomotive force)

Gilbungsgrad *m* degree of yellowing

Gilde *f* corporation, guild

Gilles-Schaltung *f* split-order wire

Gillingit *m* hisingerite

Gill-Morell-Schwingungen *pl* Gill-Morell oscillations

Gillung *f* counter

Gilsonit *m* gilsonite, uintaite

Gin-Widerstandsofen *m* Gin resistance furnace

Gipfel *m* summit, peak, top, acme, climax -**entfernung** *f* range to mask, abscissa for maximum ordinate of trajectory -**geschwindigkeit** *f* ceiling speed

Gipfelhöhe *f* maximum-trajectory ordinate, ceiling (aviation), maximum vertical ceiling **~ bei Ausfall eines Motors** ceiling with one engine out **~ mit einem stehenden Motor** ceiling with one motor stopped, emergency ceiling **errechnete ~** calculated ceiling **höchste erflogene ~** absolute ceiling **praktische ~** service ceiling

Gipfelleistung *f* top or peak performance or efficiency

gipfeln to culminate, reach a climax

Gipfel-punkt *m* maximum ordinate of trajectory, climax, culmination point, summit, vertex, zenith of trajectory -**spannung** *f* peak or crest voltage

Gipfelung *f* culmination

Gipfelwert *m* maximum (value)

Gips *m* gypsum, plaster of Paris, calcium sulfate **fetter ~** well-burnt plaster **gebrannter ~** plaster of Paris **grober ~** unsifted plaster **körniger ~** compact gypsum **schaumiger ~** scaly foliated gypsum **schuppigkörniger ~** foliated granular gypsum

Gips-abdruck *m* -**abguß** *m* plaster cast -**arbeit** *f* -**bewurf** *m* plastering -**blatt** *n* gypsum plate -**brecher** *m* gypsum crusher -**brennerei** *f* calcination of gypsum, gypsum burning, plaster burning -**diele** *f* plaster slab, gypsum deal

gipsen to plaster

Gipser *m* plasterer

Gips-erde *f* earthy gypsum -**erhärtung** *f* hardening plaster -**estrich** *m* plaster floor -**form** *f* plaster mold -**grube** *f* gypsum quarry -**kitt** *m* plaster cement -**mantel** *m* plaster lagging -**mantelbelag** *m* mantle piece of plaster -**marmor** *m* artificial marble -**mergel** *m* gypseous marl **-modell** *n* plaster-of-Paris model **-mörtel** *m* stucco, plaster **-putz** *m* plaster stucco **-spat** *m* sparry gypsum **-stein** *m* plaster, plastering **-stuck** *m* stucco **-verband** *m* plaster cast **-verputz** *m* stucco

Girant *m* endorser

Giro *n* endorsement

Girod-Ofen *m* Girod (direct-arc, conducting-hearth-, or electrode-hearth-arc) furnace

gischen to foam, froth

Gischt *m* spray, foam

Gisklappe *f* G-sharp key

Gispen *m* seed, gaseous inclusion (in glass)

Giß *f* rough estimate

gissen to estimate, make a rough calculation

Gissung *f* dead reckoning

Gitter *n* grating, lattice; (Rost) grate; (Draht) wire-lattice; (Elektro.-Röhre) grid; (Klimaanlage) grille screen, grating (of crystals), checker, plate grid (of storage batteries), mesh, trellis, fence, parallel-wire system, rack, grill, cascade **automatisch vorgespanntes ~** automatic or self-biased grid **engmaschiges ~** fine grid **freies ~** floating or free grid **kubisch raumzentriertes ~** body-centred structure **offenes ~** floating grid **weitmaschiges ~** open grid, open- or widemeshed grid **~ in der Röntgenspektroskopie** gratings in x-ray spectroscopy

Gitter-ableitung *f* grid leak (resistance) **-ableitungswiderstand** *m* grid leak (radio) **-ableitwiderstand** *m* grid return resistor, grid leak, grid resistance, field-intensity meter **-abmessungen** *pl* lattice dimensions **-abschirmhaube** *f* grid shielding can **-abstand** grating space, lattice distance, grating constant **-achse** *f* grid or lattice axis **-alarmrelais** *n* alarm relay of grid potential

Gitter-anodenkapazität *f* grid-plate capacitance, power factor of grid-plate capacity **-anodenschwingung** *f* tuned-grid, tuned-plate oscillation **-anregung** *f* excitation drive **-antenne** *f* parasol-type antenna **arbeitswiderstand** *m* field-intensity meter **-artig** latticed **-aufsatz** *m* top fencing **-aufweiterung** *f* expansion or increase in lattice spacing **-aussteuerung** *f* grid(-voltage) swing, grid sweep

Gitter-balken *m* Warren truss, lattice truss **-basis** *f* grounded grid **-basisschaltung** *f* grounded grid type circuit **-basisstufe** *f* earth grid stage **-batterie** *f* grid battery, grid-bias battery, C battery **-beeinflussung** *f* grid control or modulation **-beeinflußwert** *m* grid-influence of the modified plane **-berechnung** *f* calculation of lattice energy **-bereich** *m* lattice space **-besprechung** *f* grid modulation or control, grid-circuit modulation **-blech** *n* perforated sheet **-blende** *f* grating diaphragm **-block** *m* grid condenser, staircase-like structure of echelon grating **-blockierung** *f* negative biasing of grid, grid cutoff

Gitter-blockkondensator *m* grid-blocking or grid-bias condenser, grid condenser **-bremse** *f* (Conemaschine), washboard tension (coning machine) **-brücke** *f* lattice bridge **-brumm** *m* grid hum **-brüstung** *f* chancel, screen **-clip** *m* grid clip **-draht** *m* fence wire **-drossel** *f* grid resistance, grid resistor **-durchführung** *f* grid-seal **-durchgang** *m* checker flue, checker opening or passage **-durchgriff** *m* grid transparency, grid controllance, grid penetration factor

Gitter-ebene *f* lattice plane (of crystals) **-ebenenabstand** *m* interlattice-plane distance **-einflußbeiwert des Tragflügels** grid-influence coefficient of the airfoil **-einheit** *f* lattice unit, unit cell, elementary cell **-einsatzpunkt** *m* grid-current point, point of incipient grid-current flow **-einstellung** *f* regulable grid voltage **-elektrode** *f* grid electrode **-elektronen** *pl* lattice electrons **-emission** *f* grid emission **-energie** *f* lattice energy **-energiebänder, besetzte ~** filled lattice energy bands **-fachwerk** *n* grid or lattice construction **-fehlbau** *m* lattice disorder **-fehler** *m* lattice imperfection, lattice defects **-fehlstelle** *f* lattice imperfection **-feuerung** *f* chain-grate stokers **-filter** *n* lattice filter

gitterförmig latticed **-er Ausleger** crane arm of lattice type **-es Mauerwerk** latticed brickwork

Gitter-furchen *pl* rulings or ruling grooves (of diffraction grating) **-geber** *m* cross-bar generator **-gegenspannung** *f* inverse grid potential, reverse grid voltage **-geister** *pl* spectral grate ghosts **-gerade** *f* zone of crystal

gittergesteuert grid-controlled (radio)

gittergetastet grid-controlled

Gitter-gleichrichter *m* grid detector or rectifier **-gleichrichtung** *f* grid-current rectification or detection (in audion value)

Gittergleichstrom *m* direct-current grid current **-modulation** *f* grid-bias modulation

Gitter-gleitwiderstand *m* adjustable wire mesh resistor **-glimmröhre** *f* grid glow tube **-haltedraht** *m* grid stay wire, grid supporting wire **-halterstange** *f* side rod **-handspektroskop** *n* hand-grating spectroscope, diffraction hand-grating spectroscope **-holm** *n* grid stay or supporting member **-interferometer** *n* grating interferometer **-kammer** *f* checker chamber **-kapazität** *f* grid capacitance **-kappe** *f* grid cap **-kathodenraum** *m* grid-cathode space **-kathodenstrecke** *f* grid-cathode path

Gitter-kennlinie *f* grid characteristic, grid-current-grid-voltage characteristic **-kielschwein** *n* lattice keelson **-komplex** *m* lattice complex **-kondensator** *m* grid-blocking or grid-bias condenser, grid condenser or capacitor **-konstante** *f* lattice constant or parameter, grating constant or space **-konstruktion** *f* lattice-work girder structure **-kopfwand** *f* cross-barred end **-kopie** *f* grating replica **-korb** *m* (wooden) cage

Gitterkreis *m* grid(-filament) circuit, grid resonant circuit **-abstimmung** *f* grid tuning **-impedanz** *f* input impedance **-kapazität** *f* input capacity **-kupplung** *f* grid coupling **-reaktanz** *f* input reactance **-widerstand** *m* input resistance of a thermionic valve

Gitter-last *f* grid load **-laufzeit** *f* grid transition time **-leerstellen** *pl* lattice vacancies **-leitung** *f* grid circuit or connection, laddered telephone circuit **-leitwerte** *pl* grid conductance **-lichtmast** *m* lattice-type lamppost

Gitterlinie *f* grid line **senkrechte ~** Y line of map grid

Gitter-loch *m* lattice void (cryst.), lattice vacancy or hole **-loge** *f* latticed box **-lücke** *f* vacant position, vacant anion (cation) lattice **-masche**

f grid mesh **-maßstab** *m* grid scale **-mast** *m* lattice mast or pole, girder pole, trellis mast, (lattice) tower, latticed-girder pole, derrick-style antenna mast **-mauerwerk** *n* checker brickwork **-meßspektroskop** *n* evaluating grating spectroscope **-messung** *f* grating evaluation (optics), grating measurement **-metall** *n* a type of lead-base bearing alloy **-mikrophon** *n* grille-type microphone **-mittenabstand** *m* distance between centers of successive rulings, grating constant **-modulation** *f* grid modulation, grid-circuit modulation **-muster** *n* net pattern

gittern to grate, lattice, rail

Gitternebenschluß *m* grid leak (resistance)

Gitternetz *n* co-ordinate map grid, (measuring) grid, grid system, military grid **-karte** *f* gridded map **-linie** *f* grid line

Gitter-nord *m* grid north **-öffnung** *f* grid aperture **-ornament** *n* ornament for trellis fences **-parameter** *pl* lattice parameters **-platte** *f* grid plate **-platz** *m* lattice place or point, normal position, regular site, ion site **-pochwerk** *n* stamps or stamping mill, (wet, dry, screen, or grate, trough types, for ore) **-potentialkurve** *f* grid-potential curve **-punkte auf einer Kreisscheibe** lattice points on a circular disk **-punktmethode** *f* lattice-point method

Gitter-rad *n* skeleton wheel (of a tractor) **-rahmen** *m* lattice frame (machines) **-raum** *m* grid space **-raumladung** *f* charge of space grid **-rauschwiderstand** grid noise resistance **-relaxation** *f* lattice relaxation **-reflexe** *pl* grating reflexes **-richtung** *f* grid (base-line) direction or bearing **-rippe** *f* Warren-type rib **-rohr** *n* tube frame **-röhre** *f* radio telegraphic valve **-rost** *m* bar grate, grate **-rückleitung** *f* grid return **-rückstrom** *m* backlash **-ruhe** *f* quiescent grid **-rührer** *m* gate paddle agitator **-rumpf** *m* girder structure

Gitter-saum *m* grid skirt (TV) **-schaufel** *f* grid shovel **-schauzeichen** *n* grid indicator, shutter annunciator **-scheibe** *f* stator disk **-schieber** *m* grid-type slide valve **-schneidetechnik** *f* ruling technique **-schott** *n* batten and space bulk-head **-schranke** *f* barrier (railroad) of lattice **-schutzwiderstand** *m* grid stopper **-schwanz** *m* open tail, outrigger tail **-schwanzträger** *m* tail boom (aviation) outrigger tail boom **-schwanzstrebe** *f* tail-boom strut **-schwingung** *f* lattice vibration **-schwingungsüberlagerung** *f* lattice vibration superposition

Gitter-sieb *n* grizzly **-skelett** *n* latticework skeleton **-sockelfeld** *n* grid-socket connection **-spannung** *f* grid voltage or potential, cutoff bias **-spannungsimpuls** *m* grid voltage pulse **-spannungskennlinie** *f* grid characteristic (curve) **-spannungsmodulation** *f* grid-voltage modulation **-spektrograph** *m* lattice spectrograph **-spektrometer** *m* grating spectrometer **-spektroskop** *n* diffraction-grating spectroscope **-spektrum** *n* diffraction spectrum, grating spectrum **-sperre** *f* stake obstacle, cutoff bias **-sparkreis** *m* grid stopper **-sperrung** *f* grid extinguishing **-spule** *f* grid coil

Gitter-stab *m* lattice bar; (d. Reflektors) spine (antenna) **-ständer** *m* lattice(d) pole **-stange** *f* cast-iron paling (single bar) **-steg** *m* grid bridge or stay, solid portions forming grid meshes, grid strip used in lieu of wire, grid-support wires **-stein** *m* checker-brick **-steuerleistung** grid-driving power **-steuerung** *f* grid control (radio), grid (voltage) sweep, grid swing, excursion, excitation or modulation, grid drive **-stift** *m* grid pin **-stoff** *m* grenadine **-störstelle** *f* lattice defect or imperfection, irregularity **-störungen** *pl* lattice distortions or dislocations (cryst.) **-strebe** *f* grid stay, grid-supporting means **-strich** *m* grating line, ruling groove of a grating

Gitterstrom *m* grid current **negativer** ~ reverse or negative grid current, backlash of valve **positiver** ~ (reverse) grid current

Gitterstrom-aufnahme *f* drawing or taking of current by grid **-aussteuerung** *f* grid-current swing or sweep **-einsatzpunkt** *m* point of incipient grid-current flow **-gleichrichter** *m* grid-bias rectifier **-gleichrichtung** *f* cumulative grid detection, grid-current detection **-kennlinie** *f* grid characteristic, grid-current-grid-voltage characteristic **-modulation** *f* grid-bias modulation **-punkt** *m* grid-current point, point of incipient current flow at grid

Gitter-strömung *f* grid flow **-struktur** *f* lattice structure **-symmetrie** *f* symmetry of lattice **-tastung** *f* grid control, grid keying **-teilung** *f* grating ruling **-tor** *n* trellised gate **-träger** *m* lattice girder, frame girder, lattice gland, Warren truss **-traverse** *f* side rod **-trennungslinie** *f* line of partition between adjoining grid sections **-tür** *f* lattice gate or door

Gitter-umformer *m* grating converter **-überträger** *m* transformer **-ventil** *n* gridiron valve (slide or ordinary) **-verschiebung** *f* lattice distortion or dislocation **-verschiebungsspannung** *f* grid bias, grid priming, biasing-grid voltage, priming-grid voltage **-vervielfacher** *m* grid multiplier **-vervielfältiger** *m* mesh multiplier

Gitter-vorspannung *f* priming or biasing or initial grid voltage, grid bias, grid polarization voltage, C battery, direct-current component of grid voltage **automatische** ~ self-bias, automatic grid bias **-vorspannungsbatterie** grid battery, grid bias battery **-vorspannungsdraht** *m* bracing wire of tail girder **-vorspannungskontakt** *m* grid bias control **-vorspannungsverlagerung** *f* biasing voltage (grid bias) displacement **-vorwiderstand** *m* biasing resistor

Gitter-wärmeleitfähigkeit *f* lattice thermal conductivity **-wechselspannung** *f* grid alternating-current voltage **-werk** *n* checkerwork, braced-beam construction, latticed-girder construction, truss, lattice-work, grating

Gitterwerks-brücke *f* skeleton pier **-raum** *m* checker, checker chamber **-säule** *f* latticed-girder column **-schacht** *m* checker passage **-separator** *m* grid separator **-stein** *m* checker-brick, checker **-träger** *m* latticed girder

Gitter-werte *m pl* grid data, grid coordinates or numbers **-wickeldrähte** *pl* grid coil wires **-widerstand** *m* internal input resistance, grid (leak) resistance, grid leak or bias, C battery, direct component of grid voltage **-zaun** *m* lath fence **-zellenmodell** *n* lattice-cell model **-zellenvolumen** *n* unit cell volume (of a lattice) **-zündspannung** *f* critical grid voltage **-zündstrom** *m* cirtical grid current **-zurückspannung** *f* grid

backing
Gjerssche-Ausgleichgrube *f* Gjers soaking pit
Glacé, gebürsteter ~ bright enamel
Glacé-appretur *f* glossy finish **-papier** *n* glazed paper
glacieren to glaze, freeze, congeal
Glanz *m* brightness, brilliance, sparkle; (strahlender ~) radiance, luminosity, glow; (Glitzern) glitter; (blendender Schein) glare; (Technik) polish, luster, gloss, glory, brilliancy, splendor, glazing, sheen **-abzug** *m* glossy print **-appretur** *f* luster finish **-arsenikkies** *m* löllingite **-blech** *n* polished sheet metal **-blende** *f* alabandite **-braunstein** *m* hausmannite **-deckel** *m* flint **-decklack** *m* gloss coating lacquer
glanzdekatiert bright-finished
Glänze *f* glitter, polish, polishing material, gloss
Glanzeinfall *m* glazing incidence
Glanzeisen *n* high-silicon (pig) iron **-erz** *n* specular iron ore, hematite **-erzgrube** *f* oligist or specular iron mine **-stein** *m* oligist iron ore
glänzen to polish, burnish, buff, smooth, lap, planish
glänzend splendid, brilliant, glossy, bright **~ auftrocknende Politur** non-rub polish
Glanz-erz *n* galena, hematite, plumbago, argentite **-farbe** *f* gloss ink **-fiber** *n* glazed fiber **-firnis** *m* polishing varnish **-flor** *m* brilliant lisle **-garn** *n* glacé or glazed cotton, glazed, lustrous, or mercerized yarn **-garnumklöppelung** *f* glazed-cotton braiding **-gold** *n* burnish(ed) gold **-hammer** *m* polishing hammer
Glanzieren von Geweben cloth-piece glazing
Glanz-kalander *m* friction or glazing calender **-kobalt** *m* glance cobalt, cobaltite, smaltite **-kohle** *f* glance coal, lustrous carbon, glossy-black bituminous coal, vitrain, peacock coal, anthracite coal **-lack** *m* brilliant varnish **-leder** *n* patent leather **-leinwand** *f* trellis **-los** dull, dead **-losigkeit** *f* dullness, roughness, opacity, nontransparency
Glanz-maschine *f* glazing machine (for rice or grain) **-messer** *m* glarimeter, glossmeter **-öl** *n* gloss oil **-papier** *n* glazed paper **-pappe** *f* glazed board **-polieren** *n* ball or barrel burnishing **-presse** *f* press for glazing (textiles) **-rohr** *n* lacquered cane **-rot** *n* colcothar **-ruß** *m* shining soot **-scheibe** *f* buffing or polishing wheel **-schleifen** to polish, burnish, buff, glaze
Glanz-schuß *m* shiner **-silber** *n* burnished silver, argentite **-stärke** *f* gloss starch **-stoff** *m* celanese **-stoßen** *n* to glaze **-stoßmaschine** *f* glazing machine **-tuch** *n* glazed linen
Glänzung *f* polishing, burnishing
Glanz-verchromung *f* burnished chroming **-verkadmet** cadmium-plated, mirror-finish **-verzinkt** high-polish galvanized **-weiß** *n* talc **-welle** *f* glaze wave **-winkel** *m* glancing angle, angle of incidence **-zahl** *f* gloss value **-zwirn** *m* glacé thread
Glas *n* glass, binoculars, field glass **~ mit Gewinde** tube with screw cap **~ blind machen** to blunt glass **~ schleifen** to grind glass **acht ~** eight bells **berichtigendes ~** correcting lens **entglastes ~** devitrified glass **facettiertes ~** cut glass, edged lens
Glas, gebogenes ~ convex glass **in der Masse gefärbtes ~** glass colored in the process **gerautetes ~** lozenged glass **geschliffenes ~** cut glass **gestreiftes ~** corrugated glass **gezogenes ~** drawn glass **glattes ~** plain glass **luftleeres ~** evacuated glass
Glas, mondförmiges ~ meniscal lens **schußsicheres ~** bulletproof glass **schwer schmelzbares ~** hardly fusible glass **spannungsloses ~** strainless or strainfree glass **splitterfreies ~** splinter-proof glass **splittersicheres ~** shatterproof glass **überfangenes ~** flashed glass **ungefaßtes ~** rimless lens **zerstreuendes ~** diverging lens
Glas-achat *m* obsidian **-ähnlich** glasslike, glassy, vitreous **-akkumulatorgefäß** *n* glass accumulator jar or box
glasartig glassy, vitreous, glasslike **-e Vereisung** clear ice glaze
Glas-artikel *m pl* glassware **-ätzer** *m* glassware etcher **-ätzerei** *f* glass-etching workshop **-ätztinte** *f* diamond ink **-ätzung** *f* hyalography **-ballon** *m* (glass) bulb, carboy, demijohn, bell jar **-bandabwicklung** *f* spun-glass tape wrapping **-baustein** *m* glass tile or brick **-bedachung** *f* glass roofing **-behälter** *m* sight bowl
Glas-behang *m* (chandelier) crystals **-belegerei** *f* glass-coating factory or shop **beleuchtungsgegenstand** *m* glass light fitting **-beobachtung** *f* observation with field glass or telescope **-biegerei** *f* glass-bending workshop or factory **-bild** *n* diapositive, transparency **-bildner** *m* vitrifier **-birne** *f* (glass) bulb
Glas-blase *f* glass bubble, air bell (when of irregular shape), blister, bunch, seed, fault in the glass **-blasen** *n* glass blowing **-bläser** *m* glass blower **-bläserei** *f* glass-blowing plant **-bläserrohr** *n* bunting iron **-brillenklemmschrauben** *pl* screws for rimless mounting **-brocken** *m* **-bruch** *m* broken glass, cullet **-chemie** *f* hyalurgy **-dachsprosse** *f* trellis for glass roofs **-decke** *f* glass cover or plate
Glasdeckel *m* glass cover or top **mit ~ versehen** glass-topped
Glas-diapositiv *n* photographic glass scale, lantern slide **-druck** *m* glass printing **-eindekkung** *f* roof glazing **-elektrizität** *f* positive or vitreous electricity
glasen to strike the bell, glaze
Glasendmasse *f* optical flats
Glaser *m* glazier **-diamant** *m* glass cutter or grinder (tool), glazier's diamond
Glaserei *f* glazing
Glaserit *m* aphthitalite
Glaser-kitt *m* putty **-magnesia** *f* manganese
gläsern vitreous, glassy
Glas-erz *n* argentite **-fabrik** *f* glassworks **-faden** *m* glass thread, threadlike defect of glass **-faser** *f* glass fiber **-faßsprinkler** *m* glass bulb sprinkler, quartzoid bulb sprinkler **-federmanometer** *n* spoon-type glass manometer **-fehler** *m* glass defect, flaw, stria, or chord, bubbles (seed when small), air bell, glass crystallization bodies, cloudiness, or strain
Glasfenster *n* windowpane, glass window **Feld eines Glasfensters** area of a windowpane
Glas-fertigung *f* glassmaking **-fiber** *n* glass fiber **-filter** *m* glass filter **-flächenspiegelung** *f* glare or reflection of glass surfaces, specular reflection **-fluß** *m* vitrification **-formenschieber** *m*

mold holder **-fritte aus gesintertem Jenaer Glas** fritted Jena glass **-fühler** *m* glass probe **-füllung** *f* (Tür) glass panel **-funkenstrecke** *f* glass spark gap **-fuß** *m* glass base

Glas-galle *f* glass gall **-gebläse** *n* glass blow pipe **-gebrauchsgegenstand** *m* utility glassware **-gefäß** *n* envelope **-gehäuse** *n* glass case (showcase) **-gespinst** *n* glass thread or fiber, spun glass **-gewebe** *n* spun glass fabrics **-gießer** *m* shearer **-gießform** *f* glass **-gleichrichter** *m* glass-bull rectifier **-glocke** *f* bell jar, glass crubible, **-gießform** *f* glass mold **-gleichrichter** *m* glass-bulb rectifier **-glocke** *f* bell jar, glass bell **-gravur** *f* engraving on glass **-hafen** *m* glass crucible, meting pot, or vase **-hahn** *m* glass cock

glashart glasshard **~ machen** to chill (met) **-es Eisen** chilled iron

Glas-härte *f* glass hardness **-haube** *f* glass cap **-hauswirkung** *f* green house effect **-haut** *f* cellophane **-horizont** *m* glass horizon **-hütte** *f* glassworks

glasieren to glaze, vitrify

Glasierung *f* glaze, glazing, gloss

Glasierwalzen *f pl* papermaking machines, glazing rolls

glasig vitreous, glassy **-e Oberfläche** glaze **-e Schlacke** vitreous slag

Glasigkeit *f* flintiness, glassiness, steeliness

Glas-isolator *m* glass insulator **-kanzel** bubble **-kattun** *m* glass cloth **-keil** *m* glass prism **-kitt** *m* putty **-kirsche** *f* ampoule

glasklar-er Film pellucid film stock **-e Folie** highly transparent film

Glas-kolben *m* glass bulb or flask **-kolbenröhre** *f* glass tube **-kolbenventil** *n* glass-bulb rectifier **-kondensator** *m* glass capacitor

Glaskopf *m* (Ziegel) stock brick, globular form **brauner ~** limonite **roter ~** fibrous red iron ore, hematite iron ore, red hematite, kidney ore **schwarzer ~** psilomelane, fibrous manganese oxide

Glas-koralle *f* glass bead **-korn** *n* glass grain **-körnung** *f* glass granulations **-körper** *m* vitreous body **-kugel** *f* glass sphere or ball (bulb) **-küvette** *f* glass cell **-ladung** *f* charge of glass, glass loading **-läuterungsmittel** *n* glass-refining material **-lava** *f* obsidian, vitreous lava, volcanic glass **-leinen** *n* spun glass, glass cloth **-lichtbild** *n* positive transparance **-linse** *f* lens **-luftflächen** *pl* glass air surfaces

Glas-macherpfeife *f* blowing iron **-malz** *n* flinty, glassy, steely, or vitrified malt **-märbeln** *pl* grinding marbles **-masse** *f* glass metal **-maßstab** *m* glass scale **-metallverschmelzung** *f* glass-to-metal seal **-negativ** *n* mirror-image negative **-nutsche** *f* porcelain suction funnel **-packung** *f* glass embaling **-panzer** *m* plastic bullet-proof glass **-papier** *n* glass paper, glazed paper **-parabolspiegel** *m* parabolic glass reflector

Glasperle *f* glass bead **mit Glasperlen isoliert** beaded

Glasperlen-leinwand *f* pearl-beaded screen **-schirm** *m* pearl-beaded screen

Glas-pflaster *n* glass paving **-pinsel** *m* glass pencil **-plakat** *n* glass poster or plate **-platte** *f* disk or glass plate, focal plane glass, diapositive **-plattenbremse** *f* glass plate-brake **-plattenrahmen** *m* focal plane, glass frame **-plattensatz** *m* set of glass plates **-plattenstaffeln** *f pl* echelon spectroscope **-prisma** *n* glass prism **-prüfmaß** *n* optical flat gauge **-putzen** *m* stem press (incandescent lamps) **-reklameartikel** *pl* glass advertising goods **-ring** *m* prism

Glasrohr *n* glass tube **-scheider** *m* glass-rod separator **-schmelzeinsatz** *m* glass-tube fuse **-sicherung** *f* glass-tube fuse

Glas-sand *m* vitreous sand **-satz** *m* composition, (glass) batch, charge **-schaum** *m* glass gall **-scheibe** *f* glass pane, disk, or cover **-scheitel** *m* lens vertex **-scherben** *f pl* cullet, broken glass **-schieber** *m* glass slide **-schlange** *f* glass spiral **-schleiferei** *f* glass-grinding workshop **-schlieren** *pl* schlieren, striae, chords, reams, **-schliffverbindung** *f* ground-glass joint **-schmelz** *m* enamel **-schmelzer** *m* glass melter

Glasschmelz-einsatz *m* glass-fuse-link **-hafen** *m* melting kettle for glass **-ofen** *m* glass melting furnace **-ofenbank** *f* siege floor **-waren** *pl* vitrifications

Glas-schmutz *m* glass gall **-schnee** *m* glass decorating powder **-schneidemesser** *m* glass-cutting knife **-schneider** *n* glass cutter **-schweiß** *n* glass gall **-seide** *f* fiber glass **-sicherung** *f* glass cutout or fuse, safety fuse

Glassilber-konvexspiegel *m* silvered convex-glass reflector **-parabolspiegel** *m* silvered parabolic-glass reflector **-spiegel** *m* silvered glass mirror or reflector

Glas-spannung *f* strain or internal tension of glass **-spektrograph** *m* glass spectrograph **-spiegel** *m* glass mirror **-spritze** *f* glass syringe **-stab** *m* glass rod, stirring rod **-staub** *m* powdered glass **-stein** *m* glass brick

Glas-stopfen *m* **stöpsel** *m* glass stopper **-sturz** *m* glass bell or shade **-technisch** pertaining to glass technology **-teilkreis** *m* glass graduated circle **-temperofen** *m* annealing furnace for glass **-tiegel** *m* glass melting pot or crucible **-trübung** *f* glass muddiness or cloudiness **-überfangschicht** *f* glass lining

Glasur *f* glazing, glaze, gloss **in das Geschirr eingedrungene ~** glazing penetrated into the body of pottery **halbmatte ~** half-matt glaze **leichtflüssige ~** easily fusible glazing **strengflüssige ~** refractory glaze

glasur-bildend glazing, glaze producing **-brand** *m* glaze baking **-brecher** *m* glaze mill

Glasur-erz *n* potter's ore **-mahlen** *n* to glaze-grind **-mühle** *f* glazing mill **-sand** *m* sand for use in glazes **-ziegel** *m* glazed brick, enamelled brick

Glas-veredelung *f* decoration of glass and crystal, roughing and smoothing of glass **-vergütung** *f* refining or treating of optical glass **-verkitter** *m* glass mastic layer, cement, putty **-verschlag** *m* glass partition **-vlies** *n* glass fibre quilt **-walzenanfeuchter** *m* glass-roll dampener **-wandlung** *f* glass wall(s) **-watte** *f* wadding of glass **-wolle** *f* glass wool **-zylinder** *m* glass cylinder or globe

glatt smooth, even, polished, plain, flush, slippery **~ machen** to smooth **~ in den Rumpf übergehen lassen** to fair into the fuselage **-e Annahme** first class acceptance **-e Außenhaut** smooth skin **-e Böden** level blotch effects **-e Bohrstange** *f* polish rod **-e Erde** full earth (teleph.) **-e Färbung** level shade **-es Gewölbe** plain roof **-es Muster** plain pattern **-e Oberfläche** smooth surface **-e Ringelware** plain striped goods (textiles) **-e Rohrflansch** flange with plain face **-e Seele** smooth bore **-e Strömung** laminar flow

Glätt-ahle *f* smoothing broach **-bar** polishable

glattbehauenes Bauholz hewn timber

Glättbein *n* polishing tool, burnisher

glattbeschoren glossy, plain

glattblechbeplankt covered with stressed smooth metal skin, stressed-skin-constructed

Glatt-blechbeplankung *f* flat-sheet covering **-brand** *m* sharp fire **-deck** *n* flush deck **-dorn** *m* smoothing mandrel **-drücken** *n* planishing

Glätte *f* litharge, lead monoxide, smoothness, polish, dross

Glatteis *n* glazed frost, sleet, smooth or slippery ice

Glätteisen *n* burnishing steel, polishing iron

glätten to smooth, equalize, plane, polish, finish, stabilize

Glätten *n* smoothing, smooth finishing, filleting, glazing

Glattendrohre *pl* plain-end tubes

Glätter *m* paper glazer, folder **-walze** *f* smoothing-roller

Glattfärberei *f* plain dyeing

Glätt-faß *n* glazing barrel (for grain, etc.) **-feile** *f* smooth, silent, or spent file

Glätt-frischen *n* reduction of litharge to lead **-gasse** *f* litharge channel

glatt-hämmern to flat-hammer, flatten **-hautnietung** *f* flush riveting **-hechel** *m* intersecting, circular, or smoothing gills (textiles)

Glättheft *n* polishing tool, burnisher

Glattheitsprüfer *m* smoothness meter or tester, glossmeter, surface analyzer

Glätthobel *f* smoothing plane

Glatthobeln *n* smoothing

Glätt-holz *n* polishing stick, sleeking stick or tool **-hülse** *f* burnishing shell **-kalander** *m* friction or glazing calender

glattkalibrig smooth-bore

Glättknochen *m* polishing tool, burnisher

glattlegen to straighten out

Glattmachen der Oberfläche surfacing

Glätt-maschine *f* slating machine **-masse** *f* smoothing compound

Glätt-platte *f* round sleeker for shot molds **-presse** *f* standing or smoothing press, calender **-prozeß** *m* glazing process **-rämnadel** *f* broach

glattrichten to trim smooth

Glättschiene *f* polishing stick, sleeking stick or tool

glattschleifen to finish grinding

Glätt-stahl *m* steel rimmer, polishing tool, burnisher **-stange** *f* polishing tool, burnisher **-stein** *m* grease brick

glattstoßen to jog

Glättstraße *f* reeling mill

glattstreichen to flatten (glass mfg.) **die Fugen ~** to point up the joints

Glättung *f* fine, smooth, ground, or stoned finish, smoothing (ripples of current, potential, etc.)

Glättungs-drossel *f* smoothing reactor, smoothing choke, noise eliminator **-drosselspule** smoothing choke **-einrichtung** *f* device for flattening or smoothing rectifier currents **-kapazität** *f* equalizing capacity **-kondensator** *m* smoothing condenser or capacitor, filter condenser **-kreis** *m* smoothing circuit **-röhre** *f* glow-tube stabilizer **-selbstinduktion** *f* equalizing self-inductance **-widerstand** *m* smoothing resistance **-zwischenstück** *n* filter circuit, voltage smoothing unit

Glattwalze *f* plain or sheet roll, glazing roller

Glattwalzenstuhl *m* mill with smooth rolls

Glättwalzwerk *n* smoothing rolls, reeling machine (for tubes)

glattwandig smoothbore

Glattwasser *n* smooth sea

Glättwerk *n* calender, glazing machine for rice and grain **feuchtes ~** breaker stacks (paper mach.)

Glätt-wirkung *f* smoothing effect **-zahn** *m* polishing tool, burnisher **-zylinder** *m* machine glaze cylinder

Glauberit *n* glauberite

Glaubersalz *n* Glauber's salt, sodium sulfate

Gläubiger *m* creditor, believer **sichergestellter ~** secured creditor

Glaubwürdigkeit *f* credibility, trustworthiness, credit

Glauchherd *m* jagging board

Glaukodot *m* glaucodot

Glaukonit *m* glauconite

Glaukophan *m* glaucophane

gleich uniform, equal, even, like (in) **~ aufsetzen** to bring into phase **~ groß** equal-sized **~ schnell** isochronous **~ sein** to be equal to **~ Null setzen** to set . . . equal to zero **-e Ebene** flush **-en Abstand haben von** to be equidistant from **-e Behandlung bei** no differentiation between **vom -en Moment** equimomental **-e Neigung mit anderen Schichten** synclinal **Linien -en Potentials** equipotential surface **Linien -er Zeiten** isochrones

gleichachsig coaxial, equiaxial

gleicharmig equal-armed **-er Hebel** lever with equal arms

gleichartig homogeneous, similar, symmetrical **Reihe -er Teile** bank (mech.)

Gleichartigkeit *f* similarity, uniformity, homogeneity

Gleich-bandsender *m* moving tape transmitter **-bauen** to construct on similar lines **-beanspruchung** *f* static or constant loading **-bedeutend** equivalent, tantamount, synonymous **-beladener Kiel** even keel

gleichbelastet equally loaded **-e Phasen** balanced phases

Gleich-belastung *f* uniform load or charge **-berechtigung** *f* equality (of rights) emancipation **-beziffern** to number identically **-bleibend** constant, uniform, steady **-dauer** *f* isochronism **-deutig** synonymous, equivalent **-dick** constant-diameter, solid

Gleichdruck *m* constant pressure, balanced pressure **-anlage** *f* constant-pressure system

Gleichdruck-aufladung *f* constant-pressure boost **-axialturbine** *f* axial flow impulse turbine **-betrieb** *m* operation under constant pressure **-bombe** *f* constant-pressure bomb **-brenner** *m*

balanced-pressure torch **-gasturbine** *f* constant-pressure gas turbine **-gasturbinenanlage** *f* constant-pressure-gas-turbine plant

Gleichdruck-höhe *f* equal-pressure altitude, rated or critical altitude, supercharged height **-kondensationsturbine** *f* impulse-condensing turbine **-linie** *f* isobar, constant-pressure line **-maschine** *f* constant-pressure combustion engine **-motor** *m* constant-pressure combustion or diesel (cycle) engine **-prozeß** *m* constant-pressure cycle, even-turning cycle **-rad** *n* impulse wheel **-speicher** *m* constant pressure heat accumulator **-turbine** *f* impulse turbine, action turbine **-überdruckturbine** *f* impulse-reaction turbine **-ventil** *n* pressure-equalizing valve **-verbrennung** *f* constant-pressure combustion **-verfahren** *n* constant-pressure method or cycle

Gleich-eck *n* equiangular **-elektronisch** isoelectronic

gleichen to be equal, resemble, rectify, equalize **sich ~** to match

gleichentfernt equidistant, equally spaced

Gleich-fällig equal-falling, equal-settling **-fälligkeit** *f* equal falling, equal settling, thickening by graviation **-fälligkeitsapparat** *m* gravitational settler **-farbig** homo-chromatic, isochromatic, orthochromatic **-farbigkeit** *f* homochromatism **-feld** *n* constant or steady field

gleichförmig uniform, steady, smooth, homogeneous, even **~ verzögerte Bewegung** uniformly decreasing motion **~ wiederkehrende Bewegung** periodical uniform motion **~ verteilte Last** uniformly distributed load **-es Feld** uniform field **-e Lagerung** conformity **-e Leitung** smooth line **-er Strom** steady current **-e Strömung** streamlined flow

Gleich-förmigkeit *f* uniformity, equality, regularity, evenness, homogeneousness **-förmigkeitsgrad** *m* degree of uniformity, uniformity coefficient **-förmigkeitszahl** *f* (-wert) coefficient of uniformity **-funkelfeuer** *n* intermittent light **-gang** *m* unison, synchronism **-gängig** synchronous **-gängigkeit** *f* synchronism **-gangkondensator** *m* gang condenser **-gehend** unisonant, synchronous **-geltend** equivalent

gleichgerichtet unidirected, rectified, equiaxial, equidirectional **-er Strom** rectified current

gleich-gestaltet isomorphous **-gestaltigkeit** *f* isomorphism **-gestimmt** congenial, tuned alike, of the same mind

Gleichgewicht *n* balance, equilibrium, (equi)-poise, stability **~ der Ruhelage** static balance **aus dem ~ bringen** to unbalance **ins ~ bringen** to balance, equilibrate, trim (aviation), compensate in output circuit **im ~ erhalten, im ~ sein** to balance, poise, equilibrate **das ~ halten** to counter-balance **das ~ herstellen** to balance (circuits) **ins ~ setzen** to trim (aviation)

Gleichgewicht, devariantes ~ bivariant equilibrium **dynamisches ~** stability, dynamic equilibrium or balance **einfachfreies ~** monovariant or univariant equilibrium **einphasiges ~** monophase equilibrium **indifferentes ~** neutral equilibrium **labiles ~** unstable equilibrium **metastabiles ~** metastable equilibrium **monovariantes ~** monovariant or univariant equilibrium **nicht im ~** unbalanced **nonvariantes ~** nonvariant or unvariant equilibrium

Gleichgewicht, radioaktives ~ radioactive equilibrium **ruhendes ~** standing balance **stabiles ~ stetes ~** stable equilibrium **unfreies ~** nonvariant equilibrium **unsicheres ~** unstable equilibrium **volles ~** filled equilibrium **zweifachfreies ~** bivariant equilibrium **zweiphasiges ~** biphase or diphase equilibrium

Gleichgewichts-annäherung *f* equilibrium approach **-bahn** *f* equilibrium orbit **-bedingung** *f* equilibrium condition **-boden** *m* base of equilibrium, temporary bottom **-dichte** *f* equilibrium density (transist) **-einstellung** *f* equilibrium restoration **-energie** *f* equilibrium energy **-fall** *m* balance or equilibrium condition **-fehler** *m* unbalance, imbalance, lack of balance or equilibrium **-feldstärke** *f* equilibrium field **-flugstand** *m* balanced attitude of airplane **-flugzustand** *m* flight equilibrium

Gleichgewichts-gefühl *n* sense of equilibrium or balance **-herstellung** *f* restoration of balance or of equilibrium **-höhe** *f* height of equilibrium or static ceiling **-kammer** *f* gate recess (balancing chamber) **-konstante** *f* equilibrium constant **-kraft** *f* restoring moment **-kugelschwimmerventil** *n* equilibrium ball float valve **-kurve** *f* equilibrium or transformation curve

Gleichgewichts-lage *f* position of equilibrium, balanced position condition, state, or point of equilibrium **-lehre** *f* statics, doctrine of equilibrium **-leuchtdichte** *f* equilibrium luminance **-linie** *f* equilibrium curve **-mangel** *m* lack of equilibrium **-potential** *f* equilibrium potential **-punkt** *m* center of gravity **-sinn** *m* sense of balance **-störung** *f* unbalancing **-temperatur** *f* ignition temperature **-tor** *n* balanced gate **-ventil** *n* balance valve **-verhältnis** *n* equilibrium ratio **-verschiebung** *f* equilibrium shift

Gleichgewichts-wert *m* potential or equilibrium value **-zustand** *m* state of equilibrium, balanced condition

gleich-groß equal

Gleichheit *f* equality, evenness, sameness, par, constancy, uniformity **auf ~ einstellen** to adjust to uniformity

Gleichheits-photometer *n* equality of brightness photometer **-prüfer** *m* comparator **-prüfung** *f* parity check **-zeichen** *n* equal mark, equality sign

gleichionisch having a common ion

Gleichklang *m* unison, resonance, consonance **lokal geregelter ~** local synchronizing

gleich-kommen to equal **-kräftig** isodynamic **-lageverfahren** *n* congruent-band system **-lastig** on even keel

Gleichlauf *m* independent time control, synchronism, ganging flutter (flutter performance) **~ der Gabel** synchronism of the fork (reed) **zum ~ bringen** to synchronize **es befindet sich im ~** it is ganged **Fräsen im ~** downcut milling

Gleichlaufeinrichtung *f* synchronizing device

gleichlaufend synchronous, synchronized, parallel(ing), ganged **~ stellen** to lay reciprocally **-er Demodulator** synchronous detector **-e Kondensatoren** gang(ed) condensers, synchronized capacitors

Gleichlauf-ende *f* parallel line **-fräse** *f* downcut

miller **-fräsen** *n* climb milling, downcut milling **-fräsemaschine** climb miller **-generator** *m* synchronizing-signal generator **-getriebe** *n* synchromesh (gear)
gleichläufig running in the same direction
Gleichlauf-impuls *m* synchronizing (correcting) impulse, corrective impulse **-magnet** *m* correcting magnet **-pressen** *n* forward extruding (cold forming) **-prüfung** *f* flutter testing **-regeleinrichtung** *f* synchronous speed regulating gear
Gleichlaufregelung *f* synchronization control **örtliche, übertragene** ~ local, transmitted synchronization control
Gleichlauf-relais *n* correcting or corrector relay **-ring** *m* correcting ring **-schwankungen** *pl* wow and flutter (of tape recorder) **-segment** *n* correcting segment **-signal** *n* synchronizing pulse, synchronizing or tripping signal **-spannung** *f* synchronous voltage **-spielraum** *m* isochronous margin (telegr.) **-störung** *f* synchronization troubles
Gleichlauf-stöße *m pl* correcting currents, unison, phasing, or idle signals **-ströme** *m pl* correcting currents **-stromstoß** *m* correcting or governing impulse, unison impulse **-verfahren** *n* axial conduct of fire, reciprocal laying, method of orienting guns using the director **-verlust** *m* loss of synchronism **-winkel** *m* synchro-angle **-zeichen** *pl* correcting currents, unison, phasing, or idle signals, synchronizing signal or impulse, tripping signal **-zeitschalter** *m* synchronous timer
gleichlautend also to other addressees, to the same effect, homophonous
Gleich-licht *n* constant light **-luftstrom** *m* direct flow of air, direct-current air flow **-machen** to equalize, steady, level balance, stabilize, make even or uniform **-macher** *m* equalizer **-machung** *f* equalization
Gleichmaß *n* right proportion **-anordnung** *f* symmetry **-grenze** *f* limit of proportionality
gleichmäßig uniform, steady, constant, smooth, symmetrical, equal, homogeneous, even ~ **dicht** uniform density ~ **durchvergütet** evenly heat treated throughout ~ **erhalten** to steady, keep constant ~ **fallend oder steigend** in straight-line variation ~ **machen** to steady, equalize ~ **stetig** uniformly continuous ~ **variierende Belastung** uniformly varying load ~ **verteilt** uniformly distributed ~ **verteilte Last** uniformly distributed load
gleichmäßig-es Fliegen symmetrical flight **-e Geschwindigkeit** *f* uniform velocity **-e Lichtverteilung** equal illumination **-er Satz** *m* even charging **-e Spannung** steady voltage **-e Strömung** laminar flow **-e Teilung** uniformly divided scale **-er Wind** steady or constant wind
Gleichmäßigkeit *f* uniformity, steadiness, constancy, regularity, evenness ~ **der Beleuchtung** uniformity factor (of an illuminated surface)
Gleichmäßigkeitsprüfer *m* evenness tester
gleichnamig of the same name, similar, like, homologous, correspondent (math.) **-elektrisch** similarly electrified
Gleich-ordnung *f* co-ordination **-phasenebene** *f* equiphase surface
gleichphasig co-phasal, equal-phase, in-phase ~ **angeschlossen** connected in identical phase
Gleichphasigkeit *f* inphase condition, sympathetic phase
Gleichpol *m* homopolar **-alternator** *m* homopolar alternator
gleichpolig homopolar, unipolar
Gleichpolsynchronmaschine *f* homopolar synchronous machine
Gleichraum-prozeß *m* constant-volume cycle **-verbrennung** *f* constant-volume combustion **-verfahren** *n* constant-volume process or system
gleichrichten to rectify, redress, demodulate, straighten, detect
gleichrichtend rectifying
Gleichrichter *m* bellmouth, straightener (wind tunnel), rectifier, converter, demodulator, diode ~ **für Dauerladung** trickle charger ~ **mit Gittersteuerung** transrectifier ~ **in Grätzschaltung** bridge rectifier ~ **für Netzteil** rectifier for power supply from power mains ~ **und Überlagerröhre** intermediate-frequency detector and heterodyne ~ **mit Zündstift** ignitron **gasgefüllter** ~ gas-filled rectifier **mechanischer** ~ mechanical rectifier
Gleichrichter-anlage *f* rectifier plant ~ **oder Röhrenanordnung** *f* rectifier or tube arrangement circuit **-bahn** *f* rectifier railway **-block** *m* rectifier stack **-diffusionstheorie** diffusion theory of rectifier **-effekt** *m* rectifying action **-elektronenröhre** *f* kenotron, rectifier valve or tube **tronenröhre** *f* kenotron, rectifier valve or tube **-element** *n* crystal diode **-gitter** *n* flow straightener or honeycomb grid **-kolben** *m* rectifier bulb **-kristall** *m* rectifying crystal **-lampe** *f* rectifying tube **-pille** *f* oxide or metal rectifier of reduced size
Gleichrichterröhre *f* rectifier or rectifying valve or tube, detector tube ~ (Empfangsgleichrichter), audion, detector valve ~ (Hochleistungsgleichrichter) power rectifying valve **ungesteuerte** ~ phanotron
Gleichrichter-rückzündung *f* backfiring, arcing back, backlash **-satz** *m* rectifier stack **-säule** *f* rectifier stack **-stufe** *f* second detector **-voltmesser** *m* rectifying voltmeter **-werk** *n* rectifier substation **-widerstand** *m* rectifier resistance **-wirkung** *f* detecting or detector action, rectifying action, detection coefficient **-wirkungsgrad** *m* efficiency of rectification **-zelle** *f* rectifier cell, barrier-layer cell
Gleichrichtung *f* rectification, alignment, detection, demodulation ~ **einer Halbwelle** half-wave rectification ~ **beider Halbwellen** double-wave or fullwave rectification ~ **der Zwischenfrequenz** rectification of the intermediate frequency **lineare** ~ linear detection **unvollständige** ~ backlash
Gleichrichtungscharakteristik *f* rectification characteristic
gleichsam so to speak, as it were, almost, hardly
gleichschalig equivalve
gleichschalten to adjust, co-ordinate, synchronize
Gleichschaltung *f* coordination, synchronization, adjustment of offices, opinions
gleichschenkelig (triangle) of equal legs, equal-sided **-es Dreieck** isosceles triangle **-es Winkeleisen** equalsided angle iron

gleichseitig equilateral **-es Dreieck** equilateral triangle **-er Dreiecksquerschnitt** equilateral-triangular waveguide
Gleichseitigkeit *f* equilaterality
gleichsetzen to compare (to), equate
Gleichsetzung *f* equalization, equating, equation
gleichsignalige Zone equisignal zone
gleichsinnig synonymous, in the same direction, in sympathy **-e Blattwinkelverteilung** collective pitch **-e und periodische Blattwinkelsteuerung** collective and cyclic control of rotor blades **~ in Reihe** series-connected **zwei Spulen ~ in Reihe schalten** to connect two coils in series
gleichsinnigparallel parallel-connected
Gleichspannung *f* direct voltage or potential, D.C. or d.c., tension, continuous electromotive force
Gleichspannungs-beanspruchung *f* D. C. voltage service conditions **-generator** *m* constant voltage generator **-potential** *n* direct current voltage potential **-quelle** *f* direct-current supply, constant-potential supply **-verstärker** *m* D. C. amplifier
Gleichspulenwicklung *f* diamond winding
gleich-stellen to equalize, synchronize **-stellung** *f* (Formel) identification (von Uhren) synchronization (of watches) **-stimmen** to tune alike, tune together or uniformly **-stoffig** homogeneous **-stoffigkeit** *f* homogeneity
Gleichstrom *m* direct current, d.c., D.C. **pulsierender ~** pulsating current **zerhackter ~** interrupted or intermittent direct current
Gleichstrom-anlage *f* direct current electric plant **-antriebsmotor** *m* direct current driving motor **-bereich** *m* direct current circuit **-bogenlampe** *f* direct-current arc lamp **-doppelschlußgenerator** *m* direct current compound generator **-dosenwecker** *m* circular trembler **-drehstromeinankerumformer** *m* continuous-current-rotary-current converter **-dreileiteranlage** *f* direct-current three-wire plant **-dynamo** *f* direct-current dynamo or generator **-elektromotor** *m* direct-current motor **-empfänger** *m* direct-current-operated receiver, direct-current (mains) receiver, electric radio set **-energie** *f* direct current electric energy **-entnahme** *f* direct current output **-erregung** *f* direct current excitation **-erzeuger** *m* direct-current generator or dynamo
Gleichstrom-fahrbetrieb *m* direct-current traction **-feld** *n* continuous-current field **-fernschreiben** *n* DC teletype **-fernwahl** *f* direct-current dialing **-galvanometer** *m* direct-current galvanometer **-generator** *m* direct-current generator or dynamo **-glied des Kurzschlußstromes** aperiodic component of a short-circuit current **-heizung** *f* d.c.-heating **-impuls** *m* unidirectional pulse **-kapazitätsmessung** *f* direct-current charging test method **-kommutator** *m* direct-current commutator **-komponente** *f* direct-current (video) component, zero-frequency component **-kompressor** *m* uniflow type compressor **-kondensator** *m* parallel-flow condenser
Gleichstrom-ladeanlage *f* direct current charging unit **-leistung** *f* direct-current power **-leitung** *f* direct- or continuous-current circuit, wire, or line **-lichtbogenschweißumformer** *m* direct current arcwelding converter **-lichtmaschine** *f* direct current dynamo **-magnetapparat** *m* direct current magneto **-maschine** *f* direct current electrical machine **-meßbrücke** *f* direct-current bridge **-messer** *m* direct-current ammeter **-meßgerät** *n* direct-current meter **-meßinstrument** *n* direct-current ammeter **-messung** *f* direct-current measurement **-motor** *m* direct-current motor
Gleichstrom-nebenschlußgenerator *m* direct-current shunt-wound generator **-netz** *n* direct-current (power) supply or mains **-pol** *m* direct-current terminal **-prinzip** *n* uni-directional current principle **-quelle** *f* direct-current source **-regelmotor** *m* variable-speed direct current motor **-reihenschlußmotor** *m* direct-current series motor **-relais** *n* direct-current relay **-röhre** *f* direct-current-operated valve
Gleichstrom-schweißumformer *m* direct-current arc welder **-speisung** *f* direct-current or continuous-current supply **-spülung** *f* uniflow scavenging, end-to-end scavenging **-stoß** *m* direct-voltage impulse **-stoßabgabe** *f* direct-current pulse **-tachogenerator** *m* D. C. tachogenerator **-telegraphie** *f* direct-current telegraphy **-transformator** *m* direct-current converter **-trockner** *m* uniflow drier **-übertragung** *f* direct-current transmission
gleichstromüberlagert superposed on or with direct-current **-e Welle** pulsating wave
Gleichstrom-umformer *m* direct-current converter **-unterbrecher** *m* trembler, interrupter **-unterlagerungstelegraphie** *f* metallic polar duplex telegraphy **-ventil** *n* parallel-flow-type valve **-verhalten** *n* performance with respect to direct current **-verluste** *pl* copper (Joule) losses with direct current **-verstärker** *m* direct-current or direct-coupled amplifier **-verstärkerstufe** *f* direct-current amplifier stage **-verstärkung** *f* direct-current amplification **-vormagnetisierte Spule** direct-current controlled saturable or three-legged reactor or coil **-vormagnetisierung** *f* direct-current polarization **-wählimpulse** *pl* D. C. dialling pulses **-wärmeaustauscher** *m* parallel-flow heat exchanger
Gleichstromwechselstrom-Einankerumformer *m* direct-current alternating-current converter **-umformer** *m* inverted converter, direct-current-alternating-current converter or inverter
Gleichstrom-wecker *m* trembling or vibrating bell, trembler, direct-current bell **-widerstand** *m* direct-current or steady(-current) resistance, (ohmic) resistance **-zähler** *m* direct-current meter **-zeichengabe** *f* direct-current signaling method **-zentrierung** *f* D. C. centring **-zuschaltung** *f* direct-current restorer **-zweileiteranlage** *f* direct-current two-wire plant **-zwillingsmaschine** *f* uniflow twin engine
Gleichtakt *m* push-push (radio circuit), in phase (on film) **-aufnahme** *f* inphase recording (on film) **-feuer** *n* intermittent light **-sprossendoppelschnürspur** *f* variable-density double-squeeze track **-sprossenspur** *f* single variable-density track **-sprossenschnürspur** *f* variable-density squeeze track **-verstärker** *m* inphase amplifier **-welle** *f* symmetric wave
gleichteilig isomerous, of equal parts
Gleich-teilung *f* equipartition **-temperiert** isother-

mal, uniformly heated **-tönend** unisonant, consonant **-trittregelung** *f* synchronization **-umrichter** *m* direct-current converter

Gleichung *f* equalization, equation **eine ~ ansetzen** to form an equation **eine ~ nach N auflösen** to solve an equation with respect to *n* **einer ~ entsprechen** to fit an equation **~ 1. Grades** first order equation **2. Grades** quadratic equation **~ 4. Grades** biquadratic equation **allgemeine ~** general equation **bestimmte ~** determinate equation **quadratische ~** quadratic equation

Gleichungen, Lösungen in Kugelkoordinaten equations, solutions in spherical coordinates

Gleichungs-ansatz *m* laying down a formula **-determinate für Leitungen** determinant of the line equations **-differential** *n* differential equation **-familie** *f* equations grouped in families **-nummer** *f* number of the equation **-paar** *n* pair of equations **-system** *n* set of equations **-typ** *m* type equation

Gleich-verteilung *f* equipartition **-verteilungssatz** *m* law or principle of (energy) equipartition **-vielfach** equimultiple **-warm** isothermal, uniformly heated **-weit** equidistant

Gleichwellen *pl* continuous waves **-betrieb** *m* operation of stations on one wave, chain or network broadcast **-rundfunk** *m* common-frequency or shared-channel broadcasting

Gleich-wert *m* equivalent (value) **-wertig** equivalent, equal **-wertigkeit** *f* equivalence **-winklig** equiangular, isogonal

gleichzeitig simultaneous, coincident, synchronous, isochronous, contemporaneous **~ vorhanden sein** to coexist **~ anfallende Produkte** simultaneous products **-er Betrieb** duplex working **-e Reichweite** simultaneous range **für -es Sehen mit beiden Augen** binocular (micros.)

Gleichzeitigkeit *f* simultaneousness, coincidence, synchronism, concurrence

Gleichzeitigkeits-begriff *m* simultaneity concept **-faktor** *m* simultaneity factor

gleichzellig homocellular

Gleis *n* track, rail **durchgehendes ~** through line **festes ~** fixed track **totes ~** blind track, dead end **verlegbares ~** (contractor's) portable line **zusammengesetzte Gleise** mounted lines

Gleis-abschluß *m* buffer stops (terminal) **-abschnitt** *m* track section **-abzweigung** *f* branch line **-anlage** *f* railroad yard **-anschluß** *m* branch line, siding track, junction of lines **-balken** *m* tie (R.R.), stringer **-baumaschinen** *f pl* track laying machinery **-besetzung** *f* track circuiting for interlocking **-bettung** *f* railroad bedding **-bildstellwerk** *n* track diagram push-button system **-breite** *f* track gauge (R.R.)

Gleis-bremse *f* (electromagnetic) rail brake **-bremszeug** *n* rail brake **-brücke** *f* rail bridge **-engpaß** *m* bottleneck **-gebunden** rail-mounted, rail-guided **-hals** *m* bottleneck **-hammer** *m* drop hammer **-harfe** *f* gridiron sidings **-hebebaum** *m* crow bar **-heben** *n* jacking up the track **-heber** *m* track or rail lifter **-hebewinde** *f* rail-hoisting engine, rail-lifting jack **-joch** *n* portable line section **-kette** *f* caterpillar track

Gleisketten *pl* chain tractor

Gleisketten-antrieb *m* caterpillar drive **-fahrzeug** *n* track-laying vehicle **-gerät** *n* caterpillar, tracklayer **-kran** *m* crawler crane **-panzerfahrzeug** *n* full-track armored vehicle **-schlepper** *m* caterpillar tractor **-zugmaschine** *f* caterpillar tractor or prime mover

Gleis-klaue *f* curved track **-klemme** *f* clip for fixing light rails **-kontakt** *m* rail contact **-krümmung** *f* curvature of track, curve of line **-kurve** *f* curve, curved spur track **-los** trackless, railless **-netz** *n* network of lines, railroad network **-niveau** *n* track level

Gleis-relais *n* track relay **-rücken** *n* shifting the track **-rückmaschine** *f* rail-shifting machine **-rückvorrichtung** *f* track shifter **-sperre** *f* track lock **-stopfen** *n* track packing or tamping **-stränge** *pl* railroad tracks

Gleisstromkreis *m* track circuit **~ für Gleichstrom** track circuit with polarized relays **~ mit Ruhestrom** track circuit **~ für Wechselstrom** alternating-current track circuit

Gleis-stumpf *m* dead end (R.R.) **-tafel** *f* track diagram **-tor** *n* riding gate **-traghaken** *m* rail or track lifter **-verankerung** *f* anchoring of the track **-verlegung** *f* moving the track, plate laying **-verriegelung** *f* track locking (signal gear) **-verschlingung** *f* interlacing (of railway or tramway lines) **-verzweigung** *f* railway junction **-waage** *f* rail scales

Gleiswagen *m* car **~ mit abklappbarer Längswand** drop-side car

Gleis-weg *m* rail track **-winkel** *m* track angle **-zwischenstück** *n* interlinked piece

Gleit-angriff *m* gliding attack **-antrieb** *m* friction drive, slipping or yielding drive **-apparat** *m* airplane glider **-auflage** (für Fliehgewichte) sliding bearing (for centrifugal weights) **-auge** *n* guide sleeve of the spindle **-ausleger** *m* printed-side-up delivery **-ausrüstungsteile** *pl* slip fittings **-backe** *f* sliding or skip jaw, slide, crosshead **-backen** *m* guide block

Gleitbahn *f* slide, slideway, shoot, gliding plane, ways (shipyard), (crosshead) guide, slipway, track (for seaplanes), chute (of film) **~ von Bronze** bronze slide **~ des Ständers** face of standard or of a housing slide (tool equipment) **gezahnte ~** slide or guide with projecting teeth **glatte ~** smooth slide **zweiseitige ~** slide with two grooves

Gleitbahn-einsatz *m* aperture plate **-träger** *m* slide-bar bracket

Gleitbalken *m* launching ways, slipways

Gleitband *n* slipband **-bildung** *f* glide band formation **-ladewagen** *m* portable loader **-sender** *m* moving tape transmitter

Gleit-bedingungen *pl* slip conditions **-bewegungen** *pl* slip motions **-block** *m* sliding pulley **-bock** *m* bearing bracket **-boden** *m* planing bottom (seaplanes) **-bogen** *m* quadrant **-bohrung** *f* bore slide fit **-bolzen** *m* slide pin, thrust pin **-boot** *n* hydroplane **-vorgang** *m* wiping operation **-bruch** *m* slide fracture **-büchse** *f* sliding sleeve, slide box, floating bush(ing) **-bügel** *m* slides, guide, pantograph **-dichtring** *m* sliding packing ring

Gleitdraht *m* (differential) slide wire **-brücke** *f* slide-wire bridge **-widerstand** *m* slide-wire resistance

Gleit-drehung *f* slipping turn (aviation) **-ebene** *f* slip surface, glide plane **-eigenschaften** *pl*

antifriction properties **-element** *n* glide element

gleiten to slide, skid, glide, slip, shear, taxi; (bei einer Landung) **zu tief** ~ to undershoot (aviation) **zur Seite** ~ to sideslip

Gleiten *n* creep, sliding, slip(ping) ~ **des Laufrades** wheel spin **bildsames** ~ plastic deformation

gleitend gliding, sliding, labile, unstable ~ **regelbar** smoothly variable **-er Durchschnitt** sliding average **-es Komma** *n* floating point (info proc.) **-er Kurvenflug** gliding turn **-e** (Schrauben) **Mutter** sliding nut **-es Querhaupt** traversing saddle, traverse glide **-e Reibung** rolling or sliding friction **-er Ton** sliding note, glissando **-e Variation** continuous variation

Gleiter *m* glider, slide **-bahn** *f* gliding path

Gleit-fähigkeit *f* gliding or sliding ability **-feder** *f* sliding feather key, slide spring

Gleitfläche *f* gliding plane or surface, sliding or slip(ping) surface, slip plane, friction surface (of a brake), working surface (of cylinders), surface of rupture, cleavage plane, planing surface (cryst.), slide ~ **eines Rades** tread ~ **der Säule** face of column ~ **der Ständer** face of uprights **ebene** ~ plane failure surface **kreiszylindrische** ~ circular-cylinder failure surface, cylindrical sliding surface

Gleit-flächenmethode *f* method of slides **flieger** *m* airplane glider, glider pilot **-flosse** *f* wing float, stub plane, planing fin **-flossenstabilisator** *m* sea wings

Gleitflug *m* glide, gliding flight, volplane **-drachen** *m* glider kite **-geschwindigkeit** *f* gliding speed **-kurve** *f* gliding turn **-lastfall** *m* highspeed case, load case **-versuch** *m* gliding test **-weite** *f* gliding range **-winkel** *m* gliding angle

Gleitflugzeug *n* glider **ein** ~ **in die Luft schleudern** to catapult a glider

schleudern to catapult a glider

gleitfrei non-slipping

Gleit-fuge *f* slip joint **-führung** *f* radius link, sliding guide (guidance) **-funken** *m* slide spark, creepage spark **-funkenspannung** *f* breakdown voltage of the creep distance **-funkenstrecke** *f* creepage spark gap, surface discharge gap **-futter** *n* guide liner **-gelenk** *n* slip joint **-geschwindigkeit** *f* rubbing speed **-hang** *m* concave slope of river bend **-hängelager** *n* friction hanger bearing **-hebel** *m* sliding lever **-hebelverschluß** *m* sliding-wedge-type breech mechanism, sliding-lever breechblock

Gleit-klotz *m* shoe of crosshead, guide shoe or block **-klotzbahn** *f* rocker-arm way **-klotzlager** *n* slider bearing **-koeffizient** *m* slip coefficient **-komma** *n* floating point **-kommaprogramm** *n* floating-point routine **-kommarechnung** *f* floating point computation (comp.) **-kontakt** *m* rubbing contact, sliding contact **-kreis** *m* friction circle **-kufe** *f* landing skid **-kupplung** *f* slipper clutch

Gleit-lafette *f* sliding or rolling mount **-lager** *n* friction bearing, plain, sliding, journal, or sleeve bearing **-lagerbüchse** *f* journal-bearing bushing **-lagerschale** *f* plain bearing race **-lagerung** *f* sleeve bearing **-landung** *f* glide landing **-lauf** *m* slipway **-lineal** *n* slide rule or bar **-linie** *f* line of slide or slip, slip band **-linienbild** *n* slip line pattern **-liniennetz** *n* net of slip lines

Gleit-maß *n* modulus of shear, modulus of transverse elasticity in shear, coefficient of shear, elasticity in shear **-meßfunkenstrecke** *f* klydonograph **-mikromanipulator** *m* sliding micromanipulator **-mittel** *n* lubricant **-modul** *n* modulus of elasticity, torsion or rigidity modulus **-montage** *f* sliding fit **-mutter** *f* sliding nut, travelling sleeve **-nocken** *m* sliding cam **-passung** *f* easy or sliding fit **-pfad** *m* glide path (ILS) **-platte** *f* crosshead guide (mach.), planing surface

Gleit-rahmen *m* slide frame **-reibung** *f* sliding friction **-reibungsziffer** *f* coefficient of sliding **-reichweite** *f* gliding range **-richtung** *f* direction of slip (cryst.), glide plane **-riegel** *m* slide lock, sliding bolt **-ring** *f* slip ring, bearing ring, slide ring **-ringdichtung** *f* slide ring packing or sealing **-rippe** *f* sliding rib

Gleit-rolle *f* roller (for moving equipment), guide-pulley sheave (elec.) **-schale** *f* sliding shell **-scheibe** *f* sliding disk **-schieber** *m* slider (electrical sliding resistance) **-schiene** *f* slipway, track (for seaplanes), lower slide, skid, notched bars, guide bars (general), slide bars, slide (rails)

Gleitschienen-bock *m* slide-bar bearer or bracket **-joch** *n* carrier yoke, guide yoke (slide bars) **-träger** *m* slide-bar bearer or bracket

Gleit-schirm *m* paraglider (of spacecraft) **-schloß** *n* slide lock

Gleitschuh *m* (recoil-guide) shoe, flange, crosshead shoe, gun slide, pressure pad or guide **-kolben** *m* slipper piston

Gleitschutz *m* precaution against skidding, nonbreakable skid, nonskid tread, antiskid chain

Gleitschütze *m* sliding sluice, sliding leaf gate

Gleitschutz-greifhaken *m* mud hook **-kette** *f* nonskid chain **-mantel** *m* nonskid cover of tire **-mittel** *n pl* nonskid equipment, traction aid **-platte** *f* safety tread, nonslip plate **-reifen** *m* steel-studded tire, nonskid tire **-vorrichtung** *f* nonskid device

gleitsicher antislip **-es Trittbrett** safety tread plate **-es Wachs** no-rub wax

Gleitsicherheit *f* stability (against sliding) or resistance to sliding

Gleitsitz *m* sliding seat, fit, or thwart **saugend passender** ~ snug fit

Gleit-skala *f* sliding scale **-spiegelebene** *f* glide plane **-spiegelung** *f* glide reflection **-spur** *f* slip line **-stab** *m* guide rod **-stange** *f* catapult rail, sliding bar **-stehlager** *n* friction pillow block

Gleitstein *m* slide ring ~ **einer Kulisse** rocker arm, crank

Gleitsteine *pl*, **Fressen der** ~ friction, seizing of slides

Gleit-stößel *m* tappet rod **-strahl** *m* landing beam **-stück** *n* sliding contact, slider **-tafel** *f* sliding gate, shutter **-tensor** *m* slippage tensor **-theorie** *f* skip theory **-tisch** *m* gliding stage

Gleit- und Widerstandsbeiwert *m* lift-drag ratio

Gleitung *f* slip(ping), shearing strain, torsional-shear strain, angle of shearing deformation, sliding, transition zone, shifting

Gleitungs-ausbreitung *f* propagation of glide **-fläche** *f* sliding or gliding plane **-koeffizient** *m* slip coefficient **-zahl** *f* shear modulus

Gleit-ventil *n* slide valve **-verdeck** *n* sliding roof **-verhältnis** *n* gliding ratio, ratio of lift to drag **-vermögen** *n* gliding quality **-verschiebung** *f* displacement by slipping **-verschlußbänder** *pl* sliding fastener strips **-versuch** *m* slippage test **-vorgang** *m* whiping operation **-vorrichtung** *f* slide mechanism **-wand** *f* slide wall or plate

Gleitweg *m* glide path (aviat) **äquipotentieller ~** isopotential glide path

Gleitweg-bake *f* glide-path beacon **-landung** *f* glide-path landing **-blindlandesystem** *n* glide-path instrument landing system **-sender** *m* glide path transmitter

Gleit-welle *f* sliding shaft **-wendeflug** *m* gliding turn **-wendung** *f* slipping turn

Gleitwiderstand *m* sliding resistance, adhesion, slipping turn, planing resistance (of seaplanes) **~** (des Keilriemens) slippage (of the V belt)

Gleit-winkel *m* angle of glide or descent **-winkelbefeuerung** *f* visual approach slope indicator system **-winkelfeuer** *n* angle-of-approach ligths **-zahl** *f* lift-drag ratio, fineness ratio **-zange** *f* sliding tongs **-zollsystem** *n* gliding-scale duty system **-zone** *f* slip zone **-zuführung** *f* slide feed

Gletscher *m* glacier, snowfield **-boden** *m* soil formed by glacial action **-tal** *n* a valley through which a glacier moves or has moved **-topf** *m* pothole **-wind** *m* glacier breeze

Glied *n* (Technik) element, component; (Kette) link; (Elektr.) link; (Math.) term, file (mil.), member, rank, limb, branch, section, mesh, unit, joint **~ eines Filters** filter section **~ im Zähler** term in the numerator **~ mit konstantem Widerstand** constant-resistance network **exzentrisches ~** eccenter link **gekröpftes ~** bent link **gerades ~** straight link

gliedartig verbinden to articulate

Gliedbegriff *m* elemental term

Glieder *pl* terms, links **~ erster Ordnung** terms of the first order **äußere ~** (Proportion) extremes, extreme terms **mittlere ~** (Proportion) means, mean terms

Glieder-bandförderer *m* jointed-band conveyer **-bau** *m* structure, articulation **-breite** *f* link width (of a chain) **-egge** *f* articulated harrow

gliederförmig verbunden articulated

Glieder-hohlleiter *m* vertebrate waveguide **-kabel** *n* chain cable **-keilriemen** *m* chain belt **-kette** *f* open-link chain, link belt, chain **-kopf** *m* hook (of a chain) **-länge** *f* segment length **-maßstab** *m* folding rule

gliedern to organize, form ranks, articulate, arrange, classify, paraphrase, joint **nach der Tiefe ~** to dispose in depth

Glieder-riemen *m* link belt **-röhre** *f* articulated pipe **-rohrschneider** *m* chain pipe cutter **-säge** *f* chain saw **-schnecke** *f* sectional screw

Gliederung *f* distribution, organization, formation, structure, division, arrangement, jointing, articulation (mech.)

Glieder-versetzung *f* term displacement **-visier** jointed sighting rod **-weise** in files or ranks, by section **-welle** *f* articulated shaft **-werk** *n* linkwork, linkage **-zahl** *f* number of links (of a chain)

Glimm-abstimmanzeiger *m* neon tuning indicator **-detektor** *m* ionized gas detector

glimmen to glow, blue-glow

Glimmen *n* glow(ing), corona, ignition

Glimmentladung *f* glow discharge, corona, luminous current discharge, St. Elmo's fire

Glimmentladungs-kontinuum *n* glow-discharge continuum **-lampe** *f* glow-discharge lamp **-röhre** *f* glow (discharge) tube **-strom** *m* luminous discharge current

Glimmer *m* mica **auf ~ aufgewickelt** wound on mica **schwarzer ~** biotite, black mica **weißer ~** biaxial or potash mica, muscovite

glimmer-artig micaceous **-bruch** *m* mica mine **-dach** *n* mica cover or top **-deckel** *m* mica cover or top **-einlage** *f* mica insert **-flitter** *m* mica spangle **-folie** *f* sheet mica **-gestein** *n* micaceous rock **-haltig** micaceous **-kerze** *f* mica spark plug **-kondensator** *m* mica (dielectri) condenser

glimmern to glimmer, sparkle

Glimmer-plättchen *n* thin mica plate **-platte** *f* mica sheet, sheet mica **-sand** *m* micaceous sand **-scheibe** *f* mica washer or insulator

Glimmerscheinung *f* glow (phenomenon)

Glimmer-schiefer *m* mica schist or slate **-tafel** *f* sheet mica **-zündkerze** *f* porcelain or mica spark plug

Glimmfadenlänge *f* length of (neon) glow column

Glimmhaut *f* surface glow **anodische ~** surface glow on the anode **kathodische ~** surface glow on cathode

Glimm-kathode *f* glow discharge cathode **-kerze** *f* glow (or heater) plug **-kontrolle** *f* pilot glow plug **-lampe** *f* glow lamp, glow-discharge tube, fluorescent lamp, neon tube or lamp, semi-incandescent lamp, flashing lamp (in sound recording)

Glimmlampen-indikator *m* discharge lamp indicator **-schallaufnahme** *f* glow-lamp sound recording **-stabilisator** *m* stabilizer tube

Glimmlicht *n* blue glow, blue haze, glow (light), brush light **~ zeigen** to blue-glow **negatives ~** negative glow light **positives ~** positive glow light

Glimmlicht-anzeigeröhre *f* neon indicator **-gleichrichter** *m* glow(-discharge) rectifier **-oszillator** *n* ondoscope **-oszilloskop** *n* ondoscope, oscilloscope **-sender** *m* glow transmitter **-spannungsteiler** *m* glow-gap divider

Glimm-relais *n* ionical relay **-röhre** *f* glow lamp, glow-discharge tube **-röhrensummer** *m* dischargetube buzzer **-säule** *f* light column, glow column **-spannung** *f* glow point or potential, breakdown point or stopping anode point **-spur** *f* night tracer

Glimm-stabilisator *m* glow discharge lamp **-stift** *m* incandescent cartridge **-strecke** *f* glow-gap divider (automatic control) **-streckenspannungsteiler** *m* glow-tube voltage regulator, glow-gap divider, glow-tube potentiometer **-streckenstabilisator** *m* voltage stabilizing tube **-strom** *m* glow current **-summer** *m* glow-tube-type buzzer oscillator, neon time base **-teiler** *m* glow-gap divider **-verluste** *pl* corona losses **-zelle** *f* photoemissive gas-filled cell, photoglow tube

-zündkontakt *m* glow ignition contact
Glitscher *m* slide (of steam engine)
glitzern to glisten, gleam, glitter, sparkle
global-e Betriebsgüte overall grade of service **-er Anreicherungsfaktor** overall enrichment
Global-kontigent *n* wholesale quota of raw materials **-strahlung** *f* global radiation
Globigerinenschlamm *m* globigerina ooze
Globoidschneckentrieb *m* Hindley's screw, globoidal or hourglass worm gear
Globulit *m* globule
Globulitengefüge *n* globular structure
globulitisch globulitic, globular
Globus *m* globe
Glocke *f* bell-type distributing gear (blast furnace), bell, bell jar, jacket, bulb (radio), bell-shaped top, socket, overshot, bubble cap, arch formation in sand, globe, glass, receiver (of air pump) ~ (Dach) head of bell ~ **der Fraktionierböden** tray cap ~ **eines Kapitels** bell, basket, drum, or corbel of a capital **gezahnte** ~ bell-shaped impulse sector (Obry's gear) **graduierte** ~ graduated glass jar **mattierte** ~ frosted globe **schwimmende** ~ floating bell
Glocken-anlage *f* system of bells **-auslösehebel** *m* bell operating lever **-boden** *m* bubble tray **-boje** *f* bell buoy **-bronze** *f*, **-erz** *n* bell metal **-fänger** *m* bellmouthed socket **-fläche** *f* paraboloidal shape **-filter** *n* bell-jar filter
glockenförmig bell-shaped, bellmouthed, conoid ~ **aufgeweitet** bellmouthed
Glocken-gut *n* bell metal **-halter** *m* socket holder, gong support **-heizkessel** *m* bell-type autoclave press **-isolator** *m* bell or petticoat insulator **-klöppel** *m* bell hammer, bell striker **-kompaß** *m* bell compass **-kurve** *f* bell-shaped curve **-lager** *n* calotte (R.R.) **-läutemaschine** *f* bell-ringing apparatus
Glocken-magnet *m* bell-shaped magnet **-metall** *n* bell metal **-mühle** *f* cone mill, bell crusher **-rad** *n* (Umlaufgetriebe) ring gear **-ramme** *f* socket ram **-ring** *m* ring of bell clapper **-rückstellstab** *m* bell reset bar **-rumpf** *m* hopper with bell
Glockenschale *f* bell dome, bell gong **große flache** ~ gong
Glocken-schlag *m* bell stroke **-schwengel** *m* clapper, bell swipe **-signal** *n* bell signal **-speise** *f* bell metal **-spiel** *n* carillon, musical chimes **-stange** *f* socket stem **-stube** *f*, **-stuhl** *m* belfry **-ton** *m* bell note, peal or tune of the bell **-tonne** *f* bell buoy **-trichter** *m* bell funnel **-turm** *m* bell tower, belfry
Glocken-ventil *n* bell valve **-ventilator** *m* air pump working by means water bellows **-verfahren** *n* bell process **-verriegelungsstab** *m* bell latch bar **-verschluß** *m* bell seal (water), bell trap (sanitary) **-volumen** *n* volume of the bell jar **-wäscher** *m* bell-type wash tower **-winde** *f* bell hoist, bell-operating gear **-zählrohr** *n* end-window Geiger counter (tube) **-zählwerk** *n* bell item counter (adding mach.) **-zeichen** *n* bell or gong signal **-zwischengehäuse** *n* bell-type intermediate housing
Glonoin *n* nitroglycerin, glonoin
Glorie *f* glory, Brocken specter
Glossar *n* glossary
glucksen to bump
Glückshaken *m* wall hook, (oil-drilling) catch, finger grip, crow's-foot, fishing hook
Glucosamin *n* glucosamine
Glüh-anlage *f* annealing installation **-anlaßschalter** *m* heater plug starting switch **-anode** *f* glowing anode **-asche** *f* embers, glowing ashes **-ausdehnung** *f* annealing expansion **-bad** *n* annealing bath **-behandlung** *f* annealing (operation) **-beständig** stable at a red heat
Glüh-betrieb *m* annealing practice **-birne** *f* incandescent bulb or lamp **-dauer** *f* annealing time
Glühdraht *m* (heated) filament, annealed wire, glowing or hot wire ~ (Glühkerze) heater plug filament **-oberfläche** *f* incandescent wire surface **-verdampfung** *f* flashing (tungston) **-zündung** *f* electric firing
Glühe *f* glowing, incandescence
Glüh-eisen *n* glowing iron, red-hot iron **-elektrisch** thermionic
Glühelektronen-abgabe *f* thermionic emission **-emission** *f* thermionic emission, temperature emission of electrons **-entladung** *f* thermionic discharge **-quelle** *f* thermionic electron source **-strom** *m* thermionic current
Glühemissions-konstante *f* thermionic constant **-eigenschaften** *pl* thermionic emission properties
glühen to anneal, ignite, calcine, glow ~ **um die Eigenspannungen zu beseitigen** to strain relief
Glühen *n* annealing, calcining, glow(ing), incandescence ~ **in geschlossenen Behältern** close annealing ~ **des Fadens** incandescence of filament
glühend incandescent, glowing, red-hot **-e Kathode** incandescent cathode **-e Metalloxydkathode** incandescent metallic oxide cathode
Glüherscheinung *f* incandescence
Glühfaden *m* (heated) filament **biegsamer** ~ ductilized filament **gespritzter** ~ squirted filament **Einschmelzstellen des Glühfadens** filament seals
Glühfaden-bild *n* incandescent-filament image, cathode-ray image **-pyrometer** *m*, *n* optical, disappearing-filament, or monochromatic pyrometer **-temperatur** *f* filament temperature
Glüh-farbe *f* temper color **-feuer** *n* glowing fire, annealing furnace **-filament** *n* cathode, heated filament **-filamentbild** *n* cathode-ray image **-frischen** to malleableize **-frischen** *n* malleableizing
Glühfrisch-gut *n* material to be annealed **-hitze** *f* annealing heat, glowing heat **-kammer** *f* annealing chamber **-kasten** *m* annealing box **-kolben** *m* retort **-verfahren** *n* annealing process **-wirkung** *f* annealing action
Glüh-gasentladungsventil *n* thermionic rectifier **-gefäß** *n* annealing box **-hals** *m* venturi
Glühhaube, dunkelglühende ~ dark-red hot bulb
Glüh-haus *n* annealing house **-hitze** *f* white heat
Glühkathode *f* hot, glowing, or heated cathode, incandescent filament or cathode, hot electrode, high-vacuum rectifier, thermionic cathode **direkt geheizte** ~ directly heated cathode **indirekt geheizte** ~ indirectly heated cathode, equipotential or unipotential cathode
Glühkathoden-detektor *m* radiotelegraphic valve

-entladung *f* hot cathode discharge
Glühkathodengleichrichter *m* hot-cathode rectifier, thermionic or high-vacuum rectifier **~ mit Edelgas** tungar- (argon-tungsten-) type rectifier
Glühkathodengleichrichterröhre mit Gasfüllung hot-cathode-gas-filled rectifier tube
Glühkathoden-quecksilberdampf(welle)gleichrichter *m* hot-cathode mercury-vapor rectifier, full-wave rectifier **-röhre** *f* incandescent cathode tube, thermionic-valve vacuum tube, hot-cathode tube **-stromrichter** *m* thyratron **-verstärker** *m* thermionic amplifier
Glüh-kauter *m* electrocautery **-kerze** *f* spark plug, glow pulg, hot bulb, heater plug
Glühkerzen-anzeigewiderstand *m* heater plug indicator resistor **-schalter** *m* incandescent plug switch **-stromkreis** *m* heater plug ,circuit **-überwacher** *m* hot-bulb monitor (light) **-widerstand** *m* heater plug resistance or resistor **-zeitschalter** *m* heater plug time switch
Glüh-kohle *f* close-burning coal **-kopf** *m* hot bulb **-köpfchen** *n* hot-tube detonating head (blasting), hot-wire-bridge head
Glühkopf-maschine *f* surface-ignition engine, hot-bulb engine **-motor** *m* hot-bulb engine **-zündung** *f* hot-bulb ignition
Glühkörper *m* punk or incandescent wire (for lighting fuses or explosives), glow plug, incandescent body or mantle, Welsbach mantle **-halter** *m* mantle suspender or carrier **-schutzkorb** *m* mantle guard
Glüh-kugel *f* fire ball, flare, hot shot **-lämpchen** *n* miniature filament bulb
Glühlampe *f* (electric) bulb, incandescent or glow lamp
Glühlampen-anschluß *m* bulb connection (terminal) **-anruf** *m* lamp signal **-armatur** *f* glow-lamp fittings **-ätzpaste** *f* etching paste for incandescent lamps **-faden** *m* incandescent- or glow-lamp filament **-fassung** *f* lamp cap. lamp holder **-kolben** *m* incandescent-lamp bulb **-lichtspiegler** *m* glow-lamp reflector **-pendel** *n* counterweight-suspension fitting (elec.)
Glühlampen-schaltung *f* connection of incandescent lamps **-scheinwerfer** *m* floodlights for incandescent lamps **-schrank** *m* lamp switchboard **-schutzglas** *n* glass guard of glow lamp **-schüttelvorrichtung** *f* test vibrating device for bulbs **-signal** *n* lamp indicator **-sockel** *m* glow-lamp cap or base **-strahler** *m* floodlight unit **-träger** *m* bulb seating
Glühlicht *n* incandescent light, lighting load **-beleuchtung** *f* incandescent lighting **-brenner** *m* incandescent burner **-körper** *m* incandescent mantle or material
Glüh-masse *f* incandescent mass **-mittel** *n* cementing material (for cementation of iron)
Glühofen *m* annealing, reheating, heating, or glowing furnace **~ zur Wiederbelebung der Knochenkohle** char-revivifying kiln
Glüh-probe *f* heating test or sample, ignition test **-prozeß** *m* annealing process **-raum** *m* heating or annealing chamber
Glührohr *n* ignition or incandescent tube **-zündapparat** *m* hot-tube igniter **-zündung** *f* hot-tube ignition
Glüh-rost *m* heating grill **-rückstand** *m* residue on ignition **-sand** *m* refractory sand **-schälchen** *n* combustion capsule **-schale** *f* cupel, roasting or combustion cup **-schiffchen** *n* combustion boat **-schirm** *m* fluorescent screen (elec.) **-schlinge** *f* cautery loop or snare **-schleife** *f* (Kerze) incandescent spiral **-sender** *m* glowing transmitter **-sonde** *f* hot probe
Glüh-span *m* mill scale, hammer scale, scale **-spanbildung** *f* scaling **-spirale** *f* element wires **-spulen** *pl* glowing coils **-stahl** *m* malleable cast iron **-stahlguß** *m* casting (or pouring) of malleable (cast) iron **-stoff** *m* prepared charcoal, incandescent article **-stöpsel** *m* heater plug **-strumpf** *m* mantle (incandescent)
Glühtemperatur *f* annealing temperature **längere Zeit einer ~ aussetzen** to soak
Glüh-topf *m* annealing pot, cementing box **-tunnelofen** *m* tunnel kiln for annealing, continuous-type annealing furnace **-überwacher** *m* heater plug controller
Glüh- und Anlaßschalter *m* hot-bulb and starter switch
Glühung *f* annealing **~ auf kugeligen Zementit** spheroidizing **erste ~** black annealing, first annealing **zweite ~** white annealing, second annealing
Glüh-verfahren *n* annealing process or method **-verlust** *m* loss on ignition **-wärmegrad** *m* annealing temperature **-weise** *f* annealing method **-würmer** *pl* (slang) searchlight **-zeit** *f* annealing time or cycle **-zone** *f* zone of incandescence **-zündapparat** *m* hot-tube detonator (blasting), blasting-machine exploder
Glühzünder *m* low-tension blasting machine, electric igniter or detonator, incandescent exploder **-schloß** *n* electric lock
Glüh-zündstück *n* hot-tube detonator fuse (blasting), electric detonator or igniter, punk **-zündung** *f* ignition by incandescence
Glukometer *n* glucometer
Glukonsäure *f* gluconic acid
Glut *f* heat, glow, incandescence **-festigkeit** *f* glow resistance
Gluthitzemesser *m* ardometer
glutintrüb glutin-turbid
Glut-messer *m* pyrometer **-rot** glowing red **-schaufel** *f* fire shovel **-wirbel** *m* fiery cyclone **-wolken** *pl* hot avalanche **-zange** *f* fire tongs
Glycerin *n* glycerol, glycerin
Glycin *n* glycine
Glykohlkühlung *f* prestone cooling
Glyoxylsäure *f* glyoxal acid
Glysantin *n* Glysantine (an antifreeze)
Glyzerin *n* glycerol, glycerin **-bremse** *f* glycerin brake **-säure** *f* glyceric acid **-überzug** *m* glycerin coating
GMI-Stoff *m* nitrous oxide, rocket fuel
Gneis *m* gneiss **-formation** *f* gneissic formation
Gnomon *m* gnomon
gnomonisch gnomonic **-e Karte** gnomonic chart
Gold *n* gold **amalgamierbares ~** free gold **vererztes ~** refractory gold ore **in Anschwemmungen vorkommendes ~** alluvial gold
Gold-abfall *m* gold chips, parings of leaf gold **-ader** *f* gold vein **-amalgam** *n* gold amalgam **-ammer** *f* code for antijamming procedure

Goldanlegeöl *n* base for varnish on which to apply gold leaf **-lack** *m* varnish made with Goldanlegeöl

Gold-anstrich *m* gilding, gold coating **-artig** goldlike, golden **-äther** *m* solution of gold (chloride) in ether **-aufbereitungsanlage** *f* gold-mining machinery **-auflösung** *f* gold solution **-ausbringen** *n* gold yield **-bad** *n* gold bath **-baggern** *n* gold dredging **-barren** *m* ingot of gold **-basis** *f* gold basis, gold standard (of coinage) **-belag** *m*, **-beleg** *m* gold foil, gold coating or plating

Goldbergkeil *m* Goldberg wedge, neutral (gray) wedge

Gold-bergwerk *n* gold mine **-beryll** *m* chrysoberyl

Goldblatt *n* gold foil or leaf **~ und Aluminiumblattelektroskop** gold- and aluminium-leaf electroscope

Goldblättchen *n* small gold leaf or foil

Gold-blattelektrometer *n* gold-leaf electroscope or electrometer **-bortenwirker** *m* gold-lace maker **-bromür** *n* gold bromide **-bronze** *f* gold bronze, gilt bronze **-chlorid** *n*, **-chlorür** *n* gold chloride **-chlorwasserstoffsäure** *f* chlorauric acid **-dampfschicht** *f* evaporated gold film **-doublé** *n* rolled gold, gold-plated metal

Golddraht *m* gold wire **-relais** *n* gold-wire relay

golden golden, silver-gilt **-es Eichenblatt** gold oak leaf

Gold-druck *m* gold printing **-erde** *f* auriferous earth **-erz** *n* gold ore **-farbe** *f* gold color **-farbig** gold-colored **-feingewicht** gold carat **-firnis** *m* gold varnish **-folie** *f* gold foil **-führend** gold-bearing, auriferous **-gehalt** *m* gold content

Goldgelbbraun *n* golden brown

goldgelber Stoff canary medium (photo)

Gold-gespinst *n* gold filigree threads, spun gold **-gewicht** *n* gold weight, troy weight **-gewinnung** *f* extraction of gold **-glanz** *m* golden luster **-glätte** *f* (red) gold litharge **-glimmer** *m* yellow mica **-gräber** *m* gold digger **-granat** *m* topazolite, succinite **-graphit** *m* mixture of gold and graphite

Gold-grube *f* gold mine **-grund** *m* gold size **-haltig** auriferous, gold-bearing **-hell** bright golden, golden bright **-hornerz** *n* corneous silver **-hydroxydul** *n* aurous hydroxide **-jodür** *n* aurous iodide **-käferlack** *m* any varnish with the sheen of gold beetles **-kaliumbromür** *n* potassium aurobromide **-kaliumchlorür** *n* potassium aurochloride **-kaliumzyanür** *n* potassium aurocyanide

Gold-kalk *m* gold oxide, calcined gold **-kies** *m* auriferous pyrites, gold quartz **-klee** *m* yellow trefoil **-klumpen** *m* gold nugget **-könig** *m* regulus of gold **-körner** *pl* gold grains **-krätze** *f* gold dross, sweepings **-kupfer** *n* Mannheim gold **-lack** *m* gold varnish **-laugerei** *f* gold-leaching plant

Gold-legierung *f* gold alloy **-leim** *m* gold size **-leimflüssigkeit** *f* gold paint, chrysocol liquid **-lösung** *f* gold solution **-macherkunst** *f* alchemy **-metall** *n* gold metal, metallic gold **-natriumchlorid** *n* gold sodium chloride **-natriumchlorür** *n* sodium aurous chloride **-niederschlag** *n* gold precipitate **-ocker** *m* red ocher

Gold- oder Silberbarren *m* bullion

Gold-oxyd *n* gold oxide **-oxydsalz** *n* auric salt, aurate **-oxydul** *n* aurous oxide **-oxydverbindung** *f* auric or aurous compound **-papier** *n* gold paper, gilt paper **-plattiert** gold-plated **-plattierung** *f* gold plating, gold plate

Goldpräge-anstalt *f* gold-stamping works **-presse** *f* coining press for gold

Gold-prägung *f* gold embossing **-probe** *f* gold assay or test **-pulver** *n* gold powder, German gold **-purpur** *m* purple of Cassius **-quarz** *m* auriferous quartz **-raffination** *f* gold refining **-reich** rich in gold **-salz** *n* gold salt, sodium chloroaurate **-säure** *f* auric acid **-schale** *f* gold dish, cup, or cupel **-schaum** *n* gold leaf, imitation gold leaf

Gold-scheideanstalt *f* gold refinery **-scheiden** *n* gold refinining or parting **-scheider** *m* gold refiner **-scheideverfahren** *n* process of gold refining **-scheidewasser** *n* aqua regia **-scheidung** *f* gold refining or parting **-schlag** *m* gold leaf **-schläger** *m* goldbeater **-schlägerhaut** *f* goldbeater's skin **-schlick** *m* gold slime

Goldschmidt-hochfrequenzmaschine *f* Goldschmidt alternator **-tonrad** *n* Goldschmidt tone wheel

Gold-schmied *m* goldsmith **-schnitt** *m* gilt edge **-schreiber** *m* gold printer **-schwefel** *m* antimony pentasulfide **-seife** *f* auriferous alluvium, placer **-silber** *n* electrum **-sinter** *m* auriferous sinter **-staub** *m* flour gold, gold dust **-streichen** *n* gold test **-stück** *n* gold piece, gold coin **-sulfid** *n* gold sulfide, auric sulfide **-sulfür** *n* aurous sulfide

Gold-teilchen *n* gold particle **-thioschwefelsäure** *f* aurothiosulfuric acid **-tresse** *f* gold trimming **-unterdruckfarbe** *f* bronzing medium **-vitriol** *n* gold sulfate **-währung** *f* gold standard **-walze** *f* gold rolling **-wäsche** *f* washing of gold **-zahl** *f* gold number or figure **-zunder** *m* rags impregnated with gold solution **-zyanid** *n* gold cyanide **-zyanür** *n* aurous cyanide

Golf *m* gulf

Gonade *f* gonad

Gondel *f* car, nacelle, basket (cockspit), gondola **unter die Wolken herabsenkbare ~** subcloud car

Gondel-bremse *f* car stop or brake **-feld** *n* car bay or panel **-gerippe** *n* framework of car, car structure **-puffer** *m* pneumatic bumper **-ring** *m* car suspension frame or ring **-seil** *n* car suspension rope or cable **-schwenkvorrichtung** *f* nacelle swivelling device (power plant)

Gong *m* (time signal) chime

Goniometer *n* goniometer

Goniometrie *f* goniometry

goniometrisch goniometric

Gonios *n* goniometer

Göpel *m* drawing engine, gin, whim, horse capstan **-antrieb** *m* animal power **-betrieb** *m* horse gear, whim drive, horse-driven rig **-schacht** *m* working or winding pit

Gording *f* leach line

Gordonprozeß *m* Gordon (gashouse-liquor) process

Gordungs-pfahl *m* piling for buffer wall of a pier **-wand** *f* buffer wall

Gösch *m* jack (naut.)

Gosse *f* gutter, trench, drain, side channel, sewer

Gossen-bordstein *m* cheek stone of gutter, gutter stone **-stein** *m* gutter stone

Göthit *m* göthite

gotisch Minuskel Gothic minuscule **-er Bogen** gothic arch, pointed arch

Grab *n* grave

graben to dig, excavate

Graben *n* digging

Graben *m* ditch, trench, drain, rift valley **-aushebemaschine** *f* ditcher, trenching machine **-bagger** *m* trenching machine, ditch-digging machine, trench digger or trench excavator **-band** *n* ditch conveyor **-bekleidung** *f* trench revetment **-böschung** *f* escarp, counterscarp **-bruch** *m* trough fault **-durchfahrt** *f* crossing of trenches or ditches **-füllung** *f* trench backfill **-herstellung** *f* trenching, ditch digging

Graben-pflug *m* ditching plow **-profil** *n* trench or ditch profile **-rost** *m* trenchboard, boardwalk **-sohle** *f* trench floor or bottom, bottom of ditch **-spiegel** *m* trench periscope **-stellung** *f* trench position **-streiche** *f* caponier **-stufe** *f* firing step **-tiefe** *f* depth of trench **-wand** *f* trench wall **-wehr** *f* parapet

Gräber *m* digger, miner

Gräberei *f* open diggings

Grab-scheit *n* spade **-stichel** *m* graver, turning graver, burin **-tafel** *f* grave marker **-tiefe** *f* digging depth (dredging)

Gracht *f* canal

Grad *m* intensity, degree, grade, rank, gradation, rate, ridge, seam **vom ersten ~** linearly **~** (einer Gleichung) order **~ vom Kreuz** degrees from crossfuse setting **N ~ absolut** *n* degrees Kelvin, *n* degrees absolute **N ~ Celsius** *n* degrees centigrade **um 90 ~ drehen** to turn through 90 degrees

Gradabteilung *f* graduated scale, map square, graticule

Gradation *f* contrast

Gradations-ausgleich *m* contrast equalizer, gamma correction **-entzerrung** *f* gradation correction, gamma equalizer **-steigerung** *f* reinforcement of gradation **-verlauf** *m* linear course of gradation

Gradbogen *m* circumferentor, graduated arc, protractor, inclinometer dial, arc, bow, limb, miner's or surveyor's level, sextant, quadrant scale **-elektrometer** *n* quadrant electrometer **-teilstrich** *m* graduation mark **-transporteur** *m* protactor

Grade, in ~ einteilen to graduate

Grad-einteilung *f* graduation, division, calibration, scale **-feld** *n* map square **-führungssegment** *n* parallel guide segment

Gradiation *f* gradiation

Gradiationsverhältnis *n* overall contrast ratio

Gradient *m* gradient **~ des Potentials** potential gradient

Gradient-linie *f* grade line **-messer** *m* gradiometer **-streifen** *m* gradient strip

Gradierbeitelchen *n* dented chisel

gradieren to graduate (a scale)

Gradierung *f* graduation, grading, refining (of brine)

Gradier-waage *f* areometer, hydrometer **-werk** *n* graduation house, cooling tower

Grädigkeit *f* concentration (chem.)

Gradiometer *m* gradiometer

Grad-intervall *n* degree (grade) interval **-kreisteilung** *f* graded circle **-laufapparat** *m* stabilizer **-leiter** *f* scale of degrees **-linig** rectilineal, straight-line **-messer** *m* index, protractor **-messung** *f* graduation

Gradnetz *n* grid (map), graticule, recticle **-anmeldepunkt** *m* grid reference (mil.) **-karte** *f* air-force grid **-meldeverfahrung** *f* air-force-grid reporting

Gradometer *n* gradient recorder, gradometer

Grad-rose *f* graduated card **-schalig** slightly curved **-scheibe** *f* graduated disc **-skala** *f* tuning scale **-stein** *m* border, curbstone **-teiler** *m* vernier **-teilung** *f* graduation, scale of degrees, calibration **-zeichen** *n* degree sign

Graduator *m* graduator

Graduer *m* calibrator

graduieren to graduate

Graduierstangenführung *f* graduating stem guide

Graduierung *f* graduation or division into degrees

Grad-zahl *f* number of degrees or graduations **-zeiger** *m* arm pointer

Grahamgang *m* Graham escapement

Gramm *n* gram (metric unit of weight) **-äquivalent** *n* gram equivalent **-atom** *n* gram atom **-bruchteil** *n* fraction of a gram **-grad** *m* gram degree **-kalorie** *f* gram calorie, small calorie **-molekül** *n* gram molecule **-molekülvolumen** *n* gram-molecular volume

Grammol *n* gram molecule

Grammophon *n* gramophone **-nadel** *f* gramophone needle **-platte** *f* gramophone disk **-schalldose** *f* gramophone sound box

Granalien *pl* granulated material or metal, nonmetal shot (alloy) **-nickel** *n* nickel shot

Granat *m* garnet **böhmischer ~** pyrope Bohemian (red) garnet **roter ~** almandine **schwarzer ~** melanite

Granat-dodekaeder *n* rhombic dodecahedron

Granate *f* shell, grenade, projectile

Granat-ton *m* garnet shade **-waren** *pl* garnet-studded articles, garnetwork

Grand *m* gravel, shingle

granieren to grain

Granierstahl *m* graining steel

Granit *m* granite **-ähnlich, -artig** granitic **-gestein** *n* granitic rock **-gewebe** *n* granitic fabric **-haue** *f* granite ax

granitischer Gipfel granitic ridge or mountain

Granitwalze *f* granite roller

Granometer *m* grain counter

Granulat *n* granulated material

Granulation *f* granulation

Granulationsanlage *f* granulating plant

Granüle *f* granule

Granulierapparat *m* granulator (for chemicals, etc.)

granulieren to granulate

Granulier-rost *m* water screen, granular oxidation **-sieb** *n* graining sieve
granulierte Kunststoffe granular plastics
Granulierung *f* granulation
Granulierungsanlage *f* granulating plant
Granulit *m* granulite
Granulose *f* granulose
Grapen *m* iron or mixing pot
Graphieoszillegraph-raumdurchführung *f* indoor bushing
graphierte Electrode graphite electrode
Graphik *f* graphic arts
Graphiker *m* commercial artist
Graphikon *n* diagrammatic drawing
graphisch graphic(al), diagrammatic, surveyed, plotted **~ darstellen** to represent graphically **-e Anstalt** graphic institute **-e Bestimmung** graphic determination **-e Darstellung** diagrammatic or graphic representation, graph **-e Fachartikel** requirements for the graphical trade **-e Kräftekomposition** graphical composition of forces **-er Maßstab** graphical scale **-er Punkt** topographical point **-e Zeichnung** graph
Graphit *m* graphite, graphitic carbon **entflockter ~** deflocculated graphite **flockiger ~** flaked graphite **gereinigter ~** washed graphite
Graphit-ablagerung *f* graphite deposit **-ausbildung** *f* graphitization **-ausscheidung** *f* separation of graphite **-belag** *m* Aquadag coating **-bildung** *f* graphite formation, graphitization **-elektrode** *f* graphite electrode **-eutektikum** *n* graphite eutectic **-fett** *n* graphitized fats **-flocke** *f* graphite flake **-gewinnung** *f* graphite mine **-gitter** *n* graphite lattice **-glühen** *n* graphitizing **-haltig** graphitiferous
Graphitier-apparat *m* black-wash sprayer **-bürste** *f* black-leading brush
graphitieren to coat with graphite, graphite
graphitiert graphite-treated **-e Bronzebüchse** graphite-coated bronze **-es Fett** graphite grease **-es Schmiermittel** graphite (-treated) oil
Graphitierung *f* graphitization
graphitisch graphitic, graphitoid
graphitisieren to graphitize
Graphit-kautschuk *m* graphited rubber **-kohle** *f* graphite carbon **-lager** *n* graphite deposit
graphit-moderierter Reaktor graphite-moderated reactor **-reich** rich in graphite
Graphit-ring *m* graphite ring **-ruder** *n* jet vane **-schichtstruktur** *f* graphite layer structure **-schiffchen** *n* graphite crucible or graphite boat **-schleifring** *m* graphite slip ring **-schmierfett** *n* graphite grease **-schmiermittel** *n* graphite lubricant **-schmierung** *f* black-lead or graphite lubrication **-schuppe** *f* graphite flake **-schwärze** *f* black-lead wash, black lead, graphite blacking **-stein** *m* graphite brick **-stift** *m* conductive pencil, electrographic pen **-tiegel** *m* graphite, plumbago, or blacklead crucible, graphite pot **-widerstand** *m* graphite resistance
Graphometrie *f* graphometry
Graphostatik *f* graphical static
Gras *n* grass **-bleiche** *f* grass bleaching **-erntemaschine** *f* harvesting machine for grass
Gras-mäher *m* mower **-säapparat** *m* grass-seed attachment **-schneider** *m* grass cutter, mower **-scholle** *f* sod, turf

Grat *m* seam, burr, flash, rabbet, ridge, crest, fen, fin, spill, overflow from a mold (plastics), groin, hip, spine *n*, scoring (of barrel) **~** (der Bohrung) burr (of the hole) **~** (Spinndüse) burr (spinneret) **~ an der Schneide nach dem Anschleifen** wire edge **den ~ entfernen** to clean off burrs
Grat-abschneider *m* arris remover or cutter **-bildung** *f* formation of a shoulder or of fins, edge, ridge, burr **-blech** *n* hip lead or sheet **-bogen** *m* cross springer, diagonal arch or rib, groined arch
Gräte *f* fishbone
grätenartig herringbone
Gratentfernung *f* removel of the bur
grätenverzahnt spiral teeth
gratfrei machen to level down
Grathobel *m* dovetail plane
Gratifikation *f* gratuity, bonus
grätig overfinned
Gräting *f* grating
Gratisbeilage *f* free supplement
Gratlinie *f* edge of regression
gratlos finless **-er Schnitt** burless cut
Grat-putzer *m* bur trimmer **-seite eines Daches** hip side of a roof **-wulst** *f* hip bead **-ziegel** *m* ridge or hip tile
Grätsche *f* straddling position
Gratsparren *m* hip (of roof)
Grätzschaltung *f* Grätz (full-wave) rectifier-circuit organization
grau gray **-es Roheisen** gray or graphitic pig iron **-e Salbe** mercurial ointment **-es Zinn** gray-tin modification
Grau-braunstein *m* pyrolusite, brownstone **-eisenerz** *n* narcasite **-erz** *n* galena **-filter** *n* optic light filter (TV) **-gießerei** *f* gray-iron foundry **-glanzoxydbad** *n* stibium oxide bath
Grauglas *n* gray filter-glass **-scheibe** *f* (TV) optic light filter **-standard** *m* neutral density standard
Graugültigerz *n* mercurial gray copper ore
Grauguß *m* gray (cast) iron, cast iron **hochwertiger ~** high-test gray iron, high-strength cast iron
Grauguß-löten *n* cast-iron brazing **-riemenscheibe** *f* cast-iron pulley **-teile** *n pl* gray iron castings
Graukalk *m* lime pyrolignite, gray or meager chalk **-keil** *m* neutral (gray) wedge, Goldberg wedge, wedge filter (opt.) **-keilstufe** *f* intermediate shading value (of wedge) **-leiter** *f* (Ostwalds Farbentheorie), gray scale
gräulich grayish, grizzly
Grau-mangan *n* pyrolusite, brownstone **-manganerz** *n* manganite **-meliert** gray-mottled **-pappe** *f* paperboard stock, millboards
Graupe *f* shot, grain, hulled grain
Graupel *f* sleet, soft hail, snow **-bildung** *f* sleet formation **-bö** *f* sleet squall **-korn** *n* grain of sleet
Graupeln *pl* (meteor.) sleet
Graupel-schauer *m* sleet shower, hail or graupel shower **-schlag** *m* sleeting
Graupen-bett *n* bed of grains **-erz** *n* granular ore **-gang** *m* hulling mills (various) **-kobalt** *m* smaltite **-mühle** *f* mill for groats
graupig granular
graurötlich roan

Grau-scheibe *f* optic light filter (TV) **-schleier** *m* grey film, fog **-sandstein** *m* gray bands, gray sandstone **-silber** *n* selbite, carbonate of silver, gray silver **-skala** *f* gray scale (TV) **-spiegel** *m* gray spiegel iron **-spießglanzerz** *n* stibnite **-strahler** *m* gray body **-strahlung** *f* gray radiation **-stufe** intermediate tonal or shading value, shade of gray (TV) **-stufung** *f* gray scale (TV) **-töne** *pl* gray tints **-tonskala** *f* (Rauchgasprüfer) gray color graduation **-wacke** *f* graywacke

Graveur *m* engraver

Gravieranstalt *f* engraving establishment

gravieren to engrave, sculpture

Gravier-maschine *f* engraving machine **-schaufelbeitelchen** *n* print-cutter's spoon-bit chisel **-stichel** *m* engraving needle **-stift** *m* engraving needle

Gravierung *f* embossing, engraving, gravure

Gravierwachs *f* embossing, engraving, gravure

Gravier-wachs *n* engraving wax **-werkzeug** *n* engraving tool

Gravimetrie *f* gravimetry

gravimetrisch gravimetric **-e Unregelmäßigkeiten** gravity anomalies **-e Untersuchung** gravimetric analysis **-e Waage** gravity balance

Gravitation *f* gravitation

Gravitations-aufbereitung *f* gravity concentration, gravity dressing **-beschleunigung** *f* acceleration of gravity **-drehwaage** *f* gravity balance **-einheit** *f* gravitational unit **-feld** *n* gravitational field **-gesetz** *n* law of gravity **-konstante** *f* gravitation constant **-potential** *n* gravitational or Newtonian potential **-seigerung** *f* gravity segregation

gravitative Kristallisationsdifferentiation differentiation due to gravity sinking of crystals

Gravitätsbeschleunigung *f* acceleration of gravity

Gravitieren *n* gravitation

Graviton *n* graviton

gravoid-elastoide Wellen gravitational-compressibility waves

Gravurdruckwalze *f* engraved printing roller

Gravüre *f* engraving

Gravur-film *m* engraved sound film, embossed groove recording **-raster** *m* engraved screen

Greenockit *m* greenockite

Greenovit *m* greenovite

Greenwichzeit *f*, **mittlere ~** (MGZ) Greenwich mean time (GMT)

Greifbacke *f* gripping wedge, clamp

Greifbagger *m* single-bucket excavator, grab excavator or dredge, clamshell dredge **~ mit Wippausleger** grabbing excavator with luffing jib

greifbar seizable, substantial, palpable, tangible **-er Zucker** spot sugar

Greifdorn *m* spear **-eisen** *n* claw or dog (e.g., for lumbering)

Greifeinrichtung *f* pick-off attachment

greifen to grip (in), grasp, seize, bite, touch, cake, felt

Greifen *n* gripping, seizure

Greifer *m* gripping device, grab (of a crane), grab bucket, tappet, grip, unloader, hooking-on arm, (pull-down) claw (motion pictures), grapple claw (of in-and-out movement or feeder mechanism) **-anschlag** *m* gripper block **-backe** *f* jaw of grab **-bagger** *m* grab-bucket conveyer **-betrieb** *m* service with grabs **-bewegung** *f* operating grippers **-brücke** *f* chain gripper bar **-drehkran** *m* slewing grab crane **-einrichtung** *f* dragline equipment

Greifer-führungsspindel *f* gripper guide spindle **-füllung** (Inhalt) grab filling **-gefäß** *n* grab bucket **-gehänge** *n* spur grips **-gehäuse** *n* gripper housing **-gestell** *n* gripper **-hebel** *m* fixed gripper lever **-inhalt** *m* capacity of grab

Greifer-katze *f* bucket grab **-kopf** *m* head of the grab **-korb** *m* grab bucket **-kran** *m* grab crane **-kübel** *m* grab bucket, grab (of crane), coal grab **-kurve** *f* cam operating grippers **-laufkran** *m* overhead travelling crane with grab **-maschine** *f* step-type printer **-mechanismus** *m* pull-down claw mechanism **-rolle** *f* roller for gripper operating lever

Greifer-schale *f* grab blade or shell of a dredger **-schaufel** *f* grab spade **-schneiden** *pl* shovel teeth, edges of gripping tool **-schraube** *f* gripper bolt **-schutzstange** *f* frontguard rail **-stange** *f* gripper bar **-stift** *m* positioning or registration pin, filmfeeder or pilot pin **-system** *n* claw-feed system **-trenner** *m* pantograph isolating switch

Greifer- und Kübelbetrieb *m* grab and bucket service

Greifer-vorrichtung *f* traction device **-vorschub** *m* gripper feed **-wagen** *m* pick-up carrier **-winde** *f* winch for the grab **-windwerk** *n* grab hoist

Greif-fähigkeit *f* gripping power **-fläche** *f* gripping surface **-förderer** *m* grab transporter **-haft** *f* tangible **-haken** *m* clamp, grab hook

Greifhaufen *m* caking or rough floor, mat (brewery) **-schüttelgabel** *f* fork for separating malt

Greif-kettenantrieb *m* caterpillar drive **-klaue** *f* grip, grapple **-korb** *m* catcher, grab bucket **-kübel** *m* automatic grab **-loch** *n* finger hole **-rachen** *m* alligator grab **-ring** *m*, **-schraube** *f* grip screw **-schaufel** *f* grab bucket, grab jaw **-schaufelförderer** *m* grab transporter

Greif-vermögen *n* gripping power or capacity **-vorrichtung** *f* gripping appliance **-werkzeug** *n* gripping device **-winkel** *m* gripping angle, limiting angle of rolling, angle of contact or of nip **-zange** *f* grip(ping) tongs, pipe grip **-zirkel** *m* calipers, dividers

Greisen *m* greisen

grell bright, glaring, shrill, sharp, loud

Gremium *n* panel

Grenz-albedo *n* albedo limiting value **-amplitude** *f* oscillation amplitude limit **-arbeitslehre** *f* working-limit gauge **-auflösungsvermögen** *n* limiting resolving power **-beanspruchung** *f* limiting load or strain **-bedingung** *f* limiting, boundary, threshold, or critical condition **-befestigung** *f* border fortification **-begriff** *m* limit conception **-belastung** *f* ultimate load, limiting or critical load **-bereinigung** *f* frontier or boundary rectification **-berichtigung** *f*, **-bestimmung** *f* demarcation **-beweglichkeit** *f* limiting mobility **-bezirk** *m* frontier district **-bohrloch** *n* determining borehole **-charakteristik** *f* limit characteristics **-dämpfung** *f* ultimate damping **-durchmesser** *m* line diameter, limiting diameter (of dielectric line)

Grenze *f* junction line, bound(ary), junction, limit, frontier, limitation, cutoff (point), end, confines **unter der gefährlichen ~ bleibend** (playing) safe

Grenz-ebene *f* boundary **-eisen** *n* crown iron **-empfindlichkeit** *f* limiting sensitivity

grenzen to adjoin, border on **sie ~ ab** they mark the boundary

Grenzen *pl*, **über alle ~ wachsen** to become unbounded

Grenzenergie *f* boundary energy

grenzenlos limitless, boundless, unlimited

Grenz-erwärmung *f* temperature rise within limits **-fall** *m* border(-line), limiting, or critical case **-feld** *n* limit field **-film** *m* boundary film

Grenzfläche *f* boundary surface or layer, contact surface, interface (cryst.), cleavage plane, surface of separation **gasfeste ~** gastight membrane, wall, or partition

Grenzflächen-beziehung *f* interfacial relationships **-potential** *n* interface potential **-reibung** *f* boundary layer friction **-spannung** *f* interfacial tension, surface tension **-wellen** *pl* waves at interfaces **-winkel** *m* interfacial angle

Grenzfrequenz *f* limiting or cutoff frequency, lowest usable high frequency (LUHF) **~ eines Filters** critical or cutoff frequency of a filter **~ in Hertz** cutoff frequency, cutoff **obere** (untere) **~** upper (lower) cutoff frequency **untere ~** threshold frequency

Grenz-funkbake *f* boundary marker **-gebiet** *n* limiting area, border region, frontier area **-gedämpft** aperiodic **-gefälle** *n* limiting slope or gradient **-gegend** *f* border region **-geschwindigkeit** *f* critical velocity **-gewindelehren** *pl* limit thread gauges **-gewinderollenlehren** *pl* thread limit roll-snap gauges **-gleichung** *f* boundary equation **-höhe** *f* limiting height

Grenz-kennwert *m* limiting characteristic value **-kohlenwasserstoff** *m* limit hydrocarbon **-korn** *n* near-mesh material **-kreis** *m* limiting circle **-kreisfrequenz** *f* cutoff frequency (in terms of radians per second), cutoff angular velocity **-kugelendmaß** *n* tolerance end-measuring rod with spherical ends **-kurve** *f* limiting curve

Grenz-ladeprofil *n* limit gauge **-last** *f* maximum load **-lastspielzahl** *f* limiting value of stress cycle endured **-lastwechselzahl** *f* limiting number of load alternations **-lehrdorn** *m* tolerance-plug gauge, internal-limit gauge, cylindrical gauges, double limit **-lehre** *f* fixed gauge, plug or snap gauge, limit gauge **-leistung** *f* limiting output **-leistungskonstruktion** *f* limiting design **-licht** *n* boundary light **-lichtbake** *f* boundary light **-linie** *f* boundary line, junction line, (line of) demarcation, limiting line **-liniensingularität** *f* limit-type singularity **-lochlehre** *f* internal-limit gauge, tolerance-plug gauge

Grenz-marke *f* boundary marker **-maß** *n* limit or limiting size, extreme maximum diameter **-mauer** *f* partition or mean wall **-menge** *f* limiting set **-pegel** *m* cut-off levels **-pfahl** *m* boundary pole **-potential** *n* limiting potential **-prüfung** *f* marginal checking **-punkt** *m* cutoff point, limit point

Grenz-rachenlehre *f* limit (snap) gauge, external-limit (snap) gauge **-radius** *m* boundary radius **-regler** *m* limiting regulator **-regelung** *f* demarcation **-riegel** *m* stop bolt, limiting bolt **-schalter** *m* limit switch, overrunning switch **-scheidung** *f* demarcation

Grenzschicht *f* boundary layer or film, interface, marginal layer **-ablösung** *f* boundary breakaway separation, layer separation **-ablösungspunkt** *m* burble point, separation point **-absaugung** *f* boundary-layer control **-abspaltung** *f* boundary-layer separation **-beeinflussung** *f* boundary-layer influence **-belüftung** *f* precompression in the boundary layer

Grenzschicht-dicke *f* thickness of boundary layer **-durchflußmeßgerät** *n* boundary-layer mass flowmeter **-gebiet** *n* interface region **-lehre** *f* theory of the boundary layer **-spannungsmesser** *m* interfacial tensiometer **-steuerung** *f* boundary layer control (aerodyn.) **-wirkung** *f* boundary layer effect

Grenz-schraube *f* stop screw, locking screw (on gear), setscrew **-schwingung** *f* aperiodic vibration, maximum aperiodic oscillation **-seil** *n* check cable, safety-stop cable **-spannung** *f* limiting stress, edge stress **-sperre** *f* prohibition of trade (with foreign countries) **-stein** *m* boundary marker (stone) **-strahl** *m* border-line ray, infra-Roentgen ray **-strecke** *f* butt **-strich** *m* limit mark

Grenzstrom *m* marginal or limiting current **-betrieb** *m* marginal operation **-relais** *n* marginal-operation relay **-stärke** *f* critical current, limit of current (intensity)

Grenzübergang *m* passage to the limit (chem.) **sukzessiver ~** iterated limit

Grenz- und Kurzwellensender *m* transmitter for intermediate and short waves

Grenz-verkehr *m* frontier traffic **-viskosität** *f* limiting viscosity **-welle** *f* wave of medium to high frequency

Grenzwellen-länge *f* minimum wave length (quantum limit), critical, limiting or threshold wave length **-antennenordnung** *f* minimum wave antenna arrangement **-empfangsgerät** *n* minimum wave receiver **-funktelephon** *n* intermediate wave radio telephone

Grenzwert *m* limiting or boundary value, threshold, critical or saturation value; (bei Röhren) maximum ratings **-kontrolle** *f* off-normal check **-problem** *n* boundary-value problem **-prüfung** *f* marginal checking **-schaltereinheit** *f* limit value switch

Grenz-widerstand *m* critical, limiting or aperiodic resistance, boundary resistance **-winkel** *m* critical angle, limiting angle (of refractometer) **-zone** *f* fringe area

Greyträger *m* wide-flanged structural steel I beam, Grey girder or beam

Grezseide *f* raw silk

Gribbel *m* beet pricker

Grid-träger truss **-werk** *n* lattice **-zange** *f* grip pliers

grieselig gritty

griesig gravelly, gritty, sabulous **-es Aussehen** seediness, granulated character

Grieß *m* grit, gravel, (coarse) sand, pea coal, semolina; (Störung) grass (TV), shot noise **geputzter ~** purified semolina

Grieß-abscheider *m* sand catcher **-bildung** *f*

formation of gritty particles **-holm** *m* fender, railing

grießig gritty, gravelly

Grieß-kohle *f* pea coal **-mühle** *f* grit mill, grit tube **-pfanne** *f* ladle **-putzmaschine** *f* purifier of semolina **-sieb** *n* grits bolter

Griff *m* grip, handle, pull, touch, feel (of paper), switch, knob, hold **~ zum Schwenken des Armes** arm-swinging handle **gewellter ~** corrugated tip **~ für Indexhebel** knurled grip

Griff-arm *m* driving arm **-befestiger** *m* grip adjuster

griffbereit easily accessible, handy

Griff-brett *n* finger board (of string instrument) **-bügel** *m* handle

Griff(e)-herstellungsmaschine *f* machine for making handles

Griffel *m* slate pencil, crayon **-papier** *n* paper for slate pencils **-schiefer** *m* pencil slate **-stopfen** *m* stopper with thumb piece

Griff-feldstudium *n* time-and-motion study **-fläche** *f* curvature of the brush face

Griff-hahn mit gebogenem Auslauf grip-type cock with bent outlet **-hebel** *m* hand lever

Griffhülse *f* grip sleeve

griffig having a good feel

Griffigkeit *f* grip, gripping capacity, grip traction **~ der Reifen** tire grip **~ der Straße** non-skid property, anti-skid property, road-skid quality

Griffinmühle *f* bowl mill

Griff-klemme *f* locking handle **-kreuz** *n* star handle **-mutter** *f* knurled nut **-nocken** *pl* suction cut out lever (press) **-platte** *f* dial disk, holding plate **-rad** *n* handle **-rohr** *n* trail handspike, tubular handle

Griff-schale *f* pistol stock **-schlüssel** *m* handle wrench **-schraube** *f* ball grip screw **-sicherung** *f* grip-type fuse **-stange** *f* handle bar **-stelle** *f* point of contact **-stöpsel** *m* pinch stopper **-stück** *n* pistol stock, grip, handle, butt **-zeit** *f* handling time

grindiger Stahl spotty steel

Grindel *m* plow bean

grithaltig gritty

grob rough, coarse, uncivil, crude, gross, approximate **~ gemahlen** coarse ground **-e Ausrüstung** (Kessel) fixture **-e Dichte** coarse-grained density **-e Feuchtigkeit** surface moisture (above air dry) **-er Kies** shingle **-e Körner** large sizes **-e Mahlung** coarse ground **-er Sand** coarse-grained sand, grit **-er Titer** coarse denier **-e Werte** raw figures **in -en Zügen** approximately, roughly

Grob-abstimmung *f* coarse tuning **-abtastung** *f* coarse scanning **-ätzung** *f* macroetching

grobbearbeiten to rough-machine

Grob-beitel *m* rough chisel **-bewegung** *f* coarse motion **-bewegungsschraube** *f* quick-motion screw

Grobblech *n* heavy plate, plate, boiler plate, thick metal plate **-erzeugnisse** *pl* plate products **-lager** *n* plate store **-richtmaschine** *f* plate-straightening rolls **-straße** *f* plate mill **-walze** *f* plate roll **-walzwerk** *n* plate mill, plate rolling mill

Grob-blitzableiter *m* plate lightning rod **-brechen** to break up into pieces, grind coarsely **-bruch** *m* coarse granulation **-bürsten** *pl* coarse brushes **-dispers** coarsely dispersed **-draht** *m* coarse wire **-drahtig** coarse-threaded or -wired

Grob-einstellen *n* coarse setting **-einstellung** *f* coarse adjustment, coarse control **-eisen** *n* merchant iron **-eisenstraße** *f* breaking-down mill train **-eisenwalzwerk** *n* merchant rolls, rolls for merchant iron **-entstaubung** *f* preliminary dust extraction **-entzerrer** *m* slope equalizer **-erdig** rough **-erz** *n* coarse ore **-erzofen** *m* coarse-ore furnace

grob-fädig coarse-threaded, coarse-filamentous **-fahrlässiges Verhalten** gross negligence **-faserig** coarse-grained

Grobfeile *f* coarse file

Grob-Fein-Relais *n* coarse-fine relay

Grob-Fein-Regelung *f* coarse-fine action

Grob-filtereinsatz *m* coarse filter element **-fleyer** *m* slubbing frame **-flotation** *f* roughing flotation **-flotator** *m* rough flotation cells, initial or roughing separatory cell

grobgängiges Gewinde coarse pitch thread

Grob-gefüge *n* macrostructure, coarse or gross structure **-gelocht** coarsely perforated **-gepulvert** coarsely crushed **-gewicht** *n* gross weight **-gewinde** *n* coarse thread **-gut** *n* (Erzbergbau) oversized material **-haarig** coarse-grained

Grobheit *f* coarseness, rudeness, insolence, thickness

Grob-höhenmesser *m* standard altimeter **-horizontierung** *f* initial levelling **-jährig** coarsely ringed **-karbid** *n* coarse-sized carbide **-kegelbrecher** *m* gyratory crusher **-kennung** *f* coarse beam (in radio-controlled navigation) **-kessel** *m* tin pot **-kies** *m* coarse gravel **-kohle** *f* raw coal **-korn** *n* coarse product, coarse grain **-korneisen** *n* coarse-grain iron **-kornglühen** *n* coarse grain annealing

grobkörnig coarse-grained **-e Schleifscheibe** coarse grain grinding wheel

Grobkörnigkeit *f* coarseness

Grob-kornmaschine *f* coarse coal jig **-kornsetzmaschine** *f* coarse-grain washer **-krempel** *m* breaker or scribbler card **-kristallin** *n* coarse-crystalline, granular-crystalline, coarse-grained **-kristallinisch** coarsely crystalline

gröblich grossly

Grob-lunker *m* cavity **-mahlung** *f* crushing **-maschig** coarse-mesh(ed), wide-meshed **-meißel** *m* dressing or roughing-out chisel **-mörtel** *m* coarse-grain cement or concrete **-narbig** coarse grained **-ölfilter** *m* coarse filter **-ortung** *f* coarse radiolocation **-passung** *f* loose fit, coarse fit **-pore** *f* maeropore **-porig** coarse-pored

Grob-rasteraufnahme *f* coarse screen photograph **-rechen** *m* trash rack (water power screen), coarse rake **-regelstäbe** *pl* coarse regulating rods **-regler** *m* coarse or rough regulator (adjuster) **-sand** *m* gravel **-schlamm** *m* coarse slurry **-schleifen** to coarse-grind **-schlichten** *n* rough finishing **-schmied** *m* hammersmith, forgeman, blacksmith, edge-toolmaker **-schmiede** *f* ironware manufacture **-schotter** *m* coarse gravel **-schrot** *n* coarse-ground grist **-sicherung** *f* current-limiting fuse, glass-tube fuse, spark-gap-type arrester **-sieb** *n* coarse sieve **-sitz** *m* loose or coarse fit **-skala** *f* rough or coarse (pointer) dial or scale

Grob-spannung *f* high voltage **-spannungsschutz** *m* high-voltage protector **-spindelbank** *f* slabbing frame (textiles) **-stimmung** *f* coarse tuning **-straße** *f* breaking-down mill train, plate-rolling train, plate-mill train **-strecke** *f* breaking-down mill train **-struktur** *f* reduced, or reduction of, structure **-strukturanalyse** *f* gross, coarse, or macrostructure analysis **-strukturuntersuchung** *f* macroscopy **-stufe** *f* coarse stage **-stufenschalter** *m* coarse-adjustment switch, band switch **-stuhl** *m* stretcher mule

Grob-teilung *f* rough scale **-trieb** *m* coarse tuning drive, coarse motion **-verstellung** *f* coarse motion **-visier** *n* coarse sight **-vorschub** *m* coarse feed **-walzwerk** *n* blooming or roughing-down mill, coarse-crushing rolls **-zeiger** *m* coarse or nonsensitive indicator **-zerkleinern** to coarse crush **-zerkleinerung** *f* breaking, coarse crushing, coarse reduction **-zerkleinerungsmühle** *f* crushing mill **-zug** *m* drawing bench for thick wires, roughing block, drawing of wire, first or thick drawing, ripping, rumpling

Groden *m* false channel

Gros *n* main body (mil.), gross (twelve dozen)

groß big, large, great, tall, significant, important **gleich ~** of the same magnitude, length, height, etc. **verschieden ~** of different magnitude, length, height, etc. **-e Achse** major axis (as of an ellipse) (math.) **-er Bär** Dig Dipper **-er Dipol** code for a type of radar equipment **-er Gang** high gear **-es Gewicht** heaviness **-er Kreis** great circle **-e Kurve** gentle bank (aviation) **-e Steigung** coarse pitch **-er Zirkel** great circle

Groß-abbau *m* large-scale workings **-angelegt** large-scale **-anlage** *f* large-scale plant **-antenne** *f* giant antenna **-anzeiger** *m* large-scale indicator **-artig** grand, splendid, magnificent **-auflage** *f* large circulation **-aufnahme** *f* close-up view

Groß-backenbrecher *m* heavy-duty jaw crusher **-baggergerät** *n* heavy dredging equipment **-bauten** *pl* large-scale workings **-baustelle** *f* large-scale project site **-bereichswandler** *m* wide-range instrument transformer **-betrieb** *m* large plant, large-scale manufacturing operation

großbohriger Motor large-bore engine

Groß-bohrwerk *n* giant boring mill **-brambraß** *f* mean brace

Großbrandanlage *f* large fire installation used to simulate large-scale fires (either by themselves or in conjunction with dummy installations)

Groß-buchstabe *m* capital letter **-diesel** *m* large Diesel unit **-dimensioniert** amply dimensioned **-drehbank** *f* heavy-duty lathe

Größe *f* size, magnitude, greatness, extent, volume, quantity, value, height, dimension, amplitude, entity, format **~ der Ablenkung** amount of shift or of deflection **~ und Gewicht** size and weight **~ der Teilchen** particle size **an ~ oder Wert verlieren** to fall off (in value) **abgeleitete ~** subsidiary or derived quantity **abhängige ~** derivative **bestimmende ~** controlling factor

Größe, doppelte natürliche ~ twice full size **gerichtete ~** directional quantity **gewöhnliche ~** standard size **halbe natürliche ~** one-half full size **natürliche ~** natural or full size, full scale **periodische ~** periodic or variable quality, time space **übliche ~** standard size **unendliche kleine ~** differential or infinitesimal quantity **wirkliche ~** natural size

Großeinsatz *m* major commitment, commitment of large forces, employment of great numbers, large-scale use or operation

Größen-analyse *f* dimensional analysis **-bestimmung** *f* rating, sizing **-einfluß** *m* scale effect **-faktor** *m* variable, size factor, amplitude factor **-klasse** *f* classification according to size **-lehre** *f* mathematics, geometry **-mäßig** dimensional (as regards size or quantity) **-nummer** *f* size **-ordnung** *f* order (of magnitude), magnitude

größenordnungsmäßig according to size

Größen-skala *f* scale of surfaces or of quantities **-verhältnis** *n* relative sizes **-verteilung** *f* size distribution **-wandler** *m* quantizer **-zahl** *f* magnitude, size number

Groß-erzeugung *f* mass production, tonnage production **-fabrikation** *f* manufacture on a large scale **-fähre** *f* traject **-faserig** large-fibered **-fäustel** *n* ragging hammer **-feldabsorption** *f* broad beam **-fertigung** *f* mass production

Großflächen-lautsprecher *m* power loudspeaker, public-address loudspeaker, announce loudspeaker system **-membrane** *f* large-area diaphragm **-methandurchflußzähler** *m* large-area methane flow counter **-vermessung** *f* survey of large areas **-zählrohr** *n* large area counter tube

großflächig large surface (of), large area (of) **-e Drucke** blotch prints **-e Transistorelektrode** base electrode

Groß-flugboot *n* big flying boat **-flugzeug** *n* large aircraft **-folio** *n* large folio **-frachtflugzeug** *n* big freight carrier, super-cargo plane, flying boxcar **-funkempfangstelle** *f* receiving station **-funkstation** *f* long-distance station **-funkstelle** *f* long-distance radio station, high-power wireless station, long-distance signal station

Groß-gaskerze *f* large-size gas engine **-gasmaschine** *f* high-power, high-duty, or high-capacity gas engine **-gefäß** *n* large-size vessel, vat **-gefüge** *n* macrostructure **-gehäuse** *n* cast-metal case **-getriebe** *n* heavy gearings **-gewerbe** *n* wholesale manufacture or industry **-gewicht** *n* gross weight **-gewindeschneider** *m* large-size tapper **-handel** *m* wholesale trade **-handelspreis** *m* wholesale price **-händler** *m* wholesale dealer **-helling** *f* building for large vessels

Grossist *m* wholesaler

großkalibrig large in diameter or bore **-es Maschinengewehr** fixed machine gun

Groß-kegel *m* large body size **-kegelmatrize** *f* matrix for large body size **-kern** *m* large core **-koks** *m* furnace coke, run-of-the-oven coke, metallurgical coke, large-sized coke **-kraftwerk** *n* superpower station

Großkreis *m* great circle **-abweichung** *f* great-circle deviation **-bänderfallschirm** *m* spherical ribbon parachute **-entfernung** *f* great-circle distance **-richtung** *f* great-circle direction or course

Groß-lagertanks *pl* carload storage tanks **-lautsprecher** *m* power loud-speaker, public-address loud-speaker **-lautsprecheranlage** *f* public-address system **-leistungsanode** *f* power anode **-leistungsröhre** *f* high-power (vacuum) tube, power valve or tube **-lieferung** *f* bulk delivery **-lückig** open-grained **-luke** *f* main hatch **-maschig** large-meshed **-maßstäblich** large-scale **-molekulare Stoffe** macromolecules **-motorig** high-powered **-mars** *m* main top

Groß-oberflächenplatte *f* Planté-type plate **-ofen** *m* large-sized furnace **-orientierung** *f* orientation by large landmarks **-projektion** *f* large-picture projection **-rad** *n* greater wheel (in gears) **-raum** *m* empire, area of self-sufficiency, large area **-raumgebiet** *n* metropolitan area **-raumleuchte** *f* general ligthing **-raumwagen** *m* large capacity car **-regler** *m* highly-developed controller **-reihenfertigung** *f* large-scale or high-rate series production **-royal** *n* main royal **-rundfunksender** *m* high-power broadcast transmitter, high-power broadcasting station **-rüst** *f* main chains or channels

Groß-schallübertragungsanlage *f* public-address loud-speaker system, announser loud-speaker system **-schaufelradbagger** giant bucket wheel excavator **-scheinanlage** *f* large dummy installation **-schlächterei** *f* wholesale butchery **-schreibung** *f* capitalisation **-segler** *m* large or heavy glider **-sender** *m* high-power transmitter

Groß-serie *f* mass production **-serienbau** *m* large-scale series production **-serienanfertigung** *f* large-scale production, quantity production **-spiel** *n* maximum clearance **-stadtgebiet** *n* metropolitan area **-stapelanleger** *n* high pile combination stream **-stapelausleger** *m* extension delivery **-station** *f* long-distance station **-struktur** *f* coarse or gross structure, macro-structure

größt maximum, maximal **-e Geschwindigkeit** greatest speed **-e Höhe** greatest altitude

Großteil *n* bulky part

Größt-geschwindigkeit *f* maximum speed **-maß** *n* high limit, greatest (maximum) value, dimension size **-maßlehre** *f* high-limit gauge **-möglich** the best or the greatest possible **-moment** *n* maximum moment **-spiel** *n* maximum clearance

großstückig lumpy, large-sized, in large pieces

Größtübermaß *n* maximum interference

Großversuchsmaßstab *m* pilot plant scale

Größtwert *m* maximal value, crest value

Groß-umfangkopie *f* wide-range print **-verkauf** *m* wholesale **-vernebelung** *f* extensive smoke screen, large-area screening **-verstärkerröhre** *f* power-amplifier valve or tube **-versuch** *m* large-scale experiment or test **-wetterlage** *f* general meteorological situation **-winkelkorngrenzen** *pl* large-angle grain boundary **-wirtschaftsraum** *m* economic empire **-zahlforschung** *f* frequency research, statistics **-zahluntersuchungen** *pl* research of the probability of large groups (statistics) **-zellig** large-celled **-zentrale** *f* superstation (elec.)

Groteskschrift *f* ornamental type

Groveelement *n* Grove cell

Grubber *m* cultivator **-egge** *f* plow harrow **-sämaschine** *f* drill-grubber plow

Grübchen *n* small hole or opening, pit (of surfaces) ~ (Narben) **im Unterbau** galling (aviation)

Grübchen-bildung *f* pitting, formation of pits **-korrosion** *f* pitting

Grube *f* mine, pit, quarry, cavity, hole, well, excavation, groove (cylinder) ~ **zur Reparatur** grease (inspection) pit **eine ~ aufgeben** (auflassen, stillegen) to abandon a mine **eine ~ aufnehmen** to survey a mine **eine ~ bauen** to start a mine **eine ~ unter Wasser setzen** to flood a mine

Gruben-abbau *m* starting of a mine **-abfall** *m* mine waste **-anlage** *f* mine **-anteil** *m* share in a mine **-apparat** *m* miners' telephone station **-aufseher** *m* bottom captain, inspector **-aufsichtsbeamter** *m* inspector **-ausbau** *m* support of mines, pit arch

Grubenbahn *f* mine tramway, underground line **-fahrschalter** *m* controller for mining railway

Gruben-bau *m* mining, underground working or winning, workings **-baubogen** *m* pit arches **-beile** *pl* miners' axes **-betrieb** *m* underground pit mining **-bewetterung** *f* ventilation of mines **-bild** *n* map of mine **-bohrer** *m* mining drill **-brand** *m* mine fire, underground fire, pit fire

Gruben-direktor *m* manager **-eigner** *m* mine owner **-erz** *n* ore rough from the mine **-explosion** *f* (ausgedehnte und schwere) extensive mine fire or explosion **-fahrt** *f* descent, trip **-feld** *n* claim, ground of a mine

grubenfeucht freshly mined, green **-e Kohle** run-of-the-mine coal, green coal, freshly mined coal **-er Sand** freshly quarried sand

Gruben-fördermaschine *f* mine winder **-förderwagen** *m* mining car

Grubengas *n* marsh gas, natural gas, firedamp **-analyse** *f* analysis of mine gas **-anzeiger** *m* gas alarm (min.)

Gruben-gerbung *f* pit-tannage **-halde** *f* burrow **-haushalt** *m* economics of mine **-holz** *n* pitwood, pit prop **-holzausbau** *m* wooden support **-holzbock** *m* pine borer **-hölzer** *n pl* mine props **-hund** *m* miner's truck **-kabelwinde** *f* mining hoist **-kies** *m* pit gravel **-klein** *n* mine slack **-kleinwäsche** *f* mine-smalls separating house

Gruben-lampe *f* miner's lamp, hand lamp **-lampengläser** *pl* miners' safety-lamp glasses **-licht** *n* miner's lamp **-lokomotive** *f* mine locomotive **-maß** *n* concession of mine **-mauerung** *f* walling in mines **-messung** *f* mine survey **-muldenkipper** *m* trough tip wagon for mines **-nivellierlatte** *f* mine-leveling staff **-pächter** *m* charter master **-pumpe** *f* mine pump **-räume** *pl* mine openings

Gruben-rechnung *f* account of the mine **-rechnungsführer** *m* mining accountant **-register** *n* accounting book **-rettungsstation** *f* pit lifesaving station **-riß** *m* map of mine **-rost** *m* grizzly **-sand** *m* pit sand **-silo** *m* pit silo **-stempel** *m* mine prop **-tür** *f* mine door **-verkohlung** *f* pit burning, charring or charcoal burning in pits **-verschalung** *f* mine tubbing

Grubenvorrichtungs- und Ausrichtungsarbeiten *pl* dead works

Gruben-wagen *m* mine car, pit wagon, cart, truck, tub **-wasser** *n* pit water, mine water

-wecker *m* mining bell **-weite** *f* opening of the mine shaft **-wetter** *n* mine damp **-widerstand** *m* mine resistance **-zimmerung** *f* (vollständige) set of timbers

Grude *f* hot ashes, coke breeze (from lignite, tar), lignitic carbonization coke **-koks** *m* semicoke residue of partly carbonized lignite, small coke of lignite

Grummetstropp *m* grommet

grün green **~ fassen** to rack green **-es Holz** green wood **-er Kern** green-sand core, green core **-e Schnittlinienzone** green zone of intersection **-er Tisch** (slang) red tape

Grünablauf *m* green sirup

Grün-auszug *m* green record **-bleierz** *n* green-lead ore, green pyromorphite, mimetite

Grund *m* (Erdboden) soil; (Fundament) foundation; (Farbe) ground; (Grundierung) priming coat; (Ursache) cause, occasion, motive; (Beweis) argument; reason, base, terrain, basis, fundamental, root, whiting, background, sediment, estate **den ~ abloten** to examine or to sound the ground **auf den ~ laufen** to run aground **auf dem ~ des Meeres liegen** to lie at the bottom of the sea **der ~ ist unterspült** the foundation is undermined or blown up by water **auf ~** on the basis of **erkennbarer ~** obvious reason **von ~ auf** from the beginning, radically **im Grunde genommen** basically or fundamentally speaking, as a matter of principle

Grundablaß *m* bottom-discharge conduit, low-level outlet, sluice **-schütz** *n* bottom outlet sluice

Grund-ablösung *f* expropriation **-anker** *m* ground anchor **-anstrich** *m* prime or priming coat, flat coat, shop coat **-ausbildung** *f* basic training **-ausführung** *f* basic model or design **-ausrichtung** *f* ground layout **-bahndämpfung** *f* basic path attenuation **-balken** *m* ground beam or timber, sill **-band** *n* fundemental band

Grundbau *m* foundation structure, foundation engineering, foundation or base, basement **-rahmen** *m* foundation frame

Grund-bedeutung *f* primary meaning **-begriff** *m* basic concept, (basic) principle, fundamental principle **-bedingung** *f* primary condition **-belastung** *f* essential load **-beleuchtung** *f* priming illumination **-besitz** *m* land **-besitzer** *m* landholder, owner **-bestandteil eines Gemisches** base or vehicle of a mixture **-blatt** *n* base sheet (tables of data for rapid computation) **-bohrer** *m* bottoming tap

Grundbolzen *m* screw lag **~ der Verankerung** anchor bolt

Grundbrett *n* base(board)

Grundbruch *m* foundation failure, movement of soil **-untersuchung** *f* soil-failure investigation, pulling test

Grund-buch *n* register of land ownership **-büchse** *f* bottom bush, base bushing **-buchwesen** *n* recording of deeds **-dienstbarkeit** *f* easement, security of tenure **-drehzahl** *f* primary speed **-dreieck** *n* base triangle **-dünung** *f* ground swell **-durchschnitt** *m* (Querschnitt) **des Flügels** root section (aviation) **-ebene** *f* datum plane or level

Grund-eigenschaft *f* fundamental or basic property **-eigentum** *n* real estate **-eigentümer** *m* landowner **-einheit** *f* fundamental unit **-eis** *n* ground ice, anchor ice **-elektrode** *f* base electrode **-empfang** *m* ground reception

gründen to lay foundation, found, establish, ground

Grund-energiequelle *f* basic power source **-entstörung** *f* basic interference suppression **-entwurf** *m* basic design, ground plan, rough sketch, first draft

Gründer *m* promoter, founder

Grund-erwerb *m* ground acquisition **-exzenter** *n* main eccentric **-faden** *m* base thread or cone **-farbe** *f* basic hue or color, priming color, flat color, primary or ground color **-feuchtigkeit** *f* soil moisture **-figur** *f* basic figure, figure in horizontal plane (aerobatics) **-firnis** *m* first-coat or ground varnish **-fläche** *f* (surface) area, floor space, foundation plate, base, surface (earth), basis, basal plane or surface **-flächen** *pl* two parallel surfaces of a cube **-flächenbedarf** *m* space required (for plant) **-flüssigkeit** *f* suspending liquid

Grund-forderung *f* basic consideration **-form** *f* primary, fundamental, basic or root form **-formal** *f* fundamental formula **-forschung** *f* basic research **-frequenz** *f* fundamental frequency **-gebiet** *n* basic region **-gebühr** *f* basic rate **-gebührentarif** *m* two-part tariff **-gedanke** *m* fundamental concept or idea

Grund-gefüge *n* structure, matrix **-gehalt** *n* base pay **-geräusch** *n* background noise **-gerinne** *n* ground sluice **-geschwindigkeit** *f* ground speed **-gesetz** *n* fundamental law, law (phys.), basic principle **-gestein** *n* primitive rock **-gestell** *n* base, mount, frame **-gewebe** *n* wavy groundmass

Grund-gitterabsorption *f* fundamental lattice absorption **-gleichung** *f* fundamental or basic equation **-graben** *m* foundation ditch **-größen** *pl* fundamental quantities **-gurt** *m* inner fabric strip **-harmonische** *f* fundamental frequency **-helligkeit** *f* brightness of background, background, mean or average shading component, direct-current component **-helligkeitsregler** *m* background (brightness) control **-hieb** *m* first cut (files) **-hobel** *m* base plane

Grundier-anstrich *m* prime coat, priming coat, flat coat **-bürste** *f* bottoming brush

grundieren to prime, stop, ground

Grundierer *m* plain color, sizer

Grundier-farbe *f* flat paint, flat color, first coat of paint **-firnis** *m* ground varnish **-lack** *m* filler **-schicht** *f* priming coat **-überzug** *m* priming coat

Grundierung *f* priming

Grundierungsmittel *n* undercoat, surfacer

Grund-kapital *n* stock **-kegel** *m* pitch cone **-kenntnis** *f* basic knowledge **-kohle** *f* bottom coal **-komponente** *f* fundamental component **-körper** *m* foundation, fundamental or parent substance **-kraftwerk** *n* base-load power station **-kreis** *m* base circle, pitch circle (applied to pinions) **-kreisteilung** *f* base circle pitch **-kurs** *m* true course, head-on course **-lack** *m* base lacquer coat, filler **-ladung** *f* base charge (explosives), **-lage** *f* basis, underlying principle, fundamental, datum, foundation, base **-lagen-**

forschung *f* basic research

Grundlager *n* main bearing **-balken** *m* bedplate beam **-stühle** *pl* main-bearing support

Grund-länge *f* basic length **-last der Förderleistung** *f* base load of production **-lastbetrieb** *m* base-load operation **-läufe** *pl* culverts arranged in the floor **-lawine** *f* avalanche of earth, landslide

grundlegend fundamental **-e Bauanforderung** basic design requirements **-e Identität** basic identity **konstruktiv -es Motormuster** basic engine type **-e Sätze** basic theorems

Grundlehre *f* theory

Grundlinie *f* base (line), outline, datum line, point of reference, horizontal projection of the base

Grundloch *n* bottom hole **~ mit Innengewinde** tapped blind hole

Grund-lohn *m* base rate **-los** unfounded, baseless **-maß** *n* standard of measurement **-masse** *f* groundmass, matrix, magma base, filler (for lacquers) **-material** *n* base metal, matrix, elementary or base material, ground material, host crystal (cryst.) **-mauer** *f* tower skirt, width of the weir at the base, foundation wall, foundation of masonry **-mauerwerk** *n* foundation wall **-messer** *pl* shell bars **-metall** *n* basic or base metal

Grund-mine *f* ground mine, controlled or observation mine **-mischung** *f* master batch **-moränenlehm** *m* boulder clay **-mörtel** *m* concrete **-nachbildung** *f* basic network **-nebel** *m* ground fog **-netz** *n* trawl

Grundniveau *n* background level (TV) **~ der Beleuchtung** *f* bias lighting

Grund-norm *f* fundamental standard **-organisation** *f* ground organization **-pacht** *f* ground rent **-papier** *n* body paper (of condensers) **-partikel** *n* basic particle **-pegel** *m* settlement gauge **-periodenzahl** *f* fundamental frequency **-pfahl** *m* pile of substructure, bridge or foundation pile **-pfählung** *f* foundation piling **-pfand** *n* mortgage **-pfeiler** *m* bottom pillar, foundation plate **-plan** *m* plot, plan

Grundplatte *f* base plate, bearing plate, base slab, soleplate, lobe plate, subbase, chassis, mounting plate, base **~ der Weiche** switch plate **gemeinsame ~** common base

Grundplattenlager *n* bearing of bedplate

Grund-postulat *n* fundamental postulate **-potential** *n* basic potential **-prämie** *f* basic rate of premium **-preis** *m* base price, cost of land, prime cost (at works) **-prinzip** basic pattern **-proben** *pl* bottom samples **-prozeß** *m* random process **-punkt** *m* cardinal point (of a lens)

Grund-rahmen *m* mount base **-rauschen** *n* background noise **-reaktion** *f* essential reaction **-regel** *f* basic principle **-register** *n* main file **-reibahle** *f* rose reamer **-resonanz** *f* fundamental resonance **-richtung** *f* base-line direction, zero line

Grundrichtungs-linie *f* base line (artil.) **-punkt** *m* base point (artil.), reference point, zero point **-winkel** *m* base angle (gun.)

Grundring *m* stationary mounting ring

Grundriß *m* design, sketch, outline, ground or floor plan, cross section, horizontal projection **im ~** in plan form **polygonaler ~** polygonal trace or front

Grundriß-ansicht *f* plan view, top view (aviation) **-aufnahme** *f* planimetric survey **-form** *f* plan form **-gestalt** *f* plan form **-karte** *f* planimetric map **-lage** *f* planimetric position **-lineal** *n* (Stereoautograph) planimetric arm **-plan** *m* layout plan, general plan of arrangement **-skizze** *f* area sketch (aviation)

Grundsatz *m* principle, axiom **als ~ aufstellen** to lay down as principle **~ der geringsten Formveränderung** principle of least work

Grundsätze für die Herstellung der Verbindungen switching principles

grundsätzlich fundamental, rudimentary

Grund-schaltbild *n* basic-circuit diagram **-schaltung** *f* skeleton diagram, basic circuit, circuit element **-scheitelbrechwert** *m* primary vertex refraction **-schema** *n* (einer Schaltung) basic circuit diagram

Grundschicht *f* footing of walls, primary or fundamental layer **vorspringende ~** offset, setoff, projecting base

Grund-schieber *m* distributing slide valve **-schiene** *f* ground guide bar **-schleier** *m* inherent fog, ground fog

Grundschleifen *n* ground finishing **-flug** *m* ground loop

Grund-schrägungswinkel *m* base spiral angle **-schrift** *f* body fount **-schweißstelle** *f* basic weld **-schwelle** *f* base sill (for maintaining elevation of channel bed), cap, dam on bed of river, ground sill **-schwingung** *f* fundamental oscillation (frequency), first harmonic, fundamental period **-see** *f* undertow, ground swell, ground sea **-seife** *f* raw soap necessary for making powdered soap

Grund-signal *n* base signal **-sohle** *f* bottom sill, foundation base **-sonde** *f* main housing **-spektrum** *n* persistent spectrum **-spiel** *n* root clearance **-steigung** *f* basic pitch **-stein** *m* foundation stone, cornerstone, lower stone (in mills), pyrite (min.)

Grundstellung *f* normal position, attention position (mil.) **~** (Kartierungsgerät) zero setting (plotting apparatus) **in die ~ zurückführen** (zurückkehren) to return to normal

Grund-steuer *f* land tax **-stimmen** *pl* foundation stops (organ) **-stock** *m* foundation, matrix, basis, fund **-stoff** *m* element, raw material, base, stuff **-stollen** *m* deep adit **-straffer** *m* drawsheet

Grundstrecke *f* deep level (oil drilling), straight-line course (geol.) **obere ~** top level (min.) **untere ~** bottom level (min.)

Grund-streckenpfeiler *m* pillar of ground **-stromkreis** *m* fundamental circuit, (back)ground noise-reduction circuit, suppression or silencing circuit **-strömung der Flut** undertow, bottom or undercurrent

Grundstück *n* parcel of land, lot, site, plot, premises **anliegendes ~** adjacent land

Grund-taster *m* sounding device, sounding rod **-teil** *m* element, cell, battery, part **-teilchen** *n* smallest particle, fundamental particle, atom **-toleranz** *f* fundamental tolerance **-toleranzenreihe** *f* fundamental tolerance group **-ton** *m* fundamental tone or note, pitch, keynote, background (noise) **-translationsvektor** *m* unit-cell vector **-tuch** *n* ground panel **-überholung** *f* shop overhaul, general overhauling **-umsatz** *m* basal metabolism

Grund- und Seitenriß *m* plan and side elevation

Grund- und Sohlenstrecke *f* gallery

Gründung *f* foundation, first coat, priming, establishment, institution, footing, groundwork **~ mit Fangdämmen** foundation between crib cofferdams **~ mit Preßluft** pneumatic process of foundation **~ auf Steinschüttung** random stone foundation, riprap foundation

Gründungs-ausrüstung *f* foundation equipment **-kapital** *n* initial capital **-kosten** *pl* promotion money or expenses **-pfähle** *pl* foundation piles **-sohle** *f* bearing area, foundation level **-technik** *f* foundation practice **-tiefe** *f* foundation depth **-verfahren** *n* foundation operation

Grund-ventil *n* foot valve **-verbesserung** *f* improvement of the ground **-verfestigung** *f* basic work-hardening **-versuche** *m pl* fundamental experiments **-verstärker** *m* primary amplifier (radio) **-verteiler** *m* ground distributor **-waage** *f* level (instrument)

Grundwasser *n* ground water, underground water, water table, phreatic water **-abdichtung** *f* underground-water packing **-absenkung** *f* lowering of ground water (well-point method), lowering of the water table **-bewegung** *f* ground-water movement **-höhe** *f* sub-soil water level **-karte** *f* subsoil-water map **-spiegel** *m* ground-water level or table, phreatic nappe, water table gradient **-stand** *m* ground-water level **-strom** *m* subterranean current **-versenkung** *f* lowering of the water table

Grund-wechselräder *pl* basic change gears **-wehr** *n* submerged weir, low weir, dam on bed of river **-welle** *f* fundamental wave (length), ground wave, fundamental oscillation **-wellenfrequenz** *f* carrier (wave) frequency **-wellenlänge** *f* fundamental wave length

Grundwerk *n* beater plate, bedplate **-kasten** *m* bedplate box, den (paper mfg.) **-schiene** *f* fly bar, roll bar **-stoff** *m* base metal

Grund-wert *m* line constant, basic value **-wirkung** *f* ground cushion **-zahl** *f* cardinal number, unit, prime number (math.), reference-point reading, zero, basic uncorrected firing-table figure **-zahlen** *pl* basic data **-zehnter** *m* royalty tenth **-ziffer** *f* basic rate **-zug** *m* outline, characteristic, feature, basic trait **-zustand** *m* original state (of an atom)

grüne Welle progressive control of traffic lights

Grün-ebenholz *n* green ebony **-eisenerde** *f*, **-eisenstein** *m* dufrenite **-empfindlich** green-sensitive **-erde** *f* green earth, celadonite, glauconite **-fäule** *f* green rot **-futter-Häcksler** *m* ensilage cutter **-gewicht** *n* green weight **-kalk** *m* refuse gas lime **-kernformverfahren** *n* green core-making

grünlich greenish

Grün-sand *m* greensand **-schlick** *m* green mud **-seife** *f* soap base **-span** *m* verdigris **-spanessig** *m* acetic acid, spirit of verdigris **-stein** *m* greenstone, diorite **-stich** *m* greenish tint

Grünstrahlsystem (Elektronenstrahlsystem für grün leuchtende Teile des Bildschirms) green electron gun (TV)

Grünstreifen *m* (Straße) landscape strip, grassy median strip

Gruppe *f* section, squad, group, category, class, pursuit squadron, field (comput), digit, column, department **angeregte ~** exciton (in dielectric breakdown)

Gruppen-abschnitt *m* group section **-akkord** *m* group piece work **-antrieb** *m* series drive, group drive **-anzeigegang** *m* group indication cycle **-arbeit** *f* (am Nebenschrank) team work **-bandfilter** *n* group band filter **-bewußtsein** *n* group consciousness **-blinkfeuer** *n* group occulting light **-blitz** *m* grouped flashes **-blitzfeuer** *n* group flashing light **-bohrmaschine** *f* gang drill

Gruppen-diffusionsverfahren *n* group-diffusion method **-drehblinkfeuer** *n* group flashing light **-erscheinungen** *pl* group phenomena (cryst.) **-faktor** *m* space factor **-flugformen** *pl* pursuit-squadron flying formations, group formations **-folge** *f* rate of fire, salvo fire **-formation** *f* group formation **-fräser** *m* gang cutters, gang-type milling cutters **-frequenz** *f* group frequency, wave-train frequency, sparking frequency

Gruppen-geschwindigkeit *f* envelope velocity, group velocity, group retardation **-getriebe** *n* auxiliary range or transmission **-keil** *m* bombardment-group wedge, pursuit-squadron wedge, **-kettenführer** *m* squadron flight leader **-kontrolle** *f* automatic control **-kopplungslade** *f* group-combining drawer

Gruppenlaufzeit *f* phase (group) velocity **-ausgleich** *m* group delay equalization (elec.) **-messung** *f* group-delay measurement **-meter** group-delay meter **-verlauf** *m* group delay variation

Gruppen-leitsignal *n* pilot signal **-leitung** *f* group line (conductor) **-meldezeichen** *n* pilot indicator, pilot signal **-modulationsgeräte** *pl* group translating equipment **-montage** *f* group assembly **-notierungen** *pl* group posted prices **-relais für gerade** (ungerade) **Einer** (G.U.) group relay for the numbers with even (odd) unit digits **-schalter** *m* group switch

Gruppenschaltung *f* series-parallel arrangement of cells, series of parallel connections **~ der Verbindungsleitungen** section of multiple

Gruppen-schlüssel *m* group key **-schmierung** *f* group oiling system **-sortierung** *f* block sorting **-sperrung** *f* group locking **-stanze** *f* cluster attachment **-stellensystem** *n* party-line system (teleph.) **-sucher** *m* group detector

Gruppenteilung der Verbindungsleitungen split-trunk group (available only to certain outward positions)

gruppentheoretische Behandlung group theoretical treatment

Gruppen-theorie *f* group theory (math.) **-übergangspunkt** *m* group transfer point **-umschalter** *m* semiautomatic switch **-umsetzer** *m* group modulator **-verbindung** *f* connection in groups, group link **-verstärker** *m* group amplifier **-verstärkerlade** *f* group-repeater drawer **-verteiler** *m* group distribution frame **-verteilung** *f* group allocation **-wahl** *f* group selection

Gruppenwähler *m* (group) selector, intermediate

selector, frequency group-selector plug ~ (Keith-Vorwähler) master switch, Keith master switch ~ **mit Stromstoßübertrager** selector repeater **I. ~ in sechsstelligen Netzen** code selector, code switch **II., III., IV. ~**, tandem selector, numerical switch

Gruppen-wählerunteramt *n* group selector satellite exchange **-wechsel** *m* control change

gruppenweise in sections, in squads, by groups **-r Antrieb** group drive

Gruppen-winkel *m* group column of squadron V's (aviation) **-zahl** *f* group count

gruppieren to group (motors, cells, pipes) **Transformatoren ~** to bank transformers **übersichtlich ~** to arrange clearly

Gruppierung *f* grouping, arrangement, layout, trunking arrangement (tel.) **~ von Leitungen** arrangement of wires on pole lines **~ im Parallelogramm** parallel wiring **~ im Rechteck** rectangular wiring **waagerechte ~** straight wiring

Gruppierungsbild für Ortsfernsprechnetze pole diagram in local telephone plants

Grus *m* slack, breeze, fines, culm, fine gravel (coal slack), dross **-kohle** *f* dross (of coal, coke), slack coal, screened coal **-koks** *m* coke breeze, dross (of coal, coke)

Grützmühle *f* semolina, grits, or groats mill

Guajak *n* guaiac **-harz** *n* guaiacum resin, gum guaiac **-holz** *n* lignum vitae

Guajakol *n* guaiacol

Guck-fenster *n* window of a meter or instrument **-kasten** *m* camera obscura **-loch** *n* observation hole, peephole, bezel (in radio set panel)

Guillaume-Stahl *m* invar steel

Guillochieren *n* guilloshing

Guillochiermaschine *f* rose engine

Guillotineverschluß *m* drop shutter (phot.)

Guldinsche Regel Guldin's rule (math.)

Güldisch *n* doré silver

Gulstadrelais *n* vibration relay, Gulstad relay

gültig legal, valid, current **~ sein** to hold true, be valid, be in force

Gültigkeit *f* legality, validity, currency **~ eines Patentes anfechten** to challenge validity of a patent **Beweis, der der ~ eines Patentes Abbruch tut** evidence impeaching or prejudicial to validity of a patent

Gültigkeitsbereich *m* region of validity

Gültigkeitsdauer *f* period of validity **~ einer Gesprächsanmeldung** period during which call is active **~ einer Voranmeldung** period of validity of a prearranged call

Gültigkeits-erklärung *f* validation **-grenzen** *pl* limits of validity

Gumbildung *f* gumming

Gummi *m, n* rubber, gum, caoutchouc, vulcanized rubber **geräuchertes ~ in Blättern** smoked sheet rubber

Gummi-abdichtung *f* rubber joint, washer **-abfederung** *f* rubber shock absorber **-absatz** *m* rubber heel **-abschlußkabel** *n* bridle wire or cable **-ader** *f* vulcanized-rubber cable, rubber-covered or -insulated wire **-aderleitung** *f* rubber coated multicore line or cable **-aderschnur** *f* rubber-insulated cord **-andruckpresse** *f* proofing press for rubber plates **-andruckrolle** *f* rubber-tired pressure or pad roll (motion pictures) **-arabikum** *n* gum arabic **-ärmel** *m* rubber sleeve

gummiartig gummous, gummy **-es Harz** gummy resin, rubber latex

Gummi-auskleidung *f* rubber lining **-bahn** *f* rubber coating (sheet) **-ball** *m* rubber ball or bulb **-ballon** *m* rubber balloon **-band** *n* rubber (ed) tape, rubber band, elastic, code for an approach formula **-bandagiert** rubber-tired **-bandtransporteur** *m* rubber-belt conveyer **-behälter** *m* rubber case **-belag** *m* rubber covering **-bereift** rubber tired **-bereifung** *f* rubber tires **-bezug** *m* bronze plating or coating, rubber coating

Gummi-bleikabel *n* lead-covered rubber cable **-bleispat** *m* plumbogummite **-bodenbelag** *m* rubber flooring **-boot** *n* rubber boat **-bremsbelag** *m* rubber brake-lining **-puffer** *m* rubber buffer, rubber washer **-chromverfahren** *n* bichromated gum process **-decke** *f* rubber mat **-dichtung** *f* rubber gasket, rubber packing **-dichtungsring** *m* rubber packing ring **-draht** *m* vulcanized-rubber wire, rubber-covered or insulated wire

Gummidruck *m* offset printing **-ball** *m* rubber bulb **-farben** *pl* offset printing colors **-klischee** *n* rubber printing plate (stereo) **-kork** *m* rubber printing cork **-lack** *m* gum printing varnish **-maschine** *f* offset machine **-papier** *n* offset cartridge paper **-presse** *f* offset printing press **-walze** *f* offset roller

Gummi-durchführung *f* rubber insulator **-einlage** *f* rubber packing or core, rubber lining **-einsatzstück** *n* rubber insert **-elastikum** *n* caoutchouc, rubber, elastic gum **-elastizität** *f* rubber elasticity

gummieren to rubberize **Seide ~** to gum silk

Gummieren *n* rubberizing

Gummierrohpapier *n* gummed paper base

Gummiersatzstoff *m* rubber substitute

gummiert rubberized, gummed, adhesive, rubber covered

Gummier- und Beklebemaschine *f* glueing and labeling machine

Gummierung *f* skimming, rubberizing, rubber coating, gumming

Gummi-erz *n* pitchblende **-erzeugnis** *n* rubber product **-faden** *m* rubber strip, elastic thread **-federbein** *n* rubber shock-absorber strut **-federer** *m* rubber shock absorber **-federlager** *n* rubber spring shackle **-federung** *f* rubber suspension **-flecken** *m* rubber patch **-gelagert** rubber cushioned **-geleisekette** *f* rubber track **-gleitschutzreifen** *m* rubber-studded tire **-gewebe** *n* rubberized fabric **-gewebekupplung** *f* rubber fabric clutch

Gummi-haken *m* rubber (fixing) hook **-haltig** containing gum, gummy **-hammer** *m* rubber mallet **-handwalze** *f* rubber hand roller **-handschuh** *m* insulating glove, rubber glove **-harz** *n* gum resin **-haut** *f* rubber cover **-hülle** *f* rubber cover, rubber envelope **-hülse** *f* rubber sleeve

Gummi-industrie *f* rubber industry **-instandsetzungsmittel** *n* rubber(-tire) repair equipment **-isolation** *f* rubber insulation **-isolationsbedarf** *m* rubber insulating material **-isolator** *m* rubber insulator **-isoliert** rubber-insulated, rubber-covered **-isolierung** *f* rubber insulation

Gummi-kabel *n* rubber-insulated cable or wire **-kalander** *m* rubber calender **-keilriemen** *m* rubber V-belt **-kette** *n* rubber track **-kissen** *n* rubber pad **-klischee** *n* rubber stereo, rubber block **-kneter** *m* dough mill **-knüppel** *m* rubber truncheon or club **-konus des Füllventils** rubber filling valve **-kopie** *f* gum copy **-kordel** *n* round elastic **-kratzer** *m* rubber scraper

Gummi-lack *m* gum-lac, rubber varnish **-lager** *n* silent bloc **-lasche** *f* rubber gasket **-leinenmuffe** *f* rubber canvas hose or sleeve **-linse** *f* zoom lens (film) **-litzenfederung** *f* rubber cord springing **-lösung** *f* rubber cement, rubber solution **-lösungsbenzin** *n* benzene used as rubber solvent **-manschette** *f* rubber sleeve **-mantel** *m* mackintosh, rubber coat **-maske** *f* respirator made of rubber, rubber gas mask **-matte** *f* rubber mat

Gummimechanismus, eisentfernender ~ overshoes (aviation)

Gummi-membrane *f* rubber membrane or diaphragm **-membrankammer** *f* rubber diaphragm chamber **-metallelement** *n* vibration mount, antivibration unit **-milchsaft** *m* rubber latex **-mitnehmer** *m* rubber carrying disc

Gummimotor *m* rubber motor ~ **aufziehen** to wind the rubber motor ~ **mit Getriebe** geared rubber motor ~ **Modell** rubber-driven model

Gummi-muffe *f* rubber sleeve or hose, rubber connection **-mundstück** *n* rubber mouthpiece **-muschel** *f* rubber earpiece or eyepiece **-norm** *f* rubber standard **-packung** *f* rubber packing **-pflaster** *n* rubber patch **-pfropfen** *m* rubber stopper **-plättchen** *n* rubber pad **-platte** *f* rubber plate **-polster** *n* rubber cushion or block **-polsterunterlage** rubber cushioning pad **-preßformartikel** *m* pressed-rubber article **-profilschnüre** *pl* sectional strandrubber

Gummipuffer *m* rubber buffer ~ **der Feder** spring rebound clip **auf Gummipuffern montiert** rubber-buffer-mounted

Gummi-quetscher *m* squeegee **-rad** *n* rubber-tired wheel **-radantrieb** *m* rim drive **-raupe** *f* rubber (caterpillar) track **-regenerat** *n* regenerated rubber **-reifen** *m* rubber tire **-riemen** *m* rubber belt or belting **-ring** *m* lamp-globe cushion, rubber band **-ringdichtung** *f* rubber-ring packing or gasket **-rohr** *n* rubber tube **-schaum** *m* sponge rubber **-scheibe** *f* rubber disc

Gummischicht *f* rubber film **dünne** ~ skim (residual latex serum obtained on centrifugation of latex)

Gummischlauch *m* rubber tubing, hose, or tube **dünner** ~ thin rubber tubing, bicycle-valve tubing

Gummischlauchboot *n* rubber dinghy **aufblasbares** ~ inflatable rubber dinghy

Gummischlauch-leitung *f* rubber-tube wiring, tough-rubber-sheated cable **-muffe** *f* rubber-hose connection

Gummi-schleim *m* mucilage of gum arabic **-schnur** *f* elastic cord **-schuhe** *f* rubber boots, galoshes, rubbers **-schutzkappe** *f* rubber cap **-schwamm** *m* rubber sponge **-seil** *n* shock cord, elastic cable, rubber cord **-seilstart** *m* rubber-cord start (aviation), launch by an elastic cable, catapult launching **-spat** *m* plumbogummite **-spreizdorn** *m* expandable rubber arbor **-startseil** *n* launching elastic **-stein** *m* hyalite **-stempel** *m* rubber stamp **-stiefel** *m pl* rubber boots

Gummi-stoff *m* rubberized material **-stoffmuffe** *f* rubber sleeve **-stopfen** *m* rubber plug or stopper **-stoßdämpfer** *m*, **-stoßfänger** *m* rubber shock absorber **-torsionsfederung** *f* rubber torsion suspension **-tragant** *m* gum dragon, tragacanth **-transportband** *n* rubber apron **-treibriemen** *m* rubber belt **-tuch** *n* rubber blanket **-tülle** *f* rubber ferrule, rubber socket

Gummi-überschuhe *pl* rubber overshoes, rubber galoshes **überzug** *m* rubber tread **-unterlage** *f* insulating rubber mat, rubber washer or base **-verdickung** *f* gum thickening **-verreibwalze** *m* rubber-covered distributor roller **-walze** *f* rubber roller **-walzendruck** *m* rubber roller printing **-walzendruckmaschine** *f* offset-printing machine **-waren** *pl* rubber goods **-wäsche** *f* India-rubber linen

Gummiweb- und -wirkwaren *pl* rubber-woven goods

Gummi-wischer *m* squeegee **-zug** *m* strip of elastic, rubber webbing (aviation) **-zeugweber** *m* elastic-band weaver **-zucker** *m* arabinose **-zwischenlage** *f* rubber lining

günstig favorable, propitious, advantageous **in -eres Licht stellen** to enhance **-st** optimum, most favorable

Gur *f* guhr

Gurgel *f* throat

Gurt *m* belt, strap, chord (of truss or girder), girdle, flange, girth **-abzug** *m* belt-type capstan **-aufhängung** *f* belt suspension **-band** *n* belt, web, webbing, belt strap or band **-becherwerk** *n* band elevator **-breite** *f* width of flange **-brett** *n* girth **-dicke** *f* flange thickness

Gürtel *m* belt, cordon, zone, girdle, band **-bahn** *f* circulator or belt railroad

Gurtelevator *m* belt elevator

Gürtel-festung *f* fortress covered by outer belt of fortifications **-isolation** *f* belted insulation **-kabel** *n* belted insulation cable **-leuchte** *f* cylindric optical apparatus **-linse** *f* drum lens **-panzer** *m* belt armor **-platte** *f* saddle plate (locomotive boiler) **-radwalze** *f* tamping roller **-ring** *m* harness or belt ring

gürten to fill ammunition belts, gird, girdle

Gurt-förderband *n*, **-förderer** *m* belt or band conveyer, elevator belt **-füller** *m* belt-filling or belt-loading machine, link-loading machine **-füllmaschine** *f* belt-filling machine **-geschwindigkeit** *f* belt speed **-hebel** *m* belt-holding pawl, belt-feed guide **-holz** *n* waling **-ladung** *f* belt feed **-lasche** *f* girder fishplate **-matte** *f* girder mat

Gurt-platte *f* flange plate or sheet, chord plate, cover plate **-scheibe** *f* belt or girth pulley **-schieber** *m* belt-feed pawl **-sitz** *m* belt seat **-stab** *m* flange member, chord member **-stifte** *pl* nails with convex heads **-strippe** *f* cinch strap **-transporteur** belt conveyer, elevator belt **-trommel** *f* bobbin, reel, belt drum

Gurtung *f* flange, chord ~ **eines Brückenträgers** boom, chord, or flange of a truss

Gurtungs-blech *n* bottom or top flange **-eisen** *n* flange iron **-lamelle** *f* flange plate or sheet **-winkel** *m* angle stiffener, flange angle

Gurt-versteifung *f* flange stiffening or strengthening **-werk** *n* (Fallschirm) parachute harness **-winkel** *m* angles of the chord **-zufuhr** *f* belt feed **-zugregler** *m* belt pull regulator

Guß *m* cast iron, cast metal, cast, casting, pouring, founding, jet, fount; (gekapselt) iron-clad **fallender ~** top casting or pouring **feuerbeständiger ~** heatproof cast iron **säurebeständiger ~** acidproof cast iron **schmiedbarer ~** malleable iron or cast iron, tempered castings **schwammiger ~** spongy cast iron **steigender ~** bottom casting or pouring, group casting **undichter ~** porous cast iron **ungetemperter ~** unannealed castings, white castings

Guß-abdruck *m* stereo **-aluminium** *n* cast aluminum **-art** *f* kind of casting **-asphalt** *m* mastic or melted asphalt **-barkeit** *f* flowability **-beton** *m* concrete, concrete sufficiently wet to flow **-blase** *f* blowhole, blister, flaw or defect in a casting **-blei** *n* cast lead

Guß-block *m* ingot **-blöckchen** *n* foundry ingot **-bock** *m* cast-iron frame **-boden** *m* cast iron core **-brechmaschine** *f* casting breaker **-bronze** *f* cast bronze **-bruch** *m* broken castings, scrap iron **-dorn** *m* casting mandrel

Gußeisen *n* pig iron, cast iron, casting, gray iron, iron casting **graues ~** gray cast iron **heiß erblasenes ~** hot-blast pig iron **hochwertiges ~** high-test or high-quality cast iron **weißes ~** malleable hard cast iron, unannealed malleable iron **~ mit Stahlzusatz** semi-steel

Gußeisen-bearbeitung *f* cast-iron working or treatment **-form** *f* chill (mold) **-formkasten** *m* flask (founding) **-kaltschweißung** *f* cast-iron welding without preheating **-muffe** *f* cast-iron sleeve **-rohr** *n* cast-iron pipe **-schrott** *m* gray-iron scrap **-sockel** *m* cast-iron base **-stößel** *m* cast iron tappet **-vorwärmer** *m* cast iron economiser **-warmschweißung** *f* cast-iron welding with pre- and postheating

gußeisern cast-iron **-er Fuß** cast-iron base **-e Leitung, -es Rohr** cast-iron pipe **-er Pfahlschuh** cast iron shoe **-e Unterlagscheibe** cast washer

Guß-erzeugung *f* production of castings, output of castings **-fähig** castable **-fehler** *m* flaw in casting **-festigkeit** *f* cast-iron strength **-flasche** *f* molding flask

Gußform *f* mold (in die casting), die **die ~ anblaken** to smoke the mold **eine ~ aufstampfen** to ram up a mold **geschlossene ~** closed sand mold

Guß-fuge *f* fin **-führung** *f* method of sparging **-gattierung** *f* cast-iron mixture **-gefüge** *n* cast structure, macrostructure **-gehäuse** *n* cast-metal case or housing, cast housing **-gekapselt** in cast iron box **-gerinne** *n* casting gutter, metal drain **-gesenk** *n* die cast **-glas** *n* cast glass

Gußhaut *f* skin (of a casting), skin of metal parts, (casting) scale **~ ablösen** to dislodge casting scale

Guß-karren *m* casting cart **-kasten** *m* casting box, cast casing **-kern** *m* core (of casting) **-körper** *m* casting **-kopf** *m* feeding head **-kran** *m* casting crane **-kruste** *f* sand skin **-lager** *n* cast-iron bearing **-legierungen** *pl* casting alloys **-leuchte** *f* cast bulkhead fitting **-loch** *n* tapping hole or funnel

Guß-magazin *n* casting stores **-masse** *f* pourable compound, dope **-matrize** *f* casting matrix **-mauerwerk** *n* filling in (brickwork) **-messing** *n* cast brass **-metall** *n* cast metal, actual cast iron, founding or casting metal **-modell** *n* casting pattern

Gußmörtel *m* concrete **-stück** *n*, **-teil** *m* concrete casting

Guß-mutter *f* casting matrix **-naht** *f* fash, cast seam, feather, fin **-narbe** *f* flaw (defect) **-pfanne** *f* ladle **-pfeife** *f* runner **-platte** *f* cast plate

Gußputz-anlage *f* cleaning-room equipment **-bürste** *f* molder's brush, casting brush

Gußputz-hammer *m* casting cleansing hammer **-schleifmaschine** *f* grinding machine for cleaning castings

Gußputztisch *m* bench for cleaning castings **~ mit Staubabsaugung** exhaust bench for cleaning castings

Gußputztrommel *f* tumbling barrel

Guß-qualität *f* quality of the castings **-rad** *n* cast wheel or rotor **-regen** *m* downpour **-rinde** *f* casting crust or skin **-ringausbau** *m* tubbing **-rinne** *f* gutter **-rohr** *n* cast(-iron) pipe **-röhre** *f* jet **-schaden** *m* flaw, defect (in casting)

Gußschale *f* mold **~ eines Steckers** socket body (cast iron)

Guß-schleifer *m* castings cleaner (scraper) **-schrott** *m* cast-iron scrap, iron, iron shot **-schweißpulver** *n* cast-welding powder **-schweißung** *f* cast-iron welding **-spachtel** *f* surfacer applied by pouring **-späne** *m pl* cast-iron splinters, borings **-spannung** *f* casting strain or stress

Gußstahl *m* cast steel, crucible steel; (Elektro) electric steel; (Tiegel) crucible steel **-blech** *n* cast-steel or ingot-steel plate **-block** *m* cast-steel ingot **-draht** *m* cast-steel wire

gußstählern cast-steel

Gußstahl-fabrikation *f* cast-steel manufacture **-glocken** *pl* cast steel bells **-herzstück** *n* cast-steel crossing or frog **-kugel** *f* cast-steel bullet **-lauf** *m* cast-steel barrel **-ring** *m* cast-steel ring **-tiegel** *m* cast-steel crucible **-vollbohrer** *m* solid cast-steel bit

Gußstein *m* sink, drain, gutter **-auslauf** *m* discharging hole, spout

Gußstruktur *f* cast-iron structure, macrostructure

Gußstück *n* casting, cast piece **nicht ausgelaufenes ~** short-run casting, misrun **verwickelt gestaltetes ~** intricate or delicate casting

Gußteil *m* casting **verdichteter ~** castings with a dense structure

Gußtrichter *m* runner head, pouring ingate, casting git or gate **~ mit tangentialem Zulauf** runner gate

Guß-versetzung *f* casting displacement **-wachs** *n* casting wax **-walze** *f* cast-iron roll **-wand** *f* cast wall **-waren** *pl* cast articles, castings **-warmschweißung** *f* welding of preheated cast iron **-warze** *f* nipple **-zapfen** *m* rising head, riser, pouring head **-zerkleinerer** *m* pick breaker **-zink** *n* cast zinc **-zylinder** *m* cast-iron cylinder

gustieren to taste, approve of

gut zerspanbar free-cutting, free-machining

Gut *n* material, stock, goods, commodity, property, possessions, rigging, shrouds (navy) **aufbereitetes ~** dressed products

Gutachten *n* (expert) opinion, survey, advice, certificate, reporting, judgment, verdict ~ **eines Sachverständigen** expert's report or opinion, examination by experts

Gut-befund *m* approval **-befunden** approved **-bringen** to write off

Gutdünken *n* opinion, estimate **nach** ~ arbitrary

Güte *f* grade, class, quality, efficiency, merit, kindness, Q-factor ~ **einer Röhre** goodness of a thermionic valve ~ (Telegraphierzeichen) definition, legibility (telegraph signal) ~ (der Röhre) figure of merit ~ **des Vakuums** degree of vacuum **Maß für die** ~ gauge of excellence **gewährleistete** ~ guaranteed quality

Güte-daten *pl* efficiency dates **-eigenschaften** *pl* quality features **-einteilung** *f* grading **-faktor** *m* factor or figure of merit, quality factor **-grad** *m* efficiency factor, coefficient of excellence, quality coefficient **-gradschaubild** *n* characteristic curve

Guteinstellehre *f* "go" setting gauge

Güte-klasse *f* grade, sort **-kriterium** *n* criterion of control effectiveness **-kurve** *f* figure-of-merit curve **-maß** *n* gauge of excellence, quality gauge **-maßstab** *m* quality criterion **-prüfung** *f* soundness test

Güter *pl* goods, freight ~ **in Ballen** bale goods

Güter-abfertigung *f* freight office, clearance or dispatch of freight **-abfertigungsstelle** *f* freight depot **-aufzug** *m* freight elevator **-bahnhof** *m* freight depot, railway yard, freight yard **-beförderung** *f* forwarding of freight or of goods **-bewegung** *f* freight traffic

Güteregelung *f* end-point control, quality control

Güter-erzeugung *f* production **-flugzeug** *n* freight airplane **-ladeplatz** *m* freight platform **-lokomotive** *f* freight locomotive **-schuppen** *m* freight shed **-tarif** *m* freight tariff or rate **-transport** *m* conveyance of material **-umschlag** *m* turnover **-verkehr** *m* freight traffic, goods traffic **-vorschrift** *m* material specification **-wagen** *m* freight car, (freight) truck, van

Güterzug *m* freight train **-lokomotive** *f* freight locomotive

Güte-stelle *f* conciliation board **-stufe** *f* quality, grade (slope, quality) **-termin** *m* day of settlement **-test** *m* quality test **-verhältnis** *n* comparative quality, efficiency **-vertrag** *m* amicable agreement **-vorschrift** *f* quality specification, material specification **-wert** *m* figure of merit, quality (Q) factor, mechanical property

Güte-zahl *f* available energy (magnet), solidity index, quality or efficiency factor, figure of merit **-zeichen** *n* label (of quality) **-zeugnis** *n* certificate of quality, guarantee, works certificate **-ziffer** *f* figure of merit, quality index, efficiency factor

Gut-gewindelehrdorn *m* go-thread plug-gauge **-gewindelehrzapfen** *m* go-screw plug member **-gewinderinglehre** *f* go-thread ring gauge **-hacke** *f* first hoeing after singling **-lehrdorn** *m* "go" plug screw gauge **-lehre** *f* go gauge **-lehrring** *m* "go" ring gauge

gütlich geordnet compromised

Gutpunkt *m* good point

gutsagen to guarantee, be answerable

Gutsbesitzer *m* landholder

Gutschein *m* due bill, coupon

gutschließend tight-fitting, tightly sealed

gutschreiben to credit

Gutseite *f* (einer Lehre) go side

Guttapercha *f* gutta percha **-kabel** *n* cable in guttapercha covering **-papier** *n* gutta-percha paper, waterproof paper **-schicht** *f* gutta-percha coat(ing) **-zündschnur** *f* gutta-percha fuse

Gut- und Ausschußmaß "go" and "not go" dimension

Gütung *f* soil improvement

Gutzahl *f* acceptance number

Gypsometer *n* gypsometer

Gyrofrequenz *f* gyro-frequency

Gyrolith *m* gyrolite

gyromagnetisch-e Resonanz gyromagnetic resonance **-es Verhältnis** gyromagnetic ratio

Gyrometer *n* gyrometer

Gyrorektor *m* directional gyroscope, gyroscopic flight indicator

Gyroskop *n* gyroscope

gyroskopischer Horizont gyro horizon

Gyroskopstabilisator *m* gyroscopic stabilizer

H

Haar *n* hair **falsche Haare** false hair, dog hair (textiles)

haar-artig hairlike, capillary **-bürste** *f* hairbrush **-busch** *m* tuft of hair **-decke** *f* pile, nap **-draht** *m* Wollaston wire, capillary wire **-färbemittel** *n* hair dye, hair-dyeing tincture **-faser** *f* filament fiber **-faserig** filamentous

Haar-feder *f* hair spring **-feuchtigkeitsmesser** *m* hair hygrometer **-flechte** *f* braid of hair, plaited tress **-förmig** capillary, hair-shaped **-frost** *m* silver thaw, white frost, rime **-genau** dead-true **-gewebe** *n* structure or texture of hair, hair cloth **-hygrograph** *m* hair hygrograph **-hygrometer** *n* hair hygrometer

haarig hairy, hirsute

Haar-kalk *m* hair grout **-kanal** *m* capillary duct **-kies** *m* millerite **-kraft** *f* capillary attraction, capillarity **-krempler** *m* hair carder **-kreuz** *n* cross hairs **-kupfer** *n* capillary native copper **-linie** *f* hair line **-nadel** *f* hairpin **-nadelkurve** *f* hairpin curve (in road) **-nadelfeder** *f* hairpin spring **-pinsel** *m* fine hair brush **-riß** *m* microflaw, hairline crack, fissure craze, capillary fissure **-rissig** crazed

Haarrohr *n* capillary tube **-anziehung** *f* capillary attraction

Haarröhrchen *n* capillary tube **-kraft** *f* capillarity **-wirkung** *f* capillary attraction

haarscharf absolutely accurate, precise or correct, very (microscopically) sharp **-e Trennungslinie** sharply defined hairline

Haar-seil *n* seton **-seite** *f* grain side, hair side **-sieb** *n* (horse-) hair sieve **-silber** *n* capillary silver **-spatium** *n* hair space **-sprung** *m* hair crack **-strich** *m* hairline, serif, hair or thin stroke, upstroke **-tuch** *n* haircloth, woven hair **-wolken** *pl* mare's-tail clouds **-zange** *f* tweezers

Habann-röhre *f* type of split-anode magnetron, dynatron oscillator, Habann tube, ultra-high-frequency tube **-schwingung** *f* dynatron or Habann oscillation

Haben *n* credit **-seite** *f* credit side, creditors

Habilitation *f* appointment to a university lectureship

Habitus *m* physical appearance, habits **-wirkung** *f* habit-effect

Habutai-Seide *f* habutai silk

hachieren to hatch

Hachure (Gravierstriche) hatching on a printing roller

Hack-axt *f* chopping axe **-beil** *n* kitchen chopper **-boden** *m* soil that may be excavated with a pick **-bolzen** *m* rag bolt

Hacke *f* hoe, pick, hatchet, heel (of shoe), hock, ax

hacken to hoe, hack, chop, hew

Hacker *m* chipper, chopper

Hackmaschine *f* chipper, chopper **~ mit beweglichen Achsen** pivot-axle cultivator **~ mit Führersitz** riding cultivator **~ mit Handführung** walking cultivator **~ mit Hängesitz** (zwischen Rahmen) hammock-seat cultivator **~ mit balanziertem Rahmen** balanced-frame cultivator **~ mit beweglichem Rahmen** pivot-pole cultivator **~ mit (Führer)sitz** riding cultivator

Hack-messer *n* chopping knife, machete, meat cleaver **-säge** *f* hack-saw

Häcksel *m*, *n* chaff, chopped straw **-bank** *f* chaff or straw cutter **-lade** *f* chaffcutter **-schneider** *m* chopping machine

Hack- und Häufelpflug *m* (für ein Pferd) one-horse cultivator (scuffler)

Hackvorrichtung für Tabakkultur tobacco-hoeing attachment

Hadern *pl* (paper) rags **-brei** *m* rag-pulp **-drescher** *m* duster, willow (paper mfg.) **-karton** *m* rag board **-kocher** *m* rag boiler **-stäuber** *m* grass duster or cleaner **-wolf** *m* willow

hadrig ragged, (of iron) short, deficient for welding

Häfel *n* heddle, heald

Hafen *m* port, harbor, basin, refuge **~** (Raffinerie) berths **aus dem ~ auslaufen** to leave port **einen ~ blockieren** to blockade a port **in einen ~ einlaufen** to enter port, make port **bedeckter ~** cap pot, covered crucible, crucible with muffler (glassblowing) **eingeschlossener ~** landlocked port

Hafen-abgabe *f* harbor dues **-amt** *n* port authority

Hafenanker *m* moorings **einarmiger ~** blind or single-fluked anchor

Hafen-anlage *f* port installation **-arbeiter** *m* longshoreman **-ausrüstung** *f* port equipment or facilities **-bahn** *f* harbor railway **-bau** *m* harbor structure, harbor construction **-baum** *m* boom or bar of a harbor **-becken** *n* harbor, basin, (wet) dock (alongside a canal) **-betrieb** *m* harbor operation **-bezirk** *m* harbor district

Hafen-damm *m* dike, quay, embankment, sea wall, pier, jetty **-dienst** *m* navigation service **-dock** *n* basin, wet dock **-drehkran** *m* wharf revolving crane **-einfahrt** *f* harbor or port entrance, harbor channel **-feuer** *n* lighthouse, port light

Hafen-gebiet *n* harbor area **-gebühren** *pl* harbor dues **-haupt** *n* molehead, pier **-kapitän** *m* harbor master **-kommandant** *m* port senior officer **-kran** *m* wharf crane

Hafen-lagerhaus *n* dock or harbor warehouse **-meister** *m* harbor master **-mole** *f* quay **-mündung** *f* harbor or port entrance, harbor channel **-ofen** *m* pot furnace (glass mfg.) **-offizier** *m* port control officer **-polizeidienst** *m* harbor patrol **-schlengel** *m* boom or bar of a harbor **-schlepper** *m* harbor tugboat **-schleuse** *f* harbor lock

Hafen-schutz *m* harbor defense **-schutzboot** *n* harbor defense boat **-sperre** *f* harbor barrier, embargo **-stadt** *f* seaport town, seaport **-überwachung** *f* port control, naval control service **-wache** *f* harbor police **-wächter** *m* harbor attendant **-zange** *f* large tongs (glass mfg.) **-zeit** *f* establishment of a port, the highwater lunitidal interval at full, and change of the, moon

Hafer *m* oats **-quetsche** *f* oat crusher

Haff *n* lagoon, fresh-water lake

Hafner *m* potter

Haft *f* arrest confinement, imprisonment; clasp, hold, clamp, tie **-ahle** *f* stabbing awl **-bar** responsible, liable, accountable **-barkeit** *f* adhesion, responsibility (legal), liability **-bedingung** *f* no-slip condition **-befugnis** *f* warrant **-blei** *n* band, bands (glass mfg.) **-effekt** *m* tacking effect

haften to adhere, stick or cling to, guarantee, be liable or be responsible, bond, remain

Haften *n* adhesion, adherence **~ an der Straße** good traction, adherence of wheels

Haftenbleiben *n* adherence

Haft-fähigkeit *f* adhesion, adherence **~** (for like substances) cohesion

Haft-festigkeit *f* adhesive strength **-gläser** *pl* contact lenses **-hohlladung** *f* magnetic antitank hollow charge **-grundmittel** *n* (Farbe) wash primer, etch primer **-kleber** *m* contact adhesive **-kraft** *f* adhesion **-latte** *f* slotted batten (teleg.) **-mittel** *m* adhesive, anit-throwing agent **-pflaster** *n* adhesive tape

Haftpflicht *f* liability, responsibility **-versicherung** *f* liability on third-party insurance

Haft-pflock *m* steel picket or stake **-reibung** *f* friction of rest, static friction **-rücklaß** *m* performance bond **-schalter** *m* latching switch (relay) **-scheibe** *f* suctorial disk **-schicht** *f* adhesive layer **-sitz** *m* tight fit, transition fit **-spannung** *f* adhesive stress, bond stress, penetration tension

Haftstellen für Elektronen electron traps

Haftung *f* adhesion, liability, adsorption **~** (Beton an Eisen) bond **~ am Erdboden** stability, low center of gravity

Haft-vermögen *n* adhesive power, adhesiveness, adhesion **-wahrscheinlichkeit** sticking probability

Hag *m* bush, fence, woods, clamp of bricks

Hagel *m* sleet, hail **-bildung** *f* hail formation **-bö** *f* hail squall, hailstorm **-effekt** *m* shot effect

-korn *n* hailstone
hageln to hail
Hagel-schauer *m* hailstorm **-schlag** *m*, **-sturm** *m* sleet storm, hailstorm, damage done by hail **-wetter** *n* hailstorm **-wolken** *pl* hail clouds
Hahn *m* cock, stopcock, tap, valve, faucet, small valve hammer, cutoff (vacuum pump) **den ~ am Gewehr spannen** to cock a rifle **~ in Ruhrast** half cock **~ in Spannrast** full cock **~ am Wasserstandsanzeiger** water-gauge cock or tap **~ mit zwei Wegen** two-way cock **eingeschliffener ~** ground-in stopcock **selbsttätiger ~** self-acting cock
Hahn-batterie *f* cock system **-bolzen** *m* cocking-lever pin, hammer pin **-einstellung** *f* cock adjustment
Hahnen-fett *n* stopcock grease **-füße** *pl* spider patch, scribbling, scrawling
Hahnepot *m* arm mooring (there may be two or more arms), spider patch, crow's-foot **~ auf einem Knoten** crown knot
Hahn-fassung *f* (für Glühlampe) switch socket **-fett** *n* tap, joint, or vacuum grease **-gehäuse** *n* air control cock, aircock body **-griff** *m* valve handle
Hahnküken *n* plug of a cock **-anpreßluft** cock plug contact pressure air **-bohrungen** *pl* plug boreholes
hahn-los hammerless (said of small arms) **-öffnung** *f* (right or left) way of cock **-pot** *m* crowfoot (naut) **-schieber** *m* plug valve **-schlüssel** *m* cock or tap wrench, plug of a cock **-schraube** *f* cock pin or nail **-spitze** *f* firing pin **-ventil** *n* cock **-weg** *m* way of cock
Hain-balken *m* top or collar beam **-buche** *f* horn-beam
Häkchen *n* small hook, crook, clasp
haken to hook
Haken *m* hook, catch, clutch, fastening, clasp, clamp, hanger, lifting lug, claw **~ zum Aufheben** lifting hook **~ mit Drehgelenk** swivel hook **~ am Förderseil** clevis **~ mit Hülse** hook with socket **~ der Luftschraubenwelle** front rubber hook **~ und Ösen** hooks and eyes **~ eines Querriegels** (Schloß) staple for a bolt **~ machen** (slang) to make evasive turns **ohne ~ handhaben!** use no hooks!
haken-artig hooklike **-band** *n* hinge with hook, loop and hook, bridle wire, tie hook **-bildung** *f* turning the flank **-blatt** *n* staple plate **-bolzen** *m* hook or rag bolt **-bügel** *m* stirrup, U bolt **-eingriff** *m* hook engagement **-ende** *n* hook end
Haken-fadenführer *m* hook thread guide **-fänger** *m* fishing hook for bits **-flasche** *f* hook-type bottom block **-förmig** hooked, hook-shaped **-geschirr** *n* hook fittings **-harfe** *f* hook harp **-kehle** *f* throat of a hook **-keil** *m* nose key, gib **-kette** *f* hook-link chain, ladder chain **-klinke** *f* catch (lock) **-krone** *f* hook head (of cable)
Haken-lasche *f* hooked fishplate or fish joint **-laschung** *f* hook-and-butt joint **-last** *f* carrying capacity **-latte** *f* hook latch **-messer** *n* hook-shaped knife **-nadel** *f* spring needle **-nagel** *m* spike, hook nail **-platte** *f* hooked tie plate **-plattenoberbau** *m* hookplate track
Haken-schaft *m* shank of hook **-schalter** *m* hook switch **-scharnier** *n* hook hinge
Hakenschlag *m* doubling of hare, hitch for hooking a tackle to a rope, Blackwall hitch **einfacher** (doppelter) **~** single (double) Blackwall hitch
Haken-schloß *n* hook lock **-schlüssel** *m* hooked wrench, hook spanner, combination monkey wrench **-schraube** *f* bolt hook, screw hook, clip bolt **-schütze** *f* hook sluice **-seilmesser** *n* rope knife **-sprengring** *m* hook spring ring, snap hook **-stange** *f* hook stick **-stift** *m* dog-headed spike **-stütze** *f* hook-shaped bracket, swanneck spindle **-stützenisolator** *m* swan-neck insulator
Haken-umschalter *m* switch hook (teleph.) **-weg** *m* travel of hook **-zahn** *m* hook tooth, gullet tooth **-zapfen** *m* shank of hook **-zapfenplatte** *f* hooked tie plate with tenon
hakig hooked, hackly (fracture)
halb half **-e Fahrt** half speed **-es Gehalt** half pay **-e Kraft** half-speed **-er Looping** half loop **-e Rolle** half roll **-e schnelle Rolle** half snap roll
Halb-achse *f* seminaxis **-achsenverhältnis** *n* ellipticity coefficient **-addierer** *m* half adder **-addierwerk** *n* half adder **-amplitude** *f* semi-amplitude **-anthrazit** *m* semianthracite **-appretur** *f* semi-finish **-art** *f* subspecies **-ätze** *f* half-discharge
halbautomatisch semiautomatic, semimechanical **-er B-Platz** semi-B position
Halb-balken *m* half-beam **-ballon** *m* semiballoon type **-bandbreite** *f* midband width (electronics)
halbbasisch semibasic
halbbeständig metastable
halbbeweglich semiportable **-es Geleise** semi-portable track
Halbbild *n* (von Stereoskopbildern) half image (of stereophotographs) **-entfernungsmesser** *m* inverted-coincidence or split-field-coincidence range finder **-verfahren** *f* suppressed-frame recording
Halb-binder *m* half-truss or principal (carp.) **-blank** semibright **-bleiche** *f* semibleach **-blende** *f* half stop **-bockkran** *m* single-leg construction gantry crane **-dach** *n* shed or pent roof, lean-to **-dauernd** semipermanent **-deckend** semiopaque **-diagonalverspannung** *f* knee bracing, K truss **-dickes Profil** medium-thick profile **-diesel** *m* semi-Diesel **-direkte Gewinnung** semidirect recovery **-doppelscheibenrad** *n* halfdouble plate wheel **-dunkel** *n* twilight, semidarkness
halbdurchlässig semipermeable, semitransparent **-e Scheidewand** semipermeable partition or membrane
Halb-durchmesser *m* radius **-durchsichtig** semi-transparent **-ebene** *f* half plane, semiplane, H plane **-geviert** *n* en quadrat **-eingebettet** semiembedded, semifixed
halbeirund semioval
halbelliptisch semielliptic, halfelliptic **-er Bogen** semielliptical arch
halbempirische Formel semiempirical formula
halben to halve, bisect, mottle
Halb-erzeugnis *n*, **-fabrikat** *n* semimanufactured article, semi(finished) or intermediate product **-feder** *f* semielliptical spring **-fein** half-fine **-fernsteuerung** *f* semiremote control
halbfertig bohren semifinish bore
Halbfertigerzeugnis *n* semimanufactured pro-

duct or goods
halbfest semipermanent **-er Körper** subsolid **-er Stoff** semisolid substance (semisolid)
halbfett half-dark, medium-faced (print.) **-er Öllack** medium oil varnish
Halbflachbettfelge *f*, **Halbflachfelge** *f* semiflat-base rim
halbflächig hemihedral
Halbflächner *m* hemihedron
halbfliegend semifloating
Halbfließbandfertigung *f* semiproduction basis
Halbflügel *m* wing half **-modell** *n* half-wing test or half span model
halbflüssig semifluid **-e Masse** semiliquid mass
Halb-förderung *f* half delivery **-franzband** *m* half binding, half calf **-freitragend** semi-cantilever
Halbgas *n* halfway throttle **-feuerung** *f* semigas firing, half-gas firing
halb-gekreuzt quarter-twisted **-geleimt** half-sized **-gesättigt** partly satisfied, half saturated
halbgeschlossen half shut, semienclosed **-e Maische** semiopen crystallizer
halbgeschmolzen semifused
Halbgeschoß *n* intermediate story, mezzanine
halbgeschränkt right-angle-twisted **-er Riemen** quarter-turn belt
halb-gesintert semisintered, half-fused **-gezeit** *f* half tide **-gold** *n* imitation gold **-gruppe** *f* semigroup **-gut** *n* tin containing a great deal of lead
halbhart medium or semihard **~ entspannt** half-hard tempered **-es Gummi** semihard rubber
Halbhartwalze *f* part chill roll
Halbheit *f* imperfection, half measure, halfway step
halb-hell semiilluminated **-hochdecker** *m* mid-wing monoplane **-hochofen** *m* shaft or blast furnace of medium height **-holländer** *m* washing engine, washer, worker (paper mfg.) **-holländerführer** *m* rag cylinder driver **-holz** *n* split post, split log
halbieren to halve, bisect, mottle, dissect
Halbierende *f* bisectrix
Halbierschere *f* shears for dividing wire
halbiert mottled **-es Roheisen** mottled pig iron
Halbierung *f* bisection
Halbierungs-konus *m* bipartition cone **-linie** *f* bisector, bisectrix (line) **-winkel** *m* bipartition angle
halbindirekte Beleuchtung semi-indirect lighting
Halbinsel *f* peninsula
halb-jährlich half-yearly, semiannual **-kern** *m* half-curd soap
Halbketten-antrieb *m* half-track drive **-fahrzeug** *n* half-track vehicle **-kraftfahrzeug** *n* half-track motor vehicle **-lastkraftwagen** *m* half-track motor truck
halbklassische, ~ Bildkraftberechnung semiclassical image-force calculation **~ Näherung** semi-classical approximation
Halbkoks *m* semicoke, coalite **-staub** *m* powdered semicoke
Halbkokung *f* semicoking, partial carbonization of coal, peat, etc.
halbkontinuierlich semicontinuous **-e Walzstraße** semicontinuous rolling train **-es Walzwerk** semicontinuous mill, combination mill
Halbkonvergente *f* semiconvergent
Halbkreis *m* hemicycle, semicircle **-bogen** *m* semi-circular arch, semicircle **-einschnitt** *m* semicircular groove **-fehler** *m* constant-direction error, semi-circular error **-fehlerkomponente** *f* constant-direction error
Halbkreisformfräser *m* cutter for milling half circles **~ konkav** concave cutter **~ konvex** convex cutter
halbkreisförmig semicircular **-e Annäherung** semicircular approach
Halbkreisgradbogen *m* cemicircular protractor
halb-kreisig semicircular **-kreuzriemen** *m* quarterturn belt **-krückel** *m* half brace head
Halbkugel *f* hemisphere
halbkugelförmig hemispherical **-er Verbrennungsraum** dome-shaped combustion chamber
Halbkugelgestalt *f* hemispherical shape
halbkugelig hemispherical
Halbkugellinse *f* semicircular or hemispherical lens
Halb-kuppel *f* niche, vaulted passage **-kutsche** *f* coupe **-lasierend** semi-glazed, semi-transparent **-last** *f* half load **-laufwelle** *f* half-speed shaft **-leitend** semiconducting
Halbleiter *m* semiconductor (elec.), poor conductor; (als Bauelemente elektr.) semiconductor devices **-gerät** *n* semiconductor device **-kristall** *m* semiconducting crystal **-leckstrom** *m* channel effect **-photozelle** *f* rectifier photocell, barrier-layer, blocking-layer, or barrier-film cell, barrier-plane photocell, dry photovoltaic cell **-schicht** *f* barrier layer, film, or plane, blocking layer **-ventil** *n* semiconductor rectifier diode **-triode** *f* transistor
halbleitfähig semi-conductible
Halblinse *f* semilens, half-lens
halblogarithmische Schreibweise *f* floating-point notation (comp.) **-e Zahlendarstellung** *f* floating point representation (info proc.)
halbmagnetischer Fahrschalter semi-magnetic controller
halbmatt half matt **-glasur** *f* half-matt or semi-matt glazing **~ verchromt** semi-mat chromium plated
halb-mechanisch semimechanical **-messer** *m* radius **-messerlehre** *f* radius gauge **-metallglanz** *m* submetallic luster **-metallische Eigenschaften** metalloid properties **-muffelofen** *m* semimuffle furnace **-naßpresse** *f* semi plastic press
halboffen ajar **-es Laufrad** singlesided impeller
Halb-öffnungswinkel *m* semiapertural angle **-parabelfachwerkträger** *m* semiparabolic superstructure **-parameter** *m* half parameter
Halbperiode *f* semiperiod, halfperiod, semicycle, half cycle, semioscillation, alternation
Halbperioden-element *n* half-period element **-wechsel** *m* alternating-current, alternation or half wave
Halbpfosten *m* half-chess **-portal** *n* semi-gantry
Halbportalkran *m* semiportal crane **schwenkbarer ~** revolving one-legged gantry crane, derrick
Halbporzellan *n* feldspathic stoneware, semi-porcelain
halbpotentiometrische Methode opposition method

Halb-prisma *n* hemisprism (cryst.) **-pyritschmelzen** *n* semipyritic or partial-pyritic process **-quantenzahl** *f* half-quantum number **-quantitativ** semi-quantitative

halbraffiniertes Paraffin semirefined wax

Halbraum *m* semi-infinite body (space), half space **elastisch-isotropischer ~** elastic-isotropic semi-infinite body

halbräumliche Lichtstärke mean hemispherical candle power

Halb-reserve *f* half-resist **-riegel** *m* half the grider **-roh** semifinished

halbrund semicylindrical, semicircular, half round, hemispherical **-eisen** *n* half-round iron (bar) **-feile** *f* half-round file **-kerbnagel** *m* round-headed notched nail, round-head grooved pin (type C)

Halbrundkopf *m* roundhead, buttonhead **-schraube** *f* buttonhead screw

Halbrund-niet *n* rivet with buttonhead **-schraube** *f* roundheaded screw **-stange** *f* half-round bar

Halbschale *f* half shell

Halbschalen-bauweise *f* semimonocoque construction **-rumpf** *m* semimonocoque fuselage

Halbschappe *f* half-turn socket

Halbschatten *m* penumbra, half tone, half shade, partial shadow **-apparat** *m* half-shade apparatus, half-shadow analyzer **-grenze** *f* penumbra boundary **-kompensation** *f* penumbral compensation **-platte** *f* quarter-wavelength plate **-polarisationsapparat** *m* half-shadow polarimeter **-polarisator** *m* polarizing prism **-schleier** *m* penumbral blur

halbschlicht medium soft **-feile** *f* second-cut file **-hieb** *m* mid-cut (of a file)

Halbschmetterlingskreis *m* semi-butterfly circuit

halbschnittiges Messer semisliding knife

Halb-schott *n* partial bulkhead **-schranken** *pl* half gate (R.R.)

halbschwingende Hinterachse semifloating rear axle

Halb-seite *f* column (print.) **-seitig** semilateral, unilateral **-selbständige Entladung** semi-half-maintained discharge

halbselbsttätig semiautomatic(al), semimechanical **-es Amt** semimechanical central office (teleph.) **-e Anlage** semimechanical installation, semiautomatic exchange **-er Ruf** manually started machine ringing

Halb-spannweite *f* semispan **-sparren** *m* jack rafter **-stahl** *m* semisteel, malleable cast iron

halbstarr semirigid **-es Luftschiff** semirigid airship **-es System** semirigid system or type

Halb-steg *m* half hitch **-stehende Antriebsmaschine** semiportable engine **-steile Lagerung** semi-steep slope

Halbstich *m* half hitch (naut.) **-schurz** *m* half-hitch knot

Halb-stieler *m* semi-strut-type biplane **-stielig** halfstrut-, semistrut **-stoß** *m* scarf joint **-symmetrisch** semisymetric

halb-tägig, -täglich semidiurnal

halbtägig stehende Welle semidiurnal standing wave

Halbtags-beschäftigung *f* part-time employment **-zeit** *f* semidiurnal tide

Halbtidebecken *n* half-tide basin

Halbton *m* semitone, seminote, sharp (music) **-ätzung** *f* halftone phototypography, halftone engraving **-bild** *n* halftone picture, mezzotint **-klischee** *n* half-tone or stereotype plate **-verfahren** *n* half-tone process

Halbtotale *f* close-medium shot, medium shot

Halbtourschloß *n* German spring lock, half-turning lock

halb-tragbar semiportable **-transparent** semi-transparent **-trocken** half dry, semidry **-überzogener Flug** semistall **-ummantelt** half-shrouded **-verdeck** *n* half cover **-verkokung** *f* semicoking, partial carbonization (of coal, peat, etc.) **-versenkt** semisunk, semirecessed **-versetzung** *f* halfdislocation **-versilberter Spiegel** beam splitter (densiometer) **-vokal** *m* liquid consonant, semivowel **-vulkanisiert** semicured, semivulcanized **-wahlsystem** *n* semimechanical system, semiautomatic system **-warme Seifen** semibodied soaps

Halbwassergas *n* semiwater gas

Halbwatt-birne *f* half-watt bulb **-fadenlampe** *f* half-watt filament lamp

Halbweg-gleichrichter *m* half-wave rectifier **-gleichrichtung** *f* half-wave or single-wave rectification

halb-wegs halfway, fairly, substantially **-weiß** half white, half bleach **-weitschicht** *f* half-value layer **-welle** *f* half period, half cycle, alternation, half wave

Halb-wellen-antenne *f* half-wave antenna **-gleichrichter** *m* half wave rectifier **-länge** *f* half-wave length **-längenplättchen** *n* half-wave plate **-potential** *n* half-wave potential

Halbwert(s)breite *f* half width, width at half maximum intensity (optics), band width at 50 per cent down, halfpower width (antenna), width at half transmission; (optischer Filter) half-valve breadth **~ der Interferenzen** half width of interference maxima

Halbwert(s)-dicke *f* half-value thickness or layer **-druck** *m* half-value pressure **-periode** *f* half-decay period, half-value period **-punkt** *m* half-maximum point, half-power point **-schicht** *f* thickness for half absorption, halfthickness, half-value layer **-widerstand** *m* half-wave rectifier **-winkel** *m* half-power angle **-zeit** *f* half-crest-value time, half-life period (radioactive period), half-value life, half-time of exchange, (of radioactive element)

Halb-winkel *m* half angle **-wirkend** single-acting (mech.) **-wolle** *f* half wool, union goods

halbzahlig-e Resonanz half-integral resonance **-er Spin** half-integral of half-odd spin

Halb-zähligkeit *f* half integer **-zeit** *f* period of half life or change, semiperiod, time-to-half value

halbzeichnerische Methode semi-graphical procedure

Halb-zelle *f* half cell **-zellstoff** *m* half stuff (paper mfg.) **-zellulose** *f* hemicellulose or (in paper mfg.) half stuff **-zelt** *n* shelter-tent half

Halbzeug *n* semifinished material, products, or articles, semiproducts, semifinished steel, first stuff (paper mfg.) **-form** *f* semifabricated form **-mahlen** to break **-mutter** *f* semi-finished nut **-straße** *f* semifinishing mill train

Halbzinn *n* base tin, half tin, tin strongly mixed

with lead

Halbzug *m* half a section or detachment, a unit of troops, section **-führer** *m* half-platoon leader, section leader

Halbzylinder *m* semicylinder

Halde *f* waste dump or tip, spoil or waste heap, burrow, slags dump **auf ~ bringen** to bank out **auf ~ stürzen** to throw over the dump

Halden-material *n* dumped material **-planiermaschine** *f* spreader plow **-schlacke** *f* dump slag **-sturz** *m* dumping ground

Hälfte *f* half

hälften to halve, bisect, mottle

Halfter *m* halter **-riemen** *m* halter rope **-tasche** *f* holster

Hälftflächner *m* hemihedron

Hälftung *f* bisection

Hall *m* sound

Halle *f* hall, hangar, shed, garage

Halleffekt *m* Hall effect

hallen to reverberate, have multiple echoes

Hallen-bau *m* hangar construction **-binder** *m* truss **-dachlicht** *n* hangar skylight **-feld** *n* bay **-fenster** *n* hangar window **-gang** *m* aisle (factory construction) **-monteur** *m* hangar mechanic **-rahmen** *m* frame with the girder shaped like a gable-end roof **-stütze** *f* column **-vorplatz** *m* apron (airdome)

Hallfasthetstal *m* stability number, consistency factor

Hallformanten *m pl* resonance formants

Halligkeit *f* liveness (realistic acoustic condition)

Hallraum *m* acoustically live room, reverberating chamber or enclosure, echo chamber **-verfahren** *n* reverberation method

Hallwachseffekt *m* photoelectric emission, photoemissive, external photoelectric, or Hallwachs effect

Hallzahl *f* chamber coefficient (acoustics)

Halm *m* blade, stalk, fuse, reed, spire

Halo *m* halo **-bildung** *f* halation (television) **-chemie** *f* chemistry of salts, halochemistry **-erscheinung** *f* halo

Halogen *n* halogen

Halogene *f* halide

Halogenid *n* halide **-frei** halide free **-kristall** *n* halide crystal

halogenieren to halogenate

Halogen-lecksucher *m* halogen leak detector **-quecksilber** *n* mercury halide **-silber** *n* silver halide **-silberpapier** *n* halide silver paper **-substituiert** halogenized **-suchlampe** *f* halide torch **-wasserstoff** *m* hydrogen halides **-zählröhre** *f* halogen quenched tube

Haloidsalz *n* haloid salt, haloid, halide

Halophänomen *n* halo

Hals *m* neck, collar, throat **~ einer Bessemerbirne** neck or nose of a Bessemer converter **~ über Kopf** head over heels **~ einer Röhre** socket (end) of a pipe **~ einer Welle** neck or throat of a shaft **~ der Wendesäule eines Schleusentores** upper end of the heelpost of a lock gate **umgelegter ~** ringneck

Hals-ader *f* jugular vein **-ansatz** *m* projection (of pipe, etc.) **-ausschnitt** *m* revers **-band** *n* collar, necklace, collar strap **-bandkurve** *f* collar curve **-binde** *f* false collar **-bindung** *f* necktie, neck-groove binding (elec.)

Hals-dose *f* collar socket (petroleum) **-fläche** *f* throat area **-halter** *m* neck halter **-halfterriemen** *m* neck halter strap **-kehle** *f* flat hollow, recess head, quik head, broad channel, flat flute **-kerbe** *f* neck groove **-koppel** *f* neck strap or yoke

Halslager *n* neck journal, collar or journal bearing **~ der Schleuder** bearing of the centrifugal (sugar mfg.)

Hals-mutter *f* nut with round spigot **-naht** *f* double fillet weld **-niet** *m* web rivet **-riemen** *m* neck strap **-rille** *f* neck groove (of insulators) **-ringbremse** *f* clip (collar) brake **-senker** *m* counterbore, body counterbore **-starrig** stubborn **-tuch** *n* muffler, scarf

Hals-verankerung *f* top anchorage **-verengerung** *f* **eines Gefäßes** neck of a vessel **-zapfen** *m* top pivot (trunnion) or gudgeon pin, journal with collars, neck collar journal

Halt *m* halt, support, stop, hold **~ geben** to support **~ zum Auftanken** refuelling stop (aviat)

haltbar durable, stable, solid, lasting, strong, fast, permanent (of dyes) **-es basisches Futter** resistant basic lining

Haltbarkeit *f* life, durability, stability, service life, solidity, endurance **~ der Rüben** keeping quality of beets

Haltbarmachen *n* preserving, stabilizing

Haltbarmachung *f* preservation, conservation

Halte-anode *f* keep-alive electrode **-arm** *m* bracket, supporting arm **-band** *n* strap **-batterie** *f* locking battery **-befehl** *m* brakepoint instruction **-bereich** *m* retension range **-blech** *n* washer, sheet-metal holder, hinge socket **-bock** *m* support casting **-bolzen** *m* supporting or locking bolt, connecting pin, side stop **-bremse** *f* blocking brake **-büchse** *f* locking bush **-bügel** *m* shackle, retaining clip

Halte-draht *m* suspending wire, carrier wire **-einrichtung** *f* number-checking arrangement **-feder** *f* retaining spring **-fläche** *f* supporting surface **-form** *f* gripping form **-gerüst** *n* support (scaffolding, platform) **-gestell** *n* field handling frame, docking gear (airship) **-griff** *m* hand grip, handle **-gurt** *m* parachute harness

Halte-kabel *n* anchoring cable **-kappe** *f* holding cap **-keil** *m* wedge bolt **-kerbe** *f* pick-up groove **-kette** *f* holding with stopper (of a chain) **-klammer** *f* clamp carrier **-klemme** *f* fixing clip **-klinke** *f* holding jack **-knopf** *m* retaining button **-kraft** *f* cohesion **-kreis** *m* (Relais) locking circuit **-kreuz** *n* mooring ring

Halte-lappen *m* holding lug **-leine** *f* mooring rope or line, handling line, hawser **-leinenbund** *m* maneuvering spider **-leiste** *f* retaining strip, cleat **-loch** *n* locating hole **-magnet** *n* holding magnet **-mannschaft** *f* ground squad, handling crew **-manschette** *f* holding collar **-mutter** *f* clamping or retaining nut

halten to hold, support, keep **Kurs ~** to keep or to stand upon the course **ein Relais ~** to keep a relay excited, to hold a relay **das Relais hält sich mit eigenem Kontakt** the relay locks to its own contact

Halte-netz *n* mooring harness **-pfahl** *m* mooring post or bollard, cellular-type mooring pier **-platte** *f* carrier plate, holding plate, latch plate, supporting plate **-platz** *m* halt area, stopping or parking place, loading place **-punkt** *m* halting point, break, critical (thermal) point, change point, point of regression, point of calescence, decalescence or recalescence (point), arrest (metallography), point of aim, stopping point, stopover, instructions without force of order

Haltepunkts-bestimmung *f* critical-point determination **-dauer** *f* critical range or interval **-kurve** *f* thermal curve, S curve

Halter *m* holder, clamp, handle, support, clip, post, fixture, fastener, tie, guy, owner **~ für Bandfeder** holder for gripping tape **~ des Luftfahrzeuges** legal owner of aircraft **~ für die Schlußlaterne** rear- or tail-lamp bracket **~ für Werkzeuge** tool rack

Halterarm *m* supporting arm

Halte-relais *n* holding or locking relay, guard relay **-riemen** *m* arm strap **-ring** *m* guard ring, fastening ring, holding ring, retainer, retainer ring, snap ring, spring retainer

Halter-klammer *f* fixing clip, retaining clip **-klaue** *f* holder claw **-kopf** (Düsenhalter) holding head (nozzle holder) **-rahmen** *m* (Tragrahmen) carrier frame **-riegel** *m* retaining lug (retainer)

Halterung *f* holding, mounting, holder, mounting support **~ für Motorhaube** cowl-mounting support

Halterungs-system *n* holder, mounting or supporting system **-teile** holders

Halte-schalter *m* holding key **-scheibe** *f* holding disk **-schiene** *f* support bar, beam **-schlaufe** *f* arm strap **-schlüssel** *m* holding (retaining) spanner **-schlußleuchte** *f* stop light **-schraube** *f* clamping bolt, holding screw, check screw **-seil** *n* holding rope, guy line

Haltesignal *n*, **bedingtes ~** slowing down signal

Halte-spule *f* restraining coil, holding-on coil **-stab** *m* rod **-stange** *f* handrail **-stelle** *f* stop, stopping place, stopover, stage **-stellung** *f* holdover position (teleph.) **-stift** *m* locking pin **-strahl** *m* holding beam **-strebe** *f* tie rod

Halte-strom *m* retaining or holding current **-stromkreis** *m* retaining or holding circuit, circuit of holding coil **-stück** *n* carrier bracket **-taste** *f* holdover key (teleph.) **-tau** *n* guy rope, hauling-down cable **-verhältnis** *n* holding ratio **-vorrichtung** *f* stop device, holding device, chassis (of loud-speaker), die adapter, holding means **-wicklung** *f* holding winding or coil (teleph.) **-winkel** *m* holding angle

Halte-zapfen *m* holding plug, set pin **-zahn** *m* pilot pin **-zeichen** *n* block signal, break (print.) **-zeit** *f* halt, pause, thermal retardation, critical range or interval

Halt-knopf *m* stop button **-licht** *n* stop light **-los** unstable, unsteady, unsupported, unattached, untenable

Haltlosigkeit *f* instability, unsteadiness

Halt-netz *n* mooring harness **-schlüssel** *m* pole wrench

Haltung *f* carriage, bearing (troops), behavior, poise, attitude, level (sluice), keeping **~ eines Flusses** reach of a river **Wasserstand der oberen ~** upper pool elevation **Wasserstand der unteren ~** lower pool elevation

Haltungsschwäche *f* faulty posture

Haltzeichen *n* stop signal (traffic) **-geber** *m* autocontrol

Haltzylinderpresse *f* stop-cylinder press

Hämatachometer *n* haematachometer

Hämatit *m* hematite, red mine stone, red-slag iron-stone **-erz** *n* hematite ore **-vorkommen** *n* hematite deposit

Hämatoxylin *n* hematoxylin

Hammer *m* hammer, mallet, helve **mit dem ~ gefertigt** drop forged **~ mit gerader Finne** straight-peen hammer **~ mit gespaltener Finne** claw hammer **~ mit Kanten** sledge hammer **~ mit Kreuzfinne** cross-peen hammer **~ mit Kugelfinne** ball-peen hammer **mechanischer ~** power hammer

Hammer-arbeit *f* malleability **-auge** *n* handle or shaft hole of a hammer **-bahn** *f* hammer face **-band** *n* tilt brace **-bär** *m* hammer tup, hammer head, striker

hämmerbar malleable

Hämmerbarkeit *f* forgeability, malleability

Hammer-beil *n* hammer hatchet **-beschlag** *m* helve hoop or ring, hammer clip **-bohrmaschine** *f* drifter, stoper, sinker **-brecher** *m* hammer crusher

Hämmerchen einer Repetieruhr jack of a repeaterwatch

Hammer-eisen *n* forged or hammered iron **-finne** *f* hammer peen, striking face of a hammer **-fläche** *f* hammer face **-förmig** hammer-shaped **-führer** *m* hammer driver

hammergar tough-pitch **~ machen** to pole tough pitch **Kupfer ~ machen** to refine or to toughen copper

Hammergarmachen *n* poling tough pitch

Hammer-gebälk *n* tilt frame **-geschirr** *n* hidemill **-griff** *m* hammer handle **-helm** *m* hammer shaft **-induktor** *m* hammer-break spark coil, trembler coil **-klaue** *f* hammer claw **-klotz** *m* hammer tup

Hammerkopf *m* hammer head **-einsätze** *pl* hammer-head inserts **-filzer** *m* hammer-head felt (cover) (piano) **-schraube** *f* hammerbolt

Hammer-kran *m* hammer-head crane **-lötkolben** *m* copper bit with an edge, hammerhead soldering iron **-maschine** *f* swaging machine **-mühle** *f* hammer mill, swing-hammer mill, swing-hammer pulverizer

hämmern to hammer, hammer forge, hammer dress, peen

Hämmern *n* hammering, hammer forging or dressing, peening **~ von Lagern** knocking of (car) bearings

Hammer-nieten *n*, **-nietung** *f* hammer riveting **-risse** *pl* hammer bursts **-schlacke** *f* hammer slag, anvil dross

Hammerschlag *m* scale, mill scale, blow of the hammer, hammer finish **leichter ~** smart blow with a hammer **etwas mit leichtem ~ gestalten** to peen

Hammerschlagprobe *f* peening test

Hammer-schmied *m* forgeman, hammersmith, blacksmith **-schmiedestück** *n* drop forging **-schraube** *f* T-head bolt **-schwanz** *m* tail of a forge hammer **-schweißung** *f* hammer, horn, or forge welding **-sperre** *f* hammerlock **-sperrhebel** *m* hammerlock (long) **-spitzhaue** *f* pitching poll pick (min.)

Hammerständer, einseitiger ~ single standard of a hammer

Hammer-stiel *m* hammer handle or shaft **-stock** *m* anvil's stock **-unterbrecher** *m* hammer break, vibrating break **-walke** *f* fulling mill **-welle** *f* turning arbor of a hammer shaft **-werk** *n* forge shop, hammer mill

Hämoglobin *n* hemoglobin

Hämoglobinometer *n* haemoglobinometer

Hampelmann *m* traveling block (oil drilling)

Hand *f* hand **an ~ von** on the basis of, by means of, by reference to, by the aid of **auf der ~ liegen** to be obvious, evident, or patent, to go without saying **von der ~** offhand **zu Händen** attention of (on letters)

Hand-abblendschalter *m* hand-operated anti-dazzle switch **-abfeuerung** *f* hand-operated firing mechanism **-ablage** *f* reaping attachment **-abroller** *m* hand roller **-absperrventil** *n* hand-operated valve **-abweiser** *m* hand guard, hand rejector **-abzug** *m* hand release, hand pull **-akt** *m* official leaflet, pamphlet or document

Handamt *n* manual central office, manual exchange **~ mit selbsttätiger Schlußzeichengebung** central-battery signaling exchange

Handamtsschrank *m* manual switchboard

Hand-andrehkurbel *f* hand-starting crank **-anlage** *f* hand-feed **-anlaß** *m* hand starting **-anlaßaggregat** *n* manual start set **-anlasser** *m* hand starter

Handanlaß-magnet *m* hand-starting magneto **-magnetzünder** *m* hand booster magneto for starting

Handanlassung *f* hand starting

Handantrieb *m* hand drive, impulse by hand **~ für Schaltgeräte** manual drive for switches

Hand-apparat *m* telephone handset, microtelephone **-apparatschnur** *f* cord of hand desk telephone **-arbeit** *f* manual labor, needlework **-arbeiter** *m* manual laborer, mechanic, needleworker **-aufgabe** *f* hand feed, hand feeding (metallurgy) furnace

Hand-auflage *f* tooth rest **-aufwinder** *m* hand splitter **-auftrag** *m* coating by hand **-auftragwalze** *f* hand inking roller **-ausgabe** *f* pocket edition **-auslösung** *f* manual release or disengagement **-ausschalter** *m* manually operated circuit breaker **-ausschnitt** *m* handcut overlay **-bagger** *m* hand dredge (spoon bag) **-bandschleifmaschine** *f* hand belt sander

handbedient hand-operated **-er Block** hand-worked block system **-es Fernamt** auto-manual exchange **-er Peiler** manual direction finder

Hand-bedienung *f* manual operation, hand control **-beil** *n* hatchet **-beschickung** *f* hand stoking, hand charging

handbetätigt worked by hand, hand-operated **-er Verstellpropeller** *m* manually controllable propeller

Handbetätigung *f* hand operation

Handbetrieb *m* manual working or operation, hand power **~ in Durchgangsämtern bei Sofortverkehr** manual switching for built-up connections with no delay (or demand) service **~ mit mittelbar gesteuertem Nummernanzeiger** panel-call-indicator operation **~ mit unmittelbar gesteuertem Nummernanzeiger** step-by-step call indicator operation **den ~ einschalten** to go into hand

handbetriebsmäßig manual

Hand-blasebalg *m* single bellows **-blechschere** *f* tinner's snip, hand-operated plate shears **-bohrer** *m* hand auger, gimlet, hand drill **-bohrmaschine** *f* hand (-operated) drilling machine, drill gun, portable drill **-breit** of a hand's breadth **-bremse** *f* hand brake **-bremshebel** *m* hand-brake lever **-bremshebelwelle** *f* hand brake (lever) shaft **-brennschluß** *m* manually-given cutoff signal (missiles) **-brunnen** *m* dug well (petroleum) **-buch** *n* handbook, manual, textbook

Hand-bücherei *f* reference library **-bügelbefestigung** *f* hand clamping **-dammkulturpflug** *m* walking lister **-drahtgeflecht** *n* handmade wire cloth **-drehbank** *f* hand lathe **-drehbohrung** *f* auger boring **-drehdynamostromquelle** *f* current generated by hand-operated dynamo **-drehmaschine** *f* manual motor **-drehzähler** *m* hand revolution counter **-druck** *m* hand printing **-druckmodell** *n* printing block

Hand-durchschläger *m* nail set, drift punch **-eimer** *m* hand bucket **-einfärbung** *f* inking by hand **-einleger** *m* hand-feed attachment **-einspritzpumpenprüfvorrichtung** *f* manually-operated injection-pump testing equipment **-einstellung** *f* hand adjustment **-eisen** *n* handcuff, handling iron

Handel *m* commerce, trade **~ treiben** to trade, deal

Händel *m* knurling tool

handeln to act, deal, haggle, trade, treat, bargain

Handels-abteilung *f* commercial section (of bank) **-adreßbuch** *n* commercial or trades directory **-aluminium** *n* commercial aluminum **-baustahl** *m* commercial structural steel **-benzol** *n* commercial benzene **-bezeichnung** *f* trade designation, trade name

Handelsbilanz *f* trade balance **aktive ~** active or favorable balance of trade **passive ~** passive or unfavorable balance of trade

Handels-bleche *pl* commercial sheets **-blei** *n* commercial lead

Händelschraube *f* eyebolt

Handels-eisen *n* commercial iron or steel, merchant bar iron **-eisenwalzwerk** *n* merchant (iron) mill, guide mill **-flagge** *f* merchant (marine) flag **-flotte** *f* trading or merchant fleet **-flugzeug** *n* commercial airplane **-freiheit** *f* freedom of trade, free trade **-gängig** commercial, marketable **-gesellschaft** *f* trading company, firm, company **-gewicht** *n* avoirdupois weight **-guß** *m* commercial cast iron or casting

Handels-hafen *m* commercial harbor or port **-hochschule** *f* university or school of commerce **-kammer** *f* chamber of commerce **-kupfer** *n* merchant copper **-luftfahrt** *f* commercial aviation **-marine** *f* merchant marine **-marke** *f* trade-mark **-ministerium** *n* Board of Trade **-name** *m* trade name **-niederlassung** *f* trading settlement, factory **-produkt** *n* commercial product

Handels-qualität *f* commercial quality or grade **-recht** *n* commercial law **-schiff** *n* merchant vessel, merchantman **-schiffahrt** *f* merchant shipping, merchant marine **-schiffsraum** *m* merchant or net tonnage **-schraube** *f* commercial screw **-seehafen** *m* commercial or trading seaport **-sorte** *f* market grade **-sperre** *f* embargo on commerce **-stabeisen** *n* merchant bar iron **-stahl** *m* commercial steel

handelsüblich pertaining to commercial customs, of commercial size **auf -e Längen zerteilen** to divide into commercial lengths **-e Qualität** commercial grade or quality **-e Toleranz** mill or commercial limit

Handels-unternehmen *n* commercial enterprise **-verkehr** *m* commercial intercourse, trade, traffic **-zeichen** *n* trade-mark, trade name **-zentrum** *n* commercial center **-zerstörer** *m* raider **-zink** *n* commercial zinc

Hand-empfindlichkeit *f* hand (or body) capacity effect (electronics) **-ersatztype** *f* founder's type

Händeschutz *m* safety guard

Hand-fahrgerät *n* manually-operated conveyer **-fahrwerk** *n* hand traversing gear **-fallschirm** *m* manually operated parachute **-falzung** *f* folding by hand **-faß** *n* keg, small cask **-fäustel** *m* small hammer or mallet **-feilenkloben** *m* hand vise **-fernsprecher** *m* telephone handset, microtelephone **-fertigkeit** *f* operating skill **-fessel** *f* handcuff, manacle **-fest** sturdy

Hand-feuerlöscher *m* hand fire extinguisher **-feuerung** *f* hand firing **-feuerwaffe** *f* hand firearm, small arm **-fläche** *f* palm of the hand **-flammofen** *m* hand reverberatory furnace **-flaschenzug** *m* hand-operated block and tackle **-flügelpumpe** *f* semi-rotary hand pump **-förderung** *f* tramming **-former** *m* hand molder **-formerei** *f* hand-molding (work), hand-molding shop **-formgießerei** *f* jobbing foundry **-formguß** *m* jobbings

Handformmaschine *f* hand-molding or hand-ramming machine ~ **mit Stiftenabhebung** hand-operated flask-lifting molding machine

Handformziegel *m* hand formed brick

Handfortschaufelungsofen *m* hand-rabbled furnace, hand reverberatory roaster or calciner

Hand-fräsen *n* routing (metal) **-gaseinstellung** *f* hand throttle adjustment **-gaszug** *m* hand throttle **-geben** *n* direct or manual transmission **-geber** *m* manipulator **-gebläse** *n* hand blowpipe **-gebrauch** *m* manual use or operation **-geformt** hand-molded

Hand-gerät *n* hand-operated instrument **-geschliffen** hand cut (ground) **-geschnitten** hand cut

hand-geschöpftes Papier hand made paper **-geschorenes Leimleder** hand-cut glue stock **-gesetzter Text** hand-set text **-gesteuerter Apparat** manual controller **-getastet** key-worked

Hand-gewindebohrer *m* hand tap **-gießlöffel** *m* hand ladle **-gießmaschine** *f* hand-casting machine **-graupappe** *f* handmade gray board

Handgriff *m* (lifting) handle, handhold, manipulation, lifting strap, tiller ~ **der Bremse** brake handle ~ **mit Drückerschalter** grip handle with trigger switch ~ **für die selbsttätige Quer- und Vertikalbewegung** cross- and vertical-feed handle ~ **für die selbsttätige Tischbewegung** table-feed handle ~ **für die Zündung** ignition handle

Hand-guß *m* handcast **-habe** *f* handle **-haben** to manipulate, handle, manage, do, operate **-habung** *f* handling, use, operation, manipulation **-habungstau** *n* prolonge, drag rope **-hackmaschine** *f* walking cultivator **-hammer** *m* hand hammer, sledge **-haspel** *f* hand reel

Handhebel *m* starting handle (of an electric controller), hand lever **-betrieb** *m* operation by hand lever **-fräsmaschine** *f* hand-lever milling machine **-modellaushebung** *f* hand-lever pattern lift or draw **-presse** *f* hand-lever press **-pressung** *f* hand-lever squeezing **-reitstock** *m* hand-lever-operated tailstock **-schalter** *m* hand-lever shifter **-schaltung** *f* hand-lever control **-spannung** *f* collet chuck **-vorschub** *m* hand-lever feed

Hand-hobel *m* hand plane **-holzpappe** *f* handmade wood pulp board **-kabelwinde** *f* hand cable winch **-kalander** *m* hand-operated calender **-kammer** *f* hand-operated camera **-kapazität** *f* hand capacity, hand- or body-capacity effect **-karren** *m* handbarrow, wheelbarrow **-kette** *f* hand chain **-kettenführung** *f* hand-chain guide

Hand-kippvorrichtung *f* hand-tilting or hand-tipping device **-kleinstfunkgerät** *n* handie-talkie **-kloben** *m* hand or filling vise **-klöppel** *m* mallet **-knebel** *m* hand gag **-koffer** *m* carrying case, suitcase, attaché case **-koloriert** colored by hand **-körner** *m* center punch **-kran** *m* hand crane **-kreuz** *n* pilot wheel, cross handle **-kugeldruckprüfgerät** *n* hand ball-thrust apparatus

Handkurbel *f* crank handle, (hand) crank ~ **für den Vorschubwechsel** crank handle for changing feeds

Hand-lager *n* subsidiary store **-lampe** *f* portable lamp, hand lamp **-langer** *m* helper, handy man, hodman **-läppen** to hand-lap **-läppschliff** *m* hand-lapped finish **-laternenleitung** *f* hand lamp cable **-latte** *f* hand base staff, or pole

Handlauf *m* handrail **-katze** *f* hand-power trolley **-kran** *m* hand-power or overhead hand traveling crane

Hand-lautstärkeregler *m* manual volume control **-lederpappe** *f* handmade leather board **-leier** *f* hand drill **-leimen** *n* hand sizing **-leiste** *f* handrail (R.R.) **-lenkdeichsel** *f* hand-steering tongue

Händler *m* dealer, trader

Hand-leuchte *f* hand lamp **-leuchter** *m* candleholder, candlestick **-leuchtzeichen** *n* hand flare, ground-signal flare

handlich handy, manageable, convenient **-e Unterlage** handy reference

Handlichkeit *f* handiness **große** ~ easy handling

Handlister *m* walking lister

Handloch *n* handhole **-deckel** *m* handhole cover

Handlocher *m* hand-feed punch, key card punch, hand perforator or puncher ~ **für Kabelbetrieb** three-key perforator for cable code

Handloch-klappe *f* hand-hole or inspection flap **-maschine** *f* hand punch **-verschluß** *m* handhole stoppage

Handlot *n* hand lead **-leine** *f* hand line (naut) **-maschine** *f* hand sounding machine

Hand-lüfter *m* hand-operated blower or ventilator (min.) **-luftpumpe** *f* hand air pump
Handlung *f* action, act, business house, plot, story, theme, scenario **strafbare ~** punishable act
Hand-lupe *f* hand lens (magnifier) reading glass **-macharbeit** *f* hand-finishing **-matrizenbrett** *n* board for sorts **-meißel** *m* hand chisel **-meßkammer** *f* hand mapping camera **-mikrophon** *n* hand (-held) microphone **-mischung** *f* mixing by hand **-morsesystem** *n* key Morse system **-motor** *m* fractional motor
Hand-mühle *f* hand mule **-muster** *n* small sample **-mutter** *f* hand nut **-nachschub** *m* hand feed (regulation) **-nieten** *n* hand-riveting **-öldruckpumpe** *f* hand-operated oil pressure pump **-ölkanne** *f* hand-oil can **-ölpumpe** *f* oil handpump
Hand-Pattinson-Verfahren *n* hand-labor Pattinson process
Hand-pfanne *f* hand ladle, molder's ladle **-pferd** *n* pack horse, off horse **-pflug** *m* (Stell- oder Schwingpflug, Gangpflug) walking plow **-pinne** *f* hand tiller
Handpolierer *m*, **elektrischer ~** electric disc-type polisher
Hand-presse *f* hand press **-pressendruck** *m* hand press printing **-preßformmaschine** *f* hand-operated press-molding or squeezing machine, hand squeezer **-pressung** *f* hand pressure **-probe** *f* volatility test of the palm of the hand **-probenwechsler** *m* manual sample changer **-prüfstand** *m* hand-operated testing apparatus **-pumpe** *f* hand pump **-pumpenvorrichtung** *f* hand priming unit **-putz** *m* hand-plastering
Handrad *n* handwheel, elevation handwheel, hand valve, steering wheel **~ zum Feineinstellen der Bohrspindel** spindle slow motion, wheel to (minutely) regulate spindle **~ zur Höhenrichtung** elevating handwheel **~ zur Seitenrichtung** traversing handwheel **~ für die Tischbewegung** handwheel to move table (of a machine) **~ zum Vorschub des Rundtisches** (von Hand) rotary-attachment handwheel
Handrädchen *n* micrometer-scale knob, small handwheel
Handräder für die Vertikaleinstellung vertical-feed wheels
Handrad-schleifmaschine *f* plain grinding machine driven by a handwheel **-steuerung** *f* handwheel control **-welle** *f* handwheel shaft
Hand-ramme *f* hand rammer, hand pile driver, maul **-rauchzeichen** *n* hand smoke signal **-refraktometer** *n* hand refractionometer **-regel** *f* rough rule **-register** *n* field book (of surveyor) **-regler** *m* manual regulator (valve) **-regulierung** *f* hand regulation **-regulierbogenlampe** *f* hand-fed arc lamp
Handreibahle *f* hand reamer **~ mit verstellbaren Messern** adjustable-blade hand reamer **nachstellbare ~** expansion hand reamer
Handreichung *f* assistance
Handrüttler *m* hand-jarring pattern draw machine **~ mit Wende- und Abhebevorrichtung** hand-jarring turnover pattern draw machine
Hand-säge *f* handsaw **-sägeabrichter** *m* handsaw jointer **-satz** *m* hand composition **-schacht** *m* hand pit **-schalter** *m* lever switch, hand switch **-schaltung** *f* hand operation **-schaltverfahren** *n* manual switching system **-schaufel** *f* hand shovel **-scheiden** *n* **-scheidung** *f* hand sorting or dressing **-scheinwerfer** *m* portable searchlight **-schelle** *f* handcuff, manacle **-schere** *f* hand shears **-scherenfernrohr** *n* scissor-pattern binoculars
Hand-schlägel *m* miner's hammer for striking the borer **-schlagmater** *n* brush out (mater) matrix **-schleifarbeit** *f* freehand grinding **-schleifmaschine** *f* portable grinder **-schlepprechen** *m* drag-rakes **-schmierung** *f* hand lubrication **-schmierverfahren** *n* hand stuffing **-schnellregler** *m* manual-automatic regulator
Hand-schraubenpumpe *f* hand-screw pump **-schraubstock** *m* hand vise **-schrift** *f* handwriting manuscript **-schriftschreiber** teleautograph, telewriter **-schubkarren** *m* hand lift truck **-schuh** *m* glove **-schußwaffe** *f* hand firearm, small arm **-schutz** *m* hand guard **-schutzbügel** *m* finger guard **-schutzvorrichtung** *f* hand safety guard
Hand-schweißung *f* manual welding **-schwengel** *m* hand lever, hand walking beam **-schwungkraftanlasser** *m* hand inertia starter **-seite** *f* off side **-sender** *m* sending key or sender **-setzer** *m* hand compositor **-setzmaschine** *f* hand jig **-sieb** *n* hand sieve **-spake** *f* lever, crowbar **-spannfutter** *n* hand-operated chuck **-spannhebel** *m* feeding hand lever **-spannsäge** *f* bucksaw **-speisepumpe** *f* hand-feed pump **-spill** *n* bar capstan **-spindelpresse** *f* hand screw press
Hand-spritze *f* manual fire engine, syringe **-stampfe** *f* beetle (mech.) **-stampfen** to ram by hand **-stampfung** *f* hand ramming **-start** *m* hand launching or starting **-starter** *m* hand starter **-steuerschalter** *m* manual controller **-steuerung** *f* hand gear, hand shift **-streutrommel** *f* portable decontamination duster **-strich** *m* shaping by hand, hand molding **-strichziegel** *m* brick formed in mold **-stück** *n* geological specimen **-stütze** *f* pistol grip **-system** *n* manual system
Hand-tachometer *n* hand tachometer **-tankwagen** *m* small tank wagon **-tasche** *f* handbag **-tätig** hand-operated, manual **-teilgerät** *n* hand indexing device (tool machine) **-tempo** *n* key speed **-torf** *m* dug peat **-transportkarren** *m* hand truck
Hand-übertragung *f* transfer by hand **-umschalter** *m* hand switch **-umsteuerung** *f* hand reversing mechanism **-unterbrecher** *m* hand interrupter **-vakuumpumpe** *f* hand-operated vacuum pump **-ventil** *n* hand valve **-ventilator** *m* hand blower **-verbesserung** *f* hand correction **-vermittlung** *f* manual exchange **-vermittlungsamt** *n* manual exchange (teleph.) **-verstellhebel** *m* manual timing lever **-verstellung** *f* manual timing
Handverstellungsautomatik *f* manual automatic
Hand-versuch *m* small-scale test **-vorschub** *m* hand feed **-waffe** *f* small arm, hand arm **-wagen** *m* handcart, hand truck **-wählschalter** *m* manual selection (teleph.) **-warm** warm to touch **-wendeplattenformmaschine** *f* hand turnover molding machine **-werk** *n* handicraft, trade, profession
Handwerker *m* artisan, workman, craftsman,

manual worker

Handwerks-brauch *m* custom, way, or manner of craftsmen **-kniff** *m* mechanical dodge, knack, or trick **-mäßig** mechanical, workmanlike, by rountine **-meister** *m* master mechanic **-schulung** *f* artisan training **-zeug** *n* set of tools, instruments, implements

Hand-winde *f* hand winch, jack **-zeichnung** *f* pencil drawing, signature **-zeit** (bei Maschinenbedienung) handling time **-zellenschalter** *m* hand (-operated) battery switch

handzerkleinerter Schrott shoveling scrap

Hand-zirkel *m* dividers, compasses **-zuführung** *f* hand feed **-zug** *m* pull wire (cord, cable)

Hanf *m* hemp

Hanfantriebskabel *n*, **rundes ~** bullrope

Hanf-dichtung *f* hemp packing **-einlage** *f* hemp core

hanfen, hänfen hempen

Hanf-faser *f* hemp fiber **-isolation** *f* hemp insulation **-leine** *f* hemp rope **-leinwand** *f* canvas, hemp linen **-liderung** *f* hemp packing **-litze** *f* hemp strand **-packung** *f* hemp packing **-riemen** *m* hemp belt or belting **-seele** *f* hemp center, hemp core (of a rope)

Hanf-seil *n* sash line, hemp rope **-seilscheibe** *f* hemp-rope sheave **-seilspannbacke** *f* hemp rope holder **-tau** *n* hemp rope, hawser, manila rope **-umwickelung** *f* hemp packing **-zopf** *m* twisted hemp **-zwirnfaden** *m* hemp thread

Hang *m* slope, deep level (min) **~ einer Talsperre** side of a barrage (engin.) **gedeckter ~** defile **~ nach unten** downward trend

Hangar *m* hangar

Hangaufwind *m* upcurrent

Hängeachse *f* suspension pin **~ des Schwimmers** suspension pin of float

Hänge-anschlußdose *f* suspended contact box **-antenne** *f* trailing antenna

Hängebahn *f* overhead (chain-and-trolley) conveyer, overhead trolley, suspension or suspended railroad, monorail conveyor **~ für Handbetrieb** hand-operated trolley conveyer

Hängebahn-anlage *f* overhead-trolley equipment **-geleise** *n* overhead-trolley-conveyer rail **-gießpfanne** *f* trolley ladle **-kreuzung** *f* trolley-conveyer crossing **-kübel** *m* ropeway bucket, swing bucket **-laufkatze** *f* overhead conveyer trolley **-schiene** *f* overhead-trolley-conveyer rail **-strang** *m* overhead-trolley track **-waage** *f* overhead-trolley-track scales, overhead travelling balance **-wagen** *m* wagon for suspension railway **-weiche** *f* overhead-trolley rail switch

Hänge-balken *m* hanging beam **-band** *n* hanging tie **-bandtrockner** *m* festoon dryer

Hängebank *f* bank, eye, mouth of a shaft **-arbeiten** *pl* banking **-arbeiter** *m* pit foreman, head pitman **-lager** *n* suspension truss **-seilscheibe** *f* block pulley **-unterzug** *m* girder across landing station (min.)

Hänge-bock *m* sling or shaft hanger, drop-hanger frame, double-hanger frame, hanger bracket **-boden** *m* drying loft, suspension work **-brücke** *f* suspension bridge **-bügel** *m* suspension link **-decke** *f* suspended roof **-deckensteine** *pl* arch bricks **-dose** *f* suspension juction box

Hängedraht *m* rod support, catenary hanger, suspension wire **-antenne** *f* trailing-wire antenna

Hänge-eisen *n* hanger **-förderband** *n* overhead conveyor **-gefäß** *n* swing bucket **-gerüst** *n* hanging stage, scaffold **-gewölbe** *n* arch formed by scaffolding, scaffold, suspended roof arch **-gleiter** *m* hanging glider **-gondel** *f* suspension basket **-haken** *m* hook

Hänge-isolator *m* suspension insulator **-kabel** *n* suspension cable **-katze** *f* traveling crab **-kette** *f* suspension chain **-klemme** *f* suspension clamp **-kompaß** *m* hanging compass **-korb** *m* suspension bar, trapeze bar (aviation) **-körper** *m* suspension member **-kübel** *m* swing or suspension bucket **-kübelaufzug** *m* drop-bucket hoist

Hängekühler *m* underslung radiator **einziehbarer ~** tunnel-type or underslung radiator

Hängelager *n* drop hanger, hanger bearing **~ mit Kugelbewegung und in der Höhe verstellbarer Lagerachse** adjustable ball-and-socket hanger

Hängelager-bock *m* drop-hanger frame, hanger frame **-fuß** *m* drop-hanger shoe, hanger shoe **-körper** *m* drop-hanger frame **-schale** *f* drop-hanger bearing box, hanger bearing box

Hänge-lampe *f* suspended lamp **-lasche** *f* attachment plate **-leine** *f* suspension line **-licht** *n* drop light **-luftleiter** *m* trailing antenna **-matte** *f* hammock

Hängemeißel *m* hanging or balanced guard **~ mit Federausgleichung** guard balanced by a spring **~ mit Gewichtsausgleichung** guard balanced by a counterweight

Hänge-mine *f* hanging mine **-motor** *m* inverted engine

Hängen *n* hanging (of a criminal), suspension, scaffolding, skidding, flat turn **~ der Nadel** sticking of needle

hangen, hängen to hang (up), adhere, cling, attach, suspend, lower **an den Propeller ~** (slang) to zoom

hängen bleiben to be caught, stick, take hold (in silent tuning) **~** (Ventile) to seize (valves)

Hängenbleiben *n* scaffolding (in a blast furnace) **~ des Ventils** sticking of a valve

hängend hanging, suspended, pendent **~ angeordnet** (Ventile) overhead-type (valves) **-er Achtzylinder V-Motor** eight-cylinder inverted V engine **-e Befestigung** suspension-type mounting **-er Motor** inverted engine **-e Schicht** hanging wall, roof, upper surface **-e Scholle** upthrow side (min.) **-er Sechszylinder-Reihenmotor** six-cylinder-in-line inverted engine **-e Ventile** suspended valve array, overhead valves, valves in head, flap valves hinged at top **-er Zweizylinder-V-Motor** inverted V twin engine **Motor mit -en Zylindern** inverted-type engine

Hangende *n* roof of a seam (min.)

Hangendes hanging (in geology)

Hängendwasser *n* top water

Hänge- oder Bauchkühler *m* tunnel-type radiator

Hänge-quelle *f* slope spring **-ring** *m* suspension ring **-säule** *f* king post, queen post **-säulenhängewerk** *n* post truss **-schiene** *f* suspension rail, hanging tie **-schloß** *n* padlock **-seil** *n* suspension cable **-steckdose** *f* suspension plug socket connector **-stromschiene** *f* overhead conductor rail **-stütze** *f* hangar bracket **-system** *n* pole or suspension system **-tal** *n* hanging valley

Hänge-ventil *n* inverted valve **-verfahren** *n* airing process **-wagen** *m* cableway carriage **-wand** *f* suspended wall **-werk** *n* truss frame, bucket suspension rod, braced girder **-werksbinder** *m* joggle truss **-werksbrücke** *f* truss-framed bridge **-werksstrebe** *f* truss post **-winkel** *m* hanging or banking angle, angle of bank

Hangfaktor *m* influence of slope of the target surface upon longitudinal dispersion

hängig (hügelseitig) hill-side

Hang-mulde *f* depression on a slope **-quelle** *f* slope spring **-rutschung** *f* slope failure **-segelflug** *m* soaring over slopes, slope soaring **-segeln** *n* ridge soaring **-start** *m* start with a rubber cable **-stellung** *f* slope position (mil.) **-wasser** *n* hill water **-wind** *m* forced or mechanical up-current, upcurrent due to a slope **-winkel** *m* gradient of slope

Hankelsche Funktion Hankel function

hantelförmiger Schlitz dumb-bell slot

Hantelmodell *n* dumbbell model

hantieren to manipulate, operate, manage, handle, work

Hantierung *f* manipulation, handling, operating by hand

haploid haploid

HAPUG-Modulation floating-carrier control, variable-carrier modulation

Hardenit *m* hardenite

Hardyscheibe *f* dry disk joint, flexible disk (motor transport)

Harfe *f* (Drahtwalze) wire guides

Harfenantenne *f* harp or fan antenna

Harke *f* rake **~ zur Reinigung des Rechens** trashrack cleaner

Harkensonde *f* pressure survey rake

Harmattan *m* harmattan

Harmet Blockpreßverfahren *n* Harmet fluid-compression method **~ Prozeß** Harmet repouring or transfer process **~ Verfahren** Harmet electric-smelting process

harmonisch harmonic **-e Frequenzcharakteristik** harmonic response characteristic **-er Formfaktor** telephone harmonic form factor **-e Nährung** harmonic approximation **-e Oberschwingung** *f* overtone **-er Oszillator** harmonic oscillator **-e Punkte** harmonic points **-e Schwingung** harmonic oscillation **-e Sinusschwingungen** harmonic curves **-er Stabilisator** harmonic balancer **-e Teilschwingungen** (Komponenten) harmonics, harmonic components

Harmonische *f*, *pl* harmonic(s) **erste ~** fundamental oscillation, first harmonic **dreifache ~**, **dritte ~**, **dreizahlige ~** triple harmonics **gerade** (geradzahlige) **~** even or higher harmonics **höhere ~** higher harmonics **ungerade** (ungeradzahlige) **~** odd harmonics **untere ~** subharmonic **zweite ~** second harmonic **in einer Harmonischen schwingen** to vibrate to a harmonic

Harnisch *m* slickenside

Harnsäure *f* uric acid

Harnstoff *m* urea **-formaldehyd** *n* urea formaldehyde

hart hard, tough, servere, firm, solid; (Wasser) calcareous; (nicht nachgebend) rigid **~ anlöten** to braze **~ werden** to harden **-es Bild** crisp or harsh picture, high-contrast or hard picture **-e Drehzahl** constant speed **-er Gang des Motors** rough engine **-er Griff** harsh feel **-es Holz** hard wood **-e Komponente** penetrating or hard component **-e Landung** heavy landing **-e Röhre** hard tube, hard valve, high-vacuum tube **-e Strahlen** hard rays **magnetisch -e Werkstoffe** magnetically hard materials

Hart-achse *f* hard axle **-auftragungsschweißen** *n* hardfacing **-auftragstechnik** *f* hardsurfacing

härtbar capable of being hardened or cemented, temperable, indurable, hardenable **durch Wärme ~** (Kunstharz) thermosetting (synthetic resin) **-e Masse** (thermoplatischer Stoff) thermoplastic (substance) **-er Stahldraht** hardenable steel wire

Härtbarkeit *f* hardenability, hardening capacity

Härtbarkeitskurve *f* hardness-cooling-rate curve

Hartbelag *m* rigid pavement

Hartblei *n* hard or antimonial lead **-munition** *f* hard-lead ball ammunition

Hartborst *m* crack formed during heat-treatment or hardening

Hartbrandziegel *m* hand-burned face brick

hartbrüchig brittle

Härte *f* temper, hardness, hardship, rigor, harshness **~ einer Röntgenröhre** hardness of an X-ray tube **~ des Wassers** hardness of water **schneidhaltende ~** hardness of great cutting effect

Härte-anlage *f* hardening plant **-anleitung** *f* instruction for hardening process **-bad** *n* case-hardening or tempering bath, quenching bath **-bereich** *m* hardness range **-beständig** stable to hard water **-bestimmung** *f* hardness determination **-bild** *n* grain structure **-bildner** *m* hardening constituent, salts causing hardness (of water) **-eignungseigenschaft** *f* degree of suitability for hardening **-einheit** *f* unit of hardness **-empfindlich** sensitive to hardness

Härte-fachmann *m* hardener, heat treater **-fähigkeit** *f* hardness capacity **-fall** *m* hardship case **-flammofen** *m* tempering flame furnace **-flüssigkeit** *f* tempering liquid **-grad** *m* degree of hardness, temper (of steel)

Harteisen *n* hard iron

Härtekurve *f* hardness gradient

Härtemaß *n* measure of hardness, hardness-measuring apparatus **-stab** *m* measure of hardness

Härtemesser *m* hardness gauge, penetrometer, sclerometer **~ nach Benoist** radio chronometer of Benoist **~ mit Platte** strip penetrometer

Härte-meßlupe *f* hardness-measuring magnifier **-messung** *f* measurement of hardness **-mittel** *n* hardening or tempering agent or compound

härten to harden, temper, caseharden **im Einsatz ~** to caseharden

Härten *n* hardening (martensitic hardening), quenching, tempering **gebrochenes ~** interrupted quenching (metal)

Härte-ofen *m* casehardening or tempering furnace **-öl** *n* tallow oil, steel-hardening oil **-presse** *f* quenching press **-probe** *f* hardness test, ball or pressure test **-prüfdiamanten** *pl* hardness-testing diamonds **-prüfer** *m*, **-prüfgerät** *n* durometer, hardness tester, sclerometer, hardness testing instrument **-prüf-**

maschine *f* hardness-testing machine
Härteprüfung *f* hardness test(ing) sclerometry ~ **vornehmen** to test for hardness ~ **nach dem Ritzverfahren** scratch hardness testing
Härte-prüfverfahren *n* hardness-test procedure **-pulver** *n* cementing powder, tempering powder, case hardening compound
Härter *m* hardener; (Klebstoff) setting agent
Härterei *f* hardening room or shop, heat-treating department
Härteriß *m* crack formed during heat-treatment or hardening, quenching crack **-bildung** *f* cracking on hardening
Härterwerden *n* hardening
Härte-salz *n* carburizing agent or material **-schicht** *f* hardened case **-skala** *f* scale of hardness **-spannung** *f* hardening strain **-streuung** *f* dispersion of hardness value **-stufe** *f* hardness number in terms of Mohs' scale
Härte-technik *f* hardening technique **-tiefe** *f* depth of hardening zone, depth of case or chill **-trog** *m* hardening trough **-verfahren** *n* hardening or tempering process **-verlauf** *m* hardness curve, gradient or distribution **-versuch** *m* hardness test **-verzug** *m* distortion due to hardening **-vorgang** *m* hardening operation or process **-wert** *m*, **-zahl** *f* hardness number, coefficient of hardness **-zeittest** *m* stroke cure
Hart-faserplatte *f* molded fiber board, hard board **-feuerporzellan** *n* fused silica **-floß** *m* spiegeleisen, specular pig or cast iron **-gebrannter Ziegel** clinker **-gelötet** brazed, hard-soldered **-geschlossenes Rohr** rigidly terminated tube (acoustics) **-gewebe** *n* hard tissue or plastic, a type of laminated phenol, indurated or impregnated fabric **-gezogen** hard-drawn **-gießen** to chill-cast **-glanz** *n* hard gloss **-glas** *n* hardened glass, pyrex **-grießmühle** *f* hard semolina mill
Hartgummi *m* hard rubber, ebonite, vulcanite **-auskleidung** *f* clothing lined with ebonite **-pimpel** *m* ebonite stud **-platte** *f* ebonite plate **-preßform** *f* ebonite press mold **-scheibe** *f* hard-rubber disk **-überzug** *m* vulcanite sheating, hard-rubber coating
Hartguß *m* chilled (cast) iron, chill casting **-geschoß** *n* chilled shot **-granate** *f* chilled-cast-iron shell **-herzstück** *n* casehardened frog or crossing (R.R.)
Hartgußkörper *m* chilled-cast-iron part **Pflug mit ~ und Schar** (Schwingpflug) chilled plow
Hartguß-kreuzung *f* casehardened frog or crossing (R.R.) **-läufer** *m* chilled-iron runner **-roststab** *m* chilled fire bar **-stück** *n* chill casting **-walze** *f* chilled roll
Hart-harz *n* hardened resin **-haue** *f* granite ax (min.)
Hartholz *n* hardwood, ironwood **-pflaster** *n* hard woodblock paving **-platte** *f* table of hardwood
Hart-kautschuk *m* hard caoutchouc **-klamm** *m* hard rebel rock, hard rock or stone (min.) **-kobalterz** *n*, **-kobaltkies** *m* skutterudite
Hartkupfer- und Bronzedrähte hard drawn copper and bronze wires
Hart-lagenregler *m* regulator with constant vane angle **-lagerhärtung** *f* induction hardening **-legierung** *f* alloy
Hartley-Schaltung Hartley oscillator circuit
Härtling *m* crab apple, hard slag or head, salamander, bear, (hard) dross
Hartlot *n* brazing mixture, hard or spelter solder **kupfer-zinklegiertes ~** brazing spelter
Hartlötdraht *m* hard-solder wire
hartlöten to braze, hard-solder
Hartlöten *n* process of brazing, or hard-soldering
Hartlöt-maschine *f* brazing machine **-mittel** *n* brazing flux **-verfahren** *n* brazing process
Hartlötung *f* hard-soldering, brazing
Hart-machen *n* act or process of hardening **-manganerz** *n* psilomelane, braunite **-meißel** *m* cold chisel **-messing** *n* hard brass
Hartmetall *n* any hard alloy or metal, carbide metal **gesintertes ~** cemented-carbide
Hartmetallauflage *f* hard facing ~ **des Ventils** valve facing
hartmetallbestücktes Werkzeug carbide tipped tool
Hartmetall-bestückung cutting alloy tip **-bohrer** *m* hard metal drill **-bohrkrone** *f* carbide-tipped drill bit **-drehstahl** *m* carbide-tipped tool **-fräser** *m* tungsten-carbide milling cutter **-gepanzerte Maschinenteile** carbide-clad machine parts **-messerkopf** *m* hard-alloy inserted tooth **-plättchen** *n* carbide tip
Hartmetallsägeblatt (mit eingesetzten Hartmetallzähnen) carbide-tipped saw blade
Hartmetallschneide *f*, **Werkzeug mit ~** carbide-tipped tool
Hartmetallsorte, gesinterte ~ hard cemented-carbide grade
Hartmetallwerkzeug *n* carbide (cutting) tool, metalloid cutting tool
hart-näckig tenacious, obstinate, stubborn, inveterate **-näckigkeit** *f* rigidity, tenacity
Hartpapier *n* hard paper (bakelized paper), laminated paper **-isolation** *f* hard-paper insulation **-umpressung** *f* hard paper pressing
Hart-pappe *f* carriage panels (paper), hard-board, fiberboard **-pech** *n* hard or dry pitch **-platte** *f* hard fiber plate **-porzellan** *n* hard (-glazed) porcelain **-porzellanwalze** *f* hard-porcelain roller **-postpapier** *n* bank post paper **-preßspan** *m* hard pressboard **-riegelholz** *n* dogwood **-riegelwerkzeugheft** *n* cornelian-wood handle
Hart-salz *n* hardsalt, sylvite **-schlagen** to cool-hammer, cold-hammer, hammer-harden **-schneidemetall** *n* hard-cutting alloy **-spat** *m* andalusite **-spiritus** *m* solid spirit **-stahl** *m* hard steel **-stahlbleche** *pl* high-carbon steel plates **-strahlaufnahmen** *pl* high kilovoltage radiography **-tastung** *f* square-wave keying **-tisch** *m* vulcanite or ebonite stage (optics)
Harttrocken-glanzöl *n* hard-drying brilliant oil **-öl** *n* slow-drying oil
Härtung *f* hardening (temper), quench(ing) (metal.) **unterbrochene ~** interrupted or broken hardening ~ **durch Zug** strain hardening
Härtungs-biegeprobe *f* bending test in tempered state **-fähigkeit** *f* hardening capacity **-flüssigkeit** *f* hardening liquid **-kohle** *f* hardening carbon or carbide, cementite, soluble iron carbide, cementing carbon **-maschine** *f* tempering or hardening machine **-mittel** *n* harden-

ing agent **-öl** *n* hardening oil **-rißempfindlichkeit** *f* hardening fracture sensitivity **-spannung** *f* hardening strain, internal hardening stress, quenching stress **-verfahren** *n* hardening process **-vermögen** *n* hardening capacity **-verzug** *m* distortion on hardening **-vorgang** *m* hardening operation

hart-verchromen to deposit hard chromium **-verchromt** chromium plated, **-verchromung** *f* hard-chromium plating, electro-plating with chromium **-vernickelung** *f* hard-nickel plating **-walze** *f* chilled roll

Hartwerden einer Röntgenröhre hardening of an X-ray tube

Hartzerkleinerung *f* crushing hard materials

Hartzinn *n* (hard) pewter

Harz *n* gums; (Natur~) rosin; (Kunst~) resin **mit ~ tränken** to resin

harzähnlich resinlike

Harzbildung *f* sludge formation (in fuel), gumming **~ im Öl** resinification of the oil

Harz-destillieranlage *f* oleoresin still **-elektrizität** *f* resinous electricity

harzen to resinate

Harz-entziehung *f* extraction of resin **-ester** *m* ester gum, rosin ester **-fett** *n* rosin grease **-frei** nonresinous, resin-free **-gasleistungsschalter** *m* resin gas load isolator **-gehalt** *m* percentage of resin **-geleimt** resin-sized **-haltig** resiniferous, resinic, resinous

harzig resinous, resinic

Harz-kernseife *f* resin soap **-körper** *m* resinic body, resinous substance **-leim** *m* vegetable size **-lösung** *f* resin milk, soluble resin **-lot** *n* resin solder **-milch** *f* resin size **-öl** *n* resin or rosin oil **-pasten** *pl* paste resins **-pech** *n* common rosin, liquid pitch

harz-reich highly resinous **-reserve** *f* resin resist **-salz** *n* resinate **-sauer** resinate of **-säure** *f* resinic acid **-sikkative** *n* resin drier **-stoff** *m* resinous substance **-umhüllter Sand** resin-coated sand

haschieren to hatch, cross-shade

Haschur *f* hachure, hatching (on a printing roll)

Haselnußöl *n* hazelnut oil

Haselwurz *f* cabaric root

Haspe *f* staple, hasp, clink, cramp iron, clincher

Haspel *f* winch, windlass, spool, reel, capstan, cathead **~ und Draht** reel and wire **~ mit reduzierbarem Durchmesser** coiler with collapsible drum **~ einer Schrämmaschine** hauling mechanism

Haspel-arbeit *f* reeling **-äscher** *m* paddle lime **-farbe** *f* paddle liquor

Haspelei *f* reeling room

Haspeler *m* windlasser, winder, **-kern** *m* reel core

Haspel-holm *m* slat of reel fly **-kette** *f* spool or reel chain **-kreuz** *n* cross bars of a winch

haspeln to reel, draw up (with a windlass)

Haspel-rad *n* chain pulley or reel wheel **-seil** *n* winch or windlass rope **-streckenförderung** *f* hauling engine **-stützen** *f pl* upstanders of a windlass **-versetzer** *m* pulley winder, sheaveman **-walze** *f* draw beam **-wärter** *m* windlass driver, whim driver **-welle** *f* drawbeam, windlass **-winde** *f* hoist, chain hoist, drilling hoist (oil drilling) **-zug** *m* forward tension or pull, reel tension

Hatchettolit *m* hatchettolite

Hau *m* cut, cutting, hewing

haubar fit for hewing or cutting, fellable

Haube *f* bonnet, hood, feedhead, cap, dome **~ für Kalksteinstreuer** hood for limestone spreader **~ mit verstellbaren Luftablaßklappen** controllable flapped cowl, gilled cowling

Hauben-ausschnitte *pl* louvers **-dach** *n* capped roof **-glühofen** *m* box annealing furnace **-griff** *m* hood handle **-halter** *m* bonnet fastener, hood fastener or catch **-körper** *m* top section, upper part **-mutter** *f* cap nut, dome nut **-riemen** *m* hood strap **-schloß** *n* hood catch or fastener **-übergang** *m* cowl fairing

Haubenverkleidung *f* engine cowling, cowl **abnehmbare ~** removable cowling **aerodynamisch günstige ~** low-drag cowling **verschiebbarer zylindrischer Teil der ~** sliding-cowl skirt **zylindrischer Teil der ~** cowl skirt **ringförmige Vertiefung am Umfang der ~** cowl well

Haubenverschluß *m* bonnet latch, hood latch

Hauch *m* breath, haze (on surfaces), bloom (on varnish, blast **-laut** *m* aspirate, aspirated sound **-schutz** (bei Spaltlampengeräten) breath protection sheet (shield) **-zeichen** *n* aspirate

Haue *f* hoe, mattock, pickax, adze, spanking

Haueisen *n* mattock (min.)

hauen to strike, (in filing) cut, hew

Hauen *n* (an der Walze) ragging

Hauer *m* hewer, pikeman, miner, cutter, getter, nailsmith's chisel **-arbeit** *f* cutting, hewing **-falz** *m* blade fold

Hauespitze *f* pick point

häufeln to stack, pile, staple, heap

Häufel-pflug *m* ridge plough **-tropfpflanzmaschine** *f* hill-drop corn planter

häufen to accumulate, heap up

Haufen *m* heap, batch, bunch, mass, pile, aggregation, accumulation **in losen ~** in bulk **über den ~ werfen** to overthrow, upset

Haufenchlorierung *f* heap chlorination

häufend cumulative

Haufen-laugen *n* heap leaching **-röstung** *f* heap roasting **-sand** *m* heap sand, black sand, green sand, body sand, backing sand **-verkohlung** *f* charcoal burning in long piles, coking in ridges

Haufenwolke *f* cumulus cloud **geschichtete ~** strato-cumulus cloud

haufenwolkenartig cumuliform

häufig frequent, often, usual **-er Abstich** frequent tapping

Häufigkeit *f* frequency, abundance

Häufigkeits-anomalien *pl* abundance anomalies **-auswertung** *f* evaluation of probability **-faktor** *m* frequency factor **-funktion** *f* frequency function **-kurve** *f* frequency probability or curve **-schaubild** *n* frequency diagram **-tabelle** *f* frequency distribution (table) **-verhältnis** *n* abundance ratio **-verteilung** *f* frequency distribution **-zähler** statistical distribution counter

häufigster Leistungswert modal performance

Häufler *m* hiller (agric. mach.)

Haufröstung *f* heap roasting

Häufung *f* accumulation **~ der Einzelmessungen**

useless multiplication of measurements

Häufungspunkt *m* point of accumulation, limiting point, bottleneck

Haufwerk *n* heap of debris, feed, raw ore **angereichertes ~** enriched produce

Haumesser *n* pruning hook

Haupt *n* head, chief, principal **~ einer Schleuse** bay or crown of a sluice

Haupt-abflußgraben *m* principal eduction canal **-abmessungen** *f pl* leading or controlling dimensions **-absatzgebiet** *n* principal market **-abschlußbogen** *m* final balance sheet **-abschlußventil** *n* containment valve **-absperrventil** *n* main check valve **-absperrhahn** *m* emergency stopcock or valve **-abstimmknopf** *m* main tuning button **-achse** *f* primary or major axis, principal or transverse axis, main shaft, vertical axis (of a rhombic crystal) **-achsenkreuz** *n* system of the principal axes **-achsentransformation** *f* principal-axis transformation

Haupt-ader *f* master lode **-alarmanzeiger** *m* master warning indicator (aviat) **-alarmleuchte** *f* master warning light **-alarmlampe** *f* (HA) main fuse alarm lamp **-amt** *n* main or master office, main exchange **-amtsleiter** *m* manager of the head office **-anblaseventil** *n* main flooding valve **-anfahrventil** *n* main starting air valve **-angriff** *m* main attack or effort **-anker** *m* main or sheet or waist anchor **-anlagen** *pl* main assets

Hauptanode in einer Vakuumröhre anode plate

Hauptanschluß *m* subscriber's main station, main switchboard, trunk station **Teilnehmer ~** subscriber's main station, main set

Hauptanschlußleitung *f* direct exchange line, subscriber's line

Hauptantrieb *m* main gear, principal motive

Hauptantriebs-achse *f* main driving gear **-feder** *f* main driving spring **-kupplungshebel** *m* main-drive clutch lever **-lager** *n* main shaft bearing **-rad** *n* main driving gear, main drive wheel **-welle** *f* main drive shaft, head shaft

Haupt-apparat *m* main set (teleph) **-arm** *m* main gallery (min.)

Hauptast des Druckporenzifferdiagramms virgin curve of pressure-void ratio diagram

Haupt-aufgabe *f* principal business, chief task **-ausgangsmaterial** main basic material **-auslösetaste** *f* master release key **-ausschalter** *m* master switch **-ausschlag** *m* principal deflection or angular movement **-ausschuß** *m* central committee, main directorate **-auswanderungsstrecke** *f* distance in azimuth traveled by target during time of flight **-azimut** *m* principal azimuth

Haupt-bahn *f* main line or track, principal railway **-bahnhof** *m* main railroad station **-balken** *m* main beam **-ballasttank** *m* main ballast tank **-band** *n* master tape **-bandfilter** *n* principal channel filter **-batterie** *f* main battery **-bedingung** *f* main essential condition **-bedienungsstand** *m* main operating platform **-behälter** *m* main tank or reservoir **-beleuchtung** *f* hot-light (TV) **-beobachtungsraum** *m* main observation sector **-beobachtungsstelle** *f* main observation post **-beruf** *m* main occupation

Hauptbestandteil *m* chief constituent **~ einer Mineralölmischung** principal ingredient in a mineral-oil base

Haupt-betriebsschalter *m* main or master switch **-bewehrung** *f* main reinforcement, main bar **-binder** *m* principal truss **-blickrichtung** *f* principal line of sight **-bogen** *m* primary bow **-bolzen** *m* kingbolt **-brechungsindizes** *pl* principal indices of refraction **-buch** *n* ledger **-buchhalter** *m* auditor

Haupt-daten *pl* principal ratings **-deck** *n* main deck **-dehnungen** *pl* principal extensions **-deich** *m* main dike **-diagonale** *f* principal diagonal **-dichtung** *f* main gasket **-druckdauer** *f* duration of the principal pressure (of a shock wave) **-drücke** *pl* principal strains and stresses **-drucklager** *n* main thrust bearing **-düse** *f* main (metering) jet

Hauptebene *f* principal plane or surface **~ des Objektivs** principal plane of the lens

Hauptebenenabstand *m* distance between principal planes or points

Haupt-E-fläche *f* principal E plane

Haupt-einbruchsstelle *f* main point of penetration **-einfallwinkel** *m* angle of principal incidence **-einflugzeichen** *n* (HEZ) middle marker (of JLS)

Haupt-einheit *f* master unit **-einlaufschütze** *f* main inlet dike or sluice **-entladungsstrecke** *f* main gap **-entwässerungsgraben** *m* main drainage canal **-erfordernis** *n* primary requirement **-erregerwicklung** *f* main field coil **-erzeugnis** *n* main product **-exzenter** *m* main cam

Haupt-fahrgestell *n* main undercarriage **-fallschirm** *m* main sail or body (of parachute) **-feder** *f* master spring **-federbett** *n* top-leaf plate

Hauptfeld *n* main field **-ausgleichspule** *f* main field compensating coil **-spannung** *f* transient internal voltage (servo)

Haupt-fernamt *n* main zone center **-fesselkabel** *n* main mooring cable **-feuer** *n* strong ground light (aviation), principal airway beacon **-filter** *n* main filter **-flügel** *m* main or principal wing **-flügelrippe** *f* principal wing rib, compression rib

Haupt-fluglinie *f* trunk route, main line **-flugstreckenverkehr** *m* trunk route traffic (aviat.) **-fluß** *m* main or largest river or stream **-förderstrecke** *f* main entry, main road **-formänderung** *f* main deformation, main change in form **-formanten** *pl* main or basic formants **-frequenz** *f* primary frequency **-funkstelle** *f* station **-gang** *m* main side, champion or mother lode **-gasleitung** *f* gas main

Haupt-gebäude *n* main building **-gedinge** *n* tribute **-gedingenehmer** *m* contractor **-geleise** *n* main track **-gelenk** *n* capital link **-gemengteile** *pl* major constituents (geol.) **-geschoß** *n* principal story, main floor **-geschwindigkeit** *f* main-velocity component **-gesprächszeit** *f* busy period (teleph.) **-gestalter** *m* constructor, manufacturer, producer **-gestell** *n* headstall

Haupt-getriebe *n* main transmission gear **-gitter** *n* parent lattice **-gleichung** *f* fundamental equation **-grundlage** *f* main basis **-gruppenkontrolle** *f* intermediate control **-haken** *m* main hook **-halteleine** *f* main mooring line **-halt-**

fläche *f* main supporting surface

Haupt-H-fläche *f* principal H plane

Haupt-hohlleiter *m* main wave guide **-holm** *m* main spar **-holmgurt** *m* main-spar flange **-horchraum** *m* main listening area or sector **-horizont** *m* horizon trace (phot.) **-horizontale** *f* axis of tilt (phot.) **-horizontalebene** *f* principal horizontal plane **-hubwerk** *n* main hoisting tackle **-impulsgeber** *m* master pulse generator **-inhalt** *m* summary (book) **-invarianten** *pl* principal invariants

Haupt-kabel *n* main cable **-kammer** *f* main camera **-kanal** *m* route for subscriber's main cable, main sewer **-kartei** *f* master file **-katze** *f* main crab **-kessel** *m* main boiler **-kettbaum** *m* main beam **-keule** *f* major lobe **-kippachse** *f* main tilting axis

Haupt-kostenstellen *pl* main accounts headings **-kommandogeschwindigkeit** *f* velocity at main cutoff signal (guided missiles) **-kontrollschieber** *m* master control valve, master gate valve **-kräfte** *f pl* main forces **-kreis** *m* main circuit

Hauptkrümmungen *pl* principal stresses **~ einer Fläche** principal curvatures of a surface

Haupt-krümmungshalbmesser *m* principal radius of curvature **-richtung** *f* direction of principal curvature

Haupt-kupplung *f* main clutch **-ladung** *f* initial charge, detonator charge, primary propelling charge

Hauptlager *n* main bearing **~ der Kurbelwelle** main bearing of crankshaft

Haupt-lagerplatte *f* main bearer plate **-lagerzapfen** *m* hub gudgeon **-landungsgestell** *n* main landing gear **-längsbalken** *m* main longitudinal girder or beam **-langträger** *m* main girder **-lappen** *m* major lobe **-lastverteilungsstelle für das gesamte Netz** main load-distributing station for entire network **-lauf** *m* main runner **-lehre** *f* master gauge **-leitstand** *m* main firecontrol station (navy) **-leitung** *f* main pipe, main line, power line, trunk line

Hauptlenz-leitung *f* main pump lead **-pumpe** *f* main ballast pump

Haupt-lichtleitung *f* lighting mains **-liegehafen** *m* base harbor, main base **-linie** *f* primary or main line, trunk line, axis, main route, principal line (spectroscopy) **-linienkabel** *n* main cable **-lösung** *f* principal solution **-lotebene** *f* principal plane (phot.) **-luftdüse** *f* (Vergaser) main barrel (carburetor) **-lufteinlaß** *m* main air intake **-luftlinie** *f* trunk airway **-lüftungsrohr** *n* main ventilating pipe **-luftweg** *m* main airway (air route)

Haupt-magazin *n* main magazine **-magnetzünder** *m* main-magnet fuse **-maschine** *f* main engine **-maschinenanlage** *f* main power plant **-masse** *f* main body (army), bulk **-menge** *f* bulk **-merkmal** *n* characteristic feature, criterion **-meßmarke** *f* principal collimating mark **-meßstelle** *f* main plotting station **-minor** *n* principal minor **-moment** *n* main factor **-motor** *m* main engine **-motorenantrieb** *m* main engine drive

Haupt-nachschubstelle *f* main base of supply **-nenner** *m* common denominator **-niederlage** *f* main depot **-niederlassung** *f* registered office, principal abode **-normale einer Kurve** principal of a curve **-normalenvektor** *m* principal normal vector **-öffnung** *f* (Brücke) main span **-ölbohrung** *f* main oil gallery **-ölleitung** *f* main oil pipe

Haupt-oszillator *m* master oscillator **-patent** *n* parent specification, main or original patent **-peilstelle** *f* main direction-finding station **-periode** *f* major cycle **-pfeiler** *m* main column, principal support **-phase** *f* main phase **-planzugritzel** *f* main driving pinion

Hauptpleuel *n* master (connecting) rod, fork rod **einteiliges ~** solid master rod **geteiltes ~** two-piece master rod **ungeteiltes ~** solid master connecting rod **Gruppe von ~ und Nebenpleueln** master- and link-rod assembly

Haupt-pleuelkurbellager *n* big-end bearing **-pleuelstange** *f* master connecting rod **-poldynamoblech** *n* main pole dynamo sheet **-polunterlegblech** *n* main pole shim **-programm** *n* master program (info proc.) **-pumpe** *f* main pump **-pumpenstange** *f* main (pump) spear

Hauptpunkt *m* principal or unit point **bildseitiger** (hinterer) **~** internal perspective center (of the lens) **dingseitiger** (vorderer) **~** external perspective center (of the lens)

Hauptpunkt-brechwert *m* principal-point refraction **-marke** *f* Aero., principal (central) mark **-triangulation** *f* principal-point triangulation

Hauptquantenzahl *f* principal quantum number

Haupt-rad *n* main or bull wheel **-rädergetriebe** *n* main gearing **-rahmen** *m* main framework **-regelung** *f* principal or main adjustment **-regler** *m* master regulator, main governor or regulator (of a turbine) **-reglertafel** *f* main-regulator board **-reinigung** *f* complete cleaning **-reserve** *f* main reserve **-reservoir** *n* accumulator (air) **-resonanzfrequenz** *f* main resonance frequency **-richtung** *f* main direction **-richtungspunkt** *m* base point, primary aiming point **-riemenscheibe** *f* main pulley **-ring** *m* main traverse **-rippe** *f* main or compression rib (of wing)

Haupt-rohr *n* main pipe, main, main oscillation generator (in independent-drive system) **-rohrleitung** *f* trunk pipe line **-rolle** *f* leading or star role **-rollendarsteller** *m* principal or star performer **-rotor** *m* main rotor **-rotorkopf** *m* main rotor hub **-rückführung** *f* primary feedback **-sache** *f* chief matter, main point or item **-sächlich** principal, main, chief, essential **-sammellinse** *f* second lens (in electron gun, cathode-ray tube) **-sammelschiene** *f* main bus bar **-sanitätslager** *n* supply depot **-satz** *m* fundamental principle, law, or theorem, axiom (math.), principal theorem **-säule** *f* main column

Haupt-schacht *m* main shaft **-schachtbetrieb** *m* main pit **-schalter** *m* main, master or line switch, line breaker **-schalttafel** *f* main switchboard **-schaltung** *f* main switching or shifting **-schaltwarte** *f* main switch station **-schatten** *m* umbra (optics) **-schiene einer Weiche** main or stock rail of a siding **-schlittenhandrad** *n* carriage handwheel **-schlittenvorschubhebel** *m* carriage feed lever

Haupt-schluß *m* series-wound **-schlußdynamomaschine** *f* series-wound generator, series dynamo **-schlüssel** *m* master key **-schlüsselstollen** *m* main adit **-schlußlampe** *f* series lamp **-schlußmotor** *m* series (-wound starter),

(-wound electric) motor **-schlußschaltung** *f* series winding (elec.) **-schmierleitung** *f* main lubricating oil pipe **-schneide** *f* main cutting edge

Hauptschnitt *m* principal section, section on which principal stress occurs **erster ~** primary or tangential plane, meridional plane (optics) **zweiter ~** secondary plane, sagittal plane (optics)

Hauptschnittverfahren *n* main-station intersection method, flash spotting by leading ray

Haupt-schubstange *f* master connecting rod **-schuldiger** *m* chief offender **-schütz** *n* principal sluice, main valve, main dike or floodgate **-schutzzone** *f* main- or fighter-defense area **-schwelle** *f* main sill, principal beam (tie beam) **-schwimmer** *m* principal or main float **-sehne** *f* principal chord of an airfoil **-sehrichtung** *f* principal axis or direction of vision **-seitenband** *n* transmitted sideband **-sender** *m* main oscillator or transmitter **-senkrechte** *f* principal (vertical) line (phot.) **-separationstrommel** *f* main separation screen (min.) **-septen** *pl* major septum (geol.) **-sequenzstern** *m* star of principal sequence **-serie** *f* chief series

Haupt-sicherung *f* main fuse **-signal** *n* inner marker signal, main entrance signal, main marker (aviation) **-signalrahmen** *m* main signal frame **-skalenteilungen** *pl* major graduations **-sohle** *f* main sill **-spannung** *f* principal stress **-spannungslinie** *f* stress trajectory **-spannungsverhältnis** *n* principal-stress ratio **-spannvorrichtung** *f* main assembly jig **-spant** *n*, **-spantschnitt** *f* midships section, main frame, main bulkhead **-sparren** *m* principal rafter

Hauptspeise-graben *m* main-feeder trench (sluice) **-leitung** *f* main feeder (elec.) **-ventil** *n* main-feed check valve (navy)

Hauptspektrum *n* principal spectrum

Hauptspindel *f* main spindle **-bohrung** *f* hole through spindle **-drehzahlen** main spindle speeds **-getriebe** *n* headstock main gearing **-stillsetzung** *f* stopping of the headstock spindle

Hauptspitzenfläche (eines Quarzkristalls) major apex face (cryst.)

Haupt-spule *f* primary coil **-spülung** *f* main scavenging **-stab** *m* main strut **-ständer** *m* main standrad **-station** *f* (Funk) master station **-stelle** *f* main station **-stellung** *f* main position, main emplacement **-steuerventil** *n* main control valve **-stiel** *m* main strut **-stollen** *m* main gallery (min.)

Haupt-strahl *m* main flash, most powerful lightning discharge, principal ray, main jet **-strahlrichtung** *f* main radiation direction **-strahlzipfel** *m* main lobe of radiation **-strang** *m* main trunk line **-strangkabel** *n* main cable **-straße** *f* main rod **-strecke** *f* main level, carrying gate (petroleum), main road **-streckenfeuer** *n* main, trunk-route, or airway beacon **-streckungen** *pl* principal stretchings **-streichrichtung** *f* general direction of strike (min.) **-strick** *m* cardinal point

Hauptstrom *m* main current (elec.) **-abnehmer** *m* main pantograph **-bogenlampe** *f* series arc lamp **-dynamo** *m*, **-dynamomaschine** *f* series-wound generator, series dynamo **-erregung** *f* series excitation **-filter** *m* main current filter **-kreis** *m* main or primary circuit **-maschine** *f* series dynamo **-motor** *m* series motor, series-wound motor **-ölfilter** *n* main lubricating oil filter **-regler** *m*, **regelwerk** *n* series regulator **-thermorelais** *n* line-current thermal relay

Hauptströmung *f* main current (river), main flow

Hauptstrom-wechselrichter *m* parallel inverter **-werk** *n* differential, shunt, or series regulator

Haupt-stück *n* principal piece, body (speech, book) **-stufe** *f* main step on a flotation gear or stage **-stütze** *f* backbone, principal support **-tafel** *f* main board **-takt** *m* main stop **-taktgeberfrequenz** *f* master-impulse generator frequency **-tangentenkurven** *pl* principal tangent curves **-taste** *f* master key **-tätigkeit** *f* principal duty **-tauchtank** *m* main ballast tank **-tauchzellenventil** *n* main tank vent (torpedo) **-teil** *m* body, main part **-tippachse** *f* main tilting axis (phot.)

Hauptträger *m* longéron, main spar (aviation), main beam or girder **~ des Verfahrens** chief profit-making factor of the process

Haupt-tragfläche *f* main supporting surface **-tragflügelmoment** *n* principal moment supporting planes **-trägheitsachse** *f* main axis of inertia, principal axis of inertia **-trägheitsmomente** *pl* principal moments **-tragseil** *n* lift wire (aviation) **-trajektorien** *pl* principal trajectories **-triangulation** *f* primary triangulation **-triebrad** *n* leader (driving gear) **-triebstange** *f* main connecting rod **-trommel** *f* main cylinder **-trommelrad** *n* main drum wheel **-tubus** *m* body tube

Haupt-überwachungslampe *f* master pilot lamp **-uhr** *f* principal or master clock **-unterbau** *m* main bearing (airplane) **-unterschied** *m* main difference **-valenzkette** *f* primary valence chain **-ventil** *n* main valve **-verankerungsmastseil** *n* main mooring-mast line **-veranlagung** *f* main assessment **-verbrennungsraum** *m* main combustion chamber **-verhandlung** *f* main oral hearings, main proceedings **-verkehrsstraße** *f* main highway, thoroughfare

Hauptverkehrsstunde *f* busy hour or period, rush hour **~ des Amtes** office busy hour **~ für eine Leitung der Leitungsgruppe** circuit or circuit-group busy hour

Haupt-verkehrszeit *f* busy period **-vermittlungsstelle** *f* main exchange **-verschwindungspunkt** *m* main vanishing point **-verspannung** *f* main bracing **-verstärker** *m* main amplifier **-verstärkeramt** *n* main repeater station **-verstellhebel** *m* main adjusting lever **-verteiler** *m* main distributing frame **-verteilergestell** *n* main frame **-verteilerleitung** *f* main lubricating-oil line **-vertikalebene** *f* principal (vertical) plane (phot.) **-vertrag** *m* main contract

Haupt-verwaltung *f* administration, general offices, main office **-verwaltungsgebäude** *n* chief administrative building, head-office building **-verwendungsgebiet** *n* chief use **-vorgelege** *n* main reduction gear, transfer case **-waagerechte** *f* axis of tilt **-walze** *f* main drum or cylinder

Hauptweg *m* main leg of position vector between guided missile and cutoff ground site **-übersetzung** *f* main-leg coefficient, the difference of the two position vectors *r* and *s* in the Wolman cutoff method

Haupt-welle *f* transmission shaft, main or line shaft **-wellenlager** *n* main bearing **-wellenstrang** *m* head-shaft line **-werft** *f* main factory or yard **-werkzeugschlitten** *m* main tool slide **-wert** *m* principal value **-wetterstrecke** *f* main air head, wind or air gate **-wetterwarte** *f* main meteorological station, main weather station **-wicklung** *f* main winding **-widerstandsstellung** *f* main line of resistance **-windleitung** *f* air-distributing main, main blast line **-windrichtung** *f* prevailing direction of wind

Haupt-zahl *f* cardinal number **-zahnrad** *n* main cogwheel, main toothed wheel **-zeichen** *n* suffix **-zeile** *f* headline **-zeit** *f* productive or machining time **-ziel** *n* primary target **-zielfernrohr** *n* director (fire control) **-zipfel** *m* major lobe antenna

Haupt-zug *m* main flue (in boiler), main object, outstanding or principal feature **-züge** *pl* principal strains and stresses **-zuggraben** *m* principal ditch (canals) **-zuleitung** *f* main inlet **-zumeßdüse** *f* (Vergaser) main (metering) jet (carburetor) **-zündung** *f* primary ignition lead **-zweck** *m* main purpose

Hauptzylinder *m* main cylinder **~ beim Sternmotor** master rod cylinder

Haus *n* house, building, firm **-anlage** *f* house exchange equipment **-anschluß** *m* service line **-anschlußkasten** *m* house connecting box **-anschlußversicherung** *f* main service fuse **-bewohner** *m* lodger, tenant **-bock** *m* house beetle (longicorn varieties) **-brand** *m* domestic fuel, miner's house coal **-einführung** *f* house lead-in

Hausenblase *f* isinglass

Hausentwässerung *f* house pipe drains

Häuser-makler *m* realtor, real-estate broker

Haus-fernsprechanlage *f* house telephone plant, domestic telephone system **-fernsprecher** *m* house telephone **-flur** *m* hallway **-gerät** *n* household appliance

Haushalt *m* household, housekeeping, budget, budgetary expenses or estimates **~ und Bauten** department of finance and building

Haushaltanlage *f* domestic plant

Haushalts-geräte *pl* household appliances **-jahr** *n* fiscal year **-maschine** *f* household appliance **-ordnung** *f* budgetary instructions or regulations **-plan** *m* budget **-wesen** *n* budgetary matters **-zwecke** *pl* domestic purposes

haushoch as high as a house, huge, enormous

Haus-installation *f* home wiring **-keller** *m* cellar **-korrektur** *f* first proof **-leiterkabel** *n* indoor cable **-leitung** *f* extension, house intercommunication line

Hausmannit *m* hausmannite

Hausnebenstellenanlage mit Wählbetrieb P.A.X. (private automatic exchange)

Haus-rohrpost *f* (pneumatic) house tube(s) **-ruf** *m* house-telephone call **-schornstein** *m* chimney of a building

Hausse *f* rise or advance in prices, upward tendency, (exchange) boom **-bewegung** *f* upward movement, upswing of prices

Haussier *m* bull, bullish operator

Haus-signalvorrichtung *f* signal apparatus for domestic use **-sprechanlage** *f* intercom(munication) system **-stelle** *f* private station, extension station without exchange facilities **-strom** *m* house current

Haustein *m* ashlar, freestone **-mauerwerk** *n* ashler masonry

Haus-telephon *n* house telephone, (private) home telephone, telephone extension **-verhandlung** *f* departmental negotiation **-verteilung** *f* internal distribution **-verwaltung** *f* internal administration **-wart** *m* home air warden, custodian, janitor **-wasserleitung** *f* house water pipe or water supply **-wecker** *m* domestic electric bell

Hauszentrale *f* domestic lighting plant **automatische ~** P.A.X. (private automatic exchange)

Haut *f* skin, membrane, hide, cover, shell, film, shell plating, coating **äußere ~** shell **tragende ~** stressed skin

Haut-abdruckverfahren *n* replica process **-ableitung** *f* derivation to the skin **-abstand** *m* (focal) skin distance

hautätzend vesicant, blister-forming

Haut-aufkupferungsverfahren *n* skin coppering process **-beschädigung** *f* radiodermatitis **-bildung** *f* film formation

Hautblech *n* skin sheat, plate for the skin **-streifen** *m* covering strip

Häutchen *n* thin film

Haut-dicke *f* skin depth **-effekt** *m* skin effect, Kelvin effect **-einheitsdosis** *f* erythema dose

häuten to skin, shed skin, scalp

Haut-entgiftungsmittel *n* skin-decontamination agent **-entgiftungssalbe** *f* skin-decontamination ointment **-gift** *n* vesicant agent **-konstruktion** *f* skin construction **-krankheit** *f* skin disease **-leim** *m* hide glue **-negativ** *n* film negative **-pflege** *f* care of the skin **-pflegemittel** *n* cosmetic **-pulverschüttelmethode** *f* hide powder shaking method

Haut-reibung *f* rubbing of the skin, skin friction **-riß** *m* scratch **-spiculae** *pl* dermal spicules **-substanz** *f* hide substance **-widerstand** *m* dermal or skin resistance **-wirkung** *f* skin effect, Kelvin effect **-wirkungsverlust** *m* skin-effect losses

Havarie *f* damage (to ship or cargo), average **-arbeit** *f* salvage work

havarieren to strike the average, average

havariert damaged at sea (ship)

H-Barren *m* rolling slab

Heavisidesche Einheitsfunktion Heaviside unit function

Heavisideschicht *f* Heaviside layer

heb-bar raisable **-bewegung** *f* vertical upward motion **-drehwähler** *m* vertical and rotary selector, Strowger switch or selector, two-motion selector

Hebe-anlage *f* elevating plant **-antrieb** *m* hoist drive **-arm** *m* lever, lifting arm **-auge** *n* eyebolt **-baum** *m* lever, jack, handspike, crowbar, heaver **-block** *m* jack screw

Hebebock *m* lifting jack, jack **hydraulischer ~** hydraulic jack

Hebebockklaue *f* jack claw

Hebe-boden *m* vertically adjustable bottom **-brücke** *f* vertical-lift bridge **-bügel** *m* link **-bühne** *f* elevating platform **-bündel** *n* elevator bushing **-daumen** *m* lift, lifting cam, cam, wiper, tappet, disk with lobes **-eisen** *n* crowbar

-elektromagnet *m* lifting magnet **-feder** *f* lifting spring **-flasche** *f* hoisting jack

Hebe-gerät *n* lifting apparatus **-gerüst** *n* lifting frame **-haspel** *f* winch **-klaue** *f* hoisting clevis, runner **-klinke** *f* lifting pawl **-kloben** *m* hoisting link **-kopf** *m* tappet **-kraft** *f* lifting capacity, lifting power **-kran** *m* hoisting crane

Hebel *m* lever, jack, baffler, moment arm, pedal **~ für die Auslösung des Selbstganges** feed-trip lever **~ des Fahrschalters** controller handle **~ zum Festklemmen des Rundtisches** rotary-attachment binder **~ zum Feststellen des Konsolschlittens** saddle-clamp lever **~ zur Hebevorrichtung** handle controlling the gears for raising crossrail **~ für den schnellen Rückgang** quick-return lever

Hebel, ~ für den Spindelgeschwindigkeitswechsel speed-change lever **~ zur Verschiebung der Riemenscheibenwelle** lever for shifting friction-disk shaft **~ für den Vertikalselbstgang** power-driven elevating lever **~ für Vorlaufwerk** lever for delayed action mechanism **~ zum Auslösen des Vorschubes** feed-trip lever **~ für den Vorschubwechsel** feed-change lever **~ für den Wechsel der Spindelgeschwindigkeiten** speed-changing lever

Hebel, einen ~ umlegen to traverse a lever **einarmiger ~** one-armed lever **drehbar gelagerter ~** pivoted lever **~ ganz durchtreten** pedal fully depressed **hin- und hergehender ~** oscillating or rocking lever **T-förmiger ~** T lever **zweiarmiger ~** fulcrumed or two-armed lever

Hebel-achsenanschlag *m* lever axle stop

Hebelade *f* lighter bar, jack, crane **-fuß** *m* pry pole

Hebel-anlasser *m* lever starter **-anordnung** *f* lever arrangement **-anschlag** *m* lever stop **-anzeigevorrichtung** lever operated recorder

Hebelarm *m*, **langer ~** effort arm

Hebel-arm *m* lever arm **-armmikrometerschraube** *f* lever micro meter screw **-auge** *n* holder for lever **-auslassung** *f* lever release **-ausrüstung** *f* handle attachment **-ausschalter** *m* lever switch **-bahn** *m* lever track **-beziehung** *f* lever-relation diagram, equilibrium diagram **-block** *m* combined bomb-release levers **-bolzen** *m* bolt for lever, lever pin **-bremse** *f* lever brake

Hebel-detektor *m* lever-adjusted cat-whisker crystal detector **-dornpresse** *f* lever-operated mandrel **-drehpunkt** *m* fulcrum of lever **-druck** *m* lever pressure **-einschalter** *m* lever switch **-eisen** *n* crowbar **-fangvorrichtung** *f* lever-arresting device **-flaschen** lever-bottles **-förmig** lever-shaped **-führung** *f* lever guide

Hebel-gestänge *n* leverbar **-griff** *m* lever handle, brake lever **-hammer** *m* hammer operated on the principle of a lever **-kette** *f* lever chain **-klappenventil** *n* flap valve with levers **-kluppe** *f* sleeve twisters **-kopf** *m* lever head **-kraft** *f* leverage **-lager** *n* lever support **-lagerplatte** *f* lever bearing plate **-lochstanze** *f* lever punch **-lose Hackmaschine** leverless cultivator **-mikrometerschraube** *f* lever micrometer screw

hebeln to use levers, move with a lever

Hebel-presse *f* lever press **-pumpe** *f* lever pump **-quetsche** *f* lever-operated squeeze **-registrierkasse** *f* cash register with lever action

Hebelschalter *m* lever or fork shifter, lever switch **~ mit drei Stellungen** three-position key

Hebel-schaltung *f* lever control **-schere** *f* lever shears, alligator or crocodile shears **-schneidemaschine** *f* lever cutting machine **-schuh** *m* lever foot **-sicherheitsventil** *n* lever safety valve **-stange** *f* lever arm or rod, brake, balanced lever **-stanze** *f* lever punch **-stanzmaschine** *f* lever punching machine **-stellung** *f* lever position **-stellwerk** *n* lever-set keyboard

Hebel-steuerung *f* lever control, spring catch **-stift** *m* lever pin **-stoßdämpfer** *m* knee-action shock absorber **-system** *n* compound lever arrangement **-taste** *f* lever key **-träger** *m* fulcrum bracket **-übersetzung** *f* leverage, lever transmission **-übertragung** *f* setting arm

Hebelumschalter *m* lever switch, double-throw switch **doppelpoliger ~** double-lever switch

Hebel-unterlage *f* fulcrum, prop of a lever **-ventil** *n* lever valve **-verbindungen** *pl* system of levers **-verhältnis** *n* leverage **-verlängerungseinrichtung** *f* lever-expanding device **-verschluß** *m* lever fastener, lever breech-mechanism **-vorrichtung** *f* lever apparatus **-vorschneider** *m* double-action pliers

Hebel-waage *f* weighing lever, beam or lever scale **-weg** *m* lever path **-welle** *f* steering lever-shaft **-werk** *n* lever system, lifting appliance **-winde** *f* lever jack **-wirkung** *f* leverage, lever action, purchase

Hebe-magnet *m* vertical magnet, lifting magnet, hoisting magnet **-magnetanker** *m* lifting armature **-maschine** *f* hoisting machine **-mechanismus** *m* lifting mechanism **-mittel** *n* camel

heben to lift, raise, heave, hoist

Heben *n* raising, lift(ing), vertical upward motion **~ und Richten des Gleises** packing and ranging the permanent way (R.R.) **~ eines Wracks** refloating a wreck

Hebe-prahm *m* pontoon, lighter **-pumpe** *f* lifting pump **-punkt** *m* fulcrum

Heber *m* siphon, pipette, syringe, lever, lifter, jack

Heberad *n* wheel elevator, hoisting wheel **-gerüst** *n* frame for scoop wheel

Heber-barometer *n* siphon barometer **-einstellung** *f* control regulation **-gruppe** *f* group of battery of siphons (large dams) **-haarrohr** *n* capillary siphon

Hebering *m* ring for the lifting core

Heberlein-Verfahren *n* Heberlein (sintering) process

Heber-leitung *f* siphoning installation **-luftdruckmesser** *m* siphon barometer

Heberolle *f* pulley

Heber-pumpe mit Druckluft compressed-air lift pump **-rohr** *n* siphon pipe, siphon **-rohrverschluß** *m* trap **-säuremesser** *m* hydrometer syringe, siphon acidometer **-schieber** *m* elevator slide **-schreiber** *m* siphon recorder **-schreibermotor** *m* mouse mill

Heber-walze *f* vibrator **-welle** *f* vibrator shaft

Hebe-schiff *n* lifting or salvage ship **-schraube** *f* raising or lifting screw, screw jack, jackscrew, pressure screw **-seil** *n* lifting cable **-stange** *f* lever, crowbar **-stift** *m* lifting stud **-stück** *n* lifter

Hebetisch *m* lifting table or platform, tilting table **doppelseitiger ~** front and back elevator

Hebetrog *m* lifting trough, chute, vat, tray

Hebe- und Senkbewegung *f* upward and down-

ward motion
Hebe- und Senkvorrichtung *f* lifting and lowering arrangement
Hebevorrichtung *f* lifting device or tackle, lifting or hoisting apparatus ~ **für Schachtdeckel** manholecover hook
Hebe-walze *f* vibrator roller **-walzenbewegung** *f* lever for vibrator roller **-wäsche** *f* siphon separator **-wasserwirbel** *m* lifting-water swivel **-werk** *n* draw works, elevator, hoisting device **-werkzeug** *n* appliance for lifting or hoisting **-winde** *f* lifting jack, lever jack, screw gear, hoisting crab
Hebezeug *n* lifting appliance, hoisting or lifting apparatus or equipment, elevator, lifting unit, winding engine **-kettenrad** *n* block-chain sprocket
Hebezug *m* crab (mach.) **-kette** *f* block chain **-seil** *n* hoisting rope
Hebezwinge *f* lifting bar
Hebling *m* tappet
Heb-magnet *m* vertical magnet **-schritt** *m* vertical step
Hebung *f* raising, (frost) heaving, lift, swelling, heave, (surveying) elevation
Hebungswelle *f* wave caused by a rising stage
Hechel *f* hackle, comb, hatched
Hechelei *f* hackling room
Hechelwerg *n* hackle tow
Hechler *m* hackler **-zange** *f* comb pliers
Heck *n* stern (navy), poop, tail, rear, afterdeck, counter **nach dem ~ zu** sternward(s)
heckangetrieben rear-engine driven
Heck-anker *m* stern anchor **-antrieb** *m* rear-engine drive **-ausleger** *m* tail boom **-beschwerung bei der Verankerung** mooring drag (aviation) **-boden** *m* tail base **-düse** *f* tail nozzle
Hecke *f* hedge, fence, brushwood
Heckenschere *f* hedge clipper
Heck-explosion *f* tail explosion **-fahrwerk** *n* rear landing gear **-feuer** *n* stern light **-kanzel** *f* tail turret **-kappe** *f* stern (tail) cap **-knick** *m* stern (tail) droop **-koffer** *m* test set for steering machine **-kühler** *m* stern or rear radiator (aviation)
Heck-lampe *f* astern light **-last** *f* tail load **-lastig** stern-heavy **-laterne** *f* stern light, poop lantern **-licht** *n* (tail) stern light, rear or wake light **-motor** *m* rear engine drive **-motorwagen** *m* rear-engine motor car **-mulde** *f* exhaust depression (missiles) **-rad** *n* tail wheel
Heck-raddampfer *m* stern-wheel steamer **-ring** *m* tail ring
Heckrotor *m* tail rotor **-blattanschluß** *m* tail rotor grip **-kopflager** *pl* tail rotor hub bearings
Heck-rumpf *m* tail hull **-schränkung** *f* tail decalage **-schütze** *m* rear or tail gunner **-schwer** stern-heavy **-spitze** *f* stern (point) tip **-sporn** *m* tail skid **-träger** *m* keel girder **-welle** *f* tail or stern wave (aviat.) **-zelle ohne Einbauten** tail-hull guided missiles
Hede *f* hemp, oakum, tow **-leinen** *n* tow linen
Hedenbergit *m* hedenbergite
Hederichvernichtungspulver *n* charlock-destroying powder
Hedespinnerei *f* tow spinning
Hedyphan *m* hedyphane
Heer *n* army **stehendes ~** standing army
Heeres-druckvorschrift *f* army regulations, army manual **-einrichtung** *f* army establishment, organization, or institution **-luftwaffe** *f* army air force **-meteorologe** *m* army meteorologist **-motorisierung** *f* motorization of the army **-museum** *n* army museum **-versorgung** *f* quartermaster service, supply of arms and services **-verwaltung** *f* army administration
Hefe *f* yeast **-aufziehvorrichtung** *f* yearst-rousing or yeast-cultivating apparatus **-behälter** *m* yeast tank **-kulturapparat** *m* yeast fermenter **-pfropfen** *m* yeast stopper **-raum** *m* yeast room **-reinzucht-apparat** *m* pure-yeasting machine
Hefnerkerze *f* Hefner candle
Heft *n* handle, grip, hilt, haft, booklet, bulletin, issue or number (of a periodical) **~ mit Stützpunktbildern** *pl* pole-diagram book
Heft-apparat *m* stitching apparatus **-bolzen** *m* locating pin **-draht** *m* stitching wire, stapling wire **-eisen** *n* punty
Heftel *m* clasp, hook and eye
heften to attach, fasten, pin, tack, stitch, sew
Heften *n* stitching, sewing
Hefter *m* stitcher, sewer
Heft-faden *m* binding (sewing) thread **-gaze** *f* stitching gauze **-großvorrichtung** *f* power-stitching fixture **-haken** *m* stitching hook
heftig violent, vigorous, forcible, impetuous **-er Regen** heavy rain
Heftigkeit *f* vehemence, violence, vigor, intensity
Heft-klammer *f* wire stitch, stiching hook **-lade** *f* sewing press
Heftmaschine *f* stapling or stitching machine **~ für Drahtheftung** stapling machine **~ für Fadenheftung** thread-stitching machine
Heft-nadel *f* stitching needle **-niet** *n* tacking, binding, dummy, or temporary rivet, "stitch" rivet, rivet not transmitting a force **-nietung** *f* tack welding **-pflaster** *n* adhesive plaster **-probe** *f* stitching test **-ring** *m* binding ring **-säge** *f* pad saw **-schnur** *f* band, band string **-schraube** *f* tacking bolt **-schweißen** to tack-weld **-schweißung** *f* tack welding
Heftung *f* stitching, sewing
Heft-vorrichtung *f* stitcher **-weise** in parts or numbers **-zapfen** *m* tang **-zwecke** *f* thumbtack, drawing pin, peg for drawing boards
Hegeler-Ofen *m* Hegeler (semimechanical rabble) furnace
hegen to enclose, entertain
Heide-mehl *n*, **-kornmehl** *n* buckwheat flour
Heidenstein *m* heath stone, ericite (min.)
Heidetorf *m* peat
heilbar curable
Heilbehandlung *f* cure, treatment (med.)
heilen to heal, cure
Heil-gerät *n* therapeutic apparatus **-mittel** *n* remedy **-zweck** *m* therapeutic purpose **-wirkung** *f* healing
Heimarbeit *f* homework
Heimat *f* home, native country **-erzeugnis** *n* native manufacture **-flotte** *f* home fleet **-flugplatz** *m* home air base **-frequenz** *f* code for test-missile frequency **-gebiet** *n* homeland zone of the interior **-hafen** *m* home port, port of registry **-horst** *m* home base **-schlag** *m* pigeon loft

heimisch native, domestic **-e Rohstoffe** home-grown raw materials

Heim-lauf *m* return stroke or motion, retrace or flyback (of pencil or beam, in television tube, often gated by blanking pulse)

Heimpfahl *m* graded post fixing maximum permissible elevation of reservoir-water surface

Heim- und Tor-Fernsprechanlage *f* home converser and entrance telephone system

H-Eisen n H iron

Heising-Modulation *f* Heising or choke modulation, constant-current modulation

heiß hot, torrid **~ ausgezogen** hard driven **~ aussehen** to look hot **~ gewalzt** hot rolled **-es Eisen** hot iron **-es Ende** high side, top end **-er Stöpsel** hot plug **-e Welle** hot wave **-e Zone** torrid zone

Heiß-achsenschmiere *f* antifriction grease **-ätzversuch** *m* hot-etching test **-beschlag** *m* hoist fitting, lug **-blasen** to blow hot, blow up, airblast **-blasen** *n* blowing hot, blowing up, air blasting, air blow **-blasperiode** *f* air blow, airblasting period **-brüchig** hot-short, brittle, in the hot state

Heißdampf *m* superheated steam **-dreiradwalze** *f* three-wheel superheated steam roller **-kühler** *m* desuperheater **-regler** *m* desuperheater **-schieberring** *m* **für Lokomotiven** superheated slide for locomotives **-tandemwalze** *f* tandem superheated steam roller

Heißeisen-säge *f* hot-iron saw **-schere** *f* hot ingot shear **-hebelsäge** *f* hot-iron lever-type saw

heißen to be named, be called, order

heißerblasenes Roheisen hot-blast pig iron

Heißfixierung *f* heat-setting

Heißgas *n* hot gas **-schieber** *m* hot-gas valve, valve for superheated gases

heißgekühlt hot-cooled **-er Motor** hot-cooled engine

heißgelaufen overheated **-es Lager** heated (hot) bearing

heiß-grädig difficultly fusible **-kleber** *m* hot-setting adhesive **-korrosionsbeständig** high-temperature corrosion-resistant

Heiß-kastenverfahren *n* hot box process **-klebend** heat sealing **-korrosion** *f* hot corrosion **-kühlsystem** *n* high-boiling-point cooling system

Heißkühlung *f* high-temperature liquid-cooling, Prestone cooling, ethylene glycol cooling, evaporation cooling **Motor mit ~** glycol installation

Heiß-kühlungsvorrichtung *f* glycol installation **-lagerfett** *n* high melting-point grease **-lagerplatz** *m* hot store **-lauf** *m* hot run **-laufen** to run hot, overheat **-leiter** *m* pyroelectric conductor, hot conductor (with negative temperature coefficient), third-class conductor **-löseverfahren** *n* hot dissolving process **-löten** to hot-solder, sweat **-lötstelle** *f* hot junction (thermoelement)

Heißluft *f* hot or warm air, air rarefied by heating **-apparat** *m* hot-air apparatus **-ballon** *m* hot-air balloon **-bläser** *m* hot-air blower **-duschen** *pl* hot-air suppliers **-enteiser** *m* hot-air deicer **-erhitzer** *m* air heater

Heißluft-förderleitung *f*, **-leitung** *f* hot-air supply pipe **-mansarde** *f* hot air drying loft **-maschine** *f* hot-air engine **-schlitz** *m* hot-air slot **-speiseleitung** *f* hot-air supply pipe **-sprüher** *m* hot-air sprayer **-strahl** *m* thermal jet **-strahlantrieb** *m* jet propulsion **-strahltriebwerk** *n* jet-propilsion engine **-strahlverfahren** *n* jet-propulsion system **-zuführung** *f* hot-air conduction or delivery

Heiß-maschine *f* hoisting engine **-öse** *f* lifting eye **-prägepresse** *f* embossing press for hot process **-punkte** *pl* hoisting points **-richten** *n* hot-straightening (rails) **-satiniermaschine** *f* burnisher (photo.) **-siegelfähiges Papier** heat-sealing paper **-siegelverfahren** *n* heat-sealing **-spritzverfahren** *n* hot spraying process

Heiß-strahltriebwerk *n* thermal-jet engine **-tauchen** *n* dip-molding **-temperaturzone** *f* hot-temperature zone, soaking zone **-verfestigung** *f* hot work hardening **-verkleben** *n* heat-sealing **-vorrichtung** *f* hoisting device, hoist crane

Heißwasser-apparat *m* hot-water apparatus **-behälter** *m* hot-water tank **-entnahme** *f* hot water supply **-heizung** *f* hot-water heating **-speicher** *m* hot-water reservoir, boiler **-vulkanisation** *f* water cure

Heißwerden *n* heating, becoming hot (chem.)

Heißwind *m* hot-air blast, hot blast **-austritt** *m* hotblast outlet **-leitung** *f* hot-blast main **-ofen** *m* hot-blast furnace **-schieber** *m* hot-blast slide valve **-ventil** *n* hot-blast valve **-verschluß** *m* hot-blast valve joint

Heißzapfenfett *n* hot neck grease

heiter serene, glad, clear (weather), bright, cheerful **-er Tag** clear sky

heizabgestimmt heat-regulated **-er Strom** regulated- or adjustedfilament current

Heiz-abstimmung *f* tuning of filament circuit **-akkumulator** *m* filament accumulator **-anlage** *f* heat installation, heating installation **-anschluß** *m* heating connection

Heizanzug für Höhenflug electrically heated suit for high-altitude flying

Heizapparat *m* heater, heating apparatus

Heizband *n* strip heater

heizbares Mikroskop hot-stage microscope

Heiz-batterie *f* A battery, filament battery **-bauteil** *m* structural heater element **-behälter** *m* combustion unit, burner rocket motor **-behälterunterteil** *n* lower portion of the combustion unit **-brenner** *m* preheating torch

Heizdampf *m* steam for heating, superheated steam **-kondensat** *n* heating-steam condensate **-kühlanlage** *f* superheated-steam cooling installation **-kühler** *m* superheated-steam cooler, desuperheater **-leitung** *f* steam-heating line

Heiz-daten *pl* filament data **-draht** *m* heater, heated filament, heating wire, voltage amplifier **-drahtfaden** *m* heater wire, voltage amplifier **-drahtmanometer** *n* hot-wire gauge **-drossel** *f* heater control

Heize *f* charge of pig (smelting)

Heiz-effekt *m* heating effect, calorific intensity **-effektmesser** *m* calorimeter **-einrichtung** *f* heating installation **-einsatz** *m* heating inset (elec.) **-element** *n* heating element

heizen to heat, make a fire

Heizenergie *f* filament energy

Heizer *m* stoker, fireman **-motor** *m* (car) heater motor **-schaufel** *f* firing or stoker scoop **-stand** *m* stokehold

Heizfaden *m* heating filament (in indirectly

heated tubes), cathode ~ **mit Thoriumschicht** thoriated filament

Heizfaden-leistung *f* filament power **-spannung** *f* heater (filament) voltage **-speisung** *f* filament supply **-strom** *m* heater current **-temperatur** *f* heater temperature

Heizfähigkeit *f* heating capacity

Heizfläche *f* heating surface **feuerberührte** ~ convection heat surface

Heiz-flächenbelastung *f* heat transferred per unit surface **-flamme** *f* heating flame **-flansch** *m* heating element **-flüssigkeit** *f* heating liquid

Heizgas *n* heating or fuel gas **-brenner** *m* fuel-gas burner **-strom** *m* fuel-gas current

Heizgebläse *n* heater fan

Heizgerät *n* heating apparatus **gasbetriebenes** ~ gas heater

Heiz-gewebe *n* heating fabric **-gitter** *n* heating grill **-kammer** *f* heating chamber, firebox, stokehold **-kanal** *m* (heating) flue, subway for heating and electric mains **-kanalsystem** *n* system of heating flues **-kathode** *f* filament (of valve) **-kathodenroentgenröhre** *f* hot-cathode X-ray tube **-kessel** *m* kettle, boiler, caldron **-kesselanlage** *f* heating boiler plant **-kissen** *n* heating pad **-kopf** (Ofen) port end **-kordelträger** *m* heating cord carrier

Heizkörper *m* heating body, heater, radiator, heating element **eingehängter** ~ floating calandria **freistrahlender** ~ electric radiator

Heizkörper-anschlüsse *pl* element leads **-lack** *m* heat-resisting varnish **-verschalung** *f* radiater grill

Heiz-kraft *f* heating, calorific, thermal power **-kraftwerk** *n* heating power station **-kräftiges Gas** gas of high calorific value **-kranz** *m* ring burner **-kreis** *m* heating circuit (radio), filament circuit **-kuppelung** *f* heating-pipe coupling **-lampe** *f* heating lamp **-lampenzündung** *f* flame ignition, hottube ignition **-leistung** *f* filament power or wattage, filament energy consumption **-leiter** *m* heating conducter **-leitung** *f* heater circuit

Heiz-loch *n* fire door, stokehole **-lötstelle** *f* hot junction (of a thermocouple) **-lüfter** *m* fan-forced heater **-mantel** *m* steam jacket, heating jacket **-mantelrohr** *n* jacketed pipe **-maschine** *f* filament generator, generator for the filament supply **-maß** *n* emission efficiency **-material** *n* fuel **-messer** *m* calorimeter **-muffe** *f* heating muff **-oberfläche** *f* heating surface **-ofen** *m* heating furnace or oven, heater

Heizöl *n* fuel oil **-destillat** *n* stove distillate **-förderpumpe** *f* oil-fuel pump **-messer** *m* fuel-oil meter **-schiff** *n* fuel ship **-tank** *m* oil tank **-zufuhr** *f* fuel-oil supply

Heiz-periode *f* heating season **-platte** *f* heating plate **-punkt** *m* heating point **-quelle** *f* source of heat **-raum** *m* firebox, heating or combustion chamber **-raumschlange** *f* heating worm **-register** *n* radiator **-regler** *m* filament, variable rheostat **-ring** *m* heating collar **-rohr** *n* fire tube, heating tube, radiator pipe **-röhrenkessel** *m* firetube boiler **-röhrensystem** *n* flue system **-rohrkessel** *m* heated-tube boiler

Heiz-sammler *m* filament battery or supply, heater battery, filament accumulator, current-storage cell **-schacht** *m* heating section **-scheibe** *f* heating plate **-schicht** *f* hot layer **-schlange** *f* heating coil or worm **-schlauch** *m* air bag or tube **-schrank** *m* heating chamber **-seite** *f* filament voltage **-spannung** *f* (heater) filament voltage

Heiz-spirale *f* heating spiral (coil) **-spule** *f*, **-spulensicherung** *f* heating coil, heater **-stab** *m* rod heater, heating rod **-stiefel** *m* electrically heated boots **-stoff** *m* fuel **-strahltriebwerk** *n* thermal jet engine

Heizstrom *m* filament current, heating, heat, or heater current **-änderung** *f* heating-current variation **-automatik** *f* automatic regulation of heating current **-einstellung** *f* setting of heating current **-kontrollrelais** *n* heating-current supervisory relay **-kreis** *m* (heater) filament circuit **-quelle** *f* filament current source **-regler** *m* filament-current regulation **-stärke** *f* heating-current intensity **-verbrauch** *m* filament or heater current consumption

Heiz-system *n* heating system **-teppich** *m* heating mat **-transformator** *m* heating(-current) transformer, filament (supply) transformer **-tür** *f* fire door

Heiz- und Widerstandsdrähte *pl* **und -bänder** *pl* resistance wires and tapes

Heizung *f* heating, firing ~ **durch Gammastrahlung** gamma heating

Heizungs-anlage *f* heating plant **-gebläse** *n* heating blower **-kesselthermometer** *n* thermometer for heating boilers **-schalter** *m* heating switch **-schütz** *m* heating contactor **-sender** *m* heating transmitter **-vorrichtung** *f* heating device or apparatus

Heiz-unruhe *f* fluctuation in heating current **-verfahren** *n* heating method **-vergaser** *m* carburetor heater **-verlust** *m* heat loss **-vermögen** *n* heating capacity **-vorgang** *m* heating process **-vorrichtung** *f* heater, heating device or apparatus **-wendel** *m* (coiled) filament, heater spiral or coil **-werk** *n* heating station

Heizwert *m* calorific or heating power or value, pyrometric effect **oberer** ~ gross calorific value **unterer** ~ net calorific power

Heizwert-bestimmung *f* heating-value determination **-messer** *m* calorimeter **-zahl** *f* heating value per unit weight, calorific value, fuel ratio

Heiz-wickelung *f* filament winding **-widerstand** *m* filament rheostat or resistance, heating conductor, resistor element, resistance unit **-wirkung** *f* heating effect **-wirkungsgrad** *m* heating efficiency **-zeit** *f* heating period **-zone** *f* heating or soaking zone **-zug** *m* heating flue **-zweck** *m* heating purpose

Hektar *n* hectare

Hektograph *m* hectograph

Hektographen-blatt *n* hectographing paper **-masse** *f* copying paste, hectograph mass or pulp

hektographieren to manifold

hektographischer Abzug hectographic copy

Hekto-gramm *n* hectogram **-liter** *m* hectoliter **-meterwellen** *pl* hectometric waves **-watt** *n* hectowatt

Helberger-Ofen *m* Helberger furnace (indirect-heating type of electric smelting)

Helfe *f* heddle, heald

helfen to help, aid, assist

Helfer *m* helper, aid, assistant

Helferin *f* woman assistant or helper, nurse

Helgen *m* building slip

Helikometer *n* helicometer

Helikopter *m* helicopter

Helio-chromie *f* color photography, photochromation **-chromogravüre** *f* heliochromogravure **-chromoskop** *n* three-color photography apparatus **-graph** *m* heliograph

Heliographie *f* heliography **-papier** *n* black-line paper

Helio-gravüre *f* heliography **-meter** *n* heliometer

Helioskop *n* helioscop

Heliostat *n* heliostat

Heliothermometer *n* heliothermometer

Helipot *n* helipotentiometer

Helium *n* helium **-ähnlich** helium-like **-blasenkammer** *f* helium bubble chamber **-druckgefäß** *n* helium pressure tank **-gas** *n* helium gas **-gewinnung** *f* recovery or extraction of helium **-hauptserienkontinuum** *n* helium, continuous spectrum of principal series

Helium-ionenstoß *m* helium-ion collision **-kern** *m* helium nucleus **-niveaus** *pl* helium levels **-röhre** *f* helium tube **-schicht** *f* (dünne) helium film **-wellenfunktion** *f* helium wavefunction

Helixgetriebe *n* skew spur wheel

Helizität *f* helicity

hell light, bright, transparent, clear, brilliant, pale, shrill (acoustics) ~ **färben** to tint **-e Bildstellen** light tones **-e Klangfarbe** strident or shrill timbre **-es Öl** pale oil **-e Stelle** clear portion

Hell-adaptation *f* light adaption **-anpassung** *f* bright adaptation, light adaption, photopia **-ätzerei** *f* light etching **-bezugswert** *m* albedo **-blau** pale blue, light blue

Helldunkel *n* twilight, dusk, black and white **-feldschieber** *m* bright-dark field slider **-intervall** *n* light-dark range **-schalter** *m* dimming switch **-steuerung** *f* black-white or on-off control, brilliance control

Helle *f* luminance (TV) **spezifische** ~ luminosity (TV)

Hellebardenspitze *f* cusp of the first kind

Hellegat *n* storeroom

Hellegatsmann *m* storekeeper

Helleinformation *f* luminance information (TV)

Hellempfindlichkeit *f*, **spektrale** ~ relative luminosity factor

hellere Klangfarbe higher timbre

Helle-Signal, Helligkeitssignal *n* (gemischt aus R, G und B) luminance signal (TV)

Hellesteuerung *f*, **dynamische** ~ tracking (TV)

hellfarbig light-colored

Hellfeld *n* bright field **-abbildung** *f* bright-field illumination **-beleuchtung** *f* bright ground illumination (micros.) **-beobachtung** *f* bright-field observation **-bild** *n* bright field image **-blende** *f* bright field diaphragm

hell-gelb light yellow **-grau** light gray **-hörig** noise-propagating

Helligkeit *f* clearness, brightness, brilliancy, luminosity, intensity ~ **als photometrische Größe** luminance (TV) ~ **als physikalische Größe** photometric brightness, luminance, radiance ~ **als psychologische Größe** visual sensation ~ **eines Objektivs** speed of a lens or objective **Flächen konstanter** ~ surfaces of constant brightness **falsche** ~ apparent brightness **mittlere** ~ (average) mean brightness, average background illumination (television)

Helligkeits-änderung *f* brightness change **-angleichung** *f* brightness matching **-blende** *f* intensity diaphragm **-eindruck** *m* sensation of brightness **-einstellung** *f* brightness setting **-empfindlichkeit** *f* light sensitivity **-impuls** *m* brightening pulse **-messung** *f* brightness measurement **-modulation** *f* intensity modulation **-niveau** *n* level of brightness **-regler** *m* background control, brightness regulator

Helligkeitsregelung *f*, **selbsttätige** ~ automatic background, automatic brightness control (ABC)

Helligkeits-regulierung *f* regulation of light volume or of intensity **-schwankung** *f* brightness fluctuation **-schwebung** *f* brightness flutter **-signal** *n* luminance signal **-sinn** *m* sense of light **-skala** *f* brightness scale, tone control aperture **-sprung** *m* contrast range, jump in brightness, sudden brightening up

Helligkeitssteuerung *f* intensity modulation, brilliance modulation, brightness control ~ **des Lichtfleckes** brightness control of (light) spot

Helligkeits-stufe *f* degree of luminosity or brightness, intermediate gray value (between black and white), shading or tonal value **-übergang** *m* brightness transition (half tones) (teleph.) **-umfang** *m* contrast range of a picture, range-of-brightness contrast, key (of a picture) **-unterschiede** *pl* tones of brightness **-veränderung** *f* brightness-intensity change **-verhältnis** *n* intensity ratio **-verteilung** *f* brightness distribution **-wechsel** *m* change of brightness, frame frequency, number of illuminations of a picture point **-welle** *f* brilliance wave (electronics) **-werte** *pl* brightness values, density or shading values

Helling *f* slip, shipyard, berth **auf die** ~ **strecken** to lay down (ship) **gedeckte** ~ covered slip

Helling-anlage *f* shipbuilding plant **-gerüst** *n* slipway superstructure **-kran** *m* ship building crane **-mole** *f* berth mole **-ponton** *m* caisson of a building slip **-tisch** *m* building cradle **-winde** *f* shipyard winch

hell-klare Farbe clear light tint **-linien** *f pl* light-dark lines **-mark** *f* range-marker pip **-matt** semidull, slightly dulled **-modulation** *f* positive modulation **-rosa** light pink

hellrot light red **-glühend** bright red-hot **-glühhitze** *f*, **-glut** *f* bright-red heat

Hellschreiber *m* Siemens-Hell printer; Hell receiver

Hell-sektoren *pl* shutter openings **-sender** *m* Hell sender **-stellungen** *pl* light positions **-steuerimpuls** *m* indicator gate (rdr) **-steuerung** *f* modulation to light condition **-strohgelb** light straw color **-suchen** *n* bright search, illuminated searching **-tastimpuls** *m* unblanking pulse, intensity modulation pulse **-tönend** high pitched **-tran** *m* clear fish oil **-weiß** clear white

Helm *m* helmet, helm, shaft (of hammer), head (of still), mouth (of converter) **-decke** *f* dome, spherical vault

Helmholtzsche Kreise Helmholtz circles

Helm-keil *m* wedge for fastening helve to the

hammer **-öler** *m* oil cap **-rohr** *n*, **-schnabel** *m* nose, nozzle, beak (still) **-stange** *f* broach post **-stangenspitze** *f* hip knob **-überzug** *m* helmet cover

Helvit *m* helvite

Hematometer *n* haematometer

Hemd *n* shell (of blast furnace), shirt, chemise

Hemdbrett *n* thickness board

hemianopische Pupillenstarre *f* hemianopic pupillary rigidity

Hemiëder *n* hemihedron, hemihedral form or crystal

Hemiëdrie *f* hemihedrism, hemihedral forms

hemiëdrisch hemihedral

Hemimorphismus *m* hemihedrism, heminorphism

Hemimorphit *m* hydrous silicate of zinc, siliceous calamine

Hemisphäre *f* hemisphere

hemitrop hemitropic, twinned

hemizyklisch hemicyclic(al)

Hemmblech *n* drag plate

Hemme *f* device for stopping, locking, arresting, adjusting, or setting

hemmen to check, retard, curb, inhibit, obstruct, restrain, arrest, lock, dam, detain, maintain **ein Rad ~** to skid, chock, or scotch a wheel

hemmend lagging **-e Kraft** restraining force **-e Zusätze** retarding additives

Hemm-keil *m* recoil buffer (wedge), chock **-kette** *f* drag chain **-kurvenhindernis** *n* retarding-curve obstacle **-leisten** *pl* stops on the carriage (print)

Hemmnis *n* handicap, obstruction

Hemm-rad *n* brake wheel, escape or escapement wheel **-schraube** *f* setscrew **-schuh** *m* drag shoe, skid shoe, clog, brake, wheel drag **-seil** *n* check-rope **-stange** *f* control plunger **-stoff** *m* inhibitor

Hemmung *f* jam, stoppage, check, restraint, hindrance, inhibition, retardation, escapement, arrest, brake action **freie ~** chronometer escapement **ruhende ~** repose escapement **schleifende ~** deadbeat escapement **zurückspringende ~** recoil escapement

Hemmungen, Beseitigung von ~ immediate action (ordnance term)

Hemmungs-ebene *f* checking plane **-grund** *m* disability (law) **-körper** *m* restraining substance, decelerator **-lappen** *m* pallet of escapement **-losigkeit** *f* impetuosity **-rad** *n* escapement or balance or swing wheel

Hemm-vorrichtung *f* braking or impedance device **-werk** *n* retard mechanism **-zeug** *n* trigger, drag, wheel drag, skid

Hengst *m* stallion **-fohlen** *n* colt

Henkel *m* lug, ear, handle, hook, bail **-locheisen** *n* arch punch, wad punch

Hennegatt *n* helm port

Henry *n* henry, secohm, quadrant **-sches Gesetz** Henry's law

Hepatit *m* hepatite, liver stone

Heptaeder *n* heptahedron

Heptaldehyd *n* heptaldehyde

Heptan *n* heptane

Hepten *n* heptene

Hepthode *f* heptode, pentagrid valve

Heptin *n* heptyne

Heptylalkohol *m* heptylalcohol

Heptylen *n* heptylene

herab-arbeiten to work down **-bewegung** *f* downward motion **-drücken** to press down, minimize, depress **-fahren** to descend **-führen** to lead down **-führung** *f* leading down, downleads (of an antenna)

herab-gehen to descend, sink **-gesetzt** reduced **-gleiten** to slide down **-hängen** to depend, be pending or suspended

herablaßbares Fenster drop window

herablassen to lower

Herablaß-feder *f* lowering spring **-griff** *m* lowering handle **-stange** *f* lowering spindle

herab-mindern to minimize, reduce, diminish, lessen **-minderung der Viskosität** viscosity breaking **-rieseln** to trickle down

herabsenkbar capable of being lowered **unter die Wolken -e Gondel** subcloud car

herabsetzen to reduce, bring down, decrease, degrade, lower, disparage **~ des Wirkungsgrades** decreasing the efficiency

Herabsetzung *f* reduction, degradation, disparagement, decrease, stepping down (of potential, gearing, etc.), decrease (speed, by step-down gear), submultiplication **~ des Wertes** depreciation

Herabsetzungsbeiwert *m* reduction coefficient

herab-sinken to descend **-stimmen** to tune down **-stürzen** to plunge down **-transformieren** to step down (elec.) **-tropfen** to drip (chem.)

Herabziehung *f* depression

Heranbildung *f* training **~ von Flugzeugführern** training of pilots

heranbrausen to roar up

Heranführung *f* concentration, bringing forward, bringing up (mil.) **~ der Kräfte** concentration of forces

heran-kommend oncoming **-locken** to decoy, lure **-marschieren** to march up, come up, approach **-nahen** to approach **-schaffen** to bring up **-ziehen** to detail, bring up, draw near **-ziehung** *f* requisitioning, drawing up

Herapatit *n* herapatite

herauf-kommen to come up, to approach (said of bad weather) **-setzen** to run up, increase **-transformieren** to step up (elec.) **-ziehen** to pull up, raise

heraus-arbeiten to work out, to rough-work **-brechen** to burst forth **-bringen** to bring out, export, make available, release (e.g. new model) **-destillieren** to distill out **-diffundieren** to diffuse out **-drehen** to turn out **-drücken** to force out, push out **-fallen** to drop out

heraus-fangen to extricate from a spin (aviation) **-fließen** to flow out **-gabe** *f* giving up, surrender, issue, publication

herausgearbeitet, aus dem Vollen ~ cut or machined from solid

heraus-geben to give out, up, or back, give change, publish, edit **-geber** *m* editor, publisher **-gleiten** to slip out **-greifen** to single out, extract **-heben** to lift out, remove, emphasize, note, point out **-heber** *m* extractor **-hebung** *f* uplift, elevation **-hören** to apperceive **-klappbar** collapsible, tilted upwards

herauskommen to come out, become known, be published, recover from a spin (aviation)

heraus-kratzen to rake out, scrape out, rabble out **-kristallisieren** to crystallize out **-lassen** to let out **-lösen** to eliminate (chem.) **-manövrieren** to maneuver out of position

herausnehmbar removable **-er Einsatzkessel** removable inner boiler **-er Laufflächenteil der Reifenform** insert thread

heraus-nehmen to remove, lift out, take out **-oxydieren** to oxidize off **-pipettieren** to pipette out, remove with pipette **-pressen** to press out, extrude

Herausquetschen *n* squeezing out **seitliches ~ des Nietschaftes zwischen den Blechen** spewing

heraus-ragen to protrude, project **-reduzieren** to reduce out **-reißen** to tear out, pull out **-rollen** to take off (the printing cylinder) **-schälen** to enucleate **-schaufeln** to shovel out **-schlagen** to knock out **-schleudern** to eject, throw out, spatter **-schneiden** to cut out **-schrauben** to unscrew **-schwenken** to swing out **-setzen** to settle out

heraus-sickern to trickle out, ooze out **-springen** to trip (circuit breaker) **-spritzen** to spurt out, spray out, jet, spout out, squirt out, back out **-spülen** to wash out, rinse out, expel **-stehen** to stand out, project **-stoßen** to push out, knock out **-strömen** to stream out, pour out **-stülpen** to extrovert **-suchen** to single out **-treten** protrude, emerge, step out of **-waschen** to wash out, scrub out **-wickeln** to extricate (from an entanglement)

herausziehen to extract, draw out, march out, remove, withdraw **das Modell ~** to draw a pattern

Herausziehen *n* withdrawal

herb harsh, sharp, acrid

herbei-führen to bring about **-holen** to fetch **-rufen** to summon, call for (someone) **-schaffen** to procure, bring up

Herbertgerät *n* Herbert bridge unit

Herbheit *f* bitterness, acerbity

Herbst *m* autumn, fall **-äquinoktium -Tagundnachtgleiche** *f* autumnal equinox

Herd *m* fireplace, range, forge, hearth, furnace (bottom), firebox, smelting chamber, laboratory sole **-abmessung** *f* hearth dimension **-abteilung** *f* table section **-ansatz** *m* hearth accretion **-anschluß** *m* bottom contact **-arbeit** *f* table concentration, table work, tabling, hearth smelting

Herd-asche *f* hearth ashes **-auskleidung** *f* hearth lining **-bearbeitung** *f* table treatment **-beheizung** *f* bottom heating **-blei** *n* furnace lead **-boden** *m* hearth bottom **-bolzen** *m* stove bolt **-brücke** *f* fire bridge

Herde *f* herd, flock, drove

Herd-einsatz *m* hearth casing **-eisen** *n* double-wall box **-fläche** *f* hearth area **-flächenleistung** *f* hearth-area efficiency **-flammofen** *m* reverberatory hearth furnace **-flicken** *n* hearth patching **-form** *f* open sand mold, hearth mold **-formerei** *f* open sand molding **-frischarbeit** *f* refinery process or operation, knobbling **-frischeisen** *n* knobbled or bloomery iron

Herd-frischen *n* hearth refining, open-hearth refining **-frischprozeß** *m* refinery process **-frischroheisen** *n* pig iron for refining **-frischschlacke** *f* refinery slag or cinder **-frischstahl** *m* charcoal-hearth steel, open-hearth steel **-futter** *n* hearth lining or fettling **-gebiet** *n* focal region **-gewölbe** *n* arched roof of a hearth **-glas** *n* glass which has flown into the hearth (glass mfg.) **-guß** *m* open sand casting, furnace or stove casting **-gußform** *f* open sand mold

Herd-konzentrat *n* table concentrate **-körper** *m* furnace proper **-material** *n* hearth material **-mauer** *f* cutoff wall, upstream toe wall, curtain **-mulde** *f* saucer-shaped furnace bottom **-ofen** *m* hearth-type furnace **-ofenprozeß** *m* open-hearth process **-platte** *f* hearth plate, stove plate or lid **-rahmen** *m* test ring

Herdraum *m* heating chamber **~ des Flammofens** body of a reverberatory furnace

Herdraumdruck-regelung *f* control furnace pressure

Herdrehsperrklinke *f* double dog (in a Strowger selector)

Herd-schmelzofen *m* hearth-type smelting furnace **-schraube** *f* stove bolt **-sohle** *f* hearth or furnace bottom, base of hearth, hearth sole **-stahl** *m* fine steel **-tiefe** *f* focal depth **-tiefofen** *m* vertical-heating furnace, soaking-pit furnace **-wanderung** *f* hearth wall **-zacken** *m* hearth plate **-zug** *m* hearth flue

hereingewinnen to get, win, work

Hereingewinnung, hydraulische ~ hydraulicking

Herein-lotsen *n* piloting-in by ground-air radio communication **-schlagen** to beat into (the ground) **-treibearbeit** *f* drift work, drifting

Hergang *m* process

hergeben to yield

hergebracht conventional

hergestellt made, prepared, recovered **galvanisch ~** electroplated **serienmäßig ~ werden** to be in production

herhalten to serve as a makeshift or stopgap, submit to, endure, pay, suffice

Hering *m* herring; tent peg

herkömmlich conventional **-e, übliche Bauart** orthodox design

Her-kunft *f* origin **-leiten** to derive, deduce **-leitung** *f* deduction, return circuit, derivation (math)

hermetisch hermetic(al) **-es Rohr** blank pipe (well) **-er Verschluß** hermetic seal

Hermeto-Verschraubung *f* Hermeto screw coupling

Hermitizität *f* hermiticity

Héroult-Lichtbogenofen *m* Héroult electric-arc furnace **-Lichtbogen-Widerstandsofen** *m* Héroult direct-heating arc furnace, Héroult electrode-hearth arc furnace, Héroult series arc furnace **-Schachtofen** *m* Héroult ore-smelting furnace **-Widerstandsofen** *m* Héroult resistance furnace

Herpolhodie *f* herpolhode **-kegel** *m* herpolhode cone

herragen to extend

herrenlos ownerless, derelict

herrichten to prepare, arrange, adjust, adapt

Herrlichkeit *f* splendor, excellence

herrschen to rule, reign, prevail, govern

herrschend prevailing

herrühren to emanate, originate

herrührend due to, owing to

Herstellbarkeit *f*, **leichte ~** ease of fabrication

herstellen to manufacture, produce, prepare, process **(Anlagen) ~** to erect, set up, establish **einen Stromkreis ~** to close or make a circuit

Streifen ~ to prepare the tape **eine Verbindung** ~ to establish a connection **künstlich** ~ to synthesize **sachgemäß** ~ to make with appropriateness **serienmäßig** ~ to produce in quantity

Hersteller *m* manufacturer, maker, producer, mill owner **-firma** *f* manufacturing firm

Herstellung *f* manufacture, fitting, fixing up, construction, production, recovery, restitution ~ **einer Verbindung** establishment of a connection **fabrikationsmäßige** ~ processing **wirtschaftliche** ~ economical manufacture

Herstellungs-daten *pl* construction specification **-dauer** *f* operating time **-gang** *m* manufacturing method, process of manufacture **-genauigkeit** *f* accuracy of manufacture

Herstellungsgleichmäßigkeit *f* uniformity of reproduction **losmäßige** ~ reproducibility from run to run

Herstellungs-jahr *n* year of manufacture **-kosten** *pl* cost of construction or of production, first cost **-länge** *f* factory length **methode** *f* manufacturing program **-stückkosten** *pl* piece production costs **-summe** *f* cost of production (of building) **-verfahren** *n* manufacturing process, factory process **-weise** *f* manufacturing method

Herstellwerk *f* manufacturing plant, originating firm

Hertz Hertz (Hz), cycles per second (c/s, cps)

Hertz-Einheit *n* hertzian unit

Hertz-scher Dipol *m* infinitesimal dipole, radiating dipole **-scher Doppelpol** hertzian doublet **-sche Funktion** hertzian radiation integral **-scher Sender** hertzian oscillator **-sche Wellen** radio or wireless waves, hertzian waves or radiation, electric waves

herum-drehen to change (said of the wind) **-flikken** to tinker **-fühlen** to feel about or around, fumble **-gießen** to cast around **-holen des Windes** changing of wind direction **-irrender Strom** stray current

herum-kramen to fumble **-legen** to turn and bank (aviation) **-pfuschen** to tinker **-pressen** to press around **-schiffen** to sail about or around

herumschlagen to wrap around, right a plane **Maschinen ~ lassen** to try the engines

herum-schleudern to propel around **-schweifend** stray **-spritzen** to spray, squirt, or splash around **-ziehen** (slang) to swing the plane, set the controls for a steep turn **-züngeln** to play around (of flames)

herunter-blasen to blow down **-blocken** to cog or break down

herunterdrücken to press, push, or force down, reduce, lower, minimize **die Spannung** ~ to step down the voltage

herunter-fieren to lower or ease down **-frischen** to blow down, work down, boil down

heruntergehen to descend, let down (of an airplane) **im Gleitflug** ~ to flatten out

herunterhängend drooping **-e Hilfsflügel** drooped ailerons

herunter-holen to shoot down, haul or clew down **-klappbar** folding down, hinged **-klappen** to let down in hinges, hinge down, drop (a table leaf) **-kommen** to descend, sweep down (said of the wind) **-kühlen** to cool down **-lassen** to down, let down **-regeln** to regulate in a downward direction, regulate down

herunter-setzen to reduce **-steuern** to regulate in a downward direction, regulate down **-stoßen** to push down **-stürzen** to tumble or fall down **-tröpfeln** to trickle or drip down **-walzen** to roll, rough, or cog down **-wehender Wind** down wind or current, fall wind (aviation) **-werfen** to throw down, dump **-ziehen** (Farbe) to strip

hervor-brechen to debouch, to sally forth **-bringen** to bring forth, produce, create, yield, develop **-bringung** *f* bringing forth, production, creation **-gerufene Ströme** artificial currents **-heben** to make conspicuous or prominent, accentuate, emphasize, underscore, highlight **-kommen** to arise **-locken** to draw out, lure or entice out

hervorquellen to bubble or gush forth **unregelmäßig** ~ to flow by heads

hervor-ragen to project, stand out, be salient **-rufen** to generate **-rufungszeit** *f* developing time **-sprießen** to outshoot **-springende Punkte** salient points **-sprudeln** to bubble forth, splutter **-stechende Eigenschaften** characteristic features **-stehen** *n* offset (aviat.), joggle

hervorstehend overhanging **-e tragende Fläche** bearing land (mach.) **-er Teil zwischen zwei Nuten** land (mach.)

hervortreten to become conspicous, show up, protrude **gegenüber etwas ~ lassen** to contrast

hervortretend prominent, predominant, bold **scharf** ~ articulated

Herz *n* heart, core, cycle (elec.) ~ **eines gerösteten Erzes** core or kernel of a roasted ore

Herz-angiographie *f* angiocardiography **-bahn** *f* cardioid-shaped path **-bindsel** *n* throat seizing **-charakteristik** *f* cardioid characteristic or space pattern **-exzenter** *m* heart cam **-exzenterbewegung** *f* cam movement

herzförmig heart-shaped cardioid **-es Diagramm** cardioid space pattern

Herz-fraktion *f* heart cut (petroleum) **-kausche** *f* heart-shaped thimble or deadeye **-klaue** *f* fixed or plain toolpost **-kurve** *f* cardioid

Herzscheibe *f* heart wheel, cam **Zapfenschlüssel für die** ~ cam key

Herz-spannungskurve *f* electrocardiogram **-spitze** *f* point of a crossing, frog point (R.R.)

Herzstück *n* frog, crossing, switch point on railroad ~ **mit Flanschen** crossing with wheel-flange ramp ~ **mit geschmiedeter Flußstahlspitze** frog with forged-steel point (R.R.) ~ **einer Kreuzung** tongue of a crossing, cross frog (R.R.)

Herzstückneigung *f* angle of crossing

Herzstückspitze, im Gesenk geschmiedete ~ dieforged point of frog

Herzstückunterlagsplatte *f* base plate for frog (R.R.)

Herzwinkel *m* number or angle of the frog (R.R.)

Hessonit *m* essonite, cinnamon stone

heterochrom (heterochrome) heterochromatic

heterochromatisch heterochromatic

heterodin heterodyne **-er Empfang, -e Verständigung** heterodyne reception

Heterodyn(e) *n* heterodyne, beat method **-empfang** *m* heterodyne reception, beat reception **-empfänger** *m* heterodyne receiver, beat receiver **-röhre** *f* heterodyne tube

heterogen heterogeneous **-e Reaktion bei der Verbrennung** heterogeneous reaction in combustion **-e Röntgenstrahlung** heterochromatic or heterogenous X-radiation **-e Strahlung** heterogeneous radiation **-es Ziel** compound target

Heterogenität *f* heterogeneity, heterogeneousness

Heteroladung heterocharge

heteromorph heteromorphic

heteropolar heteropolar **-e Bindung** *f* heteropolar bond **-e Valenz** electrostatic valence

heterostatisch (Schaltung) heterostatic (method or mounting **-e Schaltung** heterostatic circuit

heterotopisch heterotopic

heterotrop heterotropic

heterozyklisch heterocyclic

Heuerbas *m* crimp

heuern to charter, hire, rent

Heuerntemaschine *f* harvesting machine for hay, haymaking machine

Heuer-rückstand *m* claims respecting the wages of a ship's crew **-vertrag** *m* The Articles (naut.)

Heugabel *f* hayfork, pitchfork

Heulboje *f* whistling or howling buoy

heulen to howl, cry, scream

Heulen *n* howling **~ der Zahnräder** humming of gears

Heuler *m* howler (electronics), diaphone **-anruf** *m* howler connection (teleph.) **-hochfrequenz** *f* high frequency

Heul-kondensator *m* wobbling, warbling, or howling condenser **-pfeife** *f*, **-signal** *n* siren

Heulton *m* howling sound, high-pitched whine, sound with large number of modes of vibration, high-frequency warble tone, multitone **-frequenz** *f* wobbling frequency

Heultonne *f* whistling buoy, howling buoy

Heu-maschine *f* haying machine **-presse** *f* hay (press) baler

Heurechen *m* hay rake **seitwärts ablegender ~** side-delivery hay rake

heuristisch heuristic

Heurtleyrelais *n* Heurtley's magnifier

Heu-scheuer *f* hay barn **-schrecke** *f* grasshopper, trolley for tailskid for moving aircraft

hexadezimal hexadecimal (info proc.)

Heuschubrechen *m* (Schlepprechen) sweep rake **kombinierter ~ und Heustapler** combined sweep rake and stacker

Heustapler *m* haystacker **~** (Überkopfwurfsystem) **mit Abladevorrichtung** overshot haystacker **~ mit Hochwinde und drehbarer Abladevorrichtung, drehbarer ~** swinging haystacker

Heu-wendemaschine *f* tedder **-wenden** *n* tedding **-wender** *m* tedder

Hevea *f* Hevea brasiliensis

Hexachloräthan *n* hexachlorethane

hexadezimale Schreibweise hexadecimal notation

Hexadezimalzahlensystem *n* hexadecimal number system

Hexadien *n* hexadiene

Hexaeder *n* hexahedron

hexaedrisch hexahedral

hexagonal hexagonal

Hexahydrobenzol *n* hexahydrobenzene

Hexakistetraeder *n* hexakistetrahedron

Hexamethylenamin *n* hexamethylenamine, formin

Hexan *n* bexane

Hexen *n* hexene

Hexode *f* hexode

Hexodenkappe *f* top cap of hexode tube

Hexogen *n* trimethylenetrinitroamine

HF-Anschluß *m* RF connection

HF-Eingangsspannung *f* signal strength

HF-Gitterwechselspannung *f* signal voltage

H-Filterglied *n* H-network

H-förmig H-shaped **-er Balken** H beam **Motor mit -er Anordnung der Zylinder** H-formation engine

H-Formstahl *m* H beam

Hickorynußbaum *m* hickory

Hieb *m* blow, slash, hit, bat, cut **-folge** *f* succession of cuttings **-ton** *m* Aeolian note **-waffe** *f* slashing weapon

Hieling *f* (des Kiels), heel (of keel)

hieven to trip, heave in

Hieven *n* tripping (anchor)

Hilfe *f* help, assistance, support, relief, remedy **-leistung** *f* assistance, help, rescue work, first aid, teamwork

Hilfs-abbildung *f* auxiliary image, auxiliary datum **-ableitung** *f* auxiliary outlet **-achse** *f* transverse strut **-aggregat für Schiffe** auxiliary unit on board **-amt** *n* satellite exchange, suboffice **-anfahrventil** *n* auxiliary starting valve **-anlage** *f* emergency set **-anode** *f* auxiliary anode, ignition or exciting anode **-antenne** *f* auxiliary antenna

Hilfsantrieb *m* accessory drive **Geräte, die durch Hilfsantriebe angetrieben werden** auxiliary-driven units

Hilfs-apparat *m* auxiliary apparatus, stand-by equipment **-arbeiter** *m* helper laborer **-arzt** *m* assistant physician in medical corps **-aufhängung** *f* auxiliary suspension **-auspuff** *m* auxiliary exhaust **-ballasttank** *m* auxiliary ballast tank **-basis** *f* auxiliary base **-behälter** *m* auxiliary tank, reserve tank (for fuel) **-beischiff** *n* tender, supply ship **-beize** *f* auxiliary mordant **-beleuchtungseinrichtung** *f* auxiliary illumination equipment **-benzinbehälter** *m* auxiliary gasoline tank

Hilfs-beobachter *m* assistant observer **-beobachtungsstelle** *f* auxiliary observation post **-betrachtung** *f* auxiliary consideration **-betrieb** *m* service department, auxiliary department **-blatt** *n* table or graphical presentation of data to aid in rapid calculation **-brennstoffbehälter** *m* fuel-reserve tank **-brunnen** *m* auxiliary manhole **-buch** *n* manual **-damm** *m* auxiliary dam or embankment, cofferdam **-düse** *f* auxiliary jet **-düsenvergaser** *m* auxiliary jet carbureter

Hilfs-ebene *f* auxiliary plane **-einrichtung** *f* auxiliary device, apparatus, mechanism, or appliance **-einschub** *m* auxiliary plug-in unit **-einstellung** *f* auxiliary scale **-elektrode** *f* auxiliary (testing) electrode **-energie** *f* auxiliary energy **-erregerwicklung** *f* auxiliary exciting winding **-fallschirm** *m* pilot parachute **-fangedamm** *m* safety cofferdam **-federung** *f* supplementary spring **-feld** *n* auxiliary field **-felge** *f* extra rim **-feuer** *n* stand-by light **-fläche** *f* auxiliary surface

Hilfsflügel *m* aileron, wing flap, slat, auxiliary wing, airfoil **~ an der Flügelspitze** wing-tip aileron **äußerer** ~ external aileron

Hilfsflügelrippe *f* former, false rib, false wing ring

Hilfsflügelschlitz *m* auxiliary wing slot **fester** (unbeweglicher) ~ fixed auxiliary wing slot

Hilfsfrequenz *f* auxiliary or stand-by frequency, quenching, pilot, or local frequency, oscillation (in superheterodyne) **-empfänger** *m* superregenerative receiver, superregenerator, periodic-trigger-type receiver **-röhre** *f* grid-bias tube **-rückkuppelung** *f* superregeneration (working with quench voltage) **-rückkuppelungsempfänger** *m* superregenerative receiver, superregenerator, periodic-trigger-type receiver

Hilfsfunkenstrecke *f* auxiliary spark gap

Hilfs-gerät *n* auxiliary device or tools ~ **für Notfall** stand-by unit

Hilfsgeräte-antrieb *m* accessory drive **-gehäuse** *n* accessory housing **-träger** *m* accessory section **-wagen** *m* breakdown wagon

Hilfsgestänge *n* (zum Aufrichten schwerer Gestänge) derrick pole

hilfsgesteuert pilot operated

Hilfs-gitter *n* space-charge grid, auxiliary grid **-gleichrichter** *m* complementary rectifier **-größe** *f* auxiliary quantity or variable **-haken** *m* auxiliary hook **-hohlleiter** *m* auxiliary waveguide **-holm** *m* auxiliary spar **-hubwerk** *n* auxiliary lift of crane, auxiliary hoisting gear or tackle **-hubwindwerk** *n* auxiliary hoist **-joch** *n* false or temporary frame (min.)

Hilfs-kabel *n* emergency cable **-katze** *f* auxiliary crab **-kette** *f* auxiliary track **-kettenfahrzeug** *n* auxiliary track vehicle, combination wheel-track vehicle **-klappe** *f* wing-tab **-klinke** *f* auxiliary lock or jack, ancillary lens (film)

Hilfs-knotenamt *n* auxiliary central office (teleph.) **-knotenfänger** *m* auxiliary strainer **-kolben** *m* auxiliary piston **-kontakt** *m* auxiliary contact; (auf Schütz) auxiliary switch **-kontaktlamelle** *f* auxiliar screw arc **-korn** *n* auxiliary front sight **-korrektionsrelais** *n* auxiliary corrector relay **-kraft** *f* auxiliary force or personnel, assistance, temporary employee, auxiliary labor **-kran** *m* auxiliary crane **-kranz** *m* temporary or false frame (min.) **-kreis** *m* subsidiary circuit, line of force, fall back circuit

Hilfs-kühler *m* booster radiator **-kurven** *pl* auxiliary contours **-lager** *n* auxiliary bearing, warehouse **-landeplatz** *m* emergency or auxiliary landing place or field **-längsträger** *m* intermediate longitudinal girder **-laufkatze** *f* auxiliary trolley **-leiter** *m* pilot wire **-leitung** *f* auxiliary conduit **-lenzleitung** *f* auxiliary suction lead **-linie** *f* auxiliary line

Hilfsluft *f* auxiliary air **-stützpunkt** *m* auxiliary air base **-verdichter** *m* auxiliary air compressor

Hilfs-marke *f* locating mark **-maschine** *f* auxiliary or emergency machine, donkey engine, jack engine **-maß** *n* reference dimension **-maßnahme** *f* remedial measure **-maßstab** *m* auxiliary scale **-mast** *m* jury mast **-metallstaub** *m* metallic powder

Hilfsmittel *n* auxiliary or supplementary means, expedient, accessories, adjuvants ~ **für die Filtration** filter aid

Hilfs-monteur *m* assistant mechanic **-motor** *m* servomotor, booster **-nebelung** *f* auxiliary smoke screen as produced by factories

Hilfsnebenwiderstand, Voltmeter mit ~ voltmeter multiplier

Hilfs-netz *n* auxiliary (control) grid, auxiliary supply (system) **-ölpumpe** *f* booster oil pump **-oszillator** *m* auxiliary oscillator radio, booster oscillator **-peilstelle** *f* auxiliary, associate or affiliated ground direction-finding station **-peilung** *f* auxiliary bearing **-phasenkreis** *m* starting-winding circuit **-platte** *f* compensating plate **-platz** *m* auxiliary position

Hilfs-pol *m* auxiliary pole **-polizei** *f* auxiliary police **-puddler** *m* underhand puddler **-pumpe** *f* auxiliary pump **-rad** *n* spare wheel **-rahmen** *m* underframe, subframe **-regelgröße** *f* objective variable **-relais** *n* all-or-nothing relay, auxiliary or booster relay **-rost** *m* auxiliary grate **-ruder** *n* auxiliary control surface (aviation), Flettner control surface, tab

Hilfs-sammelschienen *pl* auxiliary bus bars **-satz** *m* auxiliary theorem **-schacht** *m* escape (min.) **-schaltung** *f* auxiliary circuit (elec.) **-schichtfilter** *n* precoat filter **-schieber** *m* auxiliary slide valve **-schiff** *n* auxiliary vessel or skid

Hilfsschirm *m* pilot parachute (missiles), auxiliary parachute; (zur Lagestabilisierung) drogue chute **-patrone** *f* drogue gun (missiles)

Hilfs-schwimmer *m* wing-tip float (seaplane) **-schwimmkraft** *f* reserve buoyancy **-sender** *m* auxiliary transmitter, local oscillator, satellite transmitter

Hilfs-spannung *f* auxiliary voltage **-spiegel** *m* duplex mirror **-spindel** *f* high-speed auxiliary spindle **-spinner** *m* head piecer, spare spinner (textiles) **-standlinie** *f* base of verification **-starter** *m* assistent starter **-stativ** *n* manipulating stand **-stempel** *m* emergency prop **-steuerapparat** *m* co-selector **-stoff** *m* adjuvant (substance), auxiliary or accessory material or agent **-stollen** *m* auxiliary adit **-strecke** *f* subsidiary road **-stromabnehmer** *m* auxiliary pantograph **-stromkreis** *m* auxiliary circuit (teleph.)

Hilfsträger *m* auxiliary spar (aviat.), auxiliary carrier, subcarrier, adapter **-gleichlaufpuls** *m* color-burst (TV)

Hilfs-triebwerk *n* auxiliary power unit **-unterwerk** *n* auxiliary power station, substation **-variable** *f* auxiliary variable **-ventilator** *m* stand-by ventilator or fan **-voramt** *n* subcontrol office or station **-vorrichtung** *f* auxiliary implement, apparatus, or device, accessory equipment, servomechanism **-wagen** *m* emergency car **-wähler** *m* special code selector

Hilfs-wechselspannung *f* auxiliary alternating voltage **-weg** *m* emergency or alternative route **-welle** *f* intermediate or auxiliary shaft **-werk** *n* auxiliary power station, sub-station **-wert** *m* coefficient **-wicklung** *f* auxiliary winding **-winkel** *m* auxiliary angle **-zapfen** *m* arbor **-zeichen** *n* auxiliary signal

Hilfs-zentrale für Dienstverkehr parent exchange **-ziel** *n* auxiliary aiming mark or point, reference point, auxiliary target **-zug** *m* safety train, additional train section **-zündung** *f* auxiliary ignition **-zündvorrichtung** *f* auxiliary ignition device **-zusatzgerät** *n* auxiliary instrument

-zwischenplatte *f* separating plate

Himmel *m* heaven, sky **bedeckter ~** overcast sky **heiterer ~** clear sky

Himmelblau *n* blue of the sky **-messer** *m* cyanometer

Himmels-erscheinung *f* celestial phenomenon **-fernrohr** *n* astronomic or astrographic telescope **-gegend** *f* cardinal point, point of compass, quarter of the heavens **-globus** *m* celestial globe **-karte** *f* astronomical or celestial chart **-körper** *m* celestial body **-kugel** *f* celestial sphere **-licht** *n* skylight **-lichtpolarisation** *f* skylight polarization **-mechanik** *f* celestial mechanics **-mehl** *n* gypsum

Himmels-objekt *n* celestial object **-ortung** *f* celestial navigation **-richtung** *f* cardinal point, compass bearing **-schreiber** *m* skywriter **-schrift** *f* skywriting **-sphäre** *f* celestial sphere **-strahlung** *f* sky-radiation **-symbole** *n pl* celestial signs, sky symbols (meteor.) **-welle** *f* sky wave **-wölbung** *f* vault of the sky, celestial globe **-zeichen** *n* sign of the zodiac, celestial sign **-zustand** *m* sky conditions

hinablassen to lower, let down

hinauf-klettern to climb up **-pendel** *n* resonant rise **-pendeln** to rise in resonance **-pendeln** *n* gradual rise in resonance **-transformieren** to step up (elec.)

hinausdrücken to push out

hinausgehen to pass, exit

hinausgehend passing **über eine runde Zahl ~** odd

hinausragen to jut out

hinausragend jutting **-er Strukturteil** structure

hinausschießen to overshoot

hindern to prevent

Hindernis *n* obstacle, barricade, entanglement, hurdle bar, accessory defense, difficulty, estoppel (law) **~ auf der Strecke** impediment on the line **durch ~ zum Stillstand kommen** to stall **bewegliches ~** portable obstacle **elektrisches ~** electrically charged entanglement **gesetzliches ~** statutory bar, legal impediment, estoppel **versenktes ~** sunken obstacle

Hindernis-bahn *f* obstacle course **-befeuerung** *f* obstruction lighting **-beseitigung** *f* obstruction clearing **-draht** *m* entanglement wire **-feuer** *n* obstruction light (aviation) **-freifläche** *f* obstacle clearance surface **-freigrenze** *f* obstruction clearance limit (OCL) **-freiheit** *f* obstruction clearance

Hindernis-kennzeichnung *f* obstruction marking **-schlagpfahl** *m* driving-type obstacle picket **-schraubpfahl** *m* screw-type obstacle picket **-sprengtrupp** *m* obstacle-demolition squad **-strecke** *f* obstacle course **-trupp** *m* obstacle-construction squad

Hinderung *f* impediment, obstacle, distortion

Hinderungsgrund, ein ~ sein to be a bar to (law)

hindurch-fliegen to travel through **-fließen** to flow through **-geführt** passed through **-gehen** to pass through, transit **-gelassene Energie** transmitted energy **-lassen** to let through, pass, transmit **-laufen** to pass or travel through **-schlagen** to beat through **-streichen** to pass through, flow through **-strömen** to flow through, pass through, move through

hindurchströmend flowing through **durch einen Querschnitt -e Luftmenge** mass air flow

hindurch-treten to pass through **-wandern** (Gase) to diffuse **-ziehen** to pull, draw, or drag through

hinein-diffundieren to diffuse into **-dringen** to penetrate **-drücken** to push in **-fassen** to engage **-fressen** to eat into, erode **-gesteckte Arbeitsleistung** work input **-gießen** to pour into **-hören** to listen in **-passen** to fit, fit into **-ragen** to extend (into) **-schieben** to slip into **-schlagen** to insert (lead) **-spiegeln** to reflect into **-spielen** to be of influence on

hineinstecken, Geld ~ in to invest money in

hinein-tauchen to dip into, submerge partially or entirely **-treiben** to force into **-wandern** to go into, diffuse into **-ziehen** to draw in, drag in, incorporate, involve **-zwingen** to force into

hin-fällig decaying, frail, infirm, no longer in force **-flug** *m* outgoing flight **-fort** henceforth **-führen** to bring to (circuit point) **-gang** *m* (in rolling) forward pass, forward travel, death

hingestreckt, auf der Erde ~ prostrate

hinhalten to delay, retard, contain

hinhaltend holding, delaying

Hinken *n* limping, peg-legging (oil drilling)

hin-länglich sufficient **-länglichkeit** *f* sufficiency **-lauf** *m* forward move, forward-working stroke, travel, pass or journey, scansion, scanning motion, forward trace sweep (television)

Hinlauf-Rücklaufverhältnis *n* sweep-flyback ratio

hin-legen to lay down **-leiter** *m* one-way or outgoing conductor, outgoing lead or wire **nehmen** to take, accept, submit to **-reichen** to be sufficient, be adequate

hinreichend adequate

hin-richten to turn, direct; ruin

Hinsicht *f* regard, respect **in ~ auf** with respect to, in regard to, in view of **in dieser ~** in this regard

hinsichtlich concerning, regarding

hintanhalten to stop, retard, suppress, check

hinten behind, in the rear, at the end, astern, posteriorly **nach ~** to the rear

hinter behind, rear **-e Ansicht** rear elevation, rear view **-e Bremse** rear brake **-e Brennweite** back focal length **-e Brennebene** posterior focal plane **-er Brennpunkt** back focal point **-es Ende** tail end **-e Griffvorrichtung** rear handle attachment **-es Hauptlager der Kurbelwelle** rear main bearing of crankshaft

hinter-e Kante trailing edge **-es Lager** journal bearing **-e Landfeste** stern fast **-e Nabe** rear hub **-er Rand** trailing edge **-e Stütze** rear support **-e Zwischenachse** jackshaft

Hinterachs-antrieb *m* rear-axle drive **-antriebswelle** *f* rear-axle driving shaft **-bremswelle** *f* rear axle brake shaft **-brücke** *f* rear axle housing, rear axle beam **-druck** *m* rear axle load

Hinterachse *f* rear or back axle, trailing axle **kurvenbewegliche ~** radial end axle (R.R.) **vollschwingende ~** full-floating back axle

Hinterachs-gehäuse *n* rear-axle housing **-gehäusedeckel** *m* rear-axle housing cover **-getriebe** *n* differential gear **-schale** *f* hind bolster **-schub** *m* rear-axle thrust **-schubstange** *f* radius rod (automobile) **-strebe** *f* rear-axle tie bar **-träger** *m* rear axle carrier **-trichter** *m* flared tube of rear axle, reduction gear housing **-triebwerk** *n* rear axle gear **-unterzug** *m* rear-axle tie rod **-welle** *f* rear-axle shaft **-wellenrad** *n* differential side gear

Hinter-ansicht *f* back view or plan **-antrieb** *m* rear (wheel) drive **-arbeiten** *n* relieving **-beleuchtung** *f* Rembrandt illumination, half-back illumination **-boden** *m* back plate, back-end plate **-bohreinrichtung** *f* back-drilling attachment **-bohren** *n* back-drilling **-bremse** *f* back brake **-bringen** to give information **-brücke** *f* rear axle **-bügel** *m* rear anchoring clevis or stirrup **-bündelecho** *n* back echo

Hinter-damm *m* back dike **-deck** *n* quarter-deck **-docke** *f* back puppet **-dreharbeit** *f* relieving work **-drehbank** *f* relieving or backing-off lathe **-drehen** to back off, relieve (eccentrically)

Hinterdrehen, axial ~ end relieving

Hinter-drehkurve *f* relieving cam, relief curve **-drehsupport** *m* relieving rest

hinterdreht -er Fräser milling cutter backed for clearance, relieved-tooth milling cutter

Hinter-drehung *f* (eccentric) relief, backing-off **-drehvorrichtung** *f* relieving attachment, backing-off device **-drehwinkel** *m* relief angle **-ebbe** *f* end of ebb

hintereinander in series, in tandem, consecutively, serially ~ **angeordnet** tandem joined

hintereinandergeschaltet series-connected **-e Ventilatoren** fans arranged in series

hintereinanderliegend tandem (said of two engines) **zwei -e Motoren** tandem engines

hintereinander-schalten to connect or join in series **-schaltung** *f* series connection, cascading, concatenation or tandem connection (of motors), cascade connection **-triebwerkanlage** *f* tandem-type powerplant

Hinterendplandrehen *n* back-facing

Hinter-feder *f* rear spring **-federbock** *m* rear-spring bracket **-federlasche** *f* rear spring shackle **-fenster** *n* rear window **-flanke** *f* trailing edge (of pulses) **-flügel** *m* back wing, retreating part (building) **-fräsen** to reliefmill **-front** *f* back elevation **-führen** to run out with leaders **-füllung** *f* backfilling

Hinter-gabel *f* back fork (motorcycle) **-gelände** *n* rear area **-gelenk** *n* rear joint (pistol) **-gestell** *n* back stand, back part, inner crucible, hind carriage

hintergießen, das Galvano ~ to back up, back the shell (print.)

Hintergießmetall *n* backing metal (print.)

Hinterglied einer Linse back compound, back lens ~ **eines Verhältnisses** consequent of a ratio

Hintergrund *m* background, rear **-effekt** *m* background effect **-marke** *f* background collimating point **-projektion** *f* back(-ground) projection **-zählrate** *f* background counting rate **-zählstöße** *pl* background counts

hinter-halten to retard, hold back, reserve **-hand** *f* hindquarter

Hinterhang *m* reverse slope **-stellung** *f* reverse-slope position

hinterherschleifen to trail

Hinter-holm *m* rear outrigger (gun platform), rear spar (antiaircraft gun) **-kaffe** *f* stern compartment **-kante** *f* rear or trailing edge **-kantenwinkel** *m* trailing-edge angle **-kappe** *f* stiffening (shoemaking) **-keule** *f* back lobe (of antenna) **-kipper** *m* rear dumper **-kleiden** *n* backing, background (phot.) **-knobben eines Hochofens** back of a blast furnace **-lader** *m* breechloader **-lage** *f* scale board for back of small looking glasses

Hinter-lager *n* rear bearing **-lagerungsraum** *m* added area for augmenting the tidal-air effect **-land** *n* hinterland, interior of a country **-lappen** *m* posterior lobe **-lastig** tail-heavy, by the stern **-legen** to deposit, back, file, record, register **-leger** *m* depositor **-linse** *f* back lens **-linsenring** *m* rear element lens mount **-mann** *m* rear-rank man, ship next astern

Hintermauerung, Beton der ~ concrete composing the body of the wall

Hinterplatte *f* rear end plate

Hinterrad *n* rear wheel **-achse** *f* rear axle **-antrieb** *m* rear(-wheel) drive **-bremsgestänge** *n* rear wheel brake linkage **-bremswelle** *f* rear wheel brake cylinder **-einrichtung** *f* rear-wheel attachment **-federung** *f* rear-wheel spring suspension **-gabelverbindung** *f* back fork bridge **-nabe** *f* rear-wheel hub **-reifen** *m* back tire **-satz** *m* rear wheel pair

Hinter-rahmen *m* rear frame **-rand** *m* posterior end **-reifen** *m* rear tire **-schleifeinrichtung** *f* relief grinding attachment **-schleifen** to back off, relieve eccentrically, relief grind **-schleifen** *n* relief grinding **-schleifscheibe** *f* relief-grinding wheel **-schleifwinkel** *m* back-slope angle (of cutting tool), clearance angle **-schliff** *m* eccentric relief, backing-off clearance

hinterschliffen slope-back-ground **-er Fräser** eccentric relief cutter **-er Zahn** eccentrically relieved tooth

Hinter-schliffwinkel *m* back-slope angle, clearance angle **-schneidung** *f* undercut, back taper **-schnitten** undercut **-seil** *n* tail rope **-seite** *f* rear or back side **-setzer** *m* false front **-stampfung** *f* backing **-stechen** to recess **-stechwerkzeug** *n* recessing tool **-stellwinkel** *m* relief angles **-steven** *m* stern stay (aviation), rudder post **-strang** *m* hind or shaft trace **-stütze** *f* rear trail, rear support **-support** *m* rear rest, back rest

Hinterteil *m* stern sheet of boat **am** ~ abaft ~ **eines Bohrgerüstes** backframe of a rig

Hinterwagen *m* caisson

Hinterwand *f* back (end) plate, tail rack, hind board **-sperrschichtzelle** *f* backwall barrier (blocking) layer cell **-zelle** *f* back-effect cell, barrierplane rear-wall cell, photovoltaic barrier-layer cell with posterior metallic layer, back-wall photovoltaic cell

Hinter-welle *f* roach (naut.) **-zacken** *m* backplate, ash plate **-zange** *f* end screw **-zangenspindel** *f* end chap spindle **-zeug** *n* hip pad (harness), breeching **-zipfel** *m* back lobe (of antenna) **-zwiesel** *m* cantle, rear arch of saddle

hinüberreißen to carry over (distillation)

hin- und herbewegen to reciprocate, move to and fro, rock, shuttle, wag

Hin- und Herbewegung *f* reciprocating or oscillating motion, backward-and-forward movement, to-and-fro motion, rocking, shuttle

Hin- und Herbiegemaschine *f* alternation bending test machine

Hin- und Herbiegeprobe *f* backward-and-forward

bending test, alternating bending test, reverse-bending test, alternate-stress test
Hin- und Herbiegeprüfer *m* to-and-fro bending tester, forward-and-backward bending tester
Hin- und Herbiegeversuch *m* reverse-bending test
hin- und hergehen to reciprocate, shuttle
hin- und herschieben to shuffle
Hin- und Herschwanken *n* tailing or rocking motion
hin- und herschwingen to rock, surge back and forth, oscillate
Hin- und Herwallen *n* surging
hin- und herwerfen to toss
Hin- und Herwerfen *n* surging, vibration, oscillation
Hin- und Rückflugschein *m* return airplane ticket
Hin- und Rückführung *f* lead and return, scansion and flyback (television)
Hin- und Rückleitung *f* complete circuit (elec.), up-and-down line, go-and-return line
Hin- und Rückreise *f* voyage out and in
hin und zurück there and back, outward and inward, reversible (reaction)
Hinuntertasten *n* causing carrier to drop to low value (zero) by synchronizing signal
Hinverbindung *f* outgoing connection
Hinweg *m* way or journey there
hinweg off, away **-laufen über** to ride over (relay) **-streichen** to pass (across)
Hinweis *m* hint, indication, direction, inference, reference **gegenseitiger ~** cross reference
Hinweisansagegerät *n* message disseminator
hinweisen to direct
Hinweis-karte *f* cross-reference card **-leitung** *f* intercepting trunk **-stöpsel** *m* signal plug, indicating peg **-tonerzeuger** *m* no-such-number-tone generator
Hinweisung *f* hint, reference
Hinweisungsstöpsel *m* signal plug, indicating peg
Hinweis-zeichen *n* reference mark **-zeichnung** *f* reference drawing
hin-werfen to throw down **-zeichnen** to plot, draw a diagram
hinziehen to draw to, drag on, delay **sich ~ unter** to subtend
hinzu-fügen to add, associate **-geben** to add (chem.)
hinzugesellen, sich ~ to associate
hinzu-kommend accessory **-rechnen** to add
Hiorth-Ofen *m* Hiorth (induction) furnace
Hippe *f* bill hook, hedging or gardening knife, scythe, sickle
Hippursäure *f* hippuric acid
hippursaures Ammonium ammonium hippurate
Hirn-fläche *f* cross-cut end **-fuge** *f* butt joint **-holz** *n* cross-cut or end-grained wood, end grain **-leiste** *f* crosspiece, wooden clamp **-ring** *m* ferrule, ferrel, hoop **-säge** *f* crosscut saw **-schale** *f* skull **-schnitt** *m* end cut, end-grained cut, crosscut **-seite** *f* cross, end, or pin way of the grain, end grain
Hirsch *m* stag **-horn** *n* hartshorn **-leder** *n* buckskin
Hirth-Verzahnung *f* Hirth-type serrations
hissen to hoist, raise
Hiss-tau *n* halyard **-zeug** *n* lifting tackle
Hittorfsche Röhre Hittorf tube (elec.)
Hitzband-amperemesser *m* thermal or hot-wire ammeter **-strommesser** *m* hot-band ammeter
Hitzbearbeitungsofen *m* heat-treating furnace
Hitzdraht *m* hot or heated wire **-amperemeter** *n* thermal or hot-wire ammeter **-anemometer** *n* hotwire anemometer **-blinkgeber** *m* hot-wire blinker unit **-instrument** *n* hot-wire instrument (blasting), expansion instrument (hot wire) **-meßgerät** *n* hot-wire (measuring) instrument, hot-wire meter **-sonde** *f* hot-wire anemometer **-spannungsmesser** *m* hot-wire voltmeter **-spulensicherung** *f* heat coil **-strommesser** *m* thermal ammeter **-voltmeter** *n* hot-wire voltmeter **-windmesser** *m* hot-wire anemometer
Hitze *f* heat, a series of blows (by a pile driver) **in der ~ erhärtend** thermosetting **abgehende ~** waste heat
Hitze-ausgleich *m* heat balance **-beständig** refractory, heat-resisting, heatproof, thermostable **-beständigkeit** *f* heat-resisting quality, heat resistance **-breiten** *pl* horse latitudes **-dämpfer** *m* (exhaust) flame damper, heat damper **-einheit** *f* heat unit **-einwirkung** *f* influence of heat **-empfindlich** sensitive to heat **-erzeugung** *f* generation of heat **-falten** *pl* heat-creases **-festigkeit** *f* heat resistance **-gegenwert** *m* equivalent of heat
Hitzegrad *m* degree of heat, intensity of heat **-messer** *m* pyrometer
Hitze-grenze *f* thermal barrier (aviat.) **-härtbar** heat setting **-härten** *n* thermosetting **-härtung** *f* baking (resins) **-messer** *m* pyrometer **-probe** *f* heat test **-strahlungsmesser** *m* pyrometer **-welle** *f* heat wave **-wirkungsgrad** *m* thermal efficiency
hitziger Gang hot running (metal)
Hitzrolle *f* heat coil **~ mit Gleitstift** collapsible heat coil
Hitz-schlag *m* heatstroke **-wechselvorrichtung** *f* heat changer
H-Leitung *f* H circuit, I circuit
H-Mast *m* H pole (two poles connected)
H-Motor *m* H formation, H-shaped engine
Hobbock *n* large tin can for shipping materials
Hobel *m* planing tool, plane, knife of plow, shootboard (print), beveller **~ mit Nase** plane with handle **der ~ greift** the plane has iron enough **runder ~** spout plane
Hobelanschlag *m* ledge of plane **verstellbarer ~** fence of a plane
Hobel-bank *f* carpenter's bench **-bankhaken** *pl* bench dogs (carpenter's) **-beitel** *m* ripping chisel **-eisen** *n* bit, plane iron **-fläche** *f* planing surface **-kamm** *m* gear cutter **-kasten** *m* plane stock **-kopf** *m* head of a plane **-kreissäge** *f* hollow-ground circular saw
Hobel-maschine *f* planer, planing machine, shaping machine **-maschinenantrieb** *m* planer drive **-maschinenschlitten** *m* planing-machine table **-meißel** *m* planing tool **-messer** *n* planing knife, plane iron
hobeln to plane, smooth, slot
Hobeln *n* planing, shaping
Hobelspan *m* facing (of steel), (wood) shaving, chip, paring
Hobelstahl *m* planer or planing tool
Hobelstahlschleifmaschine, Dreh- und ~ lathe and planer tool grinder
Hobel- und Aussparrmaschine für Dauben stave-backing and -hollowing machine
Hobel- und Fügemaschine mit Dübellochbohr-

apparat (für Bodenbretter) head planing, jointing, and doweling machine

Hobel-vorrichtung *f* planing fixture **-werk** *n* planing mill, planing works **-zahn** *m* riptooth **-zwinge** *f* book clamp

Hobler *m* bevel gear generator

hoch high, lofty, tall, anticyclone **~ gelegen** mounted in an elevated position **~ maschinenglatt** highly machine- or millfinished **~ ohmisch** high-ohmic **~ siliziertes Eisen** high-silicon iron **~ zwei** (z. B. 10^2) second to the power

Hoch-achse *f* vertical axis of plane **-achtung** *f* regard

hochaktiv highly active **-er Abfall** high-activity waste

hochangeregte Zustände highly excited states

Hoch-antenne *f* outdoor aerial or antenna, high antenna **-ätzen** to etch in relief **-ätzung** *f* relievo-engraving, relief etching **-aufnahme** *f* vertical or upright picture or shot **-auftriebseinrichtung** *f* high-lift device

Hochbahn *f* overhead railway, elevated railway, overhead track **-kran** *m* bridge crane

Hochbau *m* any structure above the surface, building construction **~ von Leitungen** overhead-line construction

Hochbehälter *m* overhead reservoir, tank, or bin, gravity tank, high-level tank

hochbeheizt highly heated **-e Röhre** bright valve

hochbelastbare Anoden high-duty anodes

Hoch-belastbarkeit *f* high-load, heavy-load, or current-carrying capacity **-belastung** *f* high power (elec.) **-biegen** to bend up **-bild** *n* relief **-blau** bright blue, azure **-bleichfähig** high-boiled **-bocken** to jack up, put on blocks **-bohrloch** *n* upward borehole, upward-pointing hole **-brechend** highly refractive **-brisant** higly explosive **-bügel** *m* high bow

Hochdecker *m* high-wing airplane **-flügel** *m* wing of high-wing airplane **-flugmodell** *n* high-wing airplane model

hochdispers highly dispered

Hochdruck *m* high pressure, relief print **-abschmiergerät** *n* high pressure lubrication set **-apparaturen** *pl* high-pressure apparatus **-armaturen** *pl* high-pressure valves and fittings **-ballastpumpe** *f* high-pressure ballast pump **-bogen** *m* high-pressure arc **-bogenrotationsmaschine** *f* sheet-fed rotary letter press printing press **-bohröl** *n* high-pressure drilling oil **-brenner** *m* high-pressure burner **-dampf** *m* high-pressure steam **-dampfkessel** *m* high-pressure boiler **-dampfmaschine** *f* high pressure steam engine

Hochdruck-eigenschaften *pl* E. P. properties (extreme pressure) **-flasche** *f* high-pressure cylinder (vessel) **-förderung** *f* high-pressure transport or conveyance **-formgebung** *f* high-energy-rate forming **-gebiet** *n* anticyclone, high-pressure area **-gebläse** *n* high-pressure blower **-glimmentladung** *f* high pressure glow discharge **-gürtel** *m* high-pressure belt or zone **handabsperrventil** *n* manual high-pressure valve (missiles) **-heißdampfabsperrschieber** *m* H. P. steam gate valve **-heißdampfkessel** *m* high-pressure steam boiler

Hochdruck-kammer *f* high-pressure stall **-kapselgebläse** *n* high-pressure rotary blower **-keil** *m* wedge (aviation) **-kessel** *m* high-pressure tank **-kesselbatterie** *f* series or battery of high-pressure tanks **-kolben** *m* high-pressure piston **-kondensationsmaschine** *f* high-pressure condensing turbine **-kondensator** *m* pressure-type capacitor **-kreis** *m* high-pressure cycle **-läufer** *m* runner of the high pressure section **-leitung** *f* high-pressure (piping) line **-luftsystem** *n* high-pressure-air system

Hochdruck-maschine *f* high-pressure engine **-ölpresse** *f* high-pressure oil gun **-ölschmierpumpe** *f* high pressure oil pump or lubricating pump **-pumpe** *f* high-pressure pump **-reifen** *m* high-pressure tire **-rohr** *n* high-pressure tube **-rohrleitung** *f* power piping **-rücken** *m* ridge (aviation) **-satz** *m* high-pressure unit **-sauerstoff** *m* compressed oxygen **-schieber** *m* high-pressure slide valve

Hochdruck-schlauch *m* high-pressure hose, flexible high-pressure tubing **-schaufel** *f* high-pressure blade **-schmiermittel** *n* extreme-pressure lubricant **-schmiersystem für Startzwecke** high-initial-oil-pressure system **-schmierung** *f* high-pressure lubrication

Hochdruckstromwaage *f*, **elektronische ~** electronic regulating device (Hager VBT)

Hochdruck-stufe *f* high-pressure stage **-ventil** *n* high-pressure valve, main steamplant valve (guided missiles) **-ventilfüller** *m* high-pressure valve filler **-verdichter** *m* high-pressure compressor **-zentrum** *n* center of high barometric pressure, center of anticyclone **-zerstäuber** *m* high-pressure atomizer **-zylinder** *m* high-pressure cylinder

Hoch-ebene *f* elevated plain, plateau, tableland **-elastikreifen** *m* cushion tire

hochelastisch resilient

hochempfindlich highly sensitive, supersensitive; (phot. Emulsionen) high-speed extrarapid **-er Zünder** sensitive fuse

Hoch-energieformgebung *f* high-energy rate forming **-entladung** *f* heavy-current discharge **-entwickelt** highly developed **-erhaben** in high relief embossed **-explosivstoff** *m* high explosive **-fahren** to accelerate **-farbig** highly colored, saturated **-fahrwiderstand** *m* coarse control resistor **-fester Stahl** high-tensile or high-strength steel

hoch-fein superfine, exquisite, first-rate **-feuerfest** highly refractory **-flüchtig** highly volatile **-flugzahl** *f* height factor or figure **-flußreaktor** *m* high-flux reactor **-flut** *f* high tide **-flutbett** *n* river bed during flood **-fördern** to elevate **-förderung** *f* elevation **-format** *n* upright format

hochfrequent of high frequency **-es Fernsignal** radiofrequency television signal

Hochfrequenz *f* high frequency, radio frequency **-anzeiger** *m* high-frequency indicator **-ausgleich** *m* high boost **-bereich** *m* treble range, treble band (music) **-diathermie** *f* radiothermy (med.) **-drahtsystem** *n* wired radio system **-drossel** *f* high-frequency choke, radio-frequency choke coil **-durchlassend** radiofrequency-transparent **-einrichtung** *f* high-frequency equipment **-eisenkern** *m* high-frequency iron core **-entladung** *f* high-frequency discharge **-erzeuger** *m* high-frequency generator **-feld** *n* high-frequency field, radio-frequency field **-feldstärke** *f* radio field intensity

Hochfrequenz-generator *m* high-frequency generator or alternator, radio alternator **-gleichrichter** *m* radio-frequency rectifier **-härtung** *f* hardening by high-frequency current **-heilgerät** *n* short-wave therapeutic apparatus **-induktionsofen** *m* high-frequency induction furnace **-isolator** *m* high-frequency insulator **-kabel** *n* high-frequency cable, radio cable **-kamera** *f* high-speed camera

Hochfrequenz-kauter *m* electric bistoury, diathermy knife **-kreis** *m* high-frequency circuit **-lack** (verlustarm) low-loss RF lacquer **-leistung** *f* high-frequency power **-leiter** *m* radio cable **-leitung** *f* high-frequency circuit **-litze** *f* spiral-weave cable **-litzendraht** *m* high-frequency wire strand **-maschine** *f* high-frequency or radio-frequency alternator, high-frequency generator **-mäßig** for high frequency, relative to high frequency **-mehrfachfernsprechen** *n* high-frequency multiple telephony

Hochfrequenz-meßbrücke *f* high-frequency bridge **-messung** *f* high-frequency measurement **-ofen** *m* high-frequency furnace **-pentode** *f* high-frequency pentode **-schwingung** *f* high-frequency oscillation **-sender** *m* high-frequency (radio-frequency) transmitter **-sicherung** *f* high-frequency fuse or cutout **-siebgebilde** *n* high-pass selective circuit or filter **-siebkette** *f* high-pass filter

Hochfrequenz-spektroskopie *f* radiofrequency **-sperrkette** *f* low-pass filter, infrafilter, higher limiting filter **-sperrkreis** *m* low-pass selective circuit **-sprechkanal** *m*, **-sprechweg** *m* high-frequency carrier-current telephone channel **-spule** *f* high-frequency or radio-frequency coil **-störung** *f* high-frequency interference **-strom** *m* high-frequency (alternating) current, radio-frequency current **-stufe** *f* high-frequency or radio-frequency stage **-technik** *f* high-frequency or electronic engineering

Hochfrequenztelephonie *f* high-frequency telephony **leitungsgerichtete** ~ high-frequency telephony along lines, carrier-current or wire-guided radiotelephony

Hochfrequenz-transformator *m* high-frequency or radio-frequency transformer **-übertragerwelle** *f* high-frequency carrier wave **-unterbrecher** *m* high-frequency interrupter or commutator **-verbindung** *f* (über Leitungen) carrier transmission, wired or line radio

Hochfrequenzverstärker *m* high-frequency or radiofrequency amplifier, tuned radio-frequency amplifier **linearer** ~ linear high-frequency amplifier

Hochfrequenz-verstärkung *f* high-frequency or radio-frequency amplification **-verstärkungsstufe** *f* high-frequency or radio-frequency amplification stage **-vorstufe** *f* preselector **-vorstufungsröhre** *f* radio frequency preselection stage **-weg** *m* high-frequency carrier-current telephone channel **-widerstand** *m* high-frequency or radio-frequency resistance

Hoch-führung *f* downlead (of an antenna) **-führungskanal** *m* vertical wall duct (cable) **-führungsschacht** *m* vertical-wall duct **-gebirge** *n* high-mountains

Hoch-gang *m* upward movement, ascent, upward stroke **-gebogener Flansch** upturned ears **-gefahren** raised

Hochgehen *n* rise **gleichzeitiges ~ des Stempels und Niedergehen des Preßtisches** simultaneous rising of the punch and lowering of the table

hoch-gehende See heavy sea **-gekantete Stege** bridge on edge

hochgekohlt of high carbon content **-er Stahl** high-carbon steel

Hochgerüst (für Tanks) structure above the ground

hoch-gesättigt highly saturated **-geschwindigkeit** *f* high speed **-geschwindigkeitsfräsen** *n* high-speed milling

hochgespannt high-tension **-er Dampf** high-pressure steam **-er Strom** high-tension current

Hoch-gewitter *n* high-altitude thunderstorm **-gewölbt** high-domed **-gezogene Kehrkurve** Immelmann turn (aviation)

Hochglanz *m* bright luster, high mirror finish, high polish, brilliance **-abzug** *m* glossy print **-bleikristall** *n* high-polish lead crystal glass **-farbe** *f* high gloss color **-fläche** *f* mirror-finished surface **-gebung** *f* polishing **-kalander** *m* supercalender **-kaschierung** *f* high gloss lamination **-lack** *m* high-gloss lacquer

Hochglanz-oberflächenspiegel *m* high surface reflex **-papiere** *pl* bright enamels **-paste** *f* extra-glossy paste **-polieren** to burnish, planish, or finish extra-bright, mirror-finish **-politur** *f* brilliant polish, high-luster polish **-satinage** *f* high-glaze calendering **überdrucklack** *m* high gloss transfer varnish **-zurichtung** *f* high-gloss finish

Hochglühen *n* full annealing

hochgradig intense, of a high degree or grade **-e Neutronenquelle** high level sources of neutrons **-er Spaltstoff** high-grade nuclear fuel **-er Sprinkler** high test sprinkler

hochgrün bright green

Hochhalde *f* dump above track level

hochhaltig high-grade **-e Anreicherungen** rich concentrations

Hoch-haus *n* tall building, skyscraper **-hauskran** *m* rotary tower crane **-heben** to put up, lift, raise, jack up **-heben** *n* jacking up

Hochheim'sche Verspiegelung special mirror plating

Hochheißen *n* hoisting

hochhitzebeständige Legierung heat-proof alloy

hochhub-artige Presse long-stroke press **-fahrwerk** *n* retractable landing gear **-sicherheitsventil** *n* high-lift safety valve **-ventil** *n* high-lift valve **-wagen** *m* lift truck

hoch-induktives Relais high-impedance relay **-intensitätskohle** *f* high-intensity carbon (arc)

hochionisiert highly ionized

hochkant edgewide, on edge, upright **~ gewickelte Bandspule** edgewise-wound ribbon coil **-biegen** to bend on edge **-stellen** to upend, place on edge, turn upside down

Hochkante *f* (milled) edge, working edge

Hochkantförderer *m* edge-on conveyer

hochkantig edgewise, on edge

Hochkant-stellung *f* upright position **-wicklung** *f* edgewise winding

Hochkette *f* high(-twist) warp

hochkippbar easily tilted **-er Abstreifer** adjustable (tilting) stripper **-e Oberwalze** top roller with a tilting device

Hoch-kippe *f* dumping tip **-klappbar** turn-up, swing-up **-klappflügel** *m* upward-folding wing **-klopffest** high ostane **-kompression-Gasolin** high compression gasoline **-konjunktur** *f* boom **-kurbeln** to raise, run up hoist, rack up

Hoch-lage *f* high position **-land** *n* highland **-laßtau** *n* handling guy **-lastdrahtwiderstand** *m* heavy-duty (load) wire-wound resistor **-lastpotentiometer** *n* heavy-duty potentiometer **-lauf** *m* uptake; (Maschinensatz) starting **-laufbahn** *f* runway for landing, ramp **-laufen** *n* run-up **-lautsprecher** *m* tweeter or treble loudspeaker

hochlegiert high-alloyed

Hochleistung *f* high efficiency, heavy duty, large capacity

Hochleistungs-abfühlvorrichtung *f* high-speed tape reader **-anlage** *f* high-capacity plant **-antrieb** *m* heavy-duty drive **-befeuerung** *f* high intensity lighting system **-blechrichtmaschine** *f* high-capacity plate-straightening machine **-bohrmaschine** *f* heavy-duty boring and drilling machine **-dekupiermaschine** *f* high-capacity nibbling machine **-drehbank** *f* high-duty lathe

Hochleistungs-einrichtung *f* high-production equipment **-fähig** high-performance-, high-capacity-, high-powered **-falzapparat** *m* heavy duty folder **-flächenfräsmaschine** *f* heavy-duty surface-milling machine **-flugmotor** *m* high-outpout aircraft engine **-flugzeug** *n* high-performance aircraft **-fräsmaschine** *f* high-efficiency or heavy-duty milling machine **-genauigkeitsmaschine** *f* heavy-duty machine for accurate work **-gleichrichterröhre** *f* power rectifying valve

Hochleistungs-kessel *m* heavy-duty boiler **-lampe** *f* high-intensity lamp **-lautsprecher** *m* high-efficiency speaker, high-power or public address loudspeaker **-leuchte** *f* high-efficiency lamp **-locher** *m* high-speed tape punch **-maschine** *f* heavy-duty machine **-mikroskopierleuchte** *f* high performance microscope lamp **-modell** *n* high-performance model **-motor** *m* heavy-duty aeroegine, high-output or high-powered engine **-objektiv** *n* high-quality objective **-pendelzentrifuge** *f* highly efficient hydro-extractor **-pile** *n* high-power pile **-pumpe** *f* high-speed pump

Hochleistungs-reaktor *m* high-energy level reactor **-revolverautomat** *m* high-production automatic turret screw machine **-röhre** *f* (high-)power tube, high-power vacuum tube **-satz** *m* high performance set **-schalter** *m* high-capacity circuit breaker **-schneidemetalle** *pl* high-speed cutting metals **-schnellschnittstahl** *m* superspeed steel **-segelflugzeug** *n* **-segler** *m* high-performance sailplane **-sicherung** *f* capacity fuse, quick-break fuse **-spannrahmenmaschine** *f* high effect tentering and drying machine **-typ** *m* high-production type

Hochleistungs- und Kunstsegelflugzeug *n* high-performance and acrobatic sailplane

Hochleistungs-wassersegelflugzeug *n* high-performance hydrosailplane **-zentrifuge** *f* high-speed centrifuge **-zündspule** *f* high power ignition coil

hoch-leitfähig highly conductive **-leitung** *f* high electric conduit, overhead wire **-lichtstarkes Objektiv** high-speed or ultraspeed objective or lens **-liegend** elevated, high **-luftdruckgebiet** *n* high-pressure area **-modern** up-to-date, modern **-moor** *n* high moorland **-mütig** proud, arrogant, haughty **-nehmen** to get up (the tail)

Hoch-Niedrig-Prüfung hi-lo-check

Hochofen *m* blast furnace **~ mit geschlossener Brust** blast furnace with closed front **~ mit offener Brust** open-hearth furnace, blast furnace with open front **~ mit Kippgefäßbegichtung** blast-furnace with skip hoist **~ mit Kübelbegichtung** blast-furnace with bucket hoist **~ anblasen** to blow in the furnace, to put the furnace in blast **den ~ abstechen** to tap the blast furnace **dünnwandiger ~** thinwalled blast furnace **elektrischer ~** electric-smelting furnace

Hochofen-abstich *m* blast-furnace casting **-anlage** *f* blast-furnace plant **-armatur** *f* blast-furnace fittings **-aufzug** *m* blast-furnace elevator or hoist **-begichtung** *f* blast-furnace charging **-begichtungsanlage** *f* blast-furnace charging equipment **-beschickung** *f* blast-furnace charge or charging **-besitzer** *m* ironmaster **-betrieb** *m* blast-furnace practice or operation **-dampfgebläse** *n* blast-furnace steam blower

Hochofen-erzeugung *f* blast-furnace output **-führung** *f* blast-furnace melting operation or practice **-futter** *n* blast-furnace lining **-gas** *n* blast-furnace gas **-gasgebläse** *n* blast-furnace gas-driven blowing engine **-gasgebläsemaschine** *f* blowing engine worked by blast-furnace gas **-gasmaschine** *f* blast-furnace gas engine **-gasreinigungsanlage** *f* blast-furnace gas-purifying plant **-gasschieber** *m* blast-furnace gas valve

Hochofengebläse *n* blast-furnace blowing engine **-anlage** *f* blast-furnace blowing plant

Hochofen-gerüst *n* blast-furnace frame **-gestell** *n* blast-furnace hearth or well, blast-furnace crucible

Hochofengicht *f* blast-furnace throat, top, or mouth, hopper **-verschluß** *m* throat stopper for blast furnaces

Hochofen-guß *m* iron cast directly from the blast furnace **-koks** *m* blast-furnace coke, metallurgical coke, run-of-the-oven coke **-kranz** *m* throat of blast furnace **-leiter** *m* blast-furnace operator or manager **-mann** *m* blast-furnace man **-meister** *m* blast-furnace foreman **-möller** *m* blast-furnace burden **-panzer** *m* blast-furnace jacket **-profil** *n* blast-furnace lines

Hochofen-rast *f* blast-furnace bosh **-rumpf** *m* blast furnace without appendices **-sau** *f* blast-furnace salamander, bear, or sow **-schacht** *m* blast-furnace stack or shaft **-schachtpanzer** *m* blast-furnace-stack casing **-schlacke** *f* blast-furnace slag **-schlackenzement** *m* blast-furnace slag cement **-stückschlacke** *f* blast-furnace lump slag

Hochofen-tragring *m* blast-furnace ring or mantle, blast-furnace lintel plate

Hochofen-umkleidung *f* blast furnace shaft **-verfahren** *n* blast-furnace process **-vorgang** *m* blast-furnace smelting operation **-vorherd** *m* blast-furnace settler **-werk** *n* blast-furnace plant **-wind** *m* furnace blast **-windform** *f* blast-furnace tuyère **-windring** *m* blast-furnace bustle pipe **-zement** *m* cement consisting of Portland cement and finely ground blast-furnace slag, blast-furnace(-slag) cement

Hochöfner *m* blast-furnace operator or engineer

hochohmig highly resistive or resistant, high-Z (e.g. input of amplifier) **-e Röhren** high-internal-resistance tubes **-e Wickelung** high-resistance winding

Hochohmigkeit *f* high-impedance character

Hochohmwiderstand *m* high ohmic resistance

hoch-paariges Kabel large-capacity or large-sized cable **-parterre** *n* raised ground floor

Hochpaß *m* **-filter** *m* high-pass filter

Hoch-plan *m* parade, esplanade **-polieren** to burnish **-poliert** highly polished **-prägemaschine** *f* relief embossing machine **-prägen** to emboss in relief **-punkt** *m* high reference point **-quellen** to gush up **-quellenleitung** *f* water supply from springs **-räderig** high-wheeled

hochradioaktiv highly radioactive **-e Abwässer** high-activity wastes

Hoch-rahmen *m* high-level frame **-reißen** to zoom **-richten** to hoist, erect **-rot** bright red or vermillion scarlet **-rund** convex **-satiniert** highly glazed **-schäftig** high-warp **-schätzen** to esteem highly, respect

hochschmelzend high-melting, difficultly meltable **-e Legierung** high-melting-point alloy **-es Metall** refractory metal

Hochschnappen der Spannfeder upward movement of tension spring

hochschneidende Schrämm-Maschine overcutting coalcutter

Hochschnitt (Bgb.) cutting above track level **-mähbalken** *m* high cutting mover bar

Hochschubkarren *m* high lift platform truck

Hochschule *f* university, college **technische ~** technological institute, polytechnical institute, technical college

Hochschulter-kugellager *n* deep-row ball bearing **-lager** *n* single-row rigid deep-groove ball journal bearing, thrust bearing

Hochsee *f* ocean, high sea, deep water **auf ~** on the high seas

Hochsee-flugzeug *n* seagoing aircraft **-operation** *f* operation on the high seas **-pegel** *m* high-water gauge **-rundfunk** *m* overseas broadcasting, ship-to-ship or ship-to-shore radio communication **-schiffahrt** *f* deep-sea navigation **-schleppdampfer** *m* ocean-going steamship **-schlepper** *m* ocean-going tugboat **-torpedoboot** *n* seagoing torpedo boat **-U-Boot** *n* fleet submarine

Hochseitenruder *n* high rudder

hochselektiver Empfänger single-signal reception

Hoch-sicherheitstrommel *f* high-safety drum **-siedend** high-boiling **-siliziertes Roheisen** high-silicon pig iron **-sinterung** *f* final sintering operation **-spannen** to step up **-spannleitung** *f* high-tension line

Hochspannung *f* high voltage, high potential, high tension, high pressure **mit ~ geprüft** hi-tested, high voltage tested

Hochspannungs-abnehmer high voltage consumer **-abspannklemmen** *pl* anchor clamps for high tension **-anlage** *f* high-tension (voltage) plant **-anode** *f* ultor (TV) **-ausführung** *f* high tension outlet **-draht** *m* live wire, secondary wire **-durchführung** *f* high-voltage duct **-entladungsröhre** *f* high-voltage discharge tube **-erzeuger** *m* high-tension generator **-fernschalter** *m* high-tension remote-control switch **-führend** conducting a high voltage

Hochspannungs-generator *m* high-tension generator **-gerät** *n* high tension unit **-geschützt** protected against high tension **-gleichstrom** *m* high tension direct current **-gleichrichter** *m* high voltage rectifier valve **-hängeklemmen** *pl* suspension clamps for high tension **-isolator** *m* high tension insulator

Hochspannungs-kabel *n* high-tension lead **-kondensator** *m* high-tension condenser, high-potential (fixed) condenser or capacitor **-lage** *f* high-voltage set **-leitung** *f* high-voltage line (power line) **-leitungsabführung** *f* high tension cable outlet **-magnet** *m* high-tension magneto **-magnetzünder** *m* high-tension magneto **-meßbrücke** *f* high-tension bridge **-netz** *n* high voltage (or tension) grid or system **-netzgeräte** *pl* high-voltage power pack **-pfeil** *m* danger arrow **-prüfeinrichtung** *f* high-voltage testing equipment **-prüffeld** *n* high tension test(ing) field

Hochspannungs-schalter *pl* high-tension switches **-schutzapparat** *m* **-schutzvorrichtung** *f* protective apparatus for high tension **-seite** *f* high-tension side **-sicher** safe against high-potential breakdown, having high puncture strength **-speiseapparat** *m* high voltage supply **-stahl** *m* high-tension steel **-strom** *m* high-voltage or high-tension current **-stütze** *f* high-voltage insulation support **-teil** *m* high-voltage panel (radar equipment) **-transformator** *m* high-tension or high-voltage transformer

Hochspannungs-versorgung *f* high-voltage supply **-verteiler** *m* high-tension distributor **-zuführung** *f* high tension lead-in **-zündanlage** *f* high-tension ignition unit **-zündkerze** *f* high-voltage spark plug

Hoch-spant *n* high frame **-speicherbecken** *n* elevated storage basin **-sperre** *f* high-altitude balloon barrage (above 1000 meters) **-sperrend** with high reverse voltage rating

höchst maximum, peak, maximal **-er elastischer Ausgleich** highest resiliency **-e Beanspruchungen** severe service conditions **-e Nutzlast auf** *n* **Meter Höhe** greatest load carried at an altitude of *n* meters **-e Qualität** best quality, acme **-er Totpunkt** top dead center **-e Widerstandskraft** ultimate strength

Hoch-stabanker *m* high bar armature **-stabillastung** *f* peak load, maximum output **-stabläufer** *m* high bar rotor **-stämmig** fully grown **-stand** *m* observation post in a tree, elevated position on scaffold or building, high lookout post

Höchstangebot *n* highest tender

Hoch-stapelkettenausleger *m* high pile chain delivery **-start** *m* airplane model start with elastic cord

Höchst-auftrieb *m* maximum lift (aviation) **-auftriebsbeiwert** *m* maximum coefficient of lift **-ausschalter** *m* maximum cutout

Höchstausschlag *m* elongation **~ der Schwingung** maximum amplitude or maximum deflection of the oscillation

Höchst-beanspruchung *f* highest stress **-belastung** *f* maximum or peak load **-besetzungszahl** *f* maximum number of electrons in shell **-betriebsdruck** *m* maximum operating pressure **-drehmoment** *n* maximum torque

Höchstdruck *m* maximum pressure **-kompressor** hyper-compressor, super-compressor **-lademotor** *m* fully supercharged engine **-lampe** *f* ultraviolet or vapor lamp **-schmiermittel** *n* extreme-pressure lubricant

Höchstdurchschnittskrümmung *f* maximum mean camber

hoch-stetig high-webbed (girder) **-stellbar** that can be raised (vertically adjustable) **-stellen** to raise, put upright **-stellen** *n* raising

Hochstellvorrichtung *f* elevating screw **~ eines Fernrohrstativs** elevating gear of a telescope tripod

höchstempfindlich extremely sensitive (chem.)

hochstetig (Träger) deep webbed

Höchst-fahrt *f* maximum speed, top speed **-fall** *m* maximum case

Höchstform *f* **in ~ bringen** to put in best shape

Höchstfrequenz *f* maximum frequency **-massenspektrometer** *n* mass synchrometer **-röhre** *f* disc-seal tube

Höchst-gasdruck *m* maximum gas pressure **-gebot** *n* highest offer, bid, or tender **-geschwindigkeit** *f* top or maximum speed **-geschwindigkeitsflugzeug** *n* ultrahigh-speed airplane **-geschwindigkeitsregler** *m* maximum speed governor **-gewicht** *n* maximum weight **-grad** *m* maximum

Höchstkurzleistung *f* maximum-power rating

Höchst-ladedruck *m* maximum boost **-ladestrom** *m* maximum charging current **-last** *f* maximum load or stress, ultimate strength **-lastprüfung** *f* overload test

Höchstleistung *f* maximum output, peak power, maximum efficiency or power, crest power, extreme record performance **mit ~ arbeiten** to operate at maximum capacity

Höchst-leistungsvolldruckhöhe *f* maximum power altitude **-maß** *n* greatest measure, maximum **-modulationsgrad** modulation capability **-ohmwiderstand** *m* resistor of extremely high ohmic value **-pferdekraft** *f* maximum horsepower **-prozentig** at the maximum of concentration (chem.) **-reichweite** *f* maximum range

Hochstraße *f* (Brückenstraße) overhead roadway, main highway, elevated highway, expressway

Hochstrom-bahn *f* high-amperage conductors **-bogen** *m* heavy-current arc, large-current arc **-kohlebogen** *m* high current carbon arc

Höchst-schlagweite (des Funkens) *f* maximum sparking distance **-schußweite** *f* extreme or maximum range **-spannung** *f* supertension, extra-high tension, maximum voltage, maximum or ultimate stress

Höchstspannungs-anlage *f* extra-high-tension plant **-kabel** *n* supertension cable **-kreuz** *n* high-tension cross **-leitung** *f* line carrying very high voltage **-netz** *n* extra-high-voltage system **-stahlleitung** *f* steel stranded conductor for maximum tension

Höchststellung *f* maximum position

Höchststrom *m* maximum or peak current **-impuls** *m* maximum current impulse **-relais** *n* overcurrent relay, maximum current relay, overload relay **-schalter** *m* overload switch **-stärke** *f* limit of current, maximum current intensity

Höchst-strömungsgeschwindigkeit *f* maximum velocity **-umdrehungen** *f pl* maximum revolutions **-verbrauchsmesser** *m* maximum-demand meter **-verzugsstreckwerk** *n* high draft or superhigh draft system

Höchstwert *m* peak or maximum value, unipolar peak **-anzeiger** *m* crest or peak indicator **-verfahren** *n* maximum-intensity method **-zeiger** *m* maximum-impulse indicator

Höchst-zahl *f* maximum, highest number **-zeit** *f* maximum time or period **-zug** *m* maximum tension **-zugfestigkeit** *f* maximal tensile strength **-zuladung** *f* maximum useful load

höchstzulässig maximum permissible **-e Dauerleistung** maximum cruising power **-e Frequenzabweichung** maximum system deviation **-e Spannung** (Festigkeit) limiting stress **-er Wert** maximum safe value

Hoch-tastrauschdiode *f* high-level impulse noise diode **-tastung** *f* working impulse transmitted on voltage substantially above normal

hochtemperaturbeständige Metalle refractory metals

Hochtemperatur-destillation *f* high-temperature distillation **-entwicklung** *f* high-temperature approach **-kathode** bright-emitting cathode **-reaktor** *m* high-temperature reactor **-teer** *m* high-temperature tar **-verkokung** *f* high-temperature (carbonization) coking

Hochton *m* treble **-durchlasser** *m* low-frequency muffler **-einheit** *f* (Lautsprecher) tweeter

hochtonerdehaltig highly aluminous **-er Stein** high-alumina brick

Hochton-konus *m* **-lautsprecher** *m* tweeter or treble (cone) loud-speaker, tweeter, high-frequency loudspeaker **-regler** *m* treble control (tape rec.) **-strahler** *m* tweeter (loudspeaker)

hoch-tourig of high speed **-tragender Flügel** high-lift wing **-trainieren** *n* work-toughening, breaking in **-transparent** highly transparent **-treiben** to drive or raise high, push up, work or refine highly

Hoch- und Niederfrequenzverstärkung *f* high- and low-frequency amplification **gleichzeitige ~** dual or reflex amplification

Hoch- und Seitenwertgeber *m* machine giving northings and eastings

hoch- und tiefstellbar adjustable for height or up and down

Hoch- und Tiefverstellung *f* vertical adjustment

Hochvakuum *n* low absolute pressure per unit surface, high or hard vacuum (electronic tubes) **-bedämpfungsanlage** *f* high vacuum coater **-durchschlag** high-vacuum breakdown **-elektronenröhre** *f* high-vacuum electron valve **-fernsehröhre** *f* high-vacuum television tube **-gitterröhre** *f* pliotron **-gleichrichter** *m* vacuum-tube rectifier, kenotron, electron-type rectifier **-gleichrichterröhre** *f* **-glühkathodengleichrich-**

terröhre *f* kenotron, high-vacuum-rectifier valve **-röhre** *f* (Elektronenröhre) electronic valve or vacuum tube, high-vacuum (valve) tube **-technik** *f* high-vacuum engineering **-verstärker** *m* high-vacuum amplifier **-zelle** *f* vacuum photocell, high-vacuum phototube

hoch-verdichtend high-compressing **-verdichtet** highly compressed **-verdünnt** very dilute **-verschleißfest** highly wear-resistant **-verstärkend** high gain **-verstärker** *m* high-frequency amplifier **-verzug** *m* high-drafting **-verzugstreckwerk** *n* highdraft system **-viskos** highly viscous **-warmfeste Legierung** high-temperature alley

Hochvolt *m* high volts **-elektrolytkondensator** *m* high-power electrolytic capacitor **-therapie** *f* megavoltage or supervoltage therapy

Hochwasser *n* high water (level), flood (level), high tide **-bett** *n* major bed, inundation limit **-grenze** *f* **-linie** *f* limit of the normal major bed (winter) **-rad** *n* high-water turbine **-schutzdamm** *m* flood bank **-stand** *m* high-water mark **-standsmesser** *m* high-watermark gauge

Hochwert *m* Y-coordinate number

hochwertig high-class, high-grade, of high strength, quality, or valence **-es Gas** rich gas **-er Grauguß** high-test or high-quality gray iron, high-strength cast iron **-er Guß** high-quality or high-grade cast iron **-e Lebensmittel** goods of high nutritive value **-er Stahl** high-quality steel **-e Waage** precision scale

Hochwertkomponente *f* Y-component, north-south component

hoch-winden to jack up, hoist, lift up, raise, heave **-wirbeln** to whirl high, back out **-wirksam** highly active or effective **-zahl** *f* exponent **-zeiliges Bild** high-definition picture (television) **-ziehbares Fahrwerk** retractable landing gear

hochziehen to lift up, wind up, raise up, pull out or up, stall, heave, zoom **~ und drücken** to undulate

Hochzüchten *n* breaking in (armor)

hocken to crouch, squat

Hocker *m* cam (camshaft)

Höcker *m* hump (of resonance curve), bump, protuberance, pip (of cathode-ray screen tracing) **-hindernis** *n* concrete or post tank obstacle, dragon's-teeth obstruction

Hodographen-ebene *f* hodograph plane **-gleichung** *f* hodograph (differential) equation

hodographisch hodographic

Hodoskop *n* hodoscope

Hof *m* courtyard, residence; halo (astron., opt.); aureola; farmyard, circle of glass surrounding a stone, corona **-bockkran** *m* gantry crane **-laufkran** *m* travelling crane

Hofwagen mit verstärkten Achsen cast-skein farm wagon

Höhe *f* hill, latitude, level, head, absolute unit, magnitude, pitch; (über einem Bezugspunkt) elevation, height **Höhe über NN** (Seehöhe) NN = Normal Null = mittlere Seehöhe altitude above (mean) sea-level elevation, datum **~ über der Abflugstelle** altitude above starting point **~ entsprechend Barometerstand** pressure altitude **~ der Fußringrille** base register **~ der Gebühr** amount of charge **~ der Interferenzfarbe** highest polarization color **~ der Kabine** cabin height

Höhe, entsprechend der Luftdichte density altitude **~ entsprechend Normalatmosphäre** density height **~ des Potentialwalls** barrier height **~ des Schwerpunktes** height of the center of gravity **~ des Schleusenabfalls** lift of a lock **~ des Spiegels** stage **~ bei Trägerprofil** depth **~ über dem Wasserspiegel** freeboard, height of quay surface above high water **~ des Ufers über dem Wasserspiegel** height of flood bank above water line **~ des Wehrsoldes** rate of pay (mil.) **~ behalten** to retain height (aviation)

Höhe, von . . . Metern erreichen to reach a height of . . . meters **~ gewinnen** to gain height (aviation) **in gleicher ~** at or on the same level **größte erreichbare ~** ceiling (aviat) **in die ~ heben** to jack up, lift **~ nehmen** to take sights **~ verlieren** to lose height **in der ~ verstellbar** vertically adjustable **in die ~ ziehen** to hoist **auf der ~** up-to-date well-informed **auf der ~ von** off (the port of), off or abreast of, in the latitude of

Höhe, in der ~ at a height (of), vertically **in der ~ von** at the level of, on a level with **in die ~** up **in niedriger ~** low **in sicherer ~** at a safe height **absolute ~** height above sea level **künstliche** (in der Höhenkammer erzeugte) **~** artificial altitude **lichte ~** headroom under a bridge, vertical clearance **wirksame ~** effective height

hohe Schule advanced school

Hoheit *f* elevation, loftiness, sovereignty

Hoheits-gebiet *n* sovereign territory **-gewässer** *pl* territorial waters **-grenze** *f* limit of territorial sovereignty **-und-Eintragungszeichen** *n* nationality and registration marks

Höhe-gebung *f* elevation measurement **-hobel** *m* height-to-paper shoot-board

Höhen *pl* heights, high (audio) frequencies, high pitches, treble (frequencies) **-abhängig** height dependance **-ablesung** *f* height computation **-abstand** *m* vertical interval **-abweichung** *f* elevation error, elevation or vertical deviation, range deviation **-änderung** *f* change of height or altitude **-angabe** *f* altitude indication or reading **-anhebung** *f* treble lift, raise **-anordnung** *f* staggered arrangement **-anzeiger** *m* level gauge **-anzug** *m* high-altitude flying suit **-äquivalent** *n* height equivalent **-atmer** *m* **-atmungsgerät** *n* breathing or oxygen apparatus for high-altitude flying **-auswanderung** *f* displacement in elevation

Höhen-basis *f* elevation base line **-begrenzer** *m* elevation stop

Höhenberechnung *f* height computation **barometrische ~** barometric height computation

Höhenbestimmung *f* determination of height, leveling

Höhenberichtigung *f* height correction; (bei Stereo-E-Messern) image height adjustment

Höhenberichtigungs-knopf *m* image height adjustment knob or head **-teilung** *f* image height adjustment scale, halving adjustment scale **-walze** *f* image height adjustment roll, halving adjustment roll

Höhen-beschneidung *f* treble cut, top cut **-beschreibung** *f* hypsography

Höhenbewegung *f* motion in altitude (altitude

motion) **Balanzierung eines Fernrohres in ~** balancing of a telescope for motion in altitude
Höhen-brücke *f* height bridge **-darstellung** *f* relief **-diagramm** *n* diagram of heights **-differenz** *f* vertical difference, difference in height or altitude **-differenzmelder** *m* level-difference indicator **-drossel** *f* altitude throttle **-druck** *m* maximum pressure **-ebene** *f* horizontal plane through target **-ebnung** *f* de-emphasis **-effekt** *m* altitude effect **-empfänger** *m* elevation receiver **-entfernungsmesser** *m* coincidence height finder
Höheneinstellung *f* adjustment of height; (d. Befeuerung) elevation setting (of lighting)
Höhen-entzerrung *f* treble correction (rdr) **-fehler** *m* error of height **-feinbewegung des Fernrohres** slow motion of telescope in altitude **-feinverstellung** *f* vertical fine adjustment **-fest** altitude-proved or -tested **-festigkeit** *f* physical ability to stand high altitude, altitude resistance **-festpunkt** *m* bench mark **-finder** *m* height finder
Höhenflosse *f* tail plane, horizontal stabilizer, fixed horizontal fin **im Fluge verstellbare ~** adjustable tail plane
Höhenflossen-einstellung *f* stabilizer setting (aviation) **-fläche** *f* tail-plane area, area of stabilizer **-flächeninhalt** *m* tail-plane area, area of stabilizer **-spannweite** *f* span of the tail planer or stabilizer **-tiefe** *f* tail stabilizer chord **-verstellung** *f* tail-plane trimming gear
Höhenflug *m* altitude flight **-anzug** *m* high-altitude flying suit **-ausrüstung** *f* high-altitude equipment **-motor** *m* high-altitude-flying motor **-wettbewerb** *m* altitude competition **-zeug** *n* stratoplane, high-altitude aircraft
Höhen-förderer *m* elevator, lift conveyer **-forschung** *f* altitude research **-gas** *n* high-altitude gas **-gashebel** *m* altitude throttle lever (supercharger) **-gemischregler** *m* altitude mixture control **-genauigkeit** *f* vertical accuracy **-gewinn** *m* gain in altitude **-gewinnfunktion** *f* height-gain function **-gleiche** *f* altitude parallel **-gradbogen** *m* elevation quadrant, elevating sector
Höhen-hebel *m* elevation clamping handle (machine gun) **-indexlibelle** *f* vertical index level **-isothermenkarte** *f* high-altitude isothermal chart **-justierung** *f* vertical adjustment **-kabine** *f* pressure cabin **-kammer** *f* variable-density wind tunnel, altitude-test chamber, decompression chamber **-kanal** *m* elevated duct **-karte** *f* relief map, map showing altitudes, (Luftdruck) upper-air chart **-kollimation** *f* vertical collimation
Höhen-krankheit *f* mountain sickness, high-altitude nausea, aeroembolism, bends **-kreis** *m* vertical circle, altitude or height circle **-kurve** *f* altitude curve **-kurvenkarte** *f* contour map **-lader** *m* altitude, boost, high-altitude supercharger, supercharger with high blower ratio
Höhenlage *f* altitude level, position in vertical sense **~ gegen einen höher gelegenen Festpunkt** height with reference to a bench mark **~ eines Fixpunktes** the height (elevation) of a bench mark referred to a datum **in gleicher ~** at the same grade
Höhenleistung *f* altitude performance, power at altitude
Höhenleit-fläche *f* tail plane **-werk** *n* horizontal (tail surfaces) stabilizers and elevators (aviation) **-werkfläche** *f* area of horizontal tail surfaces **-werkkraft** *f* horizontal-tail-surface force **-werktiefe** *f* depth of horizontal tail surface
Höhen-libelle *f* angle-of-site level **-lineal** *n* height arm **-linie** *f* contour, level
Höhenlinien-darstellung *f* **-diagramm** *n* level diagram or chart
Höhen-lotung *f* altitude measurement, height determination **-luft** *f* high altitude, upper air **-marke** *f* height mark, bench mark **-markierung** *f* level marker **-maß** *n* measure of altitude or elevation **-maßstab** *m* height gauge, scale of height
Höhenmesser *m* altitude meter, altimeter, statoscope, terrain-clearance indicator **den ~ auf Null stellen** (einstellen) to set the altimeter **sensitiver ~** Kollsmann station barometer
Höhenmesser-einstellung *f* altimeter setting **-verzögerung** *f*, **-widerstand** *m* altimeter lag
Höhenmeß-gerät *n* statoscope, altimeter **-kunst** *f* altimetry **-plan** *m* altitude-plotting board
Höhenmessung *f* hypsometry, altimetry, leveling **barometrische ~** leveling by means of barometer
Höhenmeß-vorrichtung *f* height-measuring device **-widerstand** *m* altimeter lag
Höhen-methode *f* method by altitude **-mischregelung** *f* high-altitude mixture control **-motor** *m* (für große Nennhöhe) supercharged engine, high-altitude engine, high-level-rated engine **-navigation** *f* **von Luftschiffen** high-altitude airship navigation **-parallaxe** *f* vertical parallax **-plan** *m* elevation chart or diagram **-prüfanlage** *f* low-pressure or altitude -pressure chamber **-prüfstand** *m* altitude-test chamber **-punkte** *pl* spot heights, altitude marks, crest points **-querruder** *n* aileron
Höhen-rad *n* (Bildkartiergeräte) height wheel **-rauch** *m* haze **-raum** *m* overhead room **-regelung** *f* altitude control **-region** *f* height level **-regler** *m* treble control (rdr.) **-reihe** *f* level (teleph.) **-rekord** *m* altitude record
Höhenricht-bereich *m* limiting angle of elevation **-bogen** *m* elevating arc **-feld** *n* gun angle of elevation **-fernrohr** *n* vertical tracking scope, elevation-tracking telescope **-geschwindigkeit** *f* rate of elevation (antiaircraft artillery) **-kurbel** *f* elevating handle **-maschine** *f* elevating mechanism or gear **-rad** *n* elevating handwheel **-schraube** *f* elevation dial or screw **-spindel** *f* elevating screw **-trieb** *m* elevating drive or mechanism
Höhenrichtung *f* elevation height setting; (Neigung) inclination; (unter der Horizontalen) depression
Höhenrichtungsbogen *m* elevating arc
Höhenricht-vorrichtung *f* elevating gear **-welle** *f* shaft of elevating mechanism **-werk** *n* elevating mechanism **-zeiger** *m* elevation indicator
Höhen-rippe *f* **-rücken** *m* ridge, crest
Höhenruder *n* elevator (flipper), stabilizer tab, pitch fin **-achse** *f* elevator axis **-ausgleich** *m* compensation of the elevator **-ausgleichklappe** *f* elevator booster tab, elevator tube **-ausschlagwinkel** *m* elevator deflection angle **-endbogen** *m* elevator edge, elevator tip strip **-hebel** *m* elevator control lever **-hinterkante** *f* elevator

trailing edge **-holm** *m* elevator false spar
Höhenruder-maschine *f* elevator servomotor **-randbogen** *m* elevator edge or stringer **-steuerhebel** *m* elevator control lever **-steuerseil** *n* elevator control cable **-stoßstange** *f* elevator push-and-pull rod **-tiefe** *f* elevator chord **-trimmklappe** *f* elevator trim tab **-trimmung** *f* elevator trimming **-welle** *f* elevator rocking shaft
Höhen-schau *f* view from above **-schicht** *f* contour line, contour, altitude bracket **-schichtenkarte** *f* contour map or plan **-schichtlinie** *f* contour line **-schieber** *m* altitude slide rule **-schieblehren** *pl* vernier height gauge **-schirm** *m* range bearing display **-schlitten** *m* height slide (photo.) **-schnittlinie** *f* contour line **-schreiber** *m* barograph, recording altimeter, altigraph
Höhenschritt *m* vertical step (in automatic-telephone equipment) **unbesetzter oder freier ~** vacant level
Höhenschrittvielfach(feld) *n* level multiple
Höhen-schwenkwinkel *m* elevation of lobe (radar) **-seitenruder** *n* elever **-sicherheit** *f* altitude stability **-sichtrohr** *n* elevation tube (electronics) **-skala** *f* altitude scale or graduation, height scale **-sprengpunkt** *m* high-air burst point **-staffelung** *f* vertical separation **-stellschraube** *f* height or vertical adjustment screw, elevating screw **-stellspindel** *f* elevating screw **-stellung** *f* position on dominant height
Höhensteuer *n* flipper, elevator, horizontal or depth rudder **~ geben** to pull out
Höhensteuerung *f* elevator control, fore and aft control
Höhenstrahlen *pl* cosmic rays **-schauer** *m* **-stöße** *m pl* bursts or showers of cosmic rays, cosmic-ray track
Höhenstrahlung *f* cosmic-ray radiation **harte Komponente der ~** penetrating or hard component of cosmic rays
Höhen-streuung *f* vertical dispersion (ballistics), range dispersion on vertical target **-stufen** *pl* altitude steps **-symmetrisch** symmetrical about vertical axis **-tafel** *f* tabel of altitudes **-tauglichkeitsprüfung** *f* altitude aptitude test **-teilkreis** *m* vertical circle, elevation scale **-teilung** *f* elevation scale **-temperatur** *f* temperature at various altitudes **-thermik** *f* high-altitude heat phenomenon **-trieb** *m* elevating mechanism or gear **-trimmung** *f* longitudinal trim
Höhen-umschaltung *f* height-change-over switch (radar) **-unterdruckkammer** *f* altitude depression chamber **-unterschied** *m* difference in elevation or in altitude, difference of level or height, vertical deflection **-verbesserung** *f* altitude correction **-verfahren** *n* method by altitude **-vergaser** *m* altitude carburetor **-verlust** *m* loss of altitude **-vermessung** *f* height measurement, altimetry **-verstellbar** vertically adjustable, adjustable up and down **-verstellbereich** *m* adjustable height range **-verstellung** *f* elevation adjustment **-verteilung** *f* vertical distribution **-vorhalt** *m* altitude lead
Höhen-wandler *m* air densitiy regulator **-weiser** *m* elevation indicator (gunner) **-welle** *f* space or sky wave, downcoming wave, atmospheric or reflected wave **-weltrekord** *m* world record for altitude **-wert** *m* altitude value (in vision) **-wetterdienst** *m* altitude meteorological service **-wind** *m* wind at high altitudes, upper wind **-winde** *f* crane **-windkanal** *m* variable-density wind tunnel **-windmessung** *f* upper-wind report (radio)
Höhenwinkel *m* angle of elevation, azimuth angle, angular height, vertical visual angle **-antrieb** *m* elevation drive **-beschleunigung** *f* vertical angular acceleration **-einstellung** *f* elevation setting **-fehler** *m* elevation error **-geschwindigkeit** *f* vertical angular velocity, rate of change of angle of sight **-peiler** *m* radio-theodolite **-teilung** *f* elevation scale **-verbesserungsknopf** *m* vertical correction knob **-vorhalt** *m* true vertical deflection, elevation lead
Höhen-wirkung *f* high-altitude effects **-zahl** *f* relative elevation, altitude figure **-zähler** *m* (Aero.) altitude counter **-zeiger** *m* elevation indicator, altimeter **-zenter zum Fräsen schlanker konischer Gegenstände** adjustable center for milling slight tapers **-zirkel** *m* circle of altitude **-zug** *m* mountain chain, range or chain of hills
Höhepunkt *m* peak, critical or culminating point, summit, top, crest **seinen ~ erreichen** to culminate
höhersteigen (der Luftströme) to rise
hoher Ton tweeter, treble, high-pitched or high-frequency note
höher higher **-e Algebra** higher algebra **-e Geometrie** analytical geometry **-e Gewalt** act of God, "force majeure" **-e Instanz** superior court, court of appeals **-e Teufe** upper level
Hohl des Schiffsraumes depth of the ship's hold
hohl hollow, empty, concave (mirror), boomy, dull (sound or voice) **-e Ebbe** dead low water **-er Kern** hollow or tubular core **-er Ton** boomy or dull sound **-e Welle** hollow or tubular shaft **-e Wiedergabe** reproduction with high acoustic frequencies
Hohl-anode *f* hollow anode **-bauten** *pl* fortification chambers **-beil** *n* adze **-beitel** *m* gouge
Hohlblock *m* hollow billet or ingot; (Rohrwalzwerke) hollow blank **-stein** *m* hollow (clay) building (or masonry) block
Hohl-bohren *n* trepanning **-bohrer** *m* hollow drill, shell auger **-bohrgestänge** *n* hollow drilling rods **-bohrmaschine** *f* trepanning machine **-bolzen** *m* bushing **-dechsel** *f* hollow adze **-dielezement** *m* hollow concrete slab
Höhle *f* cave, hollow, hole, cavity
Hohleisen *n* gouge, hollow chisel
Höhlendach *n* cave roof
hohl-erhaben concavo-convex **-flächig** tapered **-flachstahl** *m* hollow flat-bar steel **-form** *f* heavy-cored casting, shell mold **-formenpresse** *f* hollow-mold press **-fräser** *m* hollow mill, concave milling cutter **-fußguß** *m* hollow mount casting **-gefäß** *n* hollow container **-geschliffen** concave or hollow ground **-geschoß** *n* hollow projectile, shell
Hohl-gestänge *n* drill pipe or tube **-gewebe** *n* tubular fabrics **-gewinde** *n* female thread (as of pipes) **-gießen** to hollowcast **-gitter** *n* concave grating **-glas** *n* hollow or concave glass **-glaserzeugung** *f* hollow-glass industry **-guß** *m* cored work, hollow casting **-gußquadrate** *pl* hollow-

cast quade **-gußständer** *m* hollow upright
Hohlheit *f* cavity, emptiness
höhlig honeycombed, having cavities or pits
Hohl-kabel *n* hollow wave-guide **-kanteisen** *n* fluted bar iron **-kastenbauweise** *f* box-type construction **-kathode** *f* cylindrical, concave or hollow cathode **-kathodenentladung** *f* hollow cathode discharge **-kehle** *f* cavetto, groove, channel, concave mold (e.g., in structural metal), fillet, spandrel
Hohlkehlen-drechsler *m* hollower **-eisen** *n* right-side round iron, round-nose iron **-halbmesser** *m* fillet radius **-schleifvorrichtung** *f* device for hollow grinding **-stahl** *m* hollow-ground or round-nosed tool
hohlkehlig concave tapered
Hohl-kehlschweißung *f* concave fillet weld **-keil** *m* saddle key, hollow key **-kern** *m* tubular or hollow core **-kolben** *m* trunk piston **-kopfgeschoß** *n* hollow-charge projectile **-körnerspitze** *f* hollow center
Hohlkörper *m* hollow body, piece, or ware, tube blank **runder ~** tubular product
Hohl-kugel *f* hollow sphere **-ladung** *f* hollow (explosive) charge **-ladungsmunition** *f* hollow-charge ammunition
Hohlleiter *m* tubular conductor, waveguide **sich erweiternder ~** tapered waveguide **~ mit Längssteg** ridge waveguide **~ mit Leitblechen** flared radiating guide **~ mit parallelen Platten** pillbox (microwaves) **~ mit axialer Scheidewand** septate waveguide
Hohlleiter-achse *f* axis of a waveguide **-anpassungsglied** *n* non-dissipative stub **-bau** *m* plumbing **-blende** *f* waveguide shutter **-bolzen** *m* waveguide post **-meßleitung** *f* waveguide slotted line **-resonanzkreis** *m* waveguide resonator **-spannungsteiler** *m* piston attenuator **-übergang** *m* doorknob transformer **-wellen** *pl* waveguide modes **-zuführung** *f* waveguide feed
Hohl-linse *f* concave lens **-maß** *n* measure of capacity, dry measure, dry or liquid meter **-mast** *m* tubular pole **-mauer** *f* (Hohlwand) cavity wall, hollow wall **-maulzange** *f* hollow-bit tongs
Hohlmeißel *m* gouge, hollow chisel or bit **-bohrer** *m* hollow chisel bit **-stemmaschine** *f* hollow-chisel mortising machine
Hohl-niet *m* tubular rivet, hollow-type rivet **-nockenform** *f* hollow cam shape **-planspiegel** *m* plane-concave mirror **-pressen** to press hollow, hollow out **-prisma** *n* hollow prism **-profil** *n* hollow section **-querschnitt** *m* hollow section **-querschnittsfläche** *f* hollow cross-section area, area of internal-hollowed section **-radsatz** *m* hollow wheel set **-räder** *pl* annular gears, internal gears **-rahmen** *m* hollow frame
Hohlraum *m* cavity, hollow space, cell, opening, excavation, pore space, reverberation chamber (acoustics), interstice **unterirdischer ~** cavern **mittels Kern im Gußstück erzeugter ~** cored hole
Hohlraum-abmessung *f* cavity dimension **-bildung** *f* cavitation (in supersonic waves) **-druck** *m* cavity pressure
Hohlräumer *m* hollow reamer
Hohlraum-feld *n* cavity field **-gehalt** *m* porosity
hohlraumgekoppeltes Filter cavity-coupled filter
Hohlraum-gestalt *f* cavity shape **-gitter** *n* resonator grid
Hohlraumkabel *n* air-space cable **~** (Papierhohl), dry-core cable, air-space paper-core cable
Hohlraum-mischerkreis *m* wave-guide circuit **-panzerung** *f* spaced armor
Hohlraumresonator *m* cavity resonator (electronics, ultrashort waves), chamber resonator, rhumbatron **abgestimmter ~** (tuned) cavity **~ mehrfach zusammenhängend** re-entrant cavity resonator
Hohlraumresonator-röhre *f* magnetron, resonant cavity x-ray tube **-schalter** *m* performeter
Hohlraum-schießen *n* cushioned blasting, cushion shot **-strahler** *m* horn-type aerial **-strahlung** *f* cavity radiation, black-body radiation **-wellenmesser** *m* cavity wavemeter
Hohl-reibahle *f* shell reamer **-ringladung** *f* hollow-ring charge **-rinne** *f* groove **-rohrabschwächer** *m* cut-off attenuator **-röhre** *f* hollow tube **-rohrleiter** *m* waveguide **-rohrleitung** *f* hollow pipe line, hollow waveguide, concentric line, coaxial line **-rohrwellen** *pl* hollow tube waves **-rundung** *f* concavity
Hohl-säule *f* hollow supporting column **-saum** *m* hem stitch **-schale** *f* cup dish **-schaufel** *f* hollow blade **-schicht** *f* airspace (aviation) **-schiene** *f* U rail **-schliff** *m* hollow edged, concave grinding **-schlüssel** *m* barrel key
Hohlschneidestahl für runde Nuten round-nose tool
Hohl-schnitt *m* hollow section **-schraube** *f* female screw, banjo bolt, hollow screw **-schraubenstutzen** *m* hollow connection plug **-seil** *n* hollow rope or cable **-setzen** *n* hollow drift **-sog** *m* cavitation (phys.) **-sonde** *f* concave sound
Hohlspat *m* chiastolite **gewürfelter ~** a tesselated type of chiastolite
Hohl-spiegel *m* concave (mirror) reflector **-spiegelkathode** *f* concave cathode **-spitze** *f* hollow point **-ständer** *m* hollow column **-stange** *f* pipe **-steg** *m* gutter (print.), hollow stay, hollow section **-stein** *m* hollow tile or block **-stelle** *f* hollow **-stempel** *m* matrix, mold, hollow drift **-stiel** *m* hollow strut **-stopfen** *m* hollow plug **-strebe** *f* hollow strut **-stütze** *f* hollow support
Hohl-träger *m* hollow girder **-trägerkonstruktion** *f* hollow-frame construction **-trieb** *m* lantern pinion
Höhlung *f* cavity, hollow, excavation, groove, recess
Höhlungsresonanz *f* cavity resonance
Hohl-visierung *f* wide open V rear sight **-walze** *f* cylinder **-walzwerk** *n* rotary piercing mill **-wand** *f* hollow wall, cavity wall **-wandig** hollow-walled **-weg** *m* sunken road, defile, narrow pass, ravine, gorge **-welle** *f* hollow shaft, quill, tubular shaft, torque tube **-wellenlager** *n* quill bearing **-ziegel** *m* hollow brick, cavity brick **-ziegelstein** *m* hollow brick **-ziehen** to hollow draw **-zirkel** *m* inside calipers **-zylinder** *m* hollow cylinder
Holeintritt *m* die mouth
holen to get, fetch
Holländer *m* native of Holland, beater, rag, or pulp engine **-grundwerkmesser** *n* bed-plate knife **-haube** *f* dome **-kropf** *m* breasting of the beater **-mahlung** *f* hollander-beating **-masse** *f*

beater stock **-messer** *n* fly bar, roll bar, rag-machine knife **-müller** *m* beaterman **-saal** *m* beater house or room **-schiene** *f* fly bar, roll bar **-wagen** *m* enddump truck, side-dump truck **-walze** *f* cylinder of the rag engine

Holländischbütten *pl* dutch paper

Hollandit *m* hollandite

Höllenstein *m* lunar caustic, silver nitrate

Hollerith-maschine *f* Hollerith machine, IBM machine **-system** *n* perforated-card system

Holleyscher Losboden Holley detachable or removable bottom

Holm *m* small hill, islet, transom, strut, spar, arm of split trail, girder (aviation), crossbeam, outrigger, ladder stringer, longeron **durchgehender ~** continuous spar (aviation) **gezogener ~** extruded spar

Holm-abstand *m* spar gap or distance **-achse** *f* lateral or transverse axis **-ansatz** *m* spar attachment **-anschluß** *m* wing attachment, spar attachment (aircr.) **-anschlußbelag** *m* wing spar connector **-auskreuzung** *f* antidrag wire, drag wire **-beschlag** *m* spar fitting **-breite** *f* spar width **-durchbiegung** *f* deflection of spar

Holme *pl* handles **die ~ spreizen** to spread the trails

Holm-feld *n* bay or panel of spar **-firnis** *m* spar varnish **-fräsemaschine** *f* spar-milling machine **-gurt** *m* spar flange **-gurtprofil** *n* spar-girder shape **-gurtung** *f* flange of the spar **-höhe** *f* spar depth

Holmium *n* holmium

Holm-kasten *m* box spar **-lage** *f* position or location of spar **-längsachse** *f* longitudinal axis of the spar **-obergurt** *m* top flange, cap strip **-querschnitt** *m* spar cross section **-querschnittsfläche** *f* spar-section area, sectional area of spar **-schuh** *m* strut socket, wing spar box

Holm-steg *m* web of spar **-stegstärke** *f* thickness of spar web **-teilung** *f* division of spar **-tiefe** *f* spar width **-untergurt** *m* bottom flange **-verschraubung** *f* screw spar coupling **-zurrung** *f* outrigger lashing (platform, lock)

holoachsial holoaxial

holoeder *n* holohedral form of crystal

Holoedrie *f* holohedrism

holoedrisch holohedral

holoisometrisch holoisometric

holokristallin holocrystalline

Holometer *n* holometer

holomorph holomorphic

holperig uneven, clumsy, bumpy

Holt-Dern-Prozeß *m* Holt-Dern (chloride-roasting and -leaching) process

Holt-Fackel *f* Holt flare

Holundermarkkugel *f* pith ball

Holz *n* wood, timber, lumber **~ abhobeln** to jack or jack down stuff, plane off or rough-plane timber **~ abschnüren** to line out stuff **~ abvieren** to square or timber wood **~ beschlagen** to square or timber wood **~ dörren** to dry wood, kiln **~ schneiden** to block out, cut up, or saw timber

Holz, das ~ wirft sich the wood is casting or warping **abgefaßtes ~** cant or canted timber **brandiges ~** dry-rotted wood **einsträhniges ~** thick wood **einwüchsiges ~** wood flawy on one side **eisklüftiges ~** wood having fissures **engjähriges ~** close-grain wood **geschältes ~** disbarked wood

Holz, gezapftes ~ tongued wood **hochgeschoßtes ~** upshot wood, very profitable wood **kernschäliges ~** circular-checked, cracked, or creviced wood **lufttrockenes ~** air-dried wood **weiches, saftreiches ~** sappy wood **widerwüchsiges ~** wood with crooked fibers **windbrüchiges ~** rolled timber, windfall **windschiefes ~** back-sided timber

Holz-abfälle *pl* wood waste, chips of wood **-abfuhr** *f* wood transport **-abhieb** *m* wood felling **-abnehmer** *m* timber auger (min.) **-abscheider** *m* wood separator **-ähnlich** woodlike, ligneous **-arbeit** *f* woodwork **-asbest** *m* ligneous asbestos, rockwood **-äther** *m* methylic ether **-auge** *n* (slang) weaver in a formation **-auskleidung** *f* inside wooden casing, horizontal timber sheeting, logging **-ausschlepper** *m* timber loader **-ausschnittarbeit** *f* marquetry cutting

Holz-balken *m* wood beam, wood frame **-bandrohr** *n* built-up or laminated wooden tube **-bast** *m* inside bark (wood bast) **-bau** *m* wooden building **-bauweise** *f* wood or frame construction **-beanspruchung** *f* strain on poles **-bearbeitung** *f* wood-working **-bearbeitungsmaschine** *f* woodworking machine **-bearbeitungswerkstatt** *f* woodworking shop **-bearbeitungswerkzeug** *n* woodworking tool

Holz-bedruckmaschine *f* wood printing press **-beilage** *f* wood packing **-bekleidung** *f* timber lining **-belag** *m* wood covering **-besäumer** *m* tail edger (sawmill) **-bestand** *m* standing crop of wood **-besteck** *n* wooden knife, fork, and spoon **-bildhauerei** *f* wood sculpture or carving **-bildschnitzer** *m* carver of figures on or of wood **birne** *f* wooden wedge **-blasinstrument** *n* woodwind instrument **-boden** *m* woodland **-bogenfachwerk** *n* timber spandrel **-bohle** *f* deal **-bohrarbeit** *f* wood boring

Holzbohrer *m* auger bit, wood bit, wood-boring drill, gimlet **~ für Bohrkurbel** bit for hand brace (wood tools)

Holz-bohrkäfer *m* wood(-boring) beetle **-brand** *m* gangrene **-brei** *m* wood pulp **-brettchen** *n* wooden board **-brücke** (Lastwagen) timber platform **-bündel** *n* fagot **-bunker** *m* log bunker, timber shelter **-deckel** *m* wooden lid or plug **-dorn** *m* wooden center **-drahtrumpf** *m* stick-and-wire fuselage **-drehbank** *f* wood-turning lathe

Holzdruck *m* xylography **Druckstempel für ~** printing stamp for block printing

Holz-dübel *m* wooden dowel or pin **-einlegearbeit** *f* marquetry

holzen to cut wood

Holzentrindungstrommel *f* drum barker

hölzern wooden **-es Daubenrohr** stave pipe **-e Luftschraube** wooden propeller **-es Probemodell in natürlicher Größe** mock-up (aviation) **-e Unterzüge** (beim Stapeln von Stangen) trestles or wooden framework (for stacking poles)

Holzessig *m* pyroligneous acid, pyrolignite **-säure** *f* pyroligneous acid **-saures Blei** pyrolignite lead

Holz-etui *n* wooden case **-fachwerk** *n* timber framing **-farbstoff** *m* vegetable color, wood dye

Holzfaser *f* excelsior, wood fiber **-bruch** *m* woody or fibrous fracture **-masse** *f* wood pulp **-platten** *pl* wood-fiber boards **-spanplatte** *f* wood-fiber chip board **-stoff** *m* lignin, cellulose, lignocellulose

Holz-faß *n* wood barrel **-fäulnis** dry rot **-fehler** *m* defect in timber **-festpropeller** *m* fixed pitch wooden propeller **-flügel** *m* wooden wing **-flugzeug** *n* wooden aircraft **-folie** *f* wooden foil

holzförmig woody, ligneous

Holz-fournierpapier *n* plywood paper **-fräser** *m* wood-milling cutter **-frästermesser** *n* wood-milling-cutter knife **-futter** *n* timber water seals **-gasanlage für Kraftwagen** wood-consuming gas generator for motor vehicles **-gasmotor** *m* wood-gas engine

Holz-geflecht *n* cribwork of wood **-gehäuse** *n* wooden baffle, cabinet **-geist** *m* wood alcohol **-geistöl** *n* wood-spirit oil (residue from wood alcohol distillation) **-gelenke** *pl* wooden shanks **-gerippe** *n* frame or box timber, timber crib **-gerüst** *n* wood scaffold, wooden frame **-geschoß** *n* wooden projectile **-gestänge** *n* wooden poles **-gestängebohrapparat** *m* pole boring apparatus

Holz-geviert *n* timber square tubbing (min.) **-gitter** *n* wooden lattice or grid **-gittermast** *m* wood lattice mast

holzhaltiges Papier *n* paper (made) from wood pulp

Holz-hammer *m* mallet **-handdrehstahl** *m* wood turning chisel **-harz** *n* wood resin **-haspel** *f* wooden winch **-haube** *f* wooden hood **-hauer** *m* woodman, lumberman, woodcutter **-heft** *n* wooden handle **-holm** *m* wooden spar **-horde** *f* wood hurdle **-hordenkonstruktion** *f* checkerwork of wooden slats **-hülle** *f* wooden envelope

Holz-imprägnierung *f* wood impregnation, lumber preservation **-jalousie** *f* wood window blind **-joch** *n* wooden bay **-karton** *m* wood pulp boards **-kassette** *f* wooden plateholder

Holzkasten *m* wood box, wood tank, wooden cabinet ~ **zum Sumpfen** wooden sump box

Holz-keil *m* wedge fillet **-kiste** *f* wooden box **-klotz** *m* wood block, log **-klotzpflaster** *n* wooden block flooring **-kocher** *m* digester **-kohle** *f* charcoal

Holzkohlen-blech *n* charcoal-iron sheet **-eisen** *n* charcoal iron, Norway iron **-feuer** *n* charcoal fire or hearth **-frischstahl** *m* charcoal-hearth steel **-gasgenerator** *m* wood-gas generator **-gestübbe** *n* charcoal breeze or dust mixed with clay **-hochofen** *m* charcoal blast furnace **-klein** *n* small pieces of charcoal **-kreosot** *n* wood creosote

Holzkohlen-lösche *f* charcoal breeze **-mehl** *n* finely ground charcoal, charcoal powder **-mehlschwärze** *f* charcoal black **-meiler** *m* charcoal pile or heap **-pfanne** *f* charcoal brazier **-pulver** *n* powdered charcoal, charcoal fines, dust, or powder **-retorte** *f* charcoal retort **-roheisen** *n* charcoal pig, iron, or pig iron **-schwärze** *f* charcoal black

Holz-konservierung *f* preservation of lumber or of wood **-konservierungsmittel** *n* wood preservative **-kranz** *m* wooden flange, wooden ring **-krebs** *m* cankerous growth in wood **-kropf** *m* tree wart, rind gall **-kupfererz** *n* wood copper, arsenate of copper, fibrous olivenite **-lage** *f* wood layer or lamina **-lager** *n* wood stores, lumberyard **-latte** *f* wood lath **-lehre** *f* wooden gauge **-leiste** *f* wood border, lath, or molding, strip of wood, wooden ledge, wooden reglet **-luftschraube** *f* wooden propeller

Holz-lutte *f* wooden air conduit or duct **-mantel** *m* wood casing **-maserung** *f* grain of wood **-mast** *m* wooden mast **-mehl** *n* wood dust or powder, wood flour **-mehlpapier** *n* oatmeal paper **-meißel** *m* wood chisel **-meßgerät** *n* caliper (lumber) **-mine** *f* wooden-box mine **-modell** *n* wood pattern, solid scale model (made of solid wood) **-nabe** *f* wooden hub **-nagel** *m* treenail

Holzöl *n* wood oil **-säure** *f* lignoleate **-schleiflack** *m* wood-oil rubbing varnish **-überzugslack** *m* wood-oil finishing varnish

Holz-papier *n* wood-pulp paper **-pappe** *f* cellular paste-board, wood-pulp board **-pech** *n* wood pitch **-pfahl** *m* timber pile, woodpile **-pfeife** *f* wood pipe (of organ) **-pfeiler** *m* chock, cog **-pfeilerfreiträger** *m* chock release **-pflaster** *n* wood-block paving

Holzpflock *m* hob, peg **kurzer ~ zur Ermittlung der Förderung** notch stick

Holz-pfosten *m* wooden peg or stake **-plattenbandförderer** *m* wood-slat conveyer **-platz** *m* lumber-yard **-querspant** *n* wooden panel **-rad** *n* wooden wheel **-rahmen** *m* wooden frame **-randsieb** *n* wooden-rim sieve **-raspel** *f* wood rasp **-riemenscheibe** *f* wood pulley **-ring** *m* annular or timber ring **-rinne** *f* wood trough or culvert **-rippe** *f* wooden rib

Holz-rohr *n* wooden tube **-röhre** *f* cellular tube **-rolle** *f* batching roller **-rost** *m* wooden grating, trench board, catwalk, boardwalk **-rumpf** *m* wooden fuselage **-säge** *f* wood saw **-schaft** *m* handrail post **-schalenrumpf** *m* wooden monocoque fuselage

Holz-schälmaschine *f* wood-peeling machine **-scheibe** *f* wooden target, wooden disk **-scheider** *m* wood separator **-schlag** *m* woodcutting, wood felling **-schlegel** *m* (wooden) mallet, maul, beetle **-schleiferei** *f* pulp factory, wood grinding **-schliff** *m* mechanical wood pulp **-schneider** *m* wood engraver **-schnitt** *m* woodcut, wood engraving, wood stock, wood block

Holzschraube *f* wood screw, wooden propeller ~ **mit metallgeschützten Kanten** wooden airscrew with metal-sheathed leading edge ~ **mit Rundkopf** lag screw ~ **mit Vierkantkopf** coach screw

Holzschrauben-gewinde *n* wood-screw thread **-messer** *n* wood-carving or wood-screw knife

Holz-schutz *m* wooden shield **-schwarte** *f* bark **-schwelle** *f* sill timber, timber tie **-schwimmer** *m* wooden float **-sims** *m* wood molding

Holzspäne *pl* wood chips, shavings **kleine weiche** ~ excelsior

Holz-spanplatte *f* wood-chip board **-speichenrad** *n* wood-spoked wheel **-spiralbohrer** *m* spiral bit **-stab** *m* wooden slat **-stabgewebe** *n* material made of wooden latticework, wooden beading material **-ständer** *m* wooden peg or stake

Holzstange *f* wooden pole **rohe oder unzubereitete** ~ untreated wooden pole

Holz-stecherkunst *f* wood engraving, xylography **-steg** *m* wood center **-stich** *m* wood engraving

Holzstock *m* **gravierter ~** wood engraving

Holz-stoff *m* lignin, wood cellulose, lignone (chem.), wood pulp **-stoß** *m* woodpile, wood stack **-struktur** *f* wood structure **-stuck** *m* ligneous stucco **-stütze** *f* poppet **-substanz** *f* cellulose (lignin) **-tafel** *f* board, wood panel **-tafeldruck** *m* woodblock printing **-täfelung** *f* wood paneling **-teer** *m* wood tar **-träger** *m* wooden support or girder **-tränkung** *f* impregnation of timber **-trichter** *m* (founding) gate stick, wooden funnel **-turm** *m* wooden tower

Holzverdämmung, die Gewässer durch ~ abhalten to keep off the waters by timbering

Holz-vergaser *m* wood-distilling apparatus **-verkleidung** *f* wood revetment **-verkohlung** *f* charcoal burning, carbonization of wood **-verschalung zum Absteifen eines Kabelgrabens** wood piling or shoring, bracing cable ditch **-verschlag** *m* wooden frame **-versenkschraube** *f* carriage bolt **-verzimmerung** *f* timberwork **-verzuckerung** *f* saccharification of wood **-wanne** *f* wooden tank **-weg** *m* path in woods, dead-end loggers' road **-werk** *n* woodwork, frame- or timberwork **-wickelrumpf** *m* wooden shell body

Holz-wolle *f* excelsior, wood fiber or wool **-wollefilter** *m* wood-wool filter **-wurm** *m* woodworm, borer, **-zellstoff** *m* wood pulp **-zellulose** *f* wood cellulose **-zement** *m* wood cement **-zerstörend** lignicidal **-zinn** *n* wood tin **-zinnerz** *n* fibrous cassiterite **-zubereitung** *f* preservation of wood **-zucker** *m* wood sugar, xylose **-zwischenlage** *f* wood separator in storage battery

Homobrenzkatechin *n* methyl pyrocatechol

homochrom of uniform color, homochromatic, homochromous

homodin homodyne **-er Empfang -e Verständigung** homodyne reception

Homodynempfang *m* homodyne reception, zero-beat reception

homogen homogeneous, smooth, uniform as to grain size **~ verzerrt** homogenously strained **-es Feld** homogeneous field **-er Hohlleiter** uniform waveguide **-e Leitung** smooth or homogeneous line **-e Röntgenstrahlen** monochromatic X-rays **-e Strahlung** homogeneous radiation **-er Verformungszustand** homogeneous strain **-er Wasserreaktor** *m* aqueous homogenous reactor

Homogenholz *n* designation of a light material used in aircraft construction

Homogenisierapparat *m* homogenizer

homogenisieren to homogenize

Homogenisieren *n* solution treatment

Homogenisiermaschine *f* homogenizer

Homogenisierung *f* homogenization

Homogenisierungsausbeute *f* mixing efficiency

Homogenisierzone *f* metering section

Homogenität *f* homogeneity, homogeneousness

Homogen-kohle *f* solid carbon **-stahl** *m* homogeneous steel

homolog homologous

Homomorphismus *m* homomorphism

homonucleares Molekül homonuclear molecule

Homöoladung *f* homocharge

homöomorph isomorphous

homöopolar homopolar **homopolar** unipolar

homozygot homozygous

Honautomat *m* honing automatic

honen to hone

Honig-säure *f* mellitic acid **-schleudergerät** *n* honey strainer **-wabenspule** *f* honeycomb coil **-wicklung** *f* honey comb winding

Honmaschine *f* honing machine

Honorar *n* fee, remuneration, honorarium

honorieren to honor, give protection, pay

Honwerkzeug *n* honing tool

Hookesches Gesetz Hooke's law

Hooperscher Draht Hooper wire

Hopfen *m* hops **-lager** *n* hops storage **-seiher** *m* hop sieve

Hopkinsonscher Streufaktor leakage (Hopkinson coefficient)

Hops *m* hop, jump, skip

Hör-anlage *f* listening set for Morse practice, listening post **-anschluß** *m* listening connection **-anzeige** *f* loudspeaker report **-apparat** *m* listening device or apparatus **-aufnahme** *f* sound (or aural) reception **-ausbildung** *f* sound-detection training

hörbar audible **~ machen** to render audible **-e Anzeigung** audible detection **leichtes, gerade noch -es Klopfen** (Verbrennungsmotor) slight audible knock (combustion engine) **-es Signal** acoustic signal **-es Zeichen** audible signal

Hörbarkeit *f* audibility

Hörbarkeits-faktor *m* audibility factor **-grenze** *f* limit of audibility **-lautstärkeregler** *m* audibility network **-schwelle** threshold of audibility

Hör-bereich *m* range of audibility, broadcasting range **-bereitschaft** *f* listening watch, monitor

Horch-apparat *m* hydrophone (for use against submarines) **-auswertestelle** *f* radio-interception or intelligence-analysis post **-dienst** *m* listening service **-empfang** *m* stand-by operation

Horcher *m* listener, sound locator

Horcherprüf- und Übungsgerät *n* binaural trainer or training instrument

Horch-fehler *m* Morse corruption or error in reception **-funk** *m* wireless-interception service, signals intelligence **-gerät** *n* sound locator, hydrophone gear, listening gear, acoustic-detecting apparatus, range- and distance-determining device, asdic (submarine detector)

Horch H *n* static H service

Horch-meldung *f* listening report **-ortung** *f* sound location, sound ranging, radio intercept service **-posten** *m* listening post **-raum** *m* acoustic-observation area using sound locators, listening room (submarine) **-stelle** *f* listening post, monitor station

Horde *f* hurdle, horde, gang

Horden-filter *m* hurdle filter **-trockenapparat** *m* rack drying apparatus **-trockner** *m* shelf drier **-wascher** *m* hurdle-type scrubber or washer, wooden checker

Hör-empfang *m* audible or aural reception, reception by sounder or buzzer **-empfindlichkeit** *f* hearing ability, auditory sensitivity **-empfindung** *f* auditory sensation

hören to hear, listen

Hören *n* hearing, listening **einohriges ~** monaural listening or reception **zweiohriges ~** binaural or plastic hearing or audition, two-channel listening, stereo reception

Hörer *m* listener; earphone, telephone receiver **den ~ abnehmen** (abheben) to remove the receiver **den ~ anhängen** to hang up or restore the receiver

Hörer-auflegesignal *n* on hook signal **-echo** *n* listener echo **-gabel** *f* hook of the receiver (teleph.) **-gehäuse** *n* receiver shell or case **-muschel** *f* receiver cap or earpiece **-stromkreis** *m* receiver circuit

Hör-fehler *m* phonetic error **-film** *m* sound-film, sound telecinematography, sound telecast **-fläche** *f* auditory-sensation area **-frequent** audible, audio

Hörfrequenz *f* audio, audible, tonal, or acoustic frequency **-kreis** *m* audio circuit **-verstärker** *m* note amplifier

Hör-gerät *n* apparatus for the deaf **-grenze** *f* auditory range **-heft** *n* radio operator's log **-hilfe** *f* audio aid, deaf aid

Horizont *m* horizon, layer, bed, datum line, skyline **künstlicher ~** artifical horizon **natürlicher ~** visible or apparent horizon **wahrer ~** true level

horizontal horizontal **-e Auswanderungsstrecke** horizontal component of target travel during time of flight **-er Koksofen** horizontal-flue coke oven **-e Last** transverse load **-e Retorte** horizontal retort **-es Rollen** Dutch roll **-er Rücklauf** (TV) horizontal flyback **-e Schwanzfläche** horizontal tail area **-er Stellungsunterschied** horizontal distance from the director to the battery center **-e Verdrängungswinde** horizontal stabilizer winds

Horizontal-ablenkgerät *n* horizontal scan generator **-ablenkung** *f* horizontal or line scan, sweep or deflection **-achse** *f* horizontal axis **-aufnahme** *f* photograph with horizontal optical axis **-balkengenerator** *m* horizontal-bar oscillator **-balkenregler** *m* H bar control **-beleuchtung** *f* horizon illumination **-beobachtungen** *pl* sights on the horizon, "shooting" the horizon **-bohrmaschine** *f* horizontal boring machine **-bohrwerk** *n* horizontal boring mill **-diagramm** *n* azimuth field pattern **-doppelpendel** *n* horizontal double pendulum

Horizontale *f* horizontal line, datum line

Horizontal-ebene *f* horizontal plane, horizontal surface (aviat) **-endpentode** *f* line output pentode **-faden** *m* horizontal wire, thread line

Horizontalfeinbewegung des Fernrohres slow motion of telescope in azimuth

Horizontalfläche *f* (Flugplatz) horizontal surface (aerodrome)

Horizontalflug *m* horizontal or level flight **-geschwindigkeit** *f* level-flying speed **-verhalten** *n* horizontal-flight behavior

Horizontal-förderband *n* horizontal-belt conveyer **-fräsmaschine** *f* horizontal milling machine **-gatter** *n* horizontal deal frame, horizontal sawmill **-gelenk** *n* horizontal hinge **-geschwindigkeit** *f* horizontal speed, ground speed of target **-intensität** *f* horizontal intensity or force **-kammerofen** *m* vertical-flue (by-product coke) oven

Horizontalkomponente *f* horizontal component **~ des Erdmagnetfeldes** earth's horizontal field

Horizontal-kopierrahmen *m* face-up printing frame **-kreis** *m* horizontal circle, limbus **-kreisel** *m* horizontal gyro **-kugelmühle** *f* (roulette) ball-and-race mill **-kurve** *f* contour line **-linie** *f* horizontal line, datum line (survey) **-magazin** *n* horizontal magazine **-magnet** *m* horizontal magnet **-parallaxe** *f* horizontal parallax **-parallaxenschlitten** *m* horizontal parallax slide **-projektion** *f* horizontal projection

Horizontal-punkt *m* point on the horizon **-räummaschine** *f* horizontal broaching machine **-regelung** *f* horizontal centring **-schleifständer** *m* hard alloy grinder **-schleiftisch** *m* horizontal abrasive machine **-schnitt** *m* horizontal section **-schub** *m* horizontal or tangential thrust or stress

Horizontal-teilkreis *m* horizontal azimuth circle **-träger** *m* horizontal rack **-transport** *m* horizontal conveyance **-verschiebung** *f* (transversale) heave, horizontal thrust **-wechsel** *m* horizontal or line synchronizing pulse or cycle **-winkel** *m* horizontal angle **-winkelmessung** *f* measuring of horizontal angles

Horizont-aufrichtung *f* vertical-erection reversing switch (auto pilot) **-bild** *n* horizon record **-ebene** *f* horizon plane **-feuer** *n* horizon light **-hauptpunkt** *m* point of intersection of principal line with horizon trace **-hügel** *m* dome-shaped horizon

horizontierbar leveling **-e Platte** tribrach

horizontieren to level

Horizontiergriff *m* outrigger leveling handle (platform) **-kopf** *m* leveling head **-schraube** screw for adjusting horizon

Horizontierung *f* leveling, setting true to the perpendicular, leveling mechanism

Horizontierungs-libelle *f* cross level **-ring** *m* base ring of gun **-vorrichtung** *f* leveling device

Horizont-kreisel *m* gyroscopic horizon **-leuchten** *pl* cyclorama lights (theater) **-mutter** *f* vertical gyro **-strich** *n* horizontal mark **-tochter** *f* horizon repeater **-zeiger** *m* horizon pointer, horizon index **-zusatzkammer** *f* auxiliary horizon camera

Hör-kappe *f* flying helmet with earphones **-kopf** *m* sound(-pickup) head, playback head **-lücke** *f* hearing interval **-minimum** *n* aural null **-muschel** *f* receiver cup, earpiece

Horn *n* horn, bugle **~ einer Röhre** lamp terminal (wireless)

Horn-abfall *m* horn parings or shavings **-abschalter** *m* horn-stopping switch **-abschaltrelais** *n* horn cut-off relay **-artig** horny **-ausgleich** *m* overhauling balance of control surface (aerodyn.) **-betätigung** *f* horn control **-blei** *n* horn lead

Hornblende *f* hornblende, amphinole **-schiefer** *m* hornblendic schist

Hornbüchse *f* horn socket

Hörnchen *n* beak (of an anvil)

Horn-druckknopfschalter *m* horn pushbutton switch **-druckring** *m* horn-press ring

Hörner *n pl* tips, points **-ausschalter** *m* horn (-type) switch **-blitzableiter** *m* horn-shaped lightning arrester **-pol** *m* horn-shaped pole **-polrelais** *n* horn-type-pole relay

Hörnerv *m* auditory nerve

Horn-erz *n* chloride of silver, cerargyrite **-fels** *m* hornfels **-förmig** horn-shaped **-haspel** *m* common windlass

Hornhautmikroskop *n* corneal microscope

hornig horny, hornlike, corneous, callous

Horn-kohle *f* horn coal, charred horn **-löffel** *m* horn ladle **-mehl** *n* horn meal **-mine** *f* horned mine **-presse** *f* horn press **-quecksilber** *n* calomel **-schalter** *m* horn switch **-schiefer** *m* hornslate **-schiene** *f* wing rail (of a crossing)

Horn-signal *n* bugle call, horn signal **-silber** *n* horn silver cerargyrite **-späne** *pl* horn chips **-stein** *m* hornstone, capel, chert **-steinartig** cherty **-strahler** *m* horn radiator **-substanz** *f* keratin **-trichter** *m* horn gate, horn sprue

Hör-peilung *f* auditory direction finding **-reichweite** *f* receiving range **-rohr** *n* stethoscope, ear trumpet

Hörsaal *m* lecture room **-summer** *m* oscillator amplifier for code practice

Hörsamkeit *f* acoustic properties, acoustics

Hör-satz *m* listening attachment **-schärfe** *f* acuity of hearing **-schärfenmesser** *m* acoumeter, audiometer **-schwelle** *f* aural threshold, threshold of hearing or of audibility **-schutz** *m* click suppressor **-spiel** *n* radioplay **-Sprech-Schalter** *m* talk-listen-switch **-spule** *f* listening coil

Horst *m* uplift, horst, heaved block; air base

Hörstellung *f* listening position

Hörstrom, ankommender ~ incoming audible current

Horstsämaschine *f* drop drill

Hör-taste *f* listening key **-vergleichmessung** *f* aural comparison **-verlust** *m* hearing loss **-wacht** *f* listening watch **-weite** *f* hearing distance **-zeichen** *n* acoustic signal **-zentrum** *n* auditory center

Hosen-boje *f* breeches buoy **-rohr** *n* (flanged) Y piece, Y pipe, siphon pipe **-rutsche** *f* breeches chute, loading funnel **-stück** *n* bifurcated pipe, Y-fitting

H-Profil *n* H section

H-Strahl *m* H ray (consisting of H particles, positive hydrogen particles or protons)

H-Teilchen *n* H particle

H-Träger *m* H girder

Hub *m* lift, (motor) stroke, draw, lifting, throw, percentage modulation **~ des Zylinders** stroke of cylinder **aufgehender ~** upstroke

Hubbegrenzer *m* stop **-anschlag** *m* stop, collar, stroke-arresting device

Hubbegrenzung *f* stroke limiter **~ eines Ventils** valve guard, valve-lift stop **~ nach unten** depression-control gear

Hub-begrenzungsstück *n* limiting rabbet **-bewegung** *f* lifting movement, movement of stroke, hoisting or lifting motion **-brücke** *f* bascule bridge **-fahrschalter** *m* derricking controller **-feilmaschine** *f* reciprocating filing machine **-flasche** *f* leveling or displacement bottle **-geschwindigkeit** *f* lifting speed, hoisting or elevating speed **-gerät** *n* lifting appliance **-getriebe** *n* hoisting gear, lifting gear **-gewicht** *n* live load **-gondel** *f* lift pod **-hebel** *m* lift arm

Hubhöhe *f* axle-inclination difference, height of level, length of stroke, height of lift **~ des Ventils** valve lift

Hub-höhenlinie *f* line of equal amplitude (of waves), line of equal rise **-inhalt** *m* cylinder capacity **-karren** *m* lift truck, elevating-platform truck, industrial truck, jack lift **-kette** *f* hoisting or lifting chain **-kippwagen** *m* dump-type lift truck **-kolben** *m* lifting cylinders **-kraft** *f* lifting power or force, lifting capacity, buoyancy **-kraftformel** *f* lift-force formula **-lader** *m* lift(er) truck, lifter **-länge** *f* length of stroke **-längenskala** *f* stroke index **-last** *f* weight-lifting capacity **-leistung** *f* lifting capacity

Hub-magnet *m* litting magnet, solenoid, vertical stepping magnet (automatic telephony) **-mechanismus** *m* hoisting or elevating mechanism **-meßgerät** *n* frequency deviation meter **-motor** *m* hoisting motor or engine **-organ** *n* lifting element or medium **-öse** *f* lifting ring **-potentiometer** *n* valve-position potentiometer (guided missiles **-presse** *f* telescopic jack **-pumpe** *f* pressure pump **-pumpenkolben** *m* bucket-valve piston of a lift pump **-rad** *n* lifting wheel

Hubraum *m* piston displacement, stroke volume, pistonhead, swept or cubic capacity, swept volume, displacement of cylinder **-druckleitung** *f* pressure line of telescopic jack (missiles) **-gewicht** *n* ratio of weight to cylinder displacement **-leistung** *f* output or power per unit of displacement

Hub-rinne *f* lifting trough **-rotor** *m* lift rotor **-säge** *f* (Decoupiersäge) scroll saw **-satz** *m* lifting set **-schaltung** *f* circuit diagram for hoist **-schaltwerk** *n* stroke operating device **-scheibe** *f* eccentric sheave, cam plate **-scheibenring** *m* eccentric strap **-schnecke** *f* lifting screw **-schraube** *f* helicopter screw

Hubschrauber *m* helicopter, helicopter screw, gyroplane, autogyro **-betrieb** *m* operation of a heliocopter **-Dachflugplatz** *m* roof (top) heliport, roof-top helicopter airport **-landeplatz** *m* heliport

Hub-schubmantelstromtriebwerk *n* lift/thrust turbofan **-schütz,** *n* **schütztafel** *f* wicket **-seil** *n* hoisting cable or rope, maneuvering line

Hub-seilrolle *f* hoisting-rope sheave **-sinn** *m* hoisting direction **-spindel** *f* litting or elevating spindle, elevating screw **-stange** *f* lifting mechanism **-stapler** *m* stacker truck **-steg** *m* walkway **-stellvorrichtung** *f* stroke adjustment device **-steuerschalter** *m* derricking controller **-stromkreis** *m* lifting magnet circuit **-taktschmierung** *f* forced-feed lubrication **-tor** *n* vertical-lift gate **-triebwerk** *n* lift engine **-trommel** *f* winch drum

Hub- und Druckpumpe *f* lifting and forcing pump

Hubventil *n* upper valve **-kegel** *m* jack-valve cone

Hubverhältnis *n* stroke ratio **~ zwischen Hub und Bohrung** stroke-to-bore ratio

Hub-verlegung *f* wandering stroke **-verlust** *m* lost motion, backlash **-verminderer** *m* reducing gear **-verminderung** *f* stroke decrease **-vermögen** *n* lifting or hoisting capacity **-verstellung** *f* adjustment of stroke **-volumen** *n* swept capacity or volume, stroke volume, piston displacement **-vorrichtung** *f* elevating mechanism, tiering attachment **-vorwähler** *m* control valve with stroke preselection

Hubwagen *m* lift (elevating-platform) truck, industrial truck ~ **mit Hebevorrichtung** tiering truck

Hubwechsel *m* reversal of stroke

Hubweg *m* height of lift ~ **eines Ventils** valve travel

Hub-welle *f* eccentric shaft, lift shaft **-werk** *n* hoisting unit, hoisting-gear train **-werksantrieb** *m* hoist **-winde** *f* pneumatic or hydraulic jack **-windwerk** *n* hoisting-gear train, hoist gearing, drum hoist **-zahl** *f* number of strokes (of a piston, etc.) **-zähler** *m* counter of strokes **-zahlwechselräder** *pl* stroke rate change gears **-zapfen** *m* crank pin **-zeit** *f* hoisting or lifting time **-zylinder** *m* lifting cylinder

Huckbindung *f* huckaback weave

Huckepackflugzeug *n* composite aircraft, pickaback airplane

Huckepack-gehäuse *n* "piggyback"-case

Huf *m* hoof **-beschlag** *m* horseshoeing **-beschlagzange** *f* farriers' pincer

Hufeisen *n* horseshoe **-flamme** *f* flame traveling in a horseshoe direction **-förmig** horseshoe-shape **-heizfaden** *m* horse-shoe filament **-magnet** *m* horseshoe magnet **-ofen** *m* horseshoe furnace **-wirbel** *m* horseshoe vortex

Huf-kratzer *m* hoof pick, hoof scraper **-krone** *f* cornet **-pflege** *f* care of the hoof **-raspel** *f* horse rasp **-schmied** *m* farrier, blacksmith **-stollenbohrer** *m* taps for horseshoe lugs

Hügel *m* hill, knob, mound **gegen einen ~ fliegen** to fly into a hill

hügelig hilly

Hügel-kette *f* range or chain of hills **-landstrecke** *f* line with heavy gradients **-seitig** (hängig) hillside

Hughes-Apparat *m* synchronized-telegraphy apparatus

Hühnerdraht *m* chicken wire

Huk *f* foreland

Hülle *f* cover, wrapping, sheath, jacket, casing, hull, shell, contour ~ (eines Luftfahrzeuges leichter als Luft) envelope **äußere ~** case

Hüllen-bahn *f* panel **-elektronen** *pl* shell electrons, atomic electrons **-gewicht** *n* weight of the hull **-kurve** *f* envelope curve **-kurvengleichrichtung** *f* envelope detection **-magazin** *n* envelope magazine **-rohr** *n* encasing tube or pipe, jacket **-spektrum** *n* shell spectrum **-stoff** *m* balloon fabric **-verstärkungsdraht** *m* antiflutter wire

Hüll-fläche des Schraubrades addendum envelope of the skew gear **-kurve** *f* envelope curve, blanketing curve **-linie** *f* (Oberflächenrauhheit) peak **-material** *n* canning material **-ring** *m* ring envelope **-röhre** *f* jacket encasing tube **-schnitte** *pl* small cuts

Hullscher Ring Hull ring (powder pattern)

Hülse *f* jacket, casing, socket, cartridge or shell case, housing case, bushing, hull, husk, tube, collar, taper ring ~ (Hohlzylinder) cylindrical shell ~ (Kupplung) sleeve ~ (für Körnerspitze) center adapter sleeve **mit einer ~ versehen** to sleeve, jacket **abgeschossene ~** fired-shell case **verschiebbare ~** sliding sleeve

Hülsen-abstechmaschine *f* tube cutting device **-auswurf** *m* ejection of cartridge case **-auszieher** *m* cartridge-case extractor **-auszieherhaken** *m* cartridge-case extractor hook **-befestigung** *f* sleeve mounting **-boden** *m* base of a cartridge case **-brücke** *f* receiver cover **-bund** *m* (twisted) sleeve joint **-ende** *n* socket end **-fänger** *m* deflector bag **-getriebe** *n* gear in a shell **-gliederung** *f* cannelure **-greifer** *m* tube gripper **-haken** *m* fishing hook for callars **-hals** *m* neck of cartridge

Hülsen-kartusche *f* cartridge case **-kasten** *m* spent-ammunition box **-kette** *f* bushing chain **-kopf** *m* cartridge flange **-kupplung** *f* sleeve coupling, friction clip, ring-compression coupling, bobbin holder **-leitung** *f* sleeve wire **-liderung** *f* obturation by means of the cartridge case **-lochdurchmesser** *m* tube diameter **-los** without spools **-lossystem** *n* tubeless system

Hülsen-mantel *m* cartridge-case jacket **-material** *n* tube material **-mutter** *f* sleeve nut **-nippelisolator** *m* sleeve nipple insulator **-papier** *n* spool paper **-perlkorn** *n* hooded bead sight **-puffer** *pl* casing buffers **-pufferpresse** *f* buffer-casing press

Hülsen-rand *m* extracting rim, cartridge-case rim **-reißer** *m* stoppage caused by broken cartridge case **-sack** *m* spent-ammunition bag **-schaufel** *f* sleeve blade **-schliff** *m* female part of ground joint **-stopfer** *m* socket plug **-stoßdämpfer** *m* telescopic shock absorber **-tiefe** *f* base depth **-verbinder** *m* jointing sleeve **-verbindung** *f* socket coupling **-wickelmaschine** *f* tube-wrapping machine **-würgebund** *m* twisted sleeve joint **-zapfen** *m* recoil lug **-zieher** *m* extractor **-zuführung** *f* tube feed

Humboldtin *m* humboldtine

humin humic **-säure** *f* humic acid

Humus *m* humus, vegetable soil **-erde** *f* arable land **-kohle** *f* humic carbon **-kolloid** *n* humus colloid **-säure** *f* humic acid **-schicht** *f* layer of mold

Hund *m* dog, hound, rammer, monkey, guard (in rolling), miner's car, hutch

Hundebalken *m* roll beam

hundert hundred **vom Hundert** per cent

hundertgradig centrigrade

Hunderterstufe *f* hundreds digit

hundert-jährig secular **-punkt** *m* hundred-degree point

Hundertsatz *m* percentage ~ **der ausgefüllten Anmeldungen** percentage of completion ~ **der Gebührenminuten je Stunde** paid-time ratio (teleph.)

Hundertstel *n* one-hundredth part, per cent

Hundertstelle *f* hundreds place

Hupe *f* hooter, horn, buzzer **elektrische ~** electric siren

Hupen-ball *m* **-birne** *f* horn bulb **-signal** *n* hooting signal **-staubschutz** *m* horn dust shield **-stimme** *f* reed for horn **-zwischenraum** *m* horn gap

hüpfen to hop, jump, porpoise

hüpfende Bewegung skipping motion

Hüpfen der Bürsten jumping of the brushes (elec.)

Hüpfer(schalter) *m* contactor

Hüpf-linie *f* line of flight between two fields less than 200 kilometers apart (aviation) **-verkehr** *m* transatlantic air traffic with floating bases

Hupsignal *n* hooting signal

Hürde *f* hurdle, fold, pen

Hüsing *f* houseline
Hut *m* hat, cap (oil drilling) **auf der ~ sein** to be on guard **eiserner ~** ferruginous outcrop of a lode, gossan
Hutaufsetzer *m* fitter of dust pipes (watchmaking)
Hütchen *n* capsule (explosives), blasting cap, cup of cartridge **-kondensator** *m* ceramic hood-shaped fixed condenser or capacitor
Hut-manschette *f* cap-type gasket **-mutter** *f* cap nut, cover nut, cap screw **-profil** *n* hat section
Hütte *f* metallurgical or smelting plant, ironworks, blast-furnace plant, mill works **~ gezogen** furnace-tapped
Hütten-after *n* dross, residuum **-aluminium** *m* primary-aluminium pig, virgin metal **-anlage** *f* smelting plant **-arbeit** *f* smelting, founding, or foundry work **-arbeiter** *m* foundry worker **-bedarf** *m* smelting-works requirements **-betrieb** *m* metallurgical plant **-bims** *m* blast furnace slag **-erzeugnis** *n* metallurgical product
Hütten-fachmann *m* metallurgist **-flur** *m* mill or shop floor, casting-floor level **-hartblei** *n* metallurgic hard lead **-industrie** *f* iron and steel industry **-kalk** *m* metallurgical lime **-koks** *m* metallurgical or blast-furnace coke, by-product or coke-oven coke **-kunde** *f* metallurgical knowledge, metallurgy
Hütten-lager *n* cantonment **-mann** *m* metallurgist, metallurgical engineer, blast-furnace man **-prozeß** *m* metallurgical process **-raum** *m* smelting room **-sohle** *f* mill floor **-technik** *f* metallurgical engineering **-weichblei** *n* metallurgic merchant lead **-werk** *n* metallurgical works or plant, smelting plant, ironworks, steel mill, foundry **-werkskrane** *pl* steel mill cranes **-wesen** *n* metallurgical engineering, metallurgy **-wolle** *f* slag wool **-zeche** *f* colliery **-zement** *m* blast furnace cement
Huttonit *m* huttonite
Hutze *f* scoop
Hybrid-bindung *f* hybrid binding **-Doppel-T** *n* hybrid T
hybridisch-e Kopplung hybrid junction **-e Matrize** hybrid matrix
Hybridisierung *f* hybridization
Hybridrohöl *n* (gemischtes Rohöl) hybrid ~ (Gemisch chemisch verschiedener Bestandteile), mixed-base crude oil
Hybrid-rechner *m* hybrid computer **-richtkoppler** *m* hybrid coupler **-verbindung** *f* hybrid junction
Hydrant *m* hydrant, fill box
Hydranten-betankung *f* pit fueling **-gehäuse** *n* hydrant casing **-säule** *f* hydrant pillar **-ventil** *n* landing or hydrant valve
Hydrargillit *m* gibbsite
Hydrat *n* hydrate
Hydratation *f* hydratization
Hydratationsgleichgewicht *n* hydratization equilibrium
Hydrathülle *f* hydrate envelope
hydratiert hydrated
Hydration *f* hydration
Hydrationswärme *f* setting heat
hydratisieren to hydrate
Hydratwasser *n* hydrate water, water of hydration
Hydraulik *f* hydraulics, collecting main, hydraulic main **-aggregat** *n* hydraulic control unit **-anlage** *f* hydraulic plant **-arbeitszylinder** *m* hydraulic power cylinder
Hydrauliker *m* hydraulic specialist or technician
Hydraulik-leitungsfilter *n* hydraulic lead filter **-motor** *m* fluid motor **-prüfer** *m* hydraulic tester **-schieber** *m* hydraulic valves **-speicher** *m* hydraulic accumulator **-steuergerät** *n* hydraulic control valve
hydraulisch hydraulic **~ einziehbares Fahrgestell** hydraulically operated retractable undercarriage **~ zu hebendes Grundwerk** hydraulic bedplates **~ betätigte Klappen** hydraulically controlled flaps **~ verstellbar** hydro-adjustable **~ verstellbare Schraube** hydraulically controlled airscrew **~ betrieben** hydraulically operated **-er Abbau** hydraulic mining **-er Abquetschfoulard** *n* hydraulic padding machine **-er Antrieb** hydraulic drive **-er Aufzug** hydraulic lift
hydraulisch-e Ausrüstung hydraulic equipment **-e Dichtung** water seal **-er Druckmesser** water gauge **-er Einachsheber** hydraulic end lift hoist **-e Etagenpresse** multiplaten hydraulic press **-e Generatorgruppe** hydro-electric generatic set **-er Grundbruch** piping (by heave) **-e Hebebühne** hydraulic elevating platform
hydraulisch-e Kernpreßvorrichtung hydraulic core extractor **-e Kraftsteuerung** hydraulic boost control **-e Kupplung** fluid coupling **-e Schleuder** hydrospinning **-e Spindel** hydraulic jack **-er Stoßdämpfer** hydraulic shock absorber **-e Streckpresse** hydraulic stretching press **-er Verschluß** liquid-seal trap **-er Widder** hydraulic ram for water lifting **-er Wirkungsgrad** hydraulic efficiency
Hydrazin *n* hydrazine **-hydrat** *n* hydrazine hydrate
Hydrazobenzol *n* hydrazobenzene
Hydrid *n* hydride
hydrieren to hydrogenate, hydrogenize
Hydrierung *f* hydrogenation, hydration
Hydrierungsverfahren *n* hydrogenation process
Hydro-chinon *n* hydroquinone, paradioxybenzene, dihydroxyl-benzene **-diffusion** *f* hydrodiffusion **-dynamik** *f* hydrodynamics **-elektrisch** hydroelectric(al)
Hydrogenerisation *f* hydrogenerization
Hydrograph *m* hydrograph
Hydrographie *f* (Meereskunde) hydrography
hydrographisch hydrographic
Hydro-ketter *f* hydrocell (electr.) **-kinetik** *f* hydrokinetics
Hydrologie *f* hydrology
Hydrolyse *f* hydrolysis
hydrolysieren to hydrolyze
hydrolytisch hydrolytic
Hydromaliumgehäuse *n* hydromalium casing
Hydrometer *n* hydrometer, hydraulic gauge
hydrometrisch hydrometric **-er Flügel** current meter
hydrophob nonhygroscopic, nonabsorbent, moisturerepellent
hydrophobieren to make water-repellent
Hydro-presse *f* hydraulic press **-spiralflachsichter** *m* flat vortex hydrosifter **-sphäre** *f* hydrosphere **-statik** *f* hydrostatics
hydrostatisch hydrostatic **-er Druck** hydrostatic

pressure **-er Überdruck** hydrostatic-pressure excess
Hydrotimeter *n* hydrotimeter
Hydroxyd *n* hydroxide
Hydroxyl *n* hydroxyl **-aminnitrat** *n* hydroxylamine nitrate
Hydroxylierung *f* hydroxylation
Hydroxylion *n* hydroxyl ion
Hydroxytoluol *n* hydroxytoluol
Hydrozyansäure *f* hydrocyanic acid, prussic acid
Hydrozyklon *m* hydro-cyclone
Hygieniker *m* hygienist
hygienisch, ~ unbedenklich harmless **-e Untersuchungsstelle** hygienic laboratory, Department of Health laboratory
Hygro-graph *m* hygrograph **-meter** *n* hygrometer **-metrie** *f* hygrometry
Hygroskop *n* hygroscope
hygroskopisch hygroscopic(al)
Hygroskopizität *f* hygroscopicity
Hygrothermograph *m* hygrothermograph
Hyperbel *f* hyperbola **-amplitude** *f* gudermannian amplitude **-bahn** *f* hyperbolic orbit **-funktion** *f* hyperbolic function **-inversor** *m* hyperbolic inverter **-plan** *m* asymptote-correction chart **-rad** *n* hyperboloidal gear
Hyperbelsystem mit Impulsmodulation pulse-modulated hyperbolic system **~ mit ungedämpften Wellen** continuous-wave hyperbolic system
hyperbolaähnlich hyperbolalike
hyperbolisch hyperbolic **-er Abstand** hyperbolic distance **-e Bewegung** hyperbolic motion **-e Ebene** hyperbolic plane **-e Funktion** hyperbolic function **-e Geometrie** hyperbolic geometry
hyperbolisch-e Krümmung hyperbolic curvature **-e Logarithmen** Napierian logarithms **-es Paraboloid** hyperbolic paraboloid **-es Radarsystem** hyperbolic radar system **-er Raum** hyperbolic space **-er Winkel** hyperbolic angle **-er Zylinder** hyperbolic cylinder
Hyperboloid *n* hyperboloid **einschaliges ~** hyperboloid of one sheet **einschaliges, bewegliches ~** collapsible hyperboloid of one sheet **zweischaliges ~** hyperboloid of two sheets
hyperboloidische Lage von *n* **Geraden** hyperboloidal position of *n* straight lines
Hyperboloidräder *pl* skew bevel gears
Hyper-ebene *f* hyperplane **-elastisch** hyperelastic **-eutektisch** hypereutectic **-eutektoidisch** hypereutectoid
Hyperfeinstrukturkopplung *f* hyperfine coupling
-multiplett *n* hyperfine-structure multiplet
Hyper-fläche *f* hypersurface **-fragment** *n* hyperfragment **-funktion** *f* hyperbolic function
hypergeometrisch hypergeometric **-e Reihe** hypergeometric series
hypergol hypergolic
Hypergole *f* spontaneously combustible substance, code for a type of rocket fuel
hyper-komplex hypercomplex **-konisch** hyperconical **-konjugation** hyperconjugation, nobond resistance
Hyperonennachweis *m* hyperon detection
Hyperschall *m* hypersonic **-erzeugung** *f* hypersound generation **-flugzeug** *n* hypersonic aircraft **-strömung** *f* hypersonic flow
hyperskopische Projektion hyperscopic view
Hyperon *n* hyperon
Hyperventilation *f* hyperventilation
hypoabyssisch hypabyssal
Hypoelastizität *f* hypo-elasticity
Hypoid-getriebe *n* hypoid gear **-verzahnung** *f* hypoid gearing
Hypophosphat *n* hypophosphate
Hypophosphit *n* hypophosphite
Hypophyse *f* pituitary body
hyposkopische Projektion hyposcopiv view
Hypotenuse *f* hypotenuse
Hypothek *f* mortgage
Hypothese *f* hypothesis
hypothetisch hypothetical
Hypotrochoide *f* hypotrochoid
Hypozentrum *n* ground zero, hypocenter, surface zero
Hypozykloide *f* hypocycloid
Hypsometer *n* hypsometer
Hypsothermometer *n* hypsometer
Hysterese *f* **Hysteresis** *f* hysteresis **dielektrische ~** dielectric hysteresis **magnetische ~** magnetic hysteresis
hysterese-artig hysteresis type **-beiwert** *m* hysteresis factor **-fehler** *m* hysteresis error **-koeffizient** *m* coefficient of hysteresis
Hysteresemesser *m* hysteresis meter **schreibender ~** hysteresigraph
Hysterese-schleife *f* hysteresis cycle or loop **-schleifenschreiber** *m* hysteresis curve **-schreiber** *m* hysteresigraph **-verlust** *m* hysteresis loss **-verlustzahl** *f* **-zahl** *f* hysteresis coefficient
Hysteresis *f* hysteresis **-schleife** *f* hysteresis loop
hysteretisch hysteretic **-e Nacheilung** hysteretic lag
Hysterosalpingographie *f* hysterosalpingography

I

I-Anker *m* shuttle-armature, H armature
I-Antenne *f* I-antenna
Ianthinit *m* ianthinite
Iaxtron-Speicherröhre *f* Jaxtron storage tube
I-Barren *m* wirebar
IBK-System *n* CIE (Commission Internationale d'Eclairage) chromaticity scale
Iconometer *n* iconometer, wire-frame view finder
ideal ideal, perfect **~ fehlgeordnet** ideally imperfect (crystal) **~ leitend** of ideal or of perfect conductance **-es Gas** perfect or ideal gas **-e Leitung** ideal or nondissipative line (teleph.)
Idealbedingung *f* ideal condition
idealisierte Substanz ideal material
Ideal-scheibe *f* lock washer (Leica) **-weiß** *n* equal-energy white (TV) **-wert** *m* ideal value (servo)

idempotent idempotent
identifizieren to identify
Identifizierung *f* identification
Identifizierungslicht *n* identification light
identisch identical **-e Abbildung** identity transformation
Identität *f* identity
Identitätsoperator *m* identity operator
idioelektrisch idioelectric
idiomorph idiomorphic, automorphic
idiostatische Schaltung idiostatic circuit
ID-Regler *m* integral plus derivative action controller
I-echt in the best possible fastness
I-Eisen *n* double-T iron, I iron **I-Eisen(-stange** *f*) I beam
I-förmiger Balken I beam
I-Formstahl *m* I beam
IFR (Instrumentenflugregeln) IFR (Instrument Flight Rules)
Igel *m* (Mischer) porcupine (mixer)
Igelit *n* a type of electric-wire insulation, a type of plastic **-separator** *m* igelit separator
Igel-transformator *m* hedgehog transformer **-walze** *f* taper foot roller
I-Gerät *n* integrator device of guided missile, integrating accelerometer
Ignitron *n* ignitron **-schütz** *m* ignitron contactor **-stromtorkombination** *f* mutator
Ikonometer *n* direct view finder, (photo.), iconometer
Ikonoskop *n* iconoscope **-sendungen** *f pl* iconoscope transmission (pickup)
Ikosaeder *n* icosahedron
Ikositetraeder *n* icositetrahedron
i. L. im Lichten clearance
Ilgner-Antrieb *m* Ilgner system
Illmenit *m* ilmenite
Illuminant *m* illuminant (TV)
Illuminationseffekt *m* collored effect
Illuminator *m* illuminator **-blende** *f* illuminator diaphragm
illuminieren to illuminate
Illuminometer *n* illuminometer
Illustration *f* illustration, diagram, figure
Illustration-druck *m* cutwork printing, printing of illustrations **-rotationsmaschine** *f* rotary press for illustration printing
illustrieren to illustrate
ILS-Anlage instrument landing system
ILS-Haupteinflugzeichen (ILS) middle marker
IL-Triebwerk *n* resonant, pulse-jet engine, intermittent-firing duct power plant
imaginär imaginary **-e Einheit** imaginary unit **-e Zahl** imaginary number
Imago-Orthokon-Kamerazug camera chain with image orthocon
im Bau under construction
Imbus-Schlüssel *m* wrench for socket head cap screws
Imitationslack *m* a coating imitating a metal or other surface
immaterielle Aktiven intangible assets
Immelmann-Kurve *f* Immelmann turn (aviation)
Immersions-linse *f*, **-objektiv** *n* immersion lens or objective, double-aperture lens **-system** *n* immersion (lens) objective **-zähler** *m* immersion counter
immobil immobile
Immunität *f* immunity
Impedanz *f* apparent resistance, impedance, impedor **~ einer mit halber Spule beginnenden Leitung** midload impedance **~ bei Parallelresonanz** dynamic impedance
Impedanzen *pl*, **konjugiert-komplexe ~** conjugate impedances
Impedanz-anpassung *f* impedance matching **-korrektor** *m* impedance corrector, impedance compensator **-messer** *m* impedometer **-methode** *f* impedance method **-schutz** *m* mismatch protection **-wandler** impedance transformer
Impeller *m* impeller
impfen to vaccinate, inoculate, inject **~** (kristallisieren) to seed, form crystals
Impf-schein *m* vaccination certificate **-stift** *m* seeding or inoculating pencil
Impfung *f* vaccination, inoculation
Impfwirkung *f* (result of) seeding (of crystals)
Implantation *f* implantation **flache ~** planar implant
Implosions-festigkeit *f*, **-sicherheit** *f* implosion safety factor
Imponderabilien *pl* imponderables
Importeur *m* importer
importierte Gebinde imported packing
Imprägnierapparate *pl* impregnating equipment
Imprägnieren *n* waterproofing
imprägnieren to impregnate, soak, saturate
Imprägniermittel *n* impregnating compound or agent
Imprägnier- oder Sättigungsmittel *n* saturant
Imprägnier-pfanne *f* impregnating pan **-schicht** *f* impregnating coat
imprägniert-er Stoff impregnated fabric **-e Vorratskathode** impregnated cathode
Imprägniertrog *m* impregnating vat
Imprägnierung *f* impregnation, preservation
Imprägnierungs-mittel *n* stiffener, impregnating agent, bonding material **-öl für Holz** wood-preservation oil
Impuls *m* impulse, pulse, momentum (in dynamics), surge (when of unidirectional polarity) **einen ~ auswerten** to strobe **~ erteilen** to impulse **scharf begrenzter ~** sharply peaked impulse **~ durch Ionenbildung** ionization pulse
Impuls-achse *f* axis of rotation **-abfallzeit** *f* pulse decay time **-abflachung** tilt **-abfragung** *f* pulse interrogation **-abstand** *m* pulse spacing **-abtrennstufe** *f* pulse clipper (TV)
Impulsamplitude *f*, **mittlere absolute ~** average absolute pulse amplitude
Impulsamplitudenmodulation *f* pulse-amplitude modulation
Impuls-änderung *f* momentum change **-art** *f* puls mode **-begrenzungsmaß** pulse limiting rate **-bestimmung** *f* momentum determination **-betrieb** *m* pulsed operation **-bilanz** *f* balance of momentum
Impulsbild *n* impulse image **stehendes ~** stationary image
Impuls-bildungsstufe *f* pulse forming stage **-breite** *f* impulse width (length) **-buchse** *f* emitter **-code** *m* pulse code **-codemodulation** pulse code modulation **-dauer** *f* duration of impulse **-dichtefunktion** *f* momentum density

function **-drehzähler** *m* impulse speedometer or tachometer

Impuls-echometer *m* pulse echo meter **-Echoverfahren** *n* pulse echo technics **-einsatz** *m* setting in of impulse **-entschlüsselung** *f* decoding

Impulserelais *n* impulsing or impulse relay

Impulserhaltungssatz *m* theorem of conservation of momentum

Impuls-erneuerung *f* pulse restoration **-erregung** *f* impulse excitation **-erzeugung** *f* supply of momentum

Impulsespeicher *m* impulse-storing device, (digitstoring) register

Impuls-federn *pl* pulse springs **-fläche** *f* pulse cam **-flanke** *f* edge of pulse **-folge** *f* impulse sequence, series of pulses, pulse train **-folgefrequenz** *f* pulse recurrence frequency, pulse repetition frequency (PRF) **-folgegrad** *m* pulse repetition rate **-former** *m* pulse shaper

Impulsfrequenz *f* impulse frequency, pulse-recurrence frequency **-fernmessung** *f* impulse-frequency telemetering **-messung** *f* count rate **-meter** *n* ratemeter **-modulation** *f* (IFM) pulse frequency modulation (PFM)

Impuls-gabe *f* impulsing, pulsing, impulse transmission or emission **-geber** *m* impulse sender or transmitter, tonal, impulse, or surge generator **-gemisch** *n* (TV) composed TV signal **-generator** *m* impulse, surge or lighting generator **-gerät** *n* pulse generator or modulator (radar) **-gewinnung** *f* impulse generation **-größenspektrum** *n* pulse height spectrum **-gruppe** *f* (periodische) periodic pulse-train

Impuls-höhe *f* pulse depth, impulse amplitude **-höhenanalysator** *m* pulse height analyser **-höhenanalysator-Einschub** *m* pulse height analyser plug-in unit **-höreinheit** *f* pulse audio unit

Impuls-instabilität *f* pulse jitter **-integral** *n* momentum integral **-integralgleichung** *f* integral equation **-intervall** *n* pulse interval **-kamm** *m* pulsing cam **-kennzeichnung** *f* impulse identification (pulses are tagged) **-korrektor** *m* pulse corrector, pulse stretcher **-kugel** *f* momentum sphere

Impuls-lagemodulation *f* pulse position modulation (PPM) **-längenmodulation** *f* pulse duration (width) modulation **-leistungsmeßgerät** *n* peak-voltage measuring device **-leistungsverhältnis** *n* pulse duty factor **-leitung** *f* stepping line, pulse power (radar)

Impuls-markengebereinheit *f* pulse mark generator unit **-messer** *m* peak or crest voltmeter **-messung** *f* momentum measurement **-mischung** *f* pulse mixing **-modulierte Wellen** pulse-modulated waves (radar) **-moment** *n* moment of momentum **-ölschalter** *m* oil-blast circuit breaker

Impuls-pause *f* pulse interval **-peilanlage** *f*, **-peiler** *m* pulse direction finder **-peilung** *f* pulse direction finding **-peilverfahren** *n* pulse direction-finding method **-phasenmodulation** *f* pulse position modulation (PPM) **-platte** *f* signal plate (iconoscope) **-produktion** *f* momentum production **-prüfer** *m* pulse tester **-prüfung** *f* flash or impulse test **-punktschweißen** *n* impulse spot welding

Impuls-quantenzahl *f* spin quantum number **-rate** *f* pulse rate **-raumdarstellung** *f* momentum space representation **-rauschen** *n* pulse noise **-regenerierung** *f* pulse regeneration **-regler** *m* impulse intervalometer **-reihe** *f* succession or train of impulses, impulse series **-relais** *n* time pulse relay

Impuls-satz *m* theorem of momentum **-schaltbedingung** *f* pulse-switching condition **-schalter** *m* pulse switch **-schütz** *m* impulse contactor **-schwanz** *m* (Nachleuchtschleppe) pulse stretching **-senden** *n* sending pulses, interrupted, continuous-wave transmission **-sender** *m* pulse transmitter **-speicher** *m* register-sender **-spektrometer** *n* pulse spectrometer

Impulsspektrums, Breite des ~ pulse bandwidth

Impuls-spitze *f* spike (rdr) **-steilheitsmodulation** *f* pulse slope modulation (rdr) **-steuerung** *f* impulse control **-stromkreis** *m* pulsing circuit **-summe** *f* sum of momenta

Impuls-tastgerät *n* echo box **-tastgerätschalter** *m* perfometer **-tastung** *f* pulse excitation **-tastverhältnis** *n* pulse time ratio **-teilung** *f* break-to-impulse duration ratio **-telegramm-Methode** (Fernwirktechnik) coded pulse train method **-tempomodulation** *f* pulse frequency modulation (PFM) **-tensor** *m* momentum tensor

Impuls-träger *m* pulse carrier **-transport** *m* transport of momentum **-transportgleichung** *f* momentum transfer equation **-transporttensor** *m* momentum flow tensor **-transporttheorie** *f* momentum-transportation theory **-trenner** *m* pulse separator **-trennung** *f* synchronizing-pulse separation

Impuls-überlagerung *f* pulse overlapping **-überschneidung** *f* pulse pile-up **-übertrag** *m* momentum transfer **-übertrager** *m* impulse repeater **-übertragung** *f* impulse repeating (in automatic telephony), transfer or momentum **-übertragungsreaktion** *f* impulse reaction **-umformer** *m* pulse lengthener **-umrechnungsverfahren** *n* method of translation of impulses

Impuls- und Zeitvorwahl preset count and time

Impuls-untersetzer *m* pulse reducer **-veränderung** *f* change of impulse or of momentum **-verbesserung** *f* pulse regneration **-verflechtung** *f* pulse interleaving **-verhältnis** *n* impulse ratio, break-to-make ratio **-verlängernd** pulse lengthening **-vernichter** *m* digit absorber **-verschlüsselung** *f* pulse coding **-verstärker** *m* pulse amplifier **-verzerrung** *f* impulse distortion **-vorwahl** *f* preset count

Impuls-wahl *f* impulse selection **-wert** *m* value of momentum **-widerstand** *m* peak resistance **-zähler** *m* impulse counter, impulse meter **-zählwerk** *n* pulse counting instrument **-zahlvorwahl** *f* pre-selected pulse count

Impuls-zeitmodulation *f* pulse-time modulation, (PTM) **-zentrale** *f* synch generator (TV) **-zunahme** *f* increase of momentum **-zündung** *f* impulse firing **-zusatz** *m* booster-power supply

Ina-Atmosphäre *f* standard air **-Leistung** *f* power corrected to standard

Inaktivierung *f* inactivation, deactivation, racemization (optics)

Inangriffnahme *f* attack **Art der ~** method of attack

Inanspruchnahme *f* requirements, demands

(load), claim
Inaugenscheinnahme *f* inspection
Inausgabegenehmigung *f* authorized permission to delete from stock record items issued
Inbegriff *m* epitome, sum, totality
inbegriffen included, inclusive(ly)
Inbesitznahme *f* occupation, act of taking possession
Inbetriebnahme *f* starting apparatus, putting apparatus into operation, time of beginning of operation ~ (eines Amtes, einer Teilnehmerleitung), cutover (exchange, subscriber's line)
inbetriebnehmen to start up, put into operation
inbetriebsetzen to start, set going
Inbetriebsetzung *f* setting going (engine, etc.), setting in motion, rendering operative, starting, initiating **heißes Öl in die Lagerstellen des Motors vor der ~ einspritzen** to prime with hot oil
Inbusschraube *f* hollow screw
Inden *n* indene
indeterministische Auffassung indeterministic conception or interpretation
Index *m* index, subscript (math.) **~ bei Maßstäben** sighting mark, index mark **tiefgestellter ~** subscript
Index-fehler *m* index error, sighting-mark error **-hebel** *m* index lever **-karte** *f* guide card **-korrektion** *f* index correction **-punkt** *m* (punktähnliche Vertiefung) index depression
Index-raste *f* index notch **-register** (IR) *n* B-tube, B-box, index register, (info proc.) **-revolverautomat** *m* index full-automatic turret screw machine **-scheibe** *f* graduated dial, index plate **-strich** *m* index mark or line, gauge mark **-zahl** *f* index number **-zeiger** *m* indicator needle, dial pointer
Indices *pl* subscripts (and superscripts)
Indiensthaltung *f* commission
Indienststellen *n* commissioning
Indienststellung *f* call or draft (mil.), commission (navy), commissioning
indifferent inert, eutral, indifferent **~ aufgehängt** neutrally mounted (as a compass mounted on gimbals) **~ statisch** in neutral equilibrium **-es Gleichgewicht** neutral air layer
Indifferenz *f* neutrality (of a gimbal or gyro mounting, phys.) **-kurve** *f* curve of neutral stability **-linie** *f* dead line (elec.) **-punkt** *m* aerodynamic center, neutral point, point of neutral stability **-stelle eines Magnetes** neutral line of a magnet **-zone** *f* neutral zone
Indigo-carmin für Titrierzwecke indigo carmine for titrating purposes **-farbig** indigo in color **-farbstoff** *m* indigo dye **-kugelmühle** *f* indigo ball mill **-pappartikel** *m* indigo resist style **-weiß** *n* deoxidized (reduced) indigo
Indikan *n* indican
Indikation *f* information, sign
Indikationsschärfe *f* (Farbumschlag) sensitivity (in color change)
Indikator *m* indicating instrument or apparatus, indicator **-anhaltsvorrichtung** *f* detent gear of an indicator **-antrieb** *m* indicator drive **-chemie** *f* tracer chemistry **-diagramm** *n* indicator diagram or chart
Indikatorenmethode *f* tracer method **-untersuchung** *f* tracer studies
Indikator-feder *f* indicator spring **-gehäuse** *n* indicator casing **-hahn** *m* indicator cock **-instrument** *n* indicating instrument, indicator
indikatorische Untersuchung indicator test
Indikator-kolben *m* indicator piston **-papier** *n* diagram paper **-schreibstift** *m* indicator stylus **-stutzen** *m* indicator connection piece **-trommel** *f* paper-carrying cylinder of the indicator **-verbindung** *f* tracer compound **-verschlußschraube** *f* indicator plug screw **-zusatz** *m* spiking
Indikatrix *f* indicatrix
indirekt indirect, secondary **~ beheizt** indirect-fired **~ geheizte Röhre** heater-type vacuum tube, indirectly heated tube **~ wirkend** pilot or relay operated **-e Beleuchtung** indirect lighting **-er Beweis** indirect demonstration **-er Dampf** closed or latent steam **-e Feuerung** indirect firing **-e Lichtbogenerhitzung** independent or indirect arc heating
indirekt-e Regelstrecke indirectly controlled system **-er Regler** integral action controller **-es Richten** indirect laying **-es Verfahren** indirect process, fire control using director and locational apparatus **-er Walzdruck** side pressure (steel mill)
Indirekttreffer *m* ricochet
Indischgelb *n* Indian yellow (a red oxide)
Indium *n* indium **-chlorid** *n* indium chloride **-oxyd** *n* indium oxide **-sulfat** *n* indium sulfate **-selenid** *n* indium selenide **-standardfolie** *f* standard indium foil
Individual-dosimeter *n* personal monitor **-monitor** *m* personal monitor
Indizes *pl* subscripts (and superscripts)
Indizienbeweis *m* circumstantial evidence
indizieren to indicate
Indizierhahn *m* indicator cock
indiziert indicated **-er mittlerer Druck** mean indicated pressure **-e Leistung** indicated output, indicated horsepower **-e Pferdestärke** indicated horsepower **-er Wirkungsgrad** indicated effi ciency
Indizierung *f* indication, indexing
Indol *n* indole
Indossament *n* endorsement
Indossant *m*, **Indossent** *m* endorser, transferrer
Indossat(ar) *m* endorsee, transferee
Indosserieeinrichtung *f* endorsing unit
indossieren to endorse
Induktanz *f* inductance, inductive, positive, or inductance reactance, inductivity **~ zum Abstimmen der Antenne** aerial-tuning inductance
Induktanzspule *f* inductance or retard(ation) coil, inductor, reactor, graduator **~ mit Eisenkern** ferric inductance coil **~ mit Luftkern** air-core inductance coil
Induktion *f* induction **elektrische ~** electrostatic induction **gegenseitige ~** mutual induction **magnetische ~** magnetic flux
Induktions-anlage *f* induction system **-apparat** *m* induction coil **-arm** of low inductance **-beheizung** *f* inductive heating **-brenner** *m* induction burner **-dauer** *f* induction period **-dehnungsmeßstreifen** *m* inductance strain gauge **-elektrizität** *f* induced electricity **-feld** *n* induction field
Induktionsfluß *m* induction flux **elektrischer ~**

electrical flux **magnetischer ~** magnetic flux

induktionsfrei noninductive (free of inductance), nonreactive **-es Kabel** screened conductor cable, antiinduction cable **-e Wicklung** non-inductive winding **-er Widerstand** plain or noninductive resistance, effective or ohmic resistance

Induktions-funken *m* induction spark **-gerät** *n* induction-coil apparatus **-geräusch** *n* induced noise **-geschützt** eliminated of induction **-geschütztes Kabel** cable protected against interference **-gesetz** *n* law of induction, Faraday's law **-härten** *n* induction hardening **-heizstrom** *m* inductive-heating current **instrument** *n* induction instrument **-kapazität** *f* inductive capacity

Induktionskoeffizient *m* induction coefficient **magnetischer ~** magnetic permeability

Induktions-koerzitivkraft *f* intrinsic coercive force **-kompaß** *m* induction compass **-kraft** *f* force of induction **-maschine** *f* induction motor **-messer** *m* inductometer **-meßgerät für das magnetische Erdfeld** earth inductor **-meßwaage** *f* comparison of two mutual inductances **-minderung durch Schienenstrom und Kabelmantelstrom** screening effect of rail and cable-sheath currents **-motor** *m* induction motor

Induktionsofen *m* induction furnace **~ mit ringförmigen Herd** ring-shaped induction furnace

Induktions-periode *f* induction period **-relais** *n* induction-current relay **-richtung** *f* inductive direction **-rinne** *f* induction channel **-rinnenofen** *m* core-type induction furnace **-rolle** *f* induction coil **-schutz** *m* mitigation of induction by means of transpositions, anti-inductive or induction arrangement or device **-spannung** *f* induced electromotive force

Induktionsspule *f* retardation coil, induction coil, inductor (coil), inductance coil **~ der Platzschaltung** induction coil of operator's telephone set **variable ~** variometer

Induktionsspannungsregler *m* induction voltage regulator **-störung** *f* inductive interference or trouble **-strom** *m* induced current **-strömungsmesser** *m* induction flowmeter **-tiegelofen** *m* coreless induction furnace

Induktions-variometer *m* variable inductor **-vermögen** *n* inductive capacity **-wicklung** *f* inductive winding **-widerstand** *m* inductive resistance **-zähler** *m* watt-hour meter, induction meter **-zug** *m* induced draft **-zünder** *m* induction fuse

induktiv inductive **~ gekuppelt** inductively coupled **~ gekuppelter Sender** inductive transmitter **~ geladen** inductively loaded **-er Blindwiderstand** inductive reactance **-e Kapazität** permittivity **-e Kupplung** inductive coupling, magnetic coupling, flux linkage (radio), transformer coupling **-er Spannungsabfall** inductive voltage drop **-er Strom** inductive current **-er Stromkreis** inductive circuit **-er Weggeber** inductive displacement pick-up **-er Widerstand** inductive resistance or reactance

Induktivität *f* inductive reactance, (acoustics) inertance, inductivity, inductance, self-inductance **~ je Längeneinheit** inductance per unit length **Drossel mit veränderlicher ~** swinging choke **durch gemeinsame ~ gekuppelt** autoinductively coupled **gleichmäßig oder stetig verteilte ~** evenly, uniformly, or continuously distributed inductance **natürliche ~** natural inductance **punktförmig verteilte ~** distributed or lumped inductance, concentrated inductance (or electrical inertia), continuous loading **veränderliche ~** variable inductance **verteilte ~** distributed inductance

Induktivitäts-änderung *f* self-inductance variation **-armut** *f* low inductance **-kasten für Meßzwecke** inductance box **-meßapparat** *m* self-inductance meter **-meßbrücke** *f* inductance bridge **-messer** *m* inducatance meter **-spule** *f* inductance coil, inductor **-symmetrie** *f* inductance balance **-unsymmetrie** *f* inductance unbalance

Induktometer *n* inductometer

Induktor *m* induction or ignition coil, primary coil, inductor, magneto (generator) **-anruf** *m* generator call, (hand-)generator ringing **-apparat** *m* magneto telephone station **-feuermeldesystem** *n* magneto-fire-alarm system **-generator** *m* inductor alternator

induktorisch inductive **-e Beeinflussung** inductive interference or trouble

Induktorium *n* induction or spark coil, Ruhmkorff coil

Induktor-kurbel *f* generator (magneto) crank or handle **-maschine** *f* inductor-type generator, inductor alternator with moving iron **-rad** *n* inductor wheel **-schlußzeichen** *n* ring-off signal **-station** *f* inductor station **-unterbrecher** *m* induction-coil interruptor

Industrie *f* industry **~ der Erdölnebenprodukte** petroleum by-product industries **~ der Kohlen- und Teernebenprodukte** coal by-product industries **~ für Notfälle** shadow industry

Industrie-abwässer *pl* industrial waste water **-alphatron** *n* alphatron for industrial use **-anlage** *f* industrial plant or installation **-bahn** *f* factory or works railway **-betrieb** *m* industrial or engineering operation **-bezirk** *m* manufacturing district **-diamant** *m* industrial diamond **-erzeugnis** *n* industrial product **-firma** *f* industrial firm **-flugplatz** *m* factory airfield **-geräte** *pl* commercial or industrial apparatus **-hafen** *m* industrial port

industriell industrial

Industrie-manometer *n* industrial pressure gauge **-messe** *f* industries fair **-netz** *n* industrial mains **-öfen** *pl* industrial furnaces **-reaktor** *m* industrial reactor **-röhre** *f* industrial tube

Industrie-vereinheitlichung *f* industrial standardization **-viertel** *n* industrial area or section **-wasser** *n* processing water **-werk** *n* industrial plant, engineering works **-zweig** *m* branch of industry

induzieren to induce

induzierend inducing, primary (elec.) **-er Magnetpol** inducing magnetic pole **-er Strom** inducing current

induziert induced **-e Geräusche** power induction or induced noise **-er Magnet** induced magnet **-e Radioaktivität** induced radioactivity **-er Strom** induced current **-er Widerstand** induced drag (aerodyn.)

Induzierung *f* induction

ineinander into one another, into each other, one

into the other ~ **lösen** to diffuse into each other, dissolve in each other ~ **löslich** soluble in one another ~ **übergehen lassen** to blend
Ineinander-falzen *n* inset **-fügen** to join, couple **-geschachtelt** emboxed in each other, telescoped; (Impulse) interlaced (pulses) **-geschlagen** in and in (method of packing in paper mfg.) **-greifen** to intermesh, interlock, gear **-greifen** *n* intermeshing, gearing, meshing (of teeth), interlock, engagement **-greifend** interlocking, engaging
ineinanderpassen to fit into each other
ineinander-schieben to encase **-schiebung** *f* telescoping **-stecken** to fit into one another
Ineinanderstecken *n*, **die Stücke sind durch ~ vereinigt** the parts have been telescoped
Ineinnahmeverfügung *f* intake order
inert inert ~ **machen** to deactivate, devitalize, deenergize
Inertanz *f* inertance
Inertgas *n* inert gas
Inertialsystem *n* inertial frame
infinitäres Verhalten asymptotic behavior
Infinitesimalrechnung *f* infinitesimal calculus
Influenz *f* influence, (electrostatic) induction, condensing **-feld** *n* electrostatic field, static field
influenzieren to influence
Influenz-maschine *f* influence machine **-wirkung** *f* (electrostatic) induction
informationsbearbeitend data processing, data handling
Informationsbelag (einer Nachrichtenquelle) information content per symbol
Informations-deckung *f* information package **-dichte** *f* information package, packing density (comput.) **-einheit** *f* item **-erschließung** *f* information retrieval
Informationsfluß (einer Nachrichtenquelle) information rate per time
Informations-gehalt *n* (Comput.) information content **-lesedraht** *m* information-read-wire, IR-wire **-maske** *f* ellipse of essential information **-schreibdraht** *m* information-write-wire, IW-wire **-streuung** *f* dissemination of information **-technik** *f* data processing **-träger** *m* input output media (tape rec.) **-übermittlung** *f* changing information **-verlust** *m* loss of information
informieren to inform, brief
infra-akustisch subaudio **-brechung** *f* subrefraction
infrarot infrared **-beseitigung** *f* infrared removal **-bildwandlerröhre** *f* infrared image converter **-ortung** *f* infra-red range and direction detection **-steuerung** *f* (Rakete) infra-red homing head **-trockenstrahlerlampe** *f* infra-red lamp for drying apparatus **-visier** *n* (Astron.) infrared sight
Infraschall *m* infrasound, infrasonic **innerer** ~ internal, intrinsic or inner infrasonic
Infraschwerewelle *f* infra-gravity wave
infratelefonische Telegraphie subaudio telegraphy
infundieren to infuse
Infusorienerde *f* infusorial earth, kieselguhr
ingangsetzen to start, set in motion, bring on stream (petroleum)
Ingangsetzen, stoßfreies ~ starting without shock **unvorhergesehenes** ~ accidental resumption of work
Ingangsetzung *f* starting
Ingangsetzungsvorrichtung *f* starting gear
Ingenieur *m* engineer, technical officer or official **leitender** ~ chief engineer
Ingenieur-büro *n* consulting engineering office **-versuchsreaktor** *m* Engineering Trial Reactor (ETR) **-wesen** *n* civil engineering
Ingerenz *f* influence
Inhaber *m* proprietor ~ **mehrerer Anschlüsse** subscriber with several lines ~ **eines Fernsprechanschlusses,** ~ **eines Hauptanschlusses** subscriber ~ **eines Nebenanschlusses** subscriber having extension stations ~ **einer öffentlichen Sprechstelle** public-telephone-station agent ~ **eines Ausweises** holder of a license
Inhalt *m* volume, content(s), capacity, substance, area ~ **des Kraftstoffbehälters** fuel level of tank **körperlicher** ~ solid or cubical contents, volume, solidity ~ **einer Fläche** area
Inhalts-angabe *f* statement of contents, table of contents, index **-anzeiger** *m* fuel-level or storage indicator, fuel gauge **-anzeigerohr** *n* gauge pipe **-auswertung** *f* analysis of contents **-bestimmung einer Fläche** quadrature **-bestimmung** *f* **eines Körpers** cubature **-manometer** *n* cylinder-pressure gauge **-messer für Behälter** contents gauge **-nachweis** *m* reference, proof of content
Inhalts-stoffe components **-treue Abbildung** area-preserving mapping **-übersicht** *f* table of contents **-vergrößerung** *f* volumetric increase **-verzeichnis** *n* list or table of contents, index
Inhibierung *f* stay of proceedings, estoppel
Inhibitor *m* inhibitor
Inholz *f* timbers
inhomogen inhomogeneous, heterogeneous
Inhomogenität *f* inhomogeneity, heterogeneousness
Initial *n* initial
Initiale *f* primer, booster charge
Initialen als Wasserzeichen cipher (paper mfg.)
Initial-kraft *f* initiating power, initial force **-schubspannung** *f* critical shear stress (cryst.) **-sprengstoffe** *pl* initiating explosives **-zacke** *f* initial wave or spike (on cardiogram) **-zünder** *m* primer of bomb or shell initiator **-zündsatz** *m* priming composition **-zündung** *f* primer detonation, initiation
Initiative *f* initiative
Initiator *m* initiator, ignition primer
initiieren to initiate, explode
Injektions-kanüle *f* hypodermic needle **-gut** *n* grout **-lösung** *f* injection solution **-spritze** *f* syringe (med.) **-verfahren** *n* injection method of grouting
Injektor *m* injector **-brenner** *m* low-pressure torch **-düse** *f* injector nozzle or cone **-ventil** *n* injector valve
injizieren to inject
Inkandeszenzbeleuchtung *f* incandescent lighting
inkaufnehmen to make allowance
Inklination *f* magnetic inclination, inclination, dip **von gleicher** ~ isoclinal
Inklinations-bussole *f* inclination compass **-messer** *m* inclinometer **-nadel** *f* inclination or dipping needle **-richtung** *f* direction of dip

-**winkel** *m* angle of inclination or of dip, magnetic inclination or dip, pitch attitude (rdr)
Inklinatorium *n* dip needle
inklinieren to incline
Inklinometer *n* (Zur Messung der Lage des Zieles) inclinometer
inklusives Oder "or" circuit (comput)
inkohärente Streuung incoherent scattering
Inkohärenz *f* incoherence
Inkohlung *f* internal condensation, aging of coal, mineralization, carbonization
inkommensurabel incommensurable
inkompatibel incompatible
Inkompatibilitätstensor *m* incompatibility tensor
inkompatible Drehungen incompatible rotations
inkompressible incompressible **~ Strömung** incompressible flow
Inkongruenz *f* incongruity
inkonstant inconstant
Inkonstanz *f* inconstancy
Inkrafttreten *n* coming into force, commencement (of an act or a law)
Inkreis *m* inscribed circle
Inkrement *n* increment **äquivalentes logarithmisches ~** equivalent logarithmic increment
inkromieren to chromium-plate
Inkurssetzung *f* circulation
inkrustieren to incrust
Inkrustierung *f* incrustation
Inkunabel *f* wood stereotype
Inlandabnehmer *m* inland customer
inländisch domestic, native, inland
Inland-markt *m* domestic market **-nachfrage** *f* home demand **-preis** *m* domestic price
Inlands-luftverkehr *m* domestic air traffic **-luftverkehrsstrecken** *pl* internal air lines
Inland-verbrauch *m* domestic consumption **-verkehr** *m* domestic traffic **-telegramm** *n* inland message
inliegend enclosed
Inmarschsetzung *f* initiation (of a procedure), dispatch
innehalten to pause, stop, observe, keep, adhere
innen internal(ly) within **-ablesung** *f* internal reading **-abmessungen** *pl* inside dimensions **-absaugung** *f* internal evacuation or exhaust **-anlage** *f* internal plant **-ansicht** *f* interior view **-anstrich** *m* interior coating **-antenne** *f* internal or indoor aerial or antenna
Innen-aufbau *m* internal structure **-aufnahme** *f* indoor shot, studio shot **-aufstellung** *f* indoor mounting **-ausgleich** *m* aerodynamic balance **-auskreuzung** *f* internal-drag bracing (aviation) **-auspolsterung** *f* inside padding **-ausstattung** *f* inside fittings or equipment
Innen-backenbremse *f* (internal) expanding brake **-ballistik** *f* interior ballistics **-becken** *n* dock, locked basin, inner harbor or basin **-belastung** *f* the load acting on the inside **-belag** *m* inner enveloppe **-beleimen** *n* inside gluing **-betrieb** *m* indoor work **-bordscharnier** *n* inboard hinge fitting **-bordschwimmer** *m* inboard float **-bremse** *f* inner brake **-dienst** *m* internal service, indoor service
Innendrall- und Durchbiegungsmesser *m* universal bore gauge
Innen-druck *m* internal pressure **-durchmesser** *m* internal or inside diameter **-düse** *f* inside nozzle **-einpaß** *m* inner fit **-einrichtung** *f* indoor furniture or fittings **-einstechen** *n* internal recessing
Innen-federung *f* internal springing **-feuerung** *f* internal firing or heating **-fühlhebel** *m* inside calipers, inside test indicator **-flanschlasche** *f* side plate **-flußturbine** *f* inward-flow turbine
innengefedert internally sprung **-es Anlaufrad** internally sprung starting wheel
innengesteuert internally controlled
Innengewinde *n* internal thread or tap, inside or female thread, box thread **-fräsapparat** *m* internal-thread milling attachment **-schleifmaschine** *f* internal thread grinder, internal thread grinding machine **-schneiden** *n* tapping **-schneidestahl** *m* inside-threading tool **-stahl** *m* inside threading tool
Innen-gitter *n* inner grid **-glied** *n* inside or block link **-grenzlehre** *f* plug gauge **-gummifederung** *f* internal rubber shock absorber **-hafen** *m* inner harbor **-haube** *f* inner cowl **-hütchen** *n* interior percussion cap, inner capsule (explosives)
Innenkabel *n* inside cable **~ für Sprechstellen** house cable (teleph.) **~ für Vermittlungsstellen** office cable (teleph.)
Innen-kaliber *n* inside caliper **-kapazität** *f* interelectrode capacity **-kante** *f* running edge (of rail) **-kippe** *f* dumping into excavation **-knagge** *f* the pins inside **-kolbenbelag** *m* wall coating **-kontakt** *m* inner or internal contact **-konus** *m* inner cone, inside taper **-kopieren** *n* internal copying **-kugelfläche** *f* internal spherical surface
Innen-lage *f* inside position **-lamelle** *f* drive disc **-längskopieren** *n* internal copying **-lasche mit runden Löchern** inner fishplate with round holes **-laufbahn** *f* inner raceway or race **-laufring** *m* inner race **-leistung** *f* indicated horsepower **-leitung** *f* internal wiring **-lenker** *m* automobile with inside drive **-lenkung** *f* inside control or drive
innenliegend lying within, enclosed **mit -em Spindelgewinde** nonrising stem (valve)
Innenloch *n* inner hole
Innenlunker *m* blowhole
Innenmaß *n* inside measurement
innenmattiert (Birne) frosted inside **-e Lampe** (halbdunkel) pearl lamp
Innenmeßeinrichtung *f* internal measuring or gauging attachment
Innenmeßgerät *n* internal-thread-measuring instrument **~ mit federndem Anschlag** internal-measuring instrument with spring-type rest
Innen-mikrometer-Stichmaß *n* inside micrometer calipers **-messung** *f* inside measure, internal measurement **-mischer** (mit Stempel) internal mixer (with floating weight) **-muffe** *f* (beim Bohrgestänge) drill-pipe flush joint **-photographieoszillograph** *m* internal-photography oscillograph **-plandreheinrichtung** *f* internal facing attachment
Innenpol-anker *m* inner-pole armature (elec.) **-dynamo** *m* internal-pole dynamo, external-armature generator **-feld** *n* revolving field **-gehäuse** *n* inner-pole frame **-generator** *m* revolving field generator
Innen-punkt *m* inner point (math.) **-rad** *n* inside

wheel **-raum** *m* interior or inside room or space **-raumausführung** *f* (Kondensator) capacitor for indoor location **-raumdurchführung** *f* indoor bushing **-riß** *m* internal shake, inside crack, crevice (house) **-rohrgenerator** *m* internal bulb generator **-rundschleifmaschine** *f* internal grinding machine

Innen-sammler *m* inner duct or collector ring jet **-schaltgerät** *n* integrating accelerometer **-schaltuhr** *f* integrator-testing-device calibrator **-schau** *f* introspection

Innen-schieber *m* inner slide **-schleifarbeit** *f* internal-grinding work **-schleifeinrichtung** *f* internal-grinding attachment **-schleifen** *n* internal grinding **-schleifmaschine** *f* internal-grinding machine **-schleifspindel** *f* internal-grinding spindle

Innenschleifvorrichtung *f* internal-grinding fixture **Vorgelege für die ~** internal-grinding countershaft

Innenschliff *m* internal grinding **~ zylindrischer Büchsen** internal grinding of straight bores **~ konischer Rundflächen** internal grinding of taper bores

Innen-sechskant *n* hexagonal recess **-sechskantschraube** *f* screw with hexagonal recessed hole **-sehrohr** *n* bore-inspection telescope

Innensegerring *m* inner seal ring

Innenseite *f* inner side, inside **~ des Hauptverteilers** exchange side of main distributing frame

Innen-sicherungsring *m* internal safety ring **-spannbacke** *f* internal chuck jaw **-spannung** *f* internal strain **-spritzzeit** *f* inside spraying period **-stauchung** *f* internal upset **-steuerung** *f* inside steering **-stiel** *m* compression strut **-strebe** *f* compression strut **-strehler** *m* inside chaser or chasing tool **-taster** *m* (Innenzirkel) inside spring caliper

Innenteile *pl* inner or inside parts **~ entfernen** to disembowel

Innen-teilung *f* internal scale or graduation **-tränkung** *f* penetration (of water) **-treibradbetrieb** *m* inside gearing **-übertragung** *f* local link **-umfang** *m* inner circumference

Innen- und Außentaster *m* caliper-compasses

Innen- und Stirnflächenschleifmaschine *f* internal- and face-grinding machine

Innen-verbindungsleitung *f* local link (P.A.B.X.) **-verbindungssatz** *m* connecting circuit (P.A.B. X.) **-verbrennungsmotor** *m* internal-combustion engine **-verbrennungstyp** *m* internal-combustion type **-verkleidung** *f* interior panelling

Innen-verspanndraht *m* internal bracing wire **-verspannung** *f* interior strutting and bracing (aviation) **-verstrebung** *f* internal bracing **-verzahntes Zahnrad** internal gear **-verzahnung** *f* internal toothing, internal teeth, internal gear or gearing **-vierkant** *n* recessed square

Innenvierkant- oder -sechskantschraube *f* hollow set-screw

Innen-vorverdichter *m* internal supercharger **-wache** *f* interior guard **-wand** *f* inwall, inside wall **-wäsche** *f* vacuum wash

Innenwiderstand *m* output resistance, source resistance, internal resistance, anode resistance or impedance **~ im Arbeitsfeld, ~ im Arbeitspunkt** ohms of internal resistance **~** (Meßgerät) inherent resistance

Innen-winkel *m* interior angle **-zahnkranz** (einer Planscheibe) internal gear **-zahnkranzantrieb** *m* inner gearing **-zahnrad** *n* annular gear **-zentriert** (cubic) body centered **-zirkel** *m* calipers **-zünder** *m* internal fuse, delayed-action fuse

inner internal, inner **-e Ausbeute** internal operating ratio **-e Ausbuchtung** fillet (inside) **-e Austrittsarbeit** inner work function **-e Bohrung** borehole made from galleries **-e Bremsstrahlung** inner bremsstrahlung **-e Eigenschaften** internal modes **-es Elektron** inner-shell electron **-e Energie** internal or intrinsic energy

innerer Fremdphotoeffekt impurity photoconduction **-e Geometrie einer Fläche** intrinsic geometry of a surface **-er Leistungswiderstand** internal resistance **-er Leitwert** anode alternating-current conductance **-er lichtelektrischer Effekt** photoconductive effect **-es Moment** internal momentum **-es Produkt** scalar product, dot product (vector)

inner, -e Quantenzahl inner quantum number **-e Reibung** solid viscosity, internal friction **-er Rohrdurchmesser** internal diameter of pipe **-er Störpegel** crosstalk **-er Strom** internal current **-e Versteifung** internal reinforcement **-e Versteifung** (des Flügels) internal reinforcing member **-e Verzahnung** internal gear **-er Widerstand** anode alternating-current resistance, internal resistance (of a cell) **-e Wölbung** intrados **-er Zylinderdurchmesser** bore

inneratomar nuclear, pertaining to internal atomic structure

innerballistisch pertaining to interior ballistics

innerbetrieblich interdepartmental

innerhalb within, inside **~ des Großkreises fliegen** to fly the great circle **~ der Schußweite** within range **~ des Staates** intrastate

innerlich internal, inner

innermolekulare Kette intermolecular chain

innernukleare Kraft intraunuclear force

innewohnend inherent, intrinsic, innate

innig sincere, tender, intimate **~ gemischt** intimately or homogeneously mixed

Innung *f* corporation, guild

in-Phase-Signal *n* in-phase signal, common-mode signal

Inplano *n* broadside, broadsheet (print.)

Inrohrschneider *m* casing cutter, casing knife

Insasse *m* occupant

insbesondere particularly

Inschrift *f* legend, inscription

Insektenpulver *n* insecticide powder

Insel *f* isle, island, band of frequencies (radar) **Inseln im Film** spots on film, cessing, running

Inselbildung *f* island formation

Inserat *n* advertisement

Inserent *m* advertiser

inserieren to advertise

Insertions-gebühr *f*, **-kosten** *pl* cost of advertisement, advertising expense(s)

insgesamt altogether, total, as a whole

Insolation *f* insolation, solarization

Inspekteur *m* inspecting officer, inspector

Inspektion *f* inspection, supervision, inspectorate **~ des Kraftfahrwesens** motor-vehicle-inspection service

Inspektions-grube *f* (inspcetion) pit or pan **-schacht** *m* inspection shaft **-stollen** *m* inspection

gallery or tunnel
Inspektor *m* inspector, supervisor, superintendent
Inspektorat *n* inspectorate
Inspizient *m* inspector
inspizieren to inspect, examine, supervise
Inspizierung *f* inspection
instabil unstable, unsteady **-er Kreis** astable circuit
Instabilität *f* instability
Instabilitätsschauer *m* instability shower
Installateur *m* plumber, electrician
Installation *f* installation
Installations-arbeiten *f pl* plumbing **-gegenstand** *m* installation implement **-plan** *m* wiring diagram, pipe layout **-schalter** *m* house wiring switch **-selbstschalter** *m* automatic cut-out **-teil** *m* part of installation material
installieren to install, equip
instandgesetzt overhauled
instandhalten to maintain, keep up
Instandhaltung *f* maintenance, upkeep, servicing
Instandhaltungs-arbeiten *pl* maintenance (routine) work **-gebühr** *f* (periodic) maintenance charge **-kosten** *pl* maintenance cost **-messung** maintenance measurement
instandsetzen to refit, repair, recondition
Instandsetzung *f* repair, restoration, repair work, reconditioning **abgekürzte ~** maintenance **~ von Kraftfahrzeugen** repair of motor vehicles **~ und Unterhaltung** repair and maintenance **nach Bedarf durchgeführte ~** march maintenance, operating maintenance **regelmäßig durchgeführte ~** scheduled maintenance
Instandsetzungsabteilung *f* maintenance unit
Instandsetzungsarbeiten *pl* repair work, maintenance **laufende ~** routine repair work
Instandsetzungs-auftrag *m* repair contract **-dienst** *m* repair and maintenance service, damage clearance **-fähig** reparable **-fähigkeit** *f* reparability **-kraftwagen** *m* maintenance or repair truck **-staffel** *f* maintenance echelon **-trupp** *m* repair gang **-werft** *f* repair yard **-werkstatt** *f* repair shop
Instanz *f* authority, court **in letzter ~** as a last resource
Instanzen-weg *m* official channels, stages of appeal **-zug** *m* successive appeal (law)
instationär intermittent, nonsteady (said of flow)
Instellung-bringen *n* emplacing, emplacement **-gehen** *n* going or moving into position
Instradierungsplan *m* routing chart
Instruktions-reise *f* preliminary visit **-schild** *n* instruction plate
Instrument *n* device, instrument, apparatus **~ mit unmittelbarer Ablesung** direct-reading instrument **~ für Absteckungen im Straßenbau** instrument for setting out roads **~ für topographische Entfernungsmessungen** topographic-tacheometric instrument for measurements of distance **~ mit quadratischer Kennlinie bzw. Skala** square-law instrument **~ zur elektrischen Messung nichtelektrischer Größen** electrically measuring instrument **~ mit Nebenwiderstand** shunted instrument **~ mit Nullpunkt in der Mitte** center-zero instrument **~ mit unterdrücktem Nullpunkt** suppressed-zero instrument **~ in gebrauchsfertig montiertem Zustande** instrument ready for use
Instrumentalkorrektion *f* index correction
Instrument-anordnung *f* instrument layout **-ausrüstung** *f* instrumentation **-beleuchtung** *f* lighting of instruments **-birne** *f* instrument bulb
Instrumenten-anflug *m* instrument approach **-anzeige** *f* instrument reading **-beleuchtung** *f* panel illumination, dashboard lighting **-brett** *n* instrument board or panel, dashboard
Instrumenten-einbau *m* instrument installation **-einzelteil** *m* measurement component **-fehler** *m* (measuring-)instrument error, instrumental error **-fliegen** *n*, **-flug** *m* blind flying, instrument flying **-höhe** *f* height of instrument **-hülle** *f* instrument shelter
Instrumenten-Lande-System *n* instrument landing system (ILS) **-laterne** *f* pilot lamp **-liste** *f* instrument schedule **-rohrleitungen** *pl* instrument piping **-schrank** *m* instrument cubicle
Instrumentierung *f* instrumentation
Instrument-konstante *f* constant of (measuring) instrument **-korb** *m* instrument basket or cage **-öl** *n* precision-instrument oil **-planchette** *f* board for instruments **-schutz** *m* instrument shelter **-stecker** *m* instrument plug **-tafel** *f* instrument board **-teil** *m* control and instrument panel **-umhüllung** *f* instrument shelter
Insulinbildung *f* insulin formation
inszenieren to stage
intakt intact
Intarsia-Imitation *f* inlay imitation
Integrabilitätsbedingung *f* integrability condition
Integral *n* integral **bestimmtes ~** definite integral **unbestimmtes ~** indefinite integral **~ wirkender Regler** (I-Regler) integral action controller (I-controller)
Integral-begriff *m* concept of the integral **-behälter** *m* integral tank **-beziehung** *f* integral relation **-darstellung** *f* integral representation **-diskriminatior** *m* integral discriminator **-dosis** *f* integral dose **-form** *f* integral form
Integral-geber *m* integral transmitter **-gleichung** *f* integral equation **-gleichungsmethode** *f* integral equation method **-invariante** *f* integral invariant **-rechnung** *f* integral calculus **-regelung** proportional reset control **-satz** *m* integral theorem **-sinusfunktion** integral sine function **-wirkung** *f* reset action **-zerlegung** *f* integral seriation
Integrand *m* integrand
Integration *f* integration **~ erhält man durch Integration zwischen den Grenzen O und t** is obtained by integrating between the limits O and t
Integrations-flächen *f* integration surfaces **-gerät** *n* integration device, integrator **-glied** *n* integrating circuit **-grenze** *f* limit of integration **-konstante** *f* constant of integration **-kreisel** *m* integration gyro
Integrationsmesser *m* integrating meter **-schritt** *m* interval of integration **-tisch** *m* integration stage **-weg** *m* path of integration **-würfel** *m* integrating cube **-zeit** *f* integration period or interval
Integrator *m* integrator
integrierbar integrable
Integrier-anlage *f* differential analyzer **-einrich-**

tung *f* integrator

integrieren to integrate ~ **über eine Periode** to integrate over a cycle

integrierend integral, integrating, integrant, or component (part) **-er Anzeiger** integrating indicator **-es Dosimeter** integrating dose meter **-er Frequenzmesser** master frequency meter **-er Nenner** integrating denominator **-es Photometer** integrating photometer (lumen meter) **-e Regelung** floating action

Integrier-gerät *n* (Integrator) ratemeter **-trieb** *m* mechanical integrating device

integrierter Neutronenfluß integrated neutron flux

Integrierung *f* integration

Integrimeter *n* integrometer, moment planimeter

Integritätsbereich *m* integral domain

Integrodifferentialgleichung *f* integro-differential equation

Intensität *f* intensity, intensiveness ~ **der Magnetisierung** intensity of magnetization ~ **des magnetischen Moments** magnetic moment density

Intensitäts-abstufung *f* intensity steps or grades **-anomalie** *f* intensity anomaly **-ausfall** *m* fading **-beeinflussung** *f* intensity modulation **-begrenzer** video-gain control **-bereich** *m* intensity region **-bilanz** *f* intensity balance **-größe** *f* intensive property, tension **-maximum** *n* maximum intensity **-marke** *f* intensity standard **-meßgerät** *n* level recorder

Intensitäts-rückgang *m* decrease in intensity **-schrift** *f* variable density tracks **-schwächung** *f* intensity decrease **-schwankung** *f* variation in intensity **-spektrum** *n* intensity spectrum **-sprung** *m* jump in intensity **-steuerung** *f* intensity modulation **-summensatz** *m* intensity sum rule

Intensitätsunterschied *m*, **minimaler** ~ just noticeable difference

Intensitäts-verfahren *n* variable-density method **-verlauf** *m* variation in intensity **-verteilung** *f* intensity distribution

Intensitometer *n* intensitometer

intensiv intensive **-er Strahlungsfluß** high-radiation flux

Intensivverfahren *n* high power process

interatomare Kraft interatomic force

interdendritisch interdendritic

Interessen-gebiet *n* sphere of interest **-gemeinschaft** *f* community of interests, combine, pool, trust

Interessent *m* prospective buyer

interessieren to interest

Interferenz *f* interference, beat

Interferenz-apparatur *f* diffraction camera **-aufnahme** *f* interference figure, exposure, interference photograph **-bild** *n* interference figure **-doppelbrechung** *f* interference in double refraction **-empfang** *m* heterodyne or beat reception **-empfänger** *m* beat or heterodyne receiver **-erscheinung** *f* interference phenomenon **-flächenprüfer** *m* interference surface tester **-frequenz** *f* frequency of beats **-gebiet** *n* mush area **-gravimeter** *n* interference gravimeter

Interferenzialrefraktor *m* interferometer

Interferenz-komparator *m* interference comparator **-schicht** *f* interference coating **-schwund** *m* fading by interference **-spektrogramm** *n* interference spectrogram

Interferenz-streifen *m* interference band, interference fringes (optics) **-ton** *m* beat or interference note or tone **-vorgang** *m* interference phenomenon, beating effect **-welle** *f* standing wave **-wellenmesser** *m* heterodyne wavemeter **-wirkung** *f* interference effect

interferieren to interfere

Interferometer *n* interferometer, interference spectroscope **-platte** interferometer plate

Interferrikum *n* air gap of a magnet

Interfrequenzwellenmesser *m* heterodyne wavemeter

intergranular intergranular

interimistisch temporary

Interimsbahn *f* temporary railway line **-lösung** *f* interim solution

Interkombinationen *pl* intersystem combinations

Interkostalplatte *f* intercostal plate

interkristallin intercrystalline **-e Brüchigkeit** intercrystalline or cleavage brittleness **-e Grundstoffbindung** intergranular penetration **-e Korrosion** intergranular corrosion, caustic embrittlement

intermediär intermediary, intermediate **-es Neutron** resonance neutrons

intermetallisch intermetallic

Intermittenz-faktor *m* intermittency factor **-schwingung** *f* relaxation or saw-tooth oscillation or wave, ratchet oscillation, time-base or tilting oscillation **-ton** *m* interruption tone

intermittieren to intermit

intermittierend intermittent, interrupted, tapping, pulsating **-es Gerät** pulsating unit, pulsating jet **-er Strom** intermittent current **-es Luftstrahltriebwerk** intermittent jet engine, pulse motor

Intermodulation *f* intermodulation

Intermodulations-faktor *f* intermodulation products (in per cent) **-rauschen** *n* intermodulation noise **-verzerrung** *f* intermodulation distortion **-verzerrungscharakteristik** *f* modulation-frequenzcy, intermodulation distortion characteristic

intermolekular intermolecular

intern interdepartmental, internal, intraoffice (call on P.A.B.X.) ~ **Fernsehanlage** closed-circuit television system ~ **Gespräch** local call

international international **-e Beleuchtungskommission** (CIE) International Commission on Illumination **-e elektrische Einheiten** international electrical units **-es Kartell** international cartel **-e Kerze** international candle **-es Luftrecht** international air law **-es Lumen** lumen (unit of luminous flux) **-e Lumenstunde** lumen-hour **-e Normalatmosphäre** standard international atmosphere **-e Normalisierungsgesellschaft** International Standardization Association **-e Wetterwarten** international réseau (aviation) **-e Wissenschaftliche Radio Vereinigung** International Scientific Radio Union

internieren to intern, detain, confine

Interphon *n* interphone system

Interpolation *f* interpolation

Interpolationsformel *f* interpolation formula

Interpolator *m* interpolator
interpolieren to interpolate
Interpolierung *f* interpolation
interpretieren to interpret
interpretatives Teilprogramm interpretative subroutine
interpretierend-es Organ interpreter **-es Programm** interpretative routine
Interpunktionszeichen *n* punctuation mark
Intersertalstruktur *f* ophitic texture
interstaatliche Durchgangszentrale zone center
interstellar interstellar
interstitiell-e Bestrahlung interstitial irradiation **-e Verbindungen** interstitial compounds
Intertemperaturkontakt *m* low-temperature contact
intertropisch intertropical
Intervall *n* interval, range **kritisches ~** critical range **stilles ~** silent period
Intervall-faktor *m* interval factor **-regel** *f* interval rule **-satz** *m* interval theorem
intervenieren to intervene, interpose, interfere
Intonation *f* voicing
intonieren to tune (a piano), intone
intrakavitäre Bestrahlung intracavitary irradation
intrakristalliner Bruch intracrystalline or transcrystalline rupture
intraperlitisch intrapearlitic
Intravitalmikroskop *n* intravital microscope
intrinsike Empfindlichkeit des Zählers intrinsic counter efficiency
Intritt-fallen *n* coming into step (of a synchronous machine) **-fallmoment** *n* pull-in torque
Intrittkommen *n* **mit der Grundfrequenz ~** paralleling (of alternators), synchronizing, phase focusing **mit einer Unterfrequenz ~** crawling
Intrusions-beben *n* cryptovolcanic earthquake **-masse** *f* intruded body
Intumeszenz *f* intumescence
Invaliditätsversicherung *f* disability insurance
Invar *n* invar (iron-nickel alloy)
Invariant *n* Invar (nickel-iron alloy)
Invariante *f* invariant
Invarianzprinzip *n* principle of invariance
Invarstahl *m* invar steel
Inventar *n* inventory, stock **-aufnahme** *f* stock taking
Inventur *f* stock taking **laufende ~** continuous inventory
invers-e Abbildung inverse mapping **-er photoelektrischer Effekt** inverse photo-electric effect
Inversion *f* inversion **~ im Raum** inversion in space
Inversions-faktor *m* inversion factor **-methode** *f* method of reversals **-schicht** *f* inversion layer
Invertentfernungsmesser *m* inversion telemeter, inverted-image range finder
Inverter *m* inverter (thyratron)
invertierbar invertible
invertieren invert (to)
Invertin *n* invertase
Inverttelemeter *n* inverted-image range finder
Invert-zeitrelais *n* inverse-time relay **-zucker** *m* invert sugar

Inverzugsetzung *f* notice of default
Investitionsgüter *pl* capital goods
Involutionssystem *n* involution system
inwendig indoors, inside
Inzidenz, letzte ~ einer Konfiguration last incidence of a configuration
Inzidenzgeometrie *f* geometry of coincidence
iodiostatische Schaltung idiostatic method or mounting
Ion *n* ion
Ionen-akzeptor *m* ion acceptor **-anhäufung** *f* ion cluster **-antrieb** *m* ion propulsion **-aspirationsapparat** *m* ion counter **-atomlinien** *pl* lines emitted by ionized atoms **-ausbeute** ion yield **-austausch** *m* ion exchange
Ionen-bahn *f* ion path **-beschleuniger** *m* ion accelerator **-beweglichkeit** *f* ionic mobility **-bewegung** *f* migration of ions, ion movement **-bildend** ionogenic **-bindung** *f* ion binding, electrostatic bond **-bremsfeld** *n* ion retarding field
Ionen-dichte *f* ionic density **-dosismesser** *m* ionic quantimeter **-falle** *f* ion trap (in electron gun of cathode-ray tube) **-fallenmagnet** *m* ion trap magnet **-fänger** *m* ion trap **-fleck** *m* ion spot (CRT) ion burn **-fluß** *m* ion flow **-flüssigkeiten** ionic liquids **-gasmodell** *n* ionic gas model **-getterpumpe** *f* ion getter pump **-gitter** *n* ion lattice
Ionengitterstrom *m* ion current **negativer ~** reverse or negative grid current, backlash of valve
Ionen-gleichung *f* ionic equation **-grenzwert** *m* ion limit **-gruppe** *f* ion cluster **-halbleiter** *m* ionic semi-conductor **-inkrement** *n* ionic increment **-kette** *f* ion chain **-komplex** *m* ion complex **-konzentration** *f* ionic concentration, density of ionization
Ionen-leitung *f* ionic conduction **-linearbeschleuniger** *m* ion linear accelerator **-loch** *n* negative-ion vacancy **-paarausbeute** *f* ion-pair yield **-paketierung** *f* bunching of ions **-prall** *m* bombardment by ions **-rakete** *f* ion rocket **-reaktion** *f* ionic reaction **-relais** *n* gas-filled relay
Ionenröhre *f* gas tube, gas-discharge tube **gittergesteuerte ~** thyratron
Ionen-rückkoppelung *f* ion feedback **-rumpf** *m* ion core **-rundlauf** *m* circulation of ions **-sättigungsstrom** *m* ionic saturation current, ion current **-schaden** *m* ion burning **-schalter** *m* gas-filled relay **-schicht** *f* ion sheath
Ionen-spaltung *f* ionic cleavage, ionization **-spektrum** *n* ionic spectrum **-spreizung** *f* ion spreading (i.e. the expanding Hofmeister series effect) **-stärke** *f* ionic strength **-stärkemesser** *m* ionometer **-steuerrohr** *n* thyratron **-strahl** *m* ion beam **-strahltriebwerk** *n* ion beam engine **-strom** *m* stream of ions, cathode influx
Ionen-theorie *f* ionic theory **-therapie** *f* ionic medication **-valenz** *f* ionic valence **-ventil** *n* electronic or ionic valve **-wanderung** *f* traveling or migration of ions **-wanderungsgeschwindigkeit** *f* ion-drift velocity **-windvoltmesser** *m* ionic wind voltmeter **-wolke** *f* ionic atmoshere **-zähler** *m* ion counter **-zustand** *m* ionic state
Ionisation *f* ionization

Ionisations-dosimeter *n* ion meter, ionization dose meter **-geschwindigkeit** *f* ionization rate **-grad** *m* ionization constant **-kammer** *f* ionization chamber **-kontinuum** *n* ionization continuum

Ionisations-manometer *n* ionization gauge **-messer** *m* ion counter **-säule** *f* columnar ionization **-schicht** *f* ionized layer **-spannung** *f* ionization voltage or potential **-störung** *f* ionic interference **-strom** *m* ionization current **-stromstärke** *f* intensity of ionization current **-wärme** *f* heat of ionization or of dissociation **-zustand** *m* ionization state

Ionisator *m* ionizator

ionisch ionic

ionisierbar ionizable

ionisieren to ionize

ionisierendes Teilchen ionizing particle

ionisiert ionized **-e Schicht** ionized layer **-e Störstelle** ionized impurity

Ionisierung *f* ionization

Ionisierungs-ausbeute *f* ionization efficiency **-bahn** *f* ionization path **-bank** *f* ledge **-elektrode** *f* ionizing electrode **-manometer** *n* ionization gauge **-potential durch Variationsmethode** variational ionization potential **-querschnitt** *m* ionization cross-sector

Ionisierungs-spannung *f* ionization voltage or potential **-spielaufbau** *m* Townsend structure or build-up **-stärke** *f* total ionization **-stufe** *f* stage of ionization **~ und Anregungswahrscheinlichkeit** probability of ionization and excitation **-verlust** *m* ionization loss **-vermögen** *n* ionizing power **-welle** *f* ionizing wave

Ionium *n* ionium

Ion-Molekül-Komplex *m* heteroion

Ionophorese *f* electrophoresis

Ionosphäre *f* ionosphere

Ionosphären-geräusch *n* ionospheric sounding **-störung** *f* ionospheric disturbance

Ionosphärsondierung durch Rückstreuung back-scatter ionospheric-sounding

Iontophorese *f* iontophoresis

Iota *n* iota, tittle

I-Profil *n* I-beam section, I section

irden earthen **-es Formstück** earthen block **-es Geschirr** earthenware

irdisch terrestrial

I-R-Draht *m* information-read-wire

I-Regelung *f* floating controller action

I-Regelwirkung *f* floating action, reset action

I-Regler *m* reset or integral-action controller

Iridium *n* iridium

Irinit *m* irinite

Irisation *f* iridescence

Iris *f* iris **-auf- und -Abblendung** *f* irising in and out **-blende** *f* iris diaphragm **-blendenphotometer** *n* iris-diaphragm photometer **-druck** *m* saddening (dyeing) **-farbe** *f* iridescent color **-fond** *m* iris ground, rainbow ground

irisieren to iridesce, iridize

Irisieren *n* iridescence

irisierend iridescent

irrationale Zahlen irrational numbers

Irrationalität *f* irrationality

Irrationalzahl *f* surd (math.)

irreführen to mislead, misdirect, confuse

irren to err, ramble, be mistaken **sich in der Rechnung ~** to be far out in calculations

irreversible Steuerung *f* irreversible controls

Irreversibilität *f* irreversibility

irrig mistaken, erroneous, false

Irr-licht *n* ignis fatuus, will-o'-the-wisp, jack-o'-lantern **-strahl** *m* false light (optics) **-strom** *m* stray or vagabond current

Irrtum *m* error, mistake

irrtümlich mistakenly, erroneously

Irrtumswahrscheinlichkeit *f* level of significance

Irrung *f* error, difference, erasure, erase signal

Irrungs-taste *f* erase key **-zeichen** *n* erase signal, rub-out signal

Irr-zacke *f*, **-zeichen** *n* ghost or phantom signal

Isakuste *f* isacoustic line

Isallobare *f* isallobar

I-Schirm *m* I scope

Ischyeten *pl* ischyetal lines

IS-Diagramm *n* total heat-entropy diagram, IS-diagram

isentrop isentropic **-e Strömung** isentropic flow

Isentropenanalyse *f* isentropic analysis

isentropisch isentropic

isländisch Icelandic **-er Doppelspat** Iceland spar, calcium carbonate **-es Tiefdruckgebiet** Icelandic low (meteor.)

Isley Kanäle *pl* Isley flues

iso . . .(gleich) iso

Isobaren *pl* curves of equal pressure, isobars **-karte** *f* barometric or isobaric chart **-kern** *m* isobaric nucleus

isobarometrischer Faßfüllapparat isobarometrical racking apparatus

Isobaten *pl* isobath or depth contours, contours of sea bed

Isobrontenkarte *f* isobrontic chart or map

Isobutyl *n* isobutyl

isochor isochoric

isochromatisch isochromatic **-er Streifen** isochromatic fringe

Isochrone *f* isochronous curve

isochron(isch) isochronous **-e Abtastung** isochronous scanning

Isochronismus *m* isochronism

Isodiapher *n* isodiaphere

Isodose *f* isodose (curve, surface)

Isoden-kurve *f* isodose contour (curve) **-oberfläche** *f* isodose surface **-tafel** *f* isodose chart

Isodromen *pl* isodromous curves (hyperbolic position-finding systems)

isodrome Regulierung isostatic regulation

Isodyname *f* isodynamic line

isodynamischer Zustand isodynamia

isoelektrisch equipotential

isoelektronisch isoelectronic

isoenergisch isoenergetic

Isogamme *f* line of equal gravity value

Isogon *n* isogon

Isogone *f* isogonic line

Isogonenkarte *f* isogonic chart or map, chart of equal variations

isogonisch isogonic **-e Karte** isogonic chart **-e (gleichwinklige) Linien** isogonic lines

Isogramm *m* isogram

Isogriven *pl* (Linien gleicher Gitternetzabweigung) isogrivs

isohydrisch isohydric

Isoimpuls-fläche *f* isocount surface **-kurven** *pl* isopulse contours

Iso-Intensitätskurve *f* iso-intensity curve

Isoklinale *f* isocline

Isoklinalfalte *f* isoclinal fold

Isokline *f* isoclinal line

Isoklinen *f pl* isoclinics

isokliner Streifen isoclinic fringe

isoklinisch isoclinic **-e Linien** isoclinic lines

Isolation *f* isolation, insulation **~ gegen Erde** insulation against ground **keramische ~** ceramic insulation

Isolations-abziehzange *f* stripping tongs **-durchschlag** *m* disruption of insulations **-fehler** *m* insulation failure or fault **-fehlerschutz** leakage protection **-haken** *m* insulation clip **-lack** *m* insulating paint **-lage** *f* insulation layer

Isolations-material *n* insulating material **-messer** *m* insulation tester **-meßgerät** *n* short-circuit reporter, applicance for measuring insulation **-messung** *f* insulation test **-mittel** *n* isolator

Isolations-pappe *f* fishpaper **-prüfeinrichtung** *f* insulation tester **-prüfer** *m* insulation indicator or tester **-prüfung** *f* insulation test **-schicht** *f* insulating layer **-stoff** *m* insulation material **-strom** *m* insulation current **-wächter** *m* earth-leakage monitor **-wege** *m pl* creep (leakage) paths **-widerstand** *m* insulation (resistance), dielectric resistance, insulance (reciporcal of leakance) **-zustand** *m* state of insulation

Isolator *m* insulator, isolator **~ mit eingebauter Sicherung** fuse insulator **~ mit gerader Stütze** pintype insulator **gesprungener ~** cracked insulator **unvollkommener ~** imperfect dielectric, leaky insulation

Isolator-einspannung *f* insulator mounting **-kette** *f* string of insulators, insulator chain **-kopf** *m* head of insulator **-material** *n* insulator material **-oberfläche** *f* insulator surface **-prüfmaschine** insulator testing machine **-säule** *f* insulator column **-stütze** *f* insulator spindle or pin, supporting insulator

Isolierabstand *m* insulator spacing

Isolierband *n* (adhesive) insulating tape, friction tape **mit ~ umwickeln** to serve with insulating tape

Isolierbandherstellungsmaschine *f* insulating-tape-producing machine

Isolier-becher *m* insulating sheath or case **-befestigung** *f* insulation clip **-büchse** *f* insulating bush

isolieren to insulate, seal, isolate

isolierend insulatory, insulating **-es Seil** strop insulator **-e Unterlage** insulating base **-e Zwischenlage** insulating layer

Isolier-fähigkeit *f* insulating quality or property **-flasche** *f* vacuum bottle or flask **-formstück** *n* molded insulation **-füllmasse** *f* insulating compound **-gerät** *n* insulating mechanism, oxygen breathing apparatus **-glocke** *f* porcelain cup, shed, petticoat (elec.) **-hülse** *f* insulation sheath or covering **-klemme** *f* insulting clamp, cleat insulator **-körper** *m* insulator radio

Isolierlack *m* insulating varnish **mit ~ überzogen** covered with insulating varnish

Isolier-leinen *n* insulating linen **-leiste** *f* insulating ledge **-mantel** *m* insulating casing

Isoliermasse *f* insulating compound or material, moldable or fictile insulating substance, dope **mit ~ getränkt** compounded **gepreßte ~** molded insulation

Isolier-material *n* insulating material **-matte** *f* insulating mat **-mittel** *n* insulator, insulating material or medium **-muffe** *f* insulating sleeve **-öl** *n* insulating oil **-papier** *n* insulating paper **-pappe** *f* insulating board **-perlen** *pl* insulation beads **-platte** *f* insulating clamp **-preßmassen** *pl* insulation material for pressed products

Isolier-ring *m* insulating ring **-rippe** *f* insulation rib **-rohr** *n* insulating tube, electric conduit **-röhre** *f* isolating pipe or valve, buffer tube **-rolle** *f* reel insulator, knob **-rost** *m* die grid

Isolier-säule *f* (Rakete) insulating mast **-scheibe** *f* insulating washer **-schemel** *m* insulating stool or chair **-schicht** *f* lagging **-schiene** *f* detector track section **-schlauch** *m* insulating sheaths or tubing, spaghetti (elec.) **-schutz** *m* insulation **-sockel** *m* insulating base

Isolier-stoff *m* insulating material, insulant **-stoffkapsel** *f* a type of electric-wire insulation **-stoffzählertafel** *f* molded plastic meter board **-stöpsel** *m* insulating plug **-stoß** *m* insulating joint **-streifen** *m* insulating strip, friction strip **-stück** *n* insulator

isoliert insulated, sealed, isolated **-es Ende einer Leitung** sealed end of a line **-er Handhebel** insulated handle **-er Leiter** insulated conductor **-er Stromabnehmerträger** trolley support, assemblage on roof of street car **-e Zange** insulated pliers

Isolierteller *m* insulating cup

Isolierung *f* insulation, covering, absolute quarantine, isolation

Isolierungs-methode *f* method of isolation **-platte** *f* insulation plate (jet)

Isolier-vermögen *n* insulating property **-werkstoff** *m* insulation material **-zwischenlage** *f* insulating separator or layer, dielectric

Isolux-diagramm *n* isolux diagram **-kurve** *f* (Beleuchtungsgleiche) isolux curve

Isomer *n* isomer

isomer isomeric

Isomerie *f* isomerism **-Insel** *f* islands of isomerism

isomerisch isomeric

isometrisch isometric(al), regular **-e Konsistenzkarte** isometric consistency chart

isomorph isomorphous

Isomorphie *f*, **Isomorphismus** *m* isomorphism

Isomylalkohol *m* isoamyl alcohol

Isooktan *n* isooctane

isoperimetrisch isoperimetric

Isophasen *pl* lines of equal phase relations (radio)

Isophoten *pl* isophots

Isophyse *f* contour lines of terrain

Isoporen *pl* isopors **-fokus** *m* isoporic focus

Isopropylalkohol *m* isopropyl alcohol

Isopropyläthergemisch *n* isopropyl ether blend

Isospin *m* isotopic spin **-Auswahlregel** *f* isospic spin selection

Isotasie *f* isostasy

Isostatik *f* isostatics
isostatisch isostatic
isosteres Molekül isosteric molecule
isotherm isothermal **-e Schicht** isothermal layer
isothermal isothermal
Isotherme *f* isotherm
Isothermen *pl* isothermal lines
isothermisch isothermal **-e Zustandsänderung** isothermal change of state (condition)
Isoton *n* isotone
isotonisch isotonic
Isotope *f* isotope
Isotopen-ersetzung *f* isotope replacement **-indikator** *m* tracer isotope **-spin** *m* isotopic spin, isobaric spin **-verhältnis** *n* isotopic composition
Isotopie-effekt *m* isotope effect **-spin** *m* isotopic spin **-verschiebung** *f* isotope effect or shift
isotopische Homogenisierung equilibration
Isotrimorphie *f* triple isomorphism
Isotron *n* isotron
isotrop isotropic **-e Streuung** isotropic scattering
Isotropie *f* isotropy
isotropisch isotropic
Isozentrum *n* isocenter
Ist-abmaß actual allowance **-anzeige** *f* actual indication **-Beschaffenheit** *f* nature (reliability) **-bestand** *m* actual state of equipment, vehicles, etc., equipment on hand **-differenz** *f* measured (actual) difference **-geber** *m* actual selsyn **-größe** *f* actual finished size
I-Stiel *m* I strut
Isthmusverfahren *n* isthmus method
Ist-leistung *f* actual output **-maß** *n* actual finished size, actual size or dimension **-menge** *f* actual quantity
I-Stoß *m* square or straight joint
I-Strebe *f* lift strut
Ist-spiel *n* acutal clearance **-stand** *m* actual strength **-stärke** *f* actual strength **-stärkenachweisung** *f* statement showing actual strength, daily strength report **-übermaß** *n* actual interference
I-Stütze *f* I bolt
Istwert *m* actual value; (der Regelgröße) actual value (of controlled condition) **~ der Regelgröße** control point **-anzeige** *f* indication of the actual value
Istzeit *f* actual time
Itabirit *m* itabirite
Iterations-methode *f* iteration method **-verfahren** *n* iteration method, successive approximation
Iterieren *n* iteration (math.)
iteriert iterated **-e Adresse** *f* indirect address (info proc.)
It-Platten *pl* high-pressure (rubberized-asbestos) packing sheets
I-Träger *m* I beam, I girder
Ivanium *n* ivanium (an aluminum alloy)
I-W-Draht *m* information-write-wire
I-Wirkungskoeffizient *m* integral action coefficient
Izettstahl *m* a type of low-carbon steel
Izod-Kerbzähigkeitsskala *f* Izod impact-figures scale

J

Jacarandaholz *n* rosewood
Jacht *f* yacht
Jacke *f* jacket
Jacken-maschine *f*, **-stuhl** *m* jacket-body machine **-wiege** *f* sleigh cradle, jacket or ring cradle
Jacobi (Reihen q) *pl* Q series
Jade *f* jade
Jadeit *m* jade (min.)
jäh steep, sudden, abrupt
Jahr, bürgerliches ~ calendar year
Jahrbuch *n* yearbook, almanac
Jahres-abrechnung *f* yearly settlement, annual reimbursement **-abschluß** *m* annual balance of account, annual statement or balance sheet **-ausgaben** *pl* annual costs **-erzeugung** *f* annual output **-gang** *m* annual progress
Jahresgebühr *f* annual subscription rate, annual fee or tax **~ für einen Fernsprechanschluß** subscriber's annual rental **~ für Zusatzeinrichtungen** subscriber's annual rental for supplementary apparatus
Jahres-mittel der Temperatur mean annual temperature **-ring** *m* annual ring, timber ring **-tonne** *f* metric ton per year **-zeit** *f* season **-zeitliche Änderungen** seasonal variations
Jahr-gang *m* year, period, class (educ.), annual publication **-gebühr** *f* annual rate or subscription **-hundert** *n* century
jährlich yearly, annual **-e Schwankungen** seasonal variations, annual variations
Jakobsleiter *f* Jacob's ladder
Jalousie *f* louver, shutter, Venetian blind **-bretter** *pl* louver boards **-laden** *f pl* louver boards **-schütz** *n* Venetian-blind-type shutter, sluice or valve with shutters
Ja-Nein-Steuerung *f* on-off-course-indication control
Japanlack *m* Japan lacquer, Japan varnish **mit ~ überzogen** japanned
Japan-papier *n* Japanese paper **-wachs** *n* Japan wax
jarowisieren to vernalize
Jaspis *m* jasper **~ mit roten Flecken** bloodstone
JEDOCH NICHT- EXCEPT- **JEDOCH NICHT-Schaltung** *f* EXCEPT-gate, INHIBITORY-gate, AND-NOT-gate
Jenaer Glas *n* Jena glass
Jennyspinnmaschine *f* spinning jenny
Jernkontor *n* (Swedish) Ironmasters' Association
Jet *m* jet
Jigger *m* jigger
Joch *n* pile bents, yoke, bay, crossbar, magnet yoke, return pole piece (of a relay), barring, wallpiece **-brücke** *f* pile bridge
Joche *pl* shaft timbers, yokes
Joch-feld *f* bay, panel **-holz** *n* wall plate **-kern** *m* yoke core **-leiste** *f* face **-pfahl** *m* trestle upright

Jod *n* iodine **-ammon** *n* ammonium iodide

Jodat *n* iodate

Jod-äthyl *n* ethyl iodide **-benzol** *n* iodobenzene **-blei** *n* lead iodide **-chlorid** *n* iodine chloride, iodine trichloride **-chlorür** *n* iodine monochloride **-haltig** iodiferous

Jodid *n* iodide

Jodieren *n* iodizing (of a negative)

Jod-kali *n* potassium iodide **-kalium** *n* potassium iodide **-kaliumpapier** *n* chemical test paper impregnated with potassium iodide **-natrium** *n* **-natron** *n* sodium iodide

Jodoform *n* iodoform

jodometrisch iodometric

Jod-pentoxyd *n* iodine pentoxide **-probe** *f* iodine test **-propionsäure** *f* iodopropionic acid **-quecksilberoxyd** *n* mercuric iodide **-quecksilberoxydul** *n* mercurous iodide **-salz** *n* iodide **-säure** *f* iodic acid **-säureanhydrid** *n* iodic anhydride

jod-saures Kali potassium iodate **-saures Salz** iodate

Jod-silber *n* iodyrite **-tinktur** *f* tincture of iodine **-wasserstoffbildung** *f* hydrogen iodide formation **-wasserstoffzersetzung** *f* hydrogen iodide decomposition **-zahl** *f* iodine number **-zinnober** *m* red mercuric iodide

Johannit *m* gilpinite

Joosten(-sche) Verfahren a chemical method of soil consolidation

Joule *n* joule **-effekt** *m* (Stromwärme) joulean effect **-sches Gesetz** Joule's law **-scher Verlust** ohmic loss **-sche Wärme** joulean heat, Joule's law effect **-scher Wärmeverlust** resistance loss, ohmic loss, Joule's heat loss **-zähler** *m* Joulemeter

J-Schirm *m* J scope

Juckstoff *m* urticant nettle agent

Jugendschorf *m* scab on young plants

jung young **-e geringwertige Braunkohle** poor lignite of recent growth **-er Brennstoff** fuel of recent geological formation **-e Kohlenvorkommen** coal supplies of recent formation

Jungfer *f* deadeye

jungfräulich-e Kurve hysteresis curve, virgin curve **-e Neutronen** virgin neutrons **-er Neutronenfluß** virgin neutron flux **-er Zustand** neutral state

Junkerskalorimeter *n* continuous-flow calorimeter

Jura-formation *f* oölitic period **-kalk** *m* Jurassic limestone

jurassisch Jurassic

juristische Person body corporate, corporation

justierbar adjustable

Justiereinrichtung *f* adjusting device

justieren to adjust, set sights

Justier-gerät *n* artificial target for calibration, bore sight **-greifer** *m* pilot claw (motion pictures) **-marke** *f* adjustment mark, test mark **-maß** *n* brazen dish **-potentiometer** *n* adjusting (setting) control **-schraube** *f* setscrew, adjusting or adjustment screw **-stand** *m* adjusting bench **-stift** *m* adjustment pin, pilot pin, registration (film print.)

Justierung *f* adjustment, setting

Justiervorrichtung *f* adjusting device

Jute *f* jute **mit ~ umwickelt** jute-served **mit Tannin getränkte ~** tanned jute

Jute-beilauf *m* jute filler (cable making) **-faser** *f* jute fiber **-garn** *n* jute yarn **-packung** *f* jute packing **-pappe** *f* jute board **-sack** *m* canvas bag, jute bag **-spinnerei** *f* jute mill **-umwicklung** *f* jute serving, jute covering **-wicklung** *f* wrapping of jute

Jütte *f* davit

Juwel *n* jewel

K

KA *n* (Knotenpunkt) main office

kabbelig choppy (sea)

Kabbelsee *f* chopping, cockling, or rippling sea

Kabbelung *f* chopping, ripple

Kabel *n* cable, lead wire, rope **~ mit geringer Adernzahl** small-capacity or small-sized cable **~ mit verschiedenen Aderstärken** composite cable **~ mit Belastung der Stamm- und Viererleitungen** composite-loaded cable **~ mit Bleimantel** lead-covered cable **~ mit erhöhter Induktivität** loaded cable **~ mit abgeschirmten Leitern** screened-conductor cable **~ mit induktionsgeschützten Leitungen** cable protected against interference **~ mit Linksdrall** left regular lay cable

Kabel, ~ mit Luftraumisolierung dry-core cable **~ (-seile) für elektrisches Schürfen** cable for electrical surveys **~ mit Umklöppelung** braid-covered cable **~ mit enger Umwicklung** tight-core cable **~ mit vier Vierern** four-quad cable **~ mit Viererseilen** quadded cable **~ mit Viererverseilung** phantom cable, duplex cable **ein ~ abrollen** to pay out a cable **ein ~ anlanden** to land a cable

Kabel, ein ~ aufnehmen to take up or pick up a cable **ein ~ aufspleißen** to fan out a cable **ein ~ ausformen** to form out a cable **ein ~ auslegen** to lay a cable **ein ~ einziehen** to draw in a cable **ein ~ herausziehen** to remove a cable **ein ~ legen** to lay a cable **ein ~ schneiden** to cut a cable **ein ~ verlegen** to relay, shift, or transfer a cable

Kabel, Ausgießen der ~ filling up cables (elec.) **achterverseiltes ~** quadruple-pair cable **belastetes ~** loaded cable **blankes ~** bare cable **dickdrähtiges ~** heavy-gauge wire cable **doppeladriges ~** twin or bifilar cable **dreiadriges ~** triple-core cable **dünndrähtiges ~** small-gauge wire cable **einadriges ~** single-core(d) cable

Kabel, fest verseiltes ~ tight cable **gemischtpaariges ~** composite cable **geschütztes ~** armored cable **getränktes ~, imprägniertes ~** impregnated cable **induktionsfreies ~** anti-induction cable, screened-conductor cable

isoliertes ~ insulated wire **koaxiales** ~, **konzentrisches** ~ coaxial or concentric cable, pipe line **künstliches** ~ artifical cable **künstliches** ~ (aus reinen Widerständen gebildet) nonreactive artificial cable

Kabel, lose verseiltes ~ loose cable **mehradriges** ~ multiwire cable **metallumsponnenes** ~ metal-braided cable **oberirdisches** ~ overland cable **punktförmig belastetes** ~ lump-loaded cable **stetig belastetes** ~ continuously loaded cable **umklöppeltes** ~, braided cable **unterseeisches** ~ submarine cable

Kabel, verseiltes ~ twisted cable **versenktes** ~ underground or buried cable **vieladriges** ~ multiple (-conductor) cable, multicore cable **vielpaariges** ~ multipair cable, multiple twin cable **vieradriges** ~ four-wire cable **vierer-pupinisiertes** ~ composite loaded cable **vierer-verseiltes** ~ duplex (telephone) cable, phantom cable, quadded cable, multiple twin cable **zweiadriges** ~ two-wire-core or twin-core cable, bifilar cable **zweipaariges** ~ two-pair-core cable

Kabel-abgang *m* cable departure, cable tap outgoing cable **-abgleichkasten** *m* cable-tuning unit (radar) **-abschluß** *m* cable terminal or termination

Kabelabzweig *m* cable joint or tap **-kasten** *m* cable joint box **-muffe** *f* cable-distribution plug **-punkt** *m* underground cable-distributing point

Kabelader *f* cable conductor or wire, core, cable line or strand **-ausgleich** *m* cable balancing **-netz** *n* cable plant without distribution boxes

Kabel-adernpaar *n* cable pair **-alphabet** *n* cable Morse code **-anlage** *f* cable plant or system **-anpaßgerät** *n* cable matching gear (radar) **-anschluß** *m* cable connection **-anschlußgestell** *n* cable terminal rack **-anschlußstück** *n* cable connector, cable terminal, clamp lug terminal, terminal connector

Kabelaring *f* messenger cable

Kabelarschäkel *m* iron nipper

Kabel-aufbau *m* cable make-up **-aufführung** *f* cable-distribution point (junction between cable system and overhead wires) **-aufführungspunkt** *m* point where overhead line is connected to underground cable, wire lead-in point **-aufhänger** *m* cable bearer or hanger **-aufhängung** *f* cable suspension **-aufnahme** *f* removal of a cable **-ausgleich** *m* cable balancing **-ausgleichsverfahren** *n* cable-balancing method **-ausgußmasse** *f* cable compound **-auskundung** *f* survey of cable route

Kabel-auslastung *f* cable fill **-auslegemaschine** *f* cable-paying-out machine **-auslegung** *f* laying of cable **-bagger** *m* cable dredger **-bahn** *f* cable railway **-bake** *f* cable beacon **-baum** *m* laced wiring harness (in communications equipment) **-bautrupp** *m* cable-laying detachment **-besetzungsbuch** *n* cable-assignment record **-bewehrungsmaschine** *f* cable-armoring machine **-boje** *f* cable buoy **-brett** *n* cable shelf **-brief** *m* cable letter, telegram **-bruch** *m* cable break or failure

Kabelbrunnen *m* (cable) manhole or pit, joint box, jointing chamber **kleiner** ~ cable jointing chamber, flush box

Kabelbuchstabe *m* (bei dem positive und negative Stromstöße abwechseln) cross letter

Kabel-dampfer *m* cable steamer **-dämpfung** *f* cable attenuation

Kabeldichtigkeitsprüfung mittels Druckluft cable test with compressed air

Kabel-draht *m* cable wire **-durchlaß** *m* cable passage **-einführung** *f* cable inlet or socket **-einführungshals** *m* cable gland **-einziehgerät** *n* cable drawing-in implement **-einziehkasten** *m* cable drawing-in box **-einziehstrumpf** *m* cable grip **-einziehwinden** *pl* cable laying winches **-endgestell** *n* cable-support rack **-endmuffe** *f* pothead terminal

Kabelendverschluß *m* terminal box, boxhead, cable terminal, cable head ~ **für Innenleitung** indoor-cable terminator

Kabelendverzweiger *m* cable-distribution head, cable terminal

Kabel-fassung *f* conductor fitting **-fehler** *m* cable fault **-fernräumgerät** *n* towed sweep

Kabelform *f* cable form **-brett** *n* lacing or forming board

Kabelformstück *n* multiple-way duct ~ **aus Zement** cement duct

Kabel-führung *f* running of cable(s) **-führungsrohr** *n* wire manifold **-führungsrolle** *f* roller **-füllgarn** *n* cable filling yarn **-garn** *n* rope yarn, (slang) bully beef **-garnituren** *pl* cable fittings **-garnsteg** *m* rope-yarn knot **-garnstropp** *m* selvagee **-gatt** *n* cable stage **-gerüst** *n* cable rack **-gerüsttrupp** *m* cable-scaffolding detachment

Kabelgeschirr *n* wire manifold, harness ~ **für Störabschirmung** screening harness

Kabel-gesellschaft *f* cable company **-gestell** *n* cable rack or shelf **-gleitfett** *n* cable grease

Kabelgraben *m* trench ditch, cable trench, wire trench **einen** ~ **herstellen** to trench

Kabel-gruppe *f* cable assembly, harness **-halter** *m* cable clamps, lug, hanger or bearer, acorn (naut.) **-halterung** *f* (Stufenschalter) cable mounting (step switch) **-halteschelle** *f* retaining strap **-haltewinkel** *m* retaining angle strap **-haspel** *m* cable reel or drum **-haus** *n* cable house **-häuschen** *n* cable hut **-herstellung** *f* wire-rope and cable manufacture **-hochbahnkran** *m* elevated-cableway crane **-hochführung** *f* cable lifting **-hochführungsschacht** *m* cable shaft **-hülle** *f* cable covering **-hütte** *f* cable hut **-innenleiter** *m* cable-core conductor

Kabelkanal *m* cable conduit or duct, cableway, electrical subway, gate chain gallery, troughing ~ **mit mehreren Einzelrohrzügen** multiple-duct conduit

Kabelkanalführung *f* duct route

Kabelkarren *m* wire cart

Kabelkasten *m* junction box, cable trough ~ **an Brücken oder in Tunneln** cable trough for bridges or tunnels

Kabel-keller *m* underground distribution chamber, cable cellar **-kern** *m* cable core **-kette** *f* chain cable **-klammer** *f* cable clip **-klemme** *f* cable clamp, binding screw **-klemmkasten** *m* cable-terminal box **-klemmschraube** *f* cable-terminal screw **-kraftwinde** *f* motor winch for cable **-kran** *m* wire-rope cableway, cable crane **-kreis** *m* cable circuit

Kabel-lader *m* conductor or wire of a cable **-lageplan** *m* plan of cable layout **-lampe** *f*

-lageplan *m* plan of cable layout **-lampe** *f* magazine hand lamp **-länge** *f* cable's length (600 feet) **-längenmesser** *m* apparatus for automatic measurement of cable lengths **-legung** *f* laying of a cable **-leitung** *f* cable line (elec.), cable conductor, wire line **-linie** *f* cable line **-liste** *f* cable-circuit diagram

Kabel-litze *f* cable strand **-lose** *f* cable slack **-lötbrunnen** *m* cable-joint box, jointing chamber **-löter** *m* (cable) jointer, splicer, cable solderer **-lötstelle** *f* cable joint **-löttrupp** *m* cable-jointing detachment **-lötung** *f* cable jointing **-mantel** *m* cable sheathing **-mantelkorrosion** *f* corrosion of the lead sheating

Kabelmaschine *f* cable-making machine **mehrspulige ~** multiheaded cable machine

Kabel-merkstein *m* cable marker **-messer** *n* chapping knife, electrician's knife **-meßgerät** *n* cable-testing instrument **-meßkarren** *m* cable-testing car

Kabelmuffe *f* cable sleeve, joint box, splice box, cable-terminal box **ausgegossene ~** filled joint

Kabelmuffenverzweigung *f* multiple joint

kabeln to cable

Kabel-nachbildung *f* cable-balancing network **-nachziehschlauch** *m* double-eye cable

Kabelnetz *n* cable system or plant, cable network **~ mit Ortsverbindungsleitungen** inter-office-trunk-cable plant

Kabel-öl *n* cable oil **-öse** *f* cable eye, cable terminal **-pfandgesetz** *n* cables mortgaging act **-plan** *m* cable layout **-planung** *f* cable project **-prüfeinrichtung** *f* cable-testing equipment **-prüfmaschine** *f* cable-testing machine **-reparaturschiff** *n* cable-repair ship, restorer **-ring** *m* coil of cable **-rinne** *f* cable trough(ing), cable channel

Kabelrohr *n* cable manifold (for ignition wires) cable pipe, cable duct or conduit **-halter** *m* **-schelle** *f* cable-duct clip or holder **-strang** *m* cable duct or conduit

Kabelrost *m* cable shelf, rack, or vault, overhead tray

Kabelschacht *m* cable chute, manhole **~ für Fahrbahn** street manhole **~ für Gehbahn** sidewalk manhole

Kabel-scheibe *f* cable disk **-schiff** *m* cable ship **-schirmleitung** *f* cable shielding conduit **-schleife** *f* thimble **-schmiere** *f* cable compound **-schoner** *m* cable armoring, acorn (naut.) **-schrank** *m* cable turning or dummy section **-schrift** *f* cable code **-schritt** *m* cable lay

Kabelschuh *m* cable eye, (connector) lug, cable socket, thimble, cable clip, cable shoe, cable grip, cord terminal, loop-tip terminal **offener ~** spade terminal

Kabelschuhanschluß *m* cable terminal (lug)

Kabelschutz-bekleidung *f* protective covering of cables **-recht** *n* provisions concerning the protection of submarine cables **-rohr** *n* cable-protection pipe **-vertrag** *m* convention concerning the protection of cables

Kabel-seele *f* cable core, core conductor **-seil** *n* cable-laid rope, cable, cable core **-seite** *f* cable side **-sonde** *f* cable sounding **-sorte** *f* type or kind of wire **-spleißung** *f* cable joint or splice **-stecker** *m* wire plug **-stein** *m* cable tile

Kabel-strecke *f* length of cable **-stumpf** *m* stub cable, sealed cable end **-stütze** *f* cable bearer, cable bracket or support **-suchgerät** *n* cable detector **-tank** *m* cable tank **-taste** *f* cable key **-tau** *n* hawser **-tonne** *f* cable buoy **-trage** *f* cable carrier, reel

Kabel-träger *m* cable bearer, cable bracket or shelf, cable hook **-traggerüst** *n* cable rack or support **-tragringe** *m pl* cable rings for antenna, cable suspenders **-tragseil** *n* messenger-cable strand **-tränkkessel** *m* cable-impregnating tank **-trommel** *f* cable reel or drum **-trommelanhänger** *m* cable trailer (guided missiles) **-tülle** *f* cable bushing or sleeve **-tunnel** *m* (begehbar) gallery **-turm** *m* cable tower

Kabelüberführungs-endverschluß *m* **-kasten** *m* cable-distribution box **-säule** *f* cable-distribution pole

Kabel-überwachungsgerät *n* cable-control set **-umflechtmaschine** *f* cable-stranding machine **-umhüllung** *f* cable covering or sheathing **-umklöppelung** *f* cable braiding **-unterbrechung** *f* cable break or interruption **-unterstützung** *f* conduit support **-verbinder** *m* cable sleeve, connecting sleeve **-verbindung** *f* cable splice, lead (tape rec.)

Kabel-verbindungsmuffe *f* cable-connecting box **-vergußmasse** *f* sealing compound **-verlegung** *f* cable laying, burying of a cable **-verlegwagen** *m* cable reel car **-verschraubung** *f* screw-type conduit fitting **-verseilmaschine** *f* cable-stranding machine **-verstärker** *m* cable amplifier, repeater **-verteiler** *m* cable-distributing box, cable-junction box **-verteilerschrank** *m* cable distributing cabinet

Kabelverteilungssystem *n* cable-distributing system **offenes ~** tapering cable-distributing

Kabel-verzweiger *m* cable-connection or -distribution box or case, cross-connecting terminal **-verzweigung** *f* cable branching **-verzweigungsmuffe** *f* cable-distribution plug **-wachs** *n* cable paraffin or wax, cable desiccant, adhesive pitch **-wagen** *m* cable-reel trailer, cable trolley **-weg** *m* cable run **-wellenwiderstand** *m* characteristic impedance

kabelweise geschlagenes Tau cable-laid rope

Kabel-werk *n* cable work(s) **-winde** *f* cable winch or elevator **-ziehschlauch** *m* split cable grip **-ziehstrumpf** *m* (mit zwei Schlaufen) double-eye cable **-zopf** *m* cable fan or form **-zug** *m* pull of the cable

Kabelzuschlag *m* slack (cable) **~** (Vorratslänge) in den Schächten lassen to leave cable slack in manholes

Kabelzwischenstück *n* intermediate cable

Kabine *f* cabin, passenger cabin, compartment, cockpit **~ mit Schalldämpfung** soundproofed cabin **unter Druck gesetzte ~ beim Höhenflug** pressure cabin

Kabinen-dach *n* cabin roof, hood **-fenster** *n* cabin window **-flugzeug** *n* cabin plane or cruiser **-haube** *f* canopy **-heizsprüher** *m* cabin-heating jet **-heizung** *f* cabin heating **-raum** *m* cabin (volume or room) **-tür** *f* cabin door **-wand** *f* cabin wall

Kablierung *f* cabling

K-Absorptionskante *f* K edge, K absorption limit

Kachel *f* tile, wall tile (isolating, protecting) **-aus-**

kleidung *f* tile jacket **-herd** *m* tile hearth

Kadaververwertungsanlage *f* carcass-utilization plant

Kaddigöl, Kadeöl *n* cade oil

Kader *m* staff (mil.), cadre

Kadmieren *n* cadmium plating

kadmiertes Eisen cadmiated iron

Kadming *n* cadmium

Kadmium *n* cadmium **-arsenit** *n* cadmium arsenite **-gelb** *n* yellow cadmium **-(oxyd)hydrat** *n* cadmium hydrate **-rhodanid** *n* cadmium sulfocyanate **-sammler** *m* cadmium storage cell **-überzug** *m* cadmium plating

Käfer *m* beetle, chafer

Kaff *n* chaff, rubbish

Kaffee *f* half of a boat (of pontoon), compartment, sponson

Käfig *m* cage, spacer, lantern (mach.) **-anker** *m* squirrel-cage rotor **-ankermotor** *m* squirrel-cage motor **-antenne** *f* cage antenna **-bauerzange** *f* grating nippers **-dipol** *m* cage dipole **-effekt** *m* cage effect **-förmig** cagelike **-gitter** *n* cage grid **-läufer** *m* cage rotor **-magnetron** *n* squirrel-cage magnetron **-spule** *f* canned or cage coil, shield coil **-transformer** *m* shielded transformer **-wickelung** *f* squirrel cage

kahl bare, bald, threadbare, barren

Kahlerit *m* kahlerite

Kahlschlag *m* clear felling **-fläche** *f* denuded area

Kahn *m* lighter, river boat, barge, rowboat, canoe, skiff, small boat **-fähre** *f* rowing, punt, or boat ferry **-fracht** *f* lighterage

Kai *m* quay, (shipping) pier, jetty, wharf **-einfassung** *f* quay wall or edge **-fläche** *f* covered quay **-gebühr** *f* wharfage **-kante** *f* arris **-mauer** *f* quay bulkhead, quay wall **-meister** *m* wharfinger **-planum** *n* surface of filling quay level, surface of esplanade (of a dock) **-schuppen** *m* quay shed

Kaisergelb *n* mineral yellow

Kajüte *f* cabin

Kajütentreppe *f* companionway

Kajütesonnensegel *n* side screen

Kakodylsäure *f* cacodylic acid

Kakoxen *n* cacoxenite

Kalamit *m* calamite

Kalander *m* glazing rollers, calender **-biegeapparat** *m* calender bending apparatus **-effekt** *m* calender grain **-fett** *n* calender grease **-führer** *m* calenderman

kalandern to calender

Kalander-reihe *f* calender train **-schaden** *m* calender spots **-walze** *f* bowl of the calender, calender roll **-walzenpapier** *n* bowl paper

kalandrieren to calender

Kalandrieren *n* calender run, calendering

Kälber *pl* whelps (mach.)

Kalblederpapier *n* calf paper

Kalbspergament *n* vellum

Kalcium (Kalzium) *n* calcium **wolframsaures ~** calcium tungstate

Kaledonit *n* caledonite

Kaleidophon *n* kaleidophon(e)

kaleidoskopisch kaleidoscopic

kalendarisch according to our calender

Kalender *m* almanac **-ersatzblock** *m* repalcement calendar block **-zeichen** *pl* astronomical signs

Kaleszenzpunkt *m* point of calescence or decalescence

Kalfater-floß *n, m* floating stage **-gasten** *pl* calker's crew **-hammer** *m* calking mallet

kalfatern to calk

Kalfaterung *f* calking **~ durch Schweißung** calk welding

Kali *n* potash, potassium hydroxide **kohlensaures ~** potassium carbonate **überchlorsaures ~** potassium perchlorate **übermangansaures ~** potassium permanganate **überschwefelsaures ~** potassium persulfate **zyansaures ~** potassium cyanate

Kalialaun *m* potassium aluminum sulfate

Kaliber *n* diameter of bore, caliber (of firearms), groove, pass (in rolling), gauge, jig **blindes ~** blind or false pass, inoperative pass **geschlossenes ~** box or closed pass, box groove **offenes ~** open pass or groove **totes ~** inoperative or dummy pass

Kaliber-anzug *m* taper of groove **-begrenzung** *f* boundary or limitation of groove **-bohrer** *m* finishing or polishing bit, polisher **-bolzen** *m* plug gauge, gauge pin **-breite** *f* width of grovve **-breitung** *f* spreading of groove **-dorn** *m* cylindrical plug gauge **-einheit** *f* unit of caliber **-fertigwalze** *f* grooved finishing roll **-fläche** *f* cross-sectional area **-folge** *f* succession of passes **-form** *f* contour or form of groove, design of pass

Kalibergwerk *n* potash mine

kaliberhaltig true to gauge

Kaliber-konstruktion *f* design of grooves or passes **-länge** *f* length of barrel expressed in calibers, caliber length **-lehre** *f* ring, shot, or shell gauge

Kaliberlinie *f* construction line or pitch line of groove **neutrale ~** center line or axis of groove

Kaliber-maß *n* **-messer** *m* caliber gauge **-maßstab** *m* ring-gauge **-öffnung** *f* clearance between collars, opening of groove **-rand** *m* collar, rolling edge (on rolled material) **-ring** *m* ring gauge, bore gauge, breech bore gauge, gauge for base **-röhre** *f* groove **-schablone** *f* pass template **-schablonenzeichnung** *f* pass-template drawing

Kaliber-streckgerüst *n* (testing) strand **-streckwalze** *f* stranding roll **-teil** *m* section of groove **-tiefe** *f* depth of groove **-walze** *f* grooved roll **-walzwerk** *n* mill for rolling shapes **-zirkel** *m* calipers **-zylinder** *m* bore gauge, breech bore gauge, cylinder gauge

Kalibreur *m* roll designer

kalibrieren to calibrate, groove (of rollers), gauge

Kalibrieren *n* roll designing

Kalibrier-hülse *f* burnishing shell **-pipette** *f* calibrating pipette **-presse** *f* sizing or coining-press

kalibriert calibrated **-er Metallpeilstab** graduated metal gauge rod **-er Schleifdraht** graduated slide-wire **-e Skala** graduated scale **-e Walze** grooved roller

Kalibriertaster *m* caliper-compresses, calipers

Kalibrierung *f* roll designing, groove designing, calibration

Kalibrierungs-block *m* gauging block **-zeichnung** *f* pass-template drawing

Kalibrier-walze *f* calibrating roll **-werkzeug** *n* calibrating tool **-zahn einer Räumnadel** sizing tooth of a broach

kalibrig calibered

Kali-dünger *m* potash fertilizer **-düngesalz** *n* potash fertilizer salt **-eisenalaun** *m* potash iron alum **-form** *f* potash mold

Kalifornium *n* californium

kali-frei potash-free **-glimmer** *m* muscovite, potash mica **-haltig** potassic **-hydrat** *n* potassium hydroxide

Kaliko *m* cloth, calico

Kali-lauge *f* potash lye, potassium hydroxide **-lösung** *f* potash solution **-patrone** *f* potash case (mask), potassium catridge **-rohsalz** *n* crude potassium salt **-salpeter** *m* potassium nitrate, saltpeter **-salzlager** *n* deposit or bed of potash salts **-schmelze** *f* potash melt, potash fusion **-seife** *f* green soap **-tonerde** *f* aluminate of potash

Kalium *n* potassium **vanadinsaures ~** potassium vanadate **xanthogensaures ~** potassium xanthogenate

Kalium-alaun *m* **aluminiumsulfat** *n* potassium aluminum sulfate, potash alum **-antimonyltartrat** *n* tartar emetic **-behälter** *m* potassium container **-bifluorid** *n* potassium bifluoride **-bioxalat** *n* acid oxalate of potassium **-boratglas** *n* potassium borate glass **-brechweinstein** *m* tartar emetic **-dichromat** *n* bichromate of potash

Kalium-eisenalaun *m* potassium ferrisulfate **-eisenzyanid** *n* potassium ferricyanide **-eisenzyanür** *n* potassium ferrocyanide **-ferrat** *n* ferrate of potash **-ferrisulfat** *n* potassium ferrisulfate, ferric potassium sulfate **-formiat** *n* potassium formate

Kalium-goldbromür *n* potassium aurobromide **-goldchlorid** *n* potassium aurichloride **-goldzyanür** *n* potassium aurocyanide **-hydrat** *n* potassium hydroxide **-hydroxyd** *n* potassium hydroxide, caustic potash **-iridiumchlorid** *n* potassium iridichloride **-karbonat** *n* potash **metabisulfat** *n* potassium meta sulfate **-metabisulfit** *n* potassium metabisulfite **natriumkarbonat** *n* potassium sodium carbonate **-natriumtartrat** *n* potassium sodium tartrate, Rochelle salt **-niobat** *n* potassium niobate

Kalium-oxyhydrat *n* hydroxide of potash **-perchlorat** *n* potassium perchlorate **-permanganat** *n* potassium permanganate **-platinchlorid** *n* potassium platinichloride, potassium chlorplatinate **-platinchlorür** *n* potassium platinochloride **-platinzyanür** *n* potassium platinocyanide **-rhodanat** *n* **-rhodanid** *n* potassium thiocyanate or sulfocyanate **-salz** *n* potash salt **-sulfozyanid** *n* potassium sulfocyanide (sulfocyanate) **-wolframat** *n* potassium tungstate **-zelle** *f* potassium cell

Kaliwasserglas *n* potash water glass, potassium silicate

Kalk *m* lime **~ totbrennen** to overburn lime **~ verlöschen** to kill lime **abgestandener ~ abgestorbener ~** lime slaked in air, dead lime **ätzender ~ gebrannter ~** caustic lime, quicklime, calcium oxide **gelöschter ~** slaked lime, hydrated lime, calcium hydroxide **ungelöschter ~** quicklime, unslaked lime **unterchlorigsaurer ~** calcium hypochlorite **verwitterter ~** lime slaked in air, dead lime

Kalk-ablagerung *f* calcareous deposit **-abscheidung** *f* lime scum **-alkalität** *f* lime alkalinity **-artig** calcareous, limy **-äscher** *m* lime pit **-bedarf** *m* lime requirement **-blau** *n* blue verditer of ashes **-borat** *n* calcium borate **-brecher** *m* limestone breaker **-brei** *m* lime paste

Kalk-brennanlage *f* lime plant **-brennen** *n* lime burning **-brennofen** *m* lime-burning kiln, lime kiln **-bruch** *m* limestone quarry **-dinas** *m* ganister **-dinasstein** *m* ganister brick **-echtheit** *f* fastness to lime **-eisensilikat** *n* andradite **-elend** *n* lime set (of blast furnaces)

kalken to lime, lime-coat, temper

Kalk-erde *f* calcareous earth, calcium oxide **-erz** *n* lime ore **-farbe** *f* whitewash, lime wash **-feldspat** *m* anorthite **-fett** *n* lime-base grease **-frei** free from lime **-grieß** *m* milk-of-lime grit **-grube** *f* lime pit **-hacke** *f* lime beater **-haken** *m* lime rake **-haltig** limy, calcareous, containing lime **-hydrat** *n* calcium hydroxide

kalkig limy, calcareous

kalkieren to trace

Kalk-katze *f* limestone-handling crane **-kern** *m* overburned particle of limestone **-kies** *m* calcareous gravel **-krücke** *f* lime rake of beater **-krumpe** *f* overburned particle of limestone, grain in the mortar **-krumpenstrich** *m* floor of lime grains **-lager** *n* lime store **-loch** *n* lime pit or basin **-löschung** *f* lime slaking **-mergel** *m* calcareous clay, lime marl **-messer** *m* calcimeter

Kalkmilch *f* lime milk, whitewash, lime solution **-grießabscheider** *m* milk-of-lime-grit separator **-probe zur Rissepriifung** chalk test for cracks

Kalk-mörtel *m* lime mortar **-ofen** *m* lime kiln **-ofengas** *n* lime-kiln gas **-pulver** *n* lime powder **-rutsche** *f* mortar funnel **-salpeter** *m* calcium nitrate **-sandstein** *m* sand-lime brick, lime sandstone **-sandziegel** *m* lime-loam brick **-schachtofen** *m* vertical lime kiln **-schieferbruch** *m* calcareous-shale quarry **-schlacke** *f* lime slag

Kalk-schlamm *m* slaked lime **-schleier** *m* chalk fog **-schotter** *m* crushed limestone **-silikat** *n* lime silica **-silikatgesteine** *pl* calc-silicate rocks **-silo** *m* limestone bin **-spat** *m* calc-spar, calcite **-spatinterferometer** *m* calcite interferometer **-sprenger** *m* limer **-staub** *m* lime dust **-stechmaschine für Wiesenkalk** lime-cutting machine for chalky soil

Kalkstein *m* calcite, limestone **totgebrannter ~** dead-burnt limestone

Kalkstein-grube *f* limestone pit **-niere** *f* spheroidal concretion of marl, cement stone **-schotter** *m* crushed limestone **-verarbeitung** *f* limestone processing **-zuschlag** *m* limestone addition

Kalk-stickstoff *m* calcium cyanamide **-streuer** *m* lime sower or spreader **-sulfat** *n* sulfate of lime, calcium sulfate **-tiegel** *m* lime crucible **-tuff** *m* tufaceous limestone **-tünche** *f* whitewash, whiting, lime milk **-überschuß** *m* surplus of lime, excess of lime

Kalkül *n* calculus

Kalkulagraph *m* calculagraph

Kalkulation *f* calculation, estimate

Kalkulator *m* computer **~** (Refa-Ingenieur)

time study man
kalkulieren to calculate, compute
kalkulierte Analyse calculated analysis
Kalk-uranglimmer *m* lime uranite autunite **-verseiftes Fett** lime-base grease **-wasser** *n* limewater **-ziegel** *m* limestone brick **-zuschlag** *m* addition of limestone or of lime
Kalligraphie *f* calligraphy
Kallitypie *f* callitype, callityping
kallös callous
Kalmen *pl* calming (of sea), doldrums, area of calms **-gürtel** *m* intertropical front, doldrums, calm belt or zone **-zone** *f* calm zone, doldrums
kalmieren to quiet
Kalmusöl *n* calamus oil
Kalomel *n* calomel, mercurous chloride
Kaloreszenz *f* calorescence
Kalorie *f* calorie, thermal unit **große ~** kilogram-calorie, large or great calorie **kleine ~** gram-calorie, small calorie
Kalorifer *m* radiator
Kaloriferendarre *f* heating-pipe system, kiln
Kalorimeter *n* calorimeter
kalorimetrisch calorimetric(al) **-e Bombe** calorimetric bomb, bomb calorimeter
Kalorisation *f* calorizing
kalorisch thermal, caloric, calorific **-e Maschine** hot-air engine
kalorisieren to calorize
Kalorisieren *n* **Kalorisierung** *f* calorizing
Kaloriskop *n* caloriscope
Kalotte *f* cup, calotte, spherical indentation, capshaped or hemispherical object
Kalotten-bogen *m* sector arc **-fläche** *f* area of ball imprint or indentation **-förmige Einsenkung** spherical indentation **-geriffelt** cup-fluted **-membran** *f* hemispheric or cap-shaped diaphragm **-oberfläche** *f* area of cup, surface of spherical indentation **-verbindung** *f* (für Schüttelrutschen) captype joint
kalt cool, cold, frigid **~ abbindend** cold-setting **~ anstauchen** to cold-upset **~ erblasen** to blow cold, coldblast **~ gehen** to become cold, work cold (blast furnace) **~ geschmiedet** cold-drawn **~ gewalzt** cold-rolled **~ gezogen** cold-drawn **~ sägen** to cold-saw **~ verformbar** workable in cold state **~ vorgeschiedener Saft** cold-predefecated juice
kalt-es Ende bottom end (of el. component in circuit) **-er Farbton** cold color hue **-e Kathode** cold cathode **-es Löten** cold joint (soldering defect) **-e Lötstelle** dry joint **-e Röhre** idle tube (radio) **-e Verformung** cold working
Kalt-absetzen *n* cold settling **-aushärtung** *f* cold aging, cold age-hardening, cold tempering
Kaltband *n* cold rolled strip **-reversierstraße** *f* reversing cold mill
Kalt-beanspruchung *f* cold straining or working **-bearbeitung** *f* cold working **-biegen** *n* cold bending **-biegeprobe** *f* cold-bending test **-biegeversuch** *m* cold-bend test **-biegung** *f* cold bend, cold bending **-bildsamkeit** *f* ductility, malleability
Kalt-blasen *n* cold blowing, steaming **-blaseperiode** *f* cooling-down period, steaming period **-bläsig** refractory (metal) **-bruch** *m* cold-shortness **-brüchig** cold-short **-brüchigkeit** *f* cold-shortness **-bruchprobe** *f* cold shortness test **-drücken** *n* cold pressing, cold compressing
Kälte *f* frost, cold, coldness **-anlage** *f* refrigeration plant **-ausbeute** *f* refrigerating effect **-behandlung** *f* cold treatment
kältebeständig nonfreezing, antifreezing, cold resisting **-es Gemisch** antifreezing mixture
Kälte-beständigkeit *f* antifreezing quality, resistance to cold **-biegeschlagfestigkeit** *f* bending brittle point **-chemie** *f* cryochemistry **-diagramm** *n* psychrometric chart **-einbruch** *m* cold air intrusion **-einfluß** *m* influence of cold **-einheit** *f* frigorific unit **-erzeugend** cryogenic, frigorific
Kälteerzeuger *m* refrigerator **-erzeugung** *f* refrigeration **-erzeugungsmaschine** *f* refrigerator
kälte-fest cold-resisting **-festigkeit** *f* strength at low temperatures **-flexibel** flexible at low temperatures **-gebläse** *n* cold blast **-gemisch** *n* freezing mixture **-grad** *m* degree below zero (centigrade), degree of coldness
Kalteinbau *m* cold application (in road construction) **-belag** *m* cold-mix surfacings of roads
Kälte-lagerraum *m* chillroom **-leistung** *f* refrigerating capacity **-maschine** *f* refrigerating machine, refrigerator **-mischung** *f* **-mittel** *n* freezing mixture **-mittelkreislauf** *m* refrigeration cycle
kälten to chill, refrigerate
Kälte-probe *f* cold test **-punkt** *m* freezing point, solidifying point (of oil)
kalterblasen cold-blast **-es Roheisen** cold-blast pig iron
Kälte-regler *m* cryostat **-reinigungsskala** *f* low-temperature purification plant **-rückfall** *m* return of cold weather, recurrent cold snap **-schließfach** *n* frozen food locker
Kälteschutz-brille *f* frost goggles **-isolierung** *f* insulation or insulator for cold **-mittel** *n* cold protective
Kälte-speicher *m* cold storage **-technik** *f* crygenics, refrigeration **-thermometer** *n* cold-test thermometer **-träger** *m* cooling agent **-verhalten** *n* low temperature behavior **-welle** *f* cold wave
Kalt-fahren des Motors cold-operation of the engine **-festigkeit** *f* strength at low temperatures **-fließpressen** *n* cold impact (press) forming **-fließverhalten** *n* cold flow property **-front** *f* cold front
kalt-geben to slacken the fire **-gebläseofen** *m* cold-blast furnace **-geformt** cold coiled **-gereckt** cold-worked, self-hooped **-gesenkdrückmaschine** *f* cold-swaging machine **-gewalzt** cold-rolled **-gewindewalze** *f* cold-thread-rolling machine **-gezogen** cold-drawn **-gießen** to cold-cast **-guß** *m* spoiled casting **-hämmerbar** malleable when cold **-hämmerbarkeit** *f* malleability when cold **-hämmern** to cold-hammer, cold-forge
Kalt-härtbarkeit *f* strain hardenability **-härte** *f* strain or wear hardness **-härten** to strain-harden **-härtend** cold-setting **-härtung** *f* cold straining **-haus** *n* cold greenhouse **-kathode** cold cathode, dull emitter **-kathodenröhre** *f* cold cathode valve **-kauter** *m* cold cautery **-klebekitt** *m* cold adhesive putty for attaching demolition charges **-kleber** *m* cold-setting adhesive
Kalt-lack *m* cold varnish **-legen** to stop, blow

out (furnace) **-leim** *m* wood cement, cold glue, cold-setting adhesive **-liegen** to be out of operation **-liegendes Fallrohr** unheated downcomer **-löseverfahren** *n* cold dissolving process **-lötstelle** *f* cold junction, cold end

Kaltluft *f* cold air **-front** *f* cold front **-gas** carbureted water gas **-kern** *m* cold-air center

Kalt-matrize *f* cold die, cold-die block **-meißel** *m* cold chisel **-milch** *f* chilled milk **-nachpressen** *n* cold pressing or finishing **-nadelradierer** *m* dry point engraver **-nietung** *f* cold riveting **-pressen** to cold-press **-pressen** *n* cold pressing **-preßmuttereisen** *n* cold stamping nut bars **-preßverfahren** *n* cold-press method

Kalt-recken *n* cold work, cold drawing, autofrettage, cold-working process **-reckung** *f* cold straining **-richten** *n* cold straightening or dressing **-rissigkeit** *f* cold-shortness **-rühren** to stir when cold **-säge** *f* cold saw **-satz** *m* cold composition **-schlag** *m* cold-heading die **-schlagen** *n* (eines Schraubenkopfes), cold-heading

Kaltschlag-matrize *f* cold-heading die **-werkzeug** *n* cold-heading tool **-werkzeugstähle** *pl* cold upsetting steels

Kalt-schliff *m* cold-ground (pulp) **-schmiedbarkeit** *f* malleability when cold **-schmieden** *n* cold-hammering, hammer-hardening **-schrottmeißel** *m* cold chisel **-schüren** *n* a cooling period (to permit glass to obtain a proper working temperature) **-schweiße** *f* **-schweißstelle** *f* cold shut, cold shot, flaw, crack, lap **-schweißung** *f* cold welding, welding without preheating

Kalt-spiel *n* cold clearance **-spritzen** *n* impact extrusion **-sprödigkeit** *f* cold-shortness, cold-brittleness **-startgerät** *n* cold starting unit **-stauchmatrize** *f* cold upsetting die **-stauchpresse** *f* cold-heading press **-strangpreßvorgang** *m* cold extrusion process **-strecken** to cold-work, cold strain **-strecken** *n* cold working, cold straining **-verarbeitung** *f* cold working **-verarbeitungsfähigkeit** *f* cold workability

Kalt-verbindung *f* cold junction, cold end **-verfestigung** *f* strain-hardening, cloud-burst hardening, cold work-hardening **-verfestigungsgrenze** *f* limit of endurance, limit of strain-hardening, limit of work-hardening **-verformbarkeit** *f* malleability, cold-forming property **-verformen** to cold-work, cold-form **-verformt** cold-worked, cold-formed

Kaltverformung *f* cold working, cold forming, cold deformation, plastic cold working, cold shaping **Empfindlichkeit gegen ~** cold-work sensitivity

kalt-vergießen to cast or pour cold **-vergossen** cold-cast **-vergütung** *f* aging (at ordinary temperature) **-verstreckt** cold-worked **-vorstauchmaschine** *f* cold upsetting machine **-vulkanisation** *f* cold cure, cold curing, acid cure **-walzbarkeit** *f* cold-rolling property **-walze** *f* roll for cold-rolling metals **-walzen** to cold-roll **-walzen** *n* cold rolling

Kalt-walzerei *f* cold-rolling mill, cold-rolling practice **-walzwerk** *n* cold reduction mill, cold rolling mill, cold strip mill **-wind** *m* cold-air blast, cold blast **-windeingang** *m* cold-blast inlet **-windleitung** *f* cold-blast main **-windschieber** *m* cold-blast sliding valve **-ziehbank** *f* cold-drawing bench **-ziehen** to cold-draw **-ziehmatrize** *f* cold-drawing die **-zug** *m* cold drawing

kalzinieren to calcine

Kalzinierofen *m* calcining kiln or furnace

kalzinierte Soda anhydrous sodium carbonate, soda ash

Kalzit *m* calcite

Kalzium *n* calcium **-antimonphosphat** *n* calcium antimony phosphate **-chlorid** *n* calcium chloride **-glyzerinphosphat** *n* calcium glycerophosphate **-haltig** calcic **-hydroxyd** *n* calcium hydroxide, calcium hydrate **-kaliumsulfat** *n* calcium potassium sulfate **-karbidschlacke** *f* calcium carbide slag

Kalzium-metall *n* metallic calcium **-natriumsulfat** *n* calcium sodium sulfate **-oxyd** *n* calcium oxide, lime **-phosphat** *n* calcium phosphate, phosphate of lime **-rhodanid** *n* calcium sulfocyanate **-samarskit** *m* calciosamarskite **-sulfhydrat** *n* calcium hydrosulfide **-thorit** *m* calciothorite **-wolframat** *n* calcium tungstate

Kamacit *m* kamacite

Kambrik *m* cotton cambric

Kamel *n* camel **-haarriemen** *m* camel's-hair belting

Kamera *f* camera **-aggregat** *m* camera chain **-auszug** *m* camera extension **-balgen** *m* camera bellows **-bühne** *f* stacker **-fahrgestell** *n* camera truck, dolly **-kontrollgerät** *n* preview monitor **-laufwerk** *n* feed mechanism **-mutterteil** *m* camera housing (aviat) **-neigung** *f* tilting **-schutzdeckel** *m* focal-plane guard (aviat) **-zug** *m* camera chain (TV)

Kamin *m* chimney, smokestack, fireplace, flue **-abzug** *m* chimney breeching **-einfassung** *f* **-gewände** *n* chimney jambs **-gitter** *n* fender **-haube** *f* chimney hood **-höhe** *f* stack height **-schieber** *m* slide valve for chimneys **-schnäpper** *m* chimney spring **-ventil** *n* chimney valve **-verlust** *m* stack loss **-ziegel** *m* crest tile **-zug** *m* chimney draft, stack draft

Kamm *m* comb, cam, cog, tooth, crest (of a wave), ridge ~ (am Lötösenstreifen) fanning strip **eiserner ~** iron jack ~ (von einer Furche) ridge

Kamm-bau *m* ridge cultivation **-blende** *f* wedge **-breite** *f* width of summit or top

kämmen to comb, mate (gears) ~ (von Zahnrädern) to mesh

Kämmen der Turbinendichtungen rubbing of labyrinth seals

Kammer *f* chamber, cabin, locker, room, compartment, regenerative chamber, checker chamber, camera, recess, clothing depot, stateroom, stockroom **handbediente ~** hand-operated camera **liegende ~** horizontal chamber

Kammer-bahn *f* bolt slide **-bau** *m* excavation **-bedienung** *f* handling of camera **-deich** *m* dike with chambers **-druckregler** *m* cabin-pressure regulator

Kämmerei *f* (wool) combing

Kammer-fang *m* machine-gun housing attachment, bolt catch **-fangstück** *n* bolt-catch piece

Kammerfilterpresse *f* chamber filter press **~ mit einfacher Auslaugung** chamber filter press without leaching with aeration

Kammer-füllung *f* checkerwork **-gericht** *n* supreme court (Prussia)

Kammergestell *n* camera mounting ~ **für den Einbau in das Flugzeug** aircraft-camera mounting ~ **für den festen Einbau** (in das Flugzeug) fixed (aircraft-)camera mounting ~ **für beweglichen Einbau** (in das Flugzeug) movable (aircraft-)camera mounting

Kammer-gewölbe *n* arch of a chamber **-griff** *m* bolt handle **-halter** *m* cell holder (optics) **-hülse** *f* central tube (shell), flash tube **-hülsenladung** *f* central-tube charge, flash-tube charge **-hülsenrohr** *n* burster tube (shell) **-knopf** *m* bolt knob **-körper** *m* chamber body (rocket)

Kammer-ladung *f* charge of a chamber **-loses Schaufelrad** cell-less bucket wheel **-mauer** *f* side wall of a lock **-mauerwerk** *n* checkerwork **-motoren** *pl* combustion chamber engines **-ofen** *m* chamber oven or furnace, chamber or compartment kiln, by-product oven (coking) **-rad** *n* cell-type bucket wheel **-ringofen** *m* round down-draft kiln **-säure** *f* (lead) chamber acid **-schießen** *n* chambering (explosives), layer blasts

Kammerschleuse *f* lock (with chamber) **doppelte** ~ lock with double opposed gates **einfache** ~ single lock

Kammer-sohle *f* oven floor **-stein** *m* checker firebrick, checker-brick **-stengel** *m* bolt handle **-tiefenmesser** *m* chamber depth micrometer **-ton** *m* A-tone of tuning fork **-trockner** *m* chamber drying oven

Kammer- und Pfeilerbau *m* room-and-pillar system

Kammer-wand *f* side wall of a lock **-warze** *f* bolt lug

Kamm-fräser *m* multiple-thread milling cutter **-führung** *f* guide comb **-garn** *n* worsted (yarn) **-getriebe** *n* cam gearing **-kies** *m* cockscomb pyrites **-kissen** *n* back pad **-kissengurt** *m* belly-band pad, belly-pad strap **-lager** *n* (concealed-collar) thrust bearing, thrust block **-länge** *f* crest length

Kämmling *m* noil, combing (textiles)

Kämmlingswollfärberei *f* noils dyeing

Kamm-linie *f* ridge line **-rad** *n* cogwheel **-relais** *n* cradle relay **rollen** *pl* grooved rollers **-stahl** *m* rack tool **-walze** *f* cogged cylinder, broad-faced steel gear, pinion **-walzengetriebe** *n* grooved roller gear **-walzenzapfen** *m* pinion neck **-walzgerüst** *n* pinion housing **-welle** *f* pinion shaft **-zahn** *m* chaser tooth **-zapfen** *m* collar journal **-zwecke** *f* tack

Kampecheholz *n* logwood

Kampfer *m* camphor

Kämpfer *m* (arch) abutment or springing, transom, point of support, combatant, fighter

Kämpfergelenk eines Brückenbogens turning joint on abutment of a bridge arch

Kampfer-harz *n* euosmite **-monobromid** *n* camphorated monobromide **-öl** *n* camphor oil

Kampfersäure *f* camphoric acid **-anhydrid** *n* camphoric anhydride

Kämpferschicht *f* springing course

Kampferspiritus *m* spirits of camphor

Kämpferstein *m* bearing block, springing stone

Kampfin *n* camphine

Kampometer *n* kampometer

Kanadabalsam *m* Canada balsam

kanadisches Hochdruckgebiet Canadian high (aviation)

Kanal *m* channel, conduit, duct, sewer, canal, drain, ditch, wind tunnel, trunk (computor) ~ **im Auftrag** canal on embankment ~ **im Einschnitt** canal in a cut **aktiver** ~ hot drain ~ **aus einem Vollrohr** single-duct conduit **einzügiger** ~ singleway duct **mehrzügiger** ~ multiple-way duct **unaktiver** ~ cold drain

Kanal-arbeiter *m* (Abwasser) sewer man **-ausgang** *m* sliver delivery **-belastung** *f* (Funkverkehr) channel loading **-bett** *n* (lining of) canal bed **-blech** *n* U-shaped plate **-breite** *f* duct width **-brücke** *f* canal aqueduct (bridge) **-damm** *m* canal embankment **-deckel** *m* sewer cover **-diele** *f* sheet iron piles **-düker** *m* culvert, siphon

Kanal-effekt *m* channeling **-filter** *n* channel filter **-flächen** *f pl* tube surfaces **-gebiet** *n* channel area **-haltung** *f* pool **-höhe** *f* duct height

Kanalisation *f* sewerage, sewer system

Kanalisations-abwässer *pl* sewage water **-kläranlage** *f* decanting plant for canalization **-pumpe** *f* sewage pump **-rohr** *n* sewer pipe

kanalisieren to canalize

Kanalisierung *f* canalization

Kanal-kapazität (Funk) channel capacity **-kennung** *f* channel identification letter

Kanal-kühlofen *m* continuous lehr **-lagenverschiebung** *f* channel position displacement **-meßpegel** *m* channel test tone level **-modulator-Demodulator** *m* channel translating equipment **-muffel** *f* muffle-type lehr **-mundstück** *n* cable shield, orifice of conduit **-ofen** *m* tunnel kiln, continuous furnace **-öffnung** *f* pipe outlet **-querschnitt** *m* ratio between the immersed cross section of a vessel and the welted section (of the canal)

Kanal-radius *m* tunnel or channel radius **-reinigungsgerät** *n* implement for drain cleansing, canal-cleaning outfit **-rohr** *n* sewer pipe **-scheibe** *f* grooved disk **-schieber** *m* canal slide valve **-schlammsauger** *m* mud exhauster for cleaning sewers **-schlepper** *m* canal tug **-schleuse** *f* canal lock **-sohle** *f* lining of canal bed

Kanal-spin *m* channel spin **-spüler** *m* drain-rinsing apparatus **-spundwand** *f* canal piling **-stein** *m* runner brick **-strahl** *m* canal ray, positive ray, diacathode ray, anode ray **-strahlentladung** *f* canal-ray discharge **-strahlionenquelle** *f* canal-ray-discharge ion source **-strahlröhre** *f* canal-ray tube **-trockner** *m* tunnel-drying oven, tunnel (type) dryer

Kanal-übergruppe *f* channel supergroup **-umsetzer** *m* channel bank, channel modulator **-unterdrückung** *f* blanking **-verlustfaktor** *m* channeling effect faktor **-verschiebung** *f* shifting of channel, channel displacement **-versetzung** *f* staggering **-verstärker** *m* window amplifier, channel width amplifier **-waage** *f* canal water level

Kanalwähler *m* channel selector **induktiver** ~ turret turner (TV)

Kanal-wasserpumpe *f* sewage-water pump **-ziegel** *m* thin or channel brick

Kandare *f* curb bit (bridle)

Kandarenzügel *m* curb rein
Kandelaber *m* chandelier, candelabrum
kandeln to groove, gutter, flute
kandieren to candy
Kandiertrommel *f* coating drum
Kandillen *pl* thin boullion
kanelliert fluted
Kanister *m* drum, can, container, canister
Kanne *f* can, pot, canister, pitcher, jug, tankard, mug
kannelieren to chamfer, channel, flute
Kanneliergutsche *f* veining gouge
kanneliert fluted
Kannelierung *f* flute, groove, chamfering
Kännelkohle *f* cannel coal
Kannen-aufgabe *f* churn entry **-rührwerk** *n* can-stirring apparatus **-tellerrahmen** *m* can turntable **-träger** *m* can carrier **-wascherbau** *m* can and churn-washing machine **-wärter** *m* can tenter (textiles) **-wendeeinrichtung** *f* gear for turning the churns
Kannette *f* cop (textiles)
kannettieren to cop
Kanone *f* cannon, gun
Kanonen-bohrer *m* tube bit, gun-core drill **-bronze** *f* gun metal, gun bronze
Kanonen-gießerei *f* gun foundry **-lafette** *f* gun mounting **-metall** *n* gun metal **-motor** *m* cannon engine **-rohr** *n* gun tube, cannon barrel
Kanonenschlag *m* exploding charge ~ **mit Knallerscheinung** firecracker, simulated fire and detonation ~ **mit Raucherscheinung** smoke-puff charge, simulated fire with development of smoke
kanonische Zerschneidung canonical dissection
kant shipshape
Kant-bewegung *f* yawing motion **-beitel** *m* cant chisel, cant firmer chisel, wheeler's chisel
Kante *f* edge, border, selvage, rim, ridge **abgeschrägte** ~ chamfer, chamfered edge, bevel cant **abgestoßene** ~ broken corner, chamfered edge **ablaufende** ~ trailing edge **bestoßene** ~ trimmed edge **geklöppelte** ~ pillow or bone lace **hintere** ~ trailing edge **vorspringende** ~ shelf, shoulder **zugeschärfte** ~ feather edge
Kante des Büttenpapiers deckle edge of hand made paper ~, **die von einem Strahl angeblasen wird** edge hit by a jet
Kantel *n* square ruler
kanteln to cant, tilt
kanten to turn on edge, edge, give a quarter or a half turn, turn over, tip
Kanten *n* edging, turning **-abschrägmaschine** *f* bevelling machine **-anleimmaschine** *f* edge gluing machine **-beschneidemaschine** *f* trimming shears **-bestoßmaschine** *f* edge trimming machine **-bezirk** *m* edge domain **-bohrung** *f* lip drilling **-brechen** *n* chamfer **-druck** *m* selvedge printing **-effekt** *m* edge effect **-eingriff** *m* edge interference
Kanten-filter *n* cut-on filter **-fräsen** *n* side (trimming) shaving **-fräsmaschine** *f* bevelling machine **-länge** *f* edge length **-pressung** *f* end pressure **-riegel** *m* flush bolt of door **-riß** *m* edge fracture **-rissigkeit** *f* tendency to crack or tear at corners **-runden** *n* corner radiusing **-schärfe** *f* resolution on border (of a picture) **-schema** *n* Deslandres diagram (of spectral-band system) **-schiene** *f* edge rail **-schrägmaschine** *f* edge bevelling machine **-schutz** *m* sheating, edge or corner protection, folded edge protection, selvedge-protected belt
Kantensystem *n* zero-line or edge system ~ **der Bande** bands of the spectrum
Kanten-umströmung *f* flow around edge **-verschleiß** *m* wear at the edges **-welle** *f* edge wave **-weise** edgewise, on edge **-wirkung** *f* edge effect, fringe effect **-zwingen** *pl* corner clamps
Kanter *m* device used for tipping or tilting, manipulator, edger, edging device
Kanthammer *m* hammer sledge (hammer)
Kanthariden1ack *m* varnish with sheen of gold beetles (cantharis)
Kantholz *n* square timber
kantige Düsenöffnung bevelled nozzle opening
Kantileverkran *m* cantilever gantry crane
Kantine *f* post exchange, canteen
Kant-kasten *m* twisting guide **-maschine** *f* edging machine **-maßstäbe** *pl* angular rules (of square, triangular or any other polygonal section)
Kant- und Verschiebevorrichtung *f* manipulator
Kantung *f* swing, tilting, squaring
Kantungswinkel *m* angle of swing
Kant-vorrichtung *f* edger, manipulator, tilter, tilting device **-wand** *f* turning wall
Kanüle *f* channel, tubular (hollow) needle
Kanzel *f* pulpit, gunner's turret (aviation), platform, cockpit, pillbox **vordere** ~ nose turret
Kanzeldach *n* soundboard; roof over a pulpit
Kanzelle *f* chancel, screen
Kanzelverkleidung *f* cockpit facing (aviat)
Kanzlei *f* chancellery **-papier** *n* brief (foolscap paper)
Kaolin *n* kaolin, china clay
Kaolinisierung *f* kaolinization
Kaolinit *m* kaolinite
Kaolin-lager *n* kaolin deposit **-sandstein** *m* arkose, kaoliniferous sandstone **-schlämmerei** *f* china-clay washing
Kap *n* cape, headland
Kapazitanz *f* capacity reactance, capacitance, condensive reactance, negative resistance
Kapazität *f* capacitance, capacity, efficiency, authority, dielectric capacity ~ **gegen Erde** earth capacity ~ **eines Kondensators** capacitance of a condenser ~ **je Längeneinheit** capacitance per unit length ~ **eines Leiters** electric capacitance of a conductor ~ **eines Sammlers** watt-hour capacity of a storage cell ~ **eines Schwingkreises** tank or total capacity ~ **zwischen den Transformatorwickelungen** interwinding capacity of a transformer
Kapazität, akustische ~ acoustic capacitance or compliance **elektrostatische** ~ electrostatic capacity **frequenzunabhängige** ~ capacity independent of frequency **gegenseitige** ~ mutual capacity **gemeinsame** ~ joint capacity **magnetische** ~ magnetic capacity or susceptibility **mechanische** ~ mechanical compliance
Kapazität, punktförmige ~, **punktförmig verteilte** ~ lumped capacity, concentrated capacity **spezifische induktive** ~ specific inductive capacity, dielectric constant **stetig verteilte** ~ continuously distributed capacity **veränderliche** ~ variable capacity or condenser **verteilte** ~ distributed capacity, self-capacitance,

distributed capacitance **wirksame ~** effective capacity

Kapazitäts-änderung *f* change in capacity, variation in capacity **-arm** of low capacity, anticapacitive

Kapazitätsausgleich *m* capacity balance **~ durch Adernkreuzen** test-balancing method, test-splicing method **~ durch Zusatzkondensatoren** condenser-balancing method

Kapazitätsausgleichsverfahren *n* capacity balancing method **~ durch Adernkreuzung** test-balancing method **~ durch Zusatzkondensatoren** condenser-balancing method

Kapazitäts-belag *m* distributed capacity **-bereich** *m* capacity range **-brücke** *f* capacitance or farad bridge, Wien bridge **-dekade** *f* capacity decade radio **-frei** noncapacitive **-kuppelung** *f* capacitive coupling, condenser coupling **-meßbrücke** *f* capacity bridge **-messer** *m* faradmeter **-messung** *f* capacity test, gauging of capacitance

Kapazitäts-probe *f* capacity test **-reaktanz** *f* negative or capacity reactance **-symmetrie** *f* capacity balance **-überschreitung** overflow of register capacity **-ungleichheit** *f*, **-unsymmetrie** *f* capacity-unbalance **-unterschiede** *pl* capacitance deviations **-wert** *m* value of capacitance **-widerstand** *m* capacitance, capacitive resistance **-widerstandsgekuppelt** resistance-capacity-coupled

Kapazitiv *n* capacitance

kapazitiv capacitive **-er Abtaster** variable capacitance pickup **~ verstimmtes Alarmgerät** capacity operated relay **-e Belastung** capacity load **-er Blindwiderstand** negative or capacity reactance, condensance **-er Dreipunktschwinger** Colpitts oscilator **-e Hochfrequenzerhitzung** capacity current heating **-e Kuppelung** capacity coupling **ungewollte -e Kuppelung** spurious capacities **-e Leitstrahldrehung** capacitance beam switching **-es Mikrophon** condenser transmitter **-e Reaktanz** negative or capacity reactance **-e Rückkuppelung** capacitive feedback **-er Schirm** electrostatic shield **-e Schirmung** electrostatic shielding

Kapazitron *n* capacitron

Kapelle *f* cupel, tuyère cooler housing, cooling-plate box; chapel; band (music)

Kapellen-form *f* cupel mold **-gold** *n* fine gold **-kluft** *f* cupel tongs **-ofen** *m* cupeling, assay, or cupola furnace **-probe** *f* cupel test, cupellation **-raub** *m* cupellation loss **-silber** *n* fine silver **-träger** *m* cupel holder **-zug** *m* loss by cupellation

kapellieren to cupel

kapern to capture, seize

kapillar capillary **-e Steighöhe** capillary rise

kapillar-aktiv surface-active, active in lowering surface tension **-aszension** *f* capillary rise **-druck** *m* capillary pressure

Kapillare *f* capillary tube

Kapillarelektrometer *n* capillary electrometer

Kapillarität *f* capillarity

Kapillaritäts-ansteigung *f* capillary rise **-gleichung** capillarity equation **-strom** *m* capillary current **-versuch** *m* capillary test

Kapillar-kraft *f* capillary force or action **-niveauschwingung** *f* capillary level oscillation **-riß** *m* hairline crack **-rohr** *n* capillary tube **-röhrchen** *n* small capillary tube **-röhre** *f* capillary tubing **-schreiber** *m* siphon recorder **-schwerewelle** *f* capillary-gravity wave **-strömung** *f* transpiration **-variometer** *n* capillary variometer **-versuch mittels Docht** wick-feed test **-wirkung** *f* capillary action

Kapital-abfindung *f* lump-sum settlement **-anlage** *f* investment **-einlage** *f* share of capital

kapitalisieren to capitalize

Kapitalisierung *f* capitalization

Kapital-kasten *m* upper case for capitals **-keil** *m* head bolt for capitals **-steg** *m* headstick for capitals

Kapitänsdiagramm *n* captain's diagram, curve diagram containing data for maximum values of lever-arm data, angles where these maxima occur or are attained, and the points of intersection of the lever-arm curves with the reference lines or curves

Kapitel *n* section, chapter

Kapitell *n* capital **Glocke eines Kapitells** bell, basket, drum, or corbel of a capital

Kaplanturbine *f* Kaplan turbine

Kapok *m* kapok

Kappa-gerät *n* predictor **-zahl** *f* kappa number

Kappe *f* cap, hood, top, dome; casing head, cap board, lid, gland, bonnet, heelplate, horn (of mine) **mit einer ~ versehen** to cap **geschlitzte ~** split cover **~ zum Festklemmen** friction held cap

Kappeisen *n* hammer band

kappen to cut (a rope), lop off

Kappen-aufleger *m* cap fitting device **-formmaschine** *f* stiffener molding machine **-geschoß** *n* capped shell **-solator** *m* cap-and-pin suspension insulator **-mutter** *f* hat nut **-schlüssel** *m* spanner for caps **-ständer** *m* closed-top roll housing **-stanze** *f* capping unit **-steife** *f* box-toe cement **-verschluß** *m* cowling clip **-verzug** *m* poling **-ziegel** *m* capping brick, gutter tile

Kapp-lehre *f* adzing gauge **-maschine** (Presse) capping machine (press) **-naht** *f* overlapping seam **-säge** *f* oscillating saw

Kappung *f* jag, notch (R.R. tie)

Kappziegel *m* gutter-tile

Kapsel *f* capsule, cap, casing, ferrule, detonator, shell, seal, cover, element of a microphone, box (print.), chill mold (foundry) **kleine ~** button **~ mit Feder** (Rückzugfeder) ring with spring (return spring)

kapsel-artig capsular **-barometer** *n* aneroid barometer, capsule aneroid **-blitz** *m* flashlight capsule **-gebläse** *n* enclosed or positive blower, lob-type blower, Root's supercharging blower, displacement compressor **-guß** *m* chilled work, casting in chills

Kapsel-kompressor *m* enclosed compressor **-lader** *m* displacement compressor **-landungsmesser** *m* capsule or diaphragm landing indicator **-liderung** *f* cap packing **-luftdruckmesser** *m* aneroid barometer, capsule aneroid **-maschine** *f* sealing machine **-mikrophon** *n* inset transmitter, button transmitter **-motor** *m* enclosed motor or engine **-mutter** *f* cap nut

kapseln to enclose, encase

Kapsel-pumpe *f* vane-type pump **-scherben** *f pl*

capsule fragments **-ton** *m* capsule clay, sagger clay

Kapselung *f* casing; (Zündapparat) metal shielding (magneto)

Kaptanz *f* captance

Karabiner *m* carbine **-haken** *m* spring safety hook, clipper, snap hook and eye

Karat *n* carat **-gewicht** *n* troy weight **-gold** *n* alloyed gold

karatieren to alloy (gold or silver)

Karatierung *f* alloying of gold or silver

karätig carat

Karbid *n* carbide **-einwurfentwickler** *m* carbide-to-water gas generator **-füllung** *f* carbide capacity **-industrie** *f* carbide industry

karbidisch carbide

Karbid-hartmetall *n* sintered hard carbide **-kohle** *f* carbide carbon **-lamelle** *f* carbide lamella **-lampe** *f* carbide lamp **-ofen** *m* carbide furnace **-schlacke** *f* carbide slag **-schlamm** *m* carbide sludge **-seigerung** *f* carbide separation (met.) **-staub** *m* carbide powder **-trommel** *f* carbide drum **-zeile** *f* carbide band or streak

Karbol *n* phenol, carbolic acid

Karbolineum *n* carbolineum

Karbolsäure *f* carbolic acid, phenol

Karbon *n* carboniferous formation, coal measures

Karbonat *n* carbonate

Karbon-druck *m* carbon ink printing **-härte** *f* carbonate hardness

karbonieren to carbonate

Karbonisation *f* carbonization

karbonisch carboniferous

Karbonisier-anlage *f* **-anstalt** *f* carbonizing plant **-druck** *m* carbon printing

karbonisieren to carbonize

Karbonisieren *n* carburizing

Karbonisiergut *n* carbonized material

karbonitrieren to dry-cyanide

Karbon-rohpapier *n* carbon base paper **-rohseidenpapier** *n* carbon base tissue paper **-säure** *f* carboxylic acid

Karbonyl *n* carbonyl

Karborund *n* carborundum, silicon carbide **-detektor** *m* carborundum detector

Karborundumscheibe *f* carborundum wheel

Karbowid(widerstand) *m* Karbowid-type resistor

Karbür *n* carbide

Karburation *f* carburetion

Karburator *m* carburetor

karburieren to carburize, carburet

Karburierung *f* carburation, carburisation, carburetting

Karburieröl *n* carbureting oil

karburiertes Wassergas carbureted water gas

Karburierung *f* carburization, carburetion

Kardan *m* Cardan, gimbal ring **-achsen** *f pl* Cardan axes **-antrieb** *m* shaft-drive **-drehzapfen** *m* knuckle joint, universal joint **-aufhängung** *f* gimbal suspension or mounting, Cardanic suspension **-drehzapfen** *m* knuckle, swivel **-gelenk** *n* Cardan joint, knuckle joint, universal joint, Hooke's joint **-getriebe** *n* Cardan gear

kardanisch Cardanic, gimbal, Cardan (rings, links, etc.) ~ **aufgehängt** hung on gimbals, Cardanic suspension ~ **aufhängen** to suspend on gimbals, hang from gimbals ~ **gelagert** mounted on gimbals **-e Aufhängung** Cardanic suspension **-es Gelenk** universal coupling **-e Lagerung** gimbal bearings **-es Stützlager** *n* gimbal mounting

Kardan-kuppelung *f* universal joint, Cardan joint **-ring** *m* gimbal ring, Cardan ring (gyro compass) **-rohr** *n* propeller tube, tubular propeller shaft **-scheibe** *f* knuckle washer **-stein** *m* trunnion block **-stützrohr** *n* drive shaft housing **-system** *n* gimbal system **-verschalung** *f* Cardan joint casing **-welle** *f* drive shaft, Cardan shaft, propeller shaft

Karde *f* teasel (Dipsacus)

Kardeel *n* strand (of cable, etc.), hawser-laid rope **ein Tau in Kardeele zerlegen** to unlay a rope

Kardeelstropp *m* grummet

Kardenbeschlag *m* card fitting (textiles)

kardieren to card (textiles)

Kardinal-punkte *pl* **-striche** *pl* cardinal points (optics)

Kardioide *f* cardioid characteristic, cardioid directive diagram

Kardioiden-bildung *f* cardioid formation **-kennlinie** *f* cardioid or heart-shaped diagram or curve (radio)

Karduspapier *n* cartridge paper

Karfunkelstein *m* almandine, almandite, garnet carbuncle, pyrope

kärglich scant

karieren to checker

kariert cross-hatched **-es Papier** quadrillé paper

Karkasse *f* carcass

Karmesin *n* crimson

Karmin *m* carmine **-zinnober** *m* carmine cinnabar

Karmoisin *n* crimson

Karnallit *m* carnallite

Karnauba-säure *f* carnaubic acid **-wachs** *n* carnauba wax

Karneol *m* carnelian

Karnieseisen *n* quirk ogee iron

Karo *n* square

Karosserie *f* carriage or automobile body **-blech** *n* automobile-body sheet iron **-pappe** *f* carriage panels

Karossier *m* carriage builder

karossiert coach-built

Karre *f* wheelbarrow, carriage, truck, cart

Karree *n* square

karren to wheel

Karren *m* wheelbarrow, carriage, truck, cart ~ **für Buschrodepflug** truck for brush breaker

Karren-begichtung *f* barrow charging **-förderung** *f* wheeling, working, or transport(ation) by cart **-läufer** *m* hauler, putter, barrowman **-rad** *n* cart wheel, barrow wheel, truck wheel **-schenkel** *m pl* wheel-barrow handles **-station** *f* cart-type radio station, wagon radio set **-tisch** *m* truck platform

karriert checked, checkered

Karst *m* prong hoe, karst

Karstenit *m* anhydrite

Kartätsche *f* case shot, canister shot

Karte *f* card, chart, map, ticket ~ **der Funkpeilung** radio-direction-finding chart ~ **des großen Kreises** great-circle chart ~ **nach Luft-**

bildaufnahmen aerophotogrammetric map, air-survey map **~ in großem Maßstabe** large-scale map **~ aufziehen** to mount a map **Einrichten einer ~** orientation of a map **gleichgradige ~** plane chart **gnomonische ~** gnomonic or straight-course chart **hydrographische ~** chart, sea chart, hydrographical map **wachsende ~** Mercator's chart

Kartei *f* card index or catalogue, filing cabinet **-karte** *f* filing card **-kasten** *m* filing cabinet **-system** *n* card-record system

Kartei- und Leitkarten card-index cards and guide cards

Kartell *n* cartel, industrial combine

Karten-abfühler *m* card reader **-ablagemagazin** *n* card receiver (punched cards) **-archiv** *n* card file **-auflage** *f* alidade base

Kartenaufnahme *f* photographic map **photographische ~** photographic mapping

Karten-ausrüstung *f* map outfit, chart equipment **-ausschnitt** *m* map section **-ausstattung** *f* map equipment **-batterie** *f* topographic or mapping section **-berichtigung** *f* map rectification

Kartenblatt *n* map or chart sheet, map quadrangle, zone map **~ mit Gitter** grid sheet

Kartenblattnummer *f* geographic index number

Karten-brett *n* map-mounting board, military sketching board **-bügler** *m* card reconditioner **-doppler mit Zeichenabfühlung** mark sensing reproducer **-druckerei** *f* map-printing office or plant **-durchlauf** *m* card run **-ebene** *f* map plane, horizontal through base of trajectory **-eintragung** *f* entry or notation on map **-einzeichnung** *f* entry on map

Kartenentfernung *f* horizontal or map range **~ zum Abschußpunkt ~ zum Meßpunkt** horizontal range to present position **~ zum Treffpunkt** horizontal range to future position **~ zum Wechselpunkt** horizontal range to mid-point, minimum horizontal range

Karten-entwurf *m* map projection **-felddruckerei** *f* field mapping section **-gesteuerter Streifenlocher** card-to-tape converter **-gitternetz** *n* map grid **-halter** *m* map holder, map carrier, card holder **-haus** *n* pilothouse, chartroom **-herstellung** *f* map plotting or drawing **-inhalt** *m* map content

Karten-kammer *f* map room **-koordinatensystem** *n* map-coordinates system **-kurs** *m* map course **-lage** *f* position on the map **-lesen** *n* map reading **-locher** *m* **-lochzange** *f* ticket nippers **-magazin** *n* stacker **-maßstab** *m* map scale **-meridian** *m* meridian line on chart **-mischer** *m* collator

Karten-nadir *m* map plumb point **-netz** *n* map grid, system of meridians and parallels, graticule **-niveau** *n* map level **-null** *n* datum (of charts) **-papier** *n* chart paper, map or plan paper **-projektion** *f* map projection **-punktviereck** *n* map point quadrilateral **-rand** *m* border of map **-raum** *m* chartroom

Kartenrichtpunkt *m* map aiming point **-verfahren** *n* firing procedure according to map

Karten-roller *m* roller map case **-schläger** *m* card cutter **-schlagmaschine** *f* card-punching machine **-schöpfer** *m* card picker knife (punched cards) **-schrank** *m* map chest **-schutzhülle** *f* map case, map cover **-signatur** *f* conventional sign (on maps) **-skizze** *f* map sketch **-spind** *m* map chest **-stecher** *m* geographical engraver **-tasche** *f* map case **-tisch** *m* map table **-trommel** *f* map case

Karten- und Vermessungstruppen *pl* topographic troops

Karten-unterlage *f* plane table **-verbesserungsbuch** *n* map-correction book **-vervollständigung** *f* map completion or complication **-vorschub** *m* card feed **-werk** *n* cartography **-winkelmesser** *m* map protractor **-zähler** *m* card counter (register) **-zeichen** *n* conventional sign for maps **-zeichner** *m* cartographer **-zuführungseinrichter** *m* card feed device

kartesische Kurve Cartesian curve

Kartiereinrichtung *f* mapping scale

kartieren to plot or draw a map

Kartierung *f* map plotting or drawing **photogrammetrische ~** survey measurement

Kartierungs-gerät *n* map-plotting apparatus **-geschwindigkeit** *f* speed of plotting maps **-leistung** *f* output of plotting maps **-maßstab** *m* plotting scale

Kartoffel *f* potato **-gräber** *m* potato digger **-häufler** *m* potato hiller **-mehl** *n* potato flour **-pflanzmaschine** *f* potato planter **-stärke** *f* farina, potato starch **-walzmehl** *n* dextrinized potato flour **-zucker** *m* starch sugar, glucose

Kartograph *m* cartographer

Kartographie *f* topographic mapping

Karton *m* cardboard, pasteboard, pasteboard box, carton, boxboard

Kartonage *f* cardboard or pasteboard box

Kartonagen-heftmaschine pasteboard-box stabbing machine

Karton-filz *m* board felt

Kartoniersystem *n* cartoning system

Karton-kreisschere *f* circular knives for cutting cardboard **-maschine** *f* cardboard machine **-papier** *n* cartridge paper **-scheibe** *f* cardboard disk

Kartothek *f* card file, index, or catalogue **-karte** *f* index card

Kartusch-beutel *m* cartridge or powder bag, silk bag (for charge) **-deckel** *m* lid of cartridge case, spacer

Kartusche *f* shell case (semifixed), cartridge case, powder bag, propelling-charge container, cartridge (unfixed or separate ammunition)

Kartusch-pappe *f* cartridge paper **-raum** *m* powder chamber **-vorlage** *f* cartridge-case wad, flash-reducing wad

Karussell *n* merry-go-round, roundabout rotary platen **-bad** *n* revolving bath **-drehbank** *f* vertical boring mill, vertical turret boring machine **-revolverdrehbank** *f* vertical turret lathe

Karvel-boot *n* carvel-built boat **-nagel** *m* belaying pin

Karzinogenese *f* carcinogenesis

Karzinom *n* carcinoma

Karzinotron *n* carcinotron; backward-wave oscillator (rdo)

Kaschier *n* passe-partout, strong wrapping paper **-anlage** *f* gluing plant **-einrichtung** *f* lining device **-eisen** *n* scraper

kaschieren to place on a support, base, or other

surface, coat with paper, line, glue, laminate, conceal

Kaschieren *n* lamination coating

Kaschier-kalander *m* lining calender **-papier** *n* lining paper

kaschierte Folie backed or lined foil

Kaschierung *f* lining

Kasein *n* casein **-farbe** *f* casein paint **-leim** *m* casein glue **-wolle** *f* casein fiber

Käselager *n* cheese storehouse or storage

Kasemattlafette *f* casemate gun mount

Käserei *f* cheese factory

Kaserne *f* barracks

Kasernen-hof *m* barracks yard

kasernierungspflichtig obliged to live in barracks

Kasino *n* clubhouse, casino, officers' mess or club

Kaskade *f* cascade **in ~ schalten** to (join in) cascade or tandem

Kaskaden-anreihung *f* cascade of cascades **-entmagnetisierung** *f* cascade demagnetization **-kernreaktion** nuclear cascade process **-nachweis** *m* cascade detection **-röhre** *f* cascade (X-ray) tube **-schaltung** *f* cascade connection or circuit, series connection cascading, concatenation or tandem connection (of motors) **-spannungswandler** *m* cascade voltage transformer

Kaskaden-übergang *m* cascade transition **-übertrag** *m* cascade carry **-umformer** *m* cascade converter, frequency changer **-verfahren** *n* cascade process **-verstärker** *m* cascade amplifier, multistage or repeating amplifier **-vorwärmer** *m* cascade preheater

Kasko *n* body, hull **-versicherung** *f* insurance on hull and appurtenances and equipment

Kasolit *m* kasolite

Kassation *f* cashiering, military degradation

Kasse *f* safe, money chest, cashier's office, cash

Kasseler Gelb Cassel yellow, lead oxychloride

Kasseler Ofen Cassel furnace

Kassen-abschluß *m* balancing of (cash) accounts or books, cash balance, cashing up **-abteilung** *f* finance section **-anweisung** *f* cash order, bank note or bill, check **-bestand** *m* cash balance **-dienst** *m* finance service **-leergang** *m* change of register **-ordnung** *f* finance regulations **-schein** *m* cash order, bank note or bill, check **-verwaltung** *f* financial administration **-wesen** *n* finance accounts

Kasserole *f* casserole

Kassette *f* film holder, plateholder (magazine), dark slide, cashbox, coffer of ceiling pan, spool box, sagger, casket **leise ~** silenced magazine **lichtdichte ~** darkroom, pan impermeable to light

Kassetten-bauweise *f* modular construction **-decke** *f* ceiling with bays, coffered ceiling **-laufwerk** *n* film transport mechanism **-platte** *f* precast (concrete) slab unit **-rahmen** *m* dark-slide carrier **-schieber** *m* shutter of dark slide **-schlitten** *m* dark-slide carriage **-verstärker** *n* plug-in amplifier

kassieren to cashier, dismiss, cancel, quash

Kassierer *m* cashier

Kassier-relais *n* coin relay (coin collet or return) **-vorrichtung** *f* coin collector, coin box

Kassiterit *m* cassiterite, tinstone, tin dioxide

Kastanienholz *n* chestnut wood

Kästchen *n* little box **-schema** block diagram

Kasten *m* case, box, chest, molding box, caisson, box magazine, crate, (slang) guardhouse, receiver, (slang) tank or airplane **~ mit Schirmwänden** screening box **auf ~ verkochen** to boil stringproof (sugar mfg.)

Kasten-absenkvorrichtung *f* flask-lowering device (foundry) **-arbeit** *f* crystallization in tanks **-artiger Stützrollenträger** supporting roller pedestal in box form **-ausbläser** *m* bellows dust extractor **-biegepresse** *f* body-forming machine **-blau** *n* pencil blue **-boden** *m* magazine, housing, or receiver floor plate

Kasten-bohrer *m* box borer, casement drill **-bohrung** *f* casement bore **-brücke** *f* bridge of airproof cases **-damm** *m* cofferdam **-deckel** *m* cover, box cover, receiver top **-drachen** *m* box kite **-einsatzverfahren** *n* pack-hardening process **-fangedamm** *m* cofferdam with double sheeting

Kastenform *f* box mold or type **zweiteilige ~** two-part mold

kastenförmig box-type design **-er Hohlkörper aus einem Stück** massive one-piece box section **-e Konstruktion** heavy box-type construction **hydraulisch gepreßtes -es Stahlblech** hydraulically pressed box-shaped steel plate

Kasten-fuß *m* cabinet leg, bed box **-futter** *n* case lining **-gebläse** *n* chest blowing machine, chest bellows **-geglüht** box-annealed, pot-annealed, close-annealed

Kastengehänge *n* bucket, bucket hanger **~ mit Bodenentleerung** bucket with bottom discharge **~ mit Seitenentleerung** side-dump bucket

Kasten-gerippe *n* body framework **-gestell** *n* box frame **-glühofen** *m* pot-annealing furnace **-glühung** *f* box, pot, or close annealing **-guß** *m* box casting, casting molded in flask **-gußform** *f* box mold, flask **-halterung** *f* multiprong plug socket case (missiles) **-holm** *m* box spar (aviation)

Kasten-kaliber *n* (in rolling) box pass, box groove **-kamera** *f* box camera **-karre** *f* box cart, trunk barrow **-kipper** *m* mine car **-konstruktion** *f* box-frame construction **-kopierrahmen** *m* printing frame **-lafette** *f* box trail, gun carriage **-leitwerk** *n* box-tail unit **-magazin** *n* box magazine **-modell** *n* box-type pattern **-öffner** *m* hopper feeder

Kasten-platte *f* box plate **-potential** *n* potential well **-profil** *n* box section **-rad** *n* cellular or chest wheel, box turbine wheel **-rinne** *f* conveying trough **-schema** *n* layout of the case **-schleuse** *f* square sluice **-schlüssel** *m* transposition cipher (signal) **-stift** *m* box pin

Kasten-spiere *f* box spar (aviat.) **-speiser** *m* hopper feeder **-stahlhalter** *m* block toolholder **-teilfläche** *f* joint face of molding box **-tisch** *m* box table **-träger** *m* box girder or beam **-untersuchungsstelle** *f* test case **-wagen** *m* box-type hand truck, box barrow or cart **-wand** *f* housing wall, box wall, side of receiver **-werkzeug** *n* block tool **-wiege** *f* body bolster **-winde** *f* box winch **-zimmerung** *f* stulls

katabatisch catabatic

katadioptrisch catadioptric

Katalanschmiede *f* Catalan forge

Katakaustik *f* catacaustics (curve or surface)
Katalog *m* catalogue
katalogisieren to tabulate, catalogue
katalonisches Rennfeuer Catalan-forge process, Catalan direct process
Katalysator *m* catalytic agent, catalyzer, catalyst
Katalyse *f* catalysis
katalysieren to catalyze
katalytisch catalytic
Kataphorese *f* cataphoresis, electrophoresis
kataphorische Wirkung electric osmosis or endosmosis
Katapult *m* catapult **preßluftgetriebener** ~ compressed-air-impulse catapult **pulvergetriebener** ~ powder-impulse catapult
katapult-fähig catapultable **-flugzeug** *n* catapult plane
Katapultier-beschläge *pl* catapult fittings **-einrichtung** *f* catapult equipment
katapultieren to catapult, launch
Katapult-schiff *n* catapult ship **-start** *m* catapult take-off or launching **-winkel** *m* catapult or launching angle
Katarakt *m* cataract, variable orifice
Kataster *m* cadastre, land register **-aufnahme** *f* cadastral survey **-vermessung** *f* cadastral survey
katastrophale Unbeständigkeit catastrophic instability
Katechin *n* catechin **-säure** *f* catechuic acid (catechol)
Katechugerbsäure *f* catechutannic acid
Kategorie *f* category
Katelektrotonus *m* catelectrotonus
Katenarienkabel *n* catenary wire
Katenoid *n* catenoid
Katgut *n* catgut
Katharometer *n* katharometer
Kathedralenwinkel *m* cathedral angle
Kathete *f* cathetus
Katheten *pl* short sides of right-angled triangle, perpendicular and base adjoining hypotenuse
Kathetometer *n* cathetometer
Kathode *f* cathode, negative electrode, filament emitter (of electrons) ~ **einer Photozelle** photocathode **direkt geheizte** ~ directly heated cathode **geschichtete** ~ (oxide-)coated cathode, photocoated with light-sensitive layer **glühende** ~ incandescent cathode **indirekt geheizte** ~ indirectly heated cathode, unipotential or isopotential cathode **kalte** ~ cold cathode **körperliche** ~ physical or material cathode **reelle** ~ actual cathode **scheinbare** ~, **virtuelle** ~ virtual cathode
Kathoden-anheizzeit *f* cathode heating time, thermal time constant **-ansatzpunkt** *m* spot (of arc) formed **-ausdehnung** *f* area of the cathode **-ausgang** *m* cathode output **-auskopplung** cathode follower output **-bändchen** *n* cathode connecting strip **-basisschaltung** *f* grounded-cathode circuit **-basisverstärker** *m* anode follower, grounded cathode amplifier **-berechnung** *f* cathode evaluation **-dunkelraum** *m* dark space around the cathode **-fackelerscheinung** *f* cathode flicker effect **-faden** *m* cathode filament
Kathodenfall *m* cathode fall (of potential) **anomaler** ~ anomalous cathode fall
Kathoden-fallableiter *m* valve arrester, cathode-drop lightning arrester **-fläche** *f* cathode surface
Kathodenfleck, fixierter ~ fixed or anchored cathode spot
Kathoden-flüssigkeit *f* catholyte **-glimmlicht** *n* cathode-glow lamp **-glimmschicht** *f* cathode sheath **-haken** *m* cathode loop or hook **-halterung** *f* cathode anchor **-heizung** *f* A-power supply **-kopplung** cathode follower **-leitwert** *m* cathode conductance **-licht** *n* **-lichthaut** *f* cathode glow **-linie** *f* cathode line **-neuaktivierung** *f* cathode reactivation, cathode rejuvenation
Kathoden-niederschlag *m* cathode deposit **-oszillograph** *m* cathode-ray oscillograph **-raum** *m* cathode space **-röhre** *f* cathode tube, thermionic valve **-röhrendetektor** *m* tube detector **-schicht** *f* cathode layer **-spitzenstrom** peak cathode current **-siedekühlung** *f* vapor cooling for cathode **-spritzen** *m* flicker or spitting of cathode **-sprung** *m* cathode jump of potential
Kathodenstrahl *m* jet or cathode-ray oscillograph, electron beam **-abtaster** *m* electron-beam scanner **-bündel** *n* cathode-ray beam or pencil
Kathodenstrahlenoszillograph *m* Braun tube or cathoderay oscillograph
Kathodenstrahl-erzeuger *m* electron gun **-fernsehen** *n* television by electronic methods **-intensität** *f* intensity of electron beam **-intensitätskontrolle** *f* cathode-ray beam-intensity modulation **-oszillograph** *m* cathode-ray oscillograph **-röhre** *f* cathode-ray, electron-beam, or Braun tube, oscilloscope, thermionic tube, iconoscope, Lenard tube **-zählröhren** *pl* decade tubes
Kathoden-strom *m* cathode current **-tastung** *f* cathode keying **-verstärker** *m* cathode follower **-vorspannung** *f* cathode bias **-wickel** *m* cathode assembly **-zerstäubung** *f* sputtering of cathode, cathodic evaporation or disintegration **-zuleitung** *f* cathode lead
kathodisch cathodic **-e Entladung** cathodic discharge
Kathodolumineszenz *f* cathodoluminescence
Kathodo-lumineszenzlampe *f* cathode-glow tube **-phon** *m* cathodophone, diaphragmless microphone, glow-discharge microphone
Kathodyn-röhre *f* phase-splitting tube **-schaltung** *f* phase-splitting tube circuit
Katholyt *m* catholyte
Kation *n* cation
katoptrisch catoptric
Katt *f* cat (navy) **-anker** *m* backing anchor **-davit** *m* cat davit
katten to cat
Kattstopper *m* cathead stopper
Kattundruckpapier *n* chintz paper, calico
Katz-bahn *f* trolley track **-brücke** *f* man-trolley unloader
Katze *f* cat, trolley, trolley carriage (for cranes), chariot, code for a type of radar equipment ~ **mit Hebezeug** trolley hoist ~ **mit Rädervorgelege** geared trolley
Katzen (im Papierstoff) strings in the pulp
katzen to trolley **-auge** *n* cat's-eye, reflector, bull's-eye (small thick lens) **-bahn** *f* trolley track **-buckel** *m* hog **-buckeln** *n* hogging **-fahrbahn** *f* trolley-beam track, trolley runway **-fahrt** *f* trolley travel or motion **-fahrwerk** *n*

trolley-travel gearing **-fang** *m* auxiliary strainer
Katzen-gang *m* trolley runway **-gestell** *n* trolley frame **-glimmer** *m* mica **-gold** *n* mosaic gold **-kopf** *m* chain toggle **-laufrad** *n* trolley wheel **-rahmen** *m* trolley frame **-schiene** *f* trolley-travel rail **-silber** *n* mica **-steig** *m* catwalk **-stellung** *f* position of trolley **-winde** *f* crab winch
Katzfahren *n* cross traversing
katz-fahren to trolley **-fahrgeschwindigkeit** *f* traversing speed of crab **-fahrmotor** *m* trolley engine or motor **-fahrwerk** *n* traveling-overhead-hoist assembly, cross traversing
kaubar masticable, chewable
Kaue *f* shed, coop, hut at pit's mouth
Kauen *n* springing (mech.)
Kauf *m* purchase
Kaufbruch *m* bought scrap
kaufen to buy, purchase
Käufer *m* buyer, customer
Kauffahrtei *f* shipping trade **-schiff** *n* merchantman
Kauf-glätte *f* commercial litharge **-haus** *n* trading house, warehouse, department store **-kraft** *f* purchasing or buying power **-laden** *m* store, merchant's shop
käuflich commercial (grade), merchantable, purchasable
Kauf-lust *f* demand **-mann** *m* merchant, tradesman, shopkeeper **-männische Erfahrung** commercial experience **-preis** *m* buying price **-schrott** *m* bought scrap **-summe** *f* purchase price **-vertrag** *m* contract
Kaukamm *m* miner's ax
Kaule *f* pit, sphere
Kauriharz *n* dammer resin
Kaurit-leim *m* kaurit glue **-verleimung** *f* kaurit gluing
Kausalität *f* causation
Kausalitäts-bedingungen *pl* causality conditions **-forderung** *f* causality requirement **-verletzung** causality violation
Kausalnexus *m* causal nexus, causal connection (phot.)
Kausche *f* grommet, thimble, cringle, bull's-eye, dead-eye, gutter ring ~ (für Ankerseile), guy thimble **eine ~ in ein Ende splissen** to put a thimble in an eye
Kauschring *m* deadeye ring
kaustifizieren to caustify
Kaustik *f* art of etching, caustic (optics) **-fläche** *f* caustic surface **-spitze** *f* caustic tip
kaustisch caustic **-e Soda** caustic soda, sodium hydroxide
Kaustizieranlage *f* causticising plants
kaustizieren to causticize, cauterize
Kaustizierung *f* caustification, causticizing
Kaustizität *f* causticity
Kaute *f* depression, pit
Kauter *m* cautery
Kauterisation *f* thermocautery (med.)
kauterisieren to cauterize, causticize
Kaution *f* bond, surety bond, bail **~ stellen** to furnish bail, bond, or security
kautions-fähig able to put up security **-wechsel** *m* guarantee bill
kautschen to couch (paper mfg.)
Kautschucin *n* caoutchoucin
Kautschuk *m* rubber, caoutchouc, gum elastic **~ niederer Sorte** off-grade rubber **entharzter ~** deresinated rubber **vulkanisierter ~** vulcanized caoutchouc
kautschuk-ähnlich rubberlike **-faden** *m* elastic thread **-milch** *f* latex **-platte** *f* sheet rubber **-schaum** *m* mousse rubber, rubber sponge or foam **-schlauch** *m* rubber tubing **-schwefeln** to vulcanize **-stempel** *m* rubber stamp or pad **-stopfen** *m* rubber stopper **-treibriemen** *m* elastic belt
Kavernenkraftwerk *n* underground hydro-electric power station
Kavitation *f* cavitation
Kavitations-beständig resistant to cavitation **-parameter** *n* cavitation parameter **-strömung** *f* cavity flow
Kavitätswiderstand *m* cavity drag
kavitierender Wasserflügel cavitating hydrofoil
K-Blink *m* portable signal lamp
K-Brückengerät *n* portable bridge unit
Keep *f* notch, channel (ship building)
Kegel *m* (bowling) pin, cone, core, plug, conical roll inside conical refiner, bevel, volute, tapered sleeve or socket **~ zweiter Ordnung** cone of second order ~ (flacher, schlanker, steiler ~) cone, taper **~ der Schärfeinlage** cone of die
Kegel-abstand *m* bevel gear blank **-abwicklung** *f* development of conical section **-achse** *f* axis of cone **-ansatz** *m* beveled end **-antenne** *f* cone antenna **-antrieb** *m* level drive **-antriebsritzel** *m* bevel-driving pinion **-band** *n* loop and hook, hinge with hook (lock) **-bohrung** *f* taper bore or hole
Kegel-brecher *m* cone crusher **-bremse** *f* cone (friction) brake **-bremsgelenk** *n* coned brake joint **-buchse** *f* conical nipple **-dichtfläche** *f* conical packing surface **-dreharbeit** *f* taper-turning operation **-dreheinrichtung** *f* taper attachment, bevel turning device **-drehen** *n* angular turning, taper turning **-drehvorrichtung** *f* taper attachment
Kegel-druckhärte *f* conical-indentation hardness **-druckprobe** *f* cone-thrust test, static cone-indentation test, cone test **-drucksonde** *f* conical penetrometer **-druckversuch** *m* cone penetration test **-eindringungsapparat** *m* cone penetrometer **-eindruck** *m* cone impression or imprint **-feder** *f* volute or conical spiral spring **-fläche** *f* conical surface **-form** *f* conicalness
kegelförmig conical, cone-shaped, tapered **~ aussenken** to countersink **~ zulaufend** tapered **-e Messerwalze** cone, core, plug, conical roll inside conical refiner
Kegel-fräser *m* beveled cutter **-gehäuse** *n* gearbox **-granulator** *m* cone granulator **-gestalt** *f* conical shape **-getriebe** *n* bevel gear **-gewinde** *n* taper thread **-griff** *m* tapered machine handle **-grund** *m* pebbly or flinty ground **-hahn** *m* conical cock **-herd** *m* round or conical buddle (min.)
Kegelhülse *f* taper sleeve **verlängerte ~** taper-drill socket
kegelig barrel-shaped, conical, tapered **-es Antriebsrad** cone pulley **-er Bolzen** taper bolt **-er Senker** countersink **-er Stift** taper pin **-e Strömung** conical flow **-er Verlauf** taper
Kegeligdrehen *n* taper turning
Kegel-innenring *m* single-row inner race with

taper bore (bearing) **-kerbstift** *m* notched conical pin, notched taper pin **-klauenkupplung** *f* conical clutch or coupling **-klingenkupplung** *f* conical latch clutch **-kopf** *m* panhead, cone-head **-kreiselmischer** *m* cone impeller mixer **-kugel** *f* skittle ball **-kugellager** *n* cup-and-cone bearing **-kuppe** *f* tapered top **-kuppelung** *f* cone coupling or clutch, cone friction clutch

Kegel-lager *n* cone bearing **-lehre** *f* taper gauge **-leitapparat** *m* taper attachment **-lineal** *n* taper turning attachment **-linie** *f* parabola **-mantel** *m* cone-shaped shell **-messer** *m* core bar **-meßgerät** *n* instrument for testing tapers **-messung** *f* taper gauging **-mühle** *f* perfecting engine

kegeln to bowl, taper

Kegel-nabe *f* cone hub **-öffnungswinkel** *m* vertex angle **-passung** *f* taper fit **-pendel** *n* conical pendulum **-pfeilradgetriebe** *n* bevel herringbone reduction gear **-probe** *f* cone test **-projektion** *f* conical projection

Kegelrad *n* bevel gear, bevel spur gear, straight bevel gear, miter gear, bevel-gear wheel, sprocket wheel, conical wheel ~ **mit fünfundvierziggrädiger Achsenstellung** miter gear ~ **mit Holzverzahnung** wood-tooth bevel gear

Kegelrad-achse *f* bevel gear shaft **-antrieb** *m* bevel-gear drive **-antriebsritzel** *n* bevel pinion **-antriebswelle** *f* bevel gear, drive shaft **-ausgleichsgetriebe** *n* bevel gear with conical pinion **-bearbeitung** *f* machining of bevel gears

Kegelräder für die Mittenwelle column driving miters

Kegelräder-gehäuse *n* bevel gear case **-getriebe** *n* miter(-wheel) gearing, bevel gearing **-wechselgetriebe** *n* bevel gear

Kegelradfräser *m* bevel-gear cutter **-schärfmaschine** *f* bevel-gear cutter grinder, bevel-gear cutter sharpening machine

Kegelrad-gehäuse *n* bevel gear case, transfer case **-getriebe** *n* bevel-gear drive jet, miter-wheel gearing, bevel gearing **-hinterachsantrieb** *m* bevel-gear rear-axle drive **-hobler** *m* bevel gear generator **-hobelmaschine** bevel gear planer **-hobelstahl** *m* bevel gear cutter **-kugellager** *n* bevel-pinion ball bearing **-montage** *f* bevel-gear alignment **-ritzel** *n* bevel pinion **-ritzelantriebswelle** *f* bevel pinion drive shaft

Kegelrad-übertragung *f* equal-ratio bevel gear **-umlaufgetriebe** *n* bevel-epicyclic-type reduction gear **-verzahnung** *f* bevel-gear-tooth system **-vorgelege** *n* countershaft **-wendegetriebe** *n* bevel-wheel reversing wheel **-werk** *n* wheel-work with conical gearing

Kegelradzahnkranz *m*, **schräg verzahnter** ~ spiral-bevel ring gear

Kegel-reibahle *f* taper-pin or taper-shank reamer **-reibrad** *n* bevel friction wheel **-reibungskuppelung** *f* cone clutch **-riemenscheibe** *f* cone pulley **-ring** *m* tapered ring **-ritzel** *n* bevel pinion **-röhren** *pl* beveled casing **-rollenlager** *n* tapered-roller bearing, conical-roller bearing **-rückschlagventil** *n* cone non-return valve

Kegel-schaft *m* taper shank **-scheibe** *f* cone pulley **-schiene** *f* taper guide bar **-schneckengetriebe** bevel helical reduction gear **-schnitt** *m* conic section **-schnittlinie** *f* ellipse, parabola, trajectory **-schnurre** *f* semi-trumpet chute **-senkschraube** *f* flat head screw **-spitze** *f* apex of the cone

Kegelspitzen, ~ **von einander** cones base to base ~ **zu einander** cones apex to apex

Kegel-stift *m* tapered pin **-stirnrad** *n* (Bagger) tapered spur wheel **-stopfen** *m* taper plug **-strahlröhre** *f* (Kestral-Röhre) cestral tube **-strömung** *f* conically distributed flow **-stumpf** *m* truncated cone, frustum

Kegel-tellerrad *n* bevel crown wheel **-toppzeichen** *n* conical top mark **-treibrad** *n* beveled driving wheel **-trommel** *f* tapered or conical drum **-(trommel-)trieb** *m* cone-pulley drive, variable drive with cone pulleys, continuous-speed cone **-ventil** *n* cone or plug valve, mushroom or miter valve, conical-wing valve, ball valve **-wellenstumpf** *m* conical shaft end

Kegelwinkel *m* angle of opening, angle of cone of dispersion (of bursting shell) ~ **der Wälzfläche** pitch-cone angle

Kegel-winkelgradskala *f* root angle scale **-wulstschmierkopf** *m* lubricator **-zahnrad** *n* bevel gear **-zapfen** *m* tapered spigot

Kehle *f* throat, larynx, gorge (fort.), fillet, channel, flute ~ **der Axt** neck of hatchet

Kehleisen *n* molding plane iron

kehlen to groove, channel, flute, gorge, slot, key

Kehl-fuge *f* keyed pointing **-hammer** *m* rounded hammer **-hobeleisen** *n* molding plane iron

kehlig grooved, chamfered

Kehlkopf-mikrophon *n* throat microphone, laryngophone, throat mike **-spiegel** *m* laryngeal mirror, laryngoscope **-telephon** *n* throat phone

Kehl-leiste *f* ogee **-linie** *f* line of striction

Kehlnaht *f* throat seam, fillet weld or joint ~ **eines überlappten Stoßes** straight flat-lap weld **durchlaufende** ~ straight flat-lap weld **einseitige** ~ single-fillet weld **leichte** ~ straight flat-lap weld

Kehl-nahtschweißung *f* fillet weld **-rad** *n* groove or gorge wheel, wheel from groove or gorge of hyperboloid **-riemen** *m* throatlatch (harness) **-rinne** *f* gutter tile, valley channel or gutter **-schifter** *m* valley rafter **-schweißnaht** *f* fillet weld **-schweißung** *f* fillet welding or weld **-sockel** *m* coved skirting **-sparren** *m* valley rafter

Kehlung *f* haunch (of beam), molding

Kehlzeug *n* gouging planes or chisels

Kehrbewegung *f* reversing motion

Kehrbild *n* film negative, inverted image, back-to-back display (radar) **-entfernungsmesser** *m* inverted-coincidence or inverted-image range finder

Kehrdoppelwendel *n* reversed double loop

Kehre *f* turn (bank) ~ **über den Flügel** wing over (aviation) **flache** ~ flat bank (aviation)

kehren to turn, sweep (up)

Kehrgetriebe *n* reversing gear

Kehrherd *m* buddle, jagging board **drehender** ~ rotating table

Kehricht *m* dust, rubbish, refuse **-ofen** *m* incinerator

Kehrkurve *f* turn (aviation) **hochgezogene** ~ Immelmann turn

Kehr-lage *f* inverted position, lower side band position **-maschine** *f* power sweeper **-pflug** *m* turnwrest plow **-punkt** *m* cusp (of a curve)

Kehrrad *n* bull wheel, rack **-antrieb** *m* bull-wheel

drive or power
Kehr-schleife *f* serpentine **-schuß** *m* reversing weft **-seite** *f* reverse (side)
kehrt-machen to face about **-schwenkung** *f* alteration of course sixteen points in succession (naut.)
Kehrtunnel *m* loop tunnel
Kehrtwendung *f* turn, about-face turn **kurze ~** banked turn, sharp turn
Kehr-walzwerk *n* reversing rolling mill **-welle** *f* reverse shaft **-wendel** *n* reversed or return spiral, helix, coil **-wert** *m* reciprocal or inverse value **-wertintegration** *f* reciprocal integration
Keigrund *m* pebbly or flinty ground
Keil *m* key, wedge gib, cotter, liner, shim, dowel, cutter, V formation, feather, wedge-type breechlock, cleat, quoin **~ des Gewölbes** key of arch **~ und Kessel** break-through and encirclement **~ mit Spindelangriff** retaining spindle wedge plate **~ null** wedge zero **den ~ anziehen** to tighten cotter **konischer ~** cotter
Keil-abschluß (Ventil) valve disc **-achshobler** *m* spline milling machine **-ähnlich** wedge-shaped **-anordnung** *f* key arrangement **-anstellung** *f* wedge pass-setting device **-anzug** *m* taper of key or of wedge **-artig** wedge-shaped **-auslösung** *f* release of space bands **-auszieher** *m* key driver
Keil-bahnhobelarbeit *f* keyseating **-bahnlänge** *f* spline length **-beilage** (Prüfmaschine) gib **-berechnung** *f* key proportioning **-bolzen** *m* key bolt **-buchse** *f* tapered sleeve **-bügelkupplung** *f* wedge stirrup coupling **-dicke** *f* key width **-druckfeder** *f* spiral key spring
keilen to key, wedge
Keil-fänger *m* fishing, slip, or combination socket **-feder** *f* coiled spring **-flach** spheroid
Keilfläche *f* wedge surface, key bed **vordere ~** front face of wedge
Keil-flachschieber *m* sluice valve with flat body, wedge-type flat side valve **-flosse** *f* vertical tail fin **-form** *f* wedge shape, V formation or shape
keilförmig wedge-shaped **-er Querschnitt** *m* wedge section or shape
Keil-fuß *m* root of spline **-gehäuse** *n* cotter case **-glas** *n* prism lens **-hahnlänge** *f* spline length **-hammer** *m* wedge hammer **-haue** *f* pick, pickax, slitter **-höhe** *f* thickness of key **-kasten** *m* space band box **-kegel** *m* split collet **-klemme** *f* wedge-rail anchor **-kopf** *m* prism head **-kopierrahmen** *m* wedge type printing frame **-kupplung** *f* vee coupling **-lehre** *f* keyway gauge **-leiste** *f* spline part, taper gib
Keilloch *n* breech recess, cotter slot **-fläche** *f* breech-recess surface **-hammer** *m* splitting hammer **-meißel** *m* key-slot chisel
Keilnabe *f* spline shaft
Keilnaben-gelenk *n* splined vole-type universal joint **-mitnehmer** *m* splined hub sleeve, splined yoke **-schiebestück** *n* splined yoke
Keilnase *f* key head
Keilnut *f* keyway, groove, slot, slat, grooved wedge, key seat **~ einer Keilverzahnung** spline
Keilnuten *pl* splines **mit ~ versehen** to spline
Keilnutenfeder, gewöhnliche, geradstirnige ~ plain feather (mach.) **rundstirnige ~** round-ended feather (mach.)
Keilnuten-fräsen *n* keyway milling **-fräser** *m* keyseat cutter **-hobeln** *n* slotting **-lineal** *n* keyseat steel rule **-profil** *n* splines **-reibrad** *n* wedge-notched friction wheel **-stoßen** *n* keyway cutting **-ziehmaschine** *f* keyseater, keyseating machine
Keilnut-platte *f* plate with wedge-shaped groove **-scheibe** *f* grooved pulley
Keil-ovalschieber *m* sluice valve with oval body **-paar** *n* double wedge, pair of wedges **-pappe** *f* cardboard **-rad** *n* wedge-friction wheel, grooved friction wheel **-rädergetriebe** *n* wedge-friction gear, multiple V gear, frictional grooved gearing
Keilriemen *m* cone belt, V belt **-antrieb** *m* V-rope or V-belt drive **-ritzel** *n* V-belt pulley **-scheibe** *f* V-belt pulley, scored pulley **-triebe** *pl* V-belt drives
Keil-rille *f* groove, slot **-ring** *m* conical ring **-rundschieber** *m* sluice valve with round body **-schablone** *f* keyway gauge **-schieber** *m* wedge (sluice) valve **-schlitz** *m* key seat **-schloß** *n* wedge lock **-schluß** *m* keying **-schlüssel** *m* key wedge **-schneide** *f* knife edge **-schraube** *f* screw cotter, cotter screw, wedge plug or screw **-schwärzungsmesser** *m* circular-wedge densitometer **-schweißen** *n* V welding with binder
Keil-sitz *m* key seat **-spundung** *f* V groove **-stabläufer** *m* key bar rotor **-stahl** *m* key steel **-stein** *m* wedge brick **-stift** *m* taper pin **-strich** *m* cuneal-line **-stück** *n* wedge-formed part **-stütze** *f* hook bracket for insulator (with wedge lug) **-tisch** *m* tilting table **-transistor** *m* wedge-type transistor **-treiber** *m* knockout key, center plug, key driver **-trichter** *m* wedge-shaped gate (founding)
Keilung *f* wedging
Keil-verbindung *f* keying **-verjüngung** *f* taper **-verschluß** *m* wedge-type breechblock **-verzahnung** *f* splines **-vorrichtung der Zugstange am Schleusentor** keying of tie of a lock gate **-welle** *f* splined shaft, key shaft, splined arbor
Keilwellen-hülse *f* splined shaft bush **-schleifeinrichtung** *f* spline-shaft grinding attachment **-stumpf** *m* splined butt, splined shaft end **-zapfen** *m* splined shaft pin
Keilwinkel *m* front rake, cutting, wedge, or lip angle
Keilzahn *m*, **breiterer ~ in sonst gleichmäßiger Teilung der Kerbverzahnung** master spline
Keilzüge *pl* rifling with increasing twist
Keim *m* nucleus or seed (cryst.), germ, embryo, bacillus **-bildung** *f* nucleus formation **-bloßlegung** *f* nucleus denudation **-dicht** germproof **-drüse** *f* reproductive gland **-frei** free from contagion, sterilized, disinfected **-isolierung** *f* nucleus isolation
Keim-kraft *f* germinating power **-kristall** *m* crystal nucleus **-ling** *m* nucleus (cryst.), germ, embryo **-pflanzenmethode** *f* seedling method **-schale** *f* germinator **-tötend** bactericidal **-wirkung** *f* nuclear action (cryst.) **-zenter** *m* grain center
kein Ruf failure of audible ringing signal
Keithvorwähler *m* Keith-line switch
Kelch *m* calyx, chalice **-decke** *f* tegmen **-glocke** *f* cup-shaped gong
Kelle *f* ladle, trowel, signaling or marking disk
Keller *m* cellar, basement, vault

Keller-armatur *f* boiler fittings **-fußboden** *m* cellar floor **-geschoß** *n* basement **-lichtbogenofen** *m* Keller arc furnace **-sinkkasten** *m* cellar sink-water trap **-ton** *m* tunnel or boom effect **-wart** *m* shelter warden

Kellogschalter *m* multiple-throw switch

Keloid *n* keloid

Kelter *f* wine press

Kelvineffekt *m* Kelvin effect

Kenn-bake *f* identification beacon **-bar** remarkable, noticeable, distinguishable **-buchstabe** *m* indicating letter, code letter, identification letter **-dämpfung** *f* iterative attenuation constant **-dämpfungswiderstand** *m* iterative or characteristic impedance **-daten** *pl* characteristic data

Kennelly-Heaviside-Schicht *f* ionosphere, Kennelly-Heaviside layer

Kennfaden *m* (colored) tracer thread or serving **farbiger** ~ cotton binder

Kenn-feld *n* performance graph **-feuer** *n* identification beacon **-frequenz** *f* assigned frequency **-gerät** *n* identification apparatus **-größe** *f* characteristic quantity or magnitude

Kenngruppe *f* identification group **falsche** ~ misrouted message

Kenn-kurven *pl* characteristic curves **-leitwert** *m* indical admittance or conductance **-licht** *n* identification or recognition light, navigation light

Kennlinie *f* characteristic, characteristic curve ~ **von Eisenwiderständen** characteristic curve of iron filament ballast lamps ~ **der Elektronenröhre** characteristic of a thermionic valve, vacuum-tube characteristic **flache** ~ level characteristic **hyperbelförmige** ~ hyperbolic characteristic

Kennlinie, idealisierte ~ idealized characteristic **nicht lineare** ~ nonlinear characteristic **normale** ~ grid-plate characteristic, plate-current-grid-voltage characteristic, grid-potential-anode-current characteristic **optische** ~ light characteristic (of a glow lamp) **schleichende** ~ tailed characteristic **unsymmetrische** ~ asymmetrical characteristic

Kennlinien-bündel *n*, **-feld** *n* family of characteristics, family of curves **-kippung** *f* characteristic straightening

Kennlinienknick *m* bend of characteristic **oberer** ~ upper bend or knee of characteristic **unterer** ~ lower bend of the characteristic

Kennlinien-schar *f* family of characteristics **-schreiber** *m* plotter

Kenn-marke *f* identification or registering mark **-merkmal** *n* criterion, index, characteristic (feature) **-pfeil** *m* index arrow **-rille** *f* space (between bands on record disc)

Kennscheinwerfer *m* identification light

Kennsignal *n* tuning note, characteristic signal, signature of a station, theme

kenntlich conspicuous, clear, distinct **-machen** *n* **-machung** *f* marking identification, characterization

Kenntnis *f* knowledge **in** ~ **setzen** to advise (of), apprise **glaubhafte** ~ reliable knowledge ~ **nehmen** to take notice of

Kennummer *f* identification number, priority rating (building trade)

Kennung *f* route-marking characteristic (aviation), code as in identification-friend-or-foe radar recognition (light), identification or marker-beacon signal (wireless telegraphy)

Kennungs-anzeige *f* IFF-indication **-feuer** *n* visual flashing beacon **-frequenz** *f* modulation frequency **-geber** *m* identification keyer **-scheibe** *f* recognition-signal disk **-signal** *n* distinctive, identifying, or code signal, signature

Kennwert *m* characteristic (value) **-linie** *f* characteristic curve

Kenn-widerstand *m* indicial, image, or characteristic impedance **-winkelmaß** *n* iterative phase constant **-wort** *n* password **-zahl** *f* (numerical) office code, modulus with gears, characteristic factor, code number

Kennzeichen *n* characteristic, symptom, mark, indication, criterion, distinguishing or registering mark **allgemeines bauliches** ~ general design feature **amtliches** ~ official registration number or designation **besonderes** ~ specific embodiment (patent)

Kennzeichenleuchte *f* licence plate illumination

kennzeichnen to mark, designate, characterize, distinguish, brand, stamp

kennzeichnend indicative, characteristic, typical, specific **-er Unterschied** distinguishing difference

Kennzeichnung *f* characterization, mark, sign, indication

Kennzeichnungsschild *n* identification plate

Kennziffer *f* coefficient, (numerical or physical) characteristics, (office) code, index ~ *f* prefix (tel.) **bewertete** ~ weighted index

Kennzifferwähler, erster ~ A-digit selector **zweiter und dritter** ~ B- and C-digit selectors

Kenotron *n* high-vacuum rectifier valve, kenotron **-gleichrichter** *m* vacuum-tube rectifier

kentern to overturn, capsize, heel over

Kentern *n* capsizing **zum** ~ **bringen** to capsize ~ **des Stromes** turn of the tide

Kenterschäkel *m* swivel block

Keppgestänge *n* tilting rods

Keramik *f* ceramics **-kondensator** *m* ceramic capacitor **-metallgemisch** *n* ceramet, metal ceramic

keramisch ceramic **-e Bindung** vitrified bond **-e Feuerhaut** ceramic liner **-er Isolator der Zündkerze** ceramic insulator of plug **-e Körper** refractory material

Kerat *n* silver chloride, horn silver, cerargyrite

Keratometer *n* keratometer

Kerb *m*, **Kerbe** *f* groove, slot, notch, jag, score, depression **scharfer** ~ V notch, sharp notch, nick, groove, slot, slit

Kerb-biegeprobe *f* notched-bar bend test, nick bend test **-block** *m* notching block **-bolzen** *m* groove pin **-dauerfestigkeit** *f* notch fatigue strength **-empfindlichkeit** *f* stress-concentration index

Kerbe *f* mark, notch

Kerbempfindlichkeit *f* notch impact strength

kerben to groove, slot, notch, nick (in roughening rollers), rag

Kerben *pl* **mit** ~ **versehen** grooved

Kerbenfüllung *f* slit-and-tongue joint

Kerb-faktor *m* stress concentration factor **-festig-**

keit *f* notch toughness **-filter** *n* notch filter **-halbmesser** *m* radius of notch **-haue** *f* pickax **-hauer** *m* cutter (min.) **-holz** *n* tally, score, notched stick (min.)

kerbig serrated, jagged, notched

Kerb-kopf *m* rag head (met.) **-linien** *pl* indented rules **-nagel** *m* ribbed or notched nail **-nute** *f* keyway **-problem** *n* indentation problem **-prüfung** *f* notching test **-säge** *f* crosscut or pit saw **-scheitel** *m* root of the notch

Kerbschlag *m* impact (test) **-biegeprobe** *f* notched-bar impact-bending-test specimen **-biegeprüfung** *f* **-biegeversuch** *m* notched-bar or notch impact-bending test **-empfindlichkeit** *f* notch sensitivity **-festigkeit** *f* notched-bar or impact strength **-meßwert** *m* impact value **-probe** *f* **-versuch** *m* notched-bar impact test, notch bending test **-prüfung** *f* Izot test (Engineer)

Kerbschlagwert *m* resilience ~ **nach dem Izod-Verfahren** Izod value

Kerbschlag-widerstand *m* resilience **-zähigkeit** *f* notch impact strength or tenacity

Kerb-schnitt *m* notch **-sprödigkeit** *f* notch-brittleness **-stellen** ingot piping **-stift** *m* slotted or notched (taper) pin, splined pin **-verbinder** *m* indented connector **-versuch** *m* impact test **-verzahnt** splined (externally or internally)

Kerbverzahnung *f* serration **Mutter mit** ~ splined nut

Kerb-wirkung *f* notch effect **-wirkungszahl** *f* fatiguestress concentration factor **-zähigkeit** *f* notched-bar toughness, notch toughness, impact value, notch impact strength or resistance, tear resistance (of rubber) by slit test

Kerbzähigkeits-probe *f*, **-prüfung** *f* notched-bar impact test

kerbzähnig indented, serrated

Kerb-zahnnabe *f* serrated hub **-zange** *f* indentor **-zugprobe** *f* notched-bar tensile test, notched-bar pull test

Kermes *m* antimony vermilion, red trisulfide of antimony

Kern *m* core, nucleus or kernel of an integral equation, kernel, core of a magnet, grain, pip, crux (of a matter) ~ **aus geblättertem Eisen** laminated (iron) core (elec.) ~ **mit niedrigem Kohlenstoffgehalt** low-carbon core ~ **aus grünem Sand** green or green-sand core ~ (Spiralbohrer), web

Kern, bandumwickelter ~ tape-wound core **geblätterter** ~ laminated core **geschlitzter** ~ split core **geschlossener** ~ closed core **offener** ~ open core **ohne** ~ coreless **ungebackener** ~ green core **unterteilter** ~ (fein), (finely) subdivided core **versetzter** ~ misplaced core (foundry)

Kern-ablage *f* core deposit **-ablegeplatte** *f* core-receiving plate or tray **-abmessung** *f* nuclear size **-absaugpumpe** *f* core pump **-abschirmung** *f* electron screening, screening of nucleus **-abstand** *m* internuclear distance **-achse** *f* epipolar axis **-anregung** *f* nuclear excitation **-auge** *n* print, core print **-ausdrücker** *m* core knockout **-ausrichtung** *f* nuclear alignment **-ausrüttler** *m* core knockout **-ausstoßmaschine** *f* core machine

Kern-baum *m* heartwood tree **-baustein** *m* nucleon **-baustoffe** *pl* core materials **-bildung** *f* germination, nucleation **-bindemittel** *n* core binder

Kernbindungs-energie *f* nuclear binding energy **-fluidum** *n* nuclear fluid **-kräfte** *pl* force constants of linkages

Kern-blasmaschine *f* core blower **-blech** *n* core lamination or tray **-böckchen** *n* chaplet, box stud **-bohren** to core

Kernbohrer *m* core bit **automatischer** ~ automatic core-breaking tool

Kern-bohrmaschine *f* core drilling machine **-brennstoff** *m* nuclear fuel **-büchse** *f* core die, core box **-chemie** *f* nuclear chemistry **-distanz** *f* internuclear distance **-drahtrichtmaschine** *f* core-wire straightening machine **-drehbank** *f* core turning lathe **-durchdringung** *f* nuclear-penetration function

Kerndurchmesser *m* core diameter, root diameter (of gearing), minor thread diameter ~ **der Schraube oder des Schraubengewindes** root, minor, or core diameter of screw

Kern-durchschnitt *m* section of core **-ebene** *f* epipolar plane **-einflußfunktion** *f* nuclear importance function **-einleger** *m* core setter **-eisen** *n* core iron, mottled white pig iron **-empfindlichkeit** *f* notch sensitiveness

Kernenergie-anlage *f* nuclear power plant **-kraftwerk** nuclear power plant **-technik** *f* nuclear engineering

Kern-explosion *f* nuclear burst **-fach** *n* basic field **-faden** *m* core thread **-fänger** *m* core catcher **-fangring** *m* ring for fishing socket **-farbe** *f* nuclear stain **-ferne Elektronen** planetary, peripheral, orbital, or outer electrons, valence or conduction electrons **-ferromagnetismus** *m* nuclear ferromagnetism **-festigkeit** *f* core strength **-fett** *n* a fat whose soap is easily salted out **-form** *f* core mold **-formeinrichtung** *f* core-making equipment **-formen** *n* core molding

Kernformmaschine *f* core-molding machine ~ **mit Druckluftpressung** air-squeezing core machine ~ **mit Handabhebung** core-turnover draw machine ~ **mit Handhebelpressung** hand-squeezing core machine ~ **mit Wendeeinrichtung** core-rollover machine

Kernform-platte *f* core plate, core die **-presse** *f* core-molding machine

Kern-forschungszwecke *pl* nuclear research purpose **-fremdes Feld** extranuclear field **-fusion** *f* nuclear fusion **-garbe** *f* effective portion of cone of fire (ballistics) **-gebunden** attached to nucleus **-gehalt** *m* nuclear concentration, content of nuclei **-gemäuer** *n* thin inwall **-geschoß** *n* armor-piercing shell **-gestreut** deflected by nucleus **-guß** *m* cored work, cored casting

kern-haltig nucleous **-härte** *f* (bei eingesetzten Teilen) core hardness **-heber** *m* core lifter **-herstellung** *f* core making, production of cores **-holz** *n* heart, heartwood, seedling **-hülse** *f* core socket

kernig substantial, firm, solid

Kern-induktion *f* nuclear induction **-isobare** *f* nuclear isobar **-isomer** *n* nuclear isomer **-isomerie** *f* nuclear isomerism **-kasten** *m* core box (met.) **-kastenfräsmaschine** *f* core-box milling machine **-kastenregal** *n* core-box shelf **-konstanten** *pl* nuclear constants **-körperchen** *n* nucleolus (biol.) **-kraftwerk** *n* nuclear power station **-kronenbohrer** *m* core drill

Kern-ladung *f* main charge, base section **-ladungsverteilung** *f* nuclear-charge distribution

-ladungszahl *f* charge on nucleus, nuclear-charge number, atomic number **-leder** *n* leather from central part of hide **-loch** *n* core print, cored hole **-lochdeckel** *m* core-hole cap **-lochverschluß** *m* core-hole cover

kernlos coreless, seedless **-er Induktionsofen** coreless induction furnace

Kern-lüftung *f* ventilation of the core **-macher** *m* core maker **-macherei** *f* core-making department, core shop **-machertisch** *m* core-making bench **-magnetische Kopplung** nuclear magnetic coupling **-magnetmeßwerk** *n* core-magnet measuring element **-magneton** *n* nuclear magneton **-marke** *f* core mark, core print **-maß** *n* caliber

Kernmauer *f* core wall, curtain **~ von Beton** concrete core wall **~ von Eisenbeton** reinforced core wall

Kern-mauerwerk *n* inwall **-mitbewegung** *f* motion of the nucleus **-moment** *n* nuclear moment **-nagel** *m* core nail, pipe nail, chaplet, molder's nail

kernnahe Elektronen inner or fixed electrons, electrons adjacent nucleus

Kern-neuanordnung *f* nuclear rearrangement **-niveaus** *pl* nuclear energy levels **-ofen** *m* core oven **-ofenanlage** *f* core-oven plant **-öl** *n* core oil **-orientierung** *f* nuclear orientation **-paramagnetismus** *m* nuclear paramagnetism **-patrone** *f* core die **-periodizität** *f* nuclear periodicity **-pfropfen** *m* core plug **-photoeffekt** *m* photonuclear reaction **-physik** *f* nuclear physics **-platte** *f* core plate

Kern-presse *f* press-type core machine **-prozeßstreuphase** *f* nuclear phase shift **-pulver** *n* coated smokeless powder, progressively burning powder **-punkt** *m* strong point, reduit, decisive point, epipole **-quadrupolresonanz** *f* nuclear quadrupole resonance

Kern-resonanzfluoreszenz *f* nuclear-resonance fluorescence **-reich** nucleated **-ring** *m* ring for lifting core **-ringheber** *m* core lifter ring **-riß** *m* heart shake (in wood) **-rissig** shaky (crevice) **-rissigkeit** *f* internal cracking **-rohr** *n* liner artillery, inner tube, core barrel, A tube **-röhrenmuffenhänger** *m* core-barrel coupling tap **-rollband** *n* core conveyor **-rückfeinen** *n* core refining (met.) **-rückstellimpuls** *m* core recovery pulse **-rüttler** *m* core jolter

Kern-schablone *f* core template **-schäle** *f* internal annular shake (in-wood) **-schatten** *m* umbra **-scheibe** *f* core disk **-schliff** *m* male part of ground-in joint **-schrott** *Q* high-grade melting scrap **-schuß** *m* point-blank shot **-schußweite** *f* point-blank range

Kernsand *m* core sand **-mischmaschine** *f* core-sand mixer

Kern-satz *m* suite of cores **-schalenmodell** *n* nuclear shell model **-schichtmethode** *f* core method **-schlagfestigkeit** *f* notch impact strength

Kernseife *f* curd soap **abgesetzte ~** settled curd soap **geschliffene ~** pitched curd soap

Kernseifen *pl* all soaps (upper layer) which form by salting out

Kernspaltung *f* nuclear fission **~ in drei Bruchstücke** ternary fission

Kern-speicher *m* core store (info proc.) **-spin** *m* nuclear spin **-spindel** *f* core spindle (straw plaiting) **-spule** *f* core coil

Kernstabilität *f*, **ungerade-gerade Regel der ~** odd-even nucleus

Kern-stift *m* core pin **-strahl** *m* epipolar ray **-strahlenbüschel** *n* epipolar pencil of rays **-strecke** *f* cored interval or distance **-stück** *n* principal item, core part **-stütze** *f* chaplet, box stud

kern-technisch nuclear **-technologie** *f* nucleonics **teilung** *f* nuclear division **-theorie** *f* neclear theory **-transformator** *m* core transformer **-trocken** flint dry (thoroughly dry) **-trockenanlage** *f* core-baking equipment **-trockenkammer** *f* core-baking oven

Kerntrockenofen *m* core-baking oven **~ mit ausziehbaren Trockenzellen** rack-type core oven, drawer-type core oven

Kern-trockenschrank *m* core-baking oven **-trokkenwagen** *m* core-oven truck **-trocknung** *f* core baking or drying **-umänderungsprozeß** *m* nuclear-disintegration process **-umwallung** *f* enceinte (fort.) **-umwandlung** *f* nuclear transmutation

Kern-verschmelzung *f* nuclear fusion **-verlust** *m* core loss, iron loss **-vierer** *m* central quad of cable, four-wire core **-wechselwirkung** *f* nuclear interaction **-werkstoff** *m* core material **-zähigkeit** *f* toughness of the core **-zahl** *f* number of centers or of nuclei **-zähler** *m* nuclei counter **-zerschmiedung** *f* forging burst(s) **-zertrümmerung** *f* nuclear fission or disintegration **-zone** *f* core zone

Kerogen *n* kerogen

Kerosin *n* kerosene

Kerr-effekt *n* Kerr effect **-kondensator** *m* **-zelle** *f* Kerr cell **-zellenschaltung** *f* Kerr-cell circuit

Kerze *f* candle (power), spark plug, taper, international-standard candle **römische ~** Roman candle, magnesium torch, smoke pot

Kerzen-elektrode *f* spark-plug electrode **-fassung** *f* candle-lamp holder **-filter** *m* filtering candle **-flamme** *f* candle flame **-gerade** as straight as a die **-gewinde** *n* spark-plug thread **-kopf** *m* spark plug head **-körper** *m* spark-plug body **-lichtstärke** *f* candle power **-masse** *f* candle composition **-prüfer** *m* plug tester

Kerzen-reihe *f* spark plug bank or series **-reiniger** spark-plug cleaner **-sitz** *m* plug seat **-spannung** *f* spark plug voltage **-stärke** *f* candle power **stärkencharakteristik** *f* candle-power characteristic **-stecker** *m* plug connector **-stein** *m* plug insulator **-zündung** *f* electric ignition, preignition, spark-plug ignition

Kescher *m* catch net

Kessel *m* kettle, boiler, caldron, copper, reservoir, basin, air bottle (torpedo), tank, depression, crater, excavation, deep hollow **~ für Augenblicksverdampfung** flash boiler **~ mit Innenfeuerung** internal-firebox boiler **~ ablassen** to empty a boiler **den ~ ausklopfen** to scale or fur boiler

Kessel-abklopfwerkzeug *n* boiler-scaling tool **-ablaßventil** *n* main boiler blow-off valve **-abnahme** *f* boiler acceptance **-abwärme** *f* boiler waste heat **-amalgamation** *f* pan amalgamation **-anlage** *f* boiler plant **-armatur** *f* **-ausrüstung** *f* boiler fittings **-bauanstalt** *f* boiler shop **-bauart**

f boiler type **-bauingenieur** *m* boilermaker **-bauwerkstatt** *f* boiler shop

Kessel-bekleidung *f* boiler casing **-bekohlungsanlage** *f* boiler-coaling plant **-betrieb** *m* boiler operation **-blech** *n* boiler plate **-block mit 3 Zügen** 3 pass boiler block **-boden** *m* end plate, airvessel end, boiler end, bottom, or head, bulkhead, cylinder head, pump head **-bodenring** *m* bottom ring of compass bowl **-bohrer** *m* boiler auger **-bruch** *m* circular subsidence (geol.) **-dampf** *m* live steam **-dampfmaschine** *f* steam-boiler or generator machine

Kessel-deich *m* half-moon dike **-dekatiervorrichtung** *f* decatizing machine **-druck** *m* boiler pressure, working pressure **-einmauerung** *f* boiler setting **-entlaugungseinrichtung** *f* boiler blow down set **-fabrik** *f* boiler factory **-feuerung** *f* boiler firing, boiler furnace **-flammrohr** *n* boiler flue **-förmig** kettle-shaped **-gas** *n* boiler flue gas **-gewindebohrer** *m* boiler tap **-gruppe** *f* battery of boilers **-gut** *n* boiler fuel

Kessel-hammer *m* boiler-scaling hammer **-haus** *n* boilerhouse **-hausbetrieb** *m* boilerhouse operation **-heizfläche** *f* boiler-heating surface **-kohle** *f* boiler or steam coal **-lager** *n* bed(ding) of boiler **-lagerung** *f* boiler setting **-lauge** *f* boiler sludge **-los** tankless **-luftfilter** *m* drum-type air filter **-mantel** *m* boiler casing, jacket of compass bowl, kettle casing, boiler or chamber envelope or wall

kesseln to ventilate with a fire kibble (mining) **~** (von Bohrlöchern) to chamber (explosives)

Kessel-niederschlag *m* boiler scale, deposit on boiler surface **-ofen** *m* pot furnace, crucible furnace **-pauke** *f* tymbal, kettledrum **-pferdestärke** *f* boiler horsepower **-platte** *f* boiler plate **-probe** *f* boiler test **-probierpumpe** *f* boiler tester or test pump **-prüfung** *f* boiler test **-raum** *m* boiler room **-reibahle** *f* square-shank taper bridge reamer **-reparaturwerkstatt** *f* boiler repair shop **-revision** *f* boiler inspection **ring** *m* ring of compass bowl **-rohr** *n* boiler tube, heating tube **-rost** *m* boiler grate

Kessel-schäumen *n* boiler priming **-schaumverhütung** *f* anti-priming **-schleuse** *f* foursquare lock, sluice or lock with circular chamber **-schluß** *m* shell ring or belt **-schmied** *m* boilermaker **-schüsse** *f pl* chambering shots, shell rings **-sohle** *f* boiler level **-spannung** *f* boiler pressure **-speisen** to boiler-feed **-speisepumpe** *f* boiler feeder

Kesselspeisewasser *n* boiler feed water **-messer** *m* boiler-feed-water meter **-pumpe** *f* boiler-water feed pump **-vorwärmer** *m* feed-water heater (boiler)

Kesselspeisung *f* boiler feed **-sprung** *m* boiler crack

Kesselstein *m* (boiler) scale, water incrustation **~ abklopfen** to scale

Kesselstein-abklopfer *m* tube cleaner, coke knocker **-abklopfhammer** *m* scaling hammer **-ablagerung** *f* boiler-scale deposit **-ansatz** *m* incrustation of boiler fur **-bildung** *f* alkali scale (in radiators), boiler-scale formation **-lösemittel** *n* boiler-cleansing compound **-mittel** *n* antiscale composition **-niederschlag** *m* scale deposit **-verhütungsmittel** *n* boiler-antiscaling or anti-incrustant composition **-zerstörer** *m* anti-crustator

Kessel-stirnwand *f* front end plate of boiler **-stuhl** *m* boiler support **-tafel** *f* boiler control panel **-trommel** *f* boiler drum **-typ** *m* type of boiler **-überwachungsapparat** *m* boiler-supervising apparatus **-verkleidung** *f* boiler jacket

Kessel-wagen *m* tank wagon or car, fuel truck **-wand** *f* boiler shell, wall of compass bowl **-warte** *f* boiler switchboard **-wartung** *f* boiler maintenance **-wasserreinigung** *f* boiler-water treatment **-wasserrohr** *n* water tube, boiler tube **-wirkungsgrad** *m* boiler efficiency **-zubehör** *n* boiler accessories **-zug** *m* (boiler) draft, boiler flue pass

Ketongruppe *f* ketonic group

Ketsch *f* ketch

Kettbaum *m* warp, warp beam **-schleuder** *f* warp beam hydroextractor

Kettdruck *m* warp print (printing)

Kette *f* chain, train, series, warp (of a fabric), circuit (elec.), cell, element, flight, network, channel, bondage, string (info proc.) **~ zum Ausbalanzieren des Querbalkens** chain for counterweighing the crossrail **~ mit eingenieteten Bolzen** riveted chain **~ mit versplinterten Bolzen** cottered chain **~ mit Einschlagkeilen** chain with spike hooks **~ ohne Ende** endless chain **~ mit gedrehten Gliedern** twist-link chain **~ mit seitlichen Laufrollen** outside-roller chain **~ und Schuß** warp and filling (cloth)

Kette, ~ abschakeln und schlippen to slip the cable **die ~ ausstecken** to veer cable **doppelsträngige ~** double-strand chain **durchlässige ~** transmission filter, acceptor circuit **einsträngige ~** single-strand chain **elektroakustische ~** channel, electroacoustic transducer **endlose ~** endless chain **Gall'sche ~** sprocket or pin chain, roller chain

Kette, gegossene ~ malleable chain **geschlossene ~** endless chain **innermolekulare ~** intramolecular chain **kurzgliedrige ~** short-link chain **langgliedrige ~** long-link chain **lose ~** slack chain **mehrsträngige ~** multiple-strand chain **zerlegbare ~** detachable chain **zweisträngige ~** double-strand chain

Kettel *f* hasp, clasp, small chain **-maschine** *f* looping, binding-off, or linking machine

ketteln to loop, stitch, bind off, link

Kettel-nadel *f* turning hook **-schiene** *f* linking bar

ketten to chain, connect, link

Ketten *pl* (dünne) bucklers **~ junger Gebirge** young mountain ranges

Ketten-abbruch *m* chain breaking **-abdeckung** *f* track shield **-abnahme** *f* chain discharge **-abweiser** *m* chain stripper **-andreher** *m* twister (textiles) **-anker** *m* chain grapplers **-anknoten** *n* chain twisting (textiles) **-antrieb** *m* chain drive **-aufhängung** *f* triatic (radio) **-aufleger** *m* chain tool **-aufzug** *m* chain lift

Ketten-bahn *f* chain road, chain tramway **-bandeinleger** *m* traveling feed table **-baum** *m* roller, warp, or yarn beam (textiles) **-becherwerk** *n* chain elevator **-befestigungsglied** *n* chain-attachment link **-beschicker** *m* chain feeder **-bindung** *f* catenary linkage **-bogen** *m* catenary **-bolzen** *m* link pin (chain), chain stud, track pin **-bruch** *m* continued fraction (math.) **-bruch-**

darstellung *f* continued fraction representation **-bruchmethode** *f* method of infinite continued fractions **-brücke** *f* chain (suspension) bridge

Kettendämpfung *f* iterative-attenuation constant ~ **je Glied** iterative attenuation per section

Ketten-dämpfungsfaktor *m* iterative-attenuation factor **-druck** *m* printing of warp (textiles) **-durchhang** *m* slack of chain **-einbau** *m* chain installation **-einleitung** *f* chain induction **-einsteller** *m* chain adjuster **-einziehen** *n* warp drawing-in (textiles) **-eisen** *n* chain steel **-elevator** *m* bucket elevator **-endbolzen** *m* chain coupler **-faden** *m* warp thread

Kettenfahrleitung *f* catenary construction, catenary suspension ~ **mit Hilfstragedraht** compound catenary construction ~ **mit doppeltem Tragseil** double catenary construction

Ketten-fahrzeug *n* tracked vehicle, track-laying vehicle **-fläche** *f* catenoid **-flaschenzug** *m* chain tackle block, chain block, pulley chain hoist **-förderband** *n* chain conveyor **-förderer** *m* chain conveyer **-förderung** *f* chain haulage (min.)

kettenförmig having the form or shape of a chain **-e Siebschaltung** ladder-type filter

Ketten-fräsmaschine *f* chain mortiser **-führer** *m* flight leader or commander **-führung** *f* chain guide, flight lead or leader **-führungsrolle** *f* chain-guide pulley **-gabel** *f* pointer **-gebläse** *n* rosary or chain trompe **-gehänge** *n* bridle mooring **-geschäft** *n* chain store **-gespräch** *n* automatic sequence call **-getriebe** *n* chain drive

Kettenglied *n* chain link, studded link, network mesh, filter section, element, track shoe or block, chain segment ~ **erster Art** mid-shunt termination, mid-shunt, π section ~ **zweiter Art** mid-series termination, mid-series, T section

Ketten-gliedbolzen *m* chain link pin **-grad** *n* half-track motorcycle **-halter** *m* picket (surveying) **-haube** *f* chain housing **-hebel** *m* chain lever **-hülse** *f* chain bushing **-hubeinrichtung** *f* chain hoisting gear **-isolator** *m* chain insulator

Ketten-kasten *m* chain locker, chain case **-keil** *m* wedge formation of three aircraft **-kernreaktion** *f* nuclear chain reaction **-klüse** *f* chain hawse **-kraftrad** *n* half-track motorcycle **-kran** *m* chain hoist **-kranz** *m* sprocket ring **-kurbel** *f* bolt link pinion

Ketten-länge *f* length of land chain or of any chain **-lasche** *f* chain side bar, fishing chain **-last** *f* chain load, cable locker **-lauf** *m* chain travel, chain path **-lauffläche** *f* chain tread **-laufrad** *n* bogie wheel **-laufrolle** *f* chain roller **-leerkuppelung** *f* chain dummy coupling **-leimer** *m* warp sizer (textiles)

Kettenleiter *m* network, filter, periodically recurrent structure, chain (system), artificial coil, iterative network ~ **erster Art** π network ~ **zweiter Art** T network **aus Impedanzen gebildeter** ~ impedance network **aus gekoppelten Kreisen bestehender** ~ coupled-circuit chain

Kettenleiter, mit einem halben Längsglied endender ~ mid-series-terminated network **mit einem halben Längsglied** (Querglied) **beginnender** ~ wave filter terminated at mid-series (mid-shunt) **mit einem halben Querglied endender** ~ mid-shunt-terminated network **mehrgliedriger** ~, **vielgliedriger** ~ multimesh or multisection network **zweigliedriger** ~ two-section network

Kettenleiterabschluß durch ein halbes Längsglied (Querglied) mid-series (mid-shunt) termination of a network

Ketten-leiterglied *n* network mesh, filter section **-leitermasche** *f* mesh, section of a network **-leitrolle** *f* chain-guide pulley, sheave **-leitung** *f* artificial line, low-pass filter **-linie** *f* catenary (curve), line of confinement **-linienförmig** catenoidal **-maß** *n* length of the land chain **-matrix** *f* iterative matrix **-matte** *f* chain mesh mat **-messung** *f* chain surveying **-molekül** *n* chain molecule

Ketten-naht *f* intermittent weld **-nuß** *f* sprocket wheel, chain wheel **-öse** *f* chain link **-phasenfaktor** *m* iterative-phase factor **-platte** *f* chain side bar **-prüfmaschine** *f* chain testing machine **-pumpe** *f* chain pump, rag pump

Kettenrad *n* chain wheel, sprocket wheel, pattern chain drum ~ **für zerlegbare Kette** detachable-chain sprocket wheel

Kettenrad-antrieb *m* chain drive **-fräser** *m* sprocket cutter **-kette** *f* sprocket chain **-reiniger** *m* sprocket scraper **-vorgelege** *n* chain-wheel gear **-walzfräser** *m* sprocket hob

Ketten-rauschzahl *f* noise measure (electr. tube) **-reibung** *f* chain friction

Kettenreihe *f* chain-line formation (aviation), flight of airplanes echeloned left or right ~ **rechts** flight echelon starboard

Ketten-rohrschraubstock *m* chain pipe vise **-rohrzange** *f* chain-pipe wrench **-rolle** *f* chain pulley, wheel, or roller **-rollenlager** *n* chain roller bearing **-rollenscheibe** *f* chain sheave **-rost** *m* chain-type traveling grate, chain grate **-rostfeuerung** *f* chain grate firing **-säge** *f* chain saw **-schächte** *pl* chain pits **-schake** *f* chain link **-schaltapparat** *m* chain-switch-apparatus **-schaltung** *f* chain (relay) circuit

Ketten-scheibe *f* sprocket wheel **-schema** *n* chain pattern **-schenkelauge** *n* chain lug eye, eye of a side bar (elec.) **-schermaschine** *f* warping mill or frame (textiles) **-schlepper** *m* chain or caterpillar tractor **-schlichten** *n* warp dressing (textiles) **-schlinge** *f* rope loop (chain loop) **-schrämmaschine** *f* chain coal cutter **-schutz** *m* gear housing, chain guard **-seitensteg** *m* chain side bar **-sorte** *f* type of chain

Ketten-spanner *m* chain tightener, chain-stretching device, track spreader, track-connective fixture, track-connecting tool, chain tension adjuster **-spannrolle** *f* chain tension adjusting roller **-spannschraube** *f* chain-adjusting screw **-spannvorrichtung** *f* chain-tension device **-spill** *n* chain windlass

Ketten-stab *m* picket (surveying) **-steg** *m* stud, bar, stay pin **-stemmaschine** *f* chain mortising machine **-stern** *m* chain drum **-steuerung** *f* chain control **-stich** *m* chain stitch **-stopper** *m* anchor-chain stopper

Kettenstrang *m* chain strand **gezogener** ~ tight strand of chain **loser** ~ slack strand of chain

Ketten-stuhl *m* warp loom **-tasche** *f* side link **-teilung** *f* chain pitch **-treibscheibe** *f* dredging tumbler **-trieb** *m* chain drive **-triebrad** *n* driving sprocket **-trommel** *f* chain drum **-trumm** *n* strand of chain **-typ** *m* type of chain **-übersetzung** *f* chain gearing **-übertragung** *f* chain transmission **-übertragungsmaß** *n* iterative-propagation constant **-umwandlung** *f* chain decay, series disintegration

Ketten-verbindungsglied *n* chain coupler link, connecting link of chain **-verstärker** *m* distributed amplifier **-verzweigung** *f* chain branching **-verzweigungswahrscheinlichkeit** *f* chain-branching probability **-waage** *f* chainomatic balance **-ware** *f* warp fabric (textiles) **-wärme-explosion** *f* chain thermal explosion **-wechselwirkung** *f* chain reciprocal action **-welle** *f* sprocket shaft **-widerstand** *m* iterative impedance (electronics, four-pole theory) **-winde** *f* chain winch or jack

Kettenwinkelmaß *n* iterative-phase constant ~ **je Glied** phase or wave-length constant per section

Ketten-wirbel *m* swivel **-zahnrad** *n* sprocket **-zange** *f* chain tongs **-zerfall** *m* chain disintegration **-zieher** *m* chain man, chain leader or follower **-zug** *m* chain pull, chain tackle block, chain hoist

Kettspanner *m* warp shiner

Kettung *f* chaining

ketzern to cleave hard rocks with quoins

Keubel *m* sieve with a wide mouth (min.)

Keule *f* club, leg of meat, brayer (print.) lobe (radar)

Keulen-aufgliederung *f* lobe splitting (ant.) **-diagramm** *n* lobe pattern (rdr) **-förmig** lobar

Keupermergel *m* red marl

Khaki *n* khaki

Khlopinit *m* khlopinite

Kiefer *f* pine, fir

Kiefer(n)-harz *n* pine resin **-holz** *n* fir wood, pine wood **-öl** *n* pine oil **-platte** *f* pine plank

Kiel *m* keel **-bank** *f* gridiron

kielen to keel

Kiel-feder *f* quill feather **-flosse** *f* vertical tail fin (aviat.), vertical stabilizer, tail or keel fin **-gording** *f* gridiron **-holen** *n* careening **-klotz** *m* keelblock **-lager** *n* keel blocking **-laschung** *f* keel scarf **-linie** *f* keel line **-pumpe** *f* bilge pump

Kielraum *m* bilge **-pumpe** *f* bilge pump

Kiel-schwein *n* keelson **-schwert** *n* drop keel **-sponung** *f* **-spündung** *f* outward keel-grooving, rabbet of keel **-stapel** *m* keelblock (locks and dry docks) **-stoßpunkt** *m* keel apex **-versteifung** *f* keel bracing **-wasser** *n* wash, wake, dead water **-wirkung** *f* keel effect

Kieme *f* gill

Kienholz *n* fir or pine wood

kienig resinous

Kien-öl *n* kien oil **-ruß** *m* lamp black **-teer** *m* pine tar

Kiepe *f* wicker basket, scuttle, dosser

Kies *m* grit, pyrites, (fine) gravel, shingle **grober** ~ broken stone, rubble

Kies-abbrand *m* roasted pyrites, purple ore **-ablagerung** *f* deposition of gravel **-ähnlich** pyritous, pyritic, gravelly **-bank** *f* gravel bank **-bettung** *f* gravel ballast **-boden** *m* gravel soil

Kiesel *m* flint, silica, silex, pebble, flint stone

kieselartig flinty, siliceous **-es** (kalkiges) **Gestein** siliceous (calcareous) deposit

Kieselerde *f* silica, silex **-gel** *n* silicagel

Kiesel-fluoraluminium *n* aluminum silicofluoride **-fluorblei** *n* lead fluosilicate **-fluorkalium** *n* potassium fluosilicate **-fluornatrium** *n* sodium fluosilicate **-fluorsalz** *n* silicofluoride

Kieselfluorwasserstoff-säure *f* hydrofluosilicic acid, silicofluoric acid **-saures Blei** lead fluosilicate

Kiesel-fluß *m* siliceous flux **-flußsäure** *f* fluosilicic acid **-flußsaures Elektrolyt** fluosilicic electrolyte **-galmei** *m* siliceous calamine **-gesteine** *pl* siliceous rocks **-glas** *n* flint glass **-grund** *m* pebbly or shingle bottom

Kieselgur *f* kieselguhr, fossil meal, diatomaceous earth, diatomite, infusorial earth **-dosiergerät** *n* kieselguhr dosing unit **-stein** *m* kieselguhr brick

kieselhaltig siliceous, siliciferous

kieselhart flint-hard

kieselig pebbly, flinty

Kiesel-kalk *m* siliceous limestone **-kalkeisen** *n* ilvaite **-kalkspat** *m* wollastonite **-kalkstein** *m* cherty limestone **-kreide** *f* chalk flint **-mangan** *n* rhodonite **-salz** *n* fluosilicate **-sandstein** *m* siliceous sandstone

kieselsauer siliceous, silicated **-es Antimonoxyd** antimony silicate **-es Kali** potassium silicate **-er Kalk** (mono)calcium silicate **-es Natron** sodium silicate **-es Salz** silicate **-e Tonerde** (hydrated) aluminium silicate

Kieselsäure *f* silica, silicic acid **-anhydrid** *n* silicic anhydride **-haltig** siliceous **-verbindung** *f* silicate

Kieselschiefer *m* cherts **schwarzer** ~ touchstone, Lydian stone

Kiesel-schlag *m* macadamizing, macadam pavement **-sinter** *m* siliceous sinter, geyserite, pearl sinter **-stein** *m* flint, pebble **-tuff** *m* siliceous sinter of geyser **-wasserstoff** *m* hydrogen silicide **-wasserstoffsäure** *f* hydrosilicic acid **-wismut** *m* bismuth silicate **-wolframsäure** *f* silicotungstic acid **-zinkerz** *n* siliceous calamine, sillemite, willemite **-zuschlag** *m* siliceous flux

Kieserit *m* kieserite

Kies-fang *m* gravel trap **-filter** *n* rubble filter **-grube** *f* gravel pit, ballast pit **-haltig** pyritiferous **-harke** *f* gravel or ballast rake

kiesig gritty

Kies-körnung *f* gravel fraction **-rechen** *m* gravel or ballast rake **-sand** *m* gravel (sand), grit, (natural) mixture of sand and gravel **-schüttung** *f* ballasting **-straße** *f* graveled road **-unterlage-schicht** *f* sub-layer of gravel **-wäsche** *f* bar mining

Kille *f* narrow channel

Kiln *m* kiln

Kilodyn *n* kilodyne

Kilo-ampere *n* (Einheit) kilo-ampere **-curie** *f* kilocurie **-elektronenvolt** kilo-electron-volt **-gauß** *n* kilogauss

Kilogramm *n* kilogram or kilo **-kalorie** *f* large calorie, kilogram-calorie **-meter** *n* kilogram-meter **-molekül** *n* kilogram molecule

Kilohertz *n* kilocycle per second (kc/s)

Kilokalorie *f* kilogram-calorie, French or large calorie

Kilometer *n* kilometer **-stein** *m* milestone **-stunde** *f* kilometers per hour **-zähler** *m* mileage meter, trip meter **-zirkel** *m* kilometer divider or circle

Kilomol *n* kilogram molecule

Kiloohm *n* kilohm

Kilovarstunde *f* kilovar-hour

Kilovolt *n* kilovolt **-ampere** *n* kilovolt-ampere

Kilowatt *n* kilowatt **-stunde** *f* kilowatt-hour

Kilozähler *m* milage recorder

Kimm *m* visible horizon, bilge, chine

Kimme *f* notch, dip, edge, border, brim, chine, sight notch, notch of rear sight, projection, rear sight on gun, bilge

Kimmbeobachtung *f* observation of the horizon

Kimme und Korn *n* notch-and-bead, notch and (barley) corn

Kimmenhalter *m* jaw blade holder

Kimm-fehler *m* dip error, losing the horizon (photogrammetry) **-kante** *f* chine **-schlitten** *m* bilge block **-schwingschaltung** *f* saw-tooth oscillator, relaxation oscillator **-sente** *f* bilge harping **-spiegel** *m* horizon glass **-tiefe** *f* dip of the horizon **-tiefenmesser** *m* horizon-inclination meter **-träger** *m* chine (seaplane) **-triefe** *f* dip of the horizon

Kimmung *f* bilge

Kimmungsplanke *f* bilge strake

Kimmweiden *pl* basket frame

Kinematik *f* kinematics

kinematisch-e Kette train **-e Zähigkeit** kinematical viscosity

Kinematographie *f* cinematography

kinematographische Aufnahme moving-picture filming

Kinemometer *n* kinemometer

kineplastisch kineplastic

Kinescop *n* kinescope

Kinestat *n* kinestate

Kinesthesie *f* kinesthesia

kinesthetisch kinesthetic **-es Empfindungsvermögen** kinesthetic sensitivity

Kinetik *f* kinetics

kinetisch kinetic **-e Deutung** kinetical explanation **-e Dichtung** kinetic seal **-e Energie** kinetic energy **-e Gastheorie** kinetic theory of gases **-er Scheinwiderstand** motional impedance (electronics) **-e Wirkung** kinetic effect

Kink *m* kink (in chain or wire rope)

Kinn *n* chin **-kette** *f* curb chain **-kettengrube** *f* chin curb socket, chin groove **-riemen** *m* chin strap **-stössel** *m* chin tug, chin strap **-stütze** *f* chin support

Kino *n* motion-picture theater **-aufnahmegerät** *n* motion-picture-making equipment **-basisgerät** *n* cinema base-line apparatus **-flecker** *m* cinematic spotter or spotting device **-gleichrichter** *m* cinema rectifier **-maschine** *f* (sound) film projector **-positiv** *n* moving-picture positive **-skala** *f* projection scale **-theodolit** *n* recording or motion-picture theodolite **-wand** *f* motion-picture screen

Kiosk *m* newsstand

Kipp *m* sweep (elec) **-ablenkung** *f* relaxation scanning **-achse** *f* axis of tilt, horizontal axis, hinge pin **-achsenfehler** *m* error (in horizontality) of axis of tilt **-amplitude** *f* sweep amplitude **-anhänger** *m* dump-body trailer **-anordnung** *f* sweep circuit **-antrieb** *m* tilting or tipping gearing **-aufzug** *m* automatic tray elevator, skip hoist **-ausschalter** *m* trip-out switch **-bandanlage** *f* belt conveyor

kippbar tiltable, inclinable **-er Konverter** tipping converter **-er Ofen** tilting furnace **-e Traverse** tiltable lifting beam

Kipp-begichtung *f* skip charging or filling **-begichtungsanlage** *f* skip-charging gear

Kipp-bolzen *m* swing bolt **-becher** *m* tipping bucket **-bestreben** *n* tendency to dip **-bewegung** *f* tilting or tipping motion **-brücke** *f* (Magnetschalter) tumbler yoke **-bühne** *f* tipping stage, tipping or dumping platform **-drossel** *f* cutoff choke

Kippe *f* stock pile, dump, hinge joint

Kippelektrometer *n* Wilson electrometer

kippen to tilt, upset, tip, incline, throw off, trip over

Kippen *n* tipping, dumping, tilting, reversal or return of pencil (in scanning) **-generator** *m* impulse generator **~ des Kolbens** piston slap, cocking of piston **~ der Mauer** overturning or collapse of wall

kippend, einmalig -e Schaltung trigger circuit

Kippentladung *f* condenser discharge

Kipper *m* tipper, dump truck; (Kippschalter) keyswitch, switching key **-brücke** *f* tipping stage **-katzenbrücke** *f* tipping stage

Kipp-erscheinung *f* jump or swing phenomenon **-fahrzeug** *n* tipper **-flanke** *f* wave front of sweep voltage

Kippfrequenz *f* sweep, relaxation or time-base frequency **Regelung der ~** holding control

Kipp-gefäß *n* tipping bucket, skip car **-gelenk** *n* tilting joint **-generator** *m* sweep generator **-gerät** *n* relaxation oscillator, saw-tooth oscillator, sweep apparatus or circuit, tilting device, time-base device **-gestänge** *n* tilting rods **-getriebe** *n* tilting gear (searchlights etc.) **-gießwerk** *n* tiltable casting machine

Kipphebel *m* rocker arm, valve rocker, tipping lever, arm-rocker lever **-achse** *f* rocker-arm shaft, rocker shaft **-block** *m* valve-rocker bracket or pedestal rocker-arm bearing, rocker-arm bracket, rocker-shaft bearing bracket **-drehpunktbolzen** *m* valve-rocker bush or bushing **-fett** *n* rocker grease

Kipphebelgehäuse *n* rocker box, rocker-support box **am Zylinderkopf angegossenes ~** rocker-box horn

Kipphebel-kugelpfanne *f* rocker-arm cup **-lagerbock** *m* rocker-shaft bearing pedestal **-lagerung** *f* rocker-arm bearing **-rolle** *f* valve-rocker roller **-rollenbolzen** *m* valve-rocker roller pin **-schalter** *m* toggle switch **-schmierung** *f* rocker-arm lubrication **-steuerung** *f* rocker gear **-welle** *f* rocker-arm shaft **-zapfen** *m* valve-rocker fulcrum pin

Kipp-impuls *m* tripping impulse **-kapazität** *f* timebase condenser **-kante** *f* tilting edge **-karre** *f* dump cart **-karren** *m* tip or dump barrow, tipping cart

Kippkasten *m* tippler **-gehänge** *n* dump bucket **-karosserie** *f* dump body (truck)

Kipp-kessel *m* swivel pan **-kette** *f* tripping chain **-kondensator** *m* sweep condenser **-kraft** *f* tilting or tipping force **-kreis** *m* time-base, trigger, or relaxation circuit **-kübel** *m* dump or tipping bucket, skip car **-lager** *n* hinged, pivot, or rocker bearing, swing support (bridge) **-lauf** *m* drop barrel

kipplig unstable, labile

Kipp-lore *f* dump car **-mechanismus** *m* tipping or tilting mechanism **-messer** *m* pitching indicator **-mischer** *m* tipping or tilting-type mixer **-moment** *n* pull-out torque (synchronous-motor practice), breakdown torque (induction-motor practice), pitching moment, maximum torque (mech.) **-mulde** *f* tipping trough or hopper **-neigung** *f* capsizing or tipping gradient **-ofen** *m* tilting furnace

Kipp-periode *f* time-base period **-pfanne** *f* lip-poured ladle, tipping or tilting ladle **-platte** *f* tipping batten **-prahm** *m* barge, scow **-problem** *n* skew problem **-punkt** *m* pullout point (AC motor) **-regel** *f* (telescopic-sighting) alidade **-regler** *m* snap-action controller **-relais** *n* trigger-action relay **-rinne** *f* troughlike edging guide **-röhre** *f* sweep tube

Kipp-schale *f* well dish (photo.) **-schallerzeuger** *m* push-pull transducer **-schalter** *m* tumbler or toggle switch, (switching) key **-schaltung** *f* saw-tooth or relaxation oscillator, sweep circuit

Kippschaltungen *pl* **~ mit Vakuumröhren** sweep circuits with high-vacuum tubes (hard tubes) **~ mit Zweipolglimmlampen** sweep circuits with two-element glow lamps

Kipp-schnecke *f* tip screw (scope mount), elevating worm **-schraube** *f* tilting screw; (Nivellierinstrument) tilting level screw **-schwimmer** *m* carburetor float, hinged-type float

Kippschwinger *m* time-base oscillator **~ mit Neonröhre** neon oscillator

Kippschwingkreisröhre *f* trigger circuit tube

Kippschwingmethode, fremdgesteuerte unselbständige ~ distant-operated time-base method **selbständige mitgenommene ~** self-running controlled time-base method

Kipp-schwingschaltung *f* saw-tooth or relaxation oscillator **-schwingung** *f* relaxation vibration, relaxation, saw-tooth, or ratchet oscillation, time-base oscillation, Kipp oscillation

Kippschwingungen *pl* saw-tooth, relaxation, tilting, or seesaw oscillations **selbständige ~** self-running time bases **unselbständige ~** dependent or controlled sweep oscillations

Kippschwingungs-dauer *f* relaxation period **-generator** *m* relaxation generator or oscillator **-gerät** *n* relaxation oscillator **-schaltung** *f* relaxation-oscillation connection **-wandler** *m* relaxation inverter

kippsicher stable **~ machen** to stabilize

Kippsicherheit *f* stability **~ der Ruhelage** stability in rest position

Kipp-sicherung *f* stabilizer **-spannung** *f* saw-tooth voltage (oscillograph), sweep voltage **-spannungsapparat** time-base unit **-spannungserzeuger** *m* saw-tooth time base **-spannungsrücklauf** *m* flyback of sweep potential, return of time-base potential to zero **-spannungsschaltung** *f* time-base circuit **-spiegel** *m* oscillating or vibrating mirror **-spule** *f* flip coil (cathode-ray oscillator) **-spulenpaar** *n* sweep-coil pair **-stange** *f* adjusting rod **-stellung** *f* rocking position

Kippstrom, sägezahnförmiger ~ saw-tooth-shaped sweep current

Kipp-stromgenerator *m* scan current generator **-strosse** *f* dumping level **-stuhl** *m* tilting chair **-tisch** *m* tilting table **-transformator** *m* sweep transformer **-umschalter** *m* tip-change switch

Kipp- und Knickmoment overturning bending moment

Kippung *f* tilt

Kippungs-anzeiger *m* tilt indicator **-winkel** *m* angle of tilt or of inclination

Kipp-verfahren *n* press-and-blow operation (for forming glassware) **-verstärker** *m* snap-action amplifier **-vorgang** *m* sweep process, time-base or ratchet action **-vorrichtung** *f* tipping or tilting, device or equipment, tipple, dumping mechanism **-vorrichtungsgetriebe** *n* tipping gearing **-waage** *f* tipping scale

Kippwagen *m* dump car or truck, skip, tipping wagon **-aufzug** *m* skip bridge or hoist **-begichtung** *f* skip charging

Kipp-wassermesser *m* tilting trap **-welle** *f* rocker shaft **-werk** *n* tilting machinery **-winkel** *m* tipping angle **-zapfen** *m* pivot pin **-zeiger** *m* pitching indicator **-zeit** *f* time of relaxation

Kirchhoffsches Gesetz Kirchhoff's law

Kirchturm *m* church tower, steeple

Kirnvorrichtung *f* churning machine

Kirschbaumholz *n* cherry wood

Kirschglut *f* cherry-red heat

Kirschrot *n* cherry red, bright red **-glühhitze** *f* **-glut** *f* cherry-red heat

Kissen *n* cushion, pad, obturator pad, gas-check pad, washer for bearings **-fallschirm** *m* seat pack (parachute) **-förmiger Raster** pillow-shaped scanning pattern

Kissen-lautsprecher *m* pillow-type speaker **-schmierung** *f* cushion lubrication **-verzeichnung** *f* negative distortion, pincushion distortion

Kiste *f* box, case, chest, plane, crate, (slang) aircraft

Kisten-ausschlagpapier *n* casing (lining) paper **-brett** *n* boxboard, case board **-glühung** *f* box, pot, or close annealing **-kühler** *m* box-type cooler **-maß** *n* box measurement, cubic contents **-öffner** *m* ripping bar **-transportanlage** *f* platform conveyer for handling cased goods **-verschlag** *m* crate

Kits *f* ketch

Kitt *m* putty, mastic, cement, lute

kitten to cement, putty, glue

Kitten *n* lutation, luting

Kitt-falz *m* puttying groove **-fläche** *f* cementing surface **-material** *n* stopping **-mittel** *n* cement **-öl** *n* putty oil **-wachs** *n* bee glue, propolis

Kjedahlkolben *m* Kjedahl flask

Kjellin-Ofen *m* Kjellin (ring-shaped induction) furnace

klaffen to spall, split, gape

Klaffen *n* gaping

klaffende Wunde gash

Klaffstelle *f* gap

Klaffung *f* (in entzerrten Luftbildplänen), gap (in aerophotographic plans)

Klafter *n* fathom, cord **-belastung** *f* span loading

klaftern to fathom

klagbar indictable, actionable **~ werden** to bring action or suit (against)

Klage *f* complaint, grievance, suit (law) **-abweisung** *f* dismissal of claim **-beantwortung** *f* reply, answer, defense (plea) **-grund** *m* grievance, cause of action

klagen to complain, bring action, sue, file a suit

Klagepatent *n* patent in issue or in suit

Kläger *m* accuser, plaintiff, complainant

Klageschrift *f* plaint, bill of charges, statement of claim

Klamm *f* glen, ravine, defile
klamm tight, close, narrow, clammy
Klammer *f* clamp, cramp, clip, brace, clasp, swivel **mit ~ befestigen** to clip (on) **runde Klammern** parentheses, round brackets **eckige Klammern** (square) brackets (print.) **zusammenfassende Klammern** braces (print.) **das in Klammern Gesetzte** (the term) in parentheses
Klammer-anpreßmaschine *f* stapling machine **-ausdruck** *m* term in parentheses, Poisson bracket **-befestigung** *f* clamp fixing **-fuß** *m* butt swivel plate **-haken** *m* square clincher, dog hook, anchor hook **-hefter** *m* clip binder
klammern to cramp, brace, clasp
Klammer-relation *f* bracket relation **-ring** *m* retaining ring **-schieber** *m* wire staple pusher **-vorrichtung** *f* grappling device
Klampblock *m* clump block
Klampe *f* cleat, clamp, chick
Klang *m* musical sound **blecherner ~** tinny sound **zusammengesetzter ~** complex musical sound
Klang-bild *n* acoustic or sound pattern **-bildveränderung** *f* change in sound impression **-blende** *f* tone control or switch, tone-shading means, tonalizer **-drossel** *f* tone-control choke (coil) **-einsatz** *m* acoustic intonation, onset of a sound **-empfindung** *f* perception of sound
Klangfarbe *f* timbre, stamp, tone (color), tone controls (tape rec.) **helle ~** strident timbre (acoust.) ringing sound
Klang-färbemittel *n* tone-shading means, tone or timbre-control means, tonalizer **-farbenregelung** *f* tone control **-farbenregler** *m* tone control, tonalizer **-färber** *m* tone control **-feder** *f* coiled-wire gong (of coin-collector stations) **-figur** *f* sound pattern, acoustic figure **-fülle** *f* sound volume **-gemisch** *n* sound spectrum **-getreu** of high fidelity, orthophonic **-güte** *f* tone quality
Klang-intensitätsbereich *m* dynamic range of sound **-lehre** *f* acoustics **-messer** *m* phonometer **-platte** *f* sounding plate **-plattenklopfer** *m* plate sounder **-probe** *f* ringing or resonance test **-regelung** *f* tone control **-regler** *m* tone control
Klangreinheit *f*, **hohe ~** hi-fi
Klang-reiniger *m* acoustic clarifier **-umfang** *m* sound volume **-voll** sonorous **-wirkung** *f* acoustics, sound effect
Klapp-arm *m* hinged arm, extension arm **-ausleger** *m* hinged jib (hinged) apron extension **-auslegereinziehwerk** *n* apron hoist engine
klappbar hinged **nach unten ~** swing-down **-es Mannloch** manhole davit
Klapp-bett *n* folding cot **-blende** *f* drop shutter, blindage, folder stop **-bootbrücke** *f* pontoon bridge **-brücke** *f* drawbridge **-deckel** *m* hinged cover
Klappe *f* trap, lid, cover, flap, valve, trap door, shutter, indicator, damper, hatch (relief and gauging), tailboard, key (of wind instrument), pallet (of harmonium) **~ zum Niederlassen** lowerable flap **~ mit Topfmagnet** tubular indicator **die ~ aufrichten** to restore the shutter **einschenkelige ~** single-coil indicator **selbsthebende ~** self-restoring indicator **zweischenkelige ~** two-coil indicator
klappen to work out, click, strike, clapper, clap, flap, fold, open, close, (e.g., lid of a chest)
Klappen *pl* flaps **-achse** *f* gate bearing **-antriebsmotor** *m* modulating motor **-ausschlag** *m* flap displacement, deflection setting **-betätigung** *f* flap control, flap actuator **-betonbüchse** *f* clack concrete box **-bohrer** *m* clack bit **-brücke** *f* bascule bridge **-büchse** *f* clack valve **-führung** *f* clapper box, flap track or guide **-halter** *m* clapper box **-horn** *n* key horn **-mechanismus** *m* key work, key action
Klappenöffnung, selbsttätige ~ self-opening flap
Klappenprahm mit seitlichen Laderäumen side-dump scow
Klappenscharnier *n* flap hinge
Klappenschrank *m* drop-indicator or drop-type switchboard, board indicator, portable switchboard, private-branch exchange **~ für Induktoranruf** magneto switchboard **~ zu sechs Leitungen** six-line switchboard **~ für Nebenstellen** telephone switchboard for private-branch exchange **~ für Reihenanlagen** switchboard for intercommunication sets **aufklappbarer ~** hinged switchboard **schnurloser ~** cordless switchboard
Klappen-seilfänger *m* socket with valve to fish for rope **-sicherung** *f* folding safety device **-signal** *n* beat or clappers **-sitzfläche** *f* valve seating **-spindel** *f* air valve **-stellschrauben** *pl* clamping bolts **-streifen** *m* strip of indicators **-stutzen** *m* valve connection **-tiefe** *f* flap chord
Klappen-ventil *n* clack or flap valve, check or leaf valve **-ventilbüchse** *f* clack bailer **-verschluß** *m* hinged cover, flap shutter **-verstellung** *f* change in flap angle **-wehr** *f* dam
klapperfrei rattleproof
klappern to chatter, rattle
Klappern *n* chatter(ing), rattle, rattling
Klapp-fenster *n* skylight **-flügel** *m* folding wing **-form** *f* folding mold **-formkasten** *m* snap flask **-gesenk** *n* collapsible die **-hacke** *f* pick mattock **-horde** *f* dumping kiln **-käfig** *m* folding cage **-kassette** *f* hinged dark slide **-korn** *n* movable gun sight **-kübel** *m* hinged or tipping bucket
Klapp-laden *m* Venetian blind **-lafette** *f* extendable mount **-lager** *n* tilting bearing **-luke** *f* hinged hatch **-maßstab** *m* pliant rule **-messer** *n* jack-knife **-öler** *m* oiler **-rahmen** *m* hinged frame **-schalttafel** *f* hinged switchboard **-scheibe** *f* bobbing target **-schloß** *n* snap lock
Klapp-schraube *f* swing bolt, hinged bolt **-schute** *f* hopper barge, bottom-dump scow **-schütz** *n* butterfly valve **-seilmesser** *n* valve rope cutter **-sitz** *m* folding seat, tip-up seat **-sitzfläche** *f* valve seating **-sonde** *f* bailer **-spant** *n* hinged bulkhead **-spiegelstereoskop** *n* folding mirror stereoscope **-sporn** *m* folding trail spade, folding leg
Klapp-stück *n* hinge piece **-stuhl** *m* folding chair **-stütze** *f* movable stanchion **-sucher** *m* folding finder **-teil** *n* hinged portion **-tisch** *m* folding table
Klapptor *n* flap gate, gate pivoting about horizontal axis along base or along top **~ im Gleichgewicht** balanced wicket gate **eisernes ~** metal hinged falling gate
Klapp-transformator *m* rotatable coaxial-coil transformer **-trommel** *f* collapsible drum **-tür** *f* trapdoor, drop door **-variometer** *n* hinged-coil variometer **-ventil** *n* mousetrap (petroleum),

flap valve **-visier** *n* leaf sight

klapsen to slap

klar clear, distinct, bright, evident, articulate, lucid, intelligible, transparent **~ ausziehen** to exhaust completely **~ halten** to keep clear, clear **~ machen** to clarify, to explain, clear decks (navy), make ready, alert **-es unverfälschtes Gasolin** straight-run gasoline **-e Linienführung** clean lines

Klär-anlage *f* clarification (or filter) plant, sewage-treatment plant, clarifying basin or plant **-apparat** *m* clarifier **-bad** *n* clearing bath **-bassin** *n* settling tank or basin, tub, vat, or reservoir **-becken** *n* settling tank, catch pit, settler **-behälter** *m* settling tank

Klärbottich *m* settling tub, settling or clearing tank, tub, vat, or reservoir

Kläre *f* clearing liquor

Klareis *n* clear ice

klären to clear (up), clarify, settle

Klärfaß *n* settling cask, settler

Klarfernschreibmaschine clear-test teleprinter

Klär-filter *n* clarifying filter **-gas** *n* sewer gas **-filtrationsaufgeben** *pl* clarifying filtration

Klargasanlage *f* clear-gas plant

Klärgefäß *n* clarifier

Klarglas-einstellscheibe *f* clear-glass (focussing) screen **-glocke** *f* clear glass globe **-scheibe** *f* clear glass lens (disk)

Klarheit *f* clearness, distinctness, articulation, transparency, visibility

klarieren to clear

Klarierungsschein *m* clearance paper

klarifizieren to clarify

Klarinol *n* a type of cleaning fluid for optical glass

Klärkasten *m* settling box

Klar-lack *m* clear varnish or lacquer **-liste** *f* checklist (aviat) **-meldelampe** *f* all-clear or all-ready signal light

Klärmittel *n* clarifier, clearing agent, fining substance

Klärpfanne *f* clarifier

Klar-scheibe *f* antidim eyepiece (gas mask) **-scheren** to underrun

Klärschichten *pl* clarification sheets

Klarschlag *m* clearing

Klärsel *n* clear of fine liquor (sugar) **-decke** *f* washing with pure-sugar solution

Klar-sichtsalbe *f* antidim compound **-scheiben** *pl* non-clouding windscreen

Klär-spänewaschmaschine *f* chips- or shavings-clarifying washer **-spitze** *f* settling cone

Klarstellung *f* explanation

Klär-sumpf *m* **-teich** *m* settling pond or basin, separating sump, clearing basin or sump

Klartext *m* text in clear (code), plain language **-funken** *n* transmitting in clear

Klartonverfahren *n* noiseless film method

Klärtopf *m* settling sump

Klärung *f* clarification, clearing, settling, purification

Klärungsmittel *n* clarifying or clearing agent, clarifier, fining substance

Klarwasserüberlauf *m* clean-water overflow

Klarzelle *f* celluloid template (photo.)

Klärzyklon *n* cyclone clarifier

Klasse *f* grade, class, sort, quality, size, order; (bei Meßgeräten) class of accuracy

Klasseberechtigung *f* class rating (aviat)

Klassen-einteilung *f* classification **-grenzen** *pl* class limits **-größe** *f* class interval **-häufigkeitstabelle** *f* frequency table **-kette** *f* chain of class **-ordnung** *f* classification

Klassier-anlage *f* grading or classifying plant **-apparat** *m* classifier **-einschub** *m* classification unit

klassieren to classify, sort, grade, screen, size, settle, separate

Klassieren *n* classifying

Klassierer *m* bowl classifier

Klassier-rost *m* classifying grate **-sieb** *n* grading, sizing, or classifying screen **-trommel** *f* sizing or classifying drum

Klassierung *f* classification, sorting, grading, screening, sizing, gravitation thickening, settling, separation

Klassierzyklon *n* cyclone classifier

Klassifikation *f* classification **~ im geschlossenen Kreislauf** closed-circuit classification

Klassifikationsanlage *f* classification mill

Klassifikator *m* classifier **~ mit Vorbehälter** bowl-type classifier

klassifizieren to grade, classify

klassifiziert classified

Klassifizierung *f* classification, grading

klassisch classical **-es System** classical system, non-quantized system

klastisch clastic (rock), fragmental

Klatsche *f* beat, clappers **~** (Bremsluftschraube), fan brake

Klatschenbild *n* beat picture

Klaubarbeit *f* hand picking, selection

Klaube-band *n* picking or sorting belt **-berge** *m pl* pickings, wailings

klauben to pick (out), separate, sort (out), pick by hand **das Erz ~** to cull ore

Klauben *n* selection

Klauber *m* picker, wailer

Klaubetisch *m* picking or sorting table

Klaub-hammer *m* sifter, picker, pick hammer **-herd** *m* frame, nicking buddle **-junge** *m* picker, wailer **-tisch** *m* picking table, sorting board

Klaubung *f* hand picking

Klaue *f* paw, grasp, prong, clutch, pawl, jaw, claw, catch, dog, talon, fluke (navy), tappet cap

Klauen-anordnung *f* jaw arrangement **-beil** *n* claw hatchet **-bohrer** *m* claw bit **-fänger** *m* alligator grab **-feder** *f* ball clip **-fett** *n* neat's-foot oil **-förmig** jaw-shaped **-futter** *n* jaw chuck, guide lining **-haken** *m* claw hook **-hammer** *m* nail or claw hammer **-kasten** *m* (Drehbank) claw box

Klauenkuppelung *f* shifting-jay clutch coupling, jaw clutch (coupling), claw coupling or clutch, dog clutch or coupling **~ mit drei Klauen** square jaw clutch **~ mit vier Klauen** spiral-jaw clutch

Klauenkuppelungsausrücker *m* clutch shifter

Klauen-kurbel *f* forked lever **-maul** *n* pinch bar **-öl** *n* neat's-foot oil **-muffe** *f* dog clutch **-polgenerator** *m* claw-pole stationary-field synchronous generator **-rad** *n* dog clutch **-ring** *m* collar (barrel), guide ring **-schaltmuffe** *f* claw-(gear-)switch collar **-schaltung** *f* dog clutch

-stange *f* clutch rod **-versetzung** *f* claw offset

Klaukuppelung *f* dog, jaw, or claw coupling

Klausel *f* clause, stipulation

Klaustalit *m* clausthalite, lead selenide

Klaviatur *f* keys, keyboard, finger board, bank of keys **-exzenter** *m* keyboard eccentric **-schreibmaschine** *f* keyboard typewriter

Klavier *n* harpsichord, clavichord, piano

Klavier-draht *m* music wire, piano wire **-harfe** *f* keyed harp, piano harp **-tastenschalter** *m* piano-key selector

Kleb-äther *m* collodion **-band** *n* friction tape, adhesive or sticky tape

Klebe-band *n* splicing tape (tape rec.) **-fähigkeit** *f* adhesiveness **-fläche** *f* adhesion surface area **-grenze** *f* limit of adhesion, sticky limit (Atterberg) **-kraft** *f* adhesive or binding power **-lack** *m* sizing (glue), dope **-masse** *f* adhesive gluing component **-mittel** *n* adhesive, agglutinant, cement

kleben to stick, glue, paste, adhere (to), cement, follow closely, trail, splice (tape rec.) **Anker ~** to stick, freeze **auf ein Formular ~** to gum to a form **das Relais klebt** the relay is sticking

Kleben *n* gumming, adhesion, sticking (of a keeper), freezing, adhering, gluing **~ des Ankers** sticking of the armature **~ der Elektronen** capturing or sticking of electrons

Klebenaht *f* gluing seam

klebenbleiben to stick fast

klebend adhesive, adherent

Klebe-presse *f* blooper, splicer **-prüfung** *f* bonding test

Kleber *m* (rolling material) sticker, gummer, adhesive

Klebe-rand *m* jointing edge **-schicht** *f* adhesive coat **-stärke** *f* dextrin **-stellengeräusch** *n* splice bump, dull sound due to blooping patch **-stoffe** *pl* adhesive materials **-stift** *m* residual stop, stop pin **-streifen** *m* adhesive tape **-tisch** *m* splicing table or bench **-vakuum** *n* vacuum to hold apparatus parts together **-verschlußrolle** *f* gummed sealing reel **-zettel** *m* gummed label, sticker

Kleb-fähigkeit *f* cohesiveness, binding property **-folie** *f* adhesive film **-fuge** *f* joint **-grenze** *f* limit of adhesion **-kitt** *m* adhesive cement

Klebkraft *f* adhesive or binding power or force **elektrische ~** electrostatic adhesion or retentive force

Kleb-lack *m* adhesive lacquer **-pflaster** *n* adhesive tape

klebrig sticky, adhesive, glutinous, viscous, ropy, pasty, viscid

Klebrigkeit *f* stickiness, viscosity, adhesiveness

Kleb-sand *m* plastic refractory clay **-stift** *m* stop, distance piece, stop pin **-stoff** *m* binding material, adhesive, gum, paste **-stoffkitte** *m pl* adhesives, cements **-streifen** *m* adhesive tape **-wachs** *n* bee glue, propolis

Klebung *f* gumming

Klecks *m* dab, ink spot **-dichte** *f* blob density

Klecksigkeit *f* blob structure

Kleckslängenmessung *f* blob length measurement

Klee *m* clover **~ und Alfalfa-Dreschvorrichtung** clover and alfalfa threshing apparatus

Kleeblatt *n* clover, webbler (mach.) **-antenne** *f* clover-leaf antenna **-aufbau** *m* clover-leaf body **-kreuzung** *f* clover-leaf (flyover) junction, clover-leaf intersection

Kleebogen *m* foiled arch

Klee-salz *n* potassium binoxalate **-säure** *f* oxalic acid **-seide** *f* clover dodder

Klei *m* clay, marl **-abreibemaschine** *f* branning machine

Kleider-ablage *f* clothes closet **-presse** *f* electric ironing press **-sack** *m* duffel bag **-schrank** *m* ward-robe, locker

Kleidkeule *f* serving mallet

Kleidung *f* clothing

Kleie *f* bran, clover **-melasse** *f* bran molasses

klein small, little, insignificant, petty, minor, fine (gravel) **-er Flügel** tar tab (aviation) **-er Kreis** small circle **-er Kreuzer** light cruiser **-er machen** to make smaller, break up (coal, stone, etc.), lower **-er werden** to become smaller, diminish, decrease **-e Steigung** fine pitch (aviat)

Klein-anlagen *pl* small unit **-automat** *m* automatic cut-out (elec) **-bahn** *f* narrow-gauge railroad, substandard gauge railroad **-bahnhof** *m* small railroad station **-beleuchtung** *f* small lighting outfit(s) **-bessemerbirne** *f* small Bessemer converter **-bessemerei** *f* baby Bessemer steel plant **-betrieb** *m* small plant, small-scale manufacturing operation **-bildaufnahme** *f* micro-photography **-bildkammer** *f* miniature camera **-bildphotographie** *f* microphotography, photomicrography **-birne** *f* small converter **-buchstabe** *m* lower case letter

Kleineisen *n* light-section iron **-waren** *pl* **-zeug** *n* small ironware, small hardware

Klein-elektromotor *m* small power electromotor **-entstauber** *m* portable unit dust collectors **-falzer** *m* small-size folding machine **-feldabsorption** *f* narrow-beam absorption **-fernhörer** *m* small receiver **-film** *m* narrow or substandard film **-flugzeug** *n* small plane **-förderanlage** *f* small conveyer

Kleinfunk-apparat *m* walkie-talkie, portable radiotelephone set **-brücke** *f* small type radio link **-gerät** *n* walkie-talkie **-kraftwagen** *m* small radio truck **-stelle** *f* field-radio station, portable-radio-transmitting station **-trupp** *m* portable-radio section

Klein-gefüge *n* fine structure, microstructure **-gefügebild** *n* (photo-)micrograph **-gerät** *n* tackle **-guß** *m* small castings **-handel** *m* retail trade **-händler** *m* retailer **-hebezeug** *n* small lifting equipment, small block

Kleinheit *f* smallness

Kleinigkeit *f* detail, trifle, small matter

Kleinkaliber-lauf *m* subcaliber tube, small-bore barrel **-munition** *f* subcaliber ammunition **-schießen** *n* small-bore target practice

kleinkalibrig small in diameter, of small bore or caliber

Klein-kammer *f* small (air) chamber, thimble **-kohle** *f* buckwheat coal, pea coal **-koks** *m* small-sized coke, nut coke, domestic coke **-konverter** *m* small converter **-kraftrad** *n* light motorcycle **-kraftwagen** *m* small motorcar, light car

Klein-kupolofen *m* small cupola furnace **-küvette** *f* miniature cell **-lader** *m* trickle charger **-lampe** *f* miniature lamp **-lastwagen** pickup truck **-lebewesen** *n* microorganism **-lichtbildkunst** *f* photomicrography, microphotography **-lückig** close-grained, of fine porosity **-luftschiff** *n* blimp **-maschinensatz** *m* small generator, portable generating unit **-messer** *m* micrometer

Kleinmotor mit Bruchteilen einer Pferdestärke fractional-horsepower motor

Klein-orientierung *f* subsidiary orientation **-periode** *f* minor cycle **-pflaster** *n* pavement of small cobblestones in interlocking pattern, pebble pavement **-phasenschieber** *m* small-size phase shifter **-regler** *m* simple or inexpensive controller **-röhre** *f* miniature tube **-rüttler** *m* small-sized jarring machine **-sandstrahlgebläse** *n* sandblast tank cabinet **-schalter** *m* installation switch **-schlag** *m* finely crushed rock, broken stone, small-sized scrap, chippings **-schmiedeofen** *m* small forging furnace **-schrauber** *m* small-size screw driver **-schütz** *m* miniature contactor

Klein-sendegerät *n* portable radio transmitter **-selbstschalter** *m* automatic cut-out, miniature automatic circuit breaker **-serienbau** *m* small-scale series production **-serienfertigung** *f* short-run production **-spannungsanlage** *f* low-tension installation **-er gemeinsamer Nenner** least common denominator (math)

kleinst minimum **-er Gleitwinkel** minimum gliding angle **-e Periode** minor cycle **die -en Quadrate** the least squares

Klein-stahlwaren *pl* small articles **-stapel** *m* small pile **-station** *f* small power station

Kleinst-bewegung *f* micromotion **-empfänger** *m* midget set **-gebilde** *n* microscopic structure **-gleitzahl** *f* minimum gliding ratio, minimum lift-drag ratio **-maschine** *f* miniature machine

Kleinstmaß *n* lower limit, smallest size, least dimension **auf das ~ zurückführen** to minimize

Kleinst-periode *f* minor cycle **-röhre** *f* acorn tube **-serienfertigung** job-lot operation **-spiel** *n* minimum clearance **-übermaß** *n* minimum interference

kleinstückig small-sized, light-sized

Kleinstwert *m* minimum value, minimum

Klein-teil *m* small part **-triangulation** *f* triangulation network not of primary order, subsidiary triangulation **-umfangkopien** *pl* low-range prints **-verkauf** *m* retail(ing), selling by retail **-vernebelung** *f* limited-area smoke screen, local smoke screening **-versuch** *m* small-scale test **-wagen** *m* light car **-wählerzentrale** *f* unit automatic exchange (U.A.X.) **-werkzeuge** *pl* small or shop tools

Kleinwinkel *m* small angle **-korngrenze** *f* small-angle-grain boundary **-streuung** *f* small-angle scattering **-streuversuch** *m* small-angle scattering experiment

Kleister *m* glue, paste, gum

kleistern to paste

Klemm-anschluß *m* clamping connection **-auge** *n* clamping eye **-backe** *f* clamping jaw, jaw, gripping (jaw) device, grip holder

Klemmbolzen *m* binder plug, clamping bolt **Kurbelwellen ~** crankpin clamping screw

Klemm-brett *n* terminal board **-buchse** *f* adapter bush **-bügel** *m* clamp strap **-druck der Kalanderwalzen** calender pressure

Klemme *f* clamp, chuck, clip, holder, terminal (elec.), connecter (battery), binding post, box clamp, binding screw, pliers, dilemma **entnehmbare ~** output-terminal noise, backfire

Klemmeffekt *m* pinch effect

klemmen to clamp, wedge, squeeze, grip, hold, pinch, cramp **sich ~** to catch, become jammed **das Korn ~** to hold right or left

Klemmen *n* wedging, squeezing, clamping, freezing (in boring)

Klemmenanschluß *m*, **verdeckter ~** covered-in terminal connection (elec.)

Klemmen-block *m* terminal box **-brett** *n* terminal panel **-deckel** *m* terminal cover **-dose** *f* connection box, terminal strip **-endverschluß** *m* terminating box **-feld** *n* terminal strip

Klemmen-halter *m* terminal holder **-kasten** *m* terminal block, connection box, plug box **-leiste** *f* terminal or connection strip **-platte** *f* clamping or connection plate **-schutzkasten** *m* terminal box **-spannung** *f* force fit, ratchet brake, terminal voltage, binding-post voltage **-streifen** *m* connection strip, terminal strip **-widerstand** *m* terminal impedance or resistance

Klemmer *m* clip, vise, terminals

Klemmfassung *f* crimper

Klemmfeder *f* retainer spring, clamping spring

Klemmfutter *n* clamping, elastic, or expanding chuck **~ zum Innenklemmen** expanding chuck

Klemm-gesperre *n* force fit, ratchet brake, terminal voltage **-gewicht** *n* pinching weight

Klemmgriff zum Ausrücken des Tischselbstganges table-travel control

Klemm-halter *m* clamping holder **-hebel** *m* clamp(ing) lever, licking clamp, binder **-hülse** *f* collet

klemmig sturdy (min.)

Klemm-isolator *m* cleat insulator **-kegel** *m* cone clamp, centering cone **-kegelverbindung** *f* compressed cone connection **-klinke** *f* clamping latch **-knopf** *m* clamp knob **-konus** *m* tapered cone, chuck **-krone** *f* wedge crown (lock, key) **-kuppelung** *f* compression or clamp coupling **-kurbel** *f* clamped-on crank

Klemmlänge *f* clamped length, grip (of rivet), length of grip **~ eines Schraubenbolzens** effective length of a bolt

Klemm-lasche *f* clamping ring **-leiste** *f* connecting or terminal strip, connecting block, lug strip **-muffe** *f* clamping sleeve **-mutter** *f* lock nut **-nute** *f* clamping notch **-platte** *f* clamping plate or ring on dial sight, clamp, cleat, clip **-plattenbolzen** *pl* clip bolts **-pratze** *f* clamping jaw

Klemmring *m* clamp collar, clamping or locking ring, collet **-hebel** *m* clamping-ring handle

Klemm-rollenkupplung *f* grip roller and expanding friction clutch **-sätze** *pl* terminal boards (electr.) **-schaltung** *f* clamping circuit **-schelle** *f* clamp strap **-schiene** *f* clamp rail **-schlitten** *m* clamp slide **-schraube** *f* setscrew, clamping or attachment screw, terminal (screw), binding post or screw, thumbscrew **-schuh** *m* clamp plate

Klemm-sitz *m* force fit, ratchet brake, terminal

voltage, clamp fit **-spannung** *f* terminal voltage **-stange** *f* clamping bar **-strom** *m* terminal current **-stück** *n* shim

Klemmung *f* clamping, jamming, flow constriction, constriction ratio **~ der Fokussierung** focal adjustment clamp

Klemm-verbindung *f* compression joint, screw fastening **-verschiebehebel** *m* displaceable clamp lever **-vorrichtung** *f* clamping or gripping device, clamping-screw handle on dial sight **-walzen** *pl* pinch rolls **-wirkung** *f* clamping effect **-zange** *f* clamping claw (cable)

Klempner *m* sheet-metal worker, plumber, tinsmith **-arbeit** *f* sheet-metal work

Klepperboot *n* collapsible boat

Klette *f* burdock

kletten to pick, cull, unbur (wool) **-erz** *n* bur ore **-öl** *n* colza oil

Kletter-drehscheibe *f* climbing turntable **-eisen** *n* climbing iron, climbers, grapnel **-fähigkeit** *f* climbing ability **-fähigkeitsversuch** *m* climbing test (welding) **-fahrt** *f* zooming **-fräsen** *n* climb milling **-kreuzung** *f* inclined-plane switch (R.R.)

klettern to climb, clamber

Kletter-prinzip *n* cascade principle **-schuhe** *pl* climbing shoes, climbers (elec.) **-sporn** *m* gaff of climbers **-verdampfer** *m* climbing-film (vertical-film) evaporator **-walze** *f* climbing (turn) roller, front roller **-weiche** *f* inclined-plane switch (R.R.)

Klick *m* click **-filter** *n* (key) click filter

Klima *n* climate **-änderung** *f* climatic change **-anlage** *f* air conditioning installation (or plant) **-gürtel** *m* climatic belt **-kammer** *f* environmental chamber **-lehre** *f* climatology **-schrank** *m* air conditioning cabinet, coolant cabinet **-technik** *f* air conditioning

klimatisch climatic

klimatisiert air-conditioned

Klimatisierung *f* air conditioning

Klimatologie *f* climatology

Klimatruhe *f* air conditioner

klimpernd harsh, strident, grating, shrill, tingling

Klinge *f* blade, knife section, sword

Klingel *f* bell **-bleikabel** *f* lead bell wire **-draht** *m* bell wire, annunciator wire **-leitung** *f* bell circuit **-schalter** *m* knife-blade switch **-taster** *m* bell push **-transformator** *m* bell transformer **-zeichen** *n* bell signal

klingen to sound

Klingen *n* sounding, ring (of a tube)

Klingenabziehapparat *m* sharpener for razor blades

klingend sounding **-e Sprache** sonorous sound

Kling-fähigkeit *f* ringing noise, microphonic noise (of a tube) **-neigung** *f* microphone effect **-stein** *m* clinkstone, phonolite

Klinke *f* pawl, latch, handle, dog, detent, jack, ratchet, catch, socket, switch spring, spring jack, jack key switch **~ zur Einschaltung des Sprechzeuges** operator's telephone-set jack **~ mit Rolle** roller pawl **besetzte ~** engaged jack **dreiteilige ~** three-way or three-point jack **freie ~** disengaged or idle jack **~ stöpseln** to plug in **unbesetzte ~** disengaged jack **zweiteilige ~** two-point or two-way jack **an Klinken endigend** terminated on jacks

Klinken-anordnung *f* jack arrangement **-apparat** *m* pawl coupling **-auflager** *n* spring rest **-auslösung** *f* pawl release **-ausrüstung** *f* jack equipment **-bolzen** *m* pawl pin **-brett** *n* jack panel **-buchse** *f* jack bush(ing), sleeve **-fanggabel** *f* boot jack **-feder** *f* jack spring

Klinkenfeld *n* jack panel, jacks **~** (Teilnehmerklinken) subscriber's multiple **~** (Vielfachklinken) (jack) multiple

Klinken-griff *m* ratchet knob **-halter** *m* pawl holder **-hebel** *m* ratchet lever **-hülse** *f* socket, sleeve or bush of jack, jack barrel **-kopplung** *f* pawl coupling **-körper** *m* jack body or socket **-kuppelung** *f* pawl coupling **-scheibe** *f* notched or ratchet disk **-spannung** *f* jack-switch spring, pawl-latch voltage **-sperre** *f* locking pawl

Klinken-stange *f* pawl operating rod **-stecker** *m* jack, plug switch **-stöpsel** *m* jack plug **-streifen** *m* strip of jacks **-sucher** *m* jack finder **-träger** *m* pawl carrier **-umschalter** *m* jack, line, or live switchboard, toll test panel **-vielfachfeld** *n* jack multiple

Klinker *m* hard-burned brick, clinker, face brick, Dutch clinker, vitrified or clinker brick **-pflasterbau** *m* brick-pavement construction

Klinkerung *f* vitrification of clay

Klinker(ziegel) *m* vitrified brick

Klinket eines Schleusentores wicket of a lock gate

Klink-griff *m* latch **-hebel** *m* ratchet lever **-maschine** *f* coping machine, nibbling machine **-motor** *m* cut-out motor, disconnecting motor **-probe** *f* clinking test **-rad** *n* ratchet wheel **-ring** *m* ferrule **-werk** *n* trip or release gear, latch

Klinometer *n* clinometer

Klippe *f* cliff, reef, crag, rock, buff **auf eine ~ stoßen** to strike a reef

Klippenbrandung *f* waves dashing against cliffs

Klippklapptelegraph *m* flipflap or to-and-fro telegraph

klirr noisy, jangly **-dämpfung** *f* harmonic distortion expressed as an attenuation, correction of nonlinear harmonic distortion

klirren to clink, clatter, scratch (loud-speaker)

Klirrfaktor *m* nonlinear harmonic-distortion coefficient or factor, distortion (factor), blur or rattle factor **~ einer Verstärkerröhre** coefficient of nonlinear distortion (of a valve)

Klirrfaktor-meßbrücke *f* distortion bridge **-messer** *m* dirtortion factor meter

Klirr-geräusch *n* rattling noise **-koeffizient** *m* harmonic distortion faktor **-verzerrung** *f* harmonic, amplitude, nonlinear, or waveform distortion

Klischee *n* stereotype plate, block **-höhenmesser** *m* block gauge **-lochapparat** *m* hole-piercing apparatus for blocks **-prüfgerät** *n* block gauge

klischieren to electrotype, dab

klöben to rive, cleave

Kloben *m* block, vise, pulley, pincers, dog, snatch block **~ mit Schäkel** shackle block **einrolliger ~** single-sheave steel block

Klobengehäuse einer Rolle shell, pulley frame

Klobenrolle *f* sheave block and tackle, sleeve

Klopfbremse *f* fuel inhibitor, antidetonation compound, knock suppressor or inhibitor

Klopf-brett *n* planer (print.) **-eigenschaft** *f* knock property

Klopfeinsatz abhängig vom Zündzeitpunkt knocking inception depending on ignition moment

Klopfeinschätzung *f* knock rating

Klöpfel *m* mallet, beater

klopfen to knock, beat, rap, tap, detonate

Klopfen *n* rapping, knock(ing), detonation, tapping sounding, pinking **~ des Kolbens** piston knock **leichtes ~ des Motors** pinking **schwaches ~** (Verbrennungsmotor) slight detonation

klopfendes Geräusch knocking

Klopfer *m* knocker, sounder, tapper, Morse receiving or sending apparatus **~ mit zwei Klangscheiben** double-plate sounder **~ mit trägem Rade** Hughes silencer

Klopfer-apparat *m* sounder **-magnet** *m* tapper magnet **-spule** *f* tapper coil **-taste** *f* sounder key

Klopffeinde *m pl* antiknocks, antiknock agents (engines)

klopffest antiknock, antidetonant, knockproof, antipinking (of fuel) **-es Benzin** antiknock gasoline **-er Betriebsstoff** antiknock fuel **-er Brennstoff** antiknock or antidetonating fuel **-er Kraftstoff** antiknock fuel

Klopffestigkeit *f* antiknocking property, rating, or quality, octane number **Bestimmung der ~** knock rating **Verfahren zur Bestimmung der ~** knock-testing method

Klopffestigkeits-grad *m*, **-wert** *m* antiknock value, octane rating

Klopf-förderer *m pl* knock promoters **-gegenmittel** *n* antiknock chemical **-gerät** *f* tapping device **-gestänge** *n* signal wire (min.) **-grenze** *f* incipient knocking, engines' detonation limit, knock limit, anti-knock value **-holz** *n* mallet, planer (print.) **-intensität** *f* knock intensity **-neigung** *f* knocking tendency, liability to detonation **-schlägel** *m* hollowing hammer

Klopfstärke *f* knock intensity **-meßgerät** *n* knock meter

Klopf-verhalten *n* knocking behavior **-vorgang** *m* knocking process **-welle** *f* beater shaft **-werk** *n* beater **-wert** *m* (Kraftstoff) detonating characteristics **-wertbestimmung** *f* fuel rating **-wolf** *m* beating opener (textiles)

Klöppel *m* pin, axial support of a pin-type insulator, clapper, hammer, bell, lever, knocker **~ des Wheatstonelochers** mallet, punching handle

Klöppel-hebel *m* strike lever **-kugel** *f* bob **-maschine** *f* braider

klöppeln to braid, weave, bone, lace

Klöppelstange *f* clapper rod or stick

Klosett *n* closet **-anlage** *f* lavatory installation

Klotz *m* log, block, bedplate, base casting, massive block, brake, plug **-bremse** *f* block brake

Klotze *f* open stamp mill

Klotz-kuppelung *f* steel-block coupling **-reserveartikel** *m* padded resist style **-vorschrift** *f* padding recipe

Kluft *f* crack, fissure, crevasse, gullet, joint, folding rule **wasser- oder erzführende ~** feeder

Kluftfläche *f* fault plane

klüftig cleft, cracked

kluftreich full of fissures

Klümpchen *n* nodule

Klumpen *m* lump, mass, bulk, clod **natürlicher ~ von gediegenem Metall** nugget **in ~** chunky

klumpig lumpy, clotted, clotty **-er Zucker** caked sugar, sticky sugar

Kluppe *f* screw plate, screwstock, pipe stock, pliers, (screwing) diestock, holder for (screwing) dies, punch drawer, jointing clamp (elec.), tongs, threading die

Kluppen-auflage *f* bearing table **-backe** *f* pipestock die, screw die

Kluppzange *f* forceps

Klüse *f* hawse, hawse hole

Klüver *n* jib (sail)

Klydonograph *m* klydonograph

Klystron *n* **-röhre** *f* klystron (ultrahigh-frequency oscillator with two rhumbatrons acting as buncher and catcher)

K-Mesonen K particles

K-Modulus *m* modulus of cubic compressibility

Knabbelkoks *m* small-sized coke, nut coke, stove coke

Knabberer *m* nibbler

knabbern to nibble, gnaw, punch

Knabbern *n* nibbling, punching

Knabberschere *f* (Nibbelmaschine) *f* nibble machine

knacken to crackle, click, crack, crepitate, (slang) sink a ship by action

Knacken *n* spluttering (radio), acoustic shock, click, cracking **~ bei der Besetztprüfung** engaged click

Knack-geräusch *n* acoustic shock, click **-probe** *f* audible test **-prüfung** *f* audible test **-störpegel** *m* static detector (elec.) **-störung** *f* clicking disturbance, set noise

Knagge *f* ledger, bracket, short projection, tappet, cam, dog, pin, lug, stay, cog, knob, prop, wedge

Knaggensteuerung *f* cam gear

Knall *m* explosion, detonation, pop, report, pistol-shot noise **unter ~ und Feuererscheinung explodieren** to fulminate

Knall-aufsatz *m* initiator (explosives) **-bild** *n* sound projection on film **-dämpfer** *m* silencer

knallen to detonate, go off with a report

Knallen *n* detonation **~ im Auspufftopf** muffler explosion

Knall-erscheinung *f* sound effect **-funken** *m* rare spark **-funkenstrecke** *f* timed spark gap

Knallgas *n* oxyhydrogen (gas) **-flamme** *f* oxyhydrogen flame **-gebläse** *n* oxyhydrogen blowpipe **-reaktion** *f* reaction of oxyhydrogen gas **-gasschweißung** *f* oxyhydrogen welding **-verbrennung** *f* oxygen-hydrogen combustion

Knall-geräusche *pl* crackling, hissing, frying (noise), acoustic shock **-kapsel** *f* torpedo **-koffer** *m* delayed-action bomb **-kork** *m* alarm cork **-körper** *m* detonator, firecracker **-meßverfahren** *n* sound ranging **-netz** *n* mine-field detonating net **-niete** *f* pop rivet **-patrone** *f* Behm detonating cartridge **-pulver** *n* fulminating powder **-pyrometer** *n* explosion pyrometer

Knall-quecksilber *n* mercury fulminate **-rot** glaring red **-satz** *m* detonating composition **-säure** *f* fulminic acid **-schutzgerät** *n* pistol-shot silencer, crack silencer, noise killer (radio) **-signal** *n* detonator **-silber** *n* fulminating silver **-tüteneffekt** *m* paper-bag effect **-welle** *f* detonation or shock wave (acoust.) **-zucker** *m* nitroglucose **-zündmittel** *n* detonator **-zündschnur** *f* ignition wire (blasting), detonating cord, instaneous fuse

knapp close-fitting, neat, narrow, accurate, scanty, brief, concise

Knappe *m* miner, pitman, pioneer, derrick (min.)

Knappeisen *n* mattock

Knappenheit *f* short waves

Knäpper-bohrer *m* boring tool **-loch** *n* pop-hole

Knäppern *n* crushing operations

Knappheit *f* shortage, scarcity

Karre *f* ratchet, ratchet stock

knarren to jar, crackle, rattle, crack (of loudspeaker), creak

Knarren *n* jar **-bohrer** *m* ratchet drill **-fräser** *m* ratchet cutter **-hebel** *m* ratchet handle **-kluppe** *f* ratchet pipe stock, ratchet die plate **-wälzfräser** *m* ratchet hob **-winden** *n* ratchet

Knarrfunken *m* rare spark

Knast im Holz knag, snag, knot, or nob in wood

knästig knaggy, snaggy, knobby, knotty

knattern to crack, rattle, detonate

Knattern *n* cracking, sizzle

Knäuel *n* beet-seed ball, skein **-bildung** *f* formation of knots

knäueln to ball up, snarl

Knauer *m* hard rebel rock, hard rock or stone (min.)

Knauf *m* knob **mit einem ~ versehen** knobbed

Knebel *m* toggle, gag, cudgel, crossbar, tongue (saw), tommy bar, clamp handle **-bolzen** *m* toggle bolt **-dichtung** *f* **-gelenk** *n* toggle joint **-griff** *m* capstan, tommy, clamp handle, locking nut **-griffschraube** *f* tommy screw **-kerbstift** *m* grooved pin (type E), slotted pin **-kopf** *m* bar head, head with tommy bar, tommy head, pointer-shaped knob **-leine** *f* toggle rope **-mutter** *f* clamping nut

knebeln to fix with a toggle

Knebel-presse *f* gag press **-schalter** *m* jack switch **-schlaufe** *f* toggle loop **-schraube** *f* tommy screw, capstan-head screw **-stropp** *m* becket

kneifen to pinch, jam, nip, squeeze

Kneifer *m* pince-nez, eyeglasses

Kneifzange *f* end-cutting pliers, nippers, pincers

Knetapparat *m* kneading mill

knetbar kneadable, plastic

kneten to pug, squeeze, knead, to masticate

Kneten *n* mastication

Kneter *m* kneader, pug and kneading machine, masticator, wet-pan mill, churn

Knet-faß *n* pugmill **-flügel** *m* kneading blade **-holz** *n* plastic wood **-legierung** *f* malleable or forgeable alloy, plastic or wrought alloy **-maschine** *f* kneader, pug and kneading machine, masticator, wet-pan mill, perfecting engine **-masse** *f* kneading mass **-mühle** *f* kneading mill, cone breaker **-prozeß** *m* kneading process

Knetung *f* remolding, kneading

Knetwalzen *pl* working rollers

Knick *m* break (in a curve), jog, bend, kink, knee, crack, quickset-hedged wall **~ am Heck** stern droop **~ in der Mitte nach unten** sag (aviation) **oberer** (unterer) **~ der Röhrenkennlinie** upper (lower) bend of valve characteristic

Knick-banddichte *f* kink band density **-beanspruchung** *f* axial compression, buckling stress or load **-biegung** *f* stress in bending **-bruchfestigkeit** *f* loop strength **-brücke** *f* hinge

knicken to buckle (column), break, kink, bend, crack, collapse, compress

Knicken *n* kinking

Knick-erscheinung *f* buckling **-festigkeit** *f* resistance (to buckling), buckling strength (of metal), strain resistance, flexibility (of a film), breaking strength **-flügel** *m* full or cranked wing, wing with two different dihedral angles, gull wing (aviation) **-formel** *f* buckling formula **-hebel** *m* articulated lever **-kennlinie** *f* voltage and current characteristics **-kraft** *f* buckling or fracturing load **-länge** *f* unsupported length over which buckling occurs, effective length, collapsing length **-last** *f* buckling, crippling or breaking load **-linie** *f* broken line

Knick-nase *f* hinged leading edge **-punkt** *m* break (in a curve), inflexion, kink or knee **-regler** *m* voltage and current regulator **-schutz** *m* protective rubber sleeve **-schwingung** *f* bending vibration **-sicherheit** *f* security or safety against buckling, buckling resistance **-spannung** *f* breaking, buckling, or crippling stress or resilience **-stelle** *f* kink or knee, break (of a curve) **-strebe** *f* radius rod or strut **-strebenschalter** *m* down-position indicator **-trommel** *f* bend pulley

Knickung *f* lateral flexure, buckling, breaking, crinkling, collapse, kink

Knick-verstärker *m* buckling amplifier **-versuch** *m* buckling or crippling test, breaking or crinkling test, flexure test **-walzwerke** *pl* buckling mill **-widerstand** *m* resistance to buckling, crinkling, or bulging **-widerstandsfähigkeit** *f* folding endurance (of film), breaking or buckling strength **-zahl** *f* coefficient of buckling

Knie *n* knee, salient, bent, angle, joint, stifle, elbow (of a pipe), bend (of a curve), cutwater, knuckle **oberes ~** top or upper bend **unteres ~** bottom or lower bend

Knieblech *n* knee (plate) (shipbuilding)

knieen to kneel **-der Anschlag** kneeling position

Knie-falte *f* anticlinal flexure **-förmig** knee-shaped, geniculate

Kniegelenk *n* knuckle joint, universal, knee, or elbow joint, toggle joint **-federung** *f* knee-action suspension **-hebel** *m* toggle joint **-presse** *f* toggle-joint press **-schloß** *n* toggle-joint lock

Kniehebel *m* bent or elbow lever, bell crank, toggle switch or lever **-bewegung** *f* toggle motion **-druck** *m* bent-lever pressure **-klemme** *f* tensioning device for light wires, wire grip, drawing tongs **-nietmaschine** *f* toggle-joint riveting machine **-prägepresse** *f* bent-lever embossing press **-presse** *f* crank or toggle-lever press, toggle-joint press **-stauchung** *f* toggle upset **-tubenpresse** *f* toggle collapsible tube press **-zange** *f* toggle-lever tongs **-zwinge** *f* toggle clamp

Knie-heber *m* knee lever **-holz** *n* knee timber

-kupplung *f* knee coupling **-pausche** *f* knee roll (saddle) **-rohr** *n* knee pipe, (square) elbow, angle, bend **-scheibe** *f* silhouette target (kneeling), knee cap **-schützer** *m* knee pad **-spannung** (Transistorkennlinie) turnover voltage **-stange** *f* knee bar **-stellung** *f* salient **-stiefel** *m* knee boot **-strumpf** *m* stocking **-stück** *n* pipe elbow, leg or elbow pipe, bootleg, penstock, tuyère stock **-stütze** *f* knee support **-ventil** *n* knee valve **-verbindung** *f* elbow joint

Kniff *m* knack, shortcut, artifice, crease, pinch; helpful hint, handy device

kniffen to crease, fold

knippen to chip, cut

Knipp-schalter *m* rotary switch **-stange** *f* pinch bar

knipsen to clip, punch (ticket), click

Knipszange *f* ticket nippers

knirschen to scroop, make a rustling sound, grind

Knirschen *n* grinding, grinders, squeak, crunching (of sand)

knistern to sizzle, crack, crackle, crepitate, rustle (silk)

Knistern *n* sizzle, crackling

Knitter *m* crimp, wrinkle **-fest** crease proof **-festigkeit** *f* creasing resistance, crumpling strength **-maschine** *f* crumbling machine

knittern to crease (crumple)

Knitter-papier *n* crinkled paper **-probe** *f* crease-resistance test **-zahl** *f* fold test

Knochen *m* bone, runners, runner waste (in pouring) **-asche** *f* bone ash **-bruch** *m* bone fracture **-entfettungsvorrichtung** *f* bone-grease-extracting apparatus **-gallerte** *f* bone gelatine **-gelenk** *n* swivel joint, ball-and-socket joint, gimbal joint **-hörer** *m* osophone

Knochenkohle *f* animal char, bone black, bone coal, charred bone **-dämpfer** *m* bone-coal steaming apparatus **-filter** *n* char filter **-wiederbelebungsofen** *m* char-revivifying kiln

Knochen-leim *m* bone glue **-leitungshörer** bone-conduction receiver **-mark** *n* bone marrow **-mehl** *m* bone meal, bone dust **-öl** *n* neat's-foot oil, bone oil **-schwarz** *n* bone black **-sucher** *m* bone seeker **-trocken** oven-dry

knöchern (made of) bone, osseous

knochig bony

Knöllchen *n* nodule, little knob or node

Knollen *m* nodule, lump, knob, node, knot

knollig knobby, knotty, bulbous

Knopf *m* button, stud, knob, pinion (head), lever ~ **für Draht** wire billet ~ **drehen** to turn a knob **mit einem** ~ **versehen** knobbed

Knopf-gabel *f* button stick **-griff** *m* knob **-halter** *m* retaining washer **-karte** *f* instruction chart **-loch** *n* buttonhole **-lochmikrophon** *n* lapel microphone **-maschine** *f* button breaker (textile finishing) **-rohling** *m* button blank **-röhre** *f* acorn tube, button tube, doorknob tube, shoe-button tube **-steuerung** *f* push-button control **-verbindung** *f* stud connection

Knoppern *pl* crushed sugar

Knorpel *m* cartilage, gristle **-kohle** *f* lump coal

Knorrbremse *f* pneumatic or Knorr air brake

Knorren *m* knag, knot, snag

knorrenfrei knotless

knorrig knotty, knaggy

Knötchen *n* nodule, knot

knoten to knot

Knoten *m* cord (in glass), vitreous inhomogeneity, knot (naut.), node, gusset, kink (in chain or wire rope), standing wave, nodule, knob, plot, joint

Knoten-abstand *m* distance between points (nodes) of support, internodal distance **-amt** *n* main or chief central office, repeating center, tandem central office **-amtssystem** *n* zone system, repeating center system **-blech** *n* gusset plate, connection plate, fishplate **-brecher** *m* disintegrator, sugar breaker

Knoten-ebene *f* nodal plane or surface (optics) **-eisen** *n* knotted bar iron **-faktor** *m* node factor **-fänger** *m* back knotter, pulp strainer **-festigkeit** *f* loop strength **-fläche** *f* nodal plane or surface **-geflecht** *n* knotted wire netting **-graphit** *m* nodular graphite **-last** *f* panel-point load (statics) **-linie** *f* neutral, common, or nodal line

Knotenpunkt *m* intersection, joint, panel point (statics), nodal point, junction, center, fuselage joint, truss (or frame) joint, hub ~ (Objektiv), node, nodal point (lens) **bildseitiger** (hinterer) ~ rear nodal point **dingseitiger** (vorderer) ~ front nodal point

Knotenpunkt-bahnhof *m* multiple junction (R.R. station) **-belastung** *f* load at nodal point **-beschlag** *m* nodal-point fitting **-last** *f* panel-point load (statics) **-tastung** *f* nodal-point keying

Knoten-regel *f* node theorem **-satz** *m* zero rule **-schiefer** *m* knotenschiefer (a spotted rock, knotted slate, in which individual minerals can be recognized) **-station** *f* branching-off station **-strahl** *m* beam or pencil of nonuniform section **-stück** *n* knot (wood) **-verbindung** *f* temporary bridge, T joint, transfer joint **-zwirn** *m* nub twist

Knotfestigkeit *f* tensile strength at knot

knotig knotty, nodular, knubbed, gnarled

Knudsen-Manometer *n* Knudsen gauge, radiometer gauge

knüpfen to tie, knot

Knüppel *m* club, winch, control column (aviation), stick (aviation), wire bar, (metal) billet ~ **für Draht** wire billet ~ **an den Bauch** stick right back ~ **in Nullage** control column central ~ (Rundbarren), round billet

Knüppel-ausschlag *m* deflection of the control stick **-bohrmaschine** *f* billet-boring machine **-bremse** *f* sprag brake **-damm** *m* corduroy road **-ende** *n* billet end, crop end (scrap) **-gerüst** *n* billet roll stand **-griff** *m* stick grip (aviation), grip of control column **-holzweg** *m* corduroy road **-isolator** *m* club-type or pin insulator **-kraft** *f* stick force **-lager** *n* billet and sheet-bar yard **-mittenschaltung** *f* spherically mounted central

knüppeln (slang) to pilot

Knüppel-putzerei *f* billet overhauling **-rost** *m* balk, round timber, duckboard **-schere** *f* billet shears **-schleifen** *n* snagging **-schrott** *m* scrap billets **-steuerung** *f* stick control (aviation) **-straße** *f* billet-rolling train **-verfahren** *n* stick coordination **-walze** *f* billet roll, billet mill **-walzwerk** *n* billet mill **-wärmofen** *m* billet-

reheating furnace **-weg** *m* corduroy road
knurren to growl, snarl, rumble
Knüttel *m* nettle
koachsial coaxial
Koagel *n* coagulum
Koagulations-messer *m* coagulometer **-schutzwirkung** *f* anti-coagulating effect **-wert** *m* coagulation value
Koagulatmasse *f* coagulum
koagulierbar coagulable
koagulieren to coagulate
Koagulierung *f* coagulation
Koagulierungsmittel *n* coagulant, coagulating agent
Koaleszenz *f* coalescence
koaleszieren to coalesce
koaxial coaxial **-es Kabel** coaxial or concentric cable **-anschluß** *m* coaxial connecter **-antenne** *f* coaxial antenna
Koaxialität der magnetischen, mechanischen und elektrischen Achse boresight
Koaxial-leitung *f* coaxial transmission line **-Link-Leitung** *f* coaxial line link
Kobalt *m* cobalt **-arseniat** *n* cobalt arsenate **-beschlag** *m* crust of cobalt, cobalt bloom, erythrite **-bleierz** *n*, **-bleiglanz** *m* clausthalite **-blume** *f* **-blüte** *f* cobalt bloom, erythrite **-bromid** *n* cobalt(ic) bromide **-bromür** *n* cobaltous bromide **-chlorür** *n* cobaltous chloride **-gitter** *n* cobalt lattice **-glanz** *m* cobaltite **-grün** *n* cobalt green, cobaltic oxide **-haltig** cobaltiferous
Kobalti-kaliumnitrat *n* potassium cobaltinitrate **-verbindung** *f* cobaltic compound **-zyankalium** *n* potassium cobalticyanide
Kobalt-kies *m* cobalt pyrites **-maganerz** *n* asbolite **-oxydul** *n* cobaltous oxide **-oxyduloxyd** *n* cobaltocobaltic oxide
Kobaltozyankalium *n* potassium cobaltocyanide
Koch *m* cook **-becher** *m* beaker **-beständig** stable when boiling (chem.) **-echt** fast to boiling (dyes) **-echtheit** *f* ability of a fabric to resist or withstand bleaching
kochen to boil, cook, back out (of iron in a mold), flutter
Kochen *n* boiling, ebullition, cooking ~ **der Form** surface blow (foundry)
kochend fuming, boiling **-er Akkumulator** agitated or gassing accumulator **-es Geräusch** boiling noise
Köcher *m* stiff upright leather case
Kocher *m* boiler, cooker, digester, hot plate **-boden** *m* charging floor **-eintrag** *m* charge (of a furnace)
kochfest boil proof
Kochflasche *f* flask (for boiling) ~ **mit umgelegtem Rand** flask with ring neck
Koch-gerät *n* cooking utensils or appliances **-geschirr** *n* cooking utensils, mess gear **-graben** *m* cooking pit **-herd** *m* range, oven **-hitze** *f* boiling heat **-kessel** *m* cooking vat, boiler, large kettle, caldron **-klare** *f* filtered syrup **-kolben** *m* boiling flask **-kontrollapparat** *m* pan-boiling control apparatus
Koch-loch *n* cooking pit **-lösung** *f* boiling agent **-maische** *f* crystallizer pan **-periode** *f* boiling period **-presse** *f* baking press **-probe** *f* boiling test **-puddeln** *n* pig boiling **-punkt** *m* boiling point **-punktmesser** *m* ebullioscope **-salz** *n* common salt **-salzlösung** *f* saline solution **-vergütung** *f* artificial aging, aging at 100 degrees
Kode-buchstabe *m* code letter **-leuchtturm** *m* code beacon **-schlüssel** *m* telegraphic code
Köder *m* sealing strip **-flugkörper** *m* decoy missile
Kodex *m* code
Kode-zahl *f* code number **-zeichen** *n* code designation
kodifizieren to codify, code
Kodurit *m* kodurite
Koeffizient *m* coefficient ~ **der Festigkeit** coefficient of hardness ~ **der gegenseitigen Induktion** coefficient of mutual induction, mutual inductance ~ **für Kettenübertragung** iterative transfer coefficient ~ **der Selbstinduktion** coefficient of self-inductance ~ **der Transformation durch Kracken** cracks per pass ~ **der Zusammenziehung** coefficient of contraction
Koeffizienten-beziehung *f* relation between coefficients **-potentiometer** *n* coefficient potentiometer
Koepe-Förderung *f* Koepe winding engine
Koerzitiv-feld *n* coercitive field **-feldstärke** *f* coercive force **-kraft** *f* coercive force, retentivity, coercivity **-kraftmesser** *m* coercimeter
Koerzimeter *n* coercimeter
Koerzivität *f* coercivity
Koexistenz von Phasen coexistence of phases
koexistieren to coexist
Koffer *m* coffer, trunk, box, layer of broken stones (dam) **-apparat** *f* box equipment, trunk unit **-artig** trunk type **-damm** *n* sheet pile bulkhead **-empfänger** *m* portable receiver **(in) -form** (in) portable form **-gerät** *n* portable set (radio) **-kessel** *m* wagon boiler **-kino** *n* portable projector equipment **-leitdamm** *m* (rock) jetty
Koffer-nietmaschine *f* trunk riveting machine **-pappe** *f* trunk board **-raum** *m* trunk (of car)
Kofferung *f* base course (base)
Kofillennagel *m* belaying pin
Kofunktion *f* (eines Winkels) cofunction
Kogasinöl *n* mixture of kerosene, Diesel oil, and paraffin wax used for fuel (Fischer-Tropsch process)
kohärent-e Drehung coherent rotation **-e Streuung** *f* coherent scattering
Kohärenz *f* coherence **-begriff** *m* concept of coherence **-länge der Wellenzüge** coherence length of wave trains **-strahlung** *f* coherent radiation
Kohärer *m* coherer
kohäriertes Videosignal cohered video
Kohäsion *f* cohesion, cohesive force
Kohäsions-eigenschaft *f* cohesive property **-festigkeit** *f* cohesion strength **-kraft** *f* cohesive force **-vermögen** *n* cohesiveness
Kohle *f* coal, carbon, charcoal, carbonaceous material, carbon brush or rod **aschereiche** ~ high-ash coal **backende** ~ bituminous or caking coal **feingemahlene** ~ pulverized coal **fette** ~ fat coal, strongly caking coal **fette** ~ **mit kurzer Flamme** short-flaming dense-coking coal of semibituminous rank, forging coal **fossile** ~ mineral coal
Kohle, geringwertige ~ poor coal **glänzende** ~

shining coal **glimmende ~** ember **grobstückige ~** lump coal **kurzflammige ~** short-flaming coal **magere ~** lean coal, hard coal, nonbaking coal, semianthracite, semibituminous coal **~ für Magnetzünder** carbon brush for magneto **milde ~** soft coal **minderwertige ~ am Ausgehenden** (inferior) crop coal

Kohle, salzgetränkte ~ mineralized or impregnated carbon **schlackende ~** clinkering coal **schlackenreine ~** nonclinkering coal **staubförmige ~** dust coal, powdered or finely divided coal **weiche ~** apple coal **weiche, nicht backende ~** cherry coal **von Hand geschiedene ~** hand-picked coal **zu ~ brennen** to char **durch Intrusion veränderte ~** cinder coal **die ~ waschen** to wash coal

Kohle-abbrand *m* (von Kohleelektroden) consumption of carbons **-aufdampfverfahren** *n* (Elektronenmikroskop) carbon replica technique **-beheizt** coal-fired **-bildung** *f* carbonization **-blitzableiter** *m* carbon lightning arrester, carbon protector **-blitzschutz** *m* carbon lightning arrester **-bogen** *m* carbon arc **-bogenlampe** *f* carbon-arc lamp **-brei** *m* coal paste **-bürste** *f* carbon brush **-bürstenfeder** *f* carbon brush spring **-druck** *m* carbon print (photo) **-druckregler** *m* carbon pile voltage regulator **-elektrode** *f* carbon electrode **-faden** *m* carbon filament **-fadenlampe** *f* carbon-filament lamp **-frei** carbon-free, noncarbonaceous **-grieß** *m* carbon granules **-halter** *m* carbon holder

Kohle-hydrat *n* carbohydrate **-klassierung** *f* grading (sizing) coal **-kleinerzeugnisse** *pl* small carbon products **-klotz** *m* carbon block **-korn** *n* carbon granule **-lager** *n* carbon bearing **-lichtbogen** *m* carbon arc **-lichtbogenschweißung** *f* carbon-arc welding **-membran** *f* carbon diaphragm **-mikrophon** *n* carbon microphone or transmitter

kohlen to carburize, recarburize, carbonize, char

Kohlen-abbau *m* coal mining **-ablagerung** *f* carbonization **-abstand** *m* carbon separation **-ähnlich, -artig** coallike, carbonlike, carbonaceous **-aufbereitung** *f* coal preparation, dressing, or separation, cleaning of coal **-aufbereitungsanlage** *f* coal-preparation plant **-aufgabeeinrichtung** *f* coal charging device **-ausbiß** *m* coal outcrop **-bansen** *m* coal stack **-batterie** *f* carbon battery **-becken** *n* coal basin, coal field **-befeuerung** *f* coal firing **-benzin** *n* benzene (benzol)

Kohlen-bergbau *m* coal mining **-bergmann** *m* collier, miner **-bergwerk** *n* coal mine, colliery **-beschickungsvorrichtung** *f* stoker, coaling equipment **-beutelelektrode** *f* carbon-bag electrode **-beutelmikrophon** *n* carbon-bag transmitter **-bleispat** *m* cerussite **-bleivitriolspat** *m* lanarkite **-blende** *f* anthracite, blind coal

Kohlen-blitzableiter *m* carbon-block protector (voltage-discharge gap), carbon lightning arrester **-bogen** *m* carbon arc **-brechanlage** *f* coal crushing plant **-brei** *m* coal paste (mixture of coal and oil) **-brenner** *m* burner **-brikett** *n* coal brick **-bruchverhütung** *f* anti-breakage device **-bunker** *m* (coal) bunker, coalbin, dump house **-bürste** *f* carbon brush, wiper **-dampfer** *m* collier **-eisenstein** *m* carbonaceous ironstone, black band

kohlender Zusatz carburizing or recarburizing addition

Kohlendioxyd *n* carbon dioxide, carbonic acid **~ und Stickstoff** (Gemisch von) blackdamp

Kohlendruckbeschleunigungsmesser *m* carbon-pile accelerometer **-säule** *f* carbon pile **-verfahren** *n* carbon granule thrust-measuring device

Kohlen-einsatz *m* coal charge **-eisen** *n* iron carbide **-eisenstein** *m* blackband, blackband ironstone, coal-measure ironstone, pottery mine **-elektrode** *f* carbon electrode **-entgasung** *f* coal carbonization **-entladekran** *m* coal-unloading crane **-faden** *m* carbon filament **-fadenlampe** *f* carbon-filament lamp

Kohlen-feuerung *f* coal firing, coal burning **-filter** *m* charcoal filter **-flamme** *f* coal flame **-flöz** *n* coal measure, coal seam, coal bed, coal vein **-förderung** *f* coal output **-förderwagen** *m* coal lorry car **-forschung** *f* coal research **-füllung** *f* coal charge **-gas** *n* coal gas **-gebiet** *n* coal region or district

Kohlengehalt *m* percentage of carbon, carbon content **Stahl mit hohem** (niedrigem) **~** high-(low-) carbon steel

Kohlen-gestübbe *n* coal slack **-gewinnung** *f* getting or digging of coal **-greifer** *m* coal grab **-grieß** *m* finely divided carbon or carbon dust **-grube** *f* colliery, coal mine, coal pit **-grus** *m* slack coal, slack, small coal **-hafen** *m* coal wharf or dock **-halter** *m* carbon holder **-haltig** carbonaceous, carboniferous.

Kohlen-handel *m* coal business **-händler** *m* coal merchant **-hauen** *n* cutting of coal **-hauer** *m* coal miner **-haufen** *m* coal pile **-hydrat** *n* carbohydrate **-kalk** *m* carboniferous limestone **-kalkstein** *m* mountain limestone **-kessel** *m* coal-fired boiler **-kippe** *f* coal tip **-kipper** *m* coal tipper **-kippkarre** *f* dump-type coal barrow **-klaubriemen** *m* coal picking belt **-klein** *n* slack coal, small coal **-korn** *n* carbon granule, carbon grain

Kohlenkörner *pl* carbon granules **-kammer** *f* carbon-granule chamber **-mikrophon** *n* carbon-granule transmitter or microphone

Kohlen-korngeräusch *n* carbon noise (of microphone) **-lader** *m* coal loader **-laderaum** *m* coal-bunker space **-lager** *n* coal storage, coalyard, coal deposit **-lagerstätte** *f* coal deposit **-löffel** *m* coal scoop **-lösche** *f* coal slack **-mächtigkeit** *f* thickness of coal seam **-magazin** *n* coal storage place

Kohlen-mahlanlage *f* coal-milling or coal-pulverizing plant **-mehl** *n* pulverized or powdered coal, coal dust **-meiler** *m* charcoal pile, coal heap, coal pile **-mikrophon** *n* carbon transmitter or microphone **-mischanlage** *f* coal-mixing installation **-mischung** *f* coal blending **-monoxyd** *n* carbon monoxide

Kohlen-mühle *f* coal crusher **-müllerei** *f* coal-pulverizing plant **-nachschub** *m* carbon feed **-nummer** *f* check number **-oxyd** *n* carbon monoxide (gas) **-oxydchlorid** *n* carbonyl chloride **-oxydkalium** *n* potassium carboxide **-oxydnickel** *n* nickel carbonyl **-oxysulfid** *n* carbon oxysulfide **-oxydverbrennung** *f* carbon monoxide combustion

Kohlen-pfanne *f* charcoal brazier **-pfeiler** *m* pillar of coal **-platz** *m* coalyard **-preßstein** *m* coal briquette **-pulver** *n* finely divided carbon or carbon dust **-pulvermikrophon** *n* carbon-powder transmitter or microphone, carbon-granule transmitter **-revier** *n* coal district, coal field, coal-mining district **-rostfeuerung** *f* coal-grate firing **-rückstand** *m* carbon residue **-rutsche** *f* face conveyer

Kohlensack *m* coal bag, in wall batter of stack (of blast furnaces), upper bosh line **zylindrischer** ~ saucer bosh

Kohlensandstein *m* carboniferous sandstone

kohlensauer carbonic, carbonate of

Kohlensäure *f* carbonic acid gas, carbon dioxide **feste** ~ dry ice **mit** ~ **sättigen** to areate

kohlensau(e)r carbonate of **-es Ammon** ammonium carbonate **-es Barium** barium carbonate **-es Bleioxyd** lead carbonate, white lead **-es Ceroxydul** cerium carbonate **-es Eisen** iron carbonate **-es Kali** potassium carbonate **-es Kali(um)** potash **-er Kalk** calcium carbonate **-es Kupfer(oxyd)** copper carbonate **-es Natron** sodium carbonate **-es Salz** carbonate **-es Wasser** aerated water **-es Zink** zinc carbonate

Kohlensäure-abscheider *m* washer for the removal of carbon dioxide **-anhydrid** *n* carbon dioxide **-anlasser** *m* carbonic acid starter **-ausbruch** *m* outburst or irruption of carbon dioxide **-flasche** *f* carbon dioxide flask **-gas** *n* carbon dioxide **-motor** *m* carbon dioxide motor **-saturation** *f* carbonation **-spiegel** *m* carbonic acid level

Kohlen-schacht *m* pit, shaft **-schalter** *m* carbon break switch (elec.) **-schaufel** *f* coal shovel, fire shovel **-schicht** *f* coal seam, coal bed **-schichte** *f* black wash, coal-dust facing **-schiefer** *m* bituminous shale **-schiff** *n* collier **-schlamm** *m* coal mud, sludge, slurry, or silt

Kohlen-schrämmung *f* coal-cutting **-schuppen** *m* coal shed **-schüttung** *f* coal charging, coal feeding **-schwelung** *f* low-temperature carbonization of coal **-sorte** *f* kind of coal, grade of coal **-spat** *m* anthraconite **-spitze** *f* carbon (elec.) **-stab** *m* carbon bar **-station** *f* coaling station

Kohlenstaub *m* coal dust, powdered or pulverized coal **-behälter** *m* powdered-coal storage bin **-betrieb** *m* powdered-coal operation **-brenner** *m* pulverized-coal burner **-bunker** *m* pulverized-coal storage bin, pulverized-coal bunker **-feuerung** *f* powdered- or pulverized-coal firing, coal-dust firing **-flamme** *f* powdered- or pulverized-coal flame

Kohlenstaub-mahlanlage *f* coal-pulverizing plant, coal-milling plant **-mikrophon** *n* carbon-dust transmitter **-motor** *m* coal-dust engine **-mühle** *f* coal pulverizer, coal-dust mill **-müllerei** *f* coal-pulverizing plant **-teilchen** *n* coal-dust particle **-verbrennung** *f* powdered-coal combustion **-wagen** *m* tank truck for powdered coal

Kohlen-stickstoff *m* cyanogen **-stift** *m* carbon (of an arc lamp)

Kohlenstoff *m* carbon ~ **erthaltend** carbonaceous, carbonic, carboniferous **fester** ~ fixed carbon **gebundener** ~ combined carbon **graphitischer** ~ graphitic carbon, graphite carbon, graphite, uncombined carbon **härtender** ~ cementite **ungebundener** ~ uncombined or free carbon

kohlenstoff-abgebend carbonaceous **-arm** low in carbon

Kohlenstoffaufnahme *f* carbon pickup ~ **förderndes Mittel** carbon raiser

Kohlenstoff-durchdringung *f* carbon penetration **-eisen** *n* iron carbide **-entziehung** *f* decarbonization, decarburization **-frei** free from carbon

Kohlenstoffgehalt *m* carbon content **Kern mit niedrigem** ~ (Einsatzhärtung) low-carbon core

Kohlenstoff-gehaltverhältnis *n* carbon ratio **-haltig** carbonaceous, carboniferous **-hydrat** *n* hydrocarbon **-isotopenhäufigkeit** *f* carbon isotope ratio **-kalium** *n* potassium carbide **-legierung** *f* carbon alloy **-metall** *n* carbide **-reich** rich in carbon **-sättigung** *f* carbon concentration **-silizium** *n* carbon silicide

Kohlenstoffstahl *m* carbon steel **unlegierter** ~ plain carbon steel

Kohlenstoff-stampfmasse *f* carbonaceous ramming mass **-stein** *m* carbon brick or block **-stickstofftitan** *n* titanium carbonitride **-tetrachlorid** *n* carbon tetrachloride **-tetrafluorid** *n* carbon tetrafluoride **-träger** *m* charcoal-mixture container (blasting) carbon filler in liquid-oxygen blasting charges **-verbindung** *f* carbon compound **-werkzeugstahl** *m* carbon tool steel **-ziegel** *m* carbon brick

Kohlen-stoß *m* face **-stück** *n* coal lump **-suboxyd** *n* **-technik** *f* coal engineering **-teer** *m* coal tar **-teeröl** *n* coal oil **-transportanlage** *f* coal-handling equipment **-transportkarren** *m* coal barrow, coal-handling car **-trockner** *m* coal drier

Kohlen-verbrauch *m* carbon consumption **-verflüssigung** *f* hydrogenation of coal **-vergasung** *f* gasification of coal **-verladeanlage** *f* coal-handling equipment or machinery **-verladebrücke** *f* bridge for loading and stocking coal **-verladekran** *m* coal-handling crane **-verlust** *m* loss or waste of coal **-verschwelungsanlage** *f* carbonization plant **-vorkommen** *n* coal deposit carbon suboxide **-sulfid** *n* carbon disulfide **-vorschub** *m* feed(ing) of carbons **-wagen** *m* coal-handling car **-wagenwipper** *m* coal-car dumper **-wäsche** *f* coal-washing plant, coal washing, coal flotation **-wäscher** *m* coal washer

Kohlenwasserstoff *m* hydrocarbon

Kohlenwasserstoffgas *n* carbureted hydrogen gas, hydrocarbon gas **leichtes** ~ methane **schweres** ~ ethylene

kohlenwasserstoff-haltig hydrocarbonaceous **-öl** *n* hydrocarbon oil **-verbindung** *f* hydrocarbide **-verbrennung** *f* hydrocarbon combustion

Kohlen-widerstand *m* carbon resister **-wischer** *m* coal damper **-zeche** *f* colliery **-zerkleinerung** *f* coal crushing **-zerstäubungsschlauch** *m* coal-sprinkler hose **-zug** *m* trip (min.) **-zuteilkolben** *m* coal-allotting piston

Kohle-papier *n* carbon paper **-pol** *m* carbon pole, carbon terminal **-puppe** *f* carbon rod (of dry cell)

Köhler *m* (charcoal) burner

Köhlerei *f* charcoal burning

Kohle-schichtpotentiometer *n* carbon-film potentiometer **-schichtwiderstand** *m* deposited carbon resistor **-schlämmen** *n* coal slimes **-stab** *m* carbon rod **-widerstandsmikrophon** *n* carbon-resistance microphone **-zeichnung** *f* charcoal drawing **-Zinkelement** *n* carbon-zinc cell **-Zinksammler** *m* carbon-zinc battery, dry cell **-zylinder** *m* carbon (elec.)

Kohlholz *n* charcoal

kohlig coaly, coal-bearing, carbonaceous

kohlschwarz coal-black, jet-black

Kohlung *f* carburization, carbonization

Kohlungsmittel *n* carbonaceous material, carbonizing or carburizing agent, carburizer, cementing medium

kohobieren to redistill, cohobate

Koinzidenz *f* coincidence **in ~ bringen** to match

Koinzidenz-antwortbake coincident transponder **-durchlaßschaltung** *f* coincidence gating circuit **-entfernungsmesser** *m* coincidence telemeter, coincidence range finder **-schaltung** *f* coincidence circuit, coincidence connection **-signal** *n* synchronization signal **-telemeter** *n* coincidence range finder **-tor** *n* coincidence gate

koinzidieren to coincide, match

Koje *f* bunk, cabin on ship

Kokerei *f* coking plant, coke-oven plant, carbonization plant, coal-carbonizing plant, coking practice, coking **-anlage** *f* carbonization plant **-gas** *n* coal gas, coke-oven gas **-ofen** *m* coke oven **-prozeß** *m* coking process, coal-carbonizing process **-technik** *f* technology of coke, coal-carbonizing practice **-wesen** *n* coke-oven-plant operation, coking practice

Kokille *f* cast-iron or iron mold, ingot mold, iron chill **in ~ gegossen** chilled **gegen ~ gießen** casting in chill **in der ~ vergießen** to chill

Kokillen-einlage *f* iron chill, densener **-form** *f* chill mold **-guß** *m* permanent-mold casting, chill casting **-gußform** *f* ingot mold **-gußstück** *n* chill casting (the product) **-kran** *m* mold-handling crane **-mann** *m* mold setter **-schleuderguß** *m* hot-mold centrifugal casting (process) **-schlichte** *f* smoothing of chilled casting **-wand** *f* surface of the mold

Kokneter *m* co-kneader

Kokon *m* cocoon **-faden** *m* silk fiber

Kokos-bast *m* coconut fiber (coir.) **-faser** *f* coco fiber, coir **-matte** *f* coconut matting

Koks *m* cinder, coke **kleinstückiger ~** breeze

Koks-abfall *m* refuse coke **-abrieb** *m* dust coke, coke dust or breeze **-abwurframpe** *f* coke wharf **-ansatz** *m* deposit of coke **-asche** *f* coke ash **-ausbeute** *f* coke yield **-ausbringen** *n* coke yield, output of coke **-ausdrückmaschine** *f*, **-ausstoßvorrichtung** *f* mechanical coke-pusher ram, coke pusher, coke-discharging machine

Koks-begichtungswagen *m* coke-charging car **-beheizung** *f* coke firing **-bereitung** *f* coke manufacture **-bett** *n* coke bed **-brennen** *n* coke burning, coking **-brocken** *m* coke lump **-bunker** *m* coke bunker, coke-storage bin **-entstehung** *f* coke formation **-erzeugung** *f* coke manufacture

Koks-feuer *n* coke fire **-feuerung** *f* coke firing **-filter** *m* coke filter **-führungsschild** *n* coke guide **-füllrumpf** *m* coke bin, coke hopper **-füllung** *f* coke packing **-gabel** *f* coke fork **-gas** *n* by-product coke-oven gas, carbon monoxide, blue(-water) gas

koks-gefeuert coke-fired **-gestübbe** *n* coke breeze **-gicht** *f* coke burden, coke charge **-greifer** *m* coke grab **-grus** *m* coke fines, fine coke, coke dust, breeze, or screenings **-güte** *f* grade of coke, coke quality **-heizung** *f* heating with or by coke **-hochofen** *m* coke blast furnace

Koks-kammer *f* coking chamber **-karren** *m* coke barrow **-klein** *n* coke breeze, small coke, coke dross **-kohle** *f* coking coal **-korb** (zum Austrocknen des Baus) smudge pot **-kübel** *m* coke bucket **-kübelkran** *m* coke-bucket-handling crane **-kuchen** *m* coking mass **-kühlung** *f* quenching of coke

Koks-löschanlage *f* extinguishing plant for coking coal **-lösche** *f* (coke) breeze, coke dust or cinder, small coke **-löschen** *n* quenching of coke **-löschseite** *f* coke-discharge side (of a coke oven) **-löschturm** *m* coke-quenching tower or station **-löschung** *f* coke quenching **-löschwagen** *m* coke-watering car, coke-quenching car **-mehl** *n* finely ground coke, crushed or powdered coke, coke dust

Koksofen *m* coke furnace, coke oven **-abgas** *n* waste coke-oven gas **-anlage** *f* coke-oven plant, coke-oven installation **-bau** *m* coke-oven construction

Koks-öfner *m* coke-oven operator **-rückstand** *m* coked residue **-satz** *m* coke ratio **-schicht** *f* coke bed **-seite** *f* (Koksofen) coke-oven discharge side

Koksskrubber *m* coke scrubber **wasserberieselter ~** vertical water scrubber

Koks-staub *m* coke dust, braise **-stein** *m* coke brick **-stück** *n* lump of coke **-verbrennlichkeit** *f* coke combustibility **-verbrauch** *m* consumption of coke **-volumen** *n* volume of coke substance **-vorratstasche** *f* coke-storage pocket or bin **-wascher** *m* coke scrubber **-werk** *n* **-zeche** *f* coking plant, coke-oven plant **-zieher** *m* coke drawer **-ziehvorrichtung** *f* coke-drawing machine

Kokung *f* coking

Kolatur *f* filtrate

Kolben *m* plunger, piston, retort, butt, mallet, club, bulb, bulb, flask, ram, soldering iron **~ zum Bogenschieber** jogger piston **~ mit Druckausgleich** balanced piston **~ mit Invarstreifen** Invar-strut piston **~ mit geteiltem Mantel** split-skirt-type piston **~ mit umgelegtem Rand** flask with ring neck **vom ~ durchlaufendes Volumen** piston displacement

Kolben, frei schwebender ~ suspended piston **langschaftiger ~** long-skirted piston **gegenläufiger ~** opposed piston **selbsttragender ~** unsupported piston **umlaufender ~** turning piston **offenes Ende des Kolbens** skirt end of a piston

Kolben-ablenker *m* deflector of piston **-abschmelzmaschine** *f* bulb cutting machine **-ansatz** *m* extension of piston **-antrieb** *m* piston drive **-aufgabevorrichtung** *f* piston feeder **-bahn** *f* working surface of a piston **-band** *n* piston ferrule **-belastung** *f* piston load **-beschleunigung** *f* piston acceleration **-blasmaschine** *f* bulb blowing machine **-blech** *n* butt plate **-boden** *m* piston-head, top of piston, piston crown **-bohrer** *m* stem bit

Kolbenbolzen *m* gudgeon pin, wrist pin **blinder ~**

slave gudgeon pin **schwimmender ~** full-floating piston pin

Kolbenbolzen-auge *n* gudgeon-pin boss **-bohrung** *f* piston-pin bore **-buchse** *f* piston-pin bushing **-ende des Hauptpleuels** small end of master rod **-kopf** *m* small end of connecting rod **-lager** *n* piston-pin bushing, wrist-pin bearing **-nabe** *f* gudgeon-pin boss **-zangen** *pl* piston pin pliers

Kolben-(Bremse)stange *f* hydraulic ram (brake) rod **-brennkraftmaschine** *f* reciprocating engine **-brett** *n* bulb tray **-bruch** *m* piston fracture **-brücke** *f* plunger crib **-büchse** *f* piston box, piston-boss bushing **-dampfmaschine** *f* piston-type steam engine **-dichtring** *m* compression or piston ring **-dichtung** *f* piston packing **-drehbank** *f* piston turning lathe **-druck** *m* piston pressure **-durchmesserstufung** *f* stepped plunger diameter

Kolben-entferner *m* bulb remover **-feder** *f* plunger spring, piston spring **-fahne** *f* plunger lug **-fläche** *f* piston area or surface **-form** *f* bulb mold **-förmig** bulb-shaped **-führung** *f* piston guide, barrel of a ram **-gasdurchlaß** *m* piston-ring blow-by **-gasring** *m* compression ring **-gebläse** *n* piston blower, piston supercharger or compressor **-geschwindigkeit** *f* piston speed

kolbengesteuert piston-controlled **-e Schlitze** (Zweitakt), ports covered and uncovered by the working piston **Motor mit -en Ein- und Auslaßschlitzen** piston-ported engine

Kolben-gleitbahn *f* piston skirt **-guß** *m* piston casting **-hals** *m* small of stock, neck of bulb, bull plate **-hieb** *m* butt stroke

Kolbenhub *m* piston stroke, stroke **beim ~ verdrängter Raum** piston displacement

Kolben-hubanzeiger *m* piston stroke indicator **-kappe** *f* butt plate **-kegel** *m* plunger poppet **-kippen** *n* piston slap **-kopf** *m* pistonhead **-kraft** *f* plunger (piston) power **-krone** *f* piston crown **-lader** *m* displacement supercharger **-lauf** *n* piston travel **-laufmantel** *m* liner (mach.) **-leder** *n* plunger leather **-lehre** *f* dead-weight gauge

Kolben-liderung *f* piston packing **-löffel** *m* piston baller **-luftpumpe** *f* scavenging air pump **-magnet** *m* solenoid **-manometer** *n* piston manometer **-mantel** *m* piston skirt **-maschine** *f* plunger- or piston-type die-casting machine, reciprocator, reciprocating engine **-meißel** *m* central bit

Kolben-membran *f* piston diaphragm **-mikrophon** *n* pistonphone **-mitnehmer** *m* plunger (driving) vane **-motor** *m* reciprocating engine **-mutter** *f* plunger-rod nut **-nabe** *f* piston boss **-niedergang** *m* piston descent **-nut** *n* ring groove **-ölpumpe** *f* piston oil pump **-ölspritzdüse** *f* cooling jet nozzle **-packung** *f* piston packing **-pistole** *f* submachine gun consisting of automatic pistol with telescope or skeleton stock **-preßspritzen** *n* flexible plunger molding

Kolbenpumpe *f* plunger pump, reciprocating pump, piston pump **stehende ~** vertical piston pump

Kolbenraum *m* space within bulb

Kolbenring *m* piston ring, segment **~ mit Phosphidnetzwerk auf der tragenden Fläche** cell-faced piston ring **~ mit erhöhtem Radialdruck an der Stoßstelle,** high-point piston ring **gegen Verbrennungsgase abdichtender ~ mit L-förmigem Querschnitt** obturator ring **fester, verklebter ~** dead ring **verklebter ~** gummed piston ring

kolbenring-ähnlicher Öldichtring piston-ring-type oil seal **-guß** *m* piston-ring casting **-nut** *n* **-riefe** *f* piston-ring groove **-schlitz** *m* split in piston ring **-zange** *f* piston-ring pliers

Kolben-rohr *n* plunger case, working barrel **-rohrpumpe** *f* cylinder pump, working-barrel pump **-rohrventil** *n* working-barrel valve **-rückholfeder** *f* piston return spring **-sandpumpe** *f* sand pump **-schaft** *m* (Bremse) piston body (shaft) **-scheibe** *f* plunger follower, plunger disk

Kolbenschieber *m* sleeve valve **-büchse** *f* piston-valve liner **-kammer** *f* piston-valve chamber **-regler** *m* piston control **-steuerung** *f* piston-valve control **-ventil** *n* piston valve

Kolben-schub *m* piston motion **-schlüssel** *m* piston wrench **-schmierung** *f* piston lubrication **-schwärzung** *f* bulb blackening **-setzmaschine** *f* piston jig, plunger jig **-sicherung** *f* wrist pin, gudgeon pin, gudgeon pin lock

Kolbenspiel *n* play or clearance of piston **-raum** *m* (piston) clearance

Kolben-spritzmaschine *f* plunger-type die casting machine **-spülmaschine** *f* bulb washing machine

Kolbenstange *f* piston rod, regulator (gun), branch rod **hydraulische ~** hydraulic ram

Kolbenstangen-bund *m* piston-rod collar **-führung** *f* piston-rod guide **-kegel** *m* piston-rod taper **-kopf** *m* head (of piston rod), small end **-kopfbüchse** *f* small end bush (piston rod) **-lager** *n* piston rod bearing **-mutter** *f* piston-rod nut

Kolbensteg *m* piston land **oberster ~** piston-top land

Kolben-stellung *f* (bei Pumpe) plunger position **-stickerei** *f* braid **-stiefel** *m* pump barrel **-strahler** *m* piston radiator **-stulp** *m* piston-packing leather **-stutzen** *m* plunger stud **-takt** *m* piston stroke **-totlage** *f* piston dead center

Kolben-ventil *n* piston or plunger valve **-verdichter** *m* reciprocating compressor **-verdrängung** *f* piston displacement **-vollhub** *m* complete stroke of plunger (or piston) **-vorlauf** *m* forward piston stroke **-vorverdichter** *m* piston blower, piston supercharger or compressor **-weg** *m* piston path or stroke, piston travel **-wegdruckdiagramm** *n* piston-position time diagram **-wulst** *m* bulb ring **-zapfen** *m* piston pin

Koleopter *m* coleopter

kolieren to filter

Koliertuch *n* cloth filter, filter cloth

kolineare Koaxialantenne colinear coaxial antenna

Kolk *m* washed-out depression, pool (in a river), scouring, pit made by floodwater **-abwehr** *f* scour prevention **-bildung** *f* scour, erosion, undermining

kolken to undermine, erode, wash away

Kolkung *f* squeezing

kollabieren to callapse

kollaborieren to collaborate

kollationieren to collate

Kolleg *n* course of (university) lectures

Kollegium *n* board (of experts) college

Kollekte *f* collection

kollektieren to collect

kollektiv collective

Kollektiv *n* convergent or collective lens, filed lens (optics) lot (quality control) ~ **des Okulars** field lens of eyepiece

Kollektiv-linse *f* collimating lens **-marken** *pl* collective marks **-modell** collective model

Kollektor *m* commutator, collector (ring), oiler (in flotation), revolving contact maker, distributor, rotary switch, condenser (lens) **-abdrehvorrichtung** *f* commutator turning-off device **-anschluß** *m* collector terminal **-basisschaltung** *f* (Transistor) grounded collector arrangement **-belüftung** *f* ventilation of commutator **-blende** *f* condenser stop or diaphragm **-büchse** *f* commutator sleeve or bush **-bürste** *f* commutator or collector brush **-fahne** *f* commutator lug

Kollektor-geräusch *n* commutator noise **-grundschaltung** common collector circuit **-lager** *n* commutator (end) bearing **-lamelle** *f* commutator segment, collector segment or bar **-nachdrehvorrichtung** *f* commutator re-turning device **-randschicht** *f* collector junction **-reststrom** *m* reverse saturation current (in transistor) **-ring** *m* collector ring **-stab** *m* commutator bar or segment **-übergang** *m* collector junction

Koller *m* **-gang** *m* pan grinder, edge or pug mill, Chile mill

Kollergangs-läufer *m* edge runner **-schale** *f* grinding pan, edge-runner pan **-teller** *m* pan bottom

Kollerläufer *m* edge runner, pug-mill runner

Kollermühle *f* pan grinder, edge-runner mill, edge or pug mill ~ **mit aufrechten Steinen** vertical edge mill, vertical crushing mill

kollern to grind and mix

Kollern *n* pan grinding

Kollerplatte *f* edge-runner plate

Kolli *pl* packages

kollidieren to collide

Kollimation *f* collimation

Kollimations-achse *f* line of collimation **-fehler** *m* error of collimation **-linie** *f* collimating mark

Kollimator *m* collimator **-fernrohr** *n* collimator telescope

kollimieren to collimate

Kollinearantenne *f* collinear antenna

Kollineation *f* collineation

Kolliquation *f* liquefaction

Kollision *f* collision ~ **mit Energieauswechslung** exchange collision

Kollisionskurs *m* collision course (aviat) **-verfahren** *n* interception chaser system **-markierung** *f* collision course indication

Kollisions-radius *m* neutron collision radius **-raum** *m* collision space **-schott** *n* collision bulkhead **-verfahren** *n* interference action or procedure

Kollizeichen *n* distinguishing marks

Kollmanns Höhenmessereinstellung Kollman's number, altimeter setting (aviation)

kollodionieren to collodionize

Kollodium *n* collodion **-fasermasse** *f* collodion cotton or wool **-haut** *f* collodion film **-schicht** *f* collodion film **-wolle** *f* pyroxylin, guncotton

Kolloid *n* colloid

kolloidal colloidal

Kolloid(al)-stoff *m* **-substanz** *f* colloidal substance or matter

Kolloid-chemie *f* colloid chemistry

Kollokation *f* collocation

Kolmation *f* deposition of soil from flowing water, colmation

Kolonial-handel *m* colonial trade **-waren** *pl* colonial produce, groceries

Kolonie *f* colony, settlement

Kolonist *m* colonist, settler

Kolonne *f* column, column of squadrons in closed-V formation (aviation), javelin (aviation), gang (of men), tower (petroleum), (supply) train ~ **zu einem** column of files ~ **zu zweien** column of twos **fliegende** ~ flying party, flying column, independent column

Kolonnen-brücke *f* portable bridge **-chef** *m* column commander **-führer** *m* foreman of plate layers **-gebiet** *n* rear area, supply zone, communications zone **-ionisation** *f* columnar ionization **-satz** *m* setting in columns **-schalter** *m* column shift unit **-spitze** *f* head of column **-spundapparat** *m* section bunging apparatus **-staffel** *f* rear-echelon train **-turm** *m* tower (refinery) **-verkehr** *m* column traffic

Kolonel *f* minion

kolonisieren to colonize

Kolophon(ium) *n* colophony, resin, rosin **-lötzinn** *n* rosin-core solder

Koloquinte *f* colocynth

kolorieren to color

Kolorimeter *n* colorimeter **lichtelektrisches** ~ photoelectric colorimeter

Kolorimetrie *f* colorimetry

kolorimetrisch colorimetric

Kolorist *m* painter

Kolorit *n* coloring, hue

Koloß *m* colossus

Kolter und Vorschneider colter and jointer

Kolumne *f* column, page

Kolumnen-breite *f* column width, measure **-maß** *n* page rule **-schiff** *n* column galley **-schnur** *f* page (cord) string **-titel** *m* heading, column head, headline, running title **-weise setzen** to set in columns **-ziffer** *f* folio

Kolzaöl rape seed oil

Koma *n* coma **-abbildung** *f* comatic image

Komareste höherer Ordnung independent coma of higher order

Kombinat *n* combine, combined unit

Kombination *f* combination, flying suit, coveralls

Kombinations-aufnahme *f* combination exposure, composite shot **-bauweise** *f* combination principle **-blende** *f* Goerz-effect shutter **-frequenz** *f* combination frequency **-linien** *pl* combination rules **-modell** *n* unified model **-register** *n* combination stop (organ) **-schloß** *n* combination or puzzle lock **-stab** *m* key-bar **-stimme** *f* mutation stop (organ) **-ton** *m* combination(al) tone **-winkelmesser** *m* combination protractor **-zange** *f* combination pliers

Kombinator *m* combiner

Kombinatorik *f* combinatorial analysis
kombinatorische Topologie combinatorial topology
Kombinatorscheibe *f* combiner wheel
kombinieren to combine, hook up
kombiniert combined **-e Bohranlage** combination rig (drilling) **-es Buntsignal** combined chromattack, simultaneous attacks at both high and low levels **-e Bohranlage** combination rig (drilling) **-es Buntsignal** combined chrominance signal **-e Chlorsuperoxydbleiche** combined chlorineperoxide bleach **-er seitwärts ablegender Heurechen und Wender** combination side rake and tedder **-er Heuschlepprechen mit Hochwinde und Abladevorrichtung** combined sweep rake and stacker **-e Loch- und Nietmaschine** combination punching and riveting machine **-e Mäh- und Dreschmaschine** harvester thresher, combine **-er Mikro-Dia-Apparat** combined micro-dia-apparatus
kombinierte Rechnungs- und Auftragsschreibung combined billing and order preparation
kombiniert-e Rüttel- und Preßformmaschine combination jarring and squeezing machine **-es Signal** (Video-Hilfsträger) combined signal **-er Verteiler** CDF (combined distribution frame) **-es Walzverfahren** combination rolling-mill practice **-er Widerstand** joint resistance
Kombi-wagen *m* station wagon **-zange** *f* combination pliers, multiple purpose pliers
Kombüse *f* galley (on ship)
Kometen-bahn *f* cometary orbit **-kern** *m* comet's nucleus **-schweif** *m* comet's tail or train
Komfortklimatisierung *f* air conditioning
Komma *n* comma, decimal point **bewegliches ~** floating decimal point **festes ~** fixed point (data processing) **gleitendes ~** floating point (data processing)
Komma-ausrichtung *f* decimal point alignment **-bildung** *f* sparking out
Kommandant *m* commander, commanding officer, major
Kommandeur *m* commander
kommandieren to command, order, detail, detach
kommandiert zu attached to
Kommanditgesellschaft *f* limited partnership, jointstock company
Kommando *n* command, order, staff, detachment, control signal **-behörde** *f* staff commanding a division or a larger unit **-brücke** *f* (pilot) bridge **-empfänger** *m* radio-control receiver **-flagge** *f* command-post flag, commander's flag, detachment pennant
Kommando-gerät *n* stereoscopic fire director, station control, predictor, automatic engine control, data computer, ballistic director **-hilfsgerät** *n* auxiliary director or predictor **-impuls** *m* command pulse **-lautsprechanlage** *f* public-address system **-platte** *f* selector station (autom.-control) **-pult** *n* control desk **-raum** *m* control room **-rechner** *m* computor **-sache** *f* military secret, confidential military document **-sender** *m* cutoff signal transmitter, radio-control transmitter
Kommando-sprachenverschlüsseler *m* vocoder **-sprachenaufzeichner** *m* vocoding recorder **-stand** *m* control station **-stelle** *f* command post, headquarters, order point, order place or station, impulsing or control-action transmitter (remote control) **-steuerstufe** *f* talkback unit **-tafel** *f* fire-control indicator, antiaircraft-range converter, immediate-firing-data table, master panel **-turm** *m* conning tower
Kommandoübertragung *f* data transmission **~ zwischen Flugzeugen** interaircraft command or voice communication
Kommando- und Ladeverzugszeit *f* command and computation lag (antiaircraft), dead time
Kommando-werk *n* control unit **-werte** *pl* fire-director data **-wort** *n* command, command of execution (drill) **-zeiger** *m* indicator, pointer on selsyn
kommen to come, approach, arrive **außer Eingriff ~** to disengage **auf Touren ~** to pick up speed **ins Trudeln ~** to fall into a spin
kommensurabel commensurable
kommensurieren to commensurate
Kommentar *n* commentary
kommerzial, kommerziell commercial
Kommissions-lager *n* consignment **-verkauf** *m* sale by agent
Kommodore *m* commodore
kommunaler Betrieb *m* municipal undertaking
Kommutation *f* commutation
Kommutationswertspalte *f* commutation column
kommutativ commutative
Kommutator *m* commutator, switch, collector (ring), current reserve **-brand** *m* burning of commutator **-buchse** *f* commutator sleeve **-bürste** *f* commutator brush, collector segment **-fahne** *f* commutator riser (lug) **-lamelle** *f* commutator segment, collector segment **-motor** *m* commutator motor **-schritt** *m* commutator pitch **-unterbrecher** *m* commutator interrupter or break
kommutieren to commutate, reverse (polarity, connections, etc.)
kommutierende Observable commuting observable
kommutierter Strom commutated current
Kommutierung *f* commutation **geräuschlose ~** noiseless commutation
Kommutierungs-anode *f* transition anode **-frequenz** *f* (commutator) ripple frequency **-kurve** *f* curve of normal magnetization **-stoß** *m* commutation impulse **-welle** *f* commutation or commutator ripple, current ripple
kompakt compact, solid, rugged, dense, close, blocky (coke), nonapertured **-heit** *f* compactness
Kompander *m* compandor
Kompanie *f* company
Komparator *m* computing recording comparator
Komparserieraum *m* extras room
Kompaß *m* compass, magnetic compass **~ mit Kompaßrose** card compass
Kompaß-ablenkung *f* compass error **-abweichung** *f* compass declination **-ausgleichung** *f* compass compensation **-büchse** *f* compass box or bowl, kettle of the compass **-bügel** *m* gimbal **-diopter** *n* sight vane **-fehler** *m* compass error **-flüssigkeit** *f* compass liquid **-gabel** *f* gimbal **-haus, -häuschen** *n* binnacle **-hütchen** *n* socket of the compass needle
Kompaß-kessel *m* compass case or bowl, kettle

of the compass **-kompensator** *m* compass corrector **-kurs** *m* compass course, heading, bearing, steered course **-kurswinkel** *m* compass azimuth **-lenkung** *f* compass deviation **-mißweisung** *f* compass declination **-nadel** *f* compass needle, magnetic needle **-norden** *m* compass north **-peilung** *f* compass bearing **-pfanne** *f* pan or cup of the rhumb card **-pinne** *f* pivot or center pin of compass

Kompaßpunkte *pl* compass points **die ~ der Reihe nach aufzählen** to box the compass (aviation)

Kompaß-richtstrecke *f* compass heading **-richtung** *f* compass bearing **-rose** *f* compass rose, compass card, rhumb card, compass scale **-säule** *f* compass pedestal **-schwimmer** *m* compass float **-strich** *m* rhumb, point of the compass **-tagebuch** *n* deviation logbook **-zahl** *f* azimuth, compass reading, bearing **-zubehör** *n* compass accessories

kompatibiles Farbfernsehverfahren compatible color television

Kompatibilität *f* compatibility

Kompatibilitätsbedingung *f* compatibility condition

kompendiöser Bau compact design

Kompensation *f* neutralization compensation **~ des Magnetkompasses** compensation for compass deviation

Kompensations-draht *m* extension (lead) wire, compensating lead wire **-druckmeßordnung** *f* compensating-pressure measuring apparatus **-einrichtung** *f* compensation device **-einsteller** *m* compensation regulator **-feld** *n* compensating field **-geschäft** *n* export or import paid through clearing, barter system **-kraft** *f* balancing force **-kreis** *m* backing circuit **-küvette** *f* compensating cell **-längsmagnet** *m* compensating fore-and-aft magnet **-leitung** *f* compensating lead wire **-quermagnet** *m* compensating thwartship or transverse magnet

Kompensations-schaltung *f* compensating circuit or network **-schleifen** *pl* compensating loops **-schreiber** *m* potentiometric recorder **-spule** *f* cancellation coil (guided missiles), compensating or bucking coil **-strom** *m* compensating current **-verfahren** *n* compensating method, balancing method (e.g. torque balancing), opposition method **-vorrichtung** *f* compensation arrangement or device **-wickelung** *f* compensating winding **-widerstand** *m* compensating resistance **-wirkung** *f* (Eigenschaft) compensating properties

Kompensator *m* compensator, potentiometer **-düse** *f* compensating jet **-feldstärkemesser** *m* magnetic potentiometer **-schaltung** *f* compensating potentiometer circuit **-schiene** *f* compensator rail

kompensieren to compensate (for), adjust

Kompensieren *n* compensation, compensating **~ des Kompasses** compensation of the compass

kompensiert-e Abtastung expanded sweep **-e Ionisationskammer** compensation chamber **-e Lautstärkeregelung** compensated volume control

Kompensierung *f* compensation (for), compass swinging

Kompensierungs-kurs *m* compensating course **-stab** *m* compensating rod or bar

Kompensograph *m* potentiometer recorder

Kompensplanokular *n* compensating plane eyepiece

kompetent authorized

Kompetenz *f* jurisdiction

kompilieren to compile

kompilierendes Programm compiling routine

Komplanare *f* coplanar line

komplanatisch complanate

komplementär complementary

Komplementärfarben *pl* complementary colors

Komplementarität *f* complementarity principle

Komplementärmenge *f* complementary set

komplementieren to complement

Komplementwinkel *m* complementary angle

komplettes Ventil valve assembly

komplettieren to replenish

Komplettierung *f* completion, completing

Komplettmaschine *f* perfecting machine

Komplex *m* aggregate

komplex complex **~ konjugiert** complex conjugated **-es Fernsehspiel** composite television signal **-es Gebiet** complex domain (math.) **-e Größe** complex quantity **-es Rechnen mit Wechselstromgrößen** application of complex quantities to alternating-current problems

Komplex-bildung *f* sequestering **-erscheinung** *f* complex phenomenon **-erz** *n* complex ore **-former** *m* complex-forming substance **-salz** *n* complex salt

komplex-schraubenartige Bewegung complex-screw motion

Komplex-stahl *m* complex alloy steel **-verbindung** *f* complex combination, complex compound

kompliziert complicated, intricate, elaborate (work) **-e Anordnung** intricate assembly **-er Satz** complicated setting

Kompliziertheit *f* complication

Kompobuchse *f* self-lubricating bush

Komponente *f* component, constituent **~ in der Bewegungsrichtung** drag component **~ senkrecht zur Bewegungsrichtung** lift component **~ einer Verbindung** constituent of a (chemical) combination **flüchtige ~** transient component **reelle ~** real component **wattlose ~** reactive component, wattless component

Komponentenwaage *f* component scale or balance

Kompositionskopf *m* composition head

Kompounddruckregler *m* compound pressure regulator

kompoundieren to compound

Kompoundierung *f* compounding

Kompoundierungseinsteller *m* compound regulator

Kompound-motor *m* compound(-wound) motor **-öl** *n* compounded oil **-panzerplatte** *f* compound armor plate, steel-faced wrought-iron armor plate **-verrohrung** *f* compound casing

Kompresser *m* compressor, supercharger

Kompressibilität *f* compressibility, pressure modulus

Kompressibilitätseinfluß *n* compressibility effect, effect of compressibility

kompressibler Strahl compressible fluid jet

kompressible Strömung compressible flow

kompressible Unterschallströmung subsonic

compressible flow
Kompression *f* compression, supercharge, bulk
Kompressions-druck *m* compression pressure **-faktor** *m* compressibility factor **-hahn** *m* compression tap, pet cock, priming cock **-hub** *m* compression stroke **-knopf** *m* compression knob **-messer** *m* compressometer **-modul** *n* bulk modulus **-nocken** *m* compression release **-pumpe** *f* compression pump **-raum** *m* compression chamber **-ring** *m* compressing ring
Kompressions-satz *m* compression ratio **-schub** *m* **-takt** *m* compression stroke **-verhältnis** *n* compression ratio **-wärme** *f* heat of compression, compression heat **-welle** *f* drift wave **-widerstand** *m* compression resistance **-wirkung** *f* compression effect **-zentrum** *n* center of compression
Kompressometer *n* compression gauge
Kompressor *m* compressor, contracter, blower, supercharger **einseitiger** ~ single-entry compressor **einstufiger** ~ single-stage compressor **zweistufiger** ~ double-stage compressor
Kompressor-aggregat *n* engine compressor set **-anlage** *f* compressor plant **-antrieb** *m* supercharger drive **-gehäuse** *n* compressor casing **-leitrohr** *n* compressor delivery pipe (jet)
kompressorlos compressionless **-er Dieselmotor** Diesel engine with solid injection **-er ortsfester Viertaktdreizylinderdieselmotor** three-cylinder airless injection stationary four-stroke Diesel engine
Kompressor-motor *m* supercharged motor, blower-fed engine **-öl** *n* compressor oil, air-compressor oil **-schütz** *m* compressor contactor **-tank** *m* air flask **-trommel** *f* compressor drum, jet gas turbine **-ventil** *n* compressor valve **-verstärker** *m* compressor, contracter
Komprimierbarkeit *f* compressibility
komprimieren to compress
Komprimieren der Laufzeit transit-time compression
komprimierende Wirkung (der Reifen) kneading action (of the tires)
Komprimierpumpe *f* compressing pump
komprimiert compressed **-er Dampf** compressed steam **-es Gas** compressed gas
Kompromißnachbildung *f* compromise balance
Kondensabscheider *m* steam or condensing trap
Kondensanz *f* condensance, capacitance, capacitive reactance
Kondensat *n* condensate, condensation product **-ablauf** *m* condensation runoff or discharge **-ableiter** *m* steam trap **-behälter** *m* condensation tank **-entspanner** *m* condensate pressure reducer
Kondensation *f* condensation
Kondensations-anlage *f* condenser system **-apparat** *m* condenser, condensation or condensing apparatus **-basis** *f* condensation basis or level **-betrieb** *m* pass-out or condensation operation **-falle** *f* cold trap **-hygrometer** *n* hygrodeik **-kalorimeter** *n* steam calorimeter **-maschine** *f* condensation machine **-produkt** *n* condensation product **-punkt** *m* condensation level **-röhre** *f* condenser tube **-turbine** *f* condensing reheat turbine **-turbosatz** *m* condensing turbo-alternator set **-wärme** *f* heat of condensation **-wasser** *n* condenser water, water of condensation
Kondensatkreiselpumpe *f* centrifugal condensate pump
Kondensator *m* condenser, capacitor ~ **mit wellengerader Kennlinie** square-law condenser ~ **für große Leistung** power condenser ~ **mit Parallelwiderstand** shunted condenser ~ **mit geteiltem Stator** split stator capacitor ~ **mit geringen dielektrischen Verlusten** low-loss condenser **einstellbarer** ~ variable or adjustable condenser **elektrolytischer** ~ electrolytic condenser **fester** ~ fixed condenser, fixed capacity **frequenzgerader** ~ straight-line frequency capacitor **gekuppelter** ~ gang condenser
Kondensator, gleichlaufender ~ ganged condenser, synchronized condenser **großer** ~ large-capacity condenser **kapazitätsgerader** ~ straight-line capacity condenser **quadratischer** ~ square-law condenser **regelbarer** ~ variable or adjustable condenser **unvollkommener** ~ leaky condenser **variabler** ~ **veränderbarer** ~, **veränderlicher** ~ variable or adjustable condenser **wellengerader** ~ straight-line wave (length) condenser
Kondensator-abgleich *m* balancing by condensers (teleph.) **-abschlußwände** *pl* end shields of ganged condenser **-achse** *f* condenser spindle **-aufladungen** *f pl* condenser charge **-ausfall** *m* condenser (or capacitor) failure **-belagverlust** *m* surface-leakage loss of a condenser **-belegung** *f* condenser armature or coating **-betriebsspannung** *f* operating voltage of capacitor **-blitzableiter** *m* carbon lightning rod protector **-blitzschutzvorrichtung** *f* condenser lightning arrester
Kondensator-durchführung *f* condenser leads **-eingang** *m* capacitor input **-elektrometer** *n* condenser meter **-elektroskop** *n* condenser electroscope
Kondensatoren in Reihe ganged condensers
Kondensatoren-batterie *f* condenser bank **-kasten** *m* condenser box or pot
Kondensator-entladung *f* condenser discharge **-entstörung** *f* condenser (capacitor) interference suppression **-fernhörer** *m* electrostatic receiver **-folie** *f* condenser (capacitor) foil **-kette** *f* high-pass filter, lower limiting filter, infra filter **-klemme** *f* condenser-type bush or terminal **-kreis** *m* condenser circuit **-leiter** *m* high-pass filter (teleph.) **-leitung** *f* high-pass filter **-linse** *f* condenser lens **-mantel** *m* condenser jacket **-mikrophon** *n* condenser transmitter or microphone, electrostatic microphone **-mikrophonschaltung** *f* condenser-microphone circuit
Kondensator-platte *f* condenser plate **-reihe** *f* condenser (capacitor) row **-rohr** *n* condenser tube **-rohrring** *m* condenser ferrule **-rückstand** *m* residual charge of condenser **-schaber** *m* condenser scaling tool **-schütz** *m* capacitor contactor **-schweißung** *f* stored energy welding **-sirene** *f* condenser siren
Kondensator-spannung *f* condenser voltage **-telephon** *n* condenser telephone **-umladung** condenser (capacitor) charge and discharge **-wanne** *f* condenser box, ganged or multiple condenser **-wickel** *m* condenser reel **-widerstandkombination** *f* grid condenser and grid

leak connected in parallel **-zünder** *m* capacitor fuse

Kondensat-pumpe *f* condensed-steam pump **-rückführungssystem** *n* condensate return system **-sammelbehälter** *m* condensate collector **-sammelgefäß** *n* condensation trap, condensation-accumulator vessel

Kondensfahne *f* vapor trail (engines)

kondensierbar condensable

Kondensierbarkeit *f* capability of condensation

kondensieren to condense

kondensiert condensed, condensated

Kondensierung *f* condensation

Kondensor *m* condenser **ausklappbarer ~** swing-out condenser

Kondensor-ansatz *m* condenser attachment (housing) **-aufnahme** *f* substage **-hülse** *f* condenser sleeve **-linse** *f* condenser lens **-schiebhülse** *f* condenser sliding sleeve **-spule** *f* condenser coil **-stellring** *m* condenser aperture setting ring **-stutzen** *m* condenser tube **-trieb** *m* condenser motion head

Kondens-rohr *n* condenser tube **-streifen** *m* vapor trail **-topf** *m* steam trap, steam separator

Kondenswasser *n* water of condensation, condenser water **-ableiter** *m* steam trap, steam separator **-abscheider** *m* condensate separator **-austritt** *m* condensed-water discharge **-hahn** *m* pet cock **-prüfer** *m* sweet tester **-rückleiter** *m* return-type steam trap **-rückspeiseanlage** *f* apparatus for returning water of condensation **-wolke** *f* condensation cloud

Konditionier-apparat *m* conditioner **-schein** *m* conditioning certificate

konditionieren to condition

Konditionierung *f* conditioning

Konduktanz conductance **-meßbrücke** *f* conductance bridge

Kondukte *f* wind trunk (of an organ)

konduktiv conductive

Konfektion *f* packaging, filling in containers, labelling

Konferenz-gespräch *n* conference call **-klinke** *f* conference jack **-schaltung** *f* conference-calling equipment **-verbindung** *f* conference call

konferieren to confer

Konfiguration *f* configuration **ebene ~** configuration in the plane **räumliche ~** configuration in space

Konfigurations-ausdehnung *f* extension on configuration **-entropie** *f* configurational entropy **-raum** *m* configuration space **-relaxation** *f* configurational relaxation **-wechselwirkung** *f* configuration interaction

Konfirmation *f* confirmation

konfiszieren to confiscate

konfluent hypergeometrisch confluent hypergeometric

Konfluenz *f* confluence

konfokale Flächen confocal surfaces

konforme Abbildung conformal representation or transformation, conformal mapping

konfrontieren to confront (with)

Konglomerat *n* conglomerate **-gefüge** *n* conglomerate structure

konglomerieren to conglomerate

Kongo-gelb *n* Congo yellow **-rot** *n* Congo red

Kongreßstoff *m* etamine, bunting

kongruent congruent **-e Dreiecke** congruent triangles

Kongruenz *f* congruence, congruency **-annahme** *f* assumption of congruence **-axiom** *n* axioms of congruence **-satz** *m* congruence theorem **-zeichen** *n* sign of equivalence

Königs-bolzen *m* kingbolt **-säule** *f* main column, center column **-stange** *f* kingbolt, lifting rod, main connecting rod **-stein** *m* (Gießerei) king block **-stück** *n* king post or strut **-stuhl** *m* center support **-wasser** *n* aqua regia **-welle** *f* vertical shaft, kingpin **-zapfen** *m* central pivot, royal post, king pillar or bolt, kingpin

Konimeter *n* konimeter

konisch conic(al), taper(ed) **~ ausgebildeter Druckring** tapered thrust ring **~ ausgedreht** conically threaded **~ erweiterte Bohrung** reverse taper ream **~ verlaufen** flared out

konisch-e Abtastung conical scanning **-e Bohrung** tapered bore **-e Färbespule** winding cone for dyeing **-es Getriebe** bevel gear **-es Gewinde** taper threads **-er Holzdorn** conically shaped wooden bobbin **-e Kreuzspule** cone **-es Lager** tapered bearing **-e Mischtonne** double-cone mixer **-es Rad** bevel wheel **-es Rohr** tapered-bore barrel **-es Rollenlager** taper roller bearing **-e Spindel** tapered spindle **-e Spule** conical coil **-er Stift** taper pin

Konischdreharbeit *f* taper-turning work

Konizität *f* conicalness, taper, draft, conicity, coning **~ des Kegels** angle of taper

konjugiert conjugate, conjugated **~ komplex** conjugate complex, contingent complex **~ komplexe Größen** conjugate-complex quantities **~ komplexer Scheinwiderstand eines Vierpols** conjugate impedance **~ komplexes Winkelmaß** conjugate phase constant **~ komplexes Übertragungsmaß** conjugate transfer contact or constant

konjugierte Funktionen conjugate functions

Konjunktur *f* conjuncture, turn of the market, trade outlook, business boom **-forschung** *f* business research

konkav concave

Konkave eines Flusses concave bank

Konkavgitter *n* concave grating

Konkavhobelvorrichtung *f* concave shaping attachment

Konkavität *f* concavity

konkavkonvexe Linse concavo-convex lens

konkordant conformable

Konkordanz *f* conformity

Konkretion *f* concretion

konkretionär concretionary

Konkurrent *m* competitor, rival

Konkurrenz *f* competition, rivalry

konkurrenz-fähig able to compete, competitive, marketable **-los** exclusive, noncompetitive

konkurrieren to compete

Konkurs *m* bankruptcy, failure, insolvency

können to be able, know, understand

Können *n* ability

Konnossement *n* bill of lading

Konoden *pl* conodes, tie lines (used in physical-chemical diagrams)

Konoide *f* conoid

Konoidierung *f* compensation

konoidisch conoidal

Konormale *f* co-normal
konoskopisch conoscopic, converting
Konsens *m* consensus
konsequent consistent
Konsequenz *f* consistency, consequence
konservative Struktur conservative or single-grain structure
Konserve *f* preserved or canned food, preserve
Konserven-büchse *f* can **-ring** *m* jar ring
konservieren to preserve, conserve
Konservierung *f* preservation, conservation
Konservierungsgleichrichter *m* preserving rectifier
Konservierungsmittel *n* preservative **mit Konservierungsmitteln behandeln** to slush (an engine)
Konservierungs-öl *n* slushing oil **-schicht** *f* preserving layer or film, pitch mastix (used to cover tank tops)
Konsignation *f* consignment
konsistent consistent **-e Fette** grease, solid lubricant
Konsistentenfett *n* consistent grease
Konsistenz *f* consistency, consistence **-maß** *n* measure of consistency **-messer** *m* viscosimeter, consistometer **-parameter** *n* consistency variables **-zahl** *f* consistency index
Konsol *n* knee **-antrieb** *m* knee drive **-ausrüstung** *f* set of brackets **-belastung** *f* load on cantilever, load on bracket **-drehlaufkran** wall crane
Konsole *f* bracket or insulator pin, cantilever ~ (für Hilfsgeräte) pad
Konsolen für Spurbegrenzung brackets for kerb
Konsolen-arm *m* arm of bracket **-ticker** *m* cantilever trembler
Konsolescharnierbolzenstift *m* carrier hinge pin
Konsol-fräsmaschine *f* knee-type miller **-hängelager** *n* bracket drop hanger
konsolidieren to consolidate, set, concrete, solidify
konsolidierte Gruppenabrechnung group consolidations
Konsolidierung *f* consolidation
Konsol-katze *f* wall crane **-klemmhebel** *m* knee clamp lever **-kran** *m* wall-bracket crane
Konsollager *n* bracket bearing ~ **für den Selbstgang** feed bracket
Konsollaufkran *m* traveling-bracket crane
Konsolschlitten *m* carriage, saddle **-spindel** *f* table bracket screw **-spindellager** *n* table bracket screw bearing
Konsol-teller *m* bracket plate **-träger** *m* cantilever beam
Konsonant *m* consonant **explosiver** ~ explosive consonant **stimmhafter** ~ sonant, voiced, or vocal consonant **stimmloser** ~ nonvocal, surd, or breathed consonant
Konsonantendeutlichkeit *f* consonant ariculation
Konsortium *n* association, syndicate, group
konstant constant, steady, invariable, fixed, stabilized **-e Energie** isoenergetic **-e Kraft** constant power (force)
Konstantan *n* constantan
Konstante *f* constant, parameter ~ **je Längeneinheit** line constant
Konstantenbeziehung *f* relation between constants
konstanthalten to keep constant, maintain constant, stabilize
Konstanthaltung *f* maintaining constant, stabilizing, stabilization
konstant-K-Netzwerk *n* constant-K-network
Konstanz *f* constancy, stability **-methode** *f* method of right and wrong cases
konstatieren to state, ascertain, find out, verify
Konstellation *f* configuration (*e.g.*, of molecules)
Konstitutions-formel *f* constitutional formula, rational formula **-wasser** *n* water of constitution
konstitutive Eigenschaften constitutive properties
konstruieren to design, construct, build, plan, project **auf gleichmäßige Beanspruchung** ~ to design for stress uniformity
konstruiert devised
Konstruierung *f* designation
Konstrukteur *m* designer, constructor, detailer, builder **-tätigkeit** *f* design engineering
Konstruktion *f* construction, structure, design **-mechanische** ~ mechanical design
Konstruktions-abteilung *f* engineering department **-ausführung** engineering design **-belastung** *f* design load **-blatt** *n* design sheet **-blattschnitt** *m* propeller-blade section **-büro** *n* design office, bureau of construction **-daten** *pl* design data **-einzelheit** *f* constructional detail **-eisen** *n* structural steel
Konstruktions-fähigkeit *f* design engineering **-fallhöhe** *f* design head **-fehler** *m* fault of construction, faulty design, structural defect **-feinheit** *f* refinement **-form** *f* structural shape **-gewicht** *n* structural weight **-glied** *n* unit or element of construction **-höhe** *f* overall height **-leiter** *m* chief designer
Konstruktions-merkblatt *n* eneineering table **-merkmale** *pl* feature of constructions, constructional or design features **-praxis** *f* design practice **-prinzip** *n* construction principle, principle of design **-profil** *n* structural shapes **-richtlinien** *pl* specification for construction **-riß** *m* construction drawing or plan **-stahl** *m* structural steel **-stück** *n* **in zerlegtem Zustand** piece of construction in dismounted state **-technisch** constructional
Konstruktionsteil, stark beanspruchter ~ structural part or member subject to highest stresses
Konstruktions-unterlagen *pl* construction data **-vereinfachung** *f* simplification of design **-zeichner** *m* designer, draftsman **-zeichnung** *f* working or construction(al) drawing
konstruktiv constructional, practical, concrete, constructive **-e Änderung** design change **-er Aufbau** design
Konstrukteur *m* builder, constructor
konsularische Beglaubigung consular certificate
Konsulat *n* consulate
Konsum *m* consumption **-artikel** *m* article for daily use **-faktor** *m* demand factor **-güterindustrie** *f* consumer goods industry
Konsument *m* consumer
konsumieren to consume, use up
Kontakt *m* contact, stud, contactor, terminal, contact mechanism **einen** ~ **aufheben** to break contact **direkter** ~ instantaneous assembly ~ **machen** to make contact, to make connection **einen** ~ **öffnen** to break a contact **einen** ~ **schließen** to make contact **fester** ~ **in der Gleismitte** fixed contact between rails **Kontakte reinigen** to clean contacts **Kontakte enger** (weiter) **stellen** to close up (open) the contacts

Kontakt, ausgefressener ~ pitted or worn contact **federnder** ~ spring contact, flexible contact, contact spring **inniger** ~ intimate contact **intermittierender** ~ tapping contact, intermittent contact, ticker **kleiner** ~ shortened segment **schlechter** ~ poor contact **weicher** ~ spring contact, flexible contact

Kontakt-abbrände *pl* burning of the contacts **-abdruck** *m* contact print (phot.) **-abnutzung** *f* contact wear **-abstand** *m* contact clearance, contact gap or spacing **-abstandprüfer** (Magnetzünder) point gap taster **-abtastung** *f* contact scanning **-abzug** *m* contact print (photo) **-anschlag** *m* electrical-contact stop **-anzeiger** *m* contact indicator

Kontaktarm *m* brush or brush spring, contact arm, wiper, selector rod ~ **für eine Sprechleitung** line brush or brush spring **C-** ~ test brush

Kontaktarm-satz *m* wiper set, wiper assembly **-träger** *m* brush or selector rod, wiper-shaft or brush rod

Kontakt-backe *f* contact jaw **-bahn** *f* deck (in switch) **-band** *n* band or bank of contacts **-bandschleifverfahren** *n* contact band grinding method

Kontaktbank *f* contact bank, (selector) bank, bank (of contacts) **-draht** *m* bank wire **-verkabelung** *f* bank-to-bank cabling

Kontakt-behandlung *f* contacting (clay treatment) **-bolzen** *m* contact stud **-büchse** *f* contact bush **-bügel** *m* contact-bridge piece **-bürste** *f* (contact) brush, wiper, brush spring **-bürstenstreifen** *m* terminal strip **-detektor** *m* contact detector or rectifier **-dose** *f* contact plug **-draht** *m* whisker **-druck** *m* contact pressure **-elektrode** *f* touch rod **-enge** *f* trapping spot **-entstörung** *f* spark-suppression means on a contact **-einrichtung** *f* contactor (elec.)

Kontaktfeder *f* contact spring ~ **des Stromstoßgebers** impulse spring

Kontakt-federsatz *m* contact spring assembly **-fehler** *m* contact fault **-feile** *f* contact file

Kontaktfeld *n* contact bank or panel **radial angeordnetes** ~ rotary selector bank

Kontakt-filtration *f* contact filtration **-finger** *m* contact finger, wiper **-fläche** *f* contact (sur)face **-flug** *m* contact flight **-flüssigkeit** *f* buffer solution **-gang** *m* contact deposit, contact lode **-geber** *m* contakt maker, contactor, time tapper, time marker, contactor, time switch **-geberzähler** *m* meter-relay **-gebung** *f* contact making **-gestein** *n* contact rock **-gleichrichter** *m* contact detector, crystal detector or rectifier, natural detector

Kontakthalbleiter-Halbleiter *m* contact semiconductor-semiconductor

Kontakthammer *m* trembler **-halbring** *m* semicircular contact, contact half ring **-hebel** *m* contact lever **-höhenmesser** *m* contact altimeter **-hülse** *f* contact bush or sleeve **-kamm** *m* contact comb **-kette** *f* chain of contacts **-kleben** *n* sticking of contacts

Kontakt-klemme *f* contact terminal, contact clamp **-klotz** *m* contact spud **-knopf** *m* contact stud (of an electric controller), push button **-kopf** *m* contact stud **-kolben** *m* bucket piston **-kopie** *f* contact print **-kranz** *m* group of contacts **-kugel** *f* contact sphere, ball **-kühlung** *f* cooling by heat sink (transistor) **-lagerstätte** *f* primary deposit, contact deposit **-lamelle** *f* contact lamination **-leiste** *f* electric terminal board

Kontaktleitungsvielfach-kabel *n* bank cable **-verdrahtung** *f* bank wires

Kontakt-licht *n* contact light **-lichtbogenschweißung** *f* contact arc-welding **-manometer** *n* contact vacuum gauge, pressure switch **-messer** *n* knife-switch prong **-metamorphose** *f* contact metamorphism **-mikrophon** *n* contact microphone **-mine** *f* contact mine **-mittel** *n* catalyst, contact agent or substance

Kontakt-nocken *m* contact-breaker cam or shoulder **-perle** *f* contact bead **-pinsel** *m* cat's whisker **-potentialwall** *m* contact-potential barrier **-prellen** *n* contact chatter **-rahmen** *m* contact carriage **-rauschen** *n* contact murmer **-reihe** *f* contact bank (in form of an arc) **-ring** *m* (Stromverteilring) distributor ring **-rolle** *f* contact trolley

Kontaktsatz *m* contact bank **a-b-**~ line contact bank **c-**~ local contact bank, private (contact) bank, testing and guarding bank

Kontakt-scheibe *f* contact disk or segment **-schelle** *f* contact clip (elec.) **-schieber** *m* adjusting slider, slide contact

Kontaktschiene *f* contact bar **vordere** (hintere) ~ **der Taste** front (back) contact of the key

Kontakt-schließdauer *f* contact closing period (or time) **-schließung** *f* closing of the circuit **-schlitten** *m* contact carriage, brush rod **-schmoren** *n* scorching, freezing, or melting together of contacts **-schraube** *f* contact screw **-sicher** contact-proof **-sicherheit** *f* contact reliability **-spannung** *f* contact potential **-spielraum** *m* range or play between contacts **-spitze** *f* contact point **-stange** *f* trolley pole **-stelle** *f* point of contact, junction (in pyrometry), confluence

Kontaktstift *m* terminal, contact pin, prong of jack, connecting lug **freier** ~ vacant terminal **kurzer** ~ contact stud

Kontakt-stöpsel *m* contact plug **-strecke** *f* contact path **-stück** *n* contact (block), (contact) stud, switch, contact piece **-stückhalter** *m* brush holder **-substanz** *f* contact substance, catalyst **-teller** *m* contact disc **-therapieröhre** *f* contact tube **-uhr** *f* contact-making clock (CMC) **-umschalter** *m* contact switch **-unstetigkeit** *f* contact discontinuity **-unterbrecher** *m* contakt breaker

Kontakt-verfahren *n* contact process **-verformung** *f* deformation (working) of contacts **-verstellung** *f* contact adjustment

Kontaktvielfachfeld, verschränktes ~ slipped banks

Kontakt-wanderung *f* contact migration (creeping) **-weite** *f* contact clearance **-werk** *n* contact device or mechanism **-widerstand** *m* contact resistance **-winkel** *m* contact angle **-wirkung** *f* contact effect, catalysis **-zone** *f* confluent zone **-zusammenschmoren** *n* scorching, freezing, or melting together of contacts

Kontamination *f* contamination

kontaminieren to contaminate

Konten-amt *n* main center **-automat** *m* automatic

account card feed device **-inhaber** *m* account holder **-sucher** *m* (Sucher für unbewegte Konten) detector of inactive accounts **-verbindung** *f* transfer joint

Konterabdruck *m* counterproof

Konterbande *f* contraband (cargo) **-fahrer** *m* vessel carrying contraband **-liste** *f* list of contraband goods

Konter-eskarpe *f* counterscarp **-mutter** *f* check nut, lock nut, counter nut

kontern to check

Konter-spulung *f* reverse circulation **-ring** *m* guard ring

kontestabel contestable

kontestieren to contest

Kontextur *f* connection

kontinental continental **-e Polarluftmasse** polar continental air mass

Kontinental-bewegung *f* continent-making movement **-rand** *m* continental margin **-schelf** *n* continental shelf **-sperre** *f* blockade of the continent **-verschiebung** *f* continental drift

Kontingent *n* contingent, quota, allotment

kontingentieren to allocate

Kontingentierung *f* apportionment, quota system

Kontingenzkoeffizient *m* coefficient of contingency

Kontinue-apparat *m* continuous machine **-betrieb** *m* continuous work

kontinuierlich continuous **-e Anlage** continuous process **-e Drahtstraße** continuous-rod mill train **-e Fertigstraße** continuous finishing mill **-e Kollektorstromzunahme** collector-current runaway **-e Staffelstraße** continuous looping-rod mill train **-er Steuervorsatz** continuously variable drive unit **-er Wärmeofen** continuous heating or reheating furnace **-e Welle** sustained or undamped wave

Kontinuitätsgleichung *f* continuity equation

Kontinuum *n* continuous spectrum **-mechanik** *f* continuum mechanics

Kontinu-verfahren *n* continue process **-verfolgung** *f* angle tracking

Konto *n* account **ein ~ belasten** to debit

Konto-buch *n* passbook **-einlage** *f* deposit **-korrent** *n* current account

Kontor *n* office

kontort twisted, contorted

Kontra-alt *m* contralto **-baß** *m* contrabass bass viol **-gewicht** *n* counter-weight

Kontrahent *m* contractor, contracting party

kontrahieren to contract

Kontrakt *m* contract **-abschlüsse** *pl* contracts placed

Kontraktion *f* contraction, shrinkage

Kontraktions-koeffizient *m* Poisson's ratio, rho ratio **-kraft** *f* contractile force **-spalte** *f* crack from contraction

kontraktlich (stipulated) by contract, contractual

kontraktmäßig gebunden to be under contract

Kontrakurve *f* reversed curve

Kontrast *m* contrast **-einlauf** *m* opaque meal **-empfindlichkeit** *f*, **-empfindung** *f* contrast sensibility or sensitivity, intensity discrimination **-farbenbeleuchtung** *f* illumination with contrasting colors **-färbung** *f* contrast staining (coloration) **-filter** *n* filter for selective contrasts, contrast screen, contrast filter **-füllung** *f* opaque meal **-hebung** *f* compandor action (to improve signal-noise ratio) **-herabsetzung** *f* contrast reduction

kontrastieren to contrast

kontrast-los lacking contrast **-mahlzeit** *f* opaque meal **-photometer mit Würfel** cube-type contrast photometer, contrast photometer with cubical cavity **-regler** *m* contrast control **-reiches Bild** contrast picture, high-gamma picture, high contrast image **-schwelle** *f* contrast threshold **-umfang** *m* contrast range, contrast ratio (TV) **-verbesserung** *f* expanded contrast **-verhältnis** *n* (TV) contrast ratio **-vermehrung** *f* pre-emphasis **-wiedergabe** *f* contrast rendition

Kontrastwirkung *f* effect of contrast **die ~ erhöhen** to accentuate contrasts

kontravariant contravariant

Kontribution *f* contribution

Kontroll-abteilung *f* inspection department **-amt** *n* control section (teleph.) **-analyse** *f* check analysis **-anker** *m* indicator armature **-anlage** *f* checking equipment, control gear **-apparat** *m* control device **-aufgabe** *f* check problem

Kontroll-bestimmung *f* check or control determination, duplicate determination **-bild** *n* monitoring picture (television) **-bildapparatur** *f* monitor **-bildgerät** *n* built-in picture monitor **-bildröhre** *f* monitor kinoscope **-buch** *n* register **-bude** *f* operator's cabin **-diode** *f* code for a type of radar equipment, transmitter-power monitor **-diskriminator** *m* monitoring discriminator **-druck** *m* monitoring print **-drucker** *m* control printer

Kontrolle *f* muster, supervision, control, check(ing), verification, inspection, monitoring, regulation, governing **von ~ abgenommen werden** to pass inspection **fliegende ~** spot check **laufende ~** continuous checking (or check), sequential monitoring **statische ~** stress-strain analysis, static strength check **visuelle ~** visual check

Kontroll-einrichtung *f* controlling device **-empfang** *m* monitoring reception **-empfänger** *m* monitoring receiver, control printer

Kontrollen in Form von Stichproben controls in the form of random checks

Kontrolleur *m* controller, supervisor

Kontroll-faden *m* sighting threads **-feld** *n* control column **-funkenstrecke** *f* telltale spark gap **-gebiet** *n* controlled area, restricted area **-gerät** *n* checking device **-hahn** *m* control nozzle or cock

kontrollierbar controllable

Kontrollierbarkeit *f* controllability

kontrollieren to control, check (up), supervise

Kontrollindexlautsprecher *m* monitoring loudspeaker **-maß** *n* checking measurement

Kontroll-instrument *n* (controlling) instrument, controller **-karte** *f* time sheet intercept board **-kasse** *f* cash register **-kohlenstift** *m* control carbon or brush **-laboratorium** *n* control laboratory **-lampe** *f* pilot lamp, supervisory lamp, telltale lamp **-lautsprecher** *m* monitoring loudspeaker **-lehre** *f* master gauge **-leitung** *f* control line **-linie** *f* control contour **-libelle** *f* master or control level **-liste** *f* muster roll, check list **-lufthafen** *m* control airport

Kontroll-maß *n* reference dimension **-mechanismus** *m* controlling mechanism, servomechanism **-muster** *n* check sample **-normalmeter** *pl* standard meter bars **-nummer** *f* check-control number **-peilung** *f* check bearing of fix **-platte** *f* test record **-platz** *m* supervisor's or monitor's position, service observing desk **-probe** *f* duplicate sample, control sample **-pult** *n* console (rdr) **-punkt** *m* point of control, check point

Kontroll-rad *n* (time)control wheel **-raum** *m* control room **-relais** *n* supervisory relay, control relay **-röhrchen** *n* inspection tube **-röhre** *f* monitoring tube (valve) **-schild** *n* dial **-schrift** *f* home record **-sender** *m* monitor or check-up transmitter, service test oscillator **-stab** *m* standard test bar **-stelle** *f* control station

Kontroll-streifen *m* home record, control slip, flight progress strip **-stromkreis** *m* checking circuit, test circuit **-system** *n* checking system **-tabulator** *m* balancing tabulator **-taste** *f* check key **-tisch** *m* (Rdr) console **-ton** *m* check tone **-turm** *m* control tower

Kontroll-uhr *f* watchman's clock, telltale clock, time clock **-ventil** *n* control valve **-vorrichtung** *f* checking device **-walze** *f* monitor reel **-wecker** *m* pilot alarm **-wiedergaberöhre** *f* monitor picture tube **-zeichen** *n* check mark **-ziffer** *f* check digit **-zone** *f* (Flugplatz) control zone

Kontur *f* contour, outline, border

Konturen-betonung *f* crispening **-schwarz** *n* black for outlines **-versteilerung** *f* improvement in resolution and black-white contrast (television)

Kontur-karte *f* contour map **-platte** *f* key plate **-schrift** *f* outline letter

Konus *m* cone, taper sleeve, tapered socket **weitgeöffneter ~** wide-open cone **~** (der Bildröhre) bell (TV)

Konus-antenne *f* cone or cage antenna **-aufnahme** *f* taper socket **-bohrung** *f* conical bore (or hole) **-drehapparat** *m* taper attachment **-dorn** *m* taper shank **-einsatz** *m* taper adapter **-futterstück** *n* draw chuck

Konushülse *f* cone core, socket, collet **~ für kegelige Schäfte** collet for taper shanks

Konus-kreiselmischer *m* cone impeller **-kuppelung** *f* cone friction clutch **-lautsprecher** *m* cone loud-speaker **-leitapparat** *m* taper attachment

Konuslineal *n* taper-turning attachment **schwenkbares ~** swivel guide bar for taper work

Konus-membran *f* cone diaphragm, diffusion cone, conical diaphragm, woofer **-mutter** *f* cone nut **-nabe** *f* cone hub **-riemen** *m* belt for conical drum drive **-riemenrückführung** *f* backshifting of cone belt **-riemenscheibe** *f* cone pulley **-schaft** *m* taper shank **-schiene** *f* taper guide bar **-trichter** *m* conical horn **-winkel** *m* cone angle

Konvektion *f* convection

Konvektionsstand *m* level of convection **freier ~** level of free convection

Konvektions-strom *m* convection current (electronics), convection **-strömung** *f* convective flow **-zone** *f* convection section

konvektiv convective, anabatic

Konvektron *n* convectron

konvenieren to suit

Konvention für die Summation summation convention

Konventionalstrafe *f* penalty for nonfulfillment of a contract, fine for nonperformance of contract

konvergent convergent **-e Lichtstrahlen** converging rays **-e Reihe** converging series

Konvergenz *f* convergence, convergency **Stärke der ~** rate of convergence

Konvergenz-fall *m* case of convergence **-fehler** *m* error of convergence **-gebiet** *n* region of convergence **-geschwindigkeit** *f* rate of convergence

Konvergenzwinkel *m* angle of convergence **-unterschied** *m* binocular parallax difference

konvergieren to converge

konvergierend convergent

Konversationslexikon *n* encyclopedia

Konversions-artikel *m* conversion style **-faktor** *m* conversion factor **-übergang** *m* conversion transition **-verhältnis** *n* conversion ratio

Konverter *m* converter **~ mit seitwärts eintretendem Wind** side-blown converter **~ mit von unten eintretendem Wind** bottom-blown converter **basischer ~** basic converter **feststehender ~** fixed or stationary converter **kippbarer ~** tilting or tipping converter **liegender ~** barrel or horizontal converter

Konverter-anlage *f* converter plant **-auskleidung** *f* converter lining **-auswurf** *m* slopping of a converter **-bauch** *m* converter belly, converter body **-betrieb** *m* converter practice, Bessemer practice **-birne** *f* converter **-boden** *m* converter bottom **-bühne** *f* converter charging platform **-einsatz** *m* converter charge **-futter** *n* converter lining

Konverter-halle *f* converter house **-hals** *m* converter nose **-helm** *m* converter mouth **-kanzel** *f* converter platform or pulpit **-kran** *m* converter **-mündung** *f*, **-öffnung** *f* converter mouth **-ring** *m* converter trunnion ring **-ringzapfen** *m* converter-ring trunnion **-schnauze** *f* converter nose **-stahl** *m* converter steel **-werk** *n* converter mill, converter shop, Bessemer plant **-windkasten** *m* converter wind or blast box, converter air box, tuyère box **-zapfen** *m* converter trunnion

Konvertierbarkeit der Währungen convertibility of currencies

konvex convex **-er Körper** convex body **-e Krümmung** convex curvature

Konvexität *f* convexity

konvexkonkave Linse meniscus

Konvex-linse *f* convex lens **-spiegel** *m* parabolic reflector

Konvoi *m* convoy

Konzenterbolzen *m* concentric shaft

Konzentrat *n* concertrate **-austrag** *m* concentrate discharge **-behälter** *m* concentrate bin

Konzentration *f* concentration, beaming, reduction **~ eines Elektronenbündels** focusing or concentration of an electron beam **~ in Gewichtsprozenten** mass abundance

konzentrationsabhängige Eigenschaft colligative property

Konzentrations-abhängigkeit *f* dependence on concentration **-elektrode** *f* focusing electrode **-element** *n* concentration cell **-grad** *m* rate or grade of concentration **-lager** *n* concentration camp **-linse** *f* concentration lens **-schlüssel** *m* grouping key **-spannung** *f* concentration potential **-spule** *f* concentrating coil, focusing coil **-stein** *m* (copper) white metal, refined garnierite (for gaining copper) **-träger** *m* concentration carrier (met.) **-verhältnis** *n* concentration ratio, partition coefficient

Konzentrattrübe *f* concentrate pulp

konzentrieren to concentrate, lump

Konzentrieren *n* focusing, concentration, fasciculation

Konzentrierspule *f* focusing coil

konzentriert concentrated, concentric **-er Angriff** concentrated attack, simultaneous approach from all sides **-er Rückstand** short residuum **-es Schaltelement** lumped circuit element

Konzentrierung *f* concentration

konzentrisch concentric(al) **-es Kabel** coaxial cable or line, concentric cable, pipe line **-e Kreise** concentric circles **-e Ringteilung** concentric circles

Konzentrizität *f* concentricity

Konzept *n* draft, sketch **-halter** *m* copyholder (for typewriters)

Konzern *m* concern, trust **-werk** *n* manufacturing affiliate

Konzession *f* concession, license

konzessionieren to make concessions, yield

Konzessions-druck *m* design pressure **-inhaber** *m* licensee

konzipieren to design, produce

Koog *m* reclaimed land

Kooperation *f* cooperation

Kooperationsmodul *m* index of co-operation

kooperieren to co-operate

Koordinate *f* coordinate

Koordinaten-achse *f* axis **-achsen** *f pl* system of coordinates **-anfangspunkt** *m* origin of coordinates **-berechnung** *f* computation of coordinates **-bild** *n* pattern of coordination **-bohrmaschine** *f* coordinate table drilling machine **-kreuz** *n* system of coordinates **-maßangaben** co-ordinate tolerance **-mäßig** co-ordinately **-meßgerät** *n* coordinate measuring apparatus **-meßtisch** *m* compound micrometermotion table **-netz** *n* true-map grid system, coordinate scheme, system of coordinates **-nullpunkt** *m* origin of coordinates

Koordinaten-papier *n* coordinate paper, ruled o graph paper, cross-section paper **-parallaxe** *f* parallax of coordinates, parallactic displacement of coordinates **-raster** *m* coordinate lattice **-schalter** *m* crossbar switch **-schleifmaschine** *f* coordinate table grinding machine **-system** *n* coordinate system, frame of reference **-transformation** *f* transformation of coordinates **-ursprung** *m* origin of coordinates **-verzeichnis** *n* table of coordinates **-wähler** *m* crossbar switch

Koordinations-achse *f* axis of coordinates **-ausgangspunkt** *m* point of origin of coordinates **-gitter** *n* coordination lattice **-kompensator** *m* coordinate potentiometer **-meldenetz** *n* coordinate reporting network **-zahl** *f* coordination number

Koordinatograph *m* coordinatograph

koordinieren to coordinate

Kopal-firnis *m* copal varnish **-mattlack** *m* copal dull varnish

Kopalin *m* mineral resin, copalite

Kopallack *m* copal lacquer, copal varnish

Köper *m* twill (fabric) **beidrechter ~** double-face twill **dreifädiger ~** three-leaved twill

Köperfördermaschine *f* endless-rope haulage (min.)

Kopf *m* head, crown, top (end), tip, port, socket head, nose cap **~ des Erdbohrers** stirrup of a boring apparatus **~ des Strompfeilers** cut nose of the pier **~ eines Telegramms** preface, preamble **~ einer Zeitung** title **auf den ~ gehen** to tip over, go into a nose-dive (sich) **auf den ~ stellen** to nose over **runder ~** fillister or cheese head **über ~ laufend** overhead **verlorener ~** dead head, feeding or lost head, crop end, waste head **versenkter ~** countersunk head

Kopf-abrundung *f* top radius **-abschlußlinie** *f* cross rule under heading **-arbeitsstunde** *f* man-hour **-bahn** *f* (gearing) tooth crest track **-bahnhof** *m* terminal (R.R.), railhead **-band** *n* head strap (mask) **-bänderung** *f* head harness **-bedeckung** *f* headdress, hat, helmet **-befestigter Fernsprecher** headset

Kopf-bild *n* (eines Kristalls) build of the apex **-bindung** *f* top binding (elec.) **-bolzen** *m* setbolt **-brenner** *m* end burner **-bügel** *m* headband **-drehbank** *f* facing lathe **-düngung** *f* top-dressing **-einsatz** *m* headpiece

köpfen to crop, top, lop off, (be)head, poll

Kopf-ende *n* top, head end **-faschine** *f* headed fascine **-fernhörer** *m* headphone, earphone, headset **-flankeneingriff** *m* face contact (mech.) **-flosse** *f* front stabilizing surface **-fräser** *m* shell-end mill **-gerüst** *n* headframe **-gestell** *n* headstall (harness) **-gesteuertes Flugzeug** canard (aviation)

Köpfhacke *f* topping hoe

Kopf-halter *m* headrest **-haube** *f* helmet

Kopfhöhe *f* head room **~ des Zahnes** addendum of the tooth (in a gear wheel)

Kopf-höhenflosse *f* front horizontal stabilizing surface **-höranschluß** *m* telephone jacks **-hörer** *m* headphone, earphone, headset **-hörerbügel** *m* headband, harness, strap **-kammer** *f* point detonator chamber **-kappe** *f* cap **-karte** *f* heading card **-kegelwinkel** *m* external cone angle **-kontakt** *m* off-normal or mechanical contact

Kopfkreis *m* addendum line or circle, crown line or circle (in a gear wheel) **~ des Nockens** high-level portion of the cam

kopf-lastig nose-heavy (aviation), bow-heavy, trim by the bow, top-heavy **-lastigkeit** *f* nose heaviness **-lastmoment** *n* moment of nose heaviness **-latte** *f* head strap (mask) **-leiste** *f* heading **-leitwerk** *n* front controls

Kopf-Lesespannungs-Abweichungs-Faktor factor defining variation in head readback voltage

Kopflinie des Zahnes outside, top or addendum line of the tooth

Kopf-macher *m* header **-mattierung** *f* with frosted head **-niet** *m* flange rivet **-oben** nose-up (aviat.) **-pinne** *f* head pin **-platte** *f* cover plate, head-strap cushion **-produkt** *n* top product **-querträger** *m* end support

Kopf-rampe *f* end ramp **-raste** *f* headrest **-rechnen** *n* mental calculations or computation **-rille** *f* top groove **-rücknahme** *f* tip relief profile ease-off (involute gears) **-ruder** *n* forward control surface **-runge** *f* end stanchion **-schalterkontakt** *m* upper connection contact **-scheibe** *f* silhouette target (prone) **-schicht** *f* course of headers, heading course **-schienenweiche** *f* line end switch **-schild** *n* tail shield, cephalon

Köpfschippe *f* topping spade

Kopf-schirm *m* reflector (photo) **-schmierung** *f* upper cylinder lubrication **-schraube** *f* screw or bolt with head, tap bolt, setbolt, set screw, cap screw **-schutz** *m* skull guard **-schutzhaube** *f* helmet **-schweiße** *f* end-lap weld **-seite** *f* end, head end **-senker** *m* head countersink **-setzer** *m* snap-tool **-spiel** *n* tip clearance (gear) **-spitze** (magn.) *f* stylus (tape rec.) **-sprechgarnitur** *f* head set **-spule** *f* head coil

Kopfstand *m* landing on nose, nose over **~ machen** to nose over

Kopf-stärke *f* strength of a unit **-station** *f* terminal, railhead **-staucher** *m* header

Kopfstein-lage *f* header course **-pflaster** *n* cobblestone, stone pavement **-verband** *m* heading bond

Kopf-stempel *m* heading die **-steuerung** *f* forward control **-strich** *m* vinculum (math.) **-stück** *n* crown piece, header, end sill, head **-stückabsperrventil** *n* screwed bonnet shut-off valve **-stückenschicht** *f* course of headers (masonry) **-sturz** *m* crash, vertical or nose dive **-stütze** *f* headrest

Kopf-teil *m* nose of shell, headpiece **-teilung** *f* graduation on head (of panoramic telescope) **-telephon** *n* headphone **-träger** *m* end piece **-treffer** *m* point hit

kopfüber nose-over (aviat.), head first or foremost **~ laufend** overhead

Kopfübergangsradius *m* radius under the head (fillet)

Köpf- und Rodemaschine *f* topper-lifter

kopfunter nose-down (aviat.), pellmell, headlong

Kopfversenkniete *f* countersunk head rivet

Köpfvorrichtung *f* topping device

Kopf-walze *f* vertical roll **-walzensystem** *n* vertical rolls **-wand** *f* tailboard, end wall **-wandrunge** *f* front board stake **-welle** *f* shock wave (ballistics), head or front wave, bow wave, impact wave **-winde** *f* lifting jack (screw form), head windlass **-winkel des Kegelrades** addendum angle of bevel gear **-wippler** *m* end tippler **-zeile** *f* headline **-zugfestigkeit** *f* direct tensile strength **-zugstück** *n* casing clamps with wedges

Kopfzünder *m* delayed-action fuse, nose fuse, point detonating fuse **empfindlicher ~** all-ways fuse **mechanischer ~** mechanical nose fuse

kophas inphase, in phase coincidence, cophasal

Kopie *f* copy, carbon copy, print, reproduction, duplicate, photoprint, dub (tape rec.)

Kopiegabe bei Bedarfsanforderungen distribution of requisition

Kopier-anlage *f* printer **-anstalt** *f* printing shop **-arbeit** *f* profiling job **-automat** *m* automatic printing machine (phot.) **-drehbank** *f* copying lathe, duplicating lathe

Kopierdrehen *n* contour turning, copy turning **~ in Längsrichtung** longitudinal copying

Kopier-drehstahl *m* copying tool **-druck** *m* profiling pressure **-druckfarbe** *f* copying ink **-effekt** *m* accidental printing (magn. tape), magnetic printing (tape rec.), print through (tape rec.) **-einrichtung** *f* copying attachment, copying mechanism, copying device

kopieren to imitate, copy, print (phot.), trace, make a tracing **direkt ~** to contact-print

Kopieren *n* copying process, contact printing

Kopierer *m* assistant for copying (phot.)

Kopier-fähigkeit *f* copying property **-fenster** *n* printing plane or station **-fräsautomat** *m* automatic profiling machine **-fräsen** to profile **-fräsen** *n* copy milling **-fräsmaschine** *f* duplicating milling machine, profiler **-frässchablone** *f* milling template or pattern **-gamma** *n* negative gamma **-genauigkeit** *f* accuracy of reproduction **-gerät** *n* copying apparatus (printer)

Kopier-hobelmaschine *f* copying shaper, duplication shaper **-leinwand** *f* tracing cloth **-lineal** *n* guide plate templet **-löschkarton** *m* copying boards **-löschpapier** *n* drying paper

Kopiermaschine *f* printer **optische ~** projection printer, projection printing machine

Kopier-mine *m* copying lead (for pencils) **-papier** *n* copying paper, sensitive paper **-presse** *f* copying press **-rahmen** *m* printing frame (photo) **-rollenpapier** *n* copying rolls **-schablone** *f* templet **-schieber** *m* copying slide **-schiene** *f* templet **-schienenhalter** *m* form plate holder **-schleifen** *n* contour grinding **-schwärzung** *f* printing density

Kopier-stahlquerschnitt *m* adjustment of toolholder **-stelle** *f* printing drum **-stift** *m* copying pencil **-stoßmaschine** *f* die shaper **-telegraph** *m* copying telegraph **-tinte** *f* copying ink **-verfahren** *n* copying process (photo) **-vorrichtung** *f* copying attachment **-werk** *n* printing studio, printing shop or plant, repeating gear **-zirkel** *m* copying calipers

Kopist *m* copyist

Koppel *f* enclosure, paddock, string, pack (of dogs), connecting rod, coupler (kinematics)

Koppel *n* belt, sword belt, couple, torque **-bild** *m* conjugate (picture) **-bogen** *m* bend coupling **-elemente** *pl* coupling members **-feld** *n* coupling field **-getriebe** *n* linkage **-kammer** *f* multiplelens camera **-kapazität** *f* coupling capacitance **-kurs** *m* compound course, traverse sailing, dead reckoning **-leitung** *f* strapping **-leitungsunterbrechung** *f* strap freaks **-loch** *n* coupling hole

koppeln to hobble, knee-halter, couple, connect, harness together, determine a course, establish a fix by dead reckoning

Koppeln *n* dead reckoning

Koppel-navigation *f* dead reckoning navigation **-navigationsort** *m* fix, dead-reckoning position (navig.) **-raum** *m* interaction space **-schlaufe** *f* belt loop **-schlitz** *m* window **-sitzventil** *n* double-seated valve **-spalt** *m* interaction gap **-spule** *f* coupling coil **-stelle** *f* transfer substation **-tischanlage** *f* arrangement of switchboard **-tischgeber** *m* switchboard transmitter

Koppelung *f* coupling

Koppelzeit *f* time at which exact position is ascertained by means of dead reckoning

koppen to top

Koppers-Verbundofen *m* Koppers combination (byproduct coke) oven **-Vertikalkammerofen** *m* Koppers vertical-flue (regenerative by-product coke) oven

Koppler *m* coupler

Kopplung *f* coupling, interlocking gear **E-H-T-** ~ E-H tee ~ **Eins** unity coupling ~ **durch gemeinsame Induktivität** autoinductive coupling ~ **durch gemeinsame Kapazität** autocapacity coupling ~ **der Kreise** hookup (radio) ~ **kurzer Reichweite** short-range coupling ~ **zwischen zwei Röhren** intervalve coupling, intervalve linkage ~ **von Schwingungskreisen** coupling of two oscillatory circuits ~ **für automatische Steuerung** autopilot coupler

Kopplung, direkte ~ direct or conductive coupling, impedance coupling **elektrische** ~ capacitive or capacity coupling, condenser coupling, electric or electrostatic coupling **feste** ~ tight, close, or strong coupling **galvanische** ~ direct coupling, conductive coupling, galvanic coupling **induktive** ~ inductive or inductance coupling, magnetic coupling, transformer coupling **kapazitive** ~ capacity coupling, condenser coupling, capacitive coupling, electric coupling, electrostatic coupling **ungewollte kapazitive** ~ spurious coupling **kritische** ~ optimum coupling

Kopplung, lose ~ loose, weak, or slack coupling **magnetische** ~ inductive or inductance coupling, magnetic coupling **mechanische** ~ ganging **reaktionslose** ~ nonreactive coupling **statische** ~ (electro)static coupling **überkritische** ~ tight coupling, close coupling **unterkritische** ~ loose coupling **veränderliche** ~ variocoupler **wilde** ~ stray, spurious, or undesired coupling

Kopplungs-apparat *m* coupler **-arm** low-coupling **-ausgleich** *m* equalization of coupling **-beiwert** *m* coupling coefficient **-block** *m* invariable- or fixed-coupling capacitor

Kopplungsfaktor *m* coefficient of coupling (of two circuits), coupling factor ~ **Eins** unity coupling

Kopplungs-fenster *n* coupling aperture **-glied** *n* coupling member or element **-grad** *m* coupling factor **-kapazität** *f* coupling capacity **-koeffizient** *m* coupling factor, coupling coefficient **-kondensator** *m* coupling condenser

Kopplungs-matrix *f* dynamic or coupling matrix **-messer** *m* capacity-unbalance meter **-parameter** *m* coupling constant **-regler** *m* coupling control **-richtwert** *m* coupling factor **-röhre** *f* coupling tube

Kopplungsschleife *f* search coil, exploring coil **zentrale** ~ center-coupled loop

Kopplungs-sonde *f* coupling probe **-schwingungen** *pl* oscillations in coupled circuits

Kopplungsspule *f* coupling coil, coupler **veränderliche** ~ variocoupler

Kopplungs-transformator *m* repeating transformer, coupling transformer, jigger (elec.) **-übertrager** *m* coupling transformer **-wechsler** *m* poling switch, coupling changer **-welle** *f* partial wave **-widerstand** *m* coupling resistance, transfer impedance, interaction impedance **-ziffer** *f* coupling factor, coupling coefficient

Kopraöl *n* coco nut oil

Kopsbasis *f* cop base

Koralle *f* coral, code for a type of radar equipment

Korallen-riff *n* coral reef **-tier** *n* coral

Korallin *n* coralline

Korb *m* basket, hamper, (drawing) cage, drop bottom bucket **-boden** *m* bottom of the basket **-bodenspule** *f* basket(-type) coil, spider-web or basket-weave coil **-bogen** *m* compound curve, catenary **-deckelspule** *f* basket-wound coil **-filter** *m* basket screen **-flasche** *f* demijohn, carboy **-flechterei** *f* basketry, osier-goods manufacture **-gerippe** *n* basket framework **-henkelbogen** *m* basket handle arch

Korb-knebel *m* basket toggle **-kreiselmischer** *m* rotor cage impeller mixer **-möbel** *pl* osier furniture **-raum** *m* interior of the basket **-ring** *m* basket ring, concentration ring **-rost** *m* basket-shape grate **-schlagbiegeversuch** *m* notched bar impact test **-sieb** *n* screen basket, carburetor intake screen **-spule** *f* basket coil, basket-weave coil **-weide** *f* (common) osier, wicker **-wicklung** *f* basket winding, low-capacitance winding **-zarge** *f* basket rim

Kordel *f* packthread, twine, string, groove **-apparat** *m* knurling tool **-griff** *m* milled knob handle, knurled knob **-knopf** *m* milled knob **-kopfschraube** *f* thumbscrew **-mutter** *f* milled nut, knurled nut

kordeln to mill, knurl

Kordeln *n* knurling

Kordel-rad *n* knurl **-rolle** *f* milled roller **-schraube** *f* milled-head screw, knurled screw, thumbscrew **-teilung** *f* knurl pitch

Kordelung *f* cord, knurl, knurling

Kordgewebe *n* cabled-cord fabrics

kordieren to knurl or mill (an edge)

Kordierung *f* knurling

Kordierwerkzeug *n* knurling tool

Kordit *n* cordite

Kordon *m* cordon

kordonnierte Seide twisted silk

Kordreifen *m* cord tire

Koreferent *m* associate principal

Kork *m* cork **-dichtung** *f* cork gasket **-druckfeder** *f* cork pressure spring **-einlegesohle** *f* cork sole

korken to cork

Korken-anpreßfeder *f* cork pressure spring **-sortierwerk** *n* cork sorting device **-zieher** *m* corkscrew, (slang) corkscrew spin (aviation), spiral (aviation) **-zieherförmig gewunden** corkscrew

Korkerfuß *m* corker base

Kork-fallrinne *f* cork chute **-klotz** *m* cork pad **-platte** *f* cork slab **-rohrbekleidung** *f* cork molds **-rührwerk** *n* cork stirrer **-säure** *f* suberic acid **-stein** *m* cork brick **-stopfen** *m* cork stopper **-zieher** *m* corkscrew **-ziehergesetz** *n* corkscrew rule **-zuführungskanal** cork chute

Korn *n* front sight, bead (sight), grain, corn, gun sight, granule, crystal, (assaying) button ~ **und Kimme** pointer sights ~ **eines Negativs** grain ~ **einer photographischen Schicht** grain of a photographic layer ~ **bilden** to grain **feines** ~ fine grain **geklemmtes** ~ incorrectly centered front sight **gestrichenes** ~ medium sight **grobes** ~ coarse grain **verwachsenes** ~ included grain

Korn-abstufung *f* granulometric gradation **-analyse** *f* mechanical analysis **-anhäufung** *f* grain aggregation **-anteil** *m* grainsize distribution, grain-size fraction **-art** *f* type of grain **-begrenzung** *f* grain boundary **-bereich** *m* range of sizes **-beschaffenheit** *f* character of grain **-bildung** *f* graining, grain formation, crystallization, granulation **-blei** *n* grain or assay lead

Körnchen *n* grain, granule **-punze** *f* freezing tool

Korn-dichte *f* closeness of grain, grain density **-durchmesser** *m* grain diameter **-eisen** *n* iron of granular fracture

körneln to granulate

Kornen *n* pitting (of metals), granulation

körnen to granulate, grind, corn, to center punch

Körner *m* gauge point, punch mark, center mark, point, center punch, granulated metal, prick, punch

Körner *pl* grain, shot, granules **verschränkte ~** twisted grains

Körner-form *f* granular form **-fritter** *n* granular coherer **-lochsenker** *m* countersink for center punch holes **-marke** *f* center mark **-markierung** *f* punch marks **-mikrophon** *n* granular transmitter **-präparat** *n* grains **-rauschen** *n* carbon-granule noise (microphone)

Körnerschlag *m* center punch mark **durch ~ gekennzeichnet** punch-marked

Körnerspitze *f* dead center **~ fest** plain dead center **~ mitlaufend** live center

Körner-spitzkegel *m* taper of center **-zählapparat** *m* kernel counting apparatus

Korn-feinheit *f* fineness of grain **-fuß** *m* front-sight base **-gefüge** *n*, **-gestalt** *f* grain structure **-grenze** *f* crystal boundary, grain boundary

Korngrenz(en)-diffusion *f* grain-boundary diffusion **-energie** *f* energy of grain boundary **-fließen** *n* grain boundary flow

Korngrenzenkorrosion *f* intergranular corrosion **~ und Versprödung nach dem Schweißen** weld decay

Korngrenz(en)leitfähigkeit *f* grain boundary conductivity **-riß** *m* intergranular cracking **-wanderung** *f* grain boundary migration **-zerfall** *m* grain boundary breakdown

Korn-grenzlinie *f* grain boundary, grain junction line **-größe** *f* grain size

Korngrößenbestimmung *f* granulometric analysis **-einteilung** *f* grain-size distribution or classification **-kontrolle** *f* grain size control **-trennung** *f* sizing, screening or grading of grain **-überwachung** *f* grain-size control **-verteilung** *f* particle-size distribution

Kornhalter *m* front-sight holder

körnig grained, granular, pebbly, gritty, globular **-er Bruch** crystalline fracture (iron) **-es Eisen** crystalline iron **-e Feststoffe** granular solids **-er Korund** emery **-er Schnee** granular snow **-er Zementit** spheroidized or nodulous cementite

Körnigkeit *f* graininess, granularity, granulation **~ des Films** grain of the film

Körnigkeitsmesser *m* granulometer

Korn-klassierung *f* screening, screen sizing **-öffnung** *f* bead aperture **-orientiert** grain-oriented (laminations) **-papier** *n* grained transfer paper **-puddeln** *n* puddling of fine-grained iron **-pulver** *n* granulated powder

Korn-raster *m* granulated screen **-rauschen** *n* film-grain noise **-reich** very granular **-rost** *m* granular oxidation **-(rüssel)käfer** *m* grain weevil (Rhynchophora) **-sand** *m* graining sand **-schwinge** *f* corn cleaner **-struktur** *f* grain structure, granulated structure

Körnung *f* range of gain sizes, granulation, coarseness, grain

Körnungs-beschaffenheit *f* nature of grain **-verfahren** *n* granulation process

Korn-untergrund *m* background grains **-verfall** *m* disintegration of grains **-verfeinerung** *f* crystalline refinement, grain refinement **-vergröberung** *f* coarsening of grain **-verteilung** *f* grain-size distribution, granulometry **-verteilungsbestimmung** *f* mechanical analysis **-verteilungskurve** *f* grain-size distribution curve **-verzerrung** *f* distortion of grain, grain deformation

Korn-waage *f* button or bullion scale **-wachstum** *n* grain growth, crystalline growth, growth of crystal **-warze** *f* front-sight stud **-zerfall** *m* grain disintegration, intergranular corrosion **-zinn** *n* grain tin, granular tin **-zucker** *f* granulated sugar **-zusammensetzung** *f* graduation or gradation of grain sizes

Korona *f* corona, corona discharge, brush discharge **~ der Zündung** pre-onset corona (streamer)

Koronadurchbruch *m* pulse corona

Koronadurchschlag *m*, **einmaliger ~** burst-pulse corona

Korona-erscheinung, -effekt *m* corona, corona effect **-entladung** *f* corona discharge **-verlust** *m* corona loss

Koronagraph *m* coronagraph

Körper *m* body, trunk, solid, substance, region of convergence, member, hull, field (math), (opt.) housing **~ von Gußstahl** cast-steel body

Körper zur Mantelkurve hub for cam piece **~ der Maschine** frame of machine **~ von Schießbaumwolle** slab of guncotton **~ der Spule** former of coil **abgeleiteter ~** derivate (chem.) **fester ~** solid body **geschütteter ~** rubble mound **feste ~** solids **hin- und hergehender ~** shuttle **optisch inaktiver ~** racemate, racemized material, racemic substance **sanker ~** body heavier than water

Körper-achse *f* body axis **-behindert** impeded **-beschaffenheit** *f* physique, constitution

Körperchen *n* corpuscle, particle

Körperfarbe *f* pigment (as distinguished from dyes) any dye forming solid particles on the fabric

körperfest fixed with respect to a body **-es System** body system

Körper-gehalt (Lack) *m* body of the lacquer **-höhlenapplikator** *m* intracavitary applicator **-länge** *f* beam of a flying boat **-lehre** *f* stereometry **-leitung** *f* earth wire

körperlich physical, bodily, solid, three-dimensional, corporeal, material, molar **-e Beobachtung** stereoscopic observation **-e Bestandsaufnahme** physical inventory **-er Gegenstand** solid object (body) **-es Sehen** stereoscopic vision **-e Untersuchung** physical examination

Körperlichkeit *f* substantiality, solidity, plasticity

Körperlichsehen *n* stereoscopic or tridimensional vision

Körper-maß *n* cubic measure, cubic measurement **-pflege** *f* personal hygiene, care of the body **-schaft** *f* body corporate, corporation **-schall** *m* sound conducted through solids

Körperschluß *m* body contact **-kabel** *n* short-circuit or earthing wire, ground cable **-klemme** *f* short-circuit or earthing terminal, ground terminal **-kohle** *f* ground carbon

Körper-schutzmittel *n* protective clothing **-stöße** *pl* body collisions

Körperverletzung *f* bodily injury **schwere ~** grave bodily injury

Körperwiderstand *m* hull or body resistance

Korpus *f* long primer (print.)

Korpuskel *n* corpuscle

Korpuskularstrahlung *f* corpuscular radiation, particle radiation

Korrektion *f* correction, rectification

Korrektions-bürste *f* correcting brush **-daumen** *m* correcting cam **-einrichtung** *f* correcting device, correction device **-faktor** *m* correction factor **-filter** *n* equalizer **-glied** *n* correction factor, corrective term

Korrektionsgrad bei automatischer Frequenzregelung AFC correction ratio

Korrektions-linse *f* correcting lens **-mangel** *m* deficiency in correction **-mittel** *n* corrective agent **-rad** *n* correcting wheel, correction wheel, corrector wheel **-schaltung** *f* corrective circuit **-schraube** *f* adjusting screw **-signal** *n* error signal **-spule** *f* correcting coil **-zeit** *f* setting time

Korrektor *m* proofreader, corrector, reviser, compensator

Korrektoreneinstellung *f* corrector adjustment **-zeichen** *n* reader's mark

Korrektur *f* correction, alternation, adjustment **erste ~** first proof **letzte ~** press proof **~ für thermische Bewegung** thermal motion correction

Korrektur-abziehbürste *f* beating brush **-abziehpresse** *f* proof-press **-abzug** *m* proof sheet or print, revised proof **-befehl** *m* patch (comput.) **-bogen** *m* first proof, proof sheet **-düse** *f* compensating jet

Korrekturen *pl* amendments

Korrektur-fahne *f* slip proof **-faktor** *m* corrective factor **-glied** *n* correction term **-impuls** *m* correcting impulse **-kommando** *n* correction signal (guided missiles) **-lesen** *n* proof-reading **-luftdüse** *f* air adjustment (jet) **-potentiometer** *n* correction potentiometer **-scheibe** *f* compensating cam **-signal** *n* error signal **-spannung** *f* correcting voltage **-taste** *f* back spacing control (tape rec.) **-verschiebung** *f* correcting displacement **-zeichen** *n* reader's mark **-zeit** *f* setting time

Korrelat *n* correlative

Korrelations-koeffizient *m* correlation factor **-matrix** correlation matrix

Korrespondent *m* correspondent

Korrespondenz *f* correlation, interdependence, correspondence **-büro** *n* press agency **-prinzip** *n* correspondence principle

korrigieren to correct

korrigierende Leertaste *f* correcting space bar

korrigiert-es Dezibel dba **-e Peilung** corrected bearing

Korrigierwinkelhaken *m* composing stick

korrodierbar corrodible, corrosive

Korrodierbarkeit *f* corrodibility

korrodieren to corrode

korrodierend corrosive

Korrosion *f* corrosion, rusting, action of rust, etching **ebenmäßige ~** general corrosion **gegen ~ schützen** to passivate **interkristalline ~** intercrystalline or intergranular corrosion, caustic embrittlement **örtliche ~** localized or selective corrosion **Dauerschwingversuch unter ~** fatigue test under corrosion

Korrosionsangriff *m* attack by corrosion **~ bei der Laufbuchse** etching of the barrel

Korrosionsbehandlung *f* rust-proofing or corrosion-proofing treatment

korrosionsbeständig corrosion-resistant or -proof, noncorrosible, rust-resisting, stainless **-er Mantel** corrosion proof surface

Korrosions-beständigkeit *f* corrosion-resisting quality, resistance to corrosion, rustproof, stainless, or rustresisting property **-bildner** *m* corroding agent, corrosive, rusting agent **-bildung** *f* formation of rust **-dauerbruch** *m* corrosion fatigue fracture **-dauerfestigkeit** *f* corrosion-fatigue strength **-einfluß** *m* corrosive effect **-element** *n* corrosion cell

Korrosions-empfindlich corrodible, sensitive to corrosion **-empfindlichkeit** *f* corrodibility, sensitiveness to corrosion **-ermüdung** *f* corrosion fatigue **-ermüdungsfestigkeit** *f* corrosion fatigue strength **-erscheinung** *f* corrosion phenomenon

korrosionsfest corrosion-resisting, rustproof, stainless **~ machen** to passivate **-e Leichtmetall-Legierung** corrosion-resistant lightmetal alloy

Korrosionsfestigkeit *f* corrosion resistance

korrosionsfördernd corroding **-es Medium** corrosive environment **-es Mittel** corroding agent or medium **-e Umstände** factors stimulating corrosion

korrosions-frei stainless, rustless, noncorroding, noncorrosive **-geschützt** protected against corrosion **-geschwindigkeit** *f* rate of corrosion **-grenze** *f* corrosion allowance **-härtemessung** *f* measurement of hardness by corrosion **-hemmende Faktoren** factors inhibiting corrosion **-hindernd** corrosion-preventing, rust-preventing **-mittel** *n* corrosive agent **-narbe** *f* corrosion pit **-neigung** *f* tendency to(ward) corrosion, tendency to rust, susceptibility to corrosion **-prüfung** *f* corrosion test

Korrosionsschutz *m* rust protection, protection against corrosion **-fett** *n* rust-proofing grease **-mittel** *n* corrosion preventative or inhibitor **-öl** *n* corrosion preventing oil **-papier** *n* anti-corrosive paper

korrosions-sicher noncorrodible, resistant to corrosion, rustproof, stainless **-sicherheit** *f* rust protection **-verhalten** *n* corrosion resistance **-verhinderung** *f* corrosion inhibition **-verlauf** *m* rate of corrosion **-versuch** *m* corrosion test **-vorgang** *m* corrosive action **-widerstand** *m* corrosion resistance, stain resistance **-wirkung** *f* corrosive effect, corrosiveness

Korrosionszeit-schwingfestigkeit *f* fatigue strength under corrosion for finite life **-standversuch** *m* corrosion creep test depending on time

Korsettenstab (Hochofen) *m* stave

Kortexstimulator *m*, **elektronischer ~** cortical stimulator

Körtingsche Streudüse Körting's spray nozzle
Korund *m* corundum **künstlicher ~** aloxite
Korund-belag *m* corundum coating **-einlage** *f* corundum inlay
Kosekante *f* cosecant
Kosekanz²-Bündel *n* cosecant-squared beam
Kosinus *m* cosine **-glied** *n* cosine term **-satz** *m* cosine law or equation
kosmische Ultrastrahlen cosmic rays **-e Häufigkeit** cosmic abundance **-er Schauer** cosmic ray shower
Kosmologie *f* cosmology
Kosmogonie *f* cosmogony
Kosmonautik *f* cosmonautics
Kosmotron *n* cosmotron
kosten to cost; taste
Kosten *pl* cost, expenses, charges **laufende ~** current expenses (not running expenses) **untragbare ~** prohibitive cost
Kosten-abweichung *f* variance analysis **-anschlag** *m* estimate, tender **-aufschlüsselung** *f* cost analysis or break down **-aufstellung** *f* cost sheet **-aufwand** *m* expenditure
Kostenberechnung *f* calculation of cost **gesonderte ~** extra charge
Kosten-ersparnis *f* savings of costs **-frei, -los** free-of-charge **-ordnung** *f* tariff **-pflichtig abweisen** to dismiss (legal action) with costs **-preis** *m* cost price **-rechnung** *f* bill, calculation, estimate **-stelle** *f* accounting department **-übersicht** *f* statement of expense **-voranschlag** *m* estimate of costs
Kotangente *f* cotangent
Kotangentenverfahren *n* cotangent method
Köte *f* fetlock, cote
Kote *f* height notation (on maps)
Kotentafel *n* table of heights
Kot-fänger *m* fender **-flügel** *m* mudguard, (auto) fender **-flügelstrebe** *f* mudguard stay **-kratze** *f* door scraper **-schutz** *m* fender, mudguard
Kötzer *m* pirn
kovalent covalent **-e Bindung** homopolar bond **-e Verbindung** covalent compound
Kovalenz *f* covalence
Kovar *n* kovar
kovariant konstant covariant constant
Kovariante *f* covariant
kovariante Ableitung covariant derivative
Kovarianz einer Wahrscheinlichkeitsverteilung covariance of a probability distribution
Kovolumen, Kovolum *n* covolume
Krabbe *f* crab
krabbenartiges Fliegen crabbing (aviation)
Krach *m* crash, noise
krachen to crack, crash, crackle, rustle
Krach-sperre *f* squelch control **-töter** *m* silent tuning, noise suppressor, noise gate
Krack-benzin *n* cracked gasoline **-gas** *n* cracked gas
kracken to crack
Kracken *n*, **Kracking** *n* cracking
Krackindustrie *f* petroleum-cracking industry
Krack-prozeß *m* (Gas) cracking process **-verfahren** *n* cracking process
Krad (Kraftrad) *n* motorcycle **-fahrer** *m* motorcyclist
Kraft *f* power, strength, force, energy, effort, work, stress, load **~ der Expansionswelle** blast loading **~ am Schaltkolben** power of operating piston **eine ~ aufbringen** to apply a force **abstoppende ~** force of repulsion **angreifende ~** acting force **atombindende ~** atomic combining power, valence **auflösende ~** resolving power **außer ~ setzen** to cease to have effect **bewegende ~** moying force **elektromotorische ~** electromotive force **gegenelektromotorische ~** back or counter electromotive force, opposing electromotive force
Kraft, nicht zentrale ~ tensor force **lebendige ~** momentum, kinetic energy **magnetische ~** magnetic force **magnetisierende ~** magnetizing force **magnetomotorische ~** magnetomotive force **photoelektromotorische ~** photoelectromotive force **resultierende ~** resultant force **rücktreibende ~** repelling force, deflecting force **schwingungserzeugende ~** vibromotive force **wieder in ~ setzen** to revive **in ~ treten** to come into force **zwischenmolekulare ~** intermolecular force
Kraftabgabe *f* power delivery (output)
Kraftabgabeseite *f* output end **~ des Motors** power end of the engine
Kraftabgabewelle *f* output shaft **-anforderung** *f* power demand **-angetrieben** power-driven **-angriff** *m* application of power, application of stress, intensity of force **-anlage** *f* power plant, power system **-anschluß** *m* power-supply connection **-anstrengung** *f* exertion **-anteil** *m* force component **-antrieb** *m* power-drive **-arm** *m* power arm **-aufwand** *m* energy consumption **-audion** *n* power grid detector, power grid-current detector
Kraft-ausbeute *f* power output, energy **-äußerung** *f* stress, strain, manifestation or effect of force **-balken** *m* corbel tree **-beanspruchung** *f* necessary power **-bedarf** *m* power required, power requirements, power consumption, input, power demand **-behälter** *m* fuel tank **-bemessung** *f* power rating
kraftbetätigt power-operated **-es Preßluftspannfutter** *n* power-operated air chuck
Kraft-betrieb *m* power installation **-betrieben** power-actuated, power-driven **-gleichung** *f* force equation **-dehnungskurve** *f* stress-strain curve **-dehnungsmesser** *m* stress-strain tester **-detektor** *m* power detector, high-amplitude detector **-dichte** *f* force density **-drehungsverhalten** *n* stress-strain curve
Kräfte *pl* forces, power, strength **~ die in einem Punkt angreifen** concurrent forces **Zusammensetzung der ~** force polygon
Kräfte-ausgleich *m* force equilibrium **-austausch** *m* interchange of power
Kraftebene *f* plane of forces
Kräfte-berechnung *f* force calculation **-bestimmung** *f* stress analysis
Krafteck *n* force diagram, force polygon
Kräfte-dreieck *n* triangle of forces **-einsatz** *m* commitment of forces **-ersparnis** *f* economy of manpower, sparing of personnel **-funktion** *f* force function **-gleichgewicht** *n* equilibrium of forces **-gruppe** *f* system of forces
Krafteinheit *f* unit of power, unit of force
Krafteinschätzung *f* power rating
Kräfte-komponente *f* force component **-komposition** *f* composition of forces **-maßstab** *m* scale

of forces

Kraftendstufe *f* power-output stage

Kräftepaar *n* couple, two equal, opposite parallel, or noncolinear forces, force couple **-dichte** *f* assigned couple

Kräfte-parallelogramm *n* parallelogram of forces **-plan** *m* Cremona diagram, stress diagram **-polygon** *n* force polygon

Krafterhaltung *f* conservation of energy or force

Kräfte-schema *n* scheme of forces, diagram of forces **-spiel** *n* play or effect of forces **-verlauf** *m* force distribution, course or curve of forces **-verschiebung** *f* shifting of forces **-verteilung** *f* distribution of forces **-vieleck** *n* force polygon

Kräfte-zerlegung *f* resolution of forces **-zersplitterung** *f* splitting, division, or dissipation of forces **-zug** *m* stress diagram **-zusammensetzung** *f* composition of forces

Kraft-fahrer *m* driver, truck driver, motorist, chauffeur

Kraftfahr-industrie *f* automotive industry **-gerät** *n* motor-transport equipment **-park** *m* motor park **-personal** *n* motor-transport personnel **-rad** *n* motorcycle **-schau** *f* automobile show or exhibition **-unfall** *m* automobile or motor-vehicle accident **-wesen** *n* motor-transport service

Kraftfahrzeug *n* motor vehicle, automobile, power craft **-aufbau** *m* automobile body **-führer** *m* motor-vehicle driver **-schein** *m* vehicle-registration certificate **-vorschrift** *f* motor-vehicle regulations

Kraft-faktor *m* force factor **-feld** *n* field (of forces) **-felder zwischen den Ionen** interionic force fields **-fleisch** *n* corned beef **-flug** *m* power flight **-flugmodell** *n* motor airplane model

Kraftfluß *m* magnetic flux, flux of force **-dichte** *f* flux density **-höhe** *f* flux level **-wechsel** *m* (magnetic) flux reversal

Kraft-formmaschine *f* power-operated molding machine **-funktion** *f* power function **-gas** *n* power gas, fuel gas **-gaserzeuger** *m* gas producer **-gebend** energizing **-gesteuert** power controlled **gewinde** *n* heavy-duty thread **-gleichung** *f* force equation **-glied** *n* pilot, relay **-hammer** *m* power hammer **-haus** *n* powerhouse **-heber** *m* power lift **-heberblock** (Hydraulik) *m* hydraulic lift unit **-hub** *m* power stroke

kräftig rigid, firm, strong, powerful, sturdy, forcible, intensive, vigorous **-e Färbung** full shade

kräftigen to reinforce

Kraft-kabel *n* power-transmission cable **-kalander** *m* power-operated calender **-karren** *m* motor truck or lorry **-kolben** *m* servo piston **-komponente** *f* force component **-konstante** *f* force constant **-lehre** *f* dynamics **-leistung** *f* power efficiency **-leitung** *f* power main, power line or circuit

Kraftlinie *f* line of force, line of action, force vector, tube of force **elektrische ~** electric line of force **magnetische ~** magnetic line of force, line of magnetic force **totale ~** line of total force

Kraftlinien schneiden to cut or intersect lines of force

Kraftlinien-ablenkung *f* deflection of lines of force **-bild** *n* magnetic figure **-dichte** *f* density of lines of force, flux density **-feld** *n* field of force, field of lines of force **-fluß** *m* magnetic flux **-länge** *f* length of lines of force **-richtung** *f* direction of lines of force **-schräglage** *f* slope of force lines **-übergang** *m* passage of lines of force **-verlauf** *m* path of lines of force **-verteilung** *f* distribution of force

Kraftlinienweg *m* path of lines of force **magnetischer ~** magnetic flux path **mittlerer ~** mean path of lines of force

Kraftlinienzahl *f* number of lines of force **gesamte ~** total flux

kraftlos powerless, weak

Kraftloserklärung *f* declaration of invalidity or cancellation

Kraft-magnet *m* driving or power magnet **-maschine** *f* prime mover, motor, (power) engine **-maß** *n* unit of force **-meßdose** *f* pressure gauge, (electric) load cell

Kraftmesser *m* dynamometer **~ in der Luftschraubennabe** hub dynamometer

Kraft-meßgerät *n* dynamometer **-messung** *f* measurement of power **-mischung** *f* power mixture **-moment** *n* moment of force **-netz** *n* power mains **-niet** *n* rivet transmitting a force **-omnibus** *m* motor bus **-packpapier** *n* kraft wrapping paper **-papier** *n* sulfate paper **-plan** *m* force diagram **-probe** *f* strength test **-prüfer** *m* stress tester **-quelle** *f* source of power, source of energy, generating unit, power supply **-quellenwagen** *m* horse-drwan generator unit

Kraftrad *n* motorcycle **-fahrer** *m* motorcyclist **-gleichstromanlage** *f* motorcycle D.C. system **-schlauch** *m* motorcycle inner tube

Kraft-radius *m* force radius **-reserve** *f* power reserve, reserve power **-resultierende** *f* resultant force **-richtung** *f* direction of a force

Kraftröhre *f* power valve, power tube, tube of force **magnetische ~** magnetic tube of force, tube of magnetic force

Kraft-rückleitung *f* return force system **-säge** *f* power saw **-sammler** *m* accumulator **-saugrohr** *n* power Venturi tube **-schalter** *m* pilot (the device regulating the servomotor), actuator **-schalttafel** *f* power (switch)board, power panel **-schlepper** *m* tractor **-schluß** *m* closed linkage, frictional connection

kraftschlüssig tensionally, connected, force-locking **~ verbunden** frictionally connected **-e Sicherung** pressure locking (of bolt) **-e Verbindung herstellen** to couple

Kraft-schrauber *m* nut-runner **-schwingröhre** *f* power oscillator **-sinn** *m* direction of the force **-skalenbogen** *m* (testing-machine) sector **-spanneinrichtung** *f* chucking equipment **-spannfutter** *n* heavy-duty chuck **-speicher** *m* terminal box (antiaircraft mount), accumulator **-speichereinrückvorrichtung** *f* vacuum with pressure spring **-spiritus** *m* motor spirit

Kraft-sprit *m* alcohol for engine operation **-spritze** *f* fire engine **-spülpumpe** *f* power slush pump **-station** *f* power station, powerhouse **-steckdose** *f* power-connection plug **-stecker** *m* power socket **-steuerung** *f* boost control **-sitz** *m* forced fit

Kraftstoff *m* fuel, propellant **~ aus aromatischen**

Bestandteilen aromatic fuel ~ **mit übermäßig hohem Bleigehalt** overdoped fuel ~ **ohne Blei- oder andere Zusätze** undoped fuel **gebleiter** ~ leaded fuel

Kraftstoff-ablagerung *f* fuel sediment **-ablaßleitung** *f* fuel delivery pipe, fuel discharge pipe **-abschneider** *m* fuel trap **-absperrschieber** *m* fuel cutoff valve **-abstellhahn** *m* fuel shut off valve **-anhäufer** *m* fuel accumulator **-anlage** *f* fuel system **-arm** lean **-ausbreitung** deposition of the fuel **-ausgabestelle** *f* gasoline distributing point **-ausnutzung** *f* fuel economy

Kraftstoffbehälter *m* fuel tank or drum ~ **nachfüllen** to refuel **selbstabdichtender** ~ leak-retardant fuel tank

Kraftstoff-behälterdeckel *m* fuel-tank cover **-brücke** *f* fueling bridge **-dichtung** *f* fuel-tank washer **-druck** *m* fuel pressure **-druckmesser** *m* fuel-pressure gauge **-druckrohr** *n* fuel feed pump

Kraftstoffdurchflußmenge *f*, **spezifische** ~ fuel flowrate

Kraftstoff-durchflußmesser *m* fuel-flow meter **-durchsatz** *m* fuel flowrate **-düse** *f* fuel jet, fuel-metering nozzle or jet **-einfüllstutzen** *m* fuel filler neck **-einspritzdüse** *f* fuel-injection nozzle **-einspritzleitung** *f* fuel injection pipe **-einspritzpumpe** *f* fuel injection pump

Kraftstoff-einspritzung *f* fuel injection **-einspritzvorrichtung** *f* fuel injector **-einstellschraube** *f* fuel adjusting screw **-einstellung** *f* fuel adjustment **-empfindlichkeit eines Motors** fuel sensitivity of an engine **-entlüfter** air-vapor eliminator or separator, fuel deaerator **-ersparnis** *f* fuel economy

Kraftstoff-filter *m* fuel strainer or filter **-filtereinsatz** *m* fuel filter element **-filtergehäuse** *n* fuel filter case **-förderpumpe** *f* fuel pump **-förderung** *f* fuel feed **-gemisch** *n* fuel mixture (blend) **-Gewicht-Verhältnis** *n* fuel-weight or fuel-structure ratio **-handpumpe** *f* manually operated fuel pump **-kesselkraftwagen** *m* fuel truck **-lager** *n* fuel dump **-leitung** *f* fuel line, fuel manifold, fuel pipe **-Luft-Gemisch** *n* fuel-air mixture

Kraftstoff-Luft-Verhältnis *n* fuel-air ratio **Meßgerät zur Bestimmung des Kraftstoff-Luft-Verhältnisses** fuel-air-ratio indicator

Kraftstoff-manometer *n* fuel pressure gauge **-messer** *m* fuel (gasoline) gauge **-meßuhr** *f* fuel meter **-nachschub** *m* bringing up of fuel **-nadelventil** *n* carburetor needle valve **-normverbrauch** *m* normal fuel consumption **-pedal** *n* accelerator **-peilvorrichtung** *f* fuel level gauge **-pumpe** *f* fuel pump **-pumpen-dichtung** *f* fuel pump gasket **-regulierung** *f* fuel control **-reiniger** *m* fuel strainer or filter **-ringbehälter** *m* annular fuel tank **-rücklaufbehälter** *m* fuel-reclaiming tank **-rücklaufleitung** *f* fuel return pipe **-rückstand** *m* fuel residue

Kraftstoff-sammelbehälter *m* fuel-controller box **-schnellablaß** *m* fuel dumping **-schnellentleerung** *f* fuel jettisoning, fuel dumping **-schwimmerhalter** *m* fuel float switch **-sparregler** *m* fuel economizing regulator **-spielabtaster** *m* fuel level sensor **-staffel** *f* gasoline supply section **-überladungspumpe** *f* fuel boost pump (jet) **-umlauf** *m* fuel circulation

Kraftstoff-verbrauch *m* fuel consumption **-verbrauchsmesser** *m* fuel-consumption gauge or meter, fuel-pressure gauge **-verbrauchsmessung** *f* fuel measuring **-verbrauchssatz** *m* rate of fuel consumption **-vorratsanzeiger** *m* fuel quantity indicator **-vorratsmesser** *m* fuel-quantity indicator or gauge **-vorreiniger** *m* fuel strainer **-zerstäubung** *f* fuel vaporization **-zuflußleitung** *f* fuel inlet pipe **-zufuhr** *f* fuel feed

Kraftstoffzuführungseinrichtung, die gesamte ~ fuel system

Kraftstoff-zug *m* fuel train **-zulaufleitung** *f* fuel feed pipe **-zumessung** *f* fuel measuring control **-zusatzmittel** *n* fuel additive

Kraft-strom *m* power current **-stromstecker** *m* power plug **-strömung** *f* flux (elec.) **-stufe** *f* power stage, final stage **-truppe** *f* motor-transport unit **-überlappung** *f* power overlap **-überschuß** *m* surplus or excess of power, reserve power **-übersetzung** *f* power ratio **-überträger** *m* transducer **-übertragung** *f* transmission (of power), power transmission, transfer of force

Kraftübertragungs-aggregate *pl* power train assemblies **-anlage** *f* power-transmission system **-leistung** *f* power-transmitting capacity **-messer** *m* transmission dynamometer **-organ** *n* power-transmission agent **-vermögen** *n* power-transmitting capacity

Kraftumlenker *m* power transmitter

kraft- und formschlüssige Verbindung zweier Teile positive coupling

Kraft- und Gewichtsverhältnis *n* strength-weight ratio

Kraft-vektor *m* force vector **-Venturirohr** *n* power Venturi tube **-verbindung** *f* positive coupling **-verbrauch** *m* absorption or dissipation of energy, power consumption, energy consumption **-vergleich** *m* force balance **-verkehr** *m* motor traffic **-verlust** *m* loss of power, power loss **-verlustquelle** *f* source of power waste **-verschwendung** *f* power waste **-versorgung** *f* power supply

Kraftverstärker *m* power amplifier, servomotor, slave unit **-kolben** *m* servo piston **-zylinder** *m* slave cylinder

Kraft-versteller *m* output governor **-verstellung** *f* power traverse **-voll** powerful **-vorschub** *m* power feed

Kraftwagen *m* automobile, motorcar, truck, motor vehicle ~ **mit Behälter** tank truck **gepanzerter** ~ armored car

Kraftwagen-fett *n* automotive grease **-führer** *m* driver **-geschütz** *n* gun mounted on a truck, truck-borne gun

Kraftwagenkolonne *f* motor-transport train ~ **für Kraftstoffe** motor-transport fuel train

Kraftwagen-steuer *f* car license fee **-steuer** *n* steering wheel **-transport** *m* motor transport **-werkstatt** *f* garage **-werkstattzug** *m* mobile repair shop

Kraft-wechsel *m* energy exchange **-werk** *n* power plant, (electric) power station, generating station, generating plant, power unit **-werkgruppe** *f* group of power stations **-winde** *f* power winch

Kraftwirkung *f* action of force **thermoelektrische** ~ thermoelectric effect

Kraft-zahnrad *n* heavy-duty gear **-zentrale** *f* power station **-zerlegung** *f* resolution of a force **-zufuhr** *f* power supply **-zug** *m* tractor **-zu-**

maschine *f* motor tractor **-zurichtung** *f* underlay
Kragarm *m* bracket, cantilever
Kragarmlast *f* load on cantilever ~ **am Stiel,** cantilever load acting at the post
Kragbalken *m* cantilever beam
Krage *f* bracket
Kragen *m* collet, collar **-bildung** *f* rimming action **-binde** *f* necktie **-dach** *n* cantilever roof **-drehzange** *f* collar tongues **-patte** *f* collar patch, tab **-spiegel** *m* collar insignia, collar patch, tab **-steckdose** *f* socket with shrouded contacts **-steckvorrichtung** *f* shrouded plug and socket **-versteifung** *f* (Rohrleitg.) ring girder
Krag-stein *m* stone corbel or console **-stück** *n* truss, corbel, console (arch.) **-stütze** *f* bracket support **-träger** *m* cantilever beam, bracket **-trägerbrücke** *f* cantilever-beam bridge
Krägungswinkel *m* angle of bank (aviation)
Kragziegel *m* corbel brick
Krähl-arbeit *f* raking operation, rabbling operation **-arm** *m* rabble arm
Krähle *f* rake, rabble
Krähl-hälter *m* rabble arm **-ofen** *m* rabble furnace, reverberatory calciner, reverberatory roaster **-rechen** *m* rabble rake
Krählung *f* rabbling
Krählwagen *m* rabble carriage
Krakbenzin *n*, **rohes** ~ pressure distillate
Krakverfahren *n* cracking process
Kralle *f* claw, talon
Krallen-feder *f* ball clip **-kabelschuh** *m* forked cable lug
Kramme *f* staple
Krammeisen *n* cramp iron, rake
Krampe *f* cramp iron, link, staple, clamp, clasp, clip ~ **mit Stiftspitze** (pointed) staple
Krämpelbank *f* carding bench
krämpen to flange, border
Krampstock *m* (slag) skimmer, skimmer bar
Kran *m* crane, traveling crane, derrick, cock, **-anlage** *f* crane apparatus, crane installation **-arm** *m* crane jib **-ausleger** *m* crane jib, crane boom or beam **-bahn** *f* crane runway **-bahnlänge** *f* length of crane runway **-balken** *m* jib (arm) of derrick **-bau** *m* crane construction
Kranbaum *m* derrick ~ **zum Aufrichten der Stangen** pole-setting derrick
Kran-bolzen *m* lifting bolt, sling pin **-bohrmaschine** *f* radial drilling machine **-brücke** *f* crane bridge **-bühne** *f* walkway **-fahrbahn** *f* runway of crane **-fahrwerk** *n* crane-travel gearing **-fahrwerksantrieb** *m* crane travel unit **-führer** *m* crane operator
krängen to heel, lean over, list, bank
Krangerüst *n* crane frame, framework of a crane, gantry
Krangießpfanne *f* crane ladle ~ **mit Getriebekippvorrichtung** geared crane ladle, crane ladle with handtipping gear ~ **mit Schneckenradkippvorrichtung** worm-geared crane ladle ~ **mit Wagen- und Handkippvorrichtung** plain crane truck ladle
Krangreifer *m* grab bucket
Krängung *f* listing, heeling, roll
Krängungs-fehler *m* heeling error **-magnet** *m* heeling magnet **-nullage** *f* zero heeling position **-pendel** *n* clinometer pendulum **-ruder** *n* antidive and rolling rudder
Kranich *m* crane, code for a type of guided missile
Kran-haken *m* crane hook **-hebediagramm** *m* hoisting diagram
Kraniometer *n* craniometer
Kran-karre *f* swivel hoist truck **-katze** *f* crane trolley **-kette** *f* crane chain
Kran-konstruktion *f* crane construction or design **-last** *f* crane load **-laufkatze** *f* crane traveling crab **-leinebagger** *m* dragline
Kranlaufwinde *f* hoist **fahrbare** ~ trolley hoist
Kran-magnet *m* crane magnet **-montage** *f* crane erection **-monteur** *m* crane fitter **-oberwagen** *m* upper carrying chassis of a crane **-pfanne** *f* crane ladle **-pfannengehänge** *n* crane-ladle bail **-plan** *m* layout of cranes **-prahm** *f* crane pontoon
Kran-säule *f* mast of derrick **-schaltkasten** *m* control panel **-schiene** *f* crane rail, holdfast for boat hooks **-schnabel** *m* cathead of crane **-schürfbagger** *m* dragline **-seil** *n* crane rope or cable **-stopfenpfanne** *f* bottomtap crane ladle **-stütze** *f* crane column (post) **-wagen** *m* crane truck **-winde** *f* crane
Kranz *m* (Rad) rim; (Scheiben ~) face; (Gesims) cornice; (Architektur) festoon, gathering ring (glass blowing), wreath, revolving gun-mount wreath ~ **aus Holz oder Eisen** crib, curb **balliger** ~ crown rim
Kranz-brenner *m* ring burner, annular-type burner, crown burner **-erscheinung** *f* halo
Kranzfläche *f* face of a rim **ballig gedrehte** ~ crown face rim
Kranz-gesims *n* cornice **-kopf** *m* rose bit, countersink **-leiste** *f* dripstone, corona, weather molding cornice **-modell** *n* rim pattern **-querschnitt** *m* section of rim **-reif** *m* cornice **-stoß** *m* rim joint **-stück** *n* flange **-wulst** *m* rim collar
Krapp *m* madder
Krappen *n* flattening tool (for window glass)
krapp-kraß marked **-lack** *m* madder lake
Krarup-ader *f* continuously loaded conductor, iron-whipped core, Krarup conductor **-bandumspinnung** *f* iron-tape winding **-drahtumspinnung** *f* iron-wire whipping
krarupieren to krarupize, load (a line) continuously
krarupisieren to load continuously, krarupize
Krarupisierung *f* Krarup loading, continuous loading (of cable), krarupization
Krarup-kabel *n* continuously loaded cable, Krarup cable **-leiter** *m* continuously loaded conductor **-leitung** *f* continuously loaded circuit **-umspinnung** *f* iron whipping, Krarup winding, continuous loading **-verfahren** *n* continuous-load method
Krater *m* crater **-aureolen** *pl* crater aureols **-bildung** *f* blotching, crater formation, pitting **-fläche** *f* crater area **-öffnung** *f* vent in the crater **-sichtscheibe** *f* crater-card
Kratte *f* crate, skeleton case
Kratzband *n* scraper flight conveyer, drag belt
Krätzblei *n* slag lead
Kratzbürste *f* wire or scratch brush
Kratze *f* rake, scraper, scraping iron, paddle, rabble, card (weaving) skimmer
Krätze *f* waste metal (dross, sprue, sweepings, scrapings, shavings, etc.)

Kratzeisen *n* scraper, scraping iron
kratzen to scrape, scratch, rake, rabble, score, rasp, grate
Kratzen *n* scratching, scraping, jar, scratch
kratzendes Geräusch scratchy noise
Kratzenzinke *f* rake tooth
Kratzer *m* scratch, (noise) jar, auger-nose shell, scraper, cleaner, skimmer, rabble
Krätzerbehälter *m* skimmer holder
Kratzer-blech *n* scraper plate **-kettenförderer** *m* scraper flight conveyer **-klassifikator** *m* drag classifier **-schaufel** *f* creeper blade **-scheibe** *f* scraper disk **-transporteur** *m* scraper flight conveyor
kratz-fest mar-proof, mar-reistant **-förderer** *m* scraper conveyor
Krätzfrischen *n* refining of waste
Kratzgeräusch *n* crackling, hissing, frying (noise), contact noise
krätzig fibrous
Kratzkettenförderer *m* scraper chain conveyor
Krätz-kupfer *n* copper obtained by melting waste copper **-löffel** *m* skimming ladle **-schlacke** *f* slag or dross of liquation **-schlich** *m* slick or slime of waste metal
Kratz-winde *f* chain conveyer **-wunde** *f* scratch (wound)
Kräuel *m* scraper
Kraurit *m* dufrenite
kraus curly
Kräuschung *f* crinkling
Kräusel-faser *f* wool-imitation staple fiber **-krankheit** *f* crinkle, curly top (disease), downy mildew **-lack** *m* wrinkle finish
kräuseln to ripple (of water), wrinkle or crystallize (of tung-oil films), curl, crisp, frill, crimp, mill (coins)
Kräuseln *n* curling, crisping, friezing; (Farbe) wrinkling
Kräusel-papier *n* crinkled paper **-stoff** *m* ripple cloth
Kräuselung *f* ripple, rippling (of direct current) **~ des Gleichstromes** direct-current ripple **~ einer Münze** impression of the edge of a coin
Kräusel-wellen *pl* ripples
Krauskopf *m* rose bit, countersink, counterbore
Krautfänger *m* leaf catcher
Kraut- oder Buschschneidebalken *m* weed or brush bar
Krautschneidevorrichtung *f* weed attachment
Kreatinin *n* creatine
Krebs *m* lobster, cancer, the Crab (constellation), code for a type of guided missile **~ im Marmor** hard grain **~ im Ton** small stone, grain
Krebsfänger *m* casing spear
Krecke *f* cut, ditch
Kredit *m* credit **widerruflicher ~** unconfirmed credit
Kredit-brief *m* letter of credit **-fähig** trustworthy, sound, solvent **-fähigkeit** *f* trustworthiness, reliability
kreditieren to give on credit, to place to the credit
kreditwürdig reliable, sound, safe, deserving (of) credit
Kreide *f* chalk **geschlämmte ~** whitewash
kreide-artig chalky **-bereitung** *f* chalk dressing **-farbe** *f* drawing chalk **-haltig** chalky, cretaceous **-kornpapier** *n* grained enamel paper **-mergel** *m* chalk marl
Kreiden *n* chalking
Kreide-papier *n* chalk overlay paper **-system** *n* cretaceous system (geol.) **-verschnitt** *m* chalk reduction **-weiß** *n* whiting
kreidig chalky
Kreis *m* circle; (Schaltung) circuit, district, sphere **~ und Spirale** circle and helix **abgestimmter ~** tuned circuit **aperiodischer ~** aperiodic circuit **durchlässiger ~** acceptor circuit, acceptor **eingeschriebener ~** inscribed circle **elektrischer ~** electric circuit **geschlossener ~** closed circuit **Großer ~** great circle **magnetischer ~** magnetic circuit **nichtschwingungsfähiger ~** aperiodic or nonoscillatory circuit **widerstandloser ~** resistanceless circuit
Kreise in beliebiger Lage circles in any position **gekoppelte Kreise** coupled circuits
Kreis-ablesestelle *f* circle reading point **-abschnitt** *m* circle segment, circular segment **-abschnittbogen** *m* segmental arch **-abtastung** *f* circular scanning **-analysator** *m* circuit analyzer **-anzeiger** *m* circle marker **-ausheber** *m* borer with circular bit **-ausschnitt** *m* sector of circle **-bahn** *f* circular path, orbit **-bahnbewegung** *f* motion in a circle or orbit, orbital or circular movement **-belastungsfläche** *f* circular load area
Kreisbewegung *f* orbital motion, rotation, circular motion **schnelle ~** gyration
Kreis-blatt *n* circular chart **-blattschreiber** *m* disc chart recorder **-blende** *f* iris diaphragm
Kreisbogen *m* arc of circle, arc, sector, circular arc (or curve) **-absteckung** *f* measuring an arc with dividers **-förmig** circular **-gitter** *n* arcuate grid **-minute** *f* minute of arc **-profil** *n* profile whose mean line is an arc of circle **-schnitt** *m* circular arc section (of drawing)
Kreis-bohrer *m* circle cutter **-buchse** *f* circle bearing
kreischen to shriek **einen schrillen, kreischenden Ton erzeugen** to shriek
Kreischen des Zinns crackling sound of tin
Kreis-diagramm *n* circle diagram, circular loci **-drehung** *f* rotation **-durchmesser** *m* diameter **-ebene** *f* rotation plane, elevation view of antenna field pattern **-einteilung** *f* circular scale, graduated circle **-einwelligkeit** *f* cycle
Kreisel *m* gyroscope, gyrostabilizer, gyrostat, top **-abfeuergerät** *n* gyro stabilizer **-achse** *f* gyroscope, gyro axis, axis of rotation **-auslauf** *m* gyro slowdown **-belastung** *f* gyroscopic torque **-bewegung** *f* movement of gyroscope **-brecher** *m* gyratory crusher, rotary breaker or crusher **-dynamik** *f* gyrodynamics
Kreiselektron *n* spinning electron
Kreisel-flansch *m* gyro mount **-frequenz** *f* gyrofrequency **-gebläse** *n* turboblower, centrifugal supercharger or blower, rotary blower, turbocompressor, rotary-blower-type supercharger **-gehäuse** *n* box or housing of the gyro(scope) **-geradlaufgerät für Torpedos** torpedo gyroscope **-gerät** *n* gyroscopic device **-gesteuert** gyrocontrolled **-gestützt** gyroscopic **-gradflugweiser** *m* gyroscopic flight direction indicator **-hori-**

zont *m* artificial or gyro horizon **-kappe** *f* gyro cap or cone

Kreiselkompaß *m* gyroscopic sextant, or gyrostatic compass, gyrocompass **-theorie** *f* gyrocompass theory **-wiederholer** *m* gyrocompass repeater

Kreisel-kompressor *m* centrifugal compressor **-kurvenzeiger** *m* gyroscopic turn indicator **-lader** *m* centrifugal supercharger **-laderrad** *n* centrifugal rotor **-lagengeber** *m* automatic pilot **-lüfter** *m* turboventilator

kreiselmagnetisch gyromagnetic

Kreisel-magnetkompaß *m* gyromagnetic compass **-maschine** *f* centrifugal machine **-mischer** *m* impeller mixer **-molekül** *n* top molecule, spinning molecule **-moment** *n* gyroscopic couple **-momentlinie** *f* curve of gyroscopic moment **-mutter** *f* master gyroscope

kreiseln to spin

Kreisel-neigungsmesser *m* gyroscope bank indicator, bank-and-turn indicator **-pendel** *n* gyroscope pendulum, spinning top **-pilot** *m* gyropilot

Kreiselpumpe *f* centrifugal pump, rotary pump, turbine pump **selbsttätig ansaugende ~** self-priming centrifugal pump

Kreisel-rad *n* turbine, impeller, gas-turbine rotor flywheel (inertial system) **-radius** *m* radius of gyration **-rührer** *m* impeller mixer **-scheibe** *f* gyroscope disk **-schwingung** *f* gyroscopic oscillation **-sextant** *m* gyroscopic sextant **-stabilisator** *m* gyro(scopic) stabilizer **-stabilität** *f* gyroscopic stability **-steueranzeiger** *m* gyrostatic turn indicator **-steuerung** *f* gyroscope control **-theorie** *f* gyroscopic theory **-tochter** *f* repeater compass **-überwachungsschalter** *m* selector switch, gyrocompass autopilot

Kreiselung *f* gyratory cycle motion

Kreisel-verdichter *m* turbocompressor, rotary compressor, centrifugal compressor **-verfahren** *n* gyro system **-vorverdichter** *m* centrifugal supercharger, rotary blower, turbocompressor, rotary-blower-type supercharger **-wasserpumpe** *f* centrifugal water pump **-wechselwirkung** *f* gyro-interaction **-wendezeiger** *m* gyroscopic turn indicator **-widerstand** *m* gyroscopic resistance **-wipper** *m* rotary dump-type separator, revolving tippler **-wirkung** *f* gyrostatic effect, gyroscopic force of the propeller

kreisen to move in a circle, circle, circulate, rotate, revolve **~** (vom Raubvogel) to hover **schnell ~** to gyrate, eddy

kreisend circulating, rotatory, gyratory, eddying, rotational, vortical (i. e., of vortex motion) **-e Flotte** circulating liquor **-es Induktionssystem** rotary induction system **-e Luftströmung** high-speed rotary air motion

Kreisevolvente *f* circular involute

Kreis-falzsäge *f* circular grooving saw **-fläche** *f* circular surface, area of a circle, propeller-disk area **-flug** *m* circular flight **-fluß** *m* circular flux **-förderer** *m* circular conveyor **-form** *f* circularity

kreisförmig circular, round **~ gebogen** curved **-e Annäherung** circular approach **-er Faltdipol** circular antenna **-e Gleitung** rational slip **-er Grundriß** circular planform **-er Punkt** circular spot

Kreis-frequenz *f* angular velocity or frequency, frequency in radians, pulsation, cyclic frequency **-frequenzbereich** *m* angular-frequency range **-funkbake** *f*, **-funkfeuer** *n* non-directional radio beacon **-funktion** *f* circular, trigonometrical or angular function **-gang** *m* circular motion, rotation **-grad** *m* degree of a circle or arc, degree of angular measure, radian **-gruppenreusenantenne** *f* circularly arranged cage antenna **-güte** *f* factor of merit (quality)

Kreis-halbmesser *m* radius **-inhalt** *m* area of a circle **-kapazität** *f* circuit capacitance **-kegel** *m* circular cone **-keilschwärzungsmesser** *m* circular-wedge densitometer **-kimme** *f* ring sight **-klemme** *f* circle clamp **-kolbengebläse** *n* disk piston blower, radial cylinder supercharger or compressor **-kolbenmotor** *m* rotating combustion engine

Kreiskorn *n* circular front sight (antiaircraft sight for machine guns), cart wheel (a type of antiaircraft sight) ring-and-bead sight **-fuß** *m* circular-front-sight base **-halter** *m* circular-front-sight frame **-visierung** *f* sighting through circular front sight

kreislabil circularly unstable

Kreislagerung *f* packing of circles

Kreislauf *m* circuit, circulation (of fluid), cycle, cyclic course, closed cycle **direkter ~** direct cycle (power plant) **indirekter ~** indirect cycle (power plant) **~ nach Hertz** single-stage recycle **~ des Kohlenstoffs** organic carbon cycle

Kreislauf-behälter *m* circulating tank **-gas** *n* recycle gas (refinery) **-größe** *f* extent of circulation **-material** *n* return scrap, sprues and returns in foundry) **-schreiber** *m* indicator of circulations **-selbstanschlußsystem** *n* by-pass automatic-telephone system **-störung** *f* circulatory disturbance **-system** *n* by-pass system

Kreis-leitung *f* closed circuit **-linie** *f* circular line, circle **-lochblende** *f* circular aperture **-lochplatte** *f* circular disc with a hole **-lochscheibe** *f* perforated dis, Nipkow disk, film-scanning disk with apertures circularly rather than spirally arranged **-magnetischer Effekt** gyromagnetic anomaly **-messer** *n* circular knife **-messung** *f* cyclometry **-minute** *f* circle minute **-mittelpunkt** *m* center of circle

Kreis-modus *m* resonator mode **-molekül** *n* top molecule **-nut** *f* recess **-nutenfräser** *m* hollow saw **-parameter** *n* circular parameter **-peilung** *f* circle bearing (aviation) **-pendel** *m* circular pendulum **-plattenkondensator** *m* straight-line-capacity condenser **-polarimeter** *n* circle polarimeter

Kreisprozeß *m* cyclic process, continuous process, cycle **magnetischer ~** magnetic cycle **thermischer ~** thermal circle

Kreisprozeßtemperatur *f* cyclical process temperature

Kreis-punkt *m* spheric point **-quadrant** *m* quadrant **-querschnitt** *m* circular cross section **-raster** *m* circular screen **-rauschpegel** *m* circuit noise level **-reißer** *m* dividers

Kreisring *m* ring-shaped area, annular shape, circular ring **ebener ~** circular ring in the plane

Kreisring-apparat *m* ring-shearing apparatus **-stück** *n* circular ring sector, part of a circle ring

Kreisrinne *f* circular trough, annular cavity

kreisrund circular **-e Löcher** circular perforation **-er Querschnitt** circular cross section **-er Rumpf** fuselage of circular section

kreisrundgeschlossene Feldlinien circular lines of force

Kreissäge *f* circular (disk) saw **~ für Brotezucker** circular saw for sugar loaves

Kreissägeblatt mit Gruppenverzahnung (Holz) combination circular saw blade

Kreis-schablone *f* circular form, circular pattern **-scheibe** *f* circular disk **-schere** *f* circle-cutting machine **-schlitz** *m* annular slot **-schneidemaschine** *f* circular cutting guide **-schneidevorrichtung** *f* circular cutting device **-schnitt** *m* circular section **-sektor** *m* circular sector **-selbstinduktion** *f* circuit selfinduction **-skala** *f* circular scale

Kreis-spannung *f* circle voltage **-spule** *f* tuning coil **-stabil** stable at higher alpha values **-stellung** *f* (eines Theodolits), position of the azimuthal circle, circle graduation **-strom** *m* circular current **-strömung** *f* cyclic flow, circular currents, flowing in a circular path **-system** *n* system of spherical co-ordinates **-teilmaschine** *f* circular dividing machine

Kreisteilung *f* circular scale, divided or graduated circle **sexagesimale ~** sexagesimal circle graduation **zentesimale ~** centisimal circle graduation

Kreis-transporteur *m* carrousel, endless-platform or endless-roller carrousel, endless conveyer **-umfang** *m* circumference, periphery **-umlauf** *m* circulation, cycle **-verkehr** *m* radio-network communication **-verwandtschaften** *pl* homographies in the plane **-viereck** *n* blunt-cornered rectangle (square) **-visier** *n* ring sight **-vorgang** *m* cyclic process **-vorschub** *m* circular feed

Kreis-walze *f* circular cylinder **-welle** *f* circular (electric) wave **-wellenleiter** *m* circular waveguide **-wirkungsgrad** *m* circuit efficiency **-zeilendüse** *f* concentric row atomizer **-zweieck** *n* lune, crescent, angle of two great circles, circular line **-zylinder** *m* circular cylinder

kremfarben cream colored

Krempe des Kesselbodens flange of boiler end

Krempel *f* card **-bezieher** *m* card clothier

Krempelei *f* cardroom

krempeln to card, burr

Krempenübertragung *f* radius of curvature at flange

Kremserweiß *n* silver or kremnitz white

krenelieren to crenelate

Kreosot *n* creosote **mit ~ getränkte Stange** creosote(d) pole **mit ~ tränken** to creosote

Kreosot-öl *n* creosote oil **-tränkung** *f* creosoting

krepieren to detonate, explode, burst

Krepp *m* crepe

Kresol *n* cresol **-säure** *f* cresylic acid

Kresotinsäure *f* cresotic acid

Kresylsäure *f* cresylic acid, cresol

Krete *f* fire crest

Kreuz *n* cross, cross gallery (min.), crown, pile (print.), lease (weaving), sharp (music), intersection

Kreuz-antenne *f* cross-coil antenna **-arm** *m* crossbar **-balken** *m* crossbeam

Kreuzband *n* (newspaper) wrapper, double garnet **unter ~** by book post

Kreuzband-scheider *m* cross belt separator **-sendung** *f* parcel sent by book post

kreuzbeweglicher Tisch table moving crosswise and endwise

Kreuz-bodenbeutel *m* block bottom bag **-bohrer** *m* cross bit **-bund** *m* crossed-timber lashing **-dipol** *m* crossed antennas **-dose** *f* junction box **-drehrahmenantenne** *f* cross loop antenna **-drehscheibe** *f* two-way turntable **-eisen** *pl* cross bars

kreuzen to intersect, cross, cruise (navy), traverse, transpose or cross-connect (wires)

Kreuzen *n* crossing, cross-connecting, transposing, cruising

Kreuzer *m* cruiser (navy) **-verband** *m* cruiser squadron

Kreuz-fadenmikrometer crossbar micrometer **-faltdipol** *n* cross-type folded dipole **-federgelenk** *n* cross spring joint **-feld** *n* intersection **-feuer** *n* cross fire or bombardment **-finne** *f* cross peen **-flügler** *m* cross-winged guided missile

kreuzförmig cross-shaped, cruciform **-e Versteifung** X-brace

Kreuzgang (Lackierung) cross-coat

Kreuzgelenk *n* knuckle joint, universal joint, Hooke's joint **-kette** *f* transversely jointed chain **-kuppelung** *f* universal joint (coupling), cross link, universal coupling, flexible coupling, cross joint **-ring** *m* Cardan or gimbal ring

Kreuz-gewebereifen *m* fabric thread tire **-gewinde** *n* cross thread **-gewölbe** *n* groined vaulting **-gitter** *n* cross grating, surface lattice **-gleis** *n* crossing track **-glied** *n* lattice-type network, lattice section (of network or filter) **-griff** *m* star knob **-gurtung** *f* diagonal ties **-hacke** *f* pickax, flat pick, cross blocking **-hahn** *m* four-way cock **-hieb** *m* crosscut **-holz** *n* cleat **-kabel** *n* diagonal-bracing wire **-klemme** *f* crossing-over clamp **-knoten** *m* reef, right or crown knot

Kreuzkopf *m* crosshead (jet) **-führung** *f* crosshead guide **-keil** *m* adjusting or tightening wedge **-maschine** *f* crosshead-type engine **-zapfen** *m* crosshead pin **-zapfenlager** *n* crosshead bearing

kreuzkörnig cross grained

Kreuz-kuppelung *f* vernier coupling **-lafette** *f* antiaircraft outrigger gun platform

Kreuzlappenzugöse, gesenkgeschmiedete ~ swaged crossbar traction eye

Kreuz-leine *f* check line, checkrein **-leitung** *f* cross-conduction **-libellen** *pl* cross levels **-linienraster** *m* cross-line screen

Kreuzloch *n* cross hole **-kopf** *m* double-holed capstan head, cheese head with two holes **-mutter** *f* cross-hole nut **-schraube** *f* capstan screw

Kreuz-marke *f* cross mark **-maß** *n* gauge, cross staff, cross (print.) **-mast** *m* mizzenmast **-meißel** *m* bolt chisel, cape chisel, star bit **-modelung** *f*, **-modulation** *f* cross modulation **-muffe** *f* triple socket, cross sleeve **-nagel** *m* lease pin or peg **-naht** *f* cross seam **-peilung** *f* cross bearing (radio), fix (navig.), bearing taken from two or more ground direction finders **-pinzette** *f* cross-forceps **-poller** *m* bitt **-propeller** *m* four-blade propeller

Kreuzrahmen *m* crossed-coil antenna **-antenne** *f* crossed-coil antenna **-peilverfahren** *n* Bellini-

Tosi system

Kreuz-ring *m* clutch ring **-rippenmutter** *f* four-ribbed nut **-riß** *m* side elevation **-rohr** *n* tension rod **-rolle** *f* junction roller **-rollenmeißel** *m* cross roller bit **-rute** *f* lease rod **-saitig** cross-strung, overstrung

Kreuz-schaltung *f* back-to-back connection (of rectifier elements), compound slides **-scheibe** *f* cross-staff head, cross-type disc **-scheibenschnapper** *m* cross-disc-type impulse coupling **-schichtung** *f* cross-bedding, false bedding **-schienenprinzip** *n* cross-bar principle **-schienenverteiler** *m* crossbar distribution panel

Kreuzschlag *m* twist in opposite direction **-hammer** *m* cross-peen sledge **-seil** *n* regular lay rope

Kreuzschlaufe *f* cross loop

Kreuzschlitten *m* cross slide, compound slide **räumlicher** ~ three-dimensional cross slide

Kreuzschlittensystem, räumliches ~ three-dimensional cross-slide system

Kreuz-schlitzschraube *f* cross-slotted screw, Phillips screw **-schlüssel** *m* 4-way wheel brace **-schneider** *m* drill bit with crosstype cutting edge **-schnitt** *m* cross cut **-schraffieren** to crosshatch **-schraffierung** *f* crosshatching **-schraube** *f* trigger-guard screw **-spreize** *f* diagonal stay **-sprossenmaschine** *f* machine for making window-sash bars **-spule** *f* cross coil **-spulenhülse** *f* tube for cheeses

Kreuzspul-gerät *n* crossed-coil device, balanced-bridge network **-maschine** *f* quick traverse winder **-meßgerät** *n* crossed-coil measuring instrument **-säule** *f* cheese pile **-transport** *m* package conveyor **-zusatz** *m* wave winding attachment

Kreuzspur, Drehscheibe mit eingegossener ~ turntable with flush rails

Kreuz-steg *m* gutter **-stein** *m* cross-stone, chiastolite **-stelle** *f* intersection, crossing **-stich** *m* cross-stitch **-strebe** *f* cross stud **-strom** *m* crosscurrent **-strombrenner** *m* nozzle-mixing burner **-stück** *n* (flanged) crosspiece; (flanged) cross

Kreuzsupport *m* cross slide, compound (slide) rest **-handrad** *n* compound rest hand wheel **-tisch** *m* compound table

Kreuz-taurolle *f* running rigging **-teil** *n* rear of receiver well **-teilung** *f* cross scale **-teilungsmast** *m* cantilever-type tower (with double-tapered mast)

Kreuztisch *m* cross-table, mechanical stage **-mikrometer** stage micrometer **-rauschen** *n* stage noise **-verschiebung** *f* compound slide motion

Kreuzträger *m* cruciform girder

kreuz und quer laufen to criss-cross

Kreuzung *f* crossing, intersection, crossbreeding, transposition or cross connection (of wires), junction ~ **der Batteriepole** reversing or crossing of battery terminals

Kreuzungs-abschnitt *m* transposition section **-abstand** *m* transposition step (elec.) **-ausgleich** *m* transposing equalization (cable) **-bahnhof** *m* over- or under-crossing station (R.R.) **-fehler** *m* intersection error **-festpunkt** *m* transposition section point **-folge** *f* scheme of crossings, transposition system, pole diagram **-gestänge** *n* transposition pole **-isolator** *m* transposition insulator **-klemme** *f* overhead crossing, crossover clamp **-mittelpunkt** *m* cross line center on intersection

Kreuzungs-punkt *m* (point of) intersection, crossing, transposition point **-stange** *f* transposition pole **-stelle** *f* passing place, tie-up basin **-stück** *n* diamond crossing, double frog **-stuhl** *m* double chair **-system** *n* cross(over) system, transposition system **-verhältnis** *n* angle of crossing **-weiche** *f* slip points, crossover

Kreuz-ventil *n* crossing valve **-verband** *m* cross bracing **-verbindung** *f* cross connection, cross joint **-vermittlung** *f* scrambler phone exchange **-verschraubung** *f* cross-type screw fitting **-verspannung** *f* cross bracing **-verstrebung** *f* diagonal cross brace **-verweisung** *f* cross reference **-verzahnt** staggered teeth **-verzapfung** *f* cross joint **-visier** *n* line ranger, double optical (prismatic) square

Kreuz-weg *m* crossroad **-weiche** *f* cross switch **-weise** crosswise, two-way, traverse, crossway **-welle** *f* Cardan wave **-wickelbildung** *f* cross winding **-wicklung** *f* criss-crossed winding **-winkel** *m* T square **-zahnscheibenfräser** *m* staggered tooth cutter **-zangen** *pl* diagonal ties **-zeichen** *n* dagger, cross

Kribbeln *n* crawling, swarming (of film)

Kriech *n* creep

Kriech-abstand *m* creep distance **-dehnung** *f* creep strain

kriechen to creep, leak (of current), crawl, sneak

Kriechen *n* surface leakage, creeping, flow or plastic flow ~ **dünner Flüssigkeiten** film creep

kriechende Abweichung drift

Kriecherholungsmodul *m* relaxation modulus

kriechfeste Legierung creep resisting alloy

Kriech-festigkeit *f* creeping strength, creep limit **-funken** *m* flashover (surface discharge across insulation) **-galvanometer** *n* fluxmeter, quantometer **-gang** *m* catwalk, crawling speed **-ganggetriebe** *n* creep speed gear **-geschwindigkeit** *f* creep rate (metal.) **-grenze** *f* creep strength **-grenzenspannung** *f* limiting creep stress **-maß** *n* creep rate **-strecke** *f* creep distance (elec.), leakage path (elec.)

Kriechstrom *m* creeping or sneak current, surface leakage current **-beständigkeit** *f* non-tracking quality **-fehler** *m* leakage errors **-fest** creepage-proof **-festigkeit** *f* track resistance

Kriech-verhalten *n* creep behavior **-weg** *m* surface-leakage path, creepage path (elec.), creep distance **-wegbildung** *f* tracking (elec.)

Krimpe *f* warp

krimpfen to shrink, crimp, back (of wind)

Krimstecher *m* field glass

Kringel *m* curl

Krippe *f* manger, crib

Krippensetzer *m* crib-biter, cribber

Krippmaschine *f* **für die Drahtweberei** crimping machine for wire netting

Krispelholz *n* crippler, graining board, pommel **-maschine** *f* crippling machine

krispeln to grain

Kristall *m* crystal **eingelöteter** ~ solder-mounted crystal **isländischer** ~ calcareous spar, carbonate of lime **piezoelektrischer** ~ piezoelectric crystal **zweiachsiger** ~ biaxial crystal **aus mehreren Kristallen bestehend** polycrystalline ~ **mit BT-Schnitt** BT cut crystal

Kristall-achse *f* crystal axis, crystallographic axis **-achsenmesser** *m* conoscope **-achsenrichtung** *f* crystallographic-axis orientation **-aggregat** *n* crystalline aggregate **-anschuß** *m* crop of crystals, crystalline or crystallographic growth, crystallization

kristall-äquivalente Schaltung crystal equivalent circuit

kristallartig crystalline, crystalliform, crystallike

Kristall-aufbau *m* crystal structure **-aufspaltung** *f* crystalline-field splitting **-ausbildung** *f* formation or developement of crystals, crystalline growth **-ausscheidung** *f* separation of crystals

Kristall-bau *m* crystalline structure or form, crystal structure **-baufehler** *m* crystal (structural) defect, crystal lattice imperfection **-bereich** *m* crystal domain **-beschauer** *m* inspectoscope **-biegungsschwingung** *f* crystal flexural vibration **-bildabblendung** *f* stopping-down of the crystal image **-bildung** *f* formation or development of crystals, crystalline growth, crystallization, granulation (of sugar) **-brei** *m* crystal sludge

Kriställchen *n* microcrystal **-flüssigkeit** *f* crystal liquid

Kristall-detektor *m* crystal detector **-detektorempfänger** *m* crystal-control receiver **-diamagnetismus** *m* crystal diamagnetism **-dickenschwingung** *f* thickness vibration of a crystal **-drehung** *f* crystal rotation **-drehungsschwingung** *f* torsional vibration **-druse** *f* cluster of crystals

Kristall-ebene *f* crystal plane or face **-ecke** *f* solid angle of a crystal, crystal angle **-einbettung** *f* dilution of a crystal **-elektrisch** piezoelectric **-empfänger** *m* crystal receiver **-endfläche** *f* base, terminal face, or end face of a crystal **-erholung** *f* grain recovery, crystal recovery **-fassung** *f* (piezoelectric) crystal holder or mount **-fehler** *m* imperfection of a crystal **-feld** *n* crystalline field **-fernhörer** *m* piezoelectric or crystal receiver **-filter** *m* crystal filter **-fläche** *f* crystal plane or face **-form** *f* form of crystal, crystalline form **-förmig** crystalliform

Kristall-forscher *m* crystallographer **-gebilde** *n* crystalline group, structure, or matter, grain colony **-gefüge** *n* crystal structure **-gerät** *n* crystal unit **-gerippe** *n* crystal skeleton, crystallite

kristallgesteuert controlled by a crystal, crystal-controlled **-er Sender** crystal-controlled transmitter

Kristallgitter *n* space lattice, crystal lattice, crystal-grating **-schwingung** *f* crystal-lattice vibration **-skala** *f* chrystal-lattice scale **-spectrograph** *m* crystal spectrograph

Kristallgrenze *f* grain boundary **längs der Kristallgrenzen verlaufender Riß** intercrystalline crack

Kristall-grenzlinie *f* crystal junction line, crystal boundary **-halterung** *f* crystal holder, crystal mount **-haufwerk** *n* crystallite aggregation **-hell** crystalline **-hub** *m* crystal elevation **-hyperfeinstruktur** *f* crystal hyperfine structure

kristallin crystalline, crystalliform **-es Material** crystalline material

Kristallinaktivierung *f*, **optische** ~ racemization

kristallinisch crystalline ~ **körnig** granular-crystalline ~ **strahlig** radiated-crystalline **-e Schwäche** crystal weakness

Kristallinität *f* crystallinity

Kristallisation *f* crystallization **primäre** ~ primary crystallization **sekundäre** ~ secondary crystallization

Kristallisations-apparat *m* crystallizer **-becken** *n* last brine pit **-beginn** *m* chilling or cloud point (chem.) **-fähig** crystallizable **-fähigkeit** *f* crystallizability **-gefäß** *n* crystallizing vessel **-geschwindigkeit** *f* rate of crystalline growth

Kristallisations-kern *m* center or nucleus of crystallization, crystal center **-kernbildung** *f* nucleation **-vermögen** *n* crystaline force **-vorgang** *m* crystallizing process **-wachstum** *n* crystalline growth, germination **-zentrum** *n* center of crystallization, nucleus of crystallization

Kristallisator *m* crystal agent

Kristallisierapparat *m* crystallizer

kristallisierbar crystallizable

kristallisieren to crystallize

Kristallisier-gefäß *n* crystallizing vessel or pan **-schale** *f* crystallizing dish

kristallisiertes Paraffin crystalline wax

Kristallisierung *f* crystallization

Kristallit *m* crystallite, allotriomorphic crystal, crystalline grain **keilförmiger** ~ cuneate

Kristall-kante *f* crystal edge **-keim** *m* crystal nucleus, seed crystal **-keimbildung** *f* nucleation **-kern** *m* crystal center, nucleus of a crystal **-kernbildung** *f* crystallization, nucleation, germination **-kollimator** *m* crystal collimator **-korn** *n* crystalline grain, crystal grain **-kornbildung** *f* formation of a crystalline grain **-körper** *m* crystal prism, crystalline (body) lens

Kristallkörperchen *n*, **rundes** ~ globulite, spherulite

Kristall-kunde *f* crystallography **-längsschwingung** *f* longitudinal vibration of a crystal **-lautsprecher** *m* piezoelectric loud-speaker **-lehre** *f* crystallography **-lichtverstärker** *m* phototransistor **-linse** *f* crystalline lens **-lumineszenz** *f* crystalloluminescence **-mikrophon** *n* piezoelectric or crystal microphone **-mischstufe** *f* crystal mixer **-modulator** *m* frequency-changer crystal **-monochromator** *m* crystal monochromator **-morphologie** *f* crystal morphology

Kristalloden *pl* crystal diodes

Kristallogramm *n* crystallogram

Kristallographie *f* crystallography

kristallographisch crystallographic, crystalline **-e Klassen** *f pl* crystallographic classes

kristalloid crystalloid, crystalloidal

Kristallometer *n* crystallometer

kristalloptisch optical crystal (examination)

Kristall-orientierung *f* crystal orientation **-oszillator** crystal oscillator, piezoelectric oscillator **-periodizität** *f* crystal periodicity **-pfanne** *f* crystal cup **-pulver** *n* powdered crystal, powder diffraction **-quantenzahl** *f* crystal quantum number **-querschwingung** *f* transverse vibration, contour vibration or oscillation **-richtröhre** *f* crystal diode

Kristall-scheibchen *n* crystal wafer **-schnitt** *m*

crystal cut **-schwingung** *f* crystal vibration **-silber** *n* crystalline silver **-skelett** *n* skeleton crystal **-soda** *f* soda crystals **-spektrograph** crystal spectrograph **-spektrometer** crystal spectrometer, ionization spectrometer **-splitter** *n* crystal grain or chip

kristallstabilisierter Sender crystal-stabilized transmitter

Kristall-stein *m* rock crystal **-steuerstufe** *f* crystal control stage **-steuerung** *f* crystal stabilizing or control, crystal drive **-stimmgabel** *f* crystal tuning fork **-streifen** *m* band of crystal **-struktur** *f* crystalline structure **-strukturuntersuchung** *f* crystal (structure) analysis **-system** *n* system of crystallization **-szintillator** crystal scintillator

Kristall-taktgeber *m* crystal monitor, crystal-control means, crystal stabilizer **-teilchen** *n* crystalline particle **-triode** *f* crystal triode **-umhüllung** *f* perimorphous crystal **-untersuchung** *f* crystal analysis **-verbindung** *f* crystal combination **-verstärker** *m* transistor **-wachstum** *n* crystal growth, crystalline growth **-wasser** *n* water of crystallization

kristallwasserfrei anhydrous ~ **machen** to dehydrate

Kristall-wechselwirkung *f* crystalline field interaction **-winkelmessung** *f* crystal goniometry **-zähler** *m* crystal counter **-ziehen** *n* crystal growing **-ziehofen** *m* crystal pulling machine **-ziehverfahren** *n* crystal pulling **-zone** *f* zone of crystal **-züchtung** *f* crystal growth

Kristall-zustand *m* crystalline condition **-zwilling** *m* twin crystal, compound twin

Kriterion *n*, **Kriterium** *n* criterion

Kritik *f* critique

Kritikalität *f* criticality

kritisch critical, delicate **-e Abmessung** critical dimension, critical size **-er Anstellwinkel** critical angle, stalling angle **-er Augenblick** emergency, critical moment **-e Drehzahl** critical speed of rotation **-er Druck** critical compression ratio, critical pressure **-e Geschwindigkeit** hump speed, critical speed, stalling speed **-e Höhe** critical altitude **-es Intervall** critical range, critical interval

kritisch-e Paketierung optimum bunching **-er Punkt** breaking point **-er Spannungsabfall** disintegration voltage (in mercury rectifier practice) **-es Verhältnis** critical rate **-er Wert** critical value **-er Widerstand** critical resistance **-er Winkel** stalling angle

kritzeln to scrawl, scribble

Kroki *n* rough or colored map sketch

krokieren to sketch

Krokierpapier *n* sketching paper

Krokodil *n* crocodile **-klemme** *f* crocodile clip **-narben** *pl* alligatoring

Krokoit *m* crocoite

krollen (kröllen) to curl, crisp

Krone *f* crown, top, head, coronet (hoof), crest ~ **der Talsperre** dam crest ~ **des Turmes** (Tiefbohranlage) top of derrick

Kronen-armatur *f* top fittings (of blast furnace) **-aufsatz** *m* crown top, rose top **-bohrer** *m* cross-mouthed chisel or borer, crown drill, crown or square bit, annular bit or borer **-breite** *f* breadth of top of summit **-brenner** *m* boiling or ring burner (chem.) **-fräser** *m* hollow mill

Kronen-korkbehälter *m* cork hopper **-korkflaschen** *pl* crown cork bottles **-korker** *m* crown corker **-korkscheiben** *pl* cork disks for crown bottle caps **-korkverschließmaschine** *f* crown cork sealing machine

Kronenmutter *f* horned nut, castle nut, crown nut ~ **ohne Hals** castle nut without turret

Kronen-rad *n* crown wheel or gear, face wheel or gear, cogwheel **-ventil** *n* cup valve, bell-shaped valve **-welle** *f* axletree, wind shaft

Kron-glas *n* crown glass **-(glas)linse** *f* crown lens **-holz** *n* cap, capping, head or top beam

Kronierung *f* castellations

Kronleuchter *m* chandelier

Kronlinie der Erdarbeiten formation level

Kron-mutter *f* castellated nut **-rad** *n* crown wheel or gear, cogwheel, face wheel or gear **-schwelle** *f* cap, capping, head or top beam

Kronwerk *n* outwork

Kropf *m* backfall weir or descent plate, crop, goiter **-achswelle** *f* crankshaft, axle **-eisen** *n* sling, cramp iron, grapnel, devil's-claw (naut.), dog, ram

kröpfen to bend at right angles, form a knee, crank, offset

Kröpfform *f* elbow shaper

Kropf-gerinne *n* circular channel **-grat** *m* miter line **-hals** *m* crankpin **-kante** *f* miter line **-loch** *n* sling hole, lewis, hole for the ram

Kröpfmaschine *f* joggling machine

Kropfrad *n* breast water wheel, breast or middle-shot wheel

Kröpf-scheibe *f* eccentric disk or sheave **-schnitt** *m* gap cut

Kropfstein *m* quoin, cornerstone

Kröpfung *f* crank, throw, bend (as axle), elbow, offset, shoulder, crimping ~ **am Vorderrahmen** sweep over front axle

Kröpfungspaar *n* double-throw

Kröse *f* croze, notching tool

Kröseisen *n* croze iron

Kröseleisen *n* rabbet or grooving iron, crumbling iron

krösen to groove, notch

Krücke *f* crowbar, iron rod, rake, oar, rabble, crutch, back prop, beater ~ (Tauchstange) plunger

Krückeisen *n* T strap

Krückel *m* brace with key, turning lever **-führer** *m* foreman **-rohr** *n* hollow brace **-stock** *m* brace head **-stück** *n* brace head on top of the bore rod

krücken-förmig crooked **-isolator** *m* spur insulator, line insulator

Krückwerk *n* crutch (apparatus)

Krug *m* jug, jar, pitcher, tankard

Krügerelement *n* Krueger cell

Kruke *f* stone bottle or jar

krümelig crumbling (crumbly) **-er Boden** friable soil

krümeln to crumble

Krümeltorf *m* lump peat

Krümelzucker *m* glucose

krumm crooked, bent, curved, buckled ~ **machen** to warp ~ **werden** (beim Härten) to get a set, cast sideways, distort, warp, bend **sich** ~

ziehen to buckle, cast, distort **-es Bohrloch** crooked hole **-er Hebel** angular lever

Krumm-achse *f* crank **-dechsel** *f* hollow adz **-eisen** *n* hollowing knife

krümmen to bend, crook, curve, warp, buckle, collar, curl **sich ~** to warp, buckle

Krümmen *n* bending, buckling

Krümmer *m* bend, elbow, cultivator, quarter bend, discharge knee **~ mit Flanschen** flanged bend **E-Krümmer** *m* flatwise bend

Krümmer-verbindung *f* elbow joint **-verlust** *m* loss in bends

Krummfingerlederhandschuh *m* leather gauntlet with bent fingers (for wire laying, etc.)

Krummhaue *f* adz, barrel howel

Krumm-holz *n* wales (shipbuilding) **-hölzer-arbeit** *f* long-wall working on small veins (min.)

krummlinig curved, curvilinear **-e Koordinaten** curvilinear coordinates **-er Rand** curved boundary **-es Vieleck** curvilinear polygon

Krumm-meißel *m* paring tool **-ofen** *m* shaft furnace, blast furnace **-rohr** *n* bend pipe, bent pipe **-schalig** curved

Krümmung *f* bend, curve, turn, curvature, bow, camber, angle, contortion, radius, sweep, buckling, twisting, undulating **~ der Charakteristik** curvature of the characteristic **~ der equipotentialen Flächen des Schwerkraftfeldes** curvature of equipotential surfaces of gravity **~ einer ebenen Kurve** curvature of a plane curve **~ einer Raumkurve** curvature of a curve in space **~ des Skeletts** mean camber **flache ~** slow sweep **räumliche ~** double curvature **seitliche ~** sweep (iron rails) **senkrechte ~** camber (iron rails) **untere ~** lower camber

Krümmungs-abhängigkeit *f* curvature dependence **-achse** *f* axis of curvature **-fehler** *m* curvature error **-freies Feld** *n* flattened field (by flattening lens) **-gleichung** *f* curvature equation **-halbmesser** *m* radius of curvature **-korrektur** *f* field flattening **-kreis** *m* circle of curvature **-linie** *f* line of curvature

Krümmungsmaß *n* curvature **~ einer Fläche** curvature of a surface

Krümmungs-messer *m* curvometer **-mittelpunkt** *m* center of curvature **-radius** *m* radius of curvature, bend radius **-reduzierend** field-flattening **-richtung** *f* principal direction **-rücklage** *f* camber position **-verhältnis** *n* ratio of curvature **-verlauf** *m* curve trend

Krumm-werden *n* buckling, crooking, bending, warping **-zapfen** *m* crank pin **-ziegel** *m* compass brick, concave brick **-zirkel** *m* calipers

krumpeln (krümpeln) to crumple, pucker up

krumpen to shrink

Krümperpferd *n* reserve horse

Krumpf-apparatur des Spannrahmens tenter **-festigkeit** *f* shrink resistance

Krumpmörtel *m* mortar of overburnt lime grains

Kruppe *f* croup

Krüppel *m* cripple **zum ~ machen** to cripple

Krüppelspillwinde *f* crab winch

Kruskal-Grenze *f* Kruskal limit

Kruste *f* crust **mit einer ~ überziehen** to incrust **dünne ~** incrustation

Krusten-bewegung *f* crustal movement **-bildung** *f* incrustation **-gestein** *n* crustal rocks **-verformung** *f* crustal deformation

krustig crusty

Krustung *f* crust formation

Kryolith *m* cryolite

kryomagnetisch cryomagnetic

Kryometer *n* cryometer

Kryoskop *n* cryoscope

Kryostat *n* cryostat

Kryotron *n* cryotron

kryptokristallin cryptocrystalline

Kryptometer *n* cryptometer

Krypton *n n* krypton

Kryptoskop *n* kryptoscope

Kryptosterin *n* kryptosterol

Kubatur *f* cubature, cubing

Kübel *m* bucket, pail, tray, pot, vat, tub **~ mit beweglichem Boden** bottom-door skip (for filling caissons), bottom-dump bucket **~ mit Bodenentleerer** bottom dumping bucket

kübelartig tray-shaped, bucketlike

Kübel-aufzug *m* bucket elevator **-begichtung** *f* bucket charging, bucket filling **-begichtungs-anlage** *f* bucket-charging gear **-betrieb** *m* bucket service **-entleerung** *f* bucket discharge **-sitz-wagen** *m* light multiple-purpose car **-stange** *f* bucket suspension rod, handling crane **-trans-portkran** *m* bucket-handling crane

kubieren to cube, raise to third power

Kubierungsformel *f* cubing formula

Kubik-berechnung *f* cubature **-dezimeter** *m, n* cubic decimeter, liter **-fuß** *m* cubic foot **-inhalt** *m* cubic contents, cubic capacity **-maß** *n* cubic measure **-meter** *m* cubic meter **-wurzel** *f* cubic root, cube root **-wurzelgesetz** *n* cube root law **-wurzelziehen** *n* extraction of cube root, process of evolution **-zahl** *f* cube, cubic number **-zenti-meter** *m* cubic centimeter **-zoll** *m* cubic inch

kubisch cubic(al) **-es Gitter** cubic lattice **-e Kurve** curve following a thirdpower law **-e Punktgruppe** cubic point group **-e Struktur** cubic structure

kubisch dichtest cubic closed-packed

kubisch-flächenzentriert cubic face centered **-raumzentrierte Metalle** body-centered cubic metals, cubic body-centered metals (cryst.) **-zentriert** bodycentered

Kubizierapparat *m* gauging apparatus

kubizieren, die Masse ~ to calculate the volume of a solid

Kubizierung *f* volume calculation, raising to third power

Kubooktaeder *n* cubo-octahedron

Kubus *m* cube, hexahedron

Küche *f* kitchen, galley

Kuchen *m* cake **-abnahmevorrichtung** *f* filter-cakeremoving device

Küchenanrichte *f* kitchen dresser

Kuchen-auswaschung *f* washing of cake **-bildung** *f* formation of cakes **-erz** *n* cake ore

Küchen-maschine *f* kitchen machine **-schrank** *m* cupboard

Kuchenstärke *f* cake thickness

Kufe *f* ski, sledge runner, skid, tub, pressure pad, or guide, calandria **~ des Segelflugzeuges** skid of the sailplane

Kufenflugzeug *n* sled plane, ski airplane

Küfer *m* cooper **-krummesser** *pl* cooper's bent shank draw knives **-messer** *n* cooper's drawing knife **-putzmesser** *n* cooper's cleaning knife **-schraber** *m* cooper's round scraper **-schroppmesser** *n* cooper's heading knife **-zugschaber** *m* cooper's drawing scraper

Kugel *f* ball, globe, sphere, bullet, bulb, ball bearing, pellet, shot, bead **dichteste ~** close-packed structure **leitende ~** conducting sphere **matte ~** spent bullet **schwebende ~** parachute flare **~ für Regelstange** control rod ball joint

Kugel-abflachung *f* oblateness **-abschnitt** *m* spherical segment or indentation, calotte, cup **-abstand** *m* sphere gap **-ähnlich** spheroidal, ball-like **-anschluß** *m* ball-and-socket joint **-antenne** *f* isotropic antenna **-artig** spheroidal, spherical, globular, nodular **-ausschnitt** *m* spherical sector, section of a sphere

Kugel-bahn *f* ball race **-ballon** *m* spherical balloon **-behälter** *n* spherical vessel **-blasen** *n* shot-blasting **-blende** *f* ball mount **-blitz** *m* ball lightning **-boden** *m* spherical bottom **-boje** *f* ball or spherical buoy **-bohrer** *m* bullet-trephine **-bolzengruppe** *f* ball pin assembly **-brennraum** *m* spherical combustion chamber **-büchse** *f* ball box

Kügelchen *n* spherule, globule, rounded grain, pellet, small bulb, globulite, small ball or shot

Kugel-densitometer *n* spherical densitometer **-diorit** *m* orbicular diorite

Kugeldreh-apparat *m* ball turner **-ring** *m* ball race **-support** *m* ball turning rest **-verbindung** *f* ball-bearing slewing gear (of a crane)

Kugeldreieck *n* spherical wedge

Kugeldruck *m* ball pressure, ball thrust **-härte** *f* ball-pressure hardness, ball-thrust hardness **-härteprüfer** *m* ball-thrust-hardness tester, ball-indentation testing apparatus **-härteuntersuchung** *f* ball-pressure or ball-indentation test, ball-thrust or ball-harness test, static-hardness or static ball-indentation test, ball-impression test **-lager** *n* ball-thrust bearing **-maschine** *f*, **presse** *f* ball (thrust) hardness tester **-probe** *f* ball-pressure or ball-indentation test, ball-thrust or ball-hardness test, static hardness or static ball-indentation test, ball-impression test, Brinell ball-hardness test **-ring** *m* ball thrust-bearing **-versuch** *m* ball indentation test, ball hardness test

Kugeldurchmesser *m* diameter of ball

Kugeleindruck *m* ball impression or indentation, ball imprint, spherical indentation, ball hardness **-durchmesser** *m* diameter of ball impression **-fläche** *f* spherical area of indentation **-versuch** *m* ball pressure (thrust) test

Kugel-einsatztastkugel *f* (steel) ball contact tip **-einsprache** *f* microphone cap, spherical mouthpiece **-eisenstein** *m* sphaerosiderite **-elektrode** *f* sparking ball **-ende** *n* ball end **-endmaß** *n* spherical end measuring rod **-endstück** *n* ball-ended strut

Kugel-faktor *m* coefficient of sphere (photometry) **-fallhammer** *m* (indentation machine with) ball drop hammer **-fallhärte** *f* dynamic ball-indentation hardness, scleroscope hardness **-fallmethode** *f* falling-ball method (viscometry) **-fallprobe** *f* dynamic ball-indentation test, scleroscope-hardness test **-fallviskosimeter** *n* falling sphere (ball) viscosimeter **-fang** *m* butt **-fassung** *f* spherical mount **-fest** bulletproof **-finne** *f* ball peen **-fläche** *f* spherical area or surface **-flächenfunktion** *f* surface harmonics **-flasche** *f* balloon flask, spherical flask **-form** *f* ball shape, spherical shape

kugelförmig ball-shaped, spherical, globular, orbicular **nicht ~** aspherical **~ gewölbte Lamellen** dished laminae **-er Brennraum** bulb type combustion chamber **-es Endstück** ball end **-es Plasmoid** ball-shaped plasmoid

Kugel-fräser *m* cherry, spherical cutter **-führung** *f* ball-bearing **-funkenstrecke** *f* sphere gap, ball gap, ball or spherical spark gap **-funktion** *f* spherical harmonic, spherical function **-funktionsentwicklung** *f* spherical harmonic analysis **-fuß** *m* ball-type base

Kugel-gasbehälter *m* spherical gas holder **-gehäuse** *n* ball housing **-gelagert** running in ball bearings **-gelenk** *n* ball-and-socket joint, ball pivot, universal, swing, or spherical joint **-gelenkgehäuse** *n* ball joint case, ball joint housing **-gelenkwelle** *f* universal-jointed shaft **-gestalt** *f* spherical shape, ball shape, bulbous shape **-gestaltsfehler** *m* spot-size distortion, spherical aberration **-gestaltswidrig** aspherical **-gewölbe** *n* spherical vault, hemispherical vault **-gleitlager** *n* spherical bearing **-gewicht** *n* weight ball

Kugel-glocke *f* globe, glass (lamp) **-griff** *m* ball handle **-halter** *m* ball support **-hammer** *m* ball-peen hammer **-handkurbel** *f* crank handle with ball **-hängelager** *n* ball-bearing drop hanger **-härteprobe** *f* Brinell hardness test **-haube** *f* gear-shift cap **-hebel** *m* ball lever **-hohlraum** *m* spherical cavity

kugelig spherical, spheroidal, globular, nodular **-ballige Unterlegscheibe** spherical washer **-e Absonderung** spheroidal jointing

Kugeligkeit *f* sphericity

Kugel-käfig *m* ball cage, ball race, ball retainer **-kaliber** *n* indentation, hollow **-kalotte** *f* spherical segment **-kammer** *f* ball race **-kappe** *f* calotte **-kardan** *n* universal ball joint **-keil** *m* spherical cone **-kimme** *f* spherical rear sight **-knopf** *m* control lever knob, spherical knob, ball head **-kocher** *m* spherical boiler **-konsolhängelager** *n* ball-bearing-bracket drop hanger **-koordinat** *m* spherical polar coordinate

Kugelkopf *m* ball end **~ der Stoßstange** push-rod ball end

Kugel-korb *m* ball race **-körperchen** *n* globulite, spherulite **-korrektor** *m* spherical or quadrantal corrector **-kreisel** *m* spherical top **-kreiselmolekül** *n* spherical top molecule **-kreislauflenkung** *f* ball joint steering **-kühler** *m* ball-form condenser, globe-shaped condenser **-kuppe** *f* ball-point **-kuppelung** *f* ball-and-socket joint, universal joint **-ladung** *f* ball load, ball charge **-lafette** *f* ball mount

Kugellager *n* ball bearing **~ mit Fettkammer für Dauerschmierung** prelubricated ball bearing **fertig montiertes ~** assembled ball bearing

Kugellager-außenring *m* ball-bearing outer race **-buchse** *f* ball bearing cage, bush **-büchse** *f* ball-bearing sleeve **-deckel** *m* ball bearing retainer **-fassung** *f* ball-bearing race **-freilaufrad** *n* free wheel with ball bearing **-gehäuse** *n* ball-bearing cup, spherical bush or brass **-gelenk** *n* ball-and-socket hinge **-innenring** *m* ball-bearing inner race or ring **-laufring** *m* ball-bearing race **-leer-**

laufbuchse *f* ball-bearing bushing **-mühle** *f* ball-bearing mill

Kugellager-packung *f* packing of the spheres **-ring** *m* ball race, ball-bearing race **-ringkäfig** *m* ball-bearing spacer or retainer **-sitz** *m* ball-bearing seat **-spindel** *f* ball-bearing type spindle **-stahl** *m* ball-bearing steel

Kugel-lagerung *f* ball bearing, packing of the spheres **-lagerverbindung** *f* ball joint swivel joint **-lagerzapfen** *m* ball-bearing pivot **-lampe** *f* spherical bulb or lamp **-längslager** *n* longitudinal ball bearing **-laufbahn** *f* raceway of balls, ball race **-laufkranz** *m* ball race **-laufrille** *f* ball groove **-laufring** *m* ball race ring, cam bearing **-lehre** *f* ball gauge, hollow **-leuchte** *f* spherical fitting **-linse** *f* spherical lens

Kugel-messer *m* spherometer **-meßhalter** *m* ball measuring stand **-richtung** *f* ball-gauging device **-mikrometer** *n* spherical micrometer **-mikrophon** *n* spherical microphone **-mikroskop** *n* ball-stage microscope **-mine** *f* spherical trench-mortar shell **-mühle** *f* ball mill, pebble mill **-mutter** *f* ball nut, capped nut

kugeln to roll, form into a ball

Kugel-neigungsmesser *m* ball inclinometer **-nickel** *n* nickel pellets **-oberfläche** *f* spherical surface **-objektiv** *n* target **-öler** *m* ball oiler **-packung** *f* packing of the spheres, close-packed structure **-panzergalvanometer** *n* ball shield galvanometer **-papier** *m* globular paper **-pendel** spherical pendulum **-pfanne** *f* ball cup or socket, base-plate socket **-photometer** *n* sphere or globe photometer

Kugel-polieren *n* ball or barrel burnishing **-probe** *f* ball-pressure or ball-indentation test, ball-thrust or ball-hardness test, static hardness or static ball-indentation test, ball-impression test **-probehahn** *m* ball gauge cock **-pyranometer** *m* spherical pyranometer

Kugel-raste *f* ball notch **-reihe** *f* ball race **-reinigungsanlage** *f* steel shot cleaning plant **-resonator** *m* spherical resonator **-revolver** *m* spherical revolver **-rille** *f* ball groove **-ring** *m* ball race **-rohr** *n* bulbed tube, tube with bulbs **-rückschlagventil** *n* ball retaining valve **-rücksprung** *m* rebound of ball, ricocheting **-rund** round, spherical, globular **-säulenkonsollager** *n* ball-bearing post hanger

Kugel-schale *f* ball cup or socket, partial sphere, cup-shaped or hemispherical part, spherical shell **-schalenlager** *n* universal (sliding) joint **-schaltung** *f* ball-and-socket gear shifting **-scharnier** *n* ball-and-socket joint **-scheibe** *f* (ballig) spherical washer **-schicht** *f* zone (spherical) **-schiebelager** *n* sliding ball bearing **-schieber** *m* globe valve **-schlaghärteprüfer** *m* ball-impact hardness tester

Kugelschliff *m* ground-in ball-and-socket joint **-magnetventil** *n* magnetic ball joint valve **-schliffventil** *n* valve with ground-in ball-and-socket joint

Kugel-schnellverschluß *m* ball cap **-schnitt** *m* spherical section **-schott** *n* dished bulkhead **-schraubung** *f* ball joint **-schreiber** *m* ball-point pen, ball pen **-schwimmer** *m* spherical float, ball float **-segment** *n* spherical segment **-sektor** *m* sector of a sphere

kugelsicher bulletproof **-es Glas** bulletproof glass

Kugel-sitz *m* ball seat **-spannungsmesser** *m* sphere gap voltmeter **-spiegel** *m* spherical mirror or reflector **-spiegelleuchte** *f* spherical mirror lamp **-spitze** *f* ball point **-spitzenfühlnadel** *f* scanning or pickup needle with spherical point (sound-engraved film) **-spitzfeder** *f* ball-point(ed) pen **-spule** *f* spherical coil **-spur** *f* ball race **-spurlager** *n* spherical thrust bearing

Kugel-stahl *m* ball steel **-stange** *f* knee-joint bar **-stehlager** *n* ball-bearing pillow block **-steuerung** *f* ball controlled distribution **-strahlen** *n* cloudburst hardening, ball-shooting hardening, shot blasting, shot hardening, ball blasting **-strahlen** *n* shot peening **-strahler** *m* spherical source (acoust.), isotropic radiator **-stück** *n* spherical bushing, ball adapter piece

Kugel-stutzen *m* ball connecting branch **-stützlager** *n* ball thrust (bearing) **-stützpunkt** *m* spherical point of support, ball contact tip **-support** *m* revolving slide rest **-symmetrie** *f* spherical geometry **-symmetrisch** spherically symmetric, spherosymmetric

Kugel-taster *m* globe or ball caliper **-taststift** *m* tracer point (feeler) **-tensor** *m* spherical tensor **-thermometer** *n* bulb thermometer **-tisch** *m* spherical table, ball stage (micros.) **-tonne** *f* ball or spherical buoy **-träger** *m* bracket (for spherical compensators) **-traglager** *n* ball-bearing mounting **-trommelpolieren** *n* barrel polishing

Kugel-T-Stück *n* (flanged) ball T or T piece, (flanged) globe T

Kugel- und Rollenlager *n* ball bearing

Kugel-variometer *n* ball variometer **-ventil** *n* ball (check) valve, globe valve **-ventilpumpe** *f* ball pump **-verblockung** *f* ball lock **-verschluß** *m* spherical shutter, ball valve or closure, ball lock **-verschlußdüse** *f* ball check nozzle **-verschlußöler** *m* ball-valve-type lubricator **-verschraubung** *f* ball joint or connection **-verwandschaft** *f* homography in space **-vorlage** *f* spherical receiver

Kugel-wandkonsollager *n* ball-bearing wall-bracket hanger **-wechsel** *m* exchange of shots **-welle** *f* spherical wave **-wellentrichter** *m* spherical wave horn **-wendezeiger** *m* cliometer **-winkel** *m* spherical angle **-wirbel** *m* ball spinner **-zange** *f* gas pliers **-zapfen** *m* ball end pin, ball pin, ball stud, bowl gudgeon, ball and socket **-zentrierung** *f* ball centering **-zone** *f* spherical zone, quadrantal zone

Kuh-fuß *m* crowbar, nail claw or drawer

kühl cool

Kühl-abteilung (Kühlfach) *f* cooling compartment **-aggregat** *f* refrigerator **-anlage** *f* refrigeration plant, cooling system **-apparat** *m* cooling apparatus, cooler, condenser, refrigerator **-bad** *n* cooling bath **-band** *n* cooling conveyer or band **-becken** *n* cooling basin **-bett** *n* cooling bed or table **-bremssubstanz** *f* moderator-coolant **-büchse** *f* cooling jacket **-chassis** *f* cooling box

Kühle *f* cooler, cooling floor

Kuhle *f* pool

Kühl-einsatz *m* cooling insert **-eisen** *n* iron chill, chill, densener

kühlen to cool, chill, anneal

Kühler *m* (automobile) radiator, cooler, refrigerator, condenser ~ **mit eingeschmolzenem Schlangenrohr** condenser with spiral tube sealed to body ~ **mit Schlangenrohr** condenser with spiral condensing tube **in Luftführung eingeschlossener** ~ tunnel-type radiator **ausziehbarer** ~ draw-out, retractable, or extractable radiator **einziehbarer** ~ retractable radiator **freifahrender** ~ externally mounted radiator

Kühler-abdeckung *f* radiator shutter or cover, radiator flap **-ablaßhahn** *m* radiator draw-off (drain)cock **-ablaßschraube** *f* radiator draw-off plug **-attrappe** *f* radiator grill **-aufsatz** *m* radiator cowl **-ausflußstutzen** *m* water outlet of radiator **-bänder** *pl* radiator strips **-block** *m* radiator core, cooling block **-düse** *f* radiator nozzle

Kühler-einfüllstutzen *m* radiator-filler cap **-einfüllverschluß** *m* radiator cap **-einfüllverschraubung** *f* radiator cap, radiator filler cap **-einguß** *m* radiator filler **-einlaßstutzen** *m* water inlet of radiator **-einlaufstutzen** *m* radiator inlet pipe **-einsatz** *m* interior cooler unit **-element** *n* cooling section **-entlüftung** *f* radiator vent pipe

Kühler-fertigung *f* radiator manufacture **-fläche** *f* cooler area or surface **-füllkappe** *f* radiator (filler) cap **-füllschraube** *f* radiator filler cap **-fuß** *m* radiator bracket, support, or standard **-gehäuse** *n* radiator box or frame **-gitter** *n* radiator grille **-halter** *m* radiator bracket **-haube** *f* radiator cover **-jalousie** *f* adjustable air louver, radiator blinds

Kühler-kappe *f* radiator cap, shutter, or flap **-kiste** *f* condenser box **-klappe** *f* radiator shutter, radiator flap **-klappjalousie** *f* radiator shutter **-klappenhebel** *m* lever for operating radiator shutter **-körper** *m* radiator box or frame **-kulisse** *f* radiator shutter **-kulissenschaltung** *f* radiator-shutter control **-lagerung** *f* radiator support **-lamelle** *f* radiator rib, lamination or segment

Kühler-mantel *m* condenser jacket, cooling jacket **-maske** *f* radiator shutter **-maul** *n* air-intake slot (for radiator) **-netz** *n* radiator core **-paket** *n* radiator element **-querträger** *m* radiator cross stay, radiator sill **-rahmen** *m* radiator shell, frame, or box **-regelung** *f* regulation of the radiator, temperature regulation **-reinigung** *f* radiator cleaning **-rippe** *f* cooling fin **-schlauch** *m* radiator hose **-rohr** *n* cooling tube

Kühlerschutz *m* radiator guard **-bügel** *m* radiator bumper rod **-decke** *f* radiator muff **-gitter** *n* radiator grill **-haube** *f* radiator cover **-muffe** *f* radiator muff **-ring** *f* radiator guard ring

Kühler-sieb *n* radiator sieve, radiator strainer **-strebe** *f* radiator stay **-stutzen** *m* radiator filler tube **-teilblock** *m* radiator element, radiator core section **-thermometer** *n* radiator thermometer

Kühler-ventil *n* radiator or thermostatic control valve **-ventilator** *m* radiator fan **-verkleidung** *f* radiator grill, radiator shell **-verschluß** *m*, **-verschlußklappe** *f*, **-verschraubung** *f* radiator cap **-verstrebung** *f* radiator strut **-vorhang** *m* curtain-type shutter **-wärmegrad** *m*, **-wärmetemperatur** *f* temperature of the radiator **-zeichen** *n* radiator emblem

Kühl-fahne *f* cooling fin **-falle** *f* cooling trap, refrigerated trap **-faß** *n* refrigerator **-fläche** *f* cooling surface or area **-flansch** *m* cooling flange **-flügel** *m* cooling vane, electrode radiator **-flüssigkeit** *f* cooling fluid or liquid, coolant **-flüssigkeitsbehälter** *m* cooling tank

Kühl-gang *m* cooling passage (rocket) **-gaskreislauf** *m* cooling-gas circuit **-gefäß** *n* cooling tank **-gehänge** *n* cooling suspension gearing **-gut** *n* chilled goods **-halle** *f* cold store **-haube** *f* cooling cap **-haus** *n* cold storage **-kammer** *f* cooling or refrigerating chamber **-kanal** *m* cooling pipe **-kasten** *m* tuyère block, tuyère arch cooler, cooling box **-kokille** *f* chill mold **-kreislauf** *m* coolant circuit **-küvette** *f* refrigerating chamber

Kühl-lamelle *f* cooling flange, fin or rib **-leistung** *f* refrigeration capacity **-leistungsaufwand** *m* power expanded in cooling **-leitung** *f* cooling pipe

Kühlluft *f* cooling air **-abführung** *f* cooling air duct **-anschluß** *m* cold air connection **-bohrloch** *n* cold air port

Kühlluftführung *f* duct ~ **in Kanälen** ducting of the air

Kühlluftgebläse *n* cooling air blower

Kühlluftleitblech *n* cooling baffle or guide vane **enges Anliegen der Kühlluftleitbleche** baffle tightness

Kühlluft-klappen *pl* cooling flaps or flanges **-mantel** *m* cooling-air jacket **-regelklappe** *f* cowl flap **-regler** *m* radiator shutter or damper **-schlitz** *m* cooling-air slot **-spalt** *m* cooling air tap **-strom** *m* cooling air flow

Kühl-mansarde *f* cooling chamber **-mantel** *m* water jacket, cooling jacket, cooling tank, condensing jacket **-maschine** *f* refrigerator **-medium** *n* coolant

Kühlmittel *n* cooling medium, cooling agent, coolant, cutting compound, freezing mixture, refrigerant **vom** ~ **umspült** wet liner ~ **aus verflüssigtem Metall** liquid-metal coolant

Kühlmittel-abfluß *m* coolant drains **-behälter** *m* coolant tank **-leitung** *f* coolant line **-pumpe** *f* coolant pump **-rinne** *f* coolant gutter **-rohr** *n* coolant tube **-vorlauf** *m* advance of refrigerant **-vorrat** *m* stock of coolant

Kühl-nische *f* cooling plate box **-oberfläche** *f* cooling surface **-ofen** *m* annealing oven, lehr **-öffnung** *f* cooling opening **-öl** *n* cooling oil, coolant, quench oil **-ölzuführung** *f* supply of coolant **-patrone** *f* cooling device or cartridge **-platte** *f* cooling disk **-raum** *m* cold-storage room, cooling chamber **-rauminhalt** *m* refrigerating storage space capacity **-ring** *m* cooling ring **-rinne** *f* water trough

Kühlrippe *f* cooling vane, cooling flange, fin, or rib, radiating fin, vane, or flange **mit Kühlrippen versehene Zündkerze** finned spark plug

Kühlrohr *n* condenser tube, cooling tube, refrigerating pipe, radiator pipe or tube ~ (eines Raketenmotors) cooling jacket

Kühl-rohrleitung *f* radiator piping **-rost** *m* water screen **-rührmaische** *f* cooling crystallizer with stirring device **-scheibe** *f* circular heat deflector, cooling disk (plate) **-schiff** *n* cooling copper, tray, or pan, cooling tank, cooler **-schlange** *f* cooling coil, spiral condensing tube or pipe, condenser coil, condensing coil **-schlitz** *m* ventilating duct **-schrank** *m* refrigerator **-schrankblende** *f* refrigerator screen **-sicke** *f* cooling fold **-sieb** *n* hopper cooler, cooling sieve **-sole** *f* cooling liquid (brine) **-spirale** *f* cooling coil **-stock** *m* cooler, cooling floor

Kühlstoff *m* coolant **-austrittstemperatur** *f* coolant exit temperature **-behälter** *m* coolant tank reservoir **-pumpe** *f* coolant pump **-raum** *m* coolant jacket **-temperaturmesser** *m* coolant temperature gauge

Kühl-substanz *f* cooling agent **-system** *n* cooling system

Kühl-teich *m* cooling pond or reservoir **-temperatur** *f* annealing point **-tisch** *m* cooling table **-truhe** *f* low temperature cooling chest **-turm** *m* cooling tower

Kühlung *f* radiation, cooling, refrigeration **~ des Heißdampfes** desuperheating **~ durch Kompression** compression refrigeration **~ durch Rückbelüftung** reverse-flow cooling **der zur ~ dienende aerodynamische Widerstandsanteil** cooling drag **~ durch Zerstäubung** spray cooling

Kühlungsart (methode) *f* cooling system or method

Kühlungskoeffizient *m* cooling coefficient **~ bei konstanter Entropie** isentropic cooling coefficient

Kühlungskreis *m* coolant loop

Kühlungsöl für Stopfbüchse gland oil

Kühlungssystem *n* cooling system or method, coolant

Kühl-ventilator *m* cooling fan **-verfahren** *n* cooling method **-verlustbeiwert** *m* blade or bucket loss factor **-verlustleistung** *f* cooling-power loss **-vermögen der Kühlanlage** refrigerator capacity **-vitrine** *f* refrigerated display case **-vorrichtung** *f* refrigerator, cooling or chilling device, cooling jig **-wagen** *m* refrigerator car or truck **-walze** *f* cooling roller **-wanne** *f* cooler box, cooling tube

Kühlwasser *n* cooling water, water for radiator **-abfluß** *m* cooling water outlet **-ablaßhahn** *m* cooling water drain cock **-ablauf** *m* cooling-water discharge **-ableitung** *f* cooling-water discharge pipe

Kühlwasseranschluß *m* cooling water connection **-stutzen** *m* cooling water flange

Kühlwasser-anzeiger *m* temperature gauge, calorimeter **-austritt** *m* cooling-or circulating-water outlet **-behälter** *m* cooling-water tank **-beschaffung** *f* cooling-water supply **-einfüllstutzen** *m* cooling water filling neck

Kühlwassereinrichtung *f* coolant equipment **~ für Drehbänke** wet turning attachment

Kühlwasser-eintritt *m* cooling or circulating water inlet **-fernthermometer** *n* cooling water remote thermometer, heat gauge (Traktoren) **-heizgerät** *n* heating apparatus for cooling system **-hochbehälter** *m* upper cooling-water tank **-kasten** *m* cooling-water tank **-kontrollschalter** *m* cooling-water safety switch **-kreislauf** *m* cooling-water circulation **-leitung** *f* cooling-water pipe line **-mangel** *m* cooling water shortage

Kühlwassermantel *m* water jacket **~ mit Kesselsteinablagerung** furred cylinder jacket

Kühlwasser-menge *f* cooling water quantity **-pumpe** *f* water-circulating pump, cooling-water pump **-raumdeckel** *m* cooling jacket cover **-regler** *m* thermostat **-relais** *n* cooling water relay **-rohr** *n*, **-rohrleitung** *f* cooling-water pipe or line **-schauglas** *n* cooling water sight glass **-tank** (Auto) radiator header tank **-teich** *m* cooling pond **-thermometer** *n* water thermometer **-thermostat** *m* cooling water thermostat **-umlauf** *m* cooling-water circulation **-umlaufpumpe** *f* coolant circulation pump

Kühlwasser-verbrauch *m* cooling-water consumption **-verbindungsschlauch** *m* radiator water hose **-verlust** *m* loss in cooling water **-verteilerrohr** *n* cooling water manifold **-vorwärmer** *m* cooling water preheater **-wärme** *f* heat in cooling water **-wärmegrad** *m* temperature of the cooling water **-wärmegradmesser** *m* cooling-water thermometer **-zufluß** *m*, **-zulauf** *m*, **-zuleitung** *f* cooling-water feed pipe or supply

Kühl-werk *n* cooling tower, cooler, refrigerating plant, cold storage **-wirkung** *f* chilling or cooling effect, refrigerating effect **-zeit** *f* cooling time

Kühlzelle *f* cooling cell **begehbare ~** walk-in cooler

Kühlzug *m* cooling train

Kühlzweck *m*, **für Kühlzwecke aufgewendeter Leistungsanteil** cooling power loss

Kuhschwanz *m* fag end (of rope)

Küken *n* key or plug of a stopcock, stopcock, chick, switching valve **-anpressung** *f* plug contact pressure **-feder** *f* gas plug spring **-hebel** *m* valve lever

Külbchen *n* ball, piece, lump (glass mfg.), parison (glass mfg.)

Külbel *m* parison (glass mfg.), partly formed bottle **-stich** *m* small protuberance (on glassware)

kulieren to sink the loops (textiles)

Kulierware *f* hosiery

Kulisse *f* coulisse, link, rocker arm, crank (sliding block), detent, gate, backdrop **~ des Gashebels** throttle gate

Kulissen-aufblendung *f* side-curtain fade-in **-bewegung** *f* crank motion **-bohrung** *f* bore-running fit **-führung** *f* connecting link guide, guide bar bracket **-hebel** *m* slotted lever, rocker arm, cam lever **-lager** *n* link bracket **-lagerung** *f* lever bearing **-platte** *f* gear change gate, guide plate

Kulissen-regler *m* sliding block governor **-rolle** *f* slot roll **-schaltung** *f* selective system of gear shifting, gate change **-schleif- und Kopiermaschine** *f* link-grinding and copying machine **-schütz** *m* paddle valve **-stein** *m* sliding block **-stellung** *f* sliding block position **-steuerung** *f* link motion, distributing-valve motion **-wähler** *m* Ericsson selector

Kullmann-Verfahren *n* Kullmann's communication system

Kulm *m* **culm**

Kulminations-höhe *f* altitude or height at culmination **-punkt** *m* culmination point

kulminieren to culminate

Kulmkalk *m* carboniferous limestone

Kultivator *m* cultivator **-zinke** *f* cultivator tooth

kultivieren to cultivate

Kultivierung *f* cultivation

Kultur *f* culture, civilization, cultivation, tilling, growing, breeding, rearing **-film** *m* cultural or educational film **-land** *n* cultivated ground **-landmarken** *pl* culture (man-made landmarks) **-technik** *f* improvement of land for cultivation by means of irrigation, drainage, or soil conservation **-techniker** *m* engineer for drainage, agricultural expert

Kumaronharz *n* coumarone resin

Kumme *f* bowl

Kummet *n* horse collar **-holz** *n* hame

Kumol *n* cumene

Kümpel-arbeit *f* dishing **-blech** *n* flanged plate

kümpeln to flange

Kümpeln *n* deep drawing (aluminum mfg.)

Kümpelpresse *f* flanging press

Kümpelstempel *m* punch die

Kümpelungstiefe *f* cupping or dishing depth

Kumpen *m* bowl

Kumteisen *n* iron hame

Kumulation *f* cumulation

kumulativ cumulative **-e Anregung** cumulative excitation

kumulieren to accumulate

Kumulonimbus *m* cumulonimbus

Kumulus *m* cumulus cloud **-bildung** *f* cumulus formation **-förmig** cumuliform **-wolke** *f* cumulus cloud

kündbar terminable

Kunde *m* client, customer

Kunde *f* news, intelligence, knowledge, information, science

Kunden-dienst *m* customer or after-sales or post-sales service **-dienstabteilung** *f* service department **-dienstrücksprachen** *pl* service calls **-gießerei** *f* jobbing foundry **-guß** *m* jobbings **-kartei** *f* customers card index **-netzdienst** *m* network of service stations

Kundgabe *f* notification, announcement

kundgeben to notify, publish (notice), advertise, announce, proclaim

Kundgebung *f* demonstration

kündigen to give notice or warning

Kündigung *f* notice, warning, cancellation, denunciation (of a treaty), termination ~ **eines Fernsprechanschlusses** cancellation of a subscriber's contract

Kündigungs-frist *f* period of notice of termination (*e.g.*, of a contract) **-grund** *m* ground for dismissal **-recht** *n* right to dismiss

Kundschaft *f* scouting, reconnoitering, reconnaissance, clientele, clients, customers, following, goodwill

Kundschafter *m* scout, spy **-dienst** *m* scouting service

künftig henceforth, in the future

Kunst *f* art, skill, trade, profession **-antenne** *f* dummy (phantom) antenna **-ausdruck** *m* technical term, art term **-bau** *m* (man-made) structure **-baumwolle** *f* artificial cotton **-benzin** *n* synthetic gasoline **-bronze** *f* art bronze **-drechsler** *m* fancy-goods turner **-druck** *m* (fine) art-print(ing) **-druckkarton** *m* body board **-druckpapier** *n* art paper, enameled or chromo paper

Künstelei *f* artificial method

Kunst-faser *f* synthetic fiber **-faserzellstoff** *m* artificial-fiber cellulose **-fertig** skillful **-fertigkeit** *f* workmanship, art, artifice, technique **-fliegen** *n* acrobatic or stunt flying **-flieger** *m* acrobatic pilot

Kunstflug *m* stunt or trick flying, acrobatics, acrobatic flight, stunt ~ **in niedriger Höhe** low acrobatics ~ **mit Raucherzeugung** acrobatics with streamers of smoke ~ **der hohen Schule** advanced acrobatics ~ **im Verband** acrobatics in formation ~ **ausführen** to carry out acrobatics

Kunstflug-eigenschaften *pl* acrobatic qualities **-erprobung** *f* acrobatic-flying trial **-figur** *f* stunt-flying figure, acrobatic maneuver **-lage** *f* acrobatic altitude **-meister** *m* acrobatic champion or expert **-staffel** *f* acrobatic squadron

kunstflug-tauglich acrobatic **-tauglichkeit** *f* fitness for stunt flying **-typ** *m* aircraft used for acrobatic training **-übungseinsitzer** *m* acrobatic-training single-seater **-vorführung** *f* acrobatic display **-wettbewerb** *m* acrobatic contest **-zeug** *n* acrobatic plane

Kunstfolienkondensator *m* synthetic foil capacitor

Kunstgewerbe *n* applied art

kunstgewerblich of applied art **-e Metallarbeiten** metalwork of applied art **-e Werkstätte** workshop for industrial art

Kunst-gießerei *f* art(istic) foundry, casting of works of art **-griff** *m* expedient, trick, artifice, mechanical dodge or knack **-guß** *m* art casting **-handwerk** *n* artistic handicrafts

Kunstharz *n* artificial or synthetic resin plastic **-basis** *f* artifical resin basis **-bindemittel** *n* synthetic or artifical resin cement **-bindung** *f* bakelite-bonded **-boden** *m* plastic floor **-erzeugnis** *n* synthetic resin product **-industrie** *f* plastics industry

Kunstharz-lack *m* synthetic resin varnish **-lager** *n* synthetic resin bearing **-leim** *m* synthetic-resin cement, synthetic resin glue **-preßholz** *n* compregnated laminated wood **-preßstoff** *m* synthetic-plastic material, synthetic plastics, synthetic molding resin **-spritzform** *f* injection mold for plastic material **-wolle** *f* resin wool

Kunst-holz *n* artificial or imitation wood **-horn** *n* artificial horn, celluloid **-kautschuk** *m* synthetic rubber **-korund** *m* aluminous abrasive, fused alumina **-kreuz** *n* cross lever (min.) **-leder** *n* artificial or imitation leather, leatherette, art leather **-lederpapier** *n* leatherette **-lederrohstoff** *m* artificial leather base **-leitung** *f* artificial line, cable, or circuit, balancing or equalizing network

Künstler *m* artist **-farbe** *f* artist's paint **-ölfarben** *pl* oil-colors for artists **-steinzeichnung** *f* lithographic design

künstlerisch artistic

künstlich artificial, synthetic, dummy ~ **herstellen** to synthesize ~ **geschaffener Kennwert** synthetic index **-e Alterung** precipitation heat-treatment, artificial aging **-e Antenne** artificial antenna, mute, dummy, or phantom antenna **-e Atmung** artificial respiration **-e Beleuchtung** artificial lighting **-es Dielektrikum** *n* artificial dielectric **-es Echo** feather

künstlich -e Gründung artificial foundation **-es**

Gummi synthetic rubber **-er Horizont** absolute inclinometer, artificial horizon **-er Kernzerfall** artificial nuclear disintegration **-er Korund** alundum, aluminox, aloxite **-e Leitung** *f* artificial line or circuit, line simulator

künstlich-er Nebel screening smoke **-es Ohr** dummy ear **-e Pozzolanerde** artificial pozzolana **-e Radioaktivität** induced or artificial radioactivity **-e Seismen** artificial earthquakes **-e Verdichtung von Erdboden** soil compaction **-er Zug** forced or artificial draft **-e Zündung** controlled ignition

Kunstlicht *n* artificial light **-aufnahme** *f* photograph taken by artificial light **-filter** *n* artificial light screen

Kunst-masse *f* plastic material, synthetic compound **-mühle** *f* merchant mill **-öl** *n* artificial crude oil **-pappe** *f* millboard **-produkt** *n* synthetic or artificial product, syntetic, plastic

Kunstschaltung *f* equivalent circuit trick circuitry ~ (Sendekunstschaltung) transmission-balancing network

Kunst-schaummasse *f* artificial foam material **-schmiedestück** *n* artistic forged piece **-schweißung** *f* (trick) welding

Kunstseide *f* imitation silk, rayon **-samt** *m* rayon velvet **-verarbeitung** *f* rayon-yarn processing

Kunst-spinnfaser *f* staple fiber **-stein** *m* artificial stone

Kunststoff *m* plastic or synthetic resin, synthetic or artificial product, synthetic, plastic **-ausrüstung** *f* plastic equipment **-beschichtetes Papier** plastic-coated paper **-bezug** *m* synthetic material **-folie** *f* plastics foil **-folienkondensator** *m* plastic foil capacitor **-herstellung** *f* manufacture of plastics

Kunststoff-presse *f* molding press **-rad** *n* plastic gear **-schaumstoffartikel** *m* expanded plastics material **-schweißverfahren** *n* plastic welding technique **-spritzgerät** *n* spraying equipment for plastics **-suspension** *f* plastics suspension **-überzug** *m* plastic coating

Kunst-straße *f* causeway **-tischlerei** *f* cabinet-making, cabinetwork, art-furniture making **-tonwaren** *pl* terra cotta **-verlag** *m* art publishers **-verlagsanstalt** *f* art-publishing establishment **-werk** *n* work of art **-werkerhütte** *f* specialist foundry of mechanics **-wolle** *f* artificial or remanufactured wool, shoddy (wool)

Kuoxam *n* cellulose solution in cuprammonium hydroxide, cuprammonium solution

Küpe *f* drum for steaming, vat, dyeing vat, boiler, copper **durchgehende** ~ decomposing vat

Kupellation *f* cupellation

Kupelle *f* cupel

kupellieren to cupel

Kupfer *n* copper ~ **polen** to pole copper ~ **schwarz machen** to get coarse copper **hammergares** ~ refined- or tough-pitch copper **harzsaures** ~ copper resinate **leinölsaures** ~ copper linoleate **rohgares** ~ first-refined copper **übergares** ~ dry or underpoled copper

Kupfer-abfall *m* waste copper **-ammoniat** *n* copper ammoniate **-antimonglanz** *m* chalcostibite **-arseniat** *n* copper arsenate **-arsenit** *n* copper arsenite, cupric arsenite **-asbest** *m* copper asbestos **-asbestdichtung** *f* copper-asbestos gasket **-asche** *f* copper ashes, copper scale **-ätzplatte** *f* copperplate for photogravure **-aufwand** *m* amount of copper used **-aushärtung** *f* precipitation of excess copper **-autotypieätzung** *f* halftone engraving on copper **-autunit** *m* cuproautunite **-azetylen** *n* copper acetylide

Kupfer-backe *f* copper jaw socket **-bad** *n* copper bath **-band** *n* copper tape or band **-barre** *f* copper bar or ingot **-bergwerk** *n* copper mine **-beschlag** *m* copper fitting **-bessemerei** *f* copper-converting plant

Kupfer-blatt *n* copper foil **-blau** *n* azurite, blue verditer **-blech** *n* copper sheet or plate, copper foil, sheet copper **-blei** *n* copper-lead alloy **-bleiglanz** *m* alisonite **-bleivitriol** *n* linarite **-blende** *f* tennantite **-blöckchen** *n* copper ingot **-blüte** *f* copper bloom, capillary red oxide of copper, chalcotrichite, cuprite **-braun** *n* tile or ferruginous red oxide of copper **-bromür** *n* cuprous bromide **-bügel** *m* copper frame

Kupfer-chlorid *n* proto-chloride of copper, cupric chloride **-chlorür** *n* hemi-chloride of copper, cuprous chloride **-dämpfung** *f* copper damping **-dichtring** *m* copper gasket **-dichtung** *f* copper packing, copper gasket **-dorn** *m* slag from liquated copper

Kupferdraht *m* copper wire **-geflecht** *n* copper mesh **-netz** *n* copper gauze

Kupferdrehspäne *pl* copper turnings

Kupferdruck *m* rotogravure **-papier** *n* etching paper **-platte** *f* copperplate **-verfahren** *n* copperplate printing

Kupfereinwirkung *f* influence of copper

Kupfereisen-kies *m* copper and iron pyrites **-vitriol** *n* copper iron sulfate

kupferempfindlich sensitive to copper

Kupfer-element *n* copper-zinc cell **-erz** *n* copper ore **-erzprobe** *f* assay of copper ore **-fahlerz** *n* tetrahedrite, gray-copper ore **-farbe** *f* copper color **-federerz** *n* plush copper, copper bloom **-feilicht** *n* copper filings **-folie** *f* sheet copper foils **-formiat** *n* copper formate, cupric formate **-frischofen** *m* copper finery **-führend** cupriferous, copper-bearing **-funken** *m* copper spark

Kupfer-garherd *m* copper furnace **-garmachen** *n* copper refining **-garschlacke** *f* copper slag **-gaze** *f* copper gauze **-gehalt** *m* copper content **-gewebe** *n* copper mesh, copper gauze **-gewebebürste** *f* copper-gauze brush **-gewicht** *n* copper weight **-gewinnung** *f* extraction of copper **-gießerei** *f* copper foundry **-glanz** *m* copper glance, chalcocite **-glas** *n* copper glance, copper sulfide, vitreous copper, cuprite **-glimmer** *m* micaceous copper **-glühspan** *m* copper scale **-gold** *n* Mannheim gold **-granalien** *pl* copper granules, shot copper **-grün** *n* copper green, verdigris, chrysocolla **-guß** *m* cast copper

Kupfer-haarlitzen *pl* hair copper wires **-halogenid** *n* cuprous halide

kupferhaltig copper-bearing, cupriferous **-es Vitriol** cupreous vitriol

Kupfer-hammer *m* copper hammer **-hammerschlag** *m* copper scale **-haut** *f* copper sheathing **-heftung** *f* copper setting **-heizschlangen** *pl* copper heating coils **-hochofen** *m* copper blast furnace **-hornerz** *n* copper horn ore **-hülse** *f* copper jointing sleeve **-hütte** *f* copper-smelting plant, copper smeltery **-hydrat** *n* copper hydroxide **-hydroxyd** *n* copper hydroxide, cupric hydroxide **-hydroxydul** *n* cuprous hydroxide

kupferig cupreous, cupriferous, coppery

Kupfer-indigo *m* covellite, indigo copper **-jodid** *n* copper iodide, cupric iodide **-jodür** *n* cuprous iodide **-kaliumchlorat** *n* copper potassium chlorate **-kaliumchlorid** *n* copper potassium chloride **-kalk** *m* copper oxide, copper calx **-kapseln** *pl* copper dishes **-karbonat** *n* copper carbonate **-kies** *m* copper pyrites, chalcopyrite, yellow-copper ore, iron copper sulfide **-klotz** *m* copper block **-kohle** *f* coppered carbon **-könig** *m* copper regulus **-konus** *m* copper cone **-konzentrat** *n* copper concentrate

Kupfer-lackdraht *m* enamel copper wire **-lahn** *m* copper tinsel **-lasur** *f* azurite **-lauge** *f* copper solution **-laugung** *f* copper leaching **-legierung** *f* copper alloy **-leitfähigkeitsnormal** *n* copper-conductivity standard **-leitungsdraht** *m* copper wire **-litze** *f* copper-stranded wire **-lösung** *f* copper solution **-lot** *n* copper solder **-mangan** *n* cupromanganese

Kupfermantel *m* copper collar, jacket, or sheath, copper head or tube **~ eines Verzögerungsrelais** copper head or tube **Draht mit ~** Dumet wire **mit einem ~ versehen** copper-jacketed

Kupfermantel-draht *m* copper-clad wire, Dumet wire **-relais** *n* coppered relay, copper-jacketed relay

kupfern to treat with copper, copper

Kupfern *n* sheathing with copper

kupfern (of) copper **-er Kabelschuh zum Anlöten** copper soldering lug

Kupfernickel *m* copper-nickel alloy **-feinstein** *m* copper-nickel (converter) matte **-legierung** *f* copper nickel alloy **-röhren** *pl* cupro-nickel tubes **-rohstein** *m* copper-nickel (blast-furnace) matte

Kupfer-niederschlag *m* copper deposit, copper precipitate **-niet** *m* copper rivet **-oxyd** *n* copper oxide, cupric oxide **-oxydammoniak** *n* ammoniacal copper oxide **-oxydgleichrichter** *m* copper oxide rectifier **-oxydhydrat** *n* cupric hydroxide **-oxydsalz** *n* cupric salt **-oxydsilikat** *n* cupric silicate

Kupferoxydul *n* cuprous oxide **-gleichrichter** *m* copper-oxide rectifier **-hydrat** *n* cuprous hydroxide **-silikat** *n* cuprous silicate **-zelle** *f* copper oxide cell

Kupfer-oxydverbindung *f* cupric compound **-plastikbad** *n* galvanoplastic copper bath **-plättchen** *n* copper plate **-platte** *f* copper plate **-plattieren** to copperplate **-pol** *m* copper pole **-prägerei** *f* copper embossing **-probe** *f* copper assay **-pyrit** *m* iron copper sulfide, chalcopyrite **-raffination** *f* copper refining **-raffinerie** *f* copper refinery, copper-refining plant **-rauch** *m* copper smoke, copper fumes, white vitriol **-rayon** *n* cuprammonium rayon

kupferreich high-copper, rich in copper **-er Stein** high-grade copper matte

Kupfer-reinigung *f* copper refining **-rhodanid** *n* copper thiocyanate, cupric thiocyanate **-rhodanür** *n* cuprous thiocyanate **-ring** *m* copper collar **-ringrelais** *n* copper-collar relay **-rohr** *n* copper tube, pipe, or sleeve **-röhrenverbindung** *f* copper sleeve joint, twisted sleeve joint **-rohstein** *m* raw copper matte **-rosette** *f* cake of rose copper **-rost** *m* copper rust, verdigris **-rot** *n* red copper, red copper ore, cuprite, copper color, copper red

Kupfer-salizylat *n* copper salicylate, cupric salicylate **-samterz** *n* velvet copper ore, cyanotrichite **-säure** *f* cupric acid **-schachtofen** *m* copper blast furnace **-schaum** *m* copper scum, tyrolite **-schicht** *f* copper coating **-schlag** *m* copper scale **-schlange** *f* copper coil **-schmied** *m* copper-smith

Kupfer-schrott *m* copper scrap **-schwamm** *m* copper sponge **-schwärze** *f* melaconite **-schwefel** *m* copper sulfide **-seide** *f* cuprammonium silk **-seil** *n* stranded copper **-silberglanz** *m* stromeyerite **-sinter** *m* copper scale, copper pyrites **-smaragd** *m* emerald copper, dioptase **-sorte** *f* grade of copper **-spat** *m* malachite **-spritzgußlegierung** *f* copper die casting alloy **-stecher** *m* copperplate engraver

Kupferstein *m* copper matte or metal **erster ~** coarse copper metal **weißer ~** (relating to copper) white metal

Kupfer-stich *m* copperplate engraving **-stift** *m* caustic pencil of copper sulfate **-stil** *m* copper cable **-streckseide** *f* Lilienfeld silk **-streifen** *m* copper strip **-sulfid** *n* copper sulfide, cupric sulfide **-sulfür** *n* cuprous sulfide **-tiefdruck** *m* copper-plate printing rotogravure, photogravure **-trommel** *f* copper cylinder **-überzug** *m* copper coat, copper coating, copper plating

Kupfer- und Glimmerblitzableiter *m* copper-block protector or lightning rod

Kupfer-uranglimmer *m* torbernite **-verbindungshülse** *f* copper jointing sleeve **-verhüttung** *f* copper smelting, metallurgy of copper **-verlust** *m* copper loss

Kupfervitriol *n* blue vitriol, copper sulfate **mit ~ tränken** to boucherize

Kupfer-vorlegierungen *pl* copper master alloys **-walzwerk** *n* copper rolling mill **-wasser** *n* copperas **-wasserstoff** *m* copper hydride **-werk** *n* copper plant **-wirkungsgrad** *m* copper efficiency **-wismuterz** *n* klaprotholite, wittichemite **-wismutglanz** *m* emplectite

Kupfer-zahl *f* copper number, copper value **-zinkelement** *n* copper-zinc cell **-zippeit** *m* cuprozippeite **-zitrat** *n* copper citrate, cupric citrate **-zyanid** *n* copper cyanide, cupric cyanide **-zyanür** *n* cuprous cyanide

kupfrig coppery

Kupholit *m* prehnite

kupieren to cut, sever

Kupolofen *m* cupola furnace **~ mit Bodenklappe** drop-bottom cupola **~ mit erweitertem Herd** reservoir cupola, tank cupola, compound cupola

Kupolofen-abbrand *m* melting loss **-anlage** *f* cupola installation **-ausfütterung** *f* cupola lining **-auskleidung** *f* cupola lining **-bediener** *m* cupola keeper **-begichtung** *f* cupola charging **-begichtungskatze** *f* cupola charging crane **-betrieb** *m* cupola operation, cupola practice **-eisen** *n* cupola metal

Kupolofen-führung *f* cupla practice **-gattierung** *f* cupola mixture **-gebläse** *n* cupola blower **-gichtgas** *n* waste top gas of a cupola furnace **-guß** *m* casting from the cupola **-herd** *m* cupola hearth **-mantel** *m* cupola shell, cupola mantle **-rinne** *f* cupola spout

Kupolofen-schacht *m* cupola shaft, cupola stack, body of a cupola **-schlacke** *f* cupola slag **-schmelzen** *n* cupola melting **-schmelzer** *m* cupola tenter **-tragsäule** *f* cupola leg, supporting column of cupola **-temperguß** *m* cupola malleable iron **-verfahren** *n* cupola process

Kupolofenvorherd *m* cupola receiver, cupola settler **beheizter ~** cupola forehearth

Kupon *m* coupon

Kuppe *f* round hilltop, knoll, prominence, dome, arch, cone, globe, cupola, cusp, crest, peak, meniscus

Kuppel *f* cupola, dome, spherical vault, reverberating roof **~ für astronomische Navigation** astrodome **~ aus durchsichtigem Werkstoff** transparent cupola

Kuppel-achse *f* coupled axle **-artig** arched **-bau** *m* dome construction **-beleuchtung** *f* dome illumination **-bolzen** *m* drag bolt, knuckle pin **-fassung** *f* globe mounting **-feder** *f* spring coupling key **-förmig** cupola-shaped **-flansch** *m* coupling flange **-gewölbe** *n* arch roof, arched dome **-haken** *m* coupling or drag hook **-halle** *f* dome

kuppelieren to cupel

Kuppel-keil *m* spring coupling catch **-klaue** *f* coupler jaw **-klinke** *f* spring coupling catch **-kompaß** *m* bell compaß **-konus** *m* clutch taper **-kopf** *m* (für Anhängerschlauch) connection for trailer hose **-kranz** *m* dome ring **-leitung** *f* interconnecting feeder, interconnector **-magnet** *n* coupling magnet **-maschine** *f* (piece-end) sewing machine **-mutter** *f* coupling nut

kuppeln to clutch, couple, connect, attach, engage, hitch, interlock, gang, join, unite

Kuppel-ofen *m* cupola furnace **-produkte** *pl* coupled products

Kuppelrad *n* coupled wheel **verschiebbares ~** coupled wheel with lateral play

Kuppel-radsatz *m* coupled wheel set **-relais** *n* coupling relay **-schalter** *m* coupling switch, section switch **-schlauch** *m* coupling hose **-spindel** *f* coupling spindle **-spule** *f* coupling coil, brake solenoid **-spurlager** *n* ball-race adjuster ring **-stange** *f* double pole (wide spread), tie rod, coupling rod **-strom** *m* control current (teleph.) **-stück** *n* coupling piece **-teil** *m* coupling element

Kuppelung *f* coupling, engaging-gear clutch

Kuppel-vorrichtung *f* coupling device **-wellenstumpf** *m* coupling shaft end **-wort** *n* hyphened word **-zapfen** *m* wobbler (mach.)

Kuppler *m* coupler, shunter

Kupplung *f* coupling, clutch, coupler, attachment, axle bearing, turn flux, linkage, flux turns **~ für den Selbstgang des Rundtisches** rotary-attachment feed clutch **~ zur Verbindung zweier Wellenenden** coupling for abutting shafts **ausrückbare ~** disengaging coupling, clutch, shifting coupling **bewegliche ~** flexible coupling **~ einbinden** to refit the coupling **~ einschalten** to engage the clutch **elastische ~** flexible coupling, elastic or resilient coupling **feste ~** solid coupling **geteilte ~** split coupling **hydraulische ~** hydraulic clutch

Kupplung, längsbewegliche ~ expansion coupling **lösbare ~** shifting coupling, cutoff coupling, disengaging coupling **magnetische ~** magnetic clutch or coupling **nachgiebige ~** flexible or elastic coupling **optimale ~** optimum or critical coupling **schaltbare ~** clutch coupling, clutch **selbsteinrückende ~** self-actuating clutch **starre ~** stationary or fixed coupling **ungeteilte ~** solid coupling

Kupplungs-anschluß *m* coupling head **-antrieb** *m* clutch drive **-armkreuz** *n* clutch spider **-auslösewelle** *f* clutch-withdrawal shaft **-ausrücker** *m* clutch shifter, clutch operator

Kupplungsausrück-gabel *f* withdrawal finger **-hebel** *m* clutch-withdrawal lever **-muffe** *f* clutch-release sleeve **-vorrichtung** *f* unclutching device **-welle** *f* clutch disengaging shaft, clutch release shaft

Kupplungs-bedienung *f* clutch operation **-belag** *m* coupling lining, clutch facing **-betätigung** *f* clutch operation **-bolzen** *m* coupling pin **-bremse** *f* clutch stop **-bremsfeder** *f* clutch brake spring **-buchse** *f* muff coupling **-daumen** *m* clutch cam **-deckel** *m* clutch cover **-dose** *f* microphone socket (tape rec.), connector socket **-druckfeder** *f* release spring **-druckplatte** *f* clutch pressure plate, pressure plate

Kupplungs-einrichtung *f* clutching device **-expansionsring** *m* clutch spreader **-feder** *f* thrust spring (clutch), clutch spring **-finger** *m* clutch finger **-flansch** *m* coupling flange **-fliehgewicht** *n* clutch weight **-fußhebel** *m* clutch pedal **-fußhebelwelle** *f* clutch pedal shaft **-futter** *n* clutch lining **-gabel** *f* clutch fork **-gehäuse** *n* clutch housing **-gelenk** *n* clutch coupling **-gestänge** *n* clutch operating device, clutch rods or linkage **-glied** *n* coupler link **-glocke** *f* coupling cage, clutch housing

Kupplungs-hahn *m* coupling dog **-hälfte** *f* clutch half, coupling half

Kupplungshälften *pl*, **aufgezogene ~** shrunk-on coupling halves

Kupplungs-handhebel *m* clutch hand lever **-hauptfeder** *f* pressure spring **-hebel** *m* clutch pedal, coupling lever, chain lever, clutch lever **-hebelschalter** *m* clutch-lever shifter **-hülse** *f* coupling sleeve

Kupplungs-kasten *m* (gun) junction box, socket (electr.) **-kegel** *m* clutch cone **-kette** *f* coupling chain **-kettenrad** *n* clutch sprocket wheel **-klaue** *f* clutch dogs **-klemme** *f* coupling terminal **-knopf** *m* (Fernschreiber) switch knob **-konus** *m* clutch cone **-kopf** *m* hose coupling, coupling head **-körper** *m* clutch **-kraft** *f* connection strength **-kreuz** *n* clutch

Kupplungs-lager *n* (radial) clutch bearing **-lamelle** *f* clutch disk **-leder** *n* clutch leather **-lenkgetriebe** *n* steering coupling **-magnet** *m* clutch magnet **-maul** *n* coupling mouth **-motor** *m* case motor **-muffe** *f* coupling box, couplings, clutch-coupling sleeve **-muffenführung** *f* clutch sleeve guide **-nabe** *f* clutch hub **-nachstellung** *f* clutch adjustment **-pedal** *n* clutch pedal **-pedalhebel** *m* clutch-pedal lever **-platte** *f* clutch plate **-rad** *n* coupling wheel, clutch ring or wheel

Kupplungsring *m* clutch ring **~ für den Fräsdorn** clutch-drive collar

Kupplungs-schalter *m* clutch shifter, clutch operator **-schalterbock** *m* clutch-shifter stand **-scheibe** *f* thrust plate (clutch), clutch disk

-scheibenbelag *m* clutch-disk lining **-schieber** *m* clutch slide **-schlupf** *m* slip in the coupling **-schlüssel** *m* coupling wrench **-schnapper** *m* clutch-driven impulse **-schutz** *m* clutch guard **-speiseleitung** *f* coupling supply line **-spindel** *f* clutch shaft **-spule** *f* coupler

Kupplungs-stange *f* coupling rod, drag bar, treadle rod **-stangenfeder** *f* drag spring **-stecker** *m* coupling plug **-strebe** *f* aileron connecting strut **-stück** *n* coupling, fitting

Kupplungsteil *m* clutch member **~ Außengewinde** male coupling **~ mit Innengewinde** female coupling

Kupplungs-tritt *m* clutch pedal **-verriegelung** *f* clutch interlock **-vorrichtung** *f* coupling arrangement **-welle** *f* clutch spindle, clutch shaft, partial wave **-zapfen** *m* wobbler (mach.)

Kupri-chlorid *n* cupric chloride **-verbindung** *f* cupric compound

Kuprit *m* red oxide of copper, red copper (ore), tile ore

Kupro-chlorid *n* cuprous chloride **-dekopierbad** *n* cuprous pickling bath **-mangan** *n* cupromanganese

Kupronelement *n* copper oxide cell, cuprous oxide cell, cupron cell

Kupro-oxyd *n* cuprous oxide **-salz** *n* cuprous salt **-verbindung** *f* cuprous compound

Kupüre *f* reduction

Kuratorium (Verwaltungsrat) board of administration or management

Kurbel *f* crank, winch, (crank) handle **die ~ aufkeilen** to key on the crank **die ~ aufpressen** to force the crank by pressure **umlegbare ~** folding crank **mit einer ~ versehen** cranked **gegenläufige Kurbeln** opposite cranks

Kurbel-achse *f* crank axle, crankshaft **-andrehvorrichtung** *f*, **-anlasser** *m* crank starter **-antenne** *f* reel antenna, trailing-wire antenna **-antrieb** *m* crank drive **-arm** *m* crank web, crank arm **-ausschalter** *m* lever switch **-betrieb** *m* motion of crank **-blatt** *n* crank disk, web **-blechtafelschere** *f* guillotine shear **-bewegung** *f* crank motion **-bohrer** *m* bit stock **-bolzen** *m* crank bolt

Kurbel-drehbank *f* crank-turning lathe **-drehung** *f* rotation of crank **-drehwinkel** *m* angle of crank rotation **-druck** *m* crank pressure **-dynamo** *m* hand generator

Kurbelei *f* machine embroidery or stitching

Kurbel-fenster *n* drop window **-fensterscheibe** *f* crank-operated window pane **-folge** *f* succession of cranks

Kurbelgehäuse *n* crank chamber, crankcase, crank guard **-bohrung** *f* crankcase gallery **-deckel** *m* crankcase cover **-entlüfter** *m* crankcase breather **-entlüftung** *f* crankcase breather pipe **-oberteil** *m* top of crankcase **-öl** *n* crankcase oil **-schmierölverdünnung** *f* crankcase dilution

Kurbelgehäuseteil *m* crankcase section **mittlerer ~ beim Doppelsternmotor** main crankcase section **vorderer ~** front crankcase section

Kurbelgehäuse-unterteil *m* bottom of crankcase **-zwischenwand** *f* diaphragm plate of the crankcase

Kurbelgestänge *n* crank arragement

Kurbelgetriebe *n* crank gear, crank drive **-schwungradpumpe** *f* crank and flywheel pump

Kurbel-griff *m* crankpin, crank handle, handle grip **-griffrohr** *n* crank handle tube **-haltehaken** *m* holding hook **-haspel** *f* crank windlass **-heft** *n* hand grip **-hub** *m* stroke of crank **-induktivität** *f* switch inductance box

Kurbelinduktor *m* hand generator, magneto (generator) **dreilamelliger ~** three-bar magneto

Kurbelkasten *m* crankcase, crank chamber; (Kurbelkammer *f*) crankcase supercharger **-explosion** *f* crankcase explosion **-gebläse** *n* crankcase supercharger **-öl** *n* crankcase oil **-spülung** *f* crankcase scavenging **-vorverdichter** *m* crankcase supercharger

Kurbel-klaue *f* crank claw **-kondensator** *m* variable (crank) condenser, switch capacitance box **-kopf** *m* crank end **-kröpfung** *f* cranked portion of shaft, crank throw, crank (of a shaft)

Kurbellager *n* crankshaft or crankpin bearing **~ des Hauptpleuels** big end bearing

Kurbel-lagerbügel *m* crankshaft bearing cover **-lochdeckel** *m* crankshaft cover **-mast** *m* telescopic mast, extension mast

kurbeln to crank

Kurbelpresse *f* crank press **~ mit schrägstellbarem Körper** inclinable single-crank power press

Kurbel-öse *f* crank rod eyelet **-pumpe** *f* reciprocating pump **-rad** *n* handwheel **-radantrieb** *m* crank wheel drive **-riegel** *m* crank latch **-schaft** *m* crankshaft **-schalter** *m* radial arm switch, lever switch **-scheibe** *f* crank disk, crank sheave, cam **-schenkel** *m* crank web **-schiene** *f* crank lever **-schlag** *m* knocking in the crank **-schleife** *f* crank guide, crankslide oscillator **-schutzhaube** *f* crank guard **-schwinge** *f* sliding pin drive, sliding block, throttle crank

kurbelseitiges Kolbenende *n* skirt end of a piston

Kurbel-stange *f* connecting rod **-stein** *m* crank block **-stellung** *f* position of crank, crank angle **-stoßbohrmaschine** *f* crank slotting machine **-tafelschere** *f* crank-operated plate shears **-trieb** *m* crank gear, crank assembly, connecting-rod assembly **-triebwerk** *n* crankshaft assembly **-tritt** *m* pedal **-trog** *m* crank race

Kurbel-umschalter *m* lever switch **-versetzung** *f* angle between cranks **-wange** *f* crank web **-wangenausrundung** *f* crank-cheek or web rounding, journal web fillet **-wanne** *f* crank chamber, crank pit **-warze** *f* crank pin

Kurbelwelle *f* crankshaft **~ aus einem Stück** one-piece crankshaft **doppelt gekröpfte ~** two-throw crankshaft **dreimal gelagerte ~** three-bearing crankshaft **einfach gekröpfte ~** one-throw crankshaft **mehrfach gekröpfte ~** multiple-throw crankshaft **zweimal gelagerte ~** two-bearing crankshaft

Kurbelwellen-abdichtung *f* crankshaft seal **-anlasser** *m* crank starter **-antrieb** *m* crankshaft drive **-bearbeitung** *f* machining of crankshafts **-bock** *m* jack post **-bund** *m* shoulder on crankshaft **-dichtung** *f* crankshaft gland, crankshaft oil seal, crankshaft seal **-drehautomat** *m* automatic crankshaft turning lathe **-drehzahl** *f* crankshaft revolutions per minute, crankshaft rotational speed

Kurbelwellenende *n* crankshaft journal **~ des Hauptpleuels** big end of master rod

Kurbelwellen-federkeil *m* crankshaft feather or

key **-gegengewicht** *n* crank back balance **-gehäuse** *n* crankshaft housing **-handanlasser** *m* hand crank starter **-hauptlager** *n* crankshaft main bearing **-hubzapfen** *m* crank pin

Kurbelwellen-kegel *m* taper end of crankshaft **-klemmbolzen** *m* crankpin clamping screw **-kopf** *m* piston bearing big end of connecting rod **-kröpfung** *f* throw of crankshaft **-kupplungsflansch** *m* shaft-coupling flange **-lager** *n* crankshaft bearing, cap for shaft bearing **-lagerdeckel** *m* crankshaft bearing cover **-loser Motor** crankless engine **-magnetzünder** *m* crankshaft driven magneto

Kurbelwellenmutter (zur Befestigung der Luftschraubennabe) hub attachment nut

Kurbelwellen-paßlager *m* crankshaft thrust bearing **-rad** *n* crankshaft gear wheel **-riemenscheibe** *f* crankshaft belt pulley, crankshaft pulley **-ritzel** *n* crankshaft pinion **-schleifmaschine** *f* crankshaft grinding machine **-schutz** *m* crankshaft cover plate **-schwingung** *f* crankshaft vibration **-schwingungsdämpfer** *m* crankshaft-vibration damper **-stumpf** *m* crankshaft end **-umdrehung** *f* turn of the crankshaft **-verlängerung** *f* crankshaft extension **-zapfen** *m* crank-shaft pin

Kurbel-widerstand *m* switch resistance box **-winkel** *m* crank angle **-wischer** *m* crank-type wiper

Kurbelzapfen *m* crankpin, crankshaft pin, trunnion **durchbohrter ~** hollow crankpin

Kurbelzapfen-lager *n* crankpin bearing **-paar** *n* double-throw pins **-sitzbohrmaschine** *f* quartering machine

Kurbel-zentrum *n* crank center **-ziehpresse** *f* crank drawing press

Kurkumapapier *n* turmeric paper

Kurrentschrift *f* running hand

Kurs *m* course, route, exchange, track (aircraft), current price or rate, heading (nav.) **~ über Grund** track **einen ~ auf einer Karte absetzen** to lay a course (on a chart) **~ im größten Kreise** great-circle route **~ halten** to keep or stand upon the course **außer ~ setzen** to recall from circulation **ablaufender ~** course or direction away from airport, out-ward course **mißweisender ~** magnetic track, magnetic course **rechtvoraus ~** head-on course **rechtweisender ~** true (north) course; (über Grund) track

Kurs-absetzen *n* laying off or plotting position lines or bearings **-abweichung** *f* deviation from course, yaw **-abweichungssignal** *n* (Leitstrahlverfahren) off-course signal **-abweichungsverhältnis** *n* ratio of deviation **-änderung** *f* change of course

Kursanzeige, Einrichtung für ~ durch Funkleitstrahl oder Peilung homing device

Kursanzeiger *m* direction indicator

Kurs-aufschaltung *f* signal mixing (guided missiles) **-befehl** *m* signal from the directional gyro (autopilot) **-berichtigung** *f* course correction **-buch** *n* timetable, railway guide **-dreieck** *n* course triangle **-ermittlung** *f* plotting (of course) **-fähig** in circulation, current **-fehler** *m* course error **-feuer** *n* course light **-finder** *m* course finder **-führungssender** *m* localizer **-funkfeuer** *n* radio range **-geber** *m* autopilot control **-geberanlage** *f* directional gyro control unit **-gleiche** *f* loxodrome, rhumb line

kursieren to be current or in circulation

Kursivschrift *f* italics

Kurs-karte *f* track chart **-koppler** *m* automatic navigator **-kreisel** *m* directional gyroscope, gyroscopic direction indicator, gyrocompass

Kurslinie *f* trace or line of the course

Kurs-linienpunkt *m* way point **-meldung** *f* track signal **-messer** *m* protractor **-meßkreisel** *m* gyroscope with angle pickoff **-mikroskop** *n* class microscope **-moment** *n* yawing moment (aviation) **-motor** *m* (Kurssteuerung) course motor (autopilot)

Kurs-peilung *f* course bearing **-pfeil** *m* course arrow **-projektion** *f* track **-rechengerät** *n* course computer **-rechner** *m* course and distance calculator **-richtung** *f* head, course bearing **-richtungslicht** *n* course light **-richtigstellung** *f* course correction **-ring** *m* grid ring

Kurs-schätzer *m* course calculator (computer) **-scheibe** *f* bearing plate **-schieber** *m* route calculator, graphic course finder **-schlußbügel** *m* overload breaker **-schreiber** *m* course recorder (aviat.) odograph **-schwankung** *f* exchange fluctuation, fluctuation on or of the course **-sender** *m* localizer **-signal** *n* on course signal **-skizze** *f* route chart **-stabilität** *f* stability of course **-steueranlage** *f* course-steering apparatus, automatic flight control **-steuerung** *f* directional control, holding of course (automatic pilot) **-tor** *n* tracking gate

Kursus *m* course of instruction

Kurs-verbesserung *f* off-course correction **-verlust** *m* depreciation (exchange) **-versetzung** *f* heading displacement (nav.) **-verwandeln** *n* reduction or conversion of the course **-visier** *n* course sight **-wähler** *m* omnibearing selector (navig.) **-wechsel** *m* course change or shift **-weiser** *m* radio beacon, radio range

Kursweisung *f*, **rechtweisende ~** true course to steer, radio guidance or pilotage

Kurswinkel *m* azimuth of course, route angle, azimuth of target (gun.), magnetic azimuth **-beschleunigung** *f* angular acceleration of course **-geschwindigkeit** *f* angular velocity of course **-vorhalt** *m* course angle lead

Kurs-zahl *f* course figure or mark **-zeiger** *m* course indicator or pointer **-zeitzeichen** *n* course time signal **-zentrale** *f* directional gyroscope **-zettel** *m* stock-exchange list, course of exchange **-zwischengerät** *n* course indicator

Kurve *f* curve, bend, bow, diagram, graph, characteristic, chart, cam, turn (aviat) **~ der spektralen Energieverteilung** relative spectral curve **~ für die Ohrempfindlichkeit** sensitivity characteristic of the ear **~ dritter Ordnung** cubic curve **in der ~ abrutschen** to skid (in the curve) **sich in einer ~ bewegen** to conform to a curve **gedrückte ~** diving turn **katenarische ~** catenary (curve) **in die ~ legen** to bank a plane **~ machen** to turn, bank **~ mit Querneigung** banked turn **~ reißen** to flatten out after a dive (curving abruptly when landing)

Kurve, ballistische ~ curve of trajectory **enge, große, oder flache ~** sharp, gentle, or flat bank **flache ~** curve of large radius, flat curve or turn, flat-topped curve (*e.g.*, in broad tuning), flat characteristic **flaue** ~ flattened curve, flat characteristic **gerissene** ~ dotted-line or broken-line curve or graph **gezogene** ~ climbing turn **jungfräuliche** ~ virgin curve

Kurve, kontinuierliche ~ continuous or jogless curve **logarithmische** ~ logarithmic curve **spitze** ~ peaky curve, peaked curve **stark gekrümmte** ~ shortradius curve **wellige** ~ corrugated curve **wendigste** ~ best turn **zweispitzige** ~ double-peaked curve, double-hump curve

Kurven gleichen Abstandes equidistant curves ~ **aufnehmen** to trace curves, plot curves ~ **im Sackflug** wing over (aviat.)

kurven to curve, turn, bank

Kurven-absteckung *f* ranging or setting-out curves **-achse** *f* axis of curve **-anfang** *m* origin of curve **-anpassen** *n* curve fitting **-anzeiger** *m* bank or turn indicator **-ast** *m* branch of a curve **-aufzeichnung** *f* recording or tracing of curves

Kurven-bahn *f* curved sector or track, cam plate or disk **-bahnmotor** *m* cam-type engine **-berechnung** *f* graphical calculation **-bewegliche Endachse** radial end axle **-bild** *n* diagram, graph, graphic representation **-blatt** *n* curve sheet, graph

Kurvendarstellung *f* graph, graphic(al) representation **graphische** ~ diagram

Kurven-durchmesser *m* curve diameter **-einebnung** *f* flattening of a curve **-familie** *f* set (family) of curves

Kurvenflug *m* banking, turn, curvilinear flight **normaler** ~ normal turn

Kurvenform *f* curvature, wave shape, curve shape ~ (Verlauf einer Kurve) shape of a curve **in** ~ **darstellen** to represent graphically

Kurven-fräsvorrichtung *f* cam milling attachment **-füllfaktor** *m* (curve) fullness factor (ferromagnetism) **-gängigkeit** *f* curve negotiating characteristic **-getriebe** *n* cam gear **-gipfel** *m* apex of curve **-gleitflug** *m* spiral gliding **-hebel** *m* cam lever **-hebelschablone** *f* cam lever template **-integral** *n* contour integral **-joch** *n* curve section

Kurven-klemmer *m* a missile that does not follow the desired path **-körper** *m* ballistic cam **-lage** *f* bank **-lagenmesser** *m* turn and bank indicator **-lampe** *f* curve lamp **-lehre** *f* curve gauge **-leuchte** *f* curve light **-licht** *n* illumination on curves **-lichtmethode** *f* variable-area recording method **-lineal** *n* (French) curve, curve template, pliant rule; (irregular) curve, bow **-linie** *f* curve

Kurven-mäßig diagrammatic(al) **-messer** *m* turn and bank indicator, curvimeter **-radius** *m* radius of curve, radius of bend, radius of turn **-reiche Linienführung** line with numerous curves **-relais** *n* turn relay **-rolle** *f* guide roller, cam roller **-rollgang** *m* curved roller conveyor **-satz** *m* set of cams

Kurven-schablone *f* cam template **-schar** *f* set of curves, family, group, or system of curves or graphs **-schaubild** *n* graph

Kurvenscheibe *f* cam plate or disk ~ **zum Versenken der Greifer** cam for guide rail

Kurven-scheibenmotor *n* cam-type engine **-scheibensatz** *m* set of cam discs **-scheinwerfer** *m* curve light **-scheitelpunkt** *m* peak of the curve **-schere** *f* curve-cutting machine **-schleife** *f* guiding cam **-schlitz** *m* cam slot, curved slot **-schnittpunkt** *m* intersection of curves **-schreiber** *m* curve-drawing recorder, oscillograph, curve tracer **-schwanzstück** *n* toe region of film characteristic **-stück** *n* curved piece or section **-tafel** *f* curve sheet, graph

Kurventeil *m*, **ovaler** ~ elliptical path

Kurven-trieb *m* cam drive, cam-throttle control **-trommel** *f* cylinder cam, cam drum **-verlauf** *m* course of curve, trace of curve **-visier** *n* leaf sight **-welle** *f* camshaft **-werte auftragen über** to plot against or versus **-widerstand** *m* resistance in curves **-winkel** *m* angle of bank **-zeichnen** *n* mapping a curve, plotting a graph **-zeiger** *m* turn indicator **-ziehfeder** *f* curve pen, swivel pen

Kurvenzug *m* series of curves, trend line, curve path **abklingender** ~ decay train

Kurverei *f* flying curves (in aerial combat)

kurz short, brief, abrupt, stiff (printer's ink) **kurz dauernd** temporary, brief ~ **zuschlagen** to hammer quickly **-e und starke Bestrahlung** acute exposure **-es Kettenglied** short link **-e Wellen** short wave

Kurz-analyse *f* proximate analysis **-antrieb** *m* short drive **-auszugsstreuung** *f* document abstract dissemination **-balken** *m* stub bar **-beschreibung** *f* précis **-betrieb** *m* intermediate service or operation **-betriebsleistung** *f* intermittent capacity **-bewitterung** *f* accelerated weathering

kurzbrennweitig of short focal distance **-es Fernrohr** telescope of short focal length **-es Objektiv** short-focus lens or objective

Kurzbrief *m* postagram

kurzbrüchig brittle, short-brittle

Kurzdipol *m* Hertz dipole

Kürze *f* shortness, brevity, conciseness

kürzen to shorten, abbreviate

kürzende oder vereinfachende Wiedergabe in anderer Fassung paraphrase

kürzeste Wellenlänge minimum wavelength

Kürzezeichen *n* short mark, breve

Kurz-fassung *f* abridgement **-faserig** short fiber **-film** *m* movie short

kurzflammig short-flaming **-e Kohle** short-flaming coal

Kurz-flammlampe *f* hard light **-formschlüssel** *m* alphabetic coding

kurzfristig for a short time, on short notice **-e Berichte** up-to the minute reports

kurz-gefaßt brief, concise, abbreviated, of reduced length or style, compendious **-geschlossen** short-circuited (elec.) **-gewindefräsen** *n* short-thread milling **-gliedrige Kette** short-link chain **-gondel** *f* short car **-halsig** short-necked **-hobler** *m* shaping machine **-hubig** short-stroke **-kämmig** short-crested **-kegel** *m* short taper **-kreisel** *m* master magnetic compass **-lebig** short-life, short-lived, periodic, transient **-leistung** *f* minimum take-off output, short-duration power output

kürzlich recent(ly), late

Kurz-meldung *f* summary report **-nachricht** *f* brief **-prüfung** *f* short-time test, accelerated test **-prüfverfahren** *n* rapid-testing method **-rechnung** *f* shortform invoice **-rechnungsmethode** *f* short method of calculation **-reichweitengrenze** *f* short range limit **-reichweitig** short-range **-säulig** short-columnar **-schließen** to short-circuit, short, close, ground **-schließen** *n* short circuit **-schließer** *m* short-circuiting device, ignition switch **-schließung** *f* short circuit

Kurzschluß *m* short circuit **im ~ arbeiten** to work on short circuit **teilweiser ~** partial short circuit **vollständiger ~** dead short circuit

Kurzschluß-admittanz *f* short-circuit admittance **-anker** *m* short-circuit armature, squirrel cage **-ankermotor** *m* squirrel-cage motor **-blindschwanz** *m* closed stub **-brücke** *f* short-circuiting bridge **-bug** *m* short-circuit bow **-bügel** *m* overload breaker or switch, short-circuiting bridge **-deckel** *m* contact-breaker or short-circuit cover **-drehbrücke** *f* short-circuiting wire bridge **-drehmoment** *m* stall torque **-druckknopf** *m* short-circuiting push button

Kurzschluß-einrichtung *f* short-circuiting device **-federn** *pl* short-circuiting springs **-fortschaltung** *f* automatic reclosing under short-circuit conditions **-funke** *m* short-circuit spark **-gefahr** *f* short circuit danger **-glied** *n* short-circuit member

Kurzschlußimpedanz *f* short-circuit impedance, closed-end impedance **elektrische ~** free impedance

Kurzschluß-kabel *n* short-circuit or earthing-wire ground cable **-kennlinie** *f* static characteristic (of tube) **-klemme** *f* shunt, short-circuit terminal, ground terminal **-knopf** *m* short-circuit bottom **-kolben** *m* piston, plunger **-kontakt** *m* short-circuit contact **-läufer** *m* short-circuited rotor, squirrel-cage rotor (of induction motor) **-läufermotor** *m* short-circuit rotor motor, squirrel-cage motor **-leitung** *f* short-circuit line **-motor** *m* squirrel-cage motor

Kurzschluß-prüfstand *m* short circuit test(ing) stand **-ring** *f* short-circuiting ring or disk **-schalter** *m* short-circuiting switch **-schaltstück** *n* short-circuiting contact **-scheibe** *f* short-circuiting disk or ring **-schieber** *m* shorting plunger, non contact piston, choke plunger (piston) **-schleifringläufer** *m* short circuit slidering rotor **-schweißung** *f* (Blankdraht schweißung) short circuit or bare wire welding **-schutz** *m* short-circuit protection

kurzschluß-sicher short circuit proof **-sicherheit** *f* short-circuit strength **-spannung** *f* short-circuit voltage **-stabil** short circuit stable **-stecker** *m* short-circuit plug (jumper) **-stöpsel** *m* short-circuit plug **-strom** *m* short-circuit current **-strombremse** *f* short-circuit brake **-stromkreis** *m* short circuit **-sucher** *m* short-circuit detector **-taste** *f* short-circuit key **-übergang** *m* short-circuit transition **-verfahren** *n* closed circuit **-wicklung** *f* short-circuited winding **-widerstand** *m* short-circuit impedance, closed-end impedance

Kurz-schrift *f* shorthand **-sichtig** nearsighted, shortsighted, myoptic **-sichtigkeit** *f* shortsightedness, myopia **-signal** *n* code **-spannend** short broken (chips) **-spleißung** *f* short splice **-stapelig** short-staple **-start** *m* short taxying start **-stop** *m* (des Bandlaufes) temporary stop (tape rec.) **-strahlung** *f* short wave radiation **-streckenstrahlflugzeug** *n* short-haul jet airliner **-tauchen** *n* (Holz) dipping **-temperung** *f* short anneal(ing)

Kürzung *f* abbreviation, reduction, shortening

Kürzungsfette *f* shortening

Kurz-versuch *m* accelerated test **-waren** *pl* haberdashery, hardware **-welle** *f* short wave

Kurzwellen-antenne *f* short-wave antenna **-antennenanordnung** *f* short wave antenna arrangement **-bereich** *m* short-wave (field) range **-empfang** *m* short-wave reception **-empfänger** *m* short-wave receiver **-filter für HF** high-pass (filter) **-funkapparat** *m* portable short-wave apparatus **-gebiet** *n* short-wave range **-gerät** *n* short-wave radio **-kleinfunkapparat** *m* portable short-wave apparatus **-linse** *f* lens

Kurzwellen-sender *m* short-wave transmitter **-spule** *f* short-wave coil **-supervorsatz** *m* short-wave converter **-übertragung** *f* short-wave transmission **-verbindung** *f* short-wave communication **-verkehrsempfänger** *m* short-wave receiver **-vorsatzgerät** *n* short-wave converter or adapter **-wandler** *m* short-wave converter

kurzwellig short-wave (length) **-e Grenze** short wavelength limit **-e Kante** high energy edge (emission band)

Kurz-wort *n* contracted or alphabetic word coinage, abbreviation **-zeichen** *n* symbol, abbreviation, initials

Kurzzeit *f*, **auf ~** on short-time basis

Kurzzeitbeobachtung *f* short-time observation

kurzzeitig momentary, temporary, temporarily **-e Belastung** intermitted load **-e Bestrahlung** acute exposure **-er Betrieb** temporary service, short-time duty **-e Impulse** pulses of a short duration

Kurzzeit-messer *m* microchronometer, Behm period meter **-messerbremse** *f* brake magnet **-messerrad** *n* microchronometer wheel, interval-recording disk **-methode** *f* short-interval ranging **-prüfung** *f* short-time test, accelerated test **-sperre** *f* short-period barrage **-temperung** *f* short-cycle annealing **-triebwerk** *n* engine with shortterm action

Kurz-zugdraht (zwischen Tasten- und Typenhebel) short link **-zwischengerät** *n* device between radio control and autopilot

Küste *f* coast, shore, seacost **längs der ~ fahren** to skirt the coast **von der ~ fort nach dem Horizont gelegener Teil der See** offing

Küsten-ablagerung *f* littoral deposit **-abschnitt** *m* coastal sector **-aufnahme** *f* coast survey **-aufnahmekammer** *f* coast-survey camera **-bauten** *pl* coastal constructions **-befestigung** *f* coast(al) fortification **-befeuerung** *f* shore lighting **-beschreibung** *f* description of coast **-brechung** *f* coast(al) refraction

Küsten-dienst *m* coastal service **-fahrt** *f* coasting trade **-feuer** *n* coastal light **-funkstelle** *f* coast(al) radio station, shore station **-gestaltung** *f* configuration of coast **-hafen** *m* coasting port **-interferometer** *n* sea interferometer **-kabel** *n* shore-end cable, shallow-water cable **-karte** *f* coastal chart or map

Küsten-leuchtfeuer *n* coast beacon **-linie** *f* shore, coast line **-meer** *n* territorial sea **-nachrichtennetz** *n* coastal communication system **-peilstelle** *f* coastal direction-finding station **-radar** *n* shore-based radar

Küsten-schiffahrt *f* piloting (navy) **-schutz** *m* coast(al) defense **-schutzgebiet** *n* coast-defense zone **-sicherungen** *f pl* coast-defense forces or establishments **-strich** *m* seaboard, country adjacent to the coast **-strömung** *f* coastal stream **-überflug** *m* landfall **-vermessung** *f* coast geodetic survey

Küsten-versetzung *f* shifting of beach sand **-wache** *f* coast guard **-wachstation** *f* coast guard station **-wacht** *f* coastal patrol

Kutonase *f* balloon-cable cutter

Kutscher *m* driver, coachman, (slang) pilot

Kutter *m* cutter **-meißel** *m* rock or drop chisel

Kutsche *f* (massecuite) wagon or carriage

Kuvelage *f* timbering, tubbing (min.)

küvelieren to timber

Kuvert *n* envelope, cover

Küvette *f* tray, cuvette, shallow trough, narrow test flume, bulb, bath, vessel, cell (photo-tube)

Küvetten-boden *m* bottom of cell **-halter** *m* (Sitz für Küvetten) cell seat **-ständer** *m* cell stand **-wechsler** *m* cell reverser

Kux *m* share in a mine

K-Verband *m* knee bracing, K truss

kyanisieren to cyanize

Kyanisierung *f* cyanization

Kyanisierwerk *n* cyanizing works

Kyanit *n* kyanite

Kymograph *m* kymograph

Kymographie *f* kymography

Kymographion *n* cymograph

kymomotorische Kraft cymomotive force

Kybernetik *f* cybernetics

L

Labialpfeife *f* flue pipe (of organ)

labil unstable, unsteady, labile

Labilität *f* instability

Labium *n* lip (music)

Laborant *m* laboratory inspector, chemist, analyst, laboratory worker or assistant

Laboratorium *n* laboratory

Laboratoriums-ausbeute *f* laboratory yield **-kraftwagen** *m* laboratory truck **-mühle** *f* laboratory crusher **-prüfung** *f* laboratory test **-versuch** *m* laboratory test

laborieren to experiment

Laborversuch *m* bench test

Labradorfeldspat *m* labradorite

Labradorisieren *n* change of colors (min.)

Labradorit *m* labradorite

Labyrinth-dichtung *f* labyrinth packing or gland (of turbine) **-ring** *m* labyrinth seal

Lache *f* pool

Lachgas *n* laughing gas, nitrous oxide gas

lachsrot salmon pink

Lacht *m* slag

Lachter *f* fathom (in mining) **-kette** *f* measuring chain **-stab** *m* surveyor's rod

Lack *m* lacquer, varnish, lac, primer, dope, enamel **schwarzer ~** japan

Lack-abbeizmittel *n* varnish remover **-abdruckmittel** *n* agent for lacquered printing **-ader** *f* varnished conductor **-aderdraht** *m* varnished wire **-anstrich** *m* varnish coat **-auftrag** *m* varnishing coat

Lack-bad *n* paint booth **-benzin** *n* mineral spirits **-bildner** *m* lake former **-bindemittel** *n* lacquer binding medium **-draht** *m* enameled or varnished wire

lacken to lacquer, paint

Lack-farbe *f* varnish color, enamel **-farbstoff** *m* dyestuff for lakemaking **-firnis** *m* lac varnish **-gewebe** *n* varnished fabric **-harz** *m* gum-lac **-haut** *f* lacquer film

lackierecht fast to overvarnishing

lackieren to lacquer, varnish, dope

Lackieren *n* japanning

Lackier-grün *n* Paris green **-ofen** *m* lacquering stove **-spritzverfahren** *n* paint-spraying system

lackiert varnished, japanned

Lackiertauchapparat *m* dip varnishing apparatus

Lackierung *f* dope (paint), finish **schwarze ~** black finish

Lack-kabel *n* enameled cable **-lasurfarbe** *f* transparent paint or varnish color **-leitung** *f* varnished wiring **-lösungsmittel** *n* lacquer solvent

Lackmus *m* litmus **-flechte** *f* litmus lichen **-flechtentinktur** *f* litmus solution **-papier** *n* litmus paper

Lack-papierdraht *m* paper-insulated enameled wire **-rohr** *n* varnished rush **-säure** *f* laccinic acid **-schuhsoldat** *m* (slang) a member of the air force **-schwarz** *n* black lake or varnish **-siegel** *n* wax seal **-spachtel** *f* varnish filler **-sud** *n* varnish boiling **-tuch** *n* oilcloth **-überzug** *m* varnish coat **-unterlage** *f* varnish base **-verdünner** *m* varnish thinner

Lactat *n* lactate

Lade *f* batten (lathe), chest, drawer, load, charge **-aggregat** *n* charging set (elec.) **-amperemeter** charging ammeter **-anlage** *f* unloading plant, charging unit **-anlage für Massengüter** unloading plant for bulk goods **-anzeigeleuchte** *f* load-indicator monitor (light), charging control lamp **-apparat** *m* loading machine **-aufzug** *m* charge hoist

Lade-band *n* conveyer **-baum** *m* derrick, boom, crane **-bereichumschalter** *m* battery charging switch **-bereit** ready for loading **-bericht** *m* cargo-intake certificate **-bock** *m* skid, skid platform, load platform **-bogen** *m* spring rest **-brücke** *f* loading bridge, handling bridge, concrete wharf, loading ramp **-büchse** *f* loading tube **-bügel** *m* loop, triangular or pear-shaped lifting eye **-bühne** *f* charging or loading platform

Lade-damm *m* jetty, landing stage **-dauer** *f* (Batterie) charging period (battery) **-dichte** *f* charge density (explosives), density of loading

Ladedruck *m* induction pressure, intake manifold boost, (intake) manifold pressure, intake pressure, supercharge pressure, boost, boost pressure, boost ratio **~ für Sparflug** economical cruising boost **Schwingen des Ladedrucks** surging of the boost control

Ladedruck-anzapfung *f* boost pickoff **-begrenzer** *m* supercharger-pressure limiting control, manifold-pressure limitating regulator **-grenzregler** *m* manifold-pressure limitating regulator **-messer** *m* boost-pressure gauge, manifold-pressure gauge

Ladedruckregelung *f* boost-pressure control **selbsttätige, dreistufige ~** three-stage automatic boost control

Ladedruckregler *m* supercharger (pressure) regulator, boost control, manifold-pressure control, boost regulator **~ mit veränderlicher Ausgangsstellung der Regeldose** variable-datum boost control **~ für drei Regelstufen** three-phase boost control **~ mit drei Stufen** three-phase or three-stage boost control

Ladedruck-umkehr *f* boost reversal **-verhältnis** *n* supercharger compression ratio, boost (pressure) ratio

Lade-dynamo *m* (battery) charging generator, charging machine **-einheit** *f* load unit, unit load **-einrichtung** *f* charging equipment, battery charger **-ende** *n* feed end **-fähig** in serviceable condition **-fähigkeit** *f* rate of charge, load(ing) capacity, serviceable condition (of ammunition)

Ladefläche, freie ~ zwischen den Drehgestellen clear charging space inside cross bearers

Lade-förderbahn *f* conveyer for loading or charging **-funkenstrecke** *f* charge spark gap **-gemisch** *n* charge of mixture **-generator** *m* charging generator **-gerät** *n* battery charger

Ladegestell *n* skid, skid or load platform, loading frame **~ mit Aufsatz** loading frame with box **~ mit Etagenaufsatz** tier-construction platform **~ mit Mulde** skid hopper **~ mit Rungen** skid platform fitted with stakes

Ladegewicht *n* gross weight, load capacity, weight of load **~ eines Wagens** carrying capacity

Lade-gleichrichter *m* charging rectifier **-gleis** *n* loading track (R.R.), loading siding **-grad** *m* charge factor **-griff** *m* (manual) loading movement **-gurt** *m* cartridge belt **-gutabfertigung** *f* cargo handling **-hebel** *m* firing lever, actuating lever, loading lever **-hemmung** *f* stoppage, jam (firearms), loading or jamming (of firearms) **-höhe** *f* dumping height **-hub** *m* intake stroke **-kammer** *f* chamber (of gun) **-kapazität** *f* loading capacity (elec.)

Ladekasten *m* tote box **~ mit geschlossenem Eisenrahmen** steel-bound tote box

Lade-kennlinie *f* charging characteristic curve (or line) **-klappe** *f* breech lock **-koeffizient** *m* charging coefficient **-kondensator** *m* charging condenser, reservoir capacitor **-kontrolle** *f* charging control **-kontrollampe** *f* charging indicator lamp **-kran** *m* loading crane **-kurbel** *f* loading key **-kurve** *f* charging curve

Lade-lampe *f* charging current control lamp **-laufrad** *n* compressor or supercharger rotor impeller **-lehre** *f* clearance-loading gauge or limit **-leistung** *f* charging power or capacity **-leitrad** *n* diffuser **-leitung** *f* induction system, manifold **-liste** *f* bill of lading **-loch** *n* chamber (of gun), loading recess or aperture **-löffel** *m* loading plate (explosives)

Ladeluft *f* manifold pressure, air charge **-durchsatz** *m* supercharger air flow **-kühler** *m* compressor or supercharger intercooler **-kühlung** *f* boost intercooling **-leitung** *f* pressure pipe (from supercharger), intake manifold **-temperatur** *f* induction-system temperature, boost temperature, blower-rim air temperature **-zwischenkühler** *m* supercharger air intercooler

Lade-luke *f* loading hatch **-marke** *f* load line, Plimsoll mark **-maschine** *f* (battery-)charging generator, battery charger, charging or loading machine **-maschinensatz** *m* battery-charging unit **-maß** *n* loading gauge **-mast** *m* derrick **-meister** *m* drill charger **-meldung** *f* manifest (cargo or passenger list, aviat and shipping)

laden to charge, to load, ship (cargo), supercharge **auf sich ~** to incur **wieder ~** to recharge **zu wenig ~** to undercharge

Laden *m* shop, shutter

Laden *n* loading, charging **~ der Batterie** battery charging **~ eines Kondensators** charging of a condenser **~ mit gleichbleibender Spannung** constant voltage charge **~ mit gleichbleibendem Strom** constant current charge

Laden-fenster *n* show window **-preis** *m* retail price **-tisch** *m* counter

Lade-öffnung *f* breech (of gun) **-pforte** *f* raft port **-pfropfen** *m* wad, wadding **-platz** *m* loading point, station, wharf, ramp, platform, pier, quay **-podest** *m* loading ramp or wharf **-profil** *n* loading gauge **-pumpe** *f* charging pump, compression pump

Lader *m* supercharger, blower, compressor, boost, loader, stevedore, mucker **~ mit übersetztem Antrieb** geared fan **~ für große Nennhöhe** high-level blower **~ der Verdrängerbauart** displacement supercharger **Motor ohne ~** normally aspirated engine

Laderampe *f* loading ramp or platform

Lader-antriebritzel *n* supercharger drive gear **-antriebsleistung** *f* supercharger drive power **-arten** *pl* types of compressors

Laderaum *m* shipping room, tonnage, hopper or well, freight space (capacity), breech, chamber (of gun), hold (naut.) **-verlängerung** *f* advance of forcing cone (on gun)

Lader-bedienhebel *m* suppercharger control lever **-drehzahl** *f* supercharger speed **-druck** *m* boost pressure, impeller or turbine pressure **-druckverhältnis** *n* supercharger compression ratio

Laderegulierkasten *m* charging control box

Lader-einlaß *m* blower eye, eye of the supercharger

Ladereintrittsspirale *f* volute **Gehäuse der ~** volute casing

Lader-enddruck *m* supercharger delivery pressure **-förderhöhenlinie** *f* compressor adiabetic work head characteristic **-gangwechsel** *m* supercharge gear change **-laufrad** *n* blower fan (rotor wheel)

Ladergang *m* supercharger gear **erster ~** (für mäßige Aufladung) medium (supercharger) gear **langsamer ~** low gear **unterer ~** low (supercharger) gear **zweiter ~** (volle Aufladung beim Höhenmotor) supercharger gear

Lader-gebläse *n* superchargine blower **-gehäuse** *n* blower casing, supercharger housing **-getriebe** *n* booster or blower drive, jet-supercharger drive **-laufrad** *n* impeller rotor **-laufradantrieb**

m impeller drive **-leitapparat** *m* diffuser section **-loser Motor** self-aspirating engine **-motor** *m* supercharged aero engine, blower-fed engine

Laderöhre *f* charging tube

Laderprüfstand *m* supercharger-testing rig

Laderrad mit kastenförmig geschlossenen Schaufelkanalen box-type impeller

Lader-ringkanal *m* supercharger distribution or diffuser chamber, blower rim **-satz** *m* supercharger assembly **-schnecke** *f* supercharger volute **-sieb** *n* supercharger screen **-spirale** *f* collector ring, supercharger or blower spiral

Laderübersetzung *f* blower ratio ~ **für volle Aufladung** supercharger ratio ~ **für mäßige Aufladung** (mittlere Nennhöhe, erster Ladergang) medium supercharger ratio

Laderutsche *f* loading chute

Lade-verteilergehäuse *n* supercharger diffuser chamber, supercharger distribution chamber **-vorsatzläufer** *m* compressor inducer rotor

Lade-satz *m* battery charger, charging set, supercharger assembly **-schale** *f* charger (for cartridges), loading tray **-schalter** *m* (battery-) charging switch **-schalttafel** *f* charging (switch)-board, charging panel **-schaltung** *f* circuit means causing slow rise of sawtooth voltage **-schein** *m* bill of lading **-schrank** *m* charging chamber (air) **-schwenger** *m* loading tray **-schwinge** *f* lorry loading crane

Lade-selbstschalter *m* automatic (battery-) charging switch **-sicher** loading-safe (said of a fuse) **-sitz** *m* gunner's seat, loader's seat **-sonde** *f* charging device for ionization meter **-spannung** *f* charging voltage, supply voltage **-spindel** *f* loading spindle

Lade-station *f* charging or loading station **-steg** *m* loading (handling) bridge, concrete wharf **-stelle** *f* battery-charging station, loading, entraining, or entrucking point, platform **-stellung** *f* loading position **-stock** *m* rammer **-stöpsel** *m* charging plug **-störung** *f* jam, stoppage in loading mechanism **-straße** *f* delivery roadway (at freight station)

Lade-streifen *m* magazine clip, cartridge clip, ammunition clip, charger (for cartridges) **-strom** *m* charging current, surge current **-stromkreis** *m* charging circuit **-stromstärke** *f* charging rate **-stromstoß** *m* charging-current impulse

Lade-takel *n* Spanish burton **-tasche** *f* loading pocket **-tätigkeit** *f* loading operations **-tisch** *m* loading tray **-trichter** *m* loading (charging) hopper, bucket **-trommel** *f* cartridge drum **-trupp** *m* loading detail **-uhr** *f* clockwork fuse **-umformer** *m* charging converter **-umschalter** *m* charging commutator

Lade- und Meßgerät *n* charger-reader

Lade- und Siebkapazität *f* reservoir and filter capacity

Lade-verlust *m* loss of charge **-vermögen** *n* loading capacity, storage capacity **-verzeichnis** *n* bill of lading **-verzug** *m*, **-verzugszeit** *f* time lag due to loading, loading lag, loading time, dead time **-vorgang** *m* loading action or process

Ladevorrichtung *f* breech mechanism, loading device, charging facilities, loading equipment ~ **zur Bekohlung von Feuerungen** mechanical stoker

Lade-wasserlinie *f* load water line **-weite** *f* (Bagger) dumping width **-wicklung** *f* charging winding **-widerstand** *m* charging resistance **-winde** *f* loading winch **-zeit** *f* loading time, entrucking time, entraining time, charging time **-zunge** *f* pier, jetty **-zustand** *m* state of charge

lädieren to damage, batter

Ladkran *m* gun hoist

Ladpumpe *f* supercharger

Ladung *f* charge, propelling charge, load, shot, loading, input, freight-charging, cargo, explosive charge, invitation ~ **mit erhöhter Abteilung** leak loading ~ **des Akkumulators** battery charging ~ **des Arbeitszylinders** charging of the working cylinder ~ **der Kathode** load of the cathode ~ **eines Leiters** charge of a conductor **geschichtete** ~ **aus reiner Luft und reichem Gemisch** pure-air-rich-mixture sandwich system

Ladung, ~ **erzeugende Rohrleitung** generating pipe ~ **eines Sammlers** charge of secondary or storage cell **erste** ~ **eines Sammlers** first or initial charge of secondary or storage cell; (beförderte) ~ **pro Tonne und Meile** load ton miles **Verhältnis von** ~ **zu Masse** charge-mass radio, specific charge **die** ~ **ist übergangen** the cargo has shifted **elektrische** ~ electric charge, load, or loading **entgegengesetzte** ~ opposite charge **freie** ~ free charge **geballte** ~ concentrated charge, pole charge (blasting), demolition charge

Ladung, gebundene ~ bound charge, induced charge **gestreckte** ~ multiple charge (explosives), bangalore torpedo (blasting), distributed charge **gleichförmige** ~ uniformly or continuously distributed loading **induzierte** ~ induced charge **kleine** ~ small charge, small load **punktförmige** ~ lumped loading **ruhende** ~ static charge **ungebundene** ~ free charge

Ladungen (im Blitz), **Größenordnungen der** ~ quantities of charge (in lightning)

Ladungs-ableitung *f* charge dissipation **-abschnitt** *m* loading-coil section, pupinization section **-art** *f* kind of charge **-ausgleich** *m* charge equalization **-austauscherscheinung** *f* charge-exchange phenomenon **-austauschoperator** *m* charge exchage operator

Ladungs-bild *n* electrical image, charge pattern, charge image **-büchse** *f* blasting-charge container **-dichte** *f* density of charge **-dichtenverteilung** *f* distribution of charge density **-dichtesteuerung** *f* charge-density modulation **-einheit** *f* unit charge

Ladungs-fähigkeit *f* charge capacity **-flasche** *f* Leyden jar **-frequenz** *f* charge frequency **-gefäß** *n* explosive container, blasting-charge container **-gewicht** *n* weight of powder charge **-gleichung** *f* charge equation **-hafen** *m* loading port **-hülle** *f* shell casing (ballistics) **-invarianz** *f* charge independence **-kasten** *m* explosive box, blasting-charge box **-konjugation** *f* charge conjugation

Ladungs-manifest *n* manifest of cargo **-meßgerät** *n* charger-reader **-multiplett** *n* charge multiplet **-neutralisation** charge neutralisation **-raum** *m* (powder) chamber (of a gun), hold **-rückstand** *m* residual charge **-renormierung** *f* charge renormalization **-potential** *n* charge potential

Ladungs-säule *f* secondary battery **-schein** *m* bill of lading **-schicht** *f* layer of charge **-schieber** *m* charger indicator **-schwingung** *f* load vibrations **-skala** *f* dead-weight scale

Ladungs-speicherbildabtaster *m* mosaic-type storage iconoscope **-speicherröhre** *f* charge-storage tube **-speicherung** *f* charge storage, charge accumulation **-spin** *m* charge spin **-seite** *f* charging, face **-summierung** *f* charge integration **-stück** *n* package

Ladungs-teilchen *n* high-speed charged particle **-träger** *m* charge carrier **-trägereinbau** *m* charge carrier injection **-trägertrennung** *f* sorting or separation of charged particles **-transport** *m* transport of charges

Ladungs-überleitung *f* transport of charge **-überschuß** *m* excess of charge **-übertragung** *f* charge transfer **-unabhängigkeit** *f* charge independance **-unveränderlichkeit** *f* charge invariance **-verformung** *f* charge distortion **-verhältnis** *n* charge weight ratio of projectile

Ladungsvermögen *n* capacity **elektrisches ~** electrostatic capacity

Ladungs-verteilung *f* load distribution **-vervielfachung** *f* multiplication of charge **-verzeichnis** *n* ship's manifest **-vorzeichenbestimmung** *f* sign of charge determination **-werfer** *m* spigot mortar projector **-wolke** *f* charge cloud **-zahl** *f* charge number **-zusammenballung** *f* bunching of charges, bunching of electrons **-zustand** *m* state of charge

Lafette *f* gun carriage, mount (artil.), gun mount or mounting, limber

Lafetten-achse *f* gun-carriage axle **-art** *f* type of gun carriage or mount **-aufbau** *m* gun carriage construction **-aufsatzstück** *n* top piece of gun carriage, antiaircraft extension for machine-gun tripod, mount adapter **-dreieck** *n* triangular base (of gun) **-fahrzeug** *n* gun carriage, trailer mount **-holm** *m* gunmount outrigger, gun-trail crosspiece **-kasten** *m* trail box **-kopf** *m* base plate of gun carriage **-kranz** *m* circular track mount **-kreuz** *n* outriggers (gun platform)

Lafetten-platte *f* trail plate **-rahmen** *m* carriage frame (artil.), traversing platform **-rücklauf** *m* recoil **-schwanz** *m* trail **-schwanzgriff** *m* trail handspike **-schwanzsporn** *m* trail spade **-sitz** *m* gunner's seat **-sporn** *m* trail spade **-stütze** *f* firing base **-tisch** *m* trail base, gun-carriage bed **-wand** *f* check (gun), cradle wall (artil.), gun-carriage side plate

Lafettierung *f* mounting (gun)

Lage *f* position; (Umstände) circumstances; (Technik, Satz) set; (Zustand) condition, state; (Haltung) attitude, posture; (Schicht) layer; (Werkstoff) ply; (Farbe) coat, situation, aspect, site, bearing (direction finder), locality, strattum, location, quire, bed(ding), lamina, course (of stone), salvo **~ des Bogensatzes** sheet of the quires **~ d. Flugzeuges** attitude **~ eines Frequenzbereichs** allocation **~ der Meßpunkte** position of test points **~ eines Pegels** site of a gauge, gauging station **~ der Trennwände** baffle locations **direkte ~** upper side-band position **in die richtige ~ bringen** to position

Lagen der Blöcke courses of blocks **zwei Lagen Papier stark** two thicknesses of paper **Lagen machen** to gather, lay down a gathering

Lage-änderung *f* change of position disalignment **-aufschaltgröße** *f* position shunt or switch factor **-aufschaltung** *f* mixing ratio of angular position signal **-bericht** *m* position report, situation report **-bestimmung** *f* determination of position, fixing of position, localization **-bestimmungsgerät** air-position indicator **-beurteilung** *f* estimate of the situation **-druck** *m* closed pressure, rock pressure **-einstellung** *f* positioning control **-empfindlichkeit** *f* sensitiveness to position **-energie** *f* (Energie der Lage) potential energy **-fehler** *m* error of position

lagefest stable **~ machen** to stabilize

Lagefestigkeit *f* stability **-gruppe** *f* position group **-kreisel** *m* position gyro **-messung** *f* planimetric measurement

Lägel *n* cringle, barrel, keg

Lagen-abstand *m* distance between layers **-änderung** *f* change in position **-ausschlag** *m* principal deflection, angular movement **-bruch** *m* plaiting fold **-drall** *m* twist of wire layers **-empfindung** *f* sense of position **-falzung** *f* folding in quires **-fehler** *m* angular deviation **-feuer** *n* continuous fire, salvo fire, troop fire **-förmig** banded

Lagen-holz *n* laminated wood **-holzleim** *m* adhesive for laminated wood **-karte** *f* situation map or report **-meldung** *f* situation report **-richtig** positionally or geometrically correct **-sicherung** *f* locking in position **-wechsel** *m* change-over of layers **-weise** in layers **-wicklung** *f* layer winding **-zeiger** *m* position indicator

Lageplan *m* plan showing position, site plan, planimetry, plan, ground plan

Lager *n* pivot; (Waren) warehouse, storehouse; (Vorrat) store, supply; (Technik) bearing; (Unterlage) support; (Kohlen ~) bed, layer, deposit, stratum, stock, (mach.), storage yard, magazine, socket, camp, depot, dump, bushing, ledge, pedestal, supply base, sheets, sills, sediment

Lager für axiale und radiale Belastung radial thrust bearing **~ für periodische Blattwinkelverstellung** feathering bearings **~ mit Bundringen** collar end bearing **mit einem ~ versehene Drehspule** unipivot moving coil **~ des Hauptantriebes** main bearing **~ zur Kegelradwelle** drive shaft bearing **~ mit Kugelbewegung** spherical bearing **~ mit Kugelgelenk** ball-and-socket bearing **~ für Sammelschienen** bus-bar supports **~ mit Schmierring** ring-oil bearing

Lager für Übertragwalze bearing for distributor roller **~ für den Verschlußbolzen** breech-bolt recess **~ mit Weißmetallfutter** babbitt-lined bearing, babbitted bearing **~ einer stehenden Welle** step bearing, step brass **~ abbrechen** to strike camp, break camp **ein ~ anlegen** to lay out a store **~ aufschlagen** to pitch camp **ein ~ ausfüttern** to line a bearing **ein ~ neu ausgießen** to remetal a bearing

Lager, ein ~ ausrichten to true a bearing **einreihiges ~** single-row bearing **einseitig wirkendes ~** single-direction bearing **einteiliges ~** solid bearing **ein ~ hat geschmiert** a bearing has wiped **geteiltes ~** split bearing **nachstellbares ~** adjustable bearing **das ~ nachstellen** to take up a bearing **zweiseitig wirkendes ~** two-direction bearing

Lager-abschlußdeckel *m* bearing side cover **-abstand** *m* distance between bearings **-arbeiter** *m*

store hand **-arm** *m* bearing bracket **-auflagefläche** *f* bearing surface **-aufnahme** *f* inventory, stocktaking **-aufseher** *m* storekeeper, storeman **-ausguß** *m* lining of the bearing **-ausrüstung** *f* **für Farben** paint-storage equipment

Lager-balken *m* bearing carrier or beam **-batterie** *f* storage battery **-bauart** *f* type of bearing **-behälter** *m* storage tank **-belastung** *f* bearing load **-bestand** *m* stock, inventory, stockage **-beständig** unaffected by storing **-blech** *n* bracket

Lager-bock *m* bearing block, floor stand, floor frame, pedestal, bearing pedestal or bracket, recoil lug, coupler recess, pillow block, hand-lever bearing, base support **-bocklager** *n* pillow block bearing **-bockverschraubung** *f* bearing bracket fixture **-bockbolzen** *m* pillow block bolt, bearing pin **-brücke** *f* bearing support **-buch** *n* stock list or book

Lagerbuchse *f* bearing bush(ing) ~ **für Anlasser** bearing bush for starter ~ **auswechseln** to rebush a bearing

Lager-büchse *f* (bearing) bush(ing), axle box, journal box, bearing, liners, hub, brass (mach.) **-bügel** *m* bearing cap, bearing bracket **-dauer** *f* time of storage **-deckel** *m* bearing cap or cover **-deckelschalen** *pl* bearing caps **-deckelschraube** *f* screw for bearing cover **-druck** *m* bearing pressure, rock pressure

Lageregelung *f* operation of an automatic pilot, positioning action

Lager-einbau *m* bearing installation **-einschleifmasse** *f* grindling paste for bearings **-element** *n* inert cell **-fachkartei** *f* stock card index **-fähigkeit** *f* storage property or stability **-festung** *f* fortified area **-fett** *n* bearing grease **-fläche** *f* bearing surface **-flansch** *m* bearing flange **-förmig** in beds (geol.) **-fuge** *f* joint of the bed **-fuß** *m* bearing base **-futter** *n* lining of the bearing

Lager-gabel *f* bearing yoke **-gang** *m* vein following bedding planes, bedded vein, sheet, sill **-gebühren** storage charges **-gehäuse** *n* bearing housing, bearing box, bearing shell or casing **-gehäusedeckel** *m* bearing or end plate **-gerüst** *n* storage-closet rack **-gestell** *n* bearing support **-getriebe** *n* increasing gear (jet) **-guß** *m* bearing surface

Lager-häfte *f* bearing half **-hals** *m* bearing neck, axle journal **-halter** *m* storekeeper **-haus** *n* storehouse, warehouse, store magazine **-hebel** *m* guide bearing **-hülse** *f* bearing cage, bearing sleeve

Lager-käfig *m* bearing cage **-kalotte** *f* ball socket **-kantenpressung** *f* bearing end pressure **-kappe** *f* bearing cap **-kasten** *m* bearing box **-keller** *m* store or storage cellar **-kopf** *m* head bearing **-korb** *m* bearing cage, bearing sleeve **-körper** *m* bearing body, bearing box, bearing house, housing **-kosten** *pl* storage expenses **-kragen** *m* bearing collar **-kran** *m* warehouse crane, storage crane **-kugel** *f* bearing ball **-laufring** *m* race

Lagerlegierung *f* bearing alloy, antifriction alloy ~ **mit Kupfergehalt** copper bearing alloy

Lager-liste *f* stock list **-luft** *f* bearing clearance or tolerance (mech.) **-meister** *m* storekeeper **-metall** *n* antifriction metal, bearing metal, babbitt (metal), white metal **-metallausguß mit Stahlstützschale** steelbacked lining (for bearing) **-mitte** *f* bearing center

lagern to store, support, be on hand, embed, deposit, fix, rest, repose **drehbar** ~ to pivot **in fester Stuhlung** ~ to carry on solid frames

Lagern *n* depositing, keeping, storage

Lager-nadel *f* bearing needle **-oberfläche** *f* bearing surface **-ölabdichtung** *f* oil-retaining packing (for bearing) **-ölung** *f* bearing lubrication **-ort** *m* camp site **-pfahl** *m* picket post **-pfanne** *f* step bearing, bushing **-platte** *f* base plate, sole plate

Lagerplatz *m* dump, depot, camp, storage place, storage yard, stockyard **-beschickung** stocking out **-brücke** *f* yard transporter crane **-kran** *m* yard crane **-meister** *m* yard foreman

Lager-prozeß *m* aging or storage process **-prüfer** *m* bearing tester **-prüfmaschine** *f* bearing testing machine **-punkt** *m* point of support **-raum** *m* store-room, stockroom, storage space, bearing frame **-reibung** *f* bearing friction **-ring** *m* ring bearing **-rolle** *f* bearing roller **-ruhe** *f* bearing support **-schaber** *m* three-square scraper

Lagerschale *f* bearing box, split section of a bearing, brass (mach.), bearing brass, (shell of) bushing, sleeve or collar, bush, axle box, bearing seat ~ **der Pleuelstange** brasses of connecting rod

Lagerschalen-ausguß *m* bearing-box lining **-bund** *m* flange of brass bearings **-gehäuse** *n* shell case **-gießvorrichtung** *f* casting device for bushes **-hälfte** *f* bearing half **-paar** *n* pair of split bearings or brasses (mach.)

Lager-schein *m* warrant, warehouse receipt **-scheine** *f* fulcrum bar **-schild** *n* bearing bracket or plate **-schlitz für die Zunge im Nadelschaft** latch slot **-schraube** *f* bearing bolt **-schuppen** *m* storage shed, depot **-schwelle des Fußbodens** dormer, sleeper **-schwund** *m* stock loss **-silo** *m* storage silo **-spesen** *pl* warehouse charges **-spiel** *n* bearing clearance, slackness **-spiel** *n* bearing play **-spitze** *f* pivot point **-stange** *f* side guard shaft

Lagerstätte *f* deposit, bed, seam (of ores), field **angeschwemmte** ~ alluvial deposit **oberflächliche** ~ superficial deposit **plattenförmige** ~ tabular deposit

Lagerstätten-kunde *f* science of mineral deposits **-lehre** *f* economic geology **-suche** *f* prospecting **-wasser** *n* oil water

Lager-stein *m* bearing jewel **-steinschraube** *f* jewel support **-stelle** *f* bearing, camp site **-stern** *m* bearing support (in turbine and jet engines) **-stift** *m* hinge pin **-strebe** *f* supporting strut **-stuhl** *m* bearing block, floor stand, floor frame, socket, cradle **-stütze** *f* bearing bracket **-stutzen** *m* support stud **-stützkraft** *f* bearing reaction force **-stützschale** *f* bearing support, shell **-tank** *m* storage tank **-träger** *m* bearing flange **-typ** *m* type of bearing, stock type

Lage und Höhe position and level, planimetry and elevation

Lagerung *f* storage, warehousing; (Alterung) seasoning; (Technik) bearing, application; (Geologie) stratification; (Abstützung) support; (Befestigung) mounting, bedding, seating, orientation (cryst.), spacing, stratification (geol.), conformity, bearing, bagging down (as a balloon), arrangement, suspension, stowage ~ **der Fasern** formation, disposition (texture) of fibers ~ **in Steinen** jeweled bearing **drehbare** ~ pivoting **elastische weiche** ~ **des Motors in Gummi** floating power **kugelige** ~ spherical seating **schichtenförmige** ~ foliation **schwimmende** ~ floating mounting **steile** ~ steep measures

Lagerungs-bedingung *f* condition of storage **-dichte** *f* degree of compaction, thickness of stratum **-fähigkeit** *f* storage capacity **-möglichkeit** *f* storage facility **-schiene** *f* hollow splint **-störung** *f* disturbance of beds, dislocation **-tisch** *m* radiographic couch **-verhältnisse** *pl* storage conditions **-verschlechterung** *f* shelf life deterioration

Lager-versuche *pl* storage tests **-vorrat** *m* storage stock, stock on hand **-wand** *f* bearing wall **-weißmetall** *n* babbitt (metal) **-zapfen** *m* trunnion, trail-spade trunnion, journal, supporting stud of telescope, pivot pin, journal pin **-zeit** *f* time of storage

Lage-steuerungsdüse *f* attitude control nozzle (rocket) **-toleranz** *f* positional tolerance **-verhalten** *n* positioning action **-wechsel** *m* transposition (teleph.), change of position **-winkel** *m* course or sight angle **-winkelkommando** *n* angular position signal **-zeichen** *n* position mark **-zuordnung** *f* controlled (angular) vane position

lagunare Ablagerung lagoon deposit

Lagune *f* lagoon

Lagunenriff *n* atoll

lahm lame

lähmen to paralyze, immobilize, neutralize

lahmgelegt tied up

lahmlegen to neutralize, render ineffective

Lahmlegung *f* neutralization

Lähmung *f* paralysis

Lahn *m* flat wire, tinsel **-litze** *f* tinsel (cord) **-litzenschnur** *f* tinsel cord **-stopfen** *m* ground stop-lock

Laibung *f* soffit

Laie *m* layman

laienhaft lay

Laken *n* linen, linen sheet, sheet

Lakepumpe zum Schnellpökeln brine pump for rapid pickling

Lakkolity *m* laccolith, igneous intrusion

Lakmoid *n* lacmoid

Lakmus *m* litmus

Laktat *n* lactate

Laktoglukose *f* lactoglucose, galactose

Laktolin *n* bilactate of potash (Lactoline)

Laktometer *n* lactometer

Laktobutyrometer *n* lactobutyrometer

Lambda-Begrenzung *f* lambda limiting process

Lambda/2-Blättchen *n* half-wave plate

Lambda/4-Blättchen *n* quarter-wave plate

Lambda/4-Verschiebung *f* quadrature

Lamberit *m* lamberite

Lambert *n* lambert (unit of brightness) **-gesetz** *n* Lambert's law, cosine emission law

Lambris *m* inlaying, paneling, wainscot

Lambsche Verschiebung *f* Lamb shift

lamellar lamellar, laminated, platelike **-gefüge** *n* laminated structure

Lamelle *f* lamination, lamina, bar, lamella, sheet of metal, disk, shim, cooling fin, segment; (Kühler) radiator rib ~ **einer Gürtung** sheet, plate **kugelförmig gewölbte Lamellen** dished laminae

lamellen-artig lamellar, laminated **-bremse** *f* multiple-plate or multiple-disk brake **-führungsring** *m* diaphram leaf guide ring **-haken** *m* laminated hook **-heizkörper** *m* laminated radiator arrangement **-isolation** *f* insulation between commitator segments **-kern** *m* laminated core **-kühler** *m* sheet-metal radiator, ribbed, gilled, flanged, or finned radiator **-kupfer** *m* copper segments **-kuppelung** *f* (multiple) disk clutch **-luftfilter** *m* multi-plate air filter

Lamellen-magnet *m* compound magnet, laminated magnet **-meißel** *m* lamellar chisel **-rippe** *f* laminate rib **-rohr** *n* gilled or ribbed tube, extended surface pipe **-röhre** *f* lamellar tube **-schluß** *m* armature short **-schraubbremse** *f* self-acting equilibrium brake operated by load itself

Lamellen-spiegel *m* striplike mirror **-struktur** *f* lamination **-technik** *f* vane technique **-teilung** *f* segment pitch **-träger** *m* (Kupplung) disc carrier **-verschluß** *m* lamellar shutter

lamellieren to laminate, flatten

lamelliert laminated

Lamellierung *f* lamination

laminar laminar **-strömung** *f* laminar flow **-es Modell mit Verzweigungen** branched laminar model **-e Schicht** laminar layer

Laminar-haltung *f* laminarization **-profil** *n* laminar airfoil **-strömung** *f* laminar flow

laminieren to laminate, draw (in spinning)

Laminierstuhl *m* drawing frame

Lämmerwolke *f* cirro-cumulus cloud

Lammfell *n* lambskin

Lampe *f* (pilot) burner, lamp, searchlight, light **punktförmige** ~ lamp with point-shaped or crater light source **weiße** ~ clear pilot burner

Lampen für Meßzwecke photometric lamps

Lampen-abzweigekasten *m* distributing box (elec.) **-aggregat** *n* bank or pillar of lamps **-anlasser** *m* arc-lamp starter **-anschluß** *m* lamp connection **-arbeit** *f* blast-lamp work **-arm** *m* lamp bracket **-brennerkapsel** *f* lamp-burner part or case **-brennstunde** *f* lamp hour (electr.) **-bude** *f* lamp cabin, lamp room **-docht** *m* lamp wick

Lampenfassung *f* lamp holder, (lamp) socket ~ **mit zentraler Drahteinführung** lamp holder with cord grip

Lampenfeld *n* lamp panel, (bank of) lamps ~ **für Rufanzeige** call indicator

Lampen-fuß *m* lamp squash, lamp press **-gehäuse** *n* lamp case, chamber, or housing **-gestell** *n* lampadary, lamppost **-glas** *n* (lamp) chimney **-glocke** *f* (lamp) globe **-halter** *m* lamp bracket **-käfig** *m* lamp cage **-kappe** *f* lamp cap or shield **-kasten** *m* lamp housing or box **-kranz** *m* lamp rim **-kuppel** *f* lamp globe **-kuppelfassung** *f* lamp-globe collar

Lampen-licht *n* artificial light **-putzer** *m* lamp cleaner **-regelwerk** *n* carbon-feeding mechanism of searchlight **-relais** *n* lamp-control relay **-ruß** *m* lampblack

Lampen-schirm *m* lamp shade **-schwarz** *n* lampblack **-signal** *n* lamp signal **-signalisierung** *f* lamp signaling **-sitz** *m* lamp seat **-sockel** *m* lamp socket **-stativ** *n* lamp tripod **-stempel** *m* (lamp) squash, press **-streifen** *m* lamp-socket mounting, lamp strip **-stromkreis** *m* lamp circuit **-stufenregler** *m* step regulator for bulb voltage

Lampen-träger *m* lamp holder or support **-überlastung** *f* overrunning of a lamp **-vorwiderstand** *m* lamp series resistance **-wart** *m* searchlight mechanic **-wendel** *n* lamp filament **-widerstand** *m* lamp resistance **-zeichenkasten** *m* signal-lamp box **-zylinder** *m* glass chimney, lamp chimney

Lancashire Frischherd *m* Lancashire hearth **~ Herdfrischprozeß** *m* Lancashire charcoal-hearth process

Lancierapparat, fest eingebauter ~ fixed launching tube (torpedoes)

lancieren to fire (torpedoes)

Land *n* (Staat) country, land, territory, (Boden) soil, state, region **~ in Sicht bekommen** to sight land or coast **nach ~ zu halten** to bear on shore **unter ~ halten** to hug the land, keep the land aboard **an ~** ashore **angespültes ~** alluvium **bewässertes ~** irrigated land

Land-abdachung *f* downstream slope **-ankertau** *n* shore anchor line

Landanschluß, ~ der Buhne root of a groin, dike **~ der Mole** root of the breakwater

Land-arbeit *f* agricultural work **-aufhöhung** *f* raising of an area by filling **-ausrüstung** *f* ground equipment **-batterie** *f* land-based antiaircraft battery **-bau** *m* agriculture, farming **-beobachter** *m* observer on land **-bord** *n* landward board (boat), shoreward side **-brücke** *f* landing bridge, landing stage **-dampfkessel** *m* stationary boiler

Lande-abstand *m* landing interval **-achse** *f* correct bearing or line for approach **-anflug** *m* approach for landing **-bereich** *m* landing area

Landebahn *f* landing path **-feuer** *n* landing direction light, contact light **-geber** *m* zero reader **-leuchte** *f* landing floodlight **-leuchtkraftwagen** *m* airfield-landing-lights tender **-scheinwerfer** *m* landing floodlight

Lande-beleuchtung *f* landing lights **-bereich** *m* landing area **-bremshaken** *m* arresting hook **-bremsvorrichtung** *f* arresting gear **-brücke** *f* pier, jetty, wharf or staging, landing stage **-deck** *n* flight deck, landing deck **-einrichtung** *f* landing installation or equipment or facilities **-erlaubnis** *f* landing permit, permission to land

Lande-fackel *f* wing-tip flare **-fallschirm** *m* air-brake parachute **-feldbeleuchtung** *f* field flood lighting **-feuer** *n* landing light, flare on lamp (for night flying) **-fläche** *f* landing surface **-folge** *f* landing sequence **-funkfeuer** *n* radio landing beacon

Lande-gebühr *f* landing tax or fee **-gelände** *n* landing field **-geschwindigkeit** *f* landing speed **-gestell** *n* docking trolley (airship); (Raumschiff) landing legs **-gewicht** *n* landing load **-hilfe** *f* landing device, high-lift device **-höhenschreiber** *m* landing height recorder

Landeklappe *f* landing flap, air brake **ausgefahrene ~** flaps down **voll ausgefahrene ~** full flaps

Landeklappenanzeiger *m* landing-flap-position indicator

Landeklappenausschlag *m* flap-deflection

Lande-klappenschiene *f* landing flap track **-kopf** *m* landing end, beachhead **-kreuz** *n* ground panel landing cross, landing T **-kufen** *pl* landing skids (spacecraft) **-kurssender** *m* localizer (ILS) **-last** *f* landing load **-leuchte** *f* (Leuchtpfad) contact light **-licht** *n* landing light (airport) **-mannschaft** *f* landing crew, ground crew **-meldung** *f* landing report **-möglichkeit** *f* landing facility or possibility

landen to land, make a landing

Landen *n* alighting, landing **~ mit großer Schnelligkeit** landing hot **~ ohne Bremsen** landing without use of brakes **~ mit stehendem Motor** landing with stopped engine

Landenge *f* isthmus, strait

Lande-kontrolle *f* landing chek **-platz** *m* landing ground or strip **-puffer** *m* undercarriage shock absorber, bumper bag **-punkt** *m* landing spot; (der Raumkapsel) *m* impact point (spacecraft) **-querschnitt** *m* landing profile **-rad** *n* landing wheel **-richtung** *f* direction of landing **-richtungsanzeiger** *m* landing direction indicator **-richtungsfeuer** *n* range light

Landes-aufnahme *f* topographical survey, ordnance survey, topographical mapping, geodetic survey **-fernwahl** *f* nationwide toll dialing **-fernwahlnetz** *n* nation-wide dialling network

Landescheinwerfer *m* landing floodlight, landing headlight **einziehbarer ~** retractable landing light

Lande-scheinwerferanhänger *m* field searchlight trailer **-schwelle** *f* landing threshold

Landes-erzeugnis *n* agricultural product **-farben** *pl* national colors **-gericht** *n* national court

Landespieß *m* landing hook

Lande-steg *m* landing ramp **-stelle** *f* landing spot **-stellung** *f* landing position, extended position of the undercarriage **-stoß** *m* impact of landing **-strecke** *f* landing distance or run **-streifen** *m* landing strip

Landes-vermessung *f* surveying the land **-vermessungsnetz** *n* triangulation network

Lande-T *n* landing T

Lande-tau *n* landing rope or line **-tetraeder** *m* landing tetrahedron **-trupp** *m* landing and saddling detail **-verbot** *n* landing restriction **-weg** *m* landing path **-weiser** *m* landing direction indicator **-winkel** *m* landing angle **-zeichen** *n* landing signal **-ziel** *n* landing point **-zone** *f* landing area or zone

Land-fahrwerk *n* wheel-type landing gear **-fahrzeug** *n* pontoon nearest to shore; land vehicle **-fernsprechnetz für Selbstanschlußbetrieb** rural telephone plant, community automatic exchange **-fest** (Station) shore-based (rdr.) **-flugplatz** *m* airport **-flugzeug** *n* landplane **-flugzeugschlepper** *m* landplane tug **-funkstelle** *f* ground (radio) station, shore or coast station **-gang** *m* shore liberty **-gangsausweis** *m* shoregoing pass

Land-gebühr *f* land (wireless or radio) charges per word, land-station charges **-gericht** *n* high court, district or county court, general court of justice **-gut** *n* estate **-kabel** *n* underground cable **-kabelmuffe** *f* underground cable box

Landkarte *f* (topographic) map **die Richtung der ~ bestimmen** orienting a map

Landkarten-aufzieher *m* map sticker **-druck-**

papier *n* chart paper, map or plan paper **-mäßig erfassen** to map

Land-kompaß *m* land compass **-krieg** *m* land warfare **-leitung** *f* landline

ländlich rural

Land-linie *f* landline **-marke** *f* landmark **-markenlicht** *n* landmark beacon **-maschinen** *f pl* agricultural machinery **-meile** *f* statute mile **-messer** *m* (land) surveyor **-messertrupp** *m* surveyor party **-meßkunst** *f* land surveying **-mine** *f* land mine **-nebel** *m* land or ground fog **-netzgruppe** *f* rural telephone network **-omnibus** *m* interurban bus

Landoreverfahren *n* Landore (pig and ore) process or method

Land-peilstation *f* land direction-finding station **-peilung** *f* shore bearing **-planke** *f* gangplank **-recht** *n* common law **-regen** *m* general rain **-rotte** *f* dew-retting

Land-schaft *f* scenery, landscape **-schaftsgestaltung** *f* landscaping, landscape treatment (or development) **-schwelle** *f* upthrust, shore beam

Landseite *f* shore side

landseitig at inland end **-e Stütze** *f* (Kran) inner leg

Land-spitze *f* point, cape (geog.), headlands **-start** *m* ground take-off **-station** *f* base or land station **-stoß** *m* abutment beam **-straße** *f* highway, road **-straßenwegweiser** *m* highway route marker **-stufe** *f* escarpment

Land-transport *m* overland transportation

Land- und Seewinde *m pl* land and sea breezes

Landung *f* arrival landing ~ **mit Durchsacken** pancake landing ~ **ohne Motor** dead-stick landing ~ **mit noch nicht erstorbenem Motor** power-stall landing, power landing ~ **mit Rückenwind** down-wind landing ~ **mit stehender Schraube** dead landing, landing with the airscrew stopped ~ **mit Seitenwind** cross-wind landing ~ **in Stampfbewegung** bouncing movement while landing on water, porpoise (aviation) **zur ~ ansetzen** to approach land **zur ~ gezwungen** forced to land **waagerechte ~** level landing

Landungs-abteilung *f* beach party or detachment **-beleuchtung** *f* landing lights **-boot** *n* landing barge, landing boat **-bremse** *f* landing brake **-brücke** *f* pier, landing stage, landing place, place of embarkation **-damm** *m* pier **-fahrzeug** *n* landing craft

Landungs-feld *n* landing field **-fühler** *m* landing-field indicator **-funkbake** *f*, **-funkfeuer** *n* landing beacon **-funkstelle** *f* portable wireless set **-gebiet** *n* landing area **-gerät** *n* landing gear **-gerüst** *n* field handling frame

Landungs-kai *n* landing quay **-kaje** *f* tidal quay **-klappe** *f* landing ramp **-korps** *n* landing detachment **-kufe** *f* landing skid **-licht** *n* landing light **-mannschaft** *f* ground crew **-platz** *m* unloading (discharge) wharf, landing area **-ponton** *n* landing, passenger landing **-puffer** *m* bumping bag **-rauchzeichen** *n* smoke signal carried by plane, landing smoke signal

Landungs-scheinwerfer *m* landing searchlight, landing projector **-steg** *m* jetty, wharf, staging, landing pier **-stelle** *f* landing place **-stoß** *m* landing shock **-strahl** *m* landing beam **-T** *n* landing T **-tonne** *f* landing buoy **-trupp** *m* landing party **-unternehmung** *f* landing operation **-vorgang** *m* landing procedure **-winkel** *m* landing angle **-zeit** *f* time of landing

Land-verankerung *f* shore mooring, guy-line anchorage **-vermessung** *f* land survey

landwärts landward

Landwind *m* land wind or breeze, off-shore wind or breeze ~ **und Seebrise** land and sea breezes

Landwirt *m* farmer, agriculturist

Landwirtschaft *f* agriculture

landwirtschaftlich agricultural **-er Betrieb** agricultural installation **-er Kleinbetrieb** small holding **-e Maschinen** agricultural machinery

Landzentrale *f* rural plant, R.A.W. (rural automatic exchange) **automatische ~** tertiary exchange, U.X.A. (unit automatic exchange)

Landzunge *f* spit (of land)

lang long **elektrisch ~** electrically long **unendlich ~** infinitely long

lang-andauernd lengthy **-anhaltend** prolonged

Langbasis *f* horizontal base **-anlage** *f* base end station, long base (range finder) **-entfernungsmesser** *m* longbase range finder **-verfahren** *n* horizontal base method

Langbaum *m* perch, reach, pole, tongue **-blech** *n* perch plate

Lang-bespulung *f* loading of cable by series coils **-bogenlampe** *f* long-arc lamp **-bohrer** *m* slot drill, long borer

langbrennweitig, -es Fernrohr long-focus telescope **-e Linse** long-focus lens or objective **-es Okular** eyepiece of long focal length

lang-dauernd protracted **-dreharbeit** *f* longitudinal or straight turning **-drehautomat** *m* swiss bush-type automatic lathe, swiss-type automatic machine **-drehbank** *f* long-turning lathe **-dreheinrichtung** *f* longitudinal turning attachement **-drehen** *n* turning along **-drehschlitten** *m* turning carriage, carriage, saddle, tool slide for turning **-drehstahl** *m* turning tool **-drehsupport** *m* turning support

Länge *f* length, sling, strap ~ **Tuchmuster** swatch (of fabric) ~ **der Anlaufstrecke** length of take-off run **freitragende ~ eines Balkens** bearing of a beam ~ **des Geigerbereiches** plateau length (geiger) ~ **der Hochführung** length of inclination ~ **auf Kielstapeln** length over keel blocks **größte ~ zwischen den Spitzen** greatest length between points **der ~ nach schneiden** to cut lengthwise

Länge, der ~ nach endways, lenthwise ~ **über alles** over-all length **äußerste ~** over-all length **einschießen nach der ~** range adjustment **geographische ~** longitude **gesamte ~** overall length **gewöhnliche ~** standard or usual length **mittlere ~** mean length **regelrechte ~** standard length **handelsübliche ~** commercial length

langeförmig of extended shape

Länge-dichte *f* line density **-durchschnittsverhältnis** *n* length-to-diameter ratio (of rocket-motor combustion chamber)

Länge-einheitsbelastung *f* uniform longitudinal load **-einheitslast** *f* load per unit of length

Langeisenwagen *m* car for transporting long iron bars

Längel *n* slack thread

längen to lengthen, extend, stretch, elongate

Längen-abhängigkeit *f* dependence on length **-abstufung** *f* longitudinal graduation

Längenabweichung *f* error in range, variation in longitude, range deviation **Festlegen der ~** range sensing or spotting

Längen-änderung *f* deformation in extension, elongation **-ausdehnung** *f* (linear) extension, linear expansion **-ausdehnungszahl** *f* coefficient of linear expansion **-begrenzung** *f* longitudinal dead limit **-bestimmung** *f* determination of longitude **-bruch** *m* longitudinal fracture **-dehnung** *f* dilatation of length **-durchschnitt** *m* longitudinal section **-einheit** *f* unit of length **-faser im Holz** grain of wood, woody fiber **-fehler** *m* longitudinal error **-gedinge** *n* fathom work

Längengrad *m* degree of longitude **-unterschied** *m* difference in (degrees of) longitude

Längengurt *m* longitudinal arch **freistehender ~** pier arch

Längenkreis *m* meridian, circle of longitude

Längenmaß *n* length dimension, linear measure(ment), long measure, standard of length **~ eines Telegraphenkabels** total distortion of a telegraph cable

Längen-maßstab *m* scale of length, longitudinal scale **-meßeinrichtung** *f* longitudinal measuring attachment **-messer** *m* instrument for measuring lengths **-meßgeräte** *pl* instruments for measuring gauging lengths **-meßmaschine** *f* measuring machine

Längenmessung *f* measuring length, linear measurement **echte und unechte ~** direct and indirect measurement of length

Längen-metazentrum *n* longitudinal metacenter **-minute** *f* longitude minute **-neigung** *f* longitudinal (lengthwise) inclination (tilt) **-nivellement** *n* levels of the ground taken along a line **-parameter** *n* length parameter **-profil** *n* longitudinal section **-quotient** *m* ratio of length, length quotient **-schnitt** *m* longitudinal section **-schrumpfung** *f* shrinkage in length

Längensprödigkeit von Kesselblechen embrittlement in steam boilers

Längen-streuung *f* error in range due to rain, longitudinal dispersion, axial dispersion or dispersion in depth (ballistics), ratio of length, length quotient **-stuhl** *m* legging frame

längentreu isometric **-e Abbildung** length-preserving mapping

Längen-treue *f* length-preserving **-übertragung** *f* transfer of the length **-unterschied** *m* difference in longitude **-verbesserung** *f* range correction **-verhältnis** *n* aspect ratio **-zuwachs** *m* elongation

Länge-rampe *f* long ramp, platform **-streuung** *f* longitudinal dispersion, error in range due to gun, length zone

Langfalz-, Biege- und Zudrückmaschine *f* folding bending, and grooving machine

Langfalzzudrückpresse *f* folding and grooving press

Langflächenschleifmaschine mit Horizontalschleifkopf planer-type horizontal-spindle grinding machine

Langflammenlampe *f* soft light

langflammig long-flaming **-e Kohle** long-flame or long-flaming coal, cannel coal

langflurig long-haired (longpiled)

Lang-format *n* oblong size **-fräser** *m* cotter mill, long-hole cutter **-fräsmaschine** *f* horizontal plane milling machine **-fräsmaschine, vierspindlig** four-spindle planertype milling machine **-fristig** for a long time, long-term **-frontbau** *m* long wall

lang-gebaute Filterpresse long filter press **-geschoß** *n* long shell **-gestreckt** extended, elongated, oblong **-gestreift** vertically striped **-gewindefräsen** *n* long-thread milling **-gewindefräsmaschine** *f* long-thread milling machine **-gliedrig** long-linked, long-membered

lang-halsig long-necked **-hobelmaschine** *f* parallel-planing machine **-holz** *n* long wood, long spar or beam **-holzlastwagen** *m* logging truck **-huber** *m* long stroke engine **-hubig** long-stroke **-jährig** of many years

Lang-kessel *m* boiler barrel or shell, cylindrical part of a boiler **-klauig** long-shanked (with long shanks) **-kopiefräsmaschine** *f* longitudinal milling machine with copying or profiling device **-kopierapparat** *m* longitudinal copying attachment **-kreis** *m* ellipse, oval **-laufzünder** *m* delayed-action fuse **-leberöhre** *f* long-service valve **-lebig** long-lived **-leitungseffekt** *m* long-line effect

länglich oblong, elongated **-e Öffnung** slotted opening

länglichrund oval, elliptical, lenticular

länglich vierkant oblong

Langloch *n* oblong hole, slotted hole, slot **-bohrer** *m* slot drill **-bohrmaschine** *f* slot-boring machine **-fräsen** *n* end milling **-fräser** *m* end mill, slot, or key cutter, longhole cutter **-hebel** *m* slotted lever

Lang-mascher *m* long-loop apparatus **-messer** *pl* straight knives **-mütig** patient

Lang-nutenfräsmaschine *f* long slot milling machine **-periodische Wellen** long-period waves **-reichweitig** long-range **-rohrleitung** *f* (oxygen) feed line (guided missiles) **-rund** oval elliptical **-rundholz** *n* long roundwood

längs lengthwise, along **-abmessung** *f* lenthwise dimension **-achse** *f* longitudinal or roll axis, major axis, fore-aft line **-addition** *f* longitudinal addition

langsam slow, idling **~ laufender Motor** slow-idling **~ laufender Motor** slow-running engine **~ abfallendes Relais** slow-to-release relay **~ bindender Zement** slow-setting cement **~ ansprechend** slow-operating, slow-response **~ landen** to land slowly **-es Elektron** cold electron **-e Neutronen** cold neutrons, thermal neutrons **-e Rolle** slow roll **-er Speicher** slow storage **-er werden** to slow down

Langsam-antrieb *m* slow speed drive **-ausschalter** *m* slow-break switch **-binder** *m* slow-setting cement **-einschaltung** *f* step-by-step starting **-flug** *m* slow flight, stalling flight **-gang** *m* slow motion

Langsamkeit *f* slowness, sluggishness

Langsamlauf *m* slow running **~ des Motors** idle engine, slow-running engine

langsamlaufend slow-speed, low-speed **-e Mühle**

low-speed mill

Langsam-läufer *m* slow-moving engine **-lösend** slow-release, slow releasing or disengaging, slow dissolving **-schaltung** *f* time-delay connection **-unterbrecher** *m* slow-speed interrupter **-wirkend** slow-acting

längsabgeströmte Platte flat plate at zero incidence

Längs-anschlag *m* longitudinal or length feed stop **-anschlagtrommel** *f* longitudinal stop drum **-ansicht** *f* longitudinal view **-arbeit** *f* longitudinal operation **-arm** *m* line arm, series arm **-aufriß** *m* longitudinal view **-ausgleich** *m* compensation of capacity deviations (telephone) **-ausgleichhebel** *m* longitudinal equalizer **-aussparung** *f* longitudinal recess

Längs-balken *m* main or longitudinal beam **-bauten** *pl* press gate, wet machine, wet press, regulating dikes **-beanspruchungen unnachgiebig widerstehen** to rigidly resist longitudinal stresses **-bedeckungsmaschine** *f* longitudinal covering machine **-belastung** *f* thrust load **-bespulung** *f* coil loading **-bestreichung** *f* enfilade fire (mil.)

Längs-bewegung *f* longitudinal travel (motion), displacement adjustment **-bewegungstrieb** *m* longitudinal or lengthwise motion head **-bewehrt** straight-reinforced **-bewehrung** *f* longitudinal bar **-bohren** *n* center drilling **-bohrung** *f* longitudinal hole or bore **-brett** *n* wood piling or shoring

lang-schäftiger Kolben long-skirted piston **-schliff** *m* long-fibered mechanical pulp **-schnürig** long-stapled **-schwelle** *f* longitudinal tie (R.R.) **-schwenktisch** *m* longitudinal swivel table

Längs-dämpfung *f* longitudinal damping **-dehnung** *f* linear elongation or expansion, extension **-dehnungszahl** *f* coefficient of (longitudinal) expansion **-divergenz** *f* longitudinal divergence **-drehschieber** *m* (Steuergerät) (combined) sliding and rotary-type spool (control valve) **-drehschwingung** *f* longitudinal torsional oscillation **-druck** *m* thrust, thrust load **-drucklager** *n* (end) thrust bearing **-durchflutung einer Synchronmaschine** direct-axis component of a magnetomotive force **-durchmesser** *m* longitudinal diameter **-durchschnitt** *m* longitudinal section **-ebene** *f* longitudinal plane **-eilrücklauf** *m* longitudinal rapid return

Langseite eines Daches long pane of a roof

Längs-entzerrer *m* attenuation-equalizer or compensator series type **-entzerrung** *f* equalization in series **-falz** *m* longitudinal fold **-falzeinrichtung** *f* lengthwise folding mechanism **-falzmaschine** *f* side-seaming machine **-falzung** *f* longitudinal folding **-feder** *f* longitudinal spring, feather key **-fehler** *m* longitudinal error **-feld** *n* longitudinal field, chase (of gun barrel), field parallel to axis, paraxial field **-feuer** *n* enfilade fire (mil.) **-fluß** *m* longitudinal flux **-fuge** *f* bed joint **-furnier** *n* longitudinal-ply grain, plain veneer

längs-genutete Welle spline shaft **-gerippt** longitudinally ribbed or grilled **-geschlitzt** longitudinally slit **-geschwindigkeit** *f* forward speed, translational velocity **-gestreift** vertically striped

Längsglied *n* series element **~ eines Filters** series element of a filter **in einem halben ~ endendes Filter** wave filter terminated at mid-series (position), mid-series terminated filter **~ einer Kette** series element of a network, series mesh of a network **Abschluß eines Filters durch ein halbes ~** termination of a filter at mid-series position, mid-series termination

Längs-heftung *f* longitudinal stiching **-holm** *m* longeron, span **-hub** *m* longitudinal travel **-hydraulikzylinder** *m* cylinder for the hydraulic cross traverse

lang-sichtig long-sighted **-sichtigkeit** *f* hypermetropia

Langsieb *n* machine wire, endless wire **-maschine** *f* Fourdrinier **-partie der Papiermaschine** wet part of the paper machine

Längs-impedanz *f* series impedance **-kanal** *m* axial canal **-keil** *m* ordinary key **-komponente** *f* longitudinal component **-kopieren** *n* longitudinal copying **-kopiervorrichtung** *f* longitudinal forming or copying attachment **-kraft** *f* stress resultant, longitudinal force **-kugellager** *n* longitudinal ball bearing

Längs-lager *n* axial bearings, thrust bearing, side bearing **-lastigkeit** *f* longitudinal trim **-leiste** *f* longitudinal batten, reinforcing strip **-leitfähigkeit** *f* longitudinal conductivity **-libelle** *f* longitudinal level, sight level **-linie** *f* down rule (under heading) **-loch** *n* oblong hole **-lochstreifen** *m* lengthways perforated tape **-luft** *f* axial play

Längs-magnetisierung *f* longitudinal magnetization **-maßeinheit** *f* measure of length, unit or standard of length **-meßinstrument** *n* length measuring (gauging) instrument **-meßmaschine** *f* measuring machine **-messungen** *pl* measurements lengthways **-moment** *n* pitching moment, longitudinal moment **-momentenbeiwert** *m* pitching moment coefficient

Längs-naht *f* longitudinal seam, straight bead (welding) **-neigung** *f* (Flugzeug, Autos) longitudinal slope, pitch, longitudinal inclination (pitching) **-neigungsmesser** *m* pitch indicator, fore-and-aft level indicator, inclinometer **-neigungswinkel** *m* angle of pitch **-normale** *f* standard of length, standard linear measure **-nut** *f* longitudinal groove or slot, transverse groove, spline **-nuten** to spline

Längs- oder Kippmoment *n* pitching moment

Längs- oder Schrägschlitz *m* vertical or oblique vent

Längs-perforation *f* longitudinal perforation **-peilung** *f* taking bearings from direction-finding station situated in direction of travel

Längs-pleißung *f* long splice

Längs-profil *n* longitudinal stringer, profile **-querspant** *m* longitudinal bulkhead **-recken** to stretch **-regulierung** *f* longitudinal regulation **-reiber** *m* longitudinal grinder, longitudinal friction device

Längsrichtung *f* longitudinal direction, sense of length **in ~** endwise **Spiel in ~** end float

Längs-rippe *f* longitudinal rib or fin **-riß** *m* longitudinal crack **-rissiger Draht** cuppy wire **-rückentitel** *m* title along the spine **-schärfe** *f* definition in line direction **-schermaschine** *f* longitudinal shearing machine **-schieber** *m*

sliding shutter; (Steuergerät) sliding spool (control valve) **-schiene** *f* (longitudinal) rail

längsschiffs fore-and-aft **-eisenmasse** *f* fore-and-aft iron mass, longitudinal iron mass **-kraft** *f* fore-and-aft force, longitudinal force **-magnet** *m* fore-and-aft ship's magnet **-pol** *m* fore-and-aft pole, longitudinal pole

Längs-schlag *m* twist in same direction, longitudinal stop **-schleife** *f* longitudinal, transverse loop **-schleifen** *n* long grinding **-schlitten** *m* longitudinal slide, turning carriage, carriage, saddle **-schlitz** *m* elongated slot

Längs-schneideeinrichtung *f* slitting arrangement **-schneidemaschine** *f* straight-line cutting machine, straight-line cutting guide **-schneidemesser** *n* slitting knife **-schneiden** to rip **-schneider** *m* longitudinal sheet cutter **-schnellverstellung** *f* longitudinal rapid traverse

Längsschnitt *m* slitting, longitudinal section or view, longitudinal cross section ~ **auf der Mittellinie** sectional elevation on center line

Längs-schott *n* longitudinal bulkhead **-schrumpfung** *f* longitudinal shrinkage **-schubkraft** *f* horizontal shear, longitudinal shear **-schwankung** *f* pitching or pitch (of aircraft) **-schweißung** *f* longitudinal weld **-schwelle** *f* longitudinal member **-schwingung** *f* longitudinal oscillation, or vibration, fore-and-aft oscillation

längsseits alongside ~ **gehen** to pull alongside ~ **schleppen** to tow alongside

Längs-selbstgang des Tisches longitudinal power traverse of the table **-sitz** *m* lengthwise seat **-span** *m* continuous ship **-spannung** *f* direct-axis component of the voltage **-spant** *n* longitudinal frame **-spiel** *n* end clearance, draw **-spiel** *n* axial play

Langspiel-band *n* long-playing tape **-platte** *f* long-playing record

Längs-spritzkopf *m* axial extruder head **-spule** *f* series coil

Längs-stabilität *f* longitudinal stability, pitching stability **-stabisolator** *m* one-piece rod-type suspension insulator **-steifig** longitudinally stiffened **-strahler** *m* end-fire array **-strahlung** *f* directional radiation, beaming

Langstrecken-gurtförderer *m* overland belt conveyor

Längs-streckung *f* elongation, extension **-streifen** *m* longitudinal stripe, longitudinal stria, longitudinal streak **-strich** *m* orienting or lengthwise line **-support** *m* tool post, tool carrier **-teilung** *f* longitudinal pitch or spacing

Längsträger *m* stringer, balk, longitudinal outrigger, longeron, long channel bar of chassis frame, side sill, longitudinal girder ~ **der Karosserie** longitudinal runner of carriage body ~ **des Rahmens** longitudinal member of frame

Längstragseil *n* longitudinal carrier cable

lang-strahliges Kristall elongated, needlelike crystal **-strähnig** long-skeined **-strecke** *f* long distance, long range

Langstrecken-dienst *m* longe-range or long-distance service **-flug** *m* long-distance flight **-flugboot** *n* long-range flying boat **-flugzeug** *n* long-range plane **-meßverfahren** *n* Loran (long-range radar system) **-postflugzeug** *n* long-range mail-plane

Längsstreckung *f* extension, elongation

Langstreifenmaschine *f* machine for vertical stripes

Längstrimm *m* longitudinal trim

Längstwelle *f* very long frequency (VLF)

Längsüberdeckung *f* longitudinal overlap

Längs- und Querverschiebung *f* axial and cross adjustment

Längs- und Querschnitt *m* slitting and sheeting

Längs-verband *m* longitudinal bond or bracing **-vergrößerung** *f* longitudinal magnification

längsverschiebbar, auf einer Welle frei ~ sliding endwise on a shaft

Längs-verschiebung *f* longitudinal movement, longitudinal displacement **-verspannung** *f* axial or longitudinal bracing or wiring **-versteifung** *f* longitudinal stiffening, stringer **-verstellbar** longitudinally adjustable **-verwerfung** *f* strike fault **-verzahnt** splined **-vorschubspindel** *f* table-feed screw **-wechselfeld** *n* longitudinal alternating field **-welle** *f* longitudinal (wave), long wave (of very low frequency)

Längs-werk *n* longitudinal dike **-widerstand** *m* series resistance, line resistance **-wind** *m* tail or head wind, parallel wind **-windanteil** *m*, **-windkomponente** *f* range wind component **-zapfen** *m* axle pivot pin **-zeile** *f* (metal) drawn-out slag streak, ghost line **-zug** *m* longitudinal (traverse) feed **-zusammenziehung** *f* contraction in length **-zweig** *m* line arm, series arm

Lang-tau *n* drag rope (gun) **-tischfräsmaschine** *f* planomiller **-tonne** *f* long ton

Längung *f* extension, elongation

Längungs-kurve *f* elongation curve, stretching curve **-messer** *m* extensometer

Langvorschub *m* longitudinal feed

Langwellen *pl* long waves (of medium frequency) **-aufzeichner** *m* phonautograph **-bereich** *m* long wave band **-kleinfunkapparat** *m* portable long-wave radio telephone, walkie-talkie **-peiler** *m* long-wave radio bearing station, long-wave direction finder **-sender** *m* long-wave transmitter **-senderanlage** *f* long-wave transmitting set or installation **-spule** *f* long-wave coil

langwellig of long wave length, long-wave **-er Ausläufer** low energy tail (emission band) **-e Grenze** long wavelength limit

langwierig lengthy, protracted, tedious, time-consuming

Langzeit-echo *n* long echo, echo of long duration, long-delay echo **-elektronenblitz** *m* delayed-time electronic flash

langzeitig-er Mittelwert *m* long-term average value **-e radioaktive Strahlung** *f* persistent radiation

Langzeit-konstanz *f* long-term constancy **-prüfung** *f* long-term exposure **-schweißung** *f* slow welding **-triebwerk** *n* propulsion unit for continuous operation **-versuch** *m* extended time or long time test, prolonged test **-zündung** *f* delayed time fuse

Langzug, Handrad für den ~ handwheel for traverse feed

Langzug-draht *m* (zwischen Typen- und Zwischenhebel) long link **-ritzel** *n* pinion **-schnecke** *f* feed worm **-schneckenrad** *n* feed-worm wheel **-übersetzungsrad** *n* gear in train **-zahnstange** *f* longitudinal feed rack

Lanosterin *n* lanosterol
L-Antenne *f* inverted-L antenna, gamma-type antenna **waagerechter Teil der ~** top spreader
Lanthan *n* lanthanum **-chlorid** *n* lanthanum chloride
Lanthaniden *pl* lanthanide elements
Lanthanit *m* lanthanite
Lanthanoxyd *n* lanthanum oxide
Lanze *f* lance
Lanzenschuh *m* lance bucket
Lanzette *f* slicker (in molding), lancet
Lanzierrohr *n* launching tube
Lapidar *f* block letter
Lapis-druck *m* lapis style **-lazuli** *m* lapis lazuli
Laplaceoperator *m* laplacian
Läpp-arbeit *f* lapping **-büchse** *f* lapping bush **-dorn** *m* arbor-type lap, lapping stick
Lappen *m* filing margin, gluing edge; (mech) fin, tongue, rag, flap, tang, lug, patch, duster, shred, tab, lobe, flange **bunter ~** colored cloth, garnish, garland **lose herabhängender ~** flap **vorspringender ~** projecting lug
Läppen *n* straight-line lapping **mit geradliniger Hin- und Herbewegung der Läppwerkzeuge** straight-line lapping
läppen to lap
Lappen-befestigung *f* patch system **-bohrung** *f* lug hole **-fläche** *f* tang face **-kopf** *m* lug head, thumb head **-messer** *n* amputation knife **-ring** *m* ring with flaps, flanged ring **-scheibe** *f* cloth mop **-schraube** *f* thumbscrew
lappig lobed, lobate, flabby, flaccid **-er Querschnitt** lobed cross section
Lappigkeit *f* sponginess
Läpp-maschine *f* lapping machine **-mittel** *n* lapping abrasive **-platte** *f* lapping compound, lapping plate **-ring** *m* external lap, ring lap **-scheibe** *f* lapping wheel, lap **-schleifen** to lap **-schliff** *m* finishing by lapping **-schweißung** *f* lap welding
Lappung *f* lap, serration
Läppwerkzeug *n* lap, lapping tool
Lärche *f* larch
Lärchen-holz *n* larch **-terpentin** *n* Venice turpentine
Lärm *m* noise, fuss **-abwehr** *f*, **-bekämpfung** *f* combating of noise, noise abatement **-pfeife** *f* alarm whistle **-signal** *n* sound signal
lärmen to create a disturbance, make a noise
Lärmorpräzession *f* Larmor precession, Larmor theorem
Lärm-schraube *f* air-driven siren **-schutzmittel** *pl* noise guards (acoust.) **-spiegel** *m* noise level **-spitze** *f* noise height
Larssenbohle *f* Larssen sheet pile
Larve *f* larva, (slang) depth charge
Lasche *f* cover plate, fishplate, splice strap, side bar, shackle, lashing, flap, butt strap, clip, tongue, bond, splice strip (R.R.) **~ der Spriebung** solder beams **~ der Stütze** lug of insulator
Laschen *n* fishing **-ausklinkung** *f* notching of the fishplate **-blech** *n* fishplate **-bohrer** *m* pole-strap bit **-bohrmaschine** *f* fishplate drilling machine **-bolzen** *m* track bolt for fastening fishplates **-federgehänge** *n* plate-link or shackle spring rigging
Laschen-gehäuse *n* fishplate seating **-gelenk** *n* universal joint with plates **-kaliber** *n* fishplate pass **-kammer** *f* fishplate seating **-kette** *f* steel side-bar chain, sprocket chain **-loch** *n* track-bolt hole, hole in the fishplate for the bolt **-lochmaschine** *f* fishplate punching machine
Laschen-mutter *f* connecting nut **-nietung** *f* butt-joint riveting, butt-joint **-profil** *n* fishplate section **-punktschweißung** *f* bridge spot weld **-schenkel** *m* flange of the fishplate **-schiene** *f* impact rail **-schraube** *f* track bolt **-spannband** *n* shackle band **-stoß** *m* strap joint **-teilung** *f* space between the links **-verbindung** *f* fishing, double-butt strap joint **-zwischengeschirr** *n* plate rope connecting tackle
Laschung *f* scarf, lashing
Laser (Lichtverstärker durch angeregte Strahlungsabgabe) Laser (light amplification by stimulated emission of radiation)
lasieren to glaze
lasierend transparent
Laßeisen *n* tapping bar, lancet
lassen to let (have)
Lassoband *n* adhesive tape
Last *f* load, weight, burden, onus, charge **bewegliche ~** live load **ruhende ~** dead load **ruhend wirkende ~** static load **~ ohne Führerbegleitung** automatic freight lift **vom Flügel getragene ~** wing loading **~ pro Pferdestärke** load per horsepower **bewegliche ~** live load **ruhende ~** dead load **ruhend wirkende ~** static load **ständige ~** dead load **mit voller ~** on full load, with full load **zur ~ schreiben** to debit
lastabhängig regelbare Fördermenge load-controlled feed(ing) quantity **~ geneigte Kennlinie** characteristic drooping in relation to load **-es Bremssystem** braking system depending on the load **-e Luftfederung** pneumatic suspension
Last-abwurf *m* load decrease **-achse** *f* load axis **-amplitude** *f* load level **-angriff** *m* distribution of load **-anhänger** *m* truck trailer **-annahme** *f* design load, load assumption **-anteil** *m* proportion or part of load **-arm** *m* leverage of load **-aufnahme** *f* bearing pressure (distribution), picking up the goods **-aufnahmemittel** *m* load lifting member
lastbar capable of assuming a load
Last-begrenzer *m* force-limiting device **-boot** *n* cargo boat
Lastbremse *f* load brake **selbsttätige ~** automatic load brake
Last-bügel *m* loop, triangular or pear-shaped lifting eye **-dampfer** *m* cargo boat **-dichte** *f* specific load **-drehzahl** *f* on-load speed **-dreieck** *n* load triangle **-druck** *m* load pressure **-druckbremse** *f* load-pressure brake
Lasten-aufzug *m* freight elevator **-frei** unencumbred, mortgage-free **-heft** *n* specification **-maßstab** *m* curve of displacement by load **-raum** *m* storage, bomb cell **-roller** *m* cargo scooter **-segelflugzeug** *n*, **-segler** *m* troop-carrying or cargo-carrying glider, freight glider **-seglerschleppen** *n* freight-glider towing **-zug** *m* series of loads, cargo train
Lastfaktor *m* load factor
Lastfall *m* **im ~** when loaded
Lastfälle *pl* loading conditions
Lastfallschirm *m* cargo parachute
Last-fläche *f* load area **-flugzeug** *n* cargo airplane, freight-carrying or cargo-transport aircraft

-geber *m* load cell **-güte** *f* Q external, loaded Q **-gewicht** *n* loading weight

Lasthaken *m* load hook **drehbarer ~** swivel hook

Lasthakenbetrieb *m* piece goods service

Last-Halte-Versuch *m* (hydr. Kraftheber) leak-test under load

Last-hebekette *f* elevating chain **-hebekraft** *f* lifting capacity, hoisting force **-hebemagnet** *m* lifting magnet **-hub** *m* lifting capacity, hoisting capacity

Lastigkeits-änderung *f* change in load distribution **-regelung** *f* trimming **-waage** *f* balance indicator, trim indicator

Last-kahn *m* barge, lighter **-kapazität** *f* (beim Tastkopf) input capacitance **-karre** *f* car, truck, barrow **-kette** *f* load chain **-kettenführung** *f* load-chain guide **-kettenrolle** *f* load-chain sheave

Lastkraftwagen *m* truck, cargo truck, lorry **geländegängiger ~** cross-country truck

Lastkraftwagen-anhänger *m* trailer of motor freight car **-zug** *m* motor freight car train

Lastladung *f* ballast

Lastmagnet *m* lifting magnet **~ mit beweglichen Polen** lifting magnet with movable pole shoes

Last-platte *f* load plate or slab **-probe** *f* load test **-rand** *m* edge of load **-raum** *m* cargo space or hold **-regelung** *f* load ratio control (elec) **-schalter** *m* circuit interruptor, load isolator **-schriftzettel** *m* debit note **-schwankung** *f* load fluctuation

Last-segelflugzeug *n* freight glider **-seil** *n* hoisting rope, load rope **-senkung** *f* reduction in load, load-settlement **-senkungsdiagramm** *n* load-settlement diagram **-senkungslinie** *f* load-settlement curve **-setzungskurve** *f* load settlement curve

Lastspiel *n* load application, stress cycle **-frequenz** *f* frequency of load cycles **-zahl** *f* load cycle **-zähler** *m* load cycle counter **-zahlverhältnis** *n* cycle ratio

Last-steigerung *f* increase in load **gleichmäßige ~** constant rate of loading

Last-stellung *f* position of load **-störung** *f* load disturbance **-stufe** *f* load increment, load range **-tier** *n* pack animal **-träger** *m* porter **-übertragung** *f* transmission of load

Last-verluste *pl* load losses **-verstimmung** *f* pulling **-verstimmungsmaß** *n* pulling figure **-verteiler** *m* load dispatcher **-verteileranlage** *f* load-dispatching plant (elec.)

Last-verteilung *f* load distribution **~ bei Doppeltraktion** tandem load sharing

Last-verteilungsstelle *f* load-distributing station **-verteilungszentrale** *f* truck control center **-vielfaches** *n* load factor

Lastwagen *m* freight car, truck, wagon **-schlepper** *m* truck tractor **-tragkraft** *f* truck capacity **-zug** *m* motor vehicle column

Lastwechsel *m* cycle of stress, load reversal, reversal of stress, stress-application cycle, load cycle **-gerät** *n* low-frequency load alternator (on a testing machine) **-zahl** *f* frequency, alternating stress number, number of load alternations

Last-weilscheibe *f* load sheave **-widerstand** *m* ballast resistor **-winde** *f* lifting jack, lever jack **-zug** *m* freight train, truck(-trailer) combination

Lasur *f* glaze **-fähigkeit** *f* opacity, transparency **-farbe** *f* azure color, transparent ink

Lasurit *m* azurite

Lasur-lack *m* glaze or transparent varnish **-schleiflack** *m* transparent flatting varnish **-spat** *m* lazulite **-stein** *m* lapis lazuli

latent latent **-es Bild** latent image **-e Gewebeschädigung** *f* latent tissue injury **-e Verdampfungswärme** latent heat of evaporation **-e Wärme** latent heat, solar heat

Latenz-periode *f* latent period **-zeit** *f* latency time incubation period, time of propagation (teleph.)

lateral lateral **-kanal** *m* lateral canal or channel

Laterit *m* laterite

Laterna magica magic lantern **-Bild** *n* magic lantern slide

Laterne *f* lantern, cage, spacer, (roof) monitor, distance piece, lamp

Laternen-bilderkasten *m* lantern-slide box **-bildermaske** *f* lantern mask **-einfaßleiste** *f* lantern-slide binding strip **-fuß** *m* pedestal (of lantern) **-kappe** *f* lamp hood **-kasten** *m* side-light screen **-pfahl** *m* lamp pole **-spiegel** *m* lamp reflector **-träger** *m* arm for side lights

Latex führende Kanäle laticiferous channels

Latexvulkanisation *f* latex cure

Läthaldosis *f* lethal dose

Latschenkiefer *f* dwarf pine

Latte *f* surveyor's staff, aligning pole, stadia, subtense bar, lath, batten, stick, slat, strip board, (slang) propeller **getrennte ~** broad lath

Latten-ablieferungstisch *m* lattice delivery table **-abschnitt** *m* staff section **-beschlag** *m* lathing **-brett** *n* window sill, elbow board **-entfernung** *f* staff distance **-führung** *f* pitch control

Latten-gerüst *n* lath frame **-gestell** *n* lathwork **-gitter** *n* lattice work **-gradierwerk** *n* lattice cooling stack **-haspel** *f* lath wince (winch) **-justierung** *f* (range) adjustment by lath

Latten-käfig *m* cradle **-kasten** *m* lattice frame **-kiste** *f* crate **-messung** *f* measuring by stadia **-profil** *n* gauge of laths **-profillehre** *f* batter gauge **-punkt** *m* bench mark, place mark

Latten-rost *m* boardwalk, duckboard **hölzerner ~** wooden grates (wooden grating)

Latten-rostschale *f* lattice plate **-schiefe** *f* staff slope **-schott** *n* batten and space bulkhead **-sitz** *m* batten-type seat **-spieker** *m* lath nail **-steg** *m* frame bridge, grating walk

Latten-teilung *f* intervals **-tisch** *m* lattice feed **-träger** *m* sight carrier, rodman **-tuch** *n* lattice **-tuchüberführung** *f* lap lattice **-untersatz** *m* foot-plate **-verschlag** *m* crate, latticework **-walze** *f* lattice-winch

Latthammer *m* lathing hammer

Latwerge *f* electuary

lau lukewarm, tepid, mild, balmy

laub-förmig leaf-like **-holz** *n* leaf wood **-holzzellstoff** *m* leaf wood cellulose **-reich** leafy **-säge** *f* fret saw **-sägearbeit** *f* fretwork **-schnittholz** *n* hardwood (sawn)

Laubung *f* vaulting, bowery

Laubungsbogen *m* discharging vault

Laubwald *m* deciduous wood, leafy wood, deciduous forest

Laue-diagramm *n* Laue diagram **-flecke, -punkte** *pl* Laue spots

Lauf *m* (Durchgang) run, heat; (Bewegung) movement, motion, travel; (Wasser) current, flow; (Bahn) course; (Technik) motion, operation, action; (des Kolbens) travel; (Maschine) operation; (Motor) running; (Schlitten) movement, travel, downgate, sprue, course, way, barrel (of gun), action, work, main gangway, path, race **~ eines Flusses** course of a river **~ mit Oberrohr** jacketed barrel **gezogener ~** rifled barrel **~ der Maschine** operation **ruhiger ~ des Motors** smooth or noiseless running of an engine **stoßfreier ~** smooth running

Lauf-achse *f* carrying, running, or dead axle **-anpassung** *f* running fit (aviation)

Laufbahn *f* roller path, runway, track, raceway, path, career, course **~ bei Kugellagern** race **~ einer Rolle mit Gummiüberzug** rubber tread of pad roller

Lauf-bandtrockner *m* screen belt drier **-bereich** *m* runnung range (aut. contr.)

Laufbild *n* moving picture **-fänger** *m*, **-kammer** *f* cinematograph, camera for taking pictures **-aufnahme** *f* moving or motion picture **-meßkammer** *f* aerial (air survey) camera **-werfer** *m* cinematograph, projecton apparatus

Lauf-boden *m* floor, catwalk **-bodenkamera** *f* base-board-extensible camera **-bohle** *f* barrow way, tramboard **-bohrer** *m* barrel fine borer **-bohrung** *f* bore running fit **-bohrungsmesser** *m* bore gauge **-breite** *f* solid center width **-brett** *n* roof platform (erected on roofs for workmen), running board, tram board **-bretträger** *m* platform support **-brettstütze** *f* tramboard bracket (elec.) **-brücke** *f* keel corridor, walkway (airship), footbridge, gangway, rising scaffold bridge, gang plank

Laufbuchse *f* bushing, bush, liner, sleeve, cylinder, barrel **aus Kopf und ~ zusammengesetzter Zylinder** built-up cylinder **Zylinder mit nicht benetzter Außenwand der ~** dry-liner-type cylinder

Laufbuchseflansche *f* liner flange

Laufbuchsen-dichtfläche *f* cylinder-barrel sealing surface **-halteschraube** *f* liner locking screw

Lauf-bühne *f* platform **-bühnenbelag** *m* slab for platforms **-bursche** *m* errand boy, messenger, office boy **-dauer** *f* operation life, recording time **-decke** *f* tire casing **-deckel** *m* revolving flat **-deckenmischung** *f* tire-tread stock **-deckenwulst** *m* bead of tire

Lauf-eigenschaft *f* operating characteristic, running feature **-einschaltung** *f* throwing in (of a gear), starting to run

laufen to go, run, circulate, travel (through), function, flow, extend, leak, turn, rotate **auf eine Mine ~** to hit a mine **~ lassen** (Flotte) to circulate the liquor

Laufen *n* running **~ der Schienen** slipping of the rails

laufend current (time), running, pending, present, permanent, continuous, steady, serial **~ numerieren von 1-** . . . to number consecutively 1-. . . **~ veränderlich** running variable **-e Aufträge** work in process **-e Bahnen** moving sheets **-es Band** endless belt system, conveyor belt **am -en Band fabrizieren** conveyer-belt manufacture, assembly-line or large-scale manufacture **-e Bestandsaufnahme** continuous check (inventory) of physical stocks **-e Bestandskartei** perpetual inventory file **-er Block** running block **der -e Dienst an Bord** ship's routine **-e Fabrikation** course of manufacture

laufend, -e Instandsetzungsarbeit routine repair work **-es Maß** linear measure **mit -em Motor** with engine running, engine-in **-e Nummer** consecutive number, serial number **-e Prüfung** cycle checking **-e Resonanz** travelling resonance **-e Spitze** live center **-e Überwachung** routining, constant supervision **-er Verstärker** rotating amplifier **-e Wartung** maintenance routine **auf dem laufenden** up-to-date

Läufer *m* driver, muller, (edge) runner, roller, crusher roll, (stone) traveler, rotor, armature, stretcher, sliding contact, slide; messenger; disk, turbine, jet **~ zum Erzmahlen** grinding disk **~ einer Erzmühle** muller, (upper) grinding surface **~ der Funkenstrecke** sparkgap rotor

Läufer-achse *f* rotor axle **-anlasser** *m* rotor starter **-anlasser** *m* rotor rheostat **-buchse** *f* rotor sleeve **-erregte Kommutatormaschine** *f* machine with inherent self excitation **-gespeister kompensierter Induktionsmotor** self-compensated motor (with primary rotor)

Läufer-gewicht *n* sliding weight **-käfig** *m* squirrel-cage rotor **-klemme** *f* rotor terminal **-körper** *m* spider **-kühlung** *f* rotor-cooling jet **-lage** *f* stretcher course **-mühle** *f* edge-runner mill, edge mill **-platte** *f* pan bottom **-polschuh** *m* rotor pole shoe **-posten** *m* runner post of message center

Läufer-rute *f* frame-leader, guide post **-schicht** *f* course laid straight endwise, course of stretchers **-spannung** *m* rotor voltage **-stein** *m* runner stone **-stellung** *f* rotor position **-stern** *m* armature spider (field spider) **-strom** *m* armature current, rotor current

Läufer-umdrehung *f* rotation of rotor **-verband** *m* stretcher bond **-welle** *f* armature shaft, rotor shaft **-werk** *n* roller pan, roller-chasing-type dry pan **-wicklung** *f* rotor winding **-windung** *f* rotor winding **-zarge** *f* runner frame

Lauf-feld *n* runway **-feldröhre** *f* traveling-wave tube **-feuer** *n* running fire

Lauffläche *f* tread, bearing or rolling surface, contact surface, journal, friction surface, sliding surface **-dessin** *n* nouskid pattern **-mischung** *f* tread compound (tread stock) **-platte** *f* tread plate **-risse** *pl* tread cracking

laufförmige Haube cannon tube shield

Lauf-gang *m* footwalk, walkway, gangway, catwalk, keel corridor **-gangträger** *m* walkway girder **-gangaufhängung** *f* suspension of gangway or walkway **-gerät** *n* drive mechanism **-geräusche** *n pl* background noise (tape rec.) **-gerüst des Titankrans** Titan crane truck or traveling pedestal

Laufgeschwindigkeit *f* speed **~ einer Welle** velocity of progression

Laufgeschwindigkeitssteuermaschine *f* steering machine with vane velocity control

Lauf-gestell *n* car frame **-gestellrahmen** *m* rear truck frame **-gewicht** *n* sliding weight or poise, rider weight, jockey weight **-gewichtbalken** *m* steel-yard **-gewichtswaage** *f* weighing lever with movable jockey, steel-yard **-gitter** *n* rotor blade **-glasur** *f* flow glaze **-gummi** *m* rubber tread

Lauf-haken *m* barrel lug **-inneres** *n* bore **-kabel** *n* running cable **-kammer** *f* chamber (of gun) **-karte** *f* process or route card **-karren** *m* cart, tram, wheel-barrow

Laufkatze *f* crane carriage, traveling crab, trolley, crane, traveling winch, chain drive ~ **mit Hebezeug** trolley hoist ~ **mit elektr. Hebe- und Fahrvorrichtung mit Zugseilbetätigung** overhead telpher with remote control ~ **mit Rädervorgelegevorschub** geared trolley

Laufkatzen-bahn *f* trolley beam track or runway **-fahrbahn** *f* trolley (beam) track, trolley runway **-fahrschiene** *f* trolley travel rail, beam trolley track **-fahrt** *f* trolley travel, trolley motion **-fahrwerk** *n*, **-gang** *m* trolley runway **-gehäuse** *n* casing for traveling crab **-stellung** *f* position of trolley

Lauf-kette *f* chain drive **-kettenkran** *m* crawler crane **-klaue** *f* guide claw **-knoten** *m* bowline **-kontrolle** *f* motion indicator **-kontrollrädchen** *n* indicating disk

Laufkraftwerk *n* river power station **selbsttätiges** ~ automatic continuous-service plant

Laufkran *m* traveling crane, overhead (traveling) crane, jenny ~ **mit elektrischem Antrieb** electric-power traveling crane ~ **für einen Hauptträger** traveling single-beam crane ~ **für Notverschluß** traveling crane for emergency gate

Laufkran-ständer *m* support of traveling crane **-träger** *m* traveling-crane girder

Lauf-kranz *m* tread, blade rim (turbines) **-kreis** *m* running circle **-kühlung** *f* barrel cooling system **-lager eines Kreisels** spin bearing **-leder** *n* leather apron **-leiste** *f* running board, footplate **-löter** *m* barrel brazer

Lauf-mantel *m* barrel jacket, tire casing, jacket tread band **-marke** *f* movable (moving) index **-masche** *f* ladder **-monteur** *m* barrel setter **-mundstück** *n* breech piece **-mutter** *f* running nut

Laufnummer *f* consecutive number ~ **eines Gesprächs** serial number of a call

Laufnummern-geber *m* routing code sender **-stempel** *m* numbering (stamping) machine

Lauf-plankenträger *m* gangway or walking way girder **-paß** *m* gangboard **-passung** *f* running fit **-pfanne** *f* trolley ladle **-planke** *f* gangplank **-platte** *f* (stair) landing slab, rotary disk **-probe** *f* running test, running-in test

Laufrad *n* wheel, track wheel, landing wheel, runner (of a turbine), impeller (of a ventilator), rotor, bogie wheel, traveling wheel, turbine wheel ~ **eines Flugzeuges** landing wheel ~ **unter der Flugzeugstirn** nose wheel **geschlossenes** ~ closed box-type impeller **halb offenes** ~ web-type impeller **beiderseits offenes** ~ star-type impeller

Laufrad-achse *f* landing-wheel axle **-beschaufelung** *f* rotor blading **-bremse** *f* landing-wheel brake, traversing wheel brake **-decke** *f* tire cover **-einleitschaufel** *f* impeller intake guide vane, nozzle guide vane (gas turbines) **-eintritt** *m* rotor inlet or entrance **-eintrittwinkel** *m* inlet angle of impeller **-schaufel** *f* rotor blade **-träger** *m* (Laufkran) end carriage **-verkleidung** *f* wheel side cover

Laufrädermaschine *f* wheel-testing machine

Laufrad-flügel *m* impeller blade **-kanal** *m* impeller passage, impeller channel, jet **-schwinge** *f* wheel-balancing device **-welle** *f* impeller shaft (of spindle jet)

Lauf-raum *m* drift space **-reifen** *m* tire cover **-richter** *m* barrel setter **-richtung** *f* grain direction (paper mfg.) formation, direction of course **-richtungskoeffizient** *m* directional effect (in film processing) **-riemen** *m* (driving) belt

Laufrille *f* groove of bearing, track (bearing) ~ **des Kugellageraußenringes** track of external ring of ball bearing

Laufring *m* race (of ball bearing), raceway, barrel ring, ball race (of bearing) **-kugellager** *n* annular ball bearing, ball race bearing

Lauf-rinne *f* channel, groove **-rohling** *m* barrel blank **-rohr** *n* launching tube **-röhre** *f* drift tube

Laufrolle *f* (Gleiskette) tread roller, (small) roller, runner **glatte** ~ straight-face roller ~ **mit Gummibandage** rubber-tired track roller

Lauf-rollentraverse *f* roller traverse **-ruhe** *f* (eines Motors) quietness (of running motor) **-ruhig** smooth running **-rute** *f* pile (driving) frame, guide beam

Laufschaufel *f* moving blade, turbine blade, rotor blade, jet, guide vane, bucket (turbine), runner blade **-austrittswinkel** *m* blade leaving angle, bucket leaving angle **-verlustbeiwert** *m* blade loss factor, bucket loss factor

Lauf-scheibe *f* rotor disk, gland washer **-schiene** *f* runway rail, track beam, track runway rail, guide rail, gate track, rib **-schlacke** *f* running slag **-schritt** *m* double time (march) **-schürze** *f* traveling apron **-schützer** *m* barrel protector **-seele** *f* bore (of gun) **-seelenprüfer** *m* barrel reflector **-seite des Riemens** contact side of the belt **-sicherungshebel** *m* barrel-locking lever

Laufsitz *m* running fit **leichter** ~ easy running fit

Lauf-sitzpassung *f* running fit **-sitzring** *m* barrel packing, barrel-locking ring **-spiel** *n* running clearance, work spindle, play **-stange** *f* handrail, carrier rod or bar **-stärkeregler** *m* volume control **-steg** *m* footpath, footbridge, gangway **-störung** *f* operational fault **-strecke** *f* distance traversed **-streckenmarkenrad** *n* range-setting wheel (torpedoes) **-term** *m* running term **-teufel** *m* go-devil **-trommel** *f* revolving head

Lauf-umschaltung *f* reversal of motion **-verriegelung** *f* barrel-locking gear **-wagen** *m* truck (of railroad car), hoisting carriage, bucket or traveling carriage **-walze** *f* roller **-wasserkraftwerk** *n* river power station **-weite** *f* caliber (of firearms) **-welle** *f* intermediate shaft

Laufwerk *n* mechanism, power plant without storage facilities, carriage, drive assembly, driving gear, running gear, working gear **-gehäuse** *n* roller casing **-panzerung** *f* track shield, armored skirting **-schwinge** *f* main balance beam

Lauf-wert *m* peripheral speed of wheel **-widerstand** *m* rolling resistance, running friction

Laufwinde *f* traveling hoist, trolley hoist, traveling winch **elektrische** ~ motor trolley hoist ~ **mit elektrischem Hub- und Fahrwerk** crane-type motor-driven trolley hoist

Lauf-winkel *m* transit angle **-winkel im Triftraum** bunching angle **-zahl** *f* variable number, running variable **-zapfen** *m* crankpin, journal, neck (of rolling mill)

Laufzeit *f* travel time (rdr), transit time (in el. tube), duration of transmission, propagation time, running time, pulse timing (radar) **Impuls mit langer ~** broad pulse **~ des Stromes über eine Leitung** line lag

Laufzeit-ausgleich *m* phase equalization (TV), transit time compensation **-ausgleichkegel** *m* delay equalizing cone **-charakteristik** *f* delay time caracteristic **-dämpfung** *f* transit-time damping **-diagramm** *n* time chart **-differenzen** *pl* differences in transit time

Laufzeit-effekt *m* velocity modulating effect **-einfluß** *m* transit-time effect **-entzerrer** *m* delay equalizer **-entzerrung** *f* rise time correction, transit time correction

Laufzeiten-steuerung *f* velocity modulation **-verhältnis** *n* ratio of transition times

Laufzeit-erscheinung *f* transit-time effect **-fehler** *m* phase delay error **-folger** *m* delay-lock discriminator (rdr.) **-figur** *f* oscillography figure **-frequenzverzerrung** *f* delay-frequency distortion **-generator** *m* ultra-high-frequency oscillator **-gerät** *n* device predicated on transit time

Laufzeitglied *n* delay line, circuit element, to influence the transit time **magnetostriktives ~** magnetostriction delay line

Laufzeit-kette *f* (lump constant) delay, delay-line network **-komprimierung** *f* transit-time compression **-korrektur** *f* echo or delay-weighting term, delay equalizing **-kurve** *f* time distance curve **-methode** *f* time-of-flight technique **-modulation** *f* velocity modulation **-modus** *m* transit-time mode

Laufzeit-oszillographie *f* transition time oscillography **-rohr** *n* velocity-modulated tube (electronics) **-röhre** *f* frequency-modulation tube, transit-time tube, drift tube, beam tube **-schwingungen** *pl* transit-time oscillations, electron oscillations **-spektrometer** *n* time-of-flight spectrometer **-störung** *f* delay distortion **-strecke** *f* transition time stretch **-verlauf** *m* delay time variation **-verzerrung** *f* transition-time distortion, phase distortion **-winkel** *m* angle of transition time, oscillography angle

Lauf-zettel *m* interoffice slip or tag, control tag, work-progress slip, clearance-chit circular **-zeug** *n* rotor runner **-zirkel** *m* caliper compasses **-zylinder** *m* cylinder liner

Laugbarkeit *f* leaching property

Lauge *f* lye solution, wash, liquor, leach, leaching solution, electrolyte, brine **abgeschleuderte ~** liquor discharge **abgestoßene ~** discard solution

Lauge-behälter *m* leaching vat or tank **-beständig** resistant to leaching solutions, alkali-proof, resistant to alkalies **-einrichtung** *f* leaching installation **-fähig** leachable **-mittel** *n* leaching agent

laugen to leach, lixiviate, steep in lye, wash **-artig** resembling lye, alkaline **-aufdruck** *m* printing-on of thickened caustic **-auflösebehälter** *m* lye-dissolving tank **-bad** *n* washing liquid bath **-bereiter** *m* soap-solution maker **-bereitungsbehälter** *m* lye graduating tank **-beständig** alkali-proof **-bürste** *f* lye brush

Laugen-durchfluß *m* solution flow **-echt** fast to (caustic) lye **-empfindlich** sensitive to caustic (lye) **-einrichtung** *f* leaching plant **-entspanner** *m* sludge pressure reducer **-entwicklungsverfahren** *n* caustic soda developing process **-fest** lye-proof **-fänger** *m* lye pot **-faß** *n* dissolving vat **-flüssigkeit** *f* liquor

Laugen-heber *m* lye siphon **-kessel** *m* lye vat, caustic pot **-kühler** *m* brine cooler **-leitungsarmatur** *f* fitting for lye pipe line **-lösung** *f* leach(ing) solution **-messer** *m* alkalimeter **-reinigung** *f* clarification of solution, electrolyte purification **-rückgewinnungsanlagen** *pl* lye recovery plants **-rückstand** *m* leach residue

Laugen-spritzung *f* washing liquid spray **-sprödigkeit** *f* caustic embrittlement **-standsanzeiger** *m* sludge level indicator **-standsregulierung** *f* regulation of the liquor level **-tank** *m* leaching tank **-tuch** *n* bucking cloth **-überführung** *f* liquor circulation **-umlauf** *m* solution circulation, electrolyte circulation **-verschleppung** *f* washing liquid picked up **-zufluß** *m* solution feed **-zusammensetzung** *f* solution composition

Laugerei *f* leaching plant, leaching **-anlage** *f* leaching plant

Lauge-trommel *f* leaching drum or barrel **-verfahren** *n* leaching method, lixiviation process **-waschanlage** *f* caustic washing

Laugflüssigkeit *f* liquor

Laugung *f* leaching **~ in situ** underground leaching, leaching in place

laugungsfähig leachable

Laugungsmittel *n* leaching agent lixiviant

Laurinsäure *f* lauric acid

Lauritsen-Elektroskop *n* Lauritsen electroscope

Lausch-dienst *m* signal intelligence service, listening service, line interception or tapping **-empfänger** *m* intercept receiver, ion receiver, line intercept

lauschen to listen (in)

Lausch-erde *f* listening earth **-gerät** *n* listening equipment, intercept set **-mikrophon** *n* pickup transmitter, detectophone (connected to headphones), pickup microphone **-schleife** *f* listening circuit or loop **-stelle** *f* telephone-interception post, listening point, intercept station **-zange** *f* wire-tapping clamp

Laut *m* sound (articulated)

laut loud, noisy, according to

Lautal *n* a type of light metal alloy used as aircraft skin

Lautbildung *f* formation of sounds

Läute-induktor *m* ringing inductor **-maschine** *f* bell-ringing machine

läuten to ring

Läuten *n* ringing, ring

lauter pure, clear, genuine, unalloyed, sheer **~ fassen** to rack clear

Läuter-batterie *f* refining battery **-beize** *f* (Türkischrotfärberei) white liquor **-boden** *m* sieve bottom, strainer **-bottich** *m* clearing vat

Läuterelais *n* ringing relay

Läuterflasche *f* washing bottle

Lauterkeit *f* pureness, transparency, clearness

Lauterkennung *f* phoneme recognition

läutern to clarify, filter (a liquid), clean, refine purge, purify, clear, rectify, wash

Läutern *n* refining

Läuter-ofen *m* refining furnace or kiln **-pfanne** clearing pan, clarifier **-trommel** *f* picking o purifying drum, clearing or washing cylinder

Läuterung *f* clarification, purification, washing, rectification, refining, clearing
Läuterungsmittel *n* refining means
Läutervorrichtung *f* straining apparatus
Läute-schaltung *f* alarm-bell circuit **-signal** *n* acoustic signal **-stromkreis** *m* ringing current circuit **-werk** *n* bell, chime, ringing device **-werksglocke** *f* alarm and signal bell
Lautfernsprecher *m* loud-speaking telephone
lautgetreu high-fidelity, orthophonic
Lautheit *f* loudness
Lautheitsempfindung *f* loudness sensitivity
Lauthörknopf *m* transmitter cutout, handset switch, amplifier knob
Lauthsches Blechtrio Lauth three-high plate mill
Lautlehre *f* phonetics
lautlich phonetic
lautlos noiseless, silent, quiet
Lautlosigkeitskegel *m* cone of silence
Lautminimum *n* (position of) silence
Lautschriftband *n* sound-recording tape
lautsprechendes Funktelephon loud-speaker (wireless)
Lautsprecher *m* loud-speaker, speaker, (sound) reproducer, megaphone, public-address system **(elektro)dynamischer ~** moving-coil speaker, dynamic loud-speaker **elektromagnetischer ~** magnetic-armature speaker, electromagnetic loud-speaker, moving-iron speaker, inductor speaker **elektrostatischer ~** condenser or capacitor speaker, electrostatic loud-speaker **fremderregter dynamischer ~** electrodynamic or moving-coil loud-speaker **gerichteter ~** directional loud-speaker **induktordynamischer ~** moving-iron loud-speaker **permanentdynamischer ~** permanent-magnet-type moving-coil speaker **piezoelektrischer ~** piezoelectric loud-speaker **pneumatischer ~** pneumatic speaker **trichterloser ~** direct-radiator loud-speaker (without horn) **~ mit Klangverteiler** *m* horn loaded loudspeaker
Lautsprecher-abstrahlfläche *f* projector or radiating surface (of loud-speaker) **-anker** *m* rotor armature **-anlage** *f* public-address system **-anschluß** *m* (Radio) speaker socket **-betrieb** *m* loud-speaker service **-dose** *f* loud-speaker unit, diaphragm **-empfänger** *m* transceiver **-gehäuse** *n* loudspeaker cabinet **-haltevorrichtung** *f* loud-speaker chassis
Lautsprecherhorn, aufgewundenes ~ twisted loud-speaker horn, coiled horn **gefaltetes ~** folded loud-speaker horn
Lautsprecher-kombination *f* multi-channel loud-speaker, composite loudspeaker **-korb** *m* chassis frame of loud-speaker **-leitfläche** *f* deflecting vane or labyrinth (of loud-speaker) **-leitwand** *f* deflecting vane or baffle (of loud-speaker) **-luftkammer** *f* air space or air chamber (of loud-speaker) **-membrane** *f* speaker cone **-schirm** *m* louver **-seide** *f* speaker cloth **-spinne** *f* spider of loud-speaker **-tonführung** *f* labyrinth of loud-speaker
Lautsprechertrichter, aufgewundener ~ twisted loud-speaker horn, coiled horn **gefalteter ~** folded loud-speaker horn
Lautsprechertrichter-hals *m* throat of loud-speaker horn **-mundöffnung** *f* mouth opening of horn **-mundstück** *n* throat (narrow inlet) of horn
Lautsprecher-truhe *f* baffle, speaker cabinet **-wagen** *m* loud-speaker car or truck, sound truck
Lautsprechtrichter *m* loud-speaker horn, cone, or trumpet
lautstark having volume
Lautstärke *f* loudness, intensity or volume of sound, sound level, audibility, signal strength, readability, volume control (marking on knob) **Kurven gleicher ~** isophons **~ der Sprache** volume of speech **~ von Funksendungen** signal strength
Lautstärke-anzeiger *m* volume indicator **-begrenzer** *m* volume limiter **-eindruck** *m* loudness **-messer** *m* sound-measuring device, audibility meter **-messer** (DIN) loudness-level meter **-messung** *f* sound measurement, audibility test, telephonometry
Lautstärkenausgleich, selbsttätiger ~ automatic gain control, automatic volume control
Lautstärkenbereich *m* volume range **~ der Stimme** human-voice intensity, dynamic range (of voice)
Lautstärken-empfindung *f* aural sensitivity **-stufe** *f* loudness unit, sensation unit **-unterschied** *m* difference in sound intensity
Lautstärkeregelung *f* volume control **automatische ~** automatic gain control, automatic volume control **verzögerte automatische ~** delayed automatic volume control
Lautstärkeregler *m* volume control (system), attenuator **automatischer ~** automatic-volume-control circuit or system **logarithmischer ~** volume control with resistance varying according to a logarithmic law
Lautstärke-regulierung *f* adjustment of signal strength **-schwankungen** *pl* fadings **-umfang** *m* volume range, dynamic range **-verhältnis** *n* volume range ratio
Laut-verständlichkeit *f* articulation of letters **-verstärker** *m* amplifier **-verzerrung** *f* sound distortion
Läutwerk *n* bell, alarm
Laut-zeichen *n* phonetic symbol **-zeiger** *m* volume indicator
lauwarm lukewarm, tepid
Lava- *f* lava **schlackige ~** scorified lava
Lavender *m* lavender
Lavenderkopie *f* lavender copy, lavender print
Laveur *m* (gas) washer
lavieren to tack
Lavieren *n* tacking
Lavulkan *m* a type of synthetic rubber
Lawine *f* landslide, avalanche
lawinenartige Ionisation cumulative ionization
Lawinen-diode *f* avalanche diode **-durchschlag** *m* avalanche breakdown **-kopf** *m* head of a surge **-schutzmauer** *f* avalanche baffle works **-transistor** *m* avalanche transistor **-schwankung** *f* avalanche fluctuation **-verbauung** *f* breaking up of an avalanche at the starting point **-wind** *m* avalanche wind
Lazarett *n* hospital, sick bay
Lazulit *m* lazulite
Leatheroid *n* leatheroid
Leben *n* life, living, existence
lebend alive, living **-e Energie** inertia **-er Kalk** quicklime

lebendig alive, living, lively **-e Energie, Kraft** kinetic energy or force, momentum
Lebendigkeit *f* liveliness, liveness, realistic properties (in architectural acoustics)
Lebensdauer *f* useful life, longevity, life (span), working service, working life, durability, endurance **mittlere** ~ average life, decay modulus **sichere** ~ safe life ~ **bei voller Belastung** load life ~ **in elektrischen Feldern** lifetime in electric fields
Lebensdauer-berechnungen *pl* bearing life calculations **-kennlinie** *f* life characteristic **-probe** *f* (von Röhren) life test (of tubes) **-versuch** *m* life test
Lebens-erscheinung *f* biological phenomenon **-erwartung** *f* life expectancy **-fähig** viable **-frage** *f* vital matter **-gefahr** *f* danger to (a person's) life **-gefährlich** endangering life, perilous **-haltung** *f* standard of life
lebenslänglich lifelong, for life
Lebenslauf *m* personal record, career, course of life **-akten** *pl* (des Motors), logbook (of motor)
Lebensmittel *pl* foodstuffs, subsistence, supplies **-untersuchung** *f* food research
lebenswichtig important or vital for life **-e Anlageteile** key equipment **-er Teil** vital part **-es Ziel** vital point or goal
Lebenszeit der Träger lifetime of majority carriers
Leber-eisenerz *n* pyrrhotite **-erz** *n* hepatic ore **-kies** *m* pyrrhotite **-opal** *m* menilite **-stein** *m* hepatite **-torf** *m* black glossy fuel peat **-tran** *m* cod-liver oil
lebhaft lively, brisk, active, vivacious, bright, gay (of colors)
Lebhaftigkeit *f* liveliness
Leblancscher Phasenschieber *m* Leblanc exciter
Leblancsche Schaltung Leblanc phase advancer or connection
leblos inert, lifeless, dead, inactive, dull, flat, stagnant
Lech *m* regulus (chem.), matte
Lecher-drähte *pl* Lecher system, Lecher wires, wave guide **-drahtsystem** *n* transmission line **-kreis** *m* parallel-rod tank circuit **-leitung** *f* Lecher system, Lecher wires **-oszillator** *m* parallel-rod oscillator **-system** *n* Lecher system
leck leaky ~ **machen** to spring a leak ~ **sein** to have sprung a leak, leak ~ **werden** to leak, spring a leak
Leck *n* leakage, leak **ein** ~ **springen** to spring a leak **das** ~ **hat sich zugezogen** the leak has been stopped
Leckage *f* leakage
leckagefest leakproof
Leck-behälter *m* collector tank **-brennstoff** *m* fuel-oil leakage, leaking fuel **-dampf** *m* leakage steam **-dampfkondensator** *m* gland leak-off condenser **-dicht** leakproof
Lecken *n* leakage (of a liquid), dropping out, licking
Leck-faktor *m* leakage propability (atom. phys.) **-finder** *m* vacuum leak detector **-fluß** *m* leakage flux **-flüssigkeit** *f* seepage
Leckkraftstoff *m*, **Durchtritt von** ~ fuel creepage
Leckkraftstoffleitung *f* drip-oil pipe
Leck-leitung *f* leakage pipe, collector line, drainage tube **-leitungsrohr** *n* vent line **-leitwert** *m* leakage conductance (trans)
Lecköl *n* waste oil **-abfluß** *m* leak oil discharge **-behälter** *m* leak oil container **-bohrung** *f* leakage oil bore **-leitung** *f* overflow-oil line **-pumpe** *f* leakage pump **-rückleitung** *f* leakage oil return pipe **-sperre** *f* leakage oil stop **-stutzen** *m* leakage oil connection
Leck-rohr *n* drain pipe **-schaden** *m* leakage, damage **-sicher** self-sealing (said of fuel tanks) **-sicherheit** *f* leakproofness **-stein** *m* lick(stone) **-strom** *m* leakance current, leak(age) current **-sucher** *m* leak detector **-verlust** *m* leakage loss, leakage **-wasserpumpe** *f* bilge pump
Leclanchéelement *n* Leclanché cell
Leder *n* leather, hide ~ **abflammen** to tallow or grease leather over a charcoal fire **abgenarbtes** ~ smooth leather **alaungares** ~ alumed leather **englisches** ~ moleskin, sateen **fettgares** ~ oil leather **genarbtes** ~ corned or grained leather **gepreßtes** ~ embossed leather
Leder, gestrichenes ~ scraped leather **getriebenes** ~ cup leather **lohgares** ~ oozed leather **lohgrubengegerbtes** ~ ground oak-bark or underground tanned leather **-rohgares** ~ tanned leather **sämisches** ~ chamois, shammy, wash or oil leather **zugerichtetes** ~ curried or dressed leather ~ **für Dichtungen** hydraulic leather ~ **in der Kruste** leather in crust condition
Leder-abfälle *pl* scrap leather **-abschnitt** *m* leather cutting **-appretur** *f* leather dressing or finishing **-aufbau** *m* leather body **-balg** *m* leather bellows **-band** *m* leather binding (or belt)
Leder-beilage *f* leather shim **-beschlag** *m* leather fitting **-behälter** *m* leather case **-beschwerung** *f* weighting of leather **-bimsmaschine** *f* leather fluffing machine **-brauntöne** *pl* tan shades **-bügel** *m* (am Kopfhörer), leather headgear **-creme** *f* leather dressing **-dichtung** *f* leather packing or washer
Leder-einband *m* leather binding **-einfassung** *f* leather binding **-ersatz** *m* artificial leather **-farbig** buff **-fett** *n* dubbing **-galanteriewaren** *pl* fancy leather goods **-gamasche** *f* leather legging **-gleitschutz** *m* slide-preventing leather device **-handschuh** *m* leather glove
Lederharz *n* (India) rubber **-stulpen** *pl* leather cuffs
Leder-haut *f* sclera **-hobel** *m* spokeshave **-hörkappe** *f* leather flying helmet with built-in double headphones **-imitationspapier** *n* artificial leather paper **-industrie** *f* leather industry **-kappenbehälter** *m* leather cap case **-karton** *m* leather board **-kitt** *m* leather cement **-klappenventil** *n* leather flap valve **-klopfmaschine** *f* leather beating machine **-kohle** *f* charred leather
Leder-lappen zum Putzen von Linsen chamois leather **-leim** *m* leather glue **-leinwand** *f* dowlas **-liderung** *f* leather packing **-manschette** *f* leather (collar) cuff **-mappe** *f* leather wrapper, brief case, portfolio **-maske** *f* leather (gas) mask **-membran** *f* leather diaphragm **-nuance** *f* leather brown shade
Leder-öl *n* leather oil **-packung** *f* leather packing **-paketkupplung** *f* laminated leather coupling **-pappe** *f* leather board (paper) **-pflegemittel** *n*

leather dressing agent **-polsterung** *f* leather upholstery **-riemen** *m* leather strap or belt **-riemenfett** *n* leather-belt dressing **-ring** *m* leather washer, ring, or gasket

Lederschärf- und Spaltmaschine *f* leather-skiving and -splitting machine

Leder-scheibe *f* leather washer **-schieber** *m* leather slide **-schleifmaschine** *f* buffing machine **-schmiere** *f* dubbing (stuffing) **-schürze** *f* leather apron **-schwärze** *f* black leather dye, currier's black **-spaltmaschine** *f* splitting machine **-streifen** *m* leather strip **-strippe** *f* leather strap **-stulp** *m* leather cup, leather stuffing box **-tasche** *f* leather case or bag **-treibriemen** *m* leather belt

Leder-überanzug *m* leather combination suit **-unterlegscheibe** *f* leather washer **-walke** *f* fulling mill (stock) **-walze** *f* leather pressing roller **-walzenersatz** *m* imitation leather roller **-wichse** *f* leather polish **-zurichter** *m* leather dresser

Leducstrom *m* Leduc current

Lee *n* lee, leeward **-abhang** *m* leeward drop of a wave

leer idle (motion), (Gefäß) empty, void, blank, (Platz) vacant, hollow **~ anlaufen** to start without load, start light **~ laufen** run idle or free **~ gehen** to run light **-e Batterie** (ohne Elektrolyt) dry battery **-es Blatt** blank (sheet of) paper **-es Energieband** empty band **-er Gang** idle or lost motion **-er Raum** vacuous space, vacuum **-er Ton** flat tone

Leer-anweisung *f* dummy statement (info proc.) **-arbeit** *f* no-load work **-becher** *m* furnishing pan **-bereich** *m* skip zone, zone of silence **-befehl** *m* skip instruction, blank instruction **-bild** *n* unexposed negative **-boden** *m* bottom board (in molding), turnover board, joint board **-drücken** to drain under pressure

Leere *f* emptiness, vacuum, void, blankness, vacancy

leeren to empty, evacuate, clear out

Leer-fracht *f* dead freight **-gang** *m* idle gear, backlash, lost motion, neutral gear **-gangreibung** *f* noload friction **-gebinde** *n* empty or intermediate truss **-gehend** working without load **-gerüst** *n* scaffold, centering (of arch) **-geschoß** *n* inert missile

Leer-gewicht *n* weight empty, dead weight, dry weight, tare, net weight **-gewichtsmethode** *f* deadweight method **-gut** *n* empties **-hub** *m* no-load stroke, idle stroke **-impuls** *m* spacing pulse **-karte** *f* blank card **-kontakt** *m* vacant terminal, spare contact **-lager** *n* empty deposit **-laßbehälter** *m* dumping-type or rip-bottom tank **-laßhahn** *m* drain cock

Leerlauf *m* idling, power of idle motion, power off **ruhiger ~** smooth idling

Leerlauf-abstellvorrichtung *f* slow-running cut-out valve **-admittanz** *f* open-circuit admittance **-anschlag** *m* idling stop **-arbeit** *f* no-load work, wasted energy **-austritt** *m* idling slot **-begrenzung** *f* slow-running stop **-begrenzungsschraube** *f* throttle adjusting screw **-brennstoffdüse** *f* idle or idling jet

Leerlaufbuchse *f* loose bushing, bushing, sleeve **~ mit Bund** bushing with flange **~ mit Fettschmierung** bushing with grease-pocket feed **~ mit Ölschmiernuten** oil-grooved bushing **~ mit selbsttätiger Ölschmierung** self-lubricating bushing **~ ohne Ölumlauf** oil-less bushing **~ mit Weißmetallfutter** babbitted bushing, babbitt-lined bushing

Leerlauf-charakteristik *f* no-load characteristic **-drehzahl** *f* no-load speed, idling speed **-düse** *f* slow-running jet, idling nozzle, idling jet **-einstellschraube** *f* slow-running screw **-einstellung** *f* idling adjustment

leerlaufen to (run) idle, run empty

leerlaufend working without load **-er Kollektor** collector in open circuit **-er Motor** idling engine

Leerlauf-feder *f* idling spring **-geschwindigkeit** *f* idling speed **-güte** *f* Q unloaded **-gütefaktor** *m* basic Q, non-loaded Q **-hemmung** *f* anti-creep device **-hub** *m* return stroke, idle stroke **-impedanz** *f* open-circuit, open-end, or no-load impedance

Leerlauf-kanal *m* idling duct **-kennlinie** *f* no-load characteristic **-kontakt** *m* spare or vacant terminal or contact, dumb contact **-kuppelung** *f* slip coupling, free-wheeling clutch **-kurzschlußverhältnis** *n* short circuit ratio **-luft** *f* (Vergaser) idling air **-lufteinstellung** *f* (Vergaser) idling air adjustment **-napf** *m* slow-speed well **-nocke** *f* delayed-pulse tripping cam

Leerlauf-pfeifsicherheit *f* singing stability under no-load condition **-prüfung** *f* idling or no-load test, dry run **-rad** *n* idler **-regler** *m* mimimum speed governor **-reibung** *f* no-load friction **-riemenscheibe** *f* idler pulley **-rohr** *n* (Vergaser) idling tube

Leerlauf-scheibe *f* idler pulley or rope sheave **-scheinwiderstand** *m* open-circuit impedance **-schütz** *n* idling or no-load dike **-seilscheibe** *f* idler rope sheave **-spannung** *f* no-load voltage, open-circuit voltage **-stabil** open circuit stable **-stellung** *f* idling setting, slow-running position **-strom** *m* no-load current **-trudel** *m* tail spin with power off

Leerlauf- und Endregeler *m* idling and maximum speed governor

Leerlauf-ventil *n* no-load valve **-verbrauch** *m* no-load consumption **-verlust** *m* no-load loss, idling loss **-versuch** *m* no-load test **-vorrichtung** *f* idling device **-welle** *f* idler shaft **-widerstand** *m* open-circuit impedance, no-load impedance **-zahnrad** *n* idler gear **-zeit** *f* idle or unoccupied time **-zumeßdüse** *f* idle-metering jet

Leer-material *n* empties **-raum** *m* vacuum **-schalter** *m* isolating switch **-scheibe** *f* idler wheel, loose pulley **-schicht** *f* insulating layer, potential barrier **-schlag** *m* no-load stroke, blank blow **-schöpfen** to bail dry **-schraube** *f* drain plug

Leer-seil *n* backhaul cable **-seite** *f* blank page **-spaltensucher** *m* blank column detector **-standanzeiger** *m* low level indicator **-stecker** *m* withdrawn or feint plug **-stehend** unoccupied **-stelle** *f* hole, vacancy (in lattice), empty center, lattice point, central gap, Schottky vacancy, interstice

Leerstellen-bildung *f* vacancy formation **-konzentration** *f* vacancy concentration **-paar** *n* vacancy pair **-wahrscheinlichkeit** *f* vacancy probability **-wanderung** *f* vacancy migration

Leerstellmechanismus *m* vacancy mechanism

Leerstellung *f* feathering position, no-load position

Leer-strom *m* no-load current **-takt** *m* idle stroke **-tankgewicht** *n* zero fuel weight **-taste** *f* space bar (typewriter) **-trum** (Förd.) return strand

Leerung *f* emptying

Leer-verluste *pl* losses when idling **-versuch** *m* blank experiment, no-load test **-weg** *m* idle path, free play **-zeichen** *n* ignore (comput) **-zeit** *f* drainage time, no-load time (teleph.) **-zustand** *m* empty condition (data storage)

Leeseite *f* leeward, lee side **~ der Welle** lee of a wave

leewärts leeward

Leewirbel *m* leeward eddy

legalisieren to legalize

Legeeisen *n* hearth plate

legen to place, put, lay (cable) **sich ~** to calm, fall calm, fall (of wind), lull, subside, quiet down **in die Kurve ~** to bank a plane **zur Last ~** to impute

Legendresche Polynome Legendre polynoms

Leger *m* layering apparatus

Lege-schaufel *f* plaiting shovel **-schienenschwung** *m* movement of the guide bars **-schlüssel** *m* plate key

Legierbarkeit *f* alloying property

legieren to alloy, compound **~ mit Quecksilber** to amalgamate

Legieren *n* alloying

Legierstahl *m* alloy steel

legiert alloyed **-er Diffusionstransistor** alloy-diffused transistor **-es Gußeisen** alloy cast iron **-er Stahl** alloy steel

Legierung *f* alloy, composition, alloy metal **~ auf Aluminiumgrundlage** aluminum-base alloy **binäre ~** binary alloy **hochschmelzende ~** high-melting-point alloy **niedrigschmelzende ~** low-melting-point alloy **paramagnetische ~** paramagnetic alloy **schmelzbare ~** fusible alloy **sparstoffarme ~** alloy low in critical or scarce metals

Legierungsanteil *m* alloying contribution

Legierungsbestandteil *m* alloying constituent **Stahl mit einem ~ neben Kohlenstoff** ternary steel **Stahl, der neben Kohlenstoff drei oder mehr Legierungsbestandteile enthält** complex steel

Legierungs-blech *n* alloy sheet **-blöckchen** *n* alloy ingot **-element** *n* alloying element **-gußform** *f* alloy die casting **-körper** *m* alloying element **-pyrometer** *n* cupel pyrometer **-rohmassel** *f* alloy ingot **-schicht** *f* alloy junction

Legierungsstahl *m* alloy steel **verbleiter ~** leaded alloy steel

Legierungszusatz *m* alloying addition or metal

Legierzinn *m* tin alloy

Legitimation *f* proof of identity, power to act (law)

legitimieren, sich ~ to prove one's identity

Legschiene *f* guide bar

Legschienenschwungexzenter *m* guide bar swing shaft

Legung *f* patterning, laying (of cable)

Lehm *m* loam, mud, clay **-boden** *m* clay soil **-dichtung** *f* loam seal **-form** *f* loam mold **-formen** *n* loam molding **-formerei** *f* loam-molding shop **-formguß** *m* loam casting **-füllung** *f* clay filling **-grube** *f* clay pit, loam pit **-guß** *m* loam casting **-gußwalze** *f* loam-cast roll

lehmig loamy, clayey, muddy

Lehm-kern *m* loam core **-mergel** *m* loamy marl **-messer** *n* loam beater **-mörtel** *m* loam mortar **-sand** *m* loam sand **-schlag** *m* puddle **-schmierung** *f* luting with clay **-stampfbau** *m* rammed-loam construction **-stein** *m* air-dried brick, unburnt brick, adobe **-stopfen** *m* clay plug, butt **-ziegel** *m* clay brick, loam brick

Lehne *f* rest, armrest

lehnen to lean, recline

Lehr-amt *n* position as teacher, professorship **-anstalt** *f* educational establishment, college, professional school **-bogen** *m* center(ing) **-bolzen** *m* cylindrical plug gauge, internal gauge **-brett** *n* centering **-brief** *m* (apprentice's) indenture, card of freedom (paper mfg.) **-buch** *n* textbook **-dorn** *m* internal cylindrical gauge, plug gauge

Lehre *f* science, dogma, tenet, theory, gauge, doctrine, centering, apprenticeship, template, pattern, sample instruction, caliber **~ vom Licht** optics **~ vom Schall** acoustics **~ von der elektrischen Strömung** electrokinetics **~ zum Zusammenbau** assembling jig or fixture

Lehreinrichtung *f* training institution

lehren to caliper, gauge; teach, instruct

Lehren-abmaß *n* gauge allowance **-bauer** *m* gauge engineer or manufacturer **-bohrmaschine** *f* jig boring machine **-bohrtisch** *m* jig boring table **-bohrwerk** *n* jig drill **-haltig** true or accurate to gauge **-haltige Fertigung** manufacture to fine limits

Lehrenschleif- und Poliermaschine gauge grinding and polishing machine

Lehren-sollmaß *n* nominal gauge size **-toleranz** *f* gauge tolerance **-verschleiß** *m* gauge wear

Lehrer *m* teacher, instructor

Lehr-film *m* instruction film, educational motion picture, training film **-flugwesen** *n* training aviation

Lehrgang *m* course of instruction **einen ~ durchmachen** to take a course

Lehrgangsleiter *m* instructor, training director, supervisor

Lehr-gerüst *n* scaffold, centering (of arch), false-work **-gewindebolzen** *m* thread gauge **-gruppe** *f* instruction group, class **-hauer** *m* apprentice hewer, helper **-herr** *m* employer, master, patron **-junge** *m* apprentice **-kursus** *m* course of instruction **-laufdrehschieber** *m* slow-run rotary valve

Lehrling *m* apprentice, learner

Lehr-meinung *f* hypothesis, view **-meister** *m* employer, master **-mittel** *pl* educational appliances **-mutter** *f* template **-okular** *n* tutor eyepiece **-plan** *m* curriculum, syllabus

Lehr-ring *m* ring gauge, external gauge **-satz** *m* theorem, proposition (math.), abstract doctrine or theorem **-schau** *f* educational exhibition **-spektroskop** *m* instruction spectroscope **-stelle** *f* training place, school **-tafel** *f* instructional chart **-werkzeug** *n* gauge tool **-zeit** *f* apprenticeship, time of learning **-zeugnis** *n* graduation certificate, card of freedom (paper mfg.)

Leibung *f* intrados, soffit

Leibungsdruck *m* (bolt or rivet) bearing pressure

leicht easy, easily, light, slight ~ **siedendes Öl** low-boiling oil ~ **abschneidende Stanze** dinking die ~ **beschädigt** slightly damaged ~**-beweglich** mobile ~**-fließend** easy flow ~ **flüchtig** light, light volatile (said of fuel) ~ **gehen** to work freely ~ **gefärbt** slightly stained (or colored) ~ **konisch** slightly tapered ~ **zu fliegen** easy to fly ~ **zu reparieren** to be repaired easily ~ **verderblich** perishable ~ **verletzt** slightly injured ~ **zugänglich** of easy access

leicht-e Bedienung *f* facility of operation **-er Gang** soft running **-e Kehlnaht** light fillet **-e Kunststoffschlauchleitung** light-duty thermoplastic jacket cord **-er Nebel** mist **-e Schweißnaht** light weld, concave weld **-e Steuerbarkeit** ease of handling **-er Tiefgang** shallow draft **-e Wartung** ease of maintenance **-er als Luft** lighter-than air **-e Zerlegbarkeit** easily dismantled

Leichtbau *m* light construction **-platte** *f* plastic or wood material (for emergency constructions) **-weise** *f* weight-saving construction, lightweight construction

Leicht-benzin *n* light benzine, gasoline **-benzol** *n* light benzol **-bespulung** *f* light loading

Leichter *m* lighter, barge **-kosten** *pl* lighterage

leichtern, ein Schiff ~ to lighten a ship

Leichterschiff *n* lighter, barge

Leicht-flintprisma *n* prism of light flint **-flüchtig** volatile, easily volatilized, highly volatile **-flugmotor** *n* light aero engine **-flugzeug** *n* light plane **-flüssig** easily fusible, easily liquefiable, mobile, thin **-flüssigkeit** *f* fluidity, low viscosity

leicht-gängig of easy action or motion **-gepanzert** lightly armored **-gewicht** *n* feather-weight **-gewichtskonstruktion** *f* light-weight construction

Leichtigkeit *f* facility, ease, lightness, light weight

Leicht-kraftrad *n* light motorcycle **-kraftstoff** *m* light fuel

leicht-legiert light alloy **-legierung** *f* lightweight alloy **-löslich** easily soluble

Leichtmetall *n* light metal or alloy **-bearbeitung** *f* light-metal working **-blechwaren** *pl* aluminium sheet goods **-dieseltriebwagen** *m* lightweight Diesel rail car **-gerippe** *n* light metal framework **-guß** *m* light-metal casting

Leichtmetall-haube *f* light metal cover **-kolben** *m* light-metal piston **-kopierrahmen** *m* light-metal printing frame **-kurbelgehäuse** *n* light-alloy crankcase **-legierung** *f* light alloy **-tank** *m* Al-alloy tank **-überzug** *m* light metal coating

Leichtöl *n* light oil, light fuel **-einspritzventil** *n* light-fuel injection valve **-gewinnung** *f* light-oil recovery

leicht-schmelzbar, -schmelzlich easily fusible, easily meltable **-siedend** low-boiling **-spaltig** easy to cleave or split **-spat** *m* light spar (gypsum) (a pure white grade, finely ground) **-stoff** *m* light material **-verbrennlich** easily combustible, free-burning

Leierbohrer *m* brace drill, bit-stock drill

Leih-basis *f* trial and return basis **-bedingung** *f* lending condition **-bibliothek** *f*, **-bücherei** *f* circulating library **-frist** *f* time of loan **-gebinde** *n* cask to be returned **-mengen** *pl* loan quantities (borrow) **-weise** *f* as a loan

Leim *m* glue, adhesive substance, paste, size **Anziehen des Leimes** setting of the glue

Leimanstrich *m* size color

leimartig gluey, gelatinous, glutinous

Leim-aufstrich *m* (Lack) size brushing **-auftragmaschine** *f* glue spreading machine **-ausbreiter** *m* glue spreader **-becken** *n* glue-pot **-druck** *m* (Tapeten) size printing (wallpapers) **-email** *n* glue enamel

leimen to glue, cement

Leimen der Kette sizing the warp

Leim-fabrik *f* glue factory **-fähigkeit** *f* ability to lend itself to gluing **-farbe** *f* non washable distemper, size color **-festigkeit** *f* resistance or imperviousness due to sizing, size test, bonding strength **-fett** *n* waste fat from hide-glue manufacture, fat of coconut-oil and palm-kernel-oil group, a fat whose soap resists salting out **-folie** *f* glue foil **-fuge** *f* straight-glued joint, plain joint **-gallerte** *f* (glue) jelly **-gewebe** *n* collagen **-großvorrichtung** *f* power gluing fixture **-holländer** *m* sizing engine

leimig gluey, glutinous

Leim-kante *f* gummed edge **-kocher** *m* size boiler **-kopierverfahren** *n* gum process **-knecht** *m* glue press, gluing cramp **-kratzer** *m* scraper **-leder** *n* scrapings, parings, or shreds, scrap leather **-leiste** *f* gluing strip **-maschine** *f* dressing machine **-milch** *f* resin milk (size milk) **-niederschlag** *m* soap nigre **-presse** *f* glue press **-pulver** *n* glue powder **-seife** *f* soap not salted out, filled or semiboiled nigre, paste soap, filled soap

Leimsieder *m* glue boiler **-niederschlag** *m* soap nigre

Leim-stelle *f* glued joint **-tränken** to give a coating of glue **-trockenanlage** *f* glue drying plant

Leimung *f* tub-sizing, gelatine, glue, sizing ~ **im Bogen** sheet sizing

Leimvorrichtung *f* gluing fixture

Lein *m* flax

Leine *f* line, cord, rope, chord **geschlagene** ~ braided cord, twisted rope

Leinen *n* linen, cloth, canvas **-atlas** *m* linen damask **-bänder** *pl* linen tapes **-batist** *m* linen cambric **-bund** *m* rope lashing **-einband** *m* cloth binding **-garn** *n* flax yarn **-gewebe** *n* linen texture or woof, linen fabric **-hadern** *pl* linen rags **-halbstoff** *m* linen pulp

Leinen-post *f* canvas note **-postpapier** *n* cambric paper **-prägung** *f* linen finish **-schleifblatt** *n* linen grinding blade **-stoff** *m* canvas, linen cloth **-strickerei** *f* linen hosiery **-system** *n* shroud lines, rigging system **-umschlag** *m* cloth-lined envelope **-umwicklung** *f* fabric binding

Leinen- und Drahtbund *m* rope-and-cable lashing

Leinen-velinpapier *n* linen wove paper **-werggespinst** *n* flaxen tow yarn **-werk** *n* cordage, rope **-wurfapparat** *m* line-throwing apparatus

Leinöl *n* linseed oil **-bindemittel** *n* linseed-oil vehicle **-firnis** *m* boiled (linseed) oil **-säure** *f* linoleate **-saures Bleioxyd** lead linoleate **-saures Salz** linoleate **-schlichte** *f* linseed oil size **-wand** *f* linen, cloth

Lein-pfad *m* towpath **-saat** *f* linseed

Leinsamenschleim *m* linseed mucilage

Leinwand *f* linen, screen, canvas, linen cloth, cloth, projection screen **-bindung** *f* basket weave, binding cloth **-kappe** *f* fabric cap, linen flap **-reifen** *m* canvas tire **-pause** *f* cloth print **-zeichnung** *f* cloth tracing

leise (Stimme) low, soft, silenced

Leiseabstimmung *f* silent tuning

Leistchen *n* fillet

Leiste *f* ledge, border, cleat, strip, bar, ledger, band, fillet, batten, ridge, molding

Leisten zum Festhalten des Tisches auf den Führungen gibs for holding the table

leisten to perform, do, carry out, effect

Leisten-arbeit *f* cleat work **-aufroller** *m* selvedge straightener **-bau** *m* working by overhand stopes **-bildung** *f* formation of bad selvedges **-bruch** *m* hernia **-fläche** *f* raised face **-führung** *f* selvedge guide **-gegend** *f* groin **-hobel** *m* molding of fillet plane **-macher** *m* wood molder **-neutralisiervorrichtung** *f* selvedge neutralizing device **-stein** *m* curbstone **-zelle** *f* strip cell

Leistung *f* (Großtat) achievement; (Errungenschaft) accomplishment, attainment; (Geleistetes) work done; (Technik-Wirkungsgrad) efficiency, performance; (Arbeit) power; (Maschine) capacity; (Fabrik, Ausstoß) output, production; (Elektr.) power, wattage; (Motor) performance; (Beitrag) contribution; (Dienst) service; achievement, proficiency, service, efficiency, duty, work, work done, result, effect, carrying capacity, load, energy **~ abgegeben** effective power **abgegebene ~** power output **aufgenommene ~** power input, incoming power **ausgestrahlte ~** radiated power **besondere ~** additional service **effektive ~** useful work, brake horsepower **entnommene ~** output **hohe ~** high power **indizierte ~** indicated work, indicated horsepower **von kleiner ~** low-power(ed) **nutzbare ~** useful work, brake horse-power **optische ~** optical power, optical performance **tatsächlich gemessene ~** observed output **zugeführte ~** power input, input

Leistung der Abteilungen departmental efficiency **~ des Flugzeuges** aircraft performance **~ eines Flugmotors** performance of aircraft engine **~ nach Internationaler Normalatmosphäre** power corrected to standard **~ pro Oberflächeneinheit** power per unit area **~ je Zeiteinheit** output capacity per unit time

Leistungen nicht angegeben performance figures not given

Leistungs-abfall *m* loss of power **-abgabe** *f* power delivery, output

leistungsabhängig-er Speicher volatile memory (comput.) **-e Speicherung** volatile storage

Leistungsabnahme *f* decline of (engine power) output **gleitende ~** power setback **schnelle ~** reactor trip

Leistungs-abstimmung *f* balancing (of worker's loads) **-abweichung** power drift **-abzeichen** *n* certificate or badge of performance **-angabe** *f* performance characteristic

Leistungsanteil, für Kühlzwecke angewendeter ~ cooling-power loss **~ in Prozenten für Luftwiderstand** percentage drag power

Leistungsaufgabe *f* input

Leistungsaufnahme *f* power required, input, power absorption or consumption, rate of power input **~ durch die Luftschraube** engine-power absorption by the airscrew

Leistungsaufwand *m* power input, power increment, power expenditure, energy dissipation **~ für Kühlzwecke** power expended in cooling

Anteil des Leistungsaufwandes für die Kühlung fractional cooling-power loss

Leistungs-ausfall *m* efficiency or production stoppage **-ausfallpunkt** *m* power failure point **-ausnutzung** *f* efficiency

Leistungsbedarf *m* required output, power consumption, power absorption or dissipation, power requirement **~ während des Versuches** power required across the test, power requirement during test

Leistungs-bedarfspegel *m* power-reference level **-bedarfszahl** *f* power coefficient **-begrenzung** *f* power output limitation **-beiwert** *m* performance coefficient **-belastung** *f* performance load, power loading **-belastungsgrad** *m* rate of power loading (in propellers) **-berechnung** *f* capacity rating, performance calculation **-bereich** *m* range of capacity

Leistungs-bericht *m* production report **-beschreibung** *f* specification **-bestimmung** *f* determination of output **-bilanz** *f* rating **-bild** *n* indicator diagram **-bremse** *f* dynamometrical brake **-brutreaktor** *m* power breed reactor **-buch** *n* service record

Leistungs-daten *pl* output (power) data **-detektor** *m* power detector **-diagramm** *n* performance chart, rating chart **-dichte** *f* power density **-einheit** *f* unit of energy, unit of power **-empfindlichkeit** *f* power sensitivity **-entfaltung** *f* deployment of production or efficiency **-entnahme** *f* taking of power, power consumption, energy output, power output, absorption of energy or power **-ertüchtigung** *f* production improvement **-fähig** efficient, serviceable, powerful, capable of (high) production

Leistungsfähigkeit *f* (operational) efficiency, capacity, capability, (brake) power, discharge, performance, serviceability, resolving power (micros) **~ eines Strahlers** meter-amperes, radiation constant **~ einer Vollbahnstrecke** capacity of a standard-gauge railroad

Leistungs-fähigkeitsprobe *f* performance testing **-faktor** *m* power factor **-faktormesser** *m* power-factor meter **-faktorzeiger** *m* power-factor indicator or meter **-fernmeßgerät** *n* telewattmeter **-flugzeug** *n* high-performance airplane **-fördernd** working-promoting **-formel** *f* performance formula

Leistungs-geschwindigkeit *f* velocity of flow (of oil) **-gewicht** *n* weight per horsepower, specific weight, unit power **-gewinn** *m* power gain **-gleichheit der einzelnen Zylinder** equal power distribution between cylinders **-gleichrichter** *m* power rectifier **-grad** *m* performance **-gradschätzen** *n* performance rating

Leistungsgrenze *f* limit of capacity **~ im Steigflug für Dauerleistung** cruising-climb limit

Leistungs-größen *pl* performance data **-hebel** *m* throttle control **-hemmend** work-hindering **-kammer** *f* energy chamber (of klystron)

Leistungskapazität *f* (traffic) capacity of a line **~ eines Sammlers** watt-hour capacity of a storage cell

Leistungs-kennlinie *f* power characteristic curve (or line) **-kennwert** *m*, **-kennzahl** *f* performance characteristic **-knick** *m* production drop **-konstante** *f* power constant **-kontrollabteilung** *f* efficiency department **-kurve** *f* performance graph or curve, power curve

Leistungs-linie *f* performance or power curve **-lohn** *m* production wages **-lohnsystem** *n* incentive plan **-lohntempo** *n* incentive pace (work-factor) **-lohnzuschlag** *m* incentive allowance

leistungslos wattless, nondissipative **-e Speicherung** non-volatile storage

Leistungsmesser *m* wattmeter, output meter, dynamometer, ergometer ~ **mit Hilfswicklung** compensated wattmeter

Leistungs-meßgerät *n* power-measuring device **-meßnabe** *f* dynamometer hub **-meßstand** *m* dynamometer test stand **-messung** *f* power measurement **-methode** *f* wattmeter method **-minderung** *f* production lag **-minute** *f* production per minute

Leistungs-netz *n* grid system **-niveau** *n* performance level, load factor **-pegel** *m* power level **-prüfer** *m* performance or line tester **-prüfmaschine** *f* efficiency-testing machine **-prüfung** *f* performance testing, efficiency test **-querschnitt** *m* cross-sectional efficiency or production

Leistungs-rate *f* output rating **-reaktor** *m* nuclear power plant **-rechnung** *f* performance calculation **-regelstab** *m* power control rod **-regelung** *f* load regulation, power control **-regler** *m* power control (apparatus) **-reserve** *f* reserve source of power, margin of power **-röhre** *f* power valve, power (amplifier) tube

Leistungs-schalter *m* heavy duty switch, circuit breaker **-schätzung** *f* power rating **-schaudiagramm** *n* power diagram **-schild** *n* rating plate, instruction plate **-schreiben** *n* high-performance typing (competition) **-schreiber** *m* output recorder **-schwingkreis** *m* tank circuit **-segelflugzeug** *n* performance-type glider **-soll** *n* production rate (standard) **-sparend** power saving

Leistungs-spektrum *n* power spectrum **-spielraum** *m* performance margin **-spitze** *f* power flash up **-steigerung** *f* increase in efficiency, performance, or output **-strecker** *m* line stretcher **-stufe** *f* output stage, power amplifier, final amplifier **-teiler** *m* power divider **-transformator** *m* power transformer **-trennschalter** *m* power isolating switch **-überschuß** *m* power margin or reserve **-übertragung** *f* power transmission, service transmission **-umsatz** *m* energy exchange, transduction **-unfähig** inefficient

Leistungs-vektor *m* power vector **-verbrauch** *m* power dissipation **-verdienstanstieg** *m*, **abgeschwächter** (reduced) incentive **-verhältnis** *n* power ratio **-verlust** *m* loss in efficiency, power loss (elec.) **-verlustkurven** *pl* derating curves **-vermögen** *n* output capacity **-verstärker** *m* power amplifier **-verstärkung** *f* power amplification, energy amplification, power magnification **-verstärkungsverhältnis** *n* power-amplification ratio **-verzug** *m* delay in performance or of obligation **-vorrichtung** *f* power absorption device **-vorschrift** *f* performance specification **-vorschriften** *pl* code of performance

Leistungs-wählhebel *m* speed-regulator lever, output-selector lever **-wicklung** *f* power winding **-widerstand** *m* external resistance **-zahl** *f* performance figure **-zähler** *m* position-peg-count register, peg-count meter **-zähltaste** *f* call-counter key (teleph.) **-zählung** *f* peg-count summary, load counting **-zeiger** *m* power-indicator, wattmeter **-zerstreuung** *f* power dissipation **-zufuhr** *f* power supply **-zulage** *f* incentive wage **-zunahme** *f* step-up in performance

Leit-achse *f* steering axle **-aluminium** *n* conducting aluminium

Leitapparat *m* distributor ~ **v. Kaplanturbine** gate mechanism ~ **beim Kreiselgebläse** diffuser ~ **Turbine** diaphragm

Leitapparatverdichter *m* vaned diffusor plate

Leit-artikel *m* leader, leading article **-arm** *m* crank **-auge** *n* guide

Leitbahn *f* transit path **-bewegung** *f* transit-path motion **-schwingungen** *pl* (electronic) oscillations of higher order **-welle** *f* transit-time or electron-path oscillation

leitbar ductile, manageable

Leitbarkeit *f* conductivity

Leit-batterie *f* master or lead battery (equipped with radar) **-baum** *m* guide rod **-befehl** *m* routing plan

Leitblech *n* fin, baffle(plate) (in furnace), sheet-metal deflector or guide, stub tube (jet), overflow pipe, pressure-type deflector or baffle, air deflector **mit ~ versehen** to baffle **zylindrisches ~** shell baffle **~ mit absichtlich erzeugter Wirbelbildung** mixing baffle **dicht anschließendes, gut passendes ~** tight-fitting baffle

Leitblech-hohlleiter *m* fin waveguide **-system** *n* system of baffles

Leit-block *m* guide pulley **-brett** *n* stabilizer, tail fin

Leitbuchstaben *pl* office code **-speicher** *m* office-code register

Leit-damm *m* jetty, training dike **-düse** *f* guide nozzle **-elektron** *n* conduction electron

leiten to conduct (away), pass over, convey, direct, carry, pipe, lead, guide, manage, pilot, route (over a line), govern, steer **einheitlich ~** to coordinate

Leiten *n* routing, directing

leitend leading, conductive **-er Angestellter** executive **-es Gas** conducting gas **-es Gebiet** conductive zone **-e Schicht** conducting layer or stratum

Leitepunkte *pl* leaders, guides (print.)

Leiter *f* ladder

Leiter *m* conductor, leader, lead, pilot, manager, director, conduit, core of a cable **biegsamer ~** flexible lead **blanker ~** bare conductor **gerader ~** straight conductor **rechteckiger ~** rectangular wire **runder ~** circular wire **schlechter ~** poor conductor **starker ~** heavy conductor **mit negativem Widerstand behafteter ~** third-class conductor, conductor with negative resistance

Leiter-absatz *m* landing **-antriebsanschluß** *m* electrical connection for retracting mechanism **-aufbau** *m* composition of conductor **-baum** *m* ladder beam **-bruchschutz** *m* open-phase protection (relay) **-brücke** *f* ladder bridge **-bündel** *n* bunched conductors, bunch of conductors

Leiter-dämpfer *m* ladder attenuator **-durchmesser** *m* conductor diameter **-erdspannung** *f* voltage to neutral **-gebilde** *n* conductor structure or system **-isolation** *f* conductor insulation **-nennquerschnitt** *m* nominal conductor (cross) section **-oberfläche** *f* conductor surface **-platte** *f* printed circuit board **-querschnitt** *m* cross-section area of conductor

Leiter-schleife *f* armature (turn) **-spannung** *f* voltage between lines of a polyphase system **-sprosse** *f* ladder rung **-stärke** *f* conductor diameter **-sternpunktspannung** *f* voltage to neutral **-stück** *n* conductor element **-system** *n* conductor system or structure **-tafel** *f* nomogram **-teil** *m* conductor part **-verseilmaschine** *f* core laying-up machine **-wagen** *m* rack wagon, lumber wagon **-widerstand** *m* conductor resistance **-zahl** *f* conductance factor (im Anker) number of conductors (in the armature)

Leitfaden *m* manual, guide(book), textbook

leitfähig conductive, conducting **-e Tinte** electrographic ink

Leitfähigkeit *f* conductance, conductivity **~ des Erdbodens** earth conductivity **dielektrische ~** leakance, dielectric conductance **einseitige ~** unilateral conductance **gegenseitige ~** grid-plate or controlled-plate transconductance, transconductance, mutual conductance **Grenzwert der molaren ~** limiting molar conductance **lichtelektrische ~** photoconductivity **magnetische ~** permeance, (magnetic) permeability, magnetic conductance **richtungsabhängige ~** asymmetrical conductivity **spezifische ~** (specific) conductivity **unipolare ~** unilateral or unidirectional conductivity **spezifische ~** earth conductivity **~ des Überzugs** coating conductivity

Leitfähigkeits-abfall *m* conductivity decay **-beeinflussung** *f* conductivity modulation **-dispersion** *f* conductance dispersion **-elektronen** *pl* conductivity electrons **-gefäß** *n* conductivity cell **-meßbrücke** *f* conductivity indicator **-messer** *m* conductimeter

Leitfähigkeitsnormal *n* conductivity standard **~ des Kupfers** copper-conductivity standard

Leitfähigkeits-prüfer *m* apparatus for testing electric conductivity, conductivity tester **-schreiber** *m* conductivity recorder **-zähler** *m* conductivity counter

Leitfehler *m* misrouting

Leitfernrohr *n* guiding telescope

Leitfeuer *n* fuse cord, leading light (marine), safety fuse **-kette** *f* guiding lights **-zündmittel** *n* cord-type fuse, cord-fuse detonation **-zündung** *f* cord-type fuse detonation

Leit-fläche *f* fin (aviation), deflector, labyrinth, baffle, deflecting vane (of loud-speaker), control surface (as in aircraft) **-flächenschirm** *m* drag and stabilization parachute **-form** *f* key form, leading form **-fossil** *n* key fossil, leading fossil, zone fossil **-frequenz** *f* control frequency, radio-directing frequency **-funkstelle** *f* net control station **-gerät** *n* guidebeam unit **-gitter** *n* guide baffles **-haspel** *f* guide winch **-isotop** *n* tracer (nuclear physics) **-isotopenverfahren** *n* tracer technique

Leit-kabel *n* pilot cable, leader cable **-kammer** *f* diffuser chamber **-kanal** *m* conduit, duct, leading or guiding channel; (Feldänderung) leader field change **-kante** *f* leading edge (aviation), leading tip (of air-plane wing) **-karte** *f* master card, tab index card **-kartensortiereinrichtung** *f* group sorting device **-klappe** *f* guide vane **-klotz** *m* guide block **-korb** *m* guide bucket **-kranz** *m* rim of guide blading, nozzle ring, stator ring, guide-vane ring (gas turbines) **-kreisfrequenz** *f* transit-time frequency **-kurve** *f* lead cam, directrix, pitch or contour (of cam compensator)

Leit-lineal *n* swivel guide bar **-linie** *f* directrix, beacon course, beam, equisignal line, course, or zone

Leitlinien der Kegelschnitte directrixes of conics

Leit-lochstreifen *m* pilot tape **-marke** *f* guide mark **-mineral** *n* zonal mineral **-motiv** *n* leitmotif **-pflock** *m* peg rail **-plattenhalter** *m* printed board holder **-programm** *n* master program (info proc.) **-punkt** *m* initial point

Leitrad *n* guide wheel, impeller, (front) idler, idler whed, diffuser **-achse** *f* idler-wheel shaft **-beschaufelung** *f* stator blading **-träger** *m* diaphragm carrier, guide-wheel carrier **-welle** *f* guide-wheel spindle

Leit-rechen *m* leading grate **-richtung** *f* course of beam or equisignal line **-ring** *m* ball race, guide wheel **-rohr** *n* guiding telescope, conduit tube **-rolle** *f* (guide) sheave or pulley, idler, guide roller, pad roller (without sprockets) **-salz** *n* conducting salt **-satz** *m* rule, guiding or basic principle **-schablone** *f* template follower

Leitschaufel *f* guide vane, entrance bucket (gas turbines), nozzle (jet) **radiale ~** flow straightener vane

Leitschaufel-apparat *m* vaned diffuser **-kranz** *m* vane ring **-ring** *m* turbine nozzle, vane ring **-träger** *m* blade ring carrier

Leit-scheibe *f* idler pulley **-scheinwerfer** *m* master searchlight, pickup light **-schicht** *f* index bed **-schiene** *f* guide rail **-selektron** *pl* pilot selectors **-sender** *m* regional broadcasting station **-signal** *n* pilot indicator

Leitspindel *f* leading spindle, lead screw, guide screw, screw spindle, engine lathe **-drehbank** *f* engine lathe **-kontrolle** *f* lead screw inspection **-steigerung** *f* pitch of lead screw

Leit-stab *m* guide rod **-stand** *m* fire control station (seacoast artillery), command post, fire-direction center **-stange** *f* conducting rod, guide rod, trolley pole, pit guide, handle bar **-stelle** *f* ticket-distributing position, routing desk, radio or net-control station, battery commander's post, ground direction-finder station; (Funk) master station

Leitstrahl *m* equisignal sector, (radius) vector, (pilot) ray or beam **-achse** *f* normal axis **-anlage** *f* guide beam installation **-antenne** *f* directional antenna **-aufschaltgröße** *f* pilot-beam shunt or switch factor **-aufschaltung** *f* signal mixing for guide beam **-bordgerät** *n* guide-beam receiver (in missile)

Leitstrahl-drehung *f* antenna or beam switching **-ebene** *f* guide-beam plane **-empfänger** *m* missile guide beam receiver, beam-control unit **-fächer** *m* guide-beam fan (radar) **-führung** *f* beam-control pilotage, control by pilot beam **-gasse** *f* guide-beam channel **-gerät** *n* beam-control apparatus

Leitstrahl-kontrollanlage *f* station for guide-beam azimuth adjustment **-lenkung** *f* (Rakete) beam-rider guidance **-linie** *f* equisignal line **-schaltung** *f* guide-beam superposition **-schärfe** *f* guide beam focus **-schwenkung** *f* guide-beam rotation **-schwingung** *f* trajectory oscillation about guide beam **-seitenführung** *f* lateral beam control **-sektor** *m* equisignal sector

Leitstrahlsender *m* directional radio beacon **akustischer ~** aural radio range **optischer ~** visual radio range

Leitstrahl-steuerung *f* (Rakete) command guidance **-umschaltung** *f* beam switching **-verfahren** *n* localizer-beam method (of landing), flying on the beam **-winkel** *m* angle of beam **-zeitschalter** *m* guide beam receiver time switch

Leit-strick *m* stay, guy **-strom** *m* conduction current, pilot current **-stück** *n* conducting piece **-stufe** *f* stator stage (of power plant) **-übersicht** *f* routing plan or bulletin

Leit- und Zugspindeldrehbank *f* toolroom lathe

Leitung *f* lead, conducting, guidance; (Beaufsichtigung) control, management, operation; (Vorsitz) chairmanship; (Einrichtung) management; (Maschine) guiding-bar; (Übertragung) transmission; (Physik) conduction; (Elektr.) lead, circuit, telephone wire; (Kabel) cable; (Rohr) pipeline; (Stromzuführung) supply lead; main, conduit, duct, flue, transmission guide, direction, (in pyrometry) lead wire, conductance, control, wiring, administration, piping convection, electric line, supervision, manifold, conductor, trunk-line feeder (elec.), supply line

Leitung, ~ ist besetzt line is busy **geschlitzte ~** slotted section **~ ist kurzgebunden** line is looped (the) **~ ist kurzgeschlossen** line is short-circuited

Leitung, ~ in Berührung mit einer anderen circuit crossed with another **~ mit Besetztlampe** circuit with busy lamp **~ ohne Besetztlampe** circuit without busy lamp **~ in den Boden verlegen** to bury a pipe line **~ für Duplexverkehr** two-way circuit **~ mit Geräusch** noisy circuit **~ mit erhöhter Induktivität** (inductively) loaded circuit **~ mit Kratzgeräuschen** noisy circuit **~ zum Ruderkontakt** fin contact wire

Leitung, ~ mit punktförmiger Ladung lump-loaded circuit **~ von endlicher Länge** finite line **~ für Verkehr in beiden Richtungen** circuit worked on up-and-down basis **~ für abgehenden Verkehr** outgoing one-way circuit **~ für ankommenden Verkehr** incoming one-way circuit **~ für gerichteten Verkehr** one-way circuit **~ für wechselseitigen Verkehr** two-way circuit **mehrere Ämter in einer ~** several stations in a circuit **Einschleifen einer ~** tapping a circuit **mit Erde arbeitende ~** ground-return circuit **an der Stangenspitze geführte ~** saddle wire

Leitung, eine ~ auf Anruf legen to remove a circuit from service for trouble investigation **eine ~ auftrennen** to interrupt a line **eine ~ wieder in Betrieb geben** to restore a circuit to service **eine ~ belegen** to seize a line **in der ~ bleiben** to hold the line **in die ~ eintreten** to answer **eine ~ erden** to ground a line **eine ~ oberirdisch führen** to run a line overhead **eine ~ isolieren** to insulate, disconnect, or isolate a line **die ~ ist kurzgeschlossen oder kurzverbunden** the line is short-circuited

Leitung, sich in der ~ melden to answer **die ~ ist normal geschaltet** the circuit is regular **eine ~ wieder normal schalten** to put a circuit regular **die ~ pfeift** the circuit is singing **eine ~ auf einen freien Platz legen** to transfer a circuit to a reserve position **eine ~ schleifen** to loop a line **die ~ mit Strom beschicken** to carry current on the line **in eine ~ (un)verstärkt eintreten** to monitor a circuit **in einer ~ (un)verstärkt mithören** to monitor a circuit

Leitung, abgehende ~ outgoing circuit **angepaßte ~** matched line **ankommende ~** incoming circuit **äquivalente ~** equivalent circuit **belastete ~** loaded circuit **gleichmäßig belastete ~** continuously loaded line **punktförmig belastete ~** lump-loaded circuit **stetig belastete ~** continuously loaded circuit **nicht berechtigte ~** restricted line **besetzte ~** busy line, engaged line

Leitung, bespulte ~ coil-loaded circuit **betriebsfähige ~** perfect or working circuit **bewegliche ~** distributing line **dünndrähtige ~** small-gauge line **durchgehende ~** through circuit **einwandfreie ~** circuit in good order **endigende ~** terminating circuit **endliche ~** finite line

Leitung, feste ~ fixed line **~ frei** disengaged **freie ~** disengaged line **gegabelte ~** forked circuit **gekreuzte ~** transposed line **gestörte ~** faulty circuit **gleichförmige ~, gleichmäßige ~** smooth line **gummiisolierte ~** rubber-insulated leader **homogene ~** smooth, uniform, or homogeneous line **konzentrische ~** coaxial line or cable, concentric cable, pipe line

Leitung, künstliche ~ artificial line, balancing network, artificial circuit **kurzgeschlossene ~** short-circuited line **lange ~** infinite line **natürliche ~** actual line **oberirdische ~** aerial line, overhead line **offene ~** open-ended line **quasiunendliche ~** semi-infinite line, quasi-infinite line **starkdrähtige ~** heavy(-gauge) line **stromdurchflossene ~** wire carrying current, live wire

Leitung, unipolare ~ unidirectional conductance **unterbrochene ~** interrupted circuit **unterirdische ~** underground circuit **verdrallte ~** twisted line **verkabelte ~** cable line, stranded-wire line **verlustlose ~** line of no loss **verzerrungsfreie ~** distortionless circuit **wichtige ~** controlling circuit **wirkliche ~** real line **zusammengesetzte ~** composite or compound circuit

Leitungen *pl* ductwork, wiring **alle ~ besetzt** „no lines", "no trunks" **~ am Verteiler schalten** to cross-connect lines **~ vertauschen** to cross lines **zwei ~ kreuzen** to cross or transpose two wires

Leitungs-abbau *m* line dismantling **-abfall** *m* line drop, main drop **-abfangschelle** *f* bracing clamp for lead **-abführung** *f* cable outlet **-abgleichverfahren** *n* balancing of circuits **-ablaß** *m* shunt current

Leitungs-abschluß *m* circuit termination **-abschnitt** *m* section of line or circuit **-abstand** *m* line separation **-abzweigung** *f* branching off of conductor **-adern** *pl* connecting flex **-alarmlampe** *f* line alarm lamp **-anlage** *f* wire plant, main system **-anpassungsgerät** *n* matching unit

Leitungsanschluß *m* pipe connection **-element** *n* line connecting element **-klemme** *f* cable connecting terminal **-stück** *n* terminal clamp **-stutzen** *m* union

Leitungsäquivalent *n* line equivalent ~ **in Meilen Standardkabel** standard cable equivalent, line equivalent in miles of standard cable

Leitungs-aufseher *m* (section) lineman, line-walker **-ausgleich** *m* line balance **-automat** *n* automatic line, current limiter **-bahn** *f* conduction path **-band** *n* conduction band (Trans.) **-bau** *m* line construction **-bauart** *f* type of line construction **-baueinheit** *f* line-construction unit **-bauweise** *f* method of line construction

Leitungsberührung *f* contact, cross **zeitweise** ~ tapping or intermittent contact

Leitungs-bezeichnung *f* marking of conductor **-blockierung** *f* lock out **-bruchwächter** *m* open-circuit monitor

Leitungsbündel *n* bunch of circuits, bundle of trunks, group of lines, trunk group **ankommendes** (abgehendes) ~ bunch of incoming (outgoing) trunks

Leitungsdämpfung *f* line loss, line attenuation, transmission equivalent

Leitungsdraht *m* lead wire, conducting wire, line wire, conductor **elektrischer** ~ electric wire **umwickelter** ~ taped wire

Leitungs-druck *m* manifold pressure, line pressure **-druckkontrolle** *f* manifold-pressure control **-druckmesser** *m* manifold-pressure gauge **-durchführung** *f* lead(ing)-in line **-durchhang** *m* sag (of cables) **-durchschalter** *m* (Telegr.) line concentrator **-eigenschaft** *f* line constant, line characteristic

Leitungseigenschaften mehrwertiger Metalle conduction properties of polyvalent metals

Leitungseinführung *f* lead-in (drop) wire ~ (einer Fernsprechstelle) entrance (teleph.) **gummiisolierte** ~ rubber-covered lead-in **oberirdische** ~ lead-in of an overhead line

Leitungs-elektron *n* conduction electron **-entzerrer** *m* line equalizer **-ergänzung** *f* extension circuit, (artificial) extension line, excess network **-fähig** conductive **-fähigkeit** *f* conductivity, conducting power, conduction, conductibility **-feder** *f* (der Klinke) line spring (of jack) **-fehler** *m* line failure, line fault

Leitungsführung *f* wiring, running of wires, conductor lead **offene** ~ open wiring **verdeckte** ~ concealed wiring

leitungsgebundene Welle *f* guided wave

Leitungs-geräusch *n* line noise, circuit noise

leitungsgerichtet along lines **-er Strom** carrier current **-e Trägerwellentelegraphie** wired-wave telegraphy, high-frequency telegraphy along lines

leitungsgesteuert line-controlled

Leitungs-gewicht *n* power,weight ratio, specific weight **-gleichung** *f* transmission equation **-grad** *m* effectiveness **-halter** *m* cable holder **-hang** *m* sag or dip (of lines) **induktivität** *f* lead inductance, line inductance **-kabel** *n* leader cable, lead **-kanal** *m* kennelstone, U-troughing

Leitungskapazität *f* line (shunt) capacity, watt-hour capacity

Leitungs-kennung *f* circuit identification **-klemme** *f* cable clamp **-klinke** *f* line jack, line-switch spring **-koeffizient** *m* conductivity **-konstante** *f* line constant, conductor constant, leakance, line-shunt conductance, leak conductance, circuit constant **-kontaktbank** *f* line bank **-kontaktsatz** *m* line-contact bank **-kosten** *pl* line costs **-kraft** *f* conducting power **-kreuzung** *f* line crossing, crossing or transposition of wires **-kupfer** *n* conductor copper, wire-bar copper **-kupplung** *f* line connector (line coupling) **-länge** *f* circuit length **-litze** *f* cord lead

Leitungs-mann *m* lineman **-mast** *m* pole for overhead lines, telephone pole **-material** *n* conducting material, electric wire **-mechanismus** *m* mechanism of the conductivity **-messer** *m* conductometer **-meßkraftwagen** *m* line-testing vehicle **-mittel** *n* types of lines or conductors **-monteur** *m* pipe fitter **-nachbildung** *f* (line) balance, artificial balancing line, balancing network **-netz** *n* line system, network, wire net, main system **-netzschema** *n* wiring scheme or diagram **-nummer** *f* circuit number **-parameter** *pl* linear electrical constants **-plan** *m* circuit plan, map of network **-probe** *f* line test **-prüfer** *m* circuit tester, line tester

Leitungs-querschnitt *m* cross-section of the conducting wire **-rauschen** *n* circuit noise **-relais** *n* line relay **-relaisgestell** *n* line-relay rack **-rohr** *n* line pipe, conducting tube, manifold conduit, pipe line, pipe leading **-rundfunk** *m* wire broadcast, audio-frequency rediffusion

Leitungs-sammelschiene *f* collecting bar **-schacht** *m* control cable opening **-schaltung** *f* line circuit **-schaubild** *n* performance chart **-schema** *n* diagram of connections or circuit diagram, hook-up **-schiene** *f* line bar **-schleife** *f* loop, metallic circuit **-schnur** *f* flexible cord **-schutzschalter** *m* circuit breaker **-schub** *m* connecting lug

Leitungs-seele *f* conductor core **-seite des Hauptverteilers** line side of the main distributing frame **-signal** *n* wire signal **-skizze** *f* (telephone-) network diagram **-spule** *f* line coil **-stab** *m* directing staff **-stecker** *m* connecting plug **-steckverbinder** *m* cable plug-type connector **-störung** *f* line fault **-strang mit Absperrvorrichtung** pipe system with shut-off device **-strom** *m* conduction current, line current **-stromdichte** *f* conduction current density **-stück** *n* stretch or portion of line element **-sucher** *m* line finder **-system** *n* wire system

Leitungs-taubheit *f* conduction loss, impairment of hearing, conduction deafness **-theorie** *f* transmission theory, line theory **-trennstelle** *f* line connection **-tülle** *f* cable socket (cable brush) **-turm** *m* transmission tower

Leitungs-übersicht *f* circuit-layout record **-überträger** *m* line-transformer or repeating coil **-übertragung** *f* wired radio, wire broadcast, carrier telephony or telegraphy **-überwachungsdienst** *m* maintenance department **-umschaltung** *f* line change

Leitungs- und Schiedsrichterdienst *m* maneuver-command and umpire service

Leitungs-unterbrechung *f* interruption of line, disconnection **-verbinder** *m* cable connector **-verbindung** junction of paths **-verbrauch** *m* power efficiency, consumption **-verlängerung** *f* excess network, extension circuit, artificial extension line

Leitungsverlegung *f* laying of cables ~ **unter Putz** buried wiring

Leitungs-verlust *m* line loss **-vermögen** *n* conductibility, conductivity **-verstärker** *m* telephone (circuit) repeater or amplifier, communication-line repeater **-verzögerung** *f* line lag

Leitungswähler *m* connector, final selector, final switch, line selector **~ mit Frequenzwahl** frequency-selecting connector **Folgeschalter und Relaissatz für ~** final-sequence switch-and-relay set

Leitungswähler-gestell *n* final-switch rack **-schaltung für Zweiganschlüsse** connection for party-line central-office equipment **-vielfach(feld)** *n* final selector (bank) multiple

Leitungs-wärme *f* heat of conduction **-wasser** *n* tap water, town water **-wechselstrom** *m* conduction alternating current **-wicklung** *f* line winding **-widerstand** *m* line resistance, resistance to the flow of current, resistance to conduction **-widerstandsgrenze** *f* pick-up limit **-windung** *f* line winding **-zahl** *f* consignment number **-zeit** *f* line time, circuit time **-zone** *f* equisignal or glide zone **-zubehör** *f* electric wiring accessories **-zug** *m* tension of cable, line (teleph.) **-zuschlag** *m* extra mileage rate (teleph.) **-zustand** *m* line condition

Leitvermögen *n* conductance, conductivity **richtungsabhängiges ~** asymmetric conductance **spezifisches ~** (specific) conductivity, specific conductance

Leit-vorrichtung *f* guide mechanism, guiding device, guide arragement, diffuser (jet) **-vorschub** *m* sliding feed **-walze** *f* guide roller **-wand** *f* upper round head, (guiding wall), training wall, baffle, deflecting vane (of loud-speaker)

Leitweg *m* (traffic) route, routing (radio) **einen ~ geben** to route **~ einer Meldung** routing

Leitweg-lenkung *f* alternate routing (tel.) **-verzeichnis** *n* routing guide **-wähler** *m* routing digits

Leitweg-lenkung *f* alternate routing (tel.) **-wähler** *m* routing digits

Leitwerk *n* tail plane (aeronautics), control; steering gear; tail unit, group, or assembly; jetty, training wall, diversion structure, piled fendering, fenders; susceptance, conductance; guard wall; controlling surfaces, rudders. empennage **~ schütteln** tail buffeting **hochliegendes ~** tail surfaces

Leitwerk-aufstockung *f* rudder enlargement **-auftrieb** *m* lift of tail unit **-belastung** *f* control surface loads, tail unit loads **-fläche** *f* controlling surface, tail surface, area of tail unit **-flächeninhalt** *m* tail group area **-flattern** *n* tail flutter **-flosse** *f* (tail) fin

Leitwerk-gerippe *n* framework of tail **-kabel** *n* control cable **-kraft** *f* force acting on tail unit, empennage or tail force **-masse** *f* mass of tail unit, tail mass **-moment** *n* moment of tail unit, tail moment **-schütteln** *n* tail buffeting **-strebe** *f* tail unit strut **-träger** *m* tail boom

Leitwert *m* admittance, conductance, susceptance **kapazitiver ~** capacity susceptance **magnetischer ~** permeance **negativer ~** negative conductance **relativer ~** reduced admittance **spezifischer ~** conductivity

Leitwert-charakteristik *f* conductance characteristic **-linie** *f* conductance curve **-messer** *m* conductometer **-prüfer** *m* conductivity tester

Leit-widerstand *m* conduction resistance **-zaun** *m* guide fence **-zelle** *f* guide bucket, control word (info proc.) **-zunge** *f* sheet guide (print.), point rail (R.R.) **-zwangschiene** *f* guardrail

Lemma *n* lemma

Lemniskate *f* lemniscate

Lemniskatenkennlinie *f* figure 8 or lemniscate (curve or characteristic) (radio)

Lenardröhre *f* Lenard tube

Lenkachse *f* steering axle

Lenkachs-schenkel *m* steering knuckle **-untergestell** *n* flexible axle frame

Lenkanschlagbegrenzung *m* steering stop limit **-ballon** *m* dirigible balloon, airship, navigable balloon

lenkbar steerable, controllable, dirigible **-es Luftschiff** dirigible, motor-driven airship

Lenkbarkeit *f* dirigibility, controllability, maneuverability

Lenk-baum *m* perch, pole, reach, tongue **-beil** *n* broad ax **-bremse** *f* steering brake **-bremstrommel** *f* steering-brake drum **-einrichtung** *f* steering gear **-einschlag** *m* maximum angle of turn, steering lock

lenken to steer, guide, direct, navigate, pilot, drive

Lenker *m* guide (gun), wheel fork, control handle or lever, guide rod **räumlicher ~** spatial rod

Lenker-bolzen *m* link pin **-gestänge** *n* guide rod **-griff** (Motorrad) guiding bar grip **-hebel** *m* steering knuckle arm **-nullstelle** *f* zero position of space rods **-welle** *f* shaft of steering arm

Lenk-finger *m* cam **-flugkörper** *m* guided missile **-gabel** *f* steering fork or arm **-gehäuse** *n* steering-gear housing or box **-gestänge** *n* tie rods, steering suspension

Lenkgestell *n* steered trailer chassis, steering control member **-lager** *n* pivot bearing **-zapfen** *m* pivot

Lenk-getriebe *n* steering gear, steering mechanism **-handrad** *n* steering wheel **-hebel** *m* steering knuckle arm, steering lever **-hebelanschlag** *m* steering-arm stop **-hebelwelle** *f* drop arm shaft **-kabel** *n* check cable **-klappe** *f* guide flap **-knüppel** *m* control stick **-luftschiff** *n* dirigible, airship **-mutter** *f* steering-gear (female) nut **-pumpe** *f* bilge or clearing pump

Lenkrad *n* caster, steering wheel, caster wheel **-abzieher** *pl* steering wheel pullers **-satz** *m* set of steering wheels

Lenkradius *m* turning circle, radius of wheel path

Lenkrad-mutter *f* steering wheel nut **-speichenkreuz** *n* steering-wheel spider

Lenkrohrlager *n* steering-column bearing

Lenkrolle *f* caster wheel, leading pulley **~ mit Blattzapfen** plate caster **~ mit Bolzenschaft** stem caster

Lenksäule *f* steering pillar, column, or shaft

Lenksäulen-abdichtung *f* steering column seal **-führung** *f* steering cam **-halter** *m* steering-column bearing

Lenk-schemel *m* riding bed or bolster, rider, transom bed **-schenkel** *m* steering worm, steering knuckle arm **-schloß** *n* steering wheel lock **-schnecke** *f* steering worm **-schraube** *f* steering-worm cam **-schubstange** *f* steering comnecting rod **-segment** *n* steering-worm sector **-spiegel** *m* articulated mirror, reflecting link **-spindel** *f* steering-wheel shaft or spindle **-spurhebel** *m* steering lever, track link steering arm **-stange** *f* steering gear, connecting rod, link, tiller, handle bar

Lenkstangen-klemmring *m* locking ring of the handle bar **-rohr** *n* handle-bar stem **-schaft** *m* handle bar shaft **-steuerung** *f* connecting gear, radial gear

Lenkstock *m* steering arm **-gehäuse** *n* steering gear box **-halter** *m* steering gear clamp **-halterung** *f* steering gear attachment, steering gear bracket **-hebel** *m* steering-gear arm, drop arm, drop hanger arm, pitman arm **-lager** *n* worm bearing **-spindel** *f* steering shaft

Lenkstoßfang *m* steering-shock suspension, anti-shimmy suspension

Lenkung *f* steering, steering gear **passive ~** passive homing

Lenkungs-anschlag *m* steering stop **-ausschlag** *m* steering lock **-einschlagwinkel** *m* angle of lock **-gehäuse** *n* steering box **-rad** *n* steering wheel **-schema** *f* steering system **-verfahren** *n* guiding method

Lenk-verbindungsstange *f* tie rod or bar **-vorrichtung** *f* steering gear, guiding or steering device or control **-waffe** *f* guided missile **-wand** *f* baffle **-welle** *f* pitman shaft **-zapfen** *m* steering pivot or journal **zugkabel** *n* check cable

lensen to run or sail before the wind, scud

lentern to clarify, filter

Lentzsteuerung *f* Lentz valve gear

lenzen to blow (tanks), pump out

Lenzen *n* lying to

Lenzin *m* light spar

Lenzpumpe *f* bilge pump, drainage pump

Lenzsches Gesetz Lenz's law

Lenzschieber *m* drain valve

Leonard-betrieb *m* Ward-Leonard operation **-satz** *m* Ward-Leonard set **-schaltung** *f* Ward-Leonard hoist

Lepidolith *m* lepidolite, lithium schist

Leptometer *n* leptometer

Lepton *n* lepton

Leptonenerhaltung *f* lepton conservation

lesbar legible

Lesbarkeit *f* legibility

Lese-band *n* (ore) picking belt conveyer, sorting belt **-brille** *f* reading glasses (spectacles) **-geschwindigkeit** *f* reading speed **-glas** *n* reading glass

Lese-impuls *m* sensing pulse (core memory) **-leitungen** *pl* sense lines **-leuchte** *f* reading lamp **-maschine** *f* reading machine, reader (comput)

lesen to read, pick (out), sort

Leseprogramm *n* input routine (info proc.) **-pult** *n* lectern

leserlich legible, easy to read

Lese-spule *f* sense coil **-störung** *f* read-disturbing **-tisch** *m* picking or reading table **-verstärker** *m* sense-amplifier **-vorgang** *m* readout **-wicklung** *f* read winding, sense winding **-zeichen** *n* bookmark

letale Dosis lethal dose

Lethargie *f* (neutron) lethargy

Lette *f* loam

Letten *m* loam, potter's clay, gouge (min.), very pure clay, fat clay **eisenschüssiger ~** ferriferous clay **ockerhaltiger ~** gossaniferous clay

Letten-besteg *m* vein walls **-bohrer** *m* claying bar **-damm** *m* layer of puddled clay **-haue** *f* grub hoe, mattock **-kluft** *f* weigh board **-nudel** *f* tamping cartridge of clay, roll of clay

Lettern-gießmaschine *f* type-casting machine **-gut** *n*, **-metall** *n* type metal **-messer** *m* typometer, type gauge **-stich** *m* letter engraving

lettig clayey, loamy, clayish

letzter Schliff master touch **~ Zeitpunkt** deadline

Leucht-anode *f* luminous anode **-anzeige** *f* pilot light **-apparat** *m* flare **-bake** *f* light beacon **-bedingung** *f* lighting condition for searchlight **-bereit** ready for action (said of a searchlight) **-bild** *n* transparency **-bildkondensator** *m* luminous-spot ring condenser **-bildwaage** *f* illuminated dial balance **-blatt** *n* luminous dial **-boje** *f* light buoy **-bombe** *f* flash bomb, flare

Leuchtbombenzeichen, neuartiges schwimmendes ~ multiple floating flare for light island

Leucht-dauer *f* illuminated period, light period, luminescence, luminosity, phosphorescence period

Leuchtdichte *f* intensity per unit of surface or intrinsic brilliance (of luminous surface), brightness of a surface, luminous density, brightness **-änderungen** *pl* changes in brightness **-kontraste** brightness difference **-skala** *f* luminance scale **-wert** *m* brightness level

Leuchtdraht *m* filament **gewendelter ~** coiled filament

Leuchte *f* light, lamp, optical apparatus, armature, fitting, lantern, beacon, lamp equipment (motion pictures) **~ an der Flügelspitze** wing-tip flare

Leuchtelektron *n* photoelectron (electron micros.), optical electron, emitting electron

leuchten to shine, (signallampe) light, gleam, illuminate, glow, luminesce **rot ~** to show red

Leuchten *n* lighting, luminescence **~ der Lampe** lighting of lamp

leuchtend luminous, bright, shining, incandescent **-er Faden** lamp filament **-e Fläche** radiant surface (area) **-e Flamme** luminous flame **-er Punkt** spot of light

Leuchtenergie erzeugend photogenic, fluorogenic, phosphorogenic

Leucht-fackel *f* illuminating torch **-faden** *m* conducting filament, luminous or glow column, streamer **-fadeneinsatz** *m* streamer onset **-fähigkeit** *f* luminosity **-fallschirm** *m* parachute flare **-farbe** *f* luminous or phosphorescent paint **-feld** *n* light halve (tape rec.) **-feldblende** *f* radiant field stop **-feldlinsen** *pl* condensor lenses

Leuchtfeuer *n* beacon, floating light, light fire **-verzeichnis** *n* beacon register, beacon list, light list

Leuchtfläche *f* illuminated area

Leuchtfleck *m* spot of light, light spot **-durchmesser** *m* spot diameter

Leuchtfolie *f* lightning foil

Leuchtgas *n* illuminating gas, coal gas, city gas, natural gas **-ballon** *m* balloon inflated with illuminating gas **-kohle** *f* illuminating-gas coal **-technik** *f* illuminating-gas engineering **-vergiftung** *f* illuminating-gas poisoning

Leucht-gebilde *n* luminous pattern **-gerät** *n* illuminating apparatus **-glimmen** *n* luminous glow **-grundwindzeiger** *m* luminous ground-wind indicator **-halle** *f* photosphere **-horizont** *m* transverse-bar airfield lighting **-hülle** *f* luminous sheath or envelope, photosphere **-kompaß** *m* luminous(-dial) compass, illuminated compass **-korn** *n* illuminated sight **-körper** *m* radiant (incandescent) body

Leuchtkraft *f* luminous power, luminosity, illuminating power **gemessene ~** luminance, photometric brightness

Leuchtkraft-bestimmung *f* photometry **-kurve** *f* candle-power curve **-verstärker** *m* phosphorogen

Leucht-kreuz *n* reticle image (reflector sight) **-kugel** *f* rocket, flare, signal rocket, Very light **-kugelposten** *m* flare-pistol-equipped outpost who warns of impending attacks **-lupe** *f* illuminating magnifier **-marke** *f* luminous mark **-masse** *f* phosphorescent compound, luminescent or phosphorescent substance **-meldung** *f* light message **-mittel** *n* illuminant, means of lighting, flare **-munition** *f* signal ammunition **-öl** *n* illuminating oil, kerosene, paraffin

Leucht-patrone *f* flare cartridge, signal cartridge **-patronensignal** *n* flare signal **-petroleum** *n* lamp oil, burning oil, kerosene, naphtha **-pistole** *f* pyrotechnic pistol, signal pistol, Very pistol **-plakat** *n* fluorescent poster

Leuchtpunkt *m* (luminous) spot **-abtaster** *m* flying spot scanner

Leucht-quarz *m* luminous quartz, glow crystal **-rakete** *f* light rocket, light flare, landing rocket **-raketengestell** *n* pyrotechnic projector **-raum** *m* light sector, area in which a search-light unit is to expose its beams **-resonator** *m* luminous resonator or quartz, glow-tube resonance indicator **-röhre** *f* fluorescent tube, arc-light source, luminous-discharge lamp or tube, soffit lamp **-röhrengleichrichter** *m* neon tube rectifier **-röhrenleitungen** *pl* neon-tube wires **-satz** *m* flare composition, tracer composition

Leuchtschaltbild *n* luminous-circuit diagram **~ mit Fernsteuerung und Fernmessung** luminous indicator panel with remote-control and telemetering devices

Leucht-scheibe *f* spot (disk) of light **-schicht** *f* phosphor (of cathode-ray tube) **-schild** *n* visual indicator, illuminated sign

Leuchtschirm *m* actinic screen, luminous or luminescent screen, fluorescent screen, phosphor screen, target **~ der Abtaströhre** screen of the scanning tube **~ einer Farbschriftröhre** dark trace screen

Leuchtschirm-abtastung *f* fluorescent-screen scanning **-material** *n* screen material **-personen-abtaster** *m* fluorescent-screen scanning of persons **-rohr** *n* projection tube **-röhre** *f* luminescent-screen tube **-strom** *m* fluorescent target current **-substanz** *f* phosphor, fluorescent substance

Leuchtschrift *f* luminous lettered text **~ einer Dunkelschriftröhre** dark trace screen

Leucht-schuß *m* tracer round **-signal** *n* luminous signal **-skala** *f* luminous dial **-spat** *m* a variety of heavy spar **-spirale** *f* filament spiral

Leuchtspur *f* tracer bullet (trajectory) **-satz** *m* tracer composition

Leucht-stab *m* flashlight **-stärke** *f* candle power, brightness **-stärkenverteilungskurve** *f* luminosity curve

Leuchtstoff *m* fluorenscent or phosphorescent substance **-lampe** *f* fluorescent lamp, luminous or luminescent lamp or tube, vacuum tube lamp **-leuchte** *f* fluorescent lamp **-punkt** *m* phosphor dot (TV) **-röhre** *f* fluorescent strip lamp **-streifen** *m* phosphor strip (TV)

Leuchtstrahl *m* rocket

Leuchtstrahlquelle, einfarbige ~ monochromatic illuminator, monochromator

Leucht-streifen *m* luminous streamer **-strich** *m* light line **-taste** *f* luminous key, luminous-headed press button **-tätigkeit** *f* lighting activity **-temperatur** *f* brightness temperature **-tonne** *f* lighted buoy **-turm** *m* lighthouse, beacon

Leucht- und Signalmittel *n* flare and signal material

Leucht-verbot *n* blackout, illumination prohibition **-visier** *n* luminous sight **-vorfeld** *n* forward light field **-vorrichtung** *f* reflector **-weiteregler** *m* light-range regulator **-wert** *m* illuminating value **-wirksamkeit** *f* luminous efficiency **-wirkung** *f* luminous effect

Leucht-zahlenfeld *n* (Telefon) luminous annunciator **-zeichen** *n* light signal, flare signal **-zeiger** *m* dial-light resonance indicator **-zielvorrichtung** *f* illuminated sight **-ziffer** *f* luminous figure **-zifferblatt** *n* luminous dial **-zone** *f* light zone, area covered by the effective ranges of searchlights

Leucit *m* leucite **-führend** leucite-bearing

Leuko-base *f* leuco base **-esterverbindung** *f* leucoester compound **-körper** *m* leuco-compound **-meter** *n* leucometer **-penie** *f* leucopaenia **-plast** *n* Leucoplast (adhesive tape) **-verbindung** *f* leuco-compound

Leukozyt *m* leucocyte, white corpuscule

Leukozytose *f* leucocytosis

Leukozyten-gesamtzahl *f* total white count **-zählung** *f* white count

Leunasalpeter *m* leuna saltpeter

Leuzit *m* leucite

levantieren to board (grain)

Levantierholz *n* cork board

Leviathanrechen *m* rake of a leviathan

levigieren to pulverize (levigate)

Lexikon *n* encyclopaedia, dictionary

Leydener, ~ Flasche Leyden jar **~ Flaschenbatterie** battery of Leyden jars

Liage *f* binding threads **-kamm** *m* binding leaf

Lias *m* Lias

Libelle *f* level, spirit level, bubble, liquid, or water level, bubble, clinometer **parallaxenfreie Beobachtung der ~ durch Prismen** seeing the bubble without parallax through prisms **die ~ ist ausgeglichen** the bubble has been levelled **die ~ einspielen lassen** to center the bubble

Libellen-aufsatz *m* clinometer sight (artil.), quadrant sight **-blase** *f* bubble of the level **-einstellung** *f* setting for matériel correction and gun displacement **-empfindlichkeit** *f* sensitiveness of the level **-gehäuse** *n* level housing **-instrument** *n* instrument with tubular level **-körper** *m* level tube or housing **-lotgerät** *n* bubble bombing sight **-quadrant** *m* spirit-level clinometer **-qua-**

drantenfläche *f* quadrant seat **-sextant** *m* bubble sextant **-spiegel** *m* level (bubble) mirror

Libethenit *m* copper phosphate

Licht *n* light, transparent spot or area (phot., print.), illumination, lamp ~ **des Nachthimmels** light of the night sky **auffallendes** ~ incident light **ausfallendes** ~ emergent light, transmitted light **direktes** ~ specular light **durchfallendes** ~ transmitted or transcident light **einfallendes** ~ sky light, incident light **einfarbiges** ~ monochromatic or homogeneous light **eingestrahltes** ~ incident light, exciting light **elliptisch polarisiertes** ~ elliptically polarized light

Licht, ~ **bündeln** to concentrate light **falsches** ~ light fog, leakage light, stray light **gegossenes** ~ molded candle, mold candle, mold **gerichtetes** ~ concentrated light, parallel light rays **gewöhnliches rothaltiges** ~ ordinary light containing red rays **gezogenes** ~ dip, dipped candle **linear polarisiertes** ~ plane polarized light **monochromatisches** ~ monochromatic light **spektral zerlegtes** ~ spectroscopically dispersed or separated light **unzerlegtes** ~ undispersed light ~ **zerstreuen** to disperse light **zirkular polarisiertes** ~ circulary polarized light

licht clear, unobstructed, interior, in the clear, pale, bright, luminous, light **-e Breite** breadth of the day **-er Durchmesser** inside diameter **-e Höhe** vertical clearance, clear height **-er Raum** space in the clear, clearance **-e Weite** inside diameter, inside width, lumen, clear aperture (of lens), useful or effective diameter

Licht-abbeugung *f* diffraction, diffractive properties **-abfall** *m* decrease of light **-abhängiger Widerstand** light-dependent resistor (LDR) **-ablenkung** *f* light ray bending

Lichtabschluß *m* light-tight (lightproof) connection **unter** ~ in the absence of light

Lichtabschluß-hülse *f* light screen, light guard **-trichter** *m* light guard funnel, lightproof funnel

Licht-abschwächung *f* attenuation device **-abstufung** *f* gradation of light **-abtastung** *f* flying-spot method of scanning **-aggregat** *n* lighting set **-alterung** *f* light ageing **-anker** *m* dynamo armature **-anlage** *f* light plant or installation **-anlaßbatteriezünder** *m* starter and battery-ignition unit **-anlasser** *m* light generator **-anlaßmaschine** *f* combined lighting and starting dynamo **-anschlußdose** *f* light socket **-antenne** *f* mains or light-line antenna **-antennenbauch** *m* loop antenna **-art** *f* type of light **-aufnahmewinkel** *m* light-collection angle

Lichtausbeute *f* efficiency of a luminous source, light yield or efficiency ~ **der Leuchtstoffe** light yield or efficiency of fluorescent material

Lichtausbreitung *f* distribution of exposure

Lichtausschluß, unter ~ in the absence of light

Licht-ausstrahlung *f* light radiation **-ausstrahlungsvermögen** *n* power of radiating light **-austritt** *m* exit of light, lens opening **-auswertekraftwagen** *m* flash-ranging truck **-auswertung** *f* utilization of light **-batteriezünder** *m* dynamo battery ignition unit **-beständig** stable to light **-beständigkeit** *f* fastness to light **-beugung** *f* diffraction of light **-beugungsmethode** *f* light diffraction method

Lichtbild *n* photograph, photography, photographic image ~ **aus der Luft aufgenommen** photograph taken from the air **unvergängliches** ~ imperishable picture or photograph

Lichtbild-anlage *f* photographic plant **-aufnahme** *f* photography, photograph **-aufnahmegerät** *n* camera **-auftrag** *m* photographic mission **-ausrüstung** *f* photographic equipment **-auswertung** *f* interpretation of (aerial) photograph **-einrichtung** *f* photographic equipment **-entzerrung** *f* rectification of aerial photographs **-erkundung** *f* photographic reconnaissance **-gerät** *n* photographic apparatus, camera **-kompaß** *m* photographic compass **-kunst** *f* photography

Lichtbildner *m* photographer

Lichtbildnerei *f* photography

lichtbildnerisch photographic

Lichtbild-pause *f* photographic overlay **-schale** *f* photographic basin **-typendrucker** *m* sparking printer **-werfer** *m* projector **-wesen** *n* photography **-zeichnung** *f* photogrammetry

licht-blau pale blue **-blende** *f* light stop, diaphragm, light shield

Lichtblitz *m* pulse of light, flash of light, scintillation **-analysator** *m* flashometer **-anlage** *f* photoelectric control set **-röhre** *f* high speed flash tube **-signal** *n* flash signal

Lichtbogen *m* arc, electric arc, arc lamp **flackernder** ~ unsteady arc **singender** ~ singing arc **sprechender** ~ speaking arc ~ **mit Fremdheizkathode** externally heated arc **Poulsenscher** ~ Poulsen arc

Lichtbogen-abfall *m* arc-drop (voltage) **-aureole** *f* arc flame **-beheizung** *f* arc heating **-bereich** *m* arc zone (elec.) **-beständig** arc-proof, arc-resistant **-bildung** *f* arcing **-elektroofen** *m* electric-arc furnace **-elektrostahlofen** *m* electric-arc furnace for making steel **-entladung** *f* arc discharge **-erdung** *f* arcing ground

Lichtbogen-generator *m* oscillating arc, arc generator, arc converter **-geschweißt** flash-welded **-gleichrichter** *m* arc rectifier **-heizung** *f* arc heating **-hülle** *f* arc shield **-kammer** *f* arcing chamber **-kern** *m* arc core **-kopf** *m* arc terminal **-leitfläche** *f* arc-baffles **-löschkammer** *f* arc quench chamber **-löschung** *f* arc extinction, arc extinguishing

Lichtbogenofen *m* (electric-)arc furnace ~ **mit der Widerstandserhitzung vereinigt** series-arc furnace **unmittelbarer** ~ **ohne Herdbeheizung** direct-arc nonconducting-hearth furnace

Lichtbogen-physik *f* arc physics **-rückzünder** *m* arc-back igniter **-saum** *m* arc seam **-schneidemaschine** *f* arc cutting machine **-schritt** *m* arcing step, step of the arc **-schweißautomat** *m* automatic arc-welding machine **-schweißelektroden** *pl* arc-welding electrodes **-schweißnaht** *f* arc-welding seam

Lichtbogenschweißung *f* arc welding, spark welding ~ **unter Schutzglas** shielded-metal arc welding

Lichtbogen-schweißverfahren *n* arc-welding method **-schwingung** *f* arc oscillation **-schwingungserzeuger** *m* arc generator **-sender** *m* arc transmitter **-sicherheit** *f* nonarcing property **-spannung** *f* (arc) voltage **-stahlofen** *m* electric-arc steel melting furnace **-triebwerk** *n* arc motor, (short for) arc rocket motor **-überschlag** *m* (Durchschlag) arc-back **-umhüllung** *f* arc shielding **-verlust** *m* arc-drop loss **-wärme** *f* heat of an electric arc **-widerstandsofen** *m* resistance-arc furnace, direct-heating arc furnace **-zündung** *f* arc ignition

lichtbrechend refractive, dioptric(al), refracting, refringent

Lichtbrechkraft einer Linse diopter

Lichtbrechung *f* refraction of light

Lichtbrechungs-körper *m* refractor **-lehre** *f* dioptrics **-vermögen** *n* refractivity, molecular refraction, (optical) refractive power

Licht-brücke *f* light arc **-bündel** *n* light beam, luminous beam, pencil of rays **-bündelvignettierung** *f* vignetting of cone of light **-büschel** *n* illuminating pencils **-chemisch** photochemical, actinic **-dämpfer** *m* silk, light softener (motion pictures) **-dämpfung** *f* light subduing

lichtdicht lighttight, airtight, impervious **-er Abschluß** lighttight (lightproof) connection or seal **-e Kassette** dark-room pan impermeable to light

Licht-dichte *f* light density **-dichtigkeit** *f* lightproofness, opacity **-dielektrisch** photodielectric **-dosiergerät** *n* exposure control unit **-draht** *m* light wire

Licht-druck *m* phototype, photograph, photoengraving, photolithography, photogravure, photomechanical printing, photograph printing, radiometer-vane effect **-farbe** *f* collotype printing ink **-gelatine** *f* collotype gelatine **-karton** *m* gelatine board **-korn** *n* collotype grain **-manier** *f* collotype process **-verfahren** *n* photograving

Licht-durchlässig light-transmissive or -transmitting, pervious or permeable to light rays, transparent, translucent **-durchlässigkeit** *f* transparency, light diffusion, light transmittance, (specific) light transmittancy **-durchlässigkeitsprüfer** *m* diaphanometer, opacity tester **-durchsichtigkeit** *f* transparency

Lichte *n* clear, intermediate space

lichtecht fast to light, fast (color), nonfading

Lichtechtheit *f* ability of a fabric to resist or withstand bleaching

Licht-echtheitsprobe *f* exposure test **-effekt** *m* luminous or lighting effect

Lichteindruck *m* visual impression **Verschmelzen der Lichteindrücke** merging of light impressions

Licht-einfall *m* light leak **-einheit** *f* primary luminous standard **-einlaß** *m* light entry opening (aperture) **-eintrittfenster** *n* light-admission window **-einwirkung** *f* action of light

lichtelektrisch photoelectric, radioelectric, electronogenic **-e Ausbeute, äußerer -er Effekt** photoelectric emission, photoemissive effect, external photoelectric effect, Hallwachs effect **innerer -er Effekt** photo-conductive effect **-es Remissionsphotometer** *n* photoelectric reflection photometer **-er Widerstand** photocell resistance **-e Widerstandszelle** photoresist(or) **-e Wirkung** photoelectric effect **-e Zelle** photoelectric cell, light microphone, photo cell

Licht-elektrizität *f* photoelectricity **-element** *n* photoelectric cell or tube, photocell, phototube

lichtempfindlich (photo-)sensitive, light-reactive, sensitive to light, sensitized **~ machen** to sensitize, photosensitize **-e Oberfläche** photosensitive surface **-es Papier** photographic paper **-e Platte** sensitized plate **-e Schicht** coating **-er Transistor** photistor **-e Zelle** light-reactive cell, photo(electric) cell, light microphone

Lichtempfindlichkeit *f* sensitivity, speed (phot.), photosensitivity, actinism

Lichtempfindlichkeitskurve *f* response curve

Lichtempfindung *f* light sensation

lichten to thin, clear (a forest) **einen Anker ~** to weigh anchor

Lichten *n* hoisting

Lichtenergie *f* luminous energy

Lichtenmaß *n* measures of the day

lichtentwickelnd emitting light, producing light, photogenic

Lichtentwicklung *f* light development

Lichter *pl* high-lights (TV)

Lichter *m* lighter, barge **-führung** *f* navigation lights

lichterloh ablaze

Licht-erreger *m* light producer **-erscheinung** *f* optical phenomenon, light effect **-erzeugend** light-emitting, light-producing, photogenic **-falle** *f* light trap **-fangleistung** *f* light gathering power **-farbe** *f* light coloration **-farbendruck** *m* photochemical color printing **-fenster** *n* light window **-filter** *m* light filter, ray filter, colored screen, color filter

Lichtfleck *m* light spot, hot spot (on film) **abtastender ~** scanning spot, exploring spot **wandernder ~** flying spot

Licht-fleckverzerrung *f* spot distortion **-fluß** *m* luminous or light flux **-freundlich** favoring high lights over shadows, photophilic, photophilous **-freundlichkeit** *f* light transmittancy, light transmissivity **-fülle** *f* light abundance **-funk** *m* telephoto

Licht-garn *n* wick yarn **-gebend** light-giving or -emissive, luminous, photogenic **-gebilde** *n* light effect **-geschwindigkeit** *f* velocity of light, electromagnetic wave velocity **-gewinn** *m* light increment, light gain **-gitter für Pressensteuerung** safety beam gate for controlling presses **-gitterbelag** *m* grating floor **-gitterrost** *m* egg crate decking **-grammophon** *n* sound-track film player **-grün** light green **-hahn** *m* electromagnetic mirror vibrator

Lichtheilapparat *m* salutary lighting apparatus **elektrischer ~** electrotherapeutic light apparatus

Lichtheilstation *f* establishment for light treatment

Lichthof *m* halo, halation, (glass-roofed) court **-bildung** *f* halation

lichthoffrei antihalo, nonhalating **-e Platte** *f* plate free from halation (photo) **-e Schicht** *f* antihalation backing

Lichthof-schutz *m* antihalo base **-schutzmittel** *n* antihalo means, antihalation substance **-schutzschicht** *f* backing (photo) **-sicher** nonhalating **-störung** *f* halo disturbance

Licht-höhe *f* interior height **-hupe** *f* by-pass light signal, impulse transmitter for light signal **-intensitätsschwankung** *f* light-intensity variation **-interferenz** *f* light-wave interference

Licht-kabel *n* lighting cable **-kegel** *m* cone of light, illuminating pencil, cone of rays, searchlight beam, pencil of light, luminous cone, null cone **-kenngerät** *n* optical IFF apparatus **-klappe** *f* light gate lid (cover) **-kohle** *f* electric-lighting carbon **-korpuskel** *n* photon **-kraft** *f* rapidity of lens **-kräftig** luminous **-kranz** *m* corona **-kreis** *m* circle of light **-kreuz** *n* light cross

Licht-kunde *f*, **-lehre** *f* optics, photology **-leistung** *f* light efficiency **-leitender Wandler** photo conductive transducer **-leiter** *m* photoconductor **-leitsystem** *n* condenser relay system **-leitung** *f* light wiring, lighting circuit, lighting mains **-leitungsrohr** *n* lighting conduit **-linie** *f* meter

Lichtmeß-gerät *n* amplifier, photometer **-kunst** *f* photometry **-stelle** *f* flash-ranging station **-system** *n* flash-ranging system **-theodolit** *m* flash-ranging theodolite

Lichtmessung *f* flash ranging, photometry, optometry

Lichtmeßverfahren *n* flash ranging, flash spotting

Lichtmikroskop *n* optical or light microscope, light-optical microscope

Lichtmodulator *m* light relay **selbstleuchtender** ~ light relay of the glow tube, neon arc lamp, sodium lamp

Lichtmühle *f* radiometer

Licht-nebel *m* luminous haze **-negativ** *n* light-negative

Lichtnetz *n* supply line, lighting circuit, lighting mains **-antenne** *f* mains antenna, light-line antenna, light-socket antenna, light-circuit antenna **-empfänger** *m* mains receiver, mains set, mains-driven receiver, electric radio receiver **-leitungsbelastung** *f* lighting load

Licht-öffnung *f* opening to admit light **-optik** *f* photo-optics, light optics, physical optics, geometrical optics of light rays **-orgel** *f* illumination desk **-papier** *n* photographic paper

Lichtpaus-anstalt *f* light-tracing establishment **-apparat** *m* copying apparatus, printing machine **-bogenlampe** *f* copying arc lamp

Lichtpause *f* heliographic print, blueprint, photographic tracing

Lichtpaus-gerät *n* blue printer **-lampe** *f* blueprint lamp **-leinen** *n* blue-printing linen **-papier** *n* blue-print paper, photoprinting paper, photostat paper **-rohpapier** *n* dyeline paper **-verfahren** *n* photographic or heliographic printing

Licht-pfeil *m* luminous arrow **-pforte** *f* light port, light band **-loch** *n* air hole, pupil (of eye), opening for light **-los** dark

Licht-magnetzünder *m* dynamo magneto **-manschette** *f* lightproof connecting sleeve **-marke** *f* spot **-markengalvanometer** *n* light-spot galvanometer **-markeninstrument** *n* instrument with optical pointer **-maschine** *f* dynamo, generator, lighting dynamo

Lichtmaschinen-gehäuse *n* dynamo yoke **-halterung** *f* dynamo bracket **-rad** *n* generator (dynamo) gear wheel **-träger** *m* dynamo carrier

Licht-maß *n* clearance **-maßeinheit** *f* photometric unit **-mastaufsätze** *pl* postlanters **-menge** *f* quantity of light

Lichtmeß-ausbildungsbatterie *f* flash-ranging training battery **-batterie** *f* flash-ranging battery **-beobachtung** *f* flash spotting **-dienst** *m* flash-ranging service

Licht-messen *n* flash ranging **-messer** *m* photo-dead light **-phonograph** *m* sound-track film player **-positiv** light-positive

Lichtpunkt *m* focus, light spot, point or dot of light **wandernder** ~ flying spot

Lichtpunkt-abtaster *m* flying spot scanner, light spot scanner **-abtaströhren** *pl* flying spot scanners **-abtastung** *f* flying-spot method of scanning **-durchmesser** spot diameter **-steuergerät** *n* target projector

Lichtquantum *n* light quantum, photon

Lichtquelle *f* luminous source, source of light, modulated light source, illuminant ~ **mit Struktur** source of light exhibiting structural markings **punktförmige** ~ punctiform light source, tungsten-arc lamp

Lichtquellen-ausbeute *f* light-source efficiency **-bild** *n* light source image **-spalt** *m* light source slit **-stärke** *f* light-source efficiency

Licht-rakete *f* flare **-rand** *m* bright rim **-raster** *m* light value **-raummaß** *n* clearance **-raumprofil** *n* railway loading gauge **-reaktion** *f* photoreaction **-reflexion** *f* reflection of light **-reflexionsvermögen** *n* light reflectance, light reflexivity **-regler** *m* light modulator, light relay, light-control means **-reich** bright **-reiz** *m* sensation of light, luminous stimulus **-reklame** *f* luminous advertising, illumination advertisements

Lichtrelais *n* photorelay, light modulator, light relay, device converting current into light variations **elektrooptisches** ~ electro-optical or Faraday cell, light relay depending on Faraday effect

Licht-rißbildung *f* sun cracking **-risse** *pl* light cracks **-rufanlage** *f* light-signalling system **-sammelnd** light gathering

Lichtsatz *m* photo-composition, film setting **-schachtverriegelung** *f* hood and magnifier release **-schallmessen** *n* sound-flash ranging **-scheibe** *f* transparent pane **-scheu** photophobic, obscure **-schirm** *m* light screen, light shield

Lichtsäule *f* luminous column **positive** ~ positive column

Licht-schacht *m* air shaft, light tunnel (of sensitometer) **-schachtaufsatz** *m* focusing hood unit **-schalter** *m* lighting switch **-schalttafel** *f* lighting panel **-schauzeichen** *n* electric-lamp signal **-schein** *m* blaze **-scheue** *f* photophobia **-schleier** *m* light-struck plates (phot.) **-schleusen** *f* light trap **-schluckend** light-absorbing, optically absorptive or absorbing

Lichtschnitt *m* light intersection **-mikroskop** *n* light section microscope **-verfahren** *n* light section method

Licht-schranke *f* light barrier **-schreiber** *m* photographical recorder **-schreiberempfang** *m* photographic or arc writing reception

Lichtschutz *m* lightguard (screen) **-gehäuse** *n* lamp housing **-kappe** *f* light hood (phot.) **-klappe** *f* light protection flap **-rohr** *n* tube serving as light excluding hood **-trichter** *m* light funnel

lichtschwach of low light intensity **-es Bild** low-luminosity picture, picture of low brightness **-e Erscheinung** faint luminosity

Licht-schwächung *f* light absorption, light loss, light diffusion, light dimming, light-intensity drop **-schwankung** *f* light variation or fluctuation **-schwerpunkt** *m* light center position

-schwingung *f* light vibration **-seite** *f* bright side **-setzen** *n* photo-composition, film setting **-setzmaschine** *f* photo-composing machine **-sicherung** *f* lamp fuse

Lichtsignal *n* light signal, signal flare, luminous signal **festes ~** fixed light

Lichtsignal-anlage *f* signaling plant **-geber** *m* impulse transmitter for light signal **-säule** *f* signal indicator pillar

Lichtsinn *m* light sense **-prüfer** *m* retinal or visual photometer

Licht-sirene *f* photoaudio generator, photoelectric tone generator, light siren, light chopper, chopper wheel **-sonde** *f* light probe **-sondentechnik** *f* light probe techniques **-sonne** *f* light spot **-spalt** *m* light slit, light aperture or opening **-spalter** *m* prism **-spaltprüfung** *f* light-gap testing **-spannung** *f* voltage of the lighting circuit

Licht-speicherung *f* light storage **-spender** *m* light dispenser **-spiegeln** to reflect **-spiegler** *m* reflector **-spiel** *n* motion picture **-spielhaus** *n* **-spieltheater** *n* moving-picture theater

licht-sprechen to optophone **-sprecher** *m* modulated-light speech equipment (superimposed on normal or infrared light beams) **-sprechgerät** *n* heliograph, blinker apparatus, infra-red-ray telephone, modulated-light speech equipment **-sprechgerät** *n* optophone **-sprechstelle** *f* optophone terminal **-spritze** *f* crater lamp, crater, tube, crater point lamp, recorder lamp with constricted neon arc

Lichtspritzen-lampe *f* crater(-point) lamp **-röhre** *f* crater(-point) tube

Licht-spruch *m* light-signal message **-spucker** *m* star-shell gun, marker gun **-spur** *f* light track or pattern, light tracing **-stabphotometer** *m* shadow photometer

lichtstark of high luminosity of high intensity **-e Linse** powerful wide-aperture lens **-es Objektiv** high-speed or high-power objective, fast objective

Lichtstärke *f* light intensity, luminous intensity (of a point source), candle power, power, speed, or F number (of a lens) **~ eines Objektives** strength of illumination of a lens **gemessene ~** luminance, photometric brightness **mittlere horizontale ~** mean horizontal candle power **mittlere räumliche ~** mean spherical candle power **~ in Candela** candlepower **Kurve gleicher ~** isocandela chart

Lichtstärke-messer *m* photometer **-messung** *f* photometry

Lichtstärkenkennlinie *f* light characteristic **-regelung** *f* intensity control

Licht-stärkeverteilung *f* light-intensity distribution **-starre** *f* stiff pupil **-staub** *m* luminous dust **-steckdose** *f* light socket **-steindruck** *m* photolithography **-stelle** *f* light station

Lichtsteuer-elektrode *f* (einer Braunschen Röhre) control electrode (of a cathode-ray tube), modulating electrode, shield, Wehnelt cylinder **-gerät** *n* light modulator **-kennlinie** *f* light-control characteristic

Licht-steuerung *f* light modulation, light scanning **-steuerungseinrichtung** *f* light valve, light relay **-steuerzelle** *f* light valve

Lichtstrahl *m* beam of light, light ray, luminous ray **rückgestrahlter ~** reflected ray **wandernder ~** flying spot

Lichtstrahl-abtaster *m* spotlight scanner, scanning brush or pencil **-abtastender** *m* spotlight transmitter, light-beam transmitter **-anzeiger** *m* light-ray indicator

Lichtstrahlen-bündel *n* beam of light **-büschel** *m* pencil of light **-gang** *m* path of light ray (beam) **-messer** *m* actionometer

Lichtstrahl-instrument light-beam instrument **-schweißen** *n* plasma arc torch welding **-tiefenlot** *n* light beam depth finder

Licht-strahlung *f* radiation of light **-streifen** *m* light beam **-streuend** light-dispersing (diffusing) **-streuung** *f* light scatter, diffusion **-streuungskörper** *m* diffuser **-strich** *m* line of light wave of oscilloscope

Lichtstrom *m* light or luminous flux (in lumen units), lighting or lamp current **-dichte** *f* luminous-flux density **-drosselung** *f* throttling of the light-stream, reduction of flux **-messer** *m* lumen meter, photometer **-quelle** *f* source of lighting current **-umformer** *m* light stream converter (transformer)

Licht-summe *f* total light emitted, light sum **-tableau** *n* luminous indicator board **-tag** *n* signal, light signal **-täuschung** *f* optical illusion **-technik** *f* light engineering **-technische Bewertung** photometric evaluation **-teil** *m* lighting part **-telegraphie** *f* heliograph signaling **-telephonie** *f* phototelephony

Lichtton *m* photographic sound recording **-abtastkopf** *m* photographic sound pick-up head **-ansatz** *m* photographic sound-film head **-aufnahme** *f* photographic sound-film recording **-film** *m* film with photographed sound **-generator** *m* photoaudio generator, photoelectric tone generator **-gerät** *n* light-sound apparatus, sound-film head or attachment **-punkt** *m* elementary shading or density value **-schicht** *f* photographic sound track **-spalt** *m* recording slit **-streifen veränderlicher Breite** squeeze track **-verstärker** *m* head amplifier **-wert** *m* printer factor (film) **-zusatz** *m* sound-film head or attachment

Licht-trübung *f* turbidity or optical opacity of the air **-tubusblende** *f* light beam diaphragm **-umfang** *m* range of light oscillations **-undurchlässig** lighttight, opaque, impervious to light, nondiaphanous **-undurchlässigkeit** *f* opacity **-unecht** pervious to light **-unempfindlich** not sensitive to light

Lichtung *f* clearing, opening

Licht-ventil *n* light valve, light relay **-verlust** *m* loss of light **-verkehr** *m* light traffic **-verschlußtrichter** *m* lightproof connecting funnel **-verstärkung** *f* amplified luminous intensity **-verteiler** *m* beam splitter (motion pictures) **-verteilung** *f* composition (of light beams)

Lichtverteilungs-fläche *f* luminosity curve **-körper** *m* polar surface of light distribution **-kurve** *f* (polar) curve of light distribution **-schirm** *m* concentric light diffuser

Licht-visier *m* light visor **-vorhang** *m* light curtain **-wagen** *m* light truck **-warnungssystem** *n* telltale indicating system **-wechsel** *m* variation of exposure **-weg** *m* optical path **-weite** *f* internal width, inside width, internal diameter, span, clear width, light range (optics) **-welle** *f* light wave **-werbung** *f* light advertising propaganda using light effects

Licht-werfer *m* reflector, (light) projector **-wertautomatik** *f* automatic light-figure selector **-wicklung** *f* dynamo (lighting) winding **-widerstand** *m* light resistance **-wirkung** *f* action or effect of light, actinic effect, luminous effect **-wirkungsgrad** *m* shutter efficiency **-wissenschaft** *f* optics, photology **-zähler** *m* counter tube **-zeichen** *n* luminous signal

Lichtzeiger *m* spot of light **-ablesevorrichtung** *f* light mark deflection reader **-gerät** *n* optical pointer equipment **-instrument** *n* light-spot meter, mirror instrument **-kurzzeitmesser** *m* high-speed photorecording gauge (for echo-sounding devices such as Behmlot) **-steuerinstrument** *n* (Mischpult) reflecting volume indicator

Licht-zelle *f* photo(electric) cell **-zentrale** *f* light and power station **-zentrum** *n* photocenter **-zerhacker** *m* light(-beam) chopper **-zerlegung** *f* dispersion or decomposition of light (into primary colors) **-zerstreuend** light-diffusive, -dispersive, or -scattering **-zerstreuung** *f* diffusion of light **-ziehen** *n* dipping of candles **-zufuhr** *f* admission of light **-zündmaschine für Kraftfahrzeuge** lighting dynamo **-zündschaltkasten** *m* combined light and ignition switch bow

Licker-bad *n* fat-liquoring bath **-material** *n* fat-liquor

lidern to obturate

Liderung *f* obturation (artil.), gas check, packing

Liderungs-bolzen *m* packing bolt or stud **-deckel** *m* packing washer **-druck** *m* pressure on the joint, packing (tightening) **-fläche** *f* face of joint **-klappe** *f* leather packer cap **-kopf** *m* obturator head (artil.), mushroom head (obturator) **-lager** *n* obturator pad seat (artil.) **-platte** *f* gas (check) plate **-ring** *m* obturator ring, packing ring

Lidsperrer *m* lid opener

Liebenröhre *f* Lieben valve

Liebigit *m* liebigite

Liebig-Kühler *m* Liebig condenser

Lieferant *m* dealer delivering materials, supplier, contractor

Lieferanzeiger *m* delivery indicator

lieferbar to be delivered, salable, marketable **in großen Mengen ~** to be supplied in bulk

Liefer-bedingung *f* term of delivery **-firma** *f* supplier **-frist** *f* date or term of delivery **-gewicht** *n* weight of material to be supplied

Liefergrad *m* delivery rate or priority **~ des Saughubes** supply efficiency (ratio of actual suction volume to stroke volume)

Liefer-hafen *m* delivery port **-industrie** *f* supply industry **-länge** (Maß) stock length **-menge** *f* delivery, quantity delivered

liefern to supply, furnish, deliver, render, yield

Liefer-posten *m* consignment **-preis in Tank** (in Behälter) tank cession price **-schein** *m* delivery bill, shipping slip, invoice **-termin** *m* delivery date **-umfang** *m* supply schedule

Lieferung *f* delivery, supply, shipment, carload, cargo, parcel, lot, issue, number (journal) **~ frei Schiff** free on board

Lieferungs-abnahme *f* acceptance of supply, shortage of supply **-angebot** *n* tender **-bedingung** *f* specification or condition of sale, term of delivery, delivery requirement or specification **-kontrakt** *m* supply contract **-preis in Wagen** wagon cession price **-umfang** *m* items covered by the contract

Lieferungs- und Fakturierungsverfahren *n* delivery and invoicing procedure

Lieferungs-vertrag *m* supply contract **-verzögerung** *f* delay in delivery **-wagen** *m* delivery truck **-weise** in issues or numbers **-zustand** *m* condition as supplied

Liefer-vorschrift *f* delivery specification **-wagen** *m* delivery wagon or truck **-walze** *f* feed roller **-werk** *n* creel, delivery system **-werkantrieb** *m* delivery roller drive **-zahl** *f* capacity or flow coefficient **-zeit** *f* time of delivery **-zylinder** *m* fluted delivery roller

Liege-falten *pl* creases **-geld** *n* demurrage

liegen to lie, repose **sie ~ bei einigen Millimetern** they are of the order of a few millimeters

liegend horizontal, lying, prone **-e Dampfmaschine** horizontal steam engine **-e Falte** inverted or overturned fold, (fault) overfold **-er Kristallisator** horizontal crystallizer **-er Motor** horizontally opposed engine, horizontal engine **-e Naht** horizontal weld **-e Scholle** downthrow side **-es Strichkreuz** tilted line cross or cross lines **-er Vakuumapparat** horizontal vacuum pan **-er Vierzylinder, mit paarweise gegenüberliegenden Zylindern** engine with four cylinders horizontally opposed **-e Welle** horizontal shaft

Liegende *n* (eines Flözes) sill or floor of a seam

Liegendwasser *n* bottom water

Liegenschaft *f* real estate

Liege-platz *m* (in Zügen) berth, mooring area (aviat.), parking space **-stelle** *f* anchorage basin **-zeiten** *pl* turnround time

Ligatur *f* tie piece

Lignit *m* lignite, bituminous wood, woody brown coal **schwarzer ~** black lignite, subbituminous coal

lignitartig ligneous

Lignose *f* cellulose, lignose

Ligroin *n* ligroine, petroleum spirit, mineral spirits

Lilie *f* key or plug of a stopcock **~ eines Faßhahns** plug of a tap

Limbus *m* limbus, horizontal circle, lower plate of transit **-teilstrich** *m* divided or graduated arc

limes inferior lower limit

Limnograf *m* self-registering tide gauge

Limonit *m* limonite, brown iron ore

Linde *f* linden tree **amerikanische ~** basswood

Lindemann-fenster *n* transparent window **-glas** *n* Lindemann glass

Linden-bast *m* lime tree bast **-holz** *n* linden wood, basswood, lime

lindern to relieve, ease, alleviate, soften, mitigate

Linderungsmaßnahme *f* palliative action

Lineal *n* straightedge, ruler, arm **~ mit abgeschrägter Kante** beveled rule **~ b. Manipulator** guide bar **~ mit Teilung** divided ruler

Linealvisier *n* a type of antiaircraft sight

linear linear **~ polarisiert** plane-polarized **nicht**

~ nonlinear ~ **unabhängig** linearly independent **-er Akkord** *m* straight piecework system **-es Ansprechen** linearity of response **-er Ausdehnungskoeffizient** coefficient of linear expansion

linear-e Elektrode linear electrode **-e Funktion** linear function **-er Gleichrichter** linear rectifier **-e Gleichrichtung** square-law detection **-e Größe** linear dimension **-er Impuls** linear momentum **-er Leistungsverstärker** linear power amplifier **-e Methode** linear framework **-es Netz** linear graph **-e Skalenteilung** logarithmic scale **-e Spannungsverteilung** linear stress distribution **-e Zunahme der Aufwindgeschwindigkeit** linear increase of velocity of ascending or upward currents

Linear-antenne *f* plain or straight (one-wire) antenna **-beschleuniger** *m* linear accelerator **-gleichungslöser** *m* equation solver

linearisiert linearized **-e Näherung** linearized approximation

Linearisierung *f* linearizing action, correction of nonlinear distortions

Linearisierungs-parameter *n* linearization parameter **-widerstand** *m* linearizing resistance, peaking resistance

Linearität *f* linearity

Linearitäts-bedingung *f* condition of linearity **-regelung** *f* linearity control **-testbild** *n* space pattern

Linear-maß *n*, **-maßstab** *m* linear measure

linearveränderlicher Widerstand linear taper

Linearverstärker *m* linear amplifier **-einschub** *m* plug-in linear amplifier

Linearzeichnung *f* line-drawing

Lineatur *f* screen plate (photo), ruling

Linie *f* line, curve, lead, reglet (print.) ~ **des Datumwechsels** international date line ~ **mit Doppelgestänge** A or H fixture line ~ **mit Hakenstützen** line with hook-shaped brackets, line carried on brackets ~ **auf Kante** bevelled rule ~ **mit gekreuzten Leitungen** transposition line ~ **gleichen Luftdrucks** line of equal barometric pressure, isobar ~ **gleicher Mißweisung** isogon, isogonic line

Linie, ~ **gleichen Potentials** equipotential line ~ **gleichen Rauminhaltes** constant-volume line ~ **der Sättigung** phreatic line, saturation line **eine** ~ **abpfählen** to stake out or peg out a line **die** ~ **abstecken** to set out or peg out the line **in eine** ~ **bringen** to line, align with **in gerader** ~ **mit** in alignment with

Linie, abgewickelte ~ evolute **(aus)gehackte** ~ jagged, serrated, notched, or dented line (voll) **ausgezogene** ~ solid line, full line, whole line (in graphs, etc.) **äußere** ~ exterior line **dünne** ~ light line **durchstreichende** ~ trajectory **einfach gekrümmte** ~ plane curve **elastische** ~ curved line **falsche** ~ grating ghost **gepunktete** ~ dotted line **gestrichelte** ~ dashed or dotted line

Linie, halbfette ~ mid-faced rule, medium rule **innere** ~ interior line **kurze** ~ break line **normale** ~ perpendicular line **oberirdische** ~ overhead line **punktierte** ~ dotted line **strichpunktierte** ~ chain-dotted line, dash-dotted line **unterirdische** ~ underground line **verbotene** ~ forbidden line **versenkte** ~ underground line, covered line **zusammengesetzte** ~ multiplet (in complex spectrum)

Linie, letzte Linien ultimate lines **Linien gleicher Beleuchtungsstärke** isophotic or isolux lines **Linien gleicher Kraftwirkung** isodynamic lines **Linien gleicher Neigung** isoclinal lines **Linien gleicher Spannung** isoclines, isoclinal lines, aclinic lines **Linien gleicher Winkel** isogonic lines **Linien des gleichen Wertes der Unregelmäßigkeit** lines of equal anomaly **durch Linien festlegen** to delineate

Liniehalten *n* alignement, alinement

Linien-abschnitt *m* section (of line) **-abstand** *m* line interval **-anker** *m* longitudinal stay, head guy **-arm** (Spektrum) having few lines **-aufspaltung** *f* line splitting **-aufstellung** *f* line formation **-belastung** *f* strip load **-berührung** *f* line contact **-biegeapparat** *m* rule bender **-bild** *n* line scheme or pattern **-blatt** *n* ink lines, transparent lines **-blitz** *m* streak lightning **-bö** *f* line squall, cold-front squall **-breite** *f* space between two lines, breadth or width of line, spot diameter

Linien-dampfer *m* liner **-dichte** *f* line density **-dipol** *n* line-dipole **-drossel** *f* line choke **-einfassung** *f* rule border **-fabrik** *f* brass-rule manufacturer **-festpunkt** *m* storm guyed pole, pole with line stays **-folgesystem** *n* line sequential system **-form** *f* line shape, line form **-förmig** linear **-frei** line-free

Linienführung *f* route, outline, location (R.R.), direction of the line, lines, form, shape, telephone line, intercommunication ~ **durch eine Ortschaft** passage of a line through a town ~ **festlegen** to mark out, stake out, trace

Linien-gebilde *n* linear figure or configuration **-gießblock** *m* rule slide **-glas** *n* ruled glass **-hobel** *m* ruled shooting board **-höhe** *f* peak height **-integral** *n* line integral (of a vector) **-intervall** *n* line interval

Linien-karte *f* network diagram **-kasten** *m* rule case **-komplex** *m* multiplet **-koordinaten** *pl* line coordinates **-kraft** *f* line force **-kreuzung** *f* crossing **-kreis** *m* line circuit

Linien-last *f* line load **-leitung** *f* line wires

Linien-manier *f* rule setting **-maß** *n* linear measure **-material** *n* line material **-nachweis** *m* line records, statement of lines **-netz** *n* ruled paper, grid **-papier** *n* point, squared, design, drafting, cartridge, or ruled paper **-platte** *f* ruled plate **-rand** *m* rule border **-raster** *m* ruled plate, line screen or grating, raster

linienreich rich in lines, with abundance of lines **-es Element** element with large number of spectrum lines

Linien-reißer *m* ruler **-relais** *n* line relay, main (-line) relay **-relais** *n* calling relay **-revision** *f* examination of the line **-riß** *m* outline **-rufstrom** *m* line calling current

Linien-schar *f* set of lines (or curves) **-schärfe** *f* definition of lines **-schneideapparat** *m* rule cutter **-schreiber** *m* curve-drawing recorder, continuous-line-recording instrument **-spannung** *f* line stress **-spektrum** *n* line spectrum **-steuerung** *f* velocity modulation

Linienstrecke *f* line extent (in length) **gerade** ~ alignment

Linien-strom *m* line current or signal **-stück** *n*

piece of rule **-sucher** *m* line finder **-summe** *f* line integral **-umkehr** *f* line reversal **-umkehr** *f* reversal dip **-umkehrmethode** *f* line-reversal method **-umschalter** *m* line switchboard or commutator

Linien- und Punktgitter *n* bar- and dot raster

Linien-unterbrecher *m* line breaker **-verbreiterung** *f* broadening or spread of line or strip (television) **-verschiebung** *f* (im Spektrum) displacement of lines **-verstärkung** *f* line consolidation (elec.) **-vertuscher** *m* line diffuser **-verzweiger** *m* cable distribution box (telec.)

Linienwähler *m* selector, connector, final selector, line-selector switch, intercommunication system, distributing switch **-anlage** *f* intercommunication system **-leitung** *f* internal intercommunication (house-telephone) line

Linien-zeichnung *f* line drawing **-zeit** *f* line time **-ziehbank** *f* rule drawing frame **-zieher** *m* ruling device, ruler

Linienzug *m* continuous series of lines, route, line curve, curve (math.), trunk route, line, trace (of a graph) **mittlerer ~** trend line

linieren to line, rule

Linierer *m* machine ruler

Linier-farbe *f* drafting ink **-gummiwalzenbezug** *m* covering for ruling rubber rollers **-maschine** *f* machine ruler **-maschinenfaden** *m* machine ruler thread **-satz** *m* ruling work

liniertes Papier ruled paper

Linke-Hand-Regel *f* left hand rule

linke Seite the left(-hand) side

linkisch awkward

Linkrusta *f* lincrusta

links left-hand (side), on or to the left, left, anticlockwise, port **~ drehen** to turn counter clockwise **~ Querruder geben** to apply left bank **~ Seitensteuer geben** to put on left rudder

Links-ablenkung *f* back (shifting of wind, aviation), deflection to the left, backing, shifting counterclockwise **-abweichung** *f* left-hand deviation **-anschlag** *m* changing on the left-hand side **-antrieb** *m* left hand drive **-appretur** *f* back finish **-draht** *m* left-hand twist **-drall** *m* left-hand twist or lay, counterclockwise rifling

linksdrehend counterclockwise, anticlockwise, levorotatory, counterclockwise rotating **~ elliptisch polarisierte Welle** counterclockwise polarized wave

Linksdrehung *f* revolution in counterclockwise direction, counterclockwise rotation, anticlockwise rotation, levorotation, turn to port, left turn, left-handed polarization

Linkser *m* left-handed arbor

Linksfärben *n* dyeing inside out

Linksgang *m* left-hand action

linksgängig left-handed, counterclockwise, left-turning **-es Gewinde** (Linksgewinde) left-hand thread **-e Schraube** left-handed screw

links-genutet left-hand notched **-gewinde** *n* left-hand thread (of screws) **-gewundene Feder** spring with left-handed helix **-händer** *m* South Paw **-händigkeit** *f* left-handedness **-kurve** *f* left turn, left-hand (or port) curve or loop (in airplane landing, etc.) **-lauf** *m* counterclockwise rotation

linkslaufend counterclockwise, left-hand rotation **-er Motor** anticlockwise revolving motor **-e Wellen** sinistropropagating traveling waves or surges

linksläufig from right to left, counterclockwise **~ zählen** to count counterclockwise or from right to left **-er Motor** left-hand engine

Links-lenker *m* car with left-hand steering **-lenkung** *f* left-hand steering **-orientiert** having a tendency to the left **-propeller** *m* left-handed propeller **-quarz** *m* left-handed quartz, levogyrate crystal **-schneidend** left-hand (drills) **-schraube** *f* left hand helix, left-hand propeller **-schweißung** *f* Swiss welding method

linksseitig left-sided **-e Appretur** back-finish **-es Gegengewicht des Querbalkens** counterweight for left side of crossrail **-er Motor** left-side engine **-er Wind** left wind

Linksspirale *f* left-hand spiral

linkssteigend inclined to the left, rising on the left

Links-system *n* left-handed system **-umlauf** *m* anti-clockwise rotation **-weiche** *f* left-hand switch, deviation, or turnout

Linneit *m* linnaeite (min.)

Linnen *n* linen (cloth)

Linoleum *n* linoleum **-unterlagspapier** *n* carpet felt (paper)

Linol-säure *f* linoleic acid **-schnittgerät** *n* linoleum-engraving tool

Linotype *f* linotype **-satz** *m* linotype composition

Linozynsäure *f* linoxynic acid

Linse *f* lens, lentil, objective glass **~ mit sichelförmigem Querschnitt** meniscus **eingekittete ~** cemented lens **elektrische ~** electrostatic lens **facettierte ~** bevel-edged lens **gefaßte ~** mounted lens **gekittete ~** cemented lens **kurzbrennweitige ~** short-focus lens

Linse, langbrennweitige ~ long-focus lens **lichtstarke ~** high-power or high-speed lens **~ magnetische ~** ring-shaped magnet **magnetische ~ mit Eisenpanzer** iron-clad magnetic lens, iron-core deflector unit **scharfzeichnende ~** achromatic lens **ungefaßte ~** rimless lens **ungekittete ~** uncemented lens, broken-contact lens **weichzeichnende ~, weitwinklige ~** soft-focus lens **zusammengesprengte ~** broken-contact lens

Linsen-abweichung *f* aberration of a lens **-achse** *f* optical axis of a lens **-ähnlich** lenticular, lenticulated, lens-shaped **-anordnung** *f* lens arrangement **-antenne** *f* lens antenna **-apparat** *m* lenticular apparatus **-artig** lenticular

Linsen-bläschen *n* lens vesicle **-blechschraube** *f* self-tapping convex fillister head screw **-deckglas** *n* anterior surface of a lens **-deckel** *m* lense hood **-dichtung** *f* convex seal **-dicke** *f* thickness of the lens **-einschiebebrett** *n* slidable lens panel **-erz** *n* oölitic limonite, liroconite

Linsen-fach *n* optical panel **-fassung** *f* lens mount, lens barrel **-fläche** *f* surface of the lens **-fehler** *m* lens defect or aberration **-folge** *f* lens combination, system of lenses **-förmig** lenticular, lenslike **-gang** *m* lenticular vein **-glas** *n* optical glass **-gleichung** *f* lens equation **-grundpunkt** *m* cardinal point (of a lens) **-halsschraube** *f* fillister-headed screw with undercut neck

Linsen-konzentration *f* lens concentration,

focusing **-kopf** *m* dome-tipped fillister head **-kopfschraube** *f* fillister-head screw, countersunk screw **-kranzabtaster** *m* lens disk scanner (scanning device), lens drum scanner **-kreuz** *n* lens holder **-krümmung** *f* lens curvature **-kühler** *m* lens cooler **-kuppe** *f* round point or tip

Linsen-lafette *f* bulletproof glass mount, lens-type machine-gun mount **-leuchte** *f* holophotal optical apparatus **-messer** *m* lensmeter **-meßgerät** *n* lensmeter **-niet** *m* countersunk rivet with shallow button head **-öffnung** *f* lens aperture **-paar** *n* pair of lenses (doublet) **-perspektive** *f* linear perspective **-profil** *n* biconvex or lenticular profile **-prüfer** *m* lensometer

Linsen-radius *m* lens radius **-raster** *m* lenticular screen **-rasterfarbverfahren** *n* lenticular or lenticulated color-printing method **-rasterfilm** *m* lenticular color screen film, lenticulated film **-rohrkompensator** *m* lentiform compensator

Linsen-satz *m* set, system, or assembly of lenses, lens combination **-scheibe** *f* lens scanning disk, lensed disk **-scheinwerfer** *m* spotlight **-scheitel** *m* vertex of lens, apex of lens **-schirm** *m* lens screen, gobo **-schleifen** *n* grinding of lenses **-schraube** *f* oval-head screw, slotted fillister head screw, cheese-head screw

Linsensenk-holzschraube *f* oval-head countersunk wood screw **-kopf** *m* lentil or countersunk (fillister) head **-kopfholzschraube** *f* oval-head wood screw **-niete** *f* round-head countersunk rivet **-schraube** *f* oval flat-head screw, slotted oval-head screw, countersunk oval-head screw

Linsen-spannung *f* lens voltage or potential **-stereoskop** *n* lens stereoscope **-strom** *m* lens current **-stutzen** *m* lens tube, lens cone **-system** *n* system of lenses **-träger** *m* lens holder **-trommel** *f* lens drum **-trübung** *f* clouding or opacity of a lens **-vergütung** *f* refining and treatment of optical glass **-vorspannung** *f* lens bias

Linsenweite, lichte ~ clear aperture of a lens

Linsen-zusammensetzung *f* lens system **-zusammenstellung** *f* lens combination, lens assembly

Lipowitzmetall *n* Lipowitz alloy

Lippen-applikator *m* lip applicator **-kuppelung** *f* wrought-iron lip union **-pfanne** (Gießerei) lip-pour ladle **-pfeife** *f* flue pipe, flute pipe **-stütze** *f* lip rest

Liquidation treten (in) ~ to go into liquidation

Liquidationspreis *m* making-up price

liquidieren to settle, liquidate

Liquidierung einer Gesellschaft winding up of a company

Liquidometer *n* liquidometer

Lirokonit *m* liroconite, oölitic ironstone (min.)

Lissajousfiguren *f pl* Lissajous figures or curves **-apparat** *n* kaleidophon

Lissajoussche Figuren, Lissajous' Schwingungsfiguren Lissajous figures

Liste *f* list, catalogue, roll, specification, table, statement, schedule, table synopsis **~ der Gesprächsanmeldungen** (eines Teilnehmers) sequence list **in Listen eintragen** to enlist

Listen-druckvorrichtung *f* lister **-förmig zusammenstellen** to tabulate **-führung** *f* keeping the roster or roll **-mäßig** scheduled **-preis** *m* list price

Lister-apparat *m* lister attachment **-kultivator mit Rädern** wheeled lister cultivator **-pflanzer für losen Boden** loose-ground lister planter

Liter *n* liter

Literaturverzeichnis *n* bibliography

Liter-inhalt (Flugmotor) capacity of an engine **-leistung** *f* output or power per unit of displacement, specific power output, power output per liter **-zähler** *m* meter

Lithion *n* lithia, lithium oxide **-glimmer** *m* lithia mica **-hydrat** *n* lithium hydroxide

Lithium *n* lithium **-deuterid** *n* lithium deuteride **-fluorid** *n* lithium fluoride **-getränkt** lithium loaded **-glimmer** *m* lepidolite, lithia mica **-haltig** containing lithium **-silikatglas** *n* lithium silicate glass **-tantalat** *n* lithium tantalate **-zitrat** *n* lithium citrate

Lithographen-blech *n* lithographic sheet

lithographieren to lithograph

lithographisch lithographic(al) **-er Farbendruck** chromolithography

Lithologie *f* lithology

Lithophanie *f* lithophany

Lithopone *f* lithopone

Lithosphäre *f* lithosphere

Litze *f* strand, stranded or flexible wire, lace, braid(ing), cable conductor, cordon (of a wire), cord, string **~ mit Perlen** bead-clad conductor (or lead)

Litzen-draht *m* litz, flexible, stranded wire **-leitung** *f* stranded cable **-maschine** *f* stranding machine **-querschnitt** *m* section of stranded cable **-schnur** *f* tinsel cord **-seil** *n* rope made of strands **-spule** *f* stranded conductor coil, stranded wire coil, litz coil **-verbinder** *m* braided connector

Lizenz *f* license **eine ~ erwerben** to acquire a license **in ~** under licence **(auf) Lizenzbasis** (on a) royalty basis

Lizenzbau *m* construction under license **~ auf Grund von Patentrechten** licensed under patents

Lizenz-erteiler *m* licenser, grantor, issuer of a license **-gebühr** *f* royalty, license fee **-inhaber** *m* **-nehmer** *m* licensee **-pflichtig** subject to license arrangements

Ljungström-Turbine *f* Ljungström type turbine

Llewellynformel *f* Llewellyn formula

Lobe *f* lobe

loben to praise **-linie** *f* suture, septal suture, suture line

Loch *n* hole, aperture, pit, leak, pinhole (optics), eye pore, pocket, opening, perforation, puncture **~ eines Mühlsteins** eye of the millstone **~ der Vierkantstange** Kelly's rat hole **~ auftreiben** to enlarge, expand, broach or ream a hole **ein ~ herstellen** to hole **blindes ~** dead hole **längliches ~** slotted hole **vorgegossenes ~** cored hole (precast hole)

Loch-absaugung *f* hole-siphoning **-abstand** *m* mounting hole separation, perforation pitch (motion pictures) **-anordnung** *f* arrangement of holes **-apparat** *m* perforator **-arbeit** *f* punching

Loch-bandvorschub *m* tape controlled carriage **-beitel** *m* mortise chisel **-bereich** *m* band width, transmission range **-bild** *n* pinhole image **-blechpresse** *f* extruding press **-blende** *f* apertured partition, anode aperture, diaphragm, shield **-blendenauflagen** *pl* perforated metal sheets **-blendenlinse** *f* apertured disk lens, simple aperture lens **-bohrapparat** *m* auger

Lochbohrer *m* auger ~ **mit Vorschneider** auger bit with advance cutter

Lochbreite *f* band width, transmission range ~ **eines Frequenzsiebes** transmitted band of frequencies, transmission range, band width of a filter, band pass (of a filter), spacing between cutoff points

Loch-brille *f* stenopaic spectacles **-dämpfung** *f* attenuation in the pass range, loss in the transmission range **-diopter** *n* pinhole sight

Lochdorn *m* piercer, mandrel, plug (gauge) **-stange** *f* piercer rod

Loch-durchmesser *m* diameter of bore **-düse** *f* hole-type nozzle **-eisen** *n* hollow punch, drift, center punch

Lochelektrode *f* apertured electrode disk (electron microscope) **Beschleunigungslinse aus zwei Lochelektroden** double-aperture accelerator lens (in cathode-ray tube)

lochen to perforate, pierce, punch

Lochen *n* perforation, punching

Locher *m* perforator, puncher, letter punch

Löcher *pl* deficit electrons, holes, cavities **versetzte** ~ staggered holes (in blasting)

löcherig honeycombed, porous, pitted, punctured, perforated, apertured

Löcherkonzentration *f* hole concentration (trans.)

Locherkupplung *f* punch clutch

Löcherleitung *f* hole conduction (trans.)

Lochermatrizeneinheit *f* punch die assembly

Löchermodell *n* hole model **-prüfer** *m* pinhole detector

Locherschlüssel *m* tap wrench

Löcher-spektrum *n* hole spectrum **-strom** *m* current of holes **-theorie** *f* hole theory

Löcherungsstellung *f* punch position

Loch-fang *m* hold capture (trans.) **-feile** *f* riffler, entering file **-feldsteuerung** *f* field selection **-fräser** *m* **verstellbar** adjustable hollow mill

Lochfraß *m* localized (selective) corrosion, pitting **-ähnliche Zerstörung** pitting, destruction in form of pits, honeycombing

Loch-grenze *f* transmission range of band pass, channel width or limit, cutoff boundary **-größe** *f* size of hole **-gurt** *m* suspension or rigging band **-hammer** *m* drift **-handwerkzeug** *n* punching tool for workmen **-hobeleisen** *pl* cut plane cutters **-hülse** *f* **für Lochzangen** punch pliers tube **-kaliber** *n* punching die **-kamera** *f* pinhole camera **-kante** *f* edge of hole **-karte** *f* punched card

Lochkarten-abtaster *m* punched-card reader **-abteilung** *f* punched card department **-doppler** *m* reproducing punch cards **-feld** *n* card field **-zusatzgerät** *n* punched card adapter

Lochkathode *f* perforated cathode

Lochkreis *m* bolt(hole) circle ~ (Flansche) *m* bolt circle **-durchmesser** *m* diameter of the bolt pitch circle or bolthole circle

Loch-lage eines Filters position of the transmission range or of band pass of a filter **-lehre** *f* internal-caliper gauge, plug gauge

Lochleibung *f* inside of hole, bearing ~ **des Niets** wall of the rivet hole

Lochleibungsdruck *m* (bolt or rivet) bearing pressure

Loch-marke *f* hole mark, puncture mark **-maschine** *f* broaching machine, punching machine, perforating machine **-maske** (am Bildröhrenschirm) shadow mask (TV)

Lochmeißel *m*, **dreikantiger** ~ three-faced burr

Loch-mutter *f* circular nut **-nadel** *f* eye-pointed needle **-naht** *f* perforation **-niete** *f* hollow or tubular rivet **-pass** *m* filter **-pfeife** *f* hollow punch, drift **-platte** *f* orifice plate swage block **-plattenzerstäuber** *m* diaphragm atomizer **-presse** *f* punching press **-probe** *f* punching test, drift test **-prüferin** *f* verifier operator **-putzen** *n* burr

Loch-querschnitt *m* cross section of hole **-räumer** *m* drift **-säge** *f* fret saw, keyhole saw **-schablone** *f* hole template **-schaufel** *f* long-handle shovel

Lochscheibe *f* perforated disk, Nipkow disk **konzentrierende** ~ focusing aperture lens or apertured disk

Lochscheiben-anode *f* apertured disk anode, ring anode **-generator** *m* light chopper **-linse** *f* aperture disk lens **-unterbrecher** *m* chopper disk

Loch-schneidemaschine *f* hole-cutting machine **-schraube** *f* lock screw **-schreiber** *m* punching recorder **-schrift** *f* perforated code **-schriftübersetzer** *m* alphabetical interpreter **-schweißung** *f* plug weld(ing), slot weld **-sitz** *m* perforated seat **-spirale** *f* Nipkow disk **-stange** *f* boring bar **-stanze** *f* hollow punch, drift, punching machine, punch press **-stein** *m* perforated brick, sleeve brick, firebrick sleeve, nozzle brick, teeming nozzle, stone marking boundary of a mine, perforated (brick or stone) block **-stelle** *f* punch position **-stellung** *f* punch position

Lochstempel *m* punch, die **-satz** *m* gang of punches

Loch-stift *m* core pin, dowel **-strecker** *m* reamer

Lochstreifen *m* perforated tape or slip, strip with holes, punched tape store (info proc.) **geschnittener** ~ torn tape

Lochstreifen-abtaster *m* tape reader **-empfänger** *m* receiving perforator, reperforator **-mater** master tape **-schnellsender** *m* high-speed tape transmitter **-schreiber** *m* tape transmitter **-sendetrieb** *m* tape relay procedure **-sender** *m* transmitter distributor, tape transmitter **-sendung** *f* tape transmission

Lochstreifen-transport *m* tape relay **-übertrager** *m* reperforator transmitter **-übertragung** *f* tape retransmission **-vermittlung** *f* tape relay center **-weitergabe** *f* (autom.) automatic tape relay **-zusatz** *m* (Fernschreiber) perforated tape sensing attachment

Lochstutzen *m* hole socket **-sucher** *m* leak detector **-taster** *m* inside calipers

Lochtasterteilung *f*, **genaue** ~ precise hole pitch

Lochteil einer Stanze matrix

Lochtrommel *f* scanning drum

Loch- und Ausklinkmaschine für I-Träger I-beam punching and coping machines

Loch- und Schermaschinen für Kraftbetrieb power punching and shearing machinery

Loch- und Tasterlehre *f* fixed-caliper gauge

Lochung *f* perforation, boring, punched holes

(in film), punching

Lochungs-folge *f* punching sequence **-geschwindigkeit** *f* rate of perforation **-presse** *f* punch press **-versuch** *m* punching test

Loch-versuch *m* punching test **-visier** *n* sight hole **-vorrichtung** *f* perforator **-walke** *f* fulling mill **-walze** *f* distributing roll **-walzwerk** *n* piercing mill **-wanderung** *f* hold ejection (trans.) **-wandung des Niets** wall of the rivet hole

Loch-weite *f* diameter of hole, aperture, inside diameter, band width, band pass, band between cutoff points **-werkzeug** *n* piercing die or tool **-winkel** *m* sliding or turning square **-zange** *f* punch pliers **-ziegel** *m* perforated brick **-zirkel** *m* inside compass

Locke *f* roll (textiles)

locker open, spongy, loose, porous, slack, soft, ephemeral **~ arbeiten** to loosen the loops (textiles) **-er Boden** loose soil **-es Gefüge** porous structure

Lockerion *n* defective ion

Lockerheit *f* looseness, laxity

lockern to loosen, unloosen, work loose, relax, slacken, slack (off)

Lockerstelle *f* (Smekal) imperfect structure, surface of misfit

Lockerung *f* loosening, slackening **~ des Gesteinszusammenhaltes** rock disintegration

Lockerungsbestreben *n* tendency to work loose

lockerwerden to get loose, loosen

Lockerwerden *n* loosening

Lockflamme *f* pilot flame

lockig curly

Lock-klingel *f* call bell **-schiff** *n* decoy

Löffel *m* spoon, bailer

Löffel-austragung *f* spoon discharge **-bagger** *m* bucket dredge, power shovel, steam shovel, digger **-baggerwindwerk** *n* winding mechanism of the shovel

Löffelbohrer *m* auger, center bit, shell auger, core drill, spoon bit **halbelliptischer ~** duck-nose bit

Löffel-breite *f* width of scoop **-büchse** *f* sand pump cup **-bug** *m* spoon-shaped prow **-dampfbagger** *m* steam shovel

löffelförmig spoon-shaped **-es Spleißwerkzeug** tucking needle

Löffel-geißfuß *m* spoon-bit parting tool **-gesenk** *n* spoon die **-gutsche** *f* spoon-bit gouge **-haspelwelle** *f* spool shaft **-klappe** *f* dipper slide **-lanzette** *f* double-ender (file)

löffeln to bail, spoon

Löffeln *n* bailing, sand pumping

Löffel-probe *f* cup test, spoon test **-räumer** *m* scraper (min.) **-rührer** *m* spoon agitator **-schaber** *m* spoon scraper **-schaufel** *f* scoop **-schreibfeder** *f* pen with turned up point **-seiltrommel** *f* sand line spool **-spiegel** *m* scoop-shaped speculum **-stange** *f* handle **-stiel** *m* dipper arm **-strebe** *f* spatular or spoon-shaped strut

Löffel-trommel *f* sand-pump spool **-vorrichtung** *f* bailing gear **-walze** *f* spoon rolling mill **-weise** by the spoonful **-welle** *f* sand-pump shaft **-werkzeug** *n* spoon tool **-zylinder** *m* bailing cylinder

Logarithmen-papier *n* logarithmic (cross-section) paper **-tafel** *f* table of logarithms

logarithmieren to look up the logarithm of

Logarithmierung *f* logarithmation

logarithmisch logarithmic(al) **~ abgestuft** graded logarithmically **-es Dekrement der Energie** logarithmic energy decrement **-er Maßstab** logarithmic scale **-e Spirale** equiangular spiral, logarithmic spiral

Logarithmus *m* logarithm **Napierscher ~** natural logarithm, Napierian logarithm **dekadischer ~** common logarithm

Logatom *n* logatome

Logatom- oder Silbenverständlichkeit *f* syllabic articulation

Logatomverständlichkeit *f* articulation for logatomes

Logbuch *n* ship's journal logbook **-eintragung** *f* log (entry)

Loge *f* lodge

Loggeber *m* log transmitter

loggen to log

Logglas *n* log glass

Logik *f* mathematical logic (comput)

logisch logical **-es Diagramm** functional diagram **-es Symbol** functional symbol **-es UND** and-operator

Logistik *f* logistics

Logleine *f* log line

Logotypematrize *f* logotype matrix

Logrechnung *f* dead reckoning by log

Logverstärker *m* logarithmic amplifier

Lohbrechmaschine *f* bark breaking machine

Lohe *f* tannin bark

Loh-gerben *n* bark tanning **-gerberei** *f* tannery **-grube** *f* tan pit, taning vat **-messer** *m* barkometer

Lohn *m* wages, pay, reward **-abbau** *m* cut in wages **-abzug** *m* deduction **-anreizend** incentive **-arbeiter** *m* common workman **-arbeitsbetrieb** *m* service bureau **-buchhalter** *m* timekeeper **-einheit** *f* unit of wages

lohnen, sich ~ to be profitable

löhnen to pay wages

lohnend worthwhile

lohnintensive Arbeit job order with excessive labor cost percentage

Lohn-liste *f* pay roll **-satz** *m* rate of wages **-steuer** *f* withholding tax **-steuerpflichtig** subject to wage tax **-streifen** *m* wage strip **-zeitverrechnung** *f* wage-time calculation

Löhnung *f* pay, wages

Lohnzettel *m* pay slip

Lohprobe *f* bark test

Lokalbahn *f* local railway, secondary line

lokal eben locally flat

lokale Wetterprognose local weather forecast

Lokalelement *n* local cell

Lokalisator *m* localizer **lokalisieren** to locate, localize

Lokalisierung von Teilchen localisation of particles

Lokalisierungssatz *m* localization theorem

Lokal-lastverteilungsstelle *f* local load-distributing station **-störung** *f* man-made static or interference, local interference, local electrical disturbances **-strom** *m* local current (electr.)

Lokomobil *n* tractor, traction engine, portable engine

Lokomobilkessel *m* (semi)portable boiler
Lokomotive *f* engine, locomotive, code for a sender type of radar equipment ~ **mit abrollbarem Leitungskabel** locomotive with cable drum ~ **mit Seilwinde** locomotive with hauling drum ~ **einer Zahnradbahn** cogwheel locomotive **kurvenbewegliche** ~ articulated locomotive
Lokomotiv-bahnhof *m* roundhouse **-fabrik** *f* car and locomotive works **-feuerkiste** *f* locomotive firebox **-führer** *m* engineer (R.R.) **-gelenkdrehscheibe** *f* articulated locomotive turntable **-hebebock** *m* locomotive heaver **-kessel** *m* engine boiler, locomotive boiler
Lokomotivkurbelachse *f* locomotive crank axle **doppelt gekröpfte** ~ two-throw locomotive crank axle
Lokomotiv-laterne *f* engine headlight **-scheibebühne** *f* locomotive traverser **-stehkessel** *m* locomotive firebox **-versatzkran** *m* locomotive shifting crane **-werk** *n* locomotive works
Löllingit *n* löllingite
Lombardgeschäft *n* deposit or loan business
lombardieren to advance or loan money on security
longitudinal longitudinal **-e elektromotorische Kraft** longitudinal electromotive force **-e Welle** longitudinal wave
Longitudinal-schwingung *f* longitudinal vibration **-welle** *f* longitudinal wave
Loofahfaser *f* luffa fiber
Looping *n* loop(ing) (aviation) ~ **aus der Rückenlage** inverted loop
Loopingacht *f* figure of eight (aviation) **senkrecht stehende** ~ vertical figure of eight
Lorentz-kontraktion *f* Lorentz contraction **-kraft** *f* Lorentz force
Lorin-antrieb *m* ram jet, duct devised by Lorin **-maschine** *f* ramjet **-triebwerk** *n* ram-jet power plant
Lory *m* cart, dumpcart, truck, lorry, flatcar, a type of neutrodyne receiver
Loryl *n*, **Rest der höheren Alkohole aus** ~ coconut fat
Los *n* lot, share, portion
Losantin *n* Losantin (decontamination agent)
losarbeiten to work loose
lösbar soluble, detachable, releasable, dissoluble **-e Fangglocke** releasing socket **-e Kuppelung** cutoff coupling **-er Zirkulations-Overshot** releasing and circulating overshot
Lösbarkeit *f* solubility, resolvability, solvability
losbinden to untie
losblättern to exfoliate, detach in leaves or scales, defoliate
Los-block *m* movable block **-boden** *m* detachable or removable bottom, plug
Losbrechdrehmoment *n* initial breakaway torque
losbrechen to break out, break up, scrape out, break off **die Gußform** ~ to open the mold
Losbrechmoment *n* initial break-away torque (engine) **das** ~ (des Motors) **beim Anlassen überwinden** to break the oil seal (of an engine)
Losbrechwiderstand *m* breakaway resistance
losbröckeln to crumble off
Löschanlage für Kalk lime-slaking plant **-apparat** *m* unloading apparatus **-arbeit** *f* charcoal process, fining in a charcoal bed, charcoal fining process
löschbar-er Pufferspeicher *m* erasable store (info proc.) **-er Speicher** erasable memory **-e Speicherung** *f* erasable storage
Lösch-bereich *m* arc quenching range **-blatt** *n* sheet of blotting paper **-block** *m* blotting-pad **-boden** *m* charcoal bed or bottom **-decke** *f* fire-extingusihing cover **-drossel** *f* quenching choke **-düse** *f* fire extinguishing nozzle
Lösche *f* slack, breeze, dust culm, charcoal dust, coal dust, cinder- or clinker-quenching trough
Lösch-eigenschaft *f* quenching property, erasure characteristic **-eimer** *m* fire bucket
löschen clear (info proc.); (Feuer) put out, extinguish; (Funken, Durst) quench; (Kalk) slake; (streichen) delate; (Forderung) cancel; (entladen) unload, cancel, slake (lime), unload (a ship), (coke), discharge, darken (lamp), clear, blot, erase, wash out (a magnetic record) ~ (Tonband) to erase (tape) ~ (Koks) to quench ~ **vor dem Schreiben** to clear before writing **einen Verstärker** ~ to turn off a repeater
Löschen des Baggerguts discharge of dredged material
Löscher *m* blotter
Löschfeld, magnetisches ~ obliterating field, erasing field
Lösch-feuer *n* charcoal hearth **-flüssigkeit** *f* extinguisher fluid **-frequenz** *f* wiping frequency, erase frequency
Löschfunken *m* quenched spark **-sender** *m* quenched-spark transmitter, quenched-gap transmitter **-strecke** *f* quenched spark gap, quench(ing) gap
Löschgas, trockenes ~ dry quencher gas
Lösch-gebühr *f* lighterage **-gerät** *n* fire-extinguishing appliances, fire extinguisher **-geschwindigkeit** erasing speed **-gestell** *n* quenching hood **-grube** *f* ash pit **-hebel** (bei Rechenmaschinen) clearing lever **-impuls** *m* deionization impulse **-kalk** *m* quicklime **-kammer** *f* explosion chamber **-karton** *m* thick blotting paper **-kohle** *f* quenched charcoal **-kondensator** *m* quenching condenser **-kontakt** *m* reset contact **-kopf** *m* erase head **-kreis** *m* quenching circuit
Lösch-magnet *m* obliterating magnet, wash-out magnet **-mittel** *pl* extinguishing agents **-papier** *n* blotting paper **-papierprüfer** *m* bibliometer **-platz** *m* pier, wharf **-quaste** *f* quenching brush **-rampe** *f* quenching bench **-schaltung** *f* quenching circuit **-schienenhebel** *m* clearing rail lever
Lösch-spannung *f* extinguishing voltage, stopping potential, extinction potential, critical potential, cutoff potential (of thyratron) **-speicherung** *f* erasable storage **-sperre** *f* erase cutout key (tape rec.) **-spieß** *m* straight poker **-spule** *f* blowout coil **-stoß** *m* extinction pulse **-taste** *f* release key, cancel key, clearing key **-trommel** *f* quenching or slaking drum **-trupp** *m* fire-fighting party or squad **-turm** *m* quenching tower, watering house
Löschung *f* quench(ing), watering, slaking, discharge, cancellation, extinguishing, extinction ~ (Löcher) erasure of errors ~ **einer Bandaufnahme** erasing (of a tape record) ~ **von Spektrallinien** quenching of lines

löschungsfrei-es Auslesen nondestructive mode **-es Datenauslesen** non-destructive readout **-er Lesevorgang** nondestructive readout **-er Lesespeicher** nondestructive readout memory

Löschungs-hafen *m* discharge port **-impuls** *m* reset pulse **-kreis** *f* quenching circuit

Lösch-versuch *m* slaking test **-vorgang** *m* quenching operation **-vorrichtung** *f* spraying device, quenching device **-wagen** *m* quencher car, watering car **-wasser** *n* quenching water, tempering water, water for fire fighting **-wedel** *m* swatter **-wesen** *n* organization of fire extinction **-widerstand** *m* quenching resistor **-wirkung** *f* quenching action, quench effect **-zeit** *f* running days for discharging, time for discharging cargo **-zündspannungsdifferenz** *f* extinction-striking potential difference

los loose, disengaged, slack **~ geben** to slacken **~ werden** to slacken, get loose, get rid of **-er Flansch** loose flange, slip-on flange **-er Sand** loose sand **-es Rad** impeller

los-drehen to unscrew, twist off **-drücken** to fire (a gun), press or pry loose

lose loose, slack, movable **~ Aufbewahrung** bulk storage **~ Koppelung** loose coupling **~ Ladung** bulk **~ Rollen** idle rollers **~ Verbindung** loose joint

Lose *f* slack or clearance on mating parts

Loseblättergeschäftsbuch *n* loose-leaf ledger

Loseblatt-katalog *m* loose-leaf catalogue **-sammelmappe** *f* loose-leaf binder

Löse-düse *f* exhaust-throttle disk **-fähigkeit** *f* solvency (plastics), dissolving property **-gefäß** *n* dissolving vessel

lose gekoppelt loosely coupled

Löse-geschwindigkeit *f* rate of dissolving **-keil** *m* cotter pin **-kraft** *f* solvent power

Lösemittel *n* solvent **-dämpfe** *pl* solvent fumes **-raffinieranlage** *f* solvent-treating plant **-rückgewinnung** *f* solvent recovery **-wiedergewinnung** *f* solvent recovery

lösen loosen; (Bremse) release; (aufgehen) come undone; (Chem.) dissolve; (Verbindlichkeiten) cancel, set aside; (Aufgabe) solve; (Frage) answer; (Versprechen) keep, fulfill (Schraube) unscrew; detach, disengage, untwist, untie, heave up, disconnect (etwas Angeklebtes) **wieder ~** to unstick

Lösen *n* loosening

lösend dissolving, solvent

Löser *m* solving agent, solubilizer **harmonischer ~** harmonic filter

Löse-stellung *f* release position **-vermögen** *n* dissolving power **-wirkung** *f* solvent effect

Losflansch *m* loose flange

Losgehen *n* explosion **verspätetes ~** hangfire **vorzeitiges ~** premature explosion

losgelassen let loose, uncontrolled, free, freed **-es Ruder** free controls **mit -em Steuer fliegen** to fly "hands-off"

Losgröße *f* lot size

loshaken to unhook

los-kaufen redeem **-keilen** to loosen the wedge **-ketten** to unchain **-kiel** *m* false keel **-kitten** to unglue **-klopfen** to rap **-klopfen** *n* rapping **-knüpfen** to untie, undo **-kommen** to become loose or free **-kuppeln** to disconnect **-lassen** to release, cast loose or adrift

löslich soluble **~ machen** to solubilize

Lösliche *n* soluble matter

Löslichkeit *f* solubility **beschränkte ~** limited or partial solubility

Löslichkeits-druck *m* solubility pressure **-kurve** *f* solubility curve **-veränderung** *f* change of solubility **-verminderung** *f* decrease of solubility **-zahl** *f* dilution value, solubility value, solubility coefficient

los-lösbar detachable **-lösen** to release, untie, loosen, liberate, set free, disengage, detach, separate

Loslösen der Lauffläche loosening of tread

Loslösung *f* disassociation

los-löten to unsolder **-machen** to unfasten, unfix, extricate, rid **-nageln** to unnail **-narbig** (rinnender Narben) hollow-grained **-nieten** to unrivet

Los- oder Leerscheibe *f* loose pulley

los-reißen to trip, heave up, tear off **-reißen** *n* tripping (anchor), heaving up **-rolle** *f* movable pulley

losrollender Block traveling block

Löss *m* loess

los-schäkeln to unshackle **-scheibe** *f* loose pulley, idler wheel **-scheibenantrieb** *m* loose-pulley drive **-schicht** *f* soft vein (geol.) **-schlagen** to beat off, knock loose, rap

losschnallen, sich ~ to undo one's belt

los-schnüren to undo, unlace **-schrauben** to unbolt, unscrew, screw off, undo **-schütteln** to shake loose or off

Lossev-Effekt *m* Lossev effect

los-sprengen to burst off **-springen** to fly or spring off

los-treibend adrift **-trennen** to separate, sever, tear apart, detach

Losung *f* password, droppings, dung

Lösung *f* approach (e.g. to design) loosening, detachment, untwisting, solution, dissolution, answer, discharge (of a gun), separation, opening (of a connection), severance **analytische ~** analytical solution **feste ~** solid solution **laugenartige ~** alkaline solution **strenge ~** rigorous solution **wässerige ~** aqueous solution **zeichnerische ~** graphical solution **~ in Schwerem Wasser** heavy water solution **zu einer Lösung gelangen** to arrive at a solution

Lösungs-benzol *n* solvent benzol or naphta **-chemie** *f* solution chemistry **-dauer** *f* resolution time **-dichte** *f* concentration **-druck** *m* solution pressure **-effekt** *m* solvent effect **-fähigkeit** *f* dissolving power, dissolving capacity **-glühen** *n* solution treatment **-kurve** *f* solubility **-magnet** *m* releasing magnet, trip magnet

Lösungsmittel *n* solvent, Stoddard solvent, mineral spirits **~ für Anstriche** paint thinner **gereinigtes ~** scrubbed solvent

Lösungsmittel-apparat *m* solvents-handling equipment **-echt** fast to solvents **-fabrikation und Rückgewinnung** solvent manufacturing and recovery **-frei** solvent free

Lösungs-potential *n* solution potential **-stärke** *f* strength of solution, solution concentration **-taste** *f* release key **-tension** *f* electrolytic solution pressure **-vermittler** *m* dissolving intermediary **-vermögen** *n* dissolving power, dissolving capacity **-wärme** *f* heat of solution

-wirkung *f* solvent action
los-weichen to soak off **-werden** to get rid of **-werfen** to cast off **-wickeln** to unwind, unravel **-winden** to unwind **-wuchten** to scrape loose, scrape out **-ziehen** to start off
Lot *n* plumb bob, plummet, sounding lead or line, perpendicular (line), normal, solder, vertical, plumb line **ein ~ fällen** to draw a perpendicular line, let fall a perpendicular **das ~ feststellen** to steady the plummet **im ~** on end, right by the plummet, perpendicular, vertical
Lot-abweichung *f* plumb-line deflection **-achse** *f* vertical axis
Löt-anlage *f* soldering installation **-anschluß** *m* soldered connection **-anschlußstück** *n* weld-on terminal, terminal clamp (electr.) **-apparat** *m* soldering apparatus **-arbeit** *f* process of soldering or brazing
Lotballon *m* sounding balloon
lötbar solderable
Lötblei *n* lead solder
Löt-brenner *m* gas or bellows blowpipe brazing torch **-bronze** *f* soldering bronze **-brücken** *f* soldering jumpers **-brunnen** *m* cable joint(ing) box, jointing chamber **-büchse** *f* borax or soldering box
Lötdraht *m* soldering wire **~** (Gußmittel) self-flux solder **voller ~** solid wire solder
Löte *f* solder (metal), soldering
Lotebene *f* vertical plane
Loteinrichtung *f* sounding installation
Löteisen *n* soldering iron
loten to plumb, project, to sound, take soundings (naut.)
Loten *n* plumbing, sounding
löten to solder, braze, burn on **weich ~** to solder **hart ~** to braze
Löten im Bade dip brazing
Löter *m* solderer
Löterei *f* soldering
Löterzelt *n* wireman's tent
Lötfahne *f* soldering lug
Löt-fett *n* mixture of tallow and sal ammoniac **-fläche** *f* soldering surface **-fläche** *f* soldering pad **-flamme** *f* blowpipe flame **-flansch** *m* braze-on flange **-flüssigkeit** *f* soldering fluid or flux **-folie** *f* soldering foil **-frei** solderless **-fuge** *f* soldered or brazed joint **-gabel** *f* soldering fork
Lot-gänger *m* leadsman **-geber** *m* vertical erection pickup (autopilot) **-gerät** *n* sounding device **-gewicht** *n* weight of the lead **-haken** *m* plumb (line) hook
Löt-kegel *m* soldering cone **-klemme** *f* tag, soldering terminal **-kolben** *m* soldering copper or iron, soldering or copper bit
Lötlampe *f* blow(-pipe) lamp, soldering lamp **kleine ~** blowtorch
Lötlappen *m* wiping cloth
Lot-leine *f* lead line **-linie** *f* plumb line, vertical **-maschine** *f* sounding machine
Lötmaschine *f* rotating soldering machine
Löt-material *n* soldering material **-metall** *n* soldering metal **-mittel** *n* soldering materials, solder **-mörtel** *m* plumber's solder **-naht** *f* soldered seam or joint **-ofen** *m* charcoal brazier, furnace
Lötöse *f* tag, (flat-type) soldering tab, (soldering) lug, soldering terminal **mit Lötösen versehen** tagged
Lötösen-leiste *f* soldering lug strip **-scheibe** *f* soldering terminal disc **-streifen** *m* tag strip, terminal strip, connection strip
Löt-paste *f* soldering paste **-pfanne** *f* soldering pan **-pistole** *f* soldering gun **-plättchen** *n* disc fuse **-probe** *f* blowpipe test **-pulver** *n* soldering powder
Lotpunkt *m* point vertically beneath a given point
lotrecht vertical, perpendicular, plumb **-e Komponente** vertical component
Lotrechte *f* vertical line
Lotrechtstarter *m* VTOL aircraft
Lotrichtung *f* plumb line, vertical direction
Lotriß *m* vertical or plumb line
Lötrohr *n* blowpipe **-besteck** *n* complete blowpipe
Lotröhre *f* sounding or lead tube
Lotröhrenmaßstab *m* scale of the sounding tube
Lötrohr-kapelle *f* blowpipe cupel **-lampe** *f* blowlamp **-probe** *f* blowpipe (test) piece **-probierkunst** *f* blowpipe assaying **-spitze** *f* blowpipe nipple, nozzle of a blowpipe **-versuch** *m* blowpipe test or experiment
Löt-salz *n* soldering salt **-säure** *f* soldering acid
Lotschnur *f* plumb line **-schieber** *m* plumb line slider
Lotschwankung *f* deflection of the vertical
Lotse *m* pilot, shadower **den Lotsen absetzen** to drop the pilot **um einen Lotsen bitten** to request a pilot
Lotsen *n* piloting
Lotsen-boot *n* pilot boat **-dienst** *m* shadowing service **-flagge** *f* pilot flag **-freiheit** *f* optional pilotage **-gebühr** *f* pilot charges **-kabel** *n* pilot cable **-station** *f* pilot station **-wesen** *n* pilot service **-zwang** *m* compulsory pilotage
Lotspindel *f* shank of the lead
Lötspitze *f* nozzle
Lotstab *m* plumb(ing) rod
Lotstand *m* position of the lead, sounding position
Lötstelle *f* (soldered) joint, seam, (soldered) junction, splice, wiped joint, end, cable joint, braze, brazing, shut **die ~ prüfen** to check the soldered connection **die ~ umwickeln** to wrap the joint
Lötstelle, äußere ~ couple **heiße ~** hot end, hot junction **kalte ~** cold end, cold junction, dry joint, faulty soldered joint **schlechte ~** dry joint
lötstellenfrei solderless
Lötstellennachweis *m* record of joints
Lötstift *m* tag, soldering pin, (wire-type) soldering tab or lug
Lotstrahl *m* sounding beam
Lötstreifen *m* tag strip, terminal or connection strip
Lötstutzen *m* solder union
Lottabelle *f* loading table
Lotte *f* ball or bloom of steel
Löttopf *m* charcoal brazier
Lotung *f* sounding, sounder key, probing (for depth) **nach Lotungen navigieren** to navigate by soundings

Lötung *f* soldering, brazing (by hard solder), agglutination, adhesion

Lotungs-gerät *n* sounding apparatus **-reihe** *f* series of soundings

Löt-verbindung *f* soldered joint or junction **-verfahren** *n* soldering or brazing method

Lotwaage *f* plumb bob

Löt-wasser *n* killed spirits, soldering fluid **-wulst** *m f* plumber's wiped joint

Lotwurf *m* cast of the lead

Löt-zange *f* soldering tongs **-zinn** *n* tin solder, soldering lead or tin **-zwinge (-zange)** *f* brazing tongs

Love-Wellen *pl* Love's waves

Loxodrome *f* rhumb line (straight course), loxodromic line

loxodromisch loxodromic

Lubschmiernippel *m* Lub grease gun nipple

Lucit *n* lucite

Lücke *f* interstice, void, gap (in wood), deficiency, space, check **~ in der Karte oder Aufnahme** gap, blank, lacuna in the map or in the survey **eine ~ ausfüllen** to supply a want **auf ~ stehen** positioned so as to fill gaps, staggered **positiv geladene ~** positive hole (cryst.)

Lücken-anteil *m* lacunarity **-bildung** *f* unsaturated linkage **-büßer** *m* stopgap **-deckel** *m* hatch cover **-fräser** *m* angular milling cutter **-haft** defective, incomplete **-haftigkeit** *f* porosity, incompleteness **-länge** *f* lacunarity, gap length **-längenmessung** *f* gap length measurement **-längenverteilung** *f* gap length distribution **-los** without interruption, consistently

Lücken-Rückstell-Impuls *m* gap reset pulse

Lücken-satz *m* vacancy principle **-synchronisierungsverfahren** *n* gap, underlap, interstice- or interval-synchronizing method **-test** *m* completion test **-verteilung** *f* gap length distribution **-wolken** *pl* hiatus clouds

lückig honeycombed, porous

Ludlum-Mehrelektrodenlichtbogenofen *m* Ludlum series-arc furnace

Ludlum-unmittelbarer Lichtbogenofen ohne Herdbeheizung Ludlum direct-arc nonconducting hearth furnace

Ludolphsches Auswertgerät Ludolph's altitude-reduction instrument or protractor

Ludwiks Kegeldruckpresse Ludwik's cone-hardness test

Lufberry-Kreis *m* Lufberry circle

Luffa *f* luffa, loofah

Luft *f* air, atmosphere, (Lager) play, (Abstand) clearance, space **~ abführen** to vent **~ auslassen** to deflate **die ~ entweichen lassen** to disinflate **die ~ über dem tropischen Meere** tropical air mass **mit ~ aufblasen** to inflate **in ~** subaerially **durch die ~** air-borne

Luft, böige ~ gusty air **feuchte ~** damp air **flüssige ~** liquid air **komprimierte ~** compressed air **leichter als ~** lighter-than-air **obere ~** upper air **verdünnte ~** rarefied air

Luft-abblaseventil *n* air-pressure relieve valve **-abflußklappe** *f* cowling flap **-abflußöffnung** *f* air opening vent **-abführung** *f* air exhaust **-abkommen** *n* air convention or agreement **-ablaß** *m* air escape **-abnahme** *f* diminution of air

Luft-absauger *m* suction ventilator **-absaugvorrichtung** *f* air-suction device **-abscheider** *m* air release, air separator, deaerator, air eliminator **-abschluß** *m* exclusion of air **-abschreckung** *f* air quenching **-abschreckungskühler** *m* air-quenching (grate) cooler **-abschluß** *m* exclusion of air, air seal, absence of air, hermetic seal **-absorption** *f* atmospheric absorption **-absperrhahn** *m* air shut-off valve (handle)

Luft-abstand *m* air separation (thickness) **-abzug** *m* vent, downwash **-abzugsöffnung** *f* air opening vent **-alarm** *m* air-raid alarm **-amt** *n* air ministry aviation board **-anfeuchter** *m* air moistener **-angriff** *m* (air) raid, aerial attack, aerial offense **-angriffspunkt** *m* center of pressure **-anker** *m* stub guy **-anlaßeinrichtung** *f* air starting equipment **-anreicherung** *f* density of gas in the air **-ansaugemeter** *n* Pitot tube

luftansaugendes Triebwerk air-breathing engine

Luftansaugekappe *f* air intake cap

Luftansauger *m* air breather

Luftansaug-hutze *f* air intake, air scoop, air horn **-leitung** *f* air intake **-ring** *m* air-intake ring **-rohr** *n* air intake **-stutzen** *m* air intake, air scoop

Luft-anschlußstutzen *m* air connecting piece **-ansicht** *f* aerial view

luftäquivalentes Material air equivalent material

luftartig gaseous

Luft-attaché *m* air attaché **-aufbereitungsanlage** *f* dry cleaning plant **-aufklärungsraum** *f* air-reconnaissance area **-aufnahme** *f* air survey, air phototopography, mosaic, air absorption, air occlusion, aerial photograph, airplane picture **-aufnehmer** *m* air receiver **-aufsicht** *f* air police **-aufsichtsdienst** *m* air police, air-control service **-aufsichtsstelle** *f* bureau of air-traffic supervision **-auftrieb** *m* air buoyancy **-ausgleicher** *m* compressed-air equilibrator, air compensator **-ausgleichklappe** *f* pressure flap **-ausgleichventil** *n* pressure relief vent

Luftauslaß *m* air outlet **-öffnung** *f* air outlet **-rohr** *n* discharge header **-trichter** *m* discharge funnel **-ventil** *n* pressure-relief vent

Luft-ausschluß *m* exclusion of air **-austauscher** *m* air interchanger **-austritt** *m* air exhaust **-austrittsloch** *n* air-exit hole

Luft-bad *n* air bath **-bahn** *f* (air) trajectory, elevated track, elevated railway, aerial track **-balg** *m* air bellows **-ballon** *m* balloon **-beaufschlagung** *f* volume of air **-bedarf** *m* air requirement, air required **-befeuchtung** *f* air moistening **-befeuchtungsanlage** *f* humidifier **-befördert** airborne **-beförderung** *f* air transport **-behälter** *m* gas cylinder (recoil), (compressed-) air tank (brake), air chamber, air bottle **-beherrschung** *f* air supremacy

Luft-beimischung *f* mixing air **-beobachtung** *f* aerial observation **-bereifung** *f* (having) pneumatic tires **-beschaffenheit** *f* composition of the air **-beschaffung** *f* air composition, air supply **-beschreibung** *f* aerography **-bespülung** *f* air scavenging **-beständig** air-resisting **-betankung** *f* air refueling **-betrieben** air driven **-bewegung** *f* air speed, movement of the air, air flow

Luftbild *n* aerial photograph, airscape **-abteilung** *f* aerophotographic section, photographic unit **-aufklärung** *f* photographic reconnaissance **-aufnahme** *f* air survey, air phototopography, aerial photograph, airplane picture **-aufnahmegerät** *n* aerophotographic apparatus **-ausmessung** *f* aerial photogrammetry **-auswertung** *f* plotting from air photographs, restitution from air photographs **-entzerrung** *f* rectification of aerial photographs **-flugzeug** *n* aerial photograph plane **-gerät** *n* aerial camera, air photographic apparatus

Luftbild-kamera *f* aerial camera **-kammer** *f* aerophotographic camera, aerial camera **-karte** *f* aerophotographic map, aerial mosaic, photographic map **-meßkamera** *f* aerial-mapping camera, air-survey camera **-meßkammer** *f* air-survey camera, aerial-mapping camera **-messung** *f* air photogrammetry, air phototopography aerial survey(ing) **-plan** *m* aerophotographic plan **-reihe** *f* photographic strip **-skizze** *f* aerophotographic sketch, aerial mosaic, unrectified mosaic **-wesen** *n* aerial photography **-technik** *f* aerial engineering **-umzeichner** *m* sketchmaster

Luftbildung *f* aerification

Luftbildvermessung *f* aerial photogrammetry

Luft-bläschen *n* air bell, air bubble **-blasdüse** *f* air-blast nozzle

Luftblase *f* air bubble, blowhole (in a cast piece), air pocket, air bell **eingeschlossene ~** air cavity

Luftblasensextant *m* bubble sextant

Luft-blitzableiter *m* air-gap lightning arrester **-bö** *f* gust **-Boden-Lenkwaffe** *f* air-to-ground missile **-bohne** *f* overflow well (die-casting) **-bremse** *f* fan brake, air brake, pneumatic brake **-bremsflügel** *m* fan-brake blade **-brennstoffgemisch** *n* fuel-air mixture **-brieftelegramm** *n* radio air letter **-brücke** *f* air lift **-buffer** *m* air buffer, pneumatic buffer **-bürste** *f* airbrush **-dämpfer** *m* air brake, air damper **-dämpfung** *f* air damping

luftdicht airtight, hermetic **~ verschlossen** hermetically sealed **-e Verbindung** airtight joint **-er Verschluß** hermetic seal

Luftdichte *f* air density, atmospheric density **die einer gegebenen ~ entsprechende Höhe** equivalent-density altitude

Luftdichte-messer *m* densimeter **-messung** *f* air-density measurement **-regler** *m* air density regulator **-schreiber** *m* recording densimeter

Luftdichtigkeit *f* air density

Luftdichtigkeitsmesser *m* aerometer

Luft-dielektrikum *n* air dielectric **-dienst** *m* air work or service **-diensttauglichkeit** *f* fitness for flying

Luftdosis *f* air dose

Luftdrehkondensator *m* air-dielectric variable capacitor

Luftdrehung *f* air vortex, turning by air

Luftdrossel *f* air-core choke, air strangler **-stellung** *f* air-mixture setting

Luftdruck *m* atmospheric pressure, barometric pressure, air pressure, blast pressure, wind pressure, pneumatic pressure **~ über Platz** air pressure at airport **statischer ~** static air pressure **-auffüllung** *f* filling, increasing pressure at the center of the low-pressure area **-ausgleichhutze** *f* air-pressure equalizing flap **-ausgleichsleitung** *f* air-balancing breather, equalizing line **-bereich** *m* atmospheric-pressure region **-bremse** *f* (compressed-)air brake, pneumatic brake **-erzeugung** *f* air-pressure system **-färbemaschine** *f* pneumatic dyeing machine **-feld** *n* pressure patters field **-fettpresse** *f* grease gun **-gebiet** *n* pressure area **-gradient** (Met.) *m* pressure gradient **-hammer** *m* compressed-air or pneumatic hammer **-höhenlinie** *f* (Met.) pressure contour

Luftdruck-kammer *f* air-lock **-karte** *f* barometric or isobaric chart **-kessel** *m* air-pressure boiler **-kontroller** *m* tire air-pressure controller **-lehre** *f* aerodynamics **-manometer** *n* air pressure gauge **-maschine** *f* pneumatic engine **-messer** *m* air-pressure gauge **-meßuhr** *f* air dial gauge **-messung** *f* barometry

Luftdruck-prüfer *m* tire gauge, tire pressure gauge **-prüfung** *f* air-pressure test **-regler** *m* air-reducing valve **-schalter** *m* pneumatic or air-pressure switch **-schreiber** *m* barograph **-senkkasten** *m* compressed air caisson **-spülung** *f* pneumatic bailing or flushing **-stampfer** *m* pneumatic rammer **-stand** *m* height of barometer **-steigung** *f* pressure gradient **-stufe** *f* pressure step, stage, or scale **-tür** *f* safety door in fortification to absorb air pressures from explosions

Luftdruck-variometer *n* air-pressure variometer **-verfahren** *n* compressed-air process **-verminderungsventil** *n* air-pressure release valve **-verteilung** *f* distribution of atmospheric pressure **-vertiefung** *f* deepening (aviation) **-welle** *f* barometric variation **-wert** *m* air-pressure coefficient **-wirkung** *f* effect of concussion, effect of air pressure

Luft-durchflußmenge *f* rate of air flow **-durchflußmesser** *m* air flow meter **-durchflußregelventil** *n* airflow modulating valve **-durchgang** *m* air passage **-durchlaß** *m* flow quantity **-durchlässig** penetrable by air, free-venting (in molding sand)

Luftdurchlässigkeit *f* venting property, or quality, permeability to air **~ der Leitbleche** baffle conductivity

Luftdurchlässigkeitsprüfer *m* densometer, air permeability tester, leakage tester

Luftdurchsatz *m* rate of air flow **-geschwindigkeit** *f* velocity of air flow

Luftdurchschlagspannung *f* breakdown voltage in air

Luftdurchströmungswiderstand *m* resistance of air flow, air-passage resistance

Luft-düse *f* air nozzle, choke tube, air jet, tuyère **-düsenplatte** *f* air-bleed plate **-echt** airproof **-echelot** *n* sound-ranging altimeter **-einblasemaschine** *f* air-injection engine **-einblasung** *f* air injection **-einbruch** *m* aeration inrush of air

Lufteinlaß *m* air inlet, intake, or passage **-gitter** *n* air-inlet screen **-klappe** *f* air damper or strangler **-leitschaufel** *f* air-intake guide vane **-öffnung** *f* air inlet **-rohr** *n* air intake **-schieber** *m* air shutter **-ventil** *n* air-inlet valve

Luft-einschluß *m* air pocket, air lock, air cavity, air bubble, air occlusion **-einspritzung** *f* air injection **-einströmung** *f* air ingress

Lufteintritt *m* air inlet, air intake **sich nach außen**

erweiternder ~ eines Leitbleches flared entrance of baffle

Lufteintrittsgitter *n* air intake grill

Lufteintrittsstutzen *m* air inlet branches, air horn **Druck im ~** air-scoop pressure

Luft-einwirkung *f* atmospheric action **-eisenstein** *m* aerosiderite

luftelektrisch static **-e Störungen** static, atmospherics **-er Stromkreis** atmospheric electric current circuit

Luft-elektrizität *f* atmospheric electricity **-elektrizitätsmesser** *m* electrometer **-empfindlich** affected by the air **-empfindlichkeit** *f* air sensitivity

lüften to ventilate, aerate, air, raise of lift (clear of something)

Lüften *n* raising, airing, weathering **~ der Bremse** easing the brake

Luftentfeuchter *m* silica gel breather, dehydrating breather

Luftentfeuchtung *f* dehumidification

Luft-entfeuchtungsanlage *f* dehumidifier **-entladung** *f* air discharge **-entnahme** *f* air bleed or extraction

Luftentnahme *f* air bleeding or tapping

luftentzündlich pyrophoric, inflammable in contact with air

Lüfter *m* ventilator, fan, blower, vent **-antrieb** *m* fan drive **-antriebsriemenscheibe** *f* fan drive pulley **-anzeigelampe** *f* ventilator indicator lamp **-einschub** *m* ventilation plug-in unit **-feld** *n* blower panel **-flügel** *m* fan blade

Lüfter-gebläse *n* ventilator **-geräusch** *n* fan running noise

Lufterguß *m* escape or effusion of air

Lufterhärtung *f* (Betonstein) air curing

Lüfterhaube *f* fan shell

Luft-erhitzer *m* air heater **-erhitzerröhre** *f* air-heater tube **-erkundung** *f* aerial reconnaissance **-erneuerung** *f* replacement of air

Lüfter-kupplung *f* fan coupling **-lagerung** *f* fan bearing **-nabe** *f* fan hub

Lufterneuerungsanlage *f* air regeneration unit (rocket)

Lüfter-rad *n* fan wheel, rotor **-riemen** *m* fan belt, releaser belt **-riemenscheibe** *f* fan pulley **-schaufel** *f* fan blade

Lufterscheinung *f* atmospheric phenomenon (meteor.)

Lufterschließung *f* accessibility to aircraft

Lüfterschraube *f* ventilator bolt

Lufterschütterung *f* air quake

Lüfter-sockel *m* blower base **-stillsetzung** *f* stopping of ventilator **-störungsentriegelung** *f* blower fault release **-störungsrelais** *n* blower fault relay **-träger** *m* fan bracket, fan carrier **-tunnel** *m* ventilator shroud **-übersetzungsgetriebe** *n* cooling-fan increasing gear **-überwachung** *f* blower control **-verkleidung** *f* fan shroud **-welle** *f* fan shaft **-wind** *m* fan wind

luftfähig airworthy

Luftfahrer *m* airman, aviator, aeronaut **-karte** *f* aeronautical map **-warnungsdienst** *m*, weather-warning service for air traffic

Luftfahrt *f* aeronautics, air navigation, aviation **-ausstellung** *f* aviation exhibition **-bedarf** *m* aviation accessories **-behörde** *f* aeronautical authorities **-bodenfeuer** *n* aeronautical (ground) light **-forschung** *f* aeronautical research **-forschungsanstalt** *f* aeronautical-research institute **-forschungsausschuß** *m* aeronautical-research committee **-funkdienst** *m* aeronautical radio-navigation service **-funkstation mit Funkbake** RLB, aeronautical radio-beacon station **-funkstelle** FA, aeronautical station

luftgefüllt filled with air **-er Abstand** air gap

Luftfahrt-gerät *n* aeronautical equipment **-gerätenorm** *f* aeronautical equipment standards **-gesellschaft** *f* airline company **-gesetzgebung** *f* air legislation **-handbuch** *n* aeronautical information publication (AIP) **-hindernis** abstraction to air-navigation **-industrie** *f* aircraft industry **-karte** *f* aeronautical chart **-kennzeichen** *n* aviation sign or symbol

Luftfahrt-kompaß *m* aviation compass **-kreise** *m pl* aeronautical circles **-leuchtfeuer** *n* aeronautical beacon **-medizin** *f* aeromedicine **-medizinisch** aeromedical **-ministerium** *n* air ministry **-navigation** *f* air navigation **-regeln** *pl* rules of the air **-rekord** *m* air record **-Rundsendedienst** *m* aeronautical broadcasting service **-sachverständiger** *m* air expert **-technik** *f* aeronautical engineering **-techniker** *m* aeronautical engineer or technician **-wetterdienst** *m* aeronautical weather service **-wissenschaft** *f* aeronautical science **-wesen** *n* aeronautics, aviation **-zeitalter** *n* air age

Luftfahrzeug *n* aircraft **~ leichter als die Luft** lighter-than-air aircraft, aerostat **~ schwerer als die Luft** aerodyne, heavier-than-air aircraft **~ mit Strahlantrieb** jet aircraft **~ mit Turbinenpropellerantrieb** (PTL) turbo-propaircraft **~ mit Turbinenstrahlantrieb** turbo-jet-aircraft

Luftfahrzeug-bau *m* aircraft construction **-bescheinigung** *f* aircraft certificate **-bordbuch** *n* aircraft log **-eintragungsschein** *m* aircraft certificate **-halter** *m* aircraft operating agency **-kennung** *f* aircraft identification **-mechanik** *f* mechanics of aircraft **-mechaniker** *m* aircraft mechanic **-motorenindustrie** *f* aircraft engine industry **-muster** *n* type of aircraft **-rufzeichen** *n* aircraft call sign **-werk** *n* aircraft factory

Luftfalle *f* air lock or trap **Buntensche ~** Buntens funnel or pipette

Luft-fang *m* ventilating duct, ventilator **-fänger** *m* air scoop **-federbein** *n* compressed-air-landing strut **-federstrebe** *f* compressed-air landing leg **-federung** *f* pneumatic cushioning or shock absorption **-feuchtigkeit** *f* humidity of the air, hygrometric condition, atmospheric moisture

Luftfeuchtigkeits-gehalt *m* hygroscopic moisture **-messer** *m* hygrometer **-zeiger** *m* hygroscope

Luft-filter *m* air filter or strainer **-filteröl** *n* air-filter oil **-lasche** *f* air container **-flaschenkopf** *m* valve head of air bottle **-flecken** *m* air stain **-floß** *n* air raft **-flotte** *f* air fleet, air-force command or division

Luft-flügel *m* impeller **-förderer** *m* air conveyer **-fördermenge** *f* quantity of air **-förderung** *f* air feed

Luft-förmig aeriform **-fracht** *f* air freight **-frach-**

ter *m* air freighter **-führung** *f* air circulation (air path) **-führungsregelklappe** *f* controllable (cooling) gill **-funkstelle** *f* aircraft or airborne station

Luft-gang *m* air passage **-gangentwicklung** *f* developing by air-passage **-gas** *n* air gas, producer gas **-gaserzeuger** *m* air gas producer **-gebietsbeschränkung** *f* restricted area **-gebilde** *n* aerial structure **-gebläse** *n* (air) compressor **-gefedert** has air suspension, airspring **-geheizter Ofen** air oven

luftgekühlt air-conditioned, air-cooled **-e Maschine** air-cooled engine **-er Transformator** air-cooled transformer

Luft-geltung *f* air power **-generatorgas** *n* producer gas, Siemens's gas **-gerät** *n* hydraulic thrustor **-gerätschaften** *pl* gas mask **-geschwindigkeit** *f* air speed, air velocity, blast velocity **-geschwindigkeitsmesser** *m* air-speed indicator, anemometer **-gesteuert** air-controlled **-gewehr** *n* air gun **-gewicht** *n* weight of the air, air density **-gitter** *n* balloon barrage **-gleichgewichtslehre** *f* aerostatics **-gleichstrom** *m* current of breath (in sound recording) **-granulation** *f* dry-method granulation **-gut** *n* air freight or goods **-gütemesser** *m* eudimeter

Luft-hafen *m* airport **-hahn** *m* air cock **-haltig** aerated **-hammer** *m* air hammer, pneumatic hammer **-hammeröl** *n* pneumatic-tool oil **-härter** *m* **-härtestahl** *m* air-hardening steel **-härtung** *f* air hardening **-härtungstahl** *m* air-hardening steel **-haspel** *f* pneumatic winch

Luft-haus *n* pavilion **-heber** *m* **-heberanlage** *f* air lift **-heer** *n* army of the air **-heizgerät** *n* air heating appliance **-heizkörper** *m* forced-fan unit heaters (electr.) **-heizung** *f* hot-air heating **-hindernis** *n* air obstacle **-hochdruck** *m* high-pressure area **-hohlraumkabel** *n* air-space cable **-horchdienst** *m* air-defense listening service **-horizontalbewegung** *f* (Met.) advection **-hülle** *f* atmosphere **-hutze** *f* air intake, air scoop

luftig airy, aerial

Luft-injektor *m* air injector **-insel** *f* still air space

Luftion *n* atmospheric ion

offene Luftionisationskammer *f* open-air ionization chamber

Luftisolation *f* air insulation

Luftkabel *n* overhead cable, aerial cable **-fahrstuhl** *m* cable car, boatswain's chair **-linie** *f* aerial cable line **-tragseil** *n* messenger wire or supporting strand for overhead cables

Luftkalk *m* hydrated lime

Luftkammer *f* air chamber, air checker, air box, airpressure space (loud-speaker) **-lautsprecher** *m* air-chamber loud-speaker

Luft-kanal *m* air duct, flue, channel, or passage, airport, ventilating duct, air hole or valve, air drain **-keil** *m* (Interferenz) wedge-shaped air space **-keilhammer** *m* pneumatic splitting hammer **-kern** *m* air core **-kernspule** *f* air-core(d) coil **-kessel** *m* air chamber **-kissen** *n* air cushion, dashpot **-kissenbelastung** *f* air cushion pressure **-kissenfahrzeug** *n* air cushion vehicle

Luftklappe *f* air flap **~ des Vergasers** choke

Luftklappen-betätigung *f* air throttle **-ventil** *n* choke valve

Luft-klassifikator *m* air classifier **-kolbenblock** *m* piston block **-kolbenhebelblock** *m* piston lever group **-kompression** *f* air compression **-kompressionsmaschine** *f* **-kompressor** *m* air compressor **-kompressoranlage** *f* air-compressor plant **-kondensator** *m* air capacitor, air condenser **-konditionierung** *f* air-conditioning **-körper** *m* body of air **-kraft** *f* useful lift (aviation), air force, aerodynamic force **-kraftangriffspunkt** *m* center of (aerodynamic) pressure **-kräfte** *pl* flight loads

Luftkraft-hebelarm *m* lever arm of aerodynamic force **-moment** *n* moment of resultant air force **-resultierende** *f* resultant air force **-verlauf** *m* distribution or variation of aerodynamic forces

Luft-krank airsick **-krankheit** *f* aeroëmbolism, airsickness **-kreislauf** *m* air circuit **-kühlanlage** *f* air coller, air cooling plant **-kühler** *m* air cooler or radiator, primary condenser or cooler **-kühlung** *f* air cooling, cooling by air, fan cooling **-kunde** *f* aerology **-kursbuch** *n* air timetable

Luft-lager *n* air suspension or bearing **-lagernd** air-cushioned **-landvermessung** *f* air or aerial surveying **-lastbedingungen** *pl* flight loading conditions **-lasten** *pl* flight loads **-lauf** *m* air passage

luftleer vacuous, evacuated, exhausted (of air), empty, void **~ machen** to evacuate, empty, exhaust **-e Barometerdose** aneroid barometer **-e Birne** vacuum-type bulb **-er Raum** vacuous space, evacuated space, vacuum, exhausted space

Luftleerblitzableiter *m* vacuum lightning arrester, vacuum lightning protector, gas-type arrester

Luftleere *f* vacuum, void

Luft-leermesser *m* vacuometer, vacuum gauge **-leerspannungssicherung** *f* vacuum arrester **-lehre** *f* aerology **-leitblech** *n* cooling baffle **-leitend** air-conducting **-leitung** *f* air line, air main, air pipe, aerial wire, air conduit, open-wire line or circuit, overhead line **-leitungseinlaßflansch** *m* air-inlet flange **-lenkwaffe** *f* air-to-airmissile **-leuchten** *n* air glow **-lichtformel** *f* formula for attenuation of light in air **-linie** *f* air line

Luftlinien *pl* air flux **-entfernung** *f* air-line distance **-schnittzone** *f* zone of airways intersection

Luft-linse *f* air (space) lens **-loch** *n* air pocket, air hole, vent hole **-löcher** *pl* (im Gehäuse) performations **-lochfallbö** *f* air pocket **-lot** *n* sound-ranging altimeter **-lotung** *f* air sounding, acoustic method of measuring altitude

Luft-Luft-Rakete *f* air-to-air rocket

Luft-mangel *m* deficiency of air **-manometer** *n* air pressure gauge **-masse** *f* air mass **-mast** *m* breathing mast, underwater air intake **-meer** *n* atmosphere **-meile** *f* air mile **-meilenzähler** *m* air-mile counter **-meißel** *m* pneumatic chisel **-meldedienst** *m* aircraft reporting service **-meldequadrat** *n* aerial reference square (on maps) **-meldesammelstelle** *f* air-report gathering station (for communications service) **-meldestation** *f* airway communication station

Luft-menge *f* wind volume, air volume, quantity of air **-meßbild** *n* aerial-survey photograph **-messer** *m* air meter **-mine** *f* land mine **-mischer**

m air interchanger **-mischung** *f* mixture of air masses **-molekül** *n* air molecule **-molluskel** *n* aerial mollusk **-momentenfeld** *n* restoring or aerodynamic moment field **-monitor** *m* air monitor **-mörser** *m* pneumatic trench mortar **-mörtel** *m* lime mortar, air mortar **-motor** *m* air motor

Luft-nadel *f* vent rod (in molding) **-navigation** *f* aerial navigation **-nitrit** *n* atmospheric nitrogen

Luftöffnung *f* air valve (intake), scuttle air bleed **kleine ~** bleed hole, air bleed

Luft-ortung *f* aerial navigation **-ozean** *m* ocean of air **-pakt** *m* air pact **-parade** *f* aerial parade or review **-park** *m* aircraft park **-pendelverkehr** *m* air shuttle service **-perspektive** *f* aerial perspective

Luftphoto-grammetrie *f* air photogrammetry **-graphie** *f* air photograph, air photography **-graphisch** aerophotographic

Luft-pinsel *m* aerograph **-plattenspektroskop** *n* Fabry-Pérot interferometer **-politik** *f* air politics **-polizei** *f* air police

Luftpolster *n* air cushion, cushioning cylinder **abgepuffertes ~** air buffer or cushion

Luftpolsterzylinder *m* air-cushion cylinder

Luftpore *f* air void

Luftporen-anteil *m* air space ratio **-beton** *m* air entrained concrete **-zusatzmittel** *n* air entraining agent

Luftpost *f* air mail **-ausgabe** *f* air mail edition **-brief** *m* air-mail letter **-dienst** *m* air-mail service **-marke** *f* air-mail stamp **-strecke** *f* air-mail route **-verkehr** *m* air mail service

Luft-presser *m* air compressor **-pressung** *f* air squeezing **-prüfer** *m* air tester **-puffer** *m* dashpot air-cushion **-pumpe** *f* air pump, pneumatic pump, air-compressor pump **-pumpenglocke** *f* air-pump receiver **-pyrometer** *n* air pyrometer **-rahmen** *m* air-cored frame (direction finder)

Luftradioaktivität-Überwachungsgerät air monitor

Luftraum *m* air space

Luftraumkontroll- und Warndienst *m* ACW (aircraft control and warning service)

Luft-raumreservat *n* air-space reservation **-raumüberwachung** *f* air space surveillance **-recht** *n* aeronautical law **-regelklappe** *f* gill **-regler** *m* air control **-regulieranlage** *f* air-conditioning plant

Luftreibung *f* air friction **durch ~ hervorgerufener Widerstand** frictional drag

Luft-reibungsverlust *m* windage loss **-reich** *n* air, air space, space **-reifen** *m* airplane tire, pneumatic tire, balloon tire **-reifenpanne** *f* puncture **-reiniger** *m* air filter, air cleaner, air purifier **-reinigungsanlage** air-conditioning plant or apparatus **-reise** *f* flight, voyage by air **-reisender** *m* air tourist or traveler **-reklame** *f* sky writing, aerial advertisement **-rektifikationsanlage** *f* air rectifier **-rennen** *n* air race

Luft-richter *m* air nozzle, choke tube, air guide **-richtung** *f* direction of air flow **-riß** *m* fissure **-riß** *m* natural crack (in wood) **-rohr** *n* air pipe, air tube, air shaft **-röhrchen** *n* (small) air tube **-röhrenkühler** *m* air-tube radiator **-röste** *f* dewretting **-rückführung** *f* air return **-ruder** *n* external control vane (rocket) **-rührer** *m* air-lift agitator

Luftsack *m* air pocket, ballonet, air lock, (air) hose, towed target, overflow well (die-casting) **-bildung** *f* formation of air pockets **-fassungsvermögen** *n* capacity or volume of ballonet **-hülle** *f* ballonet envelope **-maul** *n* air scoop **-sicherheitsventil** *n* automatic safety valve **-ventil** *n* air-scoop valve

Luft-salpetersäure *f* synthetic nitric acid **-sattel** *m* air saddle aerial arch **-sauerstoff** *m* atmospheric oxygen **-saugapparat** *m* aspirator **-sauger** *m* exhauster, exhaust fan (for air), aspirator

Luftsaug-leitung *f* air induction or intake pipe **-pumpe** *f* air suction pump **-rohr für die Luftgeschwindigkeit des Schraubenstrahles** ramming air intake **-schlauch** *m* air-supply hose **-ventil** *n* air suction valve

Luft-säule *f* air column **-säure** *f* carbonic acid **-schacht** *m* air shaft **-schall** *m* sound transmitted by air **-schal(l)lot** *n* sound-ranging altimeter **-schallsender** *m* nautophone, aerial oscillator **-schaltdüse** *f* air pilot nozzle **-schalter** *m* air circuit breaker, air break switch (Am) **-schattenbildung** *f* formation of air shadows **-schicht** *f* atmospheric layer, stratum, air layer **-schichtanker** *m* wall clamps **-schieber** *m* damper plate, air damper, air valve

Luftschiff *n* (lenkbares) airship, dirigible **ein ~ von der Vertäuung losmachen** to undock **kleines ~** blimp **unstarres ~** nonrigid dirigible **kleines unstarres ~** blimp

Luftschiffer *m* aeronaut

Luftschiffahrt *f* air navigation, air travel

Luftschiffahrts-kunde *f* navigation, aeronautics **-linie** *f* air line **-wissenschaft** *f* air navigation

Luftschiff-führer *m* airship pilot **-funkerei** *f* airship radio **-gondel** *f* gondola, nacelle **-hafen** *m* airship port **-halle** *f* dock, airship shed **-kunst** *f* aeronautics

Luftschiffsaufhängung *f* overhead suspension (for airships)

Luftschiff-träger *m* airship carrier or tender **-verkehr** *m* airship service

Luft-schippe *f* air scoop **-schirm** *m* air umbrella **-schlacht** *f* air battle **-schlauch** *m* inner tube (tire), air tube, pipe, or hose **-schlauchmischung** *f* air tubing mixing **-schlauchregenerat** *n* tube reclaim **-schlauchventil** *n* air chuck **-schleier** *m* counter-air current, air fogging **-schleuse** *f* air-lock, air sluice

Luftschlitz *m* louver, air passage, slot for air inlet **~ der Motorhaube** louver

Luftschmierungseinrichtung *f* air-line lubrication

luftschnittig streamlined, drag reducing

Luftschraube *f* (full-feathering) propeller **~ antreiben** to drive the propeller **~ mit verstellbaren Blättern** propeller with adjustable blades **~ zum Entfroster** fan screw for defroster **~ mit Freilauf** free-wheeling propeller **~ mit gleichbleibender Geschwindigkeit** constant-speed propeller **~ mit unbeweglicher Gierung** fixed-pitch propeller **~ von Hand durchdrehen** to swing the propeller by hand **~ mit Schnellverstellung** quick-feathering propeller **~ in Segelstellung** feathering, propeller in feathering position **~ mit elektrisch kontrollierter Steigung** nonselective pitch

Luftschraube, ~ mit umkehrbarer Steigung reversible-pitch propeller **~ mit verstellbarer Steigung** variable-pitch propeller **Antrieb der ~ durch den Fahrtwind** windmilling (of propeller) **frei umlaufende, vom Fahrtwind angetriebene ~** windmilling propeller **einstellbare ~** variable-pitch or adjustable propeller **untersetzte ~** geared-down propeller **verstellbare ~** adjustable propeller, variable- or controllable-pitch propeller **zweiflügelige ~** two-blade propeller **hintereinanderliegende Luftschrauben** tandem propellers

Luftschrauben-achse *f* thrust line, propeller axis **-anbauflansch** *m* propeller hub attachment flange **-antrieb** *m* propeller drive **-ätzung** *f* propeller etching **-aushöhlungskraft** *f* propeller cavitation **-automatik** automatic propeller **-befestigungsmutter** *f* propeller nut **-belastungslinie** *f* propeller load curve **-beschlag** *m* tipping of the propeller

Luftschraubenblatt, Schaft des Luftschraubenblattes propeller-blade shank

Luftschraubenblatt-breite *f* propeller-blade width **-flächeninhalt** *m* propeller-blade area **-grundtheorie** *f* propeller-blade element theory **-spitze** *f* propeller-blade tip **-spitzenschaden** *m* propeller-tip failure **-winkel** *m* propeller-blade angle

Luftschrauben-bremse *f* propeller brake, airscrew brake **-doppelflügel** *m* Siamese-twin-blade propeller **-drehmoment** *n* propeller torque **-drehrichtung** *f* (direction of) rotation of propeller **-drehzahl** *f* propeller r.p.m. **-drehzahlregler** *m* propeller-speed control **-durchschnitt** *m* propeller section **-ebene** *f* plane of propeller rotation **-einstellung** *f* propeller-pitch indexing **-eisen** *m* propeller bar **-element** *n* blade element **-fabrik** *f* propeller factory **-flächeninhalt** *m* propeller area **-flansch** *m* propeller flange hub

Luftschraubenflügel *m* propeller blade **Querschnitt des Luftschraubenflügels** propeller-blade section **Saugseite des Luftschraubenflügels** propeller-blade back

Luftschrauben-flügelschaft *m* propeller-blade shank **-förderwagen** *m* propeller trailer **-fräsmaschine** *f* propeller shaping machine **-frostschutz** *m* **-gefrierschützer** *m* propeller antiicer **-gang** *m* propeller path **-geräusch** *n* propeller noise **-halbmesser** *m* propeller-tip radius **-haube** *f* propeller spinner **-interferenz** *f* propeller interference **-kennlinie** *f* propeller characteristic curve **-kreis** *m* propeller disk **-kreisfläche** *f* propeller-disk area

Luftschraubenlager *n* propeller nosepiece **~ für Schubaufnahme** propeller thrust bearing

Luftschrauben-leistung *f* propeller efficiency **-nabe** *f* propeller area or hub, airscrew boss **-nabenhaube** *f* propeller spinner **-nabenkonus** *m* propeller-hub cone **-nabenstück** *n* propeller hub **-nabenwulst** *m* propeller boss

Luftschraubennachstrom *m* slip stream **durch den ~ auf die Pendelwaage des Prüfstandes ausgeübtes Drallmoment** torque imposed on the engine by the slip stream on the cradle frame

Luftschrauben-prüfstand *m* propeller test stand **-radius** *m* propeller radius **-regelung** *f* propeller-pitch control **-schlupf** *m* slip (aviation) **-schnitt** *m* propeller section **-schub** *m* propeller thrust **-schublager** *n* propeller thrust bearing **-schutz** *m* propeller protection **-schwankung** *f* propeller flutter **-segelstellung** *f* feathered-propeller position **-seite** *f* airscrew or propeller end **-seitenverhältnis** *n* aspect ratio of propeller **-stab** *m* propeller bar

Luftschraubensteigung *f* propeller pitch **Einstellung der ~** propeller-pitch indexing **niedrige ~** low or standard propeller pitch

Luftschrauben-steigungsmesser *m* propeller-pitch indicator **-steigungsregler** *m* propeller governor **-stellungsanzeiger** *m* propeller-pitch indicator **-steuerventil** *n* propeller regulator valve **-strahl** *m* propeller slip stream, wake **-uhr** *f* propeller-pitch gauge **-untersetzungsgetriebe** *n* propeller reduction gear **-verstellgerät** *n* pitch-control mechanism **-verstellung** *f* propeller-pitch change

Luftschrauben-welle *f* propeller shaft **-wellengetriebekreuz** *n* propeller-shaft gear spider **-wind** *m* propeller slipstream **-windstoß** *m* propeller blast **-wirkungsgrad** *m* propeller efficiency **-wölbungsverhältnis** *n* propeller camber ratio **-wurzel** *f* propeller root **-zug** *m* propeller thrust

Luft-schütz *m* air-break contactor **-schutzbezirk** *m* civilian air defense district **-schwere** *f* specific gravity of the air **-schweremessung** *f* barymetry **-schwinger** *m* diaphragm, membrane **-schwingung** *f* oscillation or vibration of air (gas) **-segel** *n* external control vane (rocket) **-segler** *m* glider, sailplane **-seide** *f* hollow rayon **-seil** *n* aerial rope **-seilbahn** *f* aerial tramway or cableway

Luftseite *f* downstream face **~ mit Kurvenprofil** face with curved profile

luftseitig downstream **-es Ende des Pfeilers** down-stream end of pier **-er Halbmesser der Krone** down-stream radius of crest **-es Profil der Mittellinie** downstream profile on center line **-e Sohlenbefestigung** downstream apron **-e Verjüngung** downstream batter

Luftspalt *m* air gap, entrefer **-drossel** *f* air gap choke **-kraftflußkopplung** *f* air-flux coupling **-magnetometer** *n* flux-gate magnetometer

Luftspannung *f* air pressure

Luftspeicher *m* air cell **-dieselmotor** *m* air-cell engine **-dieselverfahren** *n* air-cell combustion system **-kammer** *f* air-storage chamber **-maschine** *f* air-cell-type engine **-verfahren** *n* air cell system

Luft-spektrallinien *pl* air lines **-sperrgebiet** *n* prohibited area, airspace restriction

Luftspiegelung *f* fata morgana, mirage **~ nach oben** looming, direct mirage **~ nach unten** inverted mirage

Luft-spieß *m* venting wire, wire riddle, vent rod (in molding) **-sport** *m* aerial sport **-sprengpunkt** *m* point of air burst **-spritze** *f* air spray **-spule** *f* air(-core) coil, loop, or frame (direction finding), air-core solenoid **-spülungseinrichtung** *f* air-scavenging system **-station** (Bleichapparat) air plant (air station) **-staudüse** *f* pitot tube **-stauung** *f* stagnation of air **-stechen** *n* venting by piercing the rammed sand (in molding) **-stein** *m* aerolite

Luftsteuer *n* air controls **-relais** *n* relay valve **-werk** *n* air controls

Luft-stickstoff *m* atmospheric nitrogen **-stift** *m* air-piston **-störungen** *pl* atmospherics, static, strays

Luftstoß *m* blast **-dämpfer** *m* compressed-air shock absorber, pneumatic shock absorber **-winkel** *m* angle of attack

Luftstrahl *m* air draft, air jet **-triebwerk** *n* jet-propulsion unit

Luftstraße *f* airway

Luftstrecke *f* airway, air route, air gap, striking distance (elec.) **~ des Fadens** air travel of thread

Luft-streckennetz *n* aerial network, network of air routes **-streuung** *f* sky shine

Luftstrom *m* air current, air flow, air stream **~ mit hoher Geschwindigkeit** blast **durch den ~ angetrieben** windmilling (aviation) **stoßender ~** shock wave

Luftstrom-gerät *n* aerial gas-spraying apparatus (aviation) **-mahlanlage** *f* air-swept grinding plant **-motor** *m* airstream engine **-mühle** *f* air-swept mill **-neigung** *f* downwash (aviation) **-pendelung** *f* air-jet pendulation

Luftströmung *f* air current or flow

Luftströmungs-messer *m* anemometer, airflow meter **-versuch** *m* air flow test

Luft-strudel *m* air eddy **-stutzen** (Wagenheizer) air hose connector air scoop **-stützpunkt** *m* air base **-system** *n* air system **-taktik** *f* air tactics **-tanken** *n* refueling during flight **-tasche** *f* air lock, air pocket **-taufe** *f* first flight **-technik** *f* air engineering **-technisch** aero-dynamic **-temperatur** *f* air temperature

Luft-thermometer *n* air thermometer **-tiefdruck** *m* low (aviation) **-transformator** *m* air-core transformer **-transport** *m* air transportation **-transportierte Makroteilchen** airborne particulates **-treffbild** *n* air-burst pattern **-treibhammer** *m* pneumatic hammer **-trenner** *m* air fractionator **-trennungsanlage** *f* air-separation plant **-triangulierung** *f* aerotriangulation **-trichter** *m* Venturi tube, diffuser **-trichterhalteschraube** *f* choke tube stop-screw **-trimmer** *m* air-dielectric trimmer

lufttrocken air-dry, air-seasoned **-es Holz** air-dried wood

Luft-trocknen *n* air-conditioning **-trocknende Emaille** air-drying enamels **-trockner** *m* air-drying apparatus **-trocknung** *f* air drying, air seasoning (of wood) **-trübung** *f* turbidity of the air, murkiness **-tüchtigkeit** *f* airworthiness **-tüchtigkeitsschein** *m* certificate of airworthiness **-turm** *m* air tower

Luft-überdruck *m* positive air pressure **-überdruckregler** *m* regulator of effective air pressure **-überhitzer** *m* blast superheater **-überlegenheit** *f* air superiority **-überleitungsring** air transmission ring, air-passage ring **-überschuß** *m* excess air (amount of air actually required over theoretical amount to burn fuel) **-überschußzahl** *f* excess-air coefficient **-übertragungsweg** *f* air transmission path **-überwachungsgerät** air monitor

Luft-umgangsventil *n* by-pass valve **-umhüllung** air gap **-umlauf** *m* circulation of the air **-umsteuerung** *f* reversal of air **-umwälzofen** *m* furnace with recirculating air **-umwälzung** *f* air circulation **-umwälzungsofen** *m* air-circulating oven

Luft- und Öldruckschalter *m* air-and oil pressure switches

luftundurchlässig impermeable to air

Lüftung *f* ventilation, aeration, airing

Lüftungs-anlage *f* ventilation, ventilating system **-ansatz** *m* vent collar (parachute) **-art** *f* system of ventilation **-blech** *n* ventilating plate **-flügel** *m* ventilation flap **-jalousie** *f* louvre **-kanal** *m* ventilating shaft or channel **-klappe** *f* ventilator **-loch** *n* vent hole **-öffnung** *f* ventilation openings

Lüftungs-maschine *f* blower **-rohr** *n* ventilation pipe **-schacht** *m* air shaft **-schieber** *m* register, damper (ventilation) **-schlitz** *m* vent hole, ventilator **-schlot** *m* ventilating shaft or pipe **-schraube** *f* vent plug **-ventil** *n* vent valve **-vorrichtung** *f* ventilation appliance

Luft-unterdruck *m* air depression **-unterstandsmessungen** *pl* drag measurements **-untüchtigkeit** *f* air unworthiness **-variometer** *n* air-core variometer

Luftventil *n* valve, air slide, breather, blowoff cock, blast-control valve **~ des Reifens** tire valve

Luft-ventilblock *m* piston block base **-verankerung** *f* suspension mooring (of light pontoon bridges) **-verbindung** *f* air connection or service **-verbrauch** *m* air consumption **-verdichtende Maschine** air compressor **-verdichter** *m* (air) compressor, air condenser **-verdichtung** *f* (air) compression **-verdrängung** *f* air displacement

luftverdünnter Raum vacuum

Luft-verdünnung *f* rarefaction of the air, vacuum **-verdünnungsmesser** *m* vacuum-gauge **-verflüssiger** *m* air liquifier **-verflüssigung** *f* air liquefaction **-verflüssigungsanlage** *f* air liquefying plant **-vergütet** air-hardened **-verhältnisse** *pl* air conditions, state of the air

Luftverkehr *m* air traffic or commerce **~ innerhalb eines Staates** intrastate commerce (air)

Luftverkehrs-abkommen *n* air-traffic agreement, aviation convention **-anschluß** *m* airway connection **-bestimmungen** *pl* air-traffic regulations or rules **-genehmigung** *f* air-traffic concession **-gesellschaft** *f* air-line operating company, air-transport company **-gesetz** *n* air-traffic law **-kontrolle** *f* air traffic control, avigation regulation **-linie** *f* air line **-netz** *n* airline network

Luftverkehrs-regeln *pl* rules of the air **-strecke** *f* commercial airway or air line **-unternehmen** *n* civil air-line operating company **-verband** *m* air-traffic association **-vorschrift** *f* air-traffic rule **-wesen** *n* air traffic

Luft-vermessung *f* aerial survey **-vermittlung** *f* air-force signal center **-versorgung** *f* air supply **-versuch** *m* valve test run (guided missiles) **-verteiler** *m* air distributor **-verteilerdecke** *f* air manifold **-verunreinigung** *f* pollution of the air

Luft-vorhang *m* air curtain **-vorholer** *m* compressed-air counterrecoil mechanism, compressed-air recuperator, buffer **-vorlagerung** *f* tidal air **-vorreiniger** *m* air (pre)purifier **-vorwärmer** *m* air heater **-vorwärmkammer** *f* air-preheating chamber **-vorwärmung** *f* preheating of air **-vulkanisation** *f* open cure (of rubber)

Luftwalze der Papiermaschine air-roll

Luft-walzenstapelanleger *m* air-wheel pile feeder **-wandler** *m* air cooled transformer

Luftwärme *f* **-grad** *m* air temperature **-speicher** *m* hot-air generator **-gradmesser** *m* air thermometer

Luft-warte *f* aerological observatory **-wascher** *m* air washer **-wechsel** *m* ventilation, change of air **-wechselklappe** *f* air reversing valve, reversing air valve

Luftweg *m* airway, air flue **-weiche** *f* aerial frog **-welle** *f* wind wave, aerial billow, sky wave, space wave, indirect wave **-zeichner** *m* airway plotter

Luftwerterechner *m* air data computer

Luft-wichte *f* specific weight of air, density of the air, specific gravity of the air **-wichtenregelventil** *n* **-wichtregelventil** *n* air-density control valve **-widerstand** *m* air resistance, drag, ohmic resistance, aerodynamic drag (on airplane) **-widerstandsbeiwert** *m* drag factor, drag coefficient **-widerstandswaage** *f* drag balance or scale **-winkel** *m* angle of the wind **-wirbel** *m* air twirl, air swirl, turbulence, vortex, air eddy **-wirbelbremse** *f* air-eddy brake **-wirbelung** *f* air whirling

Luftwirbelkammer, Dieselmotor mit ~ Diesel engine with air cell and controlled turbulence

Luft-woge *f* wind wave, aerial billow **-zellwolle** *f* imitation wool fiber **-zeugführer** *m* pilot **-zerlegung** *f* separation of liquid air **-zerlegungsanlage** *f* air-separation plant **-zerstäubung** *f* air atomization **-ziel** *n* aerial target

Luft-zufuhr *f* admission of air, air supply **-zuführung** *f* air supply, air scoop **-zuführungsrohr** *n* air intake **-zug** *m* draft, air current, air duct, air uptake, air-uptake duct or flue, draft (of a lamp), current of air **-zünder** *m* pyrophorus **-zurichtung** *f* air-conditioning **-zusammensetzung** *f* composition of the air **-zusatz** *m* additional air

Luftzustand *m* atmospheric condition **reduzierter ~** standard air or atmosphere

Luft-zutritt *m* air access or admission, air inlet, air supply **-zwischenkühler** *m* air-cooled intercooler **-zwischenraum** *m* intermediate air space **-zyklon** *m* air cyclone **-zylinder** *m* pneumatic recuperator cylinder, air cylinder

Lügendetektor *m* lie detector, psycho-integroammeter

Luk *n* hatch (seaplane)

Luke *f* dormer or garret window, hatch **~ im Flugzeug für astronomische Ortung** astro-hatch

Luken *pl* louver boards (paper mfg.) **-deckel** *m* hatch cover

Lumen *n* lumen, internal diameter **-messer** *m* lumen meter

Lumenometer *n* lumenometer

Lumiereplatte *f* autochrome plate

Lumineszenz *f* luminescence **-anregung** *f* luminescence excitation **-gift** *n* killer, poison **-platte** *f* persistron **-schwelle** *f* luminescence threshold **-zentrum** *n* luminescent center

lumineszieren to luminesce

Lumme *f* crossbar

Lummer-Brodhun'sches Photometer Lummer-Brodhun contrast photometer or cube photometer

Lumpen *m pl* rags **-butte** *f* rag tub or bucket **-schneidemesser** *n* rag-cutting knife **-sortiertisch** *m* hurdles (paper mfg.) **-stäuber** *m* rag duster **-wolf** *m* willow (paper mfg.), rag-tearing machine **-zucker** *m* crushed sugar **-zurichter** *m* shredder

lunarisch lunar

Lünette *f* backrest, steady rest

luni-solar luni-solar

Lunker *m* shrinkage, cavity, piping (of metals), shrink hole, contraction cavity, void, sink hole, pipe, shrinking hole, shrinkage fault or hole, blowhole **primärer ~** pipe (of ingots) **sekundärer ~** axial sponginess, secondary pipe (in an ingot)

Lunker-bildung *f* shrinking, piping, developing or forming of piping **-frei** free of shrink holes, pipeless **-hohlraum** *m* shrinkage cavity, shrink hole

lunkerig honeycombed, piped

Lunkerkopf *m* top end of a pipe **abgeschöpfter ~** top discard, crop end (of an ingot)

lunkerlos free of shrink holes, pipeless

lunkern to pipe

Lunkern *n* shrinking, piping, liquid contraction

Lunkerstelle *f* porous spot or point, shrink hole

Lunkerung *f* shrinkage, piping, liquid contraction, porosity, blowhole formation, cavitation (in metals)

Lunker-verhütung *f* pipe elimination **-verhütungsmittel** *n* pipe eliminator, pipe eradicator

lunkrig vesicular (said of castings)

Lünse *f* linch pin, axle pin

Lünsscheibe *f* linch washer

Lunte *f* fuse, match (min.), slow-match, slubbing or roving (textiles)

Lunten-abzug *m* delivery of slivers **-länge** *f* sliver length

Lupe *f* magnifier, magnifying lens, magnifying glass eyepiece **stark vergrößernde ~** high-power magnifier

Lupen-aufnahme *f* magnifier work **-betrachtung** *f* observing under a lens **-mikroskop** *n* binocular stand magnifier **-rahmen** *m* viewing-lens frame **-scheitel** *m* lens vertex **-ständer** *m* lens stand **-vergrößerung** *f* single lens magnification

Lupferpunzen *m* punch for making fine flutes or grooves

Luppe *f* ball lump, puddle(d) ball, loop, (ore) bloom, lump, ingot **gezängte ~** rough bloom

Luppen *n* balling **-eisen** *n* ball iron, puddled iron, wrought iron, muck iron **-eisenpaket** *n* muck-bar pile, muck-bar faggot **-feuer** *n* Catalan furnace, bloomery **-frischfeuer** *n* bloomery fire **-frischhütte** *f* bloomery **-hammer** *m* ball press **-machen** *n* balling **-mühle** *f* rotary ball squeezer, coffee-mill squeezer, burden squeezer **-quetsche** *f* ball squeezer **-stab** *m* puddled bar, muck bar

Luppenstäbe *pl* puddled bars, muck bars **auf Sturz paketierte ~** flat and edge box-piled faggot, flat-box-piled faggot **paketierte ~** muck-bar pile, faggot

Luppen-stahl *m* bloom steel **-straße** *f* train for rolling squeezed balls **-wagen** *m* bloom wagon (met.) **-walzwerk** *n* puddle mill, muck mill

Lürmannsche Schlackenform Lürmann front, Lürmann's closed front

Lüsterklemme *f* porcelain insulator

lustlos (Börse) inactive
Lüstrier- und Glanzmaschine glossing machine
Lutetium *n* lutecium
lutieren to lute
Lutierungsmittel *n* luting agent, lute
Lutte *f* ventilating tube, air duct, pipe, launder
Lutten-apparat *m* multiple-cone classifier (with an ascending current of water) **-bewetterung** *f* duct ventilation, separate ventilation **-richt-apparat** *m* air-conduit-adjusting apparatus **-ventilator** *m* duct-type fan
Luv *n* luff, weather side, windward side, drift angle **-seite** *f* windward side, weather side **-wärts** windward **-winkel** *m* drift angle, angle of lead **-wirbel** *m* windward eddy
Lux *n* lux (unit of light) **-boje** *f* flare buoy
Luxemburg-Effekt *m* Luxembourg effect, Tellegen effect, interaction of radio waves
Luxmesser *m* light meter, light-measuring apparatus
Luxus-ausführung *f* deluxe model **-ausgabe** *f* de luxe edition
Lydit *m* touchstone
Lykopodium *n* lycopodium
Lymphe *f* lymph
Lymphglas *n* vaccine glass
Lymphocyt *m* lymphocyte
Lymphopenie *f* lymphopenia
Lyndochit *n* lyndochite
lyophile Eigenschaften lyophilic properties
lyophiles Sol lyophilic sol
lyotrope Reihe lyotropic series
Lyra *f* swivel, lyre **-maische** *f* lyre crystallizer
lysalbinsaures Natrium sodium lysalbinate
Lysoform *n* lysoform

M

Mäander *m* meander **-band** *n* meander belt or strip
mäanderförmig meander-shaped **-es Signal** square-wave signal
Mäanderlinie *f* meandering line
Maar *n* crater lake **-bildung** *f* formation of lunar seas
Machart *f* type (of manufacture), brand
machen to make, manufacture, cause, produce **Fahrt** ~ to make headway (aviat.)
Macher *m* maker, manufacturer **-lohn** *m* cost of production
Machgebiet *n* Mach region
Machmeter *n* Mach meter
Mach-sche Einheit *f* Mache unit **-scher Kegel** Mach cone, Mach front, Mach stem **-sche Streifen** Mach bands **-sches Viereck** *n* Mach quadrangle **-sche Welle** Mach line **-sche Zahl** Mach number
Machwerk *n* bungling work
Machzahl *f* Mach number
Macquistenprozess *m* Macquisten (tube) process
Made *f* setcrew, headless screw, grub screw
Maden-loch *n* pinhole **-schraube** *f* setscrew, grub screw, headless screw
Magazin *n* magazine, store, dump, depot, warehouse, storeroom **-balg** *m* reservoir bellows **-eintritt** *m* magazine opening **-gatter** *n* magazine creel **-gehäuse** *n* magazine chamber (gun) **-halt-hebel** *m* magazine retaining pin **-halter** *m* magazine catch, magazine holder, magazine frame **-speisung** *f* magazine feed **-sperre** *f* magazine stop **-verriegelung** *f* magazine release button (locking gear) **-verwalter** *m* storekeeper **-verwaltung** *f* depot administration **-zuführung** *f* magazine feed attachment
Magen *m* stomach **-pumpe** *f* stomach pump
mager thin, lean, meager **-e Fettungsmittel** short oil fat-liquors **-es Gemisch** poor, lean, weak mixture **-er Kalk** lean (poor) lime **-e Kohle** *f* lean coal, nonbituminous coal **-er Lack** low-grade varnish **-er Stoff** short pulp
Mager-beton *m* lean concrete **-erz** *n* lean ore **-kalk** *m* poor lime **-kohle** *f* lean coal, hard coal, nonbaking coal, semianthracite, nonbituminous coal, semibituminous coal, close burning coal **-korn** *n* grog particle (in a firebrick)
magern to make lean or poor, shorten, reduce plasticity (of ceramics)
Magerungsmittel *n* lean material, lean clay
magisch-es Auge electron-ray indicator tube, magic eye tube, tunoscope **-er Rahmen** luminous edge **-e Zahl** magic number
Magma *n* magma, ground mass, matrix
magmatischer Herd magma reservoir
Magmenintrusion *f* magmatic intrusion
Magnaflux-gerät *n* magnetic crack detector **-prüfen** *n* Magnaflux testing **-prüfung** *f* Magnaflux inspection
Magnalit *m* magnalite
Magnalium *n* magnalium (aluminum-magnesium alloy)
Magnarad *n* magna wheel
Magnesia *f* magnesium oxide, magnesia **gebrannte** ~ calcined magnesia
Magnesia-glimmer *m* biotite **-haltig** magnesian **-stein** *m* magnesia stone or brick **-usta** *n* magnesium oxide
Magnesit *m* magnesite **gebrannter** ~ calcined magnesite
Magnesit-auskleidung *f* magnesite lining **-herd** *m* magnesite bottom **-mehl** *n* ground magnesite **-spat** *m* magnesite **-ziegel** *m* magnesite brick **-zustellung** *f* magnesite lining
Magnesium *n* magnesium **-arseniat** *n* magnesium arsenate **-blech** *n* sheet magnesium **-draht** *m* magnesium wire **-eisen** *n* brown magnesite **-fackel** *f* magnesium torch or flare **-formiat** *n* magnesium formate **-gehalt** *m* magnesium

content **-haltig** containing magnesium

Magnesium-hyperoxyd *n* magnesium perioxide **-hypophosphit** *n* magnesium hypophosphite **-klischee** *n* magnesium (block) plate **-legierung** *f* magnesium-base alloy **-licht** *n* magnesium light **-oxydhydrat** *n* magnesium hydroxide **-perborat** *n* magnesium perborate **-rhodanid** *n* magnesium thiocyanate **-sulfat** *n* magnesium sulfate **-superoxyd** *n* peroxide of magnesium **-Titanspinell** *n* spinel

Magnet *m* magnet **fremderregter ~** nonpermanent magnet, electromagnet **induzierender ~** inducing magnet **induzierter ~** induced magnet **natürlicher ~** natural magnet, loadstone **zusammengesetzter ~** battery of magnets, compound magnet **~ mit Vorzugsrichtung** magnet with anisotropic properties

Magnet-abscheider *m* magnet separator **-abscheidetrommel** *f* magnetic pulley separator **-achse** *f* magnetic axis

Magnetanker *m* armature (of magnet) **~ des Dauermagneten** keeper (magnetism)

Magnet-anlasser *m* magnetostarter **-apparat** *m* magneto **-ausschalter** *m* field break switch **-ausscheider** *m* magnetic separator

Magnetband *n* magnetic tape **-laufwerk** *n* tape transport **-leser** *m* magnetic-tape reader **-geschwindigkeitsabweichungen** *pl* tape flutter **-speicher** *m* magnetic tape memory

Magnet-betrieb *m* magnet gear, magnet service, lifting magnet **-block** *m* magnetic block, magneto block **-bremse** *f* solenoid brake **-bremslüfter** *m* brake release solenoid **-bügel** *m* magneto strop **-bündel** *n* compound or fagot magnet **-detektor** *m* magnetic detector **-drahtgerät** *n* wire recorder **-dynamo** *m* magnetodynamo **-einstellskala** *f* magneto timing scale **-eisenerz** *n*, **-eisenstein** *m* magnetite, load-stone

magnetelektrisch magnetoelectric(al) **-e Maschine** magneto(electric) machine

Magnetfeld *n* magnetic field **ein ~ erzeugen** to produce a magnetic field **transversales ~** transverse magnetic field

Magnetfeld-kompaß *m* fluxgate compass **-regler** *m* rheostat **-röhre** *f* magnetron **-röhrenkennlinie** *f* critical-voltage parabola, cut-off parabola **-spule** *f* magnetic field coil

Magnet-förderer *m* magnetic conveyor **-formverfahren** *n* magnetic forming **-fluß** *m* magnetic flux **-gehäuse** *n* magnet case or housing **-gehäusedeckel** *m* magnet cover **-gestell** *n* magnetic frame **-gleitkupplung** *f* magnetic slide coupling **-halter** *m* magnetic specimen holder **-hydrodynamisch** magnethydrodynamic **-hysteresisschleife** *f* hysteresis loop of a magnet **-halter** *m* magnetic specimen holder **-induktion** *f* magnetic induction **-induktor** *m* magneto, hand generator

magnetisch magnetic **~ betätigter Schalter** magnetic switch **~ machen** to magnetize **-e Ablenkung** *f* magnetic deflection **-e Abweichung** magnetic deviation **-e Achse** magnetic axis **-e Aktivität der Erde** terrestrial magnetic activity **-e Änderung** magnetic variation **-er Anrißsucher** magnetic crack detector **-e Anziehungskraft** magnetic attraction **-e Aufbereitung** electro-magnetic separation **-es Aufnahmevermögen** magnetic susceptibility **-e Aufspannvorrichtung** magnetic chuck **-e Auslösung** *f* magnetic trip (on circuit breaker)

magnetisch-e Belegung *f* magnetic induction or charge, seat of magnetic induction or magnetic field **-e Blaswirkung** magnetic blow **-es Blatt** *n* magnetic shell **-e Bogenbeeinflussung** magnetic blow-out **-er Breiteneffekt** magnetic latitude effect **-er Brumm** magnetic hum **-e Deklination** dip, magnetic declination **-e Dichtigkeit** magnetic density **-e Doppelschicht** magnetic shell **-er Dünnfilm** *m* thin magnetic film **-e Durchlässigkeit, Durchdringbarkeit** permeability, magnetic inductivity, magnetic inductive capacity

magnetisch-e Einstreuung magnetic susceptibility **-e Empfindlichkeit** magnetic susceptibility **-es Erdfeld** magnetic field of earth **-es Erz** magnetic ore **-e Feldstärke** *f* magnetic-field strength, intensity of magnetic field, magnetic force **-er Fluß** magnetic flux or current **-e Flußdichte** magnetic flux density **-e Fremdfelder** foreign magnetic fields **-er Geber** magnetic pick-up **-es Gleichfeld** constant magnetic field **-e Glieder** magnetic links **-e Hysteresis** magnetic hysteresis

magnetisch-e Induktion magnetic induction, flux density **-er Induktionsfluß** magnetic flux **-e Kernausrichtung** nuclear magnetic alignment **-es Kernmoment** nuclear magic moment **-e Kopplung** magnetic power-clutch **-e Kraft** magnetic force or intensity **-er Kraftfluß** magnetic flux **-e Kraftlinie** line of magnetic force, magnetic line of force **-e Kraftwirkung** magnetic stress **-er Kreislauf** magnetic cycle or circuit **-er Kreisprozeß** magnetic cycle **-e Kupplung** *f* magnetic drive **-er Kurs** corrected compass course

magnetisch-e Leitfähigkeit permeance, magnetic conductance, permeability, magnetic conductivity **-er Leitwert** magnetic permeance **-es Magazin** compound magnet **-er Modulator** magnettor **-es Moment** magnetic dipole moment **-e Nachwirkung** magnetic viscosity, residual loss, magnetic fatigue **-er Nebenschluß** magnetic leak or shunt **-e Nordrichtung** magnetic North **-e Nord-Südrichtung** magnetic meridian **-e Oberflächenprüfung** magnafluxing

magnetisch-e Photodesintegration photomagnetic effect **-e Prüfspule** magnetic test coil **-e Pole der Erde** terrestrial magnetic poles **-e Polstärke** magnetic-pole strength **-e Reibung** magnetic friction **-e Reibungsarbeit** magnetic hysteresis **-e Remanenz** residual magnetism **-e Rotationsinvariante** invariant of magnetic rotation **-er Rückschluß** magnetic return path **-er Rücktritt** hysteresis, magnetic lag **-e Scheidung** magnetic separation **-er Schirm** magnetic shield or screen, can (of a coil) **-e Schirmung** magnetic shielding **-es Schürfen** magnetic survey

magnetisch-e Spannung magnetic potential **-er Spannungsgleichhalter** *m* magnetic voltage stabilizer **-er Speicher** *m* magnetic memory (print) **-er Spiegel** pyrotron **-es Spinmoment** spin-magnetic moment **-e Spinresonanz** spin-magnetic resonance **-e Stärke** magnetic intensity **-e Steifigkeit** magnetic rigidity **-er Streufluß** *m* magnetic stray flux **-e Streuung** *f* magnetic dispersion **-er Tonaufzeichner** *m* magnetic sound recorder, magnetophone

magnetisch-e Umhüllung magnetic bottle **-er**

Umdrehungsmesser magnetic tachometer **-er Umwandlungspunkt** point of magnetic transformation **-e Unregelmäßigkeit** magnetic anomaly **-er Verstärker** magnetic amplifier **-e Verzögerungsleitung** magnetic delay-line **-e Vorspannung** magnetic bias **-es Wechselfeld** alternating magnetic field **-e Wechselinduktion** magnetic alternating induction **-er Widerstand** (magnetic) reluctance, magnetic resistance **-e Widerstandsänderung** magneto-resistance **-es Zeitrelais** magnetic relay timer

magnetischbetätigter Schalter magnetic switch

magnetisierbar magnetizable

Magnetisierbarkeit *f* magnetizability, magnetic property

magnetisieren to magnetize

magnetisierend magnetizing **-e Wicklung** magnetizing coil

magnetisier-fähig magnetizable **-fähigkeit** *f* magnetizability

magnetisiert magnetized

Magnetisierung *f* magnetization **remanente ~** residual magnetization **überlagerte ~** superposed magnetization

Magnetisierungs-fähigkeit *f* magnetizability **-intensität** *f* intrinsic induction **-koeffizient** *m* susceptibility, magnetizability **-kopf** *m* magnetic sound-recording head **-kurve** *f* magnetization curve **-schleife** *f* hysteresis loop **-spule** *f* magnetic coil **-stärke** *f* intensity of magnetization, magnetizing force **-strom** *m* magnetizing current, polarizing current **-zyklus** *m* magnetization cycle

Magnetismus *m* magnetism **remanenter ~** residual or remanent magnetism **zurückbleibender ~** residual magnetism

Magnetismusmenge *f* intensity of magnetization, quantity of magnetism

Magnetittrübe *f* magnetite densemedium

Magnet-joch *n* yoke of a magnet **-katzbahn** *f* magnet crab **-kern** *m* pole core of a magnet, limb of a magnet, magnet core **-kernspeicher** *m* magnetic core memory **-kerzenzündung** *f* magnetic plug ignition **-kies** *m* pyrrhotite **-kran** *m* lifting-magnet-type crane **-kreis** *m* magnetic circuit **-kreuzventil** *n* magnetic solenoid valve **-kupplung** *f* magneto coupling **-kurzschlußvorrichtung** *f* magnet short circuiting device

Magnet-läufer *m* magnetic rotor **-locher** *m* electric punch **-luftventil** *n* solenoid air valve **-magazin** *n* battery of magnets **-motorzähler** (mit Stromwender) direct-current commutator meter **-nadel** *f* magnetic needle, deflecting magnet

Magneto-cord *n* magnetocord **-hydrodynamik** *f* magnetohydrodynamic

magneto-ionische Doppelbrechung magneto-ionic double refraction

magneto-kalorisch magnetocaloric

Magnetometer *n* magnetometer, dip needle **~ mit Abgleichspule** null coil magnetometer

magnetometrisch magnetometrical **-e Kraft** magnetomotive force

Magneton *n* magneton **-zahl** *f* magneton number

magneto-optische Drehung magnetic rotation

Magnetophon *n* tape recorder **-band** *n* magnetic tape

Magnetopyrit *m* pyrrhotite

Magnetorotationsspektrum *n* magnetic rotation spectrum

Magnetoskop *n* magnetoscope

magnetoskopisch magnetoscopical

Magnetostatik *f* magnetostatics

Magnetostriktion *f* magnetostriction

Magnetostriktions-generator *m*, **-oszillator** *m* magnetostriction oscillator

magnetostriktiv magnetostrictive

Magnet-paar *n* magnet couple **-plattenspeicher** *m* magnetic disc memory **-polschuhkante** *f* edge of the magnet pole shoe **-prüfer** *m* magnet-testing apparatus **-pulverkupplung** *f* magnetic clutch **-pulverprüfung** *f* magnetic particle test **-rad** *n* magnet wheel, magneto gear **-radantriebswelle** *f* magneto-gear driving shaft **-regelung** *f* magneto timing

Magnetron *n* magnetron **-cycloidhöhe** *f* cycloidal height of a magnetron **-durchschlag** *m* magnetron arcing **-generator** *m* magnetron oscillator **-leitbahnwelle** *f* transit-time or electronpath oscillation **-leitkreisfrequenz** *f* transit-time frequency of a magnetron **-schwingung** *f* magnetron oscillation **-verstärker** *m* magnetron amplifier

Magnet-rückzugseinrichtung *f* magnetic rotation device **-schale** *f* magnetic shell **-schalter** *m* ignition switch **-schalterwicklung** *f* solenoid winding **-scheider** *m* magnetic grader, separator, or cobber **-schelle** *f* magnet holder or carrier **-schenkel** *m* magnet limb, leg **-schieber** *m* sliding magnet **-schlüssel** *m* magneto wrench **-schreiblocher** *m* electric printing punch

Magnet-spannfutter *n*, **-spannschraube** *f* magnetic chuck **-spindelölfangschale** *f* magneto spindle oil cup **-spule** *f* coil, winding, solenoid, magnet coil, field coil **-spuren** *pl* recording tracks **-stab** *m* bar magnet **-stahl** *m* magnet steel **-stein** *m* magnetite **-summer** *m* electromagnetic oscillator, magnetic interrupter **-system** *n* magneto system **-taste** *f* magnetic button

Magnetton-abtastgerät *n* magnetic sound reproducer **-anlage** *f* magnetic sound-recording equipment **-band** *n* magnetic tape recording

Manettondraht *m*, **plattierter ~** magnetic plated wire

Magnetton-folie *f* magnetic tape **-gerät** *n* magnetic recorder **-kopf** *m* magnetic recording head **-verfahren** *n* magnetic or telegraphone sound-recording method

Magnet-topf *m* pot magnet **-träger** *m* magnet bracket carrier, magnet support or holder **-übertragung** *f* magnetic transmission **-umschalter** *m* magnetic change-over switch **-ventil** *n* solenoid valve **-verstärker** *m* transductor **-vorverstärker** *m* magnetic pre-amplifier **-wecker** *m* magneto-bell **-wicklung** *f* field coil, field winding exciting winding, magnetizing coil, magnet coil **-zahn** *m* field projection **-zugkraft** *f* pull of a magnet

Magnet-zünder, ~ mit Umlaufhülse magneto with rotating sleeve **-zündereinstellung** *f* magneto timing **-zünderschalter** *m* magneto ignition switch **-zündung** *f* magneto ignition

Magnolienholz *n* magnolia

Magnuseffekt *m* Magnus effect (ballistics)

mahagoni-braun mahogany brown **-holz** *n* mahogany **-lack** *m* mahogany lacquer

Mäh-antrieb *m* mower drive **-antriebsgehäuse** *n* mower drive housing **-balken** *m* mower cutter bar **-balkenaufzug** *m* mower cutter bar lift **-binder** *pl* harvester-binders

Mähdrescher *m* harvester thresher

mähen to mow, cut

Mähhebel *m* mower lever

Mahl-anlage *f* milling plant, pulverizing equipment or plant, pulverizer mill, grinding plant, crushing mill **-arbeit** *f* beat **-bahn** *f* grinding face

Mahlbarkeitskurve *f* grindability curve

Mahl-bombe *f* grinding bomb **-büchse** *f* grinder **-dauer** *f* grinding cycle

mahlen to mill, crush, grind, pulverize, beat (paper mfg.) **fein ~** to pulverise **grob ~** to crush **mittel ~** to grind

Mahlen *n* grinding, (der Luftschraube) windmilling

Mahl-fähigkeit *f* grinding property **-feinheit** *f* fineness of grinding, fineness of grain or comminution **-fläche** *f* grinding face or surface, crushing surface **-gang** *m* grinding operation, millstone arrangement **-gut** *n* material to be ground, crushed, or milled **-holländer** *m* beater **-kammer** *f* grinding chamber **-kegel** *m* grinding cone **-körper** *m* grinding or pulverizing element **-kranz** *m* grinding ring or box

Mahl-leistung *f* crushing duty, grinding capacity **-maschine** *f* roller mill **-organ** *n* grinding or pulverizing element **-platte** *f* grinding plate **-ring** *m* grinding ring, bull ring, ring die **-sand** *m* quicksand **-scheibe** *f* grinding disk **-stäbe** *pl* grinding rods **-stein** *m* grinder, millstone runner, running stone **-technik** *f* grinding technique or practice, crushing or pulverizing practice **-teiler** *m* grinding ring, bull ring, ring die **-trommel** *f* grinding drum

Mahl- und Siebanlage *f* grinding and sifting plant

Mahlung *f* pulverization, grinding, crushing

Mahlungsgrad *m* degree of beating, freeness (pulp) **-prüfer** *m* beaten-stuff tester, freeness tester (paper mach.)

Mahl-verfahren *n* milling or grinding process **-versuch** *m* grinding or pulversizing test, rattler attrition test (in a drum mill) **-vorgang** *m* grinding operation, pulverizing process **-vorrichtung** *f* grinding or milling apparatus **-walze** *f* grinding roll **-werk** *n* milling plant, crushing or grinding mill, pulverizing equipment, grinder **-wirkung** *f* pulverizing action **-zeit** *f* meal

Mähmaschine *f* reaper, mower

Mahnbrief *m* letter requesting payment, dunning letter, reminder

mahnen to exhort, remind, warn

Mähnenkamm *m* currycomb

Mahnung *f* reminder, admonition

Mahn-verfahren *n* dunning proceedings **-zettel** *m* tickler, reminder, prompt note

Mähwerk *n* mover

Mais *m* corn **-binder** *m* corn binder

Maischapparat *m* mashing apparatus, pony masher, wort masher

Maische *f* mash **~ mit oberem Schneckenradantrieb** crystallizer with upper worm drive

Maischekühler *m* mash cooler

maischen to mash

Maisch-gitter *n* stirrer, rake **-pfanne** *f* mash tub **-trog** *m* mingler

Maisdibbelmaschine *f* hill-drop corn planter **verstellbare ~** variable-drop corn planter

Maisdrillmaschine *f* corn drill

Maisenthülser *m* corn husker **~ und Elevator** corn husker and silo filler **~ und Zerschneider** corn husker and shredder

Maisflockenstuhl *m* maize-flaking mill

Maishackmaschine *f* corn cultivator **zweireihige ~** two-row corn cultivator

Maiskolben-aufschichter *m*, **-elevator** *m* cob stacker **-pflücker** *m* corn picker

Maiskolbenschäler *m* corn sheller **~ für Handbetrieb** hand corn sheller **~ mit Kraftbetrieb** power corn sheller

Mais-maschine *f* corn machine **-pflanzmaschine** *f* corn planter **-schäler** *m* corn sheller **-stärke** *f* Indian corn starch (maize-starch)

Maisstoppelzerschläger *m* stalk cutter

Maitlandit *m* maitlandite

Majolika *f* majolica

Majorana-Teilchen *n* Majorana particle

Majorante *f* majorant

majorisieren to carry by majority vote

Majorität *f* majority

Majoritäts-emitter *m* majority emitter **-ladungsträger** *m* majority charge carrier **-trägerkontakt** *m* majority carrier contact

Majuskel *f* capital, two-line letter

Makadam *n, m* macadam **-decke** *f* macadam surface

makadamisieren to macadamize

Makadamweg *m* macadam road

Makel *m* blemish, stain, defect **-los** pure, stainless, unblemished **-losigkeit** *f* spotlessness

Maker *m* (double-headed) maul, sledge

Makler *m* broker **-kosten** *pl* brokerage

Makrameearbeit *f* knotted work

Makro-achse *f* macro-axis (cryst.) **-analyse** *f* macroanalysis **-auflichttisch** *m* macro incident light stage **-beleuchtung** *f* macro stage illumination **-druck** *m* macro-imprinting **-einrichtung** *f* macro equipment **-feld** *n* macro field **-graphie** *f* macrography **-gravimetrisch** macrogravimetric **-kristallin** macrocrystalline **-meteorologie** *f* macrometerology **-meter** *n* macrometer **-molekül** *n* macromolecule

Makro-photographie *f* photomacrography **-programm** *n* macroprogram **-projektion** *f* macro projection **-rheologie** *f* macro-rheology **-skopisch** macroscopic **-struktur** *f* macrostructure **-teilchen** *n* particulate **-tisch** *m* macro stage **-turbulenz** *f* macroturbulence **-untersuchung** *f* macroanalysis

Makulatur *f* waste paper, waste, mackled sheets, lining paper

makulieren to print waste

Mal *n* sign, characteristic, time, mark, token, stigma

mal (in Multiplikationen) times

Malachit *m* malachite **blauer ~** azurite

Malachit-grün *n* malachite green **-kiesel** *m* chrysocolla

Malakolith *m* malacolite

Malblatt *n* pattern or stenciling paper

malen to paint

Maler *m* painter **-email** *f* painter's enamel **-firnis** *n* painter's varnish **-ringpinsel** *m* ring brushes

-schablone *f* stencil **-walzen** *pl* rollers for painters
Mal-karton *m* artist's cardboard **-kasten** (Farbkasten) *m* paint-box
Mall *n* mold **-boden** *m* molding loft **-kante** *f* molding edge
Malm *m* upper oölite
Malonsäure *f* malonic acid
Malotte *f* shackle
Malstein *m* boundary stone, marker
Malteserkreuz *n* Maltese cross, cross wheel, (cam and) star wheel in Geneva movement, Geneva wheel **-gesperre** *n* Geneva-stop mechanism **-getriebe** *n* Maltese-cross transmission
Maltha *m* maltha
Maltosebestimmung *f* maltose determination
Malvenfarbe *f* mauve
Malz *n* malt **-abreibeapparat** *m* malt-detrition apparatus **-aufschlag** *m* duty on malt **-darre** *f* maltdrying kiln, malt drier
Malzeichen *n* multiplication sign
malzen to malt
Mälzen *n* malting
Mälzerei *f*, **Malzhaus** *n* malthouse
Malz-schroterei *f* malt-bruising plant **-tenne** *f* malt floor
Mammatokumulus *m* mammato-cumulus, pocky cloud
Mammaturestform *f* hiatus clouds
Mammographie *f* mammography
Mammut-baum *m* giant redwood **-pumpe** *f* airlift pump
managen to manage
Manchester *m* velveteen, fustian, Manchester velvet **gestreifter ~** thickset
Manchesterbindung *f* weave for fustians and velveteens
Manchonspanner *m* Manchon stretcher
Mandant *m* customer of a lawyer
Mandarinagearbeit *f* mandarining
Mandat *n* order, power, authorization
Mandause *f* back-shaft scroll (textiles)
Mandel *f* fifteen, shock, almond **-artig** amygdaline **-förmig** amygdaloid(al) **-gummi** *n* almond gum
mandeln to set or place in heaps of fifteen
Mandel-stein *m* amygdaloid **-weise** by fifteens
Mandrill *m* mandrel
Mangal *n* Mangal (a type of light metal alloy)
Mangan *n* manganese **-abbrand** *m* loss of manganese **-alaun** *m* manganese alum **-arm** low-manganese, low in manganese
Manganat *n* manganate
Mangan-badmethode *f* manganese bath method **-bister** *n* manganese bister or brown **-bistertöne** *pl* manganese bister shades **-blende** *f* alabandite **-chlorür** *n* manganous chloride **-eisen** *n* ferromanganese **-epidot** *m* piedmontite
Manganerz *n* manganese ore **graues ~** manganite, pyrolusite **schwarzes ~** hausmannite
Mangan-gehalt *m* manganese content **-glanz** *m* alabandite **-hältig** manganiferous **-hartstahl** *m* austenitic manganese steel **-hydroxydul** *n* manganous hydroxide
Manganialuminat *n* manganic aluminate
Manganin *n* manganin
Manganiphosphat *n* manganic phosphate
Manganit *m* manganite
Mangan-karbid *n* manganese carbide **-kiesel** *m* rhodonite **-kitt** *m* manganese composition **-kupfer** *n* cupromanganese
Manganneusilber *n* manganese nickel silver
Mangano-aluminat *n* manganous aluminate **-ferrum** *n* ferromanganese **-hydroxyd** *n* manganous hydroxide
Mangan-oxyd *n* manganese sesquioxide, manganese oxide **-oxydul** *n* manganous oxide **-oxydul-oxyd** *n* manganese tetroxide **-pecherz** *n* triplite **-perchlorid** *n* manganese perchloride, manganic perchloride **-reich** manganiferous, rich in manganese **-säure** *f* manganic acid **-saures Natrium** sodium manganate **-siliziumstahl** *m* silicomanganese steel **-spat** *m* rhodochrosite
Manganstahl-herzstück *n* manganese-steel frog **-schiene** *f* manganese-steel rail
Mangan-stein *m* rhodonite **-sulfat** *n* manganic sulfate **-sulfür** *n* manganous sulfide **-superoxyd** *n* manganese peroxide, pyrolusite, pebble manganese, manganese dioxide **-verbindung** *f* manganic compound **-wolframat** *n* hübnerite
Mangel *m* scarcity, defect, deficiency, shortage, lack, penury, imperfection, want, need, privation, shortcomping
Mangel *f* calender, mangle
Mangel-baumstuhl *m* calender beam **-effekt** *m* calendering effect **-elektron** *n* hole electron (trans.)
mangelhaft defective, imperfect, faulty, deficient, insufficient **-es Stehen des Bildes** jumping or unsteadiness of picture or image **-e Verständigung** transmission trouble
Mangelhaftigkeit *f* deficiency, defectiveness, faultiness
Mangelhalbleitung *f* defect conduction, p-type conduction
Mangelleiter *pl* deficiency conductor
mangeln to lack, calender, mangle
Mangel- oder p-leitung *f* deficity or p-type conduction
Mangelradbewegung *f* mangle rack motion
mangels for want of, in default of, in the absence of, failing
Mangelware *f* scarce goods
Mangler *m* mangler
maniakalisch maniacal
Manier *f* fashion, manner
Manila-hanf *m* Manila hemp **-hanfseil** *n* Manila rope **-papier** *n* Manila paper
manipulieren to manipulate, handle
Manko *n* shortage, deficiency, deficit
Mann *m* man **an den ~ bringen** to sell
Männchen *n* whipstall, vertical stall, tail slide (aviation)
Mann-Einsteigloch *n* manhole
Mannesmannschrägwalzverfahren *n* Mannesmann roll-piercing process
Mannheimer Gold Mannheim gold
mannig-fach, -faltig manifold, varied
Mannigfaltigkeit *f* variety, diversity, multiplicity
männlich male
Mannloch *n* manhole, handhole, manhead **-boden** *m* manhole end plate **-bügel** *m* crossbar of the manhole
Mannlochdeckel *m* manhole cover **mit Bolzen befestigter ~** bolted manhole cover
Mannloch-deckelbehälter *m* manhole davit **-ver-**

schluß *m* manhole door **-versteifung** *f* manhole ring
Mannschaft *f* body of men, crew, team, gang, force
Manntau *n* life line, manrope **-sendseil** *n* drawing rope
Manograph *m* manograph
Manometer *n* pressure gauge, vacuum gauge **durch das ~ angezeigter Druck** manometer pressure
Manometerabsperrhahn mit Entlüftung pressure-gauge stopcock with air discharge
Manometeranschluß *m* pressure-gauge connection
Manometeraufnahme, drehbare ~ movable pressure-gauge connection
Manometer-dosensatz *m* manometer capsule **-druck** *m* gauge pressure **-feder** *f* pressure-gauge spring **-federrohr** *n* manometer elastic **-gehäuse** *n* pressure gauge case **-leitung** *f* gauge pipe **-prüfapparat** *m* pressure-gauge testing machine **-rohr** *n* tube of steam gauge **-stand** *m* pressure-gauge reading **-stutzen** *m* pressure-gauge tube **-ventil** *n* pressure-gauge valve **-zeiger** *m* pressure-gauge or manometer hand, pressure-gauge pointer
manometrisch manometric **-er Förderdruck** manometric pressure **-e Förderhöhe** manometric head or lifting, manometric delivery height
Manovakuum-messer *m* pressure vacuum gauge **-meter** *n* manometer vacuum gauge
Manöver *n* maneuver **-belastungsfaktor** *m* maneuvering load factor **-luftservomotor** *m* reversing-air servomotor **-pumpe** *f* reversing pump **-ventil** *n* maneuvering valve
Manövriereigenschaft *f* maneuvering capability
manövrieren to maneuver
Manövrier-ballast *m* ballast to throw overboard **-freiheit** *f* freedom of maneuver **-hebel** *m* starting handle **-stand** *m* operating platform control board **-unfähig** immobilized **-ventil** *n* gas valve (balloon)
Mansarde *f* drying loft
Mansarden-dach *n* mansard roof **-fenster** *n* dormer or attic window
Manschette *f* sleeve, collar, cuff, follower, (in butt welding of tubes) bell, packing ring, sealing member, rubber packing washer
Manschetten-dipol *m* sleeve dipole **-halter** *m* sleeve holder **-raum** *m* collar space
Mantel *m* overcoat; (Math.) convex surface; (Gießerei) cope; (Kabel) sheathing; (Muffe) sleeve; (Gehäuse) casing; (Ummantelung) jacket, shell; (Behälter) wall; (Elektrode) cover; (Geometrie) surface, sheet, case, covering, casing, sheath(ing), mantle, nappe, envelope, jacket (rocket) **~ der Schleuder** casing of the centrifugal **Kolben mit geteiltem ~** split-skirt-type piston **~** (Reifen) outer cover (tire) **nahtloser ~** seamless sheathing
Mantel-aufschlag *m* lapel **-außenoberfläche** *f* outer sidewall surface **-band** *n* hoop **-beugemaschine** *f* machine for bending casings **-blech** *n* metal sheet covering, shell plate **-boden** *m* jacket box **-daumen** *m* edge cam **-draht** *m* wrapped wire **-druck** *m* surface pressure **-düse** *f* cap jet **-elektrode** *f* coated or sheathed electrode, coated rod
Mantel-fläche *f* superficies, generated surface, shell, surface **-futter** *n* shell lining **-gehäuse** *n* shell **-gekühlt** jacket-cooled **-geschoß** *n* metallic cartridge **-gründung** *f* timber-and iron-cased concrete foundations **-haken** *m* coat peg **-heizung** *f* jacket heating **-holz** *n* wood cover **-kern** *m* shell core **-klappe** *f* tubular indicator **-knagge** *f* mantle corbel **-kopf** *m* end cap (jacket) **-korn** *n* protected front sight **-kühler** *m* shell-type cooler jacket cooler **-kühlung** *f* jacket ventilation, jacket cooling
Mantelkupfer *n* jacket copper **mit einem ~ versehen** copper-jacketed
Mantel-kurve *f* cylindrical cam **-kurvenfräsvorrichtung** *f* cylindrical cam-milling attachment **-leitungen** *pl* non-metallic sheathed wires and cables **-linie** *f* generatrix (of cylinder), surface line, directrix **-magnet** *m* pot magnet **-manschette** *f* blowout patch (tire) **-material** *n* blanket material **-pfahlgründung** *f* friction pile foundation **-prüfung** bulk test
Mantel-reibung *f* skin friction **-ring** *m* jacket ring **-ringrohr** *n* barrel of built-up gun **-riß** *m* surface crack **-rohr** *n* jacketed barrel, casing, tubular shell; (Autolenkung) outer column **-sack** *m* coat bag **-schneidzange** *f* sheath cutting pliers **-schraube** *f* enclosed or shrouded propeller; (Flugzeug) ducted fan **-sinus** *m* pallial sinus
Mantel-sprengstoff *m* sheathed explosive **-stauchprobe** *f* side wall crush test **-stromleitklappe** (Jet) *f* by-pass door **-stromtriebwerk** (Jet) *n* by-pass engine (turbojet) **-tarif** *m* skeleton agreement **-tiefe** *f* body length, ram jet, propeller shroud **-transformator** *m* shell-type or shielded transformer, ironclad transformer **-welle** *f* standing wave, wave on outer surface of coaxial cable, shell wave **-wirbelstrom** *m* sheath eddies (cable) **-zarge** *f* jacket rim
Mantisse *f* mantissa
Manual *n* field book, keyboard, manual
manuell manual **~ ausgelöster automatischer Ruf** semi-automatic ringing **-es Einsetzen** manual entry **-er Fallschirm** manually operated parachute
Manufakturwaren *pl* textile goods
Manuskript *n* scenario, script **-mappe** *f* manuscript cover **-verteiler** *m* copy cutter
Mappe *f* portfolio, leather wrapper, folder, catalogue
Mappeur *m* topographer
Mappierung *f* topographical survey
marbeln to marver, turn
Marengoeffekt *m* marengo effect
Margarinsäure *f* margaric acid
Margarit *m* margarite
Marginalnote *f* marginal note
Marienglas *n* isinglass, selenite, gypseous spar
Mariettaverfahren *n* Marietta process
Marine *f* marine, navy **-barometer** *n* marine barometer, ship's barometer **-küstenfunkstelle** *f* coastal naval radio station **-legierung** *f* Admiralty alloy **-normvorschrift** *f* navy-department specification **-peilfunkstelle** *f* navy radio-bearing station **-probe** *f* navy tear test (welding)
Marine-sender *m* naval transmitter **-signalstelle** *f* naval signal station **-station** *f* naval district or base **-werft** *f* navy yard **-wetterdienst** *m* naval meteorological

Mark *n* pith, heart, marrow, pulp, core

markant marked, striking

Markasit *m* marcasite, white iron pyrites **-glanz** *m* tetradymite

Marke *f* (Ablese-~) index mark; (Schutz-~) trade mark, brand; (Fabrik-~) brand, make, type; (Güte) sort, grade, quality, marking line, index line; mark, stamp, designation, type, kind, quality, beacon, mire, sentinel (comput), tag **kreisende** ~ circling mark **leuchtende** ~ illuminating mark **wandernde** ~ floating mark

marken to mark

Marken-artikel *m* branded product **-bezeichnung** *f* trade-mark, brand **-erzeugnis** *n* standard trade-marked merchandise **-faden** *m* identification thread **-feuchter** *m* stamp moistener **-glas** *n* branded lens **-(glas)platte** *f* registering (mark) plate **-kreuz** *n* pencilled cross on photograph used in collimation or plotting **-name** *m* trade name **-öl** *n* branded oil **-platte** *f* marking plate, index plate (of telescopic sight) **-ring** *m* graduated ring **-schutz** *m* trademark protection

Markenskala, schwebende ~ gliding mark scale

Marken-strich *m* index mark **-stück** *n* line-up stud (on gun), marking indicator **-viereck** *n* rectangle or quadrangle formed by points of collimation **-werkstoff** *m* branded material

Markerpeilfunk *m* radio-marker beacon

Markier-apparat *m* marking apparatus, marker **-bahn** (Speicher) *f* marker track **-dorn** *m* center marker **-einrichtung** *f* marking device

markieren to mark, beacon, sign, designate, brand, stamp, define, outline

Markierer-anschalterelais *n* marking connecting relay **-system** *n* marker system

Markier-kreise *pl* distance marks **-nadel** *f* scribing needle **-nägel** *pl* surveyers' steel wire arrows **-pfahl** *m* marking post, peg **-stab** *m* marking staff

markiertes Atom labeled atom, tagged atom

Markierung *f* marking, designation, delimitation, beaconing, signaling, tap, label (info proc.) **genaue** ~ accurate range marker

Markierungs-bake *f* marker beacon **-differenz** *f* rate of change **-experiment** *n* tagging experiment **-fenster** *n* strobe **-feuer** *n* marker beacon **-generator** *m* range marker generator

Markierungskreise *pl*, **eingesägte** ~ serrated range rings

Markierungs-landkarte *f* survey map **-leuchte** *f* flare **-linien** *pl* cursor lines **-scheibe** *f* disk marker **-sender** *m* marker beacon **-spalte** *f* marking column **-strich** *m* mark **-verbindung** *f* tagging compound **-vorrichtung** *f* marker, puncher, notcher (motion pictures)

Markierzahlengeberlampe (ZM) *f* marking key-sender pilot lamp

Markise *f* blind, awning, marquee

Mark-pfahl *m* boundary post **-röhre** *f* medullary tube **-scheide** *f* border, boundary **-scheidegerät** *n* inclinometer, mine-surveying instrument **-scheideinstrument** *n* mine-survey instrument, mining theodolite, mining dial

markscheiden to dial, survey underground

Mark-scheiden *n* surveying underground **-scheider** *m* mine surveyor, (land) surveyor **-scheideriß** *m* plot of a mine

Markscheider-steiger *m* assistant mine surveyor **-zeug** *n* mine-surveying appliances

Mark-scheidewesen *n* mine surveying **-scheidung** *f* boundary demarcation **-stab** *m* marking stick **-stein** *m* boundary stone, milestone, landmark **-strahl** *m* medullary ray, transverse septum **-strang** *m* medullary cord **-zelle** *f* medullary cell

Markt *m* market **auf den** ~ **bringen** to put on the market, offer for sale

Marktbericht *m* marketing report

Markteil *m* calibration unit

markt-fähig marketable **-gängig** commercial, marketable, current **-halle** *f* covered market **-lage** *f* trade, transaction, market (condition) **-kurs** *m* market quotations **-platz** *m* market place **-tasche** *f* shopping bag

Markung *f* marking

Marleisen *n* marlinespike

marlen to marl, marl down

Marl-leine *f* marline **-pfriem** *m* marlinespike **-spieker** *m* marling-spike

Marmor *m* marble

marmorieren to vein, marble

Marmorpapier *n* marbled or stained paper **getupftes** ~ marbled paper made by tipping

Marmor-platte *f* marble plate or slab **-schalttafel** *f* marble switchboard **-schnitt** *m* marbled edge **-tafel** *f* marble slab

Marocainpapier *n* morocco paper

Mars *m* mars **-bezug** *m* top cover

Marsch *m* march

Marsch *f* marsh

Marsch-antrieb *m* propulsion system (of spacecraft) **-boden** marshy soil or land **-kompaß** *m* prismatic compass **-länge** *f* road space **-leistung** *f* marching capacity **-raketenmotor** *m* sustainer motor (g/m) **-triebwerk** *n* sustainer (missiles, rockets), cruise engine

Mars-fall *n* topsail halyard **-gelb** *n* Mars yellow **-oberfläche** *f* Martian surface

Martensit *m* martensite **nadeliger** ~ acicular martensite

Martens-Ritzprobe *f* Martens surface-scratching test

Martin-entschlacker *m* Martin clinker ejector **-flußeisen** *n* open-hearth iron **-flußstahl** *m* open-hearth steel

Martinofen *m* (Siemens-)Martin furnace, Siemens (regenerative) furnace, open-hearth (steel) furnace **-anlage** *f* Siemens-Martin plant, open-hearth plant **-betrieb** *m* open-hearth practice or plant **-schlacke** *f* open-hearth cinder

Martin-prozeß *m* (Siemens-)Martin process, open-hearth process **-roheisen** *n* open-hearth pig (iron)

Martinstahl *m* open-hearth steel, Martin steel **-hütte** *f* Siemens-Martin steelworks, open-hearth steelworks **-ofen** *m* open-hearth steel furnace

Martin-verfahren *n* (Siemens-)Martin process, open-hearth process **-werk** *n* open-hearth shop

Masche *f* mesh, aperture, interstice, ore compartment, stitch ~ **eines Kabelnetzes** single cable (main, feeder, branch, or interoffice link) in a cable network

Maschen-anode *f* meshed anode **-bildung** *f* looping

-draht *m* wire mesh, wire netting, screen wire **-drahtabdeckung** *f* wire-mesh screen **-drahtzaun** *m* wire-mesh fence **-filter** *n* gauze filter **-geflecht** *n* wire mesh

Maschenleger *m* loop wheel **-rückstreifer** *m* repusher of loop wheel

Maschen-netz *n* meshed network, interconnected network, wire mesh **-netzschalter** *m* network protector **-prüfung** *f* stitch-counting **-rad** *n* looping wheel **-sieb** *n* mesh sieve, mesh screen **-weite** *f* screen aperture, mesh aperture, mesh size **-werk** *n* meshed network **-zähler** *m* stitch glass

maschig meshed, netted, reticulated

Maschine *f* machine, (steam) engine, airplane, car **~ für zweiseitigen Druck** duplex printing machine **~ zum Herstellen der Wulstringe** bead-winding machine **~ zum Zerschneiden von Gummiballen** balesplitting press **die ~ andrehen** to crank the engine **spanabhebende ~** planing or metal-cutting machine **Maschinen des Pilieraggregats** pulverizing machine (makes pellets) **~ mit Selbsterregung** self-excited machine **mit Maschinen bearbeiten, mit Maschinen herstellen** to machine

maschinell mechanical **-e Bearbeitung** machining **-e Einrichtung** mechanical equipment **-er Vorschub** mechanical, automatic **-er Vor- und Rücklauf** mechanical advance and return movement

Maschinen-abdampf *m* exhaust steam **-abnahme** *f* inspection prior to despatch **-abzug** *m* machine proof **-anlage** *f* plant, machine unit **-anordnung** *f* arragement of engines

Maschinenantrieb *m* machine drive **mit ~** machine driven

Maschinen-arbeit *f* machine work **-arbeiter** *m* machinist **-ausführung** *f* machine type **-auslösung** *f* mechanical disengagement **-auswertung** *f* machine plotting **-backenbohrer** *m* machine master tap **-backengewindebohrer** *m* tap for cutting machine dies **-band für Druckereien** printing machine web

Maschinenbau *m* machine construction, machine-building industry, constructional engineering, engine building, engineering construction **-anstalt** *f* mechanical engineering institute, engineering works **-guß** *m* castings for machinery building

Maschinen-bauer *m* machine or engine builder, mechanical engineer, machinist, manufacturer of machinery **-bäumer** *m* beaming-machine minder **-baustahl** *m* structural steel **-befehl** *m* computer instruction **-belastung** *f* machine load **-belegung** *f* machine assignment, load planning **-beleuchtung** *f* dynamo lighting **-betrieb** *m* mechanical operation **-betriebsführer** *m* engineer

Maschinenbett *n* bench **auf Füßen ruhendes ~** bench

Maschinen-bogen *m* machine proof **-bohrer** *m* machine tap **-bolzen** *m* machine bolt **-bütte** *f* machine chest **-büttenpapier** *n* mold-made paper **-charakteristik** *f* speed-load characteristic **-druck** *m* machine impression **-einheit** *f* machine unit **-einrichtung** *f* tooling **-einstellung** *f* setup

Maschinenelement *n* machine element **~ das einen Impuls erteilt** impeller

Maschinen-fabrik *f* engine works, factory for constructing machines, engineering works **-falzung** *f* machine folding **-fertig** machine-finished **-fett** *n* lubricant **-formerei** *f* molding-machine work **-führer** *m* engine driver, machinist **-gearbeitet** machine-made **-geber** *m* automatic transmitter **-geräusch** *n* generator hum **-gestell** *n* bedplate, frame of the machine, engine bed **-gestrichen** machine-coated **-getrocknetes Papier** *n* cylinder-dried paper

Maschinen-gitter *n* machine guard **-glatt** mill-finished **-gleichung** *f* machine equation **-gondel** *f* engine car **-gruppenbedienung** *f* machine battery attention **-grau** machine gray **-graukarton** *m* chip board **-guß** *m* machine casting **-halle** *f* engine room **-hammer** *m* power hammer **-haspel** *f* winch

Maschinenhaus *n* powerhouse, power station, machinery house, enginehouse **-kran** *m* power house crane

Maschinen-hefter *m* machine stitcher or sewer **-höhenmesser** *m* engine altimeter **-holzkarton** *m* wood board **-holzpappe** *f* machine pulp board **-ingenieur** *m* mechanical engineer **-kammer** *f* engine compartment, engine room **-karren** *m* engine cart **-kartierung** *f* machine plotting **-konstrukteur** *m* machine designer **-koordinatensystem** *n* coordinate system in plotting machines **-körper** *m* engine

Maschinen-lageröl *n* bearing oil **-läppen** to machine-lap **-läppschliff** *m* machine lapped finish **-laufzeit** *f* machine time **-lehre** *f* engineering **-leistung** *f* mechanical power (output) **-leuchte** *f* lighting equipment **-masse** *f* metal mass of the engine **-mäßig** mechanical, automatic **-maßstab** *m* scale of the (plotting) machine **-mischung** *f* machine mixing, mechanical mixing

Maschinenmuttergewindebohrer *m* machine-nut tap **~ mit langem Schaft** tapper tap **~ mit langem gebogenem Schaft** bent-shank tapper tap

Maschinen-öl *n* machine or engine oil, lubricating oil **-paginierer** *m* numbering-machine operator **-park** *m* stock of engines **-periode** *f* machine cycle **-personal** *n* engineering personnel **-pistole** *f* automatic pistol, machine pistol, submachine gun **-platte** *f* frame **-programm** *n* routine (info proc.) **-programmierung** *f* machine programming **-raum** *m* enginehouse, engine room **-rechnen** *n* comptometry **-regulator** *m* (engine) governor

Maschinenreibahle *f* machine reamer, chucking reamer **~ mit aufgeschraubten Messern** adjustable-blade chucking reamer

Maschinen-retusche *f* machine retouching **-säge** *f* power saw **-satz** *m* engine or power unit or set, power plant or unit, motor or field generator, machine composition, generating unit **-schacht** *m* engine or rod shaft **-schere** *f* shearing machine **-schlosser** *m* fitter, engine fitter, machinist **-schmierer** *m* engine lubricator or greaser **-schnüre** *pl* machine cords **-schraube** *f* machine screw **-schraubstock** *m* vise

Maschinenschreiben *n* typing, typewriting **blindes ~** touch typewriting

Maschinen-schreiber *m* typist **-schrift** *f* typewriting **-schrott** *m* machine scrap **-schweißung** *f* automatic weld **-seite** *f* pushing side, pusher side **-sender** *m* alternator transmitter, machine or automatic transmitter, automatic transmission **-setzer** *m* machine compositor (print) **-sieb** *n* wire cloth **-sockel** *m* engine base

Maschinen-spindel *f* machine spindle **-sprache** *f* hardware representation, machine language **-ständer** *m* column, upright **-stärke** *f* efficiency of engine **-steuerwerk** *n* engine controls **-stirnreibahle** *f* straight cut or special end mill **-strom** *m* machine current **-tagebuch** *n* engine-room log

Maschinenteil *m* machine member or part, machinery casting **arbeitender ~** moving parts

Maschinen-telegraph *m* engine order telegraph (shipboard), automatic telegraph, machine telegraph **-torf** *m* excavated peat **-transformator** *m* unit-connected transformer **-typ** *m* type of machine **-übersetztes Programm** object program **-umformer** *m* converter **-wählersystem** *n* machine switching system **-wärter** *m* operator, attendant, machinist **-welle** *f* machine shaft

Maschinen-werkstatt *f* machine shop **-werkzeug** *n* machine tool **-wert** *m* machine-value **-wesen** *n* mechanical engineering **-wirkzeit** *f* machine-available time **-zahlengeber** *m* pulse machine **-zapfenschneider** *m* tenoning machinist **-zeichnen** *n* mechanical drawing **-zeit** *f* actual running time **-zug** *m* machine platoon, set of machines **-zusammenbau** *m* unit construction

Maschinerie *f* machinery

maschinieren to machine

Maschinist *m* machinist, engine operator or attendant, engineman, engineer rating

MASD (Methylammonium-Aluminiumsulfat-Dekahydrat), **antiferro-elektrisches ~** antiferroelectric MASD

Maser *m* speckle, spot, mark

Maser *f* maser (microwave amplification by simulated emission of radiation)

MASER (Molekularverstärker durch angeregte Strahlungsabgabe) Maser (molecular amplification by stimulated emission of radiation

Maserholz *n* grained wood

maserig speckled, streaked, veined, grained, spotted

masern to vein, grain, speckle

Maserpapier *n* mottled paper

Maserung *f* veining, graining, streaking, grain, periodical flame effect

Maske *f* mask, gas mask, camouflage, screen, face shield mat (in film recording), matte (film recording)

Masken-bedampfung *f* metalizing with masks **-brecher** *m* respirator penetrant **-formverfahren** *n* shell molding process **-loch** *n* shadow mask hole (TV) **-spanner** *m* face form

maskieren to mask, screen, camouflage, conceal, cover, eclipse

Maskierung *f* camouflage, screen, masking

Maß *n* (Abmessung) dimension; (Messung) measurement; (Größe) size; (Menge) volume, quantity; (Ausmaß) degree, extent; (Werturteil) criterion, standard; (Lehre) gauge; (Lineal) rule; (Verhältnis) proportion rate; (Ausdehnung) extent, dimension; (Grad) degree; (Mäßigung) moderation; measure, index, rate, percentage, unit, equivalent, manner, scale **auf ~ drehen** to turn true (to template or gauge) **~ eintragen** to letter **eingeschriebenes ~** figured dimension **auf genaues ~ bringen** to true up, finish to template, finish to gauge **laufendes ~** linear measure **volles ~** finishing size **auf ~ ziehen** to draw to size **in höherem Maße** to a larger or fuller extent **mit gleichem Maße meßbar** commensurable

Maßabweichung *f* off-size condition, dimensional discrepancy or difference **zulässige ~** tolerance

Maß-analyse *f* volumetric analysis, quantitative analysis **-analytisch** titrimetric (volumetric) **-änderung** *f* change in dimension, change in size **-angabe** *f* dimension **-band** *n* measuring tape, line

Maßbegrenzung *f* indicator **sehr feine ~** hairline indicator

Maß-beständigkeit *f* dimensional stability **-bestimmung** *f* metric determination, mensuration **-blatt** *n* table of specifications or dimensions **-dimensional** dimensional

Masse *f* mass, matter, bulk, substance, batch, composition stock, dry sand, pulp, material, quantity, compound, composition **~ des Pendels** ball weights **~ für Wärmeisolation** insulating material **aktive ~** active paste **magnetische ~** magnetic substance **scheinbare ~** effective mass

Masse *f* (elektr.) earth (ground) connection **in großem Maße** on a large scale **in hohem ~** in a very large measure **~ der Leitungen** line sizes

Masseanschluß *m* earth or ground connection **-klemme** *f* earth(ing) terminal **-kohle** *f* ground carbon

Masseband *n* earth(ing) strap

Massebehälter für die Kabelherstellung compound tank for cable manufacturing

Masse-bolzen *m* earth(ing) pin **-bürste** *f* ground(ing) brush

Masseelektrode *f* ground electrode **drahtförmige ~ einer Zündkerze** ground wire of a plug

Masse-Energie-Äquivalenz *f* mass-energy equivalence

Masse-Energie-Beziehung *f* mass-energy relation

Masse-felder *pl* pastilles, pasted squares **-form** *f* dry-sand mold **-formerei** *f* sand molding **-frei** not grounded (radio)

Maßeinheit *f* unit (of measure) **abgeleitete ~** derived unit (of measure) **absolute ~** absolute unit **ohne gemeinsame ~** incommensurable

Maß-einteilung *f* graduation **-eintragen** *n* lettering

Masse-kabel *n* impregnated cable **-kern** *m* (dust) core, magnetic core, compressed-iron-powder core, molded core **-kernspule** *f* iron-dust-core coil, iron-cored coil, compressed-iron-core coil **-klemme** *f* earth (ground) terminal **-kontaktwinkel** *m* ground connecting angle

Massel *f* pig, shrink head, settling head, feedhead, feeder, feeding gate, header, deadhead **-bett** *n* pig bed **-brecher** *m* pig breaker **-eisen** *n* pig iron

Masseleitung *f* ground or earth wire

Massel-form *f* pig mold **-gießmaschine** *f* pig-casting machine, pig machine **-graben** *m* sow **-kammodell** *n* pig-bed pattern **-strang** *m* pig strand, pig string **-transportkran** *m* pig handling crane **-verladebrücke** *f* pig iron handling bridge

Massen *pl*, **hin- und hergehende ~** reciprocating parts **tote ~** dead weights

Massen-absorption *f* mass absorption **-absorp-**

tionskoeffizient *m* mass coefficient of absorption **-analyse** *f* routine analysis, routine method **-anfertigung** *f* mass production **-angriff** *m* massed attack, massive raid **-anschluß** *m* ground connection, earthing **-anziehung** *f* gravitation **-anziehungsgesetz** *n* law of gravity **-artikel** *pl* wholesale articles, articles in bulk **-auflage** *f* mass edition **-ausgleich** *m* balancing of the masses, mass equilibrium, counterbalance, mechanical balance **-ausgleichgewichte** *pl* counterbalance weights **-auslese** *f* mass selection

Massen-belegung *f* mass coverage, weight per unit area **-berechnung** *f* mensuration of earthwork, computation of quantities **-bestimmung** *f* mass assignment **-bildung** *f* formation of masses **-bremsvermögen** *n* mass stopping power **-defekt** *m* mass defect or deficiency (physics) **-dichte** *f* mass density **-einheit** *f* unit of mass **-einteilungsmaschine** *f* graduating machine **-ermittlung** *f* determination of mass **-erzeugung** *f* quantity production **-fabrikation** *f* quantity production, mass production **-fertigung** *f* mass production

massenfeste Ableitung material derivative

Massen-filter *n* filtration plant **-förderung** *f* bulk conveyance, mass conveyance **-form** *f* dry-sand mold **-formel** *f* mass formula **-gesteine** *pl* unstratified rocks **-güter** *pl* bulk goods, large-scale manufactured goods **-gutumschlagsanlagen** *pl* bulk handling equipment **-guß** *m* duplicate casting **-herstellung** *f* mass production, quantity production **-klemme** *f* earth terminal, earthing terminal **-kopie** *f* release print, quantity production of prints

Massenkorrektur *f* mass correction ~ **für Austausch** exchange mass correction

Massenkraft *f* force due to inertia, force due to gravity **-momente** *pl* moments of force

Massen-lötung *f* brazing of duplicate work **-mäßig** quantitative **-mittelpunkt** *m* center of inertia or of mass **-moment** *n* moment of intertia, rotational inertia **-produktion** *f* mass production, quantity production **-profil** *n* section of earthworks **-punkt** *m* mass point, particle, quantum, rotator, center of mass, center of inertia, centroid **-renormierung** *f* mass renormalization **-schwächungskoeffizient** *m* mass attenuation coefficient, mass-extinction coefficient **-schwankungskoeffizient** *m* mass absorption coefficient **-schwerpunkt** *m* mass center **-schwungrad** *n* solid flywheel

Massen-spektrograph *m* mass spectrograph, mass spectrometer **-spektrometisch** mass spectrometric **-spektrum** *n* mass spectrum **-störung** *f* derangement of masses, line faults **-strahler** *m* mass radiator **-streukoeffizient** *m* mass-scattering coefficient **-strom** *m* mass flow **-strömungsdichte** *f* mass flow **-synchrometer** *m* mass synchrometer **-teil** *n* mass-produced part **-teilchen** *n* molecule, mass element, corpuscle **-telegraph** *m* high-capacity telegraph **-trägheit** *f* mass moment of inertia **-trägheitsmoment** *n* inertia moment **-trennung** *f* mass separation

Massen-übergang *m* mass transfer **-übergangszahl** *f* mass transfer coefficient **-umsetzungsgeschwindigkeit** *f* mass conversion velocity **-verhältnis** *n* mass or weight ratio **-verlust** *m* mass decrement **-verriegelung** *f* mass-locking **-verteilung** *f* mass distribution

Massenverteilungen gleicher Trägheitsmomente equimomental mass distribution

Massen-voltameter *n* weight voltmeter **-ware** *f* production goods **-wert** *m* nuclear mass **-widerstand** *m* inertness, composition resistor **-wirkung** *f* mass action, influence of mass **-wirkungsgesetz** *n* law of mass action **-zahl** *f* nucleon number, mass number **-zentrum** *n* center of mass, center of inertia, centroid **-zustrom** *m* agglomeration

Masse-platte *f* pasted plate, mass-type plate **-pol** *m* earth pole **-rückleitung** *f* return line (or circuit) **-schiene** *f* grounding strap **-schluß** *m* earth short circuit **-schlußkohle** *f* ground carbon **-schraube** *f* earth (ground) screw

Masseteilchengeschwindigkeit *f* particle velocity

Masse-verbindung *f* earth connection **-walze** *f* composition roller **-widerstand** *m* composite resistor

Maß-faktor *m* dimensional constant, dimensional factor **-fehler** *m* dimension error **-flasche** *f* measuring flask **-flüssigkeit** *f* standard solution **-formel** *f* standard formula

Maßgabe *f*, **nach ~ von** in proportion to, in accordance with

maßgebend authoritative, governing, leading, decisive, determining, deciding, basic, competent, ruling, standard, restrictive **-er Faktor** determinative factor **-e Leitung** controlling circuit

Maß-gebung *f* measurement **-gefäß** *n* measuring vessel, graduated vessel **-genauigkeit** *f* true measurement **-gerecht** accurate to size of gauge, true to size **-gitter** *n* measuring grid **-glas** *n* graduated cylinder, measuring (cylinder) glass **-gleich** isometric **-halten** to keep within bounds or dimensions **-haltig** true to size or measure **-haltigkeit** *f* accuracy to gauge, accuracy to size

Massicot *n* litharge

massieren to mass (troops or weapons), massage

massig voluminous, bulky, molar, massive

mäßig moderate, temperate

mäßigen to temper, mitigate, allay, moderate

Mäßigkeit *f* moderation

mäßigster Preis modest cost

Mäßigung *f* moderation, mitigation

Massiv solid, massive, strong, molar **-decke** *f* reinforced-concrete floor **-schaufel** *f* solid blade blade **-wand** *f* solid wall

Maß-kanne *f* a measure equal to 1.069 liters **-kasten** *m* gaugebox **-ketten** *pl* chain tapes **-kontrolle** *f* gauging **-kunde** *f* metrology **-latte** *f* gauge **-lehre** *f* measuring gauge **-linie** *f* dimension line **-los** boundless **-lösung** *f* volumetric (usually standard) solution

Maß-nahme *f* measure, step, preventive measure, restriction measuring or graduated tube, burette **-nehmen** *n* taking measurements **-norm** *f* size **-ordnung** *f* system of measurement **-prüfung** *f* check of dimensions **-regel** *f* step, measure, expedient **-röhre** *f* measuring tube, graduated tube, burette **-scheibe** *f* graduate dial **-skizze** *f* dimensional outline, scale drawing

Maßstab *m* rule, scale, measure, rate, standard, size, criterion, representative fraction, gauge, proportion **Ausführung im kleinen ~** scaled-down version **mittlerer ~** mean scale **natürlicher**

~ plain scale, full size **perspektivischer ~** scenographical scale **verjüngter ~** reduced scale **in verkleinertem ~** scaled down, on a reduced scale **wilder ~** undefined scale, not to scale **zusammenlegbarer ~** (folding) pocket rule

Maßstab-beiwert *m* scale factor **-differenz** *f* difference of scale **-druck** *m* impression according to scale **-einfluß** *m* scale effect

maßstabgerecht in correct scale **-es Modell** *n* scale model

Maßstab-größe *f* scale size **-höhe** *f* scale height

maßstäblich full scale or size, according to scale **~ ändern** to scale **~ verkleinern** to scale down **~ zeichnen** to draw to scale **-es Modell** scale model

Maßstab-maschine *f* machine for making rules **-transformator** *m* gauge (group) transformer **-zahl** *f* scale number, measure or numerical criterion

Maß-stock *m* gauge, yardstick, (linear) measure, rule **-system** *n* system of measuring **-teil** *m* volumetric part **-teilung** *f* graduation **-theorie** *f* measure theory **-theoretische Behandlung** measure theoretical approach **-toleranz** *f* variation in dimension, tolerance in size

Maß- und Gewichtsnorm *f* standard gauge

Maßveränderung *f* change in scale or measure **gesättigte adiabatische ~** saturated adiabatic lapse rate

Maß-verkörperung *f* embodiment of a measure **-voll** reasonable **-walze** *f* sizing roll **-walzwerke** *pl* sizing mill **-zahl** *f* coefficient of measure **-zeichnung** *f* dimensional (dimensioned) or outline drawing

Mast *m* mast, pole, post, pylon, tower **abgespannter ~** stayed mast, guyed mast **freitragender ~** tower, self-supporting mast **umlegbarer ~** dismountable mast

Mast *f* fattening (pasture)

Mast-ankopplung *f* mast link **-armatur** *f* pole hardware, fittings **-baum** *m* mast **-befeuerung** *f* mast beacon **-blitzableiter** *m* lightning conductor for poles **-bügel** *m* mast hoop **-ducht** *f* mast or main thwart

mästen to fatten, cram

Mastenkran *m* guyed derrick

Mast-falte *f* fat-wrinkel crease **-feld** *n* span **-fernrohr** *n* large observation telescope on special mount, giant periscope **-fesselgeschirr** *n* mast-mooring gear **-fesselpunkt** *m* mast mooring point **-fundament** *n* pole foundation, mast foundation **-fuß** *m* pedestal, pole footing, mast base **-halterung** *f* mast support

Mastikator *m* masticator

Mastix *m* mastic **-firnis** *f* mastic varnish **-harz** *n* mastic (mastix)

mastizieren to masticate

Mast-käfig *m* fattening stable **-karren** *m* mast cart **-keil** *m* mast wedge **-kraftwagen** *m* antenna truck

Mastkran *m*, **schwimmender ~** pontoon or floating shears

Mast-lager *n* mast bearing **-leine** *f* mast line **-schalter** *m* pole switch **-schelle** *f* pole strap **-schlagen** *n* mast rapping **-seil** *n* mast line **-signal** *n* block signaling apparatus **-sockel** *m* base of pole **-spitze** *f* top of pole, masthead **-spur** *f* mast step **-stütze** *f* mast prop for careening **-toppe** *m* mast head **-wagen** *m* radio-mast truck **-zelle** *f* mast cell

Mästung *f* fattening

Mastwurf *m* clove hitch

Masut *m* petroleum spirit, fuel oil (Russian), mazout

Masuyit *m* masuyite

Mater *f* matrix

Material *n* matter, substance, material, equipment, matériel, stock **entgegenstehendes ~** anticipatory references **kürzeres ~** short staple **plastisches ~** plastic **rollendes ~** rolling stock **zertrümmerbares ~** fissionable or disintegrable substance

Material-abnahme *f* acceptance of material, stock removal **-abrechnung** *f* material accounting **-anforderung** *f* requisition for supplies **-anschlag** *m* stock stop **-antrieb** *m* surface drive **-aufteillehre** *f* finishing allowance equalizing gauge **-ausnutzung** *f* material economy **-auswahlproblem** *n* compatibility problem

Material-beanspruchung *f* material. stress **-belastung** *f* material load **-einsatz** *m* hold-up **-ermüdung** *f* fatigue of material **-fehler** *m* material defect **-festigkeit** *f* tensile strength **-fluß** *m* flow of material **-gleichung** *f* constitutive equation

Materialien-depot *n* supply depot **-verhältnis** *n* material balance

Material-konstante *f* matter constant **-nachschub** *m* stock feed **-prüfmaschine** *f* material-testing machine **-prüfung** *f* inspection of material, testing of material **-prüfungsanstalt** *f* materials testing institute **-spannung** *f* strain or tension **-trägerplatte** *f* carrier plate **-turm für Reifengewebe** batch turret for tire fabrics

Material-verbrauch *m* consumption of materials **-verknappung** *f* material shortage **-verwaltung** *f* stock records, depot administration **-vorrat** *m* material inventory **-vorschub** *m* automatic stock feed **-vorschubvorrichtung** *f* stock-feeding device **-vorräte** *pl* materials stocks **-wanderung** *f* flow or creep of material **-wölbung** *f* material buckling

Materie *f* matter, material

materiefest material

materiell material

materienlos devoid of physically interfering substances (electronics) **-e Sonde** electronic or light probe

Materie-strahlen *pl* corpuscular rays **-teilchen** *n* constituent particle **-welle** *f* matter, electron, phase or associated wave **-zertrümmerbarkeit** *f* disintegrability

matern to mold (a flong)

Matern *pl* matrices (matrix) **-trockenapparat** *m* flong dying apparatus

Mathematik *f* mathematics

Mathematiker *m* mathematician

mathematisch mathematical **~ genau** rigorously corroect **-e Begriffsbildung** mathematical concepts **-e Darstellung** mathematical representation **-e Erdkunde** geodesy, geophysics, mathematical geography **-er Satz** mathematical composition **-e Strenge** mathematical rigor

Matratzen-antenne *f* beam antenna **-turm** *m* radome

matrisieren to damp (paper)

Matrix *f* matrix **-schreibweise** *f* matrix notation

-speicher *m* matrix memory
Matrize *f* matrix, (bottom) die, stencil, mold, dry mat, female piece, metal master, master negative ~ **für Feinzug** sizing die
Matrizen *pl* female, grooved, or positive collars **-anschlag** *m* movable key **-backe** *f* matrix positioning jaw **-feilmaschine** *f* die filing machine **-fräsmaschine** *f* die-sinking machine **-funktion** *f* matrix function **-gleitschiene** *f* matrix guide **-karte** *f* master card **-karton** *m* brush matrix, flong
Matrizen-marken *pl* die marks **-papier** *n* brush matrix **-prägepresse** *f* matrix striking press, matrix embossing press **-richtlineal** *n* matrix adjusting plate **-speicher** *m* matrix storage **-technik** *f* die-matrix technique **-untersatz** *m* die (print) **-walze** *f* lower or bottom roll **-zentrierhebel** *m* matrix centering lever
Matrose *m* sailor
Matsch *m* sludge
matchen to pulp
matt dull, dead, mat, unpolished, cool (iron), feeble, weak, dim, exhausted ~ **verchromt** dull chrome plated ~ **satiniert** matt calendered ~ **vernickelt** dim-nickel-plated **-es Glas** *n* ground glass
Matt-abzug *m* dull-finish print **-anstrich** *m* lusterless paint **-blech** *n* terneplate, pickled sheet metal **-brenne** *f* mat pickle (met.), matte dip **-brennen** *n* dull pickling **-dekatur** *f* dull finish **-druck** *m* mat impression
Matte *f* mat
Matteisen *n* white pig (iron)
matten to dull
Mattendamm *m* mat dike **-preßverfahren** *n* mat molding **-rahmen** *m* matting frame **-zeug** *n* matting
matt-geschliffen ground, frosted, delustered, matted **-glanz** *m* dull finish **-glas** *n* ground glass, frosted glass **-gold** *n* dead gold
Mattheit *f* dullness
mattierbar tarnishable
Mattierbrenne *f* mat pickle (met.)
mattieren to deaden, dull, tarnish, frost, mat, grind (glass)
mattiert matted, dulled, satin-finished **-e Lampe** frosted lamp
Mattierung *f* frosting, tarnishing, dulling, matting
Mattierungs-messung *f* film-polish measurement, glossimetric measurement **-mittel** *n* delusterant, delustering agent
Mattigkeit *f* tiredness
Matt-kohle *f* dull-coal, durain **-kunstdruckpapier** *n* mat-surface paper **-lack** *m* mat varnish **-machen** to deluster
Matt-punze *f* tarnisher **-rot** dull-red **-salz** *n* matting salt
Mattscheibe *f* ground-glass plate, ground or frosted glass, mat lighting, light thrown on the base of clouds or smoke screen by searchlight, dimmer (elec.)
Mattscheiben-bild *n* ground-glass image **-ebene** *f* focal plane **-fenster** *n* ground-glass or frosted glass window **-sucher** *m* ground-glass view finder **-überdeckungsregler** *m* ground glass overlap regulator
matt-schleifen to make opaque by grinding **-vergoldung** *f* dead gilding **-schweiße** *f* scabs **-weiß** off-white **-weißblech** *n* terne plates **-zurichtung** *f* mat finish
Mauer *f* (masonry) wall **ausgebauchte** ~ battering or shrinking wall **einhäuptige** ~, **einseitig abgeglichene** ~ wall with one side worked fair **fliegende** ~ spandrel wall **fluchtlose** ~ slovenly built wall **gezinnelte** ~ battled or embattled wall **schwebende** ~ spandrel wall
Mauer-abdeckung *f* capping, coping, top course **-anker** *m* wall clamp **-block** *m* block (of masonry) **-bohrer** *m* stone drill **-brüstung** *f* cornice **-bügel** *m* short tubular pole affixed to walls for carrying wires on façades, wall bracket **-damm** *m* brickwork dam **-deckplatte** *f* capping, coping, top course **-durchführung** *f* wall channel (elec.) **-einsturz** *m* fall, failure, or destruction of a wall
Mauer-feld *n* pane of a wall **-flucht** *f* wall line or face **-isolator** *m* wall insulator **-kanal** *m* wall channel **-kasten** *m* built-in wall-box frame **-klammer** *f* clamp iron for walls **-kranz** *m* capping (of wall) **-lager** *n* wall-bracket bearing **-latte** *f* wall plate **-mantel** *m* mantle or outer stack of a wall
mauern to brick (up)
Mauer-nagel *m* tile pin **-rohr** *n* reed, thatch **-salz** *n* calcium acetate **-schwenkkran** *m* wall crane, bracket jib crane **-sockel** *m* pedestal (of a lantern) **-stein** *m* building stone, brick **-stütze** *f* wall bracket **-träger** *m* short tubular pole affixed to walls for carrying wires on façades
Mauerung *f* bricking walling
Mauerwerk *n* masonry, brickwork ~ **in Polygonverband** snail screep ~ **von behauenen Steinen** dressed-stone masonry
Mauke *f* malanders
mauken to ferment, digest
Maul *n* bit, chap, jaw ~ **des Steuersackes** lobe, baglike extension on the stern of a fixed balloon
Maul-schere *f* crocodile shears **-schlüssel** *m* fixed spanner **-tiefe** *f* depth of throat
Maulweite *f* interpolar distance, air gap (of horseshoe magnet), open-size (of wrench) ~ **des Schraubenschlüssels** opening of the screw spanner, spanner clearance
Maurer *m* mason, bricklayer **-kelle** *f* trowel
Maut *f* toll, duty
maximal maximum ~ **zulässiger Ablesewert** full-scale value ~ **zulässige Betriebsspannung** nominal circuit voltage ~ **zulässiger Betriebsstrom** rated temperature-rise current
maximal-er Ausschlag maximum deviation **-e Aussteuerung des Lichtstrahles** clash point of light valve (in sound recording) **-e Beladung, -e Belastung** maximum load **-e Brenngeschwindigkeit** maximum combustion velocity **-er Kurzschlußstrom** peak cathode fault current
Maximal-amplitude *f* maximum amplitude **-ausbeute** *f* maximum output **-ausschalter** *m* overload circuit breaker, maximum cutout **-automat** *m* maximum automatic device (elec.) **-druck** *m* maximum pressure **-fehler** *m* maximum error **-feld** *n* maximum area **-gefälle** *n* greatest gradient
Maximal-länge *f* maximum length **-melder** *m* maximum alarm (tele.) **-peilung** *f* maximum signal (strength) method (direction finding)

-skalenwert *m* maximum scale value **-spannung** *f* maximum voltage, highest pressure **-spannungsrelais** *n* overload relay **-strom** *m* maximum current **-wert** *m* maximum value **-wertigkeit** *f* maximum valence

Maximum *n* maximum, peak (of a curve) **~ des Beugungsspektrums** diffraction spectrum maximum **~ an Weiß** white peak **Maximum-zu-Maximum Verhältnis** peak-to-valley ratio

Maximum-anzeiger *m* demand attachment **-durchschnittswölbung** *f* maximum mean camber **-peilverfahren** *n* Robinson direction-finding system **-pferdekraft** *f* maximum horsepower **-wertzeiger** *m* peak indicator, crest indicator **-zähler** *m* maximum demand indicator

Maxwell *n* maxwell **-anordnung** *f* shunted condenser, reading condenser **-erde** *f* Maxwell earth **-schaltung** *f* shunted condenser, reading condenser

Maxwell-sche Gleichungen Maxwell's equations **-sche Grundgleichungen** Maxwell's electromagnetic equations **-sches Gesichtsfeld** Maxwellian view

Maxwellverteilung *f* Maxwell (statistical) distribution

Mazeration *f* maceration

mazerieren to macerate

Mechanik *f* mechanics, mechanism

Mechaniker *m* mechanic(ian) **-drehbank** *f* bench lathe

mechanisch mechanical **-er Antrieb** mechanical drive **-er Auftrieb** mechanical lift **~ betätigt** mechanically controlled or operated **~ betätigte Klappen** mechanically operated flaps **~ blokkierte Steuerung** ganged control **~ gekoppelt** ganged **~ wirkender Regler** mechanical control **mechanischer Enteiser** mechanical deicer **~ einziehbares Fahrgestell** mechanically retractable undercarriage

mechanisch-e Bearbeitung machining **-es Dynamometer** absorption dynamometer **-er Flugzeugstart** assisted take-off **-er Gleichrichter** mechanical rectifier **-e Grundgleichung** Newton's second law **-er Hitzegegenwert** mechanical equivalent of heat **-e Kippsicherung** mechanical stabilizer **-e Konvektion** mechanical convection **-e Kupplung** ganging **-e Kraft** mechanical force or power **-es Moment** momentum

mechanisch-er Regler mechanical control **-e Richtpresse** mechanical arbor press **-er Schalttisch** manipulator **-er Scheinwiderstand** mechanical impedance **~ verstellbare Schraube** mechanically controlled variable-pitch propeller **-e blockierte Steuerung** ganged control **-er Teil einer Seilmaschine** rig irons **-e Unbeständigkeit** mechanical instability **-e Verunreinigung** mechanical impurity **-es Visier** mechanical sight **-er Wirkungsgrad** mechanical efficiency **-es Zählwerk** mechanical register **-e Zahnerzeugung** gear generating

mechanisieren to mechanize

mechanisiert mechanized

Mechanisierung *f* mechanization **~ bis zur Automatisierung** increase of mechanization to complete automatic control

Mechanismus *m* mechanism, gear

Medaille *f* medal

Medailleur *m* engraver

Mediallinie *f* trunk line

Mediane *f* median line

Medianpapier *n* medium paper

Medium *n* medium, agent **brechendes ~** refracting medium

Medizin *f* medicine

Meer *n* ocean, sea **-ablagerung** *f* marine deposit **-busen** *m* bay, gulf **-enge** *f* strait(s), narrow channel

Meeres-arm *m* arm of the sea, sea inlet, estuary **-boden** *m* ocean floor **-enge** *f* narrows, straits **-gebiet** *n* sea area **-grund** *m* bottom of the sea, sea bed **-höhe** *f* altitude, height above sea level or datum, sea level **-höhenzahl** *f* relative elevation

Meeres-küste *f* seacoast, seashore **-leuchten** *n* phosphorescence of the sea **-niveau** *n*, **-spiegel** *m* sea level **-spiegelhöhe** *f* sea-level altitude **-strömung** *f* marine current **-welle** *f* sea wave, ocean wave **-wetterkunde** *f* marine meteorology

Meer-farbe *f* sea green **-sand** *m* sea sand **-schleuse** *f* harbor lock **-schweinöl** *n* porpoise oil **-wachs** *n* sea wax **-wasser** *n* sea water

Mega-dyn *n* megadyne **-elektronenvolt** *n* million electron-volts, mega-electron-volt, mev **-farad** *n* megafarad **-hertz** *n* megacycle per second, megacycle (MC/s)

Megampere *n* megampere

Megaphon *n* loud hailer, megaphone

Megaskop *n* projector

Megavolt *n* megavolt

Megerg *n* megerg

Megger *m* megger

Megohm *n* megohm **-meter** *n* megohmmeter

Mehl *n* dust, powder, meal flour **-artig** like meal or flour, farinaceous **-bunker** *m* meal hopper **-bürstmaschine** *f* brush bolter, cylindrical dressing machine **-förderschnecke** *f* flour worm conveyer **-gips** *m* earthy gypsum **-haltig** containing flour

mehlig floury

Mehl-motte *f* flour moth **-sand** *m* very fine sand, rock flour **-staub** *m* flour dust **-tau** *m* mildew **-wurm** *m* meal worm **-zug** *m* flour train

Mehr-achsantrieb *m* multiple-axle drive **-adressencode** *m* multiple-address code

mehradrig multiwire **-es Kabel** multi-conductor cable

Mehr-anodenventil *n* multi-anode rectifier **-arbeit** *f* extra work **-armig** multiarm(ed) **-atomig** polyatomic **-aufwand** *m* increased, extra, or additional expenditure **-ausgabe** *f* additional cost **-ausstoß** *m* increased yield **-bandantenne** *f* multi-band antenna **-bändertrieb** *m* multiband drive, multiple-belt drive **-basisch** polybasic **-bedarf** *m* increased demand **-belastung** *f* overload **-bildmessung** *f* measurement of photographs taken with multiple cameras

mehrblättriges Strahlungsdiagramm *n* multi-lobe radiation pattern

Mehr-decker *m* multiplane **-decklochkarte** *f* multi-deck card

mehrdeutig ambiguous, many-valued **-e Verrückung** multi-valued displacement

Mehrdeutigkeit *f* ambiguity, equivocation

mehrdimensional multidimensional **-e Flüssigkeitsbewegung** multidirectional motion of liquid

Mehr-drahtantenne *f* multiple wire antenna **-drähtig** multiple-wire **-drehung** *f* multirotation **-düsenvergaser** *m* multiple-jet carburetor **-einheitenrechner** *m* multi-unit machine

Mehrelektroden-kaltkathodenröhre *f* multi-electrode cold cathode tube **-ofen** *m* multiple-electrode furnace, series-arc furnace **-stabilisatorröhre** *f* multi-electrode voltage stabilizer **-system** *n* multielectrode system

Mehrer *m* multiplier, factor

mehrere several, sundry, diverse

Mehretagenofen *m* multiple-story furnace

mehrfach repeated, multiple, manifold, compound **~ abgestimmte Antenne** multiple-tuned aerial or antenna **~ geladen** multiple charged **~ legierter Stahl** multiple alloy steel **~ verzweigt** multi-branched **~ zusammenhängend** re-entrant **-e Funksignale** split course, multiple courses (condition of radio range signals near mountains) **-er Kondensator** ganged condenser **-e Markierung** multiple labelling **durch -e Mittelung** by repeatedly taking the mean (math.) **-er Riemen** belt composed of several layers of material, multiple belt

Mehrfach-anlage *f* multiple feed **-anschlußapparat** *m* multiple-request-line apparatus (teleph.) **-anschlußbündel** *n* private-branch-exchange junction group **-anschlüsse** *pl* auxiliary lines **-anschlußteilnehmer** *m* subscriber with several lines **-antenne** *f* multiple antenna **-antrieb** *m* multiple-axle drive **-ausnutzung** *f* multiple exploitation (of el. circuits) **-bahnentrockner** *m* multipass drier **-balkenrüher** *m* multiple paddle agitator **-belegung** *f* multiple seizure **-belichtung** *f* superimposing, multiple exposure **-beschichteter Film** sandwich film

Mehrfachbetrieb *m* multiple operation **~ auf Leitungen** multiple transmission on lines (teleph.)

Mehrfach-biegeautomat *m* automatic multiple bender **-bild** *n* multiple image (television) **-bildung** *f* multiple production **-brenner** *m* multiflame torch **-dekadenzähler** *m* multidecade counter **-drehkondensator** *m* gang condenser, neutralizing capacitor **-drehverfahren** *n* multiple turning **-druckmaschine** *f* multiple printing machine **-druckmesser** *m* multiple manometer **-düsensatz** *m* multiple-jet gear **-echo** *n* multiple echo, flutter echo **-empfang** *m* diversity (of) reception **-empfangsverfahren** *n* diversity-reception method **-erzeugung** *f* multiple production

mehrfaches multiple

Mehrfachfahrwerk *n* multiple wheel landing gear

Mehrfachfernsprechen *n* multiple telephony **Einrichtung für ~ mit hochfrequenten Trägerströmen** multichannel-carrier telephone system

Mehrfach-form *f* multi-impression mold, composite mold **-formular** *n* multiple form **-funkenstrecke** *f* multiple spark gap **-gesenk** *n* multiple die **-gleichrichterschaltung** *f* multiple rectifier circuit **-gleitung** *f* multiple slip **-kabel** *n* multistrand cable **-kammer** *f* multiple(-lens) camera **-karte** *f* fractional card **-kondensator** *m* multiple condenser, gang condenser or capacitor, tandem condenser, synchronized condenser **-kontakt** *m* hunting contact **-kopien** *f pl* multiple prints **-koppler** *m* multiplexer **-kreiselneigungsmesser** *m* compound gyrostatic level, multiple gyro-inclinometer **-kreislauf** *m* compound cycle

Mehrfach-leiterplatte *f* multiple board **-leitung** *f* multiple line **-leitungswähler** *m* private-branch-exchange final selector, rotary hunting connector **-lochstanze** *f* multiple hole punch **-manometer** *n* multiple manometer **-markierung** *f* multiple marking **-mengendüse** *f* multiple-feed nozzle **-meßkammer** *f* multiple photogrammetric camera **-modulation** *f* multiple modulation **-nachrichtensystem** *n* multiplex signal system **-nebenwiderstand** *m* universal shunt **-nietautomat** *m* automatic multiple riveter **-nutung** *f* multiple splining **-pendel** *n* multiple pendulum **-planierschleppe** *f* multiple-blade drags **-pumpe** *f* multiple pump

Mehrfach-raupen *pl* multiple beads **-rautenantenne** *f* musa antenna, multiple-unit steerable antenna **-reflexionen** *pl* zig-zag reflections **-reflexionsübertragung** *f* multihop transmission **-reihenbildkamera** *f* multiple-lens or multiple-series camera **-ringspule** *f* bulk toroid **-röhre** *f* multiple valve or tube, dual valve, multipurpose tube **-röhrenempfänger** *m* receiver for multiple tubes (teleph.) **-rollenherstellungsmaschine** *f* multiple reel machine **-rückkopplung** *f* multiple regeneration **-schall** hypersonic **-schalter** *m* multiple switch

Mehrfachschaltung *f* multiple connection **in ~ betreiben** to multiplex

Mehrfach-schaubild *n* multiple graph **-schichten** *pl* multilayers **-schlagprobe** *f* multiple blow test **-schlitzmaschine** *f* multiple slotter **-schmetterlingsantenne** *f* super-turnstile antenna **-schneckenförderer** *m* multiple-flight screw conveyer **-schneidenhalter** *m* inserted tooth cutter **-schweißmaschine** *f* multiple-operator welding machine **-senden** *n* multiple transmission **-sieb** *n* lattice-type filter **-spaltung** *f* iterated fission **-spirallochscheibe** *f* multispiral scanning disk

Mehrfachsprechen *n* multiplex telephony **~ mit hochfrequenten Trägerströmen** high-frequency multiple telephony

Mehrfach-stahlhalter *m* multi-toolholder **-stanze** *f* multiple punch **-stanzeinrichtung** *f* multiple-punching attachment **-stecker** *m* multiple contact plug **-steckverbinder** *m* multi-way connector **-strahler** *m* bank or pillar of lamps **-streuung** *f* multiple scattering **-stromerzeuger** *m* multiple-current generator **-stromrichter** *m* multiple convertor **-system** *n* multiplex operation **-tarifzähler** *m* multiple tariff meter

Mehrfachtelegraph *m* multiplex, multichannel, or multiple-way telegraph **~ in Gabelschaltung** split-or forked-multiples telegraph **~ in Staffelschaltung** series multiplex telegraph **~ mit abgestimmten Wechselströmen** harmonic-multiple telegraph

Mehrfach-telegraphie mit Verteilern multiplex telegraphy **-telephonie mit hochfrequenten Trägerströmen** high-frequency multiple telephony **-term** *m* multiple (spectral) term **-trägerfrequenzverfahren** *n* Bandôt multiplex printing telegraph **-übertragung** *f* multiplex radio transmission **-überzüge** *pl* multiple coatings **-unterputzkombinationen** *pl* multiple combinations for flush mounting **-verdampfapparat** *m* multiple-effect evaporator **-verkehr** *m* multiplex transmission **-verstärker** *m* multistage amplifier

-verteiler *m* multiplex or multichannel distributor **-wickeln** *n* multiple winding

Mehrfach-zackenschrift *f* multilateral sound track **-zahlung** *f* multiple registration **-zange** *f* combination pliers, multiple purpose pliers **-zeichen** *n* multiple or echo signal **-zeilensprung** *m* multiple interlacing **-zünder** *m* combination fuse, multiple fuse **-zwillingskabel** *n* multiple-twin cable

mehrfädige, ~ Düse multiple nozzle **~ Lampe** multiple-filament lamp

Mehrfarben-anilindruckmaschine *f* multi-color flexographic printer **-druck** *m* multicolor printing **-punktschreiber** *m* multiple-color dotted-line recorder **-schreiber** *m* multicolor recorder **-tiefdruck** *m* multi-color gravure printing

mehr-farbig polychrome, multicolored, pleochroic **-farbigkeit** *f* polychromy **-feldrig** multiple-span **-flammiger Brenner** multiple burner **-förderung** *f* increased delivery **-frequenzfernwahl** *f* through-dialing over trunk or toll circuits with multifrequency impulses **-frequenzsender** *m* multi-frequency transmitter **-funkenzündung** *f* multipoint ignition **-ganggetriebe** *n* multispeed transmission

mehrgängig multiple **-es Gewinde** multiple thread **-e Parallelwicklung** multiple parallel winding, multiplex lap

Mehr-gangkondensator *m* ganged condenser or capacitor, synchronized condenser, multiple condenser **-gebot** *n* outbidding

mehrgerüstig-e Walzstraße multi-stand mill **-es Walzwerk** multiple-stand rolling mill

Mehrgespann *n* additional yoke or team **Waage für ~** evener

Mehrgewicht *n* overweight, excess weight, advantage

Mehrgitter-mischröhre multigrid mixing valve **-rohr** *n* multiple-grid tube **-röhre** *f* multiple-grid valve

mehrgleisig multiple-track

mehrgliedrig multimesh, multisection **-e Größe** polynomial **-er Kettenleiter** multimesh network

Mehrheit *f* majority, plurality, multiplicity

Mehrheits-beschluß *m* majority rule or decision **-trägerkontakt** *m* majority carrier contact **-emitter** *m* majority emitter

mehr-herdiger Röstofen multihearth roasting furnace or roaster **-holmig** multispar **-kammerofen** *m* multichamber kiln **-kanaldecodierer** all-channel decoder **-kanalfernsehen** *n* multichannel television **-kanalig** multichannel **-kanalmethode** *f* multiple scanning **-kanalrundfunksender** *m* multi-channel radio transmitter

Mehrkantblockdrehbank *f* multiple-cornered lathe

Mehrkantensteuerung *f* multi-seating control

mehrkantig many-sided

Mehrkant-prisma *n* polyhedral prism **-stab** *m* polygonal bar

Mehrkeil-sitz *m* multisplined fit **-welle** *f* splined shaft

mehr-kernig polynuclear **-klangsignal** *n* multitone signal **-knotig** multinoded **-kolbenförderung** *f* multipiston feed

mehrköpfig multiple **-e Besatzung** multiman crew **-es Stationspersonal** multimanned station

Mehrkörper-kräfte *pl* many-body-forces **-verdampfapparat** *m* multiple-effect evaporator **-verdämpfer** *m* many-bodied vaporizer

Mehr-kristall *n* polycrystal **-ladeeinrichtung** *f* magnazine mechanism **-lader** *m* repeating rifle, magazine rifle **-ladevorrichtung** *f* magazine-feed mechanism

Mehrlagen-raupe (Schweißung) *f* multiple bead **-schweißung** *f* multipass welding, multi-run weld **-spule** *f* multilayer coil, banked or pile coil, honeycomb coil with banked winding

mehr-lagig multilayer **-lappig** multilobed **-läufig** multibarrel **-leistung** *f* increased efficiency, greater performance, increased output, surplus power **-leiterantenne** *f* multiple-wire aerial **-leiterkabel** *n* multicore cable **-linsenobjektiv** *n* multiple-lens combination **-linsiges Objektiv** objective composed of several lenses **-litzig** multistrand

Mehrloch-düse *f* multihole nozzle, diaphragm **-einspritzdüse** *f* multiport injector **-kanal** *m* multiple-duct conduit

Mehrmengen-anschlag *m* supplementary feed stop **-feder** *f* supplementary feed spring

Mehrmotoren-antrieb *m* multimotor drive **-flugzeug** *n* multiengine plane

mehrmotorig multi-motored, multi-engine

Mehrnadel-rose *f* multineedle compass rose or card **-telegraph** *m* multiple-needle telegraph

Mehrphasen-motor *m* polyphase motor **-schaltung** *f* connection of polyphase circuits **-(wechsel)strom** *m* multiphase or polyhase (alternating) current

Mehrphasensystem *n* polyphase or multiphase system **symmetrisches ~** balanced polyphase system

mehrphasig polyphase, multiphase **-es Aggregat** polyphase aggregate

mehrpolig multipolar, polyphase **-e Überschläge** oscillating flashovers

Mehr-preis *m* extra charge, increase in price **-punktschreiber** *m* multipoint recorder

mehrquantig multiple

Mehrradfahrwerk *n* multiple wheel landing gear

Mehrreihen-sternmotor *m* multibank radial engine **-zweitaktsternmotor** *m* multibank radial two-stroke engine

mehr-reihig multiple-row **-röhrenverstärker** *m* multivalve amplifier

mehrscharig with several blades **-er Obstgartenpflug** orchard gang plow **-er Pflug** gang plow **-er Pflug mit Sitz** riding gang plow **-er Pflug ohne Sitz** walking gang plow

Mehrscheiben-kuppelung *f* multiple-disk clutch **-pflug mit Führersitz** riding disk gang plow **-trockenkupplung** *f* multi-plate friction clutch

Mehrschicht *f* multilayer

Mehrschichten-glas *n* laminated glass **-isolierhülle** *f* multilayer insulating cover **-kunststoffbelag** *m* multi-layer of plastic covering

mehrschiffig (Halle) multiple-bay **-es Gebäude** multi-bayed building

Mehr-schneckenpreßverfahren *n* multi-screw extrusion **-schneiddrehbank** *f* multi-cut lathe **-schneider** *m* multiple cutter **-schnitteinrichtung** *f* multi-pass device **-schnittige Nietung** multiple-shear riveting

mehrseitig polygonal **-e Fräsmaschine** multilate-

ral molding machine
mehrsilbig polysyllabic
Mehrsitzer *m* multi-seater
Mehrspindel-automat *m* multiple-spindle automatic chucking machine **-bohrmaschine** *f* multiple-spindle drill **-futterautomat** *m* multiple-spindle chucking type, automatic lathe **-stangenautomat** *m* multiple-spindle bartype, automatic lathe
Mehrspurkopf *m* head stack (tape rec.)
Mehrstahl-arbeit *f* multiple-tool operation **-support** *m* multiple-tool holder or carrier
Mehrstellen-schalter *m* multiple switch **-verfahren** *n* multiplace method **-wirkung** *f* multi-step action
mehrstellig having more than one cipher or place
Mehr-stempellochapparat *m* multiple punching attachment **-presse** *f* multiple-die or multiple plunger press
mehrstielig multistrut
Mehrstiftstecker *m* cannon plug
mehrstimmig polyphonic (of an organ)
Mehrstoff *m* complex
Mehrstoffbetrieb *m* multifuel (drive) **Motor für ~** multifuel engine
Mehr-stofflegierung *f* multicomponent alloy **-strahlbrenner** *m* multijet burner
mehrstrahliges Funkfeuer multi(ray) beacon, multiple- or triple-modulation beacon
Mehrstrom-generator *m* multiple-current generator **-turbine** *f* multiflow turbine
Mehrstufen-dauerschwingversuch *m* multistage fatigue test **-entmagnetisierung** *f* multiple-stage demagnetization **-lader** *m* multistage supercharger
mehrstufig multistage, multiple-stage
Mehr-stutzenkamera *f* camera with exchangeable lens heads **-systemröhre** *f* multiple unit tube **-tarifzähler** *m* multi-rate meter **-teilchenwellenfunktion** *f* multiparticle wave function
mehrteilig multipart, multiple-part, multisectional
mehrteiliges Gesenk *n* split-ring mold
Mehr-ventilanordnung *f* multivalve arrangement **-walzwerke** *pl* cluster mill
mehrwegig multiway, multichannel **-er Schalter** multipoint switch **-er Telegraph** multichannel telegraph **-e Übertragung** multipath transmission
Mehrweg-schalter *m* multiplexer, traffic pilot **-übertragung** *f* multipath transmission **-umschalter** *m* multiway switch
mehr-wellig polyphase **-welligkeit** *f* multiwave property **-wert** *m* extra or surplus value **-wertig** multivalent **-wichtesortierung** *f* cleaning at several densities **-zahl** *f* plurality, multiplicity, majority
Mehrzählerhebelkontrollkasse *f* multiple-lever cash register
Mehrzeilen-abfühlsteuerung *f* multiple line read selection **-karte** *f* multiple line card **-schreibung** *f* multiple line printing
Mehrzeitformalismus *m* many-time formalism
Mehrzellenflotator *m* multiple-cell flotation machine
mehrzellig polycellular, multicellular, sectoral
mehrzügig multiple **-es Formstück** multiple tile **-er Kanal** multiple-way duct **-es Tonformstück** multiple-tile or -clay conduit
Mehr-zünder *m* multiple fuse **-zweck** *m* general purpose, dual purpose, multiple purpose
Mehrzweck-flugzeug *n* multiple-purpose or general-purpose plane **-fräsmaschine** *f* various-purpose milling machine **-mehrbereichinstrument** *n* electronic multi-meter **-rechner** *m* multipurpose computer **-stahllineal** *n* multi-use steel rule
Mehrzylinder *m* multicylinder **-maschine** *f* multicylinder engine **-selfaktor** *m* sectional-cylinder selfactor
Meidinger-Element *n* Meidinger cell
Meier *m* cattle fodderer or feeder
Meierei *f* farm, dairy
Meierhof *m* farmyard, (dairy) farm
Meile *f* mile **englische ~** British mile, statute mile **nautische ~** nautical mile
Meilen-beisteuer *f* mileage subsidy **-geld** *n*, **-länge** *f* mileage **-stein** *m* milestone **-zähler** *m* mileometer, speedometer
Meiler *m* pile, mound, charcoal pile or burning, earth-covered heap, stack **-kohle** *f* charcoal from piles **-ofen** *m* mound **-stätte** *f* site of a pile **-tisch** *m* launching platform (missiles) **-verfahren** *n*, **-verkohlung** *f* pile charring **-verkokung** *f* pile coking **-wagen** *m* trailer (missiles)
meinen to mean, believe, think, guess
M-Einheit *f* M unit
Meinung *f* opinion, mind, belief **anderer ~ sein** to dissent **verschiedener ~ sein** to differ
Meinungs-austausch *m* discussion **-verschiedenheit** *f* misunderstanding, difference of opinion
Meißel *m* chisel, cape or forged-steel chisel, bit, hardy, pledget, stylus **~ für Felsbearbeitung** steel drill for rock or stone
Meißel-absatz *m* shoulder of bit **-abschraubvorrichtung** *f* break-out plate **-ansatz** *m* pin of drilling bit **-bohrer** *m* flat chisel, pitching borer, short borer **-fanghaken** *m* bit hook, fishing hook for bits **-gestänge** *n* bit rods **-hammer** *m* chipping or calking hammer **-kopf** *m* bit head **-krone** *f* core-boring crown **-lehre** *f* bit gauge
meißeln to chisel, chip
Meißel-schablone *f* bit gauge **-schaft** *m* drill stem **-schlag** *m* stroke of bit **-schlitten** *m* tool slide **-schneide** *f* cutting edge of bit **-spiel** *n* play of bit **-spitze** *f* chisel joint **-stahl** *m* chisel steel **-winkel** *m* lip angle
meistbietend verkauft sold by auction
Meister *m* chief operator, foreman, master, champion **-lauge** *f* caustic potash solution **-negativ** *n* metal master, master negative **-positiv** *n* mother record, master positive **-räder** *pl* master gears **-schalter** *m* master controller **-welle** *f* master component **-wellenträger** *m* master carrier
Meistgebot *n* highest bid
Mékerbrenner *m* Méker burner
Melalithisolator *m* melalite insulator
Melange *f* mixture, blend
Melanglanz *m* stephanite
Melanit *m* melanite
Melanterit *m* melanterite
Melaphyr *m* melaphyre
Melasse *f* molasses **-bildend** melassigenic **-decke** *f* molasses wash **-entzuckerung** *f* extraction of sugar from molasses **-probenahme** *f* sampling of

molasses **-probestecher** *m* molasses proof stick **-schlempe** *f* molasses vinasse, molasses slop **-schlempekohle** *f* charred molasses slop

melassierte Schnitzel molasses pulp

Melde-abwurf *m* dropping a message (aviation) **-amtsbetrieb** *m* direct record working (teleph.) **-beamter** *m* record (table) operator, recorder, recording operator **-befehl** *m* reporting order or directive **-beutel** *m* message container spreading color on water, fluorescein bag **-block** *m* message book **-büchse** *f* message canister spreading color on water **-dienst** *m* signal communication service

Melde-fernplatzbetrieb *m* combined line and recording operation **-heft** *n* message book **-karte** *f* message blank **-kette** *f* relay of runners **-kontrollampe** *f* indicator lamp

Meldekopf *m* message center **vorgeschobener ~** advanced message center

Melde-lampe *f* alarm lamp, pilot lamp, telltale lamp, signal lamp, annunciator light **-läufer** *m* runner **-leitung** *f* toll record circuit, recording trunk

melden to announce, report, signal

Melde-netz *n* spotting system, warning system **-pflicht** *f* obligatory reporting **-platz** *m* registration office, reporting center, record position **-punkt** *m* reporting point (aviation) **-quadrat** *n* reference square (of map)

Melder *m* runner, orderly, signal, alarm, indicator

Melde-relais *n* pilot relay, supervisory relay **-rose** *f* air-raid-warning chart, graduated bearing arc for aircraft reporting **-sammelstelle** *f* message center **-schrank** *m* recording section **-sicherung** *f* alarm-type fuse **-spitzenplatz** *m* record-transfer position **-spitzenplatzbeamtin** *f* record-transfer operator **-stelle** *f* recording section or station **-stöpsel** *m* answering plug

Melde-tafel *f* indicator **-tasche** *f* message bag **-tisch** *m* record table **-übermittler** *m* messenger, runner **-verkehr** *m* record traffic **-verteiler** *m* position distributor **-verteileramt** *n* record section with selectors **-vorrichtung** *f* alarm apparatus **-weg** *m* messenger route **-zeichen** *n* indicator, alarm signal

Meldometer *n* meldometer

Meldung *f* information, report, advice, notice, communication, message **eine ~ abfangen** to intercept a message **freiwillige ~** voluntary enlistment

Meliereffekt *m* mottled effect

melieren to blend, mix

meliert speckled, mixed, blended, mottled **-es Papier** granite paper

Melierte *f* good-quality trough

Melinit *m* melinite

Melioration *f* improvement of land for cultivation by means of irrigation, drainage, soil conservation, amelioration

meliorieren to ameliorate

Melis-puder *n* powdered melis **-sud** *m* strike of melis

Mellit *m* honeystone, mellite, native mellitate of alumina

Membran(e) *f* diaphragm, membrane **als Ganzes schwingende ~** piston diaphragm, diaphragm moving like a piston **atmende ~** flexible, non-reflecting diaphragm

Membran-auslenkung *f* diaphragm displacement **-belastetes Ventil** membrane valve **-block** *m* diaphragm housing **-deckel** *m* diaphragm cap **-dose** *f* siphon diaphragm **-druckreduzierventil** *n* pressure reducing valve with diaphragm **-einspannung** *f* suspension of diaphragm **-feder** *f* diaphragm spring **-halteschraube** *f* diaphragm securing screw **-kapazität** *f* capacitance of the diaphragm **-kolben** *m* diaphragm piston **-leiter** *m* membrane duct **-loses Mikrophon** diaphragmless microphone, cathodophone

Membran-pumpe *f* diaphragm pump, surge pump, check-valve suction pump **-regler** *m* diaphragm governor **-saugpumpe** *f* diaphragm suction pump **-scheibe** *f* spring disk **-schwingamplitude** *f* excursion amplitude of diaphragm **-schwingung** *f* diaphragm oscillation **-spannungszustand** *m* membrane stress **-ventil** *n* diaphragm valve **-verhalten** *n* membrane behavior

menagieren to economize, manage

Mendheim-Ofen Mendheim (chamber-type) kiln

Menge *f* (quantitativ) quantity; (Raum) volume; (Gewicht) tonnage; (Vielzahl) multitude; (Haufen) heap, pile; (Masse) quantity; amount, crowd, mass, lots, discharge, water flowing past a given point, portion, aggregate, set **nach der ~** quantitative **äquivalente ~** quantivalence **leere ~** empty set **~ im Vergleichsnormal** quantity of comparative standard **Mächtigkeit einer ~** power of a set (math.)

mengen to mix, blend

Mengen-abrechnung *f* stock accounting by quantities **-bestimmung** *f* quantitative determination, quantitative analysis

Mengenbezeichnung *f* designation of quantity **Schild mit ~** quantity plate

Mengen-einheit *f* unit of quantity **-einteilungsmaschine** *f* dosing machine **-faktor** *m* multiplicity factor **-fertigung** *f* mass production **-lehre** *f* theory of sets (math.) **-leistung** *f* output, production capacity

mengenmäßig quantitative **qualitative, nicht ~ bestimmte Analyse** qualitative analysis

Mengen-messer *m* volumenometer, flowmeter **-prüfung** *f* serial testing **-regelung** *f* volume control **-regler** *m* volume governor **-strom** *m* weight velocity of flow, mass flow **-untersuchung** *f* quantitative analysis **-verhältnis** *n* quantitative relationship, proportion (of ingredients), quantitative composition **-verlust** *m* loss of volume **-verstellhebel** *m* quantity-adjustment lever (accelerator) **-wert** *m* quantile

Menger *m* mixer

Mengungsverhältnis *n* proportion of mix or ingredients, relative amounts

meniskenförmig meniscal

Meniskus *m* meniscus lens **-kante** *f* meniscus edge

Mennig *m* red lead, ochre

Mennige *f* minium, red lead oxide **-kitt** *m* red lead putty

Menschenführung *f* personal management, politico-psychological guidance, control of public opinion

Menschenleben *n* human life **~ gefährden** to en-

endanger human life
Menschenmenge *f* crowd, mob
menschlich human, humane **-e Energie aufspeichern** to store human energy
Mensel *f* plane table **-platte** *f* board of the plane table
Mensur *f* graduated vessel, graduate, measure (music), scale (music), measuring
Mercerisierverfahren *n* mercerizing process
Mergel *m* marl, clay **-artig** marly **-hältig** containing marl **-kalk** *m* marly limestone, chalky clay **-sandstein** *m* marly sandstone **-schiefer** *m* marl slate
Meridian *m* meridian **der ~ von Greenwich** meridian of Greenwich **geographischer ~** geographical meridian **der erste ~** prime meridian
Meridian-bogen *m* arc of the meridian **-ebene** *f* meridian plane **-geschwindigkeit** *f* actual speed of fluid at the center line of a closed duct **-höhe** *f* meridian altitude or height **-konvergenz** *f* grid declination **-kreisel** *m* meridian gyroscope **-kurve** *f* meridian line **-schnitt** *m* vertical center section **-streifen** *m* meridian section
Meridionalebene *f* meridional plane
meridionale Brennlinie meridional focal line
Merkantilarbeit *f* commercial work
Merkaptan *n* ethyl hydrosulfide (mercaptan)
Merkaptobenzothiazol *n* mercaptobenzothiazole
merkatorisch Mercatorial **-e Peilung** Mercatorial bearing
Merkatorkarte *f* Mercator's map or chart, Mercator's projection **nach der ~ fliegen** Mercatorial flying
Merkatorkartenprojektion *f* Mercator's or cylindrical projection, orthomorphic projection
merkbar appreciable, noticeable, perceptible
Merkblatt *n* memorandum, pamphlet, leaflet, specification
merken to mark, observe, notice
Merkkarte *f* index card
Merkleuchte *f* signal light
merklich noticeable, appreciable, perceptible
Merkmal *n* characteristic, feature, criterion, indication, mark, sign, index, work, token, connotation
Merkpunkt *m* landmark, reference point, index point, fiducial point, point de repère (in Baudot apparatus), bench mark
Merkstörung *f* disturbance of retention
Merkur *m* mercury **-blende** *f* cinnabar **-chlorid** *n* mercury or mercuric chloride **-chlorür** *n* mercurous chloride **-durchgang** *m* mercury transit **-haltig** mercurial, containing mercury **-hornerz** *n* horn quicksilver, calomel
Merkuri-ammoniumchlorid *n* mercury ammonium chloride **-bromid** *n* mercuric bromide **-rhodanid** *n* mercuric thiocyanate **-sulfozyanid** *n* mercuric sulfocyanide **-verbindung** *f* mercuric compound
Merkuro-bromid *n* mercurous bromide **-chrom** *n* mercurochrome
Merkursilber *n* silver amalgam
Merkwort *n* key word
merkwürdig remarkable, strange, peculiar
Merk-zeichen *n* (guide) mark **-zeiger** *m* adjustable index, indicator needle **-zettel** *m* data card, memo
meromorph meromorphic (function)
Merton-Ofen Merton (straight-line rabble) furnace
merzerisierecht fast to mercerizing
merzerisiert mercerized
Merzerisierung *f* mercerization
Mesatransistor *m* mesa transistor
Mesitinspat *m* mesitite
Mesitylen *n* mesitylene
Meson *n* meson (a nuclear particle)
Mesonen-bahnende *n* mesotron track end **-nachweis** *m* meson detection
mesonisches Atom mesonic atom
Meson-niveau *n* mesonic level **-paardämpfung** *f* meson-pair damping **-term** *m* mesonic level
Mesosiderit *m* siderolite
Mesothorium *n* mesothorium
Mesotrontheorie *f* meson theory, theory of mesotrons
mesozoisch mesozoic
Meß-ablesung *f* reading **-abstand** *m* measuring-point distance **-achse** *f* gauging axis **-ader** *f* second wire **-amboß** *m* measuring anvil **-amt** *n* measuring or testing office **-anordnung** *f* measuring arrangement or equipment **-antenne** *f* test antenna **-apparat** *m* measuring instrument, measuring apparatus, meter **-apparatöl** *n* meter oil **-aufbau** *m* test assembly or rig **-aufgaben** *pl* measuring tasks **-automatik** *f* automatic scanning device **-band** *n* surveyor's chain, tape measure, surveyor's tape
meßbar measurable **~ veränderlich** measurably changeable
Meß-basis *f* base line **-batterie** *f* testing battery, survey battery **-beamter** *m* test man, tester **-beobachtung** *f* ranging **-bereich** *m* measuring range **-bereichschalter** *m* (measuring) range switch **-bereichsumfang** *m* extension of measuring ranges **-bereit** ready for action (antiaircraft range finder) **-bereitschaft** *f* readiness for action (radar range finder)
Meßbild *n* scale drawing, photogram **-aufnahme** *f* photogrammetry **-kammer** *f* surveying camera, photogrammetric camera **-kunst** *f* photographic surveying **-paar** *n* steroscopic complement **-verfahren** *n* photogrammetry
Meß-bleistift *m* thermo-color crayon **-blende** *f* orifice (meas.), restrictor **-blendenkorrektoren** *pl* restrictor correctors **-boje** *f* recording buoy **-bolzen** *m* gauge pin **-brief** *m* bill or certidicate of tonnage **-brücke** *f* measuring or resistance bridge, Wheatstone's bridge, bridge **-buch** *n* field book **-büchse** *f* monitor socket **-buchsenleiste** test jack strip **-bügel** *m* continuous ring **-bügelträger** *m* contact arm hanger **-bunker** *m* measuring bin **-bürette** *f* graduated burette
Meß-demodulator *m* measuring detector **-dienst** *m* maintenance service **-diode** *f* measuring diode **-dipol** *m* antenna (radio) **-dorn** *m* plug gauge **-dose** *f* pressure cell, standardizing box, capsule-type dynamometer **-dosenträger** *m* gauge holder or support **-draht** *m* pilot or slide wire **-dreieck** *n* present-position triangle defined by zero point, present position, position in the horizontal plane **-dreieckverfahren** *n* triangulation method of surveying **-druck** *m* measuring pressure **-durchführungen** *m* measurement transmissions **-durchlauf** *m* measurement pas-

sage **-düse** *f* calibrated nozzle, metering orifice

Messe *f* ship's mess, mass, mess, fair (exposition) **technische ~** technical fair

Messebeschicker *m* exhibitor

Meß-ebene *f* working plane, plane of present position **-ei** *n* pressure gauge, manometer **-einheit** *f* unit of measurement **-einrichtung** *f* measuring device **-einsatz** *m* measuring jaw, gauge slide, measuring inset **-einschub** *m* plug-in measuring unit

Meßeinteilung *f*, **mit ~ versehen** to graduate

messen to measure, gauge, meter, test, survey, sound **eine Bohrung ~** to check a bore **mit der Kette ~** to chain **eine Leitung auf Isolation und Leitfähigkeit ~** to test a line for insulation and conductivity **mit der Schmiege ~** to bevel **mit Tastlehre ~** to caliper **einen Winkel ~** to take an angle, determine or take a bearing **Zeit ~** to time

Messen *n* (mit der Kette) chaining **~ von Neigungen im Meeresboden** measuring sea-bottom slopes **stereoskopisches ~** stereoscopic measurement **~ und Regeln** instrumentation and control

messende Pumpe measuring pump

Meßsender *m* test oscillator, signal generator

Meßentfernung *f* mid-point range, slant range to present position (aviat)

Messer *m* measuring instrument or device, meter, gauge **~ für Öl** meter for oil

Messer *n* knife, cutter, blade, doctor (paper mfg.) **~ für Drahtstiftmaschinen** knives for wire-nail machines **~ für Fräs- und Bohrköpfe** cutter for milling-machine and boring heads **~ für Lederbearbeitung** leather knives **~ für landwirtschaftliche Maschinen** knife for agricultural machines **eingesetztes ~** inserted blade **gekröpftes ~** probe-ended knife **kleines ~** scalpel

Messer-bändsel *n* knife seizing **-beilage** *f* blade chuck **-block** *m* bedplate (paper mfg.), cutter-holder support **-brecher** *m* knife crusher

Messerchen *n* scalpel

Messer-ebner *m* knife leveler **-egge** *f* scarifier **-einrichtung** *f* knife attachment **-einsatz** *m* knife contact **-falztrommel** *f* knife folding drum **-feld** *n* measuring panel **-flug** *m* flight along angle of sideslip **-fräser** *m* inserted-tooth cutter

Meßergebnis *n* result of measurement, test reading

Messer-halter *m* knife clip, blade holder **-haus** *n* lathe-tool holder **-heftfeiler** *m* knife-handle shaper or filer **-hochgang** *m* upstroke of the knife **-kantenversuch** *m* knife-edge test **-klemme** *f* cutter clamp **-klinge** *f* blade (of knife or cutter) **-kontakt** *m* knife-blade contact, switch jack **-kontaktbacke** *f* contact jaw

Messerkopf *m* inserted tooth cutter, end-milling cutter, boring block, cutter head **~ mit eingesetzten Messern** inserted-blade end-milling cutter

Messer-leiste *f* terminal strip **-niedergang** *m* down-stroke of knife **-picke** *f* pick, cutter pick, knife pick **-säge** *f* knife pruning saw **-schälmaschine** *f* disk barker (paper mfg.) **-schalter** *m* knife(-blade) switch **-scheibe** *f* cutter disk, knife disk **-schleifapparat** *m* knife-grinding attachment **-schleifer** *m* knife grinder

Messer-schmied *m* cutler, knifesmith **-schmiede** *f* cutler's workshop **-schmiedewaren** *pl* cutlery **-schnäbel** *pl* knife edge nose pieces **-schneide** *f* knife-edge **-schneideneffekt** *m* knife-edge effect **-schützer** *m* knife cover **-spitze** *f* knife point, pinch **-stecker** *m* knife plug **-stichel** *m* scorper

Messer-trommel *f* blade drum, cutter drum **-walze** *f* cutter block **-waren** *pl* cutlery **-wechsel** *m* change of blades **-welle** *f* cutter spindle, knife driving shaft **-zeiger** *m* knife-edge pointer

Messestand *m* stall at a fair

Meß-faden *m* stadia line **-fähig** measurable **-fähnchen** *n* banderole **-fahne** *f* surveyor's flag **-farbfilter** *m* precision filter **-feder** *f* measuring spring **-fehler** *m* error of measurement, measuring fault **-fehlergrenze** *f* error limit **-feld** *n* area (field) of measurement **-filmeinrichtung** *f* time recorder on film **-filter** *n* precision filter **-fläche** *f* measuring surface, measuring face

Meßflansch *m* orifice assembly, head producer; (einteilig) plain orifice flange

Meß-flasche *f* graduated flask **-fliegerobjektiv** *n* aerophotogrammetric lens **-flug** *m* photogrammetric flight, calibration flight **-flugzeug** *n* calibration aircraft **-flüssigkeit** *f* titrating solution **-form** *f* parison (glass mfg.) **-fühler** *m* primary element **-funkenstrecke** *f* spark gap **-geber** *m* sensor

Meßgebiet, kleines ~ small scale

Meßgefäß *n* measuring tank or bowl, graduated vessel or measure **sichtbares ~** visible measuring bowl

Meß-gegenstand *m* object of measurement **-gehäuse** *n* indicator cabinet **-genauigkeit** *f* precision of test, accuracy of measurement **-geometrie** *f* measuring dimensions

Meßgerät *n* surveying instruments, measuring tool, apparatus, device, indicator **~ für Bordzwecke** aircraft-type instrument **~ mit Dämpfung** quick-deadbeat instrument **~ mit Fernübertragung** transmitting-type gauge **~ zum Messen des Erdwiderstandes** earth tester **elektrodynamisches ~** electrodynamic meter **netzbetriebenes ~** measuring instrument with alternating-current power supply **schnell zur Ruhe kommendes ~** quick-deadbeat instrument **schreibendes ~** recording mechanism **thermoelektrisches ~** thermocouple meter, thermoelectric instrument

Meßgerätausrüstung *f* instrumentation

Meßgerätekapsel (Rakete) *f* instrument capsule

Meß-gerinne *n* measuring channel **-gerüst** *n* test rig or jig **-geschwindigkeit** *f* rapidity of measurement **-gestell** *n* test panel **-gewand** *n* vestment **-gitter** *n* measuring grid **-glas** *n* graduated measuring glass, gauge glass **-gleichrichter** *m* meter rectifier **-glied** *n* metering element the member measuring the departure of the condition from its prescribed value, error detector **-grenze** *f* limit of measurement **-größe** *f* quantity metered, measured variable, process variable **-größenumformer** *m* transducer, sensor **-grundlage** *f* test basis **-gut** *n* material under test **-haus** *n* instrument center **-heber** graduated pipette **-höhenwinkel** *m* present angle of sight, angular height **-hütchen** *n* feeler cap **-impuls** *m* test pulse

Messing *n* yellow brass, brass **~ abbrennen** to pickle or dip brass **poliertes ~** straightened brass **mit ~ verkleidet** brass-cased

Messing-abstrich *m*, **-abzug** *m* brass scum **-artig** brassy, like brass **-ausschluß** *m* brass spaces **-autotypieätzung** *f* halftone engraving on brass **-backe** *f* brass jaw socket

Messingband *n* brass tape **mit ~ umwickelt** brass-taped

Messing-bandumlappung *f* brass taping **-blas-instrument** *n* brass wind instrument **-blatt** *n* brass foil **-blech** *n* sheet brass, brass plate **-blüte** *f* aurichalcite **-bogenregletten** *pl* brass curves **-draht** *m* brass wire **-drahttäckse** *pl* brass tacks **-durchschuß** *m* brass spaces **-einfassung** *f* brass border **-fassung** *f* brass mounting or casing **-folie** *f* brass foil **-gehäuse** *n* brass case **-gießerei** *f* brass foundry **-guß** *m* cast brass, brass castings

Messing-hartlot brazing spelter **-hohlstift** *m* hollow brass pin **-hütte** *f* brass foundry **-käfer** *m* luffing beetle **-kartusche** *f* brass cartridge case **-klemme** *f* brass terminal or binding post **-lager** *n* brass bushing **-linie** *f* brass reglet **-lot** *n* brass solder, brazing metal **-netz** *n* brass gauze **-präge-platte** *f* brass embossing plate **-preßstück** *n* brass die pressing

Messing-rakel *n* brass doctor **-reifen** *m* brass rim **-rohr** *n* brass tubing **-schlaglot** *n* brass solder, brazing metal **-schlichtmaschine** *f* brass finishing machine **-schmied** *m* brazier **-schraube** *f* brass screw **-schrift** *f* brass types **-span** *m* brass turning or shaving **-spatien** *pl* brass spaces **-spritz-guß** *m* brass die-casting **-stöpsel** *m* brass peg **-ware** *f* brassware **-zylinder** *m* brass cylinder

Meßinstrument *n* measuring instrument or device, meter **~ mit Fernablesung** telegauge **aperiodi-sches ~** deadbeat instrument, highly damped instrument **gedämpftes ~** aperiodic or deadbeat measuring instrument **ungedämpftes ~** ballistic measuring instrument

Meß-kamera *f* recording camera **-kammer** *f* experiment chamber **-kante** *f* contact edge **-karren** *m* testing cart **-kartenentfernung** *f* horizontal range to target at present position **-kartenpunkt** *m* observed point **-kartusche** *f* measuring round (for powder temperature), key cartridge **-kelch** *m* chalice **-kette** *f* measuring chain, surveyor's chain, calibrated phase changer, ranging unit (radar), ranging delay, network of radar equipment

Meß-klemme *f* test-prong (autopilot) **-klinken-feld** *n* toll test panel **-klinkenstreifen** *m* measuring-jack strip **-klotz** *m* gauge block **-koffer** *m* checking case (radio) **-kolben** *m* graduated flask, measuring flask, gauge flask **-kondensator** *m* measuring condenser **-kreis** *m* map protractor, graduated circle, measuring or testing circuit **-kurskreisel** *m* gyroscope with angle pickoff **-kugel** *f* ball-tipped contact feeler **-kunde** *f* surveying, metrology **-kunst** *f* metrology, mensuration **-kurve** *f* calibration curve **-länge** *f* length of measurement, gauge length

Meßlängeneinheit *f* unit of length **Formänderung je ~** relative deformation

Meß-latte *f* surveyor's rod, aligning pole, stadia, subtense bar **-lauf** *m* test run **-lehre** *f* gauge **-leine** *f* measuring tape **-leinenhaspel** *m* (runder) measuring reel

Meßleiste *f* (Prüfmaschine) scantling; (Walzwerk) scale

Meß-leitung *f* circuit for sound- and flash-ranging station, instrument leads **-leuchtschirm** *m* measuring-point fluorescent screen **-lineal** *n* gauge length **-ling** *m* component or item under test **-lupe** *f* measuring magnifier, scale magnifying glass **-marke** *f* measuring mark, collimating mark, pylon, stake, stereoscopic mark **-markenskala** *f* measuring mark scale

Meß-maschine *f* measuring machine **-mechanis-mus** *m* measuring mechanism **-meister** *m* marker **-membran** *f* metering diaphragm **-methode** *f* testing method, measuring method **-methodik** *f* measuring methodology **-mikroskop** *n* measuring microscope **-moment** *n* deflecting torque, driving torque **-nabe** *f* torque indicator

Meß-objekt *n* target, object of measurement **-objektiv** *n* aerial mapping lens **-offizier** *m* instrument officer, range officer **-okular** *n* micrometer eyepiece **-organ** *n* measuring agent **-ortungslinie** *f* line of observed position **-oszil-lator** *m* test oscillator, signal generator **patrone** *f* key cartridge **-pause** *f* (Radar) plotting interval **-pegel** *m* expected level, measuring level **-pipette** *f* graduated pipette **-plan** *m* schedule of periodic tests **-prisma** *n* refractometer prism **-pumpe** *f* measuring pump

Meßpunkt *m* mid-point, measuring point, collimating point, test point, present position of target **~ in der Kartenebene** present position in the horizontal plane

Meß-rad *n* perambulator, surveyor's wheel, odometer, measuring wheel **-rahmen** *m* reference frame, mark frame, loading gauge, carriage gauge **-rahmen** *m* focal plane frame **-raum** *m* experiment chamber **-reihe** *f* series of measurements or readings, run **-reihenbildner** *m* serial air-survey camera, serial photogrammetric camera **-ring** *m* gauge ring **-rohr** *n* measuring tube, burette, gauge tube, graduated tube **-röhrenklemme** *f* burette pincer **-rohrleitung** *f* gauging hatches

Meß-schablone *f* no-go gauge **-schallplatte** *f* frequency record, phonograph record, parlophone record **-schaltung** *f* connections for measurement **-scheibe** *f* reference disk, toolmaker's flat, gauge block, measuring disk **-schenkel** *m* jaw blade **-schiene** *f* graduated straightedge **-schirm** *m* traveling screen for measuring discharge of water **-schlange** *f* elastic-loop dynamometer **-schleife** *f* measuring or test loop

Meßschnabel *m* measuring pin or jaw **~ mit Kugeln** ball-tipped contact feeler

Meß-schneide *f* contact blade **-schnitt** *m* test section, micrometer **-schnur** *f* test lead(s), measuring cord or tape **-schrank für Verstärker-ämter** repeater station test desk **-schraube** *f* dividing screw, measuring or contact screw **-schreiber** *m* recorder, recording mechanism **-seitenwinkel** *m* azimuth of target at present position, present bearing **-sender** *m* calibrating-transmitter test oscillator (radio), (test) signal generator **-sonde** *f* measuring or test probe **-spannung** *f* measuring (test) voltage **-spindel** *f* measuring screw

Meß-spinole *f* measuring spindle sleeve **-spirale** *f* search coil (radar) **-spule** *f* measuring coil, search coil (radar) **-stab** *m* scale, measuring rod, gauge stick **-stand** *m* observation post, range-finding post **-stange** *f* dip rod, perch, measuring staff **-stativ** *n* measuring stand **-stelle** *f* computing station for sound and flash ranging, measuring point, control point, observation point, plotting center **-stellenumschalter** *m* selector switch **-stereoskop** *n* measuring stereoscope **-stift** *m* mesuring peg or pin **-strang** *m* range circuit

Meßstrecke *f* explosive train (in measuring detonation velocity), measured trajectory (of projectile), measuring section, range of measurement **~ eines Windkanals** wind-tunnel throat

Meßstreifen *m* strip chart **-rolle** *f* chart roll

Meßstrich *m* measuring or indicating line

Meßstrom *m* testing current, measuring current **-kreis** *m* testing circuit **-stärke** *f* testing-current intensity

Meß-sucher *m* coincidence-type range finder **-support** *m* lathe-testing tool machine **-tafel** *f* test board **-taste** *f* testing key (teleph.) **-taster** *m* pressure foot **-tätigkeit** *f* operation of measurement **-technik** *f* testing technique, measuring technique **-teilung** *f* stadia scale (graduation) **-temperatur** *f* measuring temperature **-tiefe** *f* gauging depth

Meßtisch *m* measuring table, plane table, presentation screen (radar chart table), test desk **quer verstellbarer ~** lenthwise adjustable anvil

Meßtisch-aufnahme *f* plane-table surveying **-blatt** *n* map scale table, plane-table sheet **-photogrammetrie** *f* plane-table photogrammetry **-platte** *f* board of the plane table

Meß-transformator *m* measuring transformer **-trichter** *m* measuring hopper **-trommel** *f* measuring drum, graduated drum

Meßtrupp *m* instrument-computing detachment, ranging or measuring section **-führer** *m* leader of radar personnel **-kraftwagen** *m* flash- and sound-ranging-detail truck

Meß-übertrager *m* measuring transformer (teleph.) **-übungsgerät** *n* practice range finder

Meßuhr *f* dial gauge, (dial) extensometer, pressure capsule **-anschlag** *m* dial gauge stop **-anzeige** *f* meter reading **-dickenmesser** *m* dial thickness indicator **-tiefenlehre** *f* dial depth gauge

Meß-umformer *m* measuring transducer **-umschalter** *m* testing commutator

Meß- und Signaleinrichtung *f* measuring and signal equipment

Meß- und Versuchswerte *pl* data

Messung *f* measurement, measuring, analysis, gauging, testing, test **~ der Abflußmengen** measurement of discharges **~ bei offenem Bohrloch** open flow test **~ durch Hörvergleich mit Sprache** voice-ear measurement **~ elektromotorischer Kräfte** electromotive-force measurements **~ im Windkanal** wind-tunnel measurement **regelmäßige ~** routine test **stationäre ~** deadbeat measurement **unechte ~** indirect measurement of length

Meßungenauigkeit *f* inexactitude of measurement

Messungsgenauigkeit *f* exactitude of measurement

Messungsstelle *f* gauging station (hydr.)

Meßunsicherheit *f* uncertanity in measurement

Meßverfahren *n* measuring method, ranging, testing method **akustisches ~** sound ranging

Meß-verstärker *m* test amplifier **-vorgang** *m* measuring or gauging process **-vorrichtung** *f* measuring device, instrument, or appliance **-walze** *f* graduated or measuring drum, height-adjusting knob (height finder), range finder

Meßwandler *m* instrument transformer, measuring transformer **~ mit Kunstschaltung** phase-compensating transformer **~ in Sparschaltung** instrument autotransformer

Meß-warte *f* control room **-wasserdurchfluß** *m* evaporator unit **-wehr** *n* calibrated weir for measuring discharge, measuring weir

Meßwerk *n* measuring element, measuring means **~ des Belichtungsmessers** exposure meter mechanism

Meßwerkzeug *n* measuring instrument, measuring tool

Meßwert *m* measurement or test result, measured value, test value, datum **einen ~ von einem Meßgerät ablesen** to read a value by an instrument

Meßwertdrucker *m* data logger

Meßwerte *m pl* test data **erflogene ~** data obtained during flight, test data

Meßwert-fehler *m* datum error **-geber** *m* primary element, pick-up **-kategorie** *f* parameter **-speicher** *m* test value storage unit **-übertragung** *f* transmission of metering intelligence **-umformer** *m* signal modulator **-verarbeitungsanlage** *f* data processing equipment **-wandler** *m* transducer

Meß-widerstand *m* precision resistance for measurement purposes **-zahl** *f* number, numerical value, measuring value, measured value **-zapfen** *m* measuring point, spindle point **-zeit** *f* testing time

Meßzelle *f* analyzer **~ mit Drähten im Verbrennungsraum** exposed filement chamber **~ mit den Verbrennungsgasen ausgesetzten Meßdrähten** (Abgasprüfer) exposed filament chamber

Meß-zellenkapazität *f* cell capacitance **-zentrale** *f* central office of measurement **-zettel** *m* gauging sheet **-zeug** *n* measuring tools **-ziffer** *f* index number **-zirkel** *m* bow spacer **-zusatz** *m* range attachment **-zweig** *m* measuring arm **-zylinder** *m* graduated cylinder, measuring cylinder, measuring glass

Meta-borsäure *f* metaboric acid **-dichlorbenzol** *n* meta-dichlorobenzene

Metadyne *f* metadyne

Metall *n* (nonferrous) metal **in ~ verwandeln** to metalize **aus ~** metallic **edles ~** noble metal, precious metal **ganz aus ~** all-metal **gespritztes ~** die-cast metal **nicht eisenhaltiges ~** nonferrous metal **unedles ~** base metal

Metalle *pl*, **hochtemperaturbeständige ~** refractory metals

Metall-abfall *m* metal scrap, metal waste **-abrieb** *m* metal abrasion **-abschirmung** *f* metal shielding **-ader** *f* metallic vein **-ähnlich** metallic **-anlaßwiderstand** *m* metallic starting rheostat **-anstrich** *m* metal(lic) coating, metal(lic) paint **-arm** poor or deficient in metal **-armiert** metal-armed **-artig** submetallic, metalloid **-artigkeit** *f* similarity to metal

Metall-auflage *f* metal coating **-auftrag** *m* metal plating **-ausführung** *f* metal construction **-auskleidung** *f* metal coating **-ausschneider** *m* metal puncher, stamper, or cutter **-azid** *n* metallic azide **-backenbremse** *f* metal-to-metal brake **-bad** *n* metal bath **-band** *n* metallic ribbon, tape **-baukasten** *m* metal architectural box

Metall-bauweise *f* metal construction **-bearbeitung** *f*, **-bearbeitungstechnik** *f* metalworking **-bekleidung** *f* metal covering or sheathing **-belag** *m* metallization of a tube, metal lining or deposit **-beplankt** metal-skinned, covered with metal **-beplankung** *f* metal covering **-beschikkung** *f* metal charge

Metallbeschlag *m* metal coating, tarnish, armature ~ (am Flugzeugrumpf) metal fitting, mount (aviation)

Metall-beschreibung *f* metallography **-beschrifter** *m* etching tool **-bestand** *m* bullion or specie in hand **-betrieb** *m* metal working plant **-biegen** *n* metal bending **-blatt** *n* metallic reed, metal foil, lamina, or lamination **-blech** *n* sheet metal, metal sheet or plate **-blechstanzen** *n* sheet-metal punching or stamping **-block** *m* metal block, organization of the electrical, motor-vehicle, precision-tool, and engineering industries **-bootskörper** *m* metal hull (protected against corrosion) **-börse** *f* metal purse

Metall-brocken *m* metal fragment **-bronzieren** *n* metal bronzing **-bügel** *m* (am Kopfhörer) metal headgear **-deckel** *m* metal cover **-dichtung** *f* metallic packing, metal seal **-dichtungsleiste** *f* flashing **-dichtungsring** *f* metallic packing ring **-drahtentladung** *f* exploded wire

Metall-druckteil *m* pressed metal part **-druckverfahren** *n* woodburytype **-dünnklischee** *n* thin gauge metal block **-einfachkassette** *f* single metal plateholder **-einfassung** *f* flashing **-einkristall** *m* metal single crystal **-einlage** *f*, **-einsatz** *m* metal insert, bond (brake)

metallen metallic

Metall-faden *m* metallic filament **-fadenlampe** *f* metallic-filament lamp, tungsten lamp **-farbe** *f* metal(lic) color, a color like metal **-fassung** *f* metal mount(ing), metal casing or fitting **-festpropeller** *m* fixed pitch metal propeller **-fiberrad** *n* composite wheel **-flügel** *m* metal wing **-flugmodell** *n* metal model plane **-flugzeug** *n* metal plane

Metall-folie *f* metal foil **-formgebung** *f* metal forming **-formguß** *m* metal mold casting **-forschung** *f* metal research **-frei** non-metallic **-fühler** *m* metal probe **-fuß** *m* metal base **-galanteriewaren** *f pl* metal fancy goods **-gefäß** *n* metallic cistern or reservoir **-geflecht** *n* metal braid **-geflechtschlauch** *m* flexible braided metal sleeve **-gehalt** *m* metal content, amount of metal in ores, yield of ores

Metallgehäuse *n* metal(lic) case **im** ~ metal-cased

metall-gekapselt metal-clad **-gekrätz** *n* waste metal **-geräusche** *pl* metals "sound off" **-gerippe** *n* metal framework **-geschützt** metal-sheathed **-gespinst** *n* metal-covered yarn **-gewebe** *n* metal cloth, metal gauze, wire cloth

Metall-gewinnung *f*, **elektronische** ~ electro-winning **-gießerei** *f* metal foundry **-glanz** *m* metallic lustre **-glas** *n* metal glaze, metal enamel **-glaskitt** *m* metal-glass seal

Metall-gleichrichter *m* metal rectifier **-grau** *n* zinc gray **-grundplatte** *f* metal base **-gruppe** *f* metalliferous group **-guß** *m* cast metal **-gußstück** *n* metal casting **-halbzeuge** *pl* semi-finished metal products **-haltig** metalliferous **-hinterlegung** *f* metal backing **-höhe** *f* metal level **-holm** *m* metal spar **-hülle** *f* metal envelope **-hütte** *f* metalworks

metallisch metallic ~ **machen** to metalize **-e Dichtung** metallic packing **-es Klingen** chink

metallischklingend metallic

metallisieren to bond (elec.), to metallice

Metallisieren *n* metallizing

Metallisierung *f* lining with metal, aluminum coating **fehlerhafte** ~ black shot **galvanische** ~ galvanic metallization

Metallkappe *f* metal cover

Metallkarbid *n* metallic carbide **gegossenes** ~ cast metal carbide **gesintertes** ~ sintered or cemented metal carbides

metallkaschiert metal clad

Metall-kassette *f* tin cashbox, metal dark slide **-kasten** *m* metal hood **-keramik** *f* powder metallurgy **-klebestoffe** *pl* metal bonding agents **-knöpfe für Paßpunkte** studs for control points **-konus** *m* metal cone **-korn** *n* globule regulus **-kratze** *f* metallic teasel **-kreissäge** *f* metal-slitting saw **-kreuzschlitten** *m* metal cross slide, compound metal tool rest **-kugel** *f* metall ball **-kunde** *f* metal science, science of metals, metallography **-kunstguß** *m* artistic metal castings

Metall-läuterungsmittel *n* metal purifying medium **-legierung** *f* alloy **-leuchterdille** *f* metal socket of a candlestick

Metallichtbogen *m* metallic arc **-schweißung** *f* metallic-arc welding

Metall-liderungskolben *m* piston with metallic packing **-luftschraube** *f* metal propeller

Metall-lutte *f* metallic air conduit **-manometer** *n* metal gauge **-meldegerät** *n* metal detector **-meißel** *m* cold chisel **-membran** *f* metal diaphragm **-mischung** *f* **zum Schweißen** welding compound **-nebel** *m* metal mist

Metallograph *m* metallographer

Metallographie *f* metallography

metallographisch metallographic(al) **-es Ätzen der Laufbuchse** etching of the barrel

Metalloid *n* metalloid

metallorganische Verbindung chelate compound

Metall-öse *f* metal eyelet **-oxydkathode** *f* metallic-oxide cathode

Metall-packung *f* metal packing **-papier** *n* metal(lic) or watered paper **-pickelbildung** *f* (corrosion) pitting **-platte** *f* metal plate or sheet, sheet metal, slab **-poliermittel** *n* metal polish **-präge** *f* metal stamping press **-präger** *m* metal embosser **-probe** *f* metal assay, metal test(ing) **-putz** *m* metal cleaner **-rahmen für Beleuchtungskuppel** metal globe frame **-rieb** *m* metal particles **-ring** *m* metal ring **-rippe** *f* metal rib

Metall-röhre *f* metal tube **-röhren** *f pl* metal tubing **-rohrholm** *m* spar of metal tubing **-rumpf** *m* metal fuselage **-sackbinde** *f* metal bagging twine **-safran** *m* crocus of antimony **-säge** *f* hack saw, metal saw **-sägefeile** *f* metal saw file **-salzkontakt** *m* metal-to-salt contact **-salzlösung** *f* metallic salt solution **-schablone** *f* metal gauge or pattern **-scheibe** *f* metallic pulley **-schelle** *f* metal clamp or clip

Metall-schere *f* snips, plate shears **-schildchen** *n* metal label **-schirm** *m* metal shade **-schlauch** *m* flexible metallic tube, metal(lic) hose **-schliff** *m* metal surface, ground-metal or polished-metal surface, polished section, microsection, metal filings **-schließzeug** *n* metal quoin **-schmelze** *f* molten metal **-schmiedestück** *n* nonferrous forging **-schneidekunst** *f* engraving on metals **-schneiden** *n* metal shearing **-schnitt** *m* metal section

Metallschraube *f* metal propeller or (air)screw, cap or iron screw

Metall-schutzband *n* protective metal ribbon **-schutzschlauch** *m* protective metal covering **-schutzverfahren** *n* metal-coating or -plating process, metal-cementation process **-schwamm** *m* biscuit **-schwimmer** *m* metal pontoon, metal float **-seele** *f* metal core **-sieb** *n* metallic screen **-sockel** *m* metal base

Metall-spaltstoffelement *n* metallic fuel element **-späne** *pl* metal shavings, turnings, borings, or chips **-spritzmethode** *f* metal spray method **-spritzverfahren** *n* metalization **-stangenpresse** *f* extrusion press for metal bars **-stapelfaser** *f* metallized fiber layers **-staub** *m* metal(lic) dust **-stopfbüchsenpackung** *f* metallic packing **-stopfen** *m* metal plug **-strangpresse** *f* extrusion press, profile press for metal rods, wire-rope press **-streifen** *m* metal strip

Metall-sulfid *n* metallic sulfide **-tafel** *f* metal plate **-teil** *m* metal part **-temperofen** *m* annealing furnace **-thermometer** *n* metallic thermometer, differential thermometer **-tuch** *n* wire cloth **-überziehung** *f* metal plating or coating **-überzug** *m* plating, metal(lic) coating, metal coat

metallumklöppeltes Kabel metal-braided cable

Metall-umschmelzofen *m* metal furnace **-ummantelung** *f* metal sheathing, covering, or envelope **-umspinnen** to metal-braid

Metallurge *m* metallurgist

Metallurgie *f* metallurgy

metallurgisch metallurgic(al)

Metall-verarbeitung *f* metalworking **-verarbeitende Industrie** metalworking industry **-verbindung** *f* metallic compound **-vergiftung** *f* metal poisoning **-verkleidung** *f* metal facing **-verlust** *m* metal loss

Metall-verschalung *f* metal covering **-verschiebung** *f* displacement of metal **-vorrat** *m* metal reservoir **-waren** *f pl* metalware, hardware **-wärmebehandlung** *f* precipitation hardening (aviation) **-wellrohr** *n* corrugated metal tube **-zapon** *n* metal zapon lacquer (varnish) **-zylinder** *m* metal cylinder

metamagnetisch metamagnetic

metamer metameric

Metamerie *f* metamerism

metamikter Zustand metamict state

meta-morph metamorphic **-morphie** *f*, **-morphismus** *m* metamorphism **-morphose** *f* metamorphosis

Metanilsäure *f* metanilic acid

Metanitranilin *n* metanitraniline

Meta-pektin *n* metapectin **-phase** *f* metaphase **-phosphorig** metaphosphorous **-phosphorsäure** *f* metaphosphoric acid **-pol** *m* focal point, isocenter, metapole

Meta-rheologie *f* metarheology **-somatisch** metasomatic

metastabil metastable **-er Energiezustand** *m* metastable atomic state

Metastabilität *f* metastability

Metastabillage *f* quasi-stable state

Metastase *f* metastasis

metastatisches Elektron metastatic electron

Meta-stellung *f* metaposition **-wolframsäure** *f* metatungstic acid **-zenterhöhe** *f* metacentric height

metazentrisch metacentric **-e Höhe** metacentric height

Meta-zentrum *n* metacenter **-zinnsäure** *f* metastannic acid

Meteoreisen *n* meteoric iron

Meteorenechos *pl* meteoric scatter

Meteorit *m* meteorite

Meteorograph *m* meteorograph

Meteorologe *m* meteorologist

Meteorologie *f* meteorology

meteorologisch meteorological **-er Bestandteil** meteorological element **-e Störung** meteorological disturbance **-e Wendekreise** meteorological tropics

Meteorschauer *m* (Astron.) meteor shower **-schwarm** *m* meteor shower **-stahl** *m* meteoric steel

Meter *n* meter **-ampere** *n* meter-ampere

Meteramperezahl *f* radiation constant ~ **geteilt durch die Wellenlänge** radiation factor

Meter-gedinge *n* cordage, footage, yardage **-grenze** *f* meter limit **-kerze** *f* meter candle **-kilogramm** *n* kilogram-meter **-maß** *n* metric measure

metern to measure

Meter-sekunde *f* meters per second **-spur** *f* track gauge of one meter width (R.R.)

Meterwellen *pl* ultra short waves, very short waves **-bereich** *m* very-high frequency, VHF **-frequenz** *f* very high frequency

Meterzahl, ausgefahrene ~ reeled-out or paid-out yardage (airplane antenna)

Meterzähler *m* film-footage counter

Methan *n* methane **-durchflußzähler** *m* methane flow counter

Methanol *n* methanol **-bildung** *f* methanol formation

Methode *f* method, process ~ **des Anschlusses von Folgebildern** method of connecting successive photographs ~ **der unabhängigen Bildpaare** method of independent image pairs ~ **der punktförmigen Elektroden** point-electrode method ~ **mit unpolarisierbaren Elektroden** porous-pot method ~ **des geothermischen Grades** geothermal method ~ **der equipotentialen Linien** equipotential-line method ~ **der spontanen Polarisation** spontaneous-polarization method ~ **der kleinsten Quadrate** method of least squares ~ **der Verhältnisse der Potentiale** potential-ratio method ~ **nach dem Verhältnis der Wechselstrompotentiale** alternating-current potential-ratio method

Methoden-lehre *f* methodology **-zuschuß** *m* excess work allowance

Methodik *f* methodology

methodisch methodic(al)

Methyl *n* methyl **-alkohol** *m* methyl alcohol

methylieren to methylate
Methylierung *f* methylation
metonischer Zyklus metonic cycle
metrisch metric(al) **-es Gewinde** metric thread **-e Pferdestärke** *f* continental horsepower **-es System** metric system **das -e Maß- und Gewichtssystem** metric system of measurement
Metronom *n* metronome, time keeper
Metzgersäge *f* butcher's saw
Mettage *f* make-up section
MeV million electron volt
m-fach primitiv m-fold primitive
Mho, mho (elec.) **Maßeeinheit der Leitsamkeit** unit (of measure) of conductivity
MHz *n* megacycle MC/s
Micell *n* micelle
Micronometer *n* micronometer
Midgetempfänger *m* midget receiver
Miete *f* clamp, silo, rent
mieten to rent, lease
Mietenfäule *f* clamp rot, root-crop rot, sclerotium disease
Mieter *m* tenant, lessee
Miet-flugzeug *n* taxiplane, hired plane **-gebühr** *f* rental fee **-leitung** *f* leased or rented wire **-vertrag für eine Leitung** leased-line contract
Mignon *f* minion (print.), minim **-sockel** *m* miniature Edison screwcap, miniature or midget base
Mikafoliummaschine *f* mica-foil machine
Mikalex *n* mycalex
Mikanit *n* built-up mica, mikanite
Mikro-ampere *n* microampere **-amperemeter** *n* microammeter **-analyse** *f* microanalysis **-aufnahme** *f* microphotograph **-bar** *n* microbar = 1 dyn/cm² **-barograph** *m* microbarograph **-bild** *n* micrograph **-brenner** *m* microburner **-chemie** *f* microchemistry **-chemisch** microchemical **-chronograf** *m* microchronograph **-coulomb** microcoulomb **-curie** *f* microcurie
Mikro-dehnung *f* micro-strain **-densogramm** *n* microdensitometer record **-Dia-Apparat** *m* micro-dia-apparatus **-dichtemesser** *m* microdensitometer **-druckmesser** *m* micromanometer **-effekt** *m* microscopic effect **-einstellung** *f* micro-set **-elektronik** *f* microminiature electronics **-farad** *n* microfarad **-film** *m* microfilm **-filter** *n* filter for micrographic work **-granophyrisch** micrographic (geol.) **-graphie** *f* micrography **-graphisch** micrographic(al) **-härteprüfung** *f* microsclerometric measurement **-henry** *n* microhenry
Mikrohm *n* microhm
Mikro-joule *n* microjoule **-kanonisch** microcanonical **-kristallin** microcrystalline **-kristallographie** *f* microcrystallography **-küvette** *f* micro-cell **-lith** *m* microlite
Mikrometer *n* micrometer **-bügel** *m* micrometer caliper **-einstellskala** *f* micrometer adjusting dial **-funkenstrecke** *f* micrometric spark **-lupe** *f* micrometer magnifier **-plättchen** *n* scale micrometer **-schraube** *f* micrometer screw or gauge **-schraubeneinstellung** *f* micrometer control **-schraubenlehre** *f* micrometer-caliper gauge **-schublehre** *f* micrometer slide gauge, microcaliper square **-spalt** *m* precision slit **-stichmaß** *n* inside micrometer caliper
Mikrometertaster *m* micrometer caliper ~ **für Längenmessung** micrometer-screw extensiometer
Mikrometerverstellung *f* micrometer adjustment
Mikro-metrie *f* micrometry **-metrisch** micrometric **-mikrocurie** *f* micromicrocurie, sunshine unit **-mikrofarad** *n* micromicrofarad **-millimeter** *n* micron
Mikron *n* micron
Mikro-nernstlampe *f* Nernst lamp of a microscope **-nutsche** *f* micro suction filter **-ohm** *n* microhm
Mikrophon *n* microphone, telephone transmitter, transmitter ~ **mit Kugeleinsprache** transmitter or microphone with spherical mouthpiece ~ **mit fester Rückwand** solid-back transmitter **das ~ schütteln** to shake up or to agitate the transmitter **bewegliches ~** following microphone **dynamisches ~, elektrodynamisches ~** moving-coil or electrodynamic microphone **elektromagnetisches ~ mit Eisenanker** moving-iron microphone
Mikrophon, elektrostatisches ~ condenser microphone **entfesseltes ~** following microphone **kapazitives ~** condenser microphone **lichtempfindliches ~** light-sensitized cell, light microphone **membranloses ~** diaphragmless microphone, cathodophone, glow-discharge microphone **nichtrichtungsempfindliches ~** astatic microphone **piezoelektrisches ~** piezoelectric or crystal microphone **statisches ~** condenser microphone
Mikrophon-ansprechkonstante *f* sensitivity constant of microphone **-antenne** *f* microphone boom or outrigger **-arm** *m* transmitter arm **-atmen** *n* breathing of microphone **-batterie** *f* transmitter battery, speaking battery **-becher** *m* mouthpiece of microphone **-brodeln** *n* mike boling, microphone boling **-effekt** *m* microphone effect
Mikrophon-einblendung *f* fade-in and mixing of microphones **-einsatz** *m* transmitter inset **-einsprache** *f* acoustic inlet of microphone **-element** *n* microphone or transmitter battery **-galgen** *m* microphone boom **-geräusch** *n* microphone or transmitter noise, side tone, carbon noise, valve noise
Mikrophonie *f* microphony
mikrophonisch microphonic(al) **-e Einstreuung** microphone susceptibility
Mikrophon-kapsel *f* microphone button, transmitter inset, resistance cell, transmitter button (capsule) **-kohle** *f* microphonic carbon **-kreis** *m* microphone range or effect **-membran** *f* transmitter diaphragm **-normal** *n* transmitter standard **-relais** *n* receiver-transmitter amplifier **-relaisschaltung** *f* microphone relay circuit
Mikrophon-schmoren *n* microphone noise **-schütz** *n* microphone relay **-sender** *m* speech-input equipment, microphone transmitter **-spannung** *f* microphone or transmitter voltage **-speiseröhre** *f* speaking-current supply tube **-speisestrom** *m* microphone supply circuit **-speisung** *f* transmitter or microphone current supply
Mikrophon-stange *f* microphone-boom **-strom** *m* transmitter or microphone current **-stromkreis** *m* transmitter or microphone circuit **-summer** *m* microphone hummer, howler **-taste** *f* microphone key **-träger** *m* transmitter arm **-trans-**

formator *m* microphone transformer **-trichter** *m* transmitter or microphone mouthpiece **-übertrager** *m* microphone transformer **-verstärker** *m* microphone amplifier, speech (-input) amplifier, microphone preamplifier

Mikro-photogramm *n* photomicrograph **-photographie** *f* photomicrography, microphotography, photomicroscopy, photomicrograph, microphotograph, micrograph **-photographisch** photomicrographic, microphotographic **-photozellen** *f pl* globules of mosaic screen **-planar** *n* microplanar **-porös** microporous **-porphyritisch** microporphyritic **-projektion** *f* microscope projection **-pyrometer** *n* micropyrometer

Mikro-radiographie *f* microradiography **-radiometer** *n* microradiometer **-raffer** *m* camera for stop-motion or time-lapse motion micrography **-rheologie** *f* micro-rheology **-rille** *f* microgroove **-risse** *pl* microcracks **-röntgenbild** *n* microradiograph **-rühreffekt** *m* micro-stirring effect

Mikro-schalttechnik *f* microminiaturization **-schliffverfahren** *n* microsectioning process **-seismus** *m* micro seism **-sekunde** *f* microsecond **-siemens** *n* micromho **-skala** *f* microscale

Mikroskop *n* microscope **bildaufrichtendes ~** image-erecting microscope

Mikroskop-ablesung *f* reading by microscope **-aufbau** *m*, **-aufhängung** *f* microscope mounting **-bügel** *m* saddle or bracket of microscope

Mikroskopie *f* microscopic optics, microscopy

Mikroskopiker *m* microscopist

Mikroskopierpunktlichtlampe *f* microscope spot arc lamp (bulb)

mikroskopisch microscopic(al) **-e Untersuchung** microscopic inspection

Mikroskop-objektiv *n* object glass of microscope, microscope lens **-revolver** *m* revolving nosepiece (of microscope) **-schleuse** *f* airlock (chamber) of electron microscope **-spektralkamera** *f* microspectroscopic camera **-stativ** *n*, **-tisch** *m*, **-träger** *m* microscope stage **-tubus** *m* microscope tube **-untersuchung** *f* microscopic examination

Mikro-spektralapparat *m* microspectroscopic apparatus **-stereophotographie** *f* stereophotomicrography **-stereoskopie** *f* stereomicroscopy **-strahl** *m* microwave, microray, quasioptical wave **-streifenleiter** *m* microstrip **-strip** *m* strip line **-struktur** *f* microstructure **-stützwirkung** *f* microsupporting effect **-tasimeter** *n* microtasimeter **-technik** *f* microtechnique **-telephon** *n* microtelephone-transmitter, telephone or combination handset

Mikrotom *n* microtome

Mikro-turbulenz *f* microturbulence **-volt** *n* microvolt **-waage** *f* microbalance **-watt** *n* microwatt **-welle** *f* microwave, microray, quasioptical wave, hyperfrequency wave

Mikrowellen-durchschlag *m* microwave breakdown **-hohlraum** *m* microwave cavity **-interferometrie** *f* microwave interferometry **-relaisstrecke** *f* microwave radio link **-richtfunkverbindung** *f* (Astron.) microwave link **-strecke** *f* microwave relay link

Mikro-zeitmeßgerät *n* microchronograph **-zoll** *m* micro-inch

Mikrurgie *f* micrurgy

Mil *n* (1/6400 des Kreisumfanges) mil

Milch *f* emulsion, milk

milchen to give milk, emulsify

Milch-entrahmer *m* cream separator **-glas** *n* frosted glass, bone glass, opal glass **-glasglocke** *f* opal-glass globe **-glasskala** *f* ground-or milk-glass scale

milchig milky, lactic **-e Flüssigkeit** emulsion

Milch-kammer *f* milk storage **-kanne** *f* milk can **-kühlanlage** *f* milk-cooling plant

Milch-kühler und -lüfter milk cooler and aerator (Berieselungs) **Milchkühler für unmittelbare Verdampfung** milk (trickling) cooler with direct evaporation

Milch-messer *m* lactometer **-saft** *m* latex **-säure** *f* lactic acid **-säuregärung** *f* lactic fermentation

milchsauer-er Kalk calcium lactate **-es Salz** lactate

Milch-schicht *f* emulsion **-separator** *m* cream separator **-straße** *f* Milky Way **-waage** *f* lactometer **-weiß** *n* lead sulfate pigment **-zentrifuge** *f* cream separator **-zucker** *m* milk sugar, lactose

mild mild, gentle, soft

Milde *f* mildness, gentleness

mildern to mitigate, alleviate, temper, ease, moderate

Milderungsgründe *pl* extenuating or mitigating circumstances

mildharter Guß moderately chilled iron

Milieu *n* environment

Militär *n* army, military **-bauwesen** *n* military construction department **-behörde** *f* military authorities

militärisch military **-e Ausführung** military version **-e Verwendung** military use

Millefiori *f pl* fretwork, glass mosaics, millefiori

Millerit *m* millerite, hair pyrites

Miller-Kreis *m* Miller circuit **-Zeitbasis** *f* Miller time-base

Milli-ampere *n* milliampere (ma, mA) **-amperemeter** *n* milliamperemeter, milliammeter

Milliarde *f* billion

Milli-bar *n* millibar **-curie** *f* millicurie **-curie-détruit** *m* millicurie-destroyed **-henry** *n* millihenry **-lambert** *n* millilambert

Millimeter-gewinde *n* metric thread **-papier** *n* graph paper (graded in millimeters) **-steigung** *f* metric thread **-teilung** *f* metric graduation **-wellen** *pl* extremely high frequency (EHF)

Millionenzyklus *m* megacycle

Millisekunde *f* millisecond

Millivolt *n* millivolt **-messer** *m*, **-meter** *n* millivoltmeter **-spannung** *f* millivoltage

Milliwatt *n* milliwatt

Mimetesit *m* mimetite

Minderbewertung *f* devaluation

minder less, lesser, smaller **-einnahme** *f* decrease of or deficiency in receipts **-gewicht** *n* short weight **-haltiges Erz** low-grade ore

Minderheit *f* minority

Minder-jährigkeit *f* minority **-leistung** *f* reduced output **-maschine** *f* narrowing machine

mindern to lessen, diminish

Minderung *f* diminution, decrease, reduction, narrowing **~ der Übertragungsgüte** transmission impairment **~ der Übertragungsgüte durch Frequenzbandbegrenzung** distortion-transmission impairment ~ **der Übertragungsgüte durch Leitungsgeräusche** noise-transmission impairment ~ **der Verständlichkeit** articulation reduction

Minderungsbeiwert *m* coefficient of reduction

Minderwert *m* inferiority, depreciation (in value)

minderwertig low-grade **-e Mischung** low grade stock

Minderwertigkeit *f* inferiority

Minderzahl *f* minority, smaller amount or number

mindest least, smallest, minimum, lowest

Mindest-absaugemenge *f* minmum suction quantity **-achsiallänge** *f* minimum axial length **-anlaßspannung** *f* minimum starting voltage **-ansprechstrom** *m* minimum operating current **-auftriebsgeschwindigkeit** *f* stalling speed (aviation) **-ausschlag** *m* minimum deflection **-betrag** *m* lower limit **-betriebsdruck** *m* minimum operating pressure **-biegung** *f* minimum bend

Mindest-druck *m* minimum pressure **-flughöhe** *f* minimum flight altitude **-geschwindigkeit** *f* minimum speed **-gesprächsgebühr** *f* minimum rate **-gewicht** *n* minimum weight **-hindernisfreiheit** *f* minimum obstacle clearance **-kronenbreite** *f* smallest breadth of the top of an embankment **-lastwechselzahl** *f* minimum number of cycles

Mindestmaß *n* minimum (measure) **auf das ~ zurückführen** to minimize

Mindest-nutzbreite *f* usable minimum width **-restdämpfung** *f* minimum net loss **-rohrerhöhung** *f* minimum barrel elevation **-sicherheitsabstand** *m* close quarter situation **-sinkgeschwindigkeit** *f* minimum speed of vertical descent **-spannungsgradient** *m* minimum potential gradient **-spiel** *n* minimum clearance **-streckgrenze** *f* minimum elastic limit

Mindest-strom *m* minimum current **-stromstärke** *f* minimum current intensity **-voltgeschwindigkeit** *f* appearance or minimum potential **-wert** *m* minimum value **-wertanzeiger** *m* minimum (voltage) indicator **-zerplatzdruck** *m* minimum blowout pressure **-zugfestigkeit** *f* minimum tensile strength **-zündstrom** *m* striking current

Mine *f* mine, pit, lead **auf eine ~ laufen** to hit or strike a mine

Minen-abteilung *f* mine-laying detachment **-abwehr** *f* antimine defense

Minenabweiser *m* paravane **~ auslassen** to stream paravanes

Minen-auge *n* entrance into a gallery (min.) **-bezirk** *m* diggings **-gang** *m* gallery (min.)

Minen-halle *f* mine chamber (min.) **-halter** *m* lead holder **-herd** *m* focus or hearth of a mine **-hund** *m* mucker's car or truck **-kammer** *f* mine chamber, lead magazine **-kratze** *f* miner's hoe or scraper

Minen-sicherung *f* mine security **-sprengung** *f* blasting by means of a mine **-spitzer** *m* pencil sharpener **-stollen** *m* mine gallery

Minensuchgerät, elektronisches ~ mine detecting set

Minenwirkung *f* mine effect

Mineral *n* mineral **-bestandteil** *m* mineral or inorganic constituent **-bildner** *m* mineralizer **-brunnen** *m* mineral or thermal spring **-chemie** *f* inorganic chemistry **-feile** *f* emery stick **-gang** *m* mineral vein **beigemengte Mineralien** accessory minerals

Mineralien-kunde *f* mineralogy **-mahlanlage** *f* mineral-grinding plant

mineralisch mineral **-e Erschwerung** *f* mineral weighting **-es Harz** mineral resin

Mineral-kermes *m* kermes mineral **-lagerstätte** *f* mineral deposit **-lehre** *f* mineralogy

Mineralog *m* mineralogist

Mineralogie *f* mineralogy

mineralogisch mineralogical

Mineralöl *n* mineral oil, petroleum **leicht gefettetes ~** compound mineral oil

Mineral-ölraffinat *n* refined mineral oil **-ölraffinerie** *f* mineral-oil refinery **-pech** *n* mineral pitch asphaltum **-quelle** *f* mineral-water spring **-reich** *n* mineral kingdom **-säure** *f* mineral acid **-schmierstoff** *m* mineral lubricant **-talg** *m* mineral tallow, hatchettine **-teer** *m* mineral tar, maltha **-teilchen** *n* mineral particle **-wachs** *n* mineral wax, ozocerite **-wasser** *n* mineral water

Minette *f* minette ore, oölitic brown iron ore **-eisenstein** *m* minette

Miniatur *f* miniature **-dimensionierung** *f* miniaturisation **-gerät** *n* miniature device

Miniaturisierung *f* new dimensions system

minieren to mine

Miniergerät *n* mining tools

Minimal-abstand *m* minimum distance **-amplitude** *f* minimum amplitude **-ausschalter** *m* minimum cutout **-format** *n* minimum size **-größe** *f* minimum size **-relais** *n* no-load relay **-sätze** *pl* minimal theorems **-skalenwert** *m* minimum scale value

Minimalsuchzeit *f* minimum latency **-programmieren** *n* minimum access programming, forced coding

Minimalwert *m* minimum value

Minimeter *n* minimeter **-gerät zum Messen der Kompressionshöhe** minimeter instrument for testing the distance between pinholes and piston head

Minimum-auftriebsgeschwindigkeit *f* stalling speed **-bereinigung** *f* zero clearing (direction finder) **-fluggeschwindigkeit** *f* minimum flying speed **-gleitwinkel** *m* minimum gliding angle **-peilung** *f* minimum- or zero-signal direction-finding method **-schärfen** *n* zero cleaning, zero sharpening (direction finder) **-schärfer** *m* minimum fine tuning device **-strahldefinition** *f* definition of minimum beam **-strahlkennzeichnung** *f* marking of minimum beam **-verfahren** *n* method based on minimum deviation (optics) **-wanderung** *f* minimum degree of error (direction finder) **-wertzeiger** *m* minimum(-voltage) indicator **-wetterzustand** *m* weather minimum

Ministerium *n* ministry, department, cabinet

Minium *n* minium, red lead oxide

Minorante *f* minorant

Minoritäts-emitter *m* minority emitter **-ladungsträger** *m* minority charge carrier

Minosplattenkondensator *m* minos plate condenser

Minuendus *m* minuend

Minus-ader *f* negative wire **-bestand** *m* deficiency (in stock pile) **-bürstenhalter** *m* negative brush holder **-elektrizität** *f* negative electricity

Minuskel *f* small letter, minuscule

Minus-lehre *f* minus gauge **-leitung** *f* negative lead **-platte** *f* negative plate **-pol** *m* negative pole (elec.) **-strang** *m* reverse line **-zeichen** *n* minus sign

Minute *f* minute **in der ~** per minute

Minutenring *m* tapered compression piston ring

Minutenrose *f* minute card

Minutenzeiger *m* minute hand

minutlich per minute

minutiös minute

Miocän *n* miocene

Mipolam *n* a type of synthetic rubber

Mipolid *n* mixed polyamide

Mirabilit (Min.) sodium sulfate (mirabilit)

Miscella *f* oil solution obtained in extracting oil seeds, etc.

Mischanlage *f* proportioner, mixing installation, coal-blending plant **~ für Bodenarten** ground-mixing plant

Mischapparat *m* mixer, mixing apparatus, blending equipment (device)

mischbar mixable, miscible **gegenseitig ~** consolute **nicht ~** immiscible

Mischbarkeit *f* miscibility

Misch-behälter *m* mixing vessel, tank, or drum **-bewegung** *f* mixing motion **-bildentfernungsmesser** *m* double-image range finder **-binder** *m* emulsion **-blockschnabel** *m* nozzle feeding to carburetor venturi **-brett** *n* mixing panel, monitoring or supervising panel **-bühne** *f* gauging (mixing) platform **-düse** *f* mixing nozzle, eject-condenser

mischen to mix, mingle; (verschiedene Sorten) (Metall) alloy; (Chem.) combine; (Bestandteile) compound; (verfälschen) adulterate, fettle (metal.); temper, merge, potch (paper mfg.), poach, unite

Mischer *m* mixer, receiver, hot-metal mixer, fader, blender, mixing booth **mit der Hand regulierter ~** manually operated mixture control **fünfgliedriger ~** five-channel mixer **~ mit Wechselbehältern** change-tank mixer

Mischer-bühne *f* mixer platform **-eisen** *n* mixer metal **-kran** *m* mixing plant crane **-röhre** *f* frequency changer **-schaltung** *f* keying or mixer-tube scheme **-stufenröhre** *f* frequency changer

Misch-erz *n* mixed ore **-fähigkeit** *f* (mit Blei) lead response (fuel) **-farbe** *f* mixed color **-feldbeleuchtung** *f* combined bright and dark field illumination **-feuer** *n* alternating colored lights **-flosse** *f* secondary air mixer **-flügel** *m* mixing wing, stirring paddle, stirring wing **-flußschnellrührer** *m* mixed impeller

Mischgas *n* mixed gas, semiwater gas, combination coke-oven and blast-furnace gas **-erzeuger** *m* mixed-gas producer **-prozeß** *m* Dowson-gas process

Misch-gerät *n* mixer or mixing unit, control amplifier mixer bus **-gitter** *n* injector grid **-glied** *n* mixer **-gut** *n* material to be mixed **-heptode** *f* pentagrid converter **-hexode** *f* mixing hexode, hexode mixing valve **-impulsschaltung** *f* multiloop system (the correction variables acting upon the controller) **-kammer** *f* mixing chamber **-kegel** *m* burner cone **-kohle** *f* run-of-mine coal **-koller** *m*, **-kollergang** *m* pug mill, pan grinder, edge-runner mixer, runner for mixing

Mischkopf *m* mixer head (elec.) **~ zum Senderüberlagerer** mixer of main receiver

Mischkristall *n* solid solution, mixed crystal, crystalline solid solution **-legierung** *f* solid-solution alloy, mixed-crystal alloy **-reihe** *f* solid-solution series

Misch-last *f* mixed load **-lastabwurfbehälter** *m* supply container with parachute **-lautsprecher** *m* channel mixing loudspeaker **-lichtlampen** *pl* combined mercury vapor and incandescent lamps

Mischluft *f* secondary air **-leitung** *f* (Gasmaschine) suction air piping **-sammler** *m* combustion air collector

Misch-maschine *f* mixing machine, mixer, kneading mill **-metall** *n* mixed metal, alloy, misch metal **-molekül** *n* mixed molecule **-oktanzahl** *f* mixed octane numbers **-operationen in Rohrleitungen** in-line blending **-oxyd** *n* mixed oxide, leaded zinc **-peilung** *f* taking bearings on board **-pfanne** *f* mixing pan, reservoir ladle

Mischphase *f*, **geordnete ~** nonstochiometric compound

Mischprodukt *n* mixture product

Mischpult *n* mixing desk, monitoring or supervising desk **fahrbares ~** dolly or cart-type mixer, tea-wagon console mixer

Misch-polymerisat *n* interpolymer **-raum** *m* mixture chamber **-regler** *m* mixing control **-reibung** *f* mixed friction **-rohr** *n* mixing tube, burner pipe, carburetor choke

Mischröhre *f* mixing valve, frequency-changer valve, converter tube, detector mixer tube **selbstschwingende ~** self-heterodyning mixer tube, autodyne

Misch-satz *m* mixed setting **-schaltung** *f* mixing stage **-schnecke** *f* mixing screw **-signal** *n* signal spectrum **-steilheit** *f* conversion transconductance **-strom** *m* undulatory current **-stufe** *f* frequency changer, combined oscillator detector, mixer, converter, mixer stage, mixer-first detector stage **-tafel** *f* mixing panel, monitoring or supervising panel **-tisch** *m* mixing desk, monitoring desk **-trog** *m* mixing trough **-trommel** *f* mixing drum

Mischung *f* mix, mixture, blend, compound, blending

Mischungs-bestandteil *m* ingredient of mixture **-kalorimeter** *n* water calorimeter **-lücke** *f* gap in the range of miscibility, miscibility gap **-nebel** *m* advection fog **-rechnung** *f* alligation (math.) **-regelglieder** proportioning elements **-regler** *m* proportioning device **-temperatur** *f* mixture temperature **-verhältnis** *n* mixture ratio, mixing proportion **-vorgang** *m* mixing process **-vorschrift** *f* recipe **-weg** *m* mixing method

Mischungswertigkeitsziffer bei Oktanzahlbestimmung blending value

Misch-ventil *n* mixing valve, mixer valve **-verhältnis** *n* air fuel ratio **-verstärker** *m* mixing or boosting amplifier conversion gain **-verstärkungsgrad** *m* conversion gain ratio **-vorgang** *m* mixing process

Mischwähler *m* secondary-line switch, load-distributing switch **~ für Sammelanschlüsse** hunting switch

Misch-wald *m* mixed woods **-walze** *f* mixer **-walzwerk** *n* set of mixing rollers **-weise** *f* manner of mixing **-werk** *n* mixing mill **-wirkung** *f* mixing action **-zone** *f* mixing zone, twilight zone (navig) **-zug** *m* mixed sliver **-zylinder** *m* stoppered cylinder

Mispickel *m* arsenopyrite, mispickel

Missale *n* missal

Miß-bildung *f* deformity, malformation **-billigen** to disapprove, condemn, reprove **-billigung** *f* disapproval

Mißbrauch *m* miscuse, abuse

Miß-erfolg *m* failure **-ernte** *f* crop failure **-fallen** to displease **-farbig** discolored **-geschick** *n* misadventure **-gestaltet** deformed, misshapen **-griff** *m* blunder, error **-griffsicher** foolproof **-handlung** *f* maltreatment **-klang** *m* discord, dissonance **-klingend** dissonant

miß-leiten to misdirect **-liegen** to fail, miscarry, be unsuccessful **-lungener Teil** unsuccessful take (motion pictures) **-ratenes Stück** failed piece **-stand** *m* abnormal or faulty condition **-ton** *m* jar, distorted sound, offpitch note **-verhältnis** *n* asymmetry, disproportion, incongruity, disparity **-verständnis** *n* misunderstanding **-verstehen** to misunderstand

mißweisend magnetic (as opposed to true) **-er Kurs** uncorrected bearing, magnetic heading, magnetic course ~ **Nord** uncorrected or magnetic north

Mißweisung *f* magnetic declination, magnetic variation, deviation from the true bearing, indication error

Mißweisungs-gleiche *f* isogonic line **-karte** *f* declination map or chart **-winkel** *m* angle of declination

Mißzeichnung *f* distortion

Miszelle *f* micelle

Mit-arbeit *f* cooperation, collaboration, assistance **-arbeiten** to work together, collaborate, participate **-arbeiter** *m* collaborator, colleague, coworker, contributor, assistant **-arbeiterstab** *m* staff

mit-bestimmend of determinative influence **-bestimmung** *f* co-determination **-bewegend** geared to **-bewegt** convected **-bewegung** *f* dragging, comovement **-bewerber** *m* competitor

Mit-eigentümer *m* part owner **-einander** together, jointly **-einbegriffensein** *n* implication **-fahren** to be a passenger, ride along, sit in **-fällung** *f* coprecipitation, coseparation **-fühlen** to sympathize **-fühlend** sympathetic **-führung** *f* convection (of heat), entrainment **-führungskoeffizient** *m* coefficient of drag

mitgeliefert supplied

mitgenommene, selbständige Kippmethode self-running controlled time-base method (television) **loses mitgenommenes Zahnrad** idler gear

mitgeschleppt convected **-er Fehler** *m* inherited error (comput.)

Mitgliedschaft *f* membership

Mitgliedsfirma *f* subscribing firm

mit-halten to keep up with **-hilfe** *f* assistance

Mithör-apparat *m* special observation post **-dienst** *m* radio-monitoring service **-einrichtung** *f* monitoring device, circuit, or installation, wire tapping, side-tone device or circuit

mithören to listen in, overhear, monitor, (abhören) tap the wire

Mithörer *m* monitoring device for radio, monitor

Mithör-klinke *f* monitor(ing) jack, listening jack **-kreis** *m* tie-in circuit **-regler** *m* monitering control **-relais** *n* listening relay **-schalter** *m*, **-schlüssel** *m* listening key **-schaltung** *f* monitoring circuit **-schrank** *m* monitoring board **-stellung** *f* listening position **-stöpsel** *m* answering plug **-taste** *f* monitoring key, listening key **-übertrager** *m* monitoring coil

Mithör- und Sprechapparat *m* master station (teleph.)

Mithör-verfahren *n* intercept method **-vorrichtung** *f* monitoring facility

Mitinhaber *m* joint proprietor, partner in a firm

Mitisgrün *n* Paris green, emerald green

mit-klingen to resonate **-koppeln** *n* determining of course or fix, plotting (navig.)

Mitkopplung *f* positive regeneration, positive feedback, spurious feedback **äußere** ~ separate self-excitation (trans.) **innere** ~ auto self-excitation

Mitkopplungsschleife *f* regenerative loop (comput)

mitlaufend following **-e Brille** follower **-er Meßleitungsdetektor** traveling detector **-e Spannung** follower potential **-e Spitze** live or running center **-er Sucher** follow-focus device

Mitlauf-körnerspitze *f* life center **-wähler** *m* simultaneous-movement selector, companion-work switch **-werk** *n* switching selector repeater

Mitlaut *m* consonant

Mitlese-apparat *m* control instrument, leak instrument **-drucker** *m* control printer

mit-lesen to control **-leser** *m* monotorial device (teleph.)

Mitlese-rekorder *m* control recorder **-ring** *m* control ring **-streifen** *m* office record **-stromkreis** *m* leak circuit **-text** *m* local record

mitmachen to be closely identified with

Mitnahme *f* pulling into tune, synchronization, pull-in step, locking in, locking of circuit ~ **der Röhrenschwingung** carrying along of tube oscillation

Mitnahme-bereich *m* drag range (radio), range of forced oscillations, coherence range, pull-in-step range **-erscheinung** *f* pulling into tune, pulling in **-körner** *m* center driver **-oszillator** *m* locked oscillator

mitnehmen to drive (*e.g.*, a motor), take along, take up in plane, (Schmierstoff) pick up

Mitnehmen *n* drift (in discharge)

Mitnehmer *m* cam; (Vorrichtung) fixtures; (Drehwerkzeug) driver, carrier, dog; (Drehherz) lathe dog; catch, flight attachment (of a chain), tang, square, tappet, follower, striker, carrier plate (in axle assembly), gripper, nose clutch, engaging piece, entrainment means ~ **für das Arbeitsstück** work-driving arm and pin

Mitnehmer-bolzen *m* carrier bolt, tappet, keeper pin **-buchse** *f* driving bush **-einsatz** *m* drive bushing, drill-stem bushing **-flansch** *m* driving flange **-flügel** *m* driving blade **-hebel** *m* engaging lever

Mitnehmerherz für Arbeitsstücke work-driving cam

Mitnehmer-kasten *m* press button housing **-kette** *f* flight-attachment chain, coupling chain **-klaue**

f engaging dog **-klinke** *f* pawl **-kuppelung** *f* back-gear sliding pinion and stem gear **-kreuzscheibe** *f* cross-type driving disc **-lappen** *m* tang **-nut** *m* keyway **-platte** *f* dog plate, catch plate **-riegel** *m* plunger cam **-ring** *m* friction disk, catch ring **-rohr** *n* helical tube **-scheibe** *f* entrainer disk, driving disk, carrier plate cover **-schiene** *f* striker bar **-schraube** *f* cam stud

Mitnehmerspindel-antriebsscheibe *f* live-spindle driving pulley **-feststellstift** *m* live-spindle locking pin

Mitnehmer-spitze *f* lathe carrier center **-stange** *f* groove stem **-stift** *m* coupling through pin, follower pin, drive pin (acoust.) **-stück** *n* coupling adapter **-welle** *f* clutch shaft **-zapfen** *m* tang **-zunge** *f* driving lug (driving tongue)

Mitose *f* mitosis

mitogenetische Strahlung mitogenic radiation

mitotisch mitotic

mitrechnen to take into account

mitreißen to carry forward, carry over, prime (water) entrain, drag or pull along

Mitreißen von Gas vapor carryover

mitrotierend-es Bezugssystem co-rotational frame **-er Fluß** co-rotational time flux

mitschiffs amidships

Mitschleppdruck *m* drag pressure

mit-schleppen to carry along **-schleppfilter** *n* entrainment filter **-schleppkraft** *f* drag loading **-schreiber** *m* logger (comput)

mitschwingen to resonate, covibrate, oscillate in resonance, sympathy, or unison

Mitschwingen *n* resonance

mitschwingend resonant **nicht ~** nonresonant **-er Leiter** equifrequent conductor, resonant or covibrant conductor **-e Saite** sympathetic string or chord

Mit-schwingung *f* covibration, sympathetic vibration **-schwingungsgezeit** *f* co-oscillational tide **-schwingungsvermögen** *n* ability to follow in the oscillation **-sprechen** *n* side-to-phantom cross talk, overhearing **-sprechkoppelung** *f* cross-talk path, phantom-to-side unbalance

Mittag *m* noon, midday, mean noon **-essen** *n* dinner

mittags at noon, at midday **-kreis** *m* meridian **-linie** *f* meridian line

Mitte *f* middle, center, center line, center point **~ der Differentialspule** split point, center tapping point **~ des Sturmes** eye of the storm **auf die ~ einstellen** to center **genaue ~** dead center **von ~ zu ~** centre to centre (c-c)

mitteilen to communicate, intimate **einen Zustand ~** to impart (to)

Mitteilung *f* message, report, information, communication, note **schriftliche ~** written notice

Mittel *n* (Hilfs~) means; (Vorrichtung) device; (Verfahren) method; (Ausweg) expedient; (Maßregel) measure; (Durchschnitt) average; (Math.) mean; (Physik) medium; (Vorrat) supply; (Geld) means, funds; (Werkstoff) medium; compound, middle, expendable supply, resource, appliance, remedy, agency **~ zur Erhöhung der Klopffestigkeit** antidetonant **das ~ bilden** to take the mean, average **arithmetisches ~** arithmetic mean **brechendes ~** refractive medium **dünnes ~** rare or subtle medium **schwebendes ~** isolated mass **taubes ~** sterile mass **widerrechtliches ~** illegal measure

Mittel-abgriff *m* center tap **-abstand** *m* center distance **-achse** *f* axle center or shaft **-anzapfung** *f* center tapping, mid(-point) tap **-aufnahme** *f* medium shot **-bahnberechnung** *f* computation of mean trajectory **-balken** *m* balk, central girder

mittelbar indirect, mediate **~ wirkend** pilot or relay-operated, **-e Heizung** indirect heating **-e Lichtbogenbeheizung** indirect arc heating **-e Patentverletzung** contributory infringement of patent

Mittel-bau *m* frontage **-benzin** *n* medium heavy petrol **-bereich-Rundsicht-Radaranlage** *f* medium range surveillance radar **-betrieb** *m* medium-size enterprise **-bildhelligkeit** *f* average or background illumination, mean brightness value of picture **-bildung** *f* averaging **-blech** *n* medium plate or sheet, jobbing sheet, light plate **-blechwalzwerk** *n* light plate-rolling mill, jobbing sheet-rolling mill **-blende** *f* middle diaphragm **-brechpflug** *m* middle breaker **-breite** *f* mean latitude

Mittel-deck *n* waist **-decker** *m* mid-wing monoplane **-dicht** medium density **-ding** *n* intermediate case, compromise, cross **-draht** *m* medium gauge wire

Mitteldruck *m* mean effective pressure, mean pressure, medium pressure **effektiver ~, nutzbarer ~** brake mean effective pressure

Mitteldruck-anlage *f* hydroelectric plant of moderate head **-flasche** *f* flash-type intercooler **-ladermotor** *m* medium supercharged engine **-linie** *f* center (line) of pressure **-reifen** *m* medium-pressure tire **-stufe** *f* intermediate-pressure stage **-teil** *m* medium-pressure part **-zylinder** *m* medium-pressure cylinder

Mittelebene *f* median plane **~ des Objektivs** central plane of the lens

Mittel-elektrode *f* center electrode **-faden** *m* centerline wire, middle thread **-farbe** *f* secondary color

Mittelfeld *n* central field (of vision) **~ der Glasscheibe** center field of glass lens

Mittel-farben *pl* secondary colors **-fläche** *f* neutral plane **-flügel** *m* center section **-frequenz** *f* medium or center frequency **-fries** *m* mullion **-fristig** intermediate **-gang** *m* gangway, main aisle **-gebirge** *n* highlands, hills **-gedämpfter Raum** moderately live room **-gehäuse** *n* center housing

Mittel-gerüst *n* intermediate roll stand **-geschaltetes Sockel-Steuergerät** *n* socket control valve **-glied** *n* intermediate member (of a series) **-groß** medium-sized **-gut** *n* middlings **-hart** medium-hard **-hieb** *m* bastard cut **-hochwasser** *n* mean high water (level)

Mittel-höhe der Ebbe half-tide **-ionen** *pl* intermediate ions **-kielplatte** *f* center through plate **-klüver** *m* middle jib **-kontaktgefäß** *n* central-contact trough, middle-contact basin **-kraft** *f* resultant force, resultant **-kreuz** *n* cross or cross lines **-kufe** *f* central skid **-kurs** *m* middle price **-lage** *f* neutral position, central position, midposition, tenor (voice) **-lager** *n* center bearing **-lastfeder** *f* static loading spring **-lauf** *m* middle course **-leiste** *f* center selvedge

Mittelleiter *m* neutral wire, third wire, the neutral, center bar **geerdeter ~** grounded neutral

Mittellicht *n* half tone, average shading value

Mittellinie *f* axis, center line, neutral line, construction line **erste ~, spitze ~** acute bisectrix **stumpfe ~, zweite ~** obtuse bisectrix

Mittellinien-feuer (Flugplatz) *n* center line lights **-kondensator** *m* mid-line condenser, logarithmic condenser

mittel-los without means, destitute **-lot** *n* median perpendicular **-mäßig** medium, tolerable **-mäßigkeit** *f* mediocrity **-mauer** *f* mean wall **-meridian** *m* mid-meridian **-moräne** *f* medial moraine **-motor** *m* central engine

mitteln to average, ascertain mean value

Mittel-niedrigwasser *n* mean low water (level) **-öffnung** *f* main arch **-öl** *n* medium oil **-pfeiler** *m* central pier **-pfosten** *m* mullion **-platte** *f* center plate **-pleuel** *n* articulated connecting rod **-produkt** *n* chats (min.), middlings

Mittelpunkt *m* center, central point **vom ~ fortstrebend** centrifugal **zum ~ hinstrebend** centripetal **in einem ~ vereinigen** to centralize **~ des Auftriebs** center of buoyance

Mittelpunkt-ausbreitung *f* open center control **-gleichung** *f* equation of the center **-projektion** *f* gnomonic projection **-speisung** *f* apex drive **-sucher** *m* center punch, center-punching apparatus **-tastschaltung** *f* center-tap key-modulator scheme **-triangulation** *f* center triangulation

Mittel-quaderpfeiler *m* intermediate jamb **-quadratenmethode** *f* mid-square method **-rad** *n* middle, central, or minute wheel **-radius** *m* mean radius **-rapport** *m* center repeat **-reihe** *f* central row **-renner** *m* central runner **-riegel** *m* cross brace, middle traverse, middle crosspiece (sluice) **-rippe** *f* central web **-rohrrahmen** *m* center tubular chassis

mittels through, by, by means of

Mittel-schaft *m* intermediate jamb **-scheibe** *f* groove or intermediate disk **-schenkel** *m* center leg, center limb or bar

Mittelschiene *f* central rail **~ der Taste** center of key

Mittel-schiff *n* middle aisle **-schild** *n* center shield **-schneider** *m* plug tap **-schnelles Neutron** intermediate neutron **-schnitt** *m* cross section **-schnittmähbalken** *m* medium cutting mower bar

Mittelschrift, geneigte ~ large text

mittelschwer medium heavy **-e Bespulung** medium-heavy loading

Mittelschwert *n* centerboard

Mittelschwimmer *m* central float **-flugzeug** *n* central-float plane

Mittel-senkrechte *f* mid-vertical, median perpendicular **-spannung** *f* mean stress **-spant** *n* midship frame **-ständig** occupying a middle position **-starkes Klopfen** medium detonation **-steg** *m* long cross, cross bar **-stein** *m* central brick **-stellung** *f* mid-position **-stempel** *m* center ram **-straße** *f* intermediate rolling train (rolling mill), middle mill **-strebe** *f* mediate strut **-strecke** *f* intermediate strand of rolls

Mittelstück *n* center bit, body (of converter) **eingezogenes ~** waist

Mittel-stütze *f* intermediate support **-teil** *m* mid-portion, mid-section **-teil der Zelle** center frame **-trieb** *m* central focusing

Mittel- und Grobbleche *pl* plates

Mittel-wache *f* midwatch **-walze** *f* middle roll, center roller **-walzwerk** *n* intermediate rolling mill **-wasser** *n* mean water (level), mean stage, mean sea level **-weg zwischen zwei Geleisen** six-foot way (R.R.) **-weiß** *n* equal-signal white **-welle** *f* countershaft, medium wave (radio),

Mittelwellen-antriebsrad *n* center driving-shaft gear **-bereich** *m* medium frequency band **-empfänger** *m* medium-wave receiver **-sender** *m* medium-wave transmitter

Mittelwert *m* average, mean value, median **~ einer periodischen Größe** mean-value of a periodic quantity **~ in Umdrehungen pro Minute** average speed in revolutions per minute **auf einen ~ bringen** to equate **um einen ~ schwingen** to oscillate about an average value **quadratischer ~** virtual value, root-mean-square value

Mittelwert-bildung *f* taking the mean **-satz** *m* mean-value theorem, principle of averages **-schreiber** *m* impulse recorder **-zeiger** *m* mean-impulse or average-value indicator

Mittel-zahl *f* average **-zapfen** *m* center journal or stud **-zerkleinerung** intermediate size reduction **-zeit** *f* mean time **-zinken** *m* center tooth

mitten to center **-abstand** *m* distance between center lines, center-to-center distance, distance between successive rulings (in diffraction grating) **-achsenbewegung** *f* center line movement **-anschlag** *m* center stop or dog **-anzapfung** *f* central tapping (elec.) **-druck** *m* central pressure, pressure at center **-eindruck** *m* binaural balance **-entfernung** *f* center distance

Mitten-frequenz *f* center frequency **-maß** *n* center size (dimension) **-richtig** centered, cocentric **-richtigkeit** *f* concentricity **-schärfe** *f* central definition, sharpness of center **-schwimmer** *m* central float **-symmetrisch** centrosymmetrical **-versetzung** *f* center offset

mittig axial, centric, central, coaxial, concentric **~, einstellen** to center **-e Beanspruchung** *f* axial stress

Mittigkeit *f* centrality, centricity

mittler mean, average, medium **-e quadratische Abweichung** mean square deviation **-e Anregungsspannung** average exitation potential **-e Belastungsdichte** average density of charge **-e Bespulung** medium loading **-er Breitenflug** middle-latitude flying **-er Druck** mean effective (brake) pressure **-e Durchdringungsgeschwindigkeit** drift velocity (speed) **-er Fehler** standard deviation mean error **-e Flügeltiefe** mean chord

mittlere Geschwindigkeit mean or average speed **-e Gleitflugkurve** medium gliding turn **-e Größe** mean value **-e Helligkeit** average (background) illumination (television) **-e Impulsleitung** average pulse power (radar) **-er** (gezogener) **Kurvenflug** medium (climbing) turn **-e Längenstreuung** range dispersion **-e Leistung** mean power **-e Linie** mean line

mittler-es Profil medium-thick profile **-e Proportionale** mean proportional **-er Rumpfholm** stringer **-es Schmieröl** medium-heavy-weight oil **-e Sonne** mean sun **-er Sonnentag** mean solar

day **-e Sonnenzeit** civil time, mean solar time **-e Spulenweite** bobbin overall diameter **-e quadratische Streuung** standard deviation
mittlerer Tag mean noon **-e Tiefe** mean chord (of a wing) **-er Tiefgang** mean draft **-er Treffpunkt** center of dispersion, center of impact **-e Wartezeit auf einer zwischenstaatlichen Leitung** average international component of the speed-of-service interval (teleph.) **-er Wasserstand** mean water level **-e freie Weglänge** mean free length of path **-e Welle** medium wave **-er Wirkungsdruck** brake mean effective pressure **-e (Sonnen-)zeit** mean (solar) time
mittönen to sound simultaneously
mittragen to carry
mittragende Beplankung stressed skin
Mit- und Vorhöreinrichtung *f* feedback circuit
Mittung *f* centering
Mittungs-schneide *f* centering disk, knife-edge bearing **-stift** *m* centering screw or pin
Mittzapfen *m* spigot shaft
Mit-verantwortung *f* joint responsibility **-wind** *m* tail wind **-wirken** to cooperate, assist, help **-wirkung** *f* participation, collaboration, cooperation **-zählen** to add in, include **-zeichnung** *f* joint signature **-ziehbereich** *m* pull-in range **-zieheffekt** *m* frequency pulling **-ziehen** to draw, drag or pull along, pull in step, tug, warp
Mitziehen *n*, **Mitzieherscheinung** *f* pulling into tune, pull in
Mixtion *f* oil base for varnish on which to apply gold leaf
Mizelle *f* colloidal salt, colloidal electrolyte
Mizellenaufbau *m* micellar structure
M/N-Verhältnis *n* ion pair yield, yield per ion pair
Mnemonik *f* mnemonics (comput)
mks-Einheiten mks units
Möbel *n* piece of furniture **-ausstattung** *f* furniture **-mattierung** *f* rubbed finish of furniture **-wagen** *m* van
mobil mobile, mobilized **-funk** *m* mobile radio
mobilisieren to mobilize
Mobilometer *n* mobilometer
Möbius-netz *n* Möbius net **-prozeß** *m* Möbius (electrolytic silver-refining) process
Mockstahl *m* half-steel, semisteel
Moddergrund *m* muddy, slimy, or slick ground, soft mud ooze, oozy bottom
Mode *f* fashion, vogue
Model *n* module **-element** *n* modulation element
Modeler *m* modulator (radio)
Modelgeschwindigkeit *f* rapidity of modulation
Modell *n* pattern, model, mold, type ~ **mit Rohrrumpf** model with tubular fuselage **ein ~ entwerfen** to design a model **ein ~ losklopfen** (aus der Form) to rap the pattern **geteiltes ~, mehrteiliges ~** split pattern **verwickelt gestaltetes ~** pattern of intricate external shape, pattern with great intricacy of detail **virtuelles ~** virtual model **zweiseitiges ~** double-sided pattern plate, match plate, split pattern
Modell-abhebekolben *m* pattern-drawing piston **-abhebevorrichtung** *f* pattern-drawing contrivance **-abhebung** *f* pattern draw, pattern-drawing operation **-abhub** *m* pattern draw or lift **-aggregat** *n* model missile **-ausführung** *f* scaled form **-aushebung** *f* pattern drawing or lifting, pattern draw **-aushub** *m* pattern lift **-barograph** *m* barograph in airplane model **-bauer** *m* model builder
Modellbau-kasten *m* model construction kit **-lehrgang** *m* course of (airplane-)model construction **-lehrplan** *m* curriculum for (airplane-) model construction **-muster** *n* type of model **-schule** *f* model (aircraft) school **-werkstätte** *f* pattern making shop
Modell-bezeichnung *f* designation of the various models **-druckmaschine** *f* block-printing machine **-entwurf** *m* pattern design **-flugveranstaltung** *f* model flying meeting **-flugwesen** *n* model aeronautics, model aviation **-form** *f* contour or external shape of pattern **-formerei** *f* plate pattern molding, plate molding, plate-molding shop **-garnitur** *f* pattern set **-getreu** true to pattern **-gips** *m* casting plaster **-größe** *f* model size or scale **-hälfte** *f* half of pattern **-herstellung** *f* patternmaking
Modellierbogen *m* cutout sheet
modellieren to model, mold
Modellieren *n* molding
Modellier-masse *f* modeling clay **-ton** *m* modeling clay
Modellmacher *m* patternmaker
Modellplatte *f* pattern plate, match plate ~ **mit aufgeheftetem Modell** mounted pattern plate **doppelseitige ~** double-faced pattern plate, match plate **einfache ~** single-sided pattern plate
Modell-plattenherstellung *f* pattern-plate making **-rahmen** *m* pattern frame **-rumpf** *m* fuselage or body model **-sand** *m* facing sand **-schlosser** *m* patternmaker **-schreiner** *m* wood-pattern maker **-schreinerei** *f* wood-pattern shop
Modell-technik *f* pattern practice **-tisch** *m* pattern table **-tischler** *m* wood-pattern maker **-versuch** *m* model test, experiment on a model **-werkstatt** patternmaker **-schreiner** *m* wood-pattern
modeln to modulate
Modelton *m* modulation note
Modelung *f* modulation, modulating
Modelungsgrad *m* depth or amount of modulation, percentage modulation
Moderator *m* moderater (atom. phys.)
Moderfleck *m* mildew stain
moderfleckig foxed **-es Papier** foxed or foxy paper
moderierter Reaktor moderated reactor
modern to decay
modern modern, up-to-date, in fashion, contemporary
modernisieren to modernize
Modifikation *f* modification **allotropische ~** allotropic change
modifizieren to modify
Modler *m* modulator
Modul *m* modulus
Modulargleichung *f* modular equation
Modulation *f* modulation, control ~ **durch Änderung der Anodenspannung** plate modulation ~ **durch Änderung der Gitterspannung** grid modulation ~ **auf dunkel** modulation to dark condition, negative modulation ~ **eines Elektronenstrahles** modulation of the electron beam ~ **auf hell** modulation to light condition, positive modulation ~ **des Kathodenstrahls** modulation

of the cathode ray ~ **über Mittenanzapfung** center-tap modulation ~ **in Röhrenabsorptionsschaltung** valve-absorption modulation

Modulation, ~ der Sprache, ~ der Stimme inflection of voice ~ **des Strahlstroms** beam-current modulation ~ **durch Tonfrequenzverschiebung** audio-frequency shift modulation ~ **eines Trägerstroms** modulation of a carrier current ~ **mit veränderlichem Trägerwert** floating carrier control **additive** ~ upward modulation **gegenseitige** ~ intermodulation **prozentuale** ~ percentage of modulation **subtraktive** ~ downward modulation

Modulations-amplitude *f* modulation amplitude **-anordnung** *f* modulation circuit **-bereich** *m* white-to-black amplitude range **-drossel** *f* modulating choke, modulation reactor **-einrichtung** *f* modulation device **-frequenz** *f* modulating frequency, modulation frequency, signal frequency **-gegentaktstufe** *f* push-pull modulation stage **-gerät** *n* modulation unit **-gesteuerter Sender** audio-frequency modulated transmitter **-grad** *m* modulation factor, percentage modulation, degree or depth of modulation **-gradkontrolle** *f* modulation meter

Modulations-höchstfrequenz *f* maximum modulation frequency **-hüllkurve** *f* modulation envelope **-index** *m* deviation ratio **-kennlinie** *f* modulation characteristic **-koeffizient** *m* percentage modulation, degree or depth of modulation **-kreis** *m* strobing circuit **-kurve** *f* modulation characteristic **-messer** *m* modulation control **-messung** *f* modulation measurement

Modulations-rauschen *n* modulation noise **-regler** *m* modulation control **-röhre** *f* modulator valve or tube, modulating valve, mixer tube **-seitenbänder** *pl* side-band of modulation **-spannung** *f* modulating voltage **-strom** *m* modulating current **-stufe** *f* modulation stage **-tiefe** *f* depth of modulation, percentage modulation **-ton** *m* note of modulation **-träger** *m* modulation carrier

Modulations-überwachungsgerät *n* modulation monitor **-unterdrückung** *f* demodulation effect **-verfahren** *n* method of modulation, modulating method **-verstärker** *m* modulating amplifier **-verstärkerröhre** *f* modulator tube **-welle** *f* wave of modulation **-zelle** *f* modulation element **-ziffer** *f* percentage modulation, degree or depth of modulation

Modulator *m* modulator **abgeglichener** ~ balanced modulator **besprochener** ~ voice-actuated or voice-impressed modulator

Modulator-röhre *f* modulator valve or tube, modulating valve **-schaltung** *f* modulating or translating circuit

Modul-bauweise *f* modular design **-funktion** *f* modular function

Modulierbarkeit *f* modulability, modulation capability

modulieren to modulate, control

modulierend-e Schwingung modulating wave **-e Welle** modulating wave

moduliert modulated **-er Farbträger** carrier color signal **-er Sender** modulated transmitter (used in radar jamming) **-e ungedämpfte Welle** modulated continuous wave (M.C.W.)

Modulierung *f* modulation

Moduln *pl* moduli

Modulteilung *f* diametral pitch

Modus *m* mode **-umformer** *m* wave converter

möglich possible

Möglichkeit *f* possibility, potentiality, chance

Mohrsche Hüllkurve Mohr's envelope

Mohrsches Salz Mohr's salt

Mohs' Härteskala Mohs' scale

Moiré *n* moiré

moiréartiges Geräusch moiré pattern of noise

moirieren to water, cloud, moiré

Mokerhammer *m* mallet

Mokkastein *m* moss agate

Mol *n* mole, gram molecule

Molalität *f* molality

molar molecular, molar **-e Siedepunktserhöhung** molar boiling-point elevation

Molargewicht *n* molar weight

Molarität *f* molecular or equivalent concentration, molarity, molality

Molar-volumen *n* molecular volume **-wärme** *f* molecular heat

Molch (Kratzer, Rohrkratzer) scraper (go-devil, swab)

Mole *f* pier, jetty, mole, dam of a harbor

Molekel, Molekül *n* molecule **unstarres** ~ nonrigid molecule **von der Dicke eines Moleküls** monomolecular

Molekül-adhäsion *f* molecular adhesion **-aggregat** *n* molecular cluster

molekular molecular **-es Bremsvermögen** *n* molecular stopping power

Molekular-anordnung *f* arrangement of molecules **-anziehung** *f* molecular attraction **-bewegung** *f* molecular motion **-brechungsvermögen** *f* molecular refraction **-druckmanometer** *n* viscosity manometer **-durchmesser** *m* molecular diameter **-gewicht** *n* molecular mass or weight, molar weight, gram-molecular weight

Molekularität *f* molecularity, molecular concentration

Molekular-kraft *f* molecular force or energy **-manometer** *n* molecular gauge **-reibung** *f* molecular friction **-strahl** *m* molecular ray, molecular beam **-strahlexperiment** *n* molecular beam experiment **-streugesetz** *n* molecular scattering law **-zertrümmernde Stoßkraft** molecule disintegrating impact

Molekül-abbildung *f* molecular diagram **-bahnmethode** *f* method of molecular orbitals **-emissionskontinuum** *n* continuous molecular emission spectrum **-geschwindigkeit** *f* molecular velocity **-gitter** *n* molecular lattice **-haufen** *m* molecular clusters **-ionisationskontinuum** *n* continuous molecular ionization spectrum

Mole-knäuel *n* coiled molecule **-komplex** *m* molecular cluster **-masse** *f* mole, molecular mass **-rekombinationsspektrum** *n* molecular recombination spectrum **-rückstoß** *m* aggregate recoil **-schwingung** *f* vibration of a molecule **-sieb** *n* microfilter **-spektrum** *n* molecular spectrum **-streuung** *f* molecular scattering

Molenbruch *m* mole fraction, collapse or breaking up of a mole or pier **-kopf** *m* round head, pier head **-verhältnis** *n* molar ratio, mole ratio

Moleskin *m* moleskin

Mol-gewicht *n* molar weight, gram-molecular

weight **-größe** *f* molar magnitude
Molisierung *f* recombination (of ions in gas)
Molken *m* whey
Molkerei *f* dairy
Möller *m* blast-furnace burden, burden **-ausbringen** *n* burden yield **-berechnung** *f* burdening, burden calculation **-gicht** *f* burden charge
möllern to mix ores and additions for a furnace charge
Möllerung *f* mixture of ores
Möllerwagen *m* burden-charging carriage
molletieren to mill, knurl (coins)
Molette *f* grooved roller
Mol-verhältnis *n* molar ratio, mole ratio **-volumen** *n* gram-molecular or molar volume **-wärme** *f* molar heat
Molybdän *n* molybdenum **-bleispat** *m* wulfenite **-eisen** *n* ferromolybdenum **-erz** *n* molybdenum ore **-glanz** *m* molybdenite **-haltig** containing molybdenum, molybdeniferous
Molybdänit, Molybdänkies *m* molybdenite
Molybdän-oxyd *n* molybdenum oxide **-säure** *f* molybdic acid **-säureanhydrid** *n* molybdic anhydride **-saures Ammon** ammonium molybdate
Molzustand *m* molecular or molar state
Moment *n* moment, momentum, factor, quantity of motion ~ **der Bewegungsgröße** moment of momentum ~ **um die Ruderdrehachse** hinge moment **größtes** ~ maximum moment **mechanisches** ~ momentum **rückdrehendes** ~ restoring moment **statisches** ~ moment of a force **verdrehendes** ~ torsional or twisting moment
Momentabstellung *f* instant stopping
momentan instantaneous **-e Schraubungsachse** instantaneous axis
Momentan-achse *f* axis of instantaneous rotation **-reserve** *f* instantaneous stand-by **-spannung** *f* instantaneous voltage
Momentanstellung *f* instant starting
Momentan-strom *m* instantaneous current **-wert** *m* instantaneous value **-zentrum** *n* instantaneous center
Moment-aufnahme *f* instantaneous photograph, snapshot **-ausgleich** *m* equilibrium of moments **-ausgleichsverfahren** *n* moment distribution method **-ausrückung** *f* discharge control **-beiwert** *m* moment coefficient **-betrieb** *m* momentary running **-bild** *n* instantaneous photograph, snapshot **-deckung** *f* satisfying of moment requirements (with regard to the necessary length of cover plates or tension bars)
Momenten-diagramm *n* moment diagram **-drehpunkt** *m* point about which the moment turns (statics) **-erzeuger** *m* torque-producing element **-fläche** *f* moment area, area under moment curve **-gleichgewicht** *n* balance of moments **-gleichung** *f* equation of moments **-linie** *f* moment curve, moment line **-nullpunkt** *m* point of zero moment, inflection point **-punkt** *m* center of rotation, moment pole **-schaubild** *n* moment diagram
Moment-entlastung *f* instantaneous release of load **-feststellung** *f* instantaneous locking
Momentklauenkupplung *f*, **selbsttätig ausrückende** ~ self-acting instantaneous gear clutch
Moment-klemme *f* instantaneous clamp **-kontakt** *m* momentary contact **-kontaktgeber** *m* momentary contactor **-kupplung** *f* torque coupling **-objektiv** *n* highspeed lens **-prozeß** *m* moment process, evanescence process **-schalter** *m* quick-break switch **-schaltung** *f* quick break action **-stillstand** immediate stopping **-stütze** *f* torque stay rod **-transport** *m* momentum transfer
Momentum *n* momentum
Moment-unterbrechung *f* quick break (elec.) **-verschluß** *m* instantaneous or high-speed shutter **-wert** *m* magneton **-zünder** *m* instantaneous fuse (detonator) **-zündpille** *f* flash composition **-zündung** *f* instantaneous firing
Monat *m* month
monatlich monthly
Monats-auszug *m* monthly statement **-gespräch** *n* subscription call **-karte** *f* monthly subscription, commutation ticket **-tonne** *f* metric ton per month
monatweise by the month
monaurales Hören monaural reception, monaural listening
Monazit *m* monazite
Mönch *m* die, punch, stamp, friar
Mönchs-bogen *m* friar, blank sheet (print.) **-kolben** *m* ram, plunger
Möndchen *n* lune, meniscus
Mond-bewegung *f* lunar vibration **-finsternis** *f* lunar eclipse **-förmig** meniscal, crescent-shaped, lunate **-gas** *n* Mond gas **-gaserzeuger** *m* Mond-gas producer **-getriebe** *n* moon motion mechanism **-glas** *n* crown glass, bull's-eye glass **-halo** *n* lunar halo **-hof** *m* lunar aurora **-krater** *m* lunar crater
Mond-landefahrzeug *n* lunar excursion module (LEM) **-länge** *f* moon's longitude **-maare** *pl* lunar seas **-raumsonde** *f* lunar probe **-ring** *m* lunar halo, false sap or moon ring **-sichelförmig** half-moon-shaped **-umlauf** *m* lunation **-umlaufbahn** *f* lunar orbit
Monel-metall *n* Monel metal **-verfahren** *n* Monel process
Monier-bau *m* Monier's building **-eisen** *n* fastening iron
monieren to find fault with
Monier-gewölbe *n* Monier's arch or vault **-platte** *f* Monier slab
Monitor *m* monitor **-instrumente** *pl* radiac instruments
Mono-ammoniumphosphat-Kristall *m* ammonium dihydrogen phosphate crystal (adp crystal) **-atomar** monatomic **-chloressigsäure** *f* monochloracetic acid **-chord** *m* monochord, sonometer **-chrom** monochromic **-chromasie** *f* monochromatism, monochromasia **-chromat** *n* monochromatic objective
monochromatisch monochromatic **-es Licht** monochromatic light
Mono-chromator *m* monochromator **-chromie** *f* camaïeu **-chromübertragung** *f* monochrome transmission
monodimetrisch monodimetric
monoenergetisch monoenergetic
monogen monogenic (function)
Monogramm *n* monogram **-prägepresse** *f* press for stamping monograms **-schnürung** *f* tie up for weaving names
mono-klin, -klinisch monoclinic
Monoklinale *f* monocline, homocline

monokular monocular
Mono-line *f* monoline **-lith** *m* monolith **-lithischer Kabelkanal** monolithic conduit
monomer monomerous
mono-metrisch monometric **-molekularer Film** monolayer, monomolecular layer **-molekular** monomolecular **-molekularschicht** *f* unimolecular layer **-morphisch** monomorphic **-objektiv-binokulares Mikroskop** one-objective binocular microscope **-packverfahren** *n* monopack method
Monopol *n* monopoly
monopolisieren to monopolize
Monose *f* monosaccharide
Monoskop *n* monoscope
monostabil monostable **-e Kippschaltung** monostable multivibrator **-er Multivibrator** singelshot multivibrator
mono-symmetrisch monosymmetric **-telephon** *n* monotelephone
monoton monotonic decreasing
Monotonitätssatz *m* monotonicity theorems
monotrimetrisch monotrimetric
Monotype *f* monotype, monotype machine **-taster** *m* monotype keyboard
mono-variant monovariant, univariant **-zentrisch** monocentric **-zyklisch** monocyclic
Monsun *m* monsoon **-wechsel** *m* change of the monsoon
Montage *f* assembly, erection, mounting, installation, montage, setting up, fitting, support table, synopsis ~ (in) **Montage** under construction
Montage-abteilung *f* assembly department **-anleitung** *f* mounting instruction **-anweisung** *f* instructions for setting up (assembly) **-automat** *m* automatic assembly machine **-bahn** *f* assembly line **-band** *n* assembly line **-bauverfahren** *n* site assembly
Montagebock *m* assembly stand, jig **fahrbarer** ~ dolly
Montage-fließband *n* progressive assembly line **-folie** *f* transparent mounting foil
Montagegerüst *n* erecting scaffolding
Montagegestell *n* assembly stand **fahrbares** ~ dolly
Montage-gewicht *n* skeleton weight **-gläser** *pl* mounting glass **-gruppe** *f* assembly **-haken** *m* fixing clamp **-halle** *f* erecting bay, erecting shop, assembly room, department or plant **-instrument** *n* lineman's instrument **-kleber** *m* assembly adhesive **-kran** *m* erection crane, erecting crane **-leim** *m* structural adhesive **-leiter** *f* extension ladder **-luke** *f* building hatch, rigging hatch **-mast** *m* erecting mast
Montageplatte *f* mounting plate ~ **mit gedruckter Schaltung** printed wire board (P.W.B.)
Montage-raum *m* assembly space or room **-schraube** *f* fitting bolt **-spur** *f* mosaic **-straße** *f* assembly line **-untergruppe** *f* subassembly **-wagen** *m* assembly truck **-werk** *n* assembly plant **-werkstatt** *f* erecting shop **-werkzeug** *n* assembly tool, erecting tool **-winden** *pl* hoisting crabs **-zeichnung** *f* assembly blueprint
Montan-anstalt *f* college of mining **-industrie** *f* mining industry **-union** *f* European Coal and Steel Community **-wachs** *m* lignite wax
Montejus *m* monte-jus, juice pump
Monteur *m* mechanic, (engine) fitter, erector, assembler **ausgebildeter** ~, **geschulter** ~ trained mechanic
Montiereisen *n* mounting iron, tire lever
montieren to mount, assemble, erect, install
Montieren *n* rigging
Montierhalle *f* assembling shop
montiert, fest ~ rigidly mounted
Montierung *f* assembly, erection, mounting, installation, setting (up), erecting, equipment, fitting
Montierungshaltung *f* rigging position
Montmorillonit *n* montmorillonite
Montur *f* equipment
Moor *n* bog, moor, marsh, swamp **-boden** *m* moor(land), marshy soil, peat
Moore-'Lectromelt-Ofen *m* Moore (direct-arc) furnace
Mooring *f* mooring
Moor-kohle *f* glossy, black, subbituminous coal, trapezoidal coal **-torf** *m* bog peat
Moos *n* moss **-achat** *m* moss agate **-gummi** *m* rubber sponge **-gummidichtung** *f* foam rubber gasket **-torf** *m* surface peat
Mop *m* mop
Moräne *f*, **Moränenschutt** *m* moraine
Morast *m* bog **-erz** *n* bog (iron) ore
Morgankühlbett *n* cooling bed ~ **mit gezahnten Kipprinnen** mechanical notched-rack-type cooling bed
Morganstraße *f* Morgan (continuous-rod) mill
morgen tomorrow
Morgen *m* morning, 2.12 acres **-dämmerung** *f* **-grauen** *n* dawn **-nebel** *m* morning fog
Morpho-metrie *f* morphometry **-tropie** *f* morphotropy **-tropisch** morphotropic
morsch(ig) rotten, decomposed, frail, fragile, brittle, friable, damaged **morsches Eis** soft ice
Morse-alphabet *n* Morse code **-apparat** *m* Morse apparatus **-blende** *f* blinking stop **-farbschreiber** *m* (Morse) inker **-feuer** *n* blinker signaling in Morse code **-hebel** *m* telegraph (signaling) key **-kegel** *m* Morse taper shank **-kegellehre** *f* Morse taper gauge **-lampe** *f* flash lamp **-laterne** *f* signal lamp
morsen to blink
Morsen *n* transmission of Morse-code messages
Morsepunkt *m* dot **breite Morsepunkte** lengthened dots **spitze Morsepunkte** clipped dots
Mörser *m* mortar **gezogener** ~ rifled mortar
Mörserkeule *f* pestle
Mörser-probe *f* mortar test **-stempel** *m* pestle
Morse-schreiber *m* Morse printer **-schrift** *f* Morse code **-spruch** *m* telegraph message **-streifen** *m* Morse slip
Morsestrich *m* dash **gebrochene Morsestriche** split dashes
Morsesystem *n* Morse system
Morsetaste *f* Morse key, sounder key ~ **mit selbsttätiger Punktgebung** vibroplex key
Morsetastenlocher *m* keyboard perforator
Morsezahlen *pl*, **abgekürzte** ~ contracted Morse-figure signals
Morsezeichen *n* mark, Morse signal **die** ~ **brechen** the marks split
Mörtel *m* mortar, plaster **-fuge** *f* joint **-maschine** *f* mixer, pugging mill **-schlamm** *m* grout **-ständer** *m* mortar pillar **-trog** *m* hod trough
Mosaik *f* mosaic, mosaic plate **-block** *m* mosaic

block **-druck** *m* relief embossing **-elektrode** *f* mosaic electrode **-gold** *n* mosaic gold **-kristall** *m* ideally imperfect crystal **-platte** *f* target, mosaic plate (TV)

Mosaikröhre *f*, **doppelseitige ~** image-multiplier iconoscope

Mosaik-schirm *m* mosaic (of iconoscope) **-smalten** *pl* mosaic smalts **-verfahren** *n* mosaic telegraphy **-zierstreifen** *m* terrazzo strip

Moschus *m* musk **-körneröl** *n* amber-seed oil

Moseleysches Gesetz Moseley's law

Moskitonetz *n* mosquito net

Motiv *n* motive, theme **ausgeschnittenes ~** fretwork

motivieren to cause, motivate

Motor *m* motor, mover, engine **~ mit Drehzahlregelung** variable-speed motor **~ mit mehreren Drehzahlstufen** multispeed motor, change-speed motor **~ mit Eigenzündung** compression-ignition engine **~ mit Fehlzündungen** balky engine **~ mit Fremdbelüftung** separately air-cooled motor **~ mit Hohlwelle** quill-drive motor **~ mit veränderlichem Hub** variable-crank-throw engine **~ mit gegenläufigen Kolben** opposed-piston-type engine **~ mit Kompensationswicklung** compensated motor

Motor, ~ für Mehrstoffbetrieb multifuel engine **~ durch verklebtes Öl schwer durchdrehbar** tight engine **~ mit umschaltbarer Polzahl** pole change motor **~ mit Schlitzsteuerung** piston-ported engine **~ für Stangenantrieb** crank-drive motor **~ für die Stößelbewegung** ram reciprocating motor **~ mit Tellerventilen** poppet-valve engine **~ mit T-förmigem Verbrennungsraum** T-head-type engine **~ mit hängenden Ventilen** I-head motor **~ mit Verdichtungszündung** compression-ignition engine **~ mit Vorverdichtung** supercharged motor or engine

Motor, ~ für den Wälzvorschub generating roll feed motor **~ mit Zahnradvorgelege** back-geared motor **~ mit hängenden Zylindern** inverted motor **~ ohne Zubehör** bare engine **~ abbremsen** to test the engine **~ abdrosseln** to close the throttle **den ~ abstellen** to stop the engine **den ~ anlassen** to start the engine **den ~ auseinandernehmen** to dismantle the engine **mit abgestelltem ~** power off **mit arbeitendem ~** power on

Motor, ausgewuchteter ~ balanced motor **einziehbarer ~** retractable engine **im Fluge zugänglicher ~** engine accessible in flight **gekapselter ~** enclosed motor **gasdicht gekapselter ~** vaporproof motor **geschlossener ~** enclosed-type motor **hochverdichteter ~** high-compression engine **kolbengesteuerter ~** piston-ported engine **kompressorloser ~** solid-injection engine **luftgekühlter ~** air-cooled engine

Motor, offener ~ open-type motor **schlagwettergeschützter ~** flame-proof motor, flame tight motor **selbstansaugender ~** naturally aspirated or normally aspirated engine **sternförmiger ~** radial engine **symmetrisch entsprechender ~ auf der anderen Seite des Rumpfes** companion engine **überbemessener ~** oversize engine **übermessener ~** high-altitude engine **umsteuerbarer ~** reversible motor **untersetzter ~** geared motor **ventiliert gekapselter ~** enclosed ventilated motor **ventilloser ~** sleeve-type engine

Motor-abnahmeprotokoll *n* engine-test log **-abstützung** *f* engine support **-anlaßschalter** *m* motor-starting switch **-anlasser** *m* starter **-anschlußflansch** *m* engine flange

Motorantrieb *m* motor drive **mit ~** motor-driven

Motor-attrappe *f* dummy engine **-aufhängegerüst** *n* engine mount

Motoraufhängering, flacher ~ engine plate

Motoraufhängung *f* suspension of the motor, engine mounting **~ in vier Punkten** four-point attachment

Motor-auflage *f* engine bearer feet **-ausfall** *m* engine failure

Motorbefestigungs-anschluß *m* mounting attachment **-auge** *n* engine-mounting lug

Motorbergungsfahrzeug *n* salvaging vehicle

Motorbetrieb *m* running of a motor **~ bei niedriger Betriebstemperatur** cool running of an engine **~ mit geschichteter Ladung** sandwich system

Motor-betriebsstoff *m* motor fuel **-betriebstunden** *pl* engine hours **-bock** *m* engine bed or bearer, engine mount **-bockbeschlag** *m* engine mounting **-boot** *n* motorboat **-bremse** *f* motor brake, Cardan-shaft brake **-brummen** *n* motorhum

Motor-dauerlaufkondensator *m* motor continous duty condenser **-defekt** *m* motor failure **-drehleiter** *f* motor aerial, motor extension ladder **-drehmoment** *n* engine torque **-drehwähler** *m* motor uniselector **-drehzahl** *f* engine speed, engine revolutions **-drehzahlmesser** *m* engine-speed counter **-dynamo** *m* motor-generator set **-einheit** *f* motor unit **-einschätzung** *f* engine rating **-einsetzung** *f* engine installation

Motoren-bauer *m* engine manufacturer **-einbau** *m* engine mounting **-gondel** *f* engine nacelle or pod (aviation) **-guß** *m* engine casting **-öl** *n* motor oil **-raum** *m* motor room

Motorentlüftung *f* crankcase breather

Motoren-wart *m* engine mechanic, motor mechanic **-werk** *n* engine factory

Motor-fahrzeug *n* motor vehicle **-fliegerei** *f* powered flying **-flug** *m* power flight, engined flight **-flugbuch** *n* engine logbook **-flugmodell** *n* power-driven model **-flugzeug** *n* power plane **-fundament** *n* engine bed **-fuß** *m* engine mount **-gehäuse** *n* crankshaft housing **-generator** *m* motor generator **-generatortafel** *f* motor-generator panel **-geräusch** *n* engine noise

Motorgewicht gemäß Pferdekraft engine weight per horsepower

Motor-gleiter *m* powered glider **-gondel** *f* engine nacelle **-greifer** *m* motor grab **-grundplatte** *f* motor bracket **-hackmaschine** *f* motor cultivator **-handbuch** *n* instruction book **-haube** *f*, **-haubenblech** *n* (engine) cowling, motor hood **-haubenhalter** *m* bonnet fastener **-haubenverschluß** *m* hood fastener **-hebelbock** *m* throttle box **-heupresse** *f* power hay(press) baler **-hülse** *f* motor socket

motorisiert motorized

Motor-karren *m* motor-driven truck **-kehrmaschine** *f* motor-driven sweeper **-kenndaten** *pl* engine data **-kesselwagen** *m* motor tank truck **-klemmbrett** *n* motor terminal board **-klemmenkasten** *m* motor terminal box

Motor-kolben *m* engine piston **-kontrolloszillo-**

graph *m* engine analyser **-kopf** *m* motor head (in rockets) **-krafteinschätzung** *f* engine-power rating **-kühlung** *f* engine cooling **-lafette** *f* self-propelled mount, engine mount **-lager** *n* engine mount **-lagerung** (Auto) engine suspension **-lastkahn** *m* motor barge

Motorlastwagen *m* motor truck **schneller ~** speed truck, pickup truck

Motor-laufwinde *f* traveling motor hoist **-lebenslaufakte** *f* engine logbook **-leerlaufbereich** *m* no-load range of motor

Motorleistung *f* engine performance, engine power or output **~ bei Anschlagstellung der Drossel** throttle stop horsepower

Motor-lochprüfer *m* motor drive electric verifier **-los** motorless **-lotmaschine** *f* motor-driven sounding machine **-luftstrahltriebwerk** *n* combination reciprocating engine and jet **-magnetlocher** *m* motor drive punch **-mustertafel** *f* specification of engine type **-nennleistung** *f* motor rating **-nutzschub** *m* useful engine thrust **-öl** *n* motor oil **-panne** *f* engine trouble or breakdown **-periode** *f* engine cycle **-pratze** *f* engine bearer

Motor-protokoll *n* engine log **-prüfbericht** *m* engine-test report **-prüfschein** *m* engine-test certificate **-prüfstand** *m* engine-test stand **-pumpe** *f* motor-driven pump, power pump **-rad** *n* motorcycle **-rahmen** *m* engine frame **-rechnung** *f* motor symbolism **-regler** *m* governor, regulator **-regulierung** *f* control gear, engine control **-regulierungswelle** *f* engine governor shaft **-riemenscheibe** *f* motor pulley **-ringhaube** *f* circular cowl **-rüstung** *f* engine equipment or accessories

Motor-schalter *m* motor controller **-schiff** *n* motorboat **-schild** *n* name plate, engine plate **-schnellboot** *n* speedboat **-schutzschalter** *m* motor-protection **-segler** *m* power glider **-stirnblech** *n* end plate **-spritze** *f* motor fire engine **-störung** *f* engine trouble, engine failure **-strebe** *f* engine strut **-strom** *m* motor current **-stütze** *f* engine support **-teil** *m* engine part, motor part **-träger** *m* engine mounting, engine bearer, motor bearing

Motor-tragplatte *f* engine bedplate **-tragring** *m* engine-plate or engine-mount ring **-triebstoff** *m* motor fuel

Motorüberdrehzahl, höchste ~ maximum engine overspeed

Motor-überholung *f* engine overhaul(ing) **-überzug** *m* engine cover **-umlaufschmierung** *f* engine circulation lubrication system **-unterbrecher** *m* motor-drive make and break **-ventil** *n* engine valve **-verkleidung** *f* **-verschalung** *f* engine cowling **-verstrebung** *f* engine strutting, engine-nacelle bracing

Motorvorbau *m* engine mount **abnehmbarer ~** detachable engine mounting

Motor-wagen *m* motorcar, motor vehicle **-wähler** *m* motor uniselector **-welle** *f* motor shaft, main shaft **-winde** *f* motor winch, power-driven winch **-wippe** *f* motor switch armature **-wirkungsgrad** *m* engine efficiency **-zähler** *m* motor meter **-zugmaschine** *f* motor tractor

moussierend effervescent

Mövenflügel *m* gull wing

MP-Kondensator *m* metallized-paper capacitor

mü, mu micron

Mudde *f* mud

müde tired, fatigued

Muffe *f* socket, sleeve, box, coupling (box), bushing, box thread, thimble, flame tube, muff, bush, socket joint, clamp **~ für Bohrstangen** drill coupling **~ von Messing** brass sleeve **~ mit Ventil** casing float collar

Muffel *f* muffle, retort, flame tube **-ofen** *m* muffle furnace, retort furnace **-presse** *f* retort press **-prozeß** *m*, **-verfahren** *n* retort process, distillation process

Muffenabsperrschieber *m* sluice valve with socket ends, gate valve with bell ends

muffenartige Wiege sleeve-shaped cradle

Muffen-ausgußmasse *f* box compound **-bohrröhre** *f* casing with inserted joints, collar-joint casing **-brecher** *m* collar buster

Muffendreh- und Gewindeschneidebank *f* socket-turning and -screwing machine

Muffendruckrohr *n* socket pressure pipe

Muffenende *n* (eines Muffenrohres), bell (teleph.) **~ eines Rohres** socket end of a tube

Muffen-führung *f* sleeve guide **-gußrohr** *n* joint cast iron pipe **-hub** *m* lift of sleeve **-hülse** *f* collar socket, collar without thread **-kuppelung** *f* butt-muff coupling, cased-butt coupling, sleeve coupling **-loch** *n* orifice **-ring** *m* collar socket

Muffenrohr *n* socket(ed) pipe, socket tube **glattes Ende eines Muffenrohres** socket of pipe

Muffenrohr-spitzende *n* spigot end of a tube **-stück** *n* drainage fitting **-verbindung** *f* spigot(-and-socket) joint

Muffen-schloß *n* collar coupling **-stutzen** *m* reducing coupling **-träger** *m* clutch gear **-ventil** *n* sleeve valve **-verbindung** *f* sleeve joint, socket fitting, bell-and-spigot joint, spigot-and-socket joint **-verrohrung** *f* casing with collars

muffig moldy, musty

Mufflerie *f* pottery

Mühe *f* toil, effort **-los** effortless **-voller Versuch** wearisome experiment

Mühlbeutel *m* bolter

Mühle *f* mill, crusher, grinder, pulverizer

Mühleisen *n* stone spindle

Mühlen-bauindustrie *f* millwright industry **-diagramm** *n* flow sheet **-feuerung** *f* pulverized firing system **-gerinne** *n* millrace **-haube** *f* dome of the mill **-leistung** *f* mill capacity, mill efficiency **-sichter** *m* mill sifter **-ständer** *m* standard of mills

Mühl-gerüst *n* framing of a mill **-häuserweiß** *n* lead sulfate pigment **-kalkstein** *m* millstone rock **-picke** *f* mill-cutter pick, mill pick **-säge** *f* sash saw **-sandstein** *m* millstone grit

Mühlstein *m* millstone **-picke** *f* millstone hammer

Mühlteich *m* millpond

Mühl- und Messerpicken *pl* picks

mühsam irksome, assiduous **~ zusammentragen** to glean

Mulde *f* pan, bucket, trough, charging box, pig mold, pig, depression, hollow, reentrant, basin, syncline, ravine, cradle, tray **-linie** *f* depression line

Mulden-achse *f* axis of the trough **-band** *n* trough (of an inclined conveyer) **-beschickkran** *m* trough-charging crane **-biegung** *f* trough curve

-bildung *f* synclinal formation **-blei** *n* pig lead **-chargierkran** *m* box charging crane **-falte** *f* synclinal flexure of stratum

Muldenfeststellung, selbsttätige ~ automatic fastening device for tip trough

Mulden-flügel *m* limb of syncline **-förderband** *n* troughed belt conveyor **-förmig** synclinal **-gurt** *m* trough band, strip, or belt **-hebevorrichtung** *f* skip hoist **-kern** *m* trough core **-kipper** *m* trough tip (wagon), mine car **-kippwagen** *m* dump-type hopper truck, dump barrow, dumper, dump truck **-linie eines Flözes** basonic axis

Mulden-presse *f* cylinder press (textiles) **-reflektor** (Raumbeleuchtung) trough reflector (troffer) **-rolle** *f* trough roller **-rost** *m* trough grate **-rostfeuerung** *f* furnace with trough grate **-tasche** *f* socket of the boxes **-transportkran** *m* bucket-handling crane **-wagen** *m* hopper truck, pan car **-wascher** *m* trough washer

Muldungsfähigkeit *f* troughability

Mule-maschine *f* mule (spinning) **-spinner** *m* mule spinner

mulinieren to throw (silk)

Müll *n* rubbish, refuse, garbage

Mull *m* mull, fine muslin **-binde** *f* muslin bandage

Müller *m* miller

Müllerei *f* milling or pulverizing plant, mill grinding

Müllergaze *f* bolting cloth

Müll-kasten aus Eisenblech sheet-iron dust bin **-sauger** *m* refuse exhauster

Müll- und Abfallverbrennungsofen *m* garbage- and refuse-burning furnace

Müllverbrennungs-anlage *f* refuse incinerator, garbage disposal plant, refuse destructor **-ofen** *m* incinerator

Müll-verwertung *f* (house-)refuse dressing **-wagen** *m* dust cart

Mulm *m* rubble, dust or earthy ore, ore dust

Multicurie-Zelle intermediate cave

Multiklonentstaubung *f* multi-cyclon dust filter

Multimoment *n* multiple moment **-verfahren** *n* ratio delay method, snap-reading method

Multipaktorleitwert *m* multipactor

Multiplette *f* multiplet

Multiplex-betrieb *m* multiplex working **-sender** *m* multiplex radio transmitter **-verbindung** *f* multiplex (communication) **-verteilung von Kabeladern** multiple connection of cable wires

Multiplierröhre *f* multiplier tube

Multiplikant-Divisorregister *n* (MD) multiplicand register (info proc.)

Multiplikation *f* multiplication

Multiplikations-faktor *m* reproductive factor **-konstante** *f* multiplicative constant

multiplikative Mischung multiplicative mixture

Multiplikator *m* multiplier

Multiplikatorenbereich *m* domain of multipliers

Multiplikator-quotientenregister *n* multiplier-quotientsregister **-rahmen** *m* multiplier coil

multiplizieren to multiply

Multiplizier-locher *m* multiplier punch **-register** *n* multiplier register

Multiplizierungsfaktor multiplication constant

Multipol-entwicklung *f* multipole expansion **-ordnung** *f* multipolarity **-strahlungsübergang** *m* multipole-transition probability **-übergang** *m* multipol transition

Multivektor *m* multivector

Multivibrator *m* multivibrator **astabiler** ~ free-running or astable multivibrator **bistabiler** ~ (Flip-Flop) bistable multivibrator **monostabiler** ~ one-shot or monostable multivibrator

multizellular multicellular

Mund *m* mouth, opening, muzzle, vent, orifice

Mündelgeld *n* trust money

mündelsicher sufficiently safe for investment of trust money **-e Kapitalsanlage** safe investment

münden to open (out), discharge, empty

mundieren to make a clean copy

mündlich verbal, oral **-e Verhandlung** oral hearing

Mundloch *n* orifice, shaft mouth, fuse hole **-buchse** *f* fuse hole bush or plug **-futter** *n* gain (of fuse) **-deckel** *m* screwed plug **-gewinde** *n* adapter thread **-schraube** *f* adapter plug

Mund-ringhalter *m* die head **-schicht** *f* breath filter layer **-schraube** *f* mouth gauge

Mundstück *n* mouthpiece, nozzle, orifice, tip (of torch) **-öffnung** *f* chink between mouthpiece and reed

Mündung *f* muzzle, mouth, port, orifice, aperture

Mündungs-arbeitdruck *m* outlet pressure **-bär** *m* skull at the converter mouth, slag adhering to the converter nose **-bremse** *f* muzzle brake **-druck** *m* orifice pressure **-energie** *f* muzzle energy

Mündungs-fläche *f* face of muzzle, mouth area of nozzle **-flamme** *f* flame playing at the (converter) mouth **-gasdruck** *m* muzzle gas pressure **-gebiet** *n* lower river **-geschwindigkeit** *f* muzzle velocity **-kappe** *f* muzzle cap, muzzle cover **-knall** *m* muzzle blast, muzzle sound

Mündungs-korrektion *f* mouth correction, orifice correction **-pfropfen** *m* tampion **-rauch** *m* muzzle-blast smoke **-schoner** *m* muzzle and sight cover (rifle) **-waagerechte** *f* horizontal plane through axis of bore at zero-degree elevation **-wucht** *f* muzzle energy, kinetic energy at the muzzle

Munition *f* ammunition, munitions

Münz-amt *n* mint **-behälter** *m* coin receptacle, coin (collecting) box, cash box **-beschickung** *f* alloyage

Münze *f* medal, coin, mint **gezähnte** ~ serrated coin **stempelharte** ~ hardened coin

Münz-einheit *f* unit of coinage **-einwurf** *m* coin slot

münzen to coin or stamp money, mint

Münzen *n* coining or minting of money **-prägemaschine** *f* coining press **-prägematrize** *f* coining die

Münzfeile *f* cabinet file

Münz-fernsprecher *m* prepayment telephone coin box, public telephone, pay station, pay telephone, public call office ~ **für verschiedene Geldsorten** multicoin pay telephone

Münz-fuß *m* monetary standard **-geber** *m* coin automat **-gewicht** *n* standard weight **-gold** *n* standard gold **-krätze** *f* clippings **-kunst** *f* coinage, minting **-legierung** *f* coinage alloy **-platte** *f* plank, blank, coin plate, planchet **-prägung** *f* coinage **-recht** *n* mintage

Münz-schläger *m* coiner **-schlaghammer** *m* coining hammer **-schlitzantrieb** *m* coin slot drive **-schwengel** *m* coiner's stamp **-speicher** *m* coin storing channel **-sprecherleitung** *f* pay-station circuit **-stätte** *f* mint **-streckwerk** *n* mint mill, rolling mill for the mint **-wesen** *n* coinage **-zähler** *m* prepayment meter

mürbe weary, pliable, tender, soft, friable, brittle, short, mellow ~ **machen** to unnerve, soften up

Mürbemachemittel *pl* shortening or softening agents

Mürbigkeit *f* shortness (met.)

Mure *f* avalanche of sand and stones, rockslide

Murex-Prozeß *m* Murex (magnetic-paint) process

Murgang *m* (wet) landslide

Murmel *f* marble, marver

Murmeln *n* purling (babbling)

Murray's Reihentelegraf Murray telegraph

Musaempfang *m* multiple-unit steerable antenna reception

Muschel *f* cap, shell, nozzle ~ **des Fernhörers** telephone earpiece

Muschel-anordnung *f* mushroom form **-förmig** shell-like **-glas** *n* globular lens

muschelig conchoidal, shell-like, flinty **-er Bruch** conchoidal fracture

Muschelkalk *m* shell lime **-vorsatzbeton** *m* limestone concrete facing

Muschel-sand *m* shell sand **-schale** *f* shell **-schieber** *m* mushroom valve **-schiebersteuerung** *f* slide-valve gear

musierte Schrift rimmed letter

musikalisch musical **-er Ton** musical note or tone

Musikdrahtpoliereinrichtung *f* wire-polishing device for string wires

Musikinstrument *n* musical instrument ~ **mit direktem Schlag** musical instrument with direct percussion

Musik-leitung *f* music circuit **-meister** *m* bandmaster **-werk** *n* musical automaton, mechanical music instrument

Musivgold *n* mossaic gold, stannic sulfide

Muskat-blüte *f* mace **-butter** *f* nutmeg or mace butter **-nuß** *f* nutmeg

Muskel *m* muscle **-flug** *m* muscle-power flight

Muskelkraft *f* muscle power **-flugzeug** *n* muscle-power plane

Muskovit *m* muscovite

müssen to have to, be obliged

mussieren to effervesce

Muster *n* pattern, model, sample, example, specimen, type, standard, design ~ **ohne Wert** sample of no value **nach** ~ according to sample

Muster-ausnehmer *m* designer **-aussetzer** *m* designer, draftsman **-bauteil** *m* sample part **-berechtigung** *f* type rating **-betrieb** *m* pilot plant **-bezeichnung** *f* type designation **-bezirk** *m* muster district (draft) **-bogen** *m* sample sheet **-brennstoff** *m* reference fuel **-brett** *n* loam, modeling, template, or molding-out board **-brief** *m* pattern card **-buch** *n* book of patterns or samples, specimen book

Muster-dekoration *f* model display **-einrichtung** *f* patterning mechanism **-exemplar** *n* type specimen **-fertigung** *f* pilot production **-formkasten** *m* master flask **-flugzeug** *n* prototype aircraft **-glas** *n* display tube **-gleich** of standard quality **-gültig** exemplary, model, classic **-haft** standard, typical, exemplary **-hahn** *m* bleeder **-hebel** *m* pattern lever **-instrument** *n* prototype

Muster-karte *f* sample or pattern card **-konformität** *f* exactness of shade **-kopie** *f* master copy, master print **-mäßig** true to type or standard **-messe** *f* (sample) fair **-modell** *n* master pattern

mustern to muster, inspect, examine closely, sign the agreement

Muster-nehmer *m* (Angestellter) sampleman **-papier** *n* design, point, or rule paper **-plan** *m* layout sheet **-platinen** *m* selector **-presse** *f* tuck presser **-probe** *f* sample **-prüfung** *f* type test **-prüfungsschein** *m* approved-type certificate **-rapport** *n* repeat of design **-riß** *m* design in full size **-rolle** *f* muster roll, ship's articles

Muster-schläger *m* card cutter **-schraubenblatt** *n* propeller master blade **-schutz** *m* utility moded, registered pattern, copyright **-stopperhebel** *m* pattern selector lever **-stück** *n* test specimen, contours of the master **-tonnegativ** *n* master sound negative **-treu** perfect match **-tüll** *m* figured net

Musterung *f* mustering, quarters for muster, review, designing

Muster-vorrichtung *f* sampling device **-wähler** (am Meßgerät) pattern selector (TV) **-walze** *f* engraved brass cylinder **-wirkung** *f* design effect **-zeichner** *m* draftsman **-ziehung** *f* sampling **-zulassung** *f* type approval

Mutationsband *n* change tape

Muten *n* location of claims

Muter *m* claimant, claimholder

mutierendes Gen mutant gene

mutmaßen to guess

mutmaßliche Erstreckung der Lagerstätte probable extent of the deposit

Mutmaßung *f* guess

Mutter *f* nut, mother, mother disk, mother matrix ~ **mit Fibereinlage** nut with fiber insert, elastic stop nut ~ **mit Kerbverzahnung** splined nut ~ **mit Pinnenzapfen** screw reed and pin, screw with pivot pin **gerändelte** ~ knurled or milled nut **gesicherte** ~ lock nut

Mutter-anlage *f* master plant **-atom** *n* parent atom

Mutteraufschraubgerät *n* nut runner **elektromotorisch betriebenes** ~ nut runner

Mutter-blech *n* starting sheet, washer for bearings **-boden** *m* natural or undisturbed soil, topsoil **-bohrer** *m* nut tap **-faß** *n* mother vat **-fels** *m* bedrock **-fräsmaschine** *f* nut machine **-frequenz** *f* master frequency **-furche** *f* female groove or roll **-gestein** *n* source rock **-gewinde** *n* female screw thread, nut thread, internal thread **-gewindebohrer** *m* nut tap

Mutter-Hubbard-Meißel Mother Hubbard bit

Mutter-kaliber *n* female (mach.), matrix **-kern** *m* parent nucleus **-kompaß** *m* master compass, hydrostatic compass **-korn** *n* ergot (of rye) **-kornauszug** *m* ergot extract **-lauge** *f* mother lye, water, or liquor **-lochstreifen** *m* master tape **-magma** *n* mother liquor **-modell** *n* master pattern

Mutternabkantmaschine *f* nut-beveling machine

Mutternbohrer *m* nut tap ~ **mit** (langem) **gebogenem Schaft** bent-shank tapper tap

Muttern-draht *m* wire for nuts **-fräsautomat** *m*

automatic nut-milling machine **-gewindeschneider** *m* nut tapper

Mutternuklid *n* parent nuclide

Mutternstempel *m* nut punch

Mutter-platte *f* apron **-rohr** *n* gun tube **-rose** *f* master compass card **-rübensamen** *m* mother seed **-scheibe** *f* nut washer **-schiff** *n* repair ship

Mutterschloß-hebel *m* half nut **-exzenter** *m* half-nut cam **-oberteil** *n* upper half nut **-unterteil** *n* lower half nut

Mutter-schlüssel *m* monkey wrench, wrench, spanner, nut key **-schraube** *f* screw nut, female screw, bolt, bolt and nut **-sender** *m* key station, master station (in chain broadcasting), master transmitter **-sicherung** *f* nut locking, lock nut **-spannschloß** *n* multiple or collecting turnbuckle **-stellschlüssel** *m* adjustable wrench **-substanz** *f* parent substance **-uhr** *f* master clock **-unterlegscheibe** *f* lock washer **-verschluß** *m* nut lock

Mutung *f* application for patent of mining claims, claim, gale ~ **einlegen** to locate a claim

Mutungs-gemeinschaft *f* concession syndicate **-recht** *n* right to a concession **-riß** *m* plan of the concession **-schein** *m* certificate of permission to work a mine **-übersichtskarte** *f* general-concession map **-urkunde** *f* deed of concession

Myelographie *f* myelography

Mylonit *n* mylonite

Myon *n* muon, mu meson

Myoneneinfang *m* muon capture

Myopie *f* near(short) sightedness

myopisch near(short)sighted

Myristinsäure *f* myristic acid

Myrtenwachs *n* bayberry wax

N

Nabe *f* driving collar, boss, hub, nave ~ **des Windflügels** fan hub

Nabelpunkt *m* umbilicus (geom.)

Naben-abzieher *m* hub drawer **-anbauteil** *m* hub attaching part **-aufweiteprobe** *f* hub-widening test **-auszieher** *m* hub extractor **-bohrer** *m* hub-mortising-machine hand, nave borer **-bohrung** *f* bore of boss, bore of hub **-büchse** *f* nave or wheel box **-durchbiegeprobe** *f* deflection test by pressure on the hub

Naben-fläche *f* hub face **-flansch** *m* hub flange **-gewicht** *n* wheel weights **-haube** *f* nose spinner, spinner **-kern** *m* hub core **-konusbohrung** *f* central hub bore **-mutter** *f* nut plate **-nute** *f* keyway in the hub **-rohr** *n* wire manifold **-schaft** *m* propeller hub barrel **-schale** *f* hub barrel **-scheibe** *f* axle disk (wheel), nave disk **-sitz** *m* wheel seat or fit **-stern** *m* hub spider **-stirnfläche** *f* end of hub

Nach-abstimmung *f* fine tuning (circuit) **-ahmen** to imitate, duplicate, copy, mimic, counterfeit, adulterate **-ahmung** *f* imitation **-ahmungsprogramm** *n* simulated program **-anmeldung** *f* supplementary application **-appretur** *f* finishing

Nacharbeit *f* repair, maintenance, rectification, refinishing operation ~ **von Hand** hand finishing **Ausschuß durch** ~ **gebrauchsfähig machen** to salvage

nach-arbeiten to recondition, refinish, rework, dress, machine **-aufnahme** *f* retake **-ätzen** *n* final etching **-ausgabe** *f* post-edition **-ausgleichung** *f* subsequent compensation **-aviage** *f* after scrooping

Nachbar *m* neighbor, adjacent unit **-atom** *n* neighbor atom **-bahn** *f* neighboring trajectory **bildträger** *m* adjacent vision carrier, adjacent picture carrier **-bohrloch** *n* offsetting well **-feld** *n* adjoining concession **-gebiet** *n* adjacent domains **-gebilde** *n* adjoining formation **-kanalstörung** *f* adjacent channel interference, monkey chatter **-ortsverkehr** *m* junction traffic, neighborhood traffic **-schaft** *f* neighborhood, vicinity **-stellung** *f* neighboring position **-zone** *f* adjacent zone, heat-affected zone, refined zone

Nachbau *m* construction under license **-recht** *n* manufacturing permit

nach-bearbeiten to rework, finish, dress, machine

Nachbearbeitung *f* reworking, finishing, dressing (of tools) ~ **der Skalenteilung** dividing

Nach-behandlung *f* aftertreatment, curing, retreatment **-belichtung** *f* post-exposure **-beschleunigung** *f* post-acceleration, acceleration by second gun anode

Nachbeschleunigungs-elektrode *f* post-deflection accelerating electrode additional gun anode, accelerator electrode, after-accelerator **-röhre** *f* post deflection accelerator tube

nach-bessern to mend, touch up **-bestellen** to repeat an order **-bestellung** *f* supplementary order, resowing **-beuchen** *n* scalding (bleaching) **-bewilligung** *f* supplementary allowance, subsequent grant

nachbiegen to rebend

Nachbiegen der Elektroden readjusting the electrodes by bending

Nach-bild *n* copy, facsimile, afterimage, imitation, replica **-bildefehler** *m* balance deficiency

nachbilden to imitate, simulate, copy, reproduce, counterfeit, balance **genau** ~ to simulate closely **neu** ~ to rebalance

Nachbilden *n* simulation, balance ~ **einer Leitung** balancing of a circuit

Nachbildner *m* simulator (comput.)

Nachbildung *f* imitation, copy, replica, balance network

Nachbildungs-fehler *m* fault of balancing (teleph.) **-frequenzbereich** *m* frequency range of simulation **-gerät** *n* photostat equipment **-gestell** *n* (balancing) network rack (teleph.) **-kamera** *f* reproducing camera **-messer** *m* impedance unbalance measuring set, return-loss measuring set **-prüfer** *m* balance tester **-satz** *m* balance-testing set (teleph.) **-seite** *f* balancing side **-überträger** *m* balancing repeating coil **-verfahren** *n* method of balancing (teleph.)

Nach-bildwiderstand *m* balance resistor **-bildwirkung** *f* persistence of vision **-blasen** *n* afterblow **-bleiben** to lag **-bohren** to ream, underream, rebore, widen, drill finished holes **-bohren** *n* reboring **-bohrer** *m* broaching bit, tooth cutter **-brecher** *m* additional breaker **-brennen** *n* afterburning, late combustion **-brenner** *m* hang-fire shell or cartridge **-brennkammer** *f* secondary combustion chamber **-büchse** *f* reaming auger **-büchsen** to ream out

nach-chromieren to chrome after dyeing **-datierung** *f* post dating **-dauer** *f* persistence **-decken** to cover subsequently **-denken** to think, reflect, ponder, reason **-denklich** thoughtful, meditative

Nachdrängen *n* pursuit, pressure (on the enemy), direct pressure in pursuit **scharfes ~** close pursuit, direct pressure (pursuit)

Nachdrehbank *f* finishing lathe

nachdrehen to take the finishing cut

Nachdrehen *n* re-turning, remilling, redressing

Nachdreh-getriebe *n* vertical gyroscope, leveling motor (autopilot) **-schleuder** *f* afterworker (sugar mfg.) **-vorrichtung** *f* re-turning device

nachdrücken to restore

nachdrücklich categorically

Nachdruck *m* reprint, counterfeit **~ legen auf** to emphasize, stress

Nachdrucksrecht *n* copyright

Nachdruckverfahren *n* reprinting process

nach-dunkeln to darken (subsequently), become darker **-eichen** to recalibrate, check (the calibration) **-eichung** *f* check(ing), check calibration, recalibration, alignment **-eilen** to go behind, run slow, to lag

Nacheilen *n* lag, lagging, trail (behind) **~ des Einlaßventils** lag of air-intake valve

nacheilend behind, lagging **-e Spannung -er Strom** lagging current

Nacheilspule *f* lagging coil

Nacheilung *f* lag, lagging, phase lag, retardation, creeping (in rolling) **hysteretische ~** hysteretic lag **zeitliche ~** time lag

Nacheilungs-winkel *m* angle of lag **-zeit** *f* dead time

nacheinander one after another, successively, sequentially, consecutively, seriatim **-färben** to dye again, counterstain

Nacheinstellung *f* readjustment

Nach-empfindung *f* aftersensation **-entladung** *f* after-discharge

nacherhitzen to temper

Nacherhitzer *m* after-heater, after-burner

Nacherzeugnis *n* afterproduct

Nachfahr-genauigkeit *f* reproductive accuracy **-verhalten** *n* copying device

Nachfall *m* caving system, following

nachfallen to cave

nachfallendes Gut caving material

Nachfallpacken *m* draw slate

Nach-federung *f* hysteresis **-filtern** to refilter **fliegen** to test and check under flight conditions, make an acceptance check, final test flight **-fließen** *n* afterflow (of metals), persistence of plastic flow, elastic aftereffect **-fokussieren** to re-focus **-folgekern** *m* product nucleus **-folgen** to succeed, follow

nachfolgend following, continuous, consecutive, secondary **-er Netzstrom, -er Strom** follow-on current

Nach-folger *m* successor, follower, imitator **-fordern** to charge extra **-formdrehen** *n* copy turning **-formdrehbank** *f* copying lathe **-formen** to overform **-formkraft** *f* copying pressure

Nachformfräsmaschine *f* duplicating milling machine, profiler

nach-forschen to inquire into, investigate **-forschen** *n* quest **-forschung** *f* search, investigation, query, scrutiny, research

Nachfrage *f* demand, enquiry, requirements **~ im Inland** home demand

nach-fragen to inquire, ask **-fraktionierturm** *m* after-fractionating tower **-fräser** *m* finishing cutter **-frist** *f* respite, time extension

Nachführung *f* (des Reglers), follow-up device **~ des Fernrohres** following of the telescope **~ des Rahmens** resetting or readjustment of frame or coil (direction finder) **~** (der Rohre) following with the casing

nach-füllen to fill up, top up, refill, replenish, refuel **-füllen** *n* topping-up, filling-up, gassing-up **-füllung** *f* afteradmission **-gang** *m* retardation **-gärung** *f* afterfermentation, post-fermentation **-gasen** *n* aftergeneration

nach-geahmt counterfeit, imitated, feigned **-gebedruck** *m* yield load (aviation) **-geben** to give way, cede, yield, run slow, go behind, drag (naut.), concede

Nachgeben *n* deflection

nachgebend-e Grenzfläche yielding boundary surface **-e Rückführung** re-set feedback

Nach-gebepunkt *m* yield point **-gebezeit** *f* reset time, integral action time **-gehen** (Uhr) to go slow **-gemacht** artificial, false, bogus

nach-geschaltet subsequently added **-geschaltete Stufe** higher stage, succeeding stage, power stage

nachgestellt adjusted

Nachgetterung *f* final gettering

nachgiebig ductile, flexible, elastic, yielding, pliable **-er Bootskörper** flexible hull **-e Kennlinie** flexible characteristic curve **-e Rückführung** gentle return **-e Scheibenkuppelung** flexible disk coupling **-er Spannungsregler** yielding voltage regulator

Nachgiebigkeit *f* compliance, yieldingness, resilience

Nach-glühcharakteristik *f* persistence characteristic **-glühen** to temper, draw, reanneal **-glühen** *n* afterglow, annealing, phosphorescence **-glühtemperatur** *f* tempering temperature **-greifer** *pl* auxiliary grippers

Nachhall *m* reverberation, echo, resonance

Nachhalldauer *f* reverberation time **übertriebene ~** excessive reverberation period

nachhallen to reverberate

Nachhallen *n* reverberation

nachhallfreies Studio dead studio

Nachhall-kammer *f* **-messung** *f* measuring of the reverberation **-raum** *m* reverberation room, enclosure, or space **-reiches Studio** live studio **-vorgang** *m* reverberation phenomenon **-zeit** *f* reverberation time

nach-haltig lasting, protracted, intense, durable,

permanent, persevering **-hämmern** to flatten **-hängen** *n* lag **-härten** *n* second cure **-härtungsfrist** *f* ageing time **-heizbehälter** *m* booster heater

Nachhinken *n* hysteresis, lag, time lag ~ **der Zelle** lag of the photoelectric cell

nach-hitzen to temper, reheat **-holbedarf** *m* backlog of needs, inadequacy gap **-holen** to bring back, recover, make up for **-holzeit** *f* (Radar) recovery time **-justieren** to readjust

Nach-kalkulation *f* recalculation **-kleben** to glue **-kochen** *n* gassing after the charge **-kommen** to follow, comply with **-kompensierung** *f* subsequent or aftercompensation **-kontrollieren** to recheck **-konzentration** *f* refocusing **-körnen** to re-grain

Nach-kühler *m* aftercooler, recooler, subcooler **-kupfern** to aftertreat with copper **-kupplung** *f* aftercoupling **-kurbeln** to recrank

Nachladeerscheinung *f* residual charge or recharging phenomenon

nachladen to recharge

Nachladeschlitz *m* auxiliary scavenging port

Nachladung *f* additional scavenging air through auxiliary scavenging ports, additional charge, regeneration ~ **von Zweitaktmaschinen** scavenging of two-stroke-cycle engines

Nachlaß *m* rebate, abatement, deduction, discount, inheritance **-draht** *m* slack wire

nachlassen to weaken, decline, loosen, yield, relax, subside, abate, reduce, temper, anneal, expand

Nachlassen *n* abatement

nachlassend, nicht ~ unabating

nachlässig neglectful, negligent

Nachlässigkeit *f* carelessness, negligence, inadvertence

Nachlaß-kette *f* extension chain **-kettenwinde** *f* extension shaft **-schraube** *f* extension bolt, temper screw **-schraubenwirbel** *m* extension swivel **-spindel** *f* temper screw **-winde** *f* extension winding gear, temper reel

Nachlauf *m* camber-and-pivot inclination, tails (distilling), last runnings, faints, positive caster, wake, track alignment **-bremse** *f* slowing-down brake **-delle** *f* reciprocal depression (of curve) **-druck** *m* wake pressure **-einrichtung** *f* servomotor **-einstellung** *f* automatic resetting of direction finder to zero

nachlaufen to go behind, lag

Nachläufer *m* single-wheeled or single-axle trailer, trailer axle

Nachlauf-genauigkeit *f* accuracy of AFC **-messung** *f* wake survey **-peiler** *m* direction finder in which readjustment to zero is effected automatically **-regelkreis** *m* follow-up servo **-regelung** *f* follow-up control **-schaltung** *f* tracking circuit, **-steuerung** *f* follower control device **-stufe** *f* follower stage **-weg** *m* slowing-down path

nach-leimen to re-size **-leistungen** *pl* deferred charges

nachlesen to glean

Nachleucht-bild *n* residual image **-charakteristik** *f* decay characteristic, persistence characteristic

Nachleuchtdauer *f* afterglow time ~ **des Fluoreszenzschirmes** persistence or decay-time of the fluorescent screen

Nachleuchten *n* phosphorescence, afterglow **Verminderer des Nachleuchtens** killer, poison

Nachleucht-erscheinung *f* persistance phenomenon **-rohr** *n* afterglow tube (electronics) **-schirm** *m* persistence screen

nachliefern to deliver subsequently

Nachlieferungskoeffizient *m* production coefficient

nach-machen to counterfeit, imitate, copy **-mattieren** *n* ultimate delustering **-messen** to check the dimension, control, recheck, measure **-messung** *f* verifying (measuring) **-musterfarben** *pl* dyeing to pattern or to shade

Nachnahme *f* cash on delivery, reimbursement **gegen** ~ cash on delivery

Nachnahme-bohrer *m* underreamer, reamer **-inkasso** *n* cash-on-delivery service

nach-nehmen to ream, send for cash on delivery **-nehmer** *m* reamer **-nuancieren** to shade (shade off) **-öl** *n* refuse oil **-ordnen** to insert after **-polieren** to redress, repolish, refinish, recut **-pressen** to re-press

Nachprodukt *n* afterproduct, second product **auf** ~ **verkochen** to boil to afterproduct

Nachprodukt-füllmasse *f* low-grade massecuite **-maische** *f* afterproduct crystallizer **-sud** *m* lowgrade strike **-vakuum** *n* low-grade vacuum pan **-verkochung** *f* boiling of afterproduct **-zucker** *m* low-grade sugar

nach-prüfen to examine, test, verify, check, control, inspect **-prüfung** *f* checking, testing, verification, inspection, revision, control, review **-prüfungsversuch** *m* retest **-prüfvorrichtung** *f* quartering gauge **-rauhen** to finish roughen **-raum** *m* waste **-räumer** *m* reamer **-rechnen** to recompute, check (computations) **-rechnung** *f* calculation, costing

nach-regeln to (re)adjust **-regelung** *f* readjustment **-regulieren** to adjust, regulate **-reibahle** *f* finishing reamer **-reiben** to finish-ream **-reife** *f* ultimate ripening

Nach-reifung *f* finishing (photographic emulsion), maturing (of film) **-reiniger** *m* final purifier, cleaner **-reinigung** *f* final cleaning or purification **-reißen** to rip, stow away the roof **-reißen** *n* (des Gesteins) brushing, ripping, widening out **-reißer** *m* ripper, widener

Nachrevision *f* final inspection

Nachricht *f* report, information, communication, news, notice, intelligence, message, signal

Nachrichten-bandbreite intelligence bandwidth **-beurteilung** *f* evaluation of information **-dienst** *m* intelligence service, signals service, signal corps **-ingenieur** *m* communication engineer

Nachrichtengerät *n* signaling apparatus, signal supplies **-karren** *m* signal-equipment cart **-park** *m* signal-communication-equipment park, signal-supply dump

Nachrichtenkopf *m* message center, wire head, advance message center

Nachrichtenmenge *f* **je Zeiteinheit** (Nachrichtenfluß) information unit/sec (bits)

Nachrichtenmittel *n* channel of communication, signals equipment **optische** ~ visual means of communication

Nachrichten-netz *n* communication net, telecommunication system or network, radio network **-querverbindung** *f* liaison communication **-sender** *m* communications transmitter **-speicher** *m* message storage unit **-stelle** *f* message center, information center **-technik** *f* science of communications, communication engineering **-übermittlung** *f* **-übertragung** *f* transmission of intelligence or communications, signaling **-verband** *m* signal(-communications) unit **-verbindung** *f* channel of communication, signal communication **-verkehr** *m* communications activity, signal-communication traffic

Nachrichten-vermittler dispatch carrier, dispatch rider **-weg** *m* signal-communication channel **-weitergabe** *f* retransmission **-wesen** *n* communication (service), news-system communications, signal communications **-zentrale** *f* signal center, message center

Nach-rotte des Flachses after-retting of flax **-rücken** to move up **-ruf** *m* recall signal **-rüstteile** *pl* supplementary parts **-sacken** to sag, settle, subside **-saturation** *f* final saturation

Nachsatz *m* draw (in casting) **-konzentration** *f* concentration of the feeding liquor **-lösung** *f* feeding liquor or solution

nachsäuren to reacidulate

nachschaben to rescrape **das Lager ~** to scrape the bearing

Nach-schall *m* reverberation **-schallen** to echo **-schalten** to connect or couple at the outlet side

Nachschalt-gebläse *n* overcompression impeller **-heizfläche** *f* ancillary heating surface **-verdichter** *m* aftercompressor, booster, compressor

nach-schärfen to resharpen **-schärfen** *n* resharpening **-schäumer** *m* scavenger flotation machine **-scheidesaft** *m* postdefecation juice **-scheidung** *f* postdefecation, postliming **-schikken** to send after, forward **-schieben** to supply **-schießen** to widen by blasting **-schießen** *n* aftershooting (in quarries, to reduce size of large pieces), reshooting

Nachschlage-buch *n* reference book **-werk** *n* reference work

nachschleifen to resharpen, regrind, true, reface **mit dem Ölstein ~** to restone

Nach-schleifen *n* regrinding, finish grinding **-schleppen** to trail **-schliff** *m* regrind **-schlüssel** *m* double, false, or skeleton key, picklock, passkey

Nachschneide-bohrer *m* reamer bit **-büchse** *f* reaming bit **-eisen** *pl* re-threading dies **-kreuz** *n* crossing reamer **-meißel** *m* reaming bit

nachschneiden, ein Gewinde ~ to chase a screw thread

Nach-schneiden *n* reaming, trimming (cloth) **-schneider** *m* bottoming tap **-schnitt** *m* recutting **-schrift** *f* postscript, picture re-creation **-schrumpfen** to aftershrink **-schrumpfung** *f* aftershrinkage

Nachschub *m* bringing up of supplies, supply, replacement, reserves **-dienst** *m* service of supply **-fahrzeug** *n* supply vehicle **-gut** *n* supply, supplies **-lage** *f* supply situation **-lager** *n* supply depot, supply dump **-linie** *f* supply line **-mittel** *n* means of supply movement

Nachschub-spindeln *pl* feeding screws **-straße** *f* axis of supply, supply route, line of supply, line of communication **-stützpunkt** *m* supply base **-transport** *m* transport of supplies **-umschlagstelle** *f* supply point **-verkehr** *m* supply traffic, movement of supplies **-vorrichtung** *f* feeding gear **-weg** *m* supply road, supply route **-wesen** *n* supply services

Nach-schwaden *m* afterdamp, chokedamp **-sehen** to inspect, overhaul, attend to, look for, check, control, look after **-seigern** to liquate subsequently or again **-sendung der Telegramme** forwarding of telegrams **-senken** to recountersink **-setzen** to add, recharge, postpone, pursue

Nachsetz-kasten *m* rewash box **-maschine** *f* rewashing machine **-vorrichtung** *f* adjusting device

Nachsicherung *f* additional security

Nachsicht *f* indulgence, leniency **ohne ~** severe

Nach-sinken *n* shrinking (in putty or plastic wood for filling defects) **-spannen** to retighten

Nachspannen *n* retightening **~ der Feder** rebending of the spring **~ der Leitung** tightening up the wire

nach-spülen to flush again **-spüren** to trace

nächst next, nearest, next to **die nächsten Angehörigen** next of kin

nachstehend hereafter, following, described below **~ erwähnt** below-mentioned

nachstellbar adjustable, regulable **-er Gewindebohrer** adjustable tap **-e Reibahle** expanding reamer **-es Spindellager** adjustable spindle bearing

Nachstellbarkeit *f* adjustability

nachstellen to adjust, reset, regulate, retard, true-up, pursue **das Lager ~** to adjust or take up the bearing

Nachstell-exzenter *m* adjustable eccentric **-keil** *m* wedge bolt **-schnecke** *f* adjusting worm **-schraube** *f* adjusting screw

Nachstellung *f* adjustment

Nachstellvorrichtung *f* adjusting device **~ für das Spiel** slack adjustment

Nachstell-werkzeug *n* resetting tool **-winkel** *m* adjustable crank or right-angled brace **-zeit** *f* integral-action time, (electronics) resetting time

nachstemmen to recalk

Nachsteuergestänge *n* follow-up transmission linkage

nachsteuern to follow up (servo)

nächstfolgend next following

nach-stimmen to tune finely **-stimmung** *f* fine tuning

Nachstimmungskondensator *m* aligning condenser, trimming capacitor, vernier capacitor

nachstollen to re-stake

nachstopfen to repack, retamp **das Geleise ~** to repack or retamp the sleepers

nach-stoßen to pursue, push forward, thrust after **-strahlen** to phosphoresce **-strecken** *n* thinning

Nachstrom *m* wake, wash, slip stream **~ der Luftschraube** slip stream

Nach-strömung *f* wake **-suchen** to apply, solicit, file (a petition) **-synchronisieren** *n* post-synchronization **-synchronisierung** *f* bouncing-ball synchronization

nachtanken to refuel (especially in flight)
Nachtankkuppelung *f* refuel connection
Nacht-arbeit *f* night shift, nightwork **-aufklärung** *f* night reconnaisance **-aufnahme** *f* night photograph **-befeuerung** *f* night lighting, illumination **-belastung** *f* night load
Nachtbeleuchtung *f* night illumination **mit ~** illuminated, luminous
Nachtbeleuchtungsansatz *m* night-illumination attachment
nacht-blind night-blind **-blindheit** *f* night blindness
Nachtdienst *m* night service, night duty **-beamtin** *f* night operator **-platz** *m* night-service position
Nachteffekt *m* night effect, polarization error, directional or quadrantal errors **-frei** free from night effect or polarization errors
Nachteil *m* disadvantage, detriment, damage, cheapness, loss, prejudice, injury, demerit **erheblicher ~** serious disadvantage
nachteilig disadvantageous **-e Wirkung** ill effect
Nachtempern *n* after annealing
Nacht-erkundung *f* night reconnaissance **-fahren** *n* night movement of vehicles **-fahrtanzeiger** *m* night signal indicating ship's course to following unit **-fee** *f* code for a type of radio (set) **-frequenz** *f* night frequency
Nacht-gebühr *f* night rate **-landung** *f* night landing
nachtleuchtend luminous, illuminated **-e Instrumente** luminous instruments **-es Lande-T** illuminated landing T
Nachtluft-aufnahme *f* night (air) photograph **-post** *f* night air mail **-postdienst** *m* night-air-mail service **-verkehr** *m* night air traffic
nach-tönen reverberate **-touren** *n* veluring
Nachtplatz *m* night position
Nachtrabant *m* post-equalizing pulse (TV)
Nachtrag *m* supplement, addendum
nachtragen to complete, supplement
nachträglich supplementary, subsequent, later **-e Richtigstellung der Rechnungen** subsequent adjustment of accounts
Nachtragmappe *f* supplementary folder
Nachtrags-befehl *m* supplementary order, annex (order) **-zahlung** *f* payment after a certain date
Nachtransport *m* take-up sprocket action
Nachtreichweite *f* night range
Nachtrelais *n* night service relay
Nachtriegel *m* night bolt
Nachtropfen *n* drip
nachts at night, by night **~ fliegen** to fly at night
Nacht-schalter *m* night depository (bank), day-and-night transfer key **-schicht** *f* night shift
Nacht-sehen *n* noctovision **-sichtgerät** *n* noctoviser **-streckenbefeuerung** *f* route beacon for night-flying service **-tarif** *m* night tariff **-unternehmung** *f* night operation **-verbindung** *f* night service connection (teleph.) **-visierbeleuchtung** *f* illumination of sight, apparatus for illuminating sight
Nacht-taste *f* night service button **-wache** *f* night watch **-wächter** *m* night watchman **-wecker** *m* night bell, night alarm **-welle** *f* night wave, wave for nighttime transmission **-wind** *m* night wind **-winkelmesser** *m* night goniometer **-wirkung** *f* night effect, swing **-zentralschalter** *m* night concentrator
Nachübertrager *m* (repeater) output transformer, outlet transformer
Nachuntersuchung *f* check-up, check **ärztliche ~** medical check-up
Nach-urlaub *m* extension of leave, extended leave **-veranlagung** *f* post assessment **-verbrennung** *f* afterburning **-verdampfer** *m* complementary evaporator **-verdichtung** *f* secondary compression **-verstärker** *m* amplifier in stage above input stage, power amplifier **-verstrecken** *n* after-stretching **-vertonung** *f* dubbing, rerecording of sound track **-wahl** *f* post-selection **-wähler** *m* hunting switch **-walzen** to reroll, finish, planish, dress **-walzgerüst** *n* finishing or dressing frame **-waschen** *n* rewash, aftertreatment
Nachwasch-kohle *f* residues of coal washing **-mittelprodukt** *n* rewashed middlings **-setzmaschine** *f* clarifier
Nachweis *m* proof, inventory, index, evidence, detection, analysis, list, record, indication, direction, information, reference **für einen ~ dienende Auskünfte** evidence **~ eines Kernteilchens** detection of nuclear particle
nach-weisbar detectable, traceable **-weisen** to indicate, prove, demonstrate, inform, detect, discover, identify
Nachweis-empfindlichkeit *f* detection efficiency **-genauigkeit** *f* detection accuracy **-gerät** *n* indicating apparatus **-interferometer** *n* detection interferometer **-linie** *f* (Spektrallinien) reference line
Nachweisung *f* detection, proof, identification, indication, statement, list, account, record, strength report, stock report
Nachweiswahrscheinlichkeit *f* probability of detection
Nach-wärmofen *m* reheating furnace **-werk** *n* finishing mill **-wetzen** (mit dem Ölstein) to restone **-wickelrolle** *f* bottom sprocket, tape-up reel or spindle, hold-back sprocket **-wickler** *m* take-up sprocket **-wiegen** to check-weigh, weigh again
Nachwirkung *f* aftereffect, hysteresis, secondary effect, afterworking, lag, persistence **~ eines Effekts** hangover effect **~ eines Einflusses** overhang effect, hangover effect **~ des Selens** hysteresis of the selenium (photoelectric) cell **dielektrische ~** dielectric fatigue, dielectric hysteresis **elastische ~** elastic afterworking **elektrische ~** electric aftereffect **magnetische ~** magnetic fatigue, magnetic aftereffect, residual loss (of metals) **plastische ~** plastic flow persistence, afterflow, elastic aftereffect
Nachwirkungs-effekt *m* aftereffect **-erscheinung** *f* secondary-effect phenomenon **-funktion** *f* aftereffect function **-strom** *m* absorption current, current of residual charge **-veränderung** *f* hysteresis **-verlust** *m* hysteretic loss, residual loss
Nach-wirkzeit *f* hangover time, decay period **-wuchs** *m* supply of personnel **-zählen** to check **-zahlung** *f* additional payment **-zeichnen** to trace, copy **-zentrieren** to re-center **-zieheffekt** *m* smearing effect (TV) **-ziehen** to bring up, tighten (up) **-ziehschlauch** *m* cable grip split **-zuchtsamen** *m* second-class seed **-zucker** *m*

low-grade sugar **-zügler** *m* straggler, camp follower **-zugsmuster** *n* exhaust test **-zündung** *f* retarded ignition, torching, sparking retard

Nacken *m* neck, nape **~ der Keilhaue** hammer end of the pick

Nacken-band *n* neck strap (mask) **-joch** *n* neck yoke **-riemen** *m* neck strap (harness)

nackt naked, bare, stripped **-es Atom** stripped atom **-er Draht** bare wire **-e Elektrode** bare electrode **-es Spaltstoffelement** uncanned fuel element

Nacktheit *f* nakedness, bareness

Nadel *f* needle, taper pin (of converter bottom), rod, fuse striker, hand, pointer, firing pin **-abnutzung** *f* needle or stylus wear (phono) **-abweichung** *f* magnetic declination **-arm** *m* needle arm **-artig** acicular, needlelike **-aufreiher** *m* needle splitter **-ausschlag** *m* deflection of the needle, needle throw

Nadel-barre *f* needle bar **-bett** *n* needle board **-bewegung** *f* stylus trajectory **-biegezange** *f* nipper for needle bending **-boden** *m* pinhole plug (of converter), needle or perforated bottom **-büchse** *f* needle case **-druck** *m* tracking force (phono), needle force **-düse** *f* pin-type nozzle **-eisenerz** *n* göthite **-eisenstein** *m* needle ironstone **-erz** *n* aikinite **-fadenzug** *m* needle thread take-up **-feile** *f* neelde point file

nadelförmig needle-shaped, acicular, needlelike **-es Gefüge** needle fracture

Nadel-funkenstrecke *f* needle-point spark gap, needle gap **-galvanometer** *n* moving-magnet galvanometer, needle galvanometer **-geräusch** *n* needle scratch (phono) **-geräuschfilter** *m* needle-scratch filter **-gesteuert** needle-controlled (valve) **-halter** *m* suture-needle holder **-hammer** *m* needle hammer **-holz** *n* pine wood **-hubregulierung** *f* needle lift control **-hülse** *f* needle bushing (sleeve)

nadelig acicular, needlelike **-er Martensit** acicular martensite

Nadel-induktion *f* needle induction **-käfig** *m* needle cage **-kanüle** *f* hollow (tubular) needle **-klappe** *f* needle valve **-kopf** *m* head of needles **-lager** *n* needle (roller) bearing, pin bearing **-lagerbüchse** *f* needle bearing bush **-lagerstützrollen** *pl* needle-bearing support-roller **-lamelle** *f* needle lamina **-länge** *f* length of wire for pins, pin length **-leiste** *f* pin plate **-maß** *n* needle gauge **-matrize** *f* needle die **-öhr** *n* needle eye, pinhole

Nadelpaar, astatisches ~ astatic couple, two compound needles

Nadel-punktanguß *m* pin point gating **-reibung** *f* needle friction **-richtzange** *f* needle dressing pliers **-rollenlager** *n* needle roller bearing **-schalter** *m* vibrating-reed rectifier **-schiene** *f* needle slide **-schmierglas** *n* glass grease cup **-schwankung** *f* oscillation of compass needle **-schwimmer** *m* guide

Nadel-senker *m* wing cam **-setzer** *m* needle caster **-sicht** *m* pinhole **-sitz** *m* needle seat **-spannrahmen** *m* pin stenter **-spitze** *f* stylus tip, needle point **-stich** *m* prick of a needle, stitch **-stück** *n* firing-pin guide (fuse), firing-pin support **-telegraph** *m* needle telegraph

Nadelton *m* stylus- or needle-recorded and -reproduced sound **-ansatz** *m* sound on disk attachment **-verfahren** *n* sound on disk method **-verstärker** *m* phonograph amplifier **-zusatz** *m* sound on disk attachment

Nadeltuch mit Holzlatten spiked lattice

Nadel-ventil *n* needle valve **-verfahren** *n* rapid preparation of axial-lateral fire with aiming circle compass, compass method of laying guns **-verschluß** *m* needle dam **-wald** *m* coniferous woods or forest **-walze** *f* porcupine (textiles) **-wehr** *n* needle weir, pin weir, post dam, dam with frames and needles **-zahl** *f* azimuth reading, magnetic azimuth **-zähler** *m* needle counter

Nadir *m* nadir **-aufnahme** *f* vertical photograph

Nadirdistanz *f* nadir distance, tilt **~ in Flugrichtung** fore-and-aft tilt **~ quer zur Flugrichtung** lateral tilt

Nadirpunkt *m* plumb point **-triangulation** *f* plumb-point triangulation

nadirwärts vertically downward

Nadirwinkel *m* angle of tilt, nadir angle

N-adrige Schnur n-conductor cord

Naegit *m* naegite

Nagel *m* nail, spike, tack **eingekerbter ~** fluted spike **hölzerner ~** dowel, peg, treenail, wooden pin **langer ~** spike

nagelbar nailable

Nagel-bohrer *m* gimlet, auger (pole) **-docke** *f* nail bore, mold, or tool **-eisen** *n* nail rod or iron, heading tool, bolt header **-erz** *n* columnar argillaceous red iron ore **-falz** *m* (finger) nail fold **-fänger** *m* nail catcher

Nagelfluh *f* conglomerate, Nagelfluh **-steingrube** *f* Nagelfluh quarry

Nagel-hammer *m* spike driver or hammer **-heber** *m* nail puller, claw, claw wrench **-hilfskranz** *m* spiking curb **-kaliber** *n* nail pass **-klaue** *f* spike drawer **-klotz** *m* pegwood (watchmaking)

Nagelkopf *m* nailhead **-eisen** *n* heading tool

Nagelleiste *f* molding with pins

nageln to nail, spike, tack, clinch

Nageln *n* nailing, spiking

nagelneu brand-new

Nagel-niet *m* clinch of horseshoe nail **-probe** *f* nail test (for blasting caps) **-schmied** *m* nailer, nail maker, nailsmith **-schneide** *f* edge of nail **-schnur** *f* small lace **-schrot** *m* nailsmith's chisel **-sicher** punctureproof **-sucher** *m* tack detector

Nagelung *f* nailing **~ der Schienen** fastening the rails to the sleepers with bolts and spikes

Nagel-zange *f*, **-zieher** *m* nail puller

Nagemaschine *f* nibbler

nah near, close, imminent, local, short range

Nahablesekompaß *m* direct-reading compass

Nah-aufnahme *f* close-up view **-beben** *n* neighboring earthquake **-beobachtung** *f* close-range observation, local observation

Nahbeobachtungsstelle *f* close-range observation post

Nah-bereich *m* antenna-proximity zone, very short range (rdr) **-besprechungsmikrophon** *f* close-talking microphone **-betrieb** *m* local operation

Nähdraht *m* chain wire (paper mfg.)

Nahdrehzahlmesser *m* direct revolution counter, direct-reading tachometer

nahe close, near

Nähe *f* vicinity, nearness, proximity, propinquity, contiguity **in der ~** close to **in erreichbarer ~** within striking distance, within reasonable distance

nahebei close to

Nahecho *n* near echo

Nahefeldpeiler *m* ground-wave direction finder, direction-finder equipment

Naheinstellung *f* short-range focus

naheliegen to be or lie near, border (on), be patent, obvious, evident, or self-suggesting, be adjacent or contiguous

naheliegend obvious, reasonable, adjacent

Nahempfang *m* short range receiving

nähen to sew

Nahentstörung short distance radio shielding

Nahepunkt *m* near point

Naherkundung *f* short range reconnaissance

nähern, sich ~ to approach, approximate, close in

nähernd, sich ~ oncoming

Näherung *f* situation of proximity, approximation, approach **gleichlaufende ~** parallelism

Näherungs-ansatz *m* approximation, rough formulation **-effekt** *m* proximity effect **-formel** *f* approximate or approximation formula, approximate equation **-gerade** (die) the straight approaching line **-gleichung** *f* approximation equation **-größe** *f* approximate quantity **-lösung** *f* approximate solution **-methode** *f* method of approximation **-rechnung** *f* approximate calculation, approximate methods of analysis **-relais** *n* capacitance relay **-verfahren** *n* approximation method **-weise** approximate(ly) **-wert** *m* approximate value, approximation

nahestehend intimately related or connected, affiliated

Nahewirkungstheorie *f* theory of continuous action

Nah-feld *n* vicinity, short-range field **-fernverkehr** *m* short-haul toll traffic (teleph.) **-förderer** *m* short-distance transporter, close-range conveyer **-förderwesen** *n* matters of short-distance conveyance

Nähgarn *n* sewing thread

Nähkante *f* seam

Nah-klemmer *m* reading pince-nez or eyeglass **-kompaß** *m* compass on board of airplane, direct-reading compass **-kontrollbereich** *m* terminal control aera (aviat)

Nähmaschine *f* sewing machine

Nähmaschinen-öl *n* sewing-machine oil **-schiffchen** *n* sewing-machine shuttle

Nahmethode *f* implicit method

Nah-nebensprechdämpfung *f* near-end crosstalk attenuation **-nebensprechen** *n* near-end crosstalk

Nah-ordnung *f* short-range order **-peilung** *f* close-range direction finding **-punkt** *m* near point

Nährboden *m* nutritive substratum, nutrient medium

nähren to feed, reinforce, nourisch

nahrhaft nourishing, nutritious

Nährhefe *f* yeast nutrient

Nähriemen *m* leather lace or strap

Nähr-mittel *n* food(stuff), nutriment, nourishing preparation **-präparat** *n* food(stuff) preparation **-stoffgehalt** *m* nutrient content

Nahrung *f* nourishment, food, feed

Nahrungs-bedingung *f* condition of nourishment **-freiheit** *f* food autarchy **-mangel** *m* lack of provisions **-mittel** *n* food, food supply, nutriment, provisions **-mittelchemiker** *m* food chemist **-zweig** *m* branch of trade or industry

Nahschwund *m* short-range fading **-antenne** *f* short-range fading antenna **-zone** *f* short-range fading area

Nah-sehen (Nahsicht) near vision **-selektion** *f* adjacent channel selectivity **-sender** *m* short-distance sender **-sicherung** *f* close-in security, close-in protection **-signalmittel** *n* short-distance or short-range signal means **-steuerung** *f* local-remote control **-störung** *f* near-by interference **-stoß** close collision **-streuung** *f* short-distance scatter **-teil** *m* near portion

Naht *f* seam, fin, feather, lap, edge, fissure, sector boundary, weld, suture line, joint, juncture **~ der Platten** seam of the plates **schlecht ausgeführte ~** pucker **überwendliche ~** overcast **versetzte ~** staggered seam, sock stitch **wulstlose ~** ridgeless seam

Nahthaken *m* ravehook, ripping iron

nahtlos weldless, seamless, jointless **~ gezogenes Rohr** seamless, weldless, or solid-drawn pipe **-er (Eisenbahn)radreifen** weldless tire **-es Rohr** seamless tube **-e Stahlmuffenröhre** *pl* seamless steel spigot and faucet tubes

Naht-oberfläche *f* surface of seam **-querschnitt** *m* cross-section of weld **-schweißmaschine** *f* seam welder **-schweißung** *f* seam welding **-stärke** *f* seam size, weld (throat) dimension **-stelle** *f* boundary (position) between units

Nahtransport *m* short distance transport

Nahtzone *f* zone adjacent to weld

Nah-unordnung *f* short-range disorder **-unterstützung** *f* close support **-verkehr** *m* short-distance traffic, junction traffic, junction or toll service, local traffic

Nahverkehrs-amt *n* toll exchange **-bezirk** *m* approach control zone **-bereich** *m* (Aviation) terminal control area (TMA)

Nahverkehrsleitung *f* short-haul toll circuit **~ mit Fernwahlbetrieb** toll circuit with dialing facilities

Nah-verteidigung *f* close defense **-warnring** *m* close warning ring **-wirkung** *f* close effect, proximity effect

Nähzeug *n* sewing kit

Namen-aufruf *m* roll call **-schild** *n* name plate **-geber** (Fernschreiber) call-back device

Namenverzeichnis *n* nomenclature or list of names or descriptions, index

Namenszeichen *n* enciphered call sign or name, initials

namhaft renowned, notable, famous, reputable, appreciable

Napf *m* pan, basin, bowl, cup, saucer

Näpfchen *n* blank (for blasting caps), cup

Napfziehen *n* dishing operation, cup drawing

naphtenisch naphthenic

Naphtenseife *f* naphthenic soap
Naphtha *f, n* naphtha, mineral oil, rock oil, crude oil, raw petroleum, standard solvent
Naphthalin *n* naphthalene **-reihe** *f* naphthalene series **-sulfosäure** *f* naphthalenesulfonic acid
Naphtharückstand *m* residual naphtha
Naphthazen *n* naphthacene
Naphthen *n* naphthene
Naphtolatdruckverfahren *n* naphtholate printing process
Naphthol *n* naphthol **-gelb** *n* naphthol yellow **-grün** *n* naphthol green
naphtholieren to naphtholize
Naphtolnachsatz *m* naphthol feeding addition
Naphthyl *n* naphthyl **-amin** *n* naphthylamine **-aminchlorhydrat** *n* naphthylamine hydrochloride
Narbe *f* scar seam, pit (of surfaces), scar, grain, defect, flaw
narben to grain
Narben-bildung *f* pitting **-brüchig** chapped
narbig pitted
Narbung *f* grain (leather), pocking
Narkose *f* narcosis
Narkosenmaske *f* ether mask
narrensicher foolproof
Nasalkonsonant *m* nasal consonant
nascendie in statu nascendi
Nase *f* nose, spout, stud, catch, cog, nozzle, lug, snug, lip, cap, beak, cam, tappet, projection **~ zum Festhalten** stop pin **~ eines Ringes** lug of a collar or ring **~** (an Stanzteilen) tab **gegabelte ~** forked projection **seine ~ in etwas stecken** to pry
Nasen-flachkeil *m* flat gib key **-förmiger Teil** horn
Nasenhaube *f* nose cowl, spinner
Nasenhauben-keil *m* nose key, gib-head key **-kolben** *m* deflector piston **-radius** *m* leading-edge radius
Nasenhöhe *f* height of gib head **~ des Keils** height of gib head
Nasen-hohlkeil *m* gib-headed saddle key **-kasten** *m* nose box **-keil** *m* gib (-head) key, jib **-klappe** *f* leading edge flap **-klammer** *f* nose clamp **-klemme** *f* nose clip (mask) **-klemmplatte** *f* catch-fitted clip **-kolben** *m* deflector piston **-körper** *m* re-entry head (missile) **-kühler** *m* leading-edge radiator
Nasen-leiste *f* leading-edge (strip), cap strip, wingrib former **-radius** *m* leading-edge radius **-riemen** *m* noseband **-rippe** *f* nose rib **-schlacke** *f* tuyère slag **-schraube** *f* snug bolt
Nasen-spaltschlitzhaube *f* nose-slot cowling **-spiegel** *m* nasal speculum **-steg** *m* nosepiece (goggles), bridge of nose **-stück** *n* nosepiece
Nasen- und Rachenreizstoff *m* nose-and-throat irritant, sternutator
naß wet, moist, damp **-er Dampf** wet steam, wet vapor **-es Element** wet cell **-es Erdgas** wet gas, casing-head gas **-er Gasmesser -e Gasuhr** wet gas meter **-e Partie** wet end (paper mfg.)
Naß-alarmventil *n* alarm check valve **-aufbereitung** *f* washing, wet cleaning **-aushub** *m* wet cuts **-beizung** *f* wet seed dressing **-betrieb** *m* wet practice **-binder** *m* liquid binder **-brandpulver** *n* black powder **-dampf** *m* wet steam, wet vapor **-dehnung** *f* wet elongation **-dekatiermaschine** *f* wet decatizing machine **-dreheinrichtung** *f* cooling installation for turning
Nässe *f* wetness, moisture **vor ~ (zu) schützen** keep dry **-element** *n* wet battery or cell
nässen to wet, moisten, soak, water
Naß-fäule *f* wet rot **-fest** waterproof **-festigkeit** *f* wet strength **-filter** *m* wet filter **-glasthermometer** *n* wet-bulb thermometer
Naßguß *m* green-mold casting **-form** *f* green-sand mold **-formerei** *f* green-sand molding
Naß-kalk *m* milk of lime **-kalt** damp cold, chilly **-kollergang** *m* edge runner for wet grinding **-kugelmühle** *f* ball mill for wet grinding **-kühl** damp cold, chilly **-läufer** *m* (water) meter with mechanism and indicator operating wet, wet-dial water meter **-levantiert** wet-grained **-luftfilter** *n* wet air cleaner, wet air filter **-mahlen** *n* wet crushing, wet grinding **-mahlgang** *m* wet pan grinding **-mahlverfahren** *n* wet grinding process **-mechanische Aufbereitung** wet-mill concentration **-metallurgie** *f* hydrometallurgy
Naß-niederschlagung *f* wet precipitation **-pochen** *n* wet-crushing **-pochwerk** *n* wet stamp mill **-preßwalze** *f* wet-press roll **-putztrommel** *f* wet tumbler, tumbling barrel **-reiniger** *m* wet cleaner, purifier, or washer, tower washer, scrubber **-reinigung** *f* wet cleaning, washing, or scrubbing, wet purification **-rommeln** *n* wet tumbling
Naß-sand *m* green sand **-scheider** *m* wet separator **-scheidung** *f* defecation with milk of lime **-scheuern** *n* wet tumbling **-scheuerwirkung** *f* wet abrasion effect **-schleifständer** *m* wet tool grinder **-schleifstein** *m* wet grindstone **-schliff** *m* wet grinding **-schnitzel** *n* wet pulp **-schroten** *n* wet grinding **-separator** *m* wet cobber, drum cobber **-siebung** *f* wet mechanical analysis
Naß-thermometer *n* wet-bulb thermometer **-trommel** *f* wet rolling barrel, wet tumbler **-trommelscheider** wet-type drum separator **-verfahren** *n* wet process **-wärmegrad** *m* wet-bulb temperature **-wäsche** *f* wet cleaning, washing **-zähler** *m* wet meter **-zerkleinerung** *f* wet crushing **-zug** *m* wet drawing machine **-zylinderlaufbüchse** *f* wet liner
naszierend nascent
Nationalisierung *f* nationalization
Nationalitätenzeichen *n* nationality marking, national insignia
Nationalitätszertifikat *n* certificate of nationality
Natrium *n* sodium **kohlensaures ~** sodium carbonate, soda **stearinsaures ~** sodium stearate **titansaures ~** sodium titanate **zinnsaures ~** sodium stannate
Natrium-alaun *m* sodium alum **-arseniat** *n* sodium arsenate **-benzolsulfonat** *n* sodium benzene sulfonate **-bisulfat** *n* sodium bisulfate **-bisulfidlauge** *f* sodium bisulfide liquor **-bisulfitlösung** *f* sodium bisulfite solution **-dampf** *m* sodium vapor **-draht** *m* sodium wire **-feuer** *n* sodium light **-formiat** *n* sodium formate **-gehalt** *m* sodium content **-goldchlorid** *n* sodium aurochloride **-gekühlt** sodium-cooled

Natrium-hydrat *n* sodium hydroxide **-hydroxyd** *n* sodium hydroxide, caustic soda **-hyperchlorat** *n* sodium perchlorate **-hyperjodat** *n* sodium periodate **-hyperoxyd** *n* sodium peroxide **-kaliumkarbonat** *n* sodium potassium carbonate **-kaliumtartrat** *n* sodium potassium tartrate **-karbonat** *n* sodium carbonate **-kieselfluorid** *n* sodium fluosilicate **-kuchen** *m* niter cake **-leuchte** *f* sodium lamp

Natriumlinie *f* sodium line **Temperaturbestimmung nach dem Verfahren der Natriumlinien-Umkehr** sodium-line reversal method

Natrium-metall *n* metallic sodium **-oxalat** *n* sodium oxalate **-oxydhydrat** *n* sodium hydroxide **-platinchlorid** *n* sodium chloroplatinate **-salz** *n* sodium salt **-salizylat** *n* sodium salicylate **-subsulfat** *n* sodium hyposulfate

Natriumsulfatkuchen *m* salt cake

Natrium-sulfit *n* sodium sulfite **-sulfozyanid** *n* sodium sulfocyanate, sodium thiocyanate **-superoxyd** *n* sodium superoxide, sodium peroxide **-tetraborat** *n* sodium tetraborate, sodium borate, borax **-thioantimoniat** *n* sodium thioantimoniate **-thiosulfat** *n* sodium thiosulfate, sodium hyposulfite **-valerianat** *n* sodium valerate **-verbindung** *f* sodium compound **-wasserstoff** *m* sodium hydride **-wolframat** *n* sodium tungstate

Natro-borokalzit *m* ulexite **-kalzit** *m* gaylussite **-lith** *m* natrolite

Natron *n* soda, natron, sodium hydroxide **anderthalbkohlensaures ~** sesquicarbonate of soda **doppelkohlensaures ~** sodium bicarbonate **kohlensaures ~** sodium carbonate **überborsaures ~** sodium perborate **überschwefelsaures ~** sodium persulfate **unterchlorigsaures ~** sodium hypochlorite **unterphosphoriges ~** sodium hypophosphite **unterschwefligsaures ~** sodium hyposulfite **wolframsaures ~** sodium tungstate

Natron-ablauge *f* black liquor, spent liquor, waste liquor **-alaun** *m* soda alum, aluminum sodium sulfate **-ätzlauge** *f* caustic soda solution **-feldspat** *m* albite **-hydrat** *n* sodium hydroxide **-kalk** *m* soda lime **-kraftpapier** *n* soda craft paper **-lauge** *f* soda lye, caustic soda (solution), soda liquor **-salpeter** *m* sodium nitrate **-wasserglas** *n* sodium silicate **-zellstoff** *m* soda cellulose, sulfate pulp **-zellstoffabrik** *f* soda cellulose works

Natur *f* nature, essence **von ~** inherent

naturähnlich realistic, true or similar to nature

Natural-leistung *f* payment in kind **-leistungsgesetz** *n* requisition law **-verpflegung** *f* food supplies in kind, rations in kind

Natur-bleicher *m* grass bleacher **-erscheinung** *f* natural phenomenon, natural process, natural action

Naturell *n* natural tendency

Natur-farbe *f* natural color **-farbendruck** *m* natural color print **-forscher** *m* physicist **-gas** *n* natural gas **-gasfeuerung** *f* natural-gas firing **-gasquelle** *f* natural-gas source **-gemäß** natural **-genarbt** with a natural grain **-getreu** lifelike, natural, full-scale, full-size

naturgroß actual-size, full-scale **-er Versuch** full-scale test

Naturgummi *m* natural rubber

naturhart naturally hard **-er Stahl** self-hardening steel

Natur-härte *f* temper, natural hardness **-kautschuk** *m* natural rubber **-korund** *m* corundum **-kunde** *f* natural science **-lehre** *f* natural science, physics, natural philosophy

natürlich natural, native, real **-er Ausfluß** flowing well **-e Beschaffenheit** nature, natural characteristic **-e Bleicherde** natural clay **-e Erdbodenpotentiale** natural earth potentials **-e Erdströme** (natural) earth currents **-e Größe** actual size, full size, full scale **-er Horizont** real horizon

natürlich-e Induktivität natural inductance **-e Oberfläche des Bodens** original ground surface **-er Parameter einer Kurve** natural parameter of a curve **-e tellurische Ströme** natural earth currents **-er Treibstoff** natural gasoline **-e Vaseline** petroleum jelly **-e Widerstandsfähigkeit gegen Korrosion** inherent corrosion resistance **-e Zahl** natural number **-er Zug** natural draft

Natürlichkeit *f* naturalness **~ der Wiedergabe** faith-fulness, fidelity, or realism of reproduction

Natur-modell *n* loose pattern **-nässe** *f* natural amount of moisture **-(kunstdruck)papier** *n* imitation art paper, stiff colored paper **-schutz** *m* cultivation of nature **-schutzgebiet** *n* national park **-stein** *m* stone, rock **-treue** *f* fidelity, faithfulness, realistic properties **-wissenschaft** *f* natural science **-wissenschaftler** *m* scientist

Naumannit *m* naumannite

Nautik *f* nautics, navigation

nautisch nautical **die -e Abteilung des Marineamts** hydrographic office **-e meteorologische Abteilung** nautical meteorological section **~ technische Abteilung** naval technical section

Nautophon *n* nautophone

Navigation *f* navigation, position fixing **astronomische ~** celestial navigation

Navigations-funkfeuer *n* radio beacon **-instrument** *n* navigation instrument **-hilfe** *f* navigational aid

Navigations-karte *f* navigation chart or map **-kompaß** *m* navigation compass **-kunde** *f* art of avigation **-lichter, -leuchten** *pl* navigational lights **-raum** *m* navigating compartment **-stern** *m* navigational star **-zeugnis** *n* certificate of navigation

navigieren to navigate

Nawi-Membrane *f* (nicht abwickelbar) curvilinear cone

Nebel *m* mist, fog, smoke, haze **künstlicher ~** smoke screen, artificial fog

Nebel-abblasen *n* smoke screening, release of smoke **-abblasgerät** *n* smoke-filled chemical cylinder **-abteilung** *f* smoke-producing unit **-apparat** *m* spraying apparatus, smoke-laying apparatus, smoke generator, atomizer **-ausdehnung** *f* smoke coverage **-bildung** *f* formation of fog **-bildungsgrenzwert** *m* cloud limit **-bogen** *m* fog bow **-büchse** *f* smoke generator **-decke** *f* smoke blanket, smoke screen **-dunst** *m* mist

Nebel-einsatz *m* use of smoke screen, employment of smoke **-entwicklung** *f* generation of smoke **-filter** *m* gas filter (mask) **-flugzeug** *n* smoke-laying plane **-gebiet** *n* fog area **-gerät** *n* smoke equipment, smoke-laying apparatus

-haufenbildung *f* clustering of galaxies **-horn** *n* foghorn **-hülle** *f* nebular shell
nebelig foggy, misty
Nebel-kamera *f* cloud chamber **-kammer** *f* expansion chamber, cloud chamber **-kammer-aufnahme** *f* cloud chamber photograph **-kasten** *m* smoke generator, smoke box **-kerze** *f* smoke candle **-kugel** *f* globule of fog **-landung** *f* fog landing, blind landing, instrument landing **-lichtsignal** *n* fog repeater **-mittel** *n* smoke-producing agent, smoke agent, smoke equipment
nebeln to lay down smoke
Nebel-messer *m* nephelometer **-pfeife** *f* fog whistle **-regenbogen** *m* fog bow **-reich** foggy **-scheinwerfer** *m* fog (head) lamp **-schleier** *m* smoke screen **-schmierung** *f* splash lubrication **-schutz** *m* protection by smoke screening **-schwaden** *m* streaks or swath of mist, damp fog **-signal** *n* fog signal **-sprinkler** *m* spray sprinkler
Nebelspuren *pl*, **kurze ~** fish tracks (short cloud tracks)
Nebel-spurmethode *f* Wilson cloud-track or chamber method **-stoff** *m* smoke(-producing) agent, screening agent **-topf** *m* smoke pot, smoke generator **-tornister** *m* pack smoke apparatus **-trommel** *f* smoke drum, smoke generator **-tropfen** *m* fog particle or drop
Nebel- und Antikollisionsradar *m* cloud and collision warning
Nebelwand *f* smoke screen
Nebel-wolke *f* stratus cloud, smoke cloud **-zeichen** *n* fog signal **-zerstäuber** *m* smoke cylinder, smoke spray **-zone** *f* smoke-screened area, smoke zone
neben beside, adjacent (to), adjoining, next to, close to, near, aside from, along with, subsidiary **-abschnitt** *m* adjoining sector, adjacent sector **-absicht** *f* secondary objective, hidden intention **-achse** *f* minor axis, secondary axis, conjugate axis, lateral axis (of rhombic crystal) **-amt** *n* minor office, minor exchange
nebenan alongside, next door
Nebenanlage *f* additional plant, annex
Nebenanschluß *m* extension telephone, extension line **-leitung** *f* extension (circuit), extension wire or line, local-circuit line **-teilnehmer** *m* subscriber having extension station
Neben-antrieb *m* auxiliary drive **-apparat** *m* accessory or auxiliary apparatus **-arbeit** *f* incidental work, spare-time work, auxiliary detail **-arm** *m* branch **-ausgabe** *f* extraordinary, additional, or incidental charge or expense **-ausgleich** *m* paddle balance
Nebenauslaß *m* by-pass, waste gate **~ ins Freie für zum Betrieb der Turbine nicht benötigtes Abgas** (Abgasturbolader), waste gate
Nebenauslaßklappe *f* effluent by-pass flap (jet)
Neben-ausschlag *m* secondary deflection, angular movement **-ausstrahlung** *f* spurious radiation **-bahn** *f* offcut (print.), branch line (R.R.) **-balken** *m* joist, secondary beam **-batterie** *f* secondary battery **-bau** *m* annexed building **-bauteil** *m* auxiliary member or construction part **-bedeutung** *f* connotation **-bedingung** *f* secondary condition **-berufliche Beschäftigung** spare-time engagement
Neben-beschäftigung *f* avocation **-bestandteil** *m* secondary ingredient **-bestimmung** *f* incidental provision **-betrieb** *m* secondary process, side line **-bewegung** *f* disturbance velocity **-beweis** *m* secondary proof, additional evidence **-bild** *n* ghost image **-bindung** *f* secondary union, secondary bond **-blitz** *m* false flash **-buhler** *m* rival **-durchgang** *m* by-pass **-durchmesser** *m* conjugate diameter
nebeneinander abreast, in parallel, side-by-side **~ angeordnet** placed or arranged side by side **~ schalten** to connect or join in parallel
Nebeneinander-bestehen *n* simultaneous existence **-schalten** *n* multiple arrangement, parallel connection (elec.) **-schaltung** *f* parallel connection, shunt connection, multiple connection, parallel circuit or hookup **-stellen** to juxtapose, place side by side or alongside **-stellung** *f* juxtaposition, comparsion
Neben-eingang *m* side entrance **-einkunft** *f* additional income **-elektrode** *f* secondary electrode **-entladung** *f* lateral stray, or secondary discharge **-ergebnis** *n* subsidiary result **-erscheinung** *f* attendant phenomenon **-erzeugnis** *n* by-product **-farbe** *f* complementary color **-fernamt** *n* subzone toll office **-fläche** *f* secondary face **-fluß** *m* tributary stream, affluent, confluence **-förderer** *m* subsidiary conveyor **-funkstelle** *f* radio substation, wireless-telegraph outstation
Neben-gang *m* private corridor **-gebäude** *n* additional building, annex **-gegensonne** *f* paranthelion **-geleise** *n* siding (R.R.) **-gemengteil** *m* secondary constituent of mixture **-geräusch** *n* crackling, hissing, frying (noise), strays (radio), side tone, ambient or extraneous noise **-geschlossen** shunted **-gestein** *n* country rock **-gleis** *n* siding (R.R.), shunt
Neben-impuls *m* satellite pulse **-intervenient** *m* cointervener **-kette** *f* side chain, subordinate chain **-keule** *f* minor lobe **-klage** *f* incidental action **-kläger** *m* coplaintiff **-klasse** *f* coset (math.) **-kolonne** *f* adjacent column, secondary column
Nebenkoppelung *f* **kapazitive ~** stray capacity
Neben-koppelungsschwingung *f* spurious oscillation **-kreis** *m* epicycle **-lager** *n* branch camp but-board bearing **-lappen** *m* minor lobe **-leistungen** *pl* ancillary labors **-leitung** *f* secondary pipe, by-pass **-licht** *n* false light (optics), light shot **-lichtfilter** *n* luminous edge **-linie** *f* side line, secondary line, spur (from main) line, branch line (R.R.), satellite (astron., phys.) **-luft** *f* secondary air
Neben-maximum *n* secondary or lateral radiation, secondary maximum, secondary lobe or ear **-meer** *n* sea of secondary importance **-mond** *m* paraselene **-operation** *f* secondary operation **-ordnung** *f* co-ordination **-patent** *n* subpatent, collateral or subordinate patent **-piste** *f* auxiliary runway
Nebenpleuel *n* articulated connecting rod, blade rod, link rod, auxiliary connection rod **-stange** *f* link rod, articulating rod **-zapfen** *m* link pin **-zapfenkopf** *m* link pin or rod end
Nebenprodukt *n* by-product
Nebenprodukt-anlage *f* by-product plant **-gewinnung** *f* by-product recovery **-gewinnungsan-**

lage *f* by-product-recovery plant **-kokerei** *f* by-product coking practice, by-product coking plant

Neben-rad *n* sidegear **-reaktion** *f* side or secondary reaction **-rippe** *f* form, former, false, or intermediate rib **-rohr** *n* side or branch tube or pipe **-sächlich** of secondary importance, accidental **-schacht** *m* by-pit **-scheinwerfer** *m* secondary searchlight, fog lamp, fog light **-schleife** *f* parasitic lobe, back ear **-schließen** to shunt (elec.) **-schließung** *f* leak, leakage

Nebenschließungs-weg *m* leakage path **-widerstand** *m* leak resistance, shunt resistance

Nebenschluß *m* shunt, sink, leak, leakage, shunt worm **einen ~ bilden** to shunt **in den ~ legen** to (put in) shunt **mit einem ~ versehen** to shunt **elektrischer ~** electric shunt **induktiver ~** inductive shunt **magnetischer ~** magnetic shunt, (electro)magnetic leak, inductive shunt **mit einem ~ behaftet** leaky **ohne ~** unshunted **im ~ zu** in shunt with, shunted across

Nebenschluß-bogenlampe *f* shunt-type arc lamp **-drosselspule** *f* substitutional induction coil **-dynamo** *m* shunt(-wound) dynamo **-dynamomaschine** *f* shunt-wound generator, shunt dynamo **-erregung** *f* shunt excitation **-feder** *f* off-normal spring (of dial), shunting spring **-filter** *n* by-pass filter **-gewickelt** shunt-wound **-kommutatormotor** *m* shunt-conduction motor **-kondensator** *m* by-pass condenser, shunt condenser

Nebenschluß-motor *m* shunt-wound electric motor **-regelwerk** *n* shunt regulator **-regelwiderstand** *m* shunt-regulating resistance **-regler** *m* shunt regulator, speed-regulating rheostat **-resonanz** *f* parallel resonance **-schaltung** *f* shunt connection (elec.) **-spule** *f* shunt magnetic coil **-strom** *m* induction current **-summer** *m* shunted buzzer **-unterbrecher** *m* field break switch **-verhalten** *n* shunt characteristic **-wicklung** *f* shunt-winding **-widerstand** *m* shunt resistance, leak resistance, shunt field rheostat

Neben-schubstange *f* articulated rod **-schwingung** *f* side-band oscillation **-seite** *f* adjacent side **-sender** *m* slave transmitter, repeater transmitter **-septen** *n pl* minor septa **-setzung** *f* juxtaposition **-sicherheit** *f* collateral **-skalenteilung** *f* minor graduation **-sonne** *f* sundog, parhelion **-spannung** *f* secondary stress **-spektrum** *n* side spectrum **-spitzenfläche** *f* minor apex face (cryst.)

Nebensprechdämpfung *f* cross-talk transmission equivalent, (near-end) cross-talk attenuation

Nebensprechdämpfungs-messer *m* crosstalk meter **-netzwerk** *n* anti-induction network **-zeiger** *m* crosstalk meter

Nebensprechen *n* cross pickup, (near-end) cross talk, cross-induction **~ am Anfang** near-end cross talk

nebensprech-frei cross-talk proof **-koppelung** *f* cross-talk circuit or path, unbalance **-messer** *m* cross-talk meter or measuring set **-messung** *f* cross-talk measurement **-pegel** *m* crosstalk volume **-strom** *m* unbalance current, cross-talk current **-weg** *m* cross-talk path

nebenstehend alongside **-e Abbildung** the opposite illustration **-es Bild** *n* accompanying picture (on data sheet)

Nebenstelle *f* auxiliary exchange, extension station or telephone, subscriber's extension, local station **~ mit freier Amtswahl** subscriber's extension station (with direct exchange facilities)

Nebenstellen-betrieb *m* extension-station service **-klappe** *f* extension indicator **-klinke** *f* extensionline jack **-leitung** *f* extension line **-rufleitung** P.B.X. ringing lead **-speiseleitung** *f* P.B.X. power lead **-speisung** *f* current supply to extension telephones **-teilnehmer** *m* extension user **-umschalter** *m* substation switchboard **-zentrale** *f* private branch exchange

Neben-strang *m* by-pass **-straße** *f* side road, branch road, side street, secondary or auxiliary road **-strecke** *f* subsidiary road

Nebenstrom *m* induction current **-kreis** *m* secondary circuit **-ölfilter** *n* by-pass lubricating oil filter **-regelwerk** *n* shunt

Neben-strömung *f* subsidiary or secondary flow **-stufe** *f* rear-step on-float gear **-titel** *m* subhead **-ton** *m* side tone (teleph.) **-träger** *m* minority carrier **-treffer** *m* near miss

Nebenuhr *f* auxiliary or secondary clock **~ einer elektrischen Uhrenanlage** secondary clock of an electric-clock installation

Neben-umstand *m* collateral circumstance or factor **-verkehrsweg** *m* by-pass **-verlust** *m* stand-by loss **-verschluß** *m* auxiliary shutter **-verstärkeramt** *n* secondary repeater station

Nebenwählstelle *f* PABX (private automatic branch exchange)

Nebenweg *m* side road, branch road, indirect means, shunt (circuit), by-pass, leakage path **-regler** *m* by-pass regulator

Neben-welle *f* countershaft, auxiliary shaft, intermediate shaft **-wellen** *pl* spurious emission (of radio xmtr.)

Nebenwellen-abschwächung *f* spurious wave attenuation **-leistung** *f* spurious wave attenuation

Neben-widerstand *m* shunt **-winkel** *m* adjacent or adjoining angle **-wirkung** *f* secondary effect **-zeit** *f* auxiliary process time, idle period **-zentrale** *f* parent exchange **-ziel** *n* secondary target **-zipfel** *m* minor lobe, minor ear, side lobe **-zweck** *m* ulterior motive

neblig foggy

nebst with, besides, in addition to

Negativ *n* negative **dichtes ~** dense negative **flaues ~** faint negative, negative without contrasts **hartes ~** hard negative, negative with too strong contrasts

negativ negative **-e Beschleunigung** negative acceleration, deceleration, retardation **-e Bewertung** demerit rating **-e Flügelschränkung** washin **-es Gebiet** negative area **-er Geländewinkel** angle of depression, negative angle of site **-es Glimmlicht** negative glow **-e Polarität der Sendung** negative polarity of transmission **-e V-Form** negative dihedral **-er Widerstand** negative resistance, third-class resistance

Negativ-betrachtungsgerät *n* viewing apparatus for negatives **-bild** *n* negative picture **-ebene** *f* negative plane, negative aperture **-elektrisch** electronegative **-farbauszug** *m* separation negative **-gamma** *n* negative gamma **-halter** *m* negative holder **-meßmikroskop** *n* microscope for evaluating negatives, negative-reading microscope **-pausen** *pl* negative prints **-schaukasten** *m* viewing screen negatoscope **-schrift** *f* nonrelief type **-schwärzung** *f* negative density **-umfang** *m* intensity range or latitude of a negative **-widerstandsröhre** *f* dynatron type of tube with negative resistance

Negatron *n* negatron

Negierbefehl *m* ignore instrument

Negrographiepapier *n* black-line paper

nehmen to take, capture, receive, seize

Nehmen der Seitenrichtung laying for direction

Nehrstrom *m* eddy, eddy current

Nehrung *f* tongue of land or spit of land separating the haff from the sea, coastal beach belt

neigbar inclinable **-es Hinterteil** (Phot.) swing back

Neigekopf *m* tilting head

neigen (um die Querachse) to pitch, incline, bend, lean, tend, bow, slope **~ um die Querachse** to pitch **~ zu** to be prone to

Neigen *n* inclining

Neig-kennlinie *f* drooping characteristic (line) **-lage** *f* inclined position

neigt nach dem Nullpunkt . . . tends to zero

Neigung *f* inclination, tendency, obliquity, slope, dip, trend, pitch, fall, declivity, descent **~ eines Ganges** dip slope **~ des auf Zug gestellten Gestänges** rake (of a pole) **~ zum Hängenbleiben** susceptibility to binding

Neigung der Antenne tilt (rdr) **~ der Auftriebskurve** slope of the lift curve **~ der Kamera** inclination of the camera, tilt **~ der Kurve** slope of a curve **~ der Straße** incline, tendency, grade, gradient **~ zur Überdrehzahl, ~ zum Übersteuern** tendency to hunt **~ zum Verharzen** gumminess **~ gegeneinander** toe in (aviation) **von gleicher ~** isoclinic, isoclinal

Neigungs-achse *f* axis of inclination (tilt) **änderung** *f* slope change **-anzeiger** *m* indicator of inclination, tilt indicator (camera) **-differenz** *f* difference of vergence **-ebene** *f* inclined plane

Neigungsfehler *m* error of tilt **-toleranz** *f* angularity tolerance

Neigungs-geber *m* elevator centering knob (autopilot) **-grad** *m* obliquity **-kreis** *m* dip circle **-linie** *f* gradient **-messer** *m* (in)clinometer, batter level **-meter** *n* inclinometer **-nadel** *f* dip needle **-schießen** *n* dip shooting **-tangente** *f* tangent of slope **-tendenz** *f* trend **-verhältnis** *n* relation of the inclination, gradient **-waage** *f* inclination balance **-wägevorrichtung** *f* inclination weighing device

Neigungswinkel *m* angle of gradient, angle of tilt, inclination, or slope, rake angle **~ einer Schneidekante** top back slope, back rake

Neigungswinkel-messer *m* clinometer **-messung** elevation

NEIN-Schaltung *f* NOT-circuit

Nelkenöl *n* clove oil

NE-Metall *n* non-ferrous metal

Nenn-abmaß *n* nominal allowance **-aufnahme** *f* initial or nominal acceptivity (elec.) **-belastung** *f* nominal load **-bereich** *m* nominal range of use **-betrag** *m* nominal value **-betrieb** *m* rating **-bürde** *f* rated burden (of instr. xfrm.), rated impedance **-drehkörperdurchmesser** *m* nominal rotor diameter **-drehmoment** *n* nominal torsional moment **-drehzahl** *f* rated speed **-drehzahlbereich** *m* rated (or nominal) speed of the engine **-druck** *m* nominal load or pressure **-durchmesser** *m* nominal diameter

nennen to name, call, term

nennenswert worth mentioning

Nenner *m* denominator **gemeinsamer ~** common denominator

Nenn-erregerstrom *m* nominal excitation current (of electr. machines) **-erregungsgeschwindigkeit** *f* relative voltage response of the exciter **-frequenz** *f* rated frequency, reference frequency **-geschwindigkeit** *f* rated speed **-größe** *f* nominal size **-höhe** *f* rated altitude, rated height **-kurzschlußspannung** *f* impedance voltage of a transformer **-ladedruck** *m* rated boost, rated pressure, rated manifold pressure

Nennlast *f* normal or rated or full load **~ beim Bruch** nominal stress at fracture

Nennleistung *f* normal output, rated power, normal efficiency, nominal capacity **~** (Flugmotor) maximum power for climb **~ Pferdestärke** rated horsepower

Nennleistungs-durchgang *m* nominal output **-höhe** *f* rated altitude, rated height **-wert** *m* rated power value

Nenn-luftspalt *m* nominal air gap **-maß** *n* nominal size **-polspalt des Aufzeichnungskopfes** nominal recording head pole gap **-querschnitt** *m* rated or nominal (cross) section **-reichweite** *f* nominal or rated range **-spannung** *f* rated voltage (of a cable), nominal or standard voltage **-spannungsbereich** *m* range of nominal tension **-spielraum** *m* nominal margin **-spitzenspannung am Lesekopf** nominal peak voltage at readback **-steigung** *f* standard or nominal pitch **-strom** *m* rated current, amperage rating (as of cable) **-tonfrequenz** *f* aural center frequency **-übersetzung** *f* nominal transformation ratio

Nennübersetzungs-fehler *m* nominal ratio error **-verhältnis** *n* nominal transformation ratio

Nennung *f* entry in a contest

Nenn-verlustleistung *f* rated electrode dissipation **-weite** *f* nominal width or diameter

Nennwert *m* nominal value, rated, assessed, normal, expected or face value **~ der Grenzfrequenz einer bespulten Leitung** nominal cutoff frequency of a loaded line

Nenn-wertfehler *m* error of calibration **-winkelfehler** *m* rated phase displacement or phase angle

Nennwortquerstromstärke *f* nominally transverse word current

Neodym *n* neodymium **-chlorid** *n* neodymium chloride **-gehalt** *m* nedoymium content

Neokom *n* Neocomian

Neolith *m* neolite

neolithisch neolithic

Neon *n* neon **-flächenglimmlampe** *f* plate neon lamp (television) **-glimmlampe** *f*, **-lampe** *f* neon lamp or tube **-licht** *n* neon light **-röhre** *f* neon lamp or tube

Neonröhren-aussteuerungskontrolle *f*, **-lautstärkemesser** *m* neon-tube volume indicator

Neonverflüssigungsmaschine *f* neon liquefier

Neopren *n* neoprene **-kabel** *n* neoprene cable

Neosidkernspule *f* iron-cored coil

Neotyp *m* neotype
neozoische Gruppe Neozoic group
Neper *n* neper
Nephelin *m* nephelite, eleolite
nephelometrische Analyse nephelometric analysis
Nephoskop *n* nephoscope
Nephrit *m* nephrite
Neprit *m* jade
Neptuniumreihe *f* neptunium series
Nernst-brenner *m*, **-lampe** *f* Nernst lamp **-stift** *m* Nernst needle
Neroliöl *n* neroli oil
Nerv *m* nerve
Nervenaktions-spannung *f* voltage due to nervous action **-strom** current due to nervous action
Nerven-reiz *m* nervous stimulus **-taubheit** *f* perception or nerve impairment of hearing
Nessel *f* China grass, nettle, nettle cloth **-gewebe** *n* nettle cloth **-tuch** *n* domestic cheesecloth, fine muslin
Nest *n* nest, isolated post, bunch, pocket (of ore), emplacement, cluster (atom. phys.), rosette **-weise** by groups
Nestel *f* string
netto net **-absackwaage** *f* sack net weigher **-gewicht** *n* net weight **-gewinn** *m* net profit
Netz *n* network, system, power supply, net, netting, lattice, grid, gauze, reticle, graticule, reticulation, grate, electric mains ~ **mit Ortsbatteriebetrieb** magneto exchange area ~ **mit Wahlbetrieb** dial exchange area ~ **mit Zentralbatteriebetrieb** common-battery exchange area **trigonometrisches** ~ net of triangulation **verzerrtes** ~ distorted grid
Netz-abschnitt *m* multi-office exchange area **-abstand** *m* distance of mesh or lattice, space-lattice distance **-adern** *pl* checking (slight criss-cross cracking) **-anode** *f* B-battery eliminator, B eliminator, grid anode, line connection, anode battery
Netzanschluß *m* power supply, mains supply (public electric supply system), commercial current supply, mains connection **-empfänger** *m* mains receiver or set, mains-driven receiver, electric radio receiver **-gerät** *n* socket-power unit, power pack, power supply unit, mains connection unit, radio transmitter or pulse gear, bias supply **-kontakt** *m* supply terminals **-schnur** *f* mains lead, power cable **-transformator** *m* power transformer
Netzantenne *f* mains antenna
netzartig netlike, reticular, reticulate, gratelike **-e Rißbildung** alligator cracking
Netz-ätzung *f* autotypy, process-block making **-ausgleich** *m* net equalization or compensation **-ausschalter** *m* master battery cutoff switch, mastery battery C main switch, mains switch or cutout **-bedeckung** *f* coverage factor **-behälter zum Vornetzen** pre-wetting vat for wetting **-betrieb** *m* mains power supply **-betrieben** mains-operated **-bild** *n* mimic network **-bildung** *f* reticulation, netting **-bindung** *f* covalence **-brummen** *n* hum, alternating-current or power-line hum **-brummstreifen** *m* hum band
Netz-drossel *f* ripple filter choke, rectifier filter reactor, hum-eliminator coil **-ebene** *f* crystal-lattice plane, network level **-ebenenabstand** *m* grating constant, interlattice plane distance **-ebenenverband** *m* adjacent elements of the lattice plane **-eingang** *m* mains or line input **-einschwingvorgänge** *pl* mains transients **-einspeisung** *f* mains input **-elektrode** *f* wire-gauze electrode, net-shaped electrode **-empfänger** *m* mains receiver or set, mains-driven receiver
netzen to moisten, wet, steep, soak
Netz-endstufe *f* mains final stage, mains output (radio) **-erde** *f* ground (conductor) **-ergibigkeit** *f* system capacity **-ersatzanlage** *f* spare-current source **-fähigkeit** *f* wetting-out property **-feld** *n* signal field **-filter** *m*, *n* hum eliminator, power-line filter **-flotte** *f* wetting-out liquor **-förmig** reticular, net-shaped **-frequenz** *f* line or mains frequency **-gang** *m* lode forming a network **-gefüge** *n* cancellated structure
Netzgerät *n* power-supply unit, power pack battery eliminator **-einsatz** *m* mains-unit adapter (radio) **-einschub** *m* plug-in power pack **-heizung** *f* mains heating unit
netz-gespeist mains-powered **-gestaltung** *f* network layout **-gleichrichter** *m* power rectifier **-grund** *m* lace ground **-gruppe** *f* rural telephone network, subzone network
Netzgruppen-schalter *m* prefix evaluator **-technik** (Teleph.) netgroup dial technique **-verkehr** *m* toll traffic **-wähler** *m* code selector
Netz-hälfte *f* half of the system (elec.) **-hauptschalter** *m* master powerswitch
Netzhaut *f* retina, code for a type of guided missile **-bild** *n* retinal image **-spiegel** *m* ophthalmoscope **-trägheit** *f* retinal persistence **-zentersehen** *n* foveal vision
Netz-kabel *n* power cord **-kessel** *m* steeping vat **-knoten** *m* junction **-knüpfen** *n* netting **-knüpfmaschine** *f* netting machine **-leger** *m* net layer, net-laying vessel **-linie** *f* system line **-los** without a net **-mikrometer** *n* crossline micrometer **-mittel** *n* wetting agent **-modell** *n* network analyzer **-negativ** *n* line screen (phot.) **-pinsel** *m* mason's broom or brush, sprinkling brush **-plan** *m* network plan, network map, loop-and-trunk layout **-punkt** *m* grid corner point, point of triangulation
Netz-rufmaschine *f* network calling machine (teleph.) **-schalter** *m* (v. Gerät) master switch **-schalttafel** *f* mains switchboard (radio) **-schere** *f* net cutter **-schnur** *f* line cord **-schütz** *m* mains contactor **-seite** *f* net(work) side **-sender** *m* mains transmitter (radio) **-sicherung** *f* mains fuse **-spannung** *f* power-supply voltage, mains voltage, system voltage
Netzspannungs-schwankungen *pl* fluctuations in the main voltage **-stabilisierung** *f* mains voltage stabilizer **-umschalter** *m* power-supply voltage switch **-wähler** *m* mains tapping panel
Netz-speisung *f* electric-power-supply network **-speisunggerät** *n* mains feed unit (radio) **-spinne** *f* junction network **-station** *f* transmission substation **-stecker** *m* power-supply plug, light-socket plug **-steuerleitung** *f* control line from mains **-strom** *m* current supply from public mains, line current **-stromversorgung** *f* mains current supply **-struktur** *f* cellular structure, lattice, reticular structure, reticulation **-synchronisiert** synchronized by power supply **-synchronisierung** *f* power-supply or mains

synchronization **-tafel** *f* coordinate or curve chart

Netzteil *m* socket-power unit, power pack, (mains-operated) power supply **mit eigenem ~** self-powered (said of equipment) **stabilisierter ~** regulated power supply

Netz-teilung *f* ruling **-ton** *m* alternating-current hum, network, mains, or line hum **-trafo** *m* mains transformer, power transformer **-transformator** *m* mains transformer, power transformer **-überwachung** *f* transmission-maintenance work **-umschalter** *m* main switch **-unruhe** *f* mains or supply-line ripple or fluctuation **-unterteilung** *f* subdivison of plant (elec.)

Netz-verband *m* diamond work, net masonry, reticulated work or bond **-verfahren** *n* grid method **-verkehr** *m* network communication, line communication or connection **-vermaschung** *f* closed circuit arrangement **-versorgung** *f* mains supply **-verstärker** *m* **-vervielfacher** *m* mesh multiplier, mesh amplifier **-wechselspannung** *f* alternating-current or power-supply voltage from mains

Netzwerk *n* network, meshwork, reticulum **~ mit wählbarer Trennschaltung** cut-set network

Netzwerk-artiges Gefüge network-type or cellular-type structure **-bauweise** *f* geodetic construction **-element** *n* system parameter **-gleichungslöser** *m* network analyzer **-struktur** *f* network structure, cellular, lattice, or plated structure **-vorstellung** *f* network concept

Netz-wirkung *f* wetting effect **-zahl** *f* wetting-out figure **-zentrifuge** *f* meshed bag hydro-extractor **-zuführung** *f* electrical connection **-zuführungseinschub** *m* plug-in mains section, power supply plug-in unit **-zusammenschluß** *m* grid extension

neu new, recent, novel, virgin **~ einregeln** to reregulate **~ einstellen** to readjust **~ entstanden** recent **~ stanzen** to repunch

Neu-aktivierung *f* reactivation, rejuvenation **-anlage** *f* new works, new installation **-anreicherung** *f* reenrichment **-artig** novel **-aufbau** *m* reconstruction **-aufgeschlossener Tagebau** recently opened cast working **-auflagepatent** *n* reissue patent **-aufnahme** *f* new recording **-aufstellung** *f* newly organized or reorganized formation (mil.) **-ausgabe** *f* new edition, reissue

Neubau *m* new construction or building **-kosten** *pl* cost of rebuilding

Neu-bearbeitung *f* revision **-bearbeitungsanlage** *f* reconditioning plant **-bekleiden von Walzen** refilling of rolls **-belegen** (*n*) **der Laufdecke** retiring or retreading of tire casing **-berechnung** *f* recalculation **-bilden** to form anew **-bildung** *f* re-creation, regeneration, new formation (geol.)

Neu-chromat *n* new achromatic objective, new achromat **-definition** *f* redefinition **-eichung** *f* recalibration **-einregelung** *f* reregulation **-einstellung** *f* readjustment

Neuerung *f* innovation

Neuerungsvertrag *m* renewed acknowledgement of indebtedness

neuest latest, newest

Neu-fläche *f* added area **-füllung** *f* refill

neugebildet newly formed **-e Zelle** neoplastic cell

Neu-gelb *n* massicot **-gemutetes Normalfeld einer Grubenanlage** normal field of a mine where coal was recently disclosed by borings **-gestalten** to reorganize, reform **-gestaltung** *f* reorganization, rearrangement, modification

Neugliederung des Stromversorgungsgebietes fresh grouping of the supply area

Neugrad *m* 1/400 of a circle or 16 mils **-einteilung** *f* centesimal graduation **-teilung** *f* map vernier of map protractor, centesimal graduation

Neugrün *n* Paris green

Neuheit *f* newness, novelty, originality

Neuheits-prüfung *f* novelty examination **-schädlich** anticipatory (patents), rendering novelty negative

Neuigkeit *f* news

Neu-justierung *f* readjustment **-konstruiert** recently built **-konstruktion** *f* redesign, reconstruction **-kristallisation** *f* recrystallization **-land** *n* newly won land, new field

neulich recently

Neuling *m* novice, new recruit, newcomer

Neu-messing *n* yellow brass, yellow metal **-metall** *n* virgin metal **-nachbilden** to rebalance

Neuneck *n* nonagon

Neuner-komplement *n* complement on n-1 **-übertrag** *m* high-speed carry

neunwertig nonavalent

neu-ordnen to rearrange **-punkt** *m* new point **-sand** *m* new sand **-satz** *m* re-setting **-schnee** *m* new or fresh-fallen snow **-schöpfung** *f* original creation **-silber** *n* German silver, nickel silver, argentan, pack fong **-silberspan** *m* German silver lining

neutral neutral, impartial, nonpolarized, inert; (farblos) achromatic indifferent **~ einstellen** to adjust or set to neutral **-es Blendglas** absorbing filter of neutral or tinted glass **-e Linie** center line, construction line, axis of a groove **-e Lösung** neutral solution **-e Luftschicht** neutral air layer **-er Prozeß** neutral leach, neutral process **-es Relais** nonpolarized relay **-er Schirm** neutral screen **-e Zone** neutral lines (of a machine with commutator), neutral zone

Neutral-achse *f* neutral axis **-atomlinie** *f* line emitted by neutral atoms

Neutrale *f* neutral line

neutraleingestellt neutrally adjusted

Neutral-fiber *f* neutral fiber **-filter** *n* optic light filter (TV) **-glas** *n* neutral filter

Neutralisations-becken *n* neutralization trough **-kondensator** *m* balancing or neutralizing condenser **-schaltung** *f* neutrodyne circuit organization **-zahl** *f* neutralization number

neutralisieren to neutralize, compensate (for), balance out

neutralisierende Steuerung neutralizing controls

Neutralisierung *f* neutralization, balancing-out

Neutralisierungskondensator *m* balancing condenser

Neutralität *f* neutrality

Neutralitätsabzeichen *n* badge of neutrals

Neutral-kohlenwasserstoff *m* neutral hydrocarbon **-ladung** *f* neutral goods **-punkt** *m* aerodynamic center **-rot** *n* neutral red **-schwarzes Farbglas** dense neutral (tint) glass **-stellung** *f* neutrality, neutral adjustment **-tinte** *f* neutral tint

Neutretto *n* neutretto
Neutrino-absorption *f* neutrino absorption **-impuls** *m* neutrino momentum
Neutroden *n* neutralizing condenser
Neutrodyn *n* neutrodyne **-empfänger** *m* neutrodyne receiver **-kondensator** *m* neutralizing condenser **-schaltung** *f* neutrodyne circuit, neutrodyne (hookup)
Neutrofon *n* neutrophone
Neutrogerät *n* neutro-apparatus
Neutron *n* neutron **gesteuertes** ~ scattered neutron **promptes** ~ prompt fission neutrons
Neutronen-beugung *f* neutron diffraction **-beugungsaufnahme** *f* neutron diffraction pattern **-beugungsgerät** *n* neutron diffractometer **-bremsung** *f* neutron degradation **-einfang** *m* neutron capture **-flußmessung** *f* neutron monitoring **-rücksteuerung** *f* neutron scatter **-thermsäule** *f* neutron thermopile
Neuverteilung *f* redistribution ~ **des Bodens** reallotment
Neu-wert *m* current value **-zustellung** *f* reconditioning
neu-wickeln to rewind **-wicklung** *f* rewinding
neuzeitlich modern, in modern times, up-to-date **-e Konstruktion** advanced design
neu-zugestellter Ofen freshly lined furnace **-zündung** *f* reignition **-zustellung** *f* fresh lining, new lining
Newtonsches Gravitationsgesetz Newton's law
nibbeln to nibble
nicht not ~ **ganz** fractional
nicht-abgestimmt untuned, aperiodic **-anerkennung** *f* non-acknowledgment **-angreifbar** non-corrosive **-annahme** *f* non-acceptance **-ausgehärtet** undercured **-benachbart** non-adjacent **-beobachtung** *f* non-observance **-berechtigt** disqualified, not entitled **-bevorzugte Orientierung** random orientation, nonpreferential orientation **-dezimalsystem** *n* nondecimal base **-dissoziiert** undissociated, nondissociated
nicht-drehbar nonrevolving **-eichstellungsanzeigelicht** *n* uncalibrated-licht **-eignung** *f* unsuitableness **-eingeweihter** *m* uninformed or uninitiated person **-einhaltung** *f* non-compliance **-einklemmbarer Schlauch** pinchproof tube **-einlaufen** *n* unshrinkability **-einmischung** *f* nonintervention
nichteisen nonferrous **-metall** *n* nonferrous metal **-metallegierung** *f* nonferrous-metal alloy
Nicht-elektrolyt *n* nonelectrolyte **-erfüllung** *f* nonfulfillment, nonperformance, default **-erscheinen** *n* nonappearance, nonattendance, absence, contempt, default **-euklidisch** noneuclidian **-fachmann** *m* inexperienced hand **-faserig** nonfibrous **-fliegendes maßstäbliches Modell** nonflying scale model **-fluchtend** misaligned **-flüchtig** nonvolatile **-garbrennen** *n* underfiring **-gebrauch** *m* disuse **-genormt** nonstandard(ized) **-gerichtetes Mikrophon** astatic or nondirectional microphone **-gleitfähig** sessile **-haftend** non-adhesive
nichtig void, invalid, null, annulled
Nichtigkeits-abteilung *f* annulment department **-beschwerde** *f* plea of nullity **-erklärung** *f* annulment, invalidation, cancellation **-klage** *f* invalidity suit (patents), plea of nullity, action or suit for cancellation or annulment **-verfahren** *n* invalidation suit
Nicht-in-Betrieb-Sein *n* inoperation
nicht-inklinierend aclinic **-ionisiert** unionized, nonionized **-karbonathärte** *f* non carbonate hardness **-kenterbar** noncapsizable **-klappend** anti-rattle **-kohärenter Spin** incoherent rotation **-kommutativ** non-commutative **-kondensierte Hochstromentladung** uncondensed heavy-current discharge **-kontinuierlich** noncontinuous, intermittent **-korrosiv** noncorrosive **-kristallisch** amorphous, noncrystalline **-kugelförmig** aspherical **-leitend** nonconductive, nonconducting **-leiter** *m* nonconductor, insulator, dielectric
nicht-leuchtende Flamme roaring flame **-lieferung** *f* failure to deliver **-linear elastisch** finitely elastic **-linearer Spannungsteiler** graded potentiometer **-linearität** *f* nonlinearity **-lokalisiert** non-localised **-löschbare Speicherung** nonerasable storage **-magnetisch** nonmagnetic **-mattiert** undelustered **-messende Pumpe** nonmeasuring pump **-metall** *n* nonmetal **-metallisch** nonmetallic **-mischbar** immiscible, insoluble, insolvable **-mischbarkeit** *f* immiscibility **-offenkundigkeit** *f* non-obviousness **-oxydierend** nonoxidizing
nichtperiodisch aperiodic **-e Temperaturunterschiede** nonperiodic temperature changes
nicht-permanenter Speicher volatile storage **-plattiert** unclad **-quietschend** nonsqueaking **-reduzierbar** irreducible **-reproduzierbar** nonreproducible, noncontrollable **-resonierend** aperiodic, nonresonant
nichtrostend rustproof, rust-free, stainless, noncorroding **-e Farbe** antirusting paint **-er Stahl** stainless or rustproof steel
nicht-rückkehrende Schallstärke nonreflected sound **-rußende Flamme** sootless flame
nichts nothing, nil ~ **als** mere, nothing but
nichtschleudernder Reifen nonskid tire
nicht-seefest unseaworthy **-söhlig** unleveled **-spanabhebend** chipless, swar fless **-sphärisch** nonspherical, aspherical
nichtssagend insignificant
nicht-ständig nonpermanent, temporary, transient, transitory **-stationär** nonsteady **-subventioniert** unsubsidized **-supraleitend** nonsuperconducting
nicht-symmetrisch asymmetric, nonsymmetric, unilateral **-thermisch** nonthermal **-tragende Wand** curtain wall **-tropfende Gelatine** nonexuding gelatin **-typisiert** non-standardized **-übereinstimmung** *f* incongruity **-umkehrbar** irreversible **-umwandelbar** inconvertible **-unterscheidbar** indistinguishable
nicht-vergasbar nongasifiable, nonvolatile **-vorhanden** null, nil **-wässerig** nonaqueous, anhydrous **-wirbelnde Düse** (Strangdüse) nonswirl nozzle **-zahlung** *f* nonpayment, default of payment **-zehnersystem** *n* nondecimal base **-zentralsymmetrisch** non-centrosymmetric (structure) **-zerfallbarkeit** *f* nondisintegrability, nonfissionability **-zerstörende Prüfung** nondestructive test
Nickbewegung *f* pitching motion (of engine)
Nickel *m* nickel **-aluminium** *n* nickel aluminum **-antimonglanz** *m*, **-antimonkies** *m* ullmanite **-arsenkies** *m* gersdorffite **-artig** nickel-like

-beschlag *m* nickel trimmings **-blech** *n* nickel sheet or plate **-blüte** *f* nickel bloom, nickel green, annabergite **-bromür** *n* nickelous bromide

Nickel-chlorür *n* nickelous chloride **-chromstahl** *m* chrome-nickel steel **-draht** *m* nickel wire **-eisen** *n* ferronickel, nickel iron **-eisendraht** *m* Dumet wire **-erz** *n* nickel ore **-fahlerz** *n* malinowskite **-feinsteinverarbeitung** *f* nickel-matte refining, nickel converting

Nickel-flußeisen *n* nickel steel **-führend** nickel-bearing **-galvano** *n* nickel electro **-gehalt** *m* nickel content **-gewinnung** *f* nickel recovery **-glanz** *m* gersdorffite **-granalien** *pl* nickel shot **-haltig** nickeliferous **-hydroxydul** *n* nickelous hydroxide

nickelig nickelous

Nickelin *n* nickeline, niccolite

Nickel-kies *m* millerite **-kohlenoxyd** *n* nickel carbonyl **-kupfermantel** *m* cupronickel jacket **-lauge** *f* nickel electrolyte **-legierung** *f* nickel alloy **-magnetkieslagerstätte** *f* nickeliferous pyrrhotite deposit **-mater** *f* nickel matrix **-münze** *f* nickel coin **-niederschlag** *m* nickel deposit **-ocker** *m* nickel ocher

Nickel-oxydul *n* nickelous oxide **-papier** *n* nickel foil **-sammler** *m* (Edision) storage battery, nickel-alkaline cell **-schabe** *f* nickel pan **-schwamm** *m* reduced nickel oxide **-späne** *pl* nickel pans **-speise** *f* nickel speiss **-spießglanzerz** *n* ullmanite **-stahlguß** *m* nickelsteel casing

Nickel-stein *m* nickel matte **-sulfid** *n* nickel sulfide, millerite **-sulfür** *n* nickelous sulfide **-tiegel** *m* nickel crucible **-überzug** *m* nickel plating **-vitrol** *n* nickel sulfate **-verbindung** *f* nickelous compound **-verzögerungsleitung** *f* nickel delay-line **-würfel** *m* nickel cube **-zusatz** *m* addition of nickel **-zyanür** *n* nickelous cyanide

Nicken des Fahrzeugs pitching of vehicle

Nick-moment *m* pitching moment **-winkel** *m* angle of pitch

Nicolayit *m* nicolayite, thorogummite

nieder down, low, mean, inferior **-blasen** *n* (blast furnace) blowout to blow out or down

niederbrechen to break down, fall down, collapse, depress **eine Taste ~** to depress, strike, touch a key

Nieder-brechung *f* breakdown, breaking down (into components) **-bringen des Bohrloches** sinking the bore hole

Niederdruck *m* low pressure **-anlage** *f* hydroelectric plant of low head **-brenner** *m* low-pressure burner **-dampf** *m* low-pressure steam **-dampferzeuger** *m* low-pressure steam generator

niederdrücken to press down, force down, depress or touch (a key or button) **eine Taste ~, einen Hebel ~** to depress a button or a key

Niederdrücken *n* depression

Niederdruck-förderung *f* low-pressure transport, low-pressure conveyance **-gebiet** *n* low-pressure area **-gebläse** *n* low-pressure blower **-kolben** *m* low-pressure piston **-kontaktmanometer** *n* pressure-control switch **-kreis** *m* lower cycle

Niederdruck-lüfter *m* low-pressure fan **-luftgebläse** *n* low-pressure blower **-luftsystem** *n* low-pressure air system **-manometer** *n* working-pressure gauge **-reifen** *m* low-pressure tire **-schlauch** *m* low-pressure hose, flexible low-pressure tubing **-seite** *f* low-pressure end **-stufe** *f* low-pressure stage **-turbine** *f* low-pressure turbine

Niederdrückung *f* oppression, depression

Niederdruck-zerstäuber *m* low-pressure atomizer **-zylinder** *m* low-pressure cylinder

Nieder-fahrt *f* downward journey **-fallen** to be deposited or precipitated, settle (down), separate, precipitate, fall down, deposit

niederfrequent low-frequency **-er Rufstrom** low-frequency signaling current

Niederfrequenz *f* low frequency, audio frequency **-drossel** *f* low-frequency choke **-drosselsatz** *m* low-pass filter **-fernsprechen** *n* voice-frequency telephony **-filter** *m* low-pass filter **-ofen** *m* low-frequency furnace **-oszillator** *m* audio oscillator **-röhre** *f* audio-frequency tube, low-frequency tube **-rufsatz** *m* low-frequency ringer, ringing set, signaling set

Niederfrequenz-schaltung *f* audio-frequency circuit **-siebgebilde** *n* low-pass selective circuit or filter **-siebkette** *f* low-frequency filter, low-pass filter **-sperrkette** *f* high-pass filter **-sperrkreis** *m* high-pass filter (circuit) **-störung** *f* low-frequency disturbance (radio) **-strom** *m* low-frequency current **-stufe** *f* audio-frequency stage, low-frequency stage

Niederfrequenz-teil *m* audio-frequency section **-tonselektion** *f* audio-frequency reception **-transformator** *m*, **-überträger** *m* audio-frequency transformer, low-frequency transformer **-verstärker** *m* audio-frequency amplifier, low-frequency amplifier, audio amplifier, note amplifier **-verstärkung** *f* audio-frequency amplification, low-frequency amplification, audio amplification **-verstärkungsstufe** *f* audio-frequency amplification stage, low-frequency amplification stage

Nieder-führung *f* down-lead (of aerial) **-gang** *m* ladder, downstroke, descent, fall, lowering movement, hatchway, scuttle, decline

niedergehen to descend, move down, travel down, go down, subside **den Bruch ~ lassen** to cause the roof of a mine to fall in or to fall down

Niedergehen *n* falling, descending, lowering movement **~** (des Flugzeuges) descent

nieder-geschlagen sad, depressed **-gespannter Strom** low-tension current **-gesunkenes** *n* settlings, deposit **-halten** to dominate, neutralize, keep or hold down, paralyze, suppress, immobilize **-haltefeder** *f* retaining spring

Niederhalter *m* device for holding down (a clamp or jack), press pad **~** (Blechbiegemaschine), jack

Nieder-hauen *n* driving (min.) **-hubkarren** *m* low-lift platform truck **-holen** to lower **-kämpfen** to reduce, overpower, put out of action, silence **-kämpfung** *f* reduction, destruction, putting out of action, covering with destructive fire **-klappbar** arranged to turn (swing) down **-klatschen** to pancake **-klopfen** to plane down **-kurbeln** to lower **-lage** *f* depot, magazine, agency, warehouse, storehouse, defeat, deposit, branch, reverse **-lassen** lower, settle **-lassung** *f* colony, settlement, establishment **-laßvorrichtung** *f* lowering device

niederlegen to lay down, deposit, put down **Arbeit ~** to cease work

Nieder-legung *f* abdication, deposition, lowering, opening, groove **-machen** to put down, **-mähen** to mow down **-metzeln** to massacre, slaughter **-molekulare Zwischenprodukte** low-molecular intermediate products **-periodig** low-frequent **-ohmig** low-resistance, low-impedance **-rahmenfahrgestell** *n* low-built chassis **-reißen** to demolish, pull down, dismount

Niederschlag *m* deposit, sediment, precipitate, deposition, precipitation, rainfall, condensation, downstroke, hydrometeor, strike **~ des Kühlwassers** deposit or scale of cooling water (radio) **~ von Reif auf . . .** rime build-up on . . . **galvanischer ~** electrodeposition **käsiger ~** curds, curdy precipitation **radioaktiver ~** fall-out

niederschlagen to deposit, precipitate, settle, break down, kill (flotation foam), condense (vapor), drop, quash, stop (proceedings) **sich ~** to condense

Niederschlag(s)-apparat *m* precipitator **-arbeit** *f* precipitation process, reduction process (using iron) **-arm** of light precipitation, dry **-elektrode** *f* collecting electrode **-fläche** *f* deposition area, settling area **-gebiet** *n* encatchment area **-gefäß** *n* precipitating vessel **-höhe** *f* depth of rainfall **-kammer** *f* settling chamber, chamber for collecting deposits **-kasten** *m* precipitation box **-menge** *f* rainfall, precipitation **-mittel** *n* precipitant, precipitating agent

Niederschlag(s)-potential *n* striking deposition or sedimentation potential **-probe** *f* sample of precipitation **-reich** of heavy precipitation, wet, rainy **-sammler** *m* precipitation unit **-stärke** *f* intensity of precipitation **-verteilung** *f* distribution of precipitation or rainfall **-wanne** *f* settling trough or tray **-wasser** *n* rain water, atmospheric or meteoric water, condensate **-wasserabscheider** *m* steam trap **-wert** *m* amount of precipitation **-ziffer** *f* precipitation number

Nieder-schlagung *f* settling, depositing, precipitation, deposition, quashing (lawsuit) **-schmelzen** to melt down, smelt down, fuse off **-schraubhahn** *m* tap **-schraubventil** *n* globe valve **-schrift** *f* notation **-sinken** to descend, sink, drop **-sinken der Gichten eines Hochofens** descent of the charges of a blast furnace **-spannspule** *f* primary coil or winding **-spannung** *f* low pressure, low tension, low voltage

Niederspannungs-generator *m* low-voltage generator **-kreis** *m* low-voltage circuit **-leitung** *f* low-tension line, low-frequency cable **-seite** *f* low-tension side **-transformator** *m* low-tension transformer or line **-zündleitung** *f* low-tension ignition cable

nieder-sperrende Platte low-voltage plate **-stauchen** to press down **-stoßen** to drive down **-stürzen** to tumble down **-tor** *n* tail or aft gate (sluice) **-trächtig** mean, low, impertinent **-transformieren** to step down (elec.) **-treiben** to drive down

Niederung *f* low country, marsh, low ground, depression.

Nieder-voltbogen *m* low-voltage arc **-voltlampe** *f* low-voltage lamp

Niederwasser *n* low water (level)

Niederzugvergaser *m* downdraft carburetor

niedrig humble, low, mean, vulgar, lower, shallow, squat **~ aufgehängt** low slung **~ fliegen** to fly low **-e Drehzahl** low number of revolutions **-er Gang** low gear **(die) -e Kurve** the flat curve **~ legierter Stahl** low-alloy steel **~ siedender Stoff** low boiler **-er gelegen sein** to be lower (surveying) **-er machen** to lower

Niedrigantenne *f* low antenna

niedriggekohlt low-carbon, low in carbon **-er Flußstahl** mild steel **-er Stahl** soft steel, mild steel, low-carbon steel

niedrig-schmelzende Legierung low-melting-point alloy **-siedend** low-boiling **-siliziertes Roheisen** low-silicon pig iron

niedrigste brauchbare Frequenz lowest useful high frequency

niedrigster Wasserspiegel lowest upper pool elevation

Niedrigst-gehalt *m* minimum content **-wärmegrad** *m* minimum temperature **-wasser** *n* extreme low water

niedrigverdichtender Motor low-compression engine

niedrigviskos of low viscosity

Niedrigwasser *n* low tide, low water **kleinstes ~** minimum flow at low water

Niedrigwasser-bett *n* minor bed **-grenze** *f* **-linie** *f* limit of the normal bed at low water (summer)

niellieren to inlay with black enamel, work in niello

Niere *f* bunch, pocket, nodule, spheroidal concretion

Nieren-baum *m* cashew tree **-bruch** *m* (Schiene) shatter crack **-erz** *n* kidney ore

nierenförmig drusy, drused, kidney-shaped, reniform **-er dynamischer Schwingungsdämpfer** movable kidney

Nierenplattenkondensator *m* square-law condenser, straight-line wave-length condenser, uniform wave-length condenser

nierig reniform, kidney-shaped, in nodules or in pockets

nieseln to drizzle (meteor.)

Nieselregen *m*, **Nieseln** *n* drizzle

Niesgas *n* sneeze gas

Niet *m* rivet, pin, riveted joint, assembly or seam **einen ~ eintreiben** to drive a rivet **geschlagener ~** driven rivet **~ mit versenktem Kopf** flush rivet

Niet-abstand *m* rivet spacing or pitch **-abzug** *m* deduction of rivet holes, rivet allowance **-amboß** *m* rivet anvil **-anordnung** *f* spacing (of rivets) **-anschluß** *m* rivetted connection **-arbeit** *f* driving of rivets, riveting **-bank** *f* riveting stock **-beilage** *f* rivet washer **-bild** *n* rivet arrangement

Nietbolzenkette *f* riveted drive chain, pin chain **versplintete ~** cotter-pin detachable roller chain

Niet-büchse *f* riveting socket **-druck** *m* riveting pressure

Niet-einsatz *m* rivet insertion **-eisen** *n* rivet steel

nieten to rivet

Nieten *n* rivet(ing) **-döpper** *m* dolly bar, rivet set

-draht *m* rivet wire **-einschläger** *m* riveter **-fänger** *m* fishing tool for rivets **-glühofen** *m* rivet forge or furnace **-kopfzieher** *pl* rivet headers **-schere** *f* rivet-shearing machine

Nietenhälter *m* rivet tongs

Nietenkopf *m* pinhead **-aufsetzeisen** *n* rivet set **-schneiden** *n* deriveting

Nieten-löser *m* rivet remover **-setzer** *m* rivet set **-setzkopf** *m* set **-zange** *f* rivet pliers **-zieher** *m* rivet setter

Nietentfernung *f* pitch of rivets

Nieter *m* riveter

Niet-hälter *m* rivet tongs **-hammer** *m* riveting hammer **-kanone** *f* rivet gun **-kluppe** *f* riveting tongs **-kopf** *m* rivet head or point **-kolben** *m* riveting block **-kolonne** *f* riveting gang **-kraft** *f* rivet efficiency **-kran** *m* traveller for rivetting shops **-loch** *n* rivet hole **-lochreibahle** *f* taper bridge reamer

Nietmaschine *f* riveting machine, riveter **pneumatische ~** rivet gun

Niet-meißel *m* riveting punch **-muster** *n* rivet pattern **-nagel** *m* rivet **-naht** *f* riveted seam or joint, row of rivets **-pfaffe** *m* riveting set, snap, rivet stamp **-pfanne** *f* dolly **-platte** *f* riveting stock **-presse** *f* riveting press

Nietreihe *f* row of rivets **versetzte ~** staggered row of rivets

Niet-röhre *f* riveted casing **-rolle für Kettenbolzen** riveting roll for link pins **-schaft** *m* rivet shank or steam **-schirrmeister** *m* foreman riveter **-schlag** *m* clinching stroke **-schließkopf** *m* rivet point **-schraube** *f* screwed rivet **-schweißung** *f* plug weld **-senkkopf** *m* countersunk rivet head **-setzer** *m* snap cup **-setzkopf** *m* set **-stanze** *f* riveting machine **-stempel** *m* snap set, riveting set **-stift** *m* rivet **-stiftdraht** *m* pin wire **-teilung** *f* spacing or pitch of the rivets

niet- und nagelfest clinched and riveted

Nietung *f* (Vorgang) riveting, (Verbindung) rivet joint **zweischnittige ~** double-shear riveting **zweireihige ~** double-row riveting

Niet-verbindung *f* rivet(ed) joint **-werkzeug** *n* riveting tool **-winde** *f* screw dolly **-wippe** *f* lever dolly **-zange** *f* heating tongs, structural tongs, riveting tongs **-zapfen** *m* rivet spigot or pin **-zieher** *m* plate-closing tool **-zuführung** *f* rivet insertion

Nikol *n* Nicol **Nikolsches Prisma** Nicol prism

nilpotent nilpotent

Nimbostratuswolke *f* nimbostratus cloud

Nimbus *m* nimbus cloud

Niob *n* niobium, columbium

Niobat *n* niobate, columbate

Niobium *n* niobium

Niob-pentoxyd *n* niobic (pent)oxide **-säure** *f* niobic or columbic acid **-säureanhydrid** *n* niobic anhydride

Nipkowkanalübertragung *f* Nipkow channel transmission

Nipkowscheibe *f* Nipkow disk

Nipolit-preßstück *n* disintegrating charge **-schnur** *f* detonating cord (primer cord)

Nippel *m* nipple **~ für Leckölrückleitung** leak-off connection

Nippel-gewindeschneidemaschine *f* nipple threading machine **-schlüssel** *m* nipple key **-verbindung** *f* nipple joint

nippen to sip

Nipp-flut *f* neap tide **-hochwasser** *n* high water of ordinary neap tide **-niedrigwasser** *n* low water of ordinary neap tide **-tide** *f* neap tide

Nische *f* recess, niche, gullet, chamber for tail gate, shaft

Nischenkasten *m* cooler housing

Nist *f* (Nietstanze) riveting machine

Nitrabirne *f* nitra bulb (lamp)

Nitralloynabe *f* nitralloy barrel

Nitranilin *n* nitraniline

Nitrat *n* nitrate **-anlage** *f* nitrate plant **-beize** *f* nitrate mordant

Nitration *f* nitration

Nitrid *n* nitride

Nitrier-anlage *f* nitriding equipment **-apparat** *m* nitrating apparatus

nitrierbar nitrifiable **-er Stahl** Hykro steel

Nitrierdauer *f* period of nitration, nitriding time

nitrieren to nitrate, nitrify, nitride (metal)

Nitrier-gemisch *n* nitrating mixture **-härten** *n* nitrogen-hardening, nitriding **-härteverfahren** *n* nitriding process, nitration process **-härtung** *f* hardening by nitridation, nitride hardening **-kasten** *m* nitriding box **-ofen** *m* nitriding furnace, nitration furnace **-schicht** *f* nitride case, nitration case, nitrated case **-schleuder** *m* acid hydroextractor **-sonderstahl** *m* special steel for nitriding **-stahl** *m* nitriding steel, nitralloy steel

nitriert nitrided **~ gehärtet** face-hardened **-e Schicht** nitrided case

Nitriertiefe *f* depth of nitration

Nitriertopfmantel *m* jacket of nitriding pot

Nitrierung *f* nitriding, nitration, nitrification, nitridation

Nitrierungsgrad *m* degree of nitration, nitridation

Nitrier-verfahren *n* nitriding process **-wirkung** *f* nitriding action

Nitro *n* nitro **-benzol** *n* nitrobenzene

Nitroglyzerin *n* nitroglycerin **-blättchenpulver** *n* nitroglycerin flake powder **-pulver** *n* nitroglycerin powder **-röhrenpulver** *n* tubular nitroglycerin powder

Nitro-lacke synthetic resin varnishes **-lampe** *f* nitrogen-filled lamp

Nitrolsäure *f* nitrolic acid

Nitrometer *n* nitrometer

Nitromethan *n* nitromethane

Nitron *n* nitron

Nitro-naphthalin *n* nitronaphthalene **-pentaerythrit** *n* pentaerythritol tetranitrate **-phenol** *n* nitrophenol

Nitrose *f* nitrous vitriol

nitrosieren to treat with nitrous acid

Nitroso-benzol *n* nitrosobenzene **-sulfosäure** *f* nitro-sosulfonic acid

Nitrospachtel *f* nitrocellulose filler mass

Nitrotoluol *n* nitrotoluene

Nitroxylol *n* nitroxylene

Nitrozellulose *f* nitrocellulose **-blättchenpulver** *n* nitrocellulose flake powder **-lack** *m* pyroxilin lacquer, nitrocellulose dope **-pulver** *n* guncotton

nitrozelluloser Spannlack nitrate dope

Nitschel-hub *m* rubbing stroke **-leder** *n* condenser leathers

Nitscheln *n* rubbing on the condenser
Niveau *n* level, standard, surface ~ **der Sohle** bed elevation **auf gleiches ~ einstellen** to adjust levels
Niveau-diode *f* D.C. clamp diode **-fixpunkt** *m* bench mark **-fläche** *f* equipotential surface, surface at given level **-flasche** *f* leveling bottle **-karte** *f* level diagram, level chart **-kreuzung** *f* crossing (of a river by a canal) on the level **-linie** *f* potential line, level, equipotential line **-meßapparat** *m* gauge equipment **-regelventil** *n* level regulating valve **-röhre** *f* standard or testing tube, level(ing) tube **-stufe** *f* term, energy level (of electrons) **-übergang** *m* level crossing, grade crossing **-verbreiterung** *f* level broadening
Nivellement *m* leveling
Nivellements-punkt *m* bench mark **-zug** *m* line of levels
nivellieren to level, equalize, smooth, grade, even
Nivellieren *n* boning, leveling
Nivellier-instrument *n* level, leveling instrument, transit **-kreuz** *n* leveling rod **-latte** *f* leveling staff **-libelle** *f* spirit level, sighting level **-maßstab** *m* leveling rule **-scheibe** *f* sliding vane **-schraube** *f* leveling screw
Nivellierung *f* leveling
Nivellier-vorrichtung *f* leveling device **-waage** *f* spirit level
Nivenit *m* nivenite
n-Leiter n-type conductor
nochmalig repeated
Nocke *f* cam, dog, pin, baffler, lift, lifting cog
Nocken *m* cam ~ **für die Zündung** ignition cam **harmonischer ~** tangential cam **zweistufiger ~** double-lift cam **Teil des Nockens auf dem der Hub erfolgt** high-level portion of the cam
Nockenantrieb *m* cam drive
Nockenbahn *f* cam, plate, disk **Zone der ~ bei welcher keine Änderung der Stößellage erfolgt** dwell of a cam
nocken-betätigt cam-controlled **-buchse** *f* cam sleeve **-buckel** *m* cam lobe **-bündel** *n* group of cams **-form** *f* cam contour **-gehäuse** *n* cam case, cam box **-getriebe** *n* cam-type drive **-hebel** *m* cam lever **-hocker** *m* cam lobe or boss **-hub** *m* lift of cam **-keilnut** *m* cam key-way **-konstruktion** *f* cam design **-kontakt** *m* cam contact, cam springs
Nocken-kopf *m* cam head **-laufbahn** *f* cam track **-motor** *m* cam engine **-profil** *n* cam profile **-satz** *m* battery of cams **-schale** *f* cam disk **-schalter** *m* snap switch, cam switch, double-throw single-pole switch, trip switch **-schaltwerk** *n* camshaft gear
Nocken-scheibe *f* cam, cam plate or disk **-stange** *f* cam stick **-stellung** *f* cam position **-steuerung** *f* cam steering, cam gear, tappet gear **-stößel** *m* cam follower, follower **-trommel** *f* cam ring, cam drum **-untersuchung** *f* cam examination **-versteller** *m* cam timing device **-welle** *f* camshaft, cam spindle
Nockenwellen-antriebsrad *n* camshaft timing gear **-gehäuse** *n* camshaft housing or casing **-getriebe** *n* camshaft gears **-getriebeschlüssel** *m* camshaft gear key **-lager** *n* camshaft bearing **-prüfgerät** *n* camshaft tester **-rad** *n* camshaft gear wheel **-rolle** *f* camshaft roller **-schleifeinrichtung** *f* camshaft grinding attachment
Nomenklatur *f* nomenclature
Nominal-betrag *m* nominal value **-kraft** *f* nominal power
nominiert standardized
Nomogramm *n* straight-line chart, self-computing chart, nomograph, alignment chart
Nomographie *f* nomography
Nonan *n* nonane
Nonius *m* vernier, nonius **-einrichtung** *f* vernier **-einteilung** *f* vernier scale **-nullpunkt** *m* nonius zero **-nullstrich** *m* zero line of the vernier **-röhre** *f* vernier tube **-skala** *f* vernier scale **-strich** *m* vernier scale mark **-teilstrich** *m* vernier division
Nonne *f* mold, matrix, gutter, hollow or concave tile
nonvariant nonvariant, unvariant
Noppe *f* knub, knub yarn
Noppeisen *n* burling iron, pick pincers
noppen to burl, pick, cull **-abstand** *m* interval between knubs **-muster** *n* nap pattern **-stift** *m* inking pencil
Noppmaschine *f* burling machine
Nopper *m* trimmer, burler
Noppzange *f* tweezers, weaver's tweezers or nippers
Nord *m* north **geographisch ~** geographic north, true north **mißweisend ~** uncorrected north, magnetic north **rechtweisend ~** true north
Norddrehfehler *m* northerly turning error
Norden *m* north, northern region
Nordhalbkugel *f*, **Nordhemisphäre** *f* northern hemisphere
nördlich northern, northward, northerly **-e Breite** *n*° latitude n° N **-e Halbkugel** northern hemisphere **-er Polarkreis** arctic circle **-er Querneigungsfehler** northerly turning error
Nordlicht *n* aurora borealis, northern lights **-draperie** *f* streamers or curtain of aurora **-linie** *f* green auroral line **-spektrum** *n* auroral spectrum
nordmagnetisch north-magnetic
Nordosten *m* northeast
Nordost-monsun *m* northeast monsoon **-passat** *m* northeast trade wind
Nord-pol *m* north magnetic pole, north pole **-punkt** *m* north point, north **-richtung** *f* north direction (magnetic, grid, true) **-stern** *m* North Star **-suchend** north-seeking **-wärts** northward **-westen** *m* northwest **-wester** *m* northwester
Nordwind *m* north wind **plötzlicher, starker ~** (über dem Golf von Mexiko), norther
Noria *f* paternoster work
Norm *f* standard, rule, model, norm, standard specifications, standards **~ festsetzen** to standardize **nach ~ hergestellt** standardized
normal standard, normal **-e Abweichung** standard deviation **-es Benzin für Laboratoriumsgebrauch** laboratory naphtha **-e Eingangsreihen** normal entries **-er Einfluß in gravimetrischen Messungen** normal effect in gravity measurements **-e Muffe** standard coupling **-er Nulleffekt** normal background **-es Rohr** standard pipe **-e Schweißnaht** standard weld **-er Stoßriegel** *m* standard type joining member
Normalatmosphäre *f* standard atmosphere

internationale ~ International Standard Atmosphere (ISA)

Normal-aufnahme *f* normal photograph **-aufstellung** *f* normal scheme of erection **-auftrieb** *m* normal lift **-ausbreitung** *f* standard propagation **-ausführung** *f* standard (regular) model (design, construction) **-ausrüstung** *f* standard equipment **-ausstattung** *f* regular equipment **-bahn** *f* standard trajectory **-band** *n* standard magnetic tape **-beanspruchung** *f* normal stress, direct stress **-bedingung** *f* standard condition **-belastung** *f* normal load, standard load **-bereifung** *f* standard tire **-betrieb** *m* normal operation

Normal-bildkadre *n* standard picture frame **-blatt** *n* standardizing sheet **-bohrer** *m* plug, original or master tap **-brechung** *f* standard refraction **-breite** *f* normal width **-brennweite der Objektive** standard value of focal length of object glasses **-bündel** *n* normal congruence **-drall** *m* normal twisting **-drehzahl** *f* rated full-load speed **-druck** *m* normal or standard pressure or boost **-druckhöhe** *f* standard pressure altitude

Normale *f* normal (line) ~ **einer Fläche** normal of a plane surface ~ **einer ebenen Kurve** normal of a plane curve

Normalebene einer Raumkurve normal plane of a curve in space

Normal-einstellung *f* normal adjustment **-element** *n* standard cell **-fall** *m* normal case **-fassung** *f* standard mounting **-fernhörer** *m* standard receiver **-fernkabel** *n* standard long-distance telephone cable **-flachstab** *m* standard plate specimen (in testing) **-fluglage** *f* level flight **-flüssigkeit** *f* normal or standard solution or liquid **-format** *n* standard shape or size **-frequenz** *f* standard frequency **-gashebel** *m* throttle lever for normal flight **-gattierung** *f* standard mixture, standard charge **-gefällerad** *n* normal head turbine **-gewicht** *n* standard weight

Normalgewinde *n* standard thread **-lehrring** *m* standard thread ring gauge **-profilfigur** *f* standard thread outline

Normal-gleichung *f* normal equation **-glühen** to normalize **-glühen** *n* normalizing (annealing followed by air cooling) **-grädiger Sprinkler** low test sprinker **-größe** *f* standard size

Normalienraum *m* conditioned room

Normal-impulsbuchsen *pl* normal drop-out hubs **-instrument** *n* standard (reference) instrument, master instrument

normalisieren to standardize, normalize (in heat-treating), anneal, soak, regulate

normalisiert standardized **-es Farbglas** standard-color glass **-e Prüfmethode** standard testing method **-e Versuchsdestillation** standard distillation test

Normalisierung *f* standardization

Normalität *f* molecular or equivalent concentration

Normal-kalomelektrode *f* normal calomel electrode (of Ostwald electrode) **-katze** *f* standard grab **-kette** *f* standard caterpillar track **-kinofilm** *m* standard motion-picture film **-kompaß** *m* standard compass **-kondensator** *m* reference condenser **-konzentration** *f* normal concentration **-kraft** *f* normal force, axial force, normal component of force

Normallage *f* normal flying position **aus der** ~ from normal flying position

Normal-lampe *f* photometric standard **-last** *f* normal load **-lehre** *f* standard gauge, master gauge **-lehrdorn** *m* plain cylindrical plug gauge **-lehrring** *m* standard ring gauge **-leistung** *f* nominal capacity, standard capacity **-lichtquelle** *f* luminous standard **-linie** *f* datum line **-lochungen** *pl* digit punching **-lösung** *f* standard solution, normal solution

Normalluft *f* standard air or atmosphere **-spule** *f* standard air-core coil **-zustand** *m* standard atmosphere, standard atmospheric conditions

Normal-mantelschliff standard female ground taper **-maß** *n* standard, standard measure **-meridian** *m* standard meridian **-mikrophon** *n* standard microphone or transmitter **-modul** *n* normal plane pitch **-null** *n* datum surface, mean sea level (NSL) **-nullpunkt** *m* mean sea level **-ohm** *n* standard ohm **-parallele** *f* standard parallel **-pferdestärke** *f* normal horsepower **-potential eines Metalls** normal electrode potential of a metal **-probestab** *m* standard test bar **-profil** *n* standard (cross) section, normal profile **-profilschablone** *f* standard clearance gauge

Normal-querschnitt *f* normal cross section **-raupe** *f* standard caterpillar track **-rillentaster** *m* turnover pick-up **-rundstab** *m* standard round test bar **-schalten** to set at normal **-schliff** *m* standard ground joint **-schließrahmen** *m* standard chase (print) **-schlitten** *m* carriage **-schnitt einer Fläche** normal section of a surface **-schnittgeschwindigkeit** *f* standard cutting speed **-schrift** *f* standard track (sound recording) **-schwingung** *f* normal mode

normal-sichtig normal sighted, emmetropic **-sitz** *m* standard fit **-skala** *f* normal scale **-sockel** *m* standard cap (illum.) **-spannung** *f* normal stress (in testing), direct stress, axial stress, axial force **-spur** *f* standard gauge (R.R.) **-spurbahn** *f* standard- or normal-gauge railway **-spurige Eisenbahn** standard-gauge railroad **-stab** *m* standard bar **-stärke** *f* normal strength

Normalstellung *f* normal position, zero position ~ **eines Anzeigegerätes** standardized position of indicator

Normal-stereogramm *n* normal stereogram **-stimmton** *m* standard pitch **-strahler** *m* standard radiator **-stück** *n* standard master, gauge **-tastenfeld** *n* universal keyboard **-teiler** *m* invariant subgroup, normal divider **-temperatur** *f* standard temperature **-thermometer** *n* standard thermometer, normal thermometer **-ton** *m* (= 1000 Hz) reftone (acoust.), reference tone (= 1000 c.p.s.) **-umkehrspiegel** *m* standard reversing mirror **-verspannung** *f* conventional bracing **-versuch** *m* routine test **-versuchsprobe** *f* standard test sample **-vorrichtung** *f* standard attachments **-vorschub** *m* proper feed

Normal-wassergehalt *m* normal moisture content **-wasserstoffelektrode** *f* normal hydrogen electrode **-weingeist** *m* proof spirit **-wellenmesser** *m* standard wavemeter **-widerstand** *m* standard resistance **-zeit** *f* standard time **-zement** *m* (künstlich) standard artifical cement **-zube-**

hör *n* standard equipment **-zustand** *m* standard condition, normal energy level
normativ normative
Normatron *n* normatron
Normblatt *n* specifications, standard sheet
Norm-drehzahlen *pl* standard-number series **-druck** *m* standard pressure
normen to standardize
Normen aufstellen to draw up standards
Normenaufstellung *f* standardization, normalization, formulation or laying down of standard rules or norms
Normenausschuß *m* standards association **Internationaler Verband der Nationalen Normenausschüsse** International Federation of the National Standardizing Associations
Normen-draht *m* code wire **-entwurf** *m* tentative standard specification **-kurve** *f* standard curve **-maß** *n* standard scale **-sand** *m* standard sand **-treue** *f* adherence to the norm
normentsprechend normal, standard
Normenvorschrift *f* standard specification
normgemäß standard
normgerecht normal, standard
Normhammerwerk *n* standard tapping machine (acoust.)
normierbar normable (functions)
normieren to standardize, gauge, fix, regulate
normiert normalized **-e Eigenfunktion** normalized eigenfunction
Normierung *f* normalization, standardization, gauging
normig normal, standard
Norm-kapazität *f* standard capacitance **-kompaß** *m* standard compass **-recht** normal standard **-schliff** *m* standard ground joint **-schlüssel** *m* standard spanner **-schraube** *f* screws standard **-spur** *f* standard gauge **-teil** *m* standard part
Normung *f* standardization **~ des Frequenzganges** standardization of frequency characteristic
Normungs-vorschrift *f* standard specification **-zahl** *f* standard figure, preferred number
normwidrig abnormal, anomalous, adverse
Norrish-Schema *n* Norrish pattern
Norton-Antrieb *m* quick change gear drive **-Getriebe** *n* quick change gearing, quick change gear mechanism **-Kasten** *m* Norton box quick change gearbox
Not *f* emergency, need, necessity, danger, want **äußerste ~** extreme emergency
Notablaß einer Sperrmauer emergency outlet of a dam
Notabsperr-hahn *m* emergency stop cock or valve **-ventil** *n* emergency valve
Not-aggregat *n* stand-by unit **-amt** *n* temporary exchange, emergency exchange **-anlage** *f* provisional plant, emergency plant **-antenne** *f* emergency aerial **-anwasserung** *f* forced landing (on water) **-apparat** *m* emergency apparatus
Notar *m* notary
Notariat *n* notary's office
notariell drawn up by a notary
Not-ausgang *m* emergency exit **-auslaß** *m* emergency outlet or opening **-ausrücker** *m* safety disconnecter **-ausrüstung** *f* emergency outfit **-aussaugleitung** *f* emergency suction line **-ausschalter** *m* emergency cutout **-ausstieg** *m* emergency exit or hatch **-batterie** *f* emergency battery, spare battery **-befeuerung** *f* emergency lighting **-behelf** *m* expedient, emergency device, makeshift, improvisation **-beleuchtung** *f* emergency lighting **-betätigung** *f* emergency procedure **-bremse** *f* emergency brake **-bremshandgriff** *m* grip handle for emergency brake **-brennschluß** *m* emergency propellant cutoff (guided missiles) **-dürftig** needy, poor, scanty
Note *f* note
Noteinrichtung *f* emergency set, emergency apparatus
Noten-ausgabe *f* issue of bank notes **-bank** *f* bank (of issue) **-druck** *m* music printing **-linien** *pl* (Farben) streaks, parallel streaks **-ständer** *m* music stand **-stecher** *m* music engraver **-umlauf** *m* circulation of bank notes, note circulation
Notfahrgestell *n* emergency undercarriage
Notfall *m* (case of) emergency, case of need **für Notfälle festgesetzte Leistung** emergency ratings
Not-feuer *pl* emergency lights, protective fire, standing barrage, normal barrage **-flagge** *f* flag of distress, waft flag **-floß** *n* temporary raft **-form** *f* auxiliary tuyère, auxiliary pipe for supplying air in blast furnaces **-frequenz** *f* emergency radio channel, distress frequency **-füllstutzen** *m* emergency filler neck **-gedrungen** under compulsion, forced **-gemeinschaft** *f* (research) aid society, cooperative (research) aid council **-glieder** *pl* repair links **-hafen** *m* calling harbor, harbor of refuge, port of distress **-hilfe** *f* emergency corps
Nothöchstleistung *f* maximum emergency power, military power on aircraft **Anreicherungsstellung des Gemischreglers für ~** emergency position of automatic mixture control
notieren to quote, note, take down
Notierung *f* quotation
notifizieren to notify
nötig necessary **~ haben** to need, require
nötigen to compel, force, necessitate
nötigenfalls in case of need
Notiz *f* note, notice **-block** *m* note pad **-buch** *n* notebook
Not-joch *n* false or temporary frame (building construction) **-kabel** *n* interruption cable **-kompaß** *m* emergency compass **-kompressoranlage** *f* emergency compressor installation **-kuppelung** *f* safety coupling
Notlande-feld *n* emergency landing field **-gelände** *n* emergency landing area, alternate landing field **-hafen** *m* emergency landing field
notlanden to make an emergency or forced landing, (Wasser) ditch
Not-landeplatz *m* emergency landing field or ground **-landung** *f* forced or emergency landing **-landungsplatz** *m* emergency landing field **-leine** *f* communication cord, bell pull, safety rope **-leistung** *f* maximum all-out level power, emergency power **-leitung** *f* emergency line (elec.)
Not-meldung *f* SOS, distress signal **-mittel** *n* expedient, makeshift, emergency means **-peilsender** *m* emergency transmitter beacon **-pferdekraft** *f* emergency horsepower **-piste** *f* emergency trail or path **-proviant** *m* emergency rations **-rampe** *f* temporary ramp **-reede** *f*

harbor of refuge **-rost** *m* auxiliary grate

Not-ruder *n* jury rudder **-ruf** *m* SOS call, distress call or signal **-rufwelle** *f* distress wave **-schacht** *m* escape shaft **-schalter** *m* emergency switch **-schott** *n* outlet **-schütz** *n* relief sluices, auxiliary valves **-schütze** *f* emergency gate **-schutzhilfsgeräte** *pl* auxiliary safety devices **-schwimmfläche** *f* emergency flotation gear **-sender** *m* emergency transmitter

Not-signal *n* SOS call, distress call or signal **-sinkflug** *m* emergency descent

Not-sporn *m* auxiliary skid (aviation) **-stand** *m* emergency, state of emergency, critical state, crisis, distress **-standsarbeit** *f* relief work **-start** *m* emergency or forced take-off **-steuerdruckleitung** *f* emergency air-pressure control pipe **-steuergeber** *m* emergency control unit **-steuerung** *f* emergency control (atom. phys.) **-stich** *m* auxiliary taphole

Notstrom *m* emergency power supply **-aggregat** *n* emergency power unit **-versorgung** *f* emergency power supply

Not-trage *f* emergency stretcher **-tür** *f* emergency door

Notverband *m* emergency dressing **-päckchen** *n* first-aid packet, first-aid dressing **-tasche** *f* first-aid pouch

Not-verbindung *f* temporary bridge **-verschluß** *m* bulkhead emergency sluice, valve, or gate, dam **-visier** *n* emergency sight, improvised sight, spirit level **-wassern** to make an emergency landing on water, ditch **-wasserung** *f* forced alighting, ditching

notwendig requisite, necessary

Notwendigkeit *f* necessity, urgency

Not-wurf *m* emergency salvo release **-zapfleitung** *f* emergency fill line **-zug** *m* emergency handle **-zugknopf** *m* emergency button

Novalröhre *f* tube with 9-pin glass-button base

Novation *f* novation, bailment

Novität *f* novelty

Novokonstant *n* copper-magnesium alloy with aluminum and iron

N-Stiel *m* **N-Strebe** *f* N strut

Nuance *f* shade, tint **nach ~ färben** to dye to pattern

Nuancenabstufung *f* gradation of shade

nuancieren to shade

nuanciertes Weiß corrected white

Nuklearrakete, thermische ~ thermodynamic nuclear rocket

Nuklearübungsgerät *n* nuclear training simulator

Nukleinsäure *f* nucleic acid

Nukleogenese *f* nucleogenesis

Nukleonenbreite *f* nucleon width

Nukleon-kern *m* nucleor **-nukleonstreuung** *f* scattering of nucleons

Nukleus *m* nucleus

Nuklid *n* nuclide

Null *f* zero, cipher, blank, nil, null **~** (im Koordinatensystem) origin **auf ~ stellen** to zeronize **~ und nichtig** null and void

Null-abgleich *m* null or zero balance **-ablenkung** *f* zero error **-ablesung** *f* zero reading **-achse** *f* neutral axis, neutral fiber, zero axis **-adressenbefehl** *m* zero-address instruction **-amplitude** *f* zero-carrier **-anode** *f* by-pass anode (of mercury-arc rect.) **-anodenstromeffekt** *m* magnetron cut-off **-anstellung** *f* zero-incidence

Null-aufstiegswinkel *m* zero lift angle **-auftrieb** *m* no-lift **-auftriebslinie** *f* zero-lift line **-auftriebswinkel** *m* zero-lift angle of attack **-auslösung** *f* no-load release **-ausschalter** *m* zero cutout, no-load cutout, no-voltage circuit breaker **-darstellung** *f* null representation **-druck** *m* zero pressure **-druckfläche** *f* zone of zero stress **-drucklinie** *f* line of zero pressure **-durchgang** *m* zero passage

Nulleffekt *m* natural background radiation **-messung** *f* background effect measurement **-rate** *f* background rate **-zählrate** *f* background counting rate

Null-einspielung *f* oscillation about zero **-einstellknopf** *m* zero setting

Nulleinstellung *f* initial adjustment, zero adjustment, set zero

nullen to restore, reset

Nullenzirkel *m* spring-bow compasses, bow compasses

Null-förderung *f* zero delivery **-frequenz** *f* frequency at which phase shift is zero **-frequenzabstand** *m* zero frequency spacing **-Geschwindigkeits-Position** *f* zero speed position **-hebel** *m* zero adjusting lever, unison lever **-hyperbel** *f* lane

nullifizieren to cancel

Null-impedanz *f* zero-sequence field impedance **-indikator** *m* null indicator **-instrument** *n* balancing apparatus, null indicator **-kegel** *m* (beim Funkfeuer) cone of silence

nullkehrig zero-return

Null-klemme *f* zero terminal **-kontrolle** *f* zero balancing **-konus** *m* cone of nulls **-korrektur** *f* zero adjuster **-lage** *f* zero position, zero balance, initial or neutral position

Nulleiter *m* neutral wire, return wire, neutral conductor **geerdeter ~** earthed neutral conductor, power ground wire

Nulleitung *f* neutral feeder

Nullinie *f* zero line, zero axis, neutral axis, neutral fiber, reference line, missing line, band center (spectroscope) **wandernde ~** shifting zero

Nullinienverlagerung *f* zero line displacement, zero setting, electrical biasing (in film recording)

Null-magnetostriktion *f* zero-magnetostrictive composition **-marke** *f* zero mark **-meridian** *m* meridian of Greenwich, zero or initial meridian **-methode** *f* null or zero method, balance method **-mittagskreis** *m* initial or zero meridian

Nullode *f* spark-gap tube, nullode, electrodeless tube, transmitterblocker cell

Null-phase *f* zero phase setting **-phasenmodulation** *f* zero-phase or null-phase modulation **-potential** *n* zero potential, zero bias

Nullpunkt *m* zero point, zero, null (point), freezing point, origin, neutral point, "O" on bombsight **geerdeter ~** grounded neutral point **mittlerer ~** center zero **seitlicher ~** zero at scale end **mit unterdrücktem ~** hushed, in the **~** condition (meas.) **wandernder ~** wandering, fluctuating, or shifting zero

Nullpunkt-abweichung *f* zero error or deviation **-änderung** *f* zero shift **-anomalie** *f* origin distortion **-einstellvorrichtung** *f* zero adjusting device **-einstellung** *f* zero adjustment **-empfindlichkeit** *f* zero-level sensitivity

Nullpunktfehler *m* residual deflection, zeroing error (aut. contr), origin distortion, ion cross effect **~ der Teilkreise** null point or zero point, errors of the calibrated circles

Nullpunkt-konstanz *f* constancy of zero setting *f* zero method **-schärfung** *f* zero-point clearing, cleaning or sharpening (in direction finding) **-stabilität** *f* background stability **-unruhe** *f* zero-point motion **-wanderung** *f* zero drift **-widerstand** *m* neutral-point resistance

Null-reichweite *f* zero range **-schubsteigung** (Propeller) *f* zero-thrust pitch **-setzen** to equate zero **-signal** *n* zero output

Nullspannung *f* zero voltage, zero potential

Nullspannungs-auslösung *f* no-volt release **-ausschalter** *m* no-voltage circuit breaker **-relais** *n* no-voltage relay

Null-spant *m* maximum cross section **-stabilität** *f* zero-point stability **-stelle** *f* zero position, zero **-stellenzähler** *m* resetting counter **-steller** *m* zero adjuster, zero place, abcissa that gives zero value to Bessel function **-stellknopf** *m* zero setting **-stellung** *f* zero position, zero setting, normal position, off position, neutral position, zeroing, home position, starting position **-stellungsanzeiger** *m* zero-position indicator **-strahl** *m* paraxial ray **-strich** *m* zero mark, zero line, zero graduation

Nullstrom *m* zero current **-anzeiger** *m* zero current indicator **-auslösung** *f* no-load release **-verstärker** *m* null-balance amplifier

Nullsummen-Spiel *n* zero-sum game

nullte Ordnung zeroth order

Null-teiler *m* zero divisor **-tensor der Spannung** null stress

Nullung *f* zero voltage (elec.), reducing the voltage to zero **~ eines Störers** connecting casing of interfering device with neutral

Nullungs-leitung *f* neutral feeder **-glied** *n* null balance device **-impuls** *m* reset pulse

Null-verfahren *n* null method **-vorspannung** *f* zero bias **-werden** to approach zero **-wert** *m* zero value **-wertig** avalent, nonvalent **-zacke** *f* null signal (radar), ground ray **-zeit** *f* zero time, zero hour **-zirkel** *m* bow compasses, spring bow compasses **-zone** *f* neutral plane (elec.) **-zustand** *m* no-load condition, zero state **-zweiglinie** *f* zero branch line

Numeait *n* noumeite

Numerier-achse *f* numbering axis **-anstalt** *f* workshop for numbering

numerieren to number **fortlaufend ~** to number consecutively

Numerieren *n* numbering

Numerierung *f* numbering

numerisch numeric(al), numeral **-e Kodierung** numerical coding **-e Objektivöffnung** numerical aperture of objective **-e Rechenmaschine** digital computer **-es Signal** digital signal **-e Stellensteuerung** numerical positioning control

Numerus *m* (Logarithmus) antilogarithm

numismatisch numismatic

Nummer *f* number, cipher, size, numeral, issue, lot number **~ der Verbindungsleitung ansagen oder bezeichnen** to assign a trunk **die ~ wählen** to dial **laufende ~** consecutive number, serial number **unbenützte ~** dead number **unzugeteilte ~** unallotted number

Nummeranzeiger *m* call indicator

nummern to enumerate

Nummern-anzeigeeinrichtung *f* call announcer **-anzeiger** *m* call indicator

Nummernfolge *f*, **in der ~** in consecutive order

Nummern-geber *m* number-indicating system, call sender **-gebung** *f* numbering **-hülse** *f* number sleeve **-lichttableau** *n* luminous number-indicator board **-pfahl** *m* number peg, stake marked with a number **-rad** *n* stencil wheel **-reglette** *f* take-slug **-schalter** *m* dial switch

Nummernscheibe *f* dial, dial switch, number plate, dial plate **die ~ ablaufen lassen** to release the dial **die ~ aufziehen** to wind up, dial, pull round the dial **die ~ drehen** to dial

Nummernscheiben-kästchen *n* dial box **-kontakt** *m* dial key

Nummern-schild *n* number plate, license plate **-schlägel** *m* die hammer **-schlucker** *m* digit absorbing selector **-speicher** *m* (numerical) register **-stempel** *m* numbering machine **-sucher** *m* number detector **-wahl** *f* impulse action, impulse stepping, selection, number dialling **-wähler** *m* numerical switch **-werk** *n* numberer

Nummerung *f* numbering

Nummulitenkalk *m* nummulitic limestone

Nurflügel *m* flying wing, all wing **-aggregat** *n* flying-wing missile **-flugzeug** *n* flyingwing plane, all-wing airplane, tailless airplane

Nuß *f* nut, button die (of tools) **~ eines Wirbels** nut of a swivel

Nußbaum *m* walnut tree **-holz** *n* walnut

nußbraun auburn

Nüsse *pl* pinions, casters

Nuß-gruskohle *f* buckwheat coal, dross **-klassiersieb** *n* classifying screen **-kohle** *f* nut coal **-körnung** *f* nut size **-steckschlüssel** *m* short box spanner

Nüster *f* nostril

Nut *f* (Nute) groove; (kerbartige ~) notch; (zur Aufnahme des Werkstücks) slot; (Span-Nut) flute; (zum Aufspannen) T-slot; (zur Aufnahme von Keilen) keyway; (~ eines Wälzfräsers) gash; (~ in Metall) slot and key; (~ einer Keilwelle) female spline

Nut(e) *f* furrow, keyseat, mortise, rabbet, slit **~ und Feder** slot and feather, groove-and-tongue joint **~ in der Rohrplatte** groove hole (in tube sheet) **~ fräsen** to mill groove or keyway **~ stoßen** to cut keyway or groove **mit Nuten versehen** slotted, notched, grooved

Nutanker *m* grooved armature

Nutation *f* nutation

Nutationsvorrichtung nutator

Nut-breite *f* width of keyway **-eisen** *n* cold or cope chisel, groove-cutting chisel, plough bit

Nuten von Werkstücken keyseating of parts

nuten to slot, groove, notch, flute, keyseat **eine Welle ~** to cut a keyway in a shaft, slot a shaft

Nutenbohrmaschine *f* slot-drilling machine

Nutenfräser *m* slot cutter **~ für Reibahlen** cutter for fluting reamers

Nuten-fräsmaschine *f* key-way milling machine **-frequenz** *f* slot ripple frequency **-führung** *f*

retaining slot **-keil** *m* sunk key **-ring** *m* guide ring **-scheibe** *f* grooved cam **-schleifmaschine** *f* slot grinder **-schnitt** *m* slot pitch (of drum winding)

Nuten-stanzautomat *m* notching press **-stoßen** to slot, slotting **-stoßmaschine** *f* keyway-slotting machine, grooving machine **-stoßwerkzeug** *n* slotter tool **-teilung** *f* slot pitch **-trommel** *f* grooved drum **-walze** *f* grooved roller **-welle** *f* spline shaft, slot ripple, tooth ripple **-wellenfrequenz** *f* slot ripple frequency

Nutenwicklung *f* slot winding **mit ~ versehen** slot wound

Nuten-zahl *f* number of slots **-ziehen** to broach **-ziehmaschine** *f* keyseating machine, draw-type broaching machine

Nut-Feder-Verbindung *f* groove and tongue joint

Nut-hobel *m* grooving plane **-kreissäge** *f* circular-grooving saw, circular-slitting saw **-messer** *n* keyway broach or cutter bar **-mutter** *f* nut (for keyed end) **-ringe** U and V (packing) rings **-rolle** *f* grooved pulley

Nutschapparat *m* suction apparatus

Nutsche *f* suction filter, porcelain funnel

nutschen to filter by suction, suck

Nut-stoßmaschine *f* slotter, slotting machine **-streuleitwerk** *m* slot scattering conductance **-teilung** *f* tooth pitch **-tiefe** *f* depth of keyway

Nutung *f* spline, grooving

Nutverschlußkeil *m* slot wedge

Nutz-anwendung *f* practical application **-arbeit** *f* effective or useful work **-auftrieb** *m* useful lift

nutzbar useful, usable, utilizable, realizable, available, effective, net, of use **~ machen** to make available, make useful, utilize, employ, economize **-e Grenzmasse** meter mounting limits **-e Lagerstätte** useful mineral deposits **-es Landungsgebiet** effective landing area **-er Linsendurchmesser** useful or effective aperture of a lens

Nutzbarkeit *f* usefulness

Nutzbarmachung *f* utilization

Nutz-blindwiderstand *m* useful reactance **-breite** *f* working width **-bremsung** *f* regenerative braking **-bringend** profitable

Nutzdämpfung *f* effective transmission equivalent, useful resistance, damping resulting in useful radiation or signal power **~ der Fernleitung** effective transmission equivalent of a toll circuit

Nutzdauer *f* service life

Nutzdruck *m*, **mittlerer ~** mean effective pressure

Nutzdurchmesser *m* useful diameter

Nutzeffekt *m* useful effect, efficiency, net efficiency, efficiency of utilization, mechanical efficiency, useful effort (of a machine), output, effective power, working efficiency **~ des Verschlusses** effective usefulness or efficiency of the shutter **absoluter ~** specific efficiency, absolute efficiency

Nutzeinsatz *m* working batch (of furnace)

Nutzen *m* usefulness, profit, use, advantage, profit, utility, benefit **wirtschaftlicher ~** commercial efficiency

nützen to be of use

Nutz-fahrzeug *n* commercial vehicle **-feld** *n* useful or signal field (radio) **-feldstärke** *f* signal strength, field intensity **-fläche** *f* useful area, effective area **-frequenz** *f* desired frequency **-gas** *n* impellent (gas) **-gefälle** *n* effective heat drop **-gewicht** *n* useful load

Nutz-höhe *f* effective depth or height **-holz** *n* lumber, timber **-hubende** *n* end of delivery **-hubkraft** *f* available lift or buoyancy **-kapazität** *f* useful capacity **-kraft** *f* effective power **-kreis** *m* output circuit, useful circuit, active circuit **-länge** *f* usable length

Nutzlast *f* live load, useful load, actual load, working load, effective weight, net load, service load, pay load, payload (for rockets and missiles), disposable load **zahlende ~** pay load

Nutzlastaufbaukraftstoffverhältnis *n* pay-load-structure-fuel-weight ratio (in rockets)

Nutzlast-spitze *f* war head **-zeit** *f* load factor

Nutzlautstärke *f* signal level, sound-signal volume

Nutzleistung *f* actual output (work), useful or net efficiency, effective capacity, useful work, power, or output, mechanical efficiency, brake horsepower, effective power, signal power, useful effect **an der Welle verfügbare reine ~** net brake horsepower

Nutzleistungsbelastung *f* useful-performance load

Nutzleitwert *m* useful conductance

nützlich useful, advantageous, profitable, beneficial, serviceable

Nützlichkeit *f* usefulness, utility, advantage

Nützlichkeitsgrundsatz *m* utilitarian principle

nutzlos unprofitable, without purpose, useless

Nutzlosigkeit *f* uselessness

Nutzmitteldruck *m* mean effective pressure

Nutznießer *m* usufructuary, beneficiary

Nutznießung *f* life interest

Nützpegel, Verhältnis von Nütz- zu Störpegel signal-to-noise ratio

Nutz-querschnitt *m* useful cross section **-raum** *m* work space, (permanent-magnet) air gap **-raumvolumen** *n* (Rakete) payload volume **-recht** *n* easement **-signal** *n* intelligence signal, any signal with information **-spannung** *f* working stress, useful or working voltage, signal potential **-strom** *m* useful current, signal current, **-stromkreis** *m* signal circuit, utilization circuit

Nutzung *f* utilization, exploitation

Nutzungs-dauer *f* useful life **-grad** *m* call fill **-hauptzeit** *f* controlled machine time **-recht** *n* easement **-zeit** *f* process time

Nutz-wert *m* mechanical effect **-widerstand** *m* useful resistance, signal resistance **-wirkung** *f* useful effect, useful effort (of a machine), net or mechanical efficiency, efficiency of utilization

Nylon-schnitzel *n* nylon flakes **-struktur** *f* nylon structure **-waben** *pl* honeycomb nylon

N-Zeichen *n* **auf Wetterkarten gebrauchtes ~** N (aviation)

O

OB-Anschluß *m* LB line, local battery line

OB-Betrieb *m* local battery working

Obdach *n* shelter, lodging **-los** homeless

oben upstairs, above, aloft, this side up, top **~ erwähnt** afore-mentioned **von ~ belastet** load acting at the top **wie ~** the same as above

Obendestillat *n* overhead product

obengesteuert overhead **-er Motor** valve-in-head engine **-es Ventil** overhead valve

oben-hin superficially, slightly **-liegende Nockenwelle** overhead or high-level camshaft **-schmieröl** *n* upper cylinder lubricant (oil) **-schmierung** *f* upper cylinder lubrication **-steuerung** (elektr. Kontroller) handle at top

ober upper, higher, top, superior **-es Abmaß** *n* upper deviation **-er Abschluß** top cover end **-e Bürsten** control brushes **-es Deck** upper deck **-es Drahtlager** top groove **-e Düse** upper tuyère or nozzle **-e Formfläche** cope **-e Grenze** high limit

oberer Heizwert gross or upper heating value **-e halbräumliche Lichtstärke** mean upper hemispherical candle power **-er hemisphärischer Lichtstrom** upper spherical flux **-es Magazin** *n* upper slides magazine **-e Modellhälfte** cope pattern **-e Reihe** top row **-e Schicht** upper stratum **-er Totpunkt** top dead center **-es Ventil** upper valve **-e Winkelgruppe** high firing angles **-er Zylinderabschluß** *m* top cylinder cover

Ober-antrieb *m* overhead drive **-aufseher** *m* supervisor, superintendent **-aufsicht** *f* supervision

Ober-balken *m* tie piece between uprights, arch **-band** *n* overtone absorption band

Oberbau *m* superstructure, top of roadbed (R.R.), railroad track, permanent way **-arbeiter** *m* plate, rail or track layer **-stoff** *m* material for permanent road

Ober-begriff *m* specifications, description (patents), superimposed concept, introductory part of German patent claims **-behörde** *f* superior authority **-beleuchter** *m* chief electrician, scaffold or top-light controller (studio) **-betriebsmeister** *m* chief superintendent **-bett** *n* coverlet, upper berth **-boden** *m* topsoil **-bohrmeister** *m* drilling foreman **-bund** *m* top binding **-deck** *n* upper deck **-druck** *m* top pressure **-faktor** *m* overseer

Oberfläche *f* surface **~ zum Schutz gegen Korrosion unangreifbar machen** to passivate (surface against corrosion) **eine ~ mit Wasserstoff beladen** to activate, sensitize, or charge a surface with hydrogen, form a hydrogen skin **benetzte ~** wetted surface **gasbehaftete ~** surface with adsorbed gas **kugelige ~** spherical surface **spiegelnde ~** specular surface **vertonte ~** sound-impressed surface, area bearing sound track **wirksame ~** active surface

Oberflächen-abdichtungsschicht *f* surface membrane **-ableitung** *f* surface leakage **-abtaster** *m* surface analyzer **-aufladungswärme** *f* surface heat of charging **-auftrieb** *m* surface of buoyancy **-bearbeitung** *f*, **-behandlung** *f* surface treatment, finishing the surface **-beladung** *f* activation, sensitization, or charging of a surface **-belag** *m* top surface covering

Oberflächenbeschaffenheit *f* surface finish, skin effect, Kelvin effect **~ des Bodens** character of soil at surface **durch Einlaufen entstandene ~** (Lager) running-in surface finish **Schaubild der ~** contourogram

Oberflächen-bestrahlung *f* surface irradiation **-bild** *n* surface appearance **-druck** *m* surfacing pressure, surface pressure **-effekt** *m* surface effect (of photocathode) **-einfluß** *m* surface influence **-einheit** *f* unit of area **-entkohlung** *f* surface decarburization **-entladung** *f* surface discharge **-färbung** *f* calender color (paper mfg.) **-fehler** *m* surface defect or imperfection **-festigkeit** *f* surface strength or stability

Oberflächen-fräsen *n* surface milling **-fräser** *m* surface facer, spot facer **-gehärtet** gas-carburized **-geleimt** machine-sized **-gerichtet** normal or directive surface **-geschwindigkeit** *f* surface speed **-gestalt** *f* shape of surface **-gestaltung** *f* topography **-glätte** *f* smooth surface finish

Oberflächengüte *f* surface finish, finish, surface quality **hohe ~** fine finish

Oberflächen-härte *f* surface hardness **-härtung** *f* surface hardening, superficial (face) hardening **-integral** *n* integral taken over a surface **-isolationsweg** *m* surface insulation path **-kernexplosion** *f* surface burst **-kohlung** *f* surface carburizing, cementation **-kondensation** *f* condensation by contact **-kondensator** *m* air condenser **-kühler** *m* surface cooler

Oberflächen-ladung *f* surface space-charge **-mangel** *m* surface defect **-mittelpunkt** *m* epicenter **-neigung** *f* slope of surface **-normale** *f* normal to surface **-ölkühler** *m* skin-type oil radiator **-oxydschicht** *f* oxide film **-phase** *f* surface phase

Oberflächenprüfung, magnetische ~ magnafluxing

Oberflächen-reibung *f* surface or skin friction **-riß** *m* surface crack **-rüttelung** *f* surface vibration **-schaubild** *n* contourogram **-schicht** *f* surface layer **-schleifmaschine** *f* surface-grinding machine **-schliff** *m* surface grinding **-schutz** *m* surface protection **-schwere** *f* surficial gravity (astron.) **-schwimmer** *m* surface float **-spannung** *f* surface constraint, surface stress or tension, interfacial tension, surface voltage **-spannungsmesser** *m* **-spannungsprüfer** *m* surface tensiometer **-strom** *m* superficial current **-strömung** *f* surface current

Oberflächen-taster *m* surface analyzer **-verätzung** *f* surface etching **-verbrennung** *f* surface combustion **-veredlung** *f* surface finishing **-verschiebung** *f* surface displacement **-verschönerung** *f* surface finish **-versilberung** *f* face silver coating **-vorbehandlung** *f* surface preparation

Oberflächen-wärmeübergangsbeiwert *m* surface heat-transfer coefficient **-wasser** *n* condenser

water, surface water **-wechselwirkung** *f* surface interaction **-welle** *f* ground wave, surface wave, direct wave **-widerstand** *m* surface resistance, skin-effect resistance **-wirkung** *f* skin effect, surface work, Kelvin effect, surface action or effect **-zustand** *m* finish
oberflächlich superficial, cursory, shallow, slight **-e Zerspannung** scalping
Oberflansch *m* top flange **-laufwerk** *n* overhead- or suspension-flange runway
Ober-flasche *f* top block, upper block **-fleckstiftmaschine** *f* slugging machine
Oberflügel *m* upper wing **-betankung** *f* overwing refueling (Tankw.) **-holm** *m* upper wing spar
Ober-flugzeug *n* upper component of a composite aircraft **-flurhydranten** *pl* surface hydrants **-form** *f* top-half mold, cope **-fräser** *m* routing cutter **-führungsbuchse** *f* overhead pilot sleeve **-funker** *m* chief radio operator **-gärig** top fermented **-gerinne** *n* upper channel
Ober-geschoß *n* upper story **-gesenk** *n* upper die **-gestein** *n* overburden (min.) **-gewicht** *n* top weight **-glocke** *f* upper bell, small bell **-graben** *m* surface trench **-grabensohle** *f* bottom of headrace feeder **-grund** *m* topsoil, tilled soil **-gurt** *m* safety cinch, top flange (aviation), head arch, overarch, upper boom or chord **-hafen** *m* crown port
oberhalb upstream, above **~ der Schallgeschwindigkeit liegend** supersonic
Oberhaltung *f* head water
Oberhand *f* the upper hand **die ~ haben** to prevail
Oberharmonische *f* upper or higher harmonics **dreifache ~** triple harmonics, third harmonic **fünffache ~** quintuple harmonics **gerade ~** higher even harmonics, even harmonic **siebenfache ~** septuple harmonics **ungerade ~** odd harmonics **in einer Oberharmonischen schwingen** to vibrate to a harmonic
Ober-haupt *n* upper or inner gate (of the lock), head bay **-holm** *m* head beam **-ingenieur** *m* chief engineer
oberirdisch aboveground, aerial, overhead **eine Leitung ~ führen** to run a line overhead **-e Linie** overhead line, open wire or line, open-wire circuit
Ober-kanal *m* headrace feeder **-kante** *f* top edge **-kasten** *m* cope flask, top part molding box, top box, drag flask **-kessel** *m* steam drum, upper boiler **-kette** *f* nap or pile warp **-klappe** *f* upstream valve **-kolbenpresse** *f* down stroke press
Ober-kontrolle *f* supervisory device **-lager** *n* upper cleaving grain **-lagerer** *m* heterodyne **-länge** *f* ascender, ascending letter **-lastig** top-heavy
Oberlauf *m* upper river, upper course **~ eines Wildbaches** catchment basin of a torrent
Oberleiter *m* supervisor **künstlerischer ~** art supervisor
Oberleitung *f* aerial conduit, trolley wire, overhead line (elec.)
Oberleitungs-autobus *m* trackless trolley bus **-material** *n* material for overhead lines **-omnibus** *m* trolley bus, trackless trolley car
Oberleuchtfeuerwärter *m* head keeper of a lighthouse
Ober-licht *n* skylight, overhead scoop, scaffold light **-lichter** *pl* boarder lights
Obermesser *n* upper blade **-verstellung** *f* adjustment of top cutter
Ober-moräne *f* upper moraine **-ofen** *m* superstructure (of furnace) **-pfanne der Türangel** upper frog of the hinge **-pforte** *f* upper port **-platte** *f* top plate **-rahmen** *m* top girder, top frame **-rahmstück** *n* top girder **-riegel** *m* top crosspiece, upper transom
Oberring *m* upper band **-feder** *f* upper-band spring
Ober-schale *f* skin of aircraft **-schalseife** *f* a form of soap that is cooled and slabbed in a special way (peculiar to German industry) **-schenkel** *m* thigh **-schieber** *m* compound rest **-schild** *n* upper shield (gun)
oberschlächtig overshot **-es Wasserrad** overshot wheel
Ober-schlitten *m* top slide **-schnitt** *m* male die **-schwelle** *f* summer, breastsummer
Oberschwingung *f* harmonic vibration, overtone **harmonische ~** harmonic
Oberschwingungs-erzeuger *m* harmonic generator **-freier Gleichstromerzeuger** telephonically silent generator **-frequenz** *f* harmonic frequency **-generator** *m* harmonic generator
Oberseite *f* top or upper side **~ des Wehrkörpers** upstream face
Oberspannung *f* high-tension voltage **~ der Dauerfestigkeit** maximum stress limit
oberspannungs-seitig on the high-tension or -voltage side **-wicklung** *f* secondary winding, secondary coil
Obersparren *m* curb rafter
Oberspiegelhöhe *f* headrace reference mark
oberst topmost, highest, chief, principal, supreme
oberständiger Anker overtype armature
Oberstanze *f* punch
Ober-stau *m* headrace **-steiger** *m* mine captain, foreman **-stempel** *m* punch, over or upper die **-streich** *m* upper band (radio or direction finder)
Oberstrich *m* permanent maximum current or carrier, peak carrier amplitude, maximum or black-level picture signal (television) **-leistung** *f* peak power output **-wert** *m* peak power output (radio)
Ober-strom *m* upstream, upper current **-support** *m* upper slide rest **-taste** *f* sharp (music)
Oberteil *n* top, upper part **umlaufendes ~ des Verbrennungsraumes** rotating combustion head
Oberton *m* overtone, upper harmonic **-bildung** *f* harmonic tone creation
Ober-tor *n* floodgate head or tide gate **-trempel** *m* upper port sill **-trommel** *f* top or upper drum, steam and water drum
ober- und unterirdisches Netz overhead-underground system
Ober-wagen *m* upper carrying chassis of a crane **-walze** *f* top roll, tongue roll **-wange** *f* top clamping bar
Oberwasser *n* headwater, water upstream of point in question, upstream discharge, upland water, river water, head race **niedrigstes ~** lowest upper pool elevation
Oberwasser-graben *m* feeder from headrace **-seite** *f* upstream **-spiegel** *m* upper water level,

upper pool or headwater elevation, surface-water mirror

Oberwelle *f* harmonic vibration, harmonic, overtone, harmonic (vibration) **harmonische** ~ harmonic

Oberwellen-anteil *m* harmonic content **-antenne** *f* harmonic antenna **-drossel** *f* choking coil for higher harmonics **-gehalt** *m* harmonic content **-leistung** *f* harmonic wave attenuation **-spannung** *f* ripple voltage

Objekt *n* object, subject **-ähnlich** true-to-nature **-bereich** *m* specimen region **-bildabstand** *m* object-image distance **-brennpunkt** *m* front focus **-glas** *n* slide, mount (micros.) **-halter** *m* strate heating

Objektiv *n* objective, object glass, lens **höchstlichtstarkes** ~ ultra-rapid or ultra-high-speed objective or lens **kurzbrennweitiges** ~ short-focus lens **lichtstarkes** ~ rapid lens, objective of great light-transmitting capacity or power **mehrlinsiges** ~ composite objective **schwaches** ~ low-power objective **starkes** ~ high-power objective **zusammengesprengtes** ~ broken-contact lens or objective ~ **mit Korrektur** objective with correction mount

objektiv objective **-es Photometer** physical photometer

Objektiv-abgleich *m* parfocalized objective **-anpassungsstück** *n* lens adapter **-blende** *f* objective stop **-brennpunkt** *m* focal point **-brett** *n* lens or objective panel or board **-deckel** *m* lens cover or cap **-diopter** *m* objective diopter **-einsatz** *m* objective mount **-fassung** *f* lens attachment, objective or lens mount or barrel **-fehler** *m* lens defect **-hauptpunkt** *m* perspective center (of the lens) **-höhe** *f* height of lens or objective

Objektivierung *f* objectification

Objektiv-knotenpunkt *m* node, nodal point (lens) **-lichtkraft** *f* rapidity of a lens **-mittelebene** *f* principal plane of the lens **-oberfläche** *f* face of the objective **-öffnung** *f* object-glass aperture, lens aperture **-öffnungswinkel** *m* angular aperture of objective **-revolver** *m* lens turrent **-ring** *m* object-glass collar, lens ring or adapter **-satz** *m* set of object glasses, set of lenses, lens combination **-scheibe** *f* objective revolver desk **-schlitten** *m* microscope objective changer **-schutzdeckel** *m* lens guard

Objektiv-sockel *m* objective scale ring **-spule** *f* objective coil **-träger** *m* object-glass carrier, lens carrier, microscope slide **-verschluß** *m* instantaneous shutter (camera), between-lens shutter **-verstellung** *f* lens adjustment **-wechsler** *m* revolving nosepiece **-zentriervorrichtung** *f* objective centering device **-zwischenstück** *n* objective (lens) adapter

Objekt-kammer *f* object chamber **-kartei** *f* object register **-kennung** *f* delineation of an objective **-kontrast** *m* subject contrast **-kontrastumfang** *m* subject range **-markierapparat** *m* object marker **-mikrometer** *n* stage micrometer **-polschuh** *m* object pole shoe **-punkt** *m* object point **-raum** *m* object space **-schleuse** *f* object air lock **-schlitten** *m* object (plate) slide **-schutz** *m* spring mount **-sucher** *m* object finder **-tisch** *m* microscope stage, micrometer stage, object stage or stand, manipulator

Objektträger *m* slide, object slide or support, mount stage, or stand **-halter** *m* (object) slide carrier or holder **-plättchen** *n* object-support lamina or slide

objekt-treu object preserving **-verschmutzung** *f* object fouling **-vorstellung** *f* idea of an object **-weite** *f* distance of object

Obligation *f* bond

Obligationsrecht *n* law of debentures

obliegen to be incumbent upon

Obliegenheit *f* obligation

obligatorisch compulsory

Obmann *m* chairman

Observatorium *n* observatory

Obsidian *m* obsidian

Obsorge *f* care of, inspection

Obstgarten-egge *f* orchard harrow **-schutz** *m* orchard guards or protection

Obus *m* trolley bus

obwohl (al)though

Ocelit *n* ocelit **-stab** *m* ocelit rod

Ochras *m* black salt, melted ashes, crude potash

Ochsen-anspannvorrichtung *f* ox hitch **-auge** *n* port-hole light, bull's-eye, dormer window, side light **-deichsel** *f* oxcart tongue **-frosch** *m* bullfrog **-zunge** *f* flat tile

Ocker *m* ocher **-hältig** ocherous

ockerig ocherous

Octaacetylsaccharose *f* octa-acetyl sucrose

Octanzahl *f* octane number

Öde waste, barren

Ödem *n* edema (oedema)

Odeometer *n* consolidometer

ODER-Tor *n* OR-gate

ODER-Schaltung *f* OR-circuit, buffer

Odiometer *n* odiometer

Odometer *n* odometer

Oersted *n* oersted

Ofen *m* oven, stove, mine chamber, furnace, kiln ~ **mit Dauerbetrieb** continuous working kiln ~ **mit niedergehender Flamme** downdraft-type furnace ~ **mit steigender Flamme** updraft-type furnace **gasgefeuerter** ~ gas-fired furnace, gas furnace **herdbeheizter** ~ conducting-hearth furnace, resistor-hearth furnace **hüttenmännischer** ~ metallurgical furnace

Ofen-abdeckung *f* furnace roof **-anlage** *f* furnace installation, oven plant **-ansätze** *pl* residues or remains of a furnace **-arbeit** *f* furnace maneuver, furnace work or operation **-auskleidung** *f* furnace lining **-ausmauerung** *f* furnace brick lining **-ausnutzung** *f* furnace efficiency **-batterie** *f* range of ovens **-bär** *m* salamander **-bauer** *m* furnace or oven builder

Ofen-beschickung *f* furnace charge **-betrieb** *m* furnace operation or practice, furnace plant **-block** *m* oven battery, oven block **-bruch** *m* tutty **-bühne** *f* charging floor **-druck** *m* chamber pressure **-einsatz** *m* charge (met.) **-erzeugung** *f* furnace output **-fachmann** *m* expert furnaceman, furnace expert **-fassung** *f* furnace capacity

Ofen-frischerei *f* puddling **-führung** *f* working of heat **-füllung** *f* oven charge **-futter** *n* furnace lining **-galmei** *m* zinc mush, cadmia **-gang** *m* furnace working, heat, fast-working furnace **-gewölbe** *n* furnace roof **-guß** *m* stove castings

-haltbarkeit *f* furnace life **-herd** *m* furnace hearth

Ofen-kachel *f* stove tile **-kanal** *m* furnace flue **-kegel** *m* upper shell of blast furnace **-kipp-steuerung** *f* furnace tilting control **-kolonne** *f* furnace attendants or crew **-konstruktion** *f* furnace design, furnace or oven construction **-kopf** *m* port, Venturi head (rocket) **-körper** *m* furnace body **-klappe** *f* damper **-krücke** *f* glazier's scraper, rake, stoker

Ofen-leistung *f* furnace efficiency or output **-loch** *n* flue **-mann** *m* furnaceman **-mantel** *m* furnace shell **-massiv** *n* body of a furnace **-mauerung** *f* furnace brick lining **-mauerwerk** *n* furnace or oven brickwork, furnace brick lining **-profil** *n* furnace lines **-putzmittel** *n* stove polish **-querschnitt** *m* cross section of a furnace

Ofen-raum *m* furnace chamber **-rost** *m* furnace bosh or grate **-ruß** *m* furnace soot **-sack** *m* furnace well **-sau** *f* sow, salamander **-schacht** *m* furnace shaft or stack **-schub** *m* thrust **-schwamm** *m* tutty **-schwärze** *f* black lead **-sohle** *f* furnace bottom, oven sole or floor

Ofen-stein *m* fire brick **-stock** *m* outer casing, mantle, rough walling, or ground wall of a furnace **-topf** *m* heat element (guided missiles) **-trocken** oven-dried, kiln-dried **-trocknung** *f* furnace or oven drying, kiln drying **-ver-kokung** *f* coking in ovens **-wärter** *m* furnace operator or attendant **-wirkungsgrad** *m* furnace efficiency **-wolf** *m* salamander, furnace sow **-ziegel** *m* firebrick, stove tile **-zug** *m* furnace pressure, draft, flue **-zustellung** *f* furnace lining

offen open, frank, outspoken, overt, exposed ~ **gesagt** frankly speaking **-e Antenne** open antenna **-es Boot** open boat **-er Dampf** live steam **-e Düse** open nozzle **-er Einschnitt** open cut **-es Ende** skirt-end (of a pisten) **-er Führer-sitz** open pilot's cockpit **-er Funkspruch** radio message in clear **-er Kreis** open circuit **-e Luftionisationskammer** standard ionization chamber

offen-er Motor open-type motor **-e Posten-Kartei** open-item file **-es Rohr mit einer Naht** open-seam tubing **-er Sand** open sand **-e See** open sea **-es Sportflugzeug** open sports airplane **-e Sprache** plain, open, or uncoded language **-er Stromkreis** open circuit **-es Teilprogramm** open subprogram **-er Tiegel** open cup **-es Unterprogramm** open subroutine

Offenbandhalbleiter *m* open-band semiconductor

offenbar obvious, evident, manifest

offenbaren to make known, manifest, reveal

Offenbarung *f* manifestation, disclosure

offenhalten to reserve

offenkundig public, notorious, well-known, obvious, evident **-e Vorbenutzung** public use, prior use

Offensive *f* offensive

öffentlich open, public ~ **anzeigen** to advertise **-e Ausschreibung** competitive procurement (letting) **-er Betrieb** public utility **-e Börsen-sprechstelle** stock-exchange call office **-e Fern-sprechstelle** public telephone **-er Sammel-schutzraum** public air-raid shelter **-er Verkehr** public correspondence, public use **-e Verkehrs-anstalt** enterprise for facilitating public intercourse **-e Vorbenutzung** public use, prior use

Öffentlichkeit *f* public, publicity

offerieren to offer

Offerte *f* offer

offiziell official **-es Flugzeug** official aircraft **-er Rekord** official record

offiziös unofficial

Offizin *f* laboratory, dispensary, printing office

öffnen to open, unseal, unlock, break **sich** ~ to open up **den Durchlaß** ~ to open the draft **den Fallschirm** ~ to release or open the parachute **eine Röhre** ~ to open, unlock, render conductive, allow discharge, cause breakdown of a tube

Öffnen *n* opening

Öffner-hebel *m* breech-mechanism lever **-hebel-nocken** *m* cam of breech-mechanism lever **-kurbel** *f* breech-mechanism crank **-schließer-kontakt** *m* make and break contact

Öffnung *f* opening, inlet, aperture, port, orifice ~ **des Kalibers** parting of the rolls **relative** ~ **eines Objektivs** ratio of lens aperture, relative aperture of the lens ~ (Auslaß) **des Ölbehälters** oil-tank vent **aus kleinen Öffnungen ausfließen** to bleed

Öffnungs-ausgleich *m* aperture compensation **-bildaperture** *f* aperture image **-blende** *f* diaphragm **-dauer bei Ventilen** timing of valves **-fehler** *m* apertural defect, error, or effect, aperture aberration **-funke** *m* spark at break **-geschwindigkeit** *f* lifting velocity **-impuls** *m* break impulse **-induktionsstrom** *m* induced or breaking current **-kontakt** *m* opening contact **-kraft** *f* opening force (missiles) **-signal** *n* gating signal **-spannung** *f* opening voltage **-stoß** *m* opening shock **-stromstoß** *m* break pulse

Öffnungsverhältnis *n* aperture ratio, relative aperture, on-off ratio ~ **eines Objektivs** ratio of lens aperture, relative aperture of the lens

Öffnungs-verzerrung *f* aperture distortion **-weite** *f* flare, width of opening **-winkel** *m* generating angle, angular aperture, aperture angle, dihedral angle (of navigation lights) **-winkel-messer** *m* apertometer

Offset-druck *m* offset printing **-schnellpresse** *f* offset high-speed press **-tiefverfahren** *n* offset deep printing process

Öfner *m* furnace or oven operator

Ohm *n* ohm **absolutes** ~ abohm **akustisches** ~ acoustical ohm **internationales** ~ international or standard ohm

ohmisch ohmic **-e Verluste** ohmic losses

Ohm-kreis *m* (Schalter) resistive load circuit **-meter** *n* ohmmeter, megger

ohm-sche Belastung resistive load **-sches Extenso-meter** strain gauge **-sches Gesetz** Ohm's law **-scher Verlust** resistance loss, ohmic loss, I^2R loss, Joule's heat loss

Ohmscher Widerstand ohmic resistance, steady current resistance, direct-current resistance **reiner Ohmscher Widerstand** nonreactive resistance, dissipative resistance

Ohmwicklung *f* resistance winding

ohne without, less, off (on a switch) ~ **Befund** negative (said of tests) ~ **Knebel** nongagged ~ **Lippe** o. L. inside diameter

Ohnehaltflug *m* nonstop flight

Ohr *n* ear **taubes ~** deaf ear
Öhr *n* ear, eye (of needle), catch, eyelet, lifting lug, loop, tab
Öhrchen *n* thimble
Ohrempfindlichkeitskurve *f* ear-response characteristic
Ohrempfindungsgrenze *f* loudness contour of ear, auditory sensation area
Ohren-kappe *f* ear muff **-kopf** *m* lug head, fixed tommy head **-kühler** *m* lateral radiator **-kurve** *f* auditory sensation curve **-lager** *n* closed support (of machine) **-mutter** *f* wing nut **-schneide** *f* claw bit **-schraube** *f* thumbscrew, thumb bolt **-schützer** *pl* ear muffs
Öhrfurche *f* channel for the eye (needle)
Ohr-höhle *f* ear cavity **-joch** *n* top frame, topshaft frame **-kurvenfilter** *m* psophometric filter **-muschel** *f* ear, cap, earpiece **-verschlußwatte** *f* cotton for ear plugs
okkludieren to occlude
okkludiertes Gas occluded gas
Okklusion *f* occlusion
Okonit *n* okonite
Ökonomiekoeffizient *m* efficiency of economy
ökonomisch economical
Oktaeder *n* octahedron **-fläche** *f* **in Schubspannung** octahedral shear stress **-struktur** *f* octahedron structure **-symmetrie** *f* octahedral symmetry
oktaedrisch octahedral
oktal octal (info proc.) **-e Schreibweise** octal notation **-e Zahlendarstellung** octonary notation
Oktal-fassung *f* octal base **-ziffer** *f* octal digit
Oktan *n* octane **-anspruch** *m* octane number requirement **-einschätzung** *f* octane rating **-einstellung** *f* octane control
Oktant *m* octant
Oktan-verstellhebel *m* octane control lever **-wert** *m* antiknock value, octane rating, army octane number
Oktanzahl *f* knock rating, octane value or rating **mit hoher ~** high-octane
Oktavband *m* octavo volume
Oktave *f* octave **eingestrichene ~** one-stroked octave
Oktavsieb *n* octave analyzer
Oktavkoppel *f* octave coupler (organ)
Okthode *f* octode
Oktoide *pl* octoids
Oktoidenverzahnung *f* cutting teeth of octoid form
Oktroigebühr *f* town dues
Oktupol octupole **-übergänge** *pl* octupole transitions
Okular *n* eyepiece, ocular **verzerrungsfreies ~** orthoscopic or distortion-free eyepiece
Okular-auflagefläche *f* eyepiece flange **-aufsatz** *m* eyepiece attachment **-aufsteckglas** *n* eyepiece correcting lens **-auszug** *m* eye-lens slide, draw of the eyepiece **-auszugsverstellbarkeit** *f* eyepiece draw-tube extension **-blende** *f* eyepiece diameter or stop **-diopter** *m* telescopic sight, ocular diopter
Okular-einblick *m* view through eyepiece **-einstellung** *f* focal adjustment **-fokussierung** *f* pinion head for focusing eyepiece **-kollektiv** *n* field lens of eyepiece **-linse** *f* eyepiece lens, ocular lens **-marke** *f* eyepiece mark **-mikrometer** *n* eyepiece micrometer
Okularmuschel *f* eyepiece cup **drehbare ~** focusing ring
Okular-netzmikrometer *n* eyepiece crossline micrometer **-öffnung** *f* eyepiece, pinhole **-paar** *n* pair of eyepieces (oculars) **-revolver** *m* revolving eyepiece head **-schiebhülse** *f* eyepiece (sliding) sleeve **-schraube** *f* eyepiece screw, focusing screw **-sperrfilter** *n* eyepiece suppression filter **-steckhülse** *f* eyepiece sliding sleeve **-stutzen** *m* eyepiece tube
okulieren to inoculate, bud
Okuliermesser *n* grafting or budding knife
Öl *n* oil **~ für medizinischen Gebrauch** medicinal or pharmaceutical oil **~ für Maßapparate** counter oil **~ für die Metallindustrie** metallurgical oil **das ~ ablassen** to drain the oil **geblasenes ~** oxydated oil **gehärtetes ~** hydrogenated or fixed oil **leichtflüssiges ~** light oil **schwerflüssiges ~** heavy oil
Öl-abdeckscheibe *f* oil thrower **-abdichtung** *f* oil joint, oil seal **-abdichtungsring** *m* oil retainer, oil-retaining ring **-abfluß** *m* oil outlet
Ölablaß oil drain **-hahn** *m* oil-drain valve **-pfropfen** *m* oil-drain plug **-schraube** *f* oil drain plug **-stopfen** *m* oil drain plug **-stutzen** *m* oil drain connection
Öl-abscheider *m* oil separator **-abscheidung** *f* oil separation **-ablauföffnung** *f* oil drainage hole **-absaugpumpe** *f* scavenge pump **-abscheider** *m* oil trap
Öl-abstreicher *m* oil wiper **-abstreifer** *m* oil wiper or scraper **-abstreifring** *m* oil control ring, scraper ring **-abziehstein** *m* oilstone **-ansaugventil** *n* oil breather **-anstrich** *m* oil paint(ing) **-anzeichen** *n* oil seepage **-armer Schalter** oil-poor breaker **-aufwertungsanlage** *f* oil treatment plant **-ausbeutungsrechte** *n pl* oil rights **-ausdehnungsgefäß** *n* oil conservator **-austritt** *m* oil outlet
Ölbad *n* oil bath **-luftfilter** *m* oil-bath air filter
Öl-basis *f* oil base **-befeuchten** to oil-coat **-behälter** *m* oil reservoir or tank **-beize** *f* oil mordant **-berieselung** *f* oil-flooding **-beschmierung** *f* oil-spray or -mist lubrication **-beständig** oil-resistant **-betätigt** oil-operated
ölbildend olefiant **-es Gas** olefiant gas
Ölbilderdruck *m* lithochromic print
Ölbohrloch *n* oil well
Ölbohrung *f* oil well **stoßweises Springenlassen einer ~** stop-cocking an oil well
Öl-bombe *f* oil bomb **-bremse** *f* brake running in an oil bath, dashpot
Ölbrenner *m* oil burner **~ für Dampfzerstäubung** gas- or steam-atomizing oil burner **~ für mechanische Zerstäubung** mechanical atomizing oil burner
Öl-büchse *f* oil box, oil cup **-dampf** *m* oil vapor **-dampfstrahlpumpe** *f* oil ejector booster pump **-dämpfung** *f* oil damping, oil dashpot **-deckel** *m* oil cover **-dicht** oiltight, greasetight **-dichtung** *f* oil guard, oil retainer **-dichtungsring** *m* packing, oil retainer (ring) **-diffusionspumpe** *f* oil diffusion pump **-drosseldüse** *f* oil restrictor
Öldruck *m* oil printing (phot.), oil pressure **-anzeiger** *m* oil-pressure gauge **-betätigter Hilfskolben** servo piston **-bremse** *f* (hydraulic) oil

brake **-erzeugungsanlage** *f* hydraulic oil pressure generating unit **-federung** *f* oil shock absorption **-förderpumpe** *f* oil-supply pump

Öldruck-leitung *f* oil-pressure pipe **-löseeinrichtung** *f* safety brake release **-lösezylinder** *m* hydraulic release cylinder, safety brake release cylinder **-messer** *m* oil-pressure gauge **-papier** *n* oleographic paper **-pumpe** *f* oil-feed pump, pressure-feed pump **-verstärkerpumpe** *f* booster oil pump **-vorrichtung** *f* oil-hydraulic device **-zerstäuber** *m* mechanical oil-atomizer burner **-zylinder** *m* hydraulic cylinder

Öldunstfilter *n* oil vapor vent

öldurchtränkt soaked with oil, oil-bearing **-e Schichtenfolge** oil-bearing series

Öldurchtritt *m* transference of oil

Öldüse *f* oil atomizer

Oleat *n* oleate

Olefin *n* olefin

Olein *n* olein

Öl-einfüllschraube *f* oil filler screw **-einfüllstutzen** *m* oil filler, oil funnel

Öleinfüllung *f* oil-filler inlet

Öleinfüll-stopfen *m* oil filler plug **-stutzen** *m* oil filler, oil filler neck **-verschraubung** *f* oil-filler plug

Öl-einguß *m* oil-filler pipe **-einlaß** *m* oil inlet

Öleinsäure *f* oleic acid

Öl-einschätzung *f* oil rating **-einspritzung** *f* oil injection **-einspritzvorrichtung** *f* oil-injection device **-eintritt** *m* oil inlet or feed

ölen to oil, lubricate, grease

Ölendverschluß *m* oil cable head

Öler *m* oil cup, oiler, lubricator

Öler-antriebsrad *n* lubricator wheel **-deckel** *m* oil cover

Ölersatz *m* oil substitute

Oleum *n* oleum

Ölfang-behälter *m* oil container, oil-drainage container **-blech** *n* oil tray (under motor)

Ölfänger *m* drip pan, oil cup or pan **-platte** *f* baffle plate

Ölfang-mulde *f* oil-collector tray **-ring** *m* oil seal of crankcase **-schale** *f* oil pan **-zylinder** *m* barrel oil saver

Öl-farbe *f* oil paint, oil color **-faß** *n* oil barrel **-federbein** *n*, **-federstrebe** *f* oleo leg, oleo strut, hydraulic strut **-feinfilter** *m* oil filling filter **-feld** *n* oil field, pool, oil pool **-fest** insoluble in oil **-feuerung** *f* oil burner, oil fire, oil firing, oil burning

Ölfeuerungsanlage *f* oil-burning installation

Ölfilm *m* oil film **-walzenzapfenlager** *n* oil-film roll neck bearing

Ölfilter *m* oil filter **-kopf** *m* oil-filter head

Ölfiltration *f* oil filtration

Ölflammofen *m* oil-fired (air) furnace, oil-burning furnace

Ölflammpunktprüfer *m* flash-point testing apparatus or tester for oil

Ölfontäne *f* oil fountain

Ölförderscheibe *f* lubricator disc, oil thrower

Ölförderung *f* lubrication **~ mittels Druckluft** air-drive, air-flooding

ölführend oil-bearing **-e Schichtenfolge** oil-bearing series

Ölfüllstutzen *m* oil filler

ölgar oil treated

Ölgas *n* oil gas, olefiant gas **-erzeugung** *f* oil-gas manufacture **-glühlicht** *n* incandescent oil-gas lighting **-glühlichtbrenner** *m* incandescent oil-gas burner **-teer** *m* oil-gas tar

öl-gefeuert oil-fired **-gehärtet** oil-hardened **-geheizt** oil-fired **-gekühlt** oil-immersed

ölgespeist oil-fed **Vergaser mit -em Heizmantel** oil-jacketed carburetor

Ölgestein *n*, **schiefriges ~** oil shale

ölgesteuert oil-relay

ölgetränkt oiled

Ölgetriebe, stufenlos regelbares ~ infinitely variable oil drive

Öl-gewinnung *f* oil production **-hahn** *m* oil cock **-haltering** *m* oil control ring

ölhältig containing oil, oily, oleiferous **-er Sand** oil sand **-e Sandlinse** oil lens **-er Sandstein** oil sand

Ölhärtung *f* oil hardening

Ölhärtungsstahl *m* oil-hardening steel

Öl-harz *n* oleoresin **-haut** *f* oil film **-hose** *f* oil-skin trousers

ölhydraulisch, ~ verstellen to shift by oil pressure **-e Regelvorrichtung** pressure oil unit **-er Servokolben** oil servo-piston

Oliban *n* olibanum

ölig oillike, unctuous, oily, fatty, greasy

Öligkeit *f* unctuousness, lubricative quality, oiliness

oligodynamisch oligodynamic

Oligoklas *m* oligoclase, sunstone

Oligozän *n* Oligocene

Olive *f* olive

Olivenit *m* olivenite

Oliven-öl *n* olive oil **-quetsche** *f* crusher for olives

olivgrün olive-drab

Olivin *m* olivine

Öl-jacke *f* oil-skin jacket **-kabel** *n* oil-filled cable **-kabinett** *n* oil-storage cabinet

Ölkammer *f* oil well, oil chamber **-lager** *n* oil-reservoir bearing, oil-pocket bearing

Ölkanal *m* oil duct or passage **langer ~** oil gallery

Öl-kanister *m* oil container **-kännchen** *n* oil can **-kanne** *f* oil can, oiler **-karburiert** oil-carbureted **-karburierung** *f* oil carburetion **-kasten** *m* oil tank **-katarakt** *m* oil dashpot **-kataraktzylinder** *m* series oil spring-dashpot **-kautschuk** *m* factice **-kesselwärter** *m* black-pot attendant **-kissen** *n* oil cushion **-kitt** *m* (oil) putty **-klappe** *f* oil cover

Ölkohle *f* oil carbon **von ~ befreien** to decarbonize

Ölkohle-ansatz aufweisend caked with carbon **-bildung** *f* coking of the oil **-entferner** *m* decarbonizer

Öl-koks *m* carbon residue of oil **-kondensator** *m* oil (dielectric) condenser **-kontrollschraube** *f* oil level check plug, oil level screw **-kreislaufbehälter** *m* oil-circulating tank **-kruste** *f* oil deposit, deposit of dry oil **-kuchen** *m* oil cake **-kühler** *m* (skin-type) oil radiator, oil cooler **-kühlung** *f* oil cooling

Öl-lack *m* oil varnish **-lade** *f* oil or stamper press **-lager** *n* oil-storage depot **-lagerstätte** *f* oil pool **-lagerung** *f* oil storage **-lampe** *f* (offene) coffee-pot lamp **-lappen** *m* oily rag **-laterne** *f* oil lamp **-leinen** *n* oilcloth, varnishhed cambric

Ölleitung *f* oil connection or line **äußere Ölleitungen** external oil system
Öl-leitungsrohr *n* pipe line **-loch** *n* oil hole, oil pits **-los** oilless
Ölluft-federbein *n*, **-federstrebe** *f* oleo strut **-stoßdämpfer** *m* oleo-pneumatic shock absorber **-stoßfänger** *m* oleo-pneumatic shock absorber
Öl-manometer *n* oil-pressure gauge **-mantel** *m* oilskin coat **-maschine** *f* oil engine **-meßbecher** *m* graduated oil dispenser **-messer** *m* oil gauge, oil meter **-meßstab** *m* oil-measuring stick **-mischung** *f* oil mixture **-motor** *m* oil engine **-nebel** *m* oil mist, cloud, or spray **-nute** *f* oil groove, oil run, oil-way **-nutenfräser** *m* oil groove milling cutter
Öl-papier *n* oilpaper **-pauspapier** *n* tracing paper **-prallblech** *n* oil baffle **-presse** *f* forced-feed lubricator, oil press **-probe** *f* oil test, oil sample **-prüfer** *m* oil tester **-prüfmaschine** *f* oil-testing machine **-pumpe** *f* oil(-feed) pump **-pumpenanlage** *f* oil-pumping outfit **-pumpenantriebsritzel** *n* oil pump drive pinion **-qualm** *m* oil smoke
Öl-raffinerie *f* oil refinery **-raffinieranlage** *f* oil refinery, oil-refining plant **-rauch** *m* oil smoke **-refraktometer** *n* oleorefractometer **-regelventil** *n* oil-controlling valve **-reiniger** *m* oil purifier, oil rectifier **-reinigungsapparat** *m* oil-purifying apparatus, oil filter **-retter** *m* oil saver **-ring** *m* oil ring **-rinne** *f* oilway, oil groove **-rohr** *n* lubrication or oil pipe **-röhre** *f* oil-immersed tube
Ölrück-förderschnecke *f* oil-return (feed) thread **-gewinnungsanlage** *f* oil reconditioning setup **-lauf** *m* oil-return line
Ölrücklaufleitung *f* oil-return pipe **~ der Kipphebelschmierung** cylinder-head oil drain
Ölrücklaufrohr *n* oil-return pipe
Ölrücksaugpumpe *f* oil-suction pump
Ölrückstand *m* oil residue **breiiger ~ mit Metallspänen** swarf
Ölruß *m* lamp black
Ölsammel-gefäß *n* oil container **-napf** *m* oil sump or well
Öl-sand *m* oil sand **-sauer** oleate of
Ölsaug-korb *m* oil pump screen, oil strainer **-pumpe** *f* scavenger pump **-rohr** *n* oil intake pipe
Öl-säure *f* oleic acid **-saures Salz** oleate **-schale** *f* oil cup **-schalter** *m* oil circuit breaker, oil switch **-schauglas** *n* oil-gauge glass or window **-schaum** *m* oil foam **-schicht** *f* oil layer **-schieber** *m* oil sluice valve **-schiefer** *m* oil shale **-schlamm** *m* oil sludge
Ölschlammabsonderung *f* oil sludge separation **Zusatzmittel zum Schmieröl zur Verhütung der ~** detergent
Öl-schleuderer *m* oil thrower **-schleuderring** *m* oil slinger or thrower **-schlitzring** *m* grooved piston ring **-schmierung** *f* oil lubrication, oiling **-schöpfbohrung** *f* oil distribution duct **-schöpfer** *m* bailer, oil scoop or catcher
Öl-schütz *m* oil immersed contactor
Ölschutz *m* oil protection or shield **unterer ~** undershield
Ölschwemmverfahren *n* oil flotation process
Ölschwungmasse *f* rotary stabilizer
Öl-seide *f* oiled silk **-seiher** *m* oil strainer or filter **-separator** *m* oil filter, separator-type oil purifier **-sicherheitslampe** *f* oil safety lamp **-sieb** *n* oil strainer **-sikkative** *pl* linoleate driers, oil driers **-spachtelgrund** (Lack) oil primer **-sparapparat** *m* economical oiling apparatus **-spiegel** *m* oil level, oil face
Ölspritz-blech *n* oil retainer plate **-düse** *f* cooling jet nozzle
Ölspritze *f* oil gun, oil squirt
Ölspritz-kanne *f* force-feed oiler **-ring** *m* oil slinger
Öl-spule *f* oil-immersed coil **-spur** *f* oil show or trace
Ölstand *m* oil level
Ölstand(s)-anzeiger *m* oil gauge **-glas** *n* oil level gauge glass **-hahn** *m* oil level gauge cock **-kontrolle** *f* oil-level check, oil-level indicator **-pfropfen** *m* oil-level plug **-rohr** *n* oil gauge, oil level pipe **-schraube** *f* oil-level plug **-zeiger** *m* oil gauge
Öl-staub *m* oil spray or mist, oil smoke **-staublech** *n* oil deflector, oil retainer **-stauring** *m* oil retaining ring **-steigrohr** *n* oil riser pipe **-stein** *m* oil-stone **-stoff** *m* varnished cambric, empire cloth **-stopfen** *m* oil filler plug, oil plug **-stöpsel** *m* oil plug
Ölstoß-dämpfer *m* oleo-pneumatic shock absorber, oil shock absorber **-dämpfung** *f* oil shock absorption **-fänger** *m* oleo gear
Öl-strebe *f* oleo strut **-strebenbügel** *m* oelo-strut trunnion **-sumpf** *m* sump **-süß** *n* glycerin
Öltank *m* oil tank **-batterie** *f* battery of oil tanks
Öl-tasche *f* oil well **-tasse** *f* oil cup **-tauchsystem** *n* oil-immersion system **-temperaturregler** *m* oil-temperature regulator **-thermometer** *n* oil thermometer, oil-temperature gauge **-transformator** *m* oil(-cooled) transformer, oil-immersed transformer **-treibdampfpumpe** *f* booster-type oil diffusion pump **-trennschalter** *m* oil-break switch **-trester** *m pl* oil lees **-trocknen** *n* dehydration of oil
Öl-tropfblech *n* oil-dripping plate **-tröpfchenmethode** *f* oil-drop method **-tropfer** *m* oiler **-tropfgefäß** *n* sight-feed lubricator **-tuch** *n* oilcloth, varnished cloth **-überdruckventil** *n* oil relief valve **-überlaufrohr** *n* oil overflow pipe **-überzug** *m* oil coating or film, oil varnish
Ölumlauf *m* oil circulation, oiling circuit **-schmierung** *f* pressure lubrication
Ölumsteuerventil für Zweistellungsschraube propeller regulator valve
Öl- und Feuchtigkeitsgehalt *m* expressible oil and moisture
Ölung *f* oiling, lubrication
Öl-vase *f* oil cup **-vektor** *m* position or radius vector **-verbrauch** *m* oil consumption **-verdünnung** *f* oil dilution **-vergüten** *n* oil-tempering **-versorgung** *f* oiling system, lubrication **-verteiler** *m* oil dispenser **-verträglichkeit** *f* compatibility with oil **-vorlage** *f* oil conservator **-vorrat** *m* oil supply **-vorwärmer** *m* oil heater, oil preheater, fuel oil preheater
Öl-wanne *f* oil sump or pan **-wannendichtung** *f* oil pan gasket **-wechsel** *m* oil change **-winde** *f* oil jack **-zapfanlage** *f* oil dispenser **-zentrifuge** *f* oil centrifuge **-zerstäuber** *m* oil sprayer **-zerstäubung** *f* oil atomization **-zufluß** *m* oil lines, oil feed, oil flow
Ölzufuhr *f* oil feed **-leitung** *f* oil-delivery pipe

Ölzuführung *f* oil feed, oil supply
Ölzuführungsrohr *n* oil tube
Öl-zulaufventil *n* oil inlet valve **-zündbrenner** *m* lighting oil burner **zurückhaltungsring** *m* oil-control ring **-zusatz** *m* oiliness dope
Omegatron *n* omegatron
Omnibus *m* bus, omnibus **-leitung** *f* omnibus circuit, way circuit
Omnigraph *m* omnigraph
Ondograph *m* ondograph
Ondoskop *n* ondoscope
Ondulator *m* undulator
Onyx *m* onyx
Oolith *m* oölite
Oolithkalk *m* oölitic limestone
oolitisch oölitic
opak opaque **-illuminator** *m* opaque reflector or illuminator, vertical illuminator
Opal *m* opal **-artig** opaline **-ausrüstung** *f* opal finish
Opaleszenz *f* opalescence
opaleszieren to opalesce
Opal-glas *n* opal or frosted glass, light-diffusing glass **-lampe** *f* opal lamp
Opazimeter *n* turbidimeter, opacimeter
Opazität *f* opaqueness
Operation *f* operation, surgical operation
Operations-befehl *m* operational code **-bereich** *m* processing section **-schnitt** *m* incision
operativ operational, strategic
Operatorenrechnung *f* operational calculus or manipulation
Operment *n* orpiment
Ophtalmometer *n* ophtalmometer
Oppanol *n* a synthetic substance resistant to mustard gas and lewisite
opprimieren to oppress
Optierung *f* focusing
Optik *f* optical system, optics **-auswechslung** *f* optical system (interchangeable lens barrels)
Optiker *m* optician
Optik-fassung *f* optical barrel **-tubus** *m* optical barrel
optimal best, highest, optimum, maximum **-e Ballung** optimum bunching **-e Belastungsimpedanz** optimum load impedance **-er Wert** optimum value
Optimeter *n* optimeter, optical indicator **~ für Außenmessungen** external-gauging optimeter
Optimierung *f* optimization
optimum most favorable, best, optimum **~ Anstellwinkel** optimum angle of incidence
Option *f* option
Optionserneuerung *f* renewal of option
optisch optic(al) **~ akustisch** audible and visible **~ akustischer Leitstrahlsender** visual/aural range **~ dünn** translucent **~ durchlässig** optically permeable **~ einachsig** optically uniaxial
optisch-e Abstimmung electric eye, visual tuning **-e Abtastung** optical scanning **-er Ausgleich** optical balance (equalizing) **-e Bank** optical bench (phot.) **-e Besetztprüfung** visual busy signal **-e Bodenhilfen** *pl* visual ground aids **-e Brechungsüberschreitung** optical exaltation **-er Brennpunkt** optical focus **-e Drehung** optical rotatory power, optical rotation, rotatory polarization **-e Einblendung** visual presentation **-er Horizontabstand** optical horizon distance
optisch-e Inaktivierung racemization **-es Maß** optical gauge **-e Ortung** visual-observation method **-e Rotationsdispersion** *f* ORD, optical rotatory dispersion **-er Telegraph** semaphore **-es Überwachungssystem** *n* viewing system **-e Verzeichnung** optical distortion **-er Zweig** optical (frequency) branch **-e Zwillingsbildung** optical twinning
Optophon *n* optophone
Optometer *n* optometer
O-Punkt *m* aiming point
Orange *f* orange **-farben, -farbig** orange
Orangit *m* orangite
Orbital-bahn *f* orbital path **-bewegung** *f* orbital motion
ordentlich orderly, neat
Orderscheck *m* order
Ordinate *f* ordinate
Ordinaten-abstand *m* offset **-achse** *f* axis of ordinates **-gesteuert** ordinate-controlled **-maßstab** *m* scale of ordinates
ordnen to arrange, rearrange, collect terms, order, regulate, settle
Ordner *m* file
Ordnung *f* arrangement, order, class, rank, regulation, line-up, array (mil.), accuracy, degree, power (math.) **Kurve dritter ~** cubic curve **in ~ befinden** to be in order **wieder in ~ bringen** to adjust **zur ~ zurückkehren** to return to law and order, return to military control **geöffnete ~** extended order (drill) **geschlossene ~** close order (drill) *n***te ~** *n*th degree, *n*th order **der ~ halber** for form's sake
Ordnungs-domäne *f* ordering domain **-gemäß** orderly, methodical **-gleis** *n* makeup track (R.R.) **-grad** *m* degree of order **-mäßig** in due order **-trenner** *m* order-sorter **-umwandlung** *f* ordering transition
Ordnungs- und Sicherheitsbestimmungen *f pl* order and security regulations
ordnungswidrig irregular, disorderly, contrary to order
Ordnungszahl *f* ordinal number, concentration factor (soils), ordinal index **~ der Atome** atomic number
Ordonnanz *f* orderly **-dienst** *m* orderly duty
Orford-Vorherd *m* Orford settler or receiver
Organ *n* technical agent, agency, part, organ
Organisation *f* organization
Organisationsstab *m* organizational staff
organisch einbauen to form an integral part
organisatorisch-e Operationen *pl* red-tape operations (info proc.) **-es Programm** executive program
organisch organic **-e Chemie** organic chemistry **-e Schwäche** structural failure
organisieren to organize
organogenes Sedimentgestein organogenic sedimentary rock
Organometall *n* organometallic compound
organometallisch organometallic
Organvertrag *m* deed of affiliation
Orgel *f* organ **geologische ~** sand pipe
Orgel-metall *n* organ-pipe metal **-zungenpfeife** *f* reed organ pipe
orientierbar orientable
orientieren to orient, adjust **sich ~** to take a bearing fix or find a position

orientiert aligned **-e Leerstellen** oriented voids
Orientierung *f* orientation, survey, direction, trend, inclination **~ im Gelände** orientation on the ground **~ verlieren** to lose one's bearings, become lost **äußere ~** outer orientation **bevorzugte ~** nonrandom or privileged orientation **gegenseitige ~** reciprocal orientation **innere ~** inner orientation
orientierungs-abhängig orientation-sensitive or -responsive **-abhängigkeit** *f* orientation dependence **-beziehung** *f* orientation relation **-bilder** *pl* orientation photographs **-dreieck** *n* orientation triangle **-elemente** *pl* elements of orientation, constants of the plate
Orientierungs-fehler *m* misorientation **-feuer** *n* route beacon **-linie** *f* orienting line **-marke** *f* locating mark **-ordnung** *f* orientation ordering **-punkt** *m* control point **-skala** *f* observation scale tube **-unbekannte** *f* orientation unknown **-verschmelzung** *f* orientation fusion
original original, inherent **-arbeit** *f* original test **-bereich** *m* time domain **-bild** *n* original prototype **-bohrer** *m* master or original tap, hob **-grün** *n* Paris green
Original-kristall *m* parent crystal **-leuchte** *f* missile orientation target light **-maßstab** *m* original scale **-modell** *n* master pattern **-negativ** *n* master negative **-positiv** *n* master positive **-programm** *n* source program **-punkt** *m* control or check point **-sendung** *f* live broadcast, live transmission
Orioskop *n* orioscope
Orkan *m* hurricane, storm **-artiger Sturm** heavy storm or gale **-mitte** *f* center of the hurricane **-regel** *f* rule or law of hurricanes **-zone** *f* hurricane zone
Ornamentguß *m* ornamental castings
Ornithopter *n* ornithopter
Orogenese *f* orogenesis
orogenetisch orogenetic
orographisch orographic **-er Regen** orographic rain
Orsat-apparat *m* Orsat gas-analysis or air-testing apparatus **-rauchmesser** *m* orsat gas analysis
Ort *m* place, village, site, point, locus, position, region, heading, end, face, forehead **an ~ und Stelle** in situ, in the site, on the spot **an einen anderen ~ verlegen** to move **auf einen bestimmten ~ zurückführen** to localize **geometrischer ~** locus, geometrical position, vector point **~ hoher Strahlungsdichte** hot spot **~ der Synthese** position of synthesis
Ortbauverfahren *n* site work
Ortbalken *m* stringer (R.R.)
orten to locate, plot, navigate, orient, take a bearing
Orter *m* navigator (aviation)
Örterbau *m* face workings
Orter-kompaß *m* navigation compass **-raum** *m* navigator's compartment
Örtersäge *f* framed whipsaw, turning saw, great span saw
Ortertisch *m* navigator's table
Ortgeber *m* locator
Orthikon *n* orthicon
ortho-basisch orthobasic **-chromatisch** orthochromatic **-chromatisierung** *f* orthochromatic processing **-chron** orthochronous
Ortho-diagraphie *f* orthodiagraphy **-dichlorbenzol** *n* ortho-dichlorobenzene
Orthodrome *f* orthodromy, great circle, straight or rhombic line portion of a great circle
orthogonal orthogonal **-e Flächensysteme** orthogonal systems of surfaces **-e Kurvenscharen** orthogonal families of curves **-e Parallelprojection** orthogonal parallel projection
orthogonalisiert orthogonalized
Orthogonalität *f* orthogonality
Orthogonalsystem *n* **normiertes ~** orthonormal system
Orthographie *f* spelling, orthography
orthographisch orthographic
Orthohelium *n* orthohelium **-terme** *pl* orthohelium terms
ortho-klastisch orthoclastic **-kohlensäure** *f* orthocarbonic acid **-nitranilin** *n* orthonitraniline **-nitrophenol** *n* orthonitrophenol **-phthalsäure** *f* orthophthalic acid **-polarenverfahren** *n* orthopolar method **-säure** *f* ortho acid
orthoskopisch orthoscopic
Orthotoluidin *n* orthotoluidine, orthoaminotoluene
ortho-ständig in the o-position **-test** *m* orthotest **-tropie** *f* orthotropy
Ortho- und Parawasserstoff ortho- and parahydrogen
Ortho-xylidin *n* ortho-xylidine **-zustände** *pl* ortho states
örtlich local **~ begrenzen** to localize **-e magnetische Anziehung** local magnetic attraction **-e Empfindlichkeit** local sensitivity **-e Intensivierung** seeding **-e Korrosion** local corrosion or pitting **-e Mittelzeit** local mean time **-e Parallel-Gegenkopplung** shunt-type local feed-back **-e Serien-Gegenkopplung** series local feedback **-er Tagesgang** local diurnal variation
Örtlichkeit *f* locality
Ortlinghauskuppelung *f* Ortlinghaus clutch
Ortmißweisung *f* local declination
Orts-abhängigkeit *f* local variation **-amt** *n* local exchange, local central office **-angabe** *f* direction, address **-anruf** *m* local call **-ausbesserungsanstalt** *f* local repair shop **-batterie** *f* local battery, separate battery **-beamtin** *f* local operator **-beben** *n* local earthquake **-behörde** *f* municipal authorities, local authorities **-beschreibung** *f* topography **-besetzt** local busy, engaged on local call **-besetztsein** *n* local busy condition, engagement on local call **-besichtigung** *f* local inspection **-besprechung** *f* local operation
Ortsbestimmung *f* position fixing, position finding, localization, orientation, bearing (radio) **astronomische ~** astronomical fixing of position or position finding **photogrammetrische ~** photogrammetric fixing of position or position finding **topographische ~** topographical fixing of position or position finding
orts-beweglich portable **-bezirk** *m* local area **-biwak** *n* close billet **-brett** *n* edge board
Ortschaft *f* village, place
Ortscheit *n* doubletree
Orts-diagramm *n* locus diagram, circle diagram **-eindruck** *m* sensation of direction, sound locator **-empfang** *m* local reception, local-

station reception **-fehler** *m* geometric location error **-fernleitungswähler** *m* combination (local and toll) connector

Ortsfernsprechanlage *f* local telephone plant **~ mit mehreren Ämtern** multi-office exchange

Ortsfernsprech-netz *n* exchange area (single- or multi-office) **-verkehr** *m* local telephone traffic

ortsfest stationary, permanent, fixed **-er Motor** fixed engine **-e Zelle und Batterie** stationary cell or battery

Ortsfeststellung *f* fix **~ durch Funkgerät** radio fix (aviation)

Orts-funktion *f* position function **-gang** *m* local variation **-gebiet** *n* local area **-gebrauch** *m* local custom **-gedächtnis** *n* sense of direction

Ortsgedinge *n* bargain(ing) **ein ~ übernehmen** to take an end

Orts-generator *m* local oscillator **-gespräch** *n* local call, city conversation, local message **-gruppenumschalter** *m* local group switch **-kabel** *n* subscriber's cable

Orts-kennzahl *f* area code (tel.) **-koordinat** *m* space coordinate **-kundig** familiar with a locality or area

Ortskurve *f* polar frequency response locus **~ der schwarzen Strahler** Planckian locus

Orts-kurvenschreiber *m* complex-ration tracing receiver **-landung** *f* spot landing **-leitung** *f* **-linie** *f* local line **-mißweisung** *f* local declination, magnetic variation **-name** *m* place name

Ortsnetz *n* subscriber network, local telephone network, local plant, local mains **~ mit Handbetrieb** manual telephone area **~ mit mehreren Vermittlungsämtern** multioffice exchange area

Ortsnetz-bau *m* local system network **-übersicht** *f* statement of local plant

Orts-pfahl *m* corner stake **-platz** *m* local position **-postbezirk** *m* town postal district **-querschlag** *m* crosscut **-relais** *n* local relay **-ring** *m* local ring **-ruf** *m* local call

Orts-sender *m* local sender **-sternzeit** *f* local sidereal time **-stoß** *m* face, heading (tunnel) **-strom** *m* local current **-sucher** *m* direction finder **-stromkreis** *m* local circuit **-taste** *f* local control **-teilnehmer** *m* local subscriber

Ortstein *m* meadow or swamp ore, bog-iron ore

Ortstoff *m* parent material

ortsüblich customary in a place

Orts-umbenennung *f* change of place name **-unterkunft** *f* billet **-veränderlich** portable, movable **-veränderung** *f* locomotion **-veränderliche Antenne** movable antenna **-verbindung** *f* local conversation, local call **-verbindungsendwähler** *m* trunk-offering final selector **-verbindungskabel** *n* trunk cable

Ortsverbindungsleitung *f* trunk circuit, interoffice trunk, junction trunk **ankommende ~** incoming trunk **gemischt betriebene ~** two-way trunk **zweiadrige ~** two-wire trunk

Ortsverkehr *m* local traffic **Anruf im ~** local call

Orts-verkehrsbereich *m* local service area, local rate zone in large cities **-verzug** *m* mantelet (mil.) **-vermittlungsstelle** *f* local exchange **-vorstand** *m* local administrator, mayor

Ortszeit *f* local apparent time, local (civil) time **mittlere ~** Local Mean Time (LMT)

Ortszulage *f* locality allowance

Ortung *f* orientation, location, navigation **akustische ~** acoustic orientation, sound location **astronomische ~** celestial navigation **elektrisch-optische ~** electrical-optical location

Ortungs-anforderung *f* request for a bearing **-gerät** *n* training device for guns, orientation instrument, instrument for taking bearings, acoustic sounding gear, position-finding apparatus **-karte** *f* orientation chart, bearing chart (radio) **-kartentisch** *m* navigator's chart table **-kompaß** *m* navigation compass **-leuchtzeichen** *n* marker beacon (aviation) **-linie** *f* line of position **-punkt** *m* reference point, aiming point, landmark **-werte** *pl* present-position data, plot radar

Ortziegel *m* border tile

Öse *f* ear, lug, eye, hook, ring, eyelet, loop, staple

Ösen-antenne *f* radio loop **-bildung** *f* loop formation **-blatt** *n* tongue, lip, flange **-bolzen** *m* eyebolt **-einsetzmaschine** *f* eyeletting machine **-haken** *m* eye hook **-loch** *n* eyelet **-(rahmen)-antenne** *f* radio loop **-schlager** *m* fastener setter **-schraube** *f* eyebolt, screw eye **-spannschraube** *f* tightening eyebolt **-zange** *f* eyelet pliers

Öser *pl* eskers

Oskulation *f* osculation (geom.)

oskulierend osculatory

Osmiridium *n* osmi-iridium

Osmium *n* osmium **-legierung** *f* osmium alloy **-oxydul** *n* osmious oxide **-säure** *f* osmic acid **-tetroxyd** *n* osmium tetroxide, osmic anhydride

Osmometer *n* osmometer

Osmondit *m* osmondite

osmonditisch osmonditic

Osmondsche Kurve inverse-rate curve

Osmoregeneriervorrichtung *f* osmo-regulator

Osmose *f* osmosis **-apparat** *m* osmogene **-entzuckerung** *f* osmosis process

osmotisch osmotic **-er Druck** osmotic pressure

Osram Lichtwurflampen *pl* light arrow instruments

Osseinanlage *f* ossein plant

osteogen osteogenic

östliche Länge East longitude

Ost-punkt *m* east, point east **-see** *f* Baltic Sea **-seite** *f* foreside front **-wärts** eastward **-Westlinie** *f* circle of latitude, east-west line

Oszillation *f* oscillation

Oszillationsquantumszahl *f* vibrational quantum number

Oszillator *m* oscillator, generator **durchstimmbarer ~** coherent oscillator **gerader ~** dipole, straight oscillator **leitungsgesteuerter ~** line-controlled oscillator **piezoelektrischer ~** piezoelectric oscillator **~ für Löschen und HF-Vormagnetisierung** bias and erase oscillator

Oszillator-abgleich *m* oscillator alignment **-abstimmraum** *m* oscillator cavity **-eichung** *f* oscillator calibration **-frequenz** *f* oscillator frequency

oszillatorisch vibrational

Oszillator-kreis *m* oscillatory circuit **-röhre** *f* oscillator tube **-stufe** *f* frequency-change oscillator **-triode** *f* oscillator triode

oszillieren to oscillate

oszillierend oscillating, oscillatory **-er Öler**

oscillation lubricator **-er Zähler** oscillating meter
Oszillier-Intervall *m* interval of oscillation
Oszillogramm *n* oscillogram, oscillograph curve
Oszillograph *m* oscillograph, main presentation
Oszillographen-ausnahme *f* oscillograph record **-bild** *n* oscillogram **-relais** *n* oscillographic relay **-röhre** *f* oscillograph tube **-schleife** *f* oscillograph loop, oscillograph vibrator
oszillographisch oscillographic
Oszillometer *n* oscillometer
Oszilloskop *n* ondoscope oscilloscope
Otter *f* otter, paravane, viper
Otto-motor *m* Otto carburetor engine, internal-reciprocating combustion engine, spark-ignition engine **-verfahren** *n* Otto method or procedure
oval oval **-er Flansch** oval flange **-er Rumpf** fuselage of oval section, oval-shaped body **-er Stahlhammer** raising hammer
Ovale *f* oval (line)
oval-förmig oval-shaped **-haspel** *f* oval winch **-kaliber** *n* oval groove **-lautsprecher** *m* elliptical speaker **-röhrchen** *n* oval tube or tubing **-stich** *m* oval pass **-zirkel** *m* trammel
Oxaläther *m* ethyl oxalate
Oxalit *m* humboldtine
Oxalsäure *f* oxalic acid
oxalsaurer Kalk calcium oxalate
oxalsaures Ammon ammonium oxalate ~ **Blei** lead oxalate ~ **Eisenoxyd** ferric oxalate ~ **Natrium** sodium oxalate ~ **Nickel** nickel oxalate ~ **Zinnoxydul** stannous oxalate
Oxazinium *n* a type of oxazine salts
Oxhoft *n* hogshead
Oxidationsflamme *f* oxidizing flame
oxyazetylenisches Schneidbrennen oxyacetylene cutting
Oxyazetylenschweißung *f* oxyacetylene welding
Oxybitumen *n* oxybitumen
Oxychinolin *n* hydroxyquinoline
Oxyd *n* oxide **wasserhaltiges** ~ hydroxide
Oxydations-ätzen *n* oxidation discharges **-beständigkeit** *f* oxidation stability **-fähig** oxidizable **-flamme** *f* oxidizing flame **-halbleiter** *m* oxidation semi-conductor **-mittel** *n* oxidizing agent **-schlacke** *f* oxidizing slag **-stufe** *f* degree of oxidation **-vorgang** *m* oxidation process **-wirkung** *f* oxidizing action **-ziffer** *f* oxidation number
Oxyd-belag *m* oxide film **-beschlag** *m* oxide coating **-chlorid** *n* oxychloride **-einschluß** *m* oxide inclusion **-faden** *m* oxide(-coated) filament **-frei** free from oxides **-haltig** oxidic, containing oxide **-haut** *f* oxide skin, oxidation film **-häutchen** *n* oxide film
oxydierbar oxidizable **nicht** ~ inoxidizable
Oxydierbarkeit *f* oxidizability
oxydieren to oxidize
oxydierende Flamme oxidizing flame
Oxydierstoff *m* oxidizer added to rocket fuel
oxydiertes Pech oxidized asphalt
Oxydierung *f* oxidation, oxygenation
oxydisch oxide
Oxydkathode *f* oxide cathode, Wehnelt cathode, oxide-coated filament, dull-emitting cathode
Oxydkathodenröhre *f* tube with oxide-coated filament, dull emitter tube
oxydkeramisch oxide ceramic
oxydometrische Methode potentiometric oxidation method
oxyd-reich rich in oxide **-rot** *n* purple oxide of iron **-schicht** *f* oxide film or coating, layer of oxide **oxydüberzogen** oxide coated
Oxydul *n* protoxide, suboxide
Oxyfettsäure *f* oxysebacic acid
oxygenieren to oxygenate, oxygenize
Oxygenierung *f* oxygenation
Oxyketongruppe *f* oxyketone group
Oxysäuren *pl* hydroxy acids
Oxyschwefelsäure *f* oxysulfuric acid
Oxysiloxen *n* oxysiloxene
Oxytoluol *n* hydroxytoluene
Ozean *m* ocean **Atlantischer** ~ Atlantic Ocean **Stiller** ~ Pacific Ocean
Ozean-dampfer *m* ocean liner **-fahrt** *f* ocean trip, cruise **-flug** *m* ocean flight
ozeanisch oceanic, marine **-es Klima** marine climate
Ozean-kabel *n* ocean cable, submarine cable **-karte** *f* ocean chart or map
ozeanographische Abteilung oceanographic section
Ozeanseen *pl* seas, ocean swells **schwere** ~ heavy seas
Ozeanüberfliegung *f* transoceanic flight
Ozeanwetterdienst *m* sea meteorological service
Ozokerit *m* ozocerite
Ozon *n* ozone **-betrag** *m* ozone amount **-bildung** *f* ozone formation **-fest** ozoneproof **-festigkeit** *f* ozone resistance **-gehalt** *m* percentage or amount of ozone in the air **-haltig** ozoniferous
Ozonisator *m* ozonizer
ozonisieren to ozonize
Ozon-kontinua *pl* continuous spectra **-messer** *m* ozonometer
Ozonosphärenschall *m* ozonosphere sound
Ozon-radiosonde *f* ozone radiosonde **-reagenzpapier** *n* ozone-paper **-sauerstoff** *m* ozonized oxygen **-zerstörung** *f* ozone-annihilation

P

Paar *n* pair, couple **-bildung** *f* pairing, formation of pairs, drawing together of lines **-bildungsgrad** *m* creation rate **-erzeugung** *f* pairing
Paarigerscheinen von Linien pairing of lines (television)
Paarigkeit *f* pairing, formation of pairs
Paarigstehen der Zeilen twinning
Paar-konversion *f* pair conversion **-umwandlung** *f* pair conversion
Paarungs-abmaß *n* mating allowance **-honen** *n* match honing **-maß** *n* mating size **-messen** *n* match gauging

Paar-verseilung *f* twisted pair lay up **-verseiltes Kabel** paired (nonquadded) cable
paarweise in pairs ~ **gegossen** cast in pairs ~ **verbinden** conjugate
Pachometer-dickmesser *m* pachymeter
Pacht *f* tenure, lease, rent
pachten to lease, farm
Pächter *m* lessee, tenant, landholder, farmer
Pacht-hof *m* farm **-mieter** *m* lessee **-vertrag** *m* leasehold
Pack *n* rabble, pack, packet, bale, bundle
Packanordnung *f* packing
Päckchen *n* small parcel or package
Pack-dichte *f* recording density **-eis** *n* pack ice
packen to pack, grip, stow away
Pack-faschinen *pl* layers of fascines **-feile** *f* rough file **-gefäß** *n* bulk container **-hahn** *m* gland cock **-kiste** *f* packing case **-korb** *m* crate, hamper **-lack** *m* brown sealing wax **-lage** *f* base (of pavement) **-leinwand** *f* burlap **-maschine** *f* packing or casing machine **-material** *n* packing
Packpapier *n* packing or wrapping paper
Pack-pappe *f* straw boards **-pferd** *n* pack horse **-presse** *f* baling or packing press **-raum** *m* packing room **-riemen** *m* pack strap **-ring** *m* calking ring **-rolle** *f* guide pulley **-sattel** *m* packsaddle **-strick** *m* pack rope **-system** *n* package dyeing **-tasche** *f* saddlebag, baggage pouch **-termin** *m* final date of packing parachute **-tier** *n* pack animal, sumpter
Packung *f* packing, serving, oil retainer ring, gasket, stuffing, wrapping **die ~ einbringen** to insert the packing
Packungs-dichte *f* packing density (comp.) **-erscheinung** *f* packing phenomenon **-material** *n* packing material **-typfilter** *m* pack-type filter **-zieher** *m* packing worm
Pack-wagen *m* baggage car, van **-werk** *n* wattlework, fascine filling **-zettel** *m* packing slip or invoice
Paddelboot *n* canoe
paddeln to paddle
Paddelrührer *m* paddle mixer
paginieren to page
Paginier-maschine *f* paging machine **-rad** *n* numbering wheel
Paket *n* package, parcel, briquette, muck pile, pile, pack, set
paketieren to briquette, faggot, pile, packet
Paketier-ofenmann *m* dragger-out, hooker **-presse** *f* baling or packing press **-schweißstahl** *m* merchant bar, refined iron, No. 2 iron
paketiert packaged **-er Eisenschrott** baled scrap **-e Luppeneisenstäbe** muckbar pile, faggot, puddled-bar-iron pile
Paketierung *f* briquetting, faggoting, piling, muckbar piling ~ **auf Sturz** flat-and-edge-box piling **flachliegende** ~ flat-box piling, slab piling
Paketierverfahren *n* faggoting, piling
Paket-satz *m* piecework, composition of slips or packets **-schalter** *m* Yaxley type switch **-setzer** *m* piece hand, solid compositor **-stahl** *m* merchant bar, refined iron, No. 2 iron **-verschlußmarke** *f* parcelclosing stamp **-verschlußrolle** *f* adhesive tape **-walzung** *f* pack rolling
paläolithisch paleolithic
Paläomagnetismus *m* paleomagnetism
Paläontologie *f* paleontology
paläozoisch paleozoic
Palisade *f* palisade
Palisanderholz *n* rose wood
Palladium *n* palladium **-bromür** *n* palladous bromide **-chlorür** *n* palladous chloride **-chlorwasserstoff** *m* chloropalladic acid **-jodür** *n* palladous iodide **-legierung** *f* palladium alloy **-mohr** *m* palladium black **-oxydul** *n* palladous oxide **-oxydulnitrat** *n* palladous nitrate **-oxydulsalz** *n* palladous salt **wasserstoff** *m* palladium hydride
Pallado-chlorid *n* palladous chloride **-chlorwasserstoffsäure** *f* chloropalladous acid
Pallung *f* float of seaplane
palmen to haul hand over hand or hand over fist, palm in
Palminsäure *f* palmitic acid
Palmitin *n* palmitin **-säure** *f* palmitic acid
Palm-kernöl *n* palm oil **-lilie** *f* yucca **-lilienholz** *n* yucca (wood) **-nußöl** *n* coconut oil **-öl** *n* palm oil
Palstek *m* bowline-knot
Paltrockmühle *f* windmill for drainage
panchromatisch panchromatic
Paneel *n* panel
panellieren to panel
Panfilm *m* panchromatic film
Panik *f* panic **-zustand** *m* state of panic
pankratisch-er Kondenser *m* pancratic condenser **-es Objektiv** zoom lens
Panne *f* breakdown, (motor) trouble, (tire) puncture, mishap, accident **eine ~ haben** to have a breakdown or blowout or flat tire ~ **erleiden** to break down
Panneaubekleidungspapier *n* carriage panels
pannengesichert trouble-free
Panorama *n* panoramic picture, code for a type of radar set **-aufnahme** *f* panoramic photograph **-bild** *n* panoramic picture or view, panning shot **-empfänger** *m* (Radar) panoramic receiver **-gerät** *n* air-borne all-around search apparatus, radar landscape scanner **-kamera** *f* aerial camera, panoramic camera **-scheibe** *f* full-view windscreen
pantschen to adulterate, mix
Pantelephon *n* pantelephone
Pantograph *m* pantograph
Pantographen-hauptlager *n* pantograph main joint **-träger** *m* pantograph support
pantographieren to pantograph, reproduce by autograph
Pantokarenenwert *m* value of the respective locus of a center of buoyancy or lift
Pantometer *n* pantometer
pantoskopisch pantoscopic
Pantrapezverbindung *f* plotting communications, the telephone lines over which airplane plots are passed
Pantschmaschine *f* washing machine with beetles, beater
Panzer *m* armor plate, casing, steel plate lining, steel jacket, armor, shield, iron cladding
Panzeraderleitung *f* metal-cased conductor, metal-sheathed conductor **-aktinometer** *m* shielded actinometer **-auto** *n* armored car **-blech** *n* armor plate **-draht** *m* armored cable or wire **-dynamo** *m* iron-clad dynamo

Panzer-galvanometer *n* shielded galvanometer **-glas** *n* bulletproof glass **-holz** *n* metal-plated plywood **-kabel** *n* armored cable **-lage** *f* breaker (strip) **-schlauch** *m* (Sicherheitsschloß) armored hose (safety lock) **-schutzkasten** *m* armored housing

panzern to armor

Panzerplatte *f* armor plate, ironclad plate

Panzerplatten-bearbeitungsmaschine *f* machine for the working of armor plates **-herstellung** *f* armorplate manufacture **-walzwerk** *n* armorplate rolling mill, slabbing mill for rolling armor plate

Panzer-schale *f* armor plate **-scheibe** *f* bulletproof glass **-schild** *n* armor shield **-schlauch** *m* hose woven around with wire **-schnur** *f* armored cord **-schrank** *m* strongbox, safe **-schutz** *m* armor protection

Panzer-stahl *m* armor steel **-stärke** *f* thickness of armor **-transformator** *m* shell-type transformer, shielded transformer, ironclad transformer **-trommel** *f* cartridge drum

Panzerung *f* armor, armor plating, steel-plate lining, casing, shielding, screening, iron cladding

Panzerungsart *f* type of armoring

Panzer-ventil *n* armored valve **-verschluß** *m* (keep in) safe

Papageigrün *n* Paris green and a little chrome yellow

Papier *n* paper **abziehbares** ~ transfer paper **geripptes** ~ laid paper **geschöpftes** ~ handmade paper **getupftes** ~ marbled paper made by tipping **lichtempfindliches** ~ sensitized paper **paraffiniertes** ~ paraffined paper **zu** ~ **bringen** to write down

Papier für Anhänger tag paper ~ **mit Wasserlinien** laid paper ~ **ohne Wasserlinien** unlaid paper

Papier-abdruck *m* paper rubbing **-abfall** *m* waste paper, litter **-abreißvorrichtung** *f* papertearing device **-abschlußkabel** *n* paper terminal cable **-abschnitt** *m* off-cut **-andrückstange** *f* paper rod (typewriter) **-anschlag** *m* feed pile divider **-auflegeblech** *n* paper table

Papier-auslösehebel *m* paper release lever **-ausrüstung** *f* paper-finishing **-ausschläger** *m* paper cutter **-ausschuß** *m* paper refuse **-ausstattung** *f* paper fancy goods

Papierbahn *f* web of paper **-rückeinführer für Mehrfarbendruck** insetter

Papierband *n* endless paper band, paper tape **-führung** *f* carbon ribbon feed device **-zwischenlage** *f* intermediate paper strip layer

papier-bespanntes Modell *n* paper covered model **-bespannung** *f* paper covering **-blatt** *n* paper blank

Papierblattstärke *f* thickness of paper **doppelte** ~ two thicknesses of paper

Papier-bleikabel *n* paper insulated lead covered cables **-block** *m* paper block condenser **-brei** *m* paper pulp **-bremse** *f* web brake **-bügel** *m* paper bail **-chromatographie** *f* paper chromatography **-dichtung** *f* paper gasket **-einstellung** *f* adjustment of paper

Papier-feuchte *f* wetting bench **-filtereinsatz** *m* paper filter element **-flugmodell** *n* paper model **-fortschubmagnet** *m* paper feed magnet, spacing magnet **-führung** *f* paper guide

Papierführungs-hebel *m* paper-feeding lever **-rad** *n* paper-guide wheel **-walze** *f* paper feed rollers

Papier-gewebe *n* paper texture **-halbstoff** *m* paper half stuff **-handlung** *f* stationer's shop **-hohlraumkabel** *n* dry-core cable, air-space paper-core cable **-hülse** *f* paper sleeve or tube **-isolierter Draht** paper covered wire **-kabel** *n* paper cable, dry-core cable, paper-insulated cable **-kalander** *m* paper mangle **-kohle** *f* paper coal, dark-brown laminated subbituminous coal, papyraceous lignite **-kordel** *f* paper string **-lauf** *m* run of the paper web **-laufrichtung** *f* machine direction **-locher** *m* perforator **-macherfilz** *m* paper felt **-maché** *n* papier-mâché

Papiermaschinen-ausschuß *m* machine broke, refuse paper **-öl** *n* paper-machine oil

Papier-masse *f* paper pulp **-mühle** *f* paper mill **-musterbogen** *m* sample sheet **-nachschub** *m* paper feed **-pergament** *n* parchment paper **-reißsicherung** *f* web break detector **-rohr** *n* paper tube **-röhrchen** *n* paper sleeve, paper jointing tube **-rolle** *f* web of paper, paper roll

Papierrollen-halter *m* tape roll holder **-schneidemaschine** *f* paper reel cutter **-träger** *m* tape wheel

Papier-sack *m* paper bag **-satinieranstalt** *f* paper-glazing works **-schirting** *f* cloth centered (paper) **-schlange** *f* coiled-up paper ribbon **-schlauch** *m* paper bag (for tamping)

Papierschlitten *m* paper carriage **-rückführung** *f* carriage return

Papier-schneidemesser *n* paper-cutting knife **-schnitzel** *n* clipping **-spule** *f* paper bobbin **-stampfe** *f* paper stamp **-stanzen** *n* paper cutting **-stärkemesser** *m* paper thickness gauge **-staude** *f* papyrus **-stereotypie** *f* paper stereo process **-stramin** *m* canvas for embroidery **-strang** *m* web of paper

Papierstreifen *m* paper tape, paper slip, strip of paper, teleprinter paper tape **gelochter** ~ perforated paper tape

Papierstreifen-rolle *f* chart roll, paper web **-verfahren** *n* method of evaluation of aerial photographs

Papier-sudler *m* bungler or dauber of paper **-teig** *m* papier-mâché **-transportwalzen** *pl* paper feed rollers **-trommel** *f* paper drum **-überseite** *f* felt side (paper mfg.) **-umhüllung** *f*, **-umwicklung** *f* paper wrapping **-veredelung** *f* paper finishing, conversion of paper **-vorschub** *m* paper feed(ing), chart speed, paper throw **-wagen** *m* carriage

Papierwaren *pl* paper goods, stationery **-handlung** *f* stationer's shop

Papier-wäsche *f* paper linen **-watte** *f* cellucotton **-wickelkondensator** *m* paper condenser **-wolf** *m* paper shredder **-zeichen** *n* token, water-mark **-zerfaserer** *m* cone breaker

Papillottenpapier *n* curling paper

Papp *m* paste, pap **-arbeit** *f* pasteboard work **-band** *m* book in boards **-bogen** *m* sheet of pasteboard or cardboard **-dach** *n* waterproofpaper roof **-deckel** *m* boards, pasteboards, paperboard, carton, cardboard **-druckware** *f* paste resist printed goods

Pappe *f* cardboard, board, millboard, pulp sheet, pasteboard, paperboard, carton **ge-**

formte ~ millboard
Pappeaufzug *m* cardboard lining
Pappel *f* poplar **-holz** *n* poplar (wood)
pappen to paste, work in paste
Pappen-abschärfmaschine *f* chamfering machine for pasteboard **-art** *f* pasteboard **-beklebemaschine** *f* cardboard lining machine **-biegemaschine** *f* cardboard-bending machine **-form** *f* board mold **-guß** *m* pasteboard casting, pressure-cast carton or cardboard (using paper pulp) **-gußmaschine** *f* pasteboard-casting machine **-kalander** *m* cardboard calenders **-satiniermaschine** *f* cardboard calenders
Papp-hülse *f* cardboard ferrule **-hülsenabstechmaschine** *f* cardboard tube cutting machine
pappig pasty, sticky
Papp-karte *f* pasteboard card **-karton** *m* cardboard box **-kreisschere** *f* circular cardboard cutter **-masche** *n* papier-mâché **-mater** *f* cardboard matrix **-messer** *n* paste knife **-scheibe** *f* cardboard washer (disc.) **-schere** *f* shears **-schnitzel** *pl* diced resin board **-verband** *m* starch or paste dressing **-weiß** *n* pigment white
Papyrin *n* parchment paper
Papyrolin *n* cloth-centered paper
Paraband *n* rubber tape **reines** ~ pure rubber tape
Parabel *f* parabola **-fachwerkträger** *m* inverted parabolic superstructure **-förmig** parabolic
parabolisch parabolic ~ **gekrümmt** curved in a parabola **-e Krümmung** parabolic curvature **-e Kurve** parabolic line **-er Reflektor** parabolic reflector
Parabolkonus *m* para-curve cone
Paraboloid *n* paraboloid
Parabol-reflektor *m*, **-spiegel** *m* parabolic mirror or reflector
Parachor von Treibstoffen parachor of fuels
parachsial paraxial
Paradichlorbenzol *n* paradichlorbenzene
Paradoxon *n* paradox
Paraffin *n* paraffin (wax), wax ~ **für Arzneigebrauch** medicinal wax ~ **für Blechbüchsen** wax for tin cans ~ **für Bügeleisen** wax for irons ~ **für elektrische Isolierung** insulating wax ~ **für Kaugummi** wax for chewing gum ~ **für Kerzenfabrikanten** wax for candle manufacturers ~ **für Streichhölzer** wax for matches ~ **für Wascher** wax for bleacher ~ **für Zündhölzchen** wax for matches
Paraffinbad *n* paraffin bath
paraffinfeste Farbe *f* paraffin-resistant color
paraffinhaltig containing paraffin **-es Destillat** wax distillate **-er Rückstand** wax tailings
paraffinieren to paraffin
paraffinisch paraffinic **-es Rohöl** paraffin-base crude oil
Paraffin-kohlenwasserstoffe *m pl* paraffinic hydrocarbons **-kristallisator** *m* paraffin crystallizer **-öl** *n* kerosene, paraffin oil, (fuel oil) lamp oil **-öldestillat** *n* paraffin distillate **-reihe** *f* paraffin series **-rohpapier** *n* paraffin-waxed paper (base) **-schuppe** *f* paraffin scale
Para-formaldehyd *n* paraformaldehyde, trioxymethylene **-gummischlauch** *m* black rubber tubing **-kresol** *n* paracresol
Paraldehyd *n* paraldehyde
Paralketon *n* paralketon
parallaktisch parallactic ~ **montiertes Fernrohr** equatorially mounted telescope
Parallaxe *f* parallax **tägliche** ~ diurnal or geocentric parallax
Parallaxen-bewegung *f* parallactic movement, movement in depth **-fehler** *m* parallax error **-lineal** *n* parallax rule or ruler **-schlitten** *m* parallax slide
parallaxfreier Spiegel anti-parallax mirror
parallel parallel, equidistant, paralleling ~ **ausrichten** to set parallel ~ **laufen** to run parallel ~ **zu** in parallel with, across **gleichsinnig** ~ parallel aiding **-e Ein- und Ausgabe** parallel access **-e Geraden** parallel lines **-es Lichtstrahlenbüschel** beam or pencil of parallel light
Parallel-absperrschieber *m* parallel-faced sluice valve **-anreißer** *pl* universal surface gauges **-ausdrücken** *n* line-a-type printing **-drahtleitung** *f* parallel-wire line **-drahtsperrleitung** *f* parallel-wire stop line
Parallelen-axiom *n* axiom of parallels **-zug** *m* parallel trace of lines
Parallel-betrieb *m* parallel operation **-bewegung** *f* parallel motion **-drahtleitung** *f* balanced feeder **-endmaß** *n* standard reference disk, gauge block, end block, end measuring block or rod, slip gauge **-epipedon** *n* parallelepiped, parallelepipedon
Parallel-fachwerkträger *m* reinforced parallel-truss superstructure **-feilkloben** *m* parallel hand vise **-fläche** *f* parallel surface **-flug** *m* parallel flight **-führung** *f* parallel construction
parallelgeschaltet in parallel (with), paralleled, shunted (across) **-es Helligkeitssignal** bypass monochrome signal **-er Widerstand** shunt resistance
parallelgeschichtet parallel laminated
Parallelimpedanz *f* leak impedance, shunt impedance **-klinke** *f* branching, parallel or duplicate jack **-kondensator** *m* shunting condenser
Parallelismus *m*, **Parallelität** *f* parallelism
Parallel-klinke *f* bridging jack **-kondensator** *m* bypass, bridging, or shunting condenser **-kreis** *m* parallel circuit, parallel of latitude (geog.), parallel circle, parallel **-lauf** *m* concurrent flow **-leistungsschwingkreis** *m* parallel-rod tank circuit **-lineal** *n* parallel ruler **-maße** *pl* marking gauges, precision gauge blocks **-nietung** *f* chain riveting
Parallelogramm *n* parallelogram ~ **der Geschwindigkeiten** parallelogram of velocities **schiefwinkliges** ~ rhomboid, oblique parallelogram **Zeissches** ~ Zeiss parallelogram
Parallel-ohmmethode *f* shunted-telephone method, parallel ohm method **-programmlauf** *m* time-sharing data processing **-projektion** *f* parallel projection **-recheneinheit** parallel arithmetic unit **-reißer** *m* surface gauge **-resonanz** *f* parallel resonance, antiresonance **-resonanzkreis** *m* parallel, multiple, branched resonant circuit, rejector circuit **-riß** *m* parallel projection **-röhrenmodulation** *f* choke modulation, Heising or constant-current modulation
parallelschalten to join or connect in parallel, shunt (across), tee together
Parallelschalter multiple switch
Parallelschaltung *f* parallel connection, multiple connection, shunt connection or arrangement,

parallel circuit, paralleling ~ **von Gleichrichtern** shunt rectifier circuit
Parallel-schere *f* guillotine shears **-schieber** *m* double-disk parallel-gate valves **-schneidenmeißel** *m* bit with parallel cutting edges **-schraub(en)stock** *m* parallel vise **-schreibfeder** *f* double-pointed pen **-schwingkreis** *m* parallel-resonant circuit **-serienkonverter** *m* dynamiciser
Parallel-speisung *f* parallel feeding, shunt feed **-sperrschichttransistor** planar surface barrier transistor **-spule** *f* bridging coil **-staboszillator** parallel-rod oscillator **-stabtopfkreis** *m* parallel-rod tank circuit **-stellen** to set parallel **-stellung** *f* parallel orientation or alignment **-strahlenbündel** *n* beam of light, pencil of rays **-strecke** *f* air heading (min.), parallel stretch
Parallelstrom *m* parallel flow **-kataraktkondensator** *m* parallel-flow cataract condenser
Parallel-struktur *f* parallel bedding **-träger** *m* braced girder **-umlauf** *m* parallel flow
Parallel- und Reiheneinstellung *f* shunt and series
Parallel-verlauf *m* parallelism **-verschiebung** *f* parallel gliding planes, translation, translatory motion or shift **-verstellung** *f* parallel adjustment **-versuch** *m* parallel experiment, duplicate determination, check-up experiment **-wandig** parallel-sided **-weg** *m* bypath, by-pass, shunt, path **-werk** *n* longitudinal dike **-widerstand** *m* parallel resistance, shunt resistance **-zeilendrucker** *m* line-at-a-time printer **-zeilendüse** *f* parallel row atomizer plate
Parallonrechner *m* parallax corrector
Paralysator *m* anticatalyst
paramagnetisch paramagnetic **-e Kernresonanz** nuclear paramagnetic resonance **-er Stoff** paramagnetic substance
Paramagnetismus *m* paramagnetism
Parameter *m* parameter ~ **der Lückenverteilung** parameter of gap length distribution
Parameterstellung *f* parametric representation
parametrischer Oszillator parametron
Parametron *n* parametron
paramorph paramorphic
Paramorphose *f* paramorphosis
parangonieren to align
Paraphasenverstärker *m* paraphase amplifier
Parapositronium *n* parapositronium
Pararosolsäure *f* pararosolic acid, aurin
Pararot *n* para red
parasitär parasitic
Parasitär-echos *pl* running rabbits **-frequenz** *f* (Radar), frequency splitting
Parasol *n* parasol, parasol wing of monoplane
Parastellung *f* para position
Paratoluidin *n* paratoluidine
Paraxialbahn *f* paraxial orbit
parazentrisch paracentric
Parazustand *m* para state
Pardun *n*, **Pardune** *f* span rope, guy wire or cable backstay
Pargasit *m* amphibole, hornblende
Parhelion *n* parhelion, sundog
Parhelium *n* para-helium, parhelium
pari par **Aktien stehen auf** ~ shares are at par
parieren to obey, parry, halt
Parierstange *f* bayonet guard
parierte Flugbewegung *f* checked manoeuvre
Pari-Goldwert *m* mint par rate of exchange
Pariser Blau *n* prussian blue
Pariser Rot crocus (polishing powder)
Parität *f* equality, parity
paritätisch on an equal footing, at par
Paritäts-bit *n* parity bit **-erhaltung** *f* parity conservation **-kontrolle** *f* parity check (comput) **-prüfung** *f* parity check (info proc.) **-ziffer** *f* parity digit
Pariwert *m* par value
Park *m* park, dump, depot, distributing point
Parkerisieren *n* Parkerizing
parkern (Rostschutz), to parker(ize)
Parker-Verfahren *n* Parker (rustproofing) process
Parkett *n* parquet, parquetry, inlaid floor **-abhobeln** *n* floor dressing **-boden** *m* inlaid floor
Parkettierungsproblem *n* tiling problem
Parkettstäbe *pl* strip flooring **-tafeln** *pl* parquetry
parkieren to park
Parkiermesser *n* park meter
Park-platz *m* park, parking lot **-verbot** *n* no parking
Parlamentär *m* bearer of a flag of truce, parliamentary
PAR-Radar *n* precision approach radar (PAR)
Parry-Trichter *m* bell-and-hopper arrangement **-Verschluß** *m* Parry closure, Parry cup-and-cone arrangement, Parry bell-and-hopper arrangement
Parsonsit *m* parsonsite
Partei *f* party, faction
Partial-bruchregel *f* partial fraction rule **-bruchzerlegung** *f* decomposition to partial fractions **-druck** *m* partial pressure **-funke** *m* partial discharge **-schwingung** *f* partial oscillation **-tide** *f* partial tide
Partie *f* population (statistics), batch, shipment **nasse** ~ wet end (paper tech.)
partiell partial ~ **Abgeleitete** partial derivative **-e Niveaubreite** *f* partial width **-e Veränderung** *f* fractional change **-e Verfallskonstante** *f* partial disintegration constant
Partieware *f* off-standard goods
Partikel *f* particle
Partikeldichte *f* particle density
parzellarisch in lots or parcels (surv.), segmented (of fiber structures)
Parzelle *f* lot, parcel, allotment, compartment
Parzellenvermessung *f* survey of parcels of land
parzellieren to parcel (out)
Pascal-sche Gerade Pascal's straight line **-sches Gesetz** Pascal's law
Paschen-Back-Verwandlung *f* Paschen-Back effect (magneto-optical phenomenon)
Paspel *m* braid
Paß *m* pass, permit, passport
Passage *f* draft, pass **-instrument** *n* transit
Passagier *m* passenger **-dampfer** *m* passenger steamer **-flug** *m* passenger flight **-flugzeug** *n* passenger plane **-kilometer** *m* passenger kilometer **-liste** *f* passenger list **-satz** *m* passenger rate **-schiff** *n* passenger ship
Passameter *n* passometer
Paßarbeit *f* fitting work
Passat-gebiet *n* trade-wind zone **-wind** *m* trade wind, geostrophic wind **-zone** *f* trade-wind zone
Paß-blech *n* shim **-bolzen** *m* fitted or reamed bolt, toggle bolt **-differenz** *f* register difference

(print.) **-dorn** *m* setting plug **-einheit** *f* unit of fit **-einsatz** *m* sleeve socket **-elemente** *pl* mating features

passen to fit, be suitable, match, suit, apply, adjust **aufeinander ~** to match **schlecht ~** to misfit

passend einrichten to accomodate **~ machen** to match

passend suitable, convenient, proper, relevant, pertinent, opposite to, appropriate

Passer *m* compass

Paß-fähigkeit *f* conformability **-feder** *f* adjusting spring

Paßfläche *f* fitting area, seat, surface where two parts fit together or engage (snugly) **~ einer sich nicht drehenden Lagerung** static bearing surface

Paß-form *f* skeleton form **-genauigkeit** *f* accuracy of fit **-gerecht** precise fitting **-glas** *n* graduated glass or jar

passieren to happen, occur

Passier-gewicht *n* minimum weight **-rohr** *n* indicating plug, inside gauge

Passigdrehbank *f* lathe for eccentric turning

Passimeter *n* pedometer, indicating plug gauge, inside gauge

passiv passive **-e Störung** passive jamming

Passivierung *f* passivation

Passivität *f* passivity, inertness

Passivum *n* liability

Paß-karte *f* chart, sea chart, hydrographical map **-kerbstift** *m* edged adjusting pin **-lager** *n* lapped bearing **-lehre** *f* gauge, jig, template **-leiste** *f* tongue, nesting strap **-loch** *n* reamed hole **-marke** *f* adjusting mark (in measuring apparatus) **-maß** *n* tolerance on fit **-muster** *n* fitted pattern

Paß-punkt *m* point of minor control **-ring** *m* gauge ring (elec.) **-rohr** *n* adapting piece, make-up piece **-scheibe** *f* shim **-schiene** *f* junction rail **-schraube** *f* tight-fit screw, fitted or reamed bolt **-sitz** *m* press fit, snug fit, seat **-stelle** *f* matching parts **-stift** *m* prisoner, set pin, dowel pin, fitting or adjusting pin **-streifen** *m* nesting strip

Paßstück *n* adjusting or fitting piece **hölzernes ~** wood capping

Paßtoleranz *f* tolerance on fit

Passung *f* fit **~ mit teilweiser Überschneidung der Toleranzfelder** transition fit **~ mit Übermaß** interference fit

Passungen *pl* close-tolerance work

Passungs-einheit *f* tolerance unit **-genau gefertigt** made to precision limit

Passungsliste *f* schedule of fits or of limits, table of clearances and fits **~ für Wartungszwecke** service fits and clearance chart

Passungs-maß *n* master dimension **-mechanik** *f* mechanics of fits **-richtlinien** *pl* fitting practice **-rost** *m* fretting corrosion (metal), galling **-system** *n* system of fits

Paß-werk *n* register device **-zeichen** *n* registering mark **-zwang** *m* compulsory passport system

Paste *f* paste **-kathode** *f* pasted cathode

Pastell *n* pastel **-farbig** pastel **-stift** *m* crayon

pastenartig pasty

Pasten-aufkohlen *n* paste carburizing **-farbe** *f* paste paint

pastenförmig pasty **-es Dichtungsmittel** gasket paste

Pasten-verformer *m* paste former **-zerstäubungstrockner** *m* paste atomizer

pasteurisieren to pasteurize

Pasteurisiergeschmack *m* bread or cooked or steam taste

pastieren to paste

pastierte Platte mass-type plate

Pastille *f* tablet, lozenge, button, bead

pastös pasty, soft

Patent *n* officer's commission, patent, broadside, placard **ein ~ anmelden oder beantragen** to apply for a patent **ein ~ erwirken für . . .**, to secure a patent for . . . **ein ~ nehmen** to take out a patent **~ ist erteilt worden** patent has been granted **abgelaufenes ~** expired patent **angemeldetes ~** patent applied for, filed patent, pending patent **schwebendes ~** pending patent **verfallenes ~** void patent

Patent-amt *n* patent office **-anmaßung** *f* usurpation of patent rights **-anmelder** *m* claimant

Patentanmeldung *f* patent application **~ von gewöhnlichem Umfang** straightforward patent application **eine ~ einreichen** to file a patent application

Patent-anspruch *m* claim (of the patent) **-anspruchsaufgabe** *f* (Patentanmeldung) abandonment **-anwalt** *m* patent attorney

Patentbeschreibung *f* patent specification **vorläufige ~** provisional specification

Patent-brief *m* letters patent **-bureau** *n* patent office **-dauer** *f* life of a patent, continuance of a patent **-draht** *m* patented steel wire **-erlöschung** *f* expiration or annulment of a patent **-erteilung** *f* patent grant, allowance, grant, or issue of letters patent **-fähig** patentable **-gebühr** *f* patent fee, patent tax **-gesetz** *n* patent law, patent code, patent statutes **-gesuch** *n* patent application **-grün** *n* Paris green

Patentgültigkeit anfechten to challenge validity of a patent

patentierbar patentable

patentieren to patent

Patentieren *n* patening

patentiert patent(ed), commissioned **im In- und Auslande ~** patented at home and abroad **~ vom** protected by patent from

Patent-inhaber *m* patentee, grantee, holder of letters patent **-jahresgebühr** *f* patent-renewal fee **-klage** *f* patent suit, patent action **-log** *n* patent log **-recht** *n* patent right **-register** *n*, **-rolle** *f* patent rolls **-salz** *n* antimony ammonium fluoride **-schrift** *f* patent, patent specification **-streit** *m* patent action, patent litigation **-unteranspruch** *m* subclaim of a patent **-untersuchung** *f* patent survey

Patent-urkunde *f* patent letter **-verlängerung** *f* renewal of a patent **-verlängerungsgebühr** *f* patent-renewal fee **-verletzend** patent infringing **-verletzung** *f* infringement of a patent **-verletzungsklage** *f* action or suit for infringement of patent rights **-verschluß** *m* patent closure **-vorwegnahme** *f* anticipation, anticipatory reference **-zeichnung** *f* patent-office drawing **-zement** *m* Roman cement, Parker's cement

Patera-Prozeß *m* Patera (hyposulfite-leaching) process

Paternoster *n* endless chain or bucket belt, pump, conveyer **-aufzug** *m* conveyer type elevator **-band** *n* chaplet hinge **-gebläse** *n* rosary or chain trompe **-schöpfwerk** *n* paternoster bailing work **-werk** *n* chain pump
patinieren to patinate (coat with patina)
Patrize *f* upper die, top die, punch, stamp (of various machines), male, tongued, negative collar
Patrizenwalze *f* former roll or tongue, closer roll, forming roll
Patrone *f* cartridge (fixed ammunition), semi-fixed shell, round of ammunition, die, stencil, pattern, punch, stamp (of various machines), mandrel, point paper design
Patronen-anlasser *m* cartridge starter **-anlaßvorrichtung** *f* breech starting mechanism **-auswerfer** *m* ejector **-auszieher** *m* extractor **-falzerin** *f* pattern folder **-filzpfropfen** *m* cartridge wad **-führungsleiste** *f* bolt guide **-gurt** *m* cartridge belt, bandoleer, ammunition belt **-halter** *m* extractor **-hebel** *m* loading mechanism lever
Patronen-hülse *f* cartridge case **-hülsenpapier** *n* ammunition papers **-kasten** *m* ammunition box **-korb** *m* ammunition basket **-lager** *n* cartridge chamber **-packmaschine** *f* cartridge packer **-papier** *n* cartridge papers, pattern paper, drafting paper **-rahmen** *m* clip, gun clip **-raum** *m* cartridge container **-reihe** *f* string of cartridges
Patronen-schleuse *f* cartridge cylinder **-sicherung** *f* cartridge fuse, plug-type cutout **-spannfutter** *n* collet chuck **-stöpsel** *m* plug fuse **-tasche** *f* cartridge pouch **-träger** *m* cartridge carrier **-trägerhebel** *m* belt-feed lever **-zugstempel** *m* shell-drawing die
patronieren to design, draft
Patrouillenschiff *n* patrol boat
Pattinsonieranstalt *f* crystallization works
pattinsonieren to pattinsonize, work at Pattinson's method
Pauke *f* bass drum, cymbal, kettledrum
Paukenstimmschlüssel *m* kettledrum wrench
Pauli-Prinzip *n* exclusion principle
Paulit *m* hypersthene
Pausapparat *m* copying apparatus
Pauschal-akkord *m* lump-sum contract **-gebühr** *f* flat rate
Pauschalgebühren-anschluß *m* flat-rate subscription **-tarif** *m* flat-rate tariff, bulk tariff **-teilnehmer** *m* flat-rate subscriber
Pauschal-summe *f* lump sum **-tarif** *m* flat-rate tariff
pauschen to swell, refine
Pauschherd *m* refining plate, sloping-hearth-type liquating furnace with a bed of glowing charcoal
Pauscht *m* post (a pile of sheets of wet pulp)
Pauschtarif *m* bulk tariff
Pause *f* interruption, pause, interval, stop, rest, recess, tracing, print, copy, calking, counter-drawing, pricked drawing, space, intermission **eine ~ einlegen** to pause **in Pausen** intermittently
pausen to trace, calk, pounce, duplicate
Pausen-fehler *m* interval error **-freies Signal** sequence signal
pausenlos without intervals, uninterruptedly, continuous
Pausenschritt *m* spacing pulse **-signalanlage** *f* break signaling system **-welle** *f* spacing wave **-zeichen** *n* interval signal **-zwischenruf** *m* listening through
pausfähig suitable for tracing or copy **-e Kopie** reproducible copy
pausieren to interrupt work
pausierend inactive **-er Betrieb** *m* intermittend operation
Paus-leinen *n*, **-leinwand** *f* tracing cloth **-papier** *n* tracing paper, calking paper, blue- or brown-print paper **-zeichnung** *f* duplicate, calking, counterdrawing
Pawsey-Symmetriertransformator *m* Pawsey stub
PeCe-Faser *f* polyvinyl chloride fiber, synthetic textile fiber
Pech *n* pitch, drill **~ für wasserdichte Anlagen** waterproofing asphalt **~ für Dachwerk** roofing asphalt **~ für Isolation** insulating asphalt **~ für das Pflastern der Straßen** paving asphalt **~ für die Preßkohlenindustrie** briquetting asphalt **~ für Straßenbau** road asphalt **mit Dampf behandeltes ~** steam-treated asphalt
Pech-apparat *m* pitching apparatus **-artig** pitchy **-automat** *m* automatic pitching machine
Pech-blende *f* pitchblende **-blendelager** *n* pitchblende deposit
pechen to pitch, pay
Pech-gang *m* asphalt rock **-granat** *m* colophonite
pechhaltig bituminous **-es Gestein** bituminous rock **-e Kohle** bituminous coal **-er Sand** bituminous sand **-er Schiefer** bituminous shale
Pech-harz *n* tar **-kohle** *f* pitch coal, jet **-koks** *m* pitch coke **-maschine** *f* pitching machine **-rückstand** *m* pitch residue **-schale** *f* pitch tool **-schwarz** jet-black, pitch-black **-spritzapparat** *m* jet-pitching or pitch-spraying apparatus **-stein** *m* pitchstone **-steinkohle** *f* pitch coal **-torf** *m* black fuel peat **-überzug** *m* pitch coat **-uran** *n* pitchblende
Pedal *n* pedal **-auflage** *f* foot-pedal pad **-koppler** *m* coupler **-welle** *f* pedal pin
pedantisch genau meticulous
Peddig *n* pith of rattan
Pegel *m* gauge, rod, depth indicator, tide gauge, water-depth gauge, watermark post, level, transmission level, gain **~ der Weißmodulation** level of white modulation **~ langsam anheben und halten** to fade up **mittlerer ~** mean power level **relativer ~** transmission level
Pegel-abweichung *f* level deviation **-anzeiger** *m* transmission level indicator **-ausgleich** *m* equalizing levels, level equalizer **-ausgleicher** *m* level compensator **-beziehung** *f* relationship between gauge readings at different stations **-bildgerät** *n* T.M.S. (transmission measuring set) **-diagramm** *n* level diagram **-eichung** *f* calibration **-höhe** *f* water gauge level
Pegel-latte *f* gauge, scale, water-level gauge **-linie** *f* (transmission) level diagram, hypsogram **-loch** *n* gauge rod hole **-messer** *m* T.M.S. (transmission measuring set), transmission level meter, hypsometer **-meßplatz** *m* level measuring set-up **-messung** *f* level measurement **-prüfer** *m* level testing equipment
Pegelregler *m* level control **automatischer ~**

automatic volume control

Pegel-schaulinie *f* (transmission) level diagram **-schlüssel** *m* rating curve for gauge (discharge plotted against gauge reading) **-schreiber** *m* level recorder, recording transmission measuring set **-schwankung** *f* level fluctuation **-sender** *m* level oscillator **-stab** *m* dipstick **-stabilisierung** *f* synchronization stretcher **-strom** *m* pilot current or carrier

Pegelung *f* level or volume regulation

Pegelzeiger *m* direct-reading (transmission) measuring set

Pegmatit *m* graphic granite or stone, pegmatite **-gang** *m* pegmatite vein

Pegmatolit *m* pegmatolite

Pehamesser *m* (PH-Messer) pH meter

Peil *m* water-mark post, water gauge, marker, floater, position direction finding **-abschnitt** *m* sector **-anlage** *f* direction-finding installation or facility **-antenne** *f* direction-finding antenna **-antennensystem** *n* directional antenna system

Peil-antrieb *m* frame drive, loop drive **-aufsatz** *m* pelorus, bearing plate of direction finder **-automat** *m* automatic direction finder **-bereich** *m* detection range **-berichtigungskurve** *f* deviation curve **-boot** *n* mark, beacon boat **-deck** *n* compass platform, upper deck **-dienst** *m* radio direction finding service **-drehrahmenanlage** *f* D. F. loop antenna **-einrichtung** *f* bearing finder **-empfänger** *m* directional receiver, direction finder (receiver)

peilen to take bearings, intercept, measure, sound, gauge, bear, find direction, take a fix, take sun's altitude **in eins ~** to be in transit

Peilen *n* direction finding, boring sounding (by pole)

Peiler *m* direction finder, goniometer **direkt anzeigender ~** direct-reading direction finder **selbstanzeigender ~** automatic direction finder, direct-reading direction finder **~ mit Suchspule** search coil direction finder

Peil-fadenaufroller *m* bearing string roll **-fehler** *m* direction-finding error, bearing error, distortion of bearing **-feld** *n* bearing field **-flugleiter** *m* direction-finder ground-station controller

Peilfunk *m* radio direction finding

Peilfunk-anlage *f* direction-finding plant **-betriebsstelle** *f* direction-finder station **-dienst** *m* direction-finding service **-einrichtung** *f* (radio) direction finder **-empfänger** *m* direction finder, direction-finding receiver, radio compass

Peilfunker *m* direction-finder or DF operator

Peilfunker-sender *m* direction-finding transmitter **-stelle** *f* direction-finding or DF station

Peil-genauigkeit *f* bearing accuracy **-gerade** *f* plumb

Peilgerät *n* homing device, direction finder **~ mit Kathodenstrahlrohranzeige** (HF) cathode ray HF/DF

Peil-glas *n* gauge glass **-hauptstelle** *f* main or central direction-finder station, main control direction-finder station (of an air-communication safety district) **-haus** *n* direction-finder station **-höhe** *f* altitude of bearing **-kompaß** *m* bearing or azimuth compass, variation compass, direction-finder compass, navigator's compass **-korrektur** *f* (selbsttätige) maintenance of true bearing (rdr) **-kraftwagen** *m* radio-beacon or direction-finder truck

Peil-kurve *f* space pattern, directional diagram **-leitstelle** *f* main or central direction-finding or DF station, main control direction-finder station (of an air-communication safety district) **-leitung** *f* fuel gauge **-linie** *f* line of bearing, sounding lead **-maximum** *n* position of maximum signal **-methode** *f* sounding or gauging method **-minimum** *n* position of minimum signal (in direction finder) **-nebenstelle** *f* auxiliary or subsidiary direction-finder station, associated direction-finder ground station, DF sub-station or slave station **-phase** *f* bearing phase **-platz** *m* DF site

Peilpunktmarke, schwarze ~ black dot, black mark (on scale)

Peilrahmen *m* directional loop antenna for radio, compass, direction-finding loop, direction-finder frame **-antrieb** *m* driving mechanism of loop antenna of direction finder **-schaft** *f* shaft of frame antenna for direction finder

Peilrichtung *f* direction bearing, direct course to transmitter or beacon **quer zur ~ geneigt** transverse to direction bearing

Peil-rohr *n* temperature tube, gauge pipe, sounding pipe, dip tube **-rose** *f* direction-finder dial **-schärfe** *f* sharpness of resonance gauge **-scheibe** *f* azimuth instrument **-schwankungen** *pl* bearing fluctuations

Peilseite *f* bearing sense **eindeutige ~** absolute direction

Peil-seiteschalter *m* bearing-sense switch, direction-finding sense switch, sense-finding switch **-sender** *m* directional transmitter **-spannung** *f* directional-signal potential **-spule** *f* direction-finder coil **-stab** *m* dip stock, measuring, gauging rod, gauge stick or rod, measuring stick, dip stick **-stabkappe** *f* gauge-rod cap **-stange** *f* sounding pole **-station** *f*, **stelle** *f* direction-finder station or post, beam station **-stock** *m* sounding rod

Peilstrahl *m* radio bearing beam, beacon course **-schwankung** *f*, **-wanderung** *f* variation in apparent bearing **-wegablenkung** *f* distortion of bearing, deviation due to diurnal or seasonal factors

Peil-tabelle *f* bearing chart **-tafel** *f* plane table (survey) **-tischanlage** *f* intersection table (radio) **-treue Bodenwelle** ground wave resulting in undistorted bearing **-turm** *m* radio-range beacon, radio amateur **-umlaufgerät** *n* rotary aerial switch unit

Peilung *f* radio direction finding, direction finding, bearing, radio bearing, sounding, taking bearings **~ mit Braunscher Röhre** Braun-tube direction finding **~ nach Gehör** audio method of direction finding **eine rechtweisende ~ in die Karte tragen** to lay off a true bearing

Peilung, eine ~ verbessern to correct a bearing **~ vornehmen** to take bearings with direction finder **optische ~** visual direction finding (aviation), visual bearings, pilotage **rechtweisende ~** true bearing **durch gegenseitige**

Peilungen by reciprocal bearings
Peilungs-anzeiger *m* bearing indicator **-art** *f* bearing method **-beiwert** *m* error-compensation value **-projektor** *m* bearing projector
Peilungsverbesserung *f*, **künstliche** ~ zero clearing
Peil-verfahrendrehturm *m* revolving turret of a direction finder **-verlagerung** *f* bearing shift, error, or displacement **-vorrichtung** *f* bearing arrangement, bearing plate, plane table apparatus, sighting device **-vorsatz** *m* direction-finder adapter (radar), direction-finder means added to normal receiver equipment **-welle** *f* beacon wave **-wesen** *n* direction finding **-winkel** *m* the (approximate five-degree) path (approach path) between the dot zone and dash zone (audio and video) shown on a direction finder, radio bearing **-zeichen** *n* direction-finder signal, call signal, code signal (*e.g.*, of a ground station) **-zeiger** *m* pointer of direction-finder apparatus, cursor (rdr)
Peilzeiten *pl*, **ungestörte** ~ hours of undisturbed direction finding
Peilzusatz *m* radio beacon accessory, direction-finder accessory set
Peinerträger *m* wide-flanged steel I beam
peinliche Genauigkeit, Pünktlichkeit punctiliousness
Peinlichkeit *f* carefulness
peitschen to whip (of ropes), lash
Peitschenantenne *f* whip antenna
Pelerine *f* cape
Peligom *n* a type of glue
pellen, den Hanf ~ to pull out the reed
Pelletisieranlage *f* pelletizer
pelletisieren to pelletize (ore.)
Peloteuse *f* plodder (soap mfg.)
Pelouze *m* Pelouze type of tar extractor
Peltiereffekt *m* Peltier effect
Pelton-rad *n* Pelton water wheel **-turbine** *f* Pelton turbine
Pelvimetrie *f* pelvimetry
Pelz *m* fur **-gefüttert** fur-lined **-weste** *f* fur waistcoat
Pendel *n* pendulum, pendants, cyclic or rhythmic variation **aperiodisches** ~ aperiodic pendulum **ballistisches** ~ ballistic pendulum **mathematisches** ~ ideal simple pendulum
Pendel-achse *f* jointed cross-shaft axle **-anker** *m* swinging lever (teleph.) **-anlasser** *m* oscillating starter **-antrieb** *m* oscillating drive **-artig** pendulous **-aufhängung** *f* suspension of pendulum **-ausschlag** *m* amplitude of pendulum swing **-becherwerk** *n* pivoted bucket conveyer, pendulum bucket conveyer **-betrieb** *m* shuttle service **-bewegung** *f* movement of pendulum, hunting, cycling, shutter movement **-bock** *m* aircraft jack
Pendel-changierung *f* swing arm traverse motion **-dynamo** *m* dynamometric dynamo **-einsatz** *m* float holder **-entlüfter** *m* pendulum-type barrel valve **-erscheinungen** *pl* huntings **-fallstab** *m* plumb drop rod **-feder** *f* vibrator blade, reed or spring **-fenster** *n* internal pressure plate **-förderer** *m* shuttle conveyor, jig-back conveyor **-fräsmaschine** *f* planetary milling machine
Pendelfrequenz *f* quenching frequency, electron-oscillation frequency **-generator** *m* quenching oscillator **-schaltung** *f* supergeneration circuit organization
Pendel-futter *pl* floating tool holders **-gewicht** *n* pendulum weight **-gleichrichter** *m* vibrating rectifier, tuned-reed rectifier **-hammer** *m* pendulum-type impact-testing machine, pendulum hammer **-hammerschlagwerk** *n* pendulum-impact testing machine **-heft** *n* message book **-isolator** *m* swinging isolator with suspending hook, suspended isolator
Pendel-kammer *f* inclinable (bascule) camera **-kontakt** *m* pendulum contact **-kraftmesser** *m* pendulum transmission dynamometer **-kugellager** *n* self-aligning (ball) bearing **-lager** *n* self-aligning, pivot, or swing bearing **-lagerung** *f* pendulum bearings or emplacement **-lasche** *f* hanger link **-lenkachse** *f* oscillating steering axle **-lichtanlaßbatteriezünder** *m* rocker-starter and battery-ignition unit **-linse** *f* bob, ball **-liste** *f* shuttle list
Pendel-magnet *n* pendulum magnet **-manometer** *n* (Prüfmaschine) pendulum type dynamometer **-maschine** *f* electric dynamometer **-mühle** *f* central spindle-type grinding mill, ring-roll mill, centrifugal grinder, pendulum mill
pendeln to oscillate, shuttle, swing, hunt, vibrate, pendulate, undulate, pulsate, rock
Pendeln *n* cyclic variation, swinging ~ **des Rotors** phase swinging, hunting
pendelnd swinging ~ **lagern** to arrange like a pendulum, to arrange to oscillate **-es Gegengewicht** pendulum counterweight, movable kidney **-er Halter** floating holder
Pendelneigungsmesser *m* pendulum inclinometer
Pendelrahmen *m* cradle frame **-bremsstand** *m* brake-torque bench with rocking plate
Pendel-regler *m* pendulum governor (conical) **-regelung** *f* average-position action **-reibahle** *f* floating reamer **-rollen des Tonlaufwerks** filter roller arms **-rollenlager** *n* self-aligning (radial) roller bearing **-rückkoppler** *m* superregenerative receiver, superregenerator, periodic-trigger-type receiver **-rückkoppelung** *f* superregeneration, superregenerative circuit, superretroaction
Pendelrückkoppelungs-empfänger *m* superregenerative receiver, superregenerator, periodic-trigger-type receiver **-schaltung** *f* superregenerative circuit **-spannung** *f* positive quench or biasing voltage
Pendel-säge *f* pendulum saw **-säule** *f* column with spherical end bearings **-schaltwerk** *n* pendulum switch gear **-schlaghammer** *m* pendulum hammer **-schlagprüfeinrichtung** *f* impact testing machine **-schlagwerk** *n* pendulum tup, striker, pendulum(-impact) (testing) machine **-schlauch** *m* gravity hose **-schlepper** *m* shuttle skid **-schmierer** *m* oscillation lubricator
Pendel-schurre *f* swinging shoot **-schutz** *m* out of-step protection (relay) **-schwingung** *f* swing or oscillation of a pendulum, hunting **-schwingungsdämpfer** *m* floating-kidney vibration absorber **-selbstunterbrecher** *m* pendulum self-interrupter **-sperre** *f* surge guard (of relay)
Pendel-stabilität *f* pendulum stability **-stauer** *m*

pendulum cross beam **-stütze** *f* pin-ended support, hinged support, link support, shear leg **-tauchfräsen** *n* planetary-plunge milling **-telegraph** *m* pendulum start-stop telegraph, Pendel telegraph **-umformer** *m* vibrating rectifier, buzzer-type transformer **-umschalter** *m* pendulum change-over switch

Pendelung *f* swinging, oscillation, hunting

Pendel-verkehr *m* shuttling **-vervielfacher** *m* pendulum multiplier, reciprocating and accelerating secondary-electron multiplier

Pendelwaage *f* pendulum balance **elektrische ~** cradled electric dynamometer

Pendel-wechselrichter *m* vibratory inverter **-windmesser** *m* pendulum anemometer **-winker** *m* semaphore direction indicator **-zähler** *m* clock meter **-zentrifuge** *f* pendulum hydro-extractor

Pendler *m* commutor

Penetrations-messer *m* penetrometer **-prüfung** *f* penetrant test **-versuch** *m* penetration test

Penetron *n* meson

Pensky-Martensapparat *m* Pensky Martens tester

Pentaeder *m* pentahedron

Pentagrammbezeichnung *f* pentagram notation

Pentagridhöhe *f* heptode, pentagrid valve

Pentanlampe *f* pentane lamp or Vernon-Harcourt lamp

Penten *n* pentene

Penthode *f* pentode

Pentlandit *m* pentlandite

Pentode *f* pentode **~ mit konstanter Steilheit** gated-beam tube

Pentrinit *n* pentaerythritol tetranitratenitroglycerin mixtures (also covers mixtures of pentaerythritol tetranitrate with TNT, etc.)

Pentrit *n* pentaerythritol tetranitrate

Peptonat *n* peptonate

Perazidität *f* superacidity, hyperacidity

Perbenzoesäure *f* perbenzoic acid

Perbunan *n* a Buna variety

Peressigsäure *f* peracetic acid

Perforations-fehler *m* uniformity error **-geräusch** *n* sprocket-hole modulation or noise (motion pictures) **-walze** *f* sprocket

Perforier-breitpresse *f* all-cross perforating press **-maschine** *f* perforating machine

perforieren to perforate, puncture

Perforierung *f* perforation

Pergament *n* parchment, vellum **-aufzieherin** *f* roll coverer **-ersatz** *m* artificial parchment **-ersatzpapier** *n* imitation parchment

pergamentieren to parchmentize

Pergamentpapier *n* parchment paper

Pergamin *n*, **-papier** *n* glassine, imitation parchment

Pergaminseide *f* glassine

Pergamoid *n* pergamoid

Perhydrol *n* hydrogen peroxide, perhydrol

Periastrondrehung *f* advance of periastron

Peridot *m* peridot

Peridotit *n* peridotite

Perigäum *n* perigee

perihel *n* perihelion

Perikondetektor *m* perikon detector

Perimeter *n* perimeter

Perinialelektrode *f* perineal electrode

Periode *f* cycle (elec.), period, phase **~ pro Sekunde** cycle, period per second **einzifferige ~** simple or single repetend **1,000 Perioden** kilocycle

Perioden-dauer *f* time of oscillation, period, cycle **-kontrolluhr** *f* time error indicator (in power station) **-meßgebiet** *n* instrument range **-meßgerät** *n* period range **-meter** *n* period meter **-mittelwertmessung** *f* period average measurement

Perioden-spannung *f* cycle **-uhr** *f* harmonic dial **-wähler** *m* selector of periods **-zahl** *f* frequency, periodicity, number of cycles per second, number of periods **-zähler** *m* cycle rate counter **-zeit** *f* time of vibration, time of oscillation

periodisch periodic(al), cyclical, recurrent, intermittent **~ aussetzender Betrieb mit gleichbleibender Belastung** intermittent periodic load **~ wiederholen** to cycle **~ zerhackte Wellen** interrupted waves **nicht ~** dead beat **-e Größe** periodic quantity **-es Kaliber** periodic pass **-e Kontrolle** line inspection **-er Ruf** machine ringing **-e Überholung** periodical overhaul **-e Ungleichmäßigkeit** periodical unevenness or variation **-e Untersuchung** periodic inspection

Periodizität *f* periodicity, frequency

Periost *n* periosteum

Peripherie *f* circumference, periphery **-austrag** *m* peripheral discharge **-winkel** *m* inscribed angle, angle at the periphery

peripherisch peripheral, peripheric

periplanatisch periplanatic

Periskop *n* periscope

Periston *n* a type of blood substitute

Peritektikum *n* peritectic

peritektisch peritectic

Perjodat *n* periodate

Perjodsäure *f* periodic acid

Perkal *n*, **-stoff** *m* percale

Perkolation *f* percolation

Perkolator *m* percolator

Perkussionsladung *f* detonator charge

Perlbad *n* gas-bubble bath

Perle *f* pearl, bead **mit Perlen isoliert** beaded

perlen to form bubbles, drops, or beads, sparkle, glisten (like pearls) **-wand** *f* directive or beaded screen

Perl-erz *n* pearl ore **-glänzend** lustrous **-glimmer** *m* margarite **-grat** *n* overfilled metal (welding) **-grau** *n* pearly (zinc) gray **-hammer** *m* bead hammer

Perlit *m* perlite, pearly constituent **-ähnlich** pearloid **-insel** *f* pearlite area

perlitisch pearlitic

perlitisieren to pearlitize (met.)

Perl-kohle *f* pea coal **-koks** *m* pea coke, small-sized coke

Perlmutter *f* mother-of-pearl **-artig** perlaceous, mother-of-pearl, pearly **-blech** *n* crystallized tin plate, moiré métallique **-papier** *n* nacreous paper

Perl-rohr *n* bead tube **-schnur** *f* margarite, string of beads or pearls, line of droplets **-schnurblitz** *m* beaded lightning **-sinter** *m* pearl sinter **-stab** *m* bead **-stein** *m* perlite **-spat** *m* pearl spar **-transistor** *m* bead transistor

Permalloy *n* permalloy
permanent permanent **-dynamik** *f* permanent-magnet-type moving-coil speaker **-dynamischer Lautsprecher** permanent-magnet dynamic loudspeaker **-magnet** *m* permanent magnet **-satz** *m* permanence principle, sum rule **-weiß** *n* permanent white, fast white, pearl white, barium sulfate, barytes
Permanganat *n* permanganate
permeabel permeable
Permeabilität *f* permeability, magnetic inductivity, magnetic inductive capacity **~ bei kleinen Feldstärken** permeability at low magnetizing forces **reversible ~** reversible permeability **reziproker Wert der ~** reluctivity **zusätzliche ~** incremental permeability
Permeabilitäts-abstimmung *f* permeability tuning **-anstimmungskern** *m* permeability tuner core **-messer** permeameter
Permeameter *n* permeameter **~ für Messungen bei erhöhter Temperatur** hot permeameter
Permisches Gestein Permian series
Permitivität *f* permitivity
permutieren to permute
Peroxyd *n* peroxide
peroxydieren to peroxidize
Perpendikel *n* perpendicular, pendulum **-ende** *n* **-gewicht** *n* bob
perpendikulär perpendicular
Perpropionsäure *f* perpropionic acid
Perron *m* platform
Persanerstahl *m* Brescian steel
Persäure *f* peracid
Perschwefelsäure *f* persulfuric acid
Persenning *f* tarpaulin
Persisches Rot coral red (a red oxide)
Persistenz *f* persistence **~ des Netzhauteindruckes** persistence of vision
Persistor *m* persistor
Personal *n* staff, personnel, crew
Personal-abteilung *f* personnel section **-amt** *n* personnel office (German general staff) **-ersparnis** *f* staff economies **-kosten** *pl* staff costs **-kurve** *f* schedule of hours **-prüfstelle** *f* psychometric station, tests and measurements center, aptitude-testing laboratory **-wechsel** *m* crew change
Personen-abtaster mit wanderndem Licht spotlight scanner for persons **-bahnhof** *m* passenger station **-beförderung** *f* passenger transport, service, or traffic **-bildgeber** *m* image transmitter of persons **-fähre** *f* passenger ferry **-flugzeug** *n* passenger airplane **-förderkorb** *m* man cage
Personenkraftwagen *m* passenger car or vehicle **geländegängiger ~** cross-country passenger car
Personen-luftverkehr *m* air-passenger service, passenger flying **-rufanlage** *f* staff calling or location system, personal paging system **-schaden** *m* personal damage **-schadenersatz** *m* damages for personal loss **-suchanlage** *f* staff locator installation **-verkehr** *m* passenger traffic **-wagen** *m* passenger (car), coach (R.R.), passenger automobile **-zug** *m* local passenger train **-zuglokomotive** *f* passenger locomotive
persönlich personal **-e Gleichung** personal equation **-e Gleichung des Beobachters** human equation of the observer
Persönlichkeit *f* personality
Persönlichkeitsbeurteilung *f* merit-rating
Perspektive *f* perspective **Zentrum der ~** perspective center
perspektivisch perspective **-e Zeichnung** perspective drawing
Perspektivität *f*, **Achse der ~** perspective axis
Perspektograph *m* perspectograph
Perstoff *m* diphosgene
Pertinax *n* pertinax **-schnittschraube** *f* pertinax preset control **-stäbchen** *n* pertinax screw-driver rod
Perturbometer *n* perturbometer
Perubalsam *m* Peruvian balsam
Perveanz *f* perveance
Pesenantrieb *m* belt drive
Petalit *n* lithia feldspar
Petit *f* brevier
Petrefakt *n* fossil, petrifaction
Petrischale *f* Petri dish
Petrochemie *f* petrochemistry
Petrographie *f* petrography
petrographisch petrographic, comagmatic
Petroläther *m* petroleum ether
Petrolatum *n* petrolatum
Petrolen *n* petrolene
Petroleum *n* petroleum, mineral oil, kerosene **~ für Eisenbahnlampen** illuminating oil for railways **~ raffinieren** to refine petroleum
Petroleum-anlage *f* kerosene outfit **-äther** *m* petroleum ether **-benzin** *n* benzine **-dampf** *m* petroleum vapor **-gesellschaft** *f* oil company **-glühlicht** *n* incandescent petroleum-vapor lighting **-glühlichtbrenner** *m* incandescent petroleum-vapor burner **-haltig** petroliferous **-koks** *m* oil coke, petroleum coke **-lampe** *f* kerosene lamp.
Petroleum-motor *m* petroleum engine, kerosene engine **-ofen** *m* petroleum furnace **-produkt** *n* petroleum product **-raffinerie** *f* petroleum refinery **-schlepper** *m* kerosene tractor (petroleum tractor) **-solvent** *n* mineral spirit **-traktor** *m* kerosene tractor **-vorkommen** *n* stringer (min.) **-zone** *f* oil zone
Petrolkoks *m* oil coke, petroleum coke
Petrolör *m* petroleum setoff device
Petrol-säure *f* petrolic acid **-schieber** *m* petroleum sluice valve
Petschaft *n* impression die, envelope sealer
Pfaff(e) *m* hubbing die
Pfahl *m* picket, pile, stake, prop, post, pole, stalk, peg, lath, stick **beschuhter ~** ferruled pile **schwebender ~** floating pile **stehender ~** bearing pile **der ~ sitzt auf** the pile sits on the ground **schachbrettförmig eingerammte Pfähle** staggered piling
Pfahl-abschneiden *n* cutting off of piles **-ausheber** *m* pile-withdrawing engine **-ausziehmaschine** *f* pile extractor **-bau** *m* pile work **-bewehrung** *f* pile reinforcement **-bündel** *n* dolphin (logging)
pfählen to fasten with piles or stakes
Pfählen *n* pile driving, piling
Pfahlführungsrahmen *m* pile driving frame
Pfahlgründung *f* pile foundation, pile bent **schwebende ~, schwimmende ~** floating-pile foundation **stehende ~** bearing-pile foundation
Pfahl-haube *f* cap (pile) **-joch** *n* pile bent **-joch-**

brücke *f* pile bridge **-kopf** *m* head of pile, cap, helmet **-rammanlage** *f* pile-driving plant **-reihe** *f* line or row of pegs or stakes

Pfahlrost *m* pile cluster, pile cap, raft, framing **-fundament** *n* pile foundation **-gründung** *f* foundation on a grillage

Pfahl-schlagen *n* piling, pile driving **-sperre** *f* post obstacle **-spitze** *f* pile point **-stich** *m* bowline-knot

Pfählung *f* pile work, piling, set of piles

Pfahl-wand *f* rank or row of piles **-werk** *n* pile foundation, palisade **-wurzel** *f* taproot **-zaun** *m* paling, stockade

Pfand *n* deposit

pfändbar seizable

Pfandbrief *m* mortgage bond or deed, debenture

Pfändekeil *m* miner's wedge

pfänden to seize

Pfändholz *n* repair timber

Pfandrecht *n* right of a mortgagee

Pfändung *f* seizure, execution, timber lining, breast boards, cleaning-up the attic

Pfanne *f* pan, copper, boiler, seat, lug, ladle, casting or teeming ladle, pot, kettle **~ mit Ausgußschnauze** lip-pour ladle, top-pour ladle **~ mit Gehänge und Wagen** crane truck ladle **~ mit Getriebekippvorrichtung** ladle with tipping-gear appliance, geared ladle **~ mit Krangehänge** crane ladle **~ mit Wagen** truck or buggy ladle

Pfannen-abdeckmasse *f* ladle covering compound **-amalgamation** *f* pan amalgamation **-ausgießzeit** *f* ladle emptying time **-ausguß** *m* ladle lip, nozzle of a ladle **-auskleidung** *f* ladle lining **-bär** *m* ladle skull **-behälter** *m* ladle bowl **-bolzen** *m* cup standard or bolt **-bügel** *m* ladle bail **-deckel** *m* cap piece

Pfannengabel *f* ladle shank **doppelseitige ~** double-end ladle shank

Pfannen-gehänge *n* ladle bail **-gießzeit** *f* ladle pouring or emptying time

Pfanneninhalt *m* ladle capacity **~ nach der Ausschmierung** ladle capacity inside lining

Pfannen-kappe *f* cup socket **-kruste** *f* ladle skull **-lager** *n* brass bushes **-mann** *m* ladle man **-mühle** *f* grinding pan, edge runner mill **-ofen** *m* crucible furnace **-probe** *f* ladle analysis or test, pit sample

Pfannen-rest *m* skull **-schnauze** *f* ladle lip, nozzle of a ladle **-stein** *m* ladle brick, pivot stone, boiler scales, copper fur **-tiegel** *m* ladle bowl **-tragschere** *f* ladle shank **-transporteur** *m* pan conveyer, apron conveyer **-wagen** *m* ladle truck, ladle barrow

Pfauter-Verzahnungsmaschine *f* Pfauter hobber

Pfeife *f* whistle, pipe, flute, blowhole, channel, blownout shot (blasting) **gedeckte ~** stopped pipe

pfeifen to sing, howl, whistle, squeal

Pfeifen *n* singing, whistling, howling, undesired oscillation (Telev.) beat frequency **~ der Verstärker** singing, squealing, howling, self-oscillation **~ des Windes** wind thresh

Pfeif-grenze *f* singing point (teleph.) **-neigung** *f* near-singing condition **-patrone** *f* whistling cartridge used as gas alarm

Pfeifpunkt *m* singing point **-abstand** *m* **-sicherheit** *f* singing, whistling, or stability margin

Pfeif-sicherheit *f* antisinging stability **-ton** *m* whistling **-ventil** *n* whistle valve

Pfeil *m* rise or camber of an arch, rise or height of a curve, arrow, dart, picket, upright, leg, arrow, strain **in einen ~ auslaufende Maßlinie** arrow-headed dimension line

Pfeilbohrer *m* dart bit

pfeilen to sweep-back

Pfeiler *m* pillar, post, standard, column, pier, pylon, counterfort, upright **-abbau** *m* panel-work **-bau** *m* board-and-pillar work, board-and-pillar system **-durchhieb** *m* cross board, holing, narrow place **-haupt** *n* cutwater or starling of a bridge **-kopf** *m*, **-vorkauf** *m* pier nose (in bridge piers), pier head (in a pier used to unload ships) **-stau** *m* backwater effect (due to bridge piers) **-vorlage** *f* pillar pier

Pfeilform *f* sweepback (aviation) **-flügel** *m* swept-back wing

pfeilförmig arrow-shaped, arrow-type, sagittate, sagittiform **-er Flügel** backswept wing (aviation)

Pfeilgeschoß *n* fin-stabilized projectile

Pfeilhöhe *f* camber, height of camber, sag or dip, rise, height of the meniscus, height of crown, deflection, height of an arch **~ des Bogens** height of arc, rise of arch or deflection, height of crown **~ der Feder** camber of spring

Pfeilkraft *f* force normal to chord **-treibwert** *m* coefficient of force normal to chord, normal-force coefficient

Pfeil-kreuz *n* arrow cross **-marke** *f* index arrow **-methode** *f* sagitta method **-motor** *m* V-type engine

Pfeilrad *n* herringbone gear, herringbone wheel, double helical gear **-motor** *m* double helical rotor-type air turbine, spiro-type air turbine (engine)

Pfeil-richtung *f* direction of arrow **-ring** *m* nozzle ring **-schrift** *f* arrowheaded letters or types **-spitze** *f* arrowhead **-stellung** *f* sweepback (aviation) **-stellungswinkel** *m* sweepback angle (aviation) **-verhältnis** *n* ratio of rise to span (of arch)

Pfeilung *f* sweepback

Pfeilverzahnung *f* herringbone gearing or teeth **Getriebe mit ~** herringbone gear(ing)

Pfeilwinkel *m* angle of sweepback

Pfeilzahn *m* herringbone tooth

Pfeilzahnrad *n* herringbone gear

Pfeilzeichnung *f* functional diagram

Pfennig *m* penny

Pferde-bespannt horse-drawn **-breiten** *pl* horse latitudes **-fahrzeug** *n* horse-drawn vehicle **-hacke** *f* horse hoe

Pferdekraft *f* horsepower **~ der Schraubendrehung** torque horsepower

Pferdekraft-ertrag *m* horsepower output **-nutzwert beim Fliegen** cruising horsepower output **-stunde** *f* horsepower-hour

Pferde-krankheit *f* horse disease **-park** *m* horse park **-pflege** *f* care of horses **-schutz** *m* horse respirator (mask) **-schwanzwolken** *pl* mare's-tails (a cloud formation) **-schwemme** *f* horse pond **-stall** *m* stable, stall

Pferdestärke *f* metric horsepower **effektive ~** actual horsepower, brake horsepower **indizierte ~** indicated horsepower **metrische ~** continental horsepower **normale ~** standard horsepower

Pferde-transportwagen *m* horse-transport vehicle
Pfette *f* purlin, roof beam, stringer
Pfiff *m* whistle (sound); interference (TV), beat frequency
Pfirsichholz *n* peach wood
Pflanze *f* plant
Pflanzen-butter *f* vegetable butter **-faser** *f* vegetable fiber **-fett** *n* vegetable fat **-kohle** *f* vegetable charcoal **-öl** *n* vegetable oil **-schädling** *m* (plant) pest **-schutzmittel** *n* plant protective **-talg** *m* Japan wax **-wachs** *n* vegetable wax **-wuchs** *m* vegetation **-züchtung** *f* plant breeding
Pflanzer *m* planter
pflanzlich vegetable
Pflanz-rohr *n* plant cane **-schule** *f* nursery
Pflanzung *f* plantation
Pflanzvorrichtung *f* planting attachment
Pflaster *n* plaster, pavement, paving, patch ~ **von Eisenbeton** reinforced plaster
Pflaster-arbeit *f* pavement work **-kasten** *m* (slang) apothecary
pflastern to pave
Pflaster-stein *m* paving brick, road stone, paving stone **-stoffe** *pl* adhesive plaster fabrics
Pflasterung *f* pavement ~ **der elliptischen Ebene** paving of the elliptic plane ~ **der euklidischen Ebene** paving of the Euclidean plane ~ **des euklidischen Raums** paving of the Euclidean space
Pflasterungsmaterial *n* paving material
Pflasterziegel *m* paving brick
Pflatschdruck *m* slop padding
Pflege *f* maintenance (work), routine repair work, nursing, care, serving attendance **-bedarf** *m* maintenance requirement
pflegen to attend (to), care for, cultivate, maintain, cherish
pfleglich careful, economical
Pflicht *f* duty, obligation **-arbeit** *f* compulsory work
Pflichten-blatt *n* **-heft** *n* rating, specification
Pflicht-landung *f* compulsory landing **-schutzbehandlung** *f* obligatory preventive treatment **-treue** *f* fidelity **-verletzung** *f* violation of duty **-wert** *m* specification value, contract value
Pflock *m* peg, stake, picket, wooden pin, pin, treenail, jack, plug
Pflug *m* plow, scraper ~ **für Erdnußkultur** peanut (plow) cultivator ~ **für Landstraßenbauzwecke** grading plow ~ **mit Sitz** riding plow ~ **für Wegebauzwecke** road plow ~ **für allgemeine Zwecke** general-purpose plow
Pflugeisen *n* colter
pflügen to plow
Pflughaupt *n* axletree of a plow
Pflugkörper *m* body of the plow ~ **für Mittelbrecher** middle breaker bottom ~ **für Reihenhäufler** lister bottom
Pflug-messer *n* colter **-schar** *f* plowshare **-stahldraht** *m* plow wire **-sterz** *m* plowtail **-streichbrett** *n* mo(u)ldboard
Pforte *f* gate, door, portal
Pfosten *m* upright, column, post, standard (tech.), pylon, stake, marker, picket, newel post, jamb, pillar **-fachwerk** *n* Vierendeel truss
pfostenloses Fachwerk (Brücke) Warren-type bridge girder
Pfote *f* paw
Pfriem *m* awl, bodkin
pfropfen to stopper, cork, graft
Pfropfen *m* stopper, plug, cork **-förderung** *f* air-pressure transportation or conveying
Pfropf-messer *n* grafting or budding knife **-säge** *f* pruning or grafting saw
Pfund *n* pound (1.10 American pounds) ~ **per Quadratzoll** pound per square inch
Pfundzinn *n* common stamped tin with an alloy of lead
pfuschen to bungle, blunder
Pfuscher *m* bungler, quack
Pfütze *f* pool
pfützen to scoop, pale out the water
Phakometer *n* phacometer
Phalanx *f* phalanx
Phänologie *f* phenology
Phänomen *n* phenomenon
phänomenologisch phenomenological
Phantasie *f* fancy, imagination **-profil** *n* irregular section
phantastisch fantastic, fanciful
Phantastron *n* phantastron
Phantom-ausnutzung *f* use of phantom circuits **-bild** *n* phantom view **-bildung** *f* phantoming
Phantomkreis *m* phantom circuit, combined circuit **zum ~ schalten** to phantom
Phantomkreis-leitung *f* phantom circuit **-schaltung** *f* phantom connection
Phantompupinspule *f* phantom circuit loading coil
Phantoskop *n* phantoscope
Phantron *n* phantron
Pharaoschlange *f* mercuric sulfocyanate
Pharmakochalzit *m* olivenite, prismatic arsenate of copper
Pharmakolith *m* arsenate of lime, pharmacolite
pharmazeutische Industrie pharmaceutical industry
Phase *f* phase, epoch, stage, era **außer** ~ out of phase, dephased **in die richtige ~ bringen** (Wechselstrom) to phase **in ~ mit** in phase or in step, cophasal **außer ~ bringen** to dephase **ungleiche ~ haben** to differ in phase **beständige** ~ stable phase **feste** ~ solid phase **verschobene** ~ displaced or shifted phase, dephased or out-of-phase condition **gleich belastete Phasen** balanced phases **um 90° verschobene** ~ quadrature phase (TV)
Phasenabgleichvorrichtung *f* phase balance, phase changer or shifter
phasenabhängiger Gleichrichter phase selective rectifier
Phasen-ablösung *f* phase switch **-abnahme** *f* phase decrement **-Amplituden-Verzerrung** *f* phase/amplitude distortion **-änderung** *f* phase transition or change **-anzeiger** *m* phase indicator **-ausgleich** *m* phase compensation or correction **-ausgleicher** *m* phase equalizer **-aussortierung** *f* phase focusing **-beziehung** *f* phase relation **-bilanz** *f* phase balance
Phasen-detektor *m* lock-in detector **-differenz** *f* space phasing, (antenna) difference in or of phase, phase difference **-diskriminator** *m* phase discriminator **-drehung** *f* persistence of vision, phase rotation, phase shift

Phasen-einstellung *f* phase adjustment or shift framing, phasing, phase regulation **-empfindlich** phase-sensitive **-entzerrer** *m* delay equalizer (phase corrector), phase compensator **-entzerrung** *f* phase compensation or correction, delay weighting term, delay equalizer, echo weighting term **-entzerrungskette** *f* phase compensator **-erdschluß** *m* one-phase grounding, leakage on one phase **-faktor** *m* phase factor **-falsch** misphased **-fehler** *m* error of phase, phase distortion **-fokus** *m* phase focusing

Phasen-folge *f* succession of phases **-frei** nonreactive **-gabe** *f* phasing signal **-gang** *m* phase-frequency characteristic **-geräusch** *n* phase jitter **-geschwindigkeit** *f* phase velocity, wave velocity **-gitter** *n* phase grating **-gleich** inphase **-gleichheit** *f* phase coincidence, inphase state, cophasal state **-grenze** *f* phase interface **-grenzschicht** *f* phase boundary

Phasen-hub *m* phase variation or fluctuation **-indikator** *m* phase indicator **-integral** *n* phase integral, action-variable **-kehrschleife** *f* phase displacement **-klemme** *f* line terminal **-kompaß** *m* phase compass **-konstante** *f* phase constant **-kontrastbild** *n* phase-contrast image **-kontrastverfahren** *n* phase-contrast method **-korrigierter Hornstrahler** phase-corrected horn **-kurve** *f* phase curve

Phasen-lage *f* phase relationship **-lampe** *f* phase lamp **-laufzeit** *f* time of transition, time of phase transmission, phase delay time **-lehre** *f* solution theory, doctrine of phases **-linearität** *f* phase linearity **-maß** *n* impedance angle, phase constant, wave-length constant **-mäßig** in proper phase relation **-messer** *m* phasemeter, power-factor meter **-meter** *m* power factor **-mittel** *n* phase average **-mittelwert** *m* ensemble average **-modelung** *f*, **-modulation** *f* phase modulation

Phasen-nacheilung *f* lag, phase lag **-nulldurchgang** *m* phase zero passage **-raum** *m* phase space (math.), extension in phase **-regel** *f* phase rule **-regelung** *f* phase adjustment or shift **-reinheit** *f* freedom from phase shift or angular differences **-resonanz** *f* phase or velocity resonance

phasen-richtig inphase, in proper phase relation **-rückdreher** *m* phase lagger or shifter **-schieber** *m* phase changer, phase shifter, compensator, phase advancer **-schiebertransformator** *m* phase-shifting transformer **-schleppung** *f* phase lag

Phasen-schreiber *m* phase recorder **-schwankung** *f* phase variations **-schwund** *m* phase fading **-spaltung** *f* phase splitting **-spannung** *f* phase voltage, phase-to-ground voltage **-spalter** *m* phase splitter (TV) **-spielraum** *m* phase margin **-sprung** *m* rapid phase change, shift in phase, phase-angle shift

phasenstarr rigid in phase, phase-locked, in locked phase relation **~ verkoppelt** coupled rigidly

Phasenstellung, entgegengesetzte ~ opposition of phase

Phasensteuerung *f*, **elektrische ~** synchroscope

Phasen-stufe *f* phase step **-teiler** *m* phase-splitting device, phase splitter **-teilung** *f* phase splitting **-theorie** *f* phase theory **-transformator** *m* phase-shifting transformer **-übergang** *m* phase transition **-umformer** *m* phase converter **-umkehr** *f* phase reversal, phase splitter (TV) **-umkehrer** *m* phase inverter, phase reverter **-umkehrschaltung** *f* phase inverter **-umkehrschleife** *f* phase-reversing loop **-umkehrstufe** *f* paraphase stage, phase-reverter stage **-umkehrung** *f* phase splitting (TV), phase reversal **-umschaltung** *f* phase adjustment **-umtastgerät** *n* phasing or lobe-switching system

phasenungleiche Komponente component out of phase

Phasenunterbrechungsrelais *n* phase balance relay

Phasenunterschied *m* difference of phases, phase difference, displacement, or angle **~ zwischen Geber und Empfänger** orientation

Phasenunterschiedverschiebung *f* phase displacement or difference

Phasen-variation *f* phase change **-verdrehung** *f* phase shifting, phase rotation **-verkehrt wirken** to act in reverse polarity, act in opposite phases **-verkettung** *f* interlinking of phases **-verschieber** *m* phase shifter

Phasenverschiebung *f* phase shift(ing), phase displacement, difference of phase, phase advancing (if forward), dephased condition **~ um 90 Grad** quadrature, phase quadrature, opposition **~ von 180 Grad** phase opposition

Phasenverschiebungsunterdrückung *f* referencing **-winkel** *m* phase angle, angle-of-phase difference

Phasenverschmierung *f* phase spreading

phasenverschoben displaced in phase, out-of-phase, dephased, in phase quadrature (when 90 degrees), in phase opposition (when 180 degrees) **um 90 Grad ~** in phase quadrature **-er Strom** out-of-phase current **-e Welle** out-of-phase wave

phasen-verspätet lagging **-verteilung** *f* random phase **-verzerrung** *f* phase shift, phase distortion, delay distortion **-verzögerung** *f* phase retardation or lag, phase delay **-voltmeter** *n* phase voltmeter **-vorauseilung** *f* phase lead **-voreilung** *f* lead, leading, phase lead, phase advance **-vorschieber** *m* phase advancer **-welle** *f* phase wave, electron wave **-wicklung** *f* phase winding **-winkel** *m* phase angle, (angle of) phase difference, impedance angle, impedance factor, quality factor **-zahl** *f* number of phase **-zeiger** *m* phase indicator

Phasierung *f* phasing **~ auf Weiß** phase-white

Phasometer *n* phasemeter

Phasotropie *f* phasotropy

Phenazit *m* phenacite

Phenol *n* phenol, carbolic acid **-artig** phenoloid **-extraktion** *f* phenol extraction **-fiber** *f* phenol fiber **-harz** *n* phenolic resin **-kalium** *n* potassium phenolate **-kalzium** *n* calcium phenolate

phenol-löslich phenol-soluble **-masse** *f* phenolic compounds **-natrium** *n* sodium, phenolate **-phthalein** *n* phenolphthalein **-quecksilber** *n* mercury phenolate **-sulfonsäure** *f* phenolsulfonic acid **-wismut** *m*, *n* bismuth phenolate

Phenoplast-Formteil *m* phenolic moulding

Phensäure *f* phenic acid

Phenyl *n* phenyl **-acetylen** *n* phenylacetylene **-ameisensäure** *f* phenylformic acid, benzoic

acid **-äthyl** phenylethylic **-äthylen** *n* phenylethylene
Phenylenblau *n* phenylene blue
Phenyl-essig *m* phenylacetic acid **-essigäther** *m* phenylacetic ether **-essigsäure** *f* phenylacetic acid **-hydrazinchlorhydrat** *n* phenylhydrazine hydrochloride
phenylieren to phenylate
Phenyl-säure *f* phenylic acid, phenol **-schwefelsäure** *f* phenyl sulfuric acid **-wasserstoff** *m* phenyl hydride, benzol
Philosophenwolle *f* zinc oxide
Phiole *f* vial
Phlebographie *f* phlebography
phlegmatisieren to desensitize (explosives)
Phlorogluzin *n* phloroglucinol
pH-Messer *m* pH meter
Phon *n* phon, decibel (acoustics)
phonisch phonic **-es Rad** tone wheel, phonic motor or wheel
Phono-Elektrokardiograph *m* phonoelectro-cardioscope
Phönizin *n* indigo purple, red indigo carmine
Phonograph *m* phonograph
Phonographen-drehplatte *f* phonograph turntable **-platte** *f* phonograph record **-plattenteller** *m* phonograph turntable
Phonolith *m* phonolite
Phonometer *m* phonometer
Phonon *n* phonon
Phorometer *n* phorometer
Phosgen *n* phosgene, carbonyl chloride **-gas** *n* phosgene gas
Phosphat *n* phosphate
Phosphid *n* phosphide
Phosphor *m* phosphorus **-arm** low in phosphorus **-artig** phosphorus-like **-blei** *n* lead phosphide, pyromorphite **-bromid** *n* phosphorus bromide, phosphorus pentabromide **-bromür** *n* phosphorus tribromide **-bronze** *f* phosphor bronze **-bronzedraht** *m* phosphor-bronze wire **-chlorid** *n* phosphorus chloride, phosphorus pentachloride **-chlorür** *n* phosphorus trichloride, phosphorus chloride
Phosphore *pl* phosphors, luminescent or fluorescent (screen or lamp) materials
Phosphor-eisen *n* ferrophosphorus, iron phosphide, basic pig iron **-eisensinter** *m* diadochite
Phosphoreszenz *f* phosphorescence, afterglow
phosphoreszenzerzeugend phosphorogenic
phosphoreszieren to phosphoresce
phosphoreszierend phosphorescent
phosphor-frei free of phosphorus **-gehalt** *m* phosphorus content **-hältig** phosphoric, phosphatic, phosphorated, (containing) phosphorus
phosphorig phosphorous, phosphoretic, phosphoric
phosphorisch phosphoric
phosphorisieren to phosphorize, phosphorate
Phosphorisierung *f* parkerizing
Phosphorit *m* apatite, phosphorite
Phosphor-jodid *n* phosphorus iodide, phosphorus tri-iodide **-jodür** *n* phosphorus di-iodide **-kalzium** *n* calcium phosphide **-kupfer** *n* copper phosphide, pseudomalachite **-kupfererz** *n* libethenite **-mangan** *n* phosphormanganese **-metall** *m* phosphite **-molybdänsäure** *f* phosphomolybdic acid **-natrium** *n* sodium phosphide
Phosphorogen *n* phosphorogen, activating addition (promotive of phosphorescence)
Phosphoroskop *n* phosphoroscope
Phosphor-oxychlorid *n* phosphorus oxychloride **-roheisen** *n* phosphoric pig iron **-salz** *n* sodium ammonium phosphate, microcosmic salt **-säureanhydrid** *n* phosphoric anhydride
phosphorsaures, ~ Ammon ammonium phosphate **~ Barium** barium phosphate **~ Eisenoxyd** ferric phosphate **~ Eisenoxydul** ferrous phosphate **~ Kali** potassium phosphate **~ Natron, ~ Natrium** sodium phosphate
Phosphor-segregierung *f* phosphorus segregation **-sesquisulfid** *n* sesquisulfide of phosphorus **-teigbereiter** *m* phosphorous composition attendant **-trijodid** *n* phosphorus tri-iodide **-wolframsäure** *f* phosphotungstic acid
Phosphorychlorid *n* phosphorus oxychloride
Phosphor-zink *n* zinc phosphide **-zinn** *n* tin phosphide
Phot *n* phot
Photo-ablichtung *f* photographic image **-abteilung** *f* photosection, photographic division **-anregungsquerschnitt** *m* photoexcitation cross section **-auslösung** *f* photoproduction **-blitzkondensator** *m* photoflash capacitor **-chemie** *f* photochemistry **-chemisch** photochemical
Photodissoziationskontinuum *n* continuous spectrum of photodissociation
Photoeffekt *m* photoelectric effect **äußerer ~** photoelectric emission, photoemissive effect, external photo electric effect, Hallwachs effect **innerer ~** photo-conductive effect, inner photoelectric effect, internal photoelectrical effect **normaler ~** normal photoelectric emission **selektiver ~** selective photoelectric emission
photoelektrisch photoelectric **-e Ablesung** photoelectric sensing **-e Ausbeute** photoelectric emissivity, photoelectric yield **-es Emissionsvermögen** photoelectric emissivity or yield **-e Schwellenfrequenz** photoelectric threshold frequency, critical frequency **-e Wirkung** photoelectric effect, Hertz effect **-e Zelle** photoelectric cell, electric eye
Photo-elektrizität *f* photoelectricity **-elektron** *n* photoelectron **-elektronenröhre** *f* phototube **-element** *n* photoelectric cell or tube, photocell, phototube **-flugzeug** *n* photographic plane **-gramm** *n* photograph, photoprint copy, photographic record **-grammeter** (Gerät) *n* photographic surveying apparatus
Photogrammetrie *f* photographic surveying, photogrammetry, production of maps from aerial photographs **terrestrische ~** ground or terrestrial photogrammetry
photogrammetrisches Aufnahmegerät instrument for photogrammetrical surveying
Photograph *m* photographer
Photographenapparat *m* camera
Photographie *f* photography, picture, photograph, photogram (aviation)
photographieren to photograph
Photographiesatinieren *n* glazing of photographs
photographisch photographic **~ festhalten** to record photographically **-e Dichtemessung**

photodensitometry, photographic density measurement **-e Lösung** photographic solution **-er Zeichendruck** photoprinting **-e Zeichnung** photographic layout drawing

Photogravüre *f* photoengraving

Photokathode *f* photo cathode, photoelectric cathode **zusammengesetzte ~** multilayer cathode of a phototube **zusammenhängende ~** plain mirror or continuous photocathode

photo-keramisch photoceramic **-kernspaltung** *f* photodisintegration **-kopie** *f* photostat, photostatic copy **-kopieren** to photostat **-lumineszenz** *f* photoluminescence

Photometer *n* photometer **-aufsatz** *m* photometer head **-schirm** *m* photometer screen

Photo-metrie *f* photometry **-metrierung** *f* photometric evaluation or recording

photometrisch photometric **-es Strahlungsäquivalent** luminosity factor of a monochromatic radiation

Photo-mikrographie *f* photomicrography **-montagelehre** *f* photo assembly jig **-mosaik** *n* photo mosaic

Photon *n* photon

Photonebenabsorption *f* photon sbsorption

Photo-phon *n* photophone, radiophone **-physik** *f* photophysics

Photopie *f* subjective sensation of light

Photo-planzeichner *m* photoplanigraph **-schicht** *f* light-sensitive or photoelectric surface, photosensitive surface **-sphäre** *f* photosphere **-strakschablone** *f* photoloft template **-strom** *m* photoelectric current, photocurrent, photocell current **-stromverstärker** *m* photocell amplifier

phototechnisch photographic

Photo-telegraph *m* telephotograph **-telegraphisch** telephotographic **-theodolit** *m* phototheodolite **-therapie** *f* light treatment, phototherapy **-tiefdruck** *m* photogravure (rotogravure) **-topographie** *f* phototopography **-transistor** *m* phototransistor

Phototropie *f* phototropism (phototropy)

Photo-varistor *m* photovaristor **-verstärker** *m* photomultiplier **-vervielfachungsröhre** *f* photomultiplier tube **-visuelle Methode** photovisual technique **-volteffekt** *m* photovoltaic effect **-widerstand** *m* photoconductive cell **-widerstandsaufnahmeröhre** *f* photo-conductive camera tube **-xylographie** *f* photographic woodengraving

Photozelle *f* photoelectric cell, photocell, phototube, light-sensitive tube, photoelectric tube, electric eye **~ mit äußerem lichtelektrischem Effekt** photoemissive cell, emission cell **gasgefüllte ~** gas-filled photocell, gas phototube

Photozellen mit Sekundärelektronenvervielfacher multiplier photocell

Photozellenabtastung *f* photoelectric scanning

Photozellennetzgerät *n* photocell supply unit

Photozellenstrom Null "Zero Photocurrent"

Photo-zellenverstärker *m* photocell amplifier, electron multiplier phototube, photoelectric-cell amplifier **-vorlicht** *n* priming (bias) illumination

Phthalid *n* phthalide

Phthalsäure *f* phthalic acid

Phugoidbewegung *f* phugoid motion, hunting (in airship)

phugoide Schwingung phugoid oscillation

Ph-Wert *m* index of pH

Phyllit *m* mica slate

Physik *f* physics

physikalisch physical **~ optisch** optophysical **~ sinnvoll** physically realizable **-e Definition** physical evidence **-er Indikator** physical tracer **-e Prüfung** physical test

physikalisch-chemisch physical-chemical, physico-chemical **-metallurgisch** physicometallurgical

Physiker *m* physicist

Physikochemiker *m* physical chemist

physikochemisches Gleichgewicht physico-chemical equilibrium

Physiologie *f* physiology

physiologisch physiological

physisch physical **-e Wetteranalyse** physical weather analysis

Phytochemie (Pflanzenchemie) phytochemistry

Pianodraht *m* piano wire

pichen to pitch

Picke *f* pick

Pickel *m* (Picke *f*) pickax, pick **-bildung** *f* pitting (of metal) **-flöte** *f* piccolo **-hammer** *m* mineralogist's hammer with pick

pickeln to pickle

Pickelwirkung *f* pickle action

picken to edge, redress, restore, jab **-griff** *m* pick handle **-träger** *m* pick carrier (min.)

Picket *n* peg, stake

Pick-hacke *f* pick **-hammer** *m* pneumatic pick, pick, scaling hammer **-napf** *m* (slang) canteen, mess tin **-zeug** *n* tire-repair tools

Pico *n* unit representing 10^{12} **-farad** *n* micromicrofarad

Pier *m* pier, jetty, mole, wharf, dam, dike, bank **an einen ~** (oder Kai) **gehen** to secure to a pier

Pierce-Oscillator *m* Pierce oscillator

Pierzuführungsband *n* conveyor to quay

Piezoeffekt *m* piezoelectric effect

piezoelektrisch piezoelectric **-er Dehnungsmeßstreifen** piezoelectric strain gauge **-er Druckmesser** piezoelectric manometer **-er Kristall, -er Quarz** piezoelectric crystal

Piezo-elektrizität *f* piezoelectiricty **-indikator** *m* piezoelectric gauge **-kristall** *m* piezoelectric crystal element **-metrisches Gefälle** piezometric head **-quarzzelle** *f* supersonic light valve **-resonator** *m* piezoelectric resonator

piezotrop piezotropic

Pigment *n* pigment, coloring matter **-diapositiv** *n* carbon diapositive **-farben** *pl* lake(s), lake pigments, hues, mineral pigments **-farbstoff** *m* toner, pigment **-papier** *n* carbon paper

Pikee *n* piqué, quilting (textiles)

Piket *n* picket, little marking pole

Pikettstelle *f* night extension

Pikiernadel pricking pin

Piknometer *n* paper gauge

Pikofarad *n* picofarad

Pikotit *m* chromic spinel, picotite

Pikrinsäure *f* picric acid, trinitrophenol

Pikrosmin *m* picrosmine

Pilar *m* post **-walzwerk** *n* pillar rolling mill

Pilaster *m* column, pilaster **flacher ~** inserted or imbedded pillar

Pilasterschleif- und Riffelmaschine *f* grinding and

fluting machine with a column saddle
Pilbarit *m* pilbarite
Pile *f* pile
Pilgergerüst *n* roll housing of pilgrim mill
Pilgerschritt-changierung *f* pilgrim step traverse motion **-schweißung** *f* step-back welding **-verfahren** *n* reciprocating rolling process, Mannesmann process, Perrins' rolling process **-walze** *f* pilger roll
Pilgerwalzwerk *n* pilger rolling mill
Pilieranlage *f* soap-refining outfit
pilieren to mill (soap)
pilierfähig millable (soap)
Piliermaschine *f* soap mill
pilierte Seife milled soap
Pilkontakt *m* mushroom contact
Pille *f* pill
pillen to edge, redress, restore
Pilot *m* pilot **automatischer ~** automatic pilot, robot pilot
Pilotanlagen pilot plant
Pilotballon *m* pilot balloon, meteorological balloon **-aufstieggerät** *n* radiosonde **-bahn** *f*, **-kurve** *f* **-linie** *f* path of pilot balloon
Piloten-raum *m* pilot's compartment **-windschutz** *m* pilot's windshield
Pilot-hebel *m* pilot's throttle lever **-tonverfahren** *n* pilot-tone process **-träger** *m* pilot carrier **-welle** *f* pilot wave
Pilz *m* mushroom, obturator head, mushroom head (obturator), small pillbox **-anker** *m* mushroom anchor **-artiges Sicherheitsventil** mushroom valve **-decke** *f* flat (girderless) slab **-felsen** *m* mushroom rock **-förmig** mushroom **-fräser** *m* semicircular cutter
Pilz-isolator *m* mushroom insulator, umbrella insulator **-kolben** *m* mushroom piston **-lautsprecher** *m* mushroom loud-speaker, omnidirectional (360 degree) exponential horn loudspeaker or sound radiator **-schiene** *f* double-headed rail **-stößel** *m* mushroom-type follower, mushroom tappet **-ventil** *n* mushroom-type valve **-wuchshemmend** fungistatic
Pi Meson pions
Pimpel *m* plunger armature stud, plunger, stud, nipple **-stein** *m* pimple metal (copper)
Pinakoid *n* pinacoid
pinakoidal pinacoidal
Pinasse *f* pinnace, canal boat
Pincheffekt *m* pinch effect, rheostriction
Pineytalg *m* piney tallow
Pinge *f* gravel pit, pay gravel, kettle-shaped deepening
Pingenbau *m* open diggings
Pinksalz *n* pink salt, ammonium stannic chloride
Pinne *f* pin, peg, peen (of a hammer), back center, center pin (of compass), tack
Pinnen-reibung *f* friction at the pin, pivot friction **-träger** *m* center-pin support, pivot or bearing post
Pinn-hammer *m* planishing (grooving) hammer **-planke** *f* provisional dike
Pinode *f* spindle
Pinole *f* spindle sleeve, tail spindle
Pinolenwickler *m* pivot coiler
Pion *n* pion, pi meson
Pinsel *m* brush (painting), code for a type of guided missile **-detektor** *m* cat-whisker detector **-elektrode** *f* cat whisker (radio)
pinseln to paint, brush
Pinselstrich *m* touch
Pinte *f* pint
Pintschregler *m* Pintsch regulator
Pinzette *f* forceps, pincers, tweezers, nippers, pincette **anatomische ~** plain forceps (med.) **chirurgische ~** toothed forceps (med.)
Pionierpatent *n* pioneer patent
Piotin *m* soapstone
Pipette *f* pipette
pipettieren to pipette
Piraniprinzip *n* Pirani gauge
Piseebau *m* beaten cobwork, tapia, cofferwork of loam earth
Pisekit *m* pisekite
pisolitisch pisolitic
Piste *f* runway **befestigte ~** paved runway
Pisten-befeuerung *f* runway lighting **-wagen** *m* aerodrome control van
Pistille *f* pestle
Pistole *f* pistol, torpedo fuse, code for a certain type of guided missile, welding handle **gesicherte ~** pistol with safety on
Pistolen-griff *m* pistol grip **-hahn** *m* pistol-type nozzle **-scheibe** *f* pistol target **-tasche** *f* pistol holster
Piston *n* cornet à pistons
Pistonieren *n* swabbing
Pistonierkolben *m* swab
Pistonphon *n* pistonphone
Pitchpineholz *n* pitch pine
Pitot-manometer *n* Pitot gauge, Pitot tube **-messer** *m* pitotmeter
Pitotrohr *n* pilot tube **dynamisches ~** impact tube **statisches ~** pilot-static tube
Pitotröhre *f* Pitot tube
Pitotsches Rohr Pitot tube
Pitot's statistisches Saugrohr Pitot static tube
Pitsreiniger *m* cinder pit man
Pittinit *m* pittinite
Pivot-lafette *f* pivot mounting, rotating mount (artil.) **-lager** *n* trunnion bearing **-zapfen** *m* trunnion
Plaaofen *m* blast furnace
Plache *f* canvas, tarpaulin
Plachmal *n* plachmal
Plaggenpflug *m* sod knife, turf cutter
Plagioklas *m* plagioclase
Plaindress-Spruch *m* plaindress message
Plakat *n* poster, bill, placard **-geschwindigkeit** *f* placard speed **-papier** *n* posters, paper for posters
Plakette *f* medal
plamotieren to brush off
Plan *m* plan, program, schedule, scheme, project, layout, contrivance, map, diagram, chart, design, device **~ in natürlicher Größe** full-size (scale) drawing **~ nach Luftaufnahmen** aerophotogrammetric plan, airsurvey plan **~ für die regelmäßigen Messungen** schedule of periodic tests **~ für die regelmäßige Überwachung** maintenance program
plan-e Bodenfläche *f* flat bottom **-e Fläche** *f* plane surface
plan-achromatisches Objektiv *n* flat-field achromat **-anschlag** *m* transverse stop
planar planar

Plan-bank *f* planer **-bewegung** *f* transverse rotary movement **-biegeversuch** *m* plane-bending test **-bildanzeiger** *m* plan position indicator (PPI)

Planchette *f* drawing board

Planck-sche Konstante Planck's constant **-sches Strahlungsgesetz** Planck's law of radiation

Plancks Wirkungsquantum Planck's constant

Plan-decke *f* tarpaulin **-dichtfläche** *f* plane sealing surface **-dichtung** *f* plane seal **-drehbank** *f* facing lathe **-drehen** *n* to face, surface **-drehknopf mit selbsttätigem Vorschub** continuous feed facing head **-drehrichtung** *f* direction of transverse power feed **-drehschlitten** *m* tool slide for facing **-drehspäne** *pl* facings **-drehwerkzeug** *n* facing tool **-druckpapier** *n* chart paper, map or plan paper

Plane *f* cover, tarpaulin, canvas hood

planen to plan, project, face, plane, plot, level, design, contrive, project

Pläner *m* cretaceous marly limestone

Planet *m* planet

planetarisch planetary **-e Strömung** planetary circulation **-es Untersetzungsgetriebe** planetary reduction gear

Planeten-bahn *f* orbit of a planet **-baumuster** *n* epicyclic type **-fräsmaschine** *f* planetary miller

Planetengetriebe *n* planetary gearing, epicyclic (train of) gear **kleines Zahnrad des Planetengetriebes** satellite

Planetenrad *n* planet pinion, star-wheel idler, epicyclic gear **-getriebe** *n* sun-and-planet gear **-untersetzungsgetriebe** *n* planetary-type reduction gear

Planeten-rührer *m* planet mixing arm **-rührwerk** *n* planet stirrer **-träger** *m* satellite carrier, pinion cage, epicyclic unit **-trieb** *m* epicyclic gearing, planetary gearing **-zahnrad** *n* planet pinion

Plan-fläche *f* plane surface **-formarbeit** *f* transversal forming **-fräsen** to face **-fräsen** *n* facing, face milling **-fräser** *m* face mill **-fräsmaschine** *f* surface milling machine, horizontal milling machine, planer-type milling machine **-gang** *m* transverse or cross movement **-gemäß** according to plan **-gerät** *n* plotting equipment **-gitter** *n* plane grating

Planglas *n* optical flat, plane glass disk **-fenster** *n* optical glass window **-frittenfilter** *m* (sheet) sinter-glass filter

Plan-hammer *m* planishing hammer **-herd** *m* blanket sluice, racking table

Planie *f* level plane, formation, formation level

Planierbagger *m* skimmer

planieren to level, plane, smooth, grade, planish, size (paper), even

Planierer *m* grader

Planier-löffel *m* skimmer **-maschine** *f* coke leveler **-raupe** *f* motor grader, bulldozer **-schaufel** *f* blade machine **-schild** *n* scraper blade **-schlepper** *m* dozer tractor **-stange** *f* leveler, leveling rod **-stößel** *m* combined ram and leveling machine **-stück** *n* planing or smoothing piece **-vorrichtung** *f* planing jig **-walzwerk** *n* levelling mill

Planiglob *n* planisphere

Plani-meter *n* planimeter, integrator **-metrie** *f* planimetry **-metrieren** to measure with planimeter **-metrierung** *f* planimetering

Planke *f* plank, board, table, shelf

plänkeln to skirmish

planken to sheathe, plank

Planken-gang *m* streak **-stoß** *m* plank butt

plankonkav planoconcave

Plankontur *f* face profile

plankonvex planoconvex **-e Linse** planoconvex lens

Plan-kopierapparat *m* transverse copying attachment **-kopieren** to cross-form **-kopieren** *n* face copying **-kopiervorrichtung** *f* transverse copying attachment

Plankton Mikroskop *n* plankton-microscope

Plankung *f* planking

Plan-kurve *f* face cam **-kurvenfräsapparat** *m* longitudinal profiling apparatus **-ladung** *f* computed blasting charge **-lager** *n* plate bearing **-legung** *f* flattening (of film)

planliegen in Fokusebene to flatten in focal plane

Planlosigkeit *f* absence of pattern

planmäßig according to plan, methodical, scheduled, systematic **-er Nachschub** automatic supply **-e Vermischung** blending (as of fuels)

Plan-material *n* topographical material **-mühle** *f* grinding mill, grinder

Planoausleger *m* open sheet delivery

Planoptik *f* plane optics

planparallel plane parallel, with parallel faces **-e Diode** planar diode **-e Glasprüfmasse** *f* optical parallels **-e Richtung** planar sense **-er Wellenleiter** parallel plateguide

Planparallelität *f* plane parallelism

Plan-platte *f* flat face-plate **-pause** *f* blue print **-quadrat** *n* coordinate, square, map square, grid square

Planrad *n* crown wheel or gear, face gear **-zahn** *m* basic crown wheel

Plan-rahmen *m* single layer stenter **-rätter** *m* shaking table, screen, or sieve **-richten** *n* base-point method of laying **-richtung** *f* transverse direction **-rost** *m* plane grate, horizontal grate **-rücklaufkupplung** *f* transverse-return clutch **-rückwärts** transverse return

Planscheibe *f* faceplate, chuck, table **~ einer Drehbank** faceplate **auf ~ eingespannte Werkstücke** faceplate work

Planscheiben-drehbank *f* facing lathe **-durchmesser** *m* diameter of faceplate **-getriebe** *n* right-angle friction gear **-kloben** *m* faceplate jaw **-umlauf** *m* table speed **-zahnkranz** *m* table gear rim

Planschieber *m* cross slide **~ mit T-Nuten** tee-slotted cross slide

Plan-schirm *m* flat screen **-schleifen** *n* surface grinding **-schleifmaschine** *f* surface-grinding machine, floor grinder **-schlichten** to finish-face **-schlitten** *m* cross-slide rest **-schnitt** *m* planing cut **-schruppen** to rough-face

Plan-sektor *m* map-protractor set, map sector, arm and arc protractor **-senken** to spotface **-sichter** *m* plan sifting machine **-sitzlochdüse** *f* flat valve-type nozzle **-spiegel** *m* plane mirror **-spindel** *f* cross-feed screw **-stelle** *f* map position **-support** *m* facing head **-symmetrisch** planisymmetric **-tisch** *m* rectangular table **-trapez** *n* grid (as used in plotting), grid sector **-übung** *f* map exercise

Planum *n* subgrade, surface (ground surface) **-sohle** *f* formation level, formation line (R.R.)
Plan- und Rundschleifmaschine *f* face and circular grinding machine
Planung *f* design, plan(ning), project, scheme, proposition, plan verification **operative ~** operational planning
Planungskennzeichen *n* planning mark
Plan-unterlage *f* plane table **-verzahnung** *f* toothing or cogging of surface or face
planvoll carefully planned
plan-vor cross-advance
Plan-vor-Bewegung *f* forward cross traverse **-Kontakt** *f* cross-advance-contact **-Kupplung** *f* transverse-advance-clutch
Planvorschub *m* transverse feed **-spindel** *f* cross-feed screw **-teilscheibe** *f* cross-feed dial
Plan-wellenhorn *n* phase-corrected horn **-wirtschaft** *f* planned economy **-zeichnen** *n* map-making, plotting **-zeiger** *m* coordinate scale, plotting board, map-reading scale, roamer (for maps)
Planzug *m* cross-feed **Handrad für den ~** hand wheel for cross-feed **selbsttätiger ~** power cross-feed
Planzug-führung *f* cross slides **-kurbel** *f* cross-feed handle **-rad** *n* cross-feed gear **-ritzel** *n* cross-feed pinion **-spindel** *f* cross-feed screw
plan-zurück cross return
Plasma *n* plasma
Plasmabegrenzungsfeld *n*, **magnetisches ~** confining field
Plasma-begrenzungsstabilität *f* containment stability of plasma **-beschleuniger** *m* plasma accelerator **-fackelschweißen** *n* plasma jet welding **-flammspritzen** *n* plasma gun spraying
plasmagen plasmagene
Plasma-gleichgewicht *n* plasma balance **-grenzfläche** *f* plasma boundary **-lichtbogenschweißen** plasma arc jet welding **-triebwerk** *n* plasma drive **-wechselwirkung** *f* plasma interaction
plasmische Vererbung cytoplasmic inheritance
Plasmoid *n* plasmoid
Plastik *f* plastic art, sculpture, relief, plastic effect, stereoscopic or relief effect (pictures)
Plastilin *n* plasticine
plastisch plastic, stereoscopic (film), viscous (flow) **~ starre Grenze** *f* plastic-rigid boundary **-es Kriechen** creep-buckling
plastizieren plasticize
Plastizierer *m* plasticizer
Plastizität *f* plasticity
Plastizitäts-gebiet *n* plastic range **-grenze** *f* plastic limit **-koeffizient** plastic compliance **-messer** *m* plastometer **-zahl** *f* **-ziffer** *f* plasticity index
Plastopal plastopal
Plastometer *n* plastometer
Platane *f* plane tree
Plateau *n* plateau, elevated plane **-anstieg** *m* plateau slope **-karre** *f* platform truck, live skid
platieren to plate
Platierung *f* plating
Platin *n* platinum **-abfall** *m* platinum waste **-bariumzyanür** *n* platinous barium cyanide **-blase** *f* platinum still **-blech** *n* platinum foil, platinum plate **-bromür** *n* platinous bromide **-chlorür** *n* platinous chloride **-chlorwasserstoffsäure** *f* chloroplatinic acid **-draht** *m* platinum wire **-drahtnetz** *n* platinum gauze **-drahtöse** *f* platinum-wire loop
Platine *f* sheet bar, plate bar, plate slab, billet, semifinished flat, bedplate, side plate, stop rod, notched bar (weaving), plate
Platinelement *n* platinum thermocouple
Platinenbrett *n* bottom board
Platinenexzenter *m*, **eingearbeiteter ~** nicked sinker cam
Platinen-exzenterring *m* jack cam ring **-führungsring** *m* sinker dial **-fuß** *m* sinker butt **-kranz** *m* sinker ring (textiles) **-lager** *n* sheet-bar storage **-presse** *f* sinker lifting bar (textiles) **-schere** *f* plate-slab or sheet-bar shears **-straße** *f* slabbing-mill train **-tragering** *m* sinker rest ring **-walzwerk** *n* slabbing mill, sheet bar rolling mill **-wärmeofen** *m* pair furnace (metal.)
Platin-folie *f* platinum foil **-gefäß** *n* platinum vessel **-gehalt** *m* platinum content **-gerät** *n* platinum apparatus **-gerätschaft** *f* platinum ware **-grau** *n* platinum gray **-haltig** containing platinum, platiniferous **-hydroxydul** *n* platinous hydroxide
Platinichlorid *n* platinic chloride
platinieren to platinize, platinum plate, slab (in rolling)
platiniert platinum-plated
Platinierung *f* platinization
Platini-rhodanwasserstoffsäure *f* thiocyanoplatinic acid **-salz** *n* platinic salt
Platinisieren *n* platinizing
Platinit *n* platynite
Platinizyanwasserstoffsäure *f* cyanoplatinic acid, platinicyanic acid
Platin-kaliumchlorür *n* platinous potassium chloride **-kegel** *m* platinum cone **-kohle** *f* platinized charcoal **-kontakt** *m* platinum contact piece **-kontaktperle** *f* platinum contact bead **-konus** *m* platinum cone **-magnesiumzyanür** *n* platinous magnesium cyanide **-metall** *n* noble metal **-mohr** *m* platinum black **-natriumchlorür** *n* platinous sodium chloride
Platinochlorid *n* platinous chloride
Platinoid *n* platinoid
Platino-rhodanwasserstoffsäure *f* thiocyanoplatinous acid **-verbindung** *f* platinous compound
Platin-oxyd *n* platinum oxide, platinic oxide **-oxydul** *n* platinous oxide **-oxydulverbindung** *f* platinous compound **-oxydverbindung** *f* platinic compound **-papier** *n* platinotype paper **-platinrhodiumelement** *n* platinum-platinum-rhodium couple **-punkt** *m* platinum point (elec.) **-reihe** *f* platinum series or group **-rhodium** *n* platinum rhodium **-rückstand** *m* platinum residue
Platin-salmiak *m* ammonium chloroplatinate, platinic ammonium chloride **-sand** *m* sand for cleaning platinum **-schale** *f* platinum dish **-schiffchen** *n* platinum boat **-schraube** *f* platinum screw **-schwamm** *m* platinum sponge, spongy platinum **-schwarz** *n* platinum black **-spatel** *m* platinum spatula **-spirale** *f* platinum coil
Platinspitze *f* platinum point **mit ~ versehene Schraube** platinum-tipped screw
Platin-sulfür *n* platinous sulfide **-thermometer** *n* platinum resistance thermometer **-tiegel** *m* platinum crucible **-überzug** *m* platinum coating

-verbindung *f* platinum fusion **-zyanür** *n* platinous cyanide, platino-cyanide
platonische Körper platonic polyhedra
platt flat, level, plain, low **~ drücken** to flatten
Plättbank *f* side fillister
Plättbrett *n* ironing board
Plättchen *n* small plate, lamella, tip (for soldering cutting tools), fillet, label, list, small band, platelet **dünnes ~** lamina
plattdrücken to smash
Platte *f* (Wandtafel) panel; (Blatt, Blech) plate; (dünne ~) lamina; (Stein ~) slab, flag; (Kachel) tile; (Tisch) top; (Plakette) plaque; (Schall ~) record, disk; (Fleck) patch; pane, sheet, lamella, plateau, wafer, platform, lamination, leaf (of a table) **~ eines Kondensators** vane or plate of a condenser **ebene ~** flat surface **formierte ~** formed plate **lichthoffreie ~** nonhalation plate, plate free from halo **unganze ~** dumb piece
Plätteisen *n* smoothing iron, flatiron **-bolzen** *m* heater for flatiron
Plattel *f* disk of pig iron
plätten to iron, smooth
Platten-abmessungen *pl* plate size **-amalgamation** *f* plate amalgamation **-anguß** *m* plate jet **-anordnung** *f* slab geometry **-ansatz** *m* adapter plate attachment **-apparat** *m* plate- or box-type apparatus **-archiv** *n* record library **-artig** platelike **-aufspannung** *f* plate mounting **-balken** *m* T beam, (concrete) slab
Plattenband *n* platform, slat, flight, plate conveyer **~ mit Rollenführung** flat with side rollers
Plattenbandförderer *m* platform conveyer **schrägliegender ~** inclined-platform conveyer
Platten-bandsegment *n* apron pan **-belag** *m* flag, floor of slabs, table floor, pavement of paving tiles **-belastungsversuch** *m* plate bearing test **-beschlag** *m* plate fitting **-beschuß** *m* plate test (explosives) **-blitzableiter** *m* plate lightning arrester, plate or table protector **-block** *m* element **-breite** *f* width of slab, width of flange (in T beams) **-dekatur** *f* hydraulic pressfinish
Plattendruck *m* stereotype printing, stereotypography **-maschine** *f* copperplate printing machine
Platten-durchlaß *m* culvert covered with a slab **-ebene** *f* plate plane **-einsatz** *m* storage-battery cell **-elektrometer** *n* plate electrometer **-empfindlichkeit** *f* sensitivity of the plate **-fahne** *f* plate lug
Plattenfeder *f* plate spring **-druckmesser** *m* plate-spring manometer **-lehre** *f* diaphragm gauge **-manometer** *n* diaphragm pressure gauge
Platten-filter *n* plate filter **-förderer** *m* platform conveyer, plate conveyer **-fördermechanismus** *m* plate-feed mechanism **-format** *n* plate size
plattenförmig platelike, lamellar, laminar, laminated, plate-shaped, laminiform **-e Massenelektrode** (einer Zündkerze) earth plate
Platten-führungsschnitt *m* cutter **-füllstück** *n* plate liner **-funkenstrecke** *f* disk gap transmitter **-füßchen** *n* feet of a plate **-gang** *m* strake (shipbuilding) **-geräusch** *n* record noise, surface noise **-gewicht** *n* flat weight **-gleichrichter** *m* copperplate rectifier **-glimmer** *m* sheet mica **-größe** *f* plate dimension, plate size
Platten-halter *m* plate carrier, plateholder **-hauptpunkt** *m* principal point **-hebel** *m* manhole hook, lever for slabs, valve plate lever **-hobel** *m* side fillister
Platten-interferenzspektrum *n* channeled spectrum **-kamera** *f* plate camera **-kassette** *f* plateholder, plate magazine **-kiel** *m* plate keel **-kondensator** *m* disk condenser, plate condenser **-koordinate** *f* plate coordinate **-korn** *n* grain of emulsion (phot.) **-kröpfmaschine** *f* plate-joggling machine
Platten-kuppelung *f* plate clutch **-kurzschluß** *m* short-circuit between plates **-lager** *n* plate racks **-lagerung** *f* plate bearing or bed **-lampe** *f* flat plate (neon) lamp **-leger** *m* floor tiler, paver **magazin** *n* plateholder **-material** *n* pliable sheeting **-mittelpunkt** *m* plate center **-ofen** *m* multiple-hearth roaster
Plattenpaar *n* pair of plates **~ der Braunschen Röhre** deflecting plates of cathode-ray tube
Platten-pflaster *n* flagstone pavement **-paketsystem** *n* grid system (Berkeley) **-pulver** *n* flake powder, rolled powder **-rahmen** *m* plate frame **-rand** *m* margin of the plate **-reihen(bild)kammer** *f*, **-reihenbildner** *m* serial plate camera **-säge** *f* saw for sugar slabs **-satz** *m* group or set of plates **-schicht** *f* emulsion **-schlag** *m* disk wobble **-schieber** *m* double disc valve
Platten-schleifer *m* flat hammerer **-schluß** *m* plate conjunction **-schnellspannvorrichtung** *f* rapid plate locking-up device **-schnitt** *m* plate contour, plate section **-schrift** *f* stereotype **-spannschiene** *f* plate clamping bar **-spieler** *m* phonograph, disk-type phonograph or gramophone **-spieleranschluß** *m* gramophone socket **-teller** *m* turntable (tape rec.) **-tellerdrehzahl** *f* turntable speed **-tiefdruck** *m* plate gravure **-träger** *m* plate carrier, plate sheath, tray support, radium plaque **-turm** *m* plate column or tower
Platten-überlaufswehr *n* tray weir **-ventil** *n* disk valve, plate valve **-verblendung** *f* dressing or lining with tables or slabs **-vervielfacher** *m* plate multiplier **-wechsel** *m* plate change **-wechsler** *m* record changer **-weiche** *f* switch with sliding plates **-welle** *f* plate wave **-zerstäuber** *m* plate atomizer **-zink** *n* slab zinc
Plätter *m* backwasher
Plattform *f* platform, peel **~ mit vierfachem Durchgang** fourble board, fourble
Plattform-rost *m* platform grate **-verlängerung** *f* platform extension **-wagen** *m* flatcar
Plattfuß *m* flat foot, belly landing, flat tire, puncture
Plätt-glocke *f* smoothing iron **-hammer** *m* flattening or planishing hammer, plank flattener
plattieren to plate, electroplate, plait, sandwich
Plattieren *n* plating
Plattier-faden *m* plaiting thread **-schicht** *f* plating
plattiert plated (electroplated) **-es Blech** bimetal plate **-er Kristall** plated crystal **-e Schlauchware** plaited tubular goods (textiles) **-er Stahl** clad steel
Plattierung *f* plating (of metal), veneering (of wood)
Plattierungsschicht *f* plated coat
Plattier-walzwerk *n* plating mill **-werkstoff** *m* plating material
plattig bladed (lathlike), laminated

Plattine *f* plate, mill bar, slab
Plattkarte *f* flat map
Plättmaschine *f* flatting mill
Plättmaschinenarbeiter *m* plate shearer (wool)
Plattner-Prozeß *m* Plattner (wet chlorine-gas) process
Plattschiene *f* plate rail
Plättwalze *f* smoothing roll
Plattzange *f* flat-nose pliers
Platymeter *m* platymeter
Platz *m* location, place, aid station, space, (public) square, switchboard position, room position, spot, seat, position (job), site **~ für den zwischenstaatlichen Verkehr** foreign-service position **den ~ auswählen** to select the site **besetzter ~** occupied position **fester ~** fortified place **freier ~** hole (in nuclear theory) **A-Platz mit Wahlzusatz** key-pulsing or dialing A position **B-Platz mit Wahlzusatz** dial system of cordless B position
Platz-aushilfe *f* teamwork (teleph.) **-ausnutzung** *f* utilization of space **-ausrüstung** *f* position equipment **-beamtin** *f* telephonist **-bedarf** *m* space occupied, required floor space **-belegung** *f* position wiring, booking **-beleuchtung** *f* lighting of squares, airfield lighting **-beschicken** to stockpile **-besetztrelais** *n* position busy relay **-buchungsanlage** *f* seat reservation system
Plätzchen *n* small place, little cake, lozenge, troche, tablet
Platzeinflugzeichen *n* inner marker beacon
platzen to burst, split, crack, explode, detonate, shatter, blow out, implode, break open
Platzen *n* bursting, blowout
Platz-ersparnis *f* space safing **-funkfeuer** *n* locator beacon **-gebrauch** *m* local usage **-geschäft** *n* local business, spot transactions **-grenze** *f* local boundary **-gruppe** *f* supervisor's section, switchboard **-hinderniszeichen** *n* obstruction mark **-höhe** *f* height of burst
Platz-karte *f* ticket for reserved seat **-ladeband** *n* yard belt **-lampe** *f* pilot lamp, pilot indicator, position pilot lamp **-lampenrelais** *n* pilot relay **-mangel** *m* restricted space, want of place **-membran(e)** *f* bursting diaphragm **-regen** *m* downpour, pelting rain, cloudburst **-runde** *f* aerodrome traffic circuit **-rundenführungsfeuer** *pl* circling guidance lights
Platz-schalter *m* grouping key **-schaltung** *f* operator's speaking circuit **-schnur** *f* switchboard cord **-umrandungslicht** *n* boundary light **-umschalter** *m* position-switching key, coupling key **-verkehrskontrollstelle** *f* aerodrome control tower **-vertreter** *m* representative
Platzwechsel *m* phantom transposition, transpositions, circuit, crossing, twisting, exchange of places (of electrons, etc.), interchange of sites **-folge** *f* transposition system **-gestänge** *n* transposition pole **-plastizität** *f* self-diffusion plasticity
Platz-zähler *m* position peg count register, position meter **-zusammenschaltung** *f* (mit Platzschalter), grouping of positions, coupling
Plazentographie *f* placentography
plazieren to place
p-Leiter p-type semiconductor
Pl(e)iodynatron *n* pliodynatron
Pl(e)iotron *n* pliotron
Plenarsitzung *f* general meeting
pleochroitischer Halo pleochroic halo
Plessit *m* plassite
Pleuel *n* piston rod, (Auto) connecting rod **inneres ~ eines Gabelpleuels** blade rod of a forked-rod and blade-rod assembly **~ für Zündmomentausgleich** connecting rod system with corrected dead-center angles
Pleuel-lager *n* connecting-rod bearing **-lagerzapfen** *m* crank pin **-schaft** *m* connecting-rod blade **-stange** *f* connecting rod, suspension link, driving rod
Pleuelstangen-büchse *f* connecting rod bush **-bügel** *m* connecting rod strap **-endlager** *n* connecting-rod big-end bearing **-knopf** *m* strap **-kopf** *m* head (connecting rod) **-lager** *n* connecting-rod bearing or bushing, big-end bearing **-schaft** *m* shank of connecting rod **-schauplatte** *f* connecting-rod inspection plate **-verbindung** *f* connecting-rod joint **-verhältnis** *n* stroke-connecting-rod ratio
Pleuelstern *m* master- and link-rod assembly
Pleurographie *f* pleurography
Plexiglas *n* safety glass, plexiglass **-lichtleiter** *m* plexiglass light conductor
pliant flexible
Plintziegel *m* plinth brick
Pliodynatron *n* pliodynatron
Pliotron *n* B-electrode tube, triode
plissieren to pleat
Plombe *f* seal, plumber's wiped joint, lead seal
Plombendraht und Bleiplombe seal wire and lead
Plomben-verschluß *m* lead seal **-zange** *f* lead-sealing pliers, hand metal punch
plombieren to seal, lead, fill (tooth)
plombiert lead-sealed
Plombierung *f* leading (calking), plumbing
Plombier-vorrichtung *f* sealing device **-zange** *f* lead-seating pliers
Plombitbehandlung *f* doctor treatment (petroleum)
Plötz *m* broad iron wedge
plötzlich sudden, unexpected, abrupt, precipitous **-er Lichtstrahl** glance **-er Sackflug** whipstall (aviation) **-es Schwingen** spilling over **-er Stoß** jolt **-er Zusammenstoß** dash
Plötzlichkeit *f* suddenness, abruptness
Plumbi-oxyd *n* plumbic oxide, lead dioxide **-verbindung** *f* plumbic compound
Plumboniobit *m* plumboniobite
Plumbo-salz *n* plumbous salt **-verbindung** *f* plumbous compound
plump buxom, plump, clumsy, coarse, iron-handed
plündern to plunder, pillage
Plünderung *f* pillage, looting
Plunger *m* plunger **-kolben** *m* plunger, plunger piston or bucket **-pumpe** *f* plunger pump
Plus-ader *f* positive wire **-belag** *m* positive deposit **-bestand** *m* surplus stock **-bürste** *f* positive brush
plüsen, die Wolle ~ to pick, pull, or pluck the wool
Plus-kontakt *m* positive contact **-lehre** *f* plus gauge **-leitung** *f* positive wire **-platte** *f* positive plate (of a storage battery) **-pol** *m* positive pole **-strang** *m* normal line
Plus- und Minusabmaß *n* plus and minus limits

Pluszeichen *n* plus sign
Plutoniumspaltung *f* plutonium fission
Plutonylion *n* plutonylion
Pluviometer *n* pluviometer
Pneu *n* tire (pneumatic)
Pneumatik *m* (pneumatic) tire, tube
pneumatisch pneumatic **-er Anlasser** compressed-air starter **-es Einstellrelais** pneumatic positioning relay **-e Förderung** conveying by (compressed) air, pneumatic conveying **-e Nietmaschine** rivet gun **-er Niethammer** pneumatic riveter **-es Pult** compressed-air panel **-e Regeleinrichtung** pneumatic (pressure) control device
Pneumometer *n* pneumatometer
Pneuwalze *f* pneumatic tired roller
Poch-blech *n* stamp screen **-eisen** *n* iron of the pounder, iron shoe of the stamper, stamp shoe, stamp socket, stamp head
pochen to stamp, pound, crush, knock, beat
Pochen *n* crushing, stamping
Poch-erz *n* milling ore, stamping ore, poor ore **-gänge** *m pl* impure or inferior ore **-gestein** *n* stamp rock **-hammer** *m* stamp mill **-klotz** *m* foundation timber, mortar block **-laden** *m* mortar, pounding or stamping trough **-leistung** *f* stamp capacity **-mehl** *n* pulverized or stamped ore **-mühle** *f* stamp mill **-satz** *m* stamp battery, ore slime **-säule** *f* battery post
Poch-schlamm *m* ore slime, slurry **-schlegel** *m* ore hammer **-schlich** *m* ore slime, slurry **-schuh** *m* beating, stamp, ore-crushing, or battery shoe (min.) **-schuhhülse** *f* stamp socket **-sohle** *f* stamp die **-steiger** *m* mill foreman **-stempel** *m* stamp die, stamp, battery dies **-stempelbeschwerer** *m* stamphead
Poch-stempelreihe *f* stamp battery **-stempelschaft** *m* stamp-stem guide **-stuhl** *m* stamp-battery framing **-trog** *m* stamp mortar, mortar box **-trübe** *f* stamp pulp **-unterlage** *f* stamp subbase **-werk** *n* stamp mill, steam stamp **-werkamalgamation** *f* plate amalgamation **-werkgerüst** *n* stamp-mill framing
Pockennarbe *f* pit (from corrosion)
Pockholz *n* lignum vitae **-lager** *n* lignum vitae bearing
Podest *n* platform, landing (staircase) **gesprengtes ~** trussed resting place
Podestbalken *m* joist of a landing place
Podium *n* rostrum
Pohlsche Wippe Pohl commutator
Pointierungsmikroskop *n* guiding microscope
Poise *f* poise
Poisson-sches Gesetz Poisson's law **-sche Zahl** Poisson's ratio
Poissonzahl *f* Poisson's ratio
Pokal *m* cup (award)
Pol *m* terminal of an element, pole, pile (in fabrics), origin (geom.), peak **ausgeprägter ~** salient pole **entgegengesetzter ~, gleichnamiger ~** like pole, similar pole **induzierender ~** inducing pole **induzierter ~** induced pole **magnetischer ~ der Erde** terrestrial magnetic pole **nordsuchender ~** north-seeking pole **ungleichnamiger ~** opposite pole, unlike pole
Pole (mit) Nuten crenellated poles **mit getrennten Polen** multipolar switch, with separate poles
Polabstand *m* pole distance, pole clearance **freier ~** pole clearance
Polackermast *m* pole mast
Polanker *m* armature with salient pole
Polanzeiger *m* pole finder
polar polar **-e Luftlinienentfernung** polar distance **-e Seeluftmasse** polar maritime air
Polar-achse *f* polar axis **-aufnahme** *f* polar measurement **-charakteristik** *f* polar characteristic **-diagramm** *n* polar diagram, radiation pattern
Polare *f* polar curve (aerodyn), polar (line)
Polar-front *f* polar front **-halbmesser** *m* polar semi-diameter
Polarimeter *n* polarimeter
Polarisation *f* polarization **~ eines Mediums** polarization of a medium **lineare ~** plane polarization **zirkulare ~** circular polarization
Polarisationsapparat *m* polarimeter, saccharimeter, polarizing apparatus, polariscope
Polarisationsebene *f* plane of polarization **Drehung der ~** rotation of plane of polarization, polarization error
Polarisations-effekt *m* polarization error **-einrichtung** *f* polarizing attachment **-erscheinung** *f* polarization phenomenon **-fading** *n* polarization fading **-fehlerfrei** free from polarization error (direction finder) **-kapazität** *f* polarization capacitance **-kolben** *m* sugar flask **-konstante** *f* polarizing constant **-nachweis** *m* polarization detection **-optisch** photoelastic
Polarisations-prisma *n* polarizer **-schwund** *m* polarization fading **-spannung** *f* electromotive force of polarization, polarization voltage **-spektralphotometer** *n* polarization spectrophotometer **-strom** *m* polarizing current, polarization current **-winkel** *m* angle of polarization, Brewster angle **-zelle** *f* electrolytic valve, polarization cell **-zustand** *m* state of polarization, polarization state
Polarisator *m* polarizer **-nikol** *n* polarizing Nicol
polarisch polar **-es Dreieck** polar triangle **-er Tiefdruck** polar low
polarisierbar polarizable
Polarisierbarkeit *f* polarizability
polarisieren to polarize
polarisierende Wirkung polarizing power
polarisiert polarized, polar **eben ~** (Wellenstrahlung) plane-polarized **geradlinig ~** plane-polarized **-es Licht** polarized light **-es Relais** polarized relay **-e Strahlung** polarized radiation **-e Welle** polarized wave
Polarisierung *f* polarization
Polariskop *n* polariscope
Polaristrobometer *n* polaristrobometer
Polarität *f* polarity **positive ~ der Sendung** positive polarity of transmission
Polaritätswechsel *m* alternation of polarity
Polar-jahr *n* sidereal year **-karte** *f* polar chart **-koordinate** *f* polar coordinate **-koordinatenröhre** *f* polar-coordinate tube, circular time-base tube **-kreis** *m* polar circle, Arctic Circle **-licht** *n* polar aurora, northern light **-luft** *f* polar air **-luftmasse über dem Stillen Ozean** polar Pacific air mass
Polarogramm *n* polarogram
Polarographie *f* polarography
polaroides Material polaroid material
Polar-planimeter *n* polar planimeter **-stern** *m* north star, Polaris, lodestar, Pole Star **-strom** *m*

arctic or polar current **-wirbel** *m* polar eddy or vortex

Pol-bedeckung *f* pole arc, pole-pitch percentage **-bedeckungsfaktor** *m* pitch factor **-bogen** *m* pole arc, pole-pitch percentage **-bolzen** *m* terminal pillar or post **-brücke** *f* connecting strap

Polder *m* land reclaimed from sea by means of dikes, swamps, marshes **-mühle** *f* windmill for drainage

Pol-distanz *f* polar distance **-draht** *m* connection (of cells), electrode **-dreck** *m* refining skimmings, oxide drosses

Pole *f* pile, nap, bar

Poleck *n* summit (cryst.)

Polecke *f* vertical solid angle

Poleffekt *m* pole effect

polen to pole

Polen *n* poling

Poleyöl *n* pennyroyal oil

Pol-entfernung *f* pole distance **-faden** *m* movable or turning thread of the warp **-fahne** *f* pole lug **-figur** *f* polar points

Polfläche *f* polar surface **~ einer Bewegung** axoid of a rigid body motion **wirksame ~** active polar surface

Pol-flügel *m* front standard (textiles) **-gehäuse** *n* pole casing **-gewebe** *n* pile fabrics

Polhodie *f* polhode

Polhöhe *f* polar altitude

Polhöhen-ablesung *f* polar altitude reading **-verstellung** *f* polar adjustment (teleph.)

Polhorn *n* pole tip, extreme tip of the pole shoe

Polianit *m* polianite

Police *f* policy

Polier *m* foreman, overseer **-ahle** *f* round broach **-anlage** *f* polishing plant **-bahn** *f* grinding track **-bar** capable of being polished **-bock** *m* polisher's frame **-drücken** to burnish **-eisen** *n* polishing tool

polieren to polish, burnish, buff, smooth, lap, planish, furbish, clean, glaze

Polieren *n* burnishing, ashing, polishing, grinding, rubbing

Poliererei *f* polishing room

polier-fähig polishable **-fähigkeit** *f* amenability to receive polish **-filz** *m* polishing cloth **-filzscheibe** *f* felt polishing wheel **-fläche** *f* polishing surface **-flüssigkeit** *f* polishing liquid **-gerüst** *n* planishing stand, planisher **-kaliber** *n* planishing pass, finishing groove, last groove **-masse** *f* polishing composition **-mittel** *n* polishing medium, polishing powder, polishing material **-motor** *m* polishing motor

Polier-öl *n* polishing oil **-papier** *n* polishing paper, sandpaper, abrasive paper **-pulver** *n* polishing powder **-reiber** *m* glass burnisher **-rot** *n* polishing red, colcothar, crocus, rouge **-scheibe** *f* buff(er) (polisher), polishing wheel **-schiefer** *m* infusorial earth, polishing slate **-schleifen** to polish-grind **-schleifen** *n* flexible grinding **-schleifmaschine** *f* grinding and polishing machine **-stahl** *m* engraver's burnisher **-ständer** *m* finishing stand **-stich** *m* finishing pass, final pass, planishing pass

poliert polished

Polier-trommel *f* rumble **-tuch** *n* polishing cloth **-walze** *f* finisher, polishing roll **-werkzeug** *n* burnishing tool

polig polar

Polimerie *f* polymerization

Polinduktion *f* pole induction

Politur *f* polish, glass, finish, gloss, shine, luster **-ballen** *m* polishing mop **-lack** *m* flatting varnish **-messer** *m* glossmeter

Polizei *f* police **-amt** *n* police station **-funkdienst** *m* police radio service

polizeilich police

Polizei-rufanlage *f* police signal system **-wache** *f* police station

Pol-joch *n* double yoke **-kante** *f* terminal edge **-kern** *m* pole shoe **-kette** *f* nap or pile warp (textiles)

Polklemme *f* (pole) terminal, binding post (elec.) **~ des Feldelements** binding screw

Polklemmenpapier *n* pole paper, pole-finding paper

Pol-körner *pl* pole tips **-leiste** *f* connecting strap, terminal bar

Poller *m* mooring post, bollard, double bollard

Pollücke *f* pole clearance, interpolar gap

Polonium *n* polonium

Pol-paar *n* pair of poles **-paket** *n* laminated pole **-papier** *n* phenolphthalein (test) paper **-platte** *f* pole plate, pole piece (of an electric furnace) **-prüfer** *m* polarity indicator

Polrad *n* cogwheel, magnet wheel, field spider **-scheider** *m* field spider separator **-winkel** *m* load angle

Pol-rand *m* pole tip **-reagenzpapier** *n* pole-finding paper, pole test paper **-richtung** *f* polarity **-schermaschine** *f* pile shearing cutter **-schiene** *f* pole rail **-schritt** *m* pole step (elec.)

Polschuh *m* pole shoe, pole piece, lug face **~ des Magnets** pole piece

Pol(schuh)-fläche *f* pole face **-kante** *f* edge of the pole pieces **-lamelle** *f* lamination of pole shoes **-schuhlos** poleless

Polschuhrand *m* pole tip **abgeschrägte Polschuhränder** skewed pole tips

Polschuhspaltbreite *f* shim separation

Pol-sequenz *f* polar sequence **-spalt** *m* pole gap **-spule** *f* pole coil **-stärke** *f* strength of poles **-steinkraft** *f* magnetic power or attraction

Polster *n* pillow, cushion, padding, stuffing, belt (cable), pad **-bürste** *f* upholstery brush **-gummiplatte** *f* padding rubber sheets **-holz** *n* filler, boarding or bridging joist **-leinwand** *f* scrim

polstern to cushion, upholster, line, pad, stuff

Polsternagelstempel *m* upholstery-nail die

Polster-schmiervorrichtung *f* pad lubricator **-sitz** *m* cushioned seat **-stange** *f* iron rod for stuffing collars

Polsterung *f* padding, upholstery

Pol-strahl *m* radius vector, polar line **-stück** *n* polar piece **-sucher** *m* polarity indicator **-suchglimmlampe** *f* polarity-finder glow tube, polarity indicator **-suchpapier** *n* pole-finding paper

Polteilung *f* pole pitch **~ am Stromwender** pole pitch at the commutator

poltern to remove the (etching or pickling) acid

Polterprobe *f* hammering test

polumschaltbar pole-changeable **-er Motor** two-speed motor, motor with commutable poles

Pol-umschalter *m* pole reverser **-umschaltung** *f* pole changing

Polumschaltungsregelung *f* pole changing control
Polung *f* polarity
Polungsweiser *m* polarity indicator
Pol-verdunkelung *f* polar blackout **-verfahren** *n* plotting by polar coordinates **-verschiebung** *f* polar wandering **-versetzung** *f* pole dislocation
Polwechsel *m* alternation, reversal, or change of polarity **-zahl** *f* frequency, number of alternations
Polwechsler *m* pole changer, ringing vibrator, transformer, current alternator, change-over switch **-feder** *f* pole-changing spring
Pol-weite *f* polar distance **-wender** *m* change-over switch, current reverser
Polyäthylen *n* polyethylene
Polychroismus *m* polychroism
Polycrasit *m* polycrase
Polycythemie *f* polycythemia
Polyeder *n* polyhedron, polyhedra **-struktur** *f* polyhedral structure
polyedrisch polyhedral **-er Winkel** polyhedral angle
Polyelektronen *pl* polyelectrons
Polyene *n* polyene (butadiene, etc.)
Polyganisierung *f* polyganization
Polygon *n* polygon, traverse **sich selbst ein- und umbeschriebenes ~** polygon inscribed into and circumscribed about itself
Polygon-abbildung *f* polygon mapping **-ausrüstung** *f* traverse outfit
polygoniometrische Aufgabe traverse problem
polygonisch polygonal
polygonisieren to make a traverse survey
Polygonisierung *f* polygonization, traverse surveys
Polygon-messung *f* polygoniometry, polygon measurement, traverse measuring **-punkt** *m* traverse station **-schaltung** *f* mesh (triangle or delta connection) **-zug** *m* traverse, polygonal course **-zugverfahren** *n* point-slope method
Polygraph *m* psycho-integroammeter
polygraphisches Gewerbe polygraphy
Polyhalit *m* polyhalite
Polykras *m* polycrase
polykristallin polycrystalline
polymer polymeric **-einheitlich** of the same degree of polymerization
Poly-merie *f* polymerization, polymerism **-merisat** *n* polymeride **-merisation** *f* polymerization **-merisieren** to polymerize **-meter** *n* polymeter **-methylmetakrylat** polymethyl metacrylate **-morph** polymorphous, polymorphic **-morphie** *f* polymorphism, polymorphy **-morphisch** polymorphous, polymorphic **-morphismus** *m* polymorphism, polymorphy
Polynom *n* multinominal, polynomial **-rechner** *m* equation solver
Polyose *f* polysaccharide
Poly-propylenfolie *f* polypropylene sheet **-somatisch** polysomatic
Polystyrol *n* polystyrene (polystyrole) **-schaum** *m* expanded polystyrene
Poly-sulfid *n* polysulfide **-symmetrie** *f* polysymmetry **-synthetisch** polysynthetic **-technisch** polytechnic
Polytrope *f* polytropic line
Polytropenbeziehung *f* polytropic relation
polytropisch polytropic **-e Zustandsänderung** polytropic change of state
Polytypie *f* cast
Polyxen *n* native platinum
Pol-zahl *f* number of poles **-zahn** *m* pole tooth, spoke **-zwinge** *f* screw clamp **-zwischenraum** *m* pole clearance, interpolar space or gap
Pommritzen *n* topping in the ground with the topping spade before lifting
Pompejanischrot *n* Pompeian red
Poncelet *n* poncelet **-brücke** *f* balance bridge of Poncelet **-rad** *n* Poncelet wheel
ponderomotorisch ponderomotive
Ponton *m* pontoon, barge **-brücke** *f* pontoon bridge **-fähre** *f* pontoon ferry
Ponton-kammer *f* caisson chamber **-kran** *m* floating crane **-wagen** *m* pontoon truck, pontoon carrier **-zug** *m* pontoon platoon
Poolverkehr *m* pooled air traffic, reciprocal interstate air traffic
Pore *f* pore, void, pocket
Poren-anteil *m* proportion of voids (pores) **-bildner** *m* pore forming material **-dichte** *f* porosity density **-flüssigkeitsanelastizität** *f* pore-fluid anelasticity **-frei** non porous **-füller** *m* primer (protective coatings), filler **-gehalt** *m* void content, pore content **-größe** *f* size of pore **-leitfähigkeit** *f* pore conductivity **-raum** *m* pore space, cell space, cell cavity, pore volume **-volumen** *n* volume of voids **-wasser** *n* pore water **-wasserdruck** *m* pore-water pressure **-wasserdruckhöhe** *f* pore water head
Porenwasserverlust *m*, **spezifischer ~** coefficient of volume change
Poren-zahl *f* void ratio **-ziffer** *f* void ratio (volume of voids to volume of solids) **-zwischenraum** *m* pore space
porig porous
Porigkeit *f* porosity
Porometer *n* porometer
porös porous, spongy **-es Gefäß** porous pot **-er Scheider** separator diaphragm **-e Scheidewand** diaphragm **faulige oder -e Stelle** speck **-e Wand** porous barrier **-e Zelle** *f* porous pot
Porosimeter *n* porosimeter
Porosität *f* porosity
Porositätsgrad *m* degree of porosity
Porphyr *m* porphyry
porphyrisch porphyritic **-es Gefüge** porphyritic structure
Porphyrwalze *f* porphyry roller
Portal *n* gantry (of a crane), front gate, porch **-kran** *m* gantry crane, portal crane, traveling gantry (for blocks) **-mast** *m* portal tower
Portion *f* portion, ration (man's) **eiserne ~** iron ration
Porto *n* postage **-frei** postage (carriage) paid, frank **-pflichtig** liable to postage **-satz** *m* rate of postage
Porzellan *n* porcelain, china **-artig** porcelain, porcellanic **-dampfschale** *f* porcelain evaporating basin **-doppelglocke** *f* double-shed porcelain insulator
Porzellanerde *f* porcelain clay, kaolin **geschlammte ~** kaolin
Porzellan-glasur *f* porcelain glaze **-isolator** *m* porcelain insulator **-maler** *m* painter on china **-märbel** *f* porcelain marble **-masse** *f* porcelain body **-matrize** *f* porcelain die **-rohr** *n* porcelain

tube -schiefer *m* bituminous slate -schiffchen *n* porcelain boat -ton *m* porcelain clay, kaolin

Posamentenfabrik *f* trimming manufacturing

Posamentier *m* lacemaker, laceman, trimming or loop maker

Posamentmaschine *f* lace and trimming machine

Posaune *f* trombone; (organ) trombone stop **durchschlagende ~** trombone with free reed (organ)

Posaunen-abgleich *m* trombone feeder **-artige Leitung** lobelike or telescopic condenser **-artig verschiebbar** telescoping, shiftable, trombone-fashion, or like a telescope **-auszug** *m* telescoping means, extension means **-einstellung** *f* trombone tuning **-federung** *f* telescopic shock absorber **-rohr** *n* telescopic tube (pipe) **-stopfbüchse** *f* telescopic stuffing box

Position *f* item, position (navig) **~ eines Zieles** plot

Positions-anzeiger *m* position indicator **-bestimmungsgerät** *n* air position indicator **-fadenmikrometer** *n* position filar micrometer **-indizierender Fernmesser** position telemeter **-lampe** *f* navigation light, position light **-laterne** *f* position light, running light **-licht** *n* navigation light **-linie** *f* line of position (LOP) (navig.) **-meldung** *f* position report **-winkel** *m* apex angle, angle of sight

positiv positive **-es Bild** positive (phot.) **-e Druckkabine** positive-pressure cabin **-e und negative Elektrizität** positive and negative electricity **-es Elektron** positron **-es Gebiet** positive area **-es Giermoment** positive yawing moment **-er Gitterstrom** "back-lash," inverse or reverse grid current **-es Ion** cation **-e elektrische Ladungseinheit** unit-positive charge **-e Polarität** positive polarity of transmission **-e Verwindung** wash-in (aviation)

Positiv-abtastung *f* scanning positive slides **-pause** *f* positive print **-stellung** *f* observing position of a photograph (positive position)

Positron *n* positron, positive electron, antielectron

Positronenzerfall *m* positron-decay

Positronium *n* positronium

Positronstrahler *m* positron emitter

Post *f* mail (letters), post **-abteil** *n* mail compartment or room

Postament *n* pedestal, base

Postanweisung *f* post-office money order **telegraphische ~** money telegram

Post-beihilfe *f* mail subsidy **-bote** *m* postman **-dampfer** *m* mail steamer **-dienst** *m* mail service **-direktion** *f* post-office authorities

Posten *m* place, post; (Ausstellung) situation, post, job; (Waren) lot, parcel; (Betrag) amount; item, entry, quantity, position, station sentry, sentinel, guard, picket, batch, series, ball, piece, lump (glass mfg.) **~ abtragen** to clear items

Posten-begrenzer *m* line limitating device **-destillation** *f* batch distillation **-speiser** *m* plug feeder (on a glass furnace) **-umdrucker** *m* facsimile posting machine **-verfahren** *n* batch process

Post-fach *n* post-office box **-flieger** *m* air-mail pilot **-flug** *m* mail flight **-flugboot** *n* mail flying boat **-flugzeug** *n* mail plane, postal plane **-karte** *f* postcard **-ladung** *f* mail load **-lagernd** c/o general delivery **-mikrophon** *n* solid-back transmitter, carbon-back microphone **-nachnahme** *f* post-office money order **-nebenstelle** *f* exchange extension set

Post-omnibus *m* mail bus **-ordonnanz** *f* mail orderly **-relais** *n* post-office standard relay **-sachen** *pl* mails **-sack** *m* mail bag **-schein** *m* postal receipt **-schließfach** *n* P.O.Box **-sperre** *f* interruption of postal services **-stempel** *m* postmark

postulieren to postulate

post-wendend by return mail **-wertzeichen** *n* postage stamp **-zoll** *m* postal customs

Pot *n* potentiometer

Potential *n* potential function, potential **abgeschirmtes ~** screened potential **~ mit rechteckigem Topf** square well potential **natürliche Potentiale des Erdbodens** natural earth potentials

Potential-abfall *m* fall or decrease of potential, potential drop **-anstieg** *m* increase in potential **-berg** *m* potential barrier **-bild** *n* potential diagram, electrical image

Potentialdifferenz *f* potential difference **~ an der Berührungsstelle zweier verschiedener Lösungen** electromotive force at liquid junctions

Potential-einheit *f* unit potential **-emission** *f* potential liberation **-fall** *m* fall or decrease potential

Potentialfläche *f* potential surface **konstante ~** equipotential surface, isopotential surface

potential-formabhängig shape dependent **-formunabhängig** shape independent

Potentialgefälle *n* electric-potential gradient or fall drop of potential

Potential-gleichung *f* potential equation **-gradient** *m* potential gradient **-hügel** *m* potential barrier **-kasten** *m* potential hole or well **-lage** *f* potential position **-linie** *f* equipotential or potential line **-mulde** *f* potential hole or well **-satz** *m* potential theorem **-schaubild** *n* potential diagram **-schwelle** *f* potential barrier **-senke** *f* potential trough **-sonde** *f* potentiometer

Potential-sprung *m* potential drop, change in potential (elec.) **-streuung** *f* potential leakage, stray **-strömung** *f* fluid flow without compressibility, potential flow, irrotational motion **-tiefe** *f* potential well depth **-topf** *m* potential well **-topftiefe** *f* well depth parameter

Potential-unterschied *m* potential difference **-verringerung** *f* potential drop **-verschiebung** *f* displacement in potential **-verteilung** *f* potential distribution **-vorrichtungsisolator** *m* bushing potential device **-wall** *m* potential barrier **-wert** *m* potential value **-wirbel** *m* potential vortex

potentiell potential **-e Kraft** latent energy **-e Wärme** potential heat

Potentiometer *n* potentiometer, control **-anordnung** *f* potentiometer arrangement **-anzeigeinstrument** *n* potentiometer indicator **-kreis** *m* potentiometer circuit **pyrometer** *n* potentiometer pyrometer **-regler** *m* potentiometer controller **-schreiber** *m* potentiometer recorder

potentiometrisch potentiometric

Potenz *f* power, exponent **in die *n*te ~ erheben** to raise to the *n*th power **wachsende Potenzen** ascending powers

Potenz-ansatz *m* exponential equation **-exponent** *m* exponent of power **-gefälle** *n* potential gra-

dient **-gesetz** *n* exponential law, exponential function
potenzieren to involve, raise to a higher power
Potenzierung *f* involution
Potenz-produkt *n* power product **-reihe** *f* exponential series, power series, potential equation **-reihenentwicklung** *f* power series expansion **-schwelle** *f* nuclear-penetration factor
Pottasche *f* potash, potassium carbonate, pearl-ash **-fluß** *m* black salt, melted ashes, crude potash
Pottlot *n* black lead, plumbago, graphite
Poussiere *f* blue powder
Poyntingscher Vektor Poynting vector
Pozzuolan *n*, **-erde** *f* pozzuolana
Präambel *f* preamble
Pracht-ausgabe *f* large paper edition, edition de luxe **-einband** *m* rich binding **-exemplar** *n* exceedingly fine specimen
Prädetonationsweg *m* predetonation path
Prädilektion *f* preference
Prädissoziation *f* predissociation
präformiert preformed
Präge *f* stamp, swage **-anstalt** *f* mint **-bär** *m* ram (of a press) **-druck** *m* relief print **-film** *m* engraved sound film **-form** *f* matrix, mold **-galvanos** *pl* embossing electros **-gesenk** *n* stamping tool **-latte** *f* die (printing) **-maschine** *f* coining or embossing machine
prägen to stamp, coin, strike, imprint, impress, emboss
Prägen *n* stamping
Präge-polieren *n* burnishing, roll polish, roll finish **-presse** *f* embossing machine, die stamp, screw press **-stanze** *f* coining, stamping, or embossing die **-stempel** *m* press die, stamp, stamp die **-streifen** *m* chadless tape **-werk** *n* stamping press **-zeichen** *n* embossed character
Präg-ring *m* coining ferrule **-schatz** *m* mintage **-stock** *m* matrix
Prägung *f* stamping, coining
Prahm *m* lighter, pontoon, barge **-bagger** *m* dredger transporting the ballast, hopper dredger
Präionisation *f* preionization
Präkambrium *n* precambrium
Präklusivfrist *f* preclusion period
Praktikant *m* trainee
Praktiker *m* experienced man, practical man
praktisch practically speaking, practical, practicable **~ dasselbe** virtually the same **-e Einheit** practical unit **-e Funkpeilungskarte** radio facility chart **-e Gipfelhöhe** service ceiling, practical ceiling **-es Meßsystem** practical system of measurement **-er Versuch** practical test, service test
Pralan *m* pontoon
Präliminarfrieden *m* preliminary peace
Präliminarien *pl* preliminaries
Prall *m* rebound
prall tight, taut, rigid
Prall-anzeiger *m* gas-cell alarm (airship), gas-pressure indicator, volume or fullness indicator **-blech** *n* baffle plate **-brecher** *m* coarse reduction impact crusher **-düse** *f* rebound nozzle **-elektrode** *f* electron mirror, dynode, reflecting electrode, impactor anode, target electrode, reflecting impactor
prallen to bound, rebound, bounce, be reflected **auf einander ~** to meet violently **zusammen ~** to rush together
Prall-filter *m* **für Luft mit Ölbenetzung** viscous-impingement-type air filter **-fläche** *f* breaker plate (of hammer mill) **-flächenluftfilter** *n* impingement-type air filter **-haltung** *f* maintenance pressure (balloon)
Prallheit *f* taut status
Prall-höhe *f* pressure height or altitude **-kraft** *f* resiliency, elasticity **-luftschiff** *n* pressure airship, nonrigid dirigible **-melder** *m* gas pressure alarm **-mühle** *f* impact pulverizer **-platte** *f* reflecting plate, target, baffleplate, deflecting plate, bounce plate
Prall-schirm *m* baffle plate, deflector **-stift** *m* flame spreader (in heating devices) **-stock** *m* anvil, recoil, spring beam **-stück** *n* striking piece, pecker block, die **-trommel** *f* baffle pulley **-wand** f baffle (of the separator) **-winkel** *m* angle of reflection, angle of ricocheting
Prämie *f* premium, bounty
Prämienlohnsystem *n* premium bonus system
prämiieren to award a prize or a medal
Prandtlrohr *n* pitot tube
Prandtlsche Zahl Prandtl group
pränumerieren to prepay
Präparat *n* preparation
Präparateraum *m* specimen room
Präparathalter *m* slide holder
präparativ preparatory
Präparierarbeit *f* dissecting work
Präparierdunkelfeldkondensor *m* dissecting dark-field condenser
präparieren to prepare, treat
Präparieren *n* sensitization (phot.)
Präparier-lupe *f* dissecting lens **-salz** *n* stannate of soda
präsentieren to present
Präsenzstärke *f* effectives, effective strength
Praseodym *n* praseodymium
Prasseln *n* frying (radio), crackle, rustle, rattle
Prasselschutzkugel *f* corona ball (of whip antenna)
Prätschmaschine *f* washing machine with beetles, beater
Pratze *f* claw, strap
Pratzen-kran *m* claw crane, cradle crane **-stempel** *m* claw beam
Praxis *f* practice **in die ~ überführen** to reduce to practice
Präzedierbarkeit *f* precessability
präzedieren to precess
Präzession des Kerns nuclear precession **~ eines Kreisels** precession of a gyro
Präzessionsschwingung des Kreisels precession oscillation of a gyro or gyropendulum (recording of pitching, yawing, and rolling curves of a ship in a seaway)
Präzessionsverstärker *m* precession amplifier
Präzipitat *n* precipitate
Präzipitation *f* precipitation
Präzipitationswärme *f* heat of precipitation
präzipitieren to precipitate
Präzision *f* precision, accuracy
Präzisionsanflugradar *n* precision approach radar (PAR)

Präzisionsanschluß *m* watched-impedance or precision connector (rdr)

Präzisions-drehbank *f* high-precision lathe **-drehtisch** *m* precision revolving stage **-drehvorgang** *m* precision turning operation **-futter** *n* precision chuck **-hochspannungseinheit** *f* precision high-voltage unit **-hochspannungseinschub** *m* precision high-voltage plug-in unit

Präzisions-impulsintervalgenerator *m* precise pulse interval generator **-instrument** *n* precision instrument **-kluppe** *f* precision caliper **-körnerspitzen** *n* precision center **-kreuzspulung** *f* precision crosswinding **-kurve** *f* precision turn

Präzisions-nivellement *n* precision leveling **-schmieden** *n* precision forging **-schnelldrehbank** *f* high-speed precision lathe **-stichmaß** *n* micrometer calipers **-trudeln** *n* precision spin **-waage** *f* precision balance, analytical balance **-wendung** *f* precision turn **-werkzeug** *n* precision tool **-wert** *m* precision value

Preemphase *f* pre-emphasis

P-Regler proportional action controller

Preis *m* price, cost, prize, premium ~ **im Kleinhandel** retail price **einen** ~ **aussetzen** to offer a prize **einen** ~ **gewinnen** to win a prize

Preis-abschlag *m* decrease in price **-abzug** *m* rebate, discount **-angabe** *f* quotation (of prices) **-angebot machen** to quote **-aufschlag** *m* rise in price

Preis-erhöhung *f* **von . . .** advance in price of . . . **-ermäßigung** *f* lowering of price, price reduction **-geben** to abandon, give up, hand over **-gebunden** price-controlled **-gericht** *n* (prize) jury **-hausse** *f* increase in price **-herabsetzung** *f* cutting of prices

Preis-liste *f* prospectus, price list **-nachlaß** *m* allowance, rebate, abatement **-schneiderei** *f* underselling **-speicher** *m* price storage **-(überwachungs)stelle** *f* office of price control **-übung** *f* qualification course **-verderber** *m* underseller, undercutter **-verzeichnis** *n* price list **-wert** moderate in price, cheap

Prell-anschlag *m* recoil rod (typewriter) **-blech** *n* baffle (plate) **-bock** *m* buffer, stop, fender (pile), bumper, bumping post, stop block, buffer stop **-buchse** *f* cushioning box **-dauer** *f* (Schalter) bounce time **-draht** *m* guard wire (under high-voltage cables)

prellen to chatter, vibrate, bounce, toss, thump or click (key), reflect

Prellen der Kontakte contact chatter

prellende Kontaktöffnung vibration or chatter of contacts

Prellerei *f* trickery, fraud, overcharging

Prell-erscheinung *f* relay chatter **-frei** free from thumping or click **-gerüst** *n* spring frame **-keil** *m* recoil key **-klotz** *m* recoil, spring pole, stop block **-kraft** *f* resiliency **-pfahl** *m* pole fender, bumping post, fender **-platte** *f* baffle plate, baffle **-schlag** *m* jarring blow **-stein** *m* curbstone, spring stone **-stoß** *m* bump **-träger** *m* buffer stop

Prellung *f* cushioning

Prellvorrichtung *f* bumping mechanism, cushioning

Preß-anlage *f* pressing plant **-arbeit** *f* pressing operation **-artikel** *m* press-cured article **-aufsatz** *m* pressure block **-backe** *f* open die, upsetting die, bolt die, heading die, swage for shaping trusses

preßbar pressable

Preßbarkeitsfaktor *m* compressibility factor

Preß-bengel *m* press jack, bar, or stick **-bernstein** *m* amberoid **-blanke Schraube** cold-pressed screw or bolt **-blech** *n* presser plate (textiles) **-beutel** *m* filter bag **-blei** *n* lowgrade lead obtained by the Carinthian process **-bodenröhre** *f* loktal-base tube **-bolzenschweißung** *f* stud welding **-dorn** *m* hydraulic forging die, cold-forging die, press mandrel

Preßdruck *m* amount of pressure applied, pressing effect, squeeze (with a forging hammer), ram pressure (in press fits) **-schmierung** *f* forced-feed lubrication

Presse *f* power press, journalism, the Press, (grease) gun **hydraulische** ~ hydraulic press ~ **für thermoplastische Massen** plastic press

Presseabonnementsgespräch *n* press conversation by subscription

Presseabzug *m* press proof

pressen to press, squeeze; (zusammendrücken) compress; (zwängen) force; (seihen) strain; (drängen) urge press; briquette, cone, dish, extrude, stamp, mold, jam ~ **mit Glanz** to glaze (gloss)

Pressen *n* extrusion, pressing, glassing, embossing ~ **ohne Druck** impression molding ~ **des Raketen-Treibsatzes** extruding of cannister grain

Pressen-arbeiter *m* pressman **-beleuchtung** *f* die space lights **-einsatz** *m* pressing set **-gestell** *n* press frame **-kopf** *m* die block **-körper** *m* press body **-steuerstand** *m* press control desk

Presser *m* pressman (glass mfg.), grease gun, compressor (in volume-range control)

Presser-Dehner *m* compandor

Preßerzeugnis *n* pressings

Pressetelegramm *n* news message, press message

Preß-filter *m* filter press **-finger** *m* spring finger (textiles) **-fleier** *m* presser frame **-flüssigkeit** *f* pressure fluid

Preßform *f* mold, matrix ~ **für Teile aus Bakelit** die for Bakelite parts

Preßformmaschine *f* squeezing molding machine, squeezer, press molding machine ~ **mit selbsttätigem Abhub** power-squeezing molding machine, power squeezer ~ **mit Abstreifvorrichtung** stripping squeezer, squeeze stripper, squeeze stripping machine ~ **für kastenlosen Guß** press molding machine for use with snap flasks ~ **mit Handhebelmodellaushebung** squeezing hand-lever lift machine ~ **für Luftdruckbetrieb** air-squeezing molding machine, air squeezer, power squeezer ~ **mit feststehendem Querhaupt** press molding machine with stationary yoke ~ **mit Stiftenabhebung** squeeze-flask lift machine, squeezing machine with flask-lift pins ~ **mit Wendeplatte** turnover press molding machine, power-squeezing turnover machine ~ **mit ausfahrbarer Wendeplatte** roll-over table press molding machine

Preß-führer *m* squeezer man **-fundament** *n* press stone **-futter** *n* press mold **-gas** *n* pressure gas **-gasschalter** *m* (cross) air-blast switch **-gesenk** *n* die **-gipsplatte** *f* compressed rubble

Preßglanz eines Tuches gloss of cloth **-dekatier-**

maschine *f* luster shrinking machine
Preß-glassockel *m* glass-button base, pressed glass base **-glimmer** *m* pressed mica **-guß** *m* pressure castings, pressure casting **-gußstück** *n* die pressing **-hammer** *m* pneumatic hammer **-harz** *m* compression molding resin **-haupt** *n* presser head, squeezer yoke **-hebel** *m* pressure lever **-holm** *m* squeezing plate **-hub** *m* squeezing stroke, pressure stroke **-kabelschuh** *m* stamped terminal
Preß-kalander *m* cloth finishing machine **-kernspule** *f* iron dust core coil **-kissen** *n* pressure pad **-klotz** *m* presser board, squeezing board, former, ramming block **-koffer** *m* press chamber or casing **-kohle** *f* briquetted coal, compressed fuel, briquette, patent fuel, code for a type of heterodyne receiver **-kolben** *m* press plunger **-körper** *m* pressed object or article
Preßkuchen *m* press cake, briquette, filter coke **-form** *f* briquette mold **-probe** *f* briquette sample
Preßleiste *f* clamping bar
Preßling *m* stamping, drop stamping, briquette; compact; pressed pulp (sugar mfg.); pressed object or article, blank (after pressure application or molding)
Preßluft *f* compressed air **-abbauhammer** *m* pneumatic coal pick hammer **-abklopfapparat** *m* pneumatic rapper, pneumatic descaling apparatus **-abklopfer** *m* pneumatic scaling hammer **-angesteuert** pneumatic-controlled **-angetrieben** pneumatic **-anlage** *f* compressed-air (installation) plant **-anlasser** *m* compressed-air starter, pneumatic starting device **-antrieb** *m* drive by compressed air **-aufzug** *m* air hoist
Preßluft-behälter *m* compressed-air tank **-betätigt** air-operated **-bohrer** *m* air drill **-bohrmaschine** *f* rotary pneumatic drill **-festspannung** *f* chucking by compressed air **-flasche** *f* compressed-air cylinder **-förderung** *f* air lift **-futter** *n* air chuck, air operated chuck **-gründung** *f* pneumatic process of foundation **-hammer** *m* compressedair gun, pick, rock drill, air hammer **-hebezeug** *n* compressed-air hoist
Preßluft-kolben *m* pneumatic piston, compressed-air piston **-lautsprecher** *m* compressed-air loud-speaker, pneumatic loud-speaker **-leitung** *f* compressed-air line **-meißel** *m* pneumatic clipper **-motor** *m* compressed-air engine **-motormodell** *n* compressed-air-driven model **-pumpen** *n* air pumping **-rüttler** *m* air jolter (in molding)
Preßluft-schalter *m* (cross) air-blast switch **-schrauber** *m* air impact wrench **-siebmaschine** *f* pneumatic riddle **-spanneinrichtung** *f* compressed air attachment for chuck **-spannfutter** *n* pneumatic chucking
Preßluft-stampfer *m* compressed-air rammer, pneumatic rammer **-steuerung** *f* air control **-strahl** *m* compressed-air jet **-strom** *m* compressed-air current **-verbrauch** *m* compressed-air consumption **-werkzeug** *n* compressed-air tool **-zerstäuber** *m* compressed-air atomizer **-zufuhr** *f* pressure air supply **-zuführung** *f* compressed-air supply **-zylinder** *m* compressed-air cylinder
Preßmaschine *f* tuck presser (textiles)
Preß-masse *f* molding preparation, molded articles, molded plastic, fictile substance, moldable material, plastic material, synthetic, (thermo)plastic
Preß-matrize *f* stamper (phonograph record) ~ (Strangpresse) extruding die
Preß-mischung *f* molding mixture **-mühle** *f* pressing mill **-naht** *f* burr **-öl** *n* pressure oil, hydraulic fluid, pressed distillate **-öler** *m* pressure lubricator, compression oil cup **-ölschmierung** *f* compression-oil-cup lubrication, pressure-feed lubrication **-platte** *f* pressure plate, compression plate, presser board (in molding), ramming board, squeezer board, die, pressing (phonograph record disks) **-profil** *n* extruded shapes, molding
Preß-prozeß *m* pressure-shaping or fashioning method **-pulver** *n* molding powder **-pumpe** *f* pressure pump **-raffinade** *f* pressed raffinade **-rollennocken** *m* release shaft cam **-schnecke** *f* screw press **-schmierung** *f* force-feed or pressure-feed lubrication **-schraube** *f* thrust screw, clamp(ing) screw, pressure screw **-schweißung** *f* pressure welding, plastic welding, autogenous welding by pressure **-schwitzverfahren** *n* press sweating process **-sitz** *m* force fit, press fit, driving fit
Preß-span *m* pressboard, strawboard, Fuller board, glaze board, presspan insulation material **-spritzen** *n* flow molding **-stellung** *f* squeezing position (in molding machines) **-stempel** *m* press die, dolly, press ram, die, extrusion die, press pin **-stift** *m* prisoner **-stoff** *m* plastic (material), (molded) plastic compound, molded Bakelite, molded plastics, pressed material, moldable or fictile material **-stroh** *n* baled straw **-stück** *n* stamping, pressing, pressed piece **-stumpen** *m* press body
Preßteil *m* pressing, stamping, molded piece **Preßteile aus Isoliermaterial** products pressed from insulating material
Preß-tisch *m* pressing table, squeezing table, press plate **-torf** *m* pressed peat **-träger** *m* pressed girder **-traverse** *f* press yoke, squeezing yoke (of molding machines) **-tuch** *n* filter cloth
Preß- und Hebevorrichtung *f* pressure screws
Pressung *f* compression, pressure, squeeze, squeezing operation, squeezing on either side, ventilator thrust
Pressung-Dehnung der Dynamik companding
Preß-ventil *n* squeezing valve **-vulkanisation** *f* press cure **-verfahren** *n* pressing process or method **-walze** *f* press roll
Preßwasser *n* power water **-kran** *m* hydraulic crane **-speicher** *m* hydraulic accumulator
Preß-werkzeug *n* pressing tool, pressing die, die **-zange** *f* jointing clamp **-ziegel** *m* pressed brick **-ziehen** *n* press-drawing **-zylinder** *m* press cylinder, squeezing cylinder
Preston *n* Prestone
Preußischblau *n* Prussian blue
Pricke *f* prick, prickle, perch, spear
Priel *m* small channel
primär primary, protogenic **-e aerodynamische Charaktereigenschaften** (Kennwerte) primary aerodynamic characteristics **-e Destillation** topping **-e Destillationsanlage** skimming plant **-er Fühler** primary detector **-es Gleitflugzeug** primary-type glider **-es Glied** primary member **-e Instabilität** primary instability **-es Kriechen**

initial creep

primär-e Lagerstätte primary deposit **-er Lunker** pipe (of ingots) **-e Nennspannung** rated primary voltage **-er Nennstrom** rated primary current **-e natürliche Nuklide** primary natural radionuclides **-e Schlämme** *f* primary slimes **-e Spaltausbeute** independent fission yield **-e Steuerfläche** primary control surface **-e stille Zone** primary skip zone

Primär-abstimmung *f* preselector means **-achse** *f* primary axis **-antriebsorgan** *n* prime mover **-ätzung** *f* primary etching **-batterie** *f* primary battery **-diagramm** *n* (Antenne) primary radiation pattern **-draht** *m* primary wire **-elektron** *n* primary electron **-element** *n* primary cell, voltaic cell, galvanic cell **-empfang** *m* single-circuit reception **-empfänger** *m* single-circuit receiving set, primary receiver

Primärfarben-signal *n* primary color signal (TV) **-Subtrahend** *m* subtractive primary (TV)

Primär-gefüge *n* dendritic structure **-generator** *m* primary dynamo **-induktion** *f* primary inductance **-komponente** (zur Erzeugung von Weiß) primary unit (TV) **-kreis** *m* primary circuit **-kristallisation** *f* primary crystallization **-kristallit** *m* primary crystallite **-luft** *f* primary air **-luftdruck** *m* primary air pressure **-luftleitung** *f* primary air line **-radar** *n* primary radar

Primär-reize *pl* primaries **-reizeinheit** *f* unit of a primary color **-relais** *n* main current relay **-riß** *m* primary crack **-schaltung** *f* primary circuit **-seite** *f* primary winding, primary **-spaltung** *f* original fission **-spannung** *f* primary voltage **-spule** *f* primary coil

Primär-stöpsel *m* priming plug (elec.) **-strahler** *m* primary radiator **-strom** *m* primary current or flow **-stromkreis** *m* primary circuit **-welle** *f* primary shaft **-wicklung** *f* primary winding **-widerstand** *m* primary resistance

Primordialstufe *f* primordial stage (geol.)

Primzahl *f* prime number, incommensurable number

Printergramm *n* printergram

Prinzip *n* principle **~ des kleinsten** (geringsten) **Zwanges** principle of least constraint **Porrosches ~** Porro's principle **Scheimpflugsches ~** Scheimpflug's principle, Scheimpflug's condition

prinzipielle Methode fundamental (basic) method

Prinzip-schaltbild *n* basic circuit diagram **-schaltung** *f* skeleton diagram, basic circuit diagram (showing underlying principle) **-schnitt** *m* diagrammatic section **-skizze** *f* diagrammatic sketch

Prinzmetall *n* Prince's metal, Prince Rupert's metal

Priorität *f* priority

Prioritäts-beanspruchung *f* priority claim **-beleg** *m* certified copy of application, priority proof **-datum** *n* convention date (patents) **-frist** *f* priority term **-jahr** *n* convention year **-recht** *n* priority right (patents)

Prise *f* prize **gesetzmäßige ~** good prize

Prisma *n* prism **bildumkehrendes ~** erecting prism **doppelumkehrendes ~** inversion prism, inverting prism **dreiseitiges ~** triangular prism **dreiteiliges ~** triple prism **gerades ~** right prism **geradsichtiges ~** direct-vision prism **stark fächerndes ~** highly dispersive prism **totalreflektierendes ~** totally reflecting prism

prisma-ähnlich prismlike, prismoidal **-förmig** prismshaped, prismatic **-glas** *n* prism binoculars **-lauffläche** *f* prism-shaped running surface **-oberkante** *f* Vee way

prismatisch prismatic, prism-shaped **-e Nut** VEE-groove

Prismen-bett *n* prismatic bed **-fernrohr** *n* prismatic telescope **-festigkeit** *f* prism strength **-fläche** *f* prism surface or face **-förmig** prism-shaped, prismatic **-fräser** *m* double angle milling cutter **-führung** *f* prismatic guide, vees, V way, taper gib **-glas** *n* prism glass **-illuminator** *m* prism illuminator **-kante** *f* prism edge **-kreis** *m* surveying sextant **-kreuz** *n* prismatic surveying instrument, double prism for angles of ninety degrees **-spektrum** *n* prismatic spectrum **-sucher** *m* prismatic finder, prismatic seeker

Prismen- und Flachführung *f* vee and flat way

Prisometer *n* prisometer

Prisonstift *m* dowel pin

Pritsche *f* plank bed, firing platform

pritschen to plane

privat private **-er Verkehr** private correspondence

Privat-anschluß *m* private connection (elec.) **-anschlußbahn** *f* private sidings **-aufführung** *f* preview **-auskunft** *f* exclusive information **-betrieb** *m* private telephone or telegraph service

Privatfernsprech-anlage *f* private-telephone plant, house-telephone plant **-leitung** *f* private (telephone) wire

Privatfernsprechzentrale *f* private exchange **selbsttätige ~** private automatic exchange

Privat-flieger *m* private pilot **-fliegerei** *f* civilian flying **-flugzeug** *n* private plane **-gespräch** *n* private call **-nebenstellenanlage mit Handbetrieb** private manual branch exchange **-nebenstellenanlage mit Wahlbetrieb** dial private branch exchange **-stelle** *f* private station **-telegramm** *n* private message **-telegraphenanlage** *f* private telegraph plant **-telegraphenleitung** *f* private telegraph wire **-telephon** *n* residence telephone

privatwirtschaftlich, etwas ~ ausbeuten to exploit something for private economic purposes

Privatzentrale mit Handbetrieb private manual exchange (P.M.X.)

Proaktinide *pl* proactinides

Probe *f* test, experiment, trial, proof, assay, sample, specimen, pattern, test piece, rehearsal, numerical check (info proc.) **~ durch Abtreiben** cupellation, assaying by the cupel **die ~ mit äußerster Kraft** full-power trial **~ entnehmen** to test **heiße ~** final shot **kalte ~** test shot **die ~ machen** to prove (math) **auf die ~ stellen** to test, put to the test **gereckte ~** stretched specimen **sperrige ~** bulky test piece **vergütete ~** quenched (tempered) specimen, test piece **das Nehmen von Proben** sampling, taking samples

Probe-abdruck *m* proof, proof print, proof sheet **-abzug** *m* proof, proof impression or print **-aufnahme** *f* test picture, trial shot **-auftrag** *m* trial order **-auftritt** *m* audition **-band** *n* dummy (printing) **-belastung** *f* test load, loading test **-bilanz** *f* trial balance **-bild** *n* definition chart (TV), image test, proof, resolution pattern

-**block** *m* test or torque stand -**bogen** *m* proof sheet -**brand** *m* fire test

Probe-dienstleistung *f* probationary period -**druck** *m* test pressure, proof, proof impression or print -**entnahme** *f* sampling (at random), sample taking -**fahrt** *f* trial run or trip -**fläschchen** *n* sampling vial -**flug** *m* flight test, test flight -**flüssigkeit** *f* test liquid -**gerätschaft** *f* assay apparatus -**gewicht** *n* test weight, standard weight -**gold** *n* standard gold -**gut** *n* sample material, sample

Probe-hahn *m* blow valve, blowoff valve, blowoff, test or gauge cock, sampling cock, proof cock, sample cock, sampling valve, try cock, bleeder (petroleum) -**klemme für Zähler** metering stud -**kolben** *m* test jar -**korn** *n* assay button -**körper** *m* test specimen, sample, test piece, test body -**länge** *f* sample (length) -**last** *f* proof load, test load, proof weight

Probelauf *m* green run, test run (engines), running-in test, trial run ~ **auf dem Prüfstand** test bench running ~ **bei Vollast** power test run

Probe-lieferung *f* trial shipment -**löffel** *m* sample spoon, assay spoon -**machen** *n* testing, assaying -**maß** *n* standard measure -**mäßig** according to sample or pattern standard regulation

proben to try, check, test, sample

Probenahme *f* sampling, testing, test portion

Proben-dichte *f* density of specimen -**druckmaschine** *f* test printing machine

Probe-nehmen *n* sampling, testing -**nehmer** *m* sampler

Proben-entnehmer *m* side tester -**glas** *n* specimen glass or tube -**länge** *f* length of specimen -**sammler** *m* sample collection system -**teller** *m* turntable -**wechsler** *m* sample changer

Probe-objekt *n* specimen -**pfahl** *m* test pile, trial pile -**pumpen** *n* trial pumping

Prober *m* assayer

Probe-saal *m* rehearsal hall -**säure** *f* test acid, standard acid -**scherbe** *f*, -**scherben** *m* cupel, trial piece -**schuß** *m* trial or sighting shot -**schweißung** *f* test weld -**silber** *n* standard silver

Probestab *m* test piece, specimen, test bar ~ **mit Gewindekopf** screwed test bar ~ **mit Stabköpfen** headed test bar ~ **für Kerbschlagversuche** notched specimen **durchgeschlagener** ~ broken test piece

Probestab-abmessung *f* diameter and gauged length of test bars -**teilmaschine** *f* test-piece dividing machine

Probe-stange *f* test rod, test bar -**stecher** *m* proof stick (sugar), sample taker **stoff** *m* sample material -**stück** *n* test specimen, test piece, sample -**verbindung** *f* trial connection, test call -**waage** *f* assay balance -**wäsche** *f* tare washer -**weise** on trial -**würfel** *m* test cube -**zeit** *f* qualifying period (of instruction), (time of) probation -**ziehen** *n* sampling -**zinn** *n* standard tin

Probier-bassin *n* model basin -**blei** *n* test lead

probieren to test, assay, try

Probieren *n* testing **systematisches** ~ setting by trial and error

Probierer *m* assayer

Probier-gefäß *n* testing vessel, assaying vessel -**gewicht** *n* assay weight -**glas** *n* test tube (glass) -**glätte** *f* test litharge -**gold** *n* standard gold -**hahn** *m* test or gauge cock, sampling cock, pet cock -**kluft** *f* assayer's tongs -**korn** *n* assay button -**kunst** *f* assaying

Probier-laboratorium *n* assay laboratory -**löffel** *m* assay spoon -**metall** *n* test metal -**ofen** *m* assay furnace -**röhrchen** *n* test tube, cylinder -**stand** *m* test stand

probiert tried, tested

Probier-tiegel *m*, -**tüte** *f* assay crucible -**ventil** *n* gauge valve -**waage** *f* assay balance -**zange** *f* assayer's tongs

Problem *n* problem **ebenes** (zweidimensionales) ~ two-dimensional problem

Problemstellung *f* posing the problem

Produkt *n* product, result, produce ~ **aus Ampere und Volt** product of amperes by volts

Produktdemodulator *m* product demodulator

Produktion *f* production, yield, output **zur** ~ **bringen** (to) bring in (a well)

Produktions-bescheinigung *f* production certificate -**dichte** *f* production density -**drehbank** *f* manufacturing lathe -**engpaß** *m* production bottleneck -**fähigkeit** *f* production capacity -**feinbohrmaschine** *f* precision production boring machine -**fräsmaschine** *f* production-type milling machine

Produktions-gang *m* course of production, manufacturing process, line of production -**gießerei** *f* tonnage foundry -**kosten** *pl* production cost, manufacturing costs -**leistung** *f* productive capacity -**leiter** *m* production supervisor (manager)

Produktions-möglichkeit *f* potential production -**plan** *m* production schedule -**programm** *n* production program -**schema** *n* flow sheet -**schleifarbeit** *f* manufacturing grinding -**steuerung** *f* production planing -**teil** *m* production part -**überwachung** *f* supervision of the production process -**verfahren** *n* production method -**ziffer** *f* production rate

produktiv productive

Produktivität *f* productivity

Produzent *m* producer

produzieren to produce

proeutektisch proeutectic

proeutektoid proeutectoid

Profil *n* profile, section, section shape, vertical section, construction lines, side view, form, shape of face dam **gewölbtes** ~ cambered profile, nonsymmetrical profile **kleines** ~ light section **vorgeschriebenes** ~ preparation of site for deposit of fill

Profil-bearbeitung *f* sculpture machining -**bauch** *m* lower surface -**begrenzung** *f* boundary of a section, contour line, boundary of a profile -**beiwert** *m* profile coefficient -**bewahrung** *f* armouring with interlocking wires -**dichtung** *f* profile washer -**dicke** *f* thickness of profile, wing thickness, airfoil-blade section -**draht** *m* streamlined wire -**drahtbewehrung** *f* wire armoring -**drehbank** *f* jog lathe -**durchmesser** *m* profile thickness

Profileisen *n* section(al) iron, section(al) steel, structural iron (steel), structural shapes or products sections, profile iron, structural rolled-steel member -**träger** *m* structural girder, beam girder, sectional girder -**walzen** *n* rolling of sections -**walzwerk** *n* shape rolling mill, shape mill, mill for rolling sections, section mill

Profil-form *f* profile **-fräsen** to profile mill **-fräser** *m* profile cutter, form cutter **-gerecht** true to profile **-gestaltung** *f* shaping, forming, profiling, designing of construction lines **-gleitzahl** *f* profile gliding coefficient **-graviermaschine** *f* mold engraving machine **-größe** *f* size of section **-hinterkante** *f* trailing edge (aviation) **-hobel** *m* molding plane (carp.) **-holz** *n* special-section timber, formed or shaped wood

profilieren to form, shape, forming of section, designing of section

Profilieren *n* profiling, profile

profiliert streamlined, side-faced, profilated, shaped, nonskid (said of tires) **-er Stab** profiled bar **-e Trommel** grooved drum

Profilierung *f* profiling, sectioning, fairing

Profil-instrument *n* edgewise instrument **-kalander** *m* embossing calender **-karte** *f* profile map **-lagerholz** *n* fairing **-lehre** *f* profile form **-linie** *f* vertical section, construction lines **-litze** *f* profiled strand **-messer** *n* formed cutter, **-messer** *m* profilometer **-meßgerät** *n* profiler

Profilometer *n*, **Profilprüfer** *m* profilometer

Profilradius *m* hydraulic radius (of cross-sectional area, as opposed to mean hydraulic radius of reach) **mittlerer ~** mean hydraulic depth

Profil-registrierung *f* profile recording **-rohr** *n* streamlined-section tube (aviation) **-rohrstiel** *m* profile strut **-rücken** *m* upper surface **-schleifmaschine** *f* form grinder **-schleifscheibe** *f* form wheel **-sehne** *f* chord, wing chord

Profilstahl *m* sectional steel, former **-lamelle** *f* sectional steel plate **-walzwerk** *n* structural-steel rolling mill

Profil-stange *f* bar **-stempel** *m* profile stamp (surface pressing) **-strebe** *f* streamlined-section strut **-tiefe** *f* depth of profile **-tragendes Oberteil** profiled top **-träger** *m* beam **-umkreis** *m* circumscribed circle of section

Profil-verjüngung *f* tapering in section **-verschiebung** *f* profile offset **-verschoben** with modified profile **-verzerrung** *f* distortion of profile **-vorderkante** *f* leading edge (aviat.)

Profil-walze *f* profile mill cutter **-walzen** *n* section rolling, rolling shapes **-walzung** *f* rolling of sectional iron **-walzwerk** *n* shape rolling mill, shape mill, mill for rolling sections, section mill **-widerstand** *m* parasite drag, profile resistance (aviation), profile drag **-widerstandsbeiwert** *m* profile drag coefficient

Profilwiderstandsfläche *f*, **verminderte ~** reduced profile drag area

Profilzieher *m* profile cutter

Profit *m* profit

Proformarechnung *f* pro forma invoice

Prognose *f* prognostics, forecast

Programm *n* course of cure (in vulcanizing rubber), cycle, program, procession (rockets), routine **-ablauf** *m* computer operation **-band** *n* program tape **-bedingtes Versagen** program-sensitive error

Programmberichtigung *f*, **schritthaltende ~** real-time control

Programmfehlerausmerzung *f* routine debugging

Programmfertigung *f*, **automatische ~** automatic coding, automatic programming (info proc.)

Programmgeber *m* programme transmitter

programmgesteuerte Rechenanlage *f* computor (info proc.) **digitale ~ ~** sequential computer

programmierbar programmable

Programmiereinschub *m* programming plug-in unit

programmieren to program

Programmierer *m* programmer (comput.)

Programmierung *f* programming

Programmierungsgerät programmer

Programm-läufer *m* torpedo running to preset course **-planer** *m* programmer (comput.) **-regler** *m* programme controller **-rückkehrpunkt** *m* rerun point **-schalter** *m* controller **-schaltwerk** *n* automatic cycle operation **-schritt** *m* program step **-speicherung** *f* stored program **-stellung** *f* cutoff angle (missiles) **-steuerung** *f* preset course, program device **-walze** *f* program cylinder **-zähler** *m* program scaler

Progression *n* progression

progressiv progressive **-er Leistungslohn** accelerating incentive **-e Wirkung** progressive action

Progressivdrall *m* increasing twist

Projekt *n* project, plan, scheme, proposition

projektieren to project, plan

Projektil *n* projectile, missile

Projektion *f* projection **flächentreue ~** equal-area projection (mapping) **gnomonische ~** gnomonic projection **zentrale ~** gnomonic projection

Projektions-apparat *m* projector **-aussteuerungsanzeiger** *m* projected volume indicator **-bild** *n* screen picture **-bildschreibröhre** *f* projection-type television receiver **-ebene** *f* plane of projection **-einrichtung** *f* projection apparatus, projection system **-empfänger** *m* projection receiver **-fenster** *n* projection aperture or gate **-fernsehröhre** *f* television projection tube **-fläche** *f* surface of projection

Projektions-kammer *f* camera of projection, projecting camera **-lampe** *f* recording lamp **-linse** *f* projecting lens **-mattscheibe** *f* ground-glass screen **-objektiv** *n* projecting lens **-okular** *n* projection eyepiece **-optik** *f* projection optics **-punkt** *m* zenith point **-röhre** *f* projection tube **-satz** *m* theorem of projection

Projektions-schirm *m* projection screen **-skala** *f* projected scale **-skaleninstrument** *n* projected-scale instrument **-spiegelsystem** *n* optical system for the projection **-spule** *f* projection coil **-strahl** *m* projecting beam

Projektions-tafel *f* plane of projection **-verfahren** *n* projection procedure, projection television **-vorrichtung** *f* projection apparatus, projection system **-wand** *f* projection screen **-zentrum** *n* center of projection

projektiv projective **-e Abbildung** projective mapping **-e Ebene** projective plane

Projektor *m* projector **~ für Bilder** picture projector

Projektoroptik *f* reflective optics

projizieren to project

projiziert projected **-er Flächeninhalt des Luftschraubenblattes** projected propeller-blade area **-e Kolbenfläche** projected area of piston **-e Schraubenflügelfläche** projected propeller-blade area

Prokeim *m* sensitivity speck (phot.)

Proklamation *f* proclamation

Prokura *f* procuration **per ~ zeichnen** to sign per procuration
Prokurist *m* official (agent) empowered to sign contracts for the firm (office manager)
Prolongation *f* prolongation **~ eines Wechsels** renewal of a bill of exchange
Promenadendeck *n* promenade deck
Promille *f* pars pro mille
prompt promt, punctual
Pronybremse *f* Prony brake
Pronyscher Zaum Prony brake
Propaganda *f* propaganda, publicity
Propan *n* propane, propylene hydride
Propanol *n* propanol
Propeller *m* propeller, impeller **den ~** (mit der Hand) **schwingen** swinging the propeller
Propeller-blattspitzenfreiheit *f* propeller clearance **-drehzahl** *f* propeller speed **-flügelschlag** *m* propeller-blade beat **-gebläse** *n* helical blower **-geräusch** *n* propeller noise **-haube** *f* propeller cap, spinner **-kreisfläche** *f* disc area
Propellerleistung *f*, **effektive ~** thrust horsepower
Propeller-nabe *f* propeller hub, airscrew boss **-radius** *m* tip radius **-regler** *m* propeller governor **-schleppdrehmoment** *n* windmilling torque **-schub** *m* propeller thrust **-schubkraft** *f* force of propeller thrust **-steigung** *f* propeller pitch **-steuerung** *f* propeller pitch controls **-strahl** *m* slip stream
Propeller-turbinenluftstrahlmotor *m* turboengine getting oxygen from the air and having a propeller (jet) **-turbomotor** *m* turbo-prop engine
Propellerüberdrehzahl *f*, **höchste ~** maximum propeller overspeed
Propeller-verstelleinrichtung *f* propeller pitch controls **-welle** *f* propeller shaft **-wind** *m* slip stream
Properzi-Walzdraht *m* Properzi rod
Propionsäure *f* propionic acid
Proportion *f* proportion
proportional proportional, proportionate **umgekehrt ~** inversely proportional **-es Zählrohr** proportional counter tube
Proportionalbereich *m* proportional band
Proportionale, mittlere ~ mean proportional, geometrical mean
Proportional-Integral-Regler, (PI-Regler) *m* proportional plus reset action controller
Proportionalität *f* proportionality
Proportionalitäts-gesetz *n* Hooke's law **-grenze** *f* proportional limit, Hooke's law **-koeffizient** *m*, **-konstante** *f* constant of proportionality
Proportional-regelung *f* proportional position action **-regler** *m* (P-Regler) proportional action controller **-stab** *m* proportional test bar **-zirkel** *m* sector, proportional compasses
proportionieren to proportion
Propyl-alkohol *m* propyl alcohol **-amin** *n* propylamine
Propylen *n* propylene
Prospekt *m* prospectus
prospektieren to prospect
Prospektieren *n* prospecting
Proszenium *n* fore scene, front stage, proscenium
Protaktinium *n* protactinium
Protein *n* protein
Protektoreinlage *f* breaker
proterozoisch proterozoic
Protium *n* protium
Protobitumen *n* protobitumen
Protodurkabel *n* protodurcable
Protokoll *n* certificate, report, minutes, records, signed statement **-führer** *m* registrar
Protokollierung *f* recording
Proton *n* proton **-elektronmassenverhältnis** *n* proton-electron mass ratio
Protonen-bahn *f* proton path **-beschleuniger** *m* proton accelerator **-beschuß** *m* proton bombardment **-bindungsenergie** *f* proton binding energy **-bündel** *n* proton bunch
Prototyp *m* prototype **-flugzeug** *n* prototype airplane
Protrahierung *f* protracted treatment
Protuberanz *f* prominence
Protz-achse *f* limber axle **-arm** *m* support bar on caisson
Protze *f* limber
Protzenstellung *f* limber position
Protz-gestell *n* limber frame **-haken** *m* limber hook **-kasten** *m* limber box **-öse** *f* lunette (artil.)
Proustit *m* proustite
Provenienz *f* origin
Proviant *m* supplies, provisions, stores
Provision *f* commission
provisorisch provisional, makeshift, temporary **~ reparieren** to make a temporary repair
Prozedur *f* procedure
Prozent *n* per cent **-gehalt** *m* per cent content, percentage
prozentig per cent
Prozent-satz *m* percentage
prozentual percentage **-e Änderung** percentage change **-e Aussteuerung** percentage modulation, modulation percentage **-e Steigung** percentage inclination **-e quadratische Streuung** coefficient of variation **-e Zunahme** percentage increase
Prozeß *m* lawsuit, process, method, proceeding, mode of procedure, suit **nicht umkehrbarer ~** irreversible process **~ außerhalb des Kerns** extranuclear process
Prozeßfließschema *n* process flow sheet
Prozession *f* procession
Prozeß-kosten *pl* law costs, costs of proceedings **-ladung** *f* writ of summons
Prüf-abzug *m* proof **-ader** *f* sleeve wire, test wire **-anleitung** *f* testing instructions **-anstalt** *f* laboratory **-apparat** *m* testing apparatus **-arbeit** *f* experimental work, test work **-arm** *m* private wiper **-attest** *n* test certificate **-ausführungsbestimmung** *f* test specification
Prüf-bank *f* (lens) test bench (optics) **-bar** capable of being tested or assayed **-batterie** *f* testing battery **-beamter** *m* testing officer, test clerk, checker, (am Wheatstone) key clerk **-beanspruchung** *f* proof stress **-bedingung** *f* condition of testing **-befund** *m* test report **-belastung** *f* ultimate strength **-bericht** *m* test report **-draht** *m* testing wire, pilot wire, sleeve wire, test pick **-druck** *m* test pressure **-düsensatz** *m* set of testing nozzles
Prüfeinrichtung *f* testing outfit, device, or set, circuit model **~ für Nummernscheiben** dial tester
prüfen (Schule) to examine, test; (stärker ~) scrutenize; (Technik) inspect; (Sache) investigate, analyze; (Erz) assay; (Maschine)

overhaul (untersuchen, erproben, versuchen) to test, control, check, try; check, verify, conform, explore, prove, true **auf vorschriftsmäßige Beschaffenheit** ~ to O.K. **auf Erdschluß** (Berührung, Kurzschluß) ~ to test for earth (contact, short-circuit) **den Ruf** ~ to test the signaling (ringing)

Prüfen *n* testing, checking

Prüfende *n* bunching of cable conductors for testing

prüfender Wähler test selector

Prüfer *m* tester, assayer, examiner, inspector, checker

Prüf-ergebnis *n* test result **-feld** *n* field of research, testing room or ground, test field, proving ground **-feldmonteur** *m* test fitter **-flieger** *m* test pilot **-flug** *m* test flight **-gehäuse** *n* portable test set **-generator** *m* signal generator, test oscillator

Prüfgerät *n* testing instrument or apparatus, tester, analyzer, trouble-shooting device ~ (tragbar oder fahrbar) portable test set

Prüf-gestell *n* test board or wire chief's desk, circuit model **-gitter** *n* test grid **-hahn** *m* test cock, sampling valve **-höhe** *f* vertical capacity of a testing machine **-hörer** *m* test receiver **-hülse** *f* test sleeve **-ingenieur** *m* testing engineer **-kabel** *n* test lead **-kasten** *m* test box **-klemme** *f* test clip **-klinke** *f* test jack **-knopf** *m* testing button **-kontaktarm** *m* test brush, private wiper **-kontaktbank** *f* private bank

Prüf-lampe *f* inspection light **-last** *f* test load **-lauf** (Motor) *m* ground run-up **-lauflehre** *f* reference gauge **-lehrdorn** *m* precision plug gauge, check gauge, standard gauge **-lehre** *f* standard gauge, reference gauge **-leitung** *f* test lead, test circuit, pilot wire, testing wire

Prüfling *m* test sample, specimen, applicant for an examination, test piece, test model

Prüflocher *m* verifier (punch)

Prüfmaschine *f* testing machine ~ **für Biegeversuche** testing machine for bending tests ~ **mit Differentialhebel** compound-lever testing machine ~ **für Drehversuche** testing machine for torsion test ~ **für Druckversuche** compression-test machine ~ **für Einbeulversuche** bulging-test machine ~ **für Faltversuche** bending-test machine ~ **mit Laufgewichtswaage** lever-testing machine ~ **mit Pendelwaage** weighted-pendulum testing machine ~ **für Zugversuche** tensile-test machine

Prüf-maß *n* check gauge, standard gauge **-merkmal** *n* test **-methode** *f* test method **-motor** *m* testing engine **-nachweis** *m* checking record **-nadel** *f* plasticity needle, Proctor needle **-netzgerät** *n* line test equipment **-objekt** *n* testee **-platz** *m* testing (operator's) position, test position, monitor's position, inspection crib **-programm** *n* test routine (info proc.) **-protokoll** *n* test certificate **-pult** *n* test desk **-punkte** *pl* entries

Prüf-räder *pl* test gears **-raum** *m* laboratory, testing room **-relais** *n* test(ing) relay, busy relay **-rohr** *n* monitor **-röhre** *f* (für Fernseher) phasmajector, monoscope, monotron **-schalter** *m* test key **-schaltung** *f* monitoring circuit, circuit model **-schein** *m* test certificate **-schnarre** *f* test buzzer **-schnur** *f* test cable **-schnurpaar** *n* pair of test cords

Prüf-schrank *m* test board or wire chief's desk, test desk, test box or case **-schraube** *f* check plug, test screw plug, thread gauge **-sender** *m* test oscillator, service test oscillator **-spannung** *f* testing voltage, proof stress, proof voltage **-spitze** *f* penetrator, penetrating point, probe, indenter **-spule** *f* exploration coil, pickup coil, search coil, test coil **-stabeinschnürung** *f* waist (forming in bar under tensile test)

Prüfstand *m* testing stop, test stand (test floor), torque stand, test bed, test(ing) bench

Prüfstands-anlage *f* test plant **-bedingungen** *pl* test-stand conditions **-bock** *m* testing rig **-gerät** *n* test equipment **-luftschraube** *f* test propeller

Prüfstandversuch *m* bench test

Prüfstein *m* touchstone

Prüfstelle *f* testing position ~ **für Luftfahrzeuge** aircraft testing board

Prüf-stöpsel *m* test plug **-streifen** *m* buzz track (on a film) **-stromkreis** *m* test circuit **-stück** *n* test specimen, test piece **-stumpf** *m* bunching of cable conductors for testing, test-cable stub **-taste** *f* test(ing) key, test switch (radio) **-techniker** *m* testing operator **-tisch** *m* test board or wire chief's desk, test desk

Prüfung *f* examination; (genaue ~) investigation, analysis, verification; (Technik) control, inspection; (Bücher) audit; (Chem.) determination; test(ing), overhauling, check(ing), quiz, trial, proving (of armor plate ballistically tested), perusal, consideration, reviewing, surveying, search, probe ~ **auf Betriebsfähigkeit** clear test ~ **auf Flugklarheit** preflight inspection ~ **durch Hörvergleich mit Sprache** volume comparison ~ **der Rechnungen** revision of accounts ~ **der Rufsätze** ringer test ~ **der Serienmotoren** production testing of engines ~ **der Speisestromspannungen** voltage test

Prüfung, ~ **der Speisestromstärken** current test ~ **auf Stromfähigkeit** continuity test ~ **des Triebwerks als Ganzes** unit test ~ **am ganzen Versuchsstück** full-size test ~ **machen** to take examination **in der** ~ **begriffen** under test **dynamische** ~ dynamic test, impact test **regelmäßige** ~ routine test **statische** ~ static test, slow test

Prüfungs-anstalt *f* testing laboratory, experiment station **-art** *f* test method, method of testing **-attest** *n* test certificate, certificate of accuracy **-beamter** *m* test clerk, checker **-bescheid** *m* office action test instructions, report on examination **-ergebnis** *n* test result **-luftdruckmesser** *m* test or standard barometer **-methode** *f* testing method **-versuch** *m* trial **-vorschrift** *f* test specification **-zeugnis** *n* proof certificate

Prüf-verfahren *n* test(ing) method, testing process, prosection (of a patent application) **-voltmeter** *n* test voltmeter **-vorrichtung** *f* test apparatus, testing appliance, tester **-wähler** *m* test connector or selector **-wert** *m* test value **-widerstand** *m* test resistance **-zapfen** *m* test lug **-zeichen** *n* test certificate **-ziffer** *f* check digit

Prügel *m* rocking tree, swing beam, stick, cudgel **-holz** *n* sticks **-weg** *m* corduroy road

pseudo-adiabatisch pseudoadiabatic **-adresse** *f* symbolic, floating address (info proc.) **-befehl** *m* pseudo instruction **-bild** *n* pseudo-image

-dämpfung *f* loss of selectivity by parallel internal resistance **-dichroismus** *m* pseudodichroism, diffraction polarization **-ebene Bewegung** pseudo-plane motion **-kristallin** pseudocrystalline **-morph** pseudomorphic **-morphose** *f* pseudomorphosis **-programm** *n* interpretive system (info proc.) **-schwund** *m* pseudofading

pseudoskalare Größe pseudoscalar quantity

pseudoskopische Projektion pseudoscopic view

Pseudo-spannung *f* pseudo-stress **-sphäre** *f* pseudosphere **-streuergebnis** *n* pseudo-random result **-streufolge** *f* pseudo-random sequence **-symmetrie** *f* pseudosymmetry **-thermostatik** *f* pseudo-thermostatics

Psilomelan *n* psilomelane, black iron ore

Psophometer *m* psophometer

PS-Stunde *f* horsepower-hour

Psychogalvanometer *n* psychogalvanometer

Psychrometer *n* psychrometer

PTFA-Schmiermittel *n* PTFE lubricant

Puddel-arbeiter *m* puddler **-betrieb** *m* puddling operation **-bett** *n* puddling-furnace bed **-drehofen** *m* rotary puddling furnace, rotating puddling machine **-eisen** *n* puddled iron, open-hearth steel **-eisenwalzwerk** *n* muck rolling mill, puddle rolling mill **-herd** *m* puddling hearth, puddling basin **-luppe** *f* balls of wrought iron, puddle ball

puddeln to puddle

Puddel-ofen *m* puddling furnace **-roheisen** *n* forge pig iron, forge pig, mill iron

Puddelschlacke *f* puddle (puddling) cinder, tappings, tap cinder, bulldog (metal.), puddling slag **vor dem Kochen abgestochene ~** boilings

Puddel-sohle *f* puddling-furnace bed **-spiegel** *m* specular forge pig **-spitze** *f* puddler's paddle **-stab** *m* puddler bar **-stahl** *m* puddle(d) steel, puddled iron **-verfahren** *n* puddling process **-walze** *f* puddle roll **-werk** *n* puddling works

Puddingstein *m* pudding stone, conglomerate (geol.)

Puddler *m* puddler

Puder *m* powder **-apparat** *m* powder spray apparatus **-einzug** *m* introduction of powdered sugar

puderig powdery

pudern to powder

puffen to chug

Puffer *m* pad, buffer, bumper, dashpot, cushion, grommet, shock absorber **-batterie** *f* buffer or boosting battery, floated or floating battery **-behälter** *m* working tanks **-betrieb** *m* floating, system of buffer battery, floating-battery operation **-druck** *m* buffing load **-dynamo** *m* buffer dynamo

Puffer-feder *f* buffer spring **-gefäß** *n* surge chamber **-gehäuse** *n* buffer case **-grundplatte** *f* buffer base plate or spring seating **-klotz** *m* buffer block (mach.) **-kreis** *m* buffer **-lage** *f* interlayer **-lager** *n* buffer bearing **-lösung** *f* buffer solution

puffern to float (a battery), buffer (a solution)

Puffer-querriegel *m* buffer crossbeam **-satz** *m* booster (elec.) **-schaft** *m* buffer plunger **-schaltung** *f* buffer circuit **-spannung** *f* floating electromotive force

Pufferspeicher *m* buffer store (info proc.) **äußerer ~** external store, auxiliary store, (info proc.)

Puffer-stand *m* buffer load **-stange** *f* buffer shank or plunger **-stoff** *m* buffer **-stufe** *f* isolator stage, buffer stage, separator stage **-teller** *m* buffer disk **-traverse** *f* headstock

Pufferung *f* cushioning (in explosives), buffering (chem.)

Puffer-vorrichtung *f* jumping apparatus **-wirkung** *f* balancing action, buffer effect, buffer action **-zylinder** *m* cushioning cylinder

Pulpe *f* pulp

Pulsabstandsmodulation *f* pulse-interval modulation

Pulsation *f* pulsation, beat, ripple, throb

Pulsationsdrossel *f* pulsation choke

Pulsator *m* pulsator **-setzmaschine** *f* pulsator classifier

Puls-breite *f* (Radar) pulse width **-codemodulation** *f* pulse code modulation (P.C.M.) **-düsenantrieb** *m* pulse jet drive

pulsen to pulsate

pulsend intermittent

Pulser *m* pulsator

Pulsformungsfaktor *m* response pulse shape

Pulsfrequenzmodulation (PFM) *f* pulse frequency modulation (PFM)

pulsgesteuerter Oszillator pulsed oscillator

pulsieren to pulsate

Pulsieren *n* pulsating, pulsation

pulsierend pulsating, intermittent, throbbing **-e Belastung** intermittent, variable or pulsating load **-e Größe** undulating quantity **-es Licht** synchrolite **-er Staustrahlmotor** *m* pulse-jet engine

Pulsmesser *m* sphygmograph

pulsmodulierter Träger radio-frequency pulse

Pulsometer *n* pulsometer

Pulsperiodendauer *f* pulse repetition period **-phasenmodulation** *f* pulse phase modulation **-strahlmotor** *m* pulse-jet engine

Pult *n* desk, lectern **-(be)feuerung** *f* firing on stepped grate bars **-gestell** *n* desk stand **-ofen** *m* backflame hearth

Pulver *n* powder, gunpowder **großkörniges ~** coarse-grain powder **rauchloses ~, rauchschwaches ~** smokeless powder **mit einer nichttreibkräftigen Lösung, oberflächenbehandeltes ~** deterrent or propellent powder

Pulver-art *f* type of powder **-artig** pulverous, powdery, pulverulent, dustlike **-hand** *n* powder strand **-blättchen** *n* (Stück des zerschnittenen Pulverbandes), powder grain **-diagramm** *n* powder pattern **-ementieren** *n* box carburizing **-erz** *n* gunpowder ore **-fabrik** *f* powder factory, powder mill **-förmig** pulverulent, powdery **-fritter** *m* powder coherer **-glühanode** *f* powder anode

pulverig powdery, pulverulent, pulverous, dustlike

pulverisierbar pulverizable

pulverisieren to powder, pulverize, grind, comminute

Pulverisier-maschine *f* disintegrator **-mühle** *f* pulverizer

Pulverisierung *f* pulverization

Pulver-kammer *f* (powder) magazine (navy) **-kern** *m* powder core, dust core **-korn** *n* percussion primer (fuse) **-kornsieb** *n* separating sieve, sieve for corning powder **-ladung** *f* powder charge **-länge** *f* length of cordite sticks **-magazin** *n* magazine (mil.) **-metallurgie** *f* powder metallurgy **-mikrophon** *n* powder transmitter **-mörser** *m* (powder) mortar

pulvern to powder, pound, pulverize, levigate, comminute

Pulver-preßling *m* compressed-powder charge **-rakete** *f* powder rocket **-raum** *m* powder chamber **-rückstand** *m* powder fouling of barrel **-satz** *m* powder train (fuse), ingredients or composition for powder **-schnee** *m* powdery snow **-seele** *f* powder core

Pulver-sorte *f* type of gunpowder **-streifen** *m* powder strand **-temperatur** *f* powder temperature **-temperaturmessung** *f* measuring of powder temperature **-thermometer** *n* powder-temperature thermometer (small thermometer inserted into test cartridge) **-treibladung** *f* propelling charge

Pulverung *f* pulverization

Pulver-vertreibladung *f* propelling charge of (black) powder **-zerstäuber** *m* decontaminating instrument **-zünder** *m* powder fuse

pulvrig pulverulent

Pump-anlage *f* pumping plant or installation, dewatering or drainage plant, pumping machinery **-automatik** *f* pumping automation

Pumpe *f* pump ~ **mit elektrischem Antrieb** motor-driven pump ~ **für Handbetrieb** hand-operated pump ~ **mit unterbrochener Leistung** intermitter ~ **mit Preßluftantrieb** air-operated pump ~ **mit Turbinenantrieb** turbine-driven pump **feste** ~ standing pump **sichtbarmessende** ~ visible pump **unklare** ~ choked or foul pump **die** ~ **schlägt** the pump knocks **die** ~ **zieht** the pump draws

pumpen to pump, fill up (tire)

Pumpen *n* pumping surge, surging ~ (beim Barometer) pumping ~ **der Kolbenringe** pump action of piston rings

Pumpen-aggregat *n* direct-connected motor-driven pump **-anlage** *f* pumping plant **-antriebswelle** *f* pump shaft **-bauart** *f* type of pump **-beschlag** *m* pump gear **-bock** *m* pumping jack **-element** *n* pump element **-fernsteuerung** *f* pump telecontrol **-flügel** *m* pump-impeller vane or blade **-flügelrad** *n* impeller of pump **-förderung** *f* pump feeding

Pumpen-gehäuse *n* outer barrel, working barrel, pump casing **-gestänge** *n* pump rods **-gestängerechen** *m* sucker-rod hanger, sucker-rod jack **-gestell** *n* pump jack **-haus** *n* pump house **-hebel** *m* pump lever **-herz** *n* lower pump box **-kammer** *f* pump room **-kasten** *m* pump stock **-kennlinien** *pl* (Förderhöhe) pump curves

Pumpenkolben *m* pump piston ~ **mit Klappe** pump bucket

Pumpenkolben-feder *f* plunger spring **-rohr** *n* plunger working barrel **-ventil** *n* plunger valve

Pumpen-kopf *m* pump head **-korb** *m* pump kettle or strainer, tube filter **-körper** *m* pump cover **-kühlung** *f* forced water cooling **-lamelle** *f* vane of vacuum pump **-liderung** *f* pump packing **-peilstock** *m* gauge rod of a pump **-platte** *f* pump plate **-probhahn** *m* petcock for pumps

Pumpenrad *n* pump impeller **getriebenes** ~ pump idler gear **treibendes** ~ pump drive gear

Pumpen-raum *m* pump room or chamber **-regler** *m* pump governor **-röhre** *f* tubing **-rohrhänger** *m* tubing hanger, tubing spider **-rohrkrebs** *m* tubing catcher **-satz** *m* set of pumps **-schacht** *m* sump shaft **-schwengel** *m* brake, pump handle **-selbstschalter** *m* electropneumatic regulator **-sog** *m* pump well, sog or suction

Pumpen-stange *f* sucker rod **-stempelantrieb** *m* pump plunger drive **-stiefel** *m* barrel, body or chamber of a pump **-stock** *m* pump staff **-sumpf** *m* sump **-träger** *m* bracket (of pump) **-welle** *f* pump shaft **-werk** *n* pumping gear **-winde** *f* pumping jack **-zylinder** *m* pump barrel or cylinder

pump-fähig pumpable **-getriebe** *n* pumping gear **-grenze** *f* surge limit, compressor pulsation limit **-leistung** *f* pumping capacity **-loch** *n* exhaust port **-rad** *n* pump wheel **-siel** *n* discharging culvert in a dike **-speicher** *m* pumped storage (at a hydroelectric plant) **-speicherwerk** *n* pump-fed power station, pump storage station

Pump-spill *n* windlass **-station** *f* pumping station, drainage station **-stengel** *m* pumping lead, exhaust tube, exhaust vent **-vorgelege** *n*, **-vorrichtung** *f* pump jack **-werk** *n* pump station **-wirkung** *f* pumpage

Punkt *m* point, dot, period, aid station, (surveying) monument ~ **im Gelände** terrain point ~ (Schriftzeichen) full stop **artilleristischer** ~ artillery reference point **ausgezeichneter** ~ cardinal point (optics) **graphischer** ~ graphic point **kritischer** ~ critical point **schwacher** ~ weak point **spitzer** ~ sharp dot, clipped dot **winkeltreuer** ~ (Radialtriangulation) equal-angle point, orthogonic point (radial triangulation)

Punktabbildung *f* point-to-point focusing (X-rays)

Punktallinse *f* toric lens

Punkt-angußverfahren *n* runnerless molding process **-belastung** *f* concentrated load **-belichtungszeit** *f* (Schlitzverschluß) point exposure (slotted shutter) **-bewertungsverfahren** *n* point rating system **-drucken** *n* dot printing **-durchmesser** *m* spot diameter

Punkte-Balken-Generator *m* (Meßgerät) dot-bar generator (TV)

Punkteinschaltung *f* point insertion, point interpolation

punkten to dot

Punkter *m* a yawing recording gauge

Punkt-eruption *f* explosion-pipe eruption **-fehlordnung** *f* point defect **-fehlstelle** *f* point imperfection **-festigkeit** *f* strength of a (weld) spot **-flächentransformation** *f* point-surface transformation **-folge** *f* welding period, sequence of dots **-folgefarbenverfahren** *n* dot sequential system **-form** *f* spot shape **-formanisotropie** *f* spot shape anisotropy

punktförmig in lumps, punctiform, crater-shaped **-er Brennpunkt** point focus ~ **verteilte Induktivität** lumped inductance ~ **verteilte Ladung** lumped load(ing) ~ **verteilter Widerstand** lumped capacity, lumped resistance ~ **verteilt** lumped, in lumps, concentrated **-e Anfressung** pitting **-e Induktanz** pure lumped inductance **-e Quelle** point(-shaped) source or emitter, focus lamp

Punktfrequenz *f* spot frequency **-störung** *f* (absichtliche) spot jamming

Punkt-generator *m* dot generator (TV) **-geschweißt** spot-welded **-gleichrichter** *m* point-contact rectifier

Punktgitter *n* point lattice **ebenes ~** point lattice in the plane **räumliches ~** point lattice in space

Punkt-glimmlampe *f* spot-lighting glow lamp, point or crater neon lamp, tungsten arc lamp, focus lamp **-gruppe** *f* point group **-heften** to spot-tack **-hof** *m* dot halo

punktieren to point, dot, punctuate

Punktiernadel *f* pricking pin

punktiert dotted **-e Linie** dotted line

Punkt-kathode *f* point-source cathode, crater cathode **-kurve** *f* dot curve, dot record (of a recording instrument)

Punktlage *f* point position **allgemeine ~** general position (in crystallography)

Punktlampe *f* point lamp, punctiform lamp, point source of light

pünktlich punctual, prompt, on time

Pünktlichkeit *f* punctiliousness, punctuality

Punktlichtlampe *f* point lamp, punctiform lamp, point source of light, spot-lighting lamp

Punkt-losigkeit *f* astigmatism **-marke** *f* spot reading **-mechanik** *f* mechanics of a particle **-plan** *m* range card **-quelle** *f* point source **-raster** *m* point (dot or granula) raster, screen, grating

Punktreflektor *m* spot reflector

Punkt-schirm *m* phosphor-dot face plate **-schreiber** *m* dotted-line recorder **-schreibung** *f* chopper bar recording **-schweißbar** spot-weldable **-schweißelektrode** *f* contact point, tip **-schweißen** to spot-weld **-schweißen** *n* spot welding **-schweißer** *m* spot-welder **-schweißgerät** *n* spot-welding apparatus

Punkt-schweißmaschine *f* spot-welding machine, spot welder **-schweißung** *f* (electrical) spot welding, spot weld **-schweißverfahren** *n* spot-welding process **-singularität** *f* point singularity

Punktsprung *m* dot interlace (TV) **-verfahren** *n* dot interlacing (TV)

Punkt-stärke *f* definition (radar) **-strichverfahren** *n* dot-dash mode **-symmetrisch** having point or radial symmetry **-system** *n* system of points **-tastung** *f* dot-keying **-tetrode** *f* crystal tetrode mixer

punktuelle Abbildung point-focal vision or imagery

Punktur *f* point spur, point **-loch** *n* point hole **-sicher** puncture-resisting **-zange** *f* pincers

Punkt-verflechtung *f* dot interlacing (TV) **-verschweißt** spotwelded

punktweis point-for-point, pointwise, point-by-point **-e Ausmessung** gradual or point-by-point measuring **-e Auswertung** point-by-point evaluation

Punkt-wertung *f* classification by points **-widerstand** *m* point or tip drag **-wirkung** *f* point-emission effect **-zentrisch** homocentric, stigmatic **-ziel** *n* pin-point target

Punze *f* counter

Pupille *f* pupil (med.) **erweiterte ~** dilated pupil

Pupillen-größe *f* pupillary size, pupillary diameter **-spiel** *n* response of pupil **-weitemesser** *m* coreometer

Pupin-freileitung *f* lump-loaded open circuit **-freileitungsapparat** *m* Pupin coil for open lines

Pupinisation *f* lump-loading

pupinisieren to coil-load, lump-load, pupinize

pupinisiert coil-loaded, lump-loaded **besonders leicht ~** extra-light-loaded **mittelstark ~** medium-heavy-loaded **-es Fernsprechkabel** loaded long-distance telephone cable

Pupinisierung *f* (coil) loading, pupinization, series loading, lumped loading **besonders leichte ~** extralight loading **leichte ~** light loading **mittelstarke ~** medium-heavy loading **starke ~** heavy loading

Pupinisierungsfestpunkt *m* section point

Pupin-kabel *n* coil-loaded cable **-leitung** *f* lump-loaded circuit, coil-loaded circuit

Pupinspule *f* load(ing) coil, Pupin coil, line-amplifying coil **längliche ~** elongated loading coil

Pupinverfahren *n* coil loading

Purpur-erz *n* purple ore **-gerade** *f* purple boundary **-licht** *n* purple light **-rot** purple **-schnecke** *f* purpura **-weide** *f* purple willow, red osier tree

Puscht *m* post (a pile of sheets of wet pulp)

Push-Push-Schaltung *f* push-push circuit

Pust-lampe *f* blow torch **-probe** *f* blow test, bubble test **-rohr** *n* blowpipe **-span** *m* skimmer

Putz *m*, **auf ~** on the surface **unter ~ verlegt** concealed, buried

Putz *m* plaster, coat, coating (of paint), rough-casting, plaster(ing), dressing, ornament **-arbeit** *f* cleaning and dressing operation **-baumwolle** *f* waste cotton, engine waste, cotton cleaning waste

putzen to clean, cleanse; (scheuern) scrub, scour; (polieren) polish; (schmücken) decorate; groom, rake off, coat, dress, strip off, trim

Putzen *n* cleaning, dressing, fettling, punching, trimming (candle, wick)

Putzen *m* bunch or pocket of ore, cut-out, slug stamping

Putzerei *f* cleaning room, dressing shop, cleaning shop, cleaning department

Putz-faß *n* rolling barrel, tumbling barrel, tumbler **-gut** *n* (founding) castings to be cleaned

Putzhaus *n* cleaning room, sandblast room **~ mit Bodenrostfläche** blast room with plain grated floor **~ mit Drehboden** rotary-floor sandblast room **~ mit Drehboden und Drehscheibe** turntable sandblast room with auxiliary revolving table **~ mit Drehscheibe** turntable sandblast room **~ mit Gleisanlage** sandblast room with track arrangement **~ mit Hängebahn** sandblast room with overhead trolley **~ mit Staubabsaugung nach unten** sandblast room with downdraft ventilation

Putz-holz *n* burnishing stick, emery stick **-karte** *f* tare ticket **-kasten** *m* dust box

Putzlappen *m* mop, cleaning rag, scouring cloth, tow flannel **-weberei** *f* scouring-cloth weaving mill

Putz-leder *n* chamois leather **-leistung** *f* cleaning efficiency, cleaning capacity **-loch** *n* core hole **-maschine** *f* barker or barking machine, (founding) sandblast machine **-messer** *n* back iron, cleaning knife **-mittel** *n* cleanser, detergent **-öl** *n* cleaning or polishing oil

Putz-papier *n* abrasive paper **-prozente** *n pl* dirt tare **-sand** *m* cleaning sand, sandblast sand, abrasive **-stand** *m* cleaning position **-stein** *m* brick stone, sand soap **-stern** *m* rattler star, milling star **-technik** *f* cleaning practice **-tisch** *m* cleaning or dressing table, cleaning bench

Putztrommel *f* tumbling or rolling barrel, tumbler **~ mit Saugleitung** exhaust tumbling mill **~ mit Staubabsaugung** tumbling barrel with dust exhaust

Putztuch *n* cleaning rag

Putzverfahren *n* cleaning process **nasses ~** wet cleaning process, wet tumbling

Putz-vorrichtung *f* clearer **-walze** *f* stripping roller **-werg** *n* cleaning waste **-wirkung** *f* cleaning action **-wolle** *f* cotton waste, oakum, rags (waste), waste (rags) **-zeug** *n* cleaning materials

Puzzolan *n*, **-erde** *f* pozzuolana **-zement** *m* pozzuolana cement

Pyelographie *f* pyelography

Pyknometer *n* pycnometer, specific-gravity bottle

Pylon *m* pylon

Pyramide *f* pyramid, stack **Pyramiden ansetzen** to stack arms

pyramiden-förmig pyramidal **-schrank** *m* pyramid switchboard (teleph.) **-spitze** *f* pyramidal point **-stativ** *n* pyramid stand **-stumpf** *m* truncated pyramid, frustum **-verfahren** *n* method of the pyramid, resection in space **-würfel** *m* tetrahexahedron

pyramidisch pyramidal

Pyrantimonit *m* red antimony ore, antimony ore, kermesite

Pyrargyrit *m* pyrargyrite

Pyrgeometer *n* pyrgeometer

Pyrheliometer pyrheliometer

Pyridin *n* pyridine **-base** *f* pyridine base

Pyrit *m* pyrite, ferric disulfide **-abbrände** *m pl* pyrite cinders **-artig** pyritic(al) **-detektor** *m* pyrite detector **-erz** *n* pyritic ore **-haltig** pyritiferous

pyritisch pyritic **-es Schmelzen** pyritic smelting

Pyrit-ofen *m* pyrite furnace or oven **-schmelzen** *n* pyritic smelting, pyrite smelting **-schmelzofen** *m* pyritic smelting furnace

Pyrobitumen *n* pyrobitumen

pyro-chemisch pyrochemical **-chlor** *n* pyrochlore **-elektrisch** pyroelectric(al) **-elektrizität** *f* pyroelectricity

Pyrogallöl *n* pyrogallol, pyrogallic acid

Pyrogallussäure *f* pyrogallic acid

pyrogen pyrogenic

pyrognomisch pyrognomic

Pyrokatechin *n* pyrocatechin

pyrokristallin pyrocrystalline

Pyrolusit *m* pyrolusite, manganese peroxide

Pyrolysegraphit pyrolytic graphite

pyrolytisch pyrolytic

Pyrometamorphose *f* pyrometamorphism, thermal metamorphism

Pyrometer *n* pyrometer **-anlage** *f* pyrometer equipment **-draht** *m* pyrometer lead **-eintauchende** *n* pyrometer fire end **-schutzrohr** *n* pyrometer-protecting tube

Pyrometrie *f* pyrometry

pyrometrisch pyrometric(al) **-er Wärmeeffekt** calorific intensity, temperature of combustion

pyromorph pyromorphous

Pyro-morphit *m* pyromorphite **-phor** *m* pyrophorus

pyrophore Legierung pyrophoric alloy

pyrophosphorsaures Natron sodium pyrophosphate

Pyroschwefelsäure *f* pyrosulfuric acid

pyroschweflige Säure pyrosulfurous acid

Pyroskop *n* pyroscope

Pyrotechnik *f* pyrotechnics, pyrotechny

Pyrotron *n* pyrotron

Pyroxylinfaden *m* explosive pyroxyline fiber

Pyrrhotin *m* pyrrhotite

Q

Q-Faktor Q factor, magnification factor

Q-Messer (Q = Güte d. el. Schwingkreises) magnification meter

Quaddel *f* swelling

Quader *m* board, square building stone, parallelepiped block (masonry) **-mauerwerk** *n* ashlar facing **-sandstein** *m* upper cretaceous sandstone, freestone **-verblendung** *f* facing of natural stone, ashlar facing **-verkleidung** *f* dressed-stone facing, ashlar facing

Quadrangel *n* square

Quadrant *m* quadrant, leg

Quadrantal-ausschlag *m* quadrantal deviation **-korrektur** *m* spherical or quadrantal corrector

Quadranten *pl* quadrants **-elektrometer** *n* quadrant electrometer **-fläche** *f* quadrant plate **-flughöhen** *pl* quadrantal cruising levels **-punkt** *n* quadrantal point **-signal** *n* zone signal

Quadrantzirkel *m* quadrant compass

Quadrat *n* square, second power **~ des Betrages** square of the modulus **zum ~ erheben** to square **kleinste Quadrate** least squares **Methode der kleinsten Quadrate** method of least squares

Quadrat-abstandsgesetz *n* square law of distances **-aufklärung** *f* square search

Quadratausgleich, kleinster ~ least-squares adjustment

Quadratblock *m* cube **gewalzter ~** square bloom

Quadrat-eisen *n* squares **-flagge** *f* square flag **-förmig** quadratic **-fuß** *m* square foot **-gestänge** *n* square poles

quadratisch square, quadratic, tetragonal (cryst.), quadrangular **-e Abtastung** square-law scan **-er Detektor** square-law detector **-e Form** quadratic form **-e Formen zum Spannungstensor** stress quadrics **-e Form eines Tensors** tensor quadric **-er Gleichrichter** square law, square-law rectifier or detector **-e Gleichrichtung** parabolic detection **-e Gleichung** quadratic equation **-er Kondensator** square-law condenser or capacitor **-er Mittelwert** effective or virtual value, root-mean-square value, root-sum-square value **-e Spule,** square coil **-es Verhältnis** proportion of a square (of) **-e Wicklung** square winding

Quadrat-kaliber *n* square pass, square groove,

box pass **-keil** *m* square key **-kilometer** *m* square kilometer, myriare **-lochstützblech** *n* support grid with square perforations **-meile** *f* square mile **-meter** *m* square meter **-navigations-karte** *f* square navigation chart **-netz** *n* square grid, square net, grid net **-ovalstreckkaliber** *n* square-oval roughing pass **-profil** *n* square section **-röhrchen** *n* square tube or tubing **-stahl-stange** *f* square steel bar **-summe** *f* sum of squares **-tisch** *m* square pass

Quadratur *f* quadrature, phase quadrature, quartile **-komponente** *f* quadrature component **-linien** *pl* equiquadrature lines

Quadrat-verhältnis *n* squareness ratio **-vorkaliber** *n* square roughing(-out) pass **-wellengenerator** *m* generator of square or rectangular waves

Quadratwert, mittlerer ~ mean square value

Quadratwurzel *f* square root ~ **ziehen** to extract square root

Quadrat-wurzelrechner *m* square-root calculator **-yard** *n* square yard **-zahl** *f* square number, square, map coordinate **-zentimeter** *m* square centimeter **-zoll** *m* square inch

quadrierbar squarable

quadrieren to square, raise to second power

Quadrierung *f* squaring (math)

Quadrillion *f* quadrillion

Quadrinom *n* quadrinominal

Quadruplex-betrieb *m* quadruplex working (teleph.) **-telegraph** *m* quadruplex, quad (elec.)

Quadrupol-moment *n* quadrupole moment **-ver-zerrung** *f* quadrupole distortion

Quaikran *m* quay crane

quälen to distress, afflict, deaden (colors), hook on (watchmaking), torture, torment, bother, worry, cause pain, tantalize

Quälen *n* disaggregating, milling to break down the structure

Qualifikation *f* qualification, ability, capacity

qualifizieren to qualify

Qualifizierung *f* qualification

Qualität *f* quality, class, grade, kind, sort **muster-gleiche** ~ standard quality, quality equal to sample

qualitativ qualitative, in quality

Qualitäts-abweichung *f* deviation in quality **-blech** *n* high-quality sheet steel **-guß** *m* high-quality cast iron, high-strength or high-test cast iron, precission casting process **-messer** *m* penetromerter, qualimeter **-muster** *n* type sample **-regulierung** *f* modification of quality **-stahl** *m* high-grade steel **-verbesserung** *f* improvement in quality **-vorschrift** *f* quality specification

Quallfassung *f* well shaft

Qualm *m* (dense) smoke

qualmen to emit thick smoke

Quandel *m*, **-schacht** *m* chimney, central channel (of a charcoal pile), central stake

Quant *n* quantum

quanteln to quantize

Quantelung *f* quantization (phys.)

Quanten *pl* energy elements in atoms **-ausbeute** *f* quantum yield or efficiency **-bedingung** *f* quantum condition **-haft** pertaining to quanta or the quantum theory **-optik** *f* quantum optics **-sprung** *m* quantum transition, quantum jump or leap **-stoß** *m* photo-impact **-theorie** *f* quantum theory **-zahlenvergrößerung bei Elektronen** electron promotion

Quantimeter *n* quantimeter

Quantisierung *f* quantizing

quantisch quantum mechanical

quantisierte Systeme quantized system

Quantisierung *f* quantization

Quantisierungs-pegel *m* quantization level **-rau-schen** *n* quantization distortion

Quantität *f* quantity

quantitativ quantitative **-e Messung** quantitative measurement or analysis

Quantitätsbestimmung *f* quantitative determination

Quantometer *n* quantometer

Quantübergang *m* quantum transition

Quantum *n* quantity, portion, quantum, share **-ausbeute** *f* quantum yield or efficiency **-gewicht** *n* quantum or statistical weight **-übergang** *m* quantum transition, quantum jump or leap **-vorrat** *m* mercury pool (in discharge tube) **-zustand** *m* quantum state, energy level

Quarantäne *f* quarantine **-flagge** *f* quarantine flag **-hafen** *m* quarantine port

Quart *n* quarto

Quartal *n* quarter of year

quartär quaternary

Quartärformation *f* quarternary formation

Quartband *m* quarto volume

Quarterdeck *n* quarter-deck

Quartformat *n* quarto

Quartier *n* billet, quarters

Quartierung *f* quartation

Quarto-gerüst *n* four-high stand **-walzwerk** *n* four-high mill

Quarz *m* quartz, crystal **geschmolzener** ~ fused quartz, melted quartz **optisch inaktiver** ~ racemic quartz, racemate **piezoelektrischer** ~ piezoelectric quartz

quarz-ähnlich, -artig quartzous, quartzose **-be-lastung** *f* level of drive (cryst.) **-brenner** *m* quartz tube lamp **-druckelement** *n* quartz crystal **-elektrisch** piezoelectric **-empfänger** *m* quartz detector

Quarzfaden *m* quartz thread or filament **-dosis-messer** quartz fiber dose meter

Quarz-fassung *f* crystal-mounting **-fels** *m* quartzite rock **-fluoritachromatlinse** *f* achromatic quartz fluorite lens

Quarzflußspatachromatlinse *f* achromatic quartz rock salt lens

quarzgesteuert crystal-controlled **-e Steuerstufe** crystal-stabilized drive (oscillator) stage

Quarzglas *n* quartz glass

Quarzglimmerfels *m* quartz mica rock

quarzhaltig, quarzig quartzy, quartzous, quartzose, quartziferous

Quarzhalterung *f* crystal suspension

Quarzinaktivierung *f*, **optische** ~ racemization

Quarzit *m* quartzite (rock) **-fels** *m* quartzite, quartz rock **-gestein** *n* quarzite rock or stone

Quarzkammer *f* quartz cell

Quarzkeil *m* quartz wedge **-saccharimeter** *n* Q-wedge saccharimeter

Quarzkiesel *m* quartz gravel

Quarzkristall *m* quartz crystal **fertiger** ~ piezoid, finished blank **optisch inaktiver** ~ racemate

Quarz-lager *n* quartz measure, quartz deposit

-mehl *n* powdered or finely ground quartz **-monochrometer** *m* quartz monochromator **-normal** *n* crystal standard **-oszillator** *m* quartz oscillator, quartz crystal-controlled oscillator **-platte** *f* quartz plate **-porphyr** *m* quartz porphyry **-resonator** *m* quartz resonator, piezoelectric resonator **-röhre** *f* silica tube

Quarz-sand *m* quartz sand **-schallgenerator** *m* quartz transducer **-sender** *m* piezoelectric crystal or quartz-stabilized transmitter **-sinter** *m* siliceous sinter **-stab** *m* quartz rod **-stein** *m* clay-bond silica brick **-steuervorsatz** *m* crystal-controlled drive unit **-steuerung** *f* quartz control (radio) **-stufe** *f* quartz stage, oscillator stage, crystal stage **-wellenmesser** *m* quartz wavemeter **-wind** *m* ultrasonic wind

Quasi-detonation *f* quasi detonation **-ergodenhypothese** *f* quasi-ergodic hypothesis **-molekül** *n* quasi molecule **-stationär** quasi-stationary

quasiunendlich quasi-infinite **~ lange Leitung** quasi-infinite line, semi-infinite line

Quassiaholz *n* quassia wood

Quast *m* brush

Quaste *f* tassel, mop.

quaternär quaternary **-e Legierung** quaternary alloy, four-component alloy

Quaternärstahl *m* quaternary steel

Quaternion *n* quaternion

Quebrachoholz *n* quebracho wood

Queckoxyd *n* mercuric oxide

Queckoxydulnitrat *n* mercurous nitrate

Quecksilber *n* mercury, quicksilver **-arsenitoxyd** *n* mercuric arsenite **-azetatoxydul** *n* mercurous acetate **-barometer** *n* mercurial barometer **-behälter** *m* mercury bath **-branderz** *n* idrialite **-chlorid** *n* mercury chloride, corrosive sublimate, mercuric chloride **-chlorür** *n* mercurous chloride **-chromatoxyd** *n* mercuric chromate

Quecksilberdampf *m* mercury vapor **-gleichrichter** *m* mercury-arc rectifier, mercury-vapor rectifier, hot-cathode or full-wave rectifier **-gleichrichterröhre** *f* mercury-vapor rectifier tube **-glühgleichrichter** *m* hot-cathode mercury-vapor rectifier

Quecksilberdampflampe *f* mercury-vapor lamp **~ mit Heizkathode** phanotron, tungar tube (with argon filling) **~ mit Steuerelektrode** mercury-vapor tube with control grid **~ mit Steuergitter** mercury-vapor tube of the thyratron or ignitron type

Quecksilberdampf-röhre *f* (mit Glühkathode) mercury-vapor tube (with thyratron) **-strahlpumpe** *f* mercury ejector **stromdichter** *m* mercury-arc converter **-wechselrichter** *m* mercury-arc inverter

Quecksilber-dose *f* mercury trough or box **-druck** *m* pressure in (terms of) millimeters of mercury **-erz** *n* quicksilver ore **-faden** *m* mercury stem, thread, or column **-fahlerz** *n* tetrahedrite containing mercury **-falle** *f* mercury trap (vacuum pump operaction) **-gehalt** *m* mercury content **-glanz** *m* onofrite

Quecksilber-gleichrichter *m* mercury converter **-grube** *f* quicksilver mine **-halogen** *n* mercury halide **-haltig** containing mercury, mercurial **-hochdruckentladungsrohr** *n* high-pressure mercury-discharge tube **-hornerz** *n* mercurial horn ore, horn quicksilver **-hüttenwesen** *n* metallurgy of quicksilver **-jodid** *n* mercury iodide, mercuric iodide **-jodür** *n* mercurous iodide

Quecksilber-kathode *f* mercury cathode **-kessel** *m* mercury bowl or bulb **-kontakt** *m* mercury contact **-kontaktröhre** *f* mercury contact tube **-kontinuum** *n* continuous mercury spectrum **-kuppe** *f* mercury meniscus **-laufzeitglied** *n* mercury delay line **-lebererz** *n* hepatic cinnabar **-legierung** *f* mercury alloy, amalgam **-leistungsmesser** *m* mercury watthourmeter

Quecksilber-lichtbogen *m* mercury arc **-lichtbogenkathodenfleck** *m* cathode spot of mercury arc **-lichtlampe** *f* mercury lamp

Quecksilber-luftdruckmesser *m* mercury barometer **-luftpumpe** *f* mercurial air pump **-manometer** *n* mercury gauge **-masse** *f* mercury pool or sump **-mohr** *m* black mercuric sulfide **-momentschalter** *m* solenoid **-näpfchen** *n* mercury cup

Quecksilber-oleat *n* mercury oleate **-oxalatoxydul** *n* mercurous oxalate **-oxyd** *n* mercury oxide, mercuric oxide **-oxydnitrat** *n* mercuric nitrate **-oxydul** *n* mercurous oxide **-oxydulnitrat** *n* mercurous nitrate **-oxyzyanid** *n* mercuric oxycyanide **-rhodanid** *n* mercuric sulfocyanate **-rhodanür** *n* mercurous thiocyanate, mercurous sulfocyanide **-salizylat** *n* mercury salicylate

Quecksilbersäule *f* barometric pressure, mercury column

Quecksilbersäulendruck in Millimetern pressure in terms of millimeters of mercury

Quecksilber-schalter *m* mercury contact tubes, mercury switch or circuit breaker **-schaltröhre** *f* mercury contact tube **-schienenkontakt** *m* contact treadle of mercury, rail contact-making device of mercury **-strahlunterbrecher** *m* mercury jet interrupter, mercury break **-sulfatoxydul** *n* mercurous sulfate **-sulfür** *n* mercurous sulfide

Quecksilber-tannatoxydul *n* mercurous tannate **-tropfelektrode** *f* dropping mercury electrode **-umschalter** *m* mercury switch **-verfahren** *n* mercury process **-vitriol** *n*, *m* mercuric sulfate **-zyanid** *n* mercury cyanide, mercuric cyanide **-zyanür** *n* mercurous cyanide

queck-silbrig mercurous **-sulfid** *n* mercuric sulfide **-zyanid** *n* mercuric cyanide

Quellbarkeit *f* swelling property

Quell-bottich *m* steeping trough or cistern, soaking tub **-brunnen** *m* spring well **-dichte** *f* source density

Quelle *f* spring, source, well, fountainhead, headwater, code for a type of guided missile **dicke ~** thick source **lineare ~** line source **punktförmige ~** point(-shaped) source or emitter

quellen to swell, spring, soak, steep, gush, flow

Quellen *n* (des Liegenden) heaving of the floor **~ der Emulsionen** swelling of emulsions **~ von Erdgas** seepages of natural gas

Quellen-angabe *f* reference **-belegung** *f* source distribution **-filmabstand** *m* source-to-film distance **-förmige Lösung** source type solution **-forschung** *f* original research

quellenfrei solenoidal **-es Feld** solenoidal field

Quellen-freiheit *f* freedom from poles (uniformity of normal component of magnetic induction) **-geschwindigkeit** *f* source speed **-glied** *n* source term **-leitwert** *m* source admittance (electr. tube)

quellenmäßig on good authority, authentic **-e Darstellung** integral representation

Quellen-nachweis *m* sources used **-reich** abounding in springs **-Senken-Darstellung** *f* source-sink representation

Quell-erz *n* limonite **-fassung** *f* capture of spring, well shaft **-fest** swell-proof **-gebiet** *n* source **-kuppe** *f* plug **-salz** *n* brine salt, spring salt **-sand** *m* quicksand **-schweißen** *n* solution welding **-stärke** *f* source strength

Quellung *f* expansion, swelling, welling, soaking, imbibition

Quellungs-kolloid *n* swelling colloid **-vermögen** *n* swelling property, expansive capacity

Quell-verschweißen *n* solution welding **-wasser** *n* spring water **-widerstand** *m* output impedance

quer cross, transverse, diagonal, oblique, at right angles, across, transversal, lateral, askance, athwart **~ zur Faserrichtung** cross-grain

querab abreast (of), off, athwart **~ Backbord** abeam, on the port beam **~ Steuerbord** abreast, on the starboard beam

Quer-abmessung *f* cross-sectional dimension **-abpeilung** *f* taking bearings from athwart stations **-abweichung** *f* lateral deviation

Querachse *f* transverse axis, lateral axis, y-axis, roll axis, lateral axis **um die ~** motion in pitch

Quer-anker *m* crosstie rod **-arm** *m* branch rod, crossarm, shunt arm (of network) **-aufhängung** *f* transverse suspension **-ausgleich** *m* capacity balancing **-ausgleichhebel** *m* traverse equalizer **-bahn** *f* cross-run of the fabric **-balken** *m* crossbeam, rail, traverse, arch **-balkenfeuer** *n* crossbar light **-band** *n* crosstie **-bandförderer** *m* crossover conveyor **-bau** *m* cross working **-belastung** *f* shunt loading **-baum** *m* crossbar **-belastung** *f* shunt loading **-berippung** *f* transverse finning

Querbewegung *f* lateral movement, cross feed, transverse travel, transverse movement **selbsttätige ~** (des Schleifrades) automatic cross-feed

Querbewehrung *f* lateral reinforcement

Querbiege-festigkeit *f* transverse strength **-spannung** *f* transverse strain **-versuch** *m* transverse bend test, cross-breaking test

Quer-bindung *f* cross bonding **-blech** *n* cross plate **-bohreinrichtung** *f* cross drilling attachment **-bolzen** *m* crossbolt **-bürstmaschine** *f* crossover brushing machine

Quercitin *n* quercitine

Quer-damm *m* transverse jetty (at right angles to another), spur jetty **-dämpfer mit leitender Schicht** transverse film attenuator **-dehnung** *f* transverse strain or expansion **-dehnungsempfindlichkeit** *f* transverse strain sensitivity **-dehnungsziffer** *f* Poisson's ratio, transverse strain or expansion **-draht** *m* chain wire, crosswire **-drift** *f* cross drift

querdurch across **-messer** *m* transverse diameter **-schnitt** *m* cross-sectional area

Quere *f* transverse or diagonal direction **in die ~ kommen** to interfere

Quereffekt *m* transversal effect (of crystal)

queren to cross

Quer-entzerrer *m* shunt-type attenuation equalizer, shunt-type attenuation compensator **-entzerrung** *f* shunt-admittance-type equalization (teleph.) **-faltversuch** *m* transverse flattening test **-faser** *f* cross grain **-feder** *f* transverse spring **-feilen** to file across **-feld** *n* transverse (magnetic) field, cross field **-feldverlust** *m* transverse (magnetic) field loss **-feldverstärkermaschine** *f* amplidyne **-festigkeit** *f* lateral strength

Quer-feuer *n* enfilading fire **-fläche** *f* transverse plane **-fluß** *m* transverse flux **-format** *n* broadside, broadsheet (print.) **-führung** *f* crossrail **-furnier** *n* traverse ply, cross grain, quarter-sawed veneer **-gang** *m* cross course, cross lode **-gefälle** *n* slope, crossfall (of the water) **-gerichtet** transversal **-geschliffene Faser** cross-grained fiber **-geschlitzt** cross-slotted **-geschnitten** cut across the grain **-gestein** *n* dead rock, rock crossing a lode **-gestreift** cross-striped **-gewellt** transversely corrugated **-gleitlinie** *f* cross slip line

Querglied *n* stem, shunt element **~ eines Filters** shunt element of a filter **Abschluß durch halb ~** mid-shunt termination **halbes ~** (Kabel) mid-shunt termination

Quer-gruppe *f* broadside array **-hacke** *f* cross blocking **-halter** *m* cross holder **-haupt** *n* crosshead, crossbeam, crossrail, yoke, top bridge, rod, crosstie, crossover, bar, traverse, traverse joist, crosspiece, crossbar **-hauptführung** *f* cross rail

Querholm *m* transverse spar **~ einer Presse** crosspart of a press

Quer-holz *n* end grained wood, transom, crossbar, dividers **-schraube** *f* transom screw

Querimpendanz *f* leak impedance, shunt impedance **-entzerrer** *m* shunt-admittance-type equalizer, two-terminal-type equalizer (radar)

Quer-impuls *m* transverse pulse **-induktivität** *f* shunt inductance, leak inductance

Querjoch, obenliegendes ~ einer Werkzeugmaschine (Presse) crown

Quer-kamm *m* transverse crest or cusp of waves in a seaway **-kapazität** *f* shunt capacity

Querkardanwelle, Achse mit ~ jointed cross-shaft axle

Querkegellager *n* thrust ball bearing

Querkeil *m* cotter, key **-verbindung** *f* cottered joint, keyer coupling

Quer-kippung *f* lateral tilt **-kluft** *f* crossbar, cross branch, cross fissure **-kondensator** *m* bridging or by-pass condenser or capacitor, shunt capacitor, shunting condenser **-kontraktion** *f* lateral contraction

Querkontraktions-koeffizient *m* Poisson's ratio **-zahl** *f* transverse contraction ratio **-ziffer** *f* Poisson's ratio

Quer-kontrolle *f* cross totals **-kraft** *f* transverse force, shearing force or load, shear, cross-wind force **-kraftfläche** *f* area of shearing force **-kreis** *m* transverse circuit **-kuppe** *f* transverse (wave) cusp in a broken or cross sea **-kürzung** *f* linear contraction of cross-sectional area **-lage** *f* bank (aviation) **-lagenbefehl** *m* aileron positioning signal (autopilot) **-lagenrelais** *n* aileron positioning relay (autopilot) **-lager** *n* roller bearing, radial (bearing) **-längslager** *n* transverse longitudinal bearing

Quer-last *f* transverse load **-lastig** wing-heavy **-lastigkeit** *f* asymmetrical loading **-laufend** transverse, transversal **-leine** *f* breast line **-leitfähigkeit** *f* transverse conductivity **-leitung** *f* shunt line, crossline **-leitungsbrücke** *f* transconductance bridge **-leitungsbündel** *n* first-choise trunk-group (tel.) **-libelle** *f* cross level, bubble **-leseimpuls** *m* transverse-read pulse **-libelle** *f* cross-level bubble **-linie** *f* diagonal **-lochstreifen** *m* cross-perforated tape

Quer-magnetfeld *n* transverse magnetic field **-magnetisiert** cross-magnetic, cross-magnetized **-magnetisierung** *f* cross magnetization **-maß** *n* square measurement **-messer** *m* scrap blade, chopping blade **-metazentrum** *n* latitudinal metacenter **-modulation** *f* cross modulation **-moment** *n* rolling moment (aviation) **-naht** *f* cross-seam

Querneigung *f* (Piste) transverse, slope; banking turn, bank, turn, crossfall (of the water), lateral tilt **Kurve mit ~** banked turn

Querneigungs-fehler *m* turning error **-grad** *m* degree of bank **-messer** *m* bank-and-turn indicator, cross level

Querneigungs- und Wendemesser *m* bank-and-turn indicator

Querneigungswinkel *m* angle of bank

Quer-nute *f* transverse slot **-oktav** *n* oblong octavo **-pfeife** *f* fife **-pressen** *n* angular extruding (cold forming)

Quer-profil *n* cross section, transverse section, traverse sight line or profile **~ des Tales** profile across valley (cross section)

Quer-profilaufnahmen *pl* cross section work **-rahmen** *m* cross frame **-rechnen** *n* crossfooting **-reihe** *f* crossrow **-restkontrolle** *f* modulo-n-check **-richtachse** *f* axis of traverse correction **-richtung** *f* cross direction **-richtwinkel** *m* angle of traverse correction

Querriegel *m* transom, traverse, crossbar, anchor, cotter, girder, beam **unter ~** pole cribbing, braces

Quer-riegelhaken *m* bolt staple **-ring** *m* transverse ring **-rippe** *f* chain line or mark **-rippen** *pl* transverse fins **-riß** *m* transverse crack or seam, cross-sectional view, cross section, fracture of mineral **-rohrträger** *m* cross tube (of chassis) **-rolle** *f* bridging coil

Querruder *n* aileron, wing flap **~ mit verjüngten Enden** washed-out ailerons **~ geben** to apply bank **eingelassene ~** ailerons inset from wing tips **seitlich überragendes ~** skew aileron

Querruder-ausgleich *m* aileron compensation **-ausgleichsklappe** *f* aileron-boosting tab, aileron-compensating or -balancing tab **-ausgleichteil** *m* aileron balance **-ausschlag** *m* aileron deflection, movement of the aileron **-entlastung** *f* aileron balance **-hebel** *m* aileron horn, lever, or crank **-kreuzgelenk** *n* aileron T-crank **-spannweite** *f* aileron span **-steuerseil** *n* aileron control cable **-stoßstange** *f* aileron-operating tube **-trimmklappe** *f* aileron-trim tab **-trimmung** *f* aileron trimming **-verbindungsstrebe** *f* inter-aileron strut

Quer-säge *f* crosscut saw **-satz** *m* cross composition **-schärfe** *f* definition in picture direction **-schiene** *f* crossbar **-schiff** *n* transept

querschiffs thwartships **-bunker** *m* cross bunker **-eisenmasse** *f* (a)thwartship or traverse iron mass **-kraft** *f* thwart- or cross-pole force, traverse or athwartship force **-magnet** *m* thwartship magnet, transverse ship magnet **-pol** *m* (a)thwartship or transverse pole

Quer-schlag *m* drifting (min.), cross heading, crosscut **-schläger** *m* oblique strike, ricochet **-schlaghammer** *m* cross-peen hammer **-schleifer** *m* cross grinder **-schlepper** *m* dragging or pulling in transversal direction **-schliffholzstoff** *m* cross-grained fibers **-schliffverfahren** *n* taper sectioning technique **-schlitten** *m* saddle, cross slide **-schlittenvorschubhebel** *m* cross slide feed lever **-schneiden** to cut across the grain **-schneider** *m* crosscutter

Querschnitt *m* profile, section, cross section, lateral or transverse section, sectional area, crosscut, cross-sectional area **~ mit U-Form** (U-Profil), U section **durch einen ~ hindurchströmende** (Luft-)**menge** mass flow **benetzter ~** area of waterway **freier ~** free-space sectional area **rechteckiger ~** rectangular cross section **runder ~** circular cross section

Querschnitt unelastischer Streuung inelastic cross-section

benetzter Umfang des Querschnitts wetted perimeter

Querschnitts-abnahme *f* (amount of) reduction, reduction of cross-sectional area, draft **-änderung der Rohrleitung** change of sectional area of piping **-ansicht** *f* cross-sectional view **-ausbildung** *f* form of cross section **-belastung** *f* ballistic coefficient, average load **-blende** *f* transverse shutter (blinker) **-ebene** *f* plane of cross section **-figuren** *pl* intersection figures

Querschnittsfläche *f* area of section, cross-sectional area, sectional area **~ der Kühlluftführung** duct area

Querschnittskreissäge *f* crosscut circular saw **-linie** *f* profile curve **-maße** *pl* scantlings (shipbuilding) **-messung** *f* cross-sectional-measurement **-öffnung** *f* aperture cross section **-übergang** *m* change in section

Querschnitts-verformung *f* sectional forming ratio **-verminderung** *f* reduction of (cross-section) area, necking, draft **-verlauf** *m* cross-sectional contour **-verringerung** *f* decrease in cross-sectional area, draft, necking **-zusammenziehung** *f* contraction of cross-sectional area, reduction of area, formation of a waist (in test piece under tension or tensile stress)

Quer-schnur *f* cross string (textiles) **-schott** *m* transverse bulkhead **-schotte** *f* diaphragm **-schrift** *f* lateral wave **-schwelle** *f* transverse sill, crosstie **-schrumpfung** *f* (Film) transverse shrinkage (film) **-schubeinrichtung** *f* traverse feed **-schwingen** *n* swaying **-schwingung** *f* transverse vibration, pitching motion (aviation), transverse or lateral oscillation, shear vibration, contour vibration or oscillation (cryst.) **-setzmaschine** *f* cross jig

Quer-siedekessel *m*, **-sieder** *m* cross-tube boiler **-sitz** *m* transverse seat **-spalte** *f* transverse fissure **-spaltengang** *m* cross-fissure vein **-spannstift** *m* cotter pin **-spannung** *f* transverse stress, transverse voltage **-spant** *m* bulkhead **-spießglanz** *m* jamesonite **-spindel für den rechten und**

linken Schlitten cross-feed screw
Querspule *f* leak coil, bridging coil **mit Querspulen belastet** leak-loaded
Querspulenbelastung *f* leak loading, leak load
Quer-spülung *f* cross scavenging **-spundwand** *f* transverse-sheet piling **-stabilität** *f* resistance to abrasion, resistance to lateral wave action, lateral or latent stability **-stange** *f* traverse bar, cross bar **-steg** *m* crossbar **-steuer** *n* aileron **-steuerbarkeit** *f* lateral control **-steuerröhre** *f* cross-control beam tube, drift tube **-steuerung** *f* lateral controls **-stiel** *m* cross-strut
Quer-stollen *m* transverse gallery **-stoßherd** *m* side-blow percussion table, side-bump table **-straße** *f* side street, crossroad **-strebe** *f* diagonal trussing **-streifen** *m* transverse stripe **-strich** *m* serif **-strom** *m* reactive, idle, or wattless current **-stroms** athwart the stream **-strömung** *f* cross-current
Querstück *n* cross member, compression strut, crossbeam, traverse, crosstie, crossover, bar, crosspiece, crossbar, thrust block, traverse joist **oberes ~ des festen Rahmens** upper brace of fixed frame **oberes ~ des Schützes** upper brace of gate (of dams)
Quer-stückzapfen *m* journal of crossbar **-summe** *f* sum of digits
Quersupport *m* cross-slide rest, cross slide (on a lathe) **-führung** *f* cross slide.
Quertal *n* transverse valley
Querteilung *f* transverse pitch or spacing **~** (Kennzahl) modulus in gears
Querträger *m* arm, crossarm, traverse, cross-beam, transom, crossbar, pole arm, cross member, compression strut, crossing, crosstie, bar, crossover, traverse support, traverse joist, crosspiece **~ für vier Leitungen** four-wire arm **einseitiger ~** extension arm **unterer ~** lower cross girder **mit Querträgern versehen** armed
Quertragseil und -draht transverse cable or wire.
Quer-transportband *n* crossbelt **-treiber** *m* disturber **-triebsbeiwert** *m* coefficient of lateral flow **-triebrad** *n* traversing pinion **-trimmung** *f* lateral trim **-trommel** *f* cross drum **-überschiebung** *f* overthrust traverse to the strike (geol.)
Quer- und Längsneigungsanzeiger *m* bank-and-pitch indicator
Quer-verband *m* crosspiece transverse bracing **-verbindung** *f* cross connection, cross, tie line, direct connection, grid connection
Querverbindungs-feld *n* cross-connecting block **-kabel** *n* tie cable **-leitung** *f* tie line (tel.)
Quer-vergrößerung *f* lateral magnifying power **-verkehr** *m* lateral traffic **-verschiebbar** cross-sliding **-verschiebung** *f* cross adjustment (of electron microscope) **-versetzen** to traverse **-verspannung** *f* Warren-type or wind bracing **-verstellung** *f* cross-adjustment **-verstrebung** *f* cross bracing (arch.) **-verwerfung** *f* transverse fault
Quervorschub *m* automatic cross-feed **~** (Drehbank) cross-feed, traverse **Handrad für den ~** cross-feed handwheel
Quervorschub-antrieb *m* cross-feed drive **-klinke** *f* cross-feed dog **-kurbel** *f* cross-feed handle **-spindel** *f* cross-feed screw
Quer-wand *f* partition, bulkhead, diaphragm **-weg** *m* by-road, crossroad, cross-country road **-welle** *f* transverse, transverse wave, cross shaft **-wellensystem** *n* transwerse wave system **-widerstand** *m* leak (shunt) resistance, stem, shunt element, cross resistance (of network) **-windanteil** *m*, **-windkomponente** *f* cross-wind component **-zahl** *f* Poisson's number **-zerteilen** to section (traversely) **-zitron** *n* quercitron **-zug** *m* transverse flue, transverse stress **-zusammenziehung** *f* contraction of area, necking, bottling, lateral contraction, transverse contraction **-zweig** *m* crossarm, shunt arm (of network)
Quetsche *f* presser, crusher, squeezer
quetschen to squeeze, pinch, mash, crush, squash, smash
Quetschfalte *f* calender cut
Quetschfuge der Walzen joint (slit) between the squeezing rollers
Quetschfuß *m* squash, press, base, stem, pinch of a tube or lamp, pinched base (electronics), press or foot (of a tube) **~ einer Röhre** squash, press of a valve
quetschfußfreie Röhre loktal-base tube
Quetsch-grenze *f* compression yield point, yield point under pressure, crushing limit **-hahn** *m* pinchcock, spring clip, snap valve **-kondensator** *m* compression condenser **-schweißen** *n* mash welding **-stelle** *f* pinch **-tube** *f* spreader or paste tube
Quetschung *f* crush(ing), volumetric strain, compressive load, deformation, squeeze(ing), bruise, contusion
Quetschungszahl *f* coefficient of elasticity
Quetsch-walze *f* crushing cylinder **-(walz)werk** *n* crushing mill
Quick-arbeit *f* amalgamation **-beutel** *m* amalgamating skin **-brei** *m* amalgam
quicken to amalgamate
Quick-erz *n* mercury ore **-gold** *n* gold amalgam, thin gold leaf on silver foil **-metall** *n* amalgamated metal **-mühle** *f* amalgamating mill **-wasser** *n* mercury solution
quieken to squeak, squeal
quietschen to squeak
Quillayarinde *f* quillai bark
quinär quinary **-e Schreibweise** quinary notation **-e Zahlendarstellung** quinary notation
quincunxial quincuncial
Quintessenz *f* quintessence
Quirl *m* agitator, scanning apparatus, paddle fan **~** (Maß der Wirbelgröße) curl (measure of the vortex) **-antenne** *f* turnstile antenna
quirlen to twirl, stir with a whirling motion, turn
Quirl-steine *pl* fillers **-wäsche** *f* beet washer
quittieren to quit, receipt, give a receipt
Quittung *f* receipt
Quittungs-druck *m* printing receipt on sales slips **-druckvorrichtung** *f* customer's receipt printer **-empfänger** *m* selsyn receiver **-schalter** *m* discrepancy switch **-schein** *m* receipt **-zeichen** *n* acknowledgement signal
Quote *f* quota, share, portion
Quoteneinschränkung *f* quota restriction
Quotient *m* quotient
Quotientenmesser *m* quotient meter, ratiometer
quotisieren to quote

R

Raa *f* spacer, spreader
Rabatt *m* rebate, discount, abatement ~ **bewilligen** ~ **geben** to allow discount, grant abatement, make an allowance
Rabatte *f* border, ridge
rabattieren to discount
Rabbitit *m* rabbitite
Rabitz *m* metal lath
Rachenlehre *f* external gauge, caliper gauge, snap gauge, pull-over gauge, gap gauge
rachenlehrenähnlicher Bügel bracket or frame similar in shape to that of a snap gauge for measuring cylindrical work
Rad *n* wheel, bicycle, gear, impeller, knurl ~ **mit eingegossener Nabe** wheel with hub cast integral ~ **mit eingepreßter Nabe** clamp-hub wheel ~ **mit angegossenem Reifen** wheel with tire cast on ~ **mit Schrägverzahnung** helically toothed wheel ~ **mit Winkelzähnen** double-helical gear, herringbone wheel or gear ~ **mit scharfen Zähnen** star wheel ~ **mit stumpfen Zähnen** cogwheel **einziehbares** ~ retractable wheel **gesprengtes** ~ split wheel **phonisches** ~ phonic wheel **schwenkbares** ~ swivel wheel **stirnverzahntes** ~ spur gear
Rad-(ab)stand *m* wheel base **-abstreicher** *m* wheel scraper **-abzieher** *m* wheel remover, puller **-achse** *f* wheel axle **-antrieb** *m* gear drive, wheel drive
Radar *n* radar (radio detecting and ranging) ~ **impulsmoduliertes** pulse-modulated radar **mit** ~ **führen** to vector ~ **mit Echoteilung** echo-splitting radar ~ **mit ungedämpften Wellen** continuous-wave radar
Radar-bake *f* radar beacon **-bedeckung** *f* radar coverage
Radar-bildschirm *m* radar scope **-bildübertragungsverbindung** *f* radar link
Radar-entfernungsmeßgerät *n* radar ranging equipment **-erfassung** *f* radar contact **-gesteuert** radar-controlled **-haube** *f* radome **-höhengerät** *n* radar height finder **-höhenmesser** *m* radar altimeter **-kartographie** *f* radar charts **-kuppel** *f* radome **-leuchtschirm** *m* radar scope **-lotse** *m* radar controller
Radarm *m* arm (mach.)
Radar-nase *f* radome **-schirm** *m* radar screen
Radar-Schirmbild-Fernübertragung radar link
Radar-störbeseitigung *f* detector balanced bias **-störflecke** (auf dem Bildschirm) radar clutter **-warngerät** *n* radar picket **-wiedergabe** *f* (auf dem Bildschirm) radar display **-zeichen** *n* radar trace **-zeichnung** *f* radar plotting **-ziel** *n* radar target
Rad-auflegepunkt *m* center of tire impact **-aufziehpresse** *f* tire mounting press **-ausschlag** *m* wheel deflection **-bandage** *f* wheel tire **-befestigungsmutter** *f* wheel nut **-belastung** *f* wheel load **-bewegung** *f* rotary motion, wheel motion, rotation **-bolzen** *m* wheel stud **-breite** *f* face of gear **-bremse** *f* wheel brake **-büchse** *f* bushing
Rädchen *n* wheel, roller
Rad-dampfer *m* paddle steamer **-deckel** *m* hub cap **-drehbank** *f* wheel turning lathe **-drehung** *f* torsion, torque, rotation **-druck** *m* wheel pressure **-druckwaage** *f* wheel-load weighing machine **-durchmesser** *m* wheel diameter **-effekt** *n* spoking **-eingriff** *m* gear-wheel engagement **-einschlag** *m* obliquity of the wheels
Rädelmutter *f* knurled nut
Räder *pl* wheels **mit Rädern versehen** wheeled
Räder-antrieb *m* gear drive **-bahre** *f* wheeled litter carrier **-fahrzeug** *n* vehicle mounted on wheels **-formmaschine** *f* wheel-molding machine **-fräsautomat** *m* automatic gear miller **-fräsmaschine** *f* gear-cutting machine **-haube** *f* gear case or box **-gehäuse** *n* gear casing **-getriebe** *n* gear, gearing
Räderkasten *m* gear box, gear casing **-deckel** *m* gear-box cover **-spindelstock** *m* geared headstock
Räder-kette *f* train **-kettenfahrzeug** *n* half-track vehicle **-lafette** *f* wheel mount
Rädern *n* shredded-wheat effect (motion pictures)
Räder-platte *f* apron on a lathe **-plattendrehbank** *f* apron lathe **-prüflehre** *f* wheel check gauge **-raupenantrieb** *m* convertible wheel-track drive **-raupenfahrzeug** *n* wheel-tracked vehicle **-schere** *f* gear quadrant **-schutzreifen** *m* tire bands **-stellhebel** *m* gearshift lever **-übersetzung** *f* gear reduction, geared transmission, gearing **-übertragung** *f* gearing **-untersetzung** *f* gear reduction
Rädervorgelege *n* back gears **-ziehkeil** *m* back-gear pull pin
Räder-werk *n* train of wheels, clockwork, gears, train of gears, gearing **-winde** *f* winch, windlass **-ziehpresse** *f* geared reducing press
radfahren to cycle, ride a bicycle
Radfahrer *m* bicyclist
Radfahr-gestell *n* wheel undercarriage, rolling undercarriage
Rad-felge *f* wheel rim **-flansch** *m* wheel flange **-flattern** *n* wheel shimmy **-flügelflugzeug** *n* cyclogyro **-förmig** rotate, spider-shaped, wheel-shaped, radial **-gabel** *f* wheel fork **-gewicht** *n* weight on the wheel **-gürtel** *m* caterpillar band
radial angeordnetes Kontaktenfeld rotary selector bank
Radial-achslagergehäuse *n* radial axle-box housing **-belastung** *f* radial load **-beschleunigung** *f* angular acceleration **-bohrmaschine** *f* radial drilling machine, radial drill **-bündelröhre** *f* radial-beam tube **-dichtring** *f* radial seal **-ebene** *f* radial plane **-eigenfunktion** *f* radial eigenfunction **-fräser** *m* side-milling cutter, radial-milling cutter **-geschwindigkeit** *f* radial velocity **-kompressor** *m* radial-flow compressor (jet) **-kraft** *f* radial force **-lager** *n* radial ball bearing **-laufring** *m* radial raceway **-luft** *f* radial clearance, tolerance (mech.)
Radial-methode *f* radial method **-motor** *m* radial engine **-rillenkugellager** *n* deepgroove ball-journals **-schnitt** *m* radial cut or section **-schwin-**

gung *f* radial mode **-spalt** *m* radial clearance **-spiel** *n* (Turbokompressor) gland clearance, diametrical clearance **-strahlig** radiating sheaves **-streckziehmaschine** *f* radial draw former

radial-symmetrisch radially symmetric, in radial symmetry **-täfelchen** *n* radial **-turbine** *f* radial-flow turbine **-verspannung** *f* radial wiring **-verzahnung** *f* radial serrations **-zeilendüse** *f* radial row atomizer plate

Radian *n*, **Radiant** *m*, **Radiationspunkt** *m* radian

Radiator *m* radiator

Radiaxlager *n* deep-groove-type radial ball bearing

radier-fest erasing-proof **-firnis** *m* etching varnish **-grund** *m* etching ground **-gummi** *m* rubber eraser **-kunst** *f* (art of) etching **-messer** *n* erasing knife **-nadel** *f* etching needle

Radierung *f* etching

radiieren to radiate

Radikal *n* radical **zweiwertiges ~** bivalent radical

Radikand *m* radicand (math)

Radioaktinium *n* radioactinium

radioaktiv radioactive **-e Abstammung** radioactive relationship **-er Ausfluß** radioactive effluent **-es Folgeprodukt** metabolon **-e Halbwertzeit** radioactive half-life **-er Indikator** radioactive tracer, tracer element **-es Jodisotop** radio-iodine **-er Niederschlag** fall-out (nuclear physics), radioactive deposit, film of radioactive matter **-es Produkt** metabolon **-er Rohrkratzer** radioactive go-devil **-e Strahlung** ionizing radiation **-e Zerfallsprodukte** deposits (nuclear physics)

Radioaktivität *f* radioactivity

radioaktivitätsarmes Laboratorium cold laboratory

Radio-amateur *m* radio amateur, wireless amateur, radio enthusiast **-bake** *f* radio beacon **-bastler** *m* amateur constructor, home constructor **-blei** *n* radio lead

radioelektrisch radioelectric **-er Höhenmesser** *m* absolute altimeter

Radio-empfang *m* radio reception, wireless reception **-entstörung** *f* radio interference suppression **-frequenz** *f* radio frequency **-funkeinrichtung** *f* radio kit

radiogene Wärme radioactive heat

Radio-goniometer *n* radiogoniometer **-goniometrie** *f* radiogoniometry **-goniometrisch** radiogoniometric(al) **-gramm** *n* wireless message, radiogram **-graphie** *f* radiography, roentgenography

radiographisch radiographic **-e Metalluntersuchung** radiographic examination of metals **-e Untersuchung der Metalle** X-ray inspection

Radio-großstation *f* long-distance radio station **-höhenmesser** *m* radio altimeter **-hörer** *m* broadcast listener, radio fan **-indikator** *m* radioactive tracer **-interferometer** *n* radio-interferometer **-isotope** *pl* radioactive isotopes **-jod** *n* radioactive iodine **-käfig** *m* radio control gauge **-kanal** *m* radio channel **-kompaß** *m* radio compass **-konduktor** *m* coherer, detector **-konstante** *f* band (range of frequencies) **-kopfhörer** *m* radio headphone

Radiolit *m* natrolite, feather zeolite

Radiologe *m* radiologist

Radiologie *f* radiology

Radiometer *n* radiometer **-flügel** *m* radiometer vane

Radiometerograph *m* radiometerograph

radiometrisch radiometric

Radionavigation *f* radio navigation

Radionuklid *n* radionuclide

radiooptische Reichweite *f* radio-optical range

Radioortungsgerät *n* radio direction finder

Radio-papierchromatograph *m* activated paper chromatography, automatic chromatogram scanner **-peilung** *f* radio bearing **-phon** *n* radiotelephone **-querschnitt** *m* radio channel

Radio-röhre *f* radio valve or tube **-rückwand** *f* wireless-set back panel **-skala** *f* radio dial **-skopie** *f* radioscopy **-sonde** *f* radiometeorograph, radiosonde **-sondierung** *f* radio-sounding **-spitzzirkel** *m* radio compass **-stille** *f* aural null **-stöpselkasten** *m* jack box **-störschutz** *m* screened, radio-shielded

Radiostörung *f* radiointerference

Radio-techniker *m* radio engineer **-(tele)gramm** *n* radio (tele)gram **-telegraphie** *f* radio telegraphy, wireless telegraphy **-telegraphisch** radiotelegraphic **-telephonie** *f* radiotelephony, wireless telephony **-telephonisch** radio(tele)phonic **-theodolit** *m* radiotheodolite **-thermolumineszenz** *f* radio-thermoluminscence **-truhe** *f* radio console **-warte** *f* radioguiding **-welle** *f* radio wave, wireless wave, Hertzian wave

Radium *n* radium **-ausstoßungsverfahren** *n* radium excretion **-behälter** *m* radiode **-belag** *m* luminous or radium paint, radium coating **-bestrahlung** *f* curietherapy **-bombe** *f* teleradium unit **-emanationseinheit** *f* curie unit quantity of radon **-jodid** *n* radium iodide **-sulfat** *n* radium sulfate

Radius *m* radius **~ der Abplattungszone** flattened radius **~ des Arbeitskreises** radius of action of a machine

Radius-stange *f* radius rod **-vektor** *m* radius vector

radizieren to extract the root of, evolve

Radizierung *f* evolution

Rad-kappe *f*, **-kapsel** *f* hub cap **-kasten** *m* paddle box (of a ship) **-keil** *m*, **-klüse** *f* wheel chock **-körper** *m* wheel body, hub **-kranz** *m* rim (of wheel), tire **-kranzschweißung** *f* building up of tires

Rad-lafette *f* wheeled gun carriage **-lager** *n* wheel bearing **-landung** *f* wheel landing, wheeler **-last** *f* wheel load **-lenker** *m* guide rail **-linie** *f* epicycloid, cycloid (in stroboscopic aberration) **-macher** *m* wheelwright **-mutter** *f* wheel nut **-nabe** *f* wheel hub, gear hub, nave

Radnaben-antriebszapfen *m* wheel hub drive shaft **-flansch** *m* hub flange **-kappe** *f* wheel hub cap **-lager** *n* hub bearing **-zapfen** *m* axle shaft

Radom *n* radome

Radon *n* radon, radium emanation **-folgeprodukte** *pl* radium secondary products **-hohlnadel** *f* radon seed

Radphänomen *n* wheel illusion

Radreifen *m* (wheel) tire, rim **-bohrbank** *f* tire-boring mill **-sicherung** *f* tire fastening, securing the tire **-walzwerk** *n* tire (rolling) mill

Rad-satz *m* wheel set, axle plus two (shrunk-on) wheels **-schaltung** *f* wheel escapement **-schaufel**

f wheel blade **-scheibe** *f* wheel-center disk, wheel disk, web of a wheel **-scheibenwalzwerk** *n* wheel-web rolling mill **-schlepper** *m* wheel tractor (untracked) **-schlüssel** *m* ratchet wrench **-schuh** *m* brake **-speiche** *f* spoke **-sperre** *f* wheel lock **-sporn** *m* tail wheel **-spur** *f* wheel track

Radstand *m* wheel base **schiefer ~** cant (mil.)

Radstandlibelle *f* cant level

Rad-stern *m* wheel spider, spoke wheel center **-steuerung** *f* wheel control (differentiating from stick control) **-stift** *m* wheel stud **-sturz** *m* camber (wheel), splay of wheel **-stütze** *f* wheel brace **-taster** *m* wheel-operated means **-teilung** *f* pitch of the wheel **-umfang** *m* circumference of wheel **-umformer** *m* speed transformer

Rad-verblendscheibe *f* wheel disk **-verbreiterung** *f* extension rim **-verkleidung** *f* streamlining of the wheel, wheel fairing, wheel spats, wheel casing **-vorgelege** *n* back gear **-walzwerk** *n* wheel rolling mill **-weg** *m* cycle track **-welle** *f* gear shaft **-zahn** *m* cog, tooth, cog of a wheel **-zapfen** *m* trunnion, pivot **-zugmaschine** *f* wheeled prime mover

Raffinade *f* raffinade, refined sugar **-kläre** *f* refined liquor **-kontingent** *n* refined-sugar quota **-vakuumapparat** *m* vacuum pan for refined sugar

Raffinadzink *n* refined spelter (zinc)

Raffinat *n* refined product **-blei** *n* refined lead

Raffination *f* refining **~ im Schmelzfluß** furnace refining

Raffinations-abfall *m* sludge or waste (refinery) **-anlage** *f* refining plant, refinery, refinery plant **-behandlung** *f* refinement, refining treatment **-prozeß** *m*, **-verfahren** *n*, **-vorgang** *m* refining process, treating process **-wirkung** *f* refining effect, refining action

Raffinatkupfer *n* refined copper

Raffinerie *f* refinery **-gas** *n* refinery gas **-kläre** *f* raw-sugar liquor **-melasse** *f* refinery molasses, barrel sirup **-spanne** *f* refiners' differential

Raffineur *m* refiner **-messer** *n* refiner bar

Raffinier-anlage *f* refining plant or still, refinery **-arbeit** *f* refining operation **-barkeit** *f* refinability

Raffinier-feuer *n* refining furnace **-gesellschaft** *f* refining company **-herd** *m*, **-ofen** *m* refining furnace **-stahl** *m* merchant bar, refined iron, No. 2 iron, refined steel

raffiniert refined, treated

Raffinierung *f* refining, refinery

Raffinierverfahren *n* refining process, treating processes

ragen to tower, loom, project

Rahe *f* spreader, yard **mit Rahen getakelt** squarerigged

Rahm *m* cream **-bildung** *f* formation of cream

Rahmen *m* frame; (Rand) edge, border, background; (Gefüge) framework, structure; (Grenze) limit; housing (rigid), set, registering frame, rack, picture frame, carrier, framework, scope, sphere, pack (for apparatus), coil, frame aerial, loop, stator **~ der Tafel** framework of shutter **doppelseitiger ~** double-sided rack **drehbarer ~** rotatable coil, moving frame, rotating loop **einseitiger ~** single-sided rack **magischer ~** luminous edge **schwenkbarer ~** gate **versteifter ~** trussed frame (car)

Rahmenachse *f* collimating axis

Rahmenachsenkreuzpunkt *m* point of intersection of the collimating axes

Rahmenantenne *f* frame, coil, loop, or frame antenna; **~** (mit einer Windung) loop (antenna) **abgegebene ~** balanced loop **drehbare ~** moving frame **zwei gekreuzte Rahmenantennen** cross-coil antenna

Rahmen-aufsatz *m* yoke to frame **-ausschnitt** *m* frame opening **-baustoff** *m* material of which the frame is built **-eckbeschlag** *m* corner piece of frame **-binder** *m* rigid frame **-blechschere** *f* guillotine plate shears **-brücke** *f* device for preadjustment of homing devices toward target (missiles) **-durchfederung** *f* elasticity of frame **-ebene** *f* plane of (the registering) frame **-effekt** *m* closed-loop effect **-einheit** *f* rack section **-einlage** *f* butt strap

Rahmen-empfang *m* frame-antenna reception, loop reception **-empfänger** *m* loop receiver **-entwickelung** *f* rack development, tray development **-fachwerk** *n* trussed frame **-filter** *m* frame filter **-form** *f* shape of the frame **-formel** *f* formula relating to rigid system **-förmiger Richtkoppler** loop-type directional coupler **-gestell** *n* frame, rack **-hammer** *m* drop hammer **-hauptpunkt** *m* principal point of registering frame **-hintergrundmarke** *f* background collimating mark

Rahmenkreis *m* frame circuit **-abstimmung** *f* loop-aerial circuit tuning

Rahmen-kurbel *f* loop crank **-lager** *n* main bearing **-längsträger** *m* side member, chassis longitudinal, chassis side member **-last** *f* loading of the frame **-luftleiter** *m* loop, aerial frame **-los** frameless, integral, without frame **-marke** *f* collimating mark

Rahmenmarkenviereck der Aufnahmekammer vertices of the rectangular frame holding plate or film in a surveying camera

Rahmenmittelpunkt *m* registering-frame center **optischer ~** optical center of the registering frame

Rahmen-nachstimmung *f* resetting or recheck of frame or coil tuning **-negative** *f* rack negatives

Rahmenpeiler *m*, **kompensierter ~** compensated loop direction finder

Rahmen-querspant *n* transverse frame **-querträger** *m* cross member, chassis cross member **-richtgerät** *n* frame adjusting device **-ring** *m* frame ring **-rührer** *m* gate paddle agitator **-schaft** *m* frame shaft **-schenkel** *m* frame piece **-schere** *f* guillotine shears **-schutzdeckel** *m* focal plane cover

Rahmen-spaltsäge *f* jig saw **-spannturm** *m* picture-frame cabane, cabane bracing **-spant** *n* frame bulkhead **-splissung** *f* frame splice **-ständer** *m* closed-top roll housing **-stoßmaschine** *f* frame slotting machine **-stück** *n* frame section

Rahmen-sucher *m* (wire) frame view finder, finder frame, iconometer **-symmetrieachse** *f* center line of the frame

Rahmensystem *n*, **ebenes ~** plane frame system

Rahmen-träger *m* member of frame **-tragfähigkeit** *f* cross carrying capacity **-trockner** *m* tenter drier **-unterzug** *m* trussing of the frame **-verformung** *f* sceleton forming **-verstrebung** *f* frame stay **-verteiler** *m* terminal assembly **-vordergrundmarke** *f* foreground collimating mark **-vortrieb** *m* timberwork (in blasting) **-werk** *n* framework, frame structure **-wirkung** *f* closed-loop effect **-zwischenverteiler** *m* trunk frame terminal assembly

Rahm-gewinnung *f* extraction of cream **-kammer** *f* cream storage **-kühler** *m* cream cooler

Rakel *n* wiper **-druck** *m* screen printing **-maschine, -stärkemaschine, -appretiermaschine** *f* backfilling machine or backfilling starcher (textiles) **-messerschleifmaschine** *f* doctor blade grinding machine **-träger** *m* doctor blade carrier

Rakete *f* rocket **mehrstufige ~** step-rocket

Raketenantrieb *m* rocket propulsion

raketenartig verbrennen to fuse (chem.)

Raketen-düse *f* rocket-jet nozzle **-flug** *m* rocket flight **-flugmodell** *n* rocket-driven model **-flugzeug** *n* rocket airplane **-getrieben** rocket-powered **-hülsenpapier** *n* rocket paper, rocket-case paper **-motor** *m* sustainer motor, rocket engine **-motorengehäuse** *n* rocket motor case

Raketen-satz *m* rocket composition, rocket attachment **-schleudersitz** *m* rocket ejection seat **-schleuderwaffen** *pl* missiles **-schraube** *f* rocket-driven propeller **-start** *m* rocket-assisted take-off **-starthilfe** *f* rocket-starting assist **-technik** *f* rocketry **-treibsatz** *m* rocket-propelling charge **-treibstoff** *m* missile fuel, rocket propellant **-triebwerk** *n* rocket booster **-verfahren** *n* rocket propulsion **-vortrieb** *m* rocket propulsion **-werfer** *m* rocket launcher **-zeichen** *n* flare signal **-zünder** *m* rocket booster

Ramé-isolierter Draht ramie covered wire

ramifizieren to ramify

Ramm-anlage *f* pile driving plant, piling plant **-apparat** *m* ramming apparatus **-arbeit** *f* pile driving, piling **-bahn** *f* trackage for pile driver **-bär** *m* rammer, tup, ram, monkey, steam hammer **-block** *m* pile hammer (monkey) **-bock** *m* ram **-brunnen** *m* well obtained by driving pipe into water-bearing stratum **-bühne** *f* pile-driver staging

Ramme *f* ram, rammer, pile driver, pile hammer, piling frame, pig driver

Rammeln von Gängen junction of lodes

rammen to ram, drive (piles), tamp (concrete), beat down, pound **die Erde ~** to ram or beat down the earth

Rammen *n* pile driving **stufenweises ~** drive by stages

Rammen-magnetzünder *m* power ram magneto **-schwelle** *f* sill of a pile-driving engine

Ramm-filterbrunnen *m* well points **-jungfer** *f* pile block **-klotz** *m* ram pile driver **-knecht** *m* pile block **-pfahl** *m* piling pole, pile to be driven **-rohr** *n* drive pipe **-schutz** *m* protective device **-vorrichtung** *f* pile-driving engine **-welle** *f* ram shaft, ram socket

Rampe *f* ramp, slope, platform, incline, sloping beach

Rampen-abtastung *f* floodlight scanning **-beleuchtung** *f* footlights **-gerät** *n* portable ramp **-licht** *n* running light (navy) **-licht** (Theater) footlights **-träger** ramp girder

Rampenverbinder, verriegelter ~ locked ramp connector

ramponiert damaged, injured, bulged

RAM-Speicher *m* random access storage

Rand *m* edge; (Grenze) border; (Umkreis) periphery; rim, border, tip, margin, skirt, boundary, collar (math.), brim, hem, flange **äußerer ~** extrados, outer surface **innerer ~** intrados, inner surfaces **unterer ~** skirt **vorspringender ~** shoulder, ledge **vorstehender ~** flange

Rand-anmerkung *f* marginal note, marginal annotation, marginalia **-antrieb** *m* peripheral drive **-aufbruch** *m* color fringing, edge flare (film, TV) **-ausgleich** *m* line justification **-auslösung** *f* marginal release **-aussparung** *f* setting-aside margin **-batterie** *f* outlying battery **-bedingung** *f* limiting condition, boundary condition, edge condition **-befeuerung** *f* boundary lighting (aviat)

Rand-bemerkung *f* marginal note or annotation, marginalia **-blase** *f* blowholes below the surface (in an ingot) **-bogen** *m* wing-tip former or strip, tip strip **-dämpfung** *f* surface damping **-dichte** *f* boundary density **-effekt** edge effect, fringe or marginal effect

Rändel *n* milled knob, micrometer knob, punch, knurled head **-band** *n* binding tape **-griff** *m* knurled nut

Rändelhalter, seitlicher ~ side knurl holder **verstellbarer ~** adjustable knurl holder

Rändel-knopf *m* milled knob, knurled knob **-kopf** *m* milled or knurled head **-maschine** *f* bordering machine

rändeln to edge, border, mill, brim, rim, bead, knurl

Rändel-rad *n* knurl, knurling wheel **-ring für die Entfernungseinstellung** milled distance setting ring **-rollenhalter** *m* knurling tool holder **-schraube** *f* knurled-head screw **-schwenkwerkzeug** *n* knurling swing tool **-teilung** *f* knurl pitch

Rändelung einer Münze milled edge of a coin

Ränderierbacke *f* jaws for knurling or milling machine

ränderieren to knurl

Ränderier-rad *n* knurl **-werkzeug** *n* knurling tool

rändern to edge, border, mill

Ränderscheibe *f* edge cutter

Ränderung *f* bordering (math.)

Randfaser *f* edge fiber

Rand-fassung *f* rim **-feld** *n* boundary field **-feuerpatrone** *f* rim-fire cartridge **-feuerung** *f* rim firing

Randfläche *f* lateral face (crystal) **feste ~** stationary boundary

Rand-gebiet *n* fringe area **-glosse** *f* commentation marginal or side note **-hemmung** *f* marginal stop **-integral** *n* circulation (of a vector), number of revolutions

Randit *m* randite

Rand-kaliber *n* groove at the end of the barrel **-kante** *f* lateral edge (cryst.) **-kappe** *f* wing-tip edge **-kegelgeschoß** *n* banded ogive bullet **-kraft** *f* force at edge, marginal force **-leiste** *f* cornice, rubbing strip

randliche Umwandlung peripheral change

Rand-linie *f* edge **-loch** *n* perforation hole **-lochkarte** *f* marginal punched card **-parabel** *f* marginal parabola (aviation) **-platte** *f* flange plate **-polsterung** *f* rim padding **-prägung** *f* marginal embossing (of film)

Randpunkt *m* marginal point **-satz** *m* boundary

point lemma

Rand-risse *pl* edge cracks **-rückfeinen** *n* edge refinement **-schärfe** *f* resolution border (TV) marginal definition, sharpness of edge **-schicht** *f* rim zone, external zone, outer zone, surface layer, outer layer **-schiene** *f* lining rail **-schleier** *m* veiling on the margin **-schleifer** *m* crimper

Rand-schubspannung *f* surface sheer stress **-spannung** *f* edge stress, extreme fiber stress **-sperre** *f* margin stop mechanism **-spur** *f* marginal track (tape rec.) **-stein** *m* curbstone **-steller** *m* marginal stop **-stellung** *f* defiladed position, margin stops **-strahl** *m* marginal or peripheral ray

Randstreifen-generator *m* stripe signal generator (TV) **-signal** (für Meßzwecke) stripe signal (TV)

Rand-tief *n* secondary depression or cyclone **-träger** *m* edge beam, wall beam, spandrel beam **-tropfpflanzmaschine** *f* edge-drop corn planter **-verbindung** *f* faucet joint **-verdunkelung** *f* limb darkening **-verlust** *m* tip loss **-verschmiert** having diffuse edge **-versteifung** *f* straightened border **-verzierung** *f* border, flourish, printer's flower **-wasser** *n* edge water

Randwert *m* boundary value **-aufgabe** *f* boundary value problem **-prüfung** *f* marginal checking **-schaltung** *f* clamping circuit

Rand-widerstand *m* induced resistance, induced drag (aviation) **-winkel** *m* boundary or rim angle, marginal angle, angle of contact, wetting angle **-wirbel** *m* marginal vortex, tip vortex **-wulst** *f* bead, surround, edged beading **-zeichnung** *f* marginal sketch

Randzone *f* shell zone, external zone, shell, skin, rim, case (metal.) **verstickte ~** nitrided edge, marginal zone

Randzuordnung *f* identification of boundary points

Rang *m* rank (of switches), grade, rate, row (of seats) **~** (Wichtigkeitsgrad) **einer Leitung** class of circuit for control purposes

Rang-dienstalter *n* seniority **-folge** *f* priority

Rangier-anlage *f* shunting, switching, or maneuvering device **-bahnhof** *m* assembling station, switchyard **-draht** *m* jumper wire (teleph.)

rangieren to shunt, switch

Rangierer *m* switchman

Rangier-funk *m* yard radio (R.R.) **-gleis** *n* switching track, siding **-heber** *m* service jack **-lokomotive** *f* switcher, switch engine **-schalter** *m* rewind control switch **-schnur** *f* patch cord **-stoß** *m* buffing load

Rangierung *f* switching, shunting

Rangier-verteiler *m* cross-connection field **-vorrichtung** *f* shunting installation **-winde** *f* maneuvering or shunting winch, car haulage

Rang-klasse *f* rank **-mäßig** in order (of rank) **-ordnung** *f* order of precedence

Rangoonvaseline *f* Rangoon tar

Rangvermerk *m* (von Meldungen) priority prefix

rank crank (naut.), sick

Ranock *f* yardarm

ranzig rancid

Rapidstahl *m* high-speed steel

rapport-frei without periodicity, correct but ambiguous **-punkt** *m* guide mark

Rapputz *m* rough cast, plastering

Rarität *f* rarity

rasant flat (trajectory), grazing

Rasanz *f* flatness (ballistics)

rasch quick, impetuous **-er Satz** common fuse composition, meal-powder composition

Raschel *f* double-rib loom

Raschheit *f* quickness, promptness

Rasen *m* sod, turf, grass **-abdeckung** *f* layer of sod (camouflage)

rasen to run fast

rasend raving, furious, mad

Rasen-decke *f* sodded slope **-eisenerz** *n*, **-eisenstein** *m*, **-erz** *n* bog iron ore **-erzreiniger** *m* bog-ore purifier **-hängebank** (Bg) *f* pit mouth **-stecher** *m* turf cutter **-torf** *m* light surface peat

Rasen- und Stoppelpflug *m* turf-and-stubble plow

Rasenziegel *m* sod squares (for paving)

Rasierapparat *m*, **elektrischer ~** dry shaver, electric razor

Raspe *f* rasp

Raspel *f* rasp, grater **-feile** *f* circular file **-maschine** *f* disintegrator

raspeln to rasp

Rasselglocke *f* continuously sounding bell

rasseln to rattle, rustle, clatter

Rasseln *n* rattle, rattling

Rasselwecker *m* vibrating bells

Rast *f* halt (on march), rest, stay, driving arm (mach.), top of cam, rut, bosh (of a furnace), device for stopping, locking, arresting, or adjusting, tuning lock (radio), notch, detention point **in die ~ einspringen** to jump into the groove

Rast-ankerring *m* bosh band **-bar** lockable **-bogen** *m* notched segment **-buchse** *f* guide bushing

Raste *f* notch, detend, indentation

rasten to rest, halt, spot, tune **-arretierung** *f* arrester or locking means **-bolzen** *m* index bolt **-hebel** *m* notch arm **-knopf** *m* button **-kühlkasten** *m* bosh cooling box

Rasten-loch *n* index hole **-schalter** *m* drum switch step switch, multiple-point switch **-scheibe** *f* slotted disk, star wheel, bosh casing **-schlitz** *m* slot **-spreize** *f* bracing member (of piano) **-teilscheibe** *f* index wheel with notches

Raster *m* screen, raster, grating, scanning pattern, microturner, screen, scanning field, unmodulated light spot, scan or scanned area (television), mosaic (in photocathode tube) **beweglicher ~** reciprocating grid **einfacher ~** (ohne Zeilensprung) consecutive scanning **ungeradzahliger ~** odd-line interlaced scan

Raster-abstand *m* screen line distance **-ätzung** *f* autotypy **-austastung** *f* frame-blanking value **-bild** *n* scanning-pattern image, autotype **-blende** *f* scanning device, diaphragm, scan hole, raster-screen aperture **-druckmaschine** *f* screen printing machine **-einstellung** *f* adjustment, tuning **-element** *n* picture element, scanning element, picture point, screen plate, elementary area **-feinheit** *f* definition of the image, resolution, raster detail or definition **-fläche** *f* scanning pattern (television) **-frequenz** *f* scanning frequency, field frequency **-impuls** *m* frame pulse

rastern to screen

Raster-kathode *f* photocathode, mosaic screen **-korn** *n* silver globule (of iconoscope mosaic), silver plug **-mikroskop** *n* screen or raster scan microscope, electron scan microscope **-oszilla-**

tor *m* spectrum oscillator **-platte** *f* scan pattern, field, or area, photosensitized mosaic plate, screen **-punkt** *m* picture element, scanning element, picture point, elementary area **-quadrat** *n* reticle of squares **-reflektor** *m* grating reflector **-schirm** *m* mosaic screen **-störung** *f* scanning interference **-stoß** *m* scanning impulse

Rasterung *f* definition or resolution of a picture, embossing, lenticulation

Raster-verformungsentzerrung *f* field tilt **-verzerrung** *f* distortion of scanning pattern **-verhältnis** *n* grid ratio **-wechselfrequenz** *f* field frequency (in interlaced scanning) **-wechselimpuls** *m* frame charge impulse **-zahl** *f* number of picture elements

Rasterzaun (für Selbstrücklauf) frame scanning array (TV)

Rast-feder *f* stop spring **-hebel** *m* stop lever **-klinke** *f* detent, latch, pawl **-knopf** *m* notch **-kühlkasten** *m* bosh cooling plate, bosh-plate box, bosh cooling box **-linie** *f* nodal line **-mauerwerk** *n* bosh brickwork **-nase** *f* detent, latch **-panzer** *m* bosh casing **-platte** *f* bosh plate **-polkegel** *m* herpolhode, space cone

Rastral *n* music ruling pen

Rast-stellung *f* stop location, register **-stern** *m* notched star **-stift** *m* drop-in pin

Rastung *f* catch

Rast-vorrichtung *f* click-stop device or arrangement **-welle** *f* preselected frequency **-winkel** *m* bosh angle **-zahn** *m* notch

Rat *m* advice, counsel, councilor, council

Rate *f* installment

Ratemeter-einschub *m* ratemeter plug-in unit **-meßbereich** *m* ratemeter measuring range **-schaltung** *f* ratemeter circuit **-teil** *m* ratemeter section

raten to advise, guess, assist, help **-weise** by installments **-zahlung** *f* payment in installments

Raterei *f* guesswork

Ratgeber *m* adviser

Rathaus *n* town hall

ratifizieren to ratify

ratinieren to freeze

Ration *f* ration

rational rational **-e Zahl** rational number

rationalisieren to rationalize

Rationalisierung *f* rationalization, economization

Rationalisierungsmaßnahme *f* economic measure

Rationalitätsgesetz der Flächenindizes law of rational indices

rationell expedient, rational, systematic, economical

Rationssatz *m* ratio or scale of rations

rätlich advisable

ratsam commendable, fit

Ratsch-bohrer *m* ratchet brace or drill

Ratsche *f* ratchet drill, ratchet, rattle

Ratschen-anpressung *f* ratchet tightening **-hebel** *m* ratchet dog, ratchet wrench **-kluppe** *f* ratchet screwstock **-schlüssel** *m* ratchet handle, ratchet spanner

Ratschlag *m* advice

Rätsel *n* puzzle, enigma, riddle **-haft** enigmatic, mysterious, puzzling

Ratten-loch *n* rat hole **-schwanz** *m* rat tail, rat-tailed file

Rattermarke *f* chatter mark

rattern to chatter

Rätterwäsche *f* swing sieve

Ratterwellen *pl* shatter marks

Raub *m* robbery **-bau** *m* unmethodical working of a mine **-winde** (Bg.) *f* prop-withdrawer

Rauch *m* smoke, fume, sheet metal **-absaugeanlage** *f* exhausting plant for smoke **-abzugskanal** *m* flue, ventilator **-ball** *m* smoke bomb, float light **-behälter** *m* smoke box **-bombe** *f* smoke bomb, float light **-darre** *f* direct-fire or open-fire kiln **-dicht** smoke-tight **-dichtemesser** *m* smoke meter **-düse** *f* smoke nozzle **-entwickler** *m* smoke generator

rauchen to smoke, fume

Räucheranlage *f* fumigator

Räuchermittel *n* disinfectant

räuchern to cure, smoke, smoke-dry

Räucherung *f* fumigation

Rauch-erzeuger *m* smoke generator **-faden** *m* smoke filament **-fahne** *f* smoke streamer or plume

Rauchfang *m* chimney, flue **-kamin** *m* smokestack **-mantel** *m* chimney hood or mantle, funnel air case

rauchgar smoke-cured

Rauchgas *n* flue gas, boiler or power-plant gas, fumes **-abführung** *f* (Züge) flues **-absaugung** *f* flue gas extraction **-anzeiger** *m* smoke detector **-entnahme** *f* flue gas extraction **-fahne** *f* flue gas plumes **-fuchs** *m* flue **-kappe** *f* flue gas flap **-schieber** *m* flue-gas register, smoke slide valve **-speisewasservorwärmer** *m* economizer **-vorwärmer** *m* preheater using flue gases, economizer

Rauch-gehalt *m* percentage or amount of smoke nuclei in the air **-gerät** *n* smoke apparatus, vapor unit **-geschoß** *n* smoke projectile, smoke shell **-glas** *n* tinted glass, smoked glass **-glocke** *f* smoke cap

rauchig smoky

Rauch-kalk *m* dolomite **-kammer** *f* smokebox, sky, combustion chamber **-kammertür** *f* smokebox door **-kanal** *m* smoke flue, waste-gas flue, chimney flue, air duct **-kasten** *m* smokebox **-kern** *m* smoke nucleus **-klappe** *f* (butterfly) damper, vent, stack (of projection booth) **-körper** *m*, **-ladung** *f* smoke element

rauchlos smokeless

Rauch-mantel *m* chimney hood, mantle **-meldekapsel** *f* message container with smoke signal **-meldepatrone** *f* smoke-generating message canister, smoke-signal cartridge **-ofen** *m* smudge fire **-patrone** *f* smoke-signal cartridge **-plage** *f* smoke nuisance **-quarz** *m* smoky quartz, cairngorm

Rauch-rohr *n* fire tube, smoke flue, chimney flue **-rohrkessel** *m* fire-tube boiler **-satz** *m* smoke mixture **-schacht** *m* outer casing, shell of a furnace **-schaden** *m* damage caused by smoke **-schieber** *m* flue-gas register, smoke slide valve, smoke-writing plane, smoke-flue damper **-schiff** *n* fume nave **-schleier** *m* smoke screen **-schreibflugzeug** *n* smoke-writing plane

Rauch-schrift *f* sky writing **-schwach** smokeless (of powder) **-signal** *n* smoke signal **-spurgeschoß** *n* tracer bullet, smoke-emitting projectile **-stoff** *m* reaction material (rockets) **-streifen** *m* smoke trail **-topas** *m* smoky topaz **-verzehrer** *m* smoke consumer **-wand** *f* smoke screen **-zeichen** *n* smoke signal **-zeichengerät** *n* smoke signal apparatus **-zug** *m* smoke flue, waste-gas flue

rauh coarse, raw, rough, rude, raucous

Rauhartikel *m* raised style

Rauheit *f* roughness, rudeness

Rauheits-beiwert *m* coefficient of roughness **-prüfer** *m* smoothness meter, glossmeter, profilometer

rauhen to nap (fabrics), roughen, dress, raise, tease, card

Rauhen *n* granulating, graining, roughing, roughening

Rauher *m* teaseler

Rauh-frost *m* hoarfrost **-gemäuer** *n* thick wall (of blast furnace), thick inwall

Rauhigkeit *f* roughness ~ **der Rohrwand** roughness of the pipe wall

Rauhigkeits-beiwert *m* coefficient of roughness **-messer** *m* roughness gauge

Rauh-maschine *f* raising machine **-putz** *m* rough cast

Rauhreif *m* hoarfrost, ice coating on bridges, aircraft, etc. **-bildung** *f* frozen fog formation

rauhschleifen to give the first grinding, rough, rough down

Rauh-schmelze *f* rough melt **-tester** *m* roughometer

Rauhtiefe (Oberflächenbeschaffenheit) peak-to-valley height

rauh-werden to roughen **-werden** *n* roughening **-werk** *n* coarse plaster

Raum *m* space, room, place, volume, hold (of ship), (charcoal) vent, area, clearance, scope ~ **gleichen Potentials** equipotential space **abgeschirmter** ~ screened room, screened cabin **ausgelichteter** ~ clearance **bestrichener** ~ danger zone, beaten zone **lichter** ~ clearance **-luftleerer** ~ vacuous space, vacuum, exhaust space **schädlicher** ~ noxious clearance, waste space **überakustischer** ~ exceedingly live room or space (with excessive reverberation period) **wenig** ~ **beanspruchend** small in bulk

Raum-abluft *f* compartment air exhaust **-abstand** *m* spacing **-achse** *f* space axis **-achsenkreuz** *n* system of space axes

Räumahle *f* broach

Raum-akustik *f* room acoustics, stereoacoustics, architectural acoustics **-änderung** *f* change of volume **-anker** *m* spare anchor **-antenne** *f* space antenna **-anzug** *m* (Astron.) space suit, pressure suit

Räumasche *f* retort residue (in zinc recovery)

Raum-aufteilung *f* floor plan **-ausdehnungszahl** *f* coefficient of cubical expansion **-bedarf** *m* overall dimensions, space occupied, floor space required, bulk **-bedingung** *f* condition of continuity, continuity equation **-beheizung mit Ölfeuerung** oil-fired space heating **-beleuchtung** *f* ambient light (T.V.) **-beständigkeit** *f* incompressibility, constancy of volume, resistance to expansion and contraction **-beständigkeitsprüfung** *f* volume constancy test **-bewetterung** *f* air conditioning

Raumbild *n* space image, stereoscopic picture or view, panoramic picture, space diagram, plastic picture **tiefenverkehrtes** ~ space image reversed in depth pseudoscopic space image

Raumbild-entfernungsmesser *m* stereoscopic range finder **-höhenmesser** *m* stereoscopic range-finder **-messer** *m* stereocomparator **-messung** *f* stereophotogrammetry **-vorführung** *f* stereoscopic picture projection

Raumchemie *f* stereochemistry

raumchemisch stereochemical

Raumdarstellung, photographische ~ stereophotography

Raum-deck *n* orlop (deck) **-dehnungszahl** *f* coefficient of expansion **-dichte** *f* volumetric density **-dipol** *m* corner reflector (radar) **-drehung** *f* space rotation **-druckanzug** *m* space pressure suit **-effekt** *m* stereoscopic effect (TV) **-eindruck** *m* impression of space **-einheit** *f* unit (of) volume, unit of space

Räumeisen *n* tapping bar

räumen to clear, remove, broach, remove retort residues, evacuate

Räumen *n* broaching ~ **einer Nut** broaching of a keyway or groove

Räumer *m* reamer

Raum-erfüllung *f* space filling **-erhitzer** *m* space heater **-ersparnis** *f* space saving **-fachwerk** *n* space framework **-fahrer** *m* astronaut

Raumfahrt *f* astronautics, space flight **-forschung** *f* space research **-projekt** *n* aerospace project **-technik** *f* space technology

Raum-fahrzeug *n* spacecraft **-feile** *f* bow file **-fest** space-bound, spatial **-filter** *m* wave guide **-flug** *m* astronautics, cosmonautics, space flight

Raumfolge *f* space interval, block system ~ **mit Zugmeldedienst** telephone block system

Raum-formel *f* spatial formula **-forschung** *f* (Astron.) space research **-frequenz** *f* spatial frequency **-frachter** *m* space freighter **-gebilde** *n* space diagram, solid three-dimensional structure **-gefühl** *n* space or spatial feeling (in vision) **-gehalt** *m* content by volume, tonnage, capacity **-geometrie** *f* solid geometry

raumgeradlinig orthodromic **-e Peilstrahlen** orthodromes

Raumgeräusch *n* room noise, set noise

Raumgewicht *n* density, weight per unit of volume, volumetric weight ~ (ohne Wasser) bulk specific gravity, unit weight, weight per unit volume

Raumgewinn *m* gaining of ground, progress

Raumgitter *n* atomic structure, space lattice, crystal lattice, spatial grid, space grid **kubisches** ~ cubic space lattice

Raumgitterform *f* space-lattice form

Raum-glas *n* stereoscope **-gleichung** *f* continuity equation **-größe** *f* volume

Raumgrößen-mittelwert *m* spatial average

Raum-gruppe *f* space group, point group **-gruppentabelle** *f* table of space groups **-halleffekt** *m* liveness (acoustics) **-heizung** *f* room heating **-heizvermögen** *n* space heating capacity **-helligkeit** *f* volume brightness **-höhe** *f* headroom

Räumhub (Räummaschine) broaching stroke, broach travel, cutting stroke

Raum-hundertstel *n* percentage by volume **-inhalt** *m* volume, (cubic) content, capacity

Raum-inhaltsmessung *f* cubing **-integral** *n* space integral **-ionisation** *f* volume ionization

raumisomer stereoisomeric

Raum-komponente *f* space component (rdo) **-koordinate** *f* coordinate in space, space coordinate
Räumkraft (Räummaschine) pulling capacity
Raum-krümmung *f* space curvature **-kühler** *m* space cooler, precooler **-kurve** *f* curve in space, spherical curve
Raumlade-gitter *n* space-charge grid, filament-screening grid **-gitterröhre** *f* space-charge tetrode, screen-grid tube **-gitterspannung** *f* space-charge-grid or control-grid potential **-netz** *n* space-charge grid **-strom** *m* space current, cathode current, total emission current **-wirkung** *f* space-charge effect
Raumladung *f* space charge
Raumladungs-abstoßung space charge repulsion **-anhäufung** *f* space-charge accumulation **-begrenzt** space-charge limited **-effekt** *m* space-charge effect **-gesetz** *n* three-halves-power law, emission law **-gitter** *n* space-charge grid, control grid, filament-screening grid **-gitterröhre** *f* space-charge tetrode **-gleichung** *f* space charge equation **-impuls** *m* cloud pulse **-konstante** *f* perveance (of a diode) **-netz** *n* space-charge grid **-randschicht** *f* barrier containing fixed space charges **-theorie** *f* space-charge theory
raumladungsverzerrt space-charge distorted **-e Felder** space-charge distorted fields
Raumladungs-verzerrung *f* space charge distortion **-welle** *f* space-charge wave **-wolke** *f* space-charge cloud, concentration or accumulation of space charges **-zerstreuungsgitter** *n* space-charge grid **-zustand** *m* space-charge-limited-current state
Raum-lehre *f* geometry **-lenker** *m* spatial rod, space rod, stereoscopic guide **-leuchten** *n* area illumination
räumlich spatial, in space, stereoscopic, three-dimensional, spacious **~ konzentrierter Parameter** lumped parameter **-e Anordnung** space arrangement **-es Achsenkreuz** three-dimensional coordinates **-e Behinderung** steric hindrance **-e Biegungsträger** space girder in bending **-e Dämpfung** attenuation, damping **-er Diffusionsvektor** *m* spatial diffusion vector **-es Fachwerk** *n* open framework **-e Fläche** three-dimension or stereometrical curve **-es Hören** auditory perspective
räumlich-e Krümmung double curvature **-e Ladungsdichte** spatial charge density **-e Lage** orientation (cryst.) **-e Masche** spatial mesh **-e Möglichkeiten** space facilities **-e Orientierung** spatial orientation **-es Problem** three-dimensional problem **-e Rotationsgruppe** space rotation group
räumlich-er Satz spatial theorem **-e Schallabbildung** stereofonic image forming **-e Strömung** three-dimensional flow **-e Tonwirkung** auditory perspective in sound reproduction **-e Verteilung** spatial or geometric distribution **-er Winkel** solid angle (in spheradian units) **-e Wirkung** effect of perspective **-e Zerstreuung** spatial scattering
räumlichfrei clear (of, from)
Räumlichkeit *f* accommodation
Raum-loch *n* vent
Räumlöffel *m* mining spoon, scraper, raker, paddler staff
Raum-luftschiff *n* stratosphere airship **-luftschiffahrt** *f* astronautics **-mangel** *m* space restriction, lack of space **-marke** *f* space mark, spatial mark, stereoscopic mark, collimating mark
Räummaschine *f* broaching or die-slotting machine
Raum-maß *n* dimensions, volume, stacked measure **-menge** *f* volume, contents, area, surface **-meßbilder** *pl* photographic pair (aviation phot.), stereoscopic pictures **-messung** *f* measuring in space, stereometry **-meter** *m* cubic meter **-metrik** *f* space metric **-mikrophon** *n* nondirectional or polydirectional microphone **-modell** *n* spatial model
Räumnadel *f* broach **~ zum Stoßen** push broach **~ zum Ziehen** draw broach
Räumnadel-führung *f* broach guiding tray **-halter** *m* broach holder **-heber** *m* broach elevator **-schärfmaschine** *f* broaching tool, sharpening machine **-schleifmaschine** *f* broaching tool grinding machine **-standzeit** *f* broach life **-ziehmaschine** *f* broaching machine
Raumnavigation *f* astrogation
Raumnot *f* need for space
Raum-(not)lüfter *m* compartment (emergency) ventilator (submarines)
Räumotter *f* paravane
Raum-peilstation *f* three-dimention DF station **-peilung** *f* three-dimension direction-finding **-photometer** *n* sphere photometer **-potential** *n* space potential
Räumpresse *f* broaching press
Raum-prozent *n* percentage by volume **-punkt** *m* space point **-quantelung** *f* space quantization, directional quantization **-recht** *n* space law **-schiff** *n* space ship **-schiffahrt** *f* interplanetary aviation **-schlittensystem** *n* three-dimensional cross-slide system
raumschots segeln to sail with flowing sheets or off the wind, going free
Raum-schutzanlage *f* intrusion detector system, installation for the protection of rooms (teleph.) **-sektor** *m* solid sector **-sinn** *m* space perception **-sondenbahn** *f* space probe orbit **-spiegelung** *f* space reflection **-spirale** *f* helix
Räumstahl *m* broach
Raum-strahl *m* space ray **-strahlantenne** *f* radiator **-strahlen** *n* nondirectional transmission **-strahlenstoß** *m* burst or shower of cosmic rays **-strahler** *m* direction beam **-strahlung** *f* space radiation, cosmic-ray radiation **-stromquelle** *f* space-current source (teleph.) **-strömung** *f* three-dimensional flow (aerodyn)
Räumte *f* open sea
Raum-teil *n* part by volume, volume **-telegraphie** *f* space telegraphy **-temperatur** *f* ambient temperature **-tensor** *m* space tensor **-tiefe** *f* depth of hold **-toneffekt** *m* stereophonic sound effect, binaural effect **-träger** *m* pile guide **-tragwerk** *n* three-dimension framework **-überwachung** *f* area monitoring **-überwachungsgerät** *n* area monitor
Räumung *f* evacuation
Räumungs-graben *m* evacuation trench **-trupp** *m* demolition squad or party
Raum-veränderlichkeit *f* variability of volume **-veränderung** *f* change in volume **-verhältnis** *n* volume relation, proportion by volume **-ver-**

minderung *f* volume contraction **-verspannung** *f* space bracing **-verteilung** *f* spatial distribution, geometric distribution
Raumverteilungszeitfolgeumformer *m* staticizer
Räumvorrichtung *f* broaching ficture, bulldozer attachment
Raum-wärme *f* room temperature **-welle** *f* space wave, sky wave, downcoming wave, atmospheric wave, reflected wave, propagating wave, spherical wave
Räumwerkzeug *n* broach, scraping tools
Raum-winkel *m* solid angle (in spheradian units) **-wirkung** *f* stereoscopic effect, spatial effect, auditory perspective, stereophonic effect **-zeitlich** spatio-temporal **-zeitkontinuum** space-time axiom **-zeitpunkt** *m* event
raumzentriert body-centered (cryst.), space-centered **-es kubisches Gitter** body-centered cubic lattice (cryst.)
Raum-zuluft *f* compartment air supply **-zusammenhang** *m* continuity
Raupe *f* caterpillar, worm, bead (in welding), tractor, caterpillar track
Raupen-bildung *f* formation of beads **-blech** *n* padded plate **-fahrwerk** *n* caterpillar-type landing gear **-fahrzeug** *n* full-track vehicle **-fördergerät** *n* crawler mounted conveyor **-gängig** caterpillar-tracked
Raupenketten-antrieb *m* caterpillar drive **-schuh** *m* track shoe
Raupen-kran *m* crawler crane **-lage** *f* (in welding) layer of bead **-leim** *m* insect lime **-schlepper** *m* caterpillar tractor, crawler tractor **-schütze** *f* caterpillar gate **-unterbau** *m* crawler undercarriage **-zug** *m* caterpillar traction
Rausch *m* pounded ore **-abstand** *m* signal-noise ratio **-abstimmung** *f* noise tuning **-anpassung** *f* noise matching **-anteil** *m* noise level **-arm** of low noise level **-armut** *f* noiselessness **-bandbreite** *f* noise bandwidth **-begrenzer** *m* noise limiter (elec.) **-bezugstemperatur** *f* noise standard temperature **-diode** *f* noise diode (electronics) **-effekt** *m* flicker effect
rauschen to rush, gurgle, murmur, rustle (in a tube), whistle, roar
Rauschen *n* background (noise), static (radio)
rausch-gesteuert noise controlled **-gold** *n* Dutch gold, tinsel **-impulsrate** *f* noise pulse rate **-kennwerte** *pl* noise parameters **-leistung** *f* noise power
Rauschpegel *m* noise level (thermal noise) **-regelung** *f* shading (control) (TV)
Rausch-sender *m* noise transmitter (radar) **-silber** *n* imitation silver foil **-signalgenerator** *m* noise signal generator **-spannung** *f* noise voltage, noise potential **-sperre** *f* squelch control (in radio receiver) **-störung** *f* noise jamming **-unterdrückung** *f* noise suppression **-ursache** *f* noise generator **-vierpol** *m* noise twoport (electr. tube) **-widerstand** *m* noise resistance
Räuspertaste *f* "cough" button
Raute *f* rhombus, diamond, lozenge
Rauten-antenne *f* rhombic antenna **-flach** *n* rhombohedron **-fläche** *f* rhombus **-form** *f* diamond **-förmig** rhombic, rhomboid, diamond-shaped **-glas** *n* glass lozenge, rhombic pane **-kaliber** *n* diamond pass **-kette** *f* rhomboid chain, minor control plot of rhomboidal figures **-muster** *n* rhombus design or pattern
Rauten-profil *n* diamond **-öl** *n* rue oil **-schnitt** *m* diamond cut **-spat** *m* rhomb spar **-stellung** *f* lozengelike position **-vorwalzkaliber** *n* roughing diamond pass
rautiertes Papier quadrillé paper
Rauvit *m* rauvite
Ravelin *n* ravelin
Rayleigh-Scheibe *f* Rayleigh disk
Rayon *m* rayon, district, area, ray, radius
Rayonnieren *n* radiation method of plotting (using polar coordinates from a central station)
Reagens *n* reagent **-bedarf** *m* solutions required **-glas** *n* test tube, test beaker **-lösung** *f* reagent **-mittel** *n* reagent **-papier** *n* test paper **-röhre** *f* test tube
Reagenzien *n pl* reagents, reactive means
reagieren to react
Reagier-glas *n*, **-zylinder** *m* test tube
Reaktanz *f* reactance **akustische** ~ specific acustic reactance **induktive** ~ inductance, positive reactance, inductance reactance, series resonant circuit **kapazitive** ~ capacity reactance, capacitance, condensive reactance, condensance **mit** ~ reactive
Reaktanzenraum *m* reactor room
Reaktanz-glied *n* reactor **-röhrenkreis** *m* tube reactor **-spule** *f* reactor
Reaktion *f* reaction ~ **beim Fall** drop reaction ~ **in der Front** reaction in the front ~ **mit atomarem Wasserstoff** reaction with atomic hydrogen **eine** ~ **eingehen** to react **ununterbrochene** ~ sustained reaction
Reaktions-antrieb *m* jet propulsion, reaction propulsion **-fähigkeit** *f* reactivity **-folge** *f* reaction sequence **-gas** *n* reaction gas **-geschwindigkeit** *f* reaction velocity **-gleichung** *f* equation (of a reaction) **-grad** *m* percentage reaction **-hof** *m* reaction rim **-kammer** *f* reaction chamber, soaker drum **-kraft** *f* torque, force of reaction
reaktions-los nonreactive, reactionless **-lötverfahren** *n* reaction-flux soldering **-maschine** *f* reaction alternator **-masse** *f* reaction mass, mass resulting from a reaction **-mechanismus** *m* reaction mechanism **-mittel** *n* reaction agent, reagent, reactive mixture **-moment** *m* moment of reaction **-papier** *n* test or reactive paper
Reaktionsprodukt *n* reaction product ~ **bei der Kohlenwasserstoffverbrennung** reaction products in hydrocarbon combustion
Reaktions-propeller *m* hydraulic propeller **-rand** *m* reaction rim **-röhre** *f* soaker tube **-schema** *n* reaction pattern **-spule** *f* reactor **-temperatur** *f* temperature of reaction **-träge** inert, unreactive **-turbine** *f* reaction turbine **-turm** *m* reaction tower
Reaktions- und Erhitzungsgeschwindigkeit *f* reaction and heating velocity
Reaktions-verhältnis *n* ratio of reaction **-versuch** *m* reaction test **-wärme** *f* heat of reaction **-zeit** *f* reaction time **-zeitmesser** *m* reaction-time apparatus
Reaktiv *n* reagent
reaktivieren to reactivate
Reaktivierung *f* reactivation
Reaktor *m* pile (reactor) **-belastung** *f* fuel rating **-berechnung** *f* reactor design **-betrieb mit Hilfs-**

quelle source range **-chargiermaschine** *f* charge face machine **-druckbehälter** *m* reactor pressure vessel **-eintrittstemperatur** reactor inlet temperature

Reaktor-kern *m* (nuclear) reactor core **-kuppel** *f* reactor sphere **-oszillator** *m* pile oscillator **-rohrpostanlage** *f* pneumatic sample irradiation system (in research reactor) **-verseuchung** *f* pile poisoning **-vorrichtung** *f* reactor hardware **-zeitkonstante** *f* reactor period

Real *f* eight lines pica

Realgar *n* realgar, red arsenic sulfide

Realindex *m* index of subjects

realisierter Fehler conscious error

Realisierungsfunktion *f* realisation function

Real-teil *m* real component **-wissenschaft** *f* practical science

Réaumur-Skala *f* Réaumur scale

Rebromierung *f* rebromination

Rechen *m* squeegee, rake, trash rack, comb, ratchet **-anlage** *f* computor **-ansatz** *m* rack attachment **-apparat** *m* calculating instrument **-art** *f* calculus

Rechenautomat *m*, **digitaler ~** calculator (info proc.)

Rechen-bild *n* nomogram **-blatt** *n* computer **-brett** *n* abacus **-einheit** *f* digital unit **-fehler** *m* arithmetical error, miscalculation **-flügel** *m* rake **-folge** *f* sequencing

Rechengerät *n* computer **elektronisches ~** electronic calculator **elektronisch lochendes ~** calculating punch

Rechen-gang *m* process or course of calculation **-getriebe** *n* computing mechanism **-glied** *n* electrical-pressure transmitter **-größe** *f* operand (comp.) **-gut** *n* material retained on trash rack **-hilfslinie** *f* auxiliary calculating line **-knecht** *m* ready reckoner **-kunst** *f* arithmetic **-locher** *m* calculating punch

Rechenmaschine *f* calculating machine, computing machine, adding machine **digitale ~** calculator (info proc.) **selbstschreibende ~** listing calculator **unsichtbar schreibende ~** blind calculator

Rechenprobe *f* check calculation

Rechenschaft *f* account **~ ablegen** to account for, answer for

Rechen-schaltung *f* setup for calculating machine **-scheibe** *f* calculating disk, computer, circular slide rule **-schema** *n* diagram

Rechenschieber *m* calculating rule, slide rule **-läufer** *m* slide (of a slide rule)

Rechen-stab *m* slide rule, trash-rack bar **-ständer** *m* rake stand **-stecker zum Heuaufschichten** rake stacker **-stelle** *f* instrument section position, computing center **-stufe** *f* evaluation and computer stage **-tafel** *f* alignment chart, nomographic chart, abacus, computation table, nomograph **-verfahren** *n* methode of calculation **-verstärker** *m* operational amplifier

Rechenvorgang, schritthaltender ~ on-line calculator operation

Rechen-werk *n* arithmetic unit (info proc.) **-zeit** *f* computing time **-zettel** *m* correction and computing tables

recherchieren to investigate

rechnen to count, compute, figure, calculate, rate, estimate, garrison **falsch ~** to miscalculate **im Kopf ~** to work out mentally

Rechner *m* calculator, computer **-anlage** *f* computing machinery **-betrieb** *m* computer operation **-gerät** *n* computing machine **-gleichung** *f* machine equation

rechnerisch analytically, by computation, arithmetic mathematical **~ genau bestimmt** mathematically exact **-e Erfassung** mathematical investigation

Rechner-logik *f* logic of the computer **-programmablauf** *m* computer operation **-wirkzeit** *f* available time (machine)

Rechnung *f* calculation, rating, bill, account, invoice, computation, reckoning **die ~ bezahlen** to settle an account **die ausführliche ~** detailed statement **~ mit fortschreitenden Näherungswerten** trial calculations

Rechnungs-abnahme *f* auditing **-abschluß** *m* balancing of accounts, balance sheet **-auszug** *m* abstract of accounts **-beamter** *m* auditor, accountant **-beleg** *m* voucher **-dienst** *m* accounting department **-einzahlung** *f* (money) received on account **-ergebnis** *n* result of the operation **-fehler** *m* miscalculation, error in figures **-führer** *m* accountant

Rechnungs-gang *m* rule for calculation **-gipfelhöhe** *f* theoretical or absolute ceiling **-jahr** *n* budget year, fiscal year **-legung** *f* making or submitting an accounting **-mäßiges Metergewicht** theoretic weight per meter run **-prüfer** *m* **-revisor** *m* accountant **-stelle** *f* account section **-verfahren mit fortschreitenden Näherungswerten** trial-and-error method **-wesen** *n* auditing

Recht *n* justice, right, claim, law **von Rechts wegen** by virtue of law

recht right **-er Kegel** right cone **vom -en Wege ab** astray **-er Winkel** right angle **im -en Winkel** at right angles, orthogonally, normally, transversely

Rechtbild *n* positive

(alle) Rechte Vorbehalten (all) rights reserved

Rechteck *n* quadrilateral, rectangle **-abstimmskala mit horizontaler Zeigerbewegung** slide-rule dial

Rechteck-belastung *f* uniform loading **-bezugssignale** basic signals **-flansch** *m* rectangular flange **-formgüte** *f* loop rectangularity **-förmig** rectangular, square-wave (of output voltage) **-hohlleiter** *m* rectangular waveguide

rechteckig quadrilateral, rectangle(d), four-square, square, rectangular **-er Flügel mit abgerundeten Enden** rectangular wing with rounded tips **-es Gitter** rectangular array **-e Kurvenform der elektromotorischen Kraft** square or flat-topped electromotive-force curve **-er Rumpf** fuselage of rectangular section **-e Spule** rectangular coil **-e Welle** square wave **-e V-Antenne** quadrant antenna

Rechteck-impuls *m* square-wave impulse **-kathode** *f* rectangular cathode **-korn** *n* square sight **-kreis** *m* squaring circuit **-kurve** *f* rectangular or square-wave curve **-platte** *f* rectangular plate **-rahmen** *m* rectangular frame **-rohr** *n* rectangular tube **-schwingung** *f* rectangular wave pulse **-signal** *n* rectangular or square-wave signal **-spannung** *f* rectangular or square-wave voltage **-welle** *f* rectangular wave

Rechteckwellen-Eichstufenwähler *m* square wave calibrator
rechtfertigen to justify, vindicate
Rechtfertigung *f* justification, defense, vindication, exculpation
Rechtfertigungsgrund *m* plea, excuse
rechtläufig progressive
rechtlich lawful, legal, juridical
rechtlinig rectilinear
rechtmäßig legal
Rechtmäßigkeit *f* lawfulness, legality, rightfulness, legitimacy
rechts right ~ **achteraus** right astern ~ **Querruder geben** to right-bank, apply right bank ~ **Seitensteuer geben** to right-turn ~ **und links zugleich** ambidextrous
Rechts-ablenkung *f* veering, shifting clockwise, deflection to the right **-abteilung** *f* legal department
Rechtsanspruch *m* legal claim or title ~ **auf alle technischen Daten** title to all technical data
Rechts-antrieb *m* right-side drive **-anwalt** *m* lawyer, attorney **-befugnis** *f* competence **-beistand** *m* counsel **-beugung** *f* miscarriage of justice **-beweis** *m* legal proof
rechtschaffen honest, just
Rechtschaffenheit *f* honesty, integrity
Rechtschreibung *f* spelling, orthography
Rechts-draht *m* hand twist **-drall** *m* right-hand twist or lay (of a cable), clockwise rifling **-drehend** clockwise, right-hand, dextrogyrate, dextrorotatory **-drehung** *f* clockwise rotation, dextrorotation, right-handed polarization **-einwand** *m* demurrer, plea, objection **-fall** *m* (legal) cause or case, suit
rechtsgängig clockwise, right-handed **-e Schraube** right-hand screw
rechtsgenutet right-hand(ed) notched
Rechts-gewinde *n* right-hand thread **-grund** *m* legal ground, legal reason **-gültig** legal **-gültigkeit** *f* validity (law) **-handel** *m* lawsuit, action **-händigkeit** *f* right-handedness
rechtsichtig normal-sighted, emmetropic
rechtskräftig of legal force, valid ~ **machen** to make legal or nonappealable, ratify, legalize, validate
Rechts-kurve *f* right turn, right-hand curve, starboard curve **-lauf** *m* clockwise rotation
rechtslaufend swinging right-handedly, right-hand **-er Motor** clockwise revolving motor **-e Welle** dextropropagating wave
rechtsläufig clockwise, from left to right **-er Motor** right-hand engine
Rechtslenkung *f* right-hand drive
Rechtsmittel *n* legal redress ~ **aufheben** to avoid or remove a remedy of law
Rechts-nachfolger *m* assign, legal successor, assignee **-nachfolgerungserklärung** *f* legalized copy of assignment
Rechts- oder Linksantrieb *m* right-hand or left-hand transmission
Rechts-pflege *f* administration of justice **-polarisation** *f* dextropolarisation **-punkt** *m* point in or of law **-quarz** *m* dextrogyrate quartz, right-handed quartz or piezoelectric crystal **-schlagseil** *n* right lay rope **-schneidend** right-hand (drills) **-schraube** *f* right-handed screw **-seitiger Motor** right-side engine **-spruch** *m* sentence, verdict, judgment, decision
Rechts-stahl *m* right-hand turning tool **-steigend** inclined to the right, rising on the right **-streit** *m* litigation, cause **-streitigkeit** *f* legal contest **-system** *n* clockwise-rotating system, right-handed system **-umlauf** *m* clockwise rotation
Rechts- und Linkslauf *m* clockwise and anti-clockwise running
Rechts-verhältnis *n* legal status **-verkehr** *m* right-hand traffic **-voraus** right ahead **-weg** *m* course of law, legal procedure **-weiche** *f* right-hand switch, turnoff, or frog **-widrig** illegal, contrary to law **-zuständigkeit** *f* jurisdiction, competence
rechtweisen to point true
rechtweisend true (magnetic needle) **-er Kurs** true (north) course **-e Peilung** true bearing **-er Windkurs** true heading
rechtwinklig right-angled, rectangular, orthogonal, square, at right angles, perpendicular ~ **abbildend** rectilinear ~ **abstecken** to square off **dreifach** ~ trirectangular ~ **gebogene Röhren** piping bent to form right angles ~ **schneiden** to square off **-es Achsenkreuz** rectangular coordinates **-er Doppeldecker** orthogonal biplane **-es Dreieck** right(-angled) triangle **-er Kurs** rectangular course, square course
Rechtwinkligkeitsfehlertoleranz *f* perpendicularity tolerance
rechtzeitig in time, promptly, timely, punctual
Reck *n* horizontal bar
Reckalterung *f* recrystallization due to cold working between stages of heat-treatment, strain aging
reckalterungsbeständiger Stahl non-strain aging steel
Reck-bank *f* stretcher **-belastung** *f* tensil strain **-dorn** *m* grid stretcher
recken to stretch, strain, elongate, extend, rack, flatten, hammer, pull, shingle
Recken *n* straining, working, stretching, elongating, racking ~ **des Drahtes** straightening of wire, drawing
Reck-grad *n* total reduction **-kraft** *f* stretching power
Recklegierung *f* wrought alloy **vergütbare** ~ strong alloy
Reck-modul *n* modulus of stretch **-probe** *f* pull test, stretch test, tensile test **-spannung** *f* strain, tensile stress, tensile strain **-vorrichtung** *f* rack **-walzwerk** *n* stretching rolls, finishing or merchant rolls or rollers **-schmieden** *n* hammer forging **-streifen** *m* strain gauge
Reckung *f* stretching
Redaktion *f* editorial office
Redan *n* redan
Redegeschwindigkeit *f* rate of speaking
Redensart *f* phrase, phraseology, idiom
Redestillation *f* redistillation
Redestillationsrückstand von Krackbenzin pressure-distillate bottoms
redestillieren to rectify
Redewendungen *pl* phraseology (aviat.)
redigieren to edit
Redler *m* coal feeder, drag-link conveyor
Redoute *f* redoubt
Reduit *n* reduit

Reduktion *f* reduction **~ der Massen** reduction of masses

reduktions-beständig reduction-proof **-fähig** capable of reduction **-fähigkeit** *f* reducibility **-faktor** *m* reduction factor **-gas** *n* reducing or reduction gas **-geschwindigkeit** *f* rate of reduction **-getriebe** *n* reduction gear(ing), stepdown gear **-halbleiter** *m* reduction semiconductor **-hütte** *f* reduction works

Reduktions-klemme *f* coupling or union reducer **-koeffizient** *m* coefficient of reduction **-kohle** *f* reduction coal **-kraft** *f* reducing power **-kuppelung** *f* reducing coupling **-mittel** *n* reducing agent, reducing medium, reducer, deoxidizing agent **-muffe** *f* reducing sleeve or socket, reducing coupling or bush **-ofen** *m* reduction furnace **-sätze** *pl* reduction discharge **-schema** *n* reduction scheme **-schlacke** *f* reduction slag, reducing slag, white slag, final slag, deoxidizing slag **-schmelzen** *n* reduction smelting **-stoff** *m* reducing agent

Reduktions-T-Stück *n* reducing T

Reduktions-tachymeter *n* reducing tachymeter **-tiegel** *m* reduction crucible **-transformator** *m* step-down transformer **-verhältnis** *n* reduction ratio **-vermögen** *n* reducing power, reducibility **-vorgang** *m* reducing process **-wärme** *f* heat of reduction, heat absorbed in reduction **-wirkung** *f* reducing action **-ziffer** *f* reduction point **-zirkel** *m* proportional compass or divider **-zone** *f* zone or region of reduction

reduktometrische Methode potentiometric-reduction method

Reduktorlampe *f* adapter-transformer lamp

Redundanz *f* redundancy

reduplizieren to reduplicate

Reduzibilität *f* reducibility

reduzibler geschlossener Weg reducible circuit

Reduzier-backe *f* reduction jaw **-bar** reducible **-barkeit** *f* reducibility **-büchse** *f* reducing bushing **-einsatz** *m* taper sleeve, reducing socket

reduzieren to reduce, decrease, lower, step down **~ auf** to reduce to **~ um** to reduce by

reduzierend reducing **~ schmelzen** melt with reducing flame **-e Flamme** carbonizing flame **-e Gleichung** reduced equations **-er Schachtofenprozeß** reducing smelting process

Reduzier-futter *n* reducing chuck **-getriebe** *n* reducing gear **-muffe** *f* reducing coupling **-nippel** *m* swadged nipple **-stahl** *m* reducing steel **-station** *f* filter regulator (for pneumatic control system) **-stück** *n* reducer, reducing socket

reduziert auf corrected to

reduziertes Kernmodell nuclear mock-up

reduziertes T-Stück (flanged) reducing T, (flanged) unequal T

Reduziertransformator *m* step-down transformer

Reduzierung *f* reduction

Reduzier-ventil *n* pressure-reducing valve **-vorgelege** *n* reducing gear **-walzwerk** *n* reducing mill **-zug** *m* reducing pass

Reede *f* roadstead, roads (navy)

Reeder *m* shipowner

Reederei *f* shipping company (merchant marine)

reell real (math.)

Refa time study

Referat *n* review, report

Referent *m* reviewer

Referenzellipsoid *n* reference ellipsoid

Referierdienst *m* abstracting service, reporting service, press-clipping service

referieren to review

reffen to reef, ripple (flax)

reflektieren to reflect

reflektierend, -e Brennfläche catacaustic **-e Dipolebene** reflecting curtain **-e Treffplatte** reflection target

reflektiert reflected **-er Strahl** reflected ray **-e Welle** reflected or indirect wave **-e seismische Welle** reflection of seismic wave

Reflektierstrahl *m* reflected ray

Reflektion *f* reflection

Reflektions-faktor *m* reflection coefficient **-messer** *m* reflectometer **-seismik** *f* reflexion-seismics **-vermögen** *n* reflective power

Reflektor *m* reflector, mirror, floodlight, lamp shade, parabolic reflector **~ für Standrohr** gauge-glass reflector **direkt erregter ~, gespeister ~** fed reflector **strahlungserregter ~, strahlungsgekoppelter ~** parasitic reflector, radiation coupled reflector

Reflektorengläser *pl* reflector glasses

Reflektor-schale *f* paraboloid dish (ant.) **-wand** *f* reflector

Reflex *m* false flash **-bewegung** *f* reflex **-druck** *m* reflected pressure **-empfänger** *m* (regenerative) reflex receiver, dual receiver **-glas** *n* transparent reflector

Reflexion *f* reflection **integrierte ~** integrated reflection **rückweisende ~** retrodirective reflection **troposphärische ~** tropospheric reflection **zerstreute ~** diffuse reflection **~ durch Polarlicht** auroral reflection **~ einer Welle** traveling-wave reflection

Reflexions-abtastung *f* reflected-light principle of scanning **-brennfläche** *f* catacaustic **-ebene** *f* plane of reflection **-faktor** *m* reflection factor or coefficient, back-scattering coefficient **-fleck** *m* flare ghost, flare (phot.)

reflexionsfrei without spatter **-er Abschluß** matched termination **-er Abschluß** non-reflecting termination

Reflexion-goniometer *n* reflecting goniometer **-höhe** *f* virtual height, effective height, level of reflection **-klystron** *n* reflex klystron **-koeffizient** *m* mismatch factor, reflectivity **-kraft** *f* reflective power **-kreis** *m* surveying sextant **-kugel** *f* sphere of reflection

Reflexions-laufzeitröhre *f* reflex-klystron **-lichthof** *m* halation by reflection **-messer** *m* reflectometer **-messung** *f* reflectance measurement, reflectometry **-methode** *f* reflectance method **-prisma** *n* reflecting prism **-röhre** *f* velocity modulation valve, reflex klystron **-schwerpunkt** *m* effective reflection point **-schwingartfilter** *n* reflection mode filter

Reflexions-verlust *m* reflection attenuation **-verlustfaktor** *m* mismatch factor **-vermögen** *n* reflectance reflecting power, reflectivity **-wattmeter** *m* reflecting wattmeter **-winkel** *m* angle of reflection **-zahl** *f* number of reflections

Reflex-klystron *n* reflex klystron **-modulation** *f* reflex bunching **-schaltung** *f* reflex circuit, double-amplification circuit **-schutzfilter** *n*

optical light filter **-verstärkung** *f* reflex amplification, dual amplification **-visier** *n* reflex sight, reflector sight **-zeichenvorrichtung** *f* reflection plotter

reformiertes Benzin re-formed gasoline

Reformierung *f* re-forming

refraktär refractory

Refraktion *f* refraction

Refraktionometer *n* refractionometer

Refraktions-index *m* index of refraction **-koeffizient** *m* coefficient of refraction **-säule** *f* refraction unit **-seismik** *f* fraction seismics **-winkel** *m* angle of refraction

Refraktometer *n* refractometer **-grenzwinkel** *m* critical or limiting angle of a refractometer

Refraktor *m* refractor **-säule mit parallaktischem Achsensystem** refractor standard with equatorial head

Refrigerant *m* refrigerator

Regal *n* shelf, partition

rege very active, intense

Regel *f* rule, regulation **-anlasser** *m* adjustable or regulating starter

Regelabweichung *f* deviation, output error (comput) **bleibende ~** offset **vorübergehende ~** oscillation **zulässige ~** specified maximum permissible deviation (aut. control.)

Regel-abweichungsanzeiger *m* deviation indicator **-anlagen** *pl* controlling equipment **-anlasser** *m* rotor rheostat **-antrieb** *m* variable-speed drive **-apparatur** *f* regulating apparatus

Regelation *f* regelation, refreezing

Regel-ausführung *f* standard design **-backen** *m* controller shutter **-band** *n* zone of action, control range

regelbar controllable, adjustable **-e Hochfrequenz** radio-frequency amplifier **-e Belüftung** controllable ventilation **-e Induktivität** continuously adjustable inductor **-er Kondensator** variable condenser, variable capacitor **-er Widerstand** variable resistance, adjustable resistance, rheostat **-er Zusatztransformator** *m* induction voltage regulator

Regelbarkeit *f* controllability, adjustability **leichte ~** ease of control

Regel-bauart *f* standard type **-belastung** *f* normal load **-belastungsfall** *m* normal-load case **-bereich** *m* range of regulation, range of adjustment **-detri** *f* rule of three, rule of proportion **-drossel** *f* regulating inductor, transductor **-einrichtung** *f* regulator, regulating device, control device

Regel-fähigkeit *f* adjustability **-faktor** *m* control factor **-feder** *f* governing spring **-fehler** *m* control error, deviation **-fläche** *f* ruled surface **-fußhebel** *m* control pedal **-genauigkeit** *f* control accuracy **-gerät** *n* regulator, controller, governor **-geschwindigkeit** *f* control rate **-gestänge** *n* governor rod

Regelgetriebe *n* variable speed gearing **stufenloses ~** infinitely variable speed transmission

Regel-glied *n* final control element, regulating member, regulating attenuator **-grad** *m* degree of dynamic-range or contrast regulation, maximum range of gain variation **-größe** *f* standard or normal size **-güte** *f* control effectiveness, quality of control **-hahn** *m* control **-hülse** *f* control sleeve, governor sleeve **-instrument** *n* standard instrument

Regel-kennlinie *f* regulating characteristic **-kolben** *m* operating piston **-kompaß** *m* standard compass **-kontakt** *m* control contact **-kreis** *m* control loop, automatic control system **-kurve** *f* regulation curve **-lamelle** *f* control arm **-last** *f* permissible load **-leistung** *f* normal or standard capacity or output **-licht** *n* regulation light **-lichtraum an Eisenbahnen** side clearance

regellos irregular, not following a rule, chaotic **~ geordnet** with random orientation **-e Anordnung** *f* irregular or haphazard arrangement **-e Orientierung** random orientation

Regellosigkeitsproblem *n* random or haphazard problem

regelmäßig regular, according to a rule, routine, clockwise, normal **~ aufblitzendes Gruppenlicht** group flashing light **~ aufblitzendes Licht** flashing light **-es Achteck** regular octagon **-e Luftverbindung** regular air service **-er Luftverkehr** regular air traffic **-e Strömung** laminar flow **-e Überholung** periodical overhaul **-es Vieleck** regular polygon **-er Windwechsel** back (shifting of wind counterclockwise)

Regelmäßigkeit *f* regularity

Regel-metall *n* standard metal **-mischröhre** *f* fading-mix hexode **-möglichkeit** *f* possibility of adjustment **-motor** *m* variable-speed motor **-muffe** *f* control or regulating sleeve

regeln to regulate, adjust, control, govern, arrange, settle

Regel-organ *n* regulating apparatus **-pentode** *f* variable mu-valve, supercontrol tube, remote cut-off tube **-preßpumpe** *f* variable delivery pressure pump **-punkt** *m* control point **-raum** *m* control room

regelrecht normal, regular, true, methodical, correct **~ schalten** to set at normal **-e Peilung** true bearing

Regel-röhre *f* variable-mu valve or tube, exponential tube, (super-)control tube, variable mutual-conductance valve, fading hexode **-sätze** *pl* regulating machine sets **-schalter** *m* regulating switch **-schaltung** *f* control circuit **-scheibe** *f* regulating pulley **-schieber** *m* governor slide valve **-schraube** *f* regulator **-schwankung** *f* hunting (elec.) **-schwingung** *f* control oscillation, hunting (servo) **-segment** *n* regulating sector

Regel-spannung *f* automatic-volume-control potential, control potential **-spannungsverstärkerröhre** *f* control-voltage amplifier **-spur** *f* standard or normal gauge **-stab** *m* control rod **-stange** *f* adjusting or actuating rod, recoil piston rod **-stangenanschlag** *m* governor rod stop **-stangenhülse** *f* governor rod sleeve **-stärke** *f* nominal rating **-stellung** *f* normal position **-strecke** *f* controlled system **-strom** *m* normal operating current **-stufe** *f* regulation step, beat-frequency oscillator

Regelsystem *n* controlled system **~ mit Verzögerungsgliedern** retarded control system (servo)

Regel-tafel *f* control panel **-transformator** *m* (autom.) regulating transformer **-tritt** *m* pedal, accelerator **-umfang** *m* automatic gain control

Regelung *f* adjustment, control, setting or timing, arrangement, settlement **~** (Regeleinrichtung), control device **~ der Bilddrehung** picture-rotate control **~ durch Federgegenkraft**

spring control ~ **der Kippfrequenz** hold control ~ **der Neutronenabsorption** absorption control ~ **durch Reihenparallelschaltung** series-parallel control ~ **mit Rückführung** feedback control system ~ **des Steuersignals** drive control ~ **der Verbrennung** control of combustion ~ **des horizontalen Verlaufs** improvement of the alignment **feinstufige** ~ sensitive control **gleichförmige** ~ smooth regulation **stufenweise** ~ regulation in steps

Regelungs-art *f* controller action **-genauigkeit** *f* control precision **-größe** *f* control variables **-technik** *f* automatic control technology **-vorgang** *m* regulation process **-vorrichtung** *f* regulating equipment

Regelunterschied *m* deviation

Regelventil *n* regulating or controlling valve **gesteuertes** ~ automatic regulator

Regel-verhalten *n* controller action **-verlauf** *m* control action, recovery curve **-verstärker** *m* variable-gain amplifier, automatic-volume-control amplifier, noise or silencing amplifier **-vieleck** *n* regular polygon **-vorgang** *m* control action, recovery curve

Regelvorrichtung *f* control equipment, control device, regulator **selbsttätige** ~ automatic control equipment

Regel-weg *m* first route **-werk** *n* control installation, control equipment **-wicklung** *f* control winding **-widerstand** *m* rheostat, variable or adjustable resistor or resistance

Regel-widerstandskennlinie *f* control-resistance characteristics **-widrig** irregular, contrary to rule, abnormal **-widrigkeit** *f* abnormality **-zeit** *f* recovery time **-zelle** *f* (Heißdampfregler) diaphragm chamber **-zug** *m* control pass (of boiler) **-zustand** *m* controlled condition

Regen *m* rain, precipitation **feiner** ~ drizzle

Regen-anlage *f* raining or watering plant **-arm** rainless, dry **-band** *n* rain band **-blende** *f* rain shutter **-bö** *f* rain squall

Regenbogen *m* rainbow **-farbig** rainbow-colored, iridescent **-haut** *f* iris

Regen-dicht rainproof (waterproof) **-dichte** *f* rainfall intensity **-dichtigkeit** *f* intensity of rain **-echos** *pl* rain clutter **-einlaß** *m* gully

Regenerat *n* regenerated material (rubber or oil), reclaimed product (rubber) **-gummi** *m* regenerated rubber

Regeneration *f* regeneration

Regenerationsmarke *f* regeneration mark

Regenerativ-feuerung *f* regenerative furnace or hearth, regenerative firing, regenerator **-flammofen** *m*, **-gasofen** *m* regenerative gas furnace **-kammer** *f* regenerative chamber **-ofen** *m* regenerative furnace or oven, regenerative open-hearth furnace **-prinzip** *n* principle of regeneration **-tiefofen** *m* regenerative soaking pit

Regenerator *m* regenerator ~ **mit Wechselbetrieb** reversing-type regenerator

Regeneratorengasturbotriebwerk *n* gas-turbine power-plant-utilizing regeneration

regenerierbar regenerable

regenerieren to regenerate, reclaim, recover

Regenerierstrahl *m* holding beam

regeneriertes Schmieröl reclaimed lubricating oil

Regenerierung *f* regeneration, reclaiming, recovery

Regenerierungsintervall *m* scan period

Regen-fall *m* rainfall, precipitation **-fallrohr** *n* down pipe **-guß** *m* shower **-haube** *f* rain cap **-häufigkeit** *f* frequency of rain **-höhe** *f* depth of rainfall **-jahr** *n* rainy year **-kammer** *f* rain chamber **-kappe** *f* rain cap or hood

Regen-karte *f* rain chart **-kern** *m* point of maximum rainfall during a rainstorm **-kondensator** *m* rain-type condenser **-leiste** *f* rainwater deflector **-los** rainless **-machen** *n* rain making **-menge** *f* amount of rain **-messer** *m* rain gauge, pluviometer **-messung** *f* rain measurement, pluviometry **-periode** *f* rain spell

regen-reich rainy, having a heavy rainfall **-röhre** *f* rain gutter **-schatten** *m* rain shadow, rainless side **-schauer** *m* shower **-schirm** *m* umbrella **-schreiber** *m* pluviograph, rainfall recorder, hyetograph **-schutzkappe** *f* rain-shield cap (waterproof cover) **-schutzrohr** *n* rain visor **-seite** *f* rainy side **-spritze** *f* Holman projector **-statik** *f* rain static

Regen-störung *f* rain clutter (rdr.) **-tag** *m* wet day, rainy day **-traufe** *f* drip flap **-tropfen** *m* raindrop **-verschluß** *m* raintrap **-versuch** *m* rain test, wet test **-wandbrause** *f* drencher **-wasser** *n* rain water **-wetter** *n* rainy weather **-wolke** *f* rain cloud **-zeit** *f* rainy period

Regie *f* master control **-arbeit** *f* building in day work, force-account work **-betrieb** *m* public works **-pult** *n* mixing table, mixing desk, control desk **-raum** *m* control room **-signal** *n* cue **-tisch** *m* control desk, console

Regierungs-behörde *f* government authority

regional, -e Gebietskarte regional chart **-e Wachfrequenz** regional guard frequency

Regisseur *m* director

Register *n* register, index, impulse-storing device, stop (organ), fast register (info proc.) **-aufbewahrung** record storage **-gesteuertes Wählsystem** register controlled system **-haltigkeit** *f* registration stability **-kapazität** *f* register length **-schütz** *n* paddle valve **-sucher** *m* register finder, sender selector **-übertragung** *f* transfer of registry **-wähler** *m* sender selector **-walze** *f* tube roll **-werk** *n* recording unit **-zug** *m* draw stop (of organ)

Registrator *m* recorder

Registratur *f* filing department

Registratursystem *n* filing system

Registrier-anemometer *n* anemograph, gust recorder, recording anemometer

Registrieranlage *f* recording arrangement ~ (Messung von Zielabweichung verfeuerter Raketen) (Astron.) scorer (astron.)

Registrier-apparat *m* recording instrument or apparatus, recorder **-ballon** *m* sounding or registering balloon **-bild** *n* recorded image **-einrichtung** *f* recorder

registrieren to register, record, index, store, file

Registrier-einrichtung *f* recording device **-einschub** *m* recording plug-in unit

registrierend-es Barometer recording barometer **-es Meßgerät** *n* graphic instrument **-er Schreiber** printing reader **-er Spannungsteiler** potentiograph **-er Strommesser** recording ammeter **-es Wattmeter** recording wattmeter

Registrier-feder *f* recorder pen **-galvanometer** *n* recording galvanometer
Registriergerät *n* recorder, recording mechanism **photographisches ~** photographic observer
Registrier-instrument *n* recording instrument, recorder **-kasse** *f* cash register **-kurve** *f* recording curve **-manometer** *n* manograph **-mechanismus** *m* recording mechanism **-papier** *n* record paper, recording paper, recorder paper, recording chart **-scheibe** *f* recording disk **-schreiber** *m* monochromator **-streifen** *m* recorder chart, record, chart **-strommesser** *m* recording ammeter **-theodolit** *m* recording theodolite **-verfahren** *n* filing method **-werk** *n* recording unit or output
Registrier- und Diagrammpapier *n* recording and diagram paper
Registrierung *f* recording, graphic recording, record
Registriervorrichtung *f* indicator, recorder, recording mechanism
Regler *m* fader (as an input control in audio control console), regulator, governor, controller, corrector, control **~ mit Angleichung** governor fitted with adapting device **~ für gleichbleibende Drehzahl** constant-speed control (unit) **~ mit Hilfsenergie** relay-operated or pilot controller **~ ohne Hilfsenergie** self-operated controller **~ mit zwei Regelstellungen** two-stage control **~ mit PI-Verhalten** compensated proportional action governor **hydraulischer ~** pressure oil unit **labiler ~** unstable governor **statischer ~** static governor **-zweistufiger ~** two-position regulator
Regler-angriff *m* place of governor attachment **-ausschlag** *m* throw of governor **-dose** *f* control aneroid (for engine) **-feder** *f* governor spring **-gehäuse** *n* governor housing, regulator housing **-gestänge** *n* plunger **-getriebe** *n* governor gearing **-hebel** *m* speed lever **-kasten** *m* regulator box **-kennlinie** *f* regulator characteristic (curve) **-knopf** *m* heat control knob **-kolben** *m* (Kompressor) pilot valve **-kontrollhebel** *m* governor control handle **-korrektur** *f* correction **-leitung** *f* pilot wire **-linie** *f* regulating line, control line
Regler-muffe *f* governor sleeve **-nabe** *f* governor hub **-propeller** *m* constant speed propeller **-pult** *n* control desk, monitoring desk **-punkt** *m* regulating point, control point **-punkthöhenwinkel** *m* altitude of target at control point **-schalter** *m* voltage regulator **-schieber** *m* governor slide valve **-spannungsspule** *f* regulator voltage coil **-stange** *f* governor control rod **-stellung** *f* fader setting **-stromspule** *f* regulator current coil **-teilung** *f* correction scale on sight **-ventil** *n* governor valve, regulator valve, throttle valve **-welle** *f* regulating or governing shaft **-widerstand** *m* rheostat **-winkel** *m* principal vertical deflection angle
Reglette *f* feeler gauge
Reglettengießform *f* reglet casting mold
Reglung *f* control, regulation, arrangement, settlement, timing, regularity, adjustment
Reglungsvorrichtung *f* control equipment
regnen to rain
Regner *m* sprinkler **-düse** *f* large sprinkler for irrigating, spray nozzle
regnerisch rainy
regredient-e Beleuchtung transmitted illumination **-es Licht** regressive light
Regressanspruch *m*, **sich den ~ vorbehalten** to reserve right of recourse
Regressionslinie *f* regression line
regreßpflichtig liable to recourse
Regreßrecht *n* recourse
regsam active
Regstoff *m* ferment
regulär regular **-er Flächenpunkt** regular point of a surface **-er Kurvenpunkt** regular point of a curve **-es Punktsystem** regular system of points
Regulator *m* regulator, controller, governor, compensator **-achse** *f* governor spindle
Regulier-apparat *m* regulating gear **-bar** controllable, adjustable **-brett** *n* adjuster board **-buchse** *f* control bushing **-einsatz** *m* starting of control or regulation
regulieren to govern, regulate, control, adjust, settle, arrange
Regulieren der Drähte adjustment of tension in wires
Regulier-exzenter *m* governor eccentric control **-fähigkeit** *f* adjustability **-fallenzug** *m* falling sluice **-gewicht** *n* governor weight **-hahn** *m* regulating cock **-hebel** *m* choke arm **-keil** *m* adjusting wedge **-kerntrockenofen** *m* drawer-type core-baking oven **-kulisse** *f* adjusting gear
Regulier-mutter *f* adjusting nut **-schalter** *m* regulating switch **-schema der Brennstoffpumpe** control method of fuel-oil pump **-schleifringläufermotor** *m* slip-regulator induction motor **-schraube** *f* adjusting screw, regulator, setscrew **-spule** *f* regulating coil **-stößel** *m* governor tap pen, lifter, valve lifter **-transformator** *m* regulating transformer
Regulierung *f* control, adjustment, regulation, settlement **~ der Leistung** regulating of performance **~ des Vergasers** carburetor adjustment **feinstufige ~** sensitive control
Regulierungs-schieber *m* regulating gate **-ventil** *n* regulating valve **-vorrichtung** *f* regulating or adjusting device
Regulierventil *n* valve regulator, check valve, regulating valve **~ zur Regelung des Zuflusses** flow-control valve
Regulier-vorgelege *n* regulating-speed gear **-wert des Spannungsreglers** regulating value of voltage regulator **-widerstand** *m* regulating resistance or cathode, control rheostat, variable resistance, regulating switch **-winkel** *m* timing angle
regulinisch reguline
Regulus *m* button (metal.), regulus **-ofen** *m* regulus furnace, reduction reverbatory, reduction crucible
Regung *f* motion, movement, impulse
Regungskraft *f* power of movement
regungslos motionless, still
Regungslosigkeit *f* calm
Rehabilitierung *f* rehabilitation
Rehbock *m* code for a type of radar equipment
Reibahle *f* reamer, reaming bit, broach **~ mit eingesetzten Messern** adjustable-blade reamer **nachstellbare ~** expanding reamer
Reibahlen mit Spiralzähnen spiral-fluted reamers **~ mit Stirnzähnen** end-cutting reamers
Reibantrieb *m* friction drive **nachgiebiger ~** slipping drive, yielding drive

Reib-band *n* skid band **-bandbremse** *f* friction brake **-belag** *m* friction facing, friction lining
Reibe *f*, **Reibeisen** *n* rasp, grater
reib-echt fast to rubbing **-eisen** *n* grater
reiben to rub, grate, cause friction, grind, ream, abrade **sich ~** to rasp, chafe
Reibepulver *n* abrasive powder
Reiber *m* brayer (print.), ink block, stage **-hahn** *m* plug cock
Reib-festigkeit *f* resistance to abrasion, chafing resistance **-fläche** *f* rubbing surface, friction area, friction contact, cartridge-base head **-getriebe** *n* friction drive or gear **-gummi** *m* eraser **-gut** *n* material to be ground **-holz** *n* timber fender **-kasten** *m* grinding mill, grinder **-kegel** *m* clutch, friction cone **-keule** *f* pestle **-korrosion** *f* brinnelling, fretting corrosion **-kuppelung** *f* friction clutch **-löten** *n* tinning
Reib-maschine *f* mill (grating or grinding) **-mittel-** *n* abrasive **-oxydation** *f* rubbing corrosion, frictional oxidation **-pfahl** *m* fender pile **-rad** *n* friction wheel **-räderantrieb** *m* friction drive **-radgetriebe** *n* friction gear **-rolle** *f* friction disk or roller **-rollenspindelpresse** *f* friction screw press **-satz** *m* fulminate **-schale** *f* mortar **-scheibe** *f* friction disk **-schiene** *f* friction band **-schleifen** *n* honing
Reibsel *n* gratings
Reibsitz, im ~ sein to be friction-tight
Reib-spindelpresse *f* friction-crew-driven press **-stein** *m* ink block, brayer **-technik** *f* grinding technique **-teller** *m* friction disk **-triebpresse** *f* friction-driven press **-triebspindelziehpresse** *f* friction-screw-drawing press
Reibtrommel *f* friction roller, friction drum **kegelige ~** conical friction roller or drum
Reib- und Hebwalze *f* vibrator and distributor roller
Reibung *f* friction, rubbing, abrasion, rolling friction **~ auf Fundamentsohle** base friction **~ der Ruhe** friction of rest **gleitende ~** rolling or sliding friction **innere ~** viscosity or internal friction, solid viscosity **rollende ~, wälzende ~** rolling or sliding friction **ruhende ~** static friction
Reibungs-anteil *m* frictional portion **-antrieb** *m* friction drive
Reibungsarbeit *f* work due to friction, frictional work, magnetic hysteresis **magnetische ~** hysteresis
Reibungs-aufwind *m* ascending current due to topography **-band** *n* friction or brake band **-beiwert** *m* coefficient of friction **-belag** *m* friction covering or lining **-brandstelle** *f* friction burns **-breccie** *f* fault breccia **-bremse** *f* friction brake **-dämpfer** *m* friction damper **-drehmoment** *n* frictional couple **-drehzahlenmesser** *m* friction revolution counter, tachometer **-elektrizität** *f* frictional electricity, static electricity **-erscheinungen** *pl* phenomena of friction **-erwärmung** *f* friction heating
Reibungs-faktor *m* friction factor **-fehler** *m* frictional error (aut.-contr.) **-fläche** *f* friction surface
reibungsfrei abrollen to turn without rubbing **-e Flüssigkeit** perfect or inviscid fluid **-es Gas** inviscid gas **-e Übertragung der Betätigungskraft** (Bremsen) frictionless transmission of operating force (brakes)
Reibungs-gewindeschneidvorrichtung *f* friction tapping device **-getriebe** *n* friction drive **-hebel** *m* friction lever **-kabel von Kokosfasern** coir fender **-kegel** *m* friction cone **-klinke** *f* friction pawl **-koeffizient** *m* coefficient of friction, friction constant **-konglomerat** *n* fault conglomerate **-kraft** *f* frictional force
Reibungskuppelung *f* friction clutch, friction-clutch coupling **lösbare ~** friction-clutch cutoff coupling
Reibungs-kuppelungsmuffe *f* friction-clutch sleeve **-lamellenkuppelung** *f* friction disk clutch **-last** *f* friction(al) load
Reibungsleistung *f* friction horsepower **Motorlauf zur Ermittlung der ~** friction run
Reibungsleistungsanteil, dem ~ entsprechender Mitteldruck friction mean effective pressure
reibungs-los frictionless **-messer** *m* tribometer **-moment** *n* friction torque **-mutter** *f* friction nut **-oxydation** *f* frictional oxydation **-pferdekraft** *f* friction horsepower **-platte** *f* wearing plate **-probe** *f* friction test, wearing test
Reibungs-rad *n* friction wheel or pulley **-räderwendegetriebe** *n* friction-wheel reversing gear **-schicht** *f* friction layer **-scheibenwelle** *f* friction-disk shaft **-schluß** *m* friction contact **-schwenkwiderstand** *m* resistance to frictional swivel movement **-schwingungsdämpfer** *m* friction vibration damper **-spannung** *f* friction stress
Reibungssperre *f*, **verstellbare ~** adjustable friction clamp
Reibungs-spitze *f* friction peak **-trommel** *f* friction roller or drum **-verhalten** *n* friction characteristics **-verhältnis** *n* ratio of friction **-verlust** *m* friction load, friction(al) loss **-versuch** *m* shear test **-vorgelege** *n* frictional countershaft
Reibungs-walze *f* friction roller, friction drum **-wärme** *f* frictional heat **-wendegetriebe** *n* friction change gear **-wert** *m* coefficient of friction, friction value **-widerstand** *m* frictional resistance, tractive stress **-winkel** *m* angle of (internal) friction, angle of repose **-wirbel** *m* friction vortex **-wirkung** *f* rubbing action **-zahl** *f*, **-ziffer** *f* coefficient of friction, angle of internal friction
Reib-versuch *m* smear test **-vorrichtung** *f* reaming fixture
Reibwalze *f*, **kegelige ~** conical friction roller or drum
Reib-wendegetriebe *n* friction change gear **-werkzeug** *n* reaming tools **-zahl** *f* coefficient of friction **-zeug** *n* rubber, cushion (mach.) **-ziffer** *f* coefficient of friction **-zunder** *m* friction primer **-zündhölzchen** *n* friction match **-zündmasse für Streichhölzchen** matchbox paste **-zündschraube** *f* friction primer **-zylinder** *m* distributing cylinder
reich rich, abundant, wealthy, imperial **-e und beste Kraftmischung** rich, best power mixture **-e Mischung** rich mixture
Reichblei *n* rich lead
reichen to reach, suffice
Reichenbeiwert *m* range coefficient
Reich-frischen *n* enriching (of copper) **-gas** *n* rich gas **-haltig** abundant, plentiful **-haltigkeit** *f* abundance, plentifulness, copiousness **-höhe** *f* cutting height
reichlich plentiful, copious, ample, abundant

Reich-schaum *m* zinc crust formed during the Parkes process **-schlacke** *f* rich slag **-schmelzen** *n* smelting of precious metals

Reichweite *f* range, range of transmission, radius of action, outer or cantilever arm, radius of influence, coverage, distance range, operating span **außer ~** out of range **optische ~** line of sight range (radio) **~ bei Reisegeschwindigkeit** range at cruising speed **~ eines Teilchens** mass range **~ eines Senders** radius of service area **große ~** long range **die ~ verlassen** to pass out of range

Reichweite-effekt *m* range effect **-energiebeziehung** *f* range-energy relation

Reichweiten-behälter *m* crusing fuel tank **-flug** *m* maximum flight range **-messung** *f* range measurement **-steigerung** *f* increase of range **-streuung** *f* range straggling **-verkürzung** *f* range reduction **-verteilung** *f* range distribution

Reif *m* rime, frozen fog, hoop, collar, ring, tire

reif ripe, mature, ready **-es, abgelagertes Papier** mature paper

Reifbildung *f* frozen-fog formation

Reife *f* ripeness, maturity

Reifeisen *n* hoop or tire iron

reifen to mature

Reifen *m* tire, hoop, rim, clip **~ mit Stahldrahtbefestigung** wired-on tire **~ mit Wulst** beaded-edge tire **~ mit geradem Wulst** beadless tire **flacher ~** soft or flat tire

Reifen-bahre *f* hooped bed cradle **-biegemaschine** *f* tire-bending machine **-cord** *m* tire cord **-cordrayon** *n* rayon tire cord

Reifendruck *m* tire pressure **-anzeigelampe** *f* tire pressure indicator lamp **-prüfer** *m* tire gauge

Reifen-einsenkung *f* tire deflection **-erneuerung** *f* retreading **-flickzeug** *n* tire-repair kit **-füllanlage** *f* tire inflating set **-füller** *m* tire inflator

Reifenfüll-flasche *f* tire-inflator cylinder **-hahn** *m* tire-inflator cock **-ventil** *n* tire inflator cylinder

Reifen-gewebe *n* tire canvas **-griffigkeit** *f* tire grip **-hebel** *m* tire tool **-hülle** *f* tire casing **-lauffläche** *f* tire contact area **-luftständer** *m* air tower, air pump **-mantel** *m* outer cover, casing, tire cover **-montierhebel** *m* tire lever **-profil** *n* tread **-pumpe** *f* tire pump

Reifen-regenerat *n* tire reclaim **-schlauch** *m* tire tube **-spur** *f* tire track **-stauchmaschine** *f* tire upsetter **-tragfähigkeit** *f* tire capacity **-vulkanisierung** *f* tire repairing or vulcanizing **-wächter** *m* tire control, tire guard **-walzwerk** *n* tire mill **-wulst** *m* bead of tire

Reifezustand der Viskose ripeness of the viscose

Reif-keim *m* digestion nucleus **-kloben** *m* vise jaw, vise clamps **-kratzer** *m* ice scraper

Reifung *f* ripening, digestion of emulsion

Reifungs-dauer *f* time for ripening **-körper** *m* ripening or accelerator substance, sensitizer

Reihe *f* row; (hintereinander) file; (nebeneinander) rank; (Linie) line; (Folge) series; (Aufeinanderfolge) succession; (Math.) progression; number, order, series, range, turn, file, column, progression (math.), array, sequence, train, bank (of contacts, keys, etc.) **in ~** in cascade, in tandem, series **in einer ~** in a (one) row **in ~ geschaltet** aerially connected

Reihe, an die ~ kommen take (one's) turn **in ~ schalten** to connect in series, join in series **der ~ nach** in series, successively **arithmetische ~** arithmetical progression **benachbarte ~** adjacent row **gegensinnig in ~** series-opposing **geometrische ~** geometrical progression **gleichsinnig in ~** series-aiding

Reihe, konvergente ~ convergent series **obere (untere) ~** top (bottom) row **senkrechte ~** vertical row, column, progression, succession **unendliche ~** infinite series **waagrechte ~** horizontal row, level **zurücklaufende ~** recurring series (math.) **auseinanderlaufende Reihen** diverging series (math.) **zusammenlaufende Reihen** converging series (math.)

Reihenanlage *f* intercommunication system **-fernsprechreihen** *f pl* intercommunication-telephone plant, house-telephone system

Reihen-anmeldung *f* sequence calling, sequence calls **-anordnung** *f* serial arrangement, tandem arrangement, series connection (of resistances) **-ansatz** *m* progression (math.), sequence, (infinite) series **-arbeit** *f* repetition work **-aufnahme** *f* serial survey, survey by serial photographs **-bau** *m* series production, series transformer, series-wound motor, series connections **-beförderung** *f* batch working **-bestimmung** *f* routine determination **-betrieb** *m* tandem operation **-bild** *n* serial photograph, aerial-photography mosaic, line-overlap photograph **-bilder** *pl* sequence of pictorial actions or pictures, motion pictures

Reihenbild-flug *m* series photograph flight **-gerät** *n* automatic aerial camera **-kamera** *f* serial camera, series camera, automatic (aerial) camera **-meßkamera** *f* serial air-survey camera, serial photogrammetry camera

Reihenbildner *m* aerial camera, series camera, automatic camera, mosaic camera

Reihen-bildzug *m* mapping group **-böe** *f* line squall **-bohrmaschine** *f* series-drilling machine **-entwicklung** *f* progressive development, progression, serial development, expansion in a power series **-entwicklungslösung** *f* series development solution

Reihenfertigung *f* repetition work, mass production, assembly-line production **Erprobung der Erzeugnisse der ~** production testing

Reihen-feuer *n* bursts of fire **-flug** *m* line formation

Reihenfolge *f* sequence, order, succession, arrangement, series **~ der Gespräche** order of calls **~ der Harmonischen** overtone order **~ der Wichtigkeit** order of merit **der ~ nach** in sequence, in succession

Reihenfolge-programmierung *f* sequential programming **-schalter** *m* sequence alternator

Reihen-formel *f* series formula (math.) **-förmige Anordnung** arrangement in straight rows **-funkenstrecke** *f* multiple spark gap **-glied** *n* series element **-großfertigung** *f* large-scale production **-haus** *n* row house **-herstellung** *f* series production, duplicate or multiple production

Reihenimpedanz *f* (line) series impedance **-entzerrer** *m* series-impedance-type equalizer **-glied** *n* series-impedance element, series impedor

Reiheninduktivität *f* series inductance

Reihenkamera *f* serial camera, series camera, automatic camera **~ mit Uhrwerksantrieb** serial camera with clockwork **~ mit Wind-**

flügelantrieb serial camera with wind motor **senkrechte ~** vertical-strip camera, camera for strip photograph on vertical axis

Reihen-kaskadenverhalten *n* series cascade action **-klemmen** *pl* line-up terminals **-kultivator auf Schlitten** sled lister cultivator **-ladung** *f* blasting charges in series **-lampe** *f* series lamp **-lochmaschine** *f* rectilinear punching machine **-maschine** *f* tandem engine **-meßkamera** *f* sarial air-survey camera, serial photogrammetric camera, mapping camera

Reihenmotor *m* in-line engine or motor, vertical engine **~ mit hängenden Zylindern** inverted in-line engine, inlet motor (inverted) **~ mit mehreren Zylinderreihen** in-line multibank engine

Reihen-näherung *f* series approach **-nietung** *f* line riveting **-nummer** *f* serial number **-parallel-regelung** *f* series-parallel control

Reihenparallelschaltung *f* series-parallel transition **~ mit Brückenschaltung** bridge transition **~ mit Leistungsunterbrechung** series-parallel change by opening the circuits in the network **~ mit Widerstandsschaltung** series-parallel shunt transition **in ~** series-parallel

Reihenparallelwicklung *f* series-parallel winding (multiplex wave)

Reihen-produktion *f* batch production, series production **-prüfung** *f* production testing **-punktschweißung** *f* straight-line spot welding **-resonanz** *f* series resonance **-resonanzkreis** *m* series-resonant circuit **-röhrenmodulation** *f* series modulation, constant-voltage modulation

Reihensä- und Zudeckmaschine *f* corn lister **kombinierte ~** combined lister

Reihen-schalter *m* intercommunication system **-schaltung** *f* series connections, series arrangement, series

Reihenschluß-dynamo *m* series(-wound) dynamo **-dynamomaschine** *f* series-wound generator, series dynamo **-erregerwicklung** *f* series exciter coil **-erregung** *f* series excitation **-gleichstrommotor** *m* series direct current motor **-maschine** *f* series dynamo **-motor** *m* series-wound motor **-spule** *f* series magnetic coil **-verhalten** *n* series characteristic

Reihen-schweißmaschine *f* series welding machine **-speisung** *f* series feeding

Reihenspule *f* series coil **Belastung durch Reihenspulen** lumped-series loading

Reihen-standmotor *m* in-line engine **-stelle** *f* series-connected station **-steller** *m* series servo **-sternmotor** *m* multibank radial engine **-teil** *m* duplicate piece **-telegraph** *m* automatic telegraph, high-speed telegraph **-transformator** *m* series transformer **-verbundmaschine** *f* tandem compound engine **-verlustwiderstand** *m* equivalent series resistance **-weise** in-series **-wicklung** *f* series winding (simplex wave) **-widerstand** *m* series resistance **-zählapparat** *m* counter

Reih und Glied rank and file, array

rein concentrated, clean, pure, clear, fine, rectified **chemisch ~** chemically pure **-e sinusförmige Bewegung** plain harmonic or sinuous motion **-es Eisen** pure iron **-es farbengleiches Gelb** psychologically unique yellow **-e Mathematik** pure mathematics **-er Segelflug** real sailing flight **-e Skala** true scale **-e Sprache** clear voice **-er Ton** pure note, pure or simple tone

Rein-aluminium *n* pure aluminum **-anthrazen** *n* pure anthracene

Reinartzschaltung *f* Reinartz circuit, special short-wave receiver-circuit scheme

Rein-ausfuhr *f* net export **-benzin** *n* unleaded gasoline

Reindarstellung *f* rectification **~ des Gases** production of pure gas

Rein-dichte *f* net density **-druck** *m* clean proof **-durchlaßgrad** *m* internal transmittance **-einnahme** *f* net gain or profit **-ertrag** *m* net profit, net proceeds **-gewicht** *n* net weight

Reinheit *f* cleanliness, purity, clearness **~ der Wiedergabe** fidelity of the reproduction

Reinheits-abfall *m* purity drop **-grad** *m* degree of purity **-messer** *m* purity indicator **-spule** *f* purity coil (TV)

reinigen to clean, wash, purify, scour, separate, refine, purge, rid

Reinigen *n* cleaning, purification

Reiniger *m* cleaner, strainer, concentrator, purifier, washer **-masse** *f* purifying material **-plättchen** *n* clearer plate (cleansing)

Reinigung *f* cleaning, washing, purification, separation, purging

Reinigungs-anlage *f* purifying plant, cleaning plant, cleaning equipment, washing plant **-apparat** *m* scourer, purifier, washer, cleaning apparatus **-behälter** *m* filter tank **-bottich** *m* purifying tank **-feld** *n* clearing field **-feuer** *n* refining fire **-fräser** *m* cleaning milling cutter **-grube** *f* cleaning pit **-hahn** *m* purging cock **-kasten** *m* mud box **-klappe** *f* cleaning port **-kreis** *m* smoothing circuit, filter circuit, low-pass filter

Reinigungs-luke *f* cleaning hole **-mittel** *n* cleansing or purifying agent, cleaner, purifier, detergent **-öffnung** *f* cleanout hole, cleaning hole **-prozeß** *m* refining or purification process **-schaber** *m* (beim Spaltfilter) cleaning knife **-schraube** *f* tapered washout plug **-stock** *m* cleaning rod **-tür** *f* cleanout door **-verfahren** *n* refining or purification process **-wirkung** *f* cleaning capability

Rein-kathode *f* bright emitter **-kohle** *f* clean coal, solid carbon **-kohlenbetrieb** *m* low intensity carbon service

Reinkohlen(bogen)lampe *f* lamp with solid carbons

Reinkultur *f* pure culture

reinlich tidy

Reinlichkeit *f* cleanliness

Reinluftraum *m* clean-air receiver

Reinöl-kreislauf *m*, **-zirkulation** *f* clean-oil-circulation cracking process

rein-pullen (slang) to flatten out **-schrift** *f* clean copy, final copy **-spülen** to rinse

Reinsteisen *n* high-purity iron

Reinton *m* note with one mode of vibration, single-frequency tone **-blende** *f* biasing stop, noise-reducing stop, shutter, gate **-verfahren** *n* noiseless recording (on film)

Reinwasser *n* pure water **-pumpe** *f* pump for clean water

Rein-weiß (Leder) clear white **-wismut** *n* pure bismuth **-zuchthefe** *f* pure yeast

Reis *n* twig, sprig, scion

Reis *m* rice **-apparat** *m* rice attachment **-binder** *m*

rice binder **-dreschmaschine** *f* rice thresher **-dreschvorrichtung** *f* rice attachment

Reise *f* voyage, trip, campaign, cruising **auf die ~ schicken** to launch

Reiseartikel *m* traveling article

Reisedauerleistung *f* cruising power **größtzulässige ~ mit armem Gemisch** maximum economy cruising power with a weak mixture

Reise-empfänger *m* traveling receiver **-fluchtstab** *m* traveling ranging pole

Reiseflug *m* cruise **~ mit Spargemisch** weak-mixture cruising conditions **Kraftstoffverbrauch bei ~** cruising fuel consumption

Reise-flughöhe *f* cruising level **-fluggipfelhöhe** *f* cruising ceiling **-flugleistung** *f* cruising power or performance **-gebührnis** *f* travel allowance **-geschwindigkeit** *f* mean traveling speed, cruising speed **-kompaß** *m* route compass **-kosten** *pl* travel expenses

Reiseleistung *f* cruising output **Ladedruck bei ~** cruising manifold pressure, cruising boost **empfohlene ~** recommended cruising output

Reise-marsch *m* cross-country march **-monteur** *m* service mechanic

reisen to travel, journey, cruise

Reisender *m* traveler, tourist

Reisequartier *n* march billet

Reise-tasche *f* traveling bag, wallet **-wagen** *m* touring car **-weg** *m* itinerary, route

Reis-faser *f* rice fiber **-holz** *n* brushwood

Reisig *n* loose sticks, dead wood, faggots, brushwood **-besen** *m* broom **-bündel** *n* fascine **-gradierwerk** *n* faggot-type cooler, brushwood cooling stack

Reis-kocher *m* rice cooker **-papier** *n* rice paper

Reiß-bahn *f* rip(ping) panel **-belastung** *f* breaking load **-blei** *n* black lead, graphite **-boden** *m* marking-off board **-bogengerät** *n* interruption arc instrument **-brett** *n* drawing board, sketch board **-diagramm** *n* breakoff diagram **-draht** *m* ripping wire **-dreieck** *n* setsquare **-ebene** *f* fracture plane

reißen to rupture, break, tear, pull, trace, draw, fracture, fail, disrupt, split, crack, burst, spring, spall, range, drag, pluck (a string or chord) **einen Funken ~** to strike a spark

Reiß-entfestigung *f* weakening of tensile strength

Reißer *m* ripper, gauge, scriber, sketcher

Reißerei *f* garnetting

Reiß-erscheinung *f* breaking **-feder** *f* drawing pen **-festigkeit** *f* breaking strain or strength, tensile strength, tenacity, resistance to tearing, ratio of tensile strength to weight density, resistance breaking **-festigkeitsprobe** *f* tearing-strength test **-gebiet** *n* discontinuity, cutoff or breakoff region **-geschwindigkeit** *f* breaking speed **-gewicht** *n* breaking load (weight) **-klinke** *f* lock for safety gear **-knebel** *m* ripping toggle

Reiß-kohle *f* crayon, charcoal crayon **-kraft** *f* ultimate strength, tensile strength, maximum load or stress **-krempel** *m* breaker card **-kuppelung** *f* quick-release coupling **-lack** *m* crackle finish, crackle lacquer, brittle lacquer **-lackmethode** *f* brittle lacquer method **-länge** *f* breaking length (synthetic fibers), gauge length, tearing length **-last** *f* breaking load or strain, maximum tensile load, elongation to failure

Reißleine *f* rip or release cord, lanyard **~ für Fallschirm** (zwischen Fallschirm und Flugzeug) static line; (Fallschirm) parachute static line, rip cord

Reiß-maß *n* carpenter's marking or shifting gauge **-nadel** *f* drawing point, scribing point, scriber **-nagel** *m* thumbtack **-pflug** *m* scarifier **-probe** *f* tearing-strength test **-schiene** *f* drawing rule T square **-schlitz** *m* ripping slit or slot **-schnur** *f* plummet **-span** *m* tear chip **-spitze** *f* drawing point, marking or scribing awl **-stock** *m* scribing block **-trommel** *f* willowing drum

Reißverschluß *m* (slide) fastener, zipper (closure) **-glied** *n* slide-fastener link or part

Reiß-versuch *m* tearing test, hanging test **-widerstand** *m* breaking strain or strength **-wolle** *f* reused wool **-wolf** willowing machine **-zeug** *n* (case of) drawing instruments **-zirkel** *m* compasses with shifting points, drawing compasses **-zwecke** *f* thumbtack

Reitel *m* anvil, recoil, rabbit, spring beam

reiten to ride on horseback

Reiter *m* horseman; slide contact, slider, cursor, staple; (Waage) jockey, rider; (meist nicht abhebbar-Rechenlineal) slider

Reiterchen *n* rider (of a balance)

Reiter-gewicht *n* rider weight **-lehre** *f* straddle gauge **-libelle** *f* striding level **-lineal** *n* (graduated) rider carrier **-rädchen, -röllchen** *n* jockey roller, jockey (wheel) **-rudel** *n* flock

Reiterschaufel *f* rim-straddling turbine bucket **-turbine** *f* turbine with rim-straddling buckets

Reiter-system *n* riding system **-walze** *f* rider roller

Reit-halfter *m* halter **-hose** *f* riding breeches **-kunst** *f* equitation

Reitnagel *m* back center (of lathe), tail spindle **-klemmhebel** *m* tail-spindle lock

Reit-peitsche *f* jockey stick **-pferd** *n* riding horse, saddle horse, mount **-schule** *f* cavalry school, riding school

Reitstock *m* tailstock, headstock (of lathe) **-ausladung** *f* tailstock overhang **-feststellhebel** *m* clamping lever **-gehäuse** *n* tailstock slide **-handrad** *n* tailstock handwheel **-oberteil** *m* tailstock barrel **-pinole** *f* tailstock quill **-planscheibe** *f* faceplate-type tailstock **-platte** *f* tailstock base **-prisma** *n* vee way of the tailstock **-spindel** *f* footstock spindle

Reitstockspitze *f* footstock center, dead center, tail center **drehbare ~** running (tail) center **feststehende ~** dead center

Reitstock-untersatz *m* tailstock base **-unterteil** *m* tailstock base

Reit-vorschrift *f* equitation manual **-weg** *m* bridle path

Reiz *m* irritant, irritation, impulse, attractivness, stimulus, excitation, stimulation **-aufnahme** *f* receptivity of stimulus

Reizbarkeit *f* irritability

Reiz-bewältigung *f* mastery over a stimulus **-empfindlichkeit** *f* susceptibility to stimulus

reizen to provoke, irritate, excite

Reizgas n irritant gas

Reiz-mittel *n* stimulus, stimulant **-schwelle** *f* threshold of sensation, limiting value of the stimulus **-schwellenwert** *m* threshold of perception

Reizstoff *m* irritant (gas) **augenangreifender ~** lachrymator

Reizung *f* stimulation, irritation

Rekaleszenzpunkt *m* point of recalescence

Reklamation *f* complaint

Reklame *f* advertising **-flug** *m* advertising flight **-flugzeug** *n* advertising airplane **-schild** *n* advertising signboard

reklamieren to raise a claim, object, complain, apply for exemption from active military service

Rekognoszierung *f* reconnaissance, reconnoitering

Rekombination *f* recombination

Rekombinationskontinuum *n* recombination continuum

Rekompatibilität *f* reverse compatibility

Rekord *m* record **einen ~ aufstellen** to establish a record **einen ~ halten** to hold a record **einen ~ schlagen** to break a record

Rekorder *m* recorder

Rekord-flieger *m* record flier **-flug** *m* record-breaking flight **-inhaber** *m* holder of a record **-klasse** *f* class of record **-versuch** *m* record attempt **-zeit** *f* record time

Rekristallisation *f* recrystallization

Rekristallisations-schweißung *f* solid phase welding **-zwillinge** *pl* recristallization twins

Rektaszension *f* right ascension

Rekteseite *f* odd or uneven page

Rektifikation *f* correction, adjustment, rectification

Rektifikationssäule *f* rectifying column

Rektifizierapparat *m* rectification apparatus

rektifizierbar rectifiable

rektifizieren to rectify

rektifizierende Ebene rectifying plane

Rektifizierer *m* rectifier

Rektifizier-gerät *n* rectifier **-kolonne** *f* stripping tower or drum

Rektifizierung *f* rectification, rectifying

Rekuperativofen *m* recuperative furnace, recuperative oven

Rekuperator *m* recuperator

Rekursionsformel *f* recurrence formula

Relais *n* relay **~ mit Abfallverzögerung** slow-releasing relay **~ mit schwerem Anker** heavy-armature relay **~ mit verzögerter Anziehung** slow-operating relay **~ mit Bremszylinder** dashpot relay **~ mit Haltewicklung** relay with holding winding **~ mit magnetischem Nebenschluß** relay with magnetic shunt **~ mit Quecksilberkontakten** mercury-contact relay

Relais, ~ mit zwei Schließ-(Trenn-) **kontakten** double-make(-break) relay **~ mit Schneidenlagerung** knife-edge relay **~ mit Spuleneinrichtung** motortype relay **~ mit zwei Wechselkontakten** double-break-and-make relay **~ mit zwei Wicklungen** two-coil relay, double-wound relay **das ~ auf einen Grenzstrom von . . . einstellen** to margin a relay to pull up at . . . **mit ~ übertragen** to relay **das ~ umlegen** to reverse the relay **mit ~ ausgerüstet** relayed **gegen Wechselstrom unempfindliches ~** relay unaffected by alternating current

Relais, einspuliges ~ single-spool relay **elektrooptisches ~** electrooptical cell, light relay depending on Faraday effect **langsam abfallendes ~** slow-to-release relay, slow-releasing relay **neutrales ~, nicht polarisiertes ~** non-polarized relay **polarisiertes ~** polar(ized) relay **polarisiertes ~ mit mittlerer Ruhestellung des Ankers** neutral relay **schnell ansprechendes ~** quick-operating relay **unpolarisiertes ~** non-polarized relay **zweispuliges ~** double-spool relay

Relais, anzugverzögertes ~ time-delay relay **~ für Amtsanlassung** trunk link start relay **~ mit Scheibenwicklung** sandwich wound relay **~ fällt ab** relay (the) de-energizes **das ~ hält sich mit eigenem kontakt** the relay locks to its own contact **~ klebt** relay is sticking **~ ist betätigt** relay is energized

Relais spricht an relay operates (the) **~ mit Schutzgaskontakten** dry-reed relay **~ mit Achsenlagerung** relay with pivoted armature **~ mit Spuleneinrichtung** motor type relay **~ mit drei Stellungen** neutral relay, three positions relay **~ mit zwei Wicklungen** two-coil relay **~ mit Zeitauslösung** time-limit relay

Relais-aberregung *f* deenergization of a relay **-abfallzeit** *f* relay releasing time **-anker** *m* tongue (of a relay), armature, relay armature **-anrufsucher** *m* relay finder **-betätigt** relay-type (switch)

Relaisbrett *n*, **abgefedertes ~** spring tray

Relais-funkstelle *f* relay station **-funktion** *f* relay operating quantity **-gestell** *n* relay rack **-kern** *m* relay core **-kette** *f* relay chain **-kontakt** *m* relay contact, relay point **-mikrophon** *n* directional microphone

Relaissatz *m* relay group, set, or unit **~ und Folgeschalter für Leitungswähler** final-sequence switch and relay set

Relais-scheit *n* rule, straightedge **-schirm** *m* relay screen **-sendeanlage** *f* beam station, radio-beacon or radio-range station **-sender** *m* relay(ing) station, rebroadcast transmitter **-spannung** *f* output voltage furnished by rectifier, direct-current potential of rectifier **-spule** *f* winding, relay coil (elec.) **-station** *f* relay(ing) station, rebroadcast transmitter

Relaissystem *n* all-relay system, relay automatic telephone system

Relais-übertragung *f* relay repeater, rebroadcasting, telegraphic repeater **unterbrecher** *m* relay interrupter **-vorwähler** *m* relay preselector **-wähler** *m* all-relay selector **-zahlengeber** *m* relay sender

relativ relative **-e Bewegung** relative motion **-e Dämpfung** relative efficiency **-e Dielektrizitätskonstante** specific inductive capacity **-e Empfindlichkeit** relative sensitivity **-e Feuchtigkeit** relative humidity, relative moisture **-er Geschwindigkeitsmesser** ground-speed meter **-e Leistungsfähigkeit der Doppeldeckerflügel** relative efficiency of biplane wings **-er Neigungsmesser** relative inclinometer **-er Nutzeffekt** relative efficiency **-e Öffnung** aperture ratio **-e Ortsbestimmung** approximate determination of a point's location **-e Peilung** relative bearing **-e Permeabilität** relative permeability **-e Sinnverständlichkeit** relative intelligibility **-er Spannungs(ab)fall** relative voltage drop, inherent regulation **-e Spannungssteigerung** relative voltage rise

relativistisch relativistic
Relativ-bewegung *f* relative motion **-geschwindigkeit** *f* relative speed or velocity **-höhenmesser** *m* sonic altimeter
Relativitätstheorie *f* theory of relativity
Relativ-verschiebung *f* relative displacement **-weg** *m* relative path
Relaxations-schwingung *f* relaxation oscillation, saw-tooth wave, tilting oscillation, ratchet oscillation **-zeit der Ionenwolke** relaxation time of ionic atmosphere
relegieren to relegate
Relief *n* embossment, relief (draw), plasticity (of pictures), three-dimensional appearance of television pictures **-bild** *n* ghost image **-druck** *m* printing in relievo **-folie** *f* overlay board **-fräseinrichtung** *f* (Autokartograph) relief milling device **-gewitter** *n* orographic or mountain thunderstorm **-karte** *f* relief map **-platte** *f* double-sided pattern plate, pattern plate with half patterns mounted on both sides **-polieren** *n* relief polishing **-schieber** *m* embosser **-schreiber** *m* embosser **-träger** *m* relief support (of embossed film) **-verfahren** *n* embossed-writing picture telegraphy **-walze** *f* surface printing roller **-zurichteverfahren** *n* stereo dressing process
Reling *f* rail (naut.), guard rail
Reluktanz *f* reluctance, magnetic resistance
Reluktivität *f* reluctivity
remanent remanent, residual **-er Magnetismus** residual magnetism
Remanenz *f* remanence, residual magnetism, retentivity, remanent polarization **maximale erreichbare ~** retentivity
Remanenzspannung *f* residual voltage
Remedium am Schrot allowance in weight (coin)
Remise *f* tool shed, garage
Remission *f* reflectance spectrometry
Remissions-ansatz *m* reflectance attachment **-grad** *m* luminance factor **-messung** *f* reflection measurement
Remittende *f* slow-moving article
remittieren to send back, send, remit
remonstrieren to remonstrate, object
Remonte *f* remount
Remontage *f* reassembling
Remontoiruhr *f* keyless watch, stem-winding watch
Remotion *f* removal
removieren to remove, demote
Remtron *n* remtron
Renardit *m* renardite
Rendant *m* accountant, auditor
Rendement *n* output, yield
Renk *m*, **Renke** *f*, **Renkanschluß** *m* bayonet lock or joint
renken to wrench, twist
Renkontre *n* encounter, engagement
Renkstecker *m* cable plug, transmission cable of transmission system or equipment
Renkverband *m* bayonet joint
Renktankverschluß *m* bayonet type tank cap, bayonet joint
Renkverband *m* bayonet lock or joint
Renn-arbeit *f* direct process or extraction (with iron) **-bahn** *f* course **-eisen** *n* direct-process malleable iron
rennen to run, race, extract (malleable iron directly from ore)
Rennerfelt-Ofen *m* Rennerfelt (independent direct-arc) furnace
rennfertig machen to tune up (motor)
Rennfeuer *n* bloomery hearth, bloomery forge or fire, charcoal hearth, bloomery **-schlacke** *f* direct-process slag
Renn-flugzeug *n* racing plane, racer **-herd** *m* bloomery hearth, bloomery forge or fire, charcoal hearth, bloomery **-jacht** *f* racing yacht **-modell** *n* speed model **-schlacke** *f* direct-process slag **-spindel** *f* upright or pump drill **-stahl** *m* bloomery iron, natural steel, steel made directly from the ore **-strecke** *f* course, race track **-verfahren** *n* direct process (for production of wrought iron), bloomery process **-wagen** *m* racing car
Renode *f* renode valve
Renormalisierung *f* renormalization
Renormierung *f* renormalization formalism
renovieren to renovate
rentabel productive, lucrative
Rentabilität *f* earning capacity, productiveness, profitableness
Rentabilitätsberechnung *f* cost accounting
rentabler Sand pay sand
Rente *f* income, revenue, annuity
Rentenbrief *f* income, revenue, annuity
Rentenbrief *m* annuity bond
Rentendeckungsverfahren *n* assessment system for annuities
rentieren, sich ~ to yield an income or a revenue
Rentrant *m* reentering angle
reorganisieren reorganize
Reoxydation *f* reoxidation
Reparatur *f* repair **~ an Ort und Stelle** on-the-spot repair **~ von Rundfunkempfängern** repairing radio-receiving sets
Reparatur-ausrüstung *f* repairing outfit or kit **-betrieb** *m* repair shop **-fähig** reparable **-glied** *n* repairing mesh **-grube** *f* inspection pit **-kasten** *m* repair kit, toolbox **-schiff** *n* repair ship **-werkstatt** *f* repair shop **-werkzeug** *n* repair tools
reparieren to mend, repair
Repassierbad (Seide) *n* second boiling-off bath
repassieren to mend, trim
repetieren to repeat **~** (Theodolit) to reiterate, repeat
Repetitions-messung *f* repetition measurement **-theodolit** *m* repeater theodolite, repetition theodolite
Repetitorium *n* survey course
Reportage *f* news-reporting or -gathering work **-film** *m* newsreel, news film, topical film
repräsentable Erscheinung good appearance
repräsentatives Ensemble representative ensemble
Repressalie *f* reprisal
Reproduktions-apparat *m* reproduction equipment (camera) **-aufnahme** *f* process work **-geschwindigkeit** *f* reproduction speed **-objektiv** *n* process lens **-proben** *pl* replica specimen **-raum** *m* projection room, reproduction room **-recht** *n* copyright **-verhältnis** *n* reproduction ratio
reproduzierbar reproducible
Reproduzierbarkeit *f* reproducibility, repeatability **~ von Meßwerten** consistency of measuring values
reproduzieren to reproduce

Repulsion *f* repulsion
Repulsionsmotor *m* repulsion motor
requirieren to claim, demand
Requisitenraum *m* property room
Requisition *f* requisition
Reseau *m* réseau
Reservage *f* resist **-druck** *m* resist printing
Reservatsgrenze *f* reservation line
Reserve *f* resist (resist paste) **mit ~ bedruckt** resist-printed **bewegliche Reserven** mobile reserves
Reserve-ader *f* reserve wire, reserve pair **-anker** *m* spare armature **-anlage** *f* spare unit **-apparat** *m* spare instrument, stand-by equipment **-artikel** *m* resist style **-behälter** *m* reserve tank **-brennstoffventil** *n* reserve-fuel valve **-druck** *m* resist print **-druckfarbe** *f* resist printing paste **-einsatz** *m* reserve set of inserts **-felge** *f* spare rim **-flugzeug** *n* reserve plane, reserve aircraft **-führer** *m* relief pilot
Reserve-kessel *m* stand-by boiler **-kühlwasserbehälter** *m* emergency radiator tank **-lampe** *f* spare lamp **-leitung** *f* spare circuit, spare wire **-lüfter** *m* standby blower **-mittel** *n* resisting agent **-nummer** *f* unallotted number
Reserven, gut stehende ~ clear resists with sharp outlines **~ unter Dampffarben** resists under steam colors
Reserve-pumpe *f* emergency pump, spare pump **-randschicht** *f* reserve layer **-reifenaufzug** *m* spare tire lift **-satz** *m* spare set or unit **-schaltung** *f* emergency system or switch **-schutz** *m* backup protection
Reserve-sender *m* standby transmitter **-sicherungsstreifen** *m* spare fuse strip **-stufe** *f* standby stage **-stutzen** *m* spare branch **-teil** *m* replacement part, spare part, spare **-trommel** *f* spare drum **-verstärker** *m* spare repeater **-windung** *f* spare coil **-zeitfaktor** *m* percent-time on reserve **-zündung** *f* auxiliary ignition lead
reservierbar resistible
reservieren to reserve
Reservierungs-artikel *m* resist-printed goods **-mittel** *n* resist, reserve (in calico printing)
Reservoir für rasche Entleerung blowdown tank
residuell residual **-er Ausschlag** residual deflection
Residuum *n* residuum, residue, remainder
Resinatfirnis *f* resinate boiled oil
Resistanz *f* resistance
resistieren to resist
Resistivität *f* resistivity
Resitex *n* resitex
Resolharz *n* single stage resin
Resolvente *f* resolvent
Resonanz *f* resonance, syntony **~ und Drosselkreis in Reihe** series-multiple resonant circuit **in ~ bringen** to tune, resonate, cause to be in resonance with **in ~ sein** to resonate **auf ~ abgestimmt** tuned to resonance **außer ~ befindlich** nonresonant **in ~** resonant, resonating or in resonance with, in tune with, syntonized **in ~ befindlich** resonant, in resonance, in tune **der ~ entgegenwirkend** antiresonant
Resonanz-anpassung *f* resonance matching **-anzeiger** *m* resonance indicator, tuning indicator **-aufhebend** anti-resonant **-band** *n* resonance band **-bedingung** *f* resonant condition **-bereich** *m* resonant range **-beschleuniger** *m* magnetic resonance accelerator, induction electron accelerator, rheotron and induction accelerator **-blase** *f* resonant bubble (acoust.) **-boden** *m* sounding board **-brücke** *f* resonance bridge **-durchlaßwahrscheinlichkeit** *f* resonance escape probability
Resonanz-einfang *m* resonance capture **-erscheinung** *f* resonance phenomenon **-erschütterung** *f* resonant vibration **-fall** *m* case of resonance **-fluoreszenz** *f* resonance radiation (fluorescence) **-form** *f* mode of resonance **-frequenz** *f* resonant or resonance frequency, natural frequency **-frequenzmesser** *m* resonance-frequency meter **-galvanometer** *n* vibration galvanometer **-gebilde** *n* resonant combination **-grundfrequenz** *f* first resonating frequency **-hohlraum** *m* resonance cavity or chamber (rhumbatron) **-kammer** *f* resonant cavity in klystron chamber (radar) **-körper** *m* sound(ing) board
Resonanzkreis *m* (series-)resonant circuit, resonating circuit; **~** (Parallelresonanz) parallel- or multiple-resonant circuit; **~** (Spannungsresonanz) series-resonant circuit; **~** (Stromresonanz) parallel-resonant circuit
Resonanzkurve *f* resonance curve **schiefe ~** unsymmetric- or skew-resonance characteristic **zweihöckrige ~, zweispitzige ~, zweiwellige ~** double-hump or double-peak resonance curve **~ des Quarzkristalls** crevasse curve (cryst.)
Resonanzkurven-einsattelung *f*, **-senke** *f* crevass of resonance curve, dip
Resonanzlage *f* resonant range **aus der ~ bringen** to detune
Resonanz-maximum *n* resonance peak **-methode** *f* resonating method, resonance method **-nebenschluß** *m* resonant shunt **-relais** *n* resonance relay **-röhre** *f* resonance or tuning indicator, flashograph **-schallquelle** *f* acoustic source **-schaltung** *f* resonance circuit
Resonanzschärfe *f* magnification of the circuit, sharpness of resonance, selectivity, sharpness tuning **~ einer Spule** dissipation constant, dissipation factor
Resonanz-schwingung *f* covibration, resonant or sympathetic vibration **-spannung** *f* resonance potential, radiation potential
Resonanzspitze *f* resonance peak **abgeflachte ~** flat-topped resonance crest
Resonanz-sprung *m* transition of electron resulting in emission of radiation **-stelle** *f* resonance point **-strahlung** *f* resonance radiation **-transformator** *m* tuned transformer, resonance transformer **-überhöhung** *f* resonance rise **-übertragung** *f* resonance transfer **-verlauf** *m* resonance curve **-verstärker** *m* tuned amplifier, resonance amplifier **-wellenmesser** *m* resonance wave meter **-widerstand** *m* resonance resistance **-wirkung** *f* resonant effect, resonance effect **-wirkungsquerschnitt** *m* resonance cross-section **-zustand** *m* resonant condition
Resonator *m* resonator, vibrator **piezoelektrischer ~** piezoelectric resonator
resonieren to resonate
Resopal *n* formica
Resorber *m* reabsorber
resorbieren to reabsorb
Resorzin *n*, **-öl** *n* resorcinol
Resotank *m* microwave generator, cavity

resonator magnetron
Respiration *f* respiration
Respiro *n* grace period (patents)
Rest *m* rest, balance, remainder, remains, remnant, relics, net, radical **-ablagefach** *n* reject pocket **-ablenkung** *f* residual or remanent deviation **-abweichung** *f* residual aberration **-aktivität** *f* residual activity **-block** *m* ingot butt **-bruch** *m* fracture residual **-brumm** *m* battery supply circuit noise **-dämpfung** *f* over-all attenuation, net loss, over-all transmission loss, over-all transmission equivalent, net attenuation, net transmission equivalent **-dämpfungsfaktor** *n* net loss factor
Restdämpfungsmessung *f* over-all (toll circuit) transmission test, net-loss measurement **~ bei mehreren Frequenzen** net-loss frequency measurements **~ zwischen den Leitungsenden** over-all net-loss measurements
Rest-dämpfungsverzerrung *f* attenuation distortion **-deviation** *f* residual or remanent deviation **-drall** *m* residual twist **-druck** *m* residual stress **-fehler** *m* residual error **-feuchtigkeit** *f* residual moisture **-flugweite** *f* linear height of burst **flußdichte** *f* residual flux density **-flüssigkeit** *f* residual liquid **-gas** *n* residual gas **-gasausspülung** *f* scavenging of residual gases
Rest-glied *n* remaining term or power **-härte** *f* residual hardness (of water) **-induktivität** *f* saturation inductance **-ionisation** *f* residual ionization **-intensität** *f* residual intensity
restituieren to restore, reinstitute
Rest-keim *m* residual nucleus **-kohle** *f* carbonized residue **-kraft** *f* residual force, remanence (of magnetism) **-kern** *m* residual nucleus **-krümpfung** *f* residual shrinkage **-ladung** *f* residual charge **-ladungsanteil** *m* end gas
restlich residual
restlos absolutely, completely, without residue
Rest-lösung *f* residual liquid, rest of the magma **-luft** *f* residual air **-magnetismus** *m* remanence (of magnetism) **-melder** *m* minimum limiting gauge **-methode** *f* method of residues **-molasse** *f* third molasses, blackstrap (molasses)
Restoktantfehler *m* residual octantal error
Reston *n* ripple frequency
Rest-periode *f* recess **-plasma** *n* residual electrons, plasma **-platte** *f* single-ingot plate **-reaktanz** *f* saturation reactance **-reichweite** *f* residual range **-schmelze** *f* residual heat
Restseitenband *n* vestigial sideband **-empfang** *m* semi-single sideband reception **-verfahren** *n* assymmetric sideband transmission
Rest-spannung *f* residual stress **-strahl** *m* residual ray, ray radiation **-strom** *m* residual current **-stromstoß** *m* residual pulse **-ton** *m* ripple frequency (radio) **-verluste** *pl* residual losses **-verstärkung** *f* overall gain **-verzerrungskorrektor** *m* line residual equalizer **-widerstand** *m* residual resistance **-widerstandsfläche** *f* residual drag area
resublimieren to resublime
Resultante *f* resultant
Resultat *n* result, outcome **-tafel** *f* score board **-wert** *m* resultant or output value
resultieren to result
resultierend resultant **-e Kraft** resultant action, net force or action **-er** (Wicklungs-)**Schritt** resultant pitch of a winding **-e Windkraft** resultant wind force **-e Wirkung** net action
Resultierende *f* resultant
Resumé *n* resumé
resümieren to make a resumé
reszindieren to rescind
retablieren to reestablish
retardieren to retard, decelerate
Retardierungs-korrektur *f* retardation correction **-zeit** *f* retardation time
Retensionsfaktor *m* retension coefficient, initial body retention
Retinoscopic Hand refractionometer
Retirade *f* retreat, latrine
Retorsion *f* reverse torsion
Retorte *f* retort **~** (mit unterbrochenem Betrieb) batch still
Retorten-hals *m* neck of a retort **-helm** *m* retort head, retort helm **-kammer** *f* retort chamber **-kohle** *f* retort carbon **-koks** *m* retort coke **-kontaktverfahren** *n* retort-contact process or method **-mulde** *f* retort channel **-ofen** *m* retort oven or furnace **-paraffin** *n* still wax **-reihe** *f* bank of retorts **-schieber** *m* retort slide **-vergasung** *f* distillation in retorts **-verkohlung** *f* retort carbonization, retort coking **-verkokung** *f* retort coking **-vorstoß** *m* condenser
Retort-kohle *f* retort carbon **-mündung** *f* mouth of a retort **-rückstand** *m* retort residue **-vergasung** *f* retort gasification **-vorstoß** *f* adapter, retort condenser
Retour-dampf *m* exhaust steam **-schlacke** *f* return slag **-speiseleitung** *f* return feeder
Retraite *f* retreat, tattoo
Retraktorstrebe *f* retractor strut
Retransmetteur *m* retransmitter
retrodatieren to date back
retrovertieren to retrovert
retrozedieren to retrocede
retten to save, rescue **sich mit dem Fallschirm ~** to save oneself by parachute
Retten *n* saving
Rettung *f* rescue, escape **~ mit dem Fallschirm** escape by parachute
Rettungs-apparat *m* rescue apparatus **-arbeit** *f* rescuing operation **-boje** *f* life buoy
Rettungsboot *n* lifeboat, whaleboat **-funkeinrichtung** *f* lifeboat wireless set
Rettungs-dienst *m* crash rescue service, lifeguard service (at river crossings) **-druckanzug** *m* pressurized suit for emergency jumps **-fahrzeug** *n* rescue vehicle, lifesaving boat (at river crossings) **-floß** *n* raft **-gerät** *n* lifesaving equipment **-gürtel** *m* safety belt, buoy **-kammer** *f* rescue chamber **-kapsel** *f* escape capsule **-leute** *pl* life guards **-luke** *f* escape hatch
Rettungs-mannschaft *f* rescue party **-mittel** *n* lifesaving equipment **-ring** *m* life belt, life preserver **-schraube** *f* safety screw **-stelle** *f* first-aid station **-truppe** *f* rescue brigade, rescue squad, salvage troop
Rettungs- und Sicherheitskammer *f* rescue and refuge chamber
Rettungs-versuch *m* attempted rescue **-wagen** *m* ambulance
Retusche *f* touching up, retouching
retuschieren to touch up, retouch
Reuse *f* grid, staggered array (of antennas)

Reusen-antenne *f* prism or pyramid antenna, cage antenna **-strahler** *m* pyramidal horn
Reverberierofen *m* reverberatory furnace, air (radiation) furnace
Revers *m* bond, undertaking
reversibel reversible
Reversibilität *f* reversibility
reversibl-er Lesevorgang reversible readout **-es Magnetisieren** reversible switching **-e Magnetisierungsrichtung** rotational reversibility
reversierbar reversible **-er Motor** reversible motor
Reversier-blechstraße *f* reversing plate train **-blechwalzwerk** *n* reversing plate mill **-blockstraße** *f* reversing blooming-mill train, reversing cogging-mill train **-blockwalzwerk** *n* reversing blooming mill, reversing cogging mill **-duo** *n* two-high reversing mill **-duogrobstraße** *f* two-high reversing plate rolling train **-duowalzwerk** *n* two-high reversing mill
reversieren to reverse
Reversier-getriebe *n* reversing gear **-maschine** *f* reversible machine **-modellplatte** *f* reversible pattern plate, single-sided pattern plate **-profileisenwalzwerk** *n* reversing shape mill **-straße** *f* reversing mill train **-strecke** *f* reversing mill strand **-streckgerüst** *n* reversing strand of rolls for roughing **-ventil** *n* reversing valve **-vorrichtung** *f* reversing gear **-walzwerk** *n* reversing mill, reversing rolling mill
Reversions-libelle *f* reversible spirit level **-nivellierlibelle** *f* reversion level **-pendel** *n* reversible pendulum, Kater's pendulum
Reverskaponniere *f* reverse caponier
Revertex *m* revertex, evaporated latex
revidieren to revise, check, audit, examine
Revier *n* district **-fahrt** *f* channel or river traffic **-grenze** *f* section line
Revision *f* inspection, revision, auditing
Revisions-abteilung *f* internal audit department **-abteilungswesen** *n* auditing **-bogen** *m* clean proof, revise **-lehre** *f* factory-acceptance gauge, inspection gauge **-loch** *n* manhole (of a water conduit) **-schacht** *m* inspection shaft, manhole of a water channel
Revisor *m* reviser, controller, auditor
Revolver *m* revolver, revolving nosepiece (micros.) **-anordnung** *f* turret arrangement **-arbeit** *f* turret work
Revolverbank *f* capstan lathe, turret lathe ~ **mit Zwischenschlitten** capstan lathe
Revolver-blende *f* rotary diaphragm, revolving diaphragm, rotating shutter **-bohrbank** *f* turret-head boring mill **-bohrkopf** *m* revolving cutter head **-drehbank** *f* capstan lathe, turret lathe **-hemmschraube** *f* turret stop screw **-kamera** *f* revolver camera
Revolver-kopf *m* turrethead, turret, turret bushing, lens turret (of camera) **-kopfdrehlänge** *f* length of turret feed **-köpfe** *pl* turret heads **-kopffläche** *f* turret face **-kopfschaltscheibe** *f* turret index-disc **-kopfwelle** *f* turret shaft
Revolver-lochzangen *pl* revolving belt punches **-okularkopf** *m* templet ocular head **-presse** *f* revolving press **-querbalkensupport** *m* cross-beam turret head **-schaltapparat** *m* turret indexing mechanism **-schlitten** *m* capstan **-strichplatte** *f* revolving templet dial **-stuhl** *m* revolver loom
Revolverteller *m* dial plate **-zuführung** *f* feed for the turntable
Revolver-tisch *m* dial feed **-trommel** *f* cartridge cylinder (revolver) **-zuführung** *f* dial feed
revozieren to revoke
Reynolds'sche Zahl Reynolds number
rezensieren to review
Rezension *f* review, criticism
Rezept *n* prescription, recipe
rezeptieren to prescribe
Rezeptivität *f* receptivity
Rezidiv *n* recurrence
Rezipient *m* container
Rezipientenbüchse *f* liner
reziprok reciprocal **-e Geschwindigkeitskurve** inverse rate curve **-e Teile** reciprocating parts **-er Wert** reciprocal value **-er Wert der Kompressabilität** bulk modulus
Reziprokalprojektion *f* reciprocal projection **gnomonische** ~ gnomonic reciprocal projection
Reziprozität *f* reciprocity
Reziprozitäts-bedingung *f* reciprocity condition **-beziehung** *f* reciprocity relation **-eigenschaft** *f* reciprocity property **-parameter** *n* reciprocity coefficient **-prinzip** *n* reciprocity principle **-sätze** *pl* reciprocity theorems
R-Gerät *n* rocket-device, rocket-propulsion unit, rocket equipment
Rhachis *m* mesotergum (paleontology)
rheinisch Rhenish **-er Ofen** Rhenish (regenerative zinc distilling) furnace
Rheostat *m* rheostat, resistor
Rheotan *n* rheotan
Rhigolen *n* petroleum ether
Rhodan *n* thiocyanogen, sulfocyanogen **-aluminium** *n* aluminium sulfocyanide **-ammon(ium)** *n* ammonium rhodanide
Rhodanat *n* thiocyanate, sulfocyanate
Rhodan-calcium *n* calcium sulfocyanide **-jodkalium** *n* iodine-potassium thiocyanate **-kali** *n* potassium sulfocyanate, potassium thiocyanate **-kalium** *n* potassium thiocyanate **-kupfer** *n* cupric thiocyanate **-natrium** *n* sodium sulfocyanate, sodium thiocyanate **-salz** *n* sulfocyanide **-wasserstoffsäure** *f* thiocyanic acid, sulfocyanic acid **-zinnoxyd** *n* stannic thiocyanate **-zinnoxydul** *n* stannous thiocynate
Rhodium *n* rhodium **-metall** *n* metallic rhodium, rhodium metal
Rhodonit *m* rhodonite
Rhomben-dodekaeder *n* rhombic dodecahedron **-förmig** rhombic
rhombisch orthorhombic
Rhomboeder *n* rhombohedron, rhomboid
rhomboedrisch rhombohedral
Rhomboid *n* rhomboid
rhomboidisch rhomboid(al)
Rhombus *m* rhombus, diamond pass (in rolling), rhomb, lozenge **-antenne** *f* diamond-shaped antenna, rhombic antenna, frame aerial
Rhometer *n* rhometer
Rhönrad *n* gyrowheel
Rhumbatron *n* rhumbatron
Rhyolit *n* rhyolite
Rhumkorffscher Apparat Rhumkorff coil
Rhythmus *m* rhythm **im** ~ in tune, synchronism, rhythm, or unison with

Ricelprobe *f* olfactory test

Richt-abdrift *f* erection drift **-analyse** *f* guide analysis **-antenne** *f* directional antenna, directive antenna, beam antenna, unilateral antenna

Richt-antennenanordnung *f* antenna array **-antennennetz** *n* antenna array, beam array

Richt-apparat *m* tuning apparatus **-arbeiten** *pl* aligning works **-aufsatz** *m* sight, gun sight, telescopic sight **-aufsatzträger** *m* sight support **-ausbildung** *f* training in sighting **-bake** *f* directional radio beacon **-bank** *f* leveler (in sheet-metal rolling) **-barkeit** *f* directiveness **-baum** *m* trail handspike **-blei** *n* plumb line **-bogen** *m* elevating rack, level clinometer

Richtcharakteristik *f* directional or directive diagram, directional characteristic, space pattern **elektrische Schwenkung der ~** electrical beam swinging **achtförmige ~** figure-of-eight characteristic or pattern, bilateral characteristic

Richt-diagramm *n* directive pattern **-dipol** fishbone antenna **-dorn** *m* mandrel **-draht** *m* grid wire **-drill** *m* gun-laying drill

Richteeisen *n* steel member used for erection purposes, spacer bar

Richt-effekt *m* directional effect, rectification effect **-empfang** *m* directional or directive reception **-empfänger** *m* tune directional receiver, directional, receiving set **-empfängertrupp** *m* beam-reception detachment

Richtempfangs-anlage *f* beam-receiving station **-antenne** *f* directional receiving antenna

richten to set right, arrange, fix, adjust; (ausrichten) align; (lenken, wenden) direct at, turn on; (sich ~ nach) conform to, act according to; (abhängen) depend on; straighten, dress, turn, set, rise, conform, level (sheet metals), point, aim ~ (Bleche) to level ~ **auf** to aim, point to, train on, aim at **sich ~ nach** to be guided by, depend on **gerade ~** to straighten **Räder ~** to true up or align wheels

Richten *n* aiming, laying dressing (metals), straightening, adjusting, setting, raising **direktes ~** direct laying

richtende Eigenschaft directional property

Richter *m* judge, magistrate, justice, converter

Richtereimaschine *f* adjusting or adjustment machine

Richterspruch *m* sentence (law), judgment

richtfähig directive **stark ~** highly directive

Richt-fähigkeit *f* directional property, directivity (radio) **-faktor** *m* (einer Verstärkerröhre) curvature, rectification factor **-feld** *n* field of fire, correcting field **-fernrohr** *n* telescopic sight **-feuer** *n* leading light **-feuerlinie** *f* alignment of lights **-finder** *m* direction finder **-fläche** *f* plane of sighting **-funkanlage** *f* radio link system

Richtfunkbake *f* directive radio beacon **umlaufende ~** rotating radio beacon, rotating-loop beacon

Richtfunk-feuer *n* directive radio beacon, directive-beacon station, directive-transmitter station, radio-range station **-netz** *n* radio relay system **-relaiskette** *f* microwave-relay system **-stelle** *f* radio relay station **-strecke** *f* radio link, microwave highway **-system** *n* radio relay system **-verbindung** *f* radio link **-zwischenstelle** *f* relay station

Richtgeber *m* course compass

Richt-gehäuse *n* laying-gear housing **-gelenk** *n* cradle joint **-genauigkeit** *f* directional accuracy

Richtgerät *n* aiming or sighting mechanism, laying gear, bombsight, sight **~ für Funkpeiler** adjusting instrument for radio-bearing sender

Richtgetriebe *n* elevating and traversing mechanism

Richtglas *n* collimator **~ für Rundblickfernrohr** sighting collimator

Richt-gleichspannung *f* rectified voltage **-größe** *f* directional quantity **-handrad** *n* manual control wheel **-hebel** *m* setting lever, elevating lever **-hebelwelle** *f* elevating-arm shaft **-höhe** *f* elevation **-hörer** *m* sound locator

richtig right, correct, accurate, properly, just, true **-er Kurs** true course

Richtigbefund *m* verification

richtiggestellte Höhe corrected altitude

Richtigkeit *f* correctness, truth, faithfulness, accuracy, rightness, fairness, exactitude, fidelity (of reproduction)

richtiglastig correctly trimmed

richtigphasig true-phased, in correct phase relationship **-e Elektronen** electrons of favorable phase

Richtigstellung *f* rectifying, adjustment, correction, rectification

Richt-kalkulation *f* guiding calculation **-kennlinie** *f* rectification characteristic, directional diagram, space pattern **-konstante** *f* rectification constant

Richtkoppler *m* directional coupler **~ mit kapazitiver Schleife** capacitance-loop directional coupler

Richtkopplung *f* directional coupling

Richtkraft *f* directing or directive force, controlling force **-strömung** *f* disturbance of directional force

Richtkreis *m* transit instrument, transit, aiming circle, collimator, director **~ für Meßstellen** aiming circle for computing stations (artil.)

Richtkreis-aufsatzrohr *n* director telescope **-bussole** *f* declinator **-einteilung** *f* aiming-circle graduation **-kollimator** *m* aiming-circle collimator **-korrektur** *f* correction for displacement **-zahl** *f* director reading

Richt-lampe *f* director lamp **-latte** *f* aiming stake, level, straightedge, leveling board, extension rod for sighting **-lautsprecher** *m* directional loud-speaker **-leistung** *f* straightening capacity **-leiter** *m* crystal diode **-licht** *n* range lights **-lineal** *n* straightedge **-linie** *f* direction, directrix, directing line, guide line, outline, aim, directive, rule, instruction, axis, standard **-liniennorm** *f* tentative standard

Richt-magnet *m* setting magnet, controlling magnet **-maschine** *f* wire-straightening and cutting machine, elevating or traversing gear **-maschinenantrieb** *m* elevation handwheel **-maschinensäule** *f* elevating-gear column **-maß** *n* rule, standard gauge **-mittel** *n* sighting instrument, aiming mechanism **-moment** *n* controlling couple, directing moment **-platte** *f* surface plate, leveling block or plate, orientation plate (micros.) **-posten** *m* signpost **-presse** *f* straightening press, gag press

Richtpunkt *m* aiming point, station, base **-ver-**

fahren *n* indirect laying (artil.) **-zahl** *f* aiming-point azimuth reading

Richt-röhre *f* two-electrode vacuum tube, diode, directional oscilloscope **-rolle** *f* straightening roll **-säule** *f* large range-finding telescope **-schärfe** *f* accuracy of alignment **-scheit** *n* batten, straightedge (drawing), leveling board, level, ruler **-schienen** *pl* parallels for levelling up **-schnur** *f* guidance **-schraube** *f* elevating screw **-schütze** *m* gunner

Richt-senden *n* directional transmission **-sender** *m* directional transmitter **-sendung** *f* beam emission **-sitz** *m* azimuth setter seat, gunner's seat **-skala** *f* alignment scale **-sohle** *f* traversing bed **-spannung** *f* directional stress **-spant** *n* midship section, main frame

Richt-spule *f* control coil **-stab** *m* aiming stake **-stäbchen** *n* aiming post **-stand** *m* sighting platform (guided missiles) **-stange** *f* alignment stake, scaffold pole, standard **-stelle** *f* offset position of aiming circle in axial-lateral conduct of fire **-stock** *m* aiming post **-stollen** *m* advance heading, driftway, pilot tunnel

Richt-strahl *m* directional beam **-strahlantenne** *f* beam antenna **-strahler** *m* beam antenna, beam sender (radio navig.), beamed short-wave transmitter, directing beam, directional antenna, directional loud-speaker **-strecke** *f* heading **-strich** *m* front sight, sighting aperture (of compass) **-strom** *m* rectified current **-system** *n* beam system **-übungsgerät** *n* aiming-practice instrument

Richtung *f* direction, alignment, aim, drift, course, tendency, bearing **~ der Schichten** strike (of beds) **in der ~ des Uhrzeigers** clockwise **~ des Vektors** direction of vector **eine bestimmte ~ haben** to bear **aus der ~** skew, out of line **in einer ~** oneway **ausgepeilte ~** bearing **optische ~** optical direction **senkrechte ~** vertical direction, plumb line **aufeinander senkrechte Richtungen** orthogonal directions **abgehende ~** outgoing direction

richtungsabhängig direction-controlled **-er Widerstand** asymmetrical resistance

Richtungs-abhängigkeit *f* directional derivative **-änderung** *f* change of direction **-angabe** *f* indication of direction

Richtungsanzeige, eindeutige ~ unidirectional direction-finding

Richtungs-anzeiger *m* direction finder, indicator, course-indicating radio beacon **-aufsucher** *m* directional finder

Richtungsbestimmung *f* radio direction finding, direction finding **drahtlose ~** wireless direction finding

Richtungs-bestimmungsfehler *m* direction-finder deviation **-bohren** *n* directional drilling **-charakteristik** *f* directive or directional-characteristic or diagram space pattern **-doppelfokussierung** *f* two directional focussing **-durchschlag** *m* directional breakdown **-effekt** *m* head-and tail effect, directional action **-empfang** *m* directional reception **-empfindlich** with directional response, dependent upon direction, non-astatic **-empfindlichkeit** *f* directional sensitivity **-empfindung** *f* perception of direction **-ermittlung** *f* radio direction finding, direction finding

Richtungs-fehler *m* error of direction, deviation (of pencil or beam), directional distortion (television) **-festigkeit** *f* directional stability **-feuer** *n* beacon light **-finder** *m* direction finder **-fokussierend** direction focusing

Richtungsflügel *m* guide wing **mit Richtungsflügeln versehen** wing-guided

Richtungs-gebend indicating the direction **-geber** *m* turn control, course-setting switch, director, directive antenna **-genauigkeit** *f* accuracy of direction **-gleis** *n* classification track (R.R.) **-glied** *n* (Relais) directional element **-hebel** *m* reversing handle **-hören** *n* aural determination of direction, airplane spotting or locating **-hörer** *m* sound locator (antiaircraft direction finder) **-instabilität** *f* directional instability **-isolator** *m* directional isolator

Richtungs-koinzidenz *f* directional coincidence **-koppler mit zwei Löchern** two-hole directional coupler **-korrelation** *f* directional correlation **-kosinus** *m* direction cosine (math.) **-kreisel** *m* directional gyroscope **-krümmung** *f* curvature of the direction **-kurve** *f* directrix **-lampe** *f* direction lamp, spotlight **-licht** *n* direction light **-lineal** *n* direction arm, azimuthal lever **-linie** *f* base line **-los** directionless **-messung** *f* directional counter

Richtungs-navigation *f* directional navigation **-pfahl** *m* leading pile **-pfeil** *m* directional marker **-phasenschieber** *m* directional phase changer **-punkt** *m* bearing point **-quantelung** *f* directional quantization **-reduktion** *f* spherical correction

Richtungs-schild *n* destination sign **-schlitten** *m* direction slide **-schuß** *m* aiming shot, sighting shot **-schwankung** *f* fluctuation **-senden** *n* directional transmission **-sender** *m* beacon station, beam station, radio-range station **-sinn** *m* sense of direction **-sinnbestimmung** *f* sense finding, sensing **-stabilität** *f* directional stability (aviation) **-übertragung** *f* transfer of direction **-umkehr** *f* reversal

Richtungs- und Entfernungsbestimmung *f* ranging

richtungs-unempfindlich nondirectional, astatic **-unschärfe** *f* direction uncertainty **-unterschied** *m* directional difference **-vermögen** *n* directivity **-verteilung** *f* direction distribution **-verzerrung** *f* direction distortion **-wechsel** *m* change in or reversal of direction **-weisend** valid **-weiser** *m* signpost **-wender** *m* reverser **-werter** *m* searchlight control pillar

Richtungswinkel *m* angle of deflection, angle of sighting, angle of collimation, angle of direction, angle of elevation, bearing, azimuth

Richtungszerstreuung *f* scatter of direction (beam)

Richtverbindungs-endstelle *f* radio link terminal **-stelle** *f* radio link relay station **-station** *f* radio link station

Richt-verfahren *n* method of sighting, gun laying **-verhältnis** *n* directivity **-vermögen** *n* directivity, directive power (antenna) **-verstärker** *m* anode detector, plate-circuit or anode-bend detector, negatively biased detector, rectifier or rectifying strengthener, amplifying detector **-verstärkungsfaktor** *m* power gain **-vorgang** *m* dressing procedure **-vorrichtung** *f* laying mechanism, laying gear **-waage** *f* level **-walze** *f* straightening roll

Richtweiser, drahtloser ~ radio beacon, radio range, beam station

Richt-werkzeug *n* dressing tool **-wert** *m* determining factor, basis of valuation, standard value, coefficient data **-werteverbindung** *f* data-transmission lines for searchlights **-widerstand** *m* unidirectional resistance, valve effect, rectifier effect

Richtwirkung *f* action of directional beam, (uni)-directional effect, directivity **einseitige ~** unidirectional action

richtwirkungsfrei nondirectional

Richtwirkungsgrad *m* rectification efficiency

Richt-zähler *m* directional counter **-zahnbogen** *m* elevating rack **-zange** *f* straightening tongs **-zeug** *n* leveling instrument

riechen to smell, detect by smelling

Riech-probe *f* smelling test **-probenkasten** *m* smelling-test box **-rohr** *n* volatilizing tube **-spur** *f* scent trail **-stoff** *m* odoriferous matter **-würfel** *m* gas capsule (maneuver)

Riedelanlasser *m* Riedel starter

Riefe *f* groove, channel, furrow, flute, slot

riefeln to knurl, striate, mill, groove

Riefelung *f* chamfer, grooving

riefen to groove, flute, serrate, champfer, channel; (Walzenzapfen) to score

Riefen-abstand *f* roughness width rating **-bildung** *f* scoring **-frei** free from hair lines **-verlauf** *m* lay

Riefung *f* grooving, rifling

Riegel *m* (Schloß) key-bolt; (Baukunst) tie beam, bar, bolt, locking bar, lock bolt (of gun), latch, girth, girt, tie rod, tie bar, tie, truss, horizontal member, slip bolt, sliding bolt, fastening, set bar, pole brace, transom, girder, linter, flank-group position, lock **~ eines Hebezeugs** crossbar or transom of a gin **~ einer Schleusenzarge** crosspiece of framing of a lock gate **gebrochener ~** girder shaped like a gable-end roof **oberer ~** top girder **unterer ~** bottom girder **~ zum Schließbalken** index piece for lock-up bar

Riegel-bau *m* half-timber construction **-blech** *n* staple plate **-bohrer** *m* bar wimble **-bolzen** *m* locking bolt or pin, plunger **-feder** *f* stop spring **-haken** *m* latch

Riegelhälfte *f* half of the girder **linke ~** left half of the girder **rechte ~** right half of the girder **beider Riegelhälften** both halves of the girder

Riegel-hebel *m* locking lever **-holz** *n* crossbar **-kugel** *f* poppet ball **-mitte** *f* middle of the girder **-schiene** *f* sliding magazine lock bar **-stellung** *f* switch position **-stift** *m* locking pin **-tor** *n* balanced gate **-verschlußdeckel** *m* locking-bar cover **-wand** *f* partition **-werk** *n* frame work

Riemannscher Abbildungssatz Riemann's mapping theorem

Riemen *m* strap, sling, oar, belt, band, endless belt, thong **halbgeschränkter ~** quarter-turn belt **langer ~** single-banked oar **mehrfacher ~** multiple-ply belt **zweifacher ~** double-ply belt **geschränkter ~** cross belt **~ nähen** to lace the belt

Riemenabsteller *m* belt shifter

Riemenantrieb *m* belt transmission, belt drive **~ für den Querbalken** pulley drive for raising crossrail **mit ~** belt-driven

Riemen-appretur *f* belt dressing **-auflеger** *m* rope setter, belt mounter

Riemenausrücker *m* belt shifter **-gabel** *f* belt-shifting fingers

Riemenausrück-gabel *f* belt-shifter fingers **-vorrichtung** *f* belt-shifting device

Riemen-band *n* belt fastener **-beanspruchung** *f* belt stress **-befestiger** *m* belt tightener **-breite** *f* belt width **-bügel** *m* swivel, stock ferrule swivel, sling swivel **-dehnung** *f* stretch of a belt **-durchhang** *m* sag of a belt

Riemen-fallhammer *m* drop press **-fett** *n* belt dressing **-fluchtgerät** *n* belt-aligning device **-führer** *m* belt shifter **-führung** *f*, **-gabel** *f* belt guide **-getrieben** belt driven **-haken** *m* hook belt fastener **-haus** *n* belt tunnel, belt house **-hebelschalter** *m* belt lever shifter **-kitt** *m* leather-cement **-klammer** *f* (hook) belt fastener **-konus** *m* stepped pulley **-kralle** *f* claw belt fastener

Riemen-leder *n* belting **-leiter** *m* belt guide, mule stand, guide pulley, binder frame **-leitrolle** *f* belt-guide pulley, idler pulley, belt guide roller **-locher** *m* belt punch **-lochzange** *f* belt punch **-pumpe** *f* belt-driven pump **-querschnitt** *m* belt (cross) section **-rad** *n* belt pulley **-rückhebel** *m* shifter lever **-rutsch** *m* belt slip **-schaltvorrichtung** *f* belt-shifting device

Riemenscheibe *f* belt pulley, band pulley, pulley, drive pulley **~ mit geradem Kranz** straight-face pulley **~ für den Rücklauf** return driving pulley **ballig gedrehte ~** crown-face pulley

Riemenscheiben-antrieb *m* pulley drive **-büchse** *f* pulley bushing **-hälfte** *f* split belt pulley (for fan) **-kranz** *m* pulley rim **-lagerarm** *m* pulley stand **-lüfter** *m* fan pulley **-nabe** *f* pulley hub **-schwungrad** *n* flywheel pulley **-umfang** *m* circumference of pulley rim **-wölbung** *f* pulley crown

Riemen-schutz *m* pulley (belt) guard **-spanner** *m* belt clamp, (belt) tightener, idlers, belt stretcher **-spannrolle** *f* belt tightener **-spannung** *f* tension of belt **-spannverstellung** belt tension adjustment **-spannvorrichtung** *m* belt take-up **-transmission** *f* belt transmission **-trieb** *m* belt drive

Riementrum *n* strand (of a belt) **gespanntes ~** tight strand of belt **loses ~** slack strand of belt

Riemen-übertragung *f* belt transmission, belt drive **-verbinder** *m* belt lacer, coupler, or fastener **-verbindung** *f* belt joint **-verschiebegabel** *f* belt shifter **-verschiebung** *f* belt shifting **-verschluß** *m* belt fastener **-vorgelege** *n* belt gearing **-zeug** *n* belting **-zubehör** *n* belt appliance **-zug** *m* belt pull or tension

Riem-gabel *f* belt-shifting finger **-scheibe** *f* pulley

Ries *n* ream

Riesbeschneidemaschine *f* guillotine cutting machine

Riese *f* gravity cable

Rieselanlage *f* trickling or dripping plant

Rieseler *m* scrubber

rieselfähig fluid

Riesel-feld *n* sewage farm, sludge bed, sprinkling bed, irrigation field **-höhe** *f* packing depth (of tower) **-kondensator** *m* open-surface condenser **-kühler** *m* open-surface cooler

Rieseln *n* rippling, gushing, trickling, swarming (of film), friable or noncaking condition (of materials)

Riesel-speicher *m* spray-and-hopper granary **-trockner** *m* flighted frier **-turm** *m* scrubbing tower, scrubber, wash tower, washer, wash column, spray tower, spray column
Rieselung *f* trickling, drainage
Riesel-verdampfer *m* open-surface evaporator **-wasser** *n* trickling water
Riesen-bagger *m* giant shovel **-flugzeug** *n* giant plane **-karusseldrehbank** *f* giant vertical boring mill **-kran** *m* giant crane **-luftreifen** *m* supercushion tire, giant tire **-resonanz** *f* giant resonance **-schauer** *m* giant air shower **-würfel** *m* enormous cube **-zellenmodell** *n* giant-cell model
riesig gigantic, vast, tremendous
Riespapier *n* ream wrappers
Riester *m* mold **-pflug** *m* moldboard plow
Riff *n* reef, shelf, sandbank, shallows, ridge **-bildende Korallen** reef-building corals
Riffel *m* ridge, rise, flute **-bildung** *f* corrugation, rippling **-blech** *n* checkered (metal) plate or sheet, corrugated sheet metal, channeled plate **-blechabdeckung** *f* chequer plate covering **-blei** *n* corrugated lead sheeting **-draht** *m* checkered wire **-faltenlautsprecher** *m* loud-speaker with folded and corrugated horn **-glas** *n* holophane or frosted glass, ribbed glass **-kalander** *m* riffle calender **-kloben** *m* grooved mandrel **-kohlenblitzableiter** *m* carbon block protector
Riffel-lautsprecher *m* loud-speaker with rifled diaphragm **-membrane** *f* pleated diaphragm, diaphragm with circular corrugations **-nabe** *f* fluted hub
riffeln to channel, groove, serrate, corrugate, knurl, furrow, ripple (flax)
Riffeln von Hartgußwalzen pattern cutting of chilled cast-iron rolls
Riffel-scheibe *f* wrinkle washer **-stahl** *m* grooving tool, fluting steel
Riffelung *f* corrugation, knurl, groove
Riffelungsmuster *n* network design
Riffel-verzahnung *f* serrations **-walze** *f* grooved roll **-welle** *f* splined shaft **-zahn** *m* serration **-zylinder** *m* fluted roller
Riffzeichen *n* isolated danger signal
Righeit *f* (Geophysik) rigidity
Rigidität *f* (Geophysik) rigidity
rigolen to trench-plow, lay out ridges
Rigolpflug *m* trench(ing) plow
Rillapparat *m* scoring apparatus
Rille *f* groove, spline, furrow, grooving, riffle **~ und Nadelresonanz** stylus-groove resonance
rillen to groove
Rillen-bolzen *m* grooved pin **-breite** *f* groove width **-büchse** *f* packing sleeve **-förmig** flute-type
Rillengeschwindigkeit *f*, **konstante ~** constant groove speed
Rillen-grund *m* tread of groove **-kugellager** *n* grooved ball bearing **-herd** *m* riffled surface table **-isolator** *m* grooved insulator **-lager** *n* ball bearing **-läufer** *m* grooved muller (of an edge mill) **-mutter** *f* circular grooved nut
Rillenprofil *n* shape or contour of a groove **~ einer Seilscheibe** pulley groove contour
Rillen-rolle *f* grooved roller **-reibrad** *n* grooved friction wheel **-scheibe** *f* sheave **-schiene** *f* tramway rail **-trommel** *f* grooved drum **-verzerrung** *f* tracing distortion (phono) **-walzentrockner** *m* grooved drum dryer **-wandsteifigkeit** *f* groove wall stiffness **-winkel** *m* angle of groove
Rillung *f* scoring
Rimesse *f* remittance
Rimessengespräch *n* collect message
Rinde *f* bark
Rinden-schälmaschine *f* barker or barking machine **-schicht** *f* cortical layer **-schneidmaschine** *f* bark cutter
Rindsleder *n* neat's leather
Ring *m* ring, coil, collar, trunnion ring (of converter), casing (of converter floor), torus, washer, coiled bundle, bundle **~ zum Aufheben** lifting ring **geteilter ~** segmented ring, split ring **ungeteilter ~** solid ring **Ringe an Stange** pin of coils **~ (Konverter)** trunnion ring **~ (Walze)** collar **~ für Saugstange** air stop ring
Ring-abstreifer *m* scraper ring **-anker** *m* ring armature **-anordnung** *f* ring arrangement **-bahn** *f* loop, channel **-bank** *f* ring rail **-behälter** *m* ring container **-bildung** *f* ring formation **-blech** *n* primary-zone casing (jet) **-blende** *f* annular diaphragm **-blendenfilter** *n* diaphragm ring mode filter
Ring-bohrer *m* annular bit, annular cutter **-bolzen** *m* eyebolt **-bremse** *f* collar brake **-brenner** *m* ring burner **-brennkammer** *f* annular combustion chamber **-brennpunkt** *m* ring focus **-bügel** *m* hoop **-bund** *m* collar **-dichtung** *f* circumferential joint **-dorn** *m* round puncheon **-drehen** *n* band turning **-durchziehofen** *m* roller-hearth furnace for coils **-düse** *f* ring nozzle
Ringel *m* circle
Ringelektrode *f* annular electrode **abbildende Ringelektroden** focusing rings
Ringel-erz *n* ring ore **-kette** *f* striping chain (textiles) **-maschine** *f* stripe machine **-muster** *n* horizontal-stripe pattern
ringeln to curl, collar
ringen to wrestle, struggle
Ring-entladung *f* ring discharge **-etagentrockner** *m* turbo drier **-fallschirm** *m* ring parachute **feder** *f* circular spring, annular spring **-federbein** *n* annular-spring shock absorber **-feinschleifwiderstand** *m* ring-shaped precision wiping resistor **-feldempfänger** *m* selsyn receiver **-feldgeber** *m* selsyn transmitter **-figur** *f* zone plate, Huygens zone, Fresnel zone **-filter** *n* ring-type filter **-form** *f* annular or circular shape
ringförmig ring-shaped, annular, circular, cyclic, toroidal, toric **-er Auspuffsammler** exhaust collector ring **-er Querschnitt** annular section **-es Wellenfilter** ring mode filter
Ring-fräser *m* annular milling cutter **-fuge** *f* ring-type joint **-führung** *f* ring gearing **-gasbrenner** *m* ring-type gas burner **-gewitter** *n* circular thunderstorm **-gewölbe** *n* annular barrel vault, annular vault
Ringhaube *f* ring cowl(ing), circular cowl **~ mit Regelklappen** circular cowl with controllable gills
Ring-kabel *n* ring cable system, ring main **-käfig** *m* ball retainer ring, ball spacer **-kaliber** *n* ring gauge
Ringkammer *f* annular chamber **-flansch** *m* orifice gauge **-normblende** *f* ring-type orifice

plate

Ring-kasten *m* bezel **-kanal** *m* wind tunnel of closed-circuit type, belt canal **-kegellager** *n* tapered roller bearing **-keil** *m* tapered collar **-kern** *m* toroidal core

Ringkessel *m* annular tank **-boden** *m* annular tank bottom

Ring-klebemaschine *f* band builder **-kluft** *f* cup shake (in wood) **-kluppen** *pl* ring end stocks **-kopf** *m* annular recording head **-kolbenzähler** *m* rotary-piston meter **-kreis** *m* ring circuit **-kreuz** *n* cruciform girder (aviation) **-kugellager** *n* annular ball bearing **-küvette** *f* ring cell

Ring-lager *n* collar **-lehre** *f* ring gauge **-leitblech** *n* baffle ring **-leitung** *f* ring conduit, ring main, closed-circuit pipe line (of blast-furnace hot-air line), bustle pipe

Ringleitungs-kabel *n* perimeter cable **-netz** *n* perimeter cabling **-system** *n* closed-circuit system

Ringlichkeit *f* ring formation

Ring-linse *f* annular lens **-lochscheibe** *f* film scan disk **-luftpumpe** *f* rotary air pump **-magnet** *m* annular magnet **-maß** *n* ring gauge (aviation) **-masse-Elektrode** *f* annular ground electrode **-mikrometer** *n* circular micrometer **-modulator** *m* ring modulator **-motorhaube** *f* annular cowl **-mutter** *f* eye nut, annular nut, ring nut

Ring-nut *f* annular tee-slot **-ofen** *m* annular kiln, round-chamber kiln **-öse** *f* eye ring

Ringpendel-lager *n* (zweireihig) self-aligning double-row ball bearing **-tachometer** *n* ring-pendulum tachometer

Ring-platte *f* doughnut disk plate **-polschuh** *m* ring pole shoe **-porig** ring-porous **-prellplatte** *f* doughnut ring **-pulver** *n* ring-shaped gunpowder **-querschnitt** *m* transverse section

Ring-ratschenschlüssel *m* ratched box end wrench **-raum** *m* annulus, torus **-richtungshörer** *m* sound locator **-rillenlager** *n* radial ball bearing **-rohr** *n* built-up barrel **-röhre** (Beschleunigungsmaschine) doughnut, toroid **-säge** *f* annular saw **-sammler** *m* annular water box, round water collector

Ring-schale *f* beaker **-schäle** *f* internal annular shake (in wood) **-schaltung** *f* closed circuit arrangement **-scheibe** *f* ring target **-scherapparat** *m* ring shearing apparatus **-schieber** *m* revolving slide plate, sliding cylindrical valve **-schiftung** *f* cyclic shift **-schleifkontakt** *m* annular sliding contact **-schließung** *f* closing a ring **-schlitz** *m* circular slot **-schlüssel** *m* ring spanner box end wrench

Ring-schmierhängelager *n* ring-oiling drop hanger **-schmierhohlwellenlager** *n* ring-oiling quill bearing **-schmierlager** *n* ring-oiling bearing **-schmiersäulenarmlager** *n* ring-oiling post hanger **-schmierstehlager** *n* ring-oiling pillow block **-schmierung** *f* ring oiling

Ring-schnallverschluß *m* ring buckle **-schneide** *f* cupped gripping point **-schräglager** (selbsterhaltend, zweireihig) angular-contact single-row ball bearing **-schraube** *f* eyebolt **-schwimmer** *m* annular or concentric float **-sendung** *f* national hookup with transmissions from several stations **-sicherung** *f* lock ring **-sitz** *m* annular seat **-skala** *f* dial scale

Ringspalt *m* ring slot, annular clearance **-düse** *f* slotted rocket jet **-mischdüse** *f* ring-gap mixing nozzle **-zerstäuber** *m* annular clearance (atomizer)

Ring-spannung *f* circumferential stress, hoop tension **-sperre** *f* ring barrage **-sprengkapsel** *f* arming ring **-spule** *f* toroidal coil **-spurlager** *n* collar step bearing **-stab** *m* annular beam **-steg** *m* ring land **-steuerrad** *n* annular gear wheel

Ring-stirnelektrode *f* ring single earth electrode **-stoß** *m* gap (in a cylinder) **-strahler** *m* annular jet discharge (GEM) **-straße** *f* encircling road, perimeter track **-strecke** *f* loop line **-stutzen** *m* ring fitting **-symmetrie** *f* ring geometry **-thermoelement** *n* ring-shaped thermo-couple **-tonnenlager** *n* annular barrel bearing **-träger** *m* transverse girder **-transformator** *m* ring-type transformer

Ringtrichter *m* ring trumpet, ring-shaped horn, sound locator **-richtungshörer** *m* sound locator, annular cone, sound detector

Ring-trog *m* ring-shaped channel **-übertrager** *m* toroidal repeating coil ring transformer, torotoroideal transformer, repeating coil **-umfang** *m* circumference, ring periphery **-ungesättigt** cyclically unsaturated **-ventil** *n* mushroom valve, poppet valve, annular valve, ring valve **-verbindung** *f* ring-type joint, lacing (aviation), cyclic compound **-verkleidung** *f* engine ring cowling **-verschmelzung** *f* ring seal **-verspannung** *f* transverse ring bracing **-verstemmen** to caulk circularly **-visier** *n* ring sight

Ring-waage *f* ring balance manometer **-walzenmühle** *f* ring-roller mill **-walzwerk** *n* rolling mill for annular shapes **-welle** *f* annular wave **-wicklung** *f* ring winding **-wirbelverteilung** *f* ring vortex distribution **-wulst** *m* torus, tore, toroid

Ring-zahl *f* number of rings **-zähler** *m* ring counter **-zange** *f* round-nosed pliers **-zapfen** *m* ring pivot **-zieher** *m* ring extractor **-zugfestigkeit** (Rohr) *f* circumferential tensile strength, annular tensile strength **-zwirn** *m* ring twisting **-zylinderlager** *n* cylindrical ball bearing

rinken, einen Pfahl ~ to hoop a pile

Rinne *f* channel, groove, gutter, trough, ditch, gorge, drain, furrow, sluice, leak, chute, trench, flute; (Wasserlandebahn) channel **feste ~** fixed chute **Rinnen und Leitungen** chutes and ducts

rinnen to flow, run, leak, trickle **tropfenweise ~** to trickle

Rinnen-abschluß *m* stopping of branches **-förmiger Induktionsofen** ring-shaped induction furnace **-eisen** *n* channel or U-iron, trough-shaped iron **-kasten** *m* rain-water head, leader head **-ofen** (Induktionsofen) channel-type or core-type induction furnace **-schlacke** *f* spout slag **-schnauze** *f* spout nozzle **-schnitzel** *n* grooved slices **-sprosse** *f* gutter-shaped rolled (steel) member **-wäsche** *f* trough washer **-ziegel** *m* drain tile

Rinnsal *n* channel, gutter, run

Rinnstein *m* curbstone, gutter (stone), culvert, drain-pipe, sewer, (kitchen) sink

Rippe *f* rib, wing rib (aviation), serration, feather, fin, girth, vane, ripple, flute, corrugation, undulation **angegossene Rippen** fins cast integral **mit Rippen versehen** ribbed

Rippelblech *n* checkered plate

rippeln to ripple

Rippelwelle *f* ripple
rippen to rib, serrate **-abstand** *m* fin pitch, spacing of fins or ribs
Rippenanordnung *f*, **dichtstehende ~** close spacing of fins
Rippen-breite *f* rib or fin width **-decke** *f* groined ceiling **-endstück** *n* tail portion of rib **-feder** *f* ribbed spring leaf **-fläche** *f* cooling-fin area of cylinder **-gefäß** *n* ribbed tank **-gurt** *m* rib flange (aviation) **-heizfläche** *f* gilled pipe heating surface **-heizkörper** *m* radiator, finned heat changer **-heizrohr** *n* ribbed heating pipe, heating coil **-höhe** *f* depth of fin, fin width
Rippen-isolator *m* ribbed insulator **-kühler** *m* radiator **-nähen** *n* rib stitching **-naht** *f* rib stitching, seam **-oberfläche** *f* finned surface **-platte** *f* slab (in reinforced concrete), ribbed plate **-querschnitt** *m* ribbed cross section of frame
Rippenrohr *n* finned tube, gilled tube, externally ribbed or finned pipe, riffled tube **-kühler** *m* flanged- or gilled-tube radiator **-lufterhitzer** *m* gilled tube air preheater **-rauchgasvorwärmer** *m* economizer with ribbed pipes **-vorwärmer** *m* feed heater with ribbed pipes
Rippen-schraube *f* ribbed or feathered bolt **-spant** *n* rib frame **-spitze** *f* fin tip **-stahl** *m* multi-rib reinforcing bars
Rippensteg *m* web of rib **-stärke** *f* thickness of rib web
Rippen-streckmaterial *m* expanded material with ribs **-teilung** *f* fin pitch or spacing **-tiefe** *f* length of rib **-trichter** *m* ribbed funnel **-umriß** *m* outline of rib **-verdampfer** *m* ribbed evaporator **-versatz** *m* strip or partial stowing or packing **-vorderstück** *n* leading edge portion of rib **-walzenmühle** *f* tooth rolls **-wurzel** *f* fin root
Rippenzwischenraum *m* interfin space **Geschwindigkeit im ~** interfin velocity
Ripp-nadel *f* dial needle **-scheibe** *f* dial
Ripströmung *f* rip current
Risalit *m* projection, projecture
Risiko *n* risk **ein ~ decken** to cover a risk
Risinolsäure *f* ricinoleic acid
Riß *m* crack, flaw, fissure, scratch, tear, gap, crevice, draft (of drawings), plan, sketch, design, drawing, seam, check, projection (geom.), sectional plane, elevation (front or side) **~ im Leichtmetall, ~ im Stahl** spilly **quer durch das Kristallkorn verlaufender ~** transcrystalline crack **auf Risse prüfen** to inspect for cracks by Magnaflux
Riß-ausbreitung *f* crack propagation **-ausweitungskraft** *f* crack-extension-force
Rißbank *f* breakwater
Rißbildung *f* formation of cracks, cracking, alligatoring, fissuration **netzartige ~** alligator cracking
Risse in der Papierbahn web breaks
Riß-ebene *f* plane of projection **-empfindlichkeit** *f* susceptibility to cracking **-festigkeit** *f* crack strength, crack resistance **-formung auf der Oberfläche** surface cracking **-frei** flawless, free of cracks, flaws or tears **-härteprobe** *f* abrasion test, scratch test
rissig full of crevices, cracked, split, fissured, faulty **~ werden** to crack, get brittle
Rissigkeit *f* cracked place
Rissigwerden *n* clinking (in castings)
Riß-prüfung *f* magnaflux inspection **-tafel** *f* plane of projection **-tiefe** *f* depth of crack **-wachstum** *n* cut growth (rubber)
Ristorno *n* return of insurance premium
rittlings astride, straddling
Ritz *m* fissure, crack, crevice, scratch, slit, score **-barkeit** *f* susceptibility to scratching
Ritze *f* split, fissure, slit, crevice, interstice, gap, rift, crack, scratch
Ritzel *n* pinion, bevel gear, driver **~ für Handlangzug** hand pinion
Ritzel-antriebswelle *f* pinion drive shaft **-freilauf** *m* pinion free wheeling **-schalter** *m* pinion switch **-seite** *f* pinion side **-trieb** pinion drive
Ritzel- und Stirnradantrieb *m* pinion and spur-gear drive
Ritzel-verschraubung *f* pinion screw fastening **-vorschub** *m* pinion advance **-welle** *f* pinion shaft
ritzen to scratch, slit, crack
Ritzgerät *n* stylus recorder
Ritzhärte *f* sclerometric hardness, scratch hardness, abrasive hardness **-probe** *f* surface-scratching test, abrasive-hardness test **-prüfer** *m* scratch-hardness tester, sclerometer **-verfahren** *n* scratch test **-zahl** *f* scratch-hardness number
ritzig scratched, fissured
Ritz-maschine *f* scratching or scoring machine **-probe** *f* scratch test, abrasive hardness test **-spalt** *m* scratched slit **-stift** *m* style, stylus **-verfahren** *n* scratch method **-versuch** *m* scratch test
Rizinolsäure *f* ricinoleic acid
Rizinusöl *n* castor oil **-säure** *f* recinoleic (recinolic) acid
Robinson-brücke *f* frequency (-measuring) bridge **-system** *n* Robinson direction-finding system
Roboter *m* robot
Robotpilot *m* automatic pilot
robust sturdy
Robustheit *f* rigidity
Rochellesalz *n* sodium potassium tartrate, Rochelle salt **-kristall** *m* Rochelle salt crystal **-schwinger** *m* Rochelle salt transducer
Röchling-Rodenhauserofen *m* Röchling-Rodenhauser furnace (reservoir-type induction)
Rock *m* coat, skirt, dress
Rocken *m* distaff
Rockwell-härte *f* Rockwell hardness **-härteprüfung** *f* Rockwell-hardness test **-härtezahl** *f* Rockwell-hardness number
Rödel *m* rack stick **-balken** *m* side rail, wheel guide **-bund** *m* side rail lashing **-keil** *m* racking wedge
Rödeln *n* racking
Rödelung *f* guard rails
Rödelzange *f* side-rail clamp
Rodemaschine *f* uprooting machine, digger, lifter
roden to dig, lift, clear (land)
Rodinal *n* rodinal
Rogen(eisen)steingrube *f* oölitic iron mine
Rogenstein *m* oölite, roestone
Rogersit *m* rogersite
roh raw, rough, crude, gross, broad (radio tuning) **~ behauen** rough hewn **-es Formstück** blank (met.) **-er Funkazimut** observed radio

bearing **-es Gleichgewicht** rough balance **-e Stange** untreated pole, plain pole

rohabgeschliffen rough-ground

Roh-analyse *f* rough analysis, approximate analysis, coking test (of coal) **-antimon** *n* crude or unrefined antimony **-arbeit** *f* ore smelting **-aufbereitung** *f* preliminary preparation **-aufbrechen** *n* first breaking-up, raising-up **-bau** *m* carcase work **-baugerüst** *n* framework **-baumwolle** *f* cotton wool

Roh-bauxit *m* crude bauxite **-benzol** *n* crude benzol **-betrag** *m* gross amount **-blei** *n* crude lead **-block** *m* raw ingot, ingot **-boden** *m* subsoil **-bramme** *f* ingot slab, slab, ingot **-braunkohle** *f* raw, crude, or rough lignite **-breite** *f* grège width **-dichte** *f* gross density

Roheisen *n* crude iron, pig iron, pig **feinkörniges** ~ close-grained pig iron, close pig **graues** ~ gray pig iron, graphitic pig iron **halbiertes** ~ mottled pig iron **heißerblasenes** ~ hot-blast pig iron **phosphorsaures** ~ low-phosphorous pig iron **synthetisches** ~ synthetic pig iron **weißes** ~ white pig iron

Roheisen-ausbringen *n* pig-iron output **-darstellung** *f* manufacture of pig iron **-einsatz** *m* pig-iron charge **-einsatzkran** *m* hot metal charging crane **-einteilung** *f* classification of pig iron **-erzeugung** *f* pig-iron production **-erzeugungsmenge** *f* pig-iron output **-erzschmelzverfahren** *n* pig-and-ore process **-frischverfahren** *n* pig-iron purifying process **-gans** *f* iron pig **-gattung** *f* pig-iron brand, class of pig iron **-gießmaschine** *f* pig machine

Roheisen-karren *m* pig-iron barrow or truck **-marke** *f* pig-iron grade, pig-iron brand **-masseln** *pl* pigs **-mischer** *m* hot-metal mixer, metal mixer, hot-metal receiver, receiver mixer, blast-furnace mixer **-pfanne** *f* hot-metal ladle **-pfannenwagen** *m* hot-metal ladle and car **-rinne** *f* iron runner **-sorte** *f* pig-iron grade **-stück** *n* pig **-verband** *m* pig iron cartel **-verfahren** *n* pig process **-wagen** *m* ladle car **-zugabe** *f* pigging

Roheit *f* coarseness, rudeness

Roh-erdöl *n* crude petroleum **-ertrag** *m* gross proceeds **-erz** *n* raw ore, green ore, crude ore, mine ore **-film** *m* blank film, raw stock **-filter** *m* coarse filter **-filzpappe** *f* crude felt **-formel** *f* empirical formula **-frischen** *n* first refining **-frischperiode** *f* boiling stage, boil

Rohgang *m* irregular working, cold working (of blast furnace), abnormally fast drive or run ~ **des Hochofens** irregular working of the blast furnace

Rohgas *n* crude gas **-brenner** *m* crude gas burner

Roh-gewicht *n* gross weight **-gips** *m* gypsum rock **-glas** *n* crude glass **-glycerin** *n* raw or crude glycerin **-gold** *n* gold bullion **-gummi** *m* raw or unvulcanized rubber **-gummimilch** *f* (rubber) latex **-guß** *m* raw castings, undressed castings

Rohhaut *f* rawhide **-aufhänger** *m* rawhide suspender **-getriebe** *n* rawhide gear **-hammer** *m* rawhide hammer **-rad** *n*, **-ritzel** *n* rawhide pinion

Roh-helium *n* crude or raw helium **-holz** *n* unhewn timber **-holzziehstein** *m* rough-cored die **-kaolin** *n* raw kaolin **-kohle** *f* raw coal, run-of-the-mine coal **-koks** *m* coke residue **-kollodium** *n* plain collodion **-kresol** *n* crude cresol **-kupfer** *n* crude copper, blister copper **-last** *f* gross load, total load **-laufstreifen** *m* untreated rubber treads **-leinen** *n*, **-leinenstoff** *m* raw flax or linen, unbleached-linen cloth **-leistung** *f* gross power

Rohling *m* blank, unworked, unfinished or unfashioned piece or part **gegossener** ~ casting, metal object cast in a mold

Roh-luppe *f* puddle ball **-magnesit** *m* raw magnesite **-maß** *n* rough size **-masseln** *pl* foundry ingots, ingot metal **-material** *n* raw material, raw stock **-merzerisation** *f* mercerizing in the grey **-messing** *n* crude brass **-muffe** *f* pipe socket

Roh-naphtha *n* crude naphtha, crude petroleum **-naphthalin** *n* crude naphthalene **-niet** *m* undriven or unclaimed rivet **-ofen** *m* ore furnace, ore-smelting furnace **-öl** *n* crude oil, crude petroleum or naphtha

Rohöl-brenner *m* crude-oil burner **-schlepper** *m* internal-combustion tractor **-stabilisierung** *f* crude stabilization **-traktor** *m* internal-combustion tractor

Rohpapier *n* backing paper, body paper

Rohparaffin *n* slack wax, asphaltic base ~ **in Schuppenform** crude scale

Rohpetroleum *n* crude petroleum, crude oil, crude naphtha

Roh-planum *n* rough grading **-platte** *f* recording blank **-probe** *f* gross sample

Rohr *n* tube, pipe, duct, conduit, valve, piping, tubing, barrel, reed, flue ~ **der Brennerwand** burner wall tube ~ **an der Feuerbrücke** bridge wall tube ~ **mit Flanschen** flanged pipe ~ **zur Messung des statischen Druckes** static tube ~ **mit Vor- und Rücksprung-Verbindung** bell-and-spigot pipe **das** ~ **auswischen** to sponge out (gun) **ein** ~ **ziehen** to draw a tube or pipe ~ **zum Reibzylinder** oil pipe for small distributing cylinder ~ **zur Seitenmarke** sliding tube ~ **zur Taststange** feed control rod ~ **zum Walzenstuhl** oil pipe for roller carriage

Rohr, äußeres (inneres) ~ outer (inner) tube **erdverlegtes** ~ underground pipe **gußeisernes** ~ cast-iron pipe **hartgeschlossenes** ~ rigidly terminated tube **indisches** ~ rattan **irdenes** ~ earthenware pipe **nahtloses** ~ seamless tube, weldless tube **nahtlos gezogenes** ~ seamless drawn tube

Rohr, schmiedeeisernes ~ wrought-iron pipe **spiralgeschweißtes** ~ spirally welded tube **stumpfgeschweißtes** ~ butt-welded tube **überlappt geschweißtes** ~ lap-welded tube **zweiteiliges** ~ split pipe **das lange Feld des Rohres** chase of the gun barrel **gezogener Teil des Rohres** rifled part of barrel

Rohr-abnutzung *f* erosion of the bore **-abschneider** *m* pipe cutter **-abschnitt** *m* pipe section **-abstechbank** *f* pipe-slicing lathe **-abzweigstück** *n* branch T of a pipe **-anbau** *m* cane culture **-anfräser** *m* burring reamer **-angel** *f* bottleneck drawing end **-anlage** *f* piping tubing, piping unit **-anordnung** *f* pipe arrangement

Rohr-ansatz *m* socket **-anschluß** *m* pipe connection **-anschlußkasten** *m* conduit box **-anspitzmaschine** *f* sharpening machine for tubes **-armaturen** pipe fittings **-aufhängung** *f* (elastisch) tube hanger or support, elastic pipe suspension **-aufmessung** *f* star gauging **-aufweiter** *m* tube expander **-aufweitung** *f* tubing expansion

Rohr-ausbeuldorn *m* barrel-dent-removing tool **-ausgleicher** *m* tube compensator **-auskleidung** *f* pipe lining **-auskratzer** *m* tube scraper **-ausrichtvorrichtung** *f* pipe straightener **-bandagierung** *f* pipe wrapping or casing **-bauweise** *f* tubular construction **-bekleidung** *f* casing of a pipe **-biegemaschine** *f* pipe bending machine

Rohrbiegen *n* pipe or tube bending

Rohrbiege-prinzip *n* tube-bending principle **-werkzeug** *n* tube bender **-zange** *f* pipe-bending tongs

Rohrbiegmaschine *f* pipe-bending machine

Rohr-bildung *f* piping **-blatt** *n* reed (of clarinet) **-block** *m* round billet, tubing or piping action **-boden** *m* tube plate

Rohrbogen *m* tube turn, L (mach.), bend **-brücke** *f* tubular arch bridge

Rohr-bolzen *m* tubular pin or bolt **-bremse** *f* recoil brake, buffer brake **-bremsflüssigkeit** *f* fluid for filling recoil buffer **-bruch** *m* pipe fracture, burst, failure, or breakage **-bruchventil** *n* self-closing valve **-brücke** *f* bridge for supporting pipe

Rohrbrunnen *m* artesian well, cased well **-pumpe** *f* artesian-well pump

Rohr-buch *n* gun-history book **-bug** *m* swept bend **-bündel** *n* nest of boiler tubes **-bündel** *n* pipe assembly **-bürste** *f* duct-cleaning tool, brush flue or tube, cylindrical brush

Röhrchen *n* tube, capillary tube **-förmig** tubular **-kühler** *m* tubular radiator **-platte** *f* tubular plate **-pulver** *n* tubular-grain powder **-widerstand** *m* tube resistor

Rohr-dach *n* thatch **-dampfkessel** *m* tubular boiler **-detonierer** *m* burst in the bore **-dichter** *m* expander **-dichtmaschine** *f* caulking machine for pipes **-dichtungskegel** *m* spherical nipple

Rohrdipol *n* sleeve dipole **-antenne** *f* cylinder dipole antenna

Rohr-doppelnippel *n* nipple joint **-doppelsitzventil** *n* double-seated sleeve valve **-draht** *m* conduit wire **-drähte** *pl* armored wires **-durchführung** *f* bushing, pipe duct **-durchlaß** *m* pipe culvert **-durchmesser** *m* diameter of tube

Röhre *f* pipe, tube, spout, duct, stem (of a thermometer), valve, gauge, conduit **~ mit veränderlichem Durchgriff** variable-mu valve, tube, or amplifier, exponential tube, supercontrol tube, multi-mu tube, variable mutual-conductance valve **~ mit dunkelrotglühendem Faden** dull emitter valve **~ mit geschirmtem Gitter** screened-grid tube **~ mit variablem Verstärkungsfaktor** variable-mu valve or tube, exponential tube, supercontrol tube, multi-mu tube, variable mutual-conductance valve **~ negativen Widerstandes** dynatron oscillator **Braunsche ~** cathode-ray tube, electron-beam tube, Braun tube

Röhre, abgeschmolzene ~ sealed-off tube **anodenlose ~** plateless valve **direkt geheizte ~** directly heated valve **fremderregte ~** separately excited tube **fremdgesteuerte ~** master-excited tube **fußlose ~** loktal tube **gasgefüllte ~** gas-content tube, gaseous or gassy tube **harte ~** hard valve or tube, highly evacuated tube **hochbeheizte ~** bright (emitting) valve

Röhre, indirekt geheizte ~ indirectly heated valve or tube, cathode-heater tube, equipotential tube, heater-type tube **luftgekühlte ~** air-cooled tube **quetschfußfreie ~** loktal-base tube **rückgekoppelte ~** self-excited valve **schwach beheizte ~** dull (emitting) valve **selbsterregte ~, selbstgesteuerte ~** self-excited valve, self-excited or self-oscillatory tube (in a direct-drive circuit) **wassergekühlte ~** water-cooled tube **weiche ~** soft valve, ionic valve, gas-filled or gassy tube **zerlegbare ~** demountable tube

Röhre, ~ einstellen to bias a tube **~ mit fester Anode** stationary-anode tube **~ mit Elektronenbündelung** aligned-grid tube **~ mit harmonischer Gradation** high gamma tube **~ mit magnetischer Steuerung** permatron **~ für Distanzzünder** proximity fuse tube

Röhre, ~ mit allen Anschlüssen am Sockel single-ended tube **~ mit veränderlichem Durchgriff** variable mu valve, mu-tube (variable), mu-valve (variable) **~ mit verlängerter Wechselwirkung** extended-interaction tube **~ mit scharf gebündeltem Elektronenstrahl** gated beam tube **~ für Leitungen** linepipe **~ mit variabler Steilheit** super-control tube

Rohre, ~ aneinanderreihen to string pipes together **~ mit Gütevorschriften** superior quality tubes **~ in Sonderausführung** special quality tubes

Röhreholm *m* tubular spar

Rohreinwalzmaschine *f* tube heading machine

Rohrelevator *m* casing elevator

Röhren-abschleifmaschine *f* tube sandpapering machine **-alterung** *f* aging of vacuum tubes **-anlage** *f* tubing, piping **-artig** tubular **-aufwalzgerät** *n* tube-rolling and-flaring equipment **-aufwand** *m* tube expenditure **-auswalzvorrichtung** *f* tube expander **-bestückung** *f* tube line-up, tube complement **-bleche** *pl* tube plates **-bussole** *f* tubular compass

Röhren-charakteristik *f* characteristic of a thermionic valve, valve characteristic, vacuum-tube characteristic **-destillationsofen** *m* pipe still **-detektor** *m* (thermionic) valve detector, audion, vacuum-tube detector, crystal detector, galena detector **-elektrometer** *n* vacuum tube electrometer

Röhrenempfang *m* valve reception **~ mit gleichzeitiger Hoch- und Niederfrequenzverstärkung** dual reception, reflex reception

Röhrenempfänger *m* thermionic valve, galena receiver, valve or tube receiver **~ ohne Anodenbatterie** solodyne receiver

Röhren-entlüftung *f* tube ventilation **-fabrikation** *f* manufacture of tubing, tube making **-fahrt** *f* pipe line

Röhrenfassung *f* socket, antimicrophonic tube or valve holder, valve socket **federnde ~** cushioned socket or antimicrophonic tube or valve holder

Röhren-federmeßwerk *n* bourdon drive **-federsystem** *n* bourdon-tube system

Röhren-fernleitung *f* pipe line **-filter** *m* pipe filter **-formlampe** *f* festoon lamp **-förmig** tubular

Röhrenführung *f* pipe guide **~ und Verkabelung einer Start- und Landebahn** runway ducting and cabling

Röhrenfuß *m* base or socket of a tube, lamp, or valve **ungebördelter ~** re-entrant squash or press

Röhren-galvanometer *n* valve or tube galvano-

meter **-gang** *m* pipe line
Röhrengenerator *m* valve oscillator, vacuum(-tube) generator, thermionic oscillator, electron-tube generator, harmonic generator **quarzgesteuerter ~** crystal-controlled tube generator **~ zur Erzeugung von Oberschwingungen** harmonic generator
Röhren-geräusch *n* vacuum-tube noise (radio) **-glättwalzwerk** *n* rolling mill for smoothing tubes **-gleichrichter** *m* (vacuum-)tube rectifier, valve rectifier **-hals** *m* neck of tube **-halter** *m* clamp **-hänger** *m* tube hanger or support **-heizkörper** *m* calandria **-heizung** *f* tube heating (radio), filament supply **-holm** *m* tubular spar **-industrie** *f* tube industry, tube branch **-kabel** *n* conduit cable
Röhrenkapazität *f* interelectrode capacity (of thermionic tube), interelectrode capacitance, internal capacity **innere ~** interelectrode capacity (of thermionic tube), interelectrode capacitance, internal capacity
Röhren-kappe *f* top cap **-kennlinie** *f* characteristic of a thermionic valve, valve characteristic vacuum-tube characteristic, radio-tube performance chart **-kessel** *m* tubular boiler, tube boiler **-kippschaltung** *f* tube-tripping circuit, relaxation circuit **-klammer** *f* pipe clamp **-klingen** *n* microphonics **-kolben** *m* bulb of a tube, vessel or container of a tube or valve **-konduktanz** *f* transconductance
Röhrenkonstante *f* tube constant **charakteristische ~** parameter of a thermionic valve, vacuum-tube constant
Röhren-kontakte *pl* base-pin contacts **-koppelung** *f* intervalve linkage, intervalve coupling **-kühler** *m* tubular radiator, tubular cooler **-lafette** *f* tubular gun carriage **-lampe** *f* tubular lamp **-legung** *f* pipe laying **-leitung** *f* pipe line, piping, tubing **-libelle** *f* tubular level **-löscher** *m* tube quench
Röhren-lot *n* pipe solder **-lötzinn** *n* resin-cored solder (for pipes) **-magnet** *m* tubular magnet **-manometer** *n* Bourdon gauge **-mehraufwand** *m* tube complement **-meßbrücke** *f* tube factor bridge **-modulator** *m* vacuum-tube modulator **-muffe** *f* pipe socket **-nadel** *f* tubular needle **-ofen** *m* pipe still, tube heater, tube furnace **-oszillator** *m* vacuum-tube oscillator, valve oscillator **-preßteller** *m* stem-press of the tube
Röhren-prüfapparat *m* pipe-testing apparatus **-prüfer** *m* tube tester, tube checker **-prüfgerät** *n* valve-testing outfit (wireless) **-prüfschalter** *m* tube-testing switch (radio) **-prüfung** *f* (im Betriebe) filament-activity test **-pulver** *n* a type of explosive (designed with maximum surface area, to increase speed of combustion), tubular powder, perforated powder **-rauschen** *n* valve or tube noise, thermal agitation of a tube, tube hiss, valve rustle **-rost** *m* tubular grate
Röhrenschaltung *f* circuit **~ mit induktiver Rückkoppelung** Hartley circuit **~ mit kapazitiver Rückkoppelung** Colpitts circuit **~ mit magnetischer Rückkoppelung** Meissner circuit
Röhren-schelle *f* clamp **-schieber** *m* cylindrical slide **-schmelzung** *f* tube melting **-schwebungsempfänger** *m* valve heterodyne receiver **-schweißtakter** *m* electronic timer
Röhren-sender *m* valve transmitter, vacuum-tube transmitter, thermionic oscillator, radio transmitter **-sockel** *m* valve or tube base, valve socket **-spannungsmesser** *m* (vacuum-)tube voltmeter, amplifying voltmeter **-sperrung** *f* cutoff of tube **-stativ** *n* telescope tripod **-stauchpresse** *f* pipe-jumping or upsetting press **-steilheit** *f* mutual conductance of tube **-stempel** *m* press or squash of a valve or tube
Röhrensteuerung *f* electronic control **~ der Gabel** tube control of the fork
Röhren-stift *m* tube pin **-stoß** *m* joint of tube **-stimme** *f* bronchophony **-straße** *f* tube rolling train **-streifen** *m* tube strip, skelp **-strom** *m* tube current **-summer** *m* electron-tube generator, vacuum-tube oscillator
Röhren-tour *f* string of casing **-träger** *m* tube or pipe support **-trockner** *m* rotary drier **-tunnel** *m* tube tunnel, tube **-übersteuerung** *f* tube overloading **-vakuum** *n* calandria-type pan **-verbindung** *f* pipe fitting **-verdampfer** *m* tubular vaporizer **-verkupp(e)lung** *f* return bend **-verstärker** *m* valve amplifier, (vacuum-)tube amplifier, thermionic amplifier, amplifying tube **-verstärkung** *f* tube amplification
Röhrenvoltmesser, selbstgleichrichtender ~ self-rectifying tube voltmeter
Röhrenvoltmeter *n* valve voltmeter, (vacuum-) tube voltmeter, thermionic voltmeter, amplifying voltmeter **~ mit direkter Ablesung** direct-reading valve voltmeter
Röhren-vorwärmer *m* preheater (boiler) **-walzen** *n* tube rolling **-walzwerk** *n* tube rolling mill **-wattmeter** *n* valve or tube wattmeter **-werk** *n* system of piping, tube mill, tubeworks **-wert** *m* tube characteristic **-wicklung** *f* tube-shaped or cylindrical winding **-widerstand** *m* tube resistance **-winderhitzungsapparat** *m* continuous-pipe stove
Röhren-wippe *f* Kipp relay, trigger circuit **-wulst** *f* tubular tore **-zange** *f* tube pliers, long-nose pliers **-zeitschalter** *m* electronic timer **-zelle** *f* tracheid **-ziehbank** *f* tube-drawing bench **-zinn** *n* (Lötzinn) cored solder **-zug** *m* conduit **-zündung** *f* electronic ignition system **-zwischenstecker** *m* valve or tube adapter
Rohrerhöhung *f* angle of elevation, quadrant elevation
Rohrerhöhungs-trommel *f* quadrant-elevation drum **-winkel** *m* elevation of barrel under firing-table conditions
Rohr-fahrstuhl *m* casing elevator **-fänger** *m* pipe dog **-fangglocke** *f* casing bowl **-fangtüte** *f* bell socket
Rohrfeder *f* bourdon tube **-druckmesser** *m* tube spring manometer, Bourdon-tube pressure gauge
Rohr-fender *m* hazel-rod fender **-fernleitung** *f* pipe line **-fittings** *pl* pipe fittings **-flansch** *m* pipe flange or socket **-förderhaken** *m* casing hook **-förmig** tubular **-formmaschine** *f* pipe-molding machine **-formstück** *n* pipe fitting or connection **-fräser** *m* burring reamer **-führung** *f* pipe layout **-futter** *n* pipe linings **-gerüst** *n* tubular frame
Rohrgewinde *n* pipe thread, pipe stock, dies, taper thread **-bohrer** *m* pipe tap **-schneidemaschine** *f* pipe-threading machine **-schneider**

m pipe tap **-schutzkappe** *f* pipe-thread protector

Rohr-greifer *m* catcher **-größe** *f* size of pipe **-guß** *m* pipe castings **-haken** *m* pipe hook, wall hook, pipe cramp **-haltehebel** *m* barrel-locking lever

Rohrhalter *m* pipe support ~ (Verbindung mit der Rücklaufbremse) coupler-key recess (artil.) crosshead key

Rohrhalterung *f* tube mounting

Rohr-härte *f* chorded cooling tube **-heber** *m* casing lifter, pipe lifter **-herstellung** *f* tube manufacture **-holm** *m* tubular spar **-holz** *n* cane **-hülse** *f* tube socket **-jack** *f* jacket **-innennietung** *f* inside tube riveting **-inneres** *n* bore

Rohr-kaliber *n* inside diameter of pipe or tube **-kanal** *m* pipe line **-kappe** *f* threaded cap **-kern** *m* tubular core **-keilkranz** *m* casing spider **-klaue** *f* muzzle guide (artil.) **-knarren** *pl* ratchet drills **-knie** *n* pipe elbow **-kolonne** *f* line of pipes **-kondensator** *m* tubular capacitor **-kopf** *m* cap or casing head, bradenhead **-kopfgasolin** *n* casing-head gasoline

Rohr-kratzer *m* pipe scraper **-krebsfänger** *m* bulldog spear **-kreuz** *n* cross-fitting **-krone** *f* manifold **-kugelstütze** *f* angle union **-krümmer** *m* (pipe) bend, bend pipe, pipe elbow or knee **-krümmung** *f* radius of pipe bend **-kühler** *m* tubular radiator **-kühlung** *f* barrel cooling **-kupplung** *f* coupling

Rohr-lager *n* conduit support **-länge** *f* length of pipe, barrel length **-legearbeit** *f* plumbing **-legebock** *m* shear legs **-legung** *f* piping, pipe laying **-längeneffekt** *m* long tube effect **-lasche** *f* tube connecting sleeve **-lauf** *m* bore **-leiter** wave guide (radio, radar)

Rohrleitung *f* pipe, conduit, tubing, pipe line, manifold, piping, pipe run ~ **zur raschen Entleerung** blowdown piping **verstopfte** ~ plugged line

Rohrleitungs-entwässerung *f* drainage **-filter** *n* pipe filter **-gehäuse** *n* pipe housing **-netz** *n* pipe system **-plan** *m* layout of pipes, pipe plan **-schema** *n* pipe diagram **-stück** *n* tubular conductor line, pipe fitting **-system** *n* piping system

Rohrloch *n* tube hole **-prüfung mit Gestänge** drill-stem test

Rohr-lot *n* pipe solder **-löter** *m* blowpipe solderer **-mantel** *m* barrel jacket **-maß** *n* tube dimension **-mast** *m* tubular pole, tube pole **-material** *n* tubular goods **-matte** *f* reed mat **-montage** *f* pipe laying, piping **-muffe** *f* (pipe) socket, pipe joint

Rohrmühle *f* tube mill, rod mill ~ **mit Kraftantrieb** belt-power cane mill ~ **mit Wasserkraftantrieb** water-power cane mill

Rohr-mündung *f* muzzle, barrel muzzle **-mutter** *f* pipe nut **-netz** *n* piping, pipe system, pipe conduit **-niet** *m* tubular rivet

Rohrnippel *m* pipe nipple ~ **für Verbindung durch Überwurfmutter** union nipple

Rohr-nut *f* tube slot **-öffnung** *f* tube aperture **pfeife** *f* reed pipe **-platte** *f* tube sheet

Rohrpost *f* pneumatic (dispatch) tube, letter shoot ~ **für die Beförderung der Gesprächsblätter oder Gesprächszettel** pneumatic-tube ticket distributor **durch** ~ by tube **einzügige** ~ single-duct conduit **mehrzügige** ~ multiple-duct conduit **nach oben verjüngte** ~ tapered-tube pole **zylindrische** ~ parallel-tube pole

Rohrpost-anlage *f* pneumatic conveyor, pneumatic-tube plant, pneumatic tubes **-büchse** *f* (pneumatic dispatch) carrier **-empfangsstelle** *f* pneumatic-tube receiving station **-kapsel** *f* pneumatic post capsule **-weiche** *f* deflector **-sendestelle** *f* pneumatic-tube dispatching station **-stutzen** *m* nozzle **-zettelverteiler** *m* pneumatic-ticket-distribution position **-zustellung** *f* delivery by pneumatic post

Rohr-presse *f* extrusion press for tubes **-pressung** *f* collapse of casing **-preßvorrichtung** *f* drive appliance **-putzturbine** *f* tube cleaner, coke knocker **-querschnitt** *m* tube diameter **-querträger** *m* tubular cross member

Rohr-rahmen *m* tubular chassis or frame **-reduktionsstück** *n* pipe reducer **-reduziermaschine** *f* pipe reducing machine **-reibung** *f* pipe friction **-reibungsglocke** *f* corrugated friction socket, friction socket **-reibungswiderstand** *m* pipe friction **-reiniger** *m* cleaning staff, barrel cleaner **-reißer** *m* tube burst **-richtmaschine** *f* tube straightening machine **-ring** *m* ring of an anchor **-rohlinge** *pl* tube rounds, tube squares

Rohrrücklauf *m* barrel recoil, gun recoil, tube recoil **-bremse** *f* recoil brake, buffer

Rohr-rumpf *m* tubular fuselage **-sattel** *m* pipe saddle, clamp, clip, or hanger **-schacht** *m* pipe-cased shaft **-schäftung** *f* tube jointing **-schäftungshülse** *f* tube-connecting sleeve **-schalter** *m* pipe switch **-schaltung** *f* casing hook

Rohr-scheibe *f* tubing disk **-scheitel** *m* pipe crown **-schelle** *f* pipe saddle, clamp, clip, or hanger, wall hook, wall clamp, pipe strap, casing clamp **-schellenverbindung** *f* sleeve joint of tubing **-schieber** *m* cylindrical slide valve, sleeve valve **-schiene** *f* rondle, muck bar

Rohrschlange *f* coil of pipe, spiral coil of pipe, spiral tube, worm (of a still) ~ **für Dampf** steam coil

Rohrschlangen-triebwerk *n* spiral tube piston unit **-verdampfer** *m* coil-type evaporator

Rohr-schlitten *m* barrel slide (artil.) **-schlitzantenne** *f* cylindrical slot antenna **-schlitzer** *m* casing ripper, casing ripper, casing splitter **-schlosser** *m* pipefitter **-schlüssel** *m* pipe wrench, socket wrench **-schneidemaschine** *f* shredder **-schneider** *m* casing cutter, casing knife, pipe cutter, tube cutter **-schneidkluppe** *f* pipe stocks **-schoner** *m* barrel protector **-schraubstock** *m* pipe vise, tube vise

Rohr-schuh *m* casing shoe **-schuß** *m* length of pipe **-schütze** tubular valve **-schutzkappe** *f* valve-protecting cap **-schweißmaschine** *f* tube welding machine **-schweißung** *f* tube welding, pipe welding **-schwimmer** *m* casing float **-seele** *f* bore of the gun, inside diameter **-sicher** bore-safe

Rohrsicherheit *f* unarmed condition of fuse in gun barrel, bore-safe fuse

Rohr-siel *n* pipe culvert or passage through a levee **-sitz** *m* cane seat **-spanner** *m* box spanner **-spinne** *f* manifold **-spirale** *f* tube coil

Rohrständer *m* steel tubes used for uprights of roof standard, tubular pole, casing support **-abdichtung** *f* cap (inserted over pipe, at point where latter penetrates roofs, to prevent entrance of water)

Rohrstauch- und Muffenmaschine *f* pipe expanding and flanging machine

Rohr-stechbeitel *m* socket chisel **-steckling** *m* cutting **-steckschlüssel** *m* socket wrench **-stemmeisen** *n* beading hand tool **-stock** *m* cane **-stopfen** *m* tube plug **-stopfstange** *f* tube plug ram

Rohrstoß *m* pipe joint **-bank** *f* tube push bench

Rohr-strang *m* pipe line (conduit), pipe string **-strebe** *f* tube stay, prop **-strecker** *m* casing straightener **-streifen** *m* skelp, strip (for forming tubes) **-strömung** *f* pipe flow

Rohrstück, T-förmiges ~ cross **kurzes ~ auf das der Schlauch aufgezogen wird** hose liner

Rohr-stummel *m* hollow bolt **-stütze** *f* barrel support **-stutzen** *m* socket, tubulure, reducing pipe, taper, tuyère, short piece of pipe (serving as an opening, outlet, socket, or connection), nipple, short cylindrical piece, bush, sleeve **-teiler** *m* cut-off attenuator **-thermoelement** *n* pipe thermocouple **-thermograph** *m* tubular thermograph **-thermometer** *n* tubular thermometer **-tour** *f* string of casing **-träger** *m* tubular girder **-tragwerke** *pl* tubular structures **-treibbirne** *f* casing swage

Rohr- und Rohrhirsemühle *f* cane-and-sorghum mill

Rohrventil *n* poppet valve

Rohrverbindung *f* pipe joint connection, or coupling ~ **mit Dehnungsausgleich** pipe expansion joint

Rohrverbindungs-hülse *f* tube-jointing or tube-connecting sleeve **-schelle** *f* pipe clamp fitting **-stück** *n* fitting

Rohr-verengung *f* narrowing the tube **-verlegböcke** *pl* pipe laying jacks **-verlegung** *f* pipe relaying **-verschalung** *f* casing, jacket **-verschluß** *m* tube closing, pipe closer, pipe seal

Rohrverschraubung *f* screw(ed) pipe joint or coupling, bolted pipe joint, union ~ **mit T-Stück** union T

Rohr-verstopfung *f* pipe clogging or choking **-verteiler** *m* manifold, pipe manifold **-verteilergrube** *f* manifold girt **-verwerfung** *f* collapsed casing **-verzweigung** *f* branching of the pipe **-wagen** *m* traveling carriage (artil.), casing wagon (dolly) **-walzapparat** *m* tube expander **-walzen** *n* tube rolling **-walzer** *m* pipe roller **-walzwerk** *n* tube rolling mill

Rohrwand *f* wall of pipe, tube sheet or plate, bore, inside diameter **-beobachtungsgerät** *n* bore searcher **-stein** *m* (Kessel) baffle plates with protecting bricks

Rohrwärmegrad-messer *m* tubular thermometer **-schreiber** *m* tubular thermograph

Rohr-weiche *f* tube switch **-weite** *f* internal diameter of tube or pipe, caliber **-weiter** *m* flue expander **-welle** *f* dielectric wave **-widerstandsziffer** *f* pipe flow, resistance coefficient **-wiege** *f* cradle (artil.) **-winkel** *m* angle tube for hose **-wischer** *m* barrel cleaner

Rohr-zange *f* pipe wrench, pipe tongs **-zeiger** *m* gun-barrel reference pointer **-ziehen** *n* pulling (the casing) **-ziehpresse** *f* extrusion press **-zucker** *m* sucrose, cane sugar **-zug** *m* tubing, tube drawing **-zuleitung** *f* tube feeder

Rohsaftpülpefänger *m* raw-juice pulp catcher

Roh-schiene *f* muck bar, muck iron, puddled iron **-schienenpaket** *n* fagot, muck-bar pile **-schienenwalze** *f* puddle-bar roll **-schlacke** *f* raw slag, ore slag **-schliff** *m* semi-pulp **-schlüssel** *m* key blank **-schmelze** *f* melt (met.) **-schmelzen** *n* raw smelting, ore smelting **-schwefel** *m* crude sulfur **-schwelle** *f* nonimpregnated sleeper

Roh-seide *f* raw silk, grège **-sieb** *n* coarse filter **-silber** *n* crude silver **-sohle** *f* crude brine **-spaltbenzin** *n* cracked gasoline **-spießglanzerz** *n* kermesite **-spiritus** *m* unrefined spirit **-stahl** *m* raw steel, natural steel **-stahleisen** *n* steel pig, pig iron for making steel **-stein** *m* first matte **-steinschlacke** *f* coarse metal slag

Rohstoff *m* raw material, raw stocks ~ **für Kracking** cracking stock

Rohstoff-grundlage *f* basic stocks of raw materials **-lage** *f* raw material supply **-not** *f* shortage of raw materials

Roh-strecker *m* gill-box minder **-stück** *n*, **-teil** *m* blank **-ton** *m* grège, unburned (plastic) clay **-uhrwerk** *n* movement in blank **-viskose** *f* raw viscose

Rohwasser *n* natural water **-pumpe** *f* pump for untreated water **-verdampfer** *m* untreated-water evaporator **-wichte** *f* apparent solid volume

Roh-wismut *n* raw or crude bismuth **-zink** *n* crude zinc, spelter

Rohzucker-erstprodukt *n* first raw sugar **-füllmasse** *f* raw masse-cuite

Rohzustand *m* raw or crude state

Roll-apparat *m* re-winder **-backe** *f* rolling die, roller jaw

Rollbahn *f* rocking path, gravity (roller) conveyor, taxi way (aviat.) **-ausrundungen** *pl* taxiway fillets **-tischsandstrahlgebläse** *n* rolling-table-type sandblast machine

Roll-ballfahrgestell *n* rolling ball banding gear **-band** *n* roller conveyor **-bandmaß** *n* roll tape measure **-bank** *f* jaw-rolling machine **-baum** *m* capstan **-bewegung** *f* rolling motion **-bock** *m* rubber-tired auxiliary gun carriage for heavy pieces, rolling fixture **-brücke** *f* swing bridge

Röllchen *n* roller **-platte** *f* rosette (Manchester) plate

Roll-dämpfung *f* rolling-damping **-deck** *n* landing deck

Rolle *f* (Walze) roller, cylinder; (Drahtrolle) coil; (Spule) reel, spool; (am Flaschenzug) pulley; (Drehrolle) mangle; roll, list, register, barrel aileron roll (aviation), sheave, sprocket, file wrapper, file, docket ~ **links** roll to the left ~ **rechts** roll to the right **feste** (am Ort bleibende) ~ simple fixed pulley, upper block **langsame** ~ slow roll **gerissene** ~ horizontal spiral (aviation) **getriebene** ~ live roller **gußeiserne** ~ cast-iron roller **schnelle** ~ flick roll **ungesteuerte** ~ horizontal spiral (aviation)

rollen to taxi, trundle, curl (of film)

Rollen, horizontales ~ Dutch roll

Rollen *pl* casters **angetriebene** ~ live rollers **lose** ~ idle rollers

Rollen-achslager axle bearings **-acht** *f* figure of eight flown while rolling (aerobatics) **-apparat** *m* multiplying-lever extensometer **-ausstoß** *m* roller ejector

Rollenbahn *f* gravity-roller conveyer, roller

train, gravity roll carrier, curved rocker, train of rollers ~ **mit Bundrollen** flanged-roller gravity conveyer ~ **mit schrägliegendem Plattenbandförderer** gravity-roller conveyer with inclined-slat-platform conveyer ~ **mit versetzten Rollen** gravity-roller conveyer with herringbone arrangement of rollers, gravity conveyer with staggered rollers **dreigleisige** ~ three-rail gravity-roller conveyer **übereinander angeordnete** ~ overlapping roller conveyer **zweigleisige** ~ two-rail gravity conveyer

Rollenbahn-spirale *f* spiral-roller conveyer, roller spiral **-stütze** *f* roller-conveyer jack

Rollen-band *n* roller conveyor, gravity conveyor **-blech** *n* roll sheet iron **-bock** *m* roller or pulley block **-bohrer** *m* drill with ferrule **-bolzen** *m* roller pin, stud for ball bearing

rollend rolling, curling **-e Abwicklung** *f* rolling contact **-er Angriff** rolling attack (aviation) **-es Material** rolling stock **-e Reibung** rolling friction, sliding friction **in -en Wellen** in waves

Rollen-doppelgelenk (G-Wagen) universal joint **-egge** *f* Norwegian or revolving harrow **-einhebevorrichtung** *f* reel-lifting device **-elektrode** *f* contact roller, roller **-fenster** *n* roller film gate **-feuchtmaschine** *f* roll damper **-förderanlage** *f* roller-conveying installation **-freilauf** overrunning clutch **-futter** *n* roller chuck

Rollen-gegenlager *n* roller turner **-gelenk** *n* universal joint **-gerüst** *n* water table **-gewicht** *n* pulley weight **-halter** *m* tape roll holder **-hängelager** *n* roller-bearing drop hanger **-hebel** *m* roller lever **-höhe** *f* sheave height

Rollen-käfig *m* (roller) cage **-kasten** *m* roller box **-kern** *m* roll (round) core **-kette** *f* roller chain **-kettenrad** *n* roller-chain sprocket **-klinke** *f* roller pawl, pawl with roller **-kloben** *m* pulley block, block **-kontaktstange** *f* trolley pole **-kopf** *m* trolley head **-korblager** *n* pin bearing **-kranz** *m* roller-carriage optical apparatus **-kreis** *m* gyroscopic roll (aerobatics) **-kuppelung** *f* roller clutch **-kurbel** *f* roller lever

Rollenlager *n* roller bearing, roller thrust bearing, roller race **elastisches** ~ flexible roller bearing

Rollenlager-kette *f* steel-bushed roller chain **-stahl** *m* roller-bearing steel

Rollen-lagerung *f* roller bearing **-laufbahn mit Gummiüberzug** rubber tread of a pad roller **-laufkranz** *m* roller race **-laufwerk** *n* roller gear **-lünette** *f* roller V-rest **-mühle** *f* crushing rollers **-nachschweißung** *f* continuous welding **-nummer** *f* docket or register number **-nute** *f* groove of pulley

Rollen-papier *n* counter reel, endless paper **-quetsche** *f* squeegee **-rest** *m* reel stump (print.) **-richtmaschine** *f* roll straightener, straightening rolls **-rille** *f* groove of pulley **-satinage** *f* web-calandered paper

Rollen-schaft *m* roll shaft **-schaltwerk** *n* roller ratchet mechanism **-scheibe** *f* chain sheave **-schlagkupplung** *f* roller striking clutch **-schnekke** *f* volute **-schranke** *f* sliding barrier **-schrittverfahren** *n* step-by-step seam welding **-schrittverfahren** *m* (Schweißen) intermittent seam welding

Rollen-schweißmaschine *f* roll-welding equipment **-schweißung** *f* roll welding **-setzstock** *m* roller steady **-spiel** *n* roller clearance **-ständer** *m* roller vat **-stehlager** *n* roller-bearing pillow block **-stern** *m* reel star (print.) **-stößel** *m* roller shaft (for cam)

Rollenstromabnehmer *m* trolley ~ **für Fahrdraht in Gleismitte** axial trolley ~ **für seitlichen Fahrdraht** nonaxial trolley

Rollen-tasterkluppe *f* roller key clip **-teilung** *f* roller pitch **-tischsandstrahlgebläse** *n* roller-table sandblast machine **-träger** *m* trolley harp **-wagen** *m* bogie-wheel suspension frame, rolling truck **-widerstand** *m* rolling resistance **-zahn** *m* roller tooth **-zug** *m* block, pulley block, tackle, block and tackle

Roller *m* roller, buckshot, calenderer

Roll-faß *n* roller vat, rolling barrel, tumbling barrel, mill barrel **-faßanlage** *f* tumbling mill **-feld** *n* manoeuvring area (aviat.) **-feldringstraße** *f* perimeter track **-film** *m* roll film **-fläche** *f* area of roller bed **-flasche** *f* cylindrical bottle **-flügel** *m* fowler flap, wing rotor **-folieneinrichtung** *f* reeled foil mechanism **-fuß** *m* caster **-gabelschlüssel** *m* Swedish wrench

Rollgang *m* table roller, roll table, roller bed, edge runner **nicht betriebsfähiger** ~ dead roller bed ~ (Schwerkraftförderer) *m* roller conveyor

Rollgang-führer *m* roll-table foreman **-gestell** *n* roller conveyor frame

Roll-geld *n* trucking charges **-genehmigung** *f* taxi clearance (aviation) **-gerade** *f* straight line along which a circle rolls when a point upon one of its radii is describing a trochoid **-geschwindigkeit** *f* landing speed roll rate (g/m), taxying speed **-gewicht** *n* take-off weight (of an aircraft **-giermoment** *n* roll-end-yaw factor **-glasschneider** *m* wheel glass cutter, glass-cutting wheel **-gut** *n* transport goods **-halteort** *m* taxi holding-position **-holz** *n* rolling pin

rollig unfixed

Roll-jalousie *f* hinged curtain, roller blind **-kalander** *m* super calender **-kardenrauhmaschine** *f* teasel-raising machine **-kassette** *f* film-roll dark slide **-keilschütz** *n* vertical trapezoidal sluice **-kette** *f* block chains **-kies** *m* round gravel **-klampe** *f* fair-lead (naut.)

Rollkolben *m* case, pulley, pulley block, drum or sheave **-verdichter** *m* rotary piston compressor

Rollkörner *pl* (mitlaufende Drehbankspitze) live center

Rollkreis-durchmesser *m* pitch diameter **-schwingung** *f* type A magnetron oscillation

Roll-kran *m* bogie crane, movable or traveling crane **-kranz** *m* rotation roller path **-kreis** *m* cycloidal path (of electrons) **-kufe** *f* rocker **-kugelkranz** *m* ball race **-kumulus** *m* roll cumulus, cumulo-stratus (clouds) **-kurve der Ellipse** roulette of an ellipse

Roll-laden *m* revolving shutter, roller blind **-lager** *n* pulley bearing, roller bearing **-leiter** *f* rolling ladder **-loch** *n* mill chute **-manöver** *n* taxiing **-maß** *n* rolling tape measure **-material** *n* (railroad) rolling stock **-meißel** *m* roller bit, rack bit **-moment** *n* rolling moment

Rollo *n* window shade

Roll-ofen *m* roller-type heating furnace, continuous-heating furnace **-pfanne** *f* roller seat **-ponton** *n* caisson or rolling lock gate **-prüfstand** *m* chassis dynamometer **-rad** *n* bed drive pinion, main pinion **-rauhmaschine** *f* roller-gig **-reibung** *f* rolling friction **-reifenfaß** *n* iron-hooped drum **-ring** *m* roller cage

Roll-schein *m* permit to taxi aircraft (aviation) **-schere** *f* circular shears **-schermesser** *n* revolving or circular shears, roll-shearing knives **-schicht** *f* upright course (bricks set on end) **-schiene** *f* sliding rail **-schlitten** *m* roller guide **-schütz** *n* rolling vertical-lift gate, sluice, or valve (trucktype) **-schütze** fixed wheel leaf gate, roller gate **-schweller** *m* crescendo pedal (organ)

Roll-stabilität *f* rolling stability **-stanze** *f* rolling press **-stein** *m* boulder **-straße** *f* taxiway **-strecke** *f* rolling distance, run **-streckenstreifen** *m* taxiing strip **-stücke** *pl* debris, rubble **-tasche aus Stoff für Werkzeug** canvas tool roll **-tisch** *m* roll-out table, run-out table, wheeled stand

Roll-tombak *m* sheet brass in rolls, red metal in rolls **-tor** *n* sliding door **-torschranke** *f* rolling gate or barrier **-treppe** *f* escalator **-tuch** *n* roller blind (phot.) roll shutter

Rollung *f* rotatory movement (of the eye)

Roll-vorhang *m* roller blind, curtain-type shutter (radiator) **-vorrichtung** *f* rolling-up device

Rollwagen *m* (farm) truck, block-carrying truck **~ mit Holzrädern** wooden-wheel truck

Rollwalze *f* roller squeeze

Rollweg *m* taxiway, take-off strip **Landung mit kurzem ~** short-stop landing

Rollwerk *n* undercarriage, landing gear

Rollwiderstand *m* rolling friction, resistance to rolling, drag when taxiing, resistance to taxiing

Rollwinkel *m* angle of roll

römische, ~ Fläche Roman surface **~ Kerze** Roman candle, magnesium torch, smoke pot

Rommel *f* rolling or tumbling barrel, mill barrel

rommeln to tumble

Ronde *f* circle, disk, ronde

Rondell *f* circle, disk

Rondell *n* cup, dome

Rondellennickel *m* nickel rondelles

Rondengang *m* rounds (mil.)

Rongalit-Pottasche-Verfahren Rongalite-potash process

Roneusil *n* stainless steel

Röntgen *n* roentgen (unit), radio **-analyse** *f* X-ray analysis **-anlage** *f* X-ray equipment **-apparat** *m* X-ray apparatus **-aufnahme** *f* radiograph, X-ray photograph or picture, skiagraph **-aufnahmeverfahren** *n* radiography **-ausrüstung** *f* radiographic equipment **-bestrahlung** *f* radiotherapy, roentgenotherapy **-beugungsaufnahme** *f* X-ray diffraction exposure or picture **-beugungsbild** *n* X-ray diffraction pattern

Röntgenabsorptionskontinuum *n* X-ray absorption band **-spektrum** *n* X-ray absorption spectrum

Röntgen-aufnahmetechnik *f* roentgenography **-belichtungseinheit** *f* radiographic exposure unit **-beugung** *f* x-ray diffraction

Röntgenbeugungs-gerät *n* X-ray diffractometer **-methode** *f* X-ray diffraction method

Röntgen-bild *n* radiograph, X-ray photograph or picture, exograph **-blitzinterferenz** *f* X-ray interference **-bremsstahl** *m* roentgen rays caused by collision and checking **-dermatitis** *f* radiodermatitis, X-ray dermatitis **-diagnostik** *f* radio diagnostics

Röntgen-dosismeter *n* X-ray dosimeter **-durchleuchtung** *f* radioscopy **-einheit** *f* roentgen (unit) **-einrichtung** *f* roentgen-ray installation, X-ray outfit **-falte** *f* high-gloss photographic paper **-feinstruktur** *f* X-ray structure **-impuls** *m* x-ray pulse

röntgenisieren to treat with X-rays

Röntgen-kunde *f*, **-lehre** *f* radiology, science of roentgen rays or X rays

Röntgenlicht *n* X ray **spektrale Zusammensetzung des Röntgenlichts** the X-ray spectrum

Röntgen-messer *m* roentgenometer **-metallographie** *f* metal radiography, radiometallography, X-ray metallography

Röntgenogramm *n* radiograph

Röntgenograph *m* X-ray photograph, skiagraph

Röntgenographie *f* radiography

röntgenographisch radiographic

Röntgenologe *m* radiologist

Röntgenologie *f* radiology, roentgenology

röntgenologisch radiological

Röntgenphotographie *f* radiophotography

Röntgenprüfung *f* X-ray examination, radiographic inspection, radiography, radiology **~ durchführen** to test by means of X rays

Röntgenröhre *f* X-ray tube, roentgen tube **~ mit Heizkathode** hot-cathode X-ray tube, Coolidge tube **fensterlose ~** windowless X-ray tube

Röntgenrohrkörper *m* bulb or body of the X-ray tube

Röntgenschichtverfahren *n* laminography, body section radiography

Röntgenschirm-bilddunkelkammerkraftwagen *m* mobile X-ray darkroom **-bildgerät** *n* photofluorograph, photo-röntgen unit

Röntgen-spektrogramm *n* radiograph **-spektrograph** *m* X-ray spectrograph **-spektralanalyse** *f* X-ray analysis **-spektrum** *n* X-ray spectrum

Röntgenstrahl *m* X-ray, roentgen ray **-benutzung** *f* use of X-rays

Röntgenstrahlen-aufnahme *f* exograph **-ausbruch der Sonne** (Astron.) solar x-ray radiation **-beugungsbild** *n* X-ray diffraction pattern **-bündel** *n* X-ray beam **-feld** *n* X-ray coverage **-härtemesser** *m* penetrometer, qualimeter **-kristalldichtemethode** *f* X-ray crystal density method (XRCD method) **-messer** *m* X-ray radiometer, intensimeter, dosimeter, roentgenometer, iontoquantimeter **-undurchlässig** radiopaque

Röntgen-strahlquelle *f* X-ray source **-strahlung** *f* X-radiation **-streuung** *f* x-ray scattering **-strukturanalyse** *f* heavy atom method **-technik** *f* X-ray technique **-term** *m* X-ray level **-therapie** *f* radiotherapy **-untersuchung** *f* X-ray examination, radiographic inspection, radiography **-verfärbung** *f* roentgenization

Roots-Gebläse Root's blower, Root's-type compressor **-Lader** *m* Root's-type compressor **-pumpe** *f* roots pump

rosa pink

rösch brittle, roasted, coarse, slightly crushed **~ gemahlen** free-beaten, free-running

Rösch-erz *n*, **-gewächs** *n* stephanite, brittle silver ore

Röschheit *f* freeness (in papermaking)

Rose *f* compass card

Roselith *m* roselite

Rosen-ablenkung *f* rose deviation **-abhebevor-**

richtung *f*, **-arretiervorrichtung** *f* device for stopping the rose or card **-blatt** *n* compass card or rose **-einteilung** *f* division of the compass card or rose **-holz** *n* rosewood **-karte** *f* compass card or rose **-körper** *m* body of the compass rose or card **-kranzzange** *f* rosary pliers **-lagerung** *f* placing of the compass rose or card **-quarz** *m* rose quartz **-rand** *m* edge, border, or rim of the compass rose or card **-säule** *f* pedestal of compass rose **-stahl** *m* rose steel **-träger** *m* compass rose, card support, or carrier

Rosette *f* collar, solid flange

Rosetten-bahn *f* rosette-shaped path (of electrons) **-herd** *m* refining hearth (for copper) **-kupfer** *n* rosette copper **-platte** *f* rosette plate **-schieber** *m* circular air grid

rosettieren to get copper cakes, lift off round crusts of copper, produce rosette copper

Rosettierherd *m* copper-refining hearth

Rosolsäure *f* rosolic acid

Roßbreiten *pl* horse latitudes

Roßbysches Diagramm Rossby chart

Roßhaar *n* horsehair

Rost *m* (Gitterwerk) grating; (Kesselunterlage) grate, rust, screen, grid, grizzly (min.), duckboard, gridiron, grillage, deck (supported on beams or bearers) **~ aus Würsten** grillage of fascine poles **den ~ fortsetzen** to put aside the roasted ore **garer ~** sufficiently roasted ore **liegender ~** spread footing

Röstabgang *m* loss of weight on or by roasting

Rostanfressung *f* corrosion, honeycombing, pitting **~ bis zu tiefen Grübchen** honeycomb corrosion **faulende ~** graphitic corrosion, spongelike decay iron cancer, graphitization **grübchenartige ~** pitting, tubercular corrosion **langadrige ~** channeling corrosion

Rostangriff *m* action of rust, corrosive action or attack

Röstanlage *f* calcining or roasting plant

Rostansatz *m* formation of rust

Röst-apparat *m* calcining or roasting apparatus **-arbeit** *f* roasting operation or process, roasting

rost-artig grate-shaped **-balken** *m* fire bearer, firebar bearer, bearing car, cross bearer **-behandlung** *f* rustproofing process **-band** *n* grate band **-belastung** *f* grate duty **-beschickung** *f* stoking **-beschickungsanlage** *f* grate stoker **-beständig** noncorrodible, corrosion-resisting, rust-resisting, rustproof, rustless **-beständigkeit** *f* resistance to corrosion, rust-resisting property, rustlessness, stainless property

Röst-betrieb *m* roasting practice **-betriebsdauer** *f* roasting time **-bett** *n* roasting bed

Rost-bildner *m* corroding agent **-bildung** *f* formation of rust, corrosion **-blech** *n* grid plate

Röstblende *f* roasted blende

Rostbrennfläche *f* effective area of grate

Röstdorn *m* ore-roasting thorn

Rostdurchfall *m* riddlings

Röste *f* roasting, roasting charge, retting, steeping

Rosteinkapselung *f* grate cover

Rösteinrichtung *f* roasting plant

Rosteinsatz *m* grate inset

rostempfindlich corrodible, sensitive to corrosion

Rostempfindlichkeit *f* corrodibility, sensitiveness to corrosion

rosten to rust, corrode, oxidize, become rusty

Rosten *n* rusting, corroding, corrosion

rösten to roast, sinter, calcine, scorch

Rösten *n* roasting, sintering, calcining **chlorierendes ~** chloridizing or chlorinating roasting **verflüchtigendes ~** volatilizing roasting

Rostentfernung *f* rust removal

Röster *m* calciner

Rösterz *n* calcined ore

Rösterzeugnis *n* product of roasting, calcining, or broiling, roasted or calcined product

Rostfarbe *f* rust color

rostfarbig rust-colored **-e Nuance** iron buff shade

rost-fest rustproof, rust-resisting, anticorrosive **-festigkeit** *f* corrosion resistance, noncorrodibility **-feuer** *n* grate fire

Rostfeuerung *f* grate firing, grate fire **selbsttätige ~** stoker firing

Rost-fläche *f* grate area or surface, area of hearth **-fleck** *m* rust spot, iron stain **-fleckig** rust-stained **-fraß** *m* corrosion

rostfrei rust-free, rustproof **-es Nadelpapier** pin paper **-er Stahl** stainless steel, rustless steel

Rost-freiheit *f* immunity to corrosion **-fuge** *f* space between the fire bars

Röstgas *n* gas from roasting

Rost-gefahr *f* danger of rusting **-gelb** *n* iron buff **-grübchen** *n* pit **-gründung** *f* foundation on timber platform

Röst-gut *n* roasting charge, material to be roasted **-haufen** *m* roast heap **-herd** *m* hearth roaster, roasting hearth

rosthindernd rust-preventing, anticorrosive

Rösthütte *f* roasting plant

rostig rusty

Rostigkeit *f* rustiness

Röstkammer *f* roasting chamber

Rost-kratze *f* cradle (met.) **-kühler** *m* grate cooler **-kühlrohre** *pl* grate water boxes **-lager** *n* fire-bar frame **-los** stainless or rustproof (steel) **-lösungsmittel** *n* rust solvent **-mittel** *n* corroding medium, corroding agent **-narbe** *f* corrosion pit **-neigung** *f* tendency to rust

Röstofen *m* roasting furnace or kiln, roaster, calcining furnace or kiln, calciner

Rost-papier *n* antitarnish paper **-papiere** *pl* abrasive papers

Röstpfanne *f* roasting or frying pan

Rostplatte *f* grate for vertical mill

Röst-posten *m* roasting charge **-probe** *f* calcination test or assay **-produkt** *n* product of roasting, calcining, or broiling, roasted or calcined product **-prozeß** *m* roasting or calcination process, roasting **-reaktionsarbeit** *f* roast-reaction process, air-reduction method of smelting **-reaktionsverfahren** *n* roasting-reaction method **-reduktionsarbeit** *f* roast-reduction process, blast-furnace method, extraction by fusion

rostrein rust-free

Röst-rückstand *m* roasting residue **-schachtofen** *m* roasting blast furnace, circular calcining kiln

Rostschalung *f* grid-type shuttering

Röstschaufel *f* rabble

Rost-schicht *f* layer of rust **-schieber** *m* gridiron valve

Röst-schlacke *f* slag from roasting **-schmelzen** *n* roasting smelting
Rostschutz *m* rust protection, anti-corrosive effect
rostschützend rust-preventing **-es Papier** anti-tarnish paper **-e Wirkung** rust-preventing quality
Rostschutz-farbe *f* rust-resisting paint **-mittel** *n* rust-preventative, anticorrosive agent **-öl** *n* slushing oil **-verfahren** *n* rustproofing process, parkerizing
Rostschwelle *f* grating beam
rostsicher noncorrodible, stainless, corrosion-resistant, nonrusting, rustproof **-er Stahl** stainless steel
Rost-sicherheit *f* rustproofing, noncorrosion property, noncorrodibility, stainless property **-spalt** *m* grate opening, air space in grate **-spaltweite** *f* fire-bar spacing
Roststab *m* fire or grate bar, rake **-eisen** *pl* fire bars **-klopfvorrichtung** *f* grate bar shaker **-träger** *m* crossbearer
Röst-stadel *m* clamp, roasting stall, calcining stall **-staub** *m* roasted-ore dust
Rostträger *m* grate bearer
Rösttrommel *f* calcining drum
Rost- und Korrosions-Schutzbehandlung für Stahl cosletizing
Rost- und Korrosions-Schutzfett *n* rustproofing grease
Rostung *f* rusting, corrosion
Röstung *f* roasting, roast, calcination **~ im Haufen** heap roasting, calcination in heaps **~ in Stadeln** stall roasting, calcination in clamps **sulfidierende ~** sulfating roasting, sulfate roast
Rostverhütungsöl *n* rust-preventive oil
Rostungsversuch *m* corrosion test
Röstverfahren *n* roasting process, calcining method
rostverhütend rust-preventing
Röst-verlust *m* loss by or from roasting **-vorgang** *m* roasting or calcining operation **-vorrichtung** *f* roasting device or apparatus
Rost-werk *n* grating **-widerstand** *m* stain resistance, resistance to corrosion **-zuschlag** *m* increase in thickness of metal to allow for rust
rot red **-e Arsenblende** realgar, red arsenic sulfide **das Rote Kreuz** the Red Cross **-es Licht** red light **-es Präzipitat** red precipitate, red mercuric oxide **-es Zinkerz** zincite
Röt *n* upper new red sandstone
Rotadurchflußmesser *m* rotameter
Rotalix-Drehanodenröhre *f* Rotalix tube
Rotamesser *m* flow meter (gas)
Rotang *m* rattan
rotarmer Filter red abstracting filter
Rotary-bohrmeißel *m* rotary bits **-bohrschlauch** *m* rotary hose **-fangdorne** *pl* rotary tapertaps **-hahn** *m* rotary valve **-kreuzmeißel** *m* rotary cross bits **-pumpe** *f* rotary pump
Rotation *f* rotation or curl (of a vector), revolution **~ eines Vektors** curl **~ der Verbrennungsluft** whirling of combustion gases **behinderte ~** hindered or inhibited rotation (of molecules)
Rotations-abplattung *f* rotational flattening **-absorptionsfrequenz** *f* rotational absorption frequency **-achse** *f* axis of rotation **-anemometer** *n* rotation anemometer **-antenne** *f* spinner (antenna) **-behinderung** *f* restricted internal rotation **-bewegung** *f* rotational motion, rotary motion **-druckmaschine** *f* rotary printing press **-durchmesser** *m* diameter of rotation **-dynamik** *f* dynamics of rotation
Rotations-ellipsoid *n* ellipsoid or revolution, spheroid **-elliptisch** spheroidal **-energie** *f* energy of rotation **-entropie** *f* rotational entropy **-feinstruktur** *f* rotational fine structure **-fläche** *f* surface of revolution **-frei** irrotational, without rotation **-freiheit** *f* rotational freedom **-gebläse** *n* rotary blower **-geschwindigkeit** *f* velocity or speed of rotation **-gesenkdrückmaschine** *f* rotary swaging machine
Rotationsgruppe, räumliche ~ space rotation group
Rotations-hyperboloid *n* hyperboloid of revolution **-integral** *n* circuital integral
Rotationsinvariante, magnetische ~ invariant of magnetic rotation
Rotations-isomere *f* rotational isomers **-kegel** *m* cone of revolution **-körper** *m* solid or body of rotation or revolution **-niveau** *n* rotational level **-parabolisch** full-parabolic **-paraboloid** *n* paraboloid of revolution **-pumpe** *f* rotary pump
Rotations-quantenzahl *f* rotational quantum number **-richtung** *f* sense or direction of rotation **-schnelldruckpresse** *f* rotary press for high speed printing **-schwingungsband** *n* rotation vibration band **-schwingungsspektrum** *n* rotation vibration spectrum **-sinn** *m* sense or direction of rotation **-symmetrie** *f* rotational symmetry
rotationssymmetrisch symmetrical with respect to rotation, axially symmetrical **-e Bewegung** rotationally symmetric motion **-er Körper** body presenting rotation symmetry
Rotations-term *n* rotational level **-tiefdruck** *m* rotary intaglio printing **-tischsandstrahlgebläse** *n* rotary-table sandblast machine **-trägheit** *f* rotational inertia **-verdichter** *m* rotary compressor **-vermögen** *n* rotatory power, Verdet's constant **-verzerrung** *f* rotational distortion **-viskosimeter** *m* rotary viscosimeter **-voltmeter** *n* rotary voltmeter
Rotations-zähler *m* revolution counter **-zeit** *f* time of rotation **-zustandssumme** *f* rotational partition function **-zylinder** *m* cylinder of revolution
Rotator *m* rotator, tube mill
Rot-auszug *m* red record (color film) **-beize** *f* red liquor or mordant
Rotblei-erz *n*, **-spat** *m* red lead ore, crocoite
Rot-braunsteinerz *n* rhodonite **-bruch** *m* red-shortness, hot-shortness **-brüchig** brittle when red-hot or red-short **-brüchigkeit** *f* red-shortness **-bruchversuch** *m* hot-bending test, hot-breaking test **-buche** *f*, **-buchenholz** *n* red beech
Röte *f* red component
Rot-eisenerz *n* red iron ore **-eisenocker** *n* red ochre **-eisenrostfarbe** *f* red iron oxide paint **-eisenstein** *m* red iron ore, red hematite
Rötel *m* red chalk, ruddle **-tönung** *f* russet toning
rotempfindlich sensitive to red light, red-sensitive
röten to redden
rotfahl tawny
Rotfilter *m* red filter (light) **-empfangsgerät** *n*

receiving apparatus for red-filter light-signal equipment **-gerät** *n* red-filter light-signal equipment

Rot-freilicht *n* red-free light **-gießer** *m* brazier **-gießerei** *f* red copper foundry **-glühen** to heat to redness **-glühend** red-hot, heated to glowing, red-heat **-glühhärte** *f* red hardness **-glühhitze** *f* red heat (of incandescence)

Rotglut *f* red heat, redness **auf ~ erhitzen** to heat to red heat **dunkle ~** dull red, low red

Rotglut-härte *f* red-hardness **-hitze** *f* red heat

Rotgültig *n* pyrargyrite, ruby blende

Rotgültigerz *n* red silver ore **dunkles ~** pyrargyrite **lichtes ~** proustite

Rotguß *m* gun metal, bronze, red brass **-lagerschale** *f* bronze bush **-schalen** *pl* brasses **-scheibe** *f* brass disk

Rot-holz *n* redwood **-hitze** *f* red heat

rotieren to rotate, revolve

rotierend rotating, rotary **-es Bezugssystem** rotating frame **-er Bläser** *m* rotary blower **-er Dämpfer** rotating stabilizer (film feed) **-e Funkenstrecke** rotary spark gap, rotary discharger **-er Gleichspannungsumformer** genemotor **-er Knotenfänger** rotary strainer

rotierend-er Kohlenhalter rotary carbon brush holder **-er Ofen** rotary kiln **-e Phasenschieber** rotating phase advancers **-e Pumpe** rotary pump **-er Schaber** rotary doctor **-es Schutzschild** rotary shield **-er Umformer mit gemeinsamem Rotor** dynamotor **-e Umlaufverschlußblende** rotary flicker shutter, rotary light cutoff

Rotierer *m*, **Rotierofen** *m* rotating kiln or furnace rotary drying kiln

Rotkali *n* potassium ferricyanide

Rot-kupfer *n* red copper **-kupfererz** *n* red copper ore, cuprite **-lauf** *m* erysipelas

rötlich reddish

Rotliegendes *n* Lower Permian (shale) sandstone

Rotmessing *n* red brass (bronze)

Rotnickelkies *m* niccolite

Rotogravüre *f* rotogravure

Roton *n* roton

Rotor *m* rotor, armature, rotator **~ der Funkenstrecke** spark-gap rotor

Rotor-belastung *f* rotor load **-blatt** *n* (Hubschr.) rotor blade **-bock** *m* rotor pylon **-ebene** *f* rotor disk **-flügel** *m* rotor blade **-flugzeug** *n* rotor plane **-funkenstrecke** *f* spark-gap rotor

Rotorkopf *m* rotor hub **-joch** *n* hub joke

Rotor-kreisfläche *f* disk area **-kreuzgelenkring** *m* rotor gimbal **-nabe** (Elektr.) armature hub **-neigung** *f* rotor tilt **-paket** *n*, **-platte** *f* moving plate of the variable condenser, rotor plate **-scheibe** *f* rotor disc **-schub** *m* rotor thrust **-spule** *f* moving or rotating coil, rotor coil **-stern** *m* armature spider (field spider) **-strom** *m* rotor current

Rot-pause *f* red print **-reserve** *f* red resist **-schlamm** *m* red mud **-schleier** *m* red fog (photo.) **-spat** *m* rhodonite

Rotspießglanz *m*, **-erz** *n* kermesite

Rot-stich *m* red cast (red tint) **-stichig** reddish

Rotstrahlsystem (Elektronenstrahlsystem für rot leuchtende Teile des Bildschirms) red electron gun (TV)

Rot-verschiebung *f* red shift **-zinkerz** *n* zincite

Rotte *f* group, file, gang, rabble

Rotten-formation *f* box formation **-führer** *m* foreman of gang

Rötung *f* redness

Rotverschiebung *f* shift of spectral lines toward red or longer waves

rotwarm red-hot **-biegeprobe** *f* hot-bending test **-härte** *f* red-hardness

Rotz *m* glanders

Rotzinkerz *n* zincite, red oxide of zinc, red zinc ore

Rouge *f* rouge

Rouleaudruck *m* roller printing

Rouleauverschluß *m* roller-blind shutter

Roulette *n* horizontal ball mill, ring-roll mill

routiniert experienced

Routine-überprüfung *f* routine check **-untersuchung** *f* routine test

Rüben-breimaschine *f* pulper **-entladen** *n* beet dumping **-gerät** *n* beet tool **-grundlieferungsrecht** *n* beet quota **-harzsäure** *f* beet sapogenin

Rübenheber *m* beet puller **~ mit Führersitz** riding beet puller **~ mit Handführung** walking beet puller **~ mit Sitz** riding beet puller

Rüben-hubrad *n* beet wheel **-krautfänger** *m* beet-leaf catcher **-lager** *n* beet bin, beet storeroom **-laub** *n* beet leaves **-müdigkeit** *f* beet sickness, beet tiredness, root knot **-quirlwäsche** *f* beet washer with revolving arm agitators **-reibe** *f* beet rasp **-säapparat** *m* beet attachment **-sämaschine** *f* beet seeder **-samenbeizmittel** *n* beet-seed disinfectant, beet-seed dressing **-samenknäuel** *n* beet-seed ball

Rübenschnitzel *n* beet slice **ausgelaugte ~** beet pulp **unausgelaugte ~** cossettes

Rüben-schrot *n* coarsely ground dried betts, beet scab **-schwemme** *f* beet flume

Rüben- und Bohnendrillmaschine *f* beet-and-bean drill

Rüben-versorgung *f* beet supply **-wirtschaft** *f* sugar-beet farm

Ruberoidbedeckung *f* rubberoid sheathing

Rubidium *n* rubidium **-alaun** *m* rubidium alum

Rubidkontakt *m* pressure switch

Rubin *m* ruby **-blende** *f* pyrargyrite **-Festkörpermaser** *m* ruby solid-state maser **-glimmer** *m* ruby mica **-laser** *m* ruby laser **-stab** *m* ruby rod

Rüböl *n* colza oil, rape oil

Rubrik *f* column, head, heading, rubric

Ruck *m* jerk, jolt, tug

Rück-anschlag *m* backstop **-anschluß** *m* back connections **-ansicht** *f* back or rear view **-anspruch** *m* counterclaim

ruckartig jerky

Rückauslösung *f* back release

rückbare Antriebsstation shiftable drive terminal **~ Bandanlage** shiftable belt conveyor

Rück-beförderung *f* evacuation to the rear, return transportation **-beförderungsrolle** *f* pull-off roll **-belüftungskühlung** *f* reverse-flow cooling **-berufung** *f* recall **-bewegung** *f* back-stroke, retrogression, return stroke, flyback (of beam, television) **-bilden** to form again **-bildung** *f* regeneration, re-formation, recovery, regression **-bleibsel** *n* remainder, residue

Rückblick *m* retrospect, backward glance **-fenster** *n* rear view window **-spiegel** *m* rear-view mirror, retrospect mirror

Rückblockungstromkreis *m* line-free circuit

Rück-brand *m* burn-back (in welding) **-brechvorrichtung** *f* book-back bending device **-buchung** *f* back entry **-dämpfung** *f* front to back ratio (antenna) **-dehnung** *f* damping capacity, elastic recovery **-destillation** *f* redistillation

Rückdiffusion von Elektronen back-diffusion of electrons

Rückdiffusionsverlust *m* back diffusion loss

rück-drehbar returnable **-drehen** to untwist **-drehendes Moment** restoring moment (aviation)

Rückdreh-moment *n* righting or restoring moment **-sicherung** *f* safety catch against reversing, reverse stop **-sperre** *f* non-reversing lock

Rückdrehung *f* untwisting

Rückdruck *m* propelling pressure, back pressure, reaction pressure, reaction (phys.) **-feder** *f* repercussive spring, return spring

Rückdrückkolben *m* draw-back ram

rücken to move, push along, jerk **aneinander ~** to come close or closer, come or move near or nearer, come together, approach

Rücken (Fräserzahn) face, back, ridge, rear **den ~ decken** to cover the back

Rücken-bau *m* mountain irrigation **-belastung** *f* inverted load **-bündigkeit** *f* flush back cones **-deckel** *m* back plate **-deckung** *f* parados **-fallschirm** *m* back-type parachute **-feld** *n* space between the backbands of a book **-flanke** *f* back of inclined face **-flosse** *f* dorsal ridge **-flossenantenne** *f* dorsal antenna

Rückenflug *m* inverted flight, inverted normal loop **-vergaser** *m* inverted-flight carburetor

Rücken-gepäck *n* pack, knapsack **-gitter** *n pl* return grilles **-gurt** *m* (Fallschirm) back strap **-kissen** *n* croup pad **-kissenfallschirm** *m* back-type parachute **-lage** *f* upside-down position **-last** *f* inverted load **-lastungsprobe** *f* loading test **-lehne** *f* back rest **-leitfläche** *f* dorsal fin (aviation) **-linie** *f* ridge line

Rücken-pack *m* pack **-polster** *n* (Flugzeug) back-pad **-polsterung** *f* back squab **-riemen** *m* leadup strap **-säge** *f* miter saw **-schale** *f* bottom of parachute pack **-schliff** *m* grinding the tooth lands **-schutz** *m* backrest **-spiel** *n* back clearance **-ständer** *m* rear lay standard

Rückentladung *f* back discharge, back kick (radio)

Rückentrage *f* pack (for carrying cable reel on back) **~ -für schweres Feldkabel** portable reel for heavy field cable

Rücken-trudeln *n* spinning upside down, inverted spin **-verkleidung** *f* back fairing

Rückenwind *m* tail wind **Landung mit ~** down-wind landing **Start mit ~** take-off with the wind **mit ~** with the wind

Rückenwinkel *m* backoff angle, rear angle

Rück-erstattung *f* restoration, return, recompensation **-fahren der Maschine** backward travel of the machine

Rückfahr-laterne *f* backing light **-leuchte** *f* reversing light **-schalter** *m* reverse driving lamp **-scheinwerfer** *m* reversing lamp

Rück-fahrt *f* return journey, downward travel, return **-fall** *m* reversion, relapse, repetition of crime **-fälle** *m*, *pl* fines (metal.), returns **-fällig** reversible **-fallstoffe** *pl* fallback

Rück-federung *f* spring-back resilience **-feuerung** *f* backfire **-fließend** with reflux (chem.) **-flanke** *f* trailing edge **-flankenverschiebung** *f* end distortion **-flug** *m* return flight

Rückfluß *m* reflux (chem.) **-dämpfung** *f* structural return loss **-dämpfungsmesser** *m* reflection-measuring set **-kühler** *m* reflux or return condenser, return-flow cooler **-spannung** *f* return voltage **-ventil** *n* return valve, relief valve

Rückförder-band für Sand sand-recovery conveyer **-gebläse** *n* return blower **-gewinde** *n* back feed thread

rückfördern to return

Rückförderpumpe *f* return pump, scavenging pump

Rückförderung *f* return

Rückfrage *f* local inquiry, reference **~ halten** to request

Rückfragegespräch *n* consultation call

Rückfrage-häufigkeit *f* repetition rate **-hilfsrelais** *n* auxiliary callback relay

rückfragen to request

Rückfragerelais *n* call-back relay

Rückführ-daumen *m* resetting cam **-drehmoment** *m* restoring torque

rückführen to lead back, pass back (in rolling)

Rückführ-feder *f* restoring, controlling, or retracting spring, retractile spring **-gestänge** *n* return mechanism **-hebel** *m* follow-up lever (jet) **-leitung** *f* return line **-moment** *n* restoring moment **-nocken** *m* return cam **-relais** *n* clear-out relay **-schieber** *m* distributor piston (jet) **-schnecke** *f* return screw, return screw conveyer, return worm

Rückführung *f* recycling, return movement, feedback (aut. contr.), return, restoring mechanism, reduction, follow-up, return lead, path, or circuit, flyback, retrace (television) **nachgebende ~** positive feedback (aut. contr) **nachgehende ~** proportional reset (control) action **~ des Papierschlittens** carriage return **~** (Regler) follow-up device

Rückführungs-band *n* reconducting belt **-fraktion** *f* middle fraction **-regler** *m* feedback controller

Rückgabe *f* return

Rückgang *m* return, decline, retrogression, return journey or stroke, backstroke, return pass (in rolling), return or reverse motion, flyback (of pencil) **~ des Verkehrs** reduction of traffic

rückgängig retrograde, retrogressive, regressive **~ machen** to cancel, annul, revoke

Rückgängigmachung *f* reversal

Rückgangmechanismus *m* return-travel mechanism

Rückgangs-dampf *m* exhaust steam **-ziffer** *f* reversible permeability factor

rückgekoppelt back-coupled, retroactive **-es Audion** regenerative grid-current detector, ultraudion **-er Verstärker** feed-back amplifier **-e Zählschaltung** ring scaler

rückgewinnbar (Satellit) recoverable (satellite)

rückgewinnen to recover

Rückgewinnung *f* reclamation, recovery, recuperation (of current or energy), regeneration **~ der Lösungsmittel** solvent recovery

Rück-gewinnungsanlage *f* recovery installation

-gitterstrom *m* reverse grid current **-gliederung** *f* reintegration **-glühung** *f* drawing, tempering

Rückgrat *n* backbone, spine, ridge **-artige Erhebung** ridge

rück-greifend retrogressive **-griff** *m* inverse-grid transparency

Rückhalt *m* backing ~ **geben** to give backing, endorse

Rückhalt-becken *n* laying-up basin **-klappe** *f* non-return or clock valve

Rückhalte-mittel *n* hold-back agent **-punkt** *m* rearward point **-träger** *m* hold-back carrier (agent)

Rückhalts-kabel *n* backstay rope **-kraft** *f* coercive force

Rück-haltvorrichtung *f* preventer mechanism **-heizung** *f* extra or additional heating **-hebel** *m* engaging or disengaging lever **-holbewegung** *f* return motion **-holer** *m* breech-mechanism connector arm

Rückhol-feder *f* return spring **-moment** *n* restoring moment **-seil** *n* backhaul cable **-stange** *f* retraction **-taste** *f* back spacing control (tape rec.) **-vorrichtung** *f* reset device

Rückhörbezugsdämpfung *f* side-tone reference equivalent

Rückhör-dämpfung *f* side-tone attenuation **-hören** *n* talker echo side tone **-hub** *m* backstroke, return stroke **-kante** *f* trailing edge **-kauf** *m* repurchase

Rückkaufs-recht *n* right of redemption or repurchase **-wert** *m* surrender value

Rückkehr *f* return ~ **der Ebbe und Flut** change of the tide ~ **zum Startpunkt** return to the starting point

rückkehrender Strahl re-entrant jet

Rückkehr-kante *f* edge of regression **-koeffizient** *m* collision coefficient, restitution coefficient **-kurve** *f* edge of regression **-linie** *f* edge of regression (geom.) **-moment** *n* restoring moment, back torque, resisting or opposing torque or moment

Rückkehrpunkt *m* cusp (radar, math.) ~ **einer Kurve** cusp or stationary point of a curve

Rückkehrungskoeffizient *m* restitution coefficient

Rückkehrzeit *f* recovery time

Rückkippgeschwindigkeit *f* flyback speed, time-base unlock speed

Rück-klappflügel *m* folding wing **-knallen** to backfire **-kohlen** to recarburize **-kohlung** *f* recarburization **-kontrolle** *f* reversive control **-kopf** *m* shift-head **-kopien** *pl* reflex prints (photog.) **-koppeln** to couple back, feed back, regenerate

Rückkoppelung *f* reaction, regeneration, reactive, or regenerative coupling, feedback, feedback coupling, return coupling, retroaction, grid-coupling control **innere** ~ inherent feedback **zu starke** ~ **im Empfänger** too much tickler ~ **mit Hilfsfrequenz** superregeneration (using quench potential) **induktive** ~ inductive feedback **kapazitive** ~ electrostatic feedback **negative** ~ negative reaction, negative feedback, negative regeneration **phasenfreie** ~ in-phase feedback **positive** ~ positive regeneration

Rückkoppelungsaudion *n* regenerative valve detector, retroactive audion, regenerative grid-current detector, ultraudion

Rückkoppelungsempfang *m* regenerative or retroactive reception ~ **mit Hilfsfrequenz** superregenerative reception

Rückkoppelungs-empfänger *m* regenerative receiver, regenerative set **-empfangsschaltung** *f* feed-back receiving circuit, retroactive receiving circuit **-erscheinung** *f* recoupling effect **-faktor** *m* regenerative coefficient of coupling, reaction coefficient **-formel** *f* feed-back or reaction formula **-frei** nonregenerative, free from feed-back action **-gefahr** *f* danger of feed-back **-generator** *m* feed-back oscillator, feedback ratio regenerative oscillator **-grad** *m* reaction coefficient, feedback ratio

Rückkoppelungs-kondensator *m* reaction condenser **-kreis** *m* reaction circuit, regenerative circuit, feed-back circuit **-magnetron** *m* feedback or regenerative magnetron oscillator **-methode** *f* reaction method, feedback method **-netzwerk** *n* feedback network **-pfeifen** *n* fringe howl **-prinzip** *n* reaction principle

Rückkopplungs-röhre *f* retroactor **-schaltung** *f* feedback circuit **-schaltung** *f* regenerative or retroactive circuit, feed-back connection **-schwingung** *f* feed-back or reaction oscillation **-spannung** *f* positive bias potential, positive quench potential **-sperre** *f* antisinging device, reaction suppressor, vodas, feedback suppressor, anti-reaction device, singing suppressor

Rückkoppelungsspule *f* reaction coil, reactance coil, feed-back or tickler coil, tickler ~ **des Schwingaudions** tickler coil

Rückkopplungs-summer *m* feedback oscillator **-transformator** *m* reaction transformer, feedback transformer **-unterdrückung** *f* decoupling, reduction, suppression, balancing out, or tuning out of feedback **-verstärker** *m* reaction amplifier **-verstärkung** *f* regeneration, regenerative amplification, retroactive amplification **-verzerrung** *f* distortion due to feedback, regeneration distortion **-weg** *m* singing path

Rück-kristallisation *f* recrystallization **-kühlwasser** *n* condensing water

Rück-kühlanlage *f* re-cooling plant **-kühlen** to return-cool **-kühler** *m* heat exchanger **-kühlturm** *m* cooling tower **-kühlung** *f* closed-circuit cooling **-kühlwasser** *n* circulating water

Rückkunft *f* return

Rücklage *f* rearward position **-konto** *n* depreciation reserve account

Rücklampe *f* rear lamp

Rücklauf *m* fly-back (TV); return trace (CRT), backstroke; return motion, kickback, reflux ratio, reversal; return travel, return pass, stroke, or movement, recoil, reflux, retrace, flyback, return (to normal) ~ **der Kippspannung** flyback of sweep potential, return of time base to zero ~ **eines Mechanismus** return stroke ~ **der Nummernscheibe** return of dial ~ **eines Wählers** return to normal **rascher** ~ quick rewind, fast reverse

Rücklauf-anschlag *m* backward stop dog **-behälter** *m* reclaiming tank, reflux drum **-bohrung** *f* return gallery **-bolzen** *m* reverse gear shaft **-bremse** *f* recoil brake, reverse brake, recoil buffer

Rücklaufbüchse *f* header **~ mit Gewindezapfen** screw-plug header **~ mit Konsolen** mule-type header **~ mit Schraubbügel** compound-plug header **~ mit konischem Verschluß** tape plus header

Rücklauf-doppelrad *n* reverse double-gear wheel **-einrichtung** *f* recoil mechanism

rücklaufen to return (to normal)

rücklaufend recurrent, retrograde, in return or opposite direction **-er Blitz** return lightning stroke

Rücklauf-entkupplung *f* rewind release **-feder** *f* recoil spring, counterrecoil spring **-gefahr** *f* reversing danger **-geschwindigkeit** *f* return speed **-getriebe** *n* return gear **-hemmung** *f* reversal prevention **-hochspannungsspeisung** *f* kickback power supply

rückläufig reverse, reversible, retrograde, recurrent **-es Ende** rear end **-e Knotendrehung** regressive mutation

Rücklauf-impuls *m* line flyback pulse **-knopf** *m* return button **-kolben** *m* follow-up piston **-kondensator** *m* reflux condenser **-leitung** *f* return pipe **-messer** *m* recoil indicator **-nadel** *f* spill piston (jet) **-öl** *n* return oil **-pumpe** *f* scavenge pump **-rad** *n* reverse wheel, reverse gear **-rinne** *f* return chute **-rohr** *n* return pipe **-rolle** *f* pull-off roll

Rücklauf-schaufel *f* return scoop **-schieber** *m* recoil-indicator slide **-sicherung** *f* sprag device **-sieb** *n* return screen **-sperre** *f* back stop, pawl stop **-sperre** *f* flyback suppressor **-spur** *f* return trace (CRT), retrace (CRT) **-stellvorrichtung** *f* recoil mechanism **-unterdrückung** *f* fly-back suppression

Rücklauf-ventil *n* by-pass valve **-verdichter** *m* reflux condenser **-verdunkelung** *f* flyback or return-trace elimination, blackout of flyback suppression **-welle** *f* reverse (gear) shaft **-wicklung** *f* reverse winding **-zahnrad** *n* reverse pinion **-zeit** *f* retrace time, flyback period, return speed, retrace interval, return time, reset time **-zylinder** *m* recoil cylinder

Rückleistung *f* reverse power

Rückleistungsschutz *m* reverse-power protection

Rückleiter *m* return, return wire, return conductor, return lead

Rückleitung *f* return conductor, return path, return circuit **~ mit besonderem Leiter** return feeder **gemeinsame ~** common return **magnetische ~** magnetic return path **metallische ~** metallic return, return wire

rückliegend rearward, backward

Rückluft-bohrung *f* return air borehole **-leitung** *f* return air pipe

Rückmagnetisierungszeit *f* (eines Kernes) core-reset

Rückmelde-feld *n* revertive signal panel **-gerät** *n* responder (iff) **-hebel** *m* reply, repeating, answering, or relief lever **-läutewerk** *n* reply bell

rückmelden to answer, acknowledge

Rückmelder *m* revertive-signal or position-repeating means, check-back position indicator

Rückmeldesignal *n* repeating signal

Rückmeldung *f* repeating or answering a signal, indication of a lever position, answer-back signal

Rückmontage *f* reassembly **~ eines Motors** (nach der Zerlegung) final assembly

Rücknahme *f* return **~ der Abwässer** reutilization of waste water

Rücknahme-streit *m* action for withdrawal **-taste** *f* canceling key **-peilung** *f* back bearing

Rück-oxydation *f* reoxidation **-phosphorisierung** *f* rephosphorization **-platte** *f* backplate

Rückprall *m* rebound, resilience, repulsion, recoil, bump, reaction, back pressure, repercussion, strike back, backstroke, backfire **-elektrode** *f* rebound electrode, target electrode, impactor electrode **-härte** *f* rebound hardness **-impuls** *m* rebound impulse

Rück-projektionsanlage *f* reprojection or back-projection equipment **-reaktion** *f* back reaction

Rückreise *f* return journey **auf der ~ begriffen** homeward bound

Rückruf *m* recall, back ring **~ auf eigene Leitung** reverting call

Rückruf-schalter *m*, **-taste** *f* ring-back key **-wähler** *m* reverting call switch

Rücksauge-einrichtung *f* return-feed equipment **-ventil** *n* return-flow valve

rückschallfrei nonresounding

Rückschalttaste (Rücktaste) back spacer (on typewriter)

Rückschaltung *f* back space mechanism

Rückschalt-verzögerungsrelais *n* reconnection delay relay

Rückschau *f* review

rück-schauend retrospective **-schlächtiges Wasserrad** high-breast water wheel

Rück-scheinwerfer *m* rear reflector **-schema** *n* shifting diagram

Rückschlag *m* rebound, repulsion, backward push, reaction, backstroke, reverse, recoil, setback **-bremse** *f* recoil brake **-dämpfung** *f* recoil cushioning device **-drossel** *f* orifice assembly

rückschlagen to backfire, rebound, recoil

Rückschlag-feder *f* retrieving spring **-gefahr** *f* kick-back danger **-impuls** *m* kick-back pulse **-klappe** *f* check, relief or nonreturn valve, nonreturn flap **-klappenventil** *n* check valve **-klotz** *m* recoil block **-löschend** nonflashing **-löschung** *f* flash back **-sicher** kick-back proof **-sicherung** *f* safety valve **-trockensicherung** *f* flash-back arrester **-ventil** *n* nonreturn valve, check valve, relief valve, back-pressure valve

Rückschluß *m* inference, conclusion **-kabel** *n* short-circuit wire, ground cable **-klemme** *f* short-circuit terminal, ground terminal **-kohle** *f* ground carbon

Rückschreiben *n* reply

Rückschreibimpuls *m* half-write pulse

rückschreitende Welle *f* regressive or reflected wave

Rück-schritt *m* retrogression, recession **-schub** *m* unshift **-schubroste** *f* reversed feed grates **-schwefelung** *f* resulfurization **-schwenkspiegel** *m* instant return mirror **-schwingung** *f* swinging back (of pendulum)

Rückseite *f* back, reverse, back side, rear **auf die ~ schreiben** to endorse

rückseitiger Anschluß rear connection

Rück-sendung *f* return motion **-setzeinrichtung** *f*

resetting mechanism

Rücksicht *f* regard, respect, attention, consideration, reference, rear view **~ nehmen auf** to allow for **mit ~ auf** in consideration of, with due regard for, because of, in the light of **ohne ~ auf** irrespective, regardless

rücksichtsloses Fliegen reckless flying

Rücksichtspiegel *m* rear-vision mirror

Rück-signal *n* back or return signal **-sitz** *m* back seat, rear seat **-speisekabel** *n* return feeder cable **-speisung** *f* feeding back **-spiegel** *m* rear-view mirror **-spiegelung** *f* specular reflection, regular reflection **-spielen** *n* playback, dubbing **-sprache** *f* consultation **-sprechdämpfung** *f* sidetone attenuation

Rücksprung *m* rebound, ricochet **-härte** *f* rebound hardness **-palette** *f* wing pallet **-verfahren** *n* rebound process (met.)

rückspulen to rewind

Rückspul-feder *f* return feed spring **-impuls** *m* half-write pulse **-instrument** *n* round-coil measuring instrument

Rückspülung *f* flushing back

Rückstand *m* still bottom heel, retention, residue, remainder, refuse, bottom arrears **~ der ersten Destillation** topped crude **harziger ~ im Kraftstoff** gum **~ der ersten Rohöldestillation** reduced crude **in ~ kommen** to fall behind, be in arrears

Rückstände (Öl) tailings

rückständig residual, residuary, overdue, old-fashioned, in arrears, backward, retrogressive, reactionary **-e Gebühr** unpaid charge

Rückstandsanalyse *f* analysis by residue

Rückstandsboden, toniger ~ residual clay soil

Rückstands-erzeugnis *n* residual product **-öl** residual oil

Rück-stange *f* pinch bar **-stau** *m* backwash **-stecher** *m* rear set trigger **-stein** *m* back stone, crucible bottom

rückstellbarer Einzelzähler set-back counter

Rückstell-beiwert *m* restoring moment coefficient **-elektromagnet** *m* release magnet

rückstellen to reset, replace

Rückstellfeder *f* return spring, restoring spring **-restkraft** *f* minimum back tension

Rückstell-feld *n* restoring moment field **-flußpegel** *m* reset flux level **-gesetz** *n* restoring moment theorem **-glied** *n* resetting member **-grad** *m* degree of reset **-halbzyklus** *m* resetting half-cycle **-hebel** *m* return lever **-intervall** *n* resetting interval

Rückstellklappe *f* plug-restored shutter, self-restoring indicator or drop **automatische ~** self-restoring drop

Rückstell-klinke *f* backspace pawl **-knopf** *m* set-back knob

Rückstellkraft *f* reestablishing or restoring force, resiliency, retractility, elastic force **~ der Nadel** stylus drag (phono), needle drag

Rückstell-magnet *m* release magnet, resetting magnet **-moment** *n* restoring moment, restoring torque **-momentbeiwert** *m* restoring moment coefficient **-muster** *n* retained sample **-regelungskreis** *m* reset control circuit **-schalter** *m* return switch **-spule** *f* reset solenoid **-strom** *m* releasing current **-taste** *f* back-space key, resetting key

Rückstellung *f* release, replacement, restoring torque, reserve, resetting **~ des Spielzeigers** cycle reset

Rückstellungen machen to set up reserves

Rückstellungs-konstante *f* control constant, restoration constant **-relais** *n* reverse-current relay

Rückstellzeit *f* restoring time

Rückstoß *m* recoil, repulsion, reaction, kick, rebound, backward push, rebuff, backstroke, shock **-antrieb** *m* reaction drive **-atom** *n* recoil atom, knocked-on atom **-bahn** *f* recoil track **-düse** *f* propulsion or propelling nozzle, thrust nozzle, reaction-propulsion jet **-elektron** *n* recoil electron, Compton electron

Rückstößer *m* reaction engine

Rückstoß-feder *f* recoil spring **-frei** recoilless, nonreacting **-hülse** *f* recoil chamber **-impuls** impulse recoil **-kerne** *pl* recoil nuclei **-kolben** *m* depression piston **-kraft** *f* jet reaction, reaction force **-lader** *m* recoil-operated gun **-masse** *f* expellant (g/m) **-motor** *m* jet propulsion

Rückstoß-nachweis *m* recoil detection **-nukleon** *n* recoil nucleus **-potential** *n* recoil potential **-proton** *n* recoil proton **-streamer** *m* recoil streamer **-teilchen** *n* recoil particle **-triebwerk** *n* reaction engine **-untersuchung** *f* recoil investigation **-verstärker** *m* recoil booster **-versuche** *pl* recoil experiments

Rückstrahl *m* echo, reflected wave, reflection **-brennfläche** *f* catacaustic **-diagramm** *n* back-reflection photogram

rückstrahlen to reflect

Rückstrahler *m* reflector, reradiator, reflex reflector

Rückstrahl-farbe *f* reflective paint **-gerät** *n* radar reflector **-kopie** *f* reflex print (phot.) **-meßkammer** *f* reflection measuring chamber **-messung** *f* backscatter gauging **-photographie** *f* back-reflection photography **-schlußleuchte** *f* reflecting tail lamp

Rückstrahlung *f* reflection **spiegelnde ~** specular or regular reflection

Rückstrahlungs-goniometer *n* reflective goniometer **-messer** *m* reflectometer **-vermögen** *n* reflecting ability

Rückstrahl-verfahren *n* back-reflection process, reflection method, backscatter process **-zacke** *f* reflection peak

Rück-streichwalze *f* evener roller **-streifschloßteil** *m* levelling cam

Rückstreuung *f* (Radar) back scatter(ing) **direkte ~** short distance backscatter **indirekte ~** long distance backscatter

Rückstreuungsfaktor *m* backscatter factor

Rückstrom *m* return current, backflow, return flow, reverse current, reflux, recurrent flow, inverse current, backward current (in rectifier) **~ der Anoden** inverse current

Rückstromausschalter *m* return-current cutout, reverse-current switch

Rückströmen *n* return flow

Rückstrom-grad *m* reflux ratio **-kanal** *m* return channel **-leitung** *f* return pipe **-relais** *n* reverse-current relay **-rohr** *n* back flow pipe **-saftvorwärmer** *m* return-current juice heater **-schalter** *m* reverse current circuitbreaker **-schütz** *n* return-current relay **-sperrrelais** *n* reverse

locking relay
Rückströmung *f* back or return current
Rückstromventil *n* nonreturn valve, check valve
Rück-taste *f* back-spacer key **-titrieren** to back-titrate **-titrieren** *n* back-titration **-treibende Kraft** repelling force, reflecting force **-trieb** *m* drag (aviation), trail (ballistics)
Rücktrift *f* trail (aviation) **~ am Boden** ground lag (aerial bombing) **räumliche ~** ground lag, drift trail **zeitliche ~** time lag
Rücktrift-strecke *f* trail distance (ballistics) **-winkel** *m* trail angle (aviation) **-zielgerät** *n* drift sight
Rücktrimmknopf *m* trimming-back knob
Rücktrittbremse *f* back-pedaling brake
Rücktrum (Förderanlagen) return belt
Rück-überhitzer *m* reheat superheater **-übersetzen** to retranslate **-übersetzung** *f* retranslation **-übertragen** to retransfer **-übertragung** *f* retransfer
Rück-ventil *f* retention valve **-verbindung** *f* return connection **-vergüten** to refund **-vergütung** *f* rebate, refund **-verlegung** *f* retardation **-versicherung** *f* reinsurance **-verwandeln** to retranslate **-verwandlung** *f* reconversion
Rückwand *f* backwall, back face **gewölbte ~** vaulted recess
rückwärtig behind the lines, rearward **-er Leitstrahl** *m* back beam (of ILS) **-e Sperrung** revertive blocking **-e Stromstöße** revertive impulses **-e Stromstoßgabe** revertive control, revertive pulsing
rückwärts backward, to the rear, astern **~ gestreut** back-scattered **~ halten** backward hold **~ liegender Antrieb** rear drive **~ gekrümmte Schaufel** back-ward-bent vane **ein Schiff fährt ~** a boat is moving astern
Rückwärts-antrieb *n* reversing motion **-ausbreitung** *f* backward propagation **-bewegung** *f* retrograde motion, backstroke, reverse movement **-differentialgleichung** *f* backward differential equation **-einschneiden** to intersect
Rückwärtseinschnitt *m* resection **~ in der Ebene** plane resection, three-point problem **~ im Raum** resection in space, three-point problem in space **ebener ~** plane resection, three-point problem
rückwärts-fahren to reverse **-fahrt** *f* reverse movement **-gang** *m* reverse, reverse motion, reverse gear **-gleitschiene** *f* astern guide **-kaliber** *n* return pass (in rolling) **-kipper** *m* end-dump truck **-lage** *f* reclining position **-lauf** *m* return movement **-lauf der Schraube** astern running of the propeller **-leitung** *f* high-resistance direction
Rückwärts-lenkung *f* rear steering system **-liegen** to recline **-regelung** *f* indirect control, backward regulation, retroactive control action, backward-acting regulator **-rückruf** *m* backward recall signal **-scheinleitwert** *m* backward transfer admittance **-schreitend** retrograde **-schreitender Rutsch** retrogressive slide **-schweißung** *f* backhand welding, retrogressive welding
Rückwärts-sperre *f* backward busying **-staffelung** *f* backward stagger **-streuung** *f* (Radar) back scatter **-verformung** *f* reverse strain **-visur** *f* backward vision **-welle** *f* backward-facing wave **-wellenoszillator** *m* backward-wave oscillator **-wellenröhre** *f* backward-wave tube **-wellenröhrenoszillator** *m* backward-wave oscillator **-wirken** to act in reverse, react
Rückwärtszeichen *n* round-the-world signal (rdo) **-gebung** *f* backward signalling
Rückwärtszielungen *pl* back sights
Rückweg *m* return path
ruckweise by jerks, intermittently, spasmodically **~ vorwärts schnellen** to advance by jerks
rück-weisende Reflexion retrodirective reflection **-werfen** to reflect **-werfende Brennfläche** catacaustic **-werfer** *m* rejector, reflector
Rückwickel-knopf *m* rewind knob **-motor** *m* rewind motor (tape rec.) **-zähler** *m* rearward turns (return) counter, return winding counter
Rückwicklung *f* rewind mechanism
rückwirken to retroact, react
rückwirkend retroactive, reactive (retrospective) **~ in Kraft treten** to have retroactive effect
Rückwirkung *f* reaction, retroaction, regeneration, feedback, reactive effect, repercussion
Rückwirkungs-feld *n* reaction field **-frei** noninteracting **-kraft** *f* reaction force **-leitwert** *m* reactive admittance, susceptance
Rückwurf *m* reflection **-winkel** *m* angle of reflection
rückzahlbar repayable
Rückzahlung *f* reimbursement, repayment, redemption
rückziehbarer Hilfssenker retractable wing cam
Rückzipfel *m* back lobe
Rückzug *m* retreat, withdrawal, retirement **-hebel** *m* withdrawal lever
Rückzugs-feder *f* restoring spring, release or retractile spring **-kolben** *m* retraction piston **-leitung** *f* retraction line **-linie** *f* line of retreat **-richtung** *f* line of retreat, line of retirement **-widerstand** *m* withdrawal resistance **-zylinder** *m* pull-back (cylinder)
Rückzugtaste *f* back-spacing key
Rückzündung *f* backfire, back-lighting, arc-back, backlash (imperfect rectification, in valves), restricking (in circuit breaker)
Rudel *n* lime rake
Ruder *n* rudder, fin, oar, helm, control surface **festgehaltenes ~** fixed controls **losgelassenes ~** free controls
Ruder-abgleichkasten *m* vane alignment box **-abstimmkasten** *m* vane alignment box **-achse** *f* control-surface axis **-anlenkung** *f* attachment of the control surface **-anschlag** *m* maximum vane deflection **-anschluß** *m* rudder connection **-antrieb** *m* vane motor (missiles) **-antriebsmaschine** *f* rudder-actuating mechanism **-ausgleich** *m* balance of controls **-ausgleichung** *f* compensation of the control surface
Ruderausschlag *m* deflection, angular displacement, or movement of control surface **-schreiber** *m* control position recorder
Ruder-befestigung *f* attachment of the control surface **-belastung** *f* control surface load **-blatt** *n* wash or blade of an oar **-blockierungszeit** *f* disable time **-bock** *m* rudder-post bracket
Ruderboot *n* rowboat **kleines ~** dinghy
Ruder-drehachse *f* rudder axis of rotation **-einrichtung** *f* steering device **-fesselung** *f* fin restraint **-fläche** *f* control surface **-flattern** *n* fin jitter **-flug** *m* bird flight

Ruder-gänger *m* steersman, helmsman **-gestänge** *n* vane linkage **-getriebe** *n* rudder drive, servomotor autopilot **-grube** *f* rudder pit **-halterung** *f* vane support **-hebel** *m* crank (rudder level, aileron lever)

Ruder-kasten *m* vane alignment box **-konstante** *f* vane coefficient **-klampe** *f* oarlock **-kraft** *f* force on control surface **-lage** *f* position of control surface, rudder angle **-lagenanzeige** *f* vane-position indication **-lagezeiger** *m* rudder-position or -setting indicator **-laufgeschwindigkeit** *f* rudder speed

Rudermaschine *f* steering engine, servo-unit **elektrische ~** telecontrol of steering gear

Rudermoment *m* hinge moment, control-surface moment

rudern to row

Ruder-normalkraft *f* normal component of force on control surface **-öse** *f* gudgeon or bracing of the rudder

Ruderpinne *f* helm, tiller **gebogene ~** crooked tiller, gooseneck tiller

Ruder-schaft *m* loom of an oar **-schlag** *m* stroke **-stellung** *f* position of control surface, rudder angle **-steven** *m* rudder post **-tiefe** *f* chord depth of control surface **-Zündkristall** *n* fin fuze crystal

Ruf *m* shout, call, hail, cry, reputation, ring, ringing **abgestimmter ~** harmonic selective ringing **handbetätigter ~** manual ringing **halbselbsttätiger ~** manually started machine ringing **intermittierender ~** interrupted ringing **mangelhafter ~** defective ringing

Ruf, selbsttätiger ~ keyless ringing, machine ringing **selbsttätig wiederholter ~** interrupted ringing **unbeantworteter ~** no-reply call **wahlweiser ~ mit abgestimmten Einrichtungen** harmonic selective ringing **wahlweiser ~ nach einem Rufschlüssel** code ringing **den ~ wiederholen lassen** to rering (on a truck) **~ mit verabredeten Zeichen** code ringing

Ruf-abschalterelais *n* tripping relay **-anlage** *f* staff location system, personal paging system **-anschalterelais** *n* ringing relay **-anzeiger** *m* demand indicator (elec.) **-batterie** *f* battery within calling distance of battalion observation post

rufen to call, shout, ring **wahlweise ~** to call selectively

Rufen *n* ringing, calling **~ mit Durchrufrelais** relayed ringing **~ in Schleifenschaltung** loop ringing **~ in Simultanschaltung** composite (through) ringing **~ mit gleichstromüberlagertem Wechselstrom** superposed ringing

rufender Teilnehmer calling party

Ruf-folge *f* calling sequence **-horn** *n* signal horn **-lampe** *f* calling lamp, calling pilot **-magnet** *m* line relay **-maschine** *f* ringing machine **-nummer** *f* subscriber's number

Rufnummernspeicher und -geber drum information assembler and dispatcher (DIAD)

Ruf-nummernsperre *f* calling number barring circuit **-ordner** *m* alotter, preselector **-phase** *f* ringing cycle **-prüfung** *f* signaling test **-relais** *n* signaling relay, calling relay, ringing relay

Rufsatz *m* (ringing) generator **einen anderen ~ einschalten** to substitute a spare (ringing) generator

Ruf-schalter *m* re-calling key, ringing key **-schaltung** *f* ringing connection **-schlüssel** *m* ringing code, calling code **-schnur** *f* calling cord

Rufsignal *n* (Fernschreiber) ringing signal **akustisches ~** audible signal

Ruf-sperrkondensator *m* block condenser for signaling purposes (teleph.) **-stellung** *f* ringing position **-stöpsel** *m* calling plug **-störung** *f* ringing failure

Rufstrom *m* ringing current **gleichstromüberlagerter ~** superposed ringing current

Rufstrom-anzeiger *m* ringing vibrator, ringing current indicator **-dynamo** *m* ringing dynamo, ringer **-frequenz** *f* signaling or ringing frequency

Ruf(strom)maschine *f* ringer, ringing machine

Rufstrom-quelle *f* ringing (current) source **-umkehrtaste** *f* ringing reversing key **-zuführung** *f* ringing lead

Ruf-taste *f* ringing key **-übertrager** *m* ringing repeater **-überwachung** *f* supervision of answering (teleph.) **-überwachungslampe** *f* ringing pilot lamp **-umschalter** *m* ring and speak key **-umsetzer** *m* ringing converter **-versuch** *m* signaling test **-wechselstromrelais** *n* alternating-current calling relay **-weite** *f* reach of call (teleph.) **-weiterschaltungslampe** *f* incoming call transfer lamp **-welle** *f* calling wave

Rufzeichen *n* call letter, calling code, code letters, call sign(al), line signal **~ für Funk- und Blinkverkehr** code designation for blinker and radio communication **hörbares ~** audible signal

Rüge *f* censure, reprimand, blame

rügen to reprimand, censure, blame

Ruhe *f* rest, calm, quiet, repose, at rest, silence **in ~ befindlich** idle, nonoperative, inoperative **zur ~ kommen** to settle **noch nicht zur ~ gekommen** unsettled

Ruhe-anschlag *m* spacing (rest) stop **-arbeitspunkt** *m* quiescent point or condition **-belichtung** *f* unmodulated lighting, no-modulation lighting, no-sound lighting, average or steady illumination **-bereich** *m* (Relais) region of non operation

Ruhedruck *m* static pressure, earth pressure at rest **-verhältnis** *n* static-pressure ratio **-ziffer** *f* static-pressure ratio, initial lateral-pressure ratio, coefficient of earth pressure at rest

Ruhe-elektrizitätslehre *f* electrostatics **-energie** *f* rest energy **-geräuschspannung** *f* no-signal noise voltage **-grad** *m* degree of rest

Ruhekontakt *m* spacing contact, rest(ing) contact, normal contact, off contact, rest or inoperating contact, contact of back part of key lever **~ des Drehmagneten** rotary interrupter contacts **~ des Hebmagneten** vertical interrupter contacts **~ des Relais** normally closed contact

Ruhelage *f* resting position, position of rest, normal or steady position, equilibrium position, balanced position **Start aus der ~** dead start **in der ~** at rest, inoperative **sich in ~ befinden** to be at rest **~ eines Wählers** normal position

Ruhelagewinkel *m* angle of friction

Ruhe-licht *n* unmodulated lighting, no-modulation lighting, average or steady illumination, no-sound illumination **-luftspalt** *m* quiescent air gap (elec.) **-masse** *f* rest mass

Ruhemassendichte *f* rest mass density

ruhen to rest ~ (lagern), to report

ruhend resting, static, inoperative, constant, steady, latent, quiescent ~ **gegossen** statically cast **-e Belastung** dead load, static load **-es Bild** still picture, unanimated picture, ordinary photograph **-e Flüssigkeit** liquid at rest, stagnant liquid **-er Frequenzwandler** static frequency converter **-er Kern** stationary nucleus **-e Konten** inactive accounts **-er Phasenschieber** (Kondensator) static phase shifter (capacitor) **-e Reibung** static friction **-e Spitze** dead center **-er Transformator** static transformer **-e Überlast** nonmovable overload **-er Umformer** static current changer, rectifier

Ruhe-potential *n* equilibrium rest potential **-punkt** *m* working point, operating point, dead center (engin.), point of rest, fulcrum **-punktspannung** *f* (production of) stress at rest, static stress **-resonanz** *f* rest resonance **-schiene** *f* backstop, spacing stop **-schwärzung** *f* unmodulated density, no-sound density **-sitz** (bei Passungen) tight fit **-spannung** *f* equilibrium potential, production of stress at rest, bias, steady, or no-signal potential

Ruhestand *m* standstill, retirement, state of rest **im** ~ retired

Ruhestellung *f* position of symmetry, unoperated position, rest(ing) position, home position, idle position, normal position **in der** ~ at rest, normal, inoperative

Ruhe-störung *f* disturbance **-streifen** *m* unmodulated track

Ruhestrom *m* quiescent current, stand-by current, holding current, feed current, spacing current, steady current **-batterie** *f* closed-circuit battery **-betrieb** *m* closed-circuit working **-kreis** *m* closed circuit **-prinzip** *n* closed circuit current principle **-schaltung** *f* closed-circuit connection **-sicher** closed-circuit proof **-system** *n* closed-circuit system

Ruhe-reibung *f* static friction **-trägerfrequenz** *f* center frequency, resting frequency **-transparenz** *f* unmodulated transmission

Ruhe- und Arbeitskontakt *m* make-and-break contact, change-over contact

Ruhe-weg *m* path of rest **-welle** *f* spacing wave **-wert** *m* equilibrium value, steady, static, stationary, no-signal, neutral, or quiescent value **-widerstand** *m* rest resistance **-winkel** *m* angle of repose or of friction **-zustand** *m* state of rest, state of quiescence

ruhig quiet, peaceful, silent, still, undisturbed, rest, dead, settled **-er Gang** smoothness of action, smooth running **-er Lauf einer Maschine** smoothness of action **-e Luft** calm air **-e See** smooth sea **-er Stahl** killed steel, quiet steel

Ruhigwerden *n* becoming quiet, killing (of a smelting bath)

Ruhmkorff-Funkeninduktor *m* Ruhmkorff coil **-sches Induktorium** Ruhmkorff coil

Rühr-apparat *m* stirring apparatus, stirrer, agitator **-arm** *m* stirrer, agitator, stirring arm **-äscher** *m* lime pit with agitator

Ruhrast *f*, **in** ~ at half cock

Rühr-blei *n* first lead removed in the Carinthian process **-bütte** *f* machine chest **-einrichtung** *f* stirring arrangement, rabbling mechanism **-eisen** *n* poker

rühren to stir, agitate, beat, strike, move, touch, puddle, pole, rabble

Rühren *n* agitating

Rührer *m* stirrer, agitator, mixer

Rühr-faß *n* churn **-flügel** *m* machine oar, scoop, stirring wing, stirring paddle, blower-agitator, agitating vane **-frischen** *n* puddling **-gebläse** *n* mixing jet **-gefäß** *n* stirrer vessel **-haken** *m* stirring implement, rake, rabble, clot **-holz** *n* stirrer

rührig busy, active

Rühr-kessel *m* agitator vessel **-krücke** *f* scrape, lime rake or beater **-kübel** *m* mixing trough **-laugung** *f* leaching by agitation **-löffel** *m* ladle **-maschine** *f* stirring machine, agitator **-ofen** *m* rabble furnace **-schaufel** *f* stirring paddle **-scheit** *n* paddle, rake, stirrer, spatula, potching stick **-stab** *m* stirring rod, stirring paddle, stirring pole, paddle, rabble **-tank** *m* agitator tank

Rührung *f* stirring, agitating, beating, striking, moving

Rühr-verfahren *n* (beim Schlämmen) tossing **-wäsche** *f* pan for dressing gold-bearing sands

Rührwerk *n* stirring apparatus, stirrer, agitator, cutter ~ **mit Motorantrieb** power agitator **handgetriebenes** ~ hand agitator

Rührzeit *f* stirring time, agitating time

Ruine *f* ruin(s)

ruinieren to ruin, demolish

Rummelfaß *n* rolling or tumbling barrel, mill barrel

Rumpeln des Papiers cockling, creasing, or wringkling of the paper

rumpeln to turn upside-down

Rumpf *m* fuselage, body, thorax, hull, trunk, core (of ions), kernel (stable inner electron group), negative unvaried portion of luminous glow (in glow tube) ~ **in Halbschalenbauweise** *f* semimonocoque fuselage ~ **aus autogen geschweißten Stahlröhren** autogenously welded steel-tube fuselage **der äußere** ~ outer hull

Rumpf-achse *f* body axis **-anordnung** *f* body arrangement **-anschlußstück** *n* fitting for attachment to fuselage **-atom** *m* kernel **-ausschnitt** *m* cockpit cutout **-außentank** *m* belly tank **-außenwand** *f* external shell **-aussparung** *f* fuselage recess or cutout section

Rumpf-behälter *m* fuselage tank **-beheizungskörper** *m* fuselage heater **-bekleidung** *f* covering of the fuselage **-beplankung** *f* fuselage covering, skin **-beschlag** *m* fuselage fitting **-bespannung** *f* fuselage-covering fabric **-bezugsebene** *f* reference plane of the fuselage

Rumpfboden *m* floor of fuselage **unter dem ~ eines Flugbootes angeordnetes Tragflügelprofil zur Erleichterung des Abhebens** hydrofoil to facilitate take-off

Rumpf-breite *f* width of fuselage **-bug** *m* (Flugzeug) nose section **-bug** (Flgzg.) *m* fuselage nose **-eindecker** *m* monoplane fuselage **-einteilung** *f* subdivision of the body or fuselage **-elektron** *n* inner electron **-ende** *n* tail of the fuselage **-endspant** *n* stern post **-endstück** *n* rear part of the fuselage

Rumpf-fachwerk *n* fuselage framework **-feld** *n* body panel **-form** *f* hull shape **-fläche** *f* pene-

plain **-flügelübergang** *m* wing-root fairing **-form** *f* shape of fuselage
Rumpf-gabelung *f* branching of the fuselage **-gerippe** *n* fuselage framework **-gerüst** *n* fuselage frame **-heckteil** *m* tail boom **-hinterteil** *n* after-portion of fuselage **-holm** *m* longeron of fuselage **-inneres** *n* interior of fuselage **-isomerie** *f* core-isomerism
Rumpf-kanzel *f* rear cockpit, rear gun turret **-kompaß** *m* cockpit or fuselage compass **-kühler** *m* body or fuselage radiator **-lager** *n* plummer, pedestal bearing **-längsholm** *m* longeron **-längsleiste** *f* longeron support **-lastig** tail-heavy **-leiter** *f* hopper beam
Rumpf-mittelstück *n* central part of the fuselage **-modell** *n* fuselage model **-nase** *f* nose (of fuselage) **-oberseite** *f* deck of fuselage **-oberstand** *m* top gun position **-querschnitt** *m* section of the body **-querstrebe** *f* body transverse member **-seite** *f*, **-seitenwand** *f* fuselage side **-spant** *m* transverse frame of the fuselage, bulkhead **-spitze** *f* nose of fuselage
Rumpf-tank *m* body tank **-unterseite** *f* underside of fuselage **-verkleidung** *f* fuselage covering **-verstärkung** *f* fuselage bracing strut **-vorderteil** *n* forward portion of fuselage **-werk** *n* fuselage body **-werkantenne** *f* skin antenna **-widerstand** *m* structural drag, body resistance **-zweidecker** *m* biplane fuselage
rund round, circular, spherical, about, rotund, even (of numbers) **~ herum** around **-e Bodenplatte** floor flange
Rund-antenne *f* omnidirectional antenna **-anzeiger** *m* circle marker **-backenzange** *f* round-nosed pliers **-bahn** *f* circular course **-ballon** *m* spherical balloon **-barren** *m* round billet **-bau** *m* rotunda **-becherkondensator** *m* cup-type condenser **-biegemaschine** *f* up-coiler **-biegen** to bend (round)
Rundbild *n* panorama, panoramic picture or view **-aufnahme** *f* panorama (phot.), panoramic exposure **-kammer** *f* panorama camera
Rundblick-aufnahme *f* panoramic exposure, view, or photograph **-fernrohr** *n* rotary telescope, panoramic telescope or sight, dial sight **-kamera** *f* panoramic camera
Rund-block *m* round or cylindrical bloom, round billet **-bogen** *m* semi circular arch **-brecher** *m* gyratory crusher, rotary breaker **-brenner** *m* annular burner **-bürste** *f* circular brush **-dosen** *pl* round containers
Runddraht *m* wire rod, round wire **-windungen** *pl* round-wire windings **-bewehrung** *f* round wire armoring
Runde *f* patrol, beat, round, lap (on track)
Rundeindicker *m* circular thickener
Rundeisen *n* round bracing and reinforcing irons, round iron, iron rod, round steel or iron bar, bar iron, rods **~ in Drahtform** wire
Rundeisen-anker *m* rigid stay **-bügel** *m* round iron strap **-kaliber** *n* rod pass **-walzung** *f* rod rolling **-walzwerk** *n* rod-rolling mill
runden to round, truncate (comput.)
runderhaben convex
runderneuerte Reifen retreaded tires
Rundfahrtswagen *m* touring car
Rund-feder *f* round-bar spiral spring **-feile** *f* rat-tailed file, round file **-feuer** *n* flashover **-feuerschutz** *m* antiarcing screen **-filz** *f* tubular felt **-flamme** *f* round flame **-flug** *m* sightseeing flight **-formstahl** *m* circular forming tool **-fräsmaschine** *f* circular milling machine **-fuge** *f* circumferential groove **-führung** *f* circular guide, circular cutting guide
Rundfunk *m* broadcast(ing), radio, wireless **durch ~ verbreiten** to broadcast **akustischer ~** sound broadcasting
Rundfunk-aufnahmeraum *m* radio studio **-bandfilter** *m* receiver (radio) band filter **-empfang** *m* broadcast reception **-empfänger** *m* broadcast receiver **-empfängerkreis** *m* broadcasting receiver circuit
rundfunken to broadcast
Rundfunk-gerät *n* broadcast apparatus, wireless equipment **-großverstärker** *m* public-address amplifier **-leitung** *f* program circuit **-netz** *n* radio network **-rede** *f* radio address **-reklame** *f* radio advertising **-reportage** *f* on-the-spot broadcast
Rundfunk-sender *m* broadcast transmitter, broadcasting station **-senderaum** *m* broadcasting studio **-sonderdienst** *m* special-messages broadcasting **-spule** *f* radio coil **-station** *f*, **stelle** *f* broadcasting station **-störschutz** *m* radio interference suppression **-störung** *f* radio interference
Rundfunk-technik *f* broadcasting or radio engineering **-teilnehmer** *m* broadcaster **-tonfilm** *m* sound telecast, sound telecine (of film) **-übertragung** *f* broadcast transmission, rebroadcast, program transmission **-übertragungsleitung** *f* programline
Rundfunkübertragungsverbindung *f* program circuit **-wagen** *m* radio mobile unit, outside broadcasting van
Rundfunk-vermittlung wire distribution radio or program distribution system **-vermittlungsanlage** *f* radio-relay exchange **-verstärker** *m* broadcast amplifier **-welle** *f* broadcast wave, medium-frequency wave **-zwischensender** *m* remotely controlled broadcast transmitter
Rund-gang *m* round trip **-gängig** round-threaded **-gehäuse** *n* circular case **-geschliffener Drehstahl** round-nosed cutting tool **-gesenk** *n* rounding tool
Rundgesprächs-einrichtung *f* conference calling equipment **-verbindung** *f* conference circuit
rund-gewickelter Typ wrap-around type **-gewinde** *n* round thread, nuckle thread **-glasschleifer** *m* polisher of convex glasses **-gliederkette** *f* round-link chain **-güsse** *pl* round ingots
Rundheit *f* concentricity
Rundherd *m* circular convex concentrator, round buddle **-mischer** *m* inactive mixer
Rundhobel *m* hollow-nosed plane **-vorrichtung** *f* rotary shaping device
Rund-höcker *m* roche moutonnée, dressed rock **-hohl** concave **-höhlung** *f* concavity **-holm** *m* cylindrical or round spar
Rundholz *n* round timber, spar
Rundiermaschine *f* rounding machine
Rund-integral *n* circulation **-kabel** *n* round (switchboard) cable **-kaliber** *n* round pass, round groove **-kanal** *m* circular passage **-kausche** *f* annular thimble
Rundkeil *m* round key **-verschluß** *m* cylindrical-

wedge breech mechanism
Rund-kerb *m* round notch, Charpy notch, notch with root radius **-kern** *m* round core **-kipp-wagen** *m* round-bottom rotary dump car **-knüppel** *m* round billet, cylindrical billet
Rundkolben *m* round-bottom flask ~ **mit umgelegtem Rand** round-bottom flask with ring neck
Rundkopf *m* round head (of screws), cheese head, fillister head, lag screw **flacher** ~ thin brazier rivet
rund-köpfig round-headed **-kopfschraube** *f* round head screw **-kopfholzschraube** *f* round-head wood screw **-kopfniet** *m* round-head rivet **-kopieren** *n* circular profiling **-körnig** globular **-kupfer** *n* copper billets **-kuppelofen** *m* circular kiln
Rundlauf *m* whirling arm **eine Welle auf** ~ **prüfen** to test a shaft for truth
rundlaufen to rotate, revolve
Rundlaufen *n* truth of rotation, circulation
rundlaufend, nicht ~ out of true
Rundlauf-fehler *f* concentricity error **-hebel** *m* lever for run out test **-lehre** *f* true-running gauge **-versuch** *m* whirling arm test
rundlich rounded off
Rund-leistenmaschine *f* circular string border machine **-maßskala** *f* measuring dial **-material** *n* round stock or material rounds **-meißel** *m* gouge **-messer** *n* revolving blade **-muffe** *f* round socket **-mutter** *f* round nut
Rundnaht *f* circumferential seam, circular bead (welding) **-schweißung** *f* circular-seam weld
Rund-nutenfräser *m* round slot milling machine **-ofen** *m* circlar furnace **-passung** *f* cylindrical fit **-passungslehre** *f* cylindrical limit gauge **-pfahl** *m* round pile **-profil** *n* round section, circular shape, rounds **-richtmaschine** *f* round-stock straightening machine **-riemen** *m* round belt
Rund-säule *f* cylinder **-schaft** *m* rudder **-schieber** *m* circular slide valve, barrel throttle **-schlag** *m* circular twist **-schleifen** *n* plain grinding, cylindrical grinding **-schleifmaschine** *f* circular grinding machine, plain grinding machine **-schlüssel** *m* hollow key **-schmelzmaschine** *f* glazing mill **-schneiden** to cut circular **-schneid-maschine** *f* circular cutter
Rundschnur *f* loop **-ring** *m* O-seal, sealing ring
Rund-schreibeanlage *f* broadcast telegraphy **-schreiben** *n* circular **-schreibsystem** *n* broadcast system **-schweißnaht** *f* circumferential welding joint
Rundschwenken, ungehindertes ~ unrestricted rotation
Rundschwenktisch *m* circular swivel table
Rundseil *n* round rope, round cable **dreilitziges** ~ three-strand round rope
Rundsichtradar *n* surveillance radar
Rundsieb *n* sifting drum **-pappenmaschine** *f* board machine (paper mfg.)
Rundsieb-entwässerungsmaschine *f* endless wet machine **-maschine** *f* cylinder paper machine
Rundsprache-anlage *f* public address system
Rundspruch *m* broadcasting **-anlage** *f* public-address system, intercommunication system **-empfänger** *m* broadcast receiver **-übertragung** programme transmission **-verstärker** *m* programme repeater
Rundstab *m* round bar, rod, rounds
Rundstahl *m* round iron, rounds, rods, round steel **-stange** *f* round steel bar
Rund-stange *f* bar of round section rod **-stauch-maschine** (Felgen) (rim) sizing machine **-steuer-technik** *f* audio-frequency powerline carrier control
Rundstrahl-antenne *f* polydirectional antenna **-bake** *f* omnidirectional radio beacon **-brenner** *m* circular section jet burner **-diagramm** *n* circular radiation pattern
rund-strahlend equi-radial **-strahler** *m* non-directional or omnidirectional antenna, circular radiation pattern
Rundstrahl-licht *n* omnidirectional light **-verteiler** *m* air cap for round spray
Rund-strecke *f* lap **-strickmaschine** *f* circular knitting machine **-stuhl** *m* circular knitting machine
Rundsuch-gerät *n* all-around search apparatus (radar) **-radar** *n* surveillance radar element **-radaranlage** *f* ground surveillance radar
Rund-support *m* circular rest **-taktbohrmaschine** *f* rotary-cycle drilling machine
Rundtisch *m* rotary attachment ~ **mit Teilkreis** round table with graduated circle
Rund-tischunterteil *m* rotary-attachment base **-tuch** *n* endless cloth
Rundumdarstellung *f* panoramic display (radar)
Rundumsuchgerät *n* panorama radar (for early warning), plan position indicator
Rundung *f* roundness, rounding **ausgewaschene** ~ **im Flußbett** pothole
Rundungs-fehler *m* rounding error (info proc.), truncation error (comput.) **-halbmesser** *m* radius of curvature **-maschine** *f* rounding machine **-ungenauigkeit** *f* truncation error
rund-walzen to roll cylindrical(ly) **-walzwerk** *n* rolling mill for circular shapes **-ware** *f* circular fabric **-weg** plainly **-welle** *f* indirect or reflected wave **-wert** *m* approximate value **-zange** *f* round-nose(d) pliers **-zellenkontroller** *m* face plate controller **-zirkel** *m* calipers
Runge *f* stake, stanchion
Rungenkette *f* stake or stanchion chain
Runse *f* gully, recently eroded valley
Runzel *f* wrinkle **-bildung** *f* shriveling or festooning (paint) **-blech** *n* corrugated sheet metal
runzelig wrinkled, puckered, shriveled, mottled, reticulated
Runzel-korn *n* distorted grain effect (phot.) **-lack** *m* wrinkle finish
runzeln to wrinkle, fold, crease
Runzeln *n* mottling, wrinkling (Farbe) rivelling
Rupertsmetall *n* Prince Rupert's metal
Rupfen *n* cracking, lifting, Hessian sack cloth
Rupffestigkeit *f* resistance to pick test
Rüsche *f* quilling, ruche
Ruß, fest gebrannt soot baked hard
Ruß *m* soot, black, lampblack, carbon black **-ablagerung** *f* carbon deposit **-bildung** *f* soot formation **-bläser** *m* soot blower, spot blower **-brennerei** *f* manufacture of lamp black
Rüssel *m* nozzle, tuyère pipe, blowpipe, belly pipe, nose, snout, (slang) oxygen mask **-strang-ablegeapparat** *m* trunk piler **-wolke** *f* funnel cloud

rußen to soot
Ruß-fänger *m* soot arrester or catcher **-farbe** *f* lampblack bister **-fleck** *m* smut **-flocke** *f* soot flake, smut **-haltig** sooty **-schwarz** *n* lampblack
rußig sooty, fuliginous
Ruß-kobalt *m* asbolite **-kohle** *f* sooty coal **-schreiber** *m* carbon recorder **-sicher** soot-proof
Rüstbaum *m* scaffolding pole, putlog, imp-pole **-bezugslinie** *f* rigging datum line
Rüste *f* setting of the sun, channel **große ~** main channel
rüsten to prepare, equip, arm, mount, erect, assemble, install
Rüsten *n* rigging, arming **-schauzeiger** *m* click stop indicator
Rüster *m* rigger (for airplane), fitter, erector
Rüst-gewicht *n* empty weight plus fixed weight (aviation) **-halle** *f* erecting shop, assembling room
rüstig active, alert, vigorous
Rüst-mann *m* fitter **-material** *n* scaffold material **-satz** *m* auxiliary apparatus, standard equipment (jet)
Rüstung *f* equipment, preparation, armament, scaffolding, armature, assembly, erection, mounting, installation, rig
Rüstungs-beschränkung *f* armament restriction **-einschränkung** *f* armament limitation **-industrie** *f* armament industry **-material** *n* armament **-verfahren** *n* rigging **-werk** *n* armament plant, armament works
Rüstzeit (Maschinenwesen) setting period **kurze ~** rapid preparation
Rüst-zeug *n* erecting tackle, equipment **-zustand** *m* equipment condition
Rute *f* pole, lug, rod, perch
Rutengänger *m* water finder or diviner
Ruthenium *n* ruthenium **-oxydul** *n* ruthenium monoxide **-säure** *f* ruthenic acid
Rutherford *n* rutherford
Rutil *m* rutile
Rutilit *m* rutilite
Rutsch-abscheider *m* chute separator **-bahn** *f* live roller bed, slide **-bohrung** *f* bore slide fit
Rutsche *f* chute, shoot, slide
Rutschen *pl* chutes
Rutschen *n* slippage **~ des Bodens** landslide
rutschen to slip, skid, slide, glide, sideslip, chute
rutschende Kuppelung slipping clutch
Rutscheneinstellung *f* chute adjustment
Rutsch-erscheinung *f* slip phenomenon **-fest** non-skid **-fläche** *f* sliding or slipping plane, surface, or area **-gefährlichkeit** *f* danger of slipping **-gewicht** *n* sliding weight **-kegel** *m* slip cone **-kuppelung** *f* slipper clutch, slipping clutch, torque overload, release clutch **-los** free of slip **-moment** *n* slide torque **-schere** *f* jars **-scherenfänger** *m* jar socket
rutschsicher antiskid, nonskid **-er Belag** *m* nonskid surfacing
Rutschung *f* slip, slide, landslide **~ einer Böschung** slide of a slope or bank **~ durch Verflüssigung** liquefaction failure
Rutsch-vorgang *m* sliding phenomenon **-winkel** *m* angle of slide
Rüttel-apparat *m* vibrator **-bewegung** *f* shaking motion **-erscheinung** *f* flutter **-feder** *f* shake spring **-feste Bauart** vibration-proof construction **-festigkeit** *f* vibration strength **-förderer** *m* shaker conveyor
Rüttelformmaschine *f* jar-ram molding machine, jarring molding machine, jolt-ramming machine, jolting molding machine, jolter **~ mit Abhebevorrichtung** jolter with mold-lift attachment **~ mit Abstreifplatte und Handhebelmodellaushebung** jolt-stripper with hand-lever lift **~ mit Abstreifvorrichtung** jar-strip molding machine, jar-ramming stripping machine, jolt stripper **~ mit Druckluftabhebung** jar-ramming power-draw machine, jarring machine with air lift **~ für Druckluftbetrieb** air-operated jarring machine, air jolter **~ mit Durchzieh- und Abhebevorrichtung** jolt-strip pattern-draw machine
Rüttelformmaschine, ~ mit Handhebelmodellabhebung jarring machine with hand-lever lift **~ mit Stiftenabhebung** jarring flask-lifting machine **~ mit Umroll- und Modellabhebeeinrichtung** jarring rollover pattern-drawing machine **~ mit Wendetisch** turnover-table jolter **~ mit ausfahrbarer Wendevorrichtung** roll-over jolter **~ mit Wende- und Abhebeeinrichtung** jar-ramming turnover pattern-drawing machine, jarring roll-over pattern-drawing molding machine **stoßfreie ~** shockless jarring machine, shockless jolter
Rüttel-herd *m* vibratory grate **-kolben** *m* jar piston, jarring piston, jolt piston **-kopf** *m* vibrating head **-leistung** *f* jarring or jolting capacity **-maschine** *f* jar-ram molding machine, jarring molding machine, jolt-ramming machine, jolting molding machine, jolter
rütteln to shake, jolt, jar ram, jar, jolt ram, vibrate, joggle
Rütteln *n* shaking, jarring, jar ramming, jolting **~ der Schalen** vibration of form
Rüttelnadel *f* vibrating point
Rüttel-ofen *m* jolting furnace **-platte** *f* vibrating plate compactor **-presser** *m* jar-and-squeeze machine
Rüttelpreßformmaschine *f* jar-squeeze machine **~ mit Stiftenabhebung** jar-squeeze flask-lift machine **~ mit Wendeplatte** jar-ramming and -squeezing turnover draw machine **~ mit Wende- und Abhebeeinrichtung** jolt roll-over squeeze pattern-draw machine
Rüttel-probe *f* shatter test **-rutsche** *f* jig-shaken tray **-schlag** *m* jolt blow **-schwingung** *f* vibration **-sieb** *n* vibrating screen, oscillating riddle, shaking screen **-stoß** *m* jolt blow, jolt, vibrating shock **-tisch** *m* jarring or jolting table, jarring plate, jolt table, bumping table **-ventil** *n* jolt valve, jarring valve **-verfahren** *n* jar-ramming process or method, vibration process **-vorgang** *m* jarring or jolting operation
Rüttelwendeformmaschine *f* jar-ramming turnover plate machine, turnover-table jolter **~ mit Abhebevorrichtung** jar-ramming turnover pattern-drawing machine, jarring roll-over pattern-drawing molding machine **~ mit Fußhebelmodellabhebung** jar-ramming turnover foot-draw machine **~ mit Preßvorrichtung** jolt-squeeze turnover machine
Rüttel-zeug *n* shaking apparatus **-zylinder** *m* jolt cylinder

Rüttler *m* jar-ram molding machine, jarring molding machine, jolt-ramming machine, jolting molding machine, jolter ~ **für Kerne** core-jarring machine

Rüttlerformmaschine *f* jarring machine

Rütt(e)lung *f* shaking, vibration

S

Saal *m* hall, room **-empfänger** *m* auditorium receiving set **-geräusch** *n* auditorium or hall or room noise **-regler** *m* auditorium volume control, theater fader (film)

Saat *f* seed (atom., phys.)

Säbel *m* saber, sword

Sabotage *f* sabotage

Sabugalith *m* sabugalite

Saccharase *f* sucrose, saccharose

Saccharat *n* saccharate

Saccharimetrie *f* saccharimetry

Saccharose *f* sucrose

Sacharin *n* saccharin

Sach-bearbeiter *m* expert, professional **-beschädigung** *f* property damage **-beweis** *m* material proof **-bezüge** *pl* payments in kind **-dienlich** relevant, appropriate, useful.

Sache *f* matter, thing, case, theme, topic, affair, docket **sich einer ~ annehmen** to take charge of (something) **einer ~ aus dem Wege gehen** to avoid (something) **freie Sachen** unrestricted or unclassified documents

sach-gemäß appropriate, expert, proper, suitable, relevant **-kenner** *m* expert **-kenntnis** *f* expert knowledge, practical experience, competence **-kunde** *f* practical experience, expert or special knowledge, competence **-kundig** expert, experienced, skilled, trained in a profession **-kundiger** *m* expert **-lage** *f* state of affairs, factual situation

sachlich pertinent, objective, real, in a matter of fact way **-es Vertragsgebiet** scope of an agreement ~ **zuständig** cognizant

Sachlichkeit *f* objectivity, reality

Sach-patentanspruch *m* article claim **-register** *n* subject index, (table of) contents **-schaden** *m* material or property damage **-schadenersatz** *m* compensation or indemnity for property damage

sacht soft, gentle, smooth, slow, scoured or boiled (silk)

Sach-verhalt *m* state or condition of affairs, facts of the case, factual situation **-verständig** adept, expert

Sachverständigenbegutachtung *f* examination by experts

Sach-verständiger *m* expert, authority, specialist **-verzeichnis** *n* subject index **-walter** *m* legal adviser, attorney, counsel **-wörterbuch** *n* encyclopedia

Sack *m* bag, sack, pocket, pouch **-ausklopfanlage** *f* sack-beating plant **-ausschüttelanlage** *f* sack-shaking plant **-bagger** *m* hand dredge, net dredger **-band** *n* sack string **-behälter** *m* self-sealing tank **-bohrer** *m* pocket drill **-bürstemaschine** *f* bag-brushing machine

sacken to bag, sack, sag, slip down, sink, subside ~ **lassen** to ease down, let come down **sich** ~ to settle

Sacken *n* sinking, sinking in, settling, subsiding

Sackfilter *n* bag filter

Sackpflug *m* stalling flight ~ **ohne Kraft** stall without power; plötzlicher ~ whipstall **vorgerückter ~**, advanced stall

Sackflug-anzeiger *m* antistall gear or indicator **-geschwindigkeit** *f* stalling speed **-landung** *f* stall landing **-schutzgerät** *n* antistall gear **-zustand** *m* stalled condition

Sack-förderer *m* bag conveyer **-füllervorrichtung** *f* bagging spout attachment **-gasse** *f* blind alley or road **-gewinde** *n* blind tapping **-gleis** *n* dead-end siding **-grube** *f* saphead **-kalk** *m* slaked lime **-kanal** *m* ditch canal **-leinen** *n* sackcloth, sacking **-leinenweberei** *f* sack-ticking weaving mill **-leinwand** *f* sackcloth, sacking **-leitung** *f* stub

Sackloch *n* blind-end bore, blind hole ~ **mit Gewinde** tapped blind hole

Sackmaß *n* measure or degree of settling, shrinkage, consolidation

Sacksches Walzwerk Sack's (universal three-high) rolling mill.

Sack-stapelförderer *m* staple conveyer for sacks **-stapler** *m* bag piler, sack elevator

Sackung *f* settling, subsidence, sagging, settlement

Sackungskeil *m* sag wedge

Sack-wendelrutsche *f* chute for sack conveyance **-zucker** *m* sugar in bags

Sä-apparat *m* seeder **-maschine** *f* sowing or seeding machine, drill, seeder

säen to sow

Saffian *m* morocco (leather)

Safflorit *m* safflorite

Safranbronze *f* tungsten bronze

Saft *m* juice, sap, (slang) electric current **-abscheider** *m* juice catcher, catchall, save-all **-absonderung** *f* secretion **-dichte** *f* juice density, juice gravity **-frisches Holz** green timber **-gewinnung** *f* juice extraction **-leitung** *f* juice piping **-probenehmer** *m* juice sampler **-pumpe** *f* juice pump **-reich** sappy **-reinigungsmittel** *n* defecant (sugar mfg.), juice purification agent **-rinne** *f* juice gutter **-vorwärmer** *m* juice (pre)heater

Säge *f* saw, saw edge ~ **für Höchstleistung** heavy-duty saw ~ **mit geradem Rücken** straight-back saw ~ **mit geschweiftem Rücken** skew-back saw

Säge-abfall *m* sawdust waste **-angel** *f* saw-blade holder

sägeartig sawlike, serrated ~ **gezackt** serrated

Säge-blatt *n* saw web, saw blade **-block** *m* sawing jack, saw log, plank log or timber **-bogen** *m* saw frame **-bügel** *m* saw bow or frame **-dach** *n* saw-tooth roof **-feile** *f* saw file **-gatter** *n* saw frame, saw-mill **-gewinde** *n* buttress thread **-mehl** *n* sawdust **-mehlfilter** *m* sawdust filter **-mühle** *f* sawmill

sägen to saw
Sägen *n* sawing **-blatt** *n* saw blade, saw web **-feile** *f* saw file **-gewinde** *n* buttress thread **-stahl** *m* saw steel
Säge-profilgewinde *n* buttress thread **-schleifstein** *m* saw whetstone or grindstone **-schlitz** *m* serrated slot **-schnitt** *m* saw cut or nick **-schränkzange** *f* saw-set pliers **-späne** *m pl* sawdust, sawmill waste **-stahl** *m* saw steel **-staub** *m* sawdust **-walze** *f* rasp cylinder **-werk** *n* sawmill
Sägezahn *m* saw tooth **-antenne** *f*, zigzag antenna, ratched aerial, saw-tooth aerial **-artig** saw-tooth shaped, saw-toothed **-erzeuger** *m* saw-tooth generator or producer **-form** *f* saw-tooth shape **-förmige Kippspannung** saw-tooth-shaped sweep voltage, saw-tooth voltage **-generator** *m* saw-tooth generator **-kurve** *f* saw-tooth curve **-spannung** *f* saw-tooth voltage, ratchet voltage **-strom** *m* saw-tooth current
sagittale Brennlinie sagittal focal line
Sagittalstrahlen *pl* sagittal rays
saigern to liquate, segregate, infiltrate, sweat out (tin).
Saigerung *f* liquation, sweating out, segregation
Saillant *m* salient
Saison *f* season **-abhängig** seasonable **-einfluß** *m* seasonal influence or inflow **-tarif** *m* seasonal tariff
Saite *f* string, cord, chord **ausgespannte ~** stretched chord or string **geschlagene ~**, percussed chord or string **gezupfte ~** plucked string **mitschwingende ~** sympathetic string covibrant string **schwingende ~** vibrating chord or string **umsponnene ~** overspun string
Saiten-aufspanner *m* string fitter **-beschleunigungsmesser** *m* vibrating string accelerometer (gyro) **-elektrometer** *n* string electrometer **-galvanometer** *n* string galvanometer, vibration galvanometer **-gravimeter** *m* string gravimeter **instrument** *n* string(ed) (musical) instrument
Saiten-näherung *f* string approximation **-oszillograph** *m* string oscillograph **-summer** *m* chord buzzer **-unterbrecher** *m* vibrating-wire interrupter **-zug** *m* string tension
säkular secular, centennial
Säkular-determinante *f* secular determinant **-gleichung** *f* secular equation
säkularisieren to secularize
Säkular-schwankung *f* secular trend or fluctuation **-verzögerung** *f* secular retardation
Salband *n* gouge (geol.), flucan, selvage
salbig salvy, unctuous
Salden-auswahl *f* balance selection **-steuerapparat** *m* balance selector
saldieren to balance, clear, settle, square
saldierende, direkt ~ Zählerstellen (net) balance counter positions
Saldo *m* balance, remainder **-konto** *n* current account book; **-vortrag** *m* balance carried forward
Saleit *m* saleite
Saline *f* salt mine, saltworks
Salinometer *n* halometer, salinometer
Salizyl-präparat *n* salicylate **saures Natrium** sodium salicylate
Salmiak *m* sal ammoniac, ammonium chloride **-element** *n* Leclanché cell, sal-ammoniac cell **-geist** *m* aqueous or liquid ammonia **-salz** *n* ammonium chloride, sal ammoniac **-stein** *m* sal ammoniac
Salpeter *m* saltpeter **-äther** *m* nitric ether, ethyl nitrate **-bildung** *f* nitrification **-fraß** *m* corrosion by niter **-haltig** nitrous
salpetersauer nitrate of, nitric
Salpetersäure *f* nitric acid **-anhydrid** *n* nitric anhydride
salpetersaur-es Ammon(ium) ammonium nitrate **-es Blei(oxyd)** lead nitrate **-es Ceroxydul** cerium nitrate **-es Eisen(oxyd)** iron nitrate, ferric nitrate **-er Kalk** calcium nitrate **-es Kupferoxyd** copper nitrate **-es Natron** sodium nitrate **-es Quecksilberoxyd** mercuric nitrate **-es Quecksilberoxydul** mercurous nitrate **-es Salz** nitrate **-es Silber(oxyd)** silver nitrate **-e Tonerde** aluminum nitrate **-es Uranoxyd** uranium nitrate **-es Wismut(oxyd)** bismuth nitrate **-es Zink(oxyd)** zinc nitrate
salpetrig nitrous **-sauer** nitrate of, nitrous
Salpetrig-säure *f* nitrous acid **-äther** *m* ethyl nitrite
salpetrigsaures Ammonium ammonium nitrite **~ Salz** nitrite
Salse *f* mud volcano, salinelle, salse
Salve *f* volley, salvo, broadside
Salz *n* salt **chlorsaures ~** chlorate **chromsaures ~** chromate **schwefelsaures ~** sulphate **unterphosphoriges ~** hypophosphite
Salzabschneider *m* salt interceptor **salz-artig** saline **-äther** *m* muriatic ether, ethyl chloride
Salzbad *n* salt bath **-aufkohlung** *f* salt bath carburizing **-einsatzhärtung** *f* salt-bath case-hardening **-härtung** *f* salt bath hardening **-tester** *m* salt immersion tester
Salz-beize *f* salt dressing **-bergwerk** *n* salt mine **-bildend** halogenous **-bildner** *m* halogen **-breiartige Masse** salt-grained sludge **-dampf** *m* salt vapor **-dom** *m* saline dome, salt dome **-diagramm** *n* salinity diagram
salz-fähige Base *f* salifiable base **-führend** saliferous
Salzgehalt *m* salinity, salt content, proportion of salt **-messer** *m* salinometer
salz-getränkte Kohle mineralized or impregnated carbon **-glasur** *f* salt glaze **-haltig** salt-bearing saliferous **-haltigkeit** *f* salinity, salt content **-haut** *f* saline encrustation
salzig salty, saline **-es Wasser** saline water
Salz-kupfererz *n* atacamite **-lauge** *f* brine **-laugung** *f* brine leaching **-lösung** *f* salt or saline solution, brine **-messer** *m* salinometer **-mutter** *f* mother of salt **-prüfversuch** *m* salt test **-quelle** *f* saline spring
Salzsäure *f* hydrochloric or muriatic acid **-gas** *n* gaseous hydrochloric acid
salzsaures Anilin aniline hydrochloride **~ Eisenoxyd** iron chloride, ferric chloride **~ Eisenoxydul** ferrous chloride **~ Kupferoxyd** copper chloride, cupric chloride **~ Kupferoxydul** cuprous chloride **~ Methylamin** methyl hydrochloride
Salz-schmelze *f* fused salt bath **-sole** *f* brine **-sprüh(nebel)versuch** *m* salt-spray test **-trichter** *m* salt hopper
Salzungsmethode *f* salt (velocity) method

Salz-umschlag *m* salting agent **-vorlage** *f* flash-reducing wad **-waage** *f* salinometer **-wasser** *n* brine, salt water **-wasserumwandlung** *f* saline water conversion

Samarium *n* samarium

Samarskit *m* samarskite

Samiresit *m* samiresite

sämisch-gares Leder chamois-dressed leather **-gerben** to chamois **-gerbung** *f* chamois tannage **-leder** *n* chamois leather

Sammel-adreßgruppe *f* collective address group **-amt** *n* smaller center **-anode** *f* collector or gathering anode, output anode, ultimate anode **-anruf** *m* trafficlist (radio)

Sammelanschluß *m* private branch exchange (teleph.), collective number **-teilnehmer** *m* subscriber with several lines

Sammel-auftrag *m* collective flight order **-bahnhof** *m* railroad collecting point, railroad supply-collecting depot **-becken** *n* collecting tank **-behälter** *m* storage bin, reservoir, sump, storage tank, accumulator (tank) **-bezeichnung** *f* collective denomination **-brunnen** *m* reservoir, cistern **-bunker** *m* storage bunker or bin

Sammeldienst-leitung *f* concentration line, split-order wire (circuit) **-leitungsbetrieb** *m* split-order wire

Sammel-drain *m* collecting pipe **-druckschrift** *f* loose-leaf catalogue **-elektrode** *f* output electrode, catcher or collector electrode, gathering electrode **-entstörung** *f* suppression **-fernplatz** *m* trunk concentration position **-flasche** *f* receptacle, collecting flask, receiver **-funkspruch** *m* collective radiogram

Sammel-gang *m* non-listing cycle **-geschwindigkeit** *f* accumulating speed, tab speed

Sammel-gebiet *n* reservoir, catchment basin, water gathering ground **-gefäß** *n* reservoir, receptacle, receiver, storage tank, collecting vessel

Sammelgespräch *n* conference call (teleph.) ~ **mit Lautsprechern** conference call with loud-speakers ~ **mit gewöhnlichen Sprechstellenapparaten** conference call between subscribers' installations without special apparatus

Sammelgesprächs-einrichtung *f* conference-calling equipment **-verbindung** *f* conference (call) circuit or connection

Sammel-getriebe *n* gear assembly or set, gearing **-glas** *n* converging lens, preparation tube, specimen tube **-gleis** *n* collecting siding **-graben** *m* drainage ditch, drainage channel, trench **-heizung** *f* central heating **-kammer** *f* storage room, stockroom **-kanal** *m* collecting main or flue,

Sammel-kasten *m* collecting tank, receiving tank or case **-kondensator** *m* loading condenser **-kondensatpumpe** *f* collected condensate pump **-kontakt** *m* hunting contact, master number contact **-kontaktstelle** *f* tie point **-ladung** *f* collective consignment or shipment

Sammelleitung *f* collecting pipe, concentration or collecting line (teleph.), omnibus circuit, common main, manifold **ringförmige** ~ collector ring

Sammel-leitungswähler *m* rotary hunting connector **-linse** *f* convergent or converging lens, collective (focusing) lens, condenser lens, positive lens **-loch** *n* catch basin, cesspool, sump **-locher** *m* summary punch **-magazin** *n* container **-meldung** *f* collective or multiple-address report **-morseeinrichtung** *f* arrangement for central code recording **-mulde** *f* collecting trough

Sammel-napf *m* sump (for oil) **-netzsystem** *n* gathering system **-nummer** *f* directory number of subscriber having more than one line **-ort** *m* place of appointment, dump, collecting dump **-öse** *f* concentration ring, load ring **-platz** *m* assembly point, concentration position, place of appointment **-prospekt** *m* master binder **-punkt** *m* center of collineation, rally, rendezvous

Sammel-raum *m* collecting chamber, receiver, receptacle, collector or catcher space (in klystron) **-ring** *m* collecting or collector ring **-rinne** *f* collecting channel **-rohr** *n* collecting pipe, main, collector, header **-ruf** *m* collective call **-rufzeichen** *n* collective call signal **-rumpf** *m* bunker, bin **-schacht** *m* collecting shaft **-schalter** *m* concentration switch **-schaltung** *f* omnibus circuit

Sammelschiene *f* bus bar, collecting bar, trunk (comput.) ~ **aus Kupfer** copper bus or bus bar

Sammelschienen-kasten *m* bus-bar chamber **-übertragungsausrüstung** *f* bus transfer equipment **-voltmeter** *n* bus-bar voltmeter

Sammel-schmierung *f* centralized lubrication **-schutz** *m* collective protection, public protection **-spannschloß** *n* multiple or collecting turnbuckle **-spiegel** *m* concave mirror **-spruch** *m* general call (radio) **-spule** *f* concentration (focusing) coil (cathode-ray oscillograph) **-stelle** *f* collecting point, salvage dump **-strahlanlage** *f* directive beacon installation **-system** *n* collective or condenser system or element, projector

Sammel-tank *m* tank, reservoir, collector **-tasche** *f* loading hopper **-tätigkeit** *f* (salvage-)collecting **-telegramm** *n* synoptic or collective telegram **-trichter** *m* collecting funnel, catchment basin **-unterbrechungen** *pl* miscellaneous delays (work-factor)

Sammel-verbindung *f* conference call, multi-address circuit **-verlegung** *f* collective wiring **-zähler** *m* continuous counter, gleaning cylinder, totalizing meter **-zylinder** *m* focusing cylinder

Sammetstoff *m* pile fabric, velvet

Sammler *m* accumulator, storage or secondary cell, collector carrier (print.), header (of boiler) **alkalischer** ~ Edison storage cell, alkaline accumulator **tragbarer** ~ portable storage cell or battery

Sammler-anlage *f* accumulator plant **-antrieb** *m* accumulator drive **-batterie** *f* accumulator battery, storage battery, secondary battery **-elektrode** *f* storage-battery **-gefäß** *n* accumulator tank **-kraftwagen** *m* battery car **-ladegerät** *n* battery-charger **-ladung** *f* charging of accumulator **-linse** *f* condenser (opt.) **-nachfüllen** to top up or fill up storage cells

Sammler-platte *f* accumulator plate **-raum** *m* battery room **-schalter** *m* junction switch box **-speisung** *f* supply by accumulators **-spirale** *f* volute collecting chamber **-stück** *n* header **-unterwerk** *n* accumulator substation

Sammlerzelle *f* accumulator cell, storage cell,

secondary cell **gegengeschaltete ~** counter cell
Sammlerzündung *f* coil (battery) ignition
Sammlung *f* collection
Sammlungswerkstatt *f* assembly plant
Samt *m* velvet **-dichtung** *f* velvet trap
sämtlich all, jointly, collectively
Sand *m* sand **~ durchwerfen** to screen or sift sand **feinkörniger ~** fine-grain sand **fester ~** compact sand **fetter ~** loamy sand **grüner ~** green sand **magerer ~, nasser ~** green sand **tonhaltiger ~** clayey sand **trockener ~** parting sand
Sand-ablagerung *f* deposition of sand **-abmeßgerät** *n* measuring device for sand **-anschwemmung** *f* encroachment by sand
Sandarak *m* sandarac
Sand-aufbereitung *f* sand preparation **-aufbereitungsanlage** *f* sand-preparing plant **-aufbruch** *m* boiling of sand **-auflockerungsmaschine** *f* sand-aerating apparatus, sand aerator **-auslaufrohr** *n* sand-discharge pipe
Sand-bad *n* sand bath **-bank** *f* sandbank **-becherwerk** *n* sand elevator **-beschaffenheit** *f* sand quality, sand property **-bestrahlung** *f* sand-blasting **-bindemittel** *n* sand agglutinant **-blasdüse** *f* sandblast nozzle **-blashaus** *n* sandblast room
Sand-blaswirkung *f* sandblast action **-boden** *m* sandy soil **-braun** *n* velvet brown **-dicht** (air-borne) dust-proof **-dichte** *f* sand density **-dornbeere** *f* sallow thorn berry **-durchgang** *m* sand passage **-düse** *f* sand nozzle **-einschluß** *m* sand pocket
Sandelholz *n* sandalwood **rotes ~** redwood
Sand-fang *m* sand trap, button trap or catcher (paper mfg.) **-fänger** *m* sand trap **-flotation** *f* sand flotation **-fluß** *m* sand flow **-förderer** *m* sand conveyer **-förderschnecke** *f* sand screw conveyer **-form** *f* sand mold **-(form)guß** *m* sand cast(ing) **-führend** sand-conveying, sand-bearing, sandy, arenaceous **-führung** *f* sand content
Sand-gebläse *n* sandblast **-gerüst** *n* sand structure or scaffolding **-gestrahlt** shot-blasted **-gießen** *n* sand casting **-gießerei** *f* sand-casting plant **-grieß** *m* coarse sand **-grube** *f* sand pit **-grund** *m* sandy bottom **-guß** *m* sand(-mold) casting, sand-mold cast iron **-haken** *m* gagger **-haufen** *m* sand pile **-hose** *f* sand spout
sandig sandy, arenaceous **-er Magneteisenstein** black iron sand
Sand-kasten *m* sand tank, sandbox, sand model **-kelle** *f* sand ladle
Sandkern *m* sand core **-blasmaschine** *f* sand core blast machine
Sand-kohle *f* nonbaking coal, free-burning coal, noncaking coal, hard coal, semianthracite, lean anthracitic coal, uninflammable coal **-korn** *n* sand grain **-kreislauf** *m* sand circulation
Sand-leiste *f* sand rib, sand-retaining flange **-leitung** *f* sand-delivery pipe **-loch** *n* sand hole **-luftgemisch** *n* air-sand mixture **-mischkessel** *m* sand-mixing chamber **-mischmaschine** *f* sand mixer **-mühle** *f* sand mill **-nest** *n* trapped sand
Sand- oder Kiesnest *n* (im Beton) honeycomb (in concrete)
Sandpapier *n* sandpaper **mit ~ schleifen** to sand-paper **-schleifmaschine** *f* sander
Sand-pressen *n* sand pressing **-prüfung** *f* static test **-radsporen** *f pl* sand-wheel lugs **-rahmen** *m* sand frame **-raum** sand(-mixing) chamber **-regulierhahn** *m* sand-feed valve, sand-control valve **-reinigung** *f* sand sifting or cleaning, sand separation **-reiße** *f* sand dike (blasting) **-rinne** *f* sand gutter, sand channel **-ruß** *m* silica black
Sandsack *m* sandbag **-aufhängöse** *f* sandbag loop **-leine** *f* sandbag line **-modell des Atomkerns** hypothesis of compound nucleus
Sand-schaber *m* sand scraper **-schlauch** *m* sand hose, shoestring sands **-schleuder** *f* sand thrower, sand disintegrator
Sandschleuderformmaschine *f* sand slinger **selbstfahrende ~** self-propelled-type sand slinger
Sand-schleudermühle *f* sand disintegrator **-schmitzen** *pl* sand streaks **-schüttelsieb** *n* sand (riddle) sifter, sand-shaking sieve **-seife** *f* sandsoap **-sichtung** *f* sand separation, sifting **-sieb** *n* sand screen, sand sifter **-siebschleudermaschine** *f* sand disintegrator with sieving arrangement **-slinger** *m* sand slinger **-sorte** *f* kind or class of sand, sand quality **-staub** *m* sand dust **-stein** *m* sandstone **-steinquader** *m* sandstone block **-stelle** *f* scab (on a casting)
Sandstrahl *m* sandblast, sand jet, stream of abrasive **mit dem ~ behandelt** sandblast finish **mit dem ~ behandelt und nachher elektrisch oxydiert** deplated finish
Sandstrahl-apparat *m* sandblast (tank) machine **-behandlung** *f* sandblasting **-blasen** *n* sand-blasting **-bläserei** *f* sandblasting installation or practice **-blasgehäuse** *n* sandblast cabinet **-druckapparat** *m* pressure-type sandblast cabinet **-drucksystem** *n* sandblast pressure system **-düse** *f* sandblast nozzle
sand-strahlen to sandblast **-strahlerei** *f* sand-blasting (shop)
Sandstrahlgebläse *n* sandblast unit, sandblasting equipment, sandblast blower **~ mit Drehboden** turntable sandblast cabinet **~ mit Drehtisch** rotary-table sandblast cabinet **~ nach dem Drucksystem** pressure-type sandblast unit **~ mit feststehender Düse** sandblast machine with stationary nozzle **~ mit Rollentisch** roller-table sandblast machine
Sandstrahlgebläse, ~ mit Sandkreislauf sand-blast tank machine with automatic return of sand **~ nach dem Saugsystem** suction-system sandblast unit **~ nach dem Schwerkraftsystem** gravity-feed-type sandblast unit **~ mit Sprossentisch** sprocket-table sandblast machine **~ mit umlaufender Trommel** sandblast barrel mill, revolving-barrel sandblast machine **Putzen mit ~** sandblast cleaning **mit dem ~ gereinigt** sand-blasted, cleaned by sandblasting
Sandstrahlgebläse-anlage *f* sandblast installation, sandblast equipment **-düse** *f* sandblast nozzle
Sandstrahlgebläsehaus *n* sandblast room, sand-blast cabinet **~ mit Drehtisch** rotary-table sandblast room
Sandstrahl-maschine *f* sandblast machine **-putzen** *n* sandblasting **-putzerei** *f* sandblast cleaning room **-putzhaus** *n* sandblast (cleaning) room **-putztrommel** *f* sandblast barrel mill, revolving-barrel sandblast machine **-reinigung** *f* sand-blast cleaning, sandblasting **-saugapparat** *m* suction-type sandblast cabinet **-saugsystem** *n* sandblast suction system **-wirkung** *f* sandblast

action or effect **-zwergtrommel** *f* sandblast mill
Sand-strake *f* crossbeam (dry docks) **-sturm** *m* sandstorm **-tasche** *f* sand pocket **-tasse** *f* sand seal **-trockenofen** *m* sand-drying oven **-uhr** *f* sandglass, hourglass **-umlauf** *m* sand circulation **-ventilsteuerung** *f* sand-valve control mechanism **-verdichtung** *f* sand packing or compacting, sand pressing
Sand-vorratsbehälter *m* sand-storage hopper **-walze** *f* emery roller **-wanderung** *f* travel of sand **-wäsche** *f* sand washery, sand-washing plant **-ziegel** *m* sandfaced brick **-zubringer** *m* sand conveyer **-zufuhr** *f* sand feed **-zuführung** *f* sand feed, sand supply **-zuleitungsmaschine** *f* sand filling machine
Sandwich-bestrahlung sandwich irradiation **-schalenbauweise** *f* sandwich monocoque construction **-schicht** *f* sandwiching
Sanforisieren *n* sanforizing (nonshirnking process)
sanft gentle, mild, smooth, soft **-er Abhang** easy gradient
Sanidin *m* sanidine
sanieren to reorganize
sanitär sanitary
Sanitäts-luftfahrzeug *n* hospital aircraft **-wagen** *m* ambulance
sanker Körper body heavier than water
Sankey-Diagramm *n* Sankey diagram
Sankt-Elms-Feuer *n* Saint Elmo's fire
Santalol *n* santalol
Santoninpräparat *n* santonin preparation
Saphir *m* sapphire **-nadel** *f* sapphire stylus **-quarz** *m* sapphire quartz **-stift** *m* sapphire stylus
Saponifikatglyzerin *n* glycerine from the fat splitting process
Saponit *m* soapstone
S-Apparat *m* S-shaped gas cooler
Sapropel *n* sapropel
Sapropelit *m* sapropelite
sapropelitisch sapropelic
Sardonyx *m* chalcedony, sardonyx
Sarkolith *m* sarcolite
Sarosperiode *f* saros period
Saß *m* pruning or gardening knife
Sastrugi *f* sastrugi
Satellit *m* satellite **-impuls** *m* satellite pulse **-sender** *m* translator **-träger** *m* satellite carrier
Satelliten-ortung *f* satellite tracking **-träger** *m* satellite vehicle
Satinage *f* finish (glaze)
Satinappretur *f* glazed or satin finish
satinieren to calender, burnish, glaze, satin-frost
Satinierfalten *pl* calender cuts
Satiniermaschine *f* glazing machine or rollers, calender **heiße ~** hot burnishing press
satiniertes Papier supercalendered paper
Satinierwerk *n* calender
satt satisfied, satiated, saturated, deep or intensive (color) **-er Druck** full (heavy) print **-er Farbton** deep or full shade **-e Wiedergabe** full clear reproduction
Sattdampf *m* saturated steam or vapor
Satte *f* bowl, dish
Sattel *m* saddle, gallows (print.), pass (mountain), descent plate (paper mfg.) **~ zwischen zwei Antizyklonen** col **~ eines Flözes** saddle of a bed **~ des Klüverbaumes** jib-boom saddle **~ eines Papierholländers** breasting backfall (paper mfg.)
Sattel-achse *f* axis of the arch or anticline **-anhänger** *m* semi-trailer **-baum** *m* saddletree **-bekleidung** *f* saddle trappings **-bildung** *f* anticlinal formation **-blech** *n* ridge lead or plate
Sattelboden *m* gable or saddle bottom **-selbstentlader** *m* saddle-bottomed self-emptying truck
Sattelbogen *m* upfold
Satteldach *n* ridged or saddle roof **-förmig geknickt** shaped like a gable-end roof
Sattel-decke *f* saddlecloth, saddle blanket **-fahrwerk** *n* saddle (undercarriage) landing gear **-fläche** *f* saddle surface
sattelförmig saddle-shaped **-e Deckplatte** saddle-backed coping
Sattel-gestell *n* saddle frame **-gurt** *m* girth **-holz** *n* transverse beam **-isolator** *m* strain or shell insulator **-kissen** *n* saddle pad **-knopf** *m* pommel **-korn** *n* ramp sight
satteln to saddle
Sattelplatte *f* waist sheet
Sattelpunkt *m* saddle point **-konfiguration** *f* configuration of saddle point **-methode** *f* steepest descent method
Sattel-rost *m* saddle grate, double-inclined fire grate **-schlepper** *m* semitrailer **-seite** *f* near side **-sitz** *m* seat **-spule** *f* saddle coil (CRT) **-tasche** *f* saddlebag **-tracht** *f* sidebar pillion
Sättespule *f* purity coil (TV)
sättigen to saturate, impregnate, satiate, satisfy
Sättiger *m* saturator, saturating device
Sättigung *f* saturation, concentration, satiation, filament saturation, emission saturation
Sättigungs-abnahme *f* color dilution **-aktivität** *f* saturation activity **-anteil** *m* fraction of saturation **-apparat** *m* saturator **-bereich** *m* saturation region **-dichte** *f* saturation density **-druck** *m* saturation pressure **-emission** *f* saturation emission
sättigungsfähig capable of saturation, saturable **-e Drosselspule** saturable reactor **-er Drosselkern** saturable core reactor **-er Reaktor** saturable reactor
Sättigungs-gebiet *n* region of saturation **-grad** *m* degree of concentration or saturation **-grenze** *f* saturation point **-induktivität** *f* saturation inductance
Sättigungs-kapazität *f* saturation capacity **-kennlinie** *f* saturation characteristic (curve) **-knie** *n* saturation bend **-linie** *f* saturation line **-magnetisierung** *f* saturation magnetization **-moment** *n*, **-punkt** *m* saturation point **-regelung** *f* saturation control, color control **-spannung** *f* saturation voltage **-strom** *m* saturation current **-unterschuß** *m* saturation deficit **-wert** *m* saturation value, valence **-zustand** *m* saturation state
Sattler *m* saddler
Saturateur *m* saturator, saturation vessel
Saturation *f*, **~ mit Kohlendioxyd** carbonation **~ mit Schwefeldioxyd** sulfitation
Saturations-apparat für Kohlendioxyd carbonation tank, carbonator **-pfanne** *f* saturation tank
saturieren to saturate **~ mit Kohlendioxyd** to carbonate **~ mit Schwefeldioxyd** to sulfurize
Satz *m* (Technik, Schub) batch, set of; (**~** von Waren) assortment; principle, law, theorem,

sediment, sentence, set, proposition, burden, charge, jump, ingredients, bound, composition, deposit, price, rate, gang, assembly, unit of machinery, pair of wheels, nest ~ (von Spulen) system (of coils) ~ **vom Antrieb** law of conservation of momentum ~ **mit viel Ausschluß** open matter (print.) ~ **z. Formfräsen** interlock form cutters ~ **z. Planfräsen** interlock helical cutters ~ **mehrerer Steuerquarze** crystal unit ~ **paarverseilter Kabel** unit twin cable

Satz, einen ~ ablegen to distribute a composition (print) **durchschossener ~** leaded matter **enger ~** solid composition (print) **enggehaltener ~** close matter (print.) **fauler ~** slow(-burning) composition **Ansetzen des Satzes** mixing or preparing of composition (pyrotechnics)

Satz-betrieb *m* batch operation **-bildend** forming sediments **-brett** *n* type board, board for composed types **-format** *n* size of matter **-fräser** *m* gang cutter **-frei** free from sediment **-gestaltung** *f* typographical design **-koks** *m* coke per charge **-kondensor** *m* convertible condenser

Satz-objektiv *n* convertible lens **-räder** *pl* interchangeable gears **-ring** *m* powder-train ring (for projectiles), time-train ring, burning composition ring **-säule** *f* composition part (of rockets) **-schale** *f* settling dish **-stück** *n* tension-setting ring or time ring of fuse, body of fuse

Satzung *f* statute, fixed rule

Satzverständlichkeit *f* phrase intelligibility

satzweise in sets ~ **Vermahlung** intermittent grinding

Satz-zeichen *n* punctuation mark **-zeit** *f* rate of charging time

Sau *f* sow, drying kiln, iron block, blot

sauber clean, neat, tidy

Sauberkeit *f* cleanliness, tidiness

säubern to clean, cleanse, inspect

Säuberung *f* clearing, cleaning

Säuberungs-aktion *f*, **-unternehmung** *f* mopping-up action

sauer acid, sour ~ **zugestellt** (Ofen) acid lined

Sauer-beize *f* sour water **-brunnen** *m* acidulous or aerated spring **-eisen** *n* iron oxide **-kasten** *m* souring tank

Sauerkeit *f* acidity, sourness

säuerlich acidulous

Säuerlichkeit *f* acidity

Säuerling *m* mineral spring charged with carbon dioxide

sauermachen to acidify

Sauermachen *n* acidification

säuern to acidify, sour

Sauerquelle *f* acidulous or aerated spring

Sauerstoff *m* oxygen **-anreicherung** *f* enriching with oxygen **-arm** poor in oxygen **-azetylenschweißung** *f* oxyacetylene weld **-behälter** *m* oxygen tank **-bordanlage** *f* aircraft oxygen installation **-druckminderer** *m* oxygen regulator **-druckschlauch** *m* oxygen pressure gauge **-entwicklung** *f* evolution of oxygen **-erzeugungsanlage** *f* oxygen producer **-flasche** *f* oxygen bottle or cylinder **-frei** containing no oxygen **-gehalt** *m* oxygen content **-gemisch** *n* oxygen mixture

Sauerstoff-gerät *n* oxygen apparatus **-gewinnung** *f* production of oxygen **-(gewinnungs)anlage** *f* oxygen plant **-haltig** oxygen-containing, oxidized **-hobeln** *n* flame gauging **-höhenatmer** *m* oxygen-breathing apparatus for high-altitude flying **-ion** *n* anion, negative ion **-kontinua** *pl* continuous oxygen spectra **-konverter** *m* oxygen furnace **-löschung** *f* oxygen quenching **-mangel** *m* oxygen deficiency **-maske** *f* oxygen mask

Sauerstoffoktaederferroelektrikum *n* oxygen-octahedron ferroelectric

Sauerstoff-pol *m* oxygen pole, anode **-reich** rich in oxygen **-rettungsapparat** *m* oxygen-inhailing apparatus, oxygen tank **-säure** *f* oxygenic acid **-schutzgerät** *n* oxygen respirator **-träger** *m* oxygen carrier, oxidant (rocket) **-umfüllwagen** *m* oxygen charging truck **-ventil** *n* oxygen valve **-verwandtschaft** *f* affinity for oxygen, oxygen relationship **-verschiebung** *f* oxygen displacement **-vorrat** *m* oxygen supply **-zuführung** *f* oxygen feed

Säuerung *f* acidification, acidulation

Saug-anode *f* first anode, first accelerator, first gun, electron gun, positive accelerator

Saug-anschluß *m* (Rohrpost) vacuum connection **-weite** *f* width of suction connection

Saug-apparat *m* suction apparatus, aspirator **-arm** *m* lower leg (dams) **-bagger** *m* suction dredge **-bogen** *m* (Ventilator) suction bend **-bohrung** *f* suction bore or hole **-bürste** *f* suction brush

Saugdrossel *f* drainage coil **-schaltung** *f* double three phase **-spule** *f* interphase transformer, sucking solenoid

Saugdruck *m* suction pressure **-messer** *m* vacuum pressure gauge **-schreiber** *m* suction-pressure recorder

Saug-düse *f* suction nozzle, Venturi tube **-elektrode** *f* drain

saugen to suck, absorb, imbibe, aspirate

Saugen *n* suction, piping

saugender Hub suction stroke

Sauger *m* suction apparatus, aspirator, exhauster, exhaust fan

Saugerohr *n* suction pipe

Saugerschiene *f* sucker bar slide

Saugestutzen *m* suction pipe connection

saugfähig absorbent, hygroscopic (chem.) **-es Papier** absorbent paper

Saug-fähigkeit *f* absorptive capacity, absorbency, imbibition power **-feld** *n* positive field, suction field, field that draws away **-festigkeit** *f* resistance to suction, suction strength **-filter** *n* suction filter, vacuum filter **-fläche** *f* suction side, upper surface of wing **-flansch** *m* suction flange **-flasche** *f* feeding bottle, aspirator, suction bottle **-flügel** *m* suction vane **-förderung** *f* lifting by suction **-freistrahlgebläse** *n* suction-type hose sandblast tank

Sauggas *n* power gas, generator gas, producer gas **-anlage** *f* suction-gas plant **-erzeuger** *m* suction(-gas) producer **-motor** *m* producer-gas engine, suction-gas motor

Saug-gebläse *n* suction fan, exhauster **-gefälle** *n* suction head **-geschwindigkeit** *f* rate of evacuation (of vacuum pump), pumping speed **-gestänge** *n* sucker rods **-gitter** *n* space-charge grid **-guß** *m* casting under suction, sink casting **-gutsch** *m* suction couch (paper) **-hahn** *m* suction valve or cock **-haube** *f* drag cowling, suction hood

Saugheber *m* siphon, pipette **-röhrenbarometer** *n* siphon barometer

Saughöhe *f* suction head, suction height or lift, capillary rise, absorptive height **~ bei leerer Pumpe und Leitung** dry suction lift

Saughöheprüfung *f* mounting test

Saug-höhle *f* cavity (in a casting) **-hub** *m* suction or intake stroke **-hutze** *f* ventilation cap **-kammer** *f* suction chamber **-kasten** *m* suction box, sucking table **-kessel** *m* priming reservoir **-klappe** *f* bottom clack, suction valve **-knotenfang** *m* suction strainer **-kolben** *m* valve piston, suction flask

Saug-kopf *m* suction head or pipe, suction basket, suction strainer **-korb** *m* rose, strainer, suction hose **-kreis** *m* impedance or absorption wave trap, acceptor circuit, induced-draught fan, filter circuit, sound trap (TV) **-krümmer** *m* suction bend **-kupolofen** *m* suction cupola furnace

Saug-leistung *f* free air capacity **-leitung** *f* suction pipe (line), suction main, vacuum pipe, intake manifold, exhaust main or pipe **-leitungsanschluß** *m* suction pipe connection **-ling** *m* pulp product

Saugluft *f* indraft, vacuum intake air **-anlage** *f* pneumatic-air plant **-anzeiger** *m* vacuum gauge **-behälter** *m* vacuum reservoir **-bremse** *f* vacuum brake **-empfänger** *m* vacuum receiver

Sauglüfter *m* exhauster

Saugluft-förderer *m* vacuum conveyer tube **-geschwindigkeit** *f* indraft velocity **-kessel** *m* vacuum vessel **-reinigung** *f* vacuum cleaning **-Servobremse** *f* vacuum servo-brake

Saug-massel *f* feedhead, sinking or shrinking head, settling or feeding head, feeder head, feeder, head, head gate, feeding gate, header, deadhead **-messer** *m* vacuometer, suction gauge **-näpfchen** *n* suction cup **-öffnung** *f* suction port, static head or opening **-papier** *n* absorbent paper **-postpapier** *n* duplicating paper **-preßwalze** *f* suction press roll **-pumpe** *f* suction pump **-raum** *m* suction chamber

Saugrohr *n* vacuum pipe, exhaust pipe, suction pipe or tube, draft tube, induction pipe, siphon, Venturi tube, Pitot tube **-filter** *n* suction blade filter **-flansch** *m* suction or induction pipe flange

Saug-röhrchen *n* pipette **-rohrleitung** *f* suction piping, suction pipe line **-satz** *m* **in einem Pumpenschacht** bucket lift **-schacht** *m* suction pit **-schlauch** *m* suction or intake tube **-seite des Flügels** suction side of wing, top or upper surface of wing **-seitiges Ventil am Manometer** low-side valve of pressure gauge **-sieb** *n* suction screen or sieve (lubricator) **-sitz** *m* minute clearing

Saug-spannung *f* accelerating voltage, anode, driving or positive potential (of photocell), saturation potential **-spitze** *f* collecting point **-spule** *f* series reactor, sucking solenoid, smoothing coil **-spülkopf** *m* suction rinsing head **-ständer** *m* suction end

Saugstangen-bewegung *f* sucker bar movement **-hebel** *m* sucker bar lever

Saug-steinbehälter *m* silicic-acid-gel (absorber) container (gas-testing apparatus) **-strahlpumpe** *f* ejector, sucking jet pump **-stutzen** *m* exhaust connection, suction stub, pump intake, pump nozzle **-system** *n* exhaust or suction system **-tiegel** *m* suction crucible **-transformator** *m* booster or suction or draining transformer **-trichter** *m* suction funnel, pipe (in a casting)

Saug- und Druckpumpe *f* spare pump, lift and delivery pump

Saug- und Staurohr *n* Venturi-Pitot tube

Saugung *f* suction, sucking

Säugungswasserstand *m* priming(-water) level

Säugung *f* **unterbrechen** breaking the priming

Saug-ventil *n* suction valve, breather, induction valve, standing valve **-ventilator** *m* exhauster, exhaust fan **-ventilregulierung** *f* **von Brennstoffpumpen** suction-valve control of fuel pumps **-vergaser** *m* suction-type carburetor **-wäsche** *f* vacuum wash **-welle** *f* surge **-widerstand** *m* resistance to suction **-windkessel** *m* suction receptacle **-wirkung** *f* suction effect, sucking action, suction, head, upward pull or draft

Saugzellen-drehfilter rotary suction cell filter **-filter** *n* suction cell filter

Saugzug *m* induced draught, head (draft), upward pull **-anlage** *f* induced-draught plant **-gebläse** *n* unduced-draught blower **-lüfter** *m* exhaust fan **-ventilator** *m* exhaust fan, exhauster

Säule *f* column, support, stand, head (of water), stanchion, pillar, pile (elec.), upright, strut, still, prism

Säulen-achse *f* prismatic axis **-arm** *m* post bracket, pillar bracket **-armlager** *n* post hanger **-artig** columnar, prismatic **-bauart** *f* column type **-bohrmaschine** *f* column-type drilling machine, post drill **-chromatographie** *f* column-type chromatography **-deckplatte** *f* abacus **-drehkran** *m* column jib crane **-echo** *n* columnar echo **-förmig** columnar, pillarlike, prismoid **-formmaschine** *f* post-type molding machine

Säulen-friktionsspindelpresse *f* column screw press **-führwerkzeuge** *pl* column guiding tools **-fundament** *n* column base **-fuß** *m* column base, pedestal **-gang** *m* peristyle **-gestell** *n* column mount **-hängelager** *n* console, wall bracket **-ionisation** *f* columnar ionization **-kappe** *f* column cap **-knauf** *m* capital **-knopf** *m* capital, column cap

Säulen-konsollager *n* post hanger **-kopf** *m* column head, capital **-kran** *m* post or pillar crane **-lampe** *f* pillar lamp **-messer** *m* stylometer **-platte** *f* plinth, abacus **-presse** *f* hydraulic press **-preßformmaschine** *f* post squeezer **-probe** *f* pillar sample

Säulen-rekombination *f* columnar recombination **-schwenkbagger** *m* derrick dredger **-ständer** *m* pedestal **-struktur** *f* columnar structure **-tischfernsprecher** *m* desk (stand) telephone set **-träger** *m* post hanger **-umschaltung** *f* column switching **-weite** *f* intercolumination **-widerstand** *m* columnar resistance

Saum *m* seam, edge, border, selvage, hem, fringe **farbiger ~** color(ed) fringe

säumen to edge, border, hem, delay, tarry

Saum-maschine *f* hemming machine **-pfad** *m* horse or mule track **-riff** *n* fringing reef **-zerkleinerungsmaschine** *f* automatic chopping machine

Sä- und Düngerstreumaschine *f* combined seed

and fertilizer drill

Säure *f* acid, sourness, acidity **von ~ angegriffen** attacked by acids **phosphorige ~** phosphorous acid **schweflige ~** sulfurous acid **selenige ~** selenious acid **unterbromige ~** hyperbromous acid **verdünnte ~** dilute acid

saur-er Farbstoff acid coloring matter **-es Fixiersalz** acid fixer **-es Futter** acid lining **-es Grubenwasser** acid mine water **-er Martinofen** acid open-hearth furnace **-er Stahl** acid steel

Säure-abfall *m* acid sludge **-absatzbehälter** *m* acid settling drum **-abspaltung** *f* splitting-off acid **-anfressung** *f* acid corrosion **-angriff** *m* attack by acid, acid corrosion **-anzug** *m* acid-proof clothing **-avivage** *f* brightening with acid **-ballon** *m* (acid) carboy **-batterie** *f* lead-acid battery **-behälter** *m* acid container **-beschleuniger** *m* acid catalyst

säurebeständig acid-resistant, acid-proof, acid-resisting **-e Kunststoffe** acid and alkali proof plastic material

Säure-beständigkeit *f* acid resistance **-bildend** acid-forming **-bindendes Mittel** acid-binding agent **-dämpfe** *m pl* acid gases or fumes **-dichte** *f* acid strength or density, acid concentration, specific gravity of acid **-dichtemesser** *m* hydrometer **-draht** *m* acidproof wire **-druckbehälter** *m* acid pressure reservoir **-echt** fast to acid **-erhitzer** *m* acid heater **-fähige Base** acidifiable base

säurefest impervious to acids, acid-resisting, acid-proof **-e Auskleidung** acidproof lining, acid seal paint **-es Bassin** acidproof tank **-e Farbe** acidproof paint

Säureflasche *f* acid bottle

säurefrei acidless **-es Fett** noncorrosive grease

Säure-gehalt *m* acid content **-gereinigt** acid-washed

säure-haltig acid-laden, acidiferous, containing acid **-harz** *n* acid sludge **-heber** *m* acid siphon, hydrometer syringe **-herstellung** *f* acid manufacture **-ion** *n* acid ion **-löslich** acid-soluble

Säuremesser *m* acidimeter

Säurenentwickler *m* acid developer

Säureniederschlagswert *m* sludging value

Säurenmesser *m* acidimeter

Säure-prüfung *f* acid test **-regenerat** *n* acid reclaim **-scheidung** *f* acid parting **-schlamm** *m* acid sludge **-schleuder** *m* acid hydroextractor **-schwellung** *f* acid plumping **-schwemmverfahren** *n* acid flotation process or method **-stand** *m* acid level **-turm** *m* acid tower **-verhältnis** *n* proportion of acid **-walkecht** fast to acid milling **-zahl** *f* neutralization number, acid number or figure **-zentrifuge** *f* acid centrifuge, acid hydroextractor

Sauschwanz *m* wire thread guide (textiles)

sausen to rush, whiz, whistle

savonieren to fine-grind (plate glass) preparatory to polishing

Sayet(te)garn *n* semiworsted or carded-worsted yarn

schabecht fast to scraping

Schabeisen *n* scraper, planing, shaving or fleshing knife

Schabemesser *n* sharping or fleshing knife, scraping knife, scraper, shaving knife

schaben to scrape, scour, pare, chafe, shave, grate, rub, abrade

Schaben *n* scraping

Schaber *m* doctor blade, scraper **-klinge** *f* scraper blade **-klingenmesser** *n* doctor blade **-vorschub** *m* advance of scraper

Schabe-vorrichtung *f* stripping comb **-werkzeug** *n* shaving tool

Schab-fräser *m* shaving tool **-hobel** *pl* scraper plane, spoke shave

Schabin *n* goldbeater s waste, parings (of leaf gold)

Schabkelle *f* notched trowel

Schablone *f* template, pattern, model, stencil, strickle, jig, form, mold **~** (f. Gesenkfräs.) master plate **~** (f. Kopiervorrichtg.) former plate

schablonenartig automatically, mechanically, according to a set or fixed pattern

Schablonen-bockspindel *m* pattern bracket screw **-bohren** *n* jig boring **-drehbank** *f* reproducing or copying lathe **-formerei** *f* template molding **-fräsmaschine** *f* profile milling machine **-führung** *f* template guide **-halter** *m* arm support for templates **-maschine** *f* designing machine **-mäßig** mechanical, automatic, according to a set or fixed pattern

Schablonen-schwenkeinrichtung *f* template swiveling device **-speicher** *m* template pool **-spule** *f* former-wound armature coil **-stechmaschine** *f* designing or pricking machine **-stiftklemmung** *f* stylus collet **-streifen** *m* controlling strip **-träger** *m* horizontal spindle arm (in molding) **-verschlüsselung** *f* spatial encoding **-wickelung** *f* former winding

schablonieren to template, strickle, stencil, copy

Schabloniervorrichtung *f* stenciling device, sweeping device (in molding)

Schabotte *f* anvil block, bedplate, base casting, stock

Schabsel *n* scrapings, parings, shavings

Schab-stelle *f* chafing mark **-stoff** *m* scraped pulp

Schachbrett *n* chessboard **-artige Aufstellung** chessboard layout

schachbrettförmig checkerboardlike, staggered **~ eingerammte Pfähle** staggered piling

Schachbrettfrequenz *f* chess-board frequency (TV)

Schachbrettmuster (auf dem Bildschirm für Meßzwecke) cross-hatch pattern (TV)

Schacht *m* pit, chute, run, stack, manhole, body (of a gas producer), (mine) shaft, well, cell, compartment, core, cored hole **den ~ mit Gebirg** (mit Abraum) **ausfüllen** to rock the well **~ des Verschlusses** gate shaft **einen ~ abseigern** to measure the depth of a shaft with a plumb line **ausziehender ~** upcast ventilating shaft **blinder ~** wince or jackhead pit **einziehender ~** downcast of a mine **gemauerter ~** brick pit **seigerer ~** vertical shaft

Schachtabdeckplatte *f* cover slab, manhole cover

Schachtabdeckung *f* manhole or joint-box cover, shaft covering **~ mit Entlüftungsschlitzen** ventilating cover **befahrbare ~** carriageway cover

Schacht-abteilung *f* compartment or division of a shaft or pit **-abteufen** *n* pit or shaft sinking **-ausbau** *m* shaft lining, timbering or walling of a shaft **-auslöser** *m* bomb-bay release gear **-band** *n* stack band **-bekleidung** *f* lining of a shaft **-be-**

trieb *m* shaft mining **-brunnen** *m* dug well **-bühne** *f* landing place, resting place, or stopping place of a pit **-deckel** *m* manhole cover, trap door of a pit **-durchmesser** *m* shaft diameter

Schachtel *f* box, case **-karton** *m*, **-körper** *m* box-shaped coil form **-pappe** *f* box-board

schachten to dig

Schacht-feld *n* bay or interval of a shaft, well pit **-fördergefäß** *n* bucket, chair, hutch **-förderung** *f* shaft hauling, raising, or hoisting **-futter** *n* stack lining, inner lining or ring wall of a furnace **-gerüst** *n* shaft tower, pit headgear **-gestänge** *n* pump spears, main rod **-geviere** *n*, **-geviert** *n* shaft frame or setting **-halle** *f* shaft sheds **-hängebank** *f* landing of a shaft **-kabelkasten** *m* manhole junction box **-mauerung** *f* stack lining or walling **-mauerwerk** *n* stack brickwork

Schachtofen *m* shaft or pit furnace, blast furnace, kiln, cupola furnace, water-jacket furnace **-arbeit** *f* blast-furnace smelting **-bau** *m* blast-furnace design **-schmelzen** *n* blast-furnace smelting, shaft-furnace melting **-trockner** *m* tunnel drier

Schacht-öffnung *f* pit mouth, manhole **-panzer** *m* stack casing **-rohr** *n* access shaft of the caisson, shaft pipe **-scheibe** *f* shaft cross section **-scheider** *m* brattice (min.), shaft partition, parting or midwall, case **-schleuse** *f* lock with high lift **-signalanlage** *f* shaft signalling plant **-sohle** *f* floor or bottom of manhole or shaft **-speicher** *m* storage bin, silo

Schacht-stoß *m* face, wall, or (short) side of a shaft **-stuhl** *m* pit frame **-sumpf** *m* sump, sink or cesspool of a pit **-trumm** *n* division of a shaft **-verrohrung** *f* tubing, a series of tubes **-verzug** *m* bay or interval of a shaft **-wand** *f* manhole wall, shaft wall **-zelle** *f* bomb chute **-ziegel** *m* radial brick

Schädel *m* skull **-messer** *m* craniometer

schaden to damage, harm, hurt, injure

Schaden *m* damage, defect, harm, injury ~ **anrichten** to cause damage **einen** ~ **ersetzen** to compensate or settle for damage ~ **nehmen** to be damaged ~ **zufügen** to damage

Schaden-abschätzung *f* appraisal of damage **-blitz** *m* destructive lightning

Schadenersatz *m* compensation, indemnification ~ **festsetzen** to assess damages or indemnity

Schadenersatz-klage *f* action for damages **-pflichtig** liable for damages

Schaden-maßstab *m* damage criteria **-schätzung** *f* damage assessment

Schadensfall *m* case of loss

Schadenversicherung *f* insurance against damages

schadhaft damaged, defective, faulty

Schadhaftigkeit *f* damage

schädigen (Material) to damage

schädigend injurious

schädlich harmful, injurious, noxious, detrimental stray (of radiations) ~ **machen** to vitiate, contaminate **-er Luftwiderstand** parasite drag **-er Raum** clearance (dead space), cylinder clearance **-er Widerstand** parasite resistance or drag, structural drag

Schädling *m* vermin, parasite

Schädlingsbekämpfung *f* pest control

schadlos unhurt ~ **halten** to indemnify

Schäfchen-himmel *m* mackerel sky **-wolken** *f pl* mackerel sky, cirro-cumulus or fleecy clouds

schaffend productive

Schaffung *f* creation

Schaft *m* shaft, shank, stem, handle, stalk, trunk, (rifle) stock ~ **eines Werkzeuges zur Befestigung im Griff** tang

Schaft-durchmesser *m* diameter of shank **-einzug** *m* draft, pass

schäften to joint, damp, furnish with a handle or stock, splice **den Holm** ~ to splice the spar

Schaftfräser *m* shank-type cutter, (shank) end mill, endmilling cutter ~ **mit Morsekegel und Anzugsgewinde** spiral cut end mill, morse taper shank tapped for drawbar ~ **mit Morsekegel und Mitnehmerlappen** spiral cut end mill, morse taper shank with tang end ~ **für T-Nuten, kreuzverzahnt** T-slot cutter, staggered teeth

Schafthalter mit Flansch flanged toolholder

Schaft-höhe *f* height of shank **-kappe** *f* butt plate **-nutenfräser** *m* slotting end mill **-maschine** *f* heald machine **-pfegemittel** *n* stock preservative **-profilfräser** *m* shank-type profile cutter

Schaft-querschnitt *m* (bei rohen Schrauben) cross section of shank **-rahmen** *m* shaft frame **-schleifscheibe** *f* rotary mounted grinding tool **-schraube** *f* shoulder stud, screwed stop pin, slotted headless screw **-skala** *f* shaft scale **-stab** *m* shaft rod or stave **-stück** *n* shaft portion

Schäftung *f* joint, splice, shaping, furnishing with a stock

Schaft-verzahnung *f* pin gear **-walzfräser** *m* shank hob

Schake *f* (chain) link

Schäkel *n* shackle, link chain **-auge** *n* shackle eye **-kette** *f* open link chain

Schäkeln *n* shackling

Schaken-buchse *f* link bush **-kette** *f* open-link chain

schal stale

Schäl-achse *f* turret axis **-anschnitt** *m* curling cut **-axt** *f* paring ax

Schalbrett *n* slab, sheeting board

Schale *f* dish, basin, (oil) cup, pan, bowl, scale (of a balance), husk, shell, saucer, peel, tray, dish, bush(ing), rind, skin **hölzerne** ~ wooden form **magnetische** ~ magnetic shell **vollbesetzte** ~ closed shell

schälen to peel, bark, pare

Schalen-abschirmungskoeffizient *m* shell-absorption coefficient **-abschluß** *m* closure of a shell **-arretierung** *f* pan arrest

Schalenbau *m* monocoque or shell construction or structure ~ **der Elektronenhülle** structure of electron shell

Schalenbauweise *f* monocoque construction or fuselage

Schalen-blende *f* fibrous sphalerite, botryoidal blende **-bretter** *n pl* form boards **-eisen** *n* sow iron, bottom iron **-elektrode** *f* dished electrode **-entwicklung** *f* dish or tray development (phot.) **-flügel** *m* cup vane, monocoque wing **-förmig** dish-shaped, saucer-shaped, shell-shaped, dished **-fuß** *m* pan base

Schalenguß *m* chill casting, die casting **-form** *f* chill **-kern** *m* chilled core **-stahl** *m* casehardened

or die-cast steel **-verfahren** *n* shell molding
Schalen-halter *m* gong support, lamp-shade holder **-hart** chilled, casehardened **-hartguß** *m* chilled cast iron **-holzzimmerung** *f* box timbering, cover binding **-kabel** *n* high-frequency cable **-kalk** *m* pisolite, aragonite **-kern** *m* shell type core **-konstruktion** *f* monocoque or shell construction, stressed-skin construction
Schalenkreuz *n* Robinson's anemometer, cup(-type) anemometer **-fahrtmesser** *m* cup-anemometer type of speed indicator **-strommesser** *m* cup-type current meter **-windmesser** *m* (Robinson's) cup anemometer
Schalen-kuppelung *f* (solid) sleeve coupling, compression or clamp coupling, split (muff) coupling **-lack** *m* shellac **-lager** *n* split bearing **-leerstelle** *f* shell vacancy **-öffnung** *f* shell aperture **-rumpf** *m* monocoque fuselage, shell body **-untergruppe** *f* subshell **-windstärkemesser** *m* cup-type anemometer
Schäler *m* barker, barking machine
Schälfestigkeit *f* peel strength
Schälfurnier *n* pared veneer
Schalholz *n* pit timber
Schälholz *n* barked wood
schalig scaly, foliated, crusted, shelled
schalken, die Luken ~ to batten the hatches
Schall *m* sound, peal, noise, ring **~ dämpfen** to
Schall-abdichtung *f* sound insulation **-abgangsempfänger** *m* initial sound receiver, impulse receiver **-abschirmung** *f*, **seitliche ~** gobo (acoust.)
Schall-absorption *f* sound absorption **-abstrahlendes Gebilde** sound reflector **-abstrahlung** *f* sound radiation or projection **-abwehr** *f* noise abatement or suppression, sound attenuation or absorption **-ampel** *f* pendant speaker arrangement **-anzeiger** *m* sound recorder
Schallaufnahme *f*, **akustische ~** direct mechanical sound recording
Schall-aufnehmen *n* sound recording, sound pickup, sound receiving **-aufzeichner** *m* sound recorder **-aufzeichnung** *f* sound recording **-ausbreitung** *f* propagation of sound **-ausschlag** *m* particle displacement (acoust.), displacement of a sound **-auswertebereitschaft** *f* readiness to locate by sound **-auszeichnung** *f* sound recording
Schall-bandaufnahme *f* (magnetic-steel) tape recording **-batterie** *f* main valve control unit (missiles) **-becher** *m* acoustic funnel (dictating machine), bell (wind instrument) **-bestrahlung** *f* sound-radiation distribution, sound irradiation **-beugung** *f* sound diffraction **-bild** *n* sound pattern, sound image **-blech** *n* diaphragm **-boden** *m* soundboard **-bombe** *f* sonic bomb **-brechung** *f* sound refraction **-brett** *n* baffle, sounding board, soundboard **-bündel** *n* sound beam **-bündelung** *f* sound transmission channel
Schall-dämmung *f* sound reduction or attenuation, sound deadening or absorption **-dämmzahl** *f* sound-transmission characteristic
schalldämpfend sound-damping or -absorbing, sound-attenuating **-e Raumverkleidung** *f* acoustic treatment (of a room) **-er Stoff** sound-absorbing material
Schalldämpfer *m* deadener (for stopping vibration of wire), muffler, silencer, damper, sound absorber
Schalldämpfung *f* muffling, silencing, sound (proofing) insulation **mit ~** soundproofed
Schalldämpfungs-einheit *f* unit of sound absorption **-mittel** *n* means or material for deadening, attenuating, or absorbing sound, sound-absorbent insulation
Schalldeckel *m* sounding top, sounding board
schalldicht soundproof **-e Zelle** soundproof cell or booth
Schall-dichte *f* sound density **-dose** *f* (phonograph) pickup, sound box
Schalldruck *m* sound pressure, sonic or acoustic pressure **-mikrophon** *n* (sound) pressure microphone **-pegel** *m* sound pressure level **-verstauung** *f* diffraction of sound
Schall-durchgang *m* transmission of sound **-durchlässigkeit** *f* sound permeability, sound transmission or transmittance
Schalleinfall *m*, **streifender ~** glancing incidence of sound wave
Schall-eisen *n* folding tool **-empfang** *m* sound collection or reception **-empfänger** *m* microphone, sound receiver, sound pickup
schallempfindliche Flamme sound-sensitive flame
Schallempfindung *f* auditory sensation
Schallempfindungsschwelle *f* threshold of audibility or of acoustic perception
schallen to sound, resound, ring
Schallenergie *f* sound energy **momentane ~** instantaneous sound energy density **momentane Dichte der kinetischen ~** instantaneous acoustic kinetic energy per unit volume
Schall-energiefluß *m* sound (energy) flux **-ereignis** *n* sound or acoustic action, audible event **-erregung** *f* sound generation, excitation **-erzeuger** *m* sound generator **-färbung** *f* timbre, tone color or quality **-feld** *n* sound field **-fluß** *m* volume velocity (acoust.) **-fokus** *m* sound focus **-fortpflanzung** *f* sound propagation **-frequenz** *f* audio-frequency, acoustic frequency **-funksender** *m* sound transmitter
Schall-geber *m* sound generator or transmitter **-gedämpfte Stoffe** sound absorbing materials **-generator** *m* sonic generator **-gerät** *n* telephone receiver **-geschwindigkeit** *f* velocity of sound **-geschwindigkeitsmessung** *f* sound velocity measurement **-geschwindigkeitsmikrophon** *n* velocity microphone **-gesteuert** autosonic **-gewölbe** *n* acoustic vault **-grenze** *f* sonic barrier **-grube** *f* sound pit
schall-hart rigid or nonabsorbing **-härte** *f* acoustic stiffness, sound hardness **-höhenmessung** *f* acoustic method of measuring altitude, air sounding **-impedanz** *f* acoustic impedance **-impuls** *m* sound impulse **-ingenieur** *m* sound engineer or technician, acoustician
Schallintensität *f* sound intensity **momentane ~** instantaneous acoustic power per unit area
Schall-intensitätsmesser *m* phonometer **-inzidenz** *f* sound incidence **-isolation** *f* soundproofing, sound isolation **-isoliert** soundproof **-kammer** *f* sound box, accoustic chamber **-lader** *m* luffer board (acoust.) **-laufzeit** *f* sound travel time **-lehre** *f* acoustics **-leistung** *f* response (of an acoustic system), acoustic power **-leiter** *m* sound conductor **-leitfähigkeit** *f* sound conductivity **-löschung** *f* sound deadening **-lot** *n*

Behm depth indicator, Behm echo depth sounder

Schall-mauer *f* sonic or sound barrier **-medium** *n* sound-propagating medium

Schallmeßaufnahmegerät *n* oscillograph **-batterie** *f* sound-ranging battery **-beobachtung** *f* sound ranging **-einrichtung** *f* sound-measuring device

Schallmessen *n* sound ranging

Schallmesser *m* sound-measuring device, sonometer

Schallmeß-gerätekraftwagen *m* sound-ranging-equipment truck **-kabel** *n* sound-ranging cable **-mikrophon** *n* sound-ranging microphone **-stelle** *f* sound-ranging station **-stellenkraftwagen** *m* mobile sound-ranging post **-stellentrupp** *m* sound-ranging detail **-system** *n* sound-ranging net or system **-trupp** *m* sound-ranging section

Schallmessung *f* sound ranging, range finding

Schallmeß-verfahren *n* sound-ranging **-wesen** *n* sound ranging

Schall-mikrophon *n* acoustic or directional microphone **-mittel** *n* sound-communication device

schallnahe Düsenströmung *f* transonic nozzle flow **~ Strömung** *f* transonic flow

Schalloch *n* aperture of a bell or belfry, sound hole, louver **~ am Glockenturm** louver

Schall-öffnung *f* sound aperture, receiver cap or earpiece, louver **-ortung** *f* sound location, sound ranging, sound radar **-pegelmesser** *m* sound level meter

Schallplatte *f* disk, record **~ mit weißem Rauschen** white noise record **eine ~ abspielen** to play a record

Schallplatten-abtastdose *f* phonographic pickup unit **-aufnahme** *f* disc recording **-entzerrer** pick-up compensation **-geräusch** *n* record noise, surface noise **-laufwerk** *n* turntable **-schnitt** *m* disc cutting **-steg** *m* wall, land, or barrier between record grooves **-verstärker** *m* grammophone amplifier

Schall-quant *m* phonon **-quantenentropie** *f* phonon entropy **-quantum** *n* phonon, quantum of sound

Schallquelle *f* acoustic source, sound generator, sound source, source of acoustic energy **strahlende ~** radiating sound source

Schallquellenortung *f* sound ranging

Schall-radiometer *n* acoustic radiometer **-raum** *m* sound box or chamber **-reaktionsrad** *n* Rayleigh disk **-reflektierend** sound-reflecting **-regler** *m* sound-corrector **-reibungswiderstand** *m* acoustic (frictional) resistance

Schallreiz *m*, **überschwelliger ~** super-threshold (sound-)intensity level

Schall-resistanz acoustic impedance **-richten** *n* sound ranging **-rille** *f* groove or track (on phonograph record) **-rohr** *n* speaking trumpet **-rückkoppelung** *f* acoustic feedback, acoustic regeneration **-rückwirkung** *f* acoustic impedance **-sammler** *m* sound or microphone concentrator **-scheinwerfer** *m* sound reflector, acoustic radiator **-schirm** *m* baffle

schallschluckend sound absorbing **-e Wandbekleidung** sound-absorbing lining

Schall-schlucker *m* sound-absorbent or -deadening material, sound absorber **-schluckschirm** *m* gobo (acoust.) **-schluckung** *f* sound or acoustic absorptivity

Schall-schnelle *f* volume current, acoustic velocity **-schnelleempfänger** *m* velocity microphone **-schreiber** *m* sound-recording stylus, sound recorder **-schutz** *m* sound-proofing, sound insulation **-schutzplatte** *f* acoustic panel **-schwellenstärke** *f* threshold-sound intensity **-schwingung** *f* sound vibration, acoustic vibration **-sender** *m* loud-speaker, (sound) reproducer, sound transmitter or emitter **-sicher** soundproof **-signal** *n* sound signal **-sonde** *f* sound probe **-spektrum** *n* sound spectrum

Schallstärke *f* sound intensity **-messer** *m* sonometer, phonometer, sound-level meter **-messerfeder** *f* sonometer spring **-messermagnet** *m* sonometer magnet

Schall-stoß *m* sympathetic vibration **-strahl** *m* sound ray **-strahlbündel** *n* pencil of sound (rays) **-strahlung** *f* sound radiation **-streuung** *f* scattering of sound **-symmetrierung** *f* balance control

Schall-technik *f* acoustics **-tilgung** *f* sound absorption, suppression, deadening, or attenuation **-tilgungsmittel** *n* gobo or baffle (motion pictures) **-tonne** *f*, **-tonnenboje** *f* sounding (cask or tun) buoy

schalltot soundproof, nonresonant, nonoscillable, acoustically inert or inactive **-er Raum** anechoic chamber **-e Werkstoffe** insonorous materials

Schall-träger *m* recording medium, film medium **-treibwerk** *n* loudspeaker operating mechanism or motor element **-trichter** *m* sound projector, bell-shaped part of trumpet, fog horn

Schall-überschlagsbasis *f* leaving-out (sound) base **-übertragungseinrichtung** *f* public-address system **-umformer** *m* transducer **-umwandlungseinrichtung** *f* electroacoustic transducer **-undurchlässig** soundproof **-verkleidung** *f* sound proofing **-verstärkung** *f* sound amplification **-verstärkungsmittel** *n* sound reinforcing means **-verteilung** *f* diffusion of sound **-verstärkungsmittel** *n* sound reinforcing means **-vertikale** *f* vertical spread or diffusion of sound **-verzug** *m* sound lag **-verzugsrechner** *m* sound-delay computor **-verzugszeit** *f* sound-lag time

Schall-vorgang *m* audio signal, sound wave **-waage** *f* balance control **-wahrnehmung** *f* tone or sound perception

Schallwand *f* baffle (partition or board), loudspeaker screen, sound panel **reflektierende ~** reflex baffle (acoust.)

Schall-wascher *m* sonic washer **-weglänge** *f* sound-path length **-weich** sound-absorbent

Schallwelle *f* sound wave, acoustic wave **sinusförmige ~** sine wave of sound

Schallwellen-aufzeichner *m* phonodeik **-ausgleich** *m* neutralization of sound waves **-widerstand** *m* acoustic impedance

Schall-wiedergabequalität *f* sound-reproduction quality **-wirkung** *f* sound effect **-wirkungswiderstand** *m* acoustic resistance **-zeichen** *n* sound signal, acoustic signal **-zeile** *f* column speaker **-zelle** *f* sound test chamber

Schälmaschine *f* barker, barking machine, decorticator

Schalmei-glocke *f* sheep gong **-wecker** *m* gong bell

Schäl-messer *n* paring or peeling knife **-pflug** *m* paring or stubbing plow **-schnitt** *m* progressive or purling cut **-stahlhalter** *m* balance turning tool

Schalstein *m* greenstone

Schaltader *f* jumper wire, cross-connecting wire

Schaltaderarm *m* (rotary) wiper

Schaltaderbild *n* circuit diagram, wiring diagram **schematisches** ~ skeleton or schematic diagram

Schaltaderdraht *m* jumper (wire), cross-connecting wire **mit** ~ **verbinden** to jumper or connect

Schaltader-einrichtung *f* switching device or equipment **-element** *n* circuit element **-feld** *n* **des Verteilers** jumpering field of distributing frame **-netz** *n* plant with distribution boxes

Schalt-anlage *f* central office, switch plant, distributing board, switch-gear **-anlagengerät** *n* switchgear **-anordnung** *f* circuit diagram **-antrieb** *m* indexing mechanism **-apparat** *m* controller, controlling apparatus or instrument, switch apparatus **-aufwand** *m* cost of circuit **-ausrüstung** *f* control equipment **-automat** *n* circuit-breaker

Schalt-band *n* controlling strip **-bewegung** *f* switch or feed motion, feed path **-begrenzer** speed selection limiter **-bild** *n* diagram of connections, wiring or circuit diagram

Schalt-blech *n* shift plate **-block** *m* gearshift-lever housing **-bock** *m* gear shift lever bracket **-bogen** *m* quadrant, switch arc **-bolzen** *m* crank rod

Schaltbrett *n* switchboard, electrical control panel **-ausrüstung** *f* instrument panel equipment **-leuchte** *f* dashboard light or lamp

Schalt-brücke *f* connecting bridge **-buchse** *f* connecting bush **-bügel** *m* escapement operating bail, function bail blade **-daumen** *m* cam **-deckel** *m* switch cover (for gear) **-diagramm** (Getriebe) shifting diagram **-dom** *m* shift-lever dust cover **-dorn** *m* switch post **-dose** *f* switch cabinet or box, switchgear distributing (junction) box

Schaltdraht *m* jumper wire **-verbindung** *f* jumper or cross connection

Schalt-effekt *m* switching effect **-einrichtung** *f* switching or shifting arrangement **-elektromagnet** *m* trip-coil magnet **-elektromagnetenstromkreis** *m* switching magnet circuit **-element** *n* circuit parameter or component, control or circuit element, initiating switch

schalten to direct, rule; (elektr.) switch; (Motor) change shift gears; (Technik, auslösen) actuate; (bedienen) operate; (steuern) control; connect, wire, change over, feed, index, trip, shift, couple, clutch, rule, join, engage **in Brücke** ~ to bridge across, place across, tee across **in Reihe** ~ to join or connect in series **gegeneinander** ~ to connect in opposition, connect differentially **gemischt** ~ to connect in series multiple, connect in multiple arc **hintereinander** ~ to join or connect in series **nebeneinander** ~ to connect or join in parallel **normal** ~ to set at normal **parallel** ~ to join or connect in parallel

Schalten *n* switching, joining, connecting, stepping, gearing ~ **für drei Stellungen** three-position switch(ing)

Schaltenden (der Wicklung) *pl* contact ends (of the winding)

Schalter *m* (Eisenbahn) ticket window; (Bank u. Post) counter, window; (elektr. ~) switch, circuit-breaker; (circuit) closer, contactor, commutator, (knife) switch, key, shifter, interrupter, cutout, controller, controlling apparatus or instrument, shutter ~ **mit fünf Ausgängen** five-point switch ~ **für Nachtwecker** night bell, night-alarm key ~ **für die Platzlampe** release key ~ **mit unabhängiger Schaltbewegung** independent switch (for opening or closing a circuit) ~ **mit festen Stellungen** locking key ~ **mit zwei Stellungen** two-way or two-position switch ~ **zur Tauchlampe** dipping switch

Schalter, einen ~ **öffnen** to open a switch **einen** ~ **schließen** to close a switch **einen** ~ **umlegen** to throw a switch **-doppelpoliger** ~ two-pole or double-pole switch **nicht festlegbarer** ~ nonlocking key **halbversenkter** ~ semisunk or semirecessed switch

Schalter, magnetisch betätigter ~ magnetic switch **mehrteiliger** ~ multiple-point switch **sechsteiliger** ~ **mit zwei Stellungen** two-position six-point switch **umlaufender** ~ rotary or revolving switch **vielstufiger** ~ multipoint switch **zweipoliger** ~ two-pole or double-pole switch

Schalter-achse *f* switch shaft **-anker** *m* switch armature **-ankerfeder** *f* switch armature spring **-arbeit** *f* switch work **-betätigung** *f* actuation of switch **-brücke** switch or contact bridge **-deckel** *m* switch cover **-diode** *f* series-efficiency diode **-dose** *f* switch outlet **-druckknopf** *m* switch push button **-element** *n* circuit element

Schalter-fall *m* tripping of circuit breaker **-fallmeldung** *f* breaker-tripped signal **-fassung** *f* switch socket **-feder** *f* switch spring **-gestell** *n* switch frame **-glimmlampe** *f* glow lamp for switch **-grundplatte** *f* key shelf, switch base plate **-halle** *f* passenger hall

Schalter-kasten *m* switch box

Schalter-kessel *m* switch tank **-kontakt** *m* contact stud **-laden** *m* fan-light shutter, Venetian blind **-leistung** *f* rupturing, circuit-opening, or circuit-breaking capacity **-öl** *n* circuit-breaker oil, oil for switches

Schalter-platte *f* switch wafer **-reihe** *f* bank or row of keys **-sockel** *m* switch base **-stellung** *f* switch position **-stromspule** *f* switch current coil **-tisch** *m* switching desk, counter **-werk** *n* electrical interlock board

Schalt-feld *n* switchgear panel **-festigkeit** *f* resistance to switching transients **-finger** *m* shift finger **-folgediagramm** *n* switching-sequence diagram **-folie** *f* automatic foil (tape rec.) **-führung** *f* (Auto) gear shifting gate

Schalt-gabel *f* striker clutch or fork, shift fork, shift claw **-gehäuse** *n* gear casing, feed box **-gerüst** *n* feeder pillar **-gestänge** *n* shifting linkage **-getriebe** *n* change-over gear, gear-shift or controlling mechanism **-glied** *n* connecting device **-griff** *m* handle, selector

Schaltgruppen *pl* speeds (gear) **-ziffer** *f* number index of the vector group

Schalthäufigkeit *f* time on in percent

Schalthebel *m* shift or switch lever, control or

clutch lever, starting handle, gearshift lever ~ (des Fahrschalters) controller handle, switch lever ~ **für Hauptgetriebe** spindle speed selector levers

Schalthebel-griff *m* knob, shift lever ball **-preßform** *f* control lever die **-welle** *f* shift lever shaft

Schalt-hub *m* length of travel (elec.) **-hülse** *f* connecting bush **-impuls** *m* switching pulse **-jahr** *n* leap year **-kamm** *m* function lever, **-kapazität** *f* capacitance of wiring, circuit capacitance

Schaltkasten *m* switch box or case **-automat** *m* timing box **-schlüssel** *m* ignition key, switch box key

Schalt-kennlinie *f* (transistor) switching characteristic **-kennzeichen** *n* switching criterium or signal **-klaue** *f* shift dog **-klinke** *f* pawl, click **-klinkengetriebe** *n* ratchet-drive mechanism **-knagge** *f* trip dog, stop dog, trip cam **-knebel** *m* switch handle or lever **-knopf** *m* switch knob, push button, selector ball **-koeffizient** *m* switching coefficient

Schaltkolben *m* operating piston **am ~ verfügbare Kraft** power of operating piston

Schalt-kommando *n* control unit **-kreise** *pl* switching network **-kugel** *f* operating ball **-kulisse** *f* gear-shifting gate **-kuppelung** *f* shifting coupling, clutch **-lader** *m* two-speed loader **-leistung** *f* contact rating **-linse** *f* field lens **-liste** *f* wiring specification sheet

Schalt-magnet *m* switching magnet, driving magnet, stepping magnet **-matrix** *f* switch matrix, wiring arrays **-mechanismus** *m* indexing mechanism, tripping or switching mechanism **-mittel** *n* switching device, switch element, circuit element, circuit means **-motor** *m* torque motor **-muffe** *f* gearshift sleeve, control sleeve **-netz** *n* combinatorial circuit **-nocke** *f*, **-nocken** *m* trip cam, trip or stop dog, trigger cam, contact cam **-organ** *n* switching relay or member, control mechanism

Schalt-periode *f* shutter period, shift period, moving period, feed stroke (motion pictures) **-plan** *m* wiring scheme, wiring or circuit diagram, toll switching plan **-pult** *n* switchboard, control desk, switch desk **-pumpe** *f* multi stage pump **-punkt** *m* switch point

Schalt-rad *n* indexing gear or wheel, notched disk, ratchet or stepping wheel **-räderkasten** *m* feed box, gear box **-radwälzfräser** *m* index gear hob **-rätsche** *f* ratched pawl **-raum** *m* switch room **-relais** *n* switching relay **-röhre** *f* mercury switch, switching tube or valve **-rolle** *f* sprocket wheel (film feed) **-satz** *m* terminal repeater **-säule** *f* switch column

Schalt-scheibe *f* indexing disk or plate, indexing ring **-schema** *n* wiring scheme or plan, wiring diagram, switch system, circuit diagram, hookup **-schieber** *m* slide valve **-schiene** *f* shift rail **-schloß** *n* locking cam **-schlüssel** *m* switching key, throw key, push key, ignition key **-schrank** *m* switch cabinet, switchboard, switch box, switchgear, control panel, switchgear cabinet **-schütz** *m* electronic contactor, relay switch **-schützmagnet** *m* relay magnet

Schalt-segment *n* gear-shifting quadrant **-signaleingang** *m* switching signal input **-skizze** *f* circuit or wiring diagram **-spanne** *f* switching period **-spannung** *f* bias-reducing potential, unblocking potential **-spiel** *n* switching cycle **-spindel** *f* shaft (jack) **-spindellager** *n* bearing carrying shaft

Schalt-stange *f* shifter rod, switching or gearshift bar, insulating rod, feed rod (textiles) **-stangenführung** *f* shift rod frame **-stellung** *f* switch position, "on" position of switch, indexing position **-stern** *m* star wheel **-stift** *m* tripping pin **-stöpsel** *m* plug **-stoß** *m* impulse **-strom** *m* current on contact **-stück** *n* throw-out mechanism, contact spud, contact **-stufe** *f* switch step, working point

Schaltsystem der Außenanlagen peripheral circuitry

Schalt-tafel *f* switchboard, switchgear, switch cabinet, panel, distribution panel or board **-tafelinstrument** *n* panel meter **-tisch** *m* switchboard **-transistor** *m* switching transistor **-übersicht** *f* circuit or wiring diagram **-uhr** *f* switch clock, economizer, time switch

Schalt- und Verteilungstafeln *f pl* switch and distribution boards

Schaltung *f* (Steuerung) control; (Motor) gear change, gearshift; (Elektr.) circuit; (Verbindungen) connections; (Umschalten) switching; wiring, star-delta, feed control, control gear, diagram, feed motion, feed path, tripping, indexing, circuit arrangement or circuit scheme, hookup

Schaltung, ~ mit Gegenkopplung degenerative circuit **~ des Ikonoskops** circuit of the iconoscope **~ zur Verminderung der Nebengeräusche** anti-side-tone device **bildweise ~** intermittent film feed or movement **gemischte ~** series-multiple connection, multiple-arc connection, parallel-series connection **geräuschdämpfende ~, rückhördämpfende ~** anti-side-tone device

Schaltungs-anordnung *f* switching arrangement, circuit **-aufbau** *m* circuit design **-bedingung** *f* switching condition **-lehre** *f* circuit studies **-plan** *m* switch system **-platte** *f* wiring plate **-schema** *n* wiring diagram **-technischer Aufbau** constructional details of circuit organization or wiring **-zeichnung** *f* circuit diagram, wiring diagram

Schalt-unterlage *f* wiring diagram **-variable** *f* logic variable, switching variable (comp.) **-ventil** *n* pilot valve **-ventilanordnung** *f* control valve arrangement **-verbindung** *f* circuit connection **-verzögerung** *f* time delay **-verzug** *m* time delay, time lag **-vorgang** *m* switching operation or process, transient **-vorrichtung** *f* switching contrivance or mechanism, switchgear **-walze** *f* controller cylinder or drum or barrel

Schaltwalzen-anlasser *m* barrel controller **-antrieb** *m* limit switch drive **-büchse** *f* (Lenkschloß) controller cylinder (drum) bush

Schalt-wand *f* switchboard **-warte** *f* switching station, control room, switchboard gallery **-weg** *m* feed motion, feed path, control distance

schaltweise Bewegung *f* intermittent movement or feed, discontinuous movement

Schalt-welle *f* interrupter or control shaft, feed shaft, gear-shift-lever shaft **-wellenhebel** *m* gear shift lever **-werk** *n* switch cabinet, switch-board, switch box, switchgear, control(ling) mechanism, ratchet wheel, feed mechanism, film feed, intermittent or shuttle mechanism (motion pictures), control-switch mechanism or gear, trip or stepping mechanism **-winkel** *m* operating angle **-wippe** *f* switching lever, control bell crank **-wirkung** *f* trigger action

Schalt-zahn *m* ratchet tooth **-zahl** *f* number of connections **-zapfen** *m* indexing bolt **-zeichen** *n* symbol of radio-circuit element, legend (list of symbols) **-zeit** *f* starting time, switching time **-zeitrelais** *n* contactor timer **-zelle** *f* (regulating) cell, end cell, cubicle **-zylinder** *m* control cylinder

Schalung *f* (concrete) form, sheathing, casing

Schalungsrütteln *n* vibration of mold

Schalung(-smauer) *f* **von trockenen Steinen** dry-stone form wall

Schaluppe *f* sloop, barge

Schälvorrichtung *f* peeling device

Schalwand *f* sheeting, board or plank partition

Schälzentrifuge *f* peeler centrifuge

Schamfielen *n* chafing

Schamotte *f* fireproof clay, (burned) fire clay **gemahlene ~** grog

Schamotte-ausfütterung *f* fire-clay lining **-brokken** *m* fire-clay brickbat **-gemäuer** *n* firebrick lining **-gut** *n* clay refractories **-haube** *f* fire-clay sleeve or nozzle **-mörtel** *m* fire-clay mortar **-retorte** *f* fire-clay retort **-stein** *m* fire-clay, firebrick **-tiegel** *m* fire-clay crucible **-ton** *m* fire-clay, refractory clay **-überhitzer** *m* carburetor, checker-brick superheater **-ziegel** *m* firebrick

Schandeck *n* gunwale, plank-sheer

Schanzarbeit *f* entrenching, construction of field-works

Schanze *f* redoubt, fieldwork, crust, entrenchment, quarter-deck

schanzen to dig, entrench

Schanz-kleid *n* bulwark, topside **-korb** *m* gabion **-tätigkeit** *f* trenchwork, entrenching

Schanz- und Werkzeugwagen *m* entrenching and tool wagon

Schanzzeug *n* entrenching tools, (slang) eating utensil (combining a spoon and a fork)

Schappe *f* (offene) auger bit, wimble (scoop)

Schappen-bohren *n* auger boring **-bohrer** *m* (shell) auger, auger bit **-kante** *f* auger edge

Schar *f* troop, host, band, herd, number, crowd, bolt, claw, blade, family (math.) **~ algebraischer Gebilde** family of algebraic loci

Schardeich *m* dike directly alongside the waterway, most exposed part of a dike

Scharegge *f* extirpator

Scharen *f pl* **von Geraden** (Kurven) bands of straight lines (curves)

scharen, sich ~ to meet, join, assemble

scharf sharp, sharp-edges; (Schneide) keen; (spitz) pointed, acute; (Kurve) sharp; (Geruch) sharp, pungent; (Essig) strong; (ätzend) caustic, mordant; (schroff) abrupt, sharp; (sorgfältig, genau) exact, precise; (streng, hart) severe, strict, rigorous; corrosive, biting, acrid, sharply defined, well-focused, strident, shrill, piercing (of sound), peaked (of a curve) **~ begrenzt** (Licht) sharply delimited **~ eingestellt** in focus **~ geschnitten** clear out (face)

scharf, -er Ansatz sharp angle of step or shoulder, abrupt sharp angle **-e Bombe** live bomb **-es Gewinde** V thread, angular thread **-e Kante** sharp or keen or feathered edge **-e Schlacke** *f* aggressive slack **-er Strahl** solid jet **-er Windstoß** sharp-edged gust

Scharf-abbildung *f* (sharp) definition, sharpness **-abbildungssteuerung** *f* definition control

Scharfabstimmung *f* frequency correction, sharp tuning **automatische ~** automatic frequency control

scharfbegrenzt highly selective (of resonance), sharply defined, sharp-edged

Schärfe *f* s. a. scharf sharpness, acutness, severity, abruptness, sharp definition, precision, clearness, keenness, resolving power, resolution, degree or measure of distinctness, acuity **gestochene ~** microscopic sharpness **~ des Lichtstrahls** focusing (of the light spot)

Schärfeinlage *f* liner

Scharfeinstellung *f* adjustment for definition, sharp focusing or setting, automatic tuning indication, focus control

Schärfemesser *n* paring knife

schärfen to sharpen, grind, whet, edge, redress, restore

Schärfenebene *f* focal plane

Schärfenfeld *n* focal field **-grenze** *f* limit of sharpness or of definition, camera line (delineating good focus area) **-tiefe** *f* depth of (focal) field

Schärfen-fläche *f* surface of sharp or distinct vision **-tiefe** *f* depth of focus or vision, definition in depth **-tiefenbereich** *m* depth of focus range **-tiefenskala** *f* depth-of-field scale **-winkel** *m* angular resolving power **-zeichnung** *f* sharpness of delineation

Schärfepunkt *m* focus

scharfgängig V-threaded, triangular-threaded **-es Gewinde** angular thread, V thread, triangular thread

scharfgeladene Granate live shell

scharfkantig sharp-edged, angular **-e Vertiefung** *f* (Kaltwalzen) pit

Scharf-kerb *m* V notch, V-shaped notch **-konturig** having sharp outlines **-manganerz** *n* hausmannite **-schliff** *m* sharpening **-schneidiges Werkzeug** *n* keenedged tool

Schärfstein *m* sharpening stone

scharfstellen to arm (bombs), make live (bombs)

Scharfstellspannung *f* focusing voltage

Schärfstempel *m* sharpening die

Schärfung *f* sharpening, grinding **~ des Peilminimums** sharpening of the minimum

scharfwinklig acute-angled

Scharlach *m* scarlet, cochineal

scharlachrot scarlet

Scharnier *n* hinge(-joint), frame joint, articulation **mit Scharnieren versehen** hinged

scharnierartige Zähne hinge teeth

Scharnier-band *n* joint or hinge frame **-bolzen** *m* hinge pin **-deckel** *m* hinged lid **-deckelkanne** *f* churn with hinged lids **-flasche** *f* hinged block **-gelenk** *n* hinge **-gelenkbolzen** *m* hinge link pin **-hülse** *f* hinge sleeve

Scharnier-kaliber *n* firmjoint caliper **-kernkasten** *m* hinged core box **-klinke** *f* joint latch **-kluppe** *f* hinge stocks **-moment** *n* vane hinge torque **-platte** *f* hinge butt **-platzfeile** *f* joint file, round-edge joint file **-rahmen** *m* hinged frame **-riegel** *m* hinge bolt

Scharnier-schraube *f* screwed rivet **-stift** *m* hinge bolt, hinge pin **-stiftschlüssel** *m* hooked wrench **-ventil** *n* swing check valve, leaf on flap valve **-verkleidung** *f* hinge cover **-zapfen** *m* pivot pin **-zirkel** *m* compasses

Schärpe *f* sash, scarf

Scharre *f* shovel, rake, scraper

Scharreisen *n* scraper

scharren to scratch, scrape

Scharrer *m* scraper

Scharrharz *n* scrape rosin or resin

Scharriereisen *n* charing chisel, scarifier, toothed chisel

scharrieren to chare **einen Stein ~** to nig or chare an ashlar

Scharte *f* indentation, notch

Scharten-blende *f* firing-port shutter **-schild** *n* firing-port shield, loophole cover **-schlitz** *m* loophole

schartig jagged, notchy, nicked, serrate

Scharung *f* linking **~ von Gängen** junction of veins

Schatten *m* shadow, shade **~ des magischen Auges** eye shadow **-anzeiger** *m* shadow tuning indicator, shadowgraph **-bandinstrument** shadow column instrument **-bereich** *m* shadow region or range **-bild** *n* silhouette, shadow image, echo **-fleck** *m* cloud

Schatten-gebiet *n* shadow region, shadow area **-generator** *m* shading generator **-maske** *f* lens mask (TV) **-mikroskop** *n* shadow microscope **-mosaik** *n* shade mosaic **-riß** *m* silhouette **-seite** *f* shady side

Schatten-sektor *m* blind sector **-stelle** *f* blind spot **-stift** *m* shadow pencil or pin **-streifen** *m* ghost line **-temperatur** *f* shade temperature **-veränderung** *f* change in shade or shading values **-verhältnis** *n* shadow ratio, cover ratio, transparency **-werk** *n* shadow factory **-wirkung** *f* shadow effect **-wurf** *m* casting of shadows **-zeiger** *m* shadowgraph (tuning indicator)

schattieren to shade, hatch, tint

Schattiertwasserzeichen *n* intaglio

Schattierung *f* shading, hatching, shade, tint

Schattierungsverfahren *n* variable-density recording method

schattig shady

Schatz *m* treasure, collection

schätzen to estimate, value, evaluate, rate, judge

Schatzmeister *m* treasurer

Schätzung *f* estimate, taxation, appraisal, evaluation, valuation, rating

Schätzungs-fehler *m* error in judging or estimating **-irrtum** *m* miscalculation **-täuschung** *f* error in calculation **-weise** by estimate

Schätzwert *m* estimate rate

Schau *f* show, exhibition **zur ~ stellen** to exhibit, display

Schaubild *n* diagram, figure, graph, perspective view **~ der Luftschraubenleistung** propeller load curve

schaubildlich graphic, diagrammatic

Schau-bildzeichner *m* autographic recorder **-blatt** *n* diagram

Schauer *m* shudder, (passing) shower, downpour, shed, shelter, penthouse **-länge** *f* shower unit **-strahlen** *m pl* shower radiations

Schaufel *f* shovel; (schöpfen) scoop; (Turbinen ~) blade, bucket, vane, turbine bucket, scoop, spade, paddle, beater, fluke (of an anchor) **~ zum Ausheben des Erdreichs aus dem Stangenloch** digging spoon **~ mit genieteter Dülle** riveted back-strap shovel **bewegliche ~** feathering paddle or float **schmale ~** narrow-mouthed shovel **zugespitzte ~** pointed shovel

Schaufel-abstand *m* circular pitch (of turbine) **-anstellung** *f* blade setting **-beiwert** *m* blade coefficient **-blatt** *n* (shovel) blade **-blech** *n* flow-guide blades **-fähiger Schrott** shoveling scrap **-form** *f* vane form **-frequenz** *f* blade frequency **-furchenöffner** *m* shovel furrow opener **-fuß** *m* bucket or blade base

Schaufel-gitter *n* cascade **-kammer** *f* vane chamber **-kette** *f* chain with paddles **-kranz** *m* bucket ring (gas turbine) **-kufe** *f* skid loader shoe **-lader** *m* tractor shovel **-lappen** *m* blade lobe **-meißel** *m* spade-type chisel **-mischer** *m* paddle mixer **-mulde** *f* bucket trough

schaufeln to shovel

Schaufelpflug *m* (single-)shovel plow

Schaufelrad *n* impeller, runner, vane wheel, rotor, paddle or bucket wheel **-bagger** *m* bucket-wheel excavator **-färbemaschine** *f* paddle dyeing machine **-lader** *m* bucket wheel loader **-mischer** *m* turbine mixer **-pumpe** *f* bucket or vane wheel pump **-rücklader** bucket wheel reclaimer

Schaufel-rührer *m* impeller **-satz** *m* set of blades **-schützer** *m* shovel coverer **-stern** *m* startype impeller **-stiel** *m* shovel handle **-tasche** *f* vane pocket **-teilung** *f* spacing of blades **-tiefe** *f* bucket depth **-träger** *m* inner nozzle ring, blade carrier **-trockner** *m* paddle dryer

Schaufelung *f* blading, shoveling buckets

Schaufel-verjüngung *f* blade taper **-verwindung** *f* blade or bucket twist **-werk** *n* shovel conveyor **-winkel** *m* blade angle **-zahl** *f* number of blades **-zeilung** *f* blade spacing **-zylinder** *m* turbine casing

Schaufenster *n* shop or show window, shop front, sash **-gestell** *n* display stand

Schaufler *m* mucker, shoveller

Schau-gang *m* inspection port **-gitter** *n* inspection screen

Schauglas *n* sight glass, inspection glass, gauge glass, display tube or glass, look box, eyepiece, ocular, specimen glass, sample glass **~ für Öl** oil-display tube, oil sight glass

Schauglaspropeller *m* sight-glass spinner

Schau-kammer *f* inspection room **-kästchen** *n* showcase

Schaukel *f* swing **-apparat** *m* oscillating or rocking device **-aufzug** *m* swinging hoist, tray elevator **-becherwerk** *n* swing-bucket elevator **-bewegung** *f* tilting or rocking motion **-breithalter** *m* oscillating stretcher **-changierung** *f* swing-arm traverse motion **-effekt** *m* jitter (TV) **-elevator** *m* tray elevator **-förderer** *m* rocker conveyer **-kurvette** *f* rocking-through dish bath, automatic rocker

schaukeln to swing, rock, oscillate, move to and fro

Schaukeln *n* rocking, swinging

Schaukel-ofen *m* tilting or tipping furnace, mechanical puddling furnace **-sortierer** *m* shaking-screen **-transporteur** *m* rocking conveyor **-welle** *f* rocker shaft

Schau-klappe *f* inspection door or flap **-linie** *f* diagram, curve, graph, sighting line **-linienzeichner** *m* graphic recorder **-linse** *f* viewing lens

Schauloch *n* inspection hole, sight opening, peephole, observation hole, aperture, inspection window **-deckel** *m* inspection or handhole cover

Schauluke *f* sight hole

Schaum *m* foam, froth, scum, dross, skimmings, crust, lather, suds **chromatischer ~** chromatic soft focus, chromatic bleeding **trockener ~** dry dross

Schaum-abheben *n* froth skimming, skimming, drossing operation, drossing **-abheber** *m* froth skimmer, drosser **-abstreifer** *m* (flotation) froth skimmer, float skimming device **-ähnlich, -artig** foamlike, foamy **-beton** *m* aeroconcrete **-bildner** *m* foamer, frothing agent, frothing oil **-bildung** *f* froth or foam formation, frothing, foaming **-bildungskennstoff** *m* antifoaming agent **-bildungsvermögen** *n* frothing quality, capacity for forming froth or foam **-blase** *f* bubble **-brecher** *m* froth breaker, froth killer

schäumen to foam, froth, effervesce, lather

Schäumen *n* effervescence, boiling (of a melting bath), violent bubbling, foaming, frothing

Schaumentnahme *f* foam removal, skimming

Schäumer *m* frother

Schaum-fähigkeit *f* lathering power **-fang** *m* skimmer gate (in casting), gate for retaining slag and dirt **-feuerlöscher** *m* foam (fire) extinguisher **-flecken** *pl* froth stains **-gemisch** *n* emulsion, foam or broth mixture, scum or lather mixture **-generator** *m* foam generator **-gold** *n* Dutch metal **-gummi** *n* expanded rubber, crepe rubber, sponge rubber

schaumig foamy, frothy, porous **-e Oberfläche** scoriaceous surface

Schaum-kalk *m* aphrite, slate spar, aragonite **-kelle** *f* skimming ladle, skimmer **-keramik** *f* foamed ceramics **-kern** *m* foam core **-kopf** *m* scum riser **-krone** *f* white cap **-latte** *f* slice (a board on a paper machine to control flow of pulp onto the Fourdrinier) **-löffel** *m* skimming spoon, skimmer **-mischkammer** *f* foam mixing chamber **-mundstück** *n* foam lance

Schaum-öl *n* antifroth oil **-säule** *f* bubble column **-schlacke** *f* granulated slag, slag pumice **-schwimmaufbereitung** *f* flotation, preparation for flotation, phenomenon involving foam

Schaumstoff *m* aerated plastics, foam (material) **-bauteil** *n* foamed structure **-isolierung** cellular plastic insulation

Schaum-ton *m* fuller's earth **-trichter** *m* scum riser **-zentrale** *f* foam(-mixing) station

Schau-öffnung *f* peephole, inspection panel **-öl-apparat** *m* sight lubricator (oil feed) **-platte** *f* inspection plate **-platz** *m* scene (of action), theater, arena **-ritze** *f* peep-hole

Schau-ständer *pl* display racks **-stellung** *f* exhibition, exposition **-stück** *n* show-piece **-tafel** *f* inspection panel, diagram, indicator, graph **-tropföler** *m* sight feed lubricator **-versuch** *m* lecture experiment, demonstration experiment

Schauzeichen *n* (visible) signal, indicator signal, (magnetic) visual signal, line marker, optical signal, telltale means **~ mit Signalkontakt** magnetic visual signal with alarm contact

Schauzeichenbatterie *f* visual-signal battery

Schawatte *f* anvil block, bedplate, base casting, stock

Scheck *m* check, ticket **-abrechnungsmaschine** *f* bank proof machine **-heft** *n* checkbook

scheckig mixed, mingled, dappled, spotted, mottled

Scheck-kontrollabschnitte *pl* cheque counter foils **-sicherheitspapier** *n* safety cheque paper

Scheel-bleierz *n*, **-bleispat** *m* scheeletine, lead tungstate

Scheelerz *n*, **Scheelit** *m*, **Scheelspat** *m* scheelite

Scheffel *m* bushel **-maß** *n* bushel measure

Scheg *n* afterpiece (shipbuilding)

Scheibe *f* (Technik) disk; (Fenster~) pane; (Wähl~) dial; (Zifferblatt) face; (Schleif~) wheel; (Dichtungs~) gasket; (Unterlage) washer; pulley, sheave, lamella, sheet, cut, slice, target, (disk) plate, reel, flange, panel

Scheibe, ~ für Riemenbetrieb belt pulley **~ für Sechskantschrauben und -muttern** washer for hexagonal bolts and nuts **~ des Verteilers** distributor disk **~ für Zylinder- und Halbrundschrauben** plain washer **bewegliche ~** movable disk **blanke ~** machined or polished washer **durchlochte ~** apertured disk (TV) **feste ~** fixed plate **halbblanke ~** semimachined washer **hintere ~** rear plate **stroboskopische ~** stroboscopic disk, stroboscope, stroboscopic pattern wheel **vordere ~** front plate

Scheibenabschwächer *m* disk attenuator (microwaves)

Scheibenachse *f* (Riemenscheibe) pulley axle **~** (Schleifmaschine) wheel arbor

Scheiben-anker *m* disk armature **-ankergenerator** *m* disk-type alternator **-antenne** *f* disk antenna **-antriebpumpstation** *f* band-wheel-powered pump **-ausgabe** *f* target office **-blende** *f* thin orifice plate **-bockschlitten** *m* wheel stand slide **-bohrung** *f* (grinding) hole **-breite** *f* width of pulley face **-bremse** *f* disk brake

Scheiben-dichtung *f* sheet gasket **-diode** *f* disc-seal diode **-drehbank** *f* surface lathe **-drillmaschine** *f* disk drill **-drossel** *f* variometer **-egge** *f* disk harrow **-elektrometer** *n* disk discharger or electrometer **-entfroster** *m* windscreen defroster

Scheiben-fassung *f* lens socket **-feder** *f* Woodruff key, disk or plate spring, spring washer **-filter** *n* disk filter **-formfräser** *m* bore shaper cutter **-förmig** disk-shaped, discoid

Scheibenfräser *m* side-milling cutter, side mill **~ mit Grobverzahnung** coarse-toothed side-milling cutter **~ mit eingesetzten Messern** inserted-tooth side-milling cutter **~ für Muttern oder Bolzenköpfe** straddle mill **~ mit hinterdrehten Zähnen** side-milling cutter with backed-off teeth **~ geradeverzahnt** (kreuzverzahnt) side milling cutter, straight teeth (staggered teeth) **verstellbarer ~** interlocking side-milling cutter

Scheiben-funkenstrecke *f* disk discharger **-furchenöffner** *m* disk furrow opener **-futter** *n* disk chuck **-gasbehälter** *m* waterless gasholder, tankless gasholder **-glas** *n* plate glass **-hackmaschine** *f* disk cultivator or hoeing machine **-häufler** *m* disk hiller **-hebel** *m* disk lever **-höhenmesser** *m* altimetric dial (disk) **-holländer** *m* disk beater **-isolator** *m* disk insulator

Scheiben-käfig *m* retainer ring (of ball bearing), cage **-kante** *f* edge of the nozzle exit **-kegelrollenlager** *n* tapered roller thrust bearing **-keil** *m* Woodruff key **-keilartig** Woodruff key-shaped **-klampe** *f* check block **-kläranlage** *f* windscreen demister **-kolben** *m* disk piston **-kolbenpumpe** *f* pump with solid piston

Scheiben-kondensator *m* disk capacitor **-konusantenne** *f* disone antenna **-kranz** *m* pulley rim **-kreiselmischer** *m* disk impeller mixer **-kühler** *m* disk cooler **-kupfer** *n* rose or rostte copper **-kuppelung** *f* flange(-face) coupling, plate coupling, disk clutch, disk coupling, plate clutch **-kurbel** *f* eccentric **-kurve** *f* discor plate cam **-küvette** *f* disk cell **-laufrad** *n* disk landing wheel **-lochwalzwerk** *n* disk piercer

Scheiben-maisdrill *m* disk corn planter **-marke** *f* index line on the dial **-markierungsapparat** *m* disk marker attachment **-meißel** *m* disk bit **-messer für Unkraut** disk weeder **-mühle** *f* disk crusher, disk mill **-nocke** *f* cam **-pfahl** *m* disk pile **-pflanzmaschine** *f* disk planter

Scheibenpflug *m* disk plow ~ **mit Führersitz** riding disk plow

Scheiben-pistole *f* target pistol **-pistolenschießen** *n* target-pistol shooting **-rad** *n* (center-)disk wheel, center-web wheel **-radwalzwerk** *n* mill for rolling center-disk-type wheels, center-web-wheel rolling mill, Schoen mill **-reibahle** *f* disk-type reamer **-reißen** *n* conversion into disks or rosettes (met.) **-relais** *n* movable-disk relay **-rille** *f* sheave groove **-rillenlager** *n* deep-groove ball bearing, axial ball bearing **-röhre** *f* disk-seal valve **-rose** *f* compass card

Scheiben-schäler *m* disk barker **-schleifmaschine** *f* disc sanders **-schlepper** *m* target-towing aircraft **-schneider** *pl* circular glass cutters **-schützer** *m* disk cover **-schwungrad** *n* driving pulley, solid or disk fly-wheel **-sech** *n* rolling colter **-signal** *n* disk or board signal **-spule** *f* pancake coil, flanged spool or bobbin **-stand** *m* rifle range **-strahl** *m* disk ray

Scheiben-teilwalze *f* divider roller **-tonnenlager** *n* spherical roller thrust bearing **-treffbild** *n* shot group or pattern **-trimmer** *m* disk trimmer **-triode** *f* disc-seal triode **-übersetzung** *f* pulley ratio, sheave ratio **-umfang** *m* circumference of cam or pulley

Scheiben- und Drillmaschine *f* disk drill

Scheiben-unterbrecher *m* chopper disc **-ventil** *n* inertia disk valve **-verschlüßler** *m* space or spatial encoder **-vorschneider** *m* rolling colter **-walze** *f* web roll, center-disk roll **-walzverfahren** *n* disk-piercing process **-walzwerk** *n* mill for rolling circular shapes **-wendepflug** *m* reversing disk plow **-wicklung** *f* pile-wound coil, disk-shaped winding, disk coil or winding **-widerstand** *m* disk type resistor **-wischer** *m* windshield wiper **-wischerschiene** wiper blade

Scheiben-zähler *m* disk indicator (missiles) **-zeigerwerk** *n* disk indicator **-zuganlage** *f* range unit with moving targets **-zylinderlager** *n* cylindrical roller thrust bearing

scheidbar separable, analyzable

Scheide *f* case, sheath, (water) divide, scabbard, isoclinal valley **-anlage** *f* screening device **-anstalt** *f* parting work, refinery **-bad** *n* separating bath **-blech** *n* baffle plate **-bogen** *m* pier arch **-erz** *n* screened or picked ore, crop **-fähig** separable

Scheide-gang *m* poor ore **-gefäß** *n* parting or separating glass, triturium **-haus** *n* sorting house **-kalk** *m* defecation lime or scum **-kapelle** *f* cupel **-kessel** *m* parting kettle **-kolben** *m* separating flask **-kühler** *m* partitioned radiator **-linie** *f* boundary or separating line **-mauer** *f* partition wall

scheiden to separate, part, decompose, sort, divide, defecate, lime, isolate, analyze, pick, sever

Scheide-ofen *m* parting furnace **-pfanne** *f* defecator, defecation tank, liming tank **-prisma** *n* separating prism

Scheider *m* separator, grader, cobber

Scheide-schlamm *m* defecation scum, press cake, molasses **-sieb** *n* separating sieve **-silber** *n* parting silver **-trichter** *m* separating funnel, separatory funnel **-verfahren** *n* refining method, separation method **-vorgang** *m* separating process, separation **-vorrichtung** *f* separating or parting device, screening or sorting device **-wand** *f* partition (wall), parting or division wall, (separating) wall, partition timber, electrolytic diaphragm, separator, bulkhead, septum (geol.), baffle (loud-speaker) **-wasser** *n* aqua fortis, aqua regia, nitric acid

Scheidung *f* separation, parting; (Chem.) analysis; (Metall) refining; decomposing, picking, sorting, clearing, clarifying, dividing, severing, extraction, defection, liming, segregation ~ **durch die Quart** (in)quartation **nasse** ~ wet separation, defecation with milk of lime

Scheidungsmittel *n* mean of separation (chem.)

Schein *m* certificate, license (permit), shine, light, flash, luster, glow **schwacher** ~ glimmer

Schein-adresse *f* dummy (comput.) **-anlage** *f* dummy emplacement, dummy position **-anlagen** *f pl* dummy works

scheinbar seeming, apparent, visible ~ **periodische Größe** pseudoperiodic quantity **-es logarithmisches Dämpfungsdekrement** effective or equivalent logarithmic or damping decrement **-e Haftfestigkeit** *f* adhesiveness **-e Höhe** virtual height, effective height **-e Masse eines Elektrons** effective mass of an electron **-er Widerstand** apparent resistance

Schein-bewegung *f* feint, simulated movement **-bild** *n* false image **-binder** *m* header **-dämpfung** *f* apparent attenuation **-diffusionskoeffizient** *m* eddy diffusivity **-diffusor** *m* dummy diffuser **-dispersion** *f* apparent dispersion **-ecke** *f* corner cramp

scheinen to shine, appear, seem

Schein-energie *f* apparent energy **-flugplatz** *m* dummy airfield **-funk** *m* dummy signal, simulated broadcast **-funkstelle** *f* deceive station **-gold** *n* imitation gold **-graben** *m* dummy trench **-hafen** *m* dummy airfield, dummy port or harbor **-komponente** *f* apparent component **-kräfte** *pl* fictitious forces **-leistung** *f* apparent power

Scheinleistungs-messer *m* volt-ampere meter **-übersetzungsverhältnis** *n* apparent-power transmission ratio **-zähler** *m* apparent-power meter, volt-ampere-hour meter, apparent-energy meter

Scheinleitfähigkeit *f* eddy conductivity

Scheinleitwert *m* admittance ~ **einer Leitung gegen Erde oder zwischen den Drähten einer Doppelleitung** line-shunt admittance

Schein-löslichkeit *f* apparent solubility **-lotrichtung** *f* direction of the apparent perpendicular (geophysics) **-lotschwankung** *f* deviation from vertical **-periode** *f* spurios period **-reibung** *f* eddy viscosity **-sender** *m* decoy transmitter **-signalrakete** *f* dummy signal rocket **-sperre** *f* dummy obstacle, dummy entanglement **-stellung** *f* dummy emplacement, dummy position **-verbrauchszähler** *m* apparent-power meter **-vernebelung** *f* diversion smoke screen

Scheinwerfer *m* searchlight, headlight, spotlight, reflector, projector, floodlight ~ **zur Bestimmung der Wolkenhöhe** ceiling projector (aviation) ~ **von . . . Kerzen** searchlight of . . . candlepower

Scheinwerfer-abwehr *f* searchlight defense **-dichte** *f* searchlight density **-einsatz** *m* head lamp unit **-einstellung** *f* head lamp adjustment **-feld** *n* optical panel **-flugzeug** *n* searchlight plane **-gerät** *n* searchlight equipment **-licht** *n* searchlight beam, flood light **-optik** *f* light unit **-richtungsweiser** *m* control station **-stand** *m* searchlight platform **-straße** *f* searchlight lane **-stütze** *f* headlamp carrier

Scheinwerfer- und Bildwerferlampe *f* projector lamp

Scheinwerferverbindungsstange *f* headlamp support tie rod

Schein-wert *m* apparent value or component (elec.) **-widerstand** *m* impedance, apparent resistance or impedance, impedor

Scheinwiderstands-angleicher *m* impedance compensator **-anpassung** *f* adaption of impedance **-meßbrücke** *f* impedance bridge **-messung** *f* apparent-resistance measuring or measurement **-nachbildung** *f* impedance imitation

Scheinwirkungsgrad *m* apparent efficiency

Scheit *m*, *n* split billet, log

Scheitel *m* apex, crown, top, vertex, mode, point of angle, summit, origin of coordinator ~ **der Brücke** bridge apex ~ **der Differentialspule** split point ~ **des Dreiecks** vertex of the triangle ~ **einer Welle** wave crest, peak ~ **eines Winkels** angle vertex, angular point

Scheitel-abstand *m* zenith distance **-ausschlag** *m* amplitude **-bogen** *m* azimuth **-brechwert** *m* vertex refraction (opt.) **-dicke** *f* crown thickness **-druckfestigkeit** *f* (Rohr) crushing strength **-faktor** *m* amplitude factor, peak or crest factor **-gebiet** *n* crest area **-gelenk** *n* crown hinge **-geschwindigkeit** *f* peak velocity

Scheitel-haltung *f* summit pool or pond **-höhe** *f* vertex **-kanal** *m* canal that crosses a water divide **-kreis** *m* azimuth **-lappen** *m* parietal lobe **-linie** *f* vertical line, zenithal line

Scheitel-messer *m* crest meter **-platte** *f* vertex plate (antenna) **-punkt** *m* vertex, apex, zenith (of trajectory) **-recht** straight, upright, vertical, perpendicular, plumb **-rille** *f* top groove **-spannung** *f* peak or crest voltage **-strom** *m* peak current **-tangente** *f* vertex tangent **-tiefe** *f* depth of vertex, vertical depth

Scheitelwert *m* peak (value), amplitude, maximum value, crest (value) ~ **des Kathodenstroms** peak cathode current

Scheitelwertspannungsmesser *m* peak voltmeter

Scheitel-winkel *m* vertical angle, opposite angle, vertex angle **-wölbung** *f* curvature at peak

scheitern to fail, be wrecked, founder, prove unavailing

Scheitersäge *f* billet saw

Scheitelholz *n* split firewood

Schelf *m* shelf

schelfen to scale, peel, shell

Schellack *m* shellac **-platte** *f* shellac disc

schellackieren to shellac

Schell-band *n* muzzle hoop **-beanspruchung** *f* unidirectional cyclic loading

Schelle *f* clamp, clip, clamping ring or collar, sliding, tap, bell, buzzer, bracket, shackle ~ **mit Handgriff** clamping collar and handle

Schelleisen *n* rivet(ing) set, snap tool

Schellenklemme *f* clamp strap

Schellhammer *m* ax, cup-shaped hammer, snap or set hammer, snap dies, rivet set, forming tool, riveting snap

Schellkopf *m* snap head **-nietung** *f* snap riveting

Schellstück *n* slab

Schema *n* scheme, schedule, form, plan, pattern, setup, model, (circuit) diagram, blank **-bild** *n* diagrammatic plan or view **-tafel** *f* graphic panel

schematisch schematic **-er Arbeitsplan** flow sheet **-e Darstellung** diagrammatic representation **-er Entwurf** *m* schematic drawing **-er Plan** outline plan **-e Zeichnung** skeleton sketch

schematisieren to schematize, standardize

Schematismus *m* formalism

Schemazeichnung *f* diagrammatic drawing (aircr.)

Schemel *m* stool **-wagen** *m* compensating truck, bogie

Schenkel *m* thigh, shank, leg, wing, blade, side (piece), foot, reins, swivel, side (of angle), arm, flank, web, haunch, limb (of transformer) ~ **eines Winkels** angle side ~ **eines Zirkels** leg

Schenkel-auge *n* eye of side bar, lug eye **-feder** *f* operating lever spring, leg spring, spring clip **-rohr** *n* bent tube, bent pipe, V tube, elbow tube, elbow pipe

Schenkelpolmaschine *f* salient-pole machine or generator

schenklig legged, limbed

Scheppern der Kuppelung rattling of the coupling

Scher-apparat *m* shearing-test apparatus **-backe** *f* shearing anvil **-balken** *m* pontoon balk **-baum** *m* shaft

Scherbe *f* fragment, piece, cupel, scorifier, body (ceramics)

Scherbeanspruchung *f* shear(ing) stress, shearing force or strain, flexing or tangential stress

Scherbelastung *f* shearing load

Scherben *f pl* cullet, body (ceramics) **-kobalt** *m* native or metallic arsenic, shard cobalt **-wand-**

verteilungsdose *f* knockout junction box

Scher-blatt *n* shear blade, blade or check of shears **-block** *m* warping block **-bolzen** *m* shear pin **-dehnung** *f* shear(ing), strain **-draht** *m* shear wire

Schere *f* scissors, shears, cutter, notch, nick, groove, shafts, claw, snips, change-gear bracket ~ (Getriebe) quadrant

Schereisen *n* fleshing knife

scheren to sheer, cut, crop, clip, yaw

Scheren *f pl* arm braces (harness)

Scheren *n* shearing **-bindung** *f* chelation, chelate combination **-blatt** *n* scissors or shear blade **-blende** *f* scissors shutter **-feder** *f* guide spring scissors spring

Scherenfernrohr *n* scissor telescope, periscope

Scheren-gerüst *n* lining frame **-klinge** *f* scissors blade **-kopf** *m* brake lever connecting rod **-kreuzung** *f* scissors junction

Scherenmesser *n* scissors or shear blade ~ **für Textilfabriken** shear knives for textile plants

Scheren-schleifer *m* knife or scissors grinder **-spreizer** *m* lazy tongs **-stahl** *m* shear steel **-strebe** *f* arm brace **-stromabnehmer** *m* pantograph, scissors-shaped collector **-system** *n* (Walzeneinstellung) jointed shank system **-trenner** *m* pantograph isolator **-verbindung** *f* slit-and-tongue **-zange** *f* wire cutter, shingling tongs, cutting forceps **zapfen** *m* forked mortice and tenon joint

Scher-festigkeit *f* shear(ing) strength, resistance to flexing, shearing resistance **-fläche** *f* plane of shear **-gerät** *n* box-shear apparatus **-gießpfanne** *f* shear ladle **-haken** *m* spacer **-kluppe** *f* hinge stocks **-kraft** *f* shearing stress, shear(ing) force, tangential stress **-maschine** *f* cutting machine

Scher-messer *n* shearing blade or knife **-modul** *m* modulus of shearing **-moment** *n* yawing moment **-niete** *f* rivet under shear stress **-pfanne** *f* shank ladle **-platt** *f* ribband **-probe** *f* shear test **-riss** *m* shearing crack

Scher-schnitt *m* shearing cut **-schwingung** *f* shear vibration **-stift** *m* shear pin **-spannung** *f* shear(ing) stress, shearing force, tangential stress, shearing resilience or strain **-spant** *m* principal frame **-stift** *m* shear pin **-tau** *n* sheer line **-tempel** *m* chearing die **-trommel** *f* warping cylinder

Scherung *f* shear(ing) action, shifting (magnetism) **zweischnittige** ~ double shear **auf** ~ **beansprucht** loaded in shear

Scherungs-anteil *m* shear-strain **-bewegung** *f* shearing **-bruch** *m* shear fracture **-druck** *m* shearing stress **-festigkeit** *f* shearing strength **-gerade** *f* straight shifting line **-grenzenmesser** *m* pachymeter

Scherungs-kegel *m* shear cone **-koeffizient** *m* rate of shear **-komponent** shear stress **-linien** *pl* shear trajectories **-modul** *m* rigidity modulus, shear modulus **-modulus** *m* shear, torsion, or rigidity modulus **-schicht** *f* shear layer **-schwingung** *f* shear vibration **-spannung** *f* shearing stress

Scherungs-stärke *f* shear intensity **-steifigkeit** *f* shear stiffness **-strömung** *f* shear flow **-übertragung** *f* shear transfer **-viskosität** *f* shearing viscosity **-welle** *f* shear wave **-winkel** *m* angle of shear **-wirkung** *f* shearing effect

Scher-verformung *f* shear strain **-versuch** *m* shear(ing) test **-werkzeuge** *pl* shearing tools **-widerstand** *m* shearing resistance **-wirkung** *f* shearing effect **-zeug** *n* shearing mechanism **-zugversuch** *m* shear tension test **-zylinderlagergehäuse** *n* shearing cylinder bearing

Scheuer-blech *n* work bar (textiles) **-bock** *m* chafe rod **-faß** *n* tumbling or rumble barrel, tumbler, rolling or shaking barrel, scouring or cleaning barrel **-fest** fast to scraping **-festigkeit** *f* abrasion resistance **-lappen** *m* scouring cloth **-leiste** *f* skirting (board)

scheuern to scour, scrub, rub, clean, wear, chafe

Scheuern *n* chafing, scouring, grinding, polishing

Scheuer-pfahl *m* chafe rod, stay, guard, vertical cattle guard **-pflaster** *n* chafing patch **-prahm** *f* copper punt **-prüfer** *m* abrasion tester, abrasimeter **-pulver** *n* scouring powder **-stein** *m* grinding stone **-stellen** *pl* chafe marks **-stück** *n* (Geländer) skirting board

Scheuertrommel *f* tumbling barrel, tumbler, rolling or shaking barrel, scouring or cleaning barrel ~ **mit Sandstrahlgebläse** sandblast rolling barrel, sandblast tumbling barrel

Scheuer-tücher *pl* floor cloths **-wirkung** *f* abrasive action or effect, scrubbing action

Scheunenestrich *m* threshing floor

Schicht *f* layer, bed; (Geolog.) stratum; (Farbe) coat; (Steine) course; (Technik, Schub) batch; (Hochofen) charge; (Bodensatz) sediment; (Arbeiter) shift, gang; (Pause) break, rest; stratum, zone, film, turn, tour, monomolecular layer, coat(ing), lamina, emulsion, roof or floor (min.), case, emulsion side, ply, pile, skin, sheath, target

Schicht, ~ **auf** ~ emulsions to emulsion **eine** ~ **anbohren** drilling in, to find a layer by boring ~ **machen** to end the work, work out a shift (min.) **eine** ~ **verfahren** to work out the task (min.) **absorbierende** ~ absorbing layer **atmosphärische** ~ atmospheric layer, sphere, stratosphere, isothermal region

Schicht, drei ~ three-ply **dünne** ~ film, thin layer (trans.) **durchlässige** ~ permeable formation **einatomige** ~ monoatomic layer **eingewanderte** ~ diffused layer (trans.) **gerasterte** ~ mosaic (photosensitized) coat or screen **lichtelektrische** ~ photoelectric layer or film **lichtempfindliche** ~ (light-)sensitive surface or layer **monoatomare** ~ monoatomic layer

Schicht, obere ~ overburden (min.), upper stratum **wasserführende** ~ water-bearing stratum ~ **endlicher Dicke** finite slab **Einfallen der Schichten** drift of strata **auf beiden Seiten mit anderen Schichten bedecken** to sandwich **aus dünnen parallelen Schichten bestehend** laminar

Schicht-abstand *m* "sandwich" spacing **-arbeit** *f* shift work **-aufnahmeverfahren** *n* planigraphy **-aufrichtung** *f* tilting of strata **-band** *n* ferrous coated tape (tape rec.) **-bildgeräte** *pl* planigraph devices **-boden** *m* mixing floor, mixing place **-breite** *f* width of layer **-dicke** *f* thickness of layer, coat, or film **-ebene** *f* contour plane or level, plane of stratification **-emulsionstechnik** *f* sandwiching

schichten to arrange in layers, stratify, stack, pile (up), pack

Schichten *n* (in Lagen) batching **supraleitende dünne ~** superconducting thin films
Schichten-abstand *m* contour interval, equidistance **-aufrichtung** *f* uplift of strata **-bau** *m* stratified or layered structure **-bildung** *f* (stratum) formation (geol.), stratification **-filter** *m* sheet filter **-filtration** *f* layer filtration **-folge** *f* oil-bearing series, succession of beds
schichtenförmig stratified **-e Lagerung** foliation
Schichten-gitter *n* layer lattice, stratified lattice **-glas** *n* laminated glass **-gruppe** *f* formation, strata group **-klasse** *f* sheet type **-kohle** *f* foliated coal **-konstruktion** *f* sandwich construction **-linie** *f* contour line **-plan** *m* relief map **-sattel** *m* anticlinal flexure (geol.) **-sorten** *pl* sheet types **-stapel** *m* stack **-störung** *f* dislocation of strata
Schichtenströmung *f* parallel flow **gleichförmige ~** steady or constant parallel flow
Schichten-struktur *f* structure of the filter sheets, layer-lattice structure **-verzeichnis** *n* boring log **-weise** stratified, in layers
Schicht-festwiderstände *pl* fixed layer resistances **-fläche** *f* bedding plane, stratification plane **-folge** *f* series or sequence of strata **-fugen** *f pl* joints of bedded rocks, bedding planes **-gefüge** *n* lamellar structure **-gemischwiderstand** *m* composition resistor **-gestein** *n* stratified rock **-gitter** *n* stratified or layer lattice **-glied** *n* stratum **-haufenwolke** *f* stratocumulus (cloud) **-höhe** *f* height of layer or stratum, height of bed **-holz** *n* plywood, stacked wood, laminated wood **-holzbelagbrettchen** *n* pile wood lag
schichtig lamellar, laminated, platelike
Schicht-kathode *f* cathode bearing a layer or coat of oxide, light-sensitive substance, coated filament **-körper** *m* stratified structure or body **-korrosion** *f* layer corrosion **-kunststoff** *m* laminated plastic **-ladung** *f* layer charge **-lage** *f* position of the coating **-länge** *f* path length (of bands), layer length
layer length
Schichtling *m* argilaceous veined agate
Schichtlinie *f* contour (line), layer line **Schichtlinien des Geländes** contour lines of terrain **Ziehen der Schichtlinien** tracing of the contours
Schichtlinien-karte *f* contour plan or map **-plan** *m* contour and elevation plot, contour map **-linienzeichnung** *f* contouring
Schicht-lücke *f* stratigraphic hiatus **-meister** *m* controller, comptroller, overseer **-mulde** *f* trough-shaped stratum **-packung** *f* compressed-sheet packing **-platte** *f* laminated record (phono) **-preßstoff** *m* moulded laminated plastics **-quelle** *f* contact or strata spring **-regler** *m* layer controller **-seite** *f* emulsion side of film
Schicht-stoff *m* laminated material or plastic **-stoffbahn** *f* laminated sheet **-strömung** *f* laminar flow **-textur** *f* stratified texture or structure, sheet intergrowth **-theorie** *f* sheat theory **-träger** *m* film base, emulsion carrier
Schichtung *f* stratification, striation, lamination, arrangement in layers, bedding, arranging in layers, piling or stacking (up) **~ der Abgase** stratification of gases
Schichtungs-fläche *f* bedding or stratification plane **-größe** *f* stratification parameter **-pendel** *n* compensation pendulum
Schicht-verteilung *f* layer distribution **-wachstum** *n* film growth **-wasser** *n* ground water **-weise** in layers or strata **-widerstand** *m* layer resistance
Schichtwolke *f* stratus (cloud) **hohe ~** altostratus (cloud)
schicken to send, ship **auf die Reise ~** to launch **auf den Weg ~** to route
Schiebe-anker *m* sliding armature **-barriere** *f* sliding barrier **-blende** *f* sliding diaphragm **-brücke** *f* traversing table, traveling platform
Schiebebühne *f* traverser, traveling platform **unversenkte ~** surface traverser
Schiebe-bühnenanlage *f* traveling platform installation **-bühnengrube** *f* pit or trench of traverser **-dach** *n* sliding roof **-deckel** *m* slip cap **-deckelöler** *m* slide-top oil cup **-dreieck** *n* (drafting) triangle **-drossel** *f* variometer **-druck** *m* separation pressure **-fahrgestell** *n* cross-wind under carriage, drift under carriage **-fahrwerk** *n* cross-wind landing gear, drift landing gear **-fenster** *n* sliding window, sash window **-fest** non-slip **-flugzustände** *pl* yawing conditions
Schiebe-gatter *n* sliding barrier **-geschwindigkeit** *f* drift velocity **-gestänge** *n* duct rod, sweep rod **-giermoment** *n* yawing moment due to slide **-haube** *f* cockpit cover **-hülse** *f* sliding sleeve **-impuls** *m* advance pulse, shift pulse
Schiebe-karren *m* (wheel)barrow **-kassette** *f* dark-slide **-kern** *m* sliding coil **-knoten** *m* running knot **-kontakt** *m* sliding contact, adjustable slide, cursor **-lager** *n* sliding bearing **-landung** *f* drift landing, lateral drift landing
Schiebe-lehre *f* sliding caliper **-leiste** *f* sliding post **-leiter** *f* traveling ladder **-linse** *f* internal focusing lens **-luke** *f* sliding hatch **-motor** *m* sleeve-valve engine **-muffe** *f* clutch sleeve, shift sleeve, sliding sleeve **-mutter** *f* sliding nut
schieben to push, slide, slip, shove, shift, thrust, crab or drift (of airplane) **nach außen ~** to squash (on turns at full throttle), skid
Schieben *n* skidding, shoving **~ in der Kurve** skidding on the turn, flat turn **~ ohne Schräglage** skidding movement without banking
schiebend-er Flügel yawed wing **-e Wirkung** heaving effect, displacing action
Schieber *m* slide, slider, slide bar, sliding plug, slide valve, slide plate, (slide) damper, pusher, extractor, cover plate, breech block, shovel, cursor, corrector, gate valve, safety bolt **~** (Rollenkühlbett) transfer frame
Schiebe-rad *n* sliding gear, wheel **-räder** *n pl* **zur Vorgelegeeinrückung** back-gear sliding pinion and stem gear
Schieberäder-getriebe *n* sliding change gear **-kupplung** *f* sliding gear clutch
Schieber-antrieb *m* sleeve drive **-boden** *m* sliding bottom **-buchse** *f* valve bush **-bund** *m* collar on slide valve **-deckung** *f* lap of the slide valve **-diagramm** *n* slide-valve diagram **-druckregler** *m* regulating feed valve **-einteilung** *f* slide division **-fläche** *f* slide or valve face **-gebläse** *n* blowing engine with slide valve **-gehäuse** *n* (slide-)valve casing **-gestänge** *n* slide-valve rod **-hub** *m* stroke of the slide valve **-hülse** *f* sliding sleeve valve
Schiebering *m* slider, sliding ring
Schieber-kassette *f* roller-blind dark slide **-kasten** *m* valve casing, slide or distributing box, steam

chest **-kerbe** *f* rod notch **-kölbchen** *n* valve piston **-körper** *m* slide valve (gate) **-lappen** *m* valve face **-luftpumpe** *f* slide-valve air pump **-motor** *m* pusher-type engine, slide- or sleeve-valve engine

Schieberollmoment *n* rolling moment due to slip, rolling and yawing moment

Schieber-platte *f* valve plate **-pumpe** *f* piston valve pump **-rad** *n* sliding gear **-rahmen** *m* lantern-slide carrier, valve buckle **-rand** *m* valve face **-register** *n* shifting register **-rohr** *n* sliding sleeve, sliding tube **-schubstange** *f* valve rod **-schütz** *n* sluice valve

Schieber-spiegel *m* slide main face, slide(-valve) face **-spindel** *m* slide screw (slide spindle) **-stange** *f* (slide-)valve rod, slide rod **-stangenführung** *f* slide rod guide **-stellung** *f* slide position **-steuerung** *f* slide-valve gear

Schieber-ventil *n* (clamp) gate valve, slide valve, cuff valve **-verbesserung** *f* deflection correction **-verschluß** *m* sliding shutter, gate-type valve joint **-widerstand** *m* slide rheostat **-zylinderkopf** *m* sliding cylinder head, junkhead

Schiebe-schachtel *f* slide carton **-schalter** *m* slider switch **-schlitten** *m* traverser truck **-schnalle** *f* slide buckle **-schranke** *f* sliding barrier **-sitz** *m* slide fit, sliding fit, wringing fit, push fit **-sitzwelle** *f* sliding-fit shaft

Schiebe-speicher *m* shift register **-spule** *f* sliding inductance or coil **-stein** *m* slide block **-tor** *n* caisson or rolling lock gate **-transformator** *m* slide transformer **-transporteur** *m* scraper conveyer **-tür** *f* sliding door **-ventil** *n* slide valve, sleeve valve **-vorrichtung** *f* slide, sliding device

Schiebe-wechselrad *n* slip change gear **-weiche** *f* sliding cross-over **-welle** *f* spline shaft **-widerstand** *m* slide resistance **-winkel** *m* angle of sideslip **-zahnrad** *n* slip gear

Schiebfach *n* drawer

schiebfeste Ausrüstung non-slip finish

Schieb-flügel *m* sliding sash **-hülse** *f* sliding sleeve **-karre** *f* wheelbarrow, handbarrow **-kasten** *m* drawer **-kraft** *f* thrusting power, thrust, shear **-kupplung** *f* sliding coupling, sleeve clutch **-lade** *f* drawer **-lehre** *f* slide caliper rule, slide gauge **-rad** *n* ratched wheel **-truhe** *f* (push)cart

Schiebung *f* shearing deformation, shifting, pushing, shoving **~ in der hyperbolischen Ebene** translation in the hyperbolic plane **spezifische ~** shearing strain

Schiebungs-fläche *f* shear plane, slip plane (cryst.) **-modulus** *m* torsion, shear or rigidity modulus

Schiebwiderstand *m* slide resistance

schiedbarer Guß semisteel

Schieds-analyse *f* arbitration or umpire analysis **-gericht** *n* court of arbitration, jury **-spruch** *m* arbitration (judgment), arbitrament

Schiedsrichter *m* umpire, referee, arbitrator, arbiter **-dienst** *m* umpire service **-liches Verfahren** arbitration **-stab** *m* umpire staff

Schiedsversuch *m* referee test

schief (schräg) oblique, slanting; (geneigt, abfallend) sloping, inclined; (hängend) lop-sided; (krumm) crooked; (e- Ebene) inclined, plane; (Hang) gradient; bias, (a)skew, sloping, tilted, sloped, warped, unsymmetric, skew-symmetric (of curves) **~ geschnitten** bias **-e Ebene** inclined plane **-er Einfall** oblique incidence **-e Falte** unsymmetrical fold **-er Hilfsflügel** skew aileron (aviation) **-er Winkel** oblique angle

schiefachsig oblique-axial

Schiefe *f* slope, inclination, obliqueness, obliquity, dissymmetric condition, skew (ness)

Schief-einfall *m* grazing incidence, oblique incidence **-eisen** *n* skew iron

Schiefensteuerung *f* horizontal steering lever

Schiefer *m* slate, schist, spangles, shale, splinter **-artig** slatelike, slaty, schistous **-bruch** *m* slaty, scaly, or laminar fracture **-dach** *n* slate roof **-farben** slate(-colored) **-grau** slate gray **-grube** *f* slate quarry **-haltig** schistose, slaty

schieferig slaty, schistous, schistose, foliated

Schiefer-kohle *f* splint coal **-letten** *m* clay shale

schiefern, sich ~ to exfoliate

Schiefer-öl *n* schist or shale oil **-paraffin** *n* shale wax **-platte** *f* slate slab **-stein** *m* slate **-stift** *m* slate pencil **-tafel** *f* slate slab, slate (board) **-teer** *m* tar from shale, slate tar **-ton** *m* clay slate, clay schist, shale, flint clay **-tonabfall** *m* spent shale

Schieferung *f* chavage, schistosity **falsche ~** oblique or transversal lamination, cleavage

Schieferweiß *n* white flake

Schiefführung eines Schornsteins bending of a chimney

Schiefheit *f* obliqueness, wryness

schief-hermetisch skew-hermetic(al) **-körper** *m* skew field **-laufen** *n* (eines Krans) twisting

schieflaufend loxodromic

Schieflaufende *f* loxodrome, rhumb line

Schieflaufschalter *m* off-track belt switch

schiefliegend inclined, sloping, obliquely positioned, slanting

schiefrig foliated, schistous

Schiefsteg *m* inclined quoin (print.)

Schiefstehen von Buchstaben inclination of letters

schiefstehend slanting, oblique **-stellen** *n* oblique setting **-stellung** *f* inclined position, angular deviation

schiefsymmetrisch skew-symmetric (of curves) **-e negative Paare** skew-symmetric negative pairs

schiefwinklig tilted, with obtuse angle, oblique-angled, skew **-es Achsenkreuz** oblique coordinates **-es Parallelogramm** rhomboid, oblique(-angled) parallelogram

Schielablenkung *f* angle of squint

Schielen *n* squinting

Schiel-fehler *m* error due to squint **-messer** *m* strabismometer **-winkel** *m* angle of strabism, angle of squint

Schienbein *n* shin bone

Schiene *f* (am Rad) iron hoop, iron band; (Eisen) bar; (Führungs~) guide rail; (Stromabnehmer) bus bar; rail, strip, beam, joist rule, tire, splint, skid, iron rail, track, rim **feste ~ einer Weiche** stock rail of a siding **Wandern der Schienen** creep of the rails

Schiene für Messingrakel bar for wash-up blade

schienen to rail, splint **den Stahl ~** to draw out and flatten steel

Schienen *m* doctor (paper mfg.) **-aggregat** *n* rail layout **-anschlußstück** *n* junction-rail end **-auftrag** *m* rail surfacing **-auszug** *m* rail overlap

-bahn *f* (rail) track -biegmaschine *f* rail bending machine -blatt *n* scarfed end of a rail

Schienenbremse *f*, **elektromagnetische ~** electromagnetic slipper brake

Schienen-bruch *m* rail breakage **-bus** *m* rail bus **-ende** *n* rail end **-fuß** *m* rail foot, rail base, flange of a rail **-geleise** *n* set of tracks

schienengleicher Wegübergang level crossing (R.R.)

Schienen-hammer *m* sledge hammer **-hebelkontakt** *m* electrical depression bar **-heber** *m* rail-lifting jack **-herzstück** *n* built-up crossing with base plate or frog

Schienen-innenkante *f* running or inner edge of rail **-kaliber** *n* rail pass **-kontakt** *m* rail contact (R.R.) **-kopf** *m* rail head **-kranz** (Kran) *m* roller path **-lager** *n* rail chair **-lasche** *f* (rail) fish plate **-lauffläche** *f* running surface or tread of rail **-laufrad** *n* rail wheel **-nagel** *m* track spike **-oberkante** *f* top (edge) of rail

Schienen-paket *n* fagot, puddle-bar pile **-paketierung** *f* fagoting **-profil** *n* rail section **-pufferfeder** *f* bar buffer spring **-putzer** *m* way cleaner **-räumer** *m* cowcatcher **-reibung** *f* rolling friction or resistance at the rails **-richtbank** *f*, **-richtmaschine** *f* rail-straightening machine **-rost** *m* grate bar **-rücker** *m* rail sluer **-rückleitung** *f* rail return **-sperre** *f* rail (angle-iron) barrier

Schienen-stahl *m* rail steel **-steg** *m* rail web **-stoß** *m* rail joint, rail bond **-strang** *m* (rail) track, beam track **-straße** *f* rail mill train (in rolling) **-strom** *m* rail current **-stromschließer für Signalsteuerung** signal pedal **-stromwandler** *m* bar-type transformer **-stuhl** *m* rail chair, cradle **-stütze** *f* track support

Schienen-traggabel *f* rail fork **-transport** *m* rail transport **-trenner** *m* bus isolator **-trio** *n* three-high rail mill **-überhöhung** *f* cant of rails **-unterkante** *f* rail bottom **-verbinder** *m* rail bond, rail joint, busbar connection (elec.) **-verbindung** *f* busbar connection, rail bond **-verkehr** *m* rail traffic **-verlegemaschine** *f* rail changing machine

Schienen-walze *f* roll for rails **-walzhütte** *f* rail mill **-walzwerk** *n* rail rolling mill **-wandern** *n* creeping of the rails **-weg** *m* railroad, tramway **-weite** *f* gauge (R.R.) **-winkel** *m* rail square **-zange** *f* rail tongs, rail clamp

Schieß-arbeit *f* blasting, shooting **-arbeiter** *m* shooter **-bahn** *f* shooting line **-baumwolle** *f* guncotton **-becher** *m* cup discharger (of rifle grenade) **-bremse** *f* firing brake **-betrieb** *m* launching operations (missiles) **-bremse** *f* firing brake

schießen to shoot, blast, flow (with velocity greater than critical value), fire, dart, emit, dash, bombard, set off **~ lassen** to let go or fly

Schießen *n* firing, shooting **~ mit Doppelzünder** fire with combination fuse, time fire **~ mit Erdbeobachtung** ground-observed fire **~ mit Karte** map firing

Schießen, ~ in der Luft air firing **~ mit Luftbeobachtung** conduct of fire with air observation **~ mit wechselnder Seitenrichtung** sweeping fire, traversing fire **~ mit hohen Sprengpunkten** fire with high bursting points **beobachtetes ~** observed fire **gefechtsmäßiges ~** combat-practice firing **das ~ beginnen** to open fire **Vorbereitung des Schießens** preparation of fire

Schieß-ergebnis *n* effect of firing **-fertigkeit** *f* marksmanship **-funkmeßgerät** *n* flak radar set **-gas** *n* gas from gas shell **-gerüst** *n* firing stand, emplacement (fort.), firing platform **-gestell** *n* firing platform **-grundlage** *f* firing data **-haken** *m* chase catch **-halter** *m* launching (switch) holder (missiles) **-hilfsmittel** *n* fire-control aid, firing accessory

Schieß-karren *m* antiaircraft rocket projector **-klotz** *m* gun-carriage wheel chock **-konstante** *f* explosive constant **-lehre** *f* ballistics, firing instructions and theory **-leitung** *f* shot-firing cable **-lineal** *n* sound- and flash-ranging slide rule **-loch** *n* shot hole **-nadel** *f* blasting needle

Schieß-ofen *m* sealed-tube furnace **-plan** *m* fire-control map, fire-direction chart **-platz** *m* firing or rifle range, shooting grounds **-pulver** *n* gunpowder **-richtung** *f* line of fire **-scharte** *f* loophole, embrasure **-scheibe** *f* target **-schlitz** *m* loophole, embrasure, firing port

Schießstand *m* rifle range, shooting range **~ für Zielmunition** miniature range

Schieß-stellung *f* shooting position **-stock** *m* anvil pillar **-übung** *f* firing practice **-unterlagen** *f pl* firing data

Schieß-verbindung *f* firing-data-transmission telephone line **-verfahren** *n* conduct of fire, method of fire **-vorschrift** *f* gunnery manual, musketry manual **-weite** *f* effective range **-wolle** *f* guncotton **-zubehör** *n* firing accessories

Schiff *n* ship, vessel, boat, nave (arch.) **ein ~ durchsuchen** to examine a vessel **~ festmachen** to moor **das ~ verlassen** to abandon ship **klar ~** decks cleared for action **neuestes ~** latest ship **veraltetes ~** obsolete ship **auf Schiffen** on board ship **festgesetzte Zeit zum Entladen eines Schiffes** lay days

schiffbar navigable **einen Fluß ~ machen** to make a river navigable

Schiffbarkeit *f* navigability

Schiffbau-werft *f* shipyard **-wesen** *n* shipbuilding, marine engineering **-wulstprofil** *n* shipbuilding bulb angle

Schiffbruch *m* shipwreck

Schiffchen *n* shuttle, little ship, composing galley (print.) **-bohrhammer** *m* cradle hammer drill

Schiffer *m* sailor, seaman, mariner, skipper **-knoten** *m* double half or clove hitch, slipknot

schiffern (slang) to cruise without sighting the enemy

Schifferpatent *n* master's certificate

Schiffahrt *f* navigation, shipping

Schiffahrts-erlaubnis *f* sailing permit **-kunde** *f* navigation **-linie** *f* steamship line **-öffnung** *f* navigable pass **-rinne** *f* sailing line **-signal** *n* navigation or nautical signal or sign **-straße** *f* navigable waterway **-warnung** *f* navigational warnings **-weg** *m* route **-zeichen** *n* navigation or nautical signal or sign

Schiffs-abstand *m* distance or interval between ships **-antrieb** *m* marine propulsion **-arzt** *m* ship's surgeon **-ausrüster** *m* shipowner **-barometer** *n* ship's barometer, marine barometer **-bauingenieur** *m* naval architect, naval engineer **-baumeister** *m* shipbuilder **-beladeanlage** *f* shiploading plant **-beleuchtung** *f* ship's lights, ship's light plant **-bemannung** *f* ship's crew

Schiffs-blech *n* shipbuilding plate, ship's sheathing **-boden** *m* ship bottom **-boot** *n* ship's boat **-breite** *f* beam of a boat or vessel **-brücke** *f* pontoon bridge **-dampfmaschine** *f* marine (steam) engine **-eisen** *n* iron in the ship, ship's iron **-flugzeug** *n* shipboard plane **-führung** *f* navigation **-funkstelle** *f* ship radio station

Schiffs-geleit *n* convoy (navy) **-gerät** *n* nautical gear **-geschwindigkeit** *f* speed of a ship **-glocke** *f* ship's bell **-halter** *m* bollard **-hebewerk** *n* shiplifting device **-helling** *f* slipway (for a vessel) **-höhe** *f* (over-all) height of a barge or vessel

Schiffs-kessel *m* marine boiler **-kompaß** *m* mariner's compass **-körper** *m* hull **-kran** *m* derrick **-kreisel** *m* gyrostatic stabilizer **-kurs** *m* steered course **-ladewinde** *f* cargo winch **-ladung** *f* cargo lading **-lände** *f* quay **-länge** *f* over-all length of a boat or vessel **-lazarett** *n* sick bay **-leiter** *f* ship or accommodation ladder, safety ladder **-liegeplatz** *m* loading berth **-liste** *f* ship's register **-luke** *f* ships' hatch

Schiffs-magnetismus *m* ship's magnetism **-makler** *m* ship broker **-maschine** *f* marine engine **-ölmaschine** *f* marine oil engine **-ordnung** *f* shipboard regulations **-ortung** *f* position finding, dead reckoning **-panzerung** *f* ship's armor **-papiere** *n pl* ship's papers **-peilanlage** *f* ship DF installation **-pfahl** *m* bollard **-pumpe** *f* ship's pump

Schiffs-radar *n* ship-borne or ship's or naval radar **-raum** *m* tonnage, hold (of a ship) **-ring** *m* mooring-ring bolt **-schleusung** *f* lock(ing) **-schornstein** *m* funnel (of a ship) **-schott** *n* bulkhead **-schraube** *f* propeller **-schwingung** *f* oscillation of a ship **-sender** *m* ship transmitter

Schiffs-spanten *pl* ship's frame **-sparren** *m* jack rafter, hip rafter **-spur** *f* wake of a ship **-suchgerät** *n* ship-locating radar

Schiffs-umschalter *m* marine transfer switch **-unfall** *m* damage (to ship or cargo), ship's accident **-verteilerdose** *f* marine distribution box **-wacht** *f* watch aboard ship **-weg** *m* course of the ship **-welle** *f* propelling shaft **-werft** *f* shipbuilding yard, shipyard, dockyard **-zertifikat** *n* ship's certificate of registry **-zettel** *m* shipping note **-ziel** *n* enemy ship under artillery fire, naval target **-zimmermann** *m* shipwright

schiften to join rafters together

Schifter *m* jack or hip rafter, rafter trimmer

Schikane *f* baffle plate

Schild *n* label, signboard, facia, identification plate **~ für Leerlauf** plate to stop suction **~ für Saugerkippung** plate for tilting sucker bar

Schild *m* shield, (atom., phys.) shell, buckler, plate, end cover (of el. motor)

Schilder *pl* (elektr. Motor) end caps

Schilderblau *n* pencil blue

Schild-fisch *m* sucker fish, ship stayer (textiles) **-klappe** *f* shield, port cover **-knoten** *m* crown knot **-lager** *n* trunnion bearing

Schildpatt *n* real shell **-papier** *n* tortoise shell paper

Schildstütze *f* shield support

Schildzapfen *m* trunnion, gudgeon **-lage** *f* trunnion tilt **-lager** *n* trunnion bearing **-lagerdeckel** *m* trunnion-bearing cover **-lagerpfanne** *f* trunnion-bearing pan **-schraube** *f* trunnion screw

Schilf *n* reed, cane

schilfern to scale off

Schilf-glaserz *n* freieslebenite **-rohr** *n* cane, reed

Schiller *m* luster, shine, iridescence, opalescence **-farbig** iridescent with metallic color or luster display **-glanz** *m* changeable or varying luster

schillern to vary or change colors, to opalesce

Schillern *n* schillerization, iridescence

schillernd shot, glacé, shot-colored, scintillating, changeable, opalescent, chatoyant **-e Flüssigkeit** opalescent liquid

Schillerspat *m* schiller spar

Schimmel *m* mold, white film, mildew **-bildung** *f* mildewing, mould growth

schimmelig moldy musty, fusty

schimmeln to mold, get or grow mo(u)ldy

Schimmelpilz *m* mold fungus

schimmeltötend fungicidal

Schimmer *m* bloom, gleam, glimmer

schimmernd resplendent

Schindel *f* shingle

Schingsche Röhre Bourdon tube

Schippe *f* scoop

Schirm *m* umbrella, screen, shield, back, shutter, shade, shelter, visor **~ aus erschwertem Beton** loaded concrete shield **~ des Braunschen Rohres** screen in the cathode-ray tube **~ für Gasfeuerung** gas-fire front **~ langer Nachleuchtdauer** long-persistence screen **ebener ~** flat (plane) screen **kapazitiver ~** electrostatic shield or screen **magnetischer ~** magnetic shield or screen **neutraler ~** neutral screen

Schirm-antenne *f* umbrella antenna **-artige Bedeckung eines Geleitzuges durch Flugzeuge** air umbrella **-ausbeute** *f* screen efficiency **-aussteuerung** *f* full utilization of screen

Schirmbild *n* image (on screen), pattern (CRT); display (rdr) **exzentrisches ~** off-center (plan) display

Schirmbildausschnitt *m*, **vergrößerter ~** expanded scope

Schirmbildauswertung *f* image interpretation (rdr)

Schirm-breite *f* screen width **-dach** *n* penthouse, shed, cover **-dämpfung** *f* shielding efficiency **-durchmesser** *m* face diameter (CRT) **-effekt** *m* screening effect **-effektkugel** *f* screening sphere **-einbrennung** *f* screen burning (CRT) **-eindecker** *m* parasol monoplane **-elektrode** *f* shield grid

schirmen to shield (from), screen, shade

Schirm-faktor *m* shield factor **-fläche** *f* shielding surface **-geflecht** *n* screen meshing **-generator** *m* umbrella-type generator

Schirmgitter *n* screen (grid) **-block** *m* screen bypass capacitor **-endröhre** *f* screen-grid output tube **-gleichstrom** screen grid current (D.C.) **-modulation** *f* screen-grid modulation **-richtverstärker** *m* screen-grid tube with plate-current rectification

Schirmgitterröhre *f* screen-grid valve or tube, screen-grid tetrode **~ mit veränderlichem Durchgriff** variable-mu tetrode, variable-mu screen-grid tube

Schirmgitter-spannung *f* screen voltage, screen volts **-verlustleistung** *f* screen-grid dissipation or power loss **-widerstand** *m* screen dropping resistor

Schirm-herrschaft *f* patronage **-isolator** *m* umbrella-type insulator **-kennlinien** *pl* screen characteristics **-leiter** *m* screened conductor **-leuchtdichte** *f* screen brightness **-luminophore** *n pl* phosphors, fluorescent substances for screens **-membrane** *f* screened diaphragm (of microphone) **-messung** *f* screen measurement (of water)

Schirm-netz *n* umbrella aerial **-posamenten** *n pl* umbrella and parasol trimmings **-rand** *m* margin of screen, screen border or edge **-ring** *m* splash ring **-schrift** *f* line, trace **-träger** *m* (screen) carrier, foundation or support for screen, face-plate (CRT) **-tuch** *n* tilt

Schirmung *f* screening, shielding, shield **-magnetische ~** magnetic shielding

Schirm-ventil *n* valve with deflector **-wand** *f* screen(ing wall), shadow wall (of a glass tank) **-werk** *n* breakwater, sea defense **-wirkung** *f* screening effect, shielding action, sheltering effect, protection **-wirkungsgrad** *m* screen efficiency

schirren to harness

Schizolith *m* diaschistic rock

Schlabberventil *n* overflow valve

Schlacht-haus *n* slaughterhouse **-hof** *m* meat-packing plant **-hofhängebahn** *f* meat conveyor **-messer** *n* butcher knife

Schlachtviehbetäubungsapparat *m* cattle-stunning apparatus

Schlachtwolle *f* skin, pelt, or plucked wool

Schlacke *f* slag, cinder, scoria, clinker, dross, boilings, tap cinder **~ abziehen** to slag (off), tap slag, draw off or remove slag, skim off slag, rake out slag or cinder **~ bilden** to work slag, form or make slag **dünnflüssige ~** fluid slag, flue-sheet clinker, wet slag **gut kontrollierte ~** well-shaped slag **kurze ~** dry or thick slag **zähflüssige ~** sticky slag, viscous slag, semipasty slag, dry slag, soft clinker

Schlacke-bilden *n* slag or ash forming, slag working **-bildend** slag-forming, ash-forming

schlacken to clinker, slag, form slag, scum, scorify

Schlacken-abscheider *m* slag skimmer or separater **-absonderung** *f* slag separation **-abstrichrinne** *f* slag spout **-abzug** *m* slag discharge **-ähnlich** slaggy, scoriaceous, drossy **-angriff** *m* cutting action of slag, slag action, fluxing action of slag, erosion by slag **-ansammlung** *f* slag accumulation **-arbeit** *f* slag smelting, manipulation or working (of slag) **-artig** slaggy, scoriaceous, drossy **-auge** *n* slag eye **-austrager** *m* clinker remover

Schlacken-band *n* slag conveyer **-basalt** *m* scoriwceous basalt **-behandlung** *f* slag treatment **-berechnung** *f* slag calculation, calculation of fluxing **-beton** *m* slag concrete **-bett** *n* slag concrete **-bildend** slag-forming **-bildner** *m* slag-forming constituent, slag-making material, flux for making slag **-bildung** *f* formation of slag or of clinker, scorification, ash formation **-blei** *n* slag lead **-brecherwalze** *f* slag-breaker roller

schlackende Kohle clinkering coal

Schlacken-damm *m* slag dam **-decke** *f* slag cover **-einschluß** *m* slag or cinder inclusion, slag occlusion or enclosure, trapped slag **-eisen** *n* cinder iron **-form** *f* slag or cinder notch, flushing hole, slag tuyère **-frei** slagless, slagfree, free of clinker **-frischen** *n* pig boiling **-frischreaktion** *f* lime boil (in the Martin process) **-gang** *m* cinder fall, cinder pit **-graben** *m* slag trap (in gating system) **-granulation** *f* slag granulation **-grube** *f* cinder pit, slag pit

Schlacken-halde *f* slag or cinder dump, cinder yard **-haldenbahn** *f* slag-heap conveyer **-haltig** slag-bearing **-hammer** *m* deslagging hammer **-haubengehänge** *n* slag pot cradle **-herd** *m* slag hearth, slag furnace **-kammer** *f* slag pocket, slag catcher, dust catcher **-karre** *f* slag car **-kasten** *m* slag pocket or catcher, dust catcher, cinder box **-klotz** *m*, **-klumpen** *m* clinker, slag lump **-,kobalt** *m* safflorite **-konstitution** *f* slag composition or constitution

Schlacken-kontrolle *f* slag control **-kopf** *m* scum riser (in casting) **-korn** *n* slag globule **-kruste** *f* slag crust, layer of slag **-kübel** *m* slag ladle or pot **-kuchen** *m* cake of slag or clinker **-kühlrohr** *n* slag-cooling tube **-lava** *f* scoria **-loch** *n* slag hole or notch, cinder notch or tap, flushing hole **-machen** *n* slag working, slag forming **-mehl** *n* ground slag **-menge** *f* slag volume

Schlacken-ofen *m* slag furnace **-öffnung** *f* slag hole or notch, cinder notch or tap, flushing hole **-pfanne** *f* slag ladle **-pflasterstein** *m* slag (paving) sett **-puddeln** *n* pig boiling, slag puddling **-reich** slaggy **-rein** free of slag or clinker **-rinne** *f* cinder spout, slag trough **-roheisen** *n* cinder pig (met.) **-rost** *m* granulating ferric hydroxide **-rösten** *n* slag roasting **-sammelgefäß** *n*, **-sammler** *m* slag pocket, cinder pocket or collector **-scherbe** *f*, **-scherben** *m* scorifier, refining pan **-schmelzpunkt** *m* slag fusion point

Schlacken-schütze *f* slag bridge **-schutzkasten** *m* guard plate (over the cinder hole of a blast furnace) **-spieß** *m* cinder iron, slag iron **-stand** *m* slag line **-staub** *m* coal dust **-stein** *m* slag brick, cinder or slag stone **-stich** *m*, **-stichloch** *n* slag hole or notch, cinder notch or tap, flushing hole **-strahl** *m* slag flow **-streifen** *m* slag streak or strip

Schlacken-tasche *f* slag pocket **-topf** *m* slag pot **-tragschicht** *f* slag base (course) **-transportanlage** *f* slag-conveying machinery **-trichter** *m* slag riser **-trichter** *m* (slag) clinker hopper **-tröpfchen** *n* slag nodule **-tür** *f* clinkering door, cleanout door **-überlaut** *m* slag overflow **-verladebrücke** *f* slag handling plant **-wagen** *m* slag ladle and car, slag car **-wechsel** *m* change of slags **-weg** *m* slag track **-wehr** *n* sand stopping

Schlacken-wolle *f* slag wool, mineral wool **-wollfilter** *n* mineral-wool filter **-zacken** *m* cinder plate **-zeile** *f* slag streak or seam **-zement** *m* slag cement **-ziegel** *m* slag brick **-ziehen** *n* removal of cinder, clinkering, withdrawal of slag **-ziffer** *f* slag ration **-zinn** *n* tin obtained from slag

schlackerlos loose

Schlackertaste *f* bug (telegr)

schlackig slaggy, drossy, clinkery, cindery, scoriaceous

Schlacktür *f* clinkering door, cleanout door

Schlaeflische Doppelsechs Schlaeflis' double six

Schlafdeich *m* safety dike

schlafend dormant (geol.)

schlaff limp, loose, slack, flabby, flaccid, soft, exhausted, tired ~ **bewehrter Teil** singly reinforced member **-es Trumm** slack or driven side or end of a belt

Schlaffheit *f* looseness, slackness, limpness

Schlaff-kettenschalter slack chain switch **-machen** to slacken, slack off **-seil** *n* slackline **-seite** *f* slack-side

Schlaffwerden *n* slackening ~ **des Drahtes** slacking of wire

Schlaf-kabine *f* sleeping cabin **-kette** *f* ground mooring chain **-koje** *f* berth **-krankheit** *f* sleeping sickness **-sack** *m* sleeping bag **-stadtrandsiedlung** *f* domitory suburb **-trunken** drowsy **-wagen** *m* sleeping car **-zimmer** *n* bedroom

Schlag *m* s. a. schlagen; (~ des Kolbens) stroke; (Aufprall) impact; (Treffer) hit; (elektr. ~) electric shock; (Pendel~) oscillation, swing; blow, shock, knock, kick, percussion, stamp, cutting (of wood), beat, pigeon loft, bay (of trench), dash, out of true, out of round, lay turn, lay (of a cable), pounding, wobble (of phonograph disk), click, thump or chatter (of a key or contact), car or carriage door ~ **eines Seiles** lay of a rope (in ropemaking) ~ **einer Welle** out of true, out of round, wobble **einen ~ erhalten** to receive a shock **auf ~ prüfen** to test for warpage

Schlag, mit ~ behaftet out of true **blinder ~** ineffective blow **dumpfer ~** thump **elektrischer ~** electric shock **kalter ~** return shock or stroke **schallender ~** bang **vernichtender ~** destructive blow

Schlag-abraum *m* slashings (forestry) **-antrieb** *m* forced flapping

Schlagarbeit *f* striking energy, impact energy, energy to fracture **spezifische ~** specific energy of blow **verbrauchte ~** striking energy absorbed

Schlag-arm *m* picker (stick) **-artig** prompt (execution of orders), striking by surprise, in sudden bursts **-bär** *m* striking hammer, impact anvil **-baum** *m* barrier, turnpike **-beanspruchung** *f* impact stress or load, shock stress or load, dynamic stress, vibratory stress

Schlagbiege-festigkeit *f* impact bend or flexure strength **-probe** *f* shock, blow, or impact bending test **-prüfung** *f* compression buckling **-versuch** *m* impact bending test

Schlagbohle *f* tamping or tamper beam

Schlagbohrer *m* percussion (rope) drill

Schlagbolzen *m* firing pin, striker ~ **für Gewehre** firing pin for guns

Schlagbolzen-feder *f* firing-pin spring, striker spring **-mutter** *f* striker nut **-spitze** *f* point of firing pin **-versager** *m* hung striker

Schlag-brecher *m* jaw crusher with inclined crushing chamber **-brunnen** *m* lever pump **-buchstaben** *pl* letter stamps **-dauer** *f* duration of blow **-dauerversuch** *m* endurance impact test, repeated-impact test **-daumen** *m* entrainer cam

Schlagdruck *m* percussion **-beanspruchung** *f* compressive impact stress, dynamic compression stress **-versuch** *m* impact compression test, dynamic compression test

Schlageküpe *f* beating vat

Schlägel *m* mallet, beater, maul, beetle, hand hammer, sledge, rammer, pestle, drumstick

Schlag-elastizität *f* impact elasticity **-empfindlichkeit** *f* sensitivity to percussion

schlagen (s. a. Schlag) to strike, beat; (übertreffen) beat; knock, hit, bore, cut (wood), fell (of trees), hook (in milling), chatter (of machines), defeat, whip (of ropes), break a record **eine Brücke ~** to lay or throw a bridge **kabelweise ~** to lay cable-fashion

Schlagen *n* driving, beating, cutting ~ **des Riemens** flapping of the belt ~ **eines Werkzeuges** jarring

schlagend convincing, striking **-e Bewegung** striking movement **-e Wetter** firedamp

Schläger *m* kicker, tennis, racket, rapier, beater **-antriebsscheibe** *f* driving pulley of beater **-magnet** *m* striker magnet **-messer** *n* beater blade **-mühle** *f* pugmill, beater mill **-schaltung** *f* plunger movement **-welle** *f* beater shaft

Schlag-exzenter *n* picker cams **-feder** *f* firing-pin spring, striker spring, impact or main spring

Schlagfehler *m* eccentric error **-prüfeinrichtung** *f* eccentric error measuring device

Schlag-fest impact resistant **-festigkeit** *f* resistance to impact or shock, impact strength or resistance **-finne** *f* striking edge **-fläche** *f* striking surface, impact surface **-flügel** *m* agitating arm **-flügelflugzeug** *n*, **-flügler** *m* ornithopter **-frei** true

Schlag-gelenk *n* (Hubschr.) flapping hinge **-gelenklager** *pl* flapping bearings **-geschwindigkeit** *f* striking velocity **-gold** *n* leaf gold

Schlag-hammer *m* sledge hammer **-härte** *f* impact hardness **-härteprüfer** *m* impact hardness tester, dynamic-hardness testing machine, autopunch-impact hardness tester **-haube** *f* driving cap (on pile), pile cover **-hebel** *m* striking lever, bell hammer **-instrument** *n* instrument for ramming, percussion instrument, ram

Schlag-kasten (Schlingenkanal) *m* wire leads **-knickversuch** *m* impact buckling test **-kolben** *m* percussion piston **-kraft** *f* impact or striking force, impact stress **-kreuzmühle** *f* beater mill, hammer mill **-krone des Kolbens** serrated edge of the piston **-ladung** *f* relay charge **-länge** *f* (length of) lay, length of twist (of cable) **-längenbereich** *m* range of lays **-leine** *f* carpenter's line

Schlag-licht *n* directed ray of light **-lichter** *pl* high-lights **-loch** *n* road hole **-locher** *m* punch **-lot** *n* spelter solder, hard solder, copper-zinc brazing mixture or spelter **-maschine** *f* ramming machine, stamper, beater **-matrize** *f* stamping die **-meißel** *f* spudding bit **-messung** *f* measuring eccentricity **-mühle** *f* beater mill, impact pulverizer, disintegrator, hammer mill, crushing mill, crusher, breaker **-mutternanzeiger** *m* impact nut runner

Schlagnase für Webstühle blade or knife for loom

Schlagnasenmühle *f* edge-runner mill, pin beater mill

Schlag-nietmaschine *f* percussion riveting machine **-panzer** *m* (Hochofen) protection shell **-patrone** *f* percussion primer, priming cartridge **-presse** *f* hammering press, matrix striking press **-pressen** *n* impact molding **-preßverfahren** *n* hammer-press process (plastics) **-probe** *f* impact or percussion test, falling-weight or drop test, hammer(ing) test, impact crushing test, dynamic test **-prüfmaschine** *f* impact testing machine **-rad** *n* cam disk, striking wheel

Schlagrädchen *n* milling wheel ~ **für Kesselreinigung** hammering wheel for boiler cleaning

Schlag-radmühle *f* beater mill **-rakete** *f* bounce or maroon-headed rocket **-raum** *m* spark-gap chamber or space **-reihenfolge** *f* stroke order (lightning) **-richtung** *f* direction of application of force **-ring** *m* brass knuckles **-rohr** *n* stroke pipe **-röhre** *f* friction tube, friction igniter **-rohrstock** *m* tube spindle

Schlag-säule *f* miter post **-schatten** *m* shade, camouflage effect of shadows cast by a body **-scheibe** *f* fuse disk **-schere** *f* hammer shears **-schlüssel** *m* hammering spanner, wrench hammer **-schlüsselanstellung** *f* hand wrench adjusting gear **-schneide** *f* impact knife-edge, striking edge, breaking knife **-schnur** *f* carpenter's (chalk) line **-schraube** *f* drive-screw **-schweißung** *f* percussion welding **-schwelle** *f* miter sill (gate stop)

Schlagseite *f* (des Schiffes) list (of a ship) **einem Schiffe** ~ **geben** to list or careen a ship **mit** ~ **liegenbleiben** to remain in a listing condition

Schlag-sieb *n* vibrating screen, shatter box **-siebprobe** *f* shatter test **-spaltung** *f* impact cleaving **-spitze** *f* point of firing pin **-stärke** *f* force of the blow **-stauchversuch** *m* impact or dynamic compression test **-stein** *m* beating stone, knockstone

Schlagstempel *m* stamp **Eindruck eines Schlagstempels** mark

Schlag-stift *m* detonating rod, firing pin (of rifle), bouncing pin, instantaneous-fuse striker **-stiftmühle** *f* pin beater mill **-stock** *m* striking rod (hammer) **-stöckchen** *n* stock anvil, beak-iron, bickern **-stromkreis** *m* striking circuit **-ton** *m* strike note **-versuch** *m* impact or percussion test, falling-weight or drop test, hammer test, impact crushing test, dynamic test **-vorrichtung** *f* beating device

Schlag-wasser *n* bilge water **-weite** *f* sparking distance, spark length, spark, flashover or striking distance (of a gap) **-werk** *n* breaking machine, impact testing machine, signal device, striking mechanism **-werkskran** *m* pig breaker crane **-werkzeug** *n* striking tool

Schlagwetter *n pl* explosive atmosphere, firedamp **-grube** *f* foul pit **-sicher** gasproof, flameproof **-zehrapparat** *m* firedamp-consuming lamp

Schlag-widerstand *m* resistance to impact or shock **-wirkung** *f* impact effect **-wort** *n* catchword, slogan **-zahlen** *pl* figure stamps **-zeile** *f* headline **-zerreißbeanspruchung** *f* tensile impact stress **-zerreißversuch** *m* impact tension test, impact pulling test, impact tearing test, dynamic tensile test, tensile shock test **-zerstäubung** *f* impact atomization

Schlag-zeug *n* percussion instrument **-zugbeanspruchung** *f* impact tensile stress **-zugversuch** *m* impact tensile test **-zünder** *m* percussion fuse **-zündschraube** *f* threaded-base percussion fuse, percussion primer **-zündung** *f* percussion priming

Schlamm *m* mud, slime, mire, silt, pulp, ooze, slurry, slip (ceramics), sediment, slush, dirt **-ablagerung** *f* deposition of mud, silting up **-ablaß** *m* sludge drain **-ablaßhahn** *m* mud cock **-ablaßschraube** *f* sediment drain screw **-ablaßventil** *n* mud-discharging valve **-absatz** *m* sediment **-absüßen** *n* scum washing (sugar mfg.) **-analyse** *f* sedimentation analysis, hydrometer analysis, wet-mechanical analysis, mud, silt or sludge analysis **-anthrazit** *m* anthracite slush or silt

Schlämmapparat *m* elutriating or decanting apparatus

schlammartig muddy, slimy

Schlamm-aufbereitungsanlage *f* reconditioning plant (reclaiming sediment in petroleum industry) **-ausbeute** *f* slime yield **-bagger** *m* mud dredger **-bahn** *f* mud conveyer **-beet** *n* sludge bed **-belebung** *f* sludge activation **-berg** *m* scum pile **-bildung** *f* slime formation **-boden** *m* muddy or boggy soil

Schlammbüchse *f* bailer ~ **mit Klappventil** mud socket

Schlamm-decke *f* slime blanket **-eindicker** *m* pulp or scum thickener **-eis** *n* ground ice, anchor ice

schlämmen to wash, elutriate, levigate, buddle, bail

Schlämmen *n* washing, elutriation, ponding (a fill)

Schlammentwässerung *f* sludge draining

Schlämmerei *f* washing plant

Schlamm-fang *m* sludge trap **-fänger** *m* sludge extractor **-faulraum** *m* sludge-digestion tank **-faulung** *f* sludge digestion **-flüssigkeit** *f* mud-laden fluid **-förderung** *f* conveyance of slimes **-gefüge** *n* muddy structure

Schlämmgerät *n* elutriator

Schlamm-grund *m* mud, ooze **-hahn** *m* mud cock, sludge cock, purging cock, blowoff cock **-haltig** muddy, slimy, containing mud, sludge, or slime **-herd** *m* slime table, slime pit

schlammig oozy, muddy, slimy

Schlamm-kanal *m* (mud) feed channel **-kasten** *m* mud box, boiling tub or drum **-kohle** *f* slurry coal **-kran** *m* sand reel, bailing drum **-kratze** *f* mud scraper

Schlämmkreide *f* precipitated chalk, whiting, prepared chalk

Schlamm-kuchen *m* press cake, scum cake **-loch** *n* slush pit, slush pond, mud pit **-löffel** *m* sludger bailer, mud ladle, mud pump **-löffelkolben** *m* mudpump plunger

Schlämmaschine *f* decanting machine

Schlamm-meißel *m* mud bit **-mischapparat** *m* mud mixer **-prozeß** *m* sedimentation process **-pumpe** *f* sludge pump, mud pump **-pumpenventil** *n* mudpump valve **-räumer** *m* sludge remover **-röhre** *f* mud tube **-rolle** *f* sand sheave **-rückstände** *pl* mud residues

Schlamm-sack *m* catch pit, sludge pocket **-saft** *m* carbonation juice, scum juice **-saftrücknahme** *f* carbonation-juice return **-sammler** *m* mud collector **-sauger** *m* mud exhauster **-schaufel** *f* dredger **-scheidemaschine** *f* slime separator **-scheider** *m* slime separator **-schicht** *f* slime layer **-schlich** *m* washed-ore slime

Schlämmschuh *m* agitator shoe for wash mill

Schlamm-schwelle *f* mud sill **-seil** *n* sand line **-setzmaschine** *f* slime jig **-sieb** *n* slurry screen **-sprudel** *m* mud volcano **-sumpf** *m* slime pit

-teich *m* mud settling pond, sludge bed -topf *m* mud pan -trübe *f* slime pulp
Schlämmung *f* washing, elutriating, levigating, buddling, sedimentation
Schlamm-ventil *n* purging valve, sludge valve -verarbeitung *f* slime treatment
Schlämm-verfahren *n* washing process, elutriating process, sedimentation, elutriation method -vorgang *m* sedimentation process, elutriation process -vorrichtung *f* washing or elutriating device or apparatus
Schlamm-vulkan *m* mud volcano -wasser *n* wash water containing slime, sludge, or mud
Schlange *f* coil, worm, hose, dike, dam, groin, snake ~ (wartender Personen) queue, waiting line **zusammengesetzte** ~ built-up coil
Schlängel *m* snakelike response of permanent echo (radar)
schlängeln, sich ~ to wriggle, wind, twist
Schlängeln *n* tailing or rocking motion
Schlängelung *f* circuit, turn
Schlangen-bohrer *m* screw bit, auger bit -bohrstange *f* helical-type cutter bar
schlangenförmig winding -es **Dampfrohr** steam coil
Schlangen-horn *n* serpent -kette *f* snake track -kühler *m* coil condenser, spiral condenser, submerged-coil-type cooler, calandria -kurve *f* serpentine -linie *f* wiggle -linienartig undulated -naht *f* zigzag seam
Schlangenröhre *f* spiral coil **flache** ~ pancake coil
Schlangen-rohrvorwärmer *m* bent-tube economizer -schieber *m* sieve-part shaking clinker gate -vakuumapparat *m* coil vacuum machine -ventil *n* cranked valve
Schlankheits-grad *m*, -verhältnis *n* fineness ratio, ratio of slenderness
schlankster Träger slim, slender, or narrowest beam, girder, or bracket
Schlappe *f* reverse, check (holding back)
Schlauch *m* tube, hose, inner tube, funnel cloud, circular work (weaving), tubing, flexible pipe ~ **mit Geflechteinlagen** braided hose ~ **aus leitfähigem Gummi** conductive rubber hose ~ **mit Gummieinlage** rubber-lined canvas hose ~ **mit Metalleinlage** metal-lined hose **Schläuche von Erz** ore chimneys, ore pipes **schlitzbarer** ~ zipper tubing
Schlauchanschluß *m* hose coupling ~ **mit Verschlußkappe** hose connection and cap
Schlauch-bänder *pl* hose slips -bandschloß *n* hose strap fastener -bett *n* pneumatic bed -binder *m* connecting hose, hose clamp
Schlauchboot *n* pneumatic boat, air raft, dinghy -abwurfhebel *m* dinghy- or raft-release lever -auslösung *f* dinghy or raft release
Schlauch-bremse *f* tube brake -drähte *pl* sheathed cables -düse *f* hose nozzle -einbindung *f* hose coupling -endstück *n* lance
Schlauchentleerungsaufsatz *m* hose-draining attachment ~ **mit Schauglas** sight-discharge attachment
Schlauch-entleerungsventil *n* hose-draining valve -filter *m* bag filter -füllung *f* inflation (of tire) -gewebe *n* hose fabric -hahn *m* hose cock -haken *m* hose hook -klemme *f* hose clip, clamp or hose connection -kuppelung *f* hose coupling -leitung *f* hose line, hose pipe
schlauchloser Reifen *m* tubeless tire
Schlauch-maschine *f* tubular fabric machine -manschette *f* hose collar -muffe *f* rubber sleeve
Schlauchmundstück *n* hose tip, nozzle -tülle *f* nozzle tip
Schlauch-nippel *m* hose nipple -riemen *m* hose strap -rohr *n*, -röhre *f* hose pipe -schelle *f* hose clip -schoner *m* tire flap -stück *n* hose coupling, tubing connection -stutzen *m* nozzle
Schlauchtrommel *f* hose reel ~ **für zentrale Entnahme** hose reel unwinding from center
Schlauchtrommelstrahlrohr *n* reel lance
Schlauchtülle *f* hose liner ~ **für Griffhähne** sleeve for grip cocks
Schlauch-ventil *n* tire valve -verbinder *m* hose joint or clip -verbindung *f* union joint hose, rubber-tube connection, coupling -verschraubung *f* screwed hose connection, hose nipple, hose coupling -waage *f* hose leveling instrument -ware *f* tubular fabric -weber *m* pipe weaver -welle *f* hose nipple -zapfen *m* hose spigot
Schlauder *f* iron tie
Schlaufe *f* loop, triangular or pear-shaped lifting eye, noose, runner
Schlaufen-fadenführer *m* loop thread guide -versuch *m* loop test
Schlaufprobe *f* loop-bending test
schlecht bad, poor, foul, vicious ~ **ausgeglichen** ill-balanced ~ **evakuiert** gassy (electr. tube) -e **Abstimmung** mistuning, off-tuned position -es **Funktionieren** malfunction -e **Verständigung** line is faint; poor transmission -es **Wetter** nasty, bad, or adverse weather
schlechter werden to deteriorate
Schlechtigkeit *f* badness, wickedness
Schlechtgrenze *f* lot tolerance perfect defective (LTPD)
Schlechtwetter-flug *m* IFR-flight -landeanlage *f* bad-visibility landing aid -landung *f* bad-weather landing
Schlechtzahl *f* rejection number
Schleichantrieb *m* slow-speed drive
schleichen to crawl, creep, sneak
Schleichen *n* crawling (of a synchr. machine)
schleichend-e Bewegung slow motion -e **Verbrennung** slow or sluggish combustion
Schleich-handel *m* black market, smuggling, illicit or contraband trade -ströme *m pl* vagabond streams or currents
Schleier *m* veil; (Nebel) haze, mist; screen, fog, lawn, turbidity; reflected, double, or ghost image causing veiling (in images or pictures), set-up (tv) **dichroitischer** ~ dichroic, silver, or red fog **zweifarbiger** ~ dichromatic fog
Schleierbildung *f* (Lack) formation of haze
Schleierbildwechselwirkung *f* fog-image interaction
Schleier-entfernung *f* background eradication -förmig veillike **schleierfrei** free from mist or fog -freiheit des Bildes absence of haze in the image
schleierig foggy, fogged, hazy, misty
Schleier-korn *n* fog grain -schwärzung *f* fog density -wert *m* fog value -wolke *f* cirro-stratus cloud, scarf cloud
Schleifabrieb *m* grit
Schleifapparat *m* knife grinder ~ **für Fußbetrieb** foot-power knife grinder ~ **für Handbetrieb**

hand-power knife grinder
Schleif-arbeit *f* grinding work, grinding operation **-arm** *m* wiper
Schleifbahn-kontaktplatte *f* sliding surface contact plate **-verteiler** *m* slide distributor
Schleifbarkeit *f* polishability
Schleifband *n* endless sanding belt, endless abrasive belt
Schleifbock *m* wheel stand **-drehplatte** *f* wheel-stand revolving plate **-schlitten** *m* wheel-stand slide
Schleif-bogen *m* duct-edge shield (a cable) **-bügel** *m* release bearing sleeve, sliding bow **-bürste** *f* brush (elec.)
Schleifchen im Gewebe little loops in weaving
Schleif-dämpfungsmesser *m* loop decremeter **-daumen** *m* sliding contact cam **-dehnung** *f* extension on untwisting **-detektor** *m* sliding ticker **-dorn** *m* grinding mandrel
Schleifdraht *m* slide wire **~ der Meßbrücke** differential slide wire
Schleifdraht-brücke *f* slide-wire bridge **-kompensator** *m* slide-wire potentiometer **-meßbrücke** *f* slide-wire measuring bridge **-widerstand** *m* slide-wire resistor
Schleifdruck *m* feeding pressure
Schleife *f* loop; (Schlinge) noose; (Kurve) loop, horse-shoe bend or curve; bight, knot, slide, sled, short circuit, bow, wire loop, kink, chute, curve, sweep **feste ~** tight loop (tape rec.) **senkrechte ~** loop **über die ~ hinweg** round the loop **zur ~ schalten** to loop (lines), join or connect like a loop **zwei Leitungen zur ~ schalten** to loop two circuits **zur ~ verbunden** looped
Schleif-echtheit *f* fastness to buffing **-einrichtung** *f* sanding attachment
schleifen (schärfen) to grind, sharpen; (wetzen) whet; (glätten) grind, abrade; (feiner ~) smooth, polish; (Glas) cut; drag, trail, slip, slide, raze, (slang) drill brutally, wipe, loop (a line), rub **aufeinander ~** to fit together by grinding one on the other **blank ~** to smooth **matt ~** to frost, rough, or grind with sand and water, make opaque by grinding
Schleifen *n* grinding, cutting, reaming, scraping, honing, polishing, buffing, lapping **-antenne** *f* loop antenna, loop aerial **-ausgleich** *m* (automatic) loop compensation **-berührung** *f* loop, constant or permanent loop, short circuit **-bildner** *m* loop setter **-bildung** *f* looping **-breite** *f* loop breadth
schleifender Teil abrasive (part), dragging section
Schleifen-dipolantenne *f* folded dipole antenna **-elektrometer** *n* string electrometer **-ende** *n* loop end **-fahrt** *f* loop the loop **-fänger** *m* feed and take-up sprocket mechanism
Schleifenflug *m* loop, (U) turn (aviation) **~ in Achterform** figure of eight (turn) (aviation)
Schleifenflugüberschlag *m* roll on top of a loop (aviation)
schleifenförmige Kraftstoffverbrauchskurve fuel-consumption loop
Schleifen-galvanometer *n* loop galvanometer **-heizung** *f* siphon heating **-index** *m* cycle index **-kapazität** *f* wire-to-wire capacity **-kreuzung** *f* single-circuit transposition (elec.), phantom transposition, transposition of pairs **-leitungsbetrieb** *m* two-wire system, telephone service with two wires **-linie** *f* lemniscate (geom.) **-luftdraht** *m* radio loop **-messung** *f* loop(-resistance) measurement or test
Schleifen-oszillograph *m* loop, string or vibrator oscillograph, bifilar oscillograph **-probe** *f* echo checking (comput.) **-rohr** *n* expansion loop (bend) **-rückenflug** *m* inverted loop (aviat.)
Schleifenschaltung *f* loop connection, circuit looped back and forth **in ~** on the loop
Schleifen-schluß *m* loop short **-speicher** *m* tank **-strom** *m* loop current **-system** *n* metallic or two-wire automatic telephone system, metallic signaling system **-teile** *pl* dipole sections
Schleifen-verfahren *n* loop test **-wahl** *f* loop dialling **-wert** *m* loop value **-wicklung** *f* lap winding **-widerstand** *m* (conductor) loop resistance **-zählung** *f* cycle count
Schleifer *m* grinder, polisher, slider, slip ring, collector ring, sliding wiper
Schleiferei *f* grinding shop, grindery
Schleiferspülung *f* loop scavenging
Schleiffähigkeit *f* (Lack) polishing property
Schleiffeder *f* brush spring, wiper, slide spring **-anker** *m* slip-ring rotor
Schleif-finger *m* contact finger (electr.) **-fläche** *f* wearing face, contact surface **-flüssigkeit** (Lack) rubbing-down liquid **-futter** *n* grinding chuck **-genauigkeit** *f* sliding accuracy **-güte** *f* quality in grinding **-härte** *f* resistance to polish **-hexe** *f* portable grinder
Schleif-knoten *m* slipknot **-kohle** *f* carbon brush or wiper (elec.) **-kontakt** *m* sliding contact, wiper **-kopf** *m* grinding wheel **-korn** *n* abrasive grain
Schleif-kupplung *f* slipping clutch (coupling) **-lehre** *f* grinding gauge **-leinwand** *f* grinding cloth **-leistung** *f* grinding efficiency or performance **-leitung** *f* current collector line, electric conductor **-leitungen** *pl* trolley wires **-leitungskanal** *m* collector line trench, contact line duct
Schleifmaschine *f* grinder, grinding machine, abrasion testing machine, tool grinder, hardness tester **spitzenlose ~** centerless grinding machine
Schleif-masse *f* grinding compound **-material** *n* abrasive, grinding material **-meßvorrichtung** *f* grinding gauge
Schleifmittel *n* grinding material, abrasive **~ aus komplexen Eisen- und Aluminiumsilikaten** garnet
Schleif-motor *m* grinding motor **-nadel** *f* grinding needle **-papier** *n* abrasive paper **-paste** *f* emery paste **-probe** *f* grinddown test, grinding test **-pulver** *n* grinding or polishing powder **-rad** *n* grinding or polishing wheel **-riefe** *f* scratch, groove **-rille** *f* groove, furrow
Schleifring *m* collecting ring, sliding (contact) ring, slip ring **-anker** *m* slip-ring armature, slip-ring rotor **-ankermotor** *m* slip-ring engine **-bürste** *f* slip-ring brush **-läufer** *m* rotor with slip rings **-läufermotor** *m* slip-ring rotor engine **-motor** *m* slip-ring engine
Schleif-riß *m* grinding crack, ghost line, grinding check **-rohstoffe** *pl* abrasive raw materials **-rot** *n* rouge for polishing **-sand** *m* grinding sand
Schleifscheibe *f* grinding wheel or disk **ver-**

schmierte ~ loaded grinding wheel **zugesetzte ~** loaded grinding wheel
Schleifscheiben-abrichtdiamant *m* diamond tipped wheel dresser **-abrichtvorrichtung** *f* diamond trueing device for grinding wheels **-antriebsscheibe** *f* wheeldriving pulley **-größe** *f* standard grinding wheel size **-schutzhaube** *f* (grinding-)wheel guard **-spindel** *f* (grinding-) wheel spindle
Schleif-schiene *f* sliding contact (electr.) **-schlamm** *m* grits, grinds **-schuh** *m* collector shoe (sliding contact) **-schütze** *m* sliding shuttle **-seite** *f* facet
Schleifsel *n* slip, grindings
Schleif-sense *f* scythe **-sohlen** *f pl* brake shoes **-spalt** *m* slit stop (optics)
Schleifspindel-kasten *m* grinding head stock **-lager** *n* spindle box **-schlitten** *m* wheel slide **-stock** *m* grinding-wheel head
Schleif-sporn *m* tail skid **-spule** *f* immovable pin, pirn **-stab** *m* grinding rod **-staub** *m* grinding dust, abrasive dust, grits, swarf **-steg** *m* wearing shoe, wearing side bar **-stein** *m* grinding stone, whetstone, sharpening stone, oilstone **-stift** *m* grinding point **-stück** *n* collector-shoe gear, trolley shoe **-tasse** *f* (Topfscheibe) cup wheel **-teller** *m* grinding disc **-trommel** *f* grinder, grinding roll **-tuch** *n* abrasive cloth
Schleif- und Poliermaschine *f* grinding and polishing machine
Schleif-verfahren *n* grinding process **-verlust** *m* loss by grinding **-versuch** *m* abrasion test **-vorgang** *m* grinding operation **-vorrichtung** *f* grinding device, honing device **-wachs** *n* flatting paste **-walze** *f* grinder, grinding roll **-walzengehäuse** hub for buffing cylinder **-weg** *m* grinding wheel travel **-welle** *f* grinder spindle
Schleif-werkzeug *n* grinding tool **-widerstand** *m* slip resistance **-winkel** *m* clearance angle, lip angle, grinding clearance **-wirkung** *f* abrasive action, abrasive power, attrition **-zentrierung** *f* grinding center **-zerspannung** *f* abrasive machining **-zeug** *n* grinding roller **-zugabe** *f* grinding addition, grinding allowance **-zusatzvorrichtung** *f* grinding attachment
Schleim *m* slime, glut, mucilage **-fäule** *f* bacterioisis **-gärung** *f* viscous fermentation **-harz** *n* gum resin **-haut** *f* mucous membrane, mucosa
schleimig glutinous
Schleimsäure *f* mucic acid
Schleißblech *n* wearing plate
Schleiße *f* splint, splinter
Schleißwirkung *f* wearing action
schlemmen to saturate (with water)
Schlemmkreide *f* prepared chalk, carbonate of lime
Schlempe *f* distiller's wash, slop, vinasse **-kohle** *f* charred slop **-mischer** *m* grout or slurry mixer **-trocknung** *f* slop drying
Schlepp-antenne *f* trailing wire antenna (of airplane), trailing aerial, drag antenna **-anzeiger** *m* maximum indicator pointer **-behälter** *m* model or towing basin (aviation) **-blech** *n* (Brücke) cover plate **-bremse** *f* tow-target cable brake **-dampfboot** *n*, **-dampfer** *m* tugboat **-drehzahl** *f* windmilling
Schleppe *f* float, founder's or stove truck, truck cart, train, trail
Schlepp-einleger *m* drag feed **-einrichtung** *f* tugging device
schleppen to haul, tow, drag, pull (along), trip, heave up **ein Segelflugzeug ~** to tow a glider **achteraus ~** to tow astern **sich ~ lassen** to be towed
Schleppen *n* heaving up, towing, hauling **-pflug** *m* tractor plow
Schlepper *m* tractor, prime mover, tug(boat), tender, lighter **~** (Walzwesen) skid
Schlepper-anhängevorrichtung *f* tractor hitch **-binder** *m* tractor binder **-brachenpflug** *m* tractor grub-breaker plow **-dammkulturpflug** *m* tractor lister **-drillmaschine mit Kraftaushebung** power-lift tractor drill **-führer** *m* tractor driver **-haspel** *f* haulage winch **-heber** *m* tractor lifter **-pflug mit Kraftausbebung** power-lift tractor plow **-roder** *m* tractor digger
Schlepperscheibenegge *f*, **hebellose ~** leverless tractor disk harrow
Schlepperscheibenpflug mit Kraftaushebung power-lift tractor disk plow
Schleppertriebwerk *n* tractor transmission (A), tractor gearbox (E)
Schlepp-feder *f* drag spring **-fehler** *m* lag error **-fernsprechanlage** *f* telephone connecting plane and towed glider **-fernsprecher** *m* telephone for towed flight
Schleppflug *m* towed flight
Schlepp-flugzeug *n* tow plane **-gerüst** *n* towing gear **-geschirr** *n* marine or towing gear **-glied** *n* drag link **-größe** *f* lag constant **-haken** *m* tow hook **-hebel** *m* drag lever
Schlepp-kabel *n* trailing cable **-kahn** *m* dumb barge, lighter **-kanal** *m* towing basin **-kante** *f* trailing edge **-kette** *f* drag chain **-kontakt** *m* continuity-preserving contact, make-before-break contact, trailing contact, shorting contact **-kraft** *f* tractive force, sweeping force (of water) **-kreisel** *m* drag gyro **-kübelbagger** *m* dragline **-kupplung** *f* delayed-action switch **-kurbel** *f* lagging crankshaft
Schlepp-leine *f* tow or drag line or rope **-leistung** *f* drag power or efficiency **-lohn** *m* towage **-modell** *n* tow model **-netz** *n* dragnet **-rad** *n* sliding wheel **-rechen** *m* sweep rake **-ring** *m* inertia ring **-rinne** *f* towing basin
Schlepp-sack *m* towed sleeve target, dredge **-schacht** *m* inclined gallery or shaft **-schalter** *m* drag switch **-schaufel** *f* dragging bucket **-scheibe** *f* towed target (aviation) **-segel** *n* trailing apron, drift sail (aviation)
Schleppseil *n* hauling rope, towrope, towing cable, dragrope **das ~ ausklinken** to release the towing cable
Schleppseilöse *f* towrope eyelet
Schlepp-spannung *f* tractive stress **-stange** *f* drag link **-start** *m* towed start
Schlepptau *n* tow cable, towrope, tow **ins ~ nehmen** to tow, tug
Schlepp-träger *m* hinged girder **-trosse** *f* towing hawser **-verhau** *n* movable or portable abatis **-versuchswesen** *n* model-basin towing testing, towing-basin test practice **-wagen** *m* tow car, truck **-walze** *f* friction-driven roll, friction roll, idle roll, dummy roll **-wechsel** *m* blunt ended or stub switch **-widerstand** *m* windmilling drag, towing drag **-winde** *f* tow winch **-zeiger** *m* drag

pointer, loose pointer, trailing pointer **-zeit** *f* time lag **-zeug** *n* mining locomotive

Schleppzug *m* train of barges, air train, truck train **-schleuse** *f* lock for trains of barges or long tows

Schleuder *f* catapult, centrifugal, sling, separator, grader, cobber, centrifuge, spin-drier **~ mit oberem Antrieb** top-driven centrifugal **~ mit unterem Antrieb** underdriven centrifugal **~ mit Dampfdeckvorrichtung** centrifugal with steaming apparatus **~ mit oberer Entleerung** centrifugal with top discharge **~ mit Sicherheitsverschluß** centrifugal with safety closing device **~ mit Wasserantrieb** water-driven centrifugal **sieblose ~** centrifugal with non-perforated basket

Schleuder-ablauf *m* centrifugal running **-anlage** *f* catapult **-apparat** *m* centrifugal separator **-bahn** *f* catapult **-band** *n* centrifugal belt **-beton** *m* centrifugal concrete, spun concrete **-blech** *n* grease baffle plate **-bund** *m* rack lashing **-drehzahl** *f* centrifugal speed, overspeed

Schleuder-flügel *m* centrifugal flier **-flugzeug** *n* catapult airplane **-formung** *f* rotational molding **-gebläse** *n* centrifugal (air) blower, centrifugal air pump **-geschwindigkeit** *f* ramming rate (in sand slinging) **-grube** *f* balance test pit

Schleuderguß *m* centrifugal (casting), centrifugally cast (iron) **-form** *f* centrifugal ingot mold **-lager** *n* spun bearing **-rohr** *n* centrifugally cast pipe, spun pipe **-stück** *n* centrifugal casting **-verfahren** *n* centrifugal casting process

Schleuder-gut *n* solid material **-hebel** *m* accelerator **-kompressor** *m* centrifugal compressor **-kopf** *m* impeller head, ram head, ramming head **-korb** *m* basket of a hydroextractor **-kraft** *f* centrifugal force **-kurbel** *f* crank racing **-lader** *m* centrifugal-type supercharger, centrifugal compressor **-lüfter** *m* centrifugal fan **-maschine** *f* centrifugal machine **-mast** *m* concrete pole or tower **-mühle** *f* centrifugal mill, disintegrator

schleudern to centrifuge, sling, fling, cure, machine, spin, skid, slip, throw, sell below cost

Schleudern *n* centrifugal action, sideslip, sling, fling **~ in der Kurve** skidding on a curve

Schleuder-preis *m* ruinously or ridiculously low price **-probe** *f* whirling test **-prüfung** *f* centrifugal load test **-psychrometer** *n* sling psychrometer **-pumpe** *f* centrifugal pump **-rad** *n* fan blower **-radmischer** *m* fan-blower mixer **-ring** *m* slinger ring

Schleuder-sämaschine *f* endgate seeder **-schiene** *f* launching rail (rockets) **-schmierung** *f* centrifugal lubrication **-sieb** *n* centrifugal screen, **-sitz** *m* (Flugzeug) pilot ejector seat, catapult seat **-spur** *f* skid marks

Schleuder-stand *m* centrifugal stand **-start** *m* catapult take-off **-startvorrichtung** *f* catapult **-thermometer** *n* sling or gyrostatic thermometer **-trommel** *f* centrifugal drum

Schleuderung *f* centrifuging, curing (sugar mfg.)

Schleuder-verdichter *m* centrifugal compressor **-versuch** *m* speed test **-vorrichtung** *f* catapult launching gear **-wärmegradmesser** *m* sling thermometer **-wascher** *m* centrifugal washer, centrifugal cleaner **-winkel** *m* launching angle (rockets) **-wirkung** *f* centrifugal effect, slinging action (in molding)

Schleuse *f* lock, sluice, sluiceway, charging valve, floodgate **bewegliche ~** hydraulic elevator

Schleusen-achse *f* lock axis or center line **-boden** *m* lock floor **-einsatz** *m*, **-fall** *m* height difference of water near floodgate, lock lift **-füllung** *f* lock filling **-kammer** *f* lock chamber **-plattform** *f* coping level of lock **-rückwand** *f* back of floodgate wall **-schieber** *m* sash gate or sliding valve of floodgate **-schütz** *n*, **-schütze** *f* floodgate, draw gate

Schleusensohle *f* lock floor **ebene ~** flat lock floor **gewölbte ~** arched lock floor

Schleusen-tor *n* sluice gate, lock gate **-torflügel** *m* leaf of sluice gate **-treppe** *f* flight of locks **-trommel** *f* rotating lock **-ventil** *n* isolation valve, sluice valve **-verstärker** *m* (Regelpult) switching amplifier **-wärter** *m* lock keeper

schlicht simple, plain, straightforward, smooth, even, fine, plane **~ feilen** to file smooth **-e Faser** straight fiber **-e Strömung** laminar flow

Schlicht-arbeit *f* finish-maching **-beil** *n* chip ax **-bohrer** *m* finishing or polishing bit, polisher **-bürste** *f* dressing brush, glue brush **-drehen** *n* smoothing **-drehzahlreihe** *f* roughing speed range **-dorn** *m* smoothing drift

Schlichte *f* black wash, cinder paste, size blacking, slur, wash, facing

Schlicht-echtheit *f* fastness to sizing **-eisen** *n* scraper

Schlichtekocher *m* size maker

schlichten (ordnen) to arrange, adjust; (Technik, eben machen) level, plane; (glätten) smooth, finish; (Metall) blackwash; dress, settle, sleek, slick, face, slur, slurry, apply a wash, planish, polish, blacken, arbitrate, settle (disputes)

Schlichten *n* finishing

Schlichter *m* arbitrator, (hand) sizer

Schlicht-feile *f* smooth-cut file, fine file **-feilen** *n* smooth filing **-fläche** *f* smooth finish **-flüssigkeit** *f* size **-fräsen** *n* finish milling **-fräser** *m* finishing cutter or mill **-gleitsitz** *m* plain sliding fit **-hammer** *m* square(-face) flatter, planishing hammer **-hebel** *m* smooth plane **-hieb** *m* single cut (of a file), smooth cut **-hobel** *m* smoothing plane

Schlicht-kaliber *n* finishing pass, planisher **-laufsitz** *m* plain running fit **-leim** *m* size **-maschine** *f* finishing machine **-masse** *f* sizing paste **-messer** *n* plane knife **-mittel** *n* sizing material **-oberfläche** *f* finishing surface **-oval** *n* finishing oval pass **-passung** *f* plain fit, free fit, medium fit **-raute** *f* last diamond pass, finishing diamond pass **-reibahle** *f* finishing reamer

Schlicht-schlag *m* finishing blow **-schnitt** *m* finishing cut **-seife** *f* sizing soap **-span** *m* smooth cut, small smoothing iron or flat

Schlichtstahl *m* smoothing tool **~ für Gußeisen** smoothing tool for cast iron **~ für Schmiedeeisen oder Stahl** smoothing tool for wrought iron or steel **~ mit Seitenmesser** water polishing tool

Schlicht-stich *m* finishing pass, final pass, planishing pass **-stoffherstellung** *f* laminating

Schlichtung *f* mediation, arbitration

Schlicht-walze *f* finishing roll **-zange** *f* tanner's pincers

Schlick *m* mud, clay, muck, silt cement, ooze

Schlicker *m* dross **-arbeit** *f* drossing

schlickern to dross
Schlick-fänger *m* secondary dike, dike of wattled piles **-grund** *m* mud bottom
schlickiger Kalk oolitic limestone
schliefen to slip, creep
Schlief-kontakt *m* sliding contact **-lack** *m* body varnish
Schliere *f* streak
Schlieren *f pl* optical inhomogeneities, cords (in glass), schlieren, streaks (phot.), striae (of glass) **-anordnung** *f* schlieren arrangement **-aufnahme** *f* schlieren photograph **-bildung** *f* striation **-blende** *f* schlieren diaphragm **-methode** *f* track method, striae method **-optik** *f* schlieren **-verfahren** *n* schlieren photography process **-zone** *f* dead or skip zone, shadow (zone)
schlierig streaky
Schließ-balken *m* lock-up bar **-beschlag** *m* locking furniture, shutting, fastenings, closure **-bolzen** *m* cotter pin, eyebolt and key **-dauer** *f* closing period **-druck** *m* closing pressure
Schließe *f* catch, latch, peg, anchor, cotter
schließen to close, shut, bolt, lock, finish, conclude **kurz ~** to ground **einen Schalter ~** to close or throw a switch **einen Stromkreis ~** to close or make or complete a circuit **einen Vertrag ~** to contract, to agree
Schließen *n* make (contact), closure **~ der Form** mold closure **~ und Unterbrechen** make and break (of circuit) **~ des Ventils** valve dropping
Schließender *m* file closer
Schließer *m* contact
Schließ-fach *n* post-office box (P. o. B.) **-feder** *f* breech-closing spring, locking spring, safety-grip spring (pistol) **-funke** *m* spark at make **-gabel** *f* operating fork **-geschwindigkeit** *m* closing speed, floating rate **-geviert** *n* m quadrat **-griff** *m* closing handle **-haken** *m* bolt nab or staple, catch, lock hook **-kappe** *f* box staple, boxed or cased catch **-keil** *m* quoin, cotter **-kloben** *m* clamp **-klobenführung** *f* keeper support
Schließ-knie *n* cheek of the head, arms of the dead wood **-kontakt** *m* closing contact (elec.) **-kopf** *m* closing head, head made during process of riveting, snaphead (rivet) **-kopfgesenk** *n* snap-head die **-nagel** *m* bar of a printer's form, square bolt, iron pin **-nippel** *m* closing die **-nocken** *m* locking cam
Schließ-rahmen *m* chase (printing) **-rahmenknagge** *f* lug for holding chase **-ring** *m* lock washer **-rolle** *f* closing pulley **-säge** *f* sash saw **-setzschiffe** *pl* galleys-chases **-spule** *f* closing coil **-stelle** *f* contact point, front contact (coil) **-trommel** *f* closing drum
Schließung *f* make (contact), closing, closure **~ eines Stromkreises** closing of a circuit **Schließungen und Unterbrechungen** makes and breaks (of a circuit)
Schließungs-bogen *m* closing arc **-draht** *m* loop wire **-funke** *m* spark at make or before contact **-gleichung** *f* closing equation (math.) **-impuls** *m* make impulse
Schließ-vorrichtung *f* closing device, closing head **-zeit** *f* closing time **-zeug** *n* quoin **-zylinder** *m* lock cylinder
Schliff *m* ground section, etching, microsection surface (as of metals, for etching), cut (of a gem), grinding, polish, smoothness, sharpening, ground slide, ground-in joint **den letzten ~ geben** to touch up **letzter ~** master touch
Schliff-bild *n* polished section, micrograph, photomicrograph, grinding finish **-fläche** *f* surface of slide **-glas** *n* cut glass **-halter** *m* specimen holder **-kolben** *m* ground(ing) stopper **-presse** *f* section-press **-rohr** *n* tube with ground joint (electron microscope) **-stopfen** *m* ground(-in) stopper **-stück** *n* slide **-zone** *f* ground zone
Schlinge *f* sling, noose, loop, tie **~ im Draht** curl
Schlingen bilden to curl
schlingen to string, wind, twist, loop
Schlingen-bildung *f* looping, loop forming, formation of snarls **-führung** *f* repeater **-gewebe** *n* looped fabric **-kanal** *m* sloping hoop channel **-wände** *pl* baffle plates **-zwirn** *m* loop twist
Schlinger-anzeiger *m* roll recorder **-bewegung** *f* rolling (movement) **-dämpfungsanlage** *f* stabilizer **-kiel** *m* bilge keel
schlingern to roll
Schlingern *n* rolling (of a ship), irregular oscillating motion (of a locomotive), hunting **~** (b. Turbinenschaufeln) feathering
Schlinger-platte *f* wash plate **-stativ** *n* baffle or rolling tripod **-tank** *m* antirolling tank
Schlinger- und Stampfbewegung *f* rolling and pitching motion
Schlinger-wand *f* baffle plate **-winkel** *m* rolling angle or angle of roll of a ship or aircraft
schlippen, ein Tau ~ to slip a rope
Schlitten *m* sled; (Technik) sliding carriage, saddle, cradle; (Schreibmaschine) carriage; sleigh, skid (aviation), sliding head, carrier, support, rest, slide (rail), chariot (teleg.)
Schlitten-achse *f* vertical axis of a chariot (teleg.) **-apparat** *m* slide(-induction) apparatus **-aufsatzstück** *n* machine-gun sleigh mount **-backen** *m* cam-box **-bett** *n* guide ways **-bewegung** *f* traverse movement, slide movement **-bohrmaschine** *f* slide drilling machine **-durchgang** *m* passage of carriage
Schlitten-feststellschraube *f* saddle clamp bolt **-führung** *f* slide conveyer, carriage guide **-führungsschiene** *f* guide rail **-gang** *m* stroke **-halter** *m* slide holder **-halteschraube** *f* slide retaining screw **-hub** *m* carriage stroke
Schlitten-kufen *pl* sleigh runners, skid runners **-kurbel** *f* carriage handle **-mikroskop** *n* traversing microscope **-stellschraube** *f* carriage bolt **-stöpsel** *m* ram **-stutze** *f* sleigh trail **-verschiebung** *f* carriage travel **-wechsler** *m* carrier changer
Schlitz *m* slit, slot, slotted hole, vent, notch, groove, port, cleft **kolbengesteuerter ~** port covered and uncovered by the working piston
Schlitz-abdeckung *f* vent covering **-achse** *f* slotted shaft **-anode** *f* split anode **-anodenmagnetron** *n* split-anode magnetron **-antenne** *f* slot antenna **-arbeit** *f* undercutting (min.) **-aufsatz** *m* wing top (chem.) **-blech** *n* slotted plate **-blende** *f* slotted diaphragm, slit diaphragm, slit stop **-breite** *f* slot or slit width **-brenner** *m* batswing burner, slit burner **-brille** *f* stenopeic spectacles **-düse** *f* air jet **-effekt** *m* apertural or slit effect **-ende** *n* end of slot
schlitzen to slit, split, slot, cleave, crack, rip
Schlitzflügel *m* slotted wing **einschlitziger ~** single-slotted wing

Schlitzform *f* slot die
schlitzförmige Steueröffnung slot-shaped port
Schlitzfräsen *n* slot milling
Schlitzfräser *m* slitting cutter, slotting cutter ~ **für Holzschrauben** slitting cutter for wood screws ~ **für Scheibenfedernuten** Woodruff keyseat cutter
Schlitz-führung *f* slot guide, slit guidance **-gefäß** *n* slotting sampling vessel **-gesteuert** port-controlled **-hilfsflügel** *m* slotted-wing flap **-hohlleiterantenne** *f* slotted guide antenna **-kegel** *m* split cone **-klappe** *f* slot (for slotted wing) **-klappenquerruder** *n* slot-lip aileron **-kopiermaschine** *f* slit-type printer, contact printer (phot.) **-lampe** *f* slit lamp **-länge** *f* length of slot
Schlitz-laterne *f* slot lantern **-lochung** *f* oblong perforation **-mantelkolben** *m* slotted-type piston, split-skirt piston **-messer** *n* slitting knife **-mischer** *m* slot mixer **-momentverschluß** *m* roller-blind instantaneous shutter **-mutter** *f* slotted nut **-naht** *f* slot seam, slot weld **-niet** *m* split rivet
Schlitz-ofen *m* spring heating furnace **-probe** *f* channel sample **-querruder** *n* slotted aileron **-rohr** *n* split tube **-rohrstrahler** *m* slotted cylinder antenna **-scheibe** *f* slotted disk **-schiene** *f* slot rail **-schraube** *f* slot bolt **-schweißung** *f* slot weld **-sieb** *n* slotted sieve
Schlitz-spule *f* open slot coil **-spülmaschine** *f* port scavenging engine **-spülung** *f* port scavenging **-stift** *m* split pin **-stopfen** *m* slotted plug **-stoß** *m* slot discontinuity effect (microw.) **-strahler** *m* slot radiator (antenna) **-strahlersystem** slot array (antenna) **-tiefe** *f* slot depth
Schlitz- und -Loch-Magnetron *n* hole and slot magnetron
Schlitz- und Nutenfräsmaschine *f* slot and keyway milling machine
Schlitzverschluß *m* slotted shutter, focal-plane shutter, slit-type (rotary-disk) shutter **-kamera** *f* focal-plane shutter camera
Schlitz-wand *f* louvered slide **-weite** *f* slit opening **-wellenfilter** *n* mode filter slot **-wellenleiter** *m* leaky waveguide
Schloß *n* lock, bolt, castle, (knuckle) joint fastening, bomb release, slip **blindes** ~ false lock **eingelassenes** ~ rabbeted or flush encased lock
Schloßblech *n* lock plate
Schlößchen *n* cocking piece
Schloße *f* sleet, hailstone
Schlosser *m* locksmith, fitter, mechanic
Schlosser-hammer *m* fitter's hammer, machinist's hammer **-werkzeug** *n* machinist's tools
Schloß-fuß *m* bolt base **-gehäuse** *n* bolt housing, lock housing **-halter** *m* lock support **-hebel** *m* bolt handle, half-nut-cam **-hülle** *f* latch covering **-kasten** *m* lock box, lock case **-kurbel** *f* operating shaft, lock shaft, crank handle **-mantel** *m* cam ring **-mutter** *f* split nut
Schloß-platte *f* hinge plate, breech plate, apron **-rand** *m* hinge line, posterior end **-schraube** *f* common carriage bolt, lock nut **-schützer** *m* breech casing **-teile** *m pl* parts of breech mechanism **-teilträgerring** *m* cam retaining ring **-verbindung** *f* interlocking joint **-zuhaltung** *f* lock hasp
Schlot *m* chimney, smokestack, vent
schlottern to fit loosely, totter, shake, tremble
Schlucht *f* ravine, gorge
Schluckbeiwert *m* absorptivity (acoust)
schlucken to swallow, absorb
Schluck-fähigkeit *f* absorption capacity **-fläche** *f* absorptive surface **-leitung** *f* ballast line **-stoff** *m*
Schluckung *f* absorption
Schluckverlust *m* absorption loss (acoust)
Schluckwärmung *f* sound absorption
Schluff *m* silt, poor(-quality) clay
Schlundrohr *n* stomodaeum
Schlupf *m* slip (of propeller, generator, or asynchronous motor), slippage, backlash, drift ~ **der Luftschraube** *f* propeller slip
schlupfen, Fässer ~ to wash store casks
schlüpfen to slip **ein Tau ~ lassen** to slip a rope
Schlüpfen *n* slippage
schlupffrei free from slipping **-er Antrieb** nonslip drive, geared drive
Schlupf-geschwindigkeit *f* slip speed **-jacke** *f* sweater **-kuppelung** *f* slip clutch, slip coupling
schlüpflos slipless
Schlupf-motor *m* cumulative compound motor **-regler** *m* slip regulator
schlüpfrig slippery, oily
Schlüpfrigkeit *f* lubricity, slipperiness, oiliness
Schlüpfrigkeitsgrad *m* degree of slipperiness **Öl hohen Schlüpfrigkeitsgrades** fatty oil
Schlüpfring *m* slip ring
Schlüpfung *f* slip, slippage
Schlüpfungs-messer *m* slip meter **-reibung** *f* sliding friction, slip
Schlupf-widerstand *m* slip resistance **-zahl** *f* slip coefficient **-zeit** *f* engaging period
schlürfen to sip
Schluß *m* end, close, conclusion, termination finish, contact closing, short circuit **magnetischer** ~ magnetic shunt ~ **des Propellers** slip
Schluß-abfertigung *f* final clearance **-abrechnung** *f* final settlement **-anstrich** *m* final coat **-beleuchtung** *f* tail lighting **-bestand** *m* closing stock **-blende** *f* final diaphragm **-deckel** *m* cover **-drehzahl** *f* tipping speed, tripping speed **-eisen** *n* circuit iron
Schlüssel *m* key, wrench, code, spanner, clue, switch (elec.) ~ **zum Einziehen von Stiftschrauben** stud block ~ **ohne feste Stellung** nonlocking key
Schlüssel-auswertung *f* cryptanalysis **-bart** *m* key bit **-befehl** *m* key instruction **-bereich** *m* cryptonent **-blatt** *n* enciphering sheet, code sheet **-bolzen** *m* retaining pin, retaining bolt, clutch key **-brett** *n* keyboard, key shelf **-buchstabe** *m* cipher **-datum** *n* cryptodate **-einstellung** *f* setting by spanners **-feile** *f* warding file **-fertig** (Haus) ready for occupation **-fläche** *f* (der Mutter) flat or key face (of nut) **-fräsmaschine** *f* key milling machine
Schlüssel-griff *m* key lever (telegr) **-gruppe** *f* code group **-hebel** *m* key lever **-heft** *n* code book **-kanal** *m* cryptochannel **-keil** *m* tightening key **-knoten** *m* half-hitch knot **-kopiermaschine** *f* key profiling machine **-kranz** *m* wrench with rim **-leiste** *f* key board **-loch** *n* keyhole **-lochstreifen** *m* one-time tape (teletype) **-lochung** *f* code punching
Schlüsselmaschine cypter or crypto machine
Schlüsselmeldung *f* code (cipher) message

schlüsseln to code, (en)cipher
Schlüsseln *n* coding, encoding, enciphering
Schlüssel-punkt *m* key point **-reihe** *f* bank of keys **-ring** *m* ring spanner, key ring **-rohling** *m* key blank **-schieber** *m* key slide **-schraube** *f* lag screw **-stecker** *m* code plug **-streifenlocher** *m* jumble perforator **-stellung** *f* key position **-text** *m* cryptotext
Schlüsselung *f* (en)coding, enciphering, crytographing
Schlüssel-weite *f* width over flats of hexagonal nut **-wort** *n* key word
Schluß-ergebnis *n* end result **-folge** *f* conclusion **-härten** *n* final hardening
schlüssig determined, decided, logical
Schluß-kaliber *n* final pass **-kennzeichenleuchte** *f* tail and number plate lamp **-klappe** *f* ring-off indicator **-klappen** *f pl* clearing-out drops **-kondensator** *m* terminating condenser or capacitor, short-circuiting capacitor **-kontrolle** *f* final inspection **-kühler** *m* secondary cooler **-kurve** *f* end curve **-lampe** *f* clearing lamp, supervisory lamp, disconnecting lamp **-leiste** *f* tailpiece
Schlüßler *m* coder (comput), cryptographer
Schluß-licht *n* tail lamp **-lichtleitung** *f* tail lamp cable **-linie** *f* closing line **-organ** *n* end device **-paneel** *n* end panel **-pfropfen** *m* plug **-querträger** *m* end cross member **-rahmen** *m* end frame **-randsteller** *m* right-hand margin stop **-relais** *n* clearing relay **-ring** *m* locking ring, end ring
Schluß-scheibe *f* end disc **-schiff** *n* rear ship **-signal** *n* clearing signal **-signallaterne** *f* tail (signaling) light **-spulmaschine** *f* quill winding machine **-stein** *m* closing stone, keystone **-steinverzerrung** *f* trapezium distortion, keystone distortion **-stück** *n* short-circuit section **-vignette** *f* tailpiece
Schlußzeichen *n* clearing or supervisory signal, disconnect signal, clearing-out signal, clearing indicator **-einrichtung** *f* clearing-signal arrangement **-gabe** *f* clearing signaling
Schlußzeichengebung *f* clearing, supervision **~ für den rufenden (verlangten) Teilnehmer** answering (calling) supervisory relay **selbsttätige ~** automatic clearing, central-battery signaling
Schlußzeichen-lampe *f* clearing-signal lamp **-relais** *n* clearing relay, supervisory relay **-schaltung** *f* supervisory circuit **-strom** *m* clearing current **-übertragung** *f* clearing-lamp repeating **-wecker** *m* auxiliary signal, clearing signal bell
schmal narrow, small **-e Seite** *f* narrow dimension
Schmalbandachse *f* narrow-band axis
Schmalbandfilter *n* narrow-band filter
Schmalbündelantenne *f* pencil-beam antenna
schmälern to reduce, lessen, curtail
Schmälerung *f* diminution, curtailing, reduction
Schmalfilm *m* substandard film, narrow film
Schmalheit *f* narrowness
Schmal-kante *f* narrow edge, narrow side **-meißel** *m* narrow bit **-seite** *f* narrow side
Schmalspur *f* narrow gauge (track), small-gauge track **-bahn** *f* narrow-gauge railroad **-gleis** *n* narrow-gauge track **-wagen** *m* narrow-gauge railroad car
schmalspurig narrow-gauge **-e Eisenbahn** narrow-gauge railroad **-e Sämaschine** narrow-track seeder
Schmaltastenwerk *n* condensed keyboard (telegr)
Schmaltonfilmtechnik *f* sub-standard film technique
Schmalzöl *n* wool oil
Schmand *n* slime, sludge, mud
Schmauchfeuer *n* smoking or choked fire
Schmeißen *n* warping, distortion
Schmelz *m* melt, smelt, fusion, enamel glaze, blue powder (metal.) melting bath **-aggregat** *n* melting aggregate, melting medium, melting unit **-anlage** *f* smelting or melting plant, foundry **-arbeit** *f* smelting process or operation, melting process or operation, enameling process or operation **-arbeiter** *m* smelter, melter, founder, enameler
schmelzartig enamel-like
Schmelz-aschenfeuerung *f* slag tap furnace **-ausdehnung** *f* dilation in melting **-bad** *n* melting bath, molten bath pool **-band** *n* melting band
schmelzbar fusible, meltable, nonrefractory **schwer ~** refractory **-er Selfbogen** melting flashover
Schmelz-basalt *m* artificial basalt **-bau für Tiegelguß** crucible-steel foundry **-bedingung** *f* melting condition **-bericht** *m* heat record **-betrieb** *m* melting operation, melting practice **-blau** *n* smalt, azurite blue **-dauer** *f* duration of heat **-draht** *m* fuse wire **-druck** *m* melting pressure **-durchrechnung** *f* melt computation
Schmelze *f* melt, smelt, fusion, fused mass, fluid solution (metallography), smelting, smeltery, melting
Schmelz-einrichtung *f* melting equipment, melting installation **-einsatz** *m* fuse plug or cartridge, fuse link, fuse element, fusible element
schmelzen to melt, smelt, fuse, frit, deliquesce, liquefy, forge
Schmelzen *n* melting (down), smelting, fusion, fusing **~ ohne Oxydation** melting without oxidation, white-slag melt-down, melting under a white slag
Schmelzer *m* melter, founder, smelter, blower (in converter operation)
Schmelzerde *f* fusible earth
Schmelzerei *f* smeltery, foundry
Schmelz-erz *n* smelting ore **-farbe** *f* vitrifiable color or pigment **-feuer** *n* refinery **-fluß** *m* fused mass, melt, fusion, flux, state of fusion **-flußelektrolyse** *f* fusion electrolysis **-flüssig** fusible, molten **-führung** *f* conduct of heat, run feed grooves in automatic welding, working the heat, conduct of the furnace operation, conduct of the melting operation, smelting practice or schedule **-gang** *m* heat, blow, melt **-gefäß** *n* melting crucible, melting hearth **-geschweißt** fusion-welded
Schmelz-geschwindigkeit *f* rate of melting **-gewicht** *n* weight of charge **-glasur** *f* enamel **-grad** *m* melting point **-gut** *n* melting charge, melting stock, metal to be melted, deposit, burden **-hafen** *m* melting pot **-herd** *m* furnace hearth, smelting hearth **-hitze** *f* melting heat **-hütte** *f* smelting plant, smelting works
schmelzig fusible
Schmelzkammer *f* molten ash chamber **-feuerung**

f slag tap furnace **-kessel** *m* wet-bottom boiler
Schmelz-karte *f* heat log **-kegel** *m* melting or fusible cone **-kessel** *m* fusion kettle **-kleber** *m* fusion adhesive **-koks** *m* foundry coke, smelter coke **-krater** *m* pool of molten metal **-kuchen** *m* solidified melted material **-kurve** *f* melting-point curve, fusion curve **-legierung** *f* fusible alloy **-leistung** *f* melting efficiency, melting-down power, melting or smelting capacity, rate of melting **-leiter** *m* fusible conductor **-linie** *f* fusion curve **-löffel** *m* melting ladle
Schmelzlot-glied *n* soldered link **-melder** *m* thermal detector
Schmelz-mittel *n* flux **-ofen** *m* smelting or melting furnace **-perle** *f* blowpipe bead, enamel bead **-pfropfen** *m* fusible plug **-programm** *n* production schedule **-prozeß** *m* smelting or melting process **-pulver** *n* flux
Schmelzpunkt *m* melting or fusing point, fusion point, softening point **-ermittlung** *f* testing fusibility **-erniedrigung** *f* melting point depression **-messer** *m* meldometer
Schmelz-pyrometrie *f* fusing-point pyrometry **-raum** *m* smelting or melting chamber, hearth **-raupe** *f* annular fused-quartz spiral **-rinde** *f* (eines Meteoriten) baked crust (astron.) **-säule** *f* melting-stock column **-schaubild** *n* heat graph **-schweißung** *f* fusion welding, fuse welding, fluid welding, autogenous welding by fusion
Schmelzsicherung *f* fuse, fusible cutout, safety cutout, safety fuse ~ **mit Signalgabe** alarm fuse
Schmelzsicherungsdraht *m* fuse wire
Schmelz-spule *f* blowout coil **-stahl** *m* natural steel, German steel **-stift** *m* fusible plug **-stopfen** *m* fusible plug **-strom** *m* fusing current **-temperatur** *f* melting or fusion temperature **-tiegel** *m* melting crucible, melting pot or tank, soldering crucible **-tiegelzange** *f* melting crucible tongs **-topf** *m* melting pot, crucible **-trichter** *m* slag hopper **-überzug** *m* vitrified coating
Schmelzung *f* melt, heat (run), fusion
Schmelzungs-dauer *f* melting period **-gang** *m* melting operation **-linie** *f* fusion curve
Schmelz-verfahren *n* method of smelting, (electric) melting process **-wärme** *f* heat of fusion **-wärmegrad** *m* melting point, fusion point or temperature **-wasser** *n* melted snow and ice **-werk** *n* smeltery, foundry **-würdig** smeltable, suitable for smelting **-zeit** *f* time of smelting or melting, time of heat, charge-to-tap time **-zement** *m* aluminous cement **-zone** *f* melting zone, smelting zone, fusion zone, hearth zone **-zuschlag** *m* furnace addition
Schmergel *m* abrasive, emery
Schmerkluft *f* clay-filled fissure
Schmerstein *m* soapstone
Schmerz-grenze *f* threshold of feeling **-los** painless **-schwelle** *f* threshold of feeling
Schmetterlings-antenne *f* turnstile or batwing antenna **-kreis** *m* butterfly circuit **-leitwerk** *n* V-tail **-mutter** *f* butterfly nut
Schmied *m* blacksmith
schmiedbar forgeable, malleable, of smithing quality, capable of being wrought **-es Eisen** wrought iron, malleable iron, wrought steel **-er Guß** malleable iron, crucible steel or iron
Schmiedbarkeit *f* forging quality or property, forgeability, malleability
Schmiede *f* forge, smithy **-abfall** *m* forge scrap **-amboß** *m* smith's anvil **-arbeit** *f* forging operation, forging, metal work **-block** *m* forging, grade ingot, bloom **-drehbank** *f* forge lathe **-durchschlag** *m* blacksmith's punch **-eisen** *n* wrought iron, malleable iron, wrought steel, low-carbon steel, forging steel **-eisenschrott** *m* wrought-iron scrap
schmiedeeisern wrought-iron, wrought **-es Rohr** wrought-iron pipe **-er Vierspitz** wrought-iron fourpointed knife rest, crow's-foot (military obstacle)
Schmiede-esse *f* forge **-feuer** *n* forge fire, smith's fire **-gerät** *n* blacksmith's tool
Schmiedegesenk *n* drop-forge die, swage **im ~ anspitzen** to swage
Schmiede-gesenkfuge *f* flash (met.) **-hammer** *m* forging hammer, forge hammer, smith's hammer, sledge hammer **-herd** *m* smith's hearth, blacksmith's forge **-hitze** *f* forging temperature **-kohle** *f* forge coal, smithy coal **-kunst** *f* workmanship **-legierung** *f* wrought alloy **-maschine** *f* forging machine **-metall** *n* forging or malleable metal
schmieden to forge, fuse, smith, hammer ~ **im Gesenk** drop forge, drop stamp
Schmieden *n* forging, smithing
Schmiede-ofen *m* forging furnace **-presse** *f* forging press, drop hammer **-preßpumpe** *f* forging-press pump **-probe** *f* forging test, ladle test, pit sample **-rohling** *m* rough stamping **-schlacke** *f* blacksmith's slag **-sinter** *m* forging scale, hammer scale **-spannung** *f* forging strain
Schmiede-stahl *m* wrought steel, forged steel **-stück** *n*, **-teil** *m* forging **-temperatur** *f* forging temperature **-vorgang** *m* forging operation, smithing operation **-werkstatt** *f* forge, smithy **-werkzeug** *n* forging tool **-zange** *f* blacksmith's tongs
Schmiedung *f* forging
Schmiege *f* bevel, protractor
Schmiegebene *f* osculating plane
schmiegen to bevel
Schmiegewinkel *m* (miter) rule, bevel
schmiegsam flexible, pliant
Schmiegungs-ebene *f* osculating plane **-kugel** *f* osculating sphere
Schmier-anweisung *f* lubricating instructions **-apparat** *m* lubricator, oil cup **-behälter** *m* grease box
Schmierbüchse *f* oil cup, grease cup, lubricator, grease box ~ **mit Federdruck** spring-compression grease cup
Schmierdocht *m* oil wick
Schmiere *f* lubricant, lubricating oil or grease, tallow fat
Schmiereigenschaft *f* lubricating property
schmieren to lubricate, smear, oil, grease **das Lager ~** to oil, grease, or lubricate the bearing
Schmieren *n* lubrication
Schmierer *m* oil cup, grease cup, lubricator
Schmier-fähigkeit *f* lubricity, lubricating power, oiliness **-fänger** *m* cup collar, oil wiper **-fett** *n* (lubricating) grease **-film** *m* lubricating film **-flüssigkeit** *f* lubricant, lubricating liquid or oil **-gefäß** *n* lubricating cup

Schmier-glas *n* grease cup **-hahn** *m* grease cock
schmierig smudgy, oily, dirty ~ **gemahlen** wet-beaten (pulp)
Schmierigkeit *f* wettness (paper mfg.), unctuousness, sliminess
Schmierigkeitsgrad *m* freeness degree of grinding (wood pulp)
Schmier-kamm *m* wiper **-kanne** *f* oiler, oil can
Schmier-keilwirkung *f* wedging effect **-lager** *n* grease bearing, self-oiling bearing **-leitung** *f* lubrication piping **-loch** *n* oil hole, oil run, oiling hole **-masse** *f* lubricating paste **-material** *n* lubricant, lubricating oil or grease
Schmiermittel *n* lubricant ~ **für die spangebende Bearbeitung** cutting lubricant
Schmiermittel-kreislauf *m* lubrication system **-zusatzregler** *m* lubricant additive blender
Schmier-nippel *m* grease nipple **-nute** *f* oil groove, oilway
Schmieröl *n* lubricant, lubricating oil ~ **für die Achsenbüchsen der Eisenbahnwagen** railroad oil ~ **für den häuslichen Gebrauch** domestic lubricating oil ~ **für Kugellager** ball-bearing oil ~ **für Transmission** transmission lubricant
Schmieröl-destillat *n* lubricating-oil distillate **-entschäumer** *m* air-oil separator **-filter** *n* lubricating-oil filter **-fördereinrichtung** *f* oil-circulating device or system, oil gun **-kanne** *f* (lubricating-)oil can **-pumpe** *f* lubricating-oil pump **-sammeltank** *m* sump, lubricating-oil collector **-verschlechterung** *f* oil dilution
Schmier-pistole *f* grease gun **-plan** *m* lubrication chart or diagram **-platte** *f* lubricating pad **-presse** force-feed oiler **-pumpe** *f* grease pump or gun **-ring** *m* oil ring **-rohr** *n* lubrication pipe, oil pipe **-schema** *n* lubrication diagram **-schraube** *f* oil plug **-seife** *f* soft soap **-stelle** *f* point of lubrication, oilhole
Schmierstoff *m* lubricant, ointment **-abstreifring** *m* oil-scraper ring **-abweiser** *m* (TWK) oil baffle **-anlage** *f* lubricating system **-behälter** *m* grease sump, oil tank **-druck** *m* lubricant pressure **-druckleitung** *f* oil-pressure line **-druckmesser** *m* oil pressure gauge **-entschäumer** *m* air-oil separator, jet oil-foam separator
Schmierstoff-gewicht *n* weight of oil carried **-leitung** *f* oil piping **-messer** *m* oil-pressure gauge **-umpumpanlage** *f* oil-transfer pump system **-verbrauch** *m* lubricant consumption **-versorgung** *f* lubricant supply
Schmier-stutzen *m* lubrication connection **-system** *n* lubricating system
Schmierung *f* lubrication, oiling **selbsttätige** ~ self-oiling, automatic lubrication **nicht ausreichende** ~ underlubrication ~ **durch Schleuderöl** splash lubrication
Schmierungssystem *n* lubrication system
Schmierungsvorschriften (einer Maschine) *pl* oiling regulations
Schmier-vase *f* oil cup, grease cup, lubricator **-vorrichtung** *f* lubricating device, lubricator **-walkfaß** *n* stuffing drum **-wert** *m* lubricating value **-wirkung** *f* lubricating action **-zapfenöl** *n* journal oil
Schmirgel *m* emery, abrasive powder **-artig** abrasive **-asche** *f* putty of emery **-imprägniert** emery-impregnated **-leinen** *n* abrasive cloth, emery cloth **-leinwand** *f* emery cloth
schmirgeln to grind with emery, lap
Schmirgeln *n* polishing, glazing
Schmirgel-papier *n* abrasive paper, emery paper **-pulver** *n* emery dust or powder **-scheibe** *f* emery wheel **-schlämmapparat** *m* apparatus for the levigation of emery **-schleifmaschine** *f* emery grinding machine **-ständer** *m* emery grinding machine **-staub** *m* emery dust **-stein** *m* emery stone **-tasse** *f* (emery) cup wheel **-tuch** *n* emery cloth **-walze** *f* emery roller
schmoren to char, stew, scorch (e.g. contacts)
Schmoren *n* scorching, freezing or melting together (of contacts)
Schmorstellen *f pl* spots of arcing
Schmuck *m* jewelry **als** ~ ornamental
schmückend ornamental
Schmutz *m* mud, dirt, filth, glut
Schmutzabscheider *m* pipe-line strainer **auswechselbarer** ~ removable strainer
Schmutzabscheidergehäuse *n* strainer bow
Schmutz-abstreifring *m* sludge scraper (ring) **-anfall** *m* dirt sediment **-band** *n* dirt-belt **-bestimmung** *f* tare estimation **-blech** *n* mud guard, fender **-ecken** *pl* dirt traps
Schmutzfänger *m* mudguard, dirt trap, catch pan ~ **für wendbare Egge** dirt fender for reversible harrow ~ **für Kabelschächte** inner cover of manhole
Schmutz-flotte *f* dirty liquid **-geräusch** *n* dirt noise
schmutzig muddy, dirty, filthy, soiled, contaminated, unrefined, polluted, smutty
Schmutz-knoten *m* clotted dirt **-lauge** *f* scouring liquor **-probe** *f* dirt sample **-walke** *f* grease milling **-wasser** *n* sewage without storm water
Schnabel *m* beak, umbo, spout, jaw, nib, bill, nozzle, nose **-gießen** *n* lip pouring **-spitze** *f* cusp of second kind **-zange** *f* jaw (beak) pliers
Schnalle *f* buckle, catch
schnallen to buckle, strap
Schnallen *pl* blisters (paper mfg.)
Schnallriemen *m* leather strap
Schnappbremse *f* snatch brake
schnappen to snap, snatch
Schnapper *m* catcher, latch ~ (Abschnappkupplung, Magnetzünder) impulse starter ~ **eines Anlaßmagneten** impulse starter
Schnapper-auslösedrehzahl *f* impulse coupling releasing speed **-schlagweite** *f* impulse spark gap
Schnäpperschloß *n* spring-bolt lock
Schnapp-feder *f* wire snap **-funke** *m* impulse spark **-locher** *m* hole punch **-riegel** *m* spring catch **-ring** *m* snap ring **-schalter** *m* quick-action switch, snap switch **-schloß** *n* spring catch or lock **-schuß** *m* snapshot **-stativ** *n* self-locking tripod **-stift** *m* locking pin
Schnarchventil *n* snifting or blow valve, breather
Schnarre *f* buzzer, rattle
schnarren to jar, buzz, burr, vibrate, tremble
Schnarren der Düse buzzing of nozzle
Schnarr-schwingung der Düse buzzing vibration of nozzle **-summer** *m* buzzer **-ventil** *n* safety valve, vacuum relief valve, blow valve **-wecker** *m* buzzer (alarm)
Schnauze *f* lip, nozzle, snout, mouth, nose, spout ~ **einer Kanne** spout

Schnecke *f* snail, slug, (endless) screw, spire, helix, scroll, volute, screw conveyer, worm-(gear) ~ **zum Drehen des Spindelkopfes** head-swiveling worm **eingängige** ~ single-thread worm

Schnecken-achse *f* worm shaft **-antrieb** *m* worm (-gear) drive **-antriebswelle** *f* worm drive shaft **-artig** helicoid **-aufgabe** *f* screw feeding **-bohrer** *m* gimlet, auger **-fallvorrichtung** *f* trip worm device **-feder** *f* coil or spiral spring, coiled spring **-feinverstellung** *f* focusing mount **-flanke** *f* flank of a worm **-förderer** *m* screw or worm conveyer **-förderrinne** *f* screw-conveyer trough **-förmig** snail-formed, helical, spiral, worm-shaped **-fräser** *m* worm-thread milling cutter, worm cutter, hob cutter

Schnecken-gang *m* spiral (walk), auger **-gang-fassung** *f* helical lens mount **-gehäuse** *n* worm-gear housing **-getriebe** *n* worm gear(ing), worm drive **-gewinde** *n* worm thread, helix **-gewölbe** *n* helical or spiral vault, snail-formed vaulting **-hinterachsenantrieb** *m* worm-gear rear-axle drive **-lenkung** *f* worm and sector steering mechanism, worm gear (steering) **-linie** *f* spiral, helical line, helix **-quadrant** *m* worm-driven quadrant

Schneckenrad *n* worm gear, worm wheel, spiral wheel **-abwälzfräsmaschine** *f* worm-wheel generating machine **-achse** *f* worm-wheel axle **-erzeugung** *f* wormwheel generating **-getriebe** *n* worm gearing, worm drive **-hubschraube** *f* worm wheel lifting screw **-untersetzungsge-triebe** *n* worm reducer **-wälzfräser** *m* worm-gear hob **-welle** *f* worm-gear shaft **-zahn** *m* worm-gear tooth

Schnecken-reduziergetriebe *n* worm reduction gear **-scheibe** *f* spiral target **-schleifmaschine** *f* worm grinding machine **-schraube** *f* worm screw **-spritzgießmaschine** *f* screw injection machine (plastics) **-trieb** *m* worm (gear) drive, worm gearing, end screw, worm and wheel drive, worm-wheel drive **-triebteile** *pl* worm gear parts **-untersetzungsgetriebe** *n* worm gear reducers

Schnecken-vorgelege *n* worm gear **-wälzfräser** *m* worm generating hob **-welle** *f* worm shaft **-wellenstirnrad** *n* worm shaft spur gear **-winde** *f* worm geared winch **-zahnrad** *n* cutting worm gears **-zapfen** *m* pinion of report

Schnee *m* snow, grass (TV) ~ **und Regen gemischt** sleet

Schnee-belastung *f* snow load **-besen** *m* egg beater **-blind** snow-blind **-brille** *f* snow goggles **-dichte** *f* density of snow **-fall** *m* snowfall **-fang-gitter** *n* snow fence **-fegewagen** *m* snowplow **-flocke** *f* snowflake **-flugzeug** *n* airplane fitted with skis **-fräse** *f* snow propeller **-fräsmaschine** *f* rotary snow plow

Schnee-gestöber *n* driving snow, blizzard **-gips** *m* scaly, foliated or snowy gypsum **-gitter** *n* snow guard or fence **-grenze** *f* snow line

Schnee-kette *f* snow or tire chain, nonskid chain **-kristall** *m* snow crystal **-kufe** *f* landing skid (aviation), skis, ski runner, snow runner **-kufenfahrwerk** *n* ski undercarriage, ski landing gear **-landung** *f* snow landing **-last** *f* snow load **-mantel** *m* white coat (for camouflage in snow), coat of snow

Schneemasse, wässerige ~ sludge

Schnee-messer *m* snow gauge **-pflug** *m* snowplow **-räumgerät** *n* snow removal equipment **-roller** *m* snow roller **-schanze** *f* snowdrift, snow trench **-schaufel** *f* snow shovel **-schläger** *m* egg whisk **-schleuder** *f* rotary snowplow **-schmelze** *f* snow melt **-stern** *m* snow crystal **-sturm** *m* snow-storm blizzard

Schnee-treiben *n*, **-verwehung** *f* snowdrift **-wasser** *n* snow water **-wehe** *f* snowdrift **-weiß** snow-white **-zaun** *m* snow fence

Schneid-abfall *m* trimmings **-anker** *m* cutting grapnel **-anlage** *f* cutting plant

Schneidapparat *m*, **autogener** ~ oxyacetylene cutter

Schneid-ausrüstung *f* cutting outfit **-backe** *f* screwing jaw or die **-backen** *m* bolt die, die, screw die **-band** *n* steel band

schneidbar sectile

Schneidbohrer *m* tap

Schneidbrenner *m* cutting torch, blowpipe **-flamme** *f* cutting-torch flame **-kante** cutting-edge weld **-mundstück** *n*, **-spitze** *f* cutting-torch tip

Schneid-brust *f* face (of a tool) **-dose** *f* cutter (phonogr. rec.) **-diamant** *m* cutting diamond **-druck** *m* tool thrust, cutting pressure **-düse** *f* cutting tip

Schneide *f* (cutting) edge, tooth (of a grinder) knife edge ~ **des Senkkastens** cutting edge of the caisson **mit scharfer** ~ keen-edged

Schneide-aufhängung *f* knife-edge suspension **-haltigkeit** *f* ability to preserve keenness

Schneideisen *n* diestock die, screw die, die, cutting die ~ **für Gewindekluppen** dies for screwstock ~ **aus einem Stück** solid-bolt die ~ **mit Schlitz** split die **geteiltes** ~ split die **ungeteiltes** ~ solid die

Schneideisen-gewindebohrer *m* die hob, screw-plate tap **-gewindestrehler** *m* die chaser **-halter** *m* dies-tock, die holder **-kapsel** *f* collet **-schleif-maschine** *f* threading die grinding machine **-strehler** *m* die-stock chaser

Schneide-feile *f* hack file **-holländer** *m* grinding or chopping chamber **-kessel** *m* masticator **-kurve** *f* recording characteristic **-lade** *f* miter box **-lager** *n* knife-edge bearing

Schneiden *n* cutting, blanking, editing (film, magn.-tape) ~ **unter Wasser** underwater cutting weld

Schneiden-ankerrelais *n* knife-edge relay **-aufhängung** *f* knife-edge suspension **-berührung** *f* contact of knife edges **-blitzableiter** *m* knife-shaped or wedge-shaped lightning arrester, knife-edge lightning protector **-breite** *f* blade width

schneidend sharp, strident, cutting **-e Flamme** cutting flame **-e Gängchen** stringers, stringer leads

Schneiden-einsatz *m* bit **-geometrie** *f* cutting edge geometry **-lager** *n* knife-edge support **-lagerung** *f* knife-edge suspension, knife-edge bearings **-last** *f* collinear load

Schneideöl *n*, **wasserlösliches** ~ soluble cutting oil

Schneider *m* cutter, mechanical recording head (phono)

Schneide-raum *m* editing room **-richtung** *f* cutting

direction, cutting position
Schneide-stahllehre *f* cutter clearance gauge **-stichel** *m* cutter, cutting stylus, engraver, cutting head **-tisch** *m* editing table (tape rec.) **-ton** *m* edge tone, flue stop (of flue pipe) **-vermögen** *n* cutting capacity or power **-werk** *n* cutter
Schneidewinkel *m* cutting angle ~ **des Gewebes** bias angle
Schneidezange *f* cutting pliers, clippers
Schneidfähigkeit *f* cutting quality or ability, cutting power or property, cutting value or capacity
Schneidfläche *f* cutting surface **obere** ~ lip surface **vordere** ~ flank
Schneid-flamme *f* cutting flame **-geschwindigkeit** *f* cutting speed **-gewindebohrer** *m* screwing tap **-härte** *f* cutting hardness **-hülse** *f* cutter head
schneidig soft, yielding (rock), sharp, cutting
Schneid-kante *f* cutting edge **-kluppe** *f* pipe-threading tool, screw plate, screw (die) stock **-kluppenbacke** *f* die-stock die **-kopf** *m* cutting head, die head, nose, mechanical recording head (phono) **-legierung** *f* alloy for cutting tools or instruments **-maschine** *f* slicer, cutter **-maß** *n* trim size **-metall** *n* metal-cutting material, cutting alloy **-mühle** *f* impeller breaker **-mundstück** *n* cutting tip **-narbe** *f* cutting scar, burry condition
Schneidöl *n* mineral lard oil, cutting oil **-behälter** *m* lubricant tank
Schneidprozeß *m* intersection process
Schneidrad *n* gear shaper cutter, pinion type cutter **-schärfmaschine** *f* gear shaper cutter sharpening machine
Schneid-schlitten *m* cutter carriage **-schraube** *f* tapping screw **-späne** *m pl* cuttings **-stahl** *m* cutting tool, cutter, cutting-off tool **-stempel** *m* punch **-stichel** *m* cutting stylus **-ungswinkel** *m* angle of intersection **-verfahren** *n* cutting process (weld) **-vorgang** *m* cutting process, cutting action **-werk für autogenes Schneiden** autogenous cutting shop **-werkzeug** *n* cutting tool, cutter (tooth), edged tool **-werkzeugstähle** *pl* cutlery steels **-winkel** *m* cutting edge, cutting angle (dig-in or drag angle) **-zahn** *m* cutter tooth **-zange** *f* cutting pliers **-zeug** *n* edge tools
Schneidzunge, einsetzbare ~ adjustable or insertable cutter
Schneise *f* unaffected zone, approach path, aisle (in a forest), flying lane, radio-beacon course, equisignal track, sector, or corridor
schnell fast, quick, rapid, mobile **-e Rolle** snap roll, flick roll (aviation) ~ **drehen** to spin ~ **lösend** quickrelease, quick releasing, quick or easy solving ~ **wirkend** quick acting **schneller werden** to accelerate, speed up
Schnell-ablaß *m* jettisoning gear, quick release, emergency release, dumping **-ableggurt** *m* quick release harness (parachute) **-abtastmotor** *m* slewing motor **-alterungsversuch** *m* accelerated aging test **-amt** *n* combined line and recording toll central office **-analyse** *f* rapid or quick analysis **-anlauf** *m* high-speed start, rapid starting, high acceleration **-arbeitsstahl** *m* high-speed steel tool
Schnell-aufzug *m* rapid wind lever **-auslösung** *f* instantaneous release or relay, quick breaking **-ausrückung** *f* quick breaking
Schnellausschalter *m* quick-action release ~ **eines Motors** quick-action engine-stopping device
Schnell-automatenweichstahl *m* low-carbon free-cutting steel **-binder** *m* quick-setting cement **-bohreinrichtung** *f* high-speed drilling attachment **-bohrer** *m* speed drill **-bremsung** *f* rapid deceleration **-brücke** *f* portable footbridge **-dämpfer** *m* rapid ager **-drahthindernis** *n* portable wire entanglement **-drehbank** *f* high speed lathe **-drehmessing** *n* high-speed brass **-drehstahl** *m* high-speed (tool) steel
Schnelle *f* speed, velocity, swiftness
Schnell-einrückung *f* quick-acting engagement **-einschaltvorrichtung** *f* rapid-closing mechanism **-einspannschraubstock** *m* quick-acting screw vise **-einstellhebel** *m* quick-adjusting lever
schnellen to impel
Schnell-entladewagen *m* rapid discharger **-entlastungsventil** *n* rapid release valve **-entleerer** *m* (fuel-)jettisoning arrangement **-entleerung des Brennstoffs** dumping or emergency jettisoning of fuel (aviation) **-entregung** *f* quick or high speed de-energizing **-entwicklung** *f* high-speed development
Schnell-erhitzung *f* shock heating **-filmaufnahme** *f* high-speed photography **-flaschenzug** *m* high-speed spur-geared block **-fließend** fast-flowing, high deposition rate **-flug** *m* high-speed flight **-flugzahl** *f* high-speed (flight) figure **-flugzeug** *n* high-speed aircraft **-flüssig** easily fusible, readily meltable **-flußprofil** *n* high-velocity airfoil **-futter** *n* quick-acting chuck
Schnellgang *m* high speed, rapid power traverse, overdrive, quick motion, rapid travel, superhigh gear **-getriebe** *n* high-speed gear, overdrive **-rad** *n* superhigh gear wheel
Schnellgangsschaltklaue *f* superhigh gearshift claw
Schnell-geber *m* rapid transmitter **-gehend** fast-running **-gesenkhammer** *m* high-speed drop hammer
Schnell-gewicht *n* tilting or tumbling ball **-heizkessel** *m* quick-firing boiler **-hindernis** *n* portable obstacle, hasty obstacle
Schnelligkeit *f* speed, velocity, rapidity
Schnelligkeitsregler *m* speed regulator
Schnell-kopie *f* quick or hurry print **-kopfniet** *m* snap headed rivet **-kraft** *f* elasticity
Schnell-ladegerät *n* rapid charging unit **-lader** *m* fast charger **-ladung** *f* high charging, rapid charging **-lastwagen** *m* speed truck **-laufdrehbank** *f* high-speed turret lathe
schnellaufend high-speed **-e Dieselmaschine** high-speed Diesel engine **-er Wähler** high-speed switch
Schnelläufer *m* high-speed engine, racer **-motor** *m* high-speed engine **-wähler** *m* high-speed switch
Schnellauf-spindel *f* high-speed spindle **-spritzgießmaschine** *f* fast cycling injection machine **-verdichter** *m* centrifugal supercharger or concentrator
Schnell-lot *n* soft solder, fusible metal **-methode** *f* rapid or high-speed method, quick procedure

-morsesystem *n* automatic Morse system **-nachführung** *f* slewing (gyro) **-öffner** *m* accelerator **-photographie** *f* instantaneous photograph, snapshot **-probe** *f* rapid test **-profil** *n* fast profile **-programmierung** *f* forced coding **-punktschweißung** *f* spot welding

Schnell-rechner *m* high-speed computer **-regler** *m* quick acting regulator **-relais** *n* high-speed relay **-rücklauf** *m* fast rewind (tape rec.) **-rücklaufventil** *n* quick-return valve **-rührer** *m* impeller

Schnell-schäler *m* knife barking machine **-schalter** *m* quick-break switch **-schaltung** *f* quick-acting controls **-schlag** *m* quick blow

Schnellschluß *m* tripping mechanism, spring lock, quick shutoff **-drehzahl** *f* tripping speed **-einrichtung** *f* emergency governor **-regler** *m* safety regulator **-schieber** *m* quick opening valve **-ventil** *n* quick-acting gate valve

Schnell-schneider *pl* high speed trimmers **-schneidestahl** *m* high-speed steel

Schnellschnitt-drehbank *f* high speed lathe **-stahl** *m* high-speed tool steel

Schnell-schreibempfang *m* high-speed reception for Morse code **-schreiber** *m* stenotype machine **-schütze** *m* flying shuttle **-schwenkung** *f* (einer Kamera) zoom (film) **-schwingsieb** *n* high-speed shaker screen **-senkbremse** *f* rapid lowering brake **-spaltung** *f* fast fission **-spanner** *m* quick-action vise

Schnellspann-exzenter *m* quick-acting cam or eccentric **-futter** *n* preset collar **-mitnehmer** *m* quick-acting driver **-mutter** *f* high-speed lock nut **-reitstock** *m* quick-acting tailstock **-schraubenschlüssel** *m* quick-adjusting screw spanner or monkey wrench **-vorrichtung** *f* quick-acting clamping device

Schnell-speicher *m* zero access-store (info proc.), rapid memory **-sperre** *f* improvised obstacle, portable obstacle for speedy obstruction **-spindelpresse** *f* rapid-action screw press

Schnellstahl *m* high-speed steel, high-speed tool steel **-bohrer** *m* high-speed (steel) drill **-fräser** *m* high-speed steel cutter **-werkzeug** *n* high-speed (steel) tool

Schnell-stanzer *m* gang punch **-steg** *m* footbridge **-stop** *m* instant stop (on tape recorder) **-stopptaste** *f* stop button (tape rec.) **-stoßherd** *m* rapid percussion table **-straße** *f* express road, expressway, express highway

Schnellstromdünnsaftvorwärmer *m* high-velocity clarified juice heater

Schnell-tauchen *n* crash dive **-telegraph** *m* high-speed telegraph, automatic telegraph **-telegraphie** *f* high-speed telegraphy **-temperverfahren** *n* shortcycle annealing **-trennkupplung** *f* quick-disconnect plug **-trennstelle** *f* quick-release or snap connection **-trocknend** quick-drying, siccative **-unterbrecher** *m* ticker, rapid interrupter **-verdampfer** *m* flash boiler **-verfahren** *n* high-speed processing

Schnellverkehr *m* high-speed traffic **~ ohne direkten Anruf** "no-delay" operation

Schnellverkehrs-amt *n* no-delay telephone or traffic exchange **-platz** *m* joint trunk position **-flugzeug** *n* high-speed commercial air-plane, express air liner **-netz** *n* no-delay telephone or traffic network **-seitenamtsleitung** *f* no-delay trunk junction

Schnellverschluß *m* snap closure **-ventil** *n* quick-opening valve **-vortreiber** *m* quick-release catch

Schnell-verseilmaschine *f* high-speed stranding machine **-verstellhandreibahlen** *pl* high speed adjustable hand reamers **-verstellung** *f* quick-action adjustment **-vorlauf** *m* fast forward (tape rec.) **-vorstreckwalze** *f* roughing roll, breaking-down roll, cogging-down roll **-vorwalzkaliber** *n* roughing pass, drawing pass, breaking-down pass, cogging-down pass **-waage** *f* steel-yard **-walzwerk** *n* high-speed rolling mill

Schnellwechsel-aufnahme *f* quick-change adaptor **-einheit** *f* quick-change unit **-futter** *n* quick-change chuck **-halter** *m* quick-change holder **-stahlhalter** *m* quick-change tool post, quick-change tool block

Schnell-zähler *m* high-speed counter **-ziehwalzwerk** *n* high-speed drawing mill **-zug** *m* express train **-zünder** *m* quick fuse, instantaneous fuse **-zündschnur** *f* instantaneous fuse

Schneppe *f* spout, lip, nozzle, clip, welt

Schnepper *m* latch, tumbler, snap **-schloß** *n* spring lock

Schnippeleinrichtung *f* trimming unit

schnippeln cut into shreds

Schnipsel *n*, **Schnipselchen** *n* scrap, bit, chip, trim, shred

Schnitt *m* cutting; (Einschnitt) cut; (Kerbe) notch; (Scheibe) slice; (Schnittmuster) pattern; (Math.) intersection; (Längs~) longitudinal section, cut, profile; (Quer~) cross-section; (Durch~) average; (Zeichnung) section, sectional drawing; (Werkzeug) blanking tool; (X-Schnitt *m*) normal cut (cryst.), parallel cut (cryst.); bearing, interface, die (mach.), incision, cutting and editing (motion pictures) ~ (Stanzwerkzeug) punching tool

Schnitt-ansicht *f* sectional view, transverse section **-bau** *m* die making **-bearbeitbarkeit** *f* machinability **-bedingungen** *pl* cutting speeds **-belastung** *f* cutting load **-bewegung** *f* working motion

Schnittbild *n* sectional view **-einsatz** *m* split-image rangefinder attachment **-entfernungsmesser** *m* split-field, cut-image, or coincidence range finder

Schnittbreite *f* cutting width **~ einer Säge** kerf, width of kerf

Schnitt-brenner *m* slot burner, slit burner, batswing burner **-darstellung** *f* transverse section **-dauer** *f* duration of cut **-druck** *m* cutting pressure, pressure from or of the chip

Schnitte *f* cut, slice

Schnitte *pl* cuttings

Schnitt-ebene *f* sectional plane **-fähiger Boden** soil of medium consistency **-fänger** *m* section lifter **-film** *m* cut film **-fläche** *f* surface of cut or section, area of cut, sectional area or plane, intersecting plane, section **-gerade** *f* intersection line **-geschwindigkeit** *f* cutting speed **-geschwindigkeitsschild** *n* table of cutting speeds **-höhe** *f* depth of cut **-hub** *m* (e. Stößels) cutting stroke

schnittig racy, stylish, of elegant design, streamlined

Schnitt-kante *f* cutting edge **-kantenwinkel** *m*

lip-clearance angle **-kopie** *f* editorially cut or edited print **-kraft** *f* cutting power **-kreis** *m* (Bagger) intersection circle **-kurven zweier Flächen zweiter Ordnung** lines of intersection of two surfaces of second order **-länge** *f* chop (paper mfg.), length of a cut **-leistung** *f* cutting efficiency, cutting capacity, cutting power

Schnittlinie *f* cutting line, line of intersection, secant, intersection (of planes), profile line **~ in der roten Zone** red zone of intersection

Schnittlinien-bedingung *f* condition of intersection **-steuerung** *f* control of the intersection of the planes **-zone** *f* zone of intersection

Schnitt-matrize *f* cutting die **-messer** *n* drawknife **-modell** *n* cut-away model **-muster** *n* paper pattern **-nute** *f* groove flute **-papiere** *pl* angular papers **peilung** *f* split direction finding **-presse** *f* cutting press, punching press

Schnittpunkt *m* (point of) intersection, crossover (beam) **-peilung** *f* split direction finding **-satz** *m* theorem on incidence, intersection theorem

Schnitt-richtung *f* cutting direction, cutting position **-schraube** *f* grub screw, headless screw **-sohle** *f* floor of cut **-stahl** *m* punching tool steel **-stanze** *f* power shears **-stanzwerkzeug** *n* blanking tool **-tiefe** *f* depth of cut **-verfahren** *n* cutting procedure

Schnittweite *f* width of cut, distance between back lens and image, intercept length **~ von durch eine Linse hindurchgehenden Strahlen** distance of intersection of rays passing through a lens **konjugierte ~** conjugate intercept or distance

Schnitt-werkzeug *n* cutting tool **-winkel** *m* angle of intersection, cutting angle **-winkellehre** *f* cutting angle gauge **-wirkung** *f* cutting action **-zeichnung** *f* (cross-)sectional drawing, illustration, view, picture, figure

Schnitzel *pl* beet slices, pulp (sugar mfg.), chip, (Lochkarten) chads, chips parings, shavings **ausgelaugte ~** beet pulp **eingemietete ~, eingesäuerte ~** siloed beet pulp **frische ~, unausgelaugte ~** cossettes

Schnitzel-anwärmung *f* heating of cossettes **-bank** *f* chopping bench **-brikettierung** *f* briquetting of pulp **-einmietung** *f* **-einsäuerung** *f* siloing of pulp **-grube** *f* pulp silo **-maschine** *f* slicing machine, slicer, cutter

Schnitzelmesser *n* chopper, slicing knife

schnitzeln to cut, carve, chip, whittle

Schnitzel-preßstoff *m* macerate molding **-schnekke** *f* pulp screw conveyer **-sortierer** *m* chip screen **-speicher** *m* chip loft **-sumpf** *m* pulp silo

schnitzen to sculpture, cut, carve, chip, whittle

Schnitzer *m* cutter, carver, knife, whittle, paring tool, blunder

Schnitz-maschine *f* copying machine **-messer** *n* carving knife

Schnorchel *n* air intake, breathing mast, air funnel

Schnörkel *m* scroll

Schnüffel-loch *n* expansion port **-ventil** *n* breather, snifting valve, poppet valve, relief valve

Schnüffler *m* relief valve

Schnur *f* lace, string, (flexible) cord, filament, line, chord, twine **~ mit Drahtlitzenleiter** tinsel cord **~ mit zwei Steckern** double-plugged cord **~ mit zwei Stöpseln** double-ended cord **N-adrige ~** N-conductor cord **biegsame ~** flexible cord **doppeladrige ~** twin flex **einadrige ~** single-conductor cord **fehlerhafte ~** defective cord **zweiadrige ~** two-way cord, double-conductor cord

Schnur-anschlußklemme *f* cord connection clip, suspender clip **-antrieb** *m* string drive **-bandumschlag** *m* tie envelope **-befestigung** *f* cord fastener **-bespinnung** *f* cord covering

Schnürboden *m* loft

Schnurbund *m* timber stay lashing

schnüren to lace

Schnüren-abnahme *f* string discharge **-bespannung** *f* strings for removing

schnurgerade deadstraight, absolutely straight, in a straight line

Schnur-gewicht *n* cord weight **-klemme** *f* cord fastener **-lauf** *m* groove wheel **-laufantrieb** *m* (endless) cord drive **-leiste** *f* lashing wedge **-leitung** *f* cord line **-los** cordless

Schnürloch *n* eyelet

Schnurlot *n* plumb bob

Schnürnadel *f* bodkin

Schnur-öse *f* cord terminal **-paar** *n* pair of cords, cord circuit **-packung** *f* cord packing **-pendel** *n* cord pendant **-prüfklinke** *f* cord-testing jack

Schnurprüfung *f* cord test **~ durch Schütteln** cord shake test

Schnurre *f* chute

Schnurrolle *f* grooved roller, cord pulley

Schnürsattelgurt *m* buckled girth

Schnurschalter *m* suspension switch, pendant switch

Schnurschaltungen *pl*, **vereinfachte ~** sleeve control cord circuits

Schnurscheibe *f* rope pulley

Schnurschutz *m* cord-protecting means **-spirale** *f* cord-protecting wire helix

Schnürspur *f* squeeze or matter track (sound film)

Schnur-stecker *m* cord terminal or plug **-stromkreis** *m* cord circuit **-trommel** *f* cord barrel

Schnürung *f* cording, tying-up, binding, lacing

Schnurverstärker *m* cord circuit repeater **-amt** *n* cord-circuit-repeater central (station) **-anlage** *f* cord-circuit-repeater plant **-schrank** *m* cord-circuit-repeater switchboard **-störung** *f* cord-circuit-repeater trouble **-versicherungsstelle** *f* cord-circuit-repeater fuse rack

Schnur-werkstatt *f* cord-repairing center **-wirtel** *m* cord pulley **-zugpendel** *n* counterweight fitting **-zwischenschalter** *m* pendant switch

Schock *m* shock, color burst **-härte** *f* shock resistance **-schalter** *m* crash switch **-versuch** *m* shock test

Scholle *f* lace-holder

Scholleisen *n* folding tool

Schollen-brecher *m* clod crusher **-gebirge** *n* mountains formed by plateau-forming movements **-zerteiler** *m* clod crusher

Schöndruck *m* first form, blank paper

schonen to spare, conserve, protect

Schönen *n* clarifying, fining

schonend zerkleinern to crush gently

Schoner *m* schooner, protector

Schonfrist *f* grace period

Schongang *m* overdrive **-getriebe** *n* high-speed gear, overdrive

Schönheitsfehler *m* blemish
Schonung *f* careful treatment, young forest plantation, nursery (hort.) ~ **des Ofenfutters** care of furnace lining
Schöpf-becher *m* drag bucket **-bohrer** *m* auger **-bohrgerät** *n* bailing auger **-büchse** *f* bailer **-bütte** *f* vat **-eimer** *m* bailing bucket
schopfen to crop, top, cut crops, discard the top (of an ingot)
schöpfen to ladle out, scoop, draw (liquid, etc.), bail, dip, charge (a battery), create
Schöpfer *m* dipper, vatman, bailer
schöpferisch productive, creative
Schöpf-gefäß *n* scoop **-haspel** *f* sand reel, bailing drum **-herd** *m* casting crucible **-höhe** *f* head of the discharge **-kelle** *f* scoop **-löffel** *m* bailer, ladle **-maschine** *f* draining machine **-polle** *f* bailer **-probe** *f* cup test, ladle test or analysis, ladle sample, pit sample **-rad** *n* bucket or scoop wheel **-werk** *n* bucket elevator **-zelle** *f* bucket
Schöpit *m* schoepite
Schoppen *m* half liter, half pint, mug
Schopperriegler *m* degree of freeness (pulp)
Schore *f* bar (of molding box), prop, shore
Schöreisen *n* sharp iron, caulking iron
Schorf *m* scab
Schornstein *m* chimney, funnel, (smoke)stack, flue **-aufsatz** *m* smokestack top, chimney cowl **-fuchs** *m* breeching **-gas** *n* stack gas **-höhe** *f* stack height **-schieber** *m* chimney damper **-sockel** *m* chimney base **-wirkung** *f* stack effect, chimney effect **-zug** *m* chimney draft, stack draft, flue draft
Schoß *m* lap
schossen to run to seed, bolt
Schoß-kelle *f* forage ladder **-kissenfallschirm** *m* lap-pack parachute, lap-type parachute **-packfallschirm** *m* lap-pack parachute **-rübe** *f* bolter, seed runner
Schotbolzen *m* eyebolt with a forelock
Schott *n* bulkhead, partition, separation, compartment
Schotten-überhitzer *m* platen superheater **-signalanlage** *f* signal installation for bulkhead
Schotter *m* (road) metal, ballast, rubble, gravel, crushed rock **-anlage** *f* road metal plant, broken-stones manufacturing plant **-bahn** *f* macadam road **-becherwerk** *n* ballast elevator **-belag** *m* graveling (with broken rock) **-bett** *n* ballast, bed of broken stone, bed of road metal **-bruch** *m* ballast digging **-decke** *f* macadam surfacing **-maschine** *f* road-metal preparing machine **-masse** *f* rounded material, heap of gravel
schottern to ballast
Schotter-schlegel *m* ballast hammer **-schüttung** *f* ballast bed **-straße** *f* gravel road **-trommel** *f* ballast screener
Schotterung *f* gravelling
Schotterwerkzeug *n* ballasting tool
Schottky-Effekt *m* Schottky effect
Schottkysche Gerade Schottky line
Schottluke *f* inspection door
Schott-tür *f* bulkhead door **-überhitzer** *m* platen superheater **-wand** *f* bulkhead partition, fire wall

Schove *f* stave
schraffen to hatch
Schraffen *pl* hachures
schraffieren to hatch, hachure, shade, line
schraffiert shaded, (cross) hatched, section lined **kreuzweise** ~ crosshatched
Schraffierung *f* hatching or shading (in drawings), hachure
Schraffur *f* shaded partion drawing, shading **-platte** *f* line screen
schräg sloping, oblique, inclined, bevel, diagonal, transverse, beveled, chamfered ~ **verstellbarer Tisch** tilting table ~ **abfallend** sloping ~ **abgeflacht** chamfered ~ **aufwärts verlaufen** to slope upwards ~ **gelagert** in inclined arrangement ~ **nach links unten hin** toward the left bottom corner ~ **nach rechts oben hin** toward the right top corner ~ **verzahnt** helical **-e Bohrung** inclined bore **-er Rost** inclined grate **-e Verbindung** bevel joint
Schräg-abschneiden *n* beveling **-anflug** *m* slant approach **-ansicht** *f* three-quartier or oblique view **-ansteigend** upward-sloping **-antrieb** *m* inclined drive **-aufnahme** *f* oblique photograph
Schrägaufzug *m* inclined elevator, inclined or skip hoist ~ **mit Kippgefäß** skip hoist with tipping bucket
Schräg-aufzugbahn *f* hoist bridge, bucket-carriage track **-bahn** *f* inclined track **-bildkamera** *f* oblique (mapping) camera **-bohrung** *f* oblique drilled duct, slanting gallery **-brett** *n* angle board **-druck** *m* italics (print)
Schräge *f* slope, slant, bevel, diagonal, loop (in rolling), rhumb line, inclination, obliquity, haunch (on beam), cant
Schräg-ebene *f* slant plane **-eingriff** *m* angular meshing **-einstellbarkeit** *f* inclinable adjustment **-eisen** *n* bent-up bar, diagonal bar
Schragen *m* trestle
schrägen to slant, chamfer
Schrägentfernung *f* slant range (rdr)
Schrägewalzwerk *n* roll piercing mill
Schrägfläche *f* inclined plane
Schrägförderband *n* inclined belt conveyer ~ **mit Flachband** inclined flat-belt-type conveyer
Schrägförderer *m* inclined conveyer ~ **mit Plattenband** inclined slat conveyer, inclined pan conveyer, inclined platform conveyer
Schräg-hammer *m* mattock **-hobeln** *n* angle planing **-kabel** *n* external drag wire **-kammwalze** *f* bevel pinion **-kante** *f* bezel, chamfer **-kolonne** *f* sloping column, inclined column **-kugelmühle** *f* inclined ball mill
Schräglage *f* sloping position, banking ~ **des Flugzeuges in der Kurve** banking of plane in a curve
Schräglageanzeiger *m* bank indicator
Schräglauf (d. Bandes) tape skew (tape rec.)
schräglaufend oblique, loxodromic
schrägliegend oblique **-e Untermesserwelle** inclined bottom shaft **-e Zündkerze** inclined spark plug
Schräg-linie *f* diagonal **-maß** *n* bevel, rule **-naht** *f* circumferential or slant weld **-nocken** *m* taperer cam **-papiere** *n pl* angle papers (paper mfg.)
Schräg-rad *n* helical gear **-rampe** *f* sloping bench, inclined wharf, inclined dock **-regelung**

f regulation with phase shifting **-retortenofen** *m* coke oven with a long inclined retort **-rohrkessel** *m* inclined-tube boiler **-rohrmanometer** *n* inclined-tube manometer **-rollenlager** *n* steep-angle bearing, taper-rolling bearing **-rost** *m* inclined grate **-scheibe** *f* tapered washer

schrägschenk(e)lige Kropfachswelle oblique crank axle

schrägschichtig obliquely bedded

Schrägschliff, wechselseitiger ~ alternating bevel grind

Schräg-schlitz *m* slanting slot **-schneidemaschine** *f* angle-cutting machine **-schnitt** *m* bevel or diagonal cut **-schrift** *f* italics **-schulterfelgen** *pl* special rims **-schuß** *m* inclined ascent (rockets) **-seite** *f* slanting or inclined side **-sicht** *f* slant visual range (aviat) **-sitzventil** *n* inclined-seat valve **-spant** *m* (Flugzeug) canted bulkhead **-spinner** *m* (Papier) lapper with inclined coil carrier **-spritzkopf** *m* oblique extruder head

Schrägstab *m* sloped girder, beam or post, diagonal rod **linker ~** left-hand sloped girder **rechter ~** right-hand sloped girder **beide Schrägstäbe** both sloped girders

Schräg-stahl *m* squared-nose tool **-steg** *m* inclined path, inclined quoin

schrägstellbar inclinable, tiltable, tilting

Schrägstellbarkeit des Werkzeugtisches angular adjustment of tilting table

schrägstellen to tilt

Schräg-stellen *n* tilting **-stellung** *f* obliquity, inclination, skewing **-strahl** *m* skew ray **-strecke** *f* (length of) incline **-strebe** *f* diagonal strut **-strich** *m* slash; slant, solidus, oblique, diagonal fraction stroke **-stütze** *f* crossarm brace, inclined bracket

Schrägung *f* facet (b. Sägezahn) setting

Schrägungswinkel *m* angle of skew or slope, lead

Schräg-verblattung *f* splayed or skew joint **-verstellung** *f* angular adjustment **-verzahnt** spiral toothed, helical toothed or geared

schrägverzahntes Planetenrad helical planet pinion

Schrägverzahnung *f* helical gearing, helical gear-wheels **doppelte ~** herringbone gearing

Schräg-verzahnungsgetriebe *n* helical gear **-verzerrung** *f* skew **-walze** *f* inclined roll **-walzen** *n* diagonal rolling **-walzenrichtmaschine** *f* reeling machine **-walzverfahren** *n* roll piercing process, diagonal rolling process, Mannesmann rolling process, Perrin's rolling process **-walzwerk** *n* skew-rolling mill, piercing mill **-wand** *f* battered wall, battering wall **-zahnrad** *n* helical gear

Schrägzahnschieber *m* helical slide **-verstellung** *f* adjustment of the helical slide

Schrägzahnstirnrad *n* helical spur gear, twisted-tooth or helical-toothed spur gear

Schrägzug *m* diagonal pull

Schram *m* cutting, holing, channel, furrow, (gang) trench

Schrämarbeit *f* (under)cutting, working of trenches

schrämen to cut or hew trenches (to ore veins)

Schrämen *n* hewing

Schrämer *m* cutter, undercutter

Schramhieb *m* trench

Schräm-leitung *f* trailing cable **-maschine** *f* cutting machine, coal auger, ripping machine

Schramme *f* scratch, stria, trench, shadow scratch (film), slash, scar

Schrammenrauschen *n* scratch noise

Schrammkronen *pl* cutter bits

Schrank *m* cabinet, locker, cupboard, wardrobe, switchboard, section, case, lease (weaving)

Schränkapparat *m* saw-setting apparatus

Schrankbatterie *f* local battery

Schranke *f* enclosure, barrier, railway gate, bound **in Schranken haltend** coercive

Schränkeisen *n* saw set

schränken to cross, put across, set (a saw)

Schränken der Walzen crossing of the rolls

schrankenlos unbounded, boundless, unrestrained

Schranken-stange *f* railing bar **-stellwerk** *n* winding gear

Schrank-fachbrett *n* shelf **-feder** *f* check or drag spring

Schränkfehler *m* constructional asymmetry

Schrankkabel *n* switchboard cable

Schränklehre für Sägezähne set regulator for saw teeth

Schränkstock *m* saw clamp

Schranksystem *n* switchboard system

Schränkung *f* setting (saw), offset, décalage, crossing **~ der Fügel gegeneinander** décalage **geometrische ~** geometrical offset

Schränkungswinkel *m* longitudinal dihedral angle

Schrankwecker *m* board bell

Schränkzange *f* saw-set pliers

Schrappeisen *n* scrap iron

schrappen to scrape

Schrapper *m* scraper

Schrappvorrichtung für Bandeisen roughing device for hoop iron

Schrapsel *n* scrapings

Schratte *f* chamfer, channel

Schraub-anker *m* screw anchor (bolt) **-backe** *f* vise jaw **-bolzen** *m* screw bolt **-deckel** *m* screwed-on cover, screw cap or cover **-deckelverschluß** *m* screw cap

Schraube *f* bolt (mit Mutter), screw, propeller, worm **~ ohne Ende** worm, endless screw, threaded valve stem **~ auf Kugellager** operating screw mounted on ball bearings **~ mit Knebel** thumb screw **~ ohne Kuppe** flat-point screw **~ mit Mutter** bolt **~ ohne Mutter** screw (without nut) **~ (fest) anziehen** to tighten the screw **eine ~ etwas lösen** to back off a screw **eine ~ nachziehen** to tighten a screw

Schraube, abgesetzte ~ necked-down bolt **dreigängige ~** triple-thread screw **durchgehende ~** through bolt **eingängige ~** single-thread screw **eingelassene ~** countersunk screw **flachgängige ~** square-thread screw **freitragende ~** overhung screw **halbblanke ~** semimachined bolt **hochköpfige ~** raised screw **scharfgängige ~** screw with a triangular thread **selbstschneidende ~** self tapping screw **ummantelte ~** shrouded or circumferentially enclosed propeller **versenkte ~** countersunk screw

schrauben to screw

Schrauben-achse *f* screw axis **-anker** *m* mooring screw, screw mooring **-anschlagsockel** *m* screw stop cap **-antenne** *f* helical antenna **-antrieb** *m* propeller drive

schraubenartig helicoidal
Schrauben-ausdreher *m* screw extractors **-automat** *m* automatic screw machine
Schraubenblatt *n* propeller blade **-durchbiegung** *f* propeller-blade flexural deflection **-geschwindigkeit** *f* propeller-blade speed **-wurzel** *f* root of propeller blade
Schrauben-blech *n* screwplate **-block** *m* screw jack **-bohrer** *m* auger bit, screw tap, twist drill
Schraubenbolzen *m* (screw) bolt, propeller bolt **~ durch den eine Dämpfungswirkung erzielt wird** damping bolt **~ mit Vierkantkopf** square-head bolt
Schrauben-bolzenabschneider *m* bolt cutter **-brunnen** *m* screw aperture, screw trunk, wake grain, propeller race **-büchse** *f* box screw **-draht** *m* bolt wire **-drehbank** *f* screw-cutting lathe, automatic screw machine **-dreher** *m* screw driver **-drehmoment** *n* (propeller) torque (aviation) **-drehzahl** *f* number of propeller revolutions, airscrew speed, propeller speed
Schrauben-druck *m* propeller thrust **-druckfeder** *f* compression spring **-dübel** *m* screwed dowel **-ebene** *f* propeller plane (of rotation) **-eisen** *n* screw plate, screw steel, bolt stock
Schraubenfeder *f* spiral spring, helical spring, coil spring **-bein** *n* spring-loaded strut **-wickelmaschine** *f* spring winder
Schrauben-feld *n* screw field **-fläche** *f* helicoidal surface **-flaschenzug** *m* screw-geared pulley
Schraubenflügel *m* propeller blade **-weitenverhältnis** *n* propeller-width ratio
Schraubenförderer *m* spiral (screw) conveyer
schraubenförmig helical, twisted, spiral **-e Fläche** helicoid
Schraubenführung *f* guide screw
Schraubenführungs-ganghöhe *f* thread pitch **-holländer** *m* beater with screw motion **-kopf** *m* screw head, bolt head
Schrauben-fuß *m* earth screw, adjustable base, screw base **-futter** *n* screw chuck **-gang** *m* screw thread **-ganglenkung** *f* cam and lever steering mechanism **-gebläse** *n* screw-type compressor **-gesenk** *n* screwing die **-getriebe** *n* worm gear
Schrauben-gewinde *n* screw thread, thread (worm of a screw), fillet, worm **-gewindeschneideisen** *n* screw-threading die **-heber** *m* screw jack **-hülse** *f* screw **-kappe** *f* screw plug **-kern** *m* screw body **-klaue** *f* screw dog **-klemme** *f* screw clamp, clip, or anchor **-kluppe** *f* screw-stock **-kolbenprinzip** *n* worm piston principle
Schraubenkopf *m* screwhead, bolthead **Herstellung einer zylindrischen oder kegeligen Vertiefung für den ~** counterboring **versenkter ~** countersunk screw-head
Schraubenkopfschlitzfräser *m* screw-slotting cutter
Schraubenkraft *f* propeller thrust **-moment** *n* moment of propeller thrust
Schraubenkreis *m* porpeller disk **-belastung** *f* propeller-disk loading **-fläche** *f*, **-flächeninhalt** *m* propeller-disk area
Schrauben-kuppelung *f* screw coupling **-lehre** *f* standard, micrometer or screw gauge, caliper gauge **-leistung** *f* propeller performance, efficiency of air-screw **-lenkerventil** *n* spiral guide valve
Schraubenlinie *f* helix, spiral, screw line, double surface curvature **~ gleichbleibender Steigung** helix of constant lead
Schraubenlinienabtastung *f* helical scanning
Schraubenloch *n* screw hole **-kreis** *m* bolt-pitch circle, bolt-hole circle, bolt circle
Schrauben-lüfter *m* propeller blower **-material** *n* screw steel, bolt stock, screwstock **-mikrometer** *n* micrometer calipers, (screw-thread) micrometer **-mikroskop** *n* screw microscope **-muffe** *f* sleeve nut **-muffenverbindung** *f* screwed joint
Schraubenmutter *f* screwed nut, (bolt) nut **~ zum Festhalten** holding nut **eine ~ etwas lösen** to free a nut
Schraubenmutterschlüssel *m*, **verschiebbarer ~** wrench (adjustable)
Schrauben-nabe *f* propeller hub **-nachstrom** *m* slip stream, wake **-nippel** *m* screwed steel ferrule **-nut** *f* helical groove or slot, worm **-patrone** *f* guide screw **-pfahl** *m* screw pile **-pumpe** *f* axial pump, screw pump, rotary pump
Schrauben-quetschhahn *m* screw pinchcock **-rad** *n* spiral gear, helical gear, worm gear, worm wheel **-radgetriebe** *n* spiral gearing **-rahmen** *m* screw chase **-rohr** *n* spiral tube **-rührer** *m* propeller mixer **-schäkel** *m* cable shackle **-schaufler** *m* propeller pump **-schlepper** *m* screw tug **-schlittenwinde** *f* push-and-pull jack **-schloß** *n* sleeve nut
Schraubenschlitz *m* (screw) nick **-einrichtung** *f* screw-slotting attachment **-fräser** *m* screw-slotting cutter
Schraubenschlüssel *m* screw spanner, monkey wrench **~ mit Drehmomentanzeige** torque-indicating wrench **englischer ~** monkey wrench, coach wrench **verstellbarer ~** crescent wrench, monkey wrench
Schraubenschlüsselbrett *n* spanner board
Schrauben-schnecke *f* screw conveyer **-schneidbank** *f* screw-cutting lathe **-schneidemaschine** *f* bolt cutter, screw-cutting machine, screw cutter **-schub** *m* propeller thrust **-schubzahl** *f* thrust coefficient **-senker** *m* countersink **-sicherung** *f* nut lock, screw-locking device
Schraubenspann-platte *f* screw tieplate **-vorrichtung** *f* (Förderband) screw take-up
Schraubenspindel *f* lead screw, spindle, male screw **~ für die Höhenstellung des Tisches** elevating screw for table
Schraubenspindel-richtmaschine *f* jack-screw elevating mechanism **-steuerung** *f* screw-spindle steering gear
Schrauben-spundringeindreher *m* inserter **-stahl** *m* bolt stock **-stanze** *f* screw-punching press **-stehbolzen** *m* screw stay bolt **-steigung** *f* propeller pitch **-steigungsanzeiger** *m* propeller-pitch indicator **-steuerung** *f* screw(-reversing) gear **-steven** *m* propeller post **-stopeinrichtung** *f* screw slotting attachment
Schraubenstrahl *m* propeller wash, propeller slip stream **-ausgleich** *m* slip-stream equalization (aviation) **-geschwindigkeit** *f* slip speed
Schrauben-strebe *f* propeller strut **-strom** *m* slip stream **-stütze** *f* insulator bolt **-transporteur** *m* screw conveyer
Schrauben- und Steckschlüssel *m* screw-socket

wrench

Schrauben-verbindung *f* bolted joint, screw joint **-verschluß** *m* interrupted-screw-type breech block **-versetzung** *f* screw dislocation **-verstellung** *f* micrometer adjustment **-wälzfräser** *m* spiral gear hob **-welle** *f* propeller shaft **-winde** *f* stave holder, jack-screw (winch)

Schrauben-windung *f* turn (of a coil), screw thread **-winkel** *m* spiral angle **-wirkungsgrad** *m* propeller efficiency **-zahngetriebe** *n* helical gear, spiral gear, worm **-zahnrad** *n* helical gear **-zahnstange** *f* helical rack **-zange** *f* hand vise **-zieher** *m* screw driver

Schraubenzug *m* (propeller) thrust (aviat), set of pulleys **-feder** *f* spiral tension spring **-kraft** *f* propeller thrust **-moment** *n* moment of propeller thrust **-zahl** *f* thrust coefficient

Schraubenzwinge *f* screw clamp

Schraub-fassung *f* screw base, screwed lampholder or socket **-futter** *n* screw chuck **-gewinde** *n* screw thread **-haken** *m* hook screw **-hülse** *f* collet **-kern** *m* screw-type core **-kappe** *f* screw(ed) cap **-klemme** *f* screw terminal **-knecht** *m* screw clamp **-kupplung** *f* vise-coupling

Schraublehre *f* micrometer caliper, micrometer **~ ohne Bügel** micrometer head

Schraub-lehrenhalter *m* micrometer stand **-patrone** *f* screw (plug) cartridge **-pfahl** *m* screw post **-rad** *n* skew gear **-sockel** *m* screw base **-spindel** *f* screw spindle

Schraubstock *m* (bench) vise, box clamp **-backen** *m pl* vise jaw(s) **-klaue** *f* vise dog

Schraub-stollen *m* screw hook **-stöpsel** *m* screw(ed) plug **-stutzen** *m* threaded ferrule **-triebanlasser** *m* wormdrive starter

Schraub- und Abschraubdrehtisch *m* make-and-break rotary table

Schraubung *f* spiral axis, screw motion, screw rotation or displacement

Schraubungsachse *f*, **momentane ~** instantaneous (spiral) axis

Schraub-verbindung *f* bolted connection, screw connection, screwed pipe joint **-verschluß** *m* screw cap **-wirkung** *f* screw action, twisting **-zwinge** *f* (screw) clamp

schraubzwingenähnliche Einstellehre screw-clamp-shaped adjusting gauge

Schreckplatte *f* chill

Schrecktiefe *f*, **undefinierte ~** indefinite chilling depth

Schrei *m* lump, bloom, or cake (metal.)

Schreib-anzeige *f*, **-anzeiger** *m* printing indicator **-apparat** *m* writing mechanism **-barometer** *n* barograph **-block** *m* note pad (holder), writing pad **-breite** *f* calibrated width (of a chart)

Schreibe-einrichtung *f* recording device **-empfänger** *m* teletype, recording receiver, recorder

Schreibimpuls *m* write pulse

Schreibempfang *m* recorder reception

schreiben to write (up), record (graphically), register, type, delineate, trace, reproduce (an image or picture) store (info proc.) **formal ~** to write formally **ins Reine ~** to make a fair (final) copy

Schreiben *n* writing, letter

schreibend recording **-e Stimmgabel** tuning-fork chronoscope **-er Voltmesser** recording voltmeter **-er Schwingungsmesser** vibrograph

Schreiber *m* recorder, writer, scribe, clerk, recording pen, recording apparatus **-anschluß** *m* connection of a recorder **-ausgang** *m* output for the recorder **-einschub** *m* recorder unit **-vorschubgeschwindigkeit** *f* recorder's feed rate

Schreibewicklung *f* write winding

Schreibfeder *f* stylus, recording pen **-bandstahl** *m* band steel for pens

Schreib-feldamplitude *f* amplitude of the drive field **-fläche** *f* record sheet or surface, writing surface **-fleck** *m* recording spot **-funk** *m* broadcasting at dictation speed **-geschwindigkeit** tracing speed (oscilloscope) **-gestänge** *n* writing lever **-gerät** *n* recording instrument **-griffel** *m* style

Schreib-hebel *m* recording arm **-instrument** *n* graphic instrument recording instrument **-kopf** *m* recorder head **-lampe** *f* recording lamp **-leiste** *f* printing ledge **-leitung** *f* drive line **-locher** *m* typing perforator **-magnet** *m* magnetic marker **-maschine** *f* type-writer

Schreibmaschinen-band *n* typewriter ribbon **-schalldämpfer** *m* rubber buffers for typewriters **-schriftsetzmaschine** *f* many-copy typewriter **-tastatur** *n* typewriter keyboard **-walze** *f* platen, typewriter roller

Schreib-platte *f* tablet chart **-pult** *n* writing shelf, writing desk **-röhrchen** *n* pen or siphon (of a recorder) **-scheibe** *f* printing disk **-schlitten** *m* marker slide **-schrift** *f* script (type) **-setzmaschine** *f* linotype **-spirale** *f* printing worm **-spitze** *f* nib **-stange** *f* writing bar **-stelle** *f* printing position

Schreibsteuerungs-ausgang *m* print selection common exit **-eingangsbuchsen** *pl* print selection entry hubs

Schreibstift *m* (recording) stylus, style, pencil, cutting tool, engraving tool **-weg** *m* path of stylus

Schreibstrom *m* driving current **-messer** *m* recording ammeter **-stufe** *f* current driver

Schreib-tafel *f* writing tablet, writing slate, blackboard **-taktgeber** *m* writing timer **-thermometer** *n* thermograph, recording thermometer **-trommel** *f* recording drum

Schreib- und Papierwaren *pl* stationery

Schreib-unterlage *f* writing or blotting pad **-walze** *f* platen **-weise** *f* spelling, notation (comput) **-werk** *n* recording instrument, recording mechanism **-wicklungen** *pl* drive windings **-zeug** *n* recording mechanism, inkstand, writing materials **-zylinder** *m* recording cylinder

Schreien *n* crackling sound (of tin)

schreiende Farbe loud color

Schrein *m* press, cupboard

Schreiner *m* cabinetmaker, carpenter, joiner

Schreinerei *f* joiner's shop, joinery

Schrenz *m* scrap from sorting rags for rag-paper stock

Schrenzpapier *n* paper from Schrenz, Graupack

Schrenz- und Speltpappe chipboard

schricken to check, collide

Schrieb *m* trace made by a recording gauge

Schrift *f* writing, pamphlet, record, lettering, signals, handwriting **abgefallene ~** broken type **erhabene ~** raised letters **fließende ~** running hand **gemeine ~** lean type **geschwänzte**

~ tail type, long or descending letters **gotische** ~ block letters **richtige** ~ straight signals **umgekehrte** ~ reversed signals

Schrift-abzug *m* proof **-bild** *n* type character **-charakter** *m* type **-einblendung** *f* caption overlay **-einwalzmaschine** *f* letter rolling machine **-erz** *n* sylvanite **-fernübertragung** *f* telautography **-führer** *m* secretary

Schrift-grad *m* size of type **-granitisch** graphic (granite) **-gravieren** *n* letter engraving purpose **-guß** *m* type casting **-höhenmesser** *m* type-high gauge **-kasten** *m* type case **-kegel** *m* body, shank or depth of a letter **-leiter** *m* editor, copy writer **-leitung** *f* editing, editorial staff

Schrift-locher *m* puncher, perforator (telegr) **-malen** *n* (Lack) sign painting or writing **-metall** *n* type metal **-mutter** *f* matrix, type mold **-plattenprägemaschine** *f* reliefograph **-probe** *f* specimen book, specimen of printing type **-regal** *n* shelf for metal types **-satz** *m* matter, composition, memorial, brief **-setzer** *m* compositor

Schriftstärkenregulierung *f* (Typenhebel) impression control

Schrift-streifen *m* written or typed identification **-stück** *n* document, brief, papers

Schrifttum *n* bibliography, documentation, source material

Schrifttums-abriß *m* digest **-hinweis** *m*, **-nachweis** *m* reference to literature **-stelle** *f* (bibliographical) reference

Schrifttumverzeichnis *n* bibliographic list

Schrift-zettel *m* bill of a font, font of letter **-zeug** *n* type metal

schrill shrill

Schritt *m* pace, step, stride, pitch (of a winding), unit (of a selector), signal element (teleg) ~ **halten** (mit), to pace, keep step with **langer** ~ stride

Schritt-für-Schritt-Steuerung *f* stepping control

Schrittgeschwindigkeit *f* telegraph (transmission) speed

schritthaltend-e Programmberichtigung real-time control **-er Rechenvorgang** on-line calculator operation

Schritthalter, elektr. step-by-step switch

Schritthaltesystem mit Umrechnung director system

Schritt-länge *f* unit duration of signal, step length **-macher** *m* pacemaker, pace setter **-maß** *n* rhythm **-messer** *m* pedometer **-motor** *m* stepping motor **-regelung** *f* step control **-schaltelektromagnet** *m* stepping electromagnet **-schalter** *m* step-by-step switch **-schaltersystem** step-by-step system

Schrittschalt-rad *n* step wheel **-relais** *n* stepping relay **-selbstanschlußsystem** *n* step-by-step automatic telephone system **-stellung** *f* letter space position **-telegraph** *m* step-by-step telegraph **-wähler** *m* step-by-step selector **-werk** *n* step-by-step switch, stepping mechanism

Schritt-umsetzer *m* code converter (teleg) **-verkürzte Wicklung** short-pitch winding **-verlängerung** *f* pulse length extension **-verkürzung** *f* pulse-length reduction (teleg) **-wahl** *f* step-by-step selection **-wählersystem** *n* step-by-step selector system

schrittweise gradual **-e Näherung** mesh method

Schritt-weite *f* step width, interval (between spectral lines), step size **-wirkung** *f* step action **-zähler** *m* pedometer **-zeit** *f* step-time

Schröckingerit *m* schroeckingerite

Schröpfkopf *m* cupping glass

Schroppeisen *n* strong-jack grooving iron

schroppen to jack, plane off, rough-plane

Schropp-hobel *m* jack plane **-maschine** *f* roughing machine **-messer** *m* roughing tool **-stahl** *m* roughing tool

Schrot *m* piece, scrap, waste, scrap iron, buckshot, grit, coarse-ground corn **-anteil** *m* noise component (TV) **-axt** *f* wood-cleaver's ax **-bohren** *n* adamantine or shot drilling **-bohrer** *m* pump bit **-effekt** *m* shot effect, Schottky effect, fluctuation noise, shot noise **-eisen** *n* great chisel

schroten to bruise, chip, chisel, grind or crush coarsely, granulate, rough-grind

Schroten *n* granulation

Schroter *m* crusher

Schroterei *f* (malt-)crushing room

Schrot-feile *f* trimming file **-gewehr** *n* shotgun **-hammer** *m* cold set **-kugeln** *pl* shot **-lauf** *m* smooth-bore barrel

Schrötling *m* blank, coin plate, plank

Schrot-mehl *n* coarse meal **-meißel** *m* (scrap) chisel, scraper **-metall** *n* shot metal **-mühle** *f* bruising mill, feed grinder **-rauschen** *n* shot effect of radio **-säge** *f* crosscut saw **-schere** *f* scrap shears **-stärke** *f* grain or shot gauge

Schrott *m* scrap iron, scrap metal, cut, piece, scrap, waste, buckshot, grit, coarsely ground corn **handlich zerkleinerter** ~ shoveling scrap

Schrott-berg *m* pile of scrap **-blech** *n* waster (in tinplate manufacture) **-bühne** *f* scrapping floor **-chargierkran** *m* scrap charging crane **-entfall** *m* percentage of scrap obtained, waste material, scrap, manufacturing loss **-fabrik** *f* shot factory **-förderer** *m* crop conveyer **-geben** *n* scrapping **-geräusch** *n* shot noise **-händler** *m* scrap dealer **-haufen** *m* scrap pile

Schrottlager *n* scrap yard **-kran** *m* scrap-yard crane **-platz** *m* scrap-stock yard

Schrott-magnetkran *m* scrap-handling magnet crane **-markt** *m* scrap market **-martinieren** *n* pig-and-scrap method **-paketierpresse** *f* scrap-briquetting press **-platz** *m* scrap yard **-schautisch** *m* reject counter **-schere** *f* scrap-shearing machine, scrap cutter **-schmelze** *f* scrap melting **-stück** *n* waster (in casting) **-verfahren** *n* pig-and-scrap method **-verhüttung** *f* scrap smelting **-wert** *m* scrap value **-zugabe** *f* scrapping, addition of scrap

Schrotwaage *f* plumb rule

Schrubbelmaschine *f* breaker or scribbler card

schrubbeln to scribble

schrubben to scrub, scour, roughen, rough-plane

Schrubbfeile *f* coarse or rough file

Schrumpf-ausgleich *m* shrinkage compensation **-band** *n* shrunk-on hoop **-effekt** *m* shrinkage

schrumpfen to shrink, contract, shrivel

Schrumpf-gewinde *n* shrinking thread **-grenze** *f* shrinkage limit **-lack** *m* wrinkle or crinkle finish **-maß** *n* amount of shrinkage or contraction, shrinkage or contraction measure **-ring** *m* shrunk(-on) ring **-riß** *m* shrinkage crack, cooling crack, contraction crack **-sitz** *m* shrink fit **-sitzpassung** *f* press fit **-spannung** *f* contraction or shrinkage strain or tension, solid-shrinkage strain, shrinkage stress **-übermaß** *n* contraction allowance

Schrumpfung *f* contraction, shrinkage, solid or contraction shrinkage, shrinking

Schrumpfungs-ausgleich *m* shrinkage equalization, shrinkage compensation **-riß** *m* contraction strain

Schrumpf-verbindung *f* slip-joint **-verformung** *f* shrinkage distortion **-versuch** *m* shrinkage test **-wulst** *f* shrunk-on rim

Schrupp-abwälzfräser *m* roughing hob **-arbeit** *f* roughing work **-drehbank** *f* roughing lathe

schruppen to scrub, scour, roughen, rough

Schruppen *n* roughing, scrubbing, scouring

Schrupp-feile *f* rough file **-fläche** *f* rough finish **-fräsen** *n* rough milling **-fräser** *m* roughing cutter, stocking cutter **-hobel** *m* round-nosed plane, jack plane **-hobeleisen** *pl* jack plane cutters **-hobeln** *n* jack planing

Schrupp-maschine, für Röhren tube roughing machine **-meißel** *m* roughing steel, tool for rough turning **-oberfläche** *f* roughing surface **-reibahle** *f* roughing reamer **-schliff** *m* roughing **-schnitt** *m* roughing cut

Schruppstahl *m* roughing tool, rough-cutting tool **~ mit Halbmondspitze** bullnose tool **linker ~ mit Rhomboidspitze** left-hand diamond-point tool **~ mit Rundschneide** bullnose tool

Schub *m* thrust, push, shear, throw, shove, shift **fester ~** fixed thrust **~ im Reiseflug** *m* (Astron.) cruise thrust **versetzter ~** offset thrust

Schub-abschaltung *f* cutoff signal (missiles) **-arm** *m* shearing arm **-ankeranlasser** *m* sliding-armature starter **-aufgabevorrichtung** *f* push feeder **-beanspruchung** *f* tangential stress **-beendigung** *f* thrust termination **-beiwert** *m* thrust coefficient **-belastungsgrad** *m* thrust coefficient **-beschleunigung** *f* thrust acceleration **-bewegung** *f* drift, thrust motion **-bewehrung** *f* shear (diagonal tension) reinforcement **-changierung** *f* sliding traverse motion

Schub-drosselung *f* thrust throttling **-düse** *f* propelling, thrust, or exhaust nozzle, discharge nozzle (jet)

Schubdüsen-einsatz *m* cambered insert **-körper** *m* nozzle cone **-nadel** *f* bullet, thrust needle (jet) **-verstellpumpe** *f* nozzle pump **-verstellung** *f* variable-jet nozzle control

Schub-elastizitätsmodul *m* modulus of shearing, (shearing) modulus of elasticity **-erhöhung im Fluge** thrust augmentation (in flight) **-festigkeit** *f* critical shear stress, shear(ing) strength **-fläche** *f* slip pan **-förderrinne** *f* pushing trough **-formänderungskurve** *f* stress-strain or shear-stress deformation curve **-gebiet** *n* shear zone **-gerüst** *n* thrust frame

Schubgetriebe *n* sliding gear **~ des ersten Ganges** first-speed sliding gear

Schub-gewicht *n* (Kg/Kp) power/weight ratio (lb/lb) **-gewinn** *m* increase in thrust **-karre** *f*, **-karren** *m* wheelbarrow **-kasten** *m* drawer, chest of drawers **-kegel** *m* (Astron.) exhaust cone (power plant) **-klasse** *f* thrust class **-kolben** *m* thrust piston **-konus** *m* thrust cone

Schub-kraft *f* pushing or shearing force, shearing or tangential stress **-kraftverstärker** *m* thrust augmenter **-kugel** *f* universal joint **-kurbel** *f* crank of breech mechanism **-kurbelverschluß** *m* semiautomatic type sliding-wedge breech mechanism **-kurve** *f* sliding curve

Schublade *f* drawer

Schubladen-fach *n* drawer section **-lösung** *f* (slang) shelving a problem **-rost** *m* drawer grid

Schub-lager *n* thrust bearing **-laschen** *pl* push plates **-lehre** *f* caliper scale, slide-rule caliper, slide gauge, vernier caliper, sliding caliper or gauge

Schubleistung *f* thrust, thrust performance **~ der Luftschraube** (propeller) thrust power **~ des Schraubenstrahls** propeller thrust line

Schub-linien *pl* shearing stress lines **-meßgerät** *n* thrust recorder **-meßwaage** *f* thrust-measuring stand

Schubmodul *m* modulus of shear, modulus of elasticity for or in shear, shearing modulus of elasticity, modulus of rigidity **~ für Verdrehung** modulus of torsional shear

Schub-räderschaltgetriebe *n* sliding shift gear **-radwechselgetriebe** *n* sliding-pinion system

Schubregelung durch Abblasventile vent valve thrust control (rocket) **~ durch nicht brennbare Gase** inert gas bleed control (rocket) **~ durch Schallwellen** sonic thrust level control (rocket)

Schub-relaxationszeit *f* shear relaxation time **-richtung** *f* direction of thrust **-riegel** *m* sliding (locking) bolt, slip or sash bolt **-riegelspannung** *f* sliding or shearing stress **-rohr** *n* push rod, torque tube **-rohrtemperatur** *f* jet pipe temperature **-rost** *m* thrust grating **-rückgang** *m* decrease of thrust **-rückgewinn** *m* thrust gain

Schub-schalter *m* tumble switch **-schraubtreibanlasser** *m* screw-push starter **-schwingungsart** *f* shear mode of vibration **-sicher** secure from shear or sliding **-spannung** *f* shear(ing) strain or stress, tangential stress, torsional shearing stress, shear(ing) strength

Schub-spannungs-geschwindigkeit *f* friction velocity **-größe** *f* intensity of shearing stress **-kegel** *m* cone of shearing stress **-tensor** *m* stress tensor **-zustand** *m* shearing stress

Schubspitze *f* thrust peak

Schubstange *f* connecting rod, torque rod, driving rod, suspension link, push(er) rod, thrust rod **~ für die Schaltzahnstange** connection to feed rack **einfache ~** plain connecting rod

Schubstangen-ausschlag *m* angle of connecting rod **-bewegung** *f* connecting-rod motion **-kopf** *m* connecting-rod head **-schaft** *m* shank of connecting rod

Schub-stärke *f* thrust strength **-steif** shear resistant **-steife** *f* modulus of shear, modulus of elasticity for or in shear, shearing modulus of elasticity **-stellung** *f* propulsion position **-taste** *f* push key **-trenner** *m* sliding-blade isolating switch **-trennschalter** *m* thrust blade switch **-trieb** *m* sliding gear **-typflugzeug** *n* pusher(-type) airplane

Schub-übertragung *f* transmission of tractive force **-umkehr** *f* thrust brake, thrust reversal **-umkehrvorrichtung** *f* thrust reverser

Schub- und Leistungsprüfung *f* (Motor) calibration test

Schub-vektor *m* thrust vector (astronaut) **-neigung** *f* lift vector **-ventil** *n* slide valve **-verformung** *f* shearing deformation **-vergrößerer** *m* thrust augmenter **-verlauf** *m* thrust curve **-verlust** *m* thrust loss **-vermehrer** *m* thrust augmenter **-verstärker** *m* thrust augmenter **-versuch** *m* shear test, shearing test **-viskosität** *f* shear viscosity (acoust.)

Schub-weg *m* sliding travel **-weise** by thrusts, gradually **-welle** *f* sliding shaft, shear wave **-wert** *m* thrust value **-wicklung** *f* coupling winding **-widerstand** *m* shearing strength, resistance to shear **-winkel** *m* sliding or turning square **-zahl** *f* shear coefficient, extension per unit length, linear strain **-zentrifuge** *f* pusher centrifuge **-zylinder** *m* free cylinder

Schuh *m* shoe, boot, skid, jaw **mit einem ~ versehen** to shoe **~e** *pl* (eines Schmelzeinsatzes) fittings

Schuh-bremse *f* spoon brake **-bürste** *f* shoe brush

Schuhmacher *m* shoemaker **-wachs** *n* cobbler's wax

Schuh-maisdrill *m* runner planter **-winkellasche** *f* shoe-shaped angular fishplate

Schuko (= Schutzkontakt) provided with non-fused earthing contact **-buchse** *m* earthing contact type socket **-kupplung** *f* Schuko-type (safety) coupling piece **-steckdose** *f* socket with earth contact (Schuko) **-stecker** *m* earthing contact-type plug

Schul-bank *f* school bench or form **-bedarf** *m* school requisites **-betrieb** *m* training

Schuld *f* guilt, blame, fault, debt, cause **eine ~ ablösen** to discharge a debt

Schuld-brief *m* promissory note, note of hand **-tilgungsfond** *m* sinking fund

schulden to owe, be indebted to **-masse** *f* liabilities

schuldig guilty, culpable, indebted, due **-erklärung** *f* verdict of guilty, conviction

schuldlos guiltless

Schuldner *m* debtor

Schuldschein *m* promissory note, note of hand, bond, debenture

Schule *f* school, school of thought **~ für höhere Studien** postgraduate school

schulen to train

Schüler *m* pupil, student

Schulflugzeug *n* (primary) training plane **~ für Anfänger** primary trainer, primary training plane **~ für Fortgeschrittene** advanced trainer

Schul-gleiter *m* (elementary) training glider **-kreide** *f* blackboard chalk (sticks)

Schülpe *f* barnacle, shell

schülpen to scab, peel away

Schul-reißzeug *n* (school) set of drawing instruments **-schiff** *n* training ship, training vessel **-steuerung** *f* control for training purposes

Schulter *f* shoulder **-decker** *m* (semi) high-wing monoplane, mid-wing monoplane **-gurt** *m*, **-klappe** *f* shoulder strap **-kugellager** *n* detachable ball journal bearing

Schulternauflauf *m* shoulders

Schulter-pegel *m* pedestal level **-punkt** *m* shoulder point **-riemen** *m* crossbelt, shoulder belt **-rollenlager** *n* roller bearing with shoulders **-scheibe** *f* collar **-schraube** *f* shoulder screw **-stück** *n* epaulet, shoulder patch or piece **-stutze** *f* stock **-wehr** *f* epaulement, breastwork, traverse

Schul- und Übungsflugzeug *n* school and training plane

Schulung *f* training

Schulungsflug *m* instruction flight

Schummelloch *n* rabbling hole, working door (of a puddling furnace)

schummeln to rabble, clear, cheat

Schummeln *n* clearing, rabbling, cheating

Schummerung *f* hatching (of maps), hachures

Schund *m* trash, waste, refuse, garbage

Schuppe *f* scale, flake

Schüppe *f* shovel, scoop

schuppen to scale off, shed

Schuppen *m* shed, hangar, garage, warehouse, shelter, shak **-bildung** *f* flaking

schuppenförmig flake-shaped **-er Bogentransport** sheet-by-sheet feeder

Schuppen-glätte *f* flake litharge **-graphit** *m* flaky graphite **-kette** *f* scale chain **-paraffin** *n* scale wax

schuppig flaky, flaked, scaly

Schuppenwanderrost *m* scaled travelling grate

Schur *f* shearing, cropping

Schürbel *m* bloom, slab

Schüreisen *n* poker, fire iron

schüren to stir (up), stoke, poke, rake, rabble

Schurf *m* digging, opening, searching, trial pit

Schürf-arbeit *f* prospecting work **-befugnis** *f* authority to prospect **-betrieb** *m* prospecting operations **-bohrmaschine** *f* prospect drilling machine

Schürfbohrung *f* sampling, prospect drilling, wildcat (petroleum)

schürfen to scratch, scrape, prospect, dig, excavate, explore, search **auf gemeinschaftliche Rechnung ~** to prospect on common account

Schürfen *n* exploration, surveying, search, prospecting

Schürfer *m* prospector, searcher

Schürf-fläche *f* thrust plane **-graben** *m* trench made for discovering mineral beds **-grube** *f* test pit **-kette** *f* drag chain **-kübelbagger** *m* dragline **-loch** *n* test pit, prospect hole **-recht** *n* right of prospecting **-schacht** *m* test shaft, exploration shaft **-tätigkeit** *f* exploration

Schürfung *f* scrape, trench, prospecting, exploration, scouting

Schürfwagen *m* scraper

Schür-gerät *n* furnace tool **-haken** *m* poker, poking bar, fire hook **-loch** *n* poke hole, poking door, stoke hole,, stoker door, stirring hole **-maschine** *f* mechanical stoker **-platte** *f* dead plate (of a grate)

Schurre *f* chute, runway, jet deflector (missiles)

Schurren-ringscheider *m* chute ring separator **-verstopfung** *f* blocking of chutes

Schurz *m* apron, blanket, skirt, chimney hood or mantel

Schürze *f* apron, anchor guard plate

Schürzeug *n* poker, furnace tools

Schurzwerk *n* assemblage or joining with key piece

Schuß *m* shot, woof (in cloth), report, blast, round **~ pro Minute** rounds per minute **~ aus dem Vollen** shot from the solid (blasting) **~** (Tuch), filling (fabric), a throw of the shuttle and the thread thus shot, woof

and the thread thus shot, woof **in ~ sein** to be in running condition or ready **blinder ~** blank firing **direkter ~** aimed shot, direct fire **vereinzelte Schüsse** scattered shots

Schuß-anlage *f* disposition of weft **-bremse** *f* recoil brake **-bühne** *f* shield, platform

Schüssel *f* dish, pan, tray **-antenne** *f* dish antenna

schüsselförmig dish-shaped

Schüsser *m* stamp, tamper

Schuß-faden *m* weft, shoot, warp thread **-garn** *n* weft, woof, filling **-gatter** *m* floodgate **-gerinne** *n* straight channel, channel with a strong current **-gewicht** *n* weight of shot (casting) **-gewichtsschwankung** *f* shot-to-shot variation

Schuß-linie *f* line of sight, line of aim, line of future position, line of departure **-loch** *n* shot-hole **-niete** *f* pop rivet **-riegel** *m* putlog **-rohrerhöhung** *f* quadrant elevation **-schweißung** *f* shot welding **-schiene** *f* inlay shooting bar

schußsicher shellproof, bulletproof **-es Glas** bulletproof glass

Schuß-spule *f* (weaving) spool, weft bobbin **-wächter** *m* warp protector **-zahl** *f* number of rounds, number of picks **-zähler** *m* weft counter, rounds counter **-zünderstellung** *f* fuse setting

Schutensauger *m* pumping plant

Schutt *m* refuse, waste, sweepings, rubbish **-abladeplatz** *m* (rubbish) dump site

Schüttbeton *m* heaped concrete

Schütt-damm *m* earth bank, embankment **-dichte** *f* bulk density

Schütte *f* chute, conduit, frame for incendiary bombs

Schüttel-amplitude *f* vibration amplitude **-apparat** *m* shaker, shaking apparatus **-aufgabevorrichtung** *f* shaking feeder **-einrichtung** *f* agitator **-elektrode** *f* shaking electrode **-fest** shakeproof **-festigkeit** *f* vibrating strength **-festigkeitsversuch** *m* static-vibration test **-flasche** *f* emulsion test flask **-herd** *m* oscillating table, bumping table, shaking table

Schüttel-klappe *f* chute trap **-maschine** *f* mashing machine, shaking machine **-mikrophon** *n* granule microphone

schütteln to shake, agitate, vibrate, joggle, churn, toss

Schütteln *n* shaking, balancing, vatman's shake **~ vor dem Abreißen** (d. Strömung) pre-stall buffeting **~ eines Luftfahrzeuges** buffeting

Schüttel-prüfung *f* vibration test **-rätter** *m* jig table **-resonanz** *f* vibration resonance **-rinne** *f* shaking gutter, shaking trough, reciprocating trough, distributing chute, shaker conveyer trough **-rost** *m* shaking grate, shaking grizzly **-rutsche** *f* shaking shoot **-rutschenofen** *m* shuffle-pan furnace **-sicher** shakeproof

Schüttelsieb *n* chip screen, shaking sieve or screen, vibrating screen, shaker screen, shaking sifter, shaker, sifter, riddle, riddler **~ mit Druckluftantrieb** pneumatic riddle sifter, pneumatic riddler

Schüttelsiebmaschine *f* power riddler, power riddle sifter **~ mit Rücklaufrinne** riddle sifter with return chute

Schüttel-sortierer *m* oscillating strainer, chip screen **-spannung** *f* vibratory voltage (tension) **-speiseapparat** *m* oscillating feeding apparatus **-speiser** *m* shaking feeder **-tisch** *m* vibrating table **-trichter** *m* shaking funnel, separatory funnel **-verfahren** *n* vibration method **-versuch** *m* rattler test **-vorrichtung** *f* mashing machine, shaking device, shaking gear

Schüttel-wagen *m* shuttle carriage **-werk** *n* shaking mechanism **-wirkung** *f* shaking effect **-zuführer** *m* vibratory feeder

schütten to heap up, throw up, distribute, charge, pour (out)

Schütten *n* distributing, charging

Schüttergebiet *n* region of disturbance

Schütt-feuerung *f* self-feeding furnace with hopper above grate **-fläche** *f* charging area **-gewicht** *n* bulk weight, apparent density or bulk density **-gleichrichter** *m* vibrator rectifier **-gut** *n* loose material, bulk material or goods

Schutt-halde *f* rubble-slope, talus, accumulation of talus **-haufen** *m* dump

Schütt-höhe *f* height of layer, height of bed **-kanal** *m* charging chute **-kasten** *m* box frame or cannister, cluster box for dropping bombs

Schuttkegel *m* debris cone, alluvial cone, talus fan

Schüttklappe *f* chute trap

Schuttkriechen *n* creep

Schütt-lage *f* filling course (layer) **-last** *f* load **-ofen** *m* tile furnace, shelf furnace **-rinne** *f* chute **-rohr** *n* discharge pipe **-röstofen** *m* continuous roasting furnace **-rumpf** *m* feed bin, loading hopper, receiving hopper

Schüttstein *m* rubble **-unterlage** *f* rubble bed

Schuttstrom *m* avalanche of sand and stones

Schütttrichter *m* discharge hopper or funnel

Schütt- und Absackwaage *f* balance with sack filler and lifter

Schüttung *f* fill, embankment, ballast(ing)

Schütt-volumen *n* bulk factor **-vorrichtung** *f* stock-distributing gear, top-charging gear, charging apparatus **-winkel** *m* angle of repose, angle of friction

Schutz *m* protection, cover, defense, safeguard, shelter, isolation, insulation, screen, shield, guard **~ gegen Phasenausfall** phase-failure protection **~ gegen Phasenumkehr** phase-reversal protection **~ gegen Unterläufigkeit** cutoff walls **~ gegen Unterspülung** cutoff walls, cutoffs **verzögerter ~** time-limit protection

Schütz *n* (s. a. Schütze *f*) relay, contactor, magnetic switch **elektromagnetisches ~** magnetic contactor **~ mit Arbeitskontakten** normally-open contactor **~ mit Relais** magnetic full-voltage starter **polarisiertes ~** polarized relay

Schutz-abdeckung *f* protecting or protective cover **-anstrich** *m* anticorrosion composition antifouling paint, preservative coat, protective coating **-anwendung** *f* protective use

Schutzanzug *m* protecting clothes, protective uniform (for paratroopers), protective suit

Schutz-auflage *f* resist **-bedeckung** *f* shielding **-behandlung** *f* preservative treatment **-beizendruck** *m* resist style **-bekleidung** *f* shielding, protective clothing **-beschlag** *m* protective fitting **-blatt** *n* flyleaf **-blech** *n* guard, protecting sheet, guard plate, fender, mudguard **-blechstreben** *pl* mudguard struts **-bleiglas** *n* protective lead-glass **-block** *m* apron block **-blockstrecke**

f stopped section

Schutz-bogen *m* (äußere Lagen) cording quires (paper mfg.) **-brett** *n* baffle board **-brille** *f* protective glasses, safety goggles **-bügel** *m* bow-wing skid **-dach** *n* shelter, shed, penthouse **-decke** *f* covering, cover **-deckel** *m* guard, cover, dust cap

Schutzdraht *m* armoring wire, sheathing wire, guard wire, cattle guard **geerdeter** ~ grounded guard wire

Schutz-drossel *f* protective choke (coil), choke coil **-elektrode** *f* guard electrode

Schütze *f* (auch Schütz *m*) (Schleuse) flood gate, sluice gate, or board, dam, valve, penstock

Schützen *m* (Weberei) shuttle

schützen to protect, guard, secure, defend, shelter, shield

schützend protective, preservative, prohibitory

Schützen-nest *n* shuttle net (textiles) **-öffnung** *f* sluice, orifice

Schützenschlag *m* shot, pick (textiles) **-kraft** *f* picker-stick blow (textiles) **-vorrichtung** *f* picker-stick mechanism (textiles)

Schützen-schleuse *f* sash or sliding sluice, sash lock **-spindel** *f* shuttle peg, tongue, or spindle **-steuerung** *f* contactor equipment **-treiber** *m* shuttle driver

Schützentriegelung *f* contactor release

Schützen-umkehrsteuerung *f* magnetic reversing type controller **-wechsel** *m* shuttle change, box motion **-wehr** *n* sluice dam or weir

Schutzende *f* non-fused earth (contact)

Schutzerdung *f* protector ground, non-fused earthing

Schutzerdungs-gestell *n*, **-gitter** *n* barrier guard **-haube** *f*, **-kappe** *f* protecting (grounded) cap **-kasten** *m* (protecting) cover **-leiste** *f* grounded guard strip **-maßnahme** *f* protective grounding means **-mittel** *n* preservative

Schutzerdungsnetz *n* protecting grounding network, guard net **geerdetes** ~ earthed cradling

Schutzerdungs-platte *f* guard plate **-ring** *m* grounded guard ring **-spirale** *f* protecting wire helix **-vorrichtung** *f* protective grounding device, guarding, safety device **-widerstand** *m* protective grounding resistance

Schützfalle *f* sash gate, sliding valve

Schutz-farbe *f* protective paint **-färbung** *f* camouflage **-fassung** *f* protection mounts **-feder** *f* protective spring **-fett** *n* protecting grease **-film** *m* protective film **-flüssigkeit** *f* sealing liquid **-frequenz** *f* guard frequency **-frist** *f* term of copyright **-funkenstrecke** *f* safety (collecting) gap, spill gap **-funkstrecke** *f* protective spark gap

Schutz-gas *n* protective gas, buffer gas **-gasschweißung** *f* shielded arc welding **-gatter** *n* floodgate, sluice **-gaze** *f* protective gauze **-gebiet** *n* protectorate, reservation **-geländer** *n* guard rail, parapet **-gerät** *n* defensive equipment **-gerüst** *n* (Bau) protective hoarding **-gestell** *n* barrier guard

Schutzgitter *n* anode-screening grid, guard grille, screen grid, barrier grid, shield **-endröhre** *f* output pentode **-fanggitterröhre** *f* pentode, five-electrode tube **-röhre** *f* screened grid valve, output pentode

Schutzglas *n* glass shield, protective glass ~ **für Zifferblatt** dial glass

Schutz-glocke *f* protective globe

Schutz-gürtel *m* critical zone **-hafen** *m* harbor of refuge or shelter **-haube** *f* cover, helmet, crank guard, cockpit cover **-helm** *m* protective helmet, skull guard **-horn** *n* protective horn **-hülle** *f* sheath, casing, protective covering, tarpaulin **-hülse** *f* protection sleeve **-insel** *f* safety or traffic island (zone)

Schützkammer *f* sluice chamber

Schutz-kappe *f* air-vent protector, cap, vent protector, protecting cap or cover, grommet **-kleidung** *f* protecting clothes **-kontaktdose** *f* safety plug socket **-korb** *m* bonnet, hood (to protect valve), basket shield, stone guard (for lamps), arcing ring, guard ring (of insulator) **-krümmer** *m* suppressor elbow

Schutzladen, eiserner ~ iron shutter

Schutz-leiste *f* protection strip **-leiter** *m* protective conductor **-mantel** *m* protective shell or cover, protective casing, sheathing, cover, protective coat

Schutzmarke *f* trade-mark **eingetragene** ~ registered trade-mark

Schutz-maske *f* protective mask **-masse** *f* resist **-maßnahme** *f* preventive measure, protective measure **-mauer** *f* screen wall, shelter wall **-mittel** *n* protective agent, preservative (agent) **-muffe** *f* pipe-thread protector, protector sleeve, protective sleeve, (elastic) grommet **-mütze** *f* protective cap **-netz** *n* cradle guard, guard wires, anode-screening grid **-netzröhre** *f* suppressor grid tube

Schütznische *f* shaft or valve well

Schützöffnung *f* valve opening

Schutz-öse *f* guard ear **-papp** *m* resist paste, reserve **-pfahl** *m* fender pile **-platte** *f* guard plate, apron **-polsterung** *f* crash padding **-präparat** *n* preservative **-rand** *m* protecting edge

Schutzraum *m* shelter **unterirdischer** ~ underground shelter

Schutzraumbau *m* (air-raid) shelter construction

Schutz-rechte *pl* patent rights, trade-mark rights **-ring** *m* guard ring

Schutzrohr *n* protective pipe, shield tube **äußeres** ~ secondary or outside protection tube

Schutz-schalter *m* protective circuit breaker, protected switchgear **-schaltung** *f* protective circuit **-scheibe** *f* glass shield, windshield **-scheibenwischer** *m* windshield cleaner, window wiper **-schicht** *f* protective layer, cover, or coat, safety film **-schiene** *f* guardrail

Schutzschild *n* protective shield, dirt shield, gunshield ~ **für wendbare Egge** dirt fender for reversible harrow

Schutzschirm *m* protective screen ~ **für den Kopfübersturz** protective screen for overturn structure

Schutz-schleuse *f* safety lock or single pair of lock gates, guard gate **-schwelle** *f* guard sleeper **-skala** *f* (Feuerschutz) scale of protection **-sieb** *n* mechanical filter, protecting screen **-spindel** *f* support bar **-stange** *f* guard bar **-stecker** *m* safety plug **-stelle** *f* security digit **-strecke** *f* overlap, fully protected section **-streifen** *m* chafing patch **-system** *n* protective system

Schütztafel *f* (actual) valve blade, shutter **aufge-**

richtete ~ raised wicket **niedergelegte ~** lowered or housed wicket
Schütztafelrahmen *m* working frame
Schutz-teil *m* safety device **-transformator** *m* isolating transformer **-trichter** *m* protecting funnel **-tülle** *f* guard socket
Schutzüberzug *m* protective coating, protective covering, protective film, preservative coating
Schutz-umfang *m* circumference of protection **-umkleidung** *f* protective coating or housing **-ummantelung** *f* protective casing, sheathing **-verfahren** *n* protective process **-verkleidung** *f* protective covering
Schützverriegelung *f* contactor interlocking
Schutz-vorrichtung *f* safety device, guard **-wald** *m* shelter wood
Schutzwand *f* protective screen **~ gegen Überschläge** antiarcing screen
Schutz-walze *f* safety roller **-wartung** *f* preventive maintenance **-weiche** *f* safety switch **-werk** *n* work of defense or of protection **-widerstand** *m* protective or safety resistor **-winkel** *m* curb **-wirkung** *f* amplification factor, amplification constant, mu factor, protective effect or action
Schutz-zaun *m* protective fence **-zelle** *f* lightning arrester **-zinke** *f* guard tooth **-zoll** *m* protective tariff **-zwischenraum** *m* protective gap
Schwabbel *m* mop, swab **-arbeit** *f* buffing work **-maschine** *f* buffing machine, buffing lathe
schwabbeln to buff
Schwabbeln *n* buffing
Schwabbel-platte *f* spray arrester **-polieren** *n* cloth wheel polishing **-rad** *n* polishing wheel **-scheibe** *f* buffing wheel, buff
Schwabber *m* swab, mop
schwabbern to swab, dry with a mop
Schwabberstiel *m* swab handle
schwach weak, faint, feeble, infirm, fine- or small-gauge (wire), slightly (cohesive), low-powered, light (wind) **~ belastete Reaktoren** low-power reactors **~ drähtig** of small-gauge or light-gauge wire **~ geglättet** low machine- (or mill-)finished (paper mfg.) **~ beheizte Röhre** dull (emitting) valve **~ ausgesteuerter Tonstreifen** low-modulation track **-er Glanz** dull (weak) luster **-e Kurve** gentle turn **-er Strom** weak current **-er Verkehr** slack traffic
Schwäche *f* faintness, weakness, slackness **organische ~** structural failure
schwächen to weaken, attenuate, diminish, chamfer, impair, dilute, dim, absorb (light), mute (sound)
schwacherhitzt gently heated
Schwächerwerden der Radiosignale fading of radio signals
Schwachfederdiagramm *n* weak-spring diagram
Schwachgas *n* poor gas, lean gas, weak gas, blast-furnace gas
Schwachheit *f* weakness
Schwach-last *f* low load **-legiert** low-alloyed
schwächlich weak, feeble, sickly
schwach-mattiert satinfrosted **-sichtig** amblyopic
Schwachsichtigkeit *f* amblyopia
Schwachstellenprüfung *f* design testing for weakest points
Schwachstrom *m* low-voltage current, weak current **-kabel** *n* cable for communication circuits **-leitung** *f* signaling circuit **-technik** *f* light-current engineering
Schwächung *f* weakening, attenuation
Schwächungs-anker *m* adjusting slide **-faktor** *m* shot-noise reduction factor (electr. tube) **-filter** *n* attenuation device **-gesetz** *n* extinction law **-glied** *n* attenuator **-koeffizient** *m* attenuation coefficient **-nebenschluß** *m* attenuation shunt **-periode** *f* fading period **-vorrichtung** *f* dimmer, weakening device or apparatus **-widerstand** *m* gain controller or regulator, potentiometer
Schwaden *m* cloud of gas or smoke produced by gunfire, blasts, or explosions **-abzug** *m* suffocating-vapor discharge **-ausbreitung** *f* expansion of clouds of gas or smoke **-blase** *f* gas globe produced by underwater explosion **-blech** *n* swathe board **-geschwindigkeit** *f* vapor velocity **-heuauflader** *m* window hay loader **-kondensator** *m* vapor vent condenser **-kugel** *f* sphere of combustion gas
Schwadenrechen *m* side-delivery hay rake **kombinierter ~ und Wender** side rake and tedder
Schwadenzusammensetzung *f* composition of the gases and smoke resulting from an explosion
Schwadstellung *f* swath level position
Schwal *m* sinter slag, shingling slag, rich finery cinder **-arbeit** *f* single refining, slag washing (process)
schwalben to dovetail
Schwalben-führung *f* dovetail guide **-nestbildung** *f* honeycombing, honeycomb formation **-nester** *n pl* honeycomb clinker, honeycombs
Schwalbenschwanz *m* dovetail **-förmig** dovetailed **-fräser** *m* dovetail cutter **-keil** *m* dovetail key **-nute** *f* dovetailed groove **-verbindung** *f* dovetail joint **-verzapfung** *f* dovetailing
Schwalboden *m* slag bed or bottom
Schwall *m* swell, flood (surge), backwater surge **-blech** *n* baffle **-wand** *f* (Tankw.) splash wall **-wassergeschützt** splash-proof (US) **-wasserschutz** *m* hose-proof enclosure
Schwamm *m* sponge, fungus
Schwammgummi *n*, *m* sponge rubber, foamed latex **-hülse** *f* foam rubber sleeve **-schleifteller** *m* rubber sponge grinding disk **-unterlage** *f* rubber sponge washer
schwammig spongy, spongelike, porous **-e Zellensubstanz** parenchyma
Schwammigkeit des Gußeisens sponginess of cast iron
Schwamm-kohle *f* sponge charcoal, burned or charred sponge **-kupfer** *n* spongy copper, copper sponge
Schwanenhals *m* gooseneck, swanneck, flexible metal hose **-presse** *f* side press (open)
schwanken to waver, fluctuate, vary, reel, range, oscillate, flutter, shake, vibrate
Schwanken *n* variation, fluctuation, flutter(ing), oscillating motion
schwankend labile, variable **-e Drehzahl** fluctating speed
Schwankung *f* fluctuation, undulation, pitching, variation, oscillation **Schwankungen im Wellenwiderstand** impedance irregularities **tägliche Schwankungen** diurnal variations
Schwankungs-bereich *m* range of variation **-breite** *f* extent of the variations, measure of deviation **-dichtefeld** *n* fluctuating density **-dissipationstheorem** *n* fluctuation dissipation

theorem **-frequenz** *f* frequency of flutter **-kurve** *f* rocking curve **-photometer** *n* flicker photometer

Schwankungs-quadrat *n* square fluctuation **-regression** *f* regression of fluctuations **-spektrum** *n* fluctuation (spectrum) **-theorem** *n* fluctuation theorem **-winkel** *m* angle of fluctuation **-zeit** *f* fluctuation time

Schwanz *m* tail, tip, end, empennage, trail **den ~ von einer Seite zur andern schwingen** fishtailing, swishtailing (aviation) **~ hochnehmen** to get the tail up **~ lastige Fluglage** *f* nose up

Schwanz-bänder *pl* tail bands **-blech** *n* trail spade

Schwänze *pl* beet tails (sugar mfg)

Schwanzeinheit *f* tail group

schwänzeln to shimmy, flutter

Schwanz-ende *n* tail end (of fuselage) **-fläche** *f* empennage, tail plane, tail surface **-flächeninhalt** *m* tail-plane area **-flächenwinkel** *m* angle of tail setting **-flosse** *f* tail fin **-gesteuert** tail-controlled **-hammer** *m* tail helve, tail hammer **-kette** *f* tail chain (of buoy) **-kufe** *f* tail skid

Schwanz-lager *n* tail bearing **-landung** *f* tail landing (aviation) **-last** *f* tail load **-lastig** tail-heavy (aviation) **-lastigkeit** *f* tail-heaviness **-lastmoment** *n* tail-load moment **-leitwerk** *n* tail group **-licht** *n* tail light **-los** tailless **-oberfläche** *f* tail surface

Schwanz-rad *n* tail wheel **-ruder** *n* tail surface **-säge** *f* bow saw, whipsaw **-schild** *n* tail shield **-sporn** *m* tail skid **-stabilisator** *m* (tail) stabilizer **-steuerung** *f* tail control **-strom** *m* tail current **-stück** *n* tailpiece **-stützschwimmer** *m* tail float **-tonne** *f* tail-tube buoy **-welle** *f* tail wave **-zapfen** *m* tail journal

Schwarm *m* swarm, flight of several planes in formation, shower (of electrons) **-bindung** *f* clustering **-ionen** *pl* exchangeable cations

Schwarte *f* slab, plank, rind, skin

Schwarten-brett *n* bolster, bridging, boarding **-formerei** *f* forming or molding with clay sheets **-pfahl** *m* plank pole

schwarz black **-er Balken** blackband **-er Befall** bean aphis, black aphis, black fly **-es Blech** black sheet steel **-er Körper** black body **-e Lauge** black liquor(s), spent liquor, waste liquors **-er Lignit** black lignite, subbituminous coal **-es Öl** blackstrap

schwarz, -es Papier blacks (in paper parlance), black paper for covers **-er Sand** black(ing) sand **-e Säure** weak acid **-e Schlacke** black slag **-e Stelle** porous spot, shrink, hole, blowhole **-er Strahler** black body **-e Strahlung** black body radiation **-e Temperatur** black(-body) temperature, cavity temperature

Schwarz-abhebung *f* setup interval (TV) **-beize** *f* iron liquor **-blech** *n* black sheet, black iron plate **-blechtafel** *f* sheet-iron plate **-blei** *n* graphite **-bleierz** *n* black-lead spar **-braunstein** *m* psilomelane **-brennen** to brown **-brennofen** *m* browning (black burn) furnace **-brüchig** black-short **-decke** *f* black top pavement, hydrocarbon pavement **-druck** *m* black printing, printing, printing in black

Schwärze *f* black wash, blacking (wash), blackness, black dye **~ auftragen** to beat the ink, beat, roll the form

Schwarzeisen *n* high-silicon pig iron

Schwarzekörperfunktion *f* black-body function

schwärzen to black, slur, blacken, darken, blackwash

Schwärzen *n* blacking

Schwärzeverteiler *m* blacking swab sprayer

Schwarz-färbung *f* blackening **-guß** *m* all-black malleable cast iron **-hörer** *m* pirate listener **-kernguß** *m* black-heart malleable iron **-kerntemperguß** *m* black-heart malleable iron **-kitt** *m* boiler putty **-kohle** *f* black coal, black charcoal **-körperstrahlung** black body radiation **-kupfer** *n* black copper **-kupferschlacke** *f* roaster or coarse copper slag, blister copper slag **-kupfererz** *n* melaconite

Schwarz-lack *m* black varnish **-lackierung** *f* black varnishing

schwärzlich blackish

Schwarz-lichtfilter *n* black light filter **-manganerz** *n* hausmannite **-mehl** *n* lowgrade flour, rye flour **-ölumlauf** *m* black oil circulation **-pegel** *m* black level **-positivpapier** *n* black-line paper **-pulver** *n* black powder **-quast** *m* blacking brush

Schwärzrolle *f* ink roller

Schwartz'sches Luftschraubenblatt Schwartz-type propeller blade

Schwarzschmelze *f* black ash

Schwarzschulter *f* pedestal (TV), porch **vordere ~** front porch (TV)

Schwarz-seher *m* pirate viewer (TV)

Schwarz-sender *m* unlicensed transmitter **-silbererz** *n*, **-silberglanz** *m* stephanite **-spannung** *f* black (level) voltage **-spießglanzerz** *n* bournonite **-stein** *m* black iron mica **-steuerdiode** *f* D. C. clamp diode **-steuerung** *f* D. C. reinsertion, D. C. restoration, black level control **-strahl** *m* black(-body) radiation, cavity radiation **-strahler** *m* black-body radiator **-streif** *m* blackband **-temperatur** *f* black-body temperature, cavity temperature

Schwärzung *f* blackening, density (phot.), photographic density

Schwärzungs-abstufung *f* density graduation **-bereich** *n* density range **-dichte** *f* density (of film) **-einheit** *f* unit of (film) density **-fleck** *m* spot **-hof** *m* halo **-kurve** *f* characteristic film curve **-messer** *m* densitometer **-methode** *f* variable-intensity or blacking method **-skala** *f* density reference scale **-umfang** *m* density scale, range or latitude of density **-verfahren** *n* variable-density method **-wert** *m* density value

Schwarzweiß-bandbreite monochrome bandwidth **-bild** *n* black-and-white picture **-bildsendung** *f* black-and-white facsimile picture or phototelegraphic transmission **-empfang** *m* black-and-white reception (TV) **-kanal** *m* black-and-white channel (TV) **-signal** monochrome signal (TV) **-sprung** *f* black-to-white amplitude **-steuerung** *f* on-off course or control **-verfahren** *n* method of variable area

Schwarzwert *m* black-level value (TV) **-abhebung** *f* set up **-haltung** *f* DC restoring

Schwebe *f* suspension, suspender **-bahn** *f* suspended railway, suspension railroad, cableway, aerial railway **-baum** *m* horizontal bar **-fähigkeit** *f* suspension property or power, floating capacity or power, soaring quality, buoyancy **-fähre** *f* aerial ferry **-flug** *m* hovering flight **-flughöhe** *f* cruising hover height **-höhe** *f* hover height

Schwebe-körper *m* (im Kreisel) float(ed) element **-kreisvisier** *n* forward-area circular sight for light and medium guns, float-circle sight **-leistung** *f* soaring performance **-methode** *f* suspension method

schweben to float, be suspended, be pending, soar, hover

schwebend pending, in suspension, floating, hovering, suspended **~ fliegen** floating (aviation) **~ halten** to suspend **-es Gitter** floating-grid **-e Stimme** voix céleste **-e Stoffe** suspended matter

Schwebestoff *m* suspended substance, suspended particles, suspended matter **-führung** *f* silt content **-teilchen** *n* gaseous particle, floating particles

Schwebe-strich *m* boards suspended between two posts, rubble or wash floor upon laths **-teilchen** *n* suspended particle **-vermögen** *n* soaring quality

Schwebstoffe *pl* chemical agents that remain in suspension in the air

Schwebstoffilter *m* mechanical filter

Schwebung *f* beat, surge, surging **Schwebungen von Hörfrequenz** beats of audible frequency **mittels Schwebungen empfangen** to heterodyne

Schwebungs-amplitude *f* surging amplitude, beat amplitude **-anzeiger** *m* beat indicator **-dauer** *f* period of beat **-effekt** *m* beating effect

Schwebungsempfang *m* heterodyne reception, beat reception **~ mit Selbsterregung** self-heterodyne reception **~ mit besonderem Überlagerer** separate heterodyne reception

Schwebungsempfänger *m* (heterodyne) beat receiver, heterodyne receiver

Schwebungsfeuer *n* oscillating beacon

Schwebungsfrequenz *f* beat frequency, combination frequency **~ null** zero-beat frequency **auf ~ null eingestellt** set for zero beat

Schwebungs-generator *m* beat-frequency oscillator **-lücke** *f* dead space, zero beat **-methode** *f* beat method, vibration method **-null** *f* zero beat **-oszillator** *m* beat oscillator **-periode** *f* beat cycle **-strom** *m* beating current **-summer** *m* heterodyne warbler or oscillator, beattone oscillator, audio oscillator, beat frequency oscillator (BFO)

Schwebungs-ton *m* beat note, beat tone, heterodyne note **-tonhöhe** *f* beat-note pitch **-verfahren** *n* beat method **-verstärker** *m* hererodyne amplifier **-verzerrung** *f* beat-note distortion **-vorgang** *m* beating effect, beating process

Schwedenstraße *f* plug mill

Schwefel *m* sulfur **-abdruck** *m* brimstone or sulfur impression **-abdruckprobe** *f* sulfur print **-alkalien** *pl* alkali sulfides **-aluminium** *n* aluminum sulfide **-ammon** *n* ammonium sulfide **-antimonsäure** *f* thioantimonic acid **-arm** poor in sulfur **-arsenik** *n* trisulfide of arsenic **-artig** sulfurous **-äther** *m* sulfuric ether **-aufnahme** *f* absorption of sulfur **-blüte** *f* flowers of sulfur **-bromid** *n* sulfur bromide **-bromür** *n* sulfur monobromide

Schwefel-chlorid *n* sulfur chloride **-chlorür** *n* sulfur monochloride **-dampf** *m* sulfuric vapor **-dioxyd** *n* sulfur dioxide **-echt** fast to sulfurous acid **-entfernung** *f* removal of sulfur, desulfurization, desulfurizing **-erz** *n* sulfide or sulfur ore **-grube** *f* sulfur pit **-haltig** sulfurous, containing sulfur **-hütte** *f* sulfur refinery **-jodür** *n* sulfur moniodide **-kalium** *n* potassium sulfide

Schwefelkies *m* pyrite **-abbrand** *m* calcine, roasted sulfur ore

Schwefel-kohlensäure *f* sulfocarbonic acid **-kohlenstoff** *m* carbon disulfide **-kupferoxydul** *n* cuprous sulfide

schwefeln to sulfurize, sulfurate, match, sulfur, vulcanize

Schwefel-natrium *n* sodium sulfide **-pocken** *pl* sulfur spots **-probe** *f* sulfur test **-salz** *n* sulfur salt, sulfate

schwefelsauer of or combined with sulfuric acid, sulfate of

schwefelsaur-es Ammon ammonium sulfate **-es Eisenoxyd** ferric sulfate **-es Eisenoxydul** ferrous sulfate **-er Kalk** calcium sulfate **-es Magnesium** magnesium sulfate, Epsom salt **-es Natron** sodium sulfate **-e Tonerde** aluminum sulfate

Schwefelsäure *f* sulfuric acid **-anhydrid** *n* sulfuric anhydride, sulfur trioxide **-anlage** *f* sulfuric acid plant **-ballon** *m* glass balloon for the transport of sulfuric acid, demijohn, carboy **-fabrik** *f* sulfuric acid plant **-scheidung** *f* sulfuric acid parting

Schwefel-schlacke *f* sulfur dross **-selen** *n* selenium sulfide, selensulfur, volcanite **-silber** *n* silver sulfide, argentite **-spießglanz** *m*, **-spießglanzerz** *n* stibnite **-stange** *f* sulfur roll

Schwefelung *f* sulfurization, sulfuring, sulfur treatment, sulfitation

Schwefelungsmittel *n* sulfurizing agent

Schwefel-verbindung *f* sulfur compound **-werk** *n* sulfur refinery **-wasserstoff** *m* hydrogen sulfide **-wismut** *n* bismuth sulfide **-zieher** *m* sulfur burner **-zinkweiß** *n* lithopone **-zyanammonium** *n* ammonium sulfocyanate **-zyankalium** *n* potassium sulfocyanate **-zyansäure** *f* thiocyanic or sulfocyanic acid

schweflig sulfurous **-saurer Kalk** calcium (lime) sulfite **-saures Natron** sodium sulfite

schweifen to bevel, chamfer, rinse, warp (textiles), sweep, curve, tail

Schweif-gestell *n* bank **-haar** *n* horsehair **-säge** *f* bow saw, fret saw

Schweifung *f* sweeping, curving

Schweige-gebiet *n* skipped distance, zone of silence **-kegel** *m* cone of silence

schweigen to keep silent

Schweigen *n* silence **zum ~ bringen** to silence

Schweige-senderüberlagerer *m* silent transmitter, local oscillator unit **-trichter** *m* cone of silence **-zone** *f* skipped or skip distance, shadow region silent area

Schweiß-aggregat *n* welding unit **-anlage** *f* welding equipment **-anschluß** *m* autogenous welding connection **-apparat** *m* welding apparatus, welding machine **-arbeit** *f* welding, metal arc weld **-ausrüstung** *f* welding outfit, welding equipment **-automat** *m* automatic welding machine **-backe** *f* welding die

Schweißbad *n* welding puddle

schweißbar weldable **-er Stahl** weldable steel

Schweißbarkeit *f* weldability, weldableness

Schweiß-bart *m* icicle (weld), excess metal at root of seam weld **-bedingungen** *pl* welding data **-blase** *f* arc crater **-bogen** welding arc **-box** *f* welding bay **-brenner** *m* welding torch, blowpipe, welding burner, cutting-off burner **-brille** *f* welding goggles **-butzen** *m* core of weld **-draht** *m* welding rod, welding wire, filler rod **-druck** *m* welding upset **-düse** *f* welding tip **-düsenmundstück** *n* welding nozzle tip

Schweiße *f* weld, layer of weld

Schweiß-echtheit *f* ability of a fabric to resist or with-stand bleaching

Schweißeisen *n* wrought iron (for rolling), puddle or puddled iron, busheled or weld iron **-blech** *n* wrought-iron plate

Schweißeisenpaket *n* muck bar pile, pile, faggot **auf Sturz paketiertes ~** flat-and-edge box-piled faggot **flachliegend paketiertes ~** slab-piled faggot

Schweißeisenstab *m* wrought-iron bar

Schweißelektrode *f* welding electrode, consumable electrode

schweißen to weld, fuse **elektrisch ~** to electroweld **nach links ~** forehand welding **nach rechts ~** backhand welding **-stumpf ~** to butt-weld, jump-weld **überlappt ~** to lap-weld, scarf-weld

Schweißen *n* welding **~ von Kunststoff** heat sealing of plastics

Schweißende *n* welding end

Schweißer *m* welder, welding operator **-ausrüstung** *f* welder's outfit

Schweißerei *f* welding operation, welding practice or shop, welding plant

Schweiß-fehler *m* welding defect **-feuer** *n* reheating hearth, welding fire **-flamme** *f* welding flame **-folge** *f* welding sequence, speed travel **-fuge** *f* welding joint, line of weld, welding seam **-generator** *m* welding generator, welding dynamo **-gerät** *n* welding apparatus **-glut** *f* welding heat **-großvorrichtung** *f* mass welding fixture or jig **-gut** *n* welding material, work to be welded, weld metal, deposit **-güte** *f* welding quality, welding property **-gutverbindung** *f* welded joint

Schweiß-handschuh *m* welding glove **-härten** to weld harden **-helm** *m* welding helmet **-herd** *m* soaking hearth **-hitze** *f* welding heat **-kabel** *n* welding cable **-kappe** *f* (welding) helmet **-kern** *m* weld nugget **-kohlen** *pl* welding carbon electrodes **-kolben** *m* welding handle **-konstruktion** *f* welded structures **-kopf** *m* welding head **-kuppe** *f* weld

Schweiß-lage *f* layer of weld, position of weld, pass of welding material **-leistung** *f* welding capacity **-lichtbogen** *m* welding arc **-linse** *f* weld nugget **-löcher** *pl* pores **-lötöse** *f* welding soldering terminal **-maschine** *f* welding machine, welder **-metall** *n* wrought iron, weldable metal **-mittel** *n* welding compound, welding flux

Schweißnaht *f* line of weld, welding seam, welded joint, soldered joint, weld, seam **volle ~** reinforced weld, convex weld

Schweiß-nahthöhe *f* leg length of weld **-nahtstoß** *m* welded rail joint, butt weld **-ofen** *m* reheating furnace, heating furnace, welding furnace, balling furnace **-ofenschlacke** *f* reheating-furnace slag, heating-furnace cinder **-paket** *n* muckbar pile, faggot, pile **-paste** *f* (welding) flux **-perle** *f* globule **-pistole** *f* welding handle, welding gun **-presse** *f* (f. Kunststoffe) welding press **-prozeß** *m* welding process **-pulver** *n* welding flux or powder

Schweißpunkt *m* welding spot, welding point **-kern** *m* weld nugget **-reihe** *f* run of spot welds

Schweißrad *n* welding wheel **-welle** *f* welding-wheel shaft

Schweißraupe *f* bead, weld bead **breite ~** spread bead

Schweiß-riß *m* welding cracker fissure **-rißempfindlich** susceptible to weld-cracking **-rissig** cracking or fissuring on welding

Schweiß-rissigkeit *f* weld cracking, fissuration due to welding **-rohrherstellung** *f* manufacture of welded-steel tubing **-sand** *m* welding sand **-schalter** *m* welding interruptor **-schlacke** *f* welding cinder **-schmiedeeisen** *n* weld iron **-spannung** *f* welding-arc voltage **-stahl** *m* wrought steel, wrought iron, welding steel, weld steel, pipe steel, skelp steel, puddled steel, mild steel, single-shear steel

Schweißstab *m* welding rod, filler rod, welding electrode **ummantelter ~** sheathed electrode

Schweißstelle *f* (location of) weld, welding position, shut, welded joint, welded or welding area **überlappte ~** welded overlap joint

Schweiß-strahlen *pl* arc rays **-straße** *f* welding line **-strom** *m* welding current **-stromkreis** *m* welding circuit **-stromquelle** *f* source of welding current **-takter** *m* welding timer **-technik** *f* welding technique **-temperatur** *f* welding heat, welding temperature **-transformator** *m* welding transformer **-tropfen** *m* welding dribble, welding bead

Schweiß-überhöhung *f* weld reinforcement **-umformer** *m* welding set (generator), welding converter, low-temperature carbonising plant **-umspanner** *m* welding transformer

Schweißung *f* welding, weld, sweating **~ über Kopf** overhead weld **~ mit Schleppführung** touch welding **~ mit Spreizelektrode** poke welding **~ von oben** flat weld **autogene ~** autogenous welding, oxyacetylene welding, lead burning **elektrische ~** electrowelding, electric welding, arc welding **hydrooxygene ~** oxy-hydrogen welding **senkrechte ~** vertical weld **überlappte ~** lap weld, scarf weld

Schweiß-unterlage *f* backing strip **-verbindung** *f* welded joint

Schweißverfahren *n* welding process, method of welding **aluminothermisches ~** thermite welding process

Schweißvorrichtung *f* welding jig, welder **~ für Kontakte** contact welder

Schweiß-wachs *m* wax from suint **-walzen** *pl* roughing rolls **-wärme** *f* welding heat **-warm machen** to give welding heat **-wasser** *n* water of condensation **-werkstatt** *f* welding shop **-widerstand** *m* welding resistance or resistor, arc adjuster **-wolle** *f* greasy wool **-wulst** *m* reinforcement (weld)

Schweiß-zange *f* electrode holder, welding tongs **-zapfengelenk** *n* welding yoke type universal joint **-zapfenmitnehmer** *m* welding yoke **-zeitgeber** *m* welding timer **-zone** *f* soaking zone

Schweizerdegen *m* compositor and printer

Schwelanlage *f* low-temperature carbonizing plant

schwelen to burn slowly, smolder, carbonize (at low temperature), distill, smoulder
Schwelen *n* low-temperature carbonization, smothering, smoldering
Schweler *m* low-temperature carbonizer
Schwel-gas *n* gas from low-temperature distillation, incompletely burned gas, low-temperature retort coal gas, carbonization gas **-kerze** *f* smudge or smoke candle **-kohle** *f* high-bituminous lignite coal, brown coal for low-temperature retort process **-koks** *m* low-temperature coke
Schwell-beiwert *m* coefficient of swelling, rebound coefficient **-beize** *f* liquor for swelling hides **-belastung** *f* repetitive stress, pulsating stress **-bereich** *m* range for pulsating **-bereichs-biegedauerfestigkeit** *f* fatigue strength under pulsating bending stresses
Schwelle *f* (Tür) threshold; (Balken) beam, joist; (Eisenbahn) tie, sleeper; base plate, sill, crosstie, pole cribbing, bedplate, crest, sole, ford (water), ground beam or timber, strobe (rdr), barrier, gate
Schwelle, aufgesetzte ~ renewable sill **unterstopfte** ~ tamped tie **vollkantige** ~ full-squared tie ~ **der automatischen Frequenzregelung** AFC threshold ~ **im Tosbecken** basin sill
schwellen to swell, grow, increase, rise, heave
Schwellen *n* swelling **-bahn** *f* roadway (with ties) **-befeuerung** *f* runway threshold lighting **-bestimmung** *f* determination of the limen **-bohrer** *m* auger **-decke** *f* top of sleeper **-dörrofen** *m* drying stove, kiln (for drying sleepers or ties) **-dosis** *f* threshold dose **-feld** *n* threshold field **-festlegung** *f* fixing the threshold **-feuer** *pl* threshold lights (aviat) **-frequenz** *f* threshold or critical frequency, photoelectric threshold
Schwellen-kaliber *n* tie pass **-kappmaschine** *f* sleeper capping machine **-klammer** *f* cramp iron **-kurve** *f* threshold curve **-lasche** *f* sleeper fishplate **-profil** *n* tie section **-reiz** *m* threshold or stimulation value **-schraube** *f* screw spike **-stopfer** *m* packer or tamper of ties **-stuhl** *m* sleeper chair **-wert** *m* threshold limit or value, threshold sensitivity, limit(ing) value, exposure factor (phot.) **-wertkurve** *f* threshold field curve
Schwell-fähigkeit *f* expansibility **-festigkeit** *f* inflation strength, fatigue limit **-holz** *n* sill, sleeper
schwellig liminal, concerning threshold
Schwell-joch *n* trestle **-kasten** *m* swell box **-kurve** *f*, **-last** *f* rebound curve **-pedal** *n* swell pedal (organ) **-rost** *m* (timber) platform, grating of the foundation
Schwellung *f* swelling, heave
Schwell-vermögen *n* expansibility **-werk** *n* timber platform, grating of the foundation, swell organ
Schwellwert *m* threshold (gyro), threshold value **-geber** *m* sector-alignment indicator **-kurve** *f* threshold value curve
Schwel-nebelkerze *f* smoke candle **-ofen** *m* low-temperature carbonizing furnace **-produkt** *n* dry distillation product **-retorte** *f* retort for low-temperature distillation or carbonization **-teer** *m* tar from low-temperature carbonization
Schwelung *f* low-temperature carbonization, slow burning, smoldering ~ **von Brennstoffen** carbonization of solid fuels
Schwel-vorgang *m* carbonization process **-wasser** *n* foul water **-zone** *f* carbonization zone, smoldering zone **-zylinder** *m* partial carbonizer
Schwemmaufbereitung *f* flotation
Schwemme *f* flume, horsepond
schwemmen to float, wash, rinse
Schwemm-filterung *f* sewage purification by filtration **-kanalisation** *f* sewerage **-mulde** *f* alluvial basin **-sand** *m* drift(ing) sand **-stein** *m* concrete pumice block, pumice stone, alluvial stone, porous brick (from clay and gravel)
Schwemmstoffführung *f* silt content
Schwemm-verfahren *n* flotation method **-wasser** *n* wash water
Schwengel *m* clapper (at a bell), charging bar, charging peel, balance lever, beam **-bock** *m* Sampson post **-bohrloch** *n* beam well **-lager** *n* saddle bearing, center irons **-sattel** *m* walking-beam saddle
Schwenk-achse *f* axis of rotation, swivel axis **-achsenwinkel** *m* caster angle **-anschlag** *m* swing stop **-antrieb** *m* pivot drive
Schwenkarm *m* swivel arm, swinging lever **-lafette** *f* crank-type swivel gun mount **-zapfvorrichtung** *f* swing arm discharge
Schwenk-aufnahme *f* oscillating exposure **-ausschlag** *m* swing **-bahn** *f* slewing path
schwenkbar sluable, swingable, swiveling, revolving, sluing, tilting, orientable, hinged ~ **aufstellen** to place on dollies
schwenkbar-er Fräskopf tilting milling head **-es Gestell** (swinging) gate **-er Heber** swing clearing cam **-e Nutsägen** pivoting grooving saws **-er Rahmen** rotating rack **-e Rolle** caster **-es Spornrad** caster(ing) tail wheel, orientable tail wheel **-es Triebwerk** (Astron.) tilting engine **-e Verbindung** swivel connection
Schwenkbarkeit *f* swivel-feature
Schwenkbereich *m* field of traverse, angular freedom ~ (Bagger) boom swing, jib swing
Schwenk-betrieb *m* slewing operation **-bewegung** *f* rotating motion, swing **-bügel** *m* movable (gun) mounting **-bühne** *f* tilting or swinging platform **-einrichtung** *f* swiveling device
schwenken to turn, traverse, swing, turn around, slue, swivel, pivot, fulcrum, rotate, revolve, tilt
Schwenker *m* oscillating lever
Schwenk-flügel *m* folded wing **-gelenkdämpfer** *m* (Hubschrauber) blade lag damper **-getriebe** *n* turning gear **-hebel** *m* rocking lever **-klappe** *f* hinged door **-kran** *m* bracket jib crane, swinging crane **-kristall** *m* rotating or oscillating crystal **-lafette** *f* flexible gun mount **-leitung** *f* shifter line **-lineal** *n* swing bar **-platte** *f* swivel carriage **-prisma** *n* swiveling V-block
Schwenk-rad *n* swivel caster or castor swivel wheel **-radius** *m* turning radius **-ritzen** *m* turning-gear pinion **-rohr** *n* swing pipe **-schablone** *f* swiveling template **-schraube** *f* swiveling propeller (VTOL aircraft) **-seil** *n* guiding cable, ladder or main rope, shroud **-strebe** *f* radius rod **-taster** *m* rotating key **-tisch** *m* swing table, swing-out table, turntable **-tür** *f* hinged door
Schwenkung *f* turn, turning movement, wheeling, sluing, swinging, caster action, oscillation, deviation, sweep, long bend ~ **der Kammer**

setting, or rotation of the camera

Schwenkungs-fall *m* case of avertence, case of horizontal swing **-punkt** *m* pivot **-winkel** *m* angle of horizontal swing, angle of traverse

Schwenk-verschraubung *f* swivel joint **-vorrichtung** *f* swinging or swiveling device **-welle** *f* rocking shaft **-werk** *n* traversing gear **-winkel** *m* angle of traverse

schwer heavy, difficult, hard, severe, massive, heavily, weighty, ponderous **~ bespult** heavy loaded (teleg) **~ durchlässiger Sand** tight sand **~ beschädigt** badly damaged **~ drücken** to weigh heavily **~ schmelzbar** difficult to fuse or melt, refractory, stubborn **~ verkäuflich** difficult to sell **~ verletzt** injured seriously **-e Bewaffnung** heavy armament **-es Elektron** heavy electron, mesotron **-er Formstahl** heavy sections

schwer-es Küstenkabel (heavy) shore end of submarine cable **-er als Luft** heavier-than-air **-es Material** heavy or bottom material **-er nasser Nebel** heavy, wet fog **-er Unfall** serious accident **-er Wasserstoff** deuterium, tritium

Schwer-achse *f* centroidal axis **-achsschenkelschleifmaschine** *f* heavy axle-journal grinding machine **-bauteil** *m* heavy supporting structure

schwerbelastet heavily loaded **-e Lager** high duty bearings

Schwer-benzin *n* heavy benzene, naphtha, mineral spirits **-benzol** *n* heavy benzol **-betrieb** *m* high-duty service, heavy-duty operation or service **-bleierz** *n* plattnerite **-brennbar** slow-burning **-brennbarkeit** *f* flame resistance **-durchlässig** difficultly permeable, of low permeability or transmittance, highly opaque

Schwere *f* gravity, weight, heaviness, gravitation **~ des Musters** fullness of the design

Schwere-anomalie *f* gravity anomaly **-beobachtung** *f* gravity observation **-berichtigung** *f* correction of or for gravity **-beschleunigung** *f* acceleration due to gravity **-druck** *m* gravity force **-empfindung** *f* weight **-felder** *pl* gravitational fields, fields of gravity **-formel** *f* gravity formula **-messer** *m* barometer, gradiometer, hydrometer, aerometer, gravitometer **-netz** *n* gravity network

schwerentzündlich not easily inflammable

Schwerependel *n* gravity pendulum

Schwererde *f* barite, baryta

Schwere-vermessung *f* gravity survey **-widerlager** *n* gravity abutment **-wirkung** *f* gravimetric effect

schwer-fällig heavy, cumbersome, ponderous, slow **-fälligkeit** *f* heaviness, clumsiness **-flüchtig** difficult to volatilize, not volatile **-feld** *n* field of gravity

schwerflüssig viscous, heavy **-es Öl** heavy oil

Schwer-flüssigkeit *f* dense liquid **-flüssigkeitsversuchsaggregat** *n* heavy-liquid test unit **-fühlig** sluggish

schwergefrierbare Mischung low-freezing mixture

Schwergewichtsmauer *f* gravity retaining wall, gravity dam

Schwergewichtsventil *n* dead-weight valve

schwerhändig iron-handed

Schwerindustrie *f* heavy industry, steel industry

Schwerkraft *f* force of gravity, gravity **-anlasser** *m* inertia starter **-antrieb** *m* gravity drive **-aufbereitung** gravity concentration **-beschleunigung** *f* gravity acceleration **-energie** *f* gravitational energy **-feld** *n* gravitational field **-förderanlage** *f* gravity feed system

Schwerkraft-moment *n* moment of gravitational force **-sichter** *m* classifier **-stoffe** *m pl* heavy fuels **-system** *n* gravity system **-wirkung** *f* effect of gravity **-zentrum** *n* central gravity, center of gravity

Schwerlast-kran *m* goliath crane **-wagen** *m* heavy duty lorry, truck

Schwerlinie *f* axis of gravity, centroidal axis

schwerlöslich difficult to dissolve

Schwermaschinenbau *m* heavy machine construction

Schwermetall-aktivator *m* heavy-metal activator **-guß** *m* heavy-metal casting

Schweröl *n* heavy oil **-förderpumpe** *f* heavy fuel feed pump **-motor** *m* heavy-oil engine **-vergaser** *m* heavy-oil carburetor

Schwerpunkt *m* strong point, center of gravity or mass, point of concentration, thrust point keypoint (fig.)

Schwerpunkt(s)-abstand *m* center-to-center spacing **-achse** *f* axis through center of gravity, neutral axis **-bewegung** *f* center of mass motion **-bildung** *f* formation of strong point, massed concentration of weapons **-halbmesser** *m* radius of center of gravity **-lage** *f* (position of or at) center of gravity or center of mass **-radius** *m* radius of center of gravity

Schwerpunkt(s)-satz *m* center-of-mass law, fundamental theorem **-schwingung** *f* oscillation of the center of gravity **-system** *n* center-of-gravity system, center-of-mass system **-verlegung** *f* displacement of the center of gravity **-verschiebung** *f* displacement of the center of mass **-vorlage** *f* forward displacement of center of gravity

schwer-rostend rustless, rustproof, stainless **-schmelzbar** difficultly fusible, refractory

Schwer-sonde *f* heavy duty measuring **-spannstift** *m* spring cotter **-spat** *m* pearl white (paper mfg.), (an artificial) barium sulfate **-spatbeton** *m* barium-sulfate concrete **-stange** *f* drill stem **-stein** *m* scheelite **-stoff** *m* dense-medium material

Schwert *n* sword, lee; tongue

Schwertakel *n* winding tackle

Schwert-anhubhebel *m* sword control lever **-artiger Teil** swordlike or sword-shaped part **-balken** *m* crossbeam **-feile** *f* feature-edge file **-förmig** ensiform, swordlike

Schwertrübe *f* heavy medium

schwer-verwundet severely wounded **-wasser** *n* heavy water **-wiegend** grave, serious **-zentrisch** centrobaric

Schwibbogen *m* arched buttress

Schwiele *f* weal, welt

schwierig difficult, hard, complicated **-e Formen** (des Werkstücks) intricate sections

Schwierigkeit *f* (serious) difficulty, (versteckte) snag **~ in der Verständigung** poor transmission **Schwierigkeiten beseitigen** to remove or overcome difficulties **auf ~ stoßen** to run into difficulties **mit ~ verbunden** beset by difficulties

Schwierigkeitsgrad *m* coefficient of difficulty

Schwimm-achse *f* axis of flotation or buoyancy **-apparat** *m* floating apparatus **-aufbereitung** *f* flotation

Schwimmaufbereitungs-anlage *f* flotation plant **-verfahren** *n* buoyancy proceeding or process

Schwimm-auftrieb *m* buoyancy **-badreaktor** *m* swimming pool reactor (atom. phys.) **-bagger** *m* dredger **-bake** *f* floating beacon **-deckel** *m* floating end cover **-drehkran** *m* floating slewing crane **-dock** *n* floating dock **-ebene** *f* plane of buoyancy or of flotation

schwimmen to swim, float

Schwimmen *n* swimming, floating, lateral flicker (in overspeedy panorama work)

schwimmend floating **-er Flugstützpunkt** floating air base **-e Insel** floating island **-er Kolbenbolzen** floating gudgeon pin **-er Körper** floating body **-er Kreisel** floating gyro **-er Rüttelapparat** floating vibrator

Schwimmer *m* swimmer, float, flat, pontoon, buoyancy chamber, float gauge, carburetor **~ des Gegengewichts** counterweight float **einfacher ~** single float **einziehbarer ~** retractable float **versenkter ~** submerged plunger or float

Schwimmer-absaugung *f* floating suction **-aufbau** *m* float construction **-ausschnitt** *m* section of float **-behälter** *m* flushing tank **-breite** *f* beam of float **-einrichtung** *f* float arrangement **-entlüfter** *m* float vent **-flugzeug** *n* seaplane, pontoon, hydroplane, floatplane **-führung** *f* float guide **-führungsschiene** *f* float guide bar or rail **-füllungsanzeiger** *m* float level indicator

Schwimmer-gefäß *n* oil cup **-gehäuse** *n* float bowl, float chamber **-gestell** *n* float (landing) gear **-hahn** *m* ball cock **-hals** *m* neck of the float **-haut** *f* float skin, float planking **-kammer** *f* float chamber **-kondenstopf** *m* float trap

Schwimmer-lager *n* float support **-manometer** *n* mercury-type differential gauge **-modell** *n* floatplane model **-nadel** *f* float (valve) needle carburetor float spindle, carburetor needle **-probe** *f* float test

Schwimmerpumpe *f*, **selbsttätige ~** automatic floating pump

Schwimmer-querschnitt *m* transverse section of float **-raum** *m* float well, float chamber **-regelventil** *n* regulating float valve **-regulierung** *f* float control **-schalter** *m* float switch **-schleuse** *f* floating sluice **-stange** *f* float spindle **-strebe** *f* float strut **-stufe** *f* float step **-stummel** *m* sponson, sea wing (aviation) **-ventil** *n* float valve, ball cock **-wagen** *m* beaching carriage (aviation) **-werk** *n* flotation gear

schwimmfähig flotable **-es Gestell** flotation gear

Schwimm-fähigkeit *f* buoyancy, floatability **-kasten** *m* floating caisson or chamber **-kette** *f* riding chain **-kiesel** *m* spongiform quartz **-kompaß** *m* spirit or fluid compass, immersed compass **-kopf** *m* floating head exchanger **-körper** *m* float, floating body, pontoon **-kraft** *f* buoyancy **-kran** *m* floating crane **-kreisel** *m* floated gyro

Schwimm-methode *f* flotation method **-ponton** *n* ship caisson **-radiometer** *n* floating radiometer **-rohrplattendeckel** *m* floating tube sheet cover **-sack** *m* flotation air bag **-sand** *m* running sand, quicksand, shifting sand **-sandschicht** *f* layer of quicksand **-sinkscheider** *m* sink float separator **-spannung** *f* floating or blurring potential **-stabilität** *f* floatation stability

Schwimm-tor *n* (ship) caisson **-torbewegung** *f* maneuvering of a ship caisson **-träger** *m* supporting beam or girder **-tüchtigkeit** *f* floatability **-verfahren** *n* flotation (method) **-vorrichtung** *f* flotation gear **-werk** *n* float landing gear, flotation gear, float undercarriage **-weste** *f* lifesaving jacket

Schwindel *m* swindle, fraud, vertigo, dizziness **-erregend** vertiginous **-gefühl** *n* vertigo **-haft** swindling, fraudulent, bogus

schwinden to shrink, contract, waste, disappear, fade (away)

Schwinden *n* shrinkage, contraction, fading (radio)

Schwind-erscheinung *f* fading effect **-faktor** *m* shrinkage factor **-fuge** *f* contraction joint **-grube** *f* bog, waste or drainage well, drain **-hohlraum** *m* shrinkage cavity, shrink hole

schwindlig giddy, dizzy

Schwindlunker *m* shrinkage cavity

Schwindmaß *n* degree of shrinkage, shrinkage gauge or allowance, contraction rule, molder's rule, pattern-maker's rule, shrinkage value **-bestimmung** *f* determination of shrinkage **-stab** *m* contraction rule **-verkürzung** *f* shrinkage, contraction **-zugabe** *f* shrinkage allowance

Schwind-riß *m* shrinkage crack **-spannung** *f* contraction strain

Schwindung *f* shrinkage, contraction **feste ~** solid contraction

Schwindungs-grad *m* degree of shrinkage or contraction **-hohlraum** *m* shrinkage cavity, shrink hole, shrink cavity **-loch** *n* shrinkage cavity **-lot** *n* shrink bob **-lunker** *m* shrinkage cavity **-riß** *m* shrinkage crack **-zugabe** *f* contraction allowance

Schwindwasser *n* shrink water

Schwing-achse *f* flexible front-drive axle, independent axle, jointed cross shaft **-amplitude** *f* amplitude of oscillations **-anker** *m* oscillating armature **-ankerwerk** *n* swinging lever work **-anschlag** *m* (e. Drehautomaten) swing stop **-arm** *m* swing arm **-armlagerblock** *m* swing arm bracket

Schwingaudion *n* autodyne, auto-heterodyne, oscillating detector **-empfang** *m* autodyne reception **-empfänger** *m* autodyne beat receiver **-wellenmesser** *m* autodyne wave meter or frequency meter

Schwing-baum *m* rocking tree, swing beam **-bereich** *m* mode **-bewegung** *f* vibratory movement **-blatt** *n* diaphragm membrane **-blende** *f* chopper diaphragm **-bolzen** *m* swivel pin **-brecher** *m* jaw crusher **-breite der Spannung** range of stress **-durchmesser** *m* swing diameter

Schwinge *f* rotating shaft, wing (of a bird), rocker arm, rocking arm, balancer, beam, link **-förderrinne** *f* reciprocating-plate feeder

schwingen to swing; (handhaben) wield; (Technik, schleudern) centrifuge; (pendeln) swing, oscillate; (schwanken) vibrate, sway; undulate, wave, float, rock, pivot, reciprocate (to and fro), surge (back and forth) **um einen Mittelwert ~** to oscillate about an average value **in einer Oberharmonischen ~** to vibrate to a harmonic **hin und her ~** to surge back and forth, swing, rock

Schwingen *n* oscillating process, swing, surge **~ des Flachses** flax scutching **~ des Ladedruckreglers** surging of the boost control **plötzliches ~** sudden (undesired) oscillating **selbsterregtes ~** hunting

schwingend vibratory, vibrating, oscillatory, oscillating, undulatory, undulating, rocking **-e Bewegung** oscillatory motion **-er Draht** swinging filament, vibrating wire **-e Entladung** oscillating discharge **-er Kontakt** vibrating contact **-er Sendungskreis** oscillating transmitting circuit **-e Zunge** vibrating reed **-er Zylinder** oscillating or rocking cylinder **~ gelagert** mounted in rockers

Schwingen-flug *m* flapping flight **-flugmodell** *n* flapping-wing model **-flugzeug** *n* flapping-wing machine, performance-type glider, sailplane, soaring glider, orthopter **-lager** *n* link bracket **-stange** *f* eccentric rod **-stein** *m* sliding block

Schwingentladung *f* oscillating discharge, oscillatory discharge

Schwingen-welle *f* tumbler shaft **-wippkran** *m* level luffing crane with rocker arm

Schwinger *m* oscillator, vibrator, resonator **offener ~** open oscillator

Schwing-fähigkeit *f* ability to vibrate, activity (cryst.) **-feder** *f* vibratory spring, reed **-förderer** *m* vibrating conveyor **-förderrinne** *f* shaker loader **-grenze** *f* oscillating limit **-größe** *f* oscillating quantity, height of oscillation

Schwinghebel *m* rocking lever, valve rocker, balancer, (swing) beam **-anschlag** *m* stop for swinging lever **-antrieb mit nicht obenliegender Nockenwelle** underhead rocker gear **-block** *m* valve-rocker bracket or pedestal **-drehpunktbolzen** *m* valve-rocker fulcrum pin **-lagerbuchse** *f* valve-rocker bush or bushing **-rolle** *f* valve-rocker roller **-rollenbolzen** *m* valve-rocker roller pin **-welle** *f* rocker shaft

Schwing-herd *m* reciprocating hearth **-kennlinie** *f* oscillating characteristic, resonance characteristic

Schwingkondensator *m*, **-verstärker** oscillating condenser-amplifier **-meßverstärker** *m* dynamic condenser electron electrometer

Schwingkontaktgleichrichter *m* vibrating-reed rectifier

Schwingkraft *f* vibration force

Schwingkreis *m* resonant circuit, oscillatory circuit **-induktivität** *f* resonant-circuit inductance **-spannung** *f* oscillatory-circuit voltage or potential **-widerstand** *m* resonant-circuit resistance or impedance

Schwing-kristall *m* crystal oscillator **-lastfeder** *f* dynamic loading spring **-leistung** *f* oscillatory power **-linie** *f* lumped characteristic, total characteristic **-loch** *n* dead spot **-maschine** *f* scutching or swinging machine, scutcher **-metall** *n* vibration dampening connector (aviation), resilient cushioning, vibration mount

Schwing-motor *m* motor with reciprocating movement **-mühle** *f* ball mill **-neigung** *f* tendency towards oscillations **-plättchen** *n* diaphragm, membrane **-prüfmaschine** *f* fatigue testing machine **-quarz** *m* oscillator crystal **-radkreis** *m* flywheel circuit **-rätter** *m* jig table **-relais** *n* trigger relay **-rinnen** *pl* vibrating troughs

Schwingröhre *f* oscillating tube, oscillator valve, generator valve **fremderregte ~** separately excited oscillator valve **selbsterregte ~** self-excited oscillator valve, self-oscillatory valve

Schwing-schaltung *f* crystal circuit **-scheibe** *f* oscillating disk **-schenkel** *m* spindle **-sieb** *n* swing sieve, shaking screen **-spiegel** *m* oscillatory or vibrating mirror **-spiegelabtaster** *m* vibrating-mirror scanner **-spule** *f* moving coil, signal-current coil, voice coil, speech coil (of loud-speaker) **-spulenzähler** *m* oscillating meter **-strom** *m* oscillating current

Schwingstufe *f* heterodyne oscillator stage **erste** (zweite) **~** radio-frequency oscillator stage

Schwing-system *n* oscillatory modes **-topf** *m* cavity resonator **-transportrinne** *f* oscillating shoot **-traverse** *f* swing arm **-trichter** *m* oscillating funnel or cone

Schwingung *f* s. a. schwingen swinging, oscillation, vibration; (Radio) cycle; (harmonische ~en) subharmonics; (in ~ setzen) set swinging, cause to vibrate; undulation, flutter (in wings), surge (elec.), pulsation, wave, high-frequency alternating current **~ durch Nebenkoppelung** stray or spurious oscillation **in ~ versetzen** to throw into vibration, set into oscillation **abklingende ~** dying-out oscillation **aufgedrückte ~** forced or imposed oscillation or vibration **einfallende ~** incoming oscillation **elektromagnetische ~** electromagnetic oscillation

Schwingung, erregende ~ exciting oscillation **erzwungene ~** forced vibration, constrained or forced oscillation **freie ~** free oscillation **fremderregte ~** forced or constrained oscillation **gedämpfte ~** damped or decadent oscillation **harmonische ~** harmonic oscillation **hochfrequente harmonische ~** high-frequency (harmonic) oscillation **quasistationäre ~** quasi-stationary oscillation

Schwingung, selbsterregte ~ self-sustained oscillation **selbststeuernde ~** free oscillation **sinusförmige ~** sine oscillation **ungedämpfte ~** continuous oscillation, undamped oscillation, sustained oscillation **wilde ~** spurious or parasitic oscillation **-zusammengesetzte ~** complex (harmonic) wave or oscillation **durch Nebenkoppelungen hervorgerufene ~** stray or spurious oscillation **freie Schwingungen ausführen** to oscillate (freely)

Schwingungs-abreißen *n* quenching, suppression, or discontinuance of oscillations **-abschnitt** *m* bit or section of vibration **-abtaster** *m* vibration pick-up **-achse** *f* axis of oscillation **-amplitude** *f* vibrational amplitude, amplitude of oscillation **-analyse** *f* vibrational analysis **-anfachung** *f* starting of oscillations, setting-in of oscillations, wave generation or excitation

Schwingungs-anschläge *f* amplitudes **-anzeiger** *m* oscillation detector or indicator **-art** *f* type of oscillation **-artverschiebung** *f* mode shift **-aufnehmer** *m* vibration pickup **-aufzeichner** *m* vibrograph **-ausgleich** *m* amplitude

Schwingungsausschlag *m* amplitude or deflection of the vibration or oscillation **~ einer Seite** deflection, excursion or swing of a chord

Schwingungs-bauch *m* loop or antinode of oscillation or vibration, internode **-beanspruchung** *f* alternating stress, vibration stress **-beschleunigung** *f* acceleration of oscillatory motion **-bogen** *m* amplitude of oscillation **-bruch** *m* vibration failure

Schwingungsdämpfer *m* damper device, vibration damper, oscillation choke **als ~ wirkendes pendelndes Gegengewicht** balance-weight vibration absorber

Schwingungs-dämpfung *f* vibration or shock absorption, damping (out) of oscillations or vibrations **-dauer** *f* period (of oscillation), time of vibration, periodic time **-dekrement** *n* logarithmic decrement, champing decrement **-ebene** *f* plane of oscillation **-eigenschaft** *f* oscillating quality or property

Schwingungseinsatz *m* starting of oscillations, setting-in of oscillations **harter ~** hard start of oscillations **weicher ~** gentle or smooth start of oscillations

Schwingungseinsatzpunkt *m* point of self-oscillation

Schwingungs-energie *f* oscillation energy **-erreger** *m* oscillator **-erregung** *f* singing **-erscheinungen** *pl* vibrations

schwingungserzeugende Kraft vibromotive force

Schwingungserzeuger *m* oscillation generator, oscillator **eigenerregter ~** self-excited oscillator **fremderregter ~** separately excited oscillator **fremdgesteuerter ~** separately controlled or excited oscillator **selbsterregter ~** self-excited oscillator **selbstsperrender ~** self-blocking oscillator

Schwingungserzeugerröhre *f* oscillator tube

Schwingungserzeugung *f* generation or production of oscillations **selbständige ~** self-oscillation, spontaneous or undesired oscillating

schwingungs-fähig oscillatory, vibratory **-fest** vibration-proof

Schwingungs-festigkeit *f* fatigue strength, dynamic strength, vibration strength **-form** *f* oscillatory form, mode or form of vibration

schwingungsfrei non-oscillating **-er Vorgang** aperiodic or non-oscillating phenomenon **-er Zustand** non-oscillating condition

Schwingungs-freiheit *f* insensible for vibrations **-frequenz** *f* frequency of the oscillation **-fundament** *n* anti-vibration foundation **-gebilde** *n* oscillatory circuit, oscillating circuit, oscillatory formations **-generator** *m* circuit driver **-größe** *f* magnitude of oscillation **-höhe** *f* amplitude of oscillation **-knoten** *m* vibration node or nodal point, interference point, null point, oscillation node or nodal point

Schwingungskreis *m* oscillatory circuit, oscillating circuit, tuned circuit, tank circuit **geschlossener ~** closed oscillatory circuit **offener ~** open oscillating circuit, open radiative circuit **gekoppelte Schwingungskreise** coupled oscillatory circuits

Schwingungs-kurven *pl* sonorous figures **-läppen** *pl* oscillating lapping **-mechanismus** *m* oscillation mechanism **-messer** *m* vibration frequency meter, oscillograph, vibroscope **-mittelpunkt** *m* center of oscillation **-modell** *n* transient analyzer **-mühle** *f* vibratory mill

Schwingungs-neigung *f* tendency toward, on the verge of, oscillating or spilling over **-periode** *f* oscillation time, period of oscillation **-prüfmaschine** *f* vibratory testing machine, vibrator **-quant** *n* vibration quantum **-richtung** *f* vibration direction

Schwingungs-schleife *f* loop, antinode or internode of stationary wave or oscillation **-schreiber** *m* oscillograph **-sicher** vibration-proof **-sieb** *n* wave filter **-spektrum** *n* vibration(al) spectrum **-summer** *m* heterodyne oscillator **-technisch** relative to vibration **-transformator** *m*, **-transformer** *m* oscillation transformer **-überlagerung** *f* vibration superposition

Schwingungs-verfahren *n* oscillation method, vibration method **-versuch** *m* vibration test, repeated-stress test

Schwingungs-vorgang *m* production or phenomenon of oscillations **-weise** *f* mode of oscillation **-weite** *f* amplitude of oscillation, amplitude of vibration **-welle** *f* undulation **-winkel** *m* angle of oscillation, angle of swing **-zahl** *f* vibration or oscillation frequency **-zeit** *f* period of the oscillation, time of vibration **-zentrum** *n* center of oscillation, center of suspension

Schwing-walze *f* swinging roller **-wand** *f* diaphragm, membrane **-weite** *f* amplitude (of oscillation or vibration) **-zahl** *f* vibration frequency **-zeit** *f* vibration period **-zug** *m* cycle

schwirren to whirr, whizz

Schwirrholz *n* full roarer, thunder stick

Schwirrgeschwindigkeit *f* whirling speed

schwitzen to perspire, sweat; (Kessel) to leak

Schwitzen *n* sweating, leaking

Schwitzkammer *f* sweating stove, smokehouse **-ablauf** *m* foots oil

Schwitz-öl *n* foots oil **-roste** *f* steam retting **-wasserkorrosion** *f* dewpoint corrosion, perspiration corrosion

schwöden cleanse and lime (hides)

Schwödgrube *f* lime pit

schwoien to swing, tend (naut.)

Schwojen *n* tend

Schwund *m* fading, shrinkage, atrophy, dwindling, leakage, disappearance

Schwundausgleich *m* antifading device, automatic volume control, volume-control circuit or system **automatischer ~** automatic gain control, automatic volume control **verzögerter ~** delayed automatic volume control, delayed fading compensation

Schwundausgleicher *m* anti-fading device

Schwundausgleichschaltung *f* automatic volume control

Schwund-automatik *f* automatic volume control means **-effekt** *m* masking

Schwunderscheinung *f* fading, atrophy, or shrinkage (phenomenon), dwindling, leakage, disappearance **synchrone ~** synchronous fading, complete fading

schwundfrei fading-free

Schwundkerben *m* shrinkage cavity

schwundkompensierende Frequenzmodulation anti-fading frequency modulation

schwundmindernde Antenne fade-reducing antenna

Schwundperiode *f* fading period

Schwundregelspannung *f* (automatic) volume-control potential

Schwundregler, automatischer ~ automatic-volume-control circuit or system

Schwundregelung, automatische ~ automatic gain control, automatic volume control, fading control

Schwund-riß *m* shrinkage crack **-toleranz** *f* fading margin

Schwundverminderungsantenne *f* antifading antenna

Schwund-wirkung *f* fading (effect) **-zahl** *f* shrinkage factor

Schwung *m* swing, impulsion, vibration, oscillation, momentum **in ~ bringen** to set in motion, energize, start, accelerate

Schwung-brett *n* springboard **-brücke** *f* lever drawbridge **-gewicht** *n* balance weight, pendulum **-gewichtsregler** *m* centrifugal governor **-haft** brisk, flourishing, prosperous **-hebel** *m* fly, rocking, or tappet lever, balance beam, rocker

Schwungkraft *f* (Fliehkraft) centrifugal force or power, vibratory power, (Wucht) inertial power

Schwungkraftanlasser *m* inertia(-type) starter, momentum starter **~ für elektrischen Betrieb** electric inertia starter **~ für Handbetrieb** hand inertia starter

Schwung-kranz *m* flywheel **-kreis** *m* oscillator circuit

Schwungkugel *f* fly ball **~ des Regulators** governor ball

Schwung-leine *f* stay wire, wind brace **-lichtbatteriezünder** *m* flywheel dynamo battery ignition unit **-magnetzünder** *m* flywheel magneto **-maschine** *f* centrifugal whirler **-masse** *f* gyrating mass, working load, flywheel mass **-massenrolle** *f* rotary stabilizer, roller with flywheel effect, impedance wheel **-moment** *n* moment of inertia or gyration, flywheel moment, rotative moment, flywheel action **-momentanlasser** *m* flywheel starter

Schwungrad *n* flywheel, balance wheel **beiderseitig gestütztes ~** flywheel between two bearings **fliegendes ~** overhung flywheel

Schwungrad-anlasser *m* inertia starter, flywheel starter **-antrieb** *m* flywheel drive **-gehäuse** *n* flywheel housing **-grube** *f* flywheel pit **-kranz** *m* flywheel rim **-kreis** *m* flywheel circuit, (parallel) resonant circuit **-lichtmagnetzünder** *m* flywheel generator magneto **-los** without flywheel **-magnet** *m* flywheel magneto **-magnetzündung** *f* magneto-flywheel ignition

Schwungrad-marke *f* flywheel marking **-maschine** *f* flywheel engine **-masse** *f* mass of flywheel **-nabe** *f* flywheel hub **-pump** *f* flywheel pump **-schale** *f* flywheel housing **-schaltung** *f* flywheel circuit or connection **-starter** *m* flywheel starter **-synchronisation** *f* flywheel synchronization

Schwungrad-umdrehung *f* flywheel speed **-umformer** *m* flywheel converter **-verzahnung** *f* flywheel gearing **-widerstand** *m* inductive impedance, flywheel resistance **-zahnkranz** *m* flywheel ring gear **-zündmagnet** *m* flywheel magneto

Schwung-regler *m* centrifugal regulator **-ring** *m* rotating ring **-schaufel** *f* Dutch scoop (hydraul.) **-scheibe** *f* driven plate **-seil** *n* guiding cable, shroud, main rope **-verzahnung** *f* flywheel starter gear **-welle** *f* crank shaft

Scintillation *f* scintillation, twinkling

Scintillationszähler *m* scintillation counter

scintillieren to twinkle, scintillate

Scintillometer *n* scintillometer

Scottsche Schaltung Scott system or connection

sechsatomig hexatomic

Sechseck *n* hexagon

sechseckig hexagonal **-e Schraube** hexagon screw or nut **-e Spule** hexagonal coil

Sechselektrodenröhre *f* hexode

Sechserkontakt *m* timing signal recurring every six seconds

sechsfach sixfold, sextuple

Sechsfach-betrieb *m* sextuple system **-pumpe** *f* sextuple pump **-schablonenhalter** *m* six-way template holder **-schreiber** *m* six-point recorder **-stahlhalter** *m* six-way tool block **-steckverbindung** *f* six-way plug connection

sechsfältig sixfold

Sechs-flach *n* hexahedron, hexagon **-flächig** hexahedral **-flügelig** six-bladed **-ganggetriebe** *n* six-speed gearbox **-gitterröhre** *f* hexode

Sechskant mit Ansatz hexagon head with collar

sechskant hexagonal **-draht** *m* hexagonal wire **-eisen** *n* hexagon bar iron **-hohlschraube** *f* female hexagon screw

sechskantiger Bolzen hexagonal bolt

Sechskant-imbusschraube *f* sockethead cap screw **-kopf** *m* hexagon head

Sechskantmutter *f* (regular) hexagonal nut **flache ~** hexagonal jam nut

Sechskant-paßschraube *f* hexagon dowel bolt **-revolverkopf** *m* hexagon turret **-revolverschlitten** *m* hexagon turrent unit **-schlüssel** *m* hexagon spanner **-schlüsselweite** *f* hexagon dimension **-schraube** *f* hexagon cap screw, hexagon head screw **-stab** *m* hexagon bar (rod) **-stahl** *m* hexagons, hexagon bars **-stange** *f* bar of hexagonal section **-steckschlüssel** *m* box-end wrench (hexagon), hexagonal spanner **-stiftschlüssel** *m* hexagon pin spanner **-verschlußschraube** *f* socket head cap screw

Sechskeilwelle *f* six-spline shaft

Sechskomponentenwaage *f* six-component balance

sechsmotorig six-engined

Sechsphasengleichrichter *m* six-phase rectifier

Sechspoldreipolröhre *f* hexode-triode tube

sechspolig six-pole

Sechspol-mischröhre *f* mixing hexode, hexode mixing valve **-regelröhre** *f* fading hexode **-röhre** *f* hexode

sechsseitig hexagonal, six-sided

Sechsspindel-automat *m* six-spindle automatic lathe **-stangenautomat** *m* six-spindle bar-type automatic lathe

sechsstellig six-digit

sechsstrahlig six-pointed

Sechstel *n* sixth

Sechstelkreis *m* sextant

Sechswalzwerk *n* six-roller mill

sechs-wertig hexavalent, sexivalent **-winklig** six-angled, hexangular, hexagonal **-zählig** of sixfold symmetry

Sechzehnerleitung *f* quadruple phantom circuit

Sechzehntel-format *n* in sixteens, sixteenmo **-grad** *m* one-sixteenth degree

Sedimentationspotential *n* sedimentation potential

Sechzigerteilung *f* division of the circle

Sechszylindersternmotor *m* six-cylinder radial engine

Secken-hammer *m* seam hammer, creasing hammer **-zug** *m* creasing tool

Securit *n* triplex glass

sedezimal sedecimal (info proc.)

Sedezimalzahlensystem sexadecimal number system

Sediment *n* sediment

Sedimentation *f* sedimentation

Sedimentgestein *n* sedimentary rocks

sedimentieren to deposit sediment, settle out

Sedimentierung *f* silting, sedimentation

See *m* lake

See *f* ocean, sea **freie ~** high seas **kabbelige ~** surf (breakers) **Über~** overseas **auf hoher ~** on the high seas **die offene ~ erreichen** to stand out to sea

See-amt *n* admiralty court **-anker** *m* sea anchor **-arsenal** *n* naval dockyard **-beben** *n* seaquake, bore (phys. geog.), eagre

Seebeckeffekt *m*, **Seebeckscher Effekt** Seebeck or thermo electric effect

seebeschädigt damaged at sea

Seebeute *f* prize (navy) **-recht** *n* right of prize (navy)

Seebrise *f* sea breeze

Seedampfer *m* ocean liner

Seedienst *m* sea duty **~ haben** to be on sea duty

See-echo *n* sea return (rdr) **-erz** *n* lake iron ore, marine ore **-fähigkeit** *f* seaworthiness **-fahrer** *m* navigator, mariner **-fahrt** *f* sea voyage, navigation **-fernsprechkabel** *n* submarine telephone cable **-fest** not subject to sea-sickness, seaworthy **-festung** *f* (fortified) naval base **-feuer** *n* sea lights **-flieger** *m* naval flier

Seeflug-hafen *m* seaplane base

Seeflugzeug *n* seaplane, hydroplane, naval plane **ein ~ aussetzen** to lower a seaplane **ein ~ einsetzen** to hoist a seaplane

Seefunk *m* marine or maritime radio **-dienst** *m* marine radio service, naval wireless service **-stelle** *f* ship (radio) station

Seegang *m* motion of the sea, swell **hoher ~** heavy sea **-echos** *pl* sea clutter **-schwundeffekt** roller fading **-störung** *f* wave clutter

See-gatt *n* channel, gat, gateway **-gebiet** *n* waters, area of waters

Seeger-ring *m* Seeger ring, circlip lock ring **-sicherung** *f* Seeger circlip

See-gesetz *n* maritime law **-gras** *n* seaweed **-grün** marine green

Seehafen *m* seaport **-tanklager** *n* seaport bulk station **-technik** *f* harbor maintenance and improvement, harbor engineering

See-hahn *m* sea cock **-handbuch** *n* marine handbook, sea annual **-höhe** *f* altitude above sea level, sea level

Seekabel *n* submarine cable, ocean cable **-alphabet** *n* cable or Morse code **-leitung** *f* ocean cable line

See-kalkstein *m* lacustrine limestone **-kanal** *m* maritime canal, sea-level canal, ship canal, sea channel **-karte** *f* hydrographic chart, nautical map, marine or sea chart

seeklar ready to sail **~ sein** to be ready to go to sea

See-klima *n* marine climate **-klippe** *f* reef, shoal **-kompaß** *m* (naval) compass **-krank** seasick **-krankheit** *f* seasickness **-kreide** *f* lake marl, bog lime

Seele *f* soul, bore (gun), stem, core, newel, shaft, center web; (Kabel) helix (cable) **~ des Drahtseiles** wire-rope core **~ eines Geschützrohres** bore of a gun barrel **~ eines Kabels** core of a cable **~ eines Spiralbohrers** twist-drill stem

Seelenachse *f* axis of the bore **~ eines Torus** skeleton of a torus **verlängerte ~** prolongation of the axis of the bore

Seelen-boden *m* bottom of bore **-draht** *m* center wire, flux-core-type electrode, cored wire **-durchmesser** *m* caliber **-elektrode** *f* cored electrode **-faden** *m* core thread **-länge** *f* length of barrel (in calibers) **-messer** *m* barrel gauge

Seelenrohr *n* inner tube of gun liner **festes ~** built-up barrel

Seelen-schweißdraht *m* core welding wire **-stärke** *f* thickness of web **-wand** *f* bore surface **-weite** *f* caliber

Seelicht *n* marine phosphorescence

Seeluft *f* sea air

Seeluftstreitkräfte *f pl* naval aviation, navy air force

See-mann *m* sailor, seaman **-mannschaft** *f* ship's crew or company **-marke** *f* buoy, marker buoy **-mäßig** ready or suitable for shipment **-meile** *f* nautical mile, knot **-mine** *f* sea mine

Seenot *f* distress at sea **-dienst** *m* sea rescue service **-welle** *f* distress wave length **-zeichen** *n* distress call, SOS, distress signal

See-pegelmesser *m* limnimeter **-recht** *n* maritime law or right **-rückleitung** *f* sea return **-sand** *m* sea sand **-schaden** *m* damage to a ship or cargo **-schiffahrt** *f* maritime navigation **-schleuse** *f* sea lock, ship canal

See-stadt *f* coast town, seaside town **-straßenordnung** *f* rules of the (water) road (navy) **-triften** *f pl* wreck or other floating things in sea, strays, derelicts **-stützpunkt** *m* naval base

See-tang *m* algae **-tonne** *f* buoy

Seetransport *m* naval transport, shipment by steamer **-gesellschaft** *f* shipping company **-versicherung** *f* marine insurance

seetüchtig seaworthy **-er Lastkahn** seafaring barge

Seetüchtigkeit *f* seaworthiness

Seeuferbau *m* works for protecting the strand

See-verpackung *f* packed for ocean, shipment, seaworthy packing **-versicherungsgesellschaft** *f* marine insurance company **-wache** *f* sea watch **-warte** *f* naval observatory

Seewasser *n* sea water, brine **-echtheit** *f* ability of a fabric to resist or withstand bleaching by sea water **-kühlung** *f* sea-water cooling

Seewesen *n* nautics

Seewetteramt *n* maritime meteorological office

Seewind *m* sea wind

Seezeichen *n* sea mark **-dampfer** *m* lighthouse tender, buoy tender

Segel *n* sail **-fliegen** *n* sailplaning, sail flying

Segelflieger *m* sailplane pilot, glider or soaring

pilot **-lager** *n* gliding camp

Segelflug *m* sailing flight, gliding or soaring flight **-gelände** *n* soaring or gliding site **-institut** *n* gliding institute **-modellwettbewerb** *m* sailplane-model competition **-sport** *m* gliding for sport **-vorführung** *f* soaring demonstration, display of gliding and soaring flight

Segelflugzeug *n* sailplane, glider **~ mit Hilfsmotor** underpowered motor glider, auxiliary sailplane **mit einem ~ fliegen** to soar, glide

Segelflugzeug-bau *m* sailplane construction **-bauer** sailplane constructor **-entwurf** *m* sailplane design **-fabrik** *f* glider factory **-halle** *f* hangar shed (for gliders) **-muster** *n* type of sailplane **-transportwagen** *m* trailer for sailplanes

Segel-karte *f* sailing chart **-klar** ready to sail **-koje** *f* sail loft **-kunstflug** *m* glider aerobatics **-kunstflugzeug** *n* aerobatic sailplane **-leinen** *n* canvas **-macher** *m* sailmaker

segeln to sail, soar (aviation) **tot ~** to stem the tide

Segeln *n* sailing **~ im größten Kreise** great-circle sailing

Segel-regatta *f* sailing race **-schiff** *n* sailing vessel, sailing barge or boat

Segelstellung *f*, **~ der Luftschraube** feathered pitch of propeller **Luftschraube, die sich in volle ~ bringen läßt** full-feathering propeller **Luftschraube mit Schnellverstellung in ~** quick-feathering propeller **Verstellung in ~** feathering operation

Segeltuch *n* cloth (sail), canvas (sail), duck **-hülle** *f* canvas cover or tarpaulin **-plane** *f* tarpaulin **-stoff** *m* canvas, sailcloth

Seger-Kegel *m* Seger or pyrometric or fusion cone

Segler *m* sailplane, glider

Segment *n* section, segment, sector; (Schalter) wafer **eingefressenes ~, verbranntes ~** burnt segment **verkürztes ~** shortened segment **in Segmente geteilt** segmented

Segment-abzweig *m* segmented branch **-antenne** *f* pill-box or cheese antenna **-blech** *n* segmental core disc **-bogen** *m* segmental arch **-bogendach** *n* arched roof **-drehlager** *n* trunnion bearing **-drucklager** *n* horsehoe bearing **-förmig** segmental, segmentally shaped

segmentieren to segement

Segment-lenkung *f* worm-and-sector steering system **-ring** *m* segmented ring **-schwinge** *f* segment rocker **-schütz** *n* segmental valve, Taintor valve **-sägeblatt** *n* segmental saw blade **-stück** *n* segmental piece **-tor** *n* segmental gate, radial gate, Taintor gate

Segment-umschaltung *f* segment shift **-ventil** *n* radial valve **-verschluß** *m* segment shutter **-welle** *f* (Auto) sector shaft **-wehr** *n* segmental barrage

Sehachse *f* axis of vision

sehen to see, perceive, look

Sehen *n* seeing, sight, vison **einäugiges ~** monocular vision, nonstereoscopic vision **natürliches ~** natural vision **punktförmiges ~** point appearance of a distant light **räumliches ~** stereoscopic vision **zweiäugiges ~** binocular vision, stereoscopic vision

Seh-fehler *m* defect of vision **-feld** *n* field of vision **-feldblende** *f* field diaphragm, field stop **-funktion** *f* visual function

Sehgrößen-konstanz *f* constancy of visual size **-täuschung** *f* illusion of visual size

Seh-hilfsmittel *n* aid to vision **-kegel** *m* angle of vision, cone of vision or view **-klappe** *f* observation port **-kraft** *f* vision, visual power **-kreis** *m* (circle of the) horizon, circle of vision **-lehre** *f* optics **-linie** *f* line of sight, of vision, or of collimation

Sehne *f* fiber, chord (geom.), tendon, sinew

Sehneisen *n* fibrous iron

Sehnen-anker *m* chord-type armature **-dickeverhältnis** *n* (fiber-)thickness ratio **-ebene** *f* chordal surface, tangential plane **-fehler** *m* arc error **-konstruktion** *f* chord construction **-kraft** *f* force parallel to or along chord **-kraftbeiwert** *m* coefficient of force along chord

Sehnen-länge *f* length of chord **-schnitt** *m* chordal or tangential cut or section **-stärkeverhältnis** *n* (fiber-)thickness ratio **-vieleck** *n* polygon inscribed in a circle **-wicklung** *f* drum winding with fractional or shortened pitch, chorded winding (elec.)

Sehnepuddeln *n* puddling of fibrous iron

Seh-nerv *m* optic nerve **-nervenapparat** *m* organ of vision

sehnig fibrous

Sehnungsfaktor *m* pitch factor

Sehöffnung *f* peep-hole

Sehpurpur *m* visual purple

sehr very, highly **~ flüchtiges Benzin** wild gasoline **~ klein** minute **~ wendig** highly maneuvrable

Sehreiz *m* optical stimulus, visual stimulus or excitation

Sehrohr *n* periscope, telescope, viewing tube **-tiefe** *f* periscope depth

Sehschärfe *f* visual acuity, sharpness of vision, resolving power (of eye) **~ des Auges** keenness of vision, resolving power of eye **auf ~ einstellen** to focus

Sehschärfegrenzwinkel *m* angular resolving power, critical angle of visual acuity

Sehschärfen-bestimmung *f* ascertaining the visual acuity **-einteilung** *f* focusing dial, focusing scale

Seh-schlitz *m*, **-spalt** *m* observation slit, peephole, sight (vane), diopter

Sehschwäche *f* weakness of sight **vorgetäuschte ~** simulated amblyopia

Seh-schwelle *f* visual threshold **-stäbchen** *n* optical rod **-strahl** *m* visual ray **-streifen** *m* angle of parallax

Sehvermögen *n* resolving power (of eye), visual faculty, power of sight, power of vision **räumliches ~** power of stereoscopic vision

Seh-tiefe *f* depth of focus, depth of field **-weite** *f* visual distance or range, range of sight **-weitemesser** *m* optometer **-winkel** *m* viewing angle, visual angle **-zäpfchen** *n* visual cone **-zeichen** *n*

visual signal or sign

seicht shallow **-es Wasser** shoal water

Seichtigkeit *f* shallowness

Seichtwasser-ergebnis *n* shallow-water result **-näherung** *f* shallow-water approximation

Seide *f* silk **geklöppelte ~** braided silk **mit ~ doppelt umsponnen** double-silk-covered **mit ~ einfach umsponnen** single-silk-covered **zweifach mit ~ umsponnen** double-silk-covered

Seidebaumwolldraht *m* silk- and cotton-covered wire

seidenartiger Glanz silking, silky sheen

Seidenbespannung *f* silk covering

Seiden-draht *m* silk-covered wire **-faden** *m* silk thread, silk fiber **-fadennaht** *f* silk suture **-fallschirm** *m* silk parachute **-gewebe** *n* silk fabric, cloth, or weave **-glänzend** silky **-glanzpapier** *n* silk paper **-griff** *m* silk scroop **-isolation** *f* silk insulation **-kabel** *n* silk-covered cable **-kämmling** *m* silk noil **-lackdraht** *m* varnished silk-braided wire **-mattiert** satin-frosted

Seiden-numerierung *f* silk titration **-papier** *n* tissue paper **-spulmaschine** *f* silk-winding machine **-stoff** *m* silk fabric or cloth **-übersponnener Messingdraht** silk-covered brass wire **-werg** *n* noils of carded waste silk **-zopf** *m* silk twist or braid

seidig silky

seifen to soap

Seifen-bildung *f* saponification, formation of soap **-blase** *f* soap bubble **-blasenmethode** *f* soap-bubble method **-blasenmodell** *n* soap-bubble model **-echt** fast to soaping **-erde** *f* fuller's earth **-erz** *n* alluvial ore, stream ore **-fertigungsmaschine** *f* soapmaker's machinery **-gold** *n* placer gold **-hautgleichnis** *n* soap film analog **-lamelle** *f* plane soap film or membrane **-lauge** *f* soapsuds **-leim** *m* soap paste

Seifenplattenkühlanlage *f* soap-slab cooling plant

Seifen-pulver *n* soap powder **-sieder** *m* soapmaker **-rinde** *f* quillai, quillaya bark

Seifenspänehobelmaschine *f* soap-shaving planing machine

Seifen-spender *m* soap distributor **-spiritus** *m* soap tincture, spirit of soap **-stein** *m* saponite, soapstone **-ton** *m* fuller's earth **-wasser** *n* soapsuds, soapy water **-wurzelemulsion** *f* soap wort emulsion **-zinn** *n* stream tin

seifig soapy

seiger perpendicular, plumb, upright, vertical **-er Gang** (almost) vertical lode **-e Sprunghöhe** perpendicular throw

Seiger-apparat *m* liquation apparatus **-blei** *n* liquation lead **-gang** *m* vertical vein **-gasse** *f* sweating gutter **-herd** *m* liquation hearth **-hütte** *f* liquation works **-kessel** *m* liquating kettle **-krätze** *f* scrapings of liquation

seigern to liquate, segregate, infiltrate, sweat out (of tin)

Seigern *n* liquating, sweating (of tin)

Seiger-ofen *m* liquating furnace **-riß** *m* vertical section **-schacht** *m* perpendicular shaft **-stelle** *f* segregated spot, hot spot **-stück** *n* liquation cake

Seigerung *f* segregation, liquation

Seigerungs-härtung *f* precipitation hardening **-stelle** *f* segregated spot, segregate **-streifen** *m* segregated band, segregate, ghost line **-zeile** *f* segregation line **-zone** *f* line of segregation (in an ingot)

Seigerwerk *n* liquation works

Seignettesalz *n* Rochelle salt, Seignette salt **-kristall** *m* Rochelle-salt crystal

Seihe *f* strainer

seihen to filter

Seiher *m* strainer, filter **-presse** *f* straining press, cage press **-tuch** *n* cloth filter

Seihe-sack *m* filtering or straining bag **-trichter** *m* percolator, straining or filtering funnel

Seil *n* cable-wire rope, cable rope, line, cable (conductor), loop, strand, chord **~ für Bohrpumpenantrieb** pumping line **durchlaufendes ~** continuous rope **eintrümmiges ~** one-strand rope **offenes ~** open cable, tail rope

Seil-anker *m* stay wire **-antrieb** *m* rope drive, cable drive **-ausgleichrolle** *f* rope balancing sheave **-auskreuzung** *f* crosswire or diagonal bracing **-auslösevorrichtung** *f* cable release (gear) **-bagger** *m* stripping shovel

Seilbahn *f* cable railroad, ropeway, cableway, cord carrier **-kran** *m* ropeway crane **-lader** *m* aerial ropeman **-wagen** *m* ropeway car

seilbetätigt cable-operated, cable-powered

Seil-betrieb *m* rope driving **-birne** *f* rope socket **-bohren** *n* cable drilling or boring, cable drill, well drill, churn drill **-bohrgerät** *n* cable(-drilling) tools **-bohrung** *f* cable drilling, cable drill, well drill, churn drill **-bremse** *f* cable brake **-büchse** *f* cable shoe

Seilchenwinde *f* winch for drawing in rope

Seil-dehnung *f* elongation of cable **-draht** *m* rope wire **-ebene** *f* inclined plane with rope **-eck** *n* string polygon, funicular polygon **-eckkonstruktion** *f* construction of the funicular (link) polygon **-einband** *m* rope splice

seilen to equip with ropes

Seilentlastung *f* pull relief (of rope)

Seiler *m* roper, ropemaker

Seilerei *f* ropemaking (factory)

Seil-fallhammer *m* rope drop hammer **-fänger** *m* rope grab **-fanghaken** *m* fishing hook for rope, rope grab **-flasche** *f* pulley-case **-flaschenzug** *m* rope block or hoist **-führung** *f* rope guide

Seilführungs-buchse *f* control cable guiding bush **-rolle** *f* fairlead **-scheibe** *f* cable pulley

Seil-führung *f* rope guide **-gehänge** *n* hoisting sling **-geschwindigkeit** *f* rope speed **-hängebahn** *f* overhead rope railway, aerial ropeway **-hubeinrichtung** *f* cable hoisting gear **-hülse** *f* rope socket, rope thimble **-hülsenbohrschraube** *f* rope screw socket

Seil-kante *f* rope guide **-kausche** *f* thimble **-klemme** *f* drilling clamp, (wire-rope) clip **-kopf** *m* rope end **-kraft** *f* cable force **-kreuzungspunkt** *m* crossing point of the bracing wires **-kupplung** *f* rope coupling **-kurve** *f* catenary **-länge** *f* rope length

Seillauf *m* rope tread **-bahn** *f* cableway, ropeway **-katze** *f* cable-traveling crab

Seil-leitrolle *f* rope sheave **-leitungswiderstand** *m* rope-guiding resistance **-litze** *f* strand of cable, wire strand **-messer** *n* (wire-rope) knife **-öhr** *n* ear of a cord **-öl** *n* cordage oil

Seil-pendellänge *f* free length of rope **-pflugmaschine** *f* cable plow **-plan** *m* funicular or link polygon **-polygon** *n* link polygon, funicular polygon **-post** *f* Lamson carrier, pickup system, rope post **-postwagen** *m* Lamson carrier **-rad** *n* cable wheel **-rangierwinde** *f* capstan **-reißer** *m* wire-rope chopper **-richtmaschine** *f* wire rope straightening machine **-riese** *m* gravity cable **-rille** *f* grooved roller, rope groove **-ring** *m* cord junction ring **-rolle** *f* rope pulley or sheave, cable pulley

Seilscheibe *f* head wheel, pulley, grooved roller, rope pulley, cable pulley **kleine ~** snatch block

Seil-scheibengerüst *n* rope-pulley frame **-schelle** *f* suspension clamp **-schlag** *m* spin of rope **-schlaufe** *f* rope sling **-schleife** *f* rope eye, rope loop

Seilschlinge *f* rope loop, chain loop, dead line **einen Motor an Seilschlingen aufhängen** to sling an engine

Seil-schloß *n* cable joint **-schlupf** *m* rope slippage **-schmiere** *f* rope grease **-schürze** *f* cable apron, multiple balloon cable **-schwebebahn** *f* aerial ropeway **-seele** *f* (cable) core **-spanner** *m* rope winder **-spannung** *f* rope tension **-speer** *m* rope spear **-sperre** *f* barrage cable **-spleißung** *f* rope splicing or splice **-stärke** *f* rope diameter **-start** *m* towed take-off **-steifigkeit** *f* stiffness of cable, resistance to bending of cable **-steuerung** *f* rope control (lift) **-strang** *m* fall of rope

Seil-trieb *m* rope transmission, rope drive **-trommel** *f* rope or cable drum, hoisting drum **-trommelbremse** *f* winder brake **-trumm** *m* strand of a rope **-tülle** *f* rope socket **-umlenkrolle** *f* guide block **-unterspannung** *f* rope tensioning

Seil-verbindung *f* splice, cable connection **-ver-drillung** *f* back twist of rope **-verkleidung** *f* cable fairing **-vorhang** *m* cable curtain **-werk** *n* cordage **-winde** *f* rope or cable winch **-windung** *f* turn, coil, or spire of rope **-wirbel** *m* rope socket

Seilzug *m* tackle, tow, or cable line **-arbeitsbühne** *f* cradle winch **-messer** *m* rope or cable tensiometer **-waagen** *pl* rope-traction weighers

seimig mucilaginous (viscous)

seismisch seismic **-e Bewegung** seism, earthquake **-e Brechungsmethode** (seismic) refraction method **-e Erschütterung** seismic disturbance

Seismograph *m* seismograph, seismometer, geophone

Seismologie *f* seismology

Seismometer *n* seismometer

Seismoskop *n* seismoscope

Seite *f* page, side, flank, (Dreieck) leg, (Gleichung) member **erste ~ eines Buches** blank page or slur page of a book **hintere ~ eines Doppelflammofens** workman's side of a double reverberatory furnace **linke ~ einer Gleichung** first member or left side of an equation **rechte ~ einer Gleichung** second member or right side of an equation **auf die andere ~ einer Gleichung schaffen** to transpose **~ eines Rahmens** frame piece **die ~ pfeifen** to pipe the side (navy) **auf der ~ liegend** on her beam ends **vordere ~** (d. Blattes) facing page

Seiteisen *n* side iron(s)

Seiten-abdeckung *f* side bonnet, side cover **-ablage** *f* lateral displacement **-ablagerung** *f* spoil bank, side piling **-abrutschanzeiger** *m* side-slip indicator **-abrutschgeschwindigkeit** *f* rate of side-slipping **-abschäumvorrichtung** *f* side skimming attachment **-abstand** *m* lateral displacement, interval **-abweichung** *f* drift, deflection error, lateral deviation, deviation from trajectory **-achse** *f* lateral axis **-amt** *n* dependent or satellite exchange, sub-exchange (teleph.) **-änderung** *f* deflection correction, switch correction of traverse

Seiten-anker *m* side guy, lateral stay **-ankerrelais** *n* side armature relay **-anmerkung** *f* marginal or side note, marginal gloss **-ansatz** *m* side tube, lateral arm or appendage

Seiten-anschluß *m* side contact **-ansicht** *f* side elevation, profile, side view, end view, lateral elevation, lateral view **-antenne** *f* side aerial **-anzeiger** *m* index, register **-arm** *m* side tube, lateral arm, lateral appendage, side branch **-aufriß** *m* side elevation, lateral elevation **-ausgleich** *m* tip balance **-aussteuerung** *f* lateral compensation

Seitenband-dämpfer *m* sideband filter **-dämpfung** *f* side band attenuation **-frequenz** *f* side-band interference, side-band splashing **-senden** *n* side-band transmission **-spitzenleistung** *f* peak sideband power **-unterdrückung** *f* side-band suppression

Seiten-basis *f* azimuth baseline **-begrenzer** *m* traversing stop **-bestimmer** *m* sense finder **-bestimmung** *f* sense finding **-bewegung** *f* yawing (motion) **-blech** *n* side plate **-block** *m* lateral radiator block **-bund** *m* side binding

Seitenbündlung, Genauigkeit der ~ azimuthal accuracy

Seiten-deckel *m* side cover plate **-deckung** *f* flank guard, flank security **-destillat** *n* side stream **-druck** *m* side pressure, side thrust, side force **-drucker** *m* page printer **-drucktelegraph** *m* page-printing telegraph **-echo** *n* side lobe echo **-eck** *n* lateral summit **-einstellung** *f* lateral adjustment **-elektrode** *f* side or lateral electrode, end electrode, wing electrode (of a magnetron)

Seiten-empfänger *m* azimuth receiver **-entladung** *f* lateral discharge **-entleerer** *m* side-dumping hopper, side-tipping dump car, side-discharge car, side-tip wagon **-entleerungsschaufel** *f* (Frontlader) side dump bucket **-entnahme** *f* side cutting **-falz** *m* groove, recess **-fehler** *m* lateral deviation or error **-feinbewegung** *f* endless tangent screw **-fläche** *f* side face, lateral face or surface, flat side, facet **-flansch** *m* side flange **-flosse** *f* vertical fin or stabilizer side float

Seitenflossen-kippsicherung *f* sea wings, stabilizer **-stabilisator** *m* stub wing stabilizer **-verstellung** *f* vertical-fin adjustment

Seiten-fräser *m* side-milling cutter **-frequenz** *f* side frequency **-fuge** *f* lateral joint **-führung** *f* lateral load or guidance, side guiding (of film strip)

Seitenführungs-rollen *pl* side guide rollers **-strahl** *m* guide beam

Seiten-galvanometer *n* string galvanometer **-gang** *m* sidewalk **-gehäuse** *n* final drive housing **-geleise** *n* siding sidetrack **-geschwindigkeit** *f* rate of side slipping, lateral component of velocity **-gesteuerter Motor** side-valve engine **-getriebe** *n* final drive **-gleich** equal sided

Seiten-gleis *n* sidetrack **-gleitflug** *m* sideslip (aviation) **-gondel** *f* sidecar **-graben** *m* side channel or gutter **-griff** *m* side handle **-halter** *m* steady arm, counterbalance **-hebel** *m* traversing lever

Seiten-höhe *f* depth of page **-holm** *m* side outrigger, side member **-hut** *f* flank guard **-induktion** *f* inductive interference **-induktionsschutz** *m* anti-induction device **-kanal** *m* lateral canal or channel **-kante** *f* lateral edge **-kennungsantenne** *f* sense antenna **-keule** *f* side slobe (ant.) **-kipper** *m* side-tip car, side-dump car **-klappe** *f* side flap or vane

Seiten-klemme *f* side terminal **-kolbenstange** *f* side connecting rod **-kollimation** *f* horizontal collimation **-kontrolle** *f* lateral control **-kraft** *f* component force **-kraftachse** *f* lateral force axis **-lage** *f* lateral deflection or position **-lampe** *f* side lamp **-länge** *f* lateral length **-lastigkeit** *f* lateral trim **-leiste** *f* skirtboard, skirting **-leitung** *f* branch pipe line

Seitenleitwerk *n* rudder (assembly), vertical tail surface **doppeltes ~** dual fins and rudders, twin rudder **geteiltes ~** split-rudder assembly, divided control surfaces

Seiten-höhe *f* depth of page **-holm** *m* side outrigger, side member **-hut** *f* flank guard **-induktion** *f* inductive interference **-induktionsschutz** *m* anti-induction device **-kanal** *m* lateral canal or channel **-kante** *f* lateral edge **-kipper** *m* side-tip car, side-dump car **-klappe** *f* side flap or vane

Seiten-klemme *f* side terminal **-kolbenstange** *f* side connecting rod **-kollimation** *f* horizontal collimation **-kontrolle** *f* lateral control **-kraft** *f* component force **-kraftachse** *f* lateral force axis **-lage** *f* lateral deflection **-lampe** *f* side lamp **-länge** *f* lateral length **-lastigkeit** *f* lateral trim **-leiste** *f* skirtboard, skirting **-leitung** *f* branch pipe line

Seitenleitwerk *n* rudder (assembly) **doppeltes ~** dual fins and rudders, twin rudder **geteiltes ~** split-rudder assembly, divided control surfaces

Seiten-leitwerkskraft *f* vertical tail surface load **-leuchten** *n* side lights **-licht** *n* gauge lamp, side light or lamp **-marke** *f* side guide (gauge) **-markenhebel** *m* side guide clamping lever **-mischluftrührer** *m* side air-lift agitator **-moment** *n* yawing moment **-navigation** *f* directional or side navigation **-neigung** (Schiff) heel, list

Seiten-öffnung *f* side opening **-ortung** *f* directional (n)avigation **-parallaxe** *f* lateral (horizontal) parallax **-peilröhre** *f* azimuth of tube **-platte** *f* side plate **-profil** *n* vertical frame member **-rampe** *f* side(-loading) ramp **-reibung** *f* side friction

Seitenricht-antrieb *m* traversing gear **-feld** *n* field of fire, angle of pintle traverse, field of traverse **-fernrohr** *n* lateral tracking telescope **-geschwindigkeit** *f* rate of traverse

seitenrichtig correct left-to-right, non reversed

Seitenricht-maschine *f* traversing mechanism, traversing gear **-rad** *n* traversing handwheel **-rohr** *n* azimuth scope **-schieber** *m* deflection board **-schraube** *f* traversing handwheel shaft **-werk** *n* traversing mechanism **-winkel** *m* angle of traverse, azimuth **-teilung** *f* graduated scale or traversing gear **-trieb** *m* traversing mechanism

Seitenrichtung *f* (angle of) deflection, angle of sighting, side direction **-anzeiger** *m* right-left bearing indicator

Seitenrichtvorrichtung *f* training gear

Seiten-rinne *f* side gutter **-riß** *m* side or lateral elevation, profile

Seitenruder *n* side rudder, rudder (pedal) **-ausgleich** *m* rudder balance **-drehung** *f* rudder torque **-fußhebel** *m* rudder bar **-gelenk** *n* rudder hinge **-hebel** *m* rudder pedal **-trimmklappen** *m* rudder trim tab **-trimmung** *f* rudder trimming **-winkel** *m* rudder angle

Seiten-rutsch *m* sideslip **-schrift** *f* lateral track, horizontal track or recording **-sichtrohr** *n* bearing tube **-schalter** *m* side switch **-scheibe** *f* washer **-schiff** *n* aisle **-schild** *m* side shield, abutment **-schlag** *m* branch gallery (min.) **-schliffwinkel** *m* side-slope angle (of a cutting tool) **-schlitten** *m* lateral slides **-schneider** *m* diagonal (side) cutting pliers **-schneidrollen** *pl* side cutters **-schnitt** *m* sectional side elevation **-schraube** *f* outboard propeller, side terminal

Seitenschruppstahl mit Vierkantspitze half-diamond-point tool

Seitenschub *m* side thrust, axial thrust, axial pressure **~ eines Bogens** shoot, thrust, drift, or push of an arch **waagerechter ~** horizontal or tangential thrust or stress

Seitenschub-beschickungsanlage *f* side-feed stoker **-feuerung** *f* side-feed firing **-lager** *n* thrust bearing

Seiten-schutz *m* flank protection, flank security **-schutzblech** *n* side guard **-schwankung** *f* lateral sway **-schweißung** *f* side-lap welding **-schwimmer** *m* wing-tip float **-septum** *n* alar septum **-sicherung** *f* flank protection

Seitenstabilität *f* directional or lateral stability

Seitenstaffelung *f* lateral separation

Seitenstahl *m* side tool **gebogener ~** bent side tool **linker ~** left-hand side tool **rechter ~** right-hand side tool

Seitensteuer *n* rudder pedal or bar **~ geben** to put on rudder

Seitensteuer-fußhebel *m*, **-hebel** *m* rudder bar **-mann** *m* rudder helmsman

Seiten-steuerung *f* rudder or lateral control **-strahlprisma** *n* side reflecting prism **-strahlung** *f* secondary radiation, lateral, stray, or spurious radiation **-strang** *m* (railway) siding **-streifen** *m* side strip marking **-streuung** *f* lateral dispersion or spread **-strom** *m* slip stream **-stutzen** *m* side support **-support** *m* sidehead, tool arm

Seitenteil *m* side-panel end plate; (Motorhaube) side cover **-kreis** *m* azimuth scale **-ring** *m* graduated ring

Seiten-träger *m* side member **-trieb** *m* traversing drive **-trift** drift due to wind, (lateral) drift **-triftwinkel** *m* drift angle **-trimmung** *f* directional trim **-überdeckung** *f* side lap **-umkehr** *f* lateral inversion (video) **-verbesserung** *f* correction for drift

Seitenverhältnis *n* picture ratio, aspect ratio, picture shape **unendliches ~** infinite aspect ratio, infinitive ratio

Seitenverschiebung *f* lateral deflection, lateral deviation, lateral displacement **schußtafelmäßige ~** theorectical deflection

Seiten-versetzung *f* sidewise displacement **-verstellung** *f* lateral adjustment **-vorgelege** *n* cross shaft **-vorhalt** *m* deflection or lateral lead (distance correction for drift)

Seitenvorhalts-ebene *f* plane of deflection lead, lateral lead plane **-winkel** *m* lateral angular lead of target

Seitenvorschub *m* page feed **~ ausführen** to page (up)

Seitenwand *f* side wall **~ der Kabeltrommel** reel flange

Seitenwand-belag *m* side-wall covering **-bläser** *m* lateral blower **-kühlrohr** (Kessel) furnace cooling tube **-säule** *f* side wall upright **-sprinkler** *m* sidewall sprinkler

Seiten-wandung *f* side wall **-wangen** (Kessel) side wall water boxes **-wendung** *f* deflection, turning **-werkzeug** *n* side-working tool

Seitenwind *m* cross wind, side wind **Landung mit ~** cross-wind landing

Seitenwind-komponente *f* cross-wind component **-kraft** *f* cross-wind force **-schutz** *m* side screen

Seitenwinkel *m* angle of yaw, bearing, azimuth **-beschleunigung** *f* horizontal angular acceleration **-geschwindigkeit** *f* horizontal angular velocity **-vorhalt** *m* deflection lead, lateral angular lead (of target)

Seitenzug *m* transverse stress, lateral pull

seitlich lateral **~ abrutschen** to fall off, sideslip **~ ausrichten** to align laterally **-e Ablenkung** side-thrust effect **-es Abrutschen** sideslip **-e Abweichung** transverse aberration **-er Abzug** side delivery **-e Führung** lateral guidance **-es Gleiten** skidding **-e Schallabschirmung** (b. Mikrophonen) gobo (acoust.) **-e Stromschiene** side contact rail **-er Stützschwimmer** outboard float

seitwärts sideways, laterally

Seitwärts-abschnitt *m* method of offsets **-bewegung** *f* lateral motion, lateral movement **-einschneiden** *n* lateral resection (artil.) **-schleuderung** *f* side glide, side slip

Sekans *m*, **Sekante** *f* secant (math)

Sekarerollen *f pl* counter reel (paper mfg.)

Sektionalkessel *m* straight-tube boiler

Sektionskarte *f* sectional chart

Sektionsmesser *n* diathermy knife **elektrisches ~** electric bistouri

Sektor *m* sector, gate **~ der dominierenden Winde oder Wellen** direction of exposure (part exposed to wind or wave) **der warme ~** warm sector

Sektor-abtastung *f* sector scanning **-bild** *n* sector display **-bildung** *f* sectoring **-darstellung** *f* sector display (rdr)

Sektoren-membran *f* sectorial cone (loudspeaker) **-scheibe** *f* spinning (sector) disk **-verschluß** *m* segment shutter

Sektor-feld *n* sector field **-feuer** *n* sector light

sektorförmiges Becken sector-shaped basin

Sektor-membran *f* sector diaphragm or cone **-momentverschluß** *m* sector instantaneous shutter **-verschluß** *m* sector gate (weir) **-wehr** *n* submergible Taintor gate dam

sektorweiser Bildausfall blind sector

sekundär secondary, secondarily, subsequent(ly) **-er Aufbau** secondary structure **-e Kaltfront** secondary cold front **-es Glied** secondary member **-er Lunker** axial sponginess (in an ingot), secondary pipe **-e Ruderfläche** secondary structure **-er Tiefdruck** secondary low **-e Zusammenstellung** subassembly

Sekundär-anker *m* rotating field magnet, secondary armature **-antenne** *f* director **-bahn** *f* light railway, secondary railway **-batterie** *f* accumulator battery, storage cell, secondary cell or battery **-durchbruch** *m* secondary burst **-echos** *pl* second-trace echoes **-elektron** *n* secondary electron **-elektronenverstärker** *m* secondary electron multiplier **-element** *n* accumulator cell, storage battery, secondary cell **-emission** *f* secondary emission

Sekundäremissions-ausbeute *f* secondary-emission rate **-charakter** *m* secondary-emission characteristic **-faktor** *m* secondary- emission factor **-kathode** *f* dynode, electron mirror **-rauschen** *n* secondary emission noise **-strom** *m* secondary-emission current **-verstärkung** *f* secondary-emission amplification, electron multiplication **-vervielfacher** *m* secondary-emission multiplier, electron multiplier tube or phototube

sekundäremittierend secondary emitting

Sekundär-empfang *m* secondary reception, double circuit reception **-fluoreszenz** *f* sensitized or secondary fluorescence **-funkempfänger** *m* double-circuit receiving set **-härte** *f* secondary hardness **-kreis** *m* secondary circuit **-leistung** *f* secondary power **-lichtquelle** *f* secondary (light) source **-luftstrom** *m* by-pass airflow (of rocket) **-radar** *n* secondary radar **-saal** *m* subsidiary hall **-schaltung** *f* secondary switching **seite** *f* secondary winding, secondary **-spannung** *f* secondary stress, secondary potential, secondary voltage **-spule** *f* secondary coil

Sekundär-strahler *m* secondary radiator, parasitic element (ant.) **-strahlung** *f* secondary emission, secondary radiation **-strom** *m* secondary current, induced current **-stromkreis** *m* secondary circuit **-struktur** *f* secondary structure **-träger** *m* subcarrier **-verstärker** *m* secondary amplifier **-wechselstrom** *m* secondary alternating current **-wicklung** *f* secondary winding **-widerstand** *m* secondary resistance **-zelle** *f* secondary or storage cell

Sekunde *f* second **-meterkerze** *f* meter-candle-second

Sekunden-antrieb *m* seconds control **-bruchteil** *m* split second **-meter** *pl* meters per second **-uhr** *f* timepiece with secondhand **-verbrauchszahl** *f* rate of consumption per second **-zähler** *m* seconds counter, stop watch **-zeiger** *m* secondhand

sekundlich per second

selbst itself, self, even, spontaneous **~ umdrehend** rotational

selbstabdichtend self-sealed, self-sealing **-er Kraftstoffbehälter** leak-retardant fuel tank **-es Lager** self-sealed bearing

selbstabfallende Schlacke self-releasing slag

Selbst-abgleich *m* automatic balancing (comput.) **-abgleichend** self-balancing **-abnahmemaschine** *f* Yankee paper machine **-abschirmend** self-shielding

Selbst-abschlackung *f* self-clinkering **-absorption** *f* self-shielding **-abstellung** *f* automatic stop-(page) **-abstoßung** *f* self repulsion **-adjungiert** self-adjoint

selbständig independent, autonomous, separate,

self-reliant **-e Entladung** spontaneous discharge, self-sustained discharge **-e Funktion** self-consistent function

Selbständigkeit *f* independence

Selbständigmachen *n* making independent, loss of control

selbst-angetrieben self-propelled **-anlasser** *m* automatic starter, self-starter **-alterung** *f* ageing at room temperature **-anlauf** *m* self-sustained operation **-anpassung** *f* auto-adaptation

selbstansaugend naturally aspirated **-er Motor** normally aspirated engine, self-aspirating engine **-e Pumpe** self-priming pump

Selbstansaugevorrichtung *f* vacuum producing priming device

Selbstanschluß-amt *n* automatic or dial telehone exchange, automatic central office **-betrieb** *m* automatic dial exchange working **-nebenstellenanlage** *f* private automatic exchange **-nebenstellenzentrale** *f* private automatic branch exchange **-privatzentrale** *f* private automatic exchange

Selbstanschlußsystem *n* automatic telephone system ~ **mit Stromstoßempfängern** stored-impulse automatic telephone system ~ **mit unmittelbarer Stromstoßgebung** direct-impulse automatic telephone system

Selbst-anschlußwesen *n* automatic telephony **-antrieb** *m* self-propulsion, automatic drive **-anzeigender Peiler** automatic or direct-reading direction finder **-aufheizkathode** *f* ionic-heated cathode **-aufladung** *f* self-charge **-aufleger** *m* automatic feeding **-aufzug** *m* automatic winding

Selbst-ausgleich *m* automatic balancing, self-regulation **-ausgleichend** self-compensating **-ausleger** *m* automatic delivery **-auslöschung** *f* self-quenching **-auslöser** *m* self-timer **-auslösung** *f* automatic release or disconnection, automatic trip (ping action) **-ausrücker** *m* automatic disengaging motion **-ausrückung** *f* automatic disengagement

Selbstausschalter *m* automatic circuit breaker **elektromagnetischer** ~ electromagnetic cutout

Selbst-austausch *m* self-exchange **-benetzend** self-wetting

Selbst-beobachtung *f* introspection **-beringung** *f* self-hooping **-binder** *m* harvester **-bremsend** self-limiting **-brennend** self-baking **-demagnetisierung** *f* self-demagnitization

selbstdichtend self-sealing, self-tightening, self-packing **-e Kopplung** self-sealing coupling

Selbst-diffusion *f* autodiffusion **-doublierung** *f* automatic doubling arrangement **-durchdringung** *f* self-intersection **-einleger** *m* self-feed attachment, self-feeder

selbsteinstellend self-adjusting, self-aligning **-er Nocken** self-adjusting cam

Selbst-einstellung *f* self-alignment, self-adjustment, self-setting **-energie** *f* self-energy **-entlader** *m* automatic-discharge hopper, automatic-tipping car, self-dumper, automatic tipper **-entladewagen** *m* self-discharging truck **-entladung** *f* self-discharge, local action **-entleerende Schleuder** self-discharging centrifugal **-entleerer** *m* automatic-discharge hopper, self-dumper, automatic-tipping car, automatic tipper

Selbst-entleerung *f* automatic discharge **-entleerungsvorrichtung** *f* automatic-discharging device **-entmagnetisierungsfeld** *n* self-demagnetizing field **-entzündlich** spontaneously inflammable **-entzündlichkeit** *f* spontaneous combustibility, spontaneous inflammability **-entzündungstemperatur** *f* autogenous-ignition temperature **-erhaltend** self-maintaining **-erhaltung** *f* self-preservation **-erhitzung** *f* self-heating, spontaneous heating

selbsterregend self-exciting **-er Röhrensender** self-excited oscillator transmitter **-er Schwingungskreis** autodyne **-er Sender** self-oscillatory transmitter

selbsterregt self-exited **-e Schwingröhre** self-excited oscillator tube

Selbsterregung *f* self-excitation, self-oscillation, self-induction, self-sustained oscillation ~ **in tiefer Frequenz** motorboating (radio)

Selbst-farbe *f* self-color, solid color **-farbig** of the same tint, self-colored **-fernwahl** *f* automatic toll dialling **-fixierende Vorrichtung** equalizing fixture, self-aligning fixture **-fluchtend** self-aligning **-fokussierend** self-focusing **-fördernd** self-feeding **-frühzündung** *f* spontaneous preignition **-führung** *f* self-commutation **-füller** *m* self-filling fountain pen

Selbstgang *m* self-feed, automatic feed, automatic operation ~ **für die Höhenstellung des Tisches** power elevation of table ~ **des Vorschubes** self-feed, automatic feed

Selbstgang-einrücker *m* regulator for power feed **-einrückrad** *n* power-feed lock **-kuppelung** *f* feed clutch **-kuppelungshebel** *m* feed-clutch lever **-stufenscheibe** *f* feed driving cone **-umsteuerhebel** *m* feed reverse

selbstgehendes Erz self-fluxing ore

selbstgegossen self-cast

selbstgehend self-starting, self-fluxing **-es Erz** self-fluxing ore

selbst-gleichrichtendes Röhrenvoltmeter self-rectifying tube voltmeter **-greifer** *m* automatic-grab bucket **-haltekontakt** *m* holding or locking contact **-härtend** self-hardening **-härter** *m* self-hardening steel **-härtestahl** *m* self-hardening steel

selbsthemmend self-locking, irreversible **-es Schneckengetriebe** self-locking worm gear

Selbsthemmung *f* automatic locking ~ **des Gewindes** nonreversibility of the tread

Selbstinduktion *f* self-induction

Selbstinduktions-änderung *f* change in self-inductance **-dekade** *f* self-induction decade (radio) **-koeffizient** *m* self-inductance, coefficient of self-induction **-normal** *n* self-induction standard **-spule** *f* inductance coil, self-induction coil

selbst-induktiv self-inductive **-induktivität** *f* self-inductance, coefficient of self-induction

Selbstinduktivitätskoeffizient *m* coefficient of self-inductance, coefficient of self-induction

Selbst-kapazität *f* self-capacitance, distributed capacitance of a circuit **-klebend** self-sealing **-klemme** *f* self-clipping device **-kontrolle** *f* automatic checking (comp) **-konzentration** *f* self-focusing

Selbstkosten *pl* cost of production, net cost, factory cost **-berechnung** *f* calculation of production cost **-berechnungsabteilung** *f* cost

accounting department **-preis** *m* cost to manufacture, cost price
Selbstkühlung *f* self cooling
Selbstlaufdrehzahl *f* self-sustaining speed
Selbstlaut *m* vowel **-deutlichkeit** *f* vowel articulation
selbstleuchtend self-illuminating, luminous **-es Instrument** luminous instrument **-er Lichtmodulator** self-illuminating light modulator
Selbstleuchter *m* self-luminous substance, fluorescent substance, phosphor
Selbstleuchtverfahren *n* self-luminous or self--emissive method
selbstlöschend self-quenching **-es Zählrohr** self-quenching counter tube
Selbst-löschung des Kalkes spontaneous slaking of lime **-lötung** *f* autogenic soldering **-messend** self-measuring **-nachstellbar** self-adjustable **-öffnender Schneidkopf** self-opening die head **-polymerisieren** to auto-polymerize **-programmierung** *f* automatic programming **-prüfend** automatic checking
selbst-reduzierend self-reducing **-regelnd** automatic (controllable), self-regulating or regulative **-regelung** *f* automatic control **-regelungsgeschwindigkeit** *f* rate of self-regulation
selbstregistrierend self-recording, automatic recording **-er Pegel** fluviograph
selbstregulierend self-regulating
Selbst-regulierung *f* automatic regulation **-rücklauf** *m* self scanning (TV) **-sättigungsgleichrichter** *m* self-saturating rectifier
Selbstschalter *m* auto-switch, automatic switch **-kasten** *m* automatic switch gear
selbst-schirmende Spule self-shielded coil, astatic coil **-schließender Brennstoffbehälter** self-sealing fuel tank
Selbstschluß-dampfventil *n* self-acting steam-pipe closing valve **-klappenventil** *n* automatic flap valve **-kugel** *f* self-closing ball valve
selbstschmierend self-lubricating
Selbst-schmierlager *n* self-lubricating bearing **-schneidende Schraube** self-tapping screw **-schreiben** to register or record by instruments
selbstschreibend self-recording **-e Meßvorrichtung** autographic recorder
Selbst-schreiber *m* recording instrument, (automatic) recorder **-schwingen** *n* self-excitation, self-oscillation
selbstschwingend self-sustained **-e Mischröhre** *f* self-heterodyning mixer tube, autodyne
Selbstschwingungsvorrichtung *f* thermionic trigger device
selbstsichernd self-locking
selbstspannend self-tightening **-e Kuppelung** automatic coupling
Selbst-spanner (Kolben) self-expanding packing ring **-speisekontakt** *m* sealing-in contact
selbstsperrend self-locking **-es Getriebe** self-locking gear **-e Lenkung** irreversible steering **-er Schwingungerzeuger** self-blocking oscillator
Selbstsperrung *f* self-stopping **~ des Gewindes** nonreversibility of the thread
Selbstspinner *m* self-acting mule
selbstständig independent **-e Entladung** spontaneous discharge, self-sustained discharge **-e Funktion** self-consistent function
Selbst-starter *m* self-starter **-steuer** *n* automatic control **-steuergerät** *n* automatic pilot, automatic control device **-steuernder Kolben** self-distributing piston **-steuerung** *f* automatic control, automatic flight control (aviat) **-steuervorrichtung** *f* self-steering device **-stich** *m* siphon tap **-strahlungsverfahren** *n* self-emissive or self-illuminating method **-synchronisierend** self-synchronizing
selbsttätig self-acting, automatic **~ abgleichend** self-balancing **~ wirkend** automatically acting
selbsttätig-e Besetzthaltung *f* automatic holding device **-er Pegelregler** automatic volume control **-er Peiler** (Radar) automatic direction finder **-er Ruf** machine ringing **-es Schlußzeichen** automatic clearing **-er Schwundregler** automatic volume control **-es Seenotalarmgerät** autoalarm **-es System** dial telephone
selbsttätig-er Übertrag *m* self-instructed carry **-er Umlauf** thermosiphon, automatic circulation **-er Untersetzer** automatic scaler **-es Unterwerk** automatic substation **-e Verstärkungsregelung** automatic gain control or regulation **-er Zähler** automatic scaler **-er Zeitansager** automatic time announcer **-e Zugsteuerung** *f* automatic traction controller
Selbst-steueranlage *f* auto-pilot **-tätig** automatic, self-acting **-temperung** *f* self-annealing **-tönen** *n* squealing or ringing (of a tube) **-tonend** self-toning **-tragend** self-supporting **-überlagerer** *m* autodyne, self-heterodyne, autoheterodyne **-überlagerung** *f* autodyne, self-heterodyne **-überlagerungsempfang** *m* self-heterodyne reception, autodyne reception **-umkehr** *f* self-reversal **-umkehrung** *f* self-reversal
selbstumlaufender Synchronmotor auto-synchronous motor
Selbstunterbrecher *m* self-interrupter, buzzer, automatic interrupter, automatic circuit breaker, automatic cutout **-kontakt** *m* trembler contact, self-interrupter contact **-relais** *n* buzzer relay **-schaltung** *f* automatic circuit-breaker circuit
Selbstunterbrechung *f* self-interruption
Selbstunterbrechungsunterbrecher *m* self-interrupting interrupter
Selbstverbrauch an Kohle coal consumed at the pit
Selbst-verbrennung *f* spontaneous combustion **-verdampfung** *f* flashing, self-evaporation **-verkäufer** *m* automatic selling machine **-verladegut** *n* self-loading charge **-vernebelung** *f* smoke screening of own troops **-verriegelt** self-locking **-verspannung** *f* creation of residual stresses
selbstverstärkende Bremse servo brake
Selbst-versteller *m* automatic timer, timing device **-verstellinie** *f* automatic control characteristic (line) **-verstellung** *f* automatic control or timing **-verstellwinkel** *m* automatic control angle (timing angle) **-verwaltung** *f* self-management, self-government, autonomy **-vorspannung** *f* self-bias
Selbstwählfernverkehr *m* toll-line dialing
selbstzentrierendes Spannfutter autocentering chuck
Selbst-zersetzung *f* spontaneous decomposition **-zerlegerzünder** *f* self-destruction type fuse **-zerstörungsanlage** *f* (Rakete) self-destruction

device **-zielgerät** *n*, **(-suchgerät)** *n* homing device

Selbst-zünder *m* self-igniting lighter **-zündung** *f* compression ignition, spontaneous ignition, self-ignition, automatic ignition, autoignition

Selektion *f* selection, selectance, selective (radio)

Selektions-filter *n* switchable i-f transformer **-draht** *m* selection wire

selektiv selective **nicht ~** nonselective **-e Ablagerung** selective localization **-e Deposition** selective localization **-er Schwund** selective fading **-e Störung** selective interference

Selektivität *f* selectivity **veränderliche ~** variable selectivity

Selektivitäts-grad *m* selectivity ratio **-kurve** *f* selectivity curve, selectivity characteristic, band-width curve **-regelung** *f* selectivity control

Selektiv-kreis *m* selecting circuit, selective circuit, selector circuit **-ruf** *m* selective calling **-schutz** *m* selective protection, discriminating relay **-störung** *f* selective jamming

Selektor *m* selector

Selektron *n* selectron (comput)

Selen *n* selenium **-ammonium** *n* ammonium selenide **-antimon** *n* antimony selenide

Selenat *n* selenate

Selen-blei *n* clausthalite **-bleiwismutglanz** *m* galenobismutite **-chlorid** *n* selenium (tetra)-chloride **-chlorür** *n* selenium monochloride **-diäthyl** *n* selenium diethyl **-eisen** *n* ferrous selenide **-gleichrichter** *m* selenium rectifier **-haltig** seleniferous, containing selenium

Selenid *n* selenide

selenig selenious **-e Säure** selenious acid

selenigsaures Ammonium ammonium selenite **~ Natrium** sodium selenite

Selenit *m* selenite

Selen-kompaß *m* selenium or selenic compass **-kupfer** *n* copper selenide **-metall** *n* (metallic) selenide **-oxyd** *n* selenium oxide **-quecksilber** *n* mercury selenide **-quecksilberblei** *n* lehrbachite **-salz** *n* selenide **-säure** *f* selenic acid

selensaures Ammonium ammonium selenate

Selen-schicht *f* selenium layer **-schichtscheibe** *f* selenium (layer) disk **-schlamm** *m* selenium slime or mud **-schwefel** *m* selensulfur **-silber** *n* silver selenide **-silberglanz** *m* naumannite **-sperrschichtphotozelle** *f* selenium blocking-layer photocell, selenium barrier cell **-sulfid** *n* selenium sulfide **-tetrafluorid** *n* selenium tetrafluoride

selentisch selenitic

Selen-verbindung *f* selenium compound **-wasserstoff** *m* hydrogen selenide **-wasserstoffsäure** *f* hydroselenic acid **-widerstandzelle** *f* selenium conductive cell **-wismutglanz** *m* guanajuatite **-zelle** *f* selenious cell, selenium cell **-zyanid** *n* selenocyanate **-zyankalium** *n* potassium selenocyanate

Selfaktor *m* self-acting mule

Selfbogen *m* flashover

Sellers-Kuppelung *f* Sellers (compression) coupling

Selsyn *n* selsyn (servo)

selten rare, seldom, infrequent **-e Erde** rare earth

seltene Erden *pl* lanthanide series

Seltenheit *f* rarity, scarcity, infrequency

Seltener-Rost *m* Seltener screen

Semaphor *m* semaphore **-station** *f* semaphore station

Semet-Solvay-Ofen *m* Semet-Solvay (horizontal-flue) oven

semiholonom semi-holonomic

Semiinvariante *f* semi-invariant

semitechnische Versuche semi-technical tests

semizirkular semicircular

Senarmontit *m* senarmontite

Sende-achse *f* transmitter shaft (teleg) **-amt** *n* transmitting station **-anker** *m* sender armature **-anlage** *f* transmitting installation **-antenne** *f* transmitting antenna or aerial **-ausgangsleistung** *f* transmitter output power **-bandfilter** *n* transmitting filter

Sendebasis der Erdtelegraphie transmitting basis of earth tepegraphy

Sende-batterie *f* sending battery **-beginn** *m* sign-on (video) **-bereich** *m* range of transmission **-bezugsdämpfung** *f* reference equivalent of the transmitter **-bereitschaft** *f* readiness to transmit **-bild** *n* outgoing subject copy **-buchse** *f* output hub **-bürste** *f* sending brush **-dipol** *n* transmitter dipole **-einrichtung** *f* transmission equipment or installation

Sendeempfangs-gerät *n* transceiver **-schalter** *m* transmitting-receiving switch **-umschalter** *m* antenna change-over switch

Sende-freigabesignal *n* proceed-to-send signal **-frequenz** *f* transmitting frequency **-gerät** *n* radio transmitter

Sende-geschwindigkeit *f* speed of transmission, signaling speed **-hebel** *m* transmitting lever **-kanal** *m* transmission channel, signaling channel **-klavier** *n* key sender

Sende-kondensator *m* signaling condenser, sending condenser **-kontakt** *m* transmitter contact **-kontrollapparat** *m* transmission-control apparatus **-leistung** *f* transmitting power **-lochstreifen** *m* perforated send tape

senden to transmit, send, radio **nochmals ~** to rerun, send again

Senden *n* (radio) transmission **~ mit unterdrückter Trägerwelle** suppressed-carrier transmission **~ durch Verstimmung** compensated continuous-wave transmission **rein ungedämpftes ~** cut-in continuous-wave transmission

Sende-norm *f* transmission standard **-ortskreis** *m* local send circuit **-pause** *f* silent period, (transmission) interval, station break, transmission intermission **-pentode** *f* transmitting pentode

Sender *m* sender, transmitter, emitter, transmitting system, vibrator, oscillator, broadcasting or sending station **~ mit Tastenfeld** keyboard sender **~ mit unterdrückter Trägerwelle** quescent transmitter system **~ mit Simultankanälen** channellized transmitter **~ mit Vakuumröhre** vacuum-tube transmitter **drahtloser ~** transmitting station, (radio) transmitter, sender **gedämpfter ~** spark transmitter **gekuppelter ~** inductive transmitter **gepeilter ~** tuned-in beacon or transmitter

Sender, modulationsgesteuerter ~ audio-frequency modulated transmitter **quarzgesteuerter ~** quartzcontrolled transmitter **rückgekoppelter ~** feed-back transmitter **selbsterregender ~** self-oscillatory transmitter **tönender ~** musical-spark transmitter **ungedämpfter ~** continuous-wave transmitter **zweistufiger ~** two-stage transmitter

Sender-achse *f* transmitting shaft **-amt** *n* transmitting station **-anlage** *f* transmitter set or station **-anordnung** *f* arrangement of transmitter **-anschluß** *m* transmitter connection or hook-up **-antenne** *f* transmitting aerial

Senderaum *m* transmitter hall

Sender-aussteuerung *f* transmitter control **-bereich** *m* range of transmitter

Senderdurchmodulierung *f*, **hohe ~** operation of transmitter station at high modulation percentage

Sendereichweite *f* range of transmitter

sendereigner Ton code or tuning note

Sendereingang *m* transmitter input

Senderelais *n* transmitting relay, signaling relay

Sender-empfänger *m* transceiver, combined transmitter-receiver **-empfängerumformer** *m* transmitter-receiver converter **-erregerkreis** *m* oscillating transmitting circuit **-frequenz** *f* transmitter frequency

Sende-richtung *f* direction of transmission **-ring** *m* transmitting ring

Senderleistung *f* power of a transmitter, capacity of a (radio) transmitter

Sendermonitor *m*, **automatischer ~** signal comparator **-pendelung** *f* transmitter suring

Senderohr *n* (Rohrpost) sending tube

Senderöhre *f* transmitter valve, generator triode, power tube, transmitting valve or tube **~ mit Anodenkühlung** cooled-anode transmitting valve (CAT) **~ an laufender Pumpe** demountable valve or tube **frequenzgesteuerte ~** frequency-stabilized transmitter tube

Senderöhren-gestell *n* power-tube rack **-kühler** *m* transmitting valve cooler

Sender-rahmen *m* transmitter mounting frame **-sockel** *m* keyboard base **-spannung** *f* transmitter voltage **-speisung** *f* transmitter supply **-sperrröhre** *f* transmitter blocker cell **-sperrschalter** *m* anti-transmit/receive tube (rdr) **-sperrzelle** *f* transmitter-blocker cell **-steuerbuchse** *f* transmitting cam sleeve **-sucher** *m* sender finder

Sender-trennschrank *m* transmitter combining filter cabinet **-vorheizung** *f* transmitter preheating **-wahlschalter** *m* transmission selector (switch) **-wahltafel** *f* transmitter selection panel **-zentrale** *f* transmitter control station **-zubehör** *n* transmitter accessories

Sende-scheibe *f* transmitting disk **-schiene** *f* selector bar **-schleife** *f* transmitting loop **-schrank** *m* transmitter cubicle **-segment** *n* transmitting segment **-seite** *f* sender end, sending end, generator end (of cable), transmit branch

sendeseitig transmitting end

Sendestation *f* transmitter, transmitting station, sending station **gerichtete ~** directional transmitter

Sendestelle *f* transmitting station, (radio) transmitter, sender, sending or broadcasting station

Sende-stopsignal *n* stop-send signal **-streifen** *m* transmitting tape **-strom** *m* sending current **-system** *n* transmitting system **-taste** *f* sending key

Sende- und Empfangsgerät *n* transmitting and receiving set, two-way radio

Sende-verstärker *m* sending amplifier, transmitter amplifier **-verteiler** *m* sending or transmitting distributor **-vorlage** *f* (Bildfunk) transmitting original **-vorrichtung** *f* transmitter arrangement **-welle** *f* transmitted wave, working wave **-werte** *pl* telemetered data

Sendklavier *n* sending key

Sendung *f* transmission, broadcast, shipment, emission, signaling

Sendungskreis, schwingender ~ oscillating transmitting circuit

sengen to singe, scorch, parch, flame

Sengerei *f* singeing

Sengierit *m* sengierite

Seng-maschine *f* singeing machine **-nadel** *f* singeing pin

senkbar depressable

Senk-baum *m* ground spear **-bewegung** *f* lowering motion, lowering movement, downward motion **-blei** *n* plumb bob, lead **-boden** *m* perforated bottom **-bolzen** *m* sink bolt **-bremsschaltung** *f* generator braking **-brunnen** *m* dry open caisson, sunk well

Senke *f* depression, sink, hoop net, catcher, shallow subsidence, crevasse, dip, trough, valley, negative source

Senkel *m* depression, hollow, plummet, plumb bob

senken to lower, sink, screw down, countersink, fall off, depress, sag, slope **sich ~** to sink in, slope, settle, sag **den Förderkorb um eine Etage ~** to drop or lower the cage one level **mit Werkzeug ~** to counterbore or chamfer

Senken *n* lowering, screwing down

Senker *m* chamfering drill, rock drill, countersink, counterbore, sinker **kegeliger ~** countersink, chamfer tool

Senker-einstellschraube *f* stitch adjusting screw **-träger** *m* stitch cam post

Senk-faschine *f* fascine dam sunk by means of stones, bundles of fascines, water fascine **-grube** *f* bog, waste or draining well, drain, catch basin, sinkhole, sink trap, sump, cesspool **-hammer** *m* sledge hammer **-holzschraube** *f* flush wood screw

Senkkasten *m* (compressed-air) caisson, sunk caisson **-gründung** *f* foundation on caissons

Senk-kerbnagel *m* countersunk head grooved pin (type C), cotter pin **-kiste** *f* crib, cribwork **-kolben** *m* (polishing or finishing) bit, pointed countersink

Senkkopf-holzschraube *f* flat-head wood screw **-niet** *m* countersunk rivet **-schraube** *f* countersunk screw, slotted flat-head screw

Senkkorb *m* snore piece of a sinking pump, basket filled with gravel

Senkkörper *m* sinker, hob **~ errichten** to erect a perpendicular **~ fällen** to drop a perpendicular

Senk-küpe *f* dipping frame **-loch** *n* catch basin, sinkhole **-lot** *n* plumb bob **-mauerung** *f* pit masonry **-mutter** *f* countersunk nut **-niet** *m* flush rivet, countersunk rivet, flat-head rivet **-nietung** *f* flush riveting, countersunk riveting **-pumpe** *f* sinking pump

senkrecht vertical, normal, at right angle to, perpendicular **~ zu** square with **~ steigen** to zoom, climb vertically ~ **zueinander** in quadrature to each other, at right angles **räumlich ~ aufeinander** in space quadrature **-e Achse** vertical axis **-e Beleuchtung** scaffold lighting, overhead lighting **-e Gitterlinie** Y line of map grid **-es Hochreißen** zooming up

senkrecht, -e magnetische Kraft vertical magnetic force **-e Kurve** vertical turn **-e umgekehrte Kurve** vertical reversement **-e Luftdrucksteigung** vertical pressure gradient **-er Schachtofen** vertical-pit-type furnace **-er Schenkel** vertical side **-e Schleife** vertical loop **-e Schleife nach vorn** outside loop

senkrecht, -e Schleife für den Sandsack mooring loop **-er Schnitt** vertical section **-e Schwanzoberfläche** vertical tail area, vertical tail surface **-er Sturzflug** vertical dive **-es Temperaturgefälle** lapse rate **-er Temperaturgradient** vertical temperature gradient **-e Wendung** vertical turn **-er Windkanal** free spinning tunnel, vertical spin tunnel

Senkrecht-anemometer *m* vertical anemometer **-antrieb** *m* vertical drive **-auflösung** *f* vertical resolution **-aufstieg** *m* vertical take-off **-bild** *n* vertical photograph **-bewegung** *f* vertical travel **-bohrung** *f* vertical hole or bore

Senkrechte *f* perpendicular line, vertical, normal, plumb (line)

Senkrecht-ebene *f* vertical plane **-faden** *m* vertical center-line-wire **-fräskopf** *m* vertical spindle head **-fräsmaschine** *f* vertical milling machine **-geschwindigkeit** *f* vertical (diving) speed **-halter** *m* vertical-type support **-induktion** *f* vertical induction **-kraft** *f* normal force, vertical force **-langfräsmaschine** *f* vertical plano-milling machine **-luftaufnahme** *f* vertical aerial photograph

Senkrechträummaschine mit Abwärtszug vertical pull-down, broaching machine ~ **mit Aufwärtszug** vertical pull-up broaching machine

Senkrecht-reihenkammer *f* vertical strip camera **-schleifmaschine** *f* vertical spindle grinder **-schlitz** *m* vertical slot

Senkrechtstanze- und Schermaschine *f* vertical punching and shearing machine

Senkrecht-stärke *f* vertical intensity **-start** *m* (VTO) vertical take-off

Senkrechtstarter *m*, **Senkrechtstartflugzeug** *n* VTOL aircraft (Vertical take-off and landing)

Senkrecht-stellung *f* verticality, vertical or perpendicular position, plumb-line position **-stoßmaschine** *f* vertical slotting machine **-tauchen** *n* stationary dive **-verstellung** *f* vertical adjustment **-vorschub** *m* vertical feed **-welle** *f* vertical shaft

Senk-satz *m* sinking set **-schacht** *m* caisson, drop shaft **-schachtverfahren** *n* sinking by the caisson method **-schaufel** *f* anti-breakage shovel **-schnur** *f* sounding line

Senkschraube *f* countersunk screw ~ **mit Vierkant** countersunk carriage bolt

Senksinne (im) lowering direction

Senk-spindel *f* specific-gravity spindle, hydrometer **-stellung** *f* (Hydraulik) lowering position, vertical position **-stift** *m* countersunk wire nail, sunken peg **-stock** *m* grooved anvil **-stück** *n* mattress of fascine work, fascine dam **-tiefe** *f* sinking depth **-turm** *m* retractable turret **-verstellung** *f* vertical adjustment

Senkung *f* dropping, lowering, depression, weight, settling, sinking, subsidence, settlement, dip, subsiding, submergence, sag, droop, inclination, hollow ~ **des Grundes** settlement or subsidence of the ground ~ **für Schaltgriff** countersinking for switch handle ~ **des Wasserstandes** lowering of the water level

Senkungs-graben *m* rift valley **-maß** *n* amount of the settling **-welle** *f* wave caused by a falling stage **-winkel** *m* depression angle

Senk-verteilung *f* drop distribution (of a curve) **-verzögerung** *f* lowering delay **-vorrichtung** *f* gear for sinking shaft, lowering device **-waage** *f* hydrometer, densimeter **-weg** *m* lowering distance **-werkzeug** *n* counterbore **-winkel** *m* countersink, countersunk angle **-zimmerung** *f* wood timbering sunk in a shaft **-zylinder** *m* cylinder of sinking pit

sensibel sensitive, sensible

Sensibilisator *m* sensitizer

sensibilisieren to sensitize

Sensibilisierung *f* sensitizing, sensitization

Sensibilität *f* sensitiveness, sensibility

sensitiver Höhenmesser Kollsman station barometer, sensitive altimeter

Sensitometer *n* sensitometer, densitometer

Separatabdruck *m* reprint, separate or special impression

separater Gang by-pass

Separation *f* separation, sorting, grading

Separations-anlage *f* screening plant **-lutte** *f* separation box or trough **-trommel** *f* revolving screen, separating screen **-werk** *n* separating dam

Separator *m* separator, grader, cobber, separating layer (cable)

separieren to separate, sort, grade

Separiertrichter *m* separatory funnel

Sepia *f* sepia **-papier** *n* sepia paper, brown print paper

Septalgrube *f* fossula

Sequenzillusion *f* sequence illusion

Serie *f* series, line **in ~ liegend** in series

Serien-abgleichkapazität *f* padding capacitance **-abgleichkondensator** *m* padding capacitor **-apparat** *m* series camera **-arbeit** *f* repetition work **-aufnahme** *f* serial radiography **-ausrüstung** *f* regular equipment **-bad** *n* series tank **-bau** *m* building in series, series production, serial construction **-belastete Antenne** series loaded antenna **-belastung** *f* series loading **-bündelkessel** *m* multi-tubular boiler **-dynamomaschine** *f* series-wound generator, series dynamo

Serien-eingabe *f* serial access **-entwicklung** *f* series expansion or development **-fertigung** *f* quantity production, repetition work, manufacturing in series **-flugzeug** *n* production airplane or aircraft **-funkenstrecke** *f* multiple spark gap **-gegentaktverstärker** *m* single-ended amplifier **-gerät** *n* standard set **-gesetz** *n* series law **-herstellung** *f* series production, multiple production, quantity production **-kuppelung** *f* coupling (in series) **-linie** *f* diagram line

serienmäßig standard, in quantity, in series ~ **hergestellt werden** to be in production ~ **herstellen** to produce in quantity, mass produce **-e Ausrüstung** standard equipment **-es Flugzeug** production airplane **-e Herstellung** quantity production, large-scale manufacture, mass or batch production

Serien-modell *n* production model **-modulation** *f* constant-voltage modulation **-motor** *m* series motor, series-wound motor, production engine, engine currently in production **-muster** *n* production model **-nummer** *f* serial number **-parallelschalter** *m* series-parallel switch **-peilungen** *pl* series of bearing readings on a direction finder, group of bearing recordings **-prüfung** *f* production testing **-rechner** *m* serial digital computer **-reife** *f* production stage

Serienresonanz-frequenz *f* series-resonant frequency **-kreis** *m* acceptor circuit, series-resonance circuit

Serien-schalter *m* multicircuit switch **-schaltung** *f* series arrangement or connection **-schlußmotor** *m* series-wound motor **-schnitt** *m* serial section **-spardiode** *f* series-efficiency diode **-speisung** *f* series feeding

Serien-teil *m* duplicate piece **-trimmer** *m* padding capacitor **-vierpol** *m* series two-terminal pair network **-wagen** *m* stock car **-weise** in series **-widerstand** *m* series rheostat or resistance

Serimeter *m* serimeter

Serizitschiefer *m* sericite slate

Serpentin *m* serpentine

Serpentinieren *n* meandering

Serpentinsteinbruch *m* serpentine quarry

Serruys-Indikator *m* Serruy's indicator

Serum *n* serum

Serviceanleitung *f* maintenance manual

Servierbrett *n* tray

Serving *f* plat or thrummel mat

Servobremse *f* servo brake

Servoeinrichtung *f* servo arrangement **mit ~** servo-assisted

Servo-klappe *f* servo tab **-kolben** *m* servo piston **-luftumsteuerung** *f* auxiliary air distribution **-mechanismus** *m* servo-control mechanism

Servomotor *m* servomotor, booster, auxiliary engine **~ zum Adjustieren** auxiliary motor for adjusting **~ zum Drehen** auxiliary motor for turning

Servomotor-kolben *m* servomotor piston **-regelung** *f* servomotor regulator

servoölbetätigt oil servo-operated

Servo-ruder *n* servo tab or flap **-schreiber** *m* servo recorder **-steueranlage** *f* power-assisted, controls system **-steuerung** *f* servo control **-system** *n* servo-system **-wirkung** *f* servo-action **-zylinder** *m* slave cylinder

Sesqui-chlorid *n* perchloride **-oxyd** *n* sesquioxide **-silikat** *n* sesquisilicate

seßhaft stationary, resident, sedentary, persistent

Seßhaftigkeit *f* persistency

Setz-arbeit *f* settling operation, settling classification **-bett** *n* settling tank, washing chamber **-boden** *m* charging floor **-bord** *m* waterboard, washboard, weatherboard (naut.) **-bottich** *m* settling vat **-brett** *n* settling bottom **-eisen** *n* cutter, smithing chisel

setzen to set, put, place, erect, charge, settle, consolidate, deposit, precipitate, sit down, subside, compose **sich ~** to subside, settle, sit down **in Betrieb ~** to set to work **in Bewegung ~** to put in motion **außer Gebrauch ~** to abolish **~** (eine Größe gleich einer anderen . . .) to put

Setzen des Zwischenbaus subsidence of the substructure

Setzenlassen *n* settling

Setzer *m* compositor

Setzerei *f* composing room

Setz-faß *n* settling tub, hutch, wash trough **-fehler** *m* typographic error

Setzhammer *m* sledge hammer, set hammer, plane-bottom hammer **hohler ~** bottom or top swedge **runder ~** bottom or top fuller

Setz-kasten *m* hutch, jig, type or lettercase **-kastenspülung** *f* bagging gear **-keil** *m* key **-kolben** *m* rammer head **-kopf** *m* sethead, swaged head, die head, primary or original head, head or undriven rivet **-maschine** *f* settling tank, sloughing-off tank, typesetting machine, composing machine **-maß** *n* subsidence **-meißel** *m* set hammer, setter

Setz-probe *f* slump test **-raum** *m* (Zone), charging zone **-riß** *m* settlement crack **-schiff** *n* (composing) galley **-schlag** *m* setting blow **-schraube** *f* temper screw, setscrew **-sieb** *n* separating screen, jig screen **-stein** *m* imposing or press stone **-stempel** *m* set hammer

Setzstock *m* steady rest **einfacher ~** plain back rest

Setz-stufe *f* riser **-tank** *m* settling tank **-tisch** *m* composing table

Setz- und Ablegemaschine *f* typesetting and distributing machine

Setzung *f* settlement **~ durch Verdichtung** consolidation settlement

Setzungsunterschied *m* differential settlement

Setz-verhalten *n* setting properties **-vorgang** *m* jigging action

Setzwaage *f* mason's level, plumb bob **behelfsmäßige ~** improvised plumb bob

Setz-wäsche *f* tub washing (of ores) **-werkzeug** *n* composing tool

Sextant *m* sextant

sezernieren to separate, remove

Seziermesser *n* scalpel

S-Haken *m* "S" safety hook

Shapingmaschine *f* shaping machine

Sharpit *m* sharpite

Sheddach *n* saw-tooth roof, north-light roof

sherardisieren to sherardize, dry-galvanize

Sherardisieren *n*, **Sherardisierung** *f* sherardizing

Sherardisierverfahren *n* sherardizing process

Shimverfahren *n* shimming procedure

Shore-Fallprobe *f* Shore's dynamic indentation test **-Härte** *f* Shore hardness **-Skleroskop** *n* Shore scleroscope

Shunt mit hoher Selbstinduktion highly inductive shunt

shunten to shunt

Shuntrelais *n* shunt relay

Sialographie *f* sialography

Sibatit *n* sibatit

Siccativ *n* siccative, drier

sich, an ~ per se, basically or fundamentally speaking in or by itself

Sichel *f* sickle, reaping or pruning hook **-brille** *f* stenopeic spectacles **-elektrode** *f* curved electrode **-förmig** cresent-shaped, sickle-shaped **-spiegelgeometrie** *f* cusped geometry

sicher certain, safe, sure, reliable, secure, definite

Sicherheit *f* security, safety, margin of safety, assurance **die ~ gefährden** endangering the security **statistische ~** statistical certainty

Sicherheits-abreißvorrichtung *f* safety link **-abstand** *m* safety zone, range of effectiveness, clearance (R. R.) **-andrehkurbel** *f* safety starting crank **-anhängekupplung** *f* safety trailer coupling **-anschlag** *m* (Kohlenförderer) safety pawl **-apparat** *m* safety appliance **-auslösung** *f* safety release (mach) **-ausschalter** *m* safety cut-out **-band** *n* guard band (radio)

Sicherheits-beanspruchung *f* safe stress **-behälter** *m* safety tank, self-sealing tank **-belastung** *f* safe bearing capacity **-bestimmung** *f* safety regulation **-bolzen** *m* safety bolt **-brandlunte** *f* **für Bergwerke** safety fuse for mines **-brennstoff** *m* safety fuel **-bügel** *m* safety gripper **-bühne** *f* safety platform, safety board

Sicherheits-draht *m* safety wire **-einrichtung** *f* dead-man's-handle, safety rod or device **-einrückung** *f* safety connector **-erde** *f* safety earthing **-fahrschaltung** *f* dead-man's-handle **-faktor** *m* safety factor **-farbe** *f* safety paint

Sicherheits-flaschenzugskette *f* safety block **-förderstuhl** *m* safety elevator **-friktionsmutter** *f* safety friction adjusting shaft **-funkenstrecke** *f* safety (spark) gap **-futter** *pl* safety tap chucks **-gerät** *n* safety device **-gestängeverbinder** *m* safety joints **-glas** *n* unsplinterable glass, safety glass **-grad** *m* margin of safety, factor of safety **-grenzschalter** *m* safety-limit switch **-gürtel** *m* safety belt **-haken** *m* safety hook

Sicherheits-hebel *m* safety lever **-höhe** *f* safe altitude level **-hülse** *f* safety socket **-inspektor** *m* safety inspector **-kabelwinde** *f* safety crab **-kette** *f* safety chain **-klappe** *f* regulating valve **-klemme** *f* safety terminal **-koeffizient** *m* factor or margin of safety **-kolben** *m* pressure-control valve, safety piston **-kopfschraube** *f* binding-head screw **-kraftstoff** *m* safety fuel

Sicherheitskreis für Servoblockierung fail-safe servo disabling

Sicherheits-kurbel *f* safety crank **-lampe** *f* safety lamp or light **-leiter** *f* safety ladder **-leitplanke** *f* (Straße) safety fence, guard fence, protection fence, guard rail

Sicherheitsmaß *n* safety factor **-nahme** *f* safety precaution **-regel** *f* safety measure **-regler** *m* emergency or safety governor

Sicherheits-meldung *f* weather warning signal **-muffe** *f* safety joint **-mutter** *f* lock nut **-nadel** *f* safety pin

Sicherheits- oder Meßklappe *f* (relief and gauging) hatch

Sicherheits-papier *n* check paper **-pfeiler** *m* barrier pillar, rib barrier, safety pillar **-rasierapparat** *m* safety razor **-regler** *m* governor, safety regulator **-riegel** *m* safety catch **-ring** *m* lock washer **-schacht** *m* escape shaft **-schalter** *m* safety switch **-schaltung** *f* safety circuit **-schar(e)** *f* pin break shovel **-schiene** *f* guardrail, safety rail, side rail **-schlinge** *f* safety loop **-schloß** *n* safety lock **-schubriegel** *m* safety sliding bolt

Sicherheits-spielraum *m* margin of safety **-sprengstoff** *m* safety explosive **-spundapparat** *m* safety bunging apparatus **-stab** *m* shut-off rod **-stange** *f* safety rod **-startgeschwindigkeit** *f* take-off safety speed (V2) **-sternrad** *n* safety capstan **-streichholz** *n* safety match **-tor** *n* emergency gate **-stütze** *f* hook guard **-summe** *f* retention money

Sicherheitsventil *n* safety valve, vacuum or pressure relief valve, blowoff valve, release valve **~ für Druck und Vakuum** pressure and vacuum vent valve

Sicherheits-ventilbelastung *f* safety-valve weight **-verriegelung** *f* safety interlock **-verschraubung** *f* safety screw **-verstärkung** *f* safety shoulder **-vorlage** *f* water seal **-vorrichtung** *f* safety device, safety appliance **-vorschriften** *pl* safety rules, safety code **-winkel** *m* margin of commutation **-zahl** *f* factor of safety, coefficient of safety **-zeichen** *n* safety signal **-ziffer** *f* safety factor **-zünder** *m* safety fuse

sichern to secure, fasten, protect, guard, check, thicken, insure, fuse, guarantee, safeguard, block **mittels Draht ~** to safety-wire

Sicherschalter *m* safe-fire switch

sicherstellen to guarantee, give security, ensure

sicherstellende Vorkehrungen *pl* preventive measures, precautions, precautionary steps

Sicher-stellung *f* security, guarantee **-trog** *m* (separating) pan

Sicherung *f* safety (mechanism), security, safety fuse, cutout, protection, guarantee **~ für Kraftanschluß** fuse for power supply connection **~ für den Stillstand des Tisches** lock to prevent table from being moved **~ gegen Übersteuern** overriding control **~ für Überwachungsrelais** fuse for pilot relay **~ für Umschalteeinrichtung** fuse for commutating device **~ für Ventilhebelrolle** valve roller lock

Sicherung, die ~ auswechseln to change the fuse **~ durchbrennen** to blow fuse or cutout **formschlüssige ~** form-locking (of bolts) **kraftschlüssige ~** pressure-locking (of bolts) **träge ~** surgeresisting fuse

Sicherungen prüfen to verify the fuses

Sicherungs-anlage *f* protective device **-anschlag** *m* safety stop **-automat** *m* automatic cut-out

Sicherungsblech *n* locking plate, anti-twisting plate **~ mit Lappen** tab washer

Sicherungs-bolzen *m* safety bolt or stop **-brett** *n* fuse panel, fuseboard **-bügel** *m* safety stirrup **-dose** *f* fuse box **-draht** *m* fuse wire, locking wire, fuse link **-einsatz** *m* fuse wire insert **-element** *n* fuse element **-erdung** *f* protector ground **-feder** *f* retaining spring **-flügel** *m* protective wing or flank

Sicherungs-gestell *n* fuse rack, fuseboard, protector frame **-gewindestift** *m* small grub screw **-haken** *m* quick-release hook, safety hook **-halter** *m* fuse-carrier **-hebel** *m* safety lever, safety catch **-kappe** *f* safety cap **-kästchen** *n* (combined) protector, heat coil and fuse **-kasten** *m* fuse box **-kette** *f* safety chain **-klappe** *f* interrupter **-kleinautomat** *m* cutout **-klemmstück** *n* safety lug

Sicherungs-klinke *f*, **-knaggen** *m* safety catch **-kolben** *m* safety piston **-lampe** *f* fuse blow lamp **-lasche** *f* safety keep flange **-leiste** *f* fuse panel, fuse strip **-maßnahme** *f* security measure **-material** *n* fuses, safety material **-mutter** *f* lock nut

Sicherungs-patrone *f* cartridge **-plättchen** *n* lockwasher **-pilz für Kolbenbolzen** piston button

-rast *m* safety slot **-riegel** *m* safety catch
Sicherungsring *m* guard ring, retaining ring or nut **mittels Sicherungsringen sichern** to locate by guard rings
Sicherungs-rücklage *f* reserve fund **-scheibe** *f* locking washer **-schieber** *m* locking-slide **-schloßteil** *n* guard cam **-schraube** *f* anchor or locking or safety screw **-schraubkappe** *f* screw plug for fuse **-seil** *n* safety cable **-signallampe** *f* fuse blow lamp **-sockel** *m* fuse mounting
Sicherungs-stift *m* locking-pin **-stöpsel** *m* safety plug, fuse plug **-streifen** *m* fuse strip, fuse or tapping panel **-stück** *n* safety lug **-tafel** *f* fuse panel, fuseboard **-träger** *pl* fuse bases **-trenner** *m* fuse isolator **-überwachungseinrichtung** *f* fuse alarm devise **-unterteil** *m* fuse carrier
Sicherungs-vorrichtung *f* safety device **-vorstecker** *m* safety wire or clip cotter pin **-weiche** *f* safety switch **-zange** *f* fuse tongs **-zuschlag** *m* margin of safety
Sichsenken *n* subsidence
Sicht *f* visibility, sight, view, outlook, clearness, transparency **~ nach der Seite** view to the sides **~ nach hinten** rear view **~ nach oben** upward view **~ nach unten** downward view **~ nach vorn** forward view **außer ~ kommen** to disappear from sight **gute ~** good view, good visibility **keine ~** zero visibility **schlechte ~** poor visibility
Sicht-analyse *f* pneumatic size analysis **-anflug** *m* visual contact approach **-anlage** *f* sorting, sifting, or separating plant **-anzeige** *f* visual display **-anzeiger** *m* visual indicator, visibility indicator **-attrappe** *f* view finder **-ausschnitt** *m* cutout section, area exposed to view **-ausschnittbogen** *m* cutout sector
sichtbar visual, visible **~ machen** to visualize, render visible or visually perceptible, indicate visually or optically **~ werden** to appear **-es Signal** optical or visible signal **-es Spektrum** luminous spectrum **-es Zeichen** visible signal
Sichtbarkeit *f* visibility **überschwellige ~** superthreshold visibility
Sichtbarkeits-beiwert *m* coefficient of visibility **-häufigkeit** *f* frequency of period of light **-messer** *m* visibility meter **-schwelle** *f* threshold of visibility or vision
Sichtbarmachung *f* visualization
Sicht-begrenzung *f* optical limitation, limited vision **-bereich** *m* visual range, sight distance **-berührung** *f* visual contact **-bild** *n* perspective (rdr.) representation **-deckung** *f* sight defilade
Sichte *f* range **-arm** *m* shaking arm
sichten to sort out, separate, sift, screen, grade, classify
Sichten *n* vision, sight (of a light), sift
Sichter *m* separator, grader, sifter, cobber **-anlage** *f* sifting device
Sichtezeug *n* common bolter, shaking apparatus
Sicht-feld *n* field of vision **-flugregeln** *pl* visual flight rules (VFR) **-funkpeiler** *m* visual radio direction finder **-gerät** *n* visual apparatus indicator (radio), video receiver, display unit
Sichthöhe *f*, **bequeme ~** height convenient to the eye
sichtig clear
Sichtigkeit *f* visibility, clearness, transparency
Sichtigkeitsbeiwert *m* factor of visibility
Sicht-kammer *f* sight chamber **-kartei** *f* referenced card index or system **-kompaß** *m* direct-compass **-keule** *f* radar lobe **-linie** *f* optical path, line of sight **-maschine** *f* separator, sifter, bolting or dressing machine **-messer** *m* visibility meter **-meßgerät** *n* visibility meter **-navigation** *f* visual navigation
Sicht-peiler *m* visual or direct-reading direction finder **-peilgerät** *n* cathode ray direction finder (CRDF) **-scheibe** *f* window shield **-scheibenkondensschutz** *m* defogging **-schmierapparat** *m* sight-feed lubricator, sight-feed oil cup
Sichtschutz *m* camouflage **-anstrich** *m* camouflage paint, shadow painting
Sichtspeicherröhre *f* viewing storage tube
Sichtsteuerung *f* visual control
sichttoter Raum blind space
Sichtung *f* separation, sifting, sorting, observation, testing
Sichtungs-anlage *f* separating plant **-stelle** *f* interview station, inspection station
Sicht-verhältnisse *pl* (conditions of) visibility **-vermerk** *m* inspection signature **-weite** *f* visual range, optical range or distance, geographical range, line of sight **-winkel** *m* viewing angle, angle of sight **-wirkung** *f* sifter effect, sorting, classification **-zeichen** *n* marker
Sicke *f* stiffening corrugation, draw, bead, reinforcing seam, crease, or pleat, reinforcing fin **mit Sicken versehen** to corrugate, crimp
Sicken-hammer *m* swaging hammer **-maschine** *f* seam rolling machine **-stöcke** *pl* creasing stakes **-verbindung** *f* crimp(ed) joint **-walze** *f* seam roller
Sicker-anlage *f* sump hole **-becken** *n* filter basin **-bewegung** *f* percolation **-fläche** *f* phreatic surface **-grube** *f* soakage pit, soakaway, drainage pit **-kanal** *m* drainage culvert, catch-water drain, canal with filter bed **-kühlung** *f* trickle-type cooling **-laugung** *f* percolating leach **-leitung** *f* seepage pipe **-linie** *f* phreatic line, topmost flow line, seepage line **-loch** *n* drainage pit
sickern to trickle, ooze (out), percolate, leak, seep, exude, bead
Sicker-rohr *n* drain pipe **-schacht** *m* seepage shaft **-schlitz** *m* filter slot **-stollen** *m* filtration gallery **-strahlung** *f* leakage (radiation) **-strömung** *f* seepage flow **-tank** *m* percolating tank
Sickerung *f* percolation, seepage, trickling
Sicker-verlust *m* leakage **-wasser** *n* percolating waters, drainage ditch, seeping or seepage water **-weg** *m* path of percolation
siderisch sidereal
Sideroskop *n* sideroscope
Sieb *n* mesh, bin, strainer, sieve, screen, filter, sifter, eliminator, network, bolter **~ von gelochtem Blech** punched screen **endloses ~** machine wire, wire cloth
Sieb-abfall *m* screening refuse **-abnahme** *f* sieve discharge **-analyse** *f* screen analysis, sizing test **-anlage** *f* screening plant, screening house, sifting plant **-apparat** *m* sifter
siebartig gauze-like **~ durchlochtes Eisenblech** perforated iron plate
Sieb-ascheanalyse *f* ash analysis by size **-aufsatz** *m* gauze top
Siebband *n* machine wire, wire cloth **-wasch-**

maschine *f* traveling-screen washing machine **-trockner** *m* screen belt drier

Sieb-blech *n* sieve sheet, punched-plate screen, perforated or screening plate **-boden** *m* perforated bottom **-breite** *f* width of wire, sieve width **-brille** *f* goggles with gauze frame **-drossel** *f* filter choke **-druck** *m* screen printing **-druckschirm** *m* screen **-durchfall** *m* screenings **-durchgang** *m* undersize **-durchlaß in Prozenten** percentage passing sieve

Siebe *pl* tin skim gates

Sieb-einrichtung *f* straining or screening installation **-einsatz** *m* strainer screen

sieben to sift, select, screen, filter (out), sieve, strain

Sieben *n* bolting, sieving, sifting, straining

Siebeneck *n* heptagon

Siebenelektrodenröhre *f* heptode

Siebenfachkabelklemme *f* seven-conductor cable terminal

Siebenflächner *m* hepta-hedrow

sieben-strahlig seven-strand **-stufig** seven-stage **-wertig** heptavalent

Siebenzylinder-sternmotor *m* seven-cylinder radial engine **-umlaufmotor** *m* seven-cylinder rotary engine

Sieberei *f* screening, sifting, separation

Sieb-faktor *m* hum-reduction or smoothing factor (radio) **-feine** *n* siftings **-feinheit** *f* mesh (size) **-filtereinsatz** *m* screen filter element **-fläche** *f* screen area **-förmig** grid- or net-shaped **-gaze aus Draht** wire screen

Sieb-feine *n* siftings **-feinheit** *f* mesh (size) **-filtereinsatz** *m* screen filter element **-fläche** *f* screen area **-förmig** grid- or net-shaped **-gaze aus Draht** wire screen

Siebgebilde *n* selective system, filter (circuit or device), sifter, network ~ **von großer Lochbreite** broad-band filter **mehrgliedriges** ~ multimesh filter circuit **zweigliedriges** ~ two-section filter

Sieb-gewebe *n* sieve netting, strainer texture **-glied** *n* filter section **-hülse** *f* screen, sieve **-kapazität** *f* filter capacity **-kappe** *f* wire-gauze cap **-kasten** *m* strainer **-kern** *m* strainer (pouring) core, filter core, grate core, strainer grate core

Siebkette *f* band-pass filter, filter chain, waveband filter (signal device), transmission network, ladder-type filter, sifter ~ **von großer Lochweite** broadband filter **eingliedrige** ~ single-mesh filter **mehrgliedrige** ~ multimesh filter, multisection filter

Siebkettenleiter *m* filter, sifter

Sieb-klassierung *f* screen sizing, screening **-kondensator** *m* filter condenser **-korbeinsatz** *m* wire basket **-kranz** *m* screening frame **-kreis** *m* filter(ing) circuit, selective circuit, sifter **-kugelmühle** *f* ball mill with screen **-kurve** *f* sieve-analysis curve, grain-size curve **-leder** *n* apron (paper mfg.) **-leistung** *f* screening capacity

Sieb-leitwalze *f* guide roll or roller, lower guide roll (paper mfg.) **-löcher** *pl* screen holes **-mantel** *m* cylinder cover **-maschine** *f* screening machine, sifter **-mittel** *n* filter element or material **-nest** *n* nest of screens **-öffnung** *f* screen hole or opening **-paket** (Kühlmaschine) screening stack (cooling machine) **-partie** *f* filter section **-plansichter** *m* screen classifier **-probe** *f* sieve test, screening test or sample

Sieb-rahmen *m* riddle **-reinigungswalze** *f* copper wash roll **-rohr** *n* spray pipe **-rost** *m* mesh grating **-satz** *m* set of sieves **-schale** *f* dish with perforated bottom **-schaltung** *f* filter (network), eliminator, sifter **-schaufel** *f* sieve shovel **-schlagmühle** *f* screen beater mill **-schneckenzentrifuge** *f* sieve-worm-centrifuge

Siebsel *n* siftings, garblings

Sieb-setzarbeit *f*, **-setzen** *n* jigging **-setzer** *m* ore jigger **-setzmaschine** *f* jig **-sichtung** *f* screen separation, screening, sifting **-skala** *f* mesh gauge **-skalenkoeffizient** *m* screening capacity **-steilheit** *f* sharpness of selective network **-stutzen** *m* sieve socket

Siebtischentwässerungsmaschine *f* wet machine, pulp machine

Sieb-trog *m* screen trough **-trommel** *f* sieve drum, sizing, screening, or straining drum, cylindrical-shaped screen, willow (textile mfg.)

Siebung *f* screening, sifting, filtering, filtration, sizing, shielding, straining, sorting, bolting, classifying

Sieb-walze *f* dandy roll (paper mfg.) **-wäsche** *f* hutching (min.), sifting, riddling **-widerstände** *pl* filter resistances or resistors, contact resistances **-wirkung** *n* sieve effect, strainer effect

Siebzylinder *m* revolving-screen drum, cylindrical-shaped screen

Siede-analyse *f* analysis by boiling or by fractional distillation **-beginn** *m* boiling point **-ende** *n* end point **-erleichterer** *m* device facilitating boiling, boil adjuvant **-grad** *m* boiling point **-grenze** *f* boiling range **-hitze** *f* boiling heat or temperature **-kolben** *m* distillation flask, boiling flask **-kühlung** *f* boiling cooling **-kurve** *f* boiling-(-point) curve **-linie** *f* boiling-point curve

sieden to simmer, boil

Sieden *n*, **stoßweises** ~ bumping

siedend boiling, simmering

Siedepfanne *f* evaporating boiler

Siedepunkt *m* boiling point ~ **eines Kraftstoffanteils bei der Siedetrennung** fractional boiling point **unterer** ~ initial boiling point

Siedepunktmesser *m* ebullioscope

Siederei *f* refinery

Siederhals *m* upright tube of a boiler tube

Siederohr *n* boiler pipe, heating tube, steam tube **-bürste** *f* steam-tube brush **-dichtmaschine** *f* calking machine for boiler pipes, tube expander **-kessel** *m* water-tube boiler

Siede-salz *n* (common) salt **-steinchen** *n* bead **-thermometer** *n* hypsometer, barometric thermometer, boiling-point thermometer **-trennung** *f* (fractional) distillation, fractionization

Siede- und Rauchrohrbearbeitungsmaschine *f* boiler and smoke tube working machine

Siede-verhalten *n* distillation characteristics **-verlauf** *m* boiling progress, boiling curve, boiling rate **-verzug** *m* retardation of ebullition or boiling **-wärmegradmesser** *m* hypsometer, barometric thermometer, boiling-point thermometer **-wasserkühlung** *f* cooling by boiling water

Siegel *n* seal **-lack** *m* scaling wax **-marke** *f* embossed seal

siegeln to seal

Siegerländer-Spezialroheisen Siegerland special iron
Sieke *f* (reinforcing) seam, pleat, crease, or fin
sieken to seam, crease
Sieken *n* beading **-eisen** *n* creasing die
Siel *n* culvert, sluiceway (or other passageway) through a levee, sewer **-anlage** *f* sewer system
Sielengeschirr *n* breast harness, wheel harness
Sieltief *n* junction canal
Siemens-Einheit *f* Siemens mercury unit **-Gas** *n* Siemens gas, producer gas **-Gaswechselklappe** *f* Siemens gas-reversing valve, Siemens reversing gas valve **-Lichtbogenofen** *m* Siemens arc furnace
Siemens-Martin-Betrieb *m* open-hearth practice **-Eisen** *n* Siemens-Martin steel, open-hearth steel **-Flußeisen** *n* Siemens-Martin steel, open-hearth (furnace) steel **-Flußstahl** *m* Siemens-Martin steel, open-hearth steel
Siemens-Martin-Material, basisches ~ basic steel
Siemens-Martin-Ofen *m* Siemens-Martin furnace, open-hearth furnace **-Ofenstein** *m* open-hearth furnace brick **-Prozeß** *m* Siemens-Martin process, open-hearth process, pig-and-scrap process **-Roheisen** *n* open-hearth pig (iron) **-Stahl** *m* Siemens-Martin steel, open-hearth steel **-Verfahren** *n* Siemens-Martin process, open-hearth process, pig and-scrap process
Siemens-Prozeß *m* Siemens process, pig-and-ore process **-Regenerativfeuerung** *f* Siemens regenerative open-hearth furnace **-Schnelltelegraph** *m* Siemens high-speed telegraph printer **-Strahlungsofen** *m* Siemens independent arc furnace **-Wechselklappe** *f* Siemens reversing valve
Siggeis *n* frazil
Sigma-funktion *f* sigma function **-meson** *n* sigma meson **-monogene Funktion** sigma-monogenic function **-reaktor** *m* sigma pile
Signal *n* indicator, sign, (fixed) signal, bell **akustisches ~** sound signal **großes ~** large signal **numerisches ~** digital signal (servo) **pausenfreies ~** sequence signal **tönendes ~** tonal signal, musical (spark) signal **~ überlagern** to mask the signal
Signal-anlage *f* signaling system or installation **-antrieb** *m* signal-operating mechanism
Signalanzeiger, registrierender ~ recording signal indicator
Signal-apparat *m* signaling apparatus, alarm apparatus **-ausfall** *m* drop out (tape rec.) **-auswertung** *f* strobing (rdr.) **-batterie** *f* common signaling battery **-bild** *n* aspect of signal (R.R.) **-buch** *n* signal book, code of signals **-draht** *m* signal wire **-einrichtung** *f* signaling device **-fallscheibe** *f* annunciator **-farbe** *f* enamel for signals **-farbengerät** *n* colored signal apparatus **-feld** *n* signal area **-feldstärke** *f* signal field strength **-fläche** signal area **-flagge** *f* signal flag **-flügelkontakt** *m* signal circuit controller
signalformend-es Glied signal-shaping network **-er Verstärker** signal-shaping amplifier
Signal-frequenz *f* signal frequency **-führer** *m* signal scanner (servo) **-gabe** *f* signaling (impulses) **-geber** *m* signaler, signal transmitter **-gebung** *f* signaling **-gemisch** (TV) composite signal **-glimmlampe** *f* pilot bulb **-größe** *f* command rate **-hammer** *m* rapper **-horn** *n* signal horn, bugle
Signalisierkontakt *m* signalizing contact
Signalisierung *f* signaling **~ mit abgestimmten Einrichtungen** harmonic selective signaling **~ mittels Schleifenbildung** loop-battery pulsing
Signal-kasten *m* horn push-button box **-knopf** *m* horn button, signal button **-kode** *m* signal code **-kontakt** *m* signaling contact, signaling key
Signallampe *f* pilot lamp, supervisory lamp, signal lamp, indicating lamp, warning light, neon sign **~ beim Einschalten** closing indicating lamp
Signallampen-einschaltrelais *n* pilot-lamp connector relay **-öl** *n* signal oil **-tafel** *f* signal-lamp or annunciator board, panel annunciator
Signal-laterne *f* signal lamp, danger light **-leine** *f* signal cord **-leitung** *f* signal line, indicator lead **-leitungsnetz** *n* wire system **-licht** *n* signal light **-mast** *m* semaphore **-mischer** *m* composite signal mixer **-mittel** *n* signaling device **-mittelwert** *m* signal mean value
Signal-nebensprechverhältnis *n* signal-to-cross-talk-ratio **-patrone** *f* signal cartridge **-pegel** *m* signal level **-pegelblockierung** *f* clamping (rdr.) **-pfeife** *f* signal whistle or siren **-platte** *f* signal plate **-rakete** *f* signal rocket **-rauschverhältnis** *n* signal/noise ratio **-relais** *n* signal relay **-rohranschluß** *m* telltale pipe connection **-rückmelder** *m* signal indicator
Signal-schalter *m* signal scanner **-scheinwerfer** *m* light gun, signalling lamp **-spruch** *m* signal message **-spule** *f* dialing coil **-stärkemesser** *m* signal meter **-stein** *m* sighting pillar **-stelle** *f* signal station **-stift** *m* signal pin **-stöße** *pl* signaling impulses **-störverhältnis** *n* (Radar) signal to noise ratio
Signal-tafel *f* signal-code table, radio-code table of board **-taste** *f* transfer button **-teil** *m* signal component **-trägerfrequenz** *f* signal carrier frequency **-überdeckung** *f* blanketing or swamping of signals **-übertragung auf den Zug** train control (of signals) **-umsetzer** *m* ac-vf converter
Signal- und Weichenstellung, elektrische ~ electrical operating of signals and switches
Signal-verfolger *m* signal tracer **-verfügung** *f* available variable group (signal codes) **-verlauf** *m* signal spectrum, signal pattern **-verschiebungsverfahren** *n* offset-signal method (TV) **-verteiler** *m* cutoff control panel (missiles) **-verteilungskasten** *m* signal mixer unit **-vorrichtung** *f* signaling device **-wand** *f* wall or curtain of signals **-wandler** *m* signal converter **-werfer** *m* signal-flare projector **-wesen** *n* signal system **-zeichen** *n* signal
signieren to sign, brand, label, stamp, designate
Signier-farbe *f* marking ink **-kreide** *f* marking crayon **-stempel** *m* signature stamp **-stift** *m* marking pencil **-werkzeug** *n* branding iron
signifizieren to designate, indicate
Signum *n* mark, brand, designation
Sikkativ *n* siccative, drier
Silbe *f* syllable, logatome
Silben-abschneidung *f* clipping, obliteration or mutilation of syllables **-frequenzgerät** *n* syllable vodas **-kompansion** *f* syllabic companding **-umkehrung** *f* inversion of syllables **-verständlichkeit** *f* syllable or syllabic articulation, syllable

intelligibility, articulation for logatomes **-verständlichkeitsmessung** *f* intelligibility measurement

Silber *n* silver **lötiges ~** silver of due alloy

Silber-amalgam *n* silver amalgam **-arbeiter** *m* silver smith **-arm** poor in silver **-arsenit** *n* silver arsenite **-artig** silvery **-ätzstein** *m* silver nitrate **-barren** *m* silver bar, silver ingot **-belag** *m*, **-belegung** *f* silver coating, silver plating, silver film, silvering **-benzoat** *n* silver benzoate **-blatt** *n* silver leaf, silver foil

Silber-blech *n* silver foil, silver sheet, (thin) silver plate **-blende** *f* pyrargyrite, proustite **-blick** *m* lightening or brightening of silver **-brennen** *n* silver refining **-brennherd** *m* silver-refining hearth **-brokat** *n* silver brocade **-chlorid** *n* silver chloride **-chlorür** *n* silver subchloride **-draht** *m* silver wire **-einkristalle** *pl* silver single crystals **-eisen** *n* silvery pig iron **-elektrolyse** *f* electrolytic silver refining

Silber-erz *n* silver ore **-essigsalz** *n* silver acetate **-fahlerz** *n* argentiferous tetrahedrite **-farbig** silver-colored **-flitter** *m* silver tinsel **-folie** *f* metallized strip **-führend** silver-bearing, argentiferous **-gehalt** *m* silver content **-gespinst** *n* silver thread **-gewinnung** *f* silver extraction **-glanz** *m* argentite, silvery luster **-glänzend** silvery **-glas** *n*, **-glaserz** *n* argentite

Silber-glätte *f* silver litharge **-glimmer** *m* common or argentine mica **-gold** *n* silver electrum, argentiferous gold **-grau** silvery gray **-grube** *f* silver mine **-halogen** *n* halide of silver **-haltig** argentiferous, silver-bearing **-hell** silvery **-hornerz** *n* cerargyrite **-hütte** *f* silver works

silberig silvery

Silber-jodid *n* silver iodide **-jodür** *n* silver subiodide **-kappe** *f* silver capping **-kies** *m* white arsenical pyrite **-korn** *n* silver bead **-kupferglanz** *m* stromeyerite

Silber-lauge *f* silver solution **-laugerei** *f* silver-leaching plant **-legierung** *f* silver alloy **-letten** *m* clay mixed with silver **-lösung** *f* silver solution **-lot** *n* silver solder **-messer** *m* argentometer (photo) **-metall** *n* silver metal, metallic silver

silbern silvery, silver **-er Streifen** silver bar

Silber-niederschlag *m* silver precipitate **-nitrat** *n* silver nitrate **-nitrit** *n* silver nitrite **-oxydammoniak** *n* fulminating silver **-oxydsalz** *n* silver oxysalt **-oxydul** *n* silver suboxide **-packpapier** *n* antitarnish paper **-papier** *n* silver paper, silver foil, tinfoil **-plattierung** *f* silver plating

Silber-prägeanstalt *f* silver stamping works **-präparierer** *m* silversaltmaker **-probe** *f* silver assay **-putz** *m* silver polish **-reich** highly argentiferous, rich in silver **-rhodanid** *n* silver rhodanide **-salpeter** *m* silver nitrate **-sand** *m* fine-grained river sand, argentiferous sand, sea sand, beach sand **-sau** *f* silver ingot, silver brick **-schaltstück** *n* silver-tripped contact **-schaum** *m* silver leaf, foliated silver

Silber-scheideanstalt *f* silver refinery **-scheidung** *f* separation of silver, silver refining **-schein** *m* silver luster **-schicht** *f* silver layer or film or coating **-schlaglot** *n* silver solder **-schlamm** *m* silver tailings **-schmelzsicherung** *f* silver wire fuse **-schwärze** *f* argentite **-schweflig** argentosulfurous

Silber-spat *m* cerargyrite **-spießglanz** *m* dyscrasite **-stahl** *m* bright polished carbon steel **-sulfid** *n* silver sulfide **-tannenöl** *n* pine oil **-thiosulfat** *n* silver thiosulfate **-tiegel** *m* silver crucible **-vitriol** *m* silver sulfate **-währung** *f* silver currency **-ware** *f*, **-waren** *pl* silverware **-weiß** silver white **-wismutglanz** *m* matildite **-zitrat** *n* silver citrate

Silentblock *m* silent block

Silicium *n* silicon **-legierung** *f* silicon alloy **-verbindung** *f* silicic compound, silicide

silifiziert siliceous

Silikaaufbereitungsanlage *f* silicon dressing plant

Silikagelkristalle *pl* silicagel crystals

Silika-sand *m* silica sand **-stab** *m* silica pencil **-stein** *m* silica brick

Silikat *n* silicate **-emaille** *f* silicate enamel **-schlacke** *f* silicate slag **-schmelzlösung** *f* melted silicate solution

Silikatstein *m*, **Silikatziegel** *m* silica brick

Silikose *f* silicosis

Silit *n* silican carbide

Silizid *n* silicide

silizieren to siliconize

Silizierung *f* silication, silification, silionizing

Silizium *n* silicon **-abbrand** *m* loss of silicon **-aluminium** *n* silumin alloy **-arm** poor or low in silicon **-bromid** *n* silicon bromide **-bronzedraht** *m* silicon bronze wire **-dioxyd** *n* silicic acid **-eisen** *n* ferrosilicon

Silizium-fluorwasserstoffsäure *f* fluosilicic acid **-fluorwasserstoffsaures Blei** lead silicofluoride **-frei** nonsiliceous **-gehalt** *m* silicon content **-haltig** siliceous **-jodid** *n* silicon iodide **-karbid** *n* silicon carbide, carborundum **-kohlenstoff** *m* silicon carbide **-kupfer** *n* copper silicide, cuprosilicon

Silizium-magnesium *n* magnesium silicide **-manganstahl** *m* silicomanganese steel **-metall** *n* metallic silicide **-oxalsäure** *f* silicooxalic acid **-oxyd** *n* silicon dioxide **-oxykarbid** *n* silicon oxycarbide **-spiegel** *m* siliceous ferromangenese **-stahl** *m* silicon steel **-tetrachlorid** *n* silicon tetrachloride **-verbindung** *f* silicon compound

Sillimanitsteine *pl* sillimanite bricks

Sillometer *n* sillometer

Silo *m* silo, storage bin **-anlage** *f* silo works **-entleerung** *f* clearing of silo **-verfahren** *n* silo process **-wirkung** *f* silo or bin effect **-zelle** *f* silo compartment

Silumin *n* silumin

Silundum *n* silundum

silurisch (Silur) silurian

Simmerring *m* retaining ring, oil seal

Simmritdichtung *f* simmrit gasket

Simplex-betrieb *m* simplex operation **-leitung** *f* simplex circuit **-rohrabschneider** *m* simplex pipe cutter **-verkehr** *m* simplex operation, simplex working

Sims *m* ledge, molding, shelf, cornice **-abdekkung** *f* cornice flashing **-hobel** *m* rabbet-plane **-werk** *n* molding

Simulatorhohlraum *m* simulator cavity

simulieren to simulate, malinger

simuliert simulated

simultan simultaneous **~ schalten** to super(im)pose

Simultan-antenne *f* duplexer **-betrieb** *m* composite working, simultaneous telephone working

Simultaneinrichtung *f* (telegraph) composite set

~ **für Doppelleitung** metallic composite set
Simultan-empfang *m* simultaneous reception **-gerät** *n* a common transmitting and receiving unit **-geräusch** *n* thump **-leitung** *f* simplexed circuit, composited circuit **-schaltung** *f* composited arrangement (telegr) **-schluß** *m* superimposed short **-telegraph** *m* superposed telegraph **-telegraphenleitung** *f* telegraph superposed circuit **-überträger** *m* simplexed coil **-verbindung** *f* superposed circuit, composited circuit, phantom circuit **-verfahren** *n* simultaneous system **-zusatz** *m* attachment to the transmitting and receiving unit
sin-cos-Flächenpotentiometer flat-card resolver
singende Bogenlampe singing arc lamp
Singularität *f* singularity
Singulett-system *n* singlet system **-zustand** *m* singlet state
Singulosilikat *n* monosilicate **-schlacke** *f* monosilicate slag
sin²-Impuls *m* sine-squared pulse
sinken to sink, to go down, abate, drop, gravitate, decline, droop (of a curve), fall (off), decrease, sag, lose flying speed ~ **lassen** to lower, sink
Sinken *n* sinking, fall(ing-off), drop
sinkende Geschwindigkeit sinking speed
Sink-flug *m* descent **-geschwindigkeit** *f* rate of (vertical) descent, vertical component of velocity, velocity of descent, sinking speed **-holz** *n* wood heavier than water **-kasten** *m* box drain **-kraft** *f* downward or sinking force **-lage** *f* water fascine **-scheider** *m* heavy medium separator **-sicher** unsinkable **-stelle** *f* sink
Sinkstoff *m* sedimentary material in suspension, sediment, settlings **-ablagerung** *f* deposits
Sinkstück *n* fascine mattress
Sinn *m* sense, tendency, significance, meaning **im ~ des Uhrzeigers** clockwise **im gleichen ~ wirken** to act in the same sense
sinnähnlich substantially synonymous, in an analogous way
sinnentstellend garbling
sinngemäß analogous, rational, logical, equivalent
sinn-getreu faithful **-los** meaningless, senseless **-reich** ingenious **-verständlichkeit** *f* intelligibility **-verwandt** synonymous(ly) **-voll** meaningful, significant, intelligent, clever, ingenious, very suitable, logical **-wahrnehmung** *f* sense perception
Sinographie *f* sinography
Sinoide *f* sinoide
Sinter *m* sinter, cinder, scale, iron dross, **-anlage** *f* sintering or agglomerating plant **-apparat** *m* sintering machine **-dolomit** *m* burnt dolomite **-eisen** *n* sintering iron **-elektrode** *f* self-baking electrode **-erzeugnis** *n* agglomerate, agglomerated cake, sinter cake **-grube** *f* scale pit **-herd** *m* fritted hearth bottom, fused or sintered hearth bottom **-karbid** *n* cemented carbide **-kathode** *f* powder cathode
Sinterkohle *f* sinter(ing) coal, noncaking or hard coal **backende ~** semibituminous coal of high rank, baking coal
Sinter-korund *n* sintered corundum **-kuchen** *m* sinter cake, agglomerate **-lagerbuchse** *f* sintered metal bearing bush **-magnet** *m* sinter magnet **-metall** *n* dry powdered metal **-metallfilter** *n* sintered stainless steel filter **-metall-Lager** *n* carbide bearing **-metallurgie** *f* powder metallurgy
sintern to sinter, frit, fuse, vitrify, clinker, bake, cake, shrink, slag
Sintern *n* sintering, fritting, fusing, vitrification, clinkering, baking
Sinterungs-hitze *f* sintering or incrustation heat **-prozeß** *m* sintering operation
Sinter-vorgang *m* sintering process, slag process **-wagen** *m* roll scale car
Sinus *m* sine **hyperbolischer ~** hyperbolic sine
Sinus-bussole *f* sine galvanometer **-feld** *n* sinusoidal field **-form** *f* sine shape, sine wave
sinusförmig sine-shaped, sinusoidal, sine-wave **rein ~** simple harmonic **-e Bewegung** harmonic motion **-er Strom** sinusoidal or sine-wave current **-e Trägerwelle** sinusoidal carrier wave **-e Wechselgröße** sinusoidal quantity **-e Wellenbewegung** harmonic motion
Sinus-funktion *f* sine function **-geber** *m* sine-wave generator **-gesetz** *n* sine law **-glied** *n* sine term **-kompensator** *m* sin potentiometer **-kosinuskompensator** *m* sine-cosine potentiometer **-kurve** *f* sinusoid, sine curve **-lammelenkupplung** *f* sinus-multiple disk clutch **-lineal** *n* sine bar rule, sine (curve) rule **-linie** *f* sinous line, sine curve, sinusoid
Sinusoide *f* sinusoid, sine curve
Sinus-reihe *f* sine series **-satz** *m* sine law, theorem of the sines
Sinusschwingung *f* sinusoid, sine wave, sine oscillation, sinusoidal wave **gedämpfte ~** damped sine wave **ungedämpfte ~** sustained sinusoid
Sinus-spannung *f* sinusoidal voltage, sine voltage, sine-wave voltage **-strom** *m* sinusoidal current, sine current, sine-wave current
Sinuswelle *f* sine wave **reine ~** pure sine wave **zusammengesetzte ~** complex sine wave
Sinus-wellenerzeuger *m* sine-wave alternator, harmonic generator **-wellengenerator** *m* sinusoidal oscillator **-winkel** *m* sine of angle
Sipho *m* siphuncle
Siphon *m* siphon **-kapsel** *f* siphon head **-schmierapparat** *m* siphon lubricator **-speiser** *m* siphon feeder
Sirufer-kern *m* sirufer core, Ferrocart core **-spule** *f* sirufer (iron-dust) coil
Sirup *m* sirup **-ablaufventil** *n* sirup discharging valve **-decke** *f* sirup washing **-einzug** *m* sirup or drink **-kessel** *m* sugar sirup kettle **-konsistenz** *f* sirup consistency **-pumpe** *f* sirup or juice pump **-transporteur** *m* bagasse carrier **-trennvorrichtung** *f* sirup classifying apparatus **-verdampfer** *m* sugar sirup evaporator **-zuzug** *m* sirup draft
sistieren to stop
Situation *f* situation, position
Situations-gegenstand *m* topographical particular **-plan** *m* plan showing position, site plan, planimetry **-skizze** *f* layout plan
Sitz *m* fit, seat, lodgment, setting **~ des Kolbens** seat of piston **verstellbarer ~** adjustable seat **in der Höhe verstellbarer ~** vertically adjustable seat
Sitz-abstützung *f* seat bracket assembly **-anordnung** *f* seating arrangement **-art** *f* class of fit,

kind of fit **-aufhängung** *f* seat bracket assembly
Sitzbank *f* sofa seat **hintere ~** stern sheet of boat
Sitz-brett *n* seat **-durchmesser** *m* valve diameter
Sitzenbleiben eines Teiles einer Ladung beim Sprengen partial detonation of charge
Sitzfallschirm *m* seat-type parachute **-pack** *m* seatpack parachute
Sitzfläche *f* seating, seat, face (value) **~ des Ventiltellers** valve seat
Sitz-fräser *m* milling cutter **-gelegenheit** *f* seating accommodation **-gleiter** *m* glider with seat **-gurt** *m* seat belt **-keil** *m* seat key
Sitzkissenfallschirm *m* seat pack or seat-type parachute
Sitzstütze *f* seat bracket, seat pedestal
Sitz(um)schalter *m* socket contact
Sitzung *f* sitting, session, meeting
Sitzungsbericht *m* proceedings
Sitz-verstellung *f* seat adjustment **-vorrichtung** *f* seat or riding attachment **-zahl** *f* seating capacity
Skala *f* scale, division, graduation, dial **doppelseitig kalibrierte ~** double graduated scale **kreissegmentförmige ~** quadrant **reine ~** true scale (music) **mit einer ~ versehen** to calibrate **~ mit direkter Frequenzablesung** direct reading frequency dial **~ der Sendestationen** station dial
Skalalineal *n* graduated rule
Skalar *n* scalar property, scalar quantity
skalar scalar **-es Produkt** scalar product **-e Größe** scalar quantity
Skalen-ablesung *f* scale reading **-aräometer** *n* graduated hydrometer **-ausschlag** *m* scale deflection **-basis** *f* scale base **-bezifferung** *f* scale numbering **-blatt** *n* dial **-einteilung** *f* graduation of scale **-endwert** *m* maximum scale reading **-faktor** *m* scale factor (info proc.) **-glasscheibe** *f* chart glass **-intervall** *m* scale division, scale interval
Skalen-konstante *f* scale factor **-kontrolle** *f* ranging **-länge** *f* lineal scale length **-marke** *f* graduation mark **-meßgerät** *n* direct-reading measuring instrument **-mikroskop** *n* scale microscope **-prüfung** *f* dial test
Skalen-rahmen *m* scale retaining frame **-ring** *m* graduated ring **-rohr** *n* scale tube **-reiter** *m* indicator clip **-schablone** *f* slotted dial plate **-scheibe** *f* graduated disk or dial, scale disk **-teil** *m* scale division, scale sector or graduation **-teilstrich** *m* scale mark **-teilung** *f* scale division **-trommel** *f* micrometer collar **-verlauf** *m* scale law **-wert** *m* reading **-zeiger** *m* dial pointer
Skalpell *n* scalpel
Skandium *n* scandium
Skarpierschaufel *f* trenching shovel
Skelett *n* skeleton **-ausfachung** *f* skeleton structure **-linie** *f* mean camber line **-trommel** *f* skeleton cylinder
skandieren to scan
Skiaskop (Hand-Refraktometer) *n* hand refractionometer
Skineffekt *m* skin effect, Kelvin effect
Skiograph *m* skiograph
Skipförderung *f* skip winding
Skizze *f* sketch, outline, drawing, draft
skizzieren to sketch, outline, delineate
Sklerolampe *f* sclerotic lamp
Sklerometer *n* sclerometer
skleronom scleronomic
sklerosieren to harden
Skleroskop *n* scleroscope **-härte** *f* scleroscope or rebound hardness
Sklodowskit *m* sklodowskite
Skorie *f* scoria, dross, slag, cinder
Skrubber *m* wash tower, (gas) scrubber
S-Kurve *f* sigmoid curve
Slack *m* slack (cable)
Slalom-fokussierung *f* slalom focussing **-verstärker** *m* rippled wall amplifier
Slip *m* slip or slipway, sideslip (of airplane) **~ der Schraube** slip of propeller
slippen to release
Smaltin *m* smaltite
Smaragd *m* emerald **-grün** emerald green, emerald(-colored) **-spat** *m* green feldspar, amazonite
Smithsonit *m* smithsonite
Sockel *m* stationary base, foundation, pedestal, sode, support; (Lampe) holder, socket; (Röhre) base, cap **fünfpoliger ~** fivepin base, five-prong base **stiftloser ~** side-contact-type base
Sockel-blech *n* base sheet **-brettchen** *n* base tray **-buchse** *f* cap sleeve **-füllgerät** *n* cap filler **-gewinde** *n* base-cap screw **-kitt** *m* socket or capping cement **-kleber** *m* lamp capping cement **-lafette** *f* rotating-base mount, pivot mounting **-leiste** *f* base rail, skirting board **-mantel** *m* base covering **-platte** *f* plinth (arch.) **-ring** *m* base ring **-schraube** *f* binding bolt **-stift** *m* pin of a tube socket, base pin
Sockelung *f* equipment with a socket
Soda *f* soda, sodium carbonate **-azetat** *n* sodium acetate **-lauge** *f* soda lye **-lösung** *f* soda solution **-salz** *n* soda salt, sodium carbonate **-stein** *m* caustic soda
Soddit *m* soddite
Sode *f* sod
Soden *m* sod, rectangular piece **-decke** *f* sodwork **-pflug** *m* sod knife, turf cutter
Söderberg-Elektrode *f* Söderberg electrode
Sodium *n* sodium **-gekühlt** sodium-cooled
Sodraum *m* well room
Sofitte *f* tubular lamp **große ~** big spot **kleine ~** ashcan
Sofitten-beleuchtung *f* tubular-lamp lighting **-lampe** *f* strip lamp, overhead scoop, scaffold light or lamp, tubular lamp **-leitung** *f* tubular lamp wire
sofort instantly, at once, immediately
sofortige Anziehung quick operation
Sofortverkehr *m* no-delay operation, "no hang-up" service **~ mit Anrufbetrieb** ring-down operation of a no-delay or on-demand basis
Sog *m* undertow, wash, wake, suction (of shock wave resulting from an explosion or detonation) **-anschluß** *m* vacuum-line connection
soggen to precipitate in crystal form, crystallize out, contract (of metal)
Sog-kraft *f* suction force **-pumpe** *f* vacuum pump, rotating piston pump **-regler** *m* suction regulator **-versorgung** *f* source of suction **-wirkung** *f* suction effect
Sohldruck *m* bottom pressure, base pressure
Sohle *f* sole, floor level, base, bottom, (river)

bed, (dredged) berth, apron, foundation, sole-plate ~ **des Flözes** bottom of the bed ~ **der oberen Haltung** upstream apron ~ **der unteren Haltung** downstream apron ~ **der Schleusenkammer** floor of (lock) chamber **befestigte** ~ consolidated floor **bewehrte** ~ reinforced floor **vertiefte** ~ depressed floor, lower level

Sohlen-auftrieb *m* creep **-ausschneidemaschine** *f* sole cutting machine **-befestigung** *f* apron **-bohrloch** *n* downward borehole, down-pointing hole **-breite** *f* width at bottom **-dichtung** *f* bottom sealing **-druck** *m* bottom-hole pressure, creep (min.) **-falz** *m* groove or recess in the floor, sill of floor **-feuer** *n* bottom fire

Sohlen-höhe *f* bed elevation **-messer** *n* ground planing knife **-oberfläche** *f* level surface **-platte** *f* bottom plate, bedplate, foundation slab or plate, base plate, sole plate **-quader** *m* foot block **-querschlag** *m* bottom crosscut **-rohr** *n* floor tube **-stopfbüchse** *f* bottom-hole packer **-strecke** *f* drift, gallery, level (drift), level gang-way, main gangway **-strömung** *f* bottom current

Sohlenverkleidung *f* riprap (bottom paving) ~ **von Holz** wooden apron

Sohlfläche *f* subface

söhlig horizontal, level, bottomed

Sohl-kanal *m* sole flue, bottom flue **-platte** *f* base plate, bottom plate, bedplate

Sol *n* (kolloide Lösung) sol

solare Teilchen sol particles

Solarimeter *n* solarimeter

Solarisation *f* solarization

solarisationsfreie Platte antihalation dry plate (phot.)

Solar-konstante *f* solar constant **-öl** *n* solar oil

Solarometer *n* solarometer (navig)

Sol-bohrloch *n* salt boring **-brunnen** *m* salt well

Sole *f* brine, salt water **gradierte** ~ refined brine

Sole-austritt *m* brine outlet **-kühler** *m* brine cooler

Solenoid *n* solenoid, helix **einlagiges** ~ single-layer solenoid **eisenloses** ~ air-core solenoid

Solenoidbohrmaschine *f* solenoid rock drill

Solfatarenstadium *n* solfatara stage

Solheber *m* salt-water elevator

Solinglas *n* crown glass

Solkanal *m* brine ditch

Soll *n* debit side, debtors, required value, requirement ~ **und Haben** debtor and creditor, debit and credit

Soll-abmessung *f* nominal dimension **-anzeige** *f* true indication **-ausgabe** *f* estimated expenditure **-bahn** *f* desired path or trajectory **-betrag** *m* nominal amount (debit side)

Sollbruch-bolzen *m* safety bolt **-glied** *n* safety member **-stelle** *f* breaking point, safety limit, predetermined, preset or rated breaking point

Soll-drehzahl *f* rated speed, rated RPM **-durchmesser** *m* nominal diameter **-durchsatz** *m* required amount of flow **-einnahme** *f* estimated or supposed receipt **-flugbahn** *f* ideal or desired trajectory

Sollform *f* true shape, specified shape **der** ~ **entsprechend** true to shape

Soll-frequenz *f* correct preset or rated or nominal frequency, assigned frequency **-geberhöhe** *f* required-elevation dial (radar) **-geschwindigkeit** *f* cutoff velocity (missiles) **-höhe** *f* designed height **-kreis** *m* equilibrium orbit **-kurs** *m* desired or prescribed course **-lage** *f* ideal position, precalculated position **-leistung** *f* design capacity

Soll-maß *n* real measure, real size specified size, theoretical size **-menge** *f* theoretical quantity **-nahtdicke** *f* thickness of weld

Sol-löffel *m* brine socket **-lösung** *f* sol dispersion

Soll-schußebene *f* plane of standard trajectory **-schußweite** *f* required range

Sollseite, auf der ~ **verbuchen** to debit

Soll-stand *m*, **-stärke** *f* authorized strength and equipment **-strom** *m* rated current **-tempratur** *f* rated temperature, desired temperature **-verstellinie** *f* specified timing curve **-vorhalt** *m* correct angle of lead **-vorzugsachse** *f* nominal easy axis

Sollwert *m* theoretical value, desired value, nominal value, ideal value, rated value, face value, set point (servo) **bei der Konstruktion zugrunde gelegter** ~ design amount

Sollwert-bereich *m* available range of set-point adjustment **-geber** *m* setting means **-potentiometer** *n* nominal value setter **-skala** *f* nominal value scale **-steller** *m* desired-value or setpoint adjuster **-zeiger** *m* limit pointer

Soll-wirkungsgrad *m* declared efficiency **-zahlung** *f* rated payment

Solodynempfang *m* solodyne reception

Soloflug *m* solo flight

Sol-quelle *f* brine spring, salt spring **-salz** *n* brine salt

Solschutz *m* protection of sol

Solstitialpunkt *m* solstitial point

Solstitium *n* solstice

solvatisiertes Harz solvated resin

Solvent *n* paint thinner, solvent **-naphtha** *n* solvent naphtha, coal-tar naphtha

Solvenz *f* ability to pay, solvency

Solwaage *f* salt or brine gauge

somatische Zahl somatic number

Sommerdeich *m* dike

Sommerfeldsche Formel Sommerfeld's transmission formula or attenuation formula

Sommer-flugplan *m* summer timetable **-gewitter** *n* summer thunderstorm **-holz** *n* summer wood or timber **-monsun** *m* summer monsoon **-polder** *m* summer polder

Sommerung *f* tecalemiting

Sommerweg *m* summer road or path, seasonal road

Sonde *f* probe, sound (device), sampling device, weather-forecasting equipment, search electrode, sonde (radio) ~ **mit geringer Produktion** stripper well **einstellbare** ~ tuning probe **statische** ~ static probe ~ **mit Verstärker** probe unit

Sonden-abtaströhre *f* probe scanning tube **-abtastung** *f* probe scanning **-ausdehnung** *f* probe area **-führung** *f* scanning lead **-halterung** *f* probe-holding device **-röhre** *f* image dissector **-spule** *f* exploring or pick-up coil **-technik** *f* probe technique

Sonder-abdruck *m* reprint, seaparate print **-antrieb** *m* accessory drive **-aufbau** *m* special body **-auftrag** *m* special mission **-ausführung** *f* special type, special design **-ausrüstung** *f* special equipment **-bauart** *f* special type **-behandlung** *f*

selective treatment **-betrieb** *m* special operation **-buchstabe** *m* separate, continental, or accented letter

Sonder-dienst *m* special service **-draht** *m* special wire **-einbauten** *pl* aircraft armor **-einheit** *f* special or separate unit **-entwicklung** *f* special or separate development **-fall** *m* special case, exception **-flugzeug** *n* special-type plane **-formationen** *f pl* special auxiliary troops **-frequenz** *f* special frequency **-funkspruch** *m* special radio message

Sonder-gerät *n* special equipment **-gespräch** *n* special telephone call **-gewinde** *n* special thread **-gußeisen** *n* special cast iron **-karte** *f* special chart or map **-leitung** *f* special circuit **-maschine** *f* special machine **-metallauflage für Schaltstücke** compact tip for contacts

sondern to separate, sort out, size, assort, classify, grade, sever, segregate

Sonder-profil *n* special section, special shape **-roheisen** *n* special grade pig iron, special pig **-schlüssel** *m* specific key **-speicher** *m* zone (comput) **-stahl** *m* special steel, alloy steel

Sonderung *f* sorting

Sonder-ventilator *m* booster fan, inbye fan **-versuch** *m* probe or sounding test **-vorrichtung** *f* sounding equipment **-walzprofil** *n* special rolling-mill section **-walzwerk** *n* special(ty) rolling mill **-werkzeug** *n* special tool **-winde** *f* sounding winch **-zug** *m* special train

Sonderzweck-automat *m* single-purpose automat(ic) **-vorrichtung** *f* special-purpose fixture

Sondier-ballon *m* sounding balloon **-bohrer** *m* probing auger **-eisen** *n* sounding rod, trial boring tool

sondieren to sound (the upper air), fathom

Sondier-handbohrer *m* hand drill **-stollen** *m* exploration tunnel

Sondierung *f* sounding

Sondierungsbohrung *f* probing a bore

Sone *n* sone **~skala** *f* sone scale

Sonne *f* sun, sun arc, klieg lights **~ schießen** to take bearings on the sun

Sonnen-aufgang *m* sunrise **-ausbruch** *m* solar eruption **-bahn** *f* ecliptic **-batterie** *f* solar battery, solar converter, solar cell **-beobachtung** *f* solar observation, observation of the sun **-beständig** sun-proof **-bestrahlung** *f* solar radiation, irradiation by solar rays, exposure to sunlight **-blende** *f* sun visor, sun shield, black screen **-bö** *f* heat eddy

Sonnen-chromosphäre *f* solar chromosphere **-energie** *f* solar energy **-eruption** *f* solar flare **-fackel** *f* solar flare **-ferne** *f* aphelion **-fernrohr** *n* helioscope **-finsternis** *f* solar eclipse **-fleck** *m* sunspot **-fleckenzahl** *f* sunspot number **-fleckperiode** *f* sunspot period or cycle **-glas** *n* helioscope **-helligkeit** *f* brightness of the sun **-hof** *m* solar corona

Sonnenhöhe *f* sun's altitude **die ~ messen** to take the sun's altitude

Sonnen-kompaß *m* sun compass **-kontinuum** *n* sun continuum **-korona** *f* solar corona **-kraftmaschine** *f* solar generator **-kraftwerk** solar plant

Sonnenlicht *n* sunlight **-telegraph** *m* heliograph

sonnenlos sunless, without sunshine

Sonnen-messer *m* heliometer **-nähe** *f* perihelion **-peilung** *f* bearing by the sun **-photosphäre** *f* solar photosphere **-protuberanz** *f* solar flare **-rad** *n* sun wheel **-rand** *m* limb of the sun **-ring** *m* solar halo **-riß** *m* natural crack (in wood) **-säule** *f* sun pillar

Sonnenschein *m* sunshine **-anzeiger** *m* sunshine recorder **-autograph** *m* sunshine recorder, heliograph **-dauer** *f* duration of sunshine **-messer** *m* sunshine recorder

Sonnen-schmelzspiegel *m* solar furnace **-schutz** *m* sunshade **-schutzbrille** *f* sunglasses **-spektrum** *n* solar spectrum **-stand** *m* position or altitude of the sun **-stich** *m* sunstroke **-strahl** *m* sunray, sunbeam **-strahlung** *f* solar radiation, sun's radiation

Sonnen-strahlungsmesser *m* solarimeter, pyrheliometer, actinometer **-tag** *m* solar day **-tätigkeit** *f* solar activity **-tätigkeitsperiode** *f* solar activity period, cycle of solar activity **-untergang** *m* sunset, sundown

Sonnenuntergangserscheinungen *pl* sunset effects

Sonnen-vorhang *m* sunshade **-wärme** *f* solar heat **-wärmemesser** *m* pyrheliometer, solarimeter **-wende** *f* solstice **-zeiger** *m* gnomon

Sonnenzeit *f* solar time **mittlere ~** mean solar time

Sonnenzeitsekunde *f* solar second

Sonnen-zelle *f* solar cell or battery (astronaut) **-zelt** *n* awning

sonnig sunny

Sonometer *n* sonometer **-feder** *f* sonometer spring **-magnet** *m* sonometer magnet

sorbierender Stoff absorbent

sorbierter Stoff absorbed substance

Sorbit *m* sorbite

sorbitisch sorbitic **-es Gefüge** sorbitic structure

Sorge *f* worry, care, uneasiness, anxiety **für etwas ~ tragen** to care for something

Sorrelsalz *n* Sorrel salt

soßig spotty, bleary (of a picture)

Sorte *f* sort, kind, class, mark, brand, quality, rank, type, species **gangbarste ~** leading species, most practicable type

sorten to sort (out), separate, classify, grade

Sorten-bezeichnung *f* type description **-versuch** *m* variety trial

Sortier-anlage *f* picking plant **-apparat** *m* sizing apparatus, separator, sorting machine, sorter

sortieren to sort (out), separate, classify, grade, size

Sortieren *n* separating **rohes ~ der Erze** rough separating (of ores)

Sortierer *m* sorter (comput.)

Sortier-maschine *f* sorting machine **-mulde** *f* sorting trough **-raum** *m* sorting room, grading room **-scheibe** *f* sorting drum, sorting disc

sortiert graded, sorted

Sortiertisch *m* sorting table

Sortiertrommel *f* revolving screen (trommel), sizing trommel **~ für Hackspäne** chip screen (paper mfg.)

Sortierung *f* sorting, separation, grading, assortment **~ nach der Größe** sizing

Sortierzyklon *m* cyclone-washer

Sortiment *n* assortment

Sortimenter *m* retail-bookseller

soufflieren to prompt

Sourdine *f* sourdine, mute

Spachtel *m* spatula, smoother, float, smoothing trowel, finishing trowel, putty knife
Spachtel-kitt *m* trowel filler mastic **-masse** *f* surfacer, filler, primer, knifing glaze, priming material, mastic, paste wood filler surface
spachteln to make smooth, prime
Spachtel-schicht *f* putty or surface coat **-schliff** *m* spatula grinding
Spachtelung *f* knifing the filler
Spahnpresse *f* press containing pressboards
Spake *f* capstan bar, handspike
spakig werden to rot
Spallationsbruchstück spallation fragment
Spalt *m* split, slit, crack, gap, fissure, crevice, aperture, clearance ~ **des Stoffauflaufs** gate or slot (paper mfg.)
Spalt-abdeckung *f* aerodynamic seal **-absaugung** *f* slot-siphoning (jet) **-algen** *pl* fission algae **-anlage** *f* cracking unit **-ausbeute** *f* fission yield **-ausleuchtung** *f* slit illumination
spaltbar cleavable, fissionable (atom)
Spaltbarkeit *f* cleavability fissionability
Spalt-backen *pl* slit jaws **-benzin** *n* cracked gasoline **-bild** *n* slit image **-blende** *f* slit (diaphragm), apertured stop **-breite** *f* gap separation, gap width, apertural width **-brüchigkeit** *f* cleavage brittleness **-buchse** *f* split bushing **-bruchstück** *n* fission fragment **-buchse** *f* split bushing
Spalte *f* break, chasm, cleft, crevice, fissure, fracture, rent, split, crack, slot, column
Spaltebene *f* cleavage plane, cleavage face **-kristallfilter** *m* plate-type filter, edge filter, streamline filter
Spalt-effekt *m* aperture or apertural effect **-einrichtung** *f* slit mechanism **-einstellung** *f* discharge setting
spalten to split, cleave, slit, crack, split up, dissociate **sich** ~ to split, to break up
Spalten (im Filterpaket) *pl* slots
Spalten-eruption *f* fissure eruption **-frost** *m* frost in the cracks of rocks **-füllung** *f* fissure filling **-index** *m* column index **-matrix** *f* column matrix
Spalt-festigkeit *f* splitting resistance, cleavage strength **-filter** *n* streamline filter, plate-type (oil) filter **-fläche** *f* clearance area, cleavage surface, cleavage plane, cleavage face **-flächenzeichnung** *f* cleavage plane, crystal marking **-flügel** *m* slotted wing, wing-tip slot **-flügelklappe** *f* slotted flap **-frei** apertureless, slitless **-frequenz** *f* split frequency **-fuge** *f* cleaving split **-funkenzünder** *m* jump spark gap **-gatter** *m* cleaving machine **-geschwindigkeit** *f* slot velocity **-glühzünder** *m* high-tension cap **-hilfsflügel** *m* split flap **-höhe** *f* slit height
Spalt-kammer *f* fission chamber **-kappe** *f* slit cover **-klappe** *f* split flap, slotted flap **-keil** *m* spliting wedge **-kollimation** *f* slit collimation **-kopfschraube** *f* slotted screw **-körper** *m* cleavage substance, cleavage product **-korrosion** *f* crevice corrosion **-lagenstreuung** *f* gap scatter (tape rec.) **-lehre** *f* feeler gauge **-leitwert eines Kreises** circuit gap admittance **-loch** *n* split or wedge hole **-lupe** *f* slip magnifier
Spalt-material *n* fissionable material **-materialelement** *n* fuel element **-meißel** *m* cleaving chisel **-niet** *n* split-head rivet **-nietung** *f* split riveting **-öffnung** *f* slit aperture, chink (in clarinet) **-platten** *pl* split clinker flags **-polmotor** *m* shaded-pole motor **-probe** *f* spalling test **-produkt** *n* product of disunion or separation, fission product **-produktausbeute** *f* chain fission yield **-prozeß** *m* fission process
Spalt-querruder *n* slotted aileron **-raum** *m* reactor core **-raumverriegelung** source interlock **-reibung** *f* windage (elec.) **-ring** *m* split ring **-riß** *m* cleavage crack or fissure **-rohr** *n* collimator **-röhre** *f* slotted tube (of rocket charge) **-rohrtreibsatz** *m* slotted tube charge (rocket) **-rohstoff** *m* fertile material
Spalt-säge *f* long saw, ripping saw **-schnitte** *f* slitting knives, splits **-schnüre** *pl* split wires **-schwelle** *f* fission threshold **-stift** *m* slit pin
Spaltstoff *m* fissionable fuel **-anordnung** *f* fuel assembly **-aufarbeitung** *f* fuel reconditioning, fuel reprocessing **-kreislauf** *m* fuel cycle **-lösung** *f* fuel solution **-zentrum** *n* center of sintered cylinder
Spalt-streuung *f* slot leakage, slot stray **-stück** *n* fission product **-ton** *m* slit tone, jet tone **-typmagnetron** *n* slot-type magnetron
Spaltung *f* cleavage, division, cracking, resolution, splitting, dissociation, separation, decomposition, fission (atom), precipitation
Spaltungs-ausbeutekurve *f* fission-yield curve **-ebene** *f* cleavage plane **-einfang** *m* fission capture **-energie** *f* energy of splitting or fission **-fläche** *f* cleavage face, cleavage plane **-gestein** *n* differentiated dike rock **-impulskammer** fission counter **-interferenz** *f* fission interference **-kette** *f* fission chain **-kristall** *n* cleavage crystal
spaltungsloser Einfang non-fission capture
Spaltungs-nachweis *m* fission detection **-produkt** *n* fission product, cleavage product **-punkt** *m* stagnation point (aerodyn.), burble point, point of separation **-querschnitt** fission cross-section **-tonne** *f* bifurcation buoy **-untergrund** *m* fission background **-wahrscheinlichkeit** *f* fission probability **-zähler** *m* fission counter **-zeichen** *n* bifurcation signal
Spalt-verkleidung *f* slot covering **-verlust** *m* clearance loss, cleavage loss **-versuch** *m* cleavage test, splitting test **-weite** *f* clearance, gauge **-werkzeug** *n* splitting tool **-zähler** *m* fission counter **-zerstäuber** *m* slot-type atomizer **-zone** *f* core (nuclear physics), active lattice or zone
Span *m* chip, splinter, shaving, boring, turning, cutting **-abheben** to cut, machine
spanabhebend cutting, machining **gut** ~ free cutting **-e Arbeit** chip detaching, material detaching work **-e Bearbeitbarkeit** free-cutting machinability **-e Formgebung** shaping by machine tool with removal of chips **-e Maschine** metal-cutting machine **-e Metallbearbeitung** metal-cutting **-e Verformung** cutting shaping **-es Werkzeug** (metal-)cutting tool
Span-abfluß *m* chip flow **-abfuhr** *f* swarf disposal **-abhebung** *f* detachment of a cutting metal removal **-abnahme** *f* stock or chip removal **-absaugung** *f* chip exhaust system **-beförderung** *f* chip handling installation **-bildung** *f* formation of a cutting
Spanbrecher *m* chip breaker **-nuten** *pl* chip breaker (breaking) grooves or flutes **-stufen** *pl* chip breaker (breaking) steps

Span-breite *f* chip width **-breitenverhältnisse** *pl* relative cutting widths **-dicke** *f* depth of cut, cutting depth **-druck** *m* cut or chip pressure

Späne *m pl* turnings, borings, chips **-absauganlage** *f* shaving suction plant **-abscheider** *m* cyclone (fan), shavings exhauster **-behälter** *m* swarf box **-brikettierungspresse** *f* chip briquetting press **-bühne** *f* papering lift **-durchlaß** *m* chip space or clearance **-fang** *m* (suitable) chip chute **-fänger** *m* shavings separator **-förderanlage** *f* shaving exhaust installation **-kasten** *m* chip tray

Spanentleerung *f* chip removal

Späne-pfanne *f* chip tray **-rinne** *f* swarf gutter **-schale** *f* chip pan **-schleuder** *f* chip separator or centrifuge **-zentrifuge** *f* centrifugal oil extractor **-zerreißer** *m* apparatus for tearing off the shavings

Span-fall *m* cuttings pit or shoot **-fangschale** *f* chip tray **-fläche** *f* true rake **-formernute** *f* chip breaker

Spange *f* clasp, buckle, clip, stay bolt

spangebende Bearbeitung machining

Spangeleisen *n* crystalline pig iron

Spangen zum Montieren clamps for mounting

Span-holz *n* chip wood **-korb** *m* wood-shaving basket, chip basket **-leistung** *f* (Schruppen) cutting capacity (power) **-lenker** *m* chip deflector

spanlos non-cutting **-e Bearbeitung** metal working **-e Formgebung** forging **-e Verformung** noncutting shaping

Span-lücke *f* chip space, chip clearance, gash **-menge** *f* quantity of metal removed, volume of metal removed **-plattenpresse** chipboard press **-tiefe** *f* depth of cut

Spann *m* instep, cutting **-abfall** *m* diminution of pressure **-anker** *m* turnbuckle **-apparat** *m* stretcher **-arbeiten** *pl* clamping work, chucking work, jig work **-armierung** *f* prestressing reinforcement **-backe** *f* contact jaw, clamping jaw, chuck jaw, gripping jaw **-balken** *m* spreader bar

Spannband *n* strap, hose clamp, bond of armature, steel collar, tension band **~ für Kolbenringeinbau** piston ring clamp, ring-band tool

Spannband-aufhängung *f* taut strip suspension (meas-instr.) **-hebel** *m* clamping band lever

spannbar tensile, extensile, ductile

Spann-bereich *m* chuck capacity **-beton** *m* prestressed concrete **-betonröhre** *f* reinforced-concrete pipe **-blech** *n* clamp, vice, spring clamp **-bock** *m* stretching or tension block, cabane **-bolzen** *m* tension rod, clamp bolt, clamping stud **-breite** *f* distance between supports **-brett** *n* stretchboard **-büchse** *f* clamping bush, spring collet

Spannbügel *m* (Kraftstoffpumpe) clamp, stirrup **-verschluß** *m* clamp locking device **-vorrichtung** *f* taut tape attachment

Spanndraht *m* bracing wire, tension cable, span wire, guy **~ für seitliche Festlegung** steady span

Spann-drahtdiagonale *f* diagonal bracing wire **-druck** *m* cut pressure **-durchmesser** *m* gripping diameter **-element** *n* (Ringfeder) grip-spring tensioning element

Spanne *f* span, interval, range

Spanneinrichtung *f* gripping arrangement, clamping device

spannen to stretch; (Bogen) bend; (straff **~**) tighten; (Werkstück) grip, clamp; (beanspruchen) stress; (Feder) tension, tighten; (Schraube) tighten; (Seil) stretch; put under stress, hold, lock, chuck, extend, span, strain (a wire), set, wind **den Hahn am Gewehr ~** to cock a gun **einen Riemen ~** to stretch a belt

Spannen *n* gripping, chucking, holding, clamping, stretching

Spanner *m* rack, strainer, turnbuckle, shiner (textiles)

Spann-exzenter *m* tensioning eccentric **-faden** *m* shiner (textiles) **-falle** *f* cocking cam, ejector nut of breech mechanism

Spannfeder *f* tension spring, cocking spring **durch ~ schließender Hahn** spring-loaded nozzle

Spann-feld *n* tentering limit **-fläche** *f* gripping surface **-flansch** *m* spring flange

Spannfutter *n* chuck, lathe chuck, chuck jaws, face-plate, collet chuck **~ zum Planschleifen** face grinding chuck **selbstzentrierendes ~** scroll chuck

Spannfuttertisch *m* chuck table

Spann-getriebe *n* chucking mechanism **-gewicht** *n* counterweight **-gitterröhre** *f* frame-grid tube **-griff** *m* tightening handel **-haken** *m* tenterhook **-hammer** *m* stretching hammer **-hebel** *m* bolt lever, cocking lever, compensator lever, gripping lever **-hülse** *f* adapter sleeve, clamping sleeve, split taper sleeve **-hülsenlager** *n* adapter bearing, tapered-sleeve wedge bearing

Spann-isolator *m* strain insulator (ant.) **-kabel** *n* bracing cable **-kegel** *m* clamping cone, hub cap **-keil** *m* chucking wedge **-klammer** *f* clamp **-klemme** *f* strainer **-kloben** *m* clamp dog, hand vise, faceplate jaw **-kluppe** *f* vise clamp

Spannkopf *m* grip, specimen holder **~** (einer Spannzange) closer

Spann-kraft *f* tension, extensibility, elasticity, tension load, elastic or tensional force, clamping power **-kräftig** elastic **-kreuz** *n* feed ratchet **-lack** *m* stiffening, varnish or dope **-länge** *f* length of span **-lasche** *f* clamping coverplate **-luft** *f* top air

Spann-maschine *f* stretching machine **-menge** *f* amount of chips and swarf **-mutter** *f* adjusting or tightening nut **-mittel** *n* chucking equipment **-nute** *f* groove, flute **-nuteneinrichtung** *f* direction of flute

Spannuten *pl*, **Bohrer mit geraden ~** straight-flute drill

Spannpatrone *f* spring for grip chuck or conical grip, collet, split chuck, spring collet **auf Druck wirkende ~** push-out collet

Spannpatronen-einrichtung *f* collet chucking attachment **-futter** *n* draw-in collet chuck

Spannplatte *f* gripping or clamping plate **~ mit Kreuzschlitten** table moving across and endwise

Spannpratze *f* clamping shoe

Spannquerschnitt *m* sectional area of cut

Spann-rahmen *m* tenter, tentering frame **-rast** *f* snatch post **-riegel eines Hängewerkes** tie beam or main timber of a truss frame **-riemen** *m* tightening belt **-ring** *m* clamping ring, locking ring, set-screw ring, straining ring, expansion or tightening ring **-rohr** *n* draw-in tube, push-out tube **-rolle** *f* tightener (pulley), idler pulley or idler, tension roller, jockey pulley, tensioning pulley **-rollenarm** *m* tension roller crank **-rollenbetrieb** *m* idler-pulley drive

Spann-säge *f* frame saw **-säule** *f* (Bohrhammer) holding column **-schaft** *m* clamping cylinder **-scheibe** *f* tightening disk **-schieber** *m* cocking slide **-schiene** *f* slide rail, clamping device

Spannschloß *n* (stay) tightener, swivel, screw shackle, rod strainer, stretching screw or bolt, spanner, turnbuckle, tension lock, tie bar, tie rod **-auge** *n* eyebolt **-hülse** *f* barrel of turnbuckle **-mutter** *f* barrel nut **-öse** *f* eyebolt

Spann-schlüssel *m* tightening key **-schraube** *f* tightening screw, turnbuckle, clamp bolt, cocking screw, turnscrew, chuck **-schütze** *f* pressure shutter **-schwelle** *f* straining-sill **-seele** *f* draw-in spindle **-seil** *n* bracing wire, guy rope, tug, shackle, tedder **-seildiagonale** *f* diagonal bracing wire **-stange** *f* spreader bar, tie rod

Spannstock *m* vise **~ mit verstellbaren Füßen** adjustable pulling-in frame

Spann-stolle *f* trigger-arm guide **-stück** *n* cocking lever, cocking bolt, tripping piece **-tau** *n* span lashing **-teil** *m* work-holding device

Spannturm *m* cabane **-strebe** *f* center section or cabane strut **-verspannung** *f* pylon or cabane bracing

Spann- und Hebelkette *f* lever chain

Spannung *f* voltage, potential (difference), tension, strain, suspense, span, stress, unit stress **~** (Getriebe) tightspot (gear) yield stress **an ~ liegende Ader** negative wire **~ am Anfang** initial voltage **~ am Ende** final voltage **~ in Flußrichtung** forward voltage **~ zwischen den Phasen** line to line voltage **~ gegen den Sternpunkt** voltage against neutral (or star) point **~ führende Teile** live parts **~ der Ventilfeder** tensioning of valve spring **~ bei der eine bleibende Verformung auftritt** strain (eine Leitung) **unter ~ setzen** to make (a circuit) alive **die ~ erhöhen** to increase the power **die ~ verringern** to decrease the power

Spannung, aufgedrückte ~ impressed pressure **abgeflachte ~** flat-topped potential (wave) **bezogene ~** true ultimate stress **deformierende ~** deforming strain **elektrische ~** electrical tension, electric pressure, voltage **flüchtige ~** transient voltage **gleichmäßige ~** steady voltage **induzierte ~** induced voltage **innere ~** internal stress

Spannung, negative ~ compressive stress, compressive strain **positive ~** tensile stress, tensile strain **pulsierende ~** pulsating voltage, ripple voltage **sinusförmige ~** sine (wave of) voltage, harmonic voltage **verformende ~** deforming strain **verkettete ~** interlinked voltage, line voltage **volle ~** full voltage **wiederkehrende ~** restored voltage **mit hoher ~** high-tension **unter ~ befindlich** alive **unter ~ setzen** to energize **dauernd schwingende ~** cyclic (alternating) stress

spannungführend live, alive **-er Draht** live, charged, or hot wire

Spannungsabfall *m* voltage drop, potential difference, pressure drop, potential drop **~ zwischen Aufnehmer und Zylinder** pressure drop between receiver and cylinder **~ durch Blindwiderstand** reactance drop of voltage **kritischer ~** disintegration voltage **ohmscher ~** ohmic drop of voltage, resistance drop **räumlicher ~** potential fall

spannungsabhängig depending on the voltage **-er Widerstand** exponential resistor

Spannungsabhängigkeit *f* amplitude distortion (expressed in decibels) **~ der Dämpfung** net loss variation with amplitude

Spannungs-abnahme *f* voltage drop, potential drop, potential fall **-absenkung** *f* voltage drop **-änderung** *f* change of strain (metal.), change in voltage **-anhäufung** *f* stress concentration **-anhäufungsbeiwert** *m* stress-concentration factor **-anstieg** *m* potential rise, voltage rise **-anteil** *m* proportion or part of stress **-anzeiger** *m* tension indicator or voltmeter **-auslösung** *f* stress release, shunt tripping **-ausschlag** *m* alternating stress amplitude

Spannungs-bauch *m* potential antinode, potential loop **-begrenzer** *m* voltage-discharge cap, carbonblock protector **-dämpfung** *f* voltage attenuation **-dehnungsbeziehung** *f* stress-strain relation **-dehnungsdiagramm** *n* stress-strain diagram, tensile diagram, load-extension diagram, stress-deformation diagram **-dehnungsschaubild** *n* stress-strain or expansion-contraction diagram **-deviator** *m* stress deviator **-differenz** *f* voltage difference, potential difference **-doppelbrechung** *f* stress birefringence

Spannungs-druckdiagramm *n* load-deformation diagram in compression, compression-stress-deformation diagram **-durchbiegungsdiagramm** *n* transverse stress-strain diagram **-durchschlag** *m* dielectric break-down, surge

Spannungs-einkopplung *f* voltage feed **-eisen** *n* iron in voltage circuit **-empfindlichkeit** *f* voltage sensitivity **-entlastung** *f* stress relief, antifatigue or antivibration means **-erhöher** *m* (battery) booster, voltage step-up means **-erhöhung** *f* voltage increase, load increase **-erhöhungstransformator** *m* voltage step-up transformer **-ermäßigung** *f* reduction of stress **-ermittlung** *f* stress analysis

Spannungs-faktor *m* voltage gain **-feder** *f* tension spring **-feld** *n* stress field **-festigkeit** *f* rigging, dielectric, electric, disruptive or puncture strength **-fernmeßgerät** *n* televoltmeter **-fläche** *f* surface of tension

spannungsfrei free of tension or stress **~ glühen** to normalize (aviation) **durch Ausglühen ~ machen** to stress-anneal **-es Glas** strain-free glass **-es Glühen** strain-relief anneal or thermal treatment, stress-relief heat-treatment

spannungsführender Teil life part

Spannungs-gefälle *n* voltage drop or gradient potential drop, potential fall, electric potential gradient **-gegenknoten** *m* potential antinode **-gegenkopplung** *f* voltage feedback **-gewinn** *m* voltage gain **-glättung** *f* smoothing device, potential stabilizer **-gleichhalter** *m* voltage stabilizer **-gleichhaltungskreis** *m* voltage-stabilizing circuit **-grad** *m* degree of tension **-gradient** *m* voltage gradient, potential gradient **-größe** *f* stress intensity, unit stress

Spannungs-impulstensor *m* stress-momentum-tensor **-joch** *n* magnetomotive-force meter **-kegel** *m* pressure cone **-kegelschnitt** stress conic **-kennlinie** *f* tension characteristic **-knoten**

m voltage node, potential node **-knotenpunkt** *m* voltage or potential nodal point **-koeffizient** *m* voltage coefficient **-komponente** *f* component voltage **-konstanz** *f* voltage stability **-kreis** *m* potential circuit **-linie** *f* pressure curve

spannungslos without tension, dead (elec.) **eine Leitung ~ machen** to kill a (power) circuit

Spannungs-losigkeit *f* slack, looseness

Spannungs-messer *m* voltmeter, tension indicator, strain gauge **-modulation** *f* voltage modulation, velocity modulation **-netz** *n* voltage network, space-charge grid **-optik** *f* optics of stress and strain, photoelectricity

spannungsoptisch pertaining to mechanical stress causing optical phenomena, voltage optical, photoelastic **-es Verfahren** photoelastic method

Spannungs-pegel *m* voltage level **-prüfer** *m* voltage detector, breakdown tester, spark tester **-pulsation** *f* voltage pulsation **-punkt** *m* terminal, tap **-quelle** *f* power source, voltage source **-regelung** *f* voltage control **-regler** *m* tension or voltage regulator (coil) **-reglerrelais** *n* voltage-control relay **-regulator** *m* voltage regulator

spannungsregulierende Lichtmaschine voltage controlling dynamo

Spannungsreihe *f* electromotive series, contact potential series, electrochemical series, contact series **elektrolytische ~** series of elements (in accordance with electrochemical potentials)

Spannungs-relais *n* voltage relay, undervoltage, low-voltage or no-voltage relay **-resonanz** *f* series resonance, parellel resonance **-resonanzkreis** *m* series resonant circuit **-richtung** *f* direction of stress **-riß** *m* tension crack, drawing crack **-rißkorrosion** *f* stress corrosion **-rückgang** *m* voltage reduction

Spannungs-schalter *m* potential divider **-schiebungdiagramm** *n* shearing stress-strain diagram, torsional stress-strain diagram **-schreiber** *m* voltage recorder **-schwankung** *f* voltage fluctuation or variation **-schwelle** *f* stress threshold **-sicherheit** *f* spark-over strength, voltage strength, breakdown strength, puncture-proofness **-sicherung** *f* voltage cutout, voltage fuse, circuit breaker

Spannungs-spitze *f* voltage peak **-spitzenanzeiger** *m* voltage-peak indicator **-spitzennivellierer** *m* voltage-peak limiter **-sprung** *m* voltage jump, voltage step, voltage leap, abrupt change of voltage **-spule** *f* voltage coil, pressure coil

Spannungs-stabilisierung *f* voltage stabilization **-stabilisierungsdiode** *f* voltage reference diode **-steigerung** *f* stress or tension increase **-stoß** *m* impulse voltage, potential impulse, voltage pulse **-strom** *m* current flowing in potential circuit **-stufe** *f* voltage degree **-sucher** *m* voltage detector **-tafel** *f* wire tension table, regulation table

Spannungsteiler *m* voltage divider, potential divider, potentiometer **~ mit Gleitkontakt** slide-wire potentiometer **kapazitiver ~** capacitative voltage divider

Spannungsteiler-gitter *n* voltage grading electrode **-schalter** *m* voltage divider circuit **-schaltung** *f* voltage-divider circuit

Spannungs-tensor *m* stress tensor **-trajektorie** *f* stress trajectory **-transformator** *m* potential transformer, voltage transformer **-überbeanspruchung** *f* voltage overstress or overload **-übersetzung** *f* voltage (current) ratio **-übertragungsfaktor** *m* response to voltage **-überwachung** *f* voltage control **-umschalter** *m* voltmeter change-over switch, voltage adapter **-unterbrechung** *f* dump **-unterschied** *m* difference of potential, tension difference

Spannungs-verdoppler *m* voltage doubler, step-up transformer **-verdopplerschaltung** *f* voltage doubler **-verdreifachung** *f* voltage trebling **-verformungs-Beziehungen** *pl* stress strain relations **-verhältnis** *n* voltage ratio **-verkleinerer** voltage reducer **-verlauf** *m* voltage variation or gradient **-verlust** *m* tension loss, potential drop

Spannungs-verschiebung *f* voltage by-passing **-verstärker** *m* voltage amplifier **-verstärkung** *f* voltage amplification **-verstärkungsfaktor** *m* voltage-amplification factor **-verteiler** *m* voltage divider

Spannungsverteilung *f* voltage distribution, stress distribution **sinusförmige ~** sine-wave potential (distribution)

Spannungs-vervielfacher *m* voltage multiplier **-wächter** *m* voltage indicator **-wächterrelais** *n* voltage control relay **-wähler** *m* selector switch **-wahlschalter** *m* voltage-selecting switch

Spannungs-wandler *m* voltage transformer **-wechsel** *m* stress reversal, cyclial variation of stress, stress cycle **-welle** *f* voltage surge or wave, potential-difference ripple **-zahl** *f* stress ratio **-zeiger** *m* voltage indicator, voltmeter, voltage vector **-zulässigkeit** *f* allowable voltage

Spannungszustand *m* state of stress **ebener ~** two-dimensional stress

Spann-ventil *n* cocking valve **-verbinder** *m* connecting strainer **-vorgang** *m* gripping or clamping action **-vorrichtung** *f* work-locating fixture, chuck, jig, turnbuckle, stretching device **-wagen** *m* tension carriage **-walze** *f* hitch roll (paper mfg.)

Spannweite *f* wingspread, span width or length **~ des Bogens** span of arch **~ mit beigeklappten Flügeln** span with wings folded **~ des Oberflügels** upper-wing span **~ des Unterflügels** lower-wing span **gesamte ~** span **unendliche ~** infinite span

Spann-welle *f* cocking-lever shaft **-werk** *n* wire compensator, gantry

Spannwerkzeug *n* clamping tool, gripping appliance, chuck **zusätzliches ~** gripping attachment

Spannwinde *f* straining pulley

Spannwinkel *m* aperture of an optical panel **~ bei Räumnadel** face angle

Spann-wirbel *m* turnbuckle, rocker arm **-wirkung** *f* gripping or stretching effect **-zange** *f* collet, pliers **-zangeneinsatz** *m* draw-in collet **-zapfen** *m* truing-up trunnion **-zeit** (f. Werkstück) setting time **-zeug** *n* clamping device, chucking tool, holding fixture **-ziffer eines Zugstabes** tension index of a (tension) member **-zylinder** *m* cocking cylinder

Spanpreß-anlage *f* paper pressing plant **-pumpe** *f* papering pump **-querschnitt** *m* chip cross section (profil)

Spanraum *m* chip space

Span-schicht *f* layer of cuttings **-schneidemaschine** *f* veneer (cutting) machine **-stärke** *f* thickness of shaving or cut

Spant *n* spar element, panel, timber, frame, rib, bulkhead, former **-bogenprofil** *n* (arched) deck beam

Spantenaufrichtung *f* raising of the frames

Spant-entfernung *f* spacing of frames **-fläche** *f* cross-sectional area

Spantiefe *f* depth of cut

Spantiefen-vorschub *m* depth of cut/feed **-vorwahl** *f* preselecting the depth

Spant-profil *n* frame or cradle member **-ring** *f* frame, former **-segment** *n* frame segment

Span-versuch *m* splinter test **-waren** *pl* chip goods **-wickelluftfilter** *n* helical coil air filter

Spanwinkel *m* side rake, side slope, rake angle, topside slope **Projektion des Spanwinkels auf eine senkrechte Längsebene des Drehstahles** front rake, top rake

Spar-becken *n* basin for saving or locking water **-beize** *f*, **-beizstoff** *m* inhibitor, economical tanning extract or mordant, restrainer **-beizzusätze** *pl* inhibitors **-beton** *m* lean concrete **-brenner** *m* pilot burner **-diode** *f* efficiency diode **-düse** *f*, **-einrichtung** *f* economizer

sparen to save

Spar-faden *m* economical filament **-feuerung** *f* economizing furnace **-flamme** *f* pilot light

Sparflug *m* economical cruising **Ladedruck für ~** economical cruising boost

Sparfluggeschwindigkeit *f* economic speed

Spargemisch *n* economic mixture, lean mixture **~ für Reiseflug** economic mixture for cruising

Spar-guß *m* economy casting **-hahn** *m* stopcock, economizer or mixture control valve **-ingenieur** *m* materials control engineer, efficiency expert **-kammer** *f* (water-)saving chamber **-kathode** *f* low-consumption cathode **-kompressor** *m* economy compressor **-lauf** *m* part throttle

Sparleistung *f*, **höchste ~** maximum weak-mixture power

spärlich scanty **~ vorhanden** scarce

Spar-maßnahme *f* measure for saving or economizing **-metall** *n* critical or priority metal **-reiseflug** *m* economic cruising

Sparren *m* rafter, spar, stull **-dach** *n* simple roof truss **-holz** *n* quartering, rafter **-kopf** *m* cantilever **-sohle** *f* pole or rafter plate **-stab** *m* rafter beam or girder **-wechsel** *m* cross rafter, trimmer of rafters

Sparrzimmerung *f* rafter timbering

sparsam economical, thrifty

Sparsamkeit *f* economy

Spar-schalter *m* economy switch **-schaltung** *f* circuit organization designed to economize plate current, economy circuit, efficiency circuit (TV) **-schleuse** *f* lock in which water is re-used **-schließrahmen** *m* skeleton chase (print) **-stelle** *f* guard position (comput) **-stoff** *m* high-priority material, rationed material

sparstoffarme Legierung alloy low in scarce or critical materials

Sparterie *f* matting

Spar-transduktor *m* auto-transductor **-transformator** *m* autotransformer, economy transformer **-umformer** *m* converter with differential winding

Spar- und Abfüllapparat *m* governor and racker

Spar-ventil *n* throttling valve **-viskose** *f* savings viscose (textiles) **-vorrichtung** *f* economizer **-wandler** *m* autotransformer **-wanne** *f* economy tub **-werkstoff** *m* critical material **-würfel** *m* small cube **-zellenschalter** *m* end cell switch (battery)

Spat *m* spar, spavin

spatartig sparry, spathic

Spateisenstein *m* siderite **kohlehaltiger ~** blackband **strahliger ~** sphaerosiderite **tonhältiger ~** argillaceous siderite, clay band

Späteinspritzung *f* retarded injection

Spatel *m* trowel, spatula, cleaner

spatelförmig spatulate

Spaten *m* spade **~ mit genieteter Dülle** riveted backstrap spade

Spatenmeißel *m* drilling bit, drag bit **ausgekehlter ~** chamfered drilling bit **flacher ~** flat drilling bit

Spatenstich *m* cut with spade, breaking of ground

Spaterz *n* spathic ore

spatförmig spathic

Spatglas *n* cryolite glass

spatig spathic

Spatium *n*, **breites ~** quadrat (print.) **dünnes ~** hair space

Spat-lack *m* barytes lake **-meißel** *m* spadeshaped chisel **-produkt** *n* scalar triple product **-sand** *m* silica sand

Spätschosser *m* late bolter

Spatstein *m* selenite

Spatverschnitt *m* barytes-reduction

Spät-wirkung *f* late effect **-zerspringer** *m* retarded burst **-zündlage** *f* retarded ignition position **-zündung** *f* retarded ignition, sparking retard

speckig greasy **-er Bruch** lardaceous fracture

Specköl *n* lard oil **unbehandeltes ~** prime lard oil

Speckstein *m* whetstone, steatite **-artig** steatitic **-pulver** *n* steatite powder

Specktorf *m* pitch peat

Spediteur *m* forwarding agent, forwarder

Spedition *f* forwarding of goods, expressing

Speer *m* spear, shaft, spindle

speerförmiger Spaltstoffstab javelin-shaped fuel rod

Speerkies *m* spear pyrites

Speiche *f* spoke **~ mit verdicktem Ende** butt-ended spoke

Speichel *m* spittle, saliva **-kammer** *f* moisture chamber

Speichen-draht *m* spoke wire **-einsetzer** *m* spoke fitter **-hobel** *f* spoke shave **-messer** *m* wheelwright's compass, spoke gauge, break **-nabe** *f* spider **-nippel** *m* spoke nipple **-rad** *n* wheel with spokes, spoked wheel **-spanner** *m* spoke tightener **-stern** *m* spider (mach.) **-system** *n* system of rotor spiders **-träger** *m* spoke flange **-triebrad** *n* spider

Speichen- und Griffdrehbank *f* spoke- and handle-turning machine

Speicher *m* warehouse, storage place, reservoir, loft, storage battery, granary, elevator, store (info proc.), register, memory (math.), accumulator (elec.)

Speicher, akustischer ~ sonic delay line (comput.), acustic memory **elektrooptischer ~**

flying stop store **elektrostatischer ~** electrostatic store **leistungsabhängiger ~** volatile store **löschbarer ~** erasable memory **nichtlöschbarer ~** non-erasable storage **nichtpermanenter ~** volatile storage **periodischer ~** cyclic store **permanenter ~** non-volatile storage, permanent storage

Speicher, ~ in Knotenämtern tandem sender **~ mit Übertragung** repeating register **~ mit Wortadresse** word-organized memory **~ für stochastischen Zugriff** random access memory

Speicher-abzug *m* feeding mechanism **-antrieb** *m* battery drive, driving by accumulators **-aufzeichnungsdichte** *f* storage packing density **-becken** *n* storage basin **-binärstelle** *f* binary cell **-blase** *f* accumulator bag **-bremsung** *f* energy-storage braking **-dauer** *f* maximum retention or storage time

Speicher-einheit *f* storage unit **-elektrode** *f* energy-storage or accumulation electrode **-element** *n* storage element, element having capacity **-fähigkeit** *f* storing capacity **-fehler** *m* blemish **-feuerung** *f* regenerative firing **-flächendicke** *f* thickness of storage surface **-folgecodierung** *f* specific coding (comput)

Speicher-gas *n* bottled motor-fuel gas (such as propane, butane) **-geber** *m* storage transmitter **-gestein** *n* reservoir rock **-kammer** *f* air cell **-kammermotor** *m* air-cell-type engine **-kapazität** *f* capacity of memory **-kathode** *f* storage cathode **-kette** *f* storage chain **-kondensator** *m* reservoir or tank or storage capacitor **-kopf** *m* record head **-kraftwerk** *n* stored-water or storage power station **-lesbarkeit** *f* storage reproducibility

speichern to store, accumulate, register, record

speichernde Kameraröhre storage camera tube **-e Übertragung** retransmitting installation

Speicheroberfläche *f* storage surface

Speicheroberflächenmagnetisierungskraft *f* intensity of magnetization in storage surface

Speicher-ofen *m* regenerative furnace **-organ** *n* storing circuit **-paket** *n* storage stack **-platte** *f* storage pickup, storage plate **-plattenelement** *n* target element **-plattenoberfläche** *f* targot surface **-programm** *n* stored program

speicherprogrammierte (digitale) **Datenverarbeitungsablage** *f* stored program (digital) computer

Speicherrelais *n* storage relay, capacitive time relay

Speicherröhre *f* (electrostatic) storage tube **~ in Rechenmaschinen** memory tube

Speicher-schicht *f* storage layer **-schirm** *m* persistant screen (TV) **-spur** *f* storage track

Speicherstelle *f* location (comput.) **~ für wartende Anrufe** queue place

Speichersystem mit direktem Zugriff random-access storage system

Speicher-tankmischer *m* retention mixer **-tastatur** *f* storage keyboard

Speicherung *f* storing, storage, accumulation

Speicher-verteilung *f* allocation (info proc.) **-wechselrichter** *m* series inverter **-werk** *n* power plant with facilities for pumping to storage pond **-werke** *pl* storage units **-wirkung** *f* storage effect, signal storage, charge accumulation **-zahlengeber** *m* pulsing keysender, storing keysender **-zähler** *m* counter storage **-zelle** *f* storage location (comp.), storage register

speichig radial

Speigatten *pl* scuppers

Speise *f* speiss, bell metal, gun metal, power supply, current, food, nourishment **-absperrventil** *n* feedcheck valve, feed-stop valve **-anschluß** *m* supply connection **-apparat** *m* feed apparatus **-behälter** *m* feed tank **-bildner** *m* speiss-forming constituent **-brücke** *f* feed-retardation coil, feeding circuit, battery-supply bridge

Speise-drossel *f* feed coil, feeder reactor **-flotte** *f* replenishing liquor **-gerät** *n* feed, feeding apparatus, supply unit **-gleichrichter** *m* supply rectifier, power rectifier **-gleichspannung** *f* direct current supply voltage **-gleichstrom** *m* direct current feed, feed current **-graben** *m* feeder ditch **-hahn** *m* feed cock **-horn** *n* feed horn **-kabel** *n* feeder cable **-kanal** *m* feed(er) canal **-kobalt** *m* smaltite **-kreis** *m* supply circuit

Speiseleitung *f* feeder, feed line, supply or power line, mains, downlead **konzentrische ~** concentric-tube transmission line, concentric-pipe transmission line

Speiseleitungssystem *n* feeder-line system

speisen to feed, supply, charge, load, energize

Speise-pumpe *f* feed pump **-punkt** *m* input terminals, feeding point, distributing point

Speise-regelventil *n* feed regulating valve **-regler** *m* feed regulator **-relais** *n* (battery-)supply relay **-rohr** *n* feed pipe, supply tube **-schiene** *f* feeder bar, feeder rail **-schnecke** *f* feed screw **-seite** *f* generator end **-sirup** *m* table sirup **-spannung** *f* supply voltage **-spule** *f* battery-supply coil

Speise-stelle *f* feeding point **-strom** *m* supply current, feeding current **-stromkreis** *m* supply circuit **-transformator** *m* substation transformer, distribution transformer **-trichter** *m* hopper **-trommel** *f* feeder drum **-ventil** *n* feed valve **-vorrichtung** *f* feeding device, supplying device, feeding equipment

Speisewasser *n* feed lye or liquor, feed water **-aufbereitung** *f* feed-water conditioning, feed-water treatment **-wasserentgasung** *f* feedwater deaeration **-pumpe** *f* feed-water pump **-regler** *m* feed-water regulator

Speise-zusatzwasser *n* feed make-up water **-zylinder** *m* assisting feed roll

spektral spectroscopic, spectral **~ zerlegtes Licht** spectroscopically dispersed or separated light

spektral-e Verteilungscharakteristik spectral-response characteristic **-e Zusammensetzung des Lichtes** spectral composition of light

Spektral-analyse *f* spectroscopic analysis, spectrum analysis **-analytisch** spectroscopic, spectrometric **-apparat** *m* spectroscope, spectrometer **-aufnahme** *f* spectrograph **-bereich** *m* spectral region **-bolometer** *m* spectrobolometer **-charakteristik der Aufnahmeröhre** camera tube spectral characteristic **-darstellung** *f* spectral representation **-gerät** *n* spectroscope

Spektral-kurve *f* curve of spectrum **~** (höchster Reinheit oder Sättigung im Farbtondiagramm) spectrum locus (TV)

Spektral-linie *f* spectrum line, spectral line **-linienfaltung** *f* folding of spectral lines

Spektrallinienverbreiterung durch Ionen- und Atomstoß collision damping (of spectral lines)
Spektral-photometer *n* spectrophotometer **-radiometer** *m* spectroradiometer **-rauschzahl** *f* spot noise factor (radio) **-schwerpunkt** *m* spectral centroid **-tafel** *f* spectral chart **-untersuchung** *f* spectroscopic analysis **-verschiebung** *f* spectral shift **-werte** *pl* distribution coefficients
Spektrogramm *n* spectrogram
Spektrograph *m* spectrograph
Spektrometer *n* spectrometer **-aufnahme** *f* spectrometer absorption
Spektrometrie *f* spectrometry
Spektroskop *n* spectroscope
Spectroskopie *f* spectroscopy
spektroskopische Beobachtung spectroscopic observation
Spektrum *n* iridescence, irization, spectrum **sichtbares ~** luminous spectrum **-analysator** *m* spectrum analyzer
Spekularit *m* hematite
spekulieren to venture, speculate
Spekulum *n* speculum
Spender *m* (Elektronenspender) donor
Spengler *m* sheet-metal worker, plumber, tinsmith
Sperr-abschnitt *m* prohibited area, off limits **-abstand** *m* barrage interval **-band** *n* rejection band **-bereich** *m* attenuation band, suppression band or range, exclusion band, stop band (filter) **-bestand** *m* earmarked stocks **-beton** *m* water-repellent concrete **-blende** *f* blocking light stop **-blockierung** *f* blocking **-bolzen** *m* strain bolt
Sperr-damm *m* dam **-dampf** *m* steam barrier **-dämpfung** *f* stop-band attenuation of a filter **-daumen** *m* locking pawl **-dichte** *f* barrage density **-drachen** *m* barrage kite
Sperre *f* (Sperren) closing, closure; (Versperren) blocking, obstruction; (Stillegung) stoppage; (Schraube) barrier, gate; (Abstell- u. Feststellvorrichtung) stop; (Hindernis) obstacle; (Straße) road, block; (Strom~) power interruption; entanglement, barricade, embargo, prohibition, quarantine, ratchet, lock(ing), arresting, adjusting, headwheel, stopper, suppressor, rejector, baffle **~ eines Anschlusses** denial for nonpayment (teleph.) **~ mit rundköpfigen Strebepfeilern** round-head buttress dam **behelfsmäßige ~** makeshift obstacle **verschiedene Sperren** various types of dams
Sperreffekt *m* blockage effect
sperren s. a. Sperre (auseinander) to spread out; (Straßen~) block, obstruct, barricade, close; (blockieren) blockade; (Licht) cut off; (Technik) stop, arrest; (verbieten) stop, prohibit; (klemmen) jam, be stuck; shut, bar, lock, space, guard, exclude, adjust, stopper, busy, set, isolate, insulate, brake, dam, detain, secure, suppress **einen Platz ~** to guard a position, make a position inaccessible **einen Wähler ~** to make the line busy, busy
Sperrer *m* suppressor, trap, excluder, lock, block
Sperr-fangvorrichtung *f* (Aufzug) dead stop gripping device **-feder** *f* retaining spring, click spring **-feld** *n* obstacle field **-filter** *n* rejector circuit, stopper circuit, suppression filter
Sperrflüssigkeit *f* sealing liquid, liquid seal, packing fluid **Dichtung durch ~** fluid packing
Sperr-form *f* barrage form for balloons **-frequenz** *f* stop frequency **-frist** *f* period of embargo **-gebiet** *n* barred zone, blockade zone, prohibited zone **-gehäuse** *n* ratchet casing **-gerät** *n* suppressor **-getriebe** *n* locking mechanism **-gitter** *n* barrier grid **-gitterröhre** *f* barrier grid tube **-gleichrichter** *m* barrier-film rectifier, blocking or electronic rectifier **-glied** *n* blocking element, suppressor **-greifer** *m* pilot pin **-gut** *n* bulk freight **-hahn** *m* stopcock
Sperrhaken *m* click, latch, (locking) pawl, catch, trip, ratchet **-feder** *f* pawl spring **-gestänge** *n* up-position lock linkage rod **-schalter** *m* up-position lock switch **-stift** *m* pawl stud
Sperrhalbwelle *f* blocked semiwave
Sperrhebel *m* (locking) pawl, check lever, latch, arresting or locking lever **~ zur Verhütung des gleichzeitigen Einschaltens von mehr als einer Bewegung** interlocking lever to prevent the engagement of more than one feed at a time
Sperrhebelwelle *f* locking lever shaft **-höhe** *f* barrage height
Sperrholz *n* plywood, wedge of wood **-bekleidung** *f* plywood covering **-beplankung** *f* plywood covering **-gerippe** *n* plywood framework **-haut** *f* plywood covering
Sperrholz-platte *f* plywood panel or plate, plywood sheet **-planke** *f* plywood sheet **-rippe** *f* plywood rib **-rumpf** *m* three-ply covered fuselage, plywood fuselage (of aircraft) **-schalung** *f* plywood slab formwork **-stahlschienenvorrichtung** *f* steel rule die **-verkleidung** *f* plywood fairing **-verschalung** *f* plywood shell or covering
Sperr-horn *n* beakiron **-hülse** *f* fuse safety cap
sperrig bulky **-es Gut** bulk freight
Sperrimpuls *m* suppressor or blocking impulse, blackout pulse
Sperrkegel *m* detent, click, (locking) pawl, trigger, pin **-stahl** *m* clock steel
Sperr-kennlinie *f* blocking characteristics **-kette** *f* curb chain, low-pass filter **-kippsender** *m* blanking sweep unit, blocking oscillator
Sperrklaue der Drehscheibe turntable bolt
Sperrklinke *f* catch, pawl, ratchet, lock pawl, stop pawl, detent, click, trip dog, (stop) latch
Sperrklinken-antrieb *m* pawl drive **-hebel** *m* ratchet lever **-vorrichtung** *f* ratchet device, locking device
Sperr-klotz *m* stop block **-kondensator** *m* stopping or blocking condenser, isolating capacitor **-kontakt** *m* blocking contact **-kranz** *m* ratchet wheel
Sperrkreis *m* antiresonant circuit, (parallel-tuned) choke circuit, rejector circuit, suppression filter, buffer stage, wave trap **-bereich** *m* antiresonant band **-koppelung** *f* circuit blocking, parallel resonance coupling **-luftspule** *f* rejector-circuit air coil **-wirkung** *f* parallel resonance, antiresonance (radio)
Sperr-kreuz *n* turnstile **-kurbel** *f* excapement crank **-leitung** *f* busy wire **-leitwert** *m* back conductance **-licht** *n* barrier light **-linie** *f* obstacle line **-magnet** *m* lock(ing) magnet, closing magnet **-membrane** *f* stop diaphragm **-metall** *n* plymetal **-mitläufer** *m* code restrictor (tel.) **-mörtelschicht** *f* water-repellent mortar course

Sperr-nase *f* firing notch **-nocken** *pl* stop cam **-nut** *f* locking notch **-platte** *f* interlock **-puls** *m* locking pulse **-punkt** *m* cut-off point **-putz** *m* water-repellent plastering

Sperr-rad *n* ratchet wheel, cogwheel, pawl wheel **-radbergstütze** *f* ratchet-type sprag **-radschraube** *f* ratchet nut **-radwälzfräser** *m* ratchet hob **-raste** *f* stop notch **-raum** *m* barrage area **-rechen** *m* holding screen

Sperr-relais *n* locking relay, guard relay, lockout relay, gate relay ~ **für Generatorschalter** relay for generator switch ~ **für Netzschalter** relay for mains switch

Sperr-resonanz *f* parallel resonance, antiresonance **-richtung** *f* high-resistance direction, backward direction, inverse direction **-riegel** *m* lock bolt (steering wheel lock), line barrage, safety bolt **-ring** *m* locking ring, retainer ring, ferrule **-rohr** *n* outer steam tube **-rollenhebel** *m* tape feed roll detent **-schalter** *m* holding key **-schalttarifzähler** *m* tariff meter with locking device **-schaltung** *f* paralysis circuit **-scheibe** *f* swing check, locking disc, ratched wheel

Sperrschicht *f* barrier layer, boundary effect, pore sealer, insulating anodic coating, blocking layer, rectifying film **-gleichrichter** *m* contact rectifier, barrier-layer rectifier

Sperrschichtkondensator, keramischer ~ ceramic junction capacitor

Sperrschicht-photoeffekt *m* attenuation-layer, photoelectric effect, photovoltaic effect **-photozelle** *f* rectifier photocell, dry photovoltaic cell, barrier-layer photocell **-theorie** *f* barrier-layer theory **-zelle** *f* barrier-layer cell, barrier-type cell, solid (photo)voltaic cell, rectifier cell (operating with a blocking layer)

Sperr-schiene *f* lock bar, treadle bar **-schleuse** *f* guard gates **-schloß** *n* (control) lock **-schraube** *f* lock screw **-schritt** *m* stop signal **-schuh** *m* stop block **-schwinger** *m* blocking oscillator **-segment** *n* locking segment **-seil** *n* barrage cable **-seilvorhang** *m* barrage cable curtain **-sieb** *n* rejector (circuit) **-signal** *n* blocking signal

Sperr-spalt *m* isolation gap **-spannung** *f* inverse voltage, blocking voltage, biasing potential **-spannungsscheitelwert** *m* peak inverse voltage **-stange** *f* locking bar **-stellung** *f* topmost indexing position **-stift** *m* pin, click, stop, catch **-störung** *f* (Radar) barrage jamming

Sperr-strom *m* backward or inverse current **-stromkreis** *m* rejector circuit **-stück** *n* stop **-synchronisierung** *f* locking synchronization **-taste** *f* spacer, locking button **-topf** *m* seal connection to dipole, wave trap **-topfantenne** *f* folded top antenna **-tor** *n* inhibition gate **-trommel** *f* locking drum

Sperrung *f* barricading, blocking, obstruction, isolation, insulation, locking device, paralysis (rdr.), suspension

Sperr-ventil *n* check valve, stop valve **-verband** *m* blocking unit **-verhältnis** *n* blocking ratio **-vorrichtung** *f* (inter)locking device, device for stopping or adjusting lock **-waffe** *f* mine **-werk** *n* stop gear, locking mechanism **-wert** *m* blocking value **-widerstand** *m* backward resistance, reverse resistance **-wirkung** *f* rectifying effect, blocking or retarding action, lagging

Sperr-zahn *m* locking tooth or ratchet, detent, dog **-zahnkranz** *m* ratchet drum **-zeichen** *n* locking signal, landing-prohibited signal

Sperrzeit *f* blocking or blanking time, idle period closing time **positive** ~ blocking period

Sperr-zeitbasis *f* ratchet time base **-zelle** *f* barrier-type cell **-zunge** *f* locking tungue

Spesen *pl* expenses, charges, costs **-frei** all expenses paid, free of charge

Spezialausführung *f* special model

Spezialausklink- und Gehrungsstanzmaschine *f* special notching and miter-cutting machine

Spezial-beschneidemaschine *f* special trimming machine **-dichtungsring** *m* special washer ring **-eisen** *n* deformed bar, special rolled-steel bar, special iron, off-grade iron **-fassung** *f* special holder **-film hoher Steilheit** high-contrast emulsion film **-flugzeug** *n* special aircraft **-frachtraten** *pl* specific commodity rates **-gießereikoks** *m* special foundry coke **-gußeisen** *n* special cast iron

spezialisieren to specialize

Spezialisierung *f* specialized experience, specialization

Spezialist *m* specialist, expert

Spezialität *f* specialty

Spezial-nickelstahl *m* special nickel steel **-nutläufermotor** *m* double squirrel cage motor **-profil** *n* special section **-röhre** *f* special tube **-rost** *m* special dust bar **-schlüssel** *m* special wrench **-stahl** *m* special steel **-werk** *n* special factory

speziell specific **-hergestellt** custom-made

Spezifikation *f* specification

Spezifikationssymbol *n* specifier (info proc.)

spezifisch specific(ally) **-er Bodendruck** ground pressure per unit area **-e Dämpfung** attenuation constant **-er Fahrwiderstand** rolling friction coefficient **-e Feuchtigkeit** specific humidity **-e Fortpflanzungskonstante** propagation constant **-es Gewicht** specific gravity, density **-e Kapazität** specific capacity or energy **-e Kerbschlagarbeit** impact resistance, shock strength **-e Ladung** specific charge, charge-mass ratio **-e Leitfähigkeit** specific conductivity **-e Lichtausstrahlung** radiance

spezifisch, -e Oberflächenenergie der Flüssigkeit specific surface energy of the liquid **-e Schlagarbeit** specific energy of blow **-es Übertragungsmaß** propagation constant **-er Verbrauch** specific consumption **-e Wärme** specific heat, thermal capacity **-er Wärmepreis** cost per unit of heat **-er Widerstand** specific resistance, resistivity **-er elektrischer Widerstand** resistivity **-e Zähigkeit** speific viscosity

spezifizieren to specify, itemize

Spezifizierung *f* specification

Sphäre *f* sphere, scope

sphärisch spherical ~ **überkorrigiert** spherically overcorrected **-e Abbildung** spherical mapping, spherical image **-e Abweichung** spherical aberration **-es Dreieck** spherical triangle **-e Spule** spherical coil **-e Trigonometrie** spherical trigonometry

Sphäroguß *m* spheroidal graphite iron

Sphäroid *n* strained sphere, spheroid

sphärokonisch sphero-conical

Sphärokristall *n* spherical crystal, spherocrystal

Sphärolith *m* spherulite

Sphärosiderit *m* sphaerosiderite
spheroidaler Zustand spheroidal state
Sphygmometer *n* sphygmometer, pulsimeter
Sphygmomanometer *n* sphygmo-manometer
Spicken *n* spiking
Spiegel *m* mirror, level, speculum, reflector, water level, polished or reflecting surface, silvering **parabolischer ~** parabolic mirror **rotierender ~** revolving mirror **schwingender ~** vibrating mirror **sphärischer ~** spherical mirror **~ der Blinkleuchte** reflector of blinking light
Spiegel-ablesung *f* reading by mirror, reading by reflection **-achse** *f* axis of symmetry **-antenne** *f* mirror antenna **-apparat** *m* mirror apparatus, mirror (and scale) extensometer, optical magnifying extensometer, reflecting strain indicator **-auslenkung** *f* base-plate deflection **-band** *n* image band (radio) **-belag** *m* mirror coating, reflecting film, silvering (of a mirror) **-belegung** *f* mirror-quicksilvering **-beobachtung** *f* observation by periscope
Spiegelbild *n* mirror image, speculum image, double or reflected (ghost) image **-aufnahme** *f* reflected image pick-up (a type of practice firing) **-funktion** *f* mirror image function
spiegelbildlich homologous, mirror-inverted, specular **~ gleich** symmetric(al) **-es Verhältnis** inverse relationship
Spiegelbildmethode *f* method of electric images
spiegelblank highly polished, bright **-e Oberfläche** mirrorlike or highly polished surface
Spiegel-bogenlampe *f* reflector arc lamp **-brennpunkt** *m* (Antenne) focal point of the reflector **-bussole** *f* mirror compass, reflecfing compass **-dämpfungskoeffizient** *m* image attenuation cozfficient **-durchmesser** *m* diameter of chamfer circle
Spiegel-ebene *f* reflection plane, mirror plane **-einstellvorrichtung** *f* reflector setting device **-entfernungsmesser** *m* macrometer **-eisen** *n* spiegeleisen **-eisenkupolofen** *m* spiegel cupola **-erz** *n* specular iron ore **-feinmeßgerät** *n* (Martens) mirror and scale extensometer **-feld** *n* reflector, screen, revertive-signal panel, check-back position indicator **-fenster** *n* plate-glass window **-fläche** *f* reflector surface **-floß** *n* spiegeleisen **-folie** *f* tin foil
Spiegelfrequenz *f* second channel frequency, image frequency **-empfindlichkeit** *f* image response **-gang** image-frequency response **-sperre** *f* image-frequency stopper or rejector **-unterdrückung** *f* image frequency rejection
Spiegel-galvanometer *n* reflecting or mirror galvenometer **-gefälle** *n* slope of (water) surface, surface slope **-gerüst** *n* reflector framework **-glanz** *m* highly polished surface
Spiegel-glasplatte *f* plate-glass pane **-glatt** mirror-like, dead-smooth **-gleiches Profil** symmetrical profile or section **-gleichheit** *f* mirror symmetry **-halter** *m* mirror support **-hals** *m* reflector ring **-höhenunterschied** *m* difference in the height of liquid levels (in turbines) **-holz** *n* quarter grain
spiegelig specular, mirrorlike, symmetric(al)
Spiegel-instrument *n* mirror or reflecting instrument **-kerne** *pl* mirror nuclei **-kluft** *f* cracks in the direction of the grain, external shakes **-kompaß** *m* mirror or reflecting compass **-kranz** *m* mirror rim, row or set of mirrors (in scanner), drum scanner **-kreis** *m* reflecting circle **-kreuz** *n* optical square (for angles of 90*s*) **-kreuzlibelle** *f* optical square level, reflector-type cross-level (panoramic telescope)
Spiegel-lager *n* (Scheinwerfer) reflector bearing or mounting (head lamp) **-lampe** *f* mirror arc-lamp **-lehre** *f* mirror comparator **-leiter** *m* image line **-leuchten** *pl* reflector luminaires **-linie** *f* surface curve **-messer** *m* gauge for glasses **-metall** *n* speculum metal
spiegeln to shine, glitter, reflect, be reflected, glare
Spiegeln (von Auflageflächen für Schraubenköpfe) spot-facing
spiegelnd specular, reflecting **-e Oberfläche** specular surface **-e Reflektion** specular reflection, mirrorlike reflection
Spiegel-nullmethode *f* mirror balancing technique **-öffnung** *f* reflector aperture **-ortungsgerät** *n* mirror position finder **-oszillograph** *m* mirror oscillograph **-pfahl** *m* water mark **-platte** *f* plate glass, reflecting plate **-prisma** *n* reflecting prism **-quadrant** *m* Hadley's quadrant **-rad** *n* mirror drum, mirror wheel **-rahmen** *m* mirror frame **-reflektor** *m* mirror reflector **-reflexion** *f* specular reflection, regular reflection
Spiegelreflexkamera *f* reflex camera **einäugige ~** single lens reflex camera **zweiäugige ~** twin-lens reflex camera
Spiegel-reflexstereokamera *f* stereo-reflex camera **-rohglas** *n* rough-cast plate glass **-rohr** *n* reflector tube **-rohrhalter** *m* reflector-tube clip **-rücken** *m* reflector back
Spiegel-scheibe *f* plate glass **-scheinwerfer** *m* reflector floodlight **-schliff** *m* mirror finish **-schraube** *f* mirror screw (scanner), mirror helix **-schreiber** *m* mirror recorder **-schrift** *f* reflected face type **-selektion** *f* image suppression **-sextant** *m* Hadley's sectant **-skala** *f* reflector dial
Spiegel-stereoskop *n* reflecting sterescope **-symmetrie** *f* mirror symmetry, specular symmetry **-telegraph** *m* heliograph **-teleskop** *n* reflecting telescope **-träger** *m* reflector support **-triftrohr** *n* reflex drift sight, reflex klystron **-übertragungsverstärker** *m* optical transmission amplifier
Spiegelung *f* reflection, mirage (radio), specular effect, picture mirroring, replica (of curves), homologous condition or relation **~ am Kreis** reflection with respect to a circle **~ an Tropfen** reflexion by water drops
spiegelungleich nonsymmetrical
Spiegelungleichheit *f* dissymmetry
Spiegelungs-faktor *m* reflectance, reflection factor **-invarianz** *f* reflection invariance **-methode** *f* reflection principle **-moment** *m* parity **-verfahren** *n* method of images **-verlust** *m* loss at a junction, reflection loss **-vermögen** *n* reflective power
spiegelverkehrt mirror inverted
Spiegel-verkehrung *f* mirror inversion **-versteller** *m* reflector-adjusting device **-visier** *n* mirror sight, reflecting sight **-welle** *f* reflected wave, specular wave **-wellenabschwächung** *f* image rejection **-wirkung** *f* reflecting or mirror effect
Spiegler *m* reflector
Spieker *m* nail **-nagel** *m* brad

Spiel *n* clearance, slackness, free space, backlash, working cycle, time cycle, tolerance, free motion, play ~ **der Getrieberäder** backlash or play of gears ~ **des Kolbens** play of the piston ~ **in Längsrichtung** end play ~ **eines Pochstempels** drop of a stamp (play) ~ **der Ventile** tappet clearance, valve clearance **bezogenes** ~ specific clearance **größeres** ~ **vorhanden** more clearance available ~ **haben** to be slack, get or work loose **zulässiges** ~ permissable clearance

Spiel-art *f* variation, touch (music) **-ausgleich** *m* compensation for play **-dauer** *f* battery life (of transistor radio)

Spiel-flächenleuchten *n* stage floor lighting fixtures **-form** *f* variety

spielfrei-er Gang *m* movement free from play **-es Umsteuern** backlash-free reversal **-es Zusammenwirken** smooth working

spielfrei gefräst milled free from backlash

Spielfreiheit *f* freedom from play

Spielfrequenzstörung *f* image interference

Spiel-leiter *m* director of play **-passung** *f* clearance fit

Spielraum *m* clearance, play, backlash, tolerance, margin, free space, allowance, scope, encroachment, free motion, windage, latitude ~ **der Zähne** backlash ~ **der Zähne eines Zahnrades** side clearance of teeth of a toothed wheel

Spiel-raumsperre *f* travel stop **-raumzeichnung** *f* clearance drawing **-schwankung** *f* variation of play **-saite** *f* (fingerboard) string

Spielseil *n* capstan rope **-rolle** *f* catline sheave **-schutz** *m* catline guard

Spiel-zahl *f* cycle criterion **-zahlanzeiger** *m* cycle index (comput)

Spiere *f* rib (aviation), spindle, boom, spar

Spierentonne *f* spindle buoy, mast or pillar buoy

Spieß *m* spear, lance, spit, pointed bar, poker, long needle, venting wire, spicule (geol.)

Spießglanz *m* antimony sulfide **-artig** antimonial **-asche** *f* antimony ash **-bleierz** *n* bournonite **-blende** *f* kermesite **-butter** *f* antimony chloride **-erz** *n* antimony ore, stibnite **-kermes** *m* kermesite **-oxyd** *n* antimony oxide **-säure** *f* antimonic acid **-silber** *n* dyscrasite **-zinnober** *m* kermesite

Spießglas *n* antimony

Spießkant *f* diamond **-kaliber** *n* diamond pass **-keil** *m* square key **-profil** *n* lozenge section

Spiker *m* spike

spikern to nail, spike

Spikerung *f* nailing

Spiköl *n* spike oil

Spill *n* vertical capstan winch, windless, air lead, capstan, spindle

Spillage *f* spillage, sweepings

Spill-anlage *f* capstan installation **-arbeiter** *m* cathead man

spillen to operate a winch, capstan

Spillen-lager *n* spindle bearing **-rad** *n* spindle wheel

Spill-kopf *m* warping drum **-seil** *n* catline **-windentrommel** *f* capstan drum

Spin *m* spin, spin quantum number

Spin-ausrichtung *f* spin alignment **-austauschwechselwirkung** *f* exchange interaction

Spinbahn-aufspaltung *f* spin orbit splitting **-kuppelung** *f* spin orbit coupling **-potential** *n* spin orbit potential **-wechselwirkung** *f* spin-orbit interaction

Spindel *f* (Welle) spindle; (Presse) screw; (Wellenbaum) arbor; (Dorn) mandril, mandrel; (Spule) bobbin; (Leit~) lead screw; (Chem.) hydrometer; lifting jack, screw jack, valve rod, pivot, beam, shaft, axle, pinion, pillar, axis of revolution ~ **zum Heben des Querbalkens** screw for elevating crossrail ~ **für die Querbalkenhöhenstellung** vertical crossrail screw ~ **zur Senkrechtstellung des Tisches** table-elevating screw ~ **für Spinnmaschinen** spinning-machine spindle

Spindel-abtrieb *m* driving spindle **-achse** *f* mesotergum (paleontol.), axis of the spindle **-anordnung** *f* arrangement of spindle **-antrieb** *m* spindle drive **-antriebsscheibe** *f* spindle driving pulley **-antriebswelle** *f* spindle driving shaft **-aufzug** *m* screw elevator

Spindel-backen *m* headstock **-bank** *f* spindle rail **-blitzableiter** *m* reel protector, spindle lightning protector **-bock** *m* spindle socket **-bohrung** *f* hole through spindle, spindle hole diameter **-bremse** *f* spindle brake **-buchse** *f* spindle step **-büchse** *f* spindle sleeve

Spindel-drehbank *f* chuck lathe **-drehzahl** *f* spindle speed **-drehzahlvorwählung** *f* spindle speed selection **-endschalter** *m* lead screw limit switch **-flansch** *m* spindle flange **-förmig** spindle-shaped, fusiform **-führung** *f* stem guide, screw control (of recording cutter) **-gabel** *f* spindle yoke **-gegenlager** *n* outer end support **-getriebe** *n* geared spindle drive, spindle gearing

Spindel-hals *m* spindle collar **-hub** *m* stroke of spindle **-hubwerk** *n* spindle-type elevating mechanism **-hülse** *f* spindle sleeve

Spindelkasten *m* headstock **-fuß** *m* headstock end leg **-getriebe** *n* headstock gearing

Spindelkegelrad *n* main driving bevel gear

Spindelkopf *m* sqindlehead, sqindle nose **-anlagefläche** *f* spindle register **-gleitfläche** *f* spindlehead bearing **-klemmschraube** *f* head-clamp bolt **-schlitten** *m* sliding head **-spannzange** *f* spindle nose collet chuck **-spitze** *f* head center **-winkelstellungsanzeiger** *m* headstock index finger

Spindellager *n* spindle bearing **oberes** ~ spindle upper box **unteres** ~ spindle lower box

Spindel-lagerung *f* spindle bearing **-lenkung** *f* cam and lever steering mechanism **-mitnehmer** *m* spindle carrier **-mitte** *f* center line of spindle **-mittenentfernung** *f* distance between spindle centers **-mutter** *f* spindle nut

spindeln to test by hydrometer

Spindel-nase *f* spindle nose, spindle end **-öl** *n* spindle oil **-pinole** *f* spindle sleeve **-presse** *f* screw press **-ring** *m* spacing collar **-rohr** *n* spindle guard tube **-rückgang** *m* spindle drawback

Spindel-schieber *m* poppet valve **-schlagpresse** *f* percussion press **-schlitten** *m* saddle trough **-schlupf** *m* spindle slip **-schütze** *m* spindle shuttle **-ständer** *m* floor column **-steigung** *f* pitch (of screw) **-steuerungshebel** *m* sqindle starting lever

Spindelstock *m* headstock **-bewegung** *f* spindle

head longitudinal adjustment **-gehäuse** *n* headstock compartment **-getriebe** *n* headstock gearing **-spannpatrone** *f* headstock collet **-spitze** *f* headstock center **-untersatz** *m* headstock base
Spindel-teilung *f* sqindle pitch **-trieb** *m* worm drive, worm gear **-trommelschaltung** *f* spindle drum indexing **-übertragung** *f* spindle transmission **-umkehrnocke** *f* spindle reversing cam
Spindelung *f* hydrometry
Spindel-universalprüfmaschine *f* spindle type universal testing machine **-ventil** *n* poppet valve **-vorderkante** *f* front edge of spindle **-vorgelege** *n* back-gear mechanism, back gears **-vorschubkurve** *f* spindle feed cam **-waage** *f* hydrometer, spindle gauge **-widerstand** *m* spindle resistor **-wirtel** *m* spindle wharve **-zahl** *f* number of spindles, winding unit **-zapfen** *m* movable spindle end **-zelle** *f* aerometer
Spin-drehimpuls *m* spin angular moment **-drehung** *f* spin twisting **-dublett** *n* spin doublet **-eigenzustand** *m* spin eigen state
Spinell *m* spinel **-gitter** *n* spinel lattice **-struktur** *f* spinel structure
Spin-erscheinung *f* spin phenomenon **-glied** *n* spin term **-gitterrelaxation** *f* spin-lattice relaxation **-impulskopplung** *f* spin-orbit coupling **-konfigurationsraum** *m* isobaric space **-modell** *n* rotational model **-momentdichte** *f* spin momentum density **-multiplett** *n* spin multiplet **-verdopplung** *f* spin doubling **-verteilung** *f* spin distribution
spinnbar spinnable
Spinnbarkeit *f* spinnability
Spinn-brause *f* multiple (spinning) nozzle **-düse** *f* spinning nozzle
Spinne *f* spider, road junction ~ (Rohr) manifold
Spinnemulsion *f* spinning emulsion
spinnen to spin
Spinnenflansch *m* spider flange
Spinnerei *f* spinning (spinning factory)
Spinn-faser *f* synthetic fiber, spun fiber **-fehler** *m* spinning defect **-gewebspule** *f* spiders web coil **-kerze** *f* filtering candle (for rayon) **-knötchen** *n* fleck **-maschine** *f* spinning frame **-masse** *f* spinning solution **-papier** *n* spinning paper **-reife** *f* maturity (for spinning), ammonium chloride index **-rendement** *n* spinning output **-rocken** *m* distaff **-röhrchen** *n* revolving tube
Spinn-schema *n* spinning arrangement **-schmälze** *f* spinning emulsion or lubricant **-spulendrehbank** *f* spinning-bobbin turning machine **-stutzen** *m* gooseneck **-stuhl** *m* spinning frame
Spinntopf *m* spinning can **-spinnen** *n* spinning bucket process (synthetic fibers)
Spin-Null-Teilchen *n* spin zero particle
Spinnverfahren *n* spinning method or process
spinnwebartig cobweblike
Spinnzentrifuge *f* (Kunstseide) spinning pot
Spinole *f* spindle sleeve
Spinoperator *m* spin operator
Spinor *m* spinor **-bezeichnung** *f* spinor notation
Spinorientierung *f* spin orientation
Spinorkalkül *n* spinor calculus
Spin-raum *m* spin space **-schleife** *f* rotational loop
Spintharoskop *n* spintharoscope
Spin-umklappstreuung *f* spin flip scattering **-umklappung** *f* spin flip **-wechselwirkung** *f* spin-spin interaction **-zustandssumme** *f* spin partition function
Spion (Stärkemesser) thickness gauge
Spionen-atom *m* spy atom **-probe** *f* spy sample
Spiral-abtastung *f* spiral scanning **-antenne** *f* flat-coil or helical antenna **-aufgabevorrichtung** *f* spiral feeder **-bahnspektrometer** *m* spiral orbit spectrometer **-band** *n* helical tape **-bandkupplung** *f* helical band friction clutch **-bewehrung** *f* spiral reinforcement
Spiralbohrer *m* twist drill **dreinutiger** ~ three-grooved drill **steilgängiger** ~ slate drill, steep spiral drill, slant drill **kurz eingespannter** ~ stub drill
Spiralbohrer-ausheber *m* twist-drill lifter **-bruch** *m* drill breakage **-halter** *m* drill holder **-lehre** *f* drill gauge **-prüfgeräte** *pl* twist-drill testers **-schärfautomat** *m* automatic twist-drill grinder **-schleiflehre** *f* drillpoint or drill grinding gauge **-schleifmaschine** drill grinder **-spitzenschleifapparat** *m* twist-drill center grinding apparatus
Spiral-bohrmesser *n* twist drilling knives **-draht** *m* spiral or coiled wire **-dübel** *m* spiral dowel
Spirale *f* spiral, (turbine) scroll case, helix, volute, scroll, coil **logarithmische** ~ logarithmic spiral, equiangular spiral **eine räumliche** ~ a spiral in space **parabolische** ~ helicoid spiral **vierfache** ~ fourfold spiral
Spiralenzirkel *m* volute compasses
Spiralfaser *f* helical fiber **-struktur** *f* helical fibering
Spiralfeder *f* coil or spiral spring, helical spring ~ (eines Kristalldetektors) cat whisker (radio)
Spiralfeder-ausgleicher *m* spiral-spring equilibrator **-klemme** *f* coil-spring connector (telegr.) **-kupplung** *f* coil clutch
spiralförmig spiral, helical, spirally
Spiral-fräseinrichtung *f* spiral-milling attachment **-futter** *n* scroll chuck **-gebläse** *n* screw blast machine or blowing machine
Spiralgehäuse *n* volute, coiled casing **-schraubenradpumpe** *f* spiral-casing mixed-flow pump
spiralgenuteter Langlochfräser *m* spiral-fluted miller
spiralgeschweißt spirally welded
Spiralgetriebe *n* spiral gearing
Spiralgleitflug *m* spiral, spiral glide
Spiralhülsenwickelmaschine *f* spiral tube binder
spiralig helical, spiral
Spiral-kegel *m* spiral bevel **-kegelrad** *n* spiral bevel gear **-klemme** *f* coil-spring connector **-läufer** *m* spiral-course torpedo **-leitung** *f* armored cable **-linie** *f* spiral curve, spiral or helical line, helix **-lochscheibe** *f* disk with spiral perforations, spiral disk scanner **-nebel** *m* spiral nebula **-nute** *f* spiral slot **-öse** *f* wire loop, ferrule **-quelle** *f* spiral source **-rad** *n* spiral gear **-rohr** *n* pipe coil
Spiralrohrschlange *f* spiral coil **flache** ~ flat spiral coil, pancake coil
Spiral-saugschlauch *m* spiral suction hose **-schlauch** *m* spiral hose **-schnecke** *f* spiral worm **-seil** *n* twisted rope **-senker** *m* spiral countersink, three-lipped twist drills **-spannfutter** *n* scroll chuck **-spule** *f* spiral coil **-steigung** *f* pitch or lead of a spire or spiral, spiral lead **-strömung** *f* spiral flow **-täuschung** *f* spiral illusion
spiralverzahnt spirally fluted, spirally grooved

Spiral-verzahnung *f* spiral gearing **-vierer** *m* spiral quad **-walze** *f* roller with spiral twigging **-wattenmaschine** *f* helicoidal spreader **-welle** *f* spirally wound shaft **-wendeleiste** *f* sqiral Ginding or turning fillet **-zahnkegelrad** *n* spiral bevel gear **-zahnrad** *n* spiral gear

Spirek-Ofen *m* Spirek tile or shaft furnace

Spiritus *m* spirit, alcohol ~ **über Normalstärke** overproof spirit

Spiritus-brennerei *f* distillery **-dampf** *m* alcohol vapor **-kopallack** *m* copal spirit varnish **-lack** *m* spirit varnish **-lötlampe** *f* alcohol blow torch **-luftschraubenblattenteiser** *m* slinger ring **-maschine** *f* alcohol engine **-motor** *m* distillate engine

spitz pointed, sharp, acute ~ **zulaufend** tapered ~ **auslaufender Hohlraum** cusped cavity **-er Morsepunkt** clipped dot **-er Steinmeißel** pointed stone chisel **-er Winkel** acute angle

Spitz-arbeiten *pl* pointed hammer work **-becherglas** *n* sedimenting glass **-beutel** *m* triangular filter bag **-bock** *m* A pole **-bogen** *m* pointed or raised arch, ogive, ogival **-bogenkaliber** *n* angular or pointed groove

spitzbogige Unterlagscheibe ogive washer

Spitz-bohrer *m* pointed(-end) drill, flat drill, drill bit, common bit **-dübelautomaten** *pl* dowelling machines

Spitze *f* point, tip, top, head, peak, apex, pivot, spike, lace(work), corner, vertex ~ (eines Gewindes) top, crest **an der** ~ **stehen** to lead **handgeklöppelte** ~ handmade lace **laufende** ~ live center **mitlaufende** ~ live center **umlaufende** ~ running center ~ **eines Dreiecks** apex

Spitze zu Spitze peak-to-peak (pp)

Spitze-Spitze-Gleichrichter *m* voltage doubler circuit

Spitzeisen *n* pointed chisel

spitzen (schärfen) to point, sharpen

Spitzen und Einbrüche peaks and dips

Spitzen-abstand *m* distance between centers, length between centers **-achse** *f* axis of centers **-amt** *n* overflow exchange **-appretur** *f* lace finishing

Spitzen-aufhängung *f* point or pivot suspension **-ausgleich** *m* peak-shaving **-ausleger** *m* head jib **-beanspruchung** *f* maximum or localized stress **-bedarf** *m* peak demand **-belastung** *f* peak load, capacity load, maximum demand **-blitzableiter** *m* pointed lightning protector

Spitzenbock *m* center cradle or rest **erhöhter** ~ raised center cradle

Spitzenbockteilkreis *m* center cradle circle

Spitzende *n* spigot end (of socket tube)

Spitzen-diode *f* point contact diode **-dosis** *f* peak dose

Spitzendrehbank *f* center lathe, engine lathe **gewöhnliche** ~ engine lathe

Spitzendreherei *f* center-lathe operation

Spitzen-drehmoment *n* peak torque **-drehzahl** *f* top speed

Spitzendruck *m* peak pressure **-adjustierschraube** *f* tension-adjusting knob

Spitzen-druckmesser *m* peak pressure meter **-durchmesser** *m* over-all diameter **-effekt** *m* edge or point effect **-elektrode** *f* point electrode, needle electrode **-entfernung** *f* distance between points, center distance **-entladung** *f* point discharge, needle(-gap) discharge **-entnahme** *f* peak discharge or demand

Spitzen-faktor *m* crest factor **-feile** *f* taper file **-feuer** *n* top light **-flächentransistor** *m* point-junction transistor **-flußdichte** *f* peak flux density **-führung** *f* guide pivot **-funkenstrecke** *f* pointed spark gap

spitzen-gelagert suspended in points, journaled on points **-geschwindigkeit** *f* tip or top speed **-gewinde** *n* angular thread, sharp thread, V thread **-glas** *n* reticulated glass **-gleichrichter** *m* point-contact rectifier **-halter** *m* point holder **-hacke** *f*, (**-haue** *f*) pick **-helligkeit** *f* highlight, brightness **-höhe** *f* height of centers **-hub** *m* maximum deviation **-kapazität** *f* top capacity

Spitzen-kathode *f* pointed filament, point cathode **-kontakt** *m* point contact **-kraftwerk** *n* peak-current generating station, peak-load power station **-lager** *n* conical bearing **-lagerung** *f* point suspension, jeweled bearing, pivot jewel, point support

Spitzenlast-deckung *f* peak load service **-fahren** *n* peak-load operation

Spitzen-lehre *f* point gauge, crest or thread template **-leistung** *f* peak capacity, record achievement, performance, or accomplishment, peak power or output, maximum output **-leitungsspannung** *f* peak line voltage **-leuchtdichte** *f* highlights, peak light output

spitzenlos schleifen to grind centerless

spitzenlos-es Gewindeschleifen centerless thread grinding **-er Kolben** tipless bulb **-e Rundschleifmaschine** centerless circular grinder

Spitzen-magnetisierungskraft *f* peak magnetizing force **-marke** *f* point(ed) mark **-mitnehmereinrichtung** *f* center driver attachment **-nutzspannung** *f* peak signal voltage **-platz** *m* transfer position **-platzbeamtin** *f* transfer operator **-prüfgerät** *n* instrument-compartment test set (guided miss.) **-punkt** *m* peak point

Spitzen-schiff *n* leading ship **-schleifapparat** *m* center grinder **-senker** *m* center reamer **-signalisierung** *f* signaling of peak load of traffic **-spannung** *f* peak voltage, crest voltage **-spannungsmesser** *m* peak voltmeter **-spannungszeiger** *m* peak indicator **-spiel** *n* crest clearance, clearance at root **-spitzenwert** *m* peak-to-peak value **-störspannung** *f* peak effective noise voltage **-strom** *m* peak current **-transistor** *m* point contact transistor

Spitzen-überdruck *m* peak overpressure **-verband** *m* peak or central organization **-verkehr** *m* peak traffic **-verlust** *m* tip loss **-verrechnung** *f* accounting of balances **-wagen** *m* leading car **-weite** *f* center clearance, distance between centers **-wert** *m* peak value, crest value, maximum value **-wertzeiger** *m* peak indicator

Spitzen-widerstand *m* point or tip drag, point resistance **-winkel** *m* point(ed) angle, center angle, lip angle **-wirbel** *m* tip vortex **-wicklung** *f* needle effect **-zähler** *m* peak meter, needle counter **-zählrohr** *n* point counter tube **-zeiger** *m* peak-reading (level) indicator **-zirkel** *m* compass, divider

Spitze-platteentladung *f* point-to-plane dischcrge **-zündstrecke** *f* point-to-point gap

Spitz-fänger *m* fishing (screw) tap **-feile** *f* taper file **-gewinde** *n* sharp thread, V thread **-gewindestahl** *m* V-thread tool **-hacke** *f* pickax, pick **-hammer** *m* pick, mattock

spitzig acute, pointed, sharp, tapering

Spitz-kasten *m* box classifier, pyramidal separator **-keil** *m* wedge **-kerbe** *f* specimen with V-notch **-kopf** *m* conical head **-krampen** *m* pickax, pick **-kühler** *m* pointed radiator **-lichter** *n pl* bright lights, high lights (art), tangential lighting **-lötkolben** *m* pointed copper bit **-lutte** *f* pointed tube **-meißel** *m* pointed chisel, diamond-point bit

Spitz-senker *m* countersink **-spaten** *m* push pick **-stahl** *m* single-point thread chaser, diamond-point tool **-stichel** *m* single-point tool **-strang** *m* (Montage) hemp rope **-tonne** *f* conical buoy **-trichter** *m* funnel **-trichterapparat** *m* funnels, funnel apparatus **-verdachung** *f* gable-roofing **-winkelkreuzung** *f* diamond crossing

spitzwinklig acute-angled **-es Dreieck** acute triangle **-er Keil** wedge

Spitz-zange *f* pointed pliers, crooked crowbar **-zapfen** *m* pointed journal, conical pivot or pin **-zirkel** *m* compass, divider **-zulaufend** tapered

Spleiß *f* splice, splinter **-block** *m* jointer's vise **-eisen** *n* marline-spike

spleißen to split, cleave, splice, refine (copper), join (to)

Spleißer *m* splicer

Spleiß-gerät *n* splicing tool **-horn** *n* splicing pin or needle **-kasten** *m* splicing box **-klammer** *f* splicing clamp **-kloben** *m* splicing block **-nadel** *f* splicing pin or needle **-stange** *f* splice bar **-stelle** *f* joint, (cable) splice

Spleißung *f* (cable conductor) splice, splicing, jointing

Spleißverrichtung *f* tucking

Spleißwerkzeuge oder -geräte splicing tools

Splint *m* key, peg, bar, strip, split pin, cotter, sap, sapwood, splint **-auszieher** *m* split-pin extractor, pin punch **-baum** *m* sapwood tree **-bohrer** *m* splint bit **-bolzen** *m* eyebolt **-draht** *m* pin wire

Splinte *f* split pin

Splintentzieher *m* cotter-pin extractor

Splinter *m* splint, splinter

Splint-frei sapless **-holz** *n* sap, sapwood **-keil** *m* cotter key **-kohle** *f* splint coal **-lager** *n* key seating **-loch** *n* locking-pin hole, cotter-pin hole

Splint-mutter *f* lock nut **-rissig** liable to break off in splinters **-scheibe** *f* circlip **-treiber** *pl* pin punches **-verschluß** *m* cotter lock **-zapfen** *m* crossdrilled spigot **-zieher** *m* split-pin pliers, cotter extractors

Spliß *m* splice

splissen to splice

Splisser *m* splicer, splicing tool

Splißholz *n* marlinespike

Splissung *f* splice

Splitt *m* a fine gravel, broken stone, chipping, chip(ping)s, stone chips

Splitter *m* splinter, chip, scale, fragment **-ballistik** *f* ballistics of shell spliterns **-bild einer Ladungshülle** photograph of the fragmentation of a shell casing **-bindend** shatterproof **-boxe** *f* blast bay **-bremse** *f* brake skid **-dichte** *f* splinter density, fragment density **-fänger** *m* splinter catch or catcher

splitterfrei shatterproof **-glas** *n* safety glass

splitterig splintery **-e Papiermasse** splintered pulp

Splitterkohle *f* splint coal

splittern to splinter, shiver, shatter, split

Splittern *n* splintering

splitternd, nicht ~ nonsplintering

Splitter-pinzette *f* spliter forceps **-schutz** *m* splinterproof protection **-sicher** splinterproof **-wall** *m* blast wall **-wand** *f* splinter screen

Splitterwirkung *f* splintering effect, fragmentation effect

splittrig splintery

Splittstreuer *m* gravel-scattering equipment

Spodium *n* bone or ivory black, bone charcoal

Spongiose *f* (Graphitierung) graphitic corrosion

spontane Verbrennung spontaneous combustion

sporadisch sporadic **-e E-Schicht** sporadic E layer **-e Ionisation der E-Schicht** sporadic E ionization

Sporen, flache ~ flat lugs

Sporn *m* trail spade, tail skid (aviation), spur, skid **-blech** *n* trail spade **-bremse** *f* spur or plow brake **-druck** *m* weight on tail wheel or skid **-feder** *f* tail-skid spring **-federung** *f* tailskid springing **-hebel** *m* tail-skid control lever **-kufe** *f* tail skid

Spornrad *n* tail wheel, nose wheel **einziehbares ~** retractable tail wheel **lenkbares ~** steerable tail wheel **Flattern von Spornrädern** shimmy

Spornrad-anzeiger *m* tail-wheel position indicator **-verkleidung** *f* tail-wheel fairing

Sporn-rolle *f* tail wheel **-rückschlag** *m* tailskid arrest or stop **-schlepp** *m* tail-skid towing **-schuh** *m* tail-skid shoe **-strebenachse** *f* spindle axis on the tail wheel, tail-strut axis **-teller** *m* spike plate (tripod)

Sport- und Reiseflugzeug *n* sporting and touring plane

Sprach-aufnahme *f* speech, voice, vocal, or dialogue recording **-bedarf** *m* energy requirement **-beeinflussung** *f* voice control, modulation by voice **-bereich** *m* telephone area **-deutlichkeit** *f* articulation, intelligibility

Sprache *f* speech, voice, language, code **chiffrierte ~** cipher or coded language **deutliche ~** articulated voice, clear voice **geheime ~** secret language **offene ~** open language **in offener ~** in plain language **verabredete ~** code language **verschwommene ~** blurred voice **die ~ ist verzerrt** the conversation is distorted **mit ~ gemessener Wert** voice-test result

Sprach-energie *f* voice power **-fluß** *m* energy flow

Sprachfrequenz *f* voice frequency, speech frequency **mittlere ~** mean frequency of speech

Sprachfrequenz-band *n* speech band **-bereich** *m* speech frequency range

Sprach-galvanometer *n* mirror speaker **-geschalteter Telephoniesender** voice-modulated radiophone or telephony (signal) transmitter **-gesteuert** voice controlled **-güte** *f* speech quality **-höhenlinie** *f* transmission level **-kenntnis** *f* knowledge of a language

Sprach-komponente *f* energy component **-laute** *pl* sounds of speech, articulate speech **-lautstärke** *f* speech volume **-messung** *f* voice test(ing) **-modulator** *m* voice-actuated modulator

sprachmoduliert speech-modulated, voice- modulated **-e ungedämpfte Wellen** speech-modulated continuous waves

Sprach-niveaulinie *f* transmission level **-pegel** *m* speech level **-rohr** *n* speaking tube, megaphone **-spitze** *f* talking peak **-steuerung** *f* voice-operated or -controlled device **-steuerungsvorrichtung** *f* voice-operated device **-schwingung** *f* speech wave **-transport** *m* transport of energy **-übertragung** *f* speech transmission, transfer of energy **-untersuchung** *f* speech study, speech analysis

Sprachverbrauch *m* energy consumption, energy dissipation ~ **des Heizfadens** filament wattage

Sprach-verlauf *m* transmission level **-verlust** *m* loss of energy **-verständlichkeit** *f* articulation, intelligibility of speech or articulate sound **-verstärker** *m* speech amplifier **-verstärkungsanlage** *f* (public-)address system **-verteilung** *f* energy distribution **-verzehrung** *f* energy dissipation **-wechselströme** *pl* voice frequency **-weite** *f* reach of talk **-wellen** *pl* speech waves **-wende** *f* inverter **-wiedergabe** *f* voice reproduction, demodulation of speech

spratzen to scatter, spatter, spit, spurt, sputter, splash

Spratzen *n* scattering, spitting, spurting, splashing, splash, flicker, sputter

Spratzwiderstand (Funkenüberschlagswiderstand) spark resistance

Sprech-adern *pl* basic speaking pair, speaking wires **-apparat** *m* speaking instrument, telephone set **-aufnahme** *f* speech, voice, vocal, or dialogue recording **-batterie** *f* speaking battery **-bereich** *m* telephone area **-einrichtung** *f* speaking equipment, operator's (telephone) set

sprechen to speak, talk

Sprechen *n* speaking, talking

sprechende Bogenlampe speaking arc, Simon arc, Duddell arc

Sprecher *m* announcer, speaker, talker **synthetischer** ~ voder

Sprecherecho *n* talker echo

Sprechfrequenz *f* audio frequency, telephonic frequency **-bereich** *m* speech-frequency range

Sprechfunk *m* radio telephony (RT) **-band** *n* telephony band **-brücke** *f* point-to-point radiotelephone link

Sprech-garnitur *f* operator's (telephone) set **-hörer** *m* telephone handset, microtelephone combination, transceiver **-hörversuch** *m* voice-ear test, volume comparison **-kanal** *m* speech channel **-kapsel** *f* transmitter unit, (condenser) microphone **-kopf** *m* sound box, recording sound head **-kreis** *m* talking or speaking circuit **-lautstärke** *f* speech volume, acoustical speech **-leistung** *f* response of an electroacoustic system **-leitung** *f* call wire, speaker wire **-maschine** *f* phonograph

Sprechmaschinenlaufwerk *n* movement or spring motor of phonograph

Sprech-pegel *m* speech level **-probe** *f* signal check (rdr.) **-prüfung** *f* voice test(ing) **-reichweite** *f* speaking range **-schalter** *m* talking key, speaking key **-schlauch** *m* dictating tube, speaking tube **-schlüssel** *m* talking or speaking key **-schnur einer B-Beamtin** interception or interruption cord **-schwingung** *f* speech wave **-spule** *f* talking circuit, induction coil

Sprechstelle *f* telephone extension, call station, (telephone) station ~ **mit Rückhördämpfung** anti-sidetone set

Sprechstellen-einführung *f* drop wire **-störung** *f* subscriber's apparatus fault

Sprechstellung *f* speaking position, talking condition

Sprechstrom *m* telephone current, talking current, audio-frequency current, sound, signal current **-kreis** *m* speaking circuit, circuit carrying voice or audiofrequency current **-speisung** *f*, **-zuführung** *f* speaking-current supply **-übertragung** telephone current transmission

Sprech-taste *f* speaking key, transmitter button, microphone switch **-transformator** *m* speech transformer, audio-frequency transformer **-trichter** *m* mouthpiece **-umschalter** *m* talking key

Sprech- und Mithörschalter *m* combined listening and speaking key

Sprech- und Rufschlüssel *m* speaking and ringing key

Sprechverbindung *f* telephone communication or connection, telephone line **gegenseitige** ~ two-way telephone line

Sprech-verkehr *m* radio-telephony traffic **-verständigung** *f* talking range, articulation, intelligibility

Sprechversuch *m* talking test, speech test **vergleichender** ~ comparative speech test

Sprech-wechselspannung *f* variation of audio voltage **-weg** *m* speaking circuit, talking path, telephone channel **-zeug** *n* (operator's) telephone set **-zucht** *f* radiotelephony discipline

Spreizband *n* (inneres Bremsband) expanding band (internal brake band)

Spreiz-bügelplatte *f* expanding bracket plate **-dorn** *m* expanding mandrel or bushing **-dübel** *m* straddling dowel

Spreize *f* spreader, spacer, strut, stay, outrigger, boom

Spreizelektrode *f* gun welder

spreizen to spread, force apart, straddle **die Holme** ~ to spread the trails

Spreizen-kamera *f* strut camera, extension camera **-kopf** *m* stay head

Spreiz-feder *f* spreading or expanding spring **-flansch** *m* splayed flange **-flügelklappe** *f* split flap

Spreizhebel *m* expanding arm, spreader lever, toggle lever **-backenbremse** *f* expanding lever shoe brake **-bremse** *f* expanding lever brake

Spreizholz *n* strut

Spreizklappe *f* spreader, (split) flap, controllable gill ~ **an der Motorhaube** cowl flap **die Spreizklappen öffnen** to extend the flaps

Spreizklappenöffnungswinkel *m* flap angle

Spreizklappenhaube *f* gill **Luftaustritt der** ~ gill exit

Spreiz-klappenring *m* expanding frill cowling **-konus** *m* expanding cone **-körper** *m* spreader **-lafette** *f* split-trail carriage

Spreizring *m* expanding ring **-kupplung** *f* spring-ring clutch, expanding band clutch

Spreiz-rolle *f* expanding roller **-schloß** *n* expanding lock **-schraube** *f* spreading or adjusting screw, expansion screw **-schwelle** *f* beam

spreader **-stange** *f* spreader bar **-stoff** *m* expander **-stößel** *m* spreading wedge head
Spreizung *f* spreading, inclination ~ (Vorderräder) king pin angle ~ **des Lenkzapfens** inclination of steering knuckle pivot
Spreizungs-koeffizient *m* spreading coefficient **-kondensator** *m* vernier capacitor
Spreiz-verschluß *m* straddle closure **-winkel** *m* angle of twist **-zylinder** *m* expanding cylinder
Spreng-apparat *m* sprinkling apparatus **-arbeit** *f* blasting, shooting **-bedarf** *m* explosives **-befehl** *m* order to blast **-bohrloch** *n* shot-hole **-boje** *f* mine-field float **-brücke** *f* strut-frame bridge
Sprengelscher Sprengstoff Sprengel's explosive
sprengen to explode, blast, blow up, burst or break open, shoot, spray, sprinkle
Sprengen *n* blasting blast
Sprenger *m* sprinkler, blaster
Spreng-fachmann *m* demolitions expert **-füllung** *f* explosive charge **-gelatine** *f* blasting gelatin **-greifer** *m* cable cutter (used in mine sweeping) **-gummi** *m* blasting gelatin **-höhe** *f* height of burst **-kabel** *n* blasting ignition cable **-kammer** *f* mine chamber
Sprengkapsel *f* detonator, primer cap, detonating or blasting cap, booster charge **-röhrchen** *n* detonator tube **-sicherung** *f* detonator safety **-zünder** *m* detonator
Spreng-kegel *m* cone of burst or blast **-keil** *m* blowing wedge **-körper** *m* blasting charge, explosive charge **-kraft** *f* explosive force **-ladung** *f* bursting charge, explosive charge **-ladungsröhre** *f* burster tube **-ladungsträger** *m* demolition vehicle **-loch** *n* shot hole **-luft** *f* liquid-oxygen explosive
Spreng-masse *f* explosive charge **-mittel** *n* blasting agent, explosive charge **-niet** *m* explosion rivet, explosive rivet **-öl** *n* nitroglycerin **-patrone** *f* blasting cartridge **-plan** *m* blasting plan **-pulver** *n* blasting powder
Sprengpunkt *m* point of burst **-dichte** *f* density of burst **-entfernung** *f* burst range
Spreng-ring *m* circlip, spring or snap ring **-ringzieher** *m* spring ring driver or extractor **-rohr** *n* conduit for detonation cord **-salpeter** *m* black powder pellets, saltpeter blasting powder, nitrate explosive **-satz** *m* bursting charge
Spreng-scheibe *f* spring disk or washer **-schlag** *m* explosion **-schnur** *f* fuse **-schraube** *f* explosive rivet **-spannung** *f* bursting or opening stress **-stange** *f* rod for placing explosives **-stelle** *f* point of rupture
Sprengstoff *m* explosive, dynamite **-behälter** *m* jacket of warhead (missiles) **-füllung** *f* explosive charge or filler **-gehalt** *m* amount of bursting charge **-kugel** *f* explosive projectile, explosive bullet **-lager** *n* explosive dump **-raum** *m* war head, storage room for explosives **-schleuder** *f* powder catapult
Spreng-stück *n* splinter **-stütze** *f* king post **-technik** *f* explosive technique **-trupp** *m* blasting detachment
Sprengung *f* explosion, blasting ~ **der Feder** camber of spring
Spreng-vorgang *m* blasting process **-vorrichtung** *f* (Sprengwagen) watering equipment **-wagen** *m* water wagon, sprinkler **-wedel** *m* sprinkler **-weite** *f* deviation (artil.) **-werk** *n* structure for strengthening roofs for standards, intermediate trestle **-wirkung** *f* explosive action or effect, splitting effect **-wolke** *f* burst smoke or cloud **-zirkel** *m* fragmentation test circle **-zünder** *m* fuse
sprenkeln to sprinkle, speckle, mottle, spot
Sprenkler *m* sprinkler
Spreutlagen *f pl* brushwork revetments, dam works
Spriegel *m* stick, hoop or support (for hood or tilt) **-trennstück** *n* bow separator
Sprieß *m* brace **-brett** *n* poling board
Sprießung *f* shuttering
Spring *f* spring
Springbrunnenwirkung *f* fountain effect
Springduowalzwerk *n* jump roughing mill
springen to burst, break, crack, split, spring, spout, jump, fracture ~ (bei der Landung) to rebound
Springen *n* cracking, breaking, bursting, splitting, springing
springend bursting **-er Punkt** crucial point
Springer *m* (Erdöl), gusher oil well, open-flow well, hopper
Springfeder *f* elastic spring, control spring
Springfederndraht *m* spring wire
Springfederwaage *f* spring balance
Spring-flut *f* spring tide **-hart** brittle **-hochwasser** *n* high water of spring tides **-höhe** *f* upthrow **-keil** *m* spring coupling-catch **-kraft** *f* springiness, resiliency, elasticity, power of recoil or rebound **-niedrigwasser** *n* low water of spring tides **-punkt** *m* critical point **-quelle** *f* curb, geyser
Spring-ring *m* circlip, retaining ring, snap ring, spring retainer **-rollos** *pl* spring blinds **-schalter** *m* snap-action switch **-schaltung** *f* intermittent control or feed, jump feed **-schlüssel** *m* spring clamp key **-schreiber** *m* start-stop teleprinter or teletype-writer **-schreibverfahren** *n* start-stop system **-schwanz** *m* springtail
Springstabindikator *m* bouncing pin
Springtide *f* springtide **-verfrühung** *f* springtide prematureness **-verspätung** *f* springtide lag
Spring-zeiger *m* bouncing pin **-zeilensendung** *f* line interlace transmission
Sprinkler *m* sprinkler ~ **mit einseitiger Verteilung** sidewall sprinkler
Sprinkler-anlage *f* sprinkler installation **-hügel** *m* sprinkler yoke **-körper** *m* sprinkler frame
sprinklern to sprinkle
Sprinkler-schutzkorb *m* sprinkler guard **-verschluß** *m* sprinkler valve retaining members
Sprit *m* alcohol, (slang) fuel or oil **-beize** *f* spirit stain
spritlöslich alcohol-soluble **-e Farbe** alcohol-soluble color
Spritraffinerie *f* spirit refinery
Spritz-alitieren *n* spray calorizing (met.) **-anlage** *f* spraying plant
Spritzanstrich durch Zerstäubung mit Druckluft spraying
Spritz-apparat *m* sprinkler, sprinkling apparatus **-auftrag** *m* spray coat **-bad** *n* splashing **-bewurf** *m* coarse plaster, squirted skin, rough plaster or cast **-blech** *n* dashboard **-bohrung** *f* orifice
Spritzbrett *n* baffle board (paper mfg.), dashboard **-kühler** *m* dashboard-mounted fan

-lampe *f* dash lamp

Spritz-dichtung *f* gland seal **-druck** *m* spraying pressure, die-casting pressure (in founding) **-drucke** *pl* splutter prints **-druckfarbe** *f* spraying color **-düse** *f* spray(ing) nozzle, discharge nozzle, power jet, injector, syringe (chem)

Spritze *f* syringe, spray(er), injector

spritzen to spray, spout, spurt, spatter, die-cast, extrude, split, exude, inject **-boot** *n* fire float **-schlauch** *m* fire hose

Spritzen *n* direct injection molding **~ mit Strahlenschutz** syringes with radiation protection

Spritzentladung *f* initial discharge caused by rapid surge of ions, needle-gap discharge

Spritzer *m* spatter, splash, sprue, catch, squirt

Spritz-fangblech *n* baffle plate **-färbung** *f* spray dyeing **-fett** *n* spraying fat **-flasche** *f* washing bottle **-flüssigkeit** *f* liquid spraying **-folge** *f* injection sequence **-form** *f* jet mold **-gas** *n* gas spray **-gießen** *n* injection molding

Spritzguß *m* injection molding, injection die-casting **-fassung** *f* die-cast mount **-form** *f* die, die mold **-gesenk** *n* die-casting die **-kondensator** *m* die-cast condenser **-maschine** *f* die-casting machine **-masse** *f* injection-molding compound

Spritzguß-matrize *f* die-casting die **-metall** *n* die-cast metal **-presse** *f* injection press **-stück** *n* die-cast(ing) **-teil** *m* sprayed die casting **-verfahren** *n* injection molding, die-casting process

Spritz-gut *n* product of injection molding **-kanal** *m* metal passage to die (of die-casting machine) **-kanne** *f* injection or squirt can **-kennlinie** *f* characteristic (line) of injection **-kolben** *m* injection plunger **-korken** *m* spurt cork, sprinkler stopper **-lack** *m* spraying lacquer or varnish **-lackieren** *n* spray painting **-lackiererei** *f* dope-spraying section or shop **-legierung** *f* die-casting alloy

Spritzling *m* injection molding

Spritzloch *n* (a. d. Düse) orifice

Spritzmaschine *f* forcing or spraying or squirting machine **~ zum Gummieren von Draht** insulating machine

Spritz-masse *f* spraying compound **-matrize** *f* dies for die casting **-metallisieren** *n* metal spraying **-mulde** *f* adapter **-narben** *n* graining or pebbling in a sprayed film **-öl** *n* oil spray **-ölschmierung** *f* splash lubrication **-pistole** *f* spray gun, air gun, aerograph **-preßformung** *f* transfer molding **-pulver** *n* injecting powder **-pumpe** *f* jet pump, spraying pump **-ring** *m* oil ring, thrower, splash ring, slinger **-rohr** *n* spraying pipe **-rohrbestückung** *f* spraying tube equipment

Spritz-sand *m* sandblasting sand **-schablonen** *pl* spray painting stencils

Spritzscheibe *f* deflector, oil ring **~ auf Nockenwelle** splash ring on camshaft

Spritz-schmierung *f* splash lubrication **-schutzdeckel** *m* spray arrester (batt.) **-spachtel** *f* any surfacer or primer that is sprayed on **-speisung** *f* slash feed **-teil** *m* **aus Isoliermaterial** product molded from insulating material **-umlaufschmierung** *f* circulating splash lubrication **-ventilregulierung** *f* spray-valve regulation **-verfahren** *n* spraying method, method of injection molding, metallization **-vergaser** *m* spray carburetor **-verschluß** *m* spray closure

Spritzversteller *m* timing gear **-kupplung** *f* coupling of injection timing device **-muffe** *f* sleeve of injection timing device

Spritz-verstellung *f* injection control, injection timer, timing control unit **-versuch** *m* impingement test **-verzinkt** galvanized by the spraying method **-wand** *f* dashboard

Spritzwasser *n* spray water **-dicht** spray-proof, splash proof **-geschützt** protected against jets of water, splash proof **-leiste** *f* spray strip **-schutz** *m* splash-proof enclosure, spray water guard

Spritz-weite *f* penetration **-werkzeug** *n* extrusion die **-zapfen** *m* injection pin **-zapfenspiel** *n* clearance of injection pin

Spritz-zeitpunkt *m* moment of injection **-zeitpunktversteller** *m* injection timing device **-zeitversteller** *m* injection timer, timing gear control, timing gear **-zündung** *f* injection ignition, Dieselgasverfahren

Sprödbruch *m* brittle failure, brittle fracture

spröde obstinate, brittle, short **~ machen** to embrittle **-es Eisen** brittle iron

Sprödewerden *n* embrittlement, embrittling

Sprödglaserz *n* stephanite

Sprödigkeit *f* brittleness, shortness, friability, obstinacy

Sprosse *f* step, tread, crossbar, rafter, (ladder) rung, spoke, stave, shoot, germ

Sprossen-belag *m* lattice flooring **-linse** *f* built-up lens **-rad** *n* stave wheel **-rolle** *f* sprocket drum **-schrift** *f* variable-density track

Sprossentisch *m* sprocket table **-sandstrahlgebläse** *n* sandblast sprocket-table machine

Sprossentrommel *f* sprocket drum or wheel

Sprößling *m* shoot, sprout

Sprossung *f* germination

Sprudel-bohrung *f* gusher, spouter **-brunnen** *m* gusher **-platte** *f* bubble tray **-wascher** *m* automatic washer

Sprüh-apparat *m* sprayer **-bild** *n* spray pattern **-dose** *f* spray nozzle **-draht** *m* electrical discharge wire **-düse** *f* spraying nozzle

sprühen to spray, spit, scintillate, spark, drizzle, scatter, sprinkle

Sprühen *n* corona, corona discharge, brush discharge, scintillation, grass (radar)

Sprüh-entladung *f* corona, corona discharge, brush discharge, spray discharge, corona brushing **-festigkeit** *f* sprayproofness **-ion** *n* spray ion **-kupfer** *n* copper rain **-nebel** *m* spray **-regen** *m* drizzle **-regenlichtbogen** *m* spray type arc **-ring** *m* anti-corona ring **-rohr** *n* spray tube

Sprüh-säule *f* spray tower **-schutzisolator** *m* antispraying insulator **-schutzring** *m* spark guard **-schutzwulst** *f* anticorona collar, guard ring **-spitzen** *pl* spray points **-stellen** *pl* spray points **-teller** *m* deflector **-verlust** *m* brush-discharge loss

Sprung *m* crack, chink, fissure, flaw, fault, leap, jump (comput), break, bounce, transient **bedingter ~** conditional jump (comput)

Sprung-baum *m* spring pole **-befehl** *m* jump order (info proc.) **-bildung** *f* cracking, kink or jog formation **-bogenverstärker** *m* jumping arc amplifier **-brett** *n* spring board **-charakteristik** *f* surge characteristic, step function response

Sprünge *pl* kinks ~ **im Glas** flaws in glass
Sprung-entfernung *f* skip distance, skip zone **-feder** *f* elastic spring **-federsitz** *m* spring seat **-frequenz** *f* transition frequency **-funktion** *f* step function **-funktionsmeßgerät** *n* transient response measuring set **-gelenk** *n* hock **-generator** *m* square-wave generator
sprunghaft jerky, irregular, nonsequential, sudden **-e Temperaturabnahme** decalescence
Sprung-haftigkeit *f* violent fluctuation or jump **-härte** *f* rebound hardness, dynamic indentation test **-höhe** *f* throw of the fault, depth of the shed, pedestal level or height, amplitude of return or flyback (television) **-kennlinie** *f* jump characteristic **-leisten** *m* wave molding **-paarbildung** *f* kink pair formation **-punkt** *m* transition point
Sprung-ring *m* spring washer **-schalter** *m* quick-break switch **-schaltung** *f* independent manual operation, spring control **-schicht** *f* boundary surface (between two liquids), interface **-schienen** *pl* skip bars **-signal** *n* step function signal **-spannung** *f* initial inverse voltage **-start** *m* jump start, quick start **-stelle** *f* point of sudden irregularity, unsteadiness, change, or discontinuity
Sprung-tischfräsen *n* intermittent feed milling **-tischschaltung** *f* intermittent table feed **-tuch** *n* safety net **-turm** *m* parachute tower, high-diving board **-übergangsfunktion** *f* unit-step response **-vorschub** *m* intermittent feed **-wahrscheinlichkeit** *f* transition probability, leap probability
sprungweise by bounds, by steps or stages, intermittently, nonsequentially ~ **Querschnittänderung** abrupt change of cross section
Sprungweite *f* shift of the fault ~ **des freien Wasserstrahls** horizontal range of water jet
Sprung-welle *f* surge **-wellenprobe** *f* surge-pressure test **-wiedergabe** *f* step response **-zeilenverfahren** *n* interlace method **-zeit** *f* transit time, transition time **-zone** *f* space zone
Spucken *n* (of a converter) slop
Spudding-scheibe *f* spudding ring **-schuh** *m* spudding shoe
Spulaggregat *n* pirning layout
Spül-anlage *f* washing plant, flushing arrangement **-aufwand** *m* quantity of scavenging air required **-becken** *n* scouring or flushing basin, scouring sluice, flushing gate
Spülbetrieb *m* filling **Landaufhöhung durch** ~ raising of an area by filling
Spül-bohren *n* hydraulic circulating system **-bohrer** *m* bit with bottom flush **-bohrgerät** *n* flush boring tools, water-flush boring poles **-bohrkopf** *m* dutchman, stuffing box for water-flush system, swivel **-bohrung** *f* hydraulic boring **-druck** *m* scavenging pressure
Spule *f* spool, coil, bobbin, reel, drum ~ **mit einem Gleitkontakt** slider coil ~ **mit zwei Gleitkontakten** double slider coil ~ **ohne Kern** air cored magnet ~ **für maximale Stromstärke und minimale Spannung** overload and undervoltage protection **mit einer halben** ~ **beginnend** beginning at mid-load **angezapfte** ~ tapped coil **astatische** ~ astatic coil **drehbare** ~ moving coil, rotating coil, rotor coil, revolving coil **einlagige** ~ single-layer coil **feste** ~ fixed coil, stator (coil) **flächenhafte** ~ laminar or areal coil, nonfilamentary coil
Spule, gleichstromvormagnetisierte ~ direct-current controlled saturable coil **kleine** ~ bobbin **koaxiale** ~ coaxial coil **körperlose** ~ structure with entire mass of vibratory system contained in oil **mehrlagige** ~ multilayer coil **quadratische** ~ square coil **rechteckige** ~ rectangular coil **selbstschirmende** ~ self-shielded or astatic coil **verschiebbare** ~ sliding coil **wenig streuende gepanzerte** ~ iron-core deflection yoke unit **wirtschaftlichste** ~ most economical coil **mit Spulen belastetes Kabel** coil-loaded cable **ineinanderschiebbare Spulen** telescoping coils
Spuleffekt *m* jetting action
Spüleinrichtung *f* rinsing appliance
spulen to spool, wind, reel, coil up
Spulen *n* spooling
spülen to rinse, clean, wash, flush, scavenge
Spülen *n* sluicing, hydraulic fill, monitor dredging, flush, scavenging, rinsing ~ **einer Schleuse** scouring of a sluice
Spulen-ableitung *f* coil tap **-abschnitt** *m* (loading) coil section, loading section **-abstand** *m* (load) coil spacing **-abzweig** *m* coil tap **-achse** *f* coil axis, core of spool **-anker** *m* slip-ring (rotor) armature **-anordnung** *f* coil arrangement **-antenne** *f* coil antenna **-anzapfung** *f* coil tap, inductor tap, tapping
Spulen-arm *m* magazine or spool arm or support **-aufstecker** *m* spool feeder **-belastet** coil-loaded **-belastung** *f* coil loading, pupinization **-betätigungsspannung** *f* magnet coil voltage **-chronograf** *m* solenoid chronograph **-draht** *m* coil wire **-(draht)ende** *n* lead-in wire, lead **-durchflutung** *f* magnetic potential of coil **-durchmesser** *m* diameter of coil **-entfernung** *f* load spacing, coil spacing
Spulenfeld *n* loading (coil) section, pupinization section **mit einem halben** ~ **beginnend** beginning at mid-section
Spulen-feldergänzung *f* building-out section **-festpunkt** *m* (loading) section point **-filz** *m* yarn package **-flansch** *m* spool flange, spool head **-fluß** *m* flux linking a coil **-fuß** *m* spindle-base **-galvanometer** *n* coil galvenometer **-gestell** *n* coil rack **-halter** *m* coil holder **-halterstange** *f* package holding rod **-kabel** *n* coil(-loaded) cable **-kapazität** *f* coil capacity, self-capacity of a coil
Spulenkasten *m* bobbin, spool, former of coil, loading-coil case or pot ~ **für Freileitungen** loading pot for overhead line
Spulenkern *m* core of a coil, core of spool **-befestigung** *f* hub fittings **-material** *n* coil core material
Spulen-kette *f* low-pass filter, ultra-filter, upper limiting filter **-kopf** *m* end winding **-koppler** *m* coil coupler **-körper** *m* spool, bobbin, (coil) former, coil form **-lagerung** *f* holding the pirn **-länge** *f* bobbin height **-leiter** *m* low-filter pass **-leitung** *f* low-pass filter **-mark** *n* molded-coil core **-mitnehmer** *m* rewind fork **-papier** *n* tube paper **-plan** *m* loading plan **-punkt** *m* loading point
Spulen-rahmen *m* coil former, bobbin frame **-revolver** *m* coil switch mechanism **-satz** *m* coil

assembly, loading (coil) unit **-scheibe** *f* spool flange, spool head **-schwinger** *m* moving-coil vibrator (or oscillograph) **-seite** *f* current sheet, group of conductors (electr.) **-seitenleitung** *f* unit interval in a winding **-seitenteilung** *f* unit interval (in coil winding)

Spulen-stromversorgung *f* coil current supply **-stück** *n* coil piece **-technik** *f* technic of designing coils **-teilung** *f* unit interval (in winding) **-teller** *m* spool support (tape rec.) **-topf** *m* can, canned coil **-träger** *m* magazine, spool arm, support **-verteiler** *m* weft distributor

Spulen-wagengeschwindigkeit *f* traverse speed of the balling table **-weite** *f* slot pitch, coil width **-wicklung** *f* coil winding **-widerstand** *m* coil resistance **-windung** *f* coil winding **-windungsschlußprüfer** *m* interturn short-circuit or continuity tester **-zündanlage** *f* coil ignition system

Spuler *m* spooler

Spüler *m* scourer

Spulerei *f* spooling, winding (room)

Spülerei *f* rinsing plant

Spülfläche *f* flushing surface **Abschlußdamm der ~** retaining dike or level

Spülfluß *m* scavenger flow (jet)

Spülgas *n* cleansing or scavenging gas, flash gas **-schwelung** *f* carbonization involving gas recirculation, purging of distilled gas by rising gas

Spül-gebläse *n* scavenging (air) blower **-halle** *f* rinsing room **-haspel** *f* rinsing paddle **-kanal** *m* water course **-kasten** *m* toilet flush tank **-kastenschwimmer** *m* toilet tank float **-kippe** *f* railway car with chute for sluicing the soil from the car into the fill **-kopf** *m* swivel, flush joint **-kopfknie** *n* gooseneck **-leitung** *f* scavenging duct, rinsing line, washing pipe **-loch** *n* outlet

Spülluft *f* scavenging air **-eintritt** *m* inlet of scavenging air **-gebläse** *n* scavenging blower **-kanal** *m* scavenging air channel **-klappe** *f* scavenging air valve **-pumpe** *f* scavenging air pump

Spulmaschine *f* winding machine

Spül-motor *m* scavenger, scavenging engine **-öl** *n* flushing oil **-ölpumpe** *f* scavenge pump **-periode** *f* scavenging period **-probe** *f* ditch sample **-pumpe** *f* slush pump, scavenging pump, hydraulic pump **-rinne** (Entaschung) sluiceway **-rohr** *n* water-jet pipe

Spülrohrgestänge, hydraulisches ~ hydraulic-tubing rods

Spül-schappe *f* flushing auger or wimble **-schlamm** *m* mud-laden fluid **-schleuse** *f* flushing sluice, sluice gate

Spülschlitz *m* scavenging port **-öffnung** *f* opening of scavenging port **-reihe** *f* row of scavenging ports

Spül-schütze scour gate **-sonde** *f* wash point, penetrometer **-spaltfilter** *m* screen filter

Spulspindel *f* spool pin

Spül-stampfe *f* ram flushing **-stein** *m* sink **-teller** *m* rinsing device **-tisch** *m* rinsing table **-trommel** *f* rinsing drum

Spül- und Ladeperiode *f* scavenging and charging period

Spülung *f* circulation, flush cleaning, scavenging

Spülungschromatographie *f* elution chromatography

Spül-ventil *n* flushing gate, scavenging valve, scour valve **-verfahren** *n* water flush system, elutriation method **-verlust** *m* loss by circulation

Spülversatz *m* hydraulic packing, hydraulic stowing **-anlage** *f* stowing rinsing plant **-verfahren** *n* hydraulic packing method

Spulvorgang *m* winding process

Spülvorrichtung *f* water-jet installation

Spulwagenführung *f* bobbin rail

Spülwasser *n* wash water

Spulwinde *f* winch

Spülwirkungsgrad *m* scavenging efficiency

Spund *m* faucet, bung, plug, shutter, stopper **-apparat** *m* bunging apparatus

Spundbohle *f* sheet piling, sheet pile, bung board **~ mit Nut und Feder** twin sheet piles

Spund-bohlenwand *f* sheeting **-büchse** *f* cask bush

spunden to bung, dovetail, groove-and-tongue

Spund-futter *n* socket chuck **-hobel** *m* plow or match plane, grooving or tongue plane **-lappen** *m* bung flap **-loch** *n* bunghole **-maschine** *f* tonguing and grooving machine **-nagel** *m* plank nail **-pfahl** *m* grooved or plank pile **-putzapparat** *m* bung-cleaning apparatus

Spundung *f* bulkheading, tongue-and-groove joint, grooving, tonguing

Spundwand *f* sheet piling, bulkhead, cutoff wall, cutoff trench **hintere ~** enclosing sheet piling

Spundwand-abdichtung *f* sheet pile cut-off **-diaphragma** *n* sheet pile screen **-einfassung** *f* enclosed sheeting **-eisen** *n* sheet piling **-profile** *pl* steel sheet piling **-stahl** *m* steel-sheet piling

Spur *f* trace (radar); (Fährte) trail, track; (Abdruck) print; (Bahngeleise) gauge; (Rille) groove; (Radar) sweep; foundation hole, pass, scent, line of train, line of intersection between plane of flight and horizontal plane, alignment, vestige, gutter, channel **~ halten** to trace **~ verfolgen** to trace **vorionisierte ~** preionized track

Spürarbeit *f* tracer work

Spur-begrenzung *f* track edge **-breite** *f* track width **-eigenschaft** *f* track property

spuren to keep the ground or in the track, roll or follow run on the same track, concentrate (metals)

Spuren *n* shows, showings, traces

Spuren-band *n* channel tape **-element** *n* trace element

Spurengruppe *f*, **normale ~** normal band

Spuren-konzentration *f* trace concentration **-löschung** *f* background eradication **-sucher** *m* tracer (atom) **-untersuchung** *f* tracer study **-verunreinigung** *f* traces of impurity **-weise** in traces

Spur-erweiterung *f* amplification of gauge **-fahren** *n* track-following **-faktor** *m* tracking factor **-fehler** *m* track fault **-fühler** *m* gauge point

Spürgerät scanner

Spur-geschoß *n* tracer (bullet) **-halter** *m* tie rod **-hebel** *m* steering arm

Spurkranz *m* rim (face), tread (of a wheel), (wheel) flange **-laufrad** *n* gear wheel **-walze** *f* rim roll, tread roll

Spur-kugellager *n* circular ballbearing **-lager** *n* hemispherical-bearing support, pivot bearing, thrust bearing, (step) bearing **-latte** *f* footstep plate, guide rail, cage guide **-lehre** *f* track gauge, rail gauge template, standard gauge **-linie** *f* line of trail, the line of intersection between plane of flight and horizontal plane **-loch** *n* step (of a mast or beacon) **-lockerer** *m* track scraper **-los** without a trace **-maß** *n* width between rails, track gauge

Spürmittel *n* (Gas) gas-detection equipment

Spur-ofen *m* forehearth **-papier** *n* (gas-detection) testing paper **-planstellwerk** *n* track-diagrammatic pushbutton control system **-plantechnik** *f* geographical circuiting principle **-plättchen** *n* adjusting clip **-platte** *f* footstep, step, bearing socket, holster, guide plate or rail **-punkt** *m* track point, trace **-rad** *n* gauge wheel, spur gear **-richter** *m* gauge-setting device **-rille** *f* flange groove **-ring** *m* tracking ring

Spur-schlacke *f* concentration slag **-schuhe** *m pl* gauge shoes **-sicher** true to gauge **-stange** *f* track rod, gauge rod, crosstie, tie bar **-stangenhälfte** *f* tierod **-stangenhebel** *m* steering-knuckle arm **-stein** *m* concentrated matt (of fine metal), enriched or concentrated metal **-strahl** (Zwilling des Schreibstrahls) tracking beam (TV)

Spur-tafel *f* treadway **-teil** *m* cell size **-veränderung** *f* change of gauge **-verengung** *f* track-gauge narrowing or tightening **-verschiebungen** *f* track displacements **-verstellung** *f* track adjustment **-verteilung** *f* track pitch (tape rec.) **-verwaschung** *f* track noise **-verzerrung** *f* track(ing) distortion, tracking error **-vorrichtung** *f* tracking device

Spurweite *f* wheel track, wheel base, (track) gauge, face width **~ des Fahrgestells** wheel track, width of undercarriage **~ des Geleises** gauge of railway

Spur-winkel *m* track angle, trail angle **-zahnlager** *n* thrust bearing **-zapfen** *m* footstep, pivot journal, pivot, pin **-zapfenlager** *n* end-thrust bearing, thrust bearing, socket, pintle **-zwang** *m* self-alignment

S-Schlüssel *m* S-wrench, S-spanner

S-Stück *n* offset

S-Stütze *f* single S insulator spindle

St. Elmsfeuer *n* St. Elmo's fire, corona or brush discharge

Staats-abgabe *f* government tax **-angehöriger** *m* subject, citizen **-angehörigkeit** *f* nationality **-betrieb** *m* state service **-eigentum** *n* state property **-gespräch** *n* government call, government message

Staats- und Verwaltungsrecht *n* public and administrative law

Staats-verfassung *f* constitution **-zugehörigkeit** *f* nationality

Stab *m* bar, rod, stick, staff, slat, peg, stake, member, post, girder, headquarter's personnel **profilierter ~** profiled bar

Stab-anker *m* bar-wound armature **-anordnung** *f* rod assembly **-antenne** *f* rod antenna, stub aerial, whip antenna **-batterie** *f* torch battery **-bewehrung** *f* bar reinforcement **-biegevorrichtung** *f* bar bending device

Stäbchen-form *f* dumbell **-förmig** rod-shaped **-förmig** rod-shaped

Stab-dehnung *f* bar expansion or extension **-eck** *n* L-shaped bar, L-bar (iron) **-eindecker** *m* monoplane star model

Stabeisen *n* bar mill products, steel (iron) bar, bar iron **-bündelmaschine** *f* bar-iron bundling machine **-profil** *n* bar section **-schere** *f* bar cutter, rod cutter, bar (iron) shears **-straße** *f* bar-rolling train **-trio** *n* three-high bar mill **-verwindemaschine** *f* bar-iron twisting machine **-walzwerk** *n* bar-rolling mill

Stabfeder *f* bar spring **-indikator** *m* beam-spring indicator

Stab-filter *n* filter cartridge **-form** *f* bar shape **-förmig** bar-shaped, rod-shaped **-gitter** *n* rod lattice

stabil stable, firm, strong, rigid, sturdy, substantial, heavy, steady, rugged **-e Bahn** equilibrium orbit, stable orbit **-es Indikatorisotop** stable tracer isotope **-e Luft** stability, stable air **-er Regler** stable governor **-e Tragfläche** stable airfoil

Stabilier-anlage *f* stabilizer **-turm** *m* stabilizer tower

Stabilisationsanlage *f* stabilizer plant

Stabilisator *m* stabilizer, rod insulator, voltage stabilizing tube

stabilisieren to stabilize, steady, regularize, make constant, uniform, or normal

stabilisierend-er Innenbordschwimmer inboard stabilizing float **-e Rückführung** stabilizing feedback

Stabilisierstangendämpfer *m* stabiliser bar damper

stabilisiert-es Glas non browning glass **-e Produktion** settled production **-e Rückkopplung** *f* stabilized feedback

Stabilisierung *f* stabilization, steadying, stability **~ durch Rotation um die Längsachse** (Astron.) spin stabilization

Stabilisierungs-fläche *f* stabilizing surface **-flosse** *f* stabilizer (aviation), horizontal fin **-schaltung** *f* stabilizing circuit **-wulst** *m* stabilizer lobe (balloon)

Stabilität *f* stability, steadiness, rigidity

Stabilitäts-anteil *m* component of stability **-arm** *m* stability, lever **-ausschuß** *m* committee on ship stability **-bedingung** *f* stability condition **-beitrag** *m* component of stability **-belange** *pl* proceeding in the field of stability (of ships) **-berechnung** *f* calculation of stability **-betrachtung** *f* stability determination or investigation

Stabilitäts-diagramm *n* stability diagram **-gewicht** *n* balancing or stability weight **-grad** *m* degree of stability **-fläche** *f* acceptance area **-güte** *f* degree of stability **-hebelarm** *m* lever arm for recording stability curves of ships **-kriterium** *n* stability condition **-lehre** *f* theory of stability **-linie** *f* stability curve

Stabilitäts-maß *n* measure or degree of stability **-richtung** *f* directional stability **-schaubild** *n* stability diagram **-theorie** *f* theory of stability, theory of buckling **-untersuchung** *f* stability determination or investigation **-wert** *m* value or degree of stability

Stabistor *m* stabistor m

Stabilivolt *n* voltage-regulating valve, stabilivolt valve, voltage stabilizer

Stabisolator *m* rod insulator

Stab-kern *m* center of bar **-konstruktion** *f* bar construction

Stabkopf *m* test-bar head, rod eye **-probe** *f*

headed test piece

Stab-körper *m* main body or rule of a slide-rule **-kraft** *f* truss force, bar stress **-liniensystem** *n* line (flow) chart **-magnet** *m* (rod) bar magnet **-material** *n* bar stock, bar material, bars **-mikrophon** *n* carbon-stick microphone **-modell** *n* spar model **-mühle** *f* rod mill **-ordner** *m* bar-arranging device **-profil** *n* bar section or shape

Stabpunkt, beliebiger ~ any point of the member

Stab-querschnitt *m* cross section of a bar **-reflektor** *m* rod mirror **-riester** *m* rod-mold attachment **-röhre** *f* arcotron **-rost** *m* bar grate **-schere** *f* rod cutter, bar cutter **-seite** *f* side of the member **-sicherung** *f* cartridge fuse

Stabstahl *m* (round) bar steel, round bar, bars **-walzwerk** *n* small section rolling mill

Stab-steifigkeit *f* bar stiffness **-strahler** *m* vertical aerial, rod aerial **-straße** *f* bar-iron rolling train, merchant-mill train **-streichblech** *n* rod-mold attachment

Stab-trägheitsmoment *n* moment of inertia of the member **-walzwerk** *n* bar-rolling mill, bar mill **-werk** *n* frame with rigid joints **-wicklung** *f* bar winding **-zellen** *pl* cylindrical dry cells **-ziehen** *n* rod drawing **-zugverfahren** *n* graphical method (Müller-Breslau) for determining joint deflections in a truss **-zusammensetzmaschine** *f* rod assembling machine

Stachel *m* sharp point, thorn tongue, sting, spine, prong

Stacheldraht *m* barbed wire **-zaun** *m* low wire entanglement, barbed-wire fence

stachelig thorny

Stachel-länge *f* spike length **-rad** *n* sprocket wheel **-scheibe** *f* pin-pointed disk **-schraube** *f* pointed screw **-schwein** *n* cradle, porcupine rack, crate **-walzen** (Zackenwalzen) spiked rollers, rough rolls **-walzwerk** *n* toothed rolls

Stadel *f* stall, open rectangular kiln, open clamp, clamp **-röstung** *f* stall roasting

Stadien der Veredelung stages of finishing or of processing

Stadt-abgabe *f* town dues or tax **-bahn** *f* metropolitan railway, urban rapid transit system

Städte-bau *m* city planing **-entwurf** *m* town planning

Stadt-flughafen *m* municipal airport **-gas** *n* sewer gas **-gebiet** *n* urban area, city area

städtisch municipal, urban, urbane **-er Flughafen** municipal airport **-es Netz** (Elektrizität) town network **-e Wasserleitung** city water supply **-es Wasserleitungsnetz** municipal water main **-e Werke** municipal public works

Stadt-kanalisierung *f* town drainage **-kern** *m* (Innenstadt) town center, central district, down-town **-nebel** *m* town or urban fog **-plan** *m* town plan, city map **-planer** *m* city planner **-planung** *f* city planning **-randsiedlung** *f* suburban settlement **-rat** *m* city council, alderman **-teil** *m* section of a city or town, borough **-verkehr** *m* town driving, urban traffic

Stadtviertel *n* quarter (district) **-sprenger** *m* blockbuster

Stafette *f* messenger relay service, mounted messenger

Staffel *f* echelon, detachment, squadron (aviation), separate roll line (in rolling), line of bearing, wing, flight **motorisierte** ~ motorized rear-echelon service

Staffel-betrieb *m* echelon working **-bruch** *m* step faults

Staffelei *f* easel

Staffel-flug *m* positive stagger, staggered flight **-form** *f* squadron formation (aviation) **-förmig** echeloned **-gebühr** *f* graduated rate **-gegensprechen** *n* echelon duplexing **-keil** *m* squad wedge (aviation), V-formation of a flight **-kolonne** *f* squad column (aviation) **-leitung** *f* echelon circuit, series circuit

staffeln to stagger, grade, arrange in lines, rise by steps, separate (aviat)

Staffeln *n* staggering, grading ~ **von Gruppen** staggering of groups

Staffel-schutz *m* stepped protection **-summen** *pl* progressive totals **-tarif** *m* differential tariff, graduated tariff, diminishing tariff **-telegraph** *m* series-multiplex telegraph

Staffelung *f* progressive rate, grading, echelonment (of guns), separation (aviat) ~ **der Flächen** stagger (of wings) ~ **nach hinten** negative stagger ~ **nach vorne** positive stagger **rückwärts und vorwärts** ~ positive and negative stagger

Staffelungs-plan *m* grading scheme **-tafel** *f* echelon table **-winkel** *m* stagger angle

Staffel-walze *f* stepped drum **-wettbewerb** *m* team competition

staffieren to trim, fit out, decorate

Stag *m* stay, brace, support

stagnierend stagnant **-es Gewässer** stagnant water

Stahl *m* medium- (or high-)carbon steel, steel ~ **zum Abdrehen der Krusten** scaling tool ~ **zum Abstechen der Kruste** scaling tool ~ **zum Abdrehen von Spitzen** tool for turning up centers **im letzten Augenblick in der Blockform beruhigter** ~ steel quieted in the last moment in the ingot mold (metal.) ~ **zum Aushobeln scharfer Ecken** tool for finishing in corners ~ **mit hoher Festigkeit** high-grade steel ~ **für schräge Flächen** bevel tool ~ **mit hohem** (niedrigem) **Kohlengehalt** high- (low-)carbon steel ~ **mit niederem Kohlenstoffgehalt** low-carbon steel ~ **mit mittlerem Kohlenstoffgehalt** medium carbon steel ~ **mit Kupferbeimengung** *f* copper-bearing steel ~ **besonderer Zusammensetzung** special-analysis steel

Stahl, austenitischer ~ austenitic steel **beruhigter** ~ killed steel **beunruhigter** ~ wild steel **gehärteter** ~ hardened steel **halbberuhigter** ~ semikilled steel **hitzebeständiger** ~ heat-resistant steel **korrosionsbeständiger** ~ stainless steel **kupferhaltiger** ~ copper(ed) steel **legierter** ~ alloy steel **lufthärtender** ~ air-quenched steel, air-hardening steel, self-hardening steel

Stahl, nichtrostender ~ stainless steel **niedriggekohlter** ~ dead soft steel, low-carbon steel **niedriglegierter** ~ alloy-treated steel **polierter** ~ polished steel **rechtseitiger** ~ right-hand (steel) tool **rostfreier** ~ stainless steel **rostbeständiger** ~ rustless steel, noncorroding steel **rostsicherer** ~ stainless steel **ruhiger** ~ killed steel, quick steel **schweißbarer** ~ welding steel

Stahl, übergarer ~ overblown steel **überhitzter** ~ overheated steel **übereutektoider** ~ hypereutectoid steel **unberuhigter ~** rimming or rimmed steel **unlegierter ~** unalloyed steel, plain steel, carbon steel **unmagnetischer ~** nonmagnetic steel **verbrannter ~** burnt steel **warmfester ~** steel with high-temperature characteristic **weicher ~** mild steel, soft steel **witterungsbeständiger ~** rustless steel **wolframlegierter ~** tungsten alloyed steel, tungsten steel

Stahl-abfall *m* steel scrap, waste steel **-abschirmung** *f* steel shield **-ähnlich** steel-like

Stahlaluminiumfreileitungsseil *n* steel-reinforced aluminum cable

Stahl-anker *m* steel tie rod **-anordnung** *f* tooling, tooling lay-out **-arm** *m* steel rod **-artig** steely **-auflageuntersatz** *m* tool rest holder **-backe** *f* steel cheek

Stahlband *n* steel strip or band, steel collar, steel strap, steel hoop **-armiert, -bewehrt** steel-tape armored, ribbon-wrapped **-aufnahme** *f* magnetic steel-tape recording **-förderer** *m* steel-belt conveyer **-maß** *n* flexible steel tape **-umreifung** *f* tensional steel strapping

Stahlbau *m* steel construction **-teile** *pl* steel parts

Stahl-bauten *pl* steel frame structures **-begleiter** *pl* minute steel impurities **-bereitung** *f* steelmaking **-beton** *m* steel concrete **-betonfertigteil** *m* pre-cast reinforced concrete (structural) unit **-blau** steel-blue

Stahlblech *n* steel plate, sheet steel, sheet iron **-auskleidung** *f* steel plate lining **-bahn** *f* steel sheet

Stahl-blende *f* steel loophole cover plate **-block** *m* steel ingot, bloom

Stahlbolzen *m* steel pin, steel bolt **-kette** *f* bolted steel chain, riveted drive chain, riveted mill chain

Stahl-borste *f* steel bristle **-bronze** *f* steel bronze **-büchsenkette** *f* steel-bushed chain **-deul** *m* puddled-steel ball

Stahldraht *m* steel wire, wire, steel cable **-aufnahme** *f* sound on wire-recording system **-beklöppelung** *f* steel wire armor **-geflecht** *n* steel mesh, meshwork, grid **-seil** *n* flexible-steel cable, steel-wire rope

Stahl-dübel *m* steel dowel **-einsatz** *m* steel lining **-einschlagstempel** *m* steel stamping letters and figures **-einstellen** *n* setting tools **-einstellehre** *f* tool setting gauge **-eisen** *n* steel pig, steely iron

stählen to steel, point with steel

stählern (made of) steel, like steel

Stahl-erz *n* steel ore, siderite **-erzeuger** *m* steelmaker **-erzeugung** *f*, **-fabrikation** *f* steel production, steel manufacture **-farbig** steel-colored

Stahlfeder *f* steel spring, pen point, steel pen **-fahrgestell** *n* steel-spring landing gear **-indikator** *m* steel-spring indicator **-ring** *m* lockwasher

Stahl-flasche *f* steel cylinder **-formgießerei** *f* steel-casting foundry, steel-castings plant

Stahlformguß *m* cast steel, steel casting **-erzeugung** *f* steel-casting production **-stück** *n* steel casting

Stahl-frischfeuer *n* steel refinery **-futter** *n* steel lining **-gattung** *f* steel grade **-gefäß** *n* steel vessel **-gewinnungsverfahren** *n* steelmaking process **-gießer** *m* steel founder **-gießerei** *f* steel-casting foundry, steel foundry, steelworks, steel-melting plant **-gießpfanne** *f* steel ladle **-gittermast** *m* lattice tower **-gliederband** *m* steel-plate apron conveyor **-grau** steel-gray **-griffel** *m* scriber **-guß** *m* cast steel, steel castings, cast-steel products

Stahlgußform *f* steel mold **gebrannte ~** dry steel mold

Stahlguß-gehäuse *n* cast-steel crankcase **-knagge** *f* steel dog **-reduzierschäkel** cast-steel reducing shackles **-trommel** *f* cast-steel drum **-walze** *f* cast-steel roll

Stahlgüte *f* steel grade, steel quality

Stahlhalter *m* tool binder, tool holder, tollhead, tool post, cutter holder **schwenkbarer ~** swiveling toolholder

Stahlhalter-schlitten *m* tool slide **-support** *m* tool slide

Stahl-hammer *m* steel hammer, steel forge **-hart** as hard as steel **-härte** *f* hardness of steel **-härtung** *f* hardening of steel **-helm** *m* steel helmet **-herstellung** *f* steelmaking, manufacture of steel **-hochbau** *m* steel skeleton for multi storied buildings **-hohlwelle** *f* steel quill, hollow steel shaft **-holm** *m* steel spar **-hütte** *f* steelworks **-kabel** *n* steel cable **-keile** *pl* steel keys

Stahlkern *m* steel core

Stahl-kette *f* steel chain **-kiesstrahl** *m* steel-shot blasting **-klammer** *f* steel-wire clip **-knüppel** *m* billet, steel **-kobalt** *m* smaltite **-kohlen** *n* conversion of iron into steel by carbonization **-klaue** *f* tool block **-kolben** *m* steel impeller **-konstruktion** *f* structural steel **-korn** *m* steel short or grit **-krone** *f* steel bit

Stahlkugel *f* steel ball or bullet **-blasen** *n* steel-shot blasting **-spitze** *f* steel-ball penetrator

Stahl-lamelle *f* laminated steel **-lamellenkupplung** *f* multiple-disk steel clutch **-laufbuchse** *f* cylinder barrel **-legierung** *f* steel alloy **-luppe** *f* steel ball **-mahlkörper** *pl* steel grinding bodies **-mantel** *m* steel jacket **-marke** *f* brand of steel **-mast** *m* iron tower

Stahl-meßband *n* steel measuring tape **-muffenrohre** *pl* steel socket pipes **-mühle** *f* flint mill **-niet** *n* steel rivet **-ofen** *m* steel furnace **-panzerrohr** *n* steel-armored conduit, steel conduit **-perle** *f* steel bead **-pfahl** *m* steel piling **-pfanne** *f* steel ladle **-pflug** *m* steel plow

Stahl-platte *f* steel plate **-plattenpanzer** *m* steel plate liner **-plattenpanzerung** *f* steel plate lining **-probe** *f* steel test, steel sample **-profil** *n* steel section **-puddeln** *n* steel puddling **-punktschweißverbindung** *f* steel spotweld **-quelle** *f* chalybeate spring **-rahmen** *m* steel frame **-rakel** *n* steel doctor **-ring** *f* steel ring **-ritzel** *n* steel pinion **-roheisen** *n* open-hearth pig iron

Stahlrohr *n* steel tubing, steel tube **nahtloses ~** seamless steel tube

Stahlröhrenrumpf *m* steel-tube fuselage

Stahlrohrgerüst *n* steel-tube fuselage **rumpfgeschweißtes ~** welded steel-tube fuselage

Stahlrohr-gestell *n* tubular steel frame **-konstruktion** *f* tubular steel structure **-leitung** *f* tubing **-mast** *m* wrought-steel pole, tubular-steel mast or pole **-rumpf** *m* fuselage of steel-tubing framework **-ständer** *m* tubular-steel pole or stand **-triebwerksgerüst** *n* steel-tube engine mounting

Stahlrolle, gehärtete ~ hard-steel roller

Stahlronde *f* steel blank

Stahl-rückdrücke *pl* high back thrusts, thrusts to the cutting tool **-rückzugeinrichtung** *f* tool withdrawal mechanism, tool back-out attachments

Stahlschale *f* metal form **zerlegbare ~** knock-down metal form

Stahl-schalungen *pl* steel shuttering material **-schiene** *f* steel rail **-schienenmatrize** *f* steel rule die **-schnecke** *f* steel worm **-schneide** *f* steel cutting edge **-schneidschuh** *m* steel casing shoe **-schmelzen** *n* steel melting, steel making **-schmelzofen** *m* steelmaking furnace, steel-melting furnace **-schmelzprozeß** *m* steel-melting process

Stahl-schrot *m* steel shot **-schrott** *m* steel scrap **-schwelle** *f* steel tie **-seele** *f* steel core **-seil** *n* steel wire, steel cable or line **-sorte** *f* steel grade **-späne** *pl* steel wool, steel cuttings or turnings **-spannlasche** *f* toolholding strap

Stahlspitze *f* steel tip **mit einer ~ versehen** steel-tipped, to steel-tip

Stahl-spundbohle *f* steel sheet pile **-spundwand mit Schloßverbindung** interlocking steel sheeting

Stahlstab *m* steel bar

Stahlstäbchen zur Blitzstrommessung surge current indicator

Stahl-stange *f* steel bar **-startbahn** *f* pierced steel plank **-stechen** *n* steel engraving **-steckröhren** *pl* plug-in steel conduits **-steg** *m* steel bar **-stein** *m* siderite **-stellung beim Profilieren** position of tool during form dressing **-stempel** *m* steel prop, steel punch

Stahlstich *m* die-stamping **-prägedruck** *m* steel-plate-engraving relief printing

Stahl-stift *m* steel pin **-strahlerei** *f* steel-blasting shop

Stahlstützschale *f*, **Lager mit ~** steel-backed bearing

Stahl-teller *m* steel plate **-träger** *m* steel girder

Stahltraverse *f*, **rostfreie ~** cross beam (of stainless steel)

Stahltrosse *f* steel hawser, wire rope

Stahlturm, freitragender ~ self-supporting steel tower

Stahlwechseldrehbank *f* universal lathe

Stahlwendel *f* steel spiral

Stahl-welle *f* shaft **-werk** *n* steelworks, steel plant, steel mill **-werker** *m* steel founder, steelmaker, steelworker

Stahlwerks-anlage *f* steelmaking plant **-betrieb** *m* steelworks practice, steelmaking plant **-gießhalle** *f* casting bay **-halle** *f* steelmaking shop **-verschleißmaterial** *n* casting-pit refractories

Stahl-werkzeug *n* steel tool **-winde** *f* steel winch **-winkel** *m* steel square **-wolle** *f* steel wool **-zahnrad** *n* steel gear **-zunge** *f* steel reed **-zylinder** *m* steel cylinder

Stake *f* groin, stake

Staken *m* grappling hook

Staket *n* palisade, stockade, paling railing

Stakudraht *m* copper-sheated steel core wire

Stalagmit *n* stalagmite

Stalagmometer *n* stactometer

Stalaktit *m* stalactite

Stall *m* stable, stall **-düngerstreuer** *m* manure spreader **-halfter** *m* halter, headstall **-leine** *f* picket line, stable halter

Stalloy stalloy

Stamm *m* tribe, trunk, stem, stalk, cadre, phylum **-aktie** *f* ordinary share **-ätze** *f* stock discharge paste **-baum** *m* flow sheet, system of ore dressing, genealogical tree **-(baum)werk** *n* parent plant **-emulsion** *f* stock emulsion

stammen aus to originate at, descend from, derive from

Stammende *n* butt (end) **zubereitetes ~** treated butt

Stammergrad *m* Stammer degree

Stamm-farbe *f* primary color **-flotte** *f* stock liquor or solution **-funktion** *f* stem or system function **-gleichung** *f* Heaviside function (teleph.), stem equation, characteristic equation **-holz** *n* stem wood, heartwood, trunk wood

stämmig robust

Stamm-kabel *n* main cable **-körper** *m* parent substance, parent body **-kreis** *m* side circuit, physical circuit, combining circuit, transformer circuit, component line, trunk line **-küpenansatz** *m* preparation of a stock vat **-leitung** *f* mains, main pipes, side circuit, main circuit, trunk line, physical line **-leitungsbau** *m* trunk-line construction **-linie** *f* trunk or main line **-liste** *f* list of components **-lösung** *f* stock solution

Stamm-patent *n* parent patent **-personal** *n* cadre, permanent staff **-pupinspule** *f* side circuit loading coil **-reserve** *f* stock resist **-rolle** *f* personnel roster, unit nominal roll or register **-spule** *f* side-circuit (loading) coil **-tafel** *f* flow sheet **-tide** *f* main tide **-uhr** *f* master clock

Stampf-anlage *f* stamping-machine plant **-appretur** *f* beetle finish (beetling) **-asphalt** *m* compressed asphalt **-auskleidung** *f* rammed lining **-beton** *m* a dry mix of concrete requiring tamping **-bewegung** *f* pitching, pitching motion **-boden** *m* tamped bottom or floor

Stampfe *f* stamp, rammer, pestle, punch, ram

stampfen to stamp, ram, pound, pave, tamp, bank (of a hearth bottom), pitch (ship), consolidate

Stampfen *n* ramming, tamping, pounding, banking, packing, porpoising

Stampfer *m* tamper, ram(mer), stamper, beater, tamping iron **kannelierter ~** channeled punch

Stampf-fuß *m* rammer foot **-futter** *n* tamped lining **-hammer** *m* bumping hammer **-herd** *m* rammed bottom lining **-holz** *n* tamping bar **-kalander** *m* beating mill, beetling mill or engine **-klotz** *m* pile driver, ram

Stampf-maschine *f* ramming machine, tamping machine **-masse** *f* ramming mass, stamping mass, tamping clay **-massenauskleidung** *f* plastic refractory **-moment** *n* pitching moment **-platte** *f* crushing plate **-schicht** *f* rammed layer **-volumen** *n* (von Pigmenten) settling volume **-walke** *f* hammer fulling mill **-walzen** *pl* tamping rollers **-werk** *n* stamp or stamping mill, pounding machine **-werkzeug** *n* ramming tool **-winkel** *m* pitching angle (of ship) **-wirkung** *f* ramming effect

Stand *m* state, stand, condition, profession, level, stage, status, position, rank, phase, booth (at exposition), emplacement **in ~ setzen** to repair, enable ~ **des Zeigers** position of the pointer **nach dem heutigen** ~ up-to-date

Stand-anzeige *f* deadbeat indication or reading **-anzeiger** *m* level indicator, bearing-indicator means

Standard-band *n* standard tape **-element** *n* standard cell **-fehlerberechnung** *f* calculation of standard errors **-frequenzanlage** *f* standard frequency plant **-inventar** *n* standard equipment

Standardkabel *n* standard cable **Meile** ~ mile of standard cable

Standard-kabeläquivalent *n* standard-cable equivalant **-kapazität** *f* standard capacitor **-luftspule** *f* standard air coil **-meßgenerator** *m* standard signal generator

Standard- oder Normteil *m* common item

Standard-radiohorizontabstand *m* standard radio horizon distance **-sonderzubehör** *m* standard extra equipment **-strahlungsmeßgerät** *n* standard radiation measuring **-zusatzausrüstungen** *pl* standard equipments

Standarte *f* standard, lens carrier, baseboard

Standbahn mit Bodenentladern rail with bottom-discharge tubs

Stand-bild *n* still-film picture, inanimate picture **-bohrmaschine** *f* power drill **-bolzen** *m* stay bolt **-bücherei** *f* reference library **-entwicklung** *f* tank development (phot.)

Ständer *m* stud, post, frame, basis, bracket, stand, stator, support, pole, upright, stage, vertical girder, column, pillar, tripod, pedestal, holder, housing, bearing, pendant, pennant **-anlasser** *m* slow motion starter **-bauart** *f* floor type **-bohrmaschine** *f* column-type drilling machine **-fachwerk** *n* vertical or upright trussing **-feld** *f* stator field **-fenster** *n* housing window **-fernsprecher** *m* pedestal (desk) telephone station **-führungsfläche** *f* housing slide **-fußschraube** *f* setscrew of support **-gerüst** *n* bearers, housing frames, standards

ständergespeister Mehrphasen-Nebenschlußmotor doubly-fed polyphase shunt commutator motor

Ständer-gewindeschneidmaschine *f* upright screw cutting machine **-gleitfläche** *f* bearing on column **-holm** *m* housing post **-kettenfräsmaschine** *f* pedestal chain mortiser **-kopf** *m* housing cap **-körper** *m* inductor alternator spider, armature spider **-kran** *m* turnstile crane

Ständer-pfosten *m* housing column or upright **-rollen** *pl* breast rollers **-säule** *f* post, pillar **-support** *m* side head **-tor** *n* balanced gate **-wicklung** *f* stator winding

standfest stable, firm, strong, rigid, sturdy, substantial, heavy, steady **-es Stativ** crowfoot

Standfestigkeit *f* stability, rigidity, creep strength, steadiness. solidity ~ **der Werkzeugschneide** duration of tool edge

Standfestigkeitsgrenze *f* creep limit **-prüfung** *f* (long-time) creep test

Stand-fläche *f* base **-gefäß** *n* thickwalled beaker, stock tub, storage vessel **-gehäuse** *n* console **-geld** *n* demurrage **-gestellrahmen** *m* floor-type relay rack

Standglas *n* gauge glass, level gauge, measuring cylinder or glass **-kappe** *f* gauge head

Stand-gütegrad *m* static rating **-haft** steady, constant, firm, stable **-haftigkeit** *f* steadiness **-halten** to resist, withstand **-holm** *m* base support (missiles)

ständig settled, fixed, constant, stationary, continual, available, permanent, steady **-e Belastung** permanent load **-er Fluß** steady flow **-e Last** dead load **-e Stellung** permanent position

Standkasten *m* dust catcher, vertical scrubber **-überlauf** *m* weir box

Stand-kühler *m* upright or vertical radiator **-lehre** *f* statics **-licht** *n* parking light **-linie** *f* (radio) base line, datum line; (Nav.) line of position (LOP)

Standlinien-kammer *f* stereocamera **-peilung** *f* position-line bearing, great-circle bearing **-rechenschieber** *m* position line or reference slide rule **-richtung** *f* direction of the position line **-schlitten** *m* transversal, base carriage **-verfahren** *n* base-line method of measurement

Standmagnetzünder *m* stationary magneto

Standmesser *m* gauge glass **-hahn** *m* gauge cock

Stand-motor *m* stationary engine **-öl** *n* stand oil

Standort *m* position, stand, radio fix, camera station **gekoppelter** ~ position according to dead reckoning

Standort-bestimmung *f* position or location finding, great-circle bearing, position-line bearing **-daten** *n pl* positional information **-fehler** *m* site error **-fehleranfälligkeit** *f* site-error susceptibility **-peilung** *f* location finding, position finding or fixing

Standortszielanzeiger *m* target-position indicator

Standort-umgebungsfehler inter-site error **-verschiebung** *f* relocation

Stand-pfahl *m* point bearing pile **-prüfung** *f* torque-stand or static test

Standpunkt *m* point of view, standard, aspect, attitude ~ (Erdbildaufnahme) camera station (ground survey) **fester** ~ foothold

Standpunktslehre *f* theory of relativity

Standregelung *f* level control device

Standrohr *n* standpipe, vertical pipe, gauge pipe, conductor string, pipe riser, siphon **-spiegellinie** *f* hydraulic grade line **-ventil** *n* stand-pipe valve

Stand-säule *f* standard (upright) **-scheibenmesser** *m* orifice meter **-schraublehre** *f* bench micrometer

Standschub *m* hovering propulsion, static thrust **-messung** *f* static thrust test

Stand-schwingungsversuch *m* static vibration test **-sicher** stable, rigid

Standsicherheit *f* stability, rigidity, steadiness (to shock and vibration) ~ **gegen Drehen** stability against overturning, resistance to sliding ~ **gegen Umkippen** stability against tilting

Stand-ventil *n* retaining valve **-verbesserung** *f* correction of the barometric reading **-verbindung** *f* point-to-point circuit **-verlust** *m* storage loss **-versuch** *m* stationary or static test, creep-test **-visier** *n* fixed sight **-zeit** *f* (Maschine) service life, edge life (tool), (tool) life **-ziel** *n* fixed or permanent target

Stange *f* pole; (Pfahl) stake; (Metall~) rod, bar; (Pfosten) post; stem, shank, stick, perch, spear, hook, picket ~ **zur Abstellung** swinging gripper cutout bar ~ **mit Anker** guyed pole ~ **zum Bogenstreicher** bar for sheet steadier ~ **mit Ein-**

stellungen dividing rod ~ **mit zubereitetem Ende** butt-treated pole ~ **mit Gewinde zu zwei Enden** rod threaded at both ends ~ **mit Strebe** strutted pole ~ **für Versatzhebel** crank for racklever ~ **mit Verspannung** truss-guyed pole **eine** ~ **anschuhen** to shoe a pole **eine** ~ **ausrichten** to straighten a pole **bei der** ~ **bleiben** to persevere **eine** ~ **setzen** to set or erect a pole

Stange, angeschuhte ~ shoed pole, pole with socle **geteerte** ~ tarred or creosoted pole **getränkte** ~ treated pole **mittelstarke** ~ medium pole **rohe** ~ plain pole, untreated pole **starke** ~ stout pole **unzubereitete** ~ untreated pole, plain pole **verankerte** ~ stayed pole, pole and stay **verstrebte** ~ strutted pole **zubereitete** ~ treated pole

Stangen-abdachung *f* pole roofing **-abnützung** *f* bar wear **-abstand** *m* pole distance **-anspitzmaschine** *f* sharpening machine for bars **-arbeit** *f* bar work **-artig** rod-shaped **-aufsatz** *m* sight bar, tangent sight **-ausrüstung** *f* pole fittings **-automat** *n* automatic bar machine

Stangen-bau *m* wire laying on poles **-bild** *n* pole diagram, pole-location chart **-blei** *n* bar lead **-blitzableiter** *m* pole lightning arrester, lightning rod **-bock** *m* pole trestle **-bohrer** *m* great auger, long-eye auger **-bohrung** *f* pole drill **-drehachse** *f* bar pivot axis **-eisen** *n* bar, rod iron

Stangenende *n* pole butt **zubereitetes** ~ treated butt **mit zubereitetem** ~ butt-treated

Stangen-erdleitung *f* earth wire for poles **-feder** *f* rod spring **-flügel** *m* current meter held in position by means of a rod **-fuß** *m* pole socket, pole pedestal, pole footing, end of pole **-gebiß** *n* curb-bit set **-gold** *n* ingot gold **-halter** *m* outer stock support **-holz** *n* pole timber

Stangen-kali *n* stick potash **-kappe** *f* saddle of pole **-kohle** *f* columnar coal **-kopf** *m* connecting piece, stub head **-kupfer** *n* bar or rod copper

Stangenlager *n* bar store, storeyard **-platz** *m* pole store

Stangenleiter peg ladder

Stangenlinie *f* pole line **an einer** ~ **geführt** carried on a pole line

Stangenloch *n* post hole, pole hole **-bohrmaschine** *f* post-hole drilling machine

Stangen-lötzinn *m* bar solder **-maschine** *f* lathe for bar work

Stangenmaterial *m* rod stock **vergütetes** ~ heat-treated bar

Stangen- oder Universalzirkel trammels or universal dividers

Stangen-packung *f* rod packing **-pferd** *n* wheel horse **-presse** *f* metal press for making round bars, extrusion press **-pressen** *n* extrusion process **-ratschenvorschub** *m* ratched bar feed **-reibahle** *f* shell end reamer **-reibhammer** *m* board drop hammer **-rest** *m* bar remnant **-revolverdrehbank** *f* bar turret lathe **-rost** *m* plane grate **-rundrichtmaschine** *f* rod straightening machine

Stangen-schälmesser *pl* bar stripping knives **-schneidmaschine** *f* rod cutter **-schloß** *n* sleeve nut **-schlüssel** *m* pole wrench **-schrämmaschine** *f* bar coal cutter **-schranke** *f* barrier with a rod **-schuh** *m* pole shoe, chair (of a roof pole) **-schwefel** *m* roll sulfur **-schwimmer** *m* staff or pole float

Stangen-seezeichen *n* mark post, nautical sign on pole or post **-silber** *n* ingot silver **-spannfutter** *n* rod chuck **-spitze** *f* pole top end **-spitzmaschine** *f* bar-chamfering machine **-stahl** *m* bar or rod steel **-statistik** *f* poles statistics (elec.) **-steckschlüssel** *m* socket wrench **-stein** *m* pycnite **-steuerung** *f* rod control **-stuhl** *m* pole clamp **-triebwerk** *n* rack gear, rack and pinion

Stangen-untersuchungskasten *m* pole test box **-verbindung** *f* rod joint **-verschleiß** *m* bar wear **-verstärkung** *f* pole reinforcement **-visier** *n* tangent sight, bar sight **-visiereinrichtung** *f* tangent sighting mechanism **-vollautomat** *m* full automatic bar machine **-vorschub** *m* feed (rod), bar feed **-wachs** *m* stick polish **-wähler** *m* panel switch, panel-type selector

Stangen-ziehbank *f* rod drawing bench **-zinn** *n* bar tin **-zirkel** *m* beam compass, (beam) trammel **-zubereitung** *f* preparation of poles **-zuführung** *f* rod feeding attachment **-zug** *m* drawing bars, rods, string of poles

Stannat (zinnsaures Salz) stannate

Stanni-chlorid *n* stannic chloride **-chlorwasserstoffsäure** *f* chlorostannic acid **-hydroxid** *n* stannic hydroxide **-jodid** *n* stannic iodide

Stanniol *n* tin foil **-papier** *n* tin-foil paper **-streifen** *m* tin foil, window (radar) **-überzug** *m* tin-foil covering, sheathing

Stanni-oxalat *n* stannic oxalate **-salz** *n* stannic salt **-verbindung** *f* stannic compound

Stanno-chlorid *n* stannous chloride **-chlorwasserstoffsäure** *f* chlorostannous acid **-jodid** *n* stannous iodide **-oxyd** *n* stannous oxide **-salz** *n* stannous salt **-sulfid** *n* stannous sulfide **-verbindung** *f* stannous compound

Stanz-abfälle *pl* punchings, stampings, trimmings **-automat** *m* automatic punching machine **-beamtin** *f* perforator operator **-blech** *n* sheet steel with good punching properties **-block** *m* die block, punch block **-bügel** *m* punch bail **-dorn** *m* mandrel **-draht** *m* punching wire

Stanze *f* punch, die, stamping, punching, stamp, swage ~ **und Ausklinkmaschine für I-Träger** I-beam punch and cooper

Stanz-einrichtung *f* punching device **-eisen** *n* punch

stanzen to punch, stamp, blank, perforate **nochmals** ~ to repunch

Stanzen *n* die cutting (printing), punching, stamping, pressing **blindes** ~ touch typewriting

Stanzer *m* perforator

Stanzereitechnik *f* press working of metals

Stanz-form *f* matrix, mold **-fuge** *f* fin **-hebel** *m* punch lever **-kante** *f* punched side **-leistung** *f* punching capacity **-loch** *n* signal hole **-magnet** *m* punch(ing) magnet **-maschine** *f* punch press, stamping machine **-matrize** *f* stamping die, punching tool, (cutting) die plate **-messer** *n* punch knives, stamping gauge

Stanz-pappe *f* friction board **-presse** *f* beam cutter, punch press, stamping press, punch **-relais** *n* punching relay **-rohr** *n* sample-taking cylinder **-schere** *f* punching shear

Stanz-stahl *m* punching or blanking tool steel **-stelle** (für Lochstreifen) perforating (poking) section **-stempel** *m* punch, die **-streifen** *m* chad tape **-stück** *n* stamping, blank **-teil** *m* stamped metal part **-verfahren** *n* stamping method, punching method **-vorrichtung** *f* punching apparatus **-werkzeug** *n* punching tool, blanking tool, stamping tool, cutting tool, blanking dies

Stapel *m* pile, heap, staple, warehouse, file, stack **vom ~** (laufen) **lassen** to launch **auf ~ liegen** lying in drydock, shored up, in yard during construction

Stapel-ablage *f* pile delivery **-artikel** *m* standard or staple goods **-ausleger** *m* pile delivery **-blöcke** *pl* ways (shipbuilding) **-brett** *n* pallet

Stapeler *m* stacker

Stapel-faser *f* rayon fiber (processed to imitate wool or cotton), staple fiber **-fehler** *m* stacking fault **-förderer** *m* staple conveyor **-glasseide** *f* copped strands **-gleichrichter** *m* metallic rectifier stack **-holz** *n* store timber **-klotz** *m* keel block **-kran** *m* stacking crane **-lauf** *m* launching ceremony

Stapel-nuance *f* standard shade **-operator** *m* stacking operator **-platte** *f* pallet **-platz** *m* dump, depot, stockyard **-schacht** *m* blind pit **-stütze** *f* shore, prop **-tisch** *m* feed pile board

Stapelung *f* storing

Stapel-vorrichtung *f* piler, stacker **-wagen** *m* stacking truck **-werk** *n* stacker

stark strong; (mächtig) mighty; (Maschine) powerful; (heftig) violent; (starker Motor) high powered engine; (~ übertrieben) grossly exaggerated; robust, vigorous, high-powered, brisk, rigid, solid, heavy, durable, thick, large, marked, intense, voluminous, sturdy, fat, loud, hard, keen, wide, great, sharp, considerable **~ belastet** heavily loaded, highly loaded **~ beansprucht** exposed to stress **~ bewehrt** heavily armored **~ gebaut** rigid(ly built) **~ geleimt** (Papier) hard-sized **~ satiniert** (Papier) super-calendered **~ wirkend** efficaceous **~ halbiertes Roheisen** mottled pig iron **-er Motor** high-powered engine **-er Sturm** gale **-er Verkehr** heavy traffic **-er Wind** strong wind, high wind

Stark-brennen *n* hardening-on **-dimensioniert** amply dimensioned **-drähtig** of heavy gauge wire

Stärke *f* strength, force, power; (Technik, Leistung) stoutness; (Chem.) concentration, intensity, starch; (Tatkraft) vigour, energy; stress, violence, thickness, gauge, diameter **~ des Blattes** strength of shell or leaf **~ der Doppelbrechung** degree of double refraction **~ der lotrechten Komponente** vertical intensity **~ der Schweißnaht** throat **~ der Blechlehre** thickness of sheet gauge **~ der Stöße** intensity of chocks **~ des Tones** volume (tone intensity)

Stärke-abbau *m* peptonization **-abnahme** (Walzwerk) drafting **-begrenzer** *m* automatic noise limiter **-bestand** *m* actual strength **-glanz** *m* starching clay, brilliant starch **-grad** *m* intensity, degree of strength or of concentration **-haltig** starchy

Stärke-kalander *m* stiffening calender **-klasse** *f* diameter class, strength group **-kleister** *m* starch paste **-lösung** *f* starch solution **-maschine** *f* back filling mangle **-messung** *f* calibration

stärken to strengthen, invigorate, starch **die Kette ~** to size the warp

Stärkenabmessung *f* gauge number

Stärkenachweis *m* statement of actual strength

Stärkeregler *m* volume control

Stärkeregelung *f*, **zeitabhängige ~** suppression control

Stärkerklappe *f* choke, arrester

Stärkerumpf *m* strength hull

Stärkeverhältnis *n* strength relation **~ der Kanäle** ratio between the channels

Stärke-zucker *m* (dextro) glucose **-zunahme** *f* gain of strength

stark-farbig strongly or highly colored **-motorig** hight-powered **-holz** *n* heavy timber

starkspiraliger Hochleistungsfräser high-duty milling cutters

Starkstrom *m* heavy current, high-tension current, strong current, high-voltage current, power current **-anlage** *f* power plant **-dehnungskabel** *pl* extensible power cables **-geräusch** *n* power-induction or -induced noise **-kabel** *n* power cable **-kreuzung** *f* power-line crossing **-leitung** *f* power (transmission) line, power circuit **-mikrophon** *n* high-power transmitter

Starkstrom-netz *n* power-supply system, mains **-sperre** *f* high-voltage obstacle **-stecker** *m* mains connecting plug, high-voltage plug **-störung** *f* power failure, interference from power systems **-technik** *f* heavy-current engineering, power engineering **-wecker** *m* power bell **-zaun** *m* high-voltage fence **-zuführung** *f* power lead

Starkton-glocke *f* high-volume bell **-summer** *m* loud note buzzer

Stärkung *f* strengthening, invigoration

stark-wandig thick-walled **-wirkend** powerful

Starrachse *f* rigid axle

starr rigid, inflexible, stiff, fixed, inelastic, nonyielding **~ aufgebaut** rigidly mounted **-e Aufhängung** rigid suspension **-e Bewegung** rigid motion **-e Grundlage** rigid foundation **-er Körper** rigid body **-e Körperverschiebung** rigid-body displacement **-es Lot** centering rod, rigid plumb **~ plastische Näherung** rigid-plastic approximation

Starrfott mit hohem Tropfpunkt solid lubricant with high dropping point

Starrheit *f* rigidity, stiffness

Starrheitsmodul *m* modulus of rigidity

Starrkoppeln *n* rigid coupling

Starrkörperverschiebung *f* rigid-body displacement

Starrluftschiff *n* rigid airship

Starrolle *f* stellar rule

Starr-schlepp *m* nonflexible connection for glider towing **-schlüssig** rigidly connected **-schmiere** *f* grease, solid lubricant **-schraube** *f* fixed-pitch or fixed-blade propeller

Start *m* start, take-off (aviation), launching **~ mit Raketenhilfe** rocket-assisted take-off **~ mit Rückwind** take-off with the wind **~ mit Seitenwind** cross-wind take-off **~ mit Starthilfe** assisted take-off **kurzer ~** take-off run **nach dem ~** after take-off **stehender ~** dead start

Start-apparat *m* launching apparatus **-art** *f* take-off method

Startbahn *f* runway **befestigte ~** paved runway

Start-bahnbefeuerung *f* runway lighting **-band** *n* identification leader (film) **-befehl** *m* order to launch or take off **-bereich** *m* take-off area **-bereit** ready to start or for take off **-bereitschaft** *f* ground alert **-deck** *n* starting or launching deck (for ship planes) **-drehscheibe** *f* flying-off turntable **-druck** *m* take-off boost **-einrichtung** *f* starting device

starten to start, take off, launch **gegen den Wind** ~ to take off into the wind

Starter *m* trigger (electronics), automatic starter **-batterie** *f* starter battery **-klappe** *f* choke

Start-erlaubnis *f* clearance for take off **-fähigkeit** *f* take-off quality **-feld** *n* take-off or starting zone **-flagge** *f* starter flag **-folge** *f* order of take-off **-freigabe** *f* clearance for take off **-gebühr** *f* take-off fee **-genehmigung** *f* departure clearance **-haken** *m* release hook, take-off hook

Starthilfe *f* catapult **abwerfbare** ~ droppable starting assistance

Start-hilfeofen *m* assisted take-off combustion unit **-impuls** *m* pilot pulse **-katapult** *n* (launching) catapult **-klar** ready for take-off **-knopf** *m* starting key **-kommando** *n* starting signal, take-off signal **-ladedruck** *m* take-off boost (pressure), manifold pressure **-länge** *f* take-off distance

Startlauf *m* ground run

Startleistung *f* maximum take-off power, take-off power, take-off rating, starting performance **erhöhte** ~ **für Notfall** emergency take-off power

Start-mannschaft *f* launching crew, starting crew **-punkt** *m* starting point, take-off point **-rakete** *f* booster rocket **-raketenmotor** *m* booster motor (g/m) **-regulierungsgestänge** *n* priming rods, starting control rods **-rollstrecke** *f* take-off run **-schacht** *m* (Astron.) launching silo (missiles) **-schleuder** *f* catapult **-schub** *m* take-off thrust **-seil** *n* launching rope

Start-Stop-Apparat *m* start-stop apparatus

Start-Stop-Verzerrung *f* start-stop distortion

Startstrecke *f* take-off run

Start- und Landebahn *f* runway **befestigte Start- und Landebahn** paved runway

Start- und Landeeinrichtungen *pl* starting and landing facilities

Start- und Landemeldung *f* departure and arrival message

Start-ventil *n* kick-off valve, starting valve **-verbot** *n* flying or take-off restriction **-verhalten** *n* take-off behavior **-vermögen** *n* take-off quality **-verschluß** *m* kick-off valve, starting valve **-vorrichtung** *f* catapult mechanism (aviation), launching device **-vorsatz** *m* booster **-wagen** *m* launching carriage, starting carriage **-weg** *m* taxi strip, take-off strip **-weite** *f* distance from origin, object distance, distance from object to lens **-zeichen** *n* starting signal **-zeit** *f* unstick or take-off time **-zone** *f* take-off area **-zug** *m* starting cable

Stassano-Ofen *m* Stassano (independent-arc) furnace

Statik *f* statics, droop ~ **eines Reglers in Prozent** regulation of a governor in per cent

Statiker *m* stress analyst

Station *f* station, depot **bewegliche** ~ mobile station **ortsfeste** ~ fixed station

stationär stationary, static, fixed, steady **nicht** ~ nonuniform, unsteady **-e Anlagen** fixed installations **-e Blende** stationary grid **-e Gesamtheit** stationary ensemble **-e Messung** deadbeat measurement **-e Strömung** steady flow, stationary flow **-e rotations-symmetrische Strömung** steady-axi-symmetric flow **-es Übersprechen** steady state cross talk **-e Wirbelbewegung** steady vorticity motion **-er Zustand** steady state, stationary or stable state

stationärbleiben to stay

Stationärblendung *f* standstill dimming

Stationarität *f* principle of immobility, principle of the stationary state

Stations-melder *m* station indicator, tuning indicator **-prüfer** *m* reception test set **-punkt** *m* camera station **-schalttafel** *f* plant switchboard **-wähler** *m* station selector **-wecker** *m* telephone ringer

statisch static(al) ~ **balanzierte Ruderfläche** statically balanced control surface ~ **bestimmbar** statically determinable or definable ~ **bestimmt** statically determinate ~ **indifferent** in neutral equilibrium ~ **nicht bestimmt** statically indeterminate ~ **stabil** statically stable ~ **stabiles Flugzeug** statically stable airplane ~ **unbestimmt** static (structure) geometrically unstable (structure)

statisch-er Arbeitspunkt quiescent point **-er Auftrieb** static lift, buoyant lift **-er Ausgleich** static balance **-e Berechnung** stress analysis, structural analysis **-er Bodendruck** static bottom-hole pressure **-e Charakteristik** volt-amperes diagram **-er Druck** shut-in pressure, static pressure **-e Durchschlagsbedingung** static breakdown condition

statisch-e Elektrizität static electricity **-e Gipfelhöhe** static ceiling **-es Gleitfliegen** static soaring **-e Kennlinie** no-load characteristic (elec.) **-e Last** static load **-e Lastprobe** static load test **-er Luftdruck** static pressure **-e Kennlinie** static characteristic (of a tube) (radio) **-e Kontrolle** stress-strain analysis **-es Medium** static bed **-er Phasenschieber** static phase advancer **-es Querfeld** statical transverse field

statisch-e Röhre static tube **-er Schraubenzug** static propeller thrust **-er Segelflug** static soaring **-e Sperre** static stop **-e Stabilität** static stability **-e Steilheit** static mutual conductance **-er Sternmotor** static radial engine **-es Unterprogramm** static subroutine **-e Untersuchung bis zum Brechpunkt** destructive static test **-e Variable** random variable **-er Versuch** static test **-e Verteilung** statistic distribution **-es Voltmeter** electrostatic voltmeter **-er Wendezeiger** static turn indicator

Statistik *f* statistics ~ **über die Unbenutzbarkeit** out-of-service record

Statistiken erstellen to prepare statistics

Statistiker *m* statistician

Stativ *n* stand, support, stage, tripod ~ **mit Kippe** inclinable stand

Stativ-aufsatz *m* adapter to stand or to tripod **-kammer** *f* camera on stand, camera on tripod **-kompaß** *m* surveyor's compass **-kopf** *m* head of stand, head of tripod **-laufbodenkamera** *f* folding stand camera **-lupe** *f* stand magnifier **-meßkammer** *f* photogrammetric camera on stand **-säule eines Fernrohres** pillar of a telescope **-schuh** *m* metal protection cap for tripod **-standfläche** *f* base of stand **-wagen** *m* tripod dolly

Statometer *n* statometer

Stator *m* stator **-anschlußgerät** motor-control unit **-bleche** *pl* stator laminations **-paket** *n* stator plates, fixed bank **-platten eines Drehkondensators** stator plates, fixed bank **-spule** *f* stator coil, fixed coil **-wicklung** *f* stator winding

Statoskop *n* statoscope

Stau *m* ram, dynamic air pressure, water level, spoiler, stagnation, accumulation, deceleration **gewöhnlicher ~** normal pool elevation

Stauanlage *f* dam (construction)

Staub *m* dust, powder, code for a type of guided missile **-ablagerung** *f* dust deposit **-absauger** *m* dust aspirator **-absaugevorrichtung** *f* dust-exhausting device or equipment **-absaugung** *f* dust exhaust, dust collection, dust removal **-abscheider** *m* dust collector, dust arrester, dust separator, dust catcher **-abscheideverfahren** *n* dust-separating method **-abscheidung** *f* dust separation **-abzug** *m* dust duct

staubartig dustlike, pulverulent, powdery, dusty

Staub-aufbereitungsanlage *f* powdered-fuel preparation plant, coal-dust preparation plant **-aufgabe** *f* coal dust collecting worm **-aufwirbelung** *f* blast effect (lunar landing), raising the dust **-ausscheidung** *f* separation of dust **-behälter** *m* dust catcher **-beheizt** fired with powdered fuel, coal-dust fired **-bekämpfung** suppression dust **-belästigung** *f* dust nuisance **-betrieb** *m* pulverized-coal practice **-bildung** *f* dusting, dust formation **-bindemittel** *n* dust-trapping agent **-bö** *f* dust squall **-bunker** *m* dust bunker **-bläser** *m* dust blower

Stäubchenzahl *f* number of dust nuclei

Staub-decke *f* dust cover **-deckel** *m* dust cap, side plate

staubdicht dustproof, dust-tight **~ gekapselte Verschalung** dust-proof housing **-e Kappe** dustproof cover

Staub-dichtscheibe *f* dust seal washer **-dichtung** *f* dust seal

Staubecken *n* reservoir

stäuben to dust, powder

Stäuben *n* dusting, powdering

Stäuber *m* hopper (for crop dusting)

stauberfüllt dust-laden

Staub-fang *m* dust catcher **-fänger** *m* dust arrester, dust collector, dust chamber **-feuerung** *f* firing with powdered fuel, coal-dust firing **-figuren** *pl* powder pattern, dust figures **-filter** *n* dust filter **-flocke** *f* fluff **-förmig** finely divided, powdered, dusty **-frei** dustless, dust-free **-gehalt** *m* dust content of the air, atmospheric pollution **-gemisch** *n* dust mixture **-geschützt** dustproof **-geschwängert** dustladen **-grün** *n* Paris green, olive drab

staubhaltig dust-laden **-e Luft** dust-laden air **stark -er Teer** tar carrying a large amount of dust

Staubhaltiggrün *n* Paris green

Staubhaube *f* dust hood

staubig dusty, powdery

Staub-kalk *m* lime powder **-kammer** *f* dust catcher, dust-collecting chamber **-kappe** *f* dust hood, dust cover **-kapsel** *f* dust box or cap

Staubkern *m* dust core, molded core **-spule** *f* irondust core coil

Staubkohle *f* coal dust, powdered coal, fine coal

staubkohlengefeuert pulverized-coal-fired

Staub-korn *n* coarse dust particle **-lawine** *f* dust avalanche **-luft** *f* dust-laden air **-luftraum** *m* dustladen air receiver **-masse** *f* dust mass **-messer** *m* konimeter **-meßgerät** *n* dust counter **-nebel** *m* dust haze **-niederschlagung** *f* depositing the dust **-öl** *n* floor oil

Staub-pinsel *m* dusting brush **-plage** *f* dust nuisance **-probensammler** *m* portable dust sampler **-pumpensystem** *n* pneumatic conveying system **-räumer** *m* dust catcher **-rauschen** *n* dust noise (of film) **-regen** *m* mist, drizzling rain **-reiniger** *m* vacuum (dust) cleaner **-ring** *m* dust shield **-sack** *m* dust pocket or collector dust catcher **-sammelraum** *m* dust chamber **-sammler** *m* dust collector, dust arrester **-sand** *m* very fine sand

Staubsauger *m* dust exhauster, vacuum cleaner **trockner ~** dry dust exhauster, cloth-screen dust arrester

Staub-säule *f* sand pillar **-schild** *n* dust shield **-schlamm** *m* dust sludge **-schleifen** *n* honing

Staubschutz-abdeckung *f* dust-proof cover **-blech** (Lager) dust washer **-gerät** *n* respirator **-helm** *m* protective helmet against dust or sand-blast **-hülle** *f* dust protecting envelope **-sieb** *n* (Hupe) dust cap

Staub-separation *f* dust separation **-separationsanlage** *f* dust-reclaiming mill **-sicher** dustproof **-streuendes Flugzeug** duster (for crop dusting), insecticide plane used for crop dusting **-trocken** to dry so that dust will not cling, bone-dry

Stäubungsverlust *m* dusting loss

Staub-verschluß *m* dust shield **-verschmutzt** dust-contaminated **-vorabscheider** *m* preliminary dust separator **-wedel** *m* feather duster **-welle** *f* acoustic dust pattern

Staubwirbel *m* dust devil **-wind** *m* dust devil, dust whirlwind

Staub-zähler *m* dust counter **-zufuhr** *f* pulverized fuel supply (in firing), dust supply **-zuteiler** *m* dust allotter **-zyklop** *m* dusting willey

Stauch-alterung *f* strain-aging **-arbeit** *f* work of upsetting **-backen** *pl* heading dies, swaging mandrels, jaws for jolting machine **-barkeit** *f* upsetting property **-bohrer** *m* percussion drill **-druck** *m* operation to maintain the edges true (in rolling), bearing pressure, compression, upsetting pressure

stauchen to upset, jump, compress, bulge, head, roll on edge (in rolling), cobble, buckle, forge, swell, beat, clinch (a rivet)

Stauchen *n* crushing

Stauch-faktor *m* upsetting factor **-frischluftheizung** *f* pitot-head fresh-air heating **-gerüst** *n* edging stand **-glied** *n* shock absorber **-hammer** *m* jumper **-härtung** *f* wear hardening

Stauchkaliber *n* edging pass (in rolling), upset pass, groove in which material is rolled on edge **geschlossenes ~** tongue-and-groove pass

Stauch-lafette *f* telescopic carriage **-maschine** *f* upsetting machine **-matrize** *f* upsetting die, heading die **-presse** *f* bulldozer **-probe** *f* bulging test, bulging-test specimen, upsetting test, hammering test **-richtung** *f* compression direction **-rundschlag** *m* rotary blow **-schlitten** *m* upsetting slide (in welding) **-schweißung** *f* upset welding **-setzmaschine** *f* percussion jig **-sieb** *n* hand jigging sieve **-spannung** *f* bearing stress of a rivet **-stanze** *f* upsetting press **-stich** *m* edging pass, reduction on edge

Stauchung *f* compression, upsetting, shortening, cobbling, buckling, bearing, slaving, compressive strain

Stauch-verschränkung *f* joggling **-verschränkungswalze** *f* joggling roll **-versuch** *m* compression test, crushing test, bulging test, upsetting test **-vorrichtung** *f* upsetting device **-wert** *m* crusher index **-wirkung** *f* upsetting effect, crushing effect **-wulst** *f* upsetting bulge **-zylinder** *m* crusher gauge

Staudamm *m* earth dam or dike, earth-fill dam

Staudruck *m* velocity head, pressure head, ramming pressure, dynamic pressure or impact pressure (aerodyn.), atmospheric pressure, thrust (ant) **-anschluß** *m* dynamic pressure nozzle **-düse** *f* pitot tube **-einrichtung** *f* stem pressure device **-erzeugung** *f* air-pressure system **-fahrtmesser** *m* pressure-head speed indicator, velocity-head speed indicator (aviation) **-fahrtschreiber** *m* pressure-head speed recorder **-heizung** *f* retaining pressure heating system **-kurve** *f* dynamic pressure curve

Staudruck-leitung *f* pressurizing line **-messer** *m* Pitot static airspeed indicator, pressure-head indicator, air-speed indicator, Pitot tube, dynamic indicator **-messeranzeige** *f* air-speed indicator, impact-pressure reading **-regelung** *f* dynamic pressure regulation **-rohr** *n* pressurizing pipe **-tachometer** *n* velocity-head tachometer **-tafel** *f* static table or chart **-tendenzmesser** *m* dynamic pressure tendency meter

Staudruck-ventil *n* pressurizing valve **-verbindung** *f* Pitot pressure connection **-verhältnis** *n* (relative) dynamic pressure ratio **-verteilung** *f* dynamic pressure distribution **-wert** *m* value of dynamic pressure **-zünder** *m* air-pressure fuse

Staudüse *f* pitot head or tube

Staudüsen-antrieb *m* ramjet propulsion **-flugzeug** *n* ramjet airplane **-heizung** *f* pitot-head heating

stauen to stow, dam up, choke, pack, impound, baffle

Stauer *m* stevedore

Stauen *n* stowage

Stau-fahrtmesser *m* pressure speed indicator **-fangbohrung** *f* ram receiver port

Stauffer-büchse *f* grease box, grease cup **-fett** *n* cup grease

Stau-fläche *f* area of dammed water **-flügel** *m* wicket **-frei** unrestricted **-gebiet** *n* pressure region **-gerät** *n* pressure reading device **-gitter** *n* suppressor grid, baffle grid **-höhe** *f* local swelling of water, fall or head of water (on weir), overflow level (dam), lift **-hutze** *f* ram tube or scoop

Stau-inhalt einer Talsperre volume of the reservoir of a barrage **-kasten** *m* weir box **-keil** *m* chock **-körper** *m* baffle barrier **-kugel** *f* pressure sphere **-kurve** *f* backwater curve **-lage** *f* damming position **-linie** *f* back water curve

Stauluft *f* ram air **-eintritt** *m* (bei Ballonschirm) ram air inlet **-temperatur** *f* ram air temperature **-turbine** *f* ram air turbine

Stau-mauer *f* (small low) dam, earth dam, masonry dam **-pendelfeuerbrücke** *f* fire bridge with swing-type ash bars **-plan** *m* loading plan **-plane** *f* tarpaulin **-punkt** *m* stagnation point, stem point, ram point **-quelle** *f* spring due to damming of underground water **-rand** *m* orifice plate, calibrated orifice (hydr.) **-randmesser** *m* orifice meter **-rand(scheibe)** *f* thin plate orifice **-raum** *m* air scoop

Stau-rohr *n* static tube, pressure nozzle, flowmeter, Pitot tube, pressure tube, impact tube **-röhre** *f* Pitot tube

Staurohr-heizung *f* Pitot-head heating **-kopf** *m* Pitot-static head **-windmesser** *m* pressure-tube anemometer

Stauscheibe *f* measuring aperture or orifice, diaphragm plate, diaphragm, baffle plate, static plate

Stauscheiben-druckmeßrohr *n* static-plate manometer **-variometer** *n* diaphragm-type rate-of-climb indicator

Stau-schütz *n* sliding sluice or valve, hatch, sliding lock gate **-schild an Walzen** damming skirt **-see** *m* storage pond **-spiegel** *m* level of upper pool, pool elevation, retained or impounded water level

Staustrahlmotor *m* ram jet engine

Staustrahltriebwerk *n* ram jet engine (aviat)

Stau-teich *m* reservoir, storage pond **-temperatur** *f* ram temperature

Stauung *f* obstruction, damming up

Stau-ventil *n* stop valve **-verdichtung** *f* impact ram compression **-vorrichtung** *f* slice or slicer (paper mfg.), stowing arrangement **-wand** *f* baffle plate **-wasser** *n* backwater, slack water **-wehr** *n* control dam **-weiher** *m* reservoir, storage pond **-werk** *n* barrage, dam **-wirkung** *f* baffle or accumulator effect, damming effect, resistance **-ziel** *n* maximum permissible water level in reservoir

Stearat *n* stearate

Stearin *n* stearin, stearine **-kerze** *f* stearin candle **-kuchen** *m* stearin cake **-öl** *n* oleic acid **-pech** *n* stearin pitch **-sauer** stearic **-säure** *f* stearic acid

stearinsaures Kalium potassium stearate **~ Natrium** sodium stearate

Steatit *m* steatite

Stech-beitel *m* ripping chisel, firmer chisel **-beutel** *m* former, (ripping) chisel **-eisen** *n* chisel, bradawl

stechen to prick, pierce, cut, dig, stab, sting, prod, tap, engrave

stechend (Geruch) pungent

Stecher (Stock) pin, stock

Stechflug *m* shallow dive (of bomb) **-klappe** *f* dive flap

Stech-heber *m* siphon, pipette **-kontakt** *m* connector **-kolben** *m* pipette **-lot** *n* grain spelter **-maschine** *f* punching machine **-ruder** *n* paddle **-schloß** *n* hair-trigger lock **-schlüssel** *m* box key or spanner

Stech-spitze *f* contact piercing point **-spitzenanschluß** *m* (Zündanker) piercing point connection (magneto armature) **-stahl mit Rundschneide** finishing or threading tool **-uhr** *f* time clock, stop watch **-zirkel** *m* dividers

Steck-achse *f* knockout spindle **-anordnung** *f* connecting panel **-anschluß** *m* plug junction

steckbar plug-in (type)

Steckblende *f* stop plug

Steckbolzen *m* cotter pin, linch pin, pintle **-sicherung** *f* pintle cotter
Steck-brett *n* pre-patch board (comput.) **-buchse** *f* plug socket, connector socket, sleeve, bush **-bügel** *m* tie **-dorn** *m* pin wrench **-dose** *f* (plug) socket, plug box, wall socket, wall plug, jack
Steckdosen-halteblech *n* dummy socket **-platte** *f* female insulator plate **-verbindung** *f* socket-switch connection
Steckeinheit *f* plug-in-unit
stecken to pin, lay out (a cable), plug, insert **in Brand ~** to set afire **ineinander ~** to fit into one another
Stecker *m* plug, operator's telephone set plug, tommy bar **~ mit Büchse** double plug and jack **~ mit Schutzkragen** plug with protection collar **~ für Voltmeter** voltmeter plug **berührungssicherer ~** shockproof plug **dreiteiliger ~** three-point or threeway plug **unverwechselbarer ~** noninterchangeable plug **~ mit Schalter** switch plug
Stecker-anschluß *m* plug connection **-buchse** *f* plug socket, connector socket, sleeve, bush **-hülse** *f* plug socket, connector socket **-leiste** *f* plug board **-säule** *f* multi(way) socket and plug device **-schnur** *f* cord and plug, plug cord **-spitze** *f* tip (of telephone plug) **-stift eines Röhrensockels** pin of the tube base, prong of the tube base **-tafel** *f* busbar or plug board
Steck-fassung *f* (lamp) jack, (plug-in) socket **-formmaschine** *f* strap-wrap-machine (forming press) **-glied** *n* connector link **-hülse** *f* adapter plug, socket **-hülsenverbindung** *f* socket connection **-kerbstift** *m* grooved pin (type D), slotted pin **-kontakt** *m* plug (contact) **-kurbel** *f* starting crank **-lager** *n* closed bearing **-lampe** *f* jack lamp
Stecklasche *f* fishplate **Stoßverbindung mit innen angenieteten Stecklaschen** joint with inside-riveted fishplates for portable lines
Stecklehre *f* plug gauge
Steckleisten *pl* contact strips
Steckling *m* layer
Steck-loch *n* hole for pinning **-lot** *n* grain spelter **-manometer** *n* tire pressure gauge **-mast** *m* dismountable antenna, collapsible radio mast
Stecknadel *f* pin **-kopf** *m* pinhead **-programmierung** *f* pinboard programming
Steck-okular *n* sliding eyepiece **-patrone** *f* plug cartrige **-platte** *f* male insulator plate **-quarz** *m* plug-in crystal **-regler** *m* plug-in and socket control
Steckschlüssel *m* box spanner, socket wrench **~ für Ablaß** discharge key **~ aus Rohr** tubular socket wrench
Steck-schlüsselschrank *m* multishape key plug switchboard **-schnur** *f* patchcord **-spule** *f* plug-in coil, plug inductor, demountable magazine or reel, detachable coil **-stift** *m* guide pin **-tafel** *f* plugboard **-uhr** *f* control clock **-umschalter** *m* plug-in switch **-verbindung** *f* plug connection **-vorrichtung** *f* plug device **-welle** *f* stub shaft **-zirkel** *m* compass with shifting points, drawing compass
Steffenfabrik *f* sugar factory with Steffen scalding process
Steg *m* (Maschinen) catwalk; (Technik) cross-piece, bar; walkway, passage, web, stem, bridge, strap, fillet, flange, leg, arm, footbridge, footpath, barrier or land (elec.) **durch Stege verbinden** to strap together
Steg-abstand *m* distance between grid wires **-blech** *n* web plate **-blechbeule** *f* buckling of the web **-blechstoß** *m* web plate joint **-dorn** *m* bridge die **-gliedrig** stud-link **-hohlleiter** *m* ridge waveguide (microw.) **-kante** *f* edge of bridge **-kette** *f* stud-link chain, stud-link cable **-kreuz** *n* turnstile **-leitung** *f* (zweiadrige) twin lead **-linien** *pl* chain lines or marks (paper mfg.) **-leitung** *f* tape conduit, twin-lead transmission line **-lochung** *f* web punching **-rad** *n* webbed wheel, web gear
Stegrippe *f* web rib
Stegverlaschung *f*, **doppelte ~** double-strap web joint
Steg-stärke *f* web thickness **-teil** *m* leg section **-träger** *m* web girder, I-beam girder **-versteifung** *f* stiffening of the web **-zahl** *f* number of grid wires, stays, or supports
Steh-achse *f* supporting axis, vertical axis **-bild** *n* still picture, nonanimated picture **-bildverfahren** *n* lantern-slide projection method **-blech** *n* vertical plate, stiffening plate, web girder, web plate **-bock** *m* bearing block, floor stand, floor frame
Stehbolzen *m* separator or spacer bolt, stay bolt, stud, dowel pin **-bohrer** *m* stay-bolt drill **-drehbank** *f* stud lathe **-schrauber** *m* staybolt driver
stehen to stand, be, become, fit, be (vertical) upright **~** (von Kleidern) to suit **~ bleiben** to stop **an der Spitze ~** to be at the head of **in einer Stellung ~ bleiben** to stop at a position
Stehen *n* steadiness **~ des Bildes** steadiness of image **mangelhaftes ~** jumping or unsteadiness of image
stehend stationary, fixed, standing, vertical **~ abgießen** to cast on end, pour on end **~ anbauen** to mount or fit vertically **~ gießen** to cast on end **-e Appretur** lasting finish **-e Dampfmaschine** motor- or marine-type steam engine **-es Echo** standing echo **-e Falte** upright fold **-e Figur** stationary pattern of figure
stehend -er Konverter upright converter **-er Kristallisator** vertical crystallizer **-er Motor** vertical engine **-e Naht** vertical weld **-e Pumpe** vertical pump **-e Retorte** vertical retort **-er Sechszylinderreihenmotor** six-cylinder in-line engine **-e Ventile** side-by-side valves **-e Welle** standing wave, vertical shaft **-e Winde** capstan **-e Zentralwelle** vertical central shaft
Steh-faden *m* stationary thread **-feldbestrahlung** *f* stationary field radiation **-gurt** *m* safety strap **-holz** *n* reinforcing web or strap, stiffener
Stehkessel-decke *f* roof sheet of the outside firebox **-mantel** *m* firebox outside sheet **-seitenwand** *f* side sheet or plate of firebox shell **-vorderwand** *f* front plate of a firebox
Steh-knecht *m* support stock, standing vise **-kolben** *m* flat-bottomed flask **-kreuz** *n* upright cross **-kugellager** *n* ball-bearing pillow block
Stehlager *n* pillow block, pedestal bearing, pillow-block bearing, bracket, footstep bearing, vertical bearing, plummer block **schräges ~** angle pillow block
Stehlager-bock *m* floor stand **-gehäuse** *n* pillow-

block frame **-oberschale** *f* pillow-block cap, upper half of pillow block **-unterschale** *f* pillow-block liner

Stehlampe *f* standard or floor lamp

Stehlstange *f* thief rod

Steh-platz *m* standing room **-rollenlager** *n* roller-bearing pillow block **-schraube** *f* stud **-spannung** *f* with stand voltage **-starter** *m* tail sitter (aviat.)

Stehwellen-anzeiger *m* standing wave indicator **-indikator** voltage standing wave ratio (VSWR) **-verhältnis** *n* power standing wave ratio (elec.) **-verhältnismesser** *m* standing-wave meter

Stehzeit *f* molding time, down time

steif stiff, rigid, firm, inflexible, nonyielding **~ holen** to tighten (a cable), heave taut **-e Brise** strong breeze **-e Spannung** *f* rigid voltage

Steifbroschur *f* stiff paper binding

Steife *f* strut, prop, brace, stiffness, stay, rigidity **amplitudenabhängige ~** stiffness depending on amplitude

steifen to proof, stiffen

steifer, geklüfteter Ton stiff-fissured clay

Steifezahl *f* stiffness coefficient

Steifheit *f* stiffness, rigidity, stability, inflexibility

Steifigkeit *f* rigidity, stiffness (acoust)

Steifigkeits-koeffizient *m* coefficient of rigidity **-zahl** *f* rigidity number, modulus of elasticity, coefficient of rigidity **-ziffer** *f* stiffness coefficient

Steif-rahmen *m* braced girder, trussing, rigid frame **-säge** *f* cross-cut saw (for logs)

Steifung *f* bracing

Steifwerden *n* stiffening, hardening **~ einer Kette** strain of a mooring cable

Steig *m* footpath **-bö** *f* (Met.) rising or vertical gust, bump (aviation) **-böenanzeiger** *m* vertical gust recorder **-brunnen** *m* artesian well **-bügel** *m* stirrup **-bügelantrieb** *m* spade-handle drive **-draht** *m* rising wire **-eigenschaft** *f* climbing quality **-eisen** *n* grapnel, climbing iron, pole step, lineman's climbers

Steige-leiter *f* safety ladder **-leitung** *f* standpipe mounting pillar, riser

steigen to rise, ascend, mount, increase, run up, climb, swell, pitch, lift or dissipate (fog) **senkrecht ~** to climb or rise vertically

Steigen *n* climb, climbing, ascent, increase **~ der Preise** increase in price **~ des Wassers** rise of the water, flood

steigend gradient **~ abgießen** to bottom-pour, bottom-cast **~ gegossen** bottom-cast **~ gießen** to bottom-cast, bottom-pour **-e Flanke des Querimpulses** rise of the transverse pulse **-er Guß** bottom casting, bottom pouring, group casting **-er Karnies** ogee (arch.) **-e Potenz** ascending power **-e Spindel** (Ventil), rising stem (valve) **-e Tendenz** upward tendency **-e Umdrehung** climbing turn **-es Wasser** flood tide

Steiger *m* riser, riser gate, rising gate, vent, feeder head (riser)

steigern to raise, increase, force up

Steige-rohr *n* ascending tube or pipe **-röhre** *f* rising main

Steigerung *f* acceleration, increase, augmentation, increment, raise, boost

Steige-stütze *f* pole steps **-trichter** *m* riser, riser gate, rising gate, flow gate, whistler, vent

Steigfähigkeit *f* climbing power or ability, climbing capacity

Steigflug *m* climb, climbing flight **-geschwindigkeit** *f* rate of climb or ascent **-leistung** *f* climb-(ing) power

Steigförderer *m* ascending conveyor

Steiggeschwindigkeit *f* climbing speed, rate of climb **~ in Bodennähe** initial rate of climb

Steiggeschwindigkeitsmesser *m* rate-of-climb indicator

Steighöhe *f* height of rise, vertical range, elevation (in capillary tube), pitch (of screw) **kapilläre ~** capillary rise

Steighöhenmethode *f* sedimentation-equilibrium method (for determination of particle size)

Steig-kanal *m* uptake **-kraft** *f* upward or rising force, climbing power **-kurve** *f* climb curve **-lattentuch** *n* upright lattice **-leistung** *f* climb power, climb rating **-leistungsmesser** *m* rate-of-climb meter **-leiter** *f* ladder **-leitung** *f* standpipe, riser, rising mains, uptake, feedpipe, mounting pillar **-linie** *f* climb curve

Steig-messer *m* climb indicator **-ortshauer** *m* coal hewer (overhand stoping) **-rad** *n* ratchet wheel, escapement wheel, balance wheel **-riemen** *m* stirrup leather **-rohr** *n* standpipe, riser, rising main, uptake, feedpipe **-schacht** *m* climbing shaft

Steigstrom-vergaser *m*, **-vorrichtung** *f* updraft carburetor, vertical-type carburetor

Steig-trichter *m* rising gate **-tropfenzeiger** *m* rising drop indicator

Steigung *f* raising, rise, increase, intensification, augmentation, ascent, pitch, incline, inclination, gradient, slope, pitch (of screw thread), lead, taper, upgrade **~ bei Drehmoment Null** zerotorque pitch **~ der Federwindung** pitch of helical spring **~ des Geigerbereiches** slope of plateau (Geiger) **~ des Muttergewindes** pitch of female thread **~ bei Vorschub Null** zero-thrust pitch **~** (Ganghöhe) einer Schraube lead of a screw **große ~** coarse pitch **kleine ~** fine pitch **mittlere ~** mean pitch **prozentuale ~** percentage of inclination **relative ~** (Propeller) pitch diameter ratio **schwache ~** easy gradient

Steigungs-abweichung *f* slope deviation (rdr) **-änderung** *f* variation in slope **-anzeiger** *m* pitch indicator **-einstellung** *f* pitch setting **-fähigkeit** *f* climbing ability **-fehler** *m* pitch error **-führung** *f* lead control **-grad** *m* degree of climb **-kurve** *f* pitch cam

Steigungs-maß *n* pitch, slope **-messer** *m* gradient indicator, inclinometer, gradient meter **-prüfer** *m* lead tester **-verhältnis** *n* pitch ratio of a propeller **-verstellbereich** *m* pitch-changing range **-verstellvorrichtung** *f* pitch-setting mechanism **-widerstand** *m* resistance due to gradients **-winkel** *m* angle of lead, angle of inclination, pitch angle, angle at climb, climbing angle, helix angle

Steigvermögen *n* climbing ability **mit großem ~** with high climbing capacity

Steigwinkel *m* angle of climb, slope or inclination **~ des Flugzeuges** flight-path angle

Steig-zahl *f* criterion of climb, climb and ceiling factor **-zeit** *f* time of climb, rise time (radio)

steil steep, abrupt **zu ~** too high **-er Abhang** steep gradient or slope **-es Felsenufer** steep rocky shore, Ridges granité **-er Gleitwendeflug** steep gliding turn **-er gezogener Kurvenflug** steep climbing turn **-e Röhre** high mu tube (radio) **-er Wendeflug** steep turn

Steilabfall *m* abrupt drop

Steilaufnahme *f* low-oblique photograph **konvergente ~** low-oblique convergent photograph

Steilaufzug *m* vertical elevator

Steildüne *f* shelving or steep dune

steilgängiger Spiralbohrer steep spiral drill

steilgängiges Gewinde coarse thread

Steilgewinde *n* coarse thread **-nuß** *f* coarse-pitch thread nut **-schneideinrichtung** *f* coarse threading attachement

Steil-hang *m* abrupt slope **-hauer** *m* vertical cutters

Steilheit *f* grid-plate transconductance, transconductance, slope, controlled plate conductance, steepness, slope of the emission characteristic, gradient, contrast (film) **~ einer Kurve** slope of curve **~ von Röhrenkennlinien** slope of valve characteristics (teleph.)

Steilheits-abweichung *f* deviation in slope **-messer** *m* derivator, tangent meter **-röhre** *f* transconductance

Steil-kegel *m* steep-angle taper **-kurve** *f* vertical bank, sharp curve, steep turn **-küste** *f* shelving or steep coast **-nocken** *m* steep cam **-rampe** *f* steep gradient

Steilrohr-kessel *m* water-tube boiler, bent-tube boiler, vertical-tube boiler **-verdampfer** *m* vertical-tube evaporator

steil-schießen to fire at high angle **-schrauber** *m* helicopter

Steilsicht *f* steep sighting **-prisma** *n* steep sighting prism

Steil-strahlung *f* high-angle or vertical radiation, space radiation **-trudeln** *n* spin **-ufer** *n* steep bank, steep shore **-zielung** *f* high shot

Stein *m* stone, rock, block, brick, matte, jewel **allseitig bearbeiteter ~** stone pared on every side **armer ~** low-grade matte **gebrannter ~** brick **gezähnelter ~** hatched stone **reicher ~** high-grade matte

Steinabdruck *m* lithographic print

Steinabricht- und Hobelmaschine *f* stone smoothing and planing machine

Stein-abrunder *m* wheel dresser **-ansatz** *m* scale **-arbeit** *f* metal smelting, stonework **-artig** stony **-ausklaubung** *f* picking out slate **-auswechslung** *f* die change **-bearbeitung** *f* stoneworking **-beschreibung** *f* petrography **-bettung** *f* roadbed **-bewurf** *m* grit layer **-bildung** *f* matte formation

Stein-block *m* boulder **-bohrer** *m* wall chisel, stone drill, stone bit, rock drill, star drill **-bohrmaschine** *f* rock drill **-böschung** *f* riprapped slope, stone paving **-bottich** *m* stoneware vat **-brand** *m* smut (of grain crops)

Steinbrecher *m* stone crusher, rock breaker or crusher, quarryman, jaw crusher **~ mit unterer Schwingungsachse** rock crusher with movable jaw pivoted at lower end

Steinbrecherwalzenmühle *f* combined stone breaker and roller mill

Steinbrocken *m* brickbat, chippings of stone

Steinbruch *m* quarry face, quarry, stone pit **-abraum** *m* quarry rubbish **-lager** *n* quarry bed

Steinchen *n* stone, nonvitreous inclusion (in glass)

Stein-decke *f* concrete and hollow tile slab **-dolle** *f* lewis bolt **-druck** *m* lithography **-druckerei** *f* lithography, lithographic printing

Steinebehauen *n* stone picking

Stein-fall *m* matte fall **-fängervorlage** *f* counter-blade stone remover **-flachs** *m* stone hemp **-fuß** *m* ceramic foot **-geschiebe** *n* boulder shingle **-glätte** *f* flint-stone glazing machine **-glättung** *f* flint glazing

Steingut *n* stoneware, pottery, earthenware, crockery **-formstück** *n* tile **-gebrauchsgeschirr** *n* household (utensils of) earthenware **-isolator** *m* stone insulator **-rohr** *n* earthenware duct

Stein-hammer *m* stone hammer **-hart** hard as stone **-härtekessel** *m* pan for roasting limestone **-hauer** *m* stonemason, stonecutter

Steinholz *n* magnesium oxychloride, xylolith (plastic from sawdust and Sorel cement)

steinig stony

Steinisolator, keramischer ~ der Zündkerze ceramic insulator of spark plug

Stein-kern *m* internal mold or cast (refinery) **-kerze** *f* stone or ceramic plug **-kiste** *f* wooden crib filler with riprap **-kitt** *m* mastic cement **-klopfer** *m* crusher **-kohle** *f* pit coal, mineral coal, stone coal, bituminous coal, soft coal, sea coal

Steinkohlen-asche *f* coal ashes **-bergwerk** *n* colliery, coal mine **-brikett** *n* coal briquette **-destillation** *f* distillation or carbonization of bituminous coal, carbonization plant **-entgasung** *f* distillation of bituminous coal, bituminous-coal carbonization **-gas** *n* bituminous-coal gas, coal gas **-gaserzeugung** *f* coal-gas manufacture, gasification of coal **-gebirge** *n* carboniferous rock **-generatorgas** *n* producer gas

Steinkohlen-hochtemperaturteer *m* high-temperature coal tar **-klein** *n* slack, culm **-kraftwerk** *n* pit-coal power station, pit-coal plant **-kreosot** *n* coal-tar creosote **-lager** *n* coal deposit **-öl** *n* coal-tar oil **-pech** *n* coal-tar pitch **-schicht** *f* coal seam **-schlacke** *f* coal cinders

Steinkohlen-schwelteer *m* low-temperature coal tar **-schwelung** *f* coal carbonization **-staub** *m* coal dust

Steinkohlenteer *m* coal tar, bituminous coal tar **-benzin** *n* benzene, benzol **-öl** *n* coal-tar oil **-pech** *n* coal-tar pitch

Steinkohlen-verkokung *f* coal carbonization, coking **-vorkommen** *n* coal deposit, coal area, coal region

Stein-körner *m* stone grainer **-krug** *m* stone mug **-kunde** *f* mineralogy **-lager** *n* jeweled bearing **-läufer** *m* stone runner **-leistung** *f* tonnage per diem **-lupe** *f* magnifying lens for precious stones **-mark** *n* lithomarge, porcelain earth **-mauer** *f* masonry or stone wall **-mehl** *n* very fine sand, rock flour, rock dust

Steinmeißel *m* star drill, rock bit, mason's chisel **flacher ~** flat stone chisel

Stein-metz *m* stonecutter, stonemason **-mörtel** *m* concrete **-nuß** *f* ivory nut **-öl** *n* petroleum, naphtha **-packung** *f* dry stone pitching **-pech** *n* asphalt **-porzellan** *n* hard porcelain **-presse** *f* brickmaking press **-quader** *m* dressed stone **-rösten** *n* roasting of matte or regulus

Stein-sägegatter *n* stone frame saws **-salz** *n* rock salt, mineral salt **-satz** *m* dry stone pitching **-schicht** *f* stratum

Steinschlag *m* broken stone, gravel, crushed rock, small stone filling, riprap **-gabel** *f* fork for mixing broken stones **-gitter** *n* protection grille, stone guard

Stein-schleifer *m* lithographic stone dresser **-schliff** *m* stone grinding **-schmelzen** *n* matte smelting **-schnitt** *m* lithotomy

Steinschotter *m* rubble, croshed rock **mit ~ belegen** to layout a road with rubble

Stein-schraube *f* screw or bolt for anchorage in masonry, stone bolt, wall screw, rag bolt **-schrotmühle** *f* stone burr mill **-schutt** *m* rubble, debris **-schüttdamm** *m* rock-fill dam **-schüttung** *f* rock filling, rubble, rubble bed, riprap **-setzer** *m* paver, stone setter **-spaltmaschine** *f* stone-splitting machine **-spaltmesser** *n* stone-splitting tools, quarry picks **-spiller** *m* spalls

Stein-stellung *f* millstone adjusting gear **-strahlbrenner** *m* multijet brick burner **-strahlofen** *m* stone radiating oven **-tafel** *f* slab **-verblendung** *f* facing of natural stone **-verkleidung** *f* facing, revetment **-winkeln** to square an ashlar **-wolf** *m* wedges for lifting stones, lewis pins **-zeichnung** *f* construction lines of brickwork (of blast furnace)

Steinzeug *n* stoneware, clayware, clay tile, stoneware **-flasche** *f* stoneware bottle **-rohr** *n* clay pipe

Stellage *f* rack, contrivance

Stellarator-geometrie *f* stellarator-geometry

stellare Materie stellar matter

Stell-becher *m* mouth of fuse setter **-bereich** *m* total range of controller output **-bock** *m* trestle, lever stand **-detektor** *m* adjustable detector

Stelle *f* place; (Fleck) spot; (Punkt) point; (Standort) stand, position; (Bau~) site; (Behörde) agency; (Arbeits~) employment, position; situation, aid station (med.), post, passage, site, billet, location **~ der Bestimmtheit** point of determination, regular point (of a differential equation) **~ in einem Buch** passage **~ mit Sprechdrahtsignalisierung** bridge-control switchboard **abgeschirmte ~** dead spot, radio shadow, radio pocket **an ~** in lieu of **auf der ~** on the spot, there and then, at once **an einer beliebigen ~** at any point **offene ~** vacant situation or post, vacancy

Stelleisen *n* change-gear bracket

stellen to place, put, adjust, supply, set, point, regulate

Stellen, auf 5 ~ genau with five-digit accuracy

Stellen-bit *n* sprocket bit **-dichte** *f* bit density **-feldgrenze** *f* digit field limit **-impuls** *m* digit pulse **-leiter** *m* digit conductor **-lesekanal** *m* digit-sense channel **-richtungskanal** *m* digit-sense channel

Stellen-schreibsteuerung *f* positions transfer print entry **-schreibweise** *f* positional notation (comp.) **-spur** *f* sprocket channel **-versetzen** *n* shift (comput.)

Stellen-wert *m* column, place or local-value **-(wert)verschiebung** *f* arithmetic shift

stellenweise here and there, in places **~ Abnutzung** spotty wear

Stellenzahl *f* index. index numbers, (number of) digits, position number, atomic number

Stellenziffer *f* index number, place digit

Steller *m* final control element, regulating unit

Stell-falle *f* sluice board or stay, lock hatch **-farbstoff** *m* shading dyestuff **-feder** *f* adjusting spring **-fläche** *f* charging space **-geschwindigkeit** *f* regulating speed (aut. contr.), maximum possible rate of change of controller **-glied** *n* final control element, correcting element **-grad** *m* regulation ratio (servo), ratio of actual steady-state controller output to maximum possible controller output **-größe** *f* regulated quantity (servo), controller output **-hahn** *m* regulating cock

Stellhebel *m* lever for tilt control (print), adjustable lever, switch lever **~ für die Höhenstellung** elevating tumble-plate segment

Stellhemmung *f* setting

Stellingsanlage *f* iron structure

Stellit *m* stellite

stellitiert stellited

Stellkegel *m* adjusting or tightening wedge

Stellkeil *m* adjusting key or wedge **~ zur Bewegung des Winkeltisches in gerader Richtung** adjustable V key to move knee in straight line

Stell-klaue *f* adjusting dog **-knopf** *m* adjustment knob **-kraft** *f* displacement force, controlling force **-kronen** *pl* adjusting wheels **-kulisse** *f* regulating slot **-leiste** *f* adjusting plate

Stellmacher *m* wheelwright

Stellmacherei *f* wheelwright's shop

Stellmacherschraube *f* coach screw

Stell-magnet *m* torquer magnet, operating magnet **-marke** *f* pointer, marker **-mittel** *n* adulterant (standardizing agent) **-motor** *m* servomotor, power device adjusting the final control element, actuator **-mutter** *f* lock nut, adjusting key, adjusting nut, setting ring **-nocken** *m* adjusting cam **-organ** *n* regulating unit **-ort** *m* regulating point, control point

Stell-rad *n* regulator or set wheel **-relais** *n* valve positioner **-ring** *m* tension ring (fuse), setting ring, adjusting ring, set collar, guide ring, cursor **-rose** *f* adjustable compass card **-scheibe** *f* adjusting disk **-schiene** *f* slide rail **-schlitten** *m* adjusting slide block **-schlüssel** *m* hand fuse setter, adjusting wrench or key **-schraube** *f* binding screw, setscrew, adjusting screw, regulating screw, leveling screw, screw jack **-schraubenhülse** *f* thumbscrew sleeve

Stell-spindel *f* adjusting spindle **-stift** *m* capstan spike, tommy (mech.), adjusting pin **-strom** *m* regulating quantity **-transformator** *m* variable-ratio transformer

Stell- und Übergangsfunktion *f* transient response of process for step change

Stellung *f* position; (Berufs~) employment, situation, job; (Eigenschaft) capacity; (Anordnung) arrangement; emplacement, line, setting, station, post, rank, attitude, place, standing **~ der Aufgabe** statement of the problem ~ **zum Bruch bringen** to break down a position ~ **Kein Stromschritt** no-impulse setting ~ **des Reglungswiderstandes** potentiometer step ~ **des Schwächungswiderstandes** stud of the potentiometer ~ **behaupten** to hold a position **in** ~ **bringen** to position, (bring into) position

Stellung, befestigte ~ fortified position, prepared position **überzogene** ~ nose high (aviation) **in** ~, **in der** ~ normal, idle, inoperative

Stellungnahme *f* comment

Stellungsanzeigegerät *n* position indicator

Stellungsanzeiger für die Luftschraubeneinstellung pitch indicator (aviation)

Stellungs-bau *m* construction of a position **-geber** *m* remote-position indicator **-güteziffer** *f* displacement figure of merit (comput.) **-karte** *f* position map **-licht** *n* navigation light **-lichtsignal** *n* position light signal **-macher** *m* positioner (servo)

Stellungs-prüfer *m* testing bar **-regelung** *f* control of position **-relais** *n* valve positioner **-rückmelder** *m* position repeating device **-schalter** *m* throw-switch **-wahl** *f* choice of position **-wechsel** *m* shift or change of position **-winkel** *m* angle of position, angular position

stellvertretend deputy, acting **-er Geschäftsführer** deputy managing director

Stellvertreter *m* second in command, representative, deputy, proxy

Stellvertretung *f* substitution

Stellvorrichtung *f* adjusting device, setting device, adjusting apparatus, switch lever, control gear ~ **für den Auf- und Niedergang** regulator for vertical feed ~ **für den Quervorschub** regulator for cross-feed ~ **für den Tisch** adjustable table dogs

Stellweg *m* regulating distance (servo)

Stellwerk *n* signaling device (R.R.), switch box, locking frame

Stellwerkanlage *f* interlocking installation **elektrische** ~ electrical interlocking post

Stell-widerstand *m* variable resistance, rheostat (servo) **-winkel** *m* bevel, bevel rule **-zapfen** *m* adjustable pin, pivot **-zeit** *f* regulating time (servo) **-zeug** *n* adjusting gear **-zylinder** *m* operating magnet, operating cylinder

Stelze *f* shoe (plow)

Stelzen *pl* stilts **-bohrer** *m* stilted bit **-unterbau** *m* elevated pile foundation grill

Stemm-arbeiten *pl* chipping or chiseling work **-draht** *m* calking wire **-eisen** *n* chisel, crowbar **-lochen** *n* mortising (of wood)

stemmen to chisel, calk

Stemmen *n* calking, fullering

Stemmer *m* punch, drift

Stemm-fuge *f* calked joint **-hammer** *m* calking hammer **-kante** *f* calking edge **-lasche gegen Schienenwandern** splice bar to prevent creeping of the rails **-loch** *n* mortise **-maschine** *f* mortising machine **-meißel** *m* (calking) chisel **-naht** *f* calk weld **-säule** *f* miter or meeting post (sluice) **-setze** *f* calking tool

Stemmtor *n* gate pivoting about vertical axis along one edge, miter gate **hölzernes** ~ wooden mitering gate

Stemmung *f* calking

Stemmwinkel *m* angle stop

Stempel *m* stamp, stemple, prop, stay, stanchion, punch, brand, mark, post, strut, die, stamper, pestle, piston, ram, press, matrix, plunger **-abgabe** *f* stamp duty **-artiger Andruck** stamp-like thrust **-bogen** *m* stamped sheet of paper **-druck** *m* stamp printing **-einschlag** *m* die mark **-frei** free from stamp duty **-gebühr** *f* stamp duty **-guß** *m* die casting **-halter** *m* stamp bearer **-holz** *n* pit prop, bar timber **-kissen** *n* ink pad, stamp(ing) pad, stamp ink cushion **-kissendose** *f* rubber stamp box **-matrize** *f* cutting die plate

stempeln to stamp, mark, letter

Stempeln *n* punching

stempel-pflichtig subject to stamp duty **-platte** *f* proof mark **-presse** *f* hand press **-richtpresse** *f* gag press **-rohr** *n* plunger tube, piston tube **-satz** *m* gang of punches **-schaft** *m* die stamp **-schneider** *m* punch cutter **-setzer** *m* timberman, rubber stamp compositor **-stange** *f* shaft of the stamp **-tinte** *f* rubber stamp ink **-uhr** *f* time recorder **-verschiebung** *f* (Presse) ram displacing device

Stengel *m* stalk

Stengelansatzmaschine tubulating machine

stengelig spiky, stalked

Stengel-kristallisation *f* radial crystallization **-schneider** *m* stalk cutter **-haken** *m* (zum Aufhängen des Lotes) stem hook

Stenographie *f* shorthand

stenographieren to write (in) shorthand

Stenzilpapier *n* cyclostyle paper

Stephanit *m* stephanite

Steppen *n* metal stiching

steppen to quilt

Steppmaschine *f* stitching machine

Stereo-aufnahme *f* stereophotograph, stereo-exposure **-betrachter** *m* viewing stereoscope **-bild** *n* stereo-pair **-blende** *f* stereostop **-chemie** *f* stereochemistry **-chemisch** stereochemical **-durchleuchtung** *f* stereo-radioscopy, stereo-fluoroscopy **-grammbeschreibung** *f* stereogram description **-grammetrie** *f* stereophotogrammetry **-graphie** *f* descriptive geometry **-graphisch** stereographic **-isomer** *n* stereoisomer

Stereokomparatur, windschiefer ~ wind-tipped stereocomparator ~ **mit Blinkmikroskop** stereocomparator with flicker microscope

Stereo-meßkammer *f* photogrammetric stereo-camera **-metrie** *f* solid geometry **-phonisch** stereophonical **-photogrammetrie** *f* stereo-photogrammetry **-photographie** *f* stereoscopic photography **-planigraph** *m* stereophotographic plotting machine **-plastik** *f* relief mapping

Stereos *pl* stereotypes

Stereoskop *n* stereoscope

Stereoskopie *f* stereoscopy

Stereotypie-metall *n* stereo metal

stereoskopisch stereoscopic **-es Sehen und Messen** stereoscopic vision and measurement

Stereotelemeter *n* stereoscopic range finder

Stereotyp *m* stereotype

Stereotypie-anstalt *f* stereotyping workshop **-papier** *n* backing paper, flong

Stereotypieverhärtungsanlage *f* stereotype tempering plant
Stereo-vorhalter *m* stereo holder **-züge** *pl* stereo paths
Sterilisator *m* sterilizer
Sterilisierapparat *m* sterilizer
sterilisieren to sterilize
Sterilisier-fähigkeit *f* resistance to sterilization **-maschine** *f* sterilizer
Sterin *n* sterol
sterischer Faktor steric factor
Stern *m* star, asterisk, spring holder (print.) **~ mit vielen Spuren** multiprong star **im ~ geschaltet** star-connected
Stern (Kernexplosion) nuclear star
Stern-anker *m* radial or pole armature **-antenne** *f* star antenna **-artig gelagerte Typenhebel** radially arranged type bars **-ausgleichsstück** *n* differential star piece **-bedeckung** *f* occultation **-bildfigur** *f* zodiacal figure
Sternchen *n* asterisk
Sterndreieck *n* star delta (elec.) **-schalter** *m* star-delta switch **-übertragung** *f* star-mesh transformation
Sterndynamik *f* stellar dynamics
Sterne schießen to take bearings on the stars
Sternen *n* starring **-himmel** *m* stellar sky
Stern-flug *m* flight converging on one point, aviation rally, star flight **-förmig** radial, star-shaped, stellate **-forscher** *m* astronomer **-geschaltet** Y-connected, star-connected **-glied** *n* star circuit, T mesh **-glied(er)kette** *f* T-mesh network **-griff** *m* grip for clamp screw **-halle** *f* star-shaped shed **-haufen** *m* star cluster, stellar cluster
Stern-kabel *n* spiral-eight cable, quad-pair cable **-keilwelle** *f* multispline shaft **-korn** *m* revolving front sight **-kunde** *f* astronomy **-kundlich** astronomical **-leuchtkugel** *f* star shell **-meißel** *m* star bit **-mikrofon** *n* radial current transmitter **-motor** *m* radial engine, radial motor **-nähe** *f* periastron (astr.) **-netz** *n* radial network **-ortung** *f* celestial navigation **-platte** *f* tripod headplate
Sternpunkt *m* neutral or star point **-klemme** *f* neutral terminal
Stern-rad *n* star wheel, pin feed wheel, planetary pinion, turnstile **-rohr** *n* astronomical telescope **-schaltung** *f* Y connection, star circuit, star (polyphase) connection, star grouping **-schauzeichen** *n* (white) star indicator **-schlacke** *f* antimony flux
Stern-schnuppenschwarm *m* meteor shower **-schreiber** *m* plane-position indicator (PPI) **-signal** *n* star signal **-spannung** *f* Y voltage, star voltage **-standmotor** *m* fixed radial engine **-symbolschutzeinrichtung** *f* asterisk protection device **-system** *n* galaxy **-tag** *m* sidereal day **-umlaufmotor** *m* rotary-type or radial engine **-verkehr** *m* network radio communication **-verseilung** *f* star twisting **-vieleck** *n* star polygow
Sternvierer *m* spiral quad, spiral four, spiral four quad **-kabel** *n* spiral(ed) four cable, spiral quad cable
Stern-warte *f* observatory **-zahnrad** *n* star pinion **-zeit** *f* sidereal time
Steroid *n* steroid
Stert *m* tail
stet constant, continuous, stable, steady
Stethoskop *n* stethoscope
stetig steady, constant, perpetual, uniform, firm, rigid, sturdy, substantial, heavy **~ ähnliche Regelung** step control **-e Abbildung** continuous mapping **-e Belastung** continuous loading **-er Bildwechsel** continuous, steady, nonintermittent feed or motion of picture strip **-e Destillation** continuous distillation **-er Regler** continuous controller (servo)
stetigen to stabilize
Stetigförderer *m* continuous conveyer
Stetigkeit *f* uniformity, stability, continuity **~ des Spannungszustandes** stress continuity
Stetigkeits-bedingung *f* equation or condition of continuity **-begriff** *m* continuity concept **-methode** *f* continuity method **-rechner** *m* analogue computer
Steuer *f* tax, rate, duty, assessment
Steuer *n* rudder, (helm) controls, steering wheel, fixed planes, control surfaces **mit losgelassenem ~ fliegen** to fly hands off
Steuer-abläufe *pl* control measures **-änderungsgeschwindigkeit** *f* (eines Kreisels) command rate (gyro) **-anlage** *f* control arrangement, steering mechanism **-apparat** *m* controller, steering gear, control gear **-arm** *m* steering arm **-ausbeute** *f* control ratio **-ausschlag** *m* control deflection, angular displacement or movement of control surface **-ausweis** *m* license, permit **-automatik** *f* automatic flight control
steuerbar controllable, modulable, maneuverable, manageable. steerable **-er Sporn** steerable tail skid
Steuerbarkeit *f* maneuverability, handling
Steuer-batterie *f* control battery **-befehl** *m* control command **-befehlspeicher** *m* program counter or register **-begrenzung** *f* control limitation **-beschläge** *pl* control fittings **-betätigung** *f* actuating mechanism **-blende** *f* modulating electrode, modulation shield, modulation grid, double-ended grid
Steuerbord *n* starboard **-dalbe** *f* starboard dolphin or pale **-korrektor** *m* starboard corrector **-kurve** *f* starboard curve **-licht** *n* starboard light **-maschine** *f* starboard engine
Steuerbordmotor *m* starboard motor or engine **der äußere ~** starboard outer engine
Steuerbord-seitenlicht *n* starboard light **-voraus** *n* starboard bow **-zeichen** *n* starboard signal
Steuer-bühne *f* platform **-daumen** *m* sequence switch cam **-diagramm** *n* valve-timing diagram **-dose** *f* receptacle, socket **-draht** (am Leuchtstoffschirm) grid wire (TV) **-drossel** *f* modulating choke, modulation reactor, magnetic modulator **-druck** *m* control pressure, controller output pressure
Steuer-eigenschaften *pl* handling qualities **-einrichtung** *f* control **-einschub** *m* control unit, plug-in timer **-elektrode** *f* control electrode **-faktor** *m* control ratio **-fähigkeit** *f* controllability, maneuverability
Steuerfläche *f* control surface, vane (aviation), rudder surface, movable surface **kleine ~** trimming tab (auxiliary control)
Steuer-flossenwurzel *f* base of vertical stabilizer **-flügel** *m* control fin **-formel** *f* rating formula

-frequenz *f* pilot frequency, synchronizing frequency, control frequency **-funken** *m* timed spark **-gehäuse** *n* steering-gear case **-gelenk** *n* steering knuckle **-generator** *m* master oscillator, drive oscillator, control generator **-gerät** *n* operating mechanism, modulator unit, stearing gear, gyro pilot **-gestänge** *n* control rods or linkage **-getriebe** *n* shaft-sliding mechanism **-gewalt** *f* steering control

Steuergitter *n* control grid, signal grid, shield **-einsatzspannung** *f* grid cut-off voltage **-gleichstrom** *m* D.C. control grid current **-modulation** *f* control-grid modulation **-photozelle** *f* three-electrode cell **-sperrspannung** *f* grid cut-off voltage **-strom** *m* current flowing from grid to screen **-verspannung** *f* grid bias

Steuer-gleichspannung *f* direct-current control voltage **-gleichung** *f* steering-control equation

Steuerhebel *m* control or steering lever, stick, operating lever, rocker arm ~ **zum Heben und Senken des Querbalkens** power-control handle ~ **für die Höhenstellung** elevating lever

Steuer-hubrad *n* (Ölpumpe) control lifting cam (lubricator) **-hystereses** *f* control hysteresis

Steuerimpuls *m* control impulse ~ **für Torschaltungen** enabling pulse

Steuer-kabel *n* control cable **-kanal** *m* pilot channel **-kante** *f* leading edge, guiding edge **-kantensteigung** *f* pitch of the control edge **-kanzel** *f* pulpit **-kasten** *m* steering frame, ground control box (missiles) **-kette** *f* timing chain, control chain **-klinke** *f* control pawl **-knagge** *f* following lever

Steuerknüppel *m* control stick, control column, cyclic stic **den ~ leicht hin und her bewegen** to joggle the control stick

Steuer-knüppelfuß *m* base of control stick **-kolben** *m* control piston, ported piston valve

Steuerkraft *f* stick or control force **-schreiber** *m* control-force recorder

Steuerkreis *m* pilot or master oscillator, control circuit **-abstimmung** *f* master-oscillator tuning

Steuerkreisabstimmungs-leistung *f* output from master-oscillator stage **-röhre** *f* master-oscillator control tube **-stufe** *f* master-oscillator control stage

Steuer-kreisteil *m* master oscillator circuit **-kupplung** *f* control coupling

Steuerkurs *m* heading (aviat.) **mißweisender ~** magnetic heading **rechtweisender ~** true heading

Steuer-kurve *f* cam **-lagenanzeiger** *m* control-position indicator **-lastig** down by the stern (navy), control heavy **-lastigkeit** *f* trim (as of an airship) **-leistung** *f* rating horsepower, (grid) driving power (radio) **-leitung** *f* pilot wire (circuit), control mechanism or cables trailing, cable (lift)

Steuerleitungs-druck *m* control line pressure **-rohr** *n* steering post

Steuer-lineal *n* control-bar **-lochstreifen** *m* pilot tape **-losigkeit** *f* lack of control **-luftverteiler und Sammler** air control manifold and header **-mann** *m* helmsman, coxswain **-maschinensatz** *m* control set **-mechanismus** *m* movement control mechanism **-meßbetrag** *m* (einheitlicher) basis amount

steuern to steer, navigate, control, regulate, pilot, route, prevent

steuernde Sägezahnspannung *f* sawtooth driving voltage

Steuer-nocken *m* sequence switch cam **-öffnung** *f* port

Steuerorgan *n* control member, control, control surface, control gear, fixed plane ~ **mit Wahl der Einstellung von Hand** selective manual control

Steuer-oszillator *m* master oscillator **-pferdestärke** *f* taxable horsepower (motor vehicles) (Germany) **-pflichtig** assessable, taxable **-potential** *n* control voltage (potential) **-pult** *n* control desk **-quarz** *m* oscillator crystal, stabilizing quartz crystal **-rad** control wheel, crank wheel, derrick wheel, steering wheel

Steuerräderdeckel *m* crankcase front cover

Steuerrad-höhe *f* elevation control wheel **-seilscheibe** *f* control-wheel center plate or disk **-seite** *f* aximuth control **-verbindung** *f* steering connection

Steuer-rakete *f* small pulse jet, vernier **-raum** *m* buncher space (radio) **-relais** *n* pilot relay, control relay **-rohr** *n* steering tube **-röhre** *f* control valve, pilot oscillator, master oscillator, exciter tube, modulator tube, drive tube, drive oscillator **-rose** *f* pointer of autopilot

Steuerruder *n* rudder, steering oar ~ **mit Flettner-Hilfsruder** control surface with Flettner balance

Steuersack *m* balloon rudder **-leine** *f* rudder bag cord

Steuer-satz *m* treasury rating **-sätze** *pl* steering sets **-säule** *f* control column (aviation), steering column (electronics), cyclic control column (helicopter)

Steuersäulen-kopf *m* head of control column **-lager** *n* control column bearings or supporting base

Steuer-schalter *m* master switch, control switch, sequence switch, controller **-schaltung mit Servomotor** servomotor-operated controller **-schärfe** *f* accuracy, sharpness of control **-scheibe** *f* plate cam **-schema** *n* timing schedule **-schenkel** *m* steering knuckle or swivel

Steuerschieber *m* servo valve spool, distributing slide valve servo-piston **Motor mit nur einem ~ nach Burt-McCollum** monosleeve valve engine

Steuerschiebeventil *n*, **rückdruckfreies ~** balanced spool valve

Steuerschirm *m* drogue **-schnecke** *f* steering worm **-schütz** *m* power relay **-schraube** *f* operating or steering screw **-schwanz** *m* steering fin (naut., ball)

Steuerseil *n* control cable **-durchführung** *f* control-cable guide

Steuer-sender *m* control transmitter, pilot or master oscillator, sender control **-sessel** *m* control chair **-signalspannung** *f* drive voltage **-spannung** *f* control voltage, excitation drive **-speicher** *m* control storage **-spiel** *n* control clearance or play **-spindel** *f* steering worm gear **-stand** *m* control stand or post **-stange** *f* steering rod **-stelle** *f* sound gate (film), impulse-receiving place or point **-strich** *m* line of zero drift (aviation), lubber line

Steuerstrom *m* steering-control current **-kreis** *m* control circuit **-kupplung** *f* control-cable coupling **-nockenschalter** *m* cam switch for control current **-steckdose** *f* socket for control current **-stoß** *m* directing pulse

Steuerstufe *f* drive or power stage, control stage **fremdgesteuerte quarzgesteuerte ~** crystal-stabilized oscillator stage, master or driver stage stabilized by quartz crystal

Steuerstufenöhre *f* master oscillator

Steuer-tafel *f* navigation or steering table **-teil** *m* steering part, main transmitter modulator of radar equipment **-tisch** *m* pulpit, platform **-traverse mit Gabeln** steering tie rod with jaw ends **-trommel** *f* drum cam

Steuerung *f* (Tätigkeit) steering, piloting; (elektr.) control; (Vorrichtung) steering mechanism; (Ventil~) valve gear, open-loop control (aut. contr); controlling device, governing control, directing or routing (through selectors), pilotage, synchronization, cam, distributing gear, regulation, timing of engine **~ der Ablenkspannungen** deflecting voltage control **~ auf dunkel** modulation to dark condition, negative modulation **~ auf hell** modulation to light condition, positive modulation **~ der Punkthelligkeit** control of the spot brightness **~ durch unrunde Scheiben** cam gearing **automatische ~** (automatic) control or steering, timing of engine, automatic pilot **phasenstarre ~** phase-rigid control

Steuerungs-antrieb *m* steering force, valve gear **-art** *f* system of control **-ausschlag** *m* steering lock **-bereich** *n* drive range, swing of amplifier grid **-diagramm** *n* timing or control chart, timing diagram **-druckluftleitung** *f* valve gear air piping **-eigenschaft** *f* control or handling characteristic **-elektrode** *f* control electrode **-exzenter** *m* distributing eccentric

Steuerungs-gegenmutter *f* control head locking nut **-getriebe** *n* valve or control mechanism **-gitter** *n* control grid **-hebel** *m* starting lever, bar reversing lever, control lever **-kanal** *m* steering channel **-kupplung** *f* steering clutch **-planetenrad** *n* planetary gear (of the valve gear) **-pult** *n* steering panel **-teil** *m* link motion part **-vorrichtung** *f* synchronizing or timing gear **-welle** *f* cam or gear shaft

Steuer-ventil *n* control valve, distribution valve, pilot valve **-verstärker** *m* control amplifier **-verzögerungsrelais** *n* time lag relay **-vorgang** *m* controlling action **-vorrichtung** *f* control appliance **-wagen** *m* driving trailer **-wähler** *m* control switch **-walze** *f* drum controller **-wechsel** *m* change of control (aviation) **-wechselkreis** *m* gyration with apparently inverted control **-wechselkurve** *f* curve with (apparently) inverted controls (aerob.)

Steuerwege, zu große ~ ausführen to overtravel

Steuerwelle *f* control shaft, governing shaft, pilot wave, drive shaft, camshaft, control wave (in chain broadcasting) **~ für die Höhenstellung** elevating-lever shaft **~ für den Senkrechtvorschub** vertical power rod

Steuerwellen-antrieb *m* camshaft drive **-drehung** *f* revolution or rotation of camshaft **-drehzahl** *f* camshaft speed **-exzenterfräsmaschine** *f* cam milling machine **-exzenterschleifmaschine** *f* cam grinding machine **-gehäuse** *n* camshaft housing or casing **-kreis** *m* camshaft cycle **-lager** *n* camshaft bearing **-magnetzünder** *m* camshaft driven magento **-rad** *n* camshaft gear

Steuer-wendzeiger *m* control turn-and-bank indicator **-werk** *n* (flying) controls, control system **-wesen** *n* taxation, taxes **-wicklung** *f* control winding **-winde** *f* control capstan or winch **-winkelscheibe** *f* bearing disk **-wirkung** *f* control effect **-zeichen** *n* pilot signal **-zeiger** *m* bank or turn indicator

Steuerzeit *f* control reaction time, control period **-schalter** *m* control time switch

Steuerzug-führung *f* control cable guide **-kanal** *m* control wire or cable duct **-kupplung** *f* control-cable coupling

steuerzeiten und einstellen to time

Steuer-zug *m* control cable, control line **-zylinder** *m* control cylinder, focusing cylinder

Steven *m* stem, post

Stibnit *m* stibnite

Stich *m* stitch, sting, spot-check, rise-to-span ratio of arch, taphole (metal.), tapping, tapped metal, pass (in rolling), shrink hole, shrink, porous spot, puncture, stab, bite, tap; (Nadel~) prick; (Stoß) thrust; (Spaten~) cut; (Kupfer~) engraving; (~ halten) hold good, hold water **~ im Ton** tint

Stich-abnahme *f* reduction per pass **-anker** *m* iron tie, wall clamp **-auge** *n* taphole, iron notch, tapping hole **-axt** *f* twibil, mortise ax **-balken** *m* short tie beam **-ballon** *m* sounding or registering balloon **-beitel** *m* **für Drechsler** turner's cross-cutting chisel **-boden** *m* soil that may be excavated with a spade

Stichbogen *m* segmental arch **-gewölbe** *n* surbased vault

Stich-drehzähler *m* chronotachometer, hand tachometer **-eisen** *n* broad chisel, stocker's rod

Stichel *m* style, planing tool, cutter, stylus **-halter** *m* clapper block **-halterstift** *m* clapper block pin **-haus** *n* tool post, toolholder **-klotz** *m* tool block **-schaft** *m* tool shank **-schleifmaschine** *f* cutter-grinding machine **-schlitten** *m* tool slide **-wirkung** *f* marking on metal

stichfest punctureproof

Stich-flamme *f* torch for lighting blasting fuses, fine-pointed flame, explosive flame, flareback, shooting flame, jet of flame **-flammenwirkung** *f* blowpipe action **-flecken** *pl* blemishes **-folge** *f* succession of passes **-größe** *f* size of pitch **-haltig** lasting, sound, valid **-haltigkeit** *f* soundness, validity **-kabel** *n* branch or by-pass cable **-kanal** *m* cutoff canal, cross-intersecting canal, cross or branch culvert **-leitung** *f* tie line, open feeder, tap line, stub line or cable

Stichleitungs-träger *m* stub support **-transformator** *m* matching transformer

Stichloch *n* taphole, iron notch, tapping hole **-armatur** *f* taphole fitting **-öffner** *m* taphole opener **-stopfmaschine** *f* taphole gun, blast-furnace gun, clay gun **-versetzung** *f* taphole displacement

Stich-maß *n* inside micrometer, inside-caliper gauge, caliber, gauge, template **-pfropf** *m* taphole plug

Stichprobe *f* random test, random sample, spot check

Stichproben-kontrolle *f* method of random sampling **-messungen** *pl* tests on selected samp-

les **-prüfung mit bestimmtem Hundertsatz** percentage inspection **-zählung** *f* peg count
Stich-programm *n* succession of passes **-säge** *f* compass saw **-tag** *m* deadline, key-day **-wahl** *f* random choice **-wort** *n* cue, key word, code
Stichwörterverzeichnis *n* subject index, list of code words, key-word index
Stich-zahl *f* module **-zähler** *m* revolution counter, tachometer **-zählung** *f* peg count
Stick-apparat *m* embroidering apparatus **-dioxyd** *n* nitrogen dioxide
Sticken *n* embroidering
Stickerei *f* embroidery **-appretur** *f* embroidery finishing
Stickgas *n* carbon dioxide, asphyxiating gas, nitrogen (gas)
stickig damp, suffocating, choking
Stickkohlenstoff *m* nitrogen carbide, nitrocarbon
Stickluft *f* nitrogen
Stickmaschineneinfädlerin *f* needle filler of embroidering machines
Sticknadel *f* embroidering needle
Stickoxydul *n* nitrous oxide
Stickperle *f* glass bead
Stickstoff *m* nitrogen **-ammonium** *n* ammonium nitride **-anlage** *f* nitrogen plant **-dampf** *m* nitrous vapor **-dioxyd** *n* nitric oxide, nitrogen dioxide **-gewinnung** *f* production of nitrogen **-halogen** *n* nitrogen halide **-haltig** nitrogenous **-härten** *n* nitriding **-kalomel** *n* mercurous (azide) nitride **-lithium** *n* lithium nitride
Stickstoff-messer *m* azotometer, nitrometer **-metall** *n* metallic nitride **-natrium** *n* sodium nitride **-oxyd** *n* nitric oxide **-oxydul** *n* nitrous oxide, nitrogen monoxide **-quecksilber** *n* mercury nitride **-quecksilberoxydul** *n* mercurous azide **-silber** *n* silver nitride **-sphäre** *f* stratosphere **-tetroxyd** *n* nitrogen tetroxyde **-nadin** *n* vanadium nitride **-verbindung** *f* nitrogen compound **-zyantitan** *n* titanium cyanonitride
Stickwetter *pl* chokedamp
Stiefel *m* boot, cylinder (of pumps) **-bohrung** *f* foothole
Stiefel-Scheibenwalzprozeß *m* Stiefel disk-piercing process
Stiege *f* staircase
Stiel *m* post, stem, haft, handle, strut, shaft, stud, shank, column, stalk **linker ~** left-hand post **rechter ~** right-hand post **beide Stiele** both posts
Stiel-ansatz *n* shank **-antenne** *f* dielectric rod antenna **-breite** *f* thickness of strut **-dicke** *f* thickness of strut **-faser** *f* stalk fiber **-feilkloben** *m* hand or pin vise **-foramen** *n* pedicle foramen **-glied** *n* stem ossicle, columnal **-hammer** *m* chop hammer **-hörer** *m* hand receiver
Stiel-klappe *f* pedicle valve **-knotenpunkt** *m* strut (nodal) point **-meißel** *m* rod chisel **-neigung** *f* inclination of strut **-strahlantenne** *f* dielectric rod antenna **-strahler** *m* rod antenna **-strahlung** *f* stem radiation **-tiefe** *f* width or depth of strut **-trägheitsmoment** *n* moment of inertia of the column
Stift *m* pin; (Holz) peg; (Bolzen) bolt; (Zwecke) tack; (Zapfen) pivot; stud, nail, crayon, pencil, foundry nail, spike, terminal, lug, plug **federnder ~** spring or elastic pin **konischer ~** taper pin
Stift-abhebemaschine *f* flask-lifting post machine **-ankerwerk** (Uhr) pin lever movement **-bolzen** *m* stud bolt **-büchse** *f* pin barrel **-draht** *m* pin wire **-elektrode** *f* pin electrode
Stiftenabhebeformmaschine *f* flask-lifting post machine **~ mit Handstampfung** hand-ramming flask-lifting post machine
Stiftenabhebehandformmaschine *f* hand-operated flask-lifting molding machine
Stiften-abhebung *f* pin lifting **-dreschmaschine** *f* peg drum threshing machine **-führung** *f* pinguide, pinholder
Stift-farbe *f* pencil color **-fräser** *m* hollow mill **-führung** *f* stem guide, pin guide **-hammer** *m* tack hammer **-kette** *f* riveted or bushing chain **-kloben** *m* pin vice **-lager** *n* (hinge) pin bearing **-lagerung** *f* pin suspension, pin support **-leiste** *f* pin bar
Stiftloch *n* pin hole **-reibahle** *f* taper pin reamer
Stift-mühle *f* pinned disk mill **-nagel** *m* brad **-nietung** *f* pin riveting **-rad** *n* pin wheel **-scheibe** *f* rotating plate with fixed studs **-schlüssel** *m* socket screw wrench, pin spanner **-schmierapparat** *m* needle lubricator
Stiftschraube *f* stud, stud bolt, tap bolt, setscrew **~ am Kurbelgehäuse zur Zylinderbefestigung** cylinder stud **~ zur Befestigung** mounting stud **Schlüssel zum Einziehen von Stiftschrauben** stud driver
Stiftschrauben-mutter *f* stud nut **-schlüssel** *m* stud driver
Stift-schreiber *m* embosser **-schweißen** *n* tack welding **-sicherung** *f* pin safety device **-sockel** *m* bayonet socket **-wandler** *m* probe transformer
Stigmator *m* stigmator
Stil *m* style, manner **im großen Stile** on a large scale
Stilb *n* stilb
Stilben-Kristallszintillator *m* stilbene crystal scintillator
still still, silent, quiet, motionless, dull, stagnant **-e Entladung** corona, silent discharge
Stille *f* quiet, lull, silence, dullness, flatness, stagnant condition
Stillen *f pl* doldrums
stillgelegt standing idle
Stillhalteforderungen *pl* standstill claims
still-legen to put out of commission, put out of service, close down, shut down, abandon (mine) **-liegezeit** *f* period of inactivity or idleness **-legung** *f* shutdown, closing up, stoppage **-liegen** inoperation
stillschweigend silent, tacit, implicit, implied, quiet, calm **-es Abkommen** tacit understanding
Still-setzen *n* stopping, shut-down, switching off **-setzung** *f* arresting, stopping
Stillstand *m* standstill, stoppage, stagnation, cessation, stopping, shutdown **zum ~ bringen** to arrest **zum ~ kommen** to come to rest
Stillstands-frist *f* respite, delay, prolongation (min.) **-zeiten** *pl* periods of disuse
still-stehen to stand still, stop, arrest, be stationary **-stehend** standing still, stationary, stagnant, tied up **-stellen** to stop **-wasser** *n* slack water
Stimm-bänder *pl* vocal cords **-berechtigt** entitled to vote
Stimme *f* voice **gemischte ~** mutation stop

(organ) **schwebende** ~ voix céleste (organ)
Stimmeisen *n* tuning key; wrest
stimmen to vote, tune
Stimmen *f* tuning
Stimmenmehrheit *f* majority of votes
Stimmer *m* tuner
Stimmflöte *f* tuning pipe, pitch pipe
Stimmgabel *f* tuning fork **schreibende** ~ tuning-fork chronoscope
Stimmgabel-generator *m* tuning-fork-controlled oscillator **-kreisel** *m* tuning fork gyro **-kristall** *n* tuning fork crystal **-röhrengenerator** *m* tuning-fork-controlled (tube) oscillator **-sender** *m* tuning-fork-controlled oscillator, vibrating-reed transmitter **-steuerung** *f* tuning-fork control, tuning-fork-oscillator drive **-summer** *m* tuning fork oscillator **-unterbrecher** *m* tuning-fork circuit breaker, tuning-fork interrupter **-zinken** *m* prong or tine of a tuning fork
stimm-hafte Konsonanten sonant, voiced, or vocal consonants **-lose Konsonanten** surd, nonvocal, or breathed consonants **-pfeife** *f* tuning pipe, pitch pipe **-platte** *f* reed board, reed plate (of accordion) **-schlüssel** *m* tuning key, wrench (of kettle drum) **-stock** *m* wrest plank (piano) **-ton** *m* tuning pitch **-umfang** *m* vocal compass or range
Stimmung *f* morale (mill.), disposition, temper **hohe** ~ high pitch
Stimmungsbild *n* key or sentiment picture **dunkles** ~ low-key picture **überhelles** ~ high-key picture
Stimmungs-spruch *m* tuning message **-wechsel** *m* change of tendency or tone (stock exchange)
Stimmwirbel *m* wrest pin
stimulieren to stimulate
Stink-bombe *f* stink bomb **-schiefer** *m* fetid shale **-stein** *m* stinkstone, anthraconite
Stipendienstiftung *f* establishment of scholarships
Stipendium *n* scholarship
stippenfreie Drucke prints free from specks
stippig werden to become pricked
Stirn *f* front, head, forehead **-ansicht** *f* front view, front elevation, end elevational view **-band** *n* head strap, headband **-blatt** *n* hub plate **-blech** *n* front plate **-böschung** *f* face bank **-brett** *n* fascia **-bügel** *m* headrest **-eingriffswinkel** *m* transverse-pressure angle **-elektrode** *f* front electrode **-ende** *n* front end
Stirnfläche *f* face, frontal area, front surface, end plane, transverse plane ~ **des Kristalls** end of the crystal ~ **des Motors** frontal area of motor ~ **bearbeiten** to face
Stirnflächen *pl* spot facing ~ **fräsen** to spot-face
Stirnflächenschub *m* (Kp/m^2) thrust/frontal area ratio (1b/59 ft)
Stirn-flansch *m* front flange, end sleeve for buffing cylinder **-fräser** *m* front-milling tool, end mill, end-milling cutter **-fräsmaschine** *f* end mill, end-milling cutter **-fuge** *f* frontal joint **-gehäuse** *n* entry duct, nose cowling **-getriebe** *n* spur pinion, spur gear **-hammer** *m* front hammer **-holm** *m* head spar **-holz** *n* crosscut or end-grained wood
Stirn-kappe *f* nose cowling **-kehlnahtprobe** *f* double fillet flanged butt weld **-kipper** *m* end-tip wagon **-kollektor** *m* vertical commutator **-kühler** *m* front radiator **-kurbel** *f* overhung crank, front crank **-lager** *n* end journal bearing **-lampe** *f* headlight **-leiste** *f* wing-rib former (aviation), leading-edge strip, cap strip **-moräne** *f* terminal moraine **-motor** *m* spur-wheel air engine **-naht** *f* front seam, transverse weld
Stirnplatte *f* front plate ~ **des Überlaufs** weir dam plate
Stirnprofil des Schraubrades section of worm gear on transverse section
Stirnrad *n* spur gear, spur wheel ~ **mit Schrägverzahnung** gear with cogging, stepped gear ~ **mit Winkelverzahnung** herringbone gear, double helical-tooth gear
Stirnrad-abwälzfräsmaschine *f* spurgear generating machine **-antrieb** *m* spur-wheel drive or gear **-differential** *n* spur-wheel differential **-drehwerksgetriebe** *n* spur wheel slewing gear
Stirnräder-getriebe *n* spur gearing **-paar** *n* spur gearing, pair of spur gears **-teilkopf** *m* dividing head for spur gears **-werk** *n* right spur gearing
Stirnrad-fräser *m* spur-gear cutter **-fräsmaschine** *f* spur-gear cutting machine **-getriebe** *n* spur-gear system, right spur gearing **-hobelmaschine** *f* spur-gear planing machine **-innenstoßmaschine** *f* internal gear shaper
Stirnradritzel *n* spur pinion **-welle** *f* spur pinion shaft
Stirnrad-schleifmaschine *f* spur-gear grinding machine **-schutzkappe** *f* face-gear guard **-stoßmaschine** *f* spur-gear shaper **-übersetzung** *f* spur-gear transmission **-vorgelege** *n* spur wheel reduction gearing **-wälzfräser** *m* spur gear hob **-wendegetriebe** *n* reverse gear, spur gearing
Stirn-rampe *f* end-loading ramp **-rand** *m* anterior end (geol.) **-reifen** *m* head-band **-reihe** *f* front row **-riemen** *m* brow band **-ring** *m* front flange **-ruder** *n* spur gear **-ringkühler** *m* front radial cooler **-schattenriß** *m* front stilhouette **-seil** *n* drag wire
Stirnseite *f* interface, front side, face, front end, cross grain ~ **einer Mauer** mantle or outer stack of a wall
stirnseitiges Hinterschleifen face-relieving
Stirnsenker *m* spot facer
Stirnsitz *m* cab over engine, forward control **-antrieb** *m* forward control drive
Stirn-stoß *m* flange edge joint, front joint **-streuung** *f* overhang leakage flux **-stütze** *f* head rest **-teilung** *f* circumferential pitch (of gear) **-treibrad** *n* main (driving) wheel
Stirn- und Kegelräder *pl* spur gear, bevel gear
Stirn-verbindung *f* face connector **-verspannung** *f* (external) drag bracing **-verzahntes Rad** spur gear **-verzahnung** *f* radial serrations
Stirnwand *f* front wall, front plate, end wall, end plank, dashboard, dash (car) **-befestigung** *f* (Magnetzünder) spigot mounting **-lampenschalter** *m* panel light switch
Stirn-welle *f* front wave, impact wave, bow wave **-wetter** *n* frontal weather **-widerstand** *m* head resistance, frontal resistance, leading-end resistance **-wind** *m* headwind **-wulst** *f* forehead pad
Stirnzahn *m* gudgeon **Fräser mit Stirnzähnen** end mill, end-milling cutter
Stirn-zahnrad *n* spur gear **-zapfen** *m* faced end journal, gudgeon, trunnion, end journal

Stöberschnee *m* drifting snow
Stobie-Ofen *m* Stobie (series-arc) furnace
stochastisch stochastic **-er Zugriff** random access
Stoch-apparat *m* mechanical poker **-arbeit** *f* poking **-eisen** *n* poker bar, poking bar, poker, stoker, stirrer bar, clinkering spear, agitator, rake
stochen to poke, stir, stoke
Stocher *m* poker, poking bar, fireman **-öffnung** *f* poking door
stochern to stoke
stöchiometrisch stoichiometric(al) **-er Metalloidmangel** stoichiometric metalloid deficiency
Stochstangenspitze *f* poker tip
Stock *m* (cleaning) rod, stick, cane, story (of building), trunk, stump, stock **-anker** *m* stock anchor **-aufschläger** *m* centrifiner **-biegemaschine** *f* stick bending machine **-eisen** *n* poker
Stöckel *m* anvil inset stake
stocken to cake (paint), turn moldy, line with turf, stop (machine), falter, hesitate, slacken, hold up, arrest, decay
stockend stagnant
Stocken ins ~ geraten to be in arrears with
Stockerplatte *f* roughening plate
Stock-erz *n* ore in large lumps **-flecke** *pl* molds **-flöte** *f* stick flute **-getriebe** *n* lantern (mech.) **-gleis** *n* dead-end siding **-hammer** *m* granulating or granulated hammer
stockig rotten, moldy, stubborn, stocky, stumpy
Stock-konverter *m* stock converter **-lacksäure** *f* lacc(in)ic acid **-laterne** *f* lantern on post, cresset **-leiter** *f* peg ladder, rack **-punkt** *m* setting point, freezing point, point of congelation, pour point, solidifying point **-rübe** *f* bolter, seed runner **-schere** *f* bench shears **-schiene** *f* stock rail, rigid rail (of the switch) **-schlüssel** *m* box spanner **-schutz** *m* pole-butt reinforcement **-schwimmer** *m* staff or pole float
Stock- und Schlagpresse matrix striking press
Stockung *f* stoppage, stagnation, obstruction, standstill, loss of time
stockunklarer Anker *m* anchor fouled by the stock
Stockwalke *f* fulling mill
Stockwerk *n* floor, story, section (geol.) **im ersten ~** on the first floor **im oberen ~, im höheren ~** upstairs
Stockwerkrahmen *m* multiple-story (rigid) frame
Stockzwinge *f* ferrule
Stoff *m* stuff, material, cloth, matter, substance, stock, subject **~ für die Bespannung** fabric for covering plane parts **abgeschiedener ~** precipitate **gelöster ~** solute **fettig gemahlener ~** wet-beaten pulp **samtartiger ~** velvet (like material)
Stoff-abfall *m* shavings, chips, waste, scrap **-abflußnute** *f* flash groove, overflow groove **-achse** *f* material axis **-auflauf** *m* breast box **-aufwand** *m* expenditure or requirement of material **-ausgleich** *m* material balance
Stoffbahn *f* web of fabric or cloth **-breite** *f* gore panel width
Stoff-baum *m* cloth beam **-bedeckung** *f* draping, gobo, tormentor **-bespannt** fabric-covered
Stoffbespannung *f* cloth covering, fabric covering **absorbierende ~** space cloth
Stoff-büchse *f* stuffing box **-bütte** *f* machine chest (paper mfg.) **-dichte** *f* stock density **-druckerfuß** *m* pressure foot of a sewing machine **-durchsatz** *m* rate of flow
Stoffe *pl* materials, stores, cloth
Stoffeinlage *f* liner, packing, filler, laying in **neue ~ eines reparierten Reifens** reliner (of tire)
Stoff-einlauf *m* breast box (paper mfg.) **-fänger** *m* pulp catcher or collector **-fehler** *m* defect, flaw of material **-fluß** *m* flow of material **-gewicht** *n* (unit) weight of material, specific gravity (of material) **-gliederung** *f* classification of equipment **-gliederungsziffer** *f* materials category number
Stoff-kassette *f* magazine of woven fabrics **-kasten** *m* drainer, draining tank or chest (paper mfg.) **-ketten** *f pl* substance chains **-kiste** *f* machine chest **-kragen** *m* vent collar (parachute) **-lage** *f* layer of fabric **-leitung** *f* nutrient transmission
stofflich material
stofflos immaterial
Stoff-lutte *f* canvas pipe or drain **-mangel** *m* deficiency or shortage of material, underfill (in rolling) **-mühle** *f* beater, rag engine (paper mfg.) **-patent** *n* patent covering substance or material, product patent **-probe** *f* test of material **-prüfeinrichtung** *f* material testing device **-prüfung** *f* fabric test **-scheibe für Aufhängung** suspension patch **-scheibenbelag** *m* cloth-disk cover
stoffschlüssige Sicherung der Schraube screw retention of self substance
Stoff-spannung *f* fabric tension or tautness **-teil** *m* facepiece (gas mask), particle **-teilchen** *n* particle (of matter), corpuscle **-überschuß** *m* excess of material, overfill (in rolling) **-überzug** *m* **-umkleidung** *f* cloth covering **-ventil** *n* fabric valve **-verbindung** *f* composition of matter **-verbrauch** *m* material consumption **-verwickelung** *f* cloth winding **-vorhang** *m* (cloth) curtain **-wanderung** *f* flow of material
Stoffwechsel *m* metabolism **-bilanz** *f* metabolism balance **-vorgang** *m* combustion, metabolic process
Stoff-zahl *f* number of components **-zerfall** *m* decay, decomposition **-zustand** *m* state of aggregation
Stoker *m* stoker **-feuerung** *f* stoker firing
Stokes-Gasmörser *m* Stokes trench mortar
Stoll-block *m* staker **-eisen** *n* stake **-maschine** *f* staking machine
stollen to stake (leather mfg.)
Stollen *m* (Pfosten) post; (Stütze) support; (unterirdischer Gang) tunnel, adit; tunnel, dugout, gallery (min.), duct (for pipe lines), heading, penstock, conduit, drift, adit **-bau** *m* gallery construction **-bergbau** *m* drift mine, tunnel mining **-betrieb** *m* drift mining **-eisen** *n* horseshoe with calkings **-herstellungsmaschine** *f* cramp-iron machine **-holz** *n* quarters, props **-mundloch** *n* end of tunnel, mouth of an adit **-ort** *m* working face, end of adit **-zimmerung** *f* tunnel timbering
Stollkrücke *f* crutch
Stolperdraht *m* trip wire **-hindernis** *n* trip-wire entanglement
stolpern to stumble, trip
Stolzit *m* lead tungstate

Stoneyketten roller trains
Stoneyscher Rollschütze stoney gate
Stopf-arbeit *f* tamping performance **-büchse** *f* gland, packing box, stuffing box
Stopfbüchsen-brille *f* gland (mech.) **-deckel** *m* stuffing-box cover **-dichtung** *f* stuffing-box packing **-dichtungsring** *m* gland sealing ring **-einsatz** *m* stuffing-box packing **-führung** *f* stuffing-box guide **-kondensator** *m* gland leak-off condenser **-kühlungsöl** *n* gland oil **-packung** *f* packer, rod packing, packing gland (aviation) **-ring** *m* rod-packing gland **-rohr** *n* stuffing-box pipe **-schraube** *f* stuffing-box stud, gland stud
Stopfdichtung *f* packing washer
stopfen to stuff, darn
Stopfen *m* threaded plug, stopper, piercer, mandrel **schräg gebohrter ~** oblique-bored stopper
Stopfen *n* tamming, padding, stopping, mending **~ des Geleises** track tamping or packing
Stopfen-ausguß *m* stopper nozzle **-kopf** *m* stopper head **-lehre** *f* (Lehrdorn) plug gauge **-pfanne** *f* bottom-pour ladle; teeming ladle, bottom-tap ladle, stopper ladle **-stange** *f* stopper rod **-walzwerk** *n* piercing mill, plug mill, high mill
Stopfer *m* tamping tool **-kolben** *m* tamper cylinder
Stopf-hacke *f* packer, beater, (tamping) pick **-holz** *n* filler, plug **-maschine** *f* notch gun, blast-furnace gun, mending machine **-packing** *f* loose-fill packing **-schläger** *m* tamping rod **-stange** *f* packing rod **-ton** *m* stopped tone
Stop-gestänge *n* cutoff rod **-hebel** *m* cutoff lever
Stopp-bad *n* shortstop bath **-bahn** *f* stopway **-befehl, bedingter** conditional breakpoint instruction
Stoppel-pflug *m* stubble plow **-rohr** *n* ratoons
stoppen to stop **Zeit ~** to time
Stopper *m* stopper **seinen ~ brechen, seinen ~ abtreiben** to let go the stopper
Stopp-kette *f* stopper **-licht** *n* stop light **-lichter** *pl* tail lights (auto) **-lichtleitung** *f* stop lamp cable **-lichtdrehschalter** *m* stop light switch **-lichtschalter** *m* stop light switch **-relais** *n* stopping relay **-schalter** *m* stop light switch **-schaltuhr** *f* stop control clock **-signal** *n* stop signal **-strecke** *f* staked-off distance **-tau** *n* stopper, stop cable **-uhr** *f* stop watch **-zeit** *f* time of (flash) ranging measurement
Stöpsel *m* stopper, plug (elec.), key plug, peg **einen ~ einsetzen** to insert a plug, to plug in **einen ~ herausziehen** to withdraw a plug, disconnect **dreiteiliger ~** three-point plug, three-way plug **geschlitzter ~** split plug **mit Stöpseln einschalten** to plug in, plug up (to)
Stöpsel-brett *n* plug shelf **-brücke** *f* plug bridge, contact plate of plug **-flasche** *f* stopper bottle **-glas** *n* stoppered glass **-griff** *m* plug handle **-hahn** *m* stopper cock, cock stopper **-hals** *m* plug sleeve, plug neck, plug ring **-hülse** *f* plug cover **-hülsengewinde** *n* plug-cover thread
Stöpsel-induktivität *f* plug inductance box **-klinke** *f* trunk jack **-kondensator** *m* plug capacitance box **-kontakt** *m* plug contact **-kopf** *m* plug head, plug cap
Stöpselkörper *m* plug body, plug sleeve **Ader zum ~** test pick
Stöpsel-leitung *f* plug on sleeve wire **-linienwähler** *m* plug selector **-loch** *n* plug hole **-meßbrücke** *f* bridge with plug contacts
stöpseln to plug in, stopper, plug (up), insert a plug **eine falsche Klinke ~** to misplug
Stöpselrheostat *m* (plug-operated) resistance box
Stöpselring *m* plug ring **isolierter ~** dead or insulated plug ring
Stöpselringzuführung *f* (plug) ring wire
Stöpselschalter *m* plug switch
Stöpselschnur *f* plug-ended cord, plug cord, cord pair **lose ~** loose cord and plugs
Stöpsel-sicherung *f* cartridge fuse, plug fuse **-sitzplatte** *f* plug seat (teleph.) **-sitzschalter** *m* plug-seat switch **-spitze** *f* plug tip **-spitzenzuführung** *f* tip wire **-spule** *f* adjustable plug coil **-umschalter** *m* plug switch, plug commutator **-wähler** *m* plug commutator **-widerstand** *m* plug resistance box
Stop-welle *f* shock wave **-zug** *m* cutoff piston
Störabschirmung *f* screening **Kabelgeschirr für ~** screening harness
Stör-absperrer *m* interference suppressor **-abstand** *m* signal-to-noise ratio **-amplitude** *f* noise level **-anfälligkeit** *f* susceptibility to trouble, interference, or noise, trouble incidence **-anpassung** *f* adaptation to eliminate noise **-anzeige** *f* trouble indication **-bandleitung** *f* impurity band conduction **-befreiung** *f* elimination of interference, elimination of jamming, fading, strays, static, or atmospherics **-befreiungsdrossel** *f* stopper **-begrenzer** *m* interference limiter **-bereich** *m* disturbance range (aut. contr) **-beseitigung** *f* debugging **-bewegung** *f* perturbed motion **-breite** *f* detuning width
Storch-schnabel *m* pantograph, diagraph
Stör-draht *m* disruptor (wire) **-effekt** *m* interference effect **-einsatz** *m* nuisance raid, harassing operation, jamming
stören to annoy, disturb, harass, jam, cause interference or break down
störend disturbing **-e Begleitstoffe** contraries (paper mfg.) **-es Licht** disturbing (troublesome) light **-e Strömung** turbulent flow
Störer *m* disturber, disturbing or jamming station **durch ~ verdeckte Zeichen** swamped signals
Störernullung *f* connection of interfering-device case with neutral wire
Stör-erscheinung *f* interference factor **-faktor** *m* interference factor **-feld** *n* interference field, stray field **-festigkeit** *f* immunity from noise, disturbance, or distortion **-fleck** *m* (Radar) clutter **-folie** *f* window (radar) **-frei** immune to interference, undisturbed **-freiheit** *f* immunity from interference **-frequenz** *f* interfering frequency **-funkstelle** *f* radio jamming station **-gebiet** *n* mush area, disturbed area **-geräusch** *n* background noise, interfering noise, jamming
Stör-geräuschatmen *n* fluctuation of noise, waxing and waning of noise **-geräuschkompensation** *f* noise-bucking **-glied** *n* element (component) producing disturbance **-grieß** *m* low noise in picture background due to thermal effects, shot effect (phys.) **-größe** *f* disturbance variable **-größenaufschaltung** *f* disturbance-variable feed-forward system **-gürtel** *m* interference belt
Stör-haken *m* iron hook (for drawing charcoal)

-halbleiter *m* extrinsic semi-conductor **-höhe** *f* noise level, interference level **-impuls** *m* interference pulse **-kante** *f* hinged spoiler **-klappe** *f* disruptor flap, spoiler **-kreis** *m* interference circuit **-lautstärke** *f* noise level **-leitung** *f* extrinsic conduction **-lichtblende** (Photo) glare prevention diaphragm **-muster** *n* spurious pattern, false pattern **-nebel** *m* chief interference zone, maximum noise zone

stornieren to carry over, transfer from one account to another, cancel, withdraw

Störniveau *n* noise level

Störoberwelle *f* parasitic harmonic

Störpegel *m* noise level **atmosphärischer ~** static, atmospheric disturbance

Stör-potential *f* disturbance potential **-rasen** *m* base-line noises (radar) **-resonanz** *f* incidental resonance

Störschutz *m* noise suppression, interference elimination, radio shielding **-anordnung** *f* interference eliminator **-drossel** *f* radio interference suppression reactor **-gerät** *n* interference eliminator **-kondensator** *m* radio-shielding condenser **-mittel** *n* radio interference suppression **-packung** *f* noise suppression, shielding harness, interference-eliminator kit **-vorsatzgerät** *n* radio interference suppressor **-widerstand** *m* radio interference (or noise) suppression resistor

Stör-schwelle *f* interference threshold **-schwingung** *f* disturbing wave **-sekundärstrahler** *m* secondary interference radiator **-sender** *m* interfering transmitter, jamming station, radio jammer **-sicherheit** *f* freedom from interference **-signal** *n* spurious signal, drop in (tape rec.) **-spannung** *f* interference voltage, static **-sperre** *f* interference-suppression device, noise gate **-spiegel** *m* interference level, noise level **-spitze** *f* interference peak **-stelle** *f* interference pattern, fault, center of disturbance, discontinuity

Störstellen-beweglichkeit *f* defect mobility **-dichte** *f* volume density of impurity centers **-halbleiter** *m* impurity semiconductor **-inversionszone** *f* excess-defect contact **-leitung** *f* extrinsic conduction

Störstellenreste *pl*, **geladene ~** ionized impurity centers

Störstrahlung *f* sweep radiation

Störstrom *m* disturbance current, interference current **~ infolge schlechter Ausgleichung** unbalance current

Stör-suchaufgabe *f* trouble-location problem **-suchgerät** *n* interference search gear, interference locator, signal tracer **-ton** *m* interfering tone **-träger** *m* interference bearer, jamming **-übergangsfunktion** *f* transient response to a step change (in disturbance variable)

Störung *f* (Stören) disturbing; (Störendes) disturbance; (Eindringen) intrusion; (Einmischung) interference; (Unterbrechung) interruption; (Unordnung) disorder; (Radio, atmosphärische ~) atmospherics (~ durch Sender) jamming, interference, obstruction, breakdown, trouble, strays, (noise) fault, static, atmospherics **~ durch Drahtbruch** trouble due to an open or broken wire **~ durch Erdschluß** ground fault, ground interference, ground leak **~ durch Festzeichen** (Radar) clutter **~ durch Nebensprechen** interaction (disturbance) **~ durch Partikeln** particle static **~ durch Schneepartikeln** snow static **~ durch andere Sender** jamming, interference **~ durch Starkstrom** interference from power lines **~ der elektromagnetischen Welle** strays (aviation)

Störung, atmosphärische ~ atmospherics, static, stray **außerirdische ~** extraterrestrial or interstellar disturbance **eine ~ beheben** to clear a fault **eine ~ eingrenzen** to sectionalize a fault **luftelektrische ~** static, atmospherics **magnetische ~** magnetic perturbation, magnetic disturbance **starke ~** heavy interference **elektromagnetische Störungen** parasitic disturbance

Störungs-aufgabe *f* harassing mission **-aufsicht** *f* fault clerk **-aufzeichner** *m* trouble recorder **-begrenzer** *m* noise limiter **-bereich** *m* region of disturbance **-beseitigung** *f* clearing of a fault, trouble shooting, interference elimination **-bruch** *m* fault log **-dienst** *m* signal-repair service, fault-complaint service **-eingrenzung** *f* localization of a fault **-faktor** *m* interference factor **-faktormesser** *m* interference-factor meter

Störungs-fallkappe *f* disturbance-fall indicator **-filter** *n* hum eliminator **-frei** static-free **-funktion** *f* perturbation function **-gebiet** *n* region of disturbance, interference area **-getriebe** *n* mirror-effect eliminator **-glocke** *f* trouble bell **-los** staticless, without disturbance **-meldung** *f* fault docket **-moment** *n* disturbing moment **-netz** *n* disturbance network

Störungspersonal *n* fault staff **~ für Amtsstörungen** exchange fault staff, internal fault staff **~ für Außenstörungen** external fault staff

Störungs-platz *m* trouble desk **-rechnung** *f* perturbation calculation **-relais** *n* trouble, interference, or warning relay **-signal** *n* out-of-order or trouble tone **-stelle** *f* fault section, trouble desk **-suche** *f* interference location

Störungssucher *m* lineman, trouble man **~ im Außendienst** external faultsman **~ im Innendienst** internal faultsman

Störungs-tafel *f* trouble table **-theorie** *f* perturbance theory **-trupp** *m* repair gang **-überwachungsplatz** *m* trouble position **-verhinderung** *f* interference prevention **-vermeidungsdienst** *m* trouble-prevention service **-welle** *f* parasitic or interference wave, jamming wave **-wellenweg** *m* path of interference wave

Störwelle *f* parasitic oscillation or wave, interference wave **-wertspeicher** *f* off-normal memory

Stoß *m* push, shove; (Physik, Schub) thrust; (Schlag) blow, knock; (Ruck) jerk; (Anprall) bump, impact; (Erschütterung) shock, concussion; (Zusammen~) collision, crash; impulse, jolt, percussion, hit, recoil, pile, heap, file, joint, surge (elec.), pulse, butt joint (of rifle), stroke, jerk, count or burst (of cosmic rays), junction (of rails), post (paper mfg.) **~ auf Gehrung** miter joint **~ des Kolbenringes** gap, piston-ring gap **~ und Schlag** shock and impact **~ und Wiedervereinigung** impact and recombination

Stoß, gerader ~ direct impact **schlagartiger ~** percussion **schräger ~** scarf joint **überhängender ~** overhanging wall **überlappter ~** lap joint

verschrämter ~ carved face (min.) **winkelrechter ~** butt joint

Stoß-ablauf *m* effect of the impulse **-achse** *f* axis of thrust **-anlage** *f* power plant or supply **-anlassen** *n* shock tempering **-anregung** *f* collision excitation **-apparat** *m* slotting attachment **-appretur** *f* friction finish **-approximation** *f* impulse approximation **-arbeit** *f* shaping, impulsive motion

stoßartig intermittent (jerky)

Stoß-aufgabevorrichtung *f* percussion or bumper-plate feeder **-ausbreitung** *f* shock propagation

Stoßausgleicher *m* stroke compensator **~ mit Druckluftbelastung** shock equalizer with compressed-air cushion

Stoß-axt *f* mortise ax **-balken** *m* abutment beam, baffle **-band** *n* juncture, strip **-bank** *f* push bench **-beanspruchung** *f* impact stress, shock stress, surge stress **-bedarf** *m* emergency needs **-beiwert** *m* impact coefficient **-belastung** *f* shock load, sudden load **-belastungswiderstand** *m* instantaneous high rate resistor **-bewegung** *f* pitching motion, propulsion

Stoßbinder *m* push binder **Elevator für ~** elevator for push binder

Stoß-bläser (Kessel), retractable soot blower **-blech** *n* butt strap, cover plate, fishplate **-boden** *m* breech block **-bohle** *f* abutment beam **-bohrer** *m* thrust borer, percussion drill **-bohrmaschine** *f* rock drill **-bügel** *m* bumper, bumper rod

stoßdämpfend shock-absorbing **-e Schwingrolle** shock-absorbing spring

Stoßdämpfer *m* shock absorber, (mit Luftpolster oder Öl arbeitender) **~** dashpot

Stoßdämpferkuppelung *f*, **elastischer Antrieb mit ~** shock-absorbing drive

Stoßdämpfer-strebe *f* shock strut **-vorrichtung** *f* shock-absorbing mechanism, shock absorber

Stoß-dämpfung *f* collision damping, damping or attenuation of pulsations or vibrations, shock absorption **-dämpfungsverbreiterung** *f* collision broadening **-dauer** *f* duration of collision or shock **-daumen** *m* actuating cam, push cam **-deckung** *f* butt straps **-dichte** *f* collision density **-dorn** *m* punch

Stoßdraht-geber *m* wire impulse transmitter **-steuerung** *f* Bowden-wire control

Stoßdruck *m* percussion pressure, impact pressure **-spitze** *f* pressure peak

Stoßdurchschlag *m* impulse breakdown **-festigkeit** *f* impulse-voltage break-down strength

Stoß-echtheit *f* fastness to friction glazing **-einfluß** *m* effect of collision **-eisen** *n* double-ended crowbar

Stößel *m* tamping or ramming tool, pestle, striker, ram, sliding head, plunger, push rod, rammer, stamper (in sheet-metal testing), hemispherical cupping tool, slide tappet, stem (of valve), driver rod, pushing or impacting rod

Stößel-anschlag *m* tappet stop **-ausbalanzierung** *f* balance of slide **-ausgangsstellung** *f* plunger initial position **-betätigung** *f* manual operation of rams **-bewegung** *f* ram movement **-buchse** *f* tappet sleeve **-draht** *m* Bowden wire **-einstellhebel** *m* ram adjuster **-einstellschraube** *f* adjusting screw of the plunger **-feder** *f* tappet spring **-führung** *f* tappet or slide guide, cam-follower guide

Stößelführungs-leisten *pl* gibs for slide guides **-nut** *f* tappet finding groove

Stößel-gleitbahn *f* ram way **-halter** *m* tappet holder

Stößelhub *m* ram stroke **Drehhebel für den ~** position lever for ram stroke

Stößel-klemmer *m* tappet clamping device **-kopf** *m* head of the ram **-lamelle** *f* tappet lamination **-leerlauf** *m* idle travel of ram **-niedergang** *m* downstroke of slide **-pfanne** *f* tappet bearing **-rollenbolzen** *m* valve-tapped roller pin **-rückkehr** *f* return (stroke) of ram

Stößel-schlitten *m* ram slide **-schraube** *f* tappet screw **-spannfläche** *f* clamping surface of slide **-spiel** *n* tappet clearance **-stange** *f* (valve) push rod **-teller** *m* tappet head **-umkehr** *f* reverse of ram **-verstellmotor** *m* slide adjustment motor

Stößelverstellung *f* slide adjustment **Mutter zur ~** sleeve nut for slide adjustment

Stößelwinkel *m* ram angle

Stoßempfindlichkeit *f* susceptibility to shock

stoßen (s.a. **Stoß**); to push, shove; (schlagend) knock, strike; (rammen) ram; (treiben) drive; (stanzen) slot; hit, trim, join, butt, thrust, cut, splice, pound **~** (kochende Flüssigkeit) to bump **nach unten ~** to push down **zu Pulver ~** to pulverize

Stoßen *n* slotting, pushing, bumping

stoßender Luftstrom shock wave

Stoßentaktivierungswahrscheinlichkeit *f* collision-deactivation probability

Stoß-entladung *f* impulse discharge **-entstehung** *f* shock formation **-entwicklung** *f* shock expansion

Stößer *m* push rod, rejecter, pestle, stamper, rammer, tamper, stem (of valve), driver rod

Stoß-erregung *f* impulse excitation, shock excitation **-fahrgestell** *n* shock landing gear **-fang** *m* shock absorber, dashpot, peg gate (in casting) **-fänger** *m* pressure equalizer, shock absorber, dashpot, bumper, buffer, ram **-fangfeder** *f* shock-absorber spring **-feder** *f* shock-absorber or buffer spring **-feile** *f* sharp file **-fest** shockproof **-festigkeit** *f* resistance to shock, shock or impact, strength **-fläche** *f* abutting end, anvil face, base **-fluoreszenz** *f* impact fluorescence

stoßförmig squally, gusty (wind)

Stoßfortpflanzung *f* pulse propagation

stoßfrei jolt-free, shockless, steady, smooth **~ anlaufen** to start without jerk **~ laufend** running smoothly **-er Eintritt** shock-free entry **-er Fahrtrichtungswechsel** smooth change of driving direction **-e Umschaltung** bumpless transfer (aut. contr.)

Stoßfront *f* shock front **-krümmung** shock curvature **-schicht** *f* shock layer **-tiefe** *f* thickness of shock layer

Stoßfuge *f* expansion joint, (upright) joint, butt joint, junction **~ des Kolbenringes** piston-ring gap

Stoß-fugenüberlaschung *f* beam splicing **-funktion** *f* step function **-galvanometer** *n* ballistic galvanometer **-generator** *m* power generator, impulse or test-wave generator **-glanz** *m* friction glaze **-größenverteilung** *f* pulse size distribution **-hebel** *m* percussion lever **-herd** *m* bumping table, percussion frame, percussion table **-hubregelung** *f* pusher control

Stoßionisation *f* ionization by impact or collision **Gegenteil von ~** detailed balancing

Stoß-kalander *m* beating mill, beetle (textiles) **-keil** *m* spearhead, wedge **-kissen** *n* bumper bag, buffer **-klinke** *f* driving pawl, thrust pawl, propelling pawl **-köpfe** *pl* heading dies, rammer heads **-kraft** *f* energy of blow, percussive power, motive power **-kreis** *m* impulsing circuit **-kurzschlußstrom** *m* maximum short-circuit current **-lade** *f* shooting board

Stoßlasche *f* fishplate, butt strap **~ des Spannriegels** tie beam plate

Stoß-leiste *f* buffer protecting strip **-leistung** *f* shock output (as of rectifier) **-leistungsgenerator** surge-power generator **-linie** *f* base line for map reference, boundary line, joining line **-lotung** *f* butt welding

Stoß-maschine *f* slotter, slotting machine **-meißel** *m* impact chisel, slotting tool **-messer** *n* pinion-type cutter **-mine** *f* contact mine **-mittelpunkt** *m* center of percussion, point of impact **-mulde** *f* pushing trough **-nadel** *f* vent rod (in core forming) **-naht** *f* butt joint **-ofen** *m* gravity-discharge furnace, pusher(-type) furnace, tunnel furnace (kiln), continuous furnace, reheating furnace **-oszillator** *m* squeegeeing oscillator

Stoß-parameter *m* impact parameter **-pferdekraft** *f* thrust horsepower **-platte** *f* butt strap or plate **-plattenstifte** *pl* pins for tipping plates **-polare** *f* shock polar **-probegerät** *n* shock tester **-prüffeld** *n* impact- or impulse-testing field **-puffer** *m* disk buffer **-punkt** *m* center of percussion, point of impact, junction

Stoß-querträger (Auto) bumper cross stay **-rad** *n* truck (R.R.) **-reiniger** *m* baffle purifier or separator **-reitel** *m* anvil, recoil, rabbet, spring beam **-riegel** *m* joining member **-ring** *m* thrust washer **-rohr** *n* shock tube **-sack** *m* bumping bag (aviation) **-satz** *m* impulse motion **-scheibe** *f* axle collar (wheel), thrust washer, pole plate **-schiene** (Auto) bumper, jointing strip

Stoßschweißung *f*, **elektromagnetische ~** percussion welding (electromagnetic)

Stoß-schwelle *f* connecting traverse, joint-sleeper **-seil** *n* jerk line **-sender** *m* impulse exciter, impulse transmitter **-sieb** *n* percussion sieve **-spannung** *f* impact potential, shock potential **-spannungsfest** surge-proof **-spiel** *n* gap (in a cylinder) **-spielkolben** *m* gap in a cylinder **-stahl** *m* slotting tool

Stoßstange *f* push rod, bumper, valve, operating rod **~ und Kipphebel** push rod and rocker arm

Stoßstangen-kammerdeckel *m* push rod chamber cover, push rod cover, rod cover, valve push **-maschine** *f* push rod type actuation typewriter

Stoßstangenraum *m* tappet chamber **-deckel** *m* tappet cover

Stoßstangen-schutzrohr *n* protecting tube for pushrod **-träger** *m* bumper bar holder **-verkleidung** *f* push-rod enclosure **-verkleidungsrohr** *n* push-rod cover tube

Stoß-stecker *m* (ground) connecting plug **-stelle** *f* intersection, joint abutment, joint area or point, junction point, contact point **-stellenabstand** *m* clearance of push rods **-strahlflug** *m* ram-jet flight **-strahlung** *f* impact radiation or fluorescence **-strebe** *f* shock strut **-strom** *m* short-time current, surge or transient current

Stoß-theorie *f* collision theory **-tisch** *m* shaking table **-ton** *m* beat note, throb **-torsion** *f* torsion impact **-turbine** *f* reaction turbine **-übergangswahrscheinlichkeit** *f* collision transition probability **-überspannung** *f* surge voltage **-unempfindlich** insusceptible to shock

Stoß- und Schlagbeanspruchung *f* notch-impact test

Stoß-ventil *n* relief valve **-verbindung** *f* butt or fish joint, connection at joint **-verbindungsart** *f* forms of joints **-verbreiterung** *f* impact broadening **-verlust** *m* shock loss **-verschraubung** *f* screwed joint **-verschweißung** *f* butt welding **-versuch** *m* impact test **-vervielfachung** *f* collisional multiplication

Stoß-vielfache *f* impact multiple **-vorgang** *m* collision exchange **-vorrichtung** *f* buffer bar, ram, pushing device, pusher **-waage** *f* ballistic pendulum **-wahrscheinlichkeit** *f* collision probability **-weg** *m* dynamic spring deflection

stoßweise spasmodic, intermittent, vibratory, pulsating, jerkily **~ Beanspruchung** pulsating or intermittent stress **~ Belastung** pulsating load, intermittent shock load, vibratory shock load, live load **~ abbauen** to stope out **-r Ausbruch** flowing by heads

Stoß-weise Belastung pulsating load **-welle** *f* percussion wave, shock wave, surge, impact or impulse wave **-wellenvorderseite** (Astron.) *f* shock front **-werk** *n* screw press, fly press, stamping press **-widerstand** *m* resistance to impact **-wind** *m* gust (of wind) **-winkel** *m* butting angle, angle of impact, angle of joint **-wirkung** *f* pulsating effect, impact effect **-zahl** *f* impact number, number of collisions or bursts **-zähler** *m* bump counter

Stoßzeit *f* peak period **mittlere ~** mean free time

Stoß-zentrum *n* center of percussion **-zünder** *m* percussion fuse **-zündung** *f* contact fire

Strabometer *n* strabometer

Strafbestimmung *f* penalty, penal regulation

Strafe *f* punishment, sentence (law), penalty, fine, judgment **bei ~ der Nichtigkeit** on pain of nullity **erhöhte ~** augmented sentence **gerichtliche ~** legal punishment

strafen to punish

straff rigid, strict, taut, tight **~ spannen** tighten

straffen to tighten, stretch

Straffhaltung *f* keeping taut

Straffheit *f* strictness, discipline, tautness

straffspannen to tighten (tension)

Straf-geld *n* penalty, fine **-gesetz** *n* penal code **-gewalt** *f* penal authority, disciplinary authority **-kammer** *f* criminal court **-losigkeit** *f* immunity, indemnity **-milderungsgrund** *m* extenuating circumstances

Straf-porto *n* surcharge, additional postage, postage due **-punkt** *m* penalty **-recht** *n* penal law **-summe** *f* penalty, fine **-tat** *f* punishable act, offense **-verfahren** *n* criminal procedure **-ver-**

schärfung *f* making a sentence more severe, increasing a sentence **-vollstreckung** *f* execution of sentence **-vollzug** *m* execution of sentences

Strahl *m* ray, beam, jet, nappe, stream, frog, straight line (geom.), radiation, flash (of lightning), radius (geom.) **achsenparalleler ~** paraxial ray **ausfallender ~** emergent ray **außeraxialer ~** extraaxial or abaxial ray **außerordentlicher ~** extraordinary ray **durchfallender ~** transcident or transmitted ray **einfallender ~** incident ray

Strahl, flach auffallender ~ ray incident at small angle or oblique axle, oblique ray **geschlossener nicht aufgespaltener ~** solid jet **grüner ~** green flash **~ positiver Ionen** positive ion beam **reflektierter ~** reflected ray **schräger ~** skew ray, oblique ray **streifender ~** glancing ray **ultraroter ~** infrared or ultrared ray **unterer ~** bottom discharge or ray

Strahl-abblender *m* means to mask, stop down, occult, eclipse, gate, or diaphragm rays, blanking means, dimmer **-abfänger** *m* beam catcher **-ablenker** *m* ray or jet deflector **-ablenkring** *m* jet (rocket) (evader) **-ablenkung** *f* ray deflection or refraction, pencil deflection, beam deflection or deviation **-absaugepumpe** *f* ejector (aviation) **-abschirmung** spray shroud

Strahl-abtaster *m* noctovision scanner **-abtastung** *f* scanning or sweeping with a light or electron pencil **-abweiser** *m* blast deflector **-antrieb** *m* jet propulsion **-apparat** *m* jet or spray apparatus, injector (of steam)

strahlartige Entladung needle-point corona or streamer discharge, leader stroke discharge

Strahl-auflösung *f* jet dispersion **-ausbreitung** *f* jet expansion **-ausfall** *m* emergence of beam **-ausfluß** *m* jet flow **-ausnutzung** *f* utilization of the slip-stream **-austastung** *f* beam suppression (TV) **-austrittsdruck** *m* pressure at the jet exit

Strahl-beeinflussung *f* propeller or slip-stream interference **-belastung** *f* beam loading **-berichtigung** *f* flow correction **-bleche** *pl* radiating sheets, plates **-blende** *f* sphalerite **-bohrung** *f* jet bore **-brechung** *f* refraction or splitting of rays **-breite** *f* beam width, jet width **-bündel** *n* beam, pencil, bundle, bunch, or brush of rays **-bündelung** *f* focus

Strahl-drehgeschwindigkeit *f* angular velocity of the slipstream **-drehung** *f* slipstream rotation **-düse** *f* blast or discharge nozzle **-düsenmischer** *m* mixer with orifice for the entraining medium **-ebene** *f* jet plane, spray level **-einfluß** *m* effect of propulsive jet **-einspritzmotor** *m* jet injection-type engine **-einspritzung** *f* solid injection **-einstellung** *f* beam positioning (TV) **-eisen** *n* actinolite, amianthus **-empfänger** *m* unidirectional (beam or ray) receiver

strahlen to radiate, emit (rays)

Strahlen *m pl* (actinic) rays **infrarote ~** infrared rays **kosmische ~** cosmic rays **ultraviolette ~** ultraviolet rays, ultraviolet light

strahlenartig gelagerte Tastenhebel radially supported type bars

Strahlen-ausbeute *f* X-ray output **-austritt** *m* X-ray port **-austrittsfenster** *n* transparent window **-bahn** *f* ray path **-begrenzung** *f* stopped down radiation **-bereich** *m* region of radiation **-blende** *f* fibrous blende (min.) **-brechend** refracting **-brechung** *f* diffraction or refraction of rays **-brechungsmesser** *m* refractometer **-bündel** *n*, **-büschel** *n* pencil or beam of rays, beam (of light), brush or bundle of rays or radiations, cone of rays

strahlend radiant, radiating **-e Dipolebene** radiating curtain **-er Hohlleiter** radiating guide

Strahlen-dosisgrenzen *pl* radiation exposure limits **-durchlässigkeit** radioopacity **-düsennadel** *f* nozzle pin or needle

Strahleneinfall *m* incidence of rays **streifender ~** glancing incidence of rays

strahlen-empfindlich radiosensitive **-falle** *f* (slang) camera **-figur** *f* echo image **-filter** *n* light or ray filter, absorbing or antidiffusion screen **-fluß** *m* radiation intensity **-förmig** radiated, radiant, ray-shaped **-formung** *f* beam-emitting, beam-forming **-gang** *m* path of rays, course of beam, ray tracing, geometric configuration of rays **-härtemesser** *m* penetrometer, qualimeter (for X rays) **-interferometer** *n* beam interferometer

Strahlen-kegel *m* cone of rays **-korrektur** *f* flow correction **-krone** *f* aureole, corona **-kunde** *f* radiology **-messer** *m* actinometer, radiometer **-messung** *f* radiometry **-nachweisgeräte** *pl* radiation surveying instruments

Strahlen-optik *f* geometric optics **-pfeil** *m* sagittal ray **-prüfer** *m* actinometer, radiometer **-pumpe** *f* injector **-punkt** *m* point of beam origin **-reichweite** *f* range of rays or corpuscular emission **-riß** *m* starshake **-schnitt** *n* jet contraction **-schleuse** *f* radiation maze, radiation trap

Strahlenschutz *m* protective screen **-gläser** *pl* absorptive lenses **-röhre** *f* autoprotective tube **-überwachung** *f* protection survey

Strahlen-spülmaschine *f* jet rinsing bowl **-teiler** *m* beam splitter

Strahlentstehungsort *m* source or origin of electron pencil or gun

strahlenundurchlässig radiopaque **-er Röhrenschutzmantel** protective arrangement surrounding the bulb

Strahlen-vereinigung *f* fusion of rays **-warngeräte** radiation monitoring instruments **-weg** *m* light-path **-werfen** *n* radiation **-werfer** *m* flash beacon **-zelle** *f* ray cell **-zentrum** *n* center of pencil of rays **-zieher** *m* protractor **-zurückwerfung** *f* beam reflection

Strahler *m* radiating system, emitter, radiator, antenna, cell (photometry), heater (of cathode) **schwarzer ~** black body (phys.)

Strahler-gebilde *n* radiating system, emitter **-halterung** *f* source holder **-haltung** *f* beam survival **-kreis** *m* radiating circuit **-oberfläche** *f* surface of the source **-öffnung** *f* opening of the source cover

Strahl-erweiterung *f* spread of beam (television) **-erz** *n* clinoclasite **-erzeugung** *f* generation of beams, electron gun **-erzeugungssystem** *n* electron gun, ray radiator system **-feld** *n* slipstream zone or region **-feuer** *n* leading light **-fläche** *f* radiant area, radiator surface, radiation-emissive surface **-fliegen** *n* bracketing a beam **-flugzeug** *n* jet-propelled aircraft **-form** *f* spray pattern **-gondel** *f* jet nacelle **-haus** *n* sandblast booth **-hebelarm** *m* pencil leverage, deflectability of electron beam

Strahlhöhe *f* radiation height **~ einer Antenne**

effective height of an antenna
strahlig radiating, radiant
Strahl-intensitätskontrolle *f* modulation of beam intensity **-keil** *m* belemnite **-kies** *m* marcasite **-kippeinrichtung** *f* sweep circuit **-kompressor** *m* jet compressor **-kondensator** *m* jet condenser **-körper** *m* radiator
Strahl-länge *f* penetration (aviation) **-mischer** *m* jet agitator, jet blender **-mittelreiniger** *m* blasting medium purifier **-motor** *m* jet-propulsion engine **-mühle** *f* fluid-energy mill, jet mill **-nachahmung** *f* simulated jet effect **-neigung** *f* jet inclination in degrees, inclination of ray
Strahl-perveanz *f* beam perveance **-prallmühle** *f* nozzle pulverizer **-pumpe** *f* injector, jet pump, ejector, aspirator **-quelle** *f* cathode-ray tube (electron microscope) **-querschnitt** *m* beam cross section **-regler** *m* jet regulator **-reichweite** *f* length of jet
Strahlrohr *n* jet pipe, blast gun **-mundstück** *n* nozzle tip
Strahl-röhre *f* beam tube **-rücklauf** *m* flyback (radar) **-rückstoßprinzip** *n* jet propulsion principle
Strahlruder *n* jet spoiler (g/m), jet vane (rocket) **-haltebock** *m* jet-rudder hinge bracket
Strahl-ruhelage *f* spot zero **-sand** *m* blasting sand, shot blast **-sauger** *m* ejector **-schärfe** *f* beam focus **-schneidequelle** *f* jet-edge source **-schub** *m* jet thrust **-schutz** *m* heat-shield (of a cathode) **-sender** *m* beam or unidirectional transmitter, link transmitter **-sendestelle** *f* beam or unidirectional transmitter
Strahl-spaltung *f* split beam, beam splitting **-spannung** *f* beam voltage **-sperrung** *f* beam cutoff or eclipse, gating of the beam **-stärke** *f* radiant intensity **-starthilfe** *f* jet-assisted takeoff (JATO) **-stein** *m* actinolite **-störung** *f* propeller interference
Strahlstrom *m* beam current **-stärke** *f* intensity of the beam current
Strahl-trieb *m* jet or jet drive **-triebwerk** *n* jet power plant, jet unit **-turbine** *f* turbojet **-umkehroptik** *f* beam reversing lens (TV) **-umlenkung** *f* jet deflection (Astron.)
Strahlung *f* radiation, rays, emission, convection, beam, jet, flash (of lightning), straight line, radius (geom.) **aktinisch undurchlässige ~** adiactinic radiation **falsche ~** stray radiation **harte ~** penetrating radiation **~ mit hohem Energieniveau** high-level radiation **Hessche ~** Hessian radiation **kosmische ~** cosmic radiation **magnetische ~** magnetic (field) radiation **schwarze ~** black-body radiation, black radiation
Strahlungs-ablenkung *f* beam deflection **-abschirmend** shielding radiation **-anisotropie** *f* ray anisotropy **-auslöschung** *f* radiaton elimination **-belastung** *f* radiation load **-biologe** *m* radiobiologist **-brandwunde** *f* flash burn **-bündel** *n* pencil or shaft of rays **-büschel** *m* shaft of rays, brush (electr.) **-charakteristik** *f* radiation characteristic or pattern, field pattern **-dämpfung** *f* radiation damping, radiation resistance **-detektoren** *pl* radiation detecting instruments
Strahlungsdiagramm *n* radiation characteristic or pattern, field pattern **horizontales ~** horizontal-plane directional pattern, horizontal radiation pattern
Strahlungs-dichte *f* radiation density **-druck** *m* radiation pressure **-dunst** *m* radiation fog **-durchgang** *m* radiation transmission **-eigenschaft** *f* radiation property **-empfänger** *m* radiation receiver, record sheet or surface, radiation-sensitive or -responsive pickup **-energie** *f* radiated energy, radiant energy **-einfangquerschnitt** *m* radiative capture cross-section **-einwirkung** *f* radiation bombardment **-erzeugt** radiogenic
Strahlungs-feld *n* radiation field **-festigkeit** *f* radiation resistance, radio resistance **-fläche** *f* emitting surface, emitting area **-fluß** *m* radiation flux **-form** *f* radiation space pattern **-frei** free of radiation
Strahlungs-gefährdung *f* danger of radiation **-gegendruck** *m* radiation reaction **-gleichgewicht** *n* radiative equilibrium **-gekoppelte Antenne** parasitic antenna **-glied** *n* radiation term **-härtegrad** *m* radiation hardness
Strahlungshöhe *f* radiation height **~ einer Antenne** effective height of an antenna
strahlungs-induziert radiation induced **-intensität** *f* intensity of radiation **-kennlinie** *f* radiation characteristic or pattern, field pattern **-kopplung** *f* parasitic coupling (ant.), radiation coupling **-kreis** *m* radiating circuit **-lappen** *m* radiation lobe **-lappenbreite** *f* radiation lobe width **-last** *f* current density on the object (electron microscopy) **-lehre** *f* theory of emission **-leistung** *f* radiated power **-los** nonradiative
Strahlungs-manometer *m* radio metric gauge **-menge** *f* amount or quantity of radiation **-messer** *m* pyrometer, actinometer, radiometer, radiation dose meter **-meßgerät** *n* radiation measuring instrument, electronic scaler **-messung** *f* radiometry **-meßwagen** *m* mobile radiation laboratories **-normal** *n* radiation standard **-nullpegel** zero level of radiation
Strahlungs-ofen *m* radiation furnace, independent-arc furnace, indirect-arc furnace, reverberatory furnace **-ökonomie** *f* efficiency of radiation **-pegel** *m* level of radiation **-potential** *n* radiation potential, resonance potential **-potentiometer** *m* radiation potentiometer **-prinzip** *n* radiation principle **-pyrometer** *n* radiation pyrometer
Strahlungs-rekombination *f* radiative recombination **-richtungsanzeiger** *m* beam direction indicator **-rückwirkung** *f* radiation reaction **-schäden** *pl* radiation damage **-scheibe** *f* insulating disk against radiation heat **-scheinleitung** *f* radiation conductivity **-schirm** *m* radiation shield **-schutz** *m* protection against radiation
Strahlungsstrom *m* radiation flux, radiative transfer **-dichte** *f* radiant intendity
Strahlungs-temperatur *f* radiation temperature, effective temperature **-theorie** *f* theory of radiation **-thermometer** *n*, pyrheliometer **-trocknung** *f* infra-red drying **-type** *f* radiant type of furnace **-übergang** *m* radiative transition **-übergangswahrscheinlichkeit** *f* radiative transition probability **-überhitzer** *m* radiant superheater **-überschuß** *m* radiation surplus **-überwachung** *f* radiation survey
Strahlungs-vektor *m* Poynting's vector, vector

radiant **-verbrennung** *f* radiation burn **-verlust** *m* radiation loss, loss by radiation **-vermögen** *n* radiant or radiating power **-wandröhre** *f* radiant wall tubes **-waage** *f* radio-balance **-wandröhre** *f* radiant wall tubes

Strahlungswärme *f* radiation heat, radiant heat **-gradmesser** *m* radiation thermometer **-übergang** *m* transition or transmutation of radiation heat **-zone** *f* radiant section

Strahlungs-widerstand *m* radiation resistance or characteristic impedance **-winkel** *m* angle of radiation (ant.) **-wirkung** *f* radiation effect **-wirkungsgrad** *m* radiation efficiency **-zählrohr** *n* radiation counter tube **-zersetzung** *f* radiation decomposition, radiolysis

Strahl-verfahren *n* jet method **-vergenz** *f* vergency of rays **-verkehrsflugzeug** *n* jet airliner **-verlauf** *m* path or course of rays, trajectory of ray, ray tracing **-verteilung** *f* spreading of the blast **-vortrieb** *m* jet propulsion **-wäsche** *f* washing with a jet **-wassergeschützt** water-tight (hose-proof) **-werfer** *m* beam antenna

Strählwerkzeug *n* chasing tool

Strahl-winkel *m* beam angle, jet angle **-wirkung** *f* blast action **-wirkungsgrad** *m* jet efficiency (aviation) **-wobblung** *f* spot wobble **-zerstäubung** *f* solid injection, jet spraying **-zerstäubungsmaschine** *f* Diesel engine with solid injection

Strähn *m* hank **-hanf** *m* scutched hemp

strähnig ply

Strak *f* smooth outline of a body moving in a fluid **-abteilung** *f* loft department **-brett** *n* loft board **-gewicht** *n* sheer iron

stramm stiff, hard, rigid, severe **-es Verkochen eines Sudes** tightening of a strike of sugar

Strand *m* beach, shore, strand **auf den ~ laufen lassen** to beach **auf den ~ kommen** to make the land **sandiger ~** sand beach

Strand-bad *n* bathing beach **-becken** *n* tidal basin that dries out at low tide **-bühne** *f* groin

stranden to make the land, run aground

Strand-gut *n* jetsam **-hafen** *m* dry harbor **-linie** *f* shore line, sea coast **-mauer** *f* sea wall **-see** *m* lagoon **-terrasse** *f* raised beach **-trift** *m* jetsam **-verschiebung** *f* displacement of the coast line

Strang *m* cord, rope, trace, skein, hank, chord, web (of paper or cloth), strand, line (of drive shafts) **gerader ~** straight track (R.R.) **krummer ~** curved track or line (R.R.)

Strangausquetschapparat *m* (warp) rope-squeezing apparatus

Strängeldrillapparat *m* skein-twisting apparatus

strang-gepreßt extruded **-gießen** *n* continuous casting **-gießverfahren** *n* extrusion process **-guß** *m* continuous casting **-klemme** *f* line terminal **-preßdüse** *f* extrusion die **-presse** *f* plodder, trace, extrusion press, extruder **-pressen** to extrude

Strangpreßmischung *f* extrusion compound **-profil** *n* expression, extrusion **-werkzeuge** *pl* extrusion press tools

Strang-spannung *f* phase voltage of a winding **-säureeinrichtung** *f* rope-acidifying apparatus **-schlaufe** *f* trace loop (harness) **-träger** *m* trace support (harness)

Strang- und Fließpressen extrusion

Strang-vieleck *n* string poly gon **-walze** *f* strand roll **-waschmaschine** *f* rope-scouring or -washing machine **-ziegelpresse** *f* long-stringed brick-molding machine

Strapaze *f* hardship, fatigue

Strapazierzug von Drähten wearing out wire drawing

Straß *m* strass

Straß *n* easily fusible glass, paste

Straße *f* road, highway, street, roll train **einachsige ~** single-line roll train **eingeschnittene ~** sunken road **gepflasterte ~** paved road **gestaffelte ~** staggered rolling train, arrangement of roll stands in separate lines

Straße, gewölbte ~ barreled or cambered road **grundlose ~** loose road **kontinuierliche ~** continuous mill train **öffentliche ~** public road **zollpflichtige ~** toll road **zweigestaffelte ~** arrangement of roll stands in two separate lines

Straßen-abhobeln *n* grading **-anordnung** *f* arrangement of a mill train **-arbeit** *f* road work **-arbeiter** *m* road laborer **-aufreißer** *m* digging bars, bull points, bull chisels, machine for breaking up pavement

Straßenbahn *f* tram, tramway, trolley car, trolley line, streetcar **-haltestelle** *f* streetcar stop **-linie** *f* trolley line **-oberleitungsmaterial** *n* overhead line material for streetcars **-schiene** *f* streetcar rail **-wagen** *m* streetcar

Straßenbankett *n* road embankment

Straßenbau *m* highway engineering or construction, road building **-material** *n* roadmaking material **-öl** *n* road oil **-stelle** *f* street construction **-weise** *f* road-construction method

Straßen-befestigung *f*, **-belag** *m* road surface **-beleuchtung** *f* street lighting **-beschotterung** *f* road metal **-betonierung** *f* road reinforcement **-biegung** *f* road turn or curve **-brecher** *m* road ripper **-brücke** *f* highway bridge, viaduct **-damm** *m* embanked road, causeway **-decke** *f* paving coat, highway surface **-deckenfertiger** *m* concrete road finisher **-disziplin** *f* road discipline

Straßen-drehkran *m* swivel-hoist truck **-dreieck** *n* triangular road junction **-einlauf** *m* catch basin, street-drainage inlet **-einmündung** *f* road junction **-fertigung** *f* line production **-fläche** *f* road surface **-gabel** *f* road fork **-graben** *m* road ditch **-greifer** *m* road lugs **-hobel** *f* road planer, grader **-höhe** *f* ground floor, street level

Straßen-kanal *m* sewer **-kante** *f* curbstone **-karte** *f* road map **-kehrichtabfuhrwagen** *m* refuse-removing cart **-kehrmaschine** *f* street cleanser, motor sweeper **-kiosk** *m* street kiosk **-knie** *n* sharp road curve **-knotenpunkt** *m* road intersection, junction, crossroads **-kreuzung** *f* (street) crossing, crossroads, traverse **-lage** *f* road holding capacity, road riding **-last** *f* load on road

Straßen-markierungsfarbe *f* traffic point **-netz** *n* road network, road system **-oberbeton** *m* concrete surface pavement

Straßen-pflaster *n* pavement **-planum** *n* street level **-reinigung** *f* street cleaning **-rinne** *f* gutter, trench, drain, sewer **-rücken** *m* road shoulder

Straßen-schlepper *m* tractor with rubber tires

-schotter *m* street macadam, road ballast **-schutz** *m* road protection **-sperre** *f* street barricade **-spinne** *f* road junction **-sporen** *f pl* road lugs **-sprengung** *f* road demolition

Straßentransport *m*, **zum ~ geeignetes Flugzeug** roadable airplane

Straßenüberführung *f* road overpass or crossing

Straßen- und Wagensperre *f* road block, barricade

Straßen-unterbau *m* road foundation **-unterführung** *f* (road) underpass **-unterhaltung** *f* road maintenance **-verkehr** *m* traffic **-verkehrsordnung** *f* traffic regulations **-verstopfung** *f* road jam, traffic jam **-walze** *f* steam roller **-wesen** *n* highway system **-zustand** *m* road conditions

Stratameter *n* stratameter

stratifizieren to stratify

Stratigraphie *f* stratigraphy, laminography

Stratigraphische Folge stratigraphical succession

Stratokumulus *m* strato-cumulus clouds

Stratosphäre *f* stratosphere

Stratosphären-aufstieg *m* ascent into the stratosphere **-flug** *m* stratosphere flight **-flugzeug** *n* stratosphere plane **-motor** *m* stratosphere engine **-niederschlag** *m* stratospheric fall-out

Stratuswolke *f* stratus cloud

sträuben, sich ~ to struggle, oppose

Strauch *m* shrub, bush **-bündel** *n* fascine

straucheln to stumble

Strauchmaske *f* shrubbery screen

Streamer, Anodenkorona ~ anode stream corona

Streamer vor der Zündung pre-onset streamer

Streb-ausbau *m* face support **-bau** *m* longwall

Strebe *f* strut, stay, shore, support, bar, rod, batter or anchor pile, (cross or push) brace, horse, (back) prop, (hip) truss, post, crossbeam, traverse, crosstie, crossover **~ für Kühlerwanne** buckstay for condenser box

Strebe-balken *m* strut **-bogen** *m* (flying) buttress

streben to strive, struggle, tend, press, seek

Streben *n* endeavor, striving, aspiration, tendency **-abstand** *m* strut spacing **-anschlußring** *m* strut-attachment ring **-biegung** *f* inclination of strut **-breite** *f* thickness of strut **-ebene** *f* strut fairing (aviation) **-fachwerk** *n* strut frame, strut bracing **-knotenstück** *n* strut-attachment fitting **-kopf** *m* strut top **-kreuz** *n* diagonal members, cross struts **-kühler** *m* strut-type radiator **-los** unsupported, unstayed, unpropped

Streben-neigung *f* strut slope **-paar** *n* pair of struts **-querschnitt** *m* strut section **-scheibe** *f* strut disk **-schraube** *f* lag screw **-schuh** *m* strut socket or fitting **-teilung** *f* strut distribution or repartition **-verkleidung** *f* strut fairing

Strebe-pfeiler *m* buttress, pier, counterfort **-stütze** *f* strut beam **-werk** *n* falsework

Streck-arbeit *f* ductility **-balken** *m* stringer, balk

streckbar extensible, ductile, malleable

Streckbarkeit *f* ductility, extensibility, drawing ability

Streckbarkeitsprobe *f* tensile strength test

Streckdauer *f* (Fallsch.) deployment speed

Strecke *f* stretch; (Teil~) stage, leg; (Entfernung) distance; (Spanne) span; (Math.) straight line, line segment; drawing frame, interval, space, extent, road, route, section, line (R.R.), (rolling) train, drift (min.), drawing (metal.), (gauge) length, track, range, gallery, field, element of length **~ für elektrischen Betrieb** electric-railway line **~ abschneiden** to lay off a distance **eine ~ abtragen** to scale off a length **eine einfallende ~ treiben** to drive a gallery to the hade of a seam (min.) **eine ~ überbrücken** to span a distance **auf ~** while cruising **durchlaufende ~** distance sailed or covered **freie ~** open line (R.R.), open road **waagerechte ~** level section (R.R.), level road **ins Gestein getriebene schwebende ~** rising stone drift

Streckeisen *n* flattening tool

strecken to stretch, extend, spread; (verdünnen) dilute; (Farbe~) extend, fill; (Metall) roll, laminate; (ziehen) draw; straighten, lengthen, elongate, flatten, admix, rough, rough down, roll out, break down, cog down **kalt ~** to draw down while cold

Strecken *n* stretching, extending, lengthening, elongating, racking, drawing **-abschnitt** *m* route segment (aviat.) **-apparat** *m* lineman's telephone or handset **-arbeiter** *m* trackman, lineman **-ausrüstung** *f* line equipment **-band** *n* drift conveyor **-befeuerung** *f* airway lighting **-betrieb** *m* drifting, drift mining

Streckenblock *m* section blocking (R.R.) **~ mit Grundstellung der Signale auf Freie Fahrt** block system with track normally open **~ mit Grundstellung der Signale auf Halt** block system with track normally closed

Streckendämpfung *f* path attenuation (radio), loss per section

Streckendämpfungs-messer *m* transmission-efficiency measuring set **-messung** *f* transmission-efficiency test

Strecken-element *n* linear element **-fernsprecher** *m* portable telephone station, portable telephone set **-feuer** *n* course light **-flug** *m* air-transport flight, commercial flight, distance flight **-förderung** *f* long distance moving **-führung** *f* route survey **-funkfeuer** *n* en-route beacon **-geschwindigkeit** *f* rate of speed **-getriebe** *n* gearing of draw frame (textiles)

Strecken-haspel *f* roadway winch **-karte** *f* road or air-route map **-kennung** *f* air route marking **-last** *f* load distributed over a length, line load **-läufer** *m* chain runner, field lineman **-licht** *n* route beacon **-markierungssender** *m* marker beacon or transmitter **-krümmung** *f* curvature of a line **-meldung** *f* airway weather report **-meßgeräte** *pl* distance measuring instrument **-meßtheodolit** *m* distance-measuring theodolite, tacheometer

Streckenmessung *f* optical distance measurement, straightaway measurement, end-to-end measurement **eine ~ machen** to make a straightaway test **optische ~** optical telemetry, optical distance measurement **trigonometrische ~** trigonometric distance measurement

Strecken-navigation *f* long-distance *n* navigation **-netz** *n* air-lines network, air routes **-ort** *m* forehead (min.) **-pfeiler** *m* pillar, post **-plan** *m* map of line (teleph.) **-profil** *n* gradient profile **-radar** *n* en-route radar **-reduktion** *f* spherical correction **-rekord** *m* long-distance record, record distance **-schalter** *m* section circuit switch or section circuit breaker **-schlag** *m* choking (in a rolling mill) **-schnellvortrieb** *m* rapid face advancement **-schutz** *m* distance protection (for powerline)

Strecken-spektrum *n* continuous spectrum **-stoß** *m* side of a gallery (min.) **-teilchen** *n* linear element (math.) **-trenner** *m* section insulator **-trennung** *f* sectioning **-treue Abbildung** projection without distortion of range **-triebwerk** *n* gearing of drawing frame (textiles) **-unterbrecher** *m* section circuit-breaker, point-to-point communication **-verhältnis** *n* aspect ratio **-versuch** *m* field test **-vortrieb** *m* driving gallery

Strecken-wärter *m* lineman **-weise** by sections **-werkzeug** *n* railway implements or tools **-wettervorhersage** *f* airway weather forecast

Streckenzug *m* straight edge, traverse (artil.) **-tafel** *f* traverse table

Streckenzusatzmaschine *f* booster (electr.)

Strecker *m* stretcher **-schicht** *f* stretching course

Streck-festigkeit *f* resistance to stretching, resistance to elongation **-figur** *f* flow line, lines of stress, surface band **-fließgrenze** *f* yield point, proof stress

Streckform *f* expanding block **-maschine** *f* stretch-wrap forming press **-verfahren** *n* slip forming, drape forming

Streck-gerüst *n* rougher, roughing stand, breakdown stand **-geschwindigkeit** *f* rate of stretch or of stretching **-gesenk** *n* fuller **-gewicht** *n* weight of the stretched leather **-grenze** *f* elastic limit, yield point, proof stress, yield strength

Streckgrenzen-effekt *m* yield phenomenon **-erscheinung** *f* yield phenomenon **-kurve** *f* stress or strain characteristic **-spannung** *f* field stress **-überhöhung** *f* yield point phenomenon

Streck-grenzverhältnis *n* yield point ratio **-kaliber** *n* roughing pass, drawing pass, breaking-down pass, cogging-down pass **-kraft** *f* stretching force **-länge** *f* gauge length **-maschine** *f* stretcher, stretching machine **-mast** *m* lattice mast (elec.) **-metall** *n* expanded metal, metal mesh **-mittel** *n* (Klebstoff) extender, diluent **-mittel** *n* stretcher **-oval** *n* **-ovalkaliber** *n* oval-shaped roughing pass, oval drawing pass **-schicht** *f* course of headers **-spannung** yield stress **-spinnen** *n* stretch spinning, tension spinning **-stahl** *m* rolled sheet **-tau** *n* life line **-träger** *m* road bearer, girder

Streck- und Drehgeschwindigkeit *f* stretching and spin

Streckung *f* stretching, extending, lengthening, section, aspect ratio ~ **eines Flußbettes** diversion of a river channel

Streckungs-grenzfläche *f* limiting surface of stress **-linie** *f* line of stress **-mittel** *n* diluent **-tensor** *m* stretching tensor **-verhältnis** *n* fineness ratio

Streck-vorrichtung *f* tightening device, stretcher **-walze** *f* drawing roller, roughing roll, breaking-down roll, cogging-down roll **-weite** *f* stretch width **-werk** *n* drafting system rolling mill

Streckwerks-antrieb *m* drive of draft system **-system** *n* drafting system

Streckziehen *n* stretch-forming, stretching, drawing

Streckzieh-formen *n* stretch forming **-eigenschaften** *pl* stretch forming qualities **-maschine** *f* stretcher leveler **-presse** *f* drawing and stretching press **-verfahren** *n* drawing process

Streck-zwirnmaschine *f* draw-twister

Strehlbohrer *m* hob ~ **für Rohrgewinde** pipe hob ~ **für Schneideisen** die hob

strehlen, Gewinde ~ to chase

Strehler *m* chaser, chasing tool

Strehlwerkzeug *n* chasing tool

Streichanlage *f* paint shop ~ **für Papier** coating plant for paper

Streich-baum *m* scudding beam **-beize** *f* brush dressing or pickling **-brett** *n* moldboard **-bürste** *f* spreading brush (paper mfg.) **-eisen** *n* scraper

streichen to paint, color, cancel, cross out, annul, pass, haul down (sails or flags), strike, graze, rub, coat, varnish, bow or stroke (a string) **eine Gesprächsanmeldung ~ lassen** to cancel a call

Streichen *n* strike (the trend), coating, course, direction, cancellation, crossing off ~ **einer Schicht** direction, bearing, strike (geol.) ~ **der Schichten** drift of strata, strike (geol.)

streichend longitudinally **-e Länge** length of strike (min.)

Streichengarn *n* carded yarn

streichfähig brushable

Streichfähigkeit *f* ease of brushing (for lacquers)

Streich-farbe *f* brushing-on color **-feder** *f* sheet steadier spring **-fläche** *f* striking surface, contact surface

Streichgarn *n* carded wool or worsted yarn **-gewebe** *n* woolen goods **-spinnerei** *f* carded-wool spinning mill

Streich-holz *n* match **-instrument** *n* string instrument **-kappe** *f* friction, striking, or explosive cap **-kalander** *m* spreading calender **-karton** *m* coating paper **-kontakt** *m* rubbing contact **-lack** *m* brushing lacquer

Streichlinie *f* line of strike **Streichlinien der Flußufer** boundaries of improved river channels

Streich-maschine *f* coating or spreading machine **-maß** *n* distance from rivet center to outside of angle, scratch gauge

Streichmesser *m* doctor (mach.) spreading knife **-verstellung** *f* adjustment of the doctor blade

Streich-model *m* strickle, gauge **-modell** *n* pattern **-nadel** *f* touch needle **-papier** *n* coating paper **-pfahl** *m* mooring pile, fender pile **-rad** *n* combining wheel **-richtung** *f* strike direction

Streichriemen *m* razor strop **am ~ abziehen** (Klinge) to strop (blade)

Streichriemenpaste *f* razor paste

Streich-spachtel *f* brush or brushing filler **-stange** *f* regulating rod **-stein** *m* hone **-torf** *m* molded peat

Streichung *f* cancellation, nullification ~ **einer Gesprächsanmeldung** cancellation of a call

Streichungsgebühr *f* termination charge, charge for cancellation

Streichverspiegelung *f* painting

Streich-vorrichtung *f* coating appliance **-walze** *f* calender roll **-wand** *f* poling boards **-winkel** *m* bearing, angle of strike

Streifbandumklebeautomat *m* wrapper glueing machine

streifen to touch, graze, border upon, strip,

roam, reconnoiter, glance, skirt, brush against, stripe, streak, striate

Streifen *n* touching, grazing

Streifen *m* band, strip, streak, strap, cut, lamella, skelp, stripe, bar, sector, lane, fillet, stria, vein, sheet, plate, stretch of country, strip of ground, mounting, fringe, ribbon, tape, slip, tab **~ herstellen** to prepare the tape **in ~ schneiden** to shred **endloser ~** endless strip **unpassender ~** misfitting slip

Streifen-abschneidemaschine *f* strip cutting machine **-abschwächer** *m* vane attenuator (microw.) **-abstand** *m* interval between strips, strip interval **-abtastung** *f* rectilinear scanning (tv), zone television **-aufhängung** *f* strip suspension **-aufnahme** *f* strip survey, strip photography **-bahn** *f* tape race, tape platform **-bilder** *pl* fringe patterns **-bildung** *f* striation

Streifenblech *n* strip steel **-walzwerk** *n* strip (steel) sheet mill

Streifenbreite 1 db flat to within 1 db (frequency response), width of strip

streifend-e Beugung reflexion diffraction **-er Einfall** grazing, oblique or glancing incidence

Streifen-dichtung *f* strip sealing **-druck** *m* tape printing **-drucker** *m* tape printer **-durchmesser** *m* tape thickness **-elektroden** *pl* strip electrodes **-entladung** *f* stratified discharge **-filter** *m* banded filter

streifenförmig lamellar

Streifen-fundament *n* strip foundation **-geber** *m* (perforated) tape transmitter **-gefüge** *n* lamination, laminated structure, banded structure **-heizkörper** *m* strip heating member (elec.) **-karte** *f* sector map, strip map **-keil** *m* photometric wedge **-kohle** *f* banded bituminous coal **-kühler** *m* sheet-metal radiator, ribbed, grilled, flanged, or finned radiator **-lade** *f* slip drawer, paper drawer

Streifenlast *f* strip load

Streifenlänge, aktive ~ active gauge length (semiconductors)

Streifen-leiter *m* strip-line **-leitung** *f* microstrip, strip line **-lesekopf** *m* tape reader **-lichtverfahren** *n* variable-density recording method **-loch** *n* tape hole

Streifenlocher *m* tape perforator **kartengesteuerter ~** card-to-tape converter

Streifen-locherin *f* tape punch girl (comput) **-magazinzuführung** *f* strip feed **-material** *n* strips **-muster** *n* striated pattern (TV)

Streifen- oder Fleckenbildung streaks or spots

Streifen-presse *f* press for sugar strips **-probe** *f* strip test **-prüflehre** tape gauge **-rolle** *f* tape roll **-schere** *f* strip cutting machine, strip shear **-schirm** *m* rod screen **-schneider** *m* strip cutter **-schreiber** *m* tape printer **-schublade** *f* slip drawer **-sender** *m* (perforated) tape transmitter **-sendung** *f* tape transmission

Streifen-sicherung *f* plate fuse, strip fuse **-spektrum** *n* band spectrum **-straße** *f* strip mill train **-sucher** *m* strip finder **-system** *n* stress pattern **-teiler** *m* vane attenuator (microw.) **-theorie** *f* strip theory **-trennvorrichtung** *f* stripe slitting device **-verschiebung** *f* displacement of the bands

Streifenvorschub *m* paper feeding **-daumen** *m* paper-feeding cam **-einrichtung** *f* paper-feeding device

Streifenwalzwerk *n* strip (rolling) mill

Streifenzieher *m* tape puller

Streiffeder *f* spring separators

streifig striated, striped, banded, stripped, having cords, platelike, lamellar, laminated, streaky, streaked, veined **~ verwachsen** banded

Streifigkeit *f* streakiness

Streif-licht *n* spotlight **-schneidemaschine** *f* slitter

Streifung *f* striation, stria

Streifzug *m* raid, expedition

Streit *m* quarrel, dispute, argument **~** (wissenschaftlicher), controversy **~ beilegen** to arrange, settle a dispute **den ~ schlichten** to settle the dispute, arbitrate

Streitanmerkung *f* annotation of litigation

Streiter *m* contestant to a suit, litigant, disputant

Streit-fall *m* case at issue, matter in dispute, dispute, controversy **-frage** *f* issue, question at issue, contested case, dispute, controversy, matter at bar **-gegenstand** *m* contention

Streitpunkt *m* contention, issue, question at issue, contested case, dispute, controversy

Streitsache *f* controversial matter, dispute,

Streitverfahren *n* contest proceedings

streng severe, strict, stern, harsh, austere, rigorous, rigid **~ gehen** to work hard

streng-flüssig refractory, viscous, sluggish, semifluid, difficultly fusible **-e Glasur** refractory glaze

Streng-flüssigkeit *f* viscosity **-lot** *n* hard solder

Streu *f* litter **-amplitude** *f* scattering amplitude **-ausbreitung** *f* scatter (radio) **-bereich** *m* spread, scatter, dispersion **-begrenzt** scattering-limited **-beutel** *m* powder bag (foundry) **-büchse** *f* pounce-box dredger **-düse** *f* spray nozzle **-echo** *n* scatter echo **-elektron** *n* emission electron **-emission** *f* stray emission

streuen to scatter, strew, dust, spread, leak (elec.), stray, spray, fluctuate

streuend scattering **durch -e Versuchspunkte gelegte berichtigte Kurven** faired curves

Streuer *m* sprinkler

Streu-faden *m* fly waste, split filament **-fähigkeit** *f* throwing power **-faktor** *m* dispersion coefficient, scattering factor (of X rays), scattering value **-feld** *n* stray field, leakage field, extraneous field

Streufeldabschirmung *f* stray field screening

Streuflugzeug *n* spraying airplane **~ für Insektenbekämpfung** airplane for spraying insecticides

Streufluß *m* stray flux, leakage flux, cross flux **-transformator** *m* (high) leakage reactance transformer

Streu-garbe *f* spread of burst, cone of dispersion **-glanz** *m* brass powder **-glas** *n* spreader glass **-glied** *n* scattering term **-gold** *n* gold dust

Streugut *n* dusting material **-behälter** *m* container for dusting material

Streu-impedanz *f* leakage impedance **-induktivität** *f* stray inductance

Streujoch *n* leakage yoke **-schieber** *m* movable leakage yoke

Streu-kapazität *f* stray capacity, spurious capacity, leakage inductance, stray inductance

-kegel *m* cone of dispersion **-koeffizient** *m* coefficient of diffusion
Streu-koppelung *f* stray coupling, capricious coupling, spurious coupling **-kupfer** *n* copper rain
Streulicht *n* floodlight, stray light **-blende** *f* baffle **-meßgerät** *n* light scattering apparatus
Streu-linse *f* dispersion lens **-matrix** *f* scattering matrix **-parameter** *m* straggling parameter **-phase** *f* phase shift **-quant** *n* scatter quantum **-querschnitt** *m* scattering cross section **-richtung** *f* scattering direction **-rille** *f* (Scheinwerfer) diffusing groove
Streu-sand *m* dry or parting sand **-scheibe** *f* diffusing lens or screen **-schicht** *f* scattering layer **-schirm** *m* diffusing screen **-schwingung** *f* parasitic oscillation **-schwund** *m* scatter fading **-selbstinduktion** *f* leakage inductance
Streuselmaschine *f* cake-top strewing-machine
Streu-spannung *f* stray voltage **-strahl** *m* scattered beam
Streustrahlenblende *f* antidiffusing screen
Streustrahlung *f* scattered radiation, scattering
Streustrom *m* stray current, vagabond current, eddy current **-austrittszone** *f* anodic area, positive area
Streutransformator *m* leakage-reactance transformer
Streutrommel *f* decontamination (sprinkling) drum **fahrbare ~** decontamination cart
Streuung *f* strewing; (Abweichung) dispersion, spread; (Kernphysik) stray, scattering (of powder), deviation, scattering effect, diffusion effect, distribution, divergence, stray(ing), leakage, throwing power, dusting, spreading **~ einer Lichtquelle** spread, dispersion or scattering of a light source **~ der aufgetragenen Meßpunkte** scattering of the plotted points **~ der elektromagnetischen Wellen** scattering of electromagnetic waves **elektromagnetische ~** electromagnetic leakage **elektrostatische ~** stray capacity **magnetische ~** magnetic dispersion, magnetic cross flux, magnetic leakage
Streuung ohne effektive Ablenkung zero-scattering **~ an statischen Fehlstellen** scattering by static imperfections **~ an Fremdatomen** impurity scattering **~** (math. bei Genauigkeitsmessungen) standard deviation **~ an Gitterstörungen** scattering by imperfections **~ in den inneren Grenzen** scattering by the internal boundaries **~** (Streugrenze) scattering (limit of scattering) **~ durch eine Versetzungslinie** scattering by a dislocation line **~ in große Winkel** large angle scattering
Streuungs-amplitude *f* scattering amplitude **-bereich** *m* zone of dispersion **-bild** *n* dispersion diagram **-garbe** *f* **-kegel** *m* cone of dispersion **-kurve** *f* scatter curve **-prisma** *n* dispersion prism **-querschnitt** *m* scattering area ratio **-vorgänge** *pl* phenomena of scattering
Streuungswinkel *m* angle of divergence **-abhängigkeit** *f* angular dependence of scattering
Streu-verlust transducer dissipation loss (acoust.) **-vermögen** *n* scattering power **-vorrichtung** *f* dusting or strewing arrangement **-wachs** *n* sprinkling wax **-weglänge** *f* scattering length **-welle** *f* spot frequency (radar) **-wert** *m* standard value of deviation, erratic value **-winkel** *m* scattering angle **-zahl** *f* dispersion coefficient **-zelle** *f* scattering cell **-zentrum** *n* scattering center **-zinn** *n* tin dust **-zucker** *m* powdered sugar
Strich *m* line, dash, streak, district, stroke, coating, prime (math.), point (of compass), stria, mark, grain **~ fliegen** to fly on a straight course **einen ~ durch etwas machen** to strike or cross out a thing **einen ~ unter etwas machen** to underline a thing **kurzer ~** dash
Strichabstand *m* lines distance
strichartig pencil-line
Strich-ätzung *f* line etching (on zinc), line block **-aufnahme** *f* line photo **-bürsteneinrichtung** *f* pile-brushing device **-code** *m* bar code **-diagramm** *n* bar graph **-diapositiv** *n* line transparency, line diapositive **-einteilung** *f* graduation (scale) **-eisen** *n* touchstone
stricheln to shade, hatch, streak
Strich-fahren *n* base operation (of power plants) **-farbe** *f* streak
Strichfokus *m* line focus (of X rays) **-röhre** *f* line-focus tube
Strich-formulierung *f* chemical formula using dashes or lines **-gitter** *n* ruled grating, simple line grating
Strichindex, mit ~ versehenes Formelzeichen primed symbol
Strichkontrastmikrometer *n* line contrast micrometer
Strichkreuz *n* cross wires or hairs, cross line **-okular** *n* cross line eyepiece **-platte** *f* cross-hair plate, reticle, graticule
Strich-kurve *f* dash curve **-latte** *f* line division staff
strichliert broken (line), dash-lined, shaded
Strich-linie *f* dotted line **-liste** *f* roster **-magnetisierung** *f* magnetization by touch **-marke** *f* division or locating mark **-maß** *n* line standard **-methode** *f* stroke method, line method (paper test)
Strichmikrometer *n* line-scale micrometer **-okular** *n* cross line eyepiece
Strich-mikroskop *n* microscope with lines **-negativ** *n* line negative **-platte** *f* graduated dial, graduated plate, reticle, graticule
Strichplatten-einsatz *m* graduated dial inset **-teilkreis** *m* dial templet scale
Strichpunkt *m* semicolon
strichpunktieren to chain-dot, dash-dot
strichpunktiert indicated by a dot-dash line, dash-dotted, broken (line) **-e Linie** dash-and-dot line
Strich-Punkt-Verfahren *n* dash-dot mode
Strichraster *m* bar pattern (TV) **-scharf** critically sharp (defined) **-schärfe** *f* sharpness of focus, definition **-schicht** *f* screeding **-skale** *f* division scale **-spektograph** *m* lattice spectrograph **-stärke** *f* thickness of the lines **-wert** *m* graticule value **-zählung** *f* dash counting (teleph.) **-zeichnung** *f* (out)line drawing
Strick *m* rope, strop, cord, line **-eisen** (Montage) tugging iron, yarning chisels
stricken to knit
Strickereiindustrie *f* knitting industry
strick-förmig rope like, cord like **-garn** *n* knitting yarn **-griff** *m* rope handle **-leiter** *f* rope ladder **-maschine** *f* knitting machine, power knitting

loom **-maschinenfabrik** *f* knitting-machinery factory **-nadel** *f* knitting needle

Strickwaren *pl* knitted fabrics, knit goods **-appretur** *f* hosiery finishing

Strick-werk *n* reticulated work, network **-wolle** *f* knitting wool

Striegel *m* currycomb

Striegler *m* brusher (paper mfg.)

Striemenbildung *f* striations

Striktion *f* striction, constriction

Striktionsspule *f* stricture coil, focusing coil

Stringer *m* stringer

strippen to strip

Stripper *m* stripper **-kolben** *m* stripper ram **-kran** *m* stripper crane, ingot crane **-laufkran** *m* traveling stripper crane **-torkran** *m* stripper gantry

Strippreaktion *f* stripping reaction

strittig moot, disputed

Stroboskop *n* stroboscope

stroboskopisch stroboscopic(al) **-e Eichung** stroboscopic calibrating **-e Erscheinung** persistance of vision **-e Läuferscheibe** stroboscopic disc **-e Scheibe** stroboscopic disk, stroboscopic pattern wheel

Stroboskopröhre *f* stroboscopic tube

Stroh *n* straw **-aufschichter** *m* straw stacker **-elevator** *m* wind stacker **-fänger** *m* trash catcher, weed catcher **-feile** *f* rough or coarse file, straw file **-gebläse** *n* rake stacker **-gedeckt** thatched **-geflecht** *n* straw-plait **-gelb** straw-yellow **-hülsen** *pl* straw casings

strohig-er Griff straw-like feel **-e Narben** strawy grain

Stroh-matte *f* straw mat **-papier** *n* straw-paper **-pappe** *f* straw-board

Strohsammler *m* straw collector and dump **~ mit Abkippvorrichtung** straw collector and dump

Stroh-seilspinnmaschine *f* straw-rope making machine **-sichter** *m* grass duster **-spalter** *m* straw-splitter **-stoff** *m* straw pulp **-streuapparat** *m* straw-spreading attachment **-streuereinrichtung** *f*, **streuvorrichtung** *f* straw-spreader attachment **-zellstoff** *m* chemical straw pulp

Strom *m* current, stream, large river, flow, circuit, equalizing current **~ im Belastungswiderstand** space current **~ gleicher Richtung** unidirectional current **in der Phase nacheilender ~** lagging current **~ abgeben** to deliver current **~ abnehmen** to take current **einen ~ abzweigen** to branch a current **~ aufnehmen** to take current **mit ~ beliefern** to deliver current to **~ führen** to carry a current **~ senden** to feed current

Strom, außer ~ setzen to deenergize, cut out the circuit **unter ~ setzen** to excite **den ~ umspannen** to transform the current **abfallender ~** decreasing current **abgehender ~** outgoing current, sending current **abklingender ~** decaying current **ankommender ~** incoming current, receiving current, input current

Strom, äquivalenter ~ equivalent circuit **ausgeglichener ~** smoothed current **effektiver ~** effective current, root-mean-square current **eingeschwungener ~** steady-state current **entgegengesetzter ~** inverse current, opposed current **gittergesteuerter ~** grid-controlled current **gleichförmiger ~** steady current **gleichgerichteter ~** rectifier current, redressed or rectified current

Strom, induzierender ~ inducing current **induzierter ~** induced current **kommutierter ~** commutated current **lichtelektrischer ~** photoelectric current **nacheilender ~** lagging current **nutzloser ~** idle current **oszillierender ~** oscillating current **phasenverschobener ~** out-of-phase current, phase-displaced current, dephased current **pulsierender ~** pulsating current, ripple current

Strom, resultierender ~ resultant current **schwacher ~** weak current, feeble current **schwingender ~** oscillatory current **sinusförmiger ~** sinusoidal current, sine-wave current, harmonic current **stationärer ~** steady-state current **thermoelektrischer ~** thermoelectric current **überlagerter ~** superposed current **undulierender ~** undulating current

Strom, vagabundierender ~ leakage current, stray current, vagabond current **verketteter ~** interlinked current **verzweigter ~** branch(ed) current **voreilender ~** leading current **wattloser ~** reactive current, idle current, wattless current **welliger ~** ripple current, undulated current, pulsating current **zeitweilig unterbrochener ~** make-and-break current

stromab downstream

Strom-abfall *m* current decrease or drop **-abgabe** *f* delivery of current **-abgleid** *m* current balance **-ableitung** *f* shunt (elec.), derivation, tapping, tap

Stromabnahme *f* decrease or fall of current **-bürste** *f* current-collecting brush **-kabel** *n* feeder cable

Stromabnehmer *m* current collector, trolley brush or arm, tap **~ für (oberirdische) Stromschiene** collector-shoe gear **~ für unterirdische Stromschiene** plow (elec. R.R.)

Stromabnehmer-bügel *m* collector bow, overhead contact hoop **-drehzapfen** *m* trolley pivot **-feder** *f* spring commutator brush **-rolle** *f* wheel trolley (elec. R.R.) **-stange** *f* trolley boom

Stromabnehmerträger *m*, **isolierter ~** trolley support

strom-abwärts downstream **-abweichung** *f* current variation or fluctuation **-ader** *f* feeder **-aggregat** *n* power-supply trailer, generating unit **-amplitude** *f* current amplitude **-änderung** *f* current variation or change **-angabe** *f* current data **-angriff** *m* attack by the current **-anker** *m* current anchor **-ankerlinie** *f* stream anchor line, current-anchor line **-anlage** *f* generating plant (elec.)

Strom-anstieg *m* current rise **-anzeiger** *m* current indicator, detector, galvanometer **-arbeit** *f* electric energy, electric work **-art** *f* kind of current **-atlas** *m* hydrographic atlas **-auf** upstream **-aufnahme** *f* current consumption, charging rate

stromauf-wärts upstream **~ gerichtet** pointing upstream **-wirkung** *f* upstream effect

Strom-ausbeute *f* current yield, electrolytic efficiency **-ausfall** *m* power failure **-austausch** *m* interchange of current **-austrittszone** *f* positive or anodic area **-bahn** *f* current path, flow path **-band** *n* current lead **-bauch** *m* current loop, current antinode **-bedarf** *m* current or power requirement **-bedarfsberechnung** *f* calculation of current consumption **-begrenzer** *m* current-limiting device, current limiter

Strombegrenzungs-drossel *f* protective reactance coil **-schalter** *m* current limiting switch **-spule** *f* current-limiting reactor

Strom-belag *m* current coverage, current distribution **-belastbarkeit** *f* current carrying capacity (of conductor) **-belastung** *f* current load, electrical load **-berechnung** *f* current computation **-beschleunigung** *f* acceleration of the current **-bett** *n* stream bed **-bild** *n* flow sheet **-bezug** *m* purchase of current **-blatt** *n* stream sheet **-brechung** *f* current refraction

Strom-dämpfung *f* current attenuation, damping **-detektor** *m* current detector **-dichte** *f* current density, luminous flux **-draht** *m* conducting wire **-dreieck** *n* current or flow triangle

stromdurchflossen current-carrying, alive (elec.), traversed by current **-es Band** ribbon carrying an electric current **-er Leiter** current-carrying conductor **-e Leitung** wire carrying current, live wire

Strom-durchfluß *m* current passage **-durchflußmesser** *m* current meter **-durchführung** *f* current lead-in (lead off) **-durchgang** *m* passage or flow of current **-durchführungskondensator** *m* bypass condenser **-durchlässigkeit** *f* permeability of current **-durchlaßrichtung** *f* direction of current passage **-einheit** *f* unit (of) current **-eintrittszone** *f* negative or cathodic area **-empfindlichkeit** *f* current sensitivity

strömen to stream, pour, flow, pass, travel

strömend torrential

Strom-energie *f* effectiveness of current **-enge** *f* narrows

Strom-entnahme *f* consumption of current **-erfüllter Zeichenschritt** mark-signal pulse **-ersparnis** *f* savings in power costs **-entnahme** *f* consumption of current **-erzeuger** *m* (current or electric) generator, dynamo **-erzeugerantrieb** *m* generator drive **-erzeugung** *f* generation of current

Strom-erzeugungsaggregat *n* industrial power pack, generator set **-erzeugungsanlage** *f* electric generator, generating set, charging machine, generating plant, power station **-erzeugermaschine** *f* generator, dynamo **-faden** *m* current path, stream line, current tube, streamer (in discharge)

stromfähig (current or wire) clear

Strom-fähigkeitsprüfung *f* continuity test **-falle** *f* flux trapping **-feld** *n* field (elec.) **-fernmeßgerät** *n* teleammeter **-fläche** *f* flow plane or line **-flächenformel** *f* current-sheet formula **-fluß** *m* flow of current **-flußwinkel** *m* forward flow angle **-folge** *f* current sequence **-form** *f* streamline shape

stromführend current-carrying, current-conveying, live, charged **-er Draht oder Leiter** live wire

Strom-führung *f* power supply **-funktion** *f* flow-stream function **-gattung** *f* kind of current, system of current **-geben** *n* current transmitting, sending **-gebiet** *n* river basin **-gefälle** *n* fall or slope of a river **-gegenkopplung** *f* current feedback **-geschwindigkeit** *f* current velocity **-geschwindigkeitsmesser** *m* current meter **-gitter** *n* atomic lattice **-gleichrichter** *m* honeycomb straightener (in wind tunnel), rectifier, unidirectional current **-gleichung** *f* current equation **-großverteilung** *f* superpower distribution

Strom-impuls *m* current impulse **-indikator** *m* ammeter **-induktion** *f* current of electromagnetic induction **-karte** *f* current chart **-klemme** *f* circuit terminal **-knoten** *m* current node **-komponente** *f* current component **-kosten** *pl* cost of current

Stromkreis *m* circuit, line, electric circuit **~ mit Erdrückleitung** ground-return circuit **~ der Schutzblockstrecke** stopped-section circuit **~ für rückwärtige Stromstoßgabe** revertive pulsing circuit **einen ~ öffnen** to open or break a circuit **einen ~ schließen** to make, complete, or close a circuit **mit Blindwiderstand behafteter ~** reactive circuit **am Ende kurzgeschlossener ~** short-circuited circuit or line, end-shorted circuit **am Ende offener ~** open-ended circuit **~ mit Erdrückleitung** earth return circuit **~ des Schienenstromschließers** pedal circuit **~ der Schutzblockstrecke** stopped section circuit **aus Ohmschen Widerständen bestehender ~** resistive circuit

Stromkreis, aperiodischer ~ aperiodic circuit **anschließender ~** connecting-up circuit **äquivalenter ~** equivalent circuit **ausschaltender ~** disconnecting circuit **geschlossener ~** closed circuit **kurzer ~** short circuit **nicht induktiver ~** noninductive circuit **offener ~** open circuit **~ öffnen** to break a circuit, open a circuit **überlagerter ~** superposed circuit **unbelasteter ~** unloaded circuit **verzweigter ~** branched circuit, divided circuit **einen Stromkreis schließen** to close a circuit, complete a circuit

Strom-kreiselement *n* circuit element **-kreisunterbrecher** *m* circuit breaker, bus-bar chamber **-kurve** *f* current curve **-ladungsdichte** *f* charge-current density

Stromlauf *m* circuit diagram, flow of current **-bahn** *f* circuit wiring **-plan** *m* circuit diagram, electrical wiring plan **-schema** *f* circles diagram (radio) **-skizze** *f*, **-zeichnung** *f* circuit diagram, wiring diagram

Strom-leine *f* current stay **-leistung** *f* current capacity, electric power **-leiter** *m* (current) conductor **-leiterdicke** *f* conductor thickness **-leitung** *f* (electric) circuit **-leitvermögen** *n* current-carrying capacity **-lichtstärkecharakteristik** *f* current-illumination characteristic **-lieferung** *f* current supply, electric power supply **-lieferungsanlage** *f* power equipment **-linie** *f* streamline, flow line

Stromlinien-aufbau *m* streamlined body **-aufzeichner** *m* device to map or plot potential, fields, lines, or tubes of force on a model **-bild** *n* configuration of flow, flow pattern **-draht** *m* streamline wire **-fläche** *f* hydrofoil **-flügel** *m* streamlined wing, airfoil **-fluß** *m* streamline flow **-form** *f* streamline shape

stromlinienförmig streamlined **~ ausbilden** to streamline **-er Rumpf** streamlined fuselage **-er Übergang von der Haube zum Rumpf** cowl fairing

Stromlinien-führung *f* streamlining **-kabel** *n* streamlined cable **-karosserie** *f* streamlined body **-körper** *m* airfoil **-krümmung** *f* streamline curvature **-profil** *n* streamlined profile or section **-punkt** *m* point on or of the streamline **-querschnitt** *m* streamlined profile or section **-reifen** *m* streamlined tire **-rohr** *n* streamlined tube

stromliniert streamlined

stromlos currentless, dead, out of circuit, wattless, deenergized **~ machen** to make dead **-e Flächen** surface of no motion **-er Leiter** dead wire **-e Zeichenschrift** space-signal pulse, no-current pulse

Stromlosigkeit *f* absence of current

Strom-menge *f* strength of electrical current **-meßbereich** *m* amperage range

Strommesser *m* ammeter **~, direkt angeschalteter** whole-current ammeter **registrierender ~** recording ammeter **thermischer ~** thermocouple ammeter **~ für Wandleranschluß** transformer-operated ammeter

Strom-meßgerät *n* current-measuring instrument **-messung** *f* current measurement **-modulation** *f* convection-current modulation **-mündung** *f* river mouth **-netz** *n* electric circuit, electric-supply line **-nullpunkt** *m* current zero point **-nullstelle** *f* current node **-pfad** *m* current path **-pfeiler** *m* pier **-phase** *f* current phase **-prüfer** *m* circuit detector, ammeter **-pulsation** *f* pulsation of current **-quelle** *f* source of current

Stromregel-größe *f* ballast resistor **-röhre** *f* ballast resistor, barretter, current regulator tube

Stromregelung *f* current regulation or control **~ bei Drei-Bürstenmaschinen** third brush regulation (or control)

Stromregler *m* rheostat **-einsatz** *m* starting of current regulator **-widerstand** *m* current regulator resistance

Strom-regulator *m* current regulator **-regulatorröhre** *f* ballast tube **-regulierung** *f* current regulation **-reiniger** *m* harmonic eliminator or excluder, smoothing means, stopper **-reiz** *m* impulse

Stromresonanz *f* parallel resonance, antiresonance, series resonance **-kreis** *m* parallel-resonant circuit, antiresonance circuit, tank circuit

Strom-richter *m* static, converter, mutator, rectifier **-richtergefäß** *n* rectifier unit **-richtung** *f* direction of current

Stromrichtungs-anzeiger *m* polarity indicator **-umkehr** *f* reversing of the flow of current **-umschalter** *m* current flow reversing switch

Stromrinne *f* channel **eine ~ vertieft sich** a channel is scoured out

Strom-röhre *f* stream tube **-rückgewinnung** *f* regeneration or recuperation of current **-rückleitung** *f* return line, return wire **-sägezahn** *m* saw-tooth voltage **-sammler** *m* accumulator, collector, storage battery **-schalter** *m* (electric) switch

Stromschiene *f* live rail, third rail, bus bar, contact rail, current-collecting rail **~ in Gleismitte** central contact rail

Strom-schleife *f* current loop **-schließer** *m* contact maker **-schließstellung** *f* circuit-closing position **-schließungsstoß** *m* make pulse (teleph.) **-schluß** *m* closing of circuit **-schlüssel** *m* key switch, make and break switch

Stromschluß-hebel *m* circuit-closing lever **-hebeltaste** *f* connection key **-prüfer** *m* continuity tester **-schraube** *f* contact screw

Strom-schnelle *f* cataract, rapid, riffle **-schreiber** *m* current recorder

Stromschritt *m* signal element, unit, pulse, signal **Stellung für ~** setting for impulse

Strom-schwankung *f* current variation or fluctuation **-schwebung** *f* current beat **-schwingung** *f* current oscillation **-setzmaschine** *f* stream washer (hydr.) **-sicherung** *f* cutout fuse **-spaltung** *f* bifurcation or branching of current (stream) **-spannung** *f* (current) voltage, current potential, tension, pressure

Stromspannungs-kennlinie *f* current-voltage characteristic, volt-ampere characteristic **-kurve** *f* current-voltage characteristic, voltage curve **-messer** *m* volt-ammeter

Strom-speicher *m* accumulator **-spule** *f* current coil **-stabilisierung** *f* current stabilizing

Stromstärke *f* current intensity, amperage **~ für den Ausschlag** figure of merit

Strom-stärkeregler *m* tickler coil **-stärkeumschalter** *m* maximum current control switch **-störung** *f* fault of current

Stromstoß *m* current surge or impulse, current pulsation or pulse **flüchtiger ~** transient impulse **plötzlicher ~** current rush **vollständiger ~** complete pulse

Stromstoß-dauer *f* impulse period **-empfänger** *m* impulse receiver, impulse-storing device **-empfangsrelais** *n* pulsing relay **-feder** *f* impulse spring **-federn** *pl* pulse spring (of dial) **-folge** *f* pulse

Stromstoßgabe *f* impulsing, pulsing **rückwärtige ~** reversed impulsing, revertive pulses or pulsing **unmittelbare ~** direct impulsing, direct pulses

Stromstoß-geschwindigkeit *f* impulse frequency **-kontakt** *m* current-impulse contact **-nocke** *f* pulsing cam **-reihe** *f* series, train, or succession of impulses, pulsations **-relais** *n* impulse relay **-schalter** *m* impulsing switch, stepping relay **-sender** *m* sender

Stromstoß-serie *f* train of impulses **-speicher** *m* (digit-storing) register, impulse-storing device **-teilung** *f* impulse ratio **-übertrager** *m* (im)pulse repeater **-umformer** *m* current transformer **-unterdrücker** *m* digit-absorbing selector **-unterlagerungstelegraphie** *f* impulse polar duplex telegraphy **-verhältnis** *n* pulse ratio, impulse ratio **-wiederholung** *f* pulse repeating

Stromstoßzählung, Relais für ~ counting relay

Strom-strahler *m* electric beam transmitter **-strich** *m* thalweg (physiog.), line of most rapid flow, stream thread or course **-system** *n* distribution system (elec.) **-tor** *n* thyratron **-torröhre** *f* gate valve **-transformator** *m* electric or current transformer **-trenner** *m* switch

Strom-übergang *m* current leakage, passage, ford **-übernahme** *f* transfer of current, tapping of current **-übernahmeverhältnis** *n* partition ratio (of tubes) **-übersetzung** *f* voltage (current) ratio **-übertragungsfaktor** response to current **-umformer** *m* current converter or transformer

-umkehr *f* reversal of current **-umkehrer** *m* current reverter, commutator **-umkehrung** *f* reversal of current

Strom- und Spannungsmesser *m* volt- and ammeter

Strömung *f* current, stream, flow, flux, race, equalizing current, circulation, tendency, trend **anliegende ~** (aerodyn.) attached flow **nicht anliegende ~** (aerodyn.) separated flow **drallfreie ~** irrotational flow **freie ~** free or unrestricted flow **glatte ~** laminar flow **nach unten gerichtete ~** downdraft **schlichte ~** laminar flow **wirbelfreie ~ wirbellose ~** laminar flow, flow free from vortices, irrotational flow

Strömungsabfluß *m*, **glatter ~** wash (aviation)

Strömungs-ablösegrenze *f* flow limit **-ablösung** *f* flow separation **-abreißpunkt** *m* break-off point **-abreißwinkel** *m* angle of stall, stalling angle

Strömungsabriß *m* (durch Beschleunigen) accelerator stall **den ~ beenden** to break the stall

Strömungs-angabe *f* current data **-ausgleich** *m* balance of flow **-beeinflussung** *f* flow interference (aviation) **-bild** *n* flow pattern, flow net **-druck** *m* flow pressure, seepage pressure **-einrichtung** *f* flow direction **-energie** *f* kinetic energy, energy of flow **-feld** *n* flow field (servo) **-form** *f* configuration or shape of flow **-forschung** *f* flow research

Strömungs-gebiet *n* region or zone of flow **-gebilde** *n* configurations of flow, flow formation **-geschwindigkeit** *f* velocity of flow **-getriebe** *n* hydraulic gearing unit **-gleichrichter** *m* straightening blade **-gleichung** *f* flow equation **-haube** *f* cowling ring

Strömungs-kalorimeter *n* streaming calorimeter **-kanal** *m* wind tunnel **-karte** *f* current chart **-kolben** *m* propelling piston **-kontrollventil** *n* flow control valve **-kupplung** *f* hydraulic coupling **-lehre** *f* (theoretical) fluid dynamics **-linie** *f* flow line **-manometer** *n* transpiration manometer **-maschine** *f* fluid flow engine, jet engine **-messer** *m* current meter, flowmeter, hydrometric vane

Strömungs-pfeil *m* arrow indicating direction of current **-potential** *n* flow potential, streaming potential, stream function **-regler** *m* flow regulator, control valve **-richtung** *f* direction of the current, direction of flow **-schatten** *m* turbulent region **-schott** *m* bulkhead (to prevent flow of air in missiles) **-sicherung** *f* draft diverter (hood) **-spiralen** *pl* spirals of air stream

strömungstechnisch inflow technique **-er Entwurf** hydraulic design **-e Erkenntnisse** flow-line pattern

Strömungs-typ *m* flow type **-uhr** *f* flowmeter **-untersuchung** *f* flow test **-verhältnis** *n* flow condition **-verlauf** *m* flow **-vorgang** *m* process or mechanism of flow, flux **-wächter** *m* water-flow detector **-weg** *m* flow route **-widerstand** *m* resistance to flow, aerodynamic resistance, drag **-zustand** *m* condition of flow

Strom-unterbrecher *m* contact breaker, cutout, circuit breaker, interrupter **-unterbrecherschalter** *m* circuit breaker **-unterbrechung** *f* interruption of current **-vektor** *m* current vector **-veränderungsfrei** free of current displacement **-verbrauch** *m* current consumption **-verbraucher** *m* current-utilization device **-verdrängung** *f* skin effect, current displacement, Heaviside effect **-verdrängungsläufer** *m* skin-effect rotor **-verdrängungsmotor** *m* current-displacement motor **-vergrößerung** *f* current gain

Stromverlauf *m* course of the current, current path, current distribution **~ bei Überbelastung** excessive load characteristic

Strom-verlust *m* current loss, leakage, loss in power **-versetzung** *f* drift **-versorgung** *f* power supply, current supply **-versorgungsanlage** *f* generating plant, power equipment **-versorgungsgerät** *n* power pack **-versorgungsgeräusch** *n* battery supply circuit noise **-versorgungsschwankung** *f* power supply variation **-verstärkung** *f* current amplification **-verstimmung** *f* pushing **-verstimmungsmaß** *f* pushing figure

Strom-verteiler *m* current distributor **-verteilung** *f* (current) distribution **-verteilungsrauschen** *n* fluctuation noise, current distribution noise **-vervielfachung** *f* current multiplication **-verzweigung** *f* network of conductors, branching of currents **-wache** *f* river police **-wächter** *m* current relay **-waage** *f* current balance (weigher), ampere balance

Stromwandler *m* current transformer, series transformer **~ mit Hilfswicklung** compensated current transformer

Stromwandlerprüfeinrichtung *f* testing device for current transformer

Stromwärme *f* joulean heat **-verlust** *m* resistance loss, ohmic loss, Joule's heat loss

Stromwechsel *m* current reversal **~ pro Sekunde** cycles per second

Strom-wechsler *m* commutator, reverser **-weg** *m* current path **-weiche** *f* current divider **-weiser** *m* galvanoscope **-welle** *f* current wave or ripple **-welligkeit** *f* current ripples **-wendebrücke** *f* current-reversal bridge

Stromwender *m* (current-)reversing key, commutator (with segments), reversing switch, collector **-fahne** *f* commutator riser (lug) **-muffe** *f* sleeve of commutator **-nabe** *f* commutator sleeve **-schritt** *m* commutator pitch **-welle** *f* commutator shaft

Strom-wendung *f* commutation, reversal of current **-wert** *m* current value or characteristics, amperage **-wicklung** *f* current winding **-widerstand** *m* circuit resistance **-wippe** *f* current balance (elec.) **-zähler** *m* current meter **-zeichen** *n* impulse **-zeiger** *m* ammeter, galvanometer, current vector **-zelle** *f* electric cell **-zufuhr** *f* current or power supply **-zinn** *n* stream tin **-zufuhrtafel** *f* incoming (current) panel **-zuführung** *f* current supply, lead-in wire, power supply

Stromzuführungs-bürste *f* current-supply brush **-drähte** *pl* lead-in wires **-düse** *f* contact tube (in welding) **-feder** *f* current-carrying spring **-leitung** *f* supply leads **-schiene** *f* current-carrying rail, bus bar **-schleifleitungsstränge** *pl* third rail for trolley car or crane power supply

Strom-zuleitung *f* conduit **-zuleitungskabel** *n* current supply cable **-zunahme** *f* increase of current, rise of current

Strontian *m*, **-erde** *f* strontia **-hydrat** *n* strontium hydrate

Strontian-salpeter *m* strontium nitrate **-salz** *n*

strontium salt

Strontium *n* strontium **-azetat** *n* strontium acetate **-carbid** *n* strontium carbide **-ferrizyanid** *n* strontium ferricyanide **-gehalt** *m* strontium content **-isotop** *n* strontium isotope **-jodid** *n* strontium iodide **-nitrat** *n* strontium nitrate **-karbonat** *n* strontium carbonate

Strontium-perborat *n* strontium perborate **-salizylat** *n* strontium salicylate **-salpeter** *m* strontium nitrate **-salz** *n* strontium salt **-sulfat** *n* strontium sulfate **-sulfid** *n* strontium sulfide **-titanat** *n* strontium titanate **-wasserstoff** *m* strontium hydride

Stropp *m* sling

Strosse *f* stope, underhand stope, step, bank

Strowgerwähler *m* Strowger switch, Strowger selector

Strudel *m* eddy, vortex, whirlpool, maelstrom **-kessel** *m* pothole **-los** irrotational, noneddying **-rad** *n* agitator

Struktur *f* structure, texture, grain **~ der Kaltreckung** strained structure, structure of cold-worked metal **adrige ~** nerve structure, capillary structure **faserige ~** texture **feinschuppige magnetische ~** fine-scaled magnetic structure **schieferige ~** slaty structure **zellenartige ~** honeycombed, pitted, or cellular structure **~ außerhalb des Kerns** extranuclear structure **flächenzentrierte ~** face-centered cubic structure

struktur-abhängig structure dependent, structure sensitive **-abschluß** *m* closure of a structure (refinery) **-bedingter Befehlsroutineteil** red-tape operation **-bestandteil** *m* structural constituent **-effekt** *m* structural effect

strukturell structural **-e Bestandteile** structural members **-e Teile** structural elements **-es Versagen** structural failure **-er Widerstand** structural drag **-e Zeichnung** structural design

strukturempfindlich structure sensitive **-e Leitfähigkeit** secondary conductivity

Struktur-ermüdung *f* structural fatigue **-faktor** *m* structure factor, atom form factor **-fehler** *m* imperfection **-formel** *f* graphic formula, rational formula

strukturlos structureless, amorphous

Struktur-relaxation *f* structural relaxation **-verschiedenheit** *f* difference in structure **-viskosität** *f* intrinsic viscosity **-wandel** *m* change in structure **-zerfall** *m* structural decay

Strumpf (Gaslicht) mantle (gas burner) **-wender** *m* stocking turner

Struppe *f* strap

Stubbe *f*, **Stubben** *m* stump

Stuck *m* stucco

Stück *n* piece, portion, fragment, lump **T-Stück** *n* (flanged) T piece, (flanged) T **zwanzig ~** score **aus einem ~** one-piece

Stückanfang und Stückende start or end of a piece

Stückarbeit (Akkordarbeit) piece-work

Stuckarbeit *f* plastering (job), stuccowork

Stückbruch *m* comminuted fracture

Stückchen *n* lump, welt, bit, chip

Stückelung *f* cutting or breaking in pieces

stückeln to cut into pieces, divide up

Stuckern des Motors spluttering of the engine

Stück-erz *n* lump ore, coarse ore **-fall** *m* bringing down lumps (min.) **-färbung** *f* tissue staining, staining in toto

Stuckgips *m* flower of gypsum, plaster of Paris

Stück-größe *f* size of lump **-gut** *n* parcel, bale, bundle, piece goods **-gutkran** *m* cargo crane

stückig lumpy, in lumps **-er Kontaktkörper** (für ortfeste Katalysatoren) pellets

Stückigkeit *f* lumpiness

Stück-kalk *m* lump lime **-kohle** *f* lump coal **-koks** *m* lump coke **-kosten** *pl* piece cost **-längenmesser** *m* cut length counter **-leistung** *f* output capacity **-liste** *f* parts list, specification **-lohn** *m* wage for piecework **-lohnarbeiter** *m* pieceworker **-lohnsatz** *m* wage for piecework **-mergel** *m* bituminous marl **-metall** *n* gun metal

Stuckmörtel *m* badigeon, plaster mortar, stucco

Stück-ofen *m* iron foundry, furnace for first refining **-preis** *m* unit price **-prüfung** *f* detailed inspection **-rechnung** *f* piece calculation **-satz** *m* piecework, composition of slips or packets **-schlacke** *f* lump slag, cinder **-schliff** *m* cut **-setzer** *m* piece hand, solid compositor (print.) **-verkauf** *m* retail sale or selling **-ware** *f* piece goods

Stuckwaren *f pl* stucco works

stückweise piecemeal, piece by piece **~ glatt** piecewise smooth (math.)

Stückwerk *n* piecework, jobbing

Stuckwerkstatt *f* workshop for stucco

Stückzahl *f* quantity **Akkord nach ~** agreement by piece

Stück-zähler *m* batch counter **-zeichnung** *f* detail or component drawing

Stückzeit *f* wage for piecework **-änderung** *f* rate change **-planung** *f* (production) rate setting

Studien-plan *m* plan of study, curriculum **-reise** *f* study tour

Studio-ausrüstung *f* studio facility **-dekor** *n* abstract set **-kulisse** *f* getaway **-sendung** *f* studio pick-up, transmission, or broadcast **-signallampen** *pl* tally lights **-übertragung** *f* studio broadcast

Studtit *m* studtite

Studium *n* study

Stufe *f* (Treppe) step; (Ton~) interval; (Farb~) shade; (Antriebs~) stage; (Grad) degree, grade stair, rung, digit (automatic telephony), phase, increment, tread, rank, pitch, gradation, point (in multipoint switch) **~ des Spannungsteilers** potentiometer step **~ am Schwimmer** float step **nachgeschaltete gesteuerte ~** main oscillator stage **in Stufen von** by gradations of

Stufen ausmitteln to average out gradients

Stufen-anker *m* double-winding armature **-anordnung** *f* stepped arrangement **-antrieb** *m* cone pulley drive

stufenartig graduated, graded, gradual, echeloned, steplike, stepped

Stufen-ausbeute *f* stage efficiency **-bahn** *f* escalator **-bank** *f* graduated bank **-belag** *m* covering of step **-belastung** *f* stage load **-bohrer** *m* step drill **-breite** *f* stepped tool **-erwärmung** *f* stage heating **-fallschirm** *m* compound parachute **-feder** *f* helper spring, step spring **-folge** *f* gradation, succession or sequence of steps or stages **-förderhöhe** *f* gradual rate of delivery **-formation** *f* step formation

stufenförmig by steps ~ **angeordnete Blenden** graded stops **-e Echos** echelon formation of multiple echoes

Stufen-fräsen *n* step milling **-futter** *n* step chuck **-gang** *m* progression by stages or degrees, graduation **-gitter** *n* echelon grating **-härtemesser** *m* step penetrometer **-härtung** (Thermalhärtung) hot-quenching, time quenching **-heizung** *f* step-up cure **-höhe** *f* step height **-höhenmesser** *m* step-landing indicator **-kaskade** *f* square cascade **-keil** *m* step tablet, stepped photometric absorption wedge

Stufenkolben *m* stepped or differential piston **-pumpe** *f* differential pump

Stufen-kolonne *f* plate tower **-körper** *m* elongated twill **-kurve** *f* step-like curve **-lader** *m* multistage supercharger **-ladung** *f* speed boost **-länge** *f* step length **-leistung** *f* stage power or efficiency **-leiter** *m* progression, conductance, modulation **-leiter** *f* scale, stepladder **-linse** *f* Fresnel lens, echelon lens **-linsenkleinscheinwerfer** *m* baby key light

stufenlos ridgeless, continuous ~ **regelbar** infinitely variable ~ **regulierbar** continuously or infinitely variable ~ **einstellbare Querreibung** vibration motion infinitely adjustable **-e Leistungsregulierung** infinitely variable output control **-es Regelgetriebe** infinitely variable speed transmission **-e Regulierung** positive control

Stufen-mahlen *n* stage grinding **-meldung** *f* tap-changing signal (from tapped transformer) **-messung** *f* strata measuring **-methode** *f* gradient method

Stufenmuster *n* arrangement of steps ~ **eines selbsttragenden Luftkabels** (step) design of a self-supporting overhead cable

Stufen-nut *f* step groove or notch **-photometer** *n* step photometer **-platte** *f* sensitometer tablet **-presse** *f* gang press **-prisma** *n* chelon prism **-prozeß** *m* step process **-pumpe** *f* differential pump

Stufen-rad *n* step wheel, cone pulley **-rädergetriebe** *n* variable gearing **-rakete** *f* step rocket **-reaktion** *f* successive reaction, stepwise reaction **-relais** *n* relay with sequence action

Stufen-rolle *f* stepped roller **-rost** *m* step grate

Stufen-säule *f* plate column **-schalter** *m* step or sequence switch, stage-selector switch, multipoint switch, multicontact switch **-schaltung** *f* cascade connection **-scheibe** *f* cone pulley, step pulley, step cone, speed pulley, taper pulley **-scheibenantrieb** *m* single- or double-screw vise, pulley drive (cone), stepped pulley drive **-schwächer** *m* step-type weakener

Stufen-sender *m* multistage transmitter **-silo** *m* step-by-step bin **-spalt** *m* step slit **-spannbacke** *f* step jaw **-spannungsregler** *m* step voltage regulator **-sprung** *m* (e. Drehbank) progression **-stoß** *m* splice effected gradually over length of member **-transformator** *m* tapped transformer **-trennfaktor** *m* simple process factor **-trennung** *f* stage separation (of multi-stage rockets) **-trocknung** *f* stage drying **-turbine** *f* stage turbine

Stufen-unterteilung des Kompressors staging of the compressor **-ventil** *n* multiple-seat valve **-verkleidung** *f* step fairing **-verschmelzung** *f* gradual blending **-versetzung** *f* edge dislocation **-versuche** *pl* tests by progressive loadings **-walze** *f* step roll **-wäsche** *f* fractional washing (paper mfg.)

stufenweise gradual(ly), in stages, stepwise, by degrees, by increments, successively, progressive ~ **Anregung** step-by-step excitation ~ **Filtration** staggered filtration ~ **Geschwindigkeitsänderung** *f* gradual speed variation ~ **Zementierung** multiple-stage cementing ~ **gesteigert** increased stepwise

stufenweiser Zuwachs *m* load increment

Stufen-wicklung *f* bank(ed) winding **-widerstand** *m* step-by-step resistance **-wirkung** *f* step-by-step action **-wirkungsgrad** *m* efficiency scale **-zahl** *f* step number **-zahnrad** *n* stepped gear, cluster gear

stufig regular, graduated, having steps **-es Gebläse** stage blower

Stufung *f* step-up distance, staggering, difference of altitude (in formation flying)

Stuhl *m* chair **-lasche** *f* fish chair (R.R.) **-nagel** *m* treenail **-platte** *f* bedplate, chair plate, saddle (R.R.)

Stuhlungsbreite *f* width of the supports

Stulpe *f* cuff

stülpen to turn inside out or upside down, put in inverted position

Stulpwand *f* sheating ~ **aus Bohlen** poling-boards sheating

Stummabstimmschaltung squelch circuit

Stummabstimmung *f* quiescent automatic volume control, quiet automatic volume control, automatic incarrier noise suppression, interstation noise suppression, aural null

Stummel *m* stump **-flügel** *m* stub wings **-welle** *f* stub shaft

Stummfilm *m* silent film **-kamera** *f* silent camera

Stumpen *m* body

stumpen to pick burs, knots and fluff from cloth as it comes from the loom, stump cloth

Stümper *m* blunderer, bungler, duffer

Stumpf *m* frustum, trunk (of polygon), stump, butt end

stumpf dull, blunt, flush, apathetic, obtuse, truncated, stud ~ **aneinanderfügen** to butt-joint, butt ~ **angefügt** butt-jointed ~ **machen** to dull **-e Gehrung** miter joint **-er Kegel** frustum (of cone), truncated cone **-es Prisma** truncated prism **-e Pyramide** frustum **-e Verbindung** butt joint **-er Winkel** obtuse angle **-er Zylinder** truncated cylinder

stumpf-eckig blunt-cornered **-elektrode** *f* truncated electrode **-feile** *f* blunt file

stumpfgeschweißt butt-welded **-es Rohr** butt-welded tube or pipe

Stumpfgewinde *n* stub thread

Stumpfheit *f* dullness, absorption (acoust)

stumpf-kabel *n* stub cable **-kantig** blunt-edged **-kegel** *m* truncated cone, frustum **-kolben** *m* butt hinge **-löten** to solder end to end **-mast** *m* stub mast **-naht** *f* blunt seam, butt weld **-nahtschweißung** *f* buttseam welding **-preßschweißverfahren** *n* buttwelding process

stumpf-schweißen to butt-weld, lump-weld **-schweißen** *n* butt welding, upset welding, jump weld **-schweißmaschine** *f* butt welder, butt-welding machine **-schweißung** *f* butt or upset welding, jump weld **-stoß** *m* butt-joint **-verbindung** *f* butt joint **-verzahnung** *f* stub-tooth gearing, stub-tooth form **-werden** (Werkzeug) dulling **-winklig** obtuse-angled **-zahn** *m* stub tooth **-zahnstahl** *m* stub tooth cutter

Stunde *f* hour **die Stunden der Dunkelheit** hours of darkness (aviat.)

stunden to allow time or grant respite for payment **-achse** *f* polar axis, hour axis **-antrieb** *m* hour drive **-betrieb** *m* one hour duty **-bewegung** *f* motion in right ascension **-drehmoment** *n* one-hour-rating torque **-drehzahl** *f* revolutions per hour **-geschwindigkeit** *f* speed per hour **-glas** *n* hourglass **-kilometer** *m pl* kilometers per hour **-kreis** *m* hour circle, right ascension circle (astron.) **-kurve** *f* meridian curve

Stunden-leistung *f* hourly output **-messer** *m* hour meter **-plan** *m* assignment of hours, duty chart, timetable, schedule **-ring** *m* graduated circle of the compass **-satz** *m* hourly rate **-tonne** *f* metric tons per hour **-umlaufzeit** *f* time of rotation in hours

stundenweise hourly, by the hour

Stunden-winkelscheibe *f* hour angle disk (astron.) **-zähler** *m* hour counter **-zeiger** *m* hour hand

stündlich per hour, hourly **-e Fördermenge** quantity delivered per hour

Stundung *f* (term of) respite **~ verlangen** to apply for a term of respite

Stundungs-frist *f* time allowed for payment, respite **-gesuch** *m* request for a respite

Stupfelmaschine *f* pricking or punching machine (textiles)

Stupp *f* stupp **-kasten** *m* soot pan

Sturm *m* assault, storm, gale, tempest **die Mitte des Sturmes** eye of the storm, center of tropical cyclone

Sturmbahn *f* storm path or track **Umbiegen der ~** recurvature of storm

Sturm-ball *m* storm ball **-bock** *m* ram **-feld** *n* storm area

Sturmflut *f* storm tide, sea level in storms **Wasserstand von Sturmfluten** tide level (due to storm), sea level in storms

stürmisch stormy, turbulent, wild, violent, vivid, agitated **-e See** rough sea

Sturm-kegel *m* storm cone **-laterne** *f* hurricane lamp, wind lantern, road darger lamp

Sturm-riemen *m* chin strap **-schaden** *m* storm damage **-segler** *m* assault glider **-signal** *n* storm signal **-warnung** *f* storm warning, gale warning, weather warnings

Sturmwarnungs-dienst *m* storm-warning service **-fahne** *f* storm-warning flag **-nebenstelle** *f* storm-warning substation or secondary warning post **-radar** *n* storm spy **-stelle** *f* storm-warning station **-zeichen** *n* storm-warning signal

Sturm-wind *m* gale **-zentrum** *n* storm center

Sturz *m* collapse, crash, fall, plunge, slab, plate, pack (metal.), camber, sudden drop or decline, (Oberschwelle) lintel, chute **~ der Kraftwagenräder** camber

Sturz-acker *m* plowed land or field **-anordnung** *f* tipping arrangement

Sturzbett *n* downstream floor or apron, lower floor, spillway board (dam), tumble bay, bucket of overflow weir **~ aus geschütteten Steinen** protection stone below dam **gekrümmtes ~** curved downstream floor **gemauertes ~** masonry downstream or apron **treppenförmiges ~** downstream floor with steps

Sturzblech *n* thin sheet

Sturz-bock *m* padding **-bremse** *f* dive brake

Stürzbrücke *f* dumping bridge

Sturz-bügel *m* safety clip **-bühne** *f* tipping stage

Stürze *f* (Schalltrichter) bell

stürzen to fall, tumble, plunge, overthrow, crash, rush, tip, dump, throw **ins Meer ~** to fall into the sea **auf das Ziel ~** to dive upon the target

Stürzen *n* slipping, slip **~ der Bilder** somersaulting or tumbling of the images

stürzender Start diving start

Sturzflug *m* vertical or nose dive, diving course **~ mit Endgeschwindigkeit** terminal-velocity dive **~ mit Vollkraft** full-power dive **~ ausführen** to dive **aus dem ~ abfangen** to pull out of a dive **einen ~ machen** to dive

Sturzflug-anschlag *m* automatic nose-dive stop **-bremse** *f* dive brake, dive flap **-drehzahl** *f* terminal-velocity engine speed **-erprobung** *f* diving trial, diving test **-geschwindigkeit** *f* diving speed

Sturz-gerüst *n* tipping jetty **-helm** *m* crash helmet **-höhe** *f* dumping height

Sturz-lage *f* diving position **-lager** *n* dump (store) **-platz** *m* dumping ground **-probe** *f* slump test **-regen** *m* intense local rain of short duration **-rinne** *f* (tip) chute

Sturz-sieb *n* screening device, grizzly **-spirale** *f* spiral (aviation) **-träger** *m* lintel beam **-visier** *n*, **-vision** *f* dive-bomber's bombsight **-wehr** *n* pile lock (dam) **-welle** *f* breaker **-wind** *m* gust of wind, strong downcurrent **-winkel** *m* camber angle

Stütz-arm *m* bracket, support **-balken** *m* supporting or reinforcing beam, rest beam, brace, supporting bar, shores, props **-blech** *n* guiding plate **-block** *m* cleat **-bock** *m* (für den Einbau von Stangenfüßen), wooden framework erected to support poles during renewals **-bolzenbohrer** *m* stay-bolt tap **-bügel** *m* support yoke **-drosselspule** *f* supporting choke coil

Stütze *f* support, column, standard, pillar, upright, stay, truss, bearing, leg, pin, horse, arm (of shield), bracket **feste ~** pier leg **gerade ~** straight insulator pin, spindle (straight)

Stutzen *m* connecting piece, short feed pipe, nipple, socket, stub, nozzle, connection, shoring, stud, union

stützen to support, prop, shore up, endorse, curtail, clip, stay, rest or bear on **sich ~ auf** to rely on, depend on, base on

Stützen-bohrer *m* pole drill (elec.) **-fußhalter** *m* knee clamp (for arm braces) **-entfernung** *f* distance between legs **-gelenk** *n* joint of support **-hülse** *f* connection sleeve **-isolator** *m* pin insulator **-verteilerscheibe** *f* distributor disk with connection

Stutzenzieher *m* stud remover

Stützer *m* pin **-führung** *f* pin (elec.) **-stromwandler** *m* bushing or spreader current transformer

Stütz-feder *f* helper spring **-fläche** *f* supporting surface **-fuß** *m* support leg **-gerüst** *n* supporting frame **-hebel** *m* supporting lever **-holm** *m* waling **-isolator** *m* pin (type) insulator, rod insulator

Stütz-kettenaufzüge *pl* supporting-chain elevators **-knagge** *f* stop **-konsole** *f* supporting bracket **-kontakt** *m* gyro-setting contact **-kraft** *f* bearing pressure or reaction, supporting force **-lager** *n* step, step bearing, spindle bracket, backrest **-lagerständer** *m* end support column **-linie** *f* line of pressure (in masonry analysis) **-mauer** *f* retaining wall, supporting wall **-moment** *m* supporting moment

Stutzmotor *m* erection motor, directional gyro autopilot, (Gyro) stiffness motor

Stütz-nabe *f* supporting hub **-pfahl** *m* bearing pile, rubbing pile, stub reinforcement **-pfeiler** *m* supporting pillar, supporting column, bearing pile, bedding pile **-pfosten** *m* supporting post; prop, strut **-platte** *f* bracket plate

Stützpunkt *m* tie lug (in wiring), support, triangulation station, bracket, stop, fulcrum, bearing surface **-abstand** *m* pole distance **-kondensator** *m* anchoring-point capacitor, standoff capacitor

Stütz-räder *pl* jackwheels **-relais** *n* stick-and-latch relay, interlocking relay **-resonanz** *f* support resonance **-ring** *m* thrust ring, prop ring **-rippe** *f* stiffening or reinforcing rib **-rohr** *n* supporting tube, steadying tube, outer steering column **-rolle** *f* track-supporting roller

Stützrollen *pl* backing rolls, backing bearings **-einstellung** *f* backing-up roll adjustment **-system** *n* backing bearing system **-träger** *m* supporting roller pedestal

Stütz-säule *f* supporting column, locking pin, prop, supporting pillar **-scheibe** *f* supporting plate or disk **-schneide** *f* supporting knife edge **-schraube** *f* carrying bolt **-schwimmer** *m* outboard float (aviation), wing-tip float **-spule** *f* torque motor **-stange** *f* supporting pole **-stoff** *m* stabilizing medium **-strebe** *f* steadying strut **-träger** *m* carrier support, kingpost

Stütz-walze *f* backing roll **-weite** *f* width between support, span, trestle interval **-werk** *n* supporting frame **-widerstand** *m* reaction of support **-winkel** *m* thrust block, stopblock, upper pintle casting **-zapfen** *m* footstep, pivot journal, pivot

Styroflexkondensator *m* styroflex capacitor

Styrol *n* styrene

Subaeration *f* subaeration

subaerisch subaerial

Suberit *m* suberite

Subharmonische *f* subharmonic (radio)

subjektiv subjective **-e Lautstärke** subjective loudness **-es Photometer** visual photometer

Subkornbildung *f* subgrain formation

subkritisch-e Vermehrung subcritical multiplication **-e Zusammenstellung** subcritical assembly

Subkutanpräparat *n* hypodermic product

Sublimat *n* sublimate, mercuric chloride spray **mit ~ tränken** kyanize

Sublimation *f* sublimation

Sublimations-anlage *f* sublimation plant **-druck** *m* sublimation pressure **-kerne** *pl* sublimation nuclei **-wärme** *f* heat of sublimation

sublimierbar sublimable

sublimieren to sublime

Submikrodehnungsgebiet sub-micro strain region

Submikrometer *n* submicrometer

Subminiaturkreisel *m* sub-miniature channel gyroscope

Submission *f* submission, contract (for public works), tender

submissionieren to sublet

Submissionsbedingungen *pl* terms of contract

Submissionsofferte *f*, **eine ~ einreichen** to make a tender

Submissionsvergebung *f* sale upon sealed tenders

Submissionsweg, auf dem ~ vergeben to entrust the execution of public works by tender

Submittent *m* contractor, tenderer

submittieren to submit, tender

Subrogationsrecht *n* right of subrogation

subsekutiv following

subsidär subsidiary

Subsidien *pl* subsidies

Subsilikat *n* subsilicate

Subsistenz *f* subsistence

Subskribent *m* subscriber

subskribieren subscribe

Subskription *f* subscription

subsonisch subsonic

substantiell-e Ableitung hydrodynamical derivative **-e Form** material form

Substantivität *f* substantivity

Substanz *f* substance, matter, essence **-muster** *n* sample in kind

substituieren to substitute

Substitution *f* substitution

Substitutions-methode *f* substitution method **-teil** *m* parameter setting orders (info proc.) **-verfahren** *n* substitution method or process

Substrat *n* substratum **-fläche** *f* substrate **-oberfläche** *f* substrate surface

Substratosphäre *f* substratosphere

Subtangente *f* subtangent

Subtrahendus *m* subtrahend

subtrahieren to subtract

Subtraktion *f* subtraction, deduction

Subtraktionszähler *m* balance counter

subtraktiv subtractive **-e Division** dividing by continuous subtraction **-es Farbensystem** *n* subtractive color system **-e Modulation** downward or positive modulation

subtransitorisch-er Kurzschlußwechselstrom subtransient three-phase short-circuit current **-e Längs-EMK** direct axis subtransient electromotive force

subtropisch subtropical

subvenieren to support, relieve

Subvention *f* subsidy

subventionieren to subsidize

Subzinylsäure *f* succinic acid

Such-anker *m* grapnel **-anlage** *f* search installation

Suche *f*, **auf der ~ nach** on the lookout for, in search of

Such-arbeit *f* research, search **-blatt** *n* reference gazette **-ebene** *f* search plane **-elektrode** *f* probe electrode, exploring electrode, collector electrode **-empfang** *m* straight-ahead reception, direct reception, nonheterodyne reception, single-circuit reception **-empfänger** *m* stand-by receiver, search receiver

suchen to search, look for, seek, select, find (out) **einen Fehler ~** to trace an error **ein Seekabel ~** to drag for a submarine cable **~ gehen** to fetch **frei ~** to hunt (for)

Suchen *n* tracing, finding, selecting, hunting

Sucher *m* (view) finder, selector, seeker, spotlight, searcher, locator, detector, probe **~ mit autom. Parallaxenkorrektur** auto-parallax finder

Sucherbild *n* view finder, image seeker picture, monitoring picture

Sucherde *f* ground rod for telephone interception

Sucher-fenster *n* view-finder **-fernrohr** *n* open-sight searching telescope, telescopic finder **-fuß** *m* seeker toe **-glas** *n* spotlight lens **-hebel** *m* seeker lever, selecting lever **-korn** *n* back sight of view finder **-kontakt** *m* cat's whisker **-kreis** *m* homing loop **-lampe** *f* spotlight **-libelle** *f* finder level (bubble) **-okular** *n* focusing lens **-parallaxe** *f* seeker parallax, finder parallax **-objektiv** *n* finder lens (objective)

Suchgerät *n* searching instrument, locator, detector **-empfänger** *m* direction-finder receiver

Such-hebel *m* (Fernschreiber) seeker **-kopf** *m* seeker head **-kurve** *f* search curve **-lampe** *f* lamp detector (elec.) **-licht** *n* spotlight, searchlight **-radar** *n* search radar **-scheinwerfer** *m* searchlamp, spotlight **-schritt** *m* hunting step (tel.) **-sektor** *m* searching sector

Such-spannung *f* search voltage **-spule** *f* exploring coil, search coil, rotating coil, flip coil **-spulenrotor** *m* search coil rotor **-spulenstator** *m* search coil stator **-strahl** *m* target beam **-tonanalysator** *m* heterodyne analyzer **-tonverfahren** *n* beat-note method

Such- und Rettungsdienst *m* search and rescue service

Such-wähler *m* finder switch **-wortverzeichnis** *n* index **-zeichen** *n* inquiry signal **-zeit** *f* access time

suchzeitlose Speicherung zero-access storage

Sud *m* strike, brewing **~ von aufgelöstem Zucker** remelt strike **blank abgekochter ~** jelly

Sudbad *n* boiling bath

Süden *m* south

Südföhn *m* southern foehn

Südhalbkugel *f* southern hemisphere

Sudhaus *n* brewing house

Südlagerung *f* south pedestal

südlich southward, southerly **-e Breite** south latitude **-e Erdhälfte, -e Halbkugel** southern hemisphere

Süd-licht *n* aurora australis, southern lights **magnetisch** south-magnetic

Sudmaschine *f* crystallizer

Sudmaische *f* crystallizer

Süd-osten *m* southeast **-ostwärts** southeasterly

Süd-pol *m* south (magnetic) pole **-punkt** *m* south point, south **-wärts** southward **-westen** *m* southwest

Sudzeit *f* duration of boiling or brewing

sukzedieren to follow upon, succed

sukzessiv-e Annäherung successive approximation **-e Umstellung** successive change-over

Sukzessivlieferung *f* successive delivery, delivery by installments

Sulfanilsäure *f* sulfanilic acid

Sulfat *n* sulfate

Sulfatation *f* sulfating

sulfatieren to sulfate

sulfatierte Batterie sulfated battery

Sulfatierung *f* sulfatation

sulfatisierende Röstung sulfating roasting, sulfate roast

Sulfatierung *f*, **Sulfation** *f* sulfatization, sulfation

Sulfatisierofen *m* sulfating (roasting) furnace

Sulfatisierungsmittel *n* sulfating agent

Sulfatkocher *m* sulfate digester

Sulfat(zell)stoff *m* sulfate pulp

Sulfatzellulose *f* sulfate cellulose

Sulf-hydrat *n*, **-hydrid** *n* hydrosulfide, sulfohydrate

Sulfid *n* sulfide **-einschluß** *m* sulfide inclusion **-erz** *n* sulfide ore

sulfidieren to sulfide

Sulfidierung *f* sulfidization

sulfidisch sulfidic, sulfide **-es Erz** sulfide ore

Sulfidschwefel *m* sulfide sulfur

sulfieren to sulfonate

Sulfierung *f* sulfonation

Sulfit-anlage *f* acid plant **-ätze** *f* sulfite discharge

Sulfit-lauge *f* sulfite liquor, sulfite solution, sodium bisulfite solution **-laugenturm** *m* sulfite tower

Sulfitierung *f* sulfation

Sulfo-bleiweiß *n* basic sulfate wite lead **-fettsäure** *f* sulfo-sebacic acid **-harnstoff** *m* sulfurea **-hydrat** *n* hydrosulfide, sulfo-hydrate

Sulfolyse *f* sulfation, sulfolysis

Sulfonat *n* sulfonate

sulfoniertes Kienöl sulfonated pine oil

Sulfonsäure *f* sulfonic acid

Sulforicinat *n* Turkey-red oil

Sulfo-salizylsäure *f* sulfosalicylic acid **-salz** *n* sulfosalt, thiosalt **-verbindung** *f* sulfo compound **-zyan** *n* sulfocyanogen **-zyaneisen** *n* ferric thio-cyanate **-zyankalium** *n* potassium sulfocyanate **-zyansäure** *f* sulfocyanic acid, thiocyanic acid

sulfurieren to sulfonate (sulfurize)

sulfuriert sulfurated

Sulkydammkulturpflug *m* sulky lister

Sulky mit Sitz riding sulky

Sulkyreihensä- und Zudeckmaschine *f* sulky lister

Sulze *f*, **Sülze** *f* brine, jelly

Summand *m* term of a sum (math.)

summarische Arbeitsbewertung factor comparison system

Summation *f* addition

Summations-formel *f* summation formula **-indices** *pl* dummies **-kurve** *f* cumulative curve **-ton** *m* summation tone **-übereinkunft** *f* summation convention **-verfahren** *n* summation method

Summe *f* total, sum, summation **ganze ~** grand total **(eine) ~ ermitteln** to assess an amount **~ der Elektronenzustände** manifold of electronic states **~ von Masse und Energie** mass-energy total

summen to hum, buzz, sum up, add (up)
Summen *n* hum(ming), buzz(ing) **-ausdruck** *m* summation **-bildung** *f* sum operation, formation of sums
Summendifferenz *f* difference of summation frequencies **-verfahren** *n* superheterodyne procedure, sum-and-difference method **-verstärker** *m* superheterodyne amplifier
Summen-drucktaste *f* key for printing totals **-formel** *f* summation formula **-frequenz** *f* sum frequency, summation frequency **-gang** *m* total cycle **-gleichung** *f* summation equation **-häufigkeit** *f* cumulative frequency, integrated frequency **-index** *m* sum subscript **-instrument** *n* summation instrument
Summen-kontrolle *f* summation check, parallel balance **-kurve** *f* cumulative curve **-linie** *f* cast line **-locher** *m* summary punch (comput.) **-messung** *f* integral measurement **-probe** *f* summation check (info proc.) **-regel** *f* sum rule, permanence principle **-regler** *m* final regulator, master attenuator or control
Summen-satz *m* sum rule, permanence principle **-schreibung** *f* total printing **-spannung** *f* total or combined stress **-spitzenpegel** *m* aggregate peak level **-stanzer** *m* gang summary pinch **-tabulator** *m* rolling total tabulator **-taste** *f* total key **-ton** *m* summation ton **-trieb** *m* adding unit **-übersetzer** (Fernschreiber) aggregate motion translator
Summenübertragung *f* total transfer, total rolling **~ im Kartengang** card cycle total transfer
Summen-verstärker *m* (Mischpult) master amplifier **-wandler** *m* totalizing current transformer **-werkausgang** *m* counter total exit **-wirkung** *f* combined or compound action or effect **-zähler** *m* summation meter
Summer *m* buzzer, oscillator, vibrator **~ für Amtszeichen** buzzer for dialing tone **~ für Besetztzeichen** buzzer for busy tone or signal **durch ~ erregter Kreis** buzzer-driven circuit **~ für frei** buzzer for ringing tone **abgestimmter ~** tuned buzzer **starker ~** howler
Summer-anlaßspule *f* buzzer-type starting coil **-anlaßzündung** *f* buzzer-type starting ignition **-apparat** *m* buzzer **-aufschlaghorn** *n* buzzer (striking) horn **-erregung** *f* buzzer excitation **-generator** *m* buzzer generator **-gerät** *n* buzzer **-horn** *n* buzzer horn **-knopf** *m* buzzer key **-leitung** *f* buzzer or oscillator lead **-meldebetrieb** *m* telegraph order-wire working **-meldedienst** *m* reporting trunk telephone calls by telegraph order wire with buzzer or sounder
Summer-prüfung *f* audible test **-relais** *n* buzzer relay **-schaltung** *f* audio-oscillator circuit **-schauzeichen** *n* buzzer visual indicator **-signal** *n* pip-pip-pip-signal **-signalanlage** *f* buzzer-signal installation **-spannung** *f* buzzer voltage, synchronizing voltage **-taster** *m* buzzer key **-teil** *n* audio (oscillator) section **-ton** *m* buzzing tone or sound, humming tone **-unterbrecher** *m* buzzer interrupter **-wellenmesser** *m* buzzer wave meter
Summerzeichen *n* humming sound or tone, buzzer signal **~ zur Anzeige unbenützter Leitung** dead-number tone **~ zur Anzeige unausführbarer Verbindung** number-unobtainable tone
Summer-zündgerät *n* vibrator ignition, high-tension ignition **-zündspule** *f* ignition coil **-zusatz** *m* buzzer set
summieren to add, sum (up), totalize
summierend adding **-es Meßgerät** summation instrument **-er Verstärker** integrating amplifier
Summier-integrator *m* summing integrator **-stufe** *f* mixing stage (TV)
summiert summed
Summiertrieb *m* mechanical adding device
Summierung *f* summation
Summierungs-gerät *n* integrator **-knotenpunkt** *m* summing junction **-knotenpunktstrom** *m* summing junction current **-prüfung** *f* summation check **-regelung** *f* compound control action **-verhalten** *n* summation action **-vorschrift** summation convention
Summierverstärker *m* summing amplifier
Summpfeife *f* buzzer **-spur** *f*, **-streifen** *m* buzz track (on film) **-ton** *m* dial hum
Sumpf (Ölwanne) sump (oil pan), swamp, flood basin, pouring basin, pool, marsh, absorption layer, foam air, iron particles **-ablaß** *m* sump plug **-dicke** *f* density of sump **-ebene** *f* mud flat **-eisenstein** *m* bog iron ore
Sümpfen *n* filling a swamp
Sumpf-erz *n* bog iron ore **-gas** *n* marsh gas **-gebiet** *n* marshland
sumpfig swampy, marshy, boggy **-e Gebiete** marshy areas **-es Gelände** marshland
Sumpf-phase *f* slurry operation methane, semisolid phase **-produkt** *n* bottom product **-schicht** *f* layer of sump (electricity absorbing stratum)
Sunk *n* suction wave
Super (Benzin) premium blend (petrol) **-brechung** *f* superrefraction **-dividende** *f* special dividend, bonus
superelastisch superelastic **-er Stoß** superelastic impact
Super(het) *n* beat receiver, superheterodyne or heterodyne receiver
Superheterodynempfang *m* superheterodyne reception **~ mit selbsterregter Trägerwelle** homodyne reception
Super-heterodynempfänger *m* superheterodyne receiver, intermediate-frequency receiver, double-detection receiver **-ikonoskop** *n* supericonoscope **-leitfähigkeit** *f* superconductivity **-oxyd** *n* peroxide **-oxydation** *f* peroxydation **-oxydbleiche** *f* peroxide bleach **-oxydecht** fast to peroxide **-phantom** *n* phantom circuit (double) **-phosphat** *n* superphosphate **-ponierbar** superposable **-ponierung** *f* superimposing
Superposition *f* superposition **~ von Singularitäten** singularity superposition
Super-positionsgesetz *n* superposition theorem **-positionsnäherung** *f* superposition approximation **-regenerativer Empfang** superregenerative reception **-sonisch** supersonic
Superregenerativ-empfang *m* superregenerative reception **-empfänger** *m* superregenerative receiver, superregenerator, periodic-trigger-type receiver
Supertara *f* additional tare
Supplement *n* supplement
Supplement(är)winkel *m* supplementary angle

Support *m* support, rest, slide, head, (tool) carriage, slide rest **in der Höhe verstellbarer ~** rise and fall rest **doppelter ~** double tool post or toolholder **drehbarer ~** full swing rest **einfacher ~** plain tool post or toolholder **schwenkbarer ~** swing rest

Support-befestigungsschraube *f* clamping bolt **-drehbank** *f* slide lathe **-drehteil** *m* tool-rest swivel **-festklemmschraube** *f* screw to clamp saddle to crossrail **-feststellbolzen** *m* binder for head **-kurbel** *f* crank handle for raising tool block **-oberschieber** *m* top slide (of the rest) **-oberschlitten** *m* tool slide **-räderplatte** *f* (saddle) apron **-schleifarbeiten** *pl* tool-post grinding (operations) **-schlitten** *m* saddle **-schloßplatte** *f* (saddle) apron **-unterschlitten** *m* saddle

Supra-leitelektron *n* superconduction electron **-fluid** *n* superfluid **-fluidität** *f* superfluidity **-flüssig** superfluid

supraleitend superconductive **-er Phasenübergang** superconductive phase transition **-e Probe** superconductive specimen

Supra-leiter *m* superconductor **-leitfähigkeit** *f* supraconductivity, superconductivity **-leitungsübergang** superconducting transition **-leitvermögenrechenmaschine** *f* superconducting computer device **-refraktion** *f* superrefraction

Surren *n* humming

Surrerscheinung *f* motorboating (in radio receivers)

Surrogat *n* substitute, surrogate

Survolteur *m* positive booster

suspendieren to suspend

Suspendierung *f*, **Suspension** *f* suspension

Suspensionen *pl* suspended matter

Suspensions-luft *f* suspension air **-mittel** *n* dispersing agent

süß sweet **-es Rohöl** sweet (crude) gasoline

Süßigkeit *f* sweetness

Süßstoff *m* dulcifying material, dulcifiant

Süßwasser *n* fresh water **-ablagerung** *f* freshwater deposit **-behälter** *m* fresh-water (storage) tank **-kühler mit Solekühlung** fresh-water cooler with brine cooling

Suszeptanz *f* susceptance **kapazitive ~** capacity susceptance

Suszeptibilität *f* susceptibility, magnetizability

Suszeptibilitätsmaximum *n* susceptibility maximum **-messer** *m* susceptibility meter

S-Verzeichnung *f* S-distortion

Swan-band *n* swan band **-fassung** *f* Swan-type socket **-sockel** *m* bayonet or swan cap **-spektrum** *n* swan spectrum

Swartzit *m* swartzite

Swingaudionempfänger *m* autodyne receiver

Sykomore *f* sycamore

Sylvanit *m* sylvanite

Sylvin *n* sylvite

Symbol *n* symbol

Symboli *f* mimic diagram

symbolisch symbolic(al) **-er Addierer** half adder **-e Adresse** *f* symbolic, floating address (info proc.) **-er Befehl** *m* pseudo instruction **-e Codierung** symbolic coding **-e Darstellung** symbolic representation **-e Logik** mathematical logic

Symbol-logik *f* mathematical logic **-schreibung** *f* symbol printing

Symmetrie *f* symmetry, balanced condition **mangelnde ~** lack of symmetry **~ der Häufigkeitskurve** isokurtosis **~ bei Steuerungsfähigkeit** enabled balance

Symmetrie-achse *f* axis of symmetry, plane of symmetry, crystallographic plane **-bedingung** *f* condition for symmetry **-dämpfung** *f* balanced attenuation **-ebene** *f* crystallographic plane, plane of symmetry **-eigenschaften** *pl* properties of symmetry **-einrichtung** *f* phase balancer (balancing single-phase load over 3-phase supply) **-gesetz** *n* law of symmetry **-linie** *f* symmetric line **-operator** *m* symmetry operator **-plan** *m* symmetry plane **-prüfung** *f* symmetry test

symmetrieren to balance, symmetrize, neutralize, align

Symmetrierkondensator balance condenser

Symmetrierung *f* balancing of circuits (teleph.), symmetrization **~ der Wippspannungen** rendering symmetrical or balancing the sweep voltages

Symmetrierzusatz *m* apparatus for increasing the symmetry (teleph.)

Symmetrie-schaltung *f* symmetrical arrangement, symmetry circuit **-symbolik** *f* symmetry symbols **-topf** *m* balance-unbalance transformer **-überträger** *m* three-coil transformer (teleph.) **-wand** *f* reflection plate (in wind tunnel) **-widerstand** *m* balancing resistor **-zahl** *f* symmetry number **-zentrum** *n* inversion center

symmetrisch symmetrical **~ heterostatische Schaltung** symmetrical heterostatic circuit **eben ~** planar symmetric **-e Ablenkung** symmetrical deflection **-e Anzapfantenne** Delta-matched impedance antenna **-e Belastung** balanced load **-er Kreis** balanced wire-circuit **-er Kreisel** sleeping top **-e Lesewicklung** balanced sense windings

symmetrisch-e Mischstufe balanced mixer **-es Netzwerk** series-shunt network, ladder network **-es Profil** symmetrical profile **-e Schaltung** symmetrical arrangement **-e Ströme** balanced currents **-er Vierpol** symmetrical two-terminal pair network, symmetrical quadripole, balanced quadripole **-er Wandler** symmetrical transducer **-e Wechselgröße** symmetrical alternating quantity

Symons-Tellermühle *f* Symons disk crusher

Sympiezometer *n* sympiesometer

symplektisch symplectic **-e Gruppe** symplectic group **-e Matrix** symplectic matrix

Synchro *m* synchro **-cyclotron** FM-cyclotron **-dynempfang** *m* synchrodyne reception **-motor** *m* power synchro

synchron synchronous, in synchronism (with) **-e Längsimpedanz** direct-axis synchronous impedance **-e Querimpedanz** quadrature-axis synchronous impedance

Synchron-abtastung *f* synchronous scanning **-antrieb** *m* automatic synchronizer **-detektor** *m* lock-in amplifier **-funkenstrecke** *f* synchronous (rotating) spark gap **-generator** *m* synchronous alternator

Synchrongetriebe *n* synchronizing gear, synchromesh ~ **mit Einrichtung zur Beseitigung von Drehmomentstößen** torque check gear

Synchron-halteeinrichtung *f* interlocking system **-höhensteuer** *n* synchronised elevator **-hörer** *m* synchro receiver

Synchronisationsfehler *m* jitter **-impuls** *m* sync pulse

Synchronisator *m* synchronizer (rdr)

Synchronisier-abtrennung *f* synchronizing separation, amplitude separator, clipper **-anlage** *f* synchronizing circuit **-atelier** *n* scoring stage **-aussiebung** *f* synchronizing separation, amplitude separator, clipper **-einrichtung** *f* synchronizing device **-generator** *m* synchronizing pulse generator **-gitter** *n* synchronizing grid **-impuls** *m* synchronizing signal, synchronizing impulse **-klappe** *f* clappers to mark sound and picture track for synchronization **-knopf** *m* synchronizing knob **-pegel** *m* level of synchronization **-signal** *n* synchronizing potential

synchronisieren to dub (film), phase in, synchronize, bring into step

Synchronisieren *n* timing **lokal geregeltes** ~ local synchronization **selbständiges** ~ distance- or signal-controlled synchronization (television)

synchronisierend synchronizing **-e Pilotwelle** synchronizing pilot

synchronisiert synchronized **-er Asynchronmotor** synchronous induction motor **-e Oszillatoren** locked oscillator

Synchronisierung *f* synchronization ~ **des Trägerstroms** synchronization of the carrier frequency **lokale** ~, **örtliche** ~ independent time control **übertragene** ~ step-by-step synchronizing

Synchronisierungs-arm *m* synchronizing arm **-bereich** *m* retension range **-einrichtung** *f* synchronizing equipment **-generator** *m* synchronizing generator **-getriebe** *n* synchronizing gear **-impulse** *pl* synchronizing pulses **-motor** selsyn (motor)

Synchronisierungs-nutzeffekt *m* percentage synchronization **-organ** *n* interlock **-pegel** *m* synchronizing level **-schaltung** *f* synchronizing circuit **-sicherung** *f* fuse for synchronisation **-umschalter** *m* change-over switch for synchronisation

Synchronisier-verfahren *n* synchronizing method **-verstärker** *m* synchronizing amplifier **-vorrichtung** *f* synchronizing gear or device, synchronizer **-zeichen** *n* synchronizing signal, synchronizing impulse **-zeitmarke** *f* marking of time, synchronizing mark, time scale **-zwang** *m* locked synchronism, locked synchronization

Synchronismus *m* synchronism **-anzeiger** *m* synchronizer

synchronistisch synchronous

Synchron-kondensator *m* synchronous condenser **-lauf** *m* synchronous running **-maschine** *f* synchronous machine **-messer** *m* synchronometer **-mischstufe** *f* sanchronous mixer **-motor** *m* synchronous motor

Synchronoskop *n* synchronous position indicator, synchronoscope

Synchron-phasenschieber *m* phase shifting transformer **-pegel** *m* synchronizing amplifier **-rechner** *m* synchronous computer **-sender** *m* synchro-transmitter, synchronized transmitter **-servomechanismus** *m* automatic synchronizer **-studio** *n* dubbing studio

Synchronsignal *n*, **totales** ~ composite synchronization signal

Synchronuhr *f* synchronous electric clock, synchronous timer

Synchronuhrensystem, elektrisches ~ synchronous electric clock system

Synchron-umrichter *m* synchronous converter **-verfahren** *n* synchronous method **-zeitschalter** synchronous timer **-zerhacker** *m* synchronous vibrator

Synchrophasenmesser *m* synchro phasemeter

Synchroskop *n* synchroscope **-methode** *f* triggered oscilloscope method

Synchrotron *n* phasotron, synchrotron

Synchroskopmethode *f* triggered oscilloscope method

Synchrotronschwingungen *pl* synchrotron oscillations

Synchrozyklotron *n* synchrocyclotron, F-M cyclotron

Syndikat *n* cartel, pool, syndicate

Syndikus *m* legal adviser

Syndrom *n* syndrome

Synergismus *m* synergism

Syngenit *m* syngenite

synklinal synclinal

Synklinal *n* syncline **-tal** *n* synclinal valley

Synklinorium *n* synclinorium

synoptisch synoptic **-e Karte** synoptic chart **-e Meldung** synoptic report **-e Meteorologie** synoptic meteorology **-e Wetterkarte** synoptic chart (weather)

Synthese *f* synthesis

synthetisch synthetic **-er Brennstoff** synthetic fuel **-er Indigo** synthetic indigo **-es Roheisen** synthetic pig iron **-er Sprecher** voder

synthetisieren to synthetize

Syntonisierlampe mit Impedanzspule tuning lamp and choke coil

Syphon *n* siphon, trap **-rekorder** *m* siphon recorder

System *n* system, method, scheme ~ **mit Erdrückleiter** earth-return system ~ **mit Maschinenwählern** power-driven system ~ **mit geerdetem Mittel- oder Sternpunkt** earthed neutral system ~ **mit Motorwählern** power-driven system ~ **mit Parallelschaltung** shunt or parallel system of distribution ~ **mit Reihenschaltung** series system of distribution ~ **mit Rückwärtsstromstößen** revertive-pulsing system ~ **der dritten Schiene** third-rail system ~ **mit geerdetem Sternpunkt** earthed neutral system ~ **mit gleichbleibender Stromstärke** constant-current system

System, ~ **mit direkten Stromstößen,** ~ **mit unmittelbarer Stromstoßgabe** direct-pulsing system ~ **mit rückwärtiger Stromstoßgabe** revertive-pulsing system ~ **mit mittelbar gesteuerter Wahl** indirect-routing system ~ **mit unmittelbar gesteuerter Wahl** direct-routing system ~ **eines Zählers** driving element **abbildendes** ~ image-forming system **bewegliches** ~ moving system **gesteuertes** ~ controlled system **halbstarres ~** semirigid system

Systemarretierung *f* system locking

Systematik *f* systematology, systematics

systematisch systematic **-e Changierung** controlled build-up (textiles)

systemeigenes Signalisieren out-of-band signaling

System-forschung *f* applications department **-kabel** *n* exchange cable, switchboard cable, multiple cable **-macher** *m* platemaker **-rauschtemperatur** *f* operating noise temperature **-träger** *m* meter frame **-verhalten** *n* system performace (servo) **-verstärkerlade** *f* system-repeater drawer **-wahl** *f* out-band signaling, speech-plus signaling **-zahl** *f* file number

Synthese des Netzwerks network synthesis **~ komplexer Wellenformen** synthesis of periodic waves

Systogen *m* systogene

Syzygien *pl* syzygies

Szintigraph *m* scintiscanner

Szintillation *f* scintillation (twinkling)

Szintillations-schicht *f* scintillation layer **-spektrometer** *m* scintillation spectrometer **-substanz** *f* scintillant

Szintillationszähler *m* scintillation counter, detector scintillation, photomultiplier counter **~ mit Bohrlochkristall** well-type scintillation counter

Szintillator *m* scintillator **-schlauch** *m* tube of the scintillator

szintillieren to scintillate

T

Tabak *m* tobacco **-presser** *m* tobacco machine wringer **-ripper** *m* tobacco stripper **-schneidemesser** *n* tobacco-cutting knife

Tabakzurichter *m* tobacco manipulator or dresser

tabellarisch tabular, in tabulated form **~ ordnen oder zusammenstellen** to tabulate **läßt sich ~ darstellen** can be tabulated

tabellarisieren to tabulate, tabularize

Tabellarisierung *f* tabulation

Tabelle *f* table, list, chart, synopsis, margin release **~ der Serienlinien** table of diagram lines

Tabellen-buch *n* book of specifications **-satz** *m* tabular work **-schreibeinrichtung** *f* device for writing tables **-werk** *n* tabular compilation, tables **-zeichner** *m* cartographer

Tabelliermaschine *f* tabulating machine, tabulator

Tableau *n* indicator board **-fernseher** *m* board television apparatus

Tablett *n* tray

Tablette *f* tablet, lozenge

tablettieren to pellet

Tablettiermaschine *f* preforming press

Tabulator-knopf *m* tabulator button **-reiter** *pl* tabular inserts **-zahnstange** *f* tabulator stop rack

Tacho-dynamo *n* electric speed indicator, generator voltmeter tachometer, tacho-generator **-generator** *m* tacho-alternator **-gramm** *n* tachogram **-graph** *m* tachometer recorder, tachograph

Tachometer *n* tachometer, speedometer **-anschluß** *m* tachometer connection **-antrieb** *m* tachometer drive **-einbau** *m* tachometer mounting **-scheinwerfer** *m* head lamp with tachometer **-schnecke** *f* speedometer worm **-trieb** *m* speedometer worm

Tachoskop *n* tachoscope

Tachymeter *n* tachymeter, speedometer **-theodolit** n transit **-zug** *m* tachymetric traverse

Tachymetrie *f* tachymetry

tachymetrieren to survey by tachymeter, survey by stadia

tachymetrisch tachymetric **-e Messung** tachymetry

Täck *m* small nail, tack

Tackbolzen *m* rag bolt

Tadel *m* blame, reprimand, rebuke **-los** faultless, flawless, immaculate

Taenit *m* taenite

Tafel *f* (Anzeigen**~**) tablet; (Wandbekleidung) panel, plate, slab; (Schiefer) slate, blackboard; (geograph. Darstellung) chart; board, table, graph, diagram, synopsis, sheet (of metal), index, list, diagram, pane (of glass) **~ von Eisenblech** sheet-iron panel **~ einer Nivellierlatte** sliding vane

Tafel-aufbau *m* projecting mounting **-aufsatz** *m* table centerpiece **-blei** *n* sheet lead

Täfelchen *n* test chart

Tafel-brett *n* shelf **-druck** *m* hand printing **-einbau** *m* flush mounting **-feld** *n* panel **-förmig** tabular, flat **-glas** *n* sheet glass **-glashütten** *pl* plate and sheet glassworks

Täfelholz *n* wainscot

tafelig tabular

Tafelmessing *n* sheet brass

täfeln to panel **den Fußboden ~** to floor with boards

Tafel-schere *f* sheet shears, plate shears **-schiefer** *m* roofing slate **-schmiere** *f* table grease

Täfelung *f* wainscoting, boarding, parquetry **Feld einer ~** panel

Tafel-waage *f* platform scales **-wagen** *m* platform, hand truck

Täfelwerk *n* inlaying, paneling, wainscoting

Tafelwert *m* calculated value

Tafler *m* cuttle motion

Tag *m* day **~ des Inkrafttretens** effective date **~ und Nacht** mean day (aviation) **trüber ~** overcast day **über ~** open workings (in mining), aboveground, in the open **unter ~** below ground, underground

Tagblindheit *f* day blindness

Tagebau *m* open-work mining, surface working, openpit mining **-betrieb** *m* strip pit, open working

Tagebuch *n* diary, journal, log (navy) **ärztliches ~** medical report book

Tage-geld *n* daily allowance **-lang** for days

Tage-lohn *m* daily wages **-löhner** *m* laborer

Tages-anbruch *m* daybreak **-änderung** *f* variation of compass, diurnal variation **-arbeit** *f* day's work **-belastung** *f* day load **-dienstplan** *m* daily schedule **-durchlauf** *m* daily task

Tages-einteilung *f* agenda **-ereignis** *n* current event **-frequenz** *f* day frequency (rdo) **-gang** *m* diurnal variation **-gebühr** *f* day rate **-karte** *f* day ticket **-kurs** *m* current rate of exchange **-leistung** *f* daily output

Tageslicht *n* daylight **-aufnahme** *f* daylight exposure **-faktor** *m* daylight factor **-füllung** *f* loading (of plates or film) in daylight **-kassette** *f* daylight loading magazine (motion picture) **-lampe** *f* daylight lamp **-photometer** *n* hemera-photometer **-wechselung** *f* daylight changing

Tages-meldung *f* daily report, return **-oberfläche** *f* ground surface **-ordnung** *f* agenda, order of the day **-rate** *f* daily rate **-reichweite** *f* day range **-satz** *m* daily rate or scale, daily-ration quantity **-schicht** *f* day shift **-schub** *m* mean thrust

Tages-sehen *n* photopic vision **-spesen** *pl* daily allowance **-stunden** *pl* hours of daylight **-tonne** *f* metric ton per day **-verbesserung** *f* correction for exterior ballistic factors **-verpflegung** *f* daily ration **-vortrieb** *m* length done in a day **-wasser** *n* surface water **-welle** *f* day wave, wave for day-time transmission **-wind** *m* day wind **-zähler** *m* speedometer **-zeit** *f* time of day, day time **-zuteilung** *f* daily ration

Tagflug *m* day flight

täglich daily, diurnal **-e Erwärmung** diurnal heating **-e Schwankungen** diurnal variations, day-to-day variations **-er Temperaturwechsel** daily march of temperature (meteor.)

Tag- und Nachtgleiche *f* equinox

Tag- und Nachtpeilscheibe *f* day-and-night direction-finding panel

Tag-wasser *n* surface water **-wind** *m* wind by day

Taille *f* reduced shank diameter

Taillen-schraube *f* necked-down bolt **-wanne** *f* wasp-shaped glass tank

Tainton-Prozeß *m* Tainton (brine-leaching) process

Takel *n* tackle

Takelage *f* rigging (of any device supported by ropes or cables), rigging gear or system

takeln to rig

Takelung *f* rigging, rig, tackle, cordage

Takt *m* cycle, stroke (of engine), tact, beat (of pulses), rhythm, cadence, time, rate **im ~** in beat **~ schlagen** to beat time

Takt-betrieb *m* fixed-cycle operation **-feuer** *n* rhythmical airplane beacon, rhythmic light **-funke** *m* timed spark **-funkenstrecke** *f* rotary spark-gap **-funkensystem** *n* timed-spark system **-geben** to cadence

Taktgeber *m* time tapper, cadence tapper, impulse generator, impulsing means, impulser, time valve, metronome, synchronizing generator (TV), timing generator (comput.)

Taktgeberbetrieb *m* synchronous operation

Taktgebung *f* impulse generation

Taktimpuls *m* synchronizing or timing impulse

taktmäßige Ablenkung timed deflection or sweep

Takt-relais *n* timing relay **-spur** *f* clocktrack (tape rec.) **-steuerung** *f* fixed-cycle control **-straße** *f* assembly line **-verfahren** *n* synchronised system **-zeichen** *n* cadence signal **-zeit** *f* station time **-zeitschema** *n* frequency diagram

Tal *n* valley, vale **~ einer Welle** wave trough

Tal-bildung *f* valley formation **-boden** *m* valley floor

Talbot-Ofen *m* Talbot (tilting) furnace

Talbotscher Satz Talbot's law

Talbot-Verfahren *n* Talbot (continuous-open-hearth) process

Talbrücke *f* valley bridge, viaduct

Taleinschnitt *m* section of a valley (geol.)

Tal-fahrt *f* descent, downstream **-fuge** *f* joint **-fühler** *m* valley sensor

Talg *m* tallow, fat, grease

talgartig sebaceous

Talgehänge *n* slope

Talg-erde *f* magnesia **-öl** *n* tempering oil **-säure** *f* stearic acid, sebacic acid **-schmelzanlage** *f* tallow-melting plant

Talhang *m* valley slope

Talje *f* winding tackle **-läufer** *m* tackle fall **-reep** *n* lanyard

Talk *m* talc(um) **-erde** *f* magnesia **-glimmer** *m* mica **-granit** *m* protogine **-schiefer** *m* talc schist, magnesian slate **-spat** *m* magnesite **-stein** *m* soap-stone, steatit

Talkum *n* French chalk, talc(um)

talkumieren to powder (dust)

Tallöl *n* liquid resin (a sulfate turpentine product), tall oil

Talmigold *n* tombac

Tal-mulde *f* basin-shaped valley, hollow **-seite** *f* downstream **-sohle** *f* bottom of the valley **-sperre** *f* dam across a valley, barrage, dam **-sperrenbau** *m* building of dikes and dams across a valley **-terrasse** *f* valley terrace **-überführung** *f* viaduct

Talweg *m* line connecting points of greatest depth along stream course, thalweg **~ eines Flusses** channel of a river

Tal-wert *m* minimum value **-wind** *m* valley breeze or wind

Tamasit *m* rhomboidal arseniate of copper

Tambouriernadel *f* tambour needle

Tambourinbecken *n* tambourine jingles or cymbals

Tandem-amt *n* tandem office **-anordnung** *f* tandem arrangement, compound arrangement **-betrieb** *m* tandem operation **-doppelrad** *n* dual tandem wheel **-fahrgestell** *n* tandem wheel under carriage **-flugzeug** *n* tandem aircraft **-förderung** *f* tandem winding **-gebläse** *n* tandem blower engine **-maschine** *f* tandem engine **-schraube** *f* tandem propeller **-walke** *f* tandem mill **-wischer** *m* wind shield-wiper

Tang *m* seaweed

Tangens *m* tangent **hyperbolischer ~** hyperbolic tangent

Tangens-getriebe *n* tangential mechanism **-karte** *f* hyperbolic chart **-relief** *n* tangential net (math.)

Tangente *f* tangent (line) **~ einer ebenen Kurve** tangent line to a plane curve **~ einer Raumkurve** tangent line to a curve in space

Tangenten-bahn *f* tangent ray **-bild** *n* tangent

image **-bogen** *m* tangent arc **-bussole** *f* tangent galvanometer **-messer** *m* derivator **-punkt** *m* tangent point **-satz** *m* tangent theorem **-schnittpunkt** *m* point of intersection of tangents **-vieleck** *m* polygon circumscribed about a circle

tangential tangential (to) **-e Beaufschlagung** tangential admission **-e Reibung** tangent friction force

Tangential-beanspruchung *f* tangential stress **-beschleunigung** *f* tangential acceleration **-ebene** *f* tangent plane **-eingußkanal** *m* runner (in foundry) **-hobelmaschine** *f* parallel planing machine **-keil** *m* key wedge, tangent key **-kraft** *f* tangential force

Tangentialprofil des Schraubrades section of skew gear on transverse section

Tangential-punkt *m* point of tangency **-rad** *n* tangential wheel **-schnitt** *m* chordal or tangential cut or section **-spannband** *n* tangential clamping band **-spannung** *f* tangential stress **-spülung** *f* tangential scavenging **-stahlhalter** *m* tangential tool holder **-vorschub** *m* tangential feed

Tangentkeilnut *m* tangential key-way

tangierend tangent

Tank *m* tank, basin, reservoir, bowl **Fahrgestell für ~** tank trolley **im Flügel aufgehängter ~** tank carried in the wing **fahrbarer ~** wheel tank **genieteter ~** riveted tank **rechteckiger ~** rectangular tank **zylindrischer ~** cylindrical tank

Tank-anhänger *m* tank trailer **-anlage** *f* berth, jetty, or wharf for fuel-oil bunkering, fuel station, tank plant **-ausweis** *m* fuel permit

Tankbelüftung *f* tank pressurizing (missiles) **-leitung** *f* tank air charging or pressurizing line (missiles) **-rohr** *n* tank standpipe (missiles)

Tank-boden *m* tank head **-dampfer** *m* tank steamer **-druckregelleitung** *f* oxygen tank pressure control line **-eichungen** *pl* tank gauging **-einfüllstutzen** *pl* tank filling hole

tanken to fuel, refuel

Tanken *n* refueling

Tankentlüftung *f* tank aeration

Tanker *m* fuel ship, tanker

Tankerrohr *n* (Luftbetankung) boom

Tank-füllstutzen *m* tank filler cap **-kraftwagen** *m* tank truck **-lager** *n* fuel depot **-löschfahrzeug** *n* crash tender **-meister** *m* foreman in charge of fueling station **-motorschiff** *n* motor tanker

Tankpeilungen nachprüfen to check tank dips

Tank-prahm *m* fuel tender **rast** *f* fueling stop **-reinigungstrupp** *m* fuel-tank cleaning squad

Tank-schiff *n* tanker **-spritze** *f* fire-fighting water truck **-station** *f* service station, filling station **-stationsausrüstung** *f* filling-station equipment **-stelle** *f* filling station **-stellenverwalter** *m* filling-station attendant **-verschluß** *m* cap of tank **-vordruck** *m* initial tank pressure (missiles) **-vorrichtung** *f* refueling

Tankwagen *m* tank truck, tank car **-behälter** *m* truck tank **-zapfhahn** *m* tank truck (draw-off) faucet

Tank-wandung *f* tank shell **-wart** *m* fueling assistant, fueling orderly

Tannat *n* tannate

Tanne *f* fir

Tannenbaum-antenne *f* pine-tree array antenna, Christmas-tree antenna **-kristall** *m* dendrite

Tannenholz *n* deal wood, white pine, fir

Tannin *n* tannin, tannic acid **mit ~ getränkt** tanned (cable)

Tannin-ätzartikel *m* tannic acid resist style **-druck** *m* tannic acid print

tanningetränktes Band cotton tape saturated with tannin

Tanninreserve *f* tannic acid resist

Tanol *n* isooctane

Tantal *n* tantalum

Tantalat *n* tantalate

Tantal-elektrolytkondensator *m* tantalic capacitor **-erz** *n* tantalum ore, tantalite **-gleichrichter** *m* tantalum rectifier **-oxyd** *n* tantalum oxide, tantalum pentoxide **-pentafluorid** *n* tantalic pentafluoride

T-Antenne *f* T-antenna, T-type aerial

Tantiemen *pl* royalties

Tanz *m* dance, jigging (petroleum) **Antreten zum ~** formation of electron groups, phase focusing

Tanzeffekt *m* jumping, vertical hunting

tanzen (e. Reglers) hunting

Tanzen *n* shimmy

Tanzerwalze *f* compensating roller

Tapete *f* tapestry **gepreßte ~** embossed hangings **hochschäftige ~** high-warp tapestry **tiefschäftige ~** low-warp tapestry

Tapeten-bahn *f* single breadth of paper hangings **-präger** *m* wallpaper embosser **-(roh)papier** *n* hangings, wallpaper

Tapezierarbeit *f* paper-hanger's work

tapezieren to cover or hang with tapestry, paper

Tapezierer *m* upholsterer

Tapezier-geschäft *n* upholstery **-nagel** *m* tin tack

Tapisserie *f* tapestry work

Tappe *f* hop (aviation)

Taquet *n* cleats (on a glass-cutting table)

Tara *f* tare, dead weight **-satz** *m* tariff rate of tare

Target target

tarieren to tare

Tarierwaage *f* pharmaceutical balance

Tarif *m* tariff, rate **laut ~** according to scale

Tarif-einheit *f* tariff unit **-ordnung** *f* regulations governing rates of pay scale or allowances, tariff regulations **-politik** *f* method of making charges **-system** *n* tariff system **-vertrag** *m* industrial or trade agreement, tariff treaty

Tarnanstrich *m* camouflage paint, shadow painting

tarnen to camouflage

Tarnen *n* camouflaging

Tarn-frequenzwähler *m* phantom frequency selector plug (missiles) **-geflecht** *n* camouflage matting or netting

Tarnieren *n* leaching (of metals)

Tarn-kappe *f* camouflage cap **-mittel** *n* camouflage material **-plane** *f* camouflage tarpaulin

Tarnung *f* camouflage, masking, screening

Tarnzahl *f* code number

Tartrat *n* tartrate

Täschchen *n* fob, little pocket, pouch, bay

Tasche *f* pocket, bin, bag, pouch, bursa, trap

Taschen-ausgabe *f* pocket edition **-buch** *n* notebook, pocketbook **-bügel** *m* closing device, casing **-bussole** *f* pocket compass **-dosismesser** *m* pocket dosimeter **-fernrohr** *n* perspective glass, pocket telescope **-feuerzeug** *n* pocket lighter **-format** *n* pocket size **-herstellungsmaschine** *f* bagmaking machine **-kompaß** *m* pocket compass **-lampe** *f* torch, pocket lamp, flashlight **-lampenbatterie** *f* flashlight battery **-lampenbirne** *f* flashlight bulb

Taschen-leuchtlupe *f* pocket luminous magnifier **-lot** *n* portable plummet **-lufterhitzer** *m* plate air preheater **-messerklinge** *f* pocket-knife blade **-strommesser** *m* pocket ammeter **-wecker** *m* alarm watch **-zähler** *m* pocket counter

Tasimeter *n* tasimeter

Tasse *f* die holder, cup

Tast-anordnung *f* keying system **-anschluß** *m* Morse key connector **-arm** *m* wiper (arm)

Tastatur *f* keyboard, keys

Tast-bolzen *m* measuring pin, gauge finger, tactile part **-bolzenhalter** *m* (der Tischträger) table carrier (socket) **-detektor** *m* switch detector **-drossel** *f* magnetic modulator

Taste *f* (Druck~) press key, push button; key, key button, sender, transmitting key, push key, (character) key (typewriting), (Morse) manipulating, sending, or operating key **~ mit selbsttätiger Auslösung** locking push button with magnetic release **~ für Hochfrequenzsender** control device of radio transmitter **~ mit Rastung** locking type button **~ mit fester Stellung** locking push-button key

Tasteinrichtung *f* keying device

Tastempfindung *f* touch

tasten to key, manipulate

Tasten *n* cadence tapper (keying), modulation, feeling, exploring, scanning, probing **-arm** *m* key lever **-aufschrift** *f* key letter **-brett** *n* finger board **-druckschalter** *m* pressbutton switch **-falle** *f* drop-in pin **-feder** *f* spring for bass keys

Tastenfeld *n* key set, keyboard **~ mit Sperre** locked keyboard

Tastengeber *m* keyboard transmitter

Tasten-hebel *m* key lever **-führungsblech** *n* guide of the tabulator-key levers **-hilfsrelais** *n* (HT) auxiliary push-button relay **-hub** *m* lift of key **-impulsgeber** *m* impuse-sending key **-knopf** *m* key button **-knopfheber** *m* key-button lifter **-kopf** *m* key head **-locher** *m* key-board perforator, key punch **-nummerngeber** *m* key(-set call) sender **-registrierkasse** *f* cash register with key action **-reihe** *f* row of keys, bank of keys

Tasten-satz *m* key set **-schalter** *m* push-button switch **-schlüssel** *m* handle of key **-schnelltelegraph** *m* keyboard printing telegraph **-sperre** *f* keyboard lock **-spitze** *f* probe tip (meas.) **-stange** *f* key rod **-streifen** *m* strip of keys **-verriegelung** *f* shift lock of the keys **-zählung** *f* key metering (teleg.) **-zirkel** *m* caliper compasses

Taster *m* feeler, antenna; (Telgr.) key; (Technik) calipers, sender, operator, keying device (radio), tactile part or device, scanner, explorer (television picture) **~ mit Federspannung** spring calipers **~ mit Feinstellschraube** calipers with regulating screw **~ mit Schraubenscharnier** firm-joint calipers **~ mit Zahnbogen** back calipers

Taster-kluppe *f* roller-key-clip **-lehre** *f* caliper gauge, snap gauge **-relais** *n* keying relay **-schenkel** *m* caliper leg **-skala** *f* feeler scale **-spitze** *f* point of the feeler **-stange** *f* tracer rod **-stift** *m* feeler pin **-zirkel** *m* caliper compasses, calipers, gauging calipers

Tast-flächen *pl* points **-fleck** *m* fingermark **-frequenz** *f* keying frequency **-funk** *m* radio telegraphy, wireless telegraphy **-gefühl** *n* sense of feeling **-gerät** *n* keying apparatus (radio), stabilizer **-geräusch** *n* key clicking (caused on closing key), key chirp or thump **-geschwindigkeit** *f* keying speed **-gleichrichter** *m* keying rectifier

Tast-klick *m* key thump, key click **-kontakt** *m* sender-key contact **-kreis** *m* keying circuit **-kugel** *f* (steel) ball, (contact) tip

Tast-(Sucher)kupplung *f* probe coupling

Tastlehre *f* caliper gauge **mit ~ messen** to caliper

Tast-leitung *f* keying circuit **-maschine** *f* automatic deviation measuring machine (missiles) **-organ** *n* contact element **-prellen** *n* key chirp (after key has been opened), key thump or click (when closing key) **-punkt** *m* measuring point **-relais** *n* key(ing) relay, contactor, relay key, magnetic key **-röhre** *f* modulation tube (electronics) **-rolle** *f* feeler roll

Tast-schaltung *f* keying circuit, centertap key modulator circuit **-schlag** *m* key click, thump or chatter **-sinn** *m* touch **-spannung** *f* modulation voltage **-spindel** *f* tracer spindle **-spitze** *f* pointed pin

Tast-stange *f* cut-out plunger **-stein** *m* contact block **-stift** *m* tracer point, feeler **-stiftlagerhülse** *f* tracer head **-strecke** *f* rough spot (on glass-ware) **-teiler** *m* RC-probe **-uhr** *f* dial indicator

Tastung *f* control, keying, remote control, modulation by key action, (im)pulsing

Tast-verhältnis *n* keying ratio **-verkehr** *m* radio traffic, wireless telegraph **-versuch** *m* tentative experiment **-voltmeter** *n* diode-probe-type-voltmeter **-vorrichtung** *f* click-stop arrangement (radio) **-wahlschalter** *m* key selector switch **-welle** *f* marking wave **-werk** *n* keyboard **-zeichen** *n* (Tel. und f. Blinde) tactile indicator **-zirkel** *m* calipers **-zwischenraum** *m* keying space

Tatbestand *m* facts of a case, object, subject, factual findings **-aufnahme** *f* summary of evidence, deposition, factual statement or report

tätig active

tätigen to do (business), effect

Tätigkeit *f* action, activity **außer ~ setzen** to throw out of action

Tätigkeitsunterbrecher *m* stopper gear, stopping mechanism

Tatkraft *f* energy

tatkräftig energetic

Tatsache *f* fact

tatsächlich actual, factual, effective, real **-e Keilbreite** obtained wedge (foundry) **-e Unterlagen liefern** to substantiate, furnish evidence **-er Flugweg** flight track

Tatsächlichkeit *f* reality

Tatze *f* paw, claw, cam

Tatz-lagerbauart *f* nose (type) suspension **-motor** *m* nose-and-axle-suspended motor

Tau *m* dew, thaw, serein

Tau *n* rope, hawser, line, cable, trace (harness) **aufgeschossenes ~** coiled rope **ein ~ aufklären** to coil up a rope **dreischäftiges ~** three-stranded rope **halbgeschlissenes ~** used rope **kabelweise geschlagenes ~** laid rope **links-geschlagenes ~** left-hand rope **vierschäftiges ~** shroud-laid rope

taub barren, sterile, deaf **~** (Gestein) dead **-e Flut** *f* neap tide

Taubeschlag *m* dew

Taubeschlag *m* cable fitting

Taubetide *f* neap tide

Taub-feld *n* barren track **-heit** *f* deafness

Taubrücke *f* rope bridge

Tauch-abschreckung *f* immersion quench **-alitieren** *n* hot-dip calorizing **-anker** *m* plunger-type armature **-anlage** *f* dipping plant

Tauchbad *n* splashing **-schmierung** *f* splash lubrication

Tauch-bandscheider *m* immersion-belt separator **-bahn** *f* dip orbit (of electrons) **-bär** *m* plunger **-batterie** *f* immersion battery, plunge battery **-behälter** *m* dip tank **-beize** (Pelz) disinfecting steep **-bewegung** *f* porpoising (seaplane), dipping motion (ship) **-boot** *n* submarine, bathyscaphe **-brenner** *m* immersion heater **-bühne** *f* immerged groin **-elektrode** *f* coated electrode

tauchen to dip, steep, soak, dive, plunge, immerse, submerge

Tauchen *n* diving, dip molding **~** (Holz) steeping **zum ~ bereitmachen** to rig for diving

Taucher *m* diver **-anzug** *m* diving-bell suit **-gerät** *n* diving-bell gear **-glocke** *f* diving bell **-herz** *n* breast lead **-kolben** *m* plunger

tauchfähig submersible

Tauch-färbemaschine *f* dip dyeing machine **-fläche** *f* diving plane **-flüssigkeit** *f* dipping fluid **-förderer** *m* dipping conveyer **-form** *f* master steel pattern **-fräsen** *n* plunge-milling **-gerät** *n* diving apparatus **-gettern** *n* dip gettering **-glocke** *f* (E-Ofen) sealing cone

Tauch-härten *n* dip hardening **-hartlötung** *f* dip brazing **-höhe** *f* (degree of) immersion **-höhlung** *f* dip cavity **-hülse** *f* immersion shell

Tauchkern *m* plunger **-relais** *n* plunger relay **-spule** *f* sucking solenoid, sucking coil

Tauchkolben *m* plunger piston **-dichter** *m* plunger compressor **-heber** *m* plunger lift **-luft-presser** *m* plunger-type air compressor **-motor** *m* trunk-type piston engine

Tauch-korrosionsversuch *m* immersion test **-kugel** *f* bathysphere **-lack** *m* dipping varnish **-lafette** *f* mortar carriage **-lampe** *f* dipping lamp **-lötbad** *n* immersion soldering bath **-löten** *n* dip brazing **-lötung** *f* dip soldering

Tauch-netzzentrifuge *f* immersion meshed bag hydro extractor **-ofen für Zündspulen** immersion furnace for ignition coils **-patentieren** *n* bath-patenting (met.) **-peilanlage** *f* submarine direction-finding set **-platte** *f* plunger **-pol** *m* adjustable pole

Tauchrohr *n* immersion tube, spray-nozzle tube (carburetor), dip pipe, telescopic tube, well **-brenner** *m* tube firing burner **-stopfbüchse** *f* telescopic tube stuffing box

Tauch-schmierung *f* splash lubrication **-schwimmer** *m* float **-sicher** submersion-proof **-sieder** *m* immersion heater **-spachtel** *f* dipping filler **-spindel** *f* tail (of a thermometer)

Tauchspule *f* voice control, voice coil, plunger, moving coil, signal coil (of loud-speaker), telescoping coil

Tauchspulen-lautsprecher *m* moving-coil speaker, moving loud-speaker, dynamic loud-speaker **-mikrophon** *n* moving-coil microphone, electro-dynamic microphone

Tauch-stab *m* dip stick **-stampfen** *n* to porpoise **-stange** *f* plunger **-tank** *m* ballast tank **-tasse** *f* suction cup, pneumatic dashpot **-tiefe** *f* water level in well, depth of immersion (of a ship), draught, diving depth **-transformator** *m* telescoping-coil transformer

Tauchtrimmer *m*, **verschiebbarer ~** slide-screw tuner

Tauchung *f* plunge, dip

Tauch-verfahren *n* dipping process **-waage** *f* aerometer, hydrometer **-walzentrockner** *m* drum drier with dip tank **-wand** *f* baffle **-zelle** *f* dip cell **-zentrifuge** *f* immersion hydro-extractor for impregnating **-zylinder** *m* plunge cylinder, plunger

tauen to condense, thaw

Tauende *n* rope end

Tauenpapier *n* jute paper, casing paper, heavy drawing and wrapping paper

Tauereikette *f* immerged chain

taufen to christen **ein Schiff ~** to name a ship

Taugarn *n* rope yarn

taugen to be useful or of value

tauglich fit, proper, useful, serviceable, usable, good, appropriate, suited

Tauglichkeit *f* fitness, usefulness

Tau-kappe *f* dew cap **-kloben** *m* rope block, tackle **-kranz** *m* rope fender (navy), grommet

Taumel *m* wobble (radio) **-bewegung** *f* tumbler movement or action **-fehler** *m* tumbling error, drunkenness (of threads) **-frequenz** *f* wobble frequency

taumeln to stagger, wobble

Taumelscheibe *f* swash plate, wobbler, wobble plate

Taumelscheiben-einspritzpumpe *f* swash-plate-type injection pump **-lager** *n* swashplate bearings **-motor** *m* swash-plate engine, crank-less engine, wobble-plate engine **-pumpe** *f* wobble pump **-scherenhebel** *n* swashplate scissor lever **-steuerung** *f* swashplate control

Taumel-schwingung *f* tumbling **-sendung** *f* wobbling **-trockner** *m* tumbling drier

Tau-messer *m* drosometer **-öse** *f* ear of a cord

Taupunkt *m* point of condensation, dew point, thawing point **-fühler** *m* dew point thimble

Tau-rolle *f* cordage reel **-röste** *f* dew retting **-spiegel** *m* dew-point mirror **-zelle** *f* dip cell

Tausch *m* exchange, barter, truck

täuschen to deceive, delude

täuschend deceitful, illusory

Tauschhandel *m* exchange

tauschieren to inlay

Tauschlaufe *f* rope loop

Tauschtafel *f* substitution table

Täuschung *f* deception, fraud, illusion **optische ~** optical illusion

Tauschzersetzung *f* double decomposition
tausend thousand
Tausender-amt *n* three-figure exchange **-system** *n* three-figure system, three-digit system **-wahlstufe** *f* thousands digit
Tausendstel *n* thousandth
Tausend-stelle *f* thousands place **-teil** *m* parts per thousand, thousandth
Taustopper *m* deck or rope stopper
Tautochrone *f* isochronous or tautochronous curve
Tauwerk *n* tackle, ropes **-herstellungsmaschine** *f* cordage-making machine
Tauwetter *n* thaw, thawing weather
Taxameter *n* taximeter, taxameter
Taxator *m* appraiser, valuer, assessor
Taxe *f* tax ~ **fällig** annuity due (patent)
taxieren to estimate, value, appraise
Tax-quadrat *n* telephone (trunk) zone **-zone** *f* exchange area
Taylorsche Reihe Taylor's series
T-Balken *m* T-beam
T-Belag *m* T-coating
T-Bolzen *m* T bolt
T-Diagramm *n* T-plot
Teakholz *n* teak
Technetium *n* technetium
Technik *f* art, engineering, technics, technique, technology, dexterity
Techniker *m* technician, engineer
technisch technical, engineering, industrial **-e Angabe** specifications **-e Artikel** technical goods **-e Bereitschaft** refueling-and-maintenance-duty squad **-er Chemiker** chemical engineer **-e Einrichtung** equipment **-es Eisen** commercial iron **-e Frequenz** commercial frequency **-e Hochschule** polytechnic institute, institute of technology
technisch, -es Personal technical staff **-e Unterlagen** engineering data **-e Wechselströme** commercial or industrial alternating currents **-e Werkstoffe** industrial, commercial, or technical materials **-er Wettbewerb** technical test **-es Zinkoxyd** commercial zinc oxide
Technologe *m* technologist
Technologie *f* technology
technologisch technological
Teer *m* tar, pitch **-abscheider** *m* tar separator or extractor, detarrer, tar settler **-abscheidung** *f* tar separation or extraction, detarring **-artig** tarry **-band** *n* friction tape, tarred tape **-bestandteil** *m* tar constituent **-bildung** *f* tar formation **-büchse** *f* tar or grease box **-bürste** *f* tar brush **-dampf** *m* tar vapor, tar fumes **-decke** *f* tar surface **-dunst** *m* tar vapor or fumes
teeren to tar, pitch
Teer-entwässerungsanlage *f* water-eliminating plant for tar **-feuerung** *f* tar-fired furnace **-frei** tarless, free from tar **-gewinnungsanlage** *f* tar-extraction plant **-grube** *f* tar-storage tank, tar pit **-haltig** containing tar
teerig tarry
Teer-kondensat *n* tar condensate **-kruste** *f* tar incrustation **-küche** *f* ropemaker's stove **-kühler** *m* tar cooler box (petroleum) **-leinwand** *f* tarpaulin **-nebel** *m* tar mist **-öl** *n* tar oil, pine-oil tar, coaltar oil **-pappe** *f* tar board **-pech** *n* coal-tar asphalt(um) **-pröpfchen** *n* tar globule **-quaste** *f* tar mop or brush **-rückstand** *m* tar residue
Teer-satz *m* dregs of tar **-säure** *f* tar acid **-scheidegrube** *f* tar-separating sump **-scheider** *m* tar extractor or separator, detarrer **-schotter** *m* tar ballast **-schwelerei** *f* tar distillery **-strick** *m* oakum **-substanz** *f* tarry matter **-tuch** *n* tarpaulin **-überzug** *m* tar coat
Teerung *f* tar spraying
Teer-wäsche *f* tar extraction **-wäscher** *m* tar scrubber or washer
Teeschraube *f* tee bolt
Tegel *m* clay, marl
Teianker *m* small bower
Teich *m* pond, pool, artificial lake **-wasser** *n* pond water
Teig *m* paste, dough **-artig** pasty
teigig pasty, doughy, mellow, plastic, kneadable **-es Eisen** pasty iron
Teigigwerden *n* assuming a pasty state
Teigpreßverfahren *n* dough molding
Teikette *f* anchor chain
Teil *m* part; (Stück) piece; (Anteil) portion, share; (Abschnitt) section; (Bestand ~) element, component; (Parteien) parties, sides; top, member, section, division **eingeschnürter** ~ necked-down portion (aviation) **fester** ~ fixed section **hervorstehender** ~ male piece **spannungsführender** ~ live part **versteifender** ~ stiffener **zylindrischer** ~ cylindrical body **aufeinander arbeitende Teile** striking parts
Teil-abtastung *f* fractional scan, partial scan, coarse scan **-achse** *f* dividing head axis **-akzept** *n* partial acceptance **-amt** *n* satellite exchange (teleph.) **-amtsnetzwerke** *pl* satellite switching networks **-ansaugevorrichtung** *f* suction blank feed attachment **-ansatz** *m* indexing attachment **-ansicht** *f* partial or scrap view (aviation) **-apparat** *m* dividing head or apparatus **-aufsatz** *m* dividing attachment, indexing center **-ausbau** *m* partial extension **-automatisch** partly automatic
Teilbahn des Stirnrades pitch line or curve of spur gear
teilbar divisible
Teilbarkeit *f* divisibility
Teil-baulänge *f* partial overall length **-baum** *m* sectional beam **-bereich** *m* sub-range step **-bericht** *m* partial report **-beschädigung** *f* partial damage **-bewegung** *f* indexing movement
Teilbild *n* partial image **-ablenkung** *f* field deflection **-abtastung** *f* field sweep **-austastung** *f* frame suppression horizontal blanking **-frequenz** *f* frame frequency **-höhenregler** *m* vertical size control **-kontrollröhre** field monitoring tube
Teilbildschirm *m*, **erweiterter** ~ expanded partial plan position indicator (EPPPI)
Teilbild-wechsel *m* field (frame) change **-verzerrung** *f* frame distortion, tilt
Teil-blatt *n* insert drawing **-block** *m* sub-block **-blockkühler** *m* radiator with detachable section **-brennkammer** *f* partial or segmented combustion chamber **-bruch** *m* partial fraction
Teilchen *n* particle, small part, corpuscle, element (math.) **-bahn** *f* particle orbit **-bild** *n*

particle aspect **-dichte** *f* particle density **-feld** *n* particle field **-geschwindigkeit** *f* particle velocity **-wolke** *f* swarm of particles

Teil-demontage *f* partial dismantling (dismounting) **-dorn** *m* (einer Lehre) plug **-druck** *m* part printing or pressure **-durchprüfung** *f* cripple leap-frog test **-einheit** *f* component, homogeneous platoon, basic, self-sufficient element of a unit (mil.) **-einrichtung** *f* dividing mechanism

Teileformel *f* formula of parts

teilen to part, divide, share, split, apportion, separate, index, graduate

Teilenteignung *f* partial alienation or expropriation

Teileprüferei *f* part-checking department

Teiler *m* divisor, divider, submultiple **in einer Zahl ohne Rest aufgehender ~** submultiple

Teil-erdkapazität *f* direct earth capacitance, direct capacitance to ground **-erfolg** *m* partial success, partial result

teilerfremd aliquant

Teil-erstarrung *f* partial solidification **-fehler** *m* partial error **-fläche** *f* joint face, jointing plane, joint line, incremental area **-flankenwinkel** *m* partial thread angle **-folge** *f* subsequence **-frequenz** *f* partial or component frequency

Teilfuge *f* joint, parting line, parting **überlappte ~** lap joint **verzahnte ~** serrated joint

Teil-gebiet *n* portion, branch (of subject) **-gebietsmethode** *f* particle domain method

teilgelochtes Band chadless tape

Teil-genauigkeit *f* spacing or indexing accuracy **-getriebe** *n* dividing gear **-gitter** *n* sublattice **-gruppe** *f* subgroup, group of apparatus

teilhaben to have an interest, participate

Teilhaber *m* shareholder, partner, part owner **geschäftsführender ~** managing partner **stiller ~** silent partner

Teilhärtung *f* selective hardening, decremental hardening **~ eines Werkstückes** selective hardening

Teilhebel *m* indexing arm

Teilkammer *f* sectional chamber **-kessel** *m* sectional boiler, section chamber

Teil-kanal *m* subchannel **-kapazität** *f* partial capacity **-kegel** *m* pitch cone **-knoten** *m* partial node **-kondensation** *f* dephlegmation

Teilkopf *m* indexing head, dividing head **~ zum Spiralfräser** spiral dividing head

Teilkopf-prüfgerät *n* division testing device **-schlitten** *m* index head slide **-spindel** *f* indexing head spindle **-verschiebespindel** *f* indexing head traverse screw **-wechselräder** *pl* change gears of indexing head **-wechselradsatz** *m* indexing head change gears

Teilkörper *m* branch

Teilkraft *f* component or partial force **waagerechte ~** horizontal component

Teilkreis *m* divided circle, graduated circle, dial, lower plate of transit, pitch circle, pitch line **~ der Schnecke** pitch circle of worm

Teilkreis-bereich *m* orientation range **-durchmesser** *m* pitch diameter, diametrical pitch **-schlag** *m* error in eccentricity (of gear)

Teil-kupplung *f* indexing clutch **-ladung** *f* propelling-charge increment, boosting charge

Teillast *f* part throttle, partial load, part load, percentage load **-gebiet** *n* partial-load region

Teil-leseimpuls *m* partial-read pulse **-linie** *f* parting line **-lochung** *f* chadless perforation

Teilmarke *f* index **auf eine ~ stellen** to index

Teil-maschine *f* dividing engine or machine, ruling engine **-menge** *f* subset **-montage** *f* subassembly **-motorisiert** partly motorized **-nachwirkzeit** *f* partial restoring time **-nahme** *f* participation, sympathy

teilnehmen to participate, take part **an einem Wettbewerb ~** to partake in a competition

Teilnehmer *m* participant, (telephone) user, public subscriber **~ mit Einzelgebührenanschluß** message-rate subscriber **~ mit Pauschgebührenanschluß** flat-rate subscriber **~ antwortet nicht** there is no reply **~ hängt an** subscriber clears **angerufener ~** called party required or wanted subscriber **anrufender ~** caller, calling party **verlangter ~** called party, required or wanted subscriber

Teilnehmer-anlage *f* substation plant **-anrufzeichen** *n* subscriber's line indicator

Teilnehmeranschluß *m* substation, subscriber's station (teleph.) **-gestell** *n* subscriber rack **-leitung** *f* subscriber's line

Teilnehmer-apparat *m* subscriber's set **-doppelleitung** *f* subscriber's loop

teilnehmereigene Fernsprechhandvermittlung *f* private manual exchange (P.M.X.)

Teilnehmer-endverstärker *m* subscriber's telephone equipped with an amplifier and loudspeaker **-feststellung** *f* line identification circuit **-gebühr** *f* rate (of subscription) **-hauptanschluß** *m*, **-hauptstelle** *f* subscriber's main station **-kabel** *n* subscriber's cable **-klinke** *f* subscriber's jack

Teilnehmerleitung *f* subscriber's line or station **~ für Fernverkehr** toll terminal **~ für abgehenden Verkehr** subscriber's line reserved for outgoing calls **~ für ankommenden Verkehr** subscriber's line reserved for incoming calls

Teilnehmer-nebenanschluß *m*, **-nebenstelle** *f* subscriber's extension station **-platz** *m* home position, answering position **-rechnung** *f* subscriber's account **-(rechts)verhältnis** *n* subscriber's contract **-schaltung** *f* line circuit **-schiene** *f* subscriber's relay strip **-schleife** *f* subscriber's loop **-sprechstelle** *f* substation, common-battery telephone station, subscriber's telephone, set, or station **-station** *f* subscriber's station **-telegraphie** *f* teletypewriter service **-vertrag** *m* contract **-verzeichnis** *n* telephone directory **-vielfach(feld)** *n* subscriber's multiple

Teilnehmerzentrale *f* private branch exchange **selbsttätige ~** private automatic branch exchange

Teil-pächter *m* share tenant **-pause** *f* part print **-platte** *f* index plate, dividing disk, scale plate **-prisma** *n* component prism **-probe** *f* sub sample **-produkt** *n* subproduct **-punkt** *m* pitch point **-rad** *n* index gear

Teilraster *m* partial scanning pattern, field, fractional scan, fractional sweep (in interlaced scanning) **ungeradzähliger ~** odd-line interlace

Teilraster-frequenz *f* field frequency **-gleichlaufimpuls** *m* field-frequency synchronizing impulse

Teil-raum *m* subspace **-reihe** *f* subseries

Teilring *m* graduated ring, azimuth micrometer, quadrated drum, micrometer ring, index ring (telescopic sight) **-änderung** *f* azimuth change **-zahl** *f* azimuth reading, micrometer setting

Teil-schablone *f* dividing template **-scheibe** *f* graduated plate, azimuth circle, eye-distance scale (binoculars), index circle, index plate **-schere** *f* cross cutting shears **-schneckenrad** *n* dividing worm wheel **-schneckenwelle** *f* index worm shaft **-schnittzeichnung** *f* part-sectioned drawing **-schreibeimpuls** *m* partial-write pulse **-schritt** *m* fractional pitch **-schwingung** *f* periodic components (of a wave) **-sendung** *f* installment of a delivery

Teil-spannung *f* component voltage, partial pressure, partial voltage, submultiple voltage **-sperrzeit** *f* partial restoring time (echo suppression) **-spindel** *f* dividing spindle **-spule** *f* fractional coil, component or subdivision of a component **-stoß** *m* partial splide **-strahlungs-pyrometer** *n* optical pyrometer **-strecke** *f* section of a line, stage

Teilstrich *m* graduation (on scale), division, dividing line, scale division **-abstand** *m* scale spacing **-teilung** *f* graduation **-waage** *f* graduated scale **-zahl** *f* number of graduations

Teilstrom *m* branch or component current, partial **-lauf** *m* circuit detail

Teilstückliste *f* parts list

Teiltief *n* secondary depression or cyclone **-druck** *m* secondary low (aviation)

Teil-ton *m* partial overtone, partial note **-trommel** *f* micrometer knob, range drum, azimuth micrometer, azimuth drum, index circle, sleeve, elevation scale drum (dial sight) **-überholung** *f* top overhaul, semi-overhauling, partial overhaul

Teilung *f* spacing, division, graduation, partition, pitch, scale, dial, calibration, submultiplication **~ in drei gleiche Teile** trisection **eine ~ beziffern** to figure a graduation **eine ~ drehen** to index one division **mit einer ~ versehen** to scale, divide **~ für die Winkeleinstellung des Schleifscheibenkopfes** graduation for angular setting of wheel head **ebene ~** straight joint line, straight parting **feine ~** fine graduation **grobe ~** coarse graduation **logarithmische ~** logarithmic calibration

Teilungsbezifferung *f* figuring of graduation

Teilungsebene *f* plane of division, jointing plane, joint face or line **unregelmäßige ~** irregular joint lines

Teilungs-fehler *m* dividing or indexing error, error of graduation, faulty pitch (television), line pitch, defect **-fläche** *f* plane of division **-gesetz** *n* law of partition **-intervall** *n* scale graduation **-koeffizient** *m* distribution coefficient **-masse** *f* property divisible among the creditors **-rechen** *m* division grate

Teilungsring für Waagrechtschwenklager horizontal swivel mount index drum

Teilungs-träger *m* graduation **-verhältnis** *n* pitch ratio, spacing ratio **-wichte** *f* effective separating gravity

Teil-unternehmer *m* subcontractor **-untersatz** *m* index base **-verfahren** *n* indexing or dividing method **-verflüssigung** *f* partial liquefaction **-verhältnis** *n* ratio of division, attenuation ratio **-versetzung** *f* partial dislocation **-versorgung** *m* partial process **-vielfachfeld** *n* partial multiple **-vierpol** *m* section (of a recurrent structure) (teleph.) **-vorgang** *m* indexing cycle, divider action **-vorrichtung** *f* indexing attachment, dividing device **-wählamt** *n* (full) satellite exchange

Teil-wechselrad *n* index change gear **-weise** partial, in part **-welle** *f* partial wave **-winkel** *m* pitch angle **-(wicklungs)schritt** *m* partial pitch (winding pitch) **-wirbel** *m* partial vortex

Teil-zahl *f* indexing number **-zahlung** *f* installment, part payment **-zahnrad** *n* index gear **-zehnerübertrag** *m* partial carry **-zeichen** *n* partial signal **-zeichnung** *f* detail drawing **-zeit-höchstverbrauchsmesser** *m* restricted-hour maximum indicator **-zirkel** *m* spring-bow divider, dividing taster, dividers **-zusammenbau** *m* subassembly **-zylinder** *m* (gearing-) pitch cylinder

T-Eisen *n* T iron, T bar

Tektonik *f* tectonics (structure)

tektonisches Aussehen tectonic features

Tektur *f* label or slip for sticking on (errata slip)

Telautograph *m* telautograph, telewriter (apparatus)

Telautographie *f* telautography

Teleansatz *m* telephoto attachment

Teleaufnahme *f* telephotographic work

Telefon siehe Telephon

Telegraf siehe Telegraph

Telegramm *n* message, telegram, wire **das ~ ist abgesetzt** the message is cleared **~ zu ermäßigten Gebühren** deferred(-rate) telegram **~ mit Vergleichung** collated telegram **ein ~ annehmen** to accept a message **ein ~ aufgeben** to hand in a telegram **ein ~ aufnehmen** to write up a message **ein ~ prüfen** to check a message **verstümmeltes ~** mutilated telegram **zurückgestelltes ~** deferred telegram

Telegram-annahmestelle *f* collecting office **-anschrift** *f* telegraphic address **-aufgabe** *f* handing-in of telegrams **-austräger** *m* telegraph messenger **-beförderung** *f* transmission of telegrams **-besteller** *m* messenger **-bestellung** *f* delivery of messages **-formular** *n* message blank **-kopf** *m* preamble, preface

Telegramm-kurzanschrift *f* registered address **-pult** *n* message desk **-schalter** *m* telegram counter **-schlüssel** *m* code (telegram) **-spesen** *pl* cost of telegram **-übertrager** *m* transducer **-verteilung** *f* distribution of messages **-vordruck** *m* **-vordrucksblatt** *n* message form or blank **-zustellung** *f* delivery of telegrams

telegen telegenic

Telegraph *m* telegraph **~ mit photographischem Zeichendruck** photoprinting telegraph **~ mit (un)gleich langen Zeichen** (un)equal letter telegraph **optischer ~** optical telegraph, semaphore

Telegraphen-abschlußkabel *n* telegraph-terminal cable **-alphabet** *n* telegraphic alphabet, telegraph code **-amt** *n* telegraph office or station **-anlage** *f* telegraph system or plant **-anstalt** *f*

telegraph station **-arbeiter** *m* line(s)man, wireman

Telegraphenbau-amt *n* telegraph-construction office **-dienst** *m* line-construction service **-gerät** *n* telegraph-construction tool **-kraftwagen** *m* signal-construction truck

Telegraphen-beamter *m* telegraph clerk **-bote** *m* telegraph messenger **-draht** *m* telegraph wire **-geschwindigkeit** *f* line speed **-gleichung** *f* telegraphic equation **-hoheitsrecht** *n* state monopoly relating to telegraphy **-kabel** *n* telegraph cable **-kode** *m* telegraph code

Telegraphenleitung *f* telegraph line ~ **mit Sprechbetrieb** phonogram circuit ~ **für den inneren Verkehr** domestic telegraph circuit ~ **für den zwischenstaatlichen Verkehr** international telegraph circuit

Telegraphen-leitungsmast *m* telegraph pole **-oberbauführer** *m* telegraph-construction manager **-schlüssel** *m* telegraph code **-stange** *f* telephone or telegraph pole **-truppe** *f* signal corps

Telegraphenübertragung *f* telegraph repeater (set) ~ **mit Berichtigung der Zeichenform** regenerative repeater

Telegraphen-übertragungsamt *n* repeater station, repeating telegraph station **-umgehungseinrichtung** *f* telegraph by-pass set **-zeugamt** *n* telegraph-material store

Telegraphie *f* telegraphy **drahtlose** ~ radiotelegraphy, wireless telegraphy **einseitige** ~ simplex telegraphy **wechselseitige** ~ two-way telegraphy **unabhörbare** ~ telegraphy not to be listened to

Telegraphie-empfang *m* telegraph reception, code reception **-empfänger** *m* telegraph receiver **-leistung** *f* peak power of the transmitter

telegraphieren to telegraph, wire

Telegraphierflüchtigerstrom, kürzester ~ signal element, unit

Telegraphier-frequenz *f* signaling frequency, telegraphic or dot frequency **-geräusch** *n* (Morse) thump, telegraph noise **-geschwindigkeit** *f* (line) speed **-grundfrequenz** *f* dot frequency **-pause** *f* space (in telegraphic work) **-sender** *m* telegraphic transmitter

Telegraphierstrom *m* signal(ing) current **-schritt** *m* signal element, unit **-stärke** *f* signal strength

Telegraphierstromstoß *m* current impulse, current surge **kürzester** ~ signal element, unit

Telegraphier-weg *m* telegraph route, channel **-zeichen** *n* telegraph(ic) signal

Telegraphiesender *m* radiotelegraph transmitter, telegraphy transmitter, telegraphic transmitter

telegraphisch telegraphic

Telegraphist *m* telegraph operator, telegrapher

Telegraphon *n* telegraphone

Telemeter *n* range finder, range-finding apparatus, telemeter

Telemetrie *f* telemetry

Teleobjektiv *n* telephoto lens

Telephon *n* telephone receiver, telephone **-anlage** *f* telephone installation, plant, or equipment **-anschluß** *m* telephone extension **-apparat** *m* telephone **-draht** *m* telephone wire **-gabel** *f* cradle **-gerät** *n* radiotelephony set **-hörer** *m* telephone receiver

Telephonie *f* telephony **drahtlose** ~ radiotelephony **-drossel** *f* magnetic modulator **-empfang** *m* telephone reception **-leistung** *f* unmodulated power of the transmitter

telephonieren to telephone

Telephoniesender *m* radio telephone transmitter, telephony transmitter, telephonic transmitter (radio) **sprachgeschalteter** ~ voice-modulated telephony (signal), transmitter or radiophonic transmitter

Telephonie-signal *n* telephone signal **-trägerleitung** *f* unmodulated power of transmitter **-verkehr** *m* radiotelephony **-zeichen** *n* telephone signal

telephonisch over the telephone, telephonic

Telephonist *m* telephone operator

Telephonkurzschlußkontakt *m* telephony short-circuiting contact

Telephonograph *m* telephonograph

Telephonometer *n* time check

Telephon-schnur *f* flexible telephone cord **-sender** *m* telephone or radiotelephone transmitter **-stecker** *m* telephone plug **-wählscheibe** *f* telephone dial **-wecker** *m* telephone ringer **-zelle** *f* telephone booth

Telephotometrie *f* telephotometry

Teleskop-betätigungsstrebe *f* telescopic strut **-brücke** *f* (Flughafen) telescopic bridge **-federung** *f* telescopic shock-absorber, telescopic suspension **-flügel** *m* variable surface or area wing

teleskopisch telescopic

Teleskop-lichtmast *m* telescopic lightpole **-mast** *m* telescopic mast **-rohr** *n* telescopic tube **-schurre** *f* telescoping chute **-spindel** *f* telescopic screw **-stoßdämpfer** *m* telescopic shock absorber **-stütze** *f* telescopic support **-wagen** *m* truck with hydraulic jack **-welle** *f* telescope shaft

Telestereoskop *n* telestereoscope

Tele-sucher *m* tele-finder **-thermometer** *n* telethermometer **-type** *f* teletype **-zentrisch** telecentric

Teller *m* tray, plate, dish, disk, seat (of valve) ~ **zur Ventilklappe** clack valve

Teller-ablage *f* container for the discs **-anode** *f* disk anode **-aufgabeapparat** *m* plate feeder **-aufgeber** *m* table feeder **-boden** *m* plate end **-bohrer** *m* earth auger **-drehscheibe** *f* turntable plate **-elektrode** *f* disc electrode **-feder** *f* cup spring **-fläche** *f* ogive

tellerförmig like a plate **-e Feder** plate spring

Teller-fräser *m* plate-shape cutter **-fuß** *m* plate- or dish-shaped foot, press, or base **-gerät** *n* double turntable type of player **-hammer** *m* chasing hammer **-horn** *n* disc-type horn **-isolator** *m* dish or disk insulator for antenna supporting **-kopf** *m* pin-feathered head **-messer** *n* circular slitting knife **-mischer** *m* pan mixer **-mühle** *f* disk crusher

Teller-platte *f* bottom plate **-rad** *n* axle-drive bevel wheel, spur bevel gear **-säule** *f* float column (gun outrigger) **-scheibe** *f* disc washer **-scheibenegge** *f* disc harrow **-schleifer** *m* disc sander **-schrank** *m* cupboard, sideboard **-steuerventil** *n* mushroom control valve **-trudeln** *n* flat spin (aviation) **-ventil** *n* poppet valve, disk valve, mushroom-type valve, globe valve, flutter valve, pipe valve **-winde** *f* disk type jack

Tellur *n* tellurium **-aluminium** *n* aluminum telluride **-führend** telluriferous **-glanz** *m* tellurium glance, nagyagite **-haltig** containing tellurium
Tellurid *n* telluride
tellurig tellurous, telluric (in mining)
tellurische Ströme natural earth currents
Tellur-nickel *n* nickel telluride, melonite **-ocker** *m* tellurite
tellursaures Kalium potassium tellurate
Tellursilber *n* silver telluride **-blei** *n* lead-silver telluride, sylvanite
Tellurvorlegierung *f* tellurium prealloy
Telpherbahn *f* telpher line
Temperafarbe *f* tempering color
Temperatur *f* temperature **~ am Erdboden** ground or surface temperature
Temperatur-abfall *m* drop in temperature **-abhängig** temperature responsive, temperature dependent **-abhängigkeit** *f* functional relationship of temperature, temperature dependence **-abnahme** *f* temperature gradient
Temperaturänderung *f* variation change in temperature **plötzliche ~** thermal chock
Temperatur-anstieg *m* rise of temperature **-anstiegrate** *f* thermal response **-anzeige** *f* temperature indication **-anzeiger** *m* temperature gauge **-ausgleich** *m* equalization of temperature, temperature balance **-ausgleichskolben** *m* compensating piston
Temperatur-beiwert *m* temperature coefficient **-beständig** unaffected by changes of temperature **-beobachtung** *f* temperature observation **-bereich** *m* temperature range **-beständigkeit** *f* temperature stability, temperature constancy **-einfluß** *m* influence of temperature **-empfindlich** thermo-sensitive **-entropiediagramm** *n* temperature-entropy diagram **-erhöhung** *f* rise in temperature, temperature increase **-erniedrigung** *f* temperature drop
Temperatur-feld *n* temperature gradient, temperature field, field pattern **fläche** *f* isothermal or temperature surface **-fühler** *m* thermometer probe, feeler gauge **-gang** *m* variation or range of temperature, function or effect of temperature **-geber** *m* thermocouple
Temperaturgefälle *n* temperature drop, gradient or difference **senkrechtes ~** lapse rate
Temperaturgradient *m* temperature gradient, temperature lapse rate **-grenze** *f* temperature limit **-hysteresis** *f* temperature hysteresis **-intervall** *m* temperature interval **-jahresmittel** *n* mean annual temperature **-koeffizient** *m* temperature coefficient **-konstante Filtration** constant filtration temperature **-leitfähigkeit** *f* thermal conductivity **-leitvermögen** *n* thermal diffusivity **-leitzahl** *f* thermal conductivity, diffusivity
Temperatur-maßeinheit *f* unit of standatd of temperature **-maximum** *n* maximum temperature **-messer** *m* temperature gauge, thermometer, pyrometer **-meßkerze** *f* temperature gauge plug **-messung** *f* upper air temperature report, temperature measurement, thermometry **-minderanlage** *f* temperature reducing set **-minimum** *n* minimum temperature **-regelventil** *n* (Turbine) temperature interlock
Temperaturregistrier-anlage *f* temperature-indicating equipment **-apparat** *m* temperature recorder
Temperatur-regler *m* temperature control equipment, temperature regulator, thermoregulator, thermostat, thermostatic regulator **-spindel** *f* temperature controller shaft
Temperatur-reglung temperature control **-schichtung** *f* thermal stratification **-schreiber** *m* temperature recorder **-schwankung** *f* temperature variation, fluctuation in temperature **-skala** *f* thermometric or pyrometric scale **-spannung** *f* thermal stress **-sprung** *m* jump of temperature **-steigerung** *f* rise in temperature **-steigung** *f* temperature gradient
Temperatur-steuerwerk *n* temperature control **-strahler** *m* incandescent-light source, incandescent luminous radiator **-strahlung** *f* thermactinic radiation **-stufe** *f* temperature range **-summe** *f* accumulated temperature **-überführung** *f* heat transfer **-umkehrschicht** *f* layer of temperature inversion **-umkehrung** *f* temperature inversion **-unterschied** *m* mean temperature difference, difference in temperature
Temperatur-veränderung *f* change of temperature **-verstellbereich** *m* range of temperature regulation **-wechsel** *m* temperature cycle **-wechselbeständigkeit** *f* resistance to sudden changes of temperature **-wechsler** *m* heat exchanger **-wirbel** *m* heat or temperature eddy **-wirkung** *f* temperature effect **-zahl** *f* temperature coefficient **-zunahme** *f* temperature increase
Temper-bedingung *f* annealing condition **-eisen** *n* malleable cast iron **-erz** *n* annealing ore **-gefäß** *n* annealing pot **-gießer** *m* malleable founder **-gießerei** *f* malleable-iron foundry **-glühofen** *m* malleable-annealing furnace
Temperguß *m* malleable cast iron, malleable iron **weißer ~** white-heart malleable iron **schwarzer ~** black-heart malleable iron
Temperguß-bruch *m* malleable (iron) scrap **-eisen** *n* malleable cast iron **-stück** *n* malleable casting
Temperierbad *n* temperature or tempering bath
temperieren to temper
Temperier-mantel *m* tempering jacket **-medium** *n* tempering medium **-ofen** *m* tempering furnace **-wasser** *n* tempering water
Temper-kohle *f* temper carbon, graphitic carbon, temper graphite **-kohleabscheidung** *f* graphitization **-kohlebildung** *f* formation of temper carbon **-kohleknötchen** *n* temper-carbon nodule **-mittel** *n* tempering material or agent, packing
tempern to temper, anneal, reheat
Tempern *n* annealing, full annealing, malleableizing
Temper-ofen *m* annealing or tempering furnace, malleableizing oven **-roheisen** *n* malleable pig iron **-rohguß** *m* malleable hard iron, unannealed malleable iron, malleable white iron **-schrott** *m* malleable scrap **-stahlguß** *m* malleable cast iron **-topf** *m* annealing pot
Temperung *f* annealing
Temperungsbereich *m* annealing range
Temper-verfahren *n* annealing process **-wirkung** *f* annealing action
tempieren to set the fuse
Tempo *n* tempo, pace, speed **-knopf** *m* speed regulator (in shape of a knob)
temporär temporary **-er Magnet** temporary magnet

temporisieren to temporize
Tenazit *n* tenacite
Tenazität *f* tenacity
Tendenz *f* tendency **fallende ~** downward tendency **steigende ~** upward tendency
Tendenzthermoelement *n* trend thermocouple
Tender *m* tender **-lokomotive** *f* tender or tank locomotive **-maschine** *f* tender **-rad** *n* tender wheel **-schaufel** *f* stoker's shovel **-wasserkastenblech** *n* tender water-tank plate
Tennantit *m* tennantite
Tenne *f* thrashing floor
Tensimeter *n* tensimeter (for gas)
Tensometer *n* strain gauge, tensiometer
Tensor der Impulse tensor of momentum **~ des Vektors** magnitude of vector
Tensoralgebra *f* tensor algebra
tensorielles mittleres Quadrat tensorial mean square
Tensor-invarianten *pl* tensor invariants **-schreibweise** *f* tensor notation
Teppich *m* carpet, rug **-störung** *f* barrage jamming (rdr) **-stuhl** *m* carpet loom **-unterlagspapier** *n* carpet felt
Terbinerde *f* terbia, terbium oxide
Terbium *n* terbium
Term *m* (optical) level, term
Termanzahl *f* level numbers
Termbeeinflussung *f* level displacement
Termin *m* term, last day, deadline, closing date **~ zur Verhandlung einer Sache anberaumen** to set a date for a hearing or a case
Termin-geschäft *n* time bargain, credit transaction, futures **-handel** *m* futures trading **-kalender** *m* engagement (desk) diary, almanac of closing dates or deadlines
Terminologie *f* terminology
Termin-plan *m* production schedule **-stand** *m* delivery date **-vorgabe** *f* schedule forecast
Termite *f* termite
Term-kontinuum *n* quasi continuum of levels **-lage** *f* term value **-schema** *n* level diagram **-strukturen** *pl* level structures **-verschiebung** *f* term shift or postponement
ternar ternary **-e Legierung** ternary alloy
Ternarstahl *m* simple alloy steel, ternary steel
Terneblech *n* terne plate
terpenfrei terpeneless
Terpenkohlenwasserstoff *m* terpene hydro-carbon
Terpentin *n* turpentine **-abscheider** *m* turpentine separator **-emulsion** *f* turpentine (missiles) **-firnis** *m* crude trupentine **-öl** *n* (spirit or oil of) turpentine, terpineol **-ölersatz** *m* white spirit, adulterated turpentine
Terrain *n* terrain, ground **-aufnahme** *f* ground survey, land surveying **-stufe** *f* scarp
Terrakotta *f* terra cotta
Terrasse *f* terrace
Terrassen-dach *n* platform roof **-schnitt** *m* terracing cut **-trommel** *f* terraced sieve drum
terrassieren to terrace
terrassiertes Haus split level house
Terrazzokörnung *f* terrazzo grade
terrestrisch terrestrial **-e Navigation** terrestrial navigation
Tertiär *n* tertiary **-empfang** *m* three-circuit reception **-formation** *f* tertiary formation **-kreis** *m* tertiary circuit **-strahlen** *m pl* tertiary radiation **-wicklung** *f* tertiary winding
Tesla-spule *f* Tesla coil **-transformator** *m* Tesla transformer or coil
Tesselith *m* tesselite
tesseral tesseral **-kies** *m* skutterudite, modumite
Test *m* test, cupel, indicator **-band** *n* test tape **-benzin** *n* turpentine substitute, white spirit
Testbild *n* test pattern (TV) **-geber** *m* test-pattern generator **-röhre** *f* monoscope **-strahl** *m* test pattern beam
Testdia *n* test slide
testen to test
Testor-Härteprüfer *m* Testor hardness
Test-pegel *m* test level **-platte** *f* test record (phono) **-programm** *n* diagnostic routine (data proc.)
Tetanthren *n* tetanthrene
Tetra-araban *n* tetraaraban **-äthylblei** *n* tetraethyl lead **-borsäure** *f* tetraboric acid **-chlorid** *n* tetrachloride **-chlorkohlenstoff** *m* carbon tetrachloride, tetrachloromethane **-chlorzinn** *n* tin tetrachloride
Tetrade *f* tetrad
Tetradecan *n* tetradecane
Tetraeder *n* tetrahedron
tetraedrisch tetrahedral **-e Kugellagerung** tetrahedral packing of spheres
Tetrafluorkohlenstoff *m* carbon tetrafluoride
tetragonal tetragonal
Tetrahalide tetrahalide
Tetrahandfeuerlöscher *m* fire extinguisher
Tetralinperoxyd *n* tetralinperoxide
Tetraoxyd *n* tetroxide
Tetratriakontadien *n* tetratricontadien
Tetrode *f* tetrode
Tetryl *n* tetryl
teuer expensive, dear
Teuerung *f* dearness or scarcity (of provisions)
Teufe *f* depth
Teufelsklaue *f* nippers, devil's claw, sling
teufen to sink, deepen, bore **-anzeiger** *m* stockline indicator (of a furnace), depth indicator
Teukette *f* anchor chain
Text *m* text
Texteinfügungsschalter insert switch
Textil-antrieb *m* textile drive **-maschine** *f* textile machine
Textilose *f* textilose
Textolit (mit) Schellacküberzug chellac bonded textolite
Textschrift *f* paragon, double pica
Textur *f* texture, X-ray diffraction pattern
TFH (Trägerfrequenzübertragung auf Hochspannungsleitungen) powerline carrier
T-Glied *n* T-type section
Thalli-bromid *n* thallic bromide **-chlorat** *n* thallic chlorate
Thallium *n* thallium **-alaun** *n* thallium alum **-bromür** *n* thallous bromide **-chlorür** *n* thallous chloride **-fluorür** *n* thallous fluoride **-jodür** *n* thallous iodine **-oxydul** *n* thallous oxide **-sauer** thallic **-sulfid** *n* thallous sulfide **-sulfidzelle** *f* thallofide photoconductive cell
Thalliverbindung *f* thallic compound
Thallo-bromid *n* thallous bromide **-fidezelle** *f* thallofide cell **-hydroxyd** *n* thallous hydroxide **-jodat** *n* thallous iodate

Thalofid *n* thalofide
Theobromin *n* theobromine
Theisen-Wascher *m* Theisen washer or cleaner, Theisen disintegrator
Thema *n* subject, theme, subject matter, topic
Theodolit *m* theodolite ~ **mit Distanzmeßeinrichtung** theodolite with stadia lines
theoretisch theoretical, calculated ~ **bester Gleitwinkel** theoretical best gliding angle **-er Fluglehrer** ground instructor **-e Gipfelhöhe** calculated ceiling **-er Luftbedarf** theoretical air requirement **-e Prüfung** technical examination **-er Trennfaktor** ideal process factor **-er Unterricht** technical instruction **-er Wert** ideal value
Theorie *f* theory ~ **fünfter Ordnung** fifth order theory
Therapieröhre *f* therapy tube
Thermalhärtung *f* hot-quenching method
Thermalisierung *f* thermalization
Thermalquelle *f* thermal spring, hot spa
Thermik *f* warm air current, upcurrent due to hot air **-blase** *f* thermal bubble **-flug** *m* thermic flight **-segelflug** *m* thermal gliding
Thermionen *n pl* thermions **-relais** *n* thermionic relay **-strom** *m* thermionic current
thermionisch thermionic **-er Gleichrichter** thermionic valve
thermisch thermal, thermic ~ **gesteuerter Kontakt** (Blinkgeber) thermically controlled contact (blinker unit) ~ **vergütbar** heat-treatable
thermisch-es Aufreißen tearing up thermically **-er Aufwind** thermal upcurrent **-e Auslösung** thermal cutout **-e Behandlung** heat-treatment **-e Bewegung** thermal agitation **-e Fehlordnungserscheinung** formation of holes **-e Kopplung** thermal contact **-er Neigungsmesser** thermal gradiometer
thermisch-e Ortung thermo location **-er Segelflug** thermal soaring **-er Störungsbereich** thermal spike **-er Strommesser** thermocouple ammeter **-e Strömung** thermal transpiration **-er Wirkungsgrad** thermal efficiency
Thermistor *m* thermistor
Thermit *n* thermite **-brandbombe** *f* thermite incendiary bomb **-eisen** *n* thermite iron **-gießverfahren** *n* thermite fusion welding **-schweißung** *f* thermite welding, thermite weld **-schweißverfahren** *n* thermite welding process **-verfahren** *n* thermite process
Thermo-analyse *f* thermal analysis **-barograph** *m* thermobarograph **-chemisch** thermochemical **-detektor** *m* thermo(electric) detector **-dynamik** *f* thermodynamics
thermodynamische Wahrscheinlichkeit statistical weight
thermoelastisch thermoelastic
thermoelektrisch thermoelectric **-er Effekt** thermoelectric effect, Seebeck effect **-es Element** thermocouple **-e Kraftwirkung** thermoelectric effect **-e Lötstelle** thermojunction **-es Meßgerät** thermocouple (thermojunction) instrument **-er Strom** thermocurrent **-es Thermometer** thermoelectric thermometer **-e Umkehrung** thermoelectric inversion **-e Wirkung** thermoelectric effect, Seebeck effect
Thermoelektrizität *f* thermoelectricity
thermoelektromotorisch thermoelectromotive
Thermo-elektron *n* thermoelectron **-element** *n* thermocouple element, vacuum thermocouple **-elementendraht** *m* thermocouple wire, thermoelement wire **-elementenkreis** *m* thermocouple circuit **-elementträger** *m* thermocouple carrier **-farbe** *f* thermocolor **-galvanometer** *n* thermogalvanometer **-gramm** *n* thermogram **-graph** *m* thermograph **-hydrometer** *n* thermohydrometer **-isoplethe** *f* thermoisopleth
Thermo-kauter *m* branding iron **-kauterisation** *f* thermocautery **-kette** *f* thermoelement **-kraft** *f* thermoelectric force
Thermokreuz *n* thermocouple (detector) **-brücke** *f* thermocouple or junction, thermal cross **-instrument** *n* thermocouple meter
thermolabil thermolabile
Thermolyse *f* thermolysis
Thermo-manometer *n* thermo pressure gauge, thermogauge **-melder** *m* automatic detectors **-metallurgie** *f* thermometallurgy
Thermometer *n* thermometer ~ **mit feucht gehaltener Kugel** wet-bulb thermometer **feuchtes** ~ wetbulb thermometer
Thermometer-blase *f* thermometer bulb **-einsatz** *m* thermometer socket **-faden** *m* thermometric column **-hülse** *f* thermometer well **-korrektor** *f* stem correction **-kugel** *f* thermometer bulb **-rohr** *n* thermometer socket **-röhre** *f*, **-säule** *f* thermometer column or stem, capillary tube of thermometer **-schaft** *m* thermometer stem **-skala** *f* thermometer scale **-stutzen** *m* thermometer branch, boss for thermometer **-tasche** *f* thermometer well
Thermo-milliamperemeter *n* thermomilliammeter **-motorisch** thermomotive **-paar** *n* thermocouple **-phon** *n* thermophone
Thermophor *n* hot water bag
Thermo-phosphoreszenz *f* thermophosphorescence **-physik** *f* thermophysics **-physikalisch** thermophysical
thermoplastisch thermoplastic **-er Werkstoff** thermoplastics
thermopneumatischer Auslöser heat actuated device
Thermo-potential *n* thermal potential **-regler** *m* thermoregulator, heat regulator **-relais** *n* thermal or thermic relay **-remanent** thermoremanent **-säule** *f* thermopile, thermoelectric pile **-schalter** *m* thermal-lag switch
Thermosflasche *f* thermos bottle
Thermosiphon *m* thermosiphon **-kühlung** *f* natural circulation water cooling, thermosyphon cooling **-umlauf** *m* gravity circulation
Thermoskop *n* thermoscope
Thermospannung *f* thermoelectric voltage
Thermostat *m* thermostat, oven chamber section
Thermostatik *f* thermostatics
thermostatoplastischer Werkstoff thermosetting plastics
Thermostrom *m* thermocurrent, thermoelectric current **-messer** *m* thermoammeter
Thermotelephon *n* thermotelephone
Thermotron *n* thermotron
Thermo-umformer *m* thermal convertor **-umformermeßgerät** *n* thermocouple instrument **-viskositätszahl** *f* thermoviscous number **-voltmeter** *n* thermocouple voltmeter **-zelle** *f*

thermoelement, thermocouple
Thetafunktion *f* theta function
Thiamin *n* auerine (Thiamin)
Thiazenium *n* a type of thiazine salts
Thiocyansäure *f* thiocyanic acid
Thioessigsäure *f* thioacetic acid
Thioharnstoff *m* thiocarbamine
Thiokresol *n* thiocresol
Thionylchlorid *n* thionyl chloride
Thiophenol *n* thiophenol
Thiophten *n* thiophthene
Thio-säure *f* thio acid, thiomic acid **-schwefelsäure** *f* thiosulfuric acid **-sinamin** *n* thiosinamine **-zinnsäure** *f* thiostannic acid
Thiozyan *n* thiocyanogen **-kalium** *n* potassium thiocyanate **-säure** *f* thiocyanic acid, sulfocyanic acid
Thixotropie *f* thixotropy
Thomas-Bessemer-Anlage *f* basic Bessemer plant
Thomas-birne *f* basic-lined (Bessemer) converter, Thomas converter **-eisen** *n* Thomas steel, basic converter steel, basic Bessemer steel **-flußeisen** *n* basic converter steel, Thomas steel, Thomas low-carbon steel **-flußstahl** *m* basic converter steel, Thomas steel **-konverter** *m* Thomas converter **-material** *n* Thomas steel **-mehl** *n* ground basic slag
Thomas-roheisen *n* basic Bessemer pig iron, basic Bessemer pig **-schlacke** *f* Thomas slag **-schlakkenmehl** *n* Thomas meal **-stahl** *m* Thomas steel, basic Bessemer steel, basic converter steel **-stahlwerk** *n* Thomas steel plant, basic steelworks **-verfahren** *n* Thomas process, Thomas-Gilchrist process, basic Bessemer process
Thomson-effekt *m* Thomson effect **-kabel** *n* nonloaded (submarine) telegraph cable **-kurve** *f* Kelvin arrival curve
Thomsonsche Formel Thomson formula
Thomsonschweißverfahren *n* Thomson contact-welding process
Thor *n* thorium
Thoraxsegment *n* thoracic somite (geol.)
Thorerde *f* thoria (thorium dioxide)
thorhaltig thoriated **-er Wolframfaden** thoriated tungsten filament
Thoride *pl* thorides
thorieren to thoriate
thoriert thoriated **-er Fader** thoriated filament **-e Kathode** thoriated cathode, flashing
thorisch thoric
Thorium *n* thorium **-chlorid** *n* thorium chloride **-emanation** *f* thoron **-faden** *m* thoriated filament, deodorant **-heizfaden** *m* thoriated filament **-haltig** thoriated **-röhre** *f* thoriated filament valve **-spaltung** *f* thorium fission
Thorogummit *m* thorogummite
Thorolit *m* thorolite
Thoron *n* thoron
Thorotungstit *n* thorotungstite
Thoroxyd *n* thorium oxide
Thraulit *m* thraulite
Thrombose *f* thrombosis, clogging or stoppage in a pipeline
Thrombozyt *n* thrombocyte
Thucholit *m* thucholite
Thulium *n* thulium
Thuryuhrschraubengewinde *n* Thury thread, British Association Standard Screw Thread

Thymol-jodid *n* thymol iodide **-phthalein** *n* thymolphthalein **-säure** *f* thymic acid
Thyration *f* thyration
Thyratron *n* thyratron **-röhre** *f* mercury-vapor tube
ticken to click
Ticker *m* ticker **~ zum Blinkgeber** ticker for blinker unit
Tickerempfänger *m* ticker apparatus
Tickmanometer *n* click gauge
Tide *f* tide, half tide **-becken** *n* tidal basin **-bewegung** *f* tidal impulse **-hafen** *m* open basin harbor (tide harbor) **-hub** *m* tide lift
Tiden-fall *m* low tide **-hub** *m* tidal range, rise of the tide, amplitude **-stieg** *m* rising tide
Tideströmung *f* alternate ebb and flow of the tide, tidal current, tidal stream
tief deep, low, profound, minimum, of low pressure **~ liegen** to range low **-er Ton** low-pitch sound, bass sound or note
tiefätzen to overetch, intaglio
Tief-ätzprobe *f* deep-etch test **-ätzung** *f* deep etching
Tiefbau *m* structural work below ground level, deep workings, underground structures or workings **-arbeiten** *pl* below grade construction **-betrieb** *m* deep mining, deep mine working, allotment worked underground **-grube** *f* underground mine **-schleuse** *f* deep level sluice
Tiefbehälter *m* underground tank
Tiefbett-felge *f* drop-base rim, drop-center rim, wellbase rim **-kugellager** *n* deep-groove-type radial ball bearing, deep-race ball bearing
Tiefbohr-anlage *f* deep-well drilling plant **-apparat** *m* mechanic auger
Tief-bohren *n* drilling deep
Tiefbohrunternehmen *n* well-sinking enterprise
Tiefbrunnen *m* deep well **-pumpe** *f* low-down pump (double-acting hand-force pump)
Tiefdecker *m* low-wing monoplane **halbfreitragender ~** semicantilever low-wing monoplane
Tiefdecker-flügel *m* monoplane of low-wing-type (aviation) **-flugmodell** *n* low-wing model
tiefdringend penetrating
Tiefdruck *m* printing with a deep edge plate, depression, low pressure, intaglio printing process **-ätze** *f* gravure etchant **-bogenmaschine** *f* sheet-fed gravure machine **-furche** *f* trough **-gebiet** *n* low-pressure area (aviat), depression **-luftkrankheit** *f* bends (aviat)
Tiefdruck-maschine *f* photogravure printing machine **-papier** *n* intaglio paper **-reifen** *m* low-pressure tire **-rinne** *f* low pressure trough **-rollenmaschine** *f* photogravure press **-rollenrotationsmaschine** *f* roll-fed photogravure rotary
Tiefdruckrotationsmaschine für Bogenanlage sheetfed photogravure rotary machine
Tiefdruck-walze *f* intaglio cylinder **-wirbel** *m* cyclone low **-zentrum** *n* center of cyclone or low barometric pressure, center of low
Tiefe *f* depth, chord (of wing), depression, profundity, depth of focus (of eye) **eine ~ abmessen** to fathom **barometrische ~** depression **mittlere ~** mean chord of a wing **nutzbare ~** (practical) depth **~ unter Ansatzpunkt** depth below insertion point

Tiefebene *f* lowland

Tiefempfangsgesetz *n* law for receiving energy (acoustics)

Tiefen *pl* bass notes, low-frequency notes, low-pitch notes, dark-picture portions **-abstand** *m* (depth) distance **-angabe** *f* depth data **-anzeiger** *m* depth indicator **-aufnahmeorgan** *n* organ with depth sensibility **-ausdehnung** *f* extension in depth **-auskreuzung** *f* incidence (stagger) bracing

Tiefen-bereich *m* depth of field **-bestimmung** *f* stereoscopic radiograph for locating defects, depth determination of flaws **-bewegung** *f* movement in depth **-differenz** *f* depth difference **-dosis** *f* depth dose **-einbruch** *m* penetration in depth **-eindruck** *m* impression of depth **-einstellung** *f* depth adjustment **-einstellvorrichttung** *f* depth regulator **-fokussierung** *f* to-and-fro focussing movement

Tiefen-gestein *n* deep-seated (plutonic) rock **-gliederung** *f* distribution in depth, disposition in depth **-hervorhebung** *f* bassy condition, emphasis on bass tones **-karte** *f* bathymetric chart **-kompensation** *f* reed armature arrangement to accentuate or emphasize low frequencies (in loud-speaker) **-konus** *m* low-frequency cone loud-speaker, woofer

Tiefenkreuz-diagonale *f* incidence or stagger wire **-draht** *m* incidence wire, stagger wire **-seil** *n* incidence wire or cable **-verspannung** *f* incedence bracing, stagger wiring

Tiefenkurve *f* depth contour, contour of sea bed

Tiefenlehre *f* depth gauge, flush-pin gauge ~ **mit Nonius** vernier depth gauge **verstellbare** ~ adjustable depth gauge

Tiefen-linie *f* depth, the lowest isobathic or bottom countour line, current of a river, depth contour **-lokalisation** *f* depth perception **-lotapparat** *m* sounding apparatur **-maß** *n* depth gauge (instrument), turning square **-meßapparat** *m* depth gauge **-meßbereich** *m* depth gauging range **-messer** *m* depth indicator, depth gauge **-meßgerät** *n* depth-measuring appliance **-meßuhr** *f* dial depth gauge **-messung** *f* depth finding **-meßvorrichtung** *f* depth gauge **-mikrometer** *n* micrometer depth gauge

Tiefen-parallaxe *f* depth parallax **-paßfilter** *m* low-pass filter **-richtig** orthoscopic **-ruder** *n* flipper, elevator, low rudder, elevator control, depth regulator **-ruderkabel** *n* elevator cable

Tiefen-schärfe *f* definition in depth, depth of focus, depth of field **-schärfenrechner** *m* depth of field scale **-schlitten** *m* depth slide **-schrift** *f* hill-and-dale track, Edison track or sound groove, vertical recording **-schürfung** *f* depth test **-staffelung** *f* echelonment in depth **-steller** *m* depth control of mine (navig.) **-steuereinrichtung** *f* cherrying attachment **-streuung** *f* range dispersion on horizontal target (artil.) **-stufe** *f* gradient **-taster** *m* depth gauge

Tiefen-unschärfe *f* insufficient depth or lack of depth of focus **-unterscheidung** *f* appreciation of difference, in depth **-unterscheidungsvermögen** *n* power of appreciation of differences in depth **-vergrößerung** *f* longitudinal magnification **-verjüngung** *f* plan or chord taper **-verkehrt** pseudoscopic **-verlagerung** *f* depth dislocation **-verringerung** *f* reduction of chord **-verspannung** *f* stagger bracing (aviation), interplane bracing, longitudinal cross bracing **-verteilung** *f* chord distribution **-vorschub** *m* down-feed, depth feed motion

Tiefen-wachstum *n* growth in depth **-wahrnehmung** *f* perception of depth, perception of relief **-wasser** *n* subterranean or ground water **-winkel** *m* angle of depression, angle of elevation below horizontal **-wirkung** *f* depth effect (artil.) throwing power, plasticity of image, plastic or stereoscopic effect (of picture) **-zahl** *f* graduation mark, index mark **-zersetzung** *f* deep-seated decomposition **-zirkulation** *f* deep water circulation **-zone** *f* defensive zone

Tiefer-drehen *n* screwing-down **-stehend** inferior **-stellung** *f* lowering **-werden** *n* deepening

Tief-fach *n* lower shed **-fassung** *f* low-set type electrode holder **-flug** *m* hedgehopping, low level flight **-fußnadel** *f* low butt needle

Tiefgang *m* draft (of ships) ~ **des beladenen Schiffes** load draft ~ **haben** to draw water

Tief-garage *f* underground garage **-gegliedert** depth-distributed

tiefgehend deep-going, deeply penetrating **-e Ausladung** deep gap

tief-gekühlt chilled **-gestaffelt** echeloned in depth **-gestellter Index** subscript **-gliedern** to form ranks in depth

Tief-gründung *f* depth foundation **-hammer** *m* hollowing hammer

tiefhängend low **-e Wolke** low cloud

Tief-kälteverfahren *n* low-temperature process

Tiefkühl-anlage *f* cooling plant for low temperature **-fach** *n* deep-freezing compartment **-pumpen** *pl* low temperature cooling (chilling pumps) **-spule** *f* low-temperature coil **-truhe** *f* frozen food chest

Tiefkühlung *f* low-temperature cooling

Tiefkühlverfahren *n* low-temperature process

Tieflade-anhänger *m* flat-bed trailer **-linie** *f* freeboard, load line **-wagen** *m* well wagon

Tieflage *f* low position ~ **des Schwerpunktes** low position of center of gravity

Tief-lastenabwurfgerät *n* low-level freight-jettisoning device **-lauf** *m* sloping hoop channel (in rolling) **-liegend** low-lying, deep-seated **-lochbohrbank** *f* horizontal deep hole boring lathe **-löffelbagger** *m* ditcher **-lot** *n* deep-sea lead

Tiefofen *m* soaking pit, pit heating furnace, soaker, vertical ingot-heating furnace **-mann** *m* soaking pitman

Tief-paßfilter *n* low-pass filter **-prägen** *n* debossing **-pumpe** *f* deep well pump **-pumpenzylinder** *m* working barrel **-rot** deep red **-rund** concave

Tiefschaltungsschneckenwelle *f* feed-rack worm shaft

tief-schmelzend low-melting **-schnitt** *m* narrow pitch cut, deep cut, below grade **-schürfend** profound **-schütze** *f* deep sluice gate **-schwarz** jet black **-schwimmer** *m* composite float, ball-and-line float, depth float

Tiefsee *f* deep water, deep sea **-kabel** *n* marine cable **-lot** *n* deep-sea lead **-lotung** *f* deep-sea sounding **-messer** *m* bathymeter

tief-siedend low-boiling **-sitzend** squat **-sondiergerät** *n* deep sounding apparatus **-sperre** *f* low-altitude barrage below 1,000 meters **-spülklosett** *n* water closet with radial flush system

-staffeln to echelon in depth -stand *m* low(est) level, depression (econ.) -stanzblech *n* sheet iron for deep stamping -stellen to lower -strahler *m* floodlight, illumination by means of built-in intensive fittings

Tiefst-wert *m* minimum value **-temperaturtechnik** *f* cyrogenic engineering

Tiefteer *m* low-temperature tar

Tieftemperatur *f* low temperatur **-forschung** *f* cryogenics **-streckziehverfahren** *n* cryogenic stretch forming process

Tiefton-durchlasser *m* high-frequency muffler **-einheit** (Lautsprecher) woofer

tieftönend low pitched

Tiefton-konus *m* low-frequency cone loudspeaker **-lautsprecher** *m* woofer

Tieftrogbandförderung *f* deep trough conveying

Tiefung *f* cupping

Tiefungs-probe *f* cupping test **-versuch** *m* deep-drawing test **-wert** *m* cupping value, cupping-ductility value

Tief-vergasung *f* low-temperature carbonization or distillation, partial carbonization **-verkokung** *f* low-temperature carbonization, distillation of coal at low temperature

tiefversenkt und breitgestaucht with cone heads or lost heads

Tiefzahl *f* subscript

Tiefziehblech *n* sheet metal for deep drawing or forming

tiefziehen to deep-draw, cup, dish

Tiefziehen *n* deep drawing, shallow drawing (of metals)

Tiefzieh-fähigkeit *f* capability of being cupped **-maschine** *f* stretcher leveler **-presse** *f* drawing press **-probe** *f* cupping test, cuppability test (specimen) **-prüfmaschine** *f* cupping test machine **-qualität** *f* deep-drawing quality **-schlagpresse** *f* impact extrusion press **-stahl** *m* deep-drawing cold rolled steel **-verfahren** *n* cupping process, cupping method **-zweck** *m* deep-drawing steel **-zwecke** *pl* deep drawing purposes

Tiegel *m* crucible, pot, melting pot, bowl, pan, skillet, stew pan **-betrieb** *m* crucible (process) practice **-brenner** *m* crucible maker **-brennofen** *m* crucible oven **-drehung** *f* crucible rotation **-druckautomat** *m* automatic platen **-drucker** *m* platen machine minder **-druckpresse** *f* platen press **-einsatz** *m* crucible charge

Tiegel-flußstahl *m* crucible cast steel **-form** *f* crucible mold **-formerei** *f* crucible molding **-frei** floating (zone melting) **-futter** *n* crucible lining **-gabel** *f* crucible shank **-gießerei** *f* **-guß** *m* casting in crucibles **-gußstahl** *m* crucible cast steel, crucible steel **-hohlform** *f* crucible mold, pot mold **-hub** *m* crucible lift

tiegelloser Ofen noncrucible furnace

Tiegelofen *m* crucible furnace ~ **mit Umschaltfeuerung** regeneration crucible furnace

Tiegel-rand *m* crucible edge or rim **-schachtofen** *m* shaft crucible furnace **-schmelzbetrieb** *m* crucible melting practice **-schmelzerei** *f* crucible steel melting, crucible melting plant **-schmelzhütte** *f* crucible steel foundry **-schmelzstahlhütte** *f* crucible-steel-furnace plant **-schmelzverfahren** *n* crucible melting process **-stahl** *m* crucible steel, cast steel **-trockner** *m* crucible drier **-verkokung** *f* crucible coking test **-zange** *f* crucible tongs **-ziehverfahren** *n* crucible-pulling method

Tier-arzt *m* veterinary **-haut** *f* hide

tierisch animal **-e Leimung** animal gelatin, glue, sizing

Tierkohle *f* animal charcoal

Tierkreis *m* zodiac **-licht** *n* zodiacal light

Tier-leim *m* animal glue, size **-öl** *n* animal oil

Tigersandstein *m* mottled sandstone

Tikker *m* ticker, radio chopper, train interrupter

tilgen to amortize, eradicate, destroy, cancel, erase, blot out, delete, efface, obliterate

Tilgung *f* obliteration, quenching, amortization, write-off (commercial), extinction (of fluorescence), evanescence

Tiltometer *n* tiltometer

Tinkal *m* native borax, tincal

Tinktur *f* tincture

Tinol *n* tinol

Tinte *f* ink **magnetische** ~ magnetic ink

Tinten-füllpatrone *f* ink cartridge **-gummi** *n* ink eraser **-kuli** *m* ballpoint pen **-schreiber** *m* ink recorder, inker **-stift** *m* indelible pencil **-strahlschreiber** *m* ink-vapor recorder **-walze** *f* inker

tintig inky

Tintometer *n* tintometer

Tippbetrieb *m* inching service

tippen to type, tape

Tipper des Vergasers carburetor primer

Tipp-schaltung *f* inching operation **-vorrichtung** *f* tipping device

Tisch *m* table, counter, platen, workbench ~ **mit automatischer Einlage** traveling feed table ~ **mit Handeinlage** plain feed table **drehbarer** ~ revolving stage (opt)

Tisch-anschlag *m* table stop **-antriebsradwelle** *f* bull or driving wheel shaft **-apparat** *m* portable (telephone) set **-aufbau** *m* table-or-bench-mounting **-backe** *f* table frame **-bett** *n* master table or copyholder **-bewegung** *f* table movement or traverse table feed **-blatt** *n* table leaf **-bohrmaschine** *f* table drill press **-bohrständer** *m* bench-drill stand

Tischchen *n* bracket

Tisch-drehbank *f* bench lathe **-drehzahlanzeiger** *m* table speed-indicator **-eilgang** *m* quick table motion **-einstellungsgetriebe** *n* table adjusting gear **-empfänger** *m* table set **-entlastung** *f* table relief **-fernsprecher** *m* desk telephone set **-feststellschraube** *f* clamping bolt **-farbwerk** *n* slab inking unit **-feder** *f* stage clamp

Tischflügel, herunterklappbarer ~ drop leaf

tischförmig table-like

Tisch-fräsmaschine *f* (für Holzbearbeitung) bench milling machine, bench wood shaper **-führung** *f* table guide **-gehäuse** *n* table-telephone station, desk-telephone set **-gerät** *n* bench model **-gestell** *n* trestle **-gewindeschneidmaschine** *f* bench screw cutting machine **-gleitbahn** *f* table guides

Tisch-halter *m* stage holder **-hub** *m* table travel **-kasten** *m* drawer **-kehrmaschine** *f* table sweeper **-klappe** *f* folding table leaf **-klemmschraube** *f* table clamp screw or locking bolt

Tischkonsol *n* table arm **-klemmschraube** *f* table-arm clamping screw

Tisch-kreissäge *f* circular-saw bench **-lade** *f* drawer **-längsbewegung** *f* longitudinal travel of table **-längsweg** *m* longitudinal table traverse **-läufer** *m* table carpet

Tischler *m* cabinetmaker, carpenter, joiner **-arbeit** *f* joiner's work

Tischlerei *f* joinery, cabinetmaking, carpenter's shop

Tischler-leim *m* joiner's or carpenter's glue **-platten** *pl* plywood board, joiner plate **-steifsäge** *f* cabinet saw

Tisch-mutter *f* stage or table raising nut **-öffnung** *f* stage (table) opening **-platte** *f* squeezer plate, table plate **-rost** *m* table grid or grating **-schlitten** *m* sliding table **-schlittenwaagerechtbewegung** *f* table slide longitudinal feed screw **-schwenkplatte** *f* swivel table **-selbstgang** *m* automatic table traverse, table power traverse **-sockel** *m* desk stand

Tischspindel für Vorfräseinrichtung rough milling attachment table screw

Tisch-ständer *m* table stand **-stativ** *n* table stand **-steuerhebel** *m* table control-lever **-steuerung** *f* control of table movement **-stillsetzung** *f* table stop **-stütze** *f* table support **-träger** *m* table bracket **-umsteuerhebel** *m* reversing latch or trip **-umsteuerung** *f* reversal of table **-verstellung** *f* table adjustment

Tischvorschub *m* table feed **-hebel** *m* table-feed lever **-kuppelungshebel** *m* platen feed clutch lever **-spindel** *f* platen feed screw

Tisch-welle *f* table roller **-zapfen** *m* table center-pin **-zarge** *f* table rim, frame

Titan *n* titanium

Titanat *n* titanate

Titan-chlorid *n* titanium chloride **-dioxyd** *n* titanic oxide

titandioxydmattierte Kunstseide titanium-dioxide-dellustered rayon

Titan-eisen *n* titaniferous iron **-eisenerz** *n* titanic iron ore, ilmenite **-eisensand** *m* titaniferous iron sand **-eisenstein** *m* titanic iron ore, ilmenite **-fluorwasserstoffsäure** *f* fluotitanous acid **-führend** titaniferous **-gewinnung** *f* titanium production **-glas** *n* titanium glass **-halogen** *n* titanium halide **-haltig** titaniferous

titanig titanous

Titanit *m* sphene, titanite

Titaniumsalz *n* titanium salt

Titan-kaliumfluorid *n* titanium potassium fluoride **-kaliumoxalat** *n* titanium potassium oxalate **-kran** *m* titan crane, revolving crane **-mennige** *f* a dark titan ore pigment **-säure** *f* titanic acid, titanium dioxide **-säureanhydrid** *n* titanic anhydride

titansaures Bleioxyd lead titanate

Titan-schwefelsäure *f* titanosulfuric acid **-stickstoff** *m* titanium nitride **-verbindung** *f* titanium compound **-weiß** *n* titanium white

Titel *m* title, degree, name, heading **-blatt** *n* title page **-buchstabe** *m* capital, two-line letter **-kopf** *m* (general) heading **-seite** *f* title page, introductory page **-setzer** *m* head setter **-zeile** *f* headline

Titer *m* denier, titer ~ **einer Flüssigkeit** standard strength of a solution, titration standard

Titer-abweichung *f* denier variation **-flüssigkeit** *f* standard solution

titern to titrate

Titer-stellung *f* standardization, establishment of titer **-welle** *f* denier variation

Titration *f* titration

Titrationsvoltmeter *n* titration voltameter

Titrierapparat *m* titrating or volumetric apparatus

titrieren to titrate

Titrier-exponent *m* hydrogen-ion concentration, titration exponent **-flüssigkeit** *f* titrating solution, standard solution **-lösung** standard solution **-methode** *f* titration method

Titrierung *f* titration

Titrierwaage *f* testing balance

titrimetrisch titrimetric

T-Luftdraht *m* T-shaped aerial

T-Luftleiter *m* extended T-shaped antenna

Tobel *m* gulch, ravine, defile, glen

Toccohärtung *f* Tocco hardening

Tochter-anzeigegerät *n* slave indicator **-gerät** *n* daughter instrument, slave equipment **-gesellschaft** *f* subsidiary company **-kompaß** *m* indicator for gyrostatic compass, auxiliary (repeater) compass **-motor** *m* repeater motor **-rohr** *n* plan position indicator tube (radar) **-sender** *m* slave transmitter **-sichtgerät** *n* radar repeater

tödlich deadly, lethal, fatal

Toilette *f* lavatory

Toiletten-essig *m* aromatic vinegar, toilet vinegar **-gegenstand** *m* toilet article

Toleranz *f* tolerance, allowable variation, permissible limits, allowance ~ **der Achsengleichheits-Abweichungen** coaxiality tolerance ~ **der Mittigkeitsabweichungen** concentricity tolerance **sich summierende Toleranzen** accumulative limits

Toleranz-anzeiger *m* tolerance indicator unit **-bereich** *m* range of tolerance **-dosisrate** *f* tolerance rate **-einengung** *f* reduction of tolerance **-einstellung** *f* setting the tolerances **-feld** *n* tolerance zone **-kaliberdorn** *m* tolerance plug gauge **-ketten** *pl* cumulative tolerances **-lage** *f* tolerance zone position **-lehre** *f* limit gauge **-tasterlehre** *f* limit snap gauge **-überschreitungsanzeiger** *m* tolerance surpassing indicator

Tolerierung *f* tolerating

Tolidin *n* tolidine

Tolit *n* tolite

Toluidin *n* toluidine

Toluol *n* toluene, methylbenzene **-sulfamid** *n* toluene sulfamide **-sulfochlorid** *n* toluene sulfochloride **-vergällt** denatured with toluene

Toluylendiamnin *n* toluylene diamine

Tombak *m* tombac (copper-base zinc alloy), red brass **-wellrohr** *n* corrugated tube of tombac

Tomographie *f* tomography

Ton *m* tone, sound, note, accent, tinge, tint, shade, blast (whistle), musical note, tune, clay **bildfähiger** ~ plastic clay **dumpfer** ~ all-bottom sound **gebrannter** ~ burned clay, fire clay, chamotte, grog **gehaltener** ~ sustained sound **gleitender** ~ glissando, sliding note **hohler** ~ boomy or dull sound **krächzender** ~ rasping sound **kreischender** ~ all-top sound or voice **sendereigner** ~ note or pitch peculiar to a beacon station, code note **tiefer** ~ low-pitched note, bass note, low tone **im ~ treffen** to match **~ zum Füllen** filler clay

Tonabnahme-einrichtung *f* pickup device **-gerät** *n* sound pickup **-stelle** *f* sound aperture, sound gate

Tonabnehmer *m* phonograph pickup, pickup, sound pickup, sound head (motion picture) **elektromagnetischer ~** electromagnetic pickup **~ mit Schwingspule** (dynamischer Tonabnehmer) moving coil pick-up

Tonabnehmer-buchse *f* phone adaptor **-taste** *f* pick-up key (tape rec.) **-trommel** *f* sound take-off drum, scanning drum

Ton-abstimmung *f* tone tuning, note tuning **-abstufung** *f* grading of tones, graduation of tonal intensities **-abtastspalte** *f* sound-scanning slit **-abtaststelle** *f* sound gate, sound-scanning slit, sound-pickup point **-abtastung** *f* sound-gate **-analysator** *m* heterodyne sound analyzer

Tonangeber *m*, **chromatischer ~** chromatic pitch pipe

Tonanteil *m* clay fraction

Tonarm *m* tone or pickup arm (tape rec) **~ mit Öldämpfung** oil damped arm

Tonart *f* kind of clay, key, tune, tonality, mode (major or minor)

tonartig clayey, argillaceous, claylike

Ton-atelier *n* sound stage, studio, teletorium **-aufbau** *m* building-up of tone **-aufnahme** *f* sound recording **-aufnehmer** *m*, **-aufzeichner** *m* sound recorder **-aufzeichnung** *f* sound recording **-aufzeichnungsverstärker** *m* sound-recording amplifier **-automatisch** autosonic **-bad** *n* toning bath (motion picture) **-ballen** *m* ball of clay

Tonband *n* recording tape **-breite** *f* sound bandwidth **-gerät** *n* tape recorder

Ton-behälter *m* stoneware container **-beize** *f* aluminum acetate **-belichtungsstelle** *f* sound gate, scanning light **-bereich** *m* frequency range of voice, range of tune **-beschlag** *m* coat of clay **-beseitigungsdrossel** *f* hum-eliminator choke **-beständigkeit** *f* syntony

Tonbild *n* tonal pattern, tone spectrum **-wand** *f* transoral screen (motion picture)

Ton-bindemittel *n* clay bond **-binder** *m* clay binder **-blende** *f* tone control means, tonalizer, fader **-blendeinstellung** *f* sound adjustment **-boden** *m* clay soil

Ton-dämpfer *m* vibration damper **-detektor** *m* sound detector **-einsumpfen** *n* wetting of the clay

Toneisenstein *m* argillaceous iron ore, clay ironstone, clay band **-lager** *n* clay ironstone deposit

Ton-empfang *m* modulated or tonal reception **-empfänger** *m* sound receiver (TV) **-empfindung** *f* acoustical perception, sound sensation

tönen to sound, hum, tone **~** (Papier) to tint

Tönen *n* hum(ming), sounding **~ der Drähte** humming of wires **~ von Freileitungen** humming of wires (teleph.)

tönend sounding, reverberating, interrupted, continuous (waves) **-er Funken** musical spark **-er Funkensender** musical-spark transmitter **-e Funkerstrecke** musical spak gap

Töner *m* high-frequency buzzer (radio) **~** (Lack) toner

Tonerde *f* pure clay, alumina, argillaceous earth, alumina cream (sugar) adobe **essigsaure ~** aluminum acetate **geschlämmte ~** emulsified alumina

Tonerde-beize alum mordant (alumina mordant) **-einschluß** *m* alumina inclusion **-gehalt** *m* alumina content **-haltig** aluminiferous **-hydrat** *n* aluminum (hydroxide) hydrate **-kali** *n* potassium aluminate **-lack** *m* alumina lake **-metall** *n* aluminum **-natron** *n* sodium aluminate **-reich** rich in alumina, aluminous **-salz** *n* aluminum salt **-schamotte** *f* clay-bond fire clay **-sulfat** *n* aluminum sulfate **-zement** *m* high alumina cement

Ton-erreger *m* tone-producer **-falle** *f* sound trap (TV) **-farbe** *f* timbre, tone quality **-färbemittel** *n* tone shading means, tonalizer **-fenster** *n* sound slit, sound gate

Tonfilm *m* sound film, talking film, sound motion picture **-aufnahmegerät** *n* sound-film camera **-geber** *m* sound-film transmitter

Ton-filter *m* tone filter **-fixierbad** *n* toning or fixing bath **-folgeschalter** *m* successive tone switch **-folgeschrift** *f* sound track, sound record

Tonformstück *n* tile, clay conduit **einzügiges ~** single tile **mehrzügiges ~** multiple tile

tonfrequenter Rufstrom voice-frequency signaling current

Tonfrequenz *f* audio-frequency, acoustic, audible, or sound frequency **-amplitudenbegrenzer** *m* audio-peak limiter **-anruf** *m* voice-frequency ringing **-belastung** *f* power handling capacity **-fernsteuerung** *f* audio-frequency control **-fernwahl** *f* voice-frequency dialing **-generator** *m* (TG) aufio-frequency generator (radio), audio-oscillator **-gleichrichter** *m* sound discriminator (TV) **-kanal** *m* audio channel **-leistung** *f* audio-frequency power **-maschine** *f* voice-frequency generator

Tonfrequenz-messer *m* audio level meter **-paket** *n* group of audio-frequency **-relais** *n* tuned-reed relay, vibrating relay **-ruf** *m* voice-frequency ringing or signaling **-rufsatz** *m* voice frequency ringing set **-rufstrom** *m* voice-frequency signalling current **-rufstrommessung** *f* voice-frequency signaling test **-signalisierung** *f* tonic train signalling **-telegraphie** *f* audio-frequency or voice-frequency telegraphy

Tonfrequenz-übertrager *m* audio-frequency transformer **-verstärker** *m* audio-frequency or low-frequency amplifier, audio-amplifier, note amplifier **-verstärkung** *f* audio-frequency or low-frequency amplification, audio amplification **-wiedergabe** *f* sound reproduction **-wiedergabetreue** *f* audio fidelity **-zeichengebung** *f* voice-frequency signaling **-zerhacker** *m* audio-frequency chopper

Tonfunk *m* sound radio

Tonführung *f* labyrinth (of loud-speaker)

Tonfunken-sender *m* musical-spark transmitter, loudspeaker **-strecke** *f* quenched spark gap **-system** *n* quenched spark system

Ton-galle *f* clay gall, marl pellet **-gebend** sound generative, acoustic, sonant **-geber** *m* audio oscillator, tone filter **-geberkopf** *m* sound reproducer head **-gefäß** *n* clay or earthen vessel **-gehalt** *m* clay content

Tongehör *n*, **absolutes ~** absolute pitch

Ton-generator *m* audio-frequency oscillator or generator, tonal or musical generator **-geschwindigkeit** *f* velocity of sound **-gleichheit** *f* syntony **-glimmerschiefer** *m* mica slate **-grube** *f* clay deposit

Tongut *n* porous ceramic, earthenware **-waren** earthenware

Tonhacke *f* mattock

tonhaltig aluminous, clay-bearing, argillaceous **-er Eisenschlamm** iron sludge with clay content **-er Schiefer** clay shale

Ton-haltungspedal *n* tone-sustaining pedal **-helligkeit** *f* pitch (of sound sensation)

Tonhöhe *f* pitch, note, pitch of tone

Tonhöhen-abstimmung *f* note tuning (telegr.) **-unterschiedschwelle** *f* pitch discrimination threshold **-vergleicher** *m* tone variator, pitch pipe

tonig argillaceous, clayey, clayish **-e Erde** clayey soil **-er Schlamm** slimes

Ton-industrie *f* clay industry **-ingenieur** *m* audio (control) engineer **-injektion** *f* clay grouting

tonisieren to tone up

Ton-kabine *f* soundbooth (film) **-kalk** *m* argillaceous limestone, argillocalcite **-kamera** *f* sound-recording camera **-kanal** *m* sound or tone channel **-kegel** *m* clay cone **-kern** *m* clay core **-kinomaschine** *f* sound-film projector **-kitt** *m* clay-lute **-klebestelle** *f* blooping patch or splice **-kleister** *m* daub **-kneter** *m* wet pan for grinding and tempering brick material

Ton-konstanz *f* constancy of pitch **-kopf** *m* soundfilm head or attachment **-kopie** *f* sound film used for reproduction **-korb** *m* loudspeaker clusters **-kreis** *m* audio stage, sound range **-kühlschlange** *f* ceramic cooling coil **-lage** *f* pitch **-lager** *n* clay deposit, clay bed **-lampe** *f* exciter lamp, operating photocell **-laufwerk** *n* sound-film feed mechanism

Tonleiter *f* scale **wohltemperierte ~** equally tempered scale

Ton-lichtlampe *f* exciter lamp, operating photocell **-linse** *f* clay lens **-los** silent **-lotsender** *m* echosounding oscillator **-masse** *f* paste (ceramics) **-mehl** *n* finely ground fire clay **-meister** *m* monitoring operator, recordist, sound engineer **-mergel** *m* loam, clayey marl **-messer** *m* volume indicator,sonometer, tone variator

Tonminimum *n* critical silence **auf ~ einstellen** to silence

Ton-mischer *m* tone fader, tone mixer, clay maker **-mischpult** *n* audio mixer, sound mixer **-modulation** *f* sound modulation

tonmoduliert tone-modulated **-er Telegraphiersender** tone-modulated telegraphic transmitter

Ton-motor *m* tape drive motor **-muffel** *f* clay retort

Tonnage *f* tonnage

Tonne *f* barrel, cask, metric ton, buoy

Tonnen-abfuhrsystem *n* carrying by means of barrels **-blech** *n* arched plate **-brücke** *f* cask bridge **-dach** *n* arched roof, barrel roof **-decke** *f* compass ceiling **-fähre** *f* barrel float **-fehler** *f* barrel or positive distortion **-flechtwerk** *n* barrel vaulting or basketwork **-floß** *n* raft of casks, barrel float **-förmig** drum-shaped, barrel-shaped, cylindrical

Tonnen-gehalt *m* tonnage (loading capacity) **-gehaltskala** *f* tonnage scale **-gewölbe** *n* barrel arch **-hof** *m* buoy store **-kilometer** *m* ton-kilometer **-lager** *n* self-aligning or barrel-shaped roller bearing, tubular bearing, roller profile **-maß** *n* ton measurement **-rollenlager** *n* barrel-shaped roller bearing **-tragfähigkeit** *f* ton burden **-verfahren** *n* barrel process **-verzeichnung** *f* barrel distortion

tonnenweise by the ton

tonnlägiger Gang lode of steep dip (geol.)

Tonometer *n* tonometer

Ton-optik *f* sound-head lens or optic (motion picture) **-papier** *n* tinted paper **-pegel** *m* sound level **-pfeifenkopf** *m* earthen bowl of pipe **-platte** *f* plate of clay or earthenware **-probe** *f* sound test, tonsil test **-projektor** *m* sound projector **-propfen** *m* clay plug, bottstick **-prüfer** *m* tone tester **-quelle** *f* tone source, source of sound **-rad** *n* tone wheel **-regietisch** *m* audio control desk **-reinheit** *f* purity of tone **-reiz** *m* sound stimulus

tonrichtiges Filter true-color or correct-tone filter (optics)

Ton-richtigkeit *f* tone correctness **-rille** *f* sound track **-rohr** *n* earthenware pipe, clay conduit **-röhre** *f* singing valve **-rolle** *f* recording roll **-rückumsetzer** *m* (tone) reconverter **-rundfunk** *m* audio and video film broadcast **-sand** *m* argillaceous sand **-säule** *f* sound column **-schicht** *f* bed of clay **-schiefer** *m* clay slate or schist, argillite, argillaceous slate **-schirm** *m* sound screen

Ton-schlag *m* clay puddle **-schlämme** *f* clay wash **-schlitz** *m* reproducer slit or aperture, sound slit **-schmelztiegel** *m* clay crucible **-schneider** *m* clay cutter **-schreiber** *m* sound recorder, cutter **-schwankungsmesser** *m* flutter meter or measuring instrument (sound film) **-schwingung** *f* sound vibration **-senden** *n* modulated continuous-wave transmission **-sender** *m* sound transmitter, oscillator, modulated continuous-wave transmitter, tonic transmitter, audio transmitter **-sendung** *f* transmission of sound **-sieb** *n* tone filter, audio filter

Ton-signal *n* sound signal **-spalt** *m* sound slit or aperture **-spalte** *f* sound track **-speicher** *m* sound recorder **-spektrum** *n* tonic or sound spectrum **-sperrkreis** *m* sound trap (TV)

Tonspur *f* film strip, sound track **eingeprägte ~** track engraved in film strip

Tonspur-abtastung *f* sound scanning (film) **-breite** *f* track width

Ton-stärke *f* intensity of tone **-stärkemeßgerät** *n* sound level meter **-stechspaten** *m* clay-digging spade **-stein** *m* mud stone **-steingut** *n* rough stoneware **-steuermann** *m* operator controlling sound volume **-steuerstelle** *f* control or exciter point **-stopfen** *m* clay plug, bottstick **-stoß** *m* tonal beat

Tonstreifen *m* tone band, sound track, sound recording **ausgesteuerter ~** modulation track **doppelspuriger ~** double-edged sound track

Ton-streifenverschmälerung *f* sound-track squeezing, matting **-strom** *m* sound or signal current, voice-signal current **-substanz** *f* clay body **-summer** *m* tone oscillator **-taube** *f* clay pigeon **-technik** *f* sound engineering **-tiegel** *m* clay crucible, white pot

Tonträger *m* sound carrier, sound-track support **-frequenz** *f* sound-carrier frequency **-welle** *f* sound-carrier wave

Ton-transportrolle *f* sound-film feed roller **-trickfilm** *m* sound animated cartoon **-trommel** *f* sound takeoff drum **-überblendung** *f* sound fading **-überlagert** modulated at audible frequencies **-überlagerung** *f* tonic sine modulation, modulation at audible frequency **-umfang** *m* tonal range, band width **-umkehrung** tone reversal **-umschalter** *m* fade-out control **-umschaltungseinrichtung** *f* fading device

Tönung *f* tone, resonance, color, tint, density value, shading value

tönungsrichtiges Bild picture of proper shading

Tönungs-skala *f* tone-control scale **-wert** *m* tonal value

Ton-unterdrückung *f* sound rejection, take off **-unterlage** *f* bed of clay

Tonus *m* tone **-verringerung** *f* atony

Ton-variation *f* sound variation **-veredler** *m* high-frequency cutoff or filter, sound clarifier **-verschiebung** *f* change of shade **-verschmelzung** *f* tonal fusion **-verstärker** *m* note or sound amplifier, note magnifier **-verstärkung** *f* note magnification **-volumen** *n* volume of sound

Ton-wagen *m* sound truck, location truck or unit **-wahl** *f* in-band signaling **-wahrnehmung** *f* acoustical perception **-walzwerk** *n* clay rolling mill **-wandler** *m* mode transducer **-waren** *pl* pottery, earthenware, crockery(ware) **-wecker** *m* tone ringer **-welle** *f* sound wave **-wellenspannung** *f* audio wave potential **-wender** *m* tone converter **-werk** *n* clayworks

tonwertrichtig tonally-correct

Ton-wiedergabe *f* sound reproduction **-wiedergabeoptik** *f* sound-head lens or optic **-zeichen** *n* note **-zeitdehnung** *f* acoustic slow motion **-zelle** *f* porous pot, sound cell **-zentrum** *n* tonal or acoustic center of frequencies

Ton-zerlegung *f*, **-zersetzung** *f* sound analysis **-zeug** *n* vitreous clayware, stoneware **-ziegel** *m* clay tile, clay brick **-zusatzgerät** *n* sound-film head **-zuschlag** *m* aluminous flux **-zwischenfrequenz** *f* sound intermediary frequency

Topas *m* topaz **-geschiebe** *n* topaz pebble

Topf *m* pot, jar, top, hand-grenade casing, container, can **-anode** *f* can anode **-ballenpresse** *f* tub-mold baling press **-deckel** *m* lid

Töpfer *m* potter

Töpferei *f* pottery

Töpfer-erde *f* potter's clay **-gut** *n* coarse pottery **-scheibe** *f* potter's lathe, pallet, throwing wheel, jigger, potter's wheel **-ton** *m* potter's clay **-ware** *f* earthenware, pottery

topfförmig cup-shaped

Topf-fräser *m* cup-shaped cutter **-gehäuse** *n* vertically split casing **-gießerei** *f* casting of iron pots **-glühen** *n*, **-glühverfahren** *n* pot annealing **-kern** *m* head core **-kernspule** *f* iron-clad or steel-clad spool

Topfkolben *m* type piston **~ ohne Aussparungen** full-skirted-type piston **~ mit nicht geschlitztem Mantel** solid-skirt-type piston

Topf-kreis *m* tank circuit; cavity resonator **-magnet** *m* pot-shaped magnet, iron-clad magnet, shielded electromagnet **-mühle** *f* barrel mill **-photometer** *n* photometric integrator **-schaufel** *f* hollow turbine bucket **-scheibe** *f* cup wheel **-scherbe** *f* potsherd **-schlacke** *f* slag cake, first-run slag **-schleifscheibe** *f* crown-grinding wheel, cup-grinding wheel **-spinnverfahren** *n* spinning-pot procedure **-spule** *f* pot-core coil **-stapel** *m* stack of pots **-stein** *m* potstone, soapstone **-tiefe** *f* well depth **-zeit** *f* (Klebstoff) pot time

Topograph *m* topographer

Topographie *f* topography, topographical features

topographisch topographical **-e Einflüsse** topographical effects **-er Entfernungsmesser** topographic tacheometer

Topologie *f* topology

topologisch topological **-e Abbildung** topological mapping

Topp *m* truck (navy), head

Toppflaggen setzen to dress ship

Topping *f* topping

Topplicht *n* masthead light

Toppsente *f* top timber line

Toppzeichen n top mark

Torbanit *m* torbinate, torch oil

Torbernit *m* torbernite

Torf *m* peat, turf **~ stechen** to dig peat

torfartig like peat, peaty

Torf-asche *f* peat ashes **-bagger** *m* peat excavator **-boden** *m* peat(y) soil **-kohle** *f* peat charcoal **-lager** *n* peat bog

Torflügel *m* gate wing

Torf-mehl *n* powdered peat, peat dust **-moor** *n* peat bog, peat moor, swamp **-mull** *m* peat litter **-packung** *f* peat backfilling **-platte** *f* peat slab **-soden** *m* peat sod, rectangular piece of peat **-staub** *m* peat dust, powdered peat **-stecher** *m* peat digger **-streu** *f* peat litter **-teer** *m* peat tar **-verkohlung** *f* peat charring

Torgerüst (Kran) gantry girder

Torimpuls *m*, **mit ~ steuern oder tasten** to gate

torisch-e Brillengläser toric lenses **-e Leuchtfeldlinse** toric radiant field lens

Torkammer *f* gate chamber

torkeln to wabble, tumble, stagger

torkretieren, mit Zement ~ to inject cement

Torkretputz *m* (coat of) gunite **verstärkter ~** revetment of reinforced gunite

Torkret-verfahren *n* applying gunite **-versatzmaschine** *f* gunite pneumatic stowing machine

Tornado *m* tornado

Tornesit *n* tornesit

Tornische *f* gate recess (of lock)

Tornister *m* pack, knapsack, rucksack, haver sack **-empfänger** *m* portable receiver, pack receiver radio **-filtergerät** *n* pack-type water purification unit **-funkgerät** *n* portable radio set, man-pack radio set **-funktrupp** *m* portable radio detachment **-klappe** *f* pack flap

Toroid *n* toroid **-spule** *f* toroidal coil

torpedieren to torpedo

Torpedo *n* torpedo, shell (petroleum) **-blech** *n* scuttle **-kreisel** *m* torpedo gyro(scope) **-leitung** *f* torpedo control **-lüfter** *m* axial-flow fan **-luftkessel** *m* compressed-air chamber for torpedoes **-raum** *m* torpedo room

Torpedorohr *n* torpedo tube **-kreiselwinkelrichter** *m* torpedo gyroscopic-angle setting device

Torpfannenstein *m* pivot or pintle stone
Torportal *n* gate, superstructure
Torr (from Torricelli) 1 mm Hg pressure
Torrostat *m* torrostat
Torschaltung *f* gate circuit
Torsiograph *m* torsion meter
Torsion *f* torsion, twist
Torsions-aufhängung *f* torsion suspension **-beanspruchung** *f* torsional stress, twisting stress **-biegung** *f* torsion-flexure **-dämpfer** *m* torsional vibration damper **-dehnungsmeßstreifen** *m* torsion strain gauge **-faden** *m* torsion wire **-feder** *f* torsion spring **-festigkeit** *f* torsional strength **-frei** torsionless **-grenze** *f* yield point of torsional shear **-indikator** *m* torsion indicator, transmission dynamometer **-konstante** *f* torsion constant **-kopf** *m* torsion head **-kraft** *f* torque, torsional force
Torsions-magnetometer *n* torsion-magnetometer **-maschine** *f* torsion-testing machine **-messer** *m* torsion meter, torsional-strain indicator, torsion indicator, torquemeter **-modulus** *m* rigidity modulus, torsion modulus, shear modulus, modulus of torsional shear **-moment** *n* twisting or torsional moment, torsion couple, starting torque, moment of rotation **-nase** *f* torsional clamp (aviation) **-pendel** *n* torsion pendulum **-probe** *f* torsion test **-prüfmaschine** *f* torsion-testing machine
Torsions-schwingung *f* torsional oscillation or vibration **-seil** *n* twist rope **-spannung** *f* torsional or twisting stress, torsional resilience or strain, twisting strain
Torsionsstab *m* torsion rod **-feder** *f* torsion bar spring **-federung** *f* torsion bar springing
Torsions-strebe *f* torque arm or stay **-versuch** *m* torsion test, twisting test **-waage** *f* torsion balance **-welle** *f* torsion bar **-wellenimpulsmethode** *f* torsional wave pulse method **-widerstand** *m* twisting resistance, resistance to torsion **-winkel** *m* angle of twist, angle of torque, torsion angle
Torsteuerspannung *f* gate voltage, gating (rdr)
Torus *m* torus **-koordinat** *m* toroidal coordinate
Tos-becken *n*, **-kammer** *f* stilling basin, water cushion
Tosiklappe *f* Tosi flap valve
tot dead, lifeless **-es Feld** dead zone **-er Gang** back-lash, lost motion, (end) play, dead run(ning) **-es Gewicht** dead weight **-es Kaliber** inoperative pass, dummy pass **-es Material** inert or stable material, neutral or inactive material **-er Punkt** dead center **-er Raum** dead ground, dead space, gap (phot.) **-er Schußwinkel** blind spot **-es Spiel** backlash, lost motion **-e Spitze** dead center **-er Weg** idle movement **-e Windung** idle turn, dead end, dummy turn, dummy spire **-er Winkel** blind angle **-e Zone** skipped or skip distance, blind spot, zone of silence, dead zone **-er Zylinderraum** compression volume (of cylinder)
total complete, total **-er Druckverlust** total head **-e Kraftlinie** *f* line of total force
Total-ausfall *m* total loss **-bewölkung** *f* total cloudiness **-durchgang** *m* total transmission (acoust.)
Totale *f* medium-long shot, full shot (motion picture)
Totalixröhre *f* totalix tube
Total-nutzeffekt *m* over-all efficiency **-verlust** *m* total loss
totbrennen to dead-burn, overburn (lime), shrink (dolomite)
Totbrennen *n* dead-burning
töten to kill, deaden, soften
Totgang *m* lost motion, backlash, end play, free travel
totgar overrefined
totgebrannt dead-burned
Tot-holz *n* deadwood **-lage** *f* dead center, dead position, blind spot (aviation), stagnation point (aerodyn.) **-last** *f* dead load **-lauf** *m* dead travel **-mahlen** *n* disaggregating, milling to break down the structure, overgrinding, overbeating, overmilling **-pressen** to dead-press (explosives)
Totpunkt *m* dead center, blind spot (aviation), stagnation point (aerodyn.), bottom dead center **den Motor über einen oberen ~ hinwegdrehen** to turn the engine past a compression point **höchster ~** top dead center **oberer ~** top (dead) center, firing top center **unterer ~** bottom dead center
Totpunkt-lage *f* dead-center position **-zündung** *f* dead-center ignition
Tot-raum *m* clearance volume, region of silence **-raumspülung** *f* scavenging of the clearance space **-rösten** to dead-roast **-schläger** *m* life preserver **-speicher** *m* permanent store (info proc.)
Tot-wasser *n* dead water **-zeit** *f* dead time, idle time **-zeitverkürzung** *f* shortening of the delay period
Tour *f* turn, revolution **auf Touren** on speed
Touren-belastungskennlinie *f* speed-load characteristic **-dynamo** *n* high frequency tachometer **-konstanz** *f* constancy of speed **-messer** *m* revolution counter, speedometer **-modell** *n* touring model **-konstanz** *f* constancy of speed **-regulierung** *f* speed regulation **-schwankung** *f* speed variation **-zahl** *f* number of revolutions, speed, number of turns, rotative speed **-zähler** *m* revolution counter, speed or counter indicator, tachometer
Tourmaschine *f* rotating block for pouncing
Tournantöl *n* rancid olive oil
Tourniquet *n* tourniquet
T-Profil *n* T section
Trabant *m* satellite, equalizing pulse (TV)
Trabantenstadt *f* satellite town, satelite community center
traben to trot
Tracerchemie *f* tracer chemistry
Trachte *f* wall (hoof), side bar, hanger bar
Trachyt *m* trachyte
Track *m* track (navy) **-auflösungsversuch** *m* split detection **-beginn** *m* track initiation **-bezeichnung** *f* track designation **-verlauf** *m* track history **-zuverlässigkeit** *f* track merit
Traditor *m* traditor
Trafo *m* transformer **-blech** *n* stamping core plate **-wicklung** *f* transformer winding
Tragachse *f* bearing or carrying axle
Tragant-gummi *n* tragacanth **-schleim** *m* tragacanth mucilage
Trag-arm *m* supporting arm or mast **-backe** *f*

guide cheek **-bahre** *f* handbarrow, stretcher, litter **-balken** *m* stringer, balk, supporting beam, girder

Tragband *n* carrying strap, conveyer belt **~ für Luftkabel** cable suspender

tragbar portable **-er Apparat** portable(-telephone) set

Tragbarkeit *f* portability

Trag-bild *n* contact reflection **-blech** *n* dummy sheet, bracket, carrier, support **-bock** *m* bracket **-büchse** *f* cylindrical mask-carrying canister **-bügel** *m* carrying sling, stirrup, gimbal **-deck** *n* supporting surface, wing (aviation) **-deckanzahl** number of planes **-decke** *f* pugging (rough plastering)

Tragdeck-hälfte *f* half-wing **-kompaß** *m* wing compass **-kühler** *m* wing radiator, surface radiator

Tragdraht *m* suspending or suspension wire, lift wire, flying wire, carrying wire

Tragdübel *m* key dowel

Trage *f* stretcher, barrow

träge inert, inactive, sluggish, slow, dull, incipient, idle, lagging, lazy, indolent, neutral **~ ansprechend** sluggish in action, slow (blow) (tape rec.) **~ Sicherung** slow-blowing fuse

Trage-band *n* sling, strap, suspender **-baum** *m* beam, girder, sill **-behälter** *m* carrying case

Tragebene *f* bearing surface

tragecht fast to wear and tear

Tragegurt *m* carrying strap

Trageisen *n* iron handle, lifting handle

Trageleine *f* suspension line (aviation)

tragen to carry, wear, bear, suffer, yield, support, sustain

tragend carrying, primary, supporting, stressed (structures) **-e Außenhaut** skin stressed covering **-er Bauteil** *m* load-bearing member **-e Fläche** land, lifting surface (aerodyn.) **-e Haut** stressed skin

Träger *m* carrier; (Inhaber) holder, bearer; (Institut) responsible body, supporter; (Technik) support, supporting beam; (Pfeiler) pillar; (Eisenlängs~) girder; (Elektr.) carrier; (Chem.) vehicle; girder, beam joist, beam, bracket, carrying agent, truss, stay, arbor, wearer (mask), foundation, bed supporting means, base, vehicle, backing **armierter ~** trussed girder **durchlaufender ~** continuous beam **positiver ~** positive carrier, ion **verdübelter ~** built beam with keys **verstrebter ~** truss **vollwandiger ~** web girder, I-beam girder, tubular or plate girder **zusammengenieteter ~** riveted girder

Träger-absenkung *f* carrier drop **-achse** *f* girder axis

Trägeramplitude *f* carrier amplitude **-abweichung** *f* asymmetrical modulation **-änderung** *f* carrier amplitude regulation

Tragerand *m* rim of bearing surface

Träger-arm *m* jib arm **-auffüllung** *f* carrier replenishment **-balken** *m* girder beam, supporting beam **-beweglichkeit** *f* carrier mobility **-bolzen** *m* bed bolt **-bündel** *n* beams of carriers **-dichte** *f* carrier density **-einbau** *m* carrier injection **-eisen** *n* girder iron

Träger-fähigkeit *f* (carrying) capacity **-fahrzeug** *n* (Astron.) carrier vehicle, booster (spacecraft) **-fernsteuerungssystem** *n* carrier current control **-flansch** *m* flange of a beam **-flugzeug** *n* carrier-based plane **-follen** *pl* supporting foils

Trägerfrequenz *f* carrier frequency (phot.), theory of color **auf Überlagerung der ~ eingestellt** set for zero beat **Unterdrückung der ~** carrier suppression **örtlich überlagerte ~** local carrier

Trägerfrequenz-abstand *m* carrier interval **-abwanderung** *f* carrier shift **-fernmessung** *f* carrier telemetering **-gerät** *n* carrier terminal **-kabel** *f* (Vierfachkabel) carrier (quad) cable **-meßverstärker** *m* carrier wave amplifier **-seite** *f* carrier frequency rating

Trägerfrequenz-spannung *f* carrier-frequency voltage **-sperre** *f* line trap (for powerline carrier) **-telegraphie** *f* carrier-wave telegraphy **-telephonie** *f* carrier telephony **-überlagerer** *m* homodyne **-übertragung** *f* carrier transmission **-verbindung** *f* carrier link **-verfahren** *n* carrier-frequency principle (radio) **-verschiebung** *f* carrier shift **-wellenzug** *m* carrier-frequency wave train

Träger-fuß *m* base of the girder **-generator** *m* carrier generator **-gesteuert** carrier-controlled **-gestein** *n* carrier bed **-gruppe** *f* carrier-borne group

Trageriemen *m* carrying strap

Träger-kaliber *n* girder pass **-lager** *n* set of supporting girders **-lawine** *f* electron (ion) avalanche **-lawinendiode** *f* unidirectional breakdown (avalanche) diode **-leiste** *f* bearing jewel holder **-leistung** *f* carrier power **-leitung** *f* carrier line (teleph.)

trägerlose Decke *f* flat slab

Träger-material *n* column support **-metall** *n* cementing material or agent, binding material, binding constituent, binder **-mittellinie** *f* girder axis **-nachlieferung** *f* carrier support **-papier** *n* body paper **-platte** *f* bearer or carrier plate **-profil** *n* girder section **-punkt** *m* base point **-querschnitt** *m* girder section, cross section of a girder

Träger-rahmen *m* supporting frame **-rakete** *f* booster **-rauschen** *n* carrier noise **-rest** *m* carrier leak **-rost** *m* girder grillage **-schalung** *f* girder mold **-schwelle** *f* summer, beam

Trägerschwingung *f* carrier oscillation **impulsmodulierte ~** carrier-frequency pulse

Träger-seite *f* film base side or face **-spannung** *f* carrier voltage **-sperrende Drossel** carrier isolating choke coil **-sperröhre** *f* carrier-current suppressor **-steg** *m* web or stem of girder **-stern** *m* spider, support **-steuerung** *f* floating carrier control **-stift** *m* center-pin support, pivot or bearing post **-stoff** *m* adsorbing substance **-straße** *f* girder mill train

Trägerstrom *m* carrier (current) **modulierter ~** modulated carrier current **zeitlich veränderlicher ~** wobbled or warbled carrier current

Trägerstrom-fernsprechanlage *f* carrier telephone system **-fernsprechen** *n* carrier-current telephony, carrier telephone **-fernsprechung** *f* carrier telephone system **-kanal** *m* carrier channel **-telegraphie** *f* carrier-current telegraphy **-verstärker** *m* carrier repeater **-vielfachtelephonie** *f* multichannel carrier telephone system **-weg** *m* carrier channel

Träger-stütze *f* bearer strut **-substanz** *f* (f. Emulsionen) emulsion matrix **-unterdrückung** *f* carrier suppression (in quiescent carrier telephony) **-untersuchung** *f* tracer study **-vektor** *m* carrier vector **-verbindung** *f* carrier compound **-verstärker** *m* carrier amplifier **-vorrichtung** *f* scabbard

Träger-walzwerk *n* girder mill, joist rolling mill **-wange** *f* lonitudinal girder **-wegtastung** *f* carrier gating, carrier suppression, carrier interruption (in synchronizing work) **-weise** *f* fitting (how to wear) **-wellblech** *n* load-bearing corrugated plate

Trägerwelle *f* carrier wave **getastete ~** interrupted continuous wave **unterdrückte ~** suppressed or eliminated carrier wave (elec.)

Träger-wellenzug *m* carrier wave train **-zusatz** *m* reinsertion of carrier

Trage-sattel *m* pack saddle **-schiene** *f* supporting rail (harness) **-wert** *m* depreciated value, wear and tear **-zeit** *f* stipulated period of wear (of clothing)

tragfähig able to support load, load bearing

Tragfähigkeit *f* bearing strength, carrying capacity, supporting or load capacity, safe load, bearing capacity, productiveness, burden, tonnage, lifting power, buoyancy, lift, yield **~ beim Bruch** ultimate bearing resistance

Trag-feder *f* frame spring, bearing spring, wagon or car spring **-festigkeit** *f* breaking strength, ultimate strength

Tragfläche *f* supporting surface, bearing(-area) surface, lifting surface (aviation), wing, airfoil, deck **~ der Gewindeflanke** bearing face of thread

Tragflächen-abstand *m* wing gap (aviation) **-belastung** *f* wing loading **-haut** *f* wing skin **-holm** *m* wing spar **-inhalt** *m* wing area **-krümmung** *f* wing bow (aviation) **-kühler** *m* wing radiator **-profil** *n* airfoil section

Tragflächen-sehne *f* wing chord **-stiel** *m* interwing or interplane strut **-strebe** *f* interplane strut **-tiefe** *f* wing depth **-umriß** *m* contour of wings **-zelle** *f* wing cell

Tragflügel *m* airfoil wing, airplane wing **-befestigung** *f* wing fastening **-ende** *n* wing tip **-gerippe** *n* wing structure **-hinterkante** *f* trailing edge of wing **-holm** *m* wing spar **-kompaß** *m* wing compass **-pfeilform** *f* positive sweep-back **-pfeilung** *f* sweep of wing

Tragflügelprofil *n* airfoil **gewölbtes ~** cambered airfoil

Tragfuß *m* foot, support, base of the girder

Traggas *n* buoyant, lifting or supporting gas **-gewicht** *n* weight of lifting or inflation **-inhalt** *m* lifting-gas content or capacity **-zelle** *f* gas bag

Trag-gerüst *n* support, rack, carrying, frame, supporting framework, supporting tissue **-geschirr** *n* carrying strap **-gestell** *n* supporting structure or frame **-gitter** *n* supporting grid or grate **-gleitfeder** *f* frame spring **-griff** *m* handle **-gurt** *m* suspension band, harness, shoulder strap

Trägheit *f* (langsam) sluggishness; (Phys.) inertia; (Chem.) inactivity; inertness, idleness, slowness, laziness, lassitude, lag, persistence (of eye or retina), time lag **~ des Instruments** sluggishness

trägheitsarm poor in inertia, low-inertia

Trägheitsellipsoid *n* ellipsoid of inertia **-frei** inertialess **-halbmesser** *m* radius of gyration **-kraft** *f* inertia or mass force **-kreis** *m* circle of inertia

Trägheitskreisel *m*, **integrierender ~** inertial reference integrating gyro (IRIG)

trägheitslos inertialess

Trägheits-mittelpunkt *m* center of inertia **-moment** *n* moment of inertia **-navigation** *f* inertial navigation **-produkt** *n* product of inertia **-radius** *m* radius of gyration **-starter** *m* inertia starter **-vermögen** *n* inertia **-zentrum** *n* center of inertia

Trag-holm *m* wing spar **-isolator** *m* support insulator **-kabel** *n* lift or flying wire **-kasten** *m* carrying case **-kette** *f* suspension chain, carrying chain **-konsole** *f* bracket, cleat **-konstruktion** *f* supporting structure **-kopf** *m* supporting head (front gudgeon) **-korb** *m* scuttle, dosser **-körper** *m* outer cover, supporting body **-kraft** *f* supporting power, carrying or bearing capacity, tractive or lifting force (magnet), load, capacity **-kräftig** capable of supporting **-kraftspitze** *f* portable power pump

Tragkranz *m* lintel ring, mantle ring **-säule** *f* mantle column (of blast furnace), supporting or furnace column

Trag-kreuz *n* spider **-lager** *n* journal bearing, supporting or angular bearing **-länge** *f* bearing length **-lasche** *f* suspension clip **-last** *f* burden, load, carrying capacity **-leine** *f* shroud line, suspension line **-leiste** *f* mounting (strip) **-linse** *f* supporting lens **-mantel** *m* support-load distributing jacket, ring, or band, outer casing **-mast** *m* suspension tower, pole **-moment** *n* limit moment **-mulde** *f* hod

Trag-nabe *f* supporting nave or hub **-pfahl** *m* supporting or bearing pile **-platte** *f* mounting (plate) **-pratze** *f* supporting bracket **-rad** *n* trailing wheel **-rahmen** *m* supporting frame **-randglas** *n* lenticular lens **-riemen** *m* carrying strap **-riemenbefestigungsknopf** *m* neck strap lug **-ring** *m* cable or jumper ring, bearing ring **-rippe** *f* supporting wing rib **-rohr** *n* pylon or cabane bracing, bracing tube **-rolle** *f* bearing pulley, bogie wheel **-rost** *m* supporting grate, grate frame, steel structure

Trag-säule *f* supporting column, pillar **-scheibe** *f* supporting or framework disk **-schere** *f* shank (of casting ladle) **-schicht** *f* basis **-schiene** *f* bearing rail **-schirm** *m* recovery parachute (missiles) **-schlepp** *m* pick-a-back towing **-schlepper** *m* implement carrier **-schnur** *f* strain cord **-schraube** *f* lifter propeller **-schrauber** *m* autogiro, gyroplane **-schwelle** *f* supporting sill

Tragseil *n* suspending wire, messenger wire, suppoerting or suspension strand **-klemme** *f* messenger wire clamp, guy clamp **-schelle** *f* messenger wire clamp

Trag-sockel *m* supporting base or socket **-spindel** *f* carrying spindle **-stab** *m* supporting member, main or tensile reinforcing bar **-stange** *f* supporting rod, carrier or bearer bar **-stutze** *f* supporting bracket, stay, or prop **-stützlager** *n* thrust bearing, angular bearing, combination radial

Tragsystem, parallaktisches ~ der Fernrohr-

montierung equatorial system of carriers of the telescope mounting

Trag-tasche *f* carrying case **-teil** *n* supporting structure **-tiefe** *f* bearing depth **-tier** *n* pack animal **-vermögen** *n* carrying capacity, lifting capacity **-vorrichtung** *f* supporting frame, stowing device for bombs **-walzenroller** *m* transportation roller **-wand** *f* lift truss, supporting wall **-weite** *f* range, significance, bearings, importance

Trag-werk *n* cell(ule) (aviation), wing-truss structure, wing unit, wing assembly, underframe, tapered wings, pugging (rough plastering), main plane structure, wing assembly (aviat.) **-werkzeug** *n* holding tackle **-winkel** *m* supporting angle **-zahlen** *pl* load capacities

Tragzapfen *m* supporting journal, pivot, pin, trunnion, lifting lug **-reibung** *f* journal-bearing friction

Tragzelle *f* cellule (aviation), wing-truss structure

Traille *f* baluster

Trainieren *n* training, understressing (of industrial work materials)

Trainingsflugzeug *n* trainer airplane

Trajekt *n* ferry bridge, moving ferry

Trajektorie *f* air trajectory, trajectory

Trajektoriengurt *m* trajectory band

Trajektschiff *n* ferryboat, railway ferry

Traktionskoeffizient *m* traction coefficient

Traktor *m* tractor ~ **mit Ladefläche** tractor with platform

Traktoranhängevorrichtung *f* tractor hitch ~ **für Ährenmähmaschine zur Bedienung vom Traktorführer** one-man header control tractor hitch ~ **für Düngerstreuer** tractor hitch for manure spreader ~ **für Garbenbinder** tractor hitch for grain binder ~ **für Getreidedrillmaschine** tractor hitch for grain drill ~ **für Grasmäher** tractor hitch for mower ~ **für kombinierte Mäh- und Dreschmaschine** tractor hitch for harvester thresher ~ **für Maispflückmaschine** tractor hitch for corn picker ~ **für Stoßbinder** tractor hitch for push binder ~ **für Wagen** tractor hitch for wagon

Traktor-aufbrecherpflug *m* tractor grub breaker plow **-binder** *m* tractor binder **-drillmaschine** *f* tractor drill

Traktoren-gehäuse *n* tractor housing **-keil** (Klampen) tractor cleats **-triebstoff** *m* tractor fuel, tractor oil **-zug** *m* tractor platoon

Traktor-pflug *m* tractor plow **-scheibenegge** *f* tractor disk harrow **-scheibenpflug** *m* tractor disk plow

Traktrix *f* tractrix

Traljenschott *n* batten and space bulkhead

Trambahn *f* tramway

Trambus *m* trolleybus

Tramen *m* tie beam

Trampdampfer *m* tramp steamer

Trampel-pfad *m*, **-weg** *m* beaten path or track

Tran *m* fish oil

Tranchierbesteck *n* carving knife and fork

tranen to oil (skins)

tränen-erregend tear-exciting **-gas** *n* tear gas **-reiz** *m* irritation of the eyes, lachrymatory action **-reizend** lachrymatory **-stoff** *m* lachrymator, tear gas

Tran-füllung *f* train-stuffing **-gerbung** *f* fish oil tannage

tranig like fish oil

Tränk-anlage *f* watering device **-apparat** *m* soaking apparatus

Tränke *f* watering place

tränken to soak, saturate, water, steep, imbue, impregnate, inject **mit Teeröl** ~ to creosote **mit Kupfervitriol** ~ to boucherize **mit Zinkchlorid** ~ to burnettize

Tränk-gefäß *n*, **-kessel** *m* impregnating tank **-lack** *m* impregnating varnish **-masse** *f* impregnating compound **-mittelförderpumpe** *f* pump for introducing impregnating fluid **-öl** *n* impregnating oil

Tränkung *f* impregnation, injection, soaking, saturation, watering, preservation, doping

Tränkungsmittel *n* impregnating preparation

Tränkvorrichtung *f* impregnating device

Tranraffinieranlage *f* fish-oil refining plant

Transaktion *f* transaction

Transchmiere *f* daubing

Transduktor *m* magnetic amplifier, transductor

Transfiguration *f* transfiguration

Transfluxor *m* transfluxor

Transformation *f* transformation

Transformations-glied *n* matching pad **-konstante** *f* transformation or disintegration constant **-leitung** *f* transformation line **-matrix** *f* matrix of the transformation **-rechnung** *f*, **numerische** numerical transform calculus **-röhrenwicklung** *f* concentric windings **-scheibenwicklung** *f* sandwich windings **-stück** *n* transforming section **-zylinderwicklung** *f* concentric windings

Transformator *m* transformer ~ **mit geschlossenem Eisenkern** closed-core transformer ~ **mit offenem Eisenkern** open-core transformer ~ **mit geschlossenem magnetischem Kreise** closed-core transformer ~ **mit Luftstromkühlung** air-blast transformer ~ **für gleichbleibenden Strom** constant-current transformer **mit Transformatoren gekoppelt** transformer-coupled **abgeschirmter** ~ screened transformer **abgestimmter** ~ tuned or resonance transformer **ruhender** ~ static or stationary transformer, inoperative transformer **spannungserniedrigender** ~ step-down transformer

Transformator-anzapfung *f* transformer tap **-ausgangswicklung** *f* transformer output winding

Transformatoren-bank *f* bank of transformers (electr.) **-blech** *m* transformer stamping or sheet, transformer lamination **-kessel** *m* transformer tank **-kuppelung** *f* transformer coupling **-öl** *n* transformer oil **-säule** *f* transformer pillar **-station** *f* transformer substation **-strom** *m* transformer current **-wagen** *m* transformer truck

Transformator-gefäß *n* transformer tank **-gehäuse** *n* transformer shell, transformer container or tank **-kern** *m* transformer core **-kippgerät** *n* transformer sweep unit **-kurve** *f* amplification curve of a transformer **-leistung** *f* transformer capacity

transformatorlose Gegentaktstufe *f* single-ended push-pull stage

Transformator-ofen *m* transformer furnace **-schwerpunktsstation** *f* load-center unit substation **-spannung** *f* transformer voltage **-übersetzung** *f* transformer ratio, turn ratio **-verstärker** *m* transformer amplifier **-wicklung** *f* transformer winding

transformieren to transform **abwärts ~** to step down **aufwärts ~** to step up

Transformierung *f* transformation

Transimpedanz *f* transfer characteristic

Transinformationsfluß *m*, **mittlerer ~ einer Nachrichtenverbindung** average transinformation rate per time

Transinformationsgehalt *m* transinformation content

Transistor *m* transistor **-bestückt** transistorized **-frequenzband** transistor-circuit bandwidth **-verstärker** *m* transistor amplifier

Transit *m* transit **-hafen** *m* port of transit **-lager** *n* bonded warehouse

Transitivität *f* transitivity

transitorisch-e Interimskonten suspense accounts **-er Kurzschlußwechselstrom** transient three-phase short-circuit current **-e Längs-EMK** direct-axis transient electromotive force

Transitronschaltung *f* transitron circuit

Transitstromkreis *m* via circuit, viaduct

Transkonduktanz *f* transconductance

transkribieren to transcribe

transkristallin transcrystalline

Transkristallisation *f* transcrystallization

Translation *f* slippage, translation (cryst.)

Translations-bewegung *f* translational motion **-ebene** *f*, **-fläche** *f* translation plane, slip plane (cryst.)

Translationsgitter *n*, **raumzentriertes ~** body-centered cubic lattice

Translations-gruppe *f* group of translations **-linie** *f* slipband **-streifung** *f* slipbands, translation banding, translation gliding striae, crystal ridges **-zustandssumme** *f* translational partition function

Translator *m* translator

Translatorenschlüssel *m* translator key

translatorisch translatory

Translokationsdiastase *f* translocation diastase

Transmission *f* transmission, drive, belt, gearing

Transmissions-anlage *f* power-transmission plant **-antrieb** *m* transmission drive, line-shaft drive **-dynamometer** *m* belt dynamometer **-gliederkette** *f* transmission chain **-lager** *n* line-shaft bearing **-leder** *n* belting leather **-öl** *n* transmission lubricant or oil **-organ** *n* transmission agent **-pumpe** *f* pump rig **-querschnitt** *m* transmission cross section **-rad** *n* driving pulley **-riemen** *m* driving belt

Transmissions-scheibe *f* bull wheel **-seil** *n* transmission rope **-strang** *m* line shaft **-treibkette** *f* line-shaft drive chain, power drive chain, power-transmitting chain, transmission-power drive chain **-vorgelege** *n* transmission gear **-welle** *f* transmission shaft, driving shaft, connecting shaft, gear shaft

Transmutation *f* transmutation

transozeanisch transoceanic

Transparent *n* (f. Richtungsanzeiger) destination screen

transparent transparent, diaphanous

Transparent-ausrüstung *f* transparent finish **-bild** *n* transparent diapositive **-papierdruck** *m* diaphany

Transparenz *f* transparency, transmittancy, transmissivity (for light) **-schwankungen** *pl* modulus of transmission (film)

transponieren to transpose

Transponierungs-empfang *m* transposition reception, heterodyne reception **-empfänger** *m* superheterodyne receiver, superheterodyne **-steilheit** *f* slope or mutual conductance

Transport *m* transport, transportation, carrier, conveyance, convoy, transfer, haulage, forwarding, shipment

transportabel portable

transportabler Reaktor package reactor

Transport-achse *f* feed roll **-anhänger** *m* transport trailer

Transportanlage *f* conveying machinery, haulage equipment, conveyer plant **~ mit Schraubengewinde** screw conveyer

Transport-band *n* conveyer belt, conveyer belting **-becher** *m* conveying or transport bucket **-befehl** *m* movement table, transfer instruction (comput) **-behälter** *m* container **-bewegung** *f* transport movement **-brücke** *f* transport bridge **-daumen** *m* spacing cam **-einnahmen** *pl* transport recoveries **-einrichtung** *f* transport accessory device or equipment

Transporter *m* transport plane

Transporteur *m* transporter, conveyer, carrier, forwarder, protractor, vernier **-antrieb** *m* conveyor drive

transportfähig transportable

Transport-fähigkeit *f* forwarding capability **-fahrzeug** *n* hauling equipment **-filz** *m* conveyor band felt **-flasche** *f* carboy **-flugzeug** *n* transport airplane **-gabel** *f* conveyor fork **-gaskühler** *m* transport gas cooler **-gasverfahren** *n* inert gas method **-gefäß** *n* transport vessel **-gerät** *n* conveying implement, transport utensil, carrying apparatus **-glied** *n* transport element (comput.) **-gut** *n* goods to be conveyed **-hebel** *m* spacing pawl

transportieren to transport, convey, haul, transfer, forward, ship

Transport-karre *f* transport truck **-kasten** *m* transportation box, carrying case **-kette** *f* transfer chain, conveyer chain **-koffer** *m* packing case, trunk **-kontrolle** *f* transport check (comput.) **-kosten** *pl* cartage expenses **-loch** *n* feed hole **-makler** *m* forwarding agent **-mechanismus** *m* feed mechanism, conveyer mechanism **-mittel** *n* means of transportation, means of conveyance, material-handling equipment

Transport-lattentuch *n* lattice running **-loch** *n* (Fernschreiber) sprocket hole, feed hole **-öffnung** *f* transfer port **-pfanne** *f* transfer ladle, bull ladle **-problem** *n* handling problem, conveying problem **-rad** *n* transport cycle **-riemen** *m* conveyer belt **-rinne** *f* feeder trough **-rolle** *f* driving roller **-rollgang** *m* roller transporter

Transport-satz *m* transport theorem **-schaden** *m* damage in transit **-schiene** *f* sprocket **-schiff** *n* troop-transport ship **-schnecke** *f* worm conveyer screw, feed screw **-sperre** *f* embargo **-spesen** *pl* shipping charges

Transportspindel *f* screw drive **~ für Rücklauf** return spiral

Transport-system *n* material-handling system, conveying system, transportation system **-tisch** *m* feed table **-trommel** *f* intermittent sprocket, supply reel or spool **-übersicht** *f* transportation table **-verbot** *n* embargo **-verschluß** *m* temporary end sleeve

Transportwagen *m* transfer car or truck, car, wheel-barrow, hand trailer, cart, dolly ~ **mit Rungen** dolly truck

Transportwagenschaltwerk *n* carriage feed

Transport-walze *f* carrier roller **-weg** *m* line of communication **-welle** *f* shaft for table movement mechanism **-wesen** *n* transportation **-wirkungsgrad** transport efficiency **-wirkungsquerschnitt** *m* transport cross-section

Transschall . . . transonic . . .

transsonisch transsonic **-er Windkanal** *m* transsonic wind channel

Transurane *pl* transuranic elements

transversal transverse **-e Bindung** cross linkage

Transversal-drehung *f* rolling **-feld** *n* transverse field, cross field

Transversalitätsbedingung *f* transversality condition

Transversal-maßstab *m* coordinate reading scale, transverse scale **-methode** *f* variable-area method **-schermaschine** *f* cross-shearing machine **-schieferung** *f* cleavage **-schwingung** *f* transverse vibration **-welle** *f* transverse wave

transzendent transcendental

Trap *m* trap (trans.)

Trapez *n* suspension band or bar, trapeze, trapezium, trapezoid **-belastung** *f* trapezoidal load **-effekt** *m* keystone effect **-fachwerkträger** *m* trapeze superstructure **-fehler** *m* keystone, trapezoidal distortion **-flügel** *m* tapered wing

Trapez-gewinde *f* trapezoidal thread, acme screw thread, buttress(-type) thread **-gewindespindel** *f* buttress **-joch** *n* beveled track section

trapezoedrisch trapezohedral

Trapezoid *n* trapezoid

Trapez-rahmen *m* frame of trapezoidal shape **-raster** *m* trapezoidal raster **-regel** *f* trapezoidal rule **-ring** *m* trapezoidal washer **-stahl** *m* trapezoid tool **-verzeichnung** *f* trapezium distortion **-welle** *f* trapezoidal wave

Trappresse *f* trap press (press with two cylinders operating with different pressures)

Truss *m* trass, volcanic tuff

Traßbeton *m* trass concrete

Trasse *f* line ~ **festlegen** to plot the route of the future pipeline

Trassier-band *n* tracing tape **-buch** *n* survey book (teleph.)

trassieren to lay out on the ground, trace

Trassierleine *f* carpenter's (chalk) line

Trassierung *f* location ~ (Trassenwahl) selection of route, route selection

Traß-mischung *f* trass mixture **-mörtel** *m* trass mortar

Tratte *f* bill of exchange, draft

Trauben-blei *n* pyromorphite, mimetite **-förmig** botryoidal **-öl** *n* grape oil **-zählung** *f* cluster counting **-zucker** *m* glucose, dextrose

traubenförmig grape-like

traubig botryoidal

Traufe *f* eaves ~ (Dachrinne) down spout, gutter

träufeln to drip

Traufenwaschmaschine *f* spray washing machine

Traufplatte *f*, **bleierne** ~ eaves lead

Trauf-rinne *f* gutter **-stein** *m* gutter stone

Traverse *f* girder, traverse, crosstie rod, transom, crossover, bar, traverse guide arm (artil.), knee clamp **einseitige** ~ extension arm

Traversen-bolzen *m* traverse bolt **-gleitstück** *n* traverse glide **-gleitstück** *n* traversing saddle

Treber *pl* brewer's or distiller's grains, draff, spent grain **-dampftrockenapparat** *m* steam draff drier **-presser** *m* lees presser **-transporteur** *m* bagasse carrier **-trockenapparat** *m* draff-drying apparatus **-trockner** *m* slop runner

trecken to haul

Trecker *m* tractor

Trecksäge *f* crosscut saw, pit or trim saw

Treff-bereich *m* space within firing range **-bild** *n* impact diagram (firing) **-dreieck** *n* future-position triangle

treffen to strike, hit, meet, hit the target

treffend striking

Treffentfernung *f* future range

Treffer *m* hit (firing), wobbler, direct hit, great success ~ **erhalten** to receive or suffer hits ~ **verzeichnen** to register hits

Treffer-ablage *f* miss distance **-bild** *n* plotted hits (firing) **-dreieck** *n* future-position triangle

Treffergebnis *n* score

Treffer-methode *f* method of correct associations **-raum** *m* zone of dispersion **-theorie** *f* target theory **-wahrscheinlichkeit** *f* probability of hitting (hits)

Trefferzahl *f* number of impacts or shocks

Treff-fläche *f* impact area, target area **-genauigkeit** *f* accuracy of fire **-höhe** *f* altitude of target **-höhenwinkel** *m* angle of sight **-kartenentfernung** *f* horizontal range to target

Treffplattendeuteron *f* target deuteron

Treffpunkt *m* point of impact, objective point, future position, meeting point, rendezvous **-entfernung** *f* range of target **-höhe** *f* altitude of point of impact

Treffseitenwinkel *m* future bearing

treffsicher accurately aimed **-es Bombenabwerfen** spot bombing (aviation)

Treffsicherheit *f* accuracy of fire

Treffwahrscheinlichkeit *f* expectancy or probability of hitting

Treffweite *f* focal length (of electrons)

T-Regler *m* T-type section attenuator

Treib-achse *f* driving or live axle **-anker** *m* sea anchor, drag anchor **-apparat** *m* propeller gear **-arbeit** *f* cupellation, embossed mark **-asche** *f* cupel ashes **-bake** *f* floating beacon **-balken** *m* floating boom, floating fender **-bolzen** *m* drift bolt (or pin) **-brühe** *f* nearly exhausted tan-liquor **-dampfpumpe** *f* booster pump **-eis** *n* floating ice, floe, drift ice

treiben to drive; (Maschine) drive, work, operate; (in Bewegung setzen) put in motion, propel; (Metall) emboss, (en)chase, raise; (läutern) refine, cupel; (drängen) induce, prompt; (betreiben) practise; (Handel) carry on; force, move, urge on, impel, sublime, hammer (metals), chase, expand (cakes of coke), rush, swell, force through, float, drift, shoot, circulate, sprout, ferment **zu etwas ~** to prompt

Treiben *n* cupeling, expansion, swelling

treibend motive, adrift, driving (force) **-es Kegelrad** bevel pinion **-es Rad** pinion **-es Wrack** derelict

Treiber *m* driver; (Technik) propeller; refiner, pusher, picker (weaving), drift punch, propelling means **-röhretransformator** *m* driver-tube transformer

Treiberimpuls *m* driving pulse

Treiberscheinung *f* appearance of expansion

Treiber-signal *n* driving signal **-stufe** *f* exciter, driver **-system** *n* driver system

Treib-fahne *f* (Zettelrohrpost) ticket sailing device **-fäustel** *m* sledge hammer, striking hammer, drilling hammer **-fläche** *f* (Zettelrohrpost) sailing surface (on ticket) **-form** *f* chasing or embossing tool

Treibgas *n* fuel gas, power gas, fixed gas, wood gas, propellent gas **-armaturen** *pl* propelling-gas valves and fittings **-motor** *m* gasoline engine, wood-gas engine

Treib-hammer *m* chasing hammer **-haus** *n* hothouse greenhouse **-hebel** *m* driving lever **-herd** *m* refining hearth of furnace **-holz** *n* driftwood **-keil** *m* taper(-sunk) key **-keilverbindung** *f* driving-key coupling **-kette** *f* driving chain **-kolben** *m* driving piston **-kraft** *f* motive or propelling power **-kugel** *f* driving ball (hammer) **-kurbel** *f* driving crank

Treib-ladung *f* propellent charge, propellant **-leine** *f* floating line or rope **-mine** *f* floating mine **-mittel** *n* propellent charge, propellant, driver, driving motor, motive fluid or substance, fuel, working fluid (of vapor pump) **-mittelpumpe** *f* vapor pump **-ofen** *m* cupeling or refining furnace **-öl** *n* fuel oil, Diesel oil **-ölförderung** *f* oil feed **-probe** *f* cupping test **-prozeß** *m* refining cupellation **-rad** *n* pinion, driving gear, flywheel, drive wheel

Treibriemen *m* driving belt, transmission belt **-fett** *f* belt grease **-rückvorrichtung** *f* belt shifter

Treib-richtung *f* set, direction of drift (aviation) **-ring** *m* thrust ring **-riß** *m* expansion crack **-rolle** *f* driving roller or pulley **-sand** *m* drifting sand

Treibsatz *m* charge (of rocket), rocket composition **gehäuseverbundener ~** case-bonded charge

Treib-satzprofil *n* charge shape **-scheibe** *f* driving pulley or shaft **-scherben** *m* cupel **-schraube** *f* self-tapping screw, pusher screw, propeller **-sitz** *m* driving fit, tight fit, force fit, drive fit **-spiegel** *m* cartridge-case base **-stange** *f* connecting rod **-stock** *m* drift

Treibstoff *m* fuel, propellant, engine fuel **-behälter** *m* fuel tank **-durchflußmesser** *m* fuel flowmeter **-durchsatz** *m* fuel flowrate **-einspritzdüse** *f* fuel-injection nozzle **-fassungsvermögen** *n* fuel tankage **-förderung** *f* fuel feed **-komponente** *f* propellant ingredient **-lager** *n* fuel dump **-regelventil** *n* propellant control valve **-schnellablaß** *m* fuel dumping, fuel jettisoning **-zuladung** *f* propellent charge

Treib-strahl *m* power or driving jet, reactive jet **-welle** *f* cardan axle **-werkssteuerung** *f* engine or power-plant controls **-werkzeug** *n* chasing tool, chisel **-wirkung** *f* propulsive effect **-zapfen** *m* crank or driving pin **-zapfengeschoß** *n* thrust trunnion projectile

Treidelleine *f* towing line, tow rope

treideln to tow, track, tow boats from land

Treideln *n* towing (navy), haulage

Treidelweg *m* trackway, towpath

Treil *n* tow line, tracking rope

Trema *n* diaeresis

Tremolit *m* tremolite

Tremolostimmung *f* tremolo effect

Trenn-abschnitt *m* line of breach **-anstalt** *f* intermediate station (teleph.)

trennbar separable

Trennbarkeit *f* detectability

Trenn-batterie *f* spacing battery **-blatt** *n* septum **-brett** *n* dividing or partition wall **-bügel** *m* break link **-bühne** *f* separating dam **-dose** *f* terminal **-ebene** *f* junction (plane)

trennen to separate; (techn., chem.) sever, put asunder; (teilen) divide; (lösen) detach, disjoin; (isolieren) isolate, segregate; (auflösen) dissolve, break up; (telef.) cut off, disconnect; cut, release, part, decompose, dissociate, sunder, resolve **eine Verbindung ~** to disconnect, break or take down a connection

Trennen *n* disconnecting, disconnection

Trennendverschluß *m* cable termination

Trenner *m* garder, cobber, isolator, isolating switch

Trenn-erdungsschalter *m* earthing isolating switch **-fähigkeit** *f* selectivity **-faktor** *m* separating factor **-festigkeit** *f* separating strength, static crack strength **-filter** *m* dividing filter, separating filter **-fläche** *f* joint face **-flüssigkeit** *f* sealing liquid **-frequenz** *f* cutoff frequency **-fuge** *f* separating line, parting line, plane of separation **-genauigkeit** *f* cleaning efficiency **-gitter** *n* (Entaschung) screen grid **-glied** *n* separative element **-güte** *f* separate efficiency

Trenn-holm *m* connecting or bolting longeron (missiles) **-hub** *m* isolating motion **-isolator** *m* double-groove or test insulator **-kante** *f* separating edge **-karte** *f* guide card (in an index) **-klinke** *f* cutoff jack, break jack, disconnecting jack, transfer jack **-kolonne** *f* fractionating column **-kontakt** *m* break contact, spacing contact **-laschen** *pl* isolating links, disconnecting links **-linie** *f* separating line, parting line

Trenn-messer *n* cutting knife **-mittel** *n* parting compound **-netzwerk** *n* dividing network **-nut** *f* cutting groove **-plattenumformer** *m* baffle converter (microwaves) **-punkt** *m* jettison point **-relais** *n* cutoff relay **-rohr** *n* separation column **-röhre** *f* separator tube, isolating tube, buffer tube **-schalter** *m* cutoff key, splitting key, isolating switch, circuit breaker, disconnector, disconnection switch, isolator **-scharf** selective

Trennschärfe *f* selectivity (radio), discriminator **~ eines Filters** filter discrimination

Trenn-schärfereglung *f* automatic band-width selection **-schicht** *f* interface **-schichtmessung** *f* interface measurement **-schiene** *f* dividing strip **-schleifen** *n* cutting-off **-schleifmaschine** *f* abrasive and cutting-off machine **-schleuder** *f* centrifuge separator **-schnitt** *m* cross section **-schott** *n* terminal wall **-schutzschalter** *m* earth leakage circuit breaker

Trenn-seite *f* spacing position **-sicherung** *f* switch fuse **-spant** *m* dividing wall **-stange** *f* test pole **-stecker** *m* disconnect plug **-steg** *m* separating web

Trennstelle *f* dismantling point, disconnecting point, testing point ~ **mit Dichtpackung** packed joint

Trenn-stellung *f* spacing position **-stöpsel** *m* infinity plug **-streifen** *m* disconnecting strip (teleph.)

Trennstrom *m* spacing current ~ **senden** to space

Trenn-stromröhre *f* spacing valve (teleg.) **-stück** *n* separator **-stufe** *f* buffer(-stage) isolator, separator stage **-stützpunkt** *m* test pole **-symbol** *n* separator (info proc.) **-taste** *f* cutoff key, disconnecting knob or key **-transformator** *m* isolating transformer **-umschalter** *m* double-throw disconnecting switch

Trennung *f* (s. a. trennen) separation; (techn., chem.) severance, disconnection; severing, breaking, parting, isolation, decomposition, selection, filtering, sorting (of ions in mass spectrometer) **sofortige** ~ quick release **verzögerte** ~ slow release **vorzeitige** ~ premature disconnection

Trennungs-apparat *m* separator **-bahnhof** *m* junction **-ebene** *f* division plane, parting force **-entschädigung** *f* separation allowance **-erzeugnis** *n* product of separation **-faktor** *m* separation or fractionating factor **-festigkeit** *f* breaking strength **-fläche** *f* interface, parting or cleavage plane, surface of separation **-fuge** *f* separation joint, expansion joint **-grad** *m* efficiency of separation **-kontakt** *m* spacing (break) contact

Trennungslinie *f* dividing line, parting line, line of demarcation, boundary **Winkel an der** ~ angle of repose

Trennungs-methode *f* method of separation **-mittel** *n* means of separation **-netz** *n* isolation network **-platte** *f* diaphragm, baffle plate **-punkt** *m* discontinuity point, point of separation (aerodyn.) **-säule** *f* stripping column **-schicht** *f* layer of separation **-strich** *m* line of demarcation **-stufenkaskade** *f* cascade of separating units

Trennungs-verfahren *n* separation process **-vermögen** *n* selectivity **-vorgang** *m* separation process **-wand** *f* partition wall, dividing wall **-wärme** *f* heat of separation or decomposition **-werk** *n* dividing wall **-wichte** *f* density of separation

Trenn-ventil *n* separating valve **-verfahren** *n* separate (sanitary) system **-verstärker** *m* isolation amplifier, buffer **-wand** *f* dividing wall, partition **-werkzeug** *n* cutting off or parting tool **-wichte** *f* specific gravity of separation **-widerstand** *m* isolating resistor **-wirkung** *f* selectivity capacity **-zeichen** *n* cutoff signal (teleph.) **-zeit** *f* splitting time

Trense *f* worming, worm, filler, snaffle, lapping

trensen to worm

Trensen-adernpaar *n* worming pair **-doppelader** *f* worming pair **-gebiß** *n* snaffle bit **-zügel** *m* snaffle rein

Trepanatorium *n* bone drill (med.)

Treppe *f* stairs, steps, staircase **einläufige** ~ single-flight stairs **freitragende** ~ overhanging stairs, fliers **gebrochene** ~ stairs with landing places or with broken center line **gerade** ~ flight of stairs

Treppen-absatz *m* stair landing **-aufzug** *m* staircase lift **-belag** *m* step planking **-beleuchtungsautomat** *m* automatic device for lighting of staircases **-beschlag** *m* staircase fitting **-boden** *m* landing **-flucht** *f* flight of steps

treppenförmig in the form of stairs, stepped, echeloned, terraced **-es Absetzen** racking back

Treppen-funktion *f* step function **-geländer** *n* railing, banister, string wall **-haus** *n* staircase, stair well **-hausautomat** *n* automatic staircase lighting switch **-lichtzeitschalter** *m* staircase lighting time switch

Treppenrost *m* step grate **-feuerung** *f* furnace with stepped grate **-generator** *m* step-grate producer

Treppen-schalter *m* tumbler switch **-seitenstück** *n* stair horse **-signal** *n* gray signal (TV) **-sohle** *f* sleeper of stairs **-spannung** *f* staircase waveform **-stoß** *m* lap joint **-stufe** *f* stair **-verwerfung** *f* step fault **-vorrost** *m* primary step grate **-wange** *f* stair stringer

treppenweise in echelon, in depth

Treppenwicklung *f* stepped winding

Tresor *m* safe (deposit), treasury **-stahl** *m* steel for making safes or vaults

Tress *m* metal twist (usually of woven copper or brass wire)

Tresse *f* lace, trimming card, hawser

Tret-anlasser *m* kick starter **-dynamo** *m* pedal dynamo

Tretlager und Tretlagerteile bottom bracket bearings and parts

treten to tread, step **in Erscheinung** ~ to appear

Tret-gebläse *n* foot bellows or blower **-generator** *m* pedal generator (radio) **-kontakt** *m* treading contact **-kurbel** *f* foot pedal, treadle **-maschine** *f* pedal-operated machine **-motor** *m* pedal-operated generator **-rad** *n* treading wheel **-satz** *m* foot generator (elec.), pedal-operated generating unit **-schalter** *m* foot switch **-vorrichtung** *f* treadle arrangement

treu true, faithful, loyal **-e Wiedergabe** faithful reproduction

Treue der Wiedergabe fidelity of reproduction

Trevelyanischer mechanischer Oszillator Trevelyan rocker

Triakisoktaeder *n* triakisoctahedron

Triangulation *f* triangulation ~ **aus winkeltreuen Punkten** triangulation from equal angle points **terrestrische** ~ ground triangulation

Triangulations-netz *n* triangulation net **-punkt** *m* triangulation point, trigonometric point

Triangulierung *f* triangulation

Triangulierungsballon *m* triangulation balloon

Trias *f* Trias, triassic formation

triassisch triassic

Triäthylamin *n* triethylamine

Treu-händer *m* trustee **-handgesellschaft** *f* trust company

tribasisch (dreibasisch) tribasic

Tribrommethan *n* tribromomethane, bromoform

Tribüne *f* stand, tribune

Trichit *m* fibrous crystal, capillary crystal, fibriform hairlike crystal

Trichlor-äthylen *n* trichloroethylene **-essigsäure** *f* trichloracetic acid **-ethylen** *n* trichlorethylene

Trichter *m* funnel; (Aufgabe~) feeding hopper; (Metall) down gate; cone, hopper, gate, tun dish, horn, crater, bell (in welding tubes), shell hole, funnel cloud (meteor.), trumpet, loudspeaker **aufgewundener ~** twisted or curled exponential (loud-speaker) horn **gefalteter ~** folded exponential horn **rohrförmiger ~** tube funnel **toter ~** dead cone

Trichter-antenne *f* funnel-shaped antenna, funnel- or horn-type antenna **-auslauf** *m* hopper outlet **-bohrer** *m* funnel-shaped auger **-einlage** *f* filter cone **-einlauf** *m* gate, downgate, ingate, runner **-ende** *n* throat of the horn

trichterförmig funnel-shaped

Trichter--formöler *m* funnel-shaped lubricator **-füllgefäß** *n* hopper-charging bucket **-hals** *m* throat of (loudspeaker) horn **-horn** *n* taper **-kaltsäge** *f* cold saw for cutting of risers **-klang** *m* characteristic horn sound **-kolben** *m* funnel flask **-kopf** *m* (founding) gate, gate opening **-ladung** *f* crater charge **-lauf** *m* downgate, sprue, ingress gate, ingate, runner **-lautsprecher** *m* horn-type loud-speaker, cone speaker **-loch** *n* sprue opening, gate opening

Trichterlunker *m* pipe, axial cavity **-bildung** *f* piping (metal.)

Trichter-mühle *f* hopper mill **-mundöffnung** *f* mouth of horn, largest flare **-mundstück** *n* throat of horn, narrow inlet of horn **-mündung** *f* gate, gate opening, sprue opening, mouth of horn, largest flare **-öffnung** *f* gate opening, mouth of the horn **-rohr** *n* funnel tube, tube funnel, funnel pipe, central pipe (founding), gate pipe, central runner **-schrot** *m*, *n* sprue-and-runner scrap **-sieb** *n* cone screen **-sprengung** *f* camouflet **-vorhof** *m* air chamber of loudspeaker **-wagen** *m* hopper car, traveling loading hopper

Trichterwand *f*, **schallharte ~** rigid or nonabsorbing horn wall

Trichterzulauf *m* downgate, ingate, runner

Trick *m* trick, artifice, sleight of hand, stratagem, trick effect **-aufnahme** *f* trick exposure **-bild** *n* trick picture **-dekor** *n* breakaway **-filmzeichner** *m* animator **-kamera** *f* trick camera **-mischer** *m* special-effects mixer **-taste** *f* trick button (tape rec.)

Trieb *m* drive, drift, operation, tuning, power, driving force; impulse, instinct; driving gear, pinion **~ für schwere Beanspruchung** heavy-duty drive

Trieb-achse *f* driving or live axle **-bewegung** *f* fine adjustment (of microscope)

Triebel *n* pinion, drive pinion

Triebelement *n* motor element (of loud-speaker)

Triebelwelle *f* pinion shaft

Trieb-feder *f* driving spring, main spring **-feile** *f* pinion file **-flügel** *m* powered wing **-gaszelle** *f* power or fuel gas cell **-gehäuse** *n* gear housing or case **-gestell** *n* headstock **-kasten** *m* pinion box, motion box **-kette** *f* drive chain **-knopf** *m* milled head, pinion head (in microscope) **-kraft** *f* motive power, driving force, driving power, momentum, propelling force **-kranz** *m* scroll **-ladung** *f* propellent charge

Triebling *m* pinion

Trieb-mittel *n* driving or motor means, fuel, propellant **-motor** *m* driving motor **-ölförderung** *f* oil feed **-organ** *n* driving member, drive member **-rad** *n* driving wheel or gear, driving sprocket **-radräderwerk** *n* bullgear train **-rohr** *n* sliding tube, telescopic tube or lens **-sand** *m* drift sand

Triebscheibe *f* knob, dial, drive pulley, micrometer head **~ zum Fernrohr** telescope knob **~ zur Höhenrichtschraube** elevation-worm knob **~ zur Seitenrichtung** azimuth knob

Trieb-schraube *f* drive screw, upper prism micrometer head, coarse adjustment (in microscope) **-seil** *n* driving rope **-stahl** *m* pinion steel **-stange** *f* driving bar

Triebstock *m* drive shaft **~ eines Getriebes** leaf of a pinion

Triebstock-kranz *m* lantern or pin gear **-ring** *m* pin gear ring **-ritzel** *n* lantern gear **-verzahnung** *f* mangle gear

Triebstrahlumlenkung *f* (Astron.) slipstream deflection

Triebwagen *m* rail motorcar, self-propelled car (R.R.) **-einheit** *f* motor-driven unit **-lokomotive** *f* battery car **-zug** *m* multiple-unit train

Triebwelle *f* drive shaft

Triebwerk *n* gear (drive), mechanism, transmission; (Motor) engine, power plant; transmission machinery or gearing, driving gearing, driving mechanism, engine-propeller unit, propulsive unit, driving system, machine, motor element

Triebwerk-abzapfdruck *m* engine bleed pressure **-anlage** *f* power plant, line-shaft equipment, transmission machinery **-anlassereinspritzvorrichtung** *f* engine primer **-aufhängung** *f* engine suspension, engine mount **-bedienungsgestänge** *n* power-plant control, engine control linkage **-brandschott** *m* engine firewall **-bremse** *f* gearbox brake, propeller shaft brake, transmission brake

Triebwerk-einbau *m* motor installation, power-plant installation **-gerät** *n* motor-performance gauge **-gerätebrett** *n* propulsion-unit or power-plant instrument panel

Triebwerkgerüst *n* engine mounting **abnehmbares ~** detachable engine mounting

Triebwerk-gestänge *n* engine controls **-gondel** *f* engine pod **-güte** *f* engine performance **-klappe** *f* engine hatch door **-lager** *n* headstock bearing **-leergewicht** weight of the power plant dry **-leitung** *f* engine pipeline, transmission line, transmission **-montagewagen** *m* engine build up truck **-montagezug** *m* power-unit installing platoon

Triebwerk-pult *n* rocket-motor test panel **-regler** *m* propulsion-unit governor **-schütze** motion contactors **-schwingung** *f* engine vibration **-seil** *n* transmission rope **-teil** *m* driving part, working (wearing) part, transmission part **-überwachungsinstrument** *n* motor instrument

Triebwerkverkleidung *f* engine fairing, engine nacelle, engine cowling **verstellbare ~** controllable cowling

Triebwerk-welle *f* transmission shaft **-widerstand** *m* resistance of driving gear

Trieb-zahn *m* connector **-zahnrad** *n* driving

pinion **-zeug** *n* driving gear **-zug** *m* multiple-unit train
Trift *f* pasturage, drift, floating
triften to drift, float
triftig convincing, cogent
Trift-rechen *m* rack for collecting logs transported by steam, leading grate **-röhre** *f* transit-time tube (klystron), drift tube, beam tube **-strom** *m* drift current
Trigger-höhe *f* triggering level **-pegel** *m* triggering level **-schaltung** *f* trigger circuit **-signal** *n* trigger input
trigonal trigonal
Trigondodekaeder *n* trigonal hemitrisoctahedron, trigonal dodecahedron cuproid
Trigonometrie *f* trigonometry
trigonometrisch trigonometrical **-er Punkt** triangulation point, primary traverse station
Trigramm *n* three-digit group
triklin, triklinisch triclinic
Trilit *n* trilit
Trillerklappe *f* shake key
trillern to trill, quaver, warble
Trillernote *f* trill note, warble note
Trillion *f* trillion (10^{18})
Trimethyl-butan *n* trimethylbutane **-buten** *n* trimethylbutene **-pentan** *n* trimethylpentane **-phenylallen** *n* trimethylphenylallene
trimetrisch trimetric
Trimm *m* trim (of a vessel) **-ballast** *m* trimming or trim ballast **-behälter** *m* trim or trimming tank **-berechnung** *f* calculation of trim **-blech** *n* fixed trim or trimming tab
trimmen to trim
Trimmer *m* trimmer **-kondensator** *m* trimming condenser, trimmer **-plattenpaar** *n* trimmer pair (TV)
Trimm-fläche *f* trimming tab **-kante** *f* fixed trimming or trim tab **-klappe** *f* trimming tab, trim tab **-knopf** *m* trimming knob or button **-kondensator** *m* trimming condenser, trimmer **-lage** *f* trim (of a vessel) **-pumpe** *f* trimming pump **-ruder** *n* trimming tab (aviation), external control vane (rockets) **-segel** *n* trim tab (missiles) **-tank** *m* trimming tank **-tankrohrleitung** *f* trimming tank pipe or pipe line
Trimmung *f* trimming, trim, trim compensation
Trimmungsanzeiger *m* trim-tab position indicator
Trimmvorrichtung *f* trim gear, flight-control surface used for trimming
trimorph trimorphous, trimorphic
Trinitro-benzoësäure *f* trinitrobenzoic acid **-benzol** *n* trinitrobenzene **-phenol** *n* trinitrophenol, trinitrophenic acid **-toluol** *n* trinitrotoluene
Trinom *n* trinomina
trinkbar drinkable, potable
Trinkbecher *m* drinking cup
Trinkgerät *n* drinking set
Trinkwasser *n* potable or drinking water **-bereiter** *m* water-purification unit **-kühler** *m* water cooler **-leitung** *f* drinking-water line **-versorgung** *f* drinking-water supply
Trio *n* three-high rolling mill, three-high mill **-anordnung** *f* three-high arrangement **-blechstraße** *f* three-high plate-mill train **-blechwalzwerk** *n* three-high plate mill **-blockstraße** *f* three-high blooming-mill train **-blockwalzwerk** *n* three-high blooming mill
Triode *f* triode, three-electrode tube ~ **für Kathodensteuerung** grounded grid triode
Triodenoszillator *m* oscillion
Trio-fertigstraße *f* three-high finishing train **-gerüst** *n* three-high mill stand **-grabstraße** *f* three-high breaking down rolling mill
Trio-graph *m* electrocardiograph **-profileisenstraße** *f* three-high shape mill train **-profileisenwalzwerk** *n* three-high shape mill
Trior *m* trieur, separating cylinder, grain-cleaning machine
Trio-straße *f* three-high rolling-mill train, three-high mill **-umkehrwalzwerk** *n* three-high reversing mill **-universalstraße** *f* three-high universal mill train **-universalwalzwerk** *n* three-high universal rolling mill **-vorstraße** *f* three-high roughing-mill train **-vorwalzgerüst** *n* three-high roughing stand of rolls **-walzensystem** *n* three-high mill arrangement **-walzgerüst** *n* three-high rolling stand **-walzstraße** *f* three-high rolling train **-walzwerk** *n* three-high rolling mill, three-high mill, trio rollers, trio mill
Tripel *n*, **-erde** *f* tripoli earth, rotten stone **-punkt** *m* triple point (metallography) **-punktsdruck** *m* triple pressure **-spiegel** *m* triple reflector **-streifen** *m* special prism used to direct the beam of a signal lamp
Triplettspektrum *n* triplet spectrum
Triplex-flaschenzug *m* triple-block chain hoist **-verfahren** *n* triplex process, three-furnace process
Trisilikat *n* trisilicate
Tritiumabschätzung *f* tritium estimation
Tritol *n* tritol
Triton *n* triton
Tritonenbeschuß *m* triton bombardment
Tritoprisma *n* prism of the third order
Tritt *m* step, tread, pace, pedal **außer ~ fallen** to fall out of step **in ~ kommen** to fall in step, synchronize, come in step or phase **ohne ~** route step
Trittbrett *n* footboard, running board, treadle **-halter** *m* step hanger **-lampe** *f* step light (on running board) **-schiene** *f* step rail **-stütze** *f* step bracket **-träger** *m* support for footboard, footboard bracket
Tritt-fläche *f* walkway, tread (of a step) **-gebläse** *n* treadle bellows or blower **-halter** *m* step bracket **-hammer** *m* treadle hammer **-hebel** *m* foot lever **-hebelbremse** *f* foot brake **-klinke** *f* foot release **-leiste** *f* floorboard, kick plate **-leiter** *f* stepladder **-pedal** *n* pedal **-platte** *f* foot board
Trittplatten-bremsventil *n* pedal-type brake valve **-kupplungsventil** *n* pedal-type clutch valve
Trittschall *m* impact sound **-dämpfung** *f* footfall sound attenuation
Tritt-schutz *m* anti-slip cover **-stufe** *f* treadboard **-stufenleuchte** *f* step light
Tritylen *n* tritylene
Trizyansäure *f* tricyanic acid, cyanuric acid
Trochoide *f* trochoid
Trochotron *n* trochotron
trocken dry, arid **einen Einschnitt ~ legen** to drain a cutting **einen Schacht ~ legen** to drain a pit **~ verzinken** to sherardize

trocken, -e adiabatische Abweichungsrate dry adiabatic lapse rate (aviation) **-e Gasuhr** dry gas meter **-es Gleichgewicht** dry balance **-er Holzschliff** dry mechanical wood pulp **-er Ölfluß** dry sump **-er Saft** concrete juice **-er Schaum** dry dross **-e Scheidung** dry separation **-es Thermometer** dry-bulb thermometer **-es Verfahren** dry treatment **-er Wärmegradmesser** dry-bulb thermometer

Trocken-alarmventil *n* dry pipe (alarm) valve **-anlage** *f* drying plant, equipment, or installation

Trockenapparat *m* drier, drying apparatus, desiccator, dehydrator **~ mit Kreuzeinbau** drier with cross-shaped internal-distribution system

Trocken-appreturmaschine *f* dry-finishing machine **-aufschütten** to heap in a dry state **-aufspeichern** *n* dry storing **-aufziehverfahren** *n* dry mounting, dry-posting method **-auszug** *m* dry extract (chem.) **-bagger** *m* excavator, steam shovel **-batterie** *f* dry-cell battery **-beizung** *f* dry-seed dressing, seed dusting **-beutel** *m* drying instrument, desiccator **-bindefestigkeit** *f* dry bond strength **-binder** *m* dry binder

Trocken-blasen *n* drying by blowing **-blatt** *n* dried sugar-beet leaves **-blech** *n* drying sheet **-bleiche** *f* dry bleaching **-boden** *m* drying place or room, hanging room **-bohrer** *m* claying bar (min.) **-bohrung** *f* dry drilling **-brikett** *n* dry-pressed briquette **-bütte** *f* dry vat

Trocken-dampf *m* dry steam **-darre** *f* drying kiln, drying tunnel, kiln **-dehnung** *f* dry elongation **-dekatieren** to decatize with dry steam **-dekatur** *f* dry steaming **-destillation** *f* dry distillation, destructive distillation, carbonization **-dock** *m* drydock, graving dock **-element** *n* dry cell (battery) **-elevator** *m* drygoods elevator **-entgasung** *f* dry distillation

Trocken-farbe *f* pigment **-fäule** *f* dry rot **-feld** *n* drying bays **-festigkeit** *f* dry strength **-filz** *m* drying felt **-firnis** *m* drying oil **-fließpapier** *n* absorbent paper **-förderer** *m* drying conveyer

Trocken-gas *n* dry gas **-gehalt** *m* dry content **-gelenk** *n* dry-disk joint, flexible-disk joint **-gerät** drying instrument, desiccator **-gerüst** *n* drying shed, frame or rack (tile) **-gestell** *n* drying rack, dish drainer **-gewicht** *n* dry weight

Trocken-glattwerk *n* calender **-gleichrichter** *m* metal rectifier, dry rectifier, copper rectifier, cuprous-oxide rectifier, selenium-oxide rectifier **-gleichrichtzelle** *f* dry rectifying cell **-guß** *m* cast in dry mold, dry-sand castings **-gußform** *f* dry-sand mold **-gut** *n* material to be dried **-hänge** *f* drying chamber **-haltung** *f* keeping dry (unwatering) **-haut** *f* dried hide

Trockenheit *f* dryness, drought (aviat.)

Trocken-herd *m* drying hearth **-kammer** *f* baking oven, drying oven, drying room, baker, dryhouse **-klebeband** *n* pressure sensitive tape (tape rec.) **-klebrigkeit** *f* aggressive tack, dry tack **-kohle** *f* dry coal **-kondensator** *m* dry electrolytic condenser

Trocken-lauf *m* dry operation **-läufer** *m* water meter with mechanism and indicator operating (dry) in air, dry-dial water meter **-laufkolbenverdichter** *m* bone-dry compressor **-leergewicht** *n* dry net weight **-legen** to drain **-legung** *f* unwatering, draining **-linse** *f* dry objective, nonimmersion objective

Trockenluft-anlage *f* dry air plant **-druckmesser** *m* aneroid or dry barometer **-filter** *n* dry filter

Trocken-mahlen *n* dry crushing, dry grinding **-mahlverfahren** *n* dry-grinding process **-maschine** *f* drying machine, drier

Trockenmauerwerk *n* (dry) stone **~ von Bruchsteinen** dry rubble

Trockenmittel *n* drying agent, drier, siccative, desiccative

Trockenofen *m* baking oven, seasoning kiln, drier furnace, drying furnace or kiln, drying oven or stove **senkrechter ~** tower drier

Trocken-öl *n* siccative oil, drier oil **-partie** *f* drier section (paper mfg.) **-patrone** *f* hygroscopic element (to prevent mist-formation on lenses) **-pflaster** *n* dry pavement (laid without mortar) **-platte** *f* dry plate **-prozeß** *m* (Bauholz) seasoning process **-puddeln** *n* dry puddling

Trocken-rahmen *m* drying frame **-raum** *m* drying space, drying chamber **-raumgewicht** *n* dry bulk density **-reibung** *f* solid friction **-reiniger** *m* dry cleaner **-reinigung** *f* dry cleaning, dry purification **-rohr** *n* dry tube or pipe **-rose** *f* dry compass rose **-rückstand** *m* dry residue

Trocken-sand *m* dry sand **-schälchen** *n* dry cell **-schaltschrank** *m* oilless unit switchgear cubicle **-scheibenkuppelung** *f* dry-plate clutch **-scheidepfanne** *f* defecator for dry lime **-scheider** *m* dry separator **-schlamm** *m* dried defecation scum **-schleuder** *f* centrifugal dryer **-schliff** *m* dry grinding **-schliffpapier** *n* dry-grinding paper

Trocken-schnitzelelevator *m* dried-pulp elevator **-schnitzelschnecke** *f* dried-pulp screw conveyer **-schrank** *m* shelf drier, drying closet or chamber, drying oven, drier, compartment drier **-schwindung** *f* shrinkage in or from drying **-spannrahmen** *m* hot-air tentering machine **-speicher** *m* drying loft **-stadium** *n* dry phase **-ständer** *m* drying rack **-stoff** *m* drier, siccative, drying substance **-stuhl** *m* drying machine

Trocken-substanz *f* drying agent **-substanzgehalt** *m* percentage of solids **-sumpf** *m* dry sump **-teller** *pl* dry plates **-temperatur** *f* drying temperature **-thermometer** *n* dry-bulb thermometer

Trockentrommel *f* rotary drying kiln, drying drum, rotary drier rotating kiln **-entwicklungsverfahren** *n* drying cylinder developing process **-maschine** *f* cylinder drying machine

Trocken-turm *m* drying tower **-tunnel** *m* tunnel drier **-verfahren** *n* drying process **-vermahlung** *f* dry grinding **-verlegt** laid dry **-vorgang** *m* drying process **-vorlage** *f* dehumidifier **-vorrichtung** *f* drying device

Trocken-walken *n* milling in the stocks **-walze** *f* dry-crushing roll **-wäsche** *f* dry scrubbing **-wirkung** *f* drying effect **-zeit** *f* drying time **-zerkleinern** to dry-grind **-zylinder** *m* drying cylinder, desiccating cylinder **-zylinderlaufbüchse** *f* dry liner

trocknen to dry, desiccate, season (wood), cure, condition, bake

Trocknen *n* drying out

Trockner *m* drier, drying chamber, desiccator, loftsman (paper mfg.) **~ mit bewegtem Gut** conveyor drier **~ mit Strahlungsheizung** radiation drier **~ mit Zerstäubung** suspended

particle drier
Trocknerei *f* drying plant
Trocknergebläse *n* blower for the drier
Trocknung *f* drying, desiccating, seasoning
Trocknungs-anlage *f* drying plant **-beschleuniger** *m* drying accelerator **-grad** *m* degree of dryness **-gut** *n* goods to be dried **-mittel** *n* drying medium
Trog *m* trough, chute, vat, hod, box (of stamping machine), pan, tray, bulb ~ **der Drehscheibe** casing of the turntable **elektrolytischer** ~ electrolytic tank **kippbarer** ~ tip pan
Trog-anhänger *m* flat trailer **-batterie** *f* trough battery **-blech** *n* trough sheet **-brücke** *f* U-type bridge **-element** *n* tray cell **-endverschluß** *m* trough terminal **-förmig** trough-shaped **-kettenförderer** *m* drag chain conveyor **-linie** *f* trough line (meteor.) **-schwingwascher** *m* oscillating trough washer **-tal** *n* U-shaped valley **-tränkung** *f* (Holz) open tank steeping
Troilit *m* troilite
Trolitul Spulenkörper *m* Trolitul coil form
Trombe *f* trumpet, funnel, cone
Trommel *f* drum; (Techn.) cylinder, barrel; tambour, trommel, reel, tympanum, tumbler (cleaning drum), sleeve (with screws), swift, dial, micrometer drum, metal drum **abkuppelbare** ~ free drum **große** ~ bass drum **kleine** ~ snare drum
Trommel-abtaster *m* beltscanner **-achsenöffnung** *f* hole of the drum axle **-anker** *m* drum armature **-ankergenerator** *m* drum-type alternator **-anzeiger** *m* drum indicator **-blech** *n* drum plate **-blende** *f* drum diaphragm, drum with scanning apertures **-böckchen** *n* pattern disc housing
Trommel-decke *f* top of the drum **-drehbank** *f* roller lathe **-drehfilter** *n* rotary drum filter
Trommelfell *n* eardrum, drumhead, tympanic membrane, tympanum (of ear) **-schalter** *m* drum controller
Trommel-filter *n* revolving filter **-flöte** *f* fife **-fräsmaschine** *f* drum milling machine **-gebläse** *n* sandblast barrel, revolving barrel, sandblast machine **-gehäuse** *n* barrel housing **-kippanlage** *f* drum dumper **-knotenfänger** *m* cylindrical drainer **-kompaß** *m* barrel or drum compass **-konverter** *m* barrel converter **-kreiselrührer** *m* rotor cage impeller **-kühler** *m* drum or barrel radiator **-kurve** *f* drum-type cam
Trommel-lager *n* drum bearing, drum store **-länge** *f* drum length **-läufer** *m* drum rotor **-magazin** *n* ammunition drum **-magazinzuführung** *f* drum feed **-mantel** *m* barrel shell **-mischer** *m* double-cone blender, drum (barrel) mixer **-motor** *m* swash-plate engine, barrel-type engine **-mühle** *f* barrel or tube mill, drum mill, rattler
trommeln tumble, rattle
Trommel-nabe *f* boss or hub of drum **-ofen** *m* rotary furnace, revolving-cylinder roaster **-probe** *f* rattler test **-rad** *n* drum wheel **-rahmen** *m* container frame **-rand** *m* drum edge **-raum** *m* drum chamber **-revolverkopf** *m* drum turret **-rille** *f* drum groove or spiral **-rohr** *n* drier tube (of drier)
Trommel-säge *f* cylinder saw **-schalter** *m* drum switch **-schaltung** *f* cylinder indexing **-scheider** *m* drum separator **-schichtenfilter** *n* drum sheets filter **-schlägel** *m* drumstick **-schleuse** *f* sluice or lock with circular chamber **-schlichtmaschine** *f* cylinder sizing machine **-schieber** *m* air control drum **-schneckenrad** *n* tympan **-schreiber** *m* drum-chart recorder
Trommel-seite *f* spooling flange **-sichter** *m* drum separator **-sieb** *n* trommel revolving screen **-sinkscheider** *m* drum sink float separator **-skala** (Autosuper) drum-shaped scale **-speicher** *m* drum store (info proc.), drum memory **-standmotor** *m* barrel-type stationary engine **-stern** *m* drum spider **-stirnwand** *f* barrel-head plate **-sucht** *f* tympanites
Trommeltrockner *m* rotary drier ~ **mit Außenbeheizung** externally heated rotary drier ~ **mit Innenbeheizung** internally heated rotary drier ~ **mit Kreuzeinbau** drum drier with cross-shaped internal distribution system
Trommel-umlaufmotor *m* barrel-type rotary engine **-verfahren** *n* drum process **-versuch** *m* rattler test **-vorschubspindel** *f* drum-feed spindle **-wand** *f* barrel shell **-wascher** *m* drum washer **-wehr** *n* drum barrage or dam **-welle** *f* drum shaft **-wicklung** *f* drum winding **-winde** *f* roller wind, reel jack **-zeiger** *m* dial pointer, dial indicator, drum index
Trommler *m* drummer
Trommsdorffantrieb *m* supersonic ram jet
Trompete *f* trumpet
trompetenförmig trumpet-shaped
Troostit *n* troostite
Troostosorbit *m* troostitic sorbite
Tropadynempfänger *m* tropadyne
Tropäolinpapier *n* tropaeoline paper
Tropen *pl* tropics **-anzug** *m* white uniform
Tropenas-Konverter *m* Tropenas (side-blown) converter
Tropen-ausführung *f* tropical finish **-beständig** suitable for use in tropical climates **-binder** *m* tropical neckcloth
tropenfest tropicalized, impervious to heat, suitable for tropics **-e Verpackung** tropicalized packing
Tropenfestigkeit *f* resistance to tropical conditions, tropic proof quality
Tropen-helm *m* sun helmet, pith helmet, topee **-kraftstoff** *m* tropical gasoline **-kühler** *m* tropical radiator **-sicher** tropics-proof **-verwendungsfähigkeit** *f* fitness for service in tropical climate **-welle** *f* B-band medium wave (radio)
tropfbar liquid, capable of forming drops, capable of dripping
Tropf-becher *m* drip cup **-behälter** *m* drip pan, save-all **-benzin** *n* leaking gasoline **-blech** *n* drip pan, drain pan **-brett** *n* drainage board
Tröpfchen *n* globule, droplet, cluster, vapor particle, spherule, small bead **-bildung** *f* coaggregation **-methode** *f* drop-weight method **-methodemodell** *n* liquid drop model **-verdampfung** *f* evaporation of droplets
Tropfdüse *f* drip nozzle
Tröpfel *n* drip
tröpfeln to trickle, dribble, leak, drop
Tropfen *m* drop (water), drip, trickle
Tropfen *n* dripping
Tropfenbildung *f* formation of drops
tropfender Kern weeping core
Tropfen-elektrode dropping electrode **-fallrohr** *n*

drip pipe

Tropfenfänger *m* drip tube, drip catcher ~ **für Gasmaschine** baffle cleaner

Tropfen-form *f* drop shape (steamline) **-förmig** tear-shaped **-hahn** *m* drop tap or cock **-kurve** *f* thickness-function curve **-ladung** *f* drop charge **-messer** *m* stalagmometer, stactometer **-öler** *m* sight-feed oiler

Tropfen-probe *f* spot test **-regler** *m* sight-feed regulator **-rohr** *n* streamline section tube **-schlag** *m* impingement of drops **-statoskop** *n* drip statoscop **-tuch** *n* drip flap **-weise** dropwise, drop by drop **-zähler** *m* dropper, drop counter, stalagmometer, eye dropper **-zeiger** *m* drop indicator

Tropf-fallpumpe *f* Sprengler pump **-flasche** *f* dropping bottle **-gewichtsmethode** *f* drop-weight method **-glas** *n* dropping glass, pipette **-hahn** *m* drip cock **-körper** *m* percolating filter **-leitung** *f* drop conduit **-naß** dripping wet **-öl** *n* dribble or drip oil **-ölapparat** *m* gravity-feed lubricator **-öler** *m* drip oiler (lubricator), sight-feed oiler **-öllager** *n* drip-oiling bearing **-öl-schmierung** *f* drip feed

Tropf-pflanzmaschine *f* drop corn planter **-pipette** *f* dropping pipette **-probe** *f* pour test **-pumpe** *f* (gas) collecting pump **-punkt** *m* dropping point **-ring** *m* drip ring **-rinne** *f* drip gutter **-rohr** *n* drip tube **-röhre** *f* burette, dropping glass, dropping tube **-schale** *f* drip pan, save-all, drip tray, oil cup **-schalentraggitter** *n* drip-tray shelf **-sicher** leakproof **-stein** *m* dripstone, stalactite **-trichter** *m* dropping funnel

Tropfungszeit *f* dropping time

Tropf-ventil *n* feed regulator **-vorrichtung** *f* sight-feed lubrication **-wanne** *f* drip pan **-wannenrost** *m* drip-pan grate **-wasser** *n* dripping water **-wasserdicht** drip-proof **-wassergeschützt** drip-proof **-zink** *n* drop zinc **-zinn** *n* drop or granulated tin **-zufuhr** *f* dripfeed (oil) **-zylinder** *m* drip cup

Tropie *f* tropism

tropisch tropic(al) **-e Luft** tropical air **-e Luftmasse** tropical air mass **-er Orkan** tornado **-e Störung** tropical distrubance **-e Warmluft** tropical air **Wirbelsturm** tropical cyclone

Tropopause *f* tropopause

Troposphäre *f* troposphere

troposphärische Streuung *f* tropospheric scatter

Troposphären-niederschlag *m* tropospheric fallout **-kanal** *m* tropospheric duct

Troß *m* supply train, field train

Trosse *f* rope, warp, hawser

Trossen-rolle *f* hawser roller **-sperre** *f* hawser barrier

Troß-fahrzeug *n* train vehicle **-schiff** *n* supply ship

Trottoir *n* sidewalk

Trotyl *n* trotyl

Trotzer *n* fizzler

trübe (Flüssigkeit) cloudy, turbid, muddy; (glanzlos) dull, dim; cheerless, wretched, miserable (business), murky, thick, veiled, opaque

Trübe *f* dross, pulp, turbidity, cloudiness, sludge, slime, mud, turbid water, slush, slurry **-eindicker** *m* densifier **-elevator** *m* pulp elevator

trüben to darken (dull)

Trübe-punkt *m* cloud test, cloud point **-sieb** *n* dense-medium screen **-strom** *m* pulp stream **-umlauf** *m* medium circuit **-verdicker** *m* pulp thickener **-verdünnung** *f* pulp dilution **-zuführungsrohr** *n* pulp feed pipe

Trüb-glas *n* frosted glass, opal glass, glass diffusing light **-glasprisma** *n* turbid prism **-presse** *f* draff press **-raum** *m* filling space **-stoffanteil** *m* impurity **-stoffe** *pl* turbidities **-stoffgehalt** *m* quantity of turbid matters

Trübung *f* (trüben) rendering turbid, making muddy, dimming; blushing (of lacquer), cloudiness, milkiness, turbidity, murkiness, opacity, tarnishing, clouding (of glass), wavering of signal beam, blurring (of minimum) ~ **eines Minimums** flattening of a minimum (direction finder)

Trübungs-grad *m* degree of turbidity **-koeffizient** *m* coefficient of turbidity **-meßeinrichtung** *f* turbidity measuring device **-messer** *m* turbidimeter, opacimeter, nephelometer **-messung** *f* turbidimetry **-mittel** *n* opacifier (glass mfg.) **-spannung** *f* potential causing quadrantal errors **-stoffe** impurities

Trudel-bewegung *f* tailspin **-drehachse** *f* axis of rotation or spin **-drehgeschwindigkeit** *f* speed of rotation in tailspin **-geschwindigkeit** *f* tailspin speed or velocity **-linie** *f* spinning or tailspin curve **-modell** *n* spin model

trudeln to spin

Trudeln *n* spiral diving (aviation), spin ~ **mit der Nase nach unten** spinning nose dive (aviation) ~ **mit noch nicht erstorbenem Motor** power spin (aviation) **ins ~ bringen** to put the machine into a spin **ins ~ kommen** to fall into a spin

Trudel-schirm *m* spin chute **-sicher** nonspinning **-umdrehung** *f* turn of a spin **-windkanal** *m* spinning tunnel, vertical wind tunnel for spinning tests

Trugbild *n* illusion, phantom

Trugschluß *m* fallacy, false or erroneous conclusion, fallacious argument

Trum *n* seam, lode, vein, leader, stringer (of a chain), strand, film strip **gezogenes ~ loses ~** slack strand **ziehendes ~** tight strand **riemengezogenes ~** slack side of belt **riemenziehendes ~** taut side of belt

Trumlampe *f* branch lamp

Trumm *n* end(piece), stump, fragment **schlaffes ~** slack end of a belt or rope **straffes ~** driving or taut end (of belt)

Trümmer *n pl* fragments, clastic rocks, debris, wreckage, ruin, fission products or fragments, remains **-gestein** *n* conglomerate, breccia **-haufen** *m* rubble pile, pile of rubble **-lagerstätte** *f* detrital deposit **-masse** *f* detritus **-verwertung** *f* utilization of brick rubble

Trummsäge *f* crosscut, pit, or trim saw

Trupp *m* party, gang, detail, troop

Truppe *f* detail (mil.), troops, personnel, men, unit, arm of service

Trust *m* trust

TSC (Zweihilfsträger)-System TSC (two-carrier) system

Tschevkinit *m* tschevkinite

T-Schraube *f* T-bolt

T-Schweißung *f* jump welding, T welding

T-Schwelle *f* **einer Zugramme** T sill of a (ringing)

pile engine

T-Stoff-Anlage *f* steam plant (guided missiles)

T-Stoff-Anlagenhauptventil *n* main steam-plant valve

T-Stoff-Anlagenstecker *m* steam-plant plug

T-Stoff-Anwärmgerät *n* peroxide preheater

T-Stoff-Behälter *m* peroxide tank

T-Stoff-Entlüfter *m* peroxide vent valve

T-Stoff-Spritzkopf *m* peroxide injection nozzle

T-Stoß *m* T joint or weld **~ mit durchlaufender Naht** straight T weld

T-Stoßkehlnahtschweißung *f* T-fillet welding or weld

T-Stück *n* tee, T iron

T-Träger *m* T beam, T girder

Tübbings *pl* tubbing, lining, casing

Tube *f* tube

Tuben-druck *m* gauge pressure (missiles) **-füllmaschine** *f* tube-filling machine **-schließmaschine** *f* tube-sealing or tube-closing machine

tubulieren to tubulate

Tubus *m* tube, tubus, tubulature, localizer, cathode-ray tube, viewing hood **-aufsatz** *m* tube attachment **-schlitten** *m* tube slide **-träger** *m* tube support

Tuch *n* cloth, fabric, linen (blind) **-einsatz** *m* cloth filter **-lutte** *f* canvas or cloth air conduit **-rahmen** *m* tenter frame **-schwabbel** *f* cloth buff **-scheibe** *f* cloth buff **-scherblatt** *n* blade of cloth shears **-schere** *f* cloth shears **-schermaschine** *f* shearing or cutting or cropping machine

Tuchstreifen *m* felt strip

Tuch-vorfilter *n* cloth strainer **-zeichen** *n* ground panel (aviation), code panel

Tudorplatte *f* Tudor plate

Tuff *m* tuff **-stein** *m* calcareous tufa **-wacke** *f* decomposed trap

Tüll *m* tulle, bobbin net, network

tüllartiges Netzgewebe tull-like net tissue

Tülle *f* nozzle, mouthpiece, lip, socket, spout, funnel, thistle funnel

Tüllenverschlußapparat *m* spout closing apparatus

Tüllmaschine *f* tulle machine

tulpenförmig tulip-shaped

Tulpen-haltestange tulip supporting rod **-kontakt** *m* contact segment **-naht** *f* bell seam **-ventil** *n* tulip valve

Tumblerschalter *m* tumbler switch, trigger switch

Tümpel *m* tymp, pool, pouring basin, sump, pouring basin (in casting) **-eisen** *n* tymp plate **-gewölbe** *n* tymp arch **-stein** *m* tymp brick

tun to do, perform, place

Tünche *f* whitewash

tünchen to whitewash, linewash

Tünch-hacke *f* plaster hatchet **-kalk** *m* lime for white washing

Tungargleichrichter *m* Tungar rectifier

Tungöl *n* tung oil, Chinese wood oil, China wood oil

Tungstein *m* scheelite

tunken to dip

Tunkverfahren *n* dipping process

Tunnel *m* tunnel, subway, gallery **-bahn** *f* tunnel railway **-bau** *m* tunnel(l)ing, tunnelwork, tunnel construction **-beben** *n* earthshake due to tunneling **-beleuchtung** *f* tunnel lighting (system) **-diode** *f* tunnel diode **-effekt** *m* tunneling effect **-gang** *m* subway **-haftleitung** *f* conduction by electrons **-korn** *m* hooded front sight **-kühler** *m* tunnel radiator **-ofen** *m* tunnel kiln, continuous-type furnace **-schild** *n* shield **-schießen** *n* lay blasts **-welle** *f* intermediate shaft **-sternkorn** *m* hooded revolving front sight **-welle** *f* intermediate shaft

Tüpfel *m* phase dot (TV) **-analyse** *f* spot analysis, drop analysis **-maschine** *f* pricking machine (textile) **-methode** *f* drop method, spot method

tüpfeln to test by the spot method, dot, spot, speckle, stipple, freckle, mottle

Tüpfel-platte *f* drop plate **-probe** *f* drop or spotting test **-test** *m* drop test **-verfahren** *n* spot test method

tupfen to dab (tip)

Tupf-papier *n* design or point or rule paper **-probe** *f* spotting test

Tür *f* door **gespundete ~** plowed and tongued door **~ mit Bleieinlage** lead door

Türangel *f* hinge **-pfanne** *f* pin with round eye, pan, socket, sole

Turas *m* dredger drum, dredging tumbler or roll

Tür-band *n* hinge plate, door loop or gunnet **-beschlag** *m* door fitting or mounting

Türbetätigung, pneumatische ~ air pressure operated doors

Turbine *f* turbine (engine) **~ mit äußerer Beaufschlagung** inward-flow turbine **~ mit innerer Beaufschlagung** outward-flow turbine **~ mit voller Beaufschlagung** full-supply or full-admission turbine

Turbinen-abdampf *m* turbine exhaust steam **-abgas** *n* turbine effluent, or exhaust **-antrieb** *m* turbine drive **-dampfer** *m* turbine steamer **-dichtung** *f* turbine seal **-druckleitung** *f* penstock

Turbinendüsen-schaufel *f* turbine nozzle blade **-verlustbeiwert** *m* turbine-nozzle loss factor

Turbinen-dynamo *m* turbogenerator **-eintrittsgehäuse** *n* nozzle box **-flugzeug** *n* turbine airplane **-gebläse** *n* turbine blower **-gehäuse** *n* turbine casing, cylinder, or housing, turbine housing (jet) **-gitter** *n* turbine nozzle **-gitteranordnung** *f* guide-vane arrangement, stator arrangement **-halle** *f* turbine shop **-kammer** *f* turbine chamber **-lager** *n* turbine mounting (jet) **-lagerträger** *m* turbine bearing casing **-läufer** *m* turbine rotor, turbine disk (jet)

Turbinen-leitgitter *n* turbine stator guide vanes **-leitung** *f* penstock line **-leitungsrohre** *pl* turbine piping **-luftstaugerät** *n* pulsating turbojet **-luftstrahlmotor** *m* turboengine getting oxygen from the air (jet) **-luftstrahltriebwerk** *n* turbojet engine **-mantel** *m* turbine casing **-mischer** *m* turbine impeller mixer **-motor** *m* jet-propulsion engine

Turbinen-propellermotor *m* turbo-prop engine **-pumpenaggregat** *n* turbine compressor unit **-rad** *n* turbine wheel **-radscheibe** *f* turbine wheel disk **-öl** *n* turbine oil **-rohrleitung** *f* turbine pipe line **-satz** *m* turbogenerator **-schaufel** *f* turbine blade, turbine vane **-schaufelrad** *n* turbine rotor

Turbinen-strahlmotor *m* turbo-jet engine **-träger** *m* (Triebwerk) backbone casing **-trommel** *f* turbine drum **-überwachungstafel** *f* control board for turbine plant **-unterbrecher** *m* turbine break, turbine interrupter **-verschluß** *m* turbine lock **-vorgelege** *n* turbine gear **-welle** *f* turbine shaft

turbinieren to stir vigorously, whirl

Turbo-aggregat *n* turbine-driven auxiliary, turbine generator **-alternator** *m* turboalternator

turboelektrischer Antrieb turboelectric drive

Turbo-feile *f* milling file **-gasexhaustor** *m* turbogas exhauster **-gebläse** *n* turboblower

Türbogen *m* door arch

Turbogenerator-gruppe *f* turbine-generator set **-satz** *m* turbine-driven set

Turbo-kompressor *m*, **-lader** *m* turbosupercharger **-ladermaschine** *f* turbojet engine **-mischer** *m* impact mixer **-raketenantrieb** *m* turborocket propulsion **-R.-Transformator** *m* turbojet transformer

Turbo-satz *m* turboset **-speisepumpe** *f* turbine driven feed water pump **-strahltriebwerk** *n* turbojet engine **-transformator** *m* adjustable turbojet unit, turbojet transformer **-trockner** *m* turbo drier **-verdichter** *m* turbo compressor

turbulent-e Ströme *pl* turbulent streams **-e Strömung** *f* eddy-motion

Turbulenz *f* turbulence, eddy, vortex

turbulenzerzeugt turbulence-produced

Turbulenz-flecken turbulent spot **-fluß** *m* eddy flux **-keil** *m* turbulent wedge **-koeffizient** *m* eddy viscosity coefficient **-schichtverdampfer** *m* turbulent film evaporator **-strömung** *f* turbulent air current **-transport** *m* eddy-flux

Tür-dichtung *f* door sealing **-drücker** *m* door handle **-einfassung** *f* door case **-falle** *f* door latch **-feder** *f* drag spring, door spring **-flügel** *m* wing of door, leaf of door **-fuge** *f* door joint **-führung** *f* door guide **-futter** *n* jamb lining of a door frame, door case **-gerüst** *n* gallery frame **-griff** *m* door handle **-joch** *n* door bay **-kappe** *f* door lintel

Türkis *m* turquoise

Türkischrot *n* Turkey red **-öl** *n* sulfonated castor oil

Tür-kissen *n* door cushion **-klinke** *f* door knob or handle **-kloben** *m* pivot stud **-klopfer** *m* knocker, rapper, click **-knopfdrehbank** *f* doorknob turning machine **-kontakt** *m* door push **-kontaktschalter** *m* door switch, door contact interrupter **-laufschiene** *f* slide of a sliding door **-lochring** *m* fire-door hole ring

Turm *m* turret, tower, pylon, transformer, derrick, mast **~ zum Heben des Betons** concrete elevator **achterer ~** after turret **freistehender ~** self-supporting tower **freitragender ~** self-supporting tower

Turmalin *m* tourmaline

Turm-anschluß *m* turret connection **-artig** towerlike, towering **-aufsatz** *m* cupola **-boden** *m* floor, derrick floor **-deckdampfer** *m* turret decker, turret-deck steamer **-deckel** *m* turret latch **-decker** *m* tower slater **-drehkran** *m* rotary-tower crane **-drehmaschine** *f* turret turning machine

Turm-fernrohr *n* turret telescope **-flaschenzug** *m* crown block **-förderanlage** *f* tower-type winder **-förderung** *f* tower winding, winding from tower-type headgear **-front** *f* turret front **-haus** *n* tall building, sky-scraper **-kessel** *m* (Turmbauart) tower-type boiler **-klappe** *f* turret hatch **-kran** *m* tower crane **-kranz** *m* derrick cornice

Turm-lukendeckel *m* turret-hatch cover **-meister** *m* drilling foreman **-montagearbeiter** *m* rig builder **-rolle** *f* crown block, derrick pulley **-rollenblock** (Tiefbohranlage) crown block **-rost** *m* derrick floor **-scheibe** *f* crown pulley, head-gear pulley **-schütze** *m* turret gunner **-schwenkwerk** *n* turret traversing mechanism

Turm-seitenwand *f* turret side-plate **-sockel** *m* tower skirt **-spannseil** *n* derrick tension cable **-spitze** *f* spire **-steiger** *m* derrick man **-stellwerk** *n* control tower **-stirnwand** *f* turret front-plate **-verbindung** *f* (horizontal) derrick girt **-wagen** *m* tower car **-windmühle** *f* tower mill **-zielfernrohr** *n* turret telescope **-zurrung** *f* turret-locking clamp

Türnische *f* bay of a door

Turnus *m* cycle, rotation

Türöffner *m* door opener **lichtelektrischer ~** photoelectric door opener

Tür-öffnung *f* aperture of a door **-pfosten** *m* door-post **-puffer** *m* door check, doorstep **-riegel** *m* head rail **-rahmen** *m* doorframe **-schalter** *m* door switch **-schwelle** *f* sill

Tür-spanner *f* door checkrod **-steg** *m* door rail **-sturz** *m* lintel beam over door opening **-verdachung** *f* head molding **-verkleidung** *f* door panel or case **-verriegelungsanlage** *f* door-bolting installation **-verschluß** *m* door fastening **-zieher** *m* doorboy

Tusche *f* (india) ink **mit ~ ausziehen** to ink

Tuschieren *n* touching up, finishing

Tuschiersieb *n* corrective screen

Tuschkasten *m* color box, paintbox

Tute *f*, **Tüte** *f* paper bag, assay crucible, glass cylinder

Tütenbildung *f* piping (in ingot or casting), pipe formation

Tutia *f* tutty, furnace cadmia, furnace calamine, spodium

Tutol *n* trinitrotoluene

T-Verbindungsstück *n* tee connection

T-Verschraubung *f* T-union, T-screw fitting

Twist *m* waste wool or cotton, twist

Twistor *m* twistor

Tyndallimetrie *f* tyndallimetry

Typ *m* type, model

Type *f* type, letter, model **erhabene ~** raised type

Typen-abdruckstelle *f* printing point **-bahn** *f* track of the types **-bereinigung** *f* standardization **-bezeichnung** *f* model designation **-bildschreiber** *m* facsimile recorder **-blatt** *n* lay-out plan

Typen-druck *m* type printing **-drucker** *m* printing telegraph, type printer, teleprinter

Typendruck-fläche *f* type surface **-hebel** *m* type bar **-hebelübersetzer** *m* type-bar translator or printer **-korb** *m* type basket (of typewriter) **-druckprüfung** *f* type acceptance test **-rad** *n* type wheel **-radachse** *f* type-wheel shaft **-radübersetzer** *m* type-wheel translator **-schreibvorrichtung** *f* type-inking recording attachment **-telegraph** *m* printing telegraph, typeprinter, teleprinter

Typenführung type bar guide

Typen-gießmaschine *f* type-casting machine

-hammer *m* printing hammer
Typenhebel *m* type lever, type bar **-anschlag** *m* type bar backstop **-getriebe** *n* type bar mechanism **-zugdraht** *m* type bar link
Typenkasten (Fernschreiber) type box **-korb** *m* (Fernschreiber) type bar carriage **-lehre** *f* typology **-leistung** *f* rated output **-muster** *n* standard sample **-normung** *f* standardization **-prüfung** *f* type (prototype) test
Typen-metall *n* type metal **-normung** *f* typization **-nummer** *f* model number
Typenrad *n* type wheel **-achse** *f* type-wheel shaft **-gravierbock** *m* numbering wheel engraving device **-schreibstellen** *pl* type-wheel printing positions **-schild** *n* identification plate **-stange** *f* type bar **-teilprüfung** *f* type test
Typen-schaft *m* type shank, shaft or bar **-schiffchen** *n* shuttle type carrier **-schild** *n* nameplate
typische Abweichung standard deviation
Typisierung *f* standardization
Typlösung *f* typical solution (colorimetry)
Typographie *f* typography
typographischer Punkt typographic point = 0.376 mm
Typus *m* type **-bescheinigung** *f* type certificate
Tyrosin *n* tyrosine
Tyrotoxikon *n* tyrotoxicon
Tysonit *m* tysonite

U

übel-nehmen to take amiss or in bad part **-riechend** of disagreeable or offensive smell **-stand** *m* drawback, disadvantage
üben to practice, exercise, drill
über over, above, across, about, on, plotted against **-alles-Frequenzgang** *m* overall frequency response **-angebot** *n* oversupply **-anpassung** *f* overmatch **-anregung eines Zählrohrs** counter overshooting **-anstrengen** to overexert, strain, tax **-anzeige** *f* overswing (of volume indicator) **-anzug** *m* overalls, combination suit **-arbeiten** to touch up, rework, overwork **-arbeitung** *f* reworking, touching up (phot.) **-armhandkreuz** *n* overarm pilot wheel **-äschert** over-limed **-ätzen** to overetch **-ausgleich** *m* overbalanced **-ausgleichen** to overbalance
Überballonreifen *m* doughnut or balloon tire
Über-bau *m* superstructure **-beanspruchung** *f* overstressing (static), overvoltage (elec.), overstrain(ing), overload **-beizung** *f* overbating **-belastbarkeit** *f* resistance to overstress **-belastet** overbusy, overloaded **-belastung** *f* ultimate load, overloading, overburdening **-belichten** to overexpose **-belichtung** *f* overexposure
überbemessen to overrate
Über-besserung *f* overcorrection, overcompensation **-bestand** *m* surplus stock **-bestimmung** *f* redundancy in determination (math.) **-beton** *m* structural concrete **-biegen** to bend over, overstress **-bieten** to overbid, outbid **-blasen** to overblow **-blatten** to rebate or scarf (rails), halve, overlap **-blaston** *m* overblow tone **-blattung** *f* halving together, halved joint, halving **-bleicht** over-bleached **-bleibsel** *n* remnant, remains, residue, relics, vestige, debris, residuum **-blendeinrichtung** *f* lap dissolve shutter **-blenden** to dissolve, fade-over, mix, lap
Überblender *m* fader (motion picture), blending and mixing
Über-blendmarke *f* change-over mark **-blendmarkengeber** *m* change-over marker generator
Überblendung *f* fading ~ **für Bild und Ton** changeover for image and sound
Überblendungs-blende *f* dissolving shutter, lap-dissolving shutter **-einrichtung** *f* fading control **-zeichen** *n* change-over cue (Film)
Über-blendverstärker *m* mixing amplifier, fading amplifier **-blick** *m* general view, survey **-bord** overboard
Überbordwerfvorrichtung *f* jettison arrangement
überborsaures Natron sodium perborate
Überbrechen *n* rise drift, working in roof (min.)
über-bremsen to brake excessively **-bringen** to convey, carry **-brücken** to bridge (across), span, shunt, by-pass
überbrücktes T-Glied bridged T network
Überbrückung *f* bridging
Überbrückungs-aufnahme *f* transition shot (film) **-draht** *m* jumper **-klemme** *f* bridge connector **-kondensator** *m* by-pass condenser, bridging condenser, shunting condenser, bridging capacitor **-kredit** *m* short-term or tie-over credit **-schalter** *m* short circuiting switch **-schaltung** *f* switching selector repeater (dial system) **-taste** *f* bridging switch
überbürden to overburden, overwork
Überchlorsäure *f* perchloric acid
Überchromsäure *f* perchromic acid
überdachen to roof
überdachte Helling roofed-over building berth
Über-dämpfung *f* overdamping **-dauern** to outlast, outlive, survive
überdecken to cover, roof, overlap, mask, swamp, blanket, eclipse, conceal ~ **eines Signals** to mask the signal
Überdeckung *f* cover, overhead cover, shelter, lap, overlap, overlapping **seitliche** ~ lateral overlap
Überdeckungs-anzeiger *m* overlap indicator **-regler** *m* overlap control
überdestillieren to overdistill
überdimensionieren to make oversize
überdimensioniert oversized
Überdisposition *f* overdraft
überdrehen to overspeed (the engine), overwind **das Gewinde** ~ to strip the thread
Überdrehen *n* superspeed operation (motion picture) ~ **des Motors** overspeeding the engine
Überdrehzahl *f* excess revolutions per minute, overspeed **höchste** ~ maximum overspeed
Überdruck *m* overprint(ing) cover-print, excess or additional pressure, pressure in excess of atmospheric pressure, gauge pressure, superpressure, overpressure, positive pressure, pres-

sure difference **hydrostatischer ~** excess hydrostatic pressure
Überdruck-abblaseventil *n* pressure relief valve, "unloader" relief valve **-anzug** *m* high-pressure diving suit **-artikel** *m* cover-print style **-behälter** *m* pressure tank **-bremse** *f* air-pressure (compressed air) **-buntreserve** *f* colored overprint resist **-echt** fast to overprinting **-effekt** *m* cover-print effect
Überdrucken *n* coverprinting (overprinting)
Überdruck-feder *f* high pressure spring **-festigkeit** *f* structural strength of pressurized cabin **-gebiet** *n* range of positive pressure (phys.), superpressure **-hahn** *m* high-pressure cock (jet) **-kabine** *f* high-pressure cabin, supercharged cabin **-kammer** *f* high-pressure or altitude cabin **-kanal** *m* variable-density wind tunnel **-kühlung** (Motor) overpressure cooling (engine) **-leitung** *f* overpressure pipe, relief pipe
Überdruck-membran *f* pressure diaphragm **-presse** *f* over-pressure grease gun **-pumpe** *f* booster pump **-stelle** *f* overprinted part **-stufe** *f* reaction stage **-tank** *m* pressure tank **-turbine** *f* high-pressure turbine, reaction turbine
Überdruckventil *n* excess-pressure valve, relief pressure valve, governor relief valve, high-pressure relief valve (jet), blowoff valve **rückdruckfreies ~** balanced relief valve
Überdruckwindkanal *m* compressed-air tunnel
überdurchschnittlich better-than-average
übereck diagonal
übereignen to transfer property
übereilen to hasten too much, precipitate, scamp
Übereilung *f* rashness, precipitation, scamping
übereinander angeordnet superposed **~ anordnen** to arrange one above the other
übereinander-fallen to cover each other (lap over) **-geschichtet** superposed **-gestockte Antennenanordnung** stacked antenna array **-greifen** to overlap (television), engage over one another **-greifen** *n* overlap(ping)
übereinandergreifendes Rohr bell and spigot (pipe)
übereinanderkopieren to superimpose
übereinander-lagern to superimpose, superpose **-lagerung** *f* superposition, superimposition **-legen** to superpose **-liegend** superposed, superjacent **-pressen** *n* stack molding **-schweißung** *f* lap welding
Übereinanderwickeln mehrerer Schichten laying various coils over one another
übereinkommen to agree with, arrange, come to terms
Übereinkommen *n* contract, agreement, arrangement, compromise, conformity, convention, compact **ein ~ treffen** to enter into an agreement
Übereinkunft *f* agreement, stipulation
übereinstimmen to agree, coincide, harmonize, acquiesce in, correspond, register (one part with another), be in unison or synchronism (of phases) **mit einem gegebenen Wert ~** to check **nicht ~** to disagree
übereinstimmend corresponding, consistent, identical
Übereinstimmung *f* agreement, conformity, accord, consistency of measuring values, correlation **in ~ befinden** to conform **in ~ bringen** to accommodate, tune, synchronize, conform **~ von Schicht und Unterlage** epitaxy
über-empfindlich hypersensitive, oversensitive **-endlich** transfinite **-entladen** to run down (storage cells) **-entlüftung** *f* overventilation **-entwickelt** overdeveloped, overdone **-erlaubt** superallowed **-erregen** to overexcite **-erregung** *f* overexcitation
Über-erzeugung *f* overproduction **-eutektisch** hypereutectic **-eutektoid** *n* hypereutectoid **-exponiert** overexposed **-fahren** to cross, run over
Überfahren der Endstelle overtravelling, overwinding
Über-fahrt *f* passage **-fahrung** *f* overtravel
Überfall *m* weir, overfall, nappe, sheet of water overflowing, discharge, closing clasp or hasp (of lock) **unvollkommener ~** submerged weir **vollkommener ~** free-overfall weir
Überfall-anruf *m* emergency call **-beiwert** *m* weir coefficient, spillway coefficient
überfallende Farbe overprint color
Überfallhöhe *f* head on weir or crest
überfällig overdue
Überfall-koeffizient *m* overfall coefficient **-krone** *f* spillway crest **-rohr** *n* overflow pipe
Überfallsquelle *f* pocket spring
Überfallwehr *n* spillway, overflow weir
Überfaltung *f* overfolding (min.)
Überfaltungsgebirge *n* overfolded rocks
Überfang *m* covering
überfangen to cover **Glas ~** to plate or case glass
Überfang-glas *n* flashed glass **-scheibe** (für Begrenzungsleuchte) covering disc **-schicht** *f* glass liner or lining
Überfärbe-artikel cross-dyed style **-echt** fast to cross-dyeing **-echtheit** *f* ability of a fabric to resist or withstand bleaching
überfärben to overdye
überfegen to swoop over, buzz
überfein overrefined **-e Struktur** hyperfine structure
überfettete Seife superfatted soap
Überfettung *f* superfattening
überfirnissen to cover with varnish
überfliegen to fly over
überfließen to overflow
überfließend redundant, profuse
überflügeln to outflank
Überflügelung *f* outflanking
Überflur *m* above floor level **-feuer** *n* elevated light **-hydrant** *m* above ground (floor) hydrant **-ofen** *m* elevated furnace **-schere** *f* floor-mounted shears **-tiegelofen** *m* side-drawing-type crucible furnace
Überfluß *m* abundance, excess **im ~ vorhanden** redundant
überflüssig superfluous
Überfluß-kante *f* overflow lip **-pferdekraft** *f* excess horsepower
überfluten to flood, inundate, drown
Überfluten *n* flooding
überflutet flooded **in -em Zustand** awash
Überflutung *f* flood, flooding, inundation
Überflutungsanlage *f* deluge system
Überforderung *f* overcharge
Überfracht *f* additional freight, overfreight

überführbar convertible
überführen to carry over, lead across, transport; (befördern) convey; (überzeugen) convince; convert, transmit, transfer, pass over, reduce to a practical form, ferry, convict
Überführung *f* overhead structure (at road intersection), carrying over, conversion, transmission, conveyance, transfer, viaduct, transition, crossing, transformation, conviction **~ mit Rohrbrücke** pipe bridge crossing **~ in gleicher Weghöhe** level crossing, grade crossing
Überführungs-draht *m* jumper wire **-energie** *f* energy of transfer **-entropie** *f* entropy of transfer **-gerät** *n* terminal equipment **-geschwader** *n* wing of ferrying command **-gestänge** *n* terminal pole
Überführungsisolator *m* terminal insulator **~ mit Vergußkammer** pothead insulator
Überführungs-kasten *m* test box, cross-connecting terminals **-klinke** *f* transfer jack **-lattentuch** *n* lap lattice **-schnur** *f* patchcord **-säule** *f*, **-stange** *f* terminal or distributing pole **-stelle** *f* ferrying station **-stern** *m* transfer star **-zahl** *f* transport number (of ions), transfer number
überfüllen to overfill
Überfüllschutzventil *n* overflow-prevention valve
überfüllt congested
Überfüllung *f* congestion, overfilling
Überfunktion *f* excess function
Übergabe *f* surrender, capitulation, giving up, handing over, yielding, delivery; (einer Anlage) delivery of plant in final working order **-rutsche** *f* chute **-stelle** *f* transfer substation, point of transfer **-verhandlung** *f* negotiation for surrender
Übergang *m* passage, transition, going or passing over, dilution, transfer, crossing, changing, blending, shading (of colors) **bedingter ~** contingent reversion **erzwungener ~** forced or nonspontaneous transition **verflauter ~** softly shaded transition (television) **~ in die Autorotation** autorotation entry **~ innerhalb einer Schale** intrashell transition **~ zur Überschallgeschwindigkeit** change to transonic speed
Übergangs-ausgleichvorrichtung *f* compensating-jet device **-ballistik** *f* intermediate ballistics **-bereich** *m* transition region **-bestandteil** *m* transition substance **-bogen** *m* transition elbow or curve, reducing curve **-brücke** *f* connecting platform **-düse** *f* (Vergaser) transition jet **-einrichtung** *f* change-over device **-eisen** *n* off-grade iron
Übergangs-farbe *f* passing color (chem.) **-fläche** *f* transition level or surface (aviat.) **-flanche** *m* reducing flange **-flugzeug** *n* intermediate training aircraft, intermediate trainer **-formstück** *n* conduit coupling **-funktion** *f* transient response
Übergangs-gebiet *n* transitory region, transonic zone **-gebirge** *n* transition rock **-gebühr** *f* toll **-gefüge** *n* structure of the transition zone **-gestänge** *n* distributing pole (elec.) **-glied** *n* transition type, transition member **-gries** *m* branny fibrous stock **-höhe** *f* transition altitude (aviat.)
Übergangs-kegel *m* forcing cone **-konus** *m* forcing cone **-kurve** *f* transition curve **-lasche** *f* cranked fishplate (R.R.) **-leitwert** *m* transconductance, transfer characteristic **-mittel** *n* (stream-)crossing means **-muffe** *f* reducing socket **-muster** *n* transition type **-nippel** *m* swadged nipple
Übergangs-passung *f* transition fit **-phänomen** *n* transport phenomena **-prüfung** *f* idling test **-punkt** *m* point of separation, burble point, transition point, place of transfer **-rampe** *f* transition shore span **-roheisen** *n* off-grade iron **-rohr** *n* reducing pipe **-schaltung** *f* fading-control unit (sound film) **-scheibe** *f* traversing table (R.R.) **-schicht** *f* transition layer (optics) **-schiene** *f* ramp (section) **-stadium** *n* transition stage **-stahl** *m* transition steel **-stange** *f* junction pole (elec.)
Übergangs-stelle *f* transition point, junction point, place of transition or transfer **-stellung** *f* intermediate position **-streifen** *m* transition strip **-strom** *m* transient **-stück** *n* scantling, reducer, fillet, wing fillet, transition piece **-stufe** *f* transition stage **-stutzen** *m* transfer pipe **-temperatur** *f* transition temperature **-ton** *m* transient sound
Übergangs-verhältnis *n* transport factor **-verkehr** *m* transit traffic **-verkleidung** *f* (Rakete) interstage fairing **-verlust** *m* loss at a junction, transition loss, contact loss **-vertrag** *m* transitional agreement **-vorgang** *m* transient **-wahrscheinlichkeit** *f* transition probability **-welle** *f* intermediate wave **-widerstand** *m* contact resistance, transfer resistance, passive resistance **-winkel** *m* angle of intersection **-wirkungsquerschnitt** *m* transfer cross section **-zahl** *f* transference number (of solution) **-zeit** *f* transition period **-zone** *f* transition zone, refined zone **-zustand** *m* transient or transition stage, intermediate or intermediary stage
übergar overrefined (of metals in general), dry (of copper), too hot (of a furnace), black, burnt **-es Kupfer** dry copper **-er Stahl** overblown steel
übergeben to hand over, surrender **dem Verkehr ~** to open for traffic
übergebietlich interstate
Übergebot *n* higher bid
übergehen to change over into, be converted into, go over, pass over, change, turn (of iron during the blowing)
übergeordnetes Teilgitter superlattice
Über-gemengteil *m* excess contituent **-geschwindigkeitsbegrenzer** *m* overspeed limiter **-geschwindigkeitszustand** *m* overspeed condition
Übergewicht *n* overweight, extra weight, unbalance, disequilibrium, preponderance, predominance **das ~ habend** prevalent
übergießen to pour over, cover by pouring
überglasen to glaze, varnish, ice, vitrify, overglaze
Überglasung *f* glaze, gloss, overglaze, overglazing, vitrification
übergleiten to slide over, glide over, pass over
übergolden to gild
Übergoldung *f* gilding
übergreifen to encroach, stretch too far, overlap, skip, lap over, engage over, transgress, cross a boundary
Übergreifen *n* overlap, crossing
übergreifend overlapping

Übergreiflehre *f* sweep gauge
Übergröße *f* oversize
Übergrundgeschwindigkeitsmesser *m* ground-speed indicator
Übergruppen-bandfilter super-group band filter **-verbindung** *f* supergroup link
Überguß *m* topping **-apparat** *m* overflow apparatus
überhalbkugelig over-hemispherical
überhand-nehmend rampant **-schuh** *m* gauntlet
Überhang *m* overhang, cantilever, rake
überhängen to hang over, project
Überhängen *n* overhang, projection **das ~ eines Flügels** overhang (one wing lower than the other)
überhängend overhanging **-e Nockenwelle** overhead camshaft **-er Stoß** overhanging side (min.) **-e Walze** overhung type of roll **-e Welle** overhanging or projecting shaft **-er Zylinder** overhung cylinder
Überhangstörzeichen *n* trouble sign (elec.)
Überhauen *n* rise drift
überhäuft glutted
überheben to lift over, overlift, pull over, drag over, exceed an issue, overdraw
Überheben *n* lifting over, pulling over
Überhebevorrichtung *f* pull-over or lift-over arrangement
überheizen to overheat
Überheizung *f* overheating
überhelles Stimmungsbild high-key picture
überhitzen to overheat, superheat (beyond saturation)
Überhitzer *m* superheater **-austrittsstutzen** *m* superheater outlet **-kammer** *f* superheater header **-rohr** *n* superheater tube or pipe **-schlange** *f* superheater coil
überhitzt overheated, burnt, superheated **-er Betrieb** dry compression **-er Dampf** superheated steam, dry steam **-er Stahl** overheated steel **-e Stelle** hot spot in combustion chamber
Überhitzung *f* overheating, superheat(ing)
Überhitzungs-messer *m* superheating meter **-temperatur** *f* final steam temperature **-verfahren** *n* working on dry compression
überhöht surmounted, superelevated, increased (geom.) **-es Diagramm** condensed diagram
Überhöhung *f* magnification, increased height, superelevation, camber, crown, bank or cant (in a curve), hump, superelevation (of rails), lobe (on cam)
Überholdrehmoment *n* overrunning torque
überholen to overtake, outspeed, outstrip, override, pass, overhaul, recondition, overreach, outrun, catch up with ~ (übertreffen) to supersede **im Lauf ~** to overrun, override
Überholen *n* overtaking
Überhol-kuppelung *f* overriding clutch, overrunning **-melder** *m* passing signal
überholt outdated, obsolete
Überholung *f* overtaking, overhauling **~ des oberen Teiles eines Motors** top overhaul (of engine) **vollständige ~** complete overhaul
Überholungs-anweisung *f* overhaul handbook **-arbeit** *f* overhauling **-gebiet** (*n*) **der Elektronen** catch-up, overtake, or bunching range of electrons **-gleis** *n* passing siding **-zeichen** *n* overtaking signal **-zeit** *f* time of overhaul

überhör-frequent ultra-audible, superaudible **-frequenz** *f* ultra-audible frequency, ultra-audio frequency, supersonic, ultrasonic, or superaudible frequency
Überkämmung *f* cogging joint
überkant overedge, overlap
überkippen to overturn, tip over
Überkippen *n* overturn
überkippt iverted, overturned **-e Falte** recumbent fold
Über-kippung *f* overthrust, reverse fault **-klappvorgang** *m* diffusionless process **-klotzen** to slop-pad
überkochen to boil over
Überkochrohr *n* overflow pipe
Überkohlung *f* supercarburization
überkompensieren to overcompensate
Überkompensierung *f* overcompensation
überkomprimiert supercompressed **-er Motor** supercompression engine
Überkonduktivität *f* hyperconductivity
Überkopf-gesteinsbohrer *m* stoper **-laden** *n* overhead loading **-schaufel** *f* overhead bucket **-schweißung** *f* overhead welding
Überkopplung *f* tight coupling
Überkorn *n* too coarse grain, oversize (pieces)
überkritisch-e Dämpfung over-damping **-e Geschwindigkeit** major resonant speed
Überkorrektur *f* overcorrection, overcompensation
überkorrigieren to overcorrect
Überkorrigieren *n* overcorrection
überkragen to overhang
Überkragung *f* overhang
Überkreuzung *f* crossing over
Überkrümmung *f* excessive curvature
überkrusten to incrust
Überkrustung *f* incrustation
Überkühlung *f* overcooling, supercooling
Überladekran *m* gantry crane, material-handling crane
überladen to overload, overcharge, tranship, surcharge **nicht -er Motor** unboosted engine
Überladen *n* transshipment, transfer, bridge
Überlader *m* supercharger (of engine) **-höhe** *f* supercharge height
Überladung *f* overcharging, overloading, transshipment, overcharge, overload
Überlage *f* auxiliary thread or binder
Überlagerer *m* heterodyne, (heterodyne) oscillator **örtlicher ~** local oscillator
Überlagererfrequenz *f* local oscillation frequency
überlagern to overlay, overlie, superpose, superimpose, heretodyne
überlagert superordinated, superimposed **-e niederfrequente Schwingung** wobbling frequency
Überlagerung *f* superposition, super(im)posing, superimposition, interference, overlapping, heterodyning **~ von Schwingungen** overlapping of vibrations **~ einer Störung** interference **mittels ~ empfangen** to heterodyne
Überlagerungsempfang *m* superheterodyne reception, beat reception **~ mit Fremderregung** separate heterodyne reception **~ mit Selbsterregung** self-heterodyne reception, autodyne reception **~ mit Überhörfrequenz** supersonic

heterodyne reception

Überlagerungsempfänger *m* (super)heterodyne receiver, beat receiver, heterodyne oscillator ~ **mit Fremderregung** separate heterodyne receiver ~ **mit Selbsterregung** autodyne receiver, self-heterodyne receiver

Überlagerungsfläche *f* covering surface **zweiblättrige** ~ covering of two sheets

Überlagerungsfrequenz *f* beat or heterodyne frequency **-messer** *m* heterodyne-frequency meter

Überlagerungs-gerät *n* heterodyne mixer **-kreis** *m* heterodyne circuit, superposed circuit **-näherung** *f* superposition approximation **-pfeifen** *n* self-whistles **-prinzip** *n* superheterodyne principle **-rechnung** *f* computation of missile oscillation

Überlagerungs-satz *m* superposition theorem **-schaltung** *f* superimposed connection **-schutz** *m* back-up protection **-schwingung** *f* heterodyne oscillation **-steilheit** *f* conversion conductance **-stufe** *f* mixer stage, first detector **-summer** *m* heterodyne oscillator **-telegraphie** *f* superaudio telegraphy **-ton** *m* beat tone, beat note **-verstärkung** *f* conversion gain

Überland-anlage *f* grid supply **-bahn** *f* interurban railway **-fernkabel** *n* overland long-distance cable **-flug** *m* cross-country flight **-leitung** *f* rural subscriber line **-teilnehmerleitung** *f* rural subscriber's line **-verkehr** *m* interurban traffic **-werk** *n* super power station **-zentrale** *f* rural power station, high-tension power plant, long-distance power station, long-distance telephone exchange

überlappen to lap (over), overlap

Überlappen *n* lapping (over), overlap(ping) ~ **der Wellenzüge** overlap of wave trains

Überlapp-naht *f* lap joint (seam) **-schweißung** *f* overlap welding

überlappt overlapped ~ **schweißen** to lap-weld, scarf-weld **-e Schweißung** joint welding, lap-seam weld **-er Stoß, -e Verbindung** lap joint

Überlappung *f* overlap, lap, overlapping, lap joint, scarf

Überlappungs-bereich *m* transition region **-frequenz** *f* crossover frequency **-nietung** *f* lap riveting **-saum** *m* overlap seam **-schweißung** *f* lap weld, lap welding **-verbindung** *f* lap joint

überlaschen to place a butt strap over the joint, splice

Überlaschung *f* splicing

überlassen to leave, give up, abandon

Überlast *f* overload, excess load, overloading

Überlastbarkeit *f* overload capacity

Überlastbarkeitsbereich *m* overload margin

überlasten to overload, overburden, overstrain, operate above capacity

Überlast-faktor *m* overload capacity **-schalter** *m* circuit breaker, overload cutout **-sicherung** *f* overload safety device **-strom** *m* overload current

Überlastung *f* overload, overstrain, overcharge, overtax, overrunning (a lamp), overvolting ~ **durch Einschaltstromspitze** inrush load **Kuppelung zur Sicherung gegen** ~ overload clutch

Überlastungs-fähigkeit *f* overload capacity **-grenze** *f* overload capacity **-prüfung** *f* overload test **-relais** *n* overcurrent relay **-schutz** *m* overload protection or relief valve **-zähler** *m* congestion meter

Überlastversuch *m* overload test, overstrain test

Überlauf *m* flash, overflow, weir, waste, spillway, tray riser, weir box, run over ~ **der Sprudelplatte** tray riser

Überlauf-behälter *m* overflow tank, flushing tank **-bohrung** *f* overflow port **-deich** *m* overflow dike

überlaufen to overflow

Überlaufen *n* overflowing, overflow, flooding

Überlauf-flansch *m* overflow flange **-gefäß** *n* overflow reservoir **-hahn** *m* overflow cock **-kanal** *m* spill port **-kante** *f* lip, overflow baffle or edge **-kraftstoff** *m* bleed fuel **-leitung** *f* overflow pipe **-platz** *m* overflow or spill-over position **-quelle** *f* depression spring **-rinne** *f* overflow gutter, overflow **-rohr** *n* tray downspout, overflow pipe **-rost** *m* transfer grid

Überlauf-sammelschiene *f* scupper **-schale** *f* oil overflow cup **-schieber** *m* overflow regulator, overflow damper **-sicherheitskupplung** *f* overflow protective clutch **-sicherung** *f* overrun safety device **-standkasten** *m* weir box **-stollen** *m* (Hochwasserstollen) tunnel-type discharge carrier **-stutzen** *m* scupper **-verschluß** *m* spillway crest gate **-verschraubung** *f* overflow coupling **-vorrichtung** *f* overflow arrangement or device

Überlebungskurve *f* survival curve

Überlebenszeit *f* survival time

überlegen superior

Überlegenheit *f* superiority, preponderance

Überlegung *f* reason, reflection, consideration, deliberation

überleicht ultra-light **-es Flugzeug** ultra-light plane

Überleitamt *n* radio relay station

überleiten to conduct over, pass over **zum Wahlbetrieb** ~ to convert from manual to automatic working (teleph.)

Überleiten von Wasserdampf über glühenden Koks passing of steam over incandescent coke

überleitend transient

Überleit-fähigkeit *f* supraconductivity **-rutsche** *f* transfer chute

Überleitung eines Amtes cutover of a central office

Überleitungs-amt *n* transfer exchange **-pumpe** *f* transfer pump **-versuch** *m* throttling experiment

Überlichtung *f* overexposure

überliegen to heel over, list

überlochen to patch, (info proc.) erase

Überlochungen *pl* zone punching

Überlüftung *f* hyperventilation

Übermalung *f* new paint

Übermangansäure *f* permanganic acid

übermangansaures Kali potassium permanganate

Übermaß *n* oversize, excess, overmeasure, interference ~ **geben** to measure over **bis zum** ~ **tun** to overdo

übermäßig excessive, exorbitant, extreme, enormous

übermastizierter Gummi dead-rolled rubber

Übermatrix *f* matrix whose elements are matrices

übermessen to remeasure

Über-mikrometer *n* ultramicrometer **-mikro-**

skopie *f* electron microscopy **-mikroskopisch** ultramicroscopic
übermitteln to transmit, send forward **eine Gesprächsanmeldung ~** to pass a call
Übermittler *m* transmitter
Übermittlung *f* transmission, forwarding
Übermittlungs-geschwindigkeit *f* transmission speed **-spruch** *m* through-message
über-modeln to overmodulate **-modelung** *f* overmodulation **-modulieren** to overmodulate **-moment** *n* lifting moment
Übernahme *f* taking over, assuming, acceptance **-bedingung** *f* condition of acceptance **-bericht** *m* taking-over report **-kommando** *n* taking-over detachment **-probe** *f* acceptance test **-urkunde** *f* acceptance receipt **-werte** *pl* take-over prices
übernehmen to take charge of, incur, take possession of, take upon oneself, take in hand **einen Aktienanteil ~** to take over part of the stock **eine Funktion ~** to take charge of
Über- oder Unterdeckung over or under-recoveries
überölt over-lubricated
Überosmiumsäure *f* osmium tetroxide
Überoxyd *n* peroxide
Über-oxydation *f*, **-oxydierung** *f* peroxidation, overoxidation
überpantoffeln to cork over (regrain)
überplanmäßig in excess of authorized strength or allowance
Über-oszillieren *n* squeeging **-plastik** *f* exaggerated relief **-polen** *n* overpoling **-polieren** to surface polish **-potential** *n* superpotential **-preis** *m* supplemental cost **-produktion** *f* overproduction, oversupply, surplus production **-prüfen** to check, examine, verify
Überprüfung *f* screening, examination, revision **~ im Flug** flight check
Über-prüfwerte *pl* supervising specifications **-quellen** to flow over **-queren** to cross **-querung** *f* crossing (elec.) **-raffiniert** overrefined **-ragen** to overlap, overhang, tower above, surmount, project (above)
Überration *f* allowance for waste
überrechnen to check figures quickly, estimate
Überreduktion *f* over-reduction
über-regeln to overregulate **-regulierung** *f* excessive regulation, excessive compensation, overcompensation
überreichen to hand
überreichlich superabundant, excess, excessive
Überreichweite *f* propagation beyond the horizon **-verbindung** *f* beyond horizon communication
Überreißen *n* entrainment
Über-rest *m* residue, remainder **-rohr** *n* suction sleeve **-rosten** to become covered with rust **-rösten** to overroast, burn **-rot** infrared, ultrared **-rottet** overdone (flax, hemp)
Überrückkuppelung *f* superregeneration
Überrückkuppelungsempfänger *m* superregenerative receiver, superregenerator, periodic-trigger-type receiver
Übersäen *n* overseeding
übersättigen to supersaturate, oversaturate
Übersättigung *f* supersaturation
Übersaturation *f* oversaturation
übersauer too acid, too sour
übersäuern to overacidify, peroxidize
übersaur-es Ammon ammonium perchlorate **-es Kali** potassium perchlorate **-es Natrium** sodium perchlorate **-es Salz** perchlorate
Überschall *m* supersonic, ultrasonic **-flugkörper** *m* aero-space project **-frequenz** *f* supersonic frequency, supertonic frequency **-gerät** *n* ultrasonic equipment **-geschwindigkeit** *f* supersonic velocity or speed **-gleitflugbahn** supersonic glide **-kanal** *m* supersonic or transonic wind tunnel **-kante** *f* supersonic edge **-knall** *m* supersonic boom **-lichtzelle** *f* supersonic light relay or valve **-profil** *n* supersonic profil, airfoil for supersonic velocity
Überschall-strömung *f* supersonic flow **-taschen** *pl* supersonic pockets **-treibstrahl** *m* supersonic driving jet **-verkehr** *m* supersonic traffic **-verkehrsflugzeug** *n* supersonic transport (SST) **-welle** *f* supersonic or ultra-audio wave **-wellenanhäufung** *f* accumulation of ultrasonic waves **-wellenfrequenz** *f* supersonic frequency **-widerstand** *m* regulating resistance, variable resistance **-windkanal** *m* supersonic wind tunnel
über-schalten to switch over **-schätzen** to overrate **-schauen** to look over, survey **-schäumen** to foam over, froth over
Überschäumen *n* foaming over
Überschäumung *f* boiling over (foam)
Überschein *m* overhand appearance (overtone)
Überschicht *f* extra task (min.)
überschicken to transmit
überschieben to slip over
Überschieb-muffe *f* double socket **-rohr** *n* sleeve tube
Überschiebung *f* fault overthrust, overthrust, overlapping of influence, transvection
Überschiebungs-fläche *f* thrust plane **-masse** *f* overthrust mass (geol.) **-schmelzung** *f* superfusion, enameling **-spalte** *f* fissure of overthrust (geol.) **-wechsel** *m* reversed fault
Überschiffung *f* transshipment
überschießen to exceed, overshooting
überschießender Betrag amount in excess of balance
Überschlag *m* breakdown by surface conduction (electric insulation), ground loop, (rough) estimate, computation, wing-over, arc-over, spark-over, flash-over, somersault, nose-over (aviation) **~ auf dem Boden** ground loop **~ über den Flügel** wing-over, barrel roll **~ elektrischer Funken** disruptive discharge, flashover **~ in der Luft** loop (aviation) **~ der Sichtmaschine** tail of a dressing machine
überschlagen to compute, estimate, flashover, arc over, sparkover **sich ~** to capsize, somersault, nose-over (aviation), turn over, tumble **bei -er Rechnung** calculating roughly
überschlägig rough(ly) **~ berechnet** calculating roughly
überschlägig estimated **-e Prüfung** judgment test
Überschlag(s)-formel *f* rule of thumb, rough formula **-länge** *f* propagation distance **-probe** *f* gap test **-rechnung** *f* rough calculation **-sicher** uncapsizable
Überschlag(s)spannung *f* breakdown voltage, sparkover voltage, disruptive voltage, flashover voltage **~ (bei nassem Isolator)** wet flashover voltage

Überschlag(s)-strecke *f* spark-over path **-versuch** *m* flashover test (elec.) **-verteiler** *m* flash-over distributor **-weise** by estimation

Überschleuseventil *n* by-pass valve

Überschleusleitung *f* overflow pipe

überschlichten to plane over

überschmelzen to enamel

überschmolzen supercooled, surfused

überschneiden to overlap, cut across

Überschneiden *n* overlapping

Überschneidung *f* (point of) intersection, overlap(ping), intercept overcutting ~ **der Blattkreise** *f* (Hubschrauber) blade overlap ~ **der Ventilöffnungszeiten** valve overlap

Überschneidungs-frequenz *f* cross-over frequency **-gebiet** *n* equiphase zone

überschreiben to carry over, transfer, entitle

Überschreibungs-fehler *m* overwriting error **-urkunde** *f* deed of conveyance

Überschreien *n* overload or peak (of microphone), overmodulation

überschreiten to cross, ford, pass, exceed

Überschreitfähigkeit *f* ditch-crossing ability

Überschreitung *f* driving-out (print.), exceeding (a certain limit, mark, level, or value), transgression

Überschrift *f* title, heading, caption

Überschub *m* transferring **-feuerung** *f* overfeed stocker **-rohr** *n* sleeve tube

überschuldet deeply involved in debt

Überschuß *m* excess, surplus **-gas** *n* surplus gas **-halbleiter** *m* N-type semi-conductor **-halbleitung** *f* conduction by excess electrons (in-type conduction)

überschüssig in excess, excess, surplus, remaining **-er Aushub** *m* spoil, surplus earth, waste

Überschuß-leiter *m* type semiconductor **-protonen** *pl* surplus protons **-reaktivität** excess multiplication constant **-wasser** *n* overflow water

Überschütten *n* paving (a road)

Überschüttung *f* (earth) fill

Überschwefelsäure *f* persulfuric acid

überschwefelsau(e)r-es Ammon ammonium persulfate **-es Kali** potassium persulfate **-es Natron** sodium persulfate

überschwellig superthreshold (sound)

überschwellt overplumped

überschwemmen to flood, inundate, submerge

Überschwemmung *f* inundation, flood, flooding, submergence, freshet

Überschwemmungs-entwickler *m* water to carbide gas generator **-gebiet** *n* inundated or flooded area

überschwer exceedingly or very heavy

Überschwingdauer *f* overshoot period

Überschwingen *n* overshot (of meas. instr)

Überschwingung *f* overswing (of compass needle in aviation), overshot (television)

Überschwingweite *f* maximum overshoot (aut. contr)

Übersee *f* overseas **-empfänger** *m* transocean or transatlantic receiver **-flugzeug** *n* seagoing or oversea plane **-handel** *m* transatlantic, foreign, or oversea trade

überseeisch transoceanic

Übersee-kabel *n* transmarine or submarine cable **-verbindung** *f*, **-verkehr** *m* transoceanic communication

übersehen to overlook, omit, oversee, see at a glance, survey, sweep (with eye)

Übersendung *f* remittance

übersetzen to gear, transmit (mech.), cross; translate

Übersetzen *n* crossing

Übersetzer *m* translator, translating device, converter, transducer, decoder, printer **-rechen** *m* combine comb **-scheibe** *f* combine disk

Übersetz-fähre *f* ferry **-gerät** *n* transmission device **-gruppe** *f* crossing detail **-hebel** *m* mixing level **-hebellager** *n* mixing lever bearing **-mittel** *n* river-crossing equipment **-stelle** *f* stream-crossing point, ferrying point, crossing site

übersetzt reflected (signal through transformer), geared, translated **nicht** ~ directly driven

Übersetzung *f* mechanical "step-up", conversion, translation, reduction, gear or lever ratio, transmission, gearing, transformer ratio, ratio of windings ~ **eines Getriebes ins Grosse** step-up gearing ~ **des Hebels** lever advantage **reduzierende** ~ reduction gearing

Übersetzungs-bereich *m* range of ratios **-fehler** *m* (Meßwandler) ratio error **-getriebe** *n* speed-increaser drive, stepup gearing, transmission gear(ing) **-motor** *m* reduction gear **-rad** *n* pulley **-räderhebel** *m* compound gear handle **-rohr** *n* converter tube **-stoßdämpfer** *m* transmission shock absorber **-stufe** *f* stage **-verhältnis** *n* transformation ratio, speed ratio, gear ratio, ratio of speed reduction, transmission ratio

Übersetzungsverhältnis des Planrades ratio for the crown wheel

Übersetzungs-welle *f* jack shaft **-zahl** *f* transformation ratio or figure **-zahnrad** *n* back gear

Übersicht *f* survey, synopsis, summary, abstract, review, chart, plan, table, extract, digest

übersichtig farsighted, hyperopic

Übersichtigkeit *f* farsightedness, hyperopia

übersichtlich clear, distinct, easily followed up, easily understandable **-e Anordnung** neat grouping

Übersichtlichkeit *f* facility of inspection, (functional) clarity (e.g. of control panel)

Übersichts-aufnahme *f* photograph survey, photography **-bild** *n* general view, index map **-karte** *f* index map to a map series, general map **-lupe** *f* survey lens **-plan** *m* general or principal plan **-rohr** *n* main range tube (electronics), general-view tube or oscilloscope **-röhre** *f* general viewing tube **-schema** *n* block diagram **-skizze** *f* general sketch, synoptical sketch, scheme, plan **-spektrum** *n* general spectrum **-tabelle** *f* synoptic table **-tafel** *f* synoptic table **-zeichnung** *f* survey diagram

Übersieb *n* superposed sieve

übersieden to boil over, distill

Übersieden *n* boiling over, distillation

übersilbern to silver-plate, silver

überspannen to overstress

überspannt overstrained, overvolted **-er Betrieb** overvoltage or overvolted operation, overrunning **-er Dampf** compressed steam **-er Zustand** overstrained state, state of supertension or overvoltage

Überspannung *f* overtension, excessive voltage, flashover voltage, surge, overload, overpressure, overrunning

Überspannungs-ableiter *m* lightening arrester or protector, surge or voltage arrester **-ausschalter** *m* over-voltage trip-out **-durchschlag** *m* breakdown due to overvoltage **-funkenstrecke** *f* surge arrester, surge gap, surge absorber **-schalter** over-voltage trip-out **-schutz** *m* surge arrester or protection, overvoltage protection **-schutzdrossel** *f* choke coil **-schutzkondensator** *m* protective capacitor for overvoltages **-schutzschalter** *m* overload safety switch **-sicherung** *f* excess-voltage cutout, lightning arrester (on mast bases), fuse **-verhältnis** *n* magnification of the circuit **-welle** *f* excess-voltage wave

überspektral superspectral

Überspielen *n* rerecording

überspinnen to spin over, cover

Übersprechdämpfung *f* cross-talk transmission equivalent

übersprechen to cross-talk (television)

Übersprechen *n* (side-to-side) cross talk, inductive disturbances ~ **der Seitenfrequenzen** side band (rdr.)

Übersprech-erscheinung *f* cross talk, distortion, lack of sensitivity **-kuppelung** *f* cross-talk path, side-to-side unbalance **-weg** *m* cross-talk path

Überspring-anschlag *m* override stop

überspringen to jump over, omit, skip, spark **-der Funke** jump spark

Überspringen *n* flashing over, side flashing of lightning

Überspringvorrichtung *f* skipper

Überspritzechtheit *f* fastness to overspraying

überspritzen to cross-spray (spray over)

übersprudeln to bubble over

Überstand *m* projecting length (of bolt)

überständig overmature

überstauen to overdam, raise a dam **ein Dorf ~** to submerge a village

Überstauung *f* overdamming

Übersteckring *m* retaining ring

überstehen to endure, overcome, project, stand out

überstehend overlying, overhanging, standing over, supernatant (liquids), projecting (beam), protruding, salient, surmounting **-e Winkelsporen** extension angle lugs

übersteigen to cross, surmount, exceed

Übersteiggefäß *n* overflow vessel

übersteuern to override, overtravel (control), overdrive, overload, overmodulate, overrun

Übersteuern *n* overriding **Sicherung gegen ~** overriding control

übersteuert overexcited, overmodulated **-er Verstärker** overdriven amplifier

Übersteuerung *f* over-excitation, overmodulation (in film recording), overbias, overloading (of tubes), causing blasting, sound overshooting, blasting (of microphone)

Übersteuerungs-abschneider *m* overload chopper **-anzeiger** *m* overload indicator **-indikator** *m* overmodulation indicator **-messer** *m* overload indicator **-punkt** *m* overload point (of recorder) **-schutz** *m* overload limiter (for film) **-sicherung** *f* overriding control **-vorgang** *m* override action **-zeiger** *m* overload indicator

Überstrahlen *n* swamping or outshining (of spectral lines)

Überstrahlung *f* halation, irradiation

überstreichen to coat, dope, sweep, stroke over

Überstreichen *n* stroking over, coating ~ **des Leuchtschirmes** sweep out of television screen

Überstreichung eines Frequenzbereichs sweeping of a frequency range, coverage of a frequency band

überstreifen to slip over, pull over

Überstreif-lehre *f* pull-over gauge **-ring** *m* spring or snap piston ring

überstrichene Fläche migration area

Überström-druck *m* overflow pressure **-leitung** *f* overflow pipe **-regelung** *f* overflow control

überströmen to flow over, overflow, by-pass

Überström-kanal *m* transfer port, return passage, bypass, receiver **-stück** *n* (Pumpe) overflow piece

Überströmventil *n* overflow or relief valve, spill valve **-regulierung** *f* by-pass valve control

Überströmvorrichtung *f* overload device

Überströmweg *m* by-pass

Überstrom *m* excess current, overcurrent **-auslöser** *m* overcurrent release **-ausschalter** *m* overload circuit breaker **-nullspannungsausschalter** *m* excess-current zero-voltage cutout switch **-relais** *n* overload relay **-schalter** *m* excess-current switch, maximum cutout, high-voltage switch **-schutz** *m* overload protective device, overload protection

Überstruktur *f* superstructure **-linien** *pl* superlattice lines **-reflex** *m* superlattice reflection **-umwandlungen** superlattice transformations

überstülpen to slip over, tilt or cover over

Überstunde *f* overtime

überstürzen to overturn, upset, act rashly

Übersud *m* distillate

übersynchron hypersynchronous

übertag aboveground

Übertagebetrieb *m* open-cast workings

übertäuben to drown (a noise), deafen

Überteilung am Maßstab additional graduation on the scale

Übertemperatur *f* excess temperature

Übertiefe *f* overdepth

Übertiefung *f* renewed degradation

übertönen to sound through or above

Überton *m* overtone **-band** *n* overtone band

Übertrag *m* transfer, carry (info proc.)

übertragbar transferable, negotiable

Übertragbarkeit *f* negotiability (of securities)

übertragen to transmit, convey, send, consign to, transport, transfer, carry, relay, alienate, translate, transcribe, assign, vest in, delegate, confer, grant, cede **durch Rundfunk ~** to broadcast

Übertragender *m* assignor, grantor, transferor

Übertrager *m* transmitter (elec.), translator, repeater, transformer or repeating coil (teleph.), carrier (chem.), transducer ~ **mit Eisenkern** transformer with iron core ~ **mit unterteiltem Eisenkern** air-gap transformer ~ **mit hohem Umsetzungsverhältnis** high-ratio transformer ~ **mit zwei Wicklungen** two-winding transformer **geschirmter ~** shielded transformer **regelbarer ~** variable transformer **symmetrischer ~** symmetrical transformer (elec.)

Übertrager-amt *n* repeater or repeating station **-gestell** *n* repeating-coil rack **-kästchen** *n* translator case, repeating-coil unit **-kondensator** *m* grid condenser (in grid-current detector) **-kreis** *m* intermediate or transformer circuit

Übertragerpaar *n* line repeating coil **~ für Viererleitung und Nachbildung** matched repeating coils for phantom circuits

Übertrager-schalter *m* translatory key **-spule** *f* repeating coil **-verstärker** *m* transformer-coupled amplifier

Übertragsglimmröhre *f* glow transfer tube

Übertragung *f* relay repeater (tel.), propagation, convection, transmission, transfer, application, transcription, translation, conduction, assignment, conveyance **~** (eines Textes vom Band) transcription (tape rec.) **~ von Dias** scanning of slides **~ eines Fernsprechanschlusses** transfer of a telephone connection **~ auf Kabeln** cable transmission **~ in Telegrafenleitungen** telegraph repeater **~ mit Trägerströmen** carrier transmission **bildtelegrafische ~** telephotographic transmission **entzerrende ~** regenerative or rectifying repeater **gerichtete ~** directive transmission **mehrwegige ~** multipath or multichannel transmission **umlaufende ~** rotary repeater

Übertragungs-amt *n* repeater station, repeating (telegraph) station, transmission equipment **-anlage** *f* transmission system **-äquivalent** *n* transmission equivalent **-band** *n* signal band, communication band **-beamter** *m* relay clerk **-bereich** *m* transmission range **-einheit** *f* transmission unit **-einrichtung** *f* repeater equipment **-entfernung** *f* transmission distance **-erklärung** *f* deed of transfer **-fähigkeit** *f* transmitting capacity

Übertragungsfaktor *m* steady state gain (servo), transfer factor, image-transfer constant **~ einer glatten** (homogenen) **Leitung** propagation factor **~ eines Vierpols** iterative propagation factor

Übertragungs-filter *n* transmission filter circuit **-formel** *f* radio-transmission formula **-frequenz** *f* transmission frequency **-frequenzlinie** *f* transmission-frequency characteristic **-funkstelle** *f* relay(ing) station, rebroadcast transmitter

Übertragungs-gegenstand *m* teleview or televised object, object to be transmitted by video signals **-gerät** *n* data transmitter, transcriber **-geschwindigkeit** *f* transmission speed, signaling speed **-gestänge** *n* transmission rods **-glied** *n* transfer element **-güte** *f* transmission performance (in rating) **-kanal** *m* communication or transmission channel **-kenngröße** *f* transmission characteristic

Übertragungsklopfer *m* relaying sounder **den ~ abstellen** to silence the sounder

Übertragungs-konstante *f* transmission or transfer constant **-körper** *m* induced-detonation charge **-kurve** *f* transmission curve, transmission-frequency characteristic **-ladung** *f* propagation charge, primer charge **-leitung** *f* transmission line, cable, or system **-leitungsstück** *n* transmission line stub **-leitwert** *m* transfer admittance

Übertragungsmaß *n* transmission unit, transmission measure, transmission equivalent, propagation constant, attenuation factor, image transfer, attenuation constant **~ je Glied** propagation constant per section **~ in Meilen Standardkabel** transmission equivalent in miles of standard cable **gesamtes ~** total transmission equivalent, transmission efficiency **zulässiges ~** total permissible transmission equivalent

Übertragungs-maximum *n* transmission maximum **-medium** *n* transmitting medium **-messung** *f* transmission measurement **-mittel** *n* transmitting medium, transmission agent, transmitter, transmitting means **-niveau** *n* transmission level **-normal** *n*, **-norm** *f* transmission standard **-organ** *n* transmission agent **-pegel** *m* transmission level, intensity of magnetic field **-prinzip** *n* transfer rate

Übertragungsrad *n* feed gear **-gehäuse** *n* transmission gear case

Übertragungs-relais *n* translating or repeating relay **-riemen** *m* transmission belt **-rolle** *f* return pulley **-schwingung** *f* signal oscillation or wave **-stange** *f* transmission rod **-stoß** *m* transmission shock **-system** *n* transmission system, transducer, transductor **-technik** *f* transmission technique **-urkunde** *f* deed of conveyance, transfer deed, deed of assignment, assignment

Übertragungs-vergleichssystem *n* transmission reference system **-verhältnis** *n* transmission ratio **-verlust** *m* transmission loss **-verteiler** *m* transmitting distributor **-verzögerung** *f* transmission lag (servo) **-vorschub** *m* overflow ejection **-weg** *m* transmission path or channel, transmission system or medium **-welle** *f* wave of translation **-wirksamkeit** *f* transmission efficiency (teleph.) **-wirkungsgrad** *m* transmission efficiency **-zeit** *f* duration of transmission, transit time

Übertragwalze *f* transporter

übertreffen to exceed, excel, surpass **an Höhe ~** to surmount **an Schnelligkeit ~** to outspeed **an Zahl ~** to outnumber

über-treiben to exaggerate, overdo **-treibung** *f* exaggeration, overstatement, excess **-trieb** *m* transmission, change over **-trieben** excessive, exaggerated, overdrawn, extreme, exorbitant **-treten** to step over, overflow, go over, trespass **-tretung** *f* transgression, infringement, contravention, offense, violation **-trocknen** to dry hard (paper mfg.) **-trocknet** overdried **-trommel** *f* range drum

Überverbrauchs-tarif *m* overload tariff **-zähler** *m* excess-power or current meter

Überverbund-dynamo *m* overcompounded dynamo **-erregung** *f* overcompound excitation

überverdichten to supercharge

überverdichtender Motor supercharged engine

Überverdichter *m* supercharger

überverdichtet over-compressed

Überverdichtung *f* supercharging

Überverdichtungsgrad *m* degree of overcompaction or supercharging

Übervergrößerung *f* extra or supplementary magnification, overmagnification

übervergütet overaging

überviolett ultraviolet

Übervorratszucker *m* surplus-stock sugar

Übervorscheidung *f* overpredefecation

Übervulkanisation *f* cure, overcure
überwachen to watch, superintend, inspect, control, supervise, observe, monitor, guard, check
Überwachsung *f* overgrowth
Überwachung *f* control, supervision, check, inspection, observation, monitoring, surveillance, tell-tale device, watching ~ **durch Flugzeuge** aerial survey ~ **ohne Schlußzeichen vom angerufenen Teilnehmer** blind supervision ~ **am Ursprungsort** local supervision **laufende** ~ routine supervision
Überwachungs-anlage *f* monitoring system **-bezirk** *m* observation area **-blatt** *n* service-observing summary, circuit-usage record **-einrichtung** *f* supervisory equipment **-gerät** *n* safety device, control instrument **-gestell** *f* monitor rack **-gruppe** *f* supervisory group **-ingenieur** *m* construction superintendent **-instrument** *n* monitoring meter **-klinke** *f* monitor jack, pilot jack **-kreis** *m* monitoring circuit
Überwachungslampe *f* supervisory lamp, pilot signal, pilot lamp ~ **des rufenden (verlangten) Teilnehmers** answering (calling) supervisory lamp
Überwachungs-liste *f* check list, control roster **-messung** *f* maintenance test **-platz** *m* service-observing desk **-programm** *n* tracing routine (info proc.) **-relais** *n* pilot relay, supervisory relay **-schalter** *m*, **-schlüssel** *m* monitoring key **-schnur** *f* monitor or supervisory cord
Überwachungs-schrank *m* service-observing board **-stelle** *f* observation desk (teleph.) **-strom** *m* control current **-stromkreis** *m* supervisory circuit **-tafel** *f* control board, supervisory board **-vorrichtung** *f* control gear **-zeichen** *n* supervisory or pilot signal
überwallen to boil over
überwältigen to overcome, subdue, overpower, vanquish
überwalzen to peen over (aviation), spin over
Überwalzung *f* lap
Überwärme *f* excess heat
Überwasser *n* overflowing water **-fahrzeug** *n* surface vessel **-geschwindigkeit** *f* surface speed **-rohr** *n* torpedo tube above water, above-water tube
Überweg *m* crossing
Überweganker *m* stub guy, over-road stay
überweisen to transfer, refer, remit, transmit, allot, send, convey
Überweisung *f* transfer, allotment
Überweisungs-amt *n* toll station **-fernamt** *n* originating or terminating toll center, transfer trunk exchange **-leitung** *f* transfer line (teleph.) **-mitteilung** *f* remittance statement **-scheck** *m* transfer ticket **-taste** *f* assignment key **-verkehr** *m* tandem operation **-wähler** *m* allotting switch
Überwendlichnähmaschine *f* oversewing machine
überwerfen to throw over, overthrow (someone)
überwiegen to outweigh, outnumber, preponderate, outbalance
Überwiegen *n* preponderance, bias ~ **nach der Zeichen-(Trenn-)seite** marking (spacing) bias
überwiegend outbalance, preponderant, predominant, prevalent **einseitig** ~ biased
überwinden to conquer, overcome, surmount, master
Überwinden *n* overcoming, conquest, crossing
Überwindung *f* overcoming, surmounting **prozentueller Anteil der zur** ~ **des Luftwiderstandes erforderlichen Leistung** percentage drag power
überwölben to overarch, vault over
überwölbte Kehlnaht *f* convex fillet weld
überwuchern to overgrow
Überwucht *f* unbalanced impact
Überwurf *m* roughcast bush (mech.), hasp, clasp (lock) **-heustabler** *m* overshot hay stacker **-kapsel** *f* screw cap **-mutter** *f* screw cap, box nut, cap screw, adapter, clamping nut, retaining nut, union (mach.), connection nut, coupling nut, hinge bolt, sleeve nut, union nut **-ring** *m* screw collar ring **-schraube** *f* cap screw
Überzahl *f* majority
überzählig superfluous, redundant, spare, supernumerary **-er Stab** redundant member **-e Teile** excess parts, overs (aviation)
überzeichnet oversubscribed
überziehen to cover, coat, line, plate, overlay, incrust, put over, put on, become coated or covered, stall (aviation), dress (filter) **das Flugzeug** ~ to fly nose high
Überziehen *n* stalling (in flight), pancaking (in landing), stall covering, plating
Überzieh-handschuh *m* protective glove, overglove **-hose** *f* overalls **-jacke** *f* wind jacket
überzogen coated, plated, lined, incrusted, covered **-er Flug** stall (aviation) **-er Flug mit Motor an** power stall **-e Fluglandung** stall landing **in -er Stellung** nose high (aviation)
Überzoll *m* surtax
Überzug *m* coat, coating, film, crust, covering, lining, incrustation, overlay, cover, slip cover, serving, flashing, skin, plating, envelope **galvanischer** ~ electroplating, electrodeposit **mit einem galvanischen** ~ **versehen** to coat (with electrolytically deposited copper) **leitender** ~ conducting finish
Überzug-aktivierung *f* coating activation **-papier** *n* lining paper
Überzugs-lack *m* finishing varnish **-leitfähigkeit** *f* coating conductivity **-metall** *n* backing or cladding metal **-mischung** *f* coating compound
überzusammensetzen to overcompound
üblich usual, customary, common, normal, general, practice, in use, conventional, ordinary **allgemein** ~ common **der -en Art** standard make **-e Bauart** standard style **-e Bedingungen** usual terms **-es Gewicht** standard weight **-e Größe** standard size
U-Bogen *m* U-bend
U-Boot *n* submarine, U-boat
übrig remaining, left, residual **-bleibend** residual
Übung *f* drill, maneuver, exercise, skill **gewohnheitsmäßige** ~ routine
Übungs-absprung *m* practice jump **-anlage** *f* practice field **-bestimmung** *f* field-practice regulation **-bombe** *f* dummy bomb, practice bomb **-einsitzer** *m* training single seater (aviation) **-entgiftungsstoff** *m* training decontaminating material **-flug** *m* training flight **-flugplatz** *m* training airport or field
Übungsflugzeug *n* training plane ~ **für Fortgeschrittene** advanced training plane ~ **für**

Kunstflug aerobatic-training plane

Übungs-gerät *n* training equipment **-summer** *m* practice buzzer **-turm** *m* practice tower (for parachutists) **-verband** *m* training unit **-ziffer des Meßtrupps** practice factor **-zündmittel** *n* practice detonating equipment

U-Eisen *n* U iron, channel iron, channel bar, rolled-steel channel

U-eisenförmig U-shaped

Ufer *n* shore, beach, bank, margin **ans ~** ashore **anlandendes ~** accreting bank **einbuchtendes ~** concave bank **konvexes ~** convex bank **leeseitiges ~** leeward bank **verlandetes ~** accreting bank **vorspringendes ~** convex bank **windseitiges ~** windward bank

Ufer-abbruch *m* cliff **-anliegend** riparian **-balken** *m* shore sill **-bekleidung** *f* revetment of the banks **-böschung** *f* slope of river banks, bank **-brücke** *f* single-span stringer bridge

Ufer-deckwerk *n* revetment of the banks **-einfassung** (Kai) embankment **-gelände** *n* riparian lands **-kante** *f* shore **-linie** *f* bank line (of a stream), shore line **-mauer** *f* quay **-pflaster** *n* paving or protection stone **-schnellsteg** *m* hasty landing bridge, hasty single-span footbridge **-schutz** *m* protection of the bank, revetment of the banks, shore protection

Uferschutzwerk *n* protection of river bank **wellenbrechendes ~** sea wall

Ufer-strömung *f* littoral current, coastal stream **-umschlag** *m* transshipping of goods at the waterside **-verteidigung** *f* protection of the bank **-vorsprung** *m* outward bend of bank **-wall** *m* beach deposit

U-Flicken *m* channel patch

U-förmig U-shaped

U-förmiger Systemträger *m* U-shaped magnet-system carrier

Uhr *f* clock, watch **die Uhren vergleichen** to synchronize watches

Uhrarmband *n* wrist-watch strap

Uhraufzug *m* clock winding

Uhren-anlage *f* clock installation **-gesteuert** clock controlled

Uhren-meßstand *m* meter test bench **-scheibe** *f* target consisting of circle of silhouettes **-unterzentrale** *f* clock substation **-vergleich** *m* time check **-zentrale** *f* central clock station **-zeichen** *n* time (signal)

uhrgesteuerter Antrieb (Uhrantrieb) clockwork action

Uhr-feder *f* clock spring, flat coil spring, watch spring **-federstahl** *m* clock-spring steel **-gehäuse** *n* watch or clock case **-gestell** *n* clock case **-gewicht** *n* driving weight **-glas** *n* watch glass, beaker cover **-halter** *m* watch panel or slide

Uhrmacher *m* watchmaker **-schule** *f* horological school, watchmaking school **-werkzeug** *n* watchmaker's tool

Uhr-platte *f* disk for clocks **-prüfung** *f* chronometer test, calibration, watch test **-schraublehre** *f* micrometer calipers with dial indicator, dial micrometer **-stellung** *f* setting (of airscrew-pitch gauge) **-stempel** *m* time stamp **-taktfrequenz** *f* clock frequency **-taktimpuls** *m* clock pulse **-vergleich** *m* synchronization of watches

Uhrwerk *n* clockwork (mechanism), timing apparatus in fuse **-antrieb** *m* clockwork action **-bogenlampe** *f* clockwork arc lamp **-nachschub** *m* clockwork feed **-verzugzünder** *m* clockwork delay fuse **-zeitschalter** *m* clockwork time switch **-zünder** *m* mechanical time fuse, clockwork fuse

Uhrzapfen *m* watch or clock pivot

Uhrzeiger *m* hand of a clock, indicator **dem ~ entgegengesetzt** counterclockwise **im Sinne des Uhrzeigers** clockwise

Uhrzeigersinn, im ~ clockwise **entgegen dem ~, gegen den ~** anticlockwise

Uhrzeit *f* clock time, time **die ~ feststellen** to determine the (watch) time **gesetzliche ~** legal time

Uhr-zeitangabe *f* time announcement, time signal **-zeitzeichen** *n* clock or time signal **-zünder** *m* time fuse, clockwork fuse

Ukeleischuppe *f* scale of alburnum

UKW-Empfang *m* very-high-frequency reception (VHF-reception)

UKW-Peilanlage *f* VHF direction finder

UKW-Sprechfunk *m* VHF radio telephony

Ulbricht'sche Kugel Ulbricht sphere-type photometer

Ullmannit *m* ullmanite

Ulmenholz *n* elm wood

Ulrichit *m* ulrichite

Ultra-abschwächung *f* ultrasonic attenuation **-akustisch** super-audio, super-sonic **-audion** *n* ultra-audion **-beschleuniger** *m* ultra accelerator **-dezimeterwelle** *f* ultrahigh-frequency wave **-dynempfänger** *m* ultradyne receiver **-hoch** ultrahigh **-hochfester Stahl** ultra-high-tensile steel **-hochfrequenz** *f* ultrahigh frequency **-ionisationspotential** *n* ultraionization potential

Ultrakurzwellen *pl* very high frequencies **-anlage** *f* ultrashort-wave set **-empfänger** *m* ultrahigh-frequency receiver **-gerät** *n* ultrashort-wave apparatus **-sender** *m* ultrahigh-frequency transmitter **-teil** *m* ultrashort-wave part **-übertragung** *f* ultrashort-wave transmission **-vorverstärker** *m* ultrashort-wave preamplifier

Ultra-lampe *f* ultra-violet lamp **-leicht** ultra-lightweight, extremely light

Ultramarin *n* ultramarine **-ersatz** *m* ultramarine substitute

Ultramikroskop *n* ultramicroscope

ultramikroskopisch ultramicroscopic **-e Erforschung** studying by ultramicroscopic illumination

ultrarot ultrared, infrared **-er Strahl** infrared ray

Ultrarot-abtastung *f* noctovisor scan **-absorption** *f* infrared absorption **-durchlässigkeit** *f* ultrared or infrared transmittancy **-sperre** *f* infrared block **-strahlung** *f* ultrared radiation **-undurchlässig** opaque to infrared

Ultraschall *m* ultrasonics **Echolot mit ~** echo sounding

Ultraschall-frequenz *f* supersonic frequency **-fühler** *m* ultrasonic (sensing), tracer **-laufzeitglied** *n* ultrasonic delay-line **-laufzeitstrecke** *f* supersonic transition time **-lehre** *f* ultrasonics **-lotung** *f* ultrasonic sounding **-reinigung** *f* ultrasonic cleaning **-prüfung** *f* ultrasonic test

Ultraschall-schalter *m* ultrasonic controller **-schwingung** *f* ultrasonic vibration **-stroboskop** *n* ultrasonic stroboscope **-verzögerungsleitung** *f*

supersonic delay-line **-welle** *f* supersonic wave, ultrasonic wave **-wellenfrequenz** *f* supersonic frequency **-zelle** *f* supersonic light valve

ultra-schnelles Relais high speed relay **-schwarzpegel** *m* blacker-than-black region **-schwärzung** *f* infrablack condition **-schwerer Kern** superheavy nucleus **-schwerewelle** *f* ultra gravity wave

Ultrasonknall *m* sonic boom

Ultrastrahlenintensität, Linie gleicher ~ isochasm

Ultrastrahlung *f*, **kosmische ~** cosmic rays or radiation

Ultrateil *m* radio-frequency unit

ultraviolett ultraviolet **-e Strahlen** ultraviolet rays

Ultraviolett-bestrahlung *f* treatment by ultraviolet radiation **-durchlässig** transparent to ultraviolet light

Ultra-wasser *n* optically empty water **-weich** ultra soft **-weißgebiet** *n* ultrawhite region **-zentrifuge** *f* ultracentrifuge, highspeed centrifuge

umändern to alter, change, modify, amend (an application), vary

Umänderung *f* alteration, change, variation, conversion

umarbeiten to work over

Umbändelung *f* wrapping

Umbäumeapparat *m* rewinding machine

umbäumen to run from one to another beam

Umbau *m* rebuilding, reequipment, reconstruction; (Gebäude) structural alteration

umbauen to remodel, rebuild, redesign, convert, change, reconstruct

Umbaukosten *f* cost of conversion

umbauter Raum *m* space enclosed

umbetten change the course (of a river)

umbeugen to turn round

umbiegen to bend over, fold, deflect, camber, round or back, double back, crimp

umbilden reorganize, transform, remodel, reform

Umbildgerät *n* transformation apparatus

Umbildung *f* transformation, reorganization

umbinden to tie or wrap around

Umblenden *f* cross fading (TV)

Umblick *m* back-glance (unobstructed view)

Umbohrung *f* drilling alongside, spudding (min.)

umbördeln to flange or bead (a tube), border, bead over **das Rohr ~** to flange the tube or pipe

Umbördelung *f* flanging

Umbra *f* umber

Umbralglas *n* umbral lens

umbrechen to make up (print.) **die Seiten ~** to impose the pages

Umbrecher *m* make-up (print.)

Umbruch *m* by-pass, brake (in a drive or gallery) **~ der Linie** line break, breakdown

Umbuchung *f* bookkeeping transfer

Umcodierer *m* code converter

Umcodierung *f* code conversion

umdecken to cover, protect **ein Dach ~** to re-lay a roof

Umdestillation *f* redistillation

umdestillieren to redistill, rectify

umdrehbar reversible, rotatable

umdrehen to turn around, rotate, revolve, twist, slacken, twirl

Umdrehung *f* revolution, rotation, turn **steigende ~** climbing turn **Umdrehungen in der Minute** revolutions per minute

Umdrehungs-achse *f* axis of rotation **-anzeiger** *m* speed indicator **-bewegung** *f* rotatory motion **-durchmesser** *m* diameter of rotation **-ellipsoid** *n* ellipsoid of revolution **-fernzeiger** *m* speed teleindicator **-fläche** *f* plane of rotation **-helipot** *n* rotary helipotentiometer **-geschwindigkeit** *f* speed of rotation **-körper** *m* solid or body of revolution or rotation **-kraft** *f* force (propelling)

Umdrehungs-messer *m* tachometer **-paraboloid** *n* paraboloid generated by rotation **-punkt** *m* center of rotation **-richtung** *f* direction of rotation **-spur** *f* revolution mark **-winkel** *m* angle of rotation **-zahl** *f* number of revolutions, speed **-zähler** *m* tachometer, revolution counter

Umdruck *m* transfer process (print.), manifold printing, mimeograph or offset reproduction, reprint, circular **-farbe** *f* reprinting ink **-flüssigkeit** *f* posting fluid **-karte** *f* copy map **-markierungseinrichtung** *f* marking device **-papier** *n* transfer paper **-presse** *f* reprinting press **-verfahren** *n* reproduction process

Umesterung *f* ester interchange, alcoholysis

umfahren to detour

Umfahrtstraße *f* by-pass road

Umfahrung *f* by-pass

Umfahrungsstrecke *f* by-pass

umfallen to tilt over, turn over on the side, tumble, dissolve and reprecipitate **nach rückwärts ~** to topple backward

Umfallen *n* overturning

umfalzen to bead, crimp over

Umfang *m* circumference, circuit; (Umkreis) periphery; (Ausdehnung) extent, size; (Reichweite) radius, range; (Rauminhalt) volume, width, scope, extent, bulk, contour, girth, perimeter, circle, compass, dimension, latitude, confines **am ~ befindlich** peripheric **in größerem ~** large scale

Umfangkraft *f* tangential force, circumferential force, peripheral force

Umfangmasse bei seemäßiger Verpackung shipping dimensions

umfangreich ample, extensive, voluminous

Umfangs-fläche *f* peripheral area **-geschwindigkeit** *f* peripheral speed, circumferential speed **-geschwindigkeitsmesser** *m* tachometer **-kabel** *f* circumferential wire **komponente** *f* tangential component **-kraft** *f* tangential force, circumferential force, peripheral force **-kreis** *m* circumferential circle **-last** *f* radial load

Umfangs-reibung *f* rolling contact **-richtung** *f* peripheral or circumferential direction **-schwingung** *f* circumferential oscillation or vibration **-spannung** *f* circumferential tension **-teilung** *f* circular pitch, transverse pitch **-verzahnung** *f* cylindrical gearing **-widerstand** *m* circumferential resistance **-winkel** *m* angle in a segment

umfärben to re-dye

Umfärbeverfahren *n* re-dyeing process

umfassen to outflank, embrace, envelop, comprise, span, encompass

umfassend extensive, far-reaching, comprehensive, embracing

Umfassung *f* envelopment

Umfassungs-mauer *f* side wall, containing or outer wall **-wand** *f* encircling or enclosing wall
Umfeld *n* outer field
Umfeldleuchtdichte *f* surrounding luminance
Umfläche *f* circumferential, contour, or ambient surface
umflechten to braid
Umflechtmaschine *f* braiding machine, braider
umfließen to flow around or in contact with, circumcirculate
Umflutkanal *m* diversion channel
Umfokussierung *f* change of focusing
Umformaggregat *n* converter set
Umformbarkeit *f* re-formability, deformability
umformen to transform, remodel, deform, shape, convert, rearrange (math.)
Umformer *m* continuous current, transformer, motor generator, (rotary) converter, transformer, dynamotor, inverter, thyratron, transducer **röhrengeregelter ~** rotary converter with tube regulator
Umformer-aggregat *n* motor converter **-anlage** *f* rotary converter **-aufhängerahmen** *m* power-unit mounting **-gruppe** *f* motor-generator set **-lüftersatz** *m* converter blower set **-satz** *m* motor generator, transformer, rotary converter, converter unit **-schalttafel** *f* converter switchboard **-stromkreis** *m* converter circuit **-unterwerk** *n* rotary sub-station **-wahlschalter** *m* alternator selection panel (radio) **-werk** *n* rotary substation
Umformung *f* transforming, remodeling, deformation, deforming, mechanical working, shaping, change, modification, transformation (of an equation), conversion, reforming **~ des Ausstoßes** conversion of yield
Umformungs-arbeit *f* deformation (met) **-faktor** *m* conversion factor **-grad** *m* conversion ratio **-verhältnis** *n* transformation ratio **-wirkungsgrad** *m* efficiency of transformation
Umfrage *f* inquiry **~ halten** to inquire, make inquiries
Umfriedigung *f*, enclosure
umführen to loop
Umführen *n* loop mill rolling
Umführer *m* repeater (in rolling)
Umführrolle *f* sheave pulley
Umführung *f* repeater, passage **Umführungen** loop troughs, loop channels
Umführungs-kanal *m* return channel **-leitung** *f* by-pass pipe
umfüllen to decant
Umfüll-gerät *n* decanting apparatus **-leitung** *f* exchange line **-pumpe** *f* transfer pump **-sammler** *m* exchange collector **-ventilator** *m* transfer blower, refill fan **-vorrichtung** *f* decanting device
Umgang *m* breeching (harness), whorl, by-pass **~ der Wicklung** convolution of the winding (elec.)
Umgangsklappe *f* by-pass clack valve
umgeändert converted, altered, changed
umgearbeitet altered, converted
umgebaut converted, rebuilt, changed
umgeben to surround, encircle
umgebördelt flanged **-er Boden** flanged end **-e Feuerbüchse** flanged fire box **-es Rohr** pipe with single bordered end
umgebrochen broken down, laid flat
Umgebung *f* surroundings, environment, region, neighborhood, ambient, ambiency
Umgebungs-flüssigkeit *f* enveloping fluid **-karte** *f* position sketch, map of the immediate environment **-licht** *n* ambient light **-lufttemperatur** *f* atmospheric temperature **-temperatur** *f* ambient temperature
umgeformt transformed
Umgegend *f* surroundings, vicinity
umgehängt slung
umgehen to flank, go around, turn, make a detour, bypass, avoid, circumvent, obviate, dodge, evade, circumnavigate
umgehen (ein Patent) to avoid (a patent)
umgehend immediate(ly) **-e Antwort** immediate reply
Umgehung *f* turning movement, flanking maneuver, detouring, by-passing **unter ~** by-passing **~ eines Patentes** evading a patent
Umgehungs-kabel *n* ring cable **-leitung** *f* by-pass line **-schaltung** *f* by-pass connection, shunt switch, by-pass circuit **-system** *n* by-pass system **-straße** *f* by-pass road, throughway branch, circumferential route, belt highway **-ventil** *n* by-pass valve
umgekehrt reciprocal, inverse, converse, obverse, inverted (image), reverse (order) **-proportional** inversely proportional **-es Bild** reversed image **-er Bogen** inverted arch **-er Fuß** reentrant squash or press (of a tube) **-er Motor** inverted engine **-es Pendel** inverted pendulum **-es Steuerwerk** reversed controls **-es Verhältnis** inverse ratio
umgelegt turned under, rounded rerouted
umgerechnet recalculated, converted, corrected
umgeschlagene Leisten curled selvedges
umgesetzte Energie converted energy
umgestalten to modify, remodel, change, transform, reorganize, reform
Umgestaltung reconstruction
umgestellt readjusted, converted
umgestülpt inverted
umgießen to recast, cast around (something), refound **~ von Flüssigkeiten** to pour from one vessel into another
Umgießvorrichtung *f* babbitting fixture
Umgitterung *f* barrier, enclosure
umgliedern to reorganize
Umgliedern *n* reorganization, regrouping, redistribution of forces
umgreifen to embrace
umgrenzen to define, limit
Umgrenzung *f* definition **~ einer Kurve** envelope **~ der Ladung** loading gauge **~ des lichten Raumes** clearance gauge **~ des lichten Raumes an örtlichen Hindernissen** gauge for goods sheds and isolated obstructions
Umgrenzungs-feuer *pl* boundary lights **-befeuerung** *f* boundary lighting **-lehre** *f* clearance gauge
Umgrenzungslinie *f* boundary line, clearance line, junction line, contour, peripheral or circumferential line, envelope **~ für Eisenbahnfahrzeuge** rolling-stock clearance gauge
Umgrößerung *f* enlargement or reduction, change in size or dimension
Umgrößerungsverhältnis *n* ratio of enlargement,

ratio of magnification
Umgruppierung *f* reorganization, regrouping
Umguß *m* recast, recasting, decantation, transfer (by pouring) **-körper** *m* recast material
umhängen to sling (packs, rifles), take up
Umhängeriemen *m* shoulder strap
Umhaspelmaschine *f* rewinding machine
umhaspeln to re-reel (re-wind)
umhauen to fell
umher-schweifen to roam **-schwimmen** to float **-spritzen** to scatter or splash around **-streuen** to scatter around **-ziehend** ambulant
umhüllen to envelop, encase, enclose, wrap (up), lap, serve, involve, jacket
Umhüllende *f* (Radar) envelope
umhüllt coated **-e Leitung** sheathed or covered wire **-er Splitt** coated chips
Umhüllung *f* envelope, jacket, casing, sheathing, box, covering, serving, lapping, wrapping, shrouding
Umhüllungs-kurve *f* enveloping curve **-linie** *f* envelope, contour line **-pseudomorphose** *f* perimorph **-ring** *m* shroud ring (gas turbine)
umkanten to cant, overturn, cant up, turn up
Umkanten *n* overturning
Umkapselung der Spulen coil jacket
Umkehr *f* reversal, inversion ~ **der Querruderwirkung** reversed aileron control
Umkehr-absorptionskante *f* reverse absorption edge or limit **-anlasser** *m* reversing starter **-anlaßwiderstand** *m* reversing and starting resistance, reversing switch **-bad** *n* reversing bath **-bandwalzwerk** *n* reversing strip mill
umkehrbar reversible, revertible, capable of being turned over or out **nicht** ~ irreversible, nonreturn **-e Kette** reversible chain **-er Kreisprozeß** reversible cycle **-er Kreisvorgang** reversible cycle **-e Luftschraube** reversible propeller **-e Permeabilität** reversible permeability **nicht -er Vorgang** irreversible cycle
Umkehrbarkeit *f* reversibility
Umkehr-blockwalzwerk *n* reversing blooming mill, reversing cogging mill **-bogen** *m* return bend **-duo** *n* double reversing mill
Umkehr-eilgang *m* reverse rapid motion **-einwand** *m* reversibility paradox
umkehren to return, invert, turn over, reverse, overturn, revert, rectify
Umkehren über den Flügel wing over (aviation)
umkehrend reversal **-e Schicht** reversing layer
Umkehrentwicklung *f* reversal development (phot.), reversal processing
Umkehrer *m* reverser (elec.)
Umkehr-erscheinung *f* photographic reversal, solarization **-film** *m* film resulting from developing by reversal **-formel** *f* inversion formula **-funktion** *f* inverse function **-getriebe** *n* reversing gear **-grenzpunkt** *m* point of no return (aviation) **-hebel** *m* reversing lever **-integral** *n* inversion integral
Umkehrkammer des Rücklaufstückes header box (petroleum)
Umkehr-kupplung *f* reversing clutch **-libelle** *f* reversible spirit level **-linse** *f* inversion lens **-maschine** *f* reversing engine **-prisma** *n* inverting prism **-punkt** *m* bending-back point, cusp or stationary point, reversal or inversion point, turning point (cryst.), point of inflection **-reibkupplung** *f* reversing friction clutch **-richtung** *f* reverse direction **-riementrieb** *m* reverse-motion belt drive **-rohr** *n* inverter electronics **-röhre** *f* converter tube **-schalter** *m* reversing switch, poling switch **-rolle** *f* reversing sheave
Umkehr-satz *m* inversion theorem **-schaltung** *f* reversible connection **-schaufel** *f* reversing blade or bucket **-scheibenverschluß** *m* reversing disk shutter **-schere** *f* reversible shear **-schleife** *f* return track curve **-schütz** *m* motor reversing contactor **-segment** *n* reversible segment **-spanne** *f* reversal error **-spannung** *f* peak reverse voltage **-spülung** *f* reverse scavenging
Umkehr-stelle *f* change point **-stellung** *f* reversed position **-strahl** *m* retrograde ray **-straße** *f* reversing mill train **-stück** *n* header box **-stückstöpsel** *m* return-bend plug **-stufe** *f* reversal stage **-system** *n* reversal lens system **-taste** *f* reversing key
Umkehrung *f* inversion, conversion, reversion, reversal, reversing (machine) ~ **des Aufnahmevorganges** reverse order of taking the photograph ~ **der Strahlen** reversal of the beams of light
Umkehrungs-prisma *n* inversion prism **-satz** *m* inversion rule, reciprocity principle
Umkehrwalzwerk *n* reversing mill, reversing rolling mill
umkippen to turn upside down, dump, tip, tilt over, upset
Umkippen *n* dumping
Umkippung *f* tipping
umklammern to embrace, clasp
Umklammerung *f* envelopment, encirclement
umklappbar folding
Umklappdiopter *n* folding peep sight
umklappen to turn about, drop down, collapse
Umklappen *n* turn about (theory of ferromagnetism), reversal (of motion) ~ **der hyperbolischen Ebene** reflection with respect to a line to the hyperbolic plane
Umklappprozeß *m* umklapp process, flip-over process
umkleiden to coat, jacket, line, sheath, cloak, surround
Umkleideräume *pl* locker rooms
umkleidete Elektrode coated electrode
Umkleidung *f* coating, covering, fireproofing, fairing, casing, jacket, sleeve
Umklemmen der Wicklung reversing of the winding
Umklöppelmaschine *f* braiding machine
umklöppeln to braid, put braiding around
Umklöppelung *f* braiding
umknicken to break in bending
Umkochen *n* reboiling
umkonstruieren to rebuild, redesign
Umkonstruktion *f* constructional change
Umkopie *f* optical-reduction print, optical print of altered dimensions
Umkopieren *n* optical printing; (Aufnahmen unter Hinzufügung neuer Aufnahmen) multiplay back (tape rec.)
umkrücken to rake
Umkreis *m* periphery, circumference, contour, perimeter, range, area, surroundings **im ~ von . . .** within a radius of . . .
umkreisen to encircle, circle, revolve, spin,

rotate, gyrate
Umkreisgeschwindigkeit *f* peripheral velocity
umkrempeln to turn inside out, flange, double over
Umkristallisation *f* crystalline transformation or modification, recrystallization, granulation, fractional crystallization
Umkristallisieren *n* recrystallizing
Umkröpfung *f* cambering
Umlade-anlage *f* unloading plant **-bahnhof** *m* transfer yard **-einrichtung** *f* transshipping device **-gebühr** *f* reloading charges
umladen to transship, shift, reload
Umlade-spesen *pl* reloading charges **-vorrichtung** *f* unloading plant
Umladung *f* transshipment, change in charge
Umladungsquerschnitt charge exchange cross section
Umlage *f* garnish, assessment, fund raising
umlagern to restore, rearrange, regroup
Umlagerung *f* rearrangement, surrounding
umlappen to lap (round), to wrap
Umlappung *f* lapping, wrapping **~ mit Band** taping
Umlauf *m* (Technik) rotation, revolution; (Zyklus) cycle; circulation, turn, recycle, recycling, diversion channel, conduit, culvert **in ~** (to be) circulated or in circulation **kurzer ~** short culvert **Umläufe** revolution per minute
Umlauf-antrieb *m* rotary drive **-apparat** *m* bypass apparatus **-aufzug** *m* circulating lift
Umlaufbahn *f* circular path, orbit **-geschwindigkeit** *f* orbital flight speed **-mechanik** *f* (Astron.) orbital mechanics
Umlauf-begrenzung *f* rotation range **-bewegung** *f* rotatory flow, eddying at the banks caused by bank friction
Umlauf-biege-maschine *f* revolving fatigue-testing machine **-probe** *f* rotating-beam test **-prüfmaschine** *f* rotating-beam testing machine **-prüfung** *f* rotating-beam test **-versuch** *m* rotating bending test
Umlauf-durchmesser *m* swing diameter **-ebene** *f* orbital plane **-einlaßverfahren** *n* rotary induction system
umlaufen to rotate, revolve, circulate, shift (wind), gyrate (spirally) **~ lassen** to circulate (oil)
umlaufend rotary, variable, swinging, current, circulating, circular, gyrating, revolving **-e Axialpumpe** rotary axial pump **-er Brennstoff** circulating fuel **-e Bürste** rotating brush **-er Funke** rotary spark **-e Funkbake** revolving radio beacon **-es Kapital** floating capital **-e Kerbe** circumferential groove **-es Langsieb** revolving endless wire **-er Peiler** *m* rotating direction finder **-es Putztuch** revolving clearer cloth **-e Radialpumpe** rotary radial pump **-e Schere** rotating shear **-e Spitze** running center (of lathe) **-er Umformer** rotary converter
Umlauf-filter *m* rotary air filter **-förderband** *n* circular conveyor **-flugzeug** *n* cyclogiro **-frequenz** *f* rotational frequency (of electrons) **-führung** *f* repeater (in rolling) **-funkenzieher** *m* rotary static spark gap
Umlauf-gebläse *n* rotary blower, centrifugal blower **-gehäuse** *n* rotating casing **-gerät** *n* revolving device, rotating device, instrument for measuring lift and drag **-geschwindigkeit** *f* rotational speed **-getriebe** *n* planetary gear, epicyclic gear(ing), sun-and-planet gear **-graben** *m* bywash **-größe** *f* cyclic or circulation constant **-heizung** *f* circulation heating
Umlauf-integral *n* contour integral **-kanal** *m* bypass, longitudinal culvert **-kette** *f* block chains **-kiste** *f* channel **-kreis** *m* circuit **-kühlung** *f* rotation cooling **-leitung** *f* circulating pipe, conducting main **-magnetzünder** *m* rotary magneto **-motor** *m* rotary engine **-öl** *n* circulating oil **-ölpumpe** *f* circulation oil pump **-periode** *f* orbited period **-produkt** *n* recycle stock **-pumpe** *f* rotary pump, circulating pump
Umlauf-rad *n* planet wheel, planetary wheel **-regler** *m* speed governor, speed-control device, speed regulator **-richtung** *f* direction of rotation **-rohr** *n* circulation pipe **-rührwerk** (Flotation) agitator **-schicht** *f* circulation layer **-schmieröl** *n* circulating lubricating oil **-schmierung** *f* constant-circulation oiling, circulation-system lubrication **-schwingungszahl** *f* rotation frequency
Umlauf-signal *n* round-the-world signal **-sinn** *m* sense of rotation **-spannung** *f* magnetomotive force **-speicher** *m* circulating memory **-sternmotor** *m* rotary engine **-stollen** *m* diversion tunnel **-übertrag** *m* end-around carry
Umlauf-ventil *n* by-pass valve, rotating valve **-ventilator** *m* centrifugal fan **-verdampfer** *m* circulation evaporator **-verdichter** *m* rotary-type compressor **-verhältnis** *n* recycle ratio **-verschluß** *m* rotary shutter **-verschlußblende** *f* rotary shutter **-verteilung** *f* distribution of circulation **-vermögen** *n* current assets **-verstärkung** *f* loop gain
Umlauf-wischermotor *m* rotary wiper motor **-zahl** *f* number of turns, number of revolutions, speed **-zähler** *m* revolution counter, cyclometer, tachometer **-zeit** *f* period **-zug** *m* bucket elevator
umlegbar reversible, inclinable **-e Ausdrückstange** hinged pushing arm **-es Fernrohr** reversible telescope **-er Klappsucher** reversible or folding finder **-e Rücklehne** hinged back **-e Wand** drop side (of cart or truck)
Umlege-diopter *m* folding peep sight **-kalender** *m* turnover (desk) calendar
umlegen to reverse, tilt, throw (a key), relay (paving), tip, lay over or around, wrap **einen Hebel ~** to traverse a lever, shift **Gemeinkosten auf das Stück ~** pro-rating of overhead costs **Schienen ~** to invert rails, turn rails upside down **vollständig ~** to relay completely
Umlegen *n* reversal, tilting, throwing (of a switch) **~ der Weichen** working of the switches
Umleger *m* shifter
Umlegeschalter *m* switch lever
Umleghebel *m* switch lever
Umlegung *f* transfer, shifting
Umlegungs-hilfsrelais *n* auxiliary call transfer relay **-relais** (W) call transfer relay **-zeichen** *n* transfer signal
umleiten to divert, deviate, reroute
Umleiter *m* director, translator, controller **-system** *n* director system
Umleit-hebel *m* switch lever (R.R.) **-kammer** *f* change-over plate **-platte** *f* change-over plate
Umleitung *f* diversion, deviation

Umleitungs-schlüssel *m* transfer key **-wähler** *m* director selector
Umleitungs-rolle *f* return pulley **-wähler** *m* director selector
Umlenk-achse *f* lateral or pitch axis **-blech** *n* baffle **-bogen** *m* turn or steer around, program path **-flügel** *m* auxiliary slat for movable surfaces **-gerät** *n* guidance unit program clock-work (missiles) **-geschwindigkeit** *f* angular program velocity **-gleichung** *f* equation of the program branch **-hebel** *m* shift lever
Umlenk-kettenrad *n* guide sprocket wheel **-kranz** *m* guide member **-prisma** *n* deviating prism **-programm** *n* climbing program (missiles) **-rolle** *f* guide pulley, guide roller, flanged idler roller, deviating roller, deflector roll **-schaufel** *f* guide vane **-scheibe** *f* deflecting pulley **-spiegel** *m* surface mirror
Umlenkung *f* returning, deflection, return, rerouting, reorientation, turn round (boiler)
Umlenkungs-düse *f* reversing nozzle **-moment** *m* deflection moment
Umlenk-walze *f* guide roller **-winkel** *m* cutoff angle
umlernen to learn anew, unlearn and relearn
umliegend surrounding
Umlötung *f* wiring change
Umluft *f* recirculated air; (Klimaanlage) return air **-heizung** *f* heating by circulating air **-schieber** *m* return air damper **-sichter** *m* air separator
ummagnetisieren to reverse the magnetism
Ummagnetisierung *f* magnetic reversal
ummanteln to surround, cover, jacket, wall off, sheath, case, encase
ummantelt lagged, covered, ducted, shrouded **-e Elektrode** sheathed electrode
Ummantelung *f* jacket, envelope, casing, sheathing, shroud
Ummantelungs-ring *m* shroud ring **-zylinder** *m* enshrouding cylinder
ummauern to surround with walls
ummodeln to remodel
Ummodelung *f* remodeling
Ummodulierung *f* remodulation
umnageln to renail
Umnormierung *f* renormalization
umordnen to rearrange, transpose
Umordnung *f* rearrangement
Umordnungsstöße *pl* rearrangement collisions
umorganisieren to reorganize
Umorientierung *f* reorientation
umpacken to repack
Umpfählung *f* fencing
umpflügen to plow up
umphotographieren to reproduce by photography
Umpolarisierung *f* reversal of polarity
umpolbar poles capable of being reversed
umpolen to reverse polarity
Umpolgefahr *f* danger of pole reversal
Umpolung *f* slope polarity, polarity reversal, reversion
umprägen to recoin
Umprägung *f* metamorphism (geol.)
umpressen to press around, put or apply (around something) by pressure
umpreßt, direkt -er Mantel extruded sheating
umprojizierend transforming
Umpump-aggregat *n* pump circulation system **-anlage** *f* pump installation **-begrenzer** *m* compensation control
Umpumpen *n* reserve pumping
Umpump-leitung *f* pump piping or line
umrahmen to frame
Umrahmung *f* framing
Umrandung *f* edge, edging, border, border strip, the coasts (of the North Sea)
Umrandungs-feuer *n* boundary lights (aviation) **-kurve** *f* envelope **-licht** *n* boundary light **-zeichen** *n*, **-zeiger** *m* boundary marker
umrangieren to rearrange, shunt
umrechnen to convert, change, reduce, translate
Umrechner *m* translator or decoder, translating device **-feld** *n* translation field **-zählwerk** *n* director meter
Umrechnung *f* translation conversion (automatic telephony), recalculation, recomputation **~ einer Gleichung** transformation of an equation
Umrechnungs-basis (Geld) conversion basis **-differenzen** *pl* differences in exchange **-faktor** *m* reduction factor, conversion rate, conversion factor, change ratio **-tabelle** *f*, **-tafel** *f* conversion table, reduction table **-weise** *f* manner of conversion
umreißen to outline
umrichten to reset
Umrichter *m* static frequency changer, transverter, inverter
Umrichtzeit *f* resetting time
umringen to surround
Umriß *m* outline, contour, ground plan, periphery, shape, schematic drawing **-bohren** *n* contour boring **-drehen** *n* circumferential contour turning **-diagramm** *n* contour diagram
umrissen defined **nicht fest ~** undefined
Umriß-form *f* outer contour **-fräsen** *n* profile or contour milling **-fühler** *m* profile tracer **-karte** *f* contour map **-kopiereinrichtung** *f* profile tracer attachment **-linie** *f* outline **-liniensteigung** *f* slope contour (math) **-skizze mit Einbaumaßen** outline drawing **-tastung** *f* profile tracing **-zeichnung** *f* (out)line drawing, linear drawing, sketch, outline illustration
Umrolleneinrichtung *f* roll-over mechanism
umrollen to roll over
Umroller *m* rewinder or rewinding machine (paper mfg.)
Umroll-maschine *f* rewinding machine, round rolling machine **-platte** *f* roll-over plate **-rüttelformmaschine** *f* jar-ramming roll-over molding machine, jolt roll-over machine **-vorrichtung** *f* rolling-over device
umrühren to stir, stir up, agitate
Umrühren *n* stirring, stirring up, puddling (of iron), poling (of copper)
Umrührstab *m* stirrer
umrüsten to change over to
umsacken to rebag, resack
umsatteln to change one's profession
Umsatz *m* conversion, reaction, exchange, turnover, sale **schneller ~** ready sale, quick returns
Umsatz-ausgleichssteuer *f* compensatory turnover tax **-geschwindigkeit** *f* sales turnover **-karte** *f* accounting detail card

umsatzlose Bestände dead or surplus stocks
Umsatz-schwankung *f* fluctuation of turnover **-statistik** *f* sales analysis **-steuer** *f* sales tax
Umsäumung *f* border
Umschaltantennenpeiler *m* commutated-antenna direction-finder
umschaltbar adapted to circuit changes, switchable, reversible, commutable **-es Vorgelege** change speed gear
Umschaltbrett *n* switchboard
Umschalte-feststeller *m* shift lock **-gestell** *n* distributing frame **-hebel** *m* change-speed lever
Umschalteinrichtung *f* shift mechanism
Umschalter für Erregung switch for excitation
Umschalte-klinke *f* transfer jack, throw-out **-kontakt** *m* make-and-break contact
umschalten to change over, throw over, reverse, change from, switch (over), commutate
Umschalten *n* reversing, switching, changing over, commutating, gear changing
Umschalter *m* throw-over switch, selector switch, reversing switch, switch commutator, double-throw switch, multiple switch, change-over switch, reverser, switchboard **~ mit zwei Stellungen** throw-over switch, two-position switch **~ mit Unterbrechung** throw-over switch with break **mehrwegiger ~** multiple-way switch **schnurloser ~** cordless private branch exchange
Umschalte-relais *n* automatic switch, switching relay
Umschaltergrundplatte *f* key shelf
Umschalterkontaktplatte (Scheinwerfer) change-over switch contact plate (head lamp)
Umschalteschnur *f* patching cord
Umschalteschrank *m* switchboard **~ eines Handamts** manual switchboard **~ für den Fernverkehr** toll switchboard
Umschaltestangenmagnet *m* changeover bar magnet
Umschaltetaste *f* shift key **Freigabe der ~** release of the shift key (typewriter)
Umschalt-feld *n* change-over panel **-feuerung** *f* regenerative furnace **-flammofen** *m* regenerator **-gasfeuerung** *f* regenerative gas furnace **-getriebe** *n* switching gear **-hahn** *m* change-over cock **-hebel** *m* shift key lever, change lever **-kette** *f* (elektron.) scanning ring **-klappe** *f* switch-over flap **-klinke** *f* elevation release catch **-kurve** *f* commutation curve
Umschalt-maßnahme *f* shift operation **-mechanismus** *m* reversing mechanism **-pause** *f* switch interval, answer lag **-periode** *f* reversing cycle, reversal period **-scheibe** *f* shift disk **-schütz** *m* change-over contactor **-steuerrelais** *n* selection relay **-stillstand** *m* shifting stoppage **-stöpsel** *m* switch plug **-system** *n* regenerative system **-taste** *f* shift key
Umschaltung *f* return pass (in boiler), shifting, changing over, reversal, commutation, cutover (teleph.), change speed, switching, cross, wiring change, shift, inversion **~ auf Empfang** change of connections for receiving **~ auf Senden** change of connections for transmitting **doppelpolige ~** double commutation **einpolige ~** single commutation
Umschaltungssystem *n* switching system
Umschaltventil *n* switch valve, reversing valve, change-over valve **-einsatz** *m* reversing-valve sleeve **-körper** *m* reversing-valve body **-spindel** *f* reversing-valve spindle
Umschalt-vorgang *m* change-over process **-vorrichtung** change-speed mechanism **-walze** *f* reversing-switch cylinder or drum **-wechselbetrieb** *m* regenerative exchange operation (in gas liquefaction) **-wicklung** *f* reversing winding **-zeichen** *n* inversion signal **-zeit** *f* change-over time
umschaufeln to turn with a shovel, stir with a spatula
umschichten to change off
umschichtig alternately
umschießen to shift **die Spalten ~** to impose the pages anew (print.)
Umschiffung *f* transshipment
Umschlag *m* (Änderung) (sudden) change, turn; (Hülle) cover, wrapper; envelope, poultice (med.), transit, travel (mach.), covering, application, turnover, sudden change, hem, collar **~ eines Buches** jacket (of a book) **den ~ nuten** to crease the cover
Umschlag-biegen *n* tangent bending **-dauer** *f* transfer period
Umschlagegenauigkeit *f* indexing accuracy
umschlagen to upset (aviation), wrap, envelop, change, shift, transload, fell, break down from bulk to unit containers, capsize, veer around suddenly **~ in** to turn into **das Papier ~** to turn up the paper
Umschlagen *n* reversal **~ der Magnetnadel** reversal of the magnetic needle
Umschlag-fertigungsmaschine *f* envelope-making machine **-form** *f* folding die **-karton** *m* cover card **-maschine** *f* folding machine **-papier** *n* packing or wrapping paper **-platte** *f* single-sided pattern plate (in molding) **-platz** *m* place of reshipment, re-handling point **-punkt** *m* change point
Umschlagseinrichtung *f* cargo-handling gear and facilities
Umschlagseite *f* cover sheet
Umschlags-farbe *f* end-point color **-gebiet** *n* transition range **-gut** *n* material to be discharged **-hafen** *m* transshipment port **-kosten** *pl* transshipment charges **-leistung** *f* rate of handling **-punkt** *m* transition point of boundary layer, point of change
Umschlagstelle *f* reloading or relay point, bulk-reduction point, transloading point
Umschlags-zahl *f* titration value, titer **-zeit** *f* transit time
Umschlag-werk *n* cover-printing unit **-werkzeug** *n* multiple-tool attachment **-zeichnung** *f* cover design
umschlämmen to move and redeposit soil by means of water
umschleiern to envelope, veil
umschließen to encircle, enclose, surround
Umschließungs-bügel *m* circumferential reinforcement **-gewicht** *n* packing weight
umschlingen to wind around, wrap around, clasp, loop, cling to, embrace
Umschlingungs-bogen *m* arc of belt contact **-winkel** *m* looping angle, angle of grip
umschlossen enclosed
Umschmelz-aluminium *n* secondary aluminum

-apparat *m* smelting unit
umschmelzen to remelt, recast, refound, redistill, melt around
Umschmelzen *n* remelting
Umschmelz-legierung *f* remelt or recast alloy **-metall** *n* remelt metal, scrap metal **-ofen** *m* remelting furnace
Umschmelzung *f* remelting, recasting, refounding
Umschmelzverfahren *n* remelting process
umschnüren to lace, thread, encircle
Umschnürung *f* threading, binding
Umschnürungsmaschine *f* wrapping machine
umschreiben to transcribe, paraphrase, circumscribe
Umschreiben *n* transcription, rewriting, circumscription, description (math.), rerecording
Umschreiber *m* transcriber
Umschreibung *f* paraphrase
Umschrift *f* legend, marginal inscription (coin)
umschulen to retrain
Umschulung *f* retraining
umschütteln to shake
Umschütteln *n* shaking
Umschweif *m* digression
umschwenken to agitate
Umschwenken *n* change-round
umschwingen to veer
Umschwung *m* turn, revulsion, rotation, revolution
Umschwungachse *f* axis of rotation
Umschwungsfaktor *m* conversion factor
Umschwungzeit *f* time of rotation
umsetzbar convertible, portable
umsetzen to convert, change, transform, sell, change over, turn, react, translate, transpose, reverse
Umsetzen *n* flitting **~ des Bohrgerätes** changing the bit
Umsetzer *m* translator, transposer, translating device, decoder **-gerät** *n* converting apparatus
Umsetzschubstange *f* reversing bar
Umsetzung *f* transformation, conversion, decomposition, reaction, translation, transposition, double decomposition, change, transduction
Umsetzungs-front *f* front along which combustion takes place **-gerät** *n* transducer, transductor **-geschwindigkeit** *f* speed or velocity of conversion, disintegration or decomposition in a chemical change, reaction rate **-grad** *m* chemical efficiency **-verhältnis** *n* conversion ratio
Umsetzvorrichtung *f* reversing apparatus
Umsichgreifen *n* spreading, expansion
Umsicht *f* circumspection, discretion, caution, wariness
umsieden to distill
umsonst gratis, gratuitously, in vain, for nothing
Umspanneinrichtung *f* rechucking device
umspannen to transform, span
Umspannen (Drehbank) re-chuck
Umspanner *m* transformer (elec.) **-belastbarkeit** *f* transformer rating **-leistung** *f* transformer capacity **-zelle** *f* transformer kiosk
Umspann-futter *n* rechucking device, adapter **-patrone** *f* rechucking collet **-station** *f* grid substation, transformer station
Umspannung *f* band of armature
Umspannungsanlage *f* transforming plant
Umspann-unterwerk *n* transformer sub-station **-vorrichtung** *f* rechucking device **-werk** *n* transformer substation **-zange** *f* external gripping device **-zeit** *f* loading time
umspeichern to exchange
umspielen to rerecord, play back
Umspielzeit *f* (eines Bandes) re-wind period (of a tape)
umspinnen to braid, cover, whip (around)
Umspinnmaschine *f* plaiting, covering, or spinning machine
Umspinnung *f* braiding, covering, whipping
Umspinnwalze *f* doffing (waste) roller
umsponnen covered **-er Draht** braided or covered wire
umspringen to veer (meteor.)
Umspringen *n* jumping, abrupt reversing, arising of sudden irregularity or unsteadiness
Umspulapparat *m* (Draht), wire-coating apparatus
umspülen to pass around, flow around, rewind, surround, skirt, circumcirculate
Umspulen *n* rewinding **~ des Bandes** fast wind (tape rec.)
Umspulmaschine *f* rewinding machine
umstampfen to ram up, bed up
Umstand *m* case, circumstance, situation **mit einem ~ rechnen** to reckon **mildernde Umstände** extenuating circumstances
umständlich circumstantial, complicated, bothersome
umsteckbar interchangeable, detachable
umstecken to commutate, change
Umsteck-kalender *m* perpetual calendar **-rad** *n* interchangeable or loose gear **-walzwerk** *f* looping-type rolling mill
Umsteigebahnhof *m* station for changing cars
umsteigen to transfer, change
umstellbar invertible, reversible, convertible **-e Kulissenbewegung** *f* link reversing motion
umstellen to shift, transpose; (Betrieb) convert, change over; reverse, readjust, readapt, invert, adjust, retrain, change (of attitude)
Umstellhebel *m* reversing lever **~ außerhalb des Geleises** switch lever outside the rails
Umstellklappe *f* reversing valve
Umstellung *f* reversal, change-over, transposition **~ des Meßbereichs** re-arranging
Umstellungs-hebel *m* reversing lever **-punkt** *m* transposition point **-zeit** *f* change-over time
Umstell-ventil *n* reversing valve **-vorrichtung** *f* change-over mechanism **-werkstoff** *m* substitute
Umsteuerautomat *m* reversing automat
umsteuerbar reversible **-e Druckwerke** reversible printing units
Umsteuerbarkeit *f* reversibility
Umsteuer-getriebe *n* reversing gear **-größe** *f* modifier
Umsteuerhebel *m* reversing handle, direction-changing lever **~ für vor- und rückwärts** transport, reversing lever
Umsteuer-klappe *f* reverse valve **-kolben** *m* reversing piston
umsteuern to change over, reverse, change direction
Umsteuern *n* reversing (machine)
Umsteuer-schieber *m* reversing slide **-schrauben-**

anlage *f* reversing propeller installation **-schraube** *f* reversing screw **-system** *n* reversing system
Umsteuerung *f* reversal, reversing gear, reversing
Umsteuer-ventil *n* reversing valve **-vorrichtung** *f* reversing device or arrangement **-welle** *f* reversing shaft **-zeichen** (Fernschreiber) shift signal
umstochen shaded (print)
umstoßen to overthrow, knock down, push over, void
umstrahlen to irradiate fully
Umstrahlung *f* luminescence
umstreichen to circulate
umstritten controversional
umströmen to flow or circulate around, flow in contact with
Umströmung *f* flow (about a body)
umstülpen to overturn, invert, put upside down or inside out
umstürzen to overturn, overthrow, demolish, upset
Umsturzmoment *m* tilting or overturning moment
Umsud *m* distillate
umtafeln to cuttle
Umtasten *n* lobe-switching
Umtastgerät *n* lobe-switching device
Umtausch *m* bartering, exchange
umtelegraphieren to retransmit
Umtelegraphierung *f* retransmission, (additional) transit, retransmitting
umtreiben to rotate, circulate
Umtrieb *m* circulation, rotation; (Riemenumführung) diverted transmission
Umtrimmen *n* retrimming
umwachsen overgrown
umwälzen to turn or roll around, revolutionize, revolve, rotate
Umwälzer *m* rolling hand
Umwälz-kühlung *f* radiator cooling **-leitung** *f* fuel-return line **-pumpe** *f* circulating pump **-regelventil** *n* circulation regulating valve
Umwälz und Sichteranlagen revolving and grading facilities
Umwälzung *f* revolution
umwandelbar convertible, transformable
Umwandelbarkeit *f* convertibility, transformability, transformation
umwandeln to change, convert, transform, modify, transpose **sich ~ in . . .** to be converted into . . . (chem.)
Umwandler *m* transformer, converter, inverter, mutator, transducer, sink **-ausbeute** *f* converter efficiency
Umwandlung *f* conversion, transformation, change, transmutation, modification, metabolism, disintegration
Umwandlungs-artikel *m* conversion style **-bereich** *m* transformation range **-elektron** *n* disintegration electron **-element** *n* sheath converter (microw.) **-fähigkeit** *f* capacity for change, metamorphism **-faktor** *m* conversion factor **-funktion** *f* transmutation function **-geschwindigkeit** *f* rate of transformation **-koeffizient** *m* conversion coefficient **-konstante** *f* disintegration constant
Umwandlungs-produkt *n* product of transformation **-punkt** *m* arrestation point, (thermal) critical point, transformation point, thermal change point, point of transition **-rad** *n* converting or translating gear **-steilheit** *f* mutual conductance or slope (electronics) **-tabelle** *f* conversion table **-technik** *f* coal-conversion or gasification industry
Umwandlungs-verfahren *n* process of conversion **-verhältnis** *n* transformation ratio **-verzögerung** *f* thermal retardation **-vorgang** *m* conversion or transformation process **-vorrichtung** *f* transducer, sink **-wärme** *f* heat of transformation, latent heat of conversion, heat of recalescence **-zone** *f* transition zone
Umwandlungstemperatur *f* equilibrium temperature **magnetische ~** magnetic transition temperature
Umwandung *f* shrouding, coating
umwechseln to exchange
Umwechs(e)lung *f* exchange
Umweg *m* detour **-anregung** *f* indirect excitation **-faktor** *m* trunk cost coefficient **-leitung** *f* bypass (elec.), additional path (missiles) **-schaltung** *f* substitute circuit, alternate routing **-steuerung** (Teleph) alternate routing
Umwehrung *f* circumferential reinforcement, breastwork
Umwelteinfluß *m* environmental influence
umwendbar reversible
umwenden to invert, reverse, turn over, turn round, turn upside down, turn about, turn sideways, revert
Umwendungspunkt *m* point of inversion
umwerfen to overthrow, upset, overturn
Umwerte-gerät *n* instrument to convert data
Umwerter *m* translator (tel.)
Umwertetrupp *m* converter section
Umwertung *f* conversion
Umwickelmaschine *f* taping machine
umwickeln to envelop, wrap around, cover, wire, coat, lap, whip (round), wind, spool, coil, wind on or over, rewind **mit Band ~** to tape **eine Spule ~** to rewind **mit Isolierband ~** to serve with insulating tape
Umwickeln *n* winding **~ des Wulstkerns** bead flipping (electronics)
umwickelt taped, covered **mit Draht ~** wire-wrapped
Umwicklung *f* lapping, serving, whipping, taping, wrapping, envelope, covering, winding
Umwicklungs-maschine *f* paper-wrapping machine, bead-covering machine **-tau** *n* winding rope
umwinden to twine or wind around
Umwindung *f* turn, convolution
Umwölkung *f* cloudiness
Umzäunung *f* fence, enclosure
Umzeichengerät *n* transformation drawing apparatus
umziehen to remove
umzingeln to encircle, envelop, invest
Umzug *m* moving, change
Umzugskosten *pl* moving expenses
Umzündstutzen *m* crossover tube
unabgeschirmt unscreened
unabgestimmt untuned, aperiodic
unabhängig independent, self-contained **~ von** irrespective of, regardless of **~ verzögerter Auslöser** time-limit release (definite) **-e Größe**

independent variable **-er Motor** self-contained motor **-es Teilchenmodell** individual-particle model **-e Veränderliche** independent variable
Unabhängige-Variable-Geber timing pulse generators
Unabhängigkeit *f* independence
Unabhängigkeitssatz *m* independence theorem
unabhörbar untapped
unabkömmlich indispensable
unabsetzbar unsalable
unabsichtlich unintentional
unachtsam careless, inattentive
Unachtsamkeit *f* carelessness, heedlessness, inadvertence
unähnlich unlike, dissimilar
Unanfachbarkeit *f* inexcitability
unangebaut uncultivated
unangegriffen unattacked, unacted
unangelassen untempered
unangelehnt unsupported **-e Flanke** exposed flank
unangemessen undue
unangenehm disagreeable, unpleasant, troublesome, undesirable
unangetastet untouched
unangreifbar unattackable, noncorrosive, nonaffected
Unannehmlichkeit *f* unpleasantness, inconvenience
unansehnlich unsightly, insignificant
unatembar irrespirable
unauffällig inconspicuous, concealed, attracting no attention
unaufgelöst undissolved, unresolved
unaufgelöst un(re)solved
unaufhörlich perpetual
unauflösbar insoluble
Unauflösbarkeit *f* insolubility
unauflöslich insoluble
unaufmerksam inattentive
unausbleiblich inevitable, unfailing
unausdehnbar inexpansible, nonductile, inextensible
unausführbar unfeasible, impracticable, impossible to execute **-e Verbindung** unobtainable number
Unausführbarkeit *f* impracticability
unausgeführt unexecuted
unausgefüllt void
unausgeglichen unbalanced, uncompensated, uneven **-er Zustand** out-of-balance condition
Unausgeglichenheit *f* unbalance
unausgelaugte Schnitzel cossettes
unausgelenkt uncompensated
unausgiebig nonyielding
unauslöschbar indelible, inextinguishable
unauslöschlich indelible
unauswechselbar noninterchangeable
unbauwürdig unworkable, inexploitable
unbeantwortet unanswered
unbearbeitbar unmachinable
unbearbeitet unwrought, unmachined, raw, crude, unfinished, in blank form, in blank condition
unbebaut not built upon, uncultivated
Unbedachtsamkeit *f* imprudence
Unbedenklichkeitsvermerk *m* license, permit
unbedeutend insignificant, trivial, unimportant, slight
Unbedeutendheit *f* smallness
unbedient unattended
unbedingt prime, indispensable, unconditional, absolute (math) **-es Haltsignal** absolute stop signal **-e Raumfolge** absolute block **-er Sprung** unconditional jump or transfer
unbedruckt blank
unbeeinfußt unaffected (by)
unbeeinträchtigt unimpaired
unbefahrbar impassable
unbefangen unprejudiced, impartial, disinterested, unbiased
unbefestigt unfixed, unfortified **-e Piste** *f* unpaved runway
unbefriedigend unsatisfactory
unbefugt unauthorized
Unbefugter *m* intruder, unauthorized person
unbeglichen unpaid
unbegrenzt unlimited, without limit, undefined **-e Bewölkungshöhe** unlimited ceiling **-e Haltbarkeit** unlimited durability
unbehaart hairless, bald
Unbehagen *n* discomfort
unbehaglich uncomfortable, uneasy
unbehandelt untreated
unbeholfen awkward, clumsy
unbekannt unknown, unexplained **-e Größe** unknown quantity **-e Ursache** unexplained cause
Unbekannte *f* unknown (quantity)
unbelastet unloaded, unstressed, nonloaded, unencumbered, no load (in specifications), off-load
unbeleuchtet nonilluminated
unbelichtet unexposed
unbemannt unmanned, pilotless
unbenannt undefined, indeterminate, nondimensional, unnamed, anonymous, indefinite (math.) **-e Zahl** nondimensional figure
unbenutzbar unserviceable
unbequem uncomfortable, uneasy
Unbequemlichkeit *f* inconvenience
unberechenbar incalculable
unberücksichtigt neglected
unberuhigter Stahl rimming or rimmed steel
unberührt unaffected
unbeschadet regardless, without prejudice
unbeschädigt undamaged
unbeschäftigt unemployed
unbeschichtet uncoated
unbeschleunigt uniform
unbeschnitten mill-cut (paper)
unbeschränkt boundless, unlimited **~ mischbar** consolute
unbeschrieben blank
unbesetzt clear, free, disengaged, idle, vacant **-es Band** empty band **-er Platz** unoccupied position
unbespannt uncovered
unbespult non-loaded
Unbestand *m* vicissitude
unbeständig unsteady, inconstant, labile, unstable, fickle, variable, unsettled **-es (pilziges) Fliegen** flying when controls go sluggish
Unbeständigkeit *f* instability, inconstancy, inconsistency
unbestimmbar indiscernible
unbestimmt undetermined, vague, undefined,

indefinite, indeterminate, uncertain, unspecified
Unbestimmte *f* variable (in algebra)
Unbestimmtheit *f* indetermination **~ der Eichung** indeterminate standard
Unbestimmtheits-beziehung *f* principle indetermination **-effekt** *m* uncertainty effect **-prinzip** *n* indetermination principle **-relation** *f* indeterminacy relation, uncertainty relation
unbeugsam unyielding
Unbeugsamkeit *f* inflexibility, rigidity
unbewachsen bare
unbewachte Endstation unattended terminal station
unbewaffnet unarmed, unaided **-es Auge** unaided eye, naked eye
unbewegbar immovable
unbeweglich motionless, immovable, stationary, fixed **-e Front** stationary front **-es Fahrgestell** fixed-type landing gear **-e Oberfläche** fixed surface
Unbeweglichkeit *f* immobility
Unbeweglichmachung *f* immobilization
unbewettert windless
unbewohnt uninhabited
unbewußt unconscious, involuntary, instinctive
unbezahlt unpaid
unbezogen unrelated
unbiegsam rigid, inflexible
unbillig unfair, unjust, unreasonable **-e Bedingungen** unreasonable terms
unbrauchbar useless, unserviceable
Unbrauchbarkeit *f* uselessness, impracticability
Unbrauchbarmachen *n* making useless, destruction
unbrechbar unbreakable
unbrennbar noncombustible, noninflammable **-er Stoff** incombustible matter
unbunt hueless **-e Farben** hueless colors, achromatic colors
Undationstheorie *f* undation theory
Undecan *n* hendecane
undehnbar inextensible, nonductile **-es Stahlband** *n* unductile (nonductile) steel band
undenklich immemorial
undeutlich indistinct, faint, indefinite, inarticulate, illegible **-e Aussprache** inarticulateness
Undeutlichkeit *f* indistinctness, inarticulateness, illegibility, indefinition
undicht leaky, unsound, untight, permeable, pervious **~ sein** to leak **-e Gewebe** loosely woven goods **-er Guß** porous casting **-es Rohr** blower
Undichtheit *f*, **Undichtigkeit** *f* leak, leakiness, porosity, perviousness, permeability, leakage
Undichtigkeitsgrad *m* degree of porosity
Undichtwerden *n* leakage
Undschaltung *f* and circuit
Undulations-strom *m* undulatory current **-theorie** *f* undulatory theory
Undulator *m* undulator
undulieren to undulate
undulierend undulating, undulatory **-er Strom** undulatory current
undulös undulatory
undurchdringbar impermeable
undurchdringlich impermeable, impervious, impenetrable
Undurchdringlichkeit *f* impenetrability, impermeability
undurchlässig impervious, impermeable, impenetrable, opaque **~ für Roentgenstrahlen** radiopaque **~ für Ultrarot** athermanous to infrared rays **-e Bodenschicht** impermeable stratum **-er Sand** close sand **-er Schutzanzug** protective suit
Undurchlässigkeit *f* impermeability, imperviousness
undurchlochbar punctureproof
undurchschossen unspaced, solid (print.)
undurchsichtig opaque, impervious to light, nontransparent, nondiaphanous
Undurchsichtigkeit *f* opaqueness
uneben uneven, not level, rough, rugged, (Blech) not flat
Unebenheit *f* unevenness, roughness, rugosity **~ ausgleichen** to true up, average out
unecht nonresisting, fading, fugitive, sham, spurious, nongenuine, imitated **~ gebrochen** improper fraction **-e Längenmessung** indirect measurement of length **-es Signal** spurious signal, shadow signal
unedel base, electronegative **unedles Metall** base metal
uneinheitlich nonuniform, inhomogeneous
Uneinheitlichkeit *f* nonuniformity
uneinnehmbar impregnable
uneinträglich unprofitable
unelastisch inelastic **~ gestreut** unelastically scattered **-e Kleinwinkelstreuung** small angle in-elastic collisions **-er Stoß** radiative collision
unelektrisch unelectric, uncharged
unempfänglich insusceptible
unempfindlich insensitive, insensible, immune, rugged, apathetic, unsusceptible, indifferent, nonreactive, inert, robust **~ gegen** insensitive or immune to **-e Zone** dead zone (servo) **~ machen** to desensitize
Unempfindlichkeit *f* insensibility, insensitiveness, robustness
unendlich unlimited, nonterminating, infinite **auf ~ eingestellt** focused for infinity **~ ferne Ebene** plane at infinity **~ kleine Größe** differential or infinitesimal quantity **~ ferne Punkte und Geraden** points and straight lines at infinity **~ klein** infinitesimal, infinitely minute **~ viele** an infinity of **~ werden** to approach infinity **~ klein weiter Punkt** far point (optics) **-e Reihe** infinite series **-e Zahl** infinity
Unendliche *n* infinity **sich ins ~ erstrecken** to extend to infinity
Unendlicheinstellung *f* infinity adjustment (optics)
Unendlichkeit *f* infinity
Unendlichkeitsstelle *f* infinity
unentflammbar flameproof, noninflammable, nonignitable, noncombustible **-er Film** safety film
unentgeltlich gratuitous, gratis, free (of charge)
unentwickelt undeveloped **-e Funktion** implicit function (math.)
unentwirrbar inextricable
unentzifferbar illegible
unentzündbar uninflammable, inert
unerfahren inexperienced
Unerfahrenheit *f* inexperience
unerforscht unexplored

unergiebig unyielding **-er Sand** barren sand
unerklärt undefined
unerläßlich indispensable
unerlaubt forbidden **-er Übergang** forbidden transition
unerledigter Anruf call on hand
unermeßlich unbounded, immeasurable, immense
unerregt unexcited
unerreichbar unobtainable; unattainable
unerreicht unattained
unerschöpflich inexhaustible
unerschüttert undisturbed
unersetzlich irreparable, irretrievable, irreplaceable
unerträglich intolerable, insufferable, unbearable
unerwartet unexpected
unerwünscht undesired, objectionable
unexplodierbar inexplosive
unfähig incompetent, disabled, unfit, incapable
Unfähigkeit *f* incompetency, disability, unfitness, incapability, inability, incapacity **~ zur Bekleidung öffentlicher Ämter** unfitness to hold public office
Unfall *m* accident **tödlicher ~** fatal accident
Unfall-anruf *m* emergency call **-bearbeitung** *f* accident investigation **-bericht** *m* accident report **-häufigkeit** *f* frequency of accident **-kran** *m* wrecking or accident crane **-meldeanlage** *f* accident signaling system **-meldung** *f* emergency call, accident report **-merkblatt** *n* accident-report sheet **-rate** *f* accident percentage **-statistik** *f* accident statistics **-stelle** *f* scene of accident **-schutz** *m* accident prevention **-sicher** accident-proof **-untersuchung** *f* accident investignation **-ursache** *f* cause of the accident **-verhütung** *f* accident prevention
Unfallverhütungs-maßregel *f* accident preventive **-verordnung** *f* safety rules **-vorrichtung** *f* safety device **-vorschrift** *f* rule for the prevention of accidents, safety rule
Unfall-verletzter *m* injured person **-versicherung** *f* accident insurance
unfertig unfinished, not ready, rough
unförmig unwieldy **-e Stücke** awkward pieces
unfrankiert, unfranko not prepaid, unfranked
unfrei restrained, constrained, engaged, tied, bound **-es Gleichgewicht** nonvariant or unvariant equilibrium
unfreiwillig unintentional, uncontrollable **-es Trudeln** uncontrollable spin
unfruchtbar unfertile, barren, sterile
unfühlbar (von Pulver) impalpable (powder)
ungangbar impassable
unganz unsound **-e Münzplatte** flawy coin plate
ungar undertanned
ungeätzt unetched
ungebeugt (Strahlen) undiffracted
ungebeutelt unshaken
ungebildet uneducated, unmannerly
ungebleicht unbleached
ungebleit unleaded
ungebraucht virgin, not used
ungebremst free wheel
ungebührlich undue
ungebunden uncombined **-e Ladung** free charge
ungedämpft undamped, sustained **-e Anzeige** ballistic or nonaperiodic reading or indication (of instrument) **-e Schwingungen** undamped, sustained, or persistent oscillations, continuous wave, persistent wave **-e Wellen** continuous waves, undamped waves **-e Zeichen** undamped wave signals, sustained signals (aviation)
ungedeckt roofless
ungeeicht uncalibrated
ungeeignet unfit, unsuited, unsuitable, improper, unqualified
ungeerdet ungrounded, not earthed, off earth **-es System** insulated system (unearthed)
ungefähr about, approximate
ungefährlich machen to render inoffensive
ungefärbte Kristalle uncolored crystals
ungefaßt frameless **-es Glas** rimless lens
ungefedert without springs, unsprung
ungefeuert unfired
ungefrierbar incongealable
ungefügig inflexible
ungegerbt untanned **-es Fell, -es Leder** rawhide
ungegoren unfermented (wine)
ungehärtet unhardened, soft
ungeheizt unfired
ungeheuer huge, monstrous **~ groß** immense
Ungehorsam *m* disobedience, insubordination
ungehört unheard
ungekerbt unnotched
ungeklärt unclear, obscure **-e Lage** obscure situation
ungekreuzt uncrossed, nonintersecting **-e Doppelleitung** nontransposed metallic circuit
ungekühlt uncooled
ungekündigt not discharged
ungeladen uncharged, nonloaded
ungelegen inopportune, inconvenient
ungeleimt (Papier) unsized
ungelernt unskilled
ungelöscht unquenched, unslaked **-er Kalk** quicklime
ungelöst unsolved
ungelüftet unventilated **-e Lichtmaschine** externally ventilated dynamo
ungemildert unmitigated
ungemischt unmixed
ungemütlich uncomfortable
ungenau inaccurate, inexact, untrue **~ werden** to get out of true
Ungenauigkeit *f* inaccuracy, discrepancy
ungenießbar unpalatable, inedible **~ machen** to denature
ungenügend insufficient
ungenutet without key-way
ungeordnet disordered **-e Bewegung** disordered motion **-e Geschwindigkeit** velocity of agitation **-er Zustand** disordered state, disordered arrangement
ungepflastert unpaved
ungeprüft unexamined
ungepuffert unbuffered **-e Lösung** unbuffered solution
ungequantelt unquantized
ungerade uneven, out of line, odd (integer), nonlinear, crooked **~ Zahl** odd number, uneven number **-s Vielfaches** odd multiple, odd harmonic (TV) **~ Zustände in gg-Kernen** odd states in even-even nuclei
ungerade-gerade-Kern odd-even nucleus

ungerade-ungerade-Kern odd-odd nucleus
Ungeradheitstoleranz *f* straightness tolerance
ung(e)radlinig nonlinear
Ung(e)radlinigkeit *f* nonlinearity
ungeradwertig of odd valence **-e Gruppen** odd-valent groups
ungeradzahlig odd-numbered
ungerandet not edged
ungerauht unraised
ungerecht unfair, unjust **-fertigt** unwarranted
ungereinigt unpurified
ungerichtet nondirectional, nondirective, equiradial **-e Antenne** nondirectional antenna **-e Geschwindigkeit** random velovity **-es Mikrophon** astatic microphone, nondirectional microphone **-e Strömung** undirected flow
ungerinnbar uncoagulable
ungerissene Abfälle (Kunstwolle) unpulled waste (shoddy)
ungeröstet unroasted, uncalcined
ungesalzen unsalted
ungesättigt unsaturated
ungesäuert unleavened
ungesäumt dull-edged
ungeschält unshelled
ungeschaltet unwired
ungeschichtet unstratified
ungeschickt clumsy, awkward
ungeschlagen unbeaten, unconquered, undefeated
ungeschliffen unpolished, unground
ungeschmolzen unfused, unmelted
ungeschränkt untwisted, without angular displacement between parts
ungeschürt whole, unstirred
ungeschützt unprotected, exposed
ungeschwächt unimpaired **-er Schroteffekt** *m* Schottky noise
ungesehnte Wicklung full-pitch winding
ungesetzlich unlawful, illegal
ungespaltene Ganggesteine undifferentiated dike rocks
ungespannt-e Federlänge unloaded spring length **-e Länge** (Feder) free height
ungesteuert uncontrolled
ungestöpselt unplugged
ungestört undisturbed **-es Einersignal** undisturbed-one output
ungesund unhealthy
ungestüm impetuous, fierce, blustering
ungeteert untarred
ungeteilt solid, undivided, whole, single **-er Ring** unsplit ring, solid ring
ungetempert unannealed
ungewalkt unmilled, unfulled, rough (cloth)
ungewaschen unwashed
ungewellt (Teilkammer) non-sinous
ungewiß uncertain, doubtful, problematic
Ungewißheitsprinzip *n* uncertainty or indetermination principle
ungewöhnlich extraordinary, uncommon, unusual, abnormal, unaccustomed
ungewollt abnormal **-e Aussendung** spurious radiation **-er Impulsmodus** spurious pulse mode **-e Strahlung** abnormal radiation
Ungeziefer *n* vermin **-vertilgungsmittel** *n* vermin destroyer
ungezielt unaimed
Ungezwungenheit *f* naturalness, spontaneity
ungiftig non-poisonous (non-toxic), nonvalid, void
unglasiert unglazed
ungleich unequal, unlike, uneven, dissimilar, unbalanced, odd, nonuniform, variable, different, unmatched **-armig** unequally armed **-artig** nonuniform, heterogeneous **-artigkeit** *f* heterogeneity, dissimilarity
ungleichförmig discontinuous, nonuniform, irregular, asymmetrical, unequal **-e Lagerung** unconformity **-er Sand** non-uniform sand
Ungleichförmigkeit *f* discontinuity, irregularity, asymmetry, nonuniformity ~ **des Wellenwiderstandes** impedance irregularity **statisch dauernde** ~ permanently drooping voltage characteristic
Ungleichförmigkeitsgrad *m* coefficient of fluctuation or of cyclic irregularity, degree of irregularity, governor regulation **Drehmoment von geringem** ~ smooth torque
Ungleich-förmigkeitsziffer *f* nonuniformity coefficient, lack of uniformity **-gewicht** *n* disequilibrium, unbalance, imbalance
ungleichgroß unequal
Ungleichheit *f* inequality, unbalance, diversity, unevenness
Ungleichheitszeichen *n* sign of inequality (math.)
Ungleichimpuls *m* unequal impulse
ungleichmäßig variable, nonuniform, asymmetrical, irregular, heterogenous, unequal, discontinuous, uneven **-e Setzungen** differential settlement
Ungleichmäßigkeit *f* nonuniformity, heterogeneity, discontinuity
ungleichnamig unlike, opposite (of poles) of different denomination ~ **elektrisch** oppositely electrified
ungleich-schalig unequivalve **-schenklig** unequal-sided **-seitig** scalene (geom.) **-stoffig** inhomogeneous **-stoffigkeit** *f* inhomogeneity
Ungleichung *f* unbalanced equation, inequality, dissimilar terms (math.)
Unglück *n* emergency, accident, misadventure
Unglücksfall *m* accident
ungrad traverse, curved, uneven, odd
ungreifbar impalpable
ungültig null, void (Patent) **für** ~ **erklären** to cancel ~ **machen** to invalidate, void, nullify, abolish
Ungültigkeit *f* invalidity, nullity, state of being void, annulled, not in force ~ **eines Patentes** nullity of a patent
Ungültigkeitserklärung *f* annulment
Ungültigmachen *n* abatement, abolition
ungummiert nonrubberized
ungünstig unfavorable, untimely ~ **einwirken** to penalize **-e Anordnung** unfavorable installation of apparatus **-er Einfluß** penalty **-es Wetter** unfavorable weather
ungünstigst most unfavorable
unhaltbar untenable
unhaltig containing no metal (min.)
unhämmerbar not malleable
unhandlich unwieldy, bulky
unheilbar incurable, irreparable
unhörbar inaudible
Unhörbarkeit *f* inaudibility
unhygroskopisch nonhygroscopic

Unifarbe *f* plain color
unifilar unifilar
Unifilaraufhängung *f* unifilar (simple) suspension
Uniform *f* uniform
unimodular unimodular (math.)
unionisiert unionized
Unionspriorität *f* convention agreement
Unipol *m* unipole
unipolar unipolar (single polar) **-er Impuls** single-polarity pulse **-e Leitung** unidirectional conductance
Unipolar-dynamo *m* homopolar or unipolar dynamo **-maschine** *f* homopolar generator
unisoliert uninsulated
unitär unitarian
Unitätssystem *n*, **praktisches ~** practical units system
Unitöne *pl* plain or solid shades
univariant univariant
universal universal **-abziehvorrichtung** *f* universal wheel dressing and profiling attachment **-anlage** *f* universal application **-antenne** *f* multiband antenna **-aufsetzkamera** *f* universal camera attachment **-aufspannplatte** *f* universal head **-ausklinkmaschine** *f* universal notching machine **-brücke** *f* universal bridge **-dämpfer** *m* universal steamer **-diode** *f* general purpose diode **-drehbank** *f* universal lathe **-drehtisch** *m* universal rotating stage **-dreibackenfutter** *n* universal chuck **-duowalzwerk** *n* universal two-high rolling mill
Universal-einstellbarkeit *f* universal adjustment, universal adjustability **-eisen** *n* universal mill plate, universal shapes **-eisenwalzwerk** *n* merchant mill, guide mill **-fallwerk** *n* universal tup machine **-fänger** *m* combination socket **-fangglocke** *f* combination fishing socket **-fertiggerüst** *n* universal finishing stand **-flanschenwalze** *f* universal flange roll **-fräskopf** *m* universal milling attachment **-fräsmaschine** *f* vertical milling machine **-führungsmaschine** *f* universal guiding machine **-futter** *n* universal chuck
Universal-gelenk *n* universal joint, flexible joint, ball-and-socket joint **-gerät** *n* universal apparatus **-gerüst** *n* universal mill stand **-gleich- und Wechselstromempfänger** *m* all-mains receiver **-glimmlampengerät** *n* universal neon-tube tester **-greifer** *m* universal grip **-handbohrer** *m* universal drill **-hinterdrehbank** *f* universal relieving lathe **-impulsregler** *m* universal-type timing impulse regulator **-instrument** *n* transit theodolite, general-purpose instrument **-lach** *m* universal varnish **-manipulator** general purpose manipulator **-mittel** *n* universal remedy **-montagebock** *m* universal trestle
Universal-lehre *f* universal gauge **-loch- und Ausklinkmaschine** *f* universal punching and notching machine **-motor** *m* universal motor **-navigationsgerät** *n* universal navigating instrument or apparatus **-nebenschluß** *m* universal shunt **-netzempfänger** *m* all-mains receiver **-objektivring** *m* universal lens adapter **-prüfer** *m* multiple-purpose tester, multimeter **-prüfmaschine** *f* universal testing machine
Universal-radar *n* general-purpose radar **-rechenmaschine** *f* general-purpose computer **-reißstock** *m* universal surface gauge **-relais** *n* general purpose relay **-röhre** *f* universal valve **-rundschleifmaschine** *f* universal cylindrical grinding machine **-rüster** *m* adapter **-schablonenhalter** *m* universal copy dial
Universal-sandpumpe *f* combination sand pump **-schleifmaschine** *f* universal grinding machine, universal grinder **-schlüssel** *m* universal screw wrench, monkey spanner **-schmiege** *f* universal bevel **-schraubenmutter** *f* plain nut **-schraubenschlüssel** *m* monkey wrench **-schrauber** *m* universal screw driver **-setzstock** *m* universal back rest **-spannfutter** *n* universal scroll chuck **-spannkopf** *m* expansion head **-spindelkopf** *m* universal head
Universal-tastatur *f* universal keyboard **-tiefenlehre** *f* universal depth gauge **-trägerwalzwerk** *n* universal mill for rolling beams **-trio** *n* three-high universal mill **-triowalzwerk** *n* universal three-high mill **-walzwerk** *n* universal mill **-werkzeugschleifmaschine** *f* universal tool and cutter grinder **-winkel** *m* universal square **-winkelmesser** *m* universal bevel protractor **-zange** *f* universal pliers **-zentrumsbohrer** *m* expanding center bit
universell universal, all-round
Universität *f* university
unkartiert unmapped
unkaschiert unlaminated
unkennbar undiscernible, unrecognizable
unkenntlich unrecognizable **-machung** *f* disguise
unklar turbid, indistinct, unclear, unserviceable, not ready for use **ein -er Anker** foul anchor
unkompensiert uncompensated **-er Abschnitt** unbalanced section (elec.)
unkompliziert straightforward
unkondensierbar uncondensable
unkontrollierbar uncontrollable
unkörperlich immaterial
unkorrigiert uncorrected
unkorrodierbar incorrodible
Unkosten *pl* cost, expense **allgemeine ~** overhead expenses **laufende ~** running cost
Unkosten-lohn *m* nonproductive wage **-verteilung** *f* expense distribution
Unkraut *n* weed
Unkraut-bekämpfung *f* weed control **-haken** *m* weed hook **-jäter** *m* weeder **-messer** *n* knife weeder **-schneidebalken** *m* weed attachment **-vertilgungsmittel** *n* weed killer
unkristallinisch noncrystalline, amorphous
unkristallisierbar uncrystallizable
unkristallisiert amorphous
unkündbar permanent
unlackiert unvarnished
unlauter unfair, dishonest
unlegiert unalloyed **-er Edelstahl** carbon steel **-er Kohlenstoffstahl** plain carbon steel **-er Stahl** simple steel, plain steel, carbon steel **-er Werkzeugstahl** unalloyed tool steel, carbon tool steel
unlenksam unmanageable
Unlinearität *f* non-linearity
unlösbar unsolvable, undissolvable, indissoluble, undetachable, locked
unlöslich insoluble
Unlösliches *n* insoluble matter
Unlöslichkeit *f* insolubility
unlötbar nonsoldering
unmagnetisch unmagnetized, nonmagnetic

Unmagnetisierungsfrequenz *f* magnetic reversal (frequency)
Unmasse *f* enormous quantity
unmäßig immoderate, excessive
unmerklich undiscernible
unmeßbar immeasurable, incommensurable (math.) **-er Niederschlag** trace of rainfall
unmischbar immiscible **-e Flüssigkeiten** immiscible fluids
unmittelbar direct(ly), immediate(ly) **~ abdestilliert** straight-run **~ angetrieben** direct-coupled **~ gekuppelt** direct-connected **-er Antrieb** direct drive **-es Einlaßventil** direct-inlet valve **-e und mittelbare Erregung** direct or indirect excitation of an aerial **-er Lichtbogenofen** direct-arc furnace **-e Unterstützung** direct support **-e Verbindung** direct circuit connection **-e Wahl** direct selection
unmodern out of fashion, obsolete
unmodifiziert unmodified
unmoduliert unmodulated **-e Rille** *f* blank groove (phono), virginal groove (phono) **-e Wellen** continuous waves
unmontiert unmounted
unmotiviert without a motive
unnachgiebig inflexible, tough, unyielding, relentless
Unnachgiebigkeit *f* rigidity
unnötig unnecessary
unnütz superfluous, useless
unofokal unofocal
unökonomisch uneconomic, inefficient, wasteful
Unordnung *f* disorder, mess **in ~** out of order, tied up, out of gear, topsy-turvy
Unordnungs-Ordnungs-Umwandlungen *pl* disorder-order transitions
unorganisch inorganic
unoxydierbar nonoxidizable
unpaarwertig of odd valence
Unparallelitätstoleranz *f* parallelism tolerance
unpassend unsuitable, improper, misplaced, inopportune, misfitting, unseemly, untimely
unpäßlich indisposed
unperiodisch aperiodic(ally), nonperiodic, deadbeat, nonrecurrent
unplatiniert unplatinized
unpolarisierbar nonpolarizing
unpolarisiert nonpolarized
unproduktiv unproductive
unpünktlich unpunctual, irregular
Unpünktlichkeit *f* unpunctuality
Unrat *m* refuse, dross (met)
Unrecht *n* wrong **-mäßig** unlawful, illegal
unregelmäßig irregular, erratic, anomalous **~ auftretende Störung** irratic trouble **-es Bruchsteinmauerwerk** random rubble **-er Gang** irregular running **-e Körperformen** three-dimensional design **-e Spannung** fluctuation voltage **-er Strom** fluctuating current **-er Untergrund** erratic subsoil **-e Verbrennung** chugging (irregular combustion due to chugging) **-e Verzerrung** fortuitous distortion
Unregelmäßigkeit *f* irregularity, anomaly
unreif raw, immature
unrein impure, crude
Unreinheit *f* impureness, impurity
Unreinigkeit *f* impurity **~ in einer Flüssigkeit** dross
unrelativistisch nonrelativistic
unrichtig incorrect, wrong **-es Arbeiten** incorrect operation (of relay)
Unrichtigkeit *f* error
unrückfällig irreversible
Unruhe *f* unrest, uneasiness, anxiety, disturbance, balance wheel, restlessness, disquiet, commotion, fluctuation, irregularity, instability, unsteadiness **-deckplatte** *f* plate covering the balance **-feder** *f* balance spring, impulse
Unruhenherstellung *f* balance-wheel manufacturing
Unruhe-polierdrehstift *m* arbor for polishing balance wheels **-welle** *f* staff, balance-wheel arbor
unruhig unquiet, restless, unsteady **-er Gang** unquiet or noisy running (eng.) **-er Lauf** uneven running (of motor) **-er Stahl** effervescent steel, running steel **-er Wagenlauf** rough running
unrund out of true, out of round, untrue, noncircular, cornered **~ werden** to come out of center **-er Zylinder** cylinder worn out of true
Unrunde *pl* oval flanges
Unrundheitstoleranz *f* circularity tolerance
Unrundlauf *m* faulty concentric running
Unrundwerden *n* ovalization **~ des Zylinders** wear or ovalization of cylinder
unsachgemäß improperly, incorrectly, irrelevant, improper
unsauber smudgy **-e Abstimmung** flat tuning **-er Abdruck** smudgy impression
unschädlich innocuous, harmless **~ machen** to render harmless, disarm, neutralize
unscharf nonsharp, out of focus, blurred, diffused, hazy, indefinite, flat, unarmed, poorly defined **~ abgestimmt** flat-tuned **~ machen** to blur **-e Kanten** diffuse boundaries **-e Prüfung** preliminary test
Unschärfe *f* lack of definition (of a picture), flat tuning condition, insufficient focus, lack of focus, haziness, diffusion, unsharpness, uncertainty, diffusiveness **Kreis der geringsten ~** circle of least confusion
Unschärfe-bedingung *f* uncertainty condition **-beziehung** *f* uncertainty relation **-ring** *m* blur circle, circle of diffusion
unscheinbar insignificant, unpretentious
unschiffbar unnavigable
Unschlitt *m* tallow
unschlüssig wavering, irresolute
Unschlüssigkeit *f* hesitation
unschmelzbar infusible
Unschmelzbarkeit *f* infusibility
Unschuld *f* innocence
unschuldig innocent
unschweißbar unweldable
unselbständig dependent, assisted, non-self-sustaining, nonspontaneous **-e Entladung** non-self-maintained discharge
Unselektivität *f* lack of selectivity, spurious response
unsicher uncertain, insecure, unsafe
Unsicherheit *f* uncertainty, drawback **~ des Impulseinsatzes** time jitter
Unsicherheitsfaktor *m* instability factor
unsichtbar invisible
unsichtig of zero visibility, hazy (meteor.)
unsinkbar insubmersible

unsolid(e) not solid

unsortiert unscreened

unstabil unstable, unsteady

Unstabilität *f* instability

unstarr nongrid, flexible, nonrigid **-es Luftschiff** blimp, nonrigid airship **-es Molekül** nonrigid molecule

Unstarrheit *f* flexibility, nonrigidity

unsteter Fehler bug (comput)

unstetig (unstät, unstet) discontinuous, intermittent, labile, unstable, uneven, nonuniform, unsteady, variable ~ **arbeitende Echosperre** relay type echo suppressor, echo suppressor **-e Lösung** discontinuous solution **-e Wirkung** discontinuous action

Unstetigkeit *f* discontinuity, nonuniformity, flutter (film pull) ~ **einer Kurve** jog

Unstetigkeits-fläche *f* discontinuity surface, surface of instability **-stelle** *f* point of discontinuity, burbling point, point of unsteadiness or instability **-strecke** *f* extent of vortex sheet or discontinuity **-stromlinie** *f* streamline of discontinuity **-typen** *pl* discontinuity types **-wechselwirkung** *f* discontinuity interaction

unstimmig discordant, nonconforming, disagreeing

Unstimmigkeit *f* variance, difference, disagreement, discrepancy, disparity, lack of harmony

unstreckbar not extensible, nonductile, nonmalleable

unsulfiert unsulfonated

Unsumme *f* immense amount

Unsymmetrie *f* asymmetry, dissymmetry, unbalance, unilateralness

unsymmetrisch unsymmetrical, asymmetrical, dissymmetric, unbalanced **-er Flug** unsymmetrical propeller thrust **-er Kreis** unbalanced wire circuit **-er Schraubenzug** unsymmetrical propeller thrust **-e Verzerrung** dyssymmetric distortion

unsystematisch at random

untadelhaft blameless, faultless

untätig idle, inactive, unoccupied

Untätigkeit *f* inactivity, inaction

untauglich unserviceable, unfit, unsuitable, useless

Untauglichkeitserklärung *f* disqualification

unteilbar indivisible

unten down, below, beneath, underneath **von ~ nach oben** from the bottom toward the top

Unten-ansicht *f* bottom view **-befüllung** bottom filling

unter under, below, among, lower ~ **null** below zero ~ **Strom** live (said of wire) ~ **Tag** underground workings (min.) ~ **Vorbehalt** with reservation **-er Boden** tank bottom of one type of guided missile **-e Bühne** lower platform **-e Bürsten** lower brushes **-es Deck** lower deck **-es Ende** bottom **-er hemisphärischer Lichtstrom** lower hemispherical flux **-er Rahmen** internal setting

Unter-abschnitt *m* subsector, subsection **-abteilen** to subdivide, make subcompartments or partitions **-abteilung** *f* subcompartment, subsection **-algebra** *f* subalgebra **-amboß** *m* anvil block **-amt** *n* suboffice, branch exchange, subexchange, minor exchange **-anspruch** *m* subclaim **-antrieb** *m* crank drive **-anzeige** *f* underswing (of volume indicator) **-art** *f* subvariety, subspecies **-ausschuß** *m* subcommittee **-bandrolle** *f* return idler

Unterbank *f* lower bench (min.) ~ **eines Flözes** bottom bench of a seam, bottom layer of a bed

Unter-bau *m* foundation, foundation or base course, substructure, earthwork, underpinning, base, support, subgrade ~ **aus Einzelschichten** sandwich slab

unter-bauen to underpin **-baut** underslung **-bauten** *pl* supporting structures **-bauvorrichtung** *f* fixture, jig (in airplane assembly) **-bauweise** *f* base construction **-belastung** *f* underload(ing) **-belegung** *f* under-assignment **-belichten** to underexpose **-belichtung** *f* underexposure

Unter-belieferung *f* shortage **-bereich** *m* complex domain, Laplace domain **-beton** *m* subconcrete, bedding concrete **-bett** *n* base **-bettung** *f* foundation **-bezeichnung** *f* dash number (aviation) **-bieten** to underbid **-bilanz** *f* short or adverse balance, deficit **-binden** to eliminate **-bindereserve** *f* tie-up resist (style)

Unterbindung *f* choking off, forestalling, preventing ~ **des Summenganges bei Einzelkartengruppen** single card total elimination

Unter-boden *m* subsoil **-brechen** to interrupt, shut off, break, disconnect, switch off, open, intermit, stop, discontinue, suspend, release **-brechend** intermittend

Unterbrecher *m* break, cutout, interrupter, buzzer, chopper, circuit breaker, contact breaker, rotor, (cutoff) switch, make and break, trembler, commutator, vibrator **elektrolytischer ~** electrolytic interrupter **schwingender ~** buzzer, vibrating contact **selbsttätiger ~** automatic contact breaker **umlaufender ~** rotary interrupter

Unterbrecher-befestigungsschraube *f* contact breaker fastening screw **-deckel** *m* contact-breaker or short-circuit cover **-drossel** *f* interrupter (jet) **-einrichtung** *f* contact breaker system **-empfänger** *m* interrupter or buzzer receiver **-feder** *f* contact spring, interrupter spring **-gehäuse** *n* magneto breaker box **-hammerkontakt** *m* hammer interruptor contact point **-hebel** *m* breaking lever, rocker arm, contact-breaker or interrupter lever, breaker arm

Unterbrecher-klappe *f* spoiler, interceptor, baffle **-klinke** *f* interrupting jack (television) **-kontakt** *m* contact-breaker point **-kontaktlehre** *f* breaker point gauge **-kontaktöffnung** *f* contact breaker opening **-maschine** *f* impulse machine **-nocken** *m* contact shoulder, breaker cam **-nockenhülse** *f* contact breaker cam sleeve

Unterbrecher-platte *f* contact breaker plate **-quersteuer** *n* spoiler control **-schalter** *m* circuit breaker **-scheibe** *f* make-and-break device, ignition cam, interrupter disk, commutator **-schlüssel** *m* contact breaker spanner **-spitze** *f* breaker point **-summer** *m* rhythmic buzzer **-steuerung** *f* spoiler control **-zugfeder** *f* contact breaker pull-type spring

Unterbrechung *f* disconnection, interruption, break, open(ing), stoppage, discontinuance, intermission, cessation, stop, clearing, discontinuity, fracture, check, delay, accident, break-away ~ **der Barprogramme** disruption of the construction schedule ~ **durch Blasenbildung** vapor lock ~ **und Schließung** break and make **funkenfreie** ~ clean break **funkenlose** ~ sparkless breaking **selbsttätige** ~ automatic break **sofortige** ~ quick release **verzögerte** ~ slow release **vorzeitige** ~ premature disconnection **zeitweilige** ~ intermittent disconnection, intermittency

Unterbrechungs-bad *n* short-stop bath **-bereich** *m* gap range **-funke** *m* break spark, circuit-opening spark, wipe spark **-geräusch** *n* disconnection or interruption noise, interfering noise **-klinke** *f* cutoff jack, break jack **-kontakt** *m* break contact

Unterbrechungs-relais *n* break relay **-schwingung** *f* quench oscillation **-stelle** *f* point of interruption **-strom** *m* current on breaking, intermittent current **-taste** *f* cutoff key, break key **-ton** *m* interruption tone **-vermögen** *n* circuit breaking, rupturing or opening capacity (of a switch) **-zahl** *f* number of interruption **-zeichen** *n* interruption signal

unterbreiten to submit

Unterbrennerofen *m* underburner-type (by-product coke) oven

unterbringen to quarter, billet, accommodate, sell, place, store, stow, house

Unterbringung *f* hangarage (of airplane), housing, billet ~ **der Belegschaft** accommodation of the workmen

Unterbringungs-gebiet *n* quartering area **-kosten** *pl* costs of housing **-möglichkeit** *f* accommodation

unterbrochen interrupted, intermittent, broken, discontinuous ~ **sein,** ~ **werden** to discontinue **-es Feuer** flashlight, occulting light, intermittent light **-es Gewinde** *n* interrupted thread **-e Härtung** interrupted hardening **-e Kehlnahtschweißung** intermitted fillet welding **-es Rauschen** impulsive noise **-er Tonfrequenzrufstrom** interrupted signaling current **-e ungedämpfte Welle** interrupted continuous wave **-e Wolken** broken clouds

unterbromig hypobromous

Unterbruch *m* interruption, shutdown

Unterbrückung *f* underbridge (R.R.)

unterchlorig hypochlorous **-e Säure** hypochlorous acid

Unterchlorsäure *f* hypochloric acid

unterchlorigsaures Calcium calcium hypochlorite

unterchlorsaurer Kalk calcium hypochloride

unterchlorigsaures Natron sodium hypochlorite

Unter-dämpfung *f* underdamping **-deck** *n* lower deck **-deckung der Kosten** under-recoveries of costs **-determinante** *f* minor determinant **-drehen** *n* low-speed shooting

Unterdruck *m* underpressure, vacuum, pressure below atmospheric, negative or reduced pressure, uplift, uplift pressure, partial vacuum, upward (hydraulic) pressure on foundations, low pressure, subpressure, depression, bottom pressure, suction head ~ **im Zerstäuber** negative pressure in the atomizer

Unterdruck-aggregat *n* vacuum unit **-anlage** *f* low-pressure chamber, altitude-pressure chamber **-anzeige** *f* low-pressure indication **-behälter** *m* vacuum reservoir **-betrieb** *m* operation at reduced pressure **-bohren** *n* pressure drilling **-bremse** *f* vacuum brake **-brennstofförderer** *m* vacuum fuel-feed device (auto.) **-dose** *f* vacuum box

Unterdrucke (Sogwirkung) depressions

unterdrücken to suppress, damp out, choke out, stifle, smother

Unterdruckentnahme *f* low-pressure extraction

Unterdrücker *m* suppressor

Unterdruck-förderer *m* vacuum fuel pump, vacuum tank; (bei Kfz.) autovac **-förderung** *f* autovac system **-gärung** *f* vacuum fermentation **-gaserzeuger** *m* suction gas producer **-gebiet** *n* low-pressure area, subpressure **-kammer** *f* air cock, pressure-testing chamber, air box, depression box, altitude test chamber, low-pressure chamber **-kanal** *m* low-pressure wind tunnel or channel **-kessel** *m* low-pressure vacuum tank **-klappe** *f* flap vacuum valve

Unterdruck-leitung *f* vacuum piping **-messer** *m* draft gauge, vacuum gauge, low-pressure gauge **-meßgerät** *n* vacuum gauge for negative pressure **-nachlauf** *m* underpressure wake **-prüfung** *f* low-pressure test **-raum** *m* vacuum space **-regler** *m* vacuum governor **-servobremse** *f* vacuum servo-brake **-speicher** *m* vacuum accumulator **-spitze** *f* minimum pressure point

unterdrückter Nullpunkt suppressed zero ~ **Träger** suppressed carrier (wave)

Unterdrückung *f* suppression, choking out, cancellation ~ **von Schwingungen** discrimination ~ **von Stromstößen** digit absorption ~ **der Trägerwelle** suppression of carrier ~ **von Wählimpulsen** digit absorption

Unterdrückungs-bereich *m* suppression range **-schwingung** *f* quench oscillation **-spannung** *f* cut-off voltage

Unterdruck-versteller *m* vacuum controller or governor **-verstellinie** *f* vacuum control curve **-verstellung** *f* vacuum advance and retard

unter-entwickelt underdeveloped **-entwicklung** *f* underdevelopment

untereutektisch hypoeutectic

Untereutektoid *n* hypoeutectoid

Unter-fach *n* lower shed **-fachgruppe** *f* subdivision **-faden** *m* lower thread

unterfahren to underrun, undercut (min.)

Unterfahrgestell *n* undercarriage

Unterfangarbeiten *pl* underpinning work

Unterfangung *f* underpinning

Unterfaß *n* coffer

Unterfeder *f* lower spring

Unter-feuer *n* front light (of lights in line) **-feuern** to underfire **-feuerung** *f* undergrate firing

Unterfilz *m* bottom-felt

Unterfläche *f* undersurface, base, underface, underside

Unterflächenwölbung *f* bottom camber

Unterflansch *m* bottom flange **-laufwerk** *n* traveling rail

Unterflasche *f* bottom sheave or block (of a flask lift), lower block

Unterflügel *m* lower wing, tail **-holm** bottom or lower wing spar **-querruder** *n* bottom or lower sileron

Unterflugzeug *n* lower component of a composite aircraft

Unterflur *m* underground, below grade **-diesel** *m* under-floor Diesel (engine) **-feuer** *pl* flush lights **-hydrant** *m* underground hydrant **-leitung** *f* underfloor duct **-leuchte** *f* flush light fitting **-ofen** *m* underground furnace, melting-hole furnace, furnace below floor level, pit fire **-rohrleitungen** *pl* underground piping **-tiegelofen** *m* pot fire, pit fire, hole furnace, pull-out-type crucible furnace **-verstärkerstelle** *f* underground repeater station

Unterform *f* bottom-half mold, subvariety, subspecies

Unterformant *m* subformant

Unterfräsmaschine *f* bottom-cutter molding machine

Unterführung *f* undercrossing structure (at road intersection), subway crossing, underbridge, underpass

Unterfunktion *f* transformed function

Unterfutter *n* lining

Untergalvanisierung *f* strike deposit

Untergang *m* decline, sinking, setting (of sun)

Untergangs-punkt *m* point of setting **-zeit** *f* time of setting

untergärig bottom-fermented **-e Hefe** bottom yeast

Untergärung *f* bottom or low fermentation

untergeben subordinate **-e Stelle** lower command

Untergebener *m* subordinate, subject

Untergehänge *n* bottom block (of flask lift)

Untergehäuseölschutz *m* base chamber oil underguard

untergehen to sink

Untergehen *n* going down, sinking, failure, swamped state, swamping ~ **der Bildspannung** swamping or blanketing of picture signal

untergeklemmter Faden underwound thread

untergeordnet subservient, secondary, subordinate, minor, subsidiary, immaterial **-e Stelle** subsidiary office

untergeordnete, ergänzende Hilfs-Aktiven ancillary assets

Unter-gericht *n* inferior court, lower court (of law) **-geschoben** spurious, supposititious **-geschoß** *n* ground floor, lower story, basement **-gesenk** *n* lower die, bottom die, bottom swage, matrix **-gestänge** *f* bottom rods

Untergestell *n* undercarriage, truck, pedestal, base, supporting frame, underframe, understructure, stand **-teil** *m* part of underframe

Untergewicht *n* short weight, underweight

untergetauchter Körper submerged body

untergießen to grout (joints)

Untergitter *n* sublattice

Unterglasur *f*, **-farbe** *f* underglaze

unterglazial subglacial

Untergliederung *f* subdivision

Unterglocke *f* lower bell, big bell, main bell

untergraben to undermine, dig in, corrupt **den Grund** ~ to sap the foundation

Untergriff beim Radreifen single flange on tire (R.R.)

Untergröße *f* undersize

Untergrund *m* sub-floor, foundation soil, subsoil, underground, underlying rock, bedrock, substratum, underlying strata, subgroup, subgrade, background **fester** ~ hardpan

Untergrund-abwässerung *f* subsurface draining **-bahn** *f* subway **-freies Spektrum** spectrum without substratum **-licht** *n* back-ground light **-lockerer** *m* subsoil attachment **-lockerung** *f* subsoiling **-malen** *n* priming (with paint) **-pflug** *m* subsoiler, subsoil plow

Untergrundquerschnitt, entnommener ~ borrow pit cross section

Untergrund-schwärzung *f* underground blackening **-strahlung** *f* background radiation **-streuung** *f* background scattering

Untergründung *f* underwater structure

Untergruppe *f* subgroup, detachment, subsidiary group, subordinate group

Untergruppenkontrolle *f* minor control

Untergurt *m* lower chord (of truss or girder), bottom flange (aviation), girt, girth

Unterguß *m* substratum (phot.)

Unterhafen *m* tail-water port

unterhalb underneath, below, downstream

Unterhalt *m* maintenance, upkeep

unterhalten to amuse, entertain, keep, maintain, support **die Feuerung** ~ to bank up fires

unterhaltener Fahrweg improved road

Unterhaltung *f* maintenance, holding under, conversation, entertainment, upkeep ~ **einer Anlage** maintenance of an installation ~ **des Fahrwassers** maintenance of the navigable channel ~ **der Tiefen** maintenance of the depth **regelmäßige** ~ routine maintenance

Unterhaltungs-arbeit *f* maintenance work **-ausgaben** *pl* cost of upkeep **-ausgaben** *pl* maintenance cost **-berechtigter** *m* dependent **-frage** *f* factor of maintenance **-kosten** *pl* maintenance (costs), expense or cost of upkeep **-unkosten** *pl* maintenance costs, overhead **-wert** *m* entertainment value

Unterhändler *m* negotiator, mediator, parliamentary, broker **-gebühr** *f* brokerage (fee)

Unterhandlung *f* parley **in** ~ **treten** to enter into negotiation

unterhängen to undersling

Unterhaupt *n* lower (or outer) gates (of lock) **-uhr** *f* auxiliary master clock

Unterhefe *f* bottom- or low-fermentation yeast

Unterhieb einer Feile first course of a file

Unterhitze *f* lower heating

unterhöhlen to hollow, underhollow, undercut

Unterholz *n* undergrowth, underbrush

unterhör-frequent subaudible, infra-audible **-frequenz** *f* subaudio frequency, infrasonic frequency

Unterhülle *f* subshell

unterirdisch subterranean, underground **-e Einlagerung** subterranean storage **-e Gewinnungsmethode** mining method **-er Leitungsweg** underground transmission path **-er Schutzraum** underground shelter

Unterkante *f* bottom edge, underside

Unterkapitel *n* subsection

Unterkasten *m* drag (flask), bottom box, lower case

Unterkellerung *f* cellaring

Unterkessel *m* water drum (engin.)

Unterkette *f* back or ground warp

Unterkloben *m* bottom block

Unterkolbenpresse *f* upstroke press

unterkompensieren to undercompensate
Unterkonoidierung *f* undercompensation
Unterkorn *n* undersize
Unterkorrektion *f* undercorrection
Unterkorrektur *f* undercorrection, undercompensation
unterkritisch subcritical **-e Ballung** underbunching **-e Geschwindigkeit** minor resonant speed **-e Masse** *f* sub-critical mass
unterkühlen to undercool
unterkühlt undercooled **-e Flüssigkeit** undercooled liquid **-er Wasserdampf** supersaturated steam
Unterkühlung *f* undercooling, subcooling, supercooling, overcooling
Unterkühlungsformgebung *f* subzero forming (process)
Unterkunft *f* billet, accommodation, shelter, quarters
Unterkunfts-bezirk *m* billeting district, shelter area, quartering area **-gebühr** *f* hangar fee, parking charge **-gruppe** *f* billeting party **-lager** *n* rest camp **-raum** *m* shelter, shed (R.R.)
unterkupfert copperplated
Unterladung *f* low charge
Unterlafette *f* lower gun carriage (artil.)
Unterlagblech *n* packing shim
Unterlage *f* base (plate) support; (Beleg) proof; (Akten) documents; (Angaben) data; (Quellen) sources, reference; foundation, basis, voucher, base, underlayer, rubble bed, packing (civil engin.), data, lining, bed, carrier, wedge, key (bookbinding), shim, underpin, substratum, backing ~ **zum Brettschneiden** saw-pit frame **erschütterungsfreie** ~ resilient support
Unterlagen *pl* data
Unterlager *n* bearing, foundation, lower bed
unterlagert subjacent, infraposed, underlying, subordinated
Unterlagerungs-fernwahl *f* low-frequency dialing **-telegraphie** *f* direct-current telegraphy over composited circuits, subaudio telegraphy, simplexed telegraphy
Unterlag-platte *f* ground or bed plate, offset plate, shim
Unterlagscheibe *f* washer, gasket, supporter **federnde** ~ spring washer
Unterlagscheibenherstellungsmaschine *f* machine for making washers
Unterlagsplatte *f* washer, base slab or plate, drop panel (in flat slab), ground plate, tie plate
Unterlagsteg *m* base (print)
Unterlängen *pl* short lengths
unterlassen to omit, abstain or refrain from, fail, default
Unterlassung *f* omission, oversight
Unterlauf *m* lower river, lower course, forefoot, stemson
unterlaufen to occur (accidentally), slip in with others, show on the surface, suffuse, run for shelter
Unterlauge spent lye (underlye)
Unterlast *f* belly load
Unterleg-blech *n* packing plate (shim) **-bogen** *m* margin sheet (print.) **-bohlen** *m* dunnage **-decke für den Sattel** saddle cloth
unterlegen to place underneath, key, wedge, underlay, adjust ~ **sein** to be inferior
Unterlegenheit *f* inferiority
Unterlegeplane *f* ground cloth or canvas
Unterleg-keil *m* wedge **-klotz** *m* support chock **-ring** *m* supporting ring, washer
Unterlegscheibe *f* supporting disk, washer, shim **federnde** ~ grower (washer), spring washer **glatte** ~ plain washer **gewellte federnde** ~ wrinkle washer **verzahnte** ~ toothed disk **verzahnte und federnde** ~ toothed spring washer **als** ~ **ausgebildetes Thermoelement** washer (thermo)couple
Unterlegestellung *f* welt position ~ **der Nadel** float position
Unterleg-gummiring *m* rubber washer **-platte** *f* washer, shim(s), liner, spacer
Unterleiter *f* lower ladder
Unterlicht *n* horizontal light
Unterlieferant *m* subcontractor
unterliegen to succumb, be defeated, be liable to, be subject to
unterliegend subjacent, underlying, placed below or underneath
Unterlitze *f* hanger, collar strap
untermalen to prime
Untermaß *n* short measure, undersize, amount of undersize ~ **aufweisend** undersized ~ **geben** to measure short
Untermeßsenker *m* undersize drills
Untermast *m* supplementary mast
untermeerisch submarine, below sea level
Untermesser *m* lower blade, bottom blade
unterminieren to undermine, sap
unternehmen to undertake
Unternehmen *n* enterprise, undertaking, operation **gemeinschaftliches** ~ joint enterprise **gewagtes** ~ adventure
Unternehmer *m* contractor, employer
Unternehmung *f* enterprise, undertaking, operation
Unterniveau *n* sublevel
unternormale Brechung substandard refraction
Unterofen *m* lower furnace
unterordnen to subordinate, make secondary or of minor rank
Unterordnung *f* subordination, submission
Unterpatent *n* subpatent
Unterpfand *n* security
Unterpflug *m* subsoil plow (plough)
unterpflügen to plow in or under
Unterpforte *f* lower port
unterphosphorig hyperphosphorous **-e Säure** hypophosphorous acid
unterphosphorigsaures Salz hypophosphite
unterpolstert padded
Unterprogramm *n* subroutine (info proc.)
Unterpulverschweißen *n* submerged arc welding
Unterputz-leitung *f* concealed wire **-leitungsverlegung** *f* buried wiring **-steckdose** *f* flush socket **-verlegung** *f* concealed wiring
Unterrahmen *m* subframe, undercarriage, bottom girder
Unterrahmenstück *n* bottom girder
Unterrandhöhe *f* altitude or height of lower rim or limb
Unterraum, invarianter ~ invariant, subspace
Unterreifen *m* rim of the wheel (R.R.)
Unterredung *f* parley, conversation, talk
Unterresonanzen *pl* subresonances

Unterresonanzfrequenz *f* submultiple resonance (of a subsynchronous frequency)
Unterricht *m* instruction, teaching
unterrichten to teach, inform, instruct
Unterrichts-blatt *n* service bulletin **-tafel** *f* demonstration chart
Unterriegel *m* earth brace, earth traverse, lower transom (elec.)
Unterring *m* lower band **-feder** *f* lower band spring
untersagen to forbid
Untersagung *f* inhibition, prohibition, forbidding, interdiction, restraint, injunction **~ der Berufsausübung** bar to practicing one's profession
Untersalpetersäure *f* nitrogen dioxide
untersättigen to undersaturate
Untersatz *m* support, base, stand, coaster, pedestal, stool **-brett** *n* supporting board
Untersäurelampe *f* cell or submersible inspection lamp
Unterschacht *m* lower shaft (of furnace)
Unterschale *f* subshell (of electrons)
Unterschallbeschaufelung *f* subsonic blading
Unterschallgeschwindigkeit *f* subsonic velocity, subacoustic speed **mit ~** subsonic
Unterschall-kanal *m* subsonic wind tunnell **-kante** *f* subsonic edge **-potentialströmung** *f* subsonic potential flow **-strahl** *m* subsonic jet **-strömung** *f* subsonic flow **-welle** *f* infrasonic wave, subaudio wave
unterschätzen to underrate, underestimate, undervalue
unterscheidbar distinguishable, discernible, discriminable, differentiable
unterscheiden to distinguish, differentiate, discriminate, differ, discern **grundlegend ~** to differ fundamentally
unterscheidend distinctive
Unterscheidung *f* distinction, discrimination **zur ~** to distinguish
Unterscheidungs-abzeichen *n* distinguishing mark **-empfindlichkeit** *f* sensitivity of discrimination **-kraft** *f* differentiating power (patent) **-kräftig** capable of distinguishing (trade-mark) **-markierung** *f* distinctive marking, telltale marking **-merkmal** *n* distinguishing feature or characteristic, characteristic feature **-signal** *n* distinguishing or recognition signal **-ton** *m* discriminating tone (teleph.) **-vermögen** *n* power of selection
Unterschenkel für Stativ side arm for stand
Unterschicht *f* lower stratum
unterschieben to push under, substitute
Unterschieber *m* cross slide; (e. Supports) bottom slide
Unterschiebungsklage *f* suit for passing off goods as though of another person
Unterschied *m* variation, difference (Relais) **auf einen ~ einstellen** to margin (a relay)
unterschiedlich diversified, variable **Stahl mit -er Korngröße** mixed-grain steel
Unterschiedsempfindlichkeit *f* sensibility to variation or difference
unterschiedslos indiscriminate
Unterschieds-schwelle *f* threshold of difference
Unterschiff *n* hull of a vessel
Unterschild *n* lower shield, apron shield **-träger** *m* lower-shield bracket
unterschlächtig undershot
unterschlägiges Seil bottom rope
Unterschleif *m* embezzlement
Unterschlagung *f* conversion (law), embezzlement
Unterschlagszeile *f* foot line, blank line (print.)
Unterschlitten *m* saddle (engin.) **-klemmhebel** *m* saddle-binding lever (engin.)
Unterschlupf *m* dugout, shelter, hiding place, cut-and-cover shelter
Unterschluß *m* lack, deficiency
unterschneiden to underream, undercut
Unterschneider *m* underreamer
Unterschneidung *f* water drip, weather groove, undercut
Unterschnitt *m* undercut
Unterschnitte *pl* female dies
unterschnitten undercut **-er Buchstabe** kerned letter (print.) **-er Zahn** undercut
unterschrämen to undercut, hole the trenches
Unterschrämung *f* undercutting
Unterschraube *f* counterscrew
unterschreiben to sign, subscribe
unterschreiten to fall below, keep within, fall short
Unterschrift *f* signature **eine ~ leisten** to subscribe
Unterschub-feuerung *f* underfeed furnace or firing **-rost** *m* underfeed grate (stoker)
Unterschuß *m* deficiency (opposite of excess), undershoot **-leitung** *f* defect conduction
Unterschutz (Auto) bottom apron plate
Unterschwefelsäure *f* hyposulfuric acid
unterschwefelsaures Salz hyposulfate
unterschweflig hyposulfurous
unterschwellig below threshold
Unterschwingen *n* precursor, underswing
Unterschwingung *f*, **subharmonische ~** subharmonics, subharmonic oscillation, subfrequency oscillation
Unterseeboot *n* U-boat, submarine
unterseeisch submarine (flat, bank, shoal)
Unterseil *n* balance rope **-führung** *f* ground-rope traction
Unterseite *f* underside, bottom side, bottom surface **mit der ~ nach oben** upside down
untersetzen to reduce (put under)
Untersetzer *m* table mat, scaler
untersetzt geared down **-e Luftschraube** geared (down) propeller **nicht -er Motor** ungeared engine
Untersetzung *f* reduction of speed **~ eines Getriebes ins Kleine** step-down gearing
Untersetzungsfaktor *m* scaling factor
Untersetzungsgetriebe *n* reducer, reduction gear, stepdown gearing, speed-reducer drive **~ mit konzentrischen An- und Abtriebswellen** concentric drive and reduction gear **Motor ohne ~** direct engine
Untersetzungsverhältnis *n* decreasing or reducing gear ratio, reduction(-gear) ratio
Untersonne *f* lower parhelion
unterspannen to subtend, subvolt
unterspannter Balken trussed beam
Unterspannung *f* low-tension voltage, underrunning voltage, undervolting **~ der Dauerfestigkeit** minimum stress limit

Unterspannungs-auslöser *m* under voltage release **-auslösung** *f* undertripping (relay) **-relais** *n* underload relay **-schalter** under-voltage switch, no-voltage tripping breaker **-seitig** on low-tension-voltage side
unterspülen to underscour
Unterspülung *f* scour (subsurface erosion), undermining, underscouring, underwashing **Schutz gegen** ~ cutoff walls, cutoffs
unterst lowermost, bottommost, lowest
Unterstand *m* dugout, (underground) shelter **unterirdischer** ~ subterranean shelter or dugout
unterständiger Anker undertype armature
Unterstanze *f* lower die, die, matrix
unterstecken to immerse (steep)
unterstehen to be subordinate to
unterstellen to attach, subordinate, park, store, put under the command of, be subordinate to, assume, presuppose, allege, impute, charge **Kraftfahrzeuge** ~ to garage
Unterstellung *f* attachment, subordination, putting under the command of, assumption
Unterstempel *m* die
Untersteuerung *f* undermodulation, insufficient modulation
unterstopfen to tamp, pack up
Unterstopfen *n* tamping
unterstreichen to underline, emphasize, underscore
Unterstreichung *f* underlining
Unterstreichvorrichtung *f* arrangement for underlining
Unterstrom *m* lower reaches of a stream
Unterströmung *f* underflow, undercurrent, seepage
Unterstruktur *f* substructure
Unterstück *n* bottom piece
Unterstufe *f* sublevel
unterstützen to support, favor, help, assist, subsidize, sustain, prop
Unterstütze, hölzerne trestles
Unterstützung *f* support, help, aid, assistance, relief ~ **eines Einspruches** support of an objection or a protest **operative** ~ indirect support
Unterstützungs-kasse *f* endowment or benevolent fund **-lager** *n* support bearing **-punkt** *m* point of suspension, point of support **-verein** *m* relief society
untersubmissionieren to sublet
untersuchen to test, examine, investigate, inspect, study, explore, trace, analyze, check up, search, inquire, scrutinize **nochmals** ~ to retest **auf Berührung** ~ to test for contact
Untersuchung *f* test(ing), examination, research, investigation, study, chemical analysis, inquiry, experiment, inspection, exploration, probing ~ **auf Gehalt an harzigen Rückständen** gum test ~ **mittels Röntgenstrahlen** X-ray analysis ~ **mit der Wünschelrute** rhabdomancy **eine** ~ **anstellen** to investigate **ärztliche** ~ medical examination **elektrische** ~ electric test **genaue** ~ scrutinizing
Untersuchungs-abschnitt *m* testing section **-amt** *n* testing office **-anstalt** *f* research institution **-apparat** *m* testing apparatus **-bereich** *m* range of investigation **-bohrer** *m* test drill **-bohrung** *f* prospecting bore
Untersuchungseinrichtung *f*, **elektromagnetisch gesteuerte** ~ remote-control testing equipment
Untersuchungs-haft *f* detention for investigation **-häuschen** *n* cable hut, test hut **-kammer** *f* test chamber **-kasten** *m* test box, test case **-klemme** *f* testing terminal **-kommission** *f* court of inquiry **-methode** *f* research method, method of investigation **-objekt** *n* test specimen, test sample, test piece **-platz** *m* test position **-raum** *m* laboratory **-säule** *f* pillar test box
Untersuchungsstand für das Schraubendrehmoment torque stand
Untersuchungsstange *f* pole test box, test pole
Untersuchungsstelle *f* testing point, examination or investigation bureau or station ~ **mit elektrischer Fernsteuerung** testing point with remote control (teleph.)
Untersuchungs-stollen *m* exploring drift **-tisch** *m* test desk
Untersuchungs- und Verteilungsstelle *f* test case (cable)
Untersupport *m* bottom slide rest
untersynchron hypersynchronous, undersynchronous **-e Resonanz** subsynchronous resonance, submultiple resonance
Untertagbau *m* underground working or mining
Untertagebetrieb *m* underground operations
untertags below-ground, underground
Untertasse *f* saucer **fliegende** ~ flying disk, saucer
Untertaste *f* long key, white key
untertauchen to immerse, submerge
Untertauchen *n* immersion, submersion, deep dip
Unterteil *n* base portion, lower part, foot, bottom, base ~ **eines Gesenks** bottom swage ~ **des Nivelliers** (nicht Dreifuß) cradle ~ **der Schmierbüchse** lower bush of the axle box (R.R.)
unterteilbar divisible
unterteilen to subdivide, section, divide **in Felder** ~ to panel
Unterteilschere *f* cross cutting shears
unterteilt subdivided, spaced **fein** ~ finely subdivided **-er Eisenkern** laminated or wire core **-e Funkenstrecke** multiple spark gap
Unterteilung *f* subdivision, compartment, submultiplication, partition, partitioning
Unterteilungspunkt *m* tap (of battery)
unterteufen to undercut
Untertitel *m* division heading
Unterton *m* undertone
untertonfrequent infra-sonic
Untertor *n* tail gate, aft gate
Untertrieb *m* negative buoyancy
Untertrum *n* empty belt
untertunneln to tunnel
Untervermittlungsstelle *f* subexchange
Unterversicherung *f* subinsurance
Unterverteiler *m* distribution terminal **-stelle** *f* subsidiary distributing point
Unterverteilung *f* secondary distribution
Untervertrag *m* subcontract
Untervollmacht *f* substitute or associate power of attorney
Unterwagen *m* lower chassis or carriage of a crane ~ **für Bremsberge** underwagon for inclined planes
Unterwagenantenne *f* undercar antenna

Unterwalze *f* bottom roll
unterwaschen undermined
Unterwaschung *f* undermining, underscouring, washing away **Schutz gegen ~** cutoffs
unterwasser below water surface
Unterwasser *n* tail water, bottom water **niedrigstes ~** lowest pool elevation
Unterwasser-abhörapparat *m* submarine detector **-anstrich** *m* antifouling painting **-antenne** *f* underwater antenna **-aufnahmen** *pl* underwater photography **-brenner** *m* underwater cutting torch **-felsbrecher** *m* subaqueous rock breaker **-geschwindigkeit** *f* submerged speed **-glocke** *f* submarine bell **-gründung** *f* underwater structure **-horchgerät** *n* submarine listening device, hydrophone **-kabel** *n* subaqueous or submarine cable
Unterwasser-kanal *m* tail race **-kraftwerk** *n* submersible power plant **-lager** *n* submerged bearing **-lautsprecher** *m* subaqueous loudspeaker **-lichtbildaufnahme** *f* underwater photograph **-lichtbogen** *m* underwater arc **-passage** *f* immersion passage **-rohr** *n* submerged tube
Unterwasser-schallanlage *f* underwater sound installation **-schallapparat** *m* hydrophone **-schallempfänger** *m* submarine sound receiver, hydrophone **-schallgeber** *m* underwater sound transmitter **-schallortungsanlage** *f* sound navigation and ranging **-schallwelle** *f* submarine sound wave **-sicher** submersion-proof (underwaterproof) **-schallsignal** *n* submarine signal **-schallzeichen** *n* submarine sound signal
Unterwasser-schiff *n* bottom (of a ship up to the water line) **-schneidbrenner** *m* underwater cutting burner or torch **-schneidetrupp** *m* underwater cutting and welding detachment **-seite** *f* downstream **-signal** *n* submarine sound signal **-spiegel** *m* lower pool or tail-water elevation, underwater reflection **-zeichen** *n* submarine signal
unterwegs en route, on the way **~ abfangen** to intercept
Unterwegsverlust *m* transmission loss
unterweisen to inform, instruct
Unterweisertafel *f* instruction chart
Unterweisung *f* information, instruction, indoctrination
unterwerfen to subject (to)
Unterwerfung *f* subjection, subjugation, submission, surrender
Unterwerk *n* substation
unterwertig inferior
Unterwind *m* downdraft, undergrate blast, draft undergrate, forced draft, lower wind
Unterwindeeinrichtung *f* doffing motion
Unterwind-feuerung *f* forced-draft furnace **-gebläse** *n* undergrate blower **-kanal** *m* forced draught duct **-ventilator** *m* forced-draught fan **-zufuhr** *f* forced-draft supply
unterworfen subject to, liable **~ sein** to underlie
Unterwühlung *f* undermining
unterzeichnen to sign
Unterzentrale *f* branch office (teleph.)
unterziehen, sich ~ to submit to, undertake, undergo **sich einer Mühe ~** to bother
Unterzug *m* beam, girder, sleeper, bearer, transom **~** (TW) unterlayer **~ eines Fußbodens** dormer or sleeper of a floor **~ des Rahmens** trussing of frame (motorcar)
Unterzugsstrebe *f* truss strut
Unterzustand *m* substate
Unterzylinder *m* lower carrier roll
untief shallow (water)
Untiefe *f* high bed, bar, shoal, bank, shallowness, shelf
untilgbar indelible
untragbare Kosten prohibitive cost
untrennbar inseparable, indivisible, unseverable, undetachable **~ verbunden** inherent
Untrennbarkeit *f* inseparability
untreu unfaithful **im Dienste ~ sein** to commit a breach of trust, be unfaithful in service
Untreue *f* disloyalty, breach of trust, malfeasance, infidelity
untrüglich unerring
unüberbrückt unbridged, unbypassed
unübersehbar uncontrollable, hard to follow up or inspect, complex, intricate, incomprehensible
unübersetzt ungeared, not translated
unübersichtlich vague
unübersteigbar insuperable
unübertragbar nontransferrable, inalienable, unassignable
unübertrefflich unexcelled, unrivaled, unsurpassable
unübertroffen unsurpassed, unexcelled
unüberwacht unattended, unguarded
unüberwindlich insuperable
ununterbrochen continuous, uninterrupted, unbroken **~ belastet** continuously loaded **-es Feuer** flash-light **-e Probeentnahme** continuous sampling
ununterscheidbar undiscernible
unveränderlich invariable, unchangeable, constant **-e Umlaufszahl** constant speed
Unveränderliche *f* constant
Unveränderlichkeit *f* invariability
unverändert unaltered, unchanged
unverantwortlich unwarranted
unverbindlich without obligation, free
unverbleit unleaded **-es Benzin** unleaded fuel
unverbrannt unburned
unverbraucht unused
unverbrennbar incombustible, fireproof **-er Film** slow-burning film, safety film
Unverbrennbarkeit *f* incombustibility
unverbrennlich incombustible **-er Bestandteil** incombustible constituent
unverbundene Niveaus unbound levels
unverdient undeserved, unmerited
unverdorben unspoiled
unverdünnt undiluted
unvereinbar contradictory
Unvereinbarkeit *f* inconsistency
Unverfallbarkeit *f* non-forfeiture
unverfaulbar unputrefiable, imputrescible
Unverformbarkeit *f* inability to deform
unvergänglich imperishable
Unvergänglichkeit *f* imperishableness, everlastingness
unvergasbar ungasifiable
unverglast unvitrified
unvergleichlich incomparable, unequaled, unparalleled
unvergrünbar not turning green
unverhältnismäßig disproportionate

unverholzt unlignified
unverhüttbar unsmeltable, unworkable
unverkennbar unmistakable
unverkittet uncemented
unverküpt unreduced (unvatted)
unverkürzt unabridged
unverlangt unsolicited
Unverläßlichkeit *f* instability
Unverletzbarkeit *f*, **Unverletzlichkeit** *f* invulnerability, inviolability, sanctity
unverletzt unhurt, uninjured
unverlierbar undetachable **-e Mutter** *f* captive nut
unverlötet not soldered
unvermeidbare Verlustzeit *f* unavoidable delay factor
unvermeidlich unavoidable
Unvermeidlichkeit *f* inevitability
unvermindert unimpaired, undiminished
unvermischbar immiscible
Unvermischbarkeit *f* immiscibility
unvermischt unadulterated (undiluted)
unvermischbares Lösungsmittel immiscible solvent
unverpackt in bulk, unpacked
unverriegelt unlocked
unverritzt untouched **-es Feld** virgin field
unverrückbar irreversible, immovable, shakefree
Unverschiebbarkeit *f* stability
unverschiebliches Gelenk fixed hinge
unverschlackt unsintered
unverschlüsselt uncoded, absolute
unverschnitten unadulterated
unversehrt undamaged, intact, sound
unverseifbar unsaponifiable
unversiegbar not running dry, inexhaustible (Energiequelle)
unversilbert unsilvered
unverspannt unbraced, braceless
unverständlich unintelligible **-es Nebensprechen** inverted cross talk, unintelligible crosstalk
Unverständlichkeit *f* unintelligibility
unverstärkt not reinforced, unamplified
unverstellbar fixed **-e Luftschraube** fixed (blade) airscrew **-e feste Motorhaube** fixed cowl **-e Steigung** fixed pitch
unversteuert duty unpaid, tax unpaid
unverstrebt unbraced
unverstrecktes Kabel undrawn tow
unvertauschbar noninterchangeable
Unvertauschbarkeit *f* noninterchangeability
unvertilgbar indelible
unverträglich inconsistent, incompatible
unverwechselbar noninterchangeable **-er Stecker** noninterchangeable plug
unverwendbar unusable
unverweslich imputrescible
unverwittert unweathered
unverwüstlich indestructible **-e Ausführung** robust construction
Unverwüstlichkeit *f* sturdy design
unverzeichnet undistorted
unverzerrt undistorted **-es Bild** undistorted picture **-er Empfang** undistorted reception
unverzinkt ungalvanized
unverzollt duty unpaid, exclusive of duty
unverzüglich immediate
unverzweigt non-branched
unviskos nonviscous **-es Öl** neutral oil
unvollendet imperfect, incomplete **-es Zylinderöl** bright stock (oil)
unvollkommen imperfect, defective, incomplete **-er Brunnen** (drainage) well that does not extend downward as far as the impermeable stratum **-er Isolator** imperfect insulation, leaky dielectric **-er Überfall** submerged weir, free discharge
Unvollkommenheit *f* imperfection
unvollständig incomplete, imperfect **-e Verbindung** incompletely dialed call **-e Wahl** mutilated selection
unvoreingenommen unprejudiced, objective
unvorschriftsmäßig contrary to regulations, not regularly prescribed
unvorsichtig careless
Unvorsichtigkeit *f* imprudence
unvorteilhaft unprofitable, disadvantageous
unwägbar unweighable
Unwägbarkeit *f* unweighability
unwahr false, untrue, fictitious
Unwahrheit *f* falsehood, lie
unwahrscheinlich improbable, unlikely
unwandelbar invariable, rigid, immutable, unchangeable, imperishable
unwegsam pathless
unwesentlich immaterial
Unwetter *n* bad weather, tempest **-bericht** *m* weather report **-warnung** *f* weather warnings
unwichtig unimportant
unwiderleglich irrefutable
unwiderrufliches Akkreditiv irrevocable credit
unwiderstehlich irresistible
unwillig reluctant, unwilling
unwirksam ineffective, inactive, inefficient, inoperative, inert ~ **machen** to kill, paralyze, render inoperative, disable, deactivate, inactivate **-e Zeit** idle time
Unwirksamkeit *f* ineffectiveness, inefficiency
unwirtschaftlich uneconomical, inefficient, unthrifty
Unwirtschaftlichkeiten beseitigen to eliminate sources of waste
unwissenschaftlich unscientific
Unwucht *f* unbalance (of shafts), unequal weighing, imbalance **-kraft** *f* out-of-balance force **-scheibe** *f* eccentric weight
unzählig innumerable, numberless, countless
Unze *f* ounce (oz.)
Unzeit *f* inopportune moment
unzeitgemäß out-of-date, untimely, unpropitious
unzeitlich untimely, immature
unzerbrechlich unbreakable, nonbreakable
unzerlegbar indecomposable, indivisible
unzerlegtes Licht undispersed light
unzerreißbar untearable
unzersetzbar indecomposable
Unzersetzbarkeit *f* indecomposability
unzersetzt undecomposed
unzerstörbar noncorrodible, noncorrosive, indestructible, imperishable
Unzerstörbarkeit *f* indestructibility
unzertrennbar inseparable
unziehbar nonductile
unziemlich unseemly
unzubereitet untreated, raw
unzugänglich inaccessible

unzugerichtet rough (rough-tanned)
unzugeteilt unallotted
unzulänglich inadequate
Unzulänglichkeit *f* shortcoming
unzulässig undue **-e Beanspruchung** undue strain
unzureichend short, insufficient **-er Schnitt** undercutting
Unzusammendrückbarkeit *f* incompressibility
Unzustellbarkeit *f* impossibility of delivery
Unzuträglichkeit *f* inconvenience, disadvantage, failure
unzuverlässig unreliable
unzweckmäßig unsuitable, improper, impracticable, inexpedient
unzweideutig explicit, unequivocal, unambiguous, clear
unzweifelhaft unquestionable
üppig wuchernd rampant
U-Profil *n*, **U-Querschnitt** *m* channel section, U section
UP-Schweißen *n* (Unterpulver-Schweißen) submerged arc welding
U.p.M., U/M (Umdrehung pro Minute) r.p.m. (revolutions per minute)
U/Q (Q-Signalspannung *f*, Buntspannung Q) *f* E/Q (Q signal voltage)
U/R (R-Signalspannung) *f* E/R (R signal voltage)
Uraconit *m* uraconite
U-Rahmen *m* U frame (tubular chassis)
Uran *n* uranium **-azetat** *n* uranium acetate **-blei** uranium lead **-blüte** *f* zippeite **-brenner** uranium pile or reactor
Urancalzit *m* uranochalcite
Uran-gehalt *m* uranium content **-gelb** *n* yellow uranium oxide, sodium uranate **-glimmer** *m* torbernite **-grün** *n* uranochalcite **-graphitgitter** *n* uranium-graphite lattice **-gummi** *n* gummite **-haltig** uraniferous **-hexafluorid** *n* uranium hexafluoride
Uraniagrün *n* urania green
Uranide *pl* uranides
uranig uranous
Urani-nitrat *n* uranic nitrate **-verbindung** *f* uranic compound
Uranit *n* uranite
Uran-karbid *n* uranium carbide **-kern** *m* uranium nucleus **-klumpen** *m* uranium slug **-molybdat** *n* uranmolybdate **-ocker** *m* uranium ocher, uraconite
Uranophan *n* uranophane
Urano-salz *n* uranous salt **-tantal** *m* samarskite **-thorit** *m* uranothorite
Urano-uranat *n* uranous uranate **-verbindung** *f* uranous compound
Uran-oxychlorid *n* uranium oxychloride, uranyl ammonium **-oxyd** *n* uranium oxide **-oxydhydrat** *n* uranium hydroxide **-oxydoxydul** *n* uranosouranic oxide **-oxydrot** *n* uranium oxide red, uranic acid **-oxydul** *n* uranous oxide **-oxydulsalz** *n* uranous salt
Uran-pechblende *f*, **-pecherz** *n* pitchblende **-phosphat** *n* uranium phosphate **-pilit** *m* uranopilite **-probe** *f* sample of uranium **-reaktor** *m* uranium pile **-rot** *n* uranium red **-säure** *f* uranic acid **-spathit** *m* uranosphathite **-spherit** *m* uranospherite **-spinit** *m* uranospinite, iranospinite **-strahlen** *m pl* uranium rays **-tonbad** *n* uranium toning bath **-uranig** uranosouranic **-verbindung** *f* uranium compound **-vitriol** *n* johannite
Uranyl-nitrat *n* uranyl nitrate **-phosphat** *n* uranyl phosphate
Urat (harnsaures Salz) urate
Uratom *n* primordial atom
Urbarmachung von Land cultivating lands
Urbaumuster *n* original model, prototype
Urbild *n* original, prototype, type
Urbohrvorrichtung *f* master drill jig
Urdestillation *f* low-temperature distillation, low-temperature carbonization
Urdeul *m* first lump (metal.)
Urdox-regler *m*, **-widerstand** *m* Urdox resistor
Ureichkreis *m* master reference system
Urfels *m* primitive rock
Urform *f* master pattern or gauge
Urgebirge *n* primary rock
Urgestein *n* mother rock, parent or igneous rock
Urgewicht *n* standard weight, primary standard weight
Urheber *m* author, writer, founder, originator **-recht** *n* privilege of the author, copyright, rights of an author or inventor **-schaft** *f* parentage **-schutzvermerk** *m* copyright mark
Urkoks *m* semicoke, low-temperature coke
Urkunde *f* letter, document ~ **ausstellen** to execute a document
Urkunden-beweis *m* documentary evidence **-fälschung** *f* falsification, forgery of documents **-papier** *n* document paper
urkundlich authentic, documentary
Urlaub *m* furlough, leave (of absence) **auf** ~ on leave
Urlehre *f* master gauge, standard gauge
Urmaß *n* standard gauge, standard measure, master gauge, primary standard
Urmeter *m* standard meter
Urmultivibrator *m* basic multivibrator
Urmuster *n* prototype, standard
Urnocke *f* master cam
Urnormale *f* primary standard
U-Rohr *n* U tube
Urortungsgerät *n* infrared position-finding set (radar)
Urplasma *n* ylem
Urpreis *m* original or cost price
Urproduction *f* raw material production
Ursache *f* cause, reason
ursächlich causal, causative
Ursächlichkeit *f* causality, causation
Urschablone *f* master template or pattern
Urschrift *f* original document, manuscript, first draft
Ursprung *m* source, origin, beginning
Ursprungs-knall *m* initial report or detonation
ursprünglich original, primitive, first, primary, parent **zu -en Bedingungen annehmen** to accept on original conditions
Ursprünglichkeit *f* originality
Ursprungs-anstalt *f* originating office, originating toll center **-bild** *n* original subject copy **-festigkeit** *f* endurance strength, fatigue limit, natural limit of stress
Ursprungsform *f* form of origin **elastische Rückkehr zur** ~ elastic restoration
Ursprungs-funkstelle *f* station of origin **-gegend** *f* source region **-land** *n* country of origin **-punkt** *m*

point of origin **-region** *f* source region **-typ** *m* prototype, original or primordial type or specimen **-verkehr** *m* originating traffic **-zeugnis** *n* certificate or origin

Urstoff *m* parent material, primary material, element

urstofflich elementary

Urteer *m* low-temperature tar, crude tar

Urteil *n* judgment, decision, opinion, sentence (law), verdict

Urteilchen *n* atom

Urteilrad *n* master dividing gear

urteilsfähig judicious

Urteils-milderung *f* mitigation of sentence **-spruch** *m* sentence, judgment **-vollstreckung** *f* execution of a sentence, carrying out a judgment

Urverkokung *f* low-temperature carbonization or distillation, low-temperature coking

Urverschwelung *f* partil carbonization at a low temperature without admission of air

Urwald *m* jungle

usancemäßig according to custom

Utelapparat *m* Fullerphone

UV-Geber *m* timing generator (comput.), timing pulse generator

Uviolflintprisma *n* uviol glass

Uviollicht *n* ultra violet rays

V

Vacon *n* vacon (metal alloy)

Vacublitz *m* flash bulb

Vadosewasser *n* vadose water

vagabundierender Strom leakage or stray current, vagabond or vagrant current

Vakat *n* white, unprinted paper of any color

Vakuole *f* pinhole, vacuole

Vakuometer vacuum gauge

Vakuskop *n* vacuoscope

Vakuum *n* vacuum **-apparat mit Heizschlangen** coil vacuum

Vakuum-anlage *f* vacuum plant **-aufdampfung** *f* vacuum deposition **-ausstoßsystem** *n* vacuum stripper **-bedampfung** *f* vacuum deposition **-behälter** *m* vacuum trap, vacuum tank **-blitzableiter** *m* vacuum-lightning arrester **-destillation** *f* vacuum topping, vacuum distillation **-dicht** hermetic, vacuum tight, sealed (airtight)

Vakuum-elektrodynamik *f* electrodynamics in vacuo **-entgasung** *f* vacuum degassing **-fett** *n* vacuum grease **-filter** *m* vacuum filter **-förderung** *f* vacuum feed **-formen** *pl* evacuated dies **-gitterspektrograph** *m* vacuum grating spectrograph **-glocke** *f* bell jar **-glühlampe** *f* incandescent lamp **-hahn** *m* vacuum tap

Vakuum-kessel *m* vacuum tank (chamber) or reservoir suction and forcing apparatus **-lampe** *f* vacuum lamp **-leitung der Diffusionspumpen** vacuum piping of diffusion pumps **-manometer** *m* vacuum gauge **-mantel** *m* vacuum jacket **-mantelgefäß** *n* thermos vessel with exhaust jacket **-messer** *m* vacuum gauge, vacuometer **-messung** *f* vacuum measurement **-metallbedampfung** *f* vacuum metallizing **-meter** *n* vacuum gauge, vacuometer, ionization gauge **-pfanne** *f* vacuum pan **-pumpsatz** *m* vacuum pump system **-quarz** *m* vacuum-sealed crystal **-regler** *m* vacuum regulator **-reiniger** *m* vacuum cleaner **-röhre** *f* vacuum tube, electron tube, thermionic tube

Vakuumröhren-empfänger *m* vacuum-valve receiver **-verstärker** *m* tube amplifier

Vakuum-schaufeltrockner *m* vacuum paddle drier **-schleuse** *f* air lock **-schranktrockner** *m* vacuum shelf drier **-servobremse** *f* booster brake **-spektrograph** *m* vacuum spectrograph **-taumeltrockner** *m* vacuum eccentric tumbling drier **-technik** *f* vacuum processing **-teer** *m* vacuum tar **-thermoelement** *n* vacuum thermocouple **-topping** *n* vacuum topping **-trebertrockenapparat** *m* vacuum draff-drying apparatus **-trockenofen** *m* vacuum drying oven **-trockner** *m* vacuum drier **-trommeltrockner** *m* vacuum rotary drier

Vakuum-verdampfer *m* vacuum evaporator **-verdampfungsapparat** *m* vacuum evaporator **-verflüchtigung** vacuum volatilization **-verformung** *f* vacuum forming **-walzentrockner** *m* vacuum drum drier **-zelle** *f* vacuum photoelectric cell **-zugwagenbremsventil** vacuum tractor brake valve

Valenz *f* valence **-bildung** *f* valence bond **-elektron** *n* outer-shell electron, conduction electron **-richtung** *f* bond direction **-schwingung** *f* stretching vibration **-stufe** *f* valence stage

valeriansau(e)r, -es Ammonium ammonium valerate **-es Kalium** potassium valerate **-es Natrium** sodium valerate

Valeriansäure *f* valeric acid

Valerylnitril *n* valeryl nitrile

Validität *f* validity

Valuta *f* standard (banking), foreign currency

Vanadat *n* vanadiate, vanadat

Vanadatbeize *f* vanadium mordant

Vanadationen *pl* vanadate ions

Vanadin-bleierz *n*, **-bleispat** *m* vanadinite **-chlorid** *n* vanadium chloride **-eisen** *n* ferrovanadium **-enthaltend** vanadiferous

Vanadin-karbid *n* vanadium carbide **-pentoxyd** *n* vanadium pentoxide **-salz** *n* vanadium salt, vanadate **-säure** *f* vanadic acid **-säureanhydrid** *n* vanadic anhydride, vanadium pentoxide

vanadinsaures Ammon ammonium vanadate

Vanadin-stahl *m* vanadium steel **-stickstoff** *m* vanadium nitride **-sulfat** *n* vanadic sulfate **-verbindung** *f* vanadium compound

Vanadium *n* vanadium **-chlorür** *n* vanadous chloride **-stahl** *m* vanadium steel **-trioxyd** *n* vanadium trioxide

Vanadolsalz *n* vanadous salt

Vanadosulfat *n* vanadous sulfate

Vanadylsulfat *n* vanadyl sulfate

Vandenbrandeit *m* uranolepidite, vandenbrandeite

Vandendriesscheit *m* vandendriesscheite

Vanoxit *m* vanoxite

V-Anker *m* V stay
V-Antenne *f* V antenna
Van Allenscher Gürtel *m* Van Allen belt
Van't-Hoffsches Gesetz van't Hoff's law
Var *n* reactive volt-ampere
variabel variable
Variabilität *f* variability **-index** *m* (mittlere Abweichung) standard deviation
Variable *f* variable
Variante *f* variant
Varianz *f* variance
Variation *f* variation
Variations-breite *f* range of variation **-messung** *f* (aviation) variation measurement **-methode** *f* variation method **-problem** *n* variation problem **-rechnung** *f* calculus of variations **-wellenfunktion** *f* variational wave function
Variator *m* variable drive
variieren to vary, alter
Variodenregler *m* variode regulator
Vario-koppler *m*, **-kuppler** *m* variocoupler
Varioplexsystem *n* varioplex system
Variometer *n* variometer, statoscope, rate-of-climb indicator, vertical-speed indicator **-kompaß** *m* variometer compass
Variometerspule *f* variometer coil **drehbare ~** variometer rotor **feste ~** variometer stator
Varioptik *f* zoom lens
Varistor *m* varistor
Varleyschleife *f* Varley's loop test (teleph.)
Var-Stunde *f* var-hour
Vaselin *n*, **Vaseline** *f* vaseline
Vaselin-herstellungsanlage *f* Vaseline plant **-öl** *n* vaseline oil
VDI (= Verein Deutscher Ingenieure) association of German engineers
V-eff V-rms
Vegetationswasser *n* vegetation moisture, water of vegetation
Vekt *m* symbol for rate of acceleration or change of target speed, remaining velocity
Vektor *m* vector, vector quantity **absoluter ~** tensor **Poyntingscher ~** Poynting's vector
Vektor-betrag *m* absolute value of modulus of vector **-bild** *n* vector diagramm **-blatt** *n* vector sheet
Vektorensatz *m* vector set
Vektor-feld *n* vector field **-gleichung** *f* vector equation **-größe** *f* vector quantity
vektoriell vectorial **~ addieren** to add vectorially **~ darstellen** to represent vectorially **-e Darstellung** vector representation **-er Schreiber** vectorial recorder
Vektor-indikation *f* vector-response index **-linie** *f* line of flux **-rechnung** *f* vector calculus **-richtung** *f* direction of vector **-röhre** *f* vector tube **-sinn** *m* sense (direction) of vector **-summe** *f* vector sum **-winkel** *m* vectorial angle **-zeichnung** *f* vector diagram
Velin *n* vellum **-form** *f* wave mold (paper)
Velourhebeapparat *m* pile- or nap-lifting apparatus
Velozipedkran *m* bicycle crane, walking jib crane
venieren to veneer
Ventil *n* valve (mech.), vent, plunger, rectifier (electr.), regulator, governor **das ~ hängt** the valve sticks **abgeschmolzenes ~** sealed rectifier **gut aufsitzendes ~** well seating valve **elektrisches ~** rectifier **elektrolytisches ~** electrolytic rectifier **entlastetes ~** balanced valve **federbelastetes ~** springloaded valve **gesteuertes ~** mechanically operated valve **hängendes ~** drop valve, inverted valve, caged valve, valve in head, overhead valve **obengesteuertes ~** valve in head **pilzförmiges ~** mushroom or poppet valve **stehendes ~** vertical valve **seitlich angeordnetes ~** valve at side **tulpenförmiges ~** tulip-type valve
Ventil mit Eisengefäß steel-tank rectifier **~ mit flüssiger Kathode** pool rectifier **~ mit Vakuumhaltung** pumped rectifier
Ventil-abdeckung *f* valve covering (seal) **-ableiter** *m* valve-type lightning arrester **-abstandsmesser** *m* valve-clearance gauge **-anhubstange** *f* valve push rod
Ventilanordnung *f* arrangement of valves **hängende ~** valve in head
Ventil-anschlag *m* valve (reed) retainer **-anschluß** *m* valve connection **-antrieb** *m* valve gear
Ventilation *f* ventilation
Ventilations-aufsatz *m* ventilation top **-flügel** *m* ventilating blade **-kamin** *m* vent (mushroom type) **-klappe** *f* ventilating aperture **-kreis** *m* vent line **-messung** *f* measurement of air currents or ventilation **-öffnungen** *f pl* ventilating ducts or apertures **-verlust** *m* windage loss
Ventilator *m* ventilator, blower, fan **blasender ~** blower, pressure fan **saugender ~** exhauster, suction fan
Ventilator-antrieb *m* fan drive **-einströmöffnung** *f* fan inlet **-flügel** *m* fan baffle **-fuß mit Gelenk** fan base with tilting device **-gebläse** *n* fan blower **-gehäuse** *n* fan casing **-kühler** *m* fan cooler **-nabe** *f* fan hub **-pressung** *f* fan pressure, blast pressure **-prüfstand** *m* fan test rig
Ventilator-rad *n* impeller **-riemen** *m* fan belt **-riemenscheibe** *f* fan pulley **-riemenschloß** *n* fan-belt fastener **-schaufel** *f* fan blade **-schlauch** *m* air duct or shaft **-schwefel** *m* a very fine sulfur **-trichter** *m* fan shell **-wind** *m* fan blast
Ventil-aufsatz *m* valve cap, valve cover **-ausgleich** *m* valve lifter **-ausrüstung** *f* valving **-auslaß** *n* valve outlet **-ausschnitt** *m* cutaway or cutout for valve **-austrittseite** *f* outlet of the valve **-batterie** *f* battery of fuel cocks **-berechnung** *f* valve computation **-betätigung** *f* actuation of valve **-bohrer** *m* shoenosed shell with valve, borehole pump, sand pump, auger **-bruch** *m* valve fracture **-büchse** *f* valve (sleeve) **-bügel** *m* valve bonnet, bridge or stirrup of valve
Ventil-deckel *m* valve (box) cover, valve cap **-deckeldichtung** *f* valve cover gasket **-dichtungsfläche** *f* valve-sealing surface **-dichtungsscheibe** *f* valve-packing disk **-drehbohrer** *m* rotary valve drill **-durchströmöffnung** *f* valve throat area
Ventil-einbau *m* valve mounting or installation **-einsatz** *m* inflation valve (for tires), valve case **-einschleifen** *n* relapping, valve grinding **-einschleifer** *m* valve (seat) grinder **-einschleifklinge** *f* valve (seat) grinding blade **-einschleifwerkzeug** *n* valve grinding tool **-einstellehren** *pl* valve setting gauges (auto) **-einsteller** *m* valve adjuster **-einstellung** *f* valve adjustment **-eintrittseite** *f* inlet side of the valve **-entwässerung**

f valve drainage **-erhebung** *f* valve spring, valve lift **-erhebungsdiagramm** *n* valve-lift diagram

Ventilfeder *f* valve spring **-berechnung** *f* valve-spring computation **-gehäuse** *n* **-haube** *f*, **-kappe** *f* valve-spring housing or cap **-hebezangen** *pl* valve spring lifting pliers **-kegelsitz** *m* valve-spring seating **-keil** *m* valve-spring cotter or key **-mitnehmer** *m* valve-spring lifter **-prüfmaschine** *f* valve-spring testing machine **-schwingung** *f* valve-spring surge **-sitz** *m* valve spring seat **-teller** *m* valve-spring washer or retainer

Ventil-flügelschraube *f* valve thumbscrew **-führung** *f* valve guide **-führungsbüchse** *f* valve-stem guide bearing **-führungsloch** *n* guide hole **-führungsreibahle** *f* valve guide reamer **-gängigkeit** *f* operating capacity of valve **-gegengewicht** *n* slide valve weight

Ventilgehäuse *n* valve housing, valve chamber, valve body **-deckel** *m* valve cover plate **-verschluß** *m* valve plug

Ventil-gestänge *n* valve gear or mechanism **-griff** *m* valve handle **-halterstück** *n* small disk holder **-haube** *f* valve bonnet, valve hood, fixed bell **-hebel** *m* valve lever, valve rocker or arm **-hebelrolle** *f* valve roller **-heber** *m* valve lifter **-herausnehmer** *m* valve remover **-hub** *m* valve lift, valve stroke, valve travel

ventilieren to ventilate, vent

ventiliert gekapselter Motor enclosed ventilated motor

Ventil-käfig *m* valve cage **-kammer** *f* valve chamber or chest **-kanal** *m* valve port **-kanone** *f* valve housing **-kappe** *f* valve hood, valve cap **-kapselfänger** *m* grab for valve clacks **-kasten** *m* slide box, steam chest or box, ground control box

Ventilkegel *m* valve cone, poppet **~ auf Schlag prüfen** to test valve cone for warpage

Ventil-kegelstück *n* valve cotter **-keil** *m* valve-spring retainer lock, valve-spring cotter **-keilpaar** *n* spring retainer keys **-kipphebel** *m* rocker arm **-kipphebelachse** *f* rocker arm bracket

Ventilklappe *f* valve flap or hood, clack **mit geschlossenen Ventilklappen und offenen Flutventilen fahren** to ride on the vents

Ventilklemmkegel *m* valve collar

Ventilklemmstück *n* valve washer lock, valve-spring split collets **geteiltes ~** split valve (spring) washer lock

Ventil-kolben *m* piston valve, plunger **-kompressor** *m* valve compressor **-korb** *m* valve cage **-körper** *m* valve body or cage, moving cylinder **-kugel** *f* ball valve **-küken** *n* plug of a valve **-leine** *f* hand valve line (balloon) **-los** valveless

Ventil-leinendurchführung *f* valve cord gland **-mitnehmer** *m* valve lifter **-nachschleifvorrichtung** *f* valve refacer **-nadel** *f* needle valve **-öffnung** *f* valve port

Ventilöffnungs-dauer *f* valve-opening duration **-geschwindigkeit** *f* valve-lifting velocity **-zeit** *f* valve-lift period

Ventil-plättchen *n* valve reed **-platte** *f* valve plate **-querschnitt** *m* valve (opening) area

Ventilröhre *f* rectifier valve or tube, rectifying valve or tube **~ mit zwei Elektroden** diode, diode valve

Ventil-röhrendetektor *m* oscillation valve detector (teleph.) **-schaft** *m* valve stem or shaft **-schaftführung** *f* valve-stem guide **-schere** *f* valve linkage, valve scissors **-schieber** *m* (hydraulisch) valve slide, valve spool **-schlauch** *m* bicycle-valve tubing **-schleifapparat** *m* valve-re-seating machine **-schleifer** *m* valve grinder **-schleifvorrichtung** *f* valve grinder

Ventil-schließen *n* valve dropping **-schluß** *m* closing of valve, valve-seat contact **-schraube** *f* suction adjusting screw **-schuh** *m* casing-float shoe **-schutz** *m* valve hood or cover **-schutzhaube** *f* valve petticoat, jam pot cover (airship) **-schwinghebel** *m* valve rocker

Ventilsitz *m* valve seat(ing), clack seat **-abschrägung** *f* cone angle of valve seat, bevel of valve seat **-breite** *f* valve face width **-buchse** *f* valve seat bush **-sitzbüchse** *f* valve case **-fläche** *f* valve seat or face **-fräser** *m* valve refacer **-ring** *m* valve seat, valve seat insert, valve-seat ring

Ventil-spalt *m* valve clearance **-spanner** *m* valve compressor **-spiel** *n* valve clearance **-spiellehre** *f* valve clearance gauge **-spindel** *f* valve stem, valve spindle, valve rod **-spülung** *f* valve scavenging **-stange** *f* valve stem or rod **-stellschraube** *f* valve-adjusting stud **-stellungsregler** *m* valve positioner

Ventilsteuerhebel-achse *f* valve-rocker fulcrum pin **-arm** *m* valve-rocking lever **-büchse** *f* valve-rocker bush **-stütze** *f* valve-rocker bracket

Ventilsteuerung *f* valve(-control) mechanism, (poppet) valve gear, valve timing

Ventilsteuerungs-organ *n*, **-teil** *m* valve gear **-vorrichtung** *f* valve operating gear, valve timing gear

Ventilsteuerzeit *f* valve timing **Einstellung der ~** valve timing

Ventil-stopfen *m* valve stopper, stopper within valve **-stoßbohrer** *m* stroke valve drill

Ventilstößel *m* valve tappet, cam follower, valve stem, valve rocker, valve lifter **~ mit automatischer Spieleinstellung** self-adjusting hydraulic tappet

Ventilstößel-anschlag *m* valve tappet stop **-führung** *f* valve-tappet guide, valve-lifter guide, tapped rod guide **-führungsbuchse** *f* tappet rod guiding bush **-rolle** *f* valve-tappet roller, valve lifter **-rollenbolzen** *m* valve-tappet roller pin

Ventilstoßstange *f* (valve) push rod

Ventilstoßstangen-auge *n* valve push-rod eye **-führung** *f* valve push-rod guide **-kammer** *f* push-rod chamber **-kugelpfanne** *f* valve push-rod ball

Ventil-tafel *f* valve-control panel **-tasche** *f* valve recess **-teil** *m* valve component **-teller** *m* valve disk, valve head, valve spring cap, poppet assembly **-tellerrand** *m* rim of the valve disk **-träger** *m* valve carrier

Ventil-überdruck *m* excessive pressure on the valve **-überschneidung** *f* valve overlap **-verkleidung** *f* valve-gear housing **-verpichung** *f* valve carbonizing **-verschluß** *m* valve shutter **-verschraubungsdichtung** *f* valve-cap gasket

ventilversehene Leitung valved line

Ventil-verzögerung *f* valve lag **-voreröffnung** *f* valve lead **-wirkung** *f* valve action **-zapfen** *m* valve plug

Ventilzelle *f* valve cell **elektrolytische ~** electrolytic valve

Ventil-zellenwirkung *f* valve effect **-ziehen** *n* pulling the valve **-zug** *m* actuation of valve **-zündeinstellung** *f* valve timing **-zylinder** *m* poppet valve cylinder

Ventriculographie *f* ventriculography

Venturi-düse *f* Venturi tube **-einsatz** *m* Venturi section

venturiförmig Venturi-shaped

Venturi-messer *m*, **-meter** *n* Venturi meter **-Pitot-rohr** *n* Venturi Pitot tube **-querschnitt** *m* calibration of Venturi **-rohr** *n* Venturi tube

Veralten *n* obsolescence

veralterungssicher obsolescence-free

veraltet obsolescent, obsolete, antiquated **-es Baumuster** obsolete model or type

veraluminieren to aluminize

veränderbar variable

veränderlich variable, varying, differential, changing, adjustable, changeable, fluctuating, unstable, unsteady **laufend ~** running variable **-e Brennweite und Größe** variable focus and variable magnification **-er Anstellwinkel** variable incidence **-e Ausdehnung** variable expansion **-e Dichte** variable density **-e Drehzahl** variable speed **-es Feld** variable area **-e Flügelfläche** airplane with variable lifting surface **-e Füllung** variable admission **-e Kuppelung** variocoupler **-e Wölbung** variable camber

Veränderliche *f* variable, variable quantity (math.) **(un)abhängige ~** (in)dependent variable

Veränderlichkeit *f* variability, unsteadiness, fluctuation

verändern to transform, vary, alter, affect, change **sich ~** to vary, change, alter **die Gestalt ~** to deform

Veränderung *f* variation, change, alteration **bleibende ~, permanente ~** permanent set

verankern to tie, stay, guy (a pole), couple, band (of a blast furnace), anchor, picket

verankerte Stange pole and stay, stayed pole

Verankerung *f* anchoring, armoring (of a blast furnace), anchor, stay(ing), mooring, anchor tie, tie beam, retaining, grappling **~ eines Hängebrückenkabels** anchorage of the backstay of a suspension bridge **~ eines Kessels** boiler brace **~ des Ofens** furnace structural steel

Verankerungs-balken *m* anchor tie, tie beam **-bolzen** *m* holding-down bolt **-bügel** *m* collar strap **-draht** *m* stay **-eisen** *n* bonding tie **-gurt** *m* mooring band (balloon) **-kabel** *n* anchor chain or cable, mooring cable **-loch** *n* anchor bolt hole **-stab** *m* bonding tie **-tau** *n* mooring rope **-verfahren** *n* anchoring system **-vorrichtung** *f* mooring gear **-wand** *f* anchor sheeting

veranlagen to estimate, assess, rate

Veranlagung *f* disposition

veranlassen to solicit (a transaction)

Veranlassung *f* cause, motive, inducement, birth **auf ~ von** at the request or suggestion of on behalf of

Veranschaulichung *f* viewpoint, view, illustration **Photographie zur ~ von Handgriffen und Arbeitsvorgängen** action photograph

veranschlagen to rate, estimate, appraise, value, compute, calculate **zu hoch ~** overrate

veranschlagt estimated **zu hoch ~** overestimated **zu niedrig ~** underestimated

Veranschlagung *f* estimation, estimate

Veranstaltung *f* event, meeting, function

Verantimonierung *f* antimony plating

verantwortlich responsible, answerable, liable, chargeable

Verantwortlichkeit *f* responsibility

Verantwortung *f* responsibility

Verantwortungs-bewußtsein *n* sense of responsibility **-freudigkeit** *f* willingness to accept responsibility

verarbeitbar workable, machinable

Verarbeitbarkeit *f* machinability, workability

verarbeiten to work, treat, use up, consume, process, manufacture, machine, handle, convert, fabricate

Verarbeiter *m* processing plant, converter, throwster

Verarbeitung *f* working (up), using up, consuming, treatment, processing, machining

Verarbeitungs-anlage *f* process unit **-fähigkeit** *f* machinability, workability **-kosten** *pl* operating costs **-punkt** *m* working point **-schutz** *m* refining protection **-stufe** *f* stage of manufacture **-ziel** *n* final processing object

verarmen to impoverish, reduce the strength, weaken

Verarmung *f* impoverishment, reduction of strength

Verarmungs-kurve *f* economy curve

veraschen to ash, incinerate

Veraschung *f* ashing, incineration

Veraschungsschale *f* incinerating dish

Verästelung *f* branching, threads

veräthern to etherify, alkoxylate

Veratrinsulfat *n* veratrine sulfate

Veratrumsäure *f* veratric acid

verauktionieren to sell by auction

verausgaben to lay out, disburse

veräußern to alienate

Veräußerungsverbot *n* receiving order against debtor in bankruptcy proceedings

Verband *m* binding, fastening, bond (masonry), task force, surgical dressing, bandage, union, connection, association, federation, bracing, formation, tie **fliegender ~** flying unit **gemischter ~** composite force, task force, mixed force, combined arms unit **leichter ~** motorized task force **motorisierter ~** motorized unit **selbständiger ~** independent unit

Verbandanode *f* regular battery connection

Verbände *pl* bracing members (steel constr.)

Verband-festigkeit *f* binding strength **-fliegen** *n* formation flying **-holz** *n* framing timber **-kasten** *m* medicine chest, first-aid box **-messung** *f* formation plotting (electronics) **-mittel** *n* dressing equipment **-mull** *m* surgical cotton **-päckchen** *n* first-aid kit

Verbandschere *f* bandage scissors

verbandsmäßig in good bond (masonry)

Verbands-stift *m* double-pointed dowel or wire nail **-stoff** *m* bandage, dressing **-stelle** *f* dressing station **-tasche** *f* first-aid bag **-watte** *f* surgical wool, compressed wadding **-zeug** *n* first-aid outfit, bandage, dressing

Verbau *m* sheeting

verbauen to crib, build up, block up

Verbauung *f* building obstacle
verbeizen to overbate
verbergen to hide, conceal
Verbergungsfläche *f* fault surface or plane
verbessern to improve, amend, correct, ameliorate
verbessert improved, corrected
Verbesserung *f* improvement, amendment, correction, adjustment, refinement, advance **freie ~** arbitrary correction
Verbesserungs-eingabe *f* application for amendment **-gerät** *n* parallax offset mechanism **-mittel** *n* corrective **-patent** *n* patent of improvement **-taste** *f* correction key **-wert** *m* correction factor or value
verbeulen to crush, dent, bump, bruise
Verbeulung *f* bulging, wrinkling, buckling
verbiegbar bendable
verbiegen to distort, deform, bend, bow, twist, buckle, warp
Verbiegen *n* buckling
Verbiegung *f* bending, twisting, deformation, warping **geringe ~ einer Achse** slight deformation of the axle **~ des Tors** warping of the gate
verbieten to forbid, prohibit
Verbildung *f* deformation
verbilligen to reduce or lower in price, cheapen
verbinden to connect, tie together, couple, pin, unite, join, combine, associate, put through **passend ~** to match **mit Anschlag und Überschlag ~** to joint by double rabbeting **Holzstücke ~** to joint timbers
Verbinden *n* jointing, connecting **~ der Kabeladern** cable-conductor splicing
Verbinder *m* binder, connector
verbindlich obliging, binding, obligatory
Verbindlichkeit *f* obligation, liability **~ eingehen** to incur liability
Verbindung *f* (Farben) blending; (Zusammenhang) connection; (Teleph., Text) context; (Beziehung) relation; (Verkehr) communucation; (Chem.) compound; (Techn., Fuge) joint, junction, union; combination, correlation, consolidation, composition, bond, assembly, contact, liaison, linkage, tie piece
Verbindung (von neuem mit älterem Beton) bond (joining new to older concrete)
Verbindung, ~ mit angeschärften Enden scarfed joint **~ durch Gelenkwellen** connection by means of cardan shafts **~ innerhalb einer Kette** intrachain connection **~ durch Schlitzzapfen** slit-and-tongue joint **~ für Theaterübertragung** electrophone call **~ mit ungedämpften Wellen** continuous wave circuit
Verbindung, eine ~ ablehnen bzw. verweigern to refuse a call **eine ~ anbieten** to announce a call **eine ~ aufheben** to release a connection, disconnect a call **eine Verbindung auflösen** to break down **eine ~ aufnehmen** to establish communication, establish contact **in ~ bringen** to connect **eine ~ eingehen** to enter into combination, form a compound **in eine ~ eintreten** to monitor
Verbindung, eine ~ halten to preserve contact **eine ~ herstellen** to set up a connection, complete a call, make a contact or connection **die ~ lösen** to disconnect **in ~ setzen** to connect **in ~ stehen** to communicate, be connected **eine ~ trennen** to cut a connection, disconnect **in ~ treten** to enter into negotiations **eine ~ umlegen** to transfer a call **eine ~ weiterleiten** to extend a call **nicht zustandegekommene ~** uncompleted call **biegsame ~** flexible coupling **drahtlose ~** radio communication, wireless communication **einfache ~** simplex (communication)
Verbindung, feste ~ rigid fastening **formschlüssige ~** positive coupling **geschäftliche ~** business relation **halbleitende ~** intermetallic compound **lösbare ~** detachable connection, soluble combination **nicht lösbare ~** permanent joint **rechtwinklige ~** square joint **schräge ~** bevel joint **stumpfe ~** butt joint **unlösbare ~** perfect or permanent junction **zeitweilige ~** (Teleph.) temporary connection **zurückgestellte ~** call filed for later completion **nicht zustandegekommene ~** uncompleted call
Verbindungen *f pl* routes of communication, connections **~ zwischen den Ämtern** (interoffice) trunks, junctions **rückwärtige ~** lines of communication
Verbindungs-achse *f* axis of communication **-aufbau** *m* trunking scheme, establishment of the connections **-aufnahme** *f* establishment of communication **-bahn** *f* connecting line, junction line, binding bond **-bestreben** *n* affinity (chem) **-blech** *n* connecting plate **-bolzen** *m* connecting bolt, tie bolt, tack bolt **-dose** *f* connection box, junction box **-draht** *m* connection wire **-fähigkeit** *f* combining ability, affinity, combining power **-fläche** *f* connecting or joining surface **-flansch** *m* connecting flange
Verbindungs-gang *m* passage **-gerade** *f* straight line connecting two points **-gerät** *n* connecting equipment **-gestänge** *n* linkage **-gestell** *n* connecting rack **-gewicht** *n* combining weight, combining equivalent **-gleichung** *f* equation of combination, chemical equation **-gleis** *n* crossover road, junction rails **-glied** *n* connecting or coupling link **-graben** *m* communication trench **-hebel** *m* connection lever **-hülse** *f* connecting or jointing sleeve, connecting casing
Verbindungs-kabel *n* junction cable, trunk(-line) cable, connecting cable **-kanal** *m* connecting passage, junction canal, connecting culvert **-kasten** *m* junction box connection or connecting box **-keil** *m* wedge coupling, fixing key **-klammer** *f* splicing clamp, brace, clip connector **-klemmbrett** *n* connection terminal board **-klemme** *f* connecting means, binding post, terminal, splicing car, connector **-klinke** *f* multiple jack **-kraft** *f* bonding strength, affinity, combining power **-kurve** *f* junction curve **-lasche** *f* connecting link **-leck** *m* joint leak
Verbindungsleitung *f* interposition trunk, lead wire, transfer circuit, connecting pipe, trunk, junction, junction line, feeder, link **~ für Dienstleitungsbetrieb** order-wire junction **~ für Tandembetrieb** tandem junction **~ für Wählerauslösung** selector-release trunk **~ für Wechselverkehr** two-way circles **abgehende ~** out(going) junction **ankommende ~** in(coming) junction **besetzte ~** busy junction, busy trunk **doppeltgerichtete ~** two-way junction, two-way trunk circuit **freie ~** idle junction,

idle trunk **gestörte ~** defective trunk (teleph.)
Verbindungsleitungsbetrieb *m* trunking
Verbindungsleitungsbündel *n* trunk group, trunk-line bundle **~ für alle Abgangsplätze** outgoing trunk multiple **~ für einen Teil der Abgangsplätze** split trunk group
Verbindungsleitungs-feld *n* junction-line panel (teleph.) **-kabel** *n* junction cable, trunk(-line) cable **-klappe** *f* junction indicator **-klinke** *f* junction jack **-netz** *n* junction network **-schrank** *m* junction board **-stöpsel** *m* junction plug **-sucher** *m* junction finder **-verkehr** *m* trunking traffic, junction service **-vielfachfeld** *n* junction multiple
Verbindungs-linie *f* line of communication, connecting line **-mann** *m* connecting file, liaison man **-mittel** *n* communication **-muffe** *f* splicing sleeve, sleeve, splice box, connecting box or sleeve, union socket **-mutter** *f* coupling nut **-netz** *n* liaison net **-organ** *n* connecting device **-platte** *f* joint plate **-platz** *m* inward position **-punkt** *m* connection point, junction, joining, connecting or union point, juncture
Verbindungs-richtung *f* main- or trunk-line telephone **-riemen** *m* backstrap **-ring** *m* locking ring, connecting ring **-rohr** *n*, **-röhre** *f* connecting pipe or tube, pipe joint **-rotte** *f* connecting file **-satz** (Teleph) connecting link or circuit **-schäkel** *m* connecting or joining shackle **-schalter** *m* position grouping key **-schema** *n* connection diagram **-schiene** *f* connecting band **-schlauch** *m* flexible connection **-schnecke** *f* connecting worm **-schnur** *f* connecting cord **-schraube** *f* assembly screw, clamping bolt **-schweißung** *f* joint weld
Verbindungsstange *f* tie rod, stretching rod **~ zum Riemenausrücken** rod to belt shifter for reversing **~ der Scheinwerfer** headlight-support tie rod **~ zur Sicherung** connections to safety lock
Verbindungsstecker *m* coupling plug, pin connector **-steg** *m* walkway **-stelle** *f* cable joint, joint, point of connection, bond, junction
Verbindungsstift *m* connecting lug, coupling pin **~ für Bohrrohr** casing fitting
Verbindungs-stöpsel *m* calling plug, ringing plug, adapter, connecting plug, junction plug **-straße** *f* communication road or route **-strebe** *f* braced link **-streifen** *m* connection strip **-strich** *m* hyphen **-stromkreis** *m* connecting circuit **-stück** *n* connector, strap, bond, tie, link, connecting piece, tie rod, stay, adapter **-stutzen** *m* connecting piece
Verbindungs-verkehr *m* trunking, junction service, junction traffic (teleph.) **-volumen** *n* combining volume **-wärme** *f* heat of combination **-weg** *m* transmission path **-wegkontrolle** *f* incomplete call and release control **-welle** *f* connection or driving shaft **-wesen** *n* liaison service or duty **-zapfen** *m* assembling pin
Verblasen *n* blowing **~ in flüssigem Zustande** bessemerizing, converting
verblasen to blow
Verblase-ofen *m* blast furnace **-röstung** *f* blast roasting, pot roasting, lime roasting **-verfahren** *n* blasting method
verblassen to fade, lose color
verblatten to frame
verblattet-e Schweißung *f* scarf weld **-er Stoß** *m* scarf joint
Verblattung *f* scarf joint, scarving
verbleibend remaining **-e Magnetisierung** residual or remant magnetization
Verbleibwahrscheinlichkeit *f* non-leakage probability
verbleichen to fade (grow pale)
verbleien to lead, fuel, plumb, lead-coat, plug
Verbleien *n* lead-coating or lining, fixing, bedding (of machines)
verbleit lead-coated **-es Blech** terne plate **-es Rohr** lead-lined pipe
Verbleiung *f* lead-lining, leading
Verbleiungsanlage *f* lead-covering or lead-plating plant
Verblendbau *m* veneer construction
verblenden to screen, face (wall), blind
Verblender *m* facing brick
Verblend-scheibe *f* wheel disk **-stein** *m* facing brick
Verblendung *f* facing, delusion, face, dressing (building)
Verblitzen des Films accidental dendriform exposure of film
verblocken to block, interlock
Verblockung *f* interlocking, locking
Verblockungssystem *n* interlocking device
verbogen crooked, bent, buckled
Verbohrschraube *f* retaining screw
verbolzen to bolt, fasten with bolts
Verbolzer *m* bolter
Verbolzung *f* bolting
verborgene Wärme latent heat
Verbot *n* interdiction, restriction, prohibition, inhibition, injunction
verboten forbidden, prohibited **-er Hafen** closed port **-e Linie** forbidden line **-er Übergang** forbidden transition
Verbots-impuls *m* inhibit pulse **-signal** *n* inhibiting input **-wicklung** *f* inhibit winding
verbrämen to trim border
verbrannt burnt, burned (off), burnt to death, torrid
Verbrauch *m* consumption, use, loss, expenditure **~ bei Reisegeschwindigkeit** cruising consumption **von geringem ~** low-consumption
verbrauchen to consume, work up, spend, dissipate, employ, use (up), be no longer available, draw
Verbraucher *m* user, consumer, buyer, customer, receiver, load, consuming device
Verbraucher-bezirk *m* area of consumption **-genossenschaft** *f* cooperative **-kreis** *m* receiver circuit, load circuit **-leitung** *f* service line **-seite** *f* receiver end **-stelle** *f* outlet **-stromkreis** *m* feeder circuit **-werk** *n* consuming works **-widerstand** *m* load resistance
Verbrauchs-abgabe *f* excise tax **-bestand** *m* consumable or expendable stocks **-faktor** *m* demand factor **-geber** *m* consumption transmitter **-gebiet** *n* area of supply **-gegenstand** *m* consumable article **-güter** *pl* consumer goods **-güterindustrie** *f* consuming branch **-kennlinie** *f* consumption characteristic **-kurve** *f* consumption curve or graph **-ladung** *f* normal charge **-last** *f* consumable load **-lenkung** *f* regulation of

consumption

Verbrauchs-magazine *pl* stores of items for internal use **-material** *n* expendable material **-messer** *m* supply meter, consumption indicator **-messung** *f* measurement of consumption **-mittel** *n* expendable stock **-prüfung** *f* consumption test **-quote** *f* consumption rate **-satz** *m* consumption unit **-stelle** *f* place of consumption

Verbrauchssteuer *f* consumption tax, excise tax **~ auf Inlandware** excise duty (consumption tax)

Verbrauchs-stoff *m* expendable supply **-verringerung** *f* decrease in fuel consumption, consumption decrease **-werkzeug** *n* perishable tool **-wettbewerb** *m* consumption test **-ziffern** *pl* consumption figures **-zweig** *m* output circuit

verbraucht spent, exhausted, used up, worn out, consumed, stale (of air), dissipated, dead

verbreiten to disseminate, broadcast (Funk)

verbreitern to widen, broaden, spread, enlarge, disperse, disseminate, propagate

Verbreiterung *f* increase of breadth, widening, extra width, expansion, enlargement, spread (of image)

Verbreiterungsreifen *m* extension rim

Verbreitung *f* distribution, propagation, spread

verbrennbar combustible

Verbrennbarkeit *f* combustibility

verbrennen to burn, be consumed by fire, burn out, deflagrate **explosionsartig ~** to deflagrate **raketenartig ~** to fuse **vollständig ~** to burn down

Verbrennen *n* burning out

verbrennlich combustible, inflammable, burnable

Verbrennlichkeit *f* combustibility

Verbrennung *f* combustion, burning, oxidation, firing stroke **beschleunigte ~** accelerated combustion **gemischte ~** mixed combustion **lebhafte ~** rapid combustion **plötzliche ~** burning off **schleichende ~** slow combustion **träge ~** slow or incipient combustion **unvollkommene ~, unvollständige ~** imperfect or incomplete combustion **verzögerte ~** retarded combustion **vollständige ~** complete combustion

Verbrennungsablauf *m* course of combustion, characteristics of combustion

Verbrennungsbereichunbeständigkeit *f* region of combustion instability

Verbrennungs-druck *m* combustion pressure, explosive thrust **-düse** *f* combustion tuyère, combustion nozzle **-ergebnis** *n* **-erzeugnis** *n* product of combustion **-formel** *f* combustion formula **-gas** *n* combustion gas, burned gas **-gefahr** *f* danger of burning **-geschwindigkeit** *f* rate or speed of combustion

Verbrennungs-intensität *f* intensity of combustion **-hilfsstoff** *m* reactant, burning agent **-hub** *m* firing stroke, explosion stroke **-kammer** *f* combustion chamber **-kapillare** *f* capillary combustion tube **-kraftmaschine** *f* internal-combustion engine **-leistung** *f* combustion efficiency **-linie** *f* combustion curve **-luft** *f* air for or of combustion, furnace air **-maschine** *f* (internal-)combustion engine **-motor** *m* internal-combustion engine **-motorenanlage** *f* internal-combustion-engine installation **-ofen** *m* combustion furnace **-produkt** *n* product of combustion

Verbrennungsraum *m* combustion space, combustion chamber, firebox, fire chamber **~ mit flachem Boden** flat-topped combustion chamber **dachförmiger ~** penthouse combustion chamber **drehbarer ~** rotary combustion chamber **flacher ~** thin combustion chamber, slab-shaped or biscuit-shaped combustion chamber **L-förmiger ~** L-head-type engine **Motor mit T-förmigem ~** T-head-type engine **rotierender ~** rotary combustion chamber

Verbrennungs-rohr *n* combustion chamber, combustion tube **-rückstand** *m* residue from combustion **-schacht** *m* combustion chamber **-schiffchen** *n* combustion boat **-system** *n* fuel system **-takt** *m* expansion stroke **-temperatur** *f* temperature of combustion, calorific intensity, pyrometer effect **-topf** *m* burner cup

Verbrennungs-verfahren *n* combustion principle system, combustion system **-verhältnis** *n* combustion condition **-verlauf** characteristics of combustion **-vorgang** *m* process of combustion **-wärme** *f* heat of combustion **-wasser** *n* water of combustion **-wirbel** *m* flame or combustion turbulence **-zone** *f* combustion zone, oxidation zone

verbriefen to confirm in writing

Verbruch *m* falling in, rupture, offense

verbrühen to scald

Verbrüstung *f* abutting

verbuchen to charge

verbüchsen to bush

Verbuchung *f* booking

Verbuchungsstelle *f* accounts section

Verbund *m* composite action **-amt** *n* minor exchange **-anordnung** *f* compound arrangement **-balken** *m* flitch(ed) beam, compound beam, sandwich compound, sandwich girder **-bauweise** *f* composite (method of) contruction **-betrieb** *m* interconnected operation, interconnection **-block** *m* compound ingot **-bügel** *m* compound bow

Verbund-dampfbackofen *m* combination baking steam oven **-dampfgebläsemaschine** *f* compound steam blowing engine **-dampfmaschine** *f* compound steam engine **-drehen** *n* combination turning **-dynamo** *m* compound(-wound) dynamo, compound-wound generator **-elektromotor** *m* compound-wound electric motor

verbunden connected **falsch ~** wrong number **untereinander ~** interconnected, connected with each other **-es Mauerwerk** bonded masonry **miteinander -e Teile** combined parts

Verbund-erregung *f* compound excitation **-fachwerkträger** *m* composite lattice beam **-federhammer** *m* compound spring hammer **-fenster** *n* composite window **-glas** *n* laminated glass, compound glass, multilayer glass **-guß** *m* compound casting, bimetal, clad metal **-gußgleitlager** *n* babbitt sleeve bearing **-heber** *m* compound lift **-höhenmotor** *m* high-altitude engine coupled with independent turbosupercharger

Verbund-kammer *f* multiple camera **-karte** *f* dual card, compound card **-kokille** *f* compound (ingot) mold **-lager** *n* babbitt bearing **-leitung** *f* tie line (power engine) **-maschine** *f* compound engine **-motor** *m* compound-wound motor, engine with independent sets of high- and low-pressure cylinders

Verbund-mühle *f* combination mill **-netz** *n* interconnection **-ofen** *m* combination oven, vertical-flued regenerative oven **-platte** *f* sandwiched layers of sheet metal and organic materials **-regelung** *f* coupled control element combination **-röhre** *f* compound tube, multipurpose tube, binode, multiple valve **-skala** *f* combination scale **-stahl** *m* compound steel **-stoff** *m* compact material, compact (metal.) **-strangpressen** *n* coextrusion **-stück** *n* fitting, coupling **-teilungssystem** *n* doublepitch system **-träger** *m* composite beam

Verbund-verfahren *n* duplexing process **-walzwerk** *n* mill tandem **-werkstoff** *m* solid solution (met.) **-wicklung** *f* compound winding **-wirkung** *f* compound effect **-wirtschaft** *f* joint or combined utilities **-zahnfräser** *m* staggered-tooth cutter **-zahnrad** *n* staggered-tooth gear **-zahnscheibenfräser** *m* staggered-tooth side mill

verbürgen to guarantee

Verchlorung *f* chlorination

verchromen to chrome-plate, chromium-plate

Verchromung *f* chrome plating, chromium plating

Verchromungs-anlage *f* chromium-plating plant **-bäder** *pl* chromium-plating baths

verdämmen to tamp, dam **einen Fluß ~** to dam up the course of a stream **die Wasser ~** to keep off the waters by timbering

Verdämmung *f* dam

Verdampf-anlage *f* evaporation plant **-apparat** *m* evaporating apparatus, evaporator, carburetor, vaporizer

verdampfbar evaporable, vaporizable, volatile

Verdampfbarkeit *f* vaporizability, volatility

Verdampfbecken *n* evaporating dish

verdampfen to vaporize, evaporate, volatilize

Verdampfen *n* evaporation by ebullition

verdampfend ablating

Verdampfer *m* evaporator, vaporizer, carburetor, drier, dehydrator **-blende** *f* evaporating screen **-fach** *n* evaporating compartment **-rippe** *f* evaporator fin **-speisepumpe** *f* evaporator feed pump **-trog** *m* evaporating tray

Verdampf-leistung *f* output **-turm** *m* evaporator tower

Verdampfung *f* vaporization, volatilization, evaporation (by ebullition) **~ durch Entspannung** flash evaporation

verdampfungs-fähig evaporable, vaporizable, volatile **-fähigkeit** *f* volatility, evaporative capacity **-kolben** *m* reducing retort **-kühlung** *f* cooling by evaporation, evaporative cooling **-kurve** *f* distillation curve **-leistung** *f* steaming capacity, evaporative power **-messer** *m* evaporimeter

Verdampfungs-ofen *m* evaporator furnace **-punkt** *m* vaporization point, steam point **-quelle** *f* source of evaporation, source of volatilization **-röstung** *f* volatilization roasting **-temperatur** *f* volatilization temperature **-vergaser** *m* vaporizing or evaporation carburetor

Verdampfungsverlust *m* volatilization loss, evaporation loss, boil-away loss **~ bei siedender Flüssigkeit** boil-away loss

Verdampfungs-vermögen *n* evaporative power **-vorwärmer** *m* steaming economiser **-wärme** *f* heat of vaporization, (latent) heat of evaporation **-ziffer** *f* rate of steaming, steam-raising coefficient, coefficient of evaporation

Verdan-Verfahren *n* Verdan system, automatic repetition

Verdeck *n* hood, top **~ des Schwimmers** float deck **aufziehbares ~** sliding roof **das ~ aufschlagen** to put the hood up, raise the hood **das ~ öffnen** to put the hood down **kurzes ~** one-man hood

verdecken to cover, mask, camouflage, cloud or mask (sound), conceal, hide, eclipse, obscure (Rdr.)

Verdeck-hülle *f* dust hood **-schutzdecke** *f* hood cover **-sitz** *m* roof seat, top

verdeckt defiladed, camouflaged, screened, masked **-er Hohlraum** concealed space **-e Leitungsführung** concealed wiring **-er Lichtbogen** submerged arc **-es Numerierungssystem** linked numbering system

Verdeckung *f* covering, clouding, masking, overriding (of noise)

Verdeckungserscheinung *f* masking effect

verderben to spoil, damage, decay, ruin, adulterate, mar, vitiate, rot

verderblich perishable **leicht -e Artikel** perishable goods

Verderbungsmittel *n* adulterant (chem.)

verdeutlichen to make evident, make clear, make apparent, illustrate, elucidate

verdichtbar condensable, compressible

Verdichtbarkeit *f* condensability, compressibility

verdichten to condense, concentrate, pack, squeeze, consolidate, compact, seal, compress, thicken, solidify **mit Schlamm ~** to mud off

Verdichten *n* compression (stroke), back-filling

verdichtendes Zündungsgeschirr supercharged ignition harness

Verdichter *m* compressor, condenser **zweistufiger ~** two-stage compressor

Verdichter-absperrventil *n* compressor throttle valve **-drehzahl** *f* r.p.m. of compressor **-ende** *n* compressor exit

Verdichterförderung *f* **gestörte ~** (Turbinenmotor) surge

Verdichter-gehäuse *n* compressor casing or housing jet **-kennfeld** *n* compressor characteristics **-lager** *n* compressor bearing jet **-läufer** *m* (TWK) compressor rotor **-leistung** *f* compressor power **-leitschaufel** *f* (TWK) stator blade **-rad** *n* impeller compressor **-regelung** *f* supercharger blast gate control **-schaufeln** *pl* compressor blades **-spirale** *f* compressor scroll (jet) **-vorkammer** *f* plenum chamber **-walzen** *pl* compactor rolls

verdichtet compressed, condensed, concentrated, consolidated **-es Ammoniakwasser** concentrated ammonia liquor **-er Gußteil** castings with a dense structure

Verdichtsteife *f* volume compression, elasticity, modulus

Verdichtung *f* compression, condensation, concentration, packing, solidification, thickening, compressing, squeezing, consolidation **~ des Baugrundes** increase in density of the subsoil

~ der Vorgangsfolge squeezing the cycle time **adiabatische ~** adiabatic compression **isothermische ~** isothermal compression

Verdichtungs-apparat *m* condenser **-arbeit** *f* work of compression **-druck** *m* compression pressure **-enddruck** *m* compression pressure (final) **-endtemperatur** *f* compression temperature **-gerät** *n* compacting equipment **-grad** *m* degree of condensation or compression, compression ratio **-hahn** *m* priming cock, compression cock

Verdichtungshub *m* compression stroke **oberer Totpunkt des Verdichtungshubes** compression point

Verdichtungs-kurve *f* compression line, compression curve **-material** *n* impermeable material **-methode** *f* compaction method **-minderer** *m* compression release, pressure-reduction device, compression relief cock **-nocken** *m* compression release **-pfahl** *m* compaction pile **-raum** *m* compression space, clearance volume, compression volume, clearance space **-rauminhalt** *m* capacity of compression chamber **-rohr** *n* condensing pipe **-stoß** *m* compression shock **-stoßwelle** *f* compression wave (explosion)

Verdichtungs-takt *m* compression cycle **-verhältnis** *n* compression ratio, degree of compression **-verminderung** *f* compression relief **-verminderungshebel** *m* decompression lever **-verminderungsnocken** *m* half-compression or compression-relief cam **-wärme** *f* heat of compression **-welle** *f* compression valve, compression wave **-ahl** *f* compression ratio

Verdichtungszündung *f* compression ignition **Motor mit ~** compression-ignition engine

verdicken to thicken, concentrate, bulge out (of tubes), coagulate, jell, curdle, become viscous

Verdicker *m* thickener

Verdickung *f* concentration, thickening

Verdickungs-behälter *m* thickener, settler **-mittel** *n* thickening substance **-trichter** *m* conical settler

verdienen to deserve, earn, merit

Verdienst *m* earnings **-bescheinigung** *f* earnings statement

verdienstvoll meritorious

verdingen to cope, adjudicate, make a contract

Verdingung *f* submission, hiring out, taking a job

Verdingungsordnung *f* (für Bauleistungen VOB) German contract procedure in the building industry

Verdingungssumme *f* sum of the contract

verdoppeln to double, duplicate

Verdoppelung *f* doubling, duplication

Verdoppler *m* doubler **-abstimmkästchen** *n* tuning box for frequency doubler (missiles) **-prüfkästchen** *n* double testbox **-stufe** *f* doubler stage (radio)

Verdopplung des Bildes doubling of the image (twin tube)

Verdopplungs-röhre *f* frequency-doubler tube **-zeitmesser** *m* doubling time meter

verdorben unsound, spoiled **-e Luft** foul air

verdorren to dry up, dry

verdrahten to wire

verdrahtet wired

Verdrahtung *f* wiring or cabling **feste ~** permanent wiring

Verdrahtungs-fehler *m* faulty wiring **-plan** wiring diagram **-stelle** *f* wiring point

verdrallen to twist, strand (together)

verdrallt twisted, stranded **-e Doppelader** twisted pair **-es zweiadriges Kabel** twisted pair (cable) **-e und abgeschirmte Zuführungen** twisted and screened leads

Verdrallung *f* twisting

Verdrallungsschema *n* twist system

Verdrang *m* displacement

verdrängen to push back, dislocate, dislodge, drive out, displace, remove, expel, supplant

Verdränger-bauaurt *f* displacement-type **Lader der ~** displacement super-charger **Pumpe der ~** positive-displacement pump **-kolben** *m* recuperator piston **-pumpe** *f* rotary pump, positive-displacement pump **-zylinder** *m* recoil cylinder

verdrängt-e Ölmenge (Quetschöl) trapped oil **-es Volumen** piston displacement

Verdrängung *f* displacement, supersession, removal

Verdrängungs-entwickler *m* recession gas generator **-körper** *m* replacement body, liquid-level displacement float **-lader** *m* displacement compressor **-messer** *m* current(-displacement) meter **-mittelpunkt** *m* center of buoyancy or displacement **-strom** *m* displacement current, dielectric current, capacitance current

Verdrehformung *f* torsional strain

verdrehen to twist, rotate, distort, wrench, turn round, subject to torsional stress, stagger (rotationally), shift (a phase)

Verdrehen *n* twisting turning

Verdrehrohr *n* torque tube **-hilfsflügelmechanismus** *m* torque-tube aileron control

Verdreh-schwingung *f* torsional vibration **-schwingungsschreiber** *m* torsiograph **-sicherung** *f* protection against torsion **-spannung** *f* torsional stress **-stab** *m* torsion rod **-steifigkeit** *f* torsional rigidity, strength or resistance

verdreht eingebaut torsionally mounted **-er Überschlag** reversement

Verdrehung *f* twist(ing), torsion, distortion, rotation, contortion, turn (of a picture), warping

Verdrehungs-beanspruchung *f* torsional stress, twisting stress **-bruch** *m* torsion failure **-dauerfestigkeit** *f* alternate torsional strength **-dauerhaltbarkeit** *f* endurance under torsion stress **-eigenfrequenz** *f* frequency of natural torsion **-fähigkeit** *f* torsibility **-festigkeit** *f* torsional strength or rigidity, resistance to twisting **-festigkeitsmaschine** *f* torsion-testing machine **-grenze** *f* yield point of torsional shear **-indikator** *m* torsion indicator **-konstante** *f* torsion constant **-kraft** *f* torsional force, torque

Verdrehungs-maschine *f* torsion-testing machine **-messer** *m* torsion meter, torsional-strain meter or indicator **-modul** *m* modulus of torsional shear **-moment** *n* twisting moment, torsional moment, starting torque, moment of rotation **-prüfmaschine** *f* torsion-testing machine **-schreiber** *m* recording torsiometer, torsiograph **-schwingung** *f* torsional oscillation or vibration **-spanne** *f* extent of torsion **-stab** *m* torsion bar

-versuch *m* torsion test, twisting test **-wechselfestigkeit** *f* strength under alternating torsion stress **-widerstand** *m* twisting resistance, torsional resistance **-winkel** *m* angle of twist, torsion angle, angle of torque
verdreifachen to treble, triple
Verdreifacher *m* frequency trebler **-stufe** *f* triplex stage
verdreifacht triplicate, trebled, tripled
Verdreifachung *f* trebling, tripling
verdrillen to twist together, twist (said of wires), strand
Verdrillen *n* twisting, transposition
verdrillt snaked (wire) (aviation) **-er Draht** *m* snaked wire
Verdrillung *f* torsion, twist, transposition, twisting
verdrosseln to provide with choke coil
Verdrosselung *f* filter choke
verdrucken to misprint
verdrücken to crumple, crush, overpress
Verdrücken *n* crush(ing) (paper mfg.)
verdrückt crushed, pinched
Verdrückung eines Flözes contraction of a seam
verdübeln to dowel, pin, peg
verdübelte Verbindung dowel joint
Verdübelung *f* doweling, pegging
verdunkeln to darken, obscure, deepen (color), black-out ~ (sich) verfinstern to occultate (astr.)
Verdunkler *m* dimming switch, dimmer
Verdunk(e)lung *f* (complete) darkening, obscuration, eclipse, blackout
Verdunklungs-anlage *f* darkening plant **-einrichtung** *f* cutting-off apparatus, screening apparatus **-kapazität** *f* shading condenser **-lampe** *f* black-out lamp or light **-maßnahme** *f* blackout measure **-rouleau** *n* black-out blind **-streifen** *m* black-out strip **-trägheit** *f* inertia to exposure to darkness (photoelectric cells)
verdünnbar rarefiable, capable of being diluted
verdünnen to dilute, rarefy (gases)
verdünnt diluted, thinned, rarefied, weak **-es Helium** low-pressure helium **-e Lösung** diluted solution (chem.) **-e Luft** rarefied air
Verdünnung *f* dilution, thinning, attenuation, rarefaction
Verdünnungs-entropie *f* entropy of dilution **-grad** *m* degree of dilution **-körper** *m* diluent **-mittel** *n* thinning agent, diluting medium, thinner, attenuant **-wärme** *f* heat of dilution **-welle** *f* rarefaction wave
verdunstbar vaporizable, volatilizable, evaporable
verdunsten to evaporate, volatilize
Verdunsten *n* evaporation, volatilization, vaporization
Verdunstrinne *f* drip tray
Verdunstungs-druck *m* vapor pressure **-gefäß** *n* atmometer **-höhe** *f* head of water vaporized **-kälte** *f* cold due to evaporation **-kühlung** *f* evaporative cooling **-messer** *m* atmometer **-verlauf** *m* course of evaporation **-verlust** *m* loss by evaporation **-zähler** *m* psychrometer
Verdüppelung *f* window or foil-jamming (Rdr.)
veredeln to refine, improve, enrich, purify, finish, ageharden, throw, elevate, ennoble, perfect
Veredeln *n* refining, improving, enriching, purifying, finishing, age-hardening
veredelt purified **-es Papier** treated paper
Vered(e)lung *f* improvement, modification, surface treatment, refinement, purification, enrichment, throwing, throwster ~ (Leichtmetall) aging
Vered(e)lungs-behandlung *f* refinement, refining treatment **-lack** *m* specialty finish **-mittel** *n* processing agent **-produkt** *n* finishing or processing agent **-prozeß** *m* anodizing operation **-verfahren** *n* refining process or procedure, purifying process, refinery process **-verkehr** *m* duty drawback **-vorgang** *m* refining process **-wirtschaft** *f* processing or finishing industry **-zeit** *f* cycle for anodizing
vereinbar compatible (TV)
vereinbaren to agree upon, stipulate, make a contract, come to an agreement **sich** ~ to agree upon **schriftlich** ~ to stipulate in writing
Vereinbarkeit *f* compatibility ~ (von Schwarz-Weiß- mit Farbempfängern für die gleiche Sendung) compatibility (TV)
vereinbart agreed, compatible
Vereinbarung *f* agreement, arrangement, accord
Vereinbarungssymbol *n* declarator, (info proc.)
vereinfachen to simplify, reduce (math.)
vereinfachte Schnurschaltungen sleeve-control cord circuits
Vereinfachung *f* simplification, reduction
vereinheitlichen to standardize, unify
Vereinheitlichung *f* standardization, unification, regularization, normalization, making for uniformity, coordination
vereinigen to unite, join, combine **an einen Punkt** ~ to centralize in one place
Vereinigung *f* fusion, amalgamation, consolidation, union, combination, junction, association, agreement, alliance
Vereinigungs-ebene *f* plane of union **-feld** *n* junction field **-koeffizient** *m* combination coefficient **-menge** *f* union of sets **-stelle** *f* junction, joining, meeting, or union point **-zeichen** *n* junction signal
Vereinslenkachse *f* flexible axle
vereinzeln to single, thin, separate (feeding)
vereinzelt isolated, sporadic, single, solitary
vereisen to frost, freeze, cover with ice
Vereisen *n* freezing up **glasartiges** ~ clear ice, glaze
vereist icy
Vereisung *f* glaciation, icing
Vereisungs-anzeiger *m* ice indicator, ice warning unit **-frei** ice-free **-gefahr** *f* danger of ice formation **-meßgerät** *n* icing measuring device
Vereisungsschutz-anlage *f* anti-icing device **-flüssigkeit** *f* anti-icer fluid **-gerät** *n* anti-icing device **-rohr** *n* ice-protection pipe **-ventil** *n* anti-icing valve
verengen to narrow, contract, constrict, squeeze
verengend convergent
Verengerungs-T-Stück *n* (flanged) reducing T, (flanged) unequal T.
verengt narrowed
Verengung *f* contraction, narrowing down, necking, reduction, stricture, constriction ~ **eines Flusses** narrowing of a river
vererzbar mineralizable

vererztes Gold encased gold
Vererzung *f* mineralization
Vererzungsmittel *n* mineralizer
verestern to convert into an ester (esterify)
Veresterung *f* esterification
Verfahreinrichtung *f* displacing device
verfahren to convey, transport, work, manage, deal, blunder, muddle, traverse **die Schicht ~** to work out the task
Verfahren procedure; (Chem.) process, method, technique; (Richtlinie) policy, system; treatment, practice, operation, principle, mode of action, processing (of film) **~ mit einfachem Anruf** combined local and toll operation **~ mit Stromstoßübertragung** sender method **direktes ~** direct method **etwas einem ~ unterwerfen** to process **~ der Wiederverwendung** salvage operations
Verfahrens-anspruch *m* method claim **-fehler** *m* error of approximation (info proc.) **-ordnung** *f* rules of procedure **-regelung** *f* (industrial) process control **-sache** *f* procedural **-stammbaum** *m* process flow-sheet **-technik** *f* industrial processing engineering, research technique **-zuschlag** *m* process allowance
Verfall *m* decay, decline, deterioration, lapse, expiration, maturity, decadence, failure
verfallen to fall, decline, decay, chance, hit, deteriorate, lapse **-es Patent** void patent
Verfall-tag *m* due date, date of maturity **-zeit** *f* time of payment
verfälschen to tamper (with), adulterate
Verfälschung *f* adulteration
Verfälschungsmittel *n* adulterant
verfärben to change color, decolorize, contaminate (TV)
Verfärbung *f* decoloration, discoloration, shading
verfassen to compose, draw up
Verfassung *f* state, condition, constitution
verfaulen to rot, decay, molder
verfault rotten, putrefied, decayed
verfehlen to miss **das Ziel ~** to miss the target
verfehlt unsuitable
verfeinern to refine, improve
Verfeinerung *f* refinement, improvement
verfertigen to manufacture, make, fabricate, prepare
Verfertigung *f* making, manufacture, fabrication, preparation
verfestigen to strengthen, solidify, stiffen, make firm, fasten, consolidate, concrete, set, harden
verfestigte Schicht concretionary horizon
Verfestigung *f* strengthening, solidifying, stiffening, dilatancy, making firm, fastening, setting, stabilization, consolidation, increase in strength and rigidity **~ durch Recken** strain hardening
Verfestigungs-grad *m* degree of consolidation **-kurve** *f* plastic stress-strain curve **-zeit** *f* time of set (of gels) **-ziffer** *f* coefficient of consolidation
verfeuern to fire, burn, use up
Verfeuerung *f* firing, heating, burning
verfilzen to felt, mat
verfilzt felted, matted, interlocked (fibers)
verfilzungsfähig proper to felt (textiles)
Verfilzungsfähigkeit felting or matting property
Verfinsterung *f* eclipse, darkening
verfirsten, ein Dach ~ to ridge a house
Verfirstung *f* ridging, ridge covering
verfitzen to tangle, perplex, embarrass
verflachen to level off, flatten, become even, smooth (down), lose selectivity, slope down, broaden
Verflachung *f* levelling, flattening, planing
verflanscht flanged
verflauter Übergang shaded-off transition
verflechten to plait, entwine, implicate, interweave, involve **ineinander ~** interlace
Verflechtung *f* entanglement, complication
verfliegen to evaporate (volatilize) **sich ~** to lose one's bearings, become lost
verfließen to elapse
Verflocken *n* lining with flocks
verflüchtigen to volatilize, evaporate
verflüchtigendes Rösten volatilizing roasting
Verflüchtiger *m* volatilizer
Verflüchtigung *f* subtilization, volatilization **~ fester Körper** sublimation
Verflüchtigungs-fähigkeit *f* volatility **-probe** *f* volatility test **-produkt** *n* volatility product **-verlust** *m* volatilization loss
verflüssigen to liquefy, dilute, thin, condense (gases)
Verflüssiger *m* condenser **-aggregat** *n* liquefier unit **-motor** *m* condenser motor
verflüssigtes Gas fixed gas
Verflüssigung *f* liquefaction, thinning, liquefying, condensation
Verflüssigungs-anlage *f* liquefying plant **-apparat** *m* liquefier **-mittel** *n* liquefacient, thinning agent **-punkt** *m* flooding point
Verfolgelenkung *f* pursuing course indication
verfolgen to pursue, persecute, trail, track (Astronaut., Rdr.)
Verfolgen *n* tracking **~ nach Echo** skin tracking
Verfolgungs-station *f* (Astron.) tracking station (spacecraft) **-stativ** *n* panoramic tripod, swivel-headed tripod
verformbar workable, deformable, plastic, kneadable, moldable **~ bleibend** permanently plastic **warm ~** thermoplastic
Verformbarkeit *f* deformability, forming property, malleability, plasticity
verformen to form, deform, work
verformt shaped, deformed
Verformung *f* deformation, distortion, working, forming, set, warping, strain **elastische und bleibende ~** stress and strain **eine ~ erleiden** to take a set **bleibende ~** permanent set **plastische ~** plastic deformation or working **spanabhebende ~** cutting shaping **spanlose ~** non-cutting shaping
Verformungs-arbeit *f* work done in deformation, resilience **-amplitude** *f* strain amplitude (level) **-behinderung** *f* resistance to deformation **-bruch** *m* ductile fracture **-einrichtung** *f* paste forming dehydrator **-ellipsoid** *n* strain magnitude **-entfestigung** *f* work-softening **-fähigkeit** *f* deformation, ductility **-funktion** *f* function of strain
Verformungs-invarianten *pl* strain invariants **-linie** *f* deflection curve **-maschine** *f* shaping machine **-varianten** *pl* strain variants **-verhältnis** *n* plastic working condition **-vermögen** *n* degree of deformation, deformability **-vor-**

gang *m* forming process **-weg** *m* strain path **-widerstand** *m* resistance to deformation, tensile strength
Verfrachtung *f* forwarding of goods, expressing **~ nach Gewicht** charter by weight **~ nach Maß** freight by measure
verfranzen, sich ~ (slang) to lose one's way (aviation), to desert, wander off course
verfrischen to refine
verfroren cold-sensitive
verfrüht premature
Verfrühung *f* prematureness
verfügbar available, at one's disposal **-es Geld** cash in hand, funds at one's disposal **-e Leistung** power available **-e Pferdekraft** actual horsepower **-e Wärme** motivity
Verfügbarkeit *f* availability
verfugen to point up (masonry)
Verfugen *n* jointing
verfügen to decree, dispose **~ über** to have at one's disposal
Verfügung *f* decree, order, disposition, disposal, instructions, action (of patent office), decision **zur ~** available, at the disposal of **zur besonderen ~** at disposal for special duty **zur ~ stellen** to place at disposal, make available
Verfügungs-frequenz *f* assigned frequency **-gut** *n* goods on consignment **-lager** *n* reserve store
Verfügungsrecht des Grundeigentümers right of disposal by the owner of the soil
verfüllen, den Fehlboden ~ to plaster the sound floor
Verfüllung *f*, **der Grundmauern** puddling of foundation walls
verfünffachen to quintuple
verfüttern to feed
vergällen to denature
Vergällung *f* discoloration, spoiling
Vergällungs-holzgeist *m* denatured or methyl alcohol **-mittel** *n* denaturant
vergänglich transient, perishable
Vergänglichkeit *f* transientness
vergärbar fermentable
vergären to ferment
Vergärung *f* fermentation, attenuation
Vergärungsgrad *m* degree of fermentation
vergasbar gasifiable, vaporizable
vergasen to gasify, vaporize
Vergasen *n* distillation
Vergaser *m* carburetor, vaporizer, gasifier, accelerating pump **~ mit Anlaßeinspritzpumpe** self-priming carburetor **~ mit Auspuffgasheizmantel** exhaust-jacketed carburetor **~ mit Druckförderung** pressurefed carburetor **~ mit ölgespeistem Heizmantel** oil-jacketed carburetor **~ mit aufsteigendem Luftzug** updraft carburetor **~ mit vollkommen selbsttätiger Regelung** master-control carburetor **~ mit gleichbleibendem Stand** constant-level carburetor **~ mit Vorwärmung** heated carburetor
Vergaser-anordnung *f* carburetion **-ansaugluft** *f* air entering the carburetor **-ansaugluftstutzen** *m* carburetor scoop ram **-berg** *m* gasification refuse **-betätigung** *f* carburetor control **-brand** *m* fire in the carburetor **-deckel** *m* lid of carburetor **-dichtung** *f* carburettor gasket **-drossel** *f* carburetor throttle **-düse** *f* carburetor jet **-einstellung** *f* carburetor adjustment **-eintrittslufttemperatur** *f* carburetor air temperature
Vergaser-eisbildung *f* carburetor icing **-enteisung** *f* deicing of carburetor **-filter** *m* carburetor filter **-frostschutzpumpe** *f* carburetor anti-icer **-gas** *n* manufactured gas **-gehäuse** *n* carburettor body **-gestänge** *n* carburetor control or linkage **-heizleitung** *f* carburetor heating pipe **-heizmantel** *m* carburetor jacket **-klappe** *f* choke
Vergaserleistung *f* carburetor capacity **~ einregeln** to time the carburetor capacity
Vergaserluft-einlaß *m* carburetor induction system **-fänger** *m* carburetor air scoop **-heizer** *m* carburetor air heater **-kontrolle** *f* carburetor air control **-schippe** *f* carburetor air scoop **-trichter** *m* carburetor throat, carburetor throttle bore, choke, barrel **-vorwärmer** *m* carburetor air heater
Vergaser-maschine *f*, **-motor** *m* carburetor engine **-regelung** *f* carburetor adjustment
Vergaserschwimmer *m* carburetor float **undichter ~** punctured carburetor float
Vergaser-seite *f* inlet or induction side **-vereisung** *f* carburetor icing **-vorwärmung** *f* carburetor hot spot **-warmluftklappe** *f* carburetor hot-air door **-zwischenstück** *n* carburetor adapter
vergastes Gebiet gassed or contaminated area
Vergasung *f* gasification, vaporization, carburetion
Vergasungs-geschwindigkeit *f* rate of gasification **-öl** *n* gas-carburetion oil **-verfahren** *n* process of gasification
vergeben to place orders, give away, let (the contract for)
Vergebung *f* subcontracting **~ eines Auftrages** placing of an order **~ von Aufträgen an Unterlieferenten** subcontracting
vergegenwärtigen to realize
Vergegenwärtigung *f* realization
Vergenz *f* vergency (opt.)
Vergesellschaftung *f* converting into an association
vergeuden to waste, dissipate
Vergeudung *f* waste, dissipation
vergewissern to ascertain **sich einer Sache ~** to make sure of a thing
vergießbar castable, ready to cast **unmittelbar -er Stahl** steel ready for casting
Vergießbarkeit *f* castability, pourability
vergießen to cast, teem, run in, fill in, fill up, cast badly, spill, shed **die Fugen mit Mörtel ~** to fill in the joints **die Klammern mit Blei ~** to run in the clamps with lead **fallend ~** to top-pour
Vergießen *n* teeming, pouring, casting
Vergießtemperatur *f* pouring or casting temperature
vergiften to poison
Vergiften *n*, **Vergiftung** *f* poisoning, contamination
vergilben to become yellow
vergipsen to plaster
vergittern to screen **mit Holz ~** to lattice
Vergitterung *f* grating, grid, lattice
verglasbar vitrifiable
verglasen to vitrify, glaze **die Scheiben in Kitt ~** to glaze, furnish with glass
Verglasen *n* glazing

verglast vitrified, glazed, glass-enclosed
Verglasung *f* glazing, vitrification
Vergleich *m* agreement, arrangement, compromise, settlement comparison, contrast, matching **zahlenmäßiger ~** *m* numerical comparison
vergleichbar comparative, comparable
Vergleichbarkeit *f* comparability
vergleichen to compare, collate, check, refer to
vergleichend comparative
Vergleicher *m* comparator (info proc.), reference input element
Vergleichs-angabe *f* reconciliation **-apparat** *m* reference instrument **-aufstellung** *f* statement of reconciliation **-ausfärbung** *f* comparative dyeing **-basis** *f* comparison basis **-brücke** *f* deviation bridge **-einrichtung** *f* comparator **-einzelversuch** *m* parallel single test **-feld** *n* matching field (photom.) **-flüssigkeit** *f* reference liquid **-frequenz** *f* standard frequency
Vergleichs-grundlage *f* basis of comparison **-horizont** *m* (Aero.) comparison (reference) horizon **-körper** *m* reference body, neutral body
Vergleichskraftstoff *m* representative fuel **~ zur Bestimmung der Klopffestigkeit** knock-reference fuel
Vergleichs-lampe *f* comparison lamp **-leitung** *f* reference circuit **-licht** *n* standard or comparison intensity of light **-linie** *f* reference line, comparison line **-lösung** *f* comparison solution, standard solution **-maß** *n* measure of comparison
vergleichsmäßig comparable, comparatively
Vergleichs-maßstab *m* standard of comparison, standard of reference, yardstick **-messung** *f* comparison measuring **-methode** *f* comparison method **-muster** *n* reference sample **-pegel** *m* reference level **-prisma** *n* comparison prism **-probe** *f* reference sample **-punkt** *m* point of comparison, check point
Vergleichs-satz *m* comparison theorem **-schaltung** *f* comparator circuit **-schwarzpegel** *m* reference black level **-spannung** *f* reference voltage **-standard** *m* standard of comparison **-stelle** *f* (bei elektrischen Meßinstrumenten) cold junction, reference junction **-stellentemperatur** *f* cold junction temperature
Vergleichs-strahlabschwächer *m* reference beam attenuator **-strahler** *m* standard radiator **-stromkreis** *m* standard reference telephone circuit **-tabelle** *f* comparative table **-termin** *m* day of settlement **-verfahren** *n* comparison method **-versuch** *m* comparative experiment
vergleichsweise Leistung comparative performance
Vergleichs-weißpegel *m* reference white level **-widerstand** *m* standard resistance **-zahl** *f* comparative figure **-ziel** *n* witness point, auxiliary target
Vergleichung *f* comparison, contrasting, matching **~ der Angaben einer Gesprächsanmeldung** repetition of particulars of call **tägliche ~** daily check
Vergleichungspunkt *m* check point
Vergleichunterlage *f* basis of comparison
verglimmen to burn, smolder
verglühen to glow, burn up (spacecraft at reentry)
Verglühen *n* faulty annealing
vergolden to gold-plate, gild
Vergoldepresse *f* gold blocking press
Vergolder *m* gilder **-grund** *m* gilding size
vergoldet gold-plated, gilded, gilt
Vergolde- und Prägepresse *f* gilding and embossing press
Vergoldung *f* gilding, gold plating **~ mit Blattgold** burnished gilding of metals **~ auf Bronze** wash gilding
Vergoldungsgrundierer *m* gold sizer
vergoren fermented
vergossen cast (into) **mit flüssiger heißer Masse ~** filled up with liquid hot material **fallend -er Stahl** top-poured steel
Vergrabungsplatz *m* ground disposal
Vergraupelung *f* granulation, joining of crystals
vergriffen exhausted, sold, out-of-print
vergröbern to coarsen
Vergröberung *f* coarsening
Vergrößerer *m* enlarger (photos), magnifier (by means of an optical lens)
vergrößern to enlarge, magnify, increase (in size) **~** (Photo) to blow up
Vergrößern *n* enlarging (phot.)
vergrößernd, stark -es Fernrohr highly magnifying telescope
vergrößert enlarged, scaled up **-e Ansicht** enlarged view
Vergrößerung *f* enlargement, extension, increase, magnification, amplification **lineare ~** magnification in diameter **~ des Durchhanges** sag magnification
Vergrößerungsapparat *m* enlarger (phot.) **~ mit selbsttätiger Einstellung** autofocus enlarger, condenser enlarger (phot.)
Vergrößerungs-bereich *m* range of magnification **-gerät** *n* enlarger **-glas** *n* magnifying lens or glass **-kraft** *f* magnifying power **-messer** *m* dynameter **-stärke** *f* magnifying power **-stufe** *f* fixed magnification value
Vergrößerungs- und Verkleinerungsspiegel *pl* magnifying and diminishing mirrors
Vergrößerungs-vermögen *n* magnifying power, magnification **-zahl** *f* coefficient of magnification, enlargement factor
vergrünen to develop a green tone on storing
vergünstigen to concede, permit, allow
Vergünstigung *f* abatement, allowance, deduction, permission, privilege, favor, concession rebate **eine ~ erweisen** to confer a favor
Verguß *m* grouting **-kammer** *f* sealing chamber **-masse** *f* sealing compound or filler **-material** *n* grout **-mittel** *n* insulating compound **-schicht** *f* layer of grouting **-stoff** *m* grouting
vergütbar age-hardenable, heat-treatable
Vergütbarkeit *f* tempering quality
Vergütekran *m* heat-treatment crane
vergüten to temper, harden, draw, allow, rebate, discount, refund, compensate, remunerate, make good, refine, improve (quality), coat (a lens) **~** (Leichtmetall) to quench-age, age-harden **Linse ~** to coat a lens **~** (Stahl) to heat-treat, quench
Vergüten *n* tempering, compensating, aging, age-hardening, sorbitizing, heat-treating
Vergüteofen *m* heat-treatment furnace
Vergüterei *f* heat-treating shop, heat-treatment

department
vergütet heat-treated (steel) **-es Holz** improved wood **-es Objektiv** coated objective **-e Probe** quenched or tempered test piece or specimen **-er Stahl** heat-treated stock, annealed steel
Vergütung *f* remuneration, age-hardening, indemnity, allowance, rebate, discount, refund, compensation, tempering, heat-treatment, annealing, recovery
Vergütungs-abrechnungsbeleg *m* commission statement **-anlage** *f* soaking pit, heat-treating plant
Vergütungsautomatenstahl, beruhigter ~ killed or deoxidized temper-hardening automatic screw-machine steel
Vergütungs-behandlung *f* solution treatment, refinement, refining treatment **-fähigkeit** *f* heat-treating quality **-gefüge** *n* annealed (grain) structure **-glühen** *n* heating just below the eutectic melting point **-satz** *m* compensation or reimbursement ratio **-stahl** *m* heat-treatable steel **-zähler** *m* two-rate meter
verhacken to block, bunch, chop out, gap
verhallen to fade away (sound)
Verhalt *m* condition, state, response
verhalten to behave, act
Verhalten *n* behavior, attitude
Verhältnis *n* relationship, relation, proportion, ratio, rate, condition, situation, connection, circumstance **~ der Fläche zu ihrem Umfang** area-perimeter ratio **~ der Hohlräume** percentage of voids in the rubble **~ von Luft zu Brennstoff** fuel-air ratio **~ Nutz- zu Störpegel** signal-to-noise ratio **~ der Spannungen und Ströme** ratio of a transformer **in keinem ~ stehend zu** unequal **akustoelektrisches ~ eines Sendesystems** acoustoelectric index **elektroakustisches ~ eines Empfangssystems** electroacoustic index **gerades ~** direct ratio **im quadratischen ~** in proportion to the square (of) **umgekehrtes ~** inverse ratio **~ von Unterspannung zu Oberspannung** ratio of minimum stress to maximum stress
Verhältnis-anteil *m* proportion **-anzeiger** *m* ratio indicator, exponent (math.) **-detektor** *m* ratio detector
Verhältniseinersignal, Teilselektionssignal one-to-partial select ratio
verhältnisgleich proportional
Verhältnis-gleichheit *f* proportionality **-gleichung** proportion
verhältnismäßig comparatively, proportion(ate), proportional, commensurable, commensurate **-e Grenze** proportional limit **~ sichere Landung** reasonably safe landing
Verhältnis-mäßigkeit *f* proportionality **-maßstab** *m* scale **-regler** *m* ratio controller **-widrig** disproportionate **-zahl** *f* proportionality factor, ratio **-zeiger** *m* ratio meter
Verhaltungs-maßregel *f* order, instruction, direction **-vorschrift** *f* instructions to be followed **-weise** *f* behavior
verhandeln to negotiate, treat, deliberate
Verhandlung *f* negotiation, trial, pleading, proceeding, hearing, argument, discussion **zur mündlichen ~ gelangen** to be called for oral hearing or argument **die ~ scheitert** the discussion deteriorates
Verhandlungsschrift *f* trouble record
verharren to persevere, remain, persist
verharschen to form a crust
verhärten to harden, indurate, set (cement)
Verhärtung *f* hardening
verharzen to resinify, resining
Verharzung *f* blurring (in X ray), gumming (valve), resinification
Verhau *m* abatis, barbed-wire obstacle
verhauen to block, bunch, chop out, gap, remove
verhauener Raum emptied space (min.)
Verhäutung *f* sheating
verheddern to tangle
verheeren to ravage, devastate
Verheerung *f* devastation, destruction, demolition
verhindern to prevent, preclude
Verhinderung *f* prevention
Verhinderungs-mittel *n* preventive **-schaltung** *f* exchange prohibitory circuit, prohibiting equipment
verholen to warp (naut.)
Verhol-klampe *f* fair-lead (naut.) **-klüse** *f* warping pipe
verholmen, ein Pfahlwerk ~ to lay the stringpieces on the top of earth piles
Verhol-spill *n* capstan, windlass **-tau** *n* warp **-tonne** *f* watch buoy **-umschalter** *m* remote-control changeover switch **-winde** *f* twoline winch
verholzen to lignify
Verholzung *f* lignification.
verhüllen to cloud, mask, cover
Verhüllen *n* clouding, masking
verhüten to prevent, obviate
verhüttbar smeltable
verhütten to smelt
Verhütten *n* smelting
Verhüttung *f* smelting, metallurgical operations
verhüttungsfähig smeltable
Verhütung *f* prevention
Verhütungs-maßnahme *f* preventive measure **-mittel** *n* preventative, inhibitor
verifizieren to verify
Verifiziergerät *n* verifier
verjährt stale, superannuated, out of date
Verjährung *f* superannuation, lapsing
Verjährungs-frist *f* statute of limitation **-gesetz** *n* law of limitations or superannuation
verjüngen to narrow, taper, reduce, diminish, chamfer, constrict, rejuvenate, renew, contract (a tensor), regenerate, point, thin **eine Zeichnung ~** to reduce a drawing
verjüngt thinned, taper(ed), conic(al), converging, beveled **nach hinten ~** backswept **-e Brettsäge** straight pit saw **-es Ende** tapered end **-e Höhenflosse** tapered tail plane **-er Maßstab** reduced scale **-e Nietung** lozenge riveting, riveting in groups
Verjüngung *f* taper cone, reduction, constriction, draft, strip, tapering, batter, rejuvenation, regeneration, contraction, narrowing **~** (b. Modellen) taper, draft, reduction **~ des Flügels** tapering of wing
Verjüngungs-grad taper ratio **-maßstab** *m* scale of reduction, reducing or tapering scale **-nippel** *m* reducing nipple **-planke** *f* diminishing

plank **-rohrstutzen** *m* reducer **-stelle** *f* tapering
verkabeln to cable **verkabelte Leitung** cable line, stranded-wire line
Verkabelung *f* cabling, wiring
Verkabelungssystem *n* cabling system **offenes ~** tapering cabling system
verkadmen to cadmium-plate
Verkadmiumierungsanlage *f* cadmium-plating plant
verkalken to calcify
verkämmen, zwei Holzstücke ~ to join timbers by cogging
Verkämmung *f* cogging joint, notching
verkanten to tilt, cant, twist
Verkanten *n* cogging of the piston, canting, tilting
verkantet swung **-e Aufnahme** canted shot
Verkantung *f* swing, cant
Verkantungs-achse *f* axis of swing **-anzeiger** *m* indicator of swing **-fehler** *m* error of swing **-libelle** *f* cant level, transverse level, cross-level bubble **-trieb** *m* cross-level drive **-winkel** *m* tipping angle
verkapseln to enclose
Verkauf *m* sale **Waren zum ~ aufstellen** to expose or display goods for sale
verkaufen to sell
Verkäufer *m* salesman, seller, sales executive
verkäuflich marketable, for sale **leicht ~** commanding a ready sale **schwer ~** hard to sell, unsalable
Verkaufs-abrechnung *f* sales account **-automat** automatic-delivery apparatus, mechanical seller **-bedingungen** *pl* terms of sale **-direktor** sales manager **-ingenieur** *m* sales engineer **-kosten** *pl* marketing expenses **-lokal** *n* store **-provision** *f* **-stand** *m* booth **-urkunde** *f* bill of sale **-vertrag** *m* sales agreement
verkauft sold **~ franko Waggon** sold free board **~ ab Lager** sold ex warehouse **~ sofortige Lieferung** sold for immediate delivery **~ für Rechnung von . . .,** sold for account of . . . **freihändig ~** sold privately **auf dem Halm ~** sold standing (on the stalk) **meistbietend ~** sold by auction **vorbehaltlich der Besichtigung ~** sold subject to inspection
Verkehr *m* traffic, communication, service, commerce **den ~ abwickeln** to carry or handle the traffic **in ~ stehen** to communicate, correspond **den ~ umleiten** to reroute **dem ~ übergeben** to open to traffic **den ~ vermitteln zwischen** to ply between **abgehender ~** outgoing traffic **ankommender ~** incoming traffic **dienstlicher ~** official communication **doppelseitiger ~, doppeltgerichteter ~** two-way or duplex traffic **einfacher ~** simplex operation **einseitiger ~** one-way traffic **gemischter ~** mixed service (teleph.) **wechselseitiger ~** two-way traffic
verkehren to communicate, intercommunicate
Verkehrs-ablauf *m* flow of traffic **-abteilung** *f* traffic branch **-abwicklung** *f* handling of traffic, handling of calls, traffic dispatch **-ader** *f* thoroughfare, principal street **-ampel** *f* traffic light (signal head) **-änderung** *f* traffic fluctuation
Verkehrsandrang *m* rush (of traffic) **Stunden starken Verkehrsandranges** rush hours
Verkehrs-anhäufung *f* accumulation of traffic **-artenschalter** *m* channel selector
Verkehrsbedürfnis *n* traffic requirements **dem ~ Rechnung tragen** to provide for traffic requirements
Verkehrs-belastung *f* traffic load **-beobachtung** *f* traffic observation **-bestimmung** *f* traffic regulation **-bewegung** *f* distribution of traffic, traffic curve **-dichte** *f* density of traffic **-einheit** *f* traffic unit **-erlaubnis** *f* traffic for general use **-erleichterung** *f* new facilities for trade **-fahrzeug** *n* passenger car **-flieger** *m* commercial pilot
Verkehrs-flugbetrieb *m* air-line work **-flugboot** *n* passenger flying boat, commercial flying boat **-flughafen** *m* airport, civil airport **-flugwesen** *n* commercial aviation **-flugzeug** *n* commercial plane, passenger plane, air liner **-flugzeugführer** *m* transport or commercial pilot **-fluß** *m* traffic flow
Verkehrsfrequenz *f*, **günstige ~** optimum working frequency (OWF)
Verkehrs-geltung *f* secondary meaning **-geschwindigkeit** *f* commercial speed **-gestaltung** *f* distribution of traffic **-gewerbe** *n* conveyance **-graben** *m* communication trench **-knotenpunkt** *m* railroad junction, center of traffic
Verkehrs-kurve *f* traffic curve **-last** *f* bridge capacity, live load **-leistung** *f* traffic load **-leitung** *f* traffic control **-luftfahrt** *f* commercial aviation, civil aviation **-luftschiff** *n* commercial airship **-meßgerät** *n* call-count meter **-mittel** *n* conveyance, vehicle, means of communication **-ordnung** *f* traffic regulation
verkehrspolizeiliche Vorschriften traffic regulations
Verkehrs-punkt *m* traffic center **-regel** *f* traffic regulation or law **-regelung** *f* traffic regulation **-rückgang** *m* reduction of traffic **-schreiber** *m* telephone-traffic recorder **-säule** *f* traffic column
verkehrsschwach having little traffic **-e Zeit** slack hours
Verkehrs-schild *n* traffic sign **-schildkröte** *f* (oder-insel) traffic island **-schwankungen** *pl* traffic fluctuations **-sicherheit** *f* traffic safety **-signal** *n* traffic signal **-sperre** *f* curfew, blockade **-spitze** *f* peak of traffic **-stärke** *f* traffic load or intensity
verkehrsstarke Zeit rush hours
Verkehrs-stauung *f* (Fernsprech-) (call) congestion **-stockung** *f*, **-störung** *f* disturbance or interruption of traffic **-tafel** *f* traffic sign **-technik** *f* science of transport **-teilnehmer** *m* road user **-überwachung** *f* traffic supervision **-umfang** *m* volume of traffic **-verteilungsübersicht** *f* traffic diagram **-vorschrift** *f* traffic rule
Verkehrs-wasserbau *m* waterway construction or engineering (for navigation) **-weg** *m* traffic route, public road **-welle** *f* traffic wave **-wert** *m* telephone-traffic unit, traffic data **-wesen** *n* transportation, traffic **-zählung** *f* peg-count summary, summary of traffic statistics **-zeichen** *n* traffic sign(al) **-zufluß** *m* flow (of traffic) **-zunahme** *f* traffic increase
verkehrt inverted **~ proportional** inversely proportional
Verkehrung *f* distortion, inversion of ratio

verkeilen to fasten, wedge, quoin, spline
verkeilt keyed
Verkeilung *f* wedging of a tubbing
verketten to link, interlink
verkettet interlinked **-e Spannung** interlinked voltage, line voltage, phase-to-phase voltage **-er Zweiphasenwechselstrom** interlinked two-phase current
Verkettung *f* interlinking, (inter)linkage, linking, concatenation, bonding **elektromagnetische ~** electromagnetic linkage
Verkettungs-punkt *m* interlinking point **-spannung** *f* interlinked voltage
verkieseln to silicify **das Holz ~** to impregnate timber with soluble glass
Verkieselung *f* silification
Verkiesen der Schwellen boxing of the ties (R.R.)
verkitten to cement, lute, seal, putty **verkittete Linse** cemented lens
Verkittung *f* luting, cementing, binding, bonding, bond
Verkittungsmaterial *n* plastering material
verklagen to take legal steps, to sue
verklammern to clamp, cotter, brace
Verklappen des Baggerguts discharge of dredged material
verkleben to lute, cement, glue, paste, cover
verklebte Einzelfäden coalesced filaments
verkleiden to case, line, cover, veneer, pave, face, disguise, mask, camouflage, coat (with paint), incrust, plank, sheath, fair (aviation), cowl **den Beton ~** to coat the concrete
verkleidet faired; spatted (of airplane), encased **aerodynamisch günstig ~** faired **-es Fahrgestell** faired undercarriage **-e Heckzelle** covered tail booth
Verkleidung *f* casing, lining, boarding, covering, cover, fairing (aviation), cowling, facing, paneling, jacket(ing), enclosure, dressing, planking, sheathing **~ von Bitumenbeton** bituminous-concrete facing **~ der wasserseitigen Böschung** revetment of upstream face or slope **~ von abwechselnder Dicke** facing of varying thickness **~ von Eisenbeton** reinforced-concrete facing **untere ~ von Eisenbeton** reinforced-concrete support **~ am Landungsgestell** spats (streamline covering of wheels) **~ der Minengänge** timbering of mine galleries **Motor ohne ~** bare engine **~ von gesiebten Steinen** revetment of screened rock
Verkleidungs-blech *n* fairing plate, covering panel **-deckel** *m* cover, flashing **-gehäuse** *n* protective housing **-mauer** *f* lining wall **-rohr** *n* protective tube, cover tube **-übergang** *m* fairing, fillet
verkleinern to decrease, reduce, diminish, lessen **maßstäblich ~** to scale down
verkleinert reduced, scaled down
Verkleinerung *f* diminution, reduction, decrease
Verkleinerungs-grad *m* attenuation **-kopie** *f* reduction print
verkleistern to paste (up), turn into paste, agglutinate
Verkleisterung *f* clogging, gelatinization (of starch), agglutination, glutinization **~ von Seide** pasting of silks
verklemmen to lock
Verklemmen *n* jamming
verklingen to decay, die out (of waves), fade out or away
verklinken to interlock
verklinkerter Schalter latch-locked switch
Verklinkung *f* latching-in
verknappen to become scarce
Verknappung *f* scarcity, shortage
verkneten to knead
verknistern to decrepitate
Verknisterungswasser *n* decrepitation water
verknoten to snarl
verknüpfen to tie, bind, connect, join, combine with
verknüpfend linking
Verknüpfung *f* connection, combination, linkage (linking)
Verknüpfungsglied *n* logic element, switching element (comp.)
verkobalten to plate with cobalt
Verkobaltung *f* cobalt plating
Verkochbarkeit *f* (Lack) compatibility with drying oils on cooking
verkochen to boil down or off, concentrate **~ auf Faden** to boil string proof **~ in Kasten** to boil blank and crystallize in tanks **~** (durch Kochen zerstören) to decompose through long boiling (overboil) **~ auf Korn** to boil to grain **~ auf Nachprodukt** to boil to afterproduct
Verkochen *n* pan boiling **~ auf Faden** string-proof boiling
Verkochungs-erscheinung *f* decomposition through long boiling **-kontrollapparat** *m* controlling apparatus for sugar boiling
verkohlen to carbonize, coke, char
Verkohlen *n* charring, carbonization, (dry) distillation, destructive distillation
verkohlt charred
Verkohlung *f* carbonization, coking, dry distillation, destructive distillation, charring
Verkohlungs-anlage *f* charring plant **-ofen** *m* carbonizing oven **-vorgang** *m* coking process
verkoken to coke, char, carbonize
Verkokung *f* coking, carbonization, coke burning **~ in Retorten** cylinder coking **~ von Steinkohle** coking of pit coal
Verkokungs-anlage *f* coking plant **-anstalt** *f* coking works **-geschwindigkeit** *f* rate of coking **-kammer** *f* coking chamber **-probe** *f* crucible test, coking test **-retorte** *f* carbonization retort **-vorgang** *m* coking process **-zahl** *f* coke test **-zeit** *f* coking time
verkollern to grind on the edge runner
verkommen to degenerate, decay
Verkoppelung *f* spurious, stray, or undesired coupling
verkorken to cork
Verkorkvorrichtung *f* corking apparatus
verkörnern to granulate
verkörpern to embody
Verkörperung *f* embodiment
verkraften to mechanize, overcome something
verkraftete Anlage mechanized plant
verkrätzt contaminated by dross
Verkröpfgesenk *n* bent or curved swage, snaker
verkrümeln to crumble
Verkrümmung *f* distortion
verkrüppeln to stunt, cripple

verkümmern to atrophy
verkrusten to incrust, crust
Verkrustung *f* incrustation
verkühlen to cool down
verkünden to announce, circulate, make known, proclaim (a judgment)
Verküpbarkeit *f* vatting property
verküpen to reduce (vat)
verkupfern to copperplate, copper
verkupfert coppered, copperplate(d)
Verkupferung *f* copperplating
verkuppeln, Telegrafenstangen ~ to frame or couple poles
verkürzen to shorten, clip, abbreviate, condense, abridge, contract, curtail
Verkürzung *f* shortening, contraction **mit perspektivischer ~ zeichnen** to foreshorten
Verkürzungsfaktor *m* velocity rate
Verkürzungskondensator *m* aerial series condenser, short-wave or shortening condenser, padding condenser, antenna condenser
verlacken to convert into a lake (produce a lake)
Verlackungsverfahren *n* process for the production of a lake
Verlade-anlage *f* handling machinery, handling equipment, loading plant **-bahnhof** *m* loading station (R.R.) **-band** *n* loading belt **-bedingungen** *f pl* shipping conditions
Verladebrücke *f* bridge crane, transporter crane **~ mit Drehkran** bridge with a slewing jib crane running on top **~ mit Führerstandslaufkatze** man-trolley transporter **~ mit Seilzuglaufkatze** rope-trolley transporter
Verlade-bühne *f* loading platform **-einrichtung** *f* loading arrangement or device **-gerüst** *n* handling platform **-greifer** *m* loading grab **-hafen** *m* loading port, port of embarkation **-klasse** *f* freight category
Verladekran *m* material-handling crane, loading crane **feststehender ~** pillar crane
verladen to ship, forward, handle, load, unload, charge, embark, entrain
Verladen *n* loading (operation)
Verlade-ort *m* loading point, entraining point **-plan** *m* loading table or plan
Verlader *m* shipper, loader, mucker
Verlade-rampe *f* material-handling ramp, loading ramp, receiving platform, loading rack **-rinne** *f* loading chute **-rollgang** *m* live roller-loading bed **-rutsche** *f* charging chute, loading chute **-schein** *m* bill of lading **-schiebe** *f* scraper flight conveyer **-stelle** *f* entraining point, loading point, point of embarkation, entrucking point **-tasche** *f* loading bunker **-vorrichtung** *f* loading plant **-zeit** *f* entraining time
Verladung *f* entraining, embarkation, embussing, shipment, loading
Verladungsschein *m* bill of lading
Verlag *m* publishing house
verlagern to shift, unbalance, displace **sich ~** to move
Verlagerung *f* displacement, path, shift, misalignment, dislocation
Verlagerungsgerüst *n* supporting frame
Verlags-buchhandlung *f*, **-haus** *n* firm of publishers, publishing house **-recht** *n* copyright **-rechtsschutz** *m* copyright protection

verlanden to silt up
Verlandung *f* silting-up
verlangen to demand, require, claim
Verlangen *n* claim (law), desire
Verlängerer *m* extension socket or part
verlängern to lengthen, prolong, extend, elongate, produce (geom.) renew (a bill of exchange) **eine Leitung ~** to extend a circuit **einen Wechsel ~** to renew a bill
verlängert extended, lengthened, elongated **-es Besetzthalten** extended guard **-e Spindel** extension stem
Verlängerung *f* elongation, extension, prolongation **~** (Gurtförderer) stringer **~ der Wartezeit** prolongation of delay
Verlängerungs-drähte extension wires **-gebühr** *f* renewal fee **-leitung** *f* extension circuit, excess network, pad (elec.) **-lineal** *n* extension ruler or straightedge **-schiene** *f* arm extension bracket **-schnur** *f* extension cord **-spule** *f* aerial loading inductance, antenna load coil, lengthening coil **-stange** *f* lengthening rod **-stanze** *f* slot extender **-stück** *n* lengthening piece, adapter **-trichter** *m* extension funnel **-welle** *f* extension shaft
verlangsamen to slow down, retard, damp (aviation) **den Gang ~** to slow down the engine
Verlangsamen *n* deceleration
verlangsamend lagging
verlangsamte oder verzögerte Verbrennung retarded combustion
Verlangsamung *f* deceleration, retardation, slowing down
verlangt demanded, wanted **-er Teilnehmer** wanted subscriber, called subscriber
verlaschen to lash, bond, splice, overlap, fish (R.R.)
Verlaschen *n* fishing
Verlaschung *f* overlapping
verlassen to leave, quit, forsake, desert, abandon, relinquish **sich ~ auf** to rely upon
Verlassen *n* abandonment, discontinue, relinquishment
verläßlich dependable, reliable
Verlasten *n* loading of pack animals
Verlauf *m* course, progress, process, development, event, flowing (of lacquer), curve, character, nature, variation, pattern, plot, path, shape, trend, slope, behavior, response **~ des Films** (Lack) flow of the film **~ der Küste** bearing of the coast **~ einer Kurve** the shape of a curve **stetiger ~ einer Linie** continuous run of a curve, continuity of a curve **~ der Materialfasern** flow of material fibers **~ einer Rohrleitung** run of a pipe **~ der Siedekurve** shape of boiling curve **~ des Verfahrens** course of the proceedings **~ des Wassers** leakage of water **gradliniger ~** straight reach **zeitlicher ~** derivative trend with respect to time
verlaufen to take a course, proceed, pass
Verlaufen *n* run
Verlauf-filter *n* sky filter **-werk** *n* delayed action release
verlegbar portable, mobile
verlegefähig semimobile, transferable
Verlegeklinke *f* transfer jack
verlegen to lay (cable), mislay, displace, transport, transfer, delay, obstruct, publish (books), introduce, shift, establish (an equilibrium or

concentration), misplace, postpone, string (wires), install, equip **auf Putz ~** to wire on the surface **in die Erde ~** to bury **oberirdisch ~** to run (a wire) overhead **offen ~** to wire on the survace **eine Rohrleitung ~** to assemble a piping **über Putz ~** exposed wiring
Verlegen *n* shift, change of position, setting, placing (of concrete) **~** (Fußboden) bedding
Verleger *m* publisher
Verlegewagen *m* cable-laying trolley car or truck
Verlegung *f* transfer(ring), postponement, shift, removal, relocation, laying (of cable), mislaying, rerouting **~ der Blöcke** setting of blocks **~ eines Fernsprechanschlusses** removal of subscriber **~ eines Flußbettes** clearing the river bed **~ in Isolierrohr** drawn-in system **~ eines Ölkabels** laying an oil-filled cable **~ auf Putz** surface wiring **~ über Putz** exposed wiring, surface interior wiring **~ von Rohren** bedding of pipes **~ in Röhren** conduit wiring
Verlegungs- oder Verarbeitungsgeschwindigkeit des Betons rate of placing concrete
verleihen to lend, bestow
Verleihkopie *f* distributing print (of film)
Verleihung *f* concession of mine, grant **die ~ aufheben** to put an end to a grant **um ~ eines Feldes nachsuchen** to apply for the grant of a concession (min.) **~ einer Genehmigung** grant of license **~ eines akademischen Grades** graduation
Verleihungsurkunde *f* document conveying the grant, license, title to mining claims **die ~ ändern** to modify the conveyance of the grant
Verleihungsverfahren *n* procedure to obtain a grant
verleimen to cement, glue
Verleimung *f* pasting
Verleimungswerkzeuge *pl* tools for glueing
Verlese-maschine *f* sorting machine **-tisch** *m* sorting table
verletten to clay
Verletten *n* **eines Bohrloches** claying of a borehole
verletzbar vulnerable
Verletzbarkeit *f* vulnerability
verletzen to wound, injure, prejudice, hurt, violate, offend, infringe (patents), transgress, contravene
verletzlich vulnerable
verletzt injured
Verletzung *f* injury, violation, infringement (of patent rights), lesion, offense
verliegen to become damaged through long storage
verlieren to lose **an Größe oder Wert ~** to fall off
verlitzen to strand
Verlitzmaschine *f* stranding machine
Verlitzung *f* stranding
verlocken to tempt
verloren lost **-e Form** sand mold **-e Gießform** dead mold **-er Kopf** feedhead, extension, finish strip, sullage head, machinery allowance, top discard (of ingots), dozzle metal, top end, crop end, blind riser, lost head, sprue (aviation), deadhead **-es Verbindungsstück** sprue (met)
verlorengehen to get lost, vanish, disappear, perish
verlorengehender Ruf uncompleted call
verlöschen to extinguish, go out, kill (lime)
verlöten to solder **mit Blei ~** to plumb
Verlöten *n* caulk welding
Verlust *m* loss, waste, damage, escape, casualty, leakage, drop, shutter, dissipation (of potential), absorption (of light) **~ ausgleichen** to make good a loss **~ bei der Destillation** distillation loss **~ an Geschwindigkeitshöhe** loss of head **Ohmscher ~** resistance or ohmic loss **~ der Steuerbarkeit durch Anschlagen des Rotors an die Rotorwelle** control rotor stop banging
verlustarm low-loss **-es Kabel** low-loss cable
verlustbehaftet dissipative
Verlust-beiwert *m* loss factor **-dämpfung** *f* loss damping **-faktor** *m* phase-angle difference (of condenser), dissipation factor **-formel** *f* lost-call formula **-frei** loss-free, free of losses **-höhe** *f* amount of loss, head loss **-kapazität** *f* imperfect capacity, leaky capacity **-konstante** *f* damping constant of a cable, attenuation constant
Verlust-leistung *f* power loss, dissipation loss **-liste** *f* casualty list
verlustlos free of losses, nondissipative **-e Leitung** dissipationless line, zero-loss circuit **-e Schaltung** reactive network (filter theory)
Verlust-maß *n* extent of losses **-meldung** *f* casualty report **-rate** *f* casualty rate **-reich** rich in losses **-spektrum** *n* leakage spectrum **-strecke** *f* loss distance **-strom** *m* watt current, active current, energy current
Verlustübersicht bei Produkten product loss analysis statement
Verlust-wärme *f* heat due to energy losses **-widerstand** *m* wasteful resistance, loss resistance, nonreactive, effective, dissipative, or ohmic resistance
Verlustwinkel *m* phase angle, difference, loss angle (of a condenser), power factor **dielektrischer ~** phase angle or difference of a condenser
Verlust-zähler *m* loss meter **-zeit** *f* delayed-pulse interval, idle time **-ziffer** *f* percentage of lost calls, grade of service, probability of loss, phase-angle difference
vermahlen to grind, crush, pulverize, comminute, spoil in grinding, mill
Vermahlung *f* grinding, vrushing, comminution, pulverizing
Vermahlungsfähigkeit *f* grindability
vermarken to mark, beacon
Vermarkung *f* marking, delimitation beaconing, signaling
vermascht intermeshed **-er Regelkreis** multiloop control system
Vermaschung *f* interconnection
vermauern to wall up
vermehren to increase, augment, multiply
Vermehrung *f* increase, addition, enlargement, multiplication
vermeidbare Verzögerung *f* avoidable delay
vermeiden to avoid, shun, eliminate, evade, elude, shirk
Vermeidung *f* avoidance
Vermeil *n* gilt silver

vermengen to mix, blend, mingle, jumble
Vermengung *f* mixture, blending, mingling
Vermerk *m* note, remark, entry, notation
vermerken to record, note, mark
vermessen to measure, gauge, survey, rate
Vermessen *n* measuring
vermessingen to brass-plate
Vermessingung *f* brass plating
Vermessung *f* measurement, measuring, survey, surveying, gauge **nautische ~** nautical surveying **~ über Tage** surface survey **eine ~ durchführen** to conduct a survey
Vermessungs-abteilung *f* survey detachment **-angabe** *f* survey data **-anstalt** *f* surveying office **-arbeit** *f* survey **-art** *f* method of surveying **-deck** *n* tonnage deck **-empfänger** *m* flight-tracking receiver **-fahrzeug** *n* surveying vessel **-flugzeug** *n* survey plane
Vermessungs-gebiet *n* area to be surveyed **-gerät** *n* measuring appliance or instrument **-gerätekraftwagen** *m* surveying-equipment truck **-gesetz** *n* tonnage law **-horizont** *m* observer's horizon **-ingenieur** *m* geodetic engineer **-instrument** *n* surveyor's transit **-kunde** *f* surveying, geodesy **-schiff** *n* surveying ship **-sender** *m* normal frequency auxiliary transmitter **-stelle** *f* evaluation receiver (missiles) **-tiefe** *f* depth for tonnage **-trupp** *m* survey detachment **-wesen** *n* surveying
vermieten to rent, let, lease
vermilchen to emulsify
vermindern to lessen, reduce, decrease, lower, cut, fall off, go down
Verminderung *f* reduction, diminution, decrease, abatement, fall, decline **~ der Verdichtung** compression relief
Verminderungsventil *n* release valve
verminen to mine
vermischbar miscible
vermischen to mix, incorporate, amalgamate **~** (verfälschen) to adulterate
Vermischung *f* mixture, comingling, alloy **eines Metalles mit Quecksilber** amalgamation
vermissen to miss
vermißt missing
vermitteln to repeat a message, mediate, intervene, settle, introduce (ins.)
Vermitteln mit Fernsprechern telephone communication
vermittelnde, ausgleichende Gerade give and take line
Vermittler *m* agent, mediator, detector **-platz** *m* junction switching position
Vermittlung *f* mediation; (Schlichtung) settlement, adjustment, negotiation; (Einschreiten) intervention; exchange, medium, switching, transmission, telephone exchange, agency, intermediary, means, interposition **einfache ~** single exchange
Vermittlungsamt *n* exchange, central office, telephone exchange **~ mit Handbetrieb** manual central office **~ mit Induktoranruf** magneto central office **~ mit Wahlbetrieb** dial central office
Vermittlungs-beamtin *f* trunk operator **-dienst** *m* telephone service **-funkstelle** *f* radio-relay station **-gebühr** *f* commission **-kästchen** *n* switch box, single switchboard unit **-klinke** *f* connecting jack **-leitung** *f* (toll) switching trunk **-platz** *m* switchboard position
Vermittlungs-schnur *f* patching cord, jumper cord with plug **-schrank** *m* switchboard **-station** *f* transmitting station **-stelle** *f* telephone exchange, central office **-techniker** telephone switching engineer **-vorschlag** *m* proposal for settlement, suggested compromise **-wählersaal** *m* automatic-telephone room **-zentrale** *f* main exchange
vermodern to decay in the open air
Vermoderung *f* rotting
Vermögen *n* capacity, power, ability
vermooren to moor
Vermooren *n* mooring (of a boat)
Vermoorung *f* transformation into peat
Vermörtelung *f* cement stabilization
vermuten to suspect, conjecture, suppose
Vermutung *f* assumption, supposition, surmise, conjecture
vernachlässigen to neglect, disregard, omit
Vernachlässigung *f* omission, neglect, approximation
vernageln to nail
verneblen to screen (by smoke), atomize (under high pressure)
Vernebelung *f* smoke screening, fine dispersion, concealment by smoke
Vernebler *m* atomizer **-düse** *f* atomization jet
Verneblungs-düse *f* atomization jet **-wand** *f* smoke screen
Vernehmbarkeit *f* audibility
vernehmlich audible, intelligible
Vernehmung *f* examination, hearing, interrogation, question
Verneinung *f* negation, denial, disavowal, contradiction
vernetzen to cross-link, interlace
Vernetzung *f* latticelike polymerization, network, reticulation
vernichten to nullify, destroy
Vernichtung *f* extermination, annihilation, destruction **~ der Energie des Gefälles** dissipation of energy of fall **~ in der Gasphase** destruction in the gas phase **Güter vor der ~ retten** to salvage
Vernichtungs-bereich *m* effective or destructive range **-strahlen** *pl* annihilation radiation
vernickeln to nickel, coat with nickel, nickel-plate
Vernickeln *n* nickeling, nickel-plating
vernickelt nickel-plate(d) **-e Armaturen** nickel fittings **-e Skalen** nickel-plated gauges
Vernickelung *f* nickel-plating
Vernier *n* vernier (condenser), vernier tuning **-kondensator** *m* vernier condenser
vernieten to rivet, fasten
Vernietung *f* riveting
Veröffentlichung *f* publication, press release
verölen to foul by oil
Verölen *n* oiling up
Verölung *f* fouling (of plugs)
Veroneserde *f* terre-verte
verordnen to order, decree, prescribe
Verordnung *f* prescription, regulation, law, order
verpachten to lease
verpacken to pack

Verpacken *n* packing
Verpacker *m* packer
Verpackung *f* packing, loading **~ nicht inbegriffen** not including packing
Verpackungs-anlage *f* packaging installation or plant **-flasche** *f* shipping flask **-gewebe** *n* packaging fabrics **-gewicht** *n* dead weight **-kiste** *f* packing case **-methode** *f* packing method **-mittel** *n* packing material **-rohr** *n* stowage or packing tube **-sack des Fallschirms** parachute pack **-straße** *f* packaging line **-technik** *f* packing engineering
verpechen to pitch
verpfählen to fasten with pales or stakes
Verpfählung *f* pile driving, paling
verpfänden pawn, assign, mortgage
Verpfändungsurkunde *f* letter of hypothecation
verpflanzen to transplant, transmit
Verpflanzung *f* transit, parallel displacement, transplanting, transmission
Verpflegung *f* food supply, ration
verpflichtet obligated, bound, under obligation
Verpflichtung *f* obligation, duty
Verpflichtungsschein *m* surety bond
verpfuschen to bungle, spoil by careless work
verpichen to pitch, stick (piston rings)
Verpichung *f* pitch formation
verplatinieren to platinum-plate
Verplatinierung *f* platinum plating
verpochen to stamp
Verpochen *n* stamp milling
verpreßbares Material extrudable material
verproviantieren to provision
verpuddeln to puddle
verpuffen to puff (off), deflagrate, detonate, crackle, (de)crepitate, fulminate (with a flame), fire, explode, vaporize, atomize
Verpuffung *f* deflagration, detonation, explosion, (de)crepitation, crackling
Verpuffungs-maschine *f* explosion engine **-motor** *m* explosion motor **-strahlrohr** *n* resonant aerothermo-dynamic duct **-verfahren** *n* constant-pressure combustion
Verpumpung *f* pumping
Verputz *m* finish, coating, veneer, stucco, plaster, plasterwork
verputzen to plaster, trim
Verputzen *n* cleaning
Verqualmung *f* fuming, smoking
verquellen to swell
verquicken to amalgamate
Verquickung *f* amalgamation
verrammeln to barricade, block
Verrastung *f* locating device
verrechnen to be accounted for in turn **sich ~** to overshoot, undershoot
Verrechnung *f* clearing, accounting
Verrechnungs-abkommen *n* clearing agreement with foreign country **-dollar** *m* clearing dollar **-konto** *n* credit account **-scheck** *m* crossed check
verregnet spoiled by rain
verreiben to grind fine, spread by rubbing, triturate
Verreib- und Auftragwalzen form- and distributor roller journals
Verreibung der Farbe ink distribution (print.)
Verreibungs- und Mischmaschinen grinding and mixing machines
Verreibwalzen *pl* distributor roller journals
verrenken to sprain, dislocate, put out of joint
Verrenkung *f* sprain
verrichten to perform, do, execute
Verrichtung des Dienstes (nontechnical) maintenance of service
verriegeln to bolt, latch, block, lock, interlock, bar, cut off, gang (condensers) **wieder ~** to relatch **~** (ein Objektiv) to lock in position
verriegelnde Spannung cutoff biasing potential
Verriegelung *f* barricade, locking mechanism, interlocking (device), clamping device, catch
Verriegelungs-bolzen *m* locking pin, lock bolt **-bremsmagnet** *m* interlocking solenoid **-bügel** *m* dislocking bracket **-glied** *n* latch member **-hebel des Spulenhalters** roll holder lock **-schalter** *m* arresting switch **-schaltung** *f* interlocking switch system **-schieber** *m* shift interlock **-stift** *m* cotter-cotter pin **-system** *n* interlocking system (elec.) **-vorrichtung** *f* locking device
Verriegler *m* suppressor **-relais** *n* locking relay
verrieseln to seep in
verringern to reduce, lessen, decrease, minimize, cut, lower, slow up, diminish
Verringerung *f* reduction, decrease, lessening, diminution, cutting **~ der Anschaffungskosten** reducing first costs **~ der Landegeschwindigkeit** reduction in landing speed
verrinnen to run off, pass
verrippen to rib, brace
verrippt webbed, wafered, ribbed
Verrippung *f* finning (of cylinders), ribbing
verrohren to case **ein Bohrloch ~** to tube a hole
verrohrtes Bohrloch cased borehole
Verrohrung *f* casing, tubbing (of shaft), string of casing, lining **volle ~** full string of casing **vorläufige ~** temporary casing
Verrohrungs-birne *f* pipe swage, swage for lowering casing **-bohrkrone** *f* blank casing bit **-büchse** *f* tubing bailer **-deckelscheibe** *f* casing disk **-haltekeil** *m* casing clamp wedge **-heber** *m* casing pressure screws **-kopf** *m* casing head **-liderung** *f* pipe packer **-reinigungsbüchse** *f* casing bailer
verrosten to rust, corrode
Verrosten *n* rusting
verrostet rusty, rusted, corroded
Verrostung *f* rusting, corrosion
verrotten to rot, decay, corrode
verrücken to shift
Verrückung *f* displacement, conjecture, disturbance, derangement, shift, dislocation, dislodgment
Verrückungs-ableitung *f* displacement derivative **-geschwindigkeit** *f* displacement speed **-gradienten** *pl* displacement gradients
verrühren to mix, stir
Verrunden *n* radiusing
Verrundung *f* roundness
verrußen to soot
Verrußung *f* sooting
Verrußungszündleistung *f* utility spark(ing) performance
versacken to bog down
versackt, das Tor ~ the gate tilts forward
Versackung *f* sagging
versagen to fail, misfire, refuse

Versagen *n* failure, refusal, breakdown
Versager *m* misfire, failure, seal, blind shell
Versalzen *n* salting
Versammlung *f* convention, assembly, gathering, meeting, concentration
Versammlungs-platz *m* assembly point **-zelt** *n* assembly tent, meeting tent
Versand *m* shipment, dispatch **-anschrift** *f* address of the consignee **-anweisung** *f* shipping instruction **-beamter** *m* shipping clerk **-betrieb** *m* dispatch facilities **-bock** *m* packing base, packing stand
versanden to silt up
versandfähig ready for shipment
Versand-faß *n* shipping cask **-gefäß** *n* dispatch jar **-karton** *m* shipping carton **-kiste** *f* shipping box **-rolle** *f* mailing tube **-station** *f* dispatch station, terminal **-vorschriften** *pl* forwarding instructions
Versandung *f* sanding up, choking up with sand, alluvion
Versatz *m* backfilling, mine filling, mixing, treating, compounding, stopping, stowing, dry packing ~ **der Keilpaare** mutual displacement of the key pair
Versatz-arbeiter *m* builder, packer, stower **-berg** *m* dirt, filling material, waste **-bolzen** *m* racking stud **-drahtgeflecht** *n* triangular-mesh gauze **-einrichtung** *f* racking mechanism **-kran** *m* shifting crane **-leiste** *f* racking bar **-mauer** *f* partition wall **-nietung** *f* staggered riveting **-pfeiler** *m* cog (min.) **-stoff** *m* filling material
Versatzung *f* gobbing
Versatzzahnrad *n* racking gear
versäuern to acidify
Versäumnis *f n* neglect **-urteil** *n* judgment by default **-verfahren** *n* proceedings by default
verschachteln to nest, insert into one another
verschachtelte Wicklung banked winding
Verschachtelung *f* agglomeration
verschaffen to get, procure
verschalen to encase, case, board, jacket, cover, plank
verschalken to batten down
verschalten to cross
Verschalten *n* faulty wiring
Verschaltung *f* wrong connection
Verschaltungsfehler beseitigen to debug a circuit
Verschalung *f* planking, boarding, revetting, revetment, casing, cowling, covering, jacketing, sheeting (with plywood), lagging, encasing, coping, form, mold
Verschanzung *f* entrenchment, fortification
verschäumen to turn into froth
verschicken to send or ship away, transport
Verschickung *f* shipment
verschiebbar slidable, sliding, movable, displaceable, adjustable, removable, shiftable **posaunenartig** ~ telescoping **-e Kuppelungsklaue** sliding dog or claw of the clutch **-e Nockenwelle** shifting camshaft **-e Schneidzunge** removable cutter **-er Schraubenmutterschlüssel** adjustable wrench **-e Spannung** slidable tension, displaceable tension or voltage **-es Zahnrad** sliding gear
Verschiebbarkeit *f* movability, displaceability
Verschiebe-anker *m* sliding armature, sliding rotor **-ankerbremse** *f* slide armature brake **-anlage** *f* shunting installation **-bahnhof** *m* switching yard (R.R.), shunting station **-dienst** *m* switching work **-einrichtung** *f* shifter (info proc.) **-fehler** *m* lack of synchronism, out-of-frame condition **-frequenz** *f* set-off frequency **-gabel** *f* striker fork **-gleis** *n* switching track **-karren** *m* shunting trolley **-körper** *m* slide part
Verschiebe-leitwerk *n* slide empennage **-lineal** *n* guide bar **-lokomotive** switching locomotive shunting-engine **-möglichkeit** *f* adjustable arrangement **-muffe** *f* shifter collar
verschieben to postpone, defer, displace, lag, shift, remove, move, shunt, slide **in der Phase** ~ to dephase
Verschieben *n* shifting ~ **des Geleises in der Längsrichtung** creep of track, pushing forward of rails in a longitudinal direction
Verschieber *m* switchman, car shunter
Verschiebe-ritzel shifting pinion **-schaltung** *f* selective system of gear shifting **-spule** *f* positioning coil, sliding coil **-stellung** *f* sliding position **-träger** *m* shuttle boom **-vorrichtung** *f* shunting installation **-wert** *m* sliding displacement value **-vorrichtung** *f* shunting installation **-widerstand** *m* resistance to motion, resistance to displacement **-winde** *f* shunting winch **-zackenspur** *f* bilateral variable-area sound track
verschieblich displaceable; subject to slide away (structure)
Verschiebung *f* displacement, movement, shifting, removing, disalignment, shift, shearing, deflection, lag, masking, dislocation, drift, slip (geol.), dephasing **bergseitige** ~ upward displacement **eingangsseitige** ~ input displacement (kinematics) **dielektrische** ~ dielectric displacement **elektrische** ~ electrostatic induction, electric displacement ~ **um 90:** quadrature (TV) ~ **auf Kugelflächen** spherical surface displacements **zyklische** ~ cyclic shift
Verschiebungs-ebene *f* slip plane **-einheit** *f* unit of displacement **-einrichtung** *f* displacement device **-faktor** shift or power factor **-feld** *n* displacement field **-fluß** *m* electric flux **-impuls** *m* (Radar) offset pulse **-konstante** *f* displacement constant, specific inductive capacity (for vacuum) **-linie** *f* line of displacement **-register** shift register **-satz** *m* displacement law, lag theorem **-spindel** *f* screw drive **-strom** *m* (dielectric) displacement current, capacitance current, electric flux
verschieden different, various, diverse, several, varied, dissimilar, separate, unlike ~ **sein** to be different, vary, alter, differ ~ **gegliederte Bildteile** picture portions of dissimilar make-up, nature, or organization **-e Böden** unclassified soil
verschiedenartig dissimilar, varied, heterogeneous, various
Verschiedenartigkeit *f* heterogeneity
Verschiedenes *n* miscellaneous
verschiedenfarbig varicolored, heterochromatic **-e Lichter** heterochromatic lights
Verschiedenheit *f* difference, variety, dissimilarity, disparity, diversity, discrepancy
Verschiedenheitsfaktor *m* diversity factor
verschiedentlich occasionally, at times
verschienen to provide with rails

verschießen to fire away, expend ammunition, change color
Verschiffer *m* shipper
Verschiffungshafen *m* port of loading
verschimmeln to get moldy, mold
verschlacken to slag, flux, scorify, sinter, scale, slake, clinker
verschlackt scorious
Verschlackung *f* slagging, sintering, clinkering, scorification, slag penetration, slag corrosion
Verschlackungs-beständigkeit *f* resistance to slagging **-fähigkeit** *f* fluxing power, capacity for forming slag **-gefahr** *f* danger of slagging **-periode** *f* slag-forming period
Verschlag *m* partition, crate, pen, booth, chute, compartment **hölzerner ~** wooden planking **abgetrennter ~** booth
verschlagen to board up, partition, cross off; tepid; (Wasser) lukewarm **mit Brettern ~** to board up
verschlämmen to fill or stop with mud
verschlämmt clogged
Verschlämmung *f* caving, choking up, clogging, siltation (with mud)
verschlechtern to deteriorate, spoil, become worse, impair, make worse
verschlechtert worsened
Verschlechterung *f* deterioration, impairment, spoiling, debasement, vitiation
verschleiern to camouflage, fog, veil, make turbid or cloudy
Verschleierung *f* masking, concealment, camouflaging, screening, fog, veiling, glare (of projected image), foggy or fogged condition (of film)
Verschleierungs-fähigkeit *f* screening or obscuring capacity or power, density of coverage **-verkehr** *m* deception signal traffic
verschleifen to obliterate
verschleimen to foul (firearms)
verschleimt obstructed with mucus
Verschleiß *m* wear, abrasion, attrition, erosion, corrosion, pitting **normaler ~** fair wear and tear **-verhindernder Zusatz** anti-wear agent **~ durch Schleifwirkung** abrasion wear
Verschleiß-ausgleich *m* compensation for wear **-beständigkeit** *f* wear resistance **-blech** *n* metal wearing plate **-eigenschaft** *f* wearing property
verschleißen to wear away, wear, wear out
verschleiß-fest wear-resistant **-festigkeit** *f* wearability, resistance to wear (and tear), wearing quality, resistance to abrasion **-härte** *f* resistance against wear and tear **-kette** *f* trash (of a mooring chain) **-maß** *n* degree of wear, rate or measure of wear and tear **-platte** *f* wearing plate **-prüfmaschine** *f* surface-endurance testing machine **-prüfung** *f* wear test, abrasion test **-schutz** *m* protection against wear and tear **-spur** *f* trace of wear **-teil** *m* part subject to wear **-verhalten** *n* wear characteristics **-widerstand** *m* wear resistance **-zäh** wear resisting **-zapfen** *m* wearing neck, wobbler
verschleppen to delay, postpone
Verschleppen des Zündzeitpunktes retarding of the ignition
verschleudern to sell at a loss or below cost price
Verschlickung *f* silting up
Verschließaggregat *n* capping unit
verschließbar fitted with lock and key
Verschließ-bereich *m* (el. Spannung) sealing range (el. voltage) **-einrichtung** *f* sealing unit
verschließen to lock (up), close, shut, seal, occlude, blind
Verschließen *n* walling off, sealing
Verschließer *m* capper **-teil** *m* capping unit
Verschließ-kopf *m* crowning head, sealing head **-maschine** *f* seaming machine, capping machine **-zylinder** *m* sealing ram
verschlingen to devour, swallow, intertwine **sich ~** (Drähte) to get entangled **eng ~** interlace
Verschlingen der Seile twisting of the ropes
Verschlingung *f* interlacing, overlapping, entanglement
verschlissen worn out, worn
verschlossen locked up, closed, shut **luftdicht ~** sealed
verschlossener Schalter locked-cover or secret or asylum switch
verschlucken to swallow, absorb
verschlungen sinuous, twisted
Verschluß *m* fastener, lock, clasp; (Flasche) stopper; (Stöpsel) plug; (Dichtung) seal; breech (mechanism), lock, breech-block, shutter, chuck, locking or closing apparatus, cutoff, trap, sluice, closure, stopping, fastening, snap, cap, closure, lock, shutter, plug, bolt
Verschluß, bedingter ~ special locking (R.R.) **elektrisch betriebener ~** electrically operated shutter **elektrooptischer ~** electrooptical shutter **luftdichter ~** airtight seal, hermetic seal **selbsttätiger ~** automatic breech mechanism **unter ~** under lock and key, in bond **~ für Flaschen** mechanical bottle stopper **~ für Röntgenröhre** tube shutter
Verschluß-art *f* type of breech mechanisms **-aufzug** *m* winding of the shutter, shutter setter **-aufzugsfeder** *f* shutter wind spring **-auslöser** *m* shutter release button **-auslösung** *f* shutter release **-band** *n* closing band **-betätigung** *f* shutter action **-blech** *n* sealing plate **-blende** *f* shutter **-block** *m* breechblock **-bolzen** *m* locking bolt, coupling pin, locking pin
Verschlußdeckel *m* cover, closure, lid **plombierter ~** welch plug
Verschlußdeckel mit Dichtplatte sealing plate with gasket **~ mit Dichtplatte für Scheinwerfer** rim for head lamp **~ mit Dichtplatte für Unterbrecher** end cap for contact breaker
Verschluß-draht *m* locking wire **-einrichtung** *f* interlocking gear **-einstellung** *f* shutter setting
verschlüsseln to encipher, code, encode
verschlüsselt in code, coded, cryptogramic **-es Sendeverfahren** privacy system **-e Sprache** scrambled speech **-er Text** secret text, ciphered message
Verschlüsselung *f* coding, cryptography
Verschlüsselungsscheibe *f* cipher disk
Verschluß-fanghebel *m* lock catch **-feder** *f* lock spring **-flansch** *m* blind flange, sealing flange **-gehäuse** *n* shutter casing **-geschwindigkeit** *f* shutter speed **-gitter** *n* interlocking gear **-glied** *n* coupler link (of a chain) **-haken** *m* locking hook **-hebel** *m* breechblock handle, bolt handle **-hülse** *f* breech casing **-hütchen** *n* bottle closure
Verschlußkappe *f* locking cap, plug, breechblock

cover, screw cap, valve cone or cap, fuse cap **~ des Rohrständers** finial **~ für Zapfhahn** nozzle cap

Verschluß-kapsel *f* inclosing capsule **-kegel** *m* male connecting nipple **-keil** *m* sliding wedge-type breechblock **-klammer** *f* locking clamp **-klappe** *f* hinged cover, tuyère latch, shutter leaf (swinging-out) **-klaue** *f* locking clamp **-klinke** *f* plunger **-knagge** *f* tappet **-knopf** *m* *m* lock knob **-kopf** *m* mushroom head (of breech), cable terminal **-körper** *m* breech body **-kugel** *f* closing ball **-kurbel** *f* breech-locking crank **-leiste** *f* backplate **-leistenachse** *f* backplate pin

Verschlüßler *m* encoder, decoder, coder (Rechner)

Verschluß-magnet *m* locking magnet **-mantel** *m* breech casing **-mechanismus** *m* locking mechanism **-muffe** *f* locking sleeve **-mutter** *f* lock nut **-nippel** *m* closing nipple **-platte** *f* breech rear plate **-pfropfen** *m* locking plug, screw plug **-pufferdorn** *m* breech buffer gear or plug **-register** *n* interlocking chart **-ring** *m* clamp collar, lock ring (of magnifier)

Verschluß-sache *f* security matter or document, classified document **-scheibe** *f* shutter disk, lock washer **-schieber** *m* shutter **-schiene** *f* breech bar or rail, guide rib **-schlitten** *m* lock frame **-schraube** *f* locking screw, threaded nose cap, fuse, screw plug, drain plug **-schraubendichtung** *f* screw-plug washer **-sockel** *m* filler neck **-spitze** *f* sealing tip

Verschluß-stellen *pl* capping heads **-stempel** *m* sealing ram **-stopfen** *m* plug, blanking plug **-streifen** *m* banderole **-stück** *n* locking piece, shutting plug, screw cap, column cap, breech ring, stopper, seal

Verschluß-teil *m* breechblock-mechanism part **-träger** *m* breechblock carrier **-überzug** *m* breechblock cover **-vorholer** *m* recuperator **-vorrichtung** *f* interlocking mechanism **-zeitenmeßgerät** *n* shutter tester, shutter speed-testing machine **-zustand** *m* watertightness

verschmälern to narrow, constrict, taper

Verschmälerung *f* narrowing

verschmelzen to smelt, melt, fuse, amalgamate, merge, coalesce, solder, blend, alloy **~ mit Sammlerplatten** to burn to storage-cell plates

Verschmelzung *f* smelting, melting, fusion, amalgamation, consolidation, merger, coalescence, blending, merging (of pictures) **~** (Glas-Metall) glass-to-metal seal **~ der Halbbilder bei stereoskopischer Betrachtung** stereoscopic fusion, correspondence (phot.)

Verschmelzungsfrequenz *f* critical flicker frequency, fusion or no-flicker frequency

Verschmiedbarkeit *f* forgeability

verschmieden to forge

verschmieren to smear, daub, lute, obliterate, blur (TV), make indistinct, plaster **sich ~** to fog, become foggy or hazy, become fouled or smeared

Verschmieren *n* smudging

verschmiert indistinct, blunt, blurred (Bild)

Verschmierung *f* smearing, daubing, luting, blurring (in X ray)

verschmoren to scorch, freeze together (of contacts)

verschmort charred

verschmutzen to contaminate, foul

Verschmutzen *n* fouling

verschmutzt foul, soil, contaminated, clogged

Verschmutzung *f* fouling (of gun barrels), contamination, pollution

Verschmutzungs-unempfindlichkeit *f* resistance to fouling **-faktor** *m* coefficient of dirtying **-gefahr** *f* danger of fouling

verschneiden to blend, mix, cut, adulterate, thin

verschneit snow covered, snowed under

Verschnitt *m* waste of timber, blend, adulteration (blending)

Verschnittansatz *m* reduction paste

verschnitten blended

verschnittfähig capable of dilution

Verschnittfähigkeit *f* dilution value (of lacquers etc.)

Verschnittmittel *n* diluent, cutting agent, filler (for lacquers, etc.) blending agent **~ für Lösungsmittel** diluent **~ für Pigmente** extender

verschnüren to lace, interlace

Verschnürungsleine *f* packing cord

verschoben displaced, shifted **~ sein** to take a heave (min.) **in der Phase ~ sein** to be out of phase **-e Phase** displaced phase, shifted phase, dephased or out-of-phase condition **-e Peilung** long-path bearing **-es Viereck** lozenge (math.)

verschollen missing

Verschollenheit *f* presumptive loss

verschonen to spare

verschossener Farbton discolored shade (faded shade)

verschrämen to trench, carve

verschrämt trenched, carved **-er Stoß** carved face

Verschränkbarkeit der Achsen radius of turn of driving axles

verschränken to cross, interlace, set (saw teeth), interconnect, traverse, skip, joggle, toggle **zwei Balken miteinander ~** to joggle two beams

verschränkt interlaced, twisted **-e Adressen-Speicherzellenzuordnung** interlaced address cell pattern **-e Doppelweiche** three-throw switch **-er Grund** (inter)laced ground **-e Numerierung** *f* interleave, interlacing **-e Vielfachschaltung** slip multiple

Verschränkung *f* crossing, interlacing, setting (of saw teeth), interconnecting, transposition

verschraubbar screwable

verschrauben to screw, bolt

Verschrauber *m* pole wrencher

verschraubt bolted **-e Enden** screwed ends

Verschraubung *f* screwing, bolting, bolted joint, screw coupling, screw cap, screwed joint, union

Verschraubungs-konus *m* union tailpiece **-mutter** *f* union nut **-stopfbüchse** *f* screwed gland **-stück** *n* locking ring

verschreiben to prescribe

Verschreibung *f* debenture

verschroten to bruise, crush, rough-grind

verschrotten to scrap, scrap

Verschrottung *f* scrapping

verschrumpfen to shrink, contract

Verschub *m* delay

Verschulden *n* fault, guilt, wrong

verschuldet indebted

verschütten to bury alive, spill, encumber

verschüttete Flüssigkeit spilt liquid

verschwächen to weaken **eine Mauer ~** to diminish a wall
verschwächter Zahn attenuated tooth
Verschwächung *f* decrease in strength, weakening
verschweißen to weld, weld together, heat-seal (plastics)
Verschweißen *n* fusing, welding
Verschweißerscheinung *f* seizing, freezing or galling (of engines)
Verschweißung *f* welding
verschwelen to carbonize or distill under vacuum at a low temperature
Verschwelung *f* low-temperature carbonization, distillation under vacuum
verschwenden to waste
Verschwendung *f* waste
verschwenken to deviate
verschwenkte Aufnahme tilted photograph
Verschwenkung *f* avertence, horizontal swing, swivelling
Verschwenkungs-fehler *m* error of avertence **-winkel** *m* angle of horizontal swing, angle of avertence
Verschwertung *f* lateral truss, sway brace
verschwimmen to blur, become indistinct, blend
Verschwimmung *f* blurring
verschwinden to fade, disappear, evanesce **~** (z. B. Koeffizient) to vanish **Ziel ~ lassen** to lower target
Verschwinden *n* disappearance, vanishing, fading **zum ~ bringen** to damp out
verschwindend disappearing, zero **-e Statik** zero steady-state output
Verschwind-linie *f* vanishing line **-scheibe** *f* disappearing target
Verschwindungs-ebene *f* vanishing-plane **-gerade** *f* vanishing line **-geschwindigkeit** *f* clearance rate **-punkt** *m* vanishing point
verschwommen blurred, indistinct, vague, foggy, indefinite, bleary **-es Aussehen** bleary, blurred, or foggy appearance (of image) **-es Bild** *f* soft picture
Versegelung *f* distance covered between two bearings, deviation from right course, yaw
versehen to provide (with), supply, furnish **mit Rippen ~** ribbed **mit Zähnen ~** to tooth
Versehen *n* error, mistake, fault, inadvertence
versehren to cripple, disable
verseifbar saponifiable
verseifen to saponify
Verseifung *f* saponification, hydrolysis
Verseifungs-grad *m* saponification factor **-mittel** *n* saponification agent **-zahl** *f* saponification number
verseilen to twist, strand, cable **zu zweien ~** to twin
Verseil-korb *m* carriage **-maschine** *f* stranding or laying up machine, twisting machine
verseilt stranded (cable) **-er Draht** twisted wire **-es Kabel** stranded cable
Verseilung *f* cable lay, twisting, stranding (of wires or leads)
versenden to ship, dispatch
versengen to scorch, singe
Versenk *n* sunk hole **-antenne** *f* disappearing antenna **-arbeit** *f* countersinking
versenkbar collapsible
Versenk-bohrer *m* countersink, rose bit **-drehturm** *m* disappearing turret
versenken to sink, send to the bottom, scuttle, plunge, countersink, dive, lay (cable), submerge, dimple **durch Anbohren ~** to scuttle
Versenken *n* sinking, immersion, counterboring, setting (by pontoon or floating sheers)
Versenker *m* rose bit, countersink, counterbore
Versenk-kopf *m* flush head, flush rivet head **-leuchten** *pl* sunken runway lights **-niet** *m* flush rivet, countersunk rivet
versenknieten to flush-rivet
Versenk-nietung *f* flush riveting, countersunk riveting **-schraube** *f* countersink bolt
versenkt sunk, countersunk **~ genietet** flush riveted **~ liegend** immerged **-er Behälter** underground tank **-er Bolzen** countersunk bolt **-er Einbau** submerged installation **-es Geleise** sunk line **-e Linie** underground line, covered line **-es Niet** countersunk or flush rivet **-e Schraube** countersunk screw **-er Schraubenkopf** countersunk screw head **-er Sprinkler** recessed sprinkler
Versenkung *f* countersink(ing), trough fault
Versenkungswinkel *m* angle of countersink(ing)
Versenkwalze *f* submersible roller
versetzbar removable, portable, capable of being treated or mixed **-es Tanklager** movable tank support
versetzen to displace; (verschieben) shift; (vermischen) mix; (Metalle) alloy; compound, treat, digest, dilute, move, stop, obstruct, misplace, alternate, transpose, transplant, stagger, reset, block, bunch, chop out, gap, transfer, weld, add (one substance to another) **gegeneinander ~** to stagger
Versetzen *n* filling up, tamping
versetzt staggered, misplaced, joggled, displaced, offset, dislocated, shifted, dephased, out of phase **~ angeordnet** in reverse order, staggered **~ werden** (Gebäude) to be transfered **-e Diagramme** transposed diagrams, draw cards **-er Kern** misplaced core **-e Nietreihe** staggered row of rivets **-e Platte** baffle plate **-er Träger** *m* offset carrier (TV) **-es Trägerwellensystem** offset carrier system **gegeneinander -e Zahnscheiben** staggered driving pinions
Versetzung *f* mixing, compounding, treating, digesting, diluting, shift(ing), moving, permutation, alligation, alloy, displacing, stopping, obstructing, misplacing, transposing, transplanting, staggering, displacement, transfer, transposition, joggle, deviation from course, drift, dislocation, (nach unten) demotion; (nach oben) promotion
Versetzungs-bewegung *f* dislocation motion **-dämpfung** *f* dislocation damping **-dichte** *f* dislocation density **-fehler** *m* linear defect of crystal matrix **-formänderung** *f* dislocation strain **-gewinn** *m* staggering advantage **-grenze** *f* dislocation line
Versetzungs-kern *m* dislocation kernel **-linie** *f* dislocation line **-sprünge** *pl* kinks in dislocations **-verteilung** *f* dislocation distribution **-vervielfachung** *f* dislocation multiplication **-winkel** *m* angle of drift
verseuchen to contaminate, infect, vitiate, poison
Verseuchen *n* contamination, poisoning

verseucht, für ~ erklärt declared infected
Verseuchung *f* contamination, infection
versicherbar insurable
Versicherer *m* insurer, assurer, underwriter
versichern to insure, assure
versichert insured
Versicherung *f* insurance, assurance **eidesstattliche ~** affirmation in lieu of oath, statutory declaration **eidliche ~** affidavit, sworn statement, testimony, or declaration
Versicherungs-anstalt *f* insurance company **-art** *f* form of insurance **-gesellschaft** *f* insurance company **-leistung** *f* benefit **-mathematik** *f* actuarial theory **-nehmer** *m* insured, assured **-police** *f* insurance policy **-vertrag** *m* insurance contract **-wert** *m* insurable value **-wesen** *n* insurance
versickern to ooze or seep away **in den Boden ~** to sink into a porous stratum **das Grubenwasser ~ lassen** to let mine water drain off
Versickerung *f* seepage
Versickerungs-becken *n* basin where percolation takes place **-verlust** *m* loss by percolation
versieden to boil away
versiegeln to seal
versiegeln, gerichtlich ~ to seal legally
versiegelt sealed-in **-e Quelle** (Bohrloch) plugged well
versiegen to be exhausted (dry up)
versilbern to silver, silver-coat, silver-plate
Versilbern *n* silvering, silver coating, silver plating
Versilberung *f* silver coating, silver plating
Versilberungs-bad *f* silver bath, silvering bath **-lösung** *f* silver-plating solution
versinken to sink
Versinkungszone *f* settlement zone
versinnbildlichen to symbolize, express or represent by symbols
Versinnbildlichung *f* symbolization
versintern to sinter
Versinterung *f* sintering process
Versitzgrube *f* percolation basin, percolation well
Verso *n* reverse side
versoffen drowned (min.)
versorgen to provide, supply, serve, take care of, feed
Versorgen *n* supplying
Versorgung *f* supply, social security, provision
Versorgungs-anspruch *m* preferential status of exservicemen **-basis** *f* source(s) of supply **-behälter** *m* aerial delivery unit **-betrieb** *m* public utility **-gebiet** *n* service area, supply district **-güter** *pl* supplies **-lage** *f* supply situation **-schiff** *n* supply ship **-spannung** *f* supply voltage
verspanbar machinable
verspanen to remove metal
Verspanndraht *m* bracing wire
verspannen to guy, span, stay, brace
Verspannen *n* arching of sand
Verspanner *m* rigger
Verspannkraft *f* expansion or restraining force
verspannt (wire-)braced, guyed **-er Schornstein** guyed stack **-e Stange** trussed pole (elec.) **-er Tiefdecker** wire-braced low-wing monoplane **-e Zahnräder** scissors or split gears **-e Zelle** wire-braced wing
Verspannung *f* bracing, wiring, rigging, guying, staying, spanning, guy, stay, supply (source), potential **innere ~** locked up stress
Verspannungs-beschlag *m* bracing wire fitting **-bezugslinie** *f* rigging datum line **-diagonale** *f* cross-bracing wire **-draht** *m* bracing wire **-faktor** *m* loading factor (explosives) **-getriebe** *n* gear rig **-kabel** *n* bracing wire
verspannungslos unbraced, braceless
Verspannungs-schema *n* rigging diagram **-seil** *n* guy wire **-seildiagonale** *f* diagonal bracing wire **-vorgang** *m* metal-removing process
verspätet late, delayed **-es Losgehen** hangfire
Verspätung *f* retardation, lag **~ eines Zuges** delay of train
verspeichen, ein Rad ~ to spoke a wheel
versperren to seal, obstruct, bar, block, lock
verspiegeln to metallize, transluce, apply a reflecting coating
verspiegelte Lampe *f* reflector lamp
Verspiegelung (Scheinwerfer) mirror-coating
verspleißen to splice, joint
Verspleißung *f* splicing, jointing
versplinten to cotter **eine Mutter ~** to fix a nut with a split pin
versplintet split
verspratzen to splatter, splash
verspreizen to strut
Verspreizung *f* strutting, bracing
versprengen to scatter, disperse
verspritzen to splash, spill, spatter
Verspritzen *n* spilling, spattering, splashing
Verspritzung *f* spraying over
Versprödung *f* embrittlement **~ nach dem Schweißen** weld decay
Versprühen *n* spraying
Versprühvorrichtung *f* (landwirtschaftliche) agricultural spray kit
verspunden to plow and tongue together, plug, bung
Verspundung *f* groove-and-tongue joint
verstaatlichen to nationalize
verstählen to convert into steel, steel, coat with steel
Verstählen *n* hard-facing
Verstählstahl *m* steel-facing steel
verstählt steel-plated
Verstählung *f* steel plating, steel or hard-facing **galvanische ~** electroplating with steel
Verstandenzeichen *n* understood signal
verständigen to transmit **sich ~** to come to an agreement
Verständigung *f* quality of reception, understanding, communication, avoidance of mistakes, intelligence, (signal) transmission, quality of reception, intelligibility, readability (Radiotel.) **~ von Flugzeug zu Flugzeug** two-way communication between aircraft **mangelhafte ~, schlechte ~** poor transmission, bad readability
Verständigungs-anlage *f* communication system **-gerät** *n* intercommunication telephone, interphone equipment **-norm** *f* terminological standard
verständlich intelligible, perspicuous understandable, clear audible (hörbar) **-es Nebentransmission** audibility
Verständlichkeit *f* intelligibility, articulation,

transmission audibility
Verständlichkeits-äquivalent *n* articulation equivalent **-verlust** *m* loss in intelligibility
Verstärkbarkeitsgrenze *f* limiting amplifiableness, maximum or practical amplification
verstärken to strengthen, reinforce; (Radio) amplify; (steigern) intensify, increase, aggravate, magnify, augment, boost (battery), truss (poles), thicken, multiply, fortify, concentrate **am Auflager ~** to reinforce at the bearing
Verstärker *m* (Radio) amplifier; (Telef.) repeater; magnifier, energizer, intensifier, amplifying means, multiplier **~ mit magnetischer Koppelung** transformer-, resistance-, or inductance-repeating amplifier **~ mit Phasenumkehrung** paraphase amplifier **~ mit 90° Phasenverschiebung** quadrature amplifier **~ mit zwei gegeneinander geschalteten Röhren** push-pull amplifier **~ mit negativem Widerstand** kalliotron, dynatron tube with negative resistance **einen ~ löschen** to turn off a repeater **~ zünden** to turn on a repeater
Verstärker, ausgeglichener ~ balanced amplifier **detonierender ~** heterodyne amplifier **entzerrender ~** equalizing amplifier **fest eingeschalteter ~** amplifier permanently in circuit **gegengekoppelter ~** feedback amplifier **linearer ~** linear amplifier **mehrstufiger ~** multistage amplifier **modulierter ~** modulated amplifier **rückgekoppelter ~** feed-back amplifier **summierender ~** integrating amplifier **untersetzender ~** scaling-down vacuum tube **zweistufiger ~** two-stage amplifier
Verstärker-abschnitt *m* repeater section **-abstand** *m* repeater spacing **-amt** *n* repeater station, amplifying relay station **-anlage** *f* amplifier installation **-anordnung** *f* arrangement of amplifier (repeaters) **-betrieb** *m* (telephonic) repeater operation **-brett** *n* amplifier rack, amplifier panel **-bucht** *f*, **-bunker** *m* amplifier or repeater rack or bay
Verstärkerdose für Kreiselkompaß gyrocompass repeater box
Verstärker-einheit *f* repeater unit **-einschub** *m* amplifier unit **-feld** *n* repeater section **-folie** *f* intensifying screen **-geräusch** *n* vacuum-tube noise, amplifier noise **-gestell** *n* repeater rack, amplifier mounting or frame **-gestellreihe** *f* repeater bay **-gleichrichter** *m* amplifying detector **-kette** *f* amplifier cascade **-lampe** *f* valve, (amplifier) lamp, amplifier valve, amplifier bulb **-netz** *n* amplifier channel **-platz** *m* repeater place **-rohr** *n*, **-röhre** *f* thermionic relay, amplifier valve, amplifying tube **-röhrenfassung** *f* amplifying-tube socket
Verstärker-saal *m* repeater room **-satz** *m* (basic) repeater unit **-schaltung** *f* repeater circuit **-schirm** *m* intensifying screen **-schrank** *m* amplifier rack **-stöpsel** *m* amplifier plug **-stufe** *f* intensifier stage, intermediate circuit **-transformator** *m* amplifier transformer
Verstärker-wirkung *f* amplification effect of the electron tube **-zug** *m* amplifier chain
verstärkt concentrated, amplified, strengthened, reinforced **-e Förderung** increased output **-es Glas** reinforced glass **-e Matrize** backed stamper **-er Träger** trussed gland **-er Zug** forced draft
Verstärkung strengthening, reinforcement; (Radio) amplification transmission gain, building up **~ Eins** unity gain **~ des Photostromes** amplification (gain) of the photocurrent; intensification, aggravation, gain, magnification, stiffening, splicing (textiles), stand-by **~ der Messer** thickening of the blades **die ~ erhöhen** to increase the gain **die ~ herabsetzen** to reduce the gain **lineare ~** linear amplification **mehrstufige ~** multistage amplification **verzerrungsfreie ~** amplifying without distortion **zeitabhängig geregelte ~** time-varied gain
verstärkungsabhängig dependent on the gain
Verstärkungs-abfall *m* loss of gain **-automatik** *f* automatic gain control **-balken** *m* stiffening rib **-batterie** *f* auxiliary battery **-begrenzer** *m* output limiter or suppressor, gain spoiler **-bereich** *m* amplification range **-blech** *n* stiffening sheet or plate, reinforcement plate **-einlage** *f* reinforcing strengthener (dentistry) **-fadenführer** *m* splicing guide
Verstärkungsfaktor *m* amplification factor, amplification constant **~ (zwischen zwei Elektroden)** voltage factor
Verstärkungs-feder *f* reinforcing spring **-folie** *f* intensifying screen
Verstärkungsgrad *m* power-amplification rate, repeater gain, degree of amplification **~ der Eingangsstufe** gain of input stage **~ und Modulationsbreite** gain and modulation width
Verstärkungsgrad *m* power-amplification rate, repeater gain, degree of amplification **~ der Eingangsstufe** gain of input stage **~ und Modulationsbreite** gain and modulation width
Verstärkungs-gradmessung *f* repeater gain measurements **-konstante** *f* amplification factor, amplification constant **-kurve** *f* amplification curve **-lasche** *f* flitch plate **-maß** *n* repeater gain (equivalent), amplification in nepers **-meßeinrichtung** *f* gain set **-messer** *m* repeater-gain measuring set, gain set **-messung** *f* gain measurement **-pfeiler** *m* counterfort **-platte** *f* reinforcing plate
Verstärkungs-regler *m* gain controler **-reglung** *f* adjustment of (repeater) gain, gain control, automatic volume control **-riegel** *m* pole brace **-ring** *m* reinforcing ring **-rippe** *f* feather, rib, strengthening or reinforcing rib **-scheitelfactor** *m* amplification or apex factor **-schirm** *m* intensifying screen (X-ray work) **-sohle** *f* reinforcing pad
Verstärkungs-steg *m* reinforcing web **-strebe** *f* stiffening brace, buckstay (for condenser box) **-streifen** *m* stiffener **-stufe** *f* amplification stage, amplifier stage **-überschuß** *m* (repeater) gain **-unterdrücker** *m* gain spoiler, output suppressor
Verstärkungs-verhältnis *n* voltage magnification, power amplification ratio **-verlauf** *m* gain characteristics **-wagen** *m* transformer truck (elec.) **-winkel** *m* angle stiffener **-wirkung** *f* amplification (effect) **-zahl** *f* amplification coefficient, amplification factor, amplification constant **-zeiger** *m* gain set **-ziffer** *f* voltage magnification, amplification coefficient
verstäuben to atomize (dust)
Verstäuben *n* dusting
Verstäuber *m* atomizer
Verstaubungsgefahr *f* danger of becoming dusty

Verstäubungsverlust *m* dust loss
Verstauchung *f* strain, sprain
verstauen to stow
Verstauen *n* stowage
Versteck *n* hiding place **-bolzen** *m* cotter bolt **-farbe** *f* duster
verstecken to conceal, hide, reset **sich ~** to disappear
Versteckhaspel *m* independent drum hoist
versteckt concealed, hidden, latent, insincere
verstehen to understand
versteifen to stiffen, strengthen, reinforce, shore up, brace, strut, prop **Schlacke ~** to thicken up slag
Versteifer *n* antisoftener (for rubber)
Versteifung *f* stiffening, strengthening, reinforcement, propping, strut, bracing
Versteifungs-balken *m* stiffening beam **-bügel** *m* stiffening strap **-draht** *m* shrouding wire **-kiel** *m* stiffening girder, suspension keel **-ring** *m* stiffening ring (coupling) **-rippe** *f* bracing rib, stiffening rib (aviation) **-schiene** *f* vertical brace **-träger** *m* crossbeam **-winkeleisen** *n* stiffening angle iron
Versteigerung *f* auction sale
Versteigerungs-bedingung *f* condition of auction **-bekanntmachung** *f* notice of sale by auction **-termin** *m* date of receipt of tenders
versteinern to petrify
versteinert petrified
Versteinerung *f* fossil, mineralization, petrifaction
Versteinerungsmittel *n* mineralizing agent
Versteinung *f* devitrification (glass), petrifaction
Verstell-achse *f* adjusting axle **-anzeiger** *m* pitch-change indicator **-backe** *f* adjusting jaw
verstellbar adjustable, controllable, movable, featherable **am Boden ~** adjustable on ground **vom Führersitz aus ~** adjustable from the cockpit **der Höhe nach ~** movable vertically **mit -er Steigung** with variable pitch **-e Ackeregge** peg-tooth harrow **-er Antrieb** movable drive **-e Flugschraube** two-position propeller **-er Führersitz** adjustable pilot's seat **-e Höhenflosse** adjustable tail plane **-e Luftschraube** feathering propeller, variable-pitch propeller, controllable-pitch propeller **-e Riemenspannvorrichtung** adjustable belt tightener **-er Schlüssel** adjustable wrench **-er Schraubenschlüssel** monkey wrench **-es Winkellineal** bevel
Verstellbarkeit *f* adjustability
Verstell-bereich *m* pitch range, range of adjustment, timing range **-bock** *m* adjusting bracket **-brett** *n* adjuster board **-diffusor** *m* adjustable diffusor **-düse** *f* adjustable nozzle **-einrichtung** *f* setting mechanism
verstellen to adjust, displace, shift, move, transpose **in Seite und Höhe ~** to traverse and elevate
Verstellen *n* shifting **~ des Zündzeitpunktes** sparking advance
Versteller *m* timing device (ignition)
Verstell-flosse *f* adjustable tail, plane or surface **-flügel** *m* variable incidence wing **-gebläse** *n* variable-pitch fan **-geschwindigkeit** *f* variable control rate, speed of rotation **-gestänge** *n* adjusting linkage **-getriebe** *n* control gear **-gitter** *n* adjustable guide vane
Verstellhebel *m* governor level **-anschlag** *m* adjusting lever stop **-befestigung** *f* adjusting (or control or timing) lever fastening
Verstellkraft *f* regulating power, adjusting power **~ einer Regelvorrichtung** power of a control device
Verstell-leiste *f* adjusting ledge **-linie** *f* (Zündung) timing curve **-linienaufnahme** *f* plotting of timing-curve **-möglichkeit** *f* adjustability **-moment** *m* trimming moment **-motor** *m* brush-shifting motor **-organ** *n* adjusting part, motor operator (Servo)
Verstell-pilz *m* mushroom-type valve, turnip-shaped valve **-profil** *n* variable camber wing profile or section
Verstellpropeller *m* feathered (variable-pitch) propeller, controllable pitch propeller **~ in Segelstellung bringen** to feather a propeller **druckölgesteuerter ~** hydrocontrollable propeller
Verstellquerschnitt *m* variable camber wing profile or section **-regler** *m* variable speed governor **-ring** *m* adjusting coller, ring **-schlüssel** *m* adjusting spanner (wrench)
Verstellschraube *f* variable-pitch propeller, controllable airscrew **~ gleichbleibender Drehzahl** constant-speed airscrew **~ für Segelstellung** full-feathered propeller **~ mit zwei Steigungsstellungen** two-position controllable airscrew
verstellt out of adjustment
Verstellturbinengitter *n* adjustable turbine or nozzle vanes
Verstellung *f* adjustment, regulation, shift, reiteration, displacement **~ der Mittellast** adjustment for static load **~ in Polhöhe** polar adjustment **~ in Segelstellung** feathering operation **feine ~** slow motion **maximale ~** high pitch **~ des Zündzeitpunktes** ignition timing control
Verstell-vorrichtung *f* adjusting device, shifter pitch-control mechanism **-weg** *m* adjusting path (timing path) **-welle** *f* control shaft (aviat.) **-winkel** *m* angle or degree of adjustment **-winkelhalter** *m* all-angle bracket **-zapfen** *m* adjusting pin **-zylinder** *m* pitchoperating cylinder
verstemmen to wedge over, pry over, tamp, stop, plug, calk, peen over
Verstemmen *n*, **Verstemmung** *f* calking, fullering
verstemmtes Niet caulked rivet
versteuern to pay duty
versteuert duty paid
versticken to nitrogenize
Verstickstahl *m* nitrided steel
verstiften to pin
Verstiftung *f* pinned fitting
verstimmbar detunable
Verstimmbarkeit *f* detunability
verstimmen to detune, to be out of tune
Verstimmen *n* detuning, mistuning
verstimmt detuned, out of tune, dissonant, untuned; disharmonious, dissyntonized, tuned off resonance **~ sein** to be out of tune **-e Antenne** dumb aerial **-e Kreise** *pl* staggered circuits (Video)
Verstimmung *f* detuning, mistuning **ungedämpftes Senden mit ~** compensated continuous-wave transmission

Verstimmungs-blindleitung *f* detuning stub **-kondensator** *m* cutoff tuning condenser **-schalter** *m* wave(length) changing switch **-welle** *f* compensation wave, spacing wave

verstocken to mold, harden, become stubborn

verstopfen to stop, plug, choke, clog, obstruct, caulk, block, become choked, become clogged, incrust (spinnerets), stopper **Fugen ~** to calk

Verstopfen, vorzeitiges ~ des Trennungsapparates precocious clogging of the separating apparatus

verstopft congested, clogged, stopped up, choked **~ werden** to clog

Verstopfung *f* choking, clogging, obstruction, congestion, blocking, lock, incrustation (of spinneret), blockage, obturation, occlusion **~ durch Dampfblasen** vapor lock

Verstoß *m* irregularity, offense, infringement

verstoßen to infringe, break, expell, reject

verstrahlen to emit radiate

verstreben to stay, reinforce, prop, strut, brace

Verstreben *n* propping, strutting

verstrebt strut-braced **-er Flügel** strutted or braced wing **-er Zeiger** truss pointer **-e Zelle** strut-braced wing

Verstrebung *f* strutting, reinforcement, prop, propping, staying, strut, bracing, backstay **~ von Gestängen** push bracing

Verstreckbarkeit *f* stretchability

verstrecken to stretch out of its natural shape

Verstreichbürste *f* distributing brush

verstreichen to fill or stop up, calk, spread or coat over, smooth, float, elapse, expire, paint, pass by **wieder ~** to repaint

Verstreichen der Fugen pointing

Verstreich-rakel *n* levelling doctor **-rauhmaschine** *f* water or laying down gig **-verfahren** *n* (Klebstoff) preliminary coating process

verstreut dispersed, scattered

verstricken to entangle

verstümmeln to mutilate, alter, maim, obliterate, clip

verstümmelte Fernmeldung garbled message

Verstümmelung *f* mutilation **~** (eines Spruchs) garble

verstürzen to fall to pieces, scatter

Versuch *m* test, trial, run, experiment, attempt, assay, effort, research **~ anstellen** to experiment **~ mit Plombit** doctor test (petroleum) **vergleichender ~** comparative test **wissenschaftlicher ~** experiment **~ mit zweifacher HF-Einstrahlung** double irradiation experiment

versuchen to test, experiment, try (out), attempt

Versuchsabbruchentscheidung *f* experiment decision procedure (reliability)

Versuchs-abteilung *f* experimental department **-aggregat** *n* experimental or test missile **-anlage** *f* testing plant, trial installation, experimental plant, pilot plant **-anordnung** *f* methods of testing, procedure, experimental arrangement **-anstalt** *f* testing laboratory, experimental plant, experiment station **-arbeit** *f* testing work **-aufbau** *m* test setup **-aufgabenerteilung** *f* experimental release **-aufschreibung** *f* logging the results of tests, test log **-auswertung** *f* method of plotting fatigue test results, test evaluation

Versuchs-bahn *f* test track or path **-ballon** *m* sounding balloon **-bank** *f* test bench **-bedingungen** *pl* test conditions **-bericht** *m* test sheet **-betriebsstufe** *f* experimental works level **-bild** *n* proof **-breite** *f* space of experiments (reliability)

Versuchs-dauer *f* duration of test **-durchführung** *f* method of test **-einrichtung** *f* testing installation, setup **-ergebnis** *n* test result, result of trial or experiment **-erlaubnis** *f* experimenter's license **-fahrt** *f* trial run **-fehler** *m* error of test, error of measurement, experimental error **-feld** *n* proving ground, field for making tests and experiments **-flamme** *f* test flame **-flieger** *m* test pilot **-flug** *m* test flight, experimental flight **-flugzeug** *n* test plane, experimental plane

Versuchs-folge *f* experimental sequence, set of experiments **-funkstelle** *f* experimental radio station **-gegenstand** *m* experimental object **-gestell** *n* test rack, test stand, trial frame **-gipfelhöhe** *f* practical or absolute ceiling **-grundlage** *f* range of tests **-ingenieur** *m* research engineer **-kanal** *m* test hole **-körper** *m* soil sample, test specimen **-laboratorium** *n* experimental laboratory, research laboratory **-last** *f* proof load, proof weight **-lauf** *m* first or test run **-lizenz** *f* experimenter's license **-luftlinie** *f* model airway

Versuchs-maschine *f* experimental engine **-mäßig** experimental **-material** *n* test material, experimental material **-methode** *f* method of testing, experimental method **-modell** *n* test model **-motor** *m* experimental engine **-muster** *n* experimental type **-ordnung** *f* order of experiment **-person** *f* patient **-protokoll** *n* log sheet, test log **-raum** *m* laboratory, room for experiments **-rechnung** *f* trial calculation **-reihe** *f* series of experiments, tests or trials **-reihenfolge** *f* program of experimental work **-röhrchen** *n* test tube

Versuchs-schacht *m* prospecting shaft **-schaltung** *f* circuit model **-schießen** *n* test firing **-serie** *f* series of experiments or tests **-stab** *m* test rod or bar **-stadium** *n* experimental stage **-stand** *m* testing stand or bed **-station** *f* research station **-stätte** *f* laboratory **-stelle** *f* experimental or testing station, testing establishment **-strecke** *f* exploring drift, trial track, measuring or experiment chamber **-stück** *n* test specimen, test piece, sample **-tätigkeit** *f* test work **-tier** *n* animal used for vivisection

Versuchs-träger *m* test stand **-verbindung** *f* test call **-vorschriften** *pl* testing directions

versuchsweise experimental(ly) **~ aufgestellte Norm** tentative standard

Versuchswert *m* experimental datum, test result

Versuchung *f* temptation, research experiment **in ~ bringen** to tempt

Versud *m* boiling or heating process

versudeln to soil

versumpft swampy, boggy

Versumpfung *f* flooding

versüßen to sweeten

Versüßungsmittel *n* sweetening chemical

vertäfeln to wainscot

Vertäfelung *f* wainscoting

Vertagung *f* adjournment, postponement

Vertakelung *f* rigging

Vertaubung *f* exhaustion, impoverishment (ore)

vertauen to moor **sich an einer Boje ~** to get

hold of a buoy **sich am Lande ~** to make fast to shore
Vertäumast *m* mooring mast
vertauschbar exchangeable, interchangeable
Vertauschbarkeit *f* interchangeability
vertauschen to interchange, permute, cross, transpose, exchange
Vertauschungsformal *f* commutation formula
Vertauschung *f* permutation, interchange, crossing, transposition, exchange
Vertauschungs-regel *f* commutation rule **-relation** commutation relation
Vertäuung *f* mooring gear, shore fast
Vertäuungspoller *m* mooring bollard
Vertäuungswinde *f* mooring winch
verteeren to tar
Verteerung *f* tarring
Verteerungszahl *f* tar value
Verteilbleimuffe *f* multiple lead cable joint
verteilen to distribute, divide, spread, apportion, peptize (chem.), disseminate, space, disperse, diffuse, scatter **von neuem ~** to redistribute
Verteiler *m* distributor, distribution frame, manifold, check table **~ mit springenden Funken** distributor with jumping sparks, jump-gap or gap-type distributor **~ des Magnetapparates** magneto distributor **drehender ~** rotating feeder **korrigierender ~** correcting or controlling distributor **mehrwegiger ~** multichannel distributor **umlaufender ~** rotary distributor
Verteiler-achse *f* distributor shaft **-amt** *n* multioffice system **-anlage** *f* distributor system **-antrieb** *m* universal drive **-antriebsspindel** *f* distributor driving spindle **-arm** *m* distributor arm **-bahnhof** *m* regulating station **-band** *n* (Versatzvorrichtung) feed drum **-bock** *m* distributor stand **-bürste** *f* distributor finger or brush
Verteiler-deckel (Motor) distributor cover **-dose** *f* junction box with plugs (radar), distributor cap **-draht** *m* jumper wire (teleph.) **-einrichtung** *f* distributing facilities **-entstörstecker** *m* suppressor plug for distributor **-feld** *n* distribution panel **-finger** *m* distributor arm **-getriebe** *n* power-drive transmission, distributor gear **-gleitbahn** *f* distributor track **-gleitlager** *n* distributor sleeve bearing
Verteiler-kabel *n* twin lead (tape rec.) **-kappe** *f* distributor cap **-kasten** *m* distribution box, terminal box, junction box **-klemmbrett** *n* terminal distribution board **-klemme** *f* distributor terminal **-kolben** *m* distributor or control piston **-kopf** *m* distributor head (engine) **-läufer** *m* distributor rotor **-laufstück** *n* distributor rotor or arm **-leiste** *f* distributor link **-leitung** *f* induction manifold, distribution conduit **-nocken** *n* distributor cam
Verteiler-platte *f* distributor plate **-relais** *n* switching relay **-ring** *m* distributor ring, crown **-rohr** *n* manifold **-scheibe** *f* distributor plate, face, head, or plateau **-schleifkontakt** *m* contact piece **-schrank** *m* distributing switchboard
Verteiler-segment *n* distributor segment **-seite** *f* jumper side **-stelle** *f* distributing point **-streife** *f* branch strip **-system** *n* call-distributing system **-tafel** *f* distributor board **-ventil** *n* diversion valve **-welle** *f* distributor shaft, timing shaft **-werk** *n* switching station, distributing substation **-zahnrad** *n* distributor cam, bossed cam, bossed wheel, distributor cogwheel
Verteil-fernamt *n* (telephone) distribution or group or zone, center, switching point **-kasten** *m* distribution terminal **-leitung** *f* distributor main **-netz** *n* distribution network **-rohr** *n* spider (petroleum) **-stück** (-Rohr) distribution header **-schiene** *f* (elektr.) distributing bar
verteilt distributed **fein ~** suspended, in continuous phase **gleichmäßig ~** evenly or continuously distributed **punktförmig ~** distributed in lumps, lumped **stetig ~** evenly or uniformly distributed **punktförmig -e Ladung** lumped capacity, concentrated capacity, lump(ed) loading **-e Induktion, -e Induktivität** distributed inductance, continuous loading **-e Kapazität** stray capacity (of wiring), distributed capacitance, self-capacitance **-e Wicklung** distributed winding
Verteil-teller *m* distributor plate **-trichter** *m* distributor, distributing device
Verteilung *f* distribution, division, dissemination, spacing, dispersion (of pigments), dissipation (of energy), allotment, partition **~ der Anrufe** call distribution **~ der Feuer** disposition of lights **~ der Gewinnrücklage des Schmutzes** dispersion of impurities **~ der Gewinnrücklage des Neutronenflusses** neutron flux distribution **~ des Verkehrs in einer bestimmten Zeit** incidence of traffic over a period **feine ~** minute distribution **feine ~ in einer Lösung** suspension **offene ~** radial distribution **man findet die ~ . . . zu** the distribution . . . is found as **unterschiedliche ~** skew distribution
Verteilungs-anlage *f* relay equipment, distribution gear **-arm** *m* distributing arm, distribution arm **-art** *f* method of distribution **-breite** *f* width of distribution (of pressure) **-eisen** *n* spacer bar, distribution reinforcement **-erlaubnis** *f* distribution license **-gesellschaft** *f* distribution company **-gesetz** *n* distribution law, partition law **-gitter** *n* distribution grid **-grad** *m* degree of distribution **-heft** *n* line records
Verteilungs-kabel *n* distribution cable **-kammer** *f* slide valve **-kanal** *m* trough for distribution cable **-kappe** *f* convection cap **-kasten** *m* distribution box or case, breast box **-konstante** *f* distribution or partition constant or coefficient **-kopf** *m* manifold **-lizenz** *f* distribution license **-mast** *m* distributing pole **-methode** *f* method of distribution, assignment method **-netz** *n* distribution network
Verteilungs-platte *f* division plate, baffle plate, partition or distribution plate, shock-dispersing beam or baffle **-punkt** *m* distributing point **-rohr** *n* intake manifold **-röhre** *f* distributing casing, distributing pipe **-satz** *m* principle of distribution, distribution law **-schieber** *m* distributing valve **-schiene** *f* distributing bus bar, distributing lens bar **-schlüssel** *m* basis for allocation **-schrank** *m* distributing cabinet **-schurre** *f* distributing chute **-sicherung** *f* distributing fuse **-stab** *m* distributing rod
Verteilungs-stelle *f* distributing agency **-system** *n* dissipative system **-tafel** *f* distributing board **-turm** *m* distributing tower **-vermögen** *n* distributing capacity (elec.) **-wert** *m* value of distribution **-winkel** *m* angle of distribution (of pressure)

Verteilzeit *f* delay allowance **-zuschlag** *m* delay allowance

vertiefen to deepen, dish, hollow

vertieft sunk **-e Fuge** recessed pointing **-e Schrift** sunk characters

Vertiefung *f* deepening, depression, cavity, recess, indentation, pit, dimple **~ des Fahrwassers** deepening of the channel **kleine ~** dimple **mit ~ versehen** to recess

vertikal vertical **-e Auswanderungsstrecke** vertical component of target travel during time of flight of projectile **-er Bildfang** vertical hold **-er Koksofen** vertical(-flue) coke oven **-e Luftströmungen** vertical wind currents **-e Querneigung** vertical bank (aviation) **-er Zwischenraum** vertical interval

Vertikal-ablenkung *f* vertical deflection **-abtastung** *f* vertical sweep **-achse** *f* vertical axis **-anemometer** *n* vertical anemometer **-antenne** *f* vertical wire aerial **-antriebswelle** *f* vertical driving shaft **-auflösung** *f* vertical definition **-aufnahme** *f* vertical photograph **-ausbreitung** *f* vertical diffusion

Vertikalbalken-generator *m* vertical-bar oscillator (TV) **-regler** *m* V bar control (TV)

Vertikalbewegung *f* downfeed (engin.), vertical motion **langsame ~** creeping **Anschlag für die ~** stop for downfeed **Einstellung der ~** downfeed adjustment **Klemmschraube für die ~** clamp for downfeed

Vertikal-bö *f* vertical gust **-bohrmaschine** *f* vertical boring mill, vertical drilling machine, upright drill **-diagramm** *n* vertical-plane directional pattern, elevation field pattern (ant.)

Vertikale *f* vertical **~ des Rahmens** upright of frame (of gate) **obere ~ des Wehrbocks** upright on upstream side of frame

Vertikal-ebene *f* vertical plane **-faden** *m* vertical wire, or thread **-flosse** *f* stabilizer **-fräsmaschine** *f* vertical milling machine **-frequenz** *f* vertical frequency **-führung** *f* vertical guide **-geschwindigkeit** *f* vertical component of speed **-hinlauf** *m* vertical scansion **-illuminator** *m* vertical illuminator **-intensität** *f* vertical force, earth's vertical field, vertical component of earth's magnetic field **-kammerofen** *m* vertical-chamber oven, vertical-flue oven **-komponente** *f* vertical component

Vertikal-kraftwaage *f* vertical dynamic balance or force scale **-kreis** *m* vertical circle **-lage** *f* vertical position **-magazin** *n* vertical magazine **-navigation** *f* vertical guidance, vertical navigation **-parallaxenschlitten** *m* vertical-parallax slide **-projektion** *f* vertical projection, elevation **-richtung** *f* vertical direction **-schaltgetriebe** *n* head-feed gear **-schaltspindel** *n* down-feed screw **-schnitt** *m* vertical section, elevation **-seismograph** *m* vertical seismograph **-sichtfernrohr** *n* vertical sighting or view telescope

Vertikal-strom *m* air-earth current **-synchronisierung** *f* vertical synchronization **-teilapparat** *m* vertical index head **-transport** *m* vertical conveyance **-verband** *m* vertical brace **-vorschubspindel** *f* vertical feed rod **-vorschubzahnrad** *n* vertical feed pinion **-walze** *f* vertical roll **-wechsel** *m* vertical or frame synchronizing pulse or cycle **-welle** *f* vertical driving shaft **-winkel** *m* vertical angle **-zug** *m* vertical flue

Vertikant *m* yaw and roll gyroscope

Vertilgung *f* destruction

vertonte Oberfläche sound-impressed surface

Vertonung *f* formation of clay, transformation of material into clay; setting to music

Vertonnung *f*, **hölzerne ~** wooden lining

Vertorfung *f* formation of peat

Vertrag *m* treaty, contract, agreement, bargain, convention **einen ~ abschließen** to make or conclude a contract **einen ~ schließen** to contract, agree

vertragen, sich ~ mit to agree with (blend well)

verträglich compatible, consistent, contractual (bound by contract)

Verträglichkeit *f* compatibilitiy, tolerance

Vertrags-abschluß *m* contract of agreement **-abschrift** *f* copy of contract **-bedingungen** *pj* conditions of contract **-bestätigung** *f* ratification of treaty **-bruch** *m* violation or breach of contract **-brüchig werden** to break a contract

Vertragschließender *m* contractor

Vertrags-dauer *f* life(time) of a patent (of an agreement) **-entwurf** *m* draft agreement **-mäßig** according to contract **-partei** *f* party to contract, contractant

Vertrags-spediteur *m* contract carriers **-staat** *m* contracting state **-strafe** *f* penalty for breach of contract **-verbindlichkeit** *f* contractual obligation **-werkstatt** *f* contractual repair shop

vertragswidrig contrary to agreement

Vertrauens-bereich *m* (Qualitätskontrolle) confidence interval **-mann** *m* confidant, trusted agent, shop deputy **-sache** *f* confidential matter

vertraulich confidential, intimate, familiar

vertraut familiar, versed **~ machen** to familiarize, acquaint

vertreiben to dispel, remove, dislodge, drift

Vertreiben *n* drift, leeway

vertreten to represent

Vertreter *m* representative agent, salesman

Vertretung *f* representation

Vertretungsvollmacht *f* power of attorney

Vertrieb *m* distribution, sale, releasing, clearance

Vertriebs-abteilung *f* sales department **-ingenieur** *m* sales engineer **-kosten** *pl* selling expenses **-spanne** *f* marketing margin **-stelle** *f* distributor

vertrimmt out of trim (Radio)

Vertrocknung *f* drying (up), desiccation

verunreinigen to soil, pollute, contaminate, vitiate, adulterate

Verunreinigung *f* impurity, contamination, pollution, contaminant **~ der Luft** atmospheric pollution **stöchiometrische ~** stoichiometric impurity

Verunreinigungs-kern *m* impurity nucleus **-photoeffekt** *m* impurity photoconduction

verunstalten to deform, disfigure

verursachen to cause, produce, occasion, result in

vervielfachen to multiply, to copy (a text)

Vervielfacher *m* multiplier **-photozelle** *f* multiplier photoelectric cell **-zelle** *f* electron multiplier phototube, photoelectric electron-multiplier tube

Vervielfachung *f* multiplication

Vervielfachungsfaktor multiplication factor

vervielfältigen to reproduce, multiply, mimeograph, manifold

Vervielfältiger *m* multiplier, duplicator, copying machine
vervielfältigte Kopie mimeographed (engrossment) copy
Vervielfältigung *f* reproduction, mimeographed copy, accurate duplication, copying, printing (of film) **photomechanische ~** photoengraving
Vervielfältigungsapparat *m* copying or duplicating apparatus **graphischer ~** manifold writer
Vervielfältigungs-arbeit *f* manifolding work **-faktor** *m* multiplication factor **-farbe** *f* duplicating or printing ink **-kondensator** *m* condensor-type directcurrent multiplier **-oberfläche** *f* dynode **-punkt** *m* multiplication point **-röhre** *f* multiplier tube
vervierfachen to quadruple
Vervierfacher *m* quadrupler (Radio)
vervollkommnen to perfect, improve
Vervollkommnung *f* perfection, accomplishment
vervollständigen to complete
Vervollständigung *f* completion, completing, complement **zur ~** for the sake of completeness
verwachsen to coalesce, grow together
verwachsen deformed, intergrown, entangled **-er Boden** natural ground **-e Kohle** combined pieces of coal and shale
Verwachsenes *n* interstratified material (true middlings)
Verwachsung *f* intergrowth, intercrescence
Verwachsungsfläche *f* composition plane (geol.), composition surface (cryst.)
verwackeln to blur (photo)
Verwackeln *n* unsteadiness
verwackelt blurred, out of focus
Verwacklung *f* blurring, judder (Bildfunk)
verwahrlosen to spoil
Verwahrungs-depot *n* custody deposit **-vertrag** *m* deposit contract
verwalten to manage, administer
Verwalter *m* administrator, manager, head **~ einer öffentlichen Sprechstelle** public-telephone-station agent **~ des Vorratslagers** stockkeeper
Verwaltung *f* administration, management
Verwaltungs-abteilung *f* administrative department **-aufsicht** *f* administrative control **-ausschuß** *m* executive comittee **-beamter** *m* administrative official **-behörde** *f* administrative authority **-büro** *n* administrative office **-bezirk** *m* administrative district **-gebäude** *n* administration building **-gebiet** *n* administrative area **-offizier** *m* supply or warrant officer **-rat** *m* advisory board **-ratsversammlung** *f* board meeting **-vorschrift** *f* administrative regulations
Verwalzbarkeit *f* milling properties, malleability
verwalzen to roll, roll into
verwandelbar transformable, convertible, transmutable
Verwandelbarkeit *f* versatility
verwandeln to transform, convert, change, turn
Verwandlung *f* transformation, conversion, change, reduction, metamorphosis
Verwandlungsflugzeug *n* convertible aircraft
verwandt related, kin, allied
Verwärmung *f* absorption
verwaschen to wash, wash out, obliterate, blur
verwaschen (part.) obliterated (Bild), blurred
Verwaschen *n* washing **~ der Farbe** weakening the color
Verwaschung *f* smear
Verwaschungs-gebiet *n* confusion region (Fdr.) **-kurve** *f* washability curve **-zone** *f* region of interference, blurred zone, bleary zone, confusion zone (TV)
verwässern to water, dilute
verwässert drowned
Verwässerung *f* flooding (petroleum), dilution
verweben to interweave
verwechselbar interchangeable, reversible
verwechseln to confuse, mix up, mistake, exchange
Verwechselung *f* mistake, confusion, mix-up
Verwehung *f* draft of air, wind
verweigern to reject, refuse, decline
Verweigerung *f* refusal, denial
Verweilweg *m* tarrying path
Verweilzeit *f* duration, period of dwell
verweisen to refer to
Verweisung *f* reference
Verweisungs-auftrag *m* skip instruction **-brennstoff** *m* reference fuel **-buchstabe** *m* reference letter **-markierung** *f* pencil marking; reference mark (rdr)
verwendbar available, usable, applicable, adaptable
Verwendbarkeit *f* usability, usefulness, utility, utilization, adaptability **vielseitige ~** versatility of service
verwenden to employ, apply, use, utilize
Verwendung *f* use, usage, utilization, application **~ des Abfalls** trash disposal **~ auf der Strecke** field use
Verwendungs-bereich *m* adaptability, field of application **-dauer** *f* period of use **-fähigkeit** *f* usefulness, employability, applicability, usability **-form** *f* form of use **-gebiet** *n* area of application **-karte** *f* qualification card **-möglichkeit** *f* range of use, variety of uses, possibility of use **-zweck** *m* applicability, duty, use, purpose
verwerfen to reject, abandon, disregard, repudiate, warp, distort, displace, twist, discard
Verwerfung *f* rejection, dislocation (min.), throw, slip, fault, faulting, break, repudiation, warping, deformation, shift (elec), thrust (geol) **gewöhnliche ~** normal fault (geol.)
Verwerfungs-kluft *f* fault, slide **-lette** *f* gouge **-linie** *f* fault line **-tal** *n* fault valley (geol.)
verwertbar utilizable
Verwertbarkeit der Wärme availability of heat
Verwertbarmachung einer Erfindung constructive reduction to practice
verwerten to utilize
Verwertung *f* utilization, use
Verwertungs-anlage *f* utilizing plant **-periode** *f* evaluation period, utilization period
Verwesung *f* putrefaction, decay
Verwetterung *f* weathering
verwickeln to tangle; **sich ~** (Drähte) entangle
verwickelt complicated, involved, complex, intricate **-er Draht** swaged wire **~ gestaltetes Modell** pattern of intricate external shape
Verwickelung *f* complication
verwiegen to weigh out **sich ~** to weigh wrongly
verwindbarer Flügel warping or winding wing
verwinden to twist, subject to torsional force, warp

Verwinde-probe *f* torsion test **-versuch** *m* twisting test

Verwindung *f* torsion, twist, distortion, rotary bending, warping **~ einer Raumkurve** twisting of a curve in space **negative ~ eines Flügels** wash out **positive ~ eines Flügels** wash in

verwindungsfrei distortion-free, faultless

Verwindungs-hebel *m* warping lever, warp control **-klappe** *f* wing flap, aileron **-probe** *f* twisting test **-seil** *n* warping wire or cable **-versuch** *m* torsion test **-winkel** *m* swirl angle **-zahl** *f* coefficient of warp

verwirbelt turbulent

Verwirbelung *f* vorticity, turbulence

verwirken to forfeit

verwirklichen to realize

Verwirklichung *f* implementation

Verwirklichungsform *f* form of construction, practical embodiment (of an invention)

verwirren to tangle, perplex, embarrass, confuse, bewilder

Verwirrung *f* confusion, disorder, trouble

Verwirrungsgebiet *n* nuisance area (Radio), interference range

verwischen to slur, smear, wipe out, obliterate, obscure, efface, blur

Verwischung *f* blur

verwittern to weather, disintegrate, effloresce

verwittertes Gestein decomposed rock

Verwitterung *f* weathering, decay, surface disintegration, efflorescence **~ der Oberfläche** surface weathering **stufenförmige ~** degradation

verwitterungsfähig disintegrable

Verwitterungsboden *m*, **unreifer ~** immature residual soil

Verwitterungs-gebilde *n* product of disintegration **-kruste** *f* crust of weathered material **-messer** *m* weatherometer **-produkt** *n* result of weathering **-rückstand** *m* residuum of weathered rocks, decomposed residuum **-schicht** *f* layer of weather-worn material

verworfen heaved **~ sein** to take a heave **-es Gestein** fault block

verworrenfaserig reticulate, fibrous (geol.)

verwundbar vulnerable

verwunden twisted **kalt ~** twisted while cold **-es Rad** buckled wheel

Verwurf *m* skipping (geol.)

verwürfeln to jumble, barble, scramble (Aut. Tel.)

Verwürfelungsschlüssel *m* jumble code

verwürgen to twist (together)

verwurzeln to take roots in

verwüsten to devastate

Verwüstung *f* devastation

verzählen to miscount

verzahnen to indent, tooth, gear, cog, joggle with (gear) teeth, serrate

Verzahnen *n* cutting the teeth

verzahnt indented, geared **-er Balken** joggled beam **-e Räder** geared wheels **-e Teilfuge** serrated joint **außen -es Zahnrad** external gear

Verzahnung *f* gear-tooth system, tooth construction, cogging, toothing, gearing, key, serration, gear, denticulation **gehauene ~** chiselled toothing **gesperrte ~** locked teeth **konische oder schiefe ~** bevel gear

Verzahnungs-arbeit *f* gear cutting work or operation **-fräser** *m* tooth-milling cutter **-genauigkeit** *f* tooth accuracy **-gesetz** *n* basic requirement of a gear tooth system **-maschine** *f* gear-cutting machine

verzapfen to mortise, joint, dispense by tap

Verzapfung *f* mortise joint

verzehren to dissipate (energy), consume, spend, abate (smoke)

verzehrend dissipative

Verzehrung *f* dissipation, corrosion

verzeichnen to deform, distort (optics), register

verzeichnet sein (auf Tabelle) to be tabulated

Verzeichnis *n* index, list, register, schedule, inventory, catalogue **~ der Vorlesungs- oder Prüfungsgegenstände** syllabus

Verzeichnung *f* distortion (phot.), poor drafting, faulty delineation or re-creation of a picture **~ einer Linse** lens distortion **anisotrope ~** anisotropic shear distortion **kissenförmige ~** cushion-shaped distortion, negative distortion **tonnenförmige ~** barrel-shaped distortion, positive distortion

Verzeichnungsfehler *m* error of distortion

verzeichnungsfrei orthoscopic, distortion-free

Verzeichnungs-freiheit *f* freedom from lens, distortion **-kurve** *f* curve of distortion **-unterschied** *m* differential distortion

verzerren to distort, contort, deform, strain

verzerrend distortional **-e Verlängerungsleitung** pad having distortion

Verzerrer *m* harmonic generator

verzerrt distorted **-e Nummernwahl** faulty selection **-e Tonwiedergabe infolge Übersteuerung** blasting

Verzerrung *f* distortion, contortion, deformation, strain **~ durch Einschwingvorgänge** transient distortion **~ durch Ein- und Ausschwingen** transient distortion, build-up and decay distortion **~ durch Feldkrümmung** distortion due to field curvature **lineare ~** linear distortion **nichtlineare ~** harmonic distortion, amplitude distortion, nonlinear distortion, wave-form distortion **stationäre ~** stationary distortion **ungradlinige ~** harmonic distortion, amplitude distortion, nonlinear distortion, wave-form distortion

verzerrungsfrei distortionless, nondistorting **-e Leitung** distortionless circuit **-es Mikrophon** distortionless microphone **-es Okular** orthoscopic eyepiece, distortion-free eyepiece

Verzerrungs-freiheit *f* absence of distortion **-konstante** *f* distortion constant **-leistung** *f* distortion power **-maß** *n* strain measure(ment) **-meßgerät** *n* transmission distortion measuring set (TDMS) **-messer** *m* distortion-measuring system **-messung** *f* distortion measurement **-tensor** *m* strain tensor **-toleranz** *f* tolerance of distortion **-verbreiterung** *f* distortion broadening

Verzicht *m* renunciation, resignation, abandonment, disclaimer, waiver **~ leisten** to renounce

verzichten abandon, drop, relinquish, disclaim, renounce, waive (rights) **~ auf** to grant exception to

Verzicht-erklärung *f* letter of renunciation **-leistung** *f* renunciation, resignation, abandonment, disclaimer, waiver

verziehen to distort, warp, buckle, strain, run out of true, shrink (steel)
Verziehen *n* distortion, warping, straining, buckling, drawing (dyes)
Verziehung *f* warpage, buckling
verzieren to decorate
Verzierung *f* ornament, decoration
Verzierungsfaden *m* ornamental thread
Verzierungsleisten an Geräten escutcheon, trimmings
verziffern to cipher, code
verzimmern to timber, plank, board, crib, line
Verzimmerung *f* boarding, timbering
verzinken to galvanize, zinc-plate, dovetail, joggle (aviation)
Verzinken *n* galvanizing, zinc coating, zinc plating
Verzinker *m* galvanizer
Verzinkerei *f* galvanizing plant, cold galvanizing
verzinkt galvanized, hot-galvanized, cold-galvanized, electroplated (with zinc), toothed **-es Blech** galvanized sheet metal **-es Eisenblech** galvanized steel plate
Verzinkung *f* galvanizing, galvanization
Verzinkungs-anlage *f* galvanizing plant **-bad** *n* galvanizing bath **-einrichtung** *f* zincing fittings **-ofen** *m* galvanizing furnace **-wanne** *f* galvanizing bath
verzinnen to tin
Verzinnen *n* tinning **kurzzeitiges oberflächliches galvanisches ~** flash tin-plating
Verzinnerei *f* tinning plant
verzinnt tinned, tin-plated **-er Draht** tinned wire **-es Eisenblech** tin plate, tinned iron sheet
Verzinnung *f* tinning, tin-plating
verzinsen to yield interest
Verzinsung *f* interest
verzogen distorted, warped, moved away
Verzögerer *m* slug, retarder, restrainer
verzögern to retard, delay, lag
verzögert retarded, delayed **-e Anziehung** slow operation **-e Auslösung** slow release **-e Kartenzuführung** delayed feed (cards) **-es Öffnen** delayed opening **-er Schutz** time-limit protection **-e Trennung** slow-release **-e Zeichengebung** delayed action alarm
Verzögerung *f* delay, delay action, retardation, lag, deceleration, negative acceleration, time lag, braking, checking **~ des Ausschlages** retardation of the deflection **~ bei der Beantwortung** speed of answer or answering interval **~ eines Impulses** pulse delay **thermische ~** thermal lag
verzögerungsarm having no appreciable time delay
Verzögerungs-bad *n* restraining bath **-demodulator** *m* delay demodulator **-dichte** *f* slowing down density **-druck** *m* retardation pressure **-einrichtung** *f* retarding device **-frei** inertialess, free from lag, delay, or sluggishness **-glied** *n* phase-shifting section, lag element
Verzögerungs-intervall *m* interval of retardation **-kette** *f* delay network **-kreis** *m* time-delay circuit **-leitungsregister** delay-line register **-leitung** *f* delay line **-linse** *f* cutoff or stopping (electron-optic) lens **-messer** *m* decelerometer **-mittel** *n* delayer **-motor** *m* time-delay motor
Verzögerungs-relais *n* slow-acting relay, copper-collar relay, coppered relay, slow-releasing relay, time-delay relay **-ring** *m* copper tube **-satz** *m* delay composition (explosives), delay pellet **-schalter** *m* delay switch, time-lag switch **-schütz** *n* time-delay relay **-spannung** *f* delay voltage, threshold bias, delayed-action voltage **-strecke** *f* delay line **-vorrichtung** *f* retarding mechanism
Verzögerungs-widerstand *m* timing resistance, retardation coil **-zeit** *f* time lag (relay) **-zeitkonstante** *f* time constant of time delay **-winkel** *m* angle of lag, retardation angle **-ziffer** *f* probability of delay, percentage of delayed calls **-zünder** *m* delay(ed)-action fuse **-zündung** *f* delayed ignition
verzollbar dutiable
verzollen to pay duty, clear
Verzollung *f* payment of duty, clearance (of goods)
Verzonung *f* zoning (Telegr.)
Verzonungskontakt *m* zone contact
verzuckern to saccharify
Verzug *m* distortion, warping, straining, delay, distortion, lagging, time delay; (Aufschub) retardation
verzugsfrei-e Fläche *f* deflection-free surface **-er Stahl** non deforming steel, non warping steel
Verzugs-getriebe *n* draft gear **-kosten** *pl* demurrage **-möglichkeit** *f* degree of draft **-rechner** *m* acoustic corrector (sound location) **-speicher** *m* delay line (acoustic) **-strafe** *f* penalty for delayed delivery
verzugstechnischer Vorteil advantage as to drafting
Verzugswechsel *m* draft change gear **-getriebe** *n* draft change wheel **-welle** *f* draft change shaft
Verzugs-zeit *f* dead time, delay time **-zinsen** *pl* interest payable on arrears **-zünder** *m* delay fuse **-zylinder** *m* draft cylinder
verzundern to flake, scale, exfoliate
Verzunderung *f* scaling
verzunderungsbeständig scaling-resistant
verzurren to clamp, seize
Verzurrstelle *f* lashing point
verzweigen to branch, derive **sich ~** to form branches
Verzweiger *m* distribution box or frame, divider
verzweigt branched **-e Ansaugleitung** induction manifold **-es Leitungssystem** manifold **-e Ströme** branched currents
Verzweigung *f* branching, tee, tap, by-pass, shunt branching (of transmutation products), ramification, fork; (Schnur) crotch **reflexionslose ~** matched junction
Verzweigungs-anteil *m* branching fraction **-glied** *n* (Heizung) branching link **-linie** *f* branch line
verzweigungslos non-branching
Verzweigungs-muffe *f* main sleeve for multiple joint, cable-distribution plug, multiple cable joint **-punkt** *m* split (point), branch(ing) point **-regel** *f* branching rule **-schaltung** *f* multiple connection **-schnitt** *m* branch line **-stromlinie** *f* branch-point stream line **-struktur** *f* lineage structure (crystals) **-stützpunkt** *m* junction pole **-verhältnis** *n* branching ratio **-wahrscheinlichkeit** *f* branching probability
verzwicken to bend or blunt the points (of nails), confuse, twist, distort, fill up the joints with

wedges or blocks
Verzwilligung *f* twinning (Kristall)
Vesiculographie *f* vesiculography
Vexier-artikel *m* puzzle article **-schloß** *n* puzzle or combination lock
V-Form *f* dihedral angle, dihedral **-motor** *m* V-type engine **-winkel** *m* dihedral
V-förmig V-shape or -type (engine), dihedral (aviation)
Viadukt *m* viaduct
Vibration *f* vibration
Vibrations-aufnahme *f* damping property **-dämpfung** *f* vibration absorption **-drahtbeschleunigungsmesser** *m* vibrating string accelerometer **-empfang** *m* reception with vibrating relay **-festigkeit** *f* vibration resistance **-freiheit** *f* absence of vibration **-galvanometer** *n* vibration galvanometer **-meßgerät** *n* vibrating reed instrument **-prüfstand** *m* vibration test stand
Vibrations-relais *n* vibrating relay **-rinne** *f* vibrating chute **-rüttler** *m* shaker **-schleifmaschine** *f* vibration sander **-schweißung** *f* pulsation welding **-schwelle** *f* vibrational threshold **-sieb** *n* vibration sifter, vibrating screen, screen riddle **-tastgerät** *n* vibrato-tactile device **-trommelschleifen** *n* vibratory (barrel) finishing
vibrations- und stoßdämpfende Lagerung shock and vibration control mounting
Vibrator *m* vibrator
vibrieren to vibrate, flutter
Vibrieren *n* vibration, flutter
vibrierend vibrating, vibratory
Vibriertisch *m* vibrating table, bench jolter (of core machine)
Vibrit *n* vibrite
Vibrograph *m* vibrograph, vibration-measuring apparatus
Vibro-meter *n* vibration meter **-pfahl** *m* vibro pile **-sichter** *m* (zum Entstäuben) vibrator-separator
Vicat-Nadel *f* Vicat needle
Vickershärte *f* Vickers hardness, diamond pyramid hardness
Vidalwagen *m* trailer (for missiles)
Video-Einblendung *f* video insertion
videofrequentes BA-Signal blanked video signal (BA)
Video-frequenz *f* video frequency **-gleichrichtung** *f* video detection **-kabel** *n* video signal cable **-signal** (TV) composite signal, video-signal
vieladrig multicore, multiwire **-es Kabel** multicore cable
vielatomiges Element polyatomic element
viel-deutig ambiguous, many-valued, multiform, non-equivocal **-doppelzackenschrift** *f* multiple double-edged variable-width track **-drahtzählrohr** *n* multi-wire counter **-drehbank** *f* multiple tool lathe **-druck** *m* cast
vieldüsiger Motor multinozzle motor
Viel-ebene *f* multiplane **-eck** *n* polygon
vieleckig polygonal, multiangular **-e Spule** polygonal coil
Vieleck-kokille *f* polygonal ingot mold **-schaltung** *f* mesh, polygon connection
vielfach in many cases, multiple, frequently, manifold, various, frequent **~ schalten** to multiply
Vielfach-abstimmgerät *n*, **-abstimmvorrichtung** *f* multiple tuner **-abtastung** *f* multiple scanning **-anschluß** *m* private branch exchange, junction, multiple connection **-anschlußdose** *f* multiple connection box **-antenne** *f* multiple antenna **-aufhängung** *f* multiple suspension **-beschleuniger** *m* cyclotron tube, betatron **-betrieb** *m* multiple operation **-dose** *f* multiple distribution box **-düse** *f* multiple nozzle **-echo** *n* multiple echo, flutter echo
Vielfaches *n* multiple **ganzes ~** integral multiple, whole multiple **gerades ~** even multiple **ungerades ~** odd multiple **das kleinste gemeinsame Vielfache** least common multiple
Vielfachfeld *n* multiple, multiple field, bank multiple **~ für die Erzeugung ungedämpfter Schwingungen** timed spark discharger
Vielfachfeld-drähte *m pl* bank wires **-kabel** *n* multiple cable
Vielfach-funkenstrecke *f* multiple spark discharger **-gerät** *n* multi-purpose appliance **-geschaltet** multiple-connected, connected in multiple, multipled (to) **-instrument** *n* multimeter, test set **-kabel** *n* multiple cable, bank cable **-kammer** *f* multiple camera **-klinke** *f* multiple jack **-klinkenfeld** *n* multiple-jack field
Vielfachkontakt *m* multiple contact **-feld** *n* multiple bank contact
Vielfach-konturen *pl* multiple outlines along edges of objects **-magnetron** *n* cavity magnetron **-manometer** *n* multiple-tubed manometer
Vielfachmeß- oder Prüfgerät *n* multitester
Vielfach-parallelklinke *f* parallel multiple jack **-punktschweißung** *f* multiple-electrode spot weld **-schalten** to multiple **-schalter** *m* multipoint switch, multiple pole switch
Vielfachschaltung *f* multiple connection, multipling **gerade ~** straight multiple **gestaffelte ~** overlapping multiple **verschränkte ~** slip multiple
Vielfach-schrank *m* multiple switchboard **-schreiber** *m* multiple-point recorder **-schwingungserzeuger** *m* multivibrator **-sicherungsdose** *f* multiple fuse box **-stecker** *m* manifold or multiple plug, polypole cable coupler **-steuerung** *f* multiple-unit control **-stoß** *m* multiple collision **-streuung** *f* multiple scattering **-telegraphie** *f* multiples telegraphy **-tonfrequenztelegraphie** *f* multichannel voice telegraphy **-übermittlung** *f* multiple transmission **-umschalter** *m* multiple switchboard **-unterbrechungsklinke** *f* series-multiple jack
Vielfach-verdrahtung *f* multiple wires, bank wiring **-verkabelung** *f* multiple cabling **-verkehr** *m* multiplex transmission **-verzögerer** *m* multiple retarder **-verzögerungsdiskriminator** *m* multiple delay discriminator **-verzweigung** *f* multiple branching **-zackenblende** *f* shutter for making multilateral sound track **-zackenschrift** *f* multilateral sound recording **-zeichengebung** *f* superimposed ringing **-zwillingskabel** *n* multiple twin cable **-zwillingsverseilung** *f* multiple twin formation
Viel-fall *m* multiplicity **-fältigkeit** *f* multiplicity, variety **-farbendruck** *m* polychromy **-farbig** multicolored, variegated, polychromatic **-flach** *n* polyhedron **-flächig** polyhedral **-gestaltig** multiform, manifold, diverse **-gestaltigkeit** *f* polymorphism

Vielfältigkeitsabwechslung *f* alternation of multiplicities
Vielfarbendruck-karton *m* multi-color printing card **-papier** *n* multi-color printing paper **-effekt** *m* multi-color effect
Vielfarbigkeit *f* diversity of colors
Vielfeldaufmerksamkeit *f* divided attention
Vielflächenverbindung *f* multiple face joint
Vielflachmantel *m* polyhedral surface
Vielflächner *m* polyhedron **-mantel** *m* polyhedral surface
vielförmiger Generator polymorphous generator
vielgliedrig polynomial (math.) **-er Kettenleiter** multimesh network
Vielgruppen multigroup
Vielhärtungsriß *m* heat crack
Vielholmflügel *m* multispar wing
Vielkammermagnetron *n* multisegment magnetron
Vielkanalübertragung *f* multichannel transmission
Vielkantscheibe *f* polyhedral mirror (of scanner)
vielkegelig polyconic
Vielkeilwelle *f* spline shaft
vielkernig multinuclear, polynuclear, polynucleate, polycyclic
Vielkörper-kraft *f* many-body force **-problem** *n* many-body problem **-verdampfapparat** *m* multiple-effect evaporator
Vielkristall *m* polycrystal
vielkuppelig multiple-domed
Viellinien-spektrum *n* discrete-band spectrum, many-line spectrum **-system** *n* many-lined system
Viellinge *m pl* conglomerate grain, crystal complexes
Viellinsenkamera *f* multiple-lens camera
viel-motorig multiengine, multimotor **-paarig** multipair **-phasig** polyphase **-polig** multipolar
Vielprobenmaschine *f* machine for simultaneous testing of several specimens
Vielpunktschweißmaschine *f* multispot-welding machine
Viel-radfahrzeug *n* convertible track-wheeled vehicle **-reihenmotor** *m* multibank engine **-röhrenkessel** *m* multitubular boiler
vielschichtig multiply, multilayered
Vielschlitzmagnetron *n* multi-segment magnetron
Vielschnittdrehbank *f* multicut lathe
vielseitig many-sided, manifold, polyhedral, versatile, extensive, comprehensive **-es Aufblasen** inflation manifold **-e Verwendbarkeit** versatility of service, manifold requirements
Vielsitzer *m* multiseater
Vielspiegelung *f* multiple of image
Vielspindel-futterautomat *m* multiple spindle chucking type, automatic lathe **-bohrmaschine** *f* multiple drilling machine **-kopf** *m* multiple-spindle head **-stangenautomat** *m* multiple spindle bartype, automatic lathe
Vielsprachenschreibmaschine *f* typewriter for several languages
Vielspurmagnetbandgerät *n* multi-channel recorder
Vielstahl-drehbank *f* multiple-cutter lathe **-halter** *m* multiple tool holder
Vielstellenschalter *m* multiposition switch
vielstellig digits, of many digits
Vielstempel-reihenlochmaschine *f* multiple rectilinear punching machine **-stanzen** *pl* multiple-die punching machines
Vielsternmotor *m* multibank radial engine
vielstimmig polyphonous, polyphonic (of organ)
Vielstoff-eignung *f* multi-fuel ability **-gemisch** *n* multi-component mixture **-motor** *m* multi-fuel engine
Vielstrahlinterferometer *n* multiple-beam interferometry
vielsträhniges Drahtkabel stranded wire cable
Vielstufen-wärmeaustauscher *m* multipass heat exchanger **-system** *n* multi-section system
vielstufig multistage **-er Schalter** multipoint switch
Vieltausendfache *n* thousands of times
vielteilig multipartite, polynomial (math.)
Vieltonsender *m* multiple-tone transmitter
Vieltypen-ausbreitung *f* multimode propagation **-schreibmaschine** *f* multiple-type typewriter
vielversprechend most promising
Vielwalzengerüst *n* cluster roll stand
Vielwegehahn *m* multiple-way stopcock
vielwertig multivalent, polyvalent
Vielwertigkeit *f* polyvalence
Vielzahl *f* plurality
Vielzellen-fernseher *m* multicell television apparatus **-lautsprecher** multicellular loudspeaker
vielzellig multicellular **-er Flügel** multicellular wing **-e Zentrifugalpumpe** multistage centrifugal pump
Vielzweckmaschine *f* universal machine tool
Vierachsseilschlepper *m* four-axle high-speed tractor
Vieradressenbefehl *m* four-address instruction
vieradrig four-wire
vierarmige aktive Brücke four-arm active bridge (semiconductors)
vieratomig tetratomic
Vierbackenfutter *n* four-jaw chuck
Vierbandlichtschleuse *f* four-band light valve, four-ribbon light valve
vierbasisch tetrabasic
Vierblatt *n* four-blade, clover leaf **-schraube** *f* four-blade propeller
Vier-bundkolben *m* four-collar piston **-bürstenlager** *n* four-brush commutator bearing
Vierfüllungstür *f* four-paneled door
vierdimensional-es Eikonal two-event characteristic function **-er Raum** four-dimensional space **-er Vektor** four dimensional vector
Vierdraht-betrieb *m* four-wire operation **-doppelstrombetrieb** *m* four-wire double current working **-gabel** *f* four-wire termination **-gabelschaltung** *f* four-wire termination **-kabel** *n* four-wire cable **-leitung** *f* four-wire circuit **-schaltung** *f* four-wire connection **-stammleitung** *f* side circuit (four wire) **-verstärker** *m* four-wire repeater **-zwischenverstärker** *m* four-wire intermediate repeater
Viereck *n* square, quadrangle, rectangle, quadrilateral **wechselseitig umschriebene Vierecke** mutually circumscribed quadrangles
Viereck-flansch *m* square flange **-flug** *m* quadrilateral or quadrangular flight
viereckig square, tetragonal, rectangular, four-cornered, quadrangular, oblong (of reading glass) ~ **oder rechtwinklig machen** to square

-er Bolzen square-headed bolt **-er Dipolrahmen** *m* square loop (antenna) **-es Gewinde** square thread **-er Turm** *m* pylon **-e Unterlegscheibe** square washer

Viereckigschmieden *n* square forging

Viereck-spant *m* square frame **-träger** *m* square girder

Vierelektroden-glimmrelais *n* glow-tetrode relay **-röhre** *f* four-electrode valve, tetrode

vieren to divide into four

Vierer *m* four-wire unit, quad, phantom **zum ~ schalten** to phantom **zum ~ verseilen** to quad

Vierer-abzweigübertrager *m* combining transformer **-ausnutzung** *f* use of phantom circuits **-belastung** *f* phantom loading **-bespulung** *f* phantom loading **-betrieb** *m* phantom-circuit operation, duplex operation **-bildung** *f* phantoming **-bündel** *n* four-wire core, quad **-fähige Leitung** phantom circuit **-folge** *f* sequence of phantom crossings

Vierer-gruppe *f* phantom group **-impuls** *m* four-momentum **-kabel** *n* multiple-twin cable **-kapazität** *f* pair-to-pair capacity, side-to-side capacity **-kolonne** *f* column of fours **-kraft** *f* four-force

Viererkreis *m* phantom or duplex circuit, superposed or combined circuit, plus circuit **~ mit Erdrückleitung** earth-phantom circuit

Viererkreisübertrager *m* phantom-circuit repeat coil

Vierer-lage *f* square, group of four wires (pairs diagonal) with twist system **-leitung** *f* phantom circuit, phantom pair **-potential** *n* four-potential **-pupinisiert** composite-loaded, phantom-loaded **-pupinisierung** *f* phantom loading, composite loading, superposed loading

Vierer-schaltung *f* phantom connection **-schleifenkapazität** *f* phantom capacity, side-to-side capacity, pair-to-pair capacity **-seil** *n* quad (elec.) **-sprechkreis** *m* superposed or combine circuit **-spule** *f* phantom coil, superimposed circuit coil, phantom-circuit loading coil **-spulensatz** *m* phantom-coil set

Vierer-stromkreis *m* phantom-circuit **-stromkpotential** *n* charge-current potential **-vektor** *m* four-component vector **-verbindung** *f* phantom circuit, plus circuit **-verseilmaschine** *f* laying-up machine, quadding machine, twisting machine

viererverseilt quaddel **-es Kabel** duplex cable, phantom cable

Viererverseilung *f* quad formation

vierfach quadruple **~ gekröpft** four-throw-(a crank) **-e Leuchte** quadriform optical apparatus **-er Meteorograph** quadruple register **-er umlaufender Nocken** four-lobed revolving cam

Vierfach-apparat *m* quadruple multiplex apparatus **-betrieb** *m* quadruplex system **-expansionsmaschine** *f* quadruple expansion engine **-gestänge** *n* quadruple pole **-kabelklemme** *f* four-conductor cable terminal **-reihenmaßkammer** *f* quadruple-serial air-survey camera, quadruple-serial photogrammetric camera **-schreiber** *m* four-point recorder, quadruple recorder, four-variable recorder **-spirallochscheibe** *f* quadruple-spiral scanning disk **-spritzgießwerkzeug** *n* four-impression injection mold

Vierfachstahlhalter *m* four-way tool block, four-way tool post **-telegraph** *m* quadruple telegraph (system) **-zwilling** *m* quadruple twin **-zwillingskabel** *n* quadruple-pair cable

vierfältig fourhold, quadruple

Vierfarben-druck *m* four-color printing **-problem** *n* four-color problem

Vierfarbsatz *m* (print) four-color process plates

Vierflach *n* tetrahedron

Vierflächendiode *f* four-layer diode

vierflächig tetrahedral, four-faced

vierflügelige Luftschraube four-bladed propeller

Vierfrequenzfernwahl *f* four-frequency dialing or signaling

Vierfüllungstür *f* four-paneled door

Vierganggetriebe *n* four-speed gear

viergängige Schnecke four-start worm

Viergangplanetengetriebe *n* four-speed planetary gear

Viergelenkkette *f* four-bar-chain

Viergitter-regelmischröhre *f* fading-mix hexode **-regelröhre** *f* fading hexode **-röhre** *f* hexode

viergleisig with four rails

viergliedrig four-membered, tetragonal (crystal) **-e Farbgleichung** four-color equation, four-stimulus equation

Viergut *n* four-product **-scheidung** *f* four-product separation

vierjährlich quadrennial

Vierkammermotor *m* four-chamber engine

Vierkanalmagnetkopf *m* four-track magnetic soundhead

Vierkant *m* square, square end, bar or key, four-cornered shaft **kegliger ~** tapered square hole

Vierkantdoppel-T-Scheibe *f* square T washer

Vierkant-einsteckschlüssel *m* square key (or box) spanner **-eisen** *n* square-bar iron, squares **-feile** *f* square file **-holz** *n* squared timber **-holzschraube** *f* square-headed coach bolt or screw

vierkantig square, square-headed, tetragonal

Vierkant-kaliber *n* box pass (met.) **-keil** *m* square key **-kohlenschaufel** *f* square coal scoop **-kopf** *m* square head, coach screw **-kopfschraube** *f* square head bolt, square head screw **-kupfer** *n* slab copper **-loch** *n* square hole **-lochung** *f* square perforation **-mutter** *f* square nut **-oberwange** *f* square upper beam

Vierkant-pfahl *m* square pile **-platting** *f* square sennit **-reibahle** *f* square broach **-revolverkopf** *m* square turret **-revolversupport** *m* square turret head, four-way toolpost **-rohr** *n* square tube or pipe

Vierkant-schaft *m* square shaft (shank) **-scheibe** *f* square washer **-schlüssel** *m* monkey wrench, spanner wrench **-schraube** *f* square-head(ed) bolt **-schraubenbolzen** *m* square-head bolt **-schraubenschlüssel** *m* square box wrench **-schubriegel** *m* flat sliding bolt **-spule** *f* square roller

Vierkant-stäbe square bar **-stahl** *m* square steel bar **-stange** *f* bar of rectangular section, square steel bar, square-section rod **-steckschlüssel** *m* square socket wrench **-stiftschlüssel** *m* allen key **-stöpsel** *m* square-headed plug

Vierkant-U-Scheibe *f* square U washer

Vierkantwelle *f* square shaft

Vierklotzbremse *f* four-shoe or four-block brake

Vierkomponentenwaage *f* four-component scale or balance

vierkomponentig four components (of)
Vierkörperverdampfapparat *m* quadruple-effect evaporator
Vierkursfunkfeuer *n* radio range
Vierkursfunkfeuer mit Sicht- und Höranzeige visual aural range
vierlappig four-cusped
Vierleiterdrehstrom *m* four-wire three-phase a-c
Vierleitungsmontage *f* four-pipe installation
Vierlippenbohrer *m* four-lipped twist drill
viermotorig four-engined
Viernetzlaufzeitmethode *f* four-gauze-shutter method
Vierpaß eines Hochofens pillars of a blast furnace
Vierphasenhalbwellenbetrieb *m* four phase half wave
vierphasig quarter-phase
Vierpol *m* quadripole, four-pole circuit, four-pole network, four-terminal network, transducer **-dämpfung** *f* image-attenuation constant **-dämpfungsfaktor** *m* image-attenuation factor **-gleichung** *f* transducer equation (quadrupole equation)
vierpolig four-pole, four-point **-er Schalter** four-point switch
Vierpol-kette *f* recurrent network **-konstante** *f* quadrupole constant **-kreuzglied** *n* bridge network, lattice network **-lautsprecher** *m* balanced-armature loud-speaker **-phasenfaktor** *m* image phase factor **-regelröhre** *f* variable-mu tetrode, variable-mu screen-grid tube **-röhre** *f* tetrode, four-electrode valve **-schirmregelröhre** *f* variable-mu tetrode, variable-mu screen-grid tube **-schirmröhre** *f* screen-grid valve or tube, screen-grid tetrode **-übertragungsmaß** *n* image-transfer constant **-winkelmaß** *n* image-phase constant
Vierprismenquarzspektrograph *m* quadruple-prism quartz spectrograph
Vierpunkt-aufhängung *f* four-point attachment or suspension **-befestigung** *f* four-point fixing (or fastening) **-lager** *n* four-point contact bearing **-verfahren** *n* four-point method
Vierrad *n* quadricycle, four-wheel **-antrieb** *m* four-wheel drive **-bremse** *f* four-wheel brake **-fahrzeug** *n* four-wheel vehicle **-lenkung** *f* four-wheel control
Vierrahmenplattform *f* four gimbal platform
Vierröhrengerät *n* four valve apparatus
Vierrollen -Illustrations -Rotationsdruckmaschine four-reel illustration rotary web press
Viersäulenpresse *f* four-column hydraulic press
Vierscheibenverschluß *m* four-disk shutter, four-flanged shutter
vierschneidig with four blades
Vierschraubendampfer *m* quadruple-screw liner
Vierseil *n* quad cable
Vierseit *n* quadrilateral
vierseitig quadrilateral, square, four-sided
Viersitzer *m* four-seater
vierspaltig in four columns (print.)
Vierspeziesrechenmaschinen *pl* calculating machines for all four fundamental operations
Vierspindelnachformfräsmaschine *f* four-spindle tracer milling machine
Vierspitz *m* four-pointed knife rest, crow's-foot
Vierstellenkochherd *m* four-hole cooking range
vierstellig four-digit **-e Kleinschmierpumpe** four-connection small-size lubricator **-e Zahl** *f* four-figure number
Vierstoffsystem *n* quaternary system
Vierstrichpeilung *f* four-point bearing
Vierstufenkeilriemenscheibe *f* four-step V-pulley
vierstufig four-stage
Viertakt *m* four-stroke cycle **-kolben** *m* four-cycle piston **-motor** *m* four-stroke (cycle) engine, four-stroke cycle, four-cylinder (cycle) engine **-prozeß** *m* Otto-cycle, four-stroke cycle **-verfahren** *n* four-stroke cycle
vierteilen to quarter
vierteilig in or consisting of four parts, four-point
Vierteilung *f* quadripartition
Viertel *n* quarter, fourth, quadrat **-drehung** *f* quarter turn **-fehler** *m* quadrantal compass error **-fläche** *f* quadrant **-geleimt** quarter-sized **-geschränkt** quarter-twisted **-jährlich** quarterly
Viertelkreis *m* quadrant, quarter circle (aviation) **~ einer Signalzone** quadrant, one of the four signal zones
Viertelkreisbogen *m* fourth part of circumference
viertelkreisig quadrantal
Viertelkreispunkte *m pl* quadrantal points
Viertellast *f* quarter load
vierteln to quarter, reduce (samples) by quartering
Viertel-periode *f* quarter period **-pinte** *f* gill **-punkt** *m* quarter point **-rohr** *n* canon pinion **-spur** *f* four track (tape rec.) **-stein** *m* (Quartier) closer
vierteltätige Welle six-hourly wave
Viertelung *f* quartering
Viertelwellen-antenne *f* quarter-wave antenna **-länge** *f* quarter wave length **-längenplättchen** *n* quarter-wave plate (optics)
Viertel-wendung *f* quarter turn **-wertszeit** *f* quarter-life span
Vierträgerbauart *f* four-girder design
Vierung *f* quadrature
Vierungsphase *f* quadrature phase (TV) **~ um 90° verschobene Phase** quadrature phase
Vierwalzen-blechbiegemaschine *f*, **-blechrundmaschine** *f* four-roller plate-bending machine **-gerüst** *n* four-high (mill) stand **-mühle** *f* four-roller cane mill
Vierwalzwerk *n* four-roller mill
Vierwege-einheit *f* four-way unit **-hahn** *m* four-way (stop)cock **-mehrspindelfeinbohrmaschine** *f* multiple spindle four-way precision boring machine **-plattform** *f* four-way platform
vierwertig quadrivalent, tetravalent
Vierwertigkeit *f* quadrivalence, tetravalence
Vierzapfenkipper *m* tipping-trough four-bolted wagon
Vierzonentransistor *m* hook transistor
Vierzylinder-einspritzpumpe *f* four-cylinder injection pump **-motor** *m* four-cylinder motor **-verteiler** *m* four-cylinder distributor **-zündverteiler** *m* four-cylinder ignition (or timing) distributor
Vietinghofit *m* vietinghofite
Vignette *f* vignette
Vignettierapparat *m* vignetter
vignettieren to vignette

Vignettieren des Lichtbündels vignetting of cone of light
Vignettiermaske *f* vignetting mask
Vignettierung *f* vignetting, mount eclipse
Vignettierwirkung *f* vignetting effect
Vignolschiene *f* Vignoles' rail
Vigopas *n* synthetic resin
Vigourexdruckmaschine *f* slubbing melange printing machine
VIKOP rectangular mechanical stage
V-Impuls eines Impulsgebers incoming control impulse
Virial *n* virial **-satz** *m* virial theorem
Viridin *n* viridine
virtue apparent, possibly
virtuell virtual
Viscoid *n* cellulose zanthogenate
Visier *n* (rear) sight, visor, view finder, gun sight **~ einstellen** to adjust the sight **starres ~** fixed sight
Visier-achse *f* line of sight **-aufsatzstange** *f* sight leaf **-bereich** *n* fanger zone **-draht** *m* sighting pendant **-ebene** *f* plane of sighting, plane of present position **-einrichtung** *f* view finder, sighting device or mechanism, (gun) sights **-einschnitt** *m* notch **-einteilung** *f* readings on the sight
visieren to sight, point, aim, adjust, gauge, take bearings
Visier-feder *f* rear-sight base spring **-fehler** *m* error of sighting **-fernrohr** *n* sighting telescope, telescopic sight, dial sight **-fuß** *m* base of rear sight **-gestänge** *n* sight bracket **-haltestift** *m* rear-sight joint pin **-höhenmesser** *m* sight height indicator, telescopic altimeter **-kenngröße** *f* sight characteristic **-kimme** *f* rear-sight notch, rear sight **-klappe** *f* sight leaf **-kreuze** *pl* boning rods **-kugel** *f* limit bar ball
Visier-latte *f* leveling board **-lineal** *n* sight vane, diopter **-linie** *f* line of sight(ing), line of present position **-linienbewegung** *f* motion of a line of a sight **-lupe** *f* sighting peep, ranging magnifier **-marke** *f* line of sight **-mattscheibe** *f* focusing screen **-richtung** *f* line of sight, direction of vision
Visier-sattel *m* base or foot of the rear sight **-scheibe** *f* sighting disk, focusing screen **-schieber** *m* slide (sight) **-schild** *n* sight shield **-schuß** *m* sighting shot **-schußweite** *f* sighting range **-spitze** *f* sighting point
Visier-stab *m* range pole, gauge rod **-stange** *f* sight leaf, sight-bar arm **-stellung** *f* sight setting or adjustment **-stift** *m* rear-sight joint pin **-tafel** *f* boning rod **-träger** *m* sight bracket **-vorrichtung** *f* sighting mechanism, view finder, ranging device, bearing plate **-winkel** *m* elevation setting, angular difference between present and future positions **-zeiger** *m* telescope-mount reference pointer **-zirkel** *m* gauging calipers
Visionspersistenz *f* persistence of vision
Visitiereisen *n* sounding rod
Viskoelastizität *f* viscoelasticity
Viskometer *n* viscosimeter
viskos viscous
Viskose *f* vixcose **-flitter** *m* viscose spangle
Viskosi-messer *m* **-meter** *m* viscometer, viscosimeter
Viskosität *f* viscosity
Viskositäts-index *m* viscosity index **-mittel** *n* viscosity average **-stufe** *f* degree of viscosity **-temperaturkoeffizient** *m* viscosity-temperature coefficient **-zahl** *f* viscosity number
Viskosometer *n* viscometer
viskothermisch viscothermal
Visolbehälter *m* visol tank
visuell visual
Visur *f* line of sight
Vitragenstab *m* curtain pole
Vitrine *f* display cabinet
Vitrinenverdampfer *m* evaporator for display cabinet
Vitriol *m, n* vitriol **weißer ~** white vitriol, zinc sulfate
Vitriol-bleierz *n*, **-bleispat** *m* anglesite **-erz** *n* vitriol ore, vitriolic ore **-hütte** *f* oil of vitriol manufacture **-kies** *m* marcasite **-küpe** *f* cold or common blue vat **-öl** *n*, **-säure** *f* vitriolic or sulfuric acid **-schiefer** *m* alum slate
Vivianit *m* vivianite
V-Kerbe *f* V notch
V-Motor *m* Vee-engine
V-Naht *f* single V groove **~ wurzelseitig nachgeschweißt** single V weld with root reinforcement
V-Nettogewicht *n* V weight
V-Null *n* muzzle velocity (ballist.)
Vocoder *m* vocoder
Vodas *m* vodas
Voder *m* voice operation demonstration equipment
Vogel-flug *m* bird flight **-perspektive** *f* bird's-eye view **-pfeife** *f* bird whistle **-schau** *f* bird's-eye view
Voglianit *m* voglianite
Voglit *m* voglite
Vokal *m* vowel **-einsatz** *m* beginning of vowel sound
vokalisieren to vocalize
Volks-wirt *m* economist **-wirtschaft** *f* political economy **-wirtschaftslehre** *f* (science of) political economy
voll full, massive, solid, entire, complete, maximum **-e Belastung** full load **-e Drehzahl** at maximum speed **-e Fahrgeschwindigkeit** full speed **-e Fracht** full cargo **-e Fuge** flush pointing, flat pointing **-e Gebühr** day rate **-es Gewicht mit voller Belastung** full load **-es Kurbelblatt** solid crank disk
Vollachse *f* solid axle
volladressierter Speicher *m* addressed memory
Voll-amt *n* main office **-analyse** *f* full or complete analysis **-anode** *f* unsplit anode, solid anode **-anschlag** *m* full stop **-ausbau** *m* ultimate capacity **-ausbruch** *m* full bore (blasting) **-ausschlag** *m* full-scale reading, full deflection (of the instrument) **-aussteuerung** *f* maximum level, maximum volume (tape rec.) **-automatisch** fully automatic
Vollast *f* full load
vollbadfeuer-verzinkt fully potgalvanized
Vollbahn *f* standard-gauge railroad, main line **-schiene** *f* standard-gauge rail
vollbelastet at full load **~ anlaufen** to start on full load
Vollbelastung *f* full load

Voll-berichtigung *f* full correction **-bestückung** *f* full capacity **-bildfrequenz** *f* frame repetition rate, frame frequency **-binder** *m* header, perpend **-boden** *m* blank head, blank end **-bogen** *m* semicircular rail **-bohrer** *m* reamer, solid bit **-bremsung** *f* full braking **-dampf** *m* full steam **-deckel** *m* blank cover
volldimensioniert fully dimensioned
Volldraht *m* solid wire
Volldruck *m* full pressure or boost, full print (full strength print) **-arbeit** *f* work done under full pressure
Volldruckhöhe *f* critical altitude, maximum boost altitude, full pressure altitude ~ **für Höchstleistung** maximum power altitude
Volldruckverhältnis *n* ratio of maximum and effective pressure, full-pressure ratio
Volleistung *f* full-power output
Volleistungshöhe *f* full-throttle altitude, maximum-power altitude
Volleiter *m* unstranded or solid conductor
vollenden to finish, complete
vollendet perfect
Vollendung *f* perfection, completion, finish, accomplishment
vollentstört, ~ **für Ultrakurzwellen** ultrahigh-frequency screened **-e Kerze** shielded plug (A), screened plug (B)
Vollentstörung *f* complete screening, ultrahigh-frequency-screening
vollfarbig of full (saturated) color
Vollfeuer *n* full fire, full heat
vollflächig holohedral
Vollflächigkeit *f* holohedry, holohedrism (cryst.)
Vollflächner *m* holoheder
Vollflansch *m* blind flange
vollfliegend full-floating
Vollförderung *f* full delivery
vollfreitragend full or pure cantilever **-er Flügel** pure-cantilever wing
vollfüllen to fill, stow, fulfill
Vollgas *n* full or open throttle, full power **mit** ~ throttle wide open ~ **geben** to shove the throttle full open
Vollgas-flug *m* flight with full throttle **-höhe** *f* critical altitude, full-throttle altitude **-meßwerte** *m pl* full-throttle calibration **-standdrehzahl** *f* full throttle bench revolutions per minute **-trudel** *m* tail-spin with power on **-sturzflug** *m* power dive
Vollgatter *n* multiple-blade saw frame
Voll-gebläse *n* complete compressor or blower **-gehalt** *n* full value, full content or strength **-geländegängig** having complete cross-country ability **-gelenkiger Rotor** fully articulated rotor **-gepfropft** stuffed full **-gerät** *n* engine at full throttle (rockets) **-geschwindigkeitsregler** *m* regulator with constant angular vane velocity
voll-gesogen saturated **-gespult** fully wound **-gießen** to pour to the top, fill up **-gummibereift** solid tired
Vollgummireifen *m* solid-rubber tire
Voll-herd *m* intermittent table (min.) **-hitzezone** *f* hot-temperature zone, soaking zone **-holm** *m* solid spar **-hub** *m* (Kolben) full stroke (piston)
völlig total, entire, thorough, full, whole, circular
Völligkeit *f* fullness, solidity
Völligkeitsgrad *m* volumetric efficiency (engine), planimetric ratio (propeller), coefficient of fineness, solidity ratio, block coefficient
vollkantig full-edged **-er Balken** squared beam **-es Brett** flatted plank **-e Schwelle** full-squared sleeper
Vollkehlnaht *f* miter fillet weld
Vollkettenfahrzeug *n* full-track vehicle
vollkommen complete, perfect ~ **streuender Körper** perfect diffuser **-e Abtrennung** exhaustion (physics) **-es Bündel** full-availability group **-e Verbrennung** perfect or complete combustion **-e und unvollkommene Polarisation** perfect and imperfect polarization **-er Überfall** free discharge over a weir **-es Überfallwehr** free-overfall weir
Vollkommenheit *f* perfection, refinement
Vollkorn *n* full sight (Visier)
Vollkörper *m* solid body
Vollkraft *f* full power
Vollkreis *m* complete circle **-gradmesser** *m* circular or circle protractor **-transporteur** *m* circle protractor, circular plotting protractor
vollkristallin holocrystalline
Vollkugel *f* solid sphere
vollkurssteuern to fly automatically
Vollkurssteuerung *f* flight with full autopilot
Voll-last *f* full load **-lastdrehzahl** *f* full-load speed **-lastmenge** *f* full-load quantity **-lastregler** *m* maximum speed governor **-lastselbstverstellinie** *f* full-load self-regulating (or self-timing) curve **-laststellung** *f* full-load position
Voll-leistung *f* full-power output **-leistungshöhe** *f* full-throttle altitude, maximum-power altitude **-leiter** *m* unstranded or solid conductor **-lüftung** *f* full ventilation
Vollmacht *f* attorney for applicant (patents), power of attorney ~ **ausstellen** to execute a power of attorney **eine** ~ **ausüben** to exercise power of attorney ~ **erteilen** to confer power of attorney
Vollmachtgeber *m* principal, mandator
Voll-mantel *m* solid jacket **-maschine** *f* full-scale model
Vollmaß *n* finishing size **-zapfen** *m* full-sized fang
vollmechanisch fully mechanical or mechanized
Vollmotor *m* multicylinder engine, engine at full throttle (rockets)
Vollmotorenversuch *m* main-engine test
vollmotorisieren to mechanize completely
Vollmotorprüfung *f* unit test
Voll-netzanschluß *m* all-electric supply, mains supply **-niet** *m* solid rivet **-opalscheibe** *f* solid opal diffuser disk **-operation** *f* complete operation **-passage** *f* immersion passage **-patrone** *f* solid collet **-pipette** *f* volumetric pipette **-pleuel** *n* plain rod **-polläufer** *m* smooth-core rotor
Vollportal-drehkran *m* portal revolving crane **-kran** *m* full gantry crane
Voll-probelauf *m* power test-run **-profil** *n* solid section **-prüffeld** *n* full-size test area or stand
Vollquerschnitt *m* solid section **-fläche** *f* sectional area of solid body, solid-cross-section area
Voll-rad *n* one-piece wheel, solid wheel **-rahmen** *m* solid frame **-raum** *m* infinite body **-reduzierbar** completely reducible **-reifen** *m* solid (rubber) tire **-riemenscheibe** *f* block pulley **-ring** *m* solid ring **-rippe** *f* solid rib
Vollrohr *n* one-piece gun barrel, monoblock

barrel **-kanal** *m* single pipe conduit
Voll-schaufel *f* solid blade **-schiene** *f* filled section rail **-schlächtiges Seil** locked or closed rope or cable **-schlagen** to be swamped **-schmieden** to forge in the solid **-schnitt** *m* full cut **-seil** *n* solid rope cable **-selbsttätig** fully automatic(al)
vollsetzen, sich ~ to clog, become stuffed up
Vollsicht *f* all-round view, all-round vision, full vision **-kanzel** *f* turret with all-around visibility, full-vision cab(in), all-round view cab(in), all-round vision cab(in) **-kuppel** *f* full-vision turret
Vollspant *m* watertight or airtight frame
Vollspule *f* solid coil **einseitig unendliche Vollspulen** semifinite solid coils
Vollspur *f* standard gauge **-bahn** *f* standard-gauge railroad **-gleisanschluß** *m* standard-gauge siding **-kopf** *m* full-track head
vollspurig (railroad track) of standard gauge
Voll-stab *m* unnotched (plain) specimen **-stahl** *m* solid tool **-stampfen** to ram up, tamp full
vollständig complete, entire **-e Gleichrichtung** full-wave rectification **-e Induktion** mathematical induction **-er Übertrag** complete carry
Vollständigkeitsrelation *f* completeness relation
Vollstange *f* bar
Voll-stangen aus Rotguß solid rods in gunmetal **-stiel** *m* solid strut **-stopfen** to cram, jam, stuff **-strebe** *f* solid strut
vollstreckbar enforceable, executable, executory
vollstrecken to carry out, execute
Voll-tastatur *f* complete keyboard **-ton** (Lack) *m* full shade (mass tone) **-tönend** round, rich in tone **-traghöhe** *f* service ceiling **-transistorisiert** fully transistorized **-treffer** *m* direct hit **-triebwerk** *n* complete installation
Voll-verband *m* force **-versammlung** *f* quota **-verstärker** *m* full-range amplifier **-verstellschraube** *f* fully controlled airscrew or propeller
vollwandig with solid web, with solid wall, massive, compact **-es Rad** solid wheel **-er Träger** web girder, I-beam girder, tubular or plate girder **-e Trägerbrücke** deck plate girder bridge
Vollweg-gleichrichter *m* full-wave rectifier **-gleichrichterröhre** *f* full-wave rectifying valve **-gleichrichtung** *f* full-wave rectification
Vollwelle *f* solid shaft
vollwertig perfect, up to standard, complete
vollzählig complete, full strength
vollzeichnen to cover with drawings, subscribe fully
Vollziegel *m* solid brick
vollzogene Flugausdehnung track distance (aviation), total ground covered
Vollzug *m* execution (orders), accomplishing
Vollzustand *m* full condition (data storage)
Vollzylinder *m* solid cylinder
Volt *n* volt **absolutes ~** abvolt
Voltaeffekt *m* Volta effect
voltaisch voltaic **-es Potential** contact potential (difference), volta potential **-e Säule** voltaic pile
Voltameter *n* voltameter, coulometer **schreibendes ~** recording voltameter
Voltampere *n* volt-ampere **-meter** *m* volt-ammeter
Voltapaar *n* voltaic couple
Voltapotential *n* Volta potential, Volta electromotive force
Voltasches Element Volta cell
Volta-spannung *f* Volta potential
Volt-drehstromnetz *n* volt system **-elementarladung** *f* equivalent electron volts
Voltmesser *m* voltmeter **-umschalter** *m* voltmeter switch
Voltmeter *n* voltmeter **-meßbereich** *n* measuring range of voltmeter **-schalter** *m* voltmeter switch **-umschalter** *m* voltmeter phase select switch **-verschaltwiderstand** *m* multiplier **-widerstand** *m* voltmeter resistor
Volt-Milliamperemeter *n* volt-milliampere meter
Voltol *n* trade name for mixed mineral and fatty oil treated with a glow discharge to impart high viscosity **-gleitöl** *n* Voltol sliding oil
Volt-sekunde *f* volt-second **-spannung** *f* voltage **-stundenzähler** *m* volt-hour meter **-verlust** *m* voltage drop **-vernichtung** *f* voltage nullifying **-zahl** *f* voltage
Volum-aräometer *n* hydrometer **-dilatation** *f* cubic dilatation, volume strain
Volumen *n* volume **verdrängtes ~** volume (of a substance) forced away
Volumen-dilatometer *n* volume dilatometer **-einheit** *f* unit volume, unit of volume **-element** *n* element of volume **-energie** *f* volume energy **-gewicht** *n* weight by volume **-gleichrichtung** *f* volume rectification **-kontraktion** *f* volume contraction **-messer** *m* volume gauge
Volumenometer *n* volumenometer
Volumen-prozent *n* per cent by volume **-schwankung** *f* volume flutter **-streuung** *f* bulk scattering **-veränderung** *f* change in volume **-verhältnis** *n* volume ratio **-verlust** *m* loss in volume **-vermehrung** *f* increase in volume, dilation **-verminderung** *f* decrease in volume **-voltameter** *n* volume voltameter **-zähler** *m* volumetric meter **-zeiger** *m* volume indicator **-zunahme** *f* growing, increase in volume
volumetrisch volumetric **-e Analyse** volumetric analysis **-er Wirkungsgrad** volumetric efficiency
Volumgewicht *n* volume weight, weight of unit volume
voluminös voluminous, bulky
Volum-integrale volume integrals **-kontraktion** *f* contraction of volume **-prozent** *n* per cent by volume **-prozentskala** *f* volume-percentage scale **-regler** *m* volume control **-verhältnis** *n* volume relation, proportion by volume **-teil** *m* partial volume
Vomhundert-anteil *m*, **-satz** *m* percentage
vorab tentatively, to begin with, before all things, first of all, especially
Vorabdruck *m* preprint
vorabgestimmt pre-plumbed
Vorabscheider *m* preliminary filter
Voraktivierungszeit *f* pre-firing
vorangehend preceding, leading, antecedent
Voranmeldungsgespräch *n* preadvice call, personal call
Voranode *f* first anode
Voranschlag *m* (preliminary) estimate, rough or provisional estimate, calculation
Voranschwemmbehälter primary flooding tank
Voranstrich *m* undercoating

Vorappretur *f* preliminary finishing
Vorarbeit *f* preparatory work, preparation, preliminary work or operation
Vorarbeiten *pl* roughing out **~ auf Rohmaß** rough machining
vorarbeiten, sich ~ to forge ahead, work one's way up
Vorarbeiter *m* foreman, gang boss, leading hand, chief operator
Vorarm *m* forearm
voraufgehen to precede
voraus ahead, forward **im ~** in advance **im ~ etwas tun** to anticipate **nicht im ~ bestimmbar** unpredictable
voraus-berechnen to predetermine **-berechnet** calculated **-berechnung** *f* predetermination **-bestellen** to order beforehand **-bestimmung** *f* predetermination **-bezahlen** to prepay **-bezahlung** *f* prepayment **-datiert** antedated **-gang** *m* headway **-gehend** preceding, leading, previous, prior, antecedent **-nehmend** anticipatory (patent law)
Vorauspuff *m* preexhaust
Voraus-raumabsuchung *f* forward area warning **-sage** *f* prediction, forecast **-schicken** to premise **-sehen** to anticipate **-setzen** to (pre)suppose, assume, postulate **-setzung** *f* premise, hypothesis, (pre)supposition, assumption, prerequisite, presumption, condition, stipulation **-sichtlich** expected, as is expected or anticipated, in all likelihood, probable, prospective
Voraus-wahl *f* screening **-wanderungsstrecke** *f* travel of target during dead time **-werteposten** *m* control filter post (CFP) **-zahlung** *f* prepayment, payment in advance or by anticipation, advance
Vorbau *m* projection
vorbauen to guard against, project, build infront
Vorbau-schnabel *m* launching nose **-stähle** *pl* cutters designed to clear gears
vorbeansprucht (vorbelastet) prestressed
vorbearbeiten to rough (work)
Vorbearbeitung *f* preliminary or rough treatment
Vorbedingung *f* prerequisite, precondition
Vorbehalt *m* reservation **unter ~** reservedly
vorbehalten to withhold, keep in reserve, reserve
vorbehaltlich with reservations
vorbehandeln to pretreat
Vorbehandlung *f* primary treatment, preliminary treatment, pretreatment, preparatory treatment
vorbei-fahren to pass **-flug** *m* passing flight, side view **-führen** to skirt, conduct or direct past (something) **-gelingen** be unsuccessful **-kommen** to pass by, clear **-rollen** pass by
Vorbeischleifungskondensator *m* by-pass capacitor
vorbei-streichen, -streifen to pass, skirt, glance, graze, brush against
vorbeizen to first pickle
Vorbeladung *f* precharge, preliminary charge
vorbelasten to prestress
Vorbelastung *f* initial loading, preconsolidation load, initial stress
Vorbelastungswiderstand *m* bleeder resistor
Vorbeleuchtung *f* priming illumination
Vorbelichtung *f* prefogging (phot.), priming exposure or illumination, preexposure
Vorbelichtungseffekt *m* pre-exposure effect
Vorbenutzung *f* prior use
Vorbenutzungsrecht *n* right (by reason) of prior use, shop right
vorberechnet precalculated
vorbereiten to prepare (a sample)
vorbereitend preparatory **-e Kontaktfeder** storage contact spring
Vorbereitung *f* preparation, preliminaries, preparatory training, line-up, readying **~ des Bauplatzes** preparation of site **~ für Bildaufnahme** lining up for shooting pictures **~ des Einschlags** preparation of the weft **~ einer Fernverbindung** notification in advance of incoming call **~ eines Ferngesprächs** advance notification of incoming call **~ des Kabelendes zum Überziehen des Ziehschlauchs** beating in of cable
Vorbereitungs-feuer *n* preparatory fire **-gebühr** *f* report charge **-kaliber** *n* preparatory pass, roughing roll **-verkehr** *m* trunk traffic
Vorbericht *m* introduction, first report
Vorbescheid *m* advance notice, preliminary action, interim decision
Vorbeschleuniger *m* pre-accelerator
vorbestimmen to allot
vorbestimmt predetermined, pre-set
Vorbetrieb *m* pre-processing shop, propulsion
vorbeugen to prevent, obviate, preclude
vorbeugend prophylactic **-e Wartung** preventive maintenance
Vorbeugungsmaßnahme *f* precautionary measure
Vorbild *n* prototype, pattern, model, copy, type, exemplar
vorbilden to preshape
Vorblasen *n* preliminary blast or blowing
Vorblcck *m* bloom, cogged ingot
vorblocken to bloom, cog
Vorblockwalze *f* blooming roll, cogging roll
Vorboden *m* upstream floor or apron
vorbohren to rough-drill
Vorbohren *n* rough drilling
Vorbohrer *m* auger, gimlet
Vorbohrloch *n* advance borehole, protection hole
Vorbohrung *f* trial bore
vorbrechen to break coarsely (of ore)
Vorbrechen *n* primary crushing, coarse crushing, preliminary breaking
Vorbrecher *m* crusher
Vorbrenne *f* preliminary pickle (met.)
vorbringen to bring up, allege, argue, plead, reason **eine Ansicht ~** to advance an opinion
Vorbringen *n* bringing up, putting forward, allegation (law)
vordatieren to antedate
Vordeck *n* forecastle, foredeck
vordecken to dye first (ground)
vorder in the front
Vorderabtastung *f* front scanning
Vorderachs-antrieb *m* front-wheel drive **-aufhängung** *f* front-axle suspension **-brücke** *f* front-axle differential casing **-druck** *m* front axle load
Vorderachse *f* front axle
Vorderachs-entlastung *f* front-axle relief **-federung** *f* spring suspension of front axle **-körper** *m* front axle beam **-schale** *f* fore-bolster (on front-axle drive of car) **-schenkel** *m* stub axle **-triebwerk** *n* front axle gear **-zapfen** *m* steering-knuckle pivot

Vorder-ansicht *f* front or panel view, front elevation **-blende** *f* anterior stop, field stop **-boden** *m* front end plate (of boiler) **-bracke** *f* trace or swingle tree bar **-endfutter** *n* collect chuck
Vorderfeder *f* front spring **-bock** *m* front-spring (hanger) bracket **-klampe** *f* front-spring clamp
Vorder-fläche *f* front face **-flanke** *f* front face **-front** *f* front, fore, anterior **-gebäude** *n* front building **-gelenk** *n* front piece of toggle joint (pistol) **-gespinst** *n* slubbing, roving **-gestell** *n* forecarriage **-glied** *n* predecessor, antecedent **-grund** *m* foreground
Vorderhang *m* positive slope, forward slope **-stellung** *f* forward-slope position
Vorder-herd *m* forehearth **-holm** *m* front outrigger, front spar, front member **-kaffe** *f* bow compartment **-kammertiefenmesser** *m* anterior chamber depth micrometer
Vorderkante *f* entering wedge, leading edge ~ **des Vorstevens** fore edge of stem
Vorderkanten-breite *f* width of front cutting edge **-einstellung** *f* setting the front cutting edge
Vorder-kipper *m*, **-kippwagen** *m* end-dump car, front tipper **-lader** *m* muzzle loader **-lastig** nose-heavy **-lastigkeit** *f* nose-heaviness **-lauf** *m* toe-in **-licht** *n* front light **-linse** *f* field lens, front lens
Vordermann *m* man in front, file leader, ship next ahead (navy) **-gitter** *n* file leader grid
Vorder-marken *pl* front stops **-maschine** *f* main machine (Scherbius sets) **-pferd** *n* lead horse
Vorderrad *n* front wheel **-achse** *f* front axle **-antrieb** *m* front-wheel drive **-bremse** *f* front-wheel brake **-bremszylinder** *m*, **-lagerung** *f* front-wheel assembly **-gabel** *f* front wheel fork **-nabe** *f* front hub **-satz** *m* front-wheel pair
Vorder-rahmen *m* wooden frame, front frame **-rand** *m* anterior end **-satz** *m* premise, antecedent **-säule** *f* front column **-schlitz** *m* forward or front slot **-schwanzflugzeug** *n* canard **-seite** *f* front, face, odd or uneven page, obverse, foreside, panel **-sieb** *n* frontal screen **-sitz** *m* front seat **-steven** *m* stem **-strebe** *f* fore or forward strut, front strut **-stufenabstand** *m* forward step position in flight formation **-stütze** *f* front tripod leg
Vorderteil *n* head, nosepiece ~ **des Getriebegehäuses** nose of the gear case
Vorderwagen *m* limber
Vorder-walze *f* front roll **-walzer** *m* roller **-wand** *f* front wall **-wandzelle** *f* front-effect cell, barrier plane front-wall cell **-zangenspindeln** *pl* front chop spindles **-zapfwelle** *f* front power take-off (shaft) **-zeug** *n* breastplate harness **-zwiesel** *m* fork of saddle, front arch of saddle **-zylinder** *m* front bottom roller
Vordestiller *m* primary still
vordornen rough punching
Vordrall initial whirl **-einrichtung** *f* pre-forming attachment
vordrehen, die Achse ~ to rough-turn the axle
VOR-Drehfunkfeuer *n* VHF omni-directional range
Vordreh-schleuder *f* crank (of car) **-supporte** *pl* turning slides
vordringen to advance, press forward, forge ahead
Vordringen *n* advance
vordringlich forward, intrusive, obtrusive, basically
Vordrossel *f* choke valve (carburetor), air-density control valve, supply restriction, input reactor (Telegr.)
Vordruck *m* first impression, proof, form, paper blank, supply pressure, inlet pressure **-buntreserve** *f* colored first printed resist **-regler** *m* admission-pressure regulator **-reserve** *f* first printed resist (preprinted resist) **-walze** *f* (Egoutteur) dandy roller **-wesen** *n* preprint system
Vordüne *f* outer down, front down
Vordüse *f* pilot jet
Vorebbe *f* ebb beginning, first quarter of the ebb
Voreil-feder *f* lead(ing) spring **-hebel** *m* combination lever (motion gear)
voreilen to lead, advance, slip forward, run fast
Voreilen *n* lead, advance, forward slip, leading
voreilend leading
Voreilung *f* lead, leading, leading of phase
Voreilungswinkel *m* angle of lead, lead angle (of phases)
Voreil-verzerrung *f* leading distortion **-winkel** *m* angle of lead, angle of advance
Voreinflugzeichen *n* outer marker (ILS)
Voreinstellstabilität preset stability
Voreinstellung *f* setting-up, zoning weighting
Voreinteilung *f* pointing
Voreinweisung *f* preadjustment of homing device (missiles)
Voreisen *n* colter
vorenthalten to withhold
Vorentladung *f* predischarge
Vorentladungskanal *m* predischarge track
Vorentwässerung *f* preliminary drying
Vorentwicklung *f* research
Vorentwicklungsabteilung *f* research division
Vorentwurf preliminary design
Vorentzerrungsglied *n* deaccentuator
Vorerhitzung *f* preheating
Voreröffnung *f* lead
vorerwähnt afore-mentioned
Vorerzeugnis *n* semifinished product
Vorfahrt *f* right-of-way
Vorfahrtsrecht *n* right of way
Vorfall *m* incident, occurrence **dienstlicher** ~ service irregularity or error
Vorfalzen *n* prefolding
Vorfärbung *f* ground dyeing
Vorfeile *f* bastard file
vorfeilen to rough-file
Vorfeld *n* (Flughafen) apron, tarmac, ramp
Vorfertigung *f* pre-fabrication
Vorfeuerung *f* prefiring
Vorfilter *m* antefilter, auxiliary filter, coarse filter, prefilter
Vorfiltration *f* prefiltration
Vorfleier *m* slubbing frame
Vorfließgeschwindigkeit strain-rate
Vorflügel *m* slat (aviation) **-führung** *f* slat track
Vorflut *f* flood beginning **die ~ stören** to disturb existing or previous drainage conditions
Vorflutanlage *f* draining plant
Vorfluter *m* main canal or ditch (in sewerage system), receiving stream
Vorflutleitung *f* outfall drain
Vorfokuserregerlampe *f* preset exciter lamp

Vorfokussierung *f* prefocusing
Vorform *f* gathering mold (glass mfg.)
Vorformen *n* tip stretching
Vorformverfahren *n* preform process
Vorfräseinrichtung *f* rough milling attachment
vorfräsen to rough-ream, rough-out
Vorfräser *m* roughing cutter
Vorfräsmaschine *f* roughing-out machine
Vorfrischen *n* primary purification
Vorfrischofen *m* primary furnace, refiner
vorfühlen to feel one's way forward
vorführen to bring up, lead forward, demonstrate, present, project (motion pictures), display, produce
Vorführer *m* projectionist, motion-picture operator
Vorführ-gerät *n* projector (phot.) **-raum** *m* operating room, projection room
Vorführung *f* demonstration, experiment **~ im Fluge** flying demonstration
Vorführungs-apparat *m* apparatus for demonstration **-film** *m* display film **-flug** *m* demonstration flight **-kabine** *f*, **-raum** *m* projection room or booth (motion pictures) **-wagen** *m* demonstration car
Vorfüll-einrichtung *f* pilot valve **-ventil** *n* preliminary feed valve
Vorfunkenstrecke (Vorschalt-Funkenstrecke) series connected spark gap
Vorgabe *f* burden (min.), handicap, turn control signal, autopilot **-zeit** *f* advance time
Vorgaffel *f* fore gaff
Vorgang *m* process, procedure, operation, act, reaction, event, phenomenon, action, proceeding, occurrence **aperiodischer ~** aperiodic phenomenon **einmaliger ~** nonrecurrent or unique action, singular action, event, or phenomenon **flüchtiger ~** transient phenomenon, transient, equilibrating process **periodischer ~** cyclic operation **umkehrbarer ~** reversible process **unperiodischer ~** nonrecurrent or nonperiodic action or phenomenon **zeitlich veränderlicher ~** action variable with time
Vorgänger *m* predecessor, antecedent, progenitor **ohne ~** unprecedented
Vorgarnspinner *m* rover
vorgearbeitet prepared **-e Röhre** prefabricated pipe **-e Welle** rough-machined shaft **-es Werkstück** blank already machined
vorgebaut in front of
vorgeben to presuppose, assume as existing, advance, allege, pretend
vorgebildeter Niederschlag preformed precipitate
Vorgebirge *n* mountain spar, foothill, promontory
vorgebrochenes Gut pre-crushed material
vorgedruckte Linie ruled line
vorgefertigt prefabricated
vorgefördert pushed forward
vorgeformt preformed
vorgefräst pre-milled, rough-milled
vorgefrischt semipurified, semifinished
vorgegeben given, specified, prescribed (math.), preset, above mentioned **-er Wert** desired value of controlled variable
vorgegossen hole-cored **-es Loch** cored hole
vorgehen to advance, precede, run fast, lead
Vorgehen *n* advance, procedure, approach **abschnittweises ~** advance by bounds
vorgeklärt pre-clarified
vorgekragt corbeled
vorgeladene (formierte) **Platte** precharged or preloaded plate (battery)
Vorgelände *n* foreground, outlying lands
Vorgelege *n* back-gearing arrangement, intermediate gear, back gear, reduction gear, gearing, transmission gear, countershaft, pinion (rim), transmission, connecting gear **~ für Tourenreduzierung** reducing gear
Vorgelege-bremse *f* brake on the transmission shaft **-einrückhebel** *m* back-gear lever **-rad** *n* countershaft wheel **-räderhaube** *f* back-gear case guard **-räderschutzkappe** *f* back-gear cover guard **-schutzkappe** *f* back-gear case **-welle** *f* jackshaft, countershaft, intermediate shaft, back gear **-zahnradblock** *m* constant mesh gear
vorgelegt given **-e Funkenlage** advanced sparking
vorgelochte Karten prepunched cards
vorgemischt premixed
vorgenannt described above
vorgeordnet marshalled
vorgepreßtes Rad rough-pressed wheel
vorgereinigt prefiltered
vorgerückter Sackflug, vorgerückter überzogener Flug advanced stall
Vorgerüst *n* rougher, roughing stand, blooming stand, breaking-down stand
vorgeschaltet superposed on, lined up
Vorgeschichte *f* antecedent, previous history
vorgeschiedener Saft predefecated juice, prelimed juice
vorgeschlagen proposed
vorgeschlitzt pre-slit
vorgeschoben advanced
vorgeschrieben positive, prescribed, specified **-e Belastung** stipulated load **-er Motorkennwert** engine specification
vorgeschroppt rough machined
vorgeschruppte Räder roughed gears
vorgesehen intended, provided
Vorgesetzter *m* principal, chief, superior, boss
vorgespannt biased, prestressed, initially tensioned **elektrisch ~** electrically biased
Vorgespinst *n* slub, roving
Vorgestell *n* first cabinet (missiles)
vorgesteuert balanced
vorgetäuscht simulated
vorgewählt preselected
vorgewalzt rough rolled **-er Block** cogged ingot, bloom
vorgewärmt preheated
vorgezogene Funkenlage salient spark position
Vorgitterfläche *f* grid-bias surface
Vorglimmlicht-gebiet *n* sustaining voltage range, prephotoglow region **-zelle** *f* photoemissive gas-filled cell
Vorglühen *n* preliminary heating, annealing
Vorglühofen *m* annealing furnace or oven
Vorgraben *m* outer trench
vorgreifen to anticipate
Vorgreifer *m* auxiliary gripper **-hebel** *m* swinging gripper lever
Vorgriff *m* anticipation
vorgrundieren to ground
Vorgruppierung *f* batch processing

vorhaben to intend
Vorhaben *n* intention, intent (law)
Vorhafen *m* outer harbor, outer basin
Vorhalle *f* entrance hall, vestibule
vorhallen to overemphasize, preverberate
Vorhalt *m* aiming-off allowance (for height, speed, lead, deflection), rate action, derivative. action, proviso
Vorhalte-einrichtung *f* lead computer **-kurs** *m* lead course **-maß** *n* amount of lead, lead value, lead figure (in charge tables)
vorhalten to lead, take a lead on
Vorhalten *n* lead, provision
Vorhalte-punkt *m* lead point, future position, predicted position **-zeit** *f* (electronics) rate-time
Vorhalter *m* holding-on tool, revetting knob
Vorhalte-schnurleitung *f* cord-junction circuit **-stöpsel** *m* plug of the trunk junction circuit **-strecke** *f* predicting interval **-winkel** *m* angle of lead, bombing angle, drift angle
Vorhaltrechner *m* delay corrector
Vorhaltswert *m* speed allowance, amount of lead
Vorhaltung *f* (Baumaschinen) furnishing (of machinery and equipment)
Vorhalt-visier *n* lead sight **-wirkung** *f* rate action, derivative action **-zeit** *f* derivative action time (aut. contr), rate time
Vorhammer *m* straight-pane sledge, sledge hammer
vorhämmern to bloom
Vorhämmern der Pakete roughing down of piles
Vorhand *f* forehand
vorhanden existing, available, at hand **-er Bestand** *m* balance on hand **-e Last** basic load **-e Pferdekraft** horsepower available
Vorhandensein *n* existence, presence
Vorhang *m* curtain, draping, drapery **-blende** *f* curtain-fading shutter
Vorhängeaufblendung *f* curtain fade-in
vorhängen to curtain
Vorhänger *m* lens attachment **-fassung** *f* slip-on mount **-gestell** *n* frame of the lens attachment
Vorhänge-schloß *n* padlock
Vorhanghalter *m* curtain clasp
Vorhaupt *n* forestarling
Vorhelling *f* breast of slipway, launch
vorher before, previously, beforehand **-bestimmen** to predetermine
Vorherd *m* forehearth, settler, receiver
vorherig previous
vorherrschen to prevail
Vorherrschen *n* predomination, prevailing, preponderance
vorherrschend prevalent, prevailing **-er Wind** prevailing wind **-e westliche Winde** prevailing westerlies **-e Windrichtung** prevailing wind direction
Vorhersage *f* forecast, prognosis **-karte** *f* (Meteorologie) prognostic chart
vorhersagen to forecast
Vorherzurichten *n* pre-sizing
vorhobeln to rough-plane
Vorhof *m* front yard, forebay
Vorholeinrichtung *f* counterrecoil or recuperator mechanism
vorholen to recuperate
Vorholer *m* counterrecoil mechanism, recuperator **-kolbenstange** *f* rod of recuperation piston **-lager** *n* counterrecoil-cylinder yoke **-stütze** *f* counterrecoil-cylinder support
Vorhol-feder *f* recoil spring, recuperator or running-out spring **-zylinder** *m* counterrecoil cylinder, recuperator cylinder
Vorhubmeßgerät *n* pre-stroke measuring instrument
vorimprägniert pre-compounded, pre-loaded
Vorimpuls *m* pretrigger, preknock impulse (rdr.)
Vorimpulserzeuger *m* preimpulse sender (generator)
vorionisiert preionized
vorjährig of last year
vorjustiert preadjusted
Vorkaliber *n* preceding pass, previous pass (in rolling) **-walze** *f* roughing roll, stranding roll, breaking-down roll, shaping roll **-walzen** *n* shaping, roughing, breaking down **-walzgerüst** *n* strand
Vorkalkulation *f* calculation of production
Vorkammer *f* antechamber, precombustion chamber, forehearth (oven) **-boden** *m* floor of the lock entrance (upstream or downstream) **-Diesel** *m* prechamber compression-ignition engine, preignition Diesel **-Dieselmotor** *m* prechamber compression ignition engine **-einspritzung** *f* antechamber system of injection **-maschine** *f* precombustion chamber engine
Vorkanal *m* basic channel
Vorkarde *f* breaker, breaking card
Vorkasten *m* ante-chamber
Vorkaufsrecht *n* right of preemption or of refusal
Vorkehr *f* precaution, provision
vorkehren to take precautions
Vorkehrung *f* precaution, provision, precautionary measure **Vorkehrungen treffen** to take precautions
Vorkeller *m* forecellar
Vorkipper *m* end-tip wagon
vorklappbar designed to swing (turn) in front
Vorklärung *f* preclarification
Vorklassiersieb *n* primary classifying screen
Vorklassierung *f* preclassification
Vorklotzung *f* pad ground
Vorkocher *m* foreboiler
vorkommen to occur, appear, happen
Vorkommen *n* presence, occurrence **stockförmiges ~** occurrence in floors (min.)
Vorkommnis *n* occurrence
Vorkondensator *m* series capacitor
Vorkonzentration *f* preliminary focusing, prefocus, first-focus action
vorkörnen to pre-grain
Vorkorrektur *f* preliminary proof (first proof)
Vorkost *f* first course, provisions
Vorkracken *n* primary cracking
Vorkragung *f* corbel
Vorkratze *f* breaker (textiles)
Vorkreis *m* input circuit
Vorkrempel *m* breaker or scribbler card
vorkühlen to precool
Vorkühler *m* forecooler, precooler, primary cooler
Vorkühlraum *m* forechill room
Vorkühlung *f* primary cooling
vorkurbeln to advance by crank

Vorlack *m* size, pore filler
vorladen to summon, cite, serve, subpoena
Vorladung *f* appointment, notice, notification, summons, subpoena, writ, citation **gerichtliche ~** summons
Vorlage *f* receiver, absorption bulb, condenser, collecting main, flash hider, tail-box water seal, original copy, pattern **-matten** *pl* rubber back velvet mats **-mündung** *f* condenser nose
vorlagern to introduce, establish (an equilibrium or concentration), store before using
Vorlagerungsrohr *n* duct that gives tidal air effect
Vorlageschneidemaschine *f* router
Vorlagestück *n*, **~ für Querträger** cross plate
Vorläppen *n* blocking down
Vorlaß *m* first runnings
Vorlast *f* initial loading
Vorlauf *m* caster, first runnings, offset (of front axle), lead or precession of sound, forward stroke **einmaliger ~** single sweep
Vorlauf-bewegung *f* counterrecoil motion **-dorn** *m* control plunger
vorlaufen to move ahead or in front of
Vorlauf-geschwindigkeit *f* cutting speed **-leitung** *f* flow line **-pumpe** *f* initial water pump
Vorläufer *m* predecessor, forerunner, stray line, precursor, sign, indication, clue
Vorlaufhemmstange *f* counterrecoil buffer
vorläufig for the time being, temporary, provisional, preliminary, advance (notice) **-er Anruf** preliminary call **-es Betriebsblatt** advance service bulletin **-e Patentbeschreibung** provisional specification
Vorlauf-scheibe *f* forward-driving pulley **-ventil** *n* retarding or recuperator valve **-zeit** *f* lead time
Vorlaugung *f* preliminary leaching
Vorlege-messer *n* carving knife **-platte** *f* wall plate **-schloß** *n* padlock
vorlegen to propose, display, submit, pose
Vorlegierung *f* key alloy, hardener
Vorleine *f* bow line
Vorlesung *f* (university) lecture
Vorlicht *n* priming or biasing illumination
Vorlickerung *f* preliminary fat-liquoring
vorliegen to be on hand, be existent
vorliegend present **der -e Fall** the case in question or under review
Vorlochdaten *pl* prepunched data
vorlochen to pre-punch, pre-pierce
vormachen to demonstrate, deceive
vormagnetisieren to polarize, bias, premagnetize, presaturate
vormagnetisierte Spule transductor
Vormagnetisierung *f* magnetization, polarization, superposed magnetization, bias magnetization
Vormagnetisierungsstrom *m* biasing current, DC magnetizing current **-wicklung** *f* bias winding
Vormahlen *n* preliminary grinding
Vormaischbottich *m* steeping trough
Vormann *m* foreman
Vormars *m* foretop
Vormarsch *m* advance
Vormarsstand *m* director foretop
Vormaterial *n* starting material, blanks
Vormeldestromkreis *m* warning circuit
Vormeldung *f* warning
vormerken to note
Vormerkgespräch *n* delayed call
vorragend projecting
Vorrang *m* priority, precedence, preeminence, superiority, first rank
Vormischung *f* premixing
Vormodelierung *f* premodulation
vorn in front, fore, ahead, forward, at the head or bow, anteriorly **von ~ nach hinten** from front to back **~ und hinten festmachen** to secure fore and aft
vornehmen to conduct, undertake, take up, deal with
vornetzen to wet out
Vornitrierungsbehandlung *f* prenitriding treatment
vornliegend ahead
Vornorm *f* tentative standard
Vorordnerschnecke *f* prearranging worm
Vorort *m* suburb **-bahn** *f* suburban railway
Vororts-gebiet *n* suburban area **-gespräch** *n* toll or suburban call **-leitung** *f* suburban junction **-netz** *n* tandem area **-platz** *m* suburban position **-schrank** *m* suburban switchboard **-verbindung** *f* toll call to suburban area, suburban connection
Vorortsverkehr *m* junction or toll traffic, suburban service or traffic **Anruf im ~** toll call to suburban area
Vororts-verkehrsbereich *m* toll area **-wagen** *m* interurban car
Vorortzug *m* suburban train
Vorpfeilung *f* negative sweep (of wing)
vorplastifizieren pre-plastify
Vorplatz mit befestigtem Boden apron (aviation), landing with solid or firm footing
vorpolieren to rough-polish
Vorpolieren *n* rough polishing
Vorpolier-kaliber *n* first-finishing pass, leader, planisher **-stich** *m* first-finishing pass, leading pass, planishing pass
Vorpolymerisat *n* pre-polymer
vorprellen to rush forward, snap forward
Vorpresse *f* baby press (paper mfg.)
Vorpreßling *m* rough-pressed block
Vorprisma *n* fore prism
Vorprobe *f* preliminary test, quick test, preliminary analysis, furnace-control test
Vorprodukt *n* intermediate or initial product, first runnings
Vorprofilieren *n* preliminary shaping
Vorprofilierungsgerüst *n* preforming stand or scaffold
Vorprüfer *m* examiner (in patent office)
Vorprüfschalter *m* precheck switch
Vorprüfung *f* previous examination
Vorprüfungsverfahren *n* preliminary examination, preliminary search or action
Vorpumpbolzen *m* priming spindle
Vorpumpe *f* forepump, backing pump (for vacuum)
Vorpumpenseite *f* fore-vacuum side
Vorpumphebel *m* priming lever
Vorpunktieren *n* pointing
Vorraffination *f* softening, improving (lead), prerefining **~ im Schmelzfluß** preliminary fire refining
vorraffinieren to soften, improve (lead)

Vorraffinierofen *m* softening furnace, improving furnace

vorragend projecting

Vorrang *m* priority, precedence, preeminence, superiority, first rank **-gespräch** *n* priority or precedence call **-ordnung** *f* order of precedence **-schaltung** *f* priority circuit **-stufe** *f* precedence

Vorrat *m* supply, store, provision, stock, spare parts, tankage **auf ~** in stock **aus ~** from stock

vorrätig on hand, in stock, in store, available

Vorrats-ader *f* spare wire **-anzeiger** *m* contents indicator (on fuel gauge) **-behälter** *m* stock bin, storage bunker, supply bin **-bunker** *m* bin **-fahrzeug** *n* supply wagon **-felge** *f* spare wheel rim **-flasche** *f* stock bottle **-gabelschaltung** *f* spare terminating set **-geber** *m* contents transmitter **-haltung** *f* maintenance of stocks or supplies **-haufen** *m* piling stores, piles

Vorrats-kabel *n* stock cable **-kathode** *f* dispenser cathode **-kessel** *m* storage tank **-kondensator** *m* tank condenser, reservoir condenser **-lagerung** *f* stockpiling **-lauf** *m* spare barrel **-leitung** *f* spare circuit, stand-by circuit **-lösung** *f* stock solution **-luftbehälter** *m* compressed air storage tank **-messer** *m* contents or quantity gauge **-platz** *m* stockyard, store yard **-raum** *m* warehouse, storeroom, magazine, stockhouse **-röhre** *f* input tube **-rolle** *f* delivery spool (wire-winding machines), magazine roll

Vorrats-sachen *pl* spares **-schrank** *m* cupboard, meat safe **-spule** *f* delivery spool (wire-winding machines) **-tank** *m* stock tank, storage tank **-tasche** *f* bunker, storage pocket, storage bin **-teil** *m* spare part **-trichter** *m* hopper **-trommel** *f* spare drum **-verstärker** *m* spare repeater **-windung** *f* spare turn **-zeiger** *m* (Luftpresser-) supply pointer (air compressor)

Vorraum *m* anteroom, outer chamber, antechamber, pedestal

Vorraute *f* first diamond pass (in rolling)

Vorreaktion *f* prereaction, preflame reactions **~ im Brenngemisch** preflame ignition

Vorrechner *m* calculator

Vorrechnung *f* calculating, costing

Vorrecht *n* privilege, prerogative, priority, exclusive right

Vorreduktion *f* preliminary reduction, prereduction

vorreduzieren to prereduce

Vorregler *m* input control (soundwaves)

Vorreibahle *f* rough(ing) reamer

vorreiben to grind beforehand, rough-ream

Vorreiber *m* turnbuckle, (Fenster) casement fastener

Vorreife *f* aging **-kasten** *m* aging hopper

Vorreiniger *m* pre-cleaner, prefilter

Vorreinigung *f* preliminary cleaning or purification

vorreißen to draw or scribe, perforate

Vorreißer *m* drawing point, marking tool **-rost** *m* taker-in grid

Vorrevision *f* preliminary inspection

vorrichten to prepare

Vorrichtung *f* device, fixture, arrangement, appliance, contrivance, equipment, apparatus, mechanism, attachment(s), installation, intrument, outfit, preparation **~ zur Herstellung bestimmter Versuchsbedingungen** conditioning device **~ zur Steigerung des Auftriebs** high-lift device **~ zur Verhütung des Leckens** antidribble device **Zusammenbau in einer ~** (Flugzeugbau) rigging **einziehbare ~** retractable gear **leicht zu bedienende ~** easy-to-operate device **nicht lineare ~** nonlinear device **zusätzliche ~** auxiliary attachment

Vorrichtungs-anschlaglehre *f* go-no-go gauge **-arbeit** *f* preparatory work **-arbeiter** *m* drifter, stoneman **-bohrmaschine** *f* jig boring machine **-formlehre** *f* block gauge **-schmiegenlehre** *f* adapter gauge **-urlehre** *f* master gauge

vorroden to predig

Vorröhre *f* input tube

Vorröhrenmodulation *f* series modulation, constant voltage modulation

vorrösten to preroast

Vorröstofen *m* preroasting furnace

Vorröstung *f* preroast, preliminary roasting

vorrücken to advance, move forward, feed (forward), progress, step forward **um einen Schritt ~** to advance one step **zu weit ~** to overfeed

Vorrücken *n* advance

Vor-Rück-Verhältnis forward-to-back ratio (Television)

Vorrüst *f* fore channels

vorsagen to prompt

Vorsammel-linse *f* first-focusing lens, cathode lens **-spule** *f* cathode-tube concentration coil

Vorsatz *m* intention, design, plan, premeditation **~ im metrischen System** prefix of the metric system **mit ~** deliberately, intentionally

Vorsatz-blatt *n* end paper (bookbinding) **-büchse** *f* front bush (supplementary bush) **-gerät** *n* converter, adapter (radio), attached or accessory device, head (motion pictures) **-gitter** *n* protection grill **-keil** *m* objective prism **-küvette** *f* light-filter trough **-läufer** *m* intake fan, inlet fan

vorsätzlich intentional, deliberate, willful, purposely, premeditatedly **-e Beschädigung** sabotage

Vorsatz-linse *f* ancillary lens (phot.), front-lens attachment, magnascope **-papier** *n* book lining paper **-platte** *f* door plate **-prisma** *n* objective prism **-stahlhalter** *m* adaptor toolpost **-stoffe** *pl* jointing pastes **-transformator** *m* series transformer

Vorschacht *m* preliminary shaft, foreshaft

Vorschäler *m* jointer

Vorschalt-anlage *f* tapping plant, superimposed plant **-drossel** (zum Entstörkondensator) series choke coil or reactor

vorschalten to connect in series, cut in circuit

Vorschalt-funkenstrecke *f* series spark gap **-gerät** *n* main connecting device, power supply unit **-getriebe** *n* twin-range case, transfer case **-leitung** *f* trunk-junction circuit **-linse** *f* swing-over lens **-turbine** *f* topping turbine, superimposed turbine **-widerstand** *m* series resistance, resistor, rheostat resistance, multiplier (of a voltmeter)

Vorschaltung *f* series connection, interposing, coupling

vorschärfen to sharpen (previously)

Vorschaumer *m* flotation rougher

vorscheiden to predefecate

Vorscheidepfanne *f* predefecation tank

Vorscheidung *f* predefecation, preliming
Vorschein *m* appearance **zum ~ kommen** to appear, emerge
vorschieben to feed (engin.), advance
Vorschiebung *f* feeding (engin.)
Vorschiff *n* forecastle
Vorschlag *m* proposal, proposition, flux **-keil** *m* range reducing wedge **-pfahl** *m* set pile
vorschlagbar capable of being moved, dropped, let, or folded down on hinges
vorschlagen to propose, suggest
Vorschlaghammer *m* sledge hammer, forehammer
vorschleifen to grind rough
Vorschleifen *n* rough grinding
Vorschleifer *m* rough grinder
Vorschleuse *f* entrance (upper or lower)
vorschlichten to first-polish, first-finish
Vorschlicht-kaliber *n* first-finishing pass, leader, planisher **-profil** *n* first-finished section
Vorschliff *m* rough grinding
Vorschmiedegesenk *n* blanker, rougher
vorschmieden to forge in the rough
Vorschmieden *n* preliminary forging, rough forge
Vorschneideisen *n* taper die
Vorschneidemesser *n* counterblade
vorschneiden to make a first cut
Vorschneider *m* (wire) cutter, taper tap (of a screw-threading device), knife cutter
Vorschneid-fräser *m* stocking cutter, roughing cutter **-stahlhalter** *m* roughing toolholder
Vorschnitt *m* part cut
Vorschnitter *m* harvester ganger
Vorschraubring *m* securing ring, locking ring
vorschreiben to specify, prescribe
vorschreibend mandatory
Vorschrift *f* regulation, prescription, instruction, provision, code, manual, rule, specification, direction **gesundheitspolizeiliche Vorschriften** department-of-health regulations **technische Vorschriften** specifications, instructions
Vorschriftenbereich *m* range (of specifications)
vorschriftsgemäß, vorschriftsmäßig according to regulations or instructions, prescribed
vorschrinken to preshrink
Vorschrinkung *f* preshrinkage
Vorschub *m* thrust, push, shear, throw, feed (Telegr.), help, assistance, furtherance, advance, traverse, conveyance ~ (Bagger) crowding **~ geben** to feed **~ leisten** to afford assistance, lend a hand, promote, support **feinstufiger ~** sensitive feed **geringer ~** fine feed **gleichmäßig ununterbrochener ~** continuous feed **maschineller ~** power feed **selbsttätiger ~** power traverse **starker ~** coarse feed
Vorschub-achse *f* (Fernschreiber) spacing shaft **-änderung** *f* change of feed **-anlage** *f* feed stop **-anschlag** *m* feed stop **-antrieb** *m* feed drive **-auslösung** *f* disengaging of the feed **-ausschaltkamm** *m* (Fernschreiber) function lever-spacing suppression **-bereich** range of feed **-bewegung** *f* feed motion, feed movement, power feed
Vorschub-daumen *m* spacing cam **-einrichtung** *f* feeder, feeding device **-getriebe** *n* feed gear, advance gear **-haltung** *f* feed control, feed mechanism **-handrad** *n* hand-feed wheel **-klinke** feed pawl **-kontrollbuchse** *f* ejection control hub **-kraft** *f* feeding power **-kuppelungshebel** *m* feed-clutch lever **-kurve** *f* feed cam **-kurventrommel** *f* feed cam drum
Vorschub-magnet *m* feeding magnet, spacing magnet **-mechanismus** *m* advance mechanism, feeding device **-patrone** *f* feed chuck **-rad** *n* feed wheel, automatic lead **-räderkasten** *m* feed gear box **-räderwerk** *n* feed gearing **-reduzierung** *f* feed reduction control **-regelung** *f* feed adjuster **-regler** *m* feed regulator
Vorschubrichtung *f* feed direction **entgegengesetzt zur ~ zurückziehen** to feed back
Vorschub-rohr *n* feed tube **-rost** *m* stoker with reciprocating grate bars **-schaltbuchse** *f* main shaft spacing gear **-schaltventil** *n* feed pilot valve **-schlitten** *m* feed slide **-schneckenradwelle** *f* feed worm (gear) shaft **-spannung** *f* feed voltage **-spindel** *f* feed screw
Vorschub-stange *f* feed bar **-stellung** *f* feed position **-stift** *m* feed pawl, feed pin, feed bolt **-umkehrhebel** *m* feed reverse lever **-umsteuerung** *f* feed reverse **-wählskala** *f* feed selection dial
Vorschubwechsel *m* feed change **-einrichtung** *f* variable feed attachment **-räderkasten** *m* feed change box
Vorschub-welle *f* feed rod **-zahnrad** *n* feed gear **-zahnstange** *f* feed rack **-zange** *f* feed collect **-zylinder** *m* feed cylinder
Vorschuß *m* deposit, money advanced, advance **-kappe** *f* fuse cap, dust excluder **-zahlung** *f* payment in advance
vorschützen to pretend, dam (up)
Vorschweißbunde *pl* welding collars
vorschweißen to preweld
Vorschweißflansch *m* blank flange
Vorschwinger *m* preshoot (TV)
vorsehen to provide for
vorseitig on the previous page
Vorselektion *f* preselection (radio), assigned frequency
Vorserienmodell *n* preproduction model
vorsetzen to place before, preset
Vorsetzzeichen *n* prefix
Vorsicht *f* care, caution, prudence, foresight, precaution
vorsichtig cautious, careful
Vorsichtsmaßregel *f* safety order, precautionary measure
Vorsieb *n* forescreen
Vorsignal *n* presignal, warning signal, first or outer marking signal, caution signal
vorsintern to presinter, semisinter
Vorsitzender *m* foreman, chairman
Vorsorge *f* foresight, early attention
vorsortieren pre-sort
Vorspann *m* team of horses, label (of print), leader (of film), screen credit (film) **-band** *n* leader-tape (tape rec.) **-bremse** *f* (Servobremse) servo brake
vorspannen to bias (elec.), prestress **eine Lokomotive ~** to put an additional locomotive to . . .
Vorspann-kraft *f* initial stressing force **-programm** *n* prologue **-rahmen** *m* saw frame
Vorspannung *f* grid potential, initial stress, polarizing potential, priming, initial or biasing potential, bias, prestressing, residual stress, bias voltage (rectifier), compression spring, pressurising, pretension **~ der Feder** initial

stress or tension in the spring **automatische ~** auto bias **~ erteilen** to bias **einseitige ~** bias **magnetische ~** magnetic polarization, magnetic bias **negative ~** negative bias **verriegelnde ~** cutoff biasing potential

Vorspannungsgerät *n* bias box (TV)

Vorspannventil *n* pressurising valve

vorspeichern to prestore

Vorspektrum *n* preliminary spectrum

Vorsperre *f* auxiliary dam

vorspinnen to slub, rove

Vorspinnen *n* slubbing, roving

Vorspinner *m* preparer

Vorspinnmaschine *f* stretching mule, billy (wool mfg.), fly frame, drawing frame

vorsprechen, bei jemandem ~ to call on a person

vorspringen to project, protrude, be salient or prominent

vorspringend salient, projecting **-e Fuge** tuck pointing

Vorspritzung *f* first spray

Vorsprung *m* projection, shoulder, boss, salient, lead, head start, overhang, key, tenon, tab, advance, protrusion, prominence, bump, dent **~ der Deckplatte** weathering **~ eines Nockens** lobe, projection of a cam **~ und Rücksprung** spigot and socket

Vorspülung *f* preliminary rinsing

Vorspur *f* toe in

Vorstadt *f* suburb

Vorstaffel *f* roughing train

Vorstand *m* directorate, managing committee **~ einer Gesellschaft** chairman of the board

vorstanzen (auf einem kleineren Durchmesser) to sub-punch

Vorstauch-apparat *m* upsetting device **-stempel** *m* top header, first upsetter

Vorstauchung *f* precompression

vorstechen to pierce

Vorstechmaschine *f* punching machine

vorstecken to plug in

Vorsteck-achse *f* pinned-on shaft **-bolzen** *m* cotter pin, pintle

Vorstecker *m* tension lock (fuse), fuse safety pin, bradawl, pawl, cotter, cotter pin, pin **-scharnierband** *n* joint hinge with pin or peg

Vorsteck-keil *m* cotter (pin) **-raster** *m* replaceable graticule (CRT) **-riemen** *m* protective strap **-scheibe** *f* take-up washer, U washer, C washer **-splint** *m* cotter split pin **-stift** *m* stop or locking pin, cotter pin (taper), temporary locking pin

vorstehen to protrude, jut out **einer Firma ~** to manage or represent a firm

vorstehend projecting, aforesaid, preceding, pending

Vorstein *m* breakdown die

vorstellen to advance, introduce **sich ~** to realize, conceive, introduce oneself

Vorstellen *n* advance (magnet)

Vorstell-platte *f* dead-plate (of grates) **-rost** *f* front bars

Vorstellung *f* introduction, performance (of a play), idea, advance, mental picture, conception, notion, representation, demonstration, display **räumliche ~** impression of space

Vorstellwinkel *m* angle of lead

Vorsteuerdruck *m* pilot pressure

Vorsteuerung *f* anticipatory control

Vorsteuerventil *n* servo valve

Vorsteven *m* stem

Vorstich *m* roughing pass, breaking-down pass, shaping pass, blooming pass, cogging pass

Vorstimmer *m* tuner

Vorstoff *m* raw material, semifinished goods

Vorstoß *m* thrust, push, piping (on uniform), adapter, advance, assault, lunge, edging, lap, projection, lug **-borte** *f* edging

Vorstrahl *m* initial jet

Vorstraße *f* roughing or shaping train (of rolls), cogging train, blooming train, breaking-down train, roughing mill

Vorstrecke *f* roughing or cogging strand (of rolls), blooming strand, shaping strand, breaking-down strand, blooming mill

vorstrecken to rough, rough down, cog, bloom, shape, break down, bolt

Vorstrecken *n* pony roughing, cogging, blooming, shaping, breaking down, bolting

Vorstreck-gerüst *n* pony roughing strand (of rolls), pony rougher **-kaliber** *n* roughing-out pass, cogging pass, blooming pass, shaping pass, breaking-down pass **-walze** *f* roughing roll, cogging roll, blooming roll, shaping roll, breaking-down roll, bolting roll

vorstreichen to prime

Vorstrom *m* dead water, indraft, dark presparking current **-anemometer** *n* corona-discharge anemometer **-entladung** *f* leakage current

Vorstudie *f* preliminary study

Vorstufe *f* driving stage, preceding stage, first step, input or first stage (of amplifier), primer

Vorstufen *n* low-stage modulation **-leistungsschalter** *m* individual bank breaker **-schalter** *m* protection switch with resistance

Vorsturzwalzwerk *n* mill for rolling breakdown, jobbing mill

Vorsud *n* first boiling

Vorsumpf *m* initial sump (electricity-absorbing layer)

Vorsynchronisieren *n* prescoring

Vortagsanmeldung *f* carried-forward call

vortäuschen to simulate, mislead

Vorteil *m* advantage, gain **~ bringen** to be advantageous

vorteilhaft advantageous, profitable

Vortexring *m* vortex

Vorticitygleichung *f* predischarge vorticity equation

Vortiegel *m* lead pot, outer basin, forehearth

Vortor *n* time basegate

Vortrab *m* vanguard, advance guard **-arten** *pl* preequalizing pulses

Vortrag *m* lecture, paper

Vortragsabdruck *m* lecture reprint

Vortransport *m* supply sprocket

vortreiben to drive **einen Stollen ~** to drive a gallery on

Vortreibepfahl *m* lath (min.)

Vortrieb *m* propulsion, forward thrust, advance, feed, positive drive, tongue **~ durch Heizstrahltriebwerk** thermal jet propulsion **im ~ umgekehrter Luftwiderstand** negative drag

Vortriebs-achse *f* line of thrust **-arbeit** *f* thrust energy **-düse** *f* propulsion nozzle **-einrichtung** *f* propulsive means **-erzeugung** *f* propulsive effort **-geschwindigkeit** *f* forward speed **-kraft** *f*

propulsive or propelling force **-mittelpunkt** *m* center of thrust **-schild** *m* driving shield **-wirkung** *f* propulsion efficiency **-wirkungsgrad** *m* propulsion efficiency, propellent efficiency
Vortrockenzylinder *m* drying cylinder in front of the machine
vortrocknen to predry
Vortrockner *m* receiving drier
Vortrocknung *f* preliminary drying
Vortrocknungskammer *f* preliminary drying chamber
Vortrommel *f* breast roller
Vortrupp *m* advance unit
vorübergehend passing, transitory, transient **schnell ~** transient **-er Vorgang** transient transaction **-er Zustand** transient state
Vorübergruppe *f* basic super-group
Vorübertrager *m* input transformer, input repeating coil
Vor- und Auslösesignal *n* presignal and release signal
Vor- und Fertigdrehen *n* roughing and finishing
Vor- und Hauptverstärker *m* preamplifier and main amplifier
Vor- und Nachbehandeln *n* preparatory and final processing
Vor- und Nachfiltration *f* pre and after filtration
Vor- und Nachprüfung *f* before and after test
Vor- und Nachwickelrolle *f* first and second sprocket wheel
Vor- und Rückgang *m* reciprocating motion
vor- und rücklaufende Blätter *pl* advancing and retreating blades
Vor- und Rücksprungverbindung *f* ball and spigot
vor- und rückwärtslaufend reversible
Vor- und Seitenschneider *m* end and side-cutting pliers
Voruntersuchung *f* preliminary investigation or test
Voruntersetzereinheit *f* preliminary frequency divider stage
Vorvakuum-anschluß *m* fore-vacuum connection **-behälter** *m* interstage reservoir **-pumpe** *f* forepump, rough-vacuum pump, backing pump
Vorventil *n* initial valve, pressure-operated valve
Vorverarbeitung *f* pre-processing
Vorverbrennung *f* (Dieselmotor) precombustion
Vorverbrennungsraum *m* (Dieselmotor) precombustion chamber
Vorverdampfer *m* preevaporator
Vorverdampfung *f* preevaporation
vorverdichten to supercharge
vorverdichtend supercharging **-er Motor** supercharge engine
Vorverdichter *m* supercharger, compressor, blower **direkt angetriebener ~** gear-driven supercharger
Vorverdichter-druckstutzen *m* blower-pressure pipe butt, pressure inlet **-laderad** *n* supercharger impeller **-motor** *m* blower motor
Vorverdichtertypus *m*, **hin- und hergehender ~** reciprocating-type supercharger
Vorverdichterwelle *f* impeller shaft, blower shaft
vorverdichtet supercharged
Vorverdichtung *f* preconsolidation, supercharging, precompression
vorverdünnen to prerarefy
Vorverfahren *n* preliminary procedure or proceedings
Vorverformung *f* pre-strain
vorverlegen advance **einen Termin ~** to shorten an agreed period
vorverlegt advanced **-es Vorsignal** advanced presignal
Vorverlegung *f* shift forward
Vorveröffentlichung *f* anticipation (patents) **gedruckte ~** printed reference (patent)
Vorverstärker *m* input amplifier, preamplifier **-stufe** *f* preamplifier stage
Vorverstärkung *f* gain amplification, preamplification
Vorversuch *m* preliminary test or trial
Vorvertrag *m* provisional agreement
Vorverzerrer *m* pre-distorter
Vorvulkanisation *f* pre-curing
Vorvulkanisationsverzögerer *m* scorch retarder
vorvulkanisieren to pre-vulcanize
Vorwachs *n* bee glue, propolis
Vorwahl *f* preselection, finding action, sender selection, assigned frequency **doppelte ~** tandem preselection, double preselection **teilweise doppelte ~** partly double preselection
vorwählbar pre-selectable
Vorwählbarkeit *f* assigned frequency
Vorwählblende *f* preselection diaphragm
Vorwahldekadenzähler *m* batching decade counter
vorwählen to preset, preselect
Vorwähler *m* preselector, line switch, individual line switch **erster ~** primary line switch **zehnteiliger ~** ten-point preselector **zweiter ~** second preselector, secondary line switch, trunk-hunting switch
Vorwähler-antrieb *m* master switch **-gestell** *n* line switchboard
Vorwählgetriebe *n* preselective gear
Vorwähl-impuls *m* preselected pulse **-schalter** *m* preset pulse switch unit **-schaltereinheit** *f* preselection pulse switch
Vorwähl-reihenzähler *m* preset row counter **-schalteinrichtung** *f* pre-selector mechanism **-schalter** *m* priority select switch **-schaltung** *f* pre-selecting control **-springblende** *f* spring-loaded preselector aperture **-stufe** *f* stage of preselection
Vorwalze *f* bloom or billet roll
vorwalzen to rough, rough down, cog down, cog, bloom, shape, break down, bolt (rolling-mill work)
Vorwalzen *n* roughing, cogging, blooming
Vorwalz-strecke *f* roughing strand of rolls, cogging strand, blooming strand, shaping strand **-trio** *n* three-high roughing mill **-werk** *n* roughing mill, cogging mill, blooming mill, shaping mill, breaking-down mill
Vorwand *m* pretext, excuse, subterfuge **als ~ brauchen** to pretend **unter dem ~** on the plea, under the pretense
Vorwärmeeinrichtung *f* hot spot
vorwärmen to preheat
Vorwärmer *m* preheater, heater, economizer, waterfeed heater, stove **~ für Speisewasser** feedwater heater
Vorwärmer-röhre *f* preheating tube **-schlange** *f* regenerator coil

Vorwärmewalze *f* feed mill

Vorwärm-kammer *f* preheating chamber **-ofen** *m* preheating furnace, forehearth

Vorwärmung *f* preliminary heating, preheating, forewarming

Vorwärmungszone *f* heating-up zone, preheating zone, distillation zone

Vorwarner *m* outpost observer, spotter **-kraftwagen** *m* spotter's lorry or truck

Vorwarnung *f* early warning, alert signal

vorwärts ahead, forward **~ bringen** to promote, advance

Vorwärts-auslösung *f* calling-party release **-belegung mit Haltekreis** forward hold **-bewegung** *f* forward motion, advance, active stroke (in film feed), translatory movement **-differentialgleichung** *f* forward differential equation **-einschneiden** to intersect **-einschnitt** *m* intersection **-gang** *m* forward speed, direct action **-geschwindigkeit** *f* forward speed **-hub** *m* forward stroke **-lauf** *m* ahead running, forward or advance movement (motion) traverse or run **-nachruf** *m* forward recall signal

Vorwärts-regelung *f* direct control, forward-acting regulation **-schalten** to step on, step up (to) **-schnellen** to impel forward **-schweißung** *f* progressive welding **-staffelung** *f* forward stagger, positive stagger **-stellung** *f* ahead position **-steuerung** *f* forward or ahead gear **-stoßen** to push forward **-strebend** going-ahead **-treiben** to propel, impel **-turbine** *f* ahead or cruising turbine, turbine running forward

Vorwärts- und Rückwärtsauslösung *f* first-party release

Vorwärtsvisur *f* forward vision

Vorwärts-zu-Rückwärtsverhältnis *n* front-to-rear ratio

Vorwäsche *f* preliminary washing

Vorweg *m* pretrajectory condition or time (electronics) **-änderungen** *f pl* pre-modifications (info proc.) **-nahmemethode** *f* anticipation mode

vorwegnehmend anticipatory

Vorwegparameter *m* preset parameter (info proc.)

vorwerfen project or push forward, reproach

Vorwerk *n* advanced work, outworks

Vorwickel *m* pull-down sprocket **-rolle** *f*, **-trommel** *f* supply reel, (upper) feed sprocket, pull-down sprocket **-zahntrommeln** *pl* pre-spooling sprockets

Vorwickler *m* upper feed sprocket

Vorwiderstand *m* compensating resistance, barrier resistance, series resistance

vorwiegen to prevail, preponderate, outweigh

vorwiegend predominant, major, preponderant, especially, chiefly

Vorwind *m* head wind

Vorwölbung *f* protrusion, anterior curvature

Vorwort *n* preface, forword

Vorwurf *m* subject (phot.), reproach, blame

Vorzeichen *n* (plus or minus) sign, sense, indication, symptom, sign digit (comput.) **entgegengesetztes ~** reversed sign **von gleichem ~** of the same sign **von verschiedenem ~** of different sign

Vorzeichen-bestimmung *f* determination of sign **-prüfsignal** *n* sign-determining signal **-umkehr** *f* sign reversal (comput.) **-ziffer** *f* sign digit (comput.)

Vorzeichner *m* tracer

Vorzeichnung *f* pattern, design, trace, example, key signature

vorzeigen to exhibit, show, present, produce

Vorzeiger *m* pointer

vorzeitig premature **-e Zündung** preignition

Vorzerkleinerung *f* preliminary breaking, jaw crushing, primary crushing, (preliminary) crushing, coarse to medium crushing

Vorzerkleinerungsmühle *f* coarse crusher, coarse-crushing grinder, preliminary grinder or crusher

Vorzerleger *m* filter for monochromator entrance slit

Vorzerlegung *f* crude fractionation (chem)

Vorziehdraht *m* redrawing wire

vorziehen to move up, prefer

Vorzug *m* advantage, special feature, virtue

Vorzugsachse *f* preferred axis

Vorzugsaktie *f* preference share **gewinnbeteiligte ~** participating preference share

Vorzugs-behandlung *f* preferential treatment **-preis** *m* preferential rate **-recht** *n* prior right **-richtung** *f* privileged direction **-system** *n* perferred frame **-wert** *m* preferred value **-zoll** *m* preferential tariff

Vorzündung *f* advanced ignition, premature ignition, preignition, spark advance

Vorzündungsgriff *m* sparking-advance handle

Vorzwirnen *n* silk spinning

Voute *f* haunch (of beam)

Voutenplatte *f* haunched slab

V-Rad *n* gear with tooth correction

V-Stellung *f* dihedral (angle) **negative ~ des Flügels** inverted V **negative ~ der Tragfläche** cathedral

V-Stiel *m* V-type strut

V-Stoß *m* V joint, double-bevel joint, single-V butt joint, weld

V-Stoß mit Stützlasche single Vee butt joint with back up

V-Strebe *f* V strut

Vulkan *m* volcano **-asbest** *m* vulcanized asbestos **-ausbruch** *m* eruption **-faser** *f* vulcanized fiber

Vulkanfiber *f* vulcanized fiber **-ersatzpappen** *pl* semi-vulcanized boards **-rohpapier** *n* vulcanised-fiber base paper **-schleifscheiben** *pl* vulcanised fiber grinding wheels

Vulkan-getriebe *n* vulcan gear **-glas** *n* tempered glass

Vulkanisat *n* vulcanisate (vulcanized goods)

Vulkanisation *f* vulcanization **~ durch trockene Hitze** open cure

Vulkanisations-artikel *pl* vulcanizing styles **-geschwindigkeit** *f* curing rate **-grenzen** *pl* curing range **-kessel** *m* vulcanizing heater or pan

vulkanisch volcanic, igneous **-es Tuffgestein** volcanic tuff

Vulkanisier-apparat *m* vulcanizer **-echtheit** *f* fastness to vulcanizing **-einrichtung** *f* vulcanizing plant

vulkanisieren to vulcanize

Vulkanisierkessel *m* vulcanizing pan
vulkanisiert vulcanized
Vulkanisierung *f* vulcanization, vulcanizing
Vulkanismus *m* vulcanicity
Vulkanit *n* vulcanite
Vulkanpapier *n* fiber paper
Vulkanschlot *m* volcanic vent
Vultex *n* vultex
VU-Meter *n* VU meter (VU = volume unit)
V-Vierkantmutter *f* square wedge or V-slot nut

W

Waage *f* scale, balance, weighing machine **chemische ~** analytical or precision balance, chemical scales **die ~** Libra, the Balance constellation
Waage-balken *m* swingletree, guide frame, beam of balance, scale balance **-balkenradiometer** *m* balance radiometer **-bühne** *f* weighing platform **-gegengewicht** *n* counterpoise
waagerecht horizontal, level **~ gießen** to cast or pour horizontally **-e Ausschleusung der Rohrpostbüchsen** *f* horizontal capsule (carrier) ejection **-er Mittelstab** center stub **-e Ruhestellung** horizontal home position
Waagerecht-bohrmaschine *f* horizontal drilling machine or drill press **-ebene** *f* horizontal plane **-einstellschraube** *f* screw for adjusting horizon **-einstellung** *f* horizontal position or adjustment **-faden** *m* horizontal wire or thread **-feinbohrwerk** *n* horizontal fine boring machine **-flächenschleifmaschine** *f* horizontal surface grinding machine **-flug** *m* level or horizontal flight **-förderung** *f* level transportation **-fräsmaschine** *f* horizontal milling machine
Waagerecht-geschwindigkeit *f* horizontal velocity or speed **-hobler** *m* horizontal planing machine **-induktion** *f* horizontal induction **-komponente** *f* horizontal component **-kraft** *f* horizontal force **-kreis** *m* horizontal circle
Waagerecht-lage *f* even or level position **-magnet** *m* horizontal magnet **-parallaxe** *f* local parallax on the horizon **-planschleifmaschine** *f* horizontal face grinding machine **-schwingung** *f* horizontal oscillation **-stoßmaschine** *f* shaping machine **-tiefbohrmaschine** *f* deep hole boring machine
Waagerecht- und Senkrechtfrässpindel *f* horizontal and vertical cutter spindles
Waagerechtwinkel *m* horizontal angle
Waage-schneide *f* balance knife-edge **-speiser** *m* (Selbstaufleger) weighing feeders **-zimmer** *n* balance room, weighing room
Waagschale *f* weighing dish, scale or balance pan
Waagskala *f* weighing scale
wabbeln to wobble
Wabbelpumpe *f* wobble pump
Wabe *f* honeycomb
waben-artig honeycombed, pitted **-gleichrichter** *m* honeycomb straightener (wind tunnel) **-kondensor** *m* comb condenser **-kühler** *m* honeycomb radiator **-spule** *f* honeycomb coil, duolateral coil, lattice-wound coil **-struktur** *f* honeycomb structure **-wicklung** *f* honeycomb winding, duolateral winding
Wache *f* guard
Wachen *n* watching
Wach-frequenz *f* frequency **-gebäude** *n* guardhouse
wachhabender Ingenieur engineer on duty
wachrufen to awake, call to life, arouse
Wachs *n* paraffin, wax **mit ~ überziehen** to wax
Wachsabdruck *m* wax impression
Wachs-anstrich *m* wax coating **-appretur** *f* wax finish **-artig, -ähnlich** waxy, waxlike **-ausschmelzkessel** *m* wax-melting boiler **-beize** *f* wax stain **-boden** *m* wax cake **-draht** *m* waxed wire, paraffined wire, waxed cotton-covered wire **-druck** *m* wax impression
wachsen to grow, increase, swell, expand, fan out, wax
Wachsen *n* growth, swelling, fanning-out, treeing, waxing, dimensional instability
wachsend growing **nach außen hin ~** exogenous **-er Drall** increasing twist **-e Karte** Mercator's chart
wächsern consisting of wax, waxy
Wachs-faden *m* wax wick **-firnis** *f* wax-varnish **-form** *f* wax mold **-glanz** *m* resinous luster **-harzreserve** *f* wax-resin resist **-kerze** *f* taper **-kitt** *m* mortar of wax, sticking wax, wax cement **-kohle** *f* waxy or lignitic coal **-leinen** *n* oilcloth **-licht** *n* wax candle
Wachsmachen des raffinierten Alauns roching of alum
Wachs-masse *f* wax composition **-matrize** *f* wax recording, stencil **-modell** *n* wax pattern
Wachspapier *n* wax paper **-verfahren** *n* wax-paper extracting process
Wachs-paste *f* cerate paste **-pauspapier** *n* waxed tracing paper **-pflaster** *n* cerate **-platte** *f* (soft) wax disk, wax master **-rohpapier** *n* waxing paper **-salbe** *f* wax ointment (wax salve) **-säure** *f* ceric acid
Wachs-schichtpapier *n* wax-coated paper **-schmelzkessel** *m* wax-melting pot **-stift** *m* wax crayon **-stock** *m* drawn taper, wax taper **-streichhölzchen** *n* wax match **-taffet** *m* oilskin, waxed or oiled silk
Wachstuch *n* oilcloth
Wachstuch-fertigungsmaschine *f* finishing machine for wax cloth **-futteral** *n* case of wax cloth **-mütze** *f* waterproof cap **-haube** *f* dust cover (oil cloth)
Wachstum *n* growth **~ in der Länge** growth in length
Wachstums-faktor *m* growth (critical) factor **-geschwindigkeit** *f* rate of growth **-kurve** *f* growth curve **-spirale** *f* growth spiral **-spitze** *f* strategic outpost, expansion base **-zentrum** *n* nucleus, center of growth, kernel
Wache *f* guard, watch
Wachen *n* watching
Wach-frequenz *f* guard frequency **-gebäude** *n*

Wacht *f* guard, watch, radar station **-dienst** *m* guard duty

Wächter *m* watchman, automatic controller, monitor (e.g. pressure, flame monitor etc.) **-kontrollanlage** *f* electric round recorder watchmen's control system **-kontrollmelder** *m* watchmen's control advertiser **-kontrolluhr** *f* watchmen's control clock, telltale watch **-uhr** *f* watchmen's time detector, controller, telltale

Wacofilter *n* waco filter

Wacht-raum *m* service room (in a lighthouse) **-turm** *m* watch tower

Wachwelle *f* stand-by frequency

Wackelchangierung *f* oscillating traverse motion

wackelig tottering, unsteady, shaky, loose

Wackelkontakt *m* defective contact, loose or variable connection

wackeln to wabble, rock, shake, be loose, totter, sway

Wad *n* wad

Wade *f* calf (textiles)

Wadelzeit *f* felling season

Waffe *f* arm, weapon, branch of service **bewegliche ~** flexible gun **blanke ~** side arms **feste ~** fixed armament **Waffen und Geräte** ordnance material

Waffel *f* wafer, waffle **-blech** *n* waffle sheet metal **-bindung** *f* honeycomb weave **-decke** *f* honeycomb covering **-gewebe** *n* honey-combed fabric **-nietung** *f* wafer-headed riveting

Waffen-amt *n* ordnance department

wägbar weighable, ponderable

Wägeapparat *m* weighing apparatus

Wagen *m* carriage, car, truck, wagon, cart, vehicle, railroad car **anlaufender ~** approaching car **auswechselbarer ~** interchangeable carriage (type-writer) **geschlossener ~** limousine, closed wagon or truck

wägen to weigh, consider, balance

Wagen-achse *f* car axle **-aufbau** *m* car body

Wagenaufschieber für Förderwagen truck to push wagons at railway stations

Wagen-aufzug *m* wagon hoist, carriage return (office machines) **-auslösetaste** *f* carriage-release key (typewriter) **-bauer** *m* carriage or car builder **-beschlag** *m* wagon fitting **-bewegung** *f* carriage movement **-bohrer** *m* carriage auger **-bolzen** *m* carriage bolt **-decke** *f* tarpaulin **-deichsel** *f* wagon tongue **-drehkran** *m* revolving wagon crane

Wagen-einstellhalle *f* garage **-elevator** *m* wagon elevator **-fähre** *f* wagon ferry, ferry for vehicles **-fänger** *m* car-catching device **-feder** *f* wagon spring **-feststeller** *m* carriage lock lever **-fett** *n* wagon grease, axle grease **-führer** *m* chauffeur, motorman, driver, car commander **-führung** *f* carriage support rails **-gestell** *n* car truck, car frame **-glühofen** *m* hearth-truck annealing furnace

Wagen-halle *f* garage, car shed **-halteplatz** *m* wagon stop, ambulance loading post **-heber** *m* wagon jack, lifting jack, carriage lever (typewriter) **-heberhalter** *m* jack holder **-hub** *m* carriage stroke **-kasten** *m* car body **-kippenbrücke** *f* car dumper **-kipper** *m* car dumper, wagon tipple, car tipper **-kontrolleur** *m* wagon checker **-kran** *m* derrick-wagon crane **-kugelkäfig** *m* carriage roll retainer **-kuppler** *m* coupler **-kuppelung** *f* railway coupling

Wagen-lader *m* wagon loader **-ladung** *f* carload, truckload, wagonload **-ladungsfrachtsatz** *m* carload rate **-laterne** *f* car headlight, carriage lantern **-macher** *m* scalemaker **-öl** *n* car oil **-park** *m* wagon park, fleet **-pfanne** *f* truck ladle **-plane** *f* tarpaulin for vehicle, awning, tilt, hood of a car **-prüfstand** *m* chassis dynamometer **-quittungskurve** *f* carriage position repeating cam disc

Wagen-rad *n* cart wheel **-raum** *m* garage **-remise** *f* coach house **-rücklauf** *m* (Fernschreiber) carriage return **-runge** *f* stud stave, stake, stanchion, pin bar **-schere** *f* shaft **-schiebebühne** *f* car-transfer platform **-schieber** *m* push pole for wagons, pusher **-schlag** *m* car door **-schlosserei** *f* carriage building, locksmith's shop **-schmied** *m* carriage blacksmith **-schmiere** *f* carriage grease **-schmierer** *m* greaser **-schuppen** *m* car shed **-schwungkraftanlasser** *m* motor vehicle inertia starter

Wagen-spinner *m* self-acting mule, spinning jenny **-spur** *f* wheel track, rut **-stößer** *m* trucker, wheelbarrower, roller, trammer **-stoßvorrichtung** *f* wagon pushing device **-stütze** *f* center-pole prop **-tritt** *m* step **-umlauf** *m* wagon circulation **-untergestell** *n* chassis, car truck **-winde** *f* screw jack, jack **-wipper** *m* car tippler

Wäge-tasche *f* weigh bin **-vorrichtung** *f* weighing appliance, scales

Waggon *m* wagon, railroad car **-ausladung** *f* car unloading **-bauteil** *m* car-construction part **-beschlagteil** *m* mounting for cars **-drehscheibe** *f* car turntable **-kipper** *m* car tipper **-kran** *m* derrick-car crane **-lader** *m* boxcar (wagon) loader **-ladung** *f* carload **-verladung** *f* car loading **-waage** *f* freight-car scales

Waghebel *m* weigh lever

Wagner *m* cartwright, wheelwright

Wagner-Hilfszweig *m* Wagner earth

Wagnersche Kennzahl structure-loading coefficient

Wägung *f* weighing

Wahl *f* choice, selection, option **~ in einer einzigen Ebene** rotary hunting **~ über verschiedene Höhenschritte** level hunting **erzwungene ~** numerical selection **freie ~** hunting, automatic hunting **unmittelbare ~** direct selection **~ auf einer Ebene** rotary search on one level **~ auf einer Stufe** rotary hunting **~ mittels Tastatur** keyboard selection

Wahlamt *n* dial central office, automatic exchange **kleines ~** unit automatic exchange, rural automatic exchange

Wahlanruf *m* selective ringing or signaling, selector calling **~ mit abgestimmten Einrichtungen** harmonic selective ringing, tuned ringing **abgestimmter ~** harmonic selective ringing

Wähl-anschluß *m* dial line **-arm** *m* selector arm (wiper)

Wahlbegleitrelais (V 2) *n* dial pulses supervising relay

Wählbereitschaftszeichen *n* proceed-to-dial signal

Wählbetrieb *m* (Teleph.) subscriber dialing, dial service **~ durch die Beamtin** operator dialing working **~ auf dem Lande** community dial service **~ zwischen Teilnehmern** full dial

service **von der Abgangsbeamtin gesteuerter ~** automatic working under control of the originating operator
Wähldaumen *m* selecting cam
Wahleinrichtung *f* dial-system installation, dial-system equipment
wählen to select, choose, elect, dial, vote
Wählen *n* selection, dialing
Wähler *m* selector, (selective or automatic) switch dial, voter **einen ~ belegen** (sperren) to busy a selector (teleph.) **~ mit einziger Bewegungsrichtung** rotary switch, uniselector (in radio) **~ für Orts- und Fernverkehr** combined local and toll selector **~ für n-Richtungen** n-point switch **~ mit Überträger** selector with repeater **~ für ankommende Verbindungsleitungen** in-junction switch **~ mit freier Wahl** selector, hunting switch **einen ~ belegen** to busy **großer ~** major switch **kleiner ~** minor switch, preselector, master switch **zehnteiliger ~** ten-point selector
Wähler-amt *n* dial central office **-anlage** *f* selector plant **-antrieb** *m* drive of selector **-berechnung** *f* calculation of the number of selectors **-bestimmungsunterlagen** *pl* traffic engineering working tables **-betrieb** *m* dial service **-bucht** *f* bay (of registers or selectors)
Wahlfernmessung *f* selective telemetering
Wahlfernsteuerung *f* trunk- or toll-line dialing
wahlfrei optional, selective, free to choose, idle
Wählerhebeschritt *m* vertical step of selector
Wähler-kontakt *m* selector contact **-kontaktfeld** *n* field of selection
Wählerlauf, ununterbrochener ~ continuous hunting
Wähler-rahmen *m* switch shelf **-raum** *m* switch-room, terminal room **-ruhekontakt** *m* normal contact **-saal** *m* switch room, terminal room **-schaltmagnet** *m* selector stepping magnet **-scheibe** *f* selector dial (teleph.) **-segment** *n* bank of (stationary) contacts **-sucher** *m* allotter **-system** *n* automatic telephone system
Wähl-hebel *m* selector lever **-impuls** *m* dialing impulse
Wahlimpulsreiheendrelais (V) *n* end-of-digit-selection relay
Wählkästchen *n* dial telephone, dial intercommunicating system
Wahlleitung *f* selector line
wahllos at random, nonselective
Wähl-magnet *m* selecting magnet, selector magnet **-mechanismus** *m*, **-organ** *n* selecting mechanism **-schalter** *m* selector switch **-scheibe** *f* dial, selector disk **-sternanschluß** *m* line multiplexing equipment **-sternschalter** *m* concentrator **-stromkreis** *m* selection circuit **-stromstoß** *m* dialing impulse **-stufe** *f* digit, stage of selection **-system** *n* dial system, automatic system
Wahl- und Verteilergerät *n* multiplex control
Wählvermittlung *f* automatic exchange or connection
Wahlvorgang *m* selection, selective process **freier ~** hunting operation
wahlweise selective, by choice, optional, directional (in signal transmission) **~ rufen** to call selectively **-r Anruf** selective call (teleph.) **-r Einzelgang** *m* selective listing **~ Leistung** *f* optional rating **~ Schreibsteuerung** *f* selective list control **-r Telegraphie- und Telefonierbetrieb** service affording either telegraph or telephone communication **-r Zugriff** *m* random access **~ Zusatzeinrichtung** *f* optional feature
Wählwerk *n* selective or selecting mechanism
wahnkantiges Holz dull-edged timber
wahr true, correct, genuine, intrinsic **-er Absorptionskoeffizient** true coefficient of absorption **-e Energie** intrinsic or interval energy **-e Geschwindigkeit** true (air) speed **-e Größe** full scale **-e Peilung** true bearing
Wahrheits-funktion *f* function of formal logic **-wert** *m* logical value (info proc.)
wahrnehmbar noticeable, perceptible, visible, perceivable **mit dem Auge ~** visible **durch Fühlen nicht ~** impalpable
Wahrnehmbarkeit *f* perceptibility, noticeability, observability, visibility, discernibility, audibility
Wahrnehmbarkeitsgrenze *f* limit of perceptibility
wahrnehmen to perceive, observe, sense, notice
Wahrnehmung *f* observation, perception, sensation
wahrscheinlich probable, likely **-er Fehler** probable error
Wahrscheinlichkeit *f* probability, likelihood, plausibility
Wahrscheinlichkeits-faktor *m* factor of probability **-gesetz** *n* probability law
Wahrscheinlichkeitshügel zweier statistischer Variablen probability hill of two random variables
Wahrscheinlichkeits-kurve *f* probability curve **-rechnung** *f* probability theory, probability calculus
wahrscheinlichster Verteilungswert *m* mode (in statistics)
wahrscheinlichster Wert most probable value
Wahrung *f* maintenance **~ der Regressrechte** reserving all rights of recourse
Wahrwert *m* intrinsic value
Wahrzeichen *n* distinctive sign or mark
Wald *m* wood, forest, woodland **-abteilung** *f* forest compartment or division **-bestand** *m* forest stand **-blöße** *f* forest clearing **-boden** *m* soil for forest growth
Wald-gelände *n* wooded area, woodland **-hammer** *m* woodman's hammer **-hüter** *m* forest ranger **-latte** *f* split lath **-lichtung** *f* forest clearing **-rand** *m* edge or fringe of forest or woods **-riß** *m* natural crack in wood
Wald-säge *f* wood saw, felling saw **-schneise** *f* aisle in a forest, firebreak, straight narrow forest clearing **-schonung** *f* young forest plantation **-schutzstreifen** *m* protective belt of trees
Waldung *f* wood
Wald-weg *m* forest road **-wolle** *f* pine-needle wool, forest wool
Wal *m* whale **-fang** *m* whaling **-fänger** *m* whaler
Walfisch-rumpf *m* monocoque fuselage **-tran** *m* whale oil
Walkbürste *f* felling brush
Walke *f* fulling mill, fulling or milling machine
walkecht fast to fulling
walken to full, mill, press, squeeze
Walkeisen *n* crimping iron
Walker *m* fuller
Walkerde *f* fuller's earth

Walkerei *f* fulling mill
Walkertischmaschine *f* (founding) Walker wheel
Walk-fett *n* fulling fat **-hammer** *m* beater **-mühle** *f* fulling mill **-penetration** *f* worked and other tests for greases **-trog** *m* fulling trough **-zylinder** *m* cylinder fulling machine
Wall *m* rampart, dam, dike, levee, wall, enclosure, mound, shore, embankment **-absatz** *m* berme
wallen to simmer
Wall-gangschott *n* wing-passage bulkhead **-graben** *m* moat, ditch
Wallonen-arbeit *f* Walloon process **-eisen** *n* Walloon iron
Wall-platte *f* dam plate **-riff** *n* barrier reef
Wallstein *m* dam, dam stone (of blast furnace) **-platte** *f* dam plate (of blast furnace)
Wallung *f* boiling, ebullition
Walm-dach *n* hip roof **-sparren** *m* jack rafter, hip rafter
Walpurgit *m* walpurgite
Walrat *m* spermaceti
Walzader *f* bar
Wälzantrieb *m* rolling motion
Walz-arbeit *f* rolling energy or work **-armaturen** *f pl* rolling equipment, fittings for rolling **-bahn** *f* path of contact or of rolling, rolling curve, centrode **-balken** *m* rolled girder, shoe (mach.) **-ballen** *m* barrel of roll, body of roll
Wälzband *n* rolling band
walzbar rollable
Walzbarkeit *f* rolling property, capacity for being rolled
Walz-barren *m* rolling ingot, sheet ingot **-bart** *m* burr **-betrieb** *m* rolling-mill practice, rolling-mill operation
Wälzbewegung *f* rolling motion
Walz-blech *n* rolled (iron) plate, sheet metal, rolled sheet metal (iron) **-blei** *n* rolled lead, sheet lead **-bleidraht** *m* rolled lead wire
Walzblock *m* bloom, cog **gestreckter ~** roughed bloom
Wälzbogen *m* rotating arc
Walz-dorn *m* roll mandrel **-draht** *m* wire rod, rolled wire
Walzdruck *m* rolling pressure, rolling draft or work **direkter ~** direct rolling pressure **indirekter ~** side pressure
Walze *f* roller, roll, drum, cylinder, shaft, wheel, roller gate, supporting cylinder, whirlpool, vortex, eddy **~ mit glattem Ballen** plain roll **ausbalanzierte ~** balanced roll **geriffelte ~** fluted roll **glasharte ~** casehardened or chilled roller **glatte ~** plain or flat roll **kalibrierte ~** grooved roll **obere ~** top roll **profilierte ~** grooved roll **schwingende ~** oscillating roll **versenkbare ~** falling or submergeable roller gate
Walzebene *f* rolling plane
Wälzeinrichtung *f* hobbing attachment
Walzeisen *n* rolled iron, rolled products **-förderkran** *m* rolled iron transporting crane **-träger** *m* rolled-iron beam
walzen to roll, mill, grind, crush, pulverize, peen, laminate **~ aus Führung** to roll by guide **~ aus freier Hand** to roll by hand **~ in langen Zügen** to roll in long lengths
wälzen to roll, turn about

Walzen *n* rolling, milling, grinding, crushing, pulverization, glaze, glazing **-abnahme** *f* roller discharge **-abschleifmaschine** *f* cylinder grinding machine **-abziehpresse** *f* press for removing roller shells **-achse** *f* axis of roll **-anlasser** *m* drum starter **-anordnung** *f* arrangement of rolls **-anstellung** *f* adjustment of rolls **-aufgabevorrichtung** *f* roller feeder **-auftrag** *m* feeding furnishing by roller **-aufziehpresse** *f.* roller press **-aushebevorrichtung** *f* lifting device for rolls **-austritt** *m* delivery side of rolls
Walzen-ballen *m* roll body, barrel of a roll **-bandage** *f* roll tire **-beschichtungsmaschine** *f* roll coating machine **-beschlagbreite** *f* length of roller clothing (cover) **-bezug** *m* roller coating, rubber cover for cylinders **-blechbiegemaschine** *f* roller plate-bending machine **-blende** *f* rotating firing post, cylindrical mount, mantlet for cylindrical mount **-blitzableiter** *m* drum lightning arrester **-brecher** *m* giratory breaker, crushing mill, rolling crusher **-breite** *f* length of roller (cover) **-bruch** *m* breakage of a roll, breakdown of a roll **-bund** *m* body of roll
wälzende Reibung rolling friction
Walzen-dekatur *f* calender or cylinder finish **-drechsler** *m* roll turner **-drehbank** *f* roll lathe **-dreher** *m* roller, roll turner **-dreherei** *f* roll-turning shop **-drehknopf** *m* platen knob
Walzendruck *m* cylinder printing **-farbe** *f* roller printing color **-maschine** *f* cylinder printing machine
Walzen-düse *f* cylindric nozzle **-egreniermaschine** *f* roller gin **-eindrücke** *pl* roller marks **-einstellung** *f* adjustment of rolls **-eintritt** *m* entering side of rolls, entrance of a pass **-empfänger** *m* drum receiver **-festigkeit** *f* roll strength **-fläche** *f* area of cylinder **-förmig** cylindrical, barrel-shaped **-foulard** *m* boul padding mangle
Walzenfräser *m* plain- or face-milling cutter **~ mit eingesetzten Messern** inserted-blade plain milling cutter **~ mit Spanbrechernuten** plain-milling cutter with nicked teeth **hinterschliffener ~** relief-ground worm hob
Walzen-freilauf (Walzenlöser) *m* platen release mechanism, free wheel **-furche** *f* pass, groove **-gatter** *n* alternating saw **-gerüst** *n* stand of rolls, housing frames **-gießen** *n* casting of rollers **-glas** *n* sheet glass **-glättwerk** *n* calender (supercalender) **-gravieranstalt** *f* cylinder engraving works **-graviervorrichtung** *f* roll engraving attachment **-gravur** *f* engraving of the roller **-griff** *m* cylindrical handle **-guß** *m* chilled roll iron, founding of rollers
Walzen-käfig *m* roller cage (of bearing) **-kaliber** *n* roll pass, pass, groove **-kalibreur** *m* roll designer **-kalibrierung** *f* roll designing **-karde** *f* roller card **-kessel** *m* cylindrical boiler **-körnmaschine** *f* granulating roller machine **-körper** *m* roll body, barrel of a roll **-kranz** *m* roller assembly **-krempel** *f* roller card
Walzen-lackierung *f* roller coating **-lafette** *f* roller-type machine-gun mount **-lager** *n* roller bearing; journal box **-lagerung** *f* roller bearing **-magnetsichter** *m* cylindrical magnetic separator **-mangel** *m* calender **-mantel** *m* roller shell **-masse** *f* printer's roller composition **-messer** (Holländer) engine knife **-mikrophon** *n* pencil transmitter **-mischer** *m* roll mill (mixing rolls)

-mühle *f* roll-jaw crusher, roll crushing mill, roll crusher, rolling mill, beater spring rolls

Walzen-paar *n* set or pair of rolls **-papier** *n* bowl paper, calender-roll paper **-park** *m* rolling-mill equipment **-presse** *f* roll press **-profil** *n* profile of a roll **-pulver** *n* roller-processed dried milk **-rad** *n* barrel wheel **-rand** *m* collar of a roll **-reibmaschine** *f* roller grinding mill **-reihe** *f* mill line **-richtmaschine** *f* roller leveller

Walzen-riffelung *f* grooving of rollers **-riffler** *m* roll grinder **-ring** *m* crushing-roll shell **-ringmühle** *f* ring-roller mill **-rost** *m* roller grate **-schablone** *f* pass template **-schalter** *m* barrel switch, drum switch **-schleifmaschine** *f* roller grinding machine, cylinder sanding machine **-schieber** *m* rotating valve **-schlacke** *f* roll or mill scale **-schnalle** *f* roller buckle

Walzen-schutzvorrichtung *f* cylinder-protecting device **-schutzwehr** *n* roller sluice weir **-schwund** *m* roller shrinkage **-senge** *f* revolving singer **-separator** *m* drum cobber **-sinter** *m* roll or mill scale **-spalte** *f* opening between rolls, roll gap or clearance **-spaltverstellung** *f* adjustment of the gap between the rolls **-spindel** *f* roll spindle or shaft **-spiralfräser** *n* plain spiral mill **-ständer** *m* roll housing, (roll) standard, holster **-steller** *m* screwman **-stirnfräser** *m* plain-milling cutter, end-face mill, face-milling cutter

Walzen-straße *f* rolling train, mill train, train of rolls, rolling-mill train **-straßenantrieb** *m* rolling-mill path drive **-strecke** *f* strand of rolls, roll train **-streckwerk** *n* drawing rollers **-stuhl** *m* roller frame, cylinder support (print.), roller carriage arm (grinding mill) **-stuhlung** *f* roller frame **-tisch** *m* roller table **-trockenmaschine** *f* cylinder-drying machine **-trockner** *m* roller or drum drier

Walzen-überzug *m* cylinder cover **-umfangsgeschwindigkeit** *f* roll-surface velocity **-verschleiß** *m* wear of rolls **-vorschub** *m* roller feed **-vorschubapparat** *m* roll-feed attachment **-walke** *f* cylinder mill **-wascheinrichtung** *f* roller washing device **-wechselkran** *m* roll changing crane **-wehr** *n* roller weir, gate, or dam, rolling gate **-winkel** *m* limiting angle of rolling **-zapfen** *m* neck of a roll, journal of a roll, roller ends **-zugmotor** *m* rolling-mill motor

Walzer *m* roller

Walz-erz *n* ore for crushing **-erzeugnis** *n* roller product, rolling-mill product **-fehler** *m* rolling defect

Wälzfeile *f* cabinet file

Walzfläche *f* rolling face

Walzflansch *m* rolled-on flange

wälzfräsen to hob

Wälzfräser *m* hob **-maschine** *f* hobbing machine, hobber

wälzgefräst hobbed

Wälzgelenk *n* rocker joint

Walzgerüst *n* roll stand, rolling stand

Walzgerüstanordnung *f* arrangement of roll stands **gestaffelte ~** roll stands arranged in separate lines

Walzgeschwindigkeit *f* speed of travel through rolls, rolling speed **horizontale ~** linear rolling speed

Walz-grat *m* fin, burr (from rolling) **-gut** *n* rolled stock **-hart** hard-rolled **-haut** *f* rolling skin, scale (aviation), outer layer or surface of rolled piece **-hobeln** *n* planing by generating

Wälzhebel *m* rolling contact lever, cam lever **-steuerung** *f* cam- or roller-lever steering

Walzhütte *f* rolling mill

walzig cylindrical, in solid rolls, roller-shaped

Walz-kaliber *n* roll groove, roll pass **-kalibrierung** *f* design of roll passes, designing of grooved rolls, grooving of rolls

Wälzkammerdüse *f* eddy chamber nozzle

Walzkante *f* rolling edge

Wälzkegel *m* rolling cone

Walz-knüppel *m* billet (met.), rolling billet

Wälz-kontakt *m* rubbing contact

Walzkörper *m* roll body, barrel of a roll

Wälzkreis *m* rolling circle, pitch circle, circle of contact

Walzkupfer *n* sheet copper

Wälz-kurve *f* contact curve **-lager** *n* antifriction bearing, roller bearing, self-adjusting bearing, ball bearing

Walzlagerteile *pl* ball and roller-bearing elements

Wälzlänge *f* cradle roll motion

Wälzlängenskala *f* cradle roll motion scale

Walz-linie *f* axis of grooves (of rolls) **-material** *n* rolling material, rolled stock **-messing** *n* rolled brass **-metall** *n* rolling or rolled metal **-motor** *m* rolling-mill motor **-mühle** *f* roller mill **-naht** *f* rolling fin or burr **-plan** *m* rolling schedule **-platte** *f* plate or slab to be rolled, rolling slab **-produkt** *n* rolled product **-profil** *n* rolled section, rolled steel section **-programm** *n* rolling schedule, rolling plan **-punkt** *m* rolling point

Wälzpunkt *m* pitch point, instantaneous center of rotation or of motion

Walz-puppe *f* billet **-rand** *m* collar, rolling edge

Wälzreibung *f* rolling friction

Walz-richtung *f* direction of rolling **-riefe** *f* rolling mark **-ring** *m* collar **-riß** *m* rolling crack **-rohr** *n* rolled tube **-rundmaterial** *n* rolled rounds **-schablone** *f* pass template

Wälzscheibe *f* rolling disc

Walz-schweißverfahren *n* sealed assembly rolling process **-sinter** *m* roll or mill scale **-spalt** *m* opening between rolls, roll gap **-splitter** *m* sliver **-stab** *m* rolled bar **-stahl** *m* rolled steel **-stange** *f* rolled steel rod

Walzsteuerung *f* cam or roller lever steering

Walz-stich *m* pass (iron and steel mfg.) **-stopfen** *m* mandrel point or plug, stopper of rolling mill

wälzstoßen to shape by generating

Wälzstoßmaschine *f* gear shaper

Walz-straße *f*, **-strecke** *f* mill train, train of rolls, rolling train, rolling mill **-tisch** *m* rolling platform, lifting platform **-toleranz** *f* rolling tolerance, mill limits **-träger** *m* rolled(-steel) beam, rolled girder

Walzung *f* rolling

Wälzung *f* rounding off, generating motion

Wälz(ungs)hebel *m* lever with rolling contact

Wälzverfahren *n* rotary-furnace method of volatilizing ores, generating principle

Walzvorgang *m* rolling operation or process, hobbing process

Wälzvorschub *m* generating feed **-geschwindig-**

keit *f* generating roll feed **-wechselräder** *pl* feed change gears, generating roll feed change gears, roll change gears, generating change gears

Walzwerk *n* rolling mill, roll-jaw crusher, crushing rolls, calender ~ **für Halbzeug** semi-finishing mill **zweigerüstiges** ~ double-stand rolling mill

Walzwerkbetrieb *m* rolling mills

Walzwerker *m* rolling-mill engineer

Walzwerks-bau *m* rolling-mill construction **-betrieb** *m* rolling-mill operation or practice **-einrichtung** *f* rolling-mill equipment **-programm** *n* rolling-mill schedule **-schere** *f* rolling-mill shears **-technik** *f* rolling-mill technique, rolling-mill construction or operation

Walzwerks- und Hüttenprodukte *n pl* rolling-mill products

Walzwerkswalzen *pl* rolling-mill rolls

Wälzwinkel *m* rolling angle

Wälzzahnrad *n* engaging or mating gear

Walz-zapfen *m* neck of a roll **-zink** *n* sheet zinc **-zinn** *n* rolled tin, sheet tin **-zunder** *m* roll or mill scale **-zustand** *m* rolled condition

Wälzzylinder *m* circle disk

Wand *f* wall, thickness (of plate), skin, partition, side, cheek, shell, panel, screen, baffle **-absaugung** *f* wall-siphoning (jet) **-abstand** *m* wall clearance **-ankerplatte** *f* wall-anchor plate **-anordnung** *f* wall brackets **-anschlußdose** *f* wall socket

Wand-apparat *m* wall telephone set **-arm** *m* angle or wall bracket **-armlager** *n* wall-bracket hanger **-auskleidung** *f* shell lining (of converter) **-aussparung** *f* recess (in wall) **-balken** *m* wall-plate **-bedeckung** *f* wall covering **-befestigung** *f* wall attachment or fixture

Wandbekleidung *f* wall facing, wainscot(ing), paneling **schallschluckende** ~ sound-absorbing wall draping or lining

Wandbekleidungs-blech *n* sheet metal for wall facing **-stoff** *m* covering for walls

Wand-belag *m* wall coating **-bespannungsstoffe** *pl* wall coverings (hangings) **-bewurf** *m* plastering **-bock** *m* wall bracket **-bohrmaschine** *f* wall drill **-dekoration** *f* mural decoration **-dicke** *f* wall thickness **-drehkran** *m* swing crane **-druck** *m* wall pressure, normal pressure **-durchführung** *f* wall entrance **-durchführungsisolator** *m* wall lead-in insulator, bushing insulator **-einfluß** *m* wall influence

wandelbar variable

wandeln to vary, alter

Wander-block *m* erratic block **-düne** *f* shifting dune **-fahren** *n* touring **-feld** *n* moving or travelling field **-feldmaser** *m* travelling-wave maser **-feldröhre** *f* travelling-wave tube **-feldröhrensender** *m* travelling vawe tube transmitter **-gerät** *n* portable projector **-geschwindigkeit** *f* speed of travel, velocity of advance, velocity of propagation (of a wave) **-hebelschiene** *f* sliding-lever bar (teleph.) **-licht** *n* spotlight scanner for persons **-marke** *f* measuring mark

wandern to diffuse, migrate, travel, wander, roam, creep, shift, crawl

Wandern *n* traveling, migration, shifting ~ **der Schienen** creep of the rails

wandernd moving, traveling **-er Lichtstrahl** flying spot, scanning spotlight **-er Sand** running sand **-e Seilrolle** floating sheave

Wandernocken travelling cam

Wanderquerruder *n* drooping aileron

Wanderrost *m* traveling grate **-beschickung** *f* traveling stoker feed, chain-grate stoker feed **-breite** *f* traveling-grate width **-feuerung** *f* traveling-grate firing **-fläche** *f* surface of traveling grate

Wander-schutzklemmen *pl* anti-creepers **-stöpsel** *m* switch plug

Wandertisch *m* platform conveyer, picking table ~ **für fließende Fertigung** picking table for line assembly

Wandertransformator *m* mobile transformer

Wandertrockner *m* multiple-pass drier

Wanderung *f* migration, creeping, diffusion, traveling, displacement, shifting, transportation, conveyance, transfer, haulage, shipment, forwarding ~ **der Kiesbänke** migration or shifting of gravel bars

Wanderungsgeschwindigkeit *f* migration velocity, travel velocity, crawl or creep (television) ~ **eines Ions** velocity of an ion

Wanderungs-richtung *f* direction of migration **-sinn** *m* direction of migration (of ions) **-tendenz** *f* (Farbe) migration tendency

Wanderwelle *f* moving wave, traveling wave, surge, transient wave

Wanderwellen-generator *m* surge generator, impulse generator **-messer** *m* surge indicator, surge recorder **-röhre** *f* travelling-wave tube **-schraube** *f* traveling wave helix **-schutz** *m* surge protection, traveling-wave protection

Wanderwiderstand *m* travel resistance, resistance to flow or deformation (of material)

Wand-fernsprecher *m* wall telephone station **-fest** attached solidly to the wall **-flächenheizung** *f* wall panel heating **-fliese** *f* wall flag **-fries** *m* molding **-futter** *n* shell lining (of converter) **-gestell** *n* wall bracket **-gleitung** *f* slippage along the wall

Wand-haken *m* wall hook **-hobel** *m* side rebate plane **-karte** *f* wall map **-kehle** *f* flashing **-kettenfräsmaschinen** *pl* post chain mortisers **-konsole** *f* wall bracket **-konsolrührer** *m* post-type (change-can) mixer **-kran** *m* wall crane **-ladungsdichte** *f* wall charge density **-laufkran** *m* traveling crane

Wandler *m* transformer, transducer, converter (television) **elektroakustischer** ~ electroacoustic transducer **lichtelektrischer** ~ photocell ~ **für Schnellregler** transformer for automatic regulator

Wandler-getriebe *n* torque converter transmission **-stromauslöser** *m* current-transformer release

Wandlüfter *m* wall ventilator

Wandlung *f* transformation, conversion

Wandlungs-bild *n* anamorphosis **-verhältnis** *n* transformation ratio

Wand-montage *f* wall mounting **-pfeiler** *m* pilaster, wall column **-platte** *f* wall plate **-pumpe** *f* wall pump **-punkt** *m* boundary point **-rahmen** *m* capping plate, coping piece, coping plate **-reibung** *f* skin friction **-reibungswinkel** *m* angle of wall friction

Wand-riegel *m* crossbar, intertie, rail of a bay work **-röhre** *f* end-wall tube, radiant wall tube **-rosette** *f* rosette **-sauger** *m* wall nozzle **-schalttafel** *f* wall switchboard **-schirm** *m* folding screen **-schrank** *m* wall chest **-stab** *m* strut, stay **-standanzeiger** *m* wall indicator

Wandstärke *f* (wall) thickness, section, thickness of (pipe) wall ~ **der Spule** thickness of the coil

Wandstärken-empfindlichkeit *f* mass influence **-kernstütze** *f* double-headed chaplet **-übergang** *m* sectional change

Wandstecker *m* wall plug ~ **mit beweglichen Kontaktstiften** wall plug with movable contact pins

Wandstärkeverlauf *m* variation of wall thickness

Wand-stoffbekleidung *f* draping, baffle, blanket, sound-absorbing material **-strom** *m* wall current (of a tube)

Wandstromverstärker *m* thyratron

Wand-stütze *f* wall bracket **-tafel** *f* wall diagram, blackboard **-täfelung** *f* wainscoting **-träger** *m* bracket **-umschalteschrank** *m* wall-pattern switchboard

Wandung *f* wall, thickness (of plate), partition

Wandungs-temperatur *f*, **-wärme** *f* wall temperature

Wand-vermittlungsschrank *m* wall-pattern switch-board **-verschiebungsbremsung** *f* wall displacement braking **-vertiefung** *f* niche **-waschbecken** *n* wall hand basin **-winde** *f* wall winch

Wange *f* side wall, cheek, side plate, frame, leg (of angle), end piece ~ **der Rollenbahn** roller-train frame

Wangen-breite *f* width of web **-höhe** *f* height of cheek **-mauer** *f* stringer (mach.), string wall

wankelhaft inconstant, unsteady, vacillatory

Wankelmotor *m* (Drehkolbenmotor) internal combustion engine with revolving piston

Wanken *n* rolling

Wanknutsäge *f* wobble-type notch saw

Wanne *f* shell e. g. of arc furnace, body, tank continuous glass-melting furnace, tub, vat, trough, underfuselage tunnel (airplane) ~ **mit Gegengewichtsausgleich** balanced gate **pneumatische** ~ pneumatic trough (in gas drying)

Wannen-befestigung *f* cradle fixation (pan mounting) **-boden** *m* hull floor **-förmig** tub-shaped, troughlike **-lage** *f* H.V. position **-ofen** *m* tank furnace (glass mfg.) **-stein** *m* tank block

Want *f* shroud **-knoten** *m* single shroud knot **-schraube** *f* rigging screw

Wappen-stecher *m* herald engraver **-ziseleur** *m* heraldic chaser

Wardein *m* assayer

wardieren to assay

Wardierschein *m* certificate of assay

Ward-Leonard-Antrieb *m* Ward-Leonard system

Ware *f* ware, commodity, merchandise, make, product, article **beschädigte** ~ damaged goods **durchbrochene** ~ lacework **geminderte** ~ narrowed goods **gerauhte** ~ fleeced goods **geringelte** ~ horizontally striped goods **geschnittene** ~ cut goods **gangbare** ~ goods commanding a ready sale **ganz und halb fertige Waren** finished and semifinished products

Waren-anstrich *m* cloth contact **-aufzug** *m* freight elevator **-beschauer** *m* inspector of products **-bestand** *m* stock in hand **-doppler** *m* piece doubler **-durchseher** *m* percher **-eingang** *m* receipt of goods **-gattung** *f* kind of goods **-gleitmulde** *f* vat, tank

Waren-lager *n* warehouse, storehouse, depot **-probe** *f* sample **-sendung** *f* shipment (of goods)

Warenverzeichnis *n* list of goods **-wechsel** *m* trade bill

Warenzeichen *n* trade-mark **eingetragenes** ~ registered trade-mark

warm warm, hot ~ **aufziehen** to shrink on ~ **laufen lassen** to warm up the engine ~ **satiniert** hot rolled ~ **werden** to heat up **das Lager läuft (sich)** ~ the bearing runs hot **-e Luftmasse** warm air mass **-e Luftschicht** stratum or layer of warm air

warm-abbindend hot setting **-abgratwerkzeug** *n* hot trimming die **-arbeitsgesenk** *n* hot-forging dies **-aufziehen** *n* shrinking on **-aushärtung** *f* artificial aging

Warmbad-härteofen *m* hot quenching furnace **-härtung** *f* hot-quenching **-walzwerk** *n* hot strip mill

warm-bearbeiten to work at red heat **-bearbeitung** *f* hot working **-behandelt** heat-treated **-behandlung** *f* heat-treatment, thermal treatment **-bett** *n* hot bed, cooling bed or table **-biegeprobe** *f* hot bending test **-biegeversuch** *m* hot bend test **-bildsamkeit** *f* forgeability

Warm-blasegas *n* hot-blast gas **-blasen** *n* hot blast, hot blow **-blaseperiode** *f* hot-blast period **-blechrichtmaschine** *f* hot-plate straightening machine **-bruch** *m* hot pull (of a cast block) **-brüchig** hot-short **-brüchigkeit** *f* hot-shortness **-dauerstandfestigkeit** *f* high-temperature creep strength **-dehnbarkeit** *f* hot ductility **-dorn** *m* hot madrel

Wärme *f* heat, temperature, warmth ~ **abführen** to eliminate heat ~ **abgeben** to give out or radiate heat ~ **abgebend** exothermic, exothermal ~ **ableiten** to carry off heat ~ **aufnehmen** to absorb heat ~ **aufnehmend** endothermic ~ **aufspeichern** to store heat ~ **durchlassen** to transmit heat ~ **erzeugend** calorific, exothermic ~ **verzehrend** heat-consuming, endothermic, endothermal

Wärme, abgegebene ~ heat given off, heat conducted off or away **freie** ~ uncombined heat **fühlbare** ~ sensible heat **gebundene** ~ latent heat **spezifische** ~ specific heat **strahlende** ~ radiant heat **zugeführte** ~ added heat, heat received **durch** ~ **härten** to thermoset

Wärme-abfall *m* heat drop **-abfluß** *m* heat transfer **-abfuhr** *f* heat flow, transmission, or dissipation, heat rejection, emission of heat, waste heat **-abführung** *f* solar radiation, emission or removal of heat, heat transmission, heat evacuation, loss of heat, heat abduction **-abgabe** *f* loss of heat, heat emission, transmission of heat **-abgabefläche** *f* heat-emitting surface **-ableitfähigkeit** *f* heat-abstracting characteristic **-ableitung** *f* dissipation of heat, heat rejection, heat conduction

Wärme-ableitungsfehler *m* heat-conduction error **-abschirmung** *f* thermal shield **-abnahme** *f* decrease in temperature **-abwertung** *f* heat devaluation **-änderung** *f* change of temperature **-anpeilung** *f* thermolocation **-ansammlung** *f*

accumulation of heat **-anschluß** *m* heat connection **-anstieg** *m* rise in temperature **-äquivalent** *n* heat equivalent **-arbeitswert** *m* mechanical equivalent of heat

Wärmeaufnahme *f* heat absorption **-fähigkeit** *f* heat-absorption capacity **-fläche** *f* heat-absorbing surface

wärme-aufnehmend heat-absorbing **-aufspeicherung** *f* accumulation of heat (heat storage) **-aufwind** *m* thermal upcurrent **-ausbeute** *f* thermal yield **-ausbreitungsvermögen** *n* thermal diffusivity **-ausdehnung** *f* thermal expansion

Wärmeausdehnungs-koeffizient *m* coefficient of thermal expansion **-vermögen** *n* thermal expansivity **-zahl** *f* coefficient of thermal expansion

Wärme-ausgleichgrube *f* soaking pit **-aushärtend** thermosetting **-aushärtung** *f* heat treatment **-ausnutzung** *f* heat efficiency, thermal efficiency, heat utilization **-ausstrahlung** *f* radiation of heat **-austausch** *m* interchange of heat, heat exchange **-austauschapparat** *m* heat exchanger or interchanger **-austauscher** *m* heat exchanger or compensator **-austrahlung** *f* heat radiation **-beanspruchung** *f* thermal strain or stress **-bedarf** *m* heat requirement, calorific requirement **-behandlung** *f* heat-treatment, thermal treatment **-belastung** *f* thermal stress **-berechnung** *f* temperature-rise computation

wärmebeständig heat-retaining, heatproof, heat-resisting **-e Schicht** stratum of constant temperature

Wärme-beständigkeit *f* heatproof quality, heat retaining capacity, thermal stability or resistivity, resistance to heat **-betrag** *m* quantity or amount of heat **-bewegung** *f* heat motion, heat transfer, thermal agitation **-bilanz** *f* heat balance, thermal balance, calorific balance **-bild** *n* temperature-entropy diagram **-bildner** *m* heat producer **-bildung** *f* production of heat **-bindung** *f* heat absorption **-dämmerung** *f* time between the lowest daily temperature and sunrise **-dämmung** *f* thermal insulation **-dehnbar** hot-ductile **-dehnung** *f* thermal expansion **-dehnungsziffer** *f* coefficient of thermal expansion

Wärme-dichte *f* quantity of heat per unit **-diffusion** *f* thermodiffusion, thermal transpiration, thermal effusion **-druckprüfung** *f* hot penetration test **-durchgang** *m* heat transmission, conduction of heat, heat transfer **-durchgangssatz** *m* heat transfer rate **-durchgangswiderstand** *m* resistivity to heat **-durchgangszahl** *f* coefficient of heat transmission, over-all coefficient **-durchgriff** *m* (Thermostat) inverse ambient temperature reduction factor **-durchlässig** diathermic **-durchlässigkeit** *f* diathermancy **-durchsatz** *m* rate of heat transfer **-durchschlag** *m* breakdown due to thermal instability **-dynamik** *f* thermodynamics **-dynamometer** *n* heat dynamometer

Wärme-einheit *f* thermal unit, heat unit, caloric unit, specific heat **-einsaugung** *f*, **-einstrahlung** *f* heat absorption **-elektrisch** thermoelectric **-elektrizität** *f* thermoelectricity **-empfindlich** sensitive to heat **-energie** *f* thermal energy, heat energy **-entbindung** *f* release of heat **-entwicklung** *f* evolution, development, or disengagement of heat, loss of heat **-erzeuger** *m* heat producer **-erzeugung** *f* generation of heat, heat production **-explosion** *f* thermal explosion

Wärme-fernsprecher *m* thermophone **-festigkeit** *f* thermal stability, heat resistance **-fluß** *m* heat flow, thermal flow or flux **-fortleitung** *f* conduction of heat, thermal conduction **-fortpflanzung** *f* propagation of heat **-fühler** *m* thermostat **-gang** *m* variation or range of temperature **-gebend** heat-yielding, exothermic, exothermal **-gefälle** *n* rate of decrease in temperature, drop in temperature, temperature or heat gradient **-gehalt** *m* heat content **-geräusch** *n* thermal noise, thermal-agitation noise **-gewicht** *n* entropy **-gewitter** *n* heat lightning, heat thunderstorm

Wärme-gleiche *f* isotherm, isothermal curve **-gleichung** *f* heat equation **-gleichwert** *m* mechanical equivalent of heat **-grad** *m* degree of heat, temperature **-gradberichtigung** *f* correction for temperature **-gradfläche** *f* isothermal or temperature surface **-gradient** *m* temperature gradient **-gradmesser** *m* thermometer **-gradmesserhülle** *f* thermometer screen **-gradschreiber** *m* thermograph **-gradunterschied** *m* temperature difference **-gradverlauf** *m* temperature lapse rate **-größe** *f* specific heat

Wärme-halter *m* thermostat **-härtender Kunststoff** *m* thermosetting plastic **-haushalt** *m* heat balance **-höchstgrad** *m* maximum temperature **-inhalt** *m* total heat, enthalpy. heat capacity, heat content **-intensität** *f* intensity of heat, calorific intensity **-ionisation** *f* thermal ionization, temperature ionization **-isolation** *f* heat insulation **-isolator** *m* heat insulator **-isoliermatte** *f* (Astron.) heat insulation blanket (missiles) **-isolierung** *f* heat insulation **-isoplethe** *f* thermoisopleth

Wärme-kapazität *f* heat capacity, thermal capacity, calorific capacity, heat-absorption capacity **-klebend** thermosetting **-koeffizient** *m* temperature coefficient **-konvektion** *f* heat convection

Wärmekraft *f* thermal power **-lehre** *f* thermodynamics **-maschine** *f* heat motor, thermal engine **-(maschinen)satz** *m* heat-engine set **-werk** *n* heat-engine generating station, thermal power station

Wärme-kumulus *m* heat or thermal cumulus **-kurve** *f* heat curve, heating curve **-lehre** *f* thermodynamics **-leistung** *f* heating efficiency, calorific efficiency, thermal efficiency **-leitend** heat-conducting **-leiter** *m* heat conductor **-leitfähigkeit** *f* heat conductivity, thermal conductivity **-leitstift** *m* heating pin

Wärme-leitung *f* heat conduction **-leitungskurve** *f* heat-conductivity curve **-leitvermögen** *n* thermal conductivity, heat conductivity **-leitzahl** *f* coefficient of thermal conductivity, heat-transfer coefficient **-liefernd** exothermal **-manko** *n* heat deficit **-mauer** *f* (Astron.) heat barrier, thermal barrier **-mechanik** *f* thermodynamics **-menge** *f* amount of heat, quantity of heat **-mengenmessung** *f* calorimetry

Wärme-meßeinrichtung *f* heat-measuring device **-messend** thermometric **-messer** *m* calorimeter, thermometer **-meßgerät** *n* pyrometer **-messung** *f* calorimetry, heat measurement **-meßwesen** *n*

pyrometry **-mitführung** *f* (heat) convection **-motor** *m* heating motor

wärmen to warm, heat

Wärme-niedrigstgrad *m* minimum temperature **-nische** *f* heating recess

Warmentgratung *f* fin-removal by heat

Wärme-nutzung *f* utilization of heat **-ofen** *m* heating furnace, brazier **-phänomen** *n* thermal phenomenon **-quelle** *f* heat source

Wärmer *m* heater

Wärme-rauschen *n* thermal-agitation noise, background noise, thermal motion of electrons **-rechnung** *f* heat calculation **-regler** *m* heat regulator, thermoregulator, thermostat **-riß** *m* heat crack **-rückgewinn** *m* heat recovery **-rückgewinnung** *f* waste heat recovery **-rückstrahlung** *f* heat reflection

Wärme-satz *m* law of thermodynamics **-saugheber** *m* thermosiphon **-schaltbild** *n* heat flow diagram **-schalter** *m* thermal switch **-schild** *n* (Astron.) heat shield (spacecraft) **-schott** *m* fireproof bulkhead **-schrank** *m* warming cupboard; steam table, bain-marie

Wärmeschutz *m* insulation against loss of heat **-blech** *n* metal heat insulator **-filter** *n* heat protection filter **-material** *n* lagging material **-masse** *f*, **mittel** *n* nonconducting or insulating material, heat insulator, insulation **-panzer** *m* heat protective covering (heat insulation)

Wärme-schwankung *f* heat fluctuation or variation **-schwingung** *f* heat vibration **-sicher** heatproof, heat-resisting **-skala** *f* thermometric scale, pyrometric scale **-spaltung** *f* heat cracking **-spannung** *f* thermal stress, heat stress **-speicher** *m* heat accumulator, heat storage, regenerator, heat reservoir, hot well **-speicherfeuerung** *f* regenerative firing **-speicherofen** *m* regenerative furnace

Wärme-speicherung *f* heat storage **-speicherungsfähig** heat-retaining **-speicherungsmasse** *f* heat-retaining mass, heat retainer **-speicherwirkung** *f* heat-retaining function **-spektrum** *n* heat spectrum, thermal spectrum **-starre** *f* heat-rigor **-stau** *m* localization of heat **-stauung** *f* accumulation of heat **-stoff** *m* caloric, thermogen **-stofftheorie** *f* corpuscular theory **-störung** *f* heat distortion **-stoß** *m* heat shock

Wärme-strahl *m* heat ray, thermal ray **-strahlung** *f* radiation of heat, thermal radiation, radiant heat, temperature radiation **-strahlungsfühler** *m* heat radiation sensing device **-strom** *m* heat flow **-stromdichte** *f* heat-flux density; heat flow vector **-strömung** *f* heat convection, heat currents **-suchmesser** *m* heat direction finder **-summe** *f* accumulated temperature

Wärme-tauscher *m* heat exchanger (spacecraft) **-technik** *f* heat engineering **-technisch** pyrometric **-tod** *m* heat death **-tönung** *f* temper color, thermal effect, evolution of heat, absorption of heat, heat of transformation, heat change, heat effect, heat tone, heat production, heat content, heat quantity **-träger** *m* heat carrier **-trägheit** *f* thermal inertia **-trocknend** thermosetting **-übergang** *m* heat transfer or transmission, passage of heat

Wärmeübergangs-beiwert *m* surface-heat-transfer coefficient **-kreislauf** *m* heat-transfer cycle **-wert** *m* coefficient of heat transfer **-widerstand** *m* heat-transmission resistance **-zahl** *f* heat-convection constant, heat transfer, heat-transfer coefficient

Wärme-überschuß *m* surplus heat, excess heat **-übertrager** *m* heat exchanger **-übertragung** *f* transmission of heat, heat transfer, convection (heat), thermal effusion, thermal transpiration, thermodiffusion **-umkehr** *f* inversion **-umkehrschicht** *f* layer of temperature inversion **-umsatz** *m* heat transformation **-undichtigkeit** *f* heat leak **-undurchlässig** athermanous, impervious to heat, heat-insulating **-unterschied** *m* drop or difference in temperature **-verbrauch** *m* heat consumption **-verbrauchend** heat-consuming, endothermal, endothermic

Wärme-verformung *f* thermal deformation **-vergangenheit** *f* thermal antecedents, prior heat treatment **-vergütung** *f* heat-treatment **-verlust** *m* heat loss, thermal loss **-verminderung** *f* cooling **-vermögen** *n* heat capacity **-vernichter** *m* heat waster **-verteiler** *m* heat exchanger or interchanger **-verteilung** *f* distribution of temperature **-verzehrend** endothermic, endothermal **-vorgang** *m* thermal process

Wärme-warte *f* thermal-control switchboard **-wechsel** *m* change of temperature **-wechselgefäß** *n* heat exchanger **-wert** *m* heat value, thermal value, calorific value, heat equivalent, thermal coefficient **-wertbereich** *m* thermovalue range **-widerstehend** heat-resistant **-wirbel** *m* heat or temperature eddy

Wärme-wirkung *f* effect of heat, action of heat, thermal effect or influence, temperature effect **-wirkungsgrad** *m* thermal efficiency, calorific efficiency **-wirtschaft** *f* heat economy **-zahl** *f* temperature coefficient, thermal coefficient **-zerstreuung** *f* heat dissipation **-zufuhr** *f* addition of heat, heat input **-zunahme** *f* increase in temperature **-zustand** *m* thermal condition **-zustandsgröße** *f* entropy **-zwang** *m* temperature stress

warmfahren to dry out, warm up

warmfest heat-resistant, high-temperature **nicht ~** hot-short **-e Legierung** refractory alloy **-er Stahl** steel with good high-temperature characteristics, steel for high-temperature service **-er Stahlguß** high-temperature steel castings

Warmfestigkeit *f* hot strength, high-temperature stability, resistance to heat **geringe ~** hot-shortness

Wärm-flasche *f* hot-water bottle **-formgebung** *f* hot forming, hot shaping, hot-working

Warmformung *f* forging

Warmfräse *f* hot milling machine

Warmfräs- und Sägemaschine *f* hot milling and sawing machine

Warmfront *f* warm front

warmgeformt warm coiled **-er Stahl** hot-worked steel

warm-gelaufenes Lager hot bearing **-gepreßt** hot-pressed, hot-press-fitted, subjected to thermoplastic treatment **-gesenkdrückmaschine** *f* hot-swaging machine **-gewalzt** hot-rolled **-gewindewalze** *f* hot thread-rolling machine **-gezogen** hot-drawn **-halteofen** *m* holding furnace **-hammer** *m* hot drop hammer **-härtbar** thermosetting **-härte** *f* hot hardness **-härten** to thermoset **-haube** *f* hot nozzle, hot top, sinkhead, hot fire-clay sleeve

Warm-kalandrieren *n* glazing **-kathodenröhre** *f* hot cathode tube **-kleber** *m* hot-setting adhesive **-kraftmaschine** *f* thermoengine **-lager** *n* cooling bed, cooling table, hot bed **-lagern** *n* artificial aging **-lagertest** *m* warm storage test

warmlaufen to run hot, run up **einen Motor ~ lassen** to run up an engine

Warm-laufen *n* hot running, running hot, heating up **-lochdorn** *m* ball (in piercing mills, reelers) mandrel **-lötstelle** *f* hot end (in pyrometry)

Warmluft *f* warm air **unter ~ erzeugtes Eisen** hot-blast cast iron

Warmluft-eintritt *m* hot-air intake **-enteisung** *f* thermal ice elimination **-front** *f* warm front **-gerät** *n* hot-air blower **-heizung** *f* hot-air heating **-kanal** *m* hot-air conduit **-klappe** *f* heater valve **-leitung** *f* hot-air pipe **-ofen** *m* heating stove **-schlauch** *m* hot-air duct **-vorhang** *m* (vertical) warm air curtain

Warm-matrize *f* hot die **-mutternpresse** *f* hot nut press **-naßspinnerei** *f* spinning with hot water **-nietung** *f* hot riveting

Wärmofen *m* heating furnace, reheating furnace, soaking furnace **kontinuierlicher ~** continuous-heating furnace

Wärmofenschlacke *f* reheating-furnace cinder

warmplastisch thermoplastic

Wärmplatte *f* warming plate

Warm-preßarbeit *f* warm pressing **-presse** *f* forging press **-pressen** to hot-press **-pressen** *n* hot pressing, drop forging **-presserei** *f* hot pressing shop

Warmpreß-formen *pl* hot-pressing dies **-guß** *m* press casting **-muttereisen** *n* hot stamping phosphorus nut bars **-stahl** *m* hot-pressing tool (steel) **-stempel** *m* hot-forging dies, hot-pressing dies, hot-press punch **-teile** *pl* hot-pressed parts **-verfahren** *n* hot-press method

Warmprüfung *f* hot inspection

warmrecken to hot-work, hot-strain

Warmrecken *n* hot working, hot straining

Warmrichten *n* hot straightening

Warmriß *m* heat crack, hot crack, thermal crack, heating crack

warmrissig hot-short

Warmrissigkeit *f* hot shortness, heat checking

Wärmröhre *f* chaffer

warm-sägen to hot-saw **-schablone** *f* hot template **-schälen** *n* hot peeling **-scheren** *n* hot shearing **-schlagmatrize** *f* hot punch die **-schmiedegesenk** *n* drop-hammer die **-schmieden** *n* hot forging **-schneidhaltigkeit** *f* red hardness **-schrottmeißel** *m* hot chisel **-schrumpfen** to press and shrink into **-schweißung** *f* welding with pre- and postheating **-sitz** *m* shrink fit

Warm-spiel *n* hot clearance **-sprödigkeit** *f* brittleness when hot, hot-shortness **-stangenpressen** *n* direct extrusion **-stauchen** *n* hot upsetting, hot heading **-stauchung** *f* hot crimping **-stoßen** *n* hot pushing **-strangpresse** *f* hot-extrusion press **-streckgrenze** *f* high temperature yield point

Wärmung *f* warming, heating

Warm-verarbeitungsfähigkeit *f* hot workability **-verformbar** hot-workable, thermoplastic **-verformbarkeit** *f* hot-forming property **-verformt** hot-formed, hot-worked **-verformung** *f* forging, hot-working, hot forming **-vergütung** *f* artificial aging **-vernietung** *f* hot riveting **-versprödung** *f* temperature embrittlement **-vulkanisation** *f* hot cure (hot vulvanization) **-walze** *f* roll for hot rolling **-walzen** to hot-roll **-walzen** *n* hot rolling **-walzwerk** *n* hot rolling mill

Warmwasser-bereiter *m* electric water heater, boiler **-bereitungsanlage** *f* hot-water plant **-heizkörper** *m* hot water radiator **-heizungsanlage** *f* hot-water heating plant **-pumpe** *f* hot-water pump

Warmwasser-raum *m* heating (water) jacket or space **-speicher** *m* hot-water tank, boiler **-schwitze** *f* warm sweating (process) **-zisterne** *f* hot-water tank

Warmwerden *n* heating (up)

Warmzerreiß-probe *f* hot tensile test **-versuch** *m* tensile test at elevated temperature, heat-strength test, hot tensile test

warmziehen to hot-draw

Warmziehen *n* hot drawing

Warmziehring *m* extrusion die for hot work, hot-piercing die

Warnanlage *f* warning indicator or device **optische akustische ~** audible and visible warning device

Warn-blinker *m* anti-collision light **-boje** *f* fairway buoy **-dienst** *m* air-raid warning service **-druckzeiger** *m* warning pressure pointer

Warner *m* warner, alarm

Warn-flagge *f* danger flag **-gebiet** *n* danger zone or area **-gerät** *n* monitor **-grenzen** *pl* (Qualitätskontrolle) warning limits **-lampe** *f* warning lamp, pilot lamp **-leuchttafel** *f* annunciator panel **-licht** *n* warning light **-meldung** *f* warning notice, alarm indication **-peilgerät** *n* DF warning set **-ring** *m* alarm area

Warnsignal *n* air-raid alarm, caution signal, warning and danger signal **~ an Wegübergängen** level-crossing signal

Warn-stelle *f* lookout post, district warning center **-ton** *m* warning signal

Warnung *f* warning, alarm

Warnungs-anzeiger *m* warning indicator **-bake** *f* aerodrome hazard beacon **-licht** *n* warning light **-ring** *m* warning ring **-schild** *n* danger signal, caution board **-schreiben** *n* cautionary letter **-schuß** *m* warning shot **-signal** *n* warning signal **-tafel** *f* danger, caution, or warning board, plate warning **-zeichen** *n* warning sign

Warn-vorrichtung *f* alarm apparatus, alarm **-zeichen** *n* (an Instrumenten) off-flag **-zeigerruhestellung** *f* warning pointer zero or end position

Warp-kette *f* warp chain **-trosse** *f* warp

Warrelschäkel *f* swivel shackle

Wart *m* ground-mechanic maintenance man, warden

Warte *f* observation tower, observatory, watch-tower **-bahn** *f* parking orbit **-feld** *n* storing up the calls **-geld** *n* separation or retaining pay **-höhe** *f* action pending altitude (for balloons) **-lampe** *f* hold signal or lamp

warten to wait, maintain, attend to, service

Wärter *m* keeper, attendant, guard

Warteraum *m* waiting room, stand-by area (for radio) **-funkfeuer** *n* holding facility

Warte-schleife *f* holding pattern (aviation), orbiting **-stand** *m* inactive status **-stelle** *f* tie-up wharf **-stellung** *f* stand-by position, waiting position **-zeichen** *n* waiting signal **-zeit** *f* delay, wait, waiting time

Wartturm *m* look-out tower

Wartung *f* attendance, care, maintenance, upkeep, service, servicing, attention **laufende ~** maintenance routine

Wartungs-aufwand *m* maintenance costs **-bereich** *m* (Flugplatz) servicing area (airport) **-frei** maintenance-free, without maintenance **-kosten** *pl* cost of attendance, maintenance costs **-vorschrift** *f* servicing schedule **-zeit** *f* engineering or servicing time

Warveton *m* varved clay

Warze *f* wart, stud, lug, pimple, boss, knob, pin, projection, nipple

warzen (Metallbearbeitung) ziehsenken to dimple

Warzen-bleche *pl* plates with projections **-förmig** mammilated **-punktschweißung** *f* projection weld **-schweißen** *n* projection welding

warzig nodular

Wasch-anlage *f* washing plant **-anstalt** *f* laundry **-apparat** *m* washer, washing apparatus **-aufsatz** *m* (gas) washing tube **-becken** *n* washing or hand basin **-behälter** *m* blow pit, tank, vat

Wasch-benzin *n* gasoline used for cleaning purposes **-benzol** *m* commercial benzol **-beständig** washproof **-bolzen** *m* washout plug **-boot** *n* floating laundry **-bottich** *m* washing vat or trough **-bütte** *f* washing tub

Wäsche *f* laundry, wash, dressing floor (min.) **-abgang** *m* washing refuse **-anlage** *f* washing plant

waschecht washable, dyed in the grain, fast

Waschechtheit *f* bleaching resistance

Wäsche-desinfektionsanlage *f* linen-disinfection plant **-fabrik** *f* lingerie factory **-fabrikationsmaschine** *f* linen-making machine **-glanzstärke** *f* brilliant starch for linen

Wascheinrichtung *f* washing accommodation, lavatory

Wäschekasten *m* washing tank

Wäschewickler *m* clothes-line winder

Wäschemangel *f* mangle

waschen to wash, clean, scrub, purify, launder

Waschen *n* washing

Wäscher *m* washer, scrubber, wash tower, scrubbing tower, wash column, disintegrator

Wäscherei *f* laundry **-anlage** *f* laundry plant

Wasch-erz *n* wash or diluvial ore **-erzeugnisse** *n pl* laundry products

Wäsche-schleuder *f* spin-drier **-zeichentinte** *f* underlinen marking ink

Wasch-filterstraße *f* filter washing plant **-flasche** *f* wash(ing) bottle **-flüssigkeit** *f* washing fluid or liquid **-gold** *n* alluvial or river gold, placer gold **-holländer** *m* washing engine **-kaue** *f* pit-head baths (min.) **-kohle** *f* coal to be washed **-leitung** *f* flushing line **-lösung** *f* wash solution **-maschine** *f* washing machine **-mittel** *n* washing agent, detergent

Waschmittelschlauch *m* tube for cleaning fluid

Wasch-öl *n* wash oil, straw oil, absorption oil **-pinsel** *m* brush for washing **-probe** *f* assay of washed or buddled ore **-prozeß** *m* washing process, cleaning process, scrubbing process **-rad** *n* dash wheel (wash wheel) **-sieb** *n* colander **-soda** *f* washing soda **-trog** *m* washing trough **-trommel** *f* washing drum or trommel

Waschung *f* washing

Wasch-verlust *m* dressing loss **-vorgang** *m* washing process, cleaning process, scrubbing process **-wasser** *n* wash water, washing water **-wasserklärung** *f* clarification of wash water

Wasser *n* water **~ entziehen** to dehydrate **~ nachgießen** to pour water again **~ zersetzen** to split up water **auf dem ~ treiben** to float **abgängiges ~** waste water **angesäuertes ~** acidulated water **destilliertes ~** distilled water **fließendes ~** running water **kohlensaures ~, moussierendes ~** aerated water **schweres ~** heavy water

Wasser-abflug *m* water take-off **-abfluß** *m* water discharge **-abhaltender Anstrich** waterproof paint **-ablaß** *m* draining, drain, water ejector, culvert **-ablaßhahn** *m* water-drawoff cock, water-discharge vent, petcock **-ablaßrohr** *n* water drain pipe **-ablaufhahn** *m* pet cock, water drain cock **-ableiter** *m* water drain **-ableitung** *f* drainage, water drain, culvert **-abperleffekt** *m* water-repellent effect **-abscheider** *m* water separator

Wasserabschluß *m* water seal, siphon **-gaserzeuger** *m* water-bottom gas producer, water-sealed gas producer **-ventil** *n* water-sealed valve

Wasser-abschreckung *f* quenching in water **-absorptionsvermögen** *n* water-absorbing capacity **-abspaltung** *f* dehydration **-abstoßend** water-repellent, nonhygroscopic, hydrofuge **-abweisring** *f* water thrower **-abziehstein** *m* waterstone **-abzug** *m* culvert **-abzugsgraben** *m* catch pit **-andrang** *m* entering of the water

Wasser-anker *m* drogue, sea anchor (aviation) **-anlage** *f* waterworks **-anschluß** *m* water connection **-anziehend** hygroscopic, water- or moisture-attracting **-anziehungsvermögen** *n* hygroscopicity

wasser-arm of low humidity **-armatur** *f* water appliance, water fitting **-artig** watery, like water, aqueous **-aufbereitung** *f* water purifying or treatment **-aufnahme** *f* absorption of water **-aufnahmefähigkeit** *f* absorptive capacity **-aufnehmend** hygroscopic **-aufsaugend** water-absorbing **-aufsaugung** *f* absorption of water **-aufzug** *m* water balance

Wasser-ausgleich *m* water distribution **-auslaß** *m* water outlet **-auslauf** *m* discharge of water **-ausströmen** *n* bleed (min.) **-austritt** *m* water outlet **-bad** *n* water bath **-baddampfumformer** *m* water-bath desuperheater **-badschießofen** *m* Carius furnace **-ballast** *m* water ballast **-ballasthosen** *pl* water trunks

Wasserbau-kunst *f* hydraulic architecture or engineering **-unternehmung** *f* enterprise of hydraulic structure

Wasser-becken *n* water basin, water reservoir, water tank, stilling basin **-bedarf** *m* water requirement **-behälter** *m* reservoir, cistern, water tank **-berieselung** *f* water-jet scrubbing, water irrigation, water spraying **-beständig**

water-resistant, waterproof **-bewegung** *f* movement of the water **-bindend** hydrophylic, water-absorbent, water-imbibent **-bindvermögen** *n* water-absorptive capacity **-blase** *f* bubble of water, vessel or container for water heating **-blei** *n* molybdenite, plumbago **-bleiocker** *m* molybdite, molybdic ocher

Wasser-blüte *f* name of several algae **-bremse** *f* water brake, hydraulic-type dynamometer **-brücke** *f* aqueduct

Wasserdampf *m* water vapor, steam, fog **~ ausscheiden** to condense water vapor **mit ~ abblasen** to distill with steam **der ~ schlägt sich nieder** the water vapor condenses

Wasserdampf-band *n* water-vapor band **-destillation** *f* steam distillation **-strahlsauger** *m* steam ejector **-strom** *m* water vapor **-verträglichkeit** *f* compatibility with water vapors **-zusatz** *m* water-vapor addition

Wasser-deckfarbe *f* water pigment finish **-destillierapparat** *m* water still

wasserdicht waterproof, watertight, impermeable **-er Abschluß** water seal **-es Abteil** watertight compartment **-er Kern** impermeable core **-e Schiffswand** bulkhead **-es Schott** watertight bulkhead **-e Verbindung** watertight joint **-e Verkleidung** impermeable facing or screen

Wasserdichtigkeit *f* watertightness, impermeability to water

Wasserdichtmachungsmittel *n* waterproofing agent

Wasserdom *n* header tank

Wasserdruck *m* hydraulic pressure, hydrostatic pressure, water pressure **-bremse** *f* hydraulic brake **-heber** *m* hydraulic lever **-höhe** *f* hydraulic-pressure head **-kolben** *m* hydraulic ram **-manometer** *n* hydraulic pressure gauge **-presse** *f* hydraulic press **-probe** *f* hydraulic test **-schere** *f* hydraulic shearing machine

Wasser-durchbruch *m* water burst **-durchflußfläche** *f* area of water-passage **-durchflußwiderstand** *m* flow resistance, resistance to passage of water **-durchlaßeinrichtung** *f* water outlet **-durchlässig** pervious to water **-durchlässigkeit** *f* permeability (water) **-durchlässigkeitsprüfer** *m* porosimeter, water permeability tester

wasser-echt unaffected by water **-ecke** *f* water pocket **-eimer** *m* water bucket **-einbruch** *m* water breaking-in **-eindampfgerät** *n* water evaporator **-einlaß** *m* water inlet **-einlaßrohr** *n* water-inlet pipe **-einspritzung** *f* water injection **-eintritt** *m* water inlet

Wasser-elektrizitätswerk *n* hydraulic central station **-enteisenung** *f* water softening, extraction of iron from water **-enteisenungsanlage** *f* water-softening plant **-enthärtung** *f* water softening **-enthärtungsanlage** *f* water softener **-entlüftungsanlage** *f* air separator for water plants **-entmanganung** *f* water demanganesing

Wasser-entnahme *f* intake (hydraulics) **-entsalzung** *f* salt water conversion, water softening **-entsäuerung** *f* water disoxydation **-entziehung** *f* abstraction of water, dehydration, removal of water, desiccation **-entziehungsmittel** *n* dehydrating agent **-ersatz** *m* water replacement **-ersparnis** *f* water saving **-faden** *m* flow filament, fluid filament, filament of water **-fahrzeug** *n* watercraft, vessel

Wasserfall *m* waterfall, type of antiaircraft rocket, type of optically or radar-guided missile

wasserfallartig herunterfallen to cascade

Wasserfalleffekt *m* breaking drop effect

Wasser-fänger *m* water guard **-fest** waterproof, watertight, resistant to water **-fläche** *f* water surface **-flachs** *m* water-retted flax **-flügel** *m* hydrofoil **-flughafen** *m* marine airport, water aerodrome

Wasserflugmodell *n* seaplane model

Wasser-flugplatz *m* seaplane aerodrome **-flugwesen** *n* marine or naval aviation

Wasserflugzeug *n* seaplane, hydroplane **ein ~ flächen** to speed a hydroplane through water

Wasserflugzeug-bassin *n* seaplane tank, towing basin **-binnenhafen** *m* seaplane basin **-führer** *m* seaplane pilot **-schleppwagen** *m* seaplane beaching trolley **-transportwagen** *m* beaching gear (for seaplanes)

Wasserflußmesser *m* rate-of-flow meter

Wasserförderung *f* raising of water **~ mit Windbetrieb** water pumping or conveying by wind

Wasser-fracht *f* discharge, water freight **-frei** dehydrated, desiccated, anhydrous, dry **-führend** water-bearing **-führung** *f* water duct or passage; water distributor, water header, river flow **-fülleinrichtung** *f* flooding device **-gang** *m* waterway

Wassergas *n* water gas **karburiertes ~** carbureted water gas

Wassergas-erzeuger *m* water-gas producer, water-gas generator **-erzeugung** *f* production or generation of water gas **-generator** *m* water-gas producer **-herstellung** *f* production or generation of water gas **-periode** *f* steaming period, steam blow **-teer** *m* water-gas tar

Wassergefäß *n* water vat

Wassergehalt *m* percentage of moisture, water content, moisture content, humidity **freier ~** free moisture

wassergekühlt water-cooled

wassergelagert, nicht ~ unsoaked

Wasser-genossenschaft *f* water company **-gewinnung** *f* procuring of water **-gierig** hygroscopic **-glas** *n* water glass **-gleitboot** *n* gliding boat **-graben** *m* ditch, channel, moat **-großreinigungsanlage** *f* water-screening plant **-guß** *m* chill casting **-hahn** *m* water cock, water tap, water faucet, water nozzle **-haltend** containing water, water-retaining

wasser-haltig hydrated, hydrous, containing water, aqueous **-haltung** *f* drainage, pit work

Wasserhaltungs-maschine *f* pumping engine **-schacht** *m* sump shaft

Wasser-härtung *f* water hardening **-härtungsstahl** *m* water-hardening steel **-haushalt** *m* water conservation, rainfall, runoff and evaporation relations **-haut** *f* water coat **-heber** *m* pulsometer **-hebewerk** *n* water-supply and -pumping station **-hebungsmaschine** *f* water-raising or pumping machine **-heilanstalt** *f* hydropathic establishment **-hell** clear as water, transparent water-white **-höhe** *f* depth of water **-höheanzeiger** *m* altitude gauge (central heating) **-hose** *f* waterspout **-hülle** *f* water film

wässerig watery, aqueous, hydrous **-e Deck-**

farben (Wasserdeckfarben) water pigment colors

Wasser-inhalt *m* volume of water **-kalander** *m* water-calender (water-mangle) **-kalk** *m* hydraulic lime **-kammer** *f* sectional chamber, water chamber

Wasserkanal *m* hydrodynamic tank **-versuch** *m* tank test

Wasser-kapazität *f* water-absorption capacity **-karte** *f* hydrographic chart **-kasten** *m* water compartment or tank, water box **-keller** *m* covered (water) reservoir at of below ground level **-kessel** *m* kettle, boiler, water tank **-kies** *m* marcasite **-kissen** *n* water cushion **-kitt** *m* hydraulic cement **-kläranlage** *f* water-clearing or water purifying plant **-klemme** *f* water shortage **-knoten** *m* crown knot

Wasserkraft *f* hydraulic power, water power **-anlage** *f* water-power plant, hydraulic power station **-generator** *m* waterwheel generator **-lehre** *f* hydrodynamics **-maschine** *f* hydraulic motor **-werk** *n* hydroelectric generating station **-wissenschaft** *f* hydraulics

Wasser-kran *m* water faucet **-kreislauf** *m* water circulation **-kristall** *m* rock crystal **-krumpe** *f* wet shrinking **-kühlanlage** *f* water-cooling installation **-kühler** *m* water cooler, water-tube cooler, water radiator **-kühlmantel** *m* water jacket **-kühlröhre** *f* water-cooled tube **-kühlung** *f* water cooling, water-cooling system **-kultur** *f* hydrophonics **-kunde** *f* hydrology **-kunst** *f* water work(s), fountain **-kuppe** *f* highest peak of the Rhone

Wasser-landebahn *f* channel **-landebahnfeuer** *n* channel light **-landflugzeug** *n* amphibian plane **-landung** *f* water landing **-lauf** *m* water-course, channel, river, stream, canal **-leck** *n* leakage of water **-leckleitung** *f* water drain **-leer** without water

Wasserleitung *f* water pipes, water conduit, water main, water system

Wasserleitungs-hahn *m* water tap, water spout **-rohr** *n* water pipe **-wasser** *n* city water

Wasser-libelle *f* water level **-linie** *f* water line, water mark (on beach), floating line **-linienmodell** *n* water-line model **-linienschwerpunkt** *m* center of flotation **-loch** *n* drain hole **-los** arid, without water **-löslich** water-soluble

Wasserlösungssohle *f* drainage level, draining level **-lösungsstollen** *m* deep adit, adit level, drainage gallery **-luftpumpe** *f* water-jet aspirator, water vacuum pump **-luke** *f* spout (of gutter)

Wassermantel *m* water jacket **~ um das Auspuffventil** water receiver around the exhaust valve

Wassermantel-generator *m* water-jacket-type producer **-ofen** *m* water-jacketed furnace

Wassermenge *f* volume or quantity of water

Wassermengen-messung *f* measurement of discharge **-registrierapparat** *m* water-quantity-recording apparatus

Wasser-messer *m* water meter, water gauge, hydrometer **-messerflügel** *m* water-measuring vane **-messungslehre** *f* hydrometry **-mörtel** *m* cement mortar **-motor** *m* hydraulic motor or engine

wassern to alight upon the water

Wassern *n* airplane traveling in contact with water

wässern to water, dilute with water, hydrate, irrigate, rinse, wash (phot.)

Wässern *n* washing

Wasser-oberfläche *f* water surface **-orgel** *f* hydraulic organ **-phantom** *n* water phantom **-polster** *n* water cushion **-presse** *f* hydraulic press **-probe** *f* water test, water sample **-prüfstand** *m* hydraulic brake test bench or torque stand **-pumpe** *f* water pump (diluting pump)

Wasserpumpen-flügelrad *n* water-pump impeller **-kühlung** *f* force-circulation cooling system **-welle** *f* water-pump shaft

Wasser-pumpkühlung *f* pressure water-cooling system **-pyrometer** *n* water pyrometer, hydropyrometer

Wasserrad *n* water wheel **mittelschlächtiges ~** breast water wheel, middle-shot water wheel **oberschlächtiges ~** overshot water wheel **rückschlächtiges ~** high-breast water wheel **unterschlächtiges ~** undershot water wheel

Wasserradschaufel *f* water-wheel paddle

Wasser-raum *m* water space or room **-recht** *n* water rights

wasserreich of high humidity **-e Luftschicht** air stratum or air layer of high humidity

Wasserreinigung *f* water purification

Wasserreinigungs-anlage *f* water-purification plant, water clarifier **-apparat** *m* detartarizer, water purifier **-sack** *m* water-sterilizing bag

Wasser-rennflugzeug *n* racing seaplane **-rieselung** *f* water spraying **-ringluftpumpe** *f* water-ring air pump **-ringpumpe** *f* liquid seal pump **-rinne** *f* gutter, water trough or channel **-rohr** *n* water pipe **-röhrenkessel** *m* **-rohrkessel** *m* water-tube boiler **-röhrenkühler** *m* water-tube-type cooler **-rollbahn** *f* taxi-channel **-rückkühlung** *f* water recooling system **-ruder** *n* water rudder

Wasser-sack *m* canvas bucket, water trap **-satt** water-saturated **-säule** *f* column of water, splash, hydrostatic head (water column) pressure in units of water height

Wassersäulen-druck *m* hydraulic head, water-column pressure **-druckmesser** *m* water-column pressure gauge

Wasser-schall *m* propagation of sound waves in water, water-borne sound **-schallsender** *m* submarine oscillator **-schalter** *m* hydroblast switch **-schaum** *m* water foam **-scheide** *f* (water) divide, watershed (boundary) **-scheu** hydrophobe **-schieber** *m* water sluice valve **-schild** *n* water guard **-schlag** *m* water-hammer(ing), water shock **-schlange** *f* water hose, water snake

Wasser-schlauch *m* water hose **-schleifmasse** *f* (in water) soluble grinding paste **-schloß** *n* surge tank **-schluß** *m* water seal, trap **-schnecke** *f* water or hydraulic screw **-schöpfmaschine** *f* water-scooping machine **-schöpfwindmühle** *f* water-pump windmill **-schwinge** *f* walking pipe **-segelflugzeug** *n* hydroglider, hydroplane **-seite** *f* upstream face **-(seiten)ruder** *n* water rudder

wasserseitig upstream **-e Stütze** waterside leg

Wasser-setzmaschine *f* water jig **-siedemesser** *m* hypsometer **-speicher** *m* water reservoir **-speicherung** *f* storage of water **-speier** *m* gargoyle **-speiser** *m* feed-water regulator, storage of water **-speisung** *f* water supply **-sperre** *f* water obstacle **-sperrkolonne** *f* water string **-sperrung** *f* water shutoff **-sperrungsprüfer** *m* casing tester

Wasserspiegel *m* water-surface, water level, water line **gestauter ~** upper pool or head-water elevation **höchster gestauter ~** highest upper pool elevation **niedrigster ~** lowest upper pool elevation

Wasserspiegel-breite *f* width at water level **-erhöhung** *f* raising of water level

Wasser-sprengwagen *m* watering car, sprinkling wagon **-spritze** *f* watering apparatus **-spritzer** *m* (water) spray **-sprühregen** *m* water spray **-sprung** *m* hydraulic jump **-spülentaschungs-anlage** *f* hydraulic ash handling plant **-spülung** *f* flushing

Wasserstand *m* water gauge, water level, height of level, stage, pool elevation, water line, sea level **höchster schiffbahrer ~** highest navigable flood stage

Wasserstands-änderung *f* change of water level **-anzeiger** *m* water gauge, water-level indicator **-fernmeldeanlage** *f* remote-operating water-level transmitting plant **-fernmelder** *m* water level tele-indicator **-glas** *n* water-gauge glass, glass gauge **-hahn** *m* water-gauge cock or tap **-marke** *f* watermark, water post **-melder** *m* water-level transmitter, water alarm **-messer** *m* water-level gauge

Wasserstands-registrierapparat *m* recorder for telehydrobarometer **-regler** *m* automatic water-level regulator **-rohr** *n* water gauge, gauge glass **-schutzglas** *n* water-gauge preserving tube **-stutzen** *m* water-gauge pocket **-tabelle** *f* tide table **-zeichen** *n* tidal signal **-zeiger** *m* gauge glass, water gauge

Wasser-start *m* rise off water **-station** *f* tank **-staub** *m* water spray, spray **-stein** *m* scale from water, incrustation **-steinsatz** *m* scale deposit **-stock** *m* hydrant

Wasserstoff *m* hydrogen **mit ~ verbunden** hydrogenated **~ mit Masse**^{3} tritium **~ mit Masse**^{2} deuterium **schwerer ~** heavy hydrogen, deuterium, tritium

Wasserstoff-abspaltung *f* dehydration **-anlage** *f* hydrogen generating plant **-anlagerung** *f* hydrogenation **-anlasser** *m* hydrogen starter **-ballon** *m* balloon inflated with hydrogen **-behälter** *m* hydrogen container or tank **-bindung** *f* hydrogen bond **-brüchigkeit** *f* hydrogen embrittlement **-brücke** *f* hydrogen bond **-entwicklung** *f* evolution of hydrogen **-erzeuger** *m* **-erzeugungsapparat** *m* hydrogen genrator **-flamme** *f* hydrogen flame **-flasche** *f* hydrogen bottle or cylinder **-funkenstrecke** *f* hydrogen spark gap

Wasserstoff-gas *n* hydrogen gas **-gasanlage** *f* hydrogen-gas plant **-gaserzeugung** *f* generation of hydrogen **-gehalt** *m* hydrogen content **-gemisch** *n* hydrogen mixture **-gewinnungsanlage** *f* hydrogen-producing plant **-haltig** hydrogenous, hydrogen-containing **-heliumgas** *n* hydrogen-helium gas **-herstellung** *f* generation of hydrogen **-hyperoxyd** *n* hydrogen peroxide

Wasserstoff-ion *n* hydrogen ion **-ionenkonzentration** *f* hydrogen-ion concentration **-kern** *m* hydrogen particle or nucleus **-knallgas** *n* detonating gas **-kontinua** *pl* continuous hydrogen **-krankheit** *f* hydrogen embrittlement **-lichtbogen** *m* hydrogen arc **-ofen** *m* hydrogen oven **-reich** rich in hydrogen **-salz** *n* hydrogen salt **-sauerstoffschweißung** *f* oxyhydrogen welding **-säure** *f* hydracid **-schacht** *m* hydrogen chimney shaft

Wasserstoff-sphäre *f* layer or stratum or the light gases **-strahl** *m* hydrogen ray **-strom** *m* current of hydrogen **-sulfid** *n* hydrogen sulfide **-superoxyd** *n* hydrogen peroxide **-supersulfid** *n* hydrogen persulfide **-thyratron** *n* hydrogen thyratron **-triebwerk** *n* hydrogen engine (g/m) **-ventil** *n* hydrogen valve, hydrogen-pressure regulator **-verbindung** *f* hydrogen compound **-versprödung** *f* hydrogen embrittlement **-zahl** *f* hydrogen-ion concentration

Wasser-stollen *m* adit drainage, drainage level **-stoß** *m* water hammer

Wasserstrahl *m* water jet **-düse** *f* water-jet nozzle **-erder** *m* water-jet type lightning arrester **-gebläse** *n* blowers actuated by water power, water blast **-mundstück** *n* nozzle **-pumpe** *f* water-jet (vacuum) pump or injector

Wasser-straße *f* canal, waterway **-streifen** *m* water streak, false sap, moon ring **-strom** *m* torrent, current or stream of water **-süchtig** hydrophilic **-tank** *m* water tank **-tasse** *f* water seal (in a gas producer) **-temperatur** *f* water temperature **-tiefe** *f* depth of water, draft **-topf** *m* water receptacle, drain tank, gully, water pot **-tragesack** *m* canvas water bucket **-transport** *m* water transportation

Wasser-treibeverfahren *n* flooding **-trense** *f* watering bridle **-triebwerk** *n* hydraulic machine **-tröpfchen** *n* water droplet or particle **-tropfempfindlich** sensitive to water-spotting **-tropfen** *m* water drop, drop of water, water particle **-turbine** *f* hydro-turbine, water turbine **-turbinenöl** *n* water-turbine oil **-turm** *m* water tower **-turmwärter** *m* reservoir keeper

Wasser-überlauf *m* water overflow **-überschwemmung** *f* water flood **-überwachungsgerät** *n* water monitor **-übungsflugzeug** *n* training seaplane **-uhr** *f* water meter **-umlauf** *m* water circulation **-umlaufkühlung** *f* cooling by means of circulating water **-undurchlässig** impervious

Wasser- und Landflugzeug *n* amphibian

Wässerung *f* irrigation, washing (phot.)

Wasserung *f* alighting on water

Wasserungsgeschwindigkeit *f* alighting speed (aviation)

Wässerungsgestell *n* washing rack (phot.)

wasser-unlöslich waterproof, insoluble in water **-ventilator** *m* hydrofoil **-ventildeckel** *m* water valve cover **-verankerung** *f* water anchorage **-verbrauch** *m* discharge of water, water consumption **-verdampfung** *f* evaporation of water **-verdrängung** *f* draft of water (seaplane), displacement of water **-vergoldung** *f* burnished or water gilding **-vergüten** *n* water tempering (met.), water hardening **-verkehrsflugzeug** *n* commercial seaplane **-verschluß** *m* water seal **-verschlußventil** *n* hopper-cock

Wasserversorgung *f* supplying of water, water supply, waterworks

Wasserversorgungs-stelle *f* water-supply plant **-tank** *m* water-supply tank **-unternehmung** *f*

water-supply enterprise

Wasserverteilungs-anlage *f* water-distribution plant **-stelle** *f* water-distribution point **-teller** *m* deflector

Wasser-verträglichkeit *f* compatibility with water **-vorlage** *f* water purifier, water seal **-vorrat** *m* water supply **-waage** *f* water balance, spirit level, (bubble) level **-walke** *f* water milling **-walze** *f* rinsing roller **-wärts** streamward **-wirbelbremse** *f* hydraulic brake **-wirtschaft** *f* hydroeconomy

Wasser-zapfpumpe *f* thief pump **-zeichen** *n* sea return (radar), water mark **-zeichenpapier** *n* water-marked paper **-zerstäuber** *m* atomizer (spray-diffuser) **-zement** *m* hydraulic cement **-ziehen der Sonne** solar tide **-zuführungskolben** *m* water feeding piston **-zulauf** *m* water supply **-zuleitungsrohr** *n* water-supply pipe **-zusatz** *m* added water quantity **-zyklon** *m* hydro-cyclone

Was-War-Wann-Apparat time and speed recorder

Watfähigkeit *f* fording power of a motor vehicle without wetting the motor, stream-crossing ability

Watt *n* watt

Watte *f* absorbent cotton, cotton batting, wadding, surgical cotton, pad **blutstillende ~** styptic cotton

Watte-band *n* ribbon of wadding **-bausch** *m* cotton plug **-färberei** *f* carded-cotton dyeing **-filter** *n* cotton filter **-herstellungsmaschine** *f* wadding-manufacturing machine **-kugel** *f* cotton-wool ball

Watten-maschine *f* set frame (textiles) **-meer** *n* shoals

Watte-pfropfen *m* wad **-rolle** *f* roll of wadding **-träger** *m* cotton-wool probe **-wickel** *m* lap (roll)

wattieren to wad

wattierte Maske padded face mask

Watt-komponente *f* active component, energy component, power component, inphase component, watt component **-leistung** *f* wattage, real-power **-los** wattless **-messer** *m*, **-meter** *n* wattmeter **-strom** *m* active current **-stunde** *f* watt-hour **-stundenverbrauch** *m* watt-hour consumption **-stundenzähler** *m* watt-hour meter **-verbrauch** *m* wattage, watt consumption **-zahl** *f* number of watts, wattage

Waustengel *m* weld stalk

Webe-blattsetzer *m* reed maker **-draht** *m* netting wire **-einlage** *f* lay (textiles) **-geschirr** *n* mounting for weaving mills **-kartenpappe** *f* Jacquard card

Webeleinensteg *m* clove hitch

Webeleinen-stich oder -steck clove hitch

weben to weave

Weber *m* weaver, weber, volt-second **-baum** *m* loom beam

Weberei *f* textile mill, weaving, weaving mill **-bedarfsartikel** *m* requirement for weaving **-erzeugnis** *n* weaving product **-geschirr** *n* weaving accessories **-mechaniker** *m* mule fitter **-vorbereitungsmaschine** *f* slubber **-zeichner** *m* textile draftsman

Weber-glas *n* cloth prover, weaver's or web glass, thread counter **-kamm** *m* reed for weaving looms **-knoten** *m* reef or weaver's knot **-schiffchen** *n* shuttle **-schiffchenflug** *m* shuttle flight **-zange** *f* weaver's tweezers or nippers

Web-fehler *m* flaw or fault in weaving **-geschirr** *n* mounting, harness **-litze** *f* heddle, harness **-schütze** *f* shuttle

Webstoff *m*, **wasserdichter ~** waterproof tissue

Webstuhl *m* Jacquard loom **-setzer** *m* weaving loom fitter **-vorrichter** *m* loom fixer, gaiter, or mounter **-vorrichtung** *f* loom fixing **-waage** *f* spring shaft

Webvogel *m* picker (weaving)

Webwaren *pl* woven goods **-fabrik** *f* weaving factory

Wechsel *m* change, shift, alternation, exchange, variation, draft, bill of exchange, inversion, reversal, trimmer (carp.), displacement, doff (textiles), reversal (Tel.) **einen ~ auslösen** to cash a bill of exchange **einen ~ ausstellen** to draw a draft **einen ~ einlösen** to honor a bill **einen ~ unterschreiben** to sign a bill **einen ~ verlängern** to renew a bill **einen ~ ziehen** to draw a bill **~ ausgestellt zu Gunsten von . . .** bill drawn in favor of . . . **~ auf kurze Sicht** short bill

Wechsel-amplitude *f* alternating-current amplitude **-bank** *f* discount house

wechselbar changeable

Wechsel-beanspruchung *f* stress reversal, alternation of stress, alternating stress, cyclic loading (in materials testing) **-belastung** *f* alternating loads **-belastungsdauerprüfmaschine** *f* machine for testing durability arranged for alternate loads **-bereich** *m* range for alternating stresses **-beschleunigung** *f* acceleration of the vibratory motion **-betauungsversuch** *m* alternating dew test **-betrieb** *m* shifting operation, reversing process (of regenerator) **-bewegung** *f* intermittent motion **-beziehung** *f* mutual relation(ship), correlation, interrelation, reciprocal relationship

Wechsel-biegeprüfung *f* alternating bending test- **-biegespannung** *f* alternating bending stress **-biegeversuch** *m* alternating bending test **-blende** *f* alternating shutter (in stereoscopy), masking disk **-blinkleuchte** *f* alternating blinker **-bogen** *m* fill-in sheets **-brenner** *m* interchangeable welding and cutting torch, variable-head torch **-brief** *m* bill of exchange **-bruchspannung** *f* endurance limit (strength of material)

Wechsel-dauer (Probenwechsler) cycle time **-diskont** *m* bill discount **-druck** *m* pulsating load pressure, alternating pressure **-drucklager** *n* alternating thrust bearing **-duo** *n* looping mill, Belgian wire mill **-einlösung** *f* cashing of a bill **-einrichtung** *f* changing device (changer) **-entladung** *f* alternating discharge **-fall** *m* alternative **-farbig** iridescent

Wechselfeld *n* alternating field **magnetisches ~** alternating magnetic field **schnelles ~** oscillatory field

Wechselfeldmagnet *m* periodic magnet(ic structure)

Wechselfestigkeit *f* fatigue strength, alternate or repeated stress

Wechselfestigkeits-prüfung *f* alternate-stress test, fatigue test **-versuch** *m* repeated stress or fatigue test

Wechsel-feuer *n* alternating flashing light, intermittent light **-fluß** *m* alternating flux **-forderung** *f* claim based on a bill of exchange **-formular** *n* draft form **-formularpapier** *n* bill paper **-geschwindigkeit** *f* angular velocity, frequency (in radians) **-getriebe** *n* change-speed gear, gear change, variable gear, transmission (gear) **-getriebehebel** *m* change gear lever **-getriebekasten** *m* change-gear box **-gleichrichter** *m* vibrator

Wechselgröße *f* alternating quantity **Amplitude einer symmetrischen ~** amplitude of a symmetrical quantity

Wechsel-hahn *m* change cock **-hebel** *m* change-gear handle **-induktion** *f* mutual inductance **-kardioide** *f* switched cardioid (direction finder) **-kassette** *f* (film-)changing magazine **-klappe** *f* butterfly valve, reversing valve **-kondensor** *m* interchangeable or changeover condenser **-kontakt** *m* make-and-break contact, two-way or double-throw contact with neutral position **-koppler** *m* variocoupler **-kredit** *m* paper credit, credit for bills **-kupplung** *f* change-over clutch **-kurs** *m* rate of exchange

Wechsel-lade *f* drop-box sley (weaving) **-lager** *n* ball-thrust bearing **-lage** *f* business cycle **-lagern** to be interbedded (geol.) **-last** *f* changing or alternating load **-lauf** *m* interchangeable barrel

Wechsellicht *n* light-intensity variations, chopped light **-empfindlichkeit** *f* dynamic luminous sensitivity **-photometer** *n* alternating light photometer

Wechsel-magazin *f* changing magazine **-möglichkeit** *f* gear change **-moment** *n* alternating moment **-motor** *m* multi-fuel engine, convertible engine **-muffe** *f* change collar

wechseln to change, exchange, interchange, alter, vary, alternate, shift

Wechseln *n* change, exchange, interchange, varying, alternating

wechselnd varying, alternating, variable, changing, changeable **-e Beanspruchung** varying stress **-e Belastung** live load

Wechselnehmer *m* taker of a bill **-nocken** *m* polar signal cam (Teleg.) **-ordnung** *f* regulations relating to exchange **-pari** *n* par of exchange **-polalternator** *m* heteropolar alternator **-polig** heteropolar **-punkt** *m* reference point, midpoint, critical point, change point **-punktentfernung** *f* slant range to mid-point or crossing point

Wechselrad *n* interchangeable gear, change gear **-anordnung** *f* arrangement of the change gears **-getriebe** *n* change gears

Wechsel-räderschere *f* change gear quadrant

Wechselrad-type *m* pick-off gear or change-gear type, change-speed gear type **-verdeck** *n* change gear cover **-verhältnisse** *pl* change gear ratios

Wechsel-recht *n* law of exchange **-reiter** *m* steel reciprocating rider **-relais** *n* center-zero relay **-richter** *m* inverted converter, direct-current-alternating-current inverter, mutator, rectifier, vibrator, static inverter (missiles) DC/AC converter **-richtungskasten** *m* reversing box **-riemenscheibe** *f* interchangeable belt pulley **-ring** *m* changing collar or ring **-satz** *m* vibrator unit, exchange principle **-schablone** *f* serial numbering holder

Wechsel-schalter *m* double-throw switch **-schaltorgan** *n* change-over switch **-schaltung** *f* two point control switch arrangement **-scheiben** *pl* pick-off gears **-schieber** *m* hunting valve **-schiene** *f* change-speed fork **-schlagbiegeversuch** *m* alternating-impact bending test **-schlagversuch** *m* alternating-impact test, alternating-stress test **-schweißbrenner** *m* variable-head welding torch

wechselseitig mutual, alternate, reciprocal, inter-changeable, two-way **-e Folge** alternation **-er Verkehr** two-way traffic (teleph.)

Wechsel-seitigkeit *f* reciprocity **-spannung** *f* alternating-current voltage, alternating voltage or stress, alternating potential, alternation of stress **-spannungsgegentaktverstärker** *m* A. C. push-pull amplifier **-spannungskomponente** *f* alternating component of voltage **-spannungsunterbrechung** *f* A. C. dump **-sperre** *f* reciprocal interlocking (RR) **-sprechanlage** *f* intercom (munication system) **-sprechen** *n* simplex (voice communication) interphone

Wechsel-stand *m* alternative position **-ständig** alternate **-stange** *f* change rod **-stelle** *f* change point, meeting **-stellung** *f* alternate position, alternative firing position, alternative implacement **-stempelsteuer** *f* exchange stamp tax **-störung** *f* operator's interference

Wechselstrom *m* alternating current AC, a-c **ausgleichender ~** rectified alternating current **erzwungener ~** forced alternating current **gleichgerichteter ~** rectified alternating current **schneller ~** oscillatory current

Wechselstrom-anker *m* alternator armature **-anlage** *f* alternating current system **-anlasser** *m* alternating-current starter **-beeinflussung** *f* alternating-current interference **-blockfeld** *n* Siemens lock and block instrument **-bogen** *m* alternating-current arc **-bogenlampe** *f* alternating-current arc lamp **-brücke** *f* bridge for alternating current **-dynamo** *m*, **-dynamomaschine** *f* alternator, alternating-current dynamo or generator **-empfänger** *m* alternating-current-operated receiver, alternating-current mains receiver, alternating-current receiver

Wechselstromerzeuger *m* alternating-current generator, alternator **~ für Meß- und Rufzwecke** oscillator for measuring and signaling purposes

Wechselstrom-fahrbetrieb *m* alternating-current traction **-feld** *n* alternating-current field **-fernwahl** *f* alternating-current dialing

Wechselstromfrequenz-transformator *m* frequency changer or converter **-umformer** *m* frequency transformer **-wandler** *m* frequency changer or converter

Wechselstromgenerator *m* alternating-current generator, alternator **~ mit rotierender Funkenstrecke** alternator with rotating spark gap **~ mit umlaufender Funkenstrecke** alternator disk set

Wechselstrom-gleichrichter *m* alternating-current rectifier **-gleichstromeinankerumformer** *m* alternating-current-continuous-current converter **-gleichstromkreis** *m* ac track circuit (R.R.) **-gleichstromruf** *m* ac/dc ringing **-gleichstromumformer** *m* alternating-current continuous dynamotor

Wechselstrom-glocke *f* magneto bell **-heizung** *f* alternating-current heating **-induktivität** *f* alternating-current induction **-kollektormotor** *m* A. C. commutator motor

Wechselstrom-kommutatormotor *m* alternating-current commutator motor **-komponente** *f* alternating-current component, alternating component of current **-kreis** *m* alternating-current circuit **-leistung** *f* alternating-current power **-leitfähigkeit** *f* alternating current conductivity **-leitung** *f* A. C. power **-lichtbogen** *m* alternating arc **-lichtnetz** *n* alternating current lighting circuit

Wechselstrom-maschine *f* alternator, ac machine **-mehrfachtelegraphie** *f* carrier-current or alternating-current multiple telegraphy **-meßbrücke** *f* alternating-current (measuring) bridge **-messer** *m* alternating-current ammeter **-meßgerät** *n* alternating-current measuring set **-messung** *f* alternating-current measurement **-motor** *m* alternating-current motor **-nebenschlußmotor** *m* alternating-current shunt motor **-netz** *n* alternating-current mains or power-supply or power-line **-periode** *f* alternating-current cycle **-phasenrelais** *n* two-phase alternating-current relay

Wechselstrom-quelle *f* alternating-current source **-relais** *n* alternating-current relay **-relaisgleichrichter** *m* alternating-current relay rectifier **-richter** *m* frequency changer or transformer **-röhre** *f* alternating-current-operated valve, alternating-current valve **-schweißumformer** *m* alternating current arc welder **-signalisierung** *f* alternating-current pulsing **-technik** *f* alternating-current engineering **-telegraphie** *f* voice-frequency telegraphy **-ton** *m* alternating-current hum **-transformator** *m* alternating-current transformer **-verluste** *pl* alternating-current losses **-wahl** *f* alternating-current selection

Wechselstromwecker *m* magneto bell, alternating-current bell or buzzer, alternating-current alarm clock or ringer **~ mit Ankerumlegefeder** biased magneto bell

Wechselstromwiderstand *m* alternating-current resistance, impedance **konjugiert-komplexe**

Wechselstromwiderstände conjugate impedances

Wechsel-stube *f* money-changer's office, banking business **-stück** *n* change-piece, substitute **-stunde** *f* hour of relief (mining) **-taste** *f* shift key **-tastverfahren** *n* reversing-switch method (in direction-finder work), make-and-break switch or keying method **-tauchversuch** *m* alternate-immersion test **-ton** *m* warble note or sound (used in airplane alarms) **-umrichter** *m* frequency changer, frequency converter or transformer **-umsetzung** *f* reciprocal conversion

Wechsel-ventil *n* two-way valve, changeover valve **-ventilkasten** *m* change-valve box, valve manifold **-verfestigung** *f* change of strengthening **-verformung** *f* alternating load deformation **-verhältnis** *n* reciprocal relation, alternate proportion **-verkehr** *m* intercommunication, two-way communication, simplex operation, simplex working, alternate two-way traffic **-verlängerung** *f* prolongation of a bill (of exchange) **-verschluß** *m* converter shutter **-verzahnung** *f* alternate-tooth construction **-vorgang** *m* changing operation, changing cycle **-vorrichtung** *f* changing device **-weibchen** *n* contact knob

wechselweise alternately, reciprocally, by turns **~ aufeinanderfolgen** to alternate

Wechsel-widerstand *m* alternating-current resistance **-winkel** *m* alternate angle, detector

Wechselwippe *f* shift rocker

wechselwirkende Kraft alternating force

Wechselwirkung *f* induction (fluorescence), reciprocal action, alternating effect, reciprocal effect, interaction, mutual action, reaction, reciprocation **in ~ stehen** to reciprocate, interact **~ zwischen Elektronenanordnungen** configuration interaction

Wechselwirkungs-aufspaltung *f* interaction splitting **-darstellung** *f* interaction representation **-effekt** *m* Luxemburg effect, Telegen effect, interaction of radio waves, total resistance **-energie** *f* mutual-potential energy **-faktor** *m* interaction factor **-gesetz** *n* Newton's third law **-glieder** *pl* interaction terms **-potential** *n* interaction potential **-widerstand** *m* interference drag

Wechsel-zahl *f* frequency, cycle, periodicity **-zeichen** *n* shift signal, reversals (teleg.)

Wechsler *m* changer (phone)

Weckanruf *m* call bell

wecken to ring, wake

Wecken *n* ringing, reveille

Wecker *m* (call) bell, (electromagnetic) alarm, ringer, buzzer, electric bell, bell set (radar) **~ mit Selbstunterbrechung** vibrating bell **~ mit Selbstunterbrecher** trembler bell **einschaliger ~** single-dome bell **polarisierter ~** polarized ringer or bell **zweischaliger ~** double-dome bell **zweiter ~** extension bell

Wecker-anruf *m* rousing alarm **-ausschalter** *m* bell stop **-fallklappe** *f* buzzer-indicator drop, bell-indicator drop **-relais** *n* relay controlling local bell circuits **-schalter** *m* ringer **-stromkreis** *m* bell circuit **-taste** *f* (Wl) button for silencing local bell **-uhr** *f* alarm clock **-umschalter** *m* ringing changeover switch **-werk** *n* alarm mechanism

Weckstrom *m* ringing current **-kreis** *m* ringing circuit, ringing loop **-taste** *f* calling key

Weckzeichenweitergabe *f* call signal

Wedel *m* brush, fan

wedeln to wag, wigwag

Wedelschwingung *f* wagging frequency

Wedge-Ofen *m* Wedge (multiple-hearth) furnace

Weftgarnspuler *m* cone winder (weaving)

Weg *m* way, path, walk, road, route, passage, trunk (comput.), course, travel, mode, manner, method, channel, displacement **~ eines drehbaren Armes** sweep **~ des vom Leitungsende herrührenden Echos** end path **gedeckter ~** defiladed route **gemeinsamer ~** common path **geschlossener ~** closed path **geteerter ~** tar road **holpreriger ~** bumpy road **öffentlicher ~** public road **toter ~** idle movement **unbefestigter ~** gravel road **zurückgelegter ~** distance covered

Weg-abschnitt *m* element of path, length, or distance, portion, fraction, or subdivision of length **-arm** lacking in roads **-aufnehmer** *m* displacement pickup, motion pickup **-ausgleichfeder** *f* travel compensating spring **-bewegen** to move (on), remove **-brücke** *f* foot bridge **-differenz** *f* path-length difference, relative retardation **-diffundieren** to diffuse away

Wege-bau *m* road building **-beschotterung** *f* road metalling **-biegung** *f* road curve or bend **-dreieck** *n* triangular road junction **-gabel** *f* road fork **-haken** *m* (f. Rohre) pipe-laying hook

Weg-einheit *f* unit path **-einmündung** *f* V fork (road), junction of side road with main road

Wege-knie *n* V-turn **-klasse** *f* type of road **-kreuzung** *f* intersection, crossroads **-messer** *m* odometer, pedometer

Wegenge *f* defile

Wege-netz *n* road network, system of roads **-plan** *m* telegraph-line plan **-posten** *m* marker **-recht** *n* wayleave, right of way

Wegerkundung *f* road reconnaissance, reconnaissance of routes

wegern to place the ceiling

Wegerung *f* inner planking (of a ship), ceiling

Wegerungsplanke *f* interior plank

Wege-skizze *f* sketched road map **-sperre** *f* road block **-spinne** *f* road junction (multiple) **-strecke** *f* stretch of road **-unterhaltungspflichtiger** *m* corporate body obliged to maintain the public roads **-vielfach** *n* space multiple

Wegfall *m* suppression, elimination, omission **in ~ kommen** to fall off or away, cease, be abolished

wegfallen to be omitted or dropped, cease, cancel (out) (math.)

Wegfeder *f* travel limiting spring

wegfieren to pay out gradually (a cable)

wegfiltrieren filter off, filter away

wegfließen to flow away, flow off

Wegflugpeilung *f* back-bearing

wegfressen to eat away, erode, cut out

weggebauter Magnetschalter separately mounted solenoid-operated switch

Weggeber *m* motion pickup, displacement pickup

weggebrochen broken away

weggesteuert path-controlled

weghauen to cut or lop off

wegheben, sich ~ to cancel out

Weg-hobel *m* concrete breaker **-karte** *f* road map **-kehren** to sweep away, turn away **-klappen** to swing out or away **-kreuzung** *f* crossroad, junction **-krümmung** *f* curvature of a road **-länge** *f* length of path, distance (covered)

Weglängenverteilung *f* path length distribution

weglassen to omit, dispense with, drop, delete

Weglassung *f* omission

weglaufen to drift

Weglaufen *n* (der Frequenz) frequency drift

weglegen to discard

Wegmarke *f* road marker

Wegmarkierung *f* trail mark

wegmeißeln to cut away with the chisel, chisel off

Wegmesser *m* odometer, mileage recorder, cydometer

Wegmeß-verfahren *n* odometrical method **-winkel** *m* angle of reference for double integration of the velocity

Wegnahme *f* deduction, removal, seizure

wegnehmen to take away, remove **Gas ganz ~** to close the throttle

Wegregelung *f* position control, road control

Wegreißen *n* tearing away

wegreißen, vom Boden ~ to make a quick steep ascent

wegrutschen, nach der Seite ~ to move sidewards (asphalt)

Wegsamkeit *f* practicability of roads

wegschaffen to remove, eliminate

Wegschaffungsgrube *f* disposal well

wegschmelzen to melt away, melt off, burn away

Wegschranke *f* railway gate

wegschwenken to swing out of the way

Wegskizze *f* strip map, sketched road map

Wegsperre *f* road barricade, road block

wegspülen to wash or flush away

Wegspur *f* track

wegstellen to put or place aside

Weg-steuer *f* toll **-strecke** *f* length of path, distance, stretch, (element of) length, length of travel

wegstreichen to cross or strike out, delete

Wegsummenverfahren (Fernschreiber) method of aggregate motion

Wegtastimpuls *m* blanking impulse

Wegüberführung *f* overhead crossing, viaduct

Wegübergang *m*, **tragbarer ~** portable line crossing

Weg-unterführung *f* underpass, underground crossing **-vergleich** *m* deflection balance, motion balance **-verhältnisse** *pl* road conditions **-vielfach** *n* (Kreuzschienenschalter) space multiple (in crossbar switches) **-wahl** *f* (Zielwahl) (Teleph) route dialling **-weiser** *m* sign-board, road sign

wegwerfen to throw away, reject

Weg-winkel *m* transit angle (of klystron) **-zeitkurve** *f* trajectory

wegziehen to pull (rip cord), move away, withdraw, strip

wehen to blow

Wehnelt-blende *f* Wehnelt control grid **-elektrode** *f* Wehnelt electrode **-röhre** *f* Wehnelt valve **-unterbrecher** *m* electrolytic interrupter **-zylinder** *m* control electrode, modulating electrode, Wehnelt cylinder, grid, or shield

Wehr *f* protection, defense, army, resistance, parapet, barrage

Wehr *n* weir, dam **bewegliches ~** movable dam **durchbrochenes ~** carved weir **festes ~** fixed dam **gemauertes ~** solid masonry weir **provisorisches ~** temporary dam **vollkommenes ~** weir with a free wall

Wehr-anlage *f* weir plant **-bau** *m* weir building **-bock** *m* frame **-damm** *m* weir

Wehr-höhe *f* height of weir, depth of still water **-körper** *m* weir, dam **-krone** *f* crest of the weir

Wehr-mauer *f* water stop wall **-rücken** *m* downstream face or back of weir or dam **-schwelle** *f* sill **-sohle** *f* foundation, sill **-überlauf** *m* overflow weir

weiblich female **-es Gewinde** box or female thread **-er Muffenteil** collar

weich soft, mild, gentle, mellow, tender, supple, yielding, pliant, weak, smooth **~ geglüht**

normalized, annealed ~ **machen** (Lack) to plasticize ~ **werden** to soften (chem.) **-e Drehzahlregelung** smooth speed regulation **-es und leichtes Fahren** smooth and easy riding **-es Holz** soft wood, sappy wood **-e Röhre** soft valve, ionic tube, gas-filled tube, gassy tube **-er Stahl** soft or mild steel **-e Strahlen** soft rays **-es Wasser** soft water

Weich-asphalt *m* soft asphalt **-bild** *n* precincts, environs, municipal area or district

Weichblei *n* refined lead, soft lead **-instrument** *n* moving-iron instrument **-kern** *m* soft-iron core **-membran** *f* ferrotype diaphragm **-strommesser** *m* soft-iron vane ammeter, moving-iron ammeter

Weich-bottich *m* soaking tub (steeping tub) **-brand** *m* place brick **-braunstein** *m* pyrolusite **-dauer** *f* steeping period **-druck** *m* yield load

Weiche *f* deflector, branch (info proc.); switch, turnout, flank, switch point, side way, siding, filter, dividing network, dividing filter, separator (for video signals); (Rohrpost) directing means, routing means; (Walzwerke) diverter, guide (Rohrpost); duplexer (rdr); mit einem Gleisstück a switch point with a length of track ~ **mit Gegengewicht** switch with counterpoise **elektrische** ~ separating filter

Weicheisen *n* soft iron, mild steel **-anker** *m* soft-iron armature **-blech** *n* ferrotype **-instrument** *n* moving-vane instrument, moving-iron instrument, trailing-wire antenna **-kern** *m* soft-iron core **-masse** *f* soft-iron mass **-spannungsanzeiger** *m* moving-iron voltmeter **-stange** *f* soft-iron bar **-stromanzeiger** *m* moving-iron ammeter **-strommesser** *m* moving-iron ammeter, soft-iron ammeter

Weichen *pl*, **HF-Weichen zur Mehrfachausnutzung** HF combining filters for multiple utilization

weichen to yield, give way, give ground, fall back, soak, steep, soften, plasticize

Weichen-antrieb *m* (elektr.) power switch machine **-antriebsmotor** *m* point motor **-back** *m* switch stand **-bauanstalt** *f* switch-construction works **-bock** *m* switch box **-bogen** *m* curve of switch **-feder** *f* leaf spring **-hebel** *m* switch lever **-hilfsrelais** *n* auxiliary key strip transfer relay **-kettenförderer** *m* power and free conveyor **-körper** *m* body of frog (elec.), switch body **-laterne** *f* signal-point indicator lamp, switch lamp **-pfahl** *m* doll, paste, stake (at R.R. switch) **-relais** *n* digit-key strip transfer relay **-rost** *m* switch and crossing ties **-schiene** *f* switch tongue **-schwelle** *f* switch tie **-sicherung** *f* point locking **-signal** *n* ground or switch signal, point indicator **-spitze** *f* point of the switch

Weichen-stellbock *m* switch lever **-stelleinrichtung** *f* (Eisenb) track switch operation mechanism **-steller** *m* switchman **-stellung** *f* operating of switches, throwing of points **-stellvorrichtung** *f* switch-stand handle, switch-operating mechanism **-steuerung** *f* point control (R.R.) **-teile** *pl* switch parts **-straße** *f* set of points **-zunge** *f* switch blade or tongue **-zungenhobelmaschine** *f* switch-blade planing machine, tongue planing machine

Weich-faß *n* steeping tub **-feuern** to melt down **-fleckigkeit** *f* weak spot (metal.) **-floß** *n* porous white pig (met.) **-fluß** *m* porous white pig **-gestellte Massen** elastomeric compounds **-gewicht** *n* soaked weight **-grube** *f* soaking pit **-glühen** *n*, **-glühung** *f* (soft) annealing, spheroidizing **-gummi** *m* rubber, caoutchouc, soft rubber **-gummidichtung** *f* soft rubber packing or gasket **-gummistreifen** *m* soft rubber strip **-guß** *m* malleable (cast) iron

Weich-haltungsmittel *n* softening agent (softener) **-harz** *n* soft resin (balsam) **-haspel** *f* soaking wheel

Weichheit *f* softness, elasticity, pliableness, resilience

Weich-kernstahl *m* soft-centered steel **-holz** *n* soft wood **-kies** *m* marcasite **-kohle** *f* soft coal **-kufe** *f* steeping trough or cistern, soaking tub **-kupfer** *n* soft copper **-kupferring** *m* soft copper gasket **-lot** *n* tin solder, soft solder **-löten** to soft-solder, solder, sweat **-löten** *n* (soft) soldering, sweating **-machen** to soften **-machen** *n* softening

weichmachende Wirkung plasticizing efficiency

Weichmacher *m* plasticizer, softener **-anteil** *m* softening agent, plasticizer

Weichmachung *f* softening

Weich-machungsmittel *n* plasticizer, softener **-mangan** *n*, **-manganerz** *n* pyrolusite **-metall** *n* soft metal **-packung** *f* soft packing **-porzellan** *n* soft porcelain **-riegelüberwachung** *f* lock proving (R.R.) **-schrot** soft shot or pellet, drop shot **-spitzengeschoß** *n* soft-nose or soft-pointed bullet **-stahl** *m* mild steel, soft steel **-stelle** *f* soft spot **-tastung** *f* rounded-wave keying **-teil** *m* soft part **-tier** *n* mollusk **-tönend** sonorous

Weich- und Feinblei *n* soft and high-grade lead

Weich- und Hartfaserplatte *f* soft and fiber board

Weich-walze *f* cast-iron roll, soft roll **-wasser** *n* soaking liquor **-zeichner** *m* butterfly (film)

weichwerden to soften

Weichwerden *n* softening

Weichwerden des Kautschuks sweetening of rubber

Weich-zeder *f* Virginia red cedar **-zeichner** *m* soft-focus lens

Weiden-flechter *m* osier plaiter **-geflecht** *n* wicker work, willow weave **-korb** *m* wicker basket **-rinde** *f* willow bark **-zweige** *pl* wicker

Weife *f* reel, saw frame, spool

weifen to wind, reel

Weifen *n* reeling

Weifer *m* cotton reeler

weigern to refuse, decline, object, reject, deny

Weigerung *f* refusal, objection, rejection

Weihnachtsbaumantenne *f* Christmas-tree antenna

Wein *m* wine **-abzieher** *m* wine tunner or racker

Weinbergpflug vineyard plow or cultivator

Weingeist *m* alcohol, spirit of niter **-messer** *m* spirit gauge

Wein-keller *m* wine cellar **-kellereimaschine** *f* wine-cellarage machine **-klärung** *f* clarifying of wine **-lagerung** *f* wine storage **-säure** *f* tartaric acid

weinsau(e)r, -es Ammon ammonium tartrate **-es Kaliumnatrium** potassium sodium tartrate **-es Natron** sodium tartrate **-es Salz** tartrate

Weinschützer *m* vine guard

Weinstein *m* tartar **-haltig** tartarous **-säure** *f* tartaric acid

Weinuntersuchungsgerät *n* wine-testing apparatus

Weise *f* manner, mode, way, method

Weiser *m* indicating apparatus, pointer, hand, guide

weiß white, blank **-er Arsenik** white arsenic, arsenic trioxide **-er Bolus** *m* (weißer Ton) porcelain clay **-es Eisenblech** tin plate **-er Elektronenstrahl** heterogeneous beam of electrons **-e Glut** white heat **-er Gummiersatz** white factice (white substitute) **-es Gußeisen** malleable hard cast iron, unannealed malleable iron **-e Kalkschlacke** white lime slag **-er Kupferstein** white metal (relating to copper) **-es Licht** white light, tail light

Weiß gleicher Energien (der Farbkomponenten) equal-energy white

Weiß-ablauf *m* high green sirup **-appretur** *f* white finishing **-äscher** *m* white lime (fresh lime) **-automatik** *f* white level control **-band** *n* tin strip

Weißblech *n* tin plate, terneplate **-abfall** *m* tin scrap **-haushaltungsgeräte** *pl* tin-plate household ware **-hersteller** *m* tin-plate manufacturer, white-smith **-kanne** *f* tin can **-stanzer** *m* tin-plate puncher **-trommel** *f* tin drum **-walzer** *m* tin-plate roller or doubler **-walzwerk** *n* tin plate mill **-waren** *pl* tinware, tin-plate ware **-werke** *n pl* tin plate mills or works

Weiß-blei *n* tin **-bleierz** *n* white lead ore, cerussite **-boden** *m* white ground **-brennen** *n* calcining at white heat **-brüchig** of white fracture, of pale fracture **-brühe** *f* tawing liquor **-buche** *f* white beech **-eichenholz** *n* white oak **-eisen** *n* white metal, white (malleable cast) iron

weißen to whitewash

Weiß-erde *f* superfine hardening **-farbe** *f* white pigment **-fäule** *f* white rot **-gar** tawed **-gebiet** (im Farbtondiagramm) achromatic locus (TV) **-gerben** to taw **-gerber** *m* alum tanner (tawer)

Weiß-glas *n* flint glass, colorless glass **-glühen** to bring to white heat **-glühen** *n* incandescence **-glühend** white hot, incandescent, bright **-glühhitze** *f*, **-glut** *f* white heat, incandescence **-gold** *n* white gold, platinum **-golderz** *n* sylvanite

Weißgrad *m* bleaching **-bestimmungsmesser** *m* leuco-meter **-messer** *m* brightness tester

Weiß-gültigerz *n* argentiferous tetrahedrite **-guß** *m* white cast iron, white malleable cast iron **-gußarmatur** *f* German-silver fittings **-hitze** *f* white heat **-kalk** *m* white lime **-kernguß** *m* white-heart malleable iron **-kocher** *m* whitener **-küferei** *f* bushel making **-kupfer** *n* German silver **-kupfererz** *n* white copper ore, cubanite **-lagermetall** *n* babbitt metal **-leder** *n* tawed leather (white leather)

weißlich whitish

Weißlot *n* soft or tin solder

Weißmessing *n* white brass

Weißmetall *n* babbitt metal, white metal, pewter, antifriction metal **-ausguß** *m* babbitt (metal) lining **-futter** *n* babbitt lining **-lager** *n* babbitted bearing, white-metal bearing **-lagerschale** *f* babbitt bushing

Weißnickel-erz *n*, **-kies** *m* white nickel ore, chloanthite

Weiß-nuancierung *f* white tint **-ofen** *m* refining furnace **-papp** *n* white resist **-pause** *f* white print **-pegel** *m* white level **-produkte** *pl* white products, refined products **-sätze** *pl* white discharge **-schliff** *m* white ground wood **-sieden** to blanch **-silbererz** *n* antimonial silver ore

Weißspies-glanz *m*, **-glanzerz** *n* white antimony, valentinite, antimony oxide

Weiß-stahl *m* white pig iron **-stein** *m* granulite **-tanne** *f* white fir **-tellur** *n* graphic tellurium, sylvanite **-tönung** *f* white tint **-verschnitt** *m* reduction with white **-warm** white hot, incandescent **-waren** *pl* linen goods, linen **-werden** *n* blushing (of lacquer or varnish) **-wert** *m* bright-level value (television) **-zuckerfüllmasse** *f* white-sugar massecuite **-zuckersichter** *m* white-sugar sifter **-zurichtung** *f* white finish

Weisung *f* order, (letter of) instruction, direction, showing, indication, guiding

weit wide, far, broad, remote **~ aussteuern** to drive hard **-er Satz** driving-out (print.)

weitausladend widely spaced

weitblickend far-sighted

Weite *f* width, breadth, largeness, amplitude, opening, range, scope, distance, beam (of ship) **~ der Ausschwingung** maximum displacement **lichte ~** inside diameter or width, bore, lumen, width in the clear

weiten to enlarge, widen, extend, stretch

weiterbelasten to charge out

Weiterbewegung *f* forward movement

weiterbefördern to retransmit, forward

Weiterbeförderung *f* transmittal, transmission, retransmission **~ von Flüssigkeiten** transfer of liquids

Weiterbehandlung *f* subsequent treatment

weiterbewegen to feed

Weiterbildung *f* advanced training, further development, evolutionary development or progress

weiterdrehen, die Schaltarme ~ to step round the wipers

weiterentwickeln to carry on development

Weiterentwicklung *f* development, outgrowth

Weiterfärben *n* continuous dyeing

weiterfliegen to continue the flight

weiterführen, eine Leitung ~ to extend a line

Weitergabe *f* retransmission **~ mit der Hand** manual retransmission **selbsttätige ~** automatic retransmission

Weitergabe-anordnung *f* repeater or retransmitting arrangement **-stelle** *f* distribution point

weitergeben to retransmit, repeat, forward, pass along, relay

Weitergeber *m* retransmitter **-relais** *n* repeating relay

weitergeschaltete Sperrzähnezahl ratchet setting

Weiterlauf *m* run-on

weiterleiten to pass on

Weiter-leitungsstelle *f* forwarding station (R.R.), supply reloading station (R.R.), forwarding point **-marsch** *m* resumed march **-rufrelais** *n* retransmission relay **-schalten** to step up, step on **-schaltleitung** *f* interposition trunk, transfer circuit **-schaltung** *f* step-by-step action **-schieben** to push forward, shuffle **-schlag** *m* redraw **-senden** to retransmit

Weitersendung *f* retransmission **~ mittels Loch-**

streifen retransmission by tape relay
Weiterungen *pl* difficulties, complications
weiterverarbeitet subsequently worked (into)
Weiterverarbeitung *f* mechanical treatment, machining, subsequent treatment
Weiterverarbeitungsbetrieb *m* finishing plant
Weiterveräußerung *f* resale
Weiterverfolgung *f* further prosecution
Weiterverladung *f* transshipment
Weiterverschmieden *n* final forging
Weiterwahl-Kontrollrelais bei einstelliger Wahl (D) subsequent digits checking relay for single-digit dialing
Weiterzerkleinerung *f* further reduction
Weiterziehen *n* successive drawing, redrawing
weitgehend largely, far-reaching, extensive, vast, substantial, thorough, appreciable
weitgeöffnet wide-open
weithalsig widemouthed, wide-necked **-e Flasche** widemouthed bottle or jar
weitläufig extensive, lengthy
weitmaschig wide-meshed **-es Gitter** open grid, widemeshed grid, coarse grid
weitreichend far-reaching, long-range
weitrohriger Steilrohrkessel boiler with vertical large tubes
weit-schweifig tedious, redundant **-schweifigkeit** *f* prolixity, redundance **-sichtig** farsighted **-sichtigkeit** *f* far-sightedness
Weitspurdammkulturpflug *m* wide-tread lister
weitspurig wide-tracked
Weitstab *m* transom of a French casement, sleeper
Weitstrahler *m* wide beam headlight
Weitstrecken-bereich *m* long range **-verkehr** *m* long-distance traffic
weittragend of far-reaching importance
Weitung *f* widening
weitverbreitet prevalent, widely circulated
Weitverkehr *m* long-distance traffic
Weitverkehrs-leitung *f* long-haul toll circuit **-pentode** *f* long-life pentode **-röhre** *f* long-range communications tube **-technik** *f* telecommunication technique **-verbindung** *f* long-distance connection or call
weitverzweigt widely extended
Weitwinkel-aufnahme *f* wide-angle photograph **-bild** *n* wide-angle picture **-feldstecher** *m* wide-angle field glass **-instrument** *n* long-scale meter **-kamera** *f* wide-angle-lens camera **-kathode** *f* wide-angle cathode **-lupe** *f* wide-angle magnifier **-objektiv** *n* wide-angle lens **-reihenbilder** *m* wide-angle aerial camera
weitwinklig wide-angled **-e Aufnahme** wide-angled picture **Bogenlampe mit -en Kohlenstiften** scissorstype arc lamp
Weizen *m* wheat **-drillmaschine** *f* wheat drill **-sieb** *n* wheat screen
Wellblech *n* corrugated iron or metal, corrugated sheet iron **-bekleidung** *f* corrugated metal wing covering **-beplankung** *f* corrugated sheet-metal covering **-boden** *m* corrugated bottom **-decke** *f* corrugated-iron cover **-haut** *f* corrugated metal wing covering **-holm** *m* beam or spar of corrugated sheet metal **-presse** *f* corrugating press **-tafel** *f* sheet of corrugated iron **-walze** *f* corrugating roll **-walzwerk** *n* corrugation rolling mill

Welle *f* wave, shaft, oscillation, axle, arbor, beam, vertical capstan, surge, surf, spindle, roll, roller, undulation **~ der Abstimmung** tuning wave **~ für die Auf- und Niederbewegung** elevating shaft **~ mit angeschmiedeten Flanschen** shaft with forged flanges **~ zum Greifer** travelling gripper shaft **~ für die Höhenstellung des Konsols** knee elevating shaft **~ mit angeschmiedeten Hubscheiben** shaft with eccentrics forged on **~ zur Leitzunge** bar for sheet guides **eine ~ auf Rundlauf prüfen** to check a shaft for truth **~ des Stromwenders** commutator shaft
Welle, akustische ~ sonic wave **antreibende ~** driving shaft **aperiodische ~** aperiodic wave **sich ausbreitende ~** traveling wave, proceeding wave, propagating wave **ausgesandte ~** transmitted wave **ballig gedrehte ~** ramp shaft **biegsame ~** flexible shaft (mech.) **direkte ~** ground wave, direct wave **durchgehende ~** shaft passing from end to end, through(-going) shaft **einfallende ~** incident wave, oncoming wave **einlagerige ~** single-bearing shaft **elektrische ~** synchro-tie **elektromagnetische ~** electromagnetic wave **elliptisch polarisierte ~** elliptically polarized wave **extremkurze ~** ultrashort wave
Welle, fortschreitende ~ moving wave, traveling wave, advancing wave, progressive wave **gedämpfte ~** damped oscillation, discontinued or decadent wave **gekröpfte ~** crank(ed) shaft **gerade ~** straight shaft **getastete ungedämpfte ~** telegraph modulated wave, key-modulated continuous wave, key-controlled continuous wave **getriebene ~** driven shaft (mech.) **gleichstromüberlagerte ~** pulsating wave, wave superposed on direct current **grüne ~** green light change **hinlaufende ~** main wave **hin- und hergehende ~** rock shaft **hochgebaute ~** overhead shaft **hohle ~** tubular shaft
Welle, impulsmodulierte ~ pulse-modulated wave **kleine ~** ripple **kontinuierliche ~** continuous wave, undamped wave, sustained wave **kurze ~** short wave, high-frequency wave **lange ~** long wave, low-frequency wave **liegende ~** horizontal wave **linear polarisierte ~** plane polarized wave **linkslaufende ~** sinistropropagating wave or surge **mittlere ~** medium-frequency wave **modulierte ~** modulated wave **modulierte ungedämpfte ~** modulated continuous wave
Welle, pendelnde ~ oscillating shaft **pulsierende ~** pulsating wave **rechteckige ~** square wave **rechtslaufende ~** dextropropagating wave or surge **reine stehende ~** stationary wave **rücklaufende ~** reflected wave, retrogressive wave
Welle, schwach beanspruchte ~ shaft subjected to slight stress **senkrechte ~** vertical shaft (mech.) **sprachmodulierte ~** speech-modulated wave **stehende ~** standing wave, stationary wave **tonmodulierte ~** tone-modulated wave **ultrakurze ~** ultrashort wave, ultrahigh-frequency wave, quasi-optic wave **ungedämpfte ~** continuous wave, undamped wave, undamped oscillation, sustained wave, persistent wave **unmodulierte ungedämpfte ~** pure

undamped wave **verzerrte ~** deformed wave
wellen to wave, corrugate, roll, boil, simmer
Wellen-abgrenzung *f* frequency and wave-band designation **-absatz** *m* chamfer of shaft **-absorbtionsaugkreis** *m* absorption wave trap **-amplitude als Näherung** wave approximation **-änderung** *f* frequency shift **-anfachung** *f* wave generation **-anregung** *f* wave generation **-anteil** *m* wave part
Wellen-antenne *f* wave antenna **-antrieb** *m* shaft drive, shaft driving **-anzeiger** *m* oscillation detector, wave detector, cymoscope, coherer **-artig** wavelike, undulatory, wavy **-auflagerebene** *f* plane of shaft support (bearing) **-aufzeichner** *m* oscillograph, phonodeik **-aufzeichnungsgerät** *n* phonodeik
Wellen-ausbreitung *f* wave propagation **-auslöschung** *f* wave quenching **-ausschlag** *m* wave extent or amplitude **-austrittsrohr** *n* stern tube **-bahnen** *pl* shafting **-bahnfunktion** *f* orbital wave function **-balken** *m* axle shaft or beam **-band** *n* wave band, spectrum, frequency band **-bauch** *m* bulge, loop, antinode **-baum** *m* axle shaft or tree
Wellenbereich *m* wave range, wave band, band pass, frequency band **-melder** *m* wave-band indicator **-schalter** *m* wave-band switch **-umschaltung** *f* wave-range switching
Wellenberg *m* (wave) crest **-lochweite** *f* distance separating peaks, intercrest distance
Wellen-bestand *m* input **-betrieb** *m* wave signals
Wellenbewegung *f* wave motion, undulation, undulatory or harmonic motion **zurückgeworfene ~** backwash
Wellenbezeichnung *f* designation of radio electric waves
Wellenbild *n* oscillogram
Wellenbildung *f* waving **~ auf den Schienen** corrugations on rails
Wellen-binderform *f* V-shaped planing bottom (seaplane hull) **-bock** *m* tail-shaft bracket **-bockbefestigung** *f* strut palm (of a propeller shaft) **-bohrbank** *f* shaft-boring machine **-bohrung** *f* corrugate opening **-brecher** *m* breakwater, breaker, wave breaker, jetty, pier, splashboard **-brechung** *f* wave diffraction **-bruch** *m* shaft failure **-bund** *m* shaft collar **-bündel** *n* wave packet, beam of electrons and ions **-bündelung** *f* beaming, directional effect of waves **-büschel** *n* fascine **-dämpfungskonstante** *f* wave-attenuation constant **-daumen** *m* cam or lift of lifting cog, lifter, wiper, or tappet of arbor
Wellen-detektor *m* cymoscope, wave detector, oscillation detector, coherer **-dichtung** *f* shaft packing **-drehmaschine** *f* shaft-turning lathe **-drehsperre** *f* shaft lock (comput.) **-drehzahlmesser** *m* shaft revolution indicator **-durchbiegung** *f* shaft deflection **-echo** *n* radio (signal or wave) echo **-einstellknopf** *m* wavepassage button **-einteilung** *f* classification of waves **-empfänger** *m* wave receiver **-ende** *n* shaft pivot or end **-erreger** *m* wave exciter, vibrator, oscillator **-erzeuger** *m* wave generator
Wellen-falle *f* wave trap, groove, ditch **-fallenrand** *m* shirt (microw.) **-faserigkeit** *f* wavy fibered growth **-federring** *m* corrugated spring washer **-feld** *n* wave field **-filter** *n* (wave) filter **-fixierung** *f* shaft alignment
Wellenfläche, Fresnelsche ~ Fresnel zone
Wellen-flächenreibung *f* shafting journal friction **-flansch** *m* shaft flange **-flug** *m* undulating flight
Wellenform *f* wave shape, wave form **-charakteristik** *f* waveform response **-wandler** *m* waveform converter
wellen-förmig wavelike, wavy, undulatory, corrugated, rippled **-fortpflanzung** *f* wave propagation **-frei** without undulations **-frequenz** *f* wave frequency
Wellenfront *f* wave front **geneigte ~** tilted wave front, tilted wave head **steile ~** steep wave front
Wellen-frontwinkel *m* wave-front angle, wave tilt **-führung** *f* wave guide (microw.)
Wellenfunktelegraphie, ungedämpfte ~ continuouswave telegraphy
Wellen-funktion *f* wave function **-furche** *f* ripple mark (geol.) **-gefüge** *n* superposition of one wave upon another (in a canal) **-generator** *m* wave generator, main-shaft mounted (auxiliary) generator
Wellen-geschwindigkeit *f* wave velocity, speed of a wave, phase velocity **-gestalt** *f* wave shape **-gipfel** *m* peak, crest, or hump of a wave **-gleichung** *f* wave equation **-gruppe** *f* wave group **-kamm** *m* top of a wave, wave crest, comb **-kegel** *m* shaft cone **-kinematische Theorie** *f* geometric interference theory **-knoten** *m* nodal point (of undulating waves) **-konstante** *f* wave constant **-kontakt** *m* rotary off-normal contact, shaft contact **-kopf** *m* wave front **-krone** *f* top of crest **-kröpfung** *f* crank of a shaft **-kuppelung** *f* (shaft) coupling (machin.)
Wellen-lage *f* shaft position **-lager** *n* bearing (of a shaft), main bearing **-länge** *f* wave length, length of an undulation **-längenkonstante** *f* wave-length constant, phase-shift constant **-längenkonstanz** *f* steadiness of the wave **-längenlinear** *n* straight line wave-length **-lehre** *f* undulating mechanics, external gauge; wave theory **-leistung** *f* shaft power, net brake horsepower, spindle capacity **-leiter** *m* wave guide, radar duct **-leitung** *f* line shaft, transmission line, shafting, shaft line, extension shaft, wave guide **-leitwert** *m* wave impedance **-linie** *f* wave line, undulatory line, sinuous line, rippled line **-linienschreiber** *m* wave-line recorder, ondograph
Wellenmechanik *f* wave mechanics **Geometrisierung der ~** geometric derivation of wave equation
wellenmechanisch wave mechanical
Wellenmesser *m* wavemeter, cymometer, wavefrequency control, ondometer, frequency meter **~ mit Summererregung** buzzer-driven wavemeter
Wellen-montage *f* line-shaft erection **-netz** *n* wave trap **-nute** *f* shaft keyseat **-nutenstoßmaschine** *f* shaft keyseater **-oberkante** *f* top of loop or shaft **-paket** *n* wave packet **-parameterfilter** *n* image-parameter filter **-periode** *f* period of a wave **-pferdekraft** *f*, **-pferdestärke** *f* shaft horsepower **-platte** *f* diaphragm **-presse** *f* corrugating press **-profil** *n* bicurve section or profile
Wellen-reflexion *f* wave clutter **-reiter** *m* radio ham, surf board **-richtmaschine** *f* shaft-straightening machine **-richtpresse** *f* shaft-

straightening press **-ritzel** *n* shaft pinion
Wellen-rohr *n* corrugated tube **-rückstrahlung** *f* wave reflection **-sauger** *m* suppressor of harmonics, series reactor, smoothing choke, wave trap **-saugkreis** *m* wave trap **-schalter** *m* wave-range switch, range switch, shaft coupling **-schalter** *m* band switch **-schalterbereich** *m* wave-switch range **-scheitel** *m* top of the wave **-schieber** *m* phase shifter **-schlag** *m* shock or beating of the waves, wave action **-schliff** *m* (plain) cylindrical grinding
Wellen-schlucker *m* wave trap, frequency sifter, frequency trap, rejector circuit **-schränkung** *f* (in Graden) angular deviation from shaft alignment **-schreiber** *m* ondograph, undulator, oscillograph, vibrograph **-schwanz** *m* wave tail **-schwingung** *f* undulation, oscillation **-sieb** *n* filter, wave screen **-spannung** *f* wave voltage **-spektrum** *n* frequency spectrum, spectrum of electromagnetic waves, radio-wave spectrum **-stern** *m* molette of turbine shaft
Wellenstirn *f* wave front, face, or head **geneigte ~** tilted wave front **steile ~** steep wave front
Wellen-störung *f* wave disturbance **-stoß** *m* wave action **-strahl** *m* wavy distortion by wave action, wave filament **-strang** *m* shafting **-stranganordnung** *f* arrangement of shafting **-strom** *m* pulsating current, ripple current, undulating current **-stromfilter** *m* ripple filter
Wellenstück, hohles ~ quill
Wellen-stummel *m* (TWK) stub shaft **-stumpf** *m* shaft butt or end **-tal** *n* wave trough
Wellentelegraphie *f* wireless telegraphy **~ längs Leitungen** wired wireless telegraphy
Wellenträger *m* shaft support
Wellentyp-wandler, ~ mit Querstab cross-bar transformer **-filter** *m* mode filter **-transformator** *m* mode changer
Wellen-umschalter *m* change-tune switch, wave-length changing switch, wave-range switch, range switch **-umschaltung** *f* wave-length switching **-vektor** *m* wave vector **-veränderliche** *f* wave variable **-verkürzung** *f* wave-length shortening **-verlängerung** *f* wave-length prolongation **-vernichtung** *f* wave reduction, reduction of range **-versetzung** *f* misalignment of shaft **-verteilung** *f* allocation of frequencies
Wellen-wechsel *m* frequency change **-weite** *f* amplitude of wave **-wicklung** *f* wave winding **-widerstand** *m* characteristic impedance, surge impedance, hump resistance (in a seaplane), oscillatory resistance, impact wave resistance (in supersonics), wave drag (of supersonic flight), iterative impedance **-zahl** *f* propagation factor, wave number **-zapfen** *m* shaft journal, pivot
Wellenzug *m* wave train, beat **-frequenz** *f* group frequency, wave-train frequency, spark frequency **-kohärenzlänge** *f* coherence length of wave trains
wellig wavy, buckled, baggy, undulating, pulsating, rippled **-es Bild** ragged picture **-e Gleichspannung** ripple voltage or potential, pulsating potential **-er Strom** ripple current
Welligkeit *f* standing-wave ratio, ripple, waviness, rippled condition, humpiness, pulsation factor **~ der Gleitlinien** wavy slip-lines
Welligkeits-entzerrung *f* elimination of standing waves **-filter** *n* ripple filter **-frequenz** *f* ripple frequency **-messer** *m* standing wave meter **-prüfung** *f* corrugation test
Wellig-liegen *n* cockling, creasing, or wrinkling of the paper **-schmieden** *n* corrugating of steel forging **-werden** *n* cockling, creasing, or wrinkling of the paper
Wellkarton *m* corrugated paper
Wellman-Kippofen *m* Wellman tilting furnace **-Rollofen** *m* Wellman rolling furnace
Wellmaschine *f* roll-forming machine
Well-papier *n*, **-pappe** *f* cellular board, corrugated paper or board **-plattenkondensator** *m* corrugated-plate condenser
Wellrohr *n* corrugated tube or tubing **-dichtung** *f* corrugated tubing seal **-kessel** *m* corrugated-flue boiler **-walzwerk** *n* rolling mill for corrugated tubes
Well-separator *m* wave-type separator **-stein** *m* corrugated brick
Wellung *f* rippling, corrugation, undulation
Wellzapfen *m* journal (of shaft), axis end, crank-pin
Welt *f* world, universe **-achse** *f* celestial axis **-all** *n* universe **-ausstellung** *f* international exhibition, world's fair **-beschreibung** *f* cosmography
Weltenraum *m* universe, interstellar space
Welt-flug *m* round-the-world flight **-funknetz** *n* world radio network, universal radio network **-handel** *m* international trade, world commerce **-höchstleistung** *f* world record **-jahr** *n* platonic year **-karte** *f* globular chart, planisphere **-körper** *m* celestial body
weltlich worldly, secular
Weltluftverkehr *m* world air traffic
Weltmarkt *m* international trade, world market **-preis** *m* world-market price
Welt-meer *n* ocean **-postkarte** *f* postal-union postcard **-postverein** *m* International Postal Union
Weltraum *m* cosmic or universal or outer space **-fahrt** *f* astronautics, cosmonautics, space navigation **-funk** *m* space radio **-rakete** *f* interplanetary rocket **-schiff** *n* interstellar craft, space ship, astronautical craft **-schiffahrt** *f* astronautics **-strahlen** *m pl* cosmic rays
Welt-rekord *m* world record **-stadt** *f* metropolis **-telegraphenverein** *m* international telegraphic union **-telegraphenvertrag** *m* international telegraphic convention **-umspannend** world wide **-verkehr** *m* world traffic, international traffic **-wirbeltensor** *m* world vorticity tensor **-wirtschaft** *f* world trade and industry **-wirtschaftskonferenz** *f* international economic conference **-zeit** *f* universal time (UT)
weltzeitlicher Anteil universal diurnal variation
Weltzeituhr *f* universal time clock
Welzel-Ofen *m* Welzel (regenerative zinc-distilling) furnace
wendbar reversible
Wende *f* turn, turning, twist **-achse** *f* axis of turn **-becken** *n* turning basin (aviat.) **-bock** *m* tilting trestle **-bogen** *m* turning arc **-bogeneinrichtung** *f* chain delivery **-bremsschütz** *n* reverse mechanism for adjustable-thrust nozzle **-dämpfung** *f* lateral damping **-eisen** *n* tap wrench
Wende-fähigkeit (Wagen) turning radius **-feldwicklung** *f* commutating winding **-flug** *m* turn

-flügel *m* pivoting sash **-formmaschine** *f* turnover-table molding machine, turnover molding machine, roll-over-type molding machine **-gabel** *f* tedding fork **-gehänge** *n* manipulator gear **-geschwindigkeit** *f* angular velocity

Wendegetriebe *n* reversing gear, turnover gear, turning gear **-hebel** *m* change-gear handle

Wende-herz *n* tumbler gear **-horizont** *m* turn-and-bank indicator combined with artificial horizon

Wendeisen *n* stock and die

Wende-kreis *m* radius of turn, turning circle, tropic **-kreisel** *m* rate gyro **-kreisradius** *m* turning radius **-kuppelung** *f* reversing gear **-kurve** *f* turn in landing, U turn

Wendel *f* helix, coil, spiral **~ des Hitzdrahts** (Blinkgeber) coil for hot wire (blinker unit)

Wendel-abtastung *f* spiral or helical scanning **-antenne** *f* helical antenna **-bohrer** *m* twist drill **-draht** *m* spiral or coiled wire **-drahtlampe** *f* coiled-up filament lamp **-einsatz** *m* (internal) spiral insert **-fläche** *f* screw surface, right helicoid **-hohlleiter** *m* helix waveguide

Wendelibelle *f* reversible spirit level

Wendel-kreis *m* circular-coil filament **-leistung** *f* turnover capacity **-mechanismus** *m* roll-over mechanism **-rohr** *n* helical tube **-rutsche** *f* spiral chute, curved or winding slide **-schwingrinnen** *pl* spiral vibrating troughs **-stufe** *f* winder **-treppe** *f* winding stairs **-zickzack** *m* zigzag spiral filament

wendeln to coil

Wende-marke *m* turning point **-maschine für Heu** hay tedder **-messer** *m* turn indicator **-moment** *n* yawing moment **-motor** *m* reversible motor, turning motor **-motorkasten** *m* reversing motor housing or box

wenden to turn (over), roll over, apply, address, yaw, veer

Wenden *n* turning over **~ eines Schiffes** swinging or turning round of a ship

Wende-nische *f* hollow quoin **-pflug** *m* hillside plow **-phase** *f* phase changer

Wendeplatte *f* pattern plate with half patterns mounted on both sides, turnover plate or table, turnplate **ausfahrbare ~** roll-over table

Wendeplattenformmaschine *f* turnover-table molding machine **~ mit Abhebevorrichtung** turnover patterndraw machine **~ für Druckluftbetrieb** compressed-air-operated turnover machine **~ mit Fußhebelmodellaushebung** turnover foot-operated draw-molding machine **~ für Handbetrieb** hand-operated turnover molding machine **~ mit Handhebelmodellaushebung** turnover hand-power draw machine, turnover molding machine with hand-lever lift **~ mit Handstampfung und Fußhebelmodellabhebung** handramming turnover foot-draw machine **~ mit eingebautem Rüttler** roll-over-table jolter **~ mit Wagen** turnover molding machine with run-out table **~ mit ausfahrbarer Wendeplatte** roll-over-table molding machine

Wendeplattenpreßformmaschine *f* turnover power squeezing machine, turnover squeezer **~ mit ausschwenkbarem Tisch** roll-over squeezer with swingout table **~ mit Modellabhebevorrichtung** squeeze roll-over pattern-draw machine

Wendeplattenrüttler *m* jar-ramming turnover molding machine, jolt turnover machine **~ mit selbsttätiger Wendevorrichtung** jar-ramming power turnover machine

Wendeplatz *m* turning basin

Wendepol *m* reversing pole, interpole, commutating pole or compensating compole **-punkt** *m* cusp **-schalter** *m* reversing key **-spule** *f* interpole winding **-unterlegblech** *n* interpole shim **-wicklung** winding of reversing pole

Wendepunkt *m* turning point, point of contraflexure, critical moment, point of inflection (math.), reversing point, cusp

Wender *m* manipulator, reverser, turning lever

Wende-radius *m* turning radius **-rahmen** *m* roll-over frame, turnover frame **-rutsche** *f* spiral chute; gravity spiral conveyer **-säule** *f* quoin post **-schalter** *m* reversing switch or key **-schemel** *m* riding bed or bolster, rider, transom bed **-schraube** *f* reversible propeller

Wende-spannvorrichtung *f* reversible clamping device **-stange** *f* turning bar **-stock** *m* (Färberei) handling pole or stick **-support** *m* reversing slide **-tangente** *f* tangent through the point of inflection, tangent to reversing point **-taste** *f* change-over button **-tisch** *m* turntable, roll-over or turnover table (of a mold machine) **-trog** *m* troughlike edging guide (in rolling) **-trommel** *f* turning drum

Wendeturm *m* pylon **-achter** *m* pylon eights, eights on pylon (aviation)

Wendeuntersetzungsgetriebe *n* reverse-reduction gear

Wendevorrichtung *f* manipulator (in rolling), pattern turnover device or arrangement **ausfahrbare ~** rollover device

Wende-walze *f* turning cylinder **-winkel** *m* angle of yaw **-zapfen** *m* trunnion (of converter) **-zeichen** *n* bank-and-turn indicator **-zeiger** *m* turn-and-bank indicator, turnmeter (of airplane) **-zeigerkreisel** *m* rate gyro

wendig maneuverable

Wendigkeit *f* maneuverability, adaptability, mobility, manageableness

Wendung *f* turning, turn, reversal (elec.), bank, turning in, facing

Wendungsfeld *n* wave range

Werbe-artikel *m* advertising article **-brief** *m* publicity letter **-drucksache** *f* advertising printed matter or print **-druckschrift** *f* prospectus **-erfolg** *m* advertising success **-fernsehen** *n* sponsored television **-gegenstand** *m* advertising article **-gespräch** *n* demonstration call **-kosten** *pl* advertising expenses **-kräftig** of advertising value, appealing **-leiter** *m* advertising manager

werben to make propaganda, advertise

Werbe-plakat *n* advertising poster **-schreiben** *n* prospectus **-schrift** *f* publication **-zeichnung** *f* propaganda drawing **-zweck** *m* advertising aim

Werbung *f* propaganda, publicity, advertising

Wer-da-Sperrhebel *m* who-are-you locking lever

Wer-da-Zeichen *n* who-are-you signal (WRU)

Werdegang *m* process of production, professional history

werden to become, grow, get, turn

werfen to throw, cast, fling, project, emit, drop bombs **über Bord ~** to dump overboard **das Log ~** to heave the log, to pay out log line **sich ~**

to warp, distort, deform
Werfen *n* throwing, emission, warpage, warping, diamonding, distortion
Werfer *m* trench mortar, projector, signal or rocket projector
Werferrahmen *m* projector frame, frame-type rocket projector
Werft *f* shipyard, dockyard, workshop **-anlage** *f* shipyard, shipbuilding installation **-direktor** *m* superintendent of shipyard **-hafenbecken** *n* careening basin **-kran** *m* shipyard or dockyard crane
Werfung *f* warping
Werg *n* cotton waste, oakum, tow **-arbeiter** *m* worker in tow or oakum waste **-dichtung** *f* hemp packing **-haken** *m* ravehook, ripping iron **-leinen** *n*, **-leinwand** *f* tow linen **-reiben** *n* tow breaking **-zupfer** *m* tow or oakum picker
Werk *n* work, production, action, mechanism, gear, works, redoubt, act, deed, performance, plant, mill, factory, manufacturing plant, labor **ab ~** ex factory
Werkbahn *f* factory or works railway
Werk(s)-angehöriger *m* employee of the firm **-anlage** *f* works
Werkbank *f* (work)bench **-bohrmaschine** *f* bench-type drilling machine **-schreiner** *m* workbench hand
Werk(s)-besitzer *m* manufacturer, maker, mill-owner **-blei** *n* work lead, crude lead bullion, softened base bullion, raw lead **-druckerei** *f* book-printing establishment **-druckpapier** *n* book paper, job office paper **-eigen** of the plant, private **-einrichtungsabteilung** *f* manufacturing engineering department **-einflieger** *m* test pilot **-ergebnis** *n* refineries proceeds
werken to manipulate, operate, manage, handle
Werk-flugplatz *m* factory airfield **-fremd** outside **-führer** *m* superintendent, foreman **-gerät** *n* tools equipment **-graben** *m* canal, ditch, open channel **-halle** *f* workshop **-holz** *n* industrial wood, timber **-instandhaltung** *f* industrial maintenance **-kanal** *m* intake **-leitung** *f* management **-luftschutz** *m* factory passive air-defence system
Werkmannsarbeit *f* craftmanship
Werk-meister *m* foreman **-norm** *f* factory standard **-nummer** *f* factory serial number, work number **-photo** *n* studio still **-platz** *m* block yard **-probe** *f* sample of metal **-platzleuchten** *pl* working area lighting fixtures
Werksatz *m* framework
Werk-schutzpolizei *f* industrial police **-siedlung** *f* workmen's dwellings **-silber** *n* silver extracted from lead ore
Werkstatt *f* workshop, factory, mill, plant, laboratory **-abnahmelehre** *f* factory-acceptance gauge, inspection gauge **-auftrag** *m* work order **-arbeit** *f* work-manship **-bank** *f* mechanical bench
Werkstätte *f* workshop
Werkstättenflächenraum *m* superficial area of shops
Werkstatt-gerätkraftwagen *m* repair-shop equipment truck, spare-parts truck **-halle** *f* workshop hall **-kraftwagen** *m* repair-shop truck, mobile machine shop **-montage** *f* shop assembly **-prüfung** *f* bench test **-schreiber** *m* timekeeper **-trupp** *m* repair-shop detachment, maintenance party **-wagen** *m* maintenance truck **-zeichnung** *f* working drawing
Werkstein *m* quarry stone, freestone
Werksteinmauerwerk in durchgehenden Lagen squared rubble course
Werkstelle *f* workshop
Werkstoff *m* material, stock, goods, construction materials, raw materials **~ über eine Kante stemmen** to peen over **~ für den Modellbau** material for constructing models **dauerhaftester ~** hardest material **filterfähiger ~** permeable material **technischer ~** industrial, technical, or commercial material **vorgearbeiteter ~** machined blank **einen ~ behandeln** to process a material **einen ~ verarbeiten** to work with a material
Werkstoff-anschlag *m* stock or material stop **-bestellung** *f* material requisition **-dämpfung** *f* damping capacity **-durchlaß** *m* diameter of work admitted **-ermüdung** *f* fatigue of material **-festigkeitslehre** *f* theory of strength of materials **-forschung** *f* materials research **-führungsring** *m* bar-guide bush **-gütegrad** *m* quality grade of materials **-liste** *f* specification
Werkstoffprüfung *f* testing of materials **zerstörungsfreie ~** nondestructive testing
Werkstoff-umstellung *f* material substitute **-verbrauch** *m* material consumption **-verfeinerung** *f* processing of any construction material **-verwalter** *m* material man **-vorschub** *m* stock feed **-wanderung** *f* transfer of material **-zufuhr** *f* feed **-zuführung** *f* feed of material
Werkstoß *m* shop splice
Werkstück *n* workpiece, production part, working part, production of small work, work, blank to be machined or tooled **ein ~ in die Vorrichtung aufnehmen** to locate a working part
Werkstückanlagefläche der Planscheibe face of the faceplate
Werkstück-auflage *f* workpiece holder **-aufspannung** *f* work-mounting
Werkstückbezeichnung, eingeätzte ~ etched identification
Werkstück-kasten *m* work tray **-rutsche** *f* work chute
Werkstudent *m* student who works his way through
Werk(s)-stufe *f* operation **-tag** *m* working day **-tätig** laboring **-umlauf** *m* internal circulation **-umschlag** *m* refinery handling **-unterricht** *m* manual training **-vertrag** *m* work contract **-vertreter** *m* work's representative **-vertriebskosten** *pl* factory selling expenses **-zeichnung** *f* working drawing or plan **-zeitschrift** *f* house organ, shop news
Werkzeug *n* tool, instrument, implement **~ für Blech- und Metallbearbeitung** tool for working tin and metal **~ für spanlose Formung** tool for noncutting shaping **~ zum Gewinderollen** thread-rolling die **scharf schneidendes ~** keen-edged tool **spanabhebendes ~** cutting tool
Werkzeug-abhebung *f* tool relief **-abteilung** *f* toolroom or tool department **-auflage** *f* adjustable tool rest **-aufnehmer** *m* tool carrier **-aufspannfläche** *f* adapter plate area **-auftragschweißung** *f* tool tipping **-ausgabe** *f* distribution of tools, crib, tool crib, toolroom **-ausrichtung** *f*

tooling **-ausrüstung** *f*, **-ausstattung** *f* tool kit, tool equipment, tooling
Werkzeug-besteck *n* set of tools **-beutel** *m* tool bag or kit **-bund** *m* tool collar **-doppelnaßschleifständer** *m* double-wet tool grinder **-drehbank** *f* tool-maker's lathe **-einrichter** *m* tool setter **-einstellung** *f* tool-setting
Werkzeug-führungstrichter *m* tool entrance bowl **-futter** *n* tool chuck **-garnitur** *f* set of tools **-gehänge** *n* string of tools **-grundform** *f* basic tool form **-halter** *m* tool binder, toolholder **-halterschlitten** *m* tool arm slide **-heft** *n* handle of tools
Werkzeug-instandhaltung *f* tool reconditioning **-instandsetzung** *f* repairs of tools **-kammer** *f* toolroom **-kasten** *m* tool kit, toolbox **-kiste** *f*, **-koffer** *m* toolbox, tool chest **-kopf** *m* cutter head, tool head **-kopfwechselräder** *pl* tool head change gears **-körper** *m* tool body
Werkzeug-lager *n* toolroom **-lehre** *f* tool gauge **-loch** *n* turret tool hole **-macher** *m* toolmaker, tool-dresser, diemaker **-macherei** *f* tool department, toolroom, tool shop **-magazin** *n* tool room, tool store **-maschine** *f* machine tool
Werkzeugmaschinen-bau *m* machine-tool industry or construction **-bauer** *m* machine-tool builder **-einrichter** *m* set-up man
Werkzeug-messer *n* knife for workman **-naßschleifmaschine** *f* wet-tool grinding machine **-rolltasche** *f* tool roll **-satz** *m* gang (aviation tools) **-schaft** *m* tool shank **-schieberführungen** *pl* spindle bearings **-schleifer** *m* tooldresser **-schleifmaschine** *f* tool-grinding machine **-schleifstein** *m* stone for grinding tools
Werkzeug-schlitten *m* tool post, tool carrier, saddle, tool slide, turret head, tool carriage **-schlosser** *m* toolmaker **-schlüssel** *m* tool wrench **-schmied** *m* toolsmith **-schneide** *f* cutting edge **-schrank** *m* tool cabinet or chest **-schraubwinde** *f* tool jack **-spind** *n* locker **-spindel** *f* tool spindle **-spindelgewinde** *n* thread of tool spindle
Werkzeugstahl *m* tool steel **~ für spanabhebende Formung** finishing pressing tool steel **hochlegierter ~** special-alloy tool steel **legierter ~** alloy tool steel **unlegierter ~** unalloyed tool steel, carbon tool steel
Werkzeug-stahlhalter *m* tool holder or block **-standzeit** *f* tool life **-stelle** *f* toolstation **-stößel** *m* slide, ram **-support** *m* tool-carrying head, tool rest
Werkzeugtasche *f* tool bag, kit, tool roll **zusammenrollbare ~** tool roll
Werkzeug-träger *m* (tool) support **-versager** *m* tool failure **-verschleiß** *m* tool wear **-verschluß** *m* boot **-vorrichtung** *f* implement
Werk-zink *n* raw zinc **-zinn** *n* raw tin
Wert *m* worth, value (price), valence **höchstzulässiger ~** maximum safe value **kritischer ~** critical value **reziproker ~** reciprocal value **zulässiger ~** admissible value, safe value **~ der inneren Reibung** (Koeffizient) coefficient of internal friction
Wert-angebe *f* declared value **-arbeit** *f* quality production, valuable work **-berichtigung** *f* revaluation (adjustment) **-beständigkeitsklausel** *f* stabilisation clause **-bestimmung** *f* valuation, evaluation, appraisal, estimate **-brief** *m* insured letter
Werte *pl* data, figures, shares, stock
Werteglättung *f* data smoothing
werten to evaluate, admit
Wertepaar *n* pair of values
Wertermittlung *f* valuation, assessment, taxation
Werte-vorrat *m* range of values **-zahl** *f* coefficient, factor
Wert-fortschreibung *f* writing-off of depreciations **-gegenstand** *m* article of value, valuable **-gelaß** *n* safe deposit **-gut** *n* article of value **-halten** to esteem, value
wertig valent
Wertigkeit *f* valence, merit, validity
Wertigkeits-abhängigkeit *f* valency dependence **-bindung** *f* valence bond (trans.) **-elektron** *n* valency eletron **-formel** *f* valence formula, structural formula, linkage formula **-stufe** *f* valency
Wertkonten *pl* value accounts
wertlos worthless
Wert-maßstab *m* measure of merit or value **-messer** *m* standard of value **-minderung** *f* diminishing value **-paket** *n* insured parcel
Wertpapier *n* security **festverzinsliches ~** security at regular interest **übertragbares ~** transferable security
Wert-schätzung *f* appreciation **-sendung** *f* consignment of valuables **-titelpapier** *n* bill paper **-umsatz** *m* sales in terms of value
Wertung *f* classification in sport, valuation, evaluation, appraisal, estimate
Wertungs-tafel *f* scoreboard **-zahl** *f* coefficient of reduction, figure of merit **-ziffer** *f* figure of merit
Wert-verhältnis *n* relative value **-verminderung** *f* depreciation **-versicherung** *f* insurance of value **-voll** valuable **-zeichenpapier** *n* security or currency paper **-ziffer** *f* factor **-zoll** *m* ad valorem duty **-zuwachssteuer** *f* tax on increment values, increment duty
Wesen *n* character, nature, matter, technique, field, practice, being, essence, substance, condition, essential feature
Wesenseinheit *f* identity
wesensgleich identical in nature
wesentlich essential, remarkable, materially intrinsic
Westdrift *f* westward drift
Westlänge *f* west longitude
westlich western, westerly, westward
Westonelement *n* Weston cell
Westpunkt *m* west, point west
westwärts westward
Westwinde *pl* prevailing westerlies, west winds
Wettbewerb *m* competition, race, meet, contest **außer ~** noncompetitive **an einem ~ teilnehmen** to compete **unlauterer ~** unfair competition
Wettbewerbs-ausschreibung *f* condition of contest **-bestimmung** *f* contest rules **-fähig** competitive **-fähigkeit** *f* competitive position **-modell** *n* competition model **-nennung** *f* entry (in a competition) **-teilnehmer** *m* competitor **-verbotsklausel** *f* restraint of trade **-vorschrift** *f* rule of the competition or contest
Wetter *n* weather, atmosphere **böiges ~** bumpy weather **helles ~** clear weather **mattes ~** oppressive air **schlagende ~** firedamp **schlechtes ~** foul air **sonniges ~** sunny weather
Wetter-ableiter *m* lightning arrestor, lightning

conductor **-amt** *n* weather bureau **-analyse** *f* weather analysis **-änderung** *f* weather change **-austausch** *m* diffusion (min.) **-beobachtung** *f* meteorological observation, weather research **-beratung** *f*, **-bericht** *m* weather report, meteorological report **-berührung** *f* weather contact **-beständig** weatherproof, weather-resistant **-beständigkeit** *f* weather stability **-damm** *m* ventilation dam (min.) **-dichte Konstruktion** weathertight construction

Wetterdienst *m* weather or meteorological service **funkentelegrafischer ~** wireless or radio weather service

Wetterdienst-geräte *pl* meteorological-service instruments **-stelle** *f* meteorological station

Wetter-dynamit *n* permissible dynamite **-echo** *n* weather echo (rdr.) **-element** *n* weather factor **-erkundung** *f* weather reconnaissance **-erkundungsflug** *f* weather-reconnaissance flight **-fahne** *f* weathervane, wind vane, wind sock

wetterfest weatherproof **-e Farbe** weatherproof paint **-es Verdeck** weatherproof hood

Wetterflugzeug *n* meteorological airplane

Wetterforschung *f* weather research **Radiosonde für ~** radiometeorographic sonde

Wetter-führung *f* air-distributing system, ventilation (service) in mines **-funkmeldung** *f*, **-funkspruch** *m* weather or meteorological message **-glas** *n* aneroid barometer, capsule aneroid

Wetter-hahn *m* weathercock **-haltung** *f* ventilation (min.) **-häuschen** *n* weather house **-karte** *f* weather map or chart **-korrosion** *f* atmospheric corrosion **-kreuz** *n* crossing

Wetterkunde *f* meteorology, weather lore, aerology **aeronautische ~** aerology

Wetterlage *f* weather or meteorological conditions, atmospheric conditions **labile ~** unstable atmospheric conditions

Wetter-lampe *f* safety lamp **-läuten** *n* ringing of bells during a thunderstorm **-leitung** *f* air channel **-leuchten** *n* summer lightning, heat or sheet lightning **-loch** *n* wind gate (min.) **-lutte** *f* air pipe (min.), air conduit **-luttenrichtapparat** *m* air-conduit adjusting apparatus (min.) **-maschine** *f* mine or colliery fan **-meldung** *f* weather report, weather message

Wettermeßinstrumente mit funktelegraphischer Fernübertragung radiotelemetric instruments

Wetter-messung *f* meteorological measurement **-nachrichten** *pl* weather report or information **-nebenschluß** *m* weather leakage **-netzsteuerstelle** *f* meteorological-network control center **-ofen** *m* air furnace, furnace for ventilating a mine **-prognose** *f* weather forecast **-rad** *n* ventilator, fan, ventilating fan **-regel** *f* weather maxim **-sammelfunkspruch** *m* radio synoptic weather message, collective weather radiogram **-schacht** *m* upcast shaft, air shaft

Wetter-scheide *f* meteorological or weather limit **-schießen** *n* weather shooting **-schleuse** *f* air lock **-schlüssel** *m* weather code **-schutzbekleidungsstoffe** *pl* weatherproof clothing materials **-sendedienst** *m* radio weather service **-sendestelle** *f* weather-service radio station **-signal** *n* weather signal **-signaldienst** *m* weather signal service **-sonde** *f* radio pilot balloon **-spinne** *f* wind-component indicator **-sprengmittel** *n*, **-sprengstoff** *m* explosives used in mining, safety mining explosive **-spruch** *m* weather maxim

Wetter-stelle *f* weather station **-störung** *f* meteorocigal disturbance or interference **-strom** *m* air current, ventilating current **-symbol** *n* weather symbol **-trupp** *m* meteorological detachment **-tuchherstellungsmaschine** *f* oilcloth-making machine **-tür** *f* air door, wind gate **-umschlag** *m* break in weather

Wetterung *f* ventilation (in mine)

Wetter-verhältnisse *pl* atmospheric conditions, meteorological or weather conditions **-voraussage** *f*, **-vorhersage** *f* weather forecast meteorological station **ortsfeste ~** permanent weather station

Wetterwarte *f* weather bureau, weather or

Wetter-wirtschaft *f* airing of mines **-zeichen** *n* weather signal

Wetterzone *f* zone of bad weather **Flug oberhalb der ~** overweather flight

wetzen to whet, sharpen, hone

Wetz-gravur *f* relief engraving **-schiefer** *m* hone-stone **-stahl** *m* whet steel **-stein** *m* grindstone, oilstone, whetstone

Wheatstone-betrieb *m* Wheatstone working **-empfänger** *m* Wheatstone receiver **-sender** *m* Wheatstone transmitter

Wheatstonesche Meßbrücke Wheastone's bridge

Whitworthgewinde *n* Whitworth tread

Wichse *f* encaustic, blacking, polishing paste

wichsen to polish (leather), shine

Wichsleder *n* blacking leather

Wichte *f* density, unit of weight, specific gravity or weight **-analyse** *f* float and sink analysis **-regler** *m* density regulator

Wichte-Sieb-Asche-Analyse *f* float-and-sink analysis by sizes with ash contents

Wichtewaage *f* density recorder

Wickel *m* package, roller, roll **-aufbau** *m* winding construction **-band** *n* winding tape **-bandwalze** *f* spiral band buffing cylinder **-bildung** *f* lap formation **-blatt** *n* winding sheet

Wickelblock *m* paper condenser or condenser **-kondensator** *m* tubular condenser, paper capacitor, wound or wrapped capacitor of fixed value

Wickel-bock *m* rolling-up bracket **-breite** *f* winding width **-dorn** *m* winding mandrel **-draht** *m* taping wire, binding wire, winding wire **-feder** *f* volute buffer spring **-filtereinsatz** *m* wound filter element

wickelfournierter Rumpf monocoque fuselage

Wickel-gitter *n* helical grid **-hammer** *m* belt drop hammer **-keule** *f* stress core (cable) **-kondensator** *m* rolltype condenser, paper condenser **-kopf** *m* coil end (elec.) **-körper** *m* coil form or core former **-lötstelle** *f* soldered joint, twist joint

Wickelmaschine *f* coiling or winding machine **~ für Schraubenfedern** spring winder

Wickelmotor *m* tape tensioning motor

wickeln to wind, coil, roll, wrap, twist, spool, roll up **neu ~** to rewind

Wickeln *n* winding, balling

Wickel-papierfilter *m* roll-type paper filter **-pappe** *f* press rolled board **-presser** *m* box prizer (tobacco) **-probe** *f* wrapping test **-prüfgerät** *m* lap tester **-rad** *n* coiled-disk wheel **-raum** *m* winding space **-rolle** *f* winding drum

-rumpf *m* monocoque

Wickel-sinn *m* winding direction **-stirnseite** *f* winding face (coil face) **-teller** *m* clutch spindle (tape rec.) **-träger** *m* lap creel **-trommel** *f* winding drum, coiler drum **-turm** *m* mandrel **-wächter** *m* lap guard **-walze** *f* batching roller (beaming roller) **-watte** *f* lap **-welle** *f* winding shaft

Wickler *m* coil winder, wrap **-messer** *n* winder's knife

Wicklung *f* winding, wrapping, casing, coiling, coil, envelopment **in der Mitte angezapfte ~** centertapped winding **bifilare ~** dual-strand winding, bifilar winding **gesehnte ~** short-pitch winding, chord winding **hochohmige ~** high resistance winding **kleine ~** bobbin **mehrlagige ~** multilayer winding **schrittverkürzte ~** short-pitch winding **verteilte ~** distributed winding **~ mit verlängertem Schritt** long-pitch winding **mit zwei Wicklungen** doublewound **zwischen den Wicklungen wirkend** interwinding

Wicklungs-baustoff *m* winding material **-element** *n* coil of a winding connected to a commutator **-faktor** *m* space factor, copper factor **-halter** *m* winding retainer or form, coil form, coil support, skeleton form, former **-klemme** *f* winding terminal

Wicklungsquerschnitt *m* cross-sectional area of winding **mit rechteckigem ~** with rectangular winding section

Wicklungs-raum *m* winding space, volume of winding **-schablone** *f* winding form (elec.) **-schritt** *m* winding pitch (elec.) **-sinn** *m* sense of winding **-tabelle** *f* winding table **-träger** *m* winding support (elec.) **-verhältnis** *n* turns ratio

Widder *m* ram (hydr.) **-hornprofil** *n* reflexed section **-kopf** *m* double ram's-horn **-punkt** *m* vernal equinox **-stoß** *m* water hammer

Widerdruck *m* reactance, inductive or capacitive reactance, counterpressure, reaction, perfecting, reiteration, second working, printing on back **-bogen** *m* perfecting sheet

widerdrücken to back, perfect

Widerdruck-form *f* perfecting or inner form **-zylinder** *m* perfecting cylinder

Wider-führung *f* down lead of an antenna **-haken** *m* barb **-hakengabel** *f* barbed fork **-hall** *m* echo, reverberation, resonance, response **-hallzeit** *f* reverberation period, reverberation time **-halt** *m* resistance (elec.), resisting force, prop, hold, grip, support, guy **-klage** *f* countersuit **-kläger** *m* cross-claim or counteraction plaintiff **-klingen** to resound, echo **-lager** *n* abutment, support, pier, thrust, block, side wall, dolly **-lagerdruck** *m* thrust **-lagspfeiler** *m* abutment **-legung** *f* rebuttal, refutation, disproof

Widermuffe *f* stop collar

widerrechtlich illegal, unlawful, contrary to law **~ betreten** to trespass

Widerrist *m* withers

widerrufen to cancel, revoke, recall, repeal

widerruflich revocable

Wider-schein *m* reflection, sheen, cast of bloom (of oil) **-setzen** to resist, oppose **-setzlich** refractory, resistible **-setzlichkeit** *f* refusal to obey orders

widersinnig in opposite or contrary sense or direction, devoid of sense of logic, irrational absurd **-e Verwerfung** reversed fault (geol.)

Widerspann-abzug *m* cocking spring catch **-feder** *f* cocking spring

widerspenstig refractory, recalcitrant, obstinat

widerspiegeln to reflect

widersprechend contrary, contradictory, inconsistent, opposite

Widerspruch *m* discrepancy (math.), contradiction, opposition, protest, objection, inconsistency **in ~ stehen** to disagree, clash **steht augenscheinlich in ~** is clearly contrary to

Widerspruchslosigkeit *f* self-consistency

Widerstand *m* resistance, drag, strength (materials), impedance, rheostat, opposition, reluctance **~ ausschalten** to cut out resistance **~ einschalten** to insert or switch in resistance **~ entgegensetzen** to impede, offer a resistance, put up opposition **~ kurzschließen** to short cut a resistor short-circuit the resistance **~ leisten** to oppose **abgestufter ~** stepped resistance **äquivalenter ~** equivalent resistance **außenliegender ~** external linebalancing resistance **effektiver ~** effective resistance **elektrischer ~** rheostat

Widerstand *m* (als physikalische Größe) resistance; (als elektr. Bauelement) resistor **~ mit achsialen Anschlüssen** axial lead style resistor **~ mit radialen Anschlüssen** tap lead style resistor **spezifischer magnetischer ~** reluctivity

Widerstand, gemeinsamer ~ common resistance **gerichteter ~** asymmetrical resistance **hinhaltender ~** delaying action, delaying resistance **induktionsfreier ~** plain or noninductive resistance, ohm resistance **induktiver ~** inductive reactance, inductance **induzierter ~** induced resistance, induced drag **innerer ~** plate resistance, anode alternating-current resistance, internal resistance (of a thermionic tube), differential resistance, output resistance **kapazitiver ~** capacitance, capacitive reactance, condensive reactance **kombinierter ~** joint or combined resistance **kritischer ~** critical resistance **lichtelektrischer ~** photoresistance

Widerstand, magnetischer ~ magnetic resistance, reluctance **negativer ~** negative resistance, third-class resistance **nützlicher ~** effective resistance **Ohm'scher ~** ohmic resistance, direct-current resistance **örtlicher ~** local resistance **punktförmig verteilter ~** lumped resistance **regelbarer ~** rheostat, adjustable resistance **reiner ~** nonreactive resistance **resultierender ~** resultant resistance **richtungsabhängiger ~** asymmetrical resistance

Widerstand, schädlicher ~ parasitic drag or resistance (aviation) **scheinbarer ~** impedance, apparent resistance **spezifischer ~** resistivity, volume resistivity, specific resistance **veränderlicher ~, verstellbarer ~** variable resistance **winkelfreier ~** resistance with zero phase angle **wirksamer ~** impedance, apparent resistance

Widerstand(s)-abbrennschweißung *f* flash welding **-abgreifer** *m* slider **-abgriff** *m* resistance tapping **-abhängig** resistance-dependent **-ableitung** *f* resistance derivation **-abschluß** *m* terminating resistance **-achse** *f* drag axis **-änderung** *f* resistance variation **-anstieg** *m* drag increase

Widerstandsanteil, aerodynamischer ~ cooling drag

Widerstands-apparat *m* resistor **-äquivalent** *n* equivalent resistance

Widerstandsatz *m* decadic resistor, standard resistance

Widerstands-ausgleich *m* resistance balance **-bahn d. Reglers** mixer (or fader) pad **-ballast** *m* resistance ballast, ballasting resistance **-begrenzt** resistively terminated **-beheizung** *f* resistance heating, resistance relation **-beiwert** *m* resistance coefficient, drag coefficient **-belag** *m* resistive lining **-bremsung** *f* rheostatic braking **-brücke** *f* Wheatstone bridge, resistance measurer, slide-wire bridge, measurement bridge **-büchse** *f* resistance box

Widerstands-dämpfung *f* resistance loss **-dehnungsmeßstreifen** *m* resistance strain gauge **-dekade** *f* resistance decade (radio) **-draht** *m* resistance wire **-drosselkuppelung** *f* resistance-choke coupling **-element** *n* heating grid **-entstörung** *f* resistor-type interference **-erhitzung** *f* resistance heating **-erhöhung** *f* increase of resistance **-fähig** resistant, refractory, proof, resisting, robust

Widerstandsfähigkeit *f* capacity for resistance, capability of resistance, load-bearing capacity, strength, resistivity, stability, resistance ~ **gegen atmosphärische Korrosion** resistance to weathering **dielektrische** ~ dielectric strength **natürliche** ~ inherent resistance

Widerstands-faktor *m* impedance factor **-fläche** *f* surface of equivalent drag **-falschanpassung** *f* mismatching of impedances **-formel** *f* resistance formula, drag formula **-gekoppelt** resistance-coupled **-gerade** *f* load line **-gerät** *n* resistor **-glied** *n* resistor, resistive element **-gruppe** *f* rear-guard troops, defense strong point, unit assigned to one sector of main line of resistance **-halter** *m* resistance holder (teleph.) **-heizung** *f* resistance heating (elec.)

Widerstands-höhe *f* loss of pressure, peak of resistance, resistance head (in filter wells), amount of resistance, friction head ~ **der Flüssigkeitsbewegung** resistance head

Widerstands-instrument *n* resistance instrument **-kapazitätsanordnung** *f* resistance-capacity arrangement **-kasten** *m* resistance box **-kessel** *m* pocket of resistance **-kette** *f* voltage divider, potentiometer **-koeffizient** *m* resistance or drag coefficient **-komponente** *f* resistance component **-koppelung** *f* resistance coupling, resistive coupling **-körper** *m* external drag body, baffle, damper **-kraft** *f* power of resistance, magnitude of resistance, defensive power, interference drag, strength

Widerstandslampe *f* resistance lamp ~ **im elektrischen Kreis** ballast lamp

Widerstands-legierung *f* resistance alloy **-leister** *m* resistor

Widerstandsleuchte im elektrischen Kreis ballast lamp

Widerstandslinie *f* line of resistance

widerstandslos resistanceless **-e Flügelnute** no-drag slot **-er Kreis** resistanceless circuit

Widerstands-messer *m* ohmmeter, electric resistance meter **-messung** *f* resistance test, measurement of resistance **-mittelpunkt** *m* center of pressure **-moment** *n* moment of resistance, section modulus (metal testing) **-nest** *n* point of resistance, island or pocket of resistance **-netz** *n* resistance lattice **-normal** *n* resistance standard **-ofen** *m* (electric) resistance furnace **-operator** *m* resistance operator **-probe** *f* nondestructive test

Widerstands-rauschen *n* thermal noise (electr. tube), circuit noise **-reaktanzverhältnis** *n* magnification factor **-regler** *m* rheostat **-reziprok** *n* inverse resistance, resistance reciprocal **-satz** *m* decadic resistor, standard resistance **-schwankung** *f* resistance variation **-schweißung** *f* resistance welding, incandescent welding **-schweißverfahren** *n* resistance welding process **-spule** *f* resistance coil **-stellung** *f* delaying position **-stufe** *f* resistance step **-symmetrie** *f* resistance balance

Widerstands-thermometer *n* resistance thermometer **-truppe** *f* delaying unit **-überanspannung** *f* overmatching of impedance **-unteranpassung** *f* undermatching of impedance **-verlust** *m* resistance loss **-vermögen** *n* resistance, defensive power, resisting power **-verringerung** *f* reduction of resistance **-verstärker** *m* resistance-coupled amplifier, resistance amplifier, resistance strengthener

Widerstands-verteilung *f* taper **-wärmegradmesser** *m* resistance thermometer **-wendel** *m* resistance windings **-werkstoff** *m* resistance metal **-wert** *m* resistance value **-zahl** *f* coefficient of resistance **-zelle** *f* photoconducting cell, photoresistance cell **-zentrum** *n* center of resistance **-ziffer** *f* resistance coefficient **-zone** *f* zone of resistance **-zunahme** *f* increase in resistance **-zündkerze** *f* resistor spark plug **-zylinder** *m* resistor tube

wider-stehen to resist, withstand, stand, hold out **-stoß** *m* reactance, countershock **-strahl** *m* reflected ray or beam **-strahlen** to reflect, radiate **-strahlend** resplendent **-streben** to oppose, resist **-strebend** reluctantly, opposing, repugnant **-streiten** to resist, oppose **-vergeltung** *f* retaliation **-wüchsig** crooked-fibered (wood) **-zeit** *f* change of the tide

Widiametall *n* (trade-mark for tungsten carbide) tungsten carbide, Widia metal

wieder again ~ **in Dienst stellen** to recommission ~ **aufbauen** to rebuild ~ **aufholen** to pick up (as of an engine) ~ **aufladen** to recharge ~ **einschiffen** to reembark ~ **instandsetzen** to repair ~ **laden** to recharge ~ **wirksam machen** to regenerate (revivify)

Wieder-abdruck *m* reprinting **-abtastender Raster** additional scanning raster **-abtastung** *f* reproduction of scanning **-abtretung** *f* reassignment **-anbau** *m* remounting (reinstallation) **-anfangen** to restart, resume **-anhalten** to rearrest **-anmeldung** *f* reissue **-anwärmen** to reheat **-anziehen** (Schrauben) to retighten **-aufarbeiten** to rework, refinish, recut **-aufarbeiten** *n* re-conditioning

Wieder-aufbau *m* reconstruction, rebuilding **-aufbauen** to rebuild, reconstruct **-aufbereitung** reprocessing **-auffinden** to retrieve **-aufgebaut** rebuilt **-aufheben** to neutralize **-aufladen** to recharge **-aufladung** *f* recharge **-auflösen** to redissolve

Wiederaufnahme *f* resumption, reopening (of a legal case), retake ~ **der normalen Drehzahl** return to normal working

wieder-aufnehmen to resume **-aufrüstung** *f* rearmament **-aufschrauben** to rescrew **-auftauen** *n* thawing **-ausfallung** *f* redeposition (geol.) **-ausfuhr** *f* reexportation **-aushärtungstemperatur** *f* annealing temperature for agehardening **-ausstrahlen** to reradiate **-ausstrahlung** *f* reradiation

wiederbearbeiteter Gummi hard rubber

wiederbeleben to reactivate, regenerate, revive, revivify

Wiederbelebung *f* reactivation, regeneration, revivification, revival (elec.) **~ der thorierten Kathode** reactivation or rejuvenation of thoriated cathode, flashing

Wiederbelebungs-apparat *m* life-restoring apparatus **-ofen** *m* revivifying kiln

Wieder-benetzen *n* reabsorbtion **-beschaffungswert** *m* replacement cost **-beschicken** to recharge, reload **-bestellung** *f* repeat order **-bewertung** *f* revaluation **-brauchbarmachen** *n* regeneration (chem.) **-einbauen** to reinstall **-einführen** to reintroduce **-einführung** *f* reinsertion, restoration **-einschalten** reclose (a switch), cut or connect in circuit again **-einschmelzen** to remelt **-einschmelzen** *n* remelting, recasting

Wieder-druck *m* reprint **-einbringen** to recover **-eingefügt** reinserted **einrücken** *n* reengaging **-einschaltrelais** *n* mains restoration relay **-einschaltsperre** *f* reclose blocking **-einschreibendes Speicherlesen** regenerative storage scanning **-einsetzen** to reinstall, replace, reinstate

Wiedereinsetzung in frühere Rechte rehabilitation

wieder-einspannen to reclamp, rechuck **-einstellen** to readjust **-eintritt** *m* reentry **-eintrittskörper** *m* re-entry body, re-entry capsule (spacecraft) **-erhitzen** to reheat **-erhitzung** *f* reheating **-erkennungsmethode** *f* recognition method **-erlangen** retrieve **-erlangung** *f* recovery **-eröffnung** *f* reopening, resumption (of a law suit)

Wieder-erreichung *f* recovery **-erstarken** *n* resuscitation, renascence **-erstatten** return, reimburse, restitute **-erstattung** *f* restitution **-erwärmen** to rewarm, reheat **-erzeugen** to regenerate, reproduce

Wiedergabe *f* play-back (tape rec.), replay, restitution, signals picked up and amplified, reproduction **flache ~** flat reproduction **flimmerfreie ~** flicker-free reproduction **genaue ~** faithful reproduction **getreue ~** good definition (of image), orthophonic reproduction (of loud speaker) **hohle ~** boomy reproduction **kontinuierliche ~** flicker-free reproduction

Wiedergabe-brillianz *f* brilliance of sound reproduction **-charakteristik** *f* playback characteristics **-dose** *f* phonograph pickup **-entzerrung** *f* playback equalization **-gerät** *n* playback unit **-güte** *f* quality of reproduction, fidelity response

Wiedergabe-kanal *m* reproduction channel **-kopf** *m* playback head **-kurve** *f* fidelity curve **-natürlichkeit** *f* faithfulness, fidelity, or realism of reproduction, brillance **-primärreize** *pl* receiver primaries **-qualität** *f* quality or faithfulness of reproduction **-röhre** *f* cathode-ray tube, electronic picture-reproducing tube **-stein** *m* reproducing stone **-treue** *f* fidelity

wiedergeben to project (motion pictures), reproduce

Wieder-gebrauch *m* reuse **-gebrauchsfähigmachen** *n* rectification **-gefrieren** to regelate **-gesetztes** *n* recomposition (print.) **-gewinnbar** recoverable **-gewinnen** to recover, regain, reclaim, recuperate **-gewinnung** *f* regeneration, recovery **-gewinnungsmotor** *m* regenerative rocket motor **-gewonnener Gummi** reclaimed rubber (by regeneration **-gutmachung** *f* restoration, reparation

wieder-herausgeben to reissue **-herstellen** to repair, rebuild, reestablish, restore, resupply, reconstruct **-herstellung** *f* restoration, reestablishment, repair, reconstruction, remaking

Wiederherstellungs-arbeit *f* repair work **-koeffizient** *m* restitution coefficient **-kraft** *f* restoring moment **-trupp** *m* repair squad

Wieder-hervorbringung *f* reproduction **-holbar** reproducible, repeatable, reiterable **-holbarkeit** *f* recurrence **-holen** to rerun (comput.) or repeat, reiterate **-holpunkt** *m* rerun point (comput.) **-holtaste** *f* back spacing control (tape rec.); repeat key (typewriter) **-holung** *f* repetition, reiteration, round of pattern (weaving)

Wiederholungs-aufnahme *f* retake **-auftrag** *m* repeat order **-einrichtung** *f* duplicating device **-frequenz** *f* repetition frequency, frequency of recurrence **-instrument** *n* slave meter **-klinke** *f* ancillary or auxiliary jack **-kreis** *m* repeating circle

Wiederholungs-lampe *f* auxiliary lamp **-lehrgang** *m* refresher course **-unterricht** *m* refresher instruction **-verfahren** *n* repeating method **-versuch** *m* retest **-zeichen** *n* repeat signal **-zwillinge** *pl* repeated or multiple twinning (geol.)

Wieder-inbesitznahme *f* reoccupation **-inbetriebnahme** *f* return to service **-inkraftsetzung** *f* re-enactment **-instandsetzen** to repair, reinstate **-instandsetzung** *f* reinstatement, reconditioning, refitment, restoration, renovation

Wiederkehr *f* period **regelmäßige ~** periodicity **~ des Schützenschlages** back pick (back shot)

wiederkehren to return

wiederkehrend recurrent (periodically or not) **regelmäßig ~** periodic, (periodically) recurrent **gleichförmige -e Bewegung** periodic uniform motion **-e Spannung** recovery voltage

Wieder-kehrsatz *m* recurrence theorem **-kehrspannung** *f* recovery voltage **-kehrzeit** *f* cycle period **-klingen** *n* resonance **-kristallisieren** to recrystallize **-kristallisierung** *f* recrystallization **-oxydation** *f* reoxidation **-schmelzen** to remelt, refuse

Wieder-spannabzug *m* double-action trigger **-spannfeder** *f* recocking spring **-spiegeln, -strahlen** to reflect **-strahlung** *f* re-radiation **-unterdrucksetzung** *f* repressuring **-verdichten** recompact

Wieder-vereinigung *f* recombination (of ions in gas), focusing (of rays, electrons) **vereinigungskoeffizient** *m* recombination coefficient **-verkäufer** *m* jobber, retailer **-verkaufspreis** *m* retail price **-verriegeln** to relatch **-verriegelung** *f* relatching

wieder-verstärken to reamplify **-verteilen** to redistribute **-verteilung** *f* redistribution **-verwendung** *f* reuse **-zulassung** *f* recommissioning **-zündbrennkammer** *f* re-igniter chamber (rocket) **-zünden** to reignite **-zündspannung** *f* reignition voltage

Wieder-zündung *f* reignition, restriking **-zurichten** to dress **-zurichtung** *f* dressing **-zusammenbau** *m* reassembly **-zusammenbauen** to reassemble **-zusammendrückung** *f* recompression **-zusammenschmelzen** to re-fuse

Wiege *f* rocker, rocking device, cradle **-arm** *m* rocker arm **-balken** *m* movable beam **-brücke** *f* weighbridge **-fehler** *m* error in weighing **-kufe** *f* rocker **-meister** *m* weigher **-messer** *n* mincing knife

wiegen to weight, rock, weigh **-artig** V-shaped **-druck** *m* incunable **-dynamometer** *m* cradle dynamometer **-gleitbahn** *f* cradle guide rails **-kipper** *m* cradle tip wagon **-träger** *m* cradle frame, cradle support **-trog** *m* cradle trough **-zurrung** *f* cradle lashing, cradle lock

Wiege-träger *m* movable beam (R.R.) **-vorrichtung** *f* weighing device

Wiener Kalk Vienna polishing chalk, French chalk

Wiesen-erz *n* bog iron ore **-grün** *n* Paris green, meadow green **-kalk** *m* chalky soil

Wigner-Effekt Wigner effect, discomposition effect

Wiikit *m* wiikite

wild wild, savage, uncultivated, uncivilized **~ gewickelt** scramble or pie-wound **-e Changierung** wild traverse motion **-e Kuppelung** stray or spurious coupling, undesired coupling **-er Maßstab** *m* undefined scale

Wildbach *m* torrent **-verbauung** *f* control or regulation of torrents

Wildleder *n* chamois leather

Wilfley-Herd *m* Wilfley table or concentrator

willkürlich arbitrary, haphazard, (at) random **~ verteilt** randomly distributed, scattered at random

Wilson-kammer *f* cloud chamber, expansion chamber **-nebelspurmethode** *f* Wilson cloud-track method

Wimmer *m* shake, cross grain (in wood)

Wimmler *m* shuffle bar

Wimpel *m* pennant, streamer

Wind *m* wind, blast, air, air blast, breeze **~ mit geringer Pressung** soft blast **~ mit starker Pressung** cutting blast **~ von hinten** tail wind **dem ~ entgegendrehen** to head into the wind, crab **am ~ liegen** to be to windward **unter ~ liegen** to be to leeward

Wind-abblaseventil *n* blowoff valve **-ablagerung** *f* wind laid deposits **-ablenkung** *f* deflection of the wind **-absperrschieber** *m* blast gate, damper **-abstellung** *f* disconnection of the blast **-abtragung** *f* deflation **-abtrift** *f* wind drift **-abwärts** downwind, leeward **-angriffsfläche** *f* wind surface, wind catching area (of antenna)

Windanker *m* downstream anchor, transversal stay (elec.), cable **-leine** *f* downstream anchor cable **-linie** *f* downstream line of anchors **-tau** *n* downstream anchor cable

Wind-anschwellung *f* wind increase **-antrieb** *m* impeller drive **-antriebsmotor** *m* winch motor, winding motor **-anzeiger** *m* weather vane, wind indicator **-ausnutzung** *f* utilization of the wind **-bahn** *f* wind course, trajectory or path of wind **-baum** *m* mare's-tail **-belastung** *f* wind load, wind pressure

Wind-bewegung *f* motion of the wind, wind movement **-bläser** *m* blower, blast apparatus **-bö** *f* squall, gust **-brett** *n* wind board **-bruch** *m* windbreak, windfall, rolled timber **-büchse** *f* wind gun **-charakter** *m* character of the wind **-dalle** *f* gust, squall **-dicht** airtight **-dichtigkeit** *f* airtightness **-docke** *f* drying horse **-dreieck** *n* wind triangle **-dreiecksrechnung** *f* airdrift triangulation

Winddruck *m* blast pressure, force, wind pressure **-formel** *f* wind-pressure formula **-krängungsmoment** *n* heeling moment (of ship) due to wind pressure **-messer** *m* wind-pressure gauge, blast-pressure meter, blast gauge

Wind-durchgang *m* blast passage **-düse** *f* blast tuyère, tuyère

Winde *f* hoist, winch, worm (gear), jack, capstan, crab, lever jack, lifting jack, screw jack, winch jack, cathead, windlass **~ zum Abnehmen von Drähten** wire reel **~ zur Handoperierung** winch for manual operation **~ auf ringförmiger Zahnstange** jack and circle

Windebock *m* lifting or screw jack

Wind-eigentümlichkeit *f* character of the wind **-einfluß** *m* wind influence **-einströmungsöffnung** *f* blast inlet **-einwirkung** *f* action of wind **-eisen** *n* twisting pliers, wrenches, tap wrench, window fastening, iron window bar, stocks and dies **-elektrizitätswerk** *n* wind-driven electric power station

Windeknüppel *m* winch lever

Windemaschine *f* winding machine

winden to wind, coil, hoist, wrap **sich ~** to turn, wriggle, wind, tack (naut.)

Winden *n* winding **-auto** *n* motorcar for winch launching **-bock** *m* lifting jack **-gehäuse** *n* winch or windlass housing **-haus** *n* winch house, winch or windlass shed or room **-kasten** *m* winch box **-rahmen** *m* winch frame **-schlepp** *m* mechanical towing, towing with a winch **-start** *m* winch launching **-stock** *m* rack bar of the jack **-trommel** *f* cable drum, hoisting drum

Winderhitzer *m* hot-blast stove, hot-air stove, regenerator, air heater, recuperator **-fachwerk** *n* hot-blast-stove checkerwork **-mantel** *m* hot-blast-stove casing

Wind-erhitzung *f* blast heating **-erhitzungsapparat** *m* hot-blast stove, regenerator **-erzeuger** *m* fan

Winde-tau *n* winding rope **-trommel** *f* drum of winch, cable drum, hoisting drum **-wagen** *m* winch wagon or truck **-welle** *f* winding shaft (milling)

Windfächer *m* fan

Windfahne *f* weather vane, wind indicator, anemoscope

Windfahnen-bewegung *f* Dutch roll (aviation) **-korn** *n* wind wave-front sight

Windfahrtrechner *m* wind direction computer

Windfang *m* clock governor (with vanes), vent hole

windfangender Gegenstand object that catches the wind

Wind-fänger *m* air scoop **-fangregler** *m* fan governor **-fest** windresistant

Windflügel *m* fan blade, vane, impeller, air vane, air wing, impeller blade **-blatt** *n* fan blade **-blech** *n* fan blade **-nabe** *f* fan hub **-riemen-**

scheibe *f* fan-driving pulley **-ring** *m* fan ring **-stütze** *f* fan support **-verstellung** *f* blade control of lifting rotors

Windform *f* blast tuyère, blowing tuyère, tuyère **-ebene** *f* tuyère line **-kühlkasten** *m* tuyère-cooling plate

Windfrischapparat *m* converter ~ **mit seitlicher Windeinströmung** side-blowing converter

Wind-frischen *n* purification, converting, air blowing, purifying **-frischverfahren** *n* purifying process **-frischvorgang** *m* blowing operation **-fühler** *m* wind antenna **-führungsblech** *n* air guiding sheet **-führungsseitenbleche** (Auto) *pl* cowl side-panels **-geber** *m* wind-speed transmitter **-gefrischt** air-cooled (said of steel) **-gebläse** *n* blower, fan

Windgeschwindigkeit *f* wind velocity, air-blast velocity, wind component

Windgeschwindigkeits-aufzeichnung *f* anemogram **-messer** *m* anemometer, wind-velocity indicator

Wind-gewölbe *n* tuyère arch **-gradient** *m* wind gradient **-haspel** *f* skeleton drums **-haube** *f* cowl **-hindernis** *n* object that catches the wind **-hose** *f* twister, whirlwind, tornado **-hutze mit Rundeinlaß** mushroom cowl

windig windy

Wind-jacke *f* windbreaker, double-breasted field jacket **-kammer** *f* air chamber

Windkanal *m* wind tunnel, wind channel ~ **für naturgroße Flugzeuge** full-scale wind tunnel ~ **für hohe Geschwindigkeiten** high-speed wind tunnel ~ **für veränderliche Luftdichte** variable-density wind tunnel ~ **für Modelle in natürlicher Größe** full-scale wind tunnel ~ **für Überschallgeschwindigkeit** supersonic tunnel **geschlossener** ~ return-flow wind tunnel

Windkanal-düse *f* wind-tunnel bell or funnel **-forschung** *f* aerodynamic flow research **-messung** *f* wind-tunnel measurements **-modell** *n* wind-tunnel model **-rückleitung** *f* wind-tunnel return flow **-untersuchung** *f* windtunnel investigation **-versuch** *m* wind-tunnel test

Wind-kanter *m* windkanter (geol.), wind-carved pebble **-karte** *f* wind chart **-kasten** *m* wind box, wind chest, blast box, air box, tuyère box, wind chest (organ) **-kastenplatte** *f* blast-box cover **-kegel** *m* wind cone **-kessel** *m* expansion chamber, air vessel, air chamber, vacuum tank (chamber), blast-pressure tank, blast box, air reservoir, surge tank **-klappe** *f* air valve **-komponente** *f* wind component **-konstanz** *f* steadiness of the wind **-korrigierungswinkel** *m* wind-correction angle **-kraftgenerator** *m* windmill generator

Windkurs *m* wind direction, course heading in wind **rechtweisender** ~ true heading

Wind-lade *f* wind chest, sound box (of organ) **-landung** *f* downwind landing **-last** *f* lateral thrust due to wind **-leine** *f* tension line **-leitung** *f* blast main, blast pipe, air line **-leitungsrohr** *n* blast pipe **-lieferung** *f* blast supply, air supply **-lose Stellung** no-wind position

Wind-mantel *m* wind box, wind belt, air belt, air chamber **-maschine** *f* fan, blower **-menge** *f* wind volume, volume of blast **-mengenmesser** *m* blast-volume meter **-meßanlage** *f* wind gauge **-messer** *m* blast gauge, air meter, wind gauge **-meßgerät** *n* wind-testing apparatus, anemometer **-meßkurve** *f* anemogram **-meßlinie** *f* anemogram **-messung** *f* wind measurement, anemometry, wind test **-motor** *m* windmill motor

Windmühle *f* windmill

Windmühlen-flügel *m* vane **-flügelverstellung** *f* anemometrically variable pitch **-flugzeug** *n* gyroplane, helicopter, autogiro

Wind-mulde *f* hollow formed by wind **-ofen** *m* air furnace **-öffnung** *f* air hole **-peilsonde** *f* radio pilot balloon for wind data **-periode** *f* period of blowing **-pfeife** *f* vent pipe, vent hole

Windpfeil *m* wind arrow **-ende** *n* wind-arrow tail **-spitze** *f* wind-arrow head

Windpressung *f* blast pressure, air pressure

Windrad *n* impeller, wind wheel **-anemograph** *m* fan-wheel or wind-wheel anemograph, rotating-wheel or wind-vane anemograph **-gebläse** *n* ventilator, fan

Windrädchen *n* instrument registering rise and fall of balloons

Windrad-sockel *m* sole plate of wind wheel **-zylinder** *m* wind-wheel drum

Wind-registrierapparat *m* anemograph, recording anemometer **-registrierung** *f* anemogram **-richtung** *f* wind direction **-richtungsanzeiger** *m* vane, wind indicator, anemoscope **-richtungsmesser** *m* wind vane **-ring** *m* bustle pipe (of blast furnace) **-riß** *m* cupping (of wood), crack, flaw **-rissig** windcracked or -shaken **-rohr** *n* blast pipe, tuyère pipe **-rohrleitung** *f* blast-pipe line **-rose** *f* wind rose, dial card

Windrosen-darstellung *f* wind compass card **-steuerung** *f* wind-governor controlling gear

Windrüssel *m* wind cone or sleeve **-stange** *f* sock pole

Wind-sack *m* wind sock, wind cone **-sammler** *m* air reservoir, compressed-air tank **-saugschacht** (Gasmaschine) air supply duct **-schacht** *m* air shaft **-schatten** *m* region sheltered from the (prevailing) winds, lee **-scheibe** *f* front shield, wind screen **-scherung** *f* wind shear **-schieber** *m* blast gate, air damper, tuyère gate, shutoff valve **-schicht** *f* wind layer

windschief wind-tipped, warped, skew, back-sided (wood), twisted (out of shape), deformed **-er Flug** crabbing

Wind-schildlager *n* wind shield bearing **-schirm** *m* windscreen, windshield **-schliff** *m* eolic gradation, eolation **-schliffe** *m pl* wind-polished rocks **-schlüpfig** streamlined **-schlüssel** *m* key to weather code numbers and symbols

windschnittig streamlined, faired, aerodynamic ~ **verkleiden** to streamline

Windschraube *f* windmill **durch** ~ **angetriebener Generator** windmill-driven generator

Windschrauben-benzinpumpe *f* windmill-driven or propeller-driven gasoline pump **-brennstoffpumpe** *f* wind-mill-driven fuel pump

Windschreiber *m* anemograph, recording anemometer

Windschubspannung *f* tangential wind stress

Windschutz *m* front shield, windscreen, wind guard **-haube** *f* protective dome **-kappe** *f* wind cap **-kasten** *m* tuyère block, tuyère arch **-korb** *m* wind screen (akust.) **-plane** *f* windbreak **-scheibe** *f* windscreen, windshield **-scheibenenteiser** *m*

windshield deicer **-scheibenwischer** *m* windshield wiper

Wind-segel *n* wind sail, air duct **-seite** *f* weather side **-seitig** windward **-semaphor** *m* aspirator

Windsenkung des Wasserspiegels lowering of the water by the effect of wind

Wind-separator *m*, **-sichter** *m* air separator, air sifter **-sichtmaschine** *f* wind-sifting machine **-sichtung** *f* air sifting, air separation **-skala** *f* wind scale **-sortierer** *m* air sifter

Wind-sprung *m* shift of wind, sudden change of wind **-stärke** *f* wind intensity, wind velocity, wind force **-stärkemesser** *m* anemometer, wind gauge

Windstärkenskala *f* **von Beaufort** Beaufort's scale

Windstau *m* (wind) pressure

Wind-stein *m* blast stone **-stern** *m* wind star

Windstille *f* calm, lull **~ des Krebses** calm of Cancer **~ des Widders** calm of Capricorn

Wind-stoß *m* gust (of wind), blast **-strahl** *m* wind jet **-strebe** *f* wind brace **-strich** *m* rhumb, lubber line **-strom** *m* air current **-strömung** *f* air flow, air current **-stufe** *f* air layer, wind layer **-stutzen** *m* blast pipe or nozzle

Wind-temperatur *f* air-blast temperature **-thermik** *f* high-speed upwinds **-träger** *m* wind truss, wind bracing **-trocknung** *f* air drying, blast drying, drying of blast **-trocknungsanlage** *f* dry-blast plant, air-drying plant **-trocknungsverfahren** *n* dry-blast process, air-drying process **-tunnel** *m* wind tunnel

Windung *f* turn, coil, twist, winding, turning, twisting, loop, convolution **~ von Stromlinien** *pl* torsion of stream-lines **~ einer Wicklung** spire **gegenläufige ~** coil in opposite direction (elec.) **tote Windungen** dead-end turns, dead end, unused turns of a coil, idle portion of a coil, idle turns

Windungs-dichte *f* closeness in winding **-ebene** *f* winding plane **-fläche** *f* turn area **-fluß** *m* turn flux, linkage (magnetic), flux turns **-ganghöhe** *f* pitch (of turns) **-isolation** *f* winding insulation **-kapazität** *f* internal capacity (of coil), interturn capacitance, self-capacitance **-linie** *f* line turn, maxwell turn **-punkt** *m* branch point **-schluß** *m* interturn short-circuit **-schlußprüfer** *m* interturn short-circuit tester, continuity tester **-spannung** *f* interturn voltage **-verhältnis** *n* ratio of the windings, turns ratio **-zahl** *f* number of turns

Wind-ventil *n* blast valve **-veränderung** *f* wind shift **-verband** *m* windbreaker, lateral wind bracing **-verbesserung** *f* windage correction **-verhältnisse** *pl* wind conditions or factors **-verteilung** *f* distribution of blast

windwärts windward, upwind

Windwechsel *m*, **regelmäßiger ~** uniform change of wind

Windwerk *n* winch, hoist, hoisting gear, lifting gear, hoisting equipment, hoisting mechanism **-anlage** *f* winch mechanism **-motor** *m* hoist motor

Wind-widerstand *m* wind resistance **-winkel** *m* wind angle, angle of drift, angle between head-on course and direction of wind, yaw angle **-woge** *f* wind wave, aerial billow **-wolke** *f* wind cloud **-zeiger** *m* anemoscope **-zufluß** *m*, **-zufuhr** *f*, **-zuführung** *f* air supply, air-blast supply **-zuführungsrohr** *n* wind pipe, blast pipe **-zug** *m* air current, ventilator **-zylinder** *m* air cylinder

Wink *m* sign, nod, hint, pointer

Winkdienst *m* flagsignalling

Winkel *m* angle, wedge formation (aviation), chevron, corner, angle guide, square (as a tool) **~ zum Anschlaghebel** angle bracket **~ in der Kurve, ~ der Schräglage** angle of bank, angle of roll **abgestumpfter ~** cutoff angle **ausspringender ~** salient, salient angle **~ durchlaufen** to travel through an angle **einspringender ~** corner notch, reentering angle, reentrant **parallaktischer ~** parallactic angle **räumlicher ~** solid angle, steradian **rechter ~** try square, right angle **spitzer ~** acute angle **stumpfer ~** obtuse angle **toter ~** dead angle, dead space **vorspringender ~** salient

Winkel-abgleich *m* angle balance **-abhängigkeit** *f* angle dependence **-ablenkung** *f* angular deflection **-abstand** *m* angular distance **-abweichung** *f* angular deflection **-änderung** *f* angular variation **-anschlag** *m* back square, angle stop **-anschluß** *m* angle connection

Winkel-antrieb *m* angle or bell-crank drive **-anzeigevorrichtung** *f* angle-indicating attachment **-arm** *m* angle or wall bracket **-aufblendung** *f* angle fade-in **-auflösung von Spuren** angular resolution of tracks **-aufspanntisch** *m* tilting table **-ausschlag** *m* angular deflection **-auswanderung** *f* angular movement, angular travel **-band** *n* angle brace, angle hinge **-bandeinlaßapparat** *m* angle-hinge sinking-in attachment

Winkelbereich *m* sector of dial **wirksamer ~** effective traverse of a beam

Winkel-beschlag *m* angle fitting **-beschleunigung** *f* angular acceleration, angular velocity **-beschleunigungsmesser** *m* angular accelerometer **-bewegung** *f* angular motion, angular movement **-beziehung** *f* angle correlation **-blech** *n* angle sheet iron, gusset (for strengthening) **-block** *m* prismatic wedge

Winkel-bogen *m* central angle **-bogensegment** *n* curved-angle segment **-bohren** *n* angle drilling **-bohrkopf** *m* angular drilling head **-bohrmaschine** *f* angular-type drill **-bügel** *m* strap **-drehmoment** *n* moment of momentum, angular momentum **-drehung** *f* angular turning **-düse** *f* angular pressure nozzle **-eikonal** *n* angle iconal (optics) **-einheit** *f* unit of angle

Winkeleisen *n* angle iron, angle steel, angles, rolled(-steel) angle **gleichschenkliges ~** equal-sided angle iron **ungleichschenkliges ~** unequal-sided angle iron

Winkeleisen-biegemaschine *f* angle-iron bending machine **-führung** *f* angle-iron guide **-richtmaschine** *f* angle-straightening machine **-ring** *m* angle-iron hoop **-scheren** *pl* double-angle shears

Winkel-entstörstecker *m* angular suppression cap or plug **-feder** *f* cock spring

Winkelfehler *m* squint (antenna) **~ beim Wandler** phase angle error, phase displacement

Winkel-fernrohr *n* elbow telescope **-flansch** *m* angle flange **-förmig** angular

Winkelfräser *m* angle cutter **~ mit doppelter Schräge** double-angle cutter **einseitiger ~** single-angle cutter

winkelfrei nonreactive **-er Widerstand** resistance with zero phase angle

Winkel-frequenz *f* angular frequency, radian frequency **-führung** *f* angular guide **-funktion** *f* circular function, trigonometric function, angular function **-gelenk** *n* angle joint **-geschwindigkeit** *f* pulsation, angular velocity, angular frequency **-geschwindigkeitsgerät** *n* angular-velocity meter **-geschwindigkeitskommandogerät** *n* angular-speed data computer **-geschwindigkeitsmesser** *m* angular velocity meter or indicator

Winkel-gestänge *n* angle poles **-getriebe** *n* miter-wheel gearing, miter gear **-gitter** *n* angle (measuring) grid **-grad** *m* degree of angle, radian **-greifer** *m* angle lugs **-größe** *f* angular ballistic variable **-gruppe** *f* firing angles **-hahn** *m* angle cock

Winkelhaken *m* composing stick (print.) ~ **für Durchhangsregelung** square for sag regulation (elec.) ~ **für Durchhangsprüfung** sag or dip gauge

Winkelhalbierende *f* angle bisector

Winkelhalbierungslinie *f* bisecting line of an angle

Winkelhebel *m* toggle lever, loading-mechanism cam, bell crank (lever), angle lever, crank **-artig** bell-crank

winkelig angular

Winkel-instrument *n* goniometer, protractor **-kabelschuh** *m* hooked cable lug **-kaliber** *n* angle groove **-kante** *f* valance **-knie** *n* square or lodging knee **-komplement** *n* complement of angle **-konsole** *f* angle or wall bracket **-konstante** *f* wave-length constant, phase constant **-konstanz** *f* constancy of the interfacial angle **-konvergenz** *f* half-convergence error

Winkel-kopf *m* head of angle-measuring instrument, cross-staff head, head of static rod **-kran** *m* angle crane **-lage** *f* angularity, angular position **-lasche** *f* angular butt strap **-lehre** *f* protractor **-libelle** *f* optical level quadrant **-linie** *f* diagonal **-lineal** *n* bevel **-lot** *n* angle plumb

Winkelmaß *n* carpenter's square, angle measurement, angle-measuring instrument, phase angle, impedance angle, (unit) phase constant, wave-length constant, set square ~ **je Längeneinheit** wave-length constant

Winkel-maßkurve *f* phase-angle curve **-mast** *m* angle tower **-meßeinsatz** *m* angle measuring inset, protractor **-messend** goniometric

Winkelmesser *m* goniometer, protractor, astrolabe, clinometer, sextant, quadrant, theodolite ~ **für konvergierende Winkel** convergence-angle gauge

Winkelmesserebene *f* quadrant seat

Winkelmeß-genauigkeit *f* accuracy of angle measurement **-gerät** *n* angle-measuring instrument, protractor **-instrument** *n* goniometer, protractor **-okularkopf** *m* protractor ocular head **-teilkreis** *m* angle measuring inset circle

Winkel-messung *f* measurement of angle, goniometry **-minute** *f* one-sixtieth of one angular degree

winkeln (slang) to square

Winkel-nippel *m* elbow grease gun nipple **-optik** *f* elbow sight **-passer** *m* curvature bevel **-peilung** *f* determination of azimuth (bearing) or elevation **-pendel** *m* crank pendulum **-platte** *f* angle plate **-presse** *f* angle molding press **-prisma** *n* angle prism, prismatic square, rectangular prism **-profil** *n* angle section, angle shape **-punkt** *m* crank point, inflection point (of curve)

Winkel-rad *n* miter gear, angular wheel, angle or bevel wheel **-randig** beveled-edge **-raum** *m* angle space **-rechnung** *f* trigonometry **-recht** right-angled, rectangular, orthogonal **-reibahle** *f* angular reamer **-richtigkeit** *f* accuracy of angle **-riementrieb** *m* angle-belt drive **-ring** *m* angle ring **-rohranschluß** *m* angular pipe connection **-rohranschlußstück** *n* angular pipe coupling **-rohrschlüssel** *m* short-elbowed box spanner **-rohrstutzen** *m* angular pipe nipple

Winkel-schere *f* cranked scissors (for trimming wicks) **-schiene** *f* L strap **-schlauchstutzen** *m* angular hose connection **-schleifer** *m* angle sander **-schmiege** *f* sliding T-bevel **-schmiernippel** *m* angle grease nipple **-schnitt** *m* angular cut **-schraubenzieher** *m* offset screw driver

Winkel-sonde flow-angle indicator **-spannung** *f* angular strain **-spant** *n* square rib **-spaten** *m* angular spade **-sperrventil** *n* angle valve **-spiegel** *m* reflecting square, sextant, periscope **-sporen** *pl* angle lugs

Winkel-stahl *m* angle bracket **-stange** *f* angle pole **-stahlschiene** *f* angle steel bar **-stecker** *m* sparkplug **-stellung** *f* angular position, angularity **-stoß** *m* corner joint, angle joint, right-angle joint **-streichmaß** *n* scribing block **-stromverlust** *m* eddy-current loss

Winkel-stück (Rohr) *n* angle plate or elbow, pipe angle **-stütze** *f* angle bracket, supporting angle piece **-stutzen** *m* elbow nipple, stay **-stützmauer** *f* cantilever retaining wall **-summe** *f* sum of the angles

Winkel-tasthebel *m* crank contact lever **-tellerschleifer** *m* angular-type disc sander **-thermometer** *n* angle or bent thermometer **-tisch** *m* knee, angle table **-träger** *m* angle support **-treu** conformal, preserving angles unaltered, (of) equal angle, orthogonic **-treue** *f* conformity, congruity, correctness of the angles **-trieb** *m* angular drive, guide-pulley drive, angle drive **-trommel** *f* cylindrical cross-staff with divided circle

Winkel-übertragung *f* angle drive **-übertreibung** *f* excess angle **-übertreibungsbeiwert** *m* deviation coefficient **-unterschied** *m* angular difference **-untersetzungsgetriebe** *n* right angle speed reducer **-ventil** *n* angle check valve **-veränderliche** *f* angle of slip **-veränderung** *f* angular displacement **-verhältnis** *n* angular ratio **-verlagerung** *f* angular displacement **-verlaschung** *f* angle butt strap **-verschiebung** *f* angular displacement **-verschraubung** *f* threaded pipe angle **-versteifung** *f* angular reinforcement **-verstellung** *f* angular adjustment

Winkel-verteilung *f* angular distribution, distribution in angle **-verzahnung** *f* double helical teeth **-verzahnungsgetriebe** *n* double helical gear **-verzerrung** *f* angular distortion **-visier** *n* goniometric sight **-voreilung** *f* angular advance **-weg** *m* angle range

Winkelwert, den ~ **ablesen** to read off the angle

Winkelwulst *f* bulb angle

Winkelzahn *m* herringbone tooth, double helical tooth **-getriebe** *n* double helical gear **-rad** *n* herringbone wheel

Winkel-zielfernrohr *n* dial sight **-zielrohr** *n* elbow

telescope **-zug** *m* evasive maneuver
winken to signal with flags and rods
Winker *m* blinker light, signal light, flag signalman, signaler using a signal disk, signal arm or light indicating direction of turn **-arm** *m* direction indicator arm **-dienst** *m* wigwagging **-flagge** *f* signaling flag, semaphore flag control, signal flag **-kelle** *f* signaling disk **-rückstellschalter** *m* automatic return switch for direction indicator **-schalter** *m* direction indicator switch **-stab** *m* signaling disk **-vorschrift** *f* signal-communication manual **-zeichen** *n* wigwag signal, flag signal
Winkflagge *f* semaphore flag control, signal flag
winklig angular
Winkligkeit *f* angularity
Wink-spruch *m* semaphore message, message transmitted by signaling disk or hand signals **-stelle** *f* flag-signaling terminal **-verbindung** *f* visual communication by flag or hand signals **-zeichen** *n* hand or flag signal
Winter-ausrüstung *f* winter equipment **-beweglichkeit** *f* mobility in winter **-gewitter** *n* winter thunderstorm **-hafen** *m* harbor or basin provided for the protection of shipping from ice during the winter **-kettenglied** *n* oversize track shoe for operations in deep snow
Wintermonsun *m* winter monsoon
wintern to season, in winter
Wintersonnenwende *f* winter solstice
Winzermaschine *f* vintager's machine
winzig extremely small, minute, tiny, miniature
Wipp-auslegerkran *m* luffing crane **-bewegung** *f* luffing movement, rocking motion **-drehkran** *m* level-luffing crane
Wippe *f* counterpoise, balance, whip, rocker; (Dachwippe) porter bar; (Wipptisch) lifting table, tilting table
Wippen *n* luffing
Wipper *m* dumper, tipper
Wipp-kran *m* luffing or whipping crane **-säge** *f* jig saw **-schalter** *m* rocker-type switch **-tisch** *m* tilting table, tilter, tumbler **-vorrichtung** *f* tilting device (typewriter)
Wirbel *m* whirl; (Luft~) turbulence; (~ einer Kette) swivel, turbulence; eddy, vortex, twirl, whirlpool, rotation or curl (of a vector), umbo, spigot, collar, sheave, gyration, bolt, button, fastener, vertebra, whorl, peg (in string instrument) **gebundener ~** bound vortex **~ und Hornsignale** ruffles and flourishes (navy)
Wirbel-ablösung *f* shedding or separating of vortices **-achse** *f* axis of eddy or vortex **-auge** *n* swivel eye **-band** *n* vortex sheet **-belegung** *f* vortex distribution **-bewegung** *f* vortex motion, turbulent or whirling motion, eddy motion, eddying whirl
Wirbelbildung *f* turbulence, eddying, vorticity, spoiling effect **~ des Ladegemisches** induction swirl (aviation)
Wirbel-blatt *n* vortex sheet **-block** *m* swivel pulley **-bö** *f* gust due to eddy **-dichte** *f* curl or rotation (of a vector) **-diffusion** *f* diffusion of vorticity **-düse** *f* spineffect nozzle **-einfluß** *m* vorticity effect **-faden** *m* vortex filament **-feld** *n* rotational field **-fläche** *f* vortex or vorticity field, surface of discontinuity **-form** *f* vorticity formula
wirbelfrei irrotational, nonvertical, having parallel flow **-es Feld** irrotational field **-e Grenzschicht** laminar layer (aerodynamics) **-e Strömung** parallel flow, laminar flow
Wirbel-freiheit *f* irrotationality **-gabel** *f* swivel wrench **-gewitter** *n* cyclonic thunderstorm **-haken** *m* shackle or swivel hook **-hals** *m* swivel neck **-hebel** *m* bell crank
Wirbeligkeit *f* vorticity, eddying
Wirbel-kammer *f* centrifugal chamber; turbulence or whirling chamber **-kammermaschine** *f* turbulent-chamber engine **-kammermotor** *m* Diesel-engine with divided combustion **-kern** *m* vortex core, center, or nucleus **-leine** *f* rope coil **-leitwerk** *n* cyclone baffles **-linienstreckung** *f* vortex line stretching
wirbellos free from eddies, nonvertical **-e Strömung** flow free from vortices, eddies, or turbulence, irrotational flow
Wirbelmittelwertsatz *m* vorticity average theorem
wirbeln to whirl, eddy, spin, warble
Wirbel-punkt *m* point of discontinuity **-quelle** *f* vortex source (aerodynamics) **-satz** *m* vorticity theorem **-säule** *f* spine, spinal column **-schichttrockner** *m* fluidized bed drier **-schleppe** *f* vortex street or trail, wake, trailing vortex **-schuh** *m* whirler shoe **-senke** *f* sink (aerodynamics), sump (engin.) **-spindel** *f* swivel spindle **-stärke** *f* vorticity **-straße** *f* vortex path **-strecke** *f* extent of vortex sheet or discontinuity
Wirbelstrom *m* eddy current, whirlpool **-bremse** *f* eddy-current brake **-drehzahlmesser** *m* eddy-current revolution counter, tachometer **-ofen** *m* high-frequency furnace **-scheibe** *f* eddy-current or electromagnetic disk or plate
Wirbel-strömung *f* whirling, flowing, metal turbulence, turbulent flow **-stromverlust** *m* eddy-current loss **-stück** *n* stirrup (of boring apparatus) **-sturm** *m* cyclone, tornado, hurricane **-transporttheorie** *f* vorticity transport theory **-trommel** *f* high side drum
Wirbelung *f* eddy formation, vorticity, whirling, eddying, spinning, turbulence
Wirbel-verlust *m* spoiling loss **-walze** *f* induced resistance **-welle** *f* rotational wave **-wert** *m* vorticity **-wind** *m* whirlwind **-wirkung** *f* propelling action, whirling effect **-wulst** *m* burble fence (parachute) **-zone** *f* eddy zone **-zopf** *m* vortex train
Wirbler *m* centrifugal separator (high-duty)
Wirk-anteil *m* active or energy component **-bild** *n* functional diagram **-dämpfung** *f* transmission efficiency, transducer loss or gain
Wirkdruck *m* effective head, differential pressure **-geber** *m* differential pressure producer **-leitung** *f* differential-pressure transmission pipe **-wandler** *m* differential-pressure transmitter
Wirkeisen *n* searcher (blacksmith), paring knife
wirken to work, effect, operate, function, act, run, knit, perform, produce, knead, result in
Wirken *n* functioning, operation, performance, action
wirkend operating, acting
Wirkenergie *f* active energy
Wirkerei *f* knitting trade
Wirkfaktormesser *m* power factor meter
Wirkkomponente *f* active component, energy component, watt component, power component, in-phase component, real component,

dissipative component ~ **des Scheinwiderstandes** dissipative impedance

Wirk-laden *m* embossing batten **-leistung** *f* actual efficiency, effective efficiency, real or active power, true power, output (in watts) **-leistungsverbrauch** *m* active (or real) power consumption **-leistungszähler** *m* watt-hour meter, active-energy meter **-leitwert** *m* conductance, active admittance

wirklich real, genuine, true, effective, actual, indeed **-e Fluggeschwindigkeit** true air speed **-er Meridian** true meridian **-er Norden** true north **-er Schlupf** linear or true slip (propeller)

Wirklichkeit *f* reality, actuality

Wirklichkeits-fall *m* actual case **-flucht** *f* flight from reality **-maßstab** *m* original or true scale

Wirkmaschine *f* knitting or weaving frame, hosiery machine **-messer** *n* buttress (blacksmith), set hammer

wirksam active, efficient, efficacious, operative, powerful, effective, practicable **chemisch** ~ actinic

Wirksamkeit *f* efficacy, efficiency, effectiveness, activity, virtue **in** ~ **setzen** to render operative, throw in gear, start

Wirk-schema *n* actual or practical operating or working diagram **-spannung** *f* active voltage **spannungskomponente** *f* active component, energy component, power component, or in-phase component of the voltage

Wirkstoff *m* effective substance ~ **aus Seide** knit or woven tissue from silk

Wirkstrom *m* energy current, active current, watt component **-komponente** *f* active component, energy component, or in-phase component of the current

Wirk-stuhl *m* knitting frame **-teil** *m* active component, real component, conductive component

Wirk- und Strickmaschine *f* stitched-stuff and knitting machine

Wirk- und Strickwaren *pl* woven and knitted goods

Wirkung *f* effect, action, efficacy, effectiveness, result **eine** ~ **aufheben** to negate an effect, neutralize **in** ~ **setzen** to make effective **psychologische** ~ moral effect **schlechte** ~ inefficiency **seitliche** ~ lateral effect

Wirkungs-ablauf *m* action sequence (aut. contr) **-art** *f* characteristic of action **-aufhebend** neutralizing

Wirkungsbereich *m* radius of action or of effect, effective range, fuse range, zone of fire

Wirkungsdauer *f* persistency, duration of effect **chemische** ~ persistency of chemical agent

Wirkungsdruck, mittlerer ~ mean effective pressure

wirkungsfähig efficient

Wirkungs-feld *n* effective field **-feuer** *n* fire for effect **-funktion** *f* characteristic function **-gebiet** *n* service area **-gehalt** *m* effective content, (percentage) active content

Wirkungsgrad *m* efficiency, effect, effectiveness, output, strength, force ~ (Wärme) thermal efficiency ~ **einer Antenne** radiation efficiency of an aerial ~ **für eine gegebene Ebene** coefficient of utilization for a given surface ~ **nach Menge und nach Energie** quantity or energy efficiency **gesamter** ~ gross efficiency, over-all efficiency **optischer** ~ optical efficiency

Wirkungsgradbestimmung *f* efficiency test

Wirkungs-größe *f* action magnitude, action quantity **-halbmesser** *m* effective radius **-kraft** *f* efficiency **-kreis** *m* radius of action, effective radius, sphere of influence **-linie** *f* line of application (of a force), line of action, point of application, effective curve **-los** ineffective, inactive, inefficient **-losigkeit** *f* inefficiency, inefficacy, ineffectiveness **-prinzip** *n* action principle **-quantum** *n* action quantum **-querschnitt** *m* effective cross section or cross-sectional area, excitation cross section

Wirkungs-richtung *f* positive direction **-sinn** *m* sense or direction of force **-sphäre** *f* sphere of operation **-variable** *f* action variables **-vermögen** *n* working power **-voll** effective, efficacious **-weise** *f* mode of operation or action, performance, operation, operating characteristics **-wert** *m* effective value **-winkel** *m* angle of action **-zeit** *f* period or duration of action **-zusammenhang** *m* casual connection

Wirkverbindung *f* operative connection, work connection

Wirkverbrauchs-messer *m* active-power meter **-zähler** *m* watt-hour meter, energy meter

Wirkverstärkung *f* transducer loss or gain

Wirkwaren *pl* woven goods **-fertigung** *f* hosiery manufacture **-presserei** *f* hosiery pressing **-walke** *f* hosiery fulling

Wirkwert *m* effective or real component

Wirkwiderstand *m* effective resistance, real resistance, active resistance, nonreactive, dissipative, or ohm resistance **-verhältnis** *n* quality factor

Wirkzeit *f* reaction time

wirr confused, irregular

Wirtel *m* whorl (textiles)

Wirtschaft *f* economy

wirtschaften to manage

wirtschaftlich economic(al), commercial ~ **gestalten** to rationalize **-e Fertigung** economic production

Wirtschaftlichkeit *f* economy ~ **im Betrieb** economy of operation, effective power **Schaulinie** größtmöglicher ~ best economy curve

Wirtschaftlichkeitsfrage *f* question of economics

Wirtschafts-abkommen *n* commercial treaty **-ausschuß** *m* economic committee **-bau** *m* economic development **-führung** *f* exploitation, management **-gebäude** *n* farm building **-gerät** *n* household implement **-gruppe** *f* working committee **-hof** *m* farm-yard **-kraft** *f* economic power **-lehre** *f* economics **-politik** *f* economic policy, economics

wirtschaftspolitische Schwankung economical fluctuation

Wirtschaftspreßglas *n* utility pressed-glas

Wirtschafts-raum *m* living space, economic domain **-verhältnis** *n* economic conditions **-zentrum** *n* commercial center

Wischbeständigkeit *f* wipe resistance

wischecht fast to wiping

wischen to wipe

Wischer *m* wiper, stump, sponge **-achse** *f* windscreen wiper shaft **-blatt** *n* wiper blade **-schneide** *f* wiper blade

Wisch-gummi *n* wiper blade **-hebel** *m* wiper arm **-kontakt** *m* self-cleaning or self-wiping contact **-lappen** *m* mop
Wischpapier für Prägestempel die-wiping paper
Wisch-stock *m* cleaning rod, spongs staff **-strick** *m* pull-through rope (for gun cleaning) **-tuch** *n* dishcloth, duster, towel
Wismut(h) *n* bismuth **-arseniat** *n* bismuth arsenate **-bleierz** *n* schapbachite **-blende** *f* bismuth blende, eulytite **-blüte** *f* bismuth ocher, bismite
wismuten to solder with bismuth
Wismut-erz *n* bismuth ore **-gehalt** *m* bismuth content **-getränkt** bismuth loaded **-glanz** *m* bismuthinite, bismuth sulfide **-glätte** *f* bismuth litharge, bismuth oxide **-gold** *n* maldonite **-haltig** bismuthiferous, containing bismuth
Wismutit *m* bismutite
Wismutlot *n* bismuth solder
Wismut-jodid *n* bismuth iodide **-kobaltkies** *m* cheleutite **-kupfererz** *n* emplectite, wittichenite **-legierung** *f* bismuth alloy **-lot** *n* bismuth solder **-niederschlag** *m* bismuth precipitate, bismuth oxynitrate **-ocker** *m* bismuth ocher, bismite **-oxychlorid** *n* bismuth oxychloride
Wismut-oxyd *n* bismuth oxide, bismuth trioxide **-oxyjodid** *n* bismuth oxyiodide **-raffination** *f* bismuth refining **-salz** *n* bismuth salt **-säure** *f* bismuthic acid **-schwamm** *m* spongy bismuth **-silber** *n* schapbachite **-spat** *m* bismutite
Wismut-spirale *f* bismuth spiral **-subbenzoat** *n* bismuth subbenzoate **-subgallat** *n* bismuth subgallate **-subjodid** *n* bismuth oxyiodide **-subkarbonat** *n* bismuth subcarbonate **-tellur** *n* tetradymite, telluric bismuth **-verbindung** *f* bismuth compound **-weiß** *n* bismuth white
Wissen *n* knowledge
Wissensbereich *n* field of knowledge
Wissenschaft *f* science, learning
Wissenschaftler *m* scientist
wissenschaftlich scientific, scholarly **-er Versuch** experiment
wissentlich knowingly, deliberately, wilfully
Wirtherit *m* witherite, barium carbonate
Witterung *f* weather, temperature, atmospheric conditions
Witterungs-beständig weather-resisting **-einfluß** *m* atmospheric influence, exterior ballistics, exposure, meteorological effect or factor **-schutz** *m* protection against weather **-umschlag** *m* sudden change of weather **-unbilden** *pl* inclemency of the weather **-verhältnis** *n* weather condition **-versuch** *m* weathering test
W-Motor *m* twelve-cylinder inverted-W engine, arrow-type engine
Wobbel-bereich *m* sweep range **-frequenz** *f* wobbling frequency **-generator** *m* swept-frequency oscillator **-hub** *m* sweep hub **-meßsender** *m* sweep generator
wobbeln to sweep (radar) ~ (zur Verschlüsselung) to warble
Wobbeln *n* wobbling, warble
Wobbler *m* Warbler (radiotel.)
Wofatitfilter *n* Wofatite filter
Woge *f* large wave
wogen to wave, billow, surge
Wöhler-kurve *f* stress-N (cycles) graph **-linie** *f* Woehler-line, stress-cycle diagram **-prüfung** *f* rotary tension-compression **-schaubild** *n* Wöhler diagram, stress-N (cycles) graph **-versuch** *m* fatigue test
Wohl-geruch *m* scent, perfume **-Klang** *m* pleasing sound
wohlklingend melodious, sweet-sounding, sonorous, euphonious
Wohlordnungssatz *m* well-orderly theorem (math)
Wohn-gegend *f* residential district **-kammer** *f* body chamber (geol.) **-ort** *m* home, place of residence **-raum** *m* living room or space **-sitz** *m* legal or postal address, residence, domicile
Wohnungs-anschluß *m* residence telephone **-bau** *m* residential construction (or housing), home building **-beschaffung** *f* housing
wölben to arch, curve, vault, make arcuate, camber
Wölb-richtscheit *n* vaulting ruler **-ring** *m* upright shell
Wölbung *f* arch, curvature, crowning, vault, camber, buckling, arching, vaulting, convexity **äußere** ~ extrados
wölbungsfrei flat, uncurved, nonbuckled, flattened
Wölbungs-klappe *f* trailing-edge flap **-lage** *f* camber position **-messer** *m* spherometer **-radius** *m* disk radius, radius of crown **-veränderlich** variable camber **-verhältnis** *n* camber ratio **-zahl** *f* coefficient of curvature
Wölbwerkzeug *n* crowning tool
Wolf *m* iron lump or bloom, mincer
Wolfer *m* willower, deviler (cotton)
Wolfram *n* tungsten, wolframite **-blau** *n* wolfram blue, mineral blue **-bleierz** *n* stolzite, lead tungstate **-bogenlampe** *f* tungsten-arc lamp **-dichlorid** *n* tungsten dichloride **-dijodid** *n* tungsten di-iodide **-disulfid** *n* tungsten disulfide **-elektrode** *f* tungsten electrode **-erz** *n* tungsten ore
Wolframat *n* tungstate
Wolframfaden *m* tungsten filament, tungsten wire **thorhaltiger** ~, **thorierter** ~ thoriated tungsten filament **wiederbelebter** ~ reactivated tungsten filament
Wolfram-gelb *n* yellow tungsten bronze **-haltig** tungsteniferous, containing tungsten
Wolframid *n* tungstide
Wolframit *m* wolframite
Wolfram-karbid *n* tungsten carbide **-ocker** *m* tungstic ocher, tungstite **-präparat** *n* tungsten preparation **-salz** *n* tungsten salt, tungstate **-säure** *f* tungstic acid, wolframic acid **-säureanhydrid** *n* tungstic anhydride **-säuresalz** *n* tungstic acid salt, tungstate
wolframsaures Ammonium ammonium tungstate ~ **Eisenmangan** ferromanganese tungstate ~ **Natron** sodium tungstate
Wolfram-silicid *n* tungsten silicide **-stahl** *m* tungsten steel **-stickstoff** *m* tungsten nitride **-sulfid** *n* tungsten sulfide **-tetrajodid** *n* tungsten tetraiodide **-trioxyd** *n* tungsten trioxide, tungstic acid
Wolfs-grube *f* obstacle pit **-ofen** *m* wolf furnace **-stahl** *m* natural steel **-zahn** *m* gullet tooth (saw)
Wolken-ausnutzung *f* making use of clouds **-automat** *m* automatic cloud instrument **-bank** *f* cloud bank **-ballen** *m* ball cloud **-basis** *f* base of the clouds **-bildung** *f* cloud formation, clouding **-bruch** *m* cloudburst **-decke** *f* cloud cover or

layer **-dichtemesser** *m* cloud-density measurement apparatus **-elektrizität** *f* cloud or atmospheric electricity **-feld** *n* cloud bank **-fetzen** *m* scud **-flug** *m* cloud flight **-formen** *pl* cloud forms **-frei** cloudiness
Wolkenhöhe *f* cloud height, ceiling **unbegrenzte ~** ceiling unlimited
Wolken-höhenmesser *m* cloud altimeter
Wolkenhöhen-meßscheinwerfer *m* light-beam projector (for determining ceiling of clouds) **-nullpunkt** *n* ceiling zero
Wolken-kappe *f* cloud cap **-karte** *f* cloud map **-kopf** *m* summit or top of the cloud **-kragen** *m* vault of cloud, arched squall **-kratzer** *m* skyscraper **-kunde** *f* nephelogy **-los** clear, cloudless **-masse** *f* cloud mass **-meer** *n* sea of clouds **-messung** *f* cloud measurement
Wolken-papier *n* fleecy paper **-rechen** *m* cloud rake **-schatten** *m* cloud shadow, shadow bank **-scheinwerfer** *m* cloud searchlight, ceiling light **-schicht** *f* cloud layer **-schleier** *m* clouds, haze **-schweif** *m* vapor trail **-segeln** *n* cloud soaring **-spiegel** *m* nepheloscope, cloud reflector or mirror **-streifen** *m* cloud banner
Wolken-tuch *n* banner cloud **-turm** *m* towering cloud **-untergrenze** *f* base of cloud **-wand** *f* bank of clouds **-zone** *f* troposphere **-zug** *f* cloud train or motion **-zugmesser** *m* nepheloscope
wolkig cloudy or broken (said of sky)
Wolkigkeit (Trübheit) *f* cloudiness
Wollabfall *m* wool waste
Wollastondraht *m* Wollaston wire
Wollastonit *m* wollastonite
Wollastonprisma *n* Wollaston prism
Woll-atlas *m* woolen satin **-aufbereitungsmaschine** *f* wool-dressing machine **-aufleger** *m* wool supplier **-baum** *m* silk-cotton tree **-beuteltuch** *n* woolen bolting cloth **-bleicher** *m* wool bleacher **-decke** *f* wool blanket **-druckerei** *f* printing of wool fabrics
Wolle *f* wool, cotton (in lacquer terminology) **~ abgiften** to loosen wool by arsenic **nitrierte ~** nitrocotton
Wollentschweißung *f* wool scouring
Wolleverwertungsanlage *f* wool-utilizing plant
Wollfett *n* degras **-gewinnungsanlage** *f* wool-grease extracting plant, yolk-producing plant
Woll-filz *m* wool felt **-filzschirm** *m* woollen felt screen **-garnfett** *n* wool-yarn grease
wollig fleecy, woolly
Woll-kotze *f* rough woolen blanket **-kratze** *f* wool card **-krempel** *m* finishing wool card **-industrie** *f* woolen industry **-sackabsonderung** *f* pillow jointing (geol.) **-schweiß** *m* wool yolk **-stärkemesser** *m* eriometer **-zupfmaschine** *f* burr- or wool-picking machine
Woltmannscher Flügel Woltmann's sailwheel
Woodmetall *n*, **Woodsches Metall** Wood's alloy
Woolffsche Flasche Woolff's bottle
Wootzstahl *m* wootz steel
Wort-abschneidung *f* clipping, obliteration, or mutilation of words (in telephony) **-abstand** *m* interword space **-angaben** *pl* annotations **-entschlüsselung** *f* word decoding
Wörterverstümmelung *f* clipping or obliteration (of words)
Wort-feldgrenze *f* word field limit **-länge** *f* capacity (comput.) **-laufzeit** *f* word time (comput.) **-laut** *m* text, wording **-leitung** *f* word line
wörtlich verbal, verbatim, literal
Wort-marke *f* word mark **-schatz** *m* vocabulary **-verständlichkeit** *f* word intelligibility **-verstümmelung** *f* clipping **-zähler** *m* word counter **-zeichen** *n* word trade mark **-zwischenraum** *m* space between words
Wrack *n* wreck, derelict **-boje** *f* wreck buoy **-guß** *m* spoiled casting **-signal** *n* wreck signal **-tonne** *f* wreck buoy
Wringeisen *n* wringing pole
wringen to wring out
Wringer *m* wringer
Wringfleck *m* stain caused by wringing
Wringholz wringing pin or stick
Wucherung *f* growth
Wuchs *m* growth
Wucht-baum *m* ram, lifter **-förderer** *m* reciprocating plate feeder
wuchtig vigorous, powerful
Wucht-kraft *f* inertia force **-steigerer** *m* dynamic expander
wühlen to dig, root, stir up
Wulfenit *m* wulfenite
Wulst *m* elevation, bead, bulb, roll, torus, beading, bulge, reinforcement, core **vorspringender ~** projecting edge (R.R.)
Wulst-band *n* rim band **-eisen** *n* bulb iron **-felge** *f* clincher rim (wheel) **-flosse** *f* flange fin, inflatable fin **-förmig** toroidal, doughnut-shaped **-gestänge** *n* rods with shoulder
wulstig stuffed (seam)
Wulstkern-belag *m* bead covering **-maschine** *f* bead-covering machine **-kumulus** *m* cumulostratus (clouds)
wulstlos ridgeless **-e Naht** ridgeless seam **-e Nahtschweißung** ridgeless-seam welding
Wulst-maschine *f* embossment machine **-naht** *f* reinforced seam or weld **-profil** *n* bulb angle **-rand** *m* beaded edge **-reifen** *m* clincher tire, heel tire **-rohrkondensator** *m* beaded-rim tubular capacitor **-schneidemaschine** *f* debeader **-schutzstreifen** *m* chafer **-stab** *m* beaded bar **-vorrichtung** *f* beading device **-winkeleisen** *n* bulb angle iron
Wundererde *f* lithomarge
Wunderlich-Röhre *f* Wunderlich valve
Wund-haken *m* retractor, wound hook **-klammer** *f* suture clip **-randhalter** *m* retractor **-verband** *m* dressing, bandage
Wünschel-rute *f* divining rod, dowsing rod **-rutengänger** *m* dowser, diviner
Wurf *m* projection, throw **-antenne** (Radio) *f* throw-out aerial **-art** *f* type of bomb release **-bahn** *f* trajectory **-beschicker** *m* sprinkler, stoker **-bewegung** *f* projectile motion **-bild** *n* projected image **-blei** *n* sounding lead
Würfel *m* cube, die, capsule, pellet, hexahedron **-alaun** *n* cubic alum **-antenne** *f* cubical antenna **-brikett** *n* cubeshaped briquette
Würfelchen *n* small cube **Abbesches ~** Abbe drawing cube
Würfel-eck *n* corner of cube, cubic summit (cryst.) **-einsatz** (Kühlschrank) *m* cube insert (refrigerator) **-festigkeit** *f* cubic strength, crushing strength of a cube **-förmig** cubic, cubical **-gambir** *n* cube gambier **-gitter** *n*

cubical lattice
würfelig cubic, checkered, tessular
Würfel-kohle *f* cobbles **-ladung** *f* powder charge of cubical shape **-muster** *n* check pattern (diamond or dice pattern)
würfeln to checker
Würfel-nickel *n* nickel cubes **-pulver** *n* prismatic powder, perforated-disk powder **-spule** *f* cube-shaped coil **-werk** *n* checkerwork (of gas producer)
Wurf-feuerung *f* spreader stoker **-förderer** *m* thrower **-förderung** *f* reciprocating plate feeding **-gerät** *n* projector, throwing device **-geschoß** *n* missile **-höhe** *f* height of projection or throw **-körper** *m* projectile **-kraft** *f* projectile force **-ladung** *f* propelling charge **-lehre** *f* ballistics
Wurfleine *f* heaving line
Wurfleinenkanone *f* line-throwing gun
Wurf-linie *f* trajectory, line or curve of projection **-netz** *n* sweep or casting net **-parabel** *f* bomb trajectory, trajectory parabola **-pfeil** *m* dart **-rad** *n* scoop wheel **-rahmen** *m* framework-type projector for high explosive or incendiary rockets **-wanderrost** *m* spreader-type travelling grate **-schaufel** *f* casting shovel, hand scoop **-weite** *f* range (phys.), forward travel, bomb ballistics, bombing range, mortar range, throwing range **-zahl** *f* ballistic coefficient
Würgebohrung *f* tapered bore, choke
Würgebund *m* twist joint (elec. line)
Würgeisen *n* twist iron
Würgekette *f* twist chain
Würgeklemme *f* twist clamp
Würgelpumpe *f* semirotary pump, wing pump
würgen to twirl
Würgerille *f* crimp in cartridge case
Würgestelle *f* twisted joint (unsoldered) **die ~ umbiegen** to bend back twisted ends of wires
Würge-verbindung *f* twist(ed) joint **-zange** *f* clamping pliers, cap crimper
Würgung *f* crimp
Wurm *m* worm (endless screw)
wurmähnlich helical
Würmerkriechen *n* swarming (motion pictures)
Wurm-getriebe *n* worm gear **-löcher** *pl* wormy or washed surface (defects on surfaces of castings) **-rad** *n* worm wheel, worm gear **-stichig** worm-eaten
Wurst *f* sausage, fascine poles **-förmig** toric, tire-shaped **-füllmaschine** *f* sausage machine
Würtel *m* whorl (textiles)
Würze *f* spice, flavoring, seasoning, wort **-ablauf-apparat** *m* wort-drawing apparatus **-kühler** *m* wort cooler
Wurzel *f* root, radix, radical, root face (welding) **~ ziehen** extraction of roots **die ~ des Luftschraubenflügels** blade root **zweite ~** square root **dritte ~** cube root, third power root **~ der Streuung** standard deviation
Wurzel-abstand *m* root gap **-ende** *n* root end **-exponent** *m* radical index, index of a root
Wurzelgröße *f* radical **~ eines Ringes** root element of a ring
Wurzel-kerbe *f* root gap **-lage** (-raupe) *f* root layer **-linie** *f* center line of rivet holes **-maß** *n* gauge distance, distance from rivet center to outside of angle **-platte** *f* anchor plate **-raupe** *f* root bead **-röhrchen** *n* rootlet tube **-schneider** *m* root cutter **-tiefe** *f* root chord **-torf** *m* fibrous peat, surface peat **-zeichen** *n* root sign, radical
Wurtzit-gitter *n* wurtzite lattice **-typ** *m* wurtzite-structure
Wüste *f* desert
Wüsten-gebiet *n* desert belt (geol.) **-sand** *m* desert sand **-sturm** *m* desert storm **-untersuchung** *f* desert test

X

X-Achse *f* X axis, axis of the abscissas
X-Amplitude *f* X-amplitude
Xanthanwasserstoff *m* hydroxanthane
Xanthat *n* xanthate
Xanthein *n* xanthein
Xanthen *n* xanthene
Xanthin *n* xanthine
Xanthit *m* xanthite
Xanthogallolsäure *f* xanthogallolic acid
Xanthogen *n* xanthogen
Xanthogenat *n* xanthate, xanthogenate
Xanthogen-oxyd *n* xanthic oxide **-säure** *f* xanthogenic acid
xanthogensaures Kalium potassium xanthogenate
Xanthonfarbstoff *m* xanthone coloring matter
X-Band *n* x-band (rdr)
X-Betrieb *m* X-operation
X-Einheit *f* unit of wave length for X rays
Xenolith *m* xenolite
xenomorph xenomorphic
Xenonblasenkammer *f* xenon bubble chamber
Xenotim *m* xenotime
Xerographie *f* xerography
X-Formmotor *m* X-type engine
X-geschnitten X-cut, X-shaped
X-Glied *n* (Kreuzglied) lattice section
X-Lochung *f* eleven-punch, X-punch
X-Motor *m* X-type engine, four-in-line engine
X-Schnitt *m* X-cut, normal-cut
X-Stoß *m* double-V (butt) joint
X-Stoßnaht *f* double-V groove
X-Strahl *m* X ray
X-Teilchen *n* x-particle
Xylidin *n* xylidine **-chlorhydrat** *n* xylene hydrochloride, xylidine hydrochloride
Xylo-graph *m* xylographer **-graphie** *f* xylography **-hydrochinon** *n* xylohydroquinone
Xylol *n* xylene, xylol
Xylolith-wand *f* partition wall of xylolite **-waren** *pl* xylolite goods, artificial wood articles
Xylometer *n* xylometer
Xylonit *m* xylonite
Xylonsäure *f* xylonic acid
Xyloplastik *f* xyloplastic
Xylose *f* xylose
Xylylsäure *f* xylic acid

Y

Y-Achse *f* Y axis, axis of the ordinates, lateral or transverse axis, time base
Yachtbau *m* yacht and small-boat building
Yangonasäure *f* yangona acid
Yard *n* yard **-maß** *n* yardstick
Yenit *m* yenite, ilcaite
Y-förmig Y-shaped
Y-geschnitten Y-cut
Y-Kettenverstärker *m* distributed vertical amplifier
Y-Kopplung *f* wye junction
Y-Legierungen *pl* hiduminium
Y-Nadel *f* Y needle
Yohimboasäure *f* yohimboa acid
Yperit *n* mustard gas, yperite
Y-Rohr *n* Y tube, Y pipe
Y-Schaltung *f* star-connected or Y-connected threephase system with neutral Y or star connection
Y-Schnitt *m* parallel cut or Y-cut
Ysop *m* hyssop
Y-Strebe *f* Y-strut, forked strut
Ytterbin *n*, **-erde** *f* ytterbia
Ytterbit *m* ytterbite, gadolinite
Ytterbium *n* ytterbium **-karbonat** *n* ytterbium carbonate
Ytter-erde *f* yttria, yttrium oxide **-flußspat** *m* yttrocerite **-haltig** yttriferous, yttric **-oxyd** *n* yttrium oxide, yttria **-salz** *n* yttrious salt **-spat** *m* xenotime, yttrium phosphate
Yttrialith *n* yttrialite
Yttrium *n* yttrium **-azetat** *n* yttrium acetate **-karbid** *n* yttrium carbide **-verbindung** *f* yttrium compound
Yttro-fluorit *m* yttrofluorite **-gummit** *m* yttrogummite **-ilmenit** *m* samarskite, yttroilmenite **-krasit** *m* yttrocrasite **-tantalit** *m* yttrotantalite **-titanit** *m* yttrotitanite **-zerit** *m* yttrocerite
Yucon *n* Yukawa particle, heavy electron (barytron, mesotron)
Yukawa-Potential *n* Yukawa potential

Z

Z-Abschluß *m* match-determination
Z-Achse *f* normal or vertical axis
Zacke *f*, **Zacken** *m* prong, tooth, jag, scallop, edging, plate, bedplate, serration, radar flip **feste(r)** ~ pip, blip, permanent echo (rdr)
Zackeisen *n* toothing iron
zacken to furnish with points, scallop
Zacken-ausstecher *m* pinking punch **-blende** *f* vane with serrated or triangular edge, triangular aperture **-förmig** toothed, pronged, jagged **-linie** *f* notched or serrated line **-marke** *f* pointed mark (stencil) **-messer** *n* serrated knife **-rad** *n* picot edge (textiles) **-reihe** *f* line of teeth **-rolle** *f* sprocket wheel **-schrift** *f* variable-width sound recording, variable-area optical sound-on-film **-tonspurbreite** *f* breadth of variable-area sound track **-trommel** *f* sprocket drum, sprocket wheel
zackig toothed, indented, jagged, serrated, ragged **am Rande ~ ausschneiden** to scallop
Zaggel *m*, *f* billet (metal.)
zäh, (zähe) viscous, tenacious, cohesive, stringy, tough, stubborn, ductile **~ machen** to toughen **~ werden** to toughen, grow fat (soap) **-e Schlacke** tough clinken **-es Gefüge** tough texture
Zähegrad *m* viscosity
Zäh-eisen *n* toughened iron **-festig** tenacious **-festigkeit** *f* toughness, tenacity, strength **-fluß** *m* viscosity
zähflüssig viscous **-e Schlacke** sticky or viscous slag, semipasty slag, soft clinker
Zähflüssigkeit *f* viscosity, viscousness, refractoriness, sluggishness, viscidity
zähgepoltes Kupfer tough-pitch copper
Zähigkeit *f* toughness, tenacity, ductility, viscosity, viscousness
Zähigkeits-beiwert *m* coefficient of viscosity **-einheit** *f* poise unit of viscosity **-grad** *m* viscosity **-index** *m* viscosity index **-kehrwert** *m* inverse of viscosity, fluidity **-maß** *n* measure of ductility **-messer** *m* viscosimeter **-probe** *f* toughness test, toughness-test specimen **-prüfmaschine** *f* toughness-testing machine **-verlust** *m* viscous loss (acoust.) **-versuch** *m* toughness test **-ziffer** *f* toughness index
Zähkupfer *n* tough-pitch copper
Zahl *f* number, factor, coefficient, numeral, figure, amount **eine ~ abrunden** to express in round numbers **eine ~ einstellen** to set up a number (on a key set) **der ~ nach** numerical
Zahl, aufgehende ~ rational number or quantity **beliebige ~** random number (comput.) **dreistellige ~** three-figure number, three-place number **eingeklammerte ~** number in brackets **ganze ~** integer, integral number **gerade ~** even number **gebrochene ~** fractional number **reelle ~** real number **reine ~** abstract number **unbenannte ~** indefinite number **ungerade ~** odd number
Zahl, Machsche ~ ratio of flow velocity to the velocity of sound, Mach number **~ veränderlicher Länge** multi-lenth number
Zählader *f* pilot wire, marked wire, meter wire
Zähladernpaar *n* key pair, pilot pair, marked pair
zahlbar payable **~ bei Lieferung** cash on delivery
zählbar computable, countable
Zahl-bereich *m* capacity (info proc.) counter range (atom) **-blatt** *n* payroll
Zähl-betrag *m* counted amount **-betragsdrucker**

m data printer **-brett** *n* counter **-dekade** *f* counting decade **-einrichtung** *f* counting device, counter **-einschub** *m* counting unit
zahlen to pay
zählen to meter, record (on a meter), count
Zahlen-angabe *f* parameter, numerical date **-aussprache** *f* enunciation of numbers **-beispiel** *n* numerical example, illustration of a problem in which actual figures are given **-blank** *n* figure space, figure blank (teleg.)
zahlend paying **-er Kurzflug** pay hop **-e Last, -e Nutzlast** pay load
Zahlen-darstellung *f* numerical notation **-drücker** *m* data printer **-druckvorrichtung** *f* number printer **-ebene** *f* plane of complex numbers, Gaussian plane **-erfaßbar** numerically evaluable **-folge** *f* numerical order, sequence of numbers
Zahlengeber *m* impuls transmitter (supervisory control), key sender **-platz** *m* key-pulsing or key-sending position, semimechanical position **-prüfeinrichtung** *f* sender test device
Zahlen-größe *f* numerical quantity **-gruppe** *f* word (comput.) **-komplex** *m* complex of figures **-körper** *m* number field (math.) **-lehre** *f* arithmetic, numerology **-lochmaschine** *f* number perforating machine **-lochstreifen** *m* number perforating machine **-lochstreifen** *m* number tape **-lochung** *f* digit punching
zahlenmäßig numerical ~ **ausdrücken** to evaluate **-e Aufstellung** tabulation **-e Menge** number set
Zahlen-punze *f* figure punch **-raum** *m* space of numbers (math.) **-reihe** *f* series **-rolle für Zählwerke** cipher roll for counters **-rollenwerk** *n* number barrel mechanism **-system** *n* number system (comput.)
Zahlentafel *f* table (of figures), numerical table or tabulation **in ~ zusammengestellte Werte** tabular data
Zahlen-tripel *n* number triple(t) **-umschaltung** *f* figure shift **-verhältnis in Form einer unbenannten Zahl** nondimensional ratio **-wechsel** *m* figure shift **-weiß** *n* figure blanc
Zahlenwert *m* numerical value **absoluter ~** nondimensional quantity, nondimensional ratio
Zahlenwurm *m* subtractor cipher
Zähler *m* numerator, counter, recorder, meter, register ~ **für direkten Anschluß** whole-current meter ~ **für die Besetzt- und Verlustfälle** overflow register ~ **mit Höchstverbrauchsangabe** maximum-demand indicator ~ **mit schreibendem Höchstverbrauchsanzeiger** maximum-demand recorder ~ **mit Münzeinwurf** prepayment meter ~ (Durchfluß) **für Summenfernmessung** remote summation meters ~ **für Wanderanschluß** transformer-operated meter **binärer ~** scale of two circuit
Zähler-ablesung *f* meter reading **-anker** *m* meter armature **-anzeige** *f* count **-batterie** *f* meter battery **-betriebsspannung** *f* counter operating voltage **-bucht** *f* bay of registers **-eicheinrichtung** *f* meter-calibrating equipment **-eichsaal** *m* calibrating room for meters, counter calibrating room **-eingang** *m* counter entry
Zahlergebnis *n* peg-count summary
Zähler-gehäuse *n* meter case or box **-gestell** *n* (service) meter rack **-grundplatte** *f* meter base
Zähler-konstante *f* constant of a meter **-kontrolllampe** *f* meter lamp **-kontrollzeichen** *n* meter indicator **-leerlauf** *m* meter creeping **-platte** *f* board for meters **-prüfeinrichtung** *f* meter-calibrating equipment **-relais** *n* meter relay **-schaltuhr** *f* meter change-over clock **-schrank** *m* meter cupbourd **-schreibung** *f* counter list
Zählerstandsaufnahme, Tag der ~ end of billing period
Zählerstellen, direkt saldierende ~ counter positions (net balance)
Zähler-tafel *f* meter board **-taste** *f* meter or register key **-transport** *m* movement of the counter **-überspannung** *f* counter overvoltage **-überwachungslampe** *f* meter lamp (teleph.) **-umschaltrelais** *n*, **-umschaltwerk** *n* discriminator **-verzögerung** *f* counter time lag **-werk** *n* train of wheels **-zündspannung** *f* counter starting potential
Zähl-faktor *m* scaling factor **-frequenz** *f* counting rate **-gebiet** *n* counter range **-gerät** *n* integrating apparatus **-gerätekanal** *m* counter tube channel **-geschwindigkeit** *f* counting rate
Zählglocke des Zeilenzählers alarm bell of line-counting machine
Zählimpuls *m* meter pulse (tel.), counting pulse **-relais** *n* metering relay
Zählkammer *f* counting chamber
Zahl-kasse *f* cash register **-kassenquittungsdrucker** *m* cash register for sales slips
Zähl-kette *f* counting chain of relays **-kopf** *m* meter head **-körper** *m* number field
Zahllast *f* pay load
Zähl-loch *n* sprocket or feed hole **-rad** *n* notch wheel, counter wheel
zahlreich numerous
Zählrelais *n* meter(ing) relay, register
Zählrohr *n* counter tube ~ **mit Abschirmung** shielded Geiger tube
Zählrohr-anschlußkabel *n* high voltage cable **-auslösungszeit** *f* counter resolving time **-blende** *f* Geiger tube shutter **-eichung** *f* counter calibration **-halterung** *f* Geiger tube holding assembly **-schutzkappen** *pl* Geiger probes
Zahlschalter *m* ticket window, shutter
Zählscheibe *f* recording disk **-stopp** *m* stop in counting
Zählstrichspeicheraufzeichnung *f* scratch pad storage
Zählstufe *f*, **binäre ~** binary counter, flip-flop circuit
Zahltag *m* pay day
Zähl-tafel *f* differential counting chart **-taste** *f* meter or register key
Zahlüberwachungslampe *f* register pilot lamp
Zähl-uhr *f* measuring counter **-umfang** *m* count(ing) capacity
Zahlung *f* payment ~ **auffordern** to press for payment, dun ~ **einstellen** to suspend payment ~ **gegen Lieferung** cash on delivery ~ **für Rechnung** payment to account
Zählung *f* metering, registering, counting, count, computation, calculation ~ **der Zeitdauer** time metering, timing ~ **durch Spannungserhöhung** booster-battery metering ~ **durch Stichproben** peg count ~ **durch Stromumkehr** reverse-battery metering
Zahlungs-aufschub *m* respite of payment **-ausgleich** *m* balance of payments in clearing

-bedingungen *f pl* terms or conditions of payment **-einstellung** *f* suspension of payment **-empfänger** *m* payee **-fähig** solvent **-mittel** *n* legal tender **-pflicht** *f* obligation to pay

Zahlungs-sperre *f* stopping of payment **-termin** *m* date of payment **-unfähig** insolvent **-unfähigkeit** *f* insolvency **-verbot** *n* prohibition of payment **-weise** *f* mode of payment

Zähl-unterdrückung *f* non-metering, non-registering **-verhinderungsrelais** *n* non-metering relay **-vorgang** *m* counting run **-vorrichtung** *f* counting mechanism **-waage** *f* counting weigher **-walze** *f* counting roll

Zählwerk *n* counter, register, meter **~ mit Zeiger** computer with pointer **~ mit springenden Ziffern** counter with click action

Zählwerk-deckel *m* counter cover **-gehäuse** *n* meter housing, dial housing **-rad** *n* counter wheel **-zifferblatt** *n* counter dial

Zahl-würfel *m* integrating cube **-zeichen** *n* numeral **-zettel** *m* dummy ticket (for statistical purposes)

Zahn *m* tooth (engin.), cog, prong **~ und Trieb** rack and pinion **~ und Triebbewegung** coarse and fine adjustment (of microscope) **eingesetzter ~** cog **gefräster ~** milled tooth **gegossener ~** cast tooth **gehobelter ~** planed tooth **geschnittener ~** cut tooth **schwalbenschwanzförmiger ~** dovetail indent **spielfreigefräster ~** tooth milled free from backlash **mit Zähnen versehen** toothed, studded

Zahnabrundfräsmaschine für Zahnräder tooth-chamfering machine for toothed wheels

Zahn-angriffstiefe *f* working depth of tooth **-anker** *m* toothed ring armature **-anlage** *f* tooth pressure **-balken** *m* indented beam

Zahnbogen *m* toothed segment or quadrant tooth sector **-richtmaschine** *f* ratchet-gear mechanism **-taster** *m* back-calipers

Zahnbreite *f* width or breadth of tooth, tooth pitch

Zahnbrust *f* (e. Fräsers) tooth face **-winkel** *m* tooth face angle

Zahn-bürste *f* toothbrush **-dicke** *f* tooth thickness

Zahndruck *m* tooth pressure **-dynamometer** *n* gear dynamometer

Zahn-eingriff *m* mesh (of tooth) **-eingriffswinkel** *m* pressure angle **-einschnitt** *m* notch **-eisen** *n* toothed chisel

zähneln to tooth, indent, denticulate, notch, mill, knurl

Zähnelung *f* serration

Zahnflächeneingriff *m* surface contact of the tooth

Zahnflanken *pl* flanks of a tooth, teeth surfaces **-schleifmaschine** *f* tooth-flank grinding machine **-spiel** *n* backlash of teeth

Zahnform *f* tooth profile **-fräser** *m* gear cutter **-vorfräser** *m* stocking cutter

Zahn-fräser *m* cutter for gear wheels **-fuß** *m* dedendum, root or shoulder of tooth **-fußabrundung** *f* root clearance **-fußtiefe** *f* depth of tooth below pitch line **-gabel** *f* cogged fork **-gesamthöhe** *f* whole depth of tooth **-gesperre** *n* ratchet and pawl **-gummi** *n* dental rubber **-heilkunde** *f* dentistry

Zahnhöhe *f* depth of tooth **wirksame ~** working depth of tooth

zahnig toothed

Zahninduktion *f* tooth induction

Zahnkanten-eingriff *m* tip contact of the tooth **-fräsmaschine** *f* chamfering machine

Zahnkette *f* gear chain **~ mit Gleitgelenk** silent or inverted tooth chain with pin link

Zahnketten-rad *n* sprocket wheel **-trieb** *m* link-belt chain drive

Zahnkopf *m* addendum, tip of tooth, face **-abrundung** *f* crest clearance **-höhe** *f* addendum **-kante** *f* edge of the tooth crest **-kreis** *m* circle which touches all extreme points of gears

Zahnkopplung *f* gear coupling

Zahnkranz *m* gear rim, toothed rim, ring gear, spur gear, toothed wheel **-abstand** *m* gear ring clearance **-drehvorrichtung** *f* toothed-rim turning arrangement **-durchdrehanlasser** *m* gear ring cranking starter **-flanke** *f* gear ring profile or face **-futter** *n* gear-wheel rim chuck **-kopfkreisdurchmesser** *m* diameter of gear ring addendum circle

Zahnkranz-nabe *f* gear ring hub **-lenkung** *f* worm-and-sector steering system **-pendelanlasser** *m* gear-ring rocker starter **-planscheibe** *f* gear-driven faceplate **-schwungkraftanlasser** *m* gear-ring inertia starter

Zahn-kreisteilung *f* circular pitch **-krümmungssinn eines Spiralkegelrades** hand of spiral gear **-kugelkopfmeißel** *m* differential bit **-kuppelung** *f* jaw clutch coupling, gear coupling, gear drive **-kurve** *f* tooth curve **-länge** *f* tooth pitch **-latte** *f* rack **-leisten** *pl* serrated slats **-lücke** *f* space or gap of tooth **-lückenbreite** *f* width of tooth space **-lückenwinkel** *m* gashing angle **-luft** *f* backlash of teeth

Zahn-meßlehre *f* tooth-measuring gauge **-meßschieblehre** *f* gear-toothed vernier **-meßschraublehre** *f* gear-toothed calipers **-meßschublehre** *f* gear-toothed vernier **-mittenlinie** *f* middle line of tooth **-motor** *m* drum motor **-paar** *n* pair of teeth

Zahnrad *n* gear wheel, cogwheel, sprocket, gear, pinion, spur wheel **~ mit Evolventenverzahnung** involute gear **~ für Geschwindigkeitsabstufung** reduction gear **~ zur Höhenstellung des Armes** elevating screw gear **~ mit Stufenzähnen** wheel with stepped teeth **~ mit innerer Verzahnung** annular toothed wheel **~ mit Winkelzähnen** mortise wheel **~ mit Zykloidenverzahnung** cycloidal toothed gear **Zähne in ein ~ einsetzen** to cog

Zahnrad, ein- und ausrückbares ~ sliding gear **gerades ~** spur pinion **geteiltes ~** split gear **konisches ~** bevel pinion **verschiebbares ~** sliding gear

Zahnrad-abteilung *f* gear cutting division **-abwälzfräser** *m*, **-abwälzfräsmaschine** *f* gear hobber **-antrieb** *m* gear drive **-auslösung** *f* cogwheel escapement **-bahn** *f* rack or cog railway **-brücke** *f* geared hind axle **-büchse** *f* gear sleeve **-entgratmaschine** *f* gear deburring machine

Zahnräder-abrundmaschine *f* gear-toothed chamfering machine **-bearbeitungsmaschine** *f* toothed-wheels milling machine

Zahnrädergetriebe *n* toothed-wheel gearing, gear, change gear **~ mit gekreuzten Wellen** skew gearing

Zahnräder-getriebegehäuse *n* gear case or housing **-laufprüfmaschine** *f* machine for testing the silent running of toothed wheels **-prüfapparat** *m* gear-testing apparatus **-schneiden** *n* toothed-gear cutting **-teilkopf** *m* gear dividing head, dividing head for toothed wheels **-werk** *n* toothed-wheel work, gear

Zahnrad-feinbewegung *f* cogwheel slow motion, slow-motion gear **-fett** *m* gear grease, pinion grease **-flaschenzug** *m* geared chain hoist, geared chain block **-formmaschine** *f* gear-wheel molding machine **-fräser** *m* gear cutter **-fräsmaschine** *f* gear hobbing, gear shaper **-gehäuse** *n* gear case or box **-getriebe** *n* gear drive, gearing, toothed-wheel gearing **-härtemaschine** *f* toothed-wheel-tempering machine **-hobelmaschine** *f* gear cutting slotter

Zahnrad-kammer *f* gear housing **-kasten** *m* gear box **-körper** *m* gear blank **-kranz** *m* rim of toothed wheel **-kupplung** *f* gear-type clutch **-nabe** *f* gear hub

Zahnradölpumpe *f* gear(-type) oil pump **getriebenes Rad der ~** oil-pump idler gear

Zahnradölpumpenantriebsrad *n* oil-pump drive gear

Zahnrad-pumpe *f* geared pump **-pumpstation** *f* geared power pump **-scheibe** *f* sprocket-wheel washer **-schmiederohteil** *m* gear forging **-schmierölpumpe** *f* geared lubricating pump **-schnapper** *m* gear-driven impulse starter **-schubgetriebe** *n* sliding mesh gearbox **-schutz** *m* gear guard **-stoßmaschine** *f* gear shaper **-übersetzung** *f* gearing, back gearing, transmission gear **-übersetzungsverhältnis** *n* transmission gear ratio

Zahnradübertragung *f* gear-wheel or cogwheel transmission **~ durch Hyperboloidräder** hyperboloidal gear

Zahnrad-unterbrecher *m* toothed-wheel circuit breaker, crown wheel, commutator **-verbindung** *f* gear trains **-verkleidung** *f* gear case **-vorgelege** *n* toothed-wheel gearing, gear train, back gearing, intermediate gearing, reduction gearing **-walzmaschine** *f* gear generator **-wechsel** *m* change gear **-wechselgetriebe** *n* change-speed gear **-welle** *f* pinion spindle **-winde** *f* windlass (toothed) **-zähne** *pl* gear teeth

Zahn-ritzel *n* pinion **-rolle** *f* sprocket **-rücken** *m* back of tooth, flank of tooth

Zahnscheibe *f* ratchet wheel, toothed or studded disk, crown wheel or gear, face gear **federnde ~** toothed spring washer **gegeneinander versetzte Zahnscheiben** staggered driving pinions

Zahnscheiben-funkenstrecke *f* studded-disk discharger **-mühle** *f* toothed attrition (or disc) mill

Zahn-schiebe *f* rack rail **-schlüssel** *m* alligator grip wrench **-schneidemaschine** *f* tooth-cutting machine **-schneider** *m* toothed cutter **-schnitt** *m* indentation **-schräge** *f* angle of tooth **-schrägstellung** *f* inclined position of tooth **-schränkung** *f* crosscut teeth (as of a saw) **-schuh** *m* milling shoe **-schwelle** *f* indented sill

Zahnsegment *n* toothed segment, segmental rack, tooth sector **~ für Farbwerk** inker drive gear segment

Zahn-segmenthebel *m* quadrant lever **-sektor** *m* toothed sector **-sirene** *f* tooth-wheel synchronizer, tone wheel **-spiel** *n* back lash **-spitze** *f* tip of a tooth **-spitzenlinie** *f* top line or edge of teeth

Zahnstange *f* rack, spur rack, gear rack, toothed rack, cog rack, shaft **~ und Ritzel** rack and pinion (gear) **~ mit Sperrzähnen** ratch **~ mit schrägen Zähnen** rack with helical teeth

Zahnstangen-antrieb *m* rack-and-pinion drive **-fräser** *m* rack tooth cutter **-führung** *f* guide frame **-gabel** *f* forked ends or horns (of a jack rack)

Zahnstangengetriebe *n* rack-and-pinion gear **~ zur Verstellung des Körpers** rack and pinion for tilting the frame

Zahnstangen-gewinde *n* track jack **-hubeinrichtung** *f* rack hoisting gear **-lager** *n* tension bar bearing **-lenkung** *f* rack steering **-presse** *f* rack-and-pinion press **-rad** *n* rack gear **-ritzel** *n* rack pinion

Zahnstangen-schutz *m* guard for rack **-steuerung** *f* rack-bar-control **-teilvorrichtung** *f* rack indexing attachment **-trieb** *m* rack and pinion, rack gear(ing) **-(wagen)winde** *f* rack jack

Zahn-stärke *f* thickness of tooth **-teilbahn** *f* pitch line, pitch circle

Zahnteilung *f* pitch, tooth pitch

Zahn-tiefe *f* cog or tooth depth **-tiefenbewegung** *f* in-feed and toolhead motion **-trieb** *m* rack-and-pinion drive, tooth-wheel drive **-trommel** *f* sprocket

Zahn und Trieb rack and pinion

Zahnung *f* teeth, toothing

Zahn-welle *f* serrated shaft **-werk** *n* gearing **-wurzel** *f* root of gear tooth **-zange** *f* alligator grip wrench **-zylinder** *m* cog roller

zähpolen to toughen by poling (metal)

zähschlackig forming tough clinker or slag

zähschleimig mucous

Zain *m* ingot, bar, rod, pig

Zaine *f* wicker work

Zaineisen *n* rods, rod iron, notched bar iron, toothed iron

zainen to make into ingots or bars, stretch, draw out

Zain-form *f* ingot mold **-silber** *n* ingot silver

Zängchen *n* small forceps, tweezers

Zange *f* tongs, pliers, pincers, nippers, tweezers, forceps, stirrup, clamp, vise, electrode holder

Zängearbeit *f* shingling, nobbing, squeezing

Zangen *n* walings (in ports)

zängen to shingle, squeeze (metals), take by means of tongs

Zängen *n* shingling, nobbing, squeezing

Zangen-apparat *m* gripper **-arm** *m* tong arm **-futter** *n* collet chuck (split chuck) **-griff** *m* handle of tongs **-hebel** *m* forked lever **-kopf** *m* collet head **-kran** *m* stock-yard crane **-maul** *n* mouth of tongs **-nietmaschine** *f* tong riveting machine **-ring** *m* coupler or ring on pliers

Zangen-schließwerk *n* closing gear of the tongs **-schloß** *n* forceps lock **-spanndrehbank** *f* lathe with draw-in attachment **-spannfutter** *n* collet chuck **-spannkopf** *m* collet chuck head or clamping head **-spannung** *f* collet chucking or gripping **-stempel** *m* tong beam **-stromwandler** *m* split-core transformer, grip current tester **-verbindung** *f* double brace (elec.) **-vorschub** *m* gripper feed

Zänger *m* shingler

Zängeschlacke *f* shingling slag

Zänghammer *m* shingling hammer
Zängwalze *f* blooming, puddling, or roughing roll
zapfen to draw, tap (trees)
Zapfen *m* plug, peg, lug, pin, pivot, journal, trunnion, cone, tenon, tap, spigot, gudgeon, faucet, wrist pin **~ mit viereckigem Loch** countersunk **einen ~ einlochen** to mortise a tenon **in ~ lagern** to pivot (on) **durchgehender ~** passing tenon **vernagelter ~** bolted tenon
Zapfen-anlagefläche *f* contact surface of the journal **-beschlag** *m* plug fitting **-bohrer** *m* pin drill, tap borer, wimble, centercock bit, teat drill **-buchse** *f* bush, sleeve **-drehgestell** *n* pivot **-drehgestellager** *n* pivot bearing
Zapfendüse *f* pivot nozzle **geschlossene ~** needle valve spray, nozzle with pilot pin
Zapfen-druck *m* pivot thrust or pressure **-feder** *f* peg feather key **-fertigungsmaschine** *f* tenoning machine
zapfenförmig cone-shaped, conical
Zapfen-fräser *m* shank cutter **-gewinde** *n* tapered thread **-hohlkehle** *f* wobbler **-kantenpressung** *f* pivot end pressure **-kipper** *m* trunnion tip wagon **-klemme** *f* stud chuck **-kragen** *m* pivot collar **-kreuz** *n* cross link, journal cross assembly **-kreuzgelenk** *n* cross and yoke type universal joint **-kurve** *f* spectral-response curve (of eye cones)
Zapfenlager *n* pivot bearing, socket, bush, collar, chock (of roller), trunnion seat, journal bearing, lower pintle casting, spindle bearing, lug, plain bearing **unteres ~** spindle bearing **wiegenartiges ~** V-shaped bearing
Zapfen-lagerung *f* pivoting **-länge** *f* pivot length
Zapfenloch *n* peg or pivot hole, mortise **-maschine** *f* mortising machine **-reibung** *f* journal friction
Zapfen-nagel *m* mortise bolt **-platte** *f* hooked tie plate with tenon **-rad** *n* pin wheel **-räderbetrieb** *m* cogwheel gearing **-reibahle** *f* pivot broach **-reibung** *f* journal friction **-reißer** *m* pin drill **-ring** *m* trunnion ring **-säge** *f* back tenon saw
Zapfen-scheibe *f* stud washer **-schleifmaschine** *f* journal grinding machine **-schloß** *n* tap lock **-schneider** *m* tenoning tenter **-schneidemaschine** *f* tenon-cutting machine, tenoning machine **-schraube** *f* trunnion screw **-senker** *m* counterbore, spot-facing cutter **-senkerabflächmesser** *n* counterboring tool **-sonde** *f* tool for sounding mortises
Zapfen-steckschlüssel *m* socket wrench **-stern** *m* satellite carrier **-streichmaß** *n* mortise gauge **-typenhebel** *m* pivoted-type bar **-verbindung** *f* mortise-and-tenon joint **-winkel** *m* angle of rudder or slope **-zähne** *pl* pin teeth, bolt teeth
Zapfer *m* feeder, delivery mechanism
Zapfgrube *f* fueling pit
Zapfhahn *m* discharge nozzle, tap **~ mit Federgriff** spring-grip-control nozzle **nichttropfender ~** antidrip nozzle **tragbarer ~** portable nozzle
Zapf-karren (AV) *m* hydrant dispenser (pit fueling) **-kolophonium** *n* gum rosin
Zapfloch *n* taphole, bunghole **-bohrer** *m* taphole borer **-büchse** *f* taphole bush
Zapf-messer *n* tapping knife **-rohr** *n* discharge pipe **-säule** *f* dispensing pump **-schlauch** *m* delivery hose, filling hose **-stelle** *f* tap, tap connection, tank station, filling station
Zapf- und Abseihvorrichtung *f* tapping and straining device
Zapf-ventil *n* hose nozzle, fill nozzle **-wellenantrieb** *m* power take off **-wellenschutzdeckel** *m* power take-off guard
Zap-Klappe *f* Zap flap
Zapon *m* varnish
zaponieren to zapon
Zaponlack *m* Zapon enamel, cellulose lacquer
Zaratit *m* emerald nickel, zaratite
Zarge *f* frame, sash, edge, border
Zargen-biegemaschine *f* body-forming machine **-bördeleinrichtung** *f* body-flanging device **-fenster** *n* frame window **-rundmaschine** *f* body-forming machine
Zartheit *f* (der Abtönung) delicate gradation (of shade)
Zasche *f* groove (eye)
Zaser *f* filament, fiber, thread
zaserig fibrous
zasern to unwind, unravel
Zäsium *n* cesium **-photozelle** *f* cesium photoelectric cell **-zelle** *f* cesium cell
Zaspel *m* hank, skein
Zaum *m* bridle, rein **Pronyscher ~** Prony brake
Zäumung *f*, **Zaumzeug** *n* bridle
Zaun *m* fence **-draht** *m* fence wire **-gitter** *n* wire fencing, fence netting **-pfosten** *m* fence post
ZB *f* (Zentralbatterie) C. B. (central battery)
ZB-Ruf *m* CBS (common battery signaling)
ZB/W-Leitung *f* CB/dial line
Z-Draht *m* distributing frame wire
Zebra *n* flame effect **-fußgängerübergang** *m* striped pedestrian crossing
Zeche *f* mine, colliery, coal pit, score, bill
Zechen-haus *n* counting house **-kohle** *f* mine coal **-koks** *m* furnace coke, by-product coke **-kraftwerk** *n* colliery power station **-teer** *m* coke tar
Zechstein *m* Zechstein
Zeder *f* cedar **rote virginische ~** red cedar
Zedernholzöl *n* cedar oil
Zeemanstruktur *f* Zeeman pattern
Zehneck *n* decagon
Zehner *m* ten **-bruch** *m* decimal fraction **-dekade** *f* tens decade **-logarithmus** *m* logarithm to the base ten **-potenz** *f* decimal power, power of ten, tenth power **-relais** (10er-Relais) *n* (Z1–Z5) "ten" relay **-ringscheibe** *f* decimal target **-satz** *m* tens digit **-stein** *m* hollow concrete block **-stelle** *f* decimal place **-stufe** *f* tens digit **-system** *n* decimal or decade system **-übertragkontakt** *m* carry contact
Zehneruntersetzer *m*, **einfacher ~** single-decade counting unit
Zehnerwellen *pl* electromagnetic waves between one hundred and ten centimeters
zehnfachnormal decinormel
Zehn-flächner *m* decahedron **-gradteilung** *f* graduation by ten-degree divisions **-tastensatz** *m* ten-button key set **-teiler** *m* (ten-)notch bar **-teilig** ten-part, ten-division
Zehntellösung *f* tenth-normal solution
zehntelnormal decinormal
Zehrungsstempel *m* drift
Zeichen *n* sign, mark, indication, signal, symbol, imprint, character (info proc.) **die ~ brechen** the marks split **die ~ laufen zusammen** the signals run together **gedämpftes ~** spark

signal **hartes** ~ crisp signal **richtiges** ~ straight signal **taktisches** ~ tactical symbol **ungedämpftes** ~ continuous-wave signal **umgekehrtes** ~ reversed signal **verschmiertes** ~ mushy signal ~ **für Zündstellung** pilot ignition marking

Zeichen-abstand *m* figure space, spacing interval **-apparat** *m* drawing apparatus **-arm** *m* drawing arm, tracing arm **-batterie** *f* marking battery **-block** *m* sketch block **-bogen** *m* drawing paper, drawing sheet **-brett** *n* drawing board **-dichte** *f* packing density **-dreieck** *n* triangle **-ebene** *f* drawing plane **-einrichtung** *f* plotter **-element** *n* code or signal element **-erklärung** *f* list of conventional signs, key, letters of reference, legend

Zeichen-feder *f* drawing pen **-feld** signal grid **-frequenz** *f* signal frequency **-gabe** *f* signaling, transmission of signals **-geber** *m* signal transmitter

Zeichengebung *f* signaling, transmission of signals ~ **mit Niederfrequenz** low-frequency signaling **sofortige** ~ immediate-action alarm **verzögerte** ~ delayed-action alarm

Zeichen-gebungsanlage *f* signaling installation **-generator** *m* character generator (comput) **-gerät** *n* drawing instrument **-gestell** *n* drawing stand **-gruppe** *f* word (computer) **-intensität** *f* signal intensity **-intervall** *n* plotting interval **-karton** *m* drawing board **-kohle** *f* drawing charcoal, charcoal or carbon pencil **-kombination** *f* (Fernschreiber) signal combination **-kontakt** *m* marking contact, marking stop **-kopf** *m* signal head, signal front **-kreide** *f* drawing chalk **-lineal** *n* drawing rule **-loch** *n* signal hole **-locher** *m* mark reading reproducer **-lochkarte** *f* mark-sensing punch card **-lochverfahren** *n* mark sensing

Zeichen-maschine *f* drafting machine **-mappe** *f* portfolio **-maßstab** *m* recording scale **-material** *n* drawing materials **-netz** *n* drawing grid, squaring, canvas reticulation **-nocken** *m* code cam (teleg) **-papier** *n* drawing paper, Bristol board **-platte** *f* reflector tracker

Zeichen-saal *m* drawing room **-schiefer** *m* pencil slate **-schlüssel** *m* key to marks and signs, signal code **-schreibung** *f* symbol printing **-seite** *f* marking side **-setzung** *f* punctuation **-spannung** *f* signal potential **-stab** *f* signal stick or baton **-stärke** *f* signal strength or intensity **-stift** *m* drawing pencil, style, stylus, crayon **-stirn** *f* signal head (teleg)

Zeichenstrom *m* marking current ~ **geben** to mark

Zeichenstrom-röhre *f* marking valve **-sendung** *f* marking current

Zeichentisch *m* drawing table, drawing board **großer** ~ loft floor

Zeichenton *m* signal note **-höhe** *f* pitch of the signal note

Zeichen-trickfilm *m* (animated) cartoon **-typenhebel** *m* sign-type bar **-übermittlungssystem** *n* signaling system **-übertragung** *f* signal transmission **-verbindung** *f* visual communication, signal communication **-verbreiterung** *f* signal spread **-vorlage** *f* drawing pattern **-vorrat** *m* character set (comp.) **-vorrichtung** *f* drawing device, tracer **-wechsel** *m* sign change, inversion (teleg), letter-figure or case shift **-welle** *f* signal wave, marking wave **-wiedergabe** *f* signal reproduction

Zeichenwinkel *m*, **rechter** ~ square rule

zeichnen to draw, design, delineate, plot, sketch, sign **eine Kurve** ~ to plot a curve, map a graph **maßstäblich** ~ to draw to scale **perspektivisch** ~ to foreshorten

Zeichner *m* draftsman, signer, designer ~ **für Einzelzeichnungen** detail draftsman **technischer** ~ tracer

zeichnerisch graphic, diagrammatic ~ **ermittelt** graphically determined

Zeichnung *f* drawing, sketch, picture, plan, design, delineation, view, layout, diagram, illustration, tracing **getuschte** ~ washed drawing, drawing in water colors **gewischte** ~ dabbed drawing **schematische** ~ skeleton sketch **schraffierte** ~ hatched drawing

zeichnungsberechtigt authorized to sign

Zeichnungs-bild *n* drawing **-formular** *n* subscription form **-kontrolle** *f* supervision of drawings **-kopiermaschine** *f* machine for reproduction of drawings **-satz** stowage chart **-vergleicheinrichtung** *f* comparison device for drawings

zeigend, direkt ~ direct reading

Zeiger *m* pointer, indicator, hand (of watch), needle, index, engraver, measuring instrument, meter, vector (math.) ~ **zur Einstellung der Steuerzeiten** timing pointer **der** ~ **schlägt aus** the pointer moves **geknickter** ~ bent pointer **optischer** ~ optical lever **springender** ~ jumping hand

Zeiger-ablesung *f* pointer reading **-apparat** *m* indicator **-ausschlag** *m* deflection of pointer, travel (aviation) **-bahn** *f* index path **-barometer** *n* dial or wheel barometer **-dämpfung** *f* (elektr. Meßgeräte) damped pointer action **-diagramm** *n* vector diagram **-frequenzmesser** *m* pointer frequency meter **-galvanometer** *n* pointer galvanometer **-instrument** *n* pointer instrument, dial gauge **-knopf** *m* dial knob **-lagerung** *f* pointer support or base

Zeiger-manometer *n* indicating pressure gauge **-maschine** *f* stylus (or pointer) operated machine **-nase** *f* indicator point, pointer tip **-okular** *n* pointer eyepiece **-platte** *f* dial **-schreibmaschine** *f* pointer typewritter **-stellung** *f* hand setting **-synchronisator** *m* dial-scoring machine (motion pictures) **-system** *n* system of arrows

Zeiger-telegraph *m* pointer or needle telegraph **-thermometer** *n* dial thermometer **-visier** *n* dial sight **-welle des Warnzeigers** pointer shaft of the warning pointer **-werk** *n* index plate **-zieleinrichtung** *f* dial sight

Zeile *f* line, scanning line (video), scanning strip, row (matrix), streak, band **Zeilen durchschießen** to interline (print.) **die Zeilen enger machen** to drive the lines (print.)

Zeile- für Zeile-Abtastung *f* progressive scanning

Zeilen drucken line-a-time printing

Zeilenablenk-gerät *n* line-deflecting (sweep) apparatus (unit) **-röhre** *f* line-deflecting (sweep) tube **-spule** *f* line-deflecting (sweep) coil

Zeilen-ablenkung *f* horizontal deflection (sweep), line scan, line sweep **-abstand** *m* distance between lines, line space or spacing, pitch **-abtastdauer** *f* trace interval **-abtastung** *f* (line) scanning **-addiertaste** *f* line adding key

Zeilenanzeiger *m*, **selbsttätiger ~** self-adjusting line finder
Zeilen-ausgangspentode *f* line output pentode **-ausgleich** *m* justification (of lines)
Zeilenaustast-impuls *m* field or line-frequency blanking impulse, horizontal blanking impulse **-lücke** *f* line blanking interval
Zeilen-austastung *f* line blanking **-automat** *m* automatic carriage **-bewegung** *f* line scan (television) **-bild** *n* line image **-breite** *f* line width, strip width, spot diameter (television) **-breitenregler** *m* line amplitude control, horizontal size control (TV)
Zeilendichte *f*, **Regelung der ~** pitch control (TV)
Zeilen-diode *f* damping diode (TV) **-drehen** *n* line copying **-drucker** *m* line printer (info proc.) **-einstellhebel** *m* line-spacing lever **-einstellung** *f* line posting **-einstellvorrichtung** *f* line-space adjusting mechanism **-entzerrung** *f* line bend, line tilt **-feld** *n* frame field **-flimmern** *n* line flickering, line crawl **-folgeimpuls** *m* fractional- or partial-scan impulse
zeilenförmig rectilinear
Zeilen-fortschaltmechanismus *m* line-spacing mechanism (typewriter) **-fortschritt** *m* line feed **-fräsen** *n* parallel-stroke or straight milling
zeilenfrequente Kippspannung *f* line output (TV)
Zeilen-frequenz *f* line frequency, horizontal scanning frequency, strip frequency **-generator** *m* line-voltage generator **-geradheit** *f* regular alignment of letters **-gießmaschine** *f* (line(s) casting machine
Zeilengleichlauf *m* line synchronism **-stoß** *m* line synchronizing impulse, horizontal synchronizing impulse
Zeilen-hinlauf *m* active line trace, scansion **-höhe** *f* line height **-impuls** *m* line-synchronizing signal, line (-synchronizing) impulse **-kippeinsatz** *m* incipient flyback **-kipper** *m* line time base, horizontal time-base generator
Zeilenkipp-gerät *n* line-sweep apparatus **-periode** *f* line-sweep period **-röhre** *f* line-sweep tube **-schwingung** *f* line-time-base impulse **-spannung** *f* line time base **-spule** *f* line-sweep coil
Zeilen-kontrollröhre *f* line monitoring tube **-länge** *f* line width **-magnet** *m* line-feed magnet **-maß** *n* ruler **-messer** *m* type gauge **-nennlänge** *f* nominal line width **-norm** *f* line standard **-raster** *m* line-scanning pattern **-rücklauf** *m* line flyback, return, retrace **-schalthebel** *m* line-space lever **-schaltung** *f* line spacing, picture traversing, vertical stepping-down movement **-schluß** *m* end of the line
Zeilensetz- und Gießmaschine *f* linotype machine
Zeilenspiegelrad *n* line-scanning mirror drum
Zeilensprung *m* interlacing, line jump **-faktor** *m* interlace factor or ratio **-methode** *f* interlaced, intermeshed, or interleaved scanning method **-sendung** *f* interlace transmission **-teilraster** *m* interlaced scanning field **-verfahren** *n* interlaced scanning **-verhältnis** *n* interlace ratio
Zeilen-spule *f* line-sweep coil, line-scan coil **-steuerung** *f* velocity modulation, variable-speed modulation
Zeilenstoß *m* line-synchronizing signal, line- (-synchronizing) impulse **-verfahren** *n* line-impulse method
Zeilen-struktur *f* banded structure **-summenprobe** *f* check column method **-synchronisier(ungs)-impuls** *m* line-synchronizing signal or impulse **-synchronisierungslücke** *f* line gap or interval **-synchronisierzeichen** *n* line-synchronizing signal **-tasten** *n* straight tracing **-teilung** *f* line pitch **-tor** *n* line gate **-transformator** *m* line transformer **-transport** *m* normal upspacing **-überdeckung** *f* line overlap, spot overlap **-überlappung** *f* overlapping of lines **-übertrager** *m* line transformer **-umsetzung** *f* line translation
Zeilen- und Bildwechselimpulsreihe *f* line- and image-change impulse series
Zeilen und Spalten rows and columns
Zeilen-verlagerung *f* migration or shift of line position **-verschiebung** *f* interlacing, line-offset scan **-verstärker** *m* line-impulse amplifier **-verzerrungskompensator** *m* tilt mixer **-vorschub** *m* line feed **-vorschubbewegung** *f* line sweep, line-traversing motion **-wähler** *m* line selector
Zeilenwechsel-frequenz *f* line frequency **-impuls** *m* line-change impulse **-zahl** *f* line frequency
zeilenweises Abtasten linear scanning
Zeilen-wobbelung *f* spot-wobbing (TV) **-zahl** *f* line frequency (number), number of lines **-zähler** *m* automatic line counter, runner (print.) **-zug** *m* line train sweep, line sequence or series **-zugwechselperiode** *f* field frequency
Z-Eisen *n* Z bar
Zeit *f* time, epoch, period **~ messen, nach der ~ abmessen** to time **die ~ abstoppen** to time, stop the time **die ~ vergleichen** to check the time of day **~ geringer Belastung** light-load period **mitteleuropäische ~** Central European Time **~ starker Belastung** heavy-load period **verkehrsschwache ~** slack or light hours **verkehrsstarke ~** busy or heavy hours **wahre ~** true time **Westeuropäische ~** Western European Time
Zeit-abhängigkeit *f* dependence on time **-ablenkfrequenz** *f* time base frequency **-ablenkung** *f* time deflection, time base, time sweep, sweep (CRT) **-ablenkungsgerät** *n* sweep unit **-abschnitt** *m* time space, period, element of time, interval of time **-abstand** *m* time interval, range **-achse** *f* time axis **-achsenfrequenz** *f* time-base frequency **-angabe** *f* time designation, statement of time, exact date and hour **-ansagegerät** *n* speaking clock
Zeitauflösung *f* time resolving or resolution **mit ~** time-limit release or relay
Zeit-auflösungsvermögen *n* time resolution **-aufnahme** *f* time exposure (phot.) **-auslöser** *m* time-limit release, timer **-auslöserelais** *n* trip switch timer **-ausschalter** *m* timing gear **-ball** *m* time ball **-bestimmung** *f* determination of time **-blinker** *m* chronograph, time-recording camera **-bogen** *m* arc of time
Zeitdauer *f* period of time, duration, term **~ des Stillsetzens** shutdown **Abstoppen von ~** stop-watch measurement of time values or intervals of time
Zeit-dehnaufnahme *f* high-speed camera shooting, high-speed picture **-dehner** *m* time extender, highspeed camera, slow-motion camera **-dehneraufnahme** *f* high-speed motion picture, slow-motion picture **-dehngrenze** *f* time yield limit **-dehnung** *f* time yield, high-speed camera

shooting, time scale **-differen** *f* time lag **-drucker** *m* fusetime measuring device **-drucker-einschub** *m* plug-in time printer
Zeiteinheit *f* unit (of) time **in der ~** per unit of time
Zeit-einstellung *f* time adjustment **-einteilung** *f* time schedule
zeiten to time
Zeitenmaßstab *m* time base or scale
Zeit-ersparnis *f* cutting and economy of time, time saving **-faktor** *m* time factor **-fernzähler** *m* distant time recorder **-festigkeit** *f* time strength, endurance strength **-folge** *f* time interval, elapsed time, time sequence **-folge-verfahren** *n* sequential or progressive scanning **-funk** *m* topics of the day
Zeitgeber *m* time-signal transmitter, timer; master clock **-betrieb** *m* fixed-cycle operation **-frequenz** *f* clock-frequency
Zeitgebühr *f* measured rate
zeitgekehrtes Pendel inverted pendulum
zeitgemäß timely, opportune, up-to-date
Zeit-gleichung *f* equation of time **-glied** *n* timing circuit **-grenze** *f* limiting date line, time limit **-härtung** *f* age-hardening, time quenching
zeitig on time
Zeit-impuls *m* clock or timing pulse **-intervall** *m* time interval **-kanalysator** *m* time-channel analyzer **-konstante** *f* time or timing constant **-kontakt** *m* intermittent contact, time closing contact **-kontakteinrichtung** *f* timing interrupter **-kontrakt** *m* period (time) contract **-kreisel-kondensator** *m* time-base condenser **-lampe** *f* chargeable-time lamp
zeitlich per unit time, timely, chronological, temporal, temporary **~ aufeinanderfolgend** chronological **~ gleichbleibend** constant in time **~ veränderlich** variable with time **-e Entwicklung** development in time **-e Kraft** lateral force **-e Reihenfolge** chronological sequence **-e Rücktrift** time lag **-es Verhalten** transient behavior, time behavior **-er Verlauf** time slope **-er Verzug** time lag **-er Zusammenfall** coincidence
Zeit-linie *f* time vector, sweep trace **-lupe** *f* slow-motion camera
Zeitlupen-anordnung *f* slow-motion arrangement **-aufnahme** *f* slow-motion pictures or photography **-kamera** *f* camera for slow-motion or retardedaction picture projection work **-tempo** *n* delayed-action timing **-verfahren** *n* slow-motion or retarded-action method
Zeit-mark *f* time mark **-marke** *f* time scale, marking of time **-markengeber** *m* time signal injector **-markenlampe** *f* time-marking lamp **-markierer** *m* time marker **-markierung** *f* time record
Zeitmaß *n* tempo, rhythm, time scale, marking of time **-faktor** *m* time scale factor (comput.) **-stab** *m* scale of time
Zeitmesser *m* chronometer, timing register, timekeeper, watch, clock **registrierender ~** chronoscope, chronograph
Zeit-meßgerät *n* chronometer, chronoscope, chronographoscope **-meßkundlich** chronometric **-messung** *f* timing **-modulation** *f* constant-frequency variable dot keying, velocity modulation, variable-speed modulation, variable-speed scanning **-mittel** *n* time average
Zeitmultiplex-system *n* time multiplex **-verfahren** *n* time-division multiple method (or system) **-verstärker** *m* time-shared amplifier
Zeit-nehmer *m* timekeeper, stopper, time-study man **-öler** *m* timed oiler **-periode** *f* duration, interval **-plan** *m* time table or schedule **-plan-regelung** *f* time pattern control **-platte** *f* deflection plate
zeitproportional time-proportional
Zeitprüfung *f* time control or check
Zeitpunkt *m* turn of call, point of time, moment, instant **letzter ~** deadline
Zeit-punkteinstellung *f* timing **-querschnitt** *m* time cross section **-rad** *n* time-control wheel
Zeitraff-aufnahmekamera *f* time-lapse camera (low-speed shooting, high-speed projection) **-aufnahmeverfahren** *n* time-lapse photography, low-speed shooting for high-speed projection
Zeitraffer *m* time-lapse motion camera, stop-motion device
Zeitraffung *f* fast motion effect (film)
zeitraubend time-consuming, wearisome, tedious
Zeitraum *m* period, age **~ der Rufstromsendung** ringing cycle
Zeit-regler *m* time regulator **-regelmaschine** *f* timing machine **-registrierapparat** *m* time recorder **-regulierband** *n* timing tape
Zeitrelais *n* timing relay, time-lag or time-limit relay **~ mit Bremszylinder** dashdot relay
Zeitrelaisanrufschaltung *f* time-relay call connection
Zeit-reserve *f* time interval **-schalter** *m* time switch, time-control unit **-schaltwerk** *n* time switch **-schnellschalter** *m* high-speed circuit breaker or switch **-schnur** *f* safety fuse **-schreiber** *m* chronograph
Zeitschrift *f*, **technische ~** technical journal
Zeitschriften-druck *m* printing periodicals **-literatur** *f* periodicals, journal literature, magazine literature
Zeit-schütz *n* time-lag relay **-schwelle** *f* threshold of time-sense **-schwingfestigkeit** *f* fatigue strength for finite life **-selektionssystem** *n* time-division multiple method (or system) **-setzungs-kurve** *f* time-settlement curve **-sicherung** *f* time fuse
Zeitsignal *n* time signal **-anlage** *f* time-signal system **-geber** *m* time-signal transmitter **-über-trager** *m* telegraphical time-signal distributor
Zeit-skaleninstrument *n* time-scale instrument **-spanne** *f* time interval **-spirale** *f* time spiral **-staffelung** *f* time characteristic (relays) **-standfestigkeit** *f* creep strength depending on time **-standversuch** *m* creep test **-stäuberkegel** *m* atomizer cone **-stempel** *m* time stamp, (automatic) calculagraph **-studie** *f* time study, record **-studienwesen** *n* cost analysis, time study **-tafel** *f* time-table, schedule **-teilchen** *n* small interval of time **-temperaturkurve** *f* time-temperature curve
Zeit- und Frequenzmesser *m* digital time and frequency meter
Zeitung *f* newspaper **kopflose ~** partly printed sheets
Zeitungs-anzeige *f* insertion, announcement **-ausschnitt** *m* newspaper clipping **-druck** *m* newspaper printing or work **-druckerei** *f*

newspaper printing plant **-druckmaschine** *f* newspaper printing machine **-falzmaschine** *f* journal folding machine
Zeitungs-rotationsdruckmaschine *f* newspaper rotary machine **-telegramm** *n* news message, press message
Zeit-unterschied *m* time difference **-verbesserung** *f* time correction **-vergeudung** *f* waste of time **-verlauf** *m* transient response, time behavior **-verlust** *m* loss of time, lost time, delay **-verschiebung** *f* time lag, time shift **-verschluß** *m* sighting disk, time shutter
Zeitverzögerung *f* time delay or lag **willkürliche ~** coding delay (rdr)
Zeit-verzögerungssicherung *f* time-delay fuse **-vorgaberelais** (W) *n* time advance relay **-vorwahl** *f* preset time, preselected pulse count **-waage** *f* watch timer **-wegschaubild** *n* time-traverse diagram
zeitweilig temporary, at times, intermittent, periodic **~ eingestellt** (temporarily) suspended
Zeitwert *m* standing value **-festsetzung** *f* rate (work-factor) **-spielraum** *m* slack time (work-factor)
Zeit-winkel *m* time angle **-zähler** *m* time meter, timing register, time recorder **-zählung** *f* timing
Zeitzeichen *n* time signal **-geber** *m* time-signal transmitter, chronopher **-stelle** *f* time-signal station
Zeitzone *f* time zone
Zeitzonen-zähler *m* time and zone meter **-zählung** *f* zone and overtime registration
Zeitzünder *m* delay-action cap, delay igniter, time fuse, igniting device **gasloser ~** ventless delay-action cap
Zeitzünderschuß *m* time fire
Zeitzündschnur *f* time fuse, long fuse cord
Zeitzuschlag bei Mehrplatzarbeit interference allowance
zellähnlich cell-like, celloid, cellular, pitted, honeycomb-like
Zellbeton *m* foam concrete
Zelle *f* segment, cell, element, battery, airframe, booth (teleph.) cellule, compartment, cabinet, cubicle, store location (info proc.) **~ verschiedener Elektrolyten** gravity cell **~ mit öffentlichem Fernsprecher** telephone booth **elektrolytische ~** electrolytic detector **gegengeschaltete ~** countercell **lichtelektrische ~** photoelectric cell, photo-electric tube **lichtempfindliche ~** light-reactive cell **photoelektrische ~** photoelectric cell **schalldichte ~** soundproof cabinet **verspannte ~** wirebraced wing **verstrebte ~** strut-braced wing
zellenartig cell-like, cellular **-e Struktur** honeycomb, pitted, or cellular structure
Zellen-aufbau *m* cell structure **-bauweise** *f* honeycomb principle **-bildschirm** *m* lamp screen **-block** *m* cellular block **-dusche** *f* fuselage shower **-einbau** *m* cellular arrangement **-einrichtung** *f* arrangement of cells **-filter** *n* plate filter **-filtereinsatz** *m* filter cell unit
zellenförmig cellular
Zellen-gefäß *n* cell box **-gerüst** *n* airplane structure **-gewebe** *n* cellular tissue **-gleichrichter** *m* honeycomb grill
zellenhaltig cellular
Zellen-heck *n* tail boom **-industrie** *f* air-frame industry **-kies** *m* cellular pyrites **-kühler** *m* cellular radiator, honeycomb radiator **-mantel** *m* gas-bag envelope **-plan** *m* allocation plan (comput) **-rad** *n* bucket wheel
Zellenschalter *m* cell switch, battery (cell) switch, charge or discharge switch, accumulator-switch regulator **-leitung** *f* battery-switch conductor
Zellenschutz *m* gas-bag or cell protection
zellenseitig on the airframe side
Zellen-spannung *f* cell voltage **-speicher** *m* silo **-stiel** *m* wing strut **-stirnwand** *f* front panel of gas bag or cell **-stoff** *m* gas-cell or -bag fabric **-stopfen für Batterie** cell plug for battery **-strebe** *f* wing strut **-struktur** *f* cellular structure, network
Zellen-tafel *f* lamp screen **-tiefofen** *m* cell pit furnace, soaking pit furnace **-verbindung** *f* cell connection **-vibration** *f* aircraft structural noise **-wand** *f* cell wall
Zell-faser *f* synthetic cellulose fiber **-faserstoff** *m* cellulose **-gewebe** *n* tissue **-glasdruckmaschine** *f* viscose foil printing press **-gummi** *n* foam rubber **-horn** *n* celluloid
zellig cellular, celled, honeycombed
Zellkern *m* nucleus **-damm** *m* earth dam with cellular core wall
Zellmasse *f* cellular substance
Zelloidinpapier *n* celloidine paper
Zellon *n* cellone **-lack** *m* cellulose acetate lacquer, cellone
Zellophan *n* cellophane
Zell-pack *m* cellulose derivate **-pech** *n* cell pitch **-plasma** *n* cytoplasm
Zellstoff *m* cellulose, pulp (paper) **-ausbeute** *f* yield of pulp **-flocken** *pl* loose pulp **-gehalt** *m* papermaking material **-karton** *m* chemical pulp card **-kocher** *m* digester **-lack** *m* cellulose lacquer **-pappe** *f* pulpboard, carton, millboard **-schleim** *m* colloidal cellulose **-watte** *f* artificial cotton, cellucotton
Zelluloid *n* celluloid **-auskleidung** *f* celluloid facing **-plakat** *n* celluloid show card **-rad** *n* celluloid wheel **-tafel** *f* celluloid disk, protractor, template
Zellulose *f* cellulose **-azetatlack** *m* cellulose acetate dope **-entwässerungsmaschine** *f* desiccating machine for wood pulp **-fabrik** *f* wood-pulp works, cellulose factory **-herstellungsmaschine** *f* wood-pulp making machine **-lack** *m* cellulose varnish
Zellulosepapier *n* wood-pulp paper, cellulose paper **geglättetes ~** cellulose paper with satin finish
Zellulose-wandung *f* cellulose wall **-watte** *f* wadding of cellulose
Zellwand *f* cell membrane, cell wall
Zellwolle *f* staple fiber, regenerated cellulose, rayon staple, synthetic wool made of cellulose
Zelt *n* tent **~ aufschlagen** to pitch a tent
Zelt-ausrüstung *f* tent equipment **-bahn** *f* shelter half **-bau** *m* tent pitching **-beschläge** *pl* tent fittings **-dach** *n* tent roof **-leinwand** *f* canvas **-pfahl** *m* tent pole **-pflock** *m* tent pin **-plane** *f* tarpaulin **-stange** *f* tent pole
Zement *m* cement **mit ~ ausgießen** to grout with cement **in ~ einschwemmen** to float in cement

mit ~ torkretieren to inject cement **hochwertiger ~** high-class cement
zementartig cementlike
Zementation *f* cementation, cementation process **~ im Salzbad** casehardening work in a cyanide bath
Zement-auftragemaschine *f* cement-laying-on machine **-ausbringer** *m* cement retainer **-beton** *m* cement concrete **-bewurf** *m* cement facing, cement plaster **-brei** *m* cement paste, neat cement, cement grout **-brennerei** *f* cement factory **-brennofen** *m* cement kiln **-darstellung** *f* cement production, cementation, converting **-drehofen** *m* rotary cement kiln
zementecht (Farbstoff) stable in cement
Zement-einpressung *f* pressure injection of cement grout **-eisen** *n* cement iron **-estrich** *m* cement floor **-fliese** *f* cement tile or flag **-förderband** *n* cement conveyer
Zementformstück *n* concrete block **einzügiges ~** single-duct concrete block **mehrzügiges ~** multiple-duct concrete block
Zement-formstückkanal *m* concrete-block conduit **-fußboden** *m* concrete floor **-gerbstahl** *m* shear steel **-gußwaren** *pl* compressed-concrete articles **-hohldiele** *f* hollow-concrete slab **-hydrat** *n* hydrated cement
zementieren to cement, carburize, caseharden, convert, cyanide
Zementieren *n* cement work, cementing **~ im Spritzverfahren** cementing by jet **Einsatzhärtung durch ~** casehardening by carburization
Zementier-faß *n* precipitation vat **-kasten** *m*, **-kiste** *f* cementing box, casehardening box, carburizing pot, converting pot **-mittel** *n* cementing agent **-muffenventil** *n* cement float collar **-ofen** *m* cementation furnace, steel-converting furnace **-packer** *m* cement retainer **-schirm** *m* basket **-schlammbüchse** *f* dump bailer **-schuh** *m* cement float shoe
zementiert cemented
Zementierung *f* cementation, carburization, cyaniding, cementing
Zementierungsofen *m* casehardening furnace
Zementierverfahren *n* cementation process, cementing process, steel-conversion process, cementation, cementing job
Zementit *m* cementite **körniger ~** granular cementite **kugeliger ~** spheroidal cementite, nodular cementite **auf kugeligen ~ glühen** to spheroidize
Zementit-zerfall *m* cementite disintegration **-zusammenballung** *f* cementite spheroidizing
Zement-kalk *m* hydraulic lime **-kalkbeton** *m* cement-lime concrete **-kalkmörtel** *m* cement-lime mortar **-kalkstein** *m* hydraulic limestone **-klinker** *m* cement clinker **-kohle** *f* cementation carbon **-kopf** *m* cementing head **-kuchen** *m* cement pat **-kunststein** *m* artificial cement stone **-kupfer** *n* cement copper **-leim** *m* cement glue
Zement-mahlanlage *f* cement-mill plant **-mast** *m* concrete pole **-mastix** *m* mastic cement **-mergelgrube** *f* cement stone quarry **-milch** *f* grout **-mörtel** *m* cement (mortar) **-mühlenantrieb** *m* cement-mill drive **-ofen** *m* cement kiln
Zement-platte *f* slab of cement **-prüfung** *f* cement testing **-pulver** *n* carburizer, cementing powder **-putz** *m* cement plaster **-putzband** *n* fillet of cement **-rohr** *n* concrete pipe **-rot** *n* English red, Venetian red **-rotierofen** *m* revolving cement drier, rotary cement kiln **-sack** *m* cement bag **-schlacke** *f* cement clinker **-schlämme** *f* cement grout **-schuppen** *m* cement shed
Zement-silber *n* cement silver **-silo** *m* cement bunker **-sockel** *m* cement foundation **-stahl** *m* blister steel, cemented steel, converter steel, casehardened steel **-stahlstab** *m* cement bar **-traßbeton** *m* cement-trass concrete **-verputz** *m* cement plaster or rendering **-waage** *f* cement scales **-werk** *n* cement plant
Zementwerks-anlage *f* cement-works installation **-einrichtung** *f* installation for cement factories
Zener-diode *f* break-down diode **-durchschlag** *m* Zener breakdown
Zenit(h) *m* zenith
Zenit-aufnahme *f* zenith photograph **-entfernung** *f* zenith distance **-distanz** *f* zenith distance, azimuth distance **-licht** *n* vertical light **-lotung** *f* zenith plumbing **-punkt** *m* zenith point **-winkel** *m* zenith angle
zentesimal centesimal **-waage** *f* centesimal weighing machine, centesimal balance
Zentibel *n* centibel (cb)
Zentigramm *n* centigram
Zentiliter *m* centiliter
Zentimeter *m* centimeter **-felderteilung** *f* centimeter division **-welle** *f* centimeter wave **-wellenfrequenz** *f* superhigh frequency **-würfel** *m* centimeter cube
Z-Entlüfter *m* safety valve (for sodium permanganate)
Zentner *m* hundredweight, quantal
zentral central **-e Erweiterung** concentric enlargement
Zentral-abstand *m* (Getriebe) distance between centers **-abzugsrohr** *n* central gas offtake **-anlage** *f* central station, central plant **-anrufschrank** *m* concentration switchboard, concentrator **-anstellung** *f* central adjusting **-aufbereitungsanlage** *f* centralized preparation plant
Zentralbatterie *f* common battery (C. B.) **-betrieb** *m* common-battery working **-speisung** *f* common-battery supply **-teilnehmer** *m* common-battery or control-battery subscriber
Zentral-bedienung *f* centralized control **-bewegung** *f* central force motion **-büchse** *f* (socket) jack
Zentrale *f* center, (telephone) exchange, control station (submarine), central office, control room, traction station, car shed **~ für die Bedienung der Maschinen** controlling cabin, control house **elektrische ~** electric power house
Zentralenspannung *f* station voltage
Zentral-fettschmierapparat *m* forced feed lubricating unit **-führung** *f* central guide **-generatoranlage** *f* central gas-producer plant **-gerät** *n* central unit **-heizung** *f* central heating
Zentralheizungs-anlage *f* central-heating plant **-armaturen** *pl* central-heating fittings **-formstück** *n* central-heating form piece **-kessel** *m* boiler for central heating **-rohr** *n* radiator pipe
zentralisieren to centralize
Zentralisierung *f* centralization
Zentral-kompensation *f* central capacitor method

(power-factor correction) **-kondensationsanlage** *f* central condensation plant **-kufe** *f* central skid **-perspektive** *f* central perspective **-projektion** *f* central projection **-pult** *n* master control **-richtanlage** *f* director system (navy) **-schärfe** *f* definition at center **-schmierung** *f* central lubrication, one-shot lubrication

Zentralschrank *m* concentrator, concentrating switchboard **in einem ~ vereinigte Leitungen** concentrated trunks

Zentral-schwimmer *m* central float **-speisung** *f* common current supply **-spindel** *f* central stem **-spindelanpressung** *f* central tightening spindle **-spurlager** *n* angular bearing **-station** *f* central station **-stellwerk** *n* CTC interlocking (centralized train control)

zentralsteuerbar centrally regulated

Zentralsteuerung *f* centralized control

Zentral-strahl *m* normal radiation, central ray **-strahlanzeige** *f* central indication **-stück** *n* centerpiece **-symmetrisch** centrosymmetrical **-träger** *m* center sill

Zentral-uhr *f* master clock **-uhrenanlage** *f* time-electrical distribution system **-umschalter** *m* intercommunication switch, concentrator **-umwertegerät** *n* main data-conversion instrument **-verschluß** *m* central shutter, between-the-lens-shutter (photo)

Zentral-wasserstation *f* central waterworks **-wasserversorgung** *f* central (hot-)water supply **-welle** *f* central fixed shaft **-werkstatt** *f* principal workshop **-wert** *m* median (statistics) **-wetterführung** *f* centralized ventilation

Zentrier-achse *f* centring spindle **-ansatz** *m* spigot **-apparat** *m* centering machine **-bank** *f* centering lathe

zentrierbar, nicht ~ noncentering

Zentrier-blende *f* centering diaphragm **-bohrer** *m* center bit or drill **-bohrung** *f* center bore **-buchse** *f* centering bush **-bund** *m* spigot **-einsatz** *m* centering insert **-einpaß** *m* centering spigot **-eisen** *n* center iron

zentrieren to center, spot

Zentrieren *n* centering

Zentrier-feder *f* centering spring **-fernrohr** *n* centering telescope

Zentrierfutter *n* centering chuck **selbsttätiges ~** self-centering chuck

Zentriergabel *f* centering fork

Zentrierglas mit Strichkreuz centering lens with ruled cross

Zentrier-hülse *f* guide sleeve **-kegel** *m* centering cone **-klemmfutter** *n* self-centering chuck **-konus** *m* propeller hub cone **-loch** *n* center hole (phono) **-rand** *m* centering shoulder **-ring** *m* centering ring

Zentrier-scheibe *f* centering disk **-schleifmaschine** *f* center grinding machine **-schneide** *f* knife-edge bearing **-schraube** *f* centering screw **-schraubenfutter** *m* centering screw chuck **-spannfutter** *n* self-centering shaft **-spitze** *f* center point **-stahl** *m* centering tool **-stift** *m* centering pin **-stock** *m* centering rod **-stück** *n* centering device

zentriert centered

Zentrier- und Anfaßvorrichtung *f* centering and chamfering toolholder

Zentrier- und Muttersenkmaschine machine for centering and countersinking nuts

Zentrier- und Plandrehwerkzeug *n* centering and facing tool

Zentrierung *f* centering, balancing

Zentrierungsfeder *f* spider (of loud-speaker coil)

Zentrierungsvorrichtung *f* centering devise, inside spider (of loudspeaker) **~ für Rundschnitte** centering attachment for circular nibbling works

Zentrier-winkel *m* center square, center head **-wulst** *f* bourrelet, shoulder of a projectile **-zapfen** *m* spigot (shaft)

Zentrifugal-abscheider *m* centrifugal separator **-beschleunigung** *f* centrifugal acceleration **-bewegung** *f* centrifugal motion **-filter** *m* centrifugal filter **-gebläse** *n* centrifugal blower or impeller **-gießen** *n* centrifugal casting **-gießverfahren** *n* centrifugal casting method or process **-guß** *m* centrifugal cast(ing)

Zentrifugal-kraft *f* centrifugal force **-kraftfeld** *n* centrifugal field **-knotenfang** *m* centrifugal strainer **-kuppelung** *f* centrifugal coupling **-laderad** *n* impeller

Zentrifugalmoment *n* product of inertia **~ der Schwimmebene** centrifugal moment of the plane of buoyancy

Zentrifugal-pumpe *f* centrifugal pump **-regler** *m* **-regulator** *m* centrifugal governor or regulator **-scheider** *m* centrifugal separator **-sichter** *m* centrifugal sifter **-sichtmaschine** *f* centrifugal dressing machine **-sortierer** *m* centrifugal strainer **-stoffmühle** *f* centrifugal beater **-stufe des Verdichters** centrifugal impeller **-tourenzähler** *m* centrifugal-force tachometer **-trockenmaschine** *f* hydroextractor **-wascher** *m* centrifugal washer **-wirkung** *f* centrifugal action

Zentrifuge *f* centrifuge, hydroextractor

Zentrifugen-boden *m* centrifugal-machine bottom **-korb** *m* extractor basket **-spinnen** *n* pot (bucket) spinning process **-verfahren** *n* pot-spinning process **-zubehör** *n* accessories of centrifugal machines

zentrifugieren to centrifuge, centrifugalize

zentripetal centripetal **-bewegung** *f* centripetal motion **-kraft** *f* centripetal force

zentrisch (con)centric, central **~ eingestellt** centered

Zentriwinkel *m* angle at the center, angle between radii, sector angle

zentrobar centrobaric

Zentrode *f* centrode

Zentrum *n* center, bull's-eye **-bohrer** *m* center bit, cutter

Zeolith *m* zeolite

Zephir *m* zephyr

Zeppelin-antenne *f* Zeppelin antenna **-verdrängungskörper** *m* streamlined blocking body

Zer *n* cerium

zerätzen to destroy by caustics, corrode

zerbersten to burst (asunder or apart)

Zerblätterungsapparat *m* hop-plucking apparatus

zerbrechen to break, fracture, rupture, smash

Zerbrechen *n* breaking, fracture

zerbrechend friable, brisant

zerbrechlich fragile, breakable, friable, brittle

Zerbrechlichkeit *f* fragility, brittleness

Zerbrechungsfestigkeit *f* strain resistance, breaking strength

zerbröckeln to crumble
zerbröckelnd crumbling, crumbly, friable
Zerdrehung *f* torsion
zerdrücken to crush, mash, grind, crumple
Zerdrücken *n* crushing
Zerdrückfestigkeit *f* resistance to crushing or compression, strain
Zerdrückungsspannung *f* crushing stress
Zereisen *n* cerium iron
Zeresin *n* ceresin
zerfahren (inf.) to crush by driving over, fly asunder
Zerfall *m* dissociation, destruction, decomposition, decay, disintegration, breaking down
zerfahren to burst or fly asunder
Zerfall *m* dissociation (of ions), destruction, decomposition, decay, disintegration, breaking down
zerfallbar, nicht ~ non-disintegrable
zerfallen to decompose, dissociate, divide, disintegrate, crumble, collapse, slake, decay (atom), split, undergo fission
Zerfall(s)-elektron *n* decay electron resulting from disintegration (mesotron) **-energie** *f* disintegration energy **-folge** *f* radioactive chain **-formel** *f* decay formula **-gebilde** *n* product of disintegration **-geschwindigkeit** *f* disintegration rate **-grenze** *f* dissociation limit **-gurt** *m* disintegrating belt
Zerfall(s)-konstante *f* constant of radioactive transformation, disintegration constant, decay coefficient **-kurve** *f* decay curve **-modul** *m* decay modulation **-prozeß** *m* decomposition process **-reihe** *f* radioactive series **-schlacke** *f* disintegrating slag, slaking slag, powdered slag **-serie** *f* radioactive decay series
Zerfall(s)-wahrscheinlichkeit *f* decay probability, decay rate **-wärme** *f* heat of dissociation, heat of radioactivity **-zeit** *f* decay time, disintegration time **-ziffer** *f* coefficient of disintegration
Zerfaserer *m* disintegrator, kneader, stuff grinder, unraveling machine
zerfasern to beat, fuzz, unravel, unthread, fray out
Zerfaserungsmaschine *f* perfecting engine (paper mfg.)
zerfetzen to tear to pieces
zerfetzt ragged, tattered
zerfleischen to lacerate
zerfließen to deliquesce, melt, dissolve, run (color)
zerfließend diffluent, melting, deliquescent
Zerfließung *f* deliquescence
zerflockt flaked, milled **-er Asbest** milled asbestos
Zerfluorid *n* cerium fluoride
zerfressen to corrode, erode, pit, attack, cauterize, gnaw, eat away
Zerfressen *n* corrosion **~ der Klemme** terminal corrosion
zerfressend corrosive
Zerfressung *f* corrosion, cauterization, erosion
zergehen to melt (away), dissolve, vanish
zergliedern to dissect, decompose, analyse
Zergliederung *f* analysis, dissection
zerhacken to chop
Zerhacker *m* chopper, vibrator **-feder** *f* synchronous reed **-spannungsverstärker** *m* chopper amplifier **-umformer** *m* vibrator converter
zerhackt flicked off, chopped **-er Gleichstrom** interrupted or intermittent DC
Zerin *m* cerine
Zeriterde *f* cerite earth
Zerium *n* cerium
Zerkleinerer *m* pulverizer, disintegrator
zerkleinern comminute, disintegrate, crush, pulverize, grind, break up
Zerkleinerung *f* size reduction, crushing, fragmentation
Zerkleinerungs-anlage *f* crushing unit, breaking plant, pulverizing plant **-maschine** *f* crushing machine, crusher, pulverizer **-mühle** *f* crushing mill **-vorrichtung** *f* crushing or grinding device **-walze** *f* crushing roll
zerklüftet full of fissures
Zerklüftung *f* crevasse, fissuring
zerknacken to crack
Zerknall *m*, **Zerknallen** *n* explosion
zerknallen to detonate, explode
Zerknallstoß *m* concussion, blast, explosion
Zerknicken *n* cracking
Zerknickungsfestigkeit *f* thrust resistance
zerknittern, zerknüllen to crumble, crush, crease
zerkörnen to granulate
Zerkratzung *f* scratching
Zerkrümeln *n* crumbling
zerlassen to melt, liquefy, dissolve
zerlaufen to run (color or liquid)
zerlegbar decomposable, capable of being detached, dismounted, split up, or resolved, collapsible **-e Antenne** sectioned antenna **-e Kurbelwelle** built-up crankshaft
Zerlegbarkeit *f* dismantling, decomposability, resolvability, factorability, collapsability, fissionability
zerlegen to split up (light beam), decompose, analyze, resolve, dissociate, dismount, decentralize, disassemble, strip, undo, scan, refract, diffract, dissect, separate, atomize
Zerlegen *n* dismantling (dismounting)
Zerleger *m* analyzer, self-destroying shell, scanner, dissector **-blende** *f* dissector aperture, scanning hole
Zerlegung *f* decomposition, resolution, dissociation, expansion, dissection, disintegration, analysis, dispersion **~ in Bestandteile** disaggregation **~ von Kräften** resolution of forces **~ eines Motors** tear-down (motor) **alternierende ~** interlaced, staggered, or interleaved scanning **Fouriersche ~** Fourier's analysis **springende ~** interlaced, staggered, or interleaved scanning
Zerlegungs-sinn *m* direction of scanning **-vorrichtung** *f* scanner, exploring means **-wärme** *f* heat of dissociation
zermahlen to crush, grind, pulverize, mill, bruise
Zermahlen *n* grinding
Zermalmen *n*, **Zermalmung** *f* grinding, crushing, squash, smash
Zermetall *n* cerium metal, cerium
zermürben to wear down, shatter
Zermürberscheinung *f* fatigue
Zermürbung *f* grinding, breaking up
Zermürbversuch *m* fatigue test
zernagen to gnaw through, corrode
zernieren to encircle, invest

Zernierung *f* encirclement, investment
Zernitrat *n* cerium nitrate
Zerograph *m* zerograph
Zeroplastik *f* ceroplastics
zerplatzen to burst, explode
Zerplatzprobe *f* bursting test
zerpulvern to pulverize
zerquetschen to crush, bruise, squeeze, squash
Zerquetschen *n* crush(ing)
Zerrbild *n* distorted picture
zerreibbar friable, triturable
Zerreibbarkeit *f* friability
zerreiben to pulverize, triturate, levigate
Zerreiben *n* comminution (of ores), powdering
Zerreibung *f* pulverization, trituration, attrition, comminution (by abrasion)
Zerreibwolf *m* crushing machine
zerreißbar capable of being torn or rent
Zerreiß-belastung *f* ultimate tensile stress, breaking stress, breaking load **-bolzen** *m* breaker bolt **-dehnung** *f* elongation at break **-diagramm** *n* load-extension diagram, stress-strain diagram
zerreißen to tear, break, rupture, pull apart, lacerate, wear out, disrupt, shred
Zerreißen *n* rupture, disruption, breaking
Zerreißer *m* apparatus for tearing off the shavings
Zerreiß-fähigkeit *f* tensile strength **-festigkeit** *f* ultimate strength, tensile strength, maximum load, maximum stress, tearing strength **-frequenz** *f* shatter oscillation **-gerät** *n* apparatus for testing the tearing strength of fabric **-geschwindigkeit** *f* rate of breaking **-grenze** *f* tearing limit, breaking limit, breaking point, destruction limit **-kegel** *m* cone of rupture **-maschine** *f* tensile-testing machine, pull-test machine **-modul** *m* modulus of rupture
Zerreiß-probe *f*, **-prüfung** *f* destructive test, tension or tensile test, tensile-test specimen, breaking test **-spannung** *f* breaking stress **-scheibe** *f* rupture or frangible disk **-stab** *m* test bar
Zerreißung *f* tearing
Zerreiß-ventil *n* rupture (frangible) disk **-verfahren** *n* tearing(-down) method **-versuch** *m* tensile test, tension test
zerren to pull, drag, tug, tear, haul
Zerrennboden *m* slag bottom
zerrennen to refine
Zerrenner *m* refiner
Zerrennfeuer *n* refining fire
zerrieben ground
zerrieseln to disintegrate (slag)
zerrinnen to dissolve, melt dwindle
zerrissen torn
Zerrlinse *f* anamorphosing lens, distorting lens (opt.)
Zerrung *f* pulling, dragging, tugging, tearing
Zerrungskreis *m* annulating network, suppressing network
zerrütten to destroy, shatter, smash
zersägen to saw
Zerschellerschicht *f* bursting or shattering layer
zerschlagen to smash, break in pieces, shatter, batter
Zerschlagen *n* crushing, grinding
zerschmelzen to melt (away)
zerschmettern to smash
Zerschmetterungsbruch *m* comminuted fracture
zerschmieden to forge badly, overstrain
Zerschmiedung *f* faulty forging
zerschneiden to cut up, dissect
Zerschneiden *n* shearing
Zerschneidezünder *m* tension-release igniter
zerschnitzeln to shred
zersetzbar decomposable
Zersetzbarkeit *f* decomposability, dissociation property
zersetzen to decompose, break up, disintegrate, dissociate, analyze **durch elektrischen Strom ~** to electrolyze
Zersetzer *m* decomposer, decomposing agent
zersetzt disintegrated, decomposed
Zersetzung *f* decomposition, disintegration, splitting up, decay, cracking, dissociation **zur ~ neigendes Öl** unstable oil
Zersetzungs-beständigkeit *f* decomposing resistance **-destillation** *f* destructive distillation, dry distillation **-geschwindigkeit** *f* rate of decomposition **-kammer** *f* dissociation or decomposition chamber **-kunst** *f* analysis, art of analyzing **-produkt** *n* decomposition product **-spannung** *f* decomposition voltage **-vorgang** *m* decomposition process **-wärme** *f* heat of decomposition **-widerstand** *m* electrolytic resistance **-zelle** *f* decomposition cell
zerspalten to split, cleave
Zerspaltung *f* splitting-up cleavage
zerspanbar machinable
Zerspanbarkeit *f* chippability, machineability, free cutting and machining property
zerspanen to splinter off, remove metal by cutting, chip
Zerspanung *f* machining, removal of metal by cutting tool
Zerspanungs-eigenschaft *f* cutting property **-festigkeit** *f* resistance to cutting **-leistung** *f* metal removal rate, dynamic stresses **-vorgang** *m* machining or cutting operation **-werkzeug** *n* cutting tool
zersplittern to splinter, break to pieces, shatter (glass)
Zersplitterung *f* dissipation of forces, splintering fire, shattering
zersprengen to burst, blow up, shatter, snap, disperse, blast
zersprengte Narben broken grain
zerspringen to crack, break, shiver, burst, explode
zerstampfen to pound, crush
Zerstampfung *f* attrition
zerstäubbar atomizable
Zerstäubegerät *n* spraying apparatus
zerstäuben to atomize, spatter, spray, pulverize, crumble, sputter, disintegrate, vaporize **fächerförmig ~** to atomize as a fan-shaped spray
Zerstäuber *m* atomizer, sprayer, diffuser, pulverizer, vaporizer **-brenner** *m* atomizing burner **-decker** *m* sprayer containing cover **-düse** *f* spray or atomizer nozzle, atomizer jet **-gerät** *n* atomizer, chemical-spray apparatus **-konus** *m* atomizing cone **-latex** *m* sprayed rubber **-lochplatte** *f* burner plate, perforated plate **-rohr** *n* atomizer pipe **-schirm** *m* atomizer cone **-ventil** *n* atomizing valve
zerstäubt vaporized

Zerstäubung *f* atomization, comminution, spattering, spraying, scattering, spray, sputtering (of a cathode)

Zerstäubungs-apparat *m* atomizer, spray apparatus **-düse** *f* spray diffuser **-gehäuse** *n* jet chamber **-gerät** *n* airplane spraying mechanism **-luft** *f* air used for atomizing **-mittel** *n* atomizing agent **-streifen** *m* spray strip **-trockner** *m* atomizing or spraying drier **-vergaser** *m* jet or spray carburetor

zerstieben to scatter

zerstörbar destructible

Zerstörbarkeit *f* destructibility, destructibleness

zerstören to destroy, demolish, ruin, corrode

zerstört wrecked, destroyed **~ werden** to decay, become wrecked

Zerstörung *f* corrosion, decay, destruction, disintegration (atom), failure **lochfräßähnliche ~** pitting, honey-combing

zerstörungsfrei non-destructive **auf magnetischem Wege ~ auf Risse prüfen** to magnaflux **-e Werkstoffprüfung** non-destructive testing

Zerstörungsstreifen *m* destructive path

zerstoßen to pound (to pieces), bruise, powder, pulverize

Zerstrahler *m* jet diffuser

Zerstrahlung *f* annihilation radiation

Zerstrahlungsphoton *n* annihilation photon

zerstreuen to disperse, scatter, dissipate, diffuse, spread, diverge

zerstreuend diverging **-es Glas** diverging lens **-e Linse** dispersing or divergent lens

Zerstreuerschaufel *f* diffuser vane

zerstreut scattered, diffuse, disseminated

zerstreutporig diffuse-porous

Zerstreuung *f* dispersion, scattering, dissipation, diffusion, diffraction

Zerstreuungsbild *n* image formed by divergent lens **Zerstreuungsbilder des Auges** blur circles of eye

Zerstreuungs-koeffizient *m* coefficient of dispersion **-kreis** *m* circle of diffusion, blur circle **-kreisdurchmesser** *m* blur circle diameter **-linse** *f* divergent or diverging lens, dispersing lens, negative lens **-punkt** *m* virtual focus **-scheibchen** *n* circle of (least) diffusion, blur circle **-vermögen** *n* dispersive power or diffusibility **-winkel** *m* angle of scattering **-wirkung** *f* scattering (of electrons)

zerstückeln to chop to pieces, crush, disintegrate

Zerstückelung *f* fracturing, breaking into small pieces

zerteilen to divide, part, split (up), disperse, separate

Zerteiler *m* distributor

zerteilt split

Zerteilung *f* dissolution, division, separation, dispersion, resolution into factors, analysis

Zerteilungs-grad *m* degree of division, dispersion **-kraft** *f* fragmentation power

zertrümmerbar fissionable, disintegrable

Zertrümmerbarkeit *f* disintegrability

zertrümmern to wreck, smash, demolish, shatter

Zertrümmerung *f* destruction, crushing, fragmentation, shattering, smashing, disintegration, fission (of atom)

Zertrümmerungsstern *m* nuclear star

Zerwalzen *n* breakdown

zerzupfen to pull to pieces, tease

Zettel *m* ticket, bill, placard, warp (weaving), voucher, label, card, check, note **-druckverfahren** *n* (Teleph. Gebühr) automatic message accounting (AMA) **-gatter** *n* magazine creel **-katalog** *m* card index or catalogue **-maschine** *f* warping machine **-kötzer** *m* warp spool

zetteln to warp (weaving)

Zettel-rohrpost *f* pneumatic ticket carrier **-spieß** *m* file spike **-spule** *f* warper's bobbin **-verteiler** *m* ticket-distribution position, bill distributor **-verteilerstelle** *f* ticket distributing position

Zettler *m* warper

Zettlerei *f* warping

Zeug *n* stuff, material, cloth, texture, implement, tool, goods, type metal, textile fabric, tissue, weft

Zeug-baum *m* cloth beam (weaving) **-druck** *m* cloth printing **-druckerei** *f* cloth-printing factory

Zeugelinie *f* generatrix, generating line

zeugen to testify, give or bear testimony

Zeugnis *n* certificate, authority, testimonial, testimony, evidence, witness

Zeug-regler *m* pulp meter **-sichter** *m* pulp strainer **-spanner** *m* temple (weaving)

Zeunerit *m* zeunerite

Zeylonit *m* ceylonite

ZF (Zwischenfrequenz) *f* intermediate frequency (i. f.)

ZF-Empfindlichkeitsverhältnis *n* intermediate-frequency response ratio

Z-Funkfeuer Z-marker (beacon)

Zickzack *m* zigzag **im ~ fahren oder laufen** to zigzag

Zickzack-antenne *f* zigzag antenna **-bewegung** *f* zigzag motion **-duostraße** *f* staggered mill

zickzackförmig staggered, zigzagged

Zickzack-linie *f* zigzag line **-lochung** *f* alternating perforation **-naht** *f* staggered seam **-nietung** *f* zigzag riveting **-presse** *f* press for zigzag feed **-punktschweißung** *f* staggered spot welding **-reflexion** *f* staggered reflection **-schaltung** *f* zigzag or interconnected star connection **-sperre** *f* zigzag barrage **-weg** *m* multiple reflection path

Ziegel *m* brick, tile, briquette **farbig glasierter ~** encaustic tile **feuerfester ~** firebrick

Ziegel-abdeckung *f* brick coping **-arbeit** *f* bricklaying **-backstein** *m* brick **-block** *m* firetile block **-brand** *m* brick or tile burning, batch of brick or tile **-brennen** *n* brick or tile burning **-brenner** *m* brick or tile burner, brickmaker, tilemaker **-brennerei** *f* brickworks **-brocken** *m* broken brick, brickbat

ziegeldachförmig imbricated

Ziegelei *f* brickkiln, brickworks **-ofen** *m* brickkiln

Ziegel-erde *f* brick clay **-erz** *n* tile ore **-fachwerk** *n* rectangular-type checkerwork **-hütte** *f* brickkiln, tile kiln **-mauer** *f* brick wall **-mauerwerk** *n* brickwork, tilework, firebrick wall

Ziegel-ofen *m* brickkiln **-presse** *f* brick press, brickmaking press **-rohbau** *m* visible or raw brickwork **-rot** brick-red **-schicht** *f* brick course **-sorte** *f* grade of brick

Ziegelstein *m* brick, tile, clay brick **-fundament** *n* brick foundation **-schicht** *f* course of bricks **-verkleidung** *f* brickwork casing

Ziegel-streicher *m* brickmaker **-stück** *n* brick bat

-ton *m* brick clay, loam, tile clay
Ziegel- und Kachelherstellungsmaschine *f* brick and slab machine
Ziegen-fuß *f* crowbar **-leder** *n* kid leather
Zieh-abnahme *f* reduction **-angel** *f* drawing-out device **-anlage** *f* drawing plant **-arm** *m* crank **-backe** *f* jaw for rifling machine or rifle bench, drawing jaw **-band** *n* clamp, strap, straining clip **-bank** *f* draw bench, skelper, skelp mill, crocodile
ziehbar ductile, stretchable
Ziehbarkeit *f* ductility, stretchability
Zieh-biegemaschine *f* draw former **-bleche** *pl* drawing sheets **-brunnen** *m* draw well **-diamant** *m* diamond die **-dorn** *m* broach, drawing mandrel **-draht** *m* drawing-in wire **-eisen** *n* drawing die, drawplate, die plate, drawing block, drawknife
ziehen to draw (out), pull, drag, suck, raise, move, tap, discharge, clinker, rake out, broach (holes), breed, train, rear, cultivate, stretch, soak, go, warp, string (wires) **Drähte ~** to string wires **einen Graben ~** to dig a ditch **Lichtbogen ~** to draw (an arc) **sich ~** to get warped, distort (steel) **nach sich ~** to drag **~ lassen** (im Bad) to allow to fill
Ziehen *n* pull, drawing, stringing, instability, pulling, dragging, haulage, coupling-hysteresis effect, oscillation hysteresis phenomena
ziehender Schnitt draw cut
Zieher *m* drawer (metal.), wire drawer
Zieherei *f* drawing installation, drawing room, steeldrawing works
Zieh-erscheinung *f* pulling (radio); locking effect, coupling-hysteresis effect, oscillation hysteresis phenomena **-fähigkeit** *f* drawing quality, capacity for being drawn **-feder** *f* drawing pen **-fett** *n* drawing grease or compound **-form** *f* draw die **-grad** *m* (amount of) reduction, ductility **-gut** *n* drawing material **-haken** *m* rake (for removing slag), drawing or pulling hook, drag hook
Zieh-kaliber *n* drawing pass **-kartei** *f* tub file **-karton** *m* molded cardboard **-keil** *m* spring-coupling key **-keilgetriebe** *n* driving-key-type transmission **-kerbstift** *m* pin **-kern** *m* drawing die, draw key **-klinge** *f* scraper, spoke shave **-kopf** *m* (Räummaschine) pull head **-kraft** *f* tensile force, pull, traction, drawing power **-kristalle** *pl* rate grown transistors
Zieh-länge *f* stroke **-loch** *n* drawing-die hole **-marken** *pl* pull guide **-masse** *f* drawing dimension **-matrize** *f* drawing die **-messer** *n* drawknife **-nadel** *f* broach **-platte** *f* drawing block **-pappe** *f* molded board **-presse** *f* extrusion press, drop(-forge) press **-probe** *f* sample drawn, sample to be drawn, tensile-test specimen **-punze** *f* tracing punch
Zieh-riefe *f* stretcher strain, fissure, drawing groove or scratch **-ring** *m* drawing die, drawing block, die plate, drawing tool **-scheibe** *f* drawing die **-schlauch** *m* single-ended cable grip **-schleifen** to hone **-schleifen** *n* stropping, honing **-schleifmaschine** *f* honing machine
Zieh-schnur *f* draw or pull cord, shutter-control line or cord **-schütz** *n* sliding sluice or valve, hatch, sliding lock gate **-spachtel** *f* surfacer applied by drawing **-stange** *f* rifling rod, broach **-stein** *m* (drawing) die **-strumpf** *m* cable grip, wire grip **-teil** *m* drawn piece, drawn metal part **-tiefe** *f* depth of drawing **-trichter** *m* bell, die (tube mfg.)
Ziehung *f* drawing, draft, traction
Zieh-vermögen *n* affinity **-vorgang** *m* drawing process, drawing out, instability **-vorgänge** *pl* pulling, oscillation hysteresis, resonance-discontinuity, -protraction, or -instability phenomena **-vorrichtung** *f* drawing device, drawing machine **-walzwerk** *n* coiler tension rolling mill **-weg** *m* towpath **-werksanlage** *f* drawing-work installation **-werkzeug** *n* drawing die, drawing tool **-wert** *m* ductility value **-winkel** *m* die angle **-zange** *f* pliers, dog (mech.) **-zeug** *n* dog and chain, dog belt (min.)
Ziel *n* target (rdr), objective, goal, destination, aim, scope, object, end, mark, boundary, limit **ins ~ gehen** to come on aim **dicht am ~** hit close to the target **übers ~ fliegen** to overshoot **bewegliches ~, fahrendes ~** moving target **feststehendes ~, festes ~** fixed or stationary target **gedecktes ~** defiladed target **gehendes ~** receding target **getarntes ~** camouflaged target
Ziel, gezogenes ~ towed target **kommendes ~** approaching target **kreisendes ~** circling target **offenes ~** visible target **widerstandsfähiges ~** resistant target
Ziel-abstand *m* target distance **-abweichung** *f* target displacement **-achse** *f* axis of collimation, axis of sight, aiming axis **-achsenfehler** *m* error of collimation **-amt** *n* (Teleph.) called destination
Zielanflug *m* homing (aviat.) **-gerät** *n* homing device **-peilanlage** homing device
Ziel-anweisungsscheinwerfer *m* target-indication searchlight **-auffassung** *f* target pickup or acquisition (rdr) **-auflösung** *f* target break-up (rdr) **-aufnahme** *f* target pickup **-aufsuchen** *n* detection of target or object (by radar) **-bestimmung** *f*, **-bezeichnung** *f* target designation **-bild** *n* target image or diagram
Ziel-darstellung *f* target designation or representation, **-darstellungsflugkörper** *m* target missile **-deckungsmethode** *f* line-of-sight system **-dreieck** *n* triangle of error **-durchgang** *m* passing the goal mark or stakes **-einrichtung** *f* sighting or aiming mechanism
zielen to sight, point, aim **~ auf** to aim at, strive for, direct or tend to, adjust (sight)
Zielen *n* sighting
Ziel-entfernung *f* distance of the target **-erfassung** *f* target acquisition (rdr) **-fehler** *m* sighting error, fault of aim **-fernrohr** *n* telescopic sight, sighting telescope, bombsight, rifle sight **-festlegung** *f* pinpointing of a target **-feststellung** *f* target designation or location
Zielflug *m* homing **-empfänger** *m* homing-receiver **-funkfeuer** *n* homing beacon, homer **-gerät** *n* homing apparatus or device, direction finder **-körper** *m* target drone **-verfahren** *n* point-to-point navigation method, homing procedure
Zielflugzeug *n* target airplane **ferngelenktes ~** remote controlled target plane
Ziel-führung *f* target tracking **-funkfeuer** *n* homing beacon **-gelände** *n* target area **-genau** accurate, precise **-genauigkeit** *f* accuracy of

sighting

Zielgerät *n* sighting mechanism, bombsight, homing adapter, sight (on gun), course indicator **optisches ~** visual sighting mechanism, visual aiming device

Ziel-geschwindigkeit *f* target speed **-gevierttafel** *f* protractor and scale, transparent decimal grid **-höhe** *f* altitude or height of target **-höhenwinkel** *m* quadrant elevation, angular height of target **-karte** *f* range table **-kern** *m* target nucleus **-kelle** *f* marking disk

Zielkopf *m* target finder or detector (electronics) **-steuerung** *f* electronic target-detecting control

Zielkreis *m* target circle or area

Ziel-landung *f* precision landing (aviation) **-latte** *f* collimating staff, target **-leuchten** *n* target illumination **-lineal** *n* orienting straightedge **-linie** *f* line of sight, finish line, line of collimation **-linienprüfer** *m* aim verifier **-löffel** *m* aiming disk, marking disk **-los** aimless, erratic **-marke** *f* measuring mark, collimating mark, sight graticule or reticule **-markierung** *f* target marking for bombers

Ziel-ortungsgerät *n* target locating set (rdr) **-peilung** *f* destination bearing (aviat.) **-photogerät** *n* photo finish apparatus **-platte** *f* cyclotron target

Zielpunkt *m* aiming point, sighting point, goal, objective, bull's-eye **-karte** *f* range card

Ziel-raumbild *n* space picture, stereoscopic view of target **-rechenmaschine** *f* predictor **-scheibe** *f* sighting disk, target **-seitenwinkel** *m* azimuth of target **-skizze** *f* target sketch **-spinne** *f* target overlay, fan **-sprache** (elektronische Übersetzung) target language **-stachel** *m* backsight **-strahl** *m* collimating ray, line of collimation

Zielstrich *m* vertical diaphragm line

Zielsuch-gerät *n* accurate position finder (apf) **-kopf** *m* homing head (g/m) **-steuerung** *f* steering control by homing device **-system** *n* (Astron.) homing system **-verfahren** *n* homing system

Ziel-tafel *f* battery chart, sighting disk **-taste** (ZT) destination key **-tastenzusatz** *m* destination key circuit **-taster** *m* autodial **-teil** *m* target sector **-unterlagen** *pl* target data **-verfolgung** *f* tracking (a target) **-vorrichtung** *f* sight, rocket, launching rack **-waagerechte** *f* horizontal **-wahl** *f* choice of target, destination or target dialling (teleph.) **-wechsel** *m* change of target

Zielweg *m* target course, path of flight, track **-aufschreibung** *f* plotting of target course **-karte** *f* target-course map

Ziel-zeichen *n* target blip (radar) **-zünder** *m* ranging fuse **-zuweisung** *f* assignment of target, indication or allotting of targets **-zuweisungsschalter** *m* assign pushbutton

Zier-band *n* ornamented hinge **-blech** *n* ornamental sheet **-eisen** *n* ornamental iron **-fuß** *m* ornamental base **-hülse** *f* decorative sleeve **-knopf** *m* knurled knob **-kreislicht** *n* zodiacal light **-leiste** *f* tailpiece (print), trim strip (on cabinets), molding **-linie** *f* fancy line (print.)

Zier-mutter *f* milled nut **-rahmen** *m* molding, decorative frame **-schiene** *f* grille bar **-schrift** *f* ornamental type **-sockel** *m* ornamental sleeve

Ziffer *f* number, factor, coefficient, cipher, numeral, digit, figure **geltende ~** significant figure

Zifferblatt *n* instrument dial **-vorderseite** *f* dial face

Ziffern-code *m* digital code **-feldimpuls** *m* numerical impulse **-kontrolle der Einrichtungen** digit control of features **-leitung** *f* digit line **-lochung** *f* numerical punching **-maschine** *f* digital computer

ziffernmäßig numerical, mathematical, digital **-e Ablesung** *f* digital readout

Ziffern-rechner *m* digital computer **-rolle** *f* counter **-schaltung** *f* figure shift **-scheibe** *f* figure dial **-schnellspeicher** high-speed digital storage **-schreiber** *m* digit driver **-schrift** *f* cipher coder **-schritt** *m* numerical increment

Ziffern-skala *f* number scale **-speicherelement** digital storage element **-summe** *f* sum of digits **-typenhebel** *m* number type bar **-umrahmung** *f* figure pattern **-vordruck** *m* preprinted figures (punched cards) **-weiß** *n* figure blank (teleph.) **-zeichen** *n* pulsing signal, pl numerical digest

Zigaretten-hülsenmaschine *f* cigarette-tube machine **-maschinenband** *n* cigarette-machine ribbon

Zigarren-abschneider *m* cigar cutter **-anzünder** *m* cigar lighter **-bändchenumleger** *m* cigar bander

Zilienpinzette *f* cilia forceps or tweezers

Zimmer-antenne *f* indoor or room antenna

Zimmerei *f* carpentry

Zimmerer *m* carpenter

Zimmer-flucht *f* suite of apartments **-kabel** *n* office cable **-lautstärke** *f* domestic volume **-leitung** *f* office wiring, office cable, internal wiring **-leitungsdraht** *m* wire for indoor installation **-mann** *m* carpenter

Zimmermannswinkel *m* carpenter's square

zimmern to frame, timber, fabricate

Zimmertemperatur *f* (normal) room temperature

Zimmerung *f* timbering, sheathing

Zimmerwerk *n* carpentry **~ eines Schachtes** pit frame

Zimmerwerkstätte *f* carpenter's workshop

Zink *n* zinc, spelter **schwefelsaures ~** sulfate of zinc

Zink-aluminiumlegierung *f* zinc-aluminum alloy **-artig** zincky, like zinc **-asche** *f* zinc ash, zinc dross **-äthyl** *n* zinc ethyl **-ätze** *f* zinc-etching solution **-auflage** *f* zinc coat **-azetat** *n* zinc acetate

Zink-badeofen *m* hot-dip galvanizing bath **-becher** *m* zinc container, zinc containing vessel, zinc cup, zinc sleeve (elec.), zinc case, zinc cylinder **-bedachung** *f* zinc roofing **-beize** *f* zinc mordant **-blech** *n* sheet zinc, zinc plate, galvanizing sheet **-blende** *f* zinc blende, sphalerite **-blendetyphalbleiter** *m* zinc blende-typ semiconductor **-blumen** *pl* flowers of zinc, zinc oxide **-blüte** *f* zinc bloom, hydrozincite **-bromid** *n* zinc bromide **-butter** *f* chloride of zinc

Zinkchlorid *n* zinc chloride **mit ~ tränken** to burnettize

Zink-chromatgrundierung *f* zinc-chromatic primer **-dampf** *m* zinc vapor **-destillation** *f* zinc distillation **-destillierofen** *m* zinc-distilling furnace

Zinkdruck-blöcke *pl* zincos **-platte** *f* zinc-printing plate **-schnellpresse** *f* high-speed zinc-printing machine **-verfahren** *n* zinc printing

Zinke *f* tenon, prong, tooth, tine, dovetail ~ **einer Stimmgabel** prong of a tuning fork **versenkte** ~ mitred dovetail
Zinkeinlage, mit ~ zinc-lined
Zinkeisen-erz *n* franklinite **-spat** *m* ferriferous smithsonite **-stein** *m* franklinite
Zink-elektrolyse *f* electrolytic zinc process **-elektrolysenanlage** *f* electrolytic zinc plant
zinken to dovetail
Zinken *n* dovetailing
zinken-fräsen to dovetail **-fräser** *m* combing tool **-fräsgerät** *n* combing attachment **-hacke** *f* pickax **-hobel** *m* dovetailing plane **-schneidmaschine** *f* dovetailing machine **-teilung** *f* pitch
Zink-entsilberung *f* zinc desilverization **-entsilberungsanlage** *f* zinc-desilverization plant
Zinkerz *n* zinc ore **rotes** ~ zincite
Zink-erzrösthütte *f* zinc ore-roasting plant **-fahlerz** *n* tennantite **-farbe** *f* zinc paint **-feile** *f*, **-feilspan** *m* zinc filing **-ferrozyanid** *n* zinc ferrocyanide **-folie** *f* zinc foil **-formiat** *n* zinc formate **-führend** zinc-bearing, zinciferous **-gehalt** *m* zinc content **-gekrätz** *n* zinc dross **-gießer** *m* zinc founder
Zink-glas *n*, **glaserz** *n* siliceous zinc oxide, hydrous zinc silicate, siliceous or electric calamine **-granalien** *pl* granulated zinc, zinc granules **-grau** *n* zinc gray **-grün** *n* zinc green **-haltig** containing zinc, zinciferous **-harz** *n* resin blende **-hütte** *f* zinc smeltery, zinc works, zinc smelting plant, zinc smelter **-hydroxyd** *n* zinc hydroxide
zinkisch zincky, of zinc
Zinkit *m* zincite
Zink-jodid *n* zinc iodide **-kalk** *m* zinc calx, zinc ash **-kiesel** *m*, **-kieselerz** *n* siliceous calamine **-kitt** *m* zinc cement **-kohle** *f* zinc carbon **-legierung** *f* zinc alloy **-lösung** *f* zinc solution **-mehl** *n* zinc powder or dust **-muffelofen** *m* zinc-distilling furnace **-muffelverfahren** *n* zinc-distilling process
Zinkofen *m* zinc furnace **-bruch** *m* tutty, cadmia
Zinkographie *f* zincography
Zinkoleat *n* zinc oleate
Zinkopapier *n* zinco paper
Zinkoxalat *n* zinc oxalate
Zinkoxyd *n* zinc oxide **technisches** ~ commercial zinc oxide
Zink-pecherz *n* sphalerite **-perborat** *n* zinc perborate **-pfeife** *f* zinc pipe **-phosphid** *n* zinc phosphide **-phyllit** *m* hopeite **-platte** *f* zinc plate **-pol** *m* zinc pole, zinc terminal **-raffinerie** *f* zinc refinery **-rauch** *m* zinc fume **-rost** *m* white rust **-röstofen** *m* zinc roaster
Zink-salizylat *n* zinc salicylate **-schaum** *m* zinc scum, zinc crust **-schlicker** *m* zinc dross **-schnitzel** *pl* zinc filings **-schutz** *m* protection by zinc **-schwamm** *m* tutty, cadmia **-schweißdrähte** *pl* zinc welding rods **-silicat** *n* zinc silicate **-span** *m* zinc shaving **-spat** *m* zinc spar, smithsonite, zinc carbonate **-spritzguß** *m* zinc die-casting **-stab** *m* zinc rod
Zinkstaub *m* zinc dust **-ätze** *f* zinc dust discharge **-fällung** *f* zinc-dust precipitation **-reinigung** *f* zinc-dust purification
Zink-stearat *n* zinc stearate **-streifen** *m* strip of zinc **-sulfat** *n* zinc sulfate **-sulfid** *n* zinc sulfide **-sulfit** *n* zinc sulfite **-tannat** *n* zinc tannate **-überzug** *m* zinc coating **-valerianat** *n* zinc valerate
Zink-verbindung *f* zinc compound **-vitriol** *n* white vitriol **-weiß** *n* zinc white **-werk** *n* zinc works **-wolle** *f* mossy zinc metal **-ziehen** *n* zinc drawing **-zieher** *m* zinc drawer **-zyanid** *n* zinc cyanide
Zinn *n* tin **-abstrich** *m* tin skimming, tin scum, tin dross **-ader** *f* tin lode, tin vein **-after** *m* tin refuse, tin-ore refuse **-ammoniumchlorid** *n* ammonium stannic chloride
zinnartig tinlike, tinny
Zinn-asche *f* tin ashes, stannic oxide **-ätzfarbe** *f* tin discharge paste **-ausbringen** *n* tin yield **-azetat** *n* tin acetate
Zinn-barren *m* tin bar or slab **-belag** *m* tin foil(ing) **-bergwerk** *n* tin mine **-blatt** *n* tin foil **-blech** *n* tin plate, sheet tin **-bleilegierung** *f* pewter **-bleilot** *n* tin-lead solder **-bromid** *n* tin bromide, stannic bromide **-bromür** *n* stannous bromide **-bromwasserstoffsäure** *f* bromostannic acid **-butter** *f* tin tetrachloride, tin butter
Zinn-charge *f* tin-weighing **-chlorammonium** *n* ammonium stannic chloride **-chlorid** *n* tin chloride, stannic chloride **-chlorür** *n* stannous chloride **-chlorwasserstoffsäure** *f* chlorostannic acid **-diphenylchlorid** *n* diphenyl tin chloride **-draht** *m* tin wire **-elektrolyseverfahren** *n* electrolytic tin-refining process
zinnen to tin
zinnen, zinnern of tin or pewter
zinnenförmig scalloped
Zinnenspannung *f* square-wave voltage
Zinnerz *n* tin ore, cassiterite **-formation** *f* tin-ore formation **-gang** *m* tin vein, tin lode **-seife** *f* tin placer deposit
Zinn-farbe *f* vermilion **-feilicht** *n*, **-feilspan** *m* tin filing **-flammofen** *m* reverberatory tin furnace **-fluorid** *n* stannic fluoride **-folie** *f* tin foil **-gehalt** *m* tin content **-gekrätz** *n* tin refuse **-geschirr** *n* tin vessels, pewter **-gießer** *m* tin founder **-glasiert** tin-glazed **-glasur** *f* tin glaze, tin glazing
Zinn-granalien *pl* granulated tin **-graupen** *pl* cassiterite **-grube** *f* tin mine **-grundierung** *f* bottoming or grounding with tin **-guß** *m* tin casting
zinnhaltig containing tin, stanniferous
Zinn-hütte *f* tins-melting plant, tinworks, tin smeltery **-hydroxyd** *n* stannic hydroxide **-hydroxydul** *n* stannous hydroxide **-jodid** *n* stannic iodide **-jodür** *n* stannous iodide
Zinn-kalk *m* stannic oxide **-kapsel** *f* tin cap **-kessel** *m* galvanizing pot, galvanizing kettle **-kies** *m* tin pyrites, stannite **-knirschen** *n* tin cry **-komposition** *f* dyer's spirit **-krätze** *f* tin dross or waste **-kreischen** *n* tin cry
Zinn-lagerstätte *f* tin deposit **-legierung** *f* tin alloy **-lösung** *f* tin solution, tin spirit **-lot** *n* tin solder **-löte** *f* soft solder, soldering **-metall** *n* metallic tin **-monoxyd** *n* stannous oxide
Zinnober *m* cinnabar **-erde** *f*, **-erz** *n* cinnabar ore **-farbe** *f* vermilion **-grün** *f* cinnabar green **-rot** *n* vermilion **-scharlach** *n* cinnabar scarlet **-spat** *m* crystallized cinnabar
Zinn-ofen *m* tin furnace **-oxychlorid** *n* stannous chloride **-oxyd** *n* cassiterite **-oxydhaltig** containing tin oxide **-oxydhydrat** *n* stannous hydroxide **-oxydnatron** *n* sodium stannate

-oxydsalz *n* stannic salt **-oxydul** *n* stannous oxide **-oxydulchlorid** *n* stannous chloride **-oxydulhydrat** *n* stannous hydroxide **-oxydulreserve** *f* stannous oxide resist **-oxydverbindung** *f* stannic compound

Zinn-pest *f* tin plague, tin pest **-pfanne** *f* tin pot **-pfeife** *f* tin pipe **-platte** *f* tin plate or sheet **-probe** *f* tin assay, tin test, sample of tin **-produktion** *f* manufacture of tin, tin output **-puder** *n* powdery tin dross or skimming **-pulver** *n* powdered tin, tin powder, grain tin **-raffination** *f* tin refining **-raffinationsanlage** *f* tin-refining plant

zinn-reich rich in tin **-rohr** *n*, **-röhre** *f* tin tube or pipe **-rückstand** *m* tin residue, tin refuse **-salmiak** *m* ammonium chlorostannate, pink salt **-salz** *n* tin salt, stannous chloride **-salzätze** *f* tin crystal discharge **-säure** *f* stannic acid **-säureanhydrid** *n* stannic anhydride

zinnsaures Natrium sodium stannate

Zinn-schere *f* tin snips **-schlich** *m* dressed or concentrated tin **-schrei** *m* tin cry **-seife** *f* stream tin **-soda** *f* sodium stannate **-staub** *m* tin dust **-stein** *m* tinstone, cassiterite

Zinn-stufe *f* lump of tin ore **-sulfid** *n* tin sulfide, stannic sulfide **-sulfür** *n* stannous sulfide **-verbindung** *f* tin compound **-waldit** *m* zinnwaldite **-wäsche** *f* tin buddle **-wolle** *f* mossy tin metal

Zipfel *m* lobe, ear, secondary beams, stray (of side radiations) **-umschaltung** *f* lobe switching

Zippeit *m* zippeit

Zirkel *m* circle, (pair of) compasses, dividers, protractor **~ mit Führungsbügel** compass with wing **~ mit Reißfeder** inking compass

Zirkel-bein *n* leg of the compasses **-bügel** *m* wing of the compasses **-feder** *f* bow pen

Zirkelit *m* zirkelite

Zirkel-schenkel *m* arm of the compasses or dividers **-schlüssel** *m* compass key **-spitze** *f* point of the compass **-stift** *m* bow pencil **-verlängerung** *f* lengthening bar of compass

Zirkon *n* zircon, zirconium

Zirkonate *pl* zirconates

Zirkon-brenner *m* zirconium filament or burner **-erde** *f* zirconium oxide, zirconia **-fluorid** *n* zirconium fluoride

Zirkonium *n* zirconium **-metall** *n* zirconium metal, metallic zirconium **-säure** *f* zirconic acid **-stahl** *m* zirconium steel **-verbindung** *f* zirconium compound

Zirkular *n* circular **-polarisiert** circularly polarized **-polariskop** *n* circular polariscope

Zirkulation *f* circulation

Zirkulations-öl *n* circulating oil **-ölpumpe** *f* circulating oil pump **-pumpe** *f* circulating pump **-steg** *m* circulating passage **-strömung** *f* circulation flow **-theorie** *f* circulation theory

zirkulieren to circulate

zirkumpolar circumpolar

Zirkumsvallationslinie *f* circumvallation line

Zirrokumulus *m* cirro-cumulus

Zirronebel *m* cirro-veil, cirro-nebula

Zirrostratus *m* cirro-stratus

Zirrus *m* cirrus **-wolke** *f* cirrus cloud

Zischeffekt *m* hiss effect

zischen to hiss, sizzle

Zischen *n* hisses, hissing, sizz, fizz, sizzle

Zisch-hahn *m* compression tap or valve, priming pump or cock, relief cock **-laut** *m* sibilant or hissing sound, friccative **-ventil** *n* compression valve

Ziselierarbeit *f* chased work, chisel work

ziselieren to chase, carve

Ziselierwerkzeug *n* engraving tool

Zissoide *f* cissoid

Zisterne *f* cistern, tank

Zisternen-wagen *m* cistern car, tank car

Zi-Taste (Fernschreiber) figure-shift key

Zitronellöl *n* citronella oil

Zitronensäure *f* citric acid

zitronensaures Ammon ammonium citrate **~ Eisenoxydammon** ferric ammonium citrate **~ Kali** potassium citrate **~ Natrium** sodium citrate

Zitter-bewegung *f* circular fluctuation movement (of spin), trembling or vibratory motion **-elektrode** *f* vibrating electrode, vibratory electrode

zittern to vibrate, chatter, shake, tremble, quiver, quake

Zittern *n* tremor, flutter, trembling

Zitter-regler *m* vibrating governor or regulator **-sieb** *n* vibrating screen **-spannung** *f* dither voltage (servo) **-spule** *f* bucking coil

Zitterung *f* vibration

Zivil-flugwesen *n* civil aviation **-flugzeug** *n* civil or private airplane

Zivilisation *f* civilization

zivilisieren to civilize

Zivilluftfahrt *f* civil aviation **amtliche Bestimmungen für die ~** civil air regulations

Z-Markierungsfunkfeuer *n* Z-marker beacon (navig.)

Zodiakallicht *n* zodiacal light (astron.)

Zodiakus *m* zodiac

Zoll *m* inch, toll, customs, duty **-abfertigung** *f* custom clearance **-amt** *n* customs office, customhouse **-barriere** *f* turnpike **-brücke** *f* toll bridge

Zoll-flughafen *m* customs airport **-frei** duty-free **-gewinde** *n* thread measured in inches (inch thread) **-grenze** *f* customs frontier **-hafen** *m* customs port

Zoll-kreuzer *m* customs launch **-kutter** *m* revenue cutter **-lagerhaus** *n* bonded warehouse **-leitspindel** *f* English-pitch lead screw **-papier** *n* customhouse document **-pflichtig** dutiable, subject to duty

Zoll-schranke *f* turnpike **-schutz** *m* tariff protection **-speicher** *m* custom warehouse **-stab** *m* inch scale **-steigung** *f* inch thread **-stock** *m* foot rule **-teilung** *f* graduation in inches

Zollverschluß *m* customs seal **unter ~** in bond

Zölostat *m* coelostat

zonal gemittelt zonally averaged

Zone *f* zone, region, district, horizon (stratigraphical) **~ der Passatwinde** trade-wind belt **~ des Schweigens** zone of silence **~ der Windstillen** doldrums **empfangslose ~** silent zone (rdr) **gemäßigte ~** temperate zone **kalte ~** frigid zone **neutrale ~** neutral zone, apron (aviation) **stille ~, tote ~** skip zone, dead zone (radio reception) **verbotene ~** prohibited area

Zonen-achse *f* zone or zonal axis **-blende** *f* limiting stop **-breite** *f* phase belt (spread) **-einbauten** *pl* compartment fittings **-entnahme** *f*

zone selection **-fehler** *m* zonal aberration **-förmig** zonal **-frei** free from zone **-gliederung** *f* zonig

Zonenhauptort *m* zone center (teleph.) **zweiter ~** subzone center

Zonen-kühler *m* cooler by stages **-mittelpunkt** *m* zone center **-rostfeuerung** *f* compartment grate stoker **-signal** *n* sone signal **-steuerungsausgang** *m* zone selection common exit **-system** *n* repeating-center system, zone system

Zonen-verband *m* crystal zone **-wähler** *m* zone selector **-wanderrost** *m* compartment-type travelling grate stoker **-zähler** *m* zone selector **-zählung** *f* zone registration **-zeit** *f* zone time

Zopf *m* plait, braid, stress, top end (wood), tress of wool (weaving) **-drehmaschine** *f* twisting machine **-durchmesser** *m* top diameter (elec.)

zopfen, zöpfen to lop (wood) **einen Baum ~** to top a timber

Zopf-ende *n* top end **-fäule** *f* top rot **-stärke** *f* top diameter

Zorgit *m* zorgite

Zottenbüschel *n* villous tuft

Z-Schiene *f* Z rail

Z-Stoff *m* Z type of rocket fuel, sodium permanganate

zubauen to add a structure, block

Zubehör *n* attachment, accessories, fittings, appurtenances, apparatus, armature, adjunct, ancillary unit **-handelsmäßiges ~** trade accessories **ohne ~** plain, bare

Zubehör-blech *n* plate for accessories **-gehäuse** *n* accessory housing **-industrie** *f* accessories industry **-stück** *n* accessory **-teil** *m* armature, fittings, accessory part, attachment, component, spare part

Zuber *m* rag tube or bucket (paper mfg.)

zubereiten to prepare, dress, finish, make ready

Zubereiter *m* pressman (print.)

zubereitet prepared, treated **-e Stange** treated pole

Zubereitung *f* preparation, dressing

zubinden to tie up, bandage

zublasen to blow shut

Zubläserrohr *n* blower pipe

zubleiben to remain closed

zublinken to give a wink

Zubrand *m* gathering up, pickup

zubrennen to roast, calcine, close by heating, cauterize

Zubringelokomotive *f* feed locomotive

zubringen to bring, spend, feed

Zubringer *m* follower (magazine), feeder, conveyer, bringer **-band** *n* delivery belt **-dienst** *m* feeder service **-feder** *f* follower spring, feeder spring **-flugzeug** *n* feeder-service airplane **-förderband** *n* delivery-belt conveyer **-haspel** *f* feed winch **-hebel** *m* belt-feed lever **-kolben** *m* feed(ing) plunger **-linie** *f* auxiliary field railroad, feeder line (air traffic) **-luftlinie** *f* feeder line airline **-pumpe** *f* transfer pump **-straße** *f* approach road, feeder road **-wagen** *m* transfer car, traveling hopper

zubruchgehen to break down

Zubruchgehen *n* breaking down, rupture, choke, falling-in

Zuchtapparat *m* breeding apparatus

züchten to breed, grow, raise, produce, cultivate

Zuchtmeiler *m* breader (atom)

Züchtung *f* growth or growing (of crystals)

Züchtungsgefäß *n* growing vessel

Zuckanzeige *f* ballistics, kick or flash reading or indication (direction finding)

zucken to jerk, quiver, flash

Zucken *n* shuttling

Zucker *m* sugar **aufgemaischter ~** magma **gedeckter ~** clayed sugar **gestoßener ~** pounded sugar **greifbarer ~** spot sugar **klumpiger ~** caked sugar **vergällter ~** denatured sugar

Zucker-bestimmung *f* sugar determination or analysis, saccharimetry **-fabrik** *f* sugar factory **-gehaltmesser** *m* saccharimeter **-grunderzeugungsrecht** *n* sugar quota **-haltig** containing sugar, sacchariferous, sugary

Zucker-kalk *m* lime sucrate **-klären** *n* sugar clearing liquors **-knoten** *m* tailings, sweets, clustered sugar **-reibemaschine** *f* sugar rasp

Zuckerrohr *n* sugar cane **-faser** *f* bagasse fiber **-maschine** *f* sugar-cane mill machinery **-mühle** *f* sugar-cane mill **-quetsche** *f* sugar-cane crusher **-walzwerk** *n* sugar-cane mill

Zucker-säure *f* saccharic acid **-siebvorrichtung** *f* sugar sifter **-sieder** *m* sugar refiner **-sortieranlage** *f* sugar-sorting plant **-spaltung** *f* splitting of sucrose

Zuckertransport-rinne *f* grasshopper conveyer for sugar **-schnecke** *f* sugar screw conveyer, sugar scroll

Zucker-untersuchungsapparat *m* sugar-testing apparatus **-vermahlungsanlage** *f* sugar-grinding plant

Zuckung *f* jerk, pull, twitch, quiver, twitching, convulsion

zudämmen to dam up

Zudampf *m* live steam

Zudecke *f* cover, blanket

zudecken to cover, cover up

zudrehen to turn off or shut off

zudringen to press (for admission), run on

zuerkennen to allot, adjudge, adjudicate, award **eine Entschädigung ~** to award damages

Zufahrt *f* approach

Zufahrts-kanal *m* access canal **-rampe** *f* approach ramp **-weg** *m* approach road

Zufälligkeitsfehler *m* (zufälliger Fehler) accidental error

Zufalls-ergebnis *n* fortuitous result, fortuitous finding **-gesetz** *n* law of chance, law of probability **-koinzidenz** *f* chance coincidence **-lösung** *f* chance solution **-maschine** *f* randomizer **-phase** *f* random phase **-treffer** *m* accidental or chance hit **-variable** *f* random variable **-wert** *m* freak value **-zahl** *f* random number

zufliegen to fly shut

zufließen to flow toward, flow in; be added

Zufluchtshafen *m* harbor of refuge, shelter, sheltered basin

Zufluß *m* supply, feed, inflow, flow, flux, afflux, influx, resources, inlet, admission **~ an Gesprächsanmeldungen** flow (of telephone calls) **höchster ~ zur Talsperre** greatest head flow to the barrage

Zufluß-behälter *m* feed tank **-gebiet** *n* basin **-menge** *f* rate of flow **-messer** *m* head meter **-regler** *m* flow regulator, admission controller **-rohr** *n* feed pipe

zufrieren to freeze up or over
zufügen to add, inflict
Zufuhr *f* addition, supply, feed, lead-in, importation, input, admission, inlet **~ abschneiden** to cut off supplies
zuführen to supply, feed, admit, convey, carry into, lead in, deliver, bring up, conduct
Zuführer *m* belt pawl, feed mechanism
Zufuhrgleis *n* leading-in line
Zuführ-greifer *m* travelling feed grippers **-lattentisch** *m* lattice feed table **-magazin** *n* feeding magazine
Zufuhr-regler *m* supply valve **-rollgang** *m* live-roller-type feeding table **-stockung** *f* interruption in supply **-straße** *f* road approach, supply road
Zuführtisch *m* feed lattice-table
Zuführung *f* feed, delivery, supply, inlet, lead (elec.), conveyance, supply line **abgeschirmte ~** shielded imput lead **~ durch Gefälle** gravity feed **in ~** in transit, on the way **lose ~** wandering lead **verdrallte und abgeschirmte ~** twisted and screened lead
Zuführungs-bewegung *f* feed movement (feed motion) **-bohrer** *m* conducting bit, guide bit **-draht** *m* lead-in or feed wire **-gehäuse** *n* feed-mechanism housing **-kabel** *n* supply or leading-in cable, feeder (cable) **-leitung** *f* supply main or lead, feeder (line) **-rohr** *n* supply pipe, feed pipe, intake **-rolle** *f* feeding pulley **-schiene** *f* conductor bar **-teller** *m* delivery plate **-vorrichtung** *f* feeding device **-walze** *f* feed roller
Zufuhrvorrichtung *f* supplying device, feeding device
zufüllen to fill in or up
Zug *m* draw; (Technik) pull, traction; (Spannung) tension, stress; (Saugkraft) suction; (Stanzwerkzeug) drawing tool; (Hebezeug) hoist; (Flaschen **~**) pully; (Eisenbahn) train; (Zugluft) draft; (U.S.) train; tug, drawing, motion, progress, impulse, tendency, drawtube, stroke, disposition, procession, feature, characteristic, flue, thrust, platoon, groove (ordnance), stand, current, pass (of boiler), trend, girder, piston, rifling, sign, stretch, whiff, course, traverse, extender, mover, negative pressure, block and tackle, strain **~ und Druck** push and pull **~ eines Kohlenmeilers** vapor channel, air hole, or funnel of a charcoal pile **~ über Tage** survey line on surface **~ unter Tage** draft underground **einen ~ ablassen** to start a train
Zuge, in einem ~ in a single operation
Zug, abfahrender ~ starting train **durchgehender ~** direct train **fahrplanmäßiger ~** scheduled train, **künstlicher ~** forced or artificial draft **leiser ~** light air **sechsfacher ~** six-line reeving **seitlicher ~** lateral pull, transverse stress **seitlich auftretender ~** side pull **verspäteter ~** delayed train
Zugabe *f* addition, extra, surplus, premium, supplement, allowance, tolerance **~ zum Einpassen** fitting allowance
Zugabeartikel *m* gift, advertising novelty
Zugabfertigungsdienst *m* train dispatch service
Zugabnahme *f* reduction
Zugang *m* access, approach, entry, entrance, opening
zugängig, zugänglich accessible
Zugänglichkeit *f* accessibility
Zugangs-leiter *f* approach ladder **-tür** *f* access door **-weg** *m* approach **-zeit** *f* access time
Zuganker *m* tie rod, tie bar, tension rod, connecting rod, through bolt, tie beam, anchoring rod, stay, adjustable bolt, iron tie **gefederter ~** adjustable spring bolt
Zuganlage *f* draft equipment
Zuganzeiger *m* draft gauge
Zugbalken *m* balk, anchor tie beam
Zugband *n* tie rod, tension member or rod, drawstring, shock cord (in parachute) **elastisches ~** elastic tie rod
Zugbandstoff *m* tie-rod material
Zugbeanspruchung *f* tensile load, tensile stress, stretching strain **~ der Vertauungen** pull of mooring ropes
Zug-begleiter *m* runner, wagon road runner (min.) **-belastung** *f* tension or tensile load
Zugbeleuchtungsausrüstung *f* train lighting equipment
Zugblechträger *m* tension-field beam
Zugbolzen *m* set or tension bolt
Zugbrücke *f* drawbridge
Zug-dämpfer *m* baffle **-dauer** *f* duration of the dip **-dehnungskurve** *f* stress-strain curve **-deckung** *f* train blocking **-diagonale** *f* tie brace, tension brace, main oblique tie, oblique suspension rod **-draht** *m* taut wire **-dreibackenfutter** *n* draw-in type three-jaw clutch
Zugdruck-dauerfestigkeit *f* tension-compression fatigue strength **-gummifederungsmittel** *n* rubber shock absorber **-maschine** *f* pulsator machine **-prüfmaschine** *f* tension and compression testing machine **-schwingungsfestigkeit** *f* alternating tension- and compression-stress fatigue strength **-schwingungsprüfmaschine** *f* fatigue machine for alternating tension and compression stresses, alternating direct stress testing machine **-verhältnis** *n* ratio of tension to thrust **-versuch** *m* tension and compression test **-wechselfestigkeit** *f* alternate tensional-compressional strength **-zünder** *m* pull-pressure igniter
Zugdynamometer *n* traction dynamometer, spring balance pull
zugeben to add, charge, feed, allow, admit, permit, grant, consent, acknowledge
zugeführt-e Leistung power input **-e Luftmenge** quantity of air supplied
Zügeführung *f* cable guides
zugehören to belong to
zugehörig belonging, accompanying, proper, inherent, associated with **-er Stecker** *m* mating plug
Zugeisen *n* drawbar, dragbar
Zügel *m* reins, bridle
zugelassen approved **behördlich ~** authorized, officially sanctioned
Zugelastizität *f* elasticity of extension or elongation
Zugelastizitätsmodul *m* modulus of elasticity in tension
Zugelektrode *f* pull electrode
zügeln to restrain, check, restrickt
Zügel- und Sattelgurt *m* rein and saddle girth
zugemischt admixed **-er Stoff** admixed substance

Zugentlastung *f* traction relief
zugeordnet associated
zugerichtetes Leder curried leather
Zugermüdungsversuch *m* tensile fatigue test
zugeschärft sharpened **-e Kante** bezel
zugeschliffen ground
zugeschnitten auf adjusted to, set up for
zugeschnittenes Feldstärkediagramm tailored pattern (antenna)
zugespitzt tapered, pointed **stark ~** heavily tapered
zugesprochenes Telegramm phonogram
zugestopft plugged
zugeteilt attached to, allotted to **-e Frequenz** assigned frequency
Zugfähre *f* cable ferry, floating bridge
Zugfalten *n* piping (paper mfg.)
Zugfeder *f* bolt spring, tension spring, draw spring, barrel spring (watch), spiral spring, sear spring, retractable spring **-haken** *m* safety-spring catch **-haus** *n* main spring drum **-schraube** *f* tension screw, safety spring **-spannschraube** *f* safety-spring tension screw
zugfest tension-proof **-er Stahl** high tensile steel
Zugfestigkeit *f* breaking strain or strength, tensile strength, tenacity, ultimate tensile strength
Zugfestigkeits-prüfmaschine *f* tensile-strength testing machine **-untersuchung** *f* tensile-strength test **-versuch** *m* tension test **-wert** *m* tensile strength
Zugflugzeug *n* tractor airplane
Zugfolge *f* block system, order of marching **-melder** *m* block system indicator **-stelle** *f* block post
Zug-führer *m* conductor (R.R.) **-funk** *m* train radio
Zuggabel *f* tow bar, towing coupling **-kraft** *f* tow bar pull
Zug-gespräch *n* train call **-gestänge** *n* shackle line **-gitter** *n* positive grid, space-charge grid **-glied** *n* tension member **-graben** *m* drainage ditch **-griff** grip, pulling handle **-gurt** *m* tension flange, tension chord
Zughaken *m* pintle, trace hook, draw hook, singletree attachment hook **fester ~** rigid draw hook
Zughakenführung *f* draw-hook guide (R.R.)
Zug-haspel *f* draw winch **-hebel** *m* draw or traction lever
zugießen to pour in, fill up by pouring
zügig speedy, free, easy, uninterupted, efficient **-er Gang** intimate or positive threading
Zügigkeit *f* elasticity (pliability), easy flow
Zug-kabeltrommel *f* tension-cable drum **-kanal** *m* (chimney) flue **-karren** *m* tractor **-kette** *f* drag chain, hauling chain **-klappe** *f* damper **-knopf** *m* pull contact, pull knob, push button **-kolben** *m* thrust piston **-kontakt** *m* draw knob, pull knob or contact
Zugkraft *f* traction, pull, tension, attraction, propelling force, propeller thrust, lifting power **~ am Radumfang** tractive effort **~ im Zugband** tension in the tie rod
Zugkraft-geber *m* dynamometer **-glied** *n* driving or power transmission medium **-messer** *m* traction dynamometer **-umwandler** *m* torque converter **-wagen** *m* half-track prime mover, prime-mover truck
Zug-kühlofen *m* blast cooling furnace **-laschen** *pl* pull straps (photography) **-laufanzeiger** *m* train indicator **-leine** *f* towline, tracking rope, safety rope, rip cord **-leistung** *f* tractive quality, tractive power, drawbar pull, draft efficiency of animals **-leitung** *f* train control office **-lichtschalter** *m* pull-type switch **-linie** *f* tractrix **-loch** *n* draft hole, air hole, vent hole, air vent
Zugluft *f* draft **vor ~ schützen** to protect from draft
Zugluft-abschließer *m* weather strip **-schraube** *f* tractor airscrew
Zugmagnete für Wechselstrom pull magnets for A. C.
Zugmaschine *f* prime mover, tractor, traction engine
Zugmesser *m* draft gauge, tension dynamometer, traction dynamometer, tensiometer, suction gauge **-lehre** *f* draft gauge
Zugmesser *n* knife with two handles, drawknife
Zugmittel *n* drawing means, tension medium
Zugnummern-melder *m* train describer **-schalter** *m* drum dial (tel.)
Zug-ofen *m* wind or draft furnace **-öffnung** *f* darft hole **-organ** *n* traction roller **-öse** *f* drag washer, clevis, loop traction eye **-pendel** *n* adjustable drawbar **-personal** *n* railway personnel or staff, train crew **-pfahl** *m* tie pile (pile subjected to tension or pull), anchor pile, tension pile **-pferd** *n* draft horse **-pferdekraft** *f* thrust horsepower **-platte** *f* draw-plate
Zugprobe *f* tensile test **-stab** *m* tensile-test rod
Zugpropeller *m* tractor propeller **-flugzeug** *n* tractor aeroplane
Zug-prüfung *f* tensile test, pull test **-prüfungsmaschine** *f* tensile-testing machine, pull-test machine **-ramme** *f* gravity ram, hand pile driver, drophammer-type pile driver **-regler** *m* draft regulator, damper **-regulierungsklappe** *f* damper **-reguliervorrichtung** *f* draft control
zugreifen to seize, grasp, lay hold of
Zug-richtung *f* direction or trajectory motion **-riemen** *m* brake strap or cable
Zugriff *m* access (data processing) **beliebiger ~** random access **~ in Speichervorgangsfolge** sequence access
Zugriff-periode *f* access cycle **-zahl** *f* read-around ratio **-zeit** *f* access time (info proc.)
zugriffzeitfreie Speicherung zero-access storage (comput.)
Zug-ring *m* tugging ring, pull ring **-rohr** *n*, **-röhre** *f* air pipe, vent pipe or tube, stack
zugrunde liegen to be at the bottom, underlie, be the basis of
Zugrute einer Zugbrücke swipe beam or counterpoise of a drawbridge
Zug-säge *f* crosscut saw **-schaber** *m* drawing scraper **-schaffner** *m* train conductor **-schalter** *m* pull switch **-scheit** *n* swingletree **-schieber** *m* chimney damper **-schnur** *f* draw or pull cord, shutter control line or cord **-schranke** *f* railway gate, barrier **-schraube** *f* tractor screw, tractor propeller, puller propeller, draw-in bolt **-schutz** *m* valve, vertical lift valve **-schütz** *n* sluice
Zugschwell-beanspruchung *f* tensile stress of varying magnitude **-bereich** *m* range for pulsating (fluctuating) tensile stresses **-festigkeit** *f*

tensile fatigue strength
Zugseil *n* traction rope, hauling or hoisting rope, hawser, load cable **geschlossenes ~** endless rope
Zug-seiltragrolle *f* rope sheave **-seite** *f* tight strand, tension side or face
Zugsicherung *f*, **induktive ~** inductive train control
Zug-sicherungsanlage *f* train protection installation **-signalvorrichtung** *f* passenger-communication apparatus **-spaltung** *f* tension cleaving **-spannspindel** *f* clamping spindle **-spannung** *f* tensile stress or strain, tractive force **-spannungsverlauf** *m* tensile stress characteristic **-spindel** *f* feed rod, draw spindle **-spule** *f* holding magnet coil **-stab** *m* tension member, tensile bar
Zugstange *f* pull rod, tie rod, draw rod, working shaft or stem, valve stem, lifting chain, lifting rod, drawbar, mooring rod **~ des Reglers** regulator valve rod **durchgehende ~** continuous drawbar (R.R.) **durchgehende federnde ~** elastic traction rod passing right through (R.R.)
Zugstangen-kopf *m* crosshead, stay head **-rohr** *n* tubular tension rod **-vierkant** *m* square shank of the drawbar
Zug-stärke *f* intensity of draft **-start** *m* launch by towing, rope start **-stempel** *m* draw punch **-steuerung** *f* multiple-unit control **-strebe** *f* hinged tie bar **-streife** *f* train patrol **-tau** *n* towrope, tug **-telephonie** *f* train telephony **-tier** *n* draft animal **-traverse** *f* straining cross head **-trommel** *f* towing drum (marine cable) **-trumm** *n* tight strand, pulling strand **-typ** *m* tractor type
Zug- und Stoßvorrichtung draw and buffer devices
Zugursprungfestigkeit *f* lower tensile limit of the fatigue cycle
Zuguß *m* infusion, addition
Zug-verformung *f* tensile strain **-verkehr** *m* railroad traffic **-verkehrsleitung** *f* train traffic line (teleph.) **-vermittlungsstelle** *f* train exchange (teleph.) **-vermögen** *n* towing capacity **-verstärker** *m* draft intensifier **-verteiler** *m* railroad allocator
Zugversuch *m* tensile test, tension test, traction test **~ mit pulsierender Beanspruchung** cyclical tensile stress test **~ mit statischer Beanspruchung** static tension test **~ mit Dauerbeanspruchung** endurance tension test, fatigue tension test **~ mit ruhender Last** static tension test **~ mit Schlagbeanspruchung** impact tension test
Zugvorheizanlage *f* train-heating plant
Zugvorrichtung *f* train drawgear **feste ~** rigid drawgear
Zug-wagen *m* tractor, automobile tractor **-wagenbremsventil** *n* tractor brake valve **-walze** *f* feed roll, delivering roller (weaving) **-welle** *f* feed shaft, feed screw **-widerstand** *m* tractional resistance, drawbar **-winde** *f* tackle, stretching screw **-wirkung** *f* pulling action, draft action, suction power
zug-zäh flexible **-zünder** *m* pull igniter **-zeitschreiber** *m* (Eisenb.) train progress recording apparatus
zuhaken to hook
Zuhaltung *f* tumbler, spring, bolt keeper
Zuhaltungs-feder *f* tumbler spring (lock) **-haken** *m* hook on the tumbler (lock) **-lappen** *m* tumbler toe (lock)
zuhängen to draw a curtain over, cover, blanket
zuhauen to rough-hew, hit or strike hard
zuheften to stitch, sew up
Zuhilfenahme *f* aid, utilization, use
zukehren to turn to, face
zukitten to cement up
zuklappen to fall shut, close
zukleben to glue together
zuklinken to latch
zuknöpfen to button up
zuknüpfen to tie up
zukorken to stop
Zuladung *f* safe load, useful load, disposable load, service load **größte ~** maximum load
Zulage *f* increase, extra, framing, platform, allowance, additional pay or allowance
Zulageklammer *f* square clincher
Zulaß *m* admission, permission, tolerance, permissible variation, allowable variation, permissible limits
zulassen to admit, permit, turn on
zulässig admissible, safe, permissible, allowable **-es Abmaß** *n* permissible deviation **-e Abweichung** tolerance, allowance, permissible or allowable variation **-er Arbeitsdruck** maximum allowable working pressure **-e Ausdehnung** limit of expansion **-er Ausschaltstrom** breaking capacity of a switch **-e Beanspruchung** design stress, permissible stress, safe stress, safe load **-e Betriebsspannung** allowable working stress **-e Frequenz** frequency tolerance **-er Heizstrom** safe filament current **-e Höchstgeschwindigkeiten** admissible flow rates **-e Spannkraft** limit of elasticity **-e Spannung** maximum safety stress, design stress **-e Stromstärke** rated current **-es Zeichen** admissible character or mark
Zulässigkeit *f* admissibility
Zulassung *f* opening of telephone service, admission, license, official authorization **amtliche ~ eines Motors** approval (of an engine)
Zulassungs-fähigkeit *f* acceptability **-frei** exempt from registration **-nummer** *f* registration number **-pflichtig** subject to registration **-prüfung** *f* acceptance test **-schein** *m* license **-zeichen** *n* registration marks **-zwang** *m* compulsory registration
Zulauf *m* supply, feed, inlet (in casting), runner, entrance, intake, inflow, lead supply **gewölbter ~** arched connection **tangentialer ~** runner
Zulauf-berg approach hump **-bohrung** *f* inlet hole
zulaufen to run in, run on, add, run, crowd, flock **spitz ~** to taper to a point
Zulauf-flotte *f* feeding or replenishing liquor **-gefälle** *n* feed(ing) height **-gehäuse** *n* feed(ing) or inlet housing **-geschwindigkeit** *f* speed of admission **-kammer** *f* filling chamber **-kanal** *m* air-inlet conduit **-leitung** *f* supply main, inlet pipe, feed line **-öffnung** *f* entrance, intake **-rohr** *n* intake or inlet pipe, feed line, supply duct **-strom** *m* inflow current **-stutzen** *m* in-feed connection **-temperatur** *f* admission temperature
Zulauf- und Ableitungselement inlet and outlet element (blank and turbid liquid plates)
zulegen to add, get, take, procure
Zulege-platte *f* attachable base plate **-vorrichtung**

f manipulator
Zulegieren *n* alloying
zuleiten to supply, lead in, feed, pipe into, route **Lochkarten ~** to route punched cards
Zuleitung *f* delivery pipe, feed pipe, feed line, supply line, conductor (elec.), lead wire, conducting rod, lead, hydraulic supply pipes, gathering line
Zuleitungs-draht *m* lead-in wire **-induktivität** *f* lead inductance **-kabel** *n* conducting cable, feeder, lead-in cord **-rohr** *n* feed pipe, inlet pipe **-schiene** *f* bus bar **-stromkreis** *m* supply circuit (elec.)
Zulieferant *m* supplier
Zulieferung *f* delivery
zulöten to solder up
Zuluft *f* supply air **-anlage** *f* induction system **-stutzen** *m* air inlet
Zulüfter *m* supply fan
zumachen to close, shut off, seal
zumauern to brick up, wall up
zumessen to allot, attribute, ascribe to, impute, meter
Zumeßdüse *f* dosing nozzle
Zumessen *n* dosing, metering
Zumeß-kennwerte *pl* metering characteristics **-kolben** *m* proportioning plunger
Zumessung *f* dose determination
Zumeßwaage *f* scale
zumischen to admix, mix with
Zumisch-pulver *n* dope (dynamite mfg.) **-stoff** *m* admixture, admixed material
Zumischung *f* admixture
Zunahme *f* growth, increase, rise, increment, head
Zünd-achse *f* detonator-plunger casing, operating piston sleeve **-akkumulator** *m* B battery **-anker** *m* ignition armature **-ankeranschluß** *m* connection of ignition armature
Zündanlage *f* ignition system, ignition device **~ mit automatischer Zündzeitpunktverstellung** automatically advanced ignition
Zünd-anlaßschalter *m* combined ignition and starting switch **-anode** *f* ignition anode, exciting anode **-apparat** *m* igniter, magneto, ignition device, primer **-ausfall** *m* misfire **-aussetzer** *m* misfiring
Zünd-anode *f* ignition anode, exciting anode **-apparat** *m* igniter, magneto, ignition device, primer **-ausfall** *m* misfire **-aussetzer** *m* misfiring
Zündband für Wetterlampen *pl* wick for miner's lamps
zündbar inflammable, ignitable, combustible
Zündbarkeit *f* inflammability
Zünd-bolzen *m* detonator percussion pellet of fuse **-brenner** *m* pilot burner **-büchse** *f* fire lighter **-draht** *m* ignition wire **-drehmoment** *n* firing torque **-drehzahl** *f* firing speed **-durchschlag** *m* penetration of ignition, complete or instantaneous ignition **-dynamo** *m* ignition dynamo **-einrichtung** *f* ignition device **-einsatz** *m* plug **-einstellung** *f* spark timing **-einstellungskette** *f* timing chain **-elektrode** *f* ignition electrode, igniter, starter **-empfindlichkeit** *f* inflammability
zünden to take fire, kindle, ignite, set fire to, prime, fuse **wieder ~** to reignite
Zünden *n* lighting **~ im schwerelosen Raum** (Astron.) zero-g start **~ im Vakuum** (Astron.) vacuum ignition
Zunder *m* scale (oxide), cinder, tinder, hammer scale
Zünder *m* igniter, lighter, fuse, detonator **~ mit Verzögerung** delay-action fuse **den ~ einstellen** to set the fuse **~ stellen** to set a fuse **empfindlicher ~** quick fuse **mechanischer ~** mechanical fuse **rohrsicherer ~** bore-safe fuse
Zünder-abstandsrohr *n* nose rod **-anzeige** *f* fuse data
Zunderausblutungen *pl* scale efflorescences
Zünderbatteriekasten *m* ignition-battery box
zunder-beständig nonscaling, scaleresistant **-beständigkeit** *f* resistance of scaling, nonscaling property **-bildung** *f* formation of scale **-brechgerüst** *n* scale breaker (stand)
Zünder-brücke *f* spark gap **-deckel** *m* false ogive **-draht** *m* detonating wire, firing wire, lead wire **-einstellung** *f* fuse setting **-einteilung** *f* fuse scale **-empfindlichkeit** *f* sensitivity of a fuse
zunderfest tinderproof
zunderfrei free of scale
Zünder-füllmasse *f* fuse composition **-gehäuse** *n* fuse casing, fuse body, fuse cover **-gerät** *n* detonator apparatus **-glocke** *f* cap chamber **-halter** *m* detonator casing, shell **-hebel** *m* ignition-spark control **-hülse** *f* fuse body, fuse cover
zunderig tindery
Zünder-kappe *f* fuse cap, closing cap head, upper cap **-kerzenreichweite** *f* reach or length of threaded end of spark plug **-kontrolle** *f* fuse check **-körper** *m* body of fuse **-laufzeit** *f* fuse setting **-motor** *m* spark-ignition engine
zundern to burn out, scale
Zündernetz *n* fuse circuit
Zunderpapier *n* tinder paper
Zünder-ring *m* time-fuse ring, fuse-setting ring **-satz** *m* fuse composition **-schaltkasten** *m* fuse switchbox **-schlüssel** *m* hand fuse setter, fuse key **-schraube** *f* threaded primer
Zunderschwamm *n* tinder, punk, spunk
Zünder-spitze *f* point or nose of fuse **-stellschlüssel** *m* manual fuse-setter, fuse-setting key **-stellen** to set a fuse **-stellmaschine** *f* automatic fuse setter **-stellsitz** *m* fuse-setter support **-stellung** *f* fuse setting **-stiel** *m* fuse steam **-stellung** *f* fuse setting **-streuung** *f* dispersion caused by fuse differences **-stutzen** *m* protruding lug (fuse) **-teller** *m* ring (of fuse)
Zunderung *f* scaling
Zünder-verstellhebel *m* spark lever **-verteileranlage** *f* ignition harness **-werte** *m pl* fuse data **-zapfen** *m* stem (of fuse)
Zünd-fackel *f* igniter **-fähig** ignitable **-fähigkeit** *f* ignitability **-feder** *f* ignition spring **-fertig** primed, fused, and ready **-flämmchen** *n*, **flamme** *f* igniting flame, pilot flame, pilot light
Zündflansch für Abreißzündung ignition flange for make and break ignition
Zündfolge *f* firing order
Zündfunken *m* ignition spark **-klopfen** *n* spark knock **-verstärker** *m* ignition spark or spark amplifier
Zünd-funker *m* sparking pilot **-gebiet** *n* ignition range **-gerät** *n* ignition coil (jet), demolition equipment **-geschwindigkeit** *f* flame-propagation velocity **-gestänge** *n* priming rods, starting

control rods **-gewölbe** *n* ignition arch **-glocke** *f* inside bottom of cartridge case **-grenze** *f* ignition limit **-hebel** *m* ignition lever, spark control **-herd** *m* ignition source or focus **-höchstdruck** *m* maximum combustion pressure

Zündholz *n* match **-draht** *m* match splint (match stalk) **-herstellung** *f* match manufacturing **-schachtel** *f* matchbox

Zündhub *m* ignition stroke

Zündhütchen *n* primer, percussion cap **-ausfall** *m* blown primer **-hülse** *f* primer cup

Zündimpuls *m* ignition impulse

Zündkabel *n* spark-plug wire, detonator cable, ignition cable, ignition wire **-führungsrohr** *n* ignition wire manifold **-geschirr** *n* ignition-wire manifold, ignition-wiring harness **-rohr** *n* ignition-wire manifold

Zünd-kanal *m* vent, detonating canal, flash hole **-kapsel** *f* detonator cap **-kasten** *m* detonator (elec.) **-kennlinie** *f* ignition characteristic

Zündkerze *f* spark plug, ignition plug **Elektrodenabstand der ~** spark-plug gap **festgeklemmte ~** frozen plug **heiße ~** hot plug **verschmutzte ~** fouled plug

Zündkerzen-abbrand *m* spark-plug erosion **-auge** *n* spark-plug boss **-bohrung** *f* spark-plug hole **-dichtung** *f* spark-plug washer **-einsatz** *m* spark-plug adapter, spark-plug bushing **-einschraubbüchse** *f* spark-plug insert **-elektrode** *f* spark-plug electrode **-gehäuse** *n* sparking-plug body

Zündkerzen-kabel *n* ignition wire **-klemmschraube** *f* spark-plug terminal **-kniestück** *n* spark-plug elbow **-öffnung** *f* passage for the plug **-prüfvorrichtung** *f* plug tester **-reichweite** *f* reach of plug **-schlüssel** plug wrench **-spannung** *f* spark-plug voltage **-thermoelement** *n* plug couple

Zünd-kipper *m* filament current key **-kirsche** *f* ignition pellet **-kohle** *f* striking carbon **-kontrolle** *f* ignition control **-köpfe** *pl* ignition heads **-kraft** *f* igniting power **-kreis** *m* ignition circuit **-ladung** *f* detonating charge, primer charge, squib (min.), explosive charge

Zündladungs-kapsel *f* detonator housing or casing **-körper** *m* detonator charge

Zünd-lage *f* ignition system **-leistung** *f* sparking power, ignition performance **-leistungsreserve** *f* reserve sparking power **-leitung** *f* firing circuit

Zündleitungs-entstörmuffe *f* ignition cable sleeve-type suppressor **-entstörstecker** *m* ignition cable plug-type suppressor **-führung** *f* arrangement of ignition cable **-system** *n* ignition wiring

Zünd-lichtmaschine *f* magneto (dynamo) generator **-lichtschalter** *m* ignition light switch **-loch** *n* flash vent **-lochstollen** *m* vent bush **-löschspannungsdifferenz** *f* striking-extinction potential difference **-lunte** *f* sparking paper (motor)

Zündmagnet *m* (ignition) magneto **-welle** *f* magneto spindle

Zünd-maschine *f* blasting detonating machine, electric detonator **-metall** *n* inflammable metal **-mittel** *n* priming substance, means of detonation (explosive), detonation agent, primer, igniter, igniting mixture **-momentverstellung** *f* ignition timing gear **-nadel** *f* primer **-papier** *n* ignition paper (phot.) **-patrone** *f* ignition cartridge **-peitsche** *f* ignition stimulant

Zündpille *f* primer capsule or pellet **~ für Annäherungszünder** influence fuse squib

Zündpunkt *m* ignition (point), firing point, burning point, flash point **-einstellung** *f* ignition timing, magneto timing **-prüfer** *m* ignition-point tester **-verstellung** *f* timing

Zünd-rakete *f* rocket booster **-regelung** *f* spark control

zundrig tindery

Zünd-rohr *n* flash tube, fuse, ignition tube, interconnector (jet) **-röhrchen** *n* interconnector (jet) **-rüssel** *m* nose piece of the fuse **-satz** *m* detonator composition, primer composition **-schaltbrett** *n* ignition switchboard **-schalter** *m* ignition switch **-schlag** *m* knock of detonation **-schlüssel** *m* ignition key

Zündschnur *f* fuse cord, fuse, lanyard, firing tape **-anzünder** *m* fuse lighter **-maschine** *f* quick-match machine

Zünd-schraube *f* threaded percussion primer **-schraubengehäuse** *n* threaded percussion-primer housing or case **-schwamm** *m* amadou **-schwellenerniedrigung** *f* threshold lowering **-seele** *f* ignition or primer core **-signalspannung** *f* firing voltage **-spannung** *f* ignition tension, initial potential, firing voltage, strikking voltage, ignition voltage, breakdown voltage, no-load voltage, striking potential **-spiegel** *m* fulminating powder **-spindel** *f* spark hand-lever tube **-spule** *f* ignition unit, coil

Zündspulen-system *n* coil-ignition system **-unterbrecher** *m* trembler coil **-zündung** *f* coil ignition

Zünd-stab *m* ignitor, ignition rod, striking rod **-steg** *m* priming-grid fuse element **-stein** *m* flint **-stelle** *f* ignition point **-stift** *m* center electrode (spark plug), ignition pin, insulated electrode **-stollen** *m* firing hole bush **-stöpsel** *m* ignition plug **-störung** *f* ignition interference **-stoß** *m* ignition impulse **-strahlverfahren** *n* ignition-ray process **-strecke** *f* starter gap

Zündstrom *m* ignition current **-abnehmer** *m* ignition current take-off **-ausschalter** *m* ignition cutout **-erzeuger** *m* ignition unit **-klappenschalter** *m* fusing circuit switch **-kreis** *m* ignition circuit

Zünd-stück *n* spark-plug point **-taste** *f* ignition-current key **-temperatur** *f* ignition temperature **-totpunkt** *m* ignition dead center **-tropfen** *m* drop of starting fuel **-übertragung** *f* induced detonation

Zünd- und Löscheinrichtung *f* make-and-break switch

Zünd- und Löschspannung *f* ignition and extinction voltage

Zünd- und Löschuhr *f* economizer

Zündung *f* ignition, priming, detonation, break-down, firing, fuse, primer, detonator **~ isolierter Tröpfchen** ignition of isolated droplets **~ ausschalten** to switch off ignition **~ einschalten** to contact **die ~ bleibt aus** the ignition fails **die ~ einstellen** to time the ignition **die ~ setzt zeitweilig aus** the ignition is intermitting **elektrische ~** electric contract, electrical ignition (firing), electrical firing mechanism **unregelmäßige ~** imperfect ignition **vorzeitige ~** preignition

Zündungs-aussetzung *f* spark failure **-draht** *m* ignition wire **-einsetzen** *n* initiation or incipience of striking or firing **-einstellung** *f* adjustment or timing of ignition **-funke** *m* jump spark **-geschirr** *n* ignition harness **-hebel** *m* ignition-control lever **-hub** *m* ignition stroke

Zündungs-potential *n* striking potential **-prüfer** *m* spark-plug tester **-schalter** *m* ignition switch **-schwierigkeit** *f*, **-störung** *f* ignition trouble **-system** *n* ignition system **-temperatur** *f* ignition temperature **-versager** *m* misfire **-verstellung** *f* ignition timing **-verteiler** *m* ignition distributor

Zünd-ventil *n* primer valve, igniting valve **-verstärker** *m* booster

Zündverstellbereich *m* ignition-timing range, spark-timing range, timing-adjustment range

Zündversteller *m* ignition timing device or timer

Zündverstell-hebel *m* spark or ignition lever, adjusting lever **-linie** *f* ignition timing curve **-stoßstange** *f* ignition-control push-and-pull rod

Zünd-verstellung *f* timing of the ignition, spark control, spark adjustment **-verteiler** *m* (ignition) distributor **-verteilerzwischenstück** *n* insert in distributor (for suppressor purposes) **-verzögerung** *f* spark lag **-verzögerungswinkel** *m* angle of grid retardation **-verzug** *m* ignition lag or delay **-vorgang** *m* ignition process **-vorrichtung** *f* ignition system or device, igniter **-wärme** *f* ignition heat **-waren** *pl* inflammables **-willigkeit** *f* ignition quality of fuel **-winkel** *m* blocking period **-zeitfolge** *f* firing or ignition order

Zündzeitpunkt *m* firing or ignition point, sparking instant ~ **verstellen** to retime **-einstellvorrichtung** *f* ignition control **-selbstverstellung** *f* automatic ignition timing **-verstellung** *f* ignition-timing adjustment **-verstellvorrichtung** *f* spark-advance and -retard mechanism

Zündzubehör *n* requirements for ignition

zunehmen to increase, grow, rise, swell, advance, improve

zunehmende Reihe ascending series

Zunge *f* switch, tongue, needle, pointer (of balance), baffle plate, reed (of horn), clasp (of lock), blade, vibrator, keeper (of magnet), slide of a sliderule **durchschlagende** ~ reed that vibrates in both directions past neutral point **schwingende** ~ vibrating reed

züngeln to lick (flames)

Zungen-angriffstange *f* stretcher rod **-bohrer** *m* bumper spud **-drehstuhl** *m* heel chair

Zungenende, angeschweißtes ~ point of blade welded to rail (R.R.)

Zungenfrequenz-indikator *m* tuned-reed indicator **-messer** *m* multivibrator, reed tachometer, vibrating-reed frequency meter **-relais** *n* tuned-reed relay, vibrating relay

Zungen-halter *m* tongue-holding forceps **-hülse** *f* tongue socket **-nadelmaschine** *f* latch-needle machine **-öffner** *m* latch opener **-paar** *n* pair of switch blades **-pfeife** *f* reed pipe, flute **-platte** *f* slide plate **-rille** *f* flangeway clearance

Zungen-schiene *f* switch point (R.R.), tongue rail, filled-section rail **-spatel** *f* tongue depressor **-stein** *m* flat tile **-stuhl** *m* heel of switch (R.R.), knee (R.R.) **-summer** *m* reed hummer **-telephon** *n* reed telephone receiver **-überwachungseinrichtung** *f* switch-position indicator **-unterbrecher** *m* vibrating-reed break **-verbindungsstange** *f* stretcher rod

Zungenvorrichtung für doppelte Kreuzungsweiche deflecting devices of double slip points

Zungenwurzel *f* tongue heel

zuordnen to assign (to), rate, translate, collate (comput.)

Zuordner *m* translator (comput.), interpreter, quantizer, collater

Zuordnung *f* coordination, correleation, assignment, allotment

Zuordnungsprogramm *n* interpretive routine (comput.)

zupacken to clutch

zupassen to fit

zupfen to pluck, pick, tug, pull

Zupf-instrument *n* plucking instrument **-maschine** *f* burling machine

zupfropfen to plug

Zupfseil *n* jerk line

zurechnen to add, hold accountable

zurecht-finden to find one's way about **-legen** to place in readiness **-machen** to prepare, adjust, get ready, line up **-schneiden** to dress

zureichen to hand, be sufficient

Zuricht-art *f* kind of finish **-axt** *f* squaring ax **-deckfarben** *pl* coating colors

Zurichtebogen *m* register sheet (print.)

zurichten to prepare, dress, make ready, fit, set, adjust, finish, trim, rough-cut, gauge, straighten **Punktur** ~ to dress the points (print.)

Zurichten der Zündleitung setting of the ignition cable

Zurichterei *f* dressing or adjusting shop **-maschine** *f* adjusting or adjustment machine

Zurichtung *f* dressing, adjustment, make-ready, finishing

Zurichtungs-maschine *f* adjusting machine **-prozedur** *f* finishing operation

zuriegeln to bolt

Zurr-bolzen *m* locking pin **-brücke** *f* locking frame, cradle lock frame

zurren to lash, tie, clamp

Zurr-griff *m* locking handle (traveling lock), cradle lock handle **-gurt** *m* clamping band **-haken** *m* locking hook **-hebel** *m* locking lever **-lager** *n* lock support **-öse** *f* securing eye

Zurr-stange *f* lock rod **-stellung** *f* locked position **-stück** *n* backplate catch, backplate latch lock

Zurrung *f* lashing, latch, clamp, clamping device

zurück-behalten to retain **-bewegen** to move back, unshift **-bilden** to re-form, form again **-bildung** *f* involution **-bleiben** to remain behind, remain over, be late or slow, lag (behind)

zurückbleibend residual, remaining behind **-er Porenwasserdruck** residual pore pressure

zurück-bringen to replace, bring back **-datieren** to antedate, back-date **-drängen** to push back, roll back

zurückdrehen to slacken, turn back, turn off, turn down **eine Schraube** ~ to slacken back a screw

Zurück-drehen *n* backing (meteor.) **-erhalten** to recover **-erstatten** to refund, return, restore **-fahren** to back up, return

zurückfallen (Licht) to be reflected; to fall back ~ **in Grundzustand** return or retransition to ground state ~ **lassen** to drop in place

zurück-federn to spring back **-federung** *f* resilience, reversion **-fließen, -fluten** to recede, ebb, flow back **-führbar** traceable, reducible

zurückführen to trace back, reduce, lead back, retract, reconvey, refer, ascribe, attribute, reconvene, return, restore **auf einen bestimmten Ort ~** to localize **auf das kleinste Maß ~** to minimize

Zurückführung *f* reduction, tracing back **~ auf eine höhere Benennung** ascending reduction (math.)

Zurückgabe *f* return, restoration, restitution

zurückgehen to go back, retreat, retire, fall back

Zurückgehen *n* return, reversion, decline, failure

zurückgelegt gone, walked, attained, made, covered **-e Entfernung** distance run or travelled **-e Meilenzahl** mileage **-e Strecke** distance covered

zurück-gestellt deferred **-gestrahlt** reflected **-gestreut** back-scattered **-gewinnbar** recoverable **-gewinnen** to recover, reclaim, recuperate **-gewinnung** *f* recuperation **-gewonnen** regenerated, restored **-geworfen** reflected **-gezogen** retired

Zurück-haltevermögen *n* retention capacity **-halten** to retain, retard, inhibit, hold back, stop, prevent (from) **-haltung** *f* reserve, holding back, reticence **-kaufen** to repurchase

zurückkehren to return **in die Ruhelage ~** to return to normal

zurück-klappen to fold back **-knallen** to backfire **-kurbeln** to crank back, to turn backward **-kurbeln** *n* to crank back **-laufen** to run back, recur, retrograde, recoil

zurücklaufend reversed **-e Strömung** backwash

zurücklegen to cover (a distance) **eine Strecke ~** to cover a distance

Zurücklegung *f* setting back

zurückleiten to reconduct, redirect, lead back, return, feed back

Zurück-nahme *f* revocation, recall, taking back

zurücknehmen, Gas ~ to throttle back

zurück-pendeln to swing back **-prallen** to rebound, recoil, be reflected **-prallen** *n* resiliency, repercussion **-rufen** to recall, ring back **-sacken** to backslide **-saugen** to suck back (draw back) **-schalten** to switch back **-schieben** to push back **-schlagen** to hit back, flash back (of a flame), strike back, beat back, repulse, retract, flare back, fold back

Zurückschlagen im Vergaser backfire in the carburetor **~ der Taste** rebound of the key

zurückschlagend repulsing **-e Flamme** flashing back of flame

zurückschnellen to jump or bounce back

Zurück-schnellen *n* spring back **-schrauben** to screw down **-schwenken** to fold, reset, swivel or swing back **-schwimmen** to float back **-senden** to redirect **-setzen** to reset **-spiegeln** to reflect **-springen** to rebound

Zurückspringen *n* resilience **~ des Windes** change of wind

zurück-stecken to put back (as a plug) **-steigen** to reflux **-stellen** to reset, release, put back, set back, defer **-stellung** *f* deferment **-stellungsantrag** *m* request for deferment **-strömen** to reflux **-stoßen** to recoil **-strahlen** to radiate back, reverberate **-strahlend** reverberatory **-strahlung** *f* reverberation

zurück-strömen to flow back, reflux **-stürzen** to rush back **-titrieren** to titrate back **-treiben** to drive back, check, repulse **-treten** to retreat, retire **-vergüten** to refund **-weichen** to fall back, retreat, give ground, give way

zurückweisen to reject, refuse, dismiss, disallow **als falsch ~** to disprove

Zurückweisung *f* repulsion, overruling, rebuttal, dismissal, disallowance, rejection

Zurückweisungsgrund *m* ground of rejection (patent)

zurückwerfen to throw back, reflect, reverberate or bend back (a ray), echo back

Zurückwerfen *n* reverberation, reflection

Zurückwerfung *f* refraction, reflection

Zurückwerfungswinkel *m* angle of reflection

zurückzahlen to pay back, reimburse, refund

zurückziehbar retractable

zurückziehen to retract, pull back, withdraw, draw back **sich ~** to withdraw, retire, fall back

Zurückziehung *f* retraction, withdrawal

Zuruf *m* call

Zurüstung *f* equipment

Zusage *f* promise, acceptance, consent **bei umgehender ~** subject to your immediate assent

Zusammen-arbeit *f* (close) cooperation, collaboration, mutual support **-arbeiten** to cooperate, collaborate, interwork **-backen** to cake, frit (together), agglomerate, conglomerate **-backen** *n* agglomeration, packing **-ballen** to agglomerate, ball up, coalesce, spheroidize, bunch **-ballen** *n* bunching (of electrons in groups), agglomeration, conglomeration, coagulation (of colloids and smoke particles)

Zusammenballung *f* agglomeration, conglomeration, balling up, bunching, coalescing, spheroidization, spheroidizing **metallographische ~** coalescence

Zusammenbau *m* erection, assemblage, building up, assembly, fitting, operation **fließender ~** progressive assembly

Zusammen-bauarbeit *f* assembly work **-bauband** *n* assembly conveyer

zusammenbauen to mount, assemble, set up, erect

Zusammenbau-großvorrichtung *f* assembly jig or rig **-lehre** *f* assembling jig, fixture **-vorrichtung** *f* assembly equipment or jig

zusammen-berufen to assemble **-brechen** to break down, crumble, collapse, subside, implode **-brennen** to burn together **-bruch** *m* breakdown, collapse, failure **-bündeln** to concentrate **-drängen** to compress **-drehen** to twist (together), twine **-drehung** *f* twisting, torsion **-drückbar** compressible **-drückbarkeit** *f* compressibility **-drücken** to compress, crush, squeeze, compact, consolidate **-drücker** *m* compressor

Zusammen-drückung *f* compression **-drückungsmodul** *m* modulus of compression **-drückungszahl** *f* (-modul) coefficient of compressibility **-dübeln** to peg **-fallen** to collapse, disintegrate, coincide (with) **-fallen** *n* collapse, coincidence **-fallend** coincident, synchronous **-falten** to fold together **-falten** *n* pleating **-fassen** to collate, combine, summarize

zusammenfassender Bericht survey, summarizing report or article

Zusammenfassung *f* recapitulation, summary, comprehension, compilation, synopsis, centralization, composition, abstract, amalgamation, fusion, résumé

zusammen-filzen to plank **-fließen** to flow together, run together (colors), coalesce
Zusammenfluß *m* confluence ~ **zweier Wasserläufe** confluence of two watercourses
zusammen-frieren to congeal, freeze together **-fritten** to frit together **-fügen** to join (together), unite, mortise **-führung** *f* junction (comp.) **-führungsband** *n* reconduction band **-geballte Wolkenmasse** ball cumulus **-gebaut** built-up **-gebolzt** assembled by bolts **-gedrängt** crowded **-gedreht** stranded or twisted together **-gefaltet** folded
zusammengefaßt concentrated, collective **-e Datenverarbeitung** integrated data processing
zusammen-gegossenes Muster bulk sample **-gehören** to belong together, fit
Zusammengehörigkeit *f* correlation (of things)
zusammengesetzt composed, combined, compound, composite, complex, complicated, assembled, resultant **aus mehreren Stoffen** ~ compound **-e Bewegung** compound motion **-e Deckoperationen** combination of movements (geol.) **-e Farbe** combination color **-e Fotokathode** multilayer cathode **-es Glas** laminated glass **-er Klang** complex musical sound **-e Leitung** compound circuit **-e Lupe** composite magnifier **-es Muster** composite sample **-e Plätze** grouped positions **-e Schwingung** complex harmonic wave **-er Träger** built up beam
zusammen-gesintert caked **-gespiegelt** reflected together **-gesprengte Prismen** broken-contact prisms **-gestellt** collected **-gewirbelter Draht** snaked wire
zusammen-gießen to pour together **-haften** to cohere **-haftvermögen** *n* cohesion
Zusammen-halt *m* consistency, cohesion, unity **-halten** to hold together, stick, be economical **-hang** *m* cohesion, coherence, connection, consistency, interrelation, mechanism, relation **-hängen** to adhere (cohere)
zusammenhängend cohesive, coherent, continuous **-er Hohlraumresonator** re-entrant cavity resonator **-e Photokathode** plain mirror or continuous (nonmosaic) photocathode
Zusammen-hangszahl *f* connectivity **-hauen** to demolish, wreck **-häufen** to aggregate, heap or pile up, accumulate, gather together **-keilen** to wedge (together) **-kitten** to bond together, cement together, putty, lute
zusammenklappbar folding, collapsible, foldable, screwed down **-es Verdeck** folding roof
zusammen-klappen to fold up, close up, fold, collapse **-kleben** to agglutinate **-kommen** to get together, assemble, meet, gather **-kuppeln** to couple **-laschen** to scarf **-lauf** *m* spontaneous gathering **-laufbütte** *f* settling tub **-laufen** to run together, converge, blend, coagulate, concur
zusammenlegbar collapsible, folding **-e Flügel** folding wings
zusammenlegen to centralize, concentrate, fold together, collapse
Zusammenlegung *f* centralization, concentration, merger, uniting, amalgamation ~ **der Leitungen** concentration of circuits
zusammen-leimen to agglutinate **-lesen** to gather **-löten** to solder up, solder together **-nähen** to sew together **-nehmen** to gather (up), collect **-passen** to adjust, fit together, match **-passend** mating, fitting **-prall** *m* collision **-preßbar** compressible
zusammenpressen to press together, compress, condense **fest** ~ to clench
Zusammenpressen *n* tightening
Zusammenpressung der Luftteilchen compression or condensation of air particles (in sound wave)
zusammen-quetschen to squeeze together **-rechnen** to add up, compute **-rollmaschine** *f* upcoiler **-rücken** to push or draw together **-sacken** to collapse, flatten out **-schalten** to bunch, patch, couple, interconnect **-schalten** *n* electrical interconnection, coupling **-scharren** to rake together **-scheren** to join by slit and tongue (carp.)
zusammenschiebbar telescopic, extensible (tripod leg) **-es Dreibeinstativ** sliding tripod
zusammen-schlagen to completely flatten out, clench together **-schleifen** to grind together **-schließen** to interlock **-schlitzen** *n* miter joint by wood split **-schluß** *m* amalgamation, consolidation, fusion, combination, merger, aggregation, organization **-schmelzen** to melt together, fuse **-schmoren** *n* scorching, freezing, or melting together of contacts
zusammen-schnüren to constrict, tie together, neck, bottle, lace togehter, lash **-schnürung** *f* constriction, tying together, necking, bottling **-schrauben** to bolt together **-schrumpfen** to shrink, contract, wrinkle, collapse, dwindle **-schrumpfen** *n* shrinkage, shrink **-schütten** to pour together **-schweißen** to weld together, weld up **-schweißvorrichtung** *f* assembly welding jig **-setzblende** *f* scanning hole, picture-recreator aperture
zusammensetzen to pile, stack, compose, assemble, make up, combine, compound **Gewehre** ~ to stack arms **aus Teilen** ~ to fabricate, assemble, fit
Zusammen-setzen *n* fitting **-setzend** constituent, component **-setzung** *f* composition, construction, combination, compound, synthesis, analysis **-setzungsgrenze** *f* composition limits **-sinken** to collapse, crumble **-sintern** to sinter together, fuse together, agglomerate, slag **-sitzen** *n* being consolidated (of sediment) **-spiel** *n* coordination, interplay **-sprengen** to join or fit together without cement **-stauchen** to upset **-stecken** to assemble (put together) **-stellarbeit** *f* assembling work
zusammenstellen to set up, to compile (a text) **einen Apparat** ~ to set up an apparatus
Zusammenstellung *f* grouping, combination, classification, compilation, association, analysis, assemblage, assembly, summary, symposium, list ~ **in ihren Einzelheiten** detail assembly (aviation) **tabellarische** ~ tabular synopsis
zusammenstimmen to harmonize, agree, conform, correspond
zusammenstimmend harmonious, concordant, congruous
Zusammenstoß *m* collision, engagement, impact, running foul ~ **am Boden** collision on the ground ~ **zweier Kartenblätter** junction of two map sheets ~ **von Warm- und Kaltfront** occlusion
zusammenstoßen to collide
zusammenstoßende Enden superposed ends

(abuting ends)

Zusammen-stoßgefahr *f* collision hazard **-stürzen** to fall down, collapse **-tragen** to compile, collect, gather up **-treffen** to meet, coincide **-treffen** *n* meeting, coincidence, collision **-treiben** to drive together, unite, collect **-wachsen** to grow together, coalesce

zusammenwirken to cooperate, collaborate, to act together, interact

Zusammenwirken *n* interaction, cooperation

zusammen-zählen to add **-zählregel** *f* rule of addition **-ziehbar** contractible **-ziehen** to draw together, contract, tighten, shrink **-ziehend** astringent

Zusammenziehung *f* contraction, shrinkage, constriction, concentration **~ eines Textes** condensing of a text

Zusammenzinken *n* dovetailing

Zusatz *m* addition, supplement, appendix, postscript, admixture, alloy, clause, auxiliary, adjunct, booster set, emergency set **flüssiger ~** liquid addition, melted addition **kohlender ~** recarburizer **ohne ~** no-alloy, pure

Zusatz-aggregat *n* additional set, booster aggregate (elec.) **-anmeldung** *f* additional application (patent) **-annahme** *f* corollary assumption, corollary

Zusatzantrieb *m*, **pneumatischer ~** pneumatic attachment

Zusatz-apparat *m* supplementary apparatus **-artikel** *m* additional article **-ausgleichsaggregat** *n* auxiliary compensation set **-batterie** *f* booster battery, bucker battery **-behälter** *m* additional tank, spare or auxiliary tank, jettisonable tank **-belüftung** *f* compressed air conditioning **-bestimmung** *f* supplementary rule or regulation **-bewegung** *f* superposed or subsidiary motion, supplementary motion **-bremswiderstand** *m* additional brake resistance **-drehkondensator** *m* attachment for shifting **-düse** *f* supplementary or auxiliary jet, speed jet **-dynamo** *m* booster (dynamo)

Zusätze *pl* additions, finishing metals, loading agents **~ zur Erhöhung der Zündwilligkeit** ignition quality improvers

Zusatz-einrichtung *f* ancillary lens system, additional instrument, auxiliary attachment or equipment, accessory **-einschub** *m* additional plug-in

Zusatz-eisen *n* additional iron, addition agent **-element** *n* alloying element **-fallschirm** *m* pilot parachute, parachute lobe **-feuer** *n* additional airport lighting, supplementary fire **-feuerung** *f* additional firing, supplementary firing **-flügel** *m* auxiliary wing flap, interceptor, spoiler **-gefälle** *n* supplementary slope **-gerät** *n* attachment, accessory instrument, supplementary or ancillary apparatus, adapter **-geräteplatte** *f* auxiliary instrument plate **-geschwindigkeit** *f* incremental velocity, velocity increment **-gespräch** *n* overtime period on private-line telephone service

Zusatz-gestell *n* additional rack **-getriebe** *n* auxiliary transmission **-gewicht** *n* additional weight **-gleichrichter** *m* booster **-heizung** *f* auxiliary heater **-impuls** *m* additional impulse **-knickkraft** *f* additional bending strength **-kühler** *m* booster or extra radiator **-ladung** *f* supercharge, additional charge **-legierung** *f* hardener

zusätzlich additional, additive, supplementary, secondary, added, incremental, accessory, subsidiary, supplemental, auxiliary, boosting **-er Drall, -e Drehung** additional twisting **-es Durchlaufen** (durch die Maschine) additional passes **-er Hilfsantrieb** spare drive **-e Kraftstoffmenge** extra fuel **-e Nachbildung** building-out section **-e Permeabilität** incremental permeability **-er Pol** consequent pole **-er Verschleiß** undue wear **-er Widerstand** additional resistance

Zusatz-linse *f* supplementary lens **-luft** *f* additional air, secondary air, supplementary air **-luftdüse** *f* additional air nozzle

Zusatzmaschine *f* emergency or auxiliary machine, booster **~ mit Differentialerregung** differential booster **~ in Gegenschaltung** negative booster **~ für Zu- und Gegenschaltung** positive and negative booster

Zusatz-material *n* filler metal **-metall** *n* filler metal, alloy, component metal

Zusatzmittel *n* blending agent, addition agent **~ zur Beschleunigung des Trocknens** siccative **~ zur Verhütung der Oxydation** antioxidant, antioxidation dope

Zusatz-nachbildung *f* building-out section (of transmission line) **-patent** *n* additional patent **-schutz** *m* backup protection **-spannung** *f* supplementary stress, additional stress or voltage, boosting voltage, booster potential **-spülung** *f* supplementary or auxiliary scavenging **-stab** *m* filler rod **-steuerwert** *m* supplementary value **-stoff** *m* material to be admixed, admixed material, addition **-tank** *m* supplementary tank **-tastatur** *f* extra keyboard **-träger** *m* supplementary carrier **-transformator** *m* boosting transformer **-trübe** *f* make-up medium

Zusatz-untersetzung *f* supplementary reduction **-venturi** *n* additional Venturi **-verbrennung** *f* stepped-up combustion **-verfahren** *n* additive process **-verlust** *m* additional loss **-verstärker** *m* booster amplifier **-verstellhebel** *m* additional adjusting (or timing) lever **-versuch** *m* supplementary-test or trial **-vorrichtung** *f* additional attachment

Zusatz-wasser *n* additional water, make-up water **-widerstand** *m* supplementary resistance, additional resistance or drag **-zahlwerk** *n* additional counting instruments **-zelle** *f* end cell

zuschalten to switch on, connect, close the circuit

Zuschaltraum *m* re-expansion chamber

Zuschaltung *f* putting in the circuit **~ einer Dämpfung** insertion of a pad

zuschärfen to sharpen, point

Zuschärfmaschine *f* beveling machine, scarfer

Zuschärfung *f* chamfer

Zuschärfungs-fläche *f* bezel, sloping edge **-verhältnis** *n* fineness or aspect ratio

Zuschärfwinkel *m* lip angle (of cutter)

Zuschauer *m* bystander, onlooker, spectator, observer, audience **-raum** *m* auditorium auditorium

zuschieben to shut, close

zuschießen to supplement, add, dart

Zuschlag *m* addition, admixture, flux, increase,

extra (charge) ~ **für Abtrieb** slack (for downward pressure) ~ **zur Leitungsdrahtlänge** slack ~ **einer Linie** slack (in the line)
zuschlagen to add, slam, hit hard **kurz** ~ to hammer quickly
Zuschläger *m* smith's assistant, striker
Zuschlag-erz *n* fluxing ore **-faktor** *m* (für Lager) bearing factor **-frei** without surcharge
Zuschlaggebühr *f* extra tax or fee, supplementary fee ~ **für Voranmeldung** préavis fee
Zuschlag-hammer *m* sledge hammer, two-handed hammer **-kalkstein** *m* limestone for flux **-material** *n* flux material **-pflichtig** surcharge required **-ration** *f* allowance for waste **-stoff** *m* aggregate (for concrete) **-zeit** *f* additional time
Zuschleifkette *f* covering chain
zuschließen to lock, close
zuschmelzen to close by melting, seal
zuschmieren to fill in (cracks or holes)
zuschnallen to buckle or snap
zuschnappen to fall or snap shut, click in place
Zuschneidemaschine *f* machine for cutting out
zuschneiden to cut to size
Zuschneider *m* cloth or clothier's cutter
Zuschneide-säge *f* frame saw **-schablone** *f* cutting stencil, lofting template or pattern
Zuschnitt *m* blank
zuschnüren to lace up, cord, tie up
zuschrauben to screw tight or up
zuschreiben to impute, attribute
Zuschuß *m* allowance, extra pay, contribution **-betrieb** *m* company with deficit budget, subsidy operation **-gebiet** *n* shortage area
zuschütten to add, pour to, fill up
zusenden to ship
zusetzen to add, mix, alloy, adulterate, obstruct, clog
zusichern to assure, promise, asseverate
zusiegeln to seal
Zuspann-kreuz *n* clamping cross **-schraube** *f* tightening screw
zusperren to bar, barricade
zuspitzen to point, taper, tip **sich** ~ to converge
Zuspitzung *f* point, tapering
zusprechen to adjudge, grant, telephone (a message)
Zusprechgebühr *f* additional charge for telephoning of telegram
Zustand *m* state, condition, position, situation, order, status, habit, phase, circumstance ~ **des Abgleitens** sideslipping (aviation) ~ **der abgerissenen Strömung** burbling stage of flow (aerodyn) **einem** ~ **anpassen** to correct **betriebsfähiger** ~ working condition **in eingebautem** ~ while installed **erzwungener** ~ forced state (phys.) **eingeschwungener** ~ steady-state oscillation **geordneter** ~ ordered state or arrangement, preferred configuration **stationärer, statischer** ~ steady state **vorübergehender** ~ transient state
zustande bringen to achieve
zustande kommen to come about, occur, mature
Zustandekommen *n* occurrence, formation, taking place
zuständig competent, authorized **-er Gerichtshof** court of competent jurisdiction or venue
Zuständigkeit authority, competence
Zuständigkeitsbereich *m* area of competency
Zustands-änderung *f* change of condition or state **-diagramm** *n* phase diagram, equilibrium diagram, fusibility curve **-feld** *n* constitutional field, equilibrium region, field of state or condition **-form** *f* configuration **-formel** *f* state formula **-funktion** *f* partition function **-gesetz** *n* law of stages **-gleichung** *f* equation of state or condition **-größe** *f* entropy, variable of state
Zustands-integral *n* partition function **-kurve** *f* constitutional curve, curve of state, curve of condition **-lampe** *f* condition signal light (guided missiles) **-raum** *m* phase space **-schaubild** *n* phase diagram, constitutional or equilibrium diagram **-summe** *f* partial function **-variable** *f*, **-veränderliche** *f* variable of state **-verschiebung** *f* change in state, displacement of state **-wahrscheinlichkeit** *f* state probability
zustellen to block up, close, deliver, prepare (a furnace), line **jemandem etwas** ~ to forward, send or deliver a thing to a person
Zustell-hebel *m* vertical feed lever **-maschine** *f* settling machine
Zustellung *f* preparation, lining, delivery, infeed, communication, service
Zustellungs-datum *n* date of service **-gebühr** *f* charges for conveyance, cartage **-masse** *f* lining mass **-schaltwerk** *n* feed mechanism
Zustellzeit *f* time of delivery (TOD)
zusteuern to contribute, steer toward
Zustich *m* half-stitch (of rope)
Zustimmung *f* consent, assent, agreement, approval, accession, acquiescence, permission
zustopfen to stop up
zustöpseln to plug or stop up
zustoßen to happen, befall, push shut
Zustrebekraft *f* centripetal force
zustreben to tend
Zustreichbürste *f* brushing device
Zustrom *m* arriving current, influx, afflux
zuströmen to flow or stream in, blow toward
Zuströmung *f* afflux
zustutzen to make shorter
zutage at day, on the surface ~ **kommen** to come to light ~ **liegen** to be evident ~ **treten** to come to light
Zutakelung *f* rigging
Zutat(en) *f, pl* lining and trimming, raw material, ingredient (cooking), addition, complement
zuteilen to allot, allocate, feed, supply, appropriate, attach, assign, delegate, adjudicate, award
Zuteiler *m* feeder
Zuteil-schalter *m* assignment key, transfer key **-schnecke** *f* feed screw **-taste** *f* assignment key
Zuteilung *f* allotment, appropriation, allocation, assignment, feed **die** ~ **des Vertrags** the award of contract
Zuteilungs-anzeige *f* letter of allotment **-auslösung** *f* selector release **-bank** *f* selector bank **-geschwindigkeit** *f* rate of feed **-gestell** *n* selector rack, switch frame, auto switch rack **-kamm** *m* permutation plate **-scheibe** *f* dial switch, permutation disk, selector plate **-schiene** *f* permutation bar, combination bar, code bar, selector bar **-system** *n* selector system, automatic telephone system **-vielfach** *n* bank multiple **-vielfachkabel** *n* bank cable
zutragen to carry (messages etc.)

zutreffen to come true, prove correct, be conclusive, hold true, be true
zutreffend striking, suitable, appropriate, conclusive
zutreiben to drive toward
Zutritt *m* access, admittance, admission, entrance
zutröpfeln lassen to add drop by drop
zuverlässig dependable, trustworthy, reliable, certain, authentic, sure **-er Anschlag** positive stop
Zuverlässigkeit *f* reliability, trustworthiness, certainty, authenticity
Zuverlässigkeits-probe *f*, **-prüfung** *f* reliability test, dependability test
zuvorkommen to forestall, anticipate, prevent, obviate **einer Sache ~** to obviate, prevent
Zuwachs *m* growth, increase, increment, extension, expansion **-bohrer** *m* timber tester, pole tester
zuwachsen to incrust
Zuwachsimpuls *m* incremental impulse
zuwägen to weigh or measure out
zuwegebringen to accomplish
zuweisen to assign, appropriate, allot
Zuweisung *f* assignment, appropriation, assignation, allotment **~ der Wellenlängen** frequency allocation or assignment
zuwiderhandeln to act against, disobey, contravene, act in opposition, counteract, break, violate
Zuwiderhandlung *f* infringement, violation, contravention
zuwiderlaufen to go against, counterrotate
zuwiderlaufend cross
zuzahlen to pay additionally or in excess, pay the surcharge
zuzählen to add
zuziehen to tighten, draw together
Zuzug *m* influx
zuzüglich with the addition of, plus, including
Zwackeisen *n* pincers
Zwang *m* force, pressure, constraint, compulsion, coercion, restraint **geringster ~** least constraint or resistance **-lauf** *m* positive movement (mach.)
Zwangs-anleihe *f* forced loan **-auslösung** *f* static line device, positive release (on parachutes) **-bedingung** *f* constraint **-belüftung** *f* pressure cooling
Zwangsdurchlauf *m* once-through **-kessel** *m* induced-single-circulation boiler, forced-through-flow boiler **-kühlung** once-through cooling **-wärmeübertrager** *m* flow-forced heat exchanger
Zwangs-einmittung *f* automatic centering **-führung** *f* guide rings on a projectile **-gekühlt** blower-cooled **-kraft** *f* compulsive force **-kurs** *m* forced rate of exchange **-lage** *f* embarrassing situation **-landung** *f* forced landing
zwangsläufig positively actuated, necessary, enforced, guided, constrained, positive (engine), by constraint, in a locked manner, nonslip (in drive), forced **~ arbeiten** to operate mechanically **~ betätigt** forcibly actuated, positively actuated
zwangsläufig-er Antrieb positive drive **-er Ferndrehzahlmesser** escapement teletachometer **-er selbsttätiger Vorschub** automatic power feed **-e Zuführung** force-feed (forced feed)
Zwangsläufigkeit *f* guided motion
Zwangslauf-kessel *m* forced-flow boiler **-lehre** *f* kinematics, determinism
Zwangs-lieferung *f* compulsory furnishing of supply **-lizenz** *f* compulsory license **-mittel** *n* coercive measure, means of restraint **-rücklauf** *m* enforced surrender **-schiene** *f* check rail **-schienenwinkel** *m* rolled section for guide and check rails **-schmierung** *f* forced-feed lubrication **-sperrung** *f* boycott
Zwangsumlauf *m* forced rotation **-erhitzung** *f* forced convection heating **-kessel** *m* forced-circulation boiler **-schmierung** *f* circulating forced lubrication **-verdampfer** *m* forced-circulation evaporator
Zwangs-verfahren *n* coercive measures **-verkauf** *m* forced sale **-versteigerung** *f* compulsory sale by auction **-vollstreckungsbefehl** *m* writ of (compulsory) execution **-zentrierung** *f* perforce-centering, compulsory centering
Zwanzigflächner *m* icosahedron
Zweck *m* purpose, objective, aim, end **-bau** *m* functional structure **-bedingt** functional **-dienlich** serviceable, useful, efficient, pertinent, convenient, apt
Zwecke *f* tack, peg, pin
zweck-entfremdet used for purposes other than originally intended **-entsprechend** serviceable, useful, efficient **-form** *f* utility form **-forschung** *f* practical research **-gebunden** reserved for special use, delimited **-los** aimless, useless **-mäßig** effective, practical, advantageous, suitable, appropriate, opportune, proper, advisable, expedient, adapted, fit **-mäßigkeit** *f* suitability, expediency **-verband** *m* utilitarian union
Zwei-abnehmerausführung *f* two doffer type design **-abrißbauart** *f* double-breaking type **-achser** *m* two-axle vehicle, four-wheel vehicle **-achsig** biaxial **-achsigkeit** *f* biaxiality **-adressenbefehl** *m* two-address instruction
zweiadrig twin, bifilar, biaxial, pair, two-wire, two-stranded **-e Ortsverbindungsleitung** two-wire trunk
Zweiankersystem *n* two-armature system
zweiarmig two-armed **-er Hebel** two-armed lever
zweiatomig diatomic
zweiäugig binocular **-es Sehen** binocular vision, stereoscopic vision
Zweibacken-ausgleichsmitnehmer *m* two-jaw equalizing driver **-bremse** *f* double-shoe-type brake **-futter** *n* box chuck, two-jaw chuck **-spannpatrone** *f* two-jawed collect chuck **-zugfutter** *n* two jaw draw-in-type chuck
zwei-badig two-bath **-ballig** double-canneled
Zweibahnenbett *n* double-track bed
zweibahnig two-ply
Zweiband-kabel *n* cable for twin-band telephony **-projektor** *m* double-film projector **-spieler** *m* two-unit dubber
zweibasisch dibasic
Zweibein *n* bipod **-fahrwerk** *n* split undercart
Zweibildmessung *f* two-image photogrammetry
Zweiblattschraube *f* two-blade propeller
Zweibrennraummotor *m* divided combustion engine

zweichoriges Piano bichord piano
Zweidecker *m* biplane
zweideutig equivocal, ambiguous, double-meaning
Zweideutigkeit *f* ambiguity
zweidimensional two-dimensional
Zweidrahtaufhängung *f* bifilar or double suspension
Zweidraht-betrieb *m* two-wire operation **-doppelrohrverstärker** *m* two-valve two-wire (intermediate) repeater **-doppelrohrzwischenverstärker** *m* two-wire two-valve intermediate repeater **-gabel** *f* two-wire termination
zweidrahtig with two wires
Zweidraht-leitung *f*, **-schaltung** *f* two-wire circuit **-speiseleitung** *f*, **symmetrische ~** balanced twin feeder **-stammleitung** *f* two-wire side circuit **-verstärker** *m* two-wire repeater **-wicklung** *f* bifilar winding **-zwischenverstärker** *m* two-wire two-way repeater
Zweidruck-dampfturbine *f* two-stage mixed-pressure steam turbine **-regelung** *f* double-pressure regulation
Zweidüsenzerstäuber *m* two-nozzle atomizer
Zweiebenenantenne *f* two-bay antenna
Zweieck *n* spindle
zweieckig spindle, fusiform
Zweieckprofil *n* streamlined profile **-haltung** *f* streamlined (mounting) strut
Zweieinhalbdecker *m* two and a half plane
Zweielektrodenröhre *f* diode, Fleming valve, kenotron
Zwei-elektronen *pl* dielectronic **-elementkristall** *m* bimorph crystal
Zweier-anschluß *m* two-party line system **bildskizze** *f* stereoscopic pair **-schalen** *pl* duplex rings **-stoß** *m* two-body collision, binary collision **-stoßassoziation** *f* double-impact association **-teiler** *m* ratio of two **-verfahren** *n* two-line series or two fractional scans per frame **-zelt** *n* two-man shelter tent
Zweietagen-korb *m* double-deck cage **-ofen** *m* two-story furnace
zweifach twofold, double, dual, twice **~ unstetig** double discontinuity **in -er Ausfertigung** in duplicate **-e Erscheinung** composite phenomenon **-e Expansionsmaschine** double-expansion engine **-e Rückkopplung** double regeneration **-e Schreibung** dual printing
Zweifach-antenne *f* two-bay or two-level antenna **-apparat** *m* double multiplex insulator **-betrieb** *m* duplex system (teleph.) **-diodengleichrichter** *m* duodiode rectifier, duodiode valve **-diodepentode** *f* double diode pentode **-drossel** *f* twin choke **-düse** *f* double nozzle **-expansionsdampfmaschine** *f* twofold expansion steam engine
zweifachfrei divariant, bivariant **-es Gleichgewicht** bivariant equilibrium, divariant equilibrium
Zweifach-kamera *f* twin camera **-konusantenne** *f* biconical antenna **-kupplung** *f* double action clutch **-meßkamera** *f* twin photogrammetric camera **-regelpumpe** *f* twin variable delivery pump **-reihenbildkamera** *f* twin aerial camera **-reihenmeßkamera** *f* two-lens aerial survey camera
Zweifach-schneide *f* double-type edge **-schwefeleisen** *n* iron disulfide **-schwefelzinn** *n* tin disulfide **-stecker** *m* two-pin-plug **-streuexperiment** *n* double scattering experiment **-steuerung** *f* two-control system, dual control **-telegraph** *m* double-telegraph set **-untersetzer** *m* binary scaler
Zweifach-verbindung *f* binary compound **-verstärker** *m* two-stage amplifier **-verteiler** *m* two-output junction box, Y-fitting **-weinsauer** bitartrate **-zündunterbrecher** *m* double ignition contact breaker **-zweipolröhre** *f* duodiode rectifier, duodiode valve
Zweifaden-aufhängung *f* bifilar or double suspension **-lampe** *f* (Bilux) two filament bulb (Bilux)
zweifadig bifilar
Zweifarben-band *n* two-colored ribbon **-druck** *m* two-color printing **-druckvorrichtung** *f* two-color printer **-schreibeinrichtung** *f* two-color-writing device
zweifarbig dichromatic, two-toned, two-colored **-es Papier** duplex paper **-er Schleier** dichroic fog, dichromatic fog, silver or red fog **-er Spiegel** dichroic mirror
Zweifarbigkeit *f* (TV) dichroism
Zweifeld-platte *f* slab continuous over two spans **-röhre** *f* drift or beam tube working with two fields
zweiflächig dihedral, two-faced
Zweiflammrohrkessel *m* double-flue boiler
Zweiflankenabrollgerät *n* two-flank rolling gear tester
zweiflanschig double-flanged
zweiflügelig two-bladed **-e Luftschraube** two-bladed propeller **-e Tür** two-leaved door
Zweiflügelluftschraube *f* two-blade propeller
Zwei-flüssigkeitelement *n* double-fluid cell **-flutige Turbine** double-flow turbine **-formpressen** *n* matched die molding
Zweifunken-doppelzündung *f* double ignition **-magnetapparat** *m* twin or double spark magneto **-spule** *f* two-spark coil **-zündung** *f* twin or double spark ignition
Zweig *m* branch, leg, twig, arm (of bridge or filter) **-amt** *n* branch exchange
Zweigang *m* two-position **-getriebe** *n* two-ratio gear
zweigängiges Gewinde double thread
Zweigang-handbohrer *m* two speed drill **-lader** *m* two-speed blower, two-speed supercharger **-planetengetriebe** *n* two-speed planetary gear **-schraube** *f* two-position controllable propeller
Zweig-anlage *f* exchange **-anstalt** *f* branch establishment **-bahn** *f* branch line, branch **-betrieb** *m* dispersal plant
Zweigelenkrahmen *m* rigid frame with two hinged supports
zweigerüstiges Walzwerk double-stand rolling mill
Zweigestaltigkeit *f* dimorphism
Zweig-fabrik *f* branch works **-gesellschaft** *f* affiliated company
Zweigitterröhre *f* tetrode, double-grid lamp, space-charge tetrode
Zweig-kabel *n* branch cable **-kanal** *m* secondary arm of a canal **-lager** *n* branch depot or camp
zweigleisig double-track **-e Bahn** double-track railway

Zweigleitung *f* branch line, branch pipe
zweigliedrig binary, two-membered, binomial (math.) **-er Kettenleiter** two-section network
Zweig-linie *f* branch line, junction line **-rohr** *n* branch pipe **-rohrleitung** *f* branch piping **-rutsche** *f* bifurcated chute **-schalter** *m* branch switch **-schaltung** *f* parallel connection **-stelle** *f* branch office, branch, substation **-stellung** *f* switch line (R.R.) **-stollen** *m*, **-strecke** *f* branch gallery (min.) **-strom** *m* branch current **-stromkreis** *m* branch circuit, divided circuit **-system** *n* tapering cabling system
Zwei-gurtträger *m* two-flanged or double-flanged girder **-gut** *n* two-product
Zweig-werk *n* branch factory **-widerstand** *m* shunt, derived or branched or shunt resistance
zweihalsig two-necked
zweihangiges Dach ridged roof
Zweiheit *f* duality, dyad, couple
zweihiebig double-cut (said of files)
Zweihilfsträgersystem *n* two sub-carrier system
zweihöckrig two-lobed **-e Resonanzkurve** *f* double-hump resonance curve
Zweiholmbauart *f* two-spar type of construction
zweiholmig two-spar
Zweihordendarre *f* two-floored drying kiln
Zweikammer-ausführung *f* twin chamber machine **-bremszylinder** *m* two-chamber brake cylinder **-sandstrahlapparat** *m* two-compartment sandblast tank machine **-wasserrohrkessel** *m* water-tube boiler with two headers
Zweikanal *m* double channel **-diskriminatoreinschub** *m* plug-in two-channel discriminator **-simplex** *m* two-way simplex system
zwei-kegelig two-cone **-kehrig** double-return **-kettig** double twist, double warp
Zweiklang-anlage *f* two-tone system **-pfeife** *f* harmony whistle, whistle with double tone **-signal** *n* two-tone signal
zweiknotige Schwingung two-noded oscillation (waves, etc.)
zweikomponentig two components (of)
Zweikontakt-regel *f* two-contact regulator (or governor) **-einfeldregler** *m* two-contact one-field regulator **-wegbauregler** *m* double-contact separately mounted regulator
Zweikörperformalismus *m* two-body formalism
Zweikraftstoffverfahren *n* bifuel system
Zweikreis-bandsiebschaltung *f* two-circuit band-pass filter **-empfang** *m* secondary reception, two-circuit reception **-empfänger** *m* two-circuit receiver, two-circuit set, double-circuit receiver
Zweikreiser *m* two-circuit receiver, two-circuit set, double-stage system, dual-flow system (aviat.)
zweikreisiges Kristallgoniometer crystal goniometer with two circles
Zweikreis-strahlantrieb *m* dual cycle jet propulsion unit **-turbinenluftstrahlwerk** *n* turbo-jet engine with regeneration **-verstärker** *m* double-tuned amplifier
Zweikristallspektrometer *n* double-crystal spectrometer
Zwei-kurbelpumpe *f* double-throw pump **-kurvenschreiber** *m* two-point curve drawing instrument
zweilagig two-layer
Zweileiter-kabel *n* twin-core cable, duplex-conductor lead wire **-netz** *n* two-wire network **-schnur** *f* double flexible cord **-system** *n* two-wire system with direct or alternating current
Zweileitungsbetrieb *m* two-line service (teleph.)
Zweilinsenobjektiv *n* (zweiteiliges Objektiv) two-component lens
Zweiloch-flansch *m* two-hole flange **-herd** *m* two-hole range **-mutter** *f* nut with two holes **-mutterschlüssel** *m* socket screw wrench **-schlüssel** *m* double-ended wrench
zweimal twice **-schmelzerei** *f* two-stage melting process, Walloon process
Zweimaschinenbetrieb *m* two-dynamo operation
Zweimengendüse *f* duplex nozzle
zweimetallisch bimetallic, alloy
Zweiminuten-verbindung *f* hundred-call second **-wendung** *f* two-minute turn
Zweimotoren-antrieb *m* two-motor or -engine drive **-flugzeug** *n* twin engine or double-engine airplane
zweimotorig twin-engined
zweiohriges Hören stereophonic or binaural hearing, two-channel listening
Zweiohrverfahren *n* binaural sound-location method
zweipaariges Kabel two-pair core cable
Zweipackverfahren *n* bipack method
Zweiphasen-anker *m* two-phase rotor **-dreileitersystem** *n* two-phase three-wire system **-generator** *m* two-phase generator or alternator **-gleichgewicht** *n* two-phase equilibrium **-komponente** *f* out-of-phase component **-raum** *m* two-phase field (metal.) **-schalter** *m* biphase connection **-strom** *m* two-phase current **-system** *n* two-phase system **-vierleitersystem** *n* two-phase four-wire system **-vorverdichter** *m* two-speed super-charger
Zweiphasenwechselstrom *m* two-phase alternating current **verketteter ~** interlinked two-phase current
zweiphasig two-phase, biphase, diphase
zweiplattig bilamellar
Zweipol *m* two-terminal network
Zweipolgleichrichtung *f* diode detection, diode rectification
zweipolig double-pole, bipolar, two-pointed **-e Dynamomaschine** bipolar dynamo **-er Hebelschalter** double-lever switch **-e Nebenschlußmaschine** two-pole shunt generator **-er Schalter** double-pole switch **-er Umschalter** double-pole change-over switch, double-throw switch
Zweipol-maschine *f* bipolar dynamo **-röhre** *f* two-circuit receiver, two-circuit set, diode tube **-spannungsbegrenzungsdiode** *f* bidirectional breakdown diode **-strecke** *f* dipole tube, dipole path
Zweiprismenspektrograph *m* two-prism spectrograph
Zweipunkt-lager *n* two-point contact bearing **-landung** *f* two-point landing **-meßverfahren** *n* two-point measuring system **-regelung** *f* two-position action **-regler** *m* two-step controller, on-off controller, two-position action controller **-verfahren** *n* two-point resection
Zweireihensternmotor *m* twin-row radial engine
zweireihig in two rows, double-row **-e Nietung** double-row riveting

Zweirichtungs-impulse *pl* bidirectional pulses **-netzwerk** *n* bilateral network
Zweirillen-scheibe *f* double-sheave pulley **-tieflochbohrer** *m* two-lipped deep hole drill
Zweirinnenofen *m* double-ring-type furance
Zweirippenmutter *f* two-ribbed nut
Zweiröhren-empfänger *m* two-valve receiver **-verstärker** *m* two-valve amplifier, two-valve repeater, double-relay repeater **-zwischenverstärker** *m* two-valve, two-way intermediate repeater **-zwischenverstärkerschrank** *m* two-wire repeater board
Zweirollenrotationsdruckmaschine *f* two-reel rotary printing machine
Zweirumpfflugzeug *n* twin-boom aircraft
Zweisäulen-apparat *m* two-column apparatus **-presse** *f* double-column press
zweischäftiger Bindfaden two-strand twine
Zweischalengreifer *m* clamp-shell grab
Zweischaler *pl* bivalves
zweischalig of two sheets, two-sheet, parted
Zweischaufelrührer *m* two-arms paddle mixer
Zweischenkelflockungsmesser *n* U-tube sedimentator
zweischenklig two-legged, having two branches or limbs
Zweischienenhängebahn *f* double-beam trolley system
zweischiffig two-span
Zweischlangendurchfluß *m* two-coil flow
Zweischlauchbrenner *m* single-oxygen-hose cutting torch
Zweischleifenoszillograph *m* two-string oscillograph
Zweischlitz-flansch *m* two-slot flange **-magnetron** *n* two-split magnetron, two-segment magnetron, split-anode magnetron
Zweischneider *m* double cutter
Zweischneidewiegemesser *n* two-blade mincing knife
zweischneidig double-edged, two-edged **-er Bohrer** double-cutting drill or bit **-er Langloch-fräser** two-lipped end miller
zweischnittig in double shear **-e Abscherung** double shearing **-e Nietung** double-shear riveting
Zweischnur-betrieb *m* double-cord operation (teleph.) **-klappenschrank** *m* double-cord switchboard **-system** *n* double-cord system
Zweischraube *f* twin propeller
Zweischrauben-flansch *m* two-bolt tube flange **-modell** *n* twin-screw model **-schiff** *n* twin-screw ship
Zweischwimmer *m* twin float **-flugzeug** *n* double-pontoon seaplane, twin-float plane
Zweiseilgreifer *m* two-cabled dredger or bucket grab
Zweiseitenband *n* double side-band **-senden** *n* double side-band transmission **-übertrager** *m* side-band transmitter with suppressed carrier
zweiseitig bilateral, two-sided **-e Appretur** finish on face and back **-es Arbeiten** two-way operation, double action **-er Druck** duplex print **-e Flottezirkulation** double circulation **-er Kippwagen** dump car tipping to either side **-er Kompressor** double-entry compressor **-es Krümmer-T-Stück** (flanged) short-sweep twin elbow, (flanged) double-sweep T **-er Prozeß** ambigenous process **-e Vollnaht** square butt weld **~ senkrecht** mutually perpendicular
Zweiseitigkeit *f* two-sidedness, bilaterality
Zweisitzer *m* two-seater airplane **geschlossener ~** coupé **offener ~** roadster
Zweisitzerflugzeug *n* two-place airplane
zweisitzig two-seat
Zweisockellampe *f* tubular lamp
zweispaltig with two columns (print.)
Zweispännerlandmaschine *f* two-horse agricultural machine
zweispanniger Pferdezug two-horse draft or pull
Zweispannungsumstecker *m* two-voltage change-over switch
Zweispannwaage *f* doubletree
Zweispindelbank *f* two-spindle lathe
zweispindelig-e Automaten two spindle automatic lathes **-e Zylinderbohrmaschine** double-spindle cylinder boring machine
Zweispitze *f* pick, mattock
zweispitzige Kurve double-peaked curve, double-hump curve
zweispulig with double spools
zweispurig double-edged (film), double-tracked
Zweistahlabwälzhobel *m* tooth generation by twin reciprocating tool
Zweiständer-bauart *f* double-column type **-blechtafelschere** *f* double-standard plate shear **-karusseldrehbank** *f* double-column vertical boring mill
Zweistandsentfernungsmesser *m* two-station range finder
Zweistärkenbrille *f* bifocal glasses
zweistegig double-webbed
Zweistellenschalter *m* two-position switch
Zweistellungs-flügel two-position wing **-hebel** *m* two-position lever **-schraube** *f* two-position controllable propeller
Zweisternmotor *m* double-row staggered radial engine (aviat.)
Zweistieler *m* biplane, double-bay
zweistielig with two columns, two-handled, two-bay **-er Doppeldecker** two-bay biplane
Zweistiftsockel *m* two-pin base
Zweistockfaltdipol-Antenne *f* two-story folded dipole antenna
zweistöckig two-story
Zweistoff *m* binary **-eutektikum** *n* two-component eutectic **-gemisch** *n* binary mixture **-legierung** *f* binary alloy, two-component alloy **-manometer** *n* two-fluid manometer **-system** *n* two-component system, binary system
Zweistrahl-betatron *n* double-ray betatron **-betrieb** *m* dual trace operation (of oscillograph)
zweistrahlig twin-jet
Zweistrahlröhre *f* double-beam cathode ray tube
Zweistraße *f* two-high rolling-mill train
Zweistrom-anordnung *f* double-flow arrangement **-triebwerk** *n* ducted fan powerplant (aviat.)
Zweistufen-gebläse *n* two-stage blower **-lader** *m* two-stage blower, two-stage supercharger **-modulation** *f* double modulation **-regler** *m* two-stage regulator, two-position regulator **-titration** *f* two-step titration **-zweiganglader** *m* two-speed two-stage supercharger **-warzenschweißen** *n* pilot projection welding
zweistufig two-stage, two-step **-e Luftpumpe**

two-stage air compressor **-er Nocken** double-lift cam (with two lobes) **-er Regelverstärker** two-stage variable amplifier **-er Verdichter** two-stage compressor **-es Relais** two-step relay
zweisystemiger Schlitten double lock carriage
Zweitakt *m* two(-storke) cycle **-boxermotor** *m* opposed piston 2-stroke engine **-diesel(motor)** *m* two-stroke oil engine (Diesel engine)
Zweitakter *m* two-stroke cycle engine
Zweitakt-flugmotor *m* two-cycle aircraft engine **-maschine** *f* two-stroke or double-stroke (cycle) engine
Zweitaktmotor *m* two-stroke engine, two-stroke cycle (engine), two-cycle engine **doppelwirkender ~** two-stroke cycle double-acting engine
Zweitakt-prozeß *m* two-stroke cycle **-verbrennungsmotor** *m* two-stroke internal combustion engine
Zweit-anzeigegerät *n* remote indicator **-arbeitsgänge** *pl* second operations **-druck** *m* reprint
Zweiteilchenoberflächendichte *f* superficial pair density
zweiteilig bipartite, two-part, two-piece **-e Büchse** two-point socket **-er Flügel** wing in two sections **-es Formstück** split duct **-e Kurbelwelle** two-piece crankshaft **-er Ring** two-part ring **-es Schwungrad** two-piece flywheel **-e Stopfbüchsenbrille** divided stuffing-box gland
Zweiteilung *f* bipartition, bisection
Zweitellergerät *n* two-turntable type player
Zweitemperatur-(Schnapp-)ventil two tempera-ture (snap action) valve
Zweitkreis *m* secondary circuit
Zweitluft *f* secondary air **-gebläse** *n* secondary-air blower **-zufuhr** *f* twin air supply
Zweitonverfahren *n* two-tone keying
Zweitourenschnellpresse *f* two-revolution printing press
Zweitpatrone *f* secondary charge
zweitrangig of secondary importance
zweitrümmig double-tracked, two-strand
Zweit-schrift *f* duplicate **-stufe** *f* (Astron.) second stage (missile rocket) **-wicklung** *f* secondary winding, coil winding
Zweiunddreißigerleitung *f* octuple-phantom circuit
Zweiwachs *m* piping
Zweiwalzen-foulard *m* two-bowl sizing and squeezing machine **-gerüst** *n* housing for two rolls, two-high stand of rolls **-straße** *f* two-high mill **-stuhl** *m* two-roller corn mill **-trockner** *m* twin-cylinder drying machine, double-drum drier
Zweiweg(e)-atmung *f* two-way respiration **-gleichrichter** *m* full-wave rectifier **-gleichrichtung** *f* full-wave rectification **-hahn** *m* two-way (stop) cock, two-way top, bypass valve **-pflug** *m* two-way plow **-plattform** *f* two-way platform **-umschalter** *m* two-way switch **-ventil** *n* two-way acting valve **-verstärker** *m* two-way repeater, duplex repeater
Zweiwellen-anordnung *f* cross-compound arrangement **-mikroskopie** *f* two-wavelength microscopy
zweiwellig on two shafts **-e Resonanzkurve** double-hump resonance curve
Zweiwelligkeit *f* two-wave property (cryst.)
zweiwertig bivalent, divalent, two-valued (math.) **-es Element** dyad **-es Radikal** bivalent radical **-es Zeichen** two-power signal
Zweiwertigkeit *f* bivalence
Zweizacken-fadenführer *m* two-pronged thread guide **-schrift** *f* bilateral track (sound film)
zweizackig bi-furcated, double-pointed, two-pronged
zweizahlig of twofold symmetry
Zweizahnwälzschrupper *m* two-tooth generating roughers
Zweizapfenlenkung *f* two-pivot steering gear
zweizeilig double-spaced
zweizeitig double-timed
Zweiziffernpolaritäten *pl* digit polarities
zweizinkig double-pronged
Zweizonenstoßofen *m* double-fired continuous furnace
zweizügig reversing, pull-and-push
Zweizweckbeleuchtung *f* dual-purpose illumination
Zweizylinder-boxermotor *m* flat-twin engine, horizontally opposed twin cylinder **-dampfdynamo** *m* double-cylinder steam dynamo **-frigenverflüssigeraggregat** *n* two-cylinder freon liquefier unit **-tauchkolbenverdichter** *m* two-cylinder plunger-type compressor **-V-Motor** *m* V-twin engine
Zwerg-lampe *f* miniature lamp, pea lamp **-packer** *m* pony packer (min.) **-röhre** *f* miniature or midget valve **-sandstrahlgebläse** *n* sandblast-tank cabinet **-spritzgußmaschine** *f* midget molder **-welle** *f* centimeter wave, microwave, microray, midget wave, dwarf wave
Zwick *m* pinch, nip
Zwickbohrer *m* twist drill
Zwicke *f* pincers
Zwickechtheit *f* fastness to lasting
Zwickel *m* wedge, gusset (plate), clock, filler (cable), try cock
zwickeln to gore, gusset
zwicken to nip, pinch
Zwickmaschine *f* lasting machine
Zwickzange *f* pincers, cutter, cutting pliers
zwiebelförmig bulb-shaped
zwiefädig bifilar
Zwielicht *n* dusk, twilight **-wirkung** *f* twilight effect **-zone** *f* twilight band or zone
Zwilling *m* twin
Zwillinge *pl* twin crystal, twin grain
Zwillings-achse *f* twinning axis **-antenne** *f* pair of aerials, twin aerial **-bereifung** *f* double tires **-bildung** *f* twin formation, twinning, twinning mechanism **-brennstoffpumpe** *f* duplex fuel pump **-dampfmaschine** *f* twin steam engine **-düse** *f* duplex nozzle **-ebene** *f* twinning plane (cryst.)
Zwilling-fläche *f* twinning plane **-flaschenzug** *f* double-hook hoist block, twin block **-flugzeug** *n* composite aircraft **-gesetz** *n* twinning law (cryst.) **-gleitung** *f* twin slipping **-gleitungsfläche** *f* twin gliding plane
Zwillings-kabel *n* twin cable **-klinke** *f* twin jack, pair of jacks **-kontrolle** *f* duplication check (info proc.) **-kristall** *m* twin crystal, hemitrope **-kufengestell** *n* twin-skid chassis or landing gear **-lafette** *f* twin machine-gun mount, twin barrels **-lamelle** *f* twin lamella, twin lamina, mechanical twin **-laufkran** *m* twin traveling crane **-leitung** *f* thermoplastic rip cords

-magnetzünder *m* dual-ignition magneto **-maschine** *f* twin-cylinder engine **-maschinengewehr** *n* twin-barreled machine gun **-naht** *f* suture of the twin plane (cryst.)

Zwillings-paradoxon *n* twin paradox **-prisma** *n* biprism **-propellerturbinemotor** (AV) twin power section turboprop engine **-rohrgruppe** *f* group of two torpedo tubes **-rollenzug** *m* twin-roller pull **-sammelstück** *n* twin collecting piece **-sammelstutzen** *m* twin-type collecting connection **-schleuse** *f* double locks (twin) **-schraubstutzen** *m* twin-type screwing connection **-schützen** *pl* twin gates

Zwillings-sockel *m* double socket, twin antiaircraft mounting for machine gun **-stecker** *m* biplug, pair of plugs **-transportorgan** *n* twin tape transporter **-triebwerk** *n* twin engine **-trommel** *f* twin drum **-trommelmischer** *m* twin-cylinder mixer **-verbundmaschine** *f* compound two cylinder engine **-walzen** *pl* duo rolls

Zwinge *f* clamp, cramp, holder, vise, hoop, collar, ferrule, thimble

zwingen to squeeze, press, force

Zwinger *m* wedge, ferrule, clamp

Zwirn *m* thread, twine, yarn **-band** *n* tape **-deckel** *m* twisting cap, twisting package

zwirnen to twist, twine

Zwirn-scheibe *f* spindle whorl (textile) **-wickel** *m* twisting cap, twisting package

Zwischen-ablesung *f* intermediate reading **-abmessungen** *pl* fractional sizes **-abwurfstelle** *f* intermediate discharge station **-addition** *f* subtotal

Zwischen-amt *n* intermediate station, way station, intermediate office, intermediate toll center **-amtliches Netz** inter-district network **-anstrich** *m* intermediate coat **-ausbesserung** *f* temporary repairs **-ausführung** *f* intermediate make or construction **-ausschalter** intermediate cut-off or switch

Zwischen-bad *n* intermediate bath **-band** *n* timing tape **-bahnhof** *m* way station, intermediate station **-bau** *m* substructure **-behälter** *m* surge tank, intermediate tank or container **-beschleuniger** *m* intermediate accelerator

Zwischen-bild *n* intermediate image, first image **-bildmodulation** *f* intermediate-image modulation **-bildorthikon** *n* image orthicon **-blech** *n* shim **-boden** *m* mezzanine, partition, false floor, false bottom, intermediate bottom, diaphragm **-bohrer** *m* double bit **-buchse** *f* intermedialte bush **-bürstenmaschine** *f* metadyne, metadynamo

Zwischen-dampf *m* reheat steam **-dampfentnahme** *f* intermediate steam utilization, steam extraction **-deck** *n* steerage, between decks, lower deck **-decke** *f* false floor, intermediate ceiling **-drucke** *pl* intermediate printed recordings **-druckverfahren** *n* regenerative cycle **-elektrodenkapazität** *f* interelectrode capacitance **-empfang** *m* intermediate reception **-entfernung** *f* intermediate range **-ergebnisspeicher** *m* working storage **-erzeugnis** *n* intermediate produce or product, intermediary product, partly finished article

Zwischenfall *m* mishap, indident **ohne ~** uneventful

Zwischen-farbe *f* intermediate color **-feld** *n* intermediate delaying position, covering position, ground between delaying positions, area between successive positions, intermediate area **-fehler** *m* zonal aberration **-filmgeber** *m* intermediate-film transmitter **-filmmethode** *f* intermediate-film method (television) **-filmsender** *m* intermediate-film transmitter **-filmverfahren** *n* intermediate-film method **-fläche** *f* interface **-flächenspannung** *f* interfacial tension **-flansch** *m* intermediate flange

Zwischen-flügel *m* flap (aviation), intermediary blade, antiflicker blade, balancing blade (motion picture) **-fluoreszenzschirm** *m* intermediate fluorescence screen **-flüssigkeit** *f* intermediate liquid **-folie** *f* organic lacquer foil **-form** *f* temporary type

Zwischenfrequenz (ZF) *f* intermediate frequency (IF), intermediate-beat or transfer frequency **-empfang** *m* superheterodyne reception

Zwischenfrequenzempfänger *m* superheterodyne receiver, intermediate-frequency receiver, double-detection receiver, transposition receiver **~ mit Kristallsteuerung** crystal-stabilized superheterodyne receiver

Zwischenfrequenz-gleichrichter *m* intermediate-frequency rectifier, second detector, audio detector **-stufe** *f* intermediate-frequency stage **-teil** *m* intermediate-frequency section of radar equipment **-transformator** *m* intermediate-frequency transformer **-verstärker** *m* intermediate-frequency amplifier, intermediate amplifier **-verstärkerstufe** *f* intermediate-frequency amplification stage

Zwischen-futter *n* interlining **-gas** *n* gas given at intervals to engine in gliding downward **-gebläse** *n* supercharger **-gefäß** *n* intermediate vessel, intermediate receptacle **-gerade** *f* straight between two curves **-geschaltet** interposed, inserted **-geschichtet** interstratified **-geschirr** *n* intermediate implement **-geschoß** *n* entresol, mezzanine floor **-gesperre** *n* empty or intermediate truss **-gestell** *n* intermediate stand **-getriebe** *n* intermediate drive or gearing **-gewebesubstanz** *f* intercellular substance

Zwischengitter-ion *n* interstitial ion **-plätze** *pl* interstices **-platzmechanismus** *m* interstitial mechanism (of alloys)

Zwischen-glied *n* connecting link, intermediary member, intermediate **-glühung** *f* intermediate annealing, intermediate softening **-handel** *m* carrying trade, commission business **-hebel** *m* (Bremsgestänge) swivel lever **-hilfsträger** *m* intermediate subcarrier **-holm** *m* false spar **-hörbetrieb** *m* duplex operation, alternate two-way communication **-hören** to intercept **-hülse** *f* adapter sleeve, intermediate sleeve **-impulspause** *f* (Zeichenpause) interdigital pause

Zwischen-kabel *n* intermediate cable **-kardinalpunkt** *m* intercardinal point **-karton** *m* middle (paper mfg.) **-kasten** *m* check (in molding), distributor box **-kern** *m* compound core, intermediate **-kette** *f* intermediate chain **-klappe** *f* floating aileron **-klemme** *f* intermediate terminal or connector **-klemmungsmasse** *f* interstitial material **-körper** *m* intermediate medium or substance, interposed medium or means

Zwischenkreis *m* harmonic suppressor, harmonic reducing circuit, intermediate circuit, link circuit, buffer (tuning) **abgestimmter ~** tuned intermediate circuit **aperiodischer ~** intermediate aperiodic circuit

Zwischenkreis-abstimmung *f* buffer tuning **-empfang** *m* intermediate circuit reception **-sender** *m* intermediate or link circuit transmitter

Zwischen-kristallin intercrystalline **-kühler** *m* intermediate cooler, intercooler **-kühlung** *f* intermediate cooling **-kultur** *f* inter-cropping **-kuppeln** to double-clutch **-ladung** *f* boosting charge, intermediate charge **-lage** *f* intermediate layer, separator, interposition, intermediate position, inset, interleaf **-lagenpapier** *n* interleaving paper

Zwischen-lager *n* intermediate layer or bearing **-lagerung** *f* interstratification **-lagplatte** *f* shim (plate) liner **-lagscheibe** *f* washer **-landeplatz** *m* intermediate landing field **-landung** *f* stop-over, intermediate landing or stop

Zwischen-längsträger *m* intermediate longitudinal girder **-last** *f* intermediat load **-läufer** (Mit-, Unter-läufer) back cloth (back grey) **-legen** to interpose, interlay, intercalate, insert **-legierung** *f* interposing alloy, hardener **-legplatte** *f* shim liner **-legscheibe** *f* shim **-leiter** *m* semi-conductor **-leitschaufel** *f* intermediate blade

Zwischen-leitung *f* intermediate line **-liegend** intermediate, intervening **-linienflimmer** *m* interline flicker, shimmer, weave **-linsenverschluß** *m* between-lens shutter **-maschine** *f* communicator **-maß** *n* intermediate size **-masse** *f* interstitial matter, matrix, cement (petrog.) **-mauer** *f* partition **-mittel** *n* intermediate medium or substance, interposed medium or means **-mittelmasse** *f* intermediate mass

Zwischen-modulation *f* intermodulation **-molekular** intermolecular **-mutter** *f* intermediate nut (intermediate lock) **-nippel** *n* intermediate disc, screwed reducing nipple **-niveau** *n* interface level **-nutzung** *f* intermediate yield **-optik** *f* intermediate optic, interposed optical means **-pause** *f* time interval **-pfeiler** *m* intermediate pillar **-phase** *f* interphase

Zwischen-platte *f* intermediate plate **-pol** *m* interpole **-positiv** *n* master positive **-produkt** *n* intermediate product **-punkt** *m* intermediate point **-punktabtastung** *f* dot interlacing (TV) **-punktflimmern** *n* interdot flickering **-querstück** *n* intermediate brace **-rad** *n* intermediate gear wheel, idler **-radbolzen** *m* gear stud **-radwelle** *f* double intermediate pinion gear **-rahmen** *m* wicket, subframe (car)

Zwischenraum *m* space, gap, interspace, interstice, interval, range, clearance, distance, intervening or interstitial space **-messer** *m* thickness gauge **-taste** *f* space key **-zeichen** *n* space signal (telegr.)

Zwischen-reaktion *f* intermediate, reaction **-rechenwert** *m* intermediate value **-registrierung** *f* extra recording image **-resultatspeicher** temporary storage **-ring** *m* special collar (Leica), intermediate ring, spacer, adapter (phot.) **-röhre** *f* intermediate-frequency tube **-rohrtransformator** *m* intervalve transformer **-rückschlagventil** *n* intermediate non-return valve (check valve) **-ruder** *n* floating or interplane aileron

Zwischen-sammler *m* intermediary header **-satzstück** *n* adapter **-schale** *f* subshell **-schalten** to interpose, interpolate, insert, include, intercalate

Zwischenschaltung *f* interposition, interpolation, mediation, intercalation, interposing, intermediate gear **unter ~ von** through the intermediary of

Zwischen-scheibe *f* center plate, distance piece, clamping washer, shim **-schicht** *f* intermediate layer, interlining **-schieben** *n* interpolation, insertion, intercalation **-schritt** *m* intermediary step or stage **-sender** *m* relay(ing) station, rebroadcast transmitter, retransmitter, repeater or repeating station **-speicherung** temporary storage (comput.)

Zwischen-sente *f* intermediate riband **-setzen** to interpose **-sockel** *m* adapter **-sorte** *f* intermediate sort or kind, intermediate quality **-spannvorrichtung** *f* intermediate stretching device **-spant** *n* intermediate frame **-spiel** *n* interlude **-spülung** *f* intermediate rinsing

zwischenstaatlich international, interstate **-es Fernamt** international terminal office **-er Luftverkehr** interstate air traffic

Zwischenständer für Anlage partition plate, feed side

Zwischenstecker *m* adapter plug, valve adapter, socket adapter **~ für Röhren** valve adapter, socket adapter

zwischenstehend intermediate

Zwischen-stein *m* (of copper) blue metal, blue stone **-stelle** *f* blinker post, relay post, intermediate telephone set, linking station **-stellenumschalter** *m* interthrough switch **-stellung** *f* intermediate position **-stiel** *m* intermediate strut **-stop** *m* breakpoint (info proc.) **-stößel** *m* intermediate tappet **-straße** *f* intermediate mill **-strecke** *f* intermediate rolling train **-stromröhre** *f* spacing valve

Zwischenstück *n* connection, distance, spacing, jumbling or intermediate piece or part, spacer, adapter **~ für Schlangenrohr** coil drag

Zwischen-stufe *f* intermediate grade or stage **-stufenkühlung** *f* interstage cooling **-stuhl** *m* intermediate chair (R.R.) **-stütze** *f* intermediate support **-summe** *f* subtotal **-summentaste** (Rechenmaschinen) sub-total key

Zwischen-taste *f* spacer **-telephon** *n* interphone system **-teller mit Deckelteiler** intermediate and top disc **-ton** *m* medium tone, intermediate tone or shade **-tor** *n* intermediate gate **-träger** *m* intermediate member, subcarrier **-trägerverfahren** *n* intercarrier sound system **-transformator** *m* intervalve transformer, intermediate transformer, interstage transformer

Zwischen-überhitzer *m* reheater, reheat superheater **-übertrager** *m* intervalve transformer, interstage transformer **-verankerung** *f* intermediate anchoring

Zwischenverfahren, im ~ gestellter Antrag interlocutory application

Zwischen-verkehr *m* intercommunication **-vermitt(e)lung** *f* intermediate exchange

Zwischenverstärker *m* telephone intermediate repeater, through-line repeater, intermediate amplifier, stage amplifier **fester ~** through-line repeater (teleph.)

Zwischen-verteiler *m* intermediate distributing

frame, cross-connection field, cross-connecting board **-vertreter** *m* intermediate agent **-wahl** *f* interdialling **-walzer** *m* cogger

Zwischenwand *f* baffle, bulkhead, partition, diaphragm **-stahlblech** *n* sheet-steel wall

Zwischen-wärmung *f* intermediate heating **-wasserung** *f* stopover of a seaplane **-wegweiser** *m* intermediate town marker **-weite** *f* distance between, interval **-welle** *f* main drive shaft, transmission line, intermediate gear or shaft, lay shaft **-werk** *n* intermediate work **-zahnrad** *n* idler gear **-zeichenstrom** *m* spacing current **-zeichenwelle** *f* spacing wave, compensation wave, back wave **-zeile** *f* interline, interlace

Zwischenzeilen-abtastung *f* interlaced scanning **-flimmer** *m* interline flicker, shimmer, weave (television)

Zwischenzeilenraster *m* interlaced scanning pattern **ungerader** ~ odd-line scanning

Zwischenzeilen-rhythmus *m* interline rhythm, interlace **-verfahren** *n* interlaced scanning, staggered scanning, interleaved scanning

Zwischen-zeit interval, interim **-zellig** intercellular **-ziel** *n* intermediate or secondary objective **-zone** *f* intermediate zone **-zünder** *m* intermediate charge, booster (explosives) **-zustand** *m* intermediate stage

Zwischenzylinder-leitring *m* intercylinder baffle ring **-ring** *m* intercylinder ring

Zwitschern *n* birdie, chirping, canaries (extraneous high-frequency noise)

Zwitter-apertur *f* split focus **-fahrzeug** *n* half-track vehicle **-ion** *n* dual ion, amphoteric ion, hybrid ion

Zwitter-apertur *f* split focus **-fahrzeug** *n* half-track vehicle **-ion** *n* dual ion, amphoteric ion, hybrid ion

Zwitterspule *f* hybrid coil **runde** ~ circular hybrid

Zwitterstecker *m* sexless connector (rdr.)

Zwölfeck *n* dodecagon

Zwölferlochung *f* twelve-punch or Y-punch (comput.)

Zwölfflach *n* dodecahedron

zwölfstufiges System duodecimal scale (tonal system)

Zwölfuhrzeiger *m* clock-dial target direction-indicator

Zwölfzylinder-V-Motor *m* twelve-cylinder V engine

zwölfteilig duodecimal

Zyan *n* cyanogen **-alkali** *n* alkali cyanide **-alkyl** *n* alkyl cyanide **-amid** *n* cyanamide **-ammonium** *n* ammonium cyanide

Zyanat *n* cyanate

Zyan-äthyl *n* ethyl cyanide **-barium** *n* barium cyanide **-bromid** *n* cyanogen bromide **-doppelsalz** *n* double cyanide **-einsatzhärtung** *f* cyaniding, cyanizing **-eisen** *n* iron cyanide **-eisenkalium** *n* potassium ferrocyanide **-eisenverbindung** *f* iron-cyanogen compound **-essigsäure** *f* cyanacetic acid

zyanessigsauer cyanacetic

Zyangas *n* cyanogen gas

Zyangold *n* gold cyanide **-kalium** *n* potassium auricyanide, potassium aurocyanide

Zyanhärten *n* cyaniding

Zyanid *n* cyanide **-frei** cyanide-free **-prozess** *m* **-verfahren** *n* cyanide process, cyanidation

Zyan-jodid *n* cyanogen iodide **-kali** *n*, **-kalium** *n* potassium cyanide **-kohlensäure** *f* cyanocarbonic acid **-laugerei** *f*, **-laugung** *f* cyaniding, cyanidation **-metall** *n* metallic cyanide **-quecksilberkalium** *n* mercury potassium cyanide **-quecksilberoxyd** *n* mercuric cyanide **-salz** *n* cyanogen salt, cyanide **-salzbad** *n* cyanide bath **-salzbadhärtung** *f* cyanide, bath hardening, cyaniding

zyansaurer Baryt barium cyanate

zyansaures Kali potassium cyanate

Zyan-schlamm *m* cyanogen sludge **-stickstoff** *m* cyanonitride **-toluol** *n* cyanotoluene

Zyanürsäure *f* cyanuric acid

Zyan-verbindung *f* cyanogen compound **-vergiftung** *f* cyanide poisoning, cyanogen poisoning **-wasserstoff** *m* hydrogen cyanide **-wasserstoffsäure** *f* hydrocyanic acid **-zink** *n* zinc cyanide

Zygote *f* zygote

Zykliden *pl* cyclids

zyklisch cyclic **-e Kohlenwasserstoffe** cyclical hydrocarbons **-e Koordinate** cyclic coordinate **-e Verschiebung** *f* cyclic shift **-e Versetzung** register rotation **-e Vertauschung** rotate register (info proc.)

zyklischbinärer Code modifiied binary code

Zyklodenverzahnung *f* cycloidal tooth system

Zyklograph *m* cyclograph

Zyklohexanol *n* cyclohexanol

Zykloid *n* cycloid

zykloidenähnlich cycloidal

zykloidisch cycloidal

zyklometrische Funktion inverse trigonometric function

Zyklon *m* cyclone, tornado, hurricane

zyklonal cyclonic

Zyklone *f* low minimum cyclone, area of low pressure

Zyklonenscheider *m* cyclone separator

Zyklon-filter *n* cyclone filter **-vorabscheider** *m* cyclonic precleaner

Zyklotron *n* cyclotron

Zyklotronumlauffrequenz *f* cyclotron frequency

Zyklus *m* cycle, loop (info proc.) **-zähler** *m* cycle counter

Zylinder *m* cylinder ~ **mit Dampfmantel** jacketed cylinder ~ **ohne Leitbleche** unbaffled cylinder ~ **mit flachem Verbrennungsraum** poultice head cylinder **einzelstehender** ~ separately cast cylinder **fächerförmig angeordnete** ~ cylinders arranged in fan shape **hängender** ~ inverted cylinder **schräger** ~ oblique cylinder **schwingender** ~ oscillating or rocking cylinder **stehender** ~ upright cylinder **stumpfer** ~ truncated cylinder **umlaufender** ~ revolving cylinder **unrunder** ~ worn cylinder

Zylinder-anordnung *f* position of the cylinders **-antenne** *f* cylindrical antenna **-auflagefläche** *f* cylinder pad **-auflager** *n* cylinder support bearing **-auskleidung** *f* cylinder liner **-ausrüstung** *f* cylinder fittings

Zylinder-bank *f* roller beam **-befestigung** *f* attachment of the cylinder **-befestigungsschraube** *f* cylinder hold-down bolt **-belastung** *f* top rollers **-berieselungsapparat** *m* cylindrical trickling apparatus **-blende** *f* cylinder diaphragm

-block *m* cylinder block, motor block **-boden** *m* bottom cylinder casting **-bodenventil** *n* cylinder bottom valve

Zylinder-bohrapparat *m* cylinder boring apparatus **-bohrer** *m* cylindrical bit **-bohrmaschine** *f* cylinder boring machine **-bohrung** *f* cylinder bore **-bolzen** *m* cylinder bolt **-büchse** *f* cylinder liner, barrel **-deckel** *m* cylinder cover, cylinder head **-dichtungsring** *m* (cylinder) packing ring **-drehbank** *f* slide lathe **-drehverschluß** *m* cylindric-prismatic breech mechanism **-druckfeder** *f* cylindrical thrust spring

Zylinderdurchmesser *m* cylinder diameter **innerer** ~ cylinder bore

Zylinder-einsatz *m* cylinder liner **-einspritzung** *f* direct injection **-elektrode** *f* cylindrical electrode, cylinder (of cathode-ray oscillograph)

Zylinderflansch *m* cylinder base **-temperatur** *f* cylinder-base temperature

zylinder-förmig cylindrical **-füllung** *f* cutoff **-funktion** *f* cylindrical function, cylindrical harmonics **-futter** *n* loose self-sealing liner (brewing), cylinder liner **-gehäuse** *n* cylinder block **-gestell** *n* cylinder foot **-guß** *m* cylinder casting, cylinder iron

Zylinder-haltebolzen *m* cylinder-holding stud **-haube** *f* cylinder fairing, cylinder **-hemmung** *f* cylinder escapement **-höhe** *f* clearance volume **-hub** *m* length of stroke **-hubvolumen** *n* piston displacement **-hülle** *f* cylinder liner **-hülse** *f* cylinder liner or sleeve

Zylinder-inhalt *m* cylinder volume or capacity, piston displacement, swept capacity, swept volume, cylinder displacement **-innendruck** *m* cylinder pressure **-kappe** *f* recoil-cylinder cap **-kerbstift** *m* cylindrical pin **-kern** *m* cylindrical-shaped core **-kessel** *m* shell-type boiler **-kolben** *m* cylinder piston **-koordinate** *f* cylindrical coordinate

Zylinderkopf *m* top cylinder casting, cylinder head **angegossener** ~ integral cylinder head

Zylinderkopf-dichtung *f* cylinder-head gasket **-haube** *f* cylinder-head cover **-schraube** *f* socket-head cap screw

Zylinder-kühlrippe *f* cylinder cooling fin **-kurvenfräseapparat** *m* circular profiling apparatus **-ladung** *f* cylindrical-shaped powder charge **-lager** *n* journal bearing **-lagerbock** *m* cylinder side frame **-lagerdeckel** *m* top portion of side frame **-lauf** *m* cylinder barrel **-laufbüchse** *f* actuator sleeve (hydr.) **-laufbuchse** *f* sleeve, sleeve valve, cylinder barrel, cylinder liner, wet liner **-lauffläche** *f* cylinder bore, working surfaces of cylinder **-leistung** *f* cylinder output **-lücke** *f* cylinder gap or interval **-mantel** *m* cylinder jacket or barrel

Zylinderöl *n* cylinder oil **-lösung** *f* cylinder stock solution

Zylinderputzwalze *f* cylinder clearer roller

Zylinderrad *n* cylinder gear

Zylinderraum *m*, **toter** ~ compression volume

Zylinder-reihe *f* bank or row of cylinders **-resonator** *m* cylindrical resonator **-ringanker** *m* cylindrical ring armature **-rollen für Zylinderrollenlager** rollers for roller-journals **-rollenlager** *n* roller bearing

Zylinder-schaft *m* straight shank **-schaftleitblech** *n* intercylinder baffle **-schleifmaschine** *f* cylinder grinder **-schlichtmaschine** *f* cylinder sizing machine **-schmierung** *f* cylinder lubrication **-schneidschraube** *f* cylindrical tap

Zylinderschraube *f* cheese-head screw ~ **mit Innensechskant** fillister socket head screw

Zylinder-schütz *n* cylindrical valve **-senge** *f* cylinder singeing machine **-spaltmagnetron** *n* hole and slot-type magnetron **-spule** *f* cylindric coil **-stegdecke** *f* armored tubular flooring **-stern** *m* radial arrangement of cylinders **-stichmaß** *n* tubular inside-micrometer gauge **-stift** *m* straight or cylindrical pin **-symmetrische TM-Welle** circular magnetic wave **-toppzeichen** *n* cylindrical top mark **-trockner** *m* can drier

Zylinderventil *n* cylinder gate or valve **niedriges** ~ shallow cylindrical valve

Zylinder-verkleidung *f* cylinder lagging **-verschluß** *m* (cylinder) breech mechanism, skin plate **-verstrebung** *f* cylinder stiffening piece **-volumen** *n* cylinder volume or capacity, piston displacement, cubic capacity of cylinder **-vorderdeckel** *m* front cover of cylinder **-walke** *f* cylindrical milling or cylindrical fulling machine **-wandung** *f* cylinder jacket, cylinder wall **-wasser** *n* jacket water

Zylinder-weite *f* cylinder diameter **-werk** *n* roller **-wicklung** *f* tube-shaped winding **-winkel** *m* angle of cylinder setting **-zahnstange** *f* cylinder gear rack **-zapfen** *m* dowel pin

zylindrieren to calender

zylindrisch cylindrical **-er Ansatz** cylindrical projection **-es Gewinde** straight thread **-e Kreuzspule** tube **-es Leitblech** shell baffle **-e Schnecke** straight thread **-es Schraubrad** cylindrical screw gear **-e Spule** cylindrical coil

Zylindrischziehen *n* drawing cylindrically

Zylindrizität, auf ~ **prüfen** to check the roundness and parallelism

Zymoskop *n* zymoscope

Zymotechnik *f* zymology

zymotechnisch zymotechnic(al)

zymotisch zymotic

Zypressenholz *n* cypress wood

Zytidinphosphat *n* cytidine phosphate

NOTIZEN — NOTES

NOTIZEN — NOTES

NOTIZEN — NOTES

NOTIZEN — NOTES

NOTIZEN — NOTES

NOTIZEN — NOTES